Roget's International Thesaurus®

Roget's International Thesaurus®

8

EIGHTH EDITION

Edited by Barbara Ann Kipfer, Ph.D.

Collins Reference
An Imprint of HarperCollins*Publishers*

Lithograph of Peter Mark Roget:
Edward Mansfield Burbank, *Sketches of the Lives & Works of the Honorary Medical Staff of the Manchester Infirmary, from 1752 to 1830*, Volume 1, 1904. Courtesy of the New York Public Library

FIRST EDITION

Library of Congress Cataloging-in-Publication Data has been applied for.

ISBN 978-0-06-284372-2 (thumb-indexed)

19 20 21 22 23 LSC 10 9 8 7 6 5 4 3 2 1

Contents

Peter Mark Roget vii

How to Use This Book xi

Peter Roget's Preface to the First Edition (1852) xv

Foreword by Barbara Ann Kipfer, Ph.D. xvii

Synopsis of Categories xix

Abbreviations Used in This Book xli

Thesaurus of English Words and Phrases 1

Index 809

How to Use This Index 810

P. M. Roget

Peter Mark Roget

1779–1869

The author of the "Treasury of Words" could hardly have thought that his name would become forever associated with a particular book, even though he hoped that he was suggesting a unique way of utilizing the richness and flexibility of the English language. But for more than 150 years Roget's work has been the constant companion of all those who aspire to use the language most effectively.

The career of Peter Mark Roget prior to the publication of his *Thesaurus* in 1852, when he was seventy-three years old, while largely devoted to science and to medicine, required of him a facility with words in the delivery of ideas and concepts. A lifetime of secretaryships for several learned societies had thoroughly familiarized him with the need for clarity and forcefulness of expression. That he was justified in his concept is made obvious by the universal acceptance of his thesaurus as an indispensable tool for all those who wish to write and speak with eloquence.

Born in London the son of a Protestant pastor who died at an early age, Roget was raised by his mother. He studied at the University of Edinburgh from 1793 to 1798 and received an M.D. after his successful defense of his Latin thesis dealing with the laws of chemical affinity. He was, however, too late to share in that institution's happy days as a stunning example of the Scottish Enlightenment. He was not to know William Cullen, the great nosologist, nor Alexander Monro primus, who brought Hermann Boerhaave's ethos of a medical school from Leyden; but he did learn anatomy from Monro secundus and medicine from John Gregory. The bright stars of David Hume, denied professorship at the university for his radical thinking, and of Adam Smith had long since blazed across the Scottish intellectual world. Moreover, Roget was too early for Sir James

Young Simpson and chloroform, or for the dexterous James Syme, who was mentor and father-in-law to the great Lord Lister. While Roget was in Edinburgh, the soil was being prepared for the phenomenon of Paris Medicine, the next wave of medical advance, which would be built on the ruins of the French Revolution.

After his graduation, the young physician looked about for the connections he would need to launch a medical career. In this he was fortunate in having the concerned attention of his uncle, Sir Samuel Romilly, whose own promising political potential, shortened by his suicide, provided an entrée to certain segments of English scientific and intellectual life. Through his uncle, Roget was introduced to Lord Lansdowne, for whom he served briefly as personal physician, and to Jeremy Bentham. On his own initiative, Roget spent some time in Bristol in Thomas Beddoes's Pneumatic Institute, devoted to the treatment of human illness using various gases. There he may have met illustrious figures Humphry Davy, James Watt, Samuel Taylor Coleridge, William Wordsworth, and Robert Southey.

In the midst of his desultory round of attendance at lectures and dispensary duties, Roget learned that his uncle had maneuvered for him an opportunity to tutor two scions of a wealthy Manchester manufacturer on a grand tour of Europe. The Peace of Amiens had been signed in 1802, and continental travel was once again open to English families anxious to provide their children with the advantages of foreign scenes.

Roget was twenty-three when he shepherded his charges across the English Channel and on to Paris, where they entered into the round of parties and dinners opened to them through letters from Sir Samuel and from the boys' family. But there was more than that. Roget hired a French tutor and supervised his charges' studies in mathematics, chemistry, and geology. He also saw to it that there were the obligatory trips to museums as well as to the theater and that the boys wrote their impressions and comments after each visit.

The little party pushed on to Geneva, not without encountering obstructions, delays, and disappointments injected by the French bureaucracy. In Geneva, although the city had recently been annexed by Napoleon, the group felt secure enough to settle down to a life of studies, parties, and local sightseeing. The respite was short-lived, however. The Peace of Amiens was abrogated by Napoleon in 1803, and the position of any Englishman in French territory was in doubt. Warned by Madame de Staël that he faced internment, Roget undertook to establish for himself Genevan citizenship on the basis of his father's birth in that city. Through prodigious effort and resourcefulness remarkable in so young a man, Roget sneaked the party, dressed as peasants, into Germany. He was successful in making his way to Denmark and thence to England, delivering his charges back to their family.

Manchester now offered the best opportunity to establish a medical practice, since Roget could count on the support of the wealthy Philips family, whose sons had shared his French experience. He quickly became associated with the local infirmary and with the Manchester Literary and Philosophical Society, before which body he gave a series of lectures on physiology that historians credit as forming the basis of what became the School of Medicine in that city. As D. L. Emblen points out in his biography of Roget, "[he] showed that his chief interest in the new science of physiology lay in the organization and order of several aspects of that subject and in the relationship of the subject to such kindred fields as anatomy" (D. L. Emblen, *Peter Mark Roget: The Word and the Man*, New York: Thomas Crowell, 1970, p. 96). It was Roget's meticulous, precise way of looking at order, at plan, and at interdependence in animal economy that would eventually find expression in his unique and practical lexicographic experiment.

But the great metropolis beckoned, and the young physician finally decided on a London career. Roget was never outstandingly successful as a medical practitioner. He had, however, become associated with the establishment of the Northern Dispensary, the quintessential Victorian expression of medical charity, to which he devoted a lifetime of practice. Roget's métier was teaching and institutional activities. He lectured in the Theory and Practice of Physic at the Great Windmill Street School, which served as the school of anatomy of Middlesex Hospital before that institution was eclipsed by the new University College on Gower Street. The Medical and Chirurgical Society, founded to bridge the gap between medicine and surgery, commanded much of Roget's attention during his London days. He served as the society's secretary for twelve years and contributed to its journal, *Transactions*. In 1814 he became a fellow in the Royal Society on the basis of a paper he wrote describing a forerunner of the slide rule. He contributed many articles to the *Encyclopaedia Britannica* that were carried through several editions. In those pages he crossed swords with George Combe, the ardent promoter of phrenology, a discipline that Roget could not support. While serving as secretary of the Royal Society he wrote the Bridgewater Treatise of Physiology, which demonstrated anew Roget's ability to organize and classify the essentials of a rapidly developing science.

Although extremely occupied during these years, as a list of his extensive memberships in scientific and cultural organizations shows, Roget seems never to have captured the attention of his peers to the extent that many of his contemporaries enjoyed. There is a hint that he was always just below the top rank, never in the front. It was, after all, an age of giants, and to be even in the midst of all that ferment was remarkable enough. His active public life came to an end when he was eased out of the secretaryship of the Royal Society after a conflict over the operation of the library, and was literally forced into retirement.

An inactive retirement was not compatible with Roget's lifestyle. Since childhood, putting ideas and concepts in writing had been second nature to him. He dwelt in a world of language, and his orderly, systematic mind lent itself to classification. More than a list of synonyms, more than a dictionary, the thesaurus Roget devised and constantly improved upon during this time was a unique ordering of the English language to be used by those desiring to impart an exacting and felicitous tone to written or spoken material. Grouped by ideas rather than by a mere alphabetical listing, the thesaurus enabled the user to find the exact word or phrase needed for a specific purpose. Roget had been keeping such a wordlist for many years. He now proposed to enlarge it and present it to the world of users of the English language.

The success of this venture was never in doubt. Roget supervised some twenty-five editions and printings of the thesaurus and was actively at work on his masterpiece when he died in 1869 at the age of ninety. *Roget's International Thesaurus* continues to be issued. For all those who deal with words and with ideas as expressed in words it has become indispensable. It remains a monument of scholarship and a tribute to the industry and breadth of knowledge of one of the lesser-known Victorian greats.

DONALD F. KENT, M.D.

How to Use This Book

Like other great reference books, *Roget's International Thesaurus* is the product of continuous improvement and long-term investment by its editors. The process began almost two centuries ago, in 1805, when Dr. Peter Mark Roget began compiling a list of useful related words for his own knowledge.

The revolutionary achievement of Dr. Roget was his development of a brand new principle: the grouping of words according to ideas. If the user cannot find something in a reference book, it is often because of the restriction of searching alphabetically by "known" headwords. Dr. Roget's thesaurus reversed the access to allow the user to find a word from another word, concept, or idea. When in 1852 Roget published the first book ever to realize this concept with thoroughness and precision, he called it a "thesaurus" (from the Greek and Latin, meaning "treasury" or "storehouse").

So successful was Roget's *Thesaurus of English Words and Phrases, Classified and Arranged so as to Facilitate the Expression of Ideas and Assist in Literary Composition* that a second edition followed one year later in 1853. By Dr. Roget's death in 1869 there had been 28 editions and printings.

Each subsequent edition introduced more efficient and useful features, all of which have contributed to the quality of the present edition. Over the years, tens of thousands of new words and phrases were added, and the scope of the book expanded to include non-formal terms, including slang and informal vocabulary used in non-business and non-educational contexts.

The eighth edition of *Roget's International Thesaurus*, prepared by Barbara Ann Kipfer, Ph.D, has a text of about 443,000 words and phrases, arranged in categories by their meanings, and a comprehensive index. (Dr. Kipfer was also the editor of the fifth, sixth, and seventh editions.)

The thesaurus is a device for finding specific words or phrases for general ideas. You use a thesaurus when you have an idea but do not know, or cannot remember, the word or phrase that expresses it best or when you want a more accurate or effective way of saying what you mean. A thesaurus gives you possibilities and you choose the one that you think is best within your particular context. The range of possibilities includes not only meaning as one usually thinks of it, but also non-formal (slang and informal) and related words and phrases.

There are many more "related terms" than there are true synonyms for vocabulary. These words and phrases are not necessarily matched in meaning to your starting term, but that is okay as there are many times when you are not looking for something that means exactly the same as the term you already have. You are looking for a word or phrase whose meaning is close but differs in a way that makes sense in your context.

The search for a word that you need is a simple, two-step process that can begin in the index. For example, you may want a word to describe something that first occurred in the past.

Step 1. In the index, look up the word *first* and pick the subentry closest to the meaning you want.

Step 2. Follow its number into the text of the thesaurus and you will find a whole paragraph of adjectives under the category.

Alternatively, the reader can start in the Synopsis of Categories, which includes a short definition of each category. *Roget's International Thesaurus* is an efficient word-finder because its structure is organized intuitively, starting with the overall arrangement of the main categories that contain many sequences of closely related categories. For example, you will see **HEARING, DEAFNESS, SOUND, SILENCE, FAINTNESS OF SOUND, LOUDNESS**, a procession of similar, contrasting, and opposing concepts, all dealing with the perception and quality of sounds. So if you are not quite satisfied with what you find in one place, take a look at nearby categories, too. Seeing related terms, and antonyms, often opens up lines of thought and chains of association.

The large categories of ideas are numbered in sequence; there are 1,075 of them in this edition of *Roget's International Thesaurus*. Within each category the terms are presented in short paragraphs by basic meaning, and these are also numbered. References from the index to the text are made with two-part numbers such as 100.2, the first part being the number of the main category, the second being the number of the paragraph within that category. This system makes for quick pinpointing of the place where you will find the word or phrase you need.

The terms within a category are organized also by part of speech, in this order: nouns, verbs, adjectives, adverbs, prepositions, conjunctions, and interjections. When you are casting about for a way of saying something, rather than looking for a specific word, expand your search to other parts of speech.

By examining any paragraph, you will recognize that few words are exactly interchangeable, and you will see that there are fine distinctions between synonyms. The sequence of terms within each paragraph is determined by semantic relationships. The words closest in meaning are offered in clusters that are set off with semicolons.

The semicolon is used to delimit sequences of words in paragraphs that share some more specific relationship with each other than they share with the words in other semicolon-delimited sequences. It guides the user as to what substitution phrases would be acceptable versus what others might not be. The semicolon-delimited groups also serve as an aid to finding other phrases that one can't recall, but knows are very much like a phrase one does recall.

In previous editions, space was conserved by using the conventions of *or* and *and* to truncate the terms. This convention can be confusing for users, especially any young or non-native English speakers, so this has been changed in the eighth edition. All terms are completely spelled out.

The number of special labels used has been reduced in this edition. See the List of Abbreviations on page xli. As with film or television (adult language, graphic language), there are words and phrases that are often considered offensive, but it is difficult to mark them in a thesaurus with no context to consider. Those marked with an asterisk (*) are considered to be offensive in most contexts.

The paragraphs are highlighted with terms in boldface type. The boldfaced words are descriptive of the meaning of the paragraphs' terms.

Roget's International Thesaurus can help you to improve your writing and speech and to enrich your active vocabulary. Please use the thesaurus in conjunction with a good dictionary whenever a selected word or phrase is unfamiliar to you.

Peter Roget's Preface to the First Edition
(1852)

It is now nearly fifty years since I first projected a system of verbal classification similar to that on which the present work is founded. Conceiving that such a compilation might help to supply my own deficiencies, I had, in the year 1805, completed a classed catalog of words on a small scale, but on the same principle, and nearly in the same form, as the Thesaurus now published. I had often during that long interval found this little collection, scanty and imperfect as it was, of much use to me in literary composition, and often contemplated its extension and improvement; but a sense of the magnitude of the task, amidst a multitude of other avocations, deterred me from the attempt. Since my retirement from the duties of Secretary of the Royal Society, however, finding myself possessed of more leisure, and believing that a repertory of which I had myself experienced the advantage might, when amplified, prove useful to others, I resolved to embark in an undertaking which, for the last three or four years, has given me incessant occupation, and has, indeed, imposed upon me an amount of labor very much greater than I had anticipated. Notwithstanding all the pains I have bestowed on its execution, I am fully aware of its numerous deficiencies and imperfections, and of its falling far short of the degree of excellence that might be attained. But, in a work of this nature, where perfection is placed at so great a distance, I have thought it best to limit my ambition to that moderate share of merit which it may claim in its present form; trusting to the indulgence of those for whose benefit it is intended, and to the candor of critics who, while they find it easy to detect faults, can at the same time duly appreciate difficulties.

P. M. Roget

April 29, 1852

Foreword

by Barbara Ann Kipfer, Ph.D.

In developing this new (eighth) edition, I chose to focus on the modernity and scope of the language coverage in *Roget's International Thesaurus*. To this end, I have included as many new words and phrases as possible from general vocabulary to scientific and technological terms.

I wish to thank my brilliant technologist, Dr. Robert A. Amsler, for his invaluable help in ensuring that this edition is the best yet.

No one is luckier than I to have the time and the environment I need to complete such a massive undertaking. To that I owe gratitude to my husband, Paul Magoulas, and Hoops, our cat, who were there every step of the way.

BARBARA ANN KIPFER, PH.D.

September 2018

Synopsis of Categories

Class One: The Body and the Senses

1	**BIRTH**	<beginning of life>
2	**THE BODY**	<physical self>
3	**HAIR**	<threadlike growth from skin>
4	**CLOTHING MATERIALS**	<cloth or fabric>
5	**CLOTHING**	<bodily covering>
6	**UNCLOTHING**	<no bodily covering>
7	**NUTRITION**	<eating for health>
8	**EATING**	<taking in food>
9	**REFRESHMENT**	<food and drink>
10	**FOOD**	<things eaten>
11	**COOKING**	<preparing food>
12	**EXCRETION**	<bodily discharge>
13	**SECRETION**	<liquid bodily discharge>
14	**BODILY DEVELOPMENT**	<body growth>
15	**STRENGTH**	<inherent power>
16	**WEAKNESS**	<lacking power>
17	**ENERGY**	<usable strength>
18	**POWER, POTENCY**	<effective force>
19	**IMPOTENCE**	<lacking strength>
20	**REST, REPOSE**	<inactive state>
21	**FATIGUE**	<tired state>
22	**SLEEP**	<unconscious rest>
23	**WAKEFULNESS**	<not sleeping>
24	**SENSATION**	<physical sensibility>
25	**INSENSIBILITY**	<physical unfeeling>
26	**PAIN**	<physical suffering>
27	**VISION**	<eyesight>
28	**DEFECTIVE VISION**	<defective eyesight>
29	**OPTICAL INSTRUMENTS**	<vision aid>
30	**BLINDNESS**	<no vision>
31	**VISIBILITY**	<ability to be seen>

32	**INVISIBILITY**	<not able to be seen>
33	**APPEARANCE**	<becoming visible>
34	**DISAPPEARANCE**	<stop being visible>
35	**COLOR**	<visual quality>
36	**COLORLESSNESS**	<lacking color>
37	**WHITENESS**	<color of snow, milk>
38	**BLACKNESS**	<color of coal, night sky>
39	**GRAYNESS**	<color between black and white>
40	**BROWNNESS**	<color of wood, chocolate>
41	**REDNESS**	<color of blood>
42	**ORANGENESS**	<color between red and yellow>
43	**YELLOWNESS**	<color of lemon, sun>
44	**GREENNESS**	<color of grass, plants>
45	**BLUENESS**	<color of clear sky>
46	**PURPLENESS**	<color between red and blue>
47	**VARIEGATION**	<diversity of colors>
48	**HEARING**	<sense of hearing>
49	**DEAFNESS**	<inability to hear>
50	**SOUND**	<something heard>
51	**SILENCE**	<lack of sound>
52	**FAINTNESS OF SOUND**	<unclear or slight sounds>
53	**LOUDNESS**	<strong sounds>
54	**RESONANCE**	<loud, deep sounds>
55	**REPEATED SOUNDS**	<reoccurring sounds>
56	**EXPLOSIVE NOISE**	<sudden loud sounds>
57	**SIBILATION**	<hissing sounds>
58	**STRIDENCY**	<harsh and shrill sounds>
59	**CRY, CALL**	<human loud sound>
60	**ANIMAL SOUNDS**	<animal cry, call>
61	**DISCORD**	<dissonant sounds>
62	**TASTE**	<sense of taste>
63	**SAVORINESS**	<pleasant taste>
64	**UNSAVORINESS**	<unpleasant taste>
65	**INSIPIDNESS**	<lacking flavor>
66	**SWEETNESS**	<sugary flavor>
67	**SOURNESS**	<acidic flavor>
68	**PUNGENCY**	<sharp flavor, smell>
69	**ODOR**	<particular smells>
70	**FRAGRANCE**	<pleasant smells>
71	**STENCH**	<very bad smells>
72	**ODORLESSNESS**	<undetectable smells>
73	**TOUCH**	<sense of touch>
74	**SENSATIONS OF TOUCH**	<physical contact>
75	**SEX**	<sexual nature>
76	**MASCULINITY**	<male qualities>
77	**FEMININITY**	<female qualities>
78	**REPRODUCTION, PROCREATION**	<producing young>
79	**CLEANNESS**	<dirt-free condition>
80	**UNCLEANNESS**	<dirty condition>
81	**HEALTHFULNESS**	<good for health>
82	**UNHEALTHFULNESS**	<bad for health>
83	**HEALTH**	<physical wellness>
84	**FITNESS, EXERCISE**	<physical conditioning>
85	**DISEASE**	<illness>

86	**REMEDY**	<relief of illness>
87	**SUBSTANCE ABUSE**	<harmful drug intake>
88	**INTOXICATION, ALCOHOLIC DRINK**	<harmful alcohol intake>
89	**TOBACCO**	<smoking substance>
90	**HEALTH CARE**	<physical and mental treatment>
91	**THERAPY, MEDICAL TREATMENT**	<physical health care>
92	**PSYCHOLOGY, PSYCHOTHERAPY**	<mental health care>

Class Two: Feelings

93	**FEELING**	<emotional states>
94	**LACK OF FEELING**	<unemotional states>
95	**PLEASURE**	<feeling satisfaction>
96	**UNPLEASURE**	<feeling dissatisfaction>
97	**PLEASANTNESS**	<feeling good>
98	**UNPLEASANTNESS**	<feeling bad>
99	**DISLIKE**	<feeling aversion>
100	**DESIRE**	<feeling attraction>
101	**EAGERNESS**	<feeling interest>
102	**INDIFFERENCE**	<feeling disinterest>
103	**HATE**	<feeling extreme dislike>
104	**LOVE**	<feeling great affection>
105	**EXCITEMENT**	<feeling eager interest>
106	**INEXCITABILITY**	<feeling nothing>
107	**CONTENTMENT**	<feeling happiness, satisfaction>
108	**DISCONTENT**	<feeling unhappiness, disapproval>
109	**CHEERFULNESS**	<feeling agreeableness>
110	**ILL HUMOR**	<feeling disagreeableness>
111	**SOLEMNITY**	<feeling seriousness>
112	**SADNESS**	<feeling grief or disappointment>
113	**REGRET**	<feeling very sorry>
114	**UNREGRETFULNESS**	<feeling no regret>
115	**LAMENTATION**	<expressing deep sadness>
116	**REJOICING**	<expressing extreme happiness>
117	**DULLNESS**	<uninteresting state>
118	**TEDIUM**	<boring state>
119	**AGGRAVATION**	<annoyed state>
120	**RELIEF**	<reduced pain state>
121	**COMFORT**	<relaxed pleasant state>
122	**WONDER**	<surprised state>
123	**UNASTONISHMENT**	<unsurprised state>
124	**HOPE**	<anticipating good>
125	**HOPELESSNESS**	<anticipating bad>
126	**ANXIETY**	<fear of future>
127	**FEAR, FEARFULNESS**	<feeling or sensing danger>
128	**NERVOUSNESS**	<feeling worry>
129	**UNNERVOUSNESS**	<feeling calm>
130	**EXPECTATION**	<anticipating a happening>
131	**INEXPECTATION**	<anticipating nothing>
132	**DISAPPOINTMENT**	<unhoped-for outcome>
133	**PREMONITION**	<dreamed outcome>
134	**PATIENCE**	<calm state>
135	**IMPATIENCE**	<agitated state>
136	**PRIDE**	<self-respecting state>
137	**HUMILITY**	<humble state>

138 **SERVILITY** <obedient state>
139 **MODESTY** <shy state>
140 **VANITY** <vain state>
141 **ARROGANCE** <overly vain state>
142 **INSOLENCE** <disrespecting state>
143 **KINDNESS, BENEVOLENCE** <kind, helpful state>
144 **UNKINDNESS, MALEVOLENCE** <unkind, harmful state>
145 **PITY** <feeling sympathy>
146 **PITILESSNESS** <feeling no sympathy>
147 **CONDOLENCE** <expressing sympathy>
148 **FORGIVENESS** <expressing no resentment>
149 **CONGRATULATION** <expressing pleasure for someone>
150 **GRATITUDE** <expressing appreciation>
151 **INGRATITUDE** <lacking appreciation>
152 **RESENTMENT, ANGER** <upset, annoyed feeling>
153 **JEALOUSY** <resentment and feeling threatened>
154 **ENVY** <wanting what another has>
155 **RESPECT** <feeling admiration and regard>
156 **DISRESPECT** <lacking regard>
157 **CONTEMPT** <open disrespect>

Class Three: Place and Change of Place

158 **SPACE** <indefinite space>
159 **LOCATION** <definite place or position>
160 **DISPLACEMENT** <removal from location>
161 **DIRECTION** <motion on course>
162 **PROGRESSION** <motion forwards>
163 **REGRESSION** <motion backwards>
164 **DEVIATION** <indirect course>
165 **LEADING** <going ahead>
166 **FOLLOWING** <going behind>
167 **APPROACH** <motion towards>
168 **RECESSION** <motion away from>
169 **CONVERGENCE** <coming together>
170 **CROSSING** <passing across>
171 **DIVERGENCE** <taking different directions>
172 **MOTION** <process of moving>
173 **QUIESCENCE** <absence of moving or action>
174 **SWIFTNESS** <fast moving>
175 **SLOWNESS** <slow moving>
176 **TRANSFERAL, TRANSPORTATION** <moving to another place>
177 **TRAVEL** <journey to another place>
178 **TRAVELER** <one who journeys>
179 **VEHICLE** <road transport machines>
180 **SHIP, BOAT** <water transport machines>
181 **AIRCRAFT** <air transport machines>
182 **WATER TRAVEL** <journey by water>
183 **MARINER** <water navigator>
184 **AVIATION** <journey by air>
185 **AVIATOR** <air navigator>
186 **ARRIVAL** <coming to or reaching>
187 **RECEPTION** <welcoming or receiving>
188 **DEPARTURE** <leaving>
189 **ENTRANCE** <entering>

190	**EMERGENCE**	<becoming known>
191	**INSERTION**	<putting in>
192	**EXTRACTION**	<taking or drawing out>
193	**ASCENT**	<motion upward>
194	**DESCENT**	<motion downward>
195	**CONTAINER**	<objects for holding>
196	**CONTENTS**	<objects held by container>
197	**ROOM**	<compartment or part of space>
198	**TOP**	<highest part>
199	**BOTTOM**	<lowest part>
200	**VERTICALNESS**	<up-and-down>
201	**HORIZONTALNESS**	<side-to-side>
202	**PENDENCY**	<hanging down>
203	**PARALLELISM**	<lined up but not touching>
204	**OBLIQUITY**	<slanting>
205	**INVERSION**	<opposite or upside-down>
206	**EXTERIORITY**	<outside>
207	**INTERIORITY**	<inside>
208	**CENTRALITY**	<centered or in the middle>
209	**ENVIRONMENT**	<conditions and influences>
210	**CIRCUMSCRIPTION**	<range or restriction>
211	**BOUNDS**	<limiting line or area>
212	**ENCLOSURE**	<surrounding>
213	**INTERPOSITION**	<putting or lying between>
214	**INTRUSION**	<infringing on>
215	**CONTRAPOSITION**	<placed over or against>
216	**FRONT**	<forward part>
217	**REAR**	<part away from front>
218	**SIDE**	<part away from center>
219	**RIGHT SIDE**	<part toward the right>
220	**LEFT SIDE**	<part toward the left>
221	**PRESENCE**	<state of being present>
222	**ABSENCE**	<state of not being present>
223	**NEARNESS**	<state of being close>
224	**INTERVAL**	<space between>
225	**HABITATION**	<living in a place>
226	**NATIVENESS**	<born in a place>
227	**INHABITANT, NATIVE**	<those born or living in place>
228	**ABODE, HABITAT**	<place where animate object lives>
229	**FURNITURE**	<large objects for rooms>
230	**TOWN, CITY**	<geographic place where people live>
231	**REGION**	<part of country or world>
232	**COUNTRY**	<political geographic place>
233	**THE COUNTRY**	<area outside town, city>
234	**LAND**	<area of ground>
235	**BODY OF LAND**	<feature of the land>
236	**PLAIN**	<flat open land>
237	**HIGHLANDS**	<hilly or mountainous land>
238	**STREAM**	<flowing body of water>
239	**CHANNEL**	<pathway for water>
240	**SEA, OCEAN**	<large body of salt water>
241	**LAKE, POOL**	<large body of fresh water>
242	**INLET, GULF**	<arm of larger or smaller body of water>
243	**MARSH**	<soft wet land>

Class Four: Measure and Shape

244	**QUANTITY**	<amount or number of>
245	**DEGREE**	<amount or level measured>
246	**MEAN**	<middle point between two things>
247	**GREATNESS**	<large in importance or size>
248	**INSIGNIFICANCE**	<small in importance or size>
249	**SUPERIORITY**	<state of high quality>
250	**INFERIORITY**	<state of poor quality>
251	**INCREASE**	<become larger or greater>
252	**DECREASE**	<become smaller>
253	**ADDITION**	<process of adding>
254	**ADJUNCT**	<something added>
255	**SUBTRACTION**	<process of taking away>
256	**REMAINDER**	<something left over>
257	**SIZE, LARGENESS**	<great in size or amount>
258	**LITTLENESS**	<small in size or amount>
259	**EXPANSION, GROWTH**	<increase in size>
260	**CONTRACTION**	<decrease in size>
261	**DISTANCE, REMOTENESS**	<space between or away from>
262	**FORM**	<having shape>
263	**FORMLESSNESS**	<having no regular form>
264	**SYMMETRY**	<having equal parts or sides>
265	**DISTORTION**	<having changing shape>
266	**STRUCTURE**	<having organized form>
267	**LENGTH**	<longest dimension>
268	**SHORTNESS**	<shortest dimension>
269	**BREADTH, THICKNESS**	<large side-to-side dimension>
270	**NARROWNESS, THINNESS**	<small side-to-side dimension>
271	**FILAMENT**	<thin thread>
272	**HEIGHT**	<bottom-to-top dimension>
273	**SHAFT**	<sticklike in shape>
274	**LOWNESS**	<low in level>
275	**DEPTH**	<deep in level>
276	**SHALLOWNESS**	<having little depth>
277	**STRAIGHTNESS**	<having no curves, angles, bends>
278	**ANGULARITY**	<having angles>
279	**CURVATURE**	<having curves>
280	**CIRCULARITY**	<having circle shape>
281	**CONVOLUTION**	<having twists, complicated curves>
282	**SPHERICITY, ROTUNDITY**	<having round or globular shape>
283	**CONVEXITY, PROTUBERANCE**	<curving or extending outward>
284	**CONCAVITY**	<curving or hollowed inward>
285	**SHARPNESS**	<having edges or points>
286	**BLUNTNESS**	<having dulled edges or points>
287	**SMOOTHNESS**	<being flat and even>
288	**ROUGHNESS**	<being uneven and broken>
289	**NOTCH**	<small cut>
290	**FURROW**	<large narrow cut>
291	**FOLD**	<part bent over another part>
292	**OPENING**	<hole or empty space>
293	**CLOSURE**	<means of closing or enclosing>
294	**TEXTURE**	<surface quality>
295	**COVERING**	<concealing or on top of>

296	**LAYER**	<covering over or under another>
297	**WEIGHT**	<having heaviness>
298	**LIGHTNESS**	<lack of heaviness>
299	**RARITY**	<lack of density, thickness>
300	**MEASUREMENT**	<process determining amount or degree>

Class Five: Living Things

301	**YOUTH**	<young time of life>
302	**YOUNGSTER**	<young person>
303	**AGE**	<time of life>
304	**ADULT OR OLD PERSON**	<older person>
305	**ORGANIC MATTER**	<living nature>
306	**LIFE**	<being alive>
307	**DEATH**	<ending of life>
308	**KILLING**	<causing a death>
309	**INTERMENT**	<burying the dead>
310	**PLANTS**	<plant kingdom>
311	**ANIMALS, INSECTS**	<animal kingdom>
312	**HUMANKIND**	<human race>

Class Six: Natural Phenomena

313	**SEASON**	<four periods of year>
314	**MORNING, NOON**	<sunrise and midday>
315	**EVENING, NIGHT**	<afternoon and night>
316	**RAIN**	<water falling from sky>
317	**AIR, WEATHER**	<states of atmosphere>
318	**WIND**	<movement of atmospheric air>
319	**CLOUD**	<water condensation in sky>
320	**BUBBLE**	<liquid ball of gas or air>

Class Seven: Behavior and the Will

321	**BEHAVIOR**	<way of acting>
322	**MISBEHAVIOR**	<behaving badly>
323	**WILL**	<determination to do something>
324	**WILLINGNESS**	<cheerful compliance>
325	**UNWILLINGNESS**	<reluctance to act>
326	**OBEDIENCE**	<willingness to obey>
327	**DISOBEDIENCE**	<unwillingness to obey>
328	**ACTION**	<voluntary action>
329	**INACTION**	<voluntary inaction>
330	**ACTIVITY**	<being active>
331	**INACTIVITY**	<not acting>
332	**ASSENT**	<agreeing to do>
333	**DISSENT**	<publicly disagreeing>
334	**AFFIRMATION**	<willing to validate>
335	**NEGATION, DENIAL**	<refusal to validate>
336	**IMITATION**	<being a copy>
337	**NONIMITATION**	<being genuine>
338	**COMPENSATION**	<balancing of good for bad>
339	**CAREFULNESS**	<close or watchful attention>
340	**NEGLECT**	<inattention or failure to do>
341	**INTERPRETATION**	<understanding meaning>
342	**MISINTERPRETATION**	<misunderstanding meaning>
343	**COMMUNICATION**	<giving information>

344	**UNCOMMUNICATIVENESS**	<not giving information>
345	**SECRECY**	<hiding something>
346	**CONCEALMENT**	<preventing disclosure>
347	**COMMUNICATIONS**	<information via technology>
348	**MANIFESTATION**	<appearing or expressing>
349	**REPRESENTATION, DESCRIPTION**	<giving true information>
350	**MISREPRESENTATION**	<giving false information>
351	**DISCLOSURE**	<making something known>
352	**PUBLICATION**	<publicizing information>
353	**MESSENGER**	<delivering message>
354	**FALSENESS**	<untruthful action>
355	**EXAGGERATION**	<enlarged description>
356	**DECEPTION**	<action of deceiving>
357	**DECEIVER**	<one who deceives>
358	**DUPE**	<one who is fooled>
359	**RESOLUTION**	<resolving something>
360	**PERSEVERANCE**	<determinedly pursuing something>
361	**OBSTINACY**	<stubbornly adhering to something>
362	**IRRESOLUTION**	<uncertainty>
363	**CHANGING OF MIND**	<change of decision or opinion>
364	**CAPRICE**	<sudden change>
365	**IMPULSE**	<sudden inclination to act>
366	**LEAP**	<jumping or springing from>
367	**PLUNGE**	<sudden falling or jumping>
368	**AVOIDANCE**	<avoiding or withdrawing>
369	**ESCAPE**	<getting free or away>
370	**ABANDONMENT**	<leaving or withdrawing support>
371	**CHOICE**	<picking or choosing>
372	**REJECTION**	<refusing to accept or consider>
373	**CUSTOM, HABIT**	<common usage or practice>
374	**UNACCUSTOMEDNESS**	<uncommon experiences>
375	**MOTIVATION, INDUCEMENT**	<giving a reason for action>
376	**PRETEXT**	<hiding real reason for action>
377	**ALLUREMENT**	<enticing to action>
378	**BRIBERY**	<offer of payment for action>
379	**DISSUASION**	<advising against action>
380	**INTENTION**	<aim or purpose for action>
381	**PLAN**	<set of actions>
382	**PURSUIT**	<following or chasing>
383	**ROUTE, PATH**	<way for traveling>
384	**MANNER, MEANS**	<way of acting>
385	**PROVISION, EQUIPMENT**	<necessary supplies>
386	**STORE, SUPPLY**	<source of supplies>
387	**USE**	<using or utilizing>
388	**CONSUMPTION**	<using up something>
389	**MISUSE**	<using incorrectly>
390	**DISUSE**	<discontinuing use>
391	**USELESSNESS**	<not being useful>
392	**IMPROVEMENT**	<making something better>
393	**IMPAIRMENT**	<making something worse>
394	**RELAPSE**	<returning to worse condition>
395	**DESTRUCTION**	<damaging something>
396	**RESTORATION**	<returning something to original condition>
397	**PRESERVATION**	<keeping something in good condition>

398	**RESCUE**	<saving from danger or harm>
399	**WARNING**	<telling of danger or trouble>
400	**ALARM**	<warning signal>
401	**HASTE**	<rapidity of action>
402	**LEISURE**	<cessation of action>
403	**ENDEAVOR**	<trying to do>
404	**UNDERTAKING**	<trying to do difficult thing>
405	**PREPARATION**	<getting ready for something>
406	**UNPREPAREDNESS**	<unready for something>
407	**ACCOMPLISHMENT**	<successful completion of something>
408	**NONACCOMPLISHMENT**	<not reaching goal>
409	**SUCCESS**	<achieving planned result>
410	**FAILURE**	<lack of success>
411	**VICTORY**	<winning competition>
412	**DEFEAT**	<failure to win competition>
413	**SKILL**	<ability to do something well>
414	**UNSKILLFULNESS**	<lack of skill>
415	**CUNNING**	<cleverness in method>
416	**ARTLESSNESS**	<simpleness in method>
417	**AUTHORITY**	<power to control>
418	**LAWLESSNESS**	<absence of authority>
419	**PRECEPT**	<rule for behavior>
420	**COMMAND**	<order for behavior>
421	**DEMAND**	<requirement for behavior>
422	**ADVICE**	<suggestion for behavior>
423	**COUNCIL**	<group making rules>
424	**COMPULSION**	<forcing to do something>
425	**STRICTNESS**	<strict control>
426	**LAXNESS**	<free from control>
427	**LENIENCY**	<allowing freedom>
428	**RESTRAINT**	<limiting freedom>
429	**CONFINEMENT**	<limiting free movement>
430	**FREEDOM**	<ability to move freely>
431	**LIBERATION**	<freeing from control>
432	**SUBJECTION**	<making others obey>
433	**SUBMISSION**	<being obedient>
434	**OBSERVANCE**	<following rules, customs>
435	**NONOBSERVANCE**	<not following rules, customs>
436	**PROMISE**	<declaration of intent to do>
437	**COMPACT**	<agreement made>
438	**SECURITY**	<thing given as a pledge>
439	**OFFER**	<presenting something for acceptance>
440	**REQUEST**	<asking for something>
441	**CONSENT**	<agreeing to something>
442	**REFUSAL**	<denying something>
443	**PERMISSION**	<formal consent>
444	**PROHIBITION**	<denying by authority>
445	**REPEAL**	<revoking by authority>
446	**PROMOTION**	<raising in position>
447	**DEMOTION, DEPOSAL**	<lowering in position>
448	**RESIGNATION, RETIREMENT**	<withdrawal from position>
449	**AID**	<giving assistance>
450	**COOPERATION**	<combined helpful action>
451	**OPPOSITION**	<contrary action>

452 **OPPONENT** <one taking opposite position>
453 **RESISTANCE** <refusing to accept>
454 **DEFIANCE** <open resistance>
455 **ACCORD** <harmonious relationship>
456 **DISACCORD** <unharmonious relationship>
457 **CONTENTION** <heated disagreement>
458 **WARFARE** <engaged conflict>
459 **ATTACK** <aggressive action>
460 **DEFENSE** <defending from an attack>
461 **COMBATANT** <entity in a war>
462 **ARMS** <weapons and ammunition>
463 **ARENA** <place of conflict>
464 **PEACE** <state of no war>
465 **PACIFICATION** <soothing conflict>
466 **MEDIATION** <intervening in conflict>
467 **NEUTRALITY** <refusal to war>
468 **COMPROMISE** <mutual concession>
469 **POSSESSION** <control or owning>
470 **POSSESSOR** <controller or owner>
471 **PROPERTY** <things owned or controlled>
472 **ACQUISITION** <attaining property>
473 **LOSS** <loss of property>
474 **RETENTION** <retaining property>
475 **RELINQUISHMENT** <giving up property>
476 **PARTICIPATION** <taking part in or having a share>
477 **APPORTIONMENT** <dividing and sharing>
478 **GIVING** <put into another's possession>
479 **RECEIVING** <getting or being given something>
480 **TAKING** <taking possession>
481 **RESTITUTION** <returning something to owner>
482 **THEFT** <taking without permission>
483 **THIEF** <one taking without permission>
484 **PARSIMONY** <unwilling to spend money>
485 **LIBERALITY** <willing to spend or be generous>
486 **PRODIGALITY** <excessive spending>
487 **CELEBRATION** <special occasions>
488 **HUMOROUSNESS** <funniness>
489 **WIT, HUMOR** <ability to be funny>
490 **BANTER** <witty communication>
491 **COWARDICE** <lack of courage>
492 **COURAGE** <mental or moral strength>
493 **RASHNESS** <undue hastiness>
494 **CAUTION** <forethought to minimize risk>
495 **FASTIDIOUSNESS** <excessive attention to detail>
496 **TASTE, TASTEFULNESS** <good judgment, taste>
497 **VULGARITY** <excessive embellishment>
498 **ORNAMENTATION** <embellishment>
499 **PLAINNESS** <undecoration>
500 **AFFECTATION** <pretense, unnaturalness>
501 **OSTENTATION** <showiness>
502 **BOASTING** <prideful talk>
503 **BLUSTER** <threatening talk>
504 **COURTESY** <respectful behavior>

505	**DISCOURTESY**	<rude behavior>
506	**RETALIATION**	<counterattack>
507	**REVENGE**	<inflicting harm in retaliation>
508	**RIDICULE**	<contemptuous talk>
509	**APPROVAL**	<positive feeling toward>
510	**DISAPPROVAL**	<negative feeling toward>
511	**FLATTERY**	<insincere praising talk>
512	**DISPARAGEMENT**	<slighting talk>
513	**CURSE**	<profane or obscene talk>
514	**THREAT**	<warning of intention to harm>
515	**FASTING**	<abstaining from food>
516	**SOBRIETY**	<abstaining from intoxicating substance>

Class Eight: Language

517	**SIGNS, INDICATORS**	<symbol or signal>
518	**MEANING**	<sense of idea conveyed>
519	**LATENT MEANINGFULNESS**	<implied or suggested meaning>
520	**MEANINGLESSNESS**	<making no sense, having no meaning>
521	**INTELLIGIBILITY**	<comprehensible meaning>
522	**UNINTELLIGIBILITY**	<incomprehensible meaning>
523	**LANGUAGE**	<communication by word>
524	**SPEECH**	<spoken word>
525	**IMPERFECT SPEECH**	<speech disability>
526	**WORD**	<terms, vocabulary>
527	**NOMENCLATURE**	<names, naming>
528	**ANONYMITY**	<namelessness>
529	**PHRASE**	<multiword expression>
530	**GRAMMAR**	<language rules>
531	**UNGRAMMATICALNESS**	<not conforming to language rules>
532	**DICTION**	<word choice and usage>
533	**ELEGANCE**	<stylish language>
534	**INELEGANCE**	<simple language>
535	**PLAIN SPEECH**	<clear language>
536	**FIGURE OF SPEECH**	<nonliteral language>
537	**CONCISENESS**	<economy in language>
538	**DIFFUSENESS**	<superfluity in language>
539	**AMBIGUITY**	<multiple meaning in language>
540	**TALKATIVENESS**	<talking a lot>
541	**CONVERSATION**	<talking between two or more>
542	**SOLILOQUY**	<talking to oneself>
543	**PUBLIC SPEAKING**	<talking to public group>
544	**ELOQUENCE**	<persuasive language>
545	**GRANDILOQUENCE**	<colorful, lofty language>
546	**LETTER**	<alphabetic unit>
547	**WRITING**	<written composition>
548	**PRINTING**	<published composition>
549	**RECORD**	<documented information>
550	**RECORDER**	<documenter of information>
551	**INFORMATION**	<knowledge or facts conveyed>
552	**NEWS**	<report of events, new information>
553	**CORRESPONDENCE**	<written communication of information>
554	**BOOK**	<published literary work>
555	**PERIODICAL**	<magazine published at regular intervals>

556 **TREATISE** <published research project>
557 **ABRIDGMENT** <shortened publication>
558 **LIBRARY** <repository for publications>

Class Nine: Human Society and Institutions

559 **RELATIONSHIP BY BLOOD** <persons related>
560 **ANCESTRY** <line of descent>
561 **POSTERITY** <future generations>
562 **LOVEMAKING, ENDEARMENT** <sexual activity>
563 **MARRIAGE** <contractual relationship>
564 **RELATIONSHIP BY MARRIAGE** <extended family>
565 **CELIBACY** <abstention from sexual activity>
566 **DIVORCE, WIDOWHOOD** <dissolution of marriage>
567 **SCHOOL** <place of teaching and learning>
568 **TEACHING** <instructing>
569 **MISTEACHING** <instructing wrongly or badly>
570 **LEARNING** <gaining knowledge, experience>
571 **TEACHER** <one who instructs>
572 **STUDENT** <one who learns>
573 **DIRECTION, MANAGEMENT** <guidance or supervision>
574 **DIRECTOR** <guide or supervisor>
575 **MASTER** <one having authority over another>
576 **DEPUTY, AGENT** <one appointed to act for another>
577 **SERVANT, EMPLOYEE** <one working for another>
578 **FASHION** <prevailing style, custom>
579 **SOCIAL CONVENTION** <prevailing social norms>
580 **FORMALITY** <conventional, formal behavior>
581 **INFORMALITY** <casual, familiar behavior>
582 **SOCIABILITY** <tending toward companionship>
583 **UNSOCIABILITY** <tending toward solitude>
584 **SECLUSION** <withdrawal from socializing>
585 **HOSPITALITY, WELCOME** <welcoming guests>
586 **INHOSPITALITY** <unfriendly to guests>
587 **FRIENDSHIP** <liking other people>
588 **FRIEND** <one who is liked>
589 **ENMITY** <unfriendly feeling>
590 **MISANTHROPY** <dislike of other people>
591 **PUBLIC SPIRIT** <willingness to help public>
592 **BENEFACTOR** <one who helps cause or another person>
593 **EVILDOER** <one who does evil deed>
594 **JURISDICTION** <administration of justice>
595 **TRIBUNAL** <court of justice>
596 **JUDGE, JURY** <decider of court case>
597 **LAWYER** <one who assists others in legal matters>
598 **LEGAL ACTION** <judicial proceeding>
599 **ACCUSATION** <charge of wrongdoing>
600 **JUSTIFICATION** <denial of wrongdoing>
601 **ACQUITTAL** <setting free from charge of wrongdoing>
602 **CONDEMNATION** <declaring guilty of wrongdoing>
603 **PENALTY** <payment for wrongdoing>
604 **PUNISHMENT** <suffering for wrongdoing>
605 **INSTRUMENTS OF PUNISHMENT** <tool for punishing>
606 **THE PEOPLE** <ordinary people>
607 **SOCIAL CLASS AND STATUS** <social and economic classes>

608	**ARISTOCRACY, NOBILITY, GENTRY**	<highest social class>
609	**POLITICS**	<government-related activity>
610	**POLITICIAN**	<one active in government>
611	**POLITICO-ECONOMIC PRINCIPLES**	<political beliefs>
612	**GOVERNMENT**	<governing systems>
613	**LEGISLATURE, GOVERNMENT ORGANIZATION**	<lawmaking bodies>
614	**UNITED NATIONS, INTERNATIONAL ORGANIZATIONS**	<international relations>
615	**COMMISSION**	<group seeking information>
616	**ASSOCIATE**	<aid to someone in power>
617	**ASSOCIATION**	<organized special-interest group>
618	**WEALTH**	<having money, possessions>
619	**POVERTY**	<lacking money, possessions>
620	**LENDING**	<loaning of money, objects>
621	**BORROWING**	<temporarily using money, objects>
622	**FINANCIAL CREDIT**	<money loaned>
623	**DEBT**	<money owed>
624	**PAYMENT**	<money paid>
625	**NONPAYMENT**	<failure to pay>
626	**EXPENDITURE**	<money spent>
627	**RECEIPTS**	<record of money spent>
628	**ACCOUNTS**	<record of monetary transaction>
629	**TRANSFER OF PROPERTY OR RIGHT**	<property delivered>
630	**PRICE, FEE**	<cost of property>
631	**DISCOUNT**	<lower cost>
632	**EXPENSIVENESS**	<higher cost>
633	**CHEAPNESS**	<lowest cost>
634	**COSTLESSNESS**	<absence of cost>
635	**THRIFT**	<money carefully spent>

Class Ten: Values and Ideals

636	**ETHICS**	<moral values and rules>
637	**RIGHT**	<the good>
638	**WRONG**	<the bad>
639	**DUENESS**	<obligation due>
640	**UNDUENESS**	<undeserved payment>
641	**DUTY**	<moral obligation>
642	**PREROGATIVE**	<right or privilege>
643	**IMPOSITION**	<excessive burden>
644	**PROBITY**	<honest behavior>
645	**IMPROBITY**	<dishonest behavior>
646	**HONOR**	<token of esteem>
647	**INSIGNIA**	<sign of rank, status>
648	**TITLE**	<named rank, status>
649	**JUSTICE**	<fair and moral treatment>
650	**INJUSTICE**	<unfair or immoral treatment>
651	**SELFISHNESS**	<stinginess and disregard for others>
652	**UNSELFISHNESS**	<generosity and regard for others>
653	**VIRTUE**	<moral goodness>
654	**VICE**	<moral badness>
655	**WRONGDOING**	<immoral or illegal behavior>
656	**GUILT**	<sin or breach of law>
657	**INNOCENCE**	<freedom from guilt or sin>

658 **ATONEMENT** <repayment for offense>
659 **GOOD PERSON** <moral person>
660 **BAD PERSON** <immoral person>
661 **DISREPUTE** <lack of good reputation>
662 **REPUTE** <good reputation>
663 **SENSUALITY** <sensual desire>
664 **CHASTITY** <abstention from sexual intercourse>
665 **UNCHASTITY** <partaking often in sexual intercourse>
666 **INDECENCY** <offensive or shocking in nature>
667 **ASCETICISM** <self-denial>
668 **TEMPERANCE** <moderation in action>
669 **INTEMPERANCE** <lack of moderation>
670 **MODERATION** <avoidance of extreme action>
671 **VIOLENCE** <physically harmful action>
672 **GLUTTONY** <excessive eating, drinking>
673 **LEGALITY** <observance of law>
674 **ILLEGALITY** <disobeyance of law>
675 **RELIGIONS, CULTS, SECTS** <belief systems>
676 **THEOLOGY** <study of religion>
677 **DEITY** <a god or worshipped being>
678 **MYTHICAL AND POLYTHEISTIC GODS AND SPIRITS** <gods, goddesses, spirits of mythology>
679 **ANGEL, SAINT** <benevolent beings>
680 **EVIL SPIRITS** <harmful presence>
681 **HEAVEN** <place where God or the good live>
682 **HELL** <place where Satan or the bad live>
683 **SCRIPTURE** <holy writings>
684 **PROPHETS, RELIGIOUS FOUNDERS** <religious leaders>
685 **SANCTITY** <the sacred>
686 **UNSANCTITY** <the profane>
687 **ORTHODOXY** <accepted religious opinions, doctrines>
688 **UNORTHODOXY** <unaccepted opinions, doctrines>
689 **OCCULTISM** <belief in supernatural>
690 **SORCERY** <magic aided by evil spirits>
691 **SPELL, CHARM** <magical words>
692 **PIETY** <religious devotion>
693 **SANCTIMONY** <hypocritical, affected religious devotion>
694 **IMPIETY** <lack of religious devotion>
695 **NONRELIGIOUSNESS** <not believing in religion>
696 **WORSHIP** <reverence for deity>
697 **IDOLATRY** <reverence for idol>
698 **THE MINISTRY** <one who ministers a church>
699 **THE CLERGY** <church service leaders>
700 **THE LAITY** <members of church>
701 **RELIGIOUS RITES** <church ceremonies>
702 **ECCLESIASTICAL ATTIRE** <religious clothing>
703 **RELIGIOUS BUILDINGS** <place of worship>

Class Eleven: Arts

704 **SHOW BUSINESS, THEATER** <theatrical performance>
705 **DANCE** <movement performance>
706 **MOTION PICTURES** <film performance>
707 **ENTERTAINER** <performer>
708 **MUSIC** <musical performance>

709 **HARMONICS, MUSICAL ELEMENTS** <study of musical sound>
710 **MUSICIAN** <musical performer>
711 **MUSICAL INSTRUMENTS** <music-producing devices>
712 **VISUAL ARTS** <art making something to be viewed>
713 **GRAPHIC ARTS** <2D visual art>
714 **PHOTOGRAPHY** <art of taking photos>
715 **SCULPTURE** <art of sculpting>
716 **ARTIST** <maker of art>
717 **ARCHITECTURE, DESIGN** <art of building and decoration>
718 **LITERATURE** <writings in prose or verse>
719 **HISTORY** <chronology of events>
720 **POETRY** <writings in verse>
721 **PROSE** <ordinary writing>
722 **FICTION** <imagined stories>
723 **CRITICISM OF THE ARTS** <artistic judgment>

Class Twelve: Occupations and Crafts

724 **OCCUPATION** <job or profession>
725 **EXERTION** <physical or mental effort>
726 **WORKER, DOER** <one who works>
727 **UNIONISM, LABOR UNION** <workers' rights organization>
728 **MONEY** <pay for goods, services>
729 **FINANCE, INVESTMENT** <money spent and invested>
730 **BUSINESSMAN, MERCHANT** <one who works in or runs business>
731 **COMMERCE, ECONOMICS** <goods and services>
732 **ILLICIT BUSINESS** <illegal activity making money>
733 **PURCHASE** <buying something>
734 **SALE** <selling something>
735 **MERCHANDISE** <goods>
736 **MARKET** <place for selling goods>
737 **STOCK MARKET** <place for trading securities>
738 **SECURITIES** <instruments of investment>
739 **WORKPLACE** <place of employment, work>
740 **WEAVING** <craft of creating fabric>
741 **SEWING** <craft of creating or repairing fabric goods>
742 **CERAMICS** <art of creating things from clay>
743 **AMUSEMENT** <entertaining activity>

Class Thirteen: Sports and Recreation

744 **SPORTS** <physical competitive activity>
745 **BASEBALL** <field game with bat and ball>
746 **FOOTBALL** <field game with spheroidal ball>
747 **BASKETBALL** <court game with ball>
748 **TENNIS** <court game with racket and ball>
749 **HOCKEY** <ice rink game with stick and puck>
750 **BOWLING** <lane game with rolled ball>
751 **GOLF** <course game with clubs and ball>
752 **SOCCER** <field game with round kicked ball>
753 **SKIING** <gliding on snow skis>
754 **BOXING** <fighting with gloved hands>
755 **TRACK AND FIELD** <running, jumping, and throwing activities>
756 **AUTOMOBILE RACING** <racing automobiles>
757 **HORSE RACING** <racing horses>
758 **CARDPLAYING** <games involving card decks>

759 **GAMBLING** <games of chance for money>
760 **OTHER SPORTS** <competitive sporting activities>

Class Fourteen: The Mind and Ideas

761 **EXISTENCE** <state of existing>
762 **NONEXISTENCE** <state of not existing>
763 **SUBSTANTIALITY** <having substance>
764 **UNSUBSTANTIALITY** <lacking substance>
765 **STATE** <mode or condition of being>
766 **CIRCUMSTANCE** <determining condition or factor>
767 **INTRINSICALITY** <essential nature of thing>
768 **EXTRINSICALITY** <external influence on thing>
769 **ACCOMPANIMENT** <going with another>
770 **ASSEMBLAGE** <gathering together>
771 **DISPERSION** <breaking apart and distributing>
772 **INCLUSION** <part of group>
773 **EXCLUSION** <left out of group>
774 **EXTRANEOUSNESS** <outside normal existence>
775 **RELATION** <connection to another>
776 **UNRELATEDNESS** <lack of relation to another>
777 **CORRELATION** <mutual, reciprocal relation>
778 **SAMENESS** <being the same as>
779 **CONTRARIETY** <being opposite or incompatible>
780 **DIFFERENCE** <being different>
781 **UNIFORMITY** <being unvarying, same as others>
782 **NONUNIFORMITY** <being diverse>
783 **MULTIFORMITY** <having many forms>
784 **SIMILARITY** <having characteristics in common>
785 **COPY** <imitating or reproducing>
786 **MODEL** <thing copied>
787 **DISSIMILARITY** <being unlike>
788 **AGREEMENT** <act of agreeing>
789 **DISAGREEMENT** <act of disagreeing>
790 **EQUALITY** <being equal>
791 **INEQUALITY** <being unequal>
792 **WHOLE** <complete amount, totality>
793 **PART** <portion or unit of whole>
794 **COMPLETENESS** <having necessary parts>
795 **INCOMPLETENESS** <lacking parts>
796 **COMPOSITION** <arrangement of parts>
797 **MIXTURE** <proportions of parts>
798 **SIMPLICITY** <without multiple, complicated parts>
799 **COMPLEXITY** <having complicated, interrelated parts>
800 **JOINING** <connecting>
801 **ANALYSIS** <breaking down into parts>
802 **SEPARATION** <disconnecting>
803 **COHESION** <sticking together>
804 **NONCOHESION** <not staying together, loosening>
805 **COMBINATION** <compounding>
806 **DISINTEGRATION** <breaking into small parts>
807 **ORDER** <way something is organized>
808 **ARRANGEMENT** <organizing things>
809 **CLASSIFICATION** <categorizing things>
810 **DISORDER** <lack of order, organization>

811 **DISARRANGEMENT** <bringing into disorder>

812 **CONTINUITY** <uninterrupted order>

813 **DISCONTINUITY** <interrupted order>

814 **PRECEDENCE** <ordered by importance>

815 **SEQUENCE** <order for related things>

816 **PRECURSOR** <one that precedes>

817 **SEQUEL** <one that follows subsequently>

818 **BEGINNING** <first part>

819 **MIDDLE** <intermediate part>

820 **END** <last part>

821 **TIME** <measure of life>

822 **TIMELESSNESS** <lasting forever>

823 **INFINITY** <unlimited time, space>

824 **PERIOD** <portion of time>

825 **SPELL** <portion of time for job, duty>

826 **INTERIM** <intermediate period>

827 **DURATION** <time something exists>

828 **TRANSIENCE** <short duration>

829 **PERPETUITY** <endless duration>

830 **INSTANTANEOUSNESS** <extremely brief duration>

831 **EVENT** <occasion or happening>

832 **MEASUREMENT OF TIME** <time-keeping system>

833 **ANACHRONISM** <error in time placement>

834 **PREVIOUSNESS** <previous time>

835 **SUBSEQUENCE** <later time>

836 **SIMULTANEITY** <occurring at the same time>

837 **THE PAST** <earlier time>

838 **THE PRESENT** <now time>

839 **THE FUTURE** <time to come>

840 **IMMINENCE** <happening soon>

841 **NEWNESS** <coming into existence recently>

842 **OLDNESS** <existing a long time>

843 **TIMELINESS** <occurring at suitable time>

844 **UNTIMELINESS** <occurring at inconvenient time>

845 **EARLINESS** <being early>

846 **LATENESS** <being late>

847 **FREQUENCY** <occurring frequently>

848 **INFREQUENCY** <occurring infrequently>

849 **REPETITION** <repeated occurrence>

850 **REGULARITY OF RECURRENCE** <reoccurring regularly>

851 **IRREGULARITY OF RECURRENCE** <reoccurring irregularly>

852 **CHANGE** <becoming different>

853 **PERMANENCE** <not changing>

854 **CHANGEABLENESS** <changing often or suddenly>

855 **STABILITY** <uneasily changed>

856 **CONTINUANCE** <continuing of action>

857 **CESSATION** <stopping of action>

858 **CONVERSION** <change to something different>

859 **REVERSION** <change to a former state>

860 **REVOLUTION** <sudden, extreme change>

861 **EVOLUTION** <gradual change>

862 **SUBSTITUTION** <change of one thing for another>

863 **INTERCHANGE** <mutual change or exchange>

864 **GENERALITY** <being general rather than specific>

865 **PARTICULARITY** <being specific rather than general>
866 **SPECIALTY** <special knowledge, interest>
867 **CONFORMITY** <behavior like most others>
868 **NONCONFORMITY** <behavior differing from most others>
869 **NORMALITY** <expected condition, situation>
870 **ABNORMALITY** <unexpected condition, situation>
871 **LIST** <series of items>
872 **ONENESS** <state of being one or united into one>
873 **DOUBLENESS** <state of two combined>
874 **DUPLICATION** <two corresponding parts>
875 **BISECTION** <divided into two equal parts>
876 **THREE** <three units or members>
877 **TRIPLICATION** <three corresponding parts>
878 **TRISECTION** <divided into three equal parts>
879 **FOUR** <four units or members>
880 **QUADRUPLICATION** <four corresponding parts>
881 **QUADRISECTION** <divided into four equal parts>
882 **FIVE AND OVER** <five or more units or members>
883 **PLURALITY** <large number or quantity>
884 **NUMEROUSNESS** <great number or quantity>
885 **FEWNESS** <very few in number or quantity>
886 **CAUSE** <reason for action, condition>
887 **EFFECT** <something resulting from cause>
888 **ATTRIBUTION** <assignment of cause>
889 **OPERATION** <performance of practical work>
890 **PRODUCTIVENESS** <operation yielding results>
891 **UNPRODUCTIVENESS** <operation lacking results>
892 **PRODUCTION** <process of making, creating>
893 **PRODUCT** <something made, created>
894 **INFLUENCE** <act or power producing effect>
895 **ABSENCE OF INFLUENCE** <lack of power to create effect>
896 **TENDENCY** <proneness to thought or action>
897 **LIABILITY** <likelihood of an action>
898 **INVOLVEMENT** <engagement in action>
899 **CONCURRENCE** <co-action with another>
900 **COUNTERACTION** <opposite action>
901 **SUPPORT** <assisting action>
902 **IMPULSE, IMPACT** <driving or striking force>
903 **REACTION** <resisting or opposing force>
904 **PUSHING, THROWING** <pressing or hurling force>
905 **PULLING** <force to draw towards>
906 **LEVERAGE** <increase force with machine>
907 **ATTRACTION** <pulling toward>
908 **REPULSION** <pushing away>
909 **EJECTION** <throwing out or away>
910 **OVERRUNNING** <going beyond or past>
911 **SHORTCOMING** <action short of>
912 **ELEVATION** <raising action>
913 **DEPRESSION** <lowering action>
914 **CIRCUITOUSNESS** <circular motion>
915 **ROTATION** <rotating motion>
916 **OSCILLATION** <motion to and fro>
917 **AGITATION** <irregular motion>
918 **SPECTATOR** <one who watches>

919	**INTELLECT**	<mental capacity for knowledge>
920	**INTELLIGENCE, WISDOM**	<mental capacity to apply knowledge>
921	**WISE PERSON**	<person with wisdom>
922	**UNINTELLIGENCE**	<lacking mental capacity>
923	**FOOLISHNESS**	<lacking good sense, judgment>
924	**FOOL**	<one lacking good sense>
925	**SANITY**	<soundness of mind>
926	**INSANITY, MANIA**	<unsoundness of mind>
927	**ECCENTRICITY**	<unusual behavior>
928	**KNOWLEDGE**	<information learned>
929	**INTELLECTUAL**	<learned person>
930	**IGNORANCE**	<lack of knowledge>
931	**THOUGHT**	<process of thinking>
932	**IDEA**	<formulated thought>
933	**ABSENCE OF THOUGHT**	<unthinking>
934	**INTUITION, INSTINCT**	<knowledge through feelings>
935	**REASONING**	<process of logical thinking>
936	**SOPHISTRY**	<clever reasoning>
937	**TOPIC**	<subject thought and talked about>
938	**INQUIRY**	<request for information>
939	**ANSWER**	<response to question>
940	**SOLUTION**	<answer to a problem>
941	**DISCOVERY**	<learning something for the first time>
942	**EXPERIMENT**	<scientific test>
943	**COMPARISON**	<looking for differences, similarities>
944	**DISCRIMINATION**	<critical examination of differences>
945	**INDISCRIMINATION**	<lack of discrimination>
946	**JUDGMENT**	<forming opinion by discerning>
947	**PREJUDGMENT**	<judging before examining>
948	**MISJUDGMENT**	<faulty judgment>
949	**OVERESTIMATION**	<estimating too high>
950	**UNDERESTIMATION**	<estimating too low>
951	**THEORY, SUPPOSITION**	<principles to explain phenomena>
952	**PHILOSOPHY**	<pursuit of wisdom and truth>
953	**BELIEF**	<something accepted or considered true>
954	**CREDULITY**	<willingness to believe>
955	**UNBELIEF**	<unwillingness to believe>
956	**INCREDULITY**	<unwillingness to accept as true or real>
957	**EVIDENCE, PROOF**	<something showing existence or truth>
958	**DISPROOF**	<evidence of falsity>
959	**QUALIFICATION**	<fitting quality or skill>
960	**NO QUALIFICATIONS**	<lack of quality or skill>
961	**FORESIGHT**	<ability to see what might happen>
962	**PREDICTION**	<statement about what might happen>
963	**NECESSITY**	<something necessary>
964	**PREDETERMINATION**	<determining in advance what will happen>
965	**PREARRANGEMENT**	<something arranged in advance>
966	**POSSIBILITY**	<chance something might happen or be true>
967	**IMPOSSIBILITY**	<no change of happening or being true>
968	**PROBABILITY**	<chance that something will happen>
969	**IMPROBABILITY**	<unlikelihood that something will happen>
970	**CERTAINTY**	<something that will definitely happen>
971	**UNCERTAINTY**	<something that is uncertain>
972	**CHANCE**	<something that happens unpredictably>

973	**TRUTH**	<real facts, things that are true>
974	**WISE SAYING**	<statement of rule or moral principle>
975	**ERROR**	<mistake or failure>
976	**ILLUSION**	<false or wrong belief>
977	**DISILLUSIONMENT**	<disenchanted by dashed belief>
978	**MENTAL ATTITUDE**	<beliefs, feelings, and values held>
979	**BROAD-MINDEDNESS**	<tolerant of varied views>
980	**NARROW-MINDEDNESS**	<intolerant of varied views>
981	**CURIOSITY**	<inquisitive interest>
982	**INCURIOSITY**	<lacking normal curiosity>
983	**ATTENTION**	<applying the mind to something>
984	**INATTENTION**	<failure to pay attention>
985	**DISTRACTION, CONFUSION**	<mental confusion and disturbance>
986	**IMAGINATION**	<ability to form original mental image>
987	**UNIMAGINATIVENESS**	<lacking imagination>
988	**SPECTER**	<haunting thought>
989	**MEMORY**	<something remembered, recalled>
990	**FORGETFULNESS**	<failure to remember>
991	**SUFFICIENCY**	<sufficient resources>
992	**INSUFFICIENCY**	<insufficient resources>
993	**EXCESS**	<more resources than necessary>
994	**SATIETY**	<feeling of enough or too much>
995	**EXPEDIENCE**	<well-suited and advisable>
996	**INEXPEDIENCE**	<unsuited and unwise>
997	**IMPORTANCE**	<having worth or consequence>
998	**UNIMPORTANCE**	<lacking worth or consequence>
999	**GOODNESS**	<good quality or effect>
1000	**BADNESS**	<bad quality or effect>
1001	**BANE**	<cause of trouble, annoyance>
1002	**PERFECTION**	<excellence or excellent quality>
1003	**IMPERFECTION**	<lack of perfection or small flaw>
1004	**BLEMISH**	<mark making imperfect>
1005	**MEDIOCRITY**	<quality or state of not being very good>
1006	**DANGER**	<threat of harm, pain, loss>
1007	**SAFETY**	<freedom from danger>
1008	**PROTECTION**	<being kept from danger>
1009	**REFUGE**	<shelter from danger>
1010	**PROSPERITY**	<thriving accompanied by money>
1011	**ADVERSITY**	<misfortune or tragedy>
1012	**HINDRANCE**	<something delaying or preventing progress>
1013	**DIFFICULTY**	<something hard to do or deal with>
1014	**FACILITY**	<something making action easier>
1015	**UGLINESS**	<unpleasant to look at>
1016	**BEAUTY**	<pleasant to look at>

Class Fifteen: Science and Technology

1017	**MATHEMATICS**	<science of numbers, quantities, shapes>
1018	**PHYSICS**	<science of matter and energy>
1019	**HEAT**	<warm, hot temperature>
1020	**HEATING**	<creating warmth, heat>
1021	**FUEL**	<material to create heat or power>
1022	**INCOMBUSTIBILITY**	<material that cannot be burned>
1023	**COLD**	<cool, cold temperature>
1024	**REFRIGERATION**	<creating cold>

1025	**LIGHT**	<energy that makes things visible>
1026	**LIGHT SOURCE**	<device creating illumination>
1027	**DARKNESS, DIMNESS**	<lack of light>
1028	**SHADE**	<blocking of light>
1029	**TRANSPARENCY**	<allowing passage of light>
1030	**SEMITRANSPARENCY**	<imperfectly transparent>
1031	**OPAQUENESS**	<blocking passage of light>
1032	**ELECTRICITY, MAGNETISM**	<form of energy creating current, power, metal attraction>
1033	**ELECTRONICS**	<devices operating using electricity>
1034	**RADIO**	<broadcast of sound using electric signals>
1035	**TELEVISION**	<electronic broadcast of images and sound>
1036	**RADAR, RADIOLOCATORS**	<use of reflecting radio waves for detection>
1037	**RADIATION, RADIOACTIVITY**	<powerful, dangerous form of energy>
1038	**NUCLEAR PHYSICS**	<science of atomic nuclei and their energy>
1039	**MECHANICS**	<science of force and motion>
1040	**TOOLS, MACHINERY**	<apparatus and instruments for power>
1041	**AUTOMATION**	<machines in production process>
1042	**COMPUTER SCIENCE**	<principles and use of computers>
1043	**ENGINEERING**	<science of engines, machines, structures>
1044	**FRICTION**	<force slowing something it touches>
1045	**DENSITY**	<relationship between weight and size, closeness of parts>
1046	**HARDNESS, RIGIDITY**	<firm, solid, unbendable>
1047	**SOFTNESS, PLIANCY**	<not hard, firm, rigid>
1048	**ELASTICITY**	<flexible, returning to shape>
1049	**TOUGHNESS**	<strong, not easily damaged or broken>
1050	**BRITTLENESS, FRAGILITY**	<easily damaged or broken>
1051	**POWDERINESS, CRUMBLINESS**	<easily crushed into tiny pieces>
1052	**MATERIALITY**	<consisting of matter>
1053	**IMMATERIALITY**	<not consisting of matter>
1054	**MATERIALS**	<substance consisting of matter>
1055	**INORGANIC MATTER**	<substance not consisting of living matter>
1056	**OILS, LUBRICANTS**	<liquid, combustible substances>
1057	**RESINS, GUMS**	<semisolid sticky substances>
1058	**MINERALS, METALS**	<substance formed under ground>
1059	**ROCK**	<hard substances on earth's surface>
1060	**CHEMISTRY, CHEMICALS**	<science of substances and their makeup>
1061	**LIQUIDITY**	<being liquid>
1062	**SEMILIQUIDITY**	<somewhat liquid>
1063	**PULPINESS**	<pulverized or mixed with water>
1064	**LIQUEFACTION**	<making or becoming liquid>
1065	**MOISTURE**	<water or liquid in or on something>
1066	**DRYNESS**	<lack of liquid or water>
1067	**VAPOR, GAS**	<substances of particles mixed with air>
1068	**BIOLOGY**	<science of living things>
1069	**AGRICULTURE**	<science of farming>
1070	**ANIMAL HUSBANDRY**	<breeding and caring for animals>
1071	**EARTH SCIENCE**	<sciences of the earth and its parts>
1072	**THE ENVIRONMENT**	<sciences of the ecosystem>
1073	**THE UNIVERSE, ASTRONOMY**	<science of matter outside earth's atmosphere>
1074	**ROCKETRY, MISSILERY**	<use of rockets, missiles>
1075	**SPACE TRAVEL**	<exploration of outer space>

Abbreviations Used in This Book

ADJS	adjectives
ADVS	adverbs
Austral	Australian
Brit	British
Can	Canada, Canadian
CONJS	conjunctions
Fr	France, French
Ger	Germany, German
Gk	Greece, Greek
Heb	Hebrew
INTERJS	interjections
Irl	Ireland, Irish
Ital	Italy, Italian
L	Latin
PHRS	phrases
pl	plural
PREP	prepositions
Russ	Russia, Russian
Scot	Scotland, Scottish
Sp	Spain, Spanish
tm	trademark
US	United States

1 BIRTH

<beginning of life>

NOUNS 1 **birth,** genesis, **nativity,** nascency, **childbirth,** childbearing, having a baby, giving birth, birthing, parturition, biogenesis, the stork, patter of tiny feet; confinement, lying-in, being brought to bed, childbed, *accouchement* <Fr>; **labor,** travail, birth throes, birth pangs; **delivery,** blessed event; the Nativity; multiparity; **hatching;** littering, whelping, farrowing; active birth, alternative birth; natural childbirth; breech birth; obstetrics

VERBS 2 **be born,** have birth, come forth, issue forth, see the light of day, come into the world; **hatch;** be illegitimate, be born out of wedlock, have the bar sinister, be born on the wrong side of the blanket, come in through a side door

3 **give birth, bear,** bear young, have young, have; **have a baby,** bear a child, have children; drop, cast, throw, pup, whelp, kitten, foal, calve, fawn, lamb, cub, yean, farrow, litter, spawn, lay eggs; lie in, be confined, labor, travail

ADJS 4 **born,** given birth, postnatal; **hatched;** bred, begotten, cast, dropped, whelped, foaled, calved; née; newborn; stillborn; **bearing,** giving birth, natal

2 THE BODY

<physical self>

NOUNS 1 **body,** bod, the person, carcass, anatomy, frame, bodily entity, corporal entity, corporeal entity, physical self, physical structure, bodily structure, physique, soma, somatotype, chronotype; torso, trunk; organism, organic complex, flesh and blood; the material, the physical part

2 **skeleton, bones** <see list>, the bones, one's bones, framework, frame, form, structure, shell, bony framework, endoskeleton, bag of bones; axial skeleton, appendicular skeleton, visceral skeleton; rib cage; skeletology; cartilage

3 **muscles** <see list>, the muscles, myon, voluntary muscle, involuntary muscle; **musculature,** physique; **connective tissue,** connectivum, fascia; thew, sinew, tendon, ligament, cartilage

4 **skin,** the skin, dermis, integument, **epidermis,** scarfskin, ecderon; hypodermis, hypoderma; derma, derm, corium, true skin, cutis, cuticle; epithelium, pavement epithelium; endothelium; mesoderm; endoderm, entoderm; blastoderm; ectoderm, epiblast, ectoblast; enderon; connective tissue; age spot, liver spot; acupuncture point, acupoint, touchpoint; stretch marks

5 castoff skin, slough, cast, desquamation, exuviae, molt

6 **membrane,** membrana, pellicle, chorion; basement membrane, membrana propria; allantoic membrane; amnion, amniotic sac, arachnoid membrane; serous membrane, serosa, membrana serosa; **eardrum,** tympanic membrane, tympanum, membrana tympana; mucous membrane; velum; peritoneum; periosteum; pleura; pericardium; meninx, meninges; perineurium, neurilemma; conjunctiva; hymen, maidenhead

7 **member, appendage,** external organ; **head,** noggin, noodle; **arm;** forearm; wrist; elbow; upper arm, biceps; **leg,** limb, shank, gam, pin, legs, wheels; shin, cnemis; ankle, tarsus; calf; knee; thigh, ham; popliteal space; **hand,** paw, finger; **foot,** dog, puppy, toe, big toe, little toe

8 **teeth,** dentition, ivories, choppers, pearly whites; periodontal tissue, alveolar ridge, alveolus; **tooth,** fang, tusk; snag, snaggletooth, peg; bucktooth; pivot tooth; cuspid, bicuspid; canine tooth, canine, dogtooth, eyetooth, carnassial, tush; molar, grinder, gnasher; premolar; incisor, cutter, foretooth; wisdom tooth; milk tooth, baby tooth, deciduous tooth; permanent tooth; crown, cusp, dentine, enamel

9 **eye,** visual organ, organ of vision, oculus, optic, orb, peeper; clear eyes, bright eyes, starry orbs; saucer eyes, banjo eyes, popeyes, goggle eyes; naked eye, unassisted eye, unaided eye; corner of the eye; epicanthus, epicanthic fold; eyeball; retina; lens; cornea; sclera; optic nerve; iris; pupil; eyelid, lid, nictitating membrane; choroid coat, aqueous humor, vitreous humor

10 **ear,** auditory apparatus, hearing organ; external ear, **outer ear;** auricle, pinna; tragus; cauliflower ear; concha, conch, shell; earlobe, lobe, lobule; auditory canal, acoustic meatus, auditory meatus; helix; **middle ear,** tympanic cavity, tympanum; eardrum, drumhead, tympanic membrane; auditory ossicles; malleus, hammer, incus, anvil; stapes, stirrup; mastoid process; eustachian tube, auditory tube; **inner ear;** round window, secondary eardrum; oval window; bony labyrinth, membraneous labyrinth, utricle; perilymph, endolymph; vestibule; semicircular canals; cochlea; basilar membrane, organ of Corti; auditory nerve, acoustic nerve

11 **nose**, nasal organ, snout, smeller, proboscis, beak, schnoz, muzzle; nostril, naris, nasal cavity; olfactory nerve

12 **mouth,** oral cavity; lips, tongue, taste buds; mandible, jaw, jawline; maw; gums, periodontal tissue; uvula; teeth

13 **genitals,** genitalia, sex organs, reproductive organs, pudenda, private parts, privy parts; privates, meat, naughty bits; crotch, groin, pubic region, perineum, pelvis; **male organs; penis,** phallus, glans penis; gonads; **testes, testicles,** balls, nuts, rocks, ballocks, nads, family jewels; spermary; scrotum, bag, basket; vas deferens; **female organs; vulva,** cunt*; **vagina;** clitoris, glans clitoridis; labia, labia majora, labia minora, lips, nymphae; cervix; ovary; uterus, womb, fallopian tubes; secondary sex characteristic; mons pubis, mons veneris, pubic hair, beard; breasts

14 **nervous system,** nerves, central nervous system, peripheral nervous system; autonomic nervous system; sympathetic nervous system, thoracolumbar nervous system; parasympathetic nervous system, craniosacral nervous system; **nerve;** neuron; nerve cell, sensory neuron, afferent neuron, sensory cell; motor neuron; association neuron, internuncial neuron; nerve fiber, axon, dendrite, myelin sheath, medullary sheath; **synapse;** effector organ; nerve trunk; **ganglion;** plexus, solar plexus; **spinal cord**

15 **brain,** encephalon; cerebrum, cerebellum, cerebral matter; right brain, left brain; neuroplasticity

16 **internal organs,** viscera, vitals, insides, innards, entrails, inwards, internals, thoracic viscera, abdominal viscera; inner mechanism, works; peritoneum, peritoneal cavity; guts, kishkes, giblets; **heart,** ticker, pump, endocardium, atria, ventricles, aorta; **lung, lungs; liver;** gallbladder; spleen; pancreas; kidney, **kidneys;** urethra, urinary tract

17 **digestion,** ingestion, assimilation, absorption; primary digestion, secondary digestion, peristalsis; predigestion; salivary digestion, gastric digestion, peptic digestion, pancreatic digestion, intestinal digestion; digestive system, alimentary canal, gastrointestinal tract; salivary glands, gastric glands, liver, pancreas; digestive secretions, saliva, gastric juice, pancreatic juice, intestinal juice, bile

18 **digestive system**, mouth, maw, salivary glands; gullet, crop, craw, **throat,** pharynx; esophagus, gorge, wizen; fauces, isthmus of the fauces; **abdomen; stomach, belly**, **midriff,** diaphragm; swollen belly, distended belly, protruding belly, prominent belly, beer belly, love handles, *embonpoint* <Fr>, **paunch,** ventripotence; underbelly; pylorus; **intestine,** intestines, entrails, **bowels;** small intestine, villus, odenum, jejunum, ileum; blind gut, cecum; foregut, hindgut; midgut, mesogaster; **appendix,** vermiform appendix, vermiform process; large intestine, colon, sigmoid flexure, rectum; anus

19 **<stomach terms>** goozle, guzzle; tum, tummy, tum-tum, breadbasket, gut, bulge, fallen chest, corporation, spare tire, bay window, pot, potbelly, potgut, beerbelly, German goiter, Milwaukee goiter, pusgut, swagbelly; guts, tripes, stuffings

20 **metabolism,** metabolic process; basal metabolism, acid-base metabolism, energy metabolism; **anabolism,** substance metabolism, constructive metabolism, assimilation; **catabolism,** destructive metabolism, disassimilation; endogenous metabolism, exogenous metabolism; pharmacokinetic metabolism; uricotelic metabolism; metabolic rate

21 **breathing, respiration,** aspiration, inspiration, **inhalation;** expiration, **exhalation;** insufflation, exsufflation; **breath,** wind, breath of air; three-part breath; pant, puff; wheeze, asthmatic wheeze; broken wind; gasp, gulp; snoring, snore, stertor; sniff, sniffle, snuff, snuffle; sigh, suspiration; sneeze, sternutation; cough, hack; hiccup; **artificial respiration,** kiss of life, mouth-to-mouth resuscitation; anaerobic respiration

22 **respiratory system, lungs,** bellows; diaphragm; **windpipe, trachea,** wizen; bronchus, bronchi <pl>, bronchial tube; epiglottis

23 **duct,** vessel, canal, passage; gland; vasculature, vascularity, vascularization; vas, meatus; thoracic duct, lymphatic; emunctory; pore; urethra, urete; vagina; oviduct, fallopian tube; salpinx; eustachian tube; ostium; fistula; **blood vessel; artery,** aorta, pulmonary artery, carotid, carotid artery; **vein,** jugular vein, vena cava, pulmonary vein; portal vein, varicose vein; venation; **capillary;** arteriole, veinlet, veinule, venule

24 **body fluid, bodily fluid,** humor, **lymph,** chyle, choler, yellow bile, black bile; rheum; serous fluid, serum; plasma; **pus, matter,** purulence; suppuration; ichor, sanies; discharge; gleet, leukorrhea, the whites; mucus; **phlegm,** snot; **saliva,** spit; **urine,** piss*; **perspiration, sweat; tear,** teardrop, lachryma; milk, mother's milk, colostrum, lactation; **semen**; cerumen, earwax

25 **blood,** whole blood, lifeblood, vital fluid, venous blood, arterial blood, gore; ichor, humor; grume; serum, blood serum; blood substitute; plasma, synthetic plasma, plasma substitute, dextran, clinical dextran; **blood cell,** blood corpuscle, hemocyte; **red corpuscle**, red blood cell, erythrocyte; **white corpuscle, white blood cell,** leukocyte, blood platelet; **hemoglobin;** blood pressure; circulation; blood group, **blood type** <see list>; Rh-type, Rh-positive, Rh-negative; **Rh factor**, Rhesus factor; antigen, antibody, isoantibody, globulin; opsonin; blood grouping; blood count; hematoscope, hematoscopy, hemometer; bloodstream; blood alcohol

ADJS 26 **skeleton, skeletal; bone,** osteal; **bony,** osseous, ossiferous; ossicular; ossified; **spinal,** myelic; **muscle, muscular,** myoid; cartilage, cartilaginous

27 **cutaneous,** cuticular; skinlike, skinny; skin-deep; **epidermal,** epidermic, ecderonic; hypodermic, hypodermal, subcutaneous; dermal, dermic; ectodermal, ectodermic; endermic, endermatic; cortical; epicarpal; testaceous; membranous

28 **optic,** eye, ophthalmic, optical; visual; **ear,** otic; aural

29 **genital;** phallic, penile, penial; testicular; scrotal; spermatic, seminal; vulvar, vulval; vaginal; clitoral; cervical; ovarian; uterine; reproductive, generative, hormonal, sexual

30 **nerve, neural,** neurological; **brain, cerebral,** cerebellar, nervous, synaptic

31 **digestive;** stomachal, stomachic, abdominal; ventral, celiac, **gastric,** ventricular; big-bellied; **metabolic,** basal metabolic, anabolic, catabolic; assimilative, dissimilative; beer-bellied

32 **respiratory,** breathing; inspiratory, expiratory; nasal, rhinal; bronchial, tracheal; **lung,** pulmonary, pulmonic, pneumonic; puffing, huffing, snorting, wheezing, wheezy, asthmatic, stertorous, snoring, panting, heaving; sniffy, sniffly, sniffling, snuffy, snuffly, snuffling; sneezy, sternutative, sternutatory, errhine; breathable

33 **circulatory, vascular,** vascularized, circulating; vasiform; venous, veinal, venose; capillary; arterial, aortic; **blood,** hematal, hematic; bloody, gory, sanguinary; lymphatic, rheumy, humoral, phlegmy, ichorous, serous, sanious; chylific, chylifactive, chylifactory; **puslike,** purulent; suppurated, suppurating, suppurative; teary, tearing, tearlike, **lachrymal,** lacrimal, lacrimatory; mucous; sweaty, perspiring; urinary

34 **blood type**

A-
A+
AB-
AB+
B-
B+
O-
O+
Rh-negative
Rh-positive

35 **bones**

acetabulum
aitchbone
alveolar bone
anvil
astragalus, anklebone
backbone, spine, spinal column, myel
basilar bone, basioccipital bone
calcaneus
cannon bone
carpal, carpus
cheekbone
chin
clavicle
coccyx
collarbone
costa
cranial bones
cranium
cuboid
edgebone
ethmoid bone
femur, thighbone
fibula, calf bone
floating rib
frontal bone
funny bone, crazy bone
gladiolus
hallux
hammer
haunch bone
heel bone
hipbone
humerus
hyoid, lingual bone
ilium
incus
inferior maxillary
innominate bone
intermaxillary, premaxillary, incisive bone
interparietal bone, incarial bone
ischium
lacrimal bone
lenticular bone, os orbiculare
lentiform bone, pisiform bone, postular bone
malar bone, zygomatic bone
malleus
mandible, maxilla, jawbones
mastoid
maxillary
metacarpal, metacarpus
metatarsal, metatarsus
multangular bone large, trapezium
multangular bone small, trapezoid
nasal bone
occipital bone
palate bone
parietal bone
patella, kneecap, whirl bone
pelvis
periotic bone, otocrane
petrosal, petrous bone
phalanx, phalanges
pterygoid bone
pubis
pyramidal bone, os triquetrum
rachidial
rachis, vertebral column
radius
rib
sacrum, resurrection bone
scaphoid bone
scapula
semilunar bone
sesamoid bones
shinbone
shoulder blade
skull
sphenoid bone
stapes
sternum, breastbone
stirrup
sutural bone, wormian bone
talus
tarsal, tarsus
temporal bone
tibia
ulna
vertebra
vomer
wristbone
zygomatic

36 **muscles**

abdominal, abs
anterior tibial
biceps brachii
biceps femoris
crural ligaments soleus
deltoid
erector
external oblique
extensor
fascia lata
flexor
gastrocnemius
gluteus maximus
gracilis
hamstring
latissimus dorsi
pectoralis major
pectoralis minor
quadriceps
rectus abdominis
rectus femoris
rotator cuff
sartorius
sternomastoid

tendon of Achilles, Achilles tendon
trapezius
triceps brachii, triceps

3 HAIR

<threadlike growth from skin>

NOUNS 1 **hairiness,** shagginess, hirsuteness, pilosity, fuzziness, frizziness, **furriness,** downiness, fluffiness, woolliness, fleeciness, bristliness, stubbliness, burrheadedness, mopheadedness, shockheadedness; crinosity, hispidity, villosity; hypertrichosis, pilosis, pilosism

2 **hair,** pile, **fur,** coat, pelt, fleece, fuzz, wool, camel's hair, horsehair, hide; **mane;** shag, tousled hair, matted hair, mat of hair; pubescence, pubes, pubic hair; hairlet, villus, capillament, cilium, ciliolum; seta, setula; bristle

3 gray hair, grizzle, silver hair, silvery hair, white hair, salt-and-pepper hair, graying temples

4 **head of hair,** head, crine; crop, crop of hair, mat, elflock, thatch, mop, shock, shag, fleece, **mane;** locks, tresses, crowning glory, helmet of hair

5 **lock, tress;** flowing locks, flowing tresses; **curl, ringlet,** wisp; earlock, payess; lovelock; frizz, frizzle; crimp; ponytail

6 **tuft,** flock, fleck; forelock, widow's peak, crest, quiff, fetlock, cowlick; bang, **bangs,** fringe

7 **braid,** plait, twist; **pigtail,** rat's-tail, rat-tail, tail; queue, cue; coil, knot; topknot, scalplock, bunches; bun, chignon; widow's peak; dreadlock, cornrow

8 **beard, whiskers,** facial hair; full beard, chin whiskers, side whiskers; **sideburns,** burnsides, muttonchops**; goatee,** tuft; imperial, Vandyke, spade beard; adolescent beard, pappus, down, peach fuzz; **stubble,** bristles, five o'clock shadow, designer stubble

9 **<plant beard>** awn, brush, arista, pile, pappus, nettle

10 **<animal and insect whiskers>** tactile process, tactile hair, feeler, antenna, vibrissa; barb, barbel, barbule, tentacle, palpus; cat whisker

11 **mustache,** mustachio, soup-strainer, mustachios, toothbrush, handlebars, handlebar mustache, Fu Manchu mustache, Zapata mustache, walrus mustache, tash

12 **eyelashes,** lashes, cilia; **eyebrows,** brows

13 false hair, hair extensions, extension, switch, fall, chignon, rat; false eyelashes

14 **wig,** peruke, **toupee,** hairpiece, rug, hair extensions, hair weave, merkin, periwig; doormat

15 **hairdo,** do, **hairstyle, haircut, coiffure,** coif, headdress; wave; marcel, marcel wave; **permanent,** permanent wave; home permanent; cold wave; blow-drying, finger-drying

16 **feather,** plume, pinion; quill; pinfeather; contour feather, penna, down feather, plume feather, plumule, tail feather; filoplume; hackle; scapular; crest, tuft, topknot; panache

17 **<feather parts>** quill, calamus, barrel; barb, shaft, barbule, barbicel, cilium, filament, filamentule, plumule

18 **plumage,** feathers, feather, feathering; contour feathers; breast feathers, mail; hackle; flight feathers; remiges, primaries, secondaries, tertiaries; covert, tectrices; speculum, wing bay

19 **down,** fluff, flue, floss, fuzz, fur, pile, fleece, fine hair; eiderdown, eider; swansdown; thistledown; lint

VERBS 20 **grow hair,** sprout hair; whisker, bewhisker

21 **feather,** fledge, feather out; sprout wings

22 **style the hair,** cut the hair, dress the hair, trim, **barber,** coiffure, coif, shape the hair; pompadour, wave, marcel; process, conk**; bob, shingle**

ADJS 23 **hairlike,** trichoid, capillary; filamentous, filamentary, filiform; bristlelike

24 **hairy,** hirsute, barbigerous, crinose, crinite, pubescent; pilose, pilous, pileous; **furry,** furred; bushy; villous; villose; ciliate, cirrose; hispid, hispidulous, setal; woolly, fleecy, lanate, lanated, flocky, flocculent, floccose; woolly-headed, woolly-haired, ulotrichous; tufty, shaggy, shagged; matted, tomentose; mopheaded, burrheaded, shockheaded, unshorn; **bristly**; fuzzy

25 **bearded,** whiskered, whiskery, **bewhiskered,** barbate, barbigerous; mustached, mustachioed; awned, awny, pappose; goateed; unshaved, **unshaven;** stubbled, stubbly, bristly

26 **wigged,** periwigged, peruked, toupeed

27 **feathery,** plumy; hirsute; featherlike, plumelike, pinnate, pennate; downy, fluffy, nappy, velvety, peachy, fuzzy, flossy, furry

28 **feathered,** plumaged, flighted, pinioned, plumed, pennate, plumate, plumose

29 **tufted,** crested, topknotted

4 CLOTHING MATERIALS

<cloth or fabric>

NOUNS 1 **material, fabric** <see list>, **cloth, textile,** textile fabric, texture, tissue, stuff, weave, weft, woof, web, goods, drapery; *étoffe, tissu* <Fr>; fiber, thread, yarn, rope; napery, table linen, felt; silk; lace; cotton; wool; polyester; nylon; rag, rags

2 **fur, pelt, hide,** coat, fell, fleece, vair <heraldry>; imitation fur, fake fur, synthetic fur; furring; peltry, skin, skins; **leather** <see list>, rawhide; imitation leather, leather paper, leatherette

3 fabric

acetate
acrylic
alpaca
angora
astrakhan
baize
balbriggan
baldachin
barathea
batik
batiste
bayadere
bengaline
bombazine
boucle
brilliantine
broadcloth
brocade
brocatel, brocatelle
buckram
bunting
burlap
byssus
calico
cambric
camel hair, camel's hair
candlewick
Canton crepe
canvas
cashmere
castor
challis
chambray
charmeuse
cheesecloth
chenille
cheviot
chiffon
chinchilla
chino
chintz
cire
cloque
cloth
combing wool
cord
corduroy
cotton
cotton wool
Courtelle
crash
crepe de Chine
cretonne
Crimplene
crinoline
Dacron
damask
denim
dimity
doeskin
Donegal tweed
drill
drugget
duck
duffel, duffle
dungaree
duetyn, duvetyne
ecru
faille
felt
flannel
flannelette
fleece
foulard
frieze
fustian
gabardine
galatea
gauze
Georgette
gingham
gossamer
grenadine
grogram
grosgrain
gunny
haircloth
Harris tweed
herringbone
homespun
honan
hopsack
horsehair
houndstooth
huckaback
jaconet
jacquard
jardiniere
jean
jersey
jute
khaki
lace
lame
lawn
leatherette
linen
linsey-woolsey
lisle
lisse
loden
Lurex
mackinaw
mackintosh, macintosh
madras
maline
marocain
marquisette
Marseille, Marseilles
mat
melton
merino
mesh
messaline
mohair
moire
moleskin
monk's cloth
moquette
mousseline
muslin
nainsook
nankeen
net, netting
ninon
nylon
oilcloth
oilskin
organdy
organza
organzine
paisley
panne
paramatta
percale
percaline
petersham
Pima
pique
plaid
plush
polar fleece
polyester
pongee
poplin
Primaloft
prunella
quilting
ragg
ratine
rayon
rep
ruched
russet
sackcloth
sacking
sailcloth
samite
sarcenet
sateen
satin
scrim
seersucker
serge
shalloon
shantung
sharkskin
sheer
Shetland wool
shoddy
shot silk
silk
spandex
stockinette
suede
sunwashed
supima
surah
swansdown
swanskin
tabaret
tabby
taffeta
tapestry
terry cloth
ticking
tiffany
toile
toweling
tricot
tricotine
tulle
tussah
tweed
twill
velour
velvet
velveteen
Venetian cloth
vicuna
voile
webbing
whipcord
wool
worsted

4 leather

alligator
buckskin
buff
cabretta
calf leather
capeskin
chamois, chammy
chamois skin
chevrette
Cordovan
cowhide
deerskin
doeskin
goatskin
grain leather
horsehide

kid
lambskin
levant morocco
mocha
morocco
nappa
nubuck
oxhide
patent leather
pebble leather
pigskin
pig suede
rawhide
Russian leather
saddle leather
shagreen
sheepskin
snakeskin
sole leather, shoe leather
stirrup leather
suède, suede
tawed leather
whitleather, white leather

5 CLOTHING

<*bodily covering*>

NOUNS 1 **clothing, clothes, apparel,** wear, wearing apparel, daywear, dress, dressing, raiment, garmenture, garb, attire, array, habit, habiliment, fashion, style, guise, costume, costumery, gear, toilette, trim, bedizenment; vestment, vesture, investment, investiture, canonicals, liturgical garment; **garments,** robes, robing, rags, drapery, finery, feathers; toggery, togs, duds, threads, sportswear; work clothes, fatigues; linen; menswear, men's clothing, womenswear, women's clothing; unisex clothing; latest fashion; retro-fashion; new black; fashion roadkill, granny chic, geek chic; fashionista, shoebie; dress code

2 **wardrobe,** furnishings, things, accouterments, trappings, gear; **outfit,** livery, harness, caparison; turnout, getup, rig, rig-out; wedding clothes, bridal outfit, trousseau; maternity clothes; wardrobe basic, standard issue

3 **garment,** vestment, vesture, robe, frock, gown, rag

4 **ready-made,** ready-to-wear, off-the-rack clothes, off-the-peg clothes, store clothes, store-bought clothes, wash-and-wear, dry goods

5 **rags,** tatters, secondhand clothes, seconds, old clothes, castoff clothes, preowned clothing, consignment clothes, Goodwill clothes; worn clothes, hand-me-downs, reach-me-downs, castoffs; slops

6 **suit** <see list>, suit of clothes, set of clothes, ensemble; frock, dress, rig, costume, habit, bib and tucker

7 **uniform** <see list>, livery, monkey suit; nurse's uniform, police officer's uniform; athletic team uniform, baseball uniform; army uniform, army fatigues, standard issue

8 **mufti,** civilian dress, civilian clothes, civvies, cits, plain clothes

9 **costume,** costumery, character dress; outfit, getup, rig; masquerade, disguise, mask; tights, leotards; ballet skirt, tutu, bodysuit; motley, cap and bells; silks; buskin

10 **finery,** frippery, fancy dress, fine feather, full feather, investiture, regalia, caparison, fig, full fig; best clothes, best bib and tucker; Sunday best, Sunday clothes, Sunday-go-to-meeting clothes, Sunday-go-to-meetings, glad rags, ostrich feathers, party dress, dress-up clothes, dressy clothes; power dressing, dressing up

11 **formal dress,** formals, evening dress, evening wear, full dress, dress clothes, white tie and tails, soup-and-fish; dinner clothes; dress suit, full-dress suit, tailcoat, tails; tuxedo, tux, dinner jacket; **regalia,** court dress; dress uniform, full-dress uniform, special full-dress uniform, social full-dress uniform; whites, dress whites, white tie; evening gown, dinner dress, dinner gown; prom dress, ball dress; morning dress, morning coat; semiformal dress; black tie, bow tie, cummerbund

12 **cloak, overgarment** <see list>

13 **outerwear; coat, jacket** <see list>; **overcoat,** greatcoat, topcoat, surcoat; rainwear; rain gear, raincoat, slicker, rainsuit, foul weather gear

14 **vest,** waistcoat, weskit; down vest

15 **shirt** <see list>, waist, shirtwaist, linen, sark; **blouse,** bodice; pullover, shell, T-shirt; dickey; **sweater** <see list>

16 **dress, skirt** <see list>, gown, frock; shift

17 **apron,** *tablier* <Fr>; pinafore, bib, tucker; smock

18 **pants, trousers** <see list>, pair of trousers, pair of pants, breeches, britches, pantaloons; jeans, designer jeans, blue jeans, dungarees; **slacks;** khakis, chinos; corduroys, cords, flannels, ducks, pinstripes, bellbottoms, hiphuggers, Capri pants, Capris, pegged pants, pedal pushers, leggings, overalls, knickers, jodhpurs, sweatpants, cargo pants, carpenter pants; shorts, short pants, Bermuda shorts, hot pants, Jamaica shorts, surfer shorts, board shorts, short shorts, cycling shorts, gym shorts

19 **waistband, belt**; sash, cummerbund; loincloth, breechcloth, breechclout, waistcloth, G-string, loinguard, dhoti, moocha

20 **dishabille,** *déshabillé* <Fr>, **undress,** something more comfortable; negligee, *négligé* <Fr>; wrap, wrapper; sport clothes, playwear, activewear, sportswear, casual wear, leisurewear, **casual clothes,** casual dress, fling-on clothes, loungewear, plain clothes, dress-down clothes, knock-around clothes, grubbies; business casual; dress-down day, casual day, Casual Friday

21 **nightwear** <see list>, nightclothes, sleepwear; nightdress, nightgown, **nightie,** negligee, nightshirt, caftan; **pajamas,** pjs, pyjamas; sleepers; robe, bed jacket

22 **underclothes,** underclothing, **undergarment** <see list>, underthings, bodywear, **underwear,** undies, skivvies, BVD <tm>, briefs, boxers, boxer briefs, bikini briefs, body clothes, smallclothes, unmentionables, tighty whities, intimate apparel, lingerie, linen, underlinen; flannels, woolens, long johns; shapewear

23 **corset,** stays, foundation garment, corselet; girdle, undergirdle, panty girdle; garter belt

24 **brassiere, bra,** sports bra, bandeau, crop top, underbodice, push-up bra; padded bras, falsies

25 **headdress,** headgear, headwear, headclothes; **millinery;** headpiece, chapeau, **cap, hat,** helmet; bonnet, stocking cap, cowboy hat, ten-gallon hat, visor, baseball cap, Panama hat, skull cap; lid; headcloth, kerchief, bandanna, coverchief; handkerchief

26 **veil,** veiling, veiler, net; yashmak, chador; mantilla

27 **footwear,** footgear, *chaussure* <Fr>; **shoes, boots,** overshoes; cowboy boots; clodhoppers, gunboats, wafflestompers, shitkickers*, work shoes; oxfords, saddle shoes, pumps, slides, flats, slingbacks, espadrilles; high heels, kitten heels, spike heels; platform shoes, penny loafers, loafers, boat shoes, deck shoes; sandals, flip-flops, zoris, jellies, jelly shoes; athletic shoes, tennis shoes, sneakers, court shoes; wooden shoes, clogs; slippers, moccasin, moc

28 **hosiery** <see list>, legwear, pantyhose, hose, stockings, nylons; **socks**

29 **swimwear; bathing suit,** swimsuit, swimming suit, swimming costume; tank suit, tank top, maillot, *maillot de bain* <Fr>, one-piece suit, two-piece suit; **trunks,** swimming trunks, swim trunks, bathing trunks, surfer shorts, surf shorts; bikini, string bikini, string, thong; wet suit; coverup

30 **children's wear;** rompers, jumpers; creepers, onesie; layette, baby clothes, infantwear, infants' wear, baby linen; swaddling clothes, swaddle

31 **clothing accessory**, accessory, scarf, belt, glove, mitten, handkerchief, sunglasses, jewelry; neckwear, tie, necktie; collar, dickey; awareness ribbon

32 garment-making, **tailoring; dressmaking,** the rag trade, fashion design, haute couture, Seventh Avenue, the garment industry, Garment District; **millinery,** hatmaking, hatting; hosiery; **shoemaking**, bootmaking, cobbling; habilimentation

33 **clothier,** haberdasher, outfitter; costumier, costumer; glover; hosier; furrier; dry goods dealer; draper, mercer <Brit>

34 **garmentmaker,** garmentworker, needleworker; cutter, stitcher, finisher

35 **tailor,** tailoress, sartor; fitter; busheler, bushelman; furrier, cloakmaker, outfitter

36 **dressmaker**, modiste; *couturière, couturier* <Fr>; fashion designer; seamstress

37 **hatter,** hatmaker, **milliner**

38 **shoemaker,** bootmaker, booter, cobbler

VERBS **39** **clothe,** enclothe, **dress,** garb, attire, tire, array, apparel, raiment, garment, habilitate, tog, tog out, dud, robe, enrobe, invest, endue, deck, bedeck, dight, rag out, rag up; drape, bedrape; wrap, enwrap, lap, envelop, sheathe, shroud, enshroud; wrap up, bundle up; swathe, swaddle

40 **cloak,** mantle; coat, jacket; gown, frock; breech; shirt; hat, coif, bonnet, cap, hood; boot, shoe; stocking, sock

41 **outfit;** equip, accouter, uniform, caparison, rig, rig out, rig up, fit, fit out, turn out, costume, habit, suit; design; **tailor,** tailor-make, custom-make, make to order

42 **dress up,** get up, doll up, spruce up, primp, prink, prank, gussy up, spiff up, fancy up, slick up, pretty up, deck out, deck up, trick out, trick up, tog out, tog up, rag out, rag up, fig out, fig up; dress to kill, titivate, bedeck, dizen, bedizen; overdress; put on the dog, style; **dress down,** underdress

43 **don, put on,** slip on, slip into, get on, get into, try on, assume, dress in, adorn, dight; change; suit up

44 **wear, have on,** dress in, be dressed in, put on, slip on, affect, sport; change into; try on

ADJS **45** **clothed,** clothing**;** dress, vestiary, sartorial; clad, dressed, attired, togged, tired, arrayed, garbed, garmented, habited, habilimented, decked, bedecked, decked-out, turned-out, tricked-out, rigged-out, vested, vestmented, robed, gowned, raimented, appareled, invested, endued, liveried, uniformed; costumed, in costume, cloaked, mantled, disguised; breeched, trousered, pantalooned; coifed, capped, bonneted, hatted, hooded; shod, shoed, booted, *chaussé* <Fr>

46 **dressed up,** dolled up, spruced up; spiffed up, fancied up, slicked up, gussied up; spruce, dressed to advantage, dressed to the nines, dressed to kill, fit to kill; in Sunday best, in one's best bib and tucker, in fine feather, in high feather; in full dress, in full feather, in white tie and tails, in tails; well-dressed, chic, *soigné* <Fr>, stylish, modish, well-turned, well turned-out, tres chic; retro-chic; dressy; overdressed

47 **in dishabille,** *en déshabillé* <Fr>, in negligee; **casual,** nonformal, dressed-down, sporty, in one's shirtsleeves; baggy, sloppy; skintight, decollete, low-necked, low-cut; underdressed, half-dressed

48 tailored, custom-made, tailor-made, made-to-order, bespoke; ready-made, store-bought, off-the-rack, ready-to-wear; vestmental; sartorial

49 cloak, overgarment

academic gown
academic hood
academic robe
Afghan coat
bachelor's gown
burnoose
caftan
cap and gown
cape
capelet
capote
capuchin
cardinal
cashmere shawl
cassock
chlamys
cowl
doctor's gown
domino
duster
frock
gaberdine
haik
houppelande
Inverness cape
judge's robe, judge's gown
kaftan
kimono
kirtle
manta
manteau
mantelet
mantelletta
mantellone
mantilla
mantle
mantua
master's gown
military cloak
monk's robe
opera cloak, opera cape
pallium
pelerine
pelisse
peplos
peplum
plaid
poncho
robe
roquelaure
sagum
serape
shador
shawl
shoulderette
slop
smock
soutane
stole
tabard
talma
tippet
toga
toga virilis
tunic
wraparound
wrapover
wrapper
wrap-up

50 coat, jacket

anorak
balmacaan
benjamin
blanket coat
blazer
blouse
body-coat
bolero
bomber jacket
box coat
Burberry <tm>
bush jacket
camelhair coat
capote
capuchin
car coat
chesterfield
clawhammer coat, clawhammer
cloth coat
coach coat
coatee
coolie jacket, cookie coat
cutaway coat, cutaway
denim jacket, jean jacket
dinner coat, dinner jacket
dolman
double-breasted jacket
doublet
down jacket
dreadnought
dress coat
dressing jacket
duffle coat
duster
Eton jacket
fearnought
fingertip coat
fitted coat
flak jacket
fleece jacket
frock coat, frock
fur coat
fur-lined coat
fur-trimmed coat
greatcoat
hacking jacket
happi coat
Inverness
jerkin
jumper
leather coat
loden coat
London Fog <tm>
long coat
lounging jacket
mackinaw, mackinaw coat
mackintosh, mac
macfarlane
Mao jacket
maxicoat
mess jacket
midicoat
monkey jacket
morning coat
Nehru jacket
Newmarket, Newmarket coat
Norfolk jacket
oilskins
paletot
parka
peacoat, pea jacket
pilot jacket
Prince Albert, Prince Albert coat
raglan
raincoat
redingote
reefer, reefer jacket
sack, sack coat
safari jacket
sanbenito
shawl
shell jacket
shirtjac, shirt jacket
shooting jacket
single-breasted jacket
ski jacket
sleeve waistcoat
slicker
slip-on
smoking jacket
sou'wester
spencer
spiketail
sports coat, sport coat
sports jacket, sport jacket
suit coat
surtout
swagger coat
swallow-tailed coat, swallowtail
sweater coat
swing coat
tabard
tailcoat, tails
topcoat
topper
trench coat
tuxedo coat, tuxedo jacket
ulster
watch coat
waterproof
windbreaker
winter coat
woolly
wraparound, wrap

51 dress, skirt

A-line skirt
ballet skirt
backwrap
ballgown
body dress
bridal gown
cheongsam
chiton
coat dress
cocktail dress
crinoline
culottes, divided skirt
dinner dress, dinner gown
dirndl
evening dress
farthingale
formal
full skirt
gown, evening gown
granny dress
grass skirt
harem skirt
hobble skirt
hoop skirt
housedress
hula skirt
jumper
kilt, filibeg, tartan
kimono
kirtle
little black dress
mantua
maternity dress
maxiskirt
microskirt, microminiskirt
midiskirt
miniskirt
Mother Hubbard

muu-muu
overdress
overskirt
pannier
pantdress
pantskirt
peplum
petticoat
pinafore
pleated skirt
poodle skirt
princess dress
prom dress
sack
sari
sarong
sheath
shift
shirtdress, shirtwaist dress
skort
slit skirt
sundress
sweater dress
tank dress
T-dress
tea gown
tent dress
tube dress
tunic dress
tutu
wedding dress
wrap dress
wrap skirt, wraparound

52 hosiery
anklets, ankle socks
argyles
athletic socks
bobbysocks
body stocking
boothose
boot socks
crew socks
dress sheers
fishnet stockings
footlets
full-fashioned stockings
garter stockings
hose
knee-highs
kneesocks
leggings
leg warmers
lisle hose
nylons
pantyhose
Peds <tm>
rayon stockings
seamless stockings
sheer stockings, sheers
silk stockings
slouch socks
socks
stocking hose
stockings
stretch stockings
support hose
sweat socks
tights
tube socks
varsity socks
wigglers, toe socks
work socks

53 nightwear
baby doll pajamas
bathrobe
bed gown
bed jacket
dishabille
dressing gown
dressing jacket
housecoat
jammies, pj's
lounging pajamas
morning dress
negligee
nightgown
nightie
nightshirt
pajamas
peignor
robe
robe de chambre
romper
sleeper
smoking jacket

54 shirt
aloha shirt, Hawaiian shirt
bandeau
basque
benjamin
blouse
blouson
body shirt
bodysuit
bush shirt
bustier
button-down, button down
camp shirt
chambray shirt
coat shirt
crop top
denim shirt
dickey
doublet
dress shirt
evening shirt
flannel shirt
garibaldi shirt
golf shirt
habit shirt
hair shirt
halter, halter top
hoodie
jersey
lawn shirt
long-sleeved shirt
middy blouse
muscle shirt
olive-drab shirt, OD shirt
overblouse
Oxford shirt
polo shirt
pourpoint
pullover
rugby shirt
sark
shell
shirt jacket, shirt jac
shirtwaist
short-sleeved shirt
sleeveless shirt
sport shirt
sweatshirt
tank top
tee-shirt, T-shirt
three-quarter sleeve shirt
top
tube top
tunic
turtleneck
workshirt

55 suit
bodysuit
boiler suit
business suit
camouflage suit, camo
casual suit
catsuit
coordinates
coveralls
double-breasted suit
dress suit
ensemble
flight suit
jumpsuit
leisure suit
livery
lounge suit
monkey suit
one-piece suit
pants suit, pantsuit
pinstripe suit
playsuit
rain suit
riding habit
romper suit, rompers
sack suit
separates
single-breasted suit
ski suit
slack suit
snowsuit
spacesuit
sports suit
summer suit
sunsuit
sweatsuit
swimsuit
tailored suit
tank suit
three-piece suit
town-and-country suit
track suit, jogging suit
tropical suit
trouser suit
tuxedo
two-piece suit
wet suit
zoot suit

56 sweater
boatneck sweater
bolero
boucle
bulky
cable-knit sweater
cardigan
cashmere sweater
coat sweater
cowlneck sweater
crewneck sweater
Fair Isle sweater
fisherman's sweater
Guernsey
hand-knit
jersey
mock turtleneck
mohair sweater
polo sweater
poor boy sweater
pull-on sweater, pull-on
pullover
rollneck sweater
shell
shoulderette

ski sweater
slip-on
slipover
sloppy Joe
sweatshirt
sweater vest
turtleneck sweater
twin sweater set, twinset
V-neck sweater
woolly

57 trousers, pants

baggies
bellbottoms
Bermuda shorts
bloomers
blue jeans
boot-cut pants
breeches
buckskins
Capri pants, Capris
cargo pants
carpenter pants
chaps
chinos
clamdiggers
corduroys, cords
cutoffs
ducks
dungarees
gaiters
harem pants
high-waters
hiphuggers
hot pants
jeans
jodhpurs
knee breeches
knickers, knickerbockers
lederhosen
Levi's <tm>
loincloth
matador pants, toreador pants
moleskins
overalls
painter's pants
pantaloons
parachute pants
pedal pushers
pegleg trousers
plus fours
riding breeches
shorts
short shorts
ski pants
slacks
stirrup pants
stretch pants
sweatpants
trunk hose
waders

58 undergarment

all-in-one
athletic supporter, jockstrap
Balmoral
bandeau
bloomers
bikini
bodice
body stocking
bodysuit
boxer shorts
brassiere, bra
breechclout, loincloth
briefs
bustle
BVD's <tm>
cami-knickers
camisole
chemise
corselet
corset
crinoline
diapers
drawers
foundation garment
full slip
garter
garter belt
girdle
G-string
half-slip
Jockey shorts <tm>
knickers
leotard
lingerie
long underwear, long johns
napkins, nappies <Brit>
pannier
panties
pants
panty girdle
peekaboo
petticoat
push-up bra
scanties
shift
shorts
singlet <Brit>
skivvies
slip
smock
soakers
sport bra, sports bra
step-ins
strapless bra
support garment
tap pants
teddy
tee-shirt, T-shirt
thermal underwear, thermals
thong
tournure <Fr>
underdrawers
underpants
undershirt
undershorts
underskirt
undervest
underwire bra
undies
union suit
unitard
unmentionables
woolens

59 uniform

battle dress
blues
continentals
dress blues
dress whites
fatigues
full dress
khaki
livery
nauticals
olive-drab (OD)
regimentals
sailor suit
school uniform
soldier suit
stripes, prison uniform
undress
whites

6 UNCLOTHING

<no bodily covering>

NOUNS 1 **unclothing,** divestment, divestiture, divesture; removal; stripping, denudement, denudation; baring, stripping bare, laying bare, uncovering, exposure, exposing; indecent exposure, exhibitionism, flashing; decortication, excoriation; desquamation, exfoliation; exuviation, ecdysis

2 **disrobing, undressing,** undress, disrobement, unclothing; uncasing, discasing; shedding, molting, peeling; striptease, stripping; skinny-dipping, mooning, flashing

3 **nudity, nakedness,** bareness; the nude, the altogether, the buff, the raw; state of nature, state of undress, full frontal, birthday suit; not a stitch, not a stitch to one's name, not a stitch on one's back; full-frontal nudity; décolleté, décolletage, toplessness; nudism, naturism, gymnosophy; nudist, naturist, gymnosophist, exhibitionist; stripper, stripteaser, ecdysiast, topless dancer, lap dancer

4 **hairlessness, baldness,** acomia, alopecia; calvities; hair loss; beardlessness, baldheadedness, bald-patedness; baldhead, baldpate, baldy, skinhead; pattern baldness; shaving, tonsure, depilation; hair remover, depilatory

VERBS 5 **divest, strip,** strip away, remove; uncover, uncloak, unveil, expose, lay open, bare, lay bare, strip bare, strip naked, denude, denudate; fleece, shear; pluck; strip-search

6 **take off, remove,** doff, off with, put off, slip out of,

step out of, slip off, slough off, cast off, throw off, drop; unwrap, undo

7 **undress, unclothe,** undrape, ungarment, unapparel, unarray, disarray; disrobe; unsheathe, discase, uncase; strip, strip to the buff, do a striptease; skinny-dip, flash, moon

8 **peel, pare, skin,** strip, flay, excoriate, decorticate, bark; scalp; depilate, shave

9 **husk, hull,** pod, **shell,** shuck

10 **shed, cast,** throw off, **slough, molt,** slough off, exuviate

11 **scale, flake,** scale off, flake off, desquamate, exfoliate

ADJS 12 **divested, stripped,** bared, denuded, denudated, exposed, uncovered, stripped bare, laid bare, unveiled, showing; unsheathed, discased, uncased

13 **unclad, undressed, unclothed,** unattired, disrobed, ungarmented, undraped, ungarbed, unrobed, unappareled, uncased; clothesless, garbless, garmentless, raimentless; half-clothed, underclothed, *en déshabillé* <Fr>, in dishabille, nudish; low-necked, low-cut, décolleté, strapless, topless; seminude, scantily clad

14 **naked, nude; bare,** peeled, raw, in the raw, in a state of nature, in nature's garb; in one's birthday suit, in the buff, in native buff, stripped to the buff, in the altogether, with nothing on, without a stitch, without a stitch to one's name, without a stitch on one's back; stark-naked, bare-ass, buck naked, bare as the back of one's hand, naked as the day one was born, naked as a jaybird, naked as a worm, starkers; topless, bare-breasted, bottomless, bare-bottomed; nudist, naturistic, gymnosophical

15 **barefoot,** barefooted, unshod; discalced, discalceate

16 bare-ankled, bare-armed, bare-backed, bare-breasted, topless, bare-chested, barefaced, bare-handed, bareheaded, bare-kneed, barelegged, bare-necked, bare-throated

17 **hairless,** depilous; **bald,** acomous; bald as a coot, bald as an egg; baldheaded, bald-pated, tonsured; beardless, whiskerless, shaven, clean-shaven, smooth-shaven, smooth-faced; smooth, glabrous

18 exuvial, sloughy; desquamative, exfoliatory; denudant, denudatory; peeling, shedding

ADVS 19 nakedly, barely, baldly

COMBINING FORMS 20 de-, dis-, un-

7 NUTRITION

<eating for health>

NOUNS 1 **nutrition, nourishment,** nourishing, feeding, nurture; alimentation, sustenance; food value, nutritive value, food intake; food chain, food cycle; food pyramid, food group, recommended daily vitamins and minerals, recommended daily allowance

2 **nutritiousness,** nutritiveness, digestibility, assimilability; healthfulness

3 **nutrient,** nutritive, **nutriment,** food; nutrilite, growth factor, growth regulator; natural food, health food; roughage, fiber, dietary fiber

4 **vitamin** <see list>, vitamin complex; provitamin; food additive, vitamin supplement

5 **carbohydrate,** carbs, carbo, simple carbohydrate, complex carbohydrate; sugar; starch; hydroxy aldehyde, hydroxy ketone, glycogen, cellulose, ketone, saccharide, monosaccharide, disaccharide, trisaccharide, polysaccharide, polysaccharose; artificial sweetener

6 **protein,** proteid, simple protein, conjugated protein, protein structure; amino acid, essential amino acid; peptide, dipeptide, polypeptide; globulin, collagen, gluten, immunoglobulin, hemoglobin

7 **fat,** glyceride, lipid, lipoid; lecithin; fatty acid; steroid, sterol; cholesterol, glycerol-cholesterol, cephalin-cholesterol; triglyceride; lipoprotein, high-density lipoprotein (HDL), low-density lipoprotein (LDL); polyunsaturated fat; saturated fat; unsaturated fat

8 **digestion,** ingestion, assimilation, absorption; primary digestion, secondary digestion; predigestion; salivary digestion, gastric digestion, peptic digestion, pancreatic digestion, intestinal digestion; digestive system, alimentary canal, gastrointestinal tract; salivary glands, gastric glands, liver, pancreas; digestive secretions, saliva, gastric juice, pancreatic juice, intestinal juice, bile

9 **digestant,** digester, digestive; pepsin; **enzyme,** proteolytic enzyme

10 **enzyme,** apoenzyme, coenzyme, isoenzyme; transferase, hydrolase, lyase, isomerase, polymerase, amylase, diastase; pepsin, rennin; proenzyme, trypsin, zymogen

11 **essential element**, macronutrient; carbon, hydrogen, oxygen, nitrogen, calcium, phosphorus, potassium, sodium, chlorine, sulfur, magnesium; trace element, micronutrient; iron, manganese, zinc, copper, iodine, cobalt, selenium, molybdenum, chromium, silicon

12 **metabolism,** basal metabolism, metabolic process, acid-base metabolism, energy metabolism; anabolism, assimilation; catabolism, disassimilation

13 **diet, dieting,** dietary; dietetics; regimen, regime; bland diet, **bland food** <see list>; soft diet,

soft food <see list>, pap, spoon food, spoon meat, spoon victuals; balanced diet; diabetic diet, allergy diet, elimination diet, reducing diet, weight-loss diet, obesity diet; high-calorie diet, low-calorie diet, reduced-calorie diet, reduced-fat diet; watching one's weight, watching one's calories, calorie-counting; liquid diet; high-protein diet, low-carbohydrate diet; low-salt diet, low-sodium diet, salt-free diet; low-fat diet, fat-free diet; low-cholesterol diet; sugar-free diet; gluten-free diet; vegetarianism, lactovegetarianism, vegan diet; macrobiotic diet; crash diet, fad diet; portion control; eating disorder, anorexia, anorexia nervosa, bulimia

14 vitaminization, **fortification,** enrichment, restoration

15 **nutritionist, dietitian,** vitaminologist, enzymologist

16 science of nutrition, **dietetics,** dietotherapeutics, dietotherapy; vitaminology; threpsology; enzymology

VERBS 17 **nourish,** feed, sustain, aliment, nutrify, nurture, provide for, fatten up; strengthen; cook for, wine and dine, regale, chef; force-feed

18 **digest,** assimilate, absorb; metabolize; predigest

19 **diet,** go on a diet; watch one's weight, watch one's calories, count calories

20 vitaminize, **fortify, enrich,** restore

ADJS 21 **nutritious,** nutritive, nutrient, **nourishing;** good for, healthful; alimentary, alimental, alimentive; organic, farm-to-table, farm-to-fork; digestible, assimilable; low-salt, low-sodium, low-calorie, low-cal, reduced-calorie, reduced-fat, low-fat, salt-free, sugar-free, fat-free

22 **digestive,** assimilative; peptic, eupeptic

23 **dietary,** dietetic, dietic; regiminal

24 **bland food**

- broth
- cake
- cooked cereal
- cookie
- cracker
- decaffeinated coffee
- egg
- fruit juice
- Jell-O <tm>
- lean meat
- marshmallow
- mild-flavored vegetable juice
- milk
- pasta
- pie
- plain rice
- potato
- pudding
- refined bread
- refined cereal
- rice pudding
- soft banana
- tofu
- yogurt

25 **soft food**

- applesauce
- breakfast drink
- canned fruit
- cooked cereal
- cooked fruit
- cooked vegetable
- cottage cheese
- couscous
- custard
- eggs
- ice cream
- Jell-O <tm>
- macaroni and cheese
- mashed potato
- meatloaf
- milkshake
- muffin
- pasta
- pastry
- pudding
- smooth peanut butter
- soft bread
- soft cheese
- soft fruit
- soft vegetable
- sorbet
- soup
- yogurt

26 **vitamin**

- **vitamin A**
- vitamin A1, antiophthalmic factor, axerophthol, retinol
- vitamin A2
- carotene
- choline
- cryptoxanthin
- **vitamin B**
- vitamin B complex
- vitamin B1, thiamine, aneurin, anti-beriberi factor
- vitamin B2, vitamin G, riboflavin, lactoflavin, ovoflavin, hepatoflavin
- vitamin M, vitamin Bc
- vitamin B6, pyridoxine, adermin
- vitamin B12, cobalamin, cyanocobalamin, extrinsic factor, pentothenic acid, lipoid acid
- folic acid, pteroylglutamic acid, para-aminobenzoic acid (PABA)
- inositol
- niacin, nicotinic acid
- **vitamin C**, ascorbic acid
- **vitamin D2**, calciferol
- ergocalciferol
- cholecalciferol, vitamin D3
- vitamin E, tocopherol
- vitamin H, biotin
- vitamin K, naphthoquinone
- menadione
- vitamin P, bioflavinoid

8 EATING

<taking in food>

NOUNS 1 **eating, feeding, dining,** messing; the nosebag; ingestion, consumption, consuming, deglutition; tasting, relishing, savoring; gourmet eating, gourment dining, fine dining, gourmandise, gastronomy; nibbling, pecking, licking, munching; snacking, ambient snacking; devouring, gobbling, wolfing, downing, gulping; gorging, overeating, gluttony, overconsumption; chewing, mastication, manducation, rumination; feasting, regaling, regalement; appetite, **hunger**; nutrition; **dieting**; carnivorism, carnivorousness, carnivority; herbivorism, herbivority, herbivorousness, grazing, browsing, cropping, pasturing, pasture; vegetarianism, phytophagy; omnivorism, omnivorousness, pantophagy; cannibalism, anthropophagy; omophagia, omophagy

2 **bite, morsel,** taste, swallow; mouthful, gob, piece, slice, scrap, tidbit; nibble, munchies; cud, quid; bolus, gobbet; chew, chaw; nip, niblet; munch; gnash; champ, chomp; appetizer, hors d'oeuvre, amuse-bouche

3 **drinking,** imbibing, imbibition, potation; lapping, sipping, tasting, nipping, tippling; quaffing, gulping, swigging, swilling, guzzling, pulling; winebibbing; compotation, symposium; barhopping; drunkenness

4 **drink,** potation, **beverage** <see list>, potion, libation, oblation, thirst-quencher; draft, dram, drench, swig, swill, guzzle, quaff, tipple, sip, sup, suck, tot, bumper, snort, slug, pull, lap, gulp, slurp; nip, peg; toast, health; mixed drink, cocktail; nightcap

5 **meal,** repast, feed, sit-down, mess, spread, menu, table, board, meat, *repas* <Fr>; **refreshment,** refection, regalement, collation, entertainment, treat; frozen meal

6 <meals> **breakfast,** *petit déjeuner* <Fr>, continental breakfast, English breakfast, American breakfast, breakfast table, *déjeuner à la fourchette* <Fr>, banquet, smorgasbord; power breakfast, power lunch, power dinner; **brunch,** Sunday brunch, elevenses; **lunch,** luncheon, tiffin, hot lunch, light lunch, box lunch, brown-bag lunch, brown-bagging, packed lunch; blue-plate special; tapas, small plate; tea, teatime, high tea, afternoon tea, cream tea; **dinner,** *diner* <Fr>, evening meal, dinner party; **supper,** *souper* <Fr>; buffet supper, buffet lunch; fast food, takeout, carryout, drive-through, drive-thru meal, to-go meal, to-go, takeaway <Brit>; precooked frozen meal, TV dinner; picnic, cookout, alfresco meal, fête champêtre, tailgate picnic, barbecue, fish fry, clambake, wiener roast, wienie roast; potluck; midnight supper, midnight snack; progressive dinner; dashboard meal, cupholder meal, cupholder cuisine

7 **light meal,** refreshments, light repast, light lunch, spot of lunch, collation, **snack,** nosh, bite, bite to eat, *casse-croûte* <Fr>; informal meal; coffee break, tea break

8 **hearty meal,** full meal, healthy meal, large meal, substantial meal, heavy meal, nosh-up, square meal, man-sized meal, large order; three squares; formal meal, sit-down meal; mom food, home-cooked meal, home cooking, comfort food

9 **feast, banquet,** regale, buffet, smorgasbord, festal board, groaning board, spread; finger buffet; Lucullan banquet, bacchanalia; Passover; blow, blowout, feeding frenzy; dinner party; bean feast

10 **serving,** service; **portion, helping,** serving suggestion; second helping, seconds; **course;** dish, plate; *plat du jour* <Fr>; antepast; first course, starter, soup, entree, *entrée* <Fr>, main course, entremets, side dish, tapas; dessert

11 <manner of service> service, table service, counter service, self-service, curb service, takeout service, drive-through; table d'hôte, ordinary; à la carte; cover, *couvert* <Fr>; cover charge; American plan, European plan; to-go

12 **tableware,** dining utensils; **silverware,** silver, silver plate, stainless-steel ware; **flatware,** flat silver; hollow ware; **cutlery,** knives, fish knife, carving knife, fruit knife, steak knife, butter knife; forks, fish fork, salad fork, fondue fork; spoons, tablespoon, teaspoon, soup spoon, dessert spoon, coffee spoon, serving spoon; spork; chopsticks; **dishware,** china, dishes, plates, cups, saucers, bowls, fingerbowls; glasses, **glassware,** tumbler, goblet, wineglass, crystal, flute; dish, salad dish, fruit dish, dessert dish; bowl, cereal bowl, fruit bowl, punchbowl; tea service, tea set, tea things, tea strainer, tea caddy, tea cozy

13 **table linen,** napery, tablecloth, table cover, table mat, table pad, placemat, setting; napkin, table napkin, serviette <Brit>

14 **menu,** bill of fare, carte, a la carte, menuboard

15 **gastronomy,** gastronomics, gastrology, epicurism, epicureanism

16 **eater,** feeder, consumer, devourer, partaker; **diner,** luncher; picnicker; mouth, hungry mouth, big eater; diner-out, eater-out; boarder, board-and-roomer; gourmet, gastronome, epicure, gourmand, connoisseur of food, bon vivant, Lucullus, foodie, chowhound; overeater, pig, wolf, trencherman, **glutton**; light eater, nibbler, picky eater, fussy eater; omnivore, pantophagist; flesh-eater, meat-eater, carnivore, omophagist, predacean; man-eater, cannibal; vegetarian, lactovegetarian, vegan, fruitarian, plant-eater, herbivore, phytophagan, phytophage; grass-eater, graminivore; grain-eater, granivore; frugivore

17 **restaurant,** eating place, eating house, dining room; eatery, beanery, hashery, hash house, greasy spoon, chain restaurant, theme restaurant; fast-food restaurant, takeout, hamburger joint; *trattoria* <Ital>; bistro; lunchroom, luncheonette, breakroom; café, *caffè* <Ital>, roadside cafe; tearoom; coffeehouse, coffeeroom, coffee shop, coffee bar; tea shop, tea garden, teahouse; pub, tavern, brewpub, gastropub; chophouse; grill, grillroom, steakhouse, carvery; brasserie; pancake house, waffle house; cookshop; buffet, smorgasbord, self-service restaurant; lunch counter, quick-lunch counter; blue-plate special; salad bar; hotdog stand, hamburger stand, drive-in restaurant, drive-in; drive-through, drive-thru; doughnut shop, breakfast restaurant; snack bar, sandwich bar, *buvette* <Fr>, *cantina* <Sp>; milk bar; sushi bar; juice bar; raw bar; pizzeria; cafeteria, automat; mess hall, dining hall, refectory; canteen; cookhouse, cookshack,

lunch wagon, chuck wagon; diner, dog wagon; delicatessen, deli; ice-cream parlor, soda fountain; dining car; vending machine; **kitchen**, breakfast nook, dinette

VERBS **18** **feed, dine,** wine and dine, mess; nibble, snack, graze; satisfy, gratify; regale; bread, meat; board, sustain; pasture, put out to pasture, browse; forage, fodder; provision

19 **nourish, nurture,** nutrify, aliment, foster; nurse, suckle, lactate, breastfeed, wet-nurse, dry-nurse; fatten, fatten up, stuff, force-feed

20 **eat, feed,** fare, take, partake, partake of, *mange* <Fr>, take nourishment, subsist, break bread, break one's fast, feast on; refresh the inner man, entertain the inner man, feed one's face, put on the feed bag, fall to, pitch in; taste, relish, savor; hunger; get the munchies, have the munchies, diet, go on a diet, watch one's weight, count calories

21 **dine,** dinner; sup, breakfast; lunch; have dinner, have lunch, have breakfast; picnic, cook out; **eat out,** dine out; board; break bread with; brown-bag

22 **devour, swallow,** ingest, **consume,** take in, tuck in, tuck away, tuck into, chow down, down, get down, scarf down, put away, snarf; eat up; dispatch, dispose of

23 **gobble,** gulp, bolt, wolf, gobble down, gulp down, bolt down, wolf down

24 **feast, banquet,** regale; eat heartily, have a good appetite, eat up, lick the platter, lick the plate, do oneself proud, do one's duty, do justice to, clean one's plate, polish the platter, put it away

25 **stuff, gorge**, pig out, oink out, engorge, glut, guttle, binge, cram, eat one's fill, stuff oneself, gorge oneself, gluttonize, eat everything in sight

26 **pick,** peck, **nibble; snack**, nosh; pick at, peck at, eat like a bird, show no appetite

27 **chew,** chew up, chaw, bite into; masticate, manducate; ruminate, chew the cud; **bite,** grind, champ, chomp; munch, crunch; gnash; gnaw; mouth, mumble; gum

28 **feed on,** feed upon, **feast on,** feast upon, batten upon, fatten on, fatten upon; prey on, prey upon, live on, live upon, pasture on, browse, graze, crop

29 **drink,** drink in, imbibe, wet one's whistle; quaff, sip, sup, bib, swig, swill, guzzle, pull, gulp; suck, suckle, suck in, suck up; drink off, drink up, toss off, toss down, knock back, drain the cup; wash down; **toast,** drink to, pledge; bar-hop; tipple, **booze**

30 **lap up,** sponge up, soak up, lick, lap, slurp

ADJS **31** **eating,** feeding, gastronomical, dining, mensal, commensal, prandial, postprandial, preprandial; nourishing, **nutritious**; empty-calorie; dietetic; omnivorous, pantophagous, **gluttonous**; flesh-eating, meat-eating, carnivorous, omophagic, omophagous, predacious; man-eating, cannibal, cannibalistic; insect-eating, insectivorous; vegetable-eating, vegetarian, lactovegetarian, vegan, fruitarian; plant-eating, herbivorous, phytivorous, phytophagous; grass-eating, graminivorous; grain-eating, granivorous; organic

32 **chewing**, masticatory, masticating, manducatory; ruminant, ruminating, cud-chewing; tasting, nibbling

33 **edible, eatable,** comestible, consumable, safe to eat, esculent, digestible, gustable; kosher; palatable, succulent, mouth-watering, **delicious,** dainty, savory, good to eat, finger-licking; fine, fancy, **gourmet;** calorific, fattening, rich

34 **drinkable,** potable, quaffable

INTERJS **35** chow down, soup's on, grub's on, come and get it; *bon appétit* <Fr>, eat hearty, eat up

COMBINING FORMS **36** phag-, phago-, -phagia, -phagy; -phage, -vore, -vora

9 REFRESHMENT

<food and drink>

NOUNS **1** **refreshment,** refection, refreshing, freshening up, bracing, exhilaration, **stimulation,** enlivenment, vivification, invigoration, reinvigoration, reanimation, rejuvenation, revival, revivification, revivescence, revivescency, renewal, recreation, rest and recreation, R and R; regalement, regale; tonic, bracer, breath of fresh air, pick-me-up, a shot in the arm, an upper; cordial; digestif

VERBS **2** **refresh,** freshen, freshen up, fresh up; revive, revivify, reinvigorate, reanimate; exhilarate, stimulate, invigorate, fortify, enliven, liven up, restore, animate, vivify, quicken, brisk, brisken; brace, brace up, buck up, pick up, perk up, chirk up, set up, set on one's legs, set on one's feet; renew one's strength, breathe new life into, put new life into, give a breath of fresh air, blow out the cobwebs, give a shot in the arm; renew, recreate, charge one's batteries, recharge one's batteries, give a break, give a breather; regale, cheer, refresh the inner man

ADJS **3** **refreshing,** refreshful, **fresh,** brisk, crisp, crispy, fortifying, zesty, zestful, bracing, tonic, cordial; analeptic; exhilarating, stimulating, stimulative, stimulatory, invigorating, rousing, energizing; regaling, cheering; rejuvenating; recreative, recreational

4 **refreshed,** restored, invigorated, exhilarated, freshened up, enlivened, stimulated, energized, recharged, animated, reanimated, revived, renewed, recreated, ready for more, ready for another round

5 **unwearied,** untired, unfatigued, unexhausted

10 FOOD

<things eaten>

NOUNS 1 **food,** foodstuff, food and drink, sustenance, kitchen stuff, victualage, comestibles, edibles, eatables, viands, **cuisine,** tucker <Austral>, ingesta <pl>; fusion cuisine; soul food; fast food, junk food; street food; fare, cheer, creature comfort; provision, provender; meat, bread, daily bread, bread and butter, staff of life; health food; board, table, feast, spread; functional food; nouvelle cuisine, designer food; tasting menu; processed food, Frankenfood, pharmafood, nonfood

2 <nonformal> **grub,** grubbery, eats, chow, chuck, grits, groceries, nosh, the nosebag, scarf, scoff, nibbles, tuck, victuals, vittles; fast food; ambient food; brown bag, brown-bagging, dashboard dining

3 **nutriment,** nourishment, nurture; **sustenance**; pabulum, pap; aliment, alimentation, fare; refreshment, refection; support, keep; brain food, ambient food

4 **feed, fodder,** provender, animal food; forage, pasture, eatage, pasturage; grain; corn, oats, barley, wheat, cereal grain, ancient grain; meal, bran, chop; hay, timothy, clover, straw; ensilage, silage; chicken feed, scratch, scratch feed, mash; slops, swill; pet food, dog food, cat food; birdseed

5 **provisions, groceries,** provender, supplies, stores, larder, food supply, food and drink, victuals; fresh foods, canned foods, frozen foods, dehydrated foods, precooked foods, convenience foods; commissariat, commissary, grocery

6 **rations,** board, meals, commons <Brit>, mess, allowance, allotment, food allotment, tucker <Austral>; short commons <Brit>; emergency rations; K ration, C ration, garrison, field rations

7 **dish**, culinary preparation, culinary concoction; cover, **course**; casserole; grill, broil, boil, roast, fry; **main dish, entree,** main course, *pièce de résistance* <Fr>, culinary masterpiece, dish fit for a king; hors d'oeuvre, starter, appetizer; side dish, side, salad, vegetables; dessert; dish of the day, soup of the day, soup de jour, soup du jour, specialty; side order

8 **delicacy,** dainty, goody, treat, kickshaw, tidbit, titbit; gourmet food; morsel, choice morsel, *bonne bouche, amuse-gueule* <Fr>; savory; **dessert** <see list>; ambrosia, nectar, cate, manna

9 **appetizer,** whet, *apéritif* <Fr>; foretaste, antepast, *antipasto* <Ital>, *Vorspeise* <Ger>; **hors d'oeuvre;** *crostato* <Ital>, starter, nibbles, tidbits; smorgasbord; crackers and cheese, crudites, dip, guacamole, salsa, pate, cheese dip, nachos, potato skins, hummus; falafel; rumaki; pickle, dill pickle; bridge mix

10 **soup,** *potage* <Fr>, *zuppa, minestra* <Ital>, cream soup, clear soup, consomme, stock, bouillon, broth, potage, bisque, borscht, gumbo, chowder, bouillabaisse, alphabet soup, avgolemono, pho, ramen

11 **stew,** olla, olio, *olla podrida* <Sp>; hot pot; meat stew, *étuvée* <Fr>; Irish stew, mulligan stew, mulligan, burgoo; goulash, Hungarian goulash; ragout; salmi; *bouillabaisse* <Fr>, *paella* <Catalan>, oyster stew; fricassee; curry; casserole, shepherd's pie

12 **sauce**; tomato sauce, ketchup, catsup; brown sauce, Worcestershire sauce, soy sauce, Bordelaise; Tabasco sauce <tm>, barbecue sauce; tartar sauce, horseradish; condiment, dip, dressing, salsa, guacamole, pesto; applesauce; mayonnaise, salad dressing, vinaigrette, balsamic vinaigrette, oil-and-vinegar; ranch dressing; white sauce, veloute, Alfredo, Bearnaise, hollandaise, bechamel, cheese sauce; dipping sauce; mustard, yellow mustard, Dijon mustard, honey mustard; vinegar, balsamic vinegar; teriyaki sauce; a la king

13 **meat,** flesh, red meat, *viande* <Fr>, white meat; butcher's meat, *viande de boucherie* <Fr>; cut of meat, **meat cut** <see list>; game, *menue viande* <Fr>; venison; roast, joint, *rôti* <Fr>; pot roast; chop, cutlet, grill; lunchmeat, cold cuts; barbecue, boiled meat, *bouilli* <Fr>; forcemeat; mincemeat, mince; hash, *hachis* <Fr>; *civet* <Fr>; pemmican, jerky; pulled meat; sausage meat, scrapple; aspic; meat substitute, soyfood, tofu, bean curd

14 **beef,** *bœuf* <Fr>; roast beef, *rosbif* <Fr>; chuck, rib roast, tenderloin, sirloin, steak, round, filet, fillet, beefsteak, boneless rump, shank, brisket; hamburger, ground beef; corned beef; dried beef; chipped beef; jerky, charqui; pastrami; beef extract, bouillon; suet

15 **veal,** *vitello* <Ital>, *veau* <Fr>; veal cutlet, *côtelette de veau* <Fr>; shoulder, rib roast, chops, loin, rump, shank, leg, cutlet, escallop, breast, neck; *poitrine de veau* <Fr>; fricandeau; calf's head, *tête de veau* <Fr>; calf's liver, *foie de veau* <Fr>; sweetbread, *ris de veau* <Fr>; calf's brains

16 **mutton,** *mouton* <Fr>; muttonchop; **lamb,** *agneau* <Fr>; breast of lamb, rack of lamb, crown roast, *poitrine d'agneau* <Fr>; leg of lamb, leg of mutton, *gigot* <Fr>, *jambe de mouton* <Fr>; saddle of mutton

17 **pork,** *porc* <Fr>, pig, pigmeat, spareribs, ribs, baby back ribs
18 **steak,** *tranche* <Fr>, beefsteak, *bifteck* <Fr>, *tranche de bœuf* <Fr>, *bistecca* <Ital>, minute steak, filet, tournedo
19 **chop, cutlet,** *côtelette* <Fr>; pork chop, *côtelette de porc frais* <Fr>; mutton chop, *côtelette de mouton* <Fr>, scallop, papillote, Saratoga chop; veal cutlet, veal chop, *côtelette de veau* <Fr>, *Wiener Schnitzel* <Ger>
20 <**variety meats**> kidneys; heart; brains; liver; gizzard; tongue; sweetbread <thymus>; beef bread <pancreas>; tripe <stomach>; marrow; cockscomb; chitterlings, chitlins <intestines>; prairie oyster, mountain oyster <testis>; haslet, giblets, *abattis* <Fr>, offal
21 **sausage,** *saucisse* <Fr>, *saucisson* <Fr>, *salsiccia* <Ital>, *Wurst* <Ger>, banger, hotdog, wiener, frankfurter, footlong; pâté
22 **poultry, fowl,** bird, edible bird, chicken, turkey, *volaille* <Fr>
23 <**poultry parts**> leg, drumstick, thigh, wing, wishbone, breast; white meat, dark meat, giblets, pope's nose, parson's nose; chicken wing, Buffalo wing
24 **fish,** *poisson* <Fr>; seafood; fruits de mer; fried fish, broiled fish, boiled fish, poached fish, smoked fish, fish cake, fish ball, fish stick, fish pie; fish and chips; food fish; finnan haddie; kipper, kippered salmon, kippered herring, gravlax; smoked salmon, lox; smoked herring, red herring; eel, *anguille* <Fr>; fish eggs, roe, caviar; ceviche, sushi; shumai; squid, calamari; flatfish, sole, lemon sole, Dover sole, flounder, fluke, dab, sanddab; white fish
25 **shellfish,** *coquillage* <Fr>; **mollusk,** mollusc, snail, *escargot* <Fr>
26 **eggs,** *œufs* <Fr>; fried eggs, *œufs sur le plat* <Fr>; hard-boiled eggs, soft-boiled eggs, *œufs à la coque* <Fr>, coddled eggs; poached eggs, over-easy, sunny-side up, *œufs pochés* <Fr>; scrambled eggs, buttered eggs, *œufs brouillés* <Fr>; dropped eggs, shirred eggs, stuffed eggs, deviled eggs; omelet, omelette; soufflé; Scotch egg, eggs Benedict; egg salad
27 **stuffing, dressing,** forcemeat, farce
28 **bread** <see list>, *pain* <Fr>, *pane* <Ital>, the staff of life; French bread, Italian bread, sourdough bread, ciabatta; loaf of bread; crust, breadcrust, crust of bread; breadstuff; leaven, leavening, ferment
29 **corn bread;** pone, ash pone, corn pone, corn tash, ash cake, hoecake, johnnycake; dodger, corn dodger, corn dab, hush puppy; cracklin' bread; *tortilla* <Sp>, lavosh
30 **biscuit,** sinker; hardtack, sea biscuit, ship biscuit, pilot biscuit, pilot bread; shortcake; **cracker,** soda cracker, saltine, graham cracker, animal cracker, *biscotto, biscotti* <Ital>, cream cracker, potato chip, potato crisp <Brit>, sultana, water biscuit, butter cracker, oyster cracker; wafer; rusk, zwieback, melba toast, Brussels biscuit; pretzel
31 **roll, bun, muffin;** bagel, everything bagel, bialy, bialystoker; brioche, croissant; English muffin; popover; scone; hard roll, kaiser roll, dinner roll, Parker House roll, Portuguese roll
32 **sandwich,** *canapé* <Fr>, *smörgasbord* <Swedish>; club sandwich, dagwood; hamburger, burger; submarine, sub, hero, grinder, hoagy, poorboy; wedge; gyro; veggieburger, vegeburger, gardenburger
33 **noodles,** pasta, Italian paste, paste; spaghetti, spaghettini, ziti, penne, fettuccine, linguine, fusilli, radiattore, vermicelli, rigatoni, tortellini, ravioli, gnocchi, macaroni, lasagne; *kreplach* <Yiddish pl>, wonton; dumpling; spaetzle, dim sum; matzo balls, *knaydlach* <Yiddish>
34 **cereal,** breakfast food, dry cereal, hot cereal; flour, all-purpose flour; meal
35 **vegetable,** vegetables, produce, *légumes* <Fr>, veg, veggies; greens; potherbs; **beans,** *frijoles* <Sp>, *haricots* <Fr>; leaf vegetable, leafy vegetable, stem vegetable, root vegetable, tuber, flower vegetable, seed vegetable, pulse; **potato,** spud, tater, *pomme de terre* <Fr>, Irish potato, pratie, white potato, baked potato, mashed potato, French fries, pommes frites; tomato, love apple; mushroom; eggplant, *aubergine* <Fr>, mad apple; rhubarb, pieplant; cabbage, *Kraut* <Ger>; ratatouille, mixed vegetables
36 **rice**, white rice, long-grain rice, brown rice, wild rice, pilaf, orzo, couscous, risotto, Arborio rice, aromatic rice
37 **salad,** *salade* <Fr>; **greens,** *crudités* <Fr>, raw food, tossed salad, chef's salad, Caesar salad; fruit salad, pasta salad, potato salad, coleslaw, Cobb salad, composed salad, mixed greens, insalata verde
38 **fruit,** fruits; produce; stone fruit, drupe, berry, pome, pepo, sorosis, syconium, hesperidium; simple fruit, true fruit, composite fruit, aggregate fruit, multiple fruit, false fruit, succulent fruit; citrus fruit; tropical fruit; dry fruit, dehiscent fruit, indehiscent fruit, fruiting body; fruit compote, fruit soup, fruit cup, fruit cocktail, fruit salad, stewed fruit
39 **nut,** *noix* <Fr>, *noisette* <Fr>; kernel, meat
40 **sweets,** sweet stuff, confectionery; sweet, sweetmeat; confection; candy, candy bar; bonbon, comfit, confiture; jelly, jam; preserve, conserve;

marmalade; toffee, butterscotch, caramel, dulce de leche, chocolate, dark chocolate, milk chocolate, fudge; white chocolate; gelatin, Jell-O <tm>; compote; pudding, custard, mousse; tutti-frutti; maraschino cherries; honey; icing, frosting, glaze; meringue; whipped cream

41 **pastry,** *patisserie* <Fr>; French pastry, Danish pastry; tart, tarlet; turnover; timbale; pie, *tarte* <Fr>, fruit pie, single-crust pie, double-crust pie, deep-dish pie, custard pie, meringue pie; *quiche, quiche Lorraine* <Fr>; cobbler, crisp, bread pudding; patty, patty shell, *vol-au-vent* <Fr>; rosette; dowdy, pandowdy; phyllo, filo, strudel, baklava; puff pastry, flake pastry; puff, cream puff, croquembouche, profiterole; cannoli, cream horn; éclair; tiramisu; croissant, scone, shortbread, brioche; toaster pastry, toaster strudel; French toast

42 **cake,** *gâteau* <Fr>, *Torte* <Ger>; *petit-four* <Fr>; layer cake, Bundt cake, pound cake, sponge cake, upside-down cake, fruitcake, gingerbread, cheesecake, shortcake, cupcake, tiramisu, brownie; petit four, madeleine; doughnut, doughnut hole

43 **cookie,** biscuit <Brit>, fortune cookie, biscotti, bar cookie, drop cookie, refrigerator cookie, icebox cookie, sandwich cookie; cereal bar, energy bar

44 **doughnut,** donut, friedcake, sinker, olykoek; French doughnut, raised doughnut; glazed doughnut; doughnut hole; fastnacht; cruller, twister; jelly doughnut, bismarck; fritter, *beignet* <Fr>; apple fritter; cronut

45 **pancake,** griddlecake, hot cake, battercake, flapcake, flapjack, flannel cake; buckwheat cake; *chapatty* <India>; **waffle;** blintz, cheese blintz, *crêpe, crêpe suzette* <Fr>, *Pfannkuchen* <Ger>, Swedish pancake, latke

46 **pudding,** custard, mousse, flan, tapioca

47 **ice,** *glace* <Fr>, frozen dessert; **ice cream,** ice milk; sherbet, water ice <Brit>, Italian ice, sorbet, bombe; gelato; tortoni; parfait; sundae, ice-cream sundae, banana split; ice-cream soda; ice-cream float, frappé; ice-cream cone; frozen pudding; frozen custard, soft ice cream; frozen yogurt; ice cream sandwich

48 **dairy product,** milk product, butter, cream, yogurt; **cheese** <see list>, *fromage* <Fr>; tofu, bean curd

49 **beverage,** drink, thirst quencher, potation, potable, drinkable, **liquor** <see list>, spirits, liquid, hard liquor, alcoholic drink, libation; **liqueur** <see list>, cordial; **mixed drink** <see list>, **cocktail** <see list>; **beer** <see list>, brew, brewski, alcopop; **wine** <see list>; **soft drink** <see list>, soda, pop, soda pop; tonic, tonic water; nonalcoholic beverage; cooler, spritzer; cold drink; water, tap water, spring water, ice water, mineral water; seltzer water, seltzer, carbonated water, soda water, club soda, sparkling water; mixer; sports drink, energy drink; milkshake, shake, frosted; hot chocolate, cocoa; smoothie, juicing; **milk** <see list>, dairy drink; buttermilk; **coffee** <see list>, java, joe; **tea** <see list>; infusion, beef tea; **fruit juice** <see list>, juice, ade, punch; **vegetable juice** <see list>; juice box

50 **<food expiration>** use-by date, best-before date, sell-by date

51 **beer**

abbey ale
ale
amber ale
barley wine
bitter
bitter stout
bittersweet
bock beer
brown ale
bruised beer
caramel malt
cask-conditioned ale
chicha
copper ale
craft-brewed beer, craft beer, craft brew
cream ale
crystal malt
dark beer
diat pils
doppelbock
draft beer, draught beer
dry beer
dunkel beer
dunkel weissbier
eisbock
faro
festbier
fire-brewed beer
fruit beer
golden ale
home brew
ice beer
India pale ale
kellerbier
kolsch
krausen
kriek
kristall weizen
kruidenbier
Kulmbacher beer
kumiss
kvass
lager
lambic beer
light beer
maibock
malt liquor
marzen
mead
melomel
microbrew, microbeer
Munchener
near beer
nonalcoholic beer
nut brown ale
oatmeal stout
obergarig
old ale
oscura
pale ale
pilsener
poker beer
pony beer
porter, porter beer
saison
Scotch ale
schwarzbier
specialty malt
spruce beer
starkbier
steam beer
stout
summer ale
Trappist
tripel beer
ur-bock
Vienna beer
weiss
weizenbier
wheat beer
white beer
winter beer
zwickelbier

52 bread

andama
bagel
baguette
breadstick
brown bread
challah
corn bread
croissant
dinner roll
egg bread
English muffin
flatbread
foccaccia
French bread
Irish soda bread
lavash
matzo
melba toast
nut bread
oatmeal bread
pita
plain white roll
poppy-seed roll
potato bread
pumpernickel bread
raisin bread
roll
rye bread
scone
sourdough bread
tortilla
Vienna bread
white bread
whole-wheat bread

53 cheese

American
Banon
beer cheese
Bel paese
bleu cheese
Bleu de Bresse
blue cheese
Blue Cheshire
Boursin
brick
Brie
Caciocavallo
Caerphilly
Camembert
Cheddar
Cheshire
chevre
Colby
cottage cheese, curds and whey
cream cheese
Danish blue
Dunlop
Edam
Emmenthaler
Epoisses
Feta
Fontina
fromage
Gjetost
Gloucester
goat cheese
Gorgonzola
Gouda
Gruyere
Havarti
hoop cheese
Jaalsberg
jack cheese
Jarlsberg
Lancashire
Leicester
Liederkranz
Limburger
Liptauer
Longhorn
Maroilles
Mimolette
Monterey Jack
mozzarella
Muenster
Neufchatel
Parmesan
Parmigiano Reggiano
pecorino
Port Salut
pot cheese
process cheese
provolone
ricotta
Romano
Roquefort
Samsoe
sapsago
Scamorze
smoked cheese
St. Marcellin
St. Nectaire
Stilton
string cheese
Swiss
Teleme
Tillamook
Trappist cheese
Vacherin
White Wensleydale

54 cocktail, mixed drink

Adam and Eve
after-dinner cocktail
Alabama slammer
Alaska cocktail
alexander
Allegheny
Americana
Bacardi cocktail
B&B cocktail
Bahama mama
banshee
Basin Street
bay breeze
beachcomber
bee stinger
Bellini
Bermuda Rose
Betsy Ross
B-52
bijou cocktail
black Maria
Black Russian
black velvet
bloody Caesar
Bloody Mary
blue Hawaiian
blue lagoon
blue whale
bocce ball
Bombay cocktail
Boston cocktail
bourbon on the rocks
brandy alexander
brandy fizz
brandy smash
Bronx cocktail
buck's fizz
bull and bear
bull's eye
bull's milk
bullshot
buttered rum
Cape Codder
champagne cocktail
champagne cooler
cherry blossom
chi-chi
clamato cocktail
coffee grasshopper
cooler
Cosmopolitan, Cosmo
daiquiri
dirty martini
dixie julep
dream cocktail
dry martini
eggnog
English highball
Fifth Avenue
firefly
fizz
flip
foxy lady
frappe
French connection
frozen daiquiri
frozen Margarita
fuzzy navel
gentleman's cocktail
Georgia mint julep
Georgia peach
Gibson
gimlet
gin and bitters
gin and sin
gin and tonic
gin fizz
gin highball
gin rickey
gin sling
gin sour
gluhwein
golden Cadillac
grasshopper
greyhound
grog
Harvard cocktail
Harvard cooler
Harvey Wallbanger
highball
hole-in-one
Hollywood
Honolulu cocktail
hot buttered rum
hot toddy
hurricane
Indian summer
Irish coffee
Jack Rose
kamikaze
Kentucky blizzard
Kentucky cocktail
kiddie cocktail, Shirley Temple, mocktail
King Alphonse
Kir
Kir royale
Long Island iced tea
Louisville lady
lover's kiss
madras
mai tai
Manhattan
Margarita

martini
melon ball
merry widow
Mexican coffee
mimosa
mint julep
Mojito
muddled drink
mudslide
Narragansett
New York cocktail
nutcracker
nutty professor
old-fashioned
orange blossom
orgeat
peach sangaree
peppermint pattie
Pimm's cup
pina colada
pink lady
pink squirrel
planter's punch
posset
pousse cafa
prairie oyster
presbyterian
punch
rickey
Rob Roy
rum and coke
rum cooler
rusty nail
salty dog
sangria
San Juan cooler
Scarlett O'Hara
Scotch and soda
scotch on the rocks
screwdriver
seabreeze
Seven and Seven
shandy
shrub
sidecar cocktail
Singapore sling
slam dunk
sloe gin fizz
smash
snakebite
snowball
sombrero
soother cocktail
southern lady
southern peach
spritzer
stinger
syllabub
tequila sunrise
thoroughbred cooler
toasted almond
toddy
Tom and Jerry
Tom Collins
velvet hammer
virgin Mary
vodka and tonic
vodka gimlet
vodka martini
Wassail
whiskey sour
white lady
White Russian
white satin
white spider
wine cooler
wu-wu
zombie

55 coffee

café au lait
café filter
café noir
café latte, latte
cappuccino
chicory
decaffeinated coffee, decaf
espresso
frappé coffee, frappé
half-caf
iced coffee
pour-over coffee
mocha
Turkish coffee

56 dessert

angel food cake
apple brown betty
apple crisp
apple pie
baked Alaska
baklava
banana split
bananas Foster
Bavarian cream
blancmange
blondie
bombe
Boston cream pie
brandy snap
bread pudding
brownie
cake
cannoli
carrot cake
charlotte
charlotte russe
cheesecake
chocolate chip cookie
clafouti
cobbler
coffeecake
compote
cookie
coupe
cream puff
crème brûlée
crème caramel
crêpe suzette
crisp
cruller
cupcake
custard
Danish
deep dish pie
devil's food cake
doughnut
eclair
egg cream
Eskimo pie
fig bar
flan
floating island
flummery
frappe
frozen custard
frozen yogurt
fruitcake
fruit cup
fruit pie
frumenty
galatoboureko
gateau
gelatin
gelato
gingerbread
gingersnap
granita
halvah
ice cream
ice cream bar
ice cream cake
ice cream float
ice cream sandwich
ice cream soda
Indian pudding
Italian ice
Jell-O
jelly roll
junket
key lime pie
kuchen
lady finger
layer cake
lemon meringue pie
macaroon
marble cake
marshmallow
mela stregata
milkshake
mousse
mud pie
napoleon
Nesselrode
pandowdy
panettone
parfait
pastry
peach Melba
pie
pound cake
profiteroles
pudding
rice pudding
root beer float
sacher torte
scone
sheet cake
sherbert
shortbread
shortcake
s'mores
snow cone
snow pudding
sorbet
souffle
spice cake
sponge cake
strawberry shortcake
streusel
strudel
sugar cookie
sundae
sweet potato pie
sweet roll
syllabub
tapioca
tart
tartlet
tiramisu
Toll House cookie
torte
tres leches cake
trifle
turnover
upside-down cake
vacherin
wafer
wedding cake
zabaglione
zuppa inglese

57 fruit juice, vegetable juice

apple juice
apricot juice
carrot juice
cider, apple cider
coconut juice, coconut water
cranberry juice
grape juice
grapefruit juice
Hawaiian Punch <tm>
lemon juice
lemonade
limeade
mulled cider
orange juice
pineapple juice
pink lemonade
pomegranate juice
prune juice
sweet cider
tomato juice
V8 Vegetable Juice <tm>

58 liqueur

absinth, absinthe
amaretto
anisette, anisette de Bordeau
Benedictine
Chartreuse
coffee liqueur
crème de cacao
crème de menthe
crème de fraise
curacao, curacoa
Drambuie
Galliano
Grand Marnier
Kahlua
kummel
maraschino, maraschino liqueur
orange liqueur
pastis
Pernod
pousse-café
ratafia, ratafee
sambuca
triple sec

59 liquor

applejack
aqua vitae, ardent spirits
aquavit, akvavit
Armagnac
arrack, arak
bathtub gin
blended whiskey, blended whisky
bitters
bourbon
Calvados
Cognac
corn whiskey, corn whisky, corn liquor
demerara, demerara rum
eau de vie
firewater
geneva, Holland gin, Hollands
gin
grappa
grog
hard cider
Irish whiskey, Irish whisky
Jamaica rum
John Barleycorn
kirsch
malt whiskey, malt whisky
marc
mescal
moonshine, bootleg
ouzo
poteen
rye, rye whiskey, rye whisky
rum
schnapps, schnaps
Scotch, Scotch whiskey, Scotch whisky, Scotch malt whiskey, Scotch malt whisky
slivovitz
sloe gin
tequila
vodka
whiskey, whisky

60 meat cut

back rib
belly slice
blade
brain
breast
brisket
butt
center loin chop
chop
chuck
collar
cubes
cutlet
escalope
filet mignon
flank
fore rib
hock
joint
knuckle
leg
loin
loin chop
medallion
middle neck
neck fillet
noisette
rack
rib
ribeye
riblet
round
rump
saddle
shank
shin
shoulder
shoulder chop
side
sirloin
skirt
spareribs
steak
T-bone
tenderloin, fillet
tournedos
undercut

61 milk

almond milk
breast milk, mother's milk
buttermilk
chocolate milk
coconut milk
condensed milk
cow's milk
dried milk
evaporated milk
fat-free milk
filtered milk
fortified milk
goat's milk, goats' milk
homogenized milk
ice milk
kefir
koumiss, kumis, kumiss, kumys
Lactaid <tm> milk
lactose-reduced milk
low-fat milk
malted, malted milk
nonfat milk
one-percent milk
organic milk
pasteurized milk
powdered milk
raw milk
rice milk
skim milk, skimmed milk
soy milk, soybean milk
sterilized milk
strawberry milk
sweetened condensed milk
two-percent milk
UHT milk, ultra-heat treatment milk, long-life milk
ultra-high temperature milk
untreated milk
whole milk

62 soft drink

birch beer
Coke <tm>, Coca Cola <tm>
cola
cream soda
diet soda
Dr. Pepper <tm>
egg cream
float
ginger ale
ginger beer
Mountain Dew <tm>
orange soda
orangeade
Pepsi <tm>, Pepsi Cola <tm>
phosphate
root beer
sarsaparilla
Seven-Up <tm>, 7-Up <tm>
tonic, tonic water

63 tea

black tea
Darjeeling tea
Earl Grey tea
ginseng tea
green tea
herb tea

iced tea
orange
pekoe tea
pearl milk tea
spice tea
tisane

64 wine

Alsace
amontillado
amoroso
apple wine
Asti spumante
Aveleda
Barbera
Bardolino
Barolo
Beaujolais
Bergerac
blanc de noir
blend
blush
Bordeaux
Bordeaux Blanc
boutique wine
Burgundy
Cabernet Sauvignon
cabinet wine
California wine
Chablis
Champagne
Chardonnay
Chateauneuf-du-Pape
Chenin Blanc
Chianti
Christi
claret
cold duck
Condrieu
Cote Rotie
Cotes de Nuit
Cotes du Rhone
dandelion wine
Dao
dessert wine
DolcettoFrascati
Douro
dry wine
Entre-deux-Mers
fortified wine
Frascati
Fume Blanc
German wine
Gewurztraminer
Graves
Grenache
Hermitage
hock
Johannisberg Riesling
jug wine
Lacrima
Lambrusco
Liebfraumilch
Macon
Madeira
Malaga
Marsala
Mateus Rose
Medoc
Merlot
Montepulciano
Moselle
Muscadet
Muscat
Muscatel
Napa Valley wine
Navarra
Nierstein
noble wine
Oporto
Orvieto
Pauillac
Pinot Blanc
Pinot Grigio
Pinot Gris
Pinot Noir
Pomerol
Pommard
port
Pouilly-Fuisse
Pouilly-Fume
red wine
retsina
Rhine
Rhone
Riesling
Rioja
rose
ruby port
sake
Sancerre
Sangiovese
Sauternes
Sauvignon Blanc
Sekt
sherry
Shiraz
Soave
sparkling wine
St. Estephe
St. Julien
sweet wine
Sylvaner
Syrah
table wine
tawny port
Tokay-Pinot Gris
Valdepenas
Valpolicella
vermouth
vinho verde
vintage wine
Vouvray
white cabernet
white wine
white zinfandel
zinfandel

11 COOKING

<preparing food>

NOUNS **1** **cooking, cookery,** cuisine, culinary art; food preparation, food processing; home economics, domestic science, home management, culinary science; haute cuisine, *nouvelle cuisine* <Fr>; gastronomy; catering; nutrition

2 **<cooking technique>** manner of preparation, style of recipe; baking, blind baking, toasting, roasting, oven-roasting, frying, deep-frying, pan-frying, stir-frying, searing, flash-frying, blackening, smoking, curing, sautéing, boiling, parboiling, simmering, steaming, stewing, basting, braising, poaching, shirring, blanching, barbecuing, steeping, brewing, grilling, chargrilling, broiling, pan-broiling, charbroiling, microwaving, pressure-cooking; canning, pickling, preserving; induction cooking, slow-cooking

3 **cook, chef,** *cuisinier, cuisinière* <Fr>, kitchener, culinarian, culinary artist; chief cook, head chef, *chef de cuisine* <Fr>, cordon bleu cook; sous chef, apprentice chef, fry cook, grease-burner, short-order cook, food preparer, prep cook; **baker,** *boulanger* <Fr>, pastry cook, pastry chef, *patissier* <Fr>, saucier; caterer

4 **kitchen,** cookroom, cookery, scullery, cuisine; back of the house; kitchenette, cooking area; galley; cookhouse; bakery, bakehouse; barbecue; cookware, kitchenware, **cooker** <see list>; pots and pans; refrigerator, fridge, freezer; cookbook, recipe, receipt; batterie de cuisine <Fr>

VERBS **5** **cook,** prepare food, prepare, prepare a meal, do, cook up, fry up, boil up, rustle up; precook; boil, heat, heat up, stew, simmer, parboil, blanch; brew; poach, coddle; bake, fire, ovenbake; microwave, micro-cook, nuke; scallop; shirr; roast; toast; fry, deep-fry, deep-fat fry, griddle, pan, pan-fry; sauté, stir-fry; frizz, frizzle; sear, blacken, braise, brown; broil, grill, pan-broil; barbecue; fricassee; steam; devil; curry; baste; do to a turn, do to perfection, whip something up, throw something together

ADJS **6** **cooking, culinary,** kitchen, gastronomic, epicurean; mealtime, mensal; preprandial, postprandial, after-dinner; au naturel, a la mode, a la carte, table d'hote

7 **cooked,** heated, stewed, fried, barbecued, curried, fricasseed, deviled, sautéed, shirred, toasted; roasted, roast; fired, pan-fried, deep-fried, deep-fat fried, stir-fried; broiled, grilled, pan-broiled; seared, blackened, braised, browned; boiled, simmered, parboiled; steamed; blanched; poached, coddled; baked, oven-baked; scalloped; country-fried

8 **done, well-done,** well-cooked; *bien cuit* <Fr>, done to a turn, done to perfection; overcooked, **overdone,** burned; medium, medium-rare; doneness

9 **underdone,** undercooked, not done, **rare,** red, raw, *saignant* <Fr>; al dente; sodden, fallen

10 **cooker**

baker
barbecue
boiler
brazier
broiler
camp stove
chafer
chafing dish, chafing pan
coffee maker
convection oven
cook stove
cooktop
corn popper
Crockpot <tm>
deep fat fryer
double boiler
Dutch oven
electric cooker
electric frying pan
electric roaster
electric toaster
field range
fireless cooker
fry-cooker
galley stove
griddle
grill
hibachi
hot plate
infrared broiler
infrared cooker
instant pot
microwave oven
oven
percolator
pots and pans
pressure cooker, autoclave
range
roaster
rotisserie
samovar
slow cooker
smoker
steamer
stove
toaster
toaster oven
waffle iron
waterless cooker

12 EXCRETION

<bodily discharge>

NOUNS 1 **excretion,** egestion, extrusion, elimination, discharge, expulsion, call of nature; emission; eccrisis; exudation, transudation; extravasation, effusion, flux, flow; ejaculation, ejection; **secretion;** bodily function

2 **defecation,** dejection, evacuation, voidance; movement, **bowel movement** (BM), number two, stool, shit*, crap; diarrhea, loose bowels, flux; trots, runs, shits*, GI's, GI shits*; turistas, tourista, Montezuma's revenge, Aztec two-step; lientery; dysentery, bloody flux; catharsis, purgation, purge

3 **excrement,** dejection, dejecta, dejecture, discharge, ejection; matter; waste, waste matter; excreta, egesta, ejecta, ejectamenta; exudation, exudate; transudation; extravasation; effluent; sewage, sewerage

4 **feces,** feculence; defecation, movement, bowel movement (BM); stool, shit*, ordure, night soil, jakes, crap, ca-ca, doo-doo, number two, poo-poo, poop; turd; dingleberry; **manure,** dung, droppings; cow pats, cow flops; cow chips, buffalo chips; guano; coprolite, coprolith; sewage, sewerage

5 **urine,** water, piss*, number one, *pish* <Yiddish>, pee, pee-pee, wee-wee, whizz, piddle, leak, stale; **urination,** micturition, emiction, a piss*, a pee, a whizz; golden shower*; urea, uric acid

6 **pus; matter,** purulence, peccant humor, discharge, ichor, sanies; pussiness; suppuration, festering, rankling, mattering, running, weeping; gleet, leukorrhea

7 **sweat, perspiration,** perspiring, sweating, water, moisture, dampness, wetness; exudation, exudate; diaphoresis, sudor, sudation, sudoresis; honest sweat, the sweat of one's brow; beads of sweat, beaded brow; cold sweat; lather, swelter, streams of sweat; body odor (BO), perspiration odor

8 **hemorrhage,** hemorrhea, **bleeding;** nosebleed; ecchymosis, petechia

9 **menstruation,** menstrual discharge, flow, flux, catamenia, catamenial discharge, the curse, the curse of Eve; Aunt Flow, Flow; menses, monthlies, courses, period, one's friend, time of the month, that time

10 **restroom,** latrine, convenience, toilet, toilet room, water closet (WC); john, johnny, can, crapper, head; loo; lavatory, washroom; **bathroom,** basement; comfort station, comfort room, commode; ladies' room, women's room, girls' room, powder room, little girls' room; men's room, boys' room, little boys' room; the ladies', the gents'; privy, outhouse, backhouse, shithouse*, johnny house, earth closet <Brit>, jakes, closet, necessary; bog <Brit>; urinal

11 **toilet,** stool, water closet; john, johnny, can, crapper, thunderbox; latrine; commode, closetstool, potty-chair; chamber pot, chamber, pisspot, potty, jerry, jordan, thunder mug; throne; chemical toilet, chemical closet; urinal; bedpan; toilet training, potty training

VERBS 12 **excrete,** egest, eliminate, discharge, emit, give off, pass, expel; ease oneself, relieve oneself, go to the bathroom, go to the toilet; exude, exudate, transude; weep; effuse, extravasate; answer the call of nature, pay a call, make a pit stop, make a comfort stop; **secrete**

13 **defecate,** shit*, crap, evacuate, void, stool, dung,

have a bowel movement, have a BM, move one's bowels, soil, take a shit*, take a crap, ca-ca, number two; have the runs, have the trots, have the shits*

14 **urinate,** pass water, make water, wet, stale, piss*, piddle, pee, tinkle; pee-pee, wee-wee, whizz, take a whizz, take a leak, spend a penny, pump bilge, do number one

15 **fester,** suppurate, matter, rankle, run, weep; ripen, come to a head, draw to a head

16 **sweat, perspire,** exude; break out in a sweat, get all in a lather; sweat like a trooper, sweat like a pig, sweat like a horse, swelter, wilt, steam

17 **bleed,** hemorrhage, lose blood, shed blood, spill blood; bloody; ecchymose, extravasate

18 **menstruate,** come sick, bleed, come around, have one's period, have the curse, have one's friend, be on the rag, flow

ADJS **19** **excretory,** excretive, excretionary; eliminative, eliminant, egestive; exudative, transudative; **secretory**

20 **excremental,** excrementary; fecal, feculent, shitty*, crappy, scatologic, scatological, stercoral, stercorous, stercoraceous, dungy; **urinary,** urinative

21 **festering,** suppurative, rankling, mattering; pussy, purulent

22 **sweaty,** perspiry; sweating, perspiring; wet with sweat, beaded with sweat, sticky, clammy; bathed in sweat, drenched with sweat, wilted; in a sweat; sudatory, sudoric, sudorific, diaphoretic

23 **bleeding, bloody,** hemorrhaging; ecchymosed; blood-borne

24 **menstrual,** catamenial, menstruating; on the rag

13 SECRETION

<liquid bodily discharge>

NOUNS **1** **secretion,** secreta, secernment; **excretion**; external secretion, internal secretion; exudation, transudation; lactation; weeping, lacrimation; ooze

2 **digestive secretion**, digestive juice, salivary secretion, gastric juice, pancreatic juice, intestinal juice; bile, gall; endocrine; prostatic fluid, seminal fluid, semen, sperm; thyroxin; autacoid, hormone, chalone; mucus; tears; rheum; sebum, musk, pheromone; milk, colostrum; gland, pituitary gland

3 **saliva,** spittle, sputum, spit, expectoration, spitting; phlegm; salivation, ptyalism, sialorrhea, sialagogue, slobber, slabber, slaver, drivel, dribble, drool; froth, foam; mouth-watering

4 endocrinology, eccrinology, hormonology

VERBS **5** **secrete,** produce, give out, give off, exude, transude, release, emit, discharge, eject; **excrete**; water; lactate; weep, tear, cry, lacrimate; sweat, perspire; ooze

6 **salivate,** ptyalize; slobber, slabber, slaver, drool, drivel, dribble; expectorate, spit, spit up; spew; hawk, clear the throat

ADJS **7** **secretory,** secretive, secretional, secretionary, secreting; **excretory**; exudative, transudatory, emanative, emanatory, emanational; lymphatic, serous; seminal, spermatic; watery, watering; lactational; lacteal, lacteous, lactating; lachrymal, lacrimatory, lachrymose; rheumy; salivary, salivant, salivous, salivating, sialoid, sialagogic; sebaceous, sebiferous; sweating, sweaty, sudatory; oozing

8 **glandular,** glandulous; endocrine, humoral, exocrine, eccrine, apocrine, holocrine, merocrine; hormonal, hormonic; adrenal, pancreatic, gonadal; ovarian; luteal; prostatic; splenetic; thymic; thyroidal

14 BODILY DEVELOPMENT

<body growth>

NOUNS **1** **physical development,** growth, bodily development, development, maturation, maturing, maturescence, coming of age, growing up, reaching one's full growth, upgrowth; growing like a weed; plant growth, vegetation, germination, pullulation; sexual maturity, pubescence, puberty; nubility, marriageability, marriageableness; adulthood, manhood, womanhood; reproduction, procreation, burgeoning, sprouting; budding, gemmation; outgrowth, excrescence; overgrowth; human growth hormone (HGH)

VERBS **2** **grow, develop,** wax, **increase**; gather, brew; grow up, mature, maturate, spring up, ripen, come of age, shoot up, sprout up, upshoot, upspring, upsprout, upspear, overtop, tower, get bigger, get taller; grow like a weed; burgeon, **sprout**, blossom, reproduce, procreate, grow out of, germinate, pullulate; vegetate; flourish, thrive; mushroom, balloon; outgrow; overgrow, hypertrophy, overdevelop, grow uncontrollably

ADJS **3** **grown,** full-grown, grown-up, developed, well-developed, fully developed, mature, adult, full-fledged, fully fledged; growing, adolescent, maturescent, pubescent; nubile, marriageable; sprouting, crescent, budding, in full bloom, flowering, florescent, flourishing, blossoming, blooming, burgeoning, fast-growing, thriving; overgrown, hypertrophied, overdeveloped

15 STRENGTH

<inherent power>

NOUNS 1 **strength, might,** mightiness, powerfulness, stamina; force, potency, **power**; **energy**; vigor, vitality, vigorousness, heartiness, lustiness, lustihood; stoutness, sturdiness, stalwartness, robustness, hardiness, ruggedness; **guts**, gutsiness, fortitude, intestinal fortitude, **toughness**, endurance, staying power, sticking power, stick-to-it-iveness, sticktoitiveness, tenacity; strength of will, decisiveness, obstinacy

2 **muscularity,** brawniness; beefiness, huskiness, heftiness, burliness, thewiness, sinewiness; brawn, beef; **muscle,** sinew, sinews, thew, thews; musculature, build, physique; tone, elasticity; brute strength

3 **firmness, soundness,** staunchness, stoutness, sturdiness, stability, solidity, **hardness**, temper

4 **impregnability,** impenetrability, **invulnerability,** inexpugnability, inviolability; unassailability, unattackableness; resistlessness, irresistibility; invincibility, indomitability, insuperability, unconquerableness, unbeatableness

5 **strengthening,** invigoration, fortification; hardening, toughening, firming; case-hardening, tempering; restrengthening, reinforcement; reinvigoration, refreshment, revivification; fortifying

6 **strong man, strong woman;** stalwart, tower of strength, muscle man, piledriver, bulldozer, hunk, hardbody; giant, Samson, Goliath; Charles Atlas, Mr. Universe; superhero, Hercules, Atlas, Antaeus, Cyclops, Briareus, colossus, Polyphemus, Titan, Brobdingnagian, Tarzan, Superman; the strong, the mighty; bouncer; he-man; Wonder Woman, queen bee, high priestess; power couple

7 <nonformal> **hulk,** powerhouse, muscle man, man mountain, big bruiser, bruiser, strapper, strong-arm man, bully, bullyboy, ape, tough, toughie, tough guy, bozo, gorilla

8 <strong as comparisons> horse, ox, lion; oak, heart of oak; rock, Gibraltar; iron, steel, nails; lumberjack

VERBS 9 **be strong,** overpower, overwhelm; have what it takes, pack a punch

10 **not weaken,** not flag; bear up, hold up, keep up, stand up; hold out, stay it out, see it out, not give up, never say die, not let it get one down, gird up one's loins

11 <nonformal> **tough it out,** hang tough, hang in, stick, take it, take it on the chin, sweat it out, go the distance, stay the distance

12 **exert strength,** put beef into it, put one's back into it; use force, get tough, muscle, manhandle, strong-arm; push around

13 **strengthen,** invigorate, fortify, beef up, brace, batten, buttress, prop, shore up, support, undergird, brace up; gird, gird up one's loins; steel, harden, case-harden, anneal, stiffen, toughen, temper, nerve; confirm, sustain; restrengthen, reinforce; reinvigorate, refresh, revive, recruit one's strength; tone; soup up

14 **insulate,** proof, weatherproof, soundproof, muffle, quietize, fireproof, waterproof, goofproof; babyproof, childproof

ADJS 15 **strong, forceful,** forcible, mighty, powerful, puissant, **potent**; hard-charging; stout, sturdy, stalwart, rugged, hale; hunky, husky, hefty, beefy, strapping, durable, doughty, hardy, hard, hard as nails, cast-iron, iron-hard, steely, hard-bodied; robust, robustious, gutty, gutsy; strong-willed, obstinate; vigorous, hearty, nervy, lusty, bouncing, full-blooded, red-blooded; bionic, sturdy as an ox, strong as a lion, strong as a horse, strong as an ox, strong as brandy, strong as pig-shit*, strong as strong; full-strength, double-strength, industrial-strength

16 **able-bodied, well-built,** well-set, well-set-up, well-knit, of good physique, of powerful physique, broad-shouldered, barrel-chested, athletic; muscular, well-muscled, heavily muscled, thickset, burly, brawny; buff, buffed; thewy, sinewy, wiry; muscle-bound, all muscle; strapping

17 **herculean,** Briarean, Antaean, cyclopean, Atlantean, gigantic, gigantesque, brobdingnagian, huge; amazonian

18 **firm, sound,** stout, sturdy, tough, hard-boiled, staunch, stable, solid; sound as a dollar, solid as a rock, firm as Gibraltar, made of iron; buffed; rigid, unbreakable, infrangible; braced, buttressed

19 **impregnable,** impenetrable, **invulnerable,** inviolable, inexpugnable; unassailable, unattackable, insuperable, unsurmountable; resistless, irresistible; invincible, indomitable, unconquerable, unsubduable, unyielding, incontestable, unbeatable, more than a match for; overpowering, overwhelming, avalanchine

20 **resistant,** proof, tight; impervious; foolproof; shatterproof; weatherproof, dampproof, watertight, hermetically sealed, vacuum-packed, leakproof; hermetic, airtight; soundproof, noiseproof; puncture proof, holeproof; bulletproof, ballproof, shellproof, bombproof; rustproof, corrosionproof; fireproof, flameproof, fire-resisting; burglarproof

21 **unweakened,** undiminished, unallayed, unbated, unabated, unfaded, unwithered, unshaken, unworn, unexhausted; unweakening, unflagging,

unbowed; in full force, in full swing, going strong; in the plenitude of power

22 <of sounds and odors> **intense, penetrating,** piercing; loud, deafening, thundering; pungent, five-alarm, three-alarm, **reeking**

ADVS 23 strongly, stoutly, sturdily, stalwartly, robustly, ruggedly; mightily, powerfully, forcefully, forcibly; vigorously, heartily, lustily; soundly, firmly, staunchly; impregnably, invulnerably, invincibly, irresistibly, unyieldingly; resistantly, imperviously; intensely; loudly, at the top of one's lungs, clamorously, deafeningly; pungently

COMBINING FORMS 24 muscul-, musculo-, my-, myo-; -eus

16 WEAKNESS

<lacking power>

NOUNS 1 **weakness,** weakliness, feebleness, enfeeblement, strengthlessness; flabbiness, flaccidity, softness; impotence, impotency; debility, debilitation, prostration, invalidism, collapse; faintness, faintishness, dizziness, lightheadedness, shakiness, gone feeling, blah feeling; **fatigue**, exhaustion, weariness, dullness, sluggishness, languor, lassitude, listlessness, tiredness, languishment, atony, burnout; anemia, bloodlessness, etiolation, asthenia, adynamia, cachexia, cachexy

2 **frailty,** slightness, **delicacy,** daintiness, lightness; flimsiness, unsubstantiality, wispiness, sleaziness, shoddiness; fragility, frangibility, frangibleness, brittleness, breakableness, destructibility; disintegration; human frailty, fatal flaw, sleaze factor; gutlessness, cowardice; moral weakness, irresolution, indecisiveness, infirmity of will, velleity, changeableness; inherent vice

3 **infirmity, unsoundness,** incapacity, unfirmness, unsturdiness, instability, unsubstantiality; decrepitude; unsteadiness, shakiness, ricketiness, wobbliness, wonkiness, weediness; caducity, senility, invalidism; wishy-washiness, insipidity, vapidity, wateriness

4 **weak point, weakness,** weak place, weak side, weak link, vulnerable point, chink in one's armor, Achilles' heel, heel of Achilles, soft underbelly; fatal flaw; feet of clay

5 **weakening,** enfeeblement, debilitation, exhaustion, inanition, attrition; languishment; devitalization, enervation, evisceration; fatigue; attenuation, extenuation; softening, mitigation, damping, abatement, slackening, relaxing, relaxation, blunting, deadening, dulling; **dilution,** watering, watering-down, thinning, reduction

6 **weakling,** weak soul, meek soul, weak sister, hothouse plant, softy, softling, jellyfish, invertebrate, gutless wonder, baby, big baby, crybaby, chicken, scaredy-cat, coward, wimp, wussy, Milquetoast, sop, milksop, namby-pamby, mollycoddle, mama's boy, mother's boy, mother's darling, teacher's pet; sissy, pansy, pantywaist, pushover, softie, lightweight; poor tool, weak tool, dull tool; nonentity, hollow man, doormat, empty suit, nebbish, sad sack

7 <weak as comparisons> kitten, reed, thread, matchwood, rope of sand; house of cards, eggshell, glass, house built on sand, sand castle, cobweb; water, milk and water, gruel, dishwater, cambric tea

VERBS 8 <be weak> **shake,** tremble, quiver, quaver, cringe, cower, totter, teeter, dodder; halt, limp; be on one's last leg, have one foot in the grave

9 <become weak> **weaken,** grow weak, grow weaker, go soft; **languish,** wilt, faint, droop, drop, dwindle, sink, decline, flag, pine, fade, tail off, fail, fall by the wayside, drop by the wayside, ebb, wane; crumble, go to pieces, disintegrate; go downhill, hit the skids, give way, break, collapse, cave in, surrender, cry uncle; give out, have no staying power, run out of gas, conk out, peter out, poop out, peg out, fizzle out; come apart, come apart at the seams, come unstuck, come unglued; yield; die on the vine; wear thin, wear away

10 <make weak> **weaken, enfeeble,** debilitate, unstrengthen, unsinew, undermine, soften up, unbrace, unman, unnerve, rattle, shake up, impair, devitalize, enervate, eviscerate; sap, sap the strength of, exhaust, gruel, take it out of; shake, unstring; reduce, lay low; attenuate, extenuate, mitigate, abate; blunt, deaden, dull, damp, dampen, take the edge off; draw the teeth, defang; cramp, cripple

11 **dilute, cut, reduce,** thin, thin out, attenuate, rarefy; water, water down, adulterate, irrigate, baptize; soften, muffle, mute; negate

ADJS 12 **weak,** weakly, feeble, debilitated, imbecile; strengthless, sapless, marrowless, pithless, sinewless, listless, out of gas, nerveless, lustless; impotent, **powerless**; spineless, lily-livered, whitelivered, wimpy, wimpish, chicken, gutless, wussy, cowardly; unnerved, shookup, unstrung, faint, faintish, lightheaded, dizzy, gone; dull, slack; soft, flabby, flaccid, unhardened; limp, limber, limp as a dishrag, floppy, rubbery; languorous, languid, drooping, droopy, pooped; asthenic, anemic, bloodless, effete, etiolated; not what one used to be

13 **weak as water**, weak as milk and water, weak as a drink of water, weak as a child, weak as a baby,

weak as a chicken, weak as a kitten, weak as a mouse, weak as a rained-on bee

14 **frail,** slight, delicate, dainty; puny; light, lightweight; effeminate; namby-pamby, sissified, pansyish; fragile, frangible, breakable, destructible, shattery, crumbly, brittle, fragmentable, fracturable; unsubstantial, **flimsy,** sleazy, skeezy, tacky, wispy, cobwebby, gossamery, papery; gimcrack, gimcracky, cheap-jack, ticky-tacky; jerry-built, jerry; gimpy

15 **unsound, infirm,** unfirm, unstable, unsubstantial, unsturdy, unsolid, decrepit, crumbling, fragmented, fragmentary, disintegrating; poor, poorish; rotten, rotten to the core

16 **unsteady, shaky,** rickety, ricketish, wonky, spindly, spidery, teetering, teetery, tottery, tottering, doddering, tumbledown, ramshackle, dilapidated, rocky; groggy, wobbly, staggery

17 **wishy-washy,** tasteless, bland, insipid, vapid, neutral, watery, milky, milk-and-water, mushy; halfhearted, infirm of will, infirm of purpose, indecisive, irresolute, changeable; limp-wristed, gutless

18 **weakened,** enfeebled, disabled, incapacitated, challenged, debilitated, infirm; devitalized, drained, exhausted, sapped, burned-out, maxed-out, used up, played out, spent, out of, outta, effete, etiolated; fatigued, enervated, eviscerated; wasted, rundown, worn, worn-out, worn to a frazzle; stressed out; on one's last legs

19 **diluted,** cut, reduced, thinned, rarefied, attenuated; adulterated; watered, watered-down

20 **weakening, debilitating,** enfeebling; devitalizing, enervating, sapping, exhausting, fatiguing, grueling, trying, draining, unnerving

21 **languishing,** drooping, sinking, declining, flagging, pining, fading, failing; on the wane

ADVS 22 **weakly,** feebly, strengthlessly, languorously, listlessly; faintly; delicately, effeminately, daintily; infirmly, unsoundly, unstably, unsubstantially, unsturdily, flimsily; shakily, unsteadily, teeteringly, totteringly

17 ENERGY

<usable strength>

NOUNS 1 **energy, vigor,** force, power, vitality, strenuousness, intensity, dynamism, demonic energy; **potency**; **strength**; actual energy, kinetic energy; dynamic energy; potential energy; **energy source**, electrical energy, hydroelectric energy, hydroelectric power, water power, nuclear energy, solar energy, wind energy, solar farm; alternative energy, alternate energy, green energy; renewable energy; energy vampire

2 **vim,** verve, fire, adrenalin, dash, drive; aggressiveness, enterprise, initiative, proactiveness, thrust, spunk; **eagerness**, zeal, heartiness, keenness, gusto, passion

3 <nonformal> **pep,** bang, biff, get-up-and-go, ginger, gism, jazz, sizzle, kick, moxie, oomph, pepper, piss and vinegar*, pizzazz, poop, punch, push, snap, spizzerinctum, spark, starch, steam, zing, zip, zizz, sparkle, wallop, balls, adrenaline rush

4 **animation, vivacity,** liveliness, energy, ardor, vitality, glow, warmth, enthusiasm, vibrancy, lustiness, robustness, mettle, zest, zestfulness, gusto, élan, éclat, impetus, impetuosity, *joie de vivre* <Fr>, *brio* <Ital>, spiritedness, briskness, perkiness, sprightliness, pertness, sensibility, life, spirit, life force, vital force, vital principle, *élan vital* <Fr>; activity

5 <energetic disapproval or criticism> **acrimony,** acridity, acerbity, acidity, bitterness, tartness, causticity, mordancy, mordacity, virulence; harshness, fierceness, rigor, roughness, severity, vehemence, violence, stringency, astringency, stridency, sharpness, keenness, poignancy, trenchancy; edge, point; bite, teeth, grip, sting; animosity; backstabbing; cheap shot

6 **energizer, stimulus,** stimulant, stimulator, vitalizer, arouser, needle, restorative; tonic; activator, motivator, motivating force, motive power; animator, sparkplug, human dynamo, ball of fire; life, life of the party; spinach

7 **<unit of energy>** atomerg, dinamode, dyne, erg, energid, foot-pound, horsepower-hour, horsepower-year, joule, calorie, kilogram-meter, kilowatt-hour, photon, quantum

8 **energizing,** invigoration, animation, enlivenment, quickening, vitalization, revival, revitalization; exhilaration, stimulation

9 **activation,** reactivation; viability

VERBS 10 **energize,** dynamize; **invigorate, animate,** enliven, liven, liven up, vitalize, quicken, goose up, jazz up; exhilarate, stimulate, hearten, galvanize, enthuse, electrify, fire, build a fire under, inflame, warm, kindle, charge, charge up, psych up, pump up, rouse, arouse, act like a tonic, be a shot in the arm, pep up, snap up, zip up, perk up, put pep into it, put zip into it

11 **have energy,** be energetic, be vigorous, **thrive,** burst with energy, overflow with energy, flourish, tingle, feel one's oats, be up and doing, be full of beans, be full of pep, be full of ginger, be full of zip, be full of piss and vinegar, champ at the bit; come on like gangbusters

12 **activate,** reactivate, recharge, reanimate; step on the gas

ADJS 13 **energetic, vigorous,** strenuous, forceful, forcible, strong, dynamic, kinetic, intense, acute, keen, incisive, trenchant, vivid, vibrant, passionate; enterprising, aggressive, proactive, activist, can-do, gung ho, take-over, take-charge, go-getting; active, lively, living, animated, spirited, go-go, vivacious, brisk, bright-eyed, bright-eyed and bushy-tailed, feisty, lusty, robust, hearty, enthusiastic, mettlesome, zesty, zestful, impetuous, spanking, smacking; pumped, pumped up, jazzed-up, charged up, switched-on, full-on, snappy, zingy, zippy, peppy, full of pep, full of pizzazz, full of piss and vinegar, full of beans; adrenaline-charged

14 **acrimonious,** acrid, acidulous, acid, acerbic, bitter, tart, caustic, escharotic, mordant, mordacious, virulent, violent, vehement, vitriolic; harsh, fierce, rigorous, severe, rough, stringent, astringent, strident, sharp, keen, sharpish, incisive, trenchant, cutting, biting, stinging, scathing, stabbing, piercing, poignant, penetrating, edged, double-edged

15 **energizing,** vitalizing, enlivening, quickening; tonic, bracing, rousing; invigorating, invigorative; animating, animative; exhilarating, exhilarative; stimulating, stimulative, stimulatory, vivifying; activating; viable; energy efficient

ADVS 16 **energetically,** vigorously, strenuously, forcefully, forcibly, intensely, like a house afire, like gangbusters, zestfully, lustily, heartily, keenly, passionately; actively, briskly; animatedly, spiritedly, vivaciously, with pep, *con brio* <Ital>

18 POWER, POTENCY

<effective force>

NOUNS 1 **power, potency**, potence, prepotency, force, might, mightiness, vigor, vitality, vim, push, drive, charge, puissance; dint, virtue; moxie, oomph, pizzazz, poop, punch, bang, clout, steam; powerfulness, forcefulness; virulence, vehemence; **strength**; **energy**; **virility**; cogence, cogency, validity, effect, impact, effectiveness, effectivity, effectuality, competence, competency; productivity, productiveness; power structure, corridors of power; **influence**, pull; **authority**, weight; **superiority**; power pack, amperage, wattage; main force, *force majeure* <Fr>, main strength, brute force, brute strength, compulsion, duress; muscle power, sinew, might and main, beef, strong arm; full force, full blast; power struggle; mana; charisma

2 **ability, capability, capacity,** potentiality, faculty, facility, fitness, qualification, talent, flair, genius, caliber, competence, competency, adequacy, sufficiency, efficiency, efficacy; **proficiency**; the stuff, the goods, what it takes; susceptibility

3 **omnipotence,** almightiness, all-powerfulness, invincibility; omnicompetence

4 manpower; horsepower, brake horsepower (bhp), electric power, electropower, hydroelectric power; hydraulic power, water power; steam power; geothermal power; solar power; atomic power, nuclear power, thermonuclear power; rocket power, jet power; propulsion, thrust, impulse

5 force of inertia, *vis inertiae* <L>, torpor; dead force, *vis mortua* <L>; living force, *vis viva* <L>; force of life, *vis vitae* <L>

6 centrifugal force, centrifugal action, centripetal force, centripetal action, force of gravity

7 <science of forces> dynamics, statics, mechanics

8 **empowerment,** enablement; investment, endowment, enfranchisement

9 **work force,** hands, men, manpower; fighting force, troops, units, forces, the big battalions, firepower; **personnel**, human resources

VERBS 10 **empower, enable;** invest, clothe, invest with power, clothe with power, commission, deputize, warrant; enfranchise; endue, endow, authorize; arm; strengthen

11 **be able,** be up to, up to, lie in one's power; can, may, can do; make it, make the grade; hack it, cut it, cut the mustard; charismatize; wield power, possess authority; **take charge**, get something under one's control, get something under one's thumb, hold all the aces, have the say-so

ADJS 12 **powerful**, potent, prepotent, powerpacked, mighty, irresistible, avalanchine, forceful, forcible, dynamic; vigorous, vital, energetic, puissant, ruling, in power; cogent, striking, telling, effective, impactful, valid, operative, in force; strong; high-powered, high-tension, high-pressure, high-performance, high-potency, bionic; authoritative; armipotent, mighty in battle; kick-ass

13 **omnipotent,** almighty, all-powerful; plenipotentiary, pre-eminent, absolute, unlimited, **sovereign**; **supreme**; omnicompetent

14 **able, capable,** equal to, up to, competent, adequate, effective, effectual, efficient, efficacious, can-do; productive; **proficient**

ADVS 15 **powerfully,** potently, forcefully, forcibly, mightily, with might and main, vigorously, energetically, dynamically; cogently, strikingly, tellingly, impactfully; effectively, effectually; productively; with telling effect, to good account, to good purpose, with a vengeance

16 **ably, capably,** competently, adequately, effectively, effectually, efficiently, well; to the best of one's ability, as lies in one's power, so far as one can, as

best one can; with all one's might, with everything that is in one

17 **by force,** by main force, by brute force, by *force majeure,* with the strong arm, with a high hand, high-handedly; **forcibly,** amain, with might and main; by force of arms, at the point of the sword, by storm

PREPS 18 by dint of, by virtue of

COMBINING FORMS 19 dynam-, dynamo-; -dynamia

19 IMPOTENCE

<lacking strength>

NOUNS 1 **impotence**, impotency, **powerlessness,** impuissance, forcelessness, feebleness, softness, flabbiness, wimpiness, wimpishness, **weakness**; power vacuum

2 **inability,** incapability, incapacity, incapacitation, incompetence, incompetency, inadequacy, insufficiency, ineptitude, **inferiority**, inefficiency, unfitness, imbecility; disability, special need, special needs, disablement, disqualification; legal incapacity, wardship, minority, infancy, no can do

3 **ineffectiveness,** ineffectualness, ineffectuality, inefficaciousness, inefficacy, counterproductiveness, counterproductivity, invalidity, futility, uselessness, inutility, bootlessness, failure; fatuity, inanity

4 **helplessness,** defenselessness, unprotectedness, vulnerability; debilitation, invalidism, effeteness, etiolation, enervation; wimpiness; learned helplessness

5 **emasculation,** demasculinization, defeminization, effeminization, neutering, maiming, castration

6 **impotent,** weakling, invalid, incompetent, unable; flash in the pan, blank cartridge, wimp, dud; eunuch, *castrato* <Ital>, gelding; pushover, easy mark

VERBS 7 **be impotent**, lack force; be ineffective, avail nothing, not work, do not take; waste one's effort, bang one's head against a brick wall, have one's hands tied, spin one's wheels, tilt at windmills, run in circles, get nowhere

8 **cannot, not be able,** be unable, not have it, not hack it, not cut it, not cut the mustard, not make it, not make the grade, not make the cut, no can do

9 **disable,** disenable, unfit, **incapacitate,** drain, de-energize; enfeeble, debilitate, **weaken**; cripple, maim, lame, hamstring, knee-cap, defang, pull the teeth of; wing, clip the wings of; inactivate, disarm, unarm, put out of action, put *hors de combat;* put out of order, put out of commission, throw out of gear; bugger, bugger up <Brit>, queer, queer the works, gum up, screw up, throw a wrench in the machinery, throw a monkey wrench in the machinery, sabotage, wreck; kibosh, put the kibosh on; spike, spike one's guns, put a spoke in one's wheels

10 put out of action, **paralyze,** prostrate, shoot down in flames, put *hors de combat*, knock out, break the neck of, break the back of; hamstring; handcuff, tie the hands of, hobble, enchain, manacle, hogtie, tie hand and foot, truss up; throttle, strangle, get a stranglehold on; muzzle, gag, silence; take the wind out of one's sails, deflate, knock the props out from under, undermine, cut the ground from under, not leave a leg to stand on

11 **disqualify;** invalidate, knock the bottom out of

12 **unman, unnerve,** enervate, exhaust, etiolate, devitalize; emasculate, cut the balls off, demasculinize, effeminize; desex, desexualize; sterilize; castrate, neuter

ADJS 13 **impotent, powerless,** forceless, out of gas; feeble, soft, flabby, **weak**, weak as a kitten, wimpy, wimpish, wussy

14 **unable, incapable,** incompetent, inefficient, ineffective; unqualified, inept, lame-o, unendowed, ungifted, untalented, unfit, unfitted; outmatched, out of one's depth, in over one's head, outgunned; **inferior**

15 **ineffective, ineffectual,** inefficacious, counterproductive, feckless, not up to scratch, not up to snuff, inadequate; invalid, inoperative, of no force; nugatory, nugacious; fatuous, fatuitous; vain, futile, inutile, useless, unavailing, bootless, fruitless; all talk and no action, all wind; empty, inane; debilitated, effete, enervated, etiolated, barren, sterile, washed-out

16 **disabled, incapacitated;** crippled, hamstrung; disqualified, invalidated; disarmed; paralyzed; hogtied; prostrate, on one's back, on one's beam-ends; challenged

17 **out of action,** out of commission, out of it, out of gear; *hors de combat* <Fr>, out of the battle, off the field, out of the running; laid on the shelf, obsolete, life-expired

18 **helpless, defenseless,** unprotected; vulnerable, like a sitting duck, dead in the water, aidless, friendless, unfriended; fatherless, motherless; leaderless, guideless; untenable, pregnable; disenfranchised

19 **unmanned, unnerved**, enervated, debilitated, devitalized; nerveless, sinewless, marrowless, pithless, lustless; castrated, emasculate, emasculated, gelded, eunuchized, unsexed, deballed, demasculinized, effeminized

ADVS 20 **beyond one,** beyond one's power, beyond

one's capacity, beyond one's ability, beyond one's depth, out of one's league, above one's head, too much for

20 REST, REPOSE

<*inactive state*>

NOUNS 1 **rest,** repose, **ease, relaxation,** leisure, slippered ease, unbuttoned ease, decompression; **comfort**; comfort zone; restfulness, quiet, tranquility; inactivity; sleep

2 **respite,** recess, **rest**, pause, chillout, halt, stay, lull, break, surcease, suspension, interlude, intermission, spell, letup, time out, time to catch one's breath; breathing spell, breathing time, breathing place, breathing space, breath; breather; coffee break, tea break, cigarette break; cocktail hour, happy hour; enforced respite, downtime; R and R, rest and recreation; maternity leave, paternity leave, parental leave

3 **vacation,** holiday <Brit>, getaway; **time off;** day off, week off, month off; paid vacation, paid holiday; personal day, personal time, personal time off; weekend; **leave,** leave of absence, furlough; liberty, shore leave; day trip, scenic route; sabbatical, sabbatical leave, sabbatical year; busman's holiday; package tour, package holiday; honeymoon; babymoon; spring break, winter break; Cook's tour; vacay

4 **holiday, day off**; red-letter day, gala day, fete day, festival day, day of festivities, field day; national holiday, legal holiday, bank holiday <Brit>; High Holiday, High Holy Day; holy day; feast, feast day, high day, church feast, fixed feast, movable feast; half-holiday; mini-break; off-hours

5 **day of rest,** *dies non* <L>; Sabbath, Sunday, Lord's day, First day

VERBS 6 **rest,** repose, take rest, take one's ease, take it easy, lay down one's tools, rest from one's labors, rest on one's oars, take life easy; go to rest, settle to rest; lie down, have a lie-down, go to bed, snuggle down, curl up, tuck up, bed, bed down, couch, recline, lounge, drape oneself, sprawl, loll; take off one's shoes, unbuckle one's belt, get a load off one's feet, take a load off one's feet, put one's feet up

7 **relax,** unlax, unbend, unwind, slack, slacken, ease; ease up, let up, slack up, slack off, ease off, let down, slow down, take it slow, take time to catch one's breath; mellow out, chill, chillax, lay back, kick back, decompress

8 **take a rest,** take a break, break, take time out, grab some R and R, pause, lay off, knock off, recess, take a recess, take ten, take five; stop for breath, catch one's breath, breathe; stop work, suspend operations, call it a day; go to bed with the chickens, sleep in; take a nap, catch some Z's; take a moment; sleep off; sleep over

9 **vacation,** get away from it all, holiday, take a holiday, make holiday; take a leave of absence, take leave, go on leave, go on furlough, take one's sabbatical; weekend; Sunday, Christmas

ADJS 10 **holiday,** vacational, ferial, festal; sabbatical; comfortable; restful, quiet; chill, chill-out; off-hours

ADVS 11 **at rest,** at ease, at one's ease; abed, in bed

12 **on vacation,** on leave, on furlough; off duty, on one's own time, having a field day

21 FATIGUE

<*tired state*>

NOUNS 1 **fatigue, tiredness,** weariness, wearifulness; burnout, end of one's tether, overtiredness, overstrain; faintness, goneness, weakness, enfeeblement, lack of staying power, enervation, debility, debilitation; jadedness; lassitude, languor; tension fatigue, stance fatigue, stimulation fatigue; fatigue disease, fatigue syndrome, post-viral fatigue syndrome, chronic fatigue syndrome; combat fatigue; mental fatigue, brain fag; strain, mental strain, heart strain, eyestrain; jet lag, sleepiness

2 **exhaustion,** exhaustedness, draining, inanition; collapse, prostration, breakdown, crack-up, nervous exhaustion, nervous prostration, burnout; blackout

3 **breathlessness,** shortness of breath, windedness, short-windedness; panting, gasping; dyspnea, labored breathing

VERBS 4 **fatigue, tire,** weary, exhaust, wilt, flag, jade, harass; wear, wear on, wear upon, wear down; tire out, wear out, burn out; use up; do in; wind, put out of breath; overtire, overweary, overfatigue, overstrain; weaken, enervate, debilitate; weary to death, tire to death, take it out of; prostrate; deprive of sleep

5 **burn out, get tired,** grow weary, tire, weary, fatigue, jade; flag, droop, faint, sink, feel dragged out, wilt; play out, run out, run down; gasp, wheeze, pant, puff, blow, puff and blow, puff like a grampus; collapse, break down, crack up, give out, drop, fall by the wayside, drop by the wayside, drop in one's tracks, succumb; need a break

6 <nonformal> **beat, poop,** frazzle, fag, tucker; tucker out, knock out, do in, do up; poop out, peter out

ADJS 7 **tired, weary, fatigued,** wearied, weariful, jaded, run-down, good and tired; unrefreshed, unrestored, in need of rest, ready to drop; faint, fainting, feeling faint, weak, rocky, enfeebled, enervated, debilitated, seedy, weakened; drooping, droopy, wilting, flagging, sagging; languid; worn, worn-down, worn to a frazzle, worn to a shadow, toilworn, weary-worn; wayworn, way-weary; foot-weary, weary-footed, footsore; tired-armed; tired-winged, weary-winged; weary-laden

8 <nonformal> **beat, pooped,** bushed, poohed, paled, frazzled, bagged, fagged, tuckered, plumb tuckered, done, done in, all in, dead, dead beat, dead on one's feet, gone; pooped out, knocked out, wiped out, tuckered out, played out, fagged out; run ragged; used up, done up, beat up, washed-up, whacked out

9 tired-looking, weary-looking, tired-eyed, tired-faced, haggard, hollow-eyed, ravaged, drawn, cadaverous, worn, wan, zombiish

10 **burnt-out,** burned-out, **exhausted,** drained, spent, unable to go on, gone; tired out, worn out, beaten; maxed-out; bone-tired, bone-weary; dog-tired, dog-weary; dead-tired, tired to death, weary unto death, dead-alive, dead-and-alive, more dead than alive, ready to drop, on one's last legs; prostrate

11 **overtired,** overweary, overwrought, overwearied, overstrained, overdriven, overfatigued, overspent; hackneyed

12 **breathless,** winded; wheezing, puffing, panting, **out of breath,** short of breath, short of wind, gasping for breath, agasp; short-winded, short-breathed, dyspneic

13 **fatiguing,** wearying, wearing, tiring, straining, stressful, trying, exhausting, draining, grueling, punishing, killing, demanding; tiresome, fatiguesome, wearisome, weariful; toilsome

ADVS 14 **out,** to the point of exhaustion

22 SLEEP

<unconscious rest>

NOUNS 1 **sleepiness, drowsiness,** kef, doziness, heaviness, lethargy, oscitation, somnolence, somnolency, yawning, stretching, oscitancy, pandiculation; languor; sand in the eyes, heavy eyelids; REM sleep, rapid-eye-movement sleep, dream sleep, dreaming sleep; dormition

2 **sleep, slumber;** repose, silken repose, *somnus* <L>, the arms of Morpheus; beddy-bye; doss, blanket drill, shuteye; light sleep, fitful sleep, doze, drowse, snoozle; beauty sleep; sleepwalking, somnambulism; somniloquy; land of Nod, slumberland, sleepland, dreamland; hibernation, winter sleep, aestivation, aestivating; bedtime, sack time; unconsciousness

3 **nap, snooze,** catnap, wink, forty winks, some Zs, zizz, wink of sleep, spot of sleep; siesta, blanket drill, sack time, rack time; power nap

4 sweet sleep, balmy sleep, downy sleep, soft sleep, gentle sleep, smiling sleep, golden slumbers; peaceful sleep, sleep of the just; restful sleep, good night's sleep

5 **deep sleep,** profound sleep, heavy sleep, **sound sleep,** cataphor, unbroken sleep, wakeless sleep, drugged sleep, dreamless sleep, the sleep of the dead; paradoxical sleep, orthodox sleep, dreaming sleep, REM sleep; synchronized sleep, S sleep, NREM sleep; lucid dreaming

6 **stupor,** sopor, **coma,** swoon, lethargy, persistent vegetative state; trance; narcosis, narcohypnosis, narcoma, narcotization, narcotic stupor, narcotic trance; sedation; high; nod; narcolepsy; catalepsy; thanatosis, shock; sleeping sickness, encephalitis lethargica

7 **hypnosis,** mesmeric sleep, hypnotic sleep, trance, somnipathy, hypnotic somnolence; lethargic hypnosis, somnambulistic hypnosis, cataleptic hypnosis, animal hypnosis; narcohypnosis; autohypnosis, self-hypnosis; hypnotherapy

8 **hypnotism, mesmerism;** hypnology; hypnotization, mesmerization; animal magnetism, od, odyl, odylic force; hypnotic suggestion, posthypnotic suggestion, autosuggestion

9 **hypnotist,** mesmerist, hypnotizer, mesmerizer; Svengali, Mesmer

10 **sleep-inducer,** sleep-producer, sleep-provoker, sleep-bringer, hypnotic, soporific, somnifacient; poppy, mandrake, mandragora, opium, opiate, morphine, morphia; nightcap; sedative; anesthetic; lullaby

11 **Morpheus,** Somnus, Hypnos; sandman, dustman

12 **sleeper,** slumberer; sleeping beauty; sleepyhead, lie-abed, slugabed, sleepwalker, somnambulist; somniloquist, dreamer

VERBS 13 **sleep, slumber,** rest in the arms of Morpheus; doze, drowse; nap, catnap, take a nap, catch a wink, sleep soundly, sleep like a log, sleep like the dead; snore, saw wood, saw logs; have an early night, go to bed betimes; sleep in; oversleep

14 <nonformal> **snooze,** get some shut-eye, get some sack time, flake out, sack out, crash, catch forty winks, catch some Z's, zizz; pound the ear, kip <Brit>, doss <Brit>, log z's

15 **hibernate,** aestivate, lie dormant

16 **go to sleep,** settle to sleep, go off to sleep, **fall asleep,** drop asleep, drop off, drift off, drift off to sleep; doze off, drowse off, nod off; close one's eyes

17 **go to bed,** retire; lay me down to sleep; bed, bed down; go night-night, go beddy-bye

18 <nonformal> **hit the hay, hit the sack,** crash,

turn in, crawl in, flop, sack out, sack up; kip down, doss down <Brit>, lights out

19 **put to bed,** bed; nestle, cradle; tuck in

20 **put to sleep;** lull to sleep, rock to sleep; hypnotize, mesmerize, magnetize; entrance, trance, put in a trance; narcotize, drug, dope; anesthetize, put under; sedate

ADJS **21** **sleepy, drowsy,** dozy, snoozy, slumberous, slumbery, dreamy, sleepful; half asleep, asleep on one's feet; sleep-filled; yawny, stretchy, oscitant, yawning, napping, nodding, ready for bed; heavy, heavy-eyed, heavy with sleep, sleep-swollen, sleep-drowned, sleep-drunk, drugged with sleep; somnolent, soporific; lethargic, comatose, narcose, narcous, stuporose, stuporous, in a stupor, out of it; narcoleptic; cataleptic; narcotized, drugged, doped, doped up; sedated; anesthetized; languid

22 **asleep, sleeping,** slumbering, in the arms of Morpheus, in the lap of Morpheus, in the land of Nod; sound asleep, fast asleep, dead asleep, deep asleep, in a sound sleep, flaked-out; unconscious, oblivious, out, out like a light, out cold; comatose; dormant; dead, dead to the world; unwakened, unawakened

23 **sleep-inducing,** sleep-producing, sleep-bringing, sleep-causing, sleep-compelling, sleep-inviting, sleep-provoking, sleep-tempting; **narcotic,** hypnotic, soporific, somniferous, somnifacient; sedative

24 **hypnotic,** hypnoid, hypnoidal, mesmeric; odylic; narcohypnotic; somnambulant, somnambulic

23 WAKEFULNESS

<not sleeping>

NOUNS **1** **wakefulness,** wake; **sleeplessness,** restlessness, tossing and turning; **insomnia,** insomnolence, insomnolency, white night; vigilance, vigil, all-night vigil, lidless vigil, *per vigilium* <L>; insomniac; consciousness, sentience; alertness

2 **awakening,** wakening, rousing, arousal, wake-up call; rude awakening, rousting out; reveille

VERBS **3** **keep awake,** keep one's eyes open; keep alert, be vigilant; stay awake, toss and turn, not sleep a wink, not shut one's eyes, count sheep; have a white night

4 **awake, awaken,** wake, wake up, get up, rouse, come alive; open one's eyes, stir

5 wake someone up, awaken, waken, **rouse,** arouse, awake, wake, wake up, shake up, roust out

6 **get up,** get out of bed, arise, rise, rise and shine, greet the day, turn out; roll out, pile out, show a leg, hit the deck

ADJS **7** **wakeful, sleepless,** slumberless, unsleeping, insomniac, insomnious; restless; watchful, vigilant, lidless

8 **awake,** conscious, up; **wide-awake,** broad awake; sentient; alert

ADVS **9** **sleeplessly,** unsleepingly; wakefully, with one's eyes open; alertly

24 SENSATION

<physical sensibility>

NOUNS **1** **sensation, sense, feeling;** sense impression, sense-datum, sense-data, percept, perception, sense perception; experience, sensory experience; sensuousness, sensuosity, sensuality; consciousness, awareness, apperception; response, response to stimuli

2 **sensibility,** sensibleness, physical sensibility, sentience, sentiency; openness to sensation, readiness of feeling, receptiveness, receptivity; sensation level, threshold of sensation, limen; impressionability, impressibility, affectibility; susceptibility, susceptivity, perceptibility; esthesia, aesthesia, esthesis; cultural awareness

3 **sensitivity, sensitiveness;** perceptivity, perceptiveness, feelings; responsiveness; tact, tactfulness, considerateness, courtesy, politeness; compassion, sympathy; empathy, identification; concern, solicitousness, solicitude; capability of feeling, passibility; delicacy, exquisiteness, tenderness, fineness; oversensitiveness, oversensibility, hypersensitivity, thin skin, hyperesthesia, hyperpathia, supersensitivity, overtenderness; irritability, prickliness, soreness, **touchiness,** tetchiness; ticklishness, nervousness; allergy, anaphylaxis; sensitization; photophobia

4 **sore spot,** sore point, soft spot, raw, exposed nerve, raw nerve, nerve ending, tender spot, the quick, where the shoe pinches, where one lives, in the gut; agitation, agita, hot spot

5 **senses, five senses,** sensorium; touch, taste, smell, sight, hearing; sixth sense, second sight, extrasensory perception (ESP); sense organ, sensory organ, sensillum, receptor; synesthesia, chromesthesia, color hearing; phonism, photism; kinesthesia, muscle sense, sense of motion; horse sense

VERBS **6** **sense, feel,** experience, **perceive,** apprehend, be sensible of, be conscious of, be aware of, apperceive; taste, smell, see, hear, touch; respond, respond to stimuli; be sensitive to, have a thing about; overreact

7 **sensitize,** make sensitive; sensibilize, sensify; sharpen, whet, quicken, stimulate, excite, stir, cultivate, refine

8 **touch a sore spot,** touch a soft spot, touch on the raw, touch a raw spot, touch to the quick, hit a nerve, touch a nerve, hit a nerve ending, touch a nerve ending, touch where it hurts, hit one where he lives, strike home, hit home

ADJS 9 **sensory,** sensorial; **sensitive,** receptive, responsive; **sensuous;** sensorimotor, sensimotor; kinesthetic, somatosensory; feeling, percipient; centripetal

10 **neural**, nervous, nerval; neurologic, neurological

11 sensible, sentient, sensile; **susceptible,** susceptive; receptive, impressionable, impressible; **perceptive**; conscious, cognizant, aware, sensitive to, alive to, clued in, sussed

12 **sensitive,** responsive, sympathetic, compassionate; empathic, empathetic; passible; delicate, tactful, considerate, courteous, solicitous, tender, refined; **oversensitive,** thin-skinned; oversensible, hyperesthetic, hyperpathic, hypersensitive, supersensitive, overtender, overrefined, overwhelmed; irritable, touchy, irascible, tetchy, quick on the draw, on the trigger, on the uptake, itchy, ticklish, prickly; goosey, skittish; nervous; allergic, anaphylactic

13 keenly sensitive, exquisite, poignant, **acute,** sharp, **keen,** biting, vivid, intense, extreme, excruciating

14 **sensate**, perceptible, audible, visible, tactile, palpable, tangible, noticeable

25 INSENSIBILITY

<physical unfeeling>

NOUNS 1 **insensibility,** insensibleness, **insensitivity,** insensitiveness, insentience, impassibility, lack of feeling; unperceptiveness, imperceptiveness, imperception, imperceptivity, impercipience, blindness, lack of concern, obtuseness; inconsiderateness; unsolicitousness; tactlessness; discourtesy, boorishness; philistinism; **unfeeling,** unfeelingness, apathy, affectlessness, lack of affect; thick skin, thick hide, callousness; numbness, dullness, hypothymia, deadness; pins and needles; hypesthesia; anesthesia, analgesia; narcosis, electronarcosis; narcotization; lack of awareness

2 **unconsciousness,** senselessness; nothingness, oblivion, obliviousness, indifference, heedlessness, unawareness; nirvana; faint, swoon, blackout, syncope, athymia, lipothymy, lipothymia; coma; torpor, stupor; trance; catalepsy, catatony, catatonia, sleep; knockout (KO), kayo; semiconsciousness, grayout; suspended animation

3 **anesthetic,** general anesthetic, local anesthetic, analgesic, anodyne, balm, ointment, painkiller, pain reliever, antiodontalgic; tranquilizer, **sedative,** sleeping pill, sleeping tablet, somnifacient, knockout drops, Mickey Finn, Mickey; drug, dope, narcotic, opiate; acupuncture; desensitization; ether

VERBS 4 **deaden, numb,** benumb, blunt, dull, obtund, **desensitize;** paralyze, palsy; **anesthetize,** put to sleep, slip one a Mickey, slip one a Mickey Finn, chloroform, etherize; narcotize, drug, dope; freeze, stupefy, stun, bedaze, besot; knock unconscious, knock senseless, knock out (KO), kayo, lay out, coldcock, knock stiff, brain; concuss

5 **faint**, swoon, drop, succumb, keel over, fall in a faint, fall senseless, **pass out,** zonk out, black out, dim, go out like a light; gray out

ADJS 6 **insensible, unfeeling, insensitive,** insentient, insensate, impassible; nerveless, senseless, unemotional; unsympathetic, uncompassionate; unconcerned, unsolicitous, non-caring, uncaring, impassive, cold-blooded, apathetic, hardhearted; tactless, boorish, heavy-handed; unperceptive, imperceptive, impercipient, blind, unmindful; thick-skinned, hardened, dull, obtuse, obdurate; numb, numbed, benumbed, dead, deadened, asleep, unfelt; affectless; stoic; deaf; callous; anesthetized, narcotized, hypnotized

7 **stupefied, stunned,** dazed, bedazed, astonied

8 **unconscious,** senseless, oblivious, unaware, comatose, asleep, dead, lifeless dead to the world, cold, out, out cold; heedless, unmindful; nirvanic; half-conscious, semiconscious; drugged, narcotized; doped, stoned, spaced out, strung out, zonked, zonked out, out of it; catatonic, cataleptic; stunned, concussed, knocked out; desensitized; out for the count

9 **deadening,** numbing, dulling; **anesthetic,** analgesic, narcotic; stupefying, stunning, mind-boggling, mind-numbing; anesthetizing, narcotizing

26 PAIN

<physical suffering>

NOUNS 1 **pain; suffering, hurt,** hurting, painfulness, misery, distress, dolor; discomfort, malaise; aches and pains; pain threshold

2 **pang,** pangs, throe, throes; seizure, spasm, paroxysm; ouch; **twinge,** twitch, wrench, jumping pain; crick, kink, hitch, cramp, cramps; nip, thrill, pinch, tweak, bite, prick, pinprick, stab, stitch, sharp pain, piercing pain, stabbing pain, acute pain, shooting pain, darting pain, fulgurant pain, lancinating pain, shooting; boring pain, terebrant pain, terebrating pain; gnawing, gnawing pain, grinding pain; stitch in the side; charley horse;

phantom limb pain; hunger pang, hunger pain; wandering pain; psychalgia, psychosomatic pain, soul pain, mind pain

3 **smart,** smarting, **sting,** stinging, urtication, **tingle,** tingling; **burn,** burning, burning pain, fire; pins and needles

4 **soreness, irritation,** inflammation, tenderness, sensitiveness; algesia; rankling, festering; sore; sore spot

5 **ache,** aching, achiness, throbbing, throbbing ache, throbbing pain, throb; **headache,** cephalalgia, misery in the head; splitting headache, sick headache, migraine, megrim, hemicrania; backache; earache, otalgia; toothache, odontalgia; **stomachache,** tummyache, bellyache, gut-ache; **colic,** collywobbles, gripes, gripe, gnawing, gnawing of the bowels, fret; **heartburn,** acid reflux, agita, pyrosis; **angina**

6 **agony,** anguish, torment, torture, ordeal, exquisite torment, exquisite torture, the rack, excruciation, crucifixion, martyrdom, martyrization, excruciating pain, agonizing pain, atrocious pain, hell on earth, punishment; pain in the neck

VERBS 7 **pain,** give pain, inflict pain, **hurt, wound,** afflict, distress, injure; burn; sting; nip, bite, tweak, pinch; pierce, prick, stab, cut, lacerate, thrash; irritate, inflame, sear, harshen, **exacerbate**, intensify; chafe, gall, fret, rasp, rub, grate; gnaw, grind; gripe; fester, rankle; torture, torment, rack, put to torture, put on the rack, lay on the rack, agonize, harrow, crucify, martyr, martyrize, traumatize, excruciate, wring, twist, contorse, convulse; wrench, tear, rend; prolong the agony, kill by inches

8 **suffer, feel pain,** feel the pangs, anguish; **hurt, ache,** have a misery, ail, be afflicted; smart, tingle; throb, pound; shoot; twinge, thrill, twitch; wince, blanch, shrink, make a wry face, grimace; agonize, writhe

ADJS 9 **pained,** in pain, **hurt,** hurting, **suffering,** afflicted, wounded, distressed, in distress; tortured, tormented, racked, agonized, harrowed, lacerated, crucified, martyred, martyrized, wrung, twisted, convulsed, anguished; on the rack, under the harrow; traumatized; stressed out, bothered

10 **painful;** hurtful, **hurting,** distressing, afflictive, miserable; acute, sharp, piercing, stabbing, shooting, stinging, biting, gnawing; poignant, pungent, burning, searing, severe, cruel, harsh, grave, hard; griping, cramping, spasmic, spasmatic, spasmodic, paroxysmal; agonizing, excruciating, exquisite, atrocious, torturous, tormenting, martyrizing, racking, harrowing, unbearable, intolerable

11 **sore, raw;** pained; smarting, tingling, burning; irritated, inflamed, tender, sensitive, fiery, angry, red; algetic; chafed, galled; festering, rankling; black-and-blue

12 **aching,** achy, throbbing; headachy, migrainous, backachy, toothachy, stomachachy, colicky, griping

13 **irritating,** irritative, irritant; chafing, galling, fretting, bothersome, rasping, boring, grating, grinding, stinging, scratchy

27 VISION
<eyesight>

NOUNS 1 **vision, sight, eyesight,** seeing; sightedness; visioning; eye, power of sight, sense of sight, visual sense; **depth perception,** perception, discernment; perspicacity, perspicuity, sharp sight, acute sight, keen sight, visual acuity, quick sight, **20/20 vision**; farsight, farsightedness; nearsightedness; astigmatism; clear sight, unobstructed vision; rod vision, scotopia; cone vision, photopia; color vision, twilight vision, daylight vision, day vision, night vision; eye-mindedness; **field of vision,** visual field, depth of field, scope, ken, purview, horizon, sweep, range; line of vision, line of sight, sightline; peripheral vision, peripheral field; field of view; sensitivity to light, phototonus

2 **observation,** observance; **looking,** watching, viewing, seeing, witnessing, espial; notice, note, respect, regard; watch, lookout; spying, espionage; trainspotting

3 **look, sight,** the eye, a look-see, a gander, glad eye, dekko, eye, view, regard; sidelong look; leer, leering look, lustful leer; sly look; look-in; preview; scene, prospect

4 **glance,** glance of the eye, flick of the eye, squiz <Austral>, slant, rapid glance, cast, side-glance; **glimpse,** flash, quick sight; peek, peep; wink, blink, flicker of an eye, twinkle of an eye; casual glance, half an eye; *coup d'œil* <Fr>

5 **gaze, stare,** gape, goggle; sharp look, piercing look, penetrating look; ogle, glad eye, come-hither look, bedroom eyes; glare, glower, glaring look, glowering look, black look, dirty look; evil eye, whammy; withering look, hostile look, chilly look, the fisheye, stinkeye, hairy eyeball; rubbernecking

6 **scrutiny,** overview, **survey,** contemplation, surveillance; **examination, inspection,** the once-over, visual examination, a vetting, ocular inspection, eyeball inspection

7 **viewpoint, standpoint, point of view,** vantage, vantage point, perspective, point of vantage, coign of vantage, where one stands; bird's-eye view, worm's-eye view, fly on the wall; outlook, angle,

slant, angle of vision, field of vision, eyeshot; mental outlook

8 observation post, observation point, observation deck; **observatory; lookout,** outlook, overlook, scenic overlook; planetarium; watchtower, tower; Texas tower; beacon, lighthouse, pharos; gazebo, belvedere; bridge, conning tower, crow's nest; peephole, sighthole, spyhole, loophole; ringside, ringside seat; grandstand, bleachers, stands; gallery, top gallery; paradise, peanut gallery; window

9 **eye,** visual organ, organ of vision, oculus, optic, orb, peeper, baby blues; clear eyes, bright eyes, starry orbs; saucer eyes, popeyes, goggle eyes, banjo eyes, googly eyes, sparklers; naked eye, unassisted eye, unaided eye; corner of the eye; eyeball; iris; pupil; eyelid, lid, nictitating membrane; eyeglasses, eyewear

10 **sharp eye,** keen eye, piercing eye, penetrating eye, gimlet eye, X-ray eye; eagle eye, hawkeye, peeled eye, watchful eye; weather eye

11 <comparisons> eagle, hawk, cat, lynx, ferret, weasel; Argus

VERBS 12 **see, behold, observe,** view, witness, perceive, discern, spy, espy, sight, have in sight, make out, pick out, descry, spot, twig, discover, notice, take notice of, have one's eye on, distinguish, recognize, ken, catch sight of, get a load of, take in, get an eyeful of, look on, look upon, cast the eyes on, cast the eyes upon, set eyes on, lay eyes on, clap eyes on; glimpse, get a glimpse of, catch a glimpse of; see at a glance, see with half an eye; see with one's own eyes

13 **look, peer,** have a look, take a gander, take a look, direct the eyes, turn the eyes, bend the eyes, cast one's eye, lift up the eyes; look at, take a look at, eye, eyeball, have a look-see, have a dekko, look on, look upon, gaze at, gaze upon; watch, observe, view, regard; keep one's eyes peeled, keep one's eyes skinned, be watchful, be observant, be vigilant, keep one's eyes open; keep in sight, keep in view, hold in view; look after; check, check out, scope, scope on, scope out; keep under observation, spy on, have an eye out, keep an eye out, keep an eye on, keep a weather eye on, follow, tail, shadow, stake out; reconnoiter, scout, get the lay of the land; peek, peep, pry, take a peep, take a peek; play peekaboo

14 **scrutinize, survey,** eye, contemplate, look over, give the eye, give the once-over; ogle, ogle at, leer, leer at, give one the glad eye; examine, vet, **inspect**; pore, pore over, peruse; take a close look, take a careful look; take a long, hard look; size up; take stock of; have eyes in the back of one's head

15 **gaze,** fix one's gaze, fix one's eyes upon, fasten one's eyes upon, rivet one's eyes upon, keep one's eyes upon, feast one's eyes on; eye, ogle; stare, stare at, stare hard, stare out, zone out, look, goggle, gape, gawk, gawp, gaze open-mouthed; crane, crane the neck, stand on tiptoe, rubberneck; strain one's eyes; look straight in the eye, look full in the face, hold one's eye, hold one's gaze, stare down

16 **glare, glower,** look daggers, look black; give one the evil eye, give one a whammy; give one the fish eye, give one a dirty look

17 **glance, glimpse,** glint, cast a glance, glance at, glance upon, give a *coup d'œil* <Fr>, take a glance at, take a squint at

18 **look askance**, look askant, give a sidelong look; squint, look asquint; cock the eye; look down one's nose

19 **look away,** look aside, avert the eyes, look another way, break one's eyes away, stop looking, turn away from, turn the back upon; drop one's eyes, drop one's gaze, cast one's eyes down; avoid one's gaze

ADJS 20 **visual,** ocular, eye, eyeball; sighted, seeing, having sight, having vision; **optic, optical;** ophthalmic; retinal; visible

21 **clear-sighted,** clear-eyed; twenty-twenty; farsighted, farseeing, telescopic; sharp-sighted, keen-sighted, sharp-eyed, eagle-eyed, hawk-eyed, ferret-eyed, lynx-eyed, cat-eyed, Argus-eyed; eye-minded, perceptive, aware

ADVS 22 **at sight,** as seen, visibly, at a glance; by sight, by eyeball, visually; at first sight, at the first blush, *prima facie* <L>; out of the corner of one's eye; from where one stands, from one's viewpoint, from one's standpoint

COMBINING FORMS 23 opto-, -opsia, -opsy, -opsis; -opy, -opia; -scopy; ocul-, oculo-, ophthalm-, ophthalmo-

28 DEFECTIVE VISION

<defective eyesight>

NOUNS 1 faulty eyesight, **bad eyesight**, visual handicap, defect of vision, defect of sight, poor sight, impaired vision, imperfect vision, blurred vision, reduced sight, partial sightedness, partial blindness; legal blindness; **astigmatism,** astigmia; nystagmus; albinism; double vision, double sight, diplopia; tunnel vision; photophobia; **blindness**

2 **dim-sightedness,** dull-sightedness, near-blindness, amblyopia, gravel-blindness, sand-blindness, purblindness, dim eyes; blurredness, bleαredness, bleariness, lippitude; eyestrain, bloodshot eyes, redness, red eyes

3 **nearsightedness,** myopia, shortsightedness, short sight

4 **farsightedness,** hyperopia, longsightedness, long sight; presbyopia

5 strabismus, heterotropia; cast, cast in the eye; **squint,** squinch; **cross-eye,** cross-eyedness; convergent strabismus, esotropia; upward strabismus, anoopsia; walleye, exotropia; detached retina; tic

6 <defective eyes> cross-eyes, cockeyes, squint eyes, lazy eye, swivel eyes, goggle eyes, walleyes, bugeyes, popeyes, saucer eyes

7 **winking, blinking,** fluttering the eyelids, nictitation; winker, blinkard; tic

VERBS **8** see badly, see poorly, barely see, be half-blind; have a mote in the eye; see double

9 **squint,** squinch, squint the eye, look asquint, screw up the eyes, skew, goggle

10 **wink, blink,** nictitate, bat the eyes

ADJS **11** poor-sighted; **visually impaired**, visually handicapped, sight-impaired; legally blind; **blind**; astigmatic, astigmatical; nystagmic; nearsighted, shortsighted, myopic; farsighted, longsighted, presbyopic; dayblind, hereralopic; nightblind, nyctalopic; colorblind; sand-blind; squinting, squinty, asquint, squint-eyed, squinch-eyed, strabismal, strabismic; winking, blinking, blinky, blink-eyed, nictating; blinkered; photophobic

12 **cross-eyed, cockeyed,** swivel-eyed, goggle-eyed, bug-eyed, popeyed, **walleyed,** saucer-eyed, glare-eyed; one-eyed, monocular, cyclopean; moon-eyed

13 **dim-sighted,** dim, dull-sighted, dim-eyed, weak-eyed, feeble-eyed, mole-eyed; purblind, half-blind, gravel-blind, sand-blind; bleary-eyed, blear-eyed; filmy-eyed, film-eyed; snow-blind; bloodshot, red-eyed; dry-eyed

29 OPTICAL INSTRUMENTS

<vision aid>

NOUNS **1** **optical instrument** <see list>, optical device, viewer; **microscope** <see list>; **spectroscope, spectrometer;** optical fiber

2 **lens,** glass; prism, objective prism; eyepiece, objective, condenser; mirror system, catadioptric system, telecentric system; **camera**; bifocal lens, progressive lens

3 **spectacles,** specs, **glasses, eyeglasses,** pair of glasses, pair of spectacles, barnacles, cheaters, peepers; reading glasses, readers; bifocals, divided spectacles, trifocals, pince-nez, nippers; progressive lenses; lorgnette, *lorgnon* <Fr>; horn-rimmed glasses; harlequin glasses; granny glasses; mini specs; colored glasses, sunglasses, sun specs, dark glasses, Polaroid <tm> glasses, shades; goggles, blinkers; eyeglass, monocle, quizzing glass; thick glasses, thick-lensed glasses, thick lenses, Coke-bottle glasses; **contacts,** contact lenses, contact lens, hard lenses, soft lenses, disposable lenses, extended-wear lenses, toric lenses

4 **telescope** <see list>, scope, spy glass, terrestrial telescope, glass, field glass; **binoculars, field glasses,** zoom binoculars, opera glasses, binocs

5 **sight;** sighthole; finder, viewfinder; panoramic sight; bombsight; peep sight, open sight, leaf sight

6 **mirror,** glass, looking glass, seeing glass, reflector, speculum; hand mirror, window mirror, rearview mirror, cheval glass, pier glass, shaving mirror; steel mirror; convex mirror, concave mirror, distorting mirror

7 **optics,** optical physics; **optometry;** microscopy, microscopics; telescopy; stereoscopy; spectroscopy, spectrometry; infrared spectroscopy; spectrophotometry; electron optics; fiber optics; **photography**

8 **oculist,** ophthalmologist, **optometrist;** microscopist, telescopist; optician

ADJS **9** **optic, optical,** ophthalmic, ophthalmologic, ophthalmological, optometrical; acousto-optic, acousto-optical; ocular, binocular, monocular

10 **microscopic; telescopic**; stereoscopic, three-dimensional, 3-D

11 **spectacled,** bespectacled, four-eyed; goggled; monocled

12 **microscope**

acoustic microscope
binocular microscope
blink microscope
comparison microscope
compound microscope
conoscope
dark-field microscope
dissecting microscope
electron microscope
field-emission microscope
field-ion microscope
fluorescence microscope
gravure microscope
high-powered microscope
interference microscope
laboratory microscope
light microscope
metallograph
metallurgical microscope
microprojector
optical microscope
oxyhydrogen microscope
phase contrast microscope, phase microscope
photomicroscope
pinion focusing microscope
polarizing microscope
power microscope
projecting microscope
scanning electron microscope
scanning microscope
scanning tunneling microscope
simple microscope, single microscope
spectromicroscope
stereomicroscope, stereoscopic microscope
surface microscope
transmission electron microscope
ultramicroscope
ultraviolet microscope
X-ray microscope

13 optical instrument

abdominoscope
amblyoscope
blink comparator
bronchoscope
camera lucida
chromatoscope
chromoscope
cystoscope
diaphanoscope
diffractometer
endoscope
epidiascope
eriometer
fiberscope
gastroscope
goniometer, gonioscope
image orthicon
kaleidoscope
laser
microfilm viewer, microfilm reader
ophthalmoscope
optometer
oscilloscope
periscope
pharyngoscope
photometer
photomultiplier
photoscope
polariscope
polemoscope
prism
pseudoscope
radarscope
radioscope
rangefinder
retinoscope
saccarimeter
sniperscope
snooperscope
spectroscope
stereopticon
stereoscope
stroboscope
telestereoscope
thaumatrope

14 telescope

astronomical telescope, Kepler telescope
Cassegrain telescope
collimator
coudé telescope
Dobsonian telescope
double-image telescope
elbow telescope
electron telescope
equatorial telescope
finder telescope
Galilean telescope
Gregorian telescope
guiding telescope
Hale telescope
heliometer
Hubble Space Telescope
inverting telescope
Maksutov telescope
mercurial telescope
Mills cross
Multiple Mirror Telescope (MMT)
Newtonian telescope
optical telescope
panoramic telescope
prism telescope, prismatic telescope
radio telescope
reflecting telescope
refracting telescope
Schmidt telescope
spotting scope
telescopic sight
terrestrial telescope
tower telescope
twin telescope
vernier telescope
water telescope
zenith telescope, zenith tube

30 BLINDNESS

<no vision>

NOUNS **1 blindness, sightlessness,** cecity, ablepsia, unseeingness, sightless eyes, lack of vision, eyelessness; stone-blindness, total blindness; darkness; legal blindness; partial blindness, reduced sight, blind side; blind spot; dimsightedness; snow blindness, niphablepsia; amaurosis, *gutta serena* <L>, drop serene; cataract; glaucoma; trachoma; mental blindness, psychic blindness, mind-blindness, soul-blindness, benightedness, unenlightenment, spiritual blindness; **blinding,** making blind, depriving of sight, putting out the eyes, excecation; blurring the eyes, blindfolding, hoodwinking, blinkering; tunnel vision

2 day blindness, hemeralopia; **night blindness,** nyctalopia; moon blindness, moon-blind

3 color blindness; dichromatism; monochromatism, achromatopsia; red blindness, protanopia, green blindness, deuteranopia, red-green blindness, Daltonism; yellow blindness, xanthocyanopia; blue-yellow blindness, tritanopia; violet-blindness

4 the blind, the sightless, the unseeing; blind man; bat, mole; blind leading the blind

5 blindfold; eye patch; blinkers, blinds, blinders, rogue's badge

6 <aids for the blind> sensory aid, **Braille,** New York point, Gall's serrated type, Boston type, Howe's American type, Moon type, Moon's type, Alston's Glasgow type, Lucas's type, sight-saver type, Frere's type; line letter, string alphabet, writing stamps; noctograph, writing frame, embosser, high-speed embosser; visagraph; talking book; optophone, Visotoner, Optacon; personal sonar, Pathsounder; ultrasonic spectacles; cane; Seeing Eye dog, hearing dog, guide dog; white stick, white cane

VERBS **7 blind,** blind the eyes, deprive of sight, strike blind, render blind, make blind, excecate; darken, dim, obscure, eclipse; put one's eyes out, gouge; **blindfold,** blinker, hoodwink, bandage; throw dust in one's eyes, benight; dazzle, bedazzle, daze; glare; snow-blind

8 be blind, not see, walk in darkness, grope in the dark, feel one's way; go blind, lose one's sight, lose one's vision, black out; be blind to, close one's eyes to, shut one's eyes to, wink at, blink at, look the other way, blind oneself to, wear blinkers, have blinders on, avert one's eyes; have a blind spot, have a blind side

ADJS **9 blind, sightless,** unsighted, ableptical, eyeless, visionless, unseeing, undiscerning, unobserving, unperceiving; in darkness, rayless, bereft of light, dark; stone-blind, stark blind, blind as a bat, blind as a mole, blind as an owl; amaurotic; dim-sighted; hemeralopic; nyctalopic; color-blind; glaucomatous; legally blind; mind-blind, soul-blind, mentally blind, psychically blind, spiritually blind, benighted, unenlightened

10 blinded, excecated, darkened, obscured; **blindfolded,** blindfold, hoodwinked, blinkered; dazzled, bedazzled, dazed; snow-blind, snow-blinded; sand-blind

11 blinding, obscuring; dazzling, bedazzling, stunning

31 VISIBILITY

<ability to be seen>

NOUNS 1 **visibility,** visibleness, perceptibility, discernibleness, observability, detectability, visuality, seeableness; exposure; manifestation; outcrop, outcropping; the visible, the seen, what is revealed, what can be seen; revelation, epiphany

2 **distinctness**, plainness, evidentness, evidence, obviousness, patentness, manifestness, recognizability; **clearness, clarity,** crystal-clearness, lucidity, limpidity; definiteness, definition, sharpness, microscopical distinctness; resolution, high resolution, hi-res, low resolution, low-res; prominence, conspicuousness, conspicuity; exposure, public exposure, high profile, low profile; high visibility, low visibility; atmospheric visibility, seeing, ceiling, ceiling unlimited, visibility unlimited, ceiling and visibility unlimited (CAVU), severe clear, visibility zero

3 **field of view,** field of vision, range of vision, scope of vision, visual range, **sight,** limit of vision, eyereach, eyesight, eyeshot, ken; **vista, view,** horizon, prospect, perspective, outlook, survey, visible horizon; range, scan, scope; line of sight, sightline, line of vision; naked eye; command, domination, outlook over; viewpoint, **observation point**

VERBS 4 **show,** show up, show through, shine out, shine, through, surface, **appear**, **be visible,** be seen, be revealed, be evident, be noticeable, be obvious, meet the gaze, impinge on the eye, present to the eye, meet the eye, catch the eye, hit the eye, strike the eye; stand out, stand forth, loom large, glare, stare one in the face, hit one in the eye, stick out like a sore thumb; dominate; emerge, come into view, materialize

5 **be exposed,** be conspicuous, have high visibility, stick out, hang out, crop out; live in a glass house; have a high profile, keep a high profile

ADJS 6 **visible,** visual, **perceptible,** perceivable, discernible, seeable, viewable, witnessable, beholdable, observable, detectable, noticeable, recognizable, to be seen, head-turning; in sight, in view, in plain sight, in full view, present to the eyes, before one's eyes, under one's eyes, open, naked, outcropping, hanging out, exposed, showing, open to view, exposed to view; **evident,** in evidence, manifest, apparent; revealed, disclosed, unhidden, unconcealed, unclouded, undisguised; high-visibility

7 **distinct, plain,** clear, obvious, evident, patent, unmistakable, unmissable, not to be mistaken, much in evidence, plain to be seen, for all to see, showing for all to see, apparent, plain as a pikestaff, plain as the nose on one's face, plain as day, clear as day, plain as plain can be, big as life, twice as ugly; definite, defined, well-defined, well-marked, well-resolved, in focus; clear-cut, clean-cut; crystal clear, clear as crystal; **conspicuous,** glaring, staring, prominent, pronounced, well-pronounced, in bold relief, in strong relief, in high relief, high-profile; identifiable, recognizable

ADVS 8 **visibly, perceptibly,** perceivably, discernibly, seeably, recognizably, observably, markedly, noticeably; manifestly, apparently, evidently; distinctly, clearly, with clarity, with crystal clarity, plainly, obviously, patently, definitely, unmistakably; conspicuously, undisguisedly, unconcealedly, prominently, pronouncedly, glaringly, starkly, staringly

32 INVISIBILITY

<not able to be seen>

NOUNS 1 **invisibility,** imperceptibility, unperceivability, undetectability, indiscernibility, unseeableness, viewlessness; nonappearance; disappearance; the invisible, the unseen; more than meets the eye; unsubstantiality, immateriality, **secrecy**, **concealment**; hidden depths, tip of the iceberg; zero visibility

2 **inconspicuousness,** half-visibility, semivisibility, low profile, latency; indistinctness, unclearness, unplainness, **faintness,** paleness, feebleness, weakness, dimness, bedimming, bleariness, darkness, shadowiness, vagueness, vague appearance, indefiniteness, obscurity, uncertainty, indistinguishability; blurriness, blur, soft focus, defocus, fuzziness, haziness, mistiness, filminess, fogginess; blackout, brownout

VERBS 3 **be invisible**, be unseen, escape notice; lie hid, blush unseen; disappear; white out, black out

4 **blur, dim,** pale, soften, film, mist, fog; defocus, lose resolution, lose sharpness, lose distinctness, go soft at the edges

ADJS 5 **invisible;** imperceptible, unperceivable, indiscernible, undiscernible, undetectable, unseeable, viewless, unbeholdable, unapparent, insensible; **out of sight,** out of range; **secret**; **unseen,** sightless, unbeheld, unviewed, unwitnessed, unobserved, unnoticed, unperceived; unsubstantial, transparent; behind the curtain, behind the scenes; disguised, camouflaged, hidden, **concealed**; undisclosed, unrevealed, *in petto* <L>; latent, unrealized, submerged

6 **inconspicuous,** half-visible, semivisible, low-profile; **indistinct,** unclear, unplain, indefinite,

undefined, ill-defined, ill-marked, faint, pale, feeble, weak, dim, dark, shadowy, vague, obscure, indistinguishable, unrecognizable; half-seen, merely glimpsed; low-definition; uncertain, confused, out of focus, **blurred, blurry,** bleared, bleary, blear, fuzzy, hazy, misty, filmy, foggy

33 APPEARANCE

<becoming visible>

NOUNS **1** **appearance, appearing,** apparition, coming, forthcoming, showing-up, coming forth, coming on the scene, making the scene, putting in an appearance, arrival; emergence, issuing, issuance; arising, rise, rising, occurrence; materialization, **materializing,** coming into being; manifestation, realization, incarnation, revelation, showing-forth; epiphany, theophany, avatar, ostent; presentation, disclosure, exposure, opening, unfolding, unfoldment, showing; rising of the curtain; comings and goings

2 **appearance,** exterior, externals, mere externals, facade, outside, show, outward show, image, display, front, outward appearance, external appearance, surface appearance, surface show, vain show, apparent character, public image, window dressing, cosmetics; whitewash; whited sepulcher; glitz, tinsel, gaudiness, speciousness, meretriciousness, superficies, superficiality; PR, flack; pretense

3 aspect, **look,** view; feature, lineaments; seeming, **semblance, image,** imago, icon, eidolon, likeness, simulacrum; guise, mien; effect, impression, total effect, total impression; **form, shape,** figure, configuration, gestalt; manner, fashion, wise, style; respect, regard, reference, light; phase; facet, side, angle, viewpoint, slant, twist, spin

4 **looks, features,** lineaments, traits, lines; countenance, face, visage, feature, favor, brow, physiognomy; cast of countenance, cut of one's jib, facial appearance, facial expression, cast, turn; look, air, mien, demeanor, carriage, bearing, port, deportment, posture, stance, poise, presence; guise, garb, dress, complexion, color

5 <thing appearing> **apparition, appearance,** phenomenon, semblance; vision, image, shape, form, figure, presence; false image, mirage, phasm, specter, **phantom**

6 **view, scene,** sight; prospect, outlook, lookout, vista, perspective; scenery, scenic view; panorama, sweep; **scape**, landscape, seascape, riverscape, waterscape, airscape, skyscape, cloudscape, cityscape, townscape, moodscape; bird's-eye view, worm's-eye view; best seat in the house

7 **spectacle, sight;** exhibit, exhibition, exposition, show, **stage show**, display, **presentation,** representation; dog and pony show; tableau, tableau vivant; panorama, diorama, cosmorama, myriorama, cyclorama, georama; *son et lumière* <Fr>, sound-and-light show; phantasmagoria, shifting scene, light show; psychedelic show; pageant, pageantry; parade, pomp

VERBS **8** **appear,** become visible; arrive, **make one's appearance,** make an appearance, put in an appearance, appear on the scene, make the scene, weigh in, appear to one's eyes, meet tye eye, catch the eye, strike the eye, **come in sight**, come into view, show, show oneself, show one's face, nip in, show up, turn up, come, materialize, pop up, present oneself, present oneself to view, manifest oneself, become manifest, reveal oneself, discover oneself, uncover oneself, declare oneself, expose oneself, betray oneself, flash; come to light, see the light, see the light of day; emerge, issue, issue forth, stream forth, come forth, come to the fore, present itself, come out, come forward, come to the surface, come one's way, come to hand, come into the picture; enter, come upon the stage; **rise, arise,** rear its head; look forth, peer out, peep out; crop out, outcrop; loom, heave in sight, appear on the horizon; crawl out of the woodwork; fade in, wax

9 **burst forth,** break forth, debouch, erupt, irrupt, explode; pop up, bob up, start up, spring up, burst upon the view; flare up, flash, gleam

10 appear to be, seem to be, **appear,** seem, look, feel, sound, look to be, appear to one's eyes, have the appearance of, present the appearance of, give the feeling of, strike one as, come on as; appear like, seem like, look like, have the look of, wear the look of, sound like; have every appearance of, have all the earmarks of, have all the features of, show signs of, have every sign of, have every indication of; assume the guise of, take the shape of, exhibit the form of

ADJS **11** **apparent,** appearing, seeming, ostensible; outward, surface, superficial; material, incarnate; **visible**

ADVS **12** **apparently,** seemingly, ostensibly, to all appearances, by all appearances, to all accounts, by all accounts, to all seeming, evidently, as it seems, to the eye; on the face of it, *prima facie* <L>; on the surface, outwardly, superficially; at first sight, at first view, at the first blush

34 DISAPPEARANCE

<stop being visible>

NOUNS **1** **disappearance,** disappearing, **vanishing,** vanishment; going, passing, **departure,**

loss; dissipation, dispersion; dissolution, dissolving, melting, evaporation, evanescence, dematerialization; fade, fadeout, fading, fadeaway, blackout; wane, ebb; wipe, wipeout, wipeoff, erasure; eclipse, occultation, blocking; sunset; delitescence; vanishing point; elimination; extinction; disappearing act

VERBS 2 **disappear, vanish,** vanish from sight, do a vanishing act, depart, fly, **flee**, go, be gone, go away, pass, pass out, pass away, pass out of sight, exit, pull up stakes, leave the scene, leave the stage, clear out, pass out of the picture, pass from sight, retire from sight, become lost to sight, be seen no more, take a powder; perish, die, die off; die out, die away, dwindle, wane, fade, fade out, fade away, do a fade-out; sink, sink away, dissolve, melt, melt away, dematerialize, evaporate, evanesce, vanish into thin air, disappear into thin air, go up in smoke; disperse, dispel, dissipate; cease, cease to exist, cease to be; cease publication, go out of print, go off the air, become obsolete, close down; leave no trace; waste, waste away, erode, be consumed, wear away; undergo an eclipse, suffer an eclipse; **hide**; blend into the background

ADJS 3 **vanishing, disappearing,** passing, fleeting, fugitive, transient, flying, fading, dissolving, melting, evaporating, evanescent, waning, here today gone tomorrow

4 **gone,** away, gone away, past, extinct, missing, no more, poof, lost, lost to sight, lost to view, long-lost, out of sight; unaccounted for; nonexistent; out of the picture

35 COLOR

<visual quality>

NOUNS 1 **color, hue; tint,** tinct, tincture, tinge, shade, tone, cast; key; **coloring,** coloration; color harmony, color balance, color scheme; decorator color; complexion, skin color, skin coloring, skin tone, pigmentation; chromatism, chromaticism, chromism; achromatism; natural color; undercolor; pallor; color perception, color vision, color blindness

2 **warmth,** warmth of color, warm color; **blush,** flush, glow, healthy glow, healthy hue

3 **softness,** soft color, subtle color, pale color, pastel, pastel color, pastel shade, cool color

4 **colorfulness,** color, bright color, pure color, brightness, brilliance, vividness, intensity, saturation; richness, gorgeousness, gaiety; riot of color, splash of color; Technicolor <tm>; Day-Glo <tm>; variegation, multicolor, polychrome; color scheme, color coordination

5 **garishness,** loudness, luridness, glitz, gaudiness; loud color, screaming color; shocking pink, jaundiced yellow, chartreuse; clashing colors, color clash

6 **color quality;** chroma, Munsell chroma, brightness, purity, saturation; **hue,** value, lightness; colorimetric quality, chromaticity, chromaticness; tint, **tone;** chromatic color; achromatic color, neutral color; warm color; cool color; tinge, shade

7 **color system,** chromaticity diagram, color triangle, Maxwell triangle; hue cycle, color disk, color wheel, color circle, chromatic circle, color cycle, color gamut, color chart; Munsell scale; color solid; fundamental colors; **primary color,** primary pigment, primary; secondary color, secondary; tertiary color, tertiary; complementary color; chromaticity coordinate; color mixture curve, color mixture function; spectral color, spectrum color, pure color, full color; metamer; **spectrum,** solar spectrum, color spectrum, chromatic spectrum, color index; rainbow; monochrome; demitint, half tint, halftone, mezzotint, half-light, patina; chromatic aberration; school colors

8 <coloring matter> **color, coloring, colorant,** tinction, tincture, **pigment, stain;** chromogen; **dye,** dyestuff, artificial coloring, food coloring, color filter, color gelatin; paint, oil paint, acrylic paint, watercolor paint, gouache, tempera, enamel, glaze; distemper; coat, coating, **coat of paint**; undercoat, undercoating, primer, priming, prime coat, ground, flat coat, dead-color; spray paint; interior paint, exterior paint, floor enamel; wash, wash coat, flat wash, colorwash, whitewash; opaque color, transparent color; medium, vehicle; drier; thinner; turpentine; additive color, subtractive color; artist's colors, colored pencils, crayons, chalk, pastels

9 <**hair color**> **brunette,** brunet; **blonde,** blond, Goldilocks; bleached blond, peroxide blond; ash blond, platinum blond, strawberry blond, honey blond, dirty blond; towhead; **redhead,** carrot-top; gray

10 <**science of color**> chromatology; chromatics, chromatography, chromatoscopy, colorimetry; spectrum analysis, spectroscopy, spectrometry, spectrography; color theory

11 <applying color> **coloring,** coloration; staining, dyeing; tie-dyeing; tinting, tinging, tinction; pigmentation; illumination, emblazonry; color printing; lithography

12 **painting,** paintwork, coating, covering; enameling, glossing, glazing; varnishing, japanning, lacquering, shellacking; staining;

calcimining, whitewashing; gilding; stippling; frescoing, fresco; undercoating, priming; watercoloring, gouache, oil painting, crayoning

13 **spectrum**, rainbow; red, orange, yellow, green, blue, indigo, violet

VERBS 14 **color,** hue, lay on color; **tinge, tint,** tinct, tincture, tone, complexion; pigment; bedizen; variegate, colorize; stain, dye, dip, tie-dye; imbue; deep-dye, fast-dye, double-dye, dye in the wool, yarn-dye; ingrain, grain; shade, shadow; illuminate, emblazon; **paint**, apply paint, paint up, coat, cover, face, watercolor, crayon; dab, daub, dedaub, smear, besmear, brush on paint, slap on paint, slop on paint; enamel, gloss, glaze; varnish, japan, lacquer, shellac; white out; calcimine, whitewash, parget; wash; gild, begild, engild; stipple; fresco; distemper; undercoat, prime; color-code

15 <be inharmonious> **clash,** conflict, collide, fight

ADJS 16 **chromatic,** colorational; **coloring,** colorific, colorative, tinctorial, tingent; pigmental, pigmentary; monochrome, monochromic, monochromatic; dichromatic; many-colored, parti-colored, medley, motley, rainbow, **variegated**, polychromatic, multicolored, kaleidoscopic, technicolored; prismatic, spectral; matching, toning, harmonious; warm, glowing; cool, cold

17 **colored,** hued, in color, colorized, in Technicolor <tm>; tinged, tinted, tinctured, tinct, toned; **painted,** enameled; stained, dyed; tie-dyed; imbued; complexioned, complected; full-colored, full; deep, deep-colored; wash-colored; washed

18 **deep-dyed,** fast-dyed, double-dyed, dyed-in-the-wool; ingrained, ingrain; permanent, colorfast, fast, fadeless, unfading, indelible, constant; semi-permanent, demi-permanent

19 **colorful,** colory; bright, vivid, intense, rich, exotic, brilliant, burning, gorgeous, gay, bright-hued, bright-colored, rich-colored, gay-colored, high-colored, deep-colored

20 **garish**, lurid, loud, screaming, shrieking, glaring, flaring, flashy, glitzy, flaunting, crude, blinding, overbright, raw, gaudy; Day-Glo <tm>, fluorescent

21 **harsh-colored,** off-color, off-tone; **inharmonious,** discordant, incongruous, harsh, clashing, conflicting, colliding

22 **soft-colored**, soft-hued, soft, softened, subdued, understated, muted, delicate, light, creamy, peaches-and-cream, **pastel, pale,** palish, subtle, mellow, quiet, tender, sweet; pearly, nacreous, mother-of-pearl, iridescent, opalescent; patinaed; somber, simple, sober, sad; flat, eggshell, semigloss, gloss; weathered, heathered

COMBINING FORMS 23 -chroia, -chromasia, chrom-, chromo-, chromat-, chromato-; -phyll; pigmento-; -chrome, -chromia, -chromy; pallidi-; -chroic, -chroous

36 COLORLESSNESS

<lacking color>

NOUNS 1 **colorlessness,** lack of color, absence of color, huelessness, tonelessness, achromatism, achromaticity; dullness, lackluster; neutral hue, neutral tint

2 **paleness,** dimness, weakness, **faintness,** fadedness; lightness, fairness; **pallor,** pallidity, pallidness, prison pallor, wanness, sallowness, pastiness, ashiness; wheyface; muddiness, dullness; grayness, griseousness; anemia, hypochromic anemia, hypochromia, chloranemia; bloodlessness, exsanguination; ghastliness, haggardness, lividness, sickly hue, sickliness, deadly pallor, deathly pallor, deathly hue, cadaverousness

3 **decoloration,** decolorizing, decolorization, discoloration, achromatization, lightening; fading, paling; dimming, bedimming; whitening, blanching, etiolation, whiteness, albinism, pigment deficiency; bleeding, bleeding white; weathering

4 **bleach,** bleaching, bleaching agent, bleaching substance; whitener; color remover, decolorant, decolorizer, achromatizer

VERBS 5 **decolor**, decolorize, discolor, achromatize, etiolate; fade, wash out; dim, dull, tarnish, tone down; pale, whiten, blanch, drain, drain of color; **bleach,** peroxide

6 **lose color, fade,** fade out; bleach, bleach out; pale, turn pale, grow pale, change color, change countenance, turn white, whiten, blanch, wan; come out in the wash; discolor

ADJS 7 **colorless,** hueless, toneless, uncolored, achromic, achromatic, achromatous, unpigmented; neutral; dull, flat, mat, dead, dingy, muddy, leaden, lusterless, lackluster; faded, washed-out, dimmed, discolored, decolored, etiolated, weathered; pale, dim, weak, faint; pallid, wan, sallow, fallow; pale around the gills, blue around the gills, green around the gills, drained of color; white, white as a sheet; crystal; **pasty,** mealy, waxen; **ashen,** ashy, ashen-hued, cinereous, cineritious, gray, griseous, mousy; **anemic,** hypochromic, chloranemic; bloodless, exsanguine, exsanguinated, exsanguineous, bled white; ghastly, livid, lurid, haggard, cadaverous, unhealthy, sickly, deadly pale, deathly pale; pale as death, pale as a ghost, pale as a corpse; pale-faced, tallow-faced, wheyfaced, white-skinned

8 **bleached,** decolored, decolorized, achromatized, whitened, blanched, lightened, bleached out, bleached white; drained, drained of color; etiolated

9 **light, fair,** light-colored, light-hued; pastel; whitish

COMBINING FORMS 10 achromat-, achromato-, achro-, achroö-

37 WHITENESS

<color of snow, milk>

NOUNS 1 **whiteness, white,** whitishness; albescence; lightness, fairness; paleness; silveriness; snowiness, frostiness; chalkiness; pearliness; creaminess, off-whiteness; blondness; hoariness, grizzliness, canescence; milkiness, lactescence; glaucousness; glaucescence; silver; albinism, achroma, achromasia, achromatosis; albino; leukoderma, vitiligo; wheyface; white race

2 <comparisons> alabaster, bone, chalk, cream, ivory, lily, lime, milk, pearl, sheet, swan, sheep, fleece, flour, foam, paper, phantom, silver, snow, driven snow, tallow, teeth, wax, wool

3 **whitening,** albification, blanching; etiolation; whitewashing; **bleaching**; silvering, frosting, grizzling

4 whitening agent, **whitener**, whiting, whitening, whitewash, calcimine; pipe clay; correction fluid, Wite-Out <tm>; bleach

VERBS 5 **whiten,** white, etiolate, **blanch; bleach**; pale, blench; decolorize; fade; silver, grizzle, frost, besnow; chalk

6 **whitewash,** white, calcimine; pipe-clay; clean

ADJS 7 **white,** pure white, white as alabaster, white as bone, white as chalk, white as snow, snow-white, snowy, niveous, frosty, frosted; hoary, hoar, grizzled, grizzly, griseous, canescent; silver, silvery, silvered, argent, argentine; platinum; chalky, cretaceous; fleece-white, fleecy-white; swan-white; foam-white; milk-white, milky, lactescent; marble, marmoreal; lily-white, white as a lily; white as a sheet, wheyfaced, ghastly; albescent; whitened, bleached, blanched, achromatic; crystal

8 **whitish,** whity, albescent; **light, fair;** pale; off-white; eggshell; glaucous, glaucescent; pearl, pearly, pearly-white, pearl-white; alabaster, alabastrine; cream, creamy; ivory, ivory-white; gray-white; dun-white

9 **blond,** blonde; flaxen-haired, fair-haired; artificial blond, bleached-blond, peroxide-blond; ash-blond, platinum-blond, strawberry-blond, honey-blond, blond-headed, blond-haired; towheaded, tow-haired; golden-haired; white-haired

10 **albino,** albinic, albinistic, albinal

COMBINING FORMS 11 alb-, albo-, leuc-, leuco-, leuk-, leuko-

12 **white color varieties**

alabaster	marble
antimony white	milk-white
argent	nacre
beige	off-white
bismuth white	oyster white
blond	Paris white
bone white	pearl, pearl white
chalk	platinum
Chinese white	pure white
columbine	putty
dove	silver
Dutch white	snow white
eggshell	strontium white
flake white	swan white
gauze	titanium white
Isabelline	white lead
ivory	whitewash
lead white	zinc white
lily white	

38 BLACKNESS

<color of coal, night sky>

NOUNS 1 **blackness,** nigritude*, nigrescence*; inkiness; **black, sable, ebony;** melanism; black race; darkness

2 **darkness, darkishness,** darksomeness, blackishness; total darkness, lightlessness; swarthiness, swartness, swarth; duskiness, duskness; pitchiness; soberness, sobriety, somberness, graveness, sadness, funereality; hostility, sullenness, anger, black mood, black looks, black words

3 **dinginess,** griminess, **smokiness,** sootiness, fuliginousness, fuliginosity, smudginess, smuttiness, blotchiness, dirtiness, muddiness, murkiness

4 <comparisons> ebony, jet, ink, sloe, pitch, tar, coal, charcoal, smoke, soot, smut, raven, obsidian, sable, crow, night, hell, sin, one's hat, ebon

5 **blackening, darkening,** nigrification, melanization, melanism, melanosis, denigration; shading; smudging, smutching, smirching; smudge, smutch, smirch, smut

6 **blacking,** blackening, blackening agent, blackwash; charcoal, burnt cork, black ink; lampblack, carbon black, stove black, gas black, soot; japan; melanin

VERBS 7 **blacken,** black, nigrify*, melanize, denigrate; darken, bedarken; shade, shadow; blackwash, ink, charcoal, cork; smudge, smutch, smirch, besmirch, murk, blotch, blot, dinge, dirty; smut, soot; smoke, oversmoke, singe, scorch, char; ebonize; **smear**, blacken one's name, blacken one's reputation, give one a black eye; japan, niello

ADJS 8 **black,** black as ink, black as pitch, black as tar, black as coal, black as night; sable, nigrous, nigrescent; ebony, ebon; deep black, of the deepest dye; **pitch-black,** pitch-dark, pitchy, dark as pitch, tar-black, tarry; night-black, night-dark, dark as night; midnight, black as midnight; inky, inky-black, atramentous, achromatic, ink-black; jet-black, jet, jetty; coal-black, coaly; sloe, sloe-black, sloe-colored; raven, raven-black, black as a crow; blue-black, brown-black; **dark**

9 **dark,** dark-colored, darkish, darksome, blackish; nigrescent; swarthy, swart; dusky, dusk; somber, sombrous, sober, grave, sad, funereal; hostile, sullen, angry; achromatic

10 **dark-skinned,** black-skinned, dark-complexioned; black, colored*; swarthy, swart; melanian, melanic, melanotic, melanistic, melanous

11 **dingy,** grimy, **smoky,** sooty, fuliginous, smudgy, smutty, blotchy, dirty, muddy, murky, smirched, besmirched, dusky; blackened, singed, charred

12 livid, **black-and-blue**

13 **black-haired,** raven-haired, raven-tressed, black-locked, dark-haired; brunet, **brunette**

COMBINING FORMS 14 atro-, mel-, mela-, melo-, melano-, melam-

15 **black color varieties**

aniline black	kohl
arsenic black	lampblack
black	melanin
blue-black	night black
Brunswick black	nigrosine
carbon black	obsidian
charcoal black	Payne's gray
chrome black	pitch-black
coal black	Prussian black
corbeau	pure black
direct black	raven black
drop black	sable
ebony	slate black
ink black	sloe black
ivory black	soot black
japan	subfusc
jet, jet black	sulfur black

39 GRAYNESS

<*color between black and white*>

NOUNS 1 **grayness, gray,** grayishness, canescence; glaucousness, glaucescence; silveriness; ashiness; neutral tint; smokiness; mousiness; slatiness; leadenness; lividness, lividity; dullness, drabness, soberness, somberness; grisaille; oyster, taupe, greige; gunmetal, iron, lead, pewter, silver, slate, steel

2 **gray-haired person,** gray-headed person, gray-hair, graybeard, grisard, salt-and-pepper, hoariness

VERBS 3 **gray**, grizzle, silver, frost

ADJS 4 **gray, grayish,** gray-colored, gray-hued, gray-toned, grayed, griseous; canescent; iron-gray, steely, steel-gray; Quaker-gray, Quaker-colored, acier, gray-drab; Oxford gray; dove-gray, dove-colored; pearl-gray, pearl, pearly; silver-gray, silver, silvery, silvered; grizzly, grizzled, grizzle; ash-gray, ashen, ashy, cinerous, cinereous, cineritious, cinereal; dusty, dust-gray; smoky, smoke-gray; charcoal-gray; slaty, slate-colored; leaden, livid, lead-gray; glaucous, glaucescent; wolf-gray; mousy, mouse-gray, mouse-colored; dapple-gray, dappled-gray; gray-spotted, gray-speckled, salt-and-pepper; gray-black, gray-brown; taupe, ecru, greige; neutral; dull, dingy, dismal, somber, sober, sad, dreary; winter-gray, hoar, hoary, frost-gray, rime-gray

5 **gray-haired,** gray-headed, silver-headed; hoar, hoary, hoary-haired, grizzled; gray-bearded, silver-bearded, salt-and-pepper, pepper-and-salt; frosty

6 **gray color varieties**

ash, ash gray	moleskin
bat	mouse
battleship gray	mushroom
blue-gray	neutral
cadet gray	nutria
charcoal gray	obsidian
cinder	olive gray
cloud	opal gray
crystal gray	Oxford gray
dark gray	oyster gray
dove	pale gray
field gray	pearl, pearl gray
flint	pelican
French gray	plumbago
glaucous gray	powder gray
granite	Quaker gray
gray, grey	salt-and-pepper, pepper-and-salt
gray-white	shell gray
greige, grege	silver
gun metal	silver-gray
iron	slate gray
lead	smoke gray
light gray	steel gray
lilac gray	taupe
merle	zinc gray
mole gray	

40 BROWNNESS

<*color of wood, chocolate*>

NOUNS 1 **brownness,** brownishness, **brown,** browning, infuscation; brown race; ochre, sepia, raw sienna, burnt sienna, raw umber, burnt umber; caramel, pumpernickel, coffee, chocolate, paper bag

VERBS 2 **brown,** embrown, infuscate; rust; **tan,** bronze, suntan; sunburn, burn; fry, sauté, scorch, braise; toast; caramelize

ADJS 3 **brown, brownish;** cinnamon, hazel; fuscous; **brunet,** brunette, brune; tawny, fulvous; dark brown; tan, tan-colored; tan-faced, tan-skinned, tanned, suntanned; khaki, khaki-colored; drab, olive-drab; dun, dun-brown, dun-drab, dun-olive; beige, grege, buff, biscuit, mushroom; chocolate, chocolate-colored, chocolate-brown; cocoa, cocoa-colored, cocoa-brown; coffee, coffee-colored, coffee-brown; toast, toast-brown; nut-brown; oatmeal; walnut, walnut-brown; seal, seal-brown; fawn, fawn-colored; grayish-brown; brownish-gray, taupe, mouse-dun, mouse-brown, tweed; snuff-colored, snuff-brown, mummy-brown; umber, umber-colored, umber-brown; olive-brown; sepia; sorrel; sable; yellowish-brown, brownish-yellow; brown as a berry, berry-brown

4 **reddish-brown,** rufous-brown, brownish-red; roan; henna; terra-cotta; rufous, foxy; livid-brown; mahogany, mahogany-brown; auburn, titian; russet, russety; rust, rust-colored, rusty, ferruginous, rubiginous; liver-colored, liver-brown; **bronze,** bronze-brown, bronze-colored, bronzed, brazen; copper, coppery, copperish, cupreous, copper-colored; chestnut, chestnut-brown, castaneous; bay, bay-colored, bayard; sunburned, adust

5 **brunette,** brunet; brown-haired; auburn-haired; xanthous

6 **brown color varieties**

acorn
alesan
amber
antique bronze
antique brown
antique drab
auburn
autumn leaf
baize
bay
beaver
beige
biscuit
Bismarck brown
bistre
bone brown
Bordeaux
brick
brindle
bronze
brown
brown madder
brunet, brunette
buckthorn brown
buff
burgundy
burnt almond
burnt ocher
burnt sienna
burnt umber
butternut
café au lait
café noir
camel
caramel
Castilian brown
chestnut
chocolate
cinnamon
cocoa
coconut
coffee
Cologne brown
copper
cordovan
dark brown
dead leaf
doeskin
drab
Dresden brown
dun
earth
ecru
fallow
fawn
foliage brown
fox
ginger
Havana brown
hazel
henna
Italian earth
Italian ocher
ivory brown
khaki
leather
light brown
light red-brown
liver brown
madder brown
mahogany
manganese brown
manila
maple sugar
Mars brown
mineral brown
mink
mocha
mummy
nougat
nut
nutmeg
nutria
oatmeal
ocher
olive brown
orange-brown
otter brown
oxblood
pale brown
peat brown
peppercorn
putty
raffia
raw sienna
raw umber
reddish-brown
roan
russet
rust
sand
sandalwood
seal brown
sepia
sienna
sorrel
suntan
tan
tanaura
taupe
tawny
terra cotta
terra sienna
terra umbra
titian
toast
topaz
tortoiseshell
umber
Vandyke brown, Verona brown
walnut
yellow-brown

7 **reddish-brown color varieties**

auburn
baize
bay
brick
burgundy
burnt ocher
burnt sienna
caramel
Castilian brown
chestnut
chocolate
cinnamon
cocoa
Columbian red
cordovan
ginger
henna
India red
light red-brown
liver
madder brown
mahogany
nutmeg
ocher

oxblood	sepia
piccolopasso red	sienna
red robin	sorrel
roan	terra cotta
russet	titian
rust	Venetian red
sand	vermilion,
sedge	vermeil

41 REDNESS

<color of blood>

NOUNS 1 **redness,** reddishness, rufosity, rubricity; **red,** *rouge* <Fr>; rubicundity, ruddiness, blushing, color, high color, floridness, floridity; rubor, erythema, erythroderma; erythrism; reddish brown; red race; carmine, crimson, henna, rouge, vermilion, cerise; cherry, ruby, fire engine

2 **pinkness,** pinkishness; **rosiness;** pink, rose

3 **reddening,** rubefaction, rubification, rubescence, erubescence, rufescence; coloring, mantling, crimsoning, **blushing,** flushing; blush, flush, glow, bloom, rosiness; hectic, hectic flush; flush syndrome, alcohol flush syndrome; rubefacient

VERBS 4 make red, **redden, rouge,** ruddle, rubefy, raddle, rubric; warm, inflame; crimson, encrimson; vermilion, madder, miniate, henna, rust, carmine; incarnadine, pinkify; **blush;** red-ink, red-pencil, lipstick

5 **redden,** turn red, grow red, color, color up, mantle, blush, flush, crimson; flame, glow

ADJS 6 **red, reddish**, red-colored, red-hued, red-dyed, red-looking; **ruddy,** ruddied, rubicund; rubric, rubrical, rubricate, rubricose; rufescent, rufous, rufulous; warm, hot, glowing; bright-red; fiery, flaming, flame-colored, flame-red, fire-red, red as fire, lurid, red as a hot coal, red as a live coal; reddened, inflamed; scarlet, vermilion, vermeil; crimson; rubiate; maroon; damask; puce; stammel; cerise; iron-red; cardinal, cardinal-red; cherry, cherry-colored, cherry-red; carmine, incarmined; ruby, ruby-colored, ruby-red; wine, port-wine, wine-colored, wine-red, vinaceous; carnation, carnation-red; brick-red, bricky, tile-red, lateritious; rust, rust-red, rusty, ferruginous, rubiginous; beet-red, red as a beet; lobster-red, red as a lobster; red as a turkey-cock; copper-red, carnelian; russet; titian, titian-red; infrared; reddish-amber, reddish-gray; reddish-brown

7 **sanguine,** sanguineous, **blood-red,** blood-colored, bloody-red, bloody, gory, red as blood

8 **pink, pinkish,** pinky; **rose, rosy,** rose-colored, rose-hued, rose-red, roseate; primrose; flesh-colored, flesh-pink, incarnadine; coral, coral-colored, coral-red, coralline; salmon, salmon-colored, salmon-pink; damask, carnation; fuchsia

9 **red-complexioned, rosy-cheeked,** rosy, ruddy-complexioned, warm-complexioned, red-fleshed, red-faced, ruddy-faced, apple-cheeked, ruddy, rubicund, florid, sanguine, full-blooded; blowzy, blowzed; glowing, blooming; hectic, blushing, rouged, flushed, flush; burnt, sunburned; erythematous

10 **redheaded,** red-haired, red-polled, red-bearded; erythristic; red-crested, red-crowned, red-tufted; ginger-haired, carroty, carrot-topped, chestnut, auburn, titian, xanthous

11 **reddening**, blushing, flushing, coloring; rubescent, erubescent; rubificative, rubrific; rubefacient

12 **pink color varieties**

amaranth pink	nymph
annatto	ombre
Baker-Miller pink	opera pink
begonia	orange-pink
blush	orchid pink
burnt rose	orchid rose
cameo pink	pale pink
carnation	peach red
casino pink	peach blossom pink
chrome primrose	petal pink
coral pink	primrose
deep pink	puce
fiesta	purplish pink
flamingo	red-pink, reddish pink
flesh pink	rose
fluorescent pink	rose pink
fuchsia	rose quartz
geranium pink	royal pink
hot pink	salmon
incarnadine	scarlet madder
livid pink	shell pink
mallow pink	shocking pink
Mountbatten pink	tea rose
neon pink	watermelon

13 **red color varieties**

alizarin crimson	burnt ocher
alpenglow	cadmium red
annatto	cardinal
beet red	carmine
blood red	carnation
blush	carnelian
bois de rose	Castilian red
bougainvillea	cerise
Bordeaux	cherry
brick red	Chinese red
bright red	chrome red
bright rose	cinnabar
brownish red	claret
burgundy	cochineal
burnt carmine	coral pink

cordovan
cranberry
crimson
damask
dark red
deep red
dragon's blood
English red
faded rose
fire red
fire-engine red
flame red
fuchsia
garnet
geranium
grenadine
gules <heraldry>
hellebore red
hematite
iron red
lake, lac
light red
lobster
madder
magenta
maroon
Mars red
murrey
old red
old rose
orange-red
oxblood
palladium red
paprika
peach
Persian red
pinkish red
ponceau
poppy
Prussian red
puce
purple-red
red ocher
rhodamine
rose madder
rosso corsa
royal red
ruby
ruddle
rust
safranine
scarlet
solferino
stammel
strawberry
terra rosa
tile red
Turkey red
Venetian red
vermeil
vermilion
wild cherry
wine

42 ORANGENESS

<color between red and yellow>

NOUNS **1** **orangeness,** oranginess; **orange**; cadmium orange, carotene

ADJS **2** **orange, orangeish,** orangey, orange-hued, reddish-yellow; ocherous, ochery, ochreous, ochroid, ocherish; old gold; saffron; pumpkin, pumpkin-colored; tangerine, tangerine-colored; apricot, peach, cantaloupe, salmon, mango; carroty, carrot-colored; orange-red, orange-yellow, red-orange, reddish-orange, yellow-orange

3 **orange color varieties**

acid orange
amber
apricot
aurora
brass
burnt ocher
burnt orange
burnt Roman ocher
burnt sienna
cadmium orange
carnelian
carotene
carrot
chrome orange
copper
copper red
dark orange
Dutch orange
Florida gold
ginger
helianthin
hyacinth
madder orange
mandarin
marigold
Mars orange
melon
methyl orange
Mikado orange
minium
neon orange
ocher
ocher orange
old gold
orange chrome yellow
orange lead
orange madder
orange mineral
orange ocher
orange vermilion
orange-red
orange-yellow
orpiment
pale orange
peach
pumpkin
raw sienna
realgar orange
red-orange
Rubens' madder
saffron
Spanish ocher
sunset orange
tangerine
Tangier ocher
terra cotta
titian
yellow carmine
yellow-orange
zinc orange

43 YELLOWNESS

<color of lemon, sun>

NOUNS **1** **yellowness,** yellowishness; goldenness, aureateness; **yellow,** gold; gildedness; fallowness; cadmium yellow, cadmium lemon

2 yellow skin, yellow complexion, sallowness; biliousness; xanthochroism; **jaundice,** yellow jaundice, icterus, xanthoderma, xanthism; yellow race

VERBS **3** **yellow,** turn yellow; gild, begild, engild; aurify; sallow; **jaundice**

ADJS **4** **yellow, yellowish,** yellowy; lutescent, luteous, luteolous; xanthic, xanthous; flavescent; **gold, golden**, gold-colored, golden-yellow, gilt, gilded, auric, aureate; sunshine-yellow; canary, canary-yellow; citron, citron-yellow, citreous; lemon, lemon-colored, lemon-yellow; sulfur-colored, sulfur-yellow; mustard, mustard-yellow; pale-yellow, sallow, fallow; cream, creamy, cream-colored; straw, straw-colored, tow-colored; flaxen, flaxen-colored, flax-colored; sandy, sand-colored; ocherous, ochery, ochreous, ochroid, ocherish; buff, buff-colored, buff-yellow; honey-colored; saffron, saffron-colored, saffron-yellow; primrose, primrose-colored, primrose-yellow; topaz-yellow; greenish-yellow, chartreuse; banana; maize

5 **yellow-haired, golden-haired,** tow-headed, tow-haired, auricomous, xanthous; blonde, blond

6 yellow-faced, **yellow-complexioned**, sallow, yellow-cheeked; **jaundiced,** xanthodermatous, icteric, icterical, bilious

7 **yellow color varieties**

acid yellow
amber
apricot yellow
arsenic yellow
auramine
aureate

aureolin
azo yellow
barium yellow
blonde
brass
brazilin
brownish-yellow
buff
butter
cadmium yellow
calendula
canary
Cassel yellow
chalcedony
chamois
champagne
chartreuse yellow
chrome lemon
chrome yellow
citron
cobalt yellow
corn
cream
crocus
dandelion
ecru
flax
gamboge
gold
golden yellow
goldenrod
green-yellow
honey
Imperial yellow
jonquil
lead-tin yellow
lemon
linen
madder yellow
maize
marigold yellow
mikado yellow
mustard
Naples yellow
ocher, ochre
oil yellow
old gold
orange-yellow
orpiment
pale yellow
palomino
Paris yellow
peach yellow
pear
primrose
purree
quince yellow
reed
saffron
sallow
sand
snapdragon
straw
sulfur
sunflower
sunshine yellow
topaz yellow
yellow madder
yellow ocher
yellowstone
yolk yellow
zinc yellow

44 GREENNESS

<color of grass, plants>

NOUNS 1 **greenness,** viridity; greenishness, virescence, viridescence; verdantness, verdancy, **verdure,** glaucousness, glaucescence; **green,** greensickness, chlorosis, chloremia, chloranemia; chlorophyll; grass, emerald

2 **verdigris,** patina, aerugo; patination

VERBS 3 **green;** verdigris, patinate, patinize

ADJS 4 **green,** virid; **verdant,** verdurous, vert; grassy, leafy, leaved, foliaged; springlike, summerlike, summery, vernal, vernant, aestival; **greenish,** viridescent, virescent; grass-green, green as grass; citrine, citrinous; olive, olive-green, olivaceous; pea-green; avocado; jade; loden green; bottle-green; forest-green; sea-green; beryl-green, berylline; leek-green, porraceous; holly, holly-green; ivy, ivy-green; emerald, emerald-green, smaragdine; chartreuse, yellow-green, yellowish-green, greenish-yellow; glaucous, glaucescent, glaucous-green; blue-green, bluish-green, green-blue, greenish-blue; greensick, chlorotic, chloremic, chloranemic

5 patinous, **patinaed,** patinated, patinized, aeruginous, verdigrisy, verdigrised

6 **green color varieties**

absinthe
apple green
aqua green
aquamarine
army green
avocado
bay
beryl
bice
blue-green
bottle green
Brunswick green
cadmium green
camouflage green
celadon
chartreuse, chartreuse green
chrome green, chromium green
chrome oxide green
chrysolite green
citron green
civette green
clair de lune
cobalt green
corbeau
cucumber
cypress
dark green
drake
duck green
eau de nil
Egyptian green
emerald
fir green, fir
flagstone
forest green
gallein
glauconite
glaucous green
grass green
gray-green
green ocher
Guinea green
gunpowder
holly green
Irish green
ivy green
jade
Janus green
jungle green
kelly green
Kendal green
leaf green
leek green
light green
lime green
Lincoln green
lizard
loden
lotus
malachite
marine
methyl green
mignonette
mint
moss
myrtle
Niagara green
Nile green
olive
pale green
Paris green
parrot
patina
pea green
pistachio green
Quaker green
reseda
sage green
sap green
Scheele's green
sea green, seawater green
serpentine
shamrock
Spanish green
spruce
teal
terre verte
tourmaline
turquoise
verdant green
verdet
verdigris
vert
Vienna green
viridian
Wedgwood green

willow green
yellow-green
yew
zinc

45 BLUENESS

<color of clear sky>

NOUNS 1 **blueness,** bluishness; azureness; **blue,** azure, cyan, indigo, ultramarine; lividness, lividity; cyanosis

VERBS 2 **blue,** azure

ADJS 3 **blue, bluish,** cerulescent, cerulean, ceruleous; cyanic, cyaneous, cyanean, cyanotic; azure, azurine, azurean, azureous, azured, azure-blue, azure-colored, azure-tinted; sky-blue, sky-colored, sky-dyed; ice-blue; light-blue, lightish-blue, pale-blue; dark-blue, deep-blue, midnight-blue, navy-blue; peacock-blue, pavonine, pavonian; beryl-blue, berylline; turquoise, turquoise-blue; aquamarine; cornflower; electric-blue; ultramarine; royal-blue; indigo; sapphire, sapphire-blue, sapphirine; Wedgwood-blue, robin's-egg blue; livid

4 **blue color varieties**

air force blue
aniline blue
aquamarine
azul, azulene
azure
azurite blue
baby blue
beryl
bice
blue
blue turquoise
blueberry
bluebonnet
blue-gray
blue-green
blue-violet
bright blue
Brunswick blue
cadet blue
calamine blue
cerulean
Chinese blue
cobalt blue
Copenhagen blue
cornflower
cyan
dark blue
daylight blue
deep blue
delft blue
denim blue
Dresden blue
Egyptian blue
electric blue
Empire blue
flag blue
French blue
gentian blue
gray-blue
greenish blue
Havana lake
Helvetia blue
huckleberry
hyacinth
hydrangea
ice blue
indigo
kingfisher blue
lapis lazuli
lavender blue
light blue
lucerne
lupine
madder blue
marine blue
midnight blue
milori blue
Napoleon blue
navy blue, navy
pale blue
peacock blue
perse
Persian blue
powder blue
Prussian blue
purple-blue
reddish blue
robin's-egg blue
royal blue
sapphire blue
Saxe blue
sea blue
sky blue
slate blue
smalt
smoke blue
steel blue
teal blue
turquoise
ultramarine
Venetian blue
violet-blue
water blue
Wedgwood blue
wisteria blue
woad
zaffer

46 PURPLENESS

<color between red and blue>

NOUNS 1 **purpleness,** purplishness, purpliness; **purple; violet,** lavender, lilac, magenta, mauve, amethyst; lividness, lividity, bruise

VERBS 2 **purple,** empurple, purpurate

ADJS 3 **purple,** purpure <heraldry>, purpureal, purpureous, purpurean, purpurate; royal purple; purplish, purply, purplescent, empurpled; **violet,** violaceous; plum, plum-colored, plum-purple; amethystine; **lavender,** lavender-blue; lilac; magenta; mauve, mauvy; mulberry; orchid; pansy-purple, pansy-violet; raisin-colored; fuchsia, puce, aubergine; purple-blue; livid

4 **purple color varieties**

amaranth
amethyst
aniline purple
archil
Argyle purple
aubergine
blue-violet
bluish purple
burgundy violet
campanula
cerise
clematis
dahlia
damson
dark purple
deep purple
eggplant
fuchsia
grape
gridelin
heliotrope
hyacinth
imperial purple
indigo
king's purple
lavender
light purple
lilac
livid purple
livid violet
madder violet
magenta
maroon
Mars violet
mauve
monsignor
mulberry
orchid
pale purple
pansy violet
periwinkle
phlox
plum
prune
puce
purple-blue
purple-red
raisin
raspberry
red-violet
reddish purple
royal purple, regal purple
rubine
solferino
tulip
Tyrian purple
violet
wine purple
wisteria

47 VARIEGATION
<diversity of colors>

NOUNS 1 **variegation, multicolor;** parti-color; medley of colors, mixture of colors, spectrum, rainbow of colors, rainbow, riot of color; polychrome, polychromatism; dichromatism, trichromatism; dichroism, trichroism

2 **iridescence,** iridization, irisation, **opalescence,** nacreousness, pearliness, chatoyancy, play of colors, play of light; light show; moiré pattern, tabby; burelé, burelage

3 **spottedness,** spottiness, maculation, freckliness, speckliness, mottledness, mottlement, dappleness, dappledness, stippledness, dottedness; fleck, speck, speckle; freckle; **spot,** dot, polka dot, macula, macule, blotch, splotch, patch, splash, bullet point; **mottle,** dapple; brindle; **stipple,** stippling, pointillism, pointillage; pinpointing; spattering

4 **check,** checker, checks, checking, checkerboard, chessboard; **plaid,** tartan; checker-work, variegated pattern, harlequin, colors in patches, crazywork, patchwork; parquet, parquetry, marquetry, mosaic, tesserae, tessellation; crazy-paving; houndstooth; inlay, damascene; graph

5 **stripe,** striping, candy-stripe, pinstripe; barber pole; streak, streaking; striation, striature, stria; striola, striga; crack, craze, crackle, reticulation; bar, band, belt, list

6 <comparisons> spectrum, rainbow, iris, chameleon, leopard, jaguar, cheetah, ocelot, zebra, barber pole, candy cane, Dalmatian, firedog, peacock, butterfly, mother-of-pearl, nacre, tortoiseshell, opal, kaleidoscope, stained glass, serpentine, calico cat, marble, mackerel sky, confetti, crazy quilt, patchwork quilt, shot silk, moiré, watered silk, marbled paper, Joseph's coat, harlequin, tapestry; bar code, checkerboard, graph paper

VERBS 7 **variegate,** motley; parti-color; polychrome, polychromize; pattern; harlequin; mottle, dapple, stipple, fleck, flake, speck, speckle, bespeckle, freckle, spot, bespot, dot, sprinkle, blot, spangle, bespangle, pepper, stud, maculate; blotch, splotch; tattoo; check, checker; tessellate; **stripe,** streak, striate, band, bar, vein, craze; marble, marbleize; engrail; tabby

8 **opalesce,** opalize; iridesce

ADJS 9 **variegated, many-colored,** many-hued, diverse-colored, **multicolored,** multicolor, multicolorous, **varicolored,** varicolorous, polychrome, polychromic, polychromatic; parti-colored, parti-color; of all manner of colors, of all the colors of the rainbow; versicolor, versicolored, versicolorate, versicolorous; engrailed; motley, medley, harlequin; colorful, colory; daedal; crazy; thunder and lightning; kaleidoscopic, kaleidoscopical; prismatic, prismatical, prismal, spectral; shot, shot through; bicolored, bicolor, dichromic, dichromatic; tricolored, tricolor, trichromic, trichromatic; two-color, two-colored, three-color, three-colored, two-tone, two-toned

10 **iridescent,** iridal, iridial, iridine, iridian, iridiated; irised, irisated, rainbowy, rainbowlike, rainbowed; **opalescent,** opaline, opaloid; nacreous, nacry, *nacré* <Fr>, nacred, pearly, pearlish, mother-of-pearl; tortoiseshell; peacocklike, pavonine, pavonian; chatoyant; moiré, burelé; watered

11 **chameleonlike,** chameleonic, changeable

12 **mottled, motley**; pied, piebald, skewbald, pinto; **dappled,** dapple; calico; marbled; clouded; salt-and-pepper

13 **spotted, dotted,** polka-dot, sprinkled, peppered, studded, pocked, pockmarked; spotty, dotty, patchy, pocky; speckled, specked, speckledy, speckly, specky; **stippled,** pointillé, pointillistic; flecked, fleckered; spangled, bespangled; maculate, maculated, macular; punctate, punctated; freckled, frecked, freckly; blotched, blotchy, splotched, splotchy; flea-bitten; tortoiseshell; foxed

14 **checked, checkered,** checkedy, check, **plaid,** plaided; tessellated, tessellate, mosaic

15 **striped,** stripy, candy-stripe, pinstripe; **streaked,** streaky; striated, striate, striatal, striolate, strigate, strigose; barred, banded, listed; veined; brindle, brindled, brinded; marbled, marbleized; reticulate; tabby

48 HEARING
<sense of hearing>

NOUNS 1 **hearing,** audition; sense of hearing, auditory sense, aural sense, auditory sensation; ear; listening, heeding, attention, hushed attention, rapt attention, eager attention, mind; auscultation, aural examination, examination by ear; audibility

2 **audition,** hearing, tryout, call, audience, interview, conference; attention, favorable attention, ear; **listening,** listening in; **eavesdropping,** overhearing, wiretapping, electronic surveillance, bugging

3 **good hearing**, refined hearing, acute sense of hearing, sensitive ear, nice ear, quick ear, sharp ear, correct ear; an ear for; musical ear, ear for music, musicality; ear-mindedness; bad ear, poor ear, no ear, tin ear

4 **earshot,** ear-reach, hearing, range, auditory

range, reach, carrying distance, sound of one's voice

5 **listener,** hearer, auditor, audient, hearkener, auditioner, earwitness; eavesdropper, overhearer, monitor; little pitcher with big ears, snoop, listener-in; fly on the wall

6 **audience,** auditory, house, congregation; studio audience, live audience, captive audience, theatregoers, gallery, crowd, grandstand; orchestra, pit; groundling, boo-bird, spectator

7 **ear**, auditory apparatus, hearing organ; external ear, outer ear; cauliflower ear, jug ear, bat ear

8 listening device; **hearing aid,** hard-of-hearing aid; electronic hearing aid, transistor hearing aid; vacuum-tube hearing aid; ear trumpet; amplifier, speaking trumpet, megaphone; stethoscope

9 **<science of hearing>** otology; otoscopy, auriscopy; audiometry; otoneurology, otopathy, otography, otoplasty, otolaryngology, otorhinolaryngology; ear, nose, and throat (ENT); audiology; acoustic phonetics, phonetics; auriscope, otoscope, auscultator, stethoscope; audiometer

VERBS 10 **listen,** hark, **hearken, heed, hear, attend,** give attention, **give ear,** give an ear, lend an ear, bend an ear; **listen to,** listen at, list, attend to, pay attention, give a hearing to, give audience to, sit in on; listen in; **eavesdrop,** wiretap, tap, intercept, bug; keep one's ears open, be all ears, listen with both ears, strain one's ears; prick up the ears, cock the ears, keep one's ear to the ground, have long ears; hang on the lips of, hang on every word; hear out; auscultate, examine by ear

11 **hear,** catch, get, take in, hear from; **overhear;** hear of, hear tell of, pick up; get an earful, get wind of, get word; have an ear for, have perfect pitch

12 **be heard**, fall on the ear, sound in the ear, catch the ear, reach the ear, carry, sound, resound, echo, reverberate, come within earshot, come to one's ear, register, make an impression, get across; have one's ear, reach, contact, get to; make oneself heard, get through to, gain a hearing, reach the ear of; ring in the ear; caress the ear; assault the ear, split the ear, assail the ear

ADJS 13 **auditory,** audio, audile, **hearing, aural,** auricular, otic, audial, auditive, auditorial; audio-visual; audible; otological, otoscopic, otopathic; acoustic, acoustical, phonic

14 **listening,** attentive, open-eared, all ears, hearing; wired

15 **eared,** auriculate; big-eared, cauliflower-eared, crop-eared, dog-eared, droop-eared, flap-eared, flop-eared, jug-earned, lop-eared, long-eared, mouse-eared, prick-eared, quick-eared; sharp-eared; tin-eared; ear-minded; ear-shaped, earlike, auriform

INTERJS 16 **hark,** hark ye, hear ye; hear ye, hear ye; hearken, hear, oyez; now hear this, list, **listen,** listen up, attend, attention, hist, whisht, psst, yo

49 DEAFNESS

<inability to hear>

NOUNS 1 **deafness, hardness of hearing,** dull hearing, deaf ears; stone-deafness; nerve-deafness; mind deafness, word deafness; tone deafness, asonia, unmusicalness; cophosis; impaired hearing, hearing impairment, auditory impairment; loss of hearing, hearing loss; deaf-muteness, deaf-mutism, surdimutism; selective hearing

2 **the deaf,** the hard-of-hearing; deaf-mute, surdomute, deaf-and-dumb person; lip reader; silent person

3 deaf-and-dumb alphabet, manual alphabet, finger alphabet, fingerspelling; dactylology, sign language, American Sign Language; lip reading, oral method; hearing aid

VERBS 4 **be deaf;** have no ears, be earless; lose one's hearing, suffer hearing loss; impairment, go deaf; shut one's ears, stop one's ears, close one's ears, turn a deaf ear; fall on deaf ears; lipread, use sign language, sign

5 **deafen,** stun, split the ears, split the eardrums

ADJS 6 **deaf, hard-of-hearing,** hearing-impaired, dull of hearing, thick of hearing, deaf-eared, dull-eared; surd; deafened, stunned; stone-deaf, deaf as a stone, deaf as a door, deaf as a doorknob, deaf as a doornail, deaf as a post, deaf as an adder; unhearing; earless; word-deaf; tone-deaf, unmusical; dealfish, half-deaf, quasi-deaf; deaf and dumb, deaf-mute

50 SOUND

<something heard>

NOUNS 1 **sound,** sonance, acoustic, acoustical phenomenon, acoustic phenomenon; auditory phenomenon, auditory stimulus, auditory effect; noise; ultrasound; sound wave, sound propagation; sound intensity, sound intensity level, amplitude, loudness; phone, speech sound; resonance; tongue twister; spoken word

2 **tone, pitch, frequency,** audio frequency (AF); monotone, monotony, tonelessness; overtone, harmonic, partial, partial tone; undertone; fundamental tone, fundamental; intonation

3 **timbre,** tonality, **tone quality,** tone color, color, coloring, clang color, clang tint, register

4 **sounding,** sonation, sonification
5 **acoustics,** phonics, radioacoustics, acoustic theory, harmonics; acoustical engineer, acoustician; radiophonics
6 **sonics;** subsonics; **supersonics,** ultrasonics; speed of sound; sound barrier, transonic barrier, sonic wall; sonic boom; ultrasonic frequency, infrasonic frequency
7 <**sound unit**> **decibel** (db); bel, phon, sone
8 **loudspeaker, speaker,** dynamic speaker; speaker unit, speaker system; crossover network; voice coil; cone, diaphragm; acoustical network; horn; personal stereo; **headphones, earphone,** stereo headset, headset, ear buds
9 **microphone, mike**; radiomicrophone; concealed microphone, bug
10 audio amplifier, **amplifier**, amp; preamplifier, preamp
11 **sound reproduction system**, audio sound system, sound system; high-fidelity system, hi-fi; record player, phonograph, gramophone, Victrola; jukebox, nickelodeon; radio-phonograph combination; monophonic system, monaural system, mono, stereophonic system, binaural system, stereo, surround sound; four-channel stereo system, discrete four-channel system, derived four-channel system, quadraphonic sound system; multitrack player, multitrack recorder, multitrack sound system; pickup, cartridge, magnetic cartridge, ceramic pickup, ceramic cartridge, crystal pickup, photoelectric pickup; stylus, needle; tone arm; turntable, transcription turntable, record changer, changer; public-address system (PA), PA system; sound truck; loud-hailer, bullhorn; intercommunication system, intercom, squawk box; tape recorder, tape deck, cassette player, cassette recorder, audiocassette player, audiocassette recorder, recording system; boom box, ghetto blaster; compact disk player, CD player; media player; iPod <tm>; hi-fi fan, hi-fi freak, audiophile
12 **record,** phonograph record, record album, liner notes; disc, wax, long-playing record (LP), vinyl; transcription, electrical transcription, digital transcription, digital recording; **recording,** wire recording, tape recording; digital stereo; digital disc; tape, audiotape, tape cassette, cassette; tape cartridge, cartridge; digital audio tape (DAT), digital video disc (DVD), Blu-ray; compact disc (CD); videocassette recorder (VCR)
13 **audio distortion,** distortion; interference, static; scratching, shredding, hum, 60-cycle hum, rumble, hissing, howling, blurping, blooping, woomping, fluttering, flutter, squeals, whistles, birdies, motorboating; feedback; cell yell

VERBS 14 **sound,** make a sound, make a noise, give forth a sound, emit a sound; noise; speak; resound, reverberate, echo; **record,** tape, tape-record; prerecord; play back; broadcast, amplify

ADJS 15 **sounding,** sonorous, soniferous; sounded; tonal; monotone, monotonic, monotonal, toneless, droning; voiced
16 **audible,** hearable, heard; distinct, clear, plain, definite, articulate; distinctive, contrastive; high-fidelity, hi-fi, stereophonic; microphonic
17 **acoustic,** acoustical, phonic, sonic; subsonic, supersonic, ultrasonic, hypersonic; transonic, transsonic, faster than sound

ADVS 18 **audibly, aloud,** out, **out loud;** distinctly, clearly, plainly

51 SILENCE

<lack of sound>

NOUNS 1 **silence,** silentness, soundlessness, noiselessness, stillness, lucid stillness, quietness, quietude, quiescence, quiet, still, peace, hush, mum; lull, rest, calm; golden silence; total silence, deathlike silence, tomblike silence, dead silence, perfect silence, solemn silence, awful silence, radio silence, the quiet of the grave, the silence of the grave, the quiet of the tomb, the silence of the tomb; dull roar; hush of hight, dead of night, dead; tacitness, taciturnity, reticence, reserve; inaudibility; tranquillity; not a sound, not a peep; Fifth Amendment
2 **muteness,** mutism, **dumbness,** voicelessness, tonguelessness; speechlessness, wordlessness; inarticulateness; anaudia, aphasia, aphonia; hysterical mutism; deaf-muteness; standing mute, refusal to speak, stonewalling, the code of silence, *omertà* <Ital>, keeping one's lip buttoned; laryngitis
3 **mute,** dummy; deaf-mute
4 **silencer, mute button,** muffler, muffle, mute, baffle, baffler, quietener, cushion; damper, damp; dampener; soft pedal, sordine, sourdine, *sordino* <Ital>; hushcloth, silence cloth; gag, muzzle; antiknock; **soundproofing,** acoustic tile, sound-absorbing material, sound-proofing insulation

VERBS 5 **be silent,** keep silent, keep silence, keep still, keep quiet; keep one's mouth shut, hold one's tongue, keep one's tongue between one's teeth, bite one's tongue, put a bridle on one's tongue, seal one's lips, shut one's mouth, close one's mouth, hold one's breath, muzzle oneself, not breathe a word, not speak, forswear speech, forswear speaking, keep mum, hold one's peace, not let a word escape one, not utter a word, not open one's mouth, not make a sound, not make a peep; make no sign, keep to oneself; not have a word to say, be mute, stand mute; choke up, have one's words stick in one's throat; be taciturn, spare one's words, have little to say, keep one's counsel, hush up

6 <nonformal> **shut up,** keep one's trap shut, keep one's yap shut, button up, button one's lip, save one's breath, shut one's bazoo, can it, dummy up, clam up, close up like a clam, knock it off, not let out a peep, say nothing, not say boo, play dumb, stonewall

7 **fall silent, hush,** quiet, quieten, quiesce, quiet down, pipe down, check one's speech, stop talking; lose one's voice, get laryngitis

8 **silence,** put to silence, hush, hush one up, hush-hush, shush, quiet, quieten, still; soft-pedal, put on the soft pedal, play down; squash, squelch, stifle, choke, choke off, throttle, put the kibosh on, put the lid on, shut down on, put the damper on, gag, muzzle, muffle, stop one's mouth, cut one short; strike dumb, strike mute, dumbfound; tongue-tie

9 **muffle,** mute, dull, soften, deaden, quietize, cushion, baffle, damp, **dampen,** deafen; subdue, stop, tone down, soft-pedal, put on the soft pedal

ADJS 10 **silent,** still, stilly, quiet, quiescent, hushed, soundless, noiseless; taciturn, uncommunicative, tight-lipped, clammed up; echoless; inaudible, subaudible, below the limen of hearing, below the threshold of hearing, unhearable; quiet as a mouse, quiet as a lamb, mousy; silent as a post, silent as a stone, so quiet that one might hear a feather drop, so quiet that one might hear a pin drop; silent as the grave, silent as the tomb, still as death; **unsounded,** unvoiced, unpronounced

11 **tacit, wordless, unspoken,** unuttered, unexpressed, unsaid, unarticulated, unvocalized; **implicit**

12 **mute,** mum, dumb, voiceless, tongueless, **speechless,** wordless, breathless, at a loss for words, choked up; inarticulate; **tongue-tied,** dumbstruck, dumbstricken, stricken dumb, dumbfounded; anaudic, aphasic, aphonic

ADVS 13 **silently,** in silence, quietly, soundlessly, noiselessly; inaudibly

INTERJS 14 **silence, hush,** shush, sh, sh-sh, whist, whish, peace, pax, be quiet, be silent, be still, keep still, keep quiet, quiet, quiet please, soft, belay that, belay there, stow it; hold your tongue, hold your jaw, hold your lip, shut up, shut your mouth, save your breath, not another word, not another peep out of you, mum, mum's the word; hush your mouth, shut your trap, shut your face, button your lip, pipe down, clam up, dry up, can it, that's enough, knock it off

52 FAINTNESS OF SOUND

<unclear or slight sounds>

NOUNS 1 **faintness, lowness, softness,** gentleness, subduedness, dimness, feebleness, weakness; indistinctness, unclearness, flatness; subaudibility, inaudibility; decrescendo; distant sound; easy listening

2 **muffled tone,** veiled voice, *voce velata* <Ital>, covered tone; mutedness; dullness, deadness, flatness; noise abatement, sound reduction, soundproofing

3 **thud,** dull thud; thump, flump, crump, clop, clump, clunk, plunk, tunk, plump, bump; pad, pat; patter, pitter-patter, pit-a-pat; tap, rap, click, tick, flick, pop, peep; tinkle, ting, clink, chink, tingaling

4 **murmur,** murmuring, murmuration; **mutter,** muttering; **mumble,** mumbling; soft voice, low voice, small voice, little voice; **undertone,** underbreath, bated breath; susurration, susurrus, undercurrent; **whisper,** whispering, stage whisper, breathy voice; breath, sigh, sough, exhalation, aspiration; purl, hum, moan, white noise, gray noise, pink noise; nonresonance

5 **ripple, splash,** ripple of laughter, ripple of applause; titter, chuckle

6 **rustle,** rustling, froufrou, swoosh

7 **hum, humming,** thrumming, low rumbling, booming, bombilation, bombination, droning, buzzing, whizzing, whirring, purring

8 **sigh,** sighing, moaning, sobbing, whining, soughing

VERBS 9 steal on the ear, waft on the ear, melt in the air, float in the air

10 **murmur,** mutter, mumble, mussitate, maffle; coo; susurrate; lower one's voice, speak under one's breath; **whisper,** whisper in the ear; breathe, sigh, aspirate

11 **ripple,** babble, burble, bubble, gurgle, guggle, purl, trill; lap, plash, splash, swish, swash, slosh, wash

12 **rustle,** crinkle; swish, whish

13 **hum,** thrum, bum, boom, bombilate, bombinate, drone, buzz, whiz, whir, burr, birr, purr

14 **sigh,** moan, sob, whine, sough; whimper

15 **thud,** thump, patter, clop, clump, clunk, plunk, flump, crump; pad, pat; tap, rap, click, tick, tick away; pop; tinkle, clink, chink

ADJS 16 **faint,** low, soft, gentle, subdued, dim, feeble, weak, faint-sounding, low-sounding, soft-sounding; soft-voiced, low-voiced, faint-voiced, weak-voiced; murmured, whispered, hushed; half-heard, barely heard, scarcely heard; distant, dying away; indistinct, unclear; barely audible, subaudible, near the limit of hearing, near the threshold of hearing; soft-pedaled, piano, pianissimo; decrescendo; unstressed, unaccented; easy listening

17 **muffled, muted,** softened, dampened, damped, smothered, stifled, bated, dulled, deadened, subdued; dull, dead, flat, *sordo* <Ital>; nonresonant

18 **murmuring,** murmurous, murmurish, muttering, mumbling; susurrous, susurrant; whispering, whisper, whispery; whimpering; rustling

19 **rippling,** babbling, burbling, bubbling, gurgling, guggling, purling, trilling; lapping, splashing, plashing, sloshing, swishing

20 **humming,** thrumming, droning, booming, bombinating, buzzing, whizzing, whirring, purring, burring

ADVS 21 **faintly, softly,** gently, subduedly, hushedly, dimly, feebly, weakly, low; piano, pianissimo; *sordo, sordamente* <Ital>, *à la sourdine* <Fr>

22 **in an undertone,** *sotto voce* <Ital>, under one's breath, with bated breath, in a whisper, in a stage whisper, between the teeth; aside, in an aside; out of earshot

53 LOUDNESS

<strong sounds>

NOUNS 1 **loudness,** intensity, volume, amplitude, fullness; sonorousness, sonority; surge of sound, surge, swell, swelling; loudishness, high volume

2 **noisiness,** noisefulness, uproariousness, racketiness, tumultuousness, thunderousness, clamorousness, clangorousness, boisterousness, obstreperousness; vociferousness; stridency, stridor; intensity

3 **noise,** loud noise, **blast**, tintamarre, **racket,** din, clamor; outcry, uproar, hue and cry, shouting, shouting match; howl; clangor, clang, clatter, clap, jangle, rattle; roar, rumble, thunder, thunderclap; crash, boom, sonic boom; bang, percussion; brouhaha, tumult, hubbub, vociferation, ululation; fracas, brawl, commotion, drunken brawl; pandemonium, bedlam, hell let loose, bedlam let loose; charivari, shivaree; discord; shattered silence; cachinnation, stertor; explosion, bombardment; crescendo, forte, fortissimo, tutti

4 <nonformal> row, flap, hullabaloo, brannigan, shindy, donnybrook, free-for-all, shemozzle, rumble, rhubarb, dustup, rumpus, ruckus, ruction, rowdydow, hell broke loose, foofooraw, hoo-ha, Katy-bar-the-door, tzimmes

5 **blare, blast,** shriek, peal; toot, tootle, honk, beep, meep, blat, trumpet, report; bay, bray; whistle, tweedle, squeal; trumpet call, trumpet blast, trumpet blare, sound of trumpets, flourish of trumpets, Gabriel's trumpet, Gabriel's horn, fanfare, tarantara, tantara, tantarara, clarion call; tattoo; taps; full blast

6 **noisemaker;** ticktack, bull-roarer, catcall, whizzer, whizgig, snapper, cricket, clapper, clack, clacker, cracker; firecracker, cherry bomb; rattle, rattlebox; horn, Klaxon <tm>; whistle, thunderer, steam whistle, siren; boiler room, boiler factory; loud-hailer, bullhorn, air gun

VERBS 7 **din; boom,** thunder; resound, ring, peal, ring in the ears, resound in the ears, din in the ear, blast the ear, pierce the ears, split the ears, rend the ears, rend the eardrums, split the eardrums, split one's head; deafen, stun; blast, bang, **crash**; rend the air, rend the skies, rend the firmament, rock the sky, fill the air, make the welkin ring; shake the windows, rattle the windows; awake the echoes, startle the echoes, set the echoes ringing, awake the dead, shatter the peace; surge, swell, rise, crescendo; **shout**

8 **drown out,** outshout, outroar, shout down, overpower, overwhelm; jam

9 **be noisy,** make a noise, **make a racket,** raise a clamor, raise a din, raise a hue and cry, noise, racket, **clamor,** roar, clangor; brawl, row, rumpus; make an uproar, kick up dust, kick up a racket, kick up a hullabaloo, raise a hullabaloo, raise the roof, raise Cain, howl like all the devils of hell, raise the devil, raise hell, whoop it up, maffick <Brit>; not be able to hear oneself think

10 **blare,** blast; shriek; toot, tootle, sound, peal, wind, blow, blat; pipe, trumpet, bugle, clarion; bay, bell, bray; whistle, tweedle, squeal; **honk,** honk the horn, sound the horn, blow the horn, beep; sound taps, sound a tattoo; go off

ADJS 11 **loud,** loud-sounding, forte, fortissimo, crescendo; loudish; resounding, ringing, plangent, pealing; full, sonorous; deafening, ear-deafening, ear-splitting, head-splitting, ear-rending, ear-piercing, piercing; thunderous, thundering, tonitruous, tonitruant; crashing, **booming**; window-rattling, earthshaking, enough to wake the dead, enough to wake the seven sleepers

12 **loud-voiced, loudmouthed,** fullmouthed, full-throated, big-voiced, clarion-voiced, trumpet-voiced, trumpet-tongued, brazen-mouthed, stentorian, stentorious, stentorophonic, like Stentor, booming

13 **noisy,** noiseful, rackety, clattery, clangorous, clanging, clamorous, clamoursome, clamant, blatant, blaring, brassy, brazen, blatting;

uproarious, tumultuous, turbulent, blustering, brawling, boisterous, rip-roaring, rowdy, mafficking <Brit>, strepitous, strepitant, obstreperous; vociferous

ADVS 14 **loudly,** aloud, loud, lustily; boomingly, thunderously, thunderingly; noisily, uproariously; ringingly, resoundingly; with a loud voice, at the top of one's voice, at the pitch of one's breath, in full cry, with one wild yell, with a whoop and a hurrah; forte, *fortemente* <Ital>, fortissimo

54 RESONANCE

<loud, deep sounds>

NOUNS 1 **resonance,** resoundingness, resonancy, sonorousness, sonority, plangency, vibrancy; mellowness, richness, fullness; deepness, lowness, bassness; hollowness; snore, snoring

2 **reverberation,** resounding; rumble, rumbling, thunder, thundering, boom, booming, growl, growling, grrr, grumble, grumbling, reboation; rebound, resound, **echo,** reecho

3 **ringing,** tintinnabulation, pealing, chiming, tinkling, tingling, jingling, dinging, donging; tolling, knelling; clangor, clanking, clanging; ring, peal, chime; toll, knell; tinkle, tingle, jingle, dingle, ding, dingdong, ding-a-ling, ting-a-ling; clink, tink, ting, ping, chink; clank, clang; jangle, jingle-jangle; campanology, bell ringing, change ringing, peal ringing; tinnitis, ringing of the ear, ringing in the ear

4 **bell** <see list>, tintinnabulum; gong, triangle, chimes, door chimes, clock chimes, Westminster chimes; clapper, tongue; carillon, set of bells; ringtone

5 **resonator,** resounder, reverberator; sounding board, soundboard, sound box; resonant chamber, resonant cavity; echo chamber; loud pedal, damper pedal, sustaining pedal

VERBS 6 **resonate,** vibrate, pulse, throb; snore

7 **reverberate,** resound, sound, rumble, roll, boom, echo, reecho, rebound, bounce back, be reflected, be sent back, echo back, send back, return

8 **ring,** tintinnabulate, peal, sound; toll, knell, sound a knell; chime; gong; tinkle, tingle, jingle, ding, dingdong, dong; clink, tink, ting, chink; clank, clang, clangor; jangle, jinglejangle; ring changes, ring peals; ring in the ear

9 <**deep voices**> bass, basso, basso profundo, baritone, bass-baritone, contralto

ADJS 10 **resonant,** reverberant, vibrant, sonorous, plangent, rolling; mellow, rich, full; resonating, reverberating, echoing, reechoing, vibrating, pulsing, throbbing

11 **deep,** deep-toned, deep-pitched, deep-sounding, deepmouthed, deep-echoing; **hollow, sepulchral; low,** low-pitched, low-toned, grave, heavy; **bass;** baritone; contralto; throaty, gravelly; oompah

12 **reverberating,** reverberant, reverberatory, reboant, **resounding,** rebounding, repercussive, sounding; **rumbling,** thundering, booming, growling; echoing, reechoing, echoic; undamped; persistent, lingering

13 **ringing,** pealing, tolling, belling, sounding, chiming; tinkling, tinkly, tingling, jingling, dinging; tintinnabular, tintinnabulary, tintinnabulous; campanological

14 **bell**

air bell
alarm bell
anchor bell
angelus bell
Big Ben
bourdon
breakfast bell
call bell
chiming bell
church bell
clinkum bell
computer bell
cowbell
dinner bell, dinner gong, dinner chimes
doorbell
fire bell
fog bell
gong bell
hand bell
harness bell
hour bell
jingle bell
Liberty Bell
minute bell
news bell
night bell
pancake bell
passing bell, death bell, end bell, mortbell
ringtone
Sanctus bell, sacring bell, saunce, sauncing bell
school bell
sheepbell
shop bell
signal bell
sleigh bell
tap bell
telephone bell
tocsin
vesper bell
watch bell
wind-bell

55 REPEATED SOUNDS

<reoccurring sounds>

NOUNS 1 **staccato; drum,** thrum, beat, pound, roll; drumming, tom-tom, beating, pounding, thumping; **throb,** throbbing, pulsation; **palpitation,** flutter; sputter, spatter, splutter; patter, pitter-patter, pit-a-pat; rub-a-dub, rattattoo, rataplan, rat-a-tat, rat-tat, rat-tat-tat, tat-tat, tat-tat-tat; clop-clop; tattoo, devil's tattoo, ruff, ruffle, paradiddle; drumbeat, drum music; drumfire, barrage; echo, re-echo; ringtone

2 **clicking, ticking,** tick, ticktock, ticktack, ticktick

3 **rattle,** rattling, brattle, ruckle, rattletybang; clatter, clitter, clunter, clitterclatter, chatter, clack, clacket; racket

VERBS 4 **drum,** thrum, beat, pound, thump, thump

out, roll; **palpitate,** flutter; sputter, splatter, splutter; patter, pitter-patter, go pit-a-pat, go pitter-patter; **throb,** pulsate; beat a tattoo, sound a tattoo, beat a devil's tattoo, ruffle, beat a ruffle

5 **tick,** ticktock, ticktack, tick away

6 **rattle,** ruckle, brattle; clatter, clitter, chatter, clack; rattle around, clatter about

ADJS 7 **staccato; drumming,** thrumming, beating, pounding, thumping; throbbing; palpitant, fluttering; sputtering, spattering, spluttering; clicking, ticking

8 **rattly,** rattling, chattering, clattery, clattering

56 EXPLOSIVE NOISE

<sudden loud sounds>

NOUNS 1 **report, crash,** crack, clap, bang, wham, slam, clash, burst; knock, rap, tap, smack, whack, thwack, whop, whap, swap, whomp, splat, crump, bump, slap, slat, flap, flop, ka-ching

2 **snap, crack;** click, clack; crackle, snapping, cracking, crackling, crepitation, decrepitation, sizzling, spitting; rale

3 **detonation,** blast, explosion, fulmination, **discharge,** burst, bang, pop, crack, bark; shot, gunshot; backfire; volley, salvo, fusillade; displosion

4 **boom,** booming, cannonade, peal, rumble, grumble, growl, roll, roar; kaboom, kablooey

5 **thunder,** thundering, clap of thunder, crash of thunder, peal of thunder, thunderclap, thunderpeal, thundercrack, thunderstroke; peal; thunderstorm; Thor, Donar, Jupiter Tonans, Indra

VERBS 6 **crack,** clap, crash, wham, slam, bang, clash; knock, rap, tap, smack, whack, thwack, whop, whap, swap, whomp, splat, crump, bump, slat, slap, flap

7 **snap, crack;** click, clack; crackle, crepitate, decrepitate; spit

8 **blast, detonate, explode,** discharge, burst, go off, bang, pop, crack, bark, fulminate; burst on the ear

9 **boom, thunder,** peal, rumble, grumble, growl, roll, roar

ADJS 10 **snapping, cracking,** crackling, crackly, crepitant

11 **banging,** crashing, bursting, exploding, explosive, blasting, cracking, popping; knocking, rapping, tapping; slapping, flapping, slatting

12 **thundering,** thunderous, thundery, fulminating, tonitruous, tonitruant, thunderlike; booming, pealing, rumbling, rolling, roaring; cannonading, volleying; tonant

INTERJS 13 bang, boom, wham, whammo, blam, kerboom, kerblam

57 SIBILATION

<hissing sounds>

NOUNS 1 sibilation, sibilance, sibilancy; **hiss, hissing,** siss, sissing, white noise; hush, hushing, shush, shushing; sizz, sizzle, sizzling; fizz, fizzle, fizzling, effervescing, effervescence; swish, whish, whoosh; whiz, buzz, zip; siffle; wheeze, *râle* <Fr>, rhonchus; whistle, whistling; sneeze, sneezing, achoo, sternutation; snort; snore, stertor; **sniff,** sniffle, snuff, snuffle; spit, sputter, splutter; squash, squish, squelch; sigmatism, lisp; assibilation; frication, frictional rustling; interference, static

VERBS 2 sibilate; **hiss,** siss; hush, shush; sizzle, sizz; fizzle, fizz, effervesce; whiz, buzz, zip; swish, whish, whoosh; whistle; wheeze; sneeze, achoo; snort; snore; sniff, sniffle, snuff, snuffle; spit, sputter, splutter; squash, squish, squelch; lisp; assibilate

ADJS 3 **sibilant; hissing,** hushing, sissing; sizzling, fizzling, effervescent; **sniffing,** sniffling, snuffling; snoring; wheezing, wheezy

58 STRIDENCY

<harsh and shrill sounds>

NOUNS 1 **stridency,** stridence, stridor, stridulousness, stridulation; **shrillness,** highness, sharpness, acuteness, arguteness; screechiness, squeakiness, creakiness, reediness, pipingness, brassiness

2 **raucousness,** harshness, raucity; discord, cacophony; coarseness, rudeness, ugliness, roughness, gruffness; raspiness, scratchiness, scrapiness, hoarseness, huskiness, dryness; stertorousness; roupiness; gutturalness, gutturalism, gutturality, thickness, throatiness; cracked voice

3 **rasp, scratch**, scrape, grind; crunch, craunch, scranch, scrunch, crump; burr, chirr, buzz; snore, snort, stertor; jangle, clash, jar; clank, clang, clangor, twang, twanging; blare, blat, bray; croak, caw, cackle; belch; growl, snarl; grumble, groan

4 **screech, shriek, scream,** squeal, shrill, keen, squeak, squawk, skirl, screak, skreak, creak; bleep; whistle, wolf-whistle; pipe; **whine, wail, howl,** ululation, yammer; vibrato; waul, caterwaul; primal scream

5 <insect sounds> **stridulation,** cricking, creaking, chirking; crick, creak, chirk, chirp, chirping, chirrup, scritch

6 <**high voices**> soprano, mezzo-soprano, treble; tenor, alto; male alto, countertenor; head register, head voice, head tone, falsetto

VERBS **7 stridulate,** crick, creak, chirk, chirp, chirrup, scritch

8 screech, shriek, screak, skreak, creak, squeak, squawk, scream, squeal, shrill, keen; whistle, wolf-whistle; pipe, skirl; whine, wail, howl, wrawl, yammer, ululate; waul, caterwaul; raise the roof

9 <sound harshly> **jangle,** clash, jar; blare, blat, bray; croak, caw, cackle; belch; burr, chirr, buzz; snore; growl, snarl; grumble, groan; clank, clang, clangor; twang

10 grate, rasp, scratch, scrape, grind; crunch, craunch, scranch, scrunch, crump

11 grate on, jar on, grate upon the ear, jar upon the ear, offend the ear, pierce the ears, split the ears, rend the ears, harrow the ear, lacerate the ear, set the teeth on edge, get on one's nerves, jangle the nerves, wrack the nerves, make one's skin crawl

ADJS **12 strident,** stridulant, stridulous; strident-voiced

13 high, high-pitched, high-toned, high-sounding; treble, soprano, mezzo-soprano, tenor, alto, falsetto, countertenor; meep

14 shrill, thin, sharp, acute, argute, keen, keening, peeping, **piercing,** penetrating, ear-piercing, ear-splitting; screechy, screeching, shrieky, shrieking, squeaky, squeaking, screaky, creaky, creaking; whistling, piping, skirling, reedy; whining, wailing, howling, ululating, ululant; vibrato

15 raucous, raucid, **harsh,** harsh-sounding; coarse, rude, rough, gruff, ragged; **hoarse**, husky, roupy, cracked, dry; guttural, thick, throaty, croaky, croaking; choked, strangled; squawky, squawking; brassy, brazen, tinny, metallic; stertorous

16 grating, jarring, grinding; jangling, jangly; rasping, raspy; scratching, scratchy; scraping, scrappy; abrasive

59 CRY, CALL

<human loud sound>

NOUNS **1 cry, call, shout, yell,** hoot; halloo, hollo, yo-ho, hello, hi, yo, hail; whoop, holler; cheer, hurrah, huzzah, hooray; howl, yowl, yawl; shout-out; bawl, bellow, roar; **scream, shriek,** screech, squeal, squall, caterwaul; yelp, yap, yammer, yawp, bark; war cry, battle cry, war whoop, rallying cry; jeer, boo, hiss, razz; guffah, cachinnation; raspberry, razzing, heckling; Bronx cheer; yelling, cheering, cheerleading

2 exclamation, ejaculation, outburst, blurt, ecphonesis; expletive

3 hunting cry; tallyho, yoicks, view halloo

4 outcry, vociferation, clamor; hullabaloo, hubbub, brouhaha, uproar; hue and cry

5 vociferousness, vociferance, clamorousness, clamorsomeness, blatancy; noisiness

VERBS **6 cry, call,** shout, yell, holler, hoot; hail, halloo, hollo; whoop; **cheer**; howl, yowl, yammer, yawl; squawk, yawp; bawl, bellow, roar, roar like a bull, bellow like a bull; cry bloody murder, yell bloody murder, scream bloody murder, cry blue murder, yell blue murder, scream blue murder; scream, shriek, screech, squeal, squall, waul, caterwaul; yelp, yap, bark; heckle

7 exclaim, give an exclamation, ejaculate, burst out, blurt, blurt out, jerk out, spout out; stammer out; shout out

8 vociferate, outcry, cry out, call out, bellow out, yell out, holler out, shout out, sing out; sound off, pipe up, clamor, make a clamor, raise a clamor; make an outcry, raise a hue and cry, make an uproar

9 cry aloud, raise up the voice, lift up the voice, give voice, give tongue, shout at the top of one's voice, cry at the top of one's voice, thunder at the top of one's voice, split the throat, split the lungs, strain the voice, strain the throat, strain the vocal cords, rend the air; cheerlead

ADJS **10 vociferous,** vociferant, vociferating; **clamorous,** clamoursome; blatant; obstreperous, brawling; noisy; crying, shouting, **yelling,** hollering, bawling, screaming; yelping, yapping, yappy, yammering; loud-voiced, loudmouthed, openmouthed, stentorian, Boanergean; booming

11 exclamatory, ejaculatory, blurting

60 ANIMAL SOUNDS

<animal cry, call>

NOUNS **1** animal noise; **call, cry;** mating call, mating cry; grunt, howl, bark, howling, waul, caterwaul, ululation, barking; birdsong, birdcall, note, woodnote, clang; stridulation; dawn chorus; warning cry

VERBS **2** cry, call; **howl,** yowl, yawp, yawl, ululate; wail, whine, pule; squeal, squall, scream, screech, screak, squeak; troat; roar; bellow, blare, bawl; moo, low; bleat, blate, blat; bray; whinny, neigh, whicker, nicker; bay, bay at the moon, bell; bark, woof, latrate, give voice, give tongue; yelp, yap, yip; mew, mewl, meow, miaow, waul, caterwaul; weal

3 grunt, gruntle, oink; **snort**

4 growl, snarl, grumble, gnarl, snap; hiss, spit

5 <birds> **warble, sing,** carol, call; pipe, whistle; trill, chirr, roll; twitter, tweet, twit, chatter, chitter; chirp, chirrup, chirk, cheep, peep, pip; quack, honk, cronk; croak, caw; squawk, scold, screech; crow, cock-a-doodle-doo; cackle, gaggle, gabble, guggle, cluck, clack, chuck; gobble; hoot, hoo; coo; cuckoo; drum; tu-whit tu-whoo; whoop

ADJS 6 **howling,** yowling, crying, wailing, whining, puling, bawling, ululant, blatant; barking; lowing, mugient, snarling, growling; singing, humming

61 DISCORD

<dissonant sounds>

NOUNS 1 **discord,** discordance, discordancy, **dissonance**, dissonancy, diaphony, **cacophony;** stridor, stridency; inharmoniousness, unharmoniousness, disharmony, inharmony; unmelodiousness, unmusicalness, unmusicality, untunefulness, tunelessness; atonality, atonalism; flatness, sharpness, sourness; dissonant chord, wolf; false note, sour note, clinker, clam, off note; cipher; dodecaphonism, dodecaphony

2 **clash, jangle**, jar; noise, mere noise, confusion of sounds, conflict of sounds, jarring of sounds, jostling of sounds; Babel, witches' chorus, devils' chorus; harshness; clamor

VERBS 3 sound a sour note, strike a sour note, hit a sour note, hit a clinker, hit a clam; not carry a tune; **clash,** jar, jangle, conflict, jostle; grate; untune, unstring; hurt the ears

ADJS 4 **dissonant,** discordant, cacophonous, absonant, disconsonant, diaphonic; strident, shrill, harsh, raucous, grating; inharmonious, unharmonious, disharmonious, disharmonic, inharmonic; unmelodious, immelodious, nonmelodious; unmusical, musicless, nonmusical, untuneful, tuneless; untunable, untuned, atonal, toneless; droning, singsong; cracked, out of tune, out of tone, out of pitch; **off-key**, off-tone, off-pitch, off; **flat**, sharp, sour

5 **clashing,** jarring, jangling, jangly, confused, conflicting, jostling, warring, ajar; harsh, **hoarse, grating**

62 TASTE

<sense of taste>

NOUNS 1 **taste,** gust, *goût* <Fr>; sense of taste; **flavor,** sapor; smack, tang; savor, relish, sapidity, deliciousness; palate, tongue, tooth, stomach; taste in the mouth, taste perception; sweetness, sourness, bitterness, bittersweetness, saltiness; sharp taste, acid taste, tart taste, salty taste, spicy taste, sweet taste, sour taste, bitter taste, pungent taste, umami; aftertaste; natural flavor, savoriness

2 **sip,** sup, lick, **bite,** try, nip

3 tinge, soupçon, smack, hint

4 **sample,** specimen, taste, taste test, taster, little bite, little smack, taste treat; tidbit, sampler; example; appetizer, hors d'oeuvre, canape, aperitif, starter, tapas, little plate, small plate

5 **taste bud**, taste bulb, taste goblet, taste cell, gustatory cell, taste hair; tongue, lingua; palate

6 **tasting,** savoring, gustation, nibble, nip, sampling

VERBS 7 **taste,** taste of, sample, degust, partake; **savor,** savor of, relish; try; sip, sup, roll on the tongue, test; lick; smack

ADJS 8 **gustatory,** gustative; tastable, gustable

9 **flavored,** flavorous, flavory, sapid, saporous, saporific; tasty, savory, flavorful; sweet, sour, bitter, bittersweet, salt; unoaked

10 **lingual,** glossal; **tonguelike,** linguiform, lingulate

63 SAVORINESS

<pleasant taste>

NOUNS 1 **savoriness,** palatableness, palatability, **tastiness,** toothsomeness, goodness, good taste, right taste, deliciousness, gustatory delightfulness, scrumptiousness, yumminess, lusciousness, delectability, flavorfulness, flavorsomeness, flavorousness, flavoriness, good flavor, fine flavor, sapidity, sapidness; full flavor, full-bodied flavor; gourmet quality; succulence, juiciness

2 **savor,** relish, zest, gusto, *goût* <Fr>; richness

3 **flavoring, flavor,** flavorer; **seasoning,** seasoner, relish, condiment, spice; flavor enhancer; artificial flavoring; dry rub

VERBS 4 **taste good,** tickle the palate, delight the palate, tempt the appetite, whet the appetite, make one's mouth water, melt in one's mouth

5 **savor, relish**, like, love, be fond of, be partial to, enjoy, delight in, have a soft spot for, appreciate; smack the lips; do justice to; taste

6 savor of, **taste of,** smack of, have a relish of, have the flavor of, taste like

7 **flavor,** savor; **season,** salt, pepper, poivre <Fr>, **spice,** sauce

ADJS 8 **tasty,** fit to eat, finger-lickin' good, good-tasting, savory, savorous, palatable, toothsome, gustable, sapid, good, good to eat, nice, agreeable, likable, pleasing, mouth-watering, to one's taste, **delicious,** delightful, delectable, exquisite; delicate, dainty; juicy, succulent, luscious, lush; for the gods, ambrosial, nectarous, nectareous; fit for a king, gourmet, fit for a gourmet, of gourmet quality, epicurean; scrumptious, yummy

9 **flavorful,** flavorsome, flavorous, flavory, well-flavored; full-flavored, full-bodied; nutty, fruity; rich, rich-flavored; sapid

10 **appetizing,** mouth-watering, tempting, tantalizing, provocative, piquant

64 UNSAVORINESS

<unpleasant taste>

NOUNS 1 **unsavoriness, unpalatableness,** unpalatability, distastefulness, untastefulness; bad taste, bad taste in the mouth; yuckiness, yuck factor

2 acridness, acridity, **tartness**, sharpness, causticity, astringence, astringency, acerbity, **sourness**; pungency; **bitterness,** bitter taste; gall, gall and wormwood, wormwood, bitter pill

3 **nastiness**, foulness, vileness, loathsomeness, repulsiveness, obnoxiousness, odiousness, offensiveness, disgustingness, nauseousness; rankness, rancidity, rancidness, overripeness, rottenness, malodorousness, fetor, fetidness; yuckiness; repugnance; nauseant, emetic, sickener

VERBS 4 **disgust,** repel, turn one's stomach, nauseate; make one's gorge rise; gross one out

ADJS 5 **unsavory, unpalatable,** unappetizing, untasteful, untasty, ill-flavored, foul-tasting, distasteful, dislikable, unlikable, uninviting, unpleasant, unpleasing, displeasing, disagreeable

6 **bitter,** bitter as gall, bitter as wormwood, amaroidal; **acrid,** sharp, caustic, tart, astringent; hard, harsh, rough, coarse; acerb, acerbic, sour; pungent

7 **nasty, offensive**, fulsome, noisome, noxious, rebarbative, mawkish, cloying, brackish, foul, vile, bad; gross, icky, yucky, sickening, nauseating, nauseous, nauseant, vomity, barfy; poisonous, toxic, ecotoxic, rank, rancid, maggoty, weevily, spoiled, overripe, high, rotten, stinking, putrid, malodorous, fetid

8 **inedible, uneatable,** not fit to eat, not fit to drink, undrinkable, impotable; unfit for human consumption

65 INSIPIDNESS

<lacking flavor>

NOUNS 1 **insipidness,** insipidity, **tastelessness,** flavorlessness, blandness, savorlessness, saplessness, unsavoriness, dullness; weakness, thinness, mildness, wishy-washiness, namby-pambyness; flatness, staleness, lifelessness, deadness; vapidity, inanity, jejunity, jejuneness; adulteration, dilution; pablum

ADJS 2 **insipid, tasteless, flavorless,** bland, nondescript, unexciting, plain, spiceless, savorless, sapless, unsavory, unflavored, unseasoned; pulpy, pappy, gruelly, pasty; weak, thin, mild, wishy-washy, milktoast, washy, watery, watered, watered-down, diluted, dilute, milk-and-water, dishwater; flat, stale, dead; vapid, inane, jejune; unappetizing; indifferent, characterless, neither one thing nor the other

66 SWEETNESS

<sugary flavor>

NOUNS 1 **sweetness,** sweet, sweetishness, saccharinity, dulcitude; **sugariness**, syrupiness; oversweetness, mawkishness, cloyingness, sickly-sweetness; sweet tooth; confectionery, sweet shop, candy store, bakery

2 **sweetening,** edulcoration; sweetener; sugar, cane sugar, beet sugar, sugar lump, sugar loaf, caster sugar, granulated sugar, powdered sugar, brown sugar, turbinado sugar, raw sugar; sweetening agent, sugar substitute, artificial sweetener, saccharin, aspartame, NutraSweet <tm>, sucralose, cyclamates, sodium cyclamate, calcium cyclamate; molasses, blackstrap, treacle <Brit>; syrup, maple syrup, cane syrup, corn syrup, sorghum, golden syrup, treacle; honey, honeycomb, honeypot, comb honey, clover honey; honeydew; nectar, ambrosia; sugarcoating; sweets, candy, dessert; sugar-making; sugaring off; saccharification

3 <words meaning **added sugar** on food packaging> agave juice, agave nectar, agave sap, agave syrup, beet sugar, brown rice syrup, brown sugar, cane juice, cane sugar, cane syrup, confectioners powdered sugar, confectioners sugar, corn glucose syrup, corn sweet, corn sweetener, corn syrup, date sugar, dextrose; drimol, dri mol, dri-mol; drisweet, dri sweet, dri-sweet; dried raisin sweetener, edible lactose; flo malt, flo-malt, flomalt; fructose, fructose sweetener, glaze and icing sugar, glaze icing sugar, golden syrup, gomme, granular sweetener, granulated sugar, hi-fructose corn syrup, high fructose corn syrup, honey; honibake, honi bake, honi-bake; honi flake, honi-flake; invert sugar, inverted sugar, isoglucose, isomaltulose; kona ame, kona-ame; lactose, liquid sweetener, malt, malt sweetener, malt syrup, maltose, maple, maple sugar, maple syrup; mizu ame, mizu-ame, mizuame; molasses, nulomoline, powdered sugar, rice syrup, sorghum, sorghum syrup, starch sweetener, sucanat, sucrose, sucrovert, sugar, sugar beet, sugar cane, sugar invert, table sugar, treacle, trehalose, turbinado sugar, versatose

VERBS 4 **sweeten,** dulcify, edulcorate, dulcorate; **sugar;** honey, nectarize; sugarcoat, glaze, candy; ice, frost; mull; saccharify; sugar off; caramelize

ADJS 5 **sweet,** sweetish, sweetened; sacchariferous,

saccharine; **sugary,** sugared, candied, honeyed, carmelized, syrupy; mellifluous, mellifluent; melliferous, nectarous, nectareous, ambrosial; honeysweet, sweet as sugar, sweet as honey; sugar-coated; bittersweet; sour-sweet, sweet-sour, sweet and sour, sweet and pungent

6 **oversweet,** saccharine, rich, cloying, mawkish, sickly-sweet

67 SOURNESS

<acidic flavor>

NOUNS 1 **sourness,** sour, sourishness, **tartness,** tartishness, acerbity, astringency, verjuice; acescency; acidity, acidulousness; hyperacidity, subacidity; vinegariness; unsweetness, dryness; **pungency**; greenness, unripeness; bitterness, sharpness

2 **sour;** vinegar, acidulant; pickle, sour pickle, dill pickle, bread-and-butter pickle; verjuice; lemon, lime, crabapple, green apple, sour cherry; aloe; sourgrass; sour balls; sourdough; sour cream, sour milk; bitters; wormwood; acid

3 **souring,** acidification, acidulation, acetification, acescence; fermentation; turning

VERBS 4 **sour,** turn sour, turn acid, go sour, sharpen, acidify, acidulate, acetify; set one's teeth on edge; curdle, spoil, turn, **ferment**, go off, go bad, molder

ADJS 5 **sour,** soured, sourish; **tart,** tartish; tangy, **pungent**; crab, crabbed; acerb, acerbic, acerbate, acrid; acescent; vinegarish, vinegary, sour as vinegar, acetic; pickled; lemony; unsweet, unsweetened, dry, sec; green, unripe

6 **acid,** acidulous, acidulent, acidulated; acetic, acetous, acetose; hyperacid; subacid, subacidulous

68 PUNGENCY

<sharp flavor, smell>

NOUNS 1 **pungency, piquancy,** poignancy, spiciness; strong flavor; sharpness, keenness, edge, causticity, astringency, mordancy, severity, asperity, trenchancy, cuttingness, bitingness, penetratingness, harshness, roughness, acridity; **bitterness**; acerbity, acidulousness, acidity, **sourness**; aroma

2 **zest,** zestfulness, zestiness, briskness, liveliness, raciness; nippiness, tanginess, snappiness; spiciness, pepperiness, hotness, fieriness; **tang,** spice, relish; nip, bite, kick; sting, punch, snap, zip, ginger, sharpness; guts; heat

3 **strength,** strongness; high flavor, highness, rankness, gaminess

4 **saltiness,** salinity, brininess; brackishness; salt; brine; pepperiness

VERBS 5 **bite, nip,** cut, penetrate, bite the tongue, sting, kick, make the eyes water, go up the nose

ADJS 6 **pungent, piquant,** poignant; sharp, keen, piercing, penetrating, nose-tickling, aromatic, stinging, biting, acrid, astringent, irritating, harsh, rough, spicy, severe, asperous, cutting, trenchant; caustic, vitriolic, mordant, escharotic; **bitter**; acerbic, acid, **sour, tart**

7 **zestful,** zesty, brisk, lively, racy, zippy, nippy, snappy, **tangy,** with a kick, strong; spiced, seasoned, high-seasoned, savory; **spicy,** curried, peppery, hot, burning, hot as pepper; mustardy; like horseradish, like Chinese mustard

8 **strong,** strong-flavored, strong-tasting; high, highly flavored, highly seasoned, high-tasted; rank, gamy, racy

9 **salty,** salt, salted, saltish, saline, briny; brackish; pickled

69 ODOR

<particular smells>

NOUNS 1 **odor, smell**, scent, aroma, savor; essence, definite odor, redolence, effluvium, emanation, exhalation, fume, breath, subtle odor, whiff, wafture, trace, detectable odor; trail, spoor; **fragrance**; **stink, stench**, funk

2 **odorousness, smelliness,** headiness, pungency; aromatherapy

3 **smelling**, olfaction, nosing, scenting; sniffing, snuffing, snuffling, whiffing, odorizing, odorization

4 **sense of smell,** smell, smelling, scent, olfaction, olfactory sense

5 olfactory organ; olfactory pit, olfactory cell, olfactory area, **nose;** nostrils, noseholes, nares, naris, nasal cavity; olfactory nerves; olfactories; scent gland, pheromone

VERBS 6 <have an odor> **smell**, be aromatic, smell of, be redolent of; emit a smell, emanate a smell, give out a smell, reach one's nostrils, yield an odor, yield an aroma, breathe, exhale; reek, **stink**; pong

7 odorize; **scent**, aromatize, perfume

8 **smell,** scent, nose; sniff, snuff, snuffle, inhale, breathe, breathe in; get a noseful of, smell of, catch a smell of, get a whiff of, take a whiff of, whiff, get wind of, follow one's nose

ADJS 9 **odorous,** odoriferous, odiferous, odored, odorant, olent, smelling, **smelly**, smellsome, redolent, aromatic; effluvious; **fragrant**; **stinking**, stinky, stanky, **malodorous**; emanative, pheromonal

10 **strong,** strong-smelling, strong-scented; **pungent,** penetrating, nose-piercing, sharp, heady; reeking, reeky; funky, foul; suffocating, stifling; noisome, noxious
11 **smellable,** sniffable, whiffable
12 **olfactory,** olfactive
13 keen-scented, quick-scented, sharp-nosed, keen-nosed, with a nose for

70 FRAGRANCE
<pleasant smells>

NOUNS **1** **fragrance, perfume, aroma,** scent, redolence, balminess, incense, bouquet, sweet smell, sweet savor; **odor**; spice, spiciness; muskiness; fruitiness; perfume dynamics, aromatherapy
2 perfumery, *parfumerie* <Fr>; **perfume,** *parfum* <Fr>, eau de parfum, **scent,** essence, extract; aromatic, ambrosia; attar, essential oil, volatile oil; aromatic water; balsam, balm, aromatic gum; myrrh; bay oil, myrcia oil; champaca oil; rose oil, attar of roses, lavender oil, heliotrope, jasmine oil, bergamot oil; fixative, musk, civet, ambergris, patchouli
3 **toilet water,** Florida water; rose water, *eau de rose* <Fr>; lavender water; cologne, cologne water, eau de Cologne; bay rum; lotion, after-shave lotion
4 **incense;** joss stick; pastille; frankincense, olibanum; agalloch, aloeswood, calambac, lignaloes, linaloa, sandalwood, frangipani, resin, myrrh, eucalyptus, attar, ambergris, patchouli
5 **perfumer,** *parfumeur* <Fr>; thurifer, censer bearer, censer, thurible; **perfuming,** censing, thurification, odorizing
6 <articles> perfumer, *parfumoir* <Fr>, fumigator, scenter, odorator, odorizer; atomizer, purse atomizer, spray; censer, thurible, incensory, incense burner; vinaigrette, scent bottle, smelling bottle, scent box, scent ball; scent strip; scent bag, sachet; pomander; potpourri; scratch-and-sniff; dryer sheet

VERBS **7** **be fragrant,** smell sweet, **smell good,** please the nostrils, smell like a rose
8 **perfume, scent,** cense, incense, thurify, aromatize, odorize, fumigate, embalm

ADJS **9** **fragrant, aromatic,** odoriferous, redolent, perfumy, **perfumed,** scented, odorate, essenced, sweet, sweet-smelling, sweet-scented, savory, balmy, ambrosial, incense-breathing; thuriferous; **odorous**; sweet as a rose, fragrant as new-mown hay; pungent, heady; flowery; fruity; musky; spicy; aromatherapeutic; breathable

71 STENCH
<very bad smells>

NOUNS **1** **stench, stink,** funk, malodor, fetidness, fetidity, fetor, foul odor, bad odor, offensive odor, unpleasant smell, offense to the nostrils, bad smell, niff, pong, rotten smell, noxious stench, smell of decay, stench of decay, **reek,** reeking, nidor; fug, frowst; mephitis, miasma, graveolence, effluvium, osmidrosis; body odor (BO); halitosis, bad breath, foul breath
2 **fetidness,** fetidity, malodorousness, **smelliness,** stinkingness, odorousness, noisomeness, rankness, foulness, putridness, offensiveness; repulsiveness; mustiness, funkiness, must, frowst, frowstiness, moldiness, mildew, fustiness, frowziness, stuffiness; staleness; rancidness, rancidity, reastiness; rottenness; putrefaction, putrescence, decay, gaminess
3 **stinker,** stinkard; skunk, polecat, rotten egg; stink ball, stinkpot, stink bomb; mothball; flatus, fart, cesspool, hydrogen sulfide, sulfur dioxide

VERBS **4** **stink,** smell, **smell bad,** niffy, pong, assail the nostrils, offend the nostrils, stink in the nostrils, stink to heaven, stink to high heaven, smell of rotten eggs; reek; smell up, stink up; stink out

ADJS **5** **malodorous, fetid,** olid, odorous, stinking, reeking, reeky, nidorous, smelling, bad-smelling, evil-smelling, foul-smelling, ill-smelling, heavy-smelling, smelly, niffy, pongy, stenchy; foul, vile, putrid, bad, fulsome, noisome, fecal, feculent, excremental, offensive, repulsive, noxious, sulfurous, graveolent; rotten; rank, strong, high, gamy; rancid; musty, funky, fusty, frowy, frowzy, frowsty, stuffy, moldy, mildewed, mildewy; mephitic, miasmic, miasmal; crappy; asphyxiating

72 ODORLESSNESS
<undetectable smells>

NOUNS **1** **odorlessness,** inodorousness, lack of smell, scentlessness, smell-lessness; inoffensiveness; anosmia
2 **deodorizing,** deodorization, fumigation, ventilation; freshness, fresh air; smoke-free area, no-smoking area
3 **deodorant,** deodorizer; antiperspirant; fumigant, fumigator; mouthwash, breath freshener; ventilator, air filter, air purifier, air freshener

VERBS **4** **deodorize,** fumigate; ventilate, freshen the air; cleanse

ADJS **5** **odorless,** inodorous, nonodorous, smell-less, scentless, **unscented**; scent-free, fragrance-free;

smoke-free, smokeless; fumigated; neutral-smelling; inoffensive; in the fresh air
6 **deodorant,** deodorizing, freshening

73 TOUCH
<*sense of touch*>

NOUNS 1 **touch;** sense of touch, tactile sense, tactual sensation, cutaneous sense; taction, **contact**; **feel,** feeling; hand-mindedness; light touch, lambency, whisper, breath, kiss, lip-clap, caress, fondling; loving touch; lick, lap; brush, graze, grazing, glance, glancing; stroke, rub; tap, flick; fingertip caress; tentative poke; point of contact
2 **touching, feeling,** fingering, palpation, palpating; handling, manipulation, manipulating; petting, caressing, stroking, massaging, rubbing, frottage, frication, friction; laying on of hands, fondling; pressure; feeling up; osteopathy, chiropractic
3 **touchableness**, tangibility, palpability, tactility, sensitivity, feel
4 **feeler,** tactile organ, tactor; tactile cell; tactile process, tactile corpuscle, antenna; tactile hair, vibrissa; cat whisker; barbel, barbule; palp, palpus; tentaculum
5 **finger,** digit; forefinger, first finger, index finger, index; ring finger, annulary; middle finger, medius, dactylion; little finger, pinkie, pinky, minimus; thumb, pollex

VERBS 6 **touch, feel,** feel of, palpate; finger, pass the fingers over, run the fingers over, feel with the fingertips, thumb; handle, palm, paw; manipulate, wield, ply; twiddle; poke at, prod; tap, flick; come in contact
7 **touch lightly,** touch upon; kiss, brush, sweep, graze, brush by, glance, scrape, skim
8 **stroke,** pet, caress, fondle; nuzzle, nose, rub noses; feel up; rub, rub against, snuggle, massage, knead
9 **lick,** lap, tongue, mouth

ADJS 10 **tactile,** tactual; hand-minded
11 **touchable**, palpable, tangible, tactile, tactual; touchy-feely
12 lightly touching, lambent, playing lightly over, barely touching, grazing, skimming, tickling

74 SENSATIONS OF TOUCH
<*physical contact*>

NOUNS 1 **tingle,** tingling, thrill, buzz; prickle, prickles, prickling, pins and needles; **sting,** stinging, urtication; paresthesia
2 **tickle,** tickling, **titillation,** pleasant stimulation, ticklishness, tickliness
3 **itch,** itching, itchiness; pruritus; prurigo
4 **creeps,** cold creeps, shivers, cold shivers, creeping of the flesh; gooseflesh, goose bumps, goose pimples; formication

VERBS 5 **tingle,** thrill; itch; scratch; prickle, prick, sting
6 **tickle, titillate,** thrill
7 **feel creepy,** feel funny, creep, crawl, have the creeps, have the cold creeps, have the heebie-jeeies, have the abdabs; have gooseflesh, have goose bumps; give one the creeps, give one the willies

ADJS 8 **tingly,** tingling, atingle; prickly, prickling
9 **ticklish,** tickling, tickly, titillative
10 **itchy,** itching; pruriginous
11 **creepy,** crawly, creepy-crawly, formicative

75 SEX
<*sexual nature*>

NOUNS 1 **sex,** gender; male, maleness, masculinity, female, femaleness, femininity; **genitals, genitalia**
2 **sexuality,** sexual nature, sexualism, sex life, love life; sex education, birds and the bees; **love**, sexual activity, lovemaking, marriage; heterosexuality; homosexuality; bisexuality, ambisexuality; cisgendered; transgender, transperson; gender fluid, gender fluidity, gender bender; carnality, **sensuality**; sexiness, voluptuousness, flesh, fleshiness; **libido,** sex drive, sexual instinct, sexual urge; **potency**; impotence; frigidity, coldness
3 **sex appeal,** sexual attraction, sexual attractiveness, sexual magnetism, sexiness, animal magnetism
4 **sex object;** piece, meat, piece of meat, ass*, piece of ass*, hot number; nooky, nookie; sex queen, sex goddess, sex kitten; hottie; skirt; hunk, sex god; beefcake, stud, stud muffin, pretty boy
5 **sexual desire,** sensuous desire, carnal desire, bodily appetite, biological urge, venereal appetite, venereal desire, sexual longing, lust, desire, lusts of the flesh, desires of the flesh, itch, horniness, lech, chemistry; erection, penile erection, hard-on; passion, carnal passion, sexual passion, fleshly lust, prurience, pruriency, concupiscence, hot blood, aphrodisia, the hots, hot pants, hot rocks, hot nuts, G-spot; lustfulness, goatishness, libidinousness; lasciviousness; eroticism, erotism; indecency; erotomania, eromania; nymphomania, andromania; satyrism, satyriasis, gynecomania; infantile sexuality, polymorphous perversity; **heat,** rut, mating instinct; frenzy of lust, fury of lust; estrus, estrum, estrous cycle, estral cycle
6 **aphrodisiac,** love potion, philter, love philter; cantharis, blister beetle, Spanish fly

7 **copulation, sex act,** having sex, having intercourse, coupling, mating, pairing, intimacy, coition, coitus, pareunia, venery, copula <law>, sex, intercourse, sexual intercourse, cohabitation, commerce, sexual commerce, congress, sexual congress, sexual union, sexual relations, relations, marital relations, marriage act, consummation, act of love, making love, sleeping together, sleeping with, going to bed with, going all the way; screwing, balling, nookie, diddling, making it with; consenting adult; meat, ass*, connection, carnal knowledge, aphrodisia; foreplay; oral sex, oral-genital stimulation, fellatio, fellation, blow job, cunnilingus, sixty-nine; anal sex, anal intercourse, sodomy, buggery*; orgasm, climax, sexual climax; unlawful sexual intercourse, adultery, hanky-panky, fornication; coitus interruptus, onanism; tantric sex; group sex, group grope; serial sex, gangbang; spouse swapping, wife swapping, husband swapping; casual sex, one-night stand, quickie; walk of shame; phone sex; safe sex; sex shop; **lovemaking**; **procreation**; germ cell, sperm, ovum

8 **masturbation,** autoeroticism, self-abuse, onanism, manipulation, playing with oneself, jacking off, jerking off, pulling off, hand job, wank; sexual fantasy; wet dream; manustupration

9 **sexlessness,** asexuality, neuterness, nonsexualness; **impotence**; frigidity; eunuch, *castrato* <Ital>, spado, neuter, gelding; steer

10 **sexual preference; sexual orientation;** sexual normality, sexual nature; heterosexuality; homosexuality, homosexualism, homoeroticism, homophilia, *l'amour bleu* <Fr>, the love that dare not speak its name, sexual inversion, lesbianism, sapphism; alternative lifestyle; autoeroticism; transsexuality; bisexuality, bisexualism, ambisexuality, ambisextrousness, amphierotism, swinging, swinging both ways, going both ways; tribadism, tribady; sexual prejudice, sexism, genderism, phallicism, heterosexism, homosexism; coming out of the closet, LGBT, GLBT, LGBTQ

11 **perversion,** sexual deviation, sexual deviance, sexual perversion, sexual abnormality; sexual pathology; psychosexual disorder; sexual psychopathy; paraphilia; zoophilia, zooerastia, bestiality; pedophilia; algolagnia, algolagny, sadomasochism, s and m; active algolagnia, sadism; passive algolagnia, masochism; satyrism; fetishism, foot fetish; narcissism; pederasty; exhibitionism; nymphomania; necrophilia; coprophilia; scotophilia, voyeurism; transvestitism, cross-dressing; incest, incestuousness, sex crime, sexual offense; sexual abuse, carnal abuse, molestation; sexual harassment; unlawful sexual intercourse, rape, date rape; cybersex

12 **intersexuality,** intersexualism, epicenism, epicenity; hermaphroditism, pseudohermaphroditism; androgynism, androgyny, gynandry, gynandrism; transsexuality, transsexualism

13 **heterosexual**, straight, breeder, cisgender

14 **homosexual,** gay person, homosexualist, homophile, invert; catamite; **bisexual,** bi-guy; lesbian, sapphist, tribade, fricatrice; gay pride, gay rights; metrosexual; transgender, transsexual, gender-fluid; pansexual

15 <offensive or nonformal> **male homosexual**, homo, queer, faggot, fag, fruit, flit, fairy, pansy, nance, auntie, queen, drag queen, closet queen, fruitcake, poof, poofter, poove; **female homosexual**, lesbie, dyke, bull dyke, butchfemme, boondagger, diesel-dyke, lesbo, lez

16 sexual pervert; **pervert,** perve, **deviant,** deviate, sex pervert, sex fiend, sex criminal, sex psychopath, sex addict; sick puppy; sodomist, sodomite, sob, bugger; pederast; paraphiliac; zoophiliac; pedophiliac; sadist; masochist; sadomasochist, algolagniac; fetishist; transvestite (TV), cross-dresser; narcissist; exhibitionist; necrophiliac; coprophiliac; scotophiliac, voyeur; erotomaniac, nymphomaniac, satyr, horndog; rapist

17 **intersex,** sex-intergrade, epicence; hermaphrodite, pseudohermaphrodite; androgyne, gynandroid; transsexual

18 **sexology,** sex study, sexologist; sexual counselor; sexual surrogate; sexual customs, sexual mores, sexual practices; sexual morality; new morality, sexual revolution; sexual freedom, sexual liberation, free love; trial marriage

VERBS **19** sex, sexualize; genderize

20 lust, **lust after,** itch for, have a lech, have hot pants for, **desire**; be in heat, be in rut, rut, come in; get physical; get an erection, get a hard-on, tumesce

21 **copulate,** couple, mate, have intercourse, unite in sexual intercourse, have sexual relations, **have sex,** pair, **make love,** sleep together; make out, perform the act of lov, perform the marriage act, come together, cohabit, cohabitate, shack up, be intimate; sleep with, lay with, lay together, lie with, go to bed with, bonk; fuck*, screw, lay, ball, frig, diddle, do it, make it with, go all the way, lie together, get laid; cover, mount; serve, service <of animals>; commit adultery, fornicate

22 **masturbate,** play with oneself, abuse oneself, jack off, whack off; fellate, suck, suck off; sodomize, bugger*, ream

23 **stimulate,** have foreplay; go down on, give head, suck, suck off

24 **climax, come,** achieve satisfaction, achieve orgasm, reach orgasm; ejaculate, get off

ADJS 25 **sexual,** sex, sexlike, gamic, coital, libidinal; **erotic,** appealing, amorous, magnetic; nuptial; venereal; carnal, **sensual**, voluptuous, fleshly; desirable, baddable; **sexy;** erogenous, erogenic, erotogenic, ginchy; sexed, oversexed, hypersexual; procreative; potent; T & A

26 **aphrodisiac,** aphroditous, **arousing,** stimulating, eroticizing, venereal

27 **lustful,** prurient, hot, steamy, sexy, concupiscent, lickerish, libidinous, salacious, passionate, hot-blooded, itching, horny, hot to trot, sexed-up, hot and bothered, excited, aroused, randy, goatish; sex-starved, unsatisfied; lascivious; orgasmic, orgastic, ejaculatory

28 **in heat,** burning, hot; in rut, rutting, rutty, ruttish; in must, must, musty; estrous, estral, estrual

29 **unsexual,** unsexed; sexless, asexual, esexual, neuter, neutral, neutered; castrated, emasculated, eunuchized; cold, **frigid; impotent;** frustrated; undersexed

30 **homosexual,** homoerotic, gay, queer, limp-wristed, faggoty; **bisexual,** bisexed, ambisexual, ambisextrous, amphierotic, AC-DC, autoerotic; lesbian, sapphic, tribadistic; butch, dykey; effeminate; transvestite; outed; gay-friendly

31 hermaphrodite, hermaphroditic, pseudohermaphrodite, pseudohermaphroditic, epicene, monoclinous; androgynous, androgynal, gynandrous, gynandrian; gender-bending; gender-based, gender-neutral, gender-related; gender-fluid; gender-sensitive, gender-specific

76 MASCULINITY

<male qualities>

NOUNS 1 **masculinity,** masculineness, maleness; **manliness,** manlihood, manhood, manfulness, manlikeness; mannishness; gentlemanliness, gentlemanlikeness; boyishness; tomboyishness; a guy thing

2 **male sex,** male sexuality, virility, virileness, virilism, potence, potency, sexual power, manly vigor, machismo; ultramasculinity; phallicism; male superiority

3 **mankind,** man, men, manhood, menfolk, menfolks, the sword side, patriarchy

4 **male,** male being, masculine; he, him, his, himself; **man,** male person, *homme* <Fr>, *hombre* <Sp>; gentleman, gent

5 <nonformal> **guy,** fellow, feller, lad, blade, chap, chappie, cat, duck, stud, joker, jasper, bugger, bastard, bloke, cove, johnny, bod, body, dude, gent, Joe, Adam, bud

6 **real man, he-man,** two-fisted man, hunk, jockstrap, jock, man with hair on his chest; caveman, bucko, beefcake

7 <forms of address> **Mister, Mr,** Messrs <pl>, Master; **sir**, my good man, gentleman, my dear sir, my dear man; esquire; *monsieur* <Fr>, *messieurs* <Fr pl>; *signor, signore, signorino* <Ital>; *señor, Sr, don* <Sp>

8 **<male animals>** cock, rooster, chanticleer; cockerel; drake; gander; peacock; tom turkey, tom, turkey-cock, gobbler, turkey gobbler; dog; boar; stag, hart, buck; stallion, studhorse, stud, top horse, entire horse, entire, colt; tomcat; he-goat, billy goat, billy; hog; ram, tup; wether; bull, bullock, top cow; steer, stot; drone

9 <mannish female> amazon, virago, androgyne; lesbian, butch, dyke; **tomboy,** hoyden, romp

10 **man of the family,** family man, married man, husband, widower, househusband, patriarch, paterfamilias, father, papa; son, brother, uncle, nephew, godfather, godson, grandfather, grandson, grandpa; biodad, sperm donor

VERBS 11 masculinize, virilize

ADJS 12 **masculine, male,** he-; **manly**, manlike, mannish, manful, andric; uneffeminate; gentlemanly, gentlemanlike; bull; yang

13 **virile, potent,** viripotent; ultramasculine, macho, he-mannish, hunky, two-fisted, broad-shouldered, hairy-chested

14 mannish, mannified; unwomanly, unfeminine, uneffeminate, viraginous; **tomboyish,** hoyden, rompish

77 FEMININITY

<female qualities>

NOUNS 1 **femininity,** feminality, feminacy, feminineness, femaleness, femineity, feminism; **womanliness,** womanlikeness, womanishness, womanhood, womanity, muliebrity; girlishness, little-girlishness; maidenhood, maidenliness; ladylikeness, gentlewomanliness; matronliness, matriarchy, matronage, matronhood, matronship; the eternal feminine; feminine wile; a girl thing

2 **effeminacy,** unmanliness, effeminateness, epicenity, epicenism, womanishness, muliebrity, **sissiness**, prissiness; androgyny, girly man; feminism

3 **womankind,** woman, women, femininity, womanhood, womenfolk, womenfolks, the distaff side; the female sex; the second sex, the fair sex, the gentle sex, the softer sex, the weaker sex, the weaker vessel

4 **female,** female being; she, her, herself
5 **woman,** Eve, daughter of Eve, Adam's rib, *femme* <Fr>, distaff, weaker vessel; *wahine* <Hawaii>; **lady,** milady, gentlewoman, *domina* <L>; feme sole, feme covert <law>; married woman, wife; matron, dame, dowager; squaw; unmarried woman, bachelor girl, single woman, spinster, maiden; old maid; lass, lassie, girl; career woman, businesswoman, working woman, working wife, working mother; superwoman; liberated woman, feminist, suffragette, women's libber, alpha girl
6 <offensive or nonformal> **gal, dame,** hen, biddy, skirt, missy, toots, jane, broad, doll, damsel, babe, chick, wench, bird, tomato, bitch*, minx, momma, mouse, sister, squaw, ballbreaker, dudette
7 **woman of the family,** married woman, wife, widow, housewife, mother, matriarch, materfamilias; daughter, sister, aunt, maiden aunt, niece, godmother, goddaughter, grandmother, granddaughter; biomom; alpha mom, tiger mother, hockey mom, soccer mom
8 <forms of address> **Ms;** Miss, miss; Mistress, **Mrs;** madam, ma'am; missus; my good lady, my dear woman, my dear lady, lady; *madame, Mme* <Fr>; *mesdames, Mmes* <Fr pl>; *signora* <Ital>, *señora* <Sp>; *donna* <Ital>, *doña* <Sp>, *mademoiselle, Mlle* <Fr>; *signorina* <Ital>, *señorita* <Sp>, Dame, Lady <Brit>
9 <**female animals**> hen, biddy; guinea hen; peahen; bitch, slut, gyp; sow, gilt; ewe, ewe lamb; she-goat, nanny goat, nanny; doe, hind, roe; jenny; mare, brood mare; filly; cow, bossy; heifer; vixen; tigress; lioness; she-bear, she-lion, queen bee
10 <nonformal> effeminate male, mollycoddle, **effeminate**; mother's darling, mother's boy, mama's boy, Lord Fauntleroy, sissy, Percy, goody-goody, goody two-shoes; pantywaist, pansy, nancy, nance, chicken, lily; cream puff, weak sister, milksop, wussy; fag, queen, swish
11 feminization, womanization, effemination, effeminization, sissification

VERBS **12** **feminize**; womanize, demasculinize, effeminize, effeminatize, effeminate, soften, sissify; emasculate, castrate, geld

ADJS **13** **feminine,** female; gynic, gynecic, gynecoid; muliebral, distaff, womanly, womanish, womanlike, petticoat; ladylike, gentlewomanlike, gentlewomanly; matronly, matronal, matronlike; girlish, little-girlish, kittenish; maidenly; yin; all-female, all girl
14 **effeminate**, womanish, fem, old-womanish, unmanly, muliebrous, soft, chicken, prissy, sissified, sissy, sissyish

78 REPRODUCTION, PROCREATION

<producing young>

NOUNS **1** **reproduction,** making, re-creation, remaking, refashioning, reshaping, redoing, reformation, reworking, rejiggering; reconstruction, rebuilding, redesign, restructuring, *perestroika* <Russ>; revision; reedition, reissue, reprinting; reestablishment, reorganization, reorg, reinstitution, reconstitution; redevelopment; rebirth, renascence, resurrection, revival; past life; regeneration, regenesis, palingenesis; **duplication**, **imitation**, **copy**, **repetition**; **restoration**, renovation; producing anew, making anew, creating anew, producing again, making over, making again, creating again, producing once more, making once more, creating once more; birth rate, fertility rate; baby boom, baby boomlet; family leave
2 **procreation, reproduction**, generation, begetting, breeding, engenderment, engendering, fathering, siring, spawning; propagation, multiplication, proliferation; linebreeding; inbreeding, endogamy; outbreeding, xenogamy; dissogeny; crossbreeding
3 **fertilization,** fecundation; impregnation, insemination, begetting, getting with child, knocking up, mating, servicing; pollination, pollinization; germination; cross-fertilization, cross-pollination; self-fertilization, internal fertilization, heterogamy, orthogamy; isogamy, artificial insemination; conjugation, zygosis; in vitro fertilization, in vitro; test-tube baby
4 **conception,** conceiving, inception of pregnancy; superfetation, superimpregnation
5 **pregnancy,** gestation, incubation, parturiency, gravidness, gravidity, heaviness, greatness, bigness, the family way; brooding, sitting, covering
6 **birth**, generation, genesis; development; procreation; abiogenesis, archigenesis, biogenesis, blastogenesis, digenesis, dysmerogenesis, epigenesis, eumerogenesis, heterogenesis, histogenesis, homogenesis, isogenesis, merogenesis, metagenesis, monogenesis, oögenesis, orthogenesis, pangenesis, parthenogenesis, phytogenesis, sporogenesis, xenogenesis; spontaneous generation; kangaroo care

VERBS **7** **reproduce,** remake, make over, do over, re-create, regenerate, resurrect, revive, re-form, refashion, reshape, remold, recast, rework, rejigger, redo, reconstruct, rebuild, redesign, restructure, revise; reprint, reissue; reestablish, reinstitute, reconstitute, refound, reorganize, reorg; redevelop; duplicate, copy, repeat, restore, renovate

8 **procreate,** generate, breed, beget, get, engender; propagate, multiply; proliferate; mother; father, sire; reproduce in kind, reproduce after one's kind; breed true; inbreed, breed in and in; outbreed; cross-pollinate, crossbreed; linebreed

9 **lay** <eggs>, deposit, drop, spawn

10 **fertilize,** fructify, fecundate, fecundify; **impregnate,** inseminate, spermatize, knock up, get with child, get with young; pollinate, pollinize, pollen; cross-fertilize, cross-pollinate, cross-pollinize

11 **conceive,** get in the family way; superfetate

12 **be pregnant,** be gravid, be great with child, be with child, be with young; be in the family way, have a bun in the oven, be expecting, anticipate a blessed event, be infanticipating, be knocked up, be blessed-eventing; gestate, breed, carry, carry young; incubate, **hatch; brood,** sit, set, cover

13 **give birth**

ADJS 14 **reproductive,** re-creative, reconstructive, re-formative; renascent, regenerative, resurgent, reappearing; reorganizational; revisional; restorative; Hydraheaded, phoenixlike

15 **reproductive,** procreative, procreant, propagative, life-giving; spermatic, spermatozoic, seminal, germinal, fertilizing, fecundative; multiparous

16 **genetic,** generative, genial, gametic; genital, genitive; abiogenetic, biogenetic, blastogenetic, digenetic, dysmerogenetic, epigenetic, eumerogenetic, heterogenetic, histogenetic, homogenetic, isogenetic, merogenetic, metagenetic, monogenetic, oögenetic, orthogenetic, pangenetic, parthenogenetic, phytogenetic, sporogenous, xenogenetic

17 **bred, impregnated,** inseminated; inbred, endogamic, endogamous; outbred, exogamic, exogamous; crossbred; linebred

18 **pregnant,** *enceinte* <Fr>, preggers, knocked-up, with child, with young, in the family way, gestating, breeding, teeming, parturient; heavy with child, heavy with young, great with child great with young, big with child, big with young, wearing her apron high, in a delicate condition, gravid, heavy, great, big-laden; carrying, carrying a fetus, carrying an embryo; **expecting**, anticipating, anticipating a blessed event, infanticipating; superfetate, superimpregnated

79 CLEANNESS

<dirt-free condition>

NOUNS 1 **cleanness, cleanliness;** purity, squeaky-cleanness, pureness; immaculateness, immaculacy; spotlessness, unspottedness, stainlessness, whiteness; freshness; fastidiousness, daintiness, cleanly habits, spit and polish; asepsis, sterility, hospital cleanliness; tidiness

2 **cleansing, cleaning,** cleaning up, detersion; purge, purging, purgation, cleanout, cleaning out, catharsis, abstersion; **purification,** purifying, lustration; expurgation, bowdlerization; housecleaning, spring-cleaning, cleanup; dry cleaning

3 **sanitation, hygiene,** hygenics; disinfection, decontamination, sterilization, sanitization, antisepsis, asepsis; pasteurization; deodorization, fumigation, disinfestation, delousing; chlorination

4 **refinement,** clarification, purification, depuration; straining, colature; elution, elutriation; extraction; filtering, filtration; percolation, leaching, edulcoration, lixiviation; sifting, separation, screening, sieving, bolting, riddling, winnowing; essentialization; sublimation; **distillation,** destructive distillation; beachcombing

5 **washing, ablution;** lavation, laving, lavage; lavabo; wash, washup; soaking, soaping, lathering; dip, dipping; rinse, rinsing; sponge, sponging; shampoo, shampooing; washout, elution, elutriation; irrigation, flush, flushing, flushing out; douche, douching; enema; scrub, scrubbing, swabbing, mopping, scouring; **cleaning up**, cleaning out, washing up, scrubbing up, scrubbing out, mopping up, mopping down, wiping up, wiping down

6 **laundering, laundry,** tubbing; wash, washing; washday

7 **bathing,** balneation

8 **bath**, tub; **shower,** shower bath, needle bath, hot shower, cold shower, bathe; douche; sponge bath, sponge; hip bath, sitz bath; footbath; sweat bath, Turkish bath, hummum, Russian bath, Swedish bath, Finnish bath, sauna, sauna bath, steam bath, Japanese bath, hot tub, whirlpool bath, Jacuzzi <tm>, plunge bath

9 **dip,** bath; acid bath, mercury bath, fixing bath; sheepdip

10 **bathing place**, bath, baths, public baths, bathhouse, bath water, bagnio, sauna, Turkish baths; *balneum, balneae, thermae* <L>; watering place, spa; lavatory, washroom, bathroom; steam room, sweat room, sudatorium, sudarium, sudatory, caldarium, tepidarium; restroom

11 **laundry,** washery; washhouse, washshed; coin laundry, Laundromat <tm>, launderette, coin-operated laundry, laundrette, washateria; automatic laundry; hand laundry; car wash

12 **washbasin, washbowl,** washdish, basin; lavatory, washstand; bathtub, tub, bath; bidet; basin and

pitcher, basin and ewer; shower, showers, shower room, shower bath, shower stall, shower head, shower curtain; sink, kitchen sink; dishwasher; washing machine, washer; piscina, lavabo, ewer, aquamanile; washtub, washboard, washpot, washing pot, wash boiler, dishpan; finger bowl; wash barrel

13 **refinery;** refiner, purifier, clarifier; filter; strainer, colander; percolator, lixiviator; sifter, sieve, screen, riddle, cribble; winnow, winnower, winnowing machine, winnowing basket, winnowing fan; cradle, rocker

14 **cleaner,** cleaner-up, cleaner-off, cleaner-out; janitor, janitress, custodian; cleaning woman, cleaning lady, cleaning man, housecleaner, housemaid, maid, daily, daily woman, charwoman, char; window cleaner, squeegee; scrubber, swabber; shoeshiner, bootblack

15 **washer,** launderer; laundress, laundrywoman, washerwoman, washwoman; laundryman, washerman, washman; dry cleaner; dishwasher, pot-walloper, pearl-diver, scullion, scullery maid; dishwiper

16 **sweeper; street sweeper,** crossing sweeper, whitewing, cleanser; **chimney sweep**, chimney sweeper, sweep, flue cleaner; scavenger, beachcomber; garbage collector, trash collector, sanitary engineer

17 **cleanser, cleaner;** cleaning agent; antiseptic, disinfectant; cold cream, cleansing cream, soap, detergent, washing powder, soap flakes, abstergent, sanitizer, hand sanitizer, hand soap; dishwashing liquid, dishwashing powder; shampoo; rinse; bubble bath, shower gel, bodywash; solvent; cleaning solvent; water softener; purifier, depurant; mouthwash, gargle; dentifrice, toothpaste, tooth powder, whitener; abrasive, pumice, pumice stone, holystone, hearthstone, scouring powder, scouring pad; polish, varnish, wax, whitewash; purge, purgative, cathartic, enema, diuretic, emetic, nauseant, laxative; cleaning device, cleaning tool, cleaning cloth

VERBS 18 **clean, cleanse,** purge, deterge, depurate; purify, lustrate, disinfect; sweeten, freshen; whiten, bleach; clean up, clean out, clear out, sweep out, clean up after; houseclean, clean house, spring-clean; spruce, **tidy**; scavenge; wipe, wipe up, wipe off, mop, mop up, swab, scrub, scour; dust, dust off; steam-clean, dry-clean; expurgate, bowdlerize

19 **wash, bathe,** bath, shower, lave, have a bath, take a bath; **launder,** tub; wash up, wash out, wash away; rinse, dip, dunk, flush, flush out, irrigate, sluice, sluice out; ritually immerse, baptize, *toivel* <Yiddish>; sponge, sponge down, sponge off; scrub, scrub up, scrub out, swab, mop, mop up; scour; hose out, hose down; rinse off, rinse out; soak, soak out, soak away; soap, lather; shampoo; syringe, douche; gargle

20 **groom,** dress, fettle, brush up; preen, plume, titivate; manicure, pedicure, mani-pedi

21 **comb,** curry, card, hackle, hatchel, heckle, rake

22 **refine,** clarify, clear, purify, rectify, depurate, decrassify; try; strain; elute, elutriate; extract; filter, filtrate; percolate, leach, lixiviate, edulcorate; sift, separate, sieve, screen, decant, bolt, winnow; sublimate, sublime; **distill,** essentialize

23 **sweep,** sweep up, sweep out, **brush,** brush off, whisk, broom; vacuum, vacuum-clean

24 **sanitize,** sanitate, hygienize; **disinfect,** decontaminate, sterilize, antisepticize, radiosterilize; autoclave, boil; pasteurize, flash-pasteurize; disinfest, fumigate, deodorize, delouse; chlorinate

ADJS 25 **clean, pure; immaculate,** spotless, stainless, pristine, white, fair, dirt-free, soil-free; unsoiled, unsullied, unmuddied, unsmirched, unbesmirched, unblotted, unsmudged, unstained, untarnished, unspotted, unblemished, unmarked, undirtied; smutless, smut-free; bleached, whitened; bright, shiny; unpolluted, nonpolluted, untainted, unadulterated, undefiled; kosher, *tahar* <Heb>, ritually pure, ritually clean; squeaky-clean, clean as a whistle, clean as a new penny, clean as a hound's tooth; sweet, fresh, fresh as a daisy; cleanly, fastidious, dainty, of cleanly habits; well-washed, well-scrubbed, tubbed

26 **cleaned, cleansed,** cleaned up, cleaned out, washed, scrubbed; purged, purified; expurgated, bowdlerized; refined, filtered; spruce, spick and span, **tidy**

27 **sanitary, hygienic,** prophylactic; sterile, aseptic, antiseptic, uninfected; disinfected, decontaminated, sterilized; autoclaved, boiled; pasteurized

28 **cleansing, cleaning;** detergent, detersive; disinfectant, antibacterial; abstergent, abstersive, depurative; **purifying,** purificatory, lustral; expurgatory; purgative, purging, cathartic, diuretic, emetic; balneal, ablutionary

ADVS 29 **cleanly,** clean; purely, immaculately, spotlessly

80 UNCLEANNESS

<dirty condition>

NOUNS 1 **uncleanness,** immundity; **impurity,** unpureness; **dirtiness,** grubbiness, dinginess, griminess, messiness, grunginess, scuzziness, scruffiness, slovenliness, sluttishness, untidiness; miriness, muddiness; uncleanliness

2 **filthiness, foulness,** vileness, scumminess, feculence, shittiness*, muckiness, ordurousness, nastiness, grossness, yuckiness, ickiness; scurfiness, scabbiness; rottenness, putridness; rankness, fetidness; odiousness, repulsiveness; nauseousness, disgustingness; hoggishness, piggishness, swinishness, beastliness

3 **squalor,** squalidness, squalidity, sordidness, slum, hellhole; slumminess; insanitation, lack of sanitation; unhealthy conditions

4 **defilement,** befoulment, dirtying, soiling, besmirchment; **pollution,** contamination, infection; abomination; ritual uncleanness, ritual impurity, ritual contamination

5 **soil,** soilure, soilage, smut; smirch, smudge, smutch, smear, spot, blot, blotch, scuff, **stain**

6 **dirt, grime;** dust; soot, smut; **mud**

7 **filth,** muck, slime, mess, sordes, foul matter; ordure, **excrement**; mucus, snot; scurf, furfur, dandruff; scuzz, mung, gronk; putrid matter, pus, corruption, gangrene, decay, carrion, **rot**; obscenity, smut

8 **slime,** slop, scum, sludge, slush; glop, gunk, muck, mire, ooze

9 **offal,** slough, offscourings, scurf, scum, riffraff, scum of the earth; residue; carrion; garbage, swill, slop, slops, sullage; dishwater, ditchwater, bilgewater, bilge; **sewage,** sewerage; rubbish, trash, **waste, refuse**

10 **dunghill,** manure pile, midden, mixen, colluvies; compost heap; kitchen midden, refuse heap; vermicompost

11 **sty,** pigsty, pigpen, hogpen; stable, Augean stables; dump, hole, shithole*, rathole; tenement; warren, **slum,** rookery; the inner city, the ghetto, the slums, asphalt jungle, concrete jungle; plague spot, pesthole; hovel

12 <receptacle of filth> sink; sump, cesspool, cesspit, septic tank; catchbasin; bilge, bilges; sewer, drain, *cloaca, cloaca maxima* <L>; sewage farm, purification plant; **dump,** garbage dump, dump site, sanitary landfill, landfill; swamp, bog, mire, quagmire, marsh

13 **pig,** swine, hog, slut, sloven, slattern; infectee

VERBS 14 wallow in the mire, live like a pig, roll in the dirt, roll in the mud

15 **dirty,** dirty up, dirt, grime, begrime; muck, muck up; muddy, bemud; mire, bemire; slime; dust; soot, smoke, besmoke

16 **soil,** besoil; black, blacken; smirch, besmirch, sully, slubber, smutch, smouch, besmutch, smut, smudge, smear, besmear, daub, bedaub; spot, **stain**; get one's hands dirty, dirty one's hands, soil one's hands

17 **defile,** foul, befoul; sully; foul one's own nest, shit where one eats*, nasty, mess, mess up, make a mess of; **pollute,** corrupt, contaminate, infect; taint, tarnish, poison; profane, desecrate, unhallow

18 **spatter,** splatter, splash, bespatter, dabble, bedabble, spot, splotch

19 **bedraggle,** draggle, drabble, bedrabble, drabble in the mud

ADJS 20 **unclean,** unwashed, unbathed, unscrubbed, unscoured, unswept, unwiped; **impure,** unpure; **polluted,** contaminated, infected, corrupted; ritually unclean, ritually impure, ritually contaminated, *tref* <Yiddish>, *terefah* <Heb>, nonkosher; not to be handled without gloves; uncleanly; septic, unhygienic, toxic; pollutable

21 **soiled,** sullied, dirtied, smirched, besmirched, smudged, spotted, tarnished, tainted, stained; defiled, fouled, befouled; draggled, drabbled, bedraggled

22 **dirty,** dirt-encrusted, grimy, grubby, grungy, scummy, smirchy, dingy, messy; scruffy, slovenly, untidy; miry, **muddy**; dusty; smutty, smutchy, smudgy; sooty, smoky; snuffy

23 **filthy,** filthied, **foul,** vile, mucky, nasty, icky, yecchy, yucky, gross, grungy, scuzzy, grotty; malodorous, mephitic, rank, fetid; putrid, rotten; pollutive; nauseating, disgusting; odious, **repulsive**; slimy; barfy, vomity, puky; sloppy, sludgy; gloppy, gunky, scurfy, scabby; wormy, maggoty, flyblown; feculent, ordurous, crappy, shitty*, excremental, excrementitious, fecal

24 **hoggish,** piggish, swinish, beastly

25 **squalid,** sordid, wretched, shabby; slumlike, slummy

ADVS 26 **uncleanly,** impurely, unpurely; dirtily, grimily; filthily, foully, nastily, vilely

81 HEALTHFULNESS

<good for health>

NOUNS 1 **healthfulness, healthiness,** salubrity, salubriousness, salutariness, wholesomeness, beneficialness, goodness

2 **hygiene,** hygienics; sanitation; public health, epidemiology; health physics; preventive medicine, prophylaxis, preventive dentistry, prophylactodontia; prophylactic psychology, mental hygiene; **fitness, exercise**; cleanliness

3 **hygienist,** hygeist, sanitarian; public health doctor, public health physician, epidemiologist; health physicist; preventive dentist, prophylactodontist; dental hygienist

VERBS **4** make for health, conduce to health, **be good for,** agree with

ADJS **5** **healthful, healthy,** salubrious, salutary, wholesome, health-preserving, health-enhancing, health-giving, life-promoting, beneficial, benign, good, good for; nutritious, nourishing, roborant; **hygienic**, hygienical, hygeian, sanitary; constitutional, for one's health; conditioning; bracing, refreshing, invigorating, tonic; what the doctor ordered

82 UNHEALTHFULNESS

<bad for health>

NOUNS **1** **unhealthfulness, unhealthiness,** insalubrity, insalubriousness, unsalutariness, ill health, poor health, unwholesomeness, badness; noxiousness, noisomeness, injuriousness, harmfulness; pathenogenicity; chronic ill health, valetudinarianism; health hazard, threat to health, danger to health, menace to health; contamination, pollution, environmental pollution, air pollution, water pollution, noise pollution

2 innutritiousness, indigestibility

3 **poisonousness,** toxicity, venomousness; virulence, virulency, malignancy, noxiousness, destructiveness, deadliness, morbidity; infectiousness, infectivity, contagiousness, communicability; poison, venom

VERBS **4** disagree with, **not be good for**, sicken; decondition

ADJS **5** **unhealthful, unhealthy,** insalubrious, unsalutary, unwholesome, peccant, bad, bad for; noxious, noisome, injurious, baneful, harmful; polluted, contaminated, tainted, foul, septic, stagnant; unhygienic, unsanitary, insanitary; morbific, pathogenic, pestiferous

6 **unnutritious,** indigestible, unassimilable

7 **poisonous,** toxic, toxicant; venomous, envenomed, venenate, venenous; veneniferous, toxiferous; pollutive; virulent, noxious, malignant, malign, destructive, deadly; pestiferous, pestilential, pestilent; mephitic, miasmal, miasmic, miasmatic; **infectious,** infective, contagious, communicable, catching, germ-laden; lethal

83 HEALTH

<physical wellness>

NOUNS **1** **health, well-being;** fitness, health and fitness, physical fitness; bloom, flush, pink, glow, rosiness; mental health, emotional health; physical condition; Hygeia

2 **healthiness,** healthfulness, soundness, wholesomeness; healthy body, good constitution, healthy constitution; good health, good state of health; robust health, rugged health, rude health, glowing health, picture of health; fine fettle, fine whack, fine feather, high feather, good shape, good trim, fine shape, top shape, good condition, mint condition; eupepsia, good digestion; clean bill of health; immune system, immune response

3 **haleness, heartiness,** robustness, vigorousness, ruggedness, vitality, lustiness, hardiness, strength, vigor; longevity

4 **immunity,** immune system, resistance, nonproneness to disease, nonsusceptibility to disease; immunization; antibody, antigen

5 **health care,** health protection, health management, medical management, health maintenance, **medical care**; **wellness,** wellness program, disease prevention, preventive medicine; health awareness program; health policy, health-care policy; allied health care; ambulatory care; palliative care; health plan, health insurance, medical insurance, health service, health-care delivery service, health-care delivery plan, health maintenance organization (HMO), Medicare, Medicaid; socialized medicine; health department, health commissioner; health club, health spa; self-care

VERBS **6** **enjoy good health,** have a clean bill of health, be in the pink; be in the best of health; **feel good,** feel fine, feel fit, feel like a million dollars, feel like a million, never feel better; feel one's oats, be full of pep; burst with health, bloom, glow, flourish; keep fit, stay in shape; wear well, stay young, be well-preserved

7 **get well, recover**, mend, get healthy, be oneself again, feel like a new person, get back on one's feet, bounce back, get over it, perk up, get the color back in one's cheeks; recuperate

ADJS **8** **healthy, healthful,** enjoying health, fine, in health, in shape, in condition, fit, fit and fine; in good health, in the pink of condition, in mint condition, in good case, in good shape, in fine shape, in fine fettle, in A-1 condition, bursting with health, full of life and vigor, feeling one's oats; eupeptic

9 <nonformal> **in the pink,** in fine whack, in fine feather, in high feather, chipper, **fit as a fiddle;** alive and kicking, bright-eyed and bushy-tailed; full of beans, full of of piss and vinegar

10 **well,** unailing, unsick, unsickly, unfrail; all right, doing nicely, up and about, sitting up and taking nourishment, alive and well

11 **sound,** whole, wholesome; unimpaired; sound of mind and body, sound in wind and limb, sound as a dollar

12 **hale, hearty,** hale and hearty, robust, robustious, robustuous, vital, vigorous, strong, strong as a horse, strong as an ox, bionic, stalwart, stout, sturdy, rugged, rude, hardy, lusty, bouncing, well-knit, flush; fit, in condition, in shape; of good constitution
13 **fresh,** green, youthful, blooming; flush, flushed, rosy, rosy-cheeked, apple-cheeked, ruddy, pink, pink-cheeked; fresh-faced, fresh as a daisy, fresh as a rose, fresh as April
14 **immune, resistant,** nonprone to disease, nonsusceptible to disease; health-conscious, health-protecting

84 FITNESS, EXERCISE

<physical conditioning>

NOUNS 1 **fitness,** physical fitness, physical conditioning, condition, shape, trim, tone, fettle, aerobic fitness, anaerobic fitness, cardiovascular fitness, cardiorespiratory fitness, cardio; gymnasium, gym, fitness center, health club, health spa, workout room, weight room, exercise track, trail; weight, barbell, dumbbell, exercise machine, Nautilus <tm>, multi-gym, bench, exercise bike, rowing machine, stair-climbing machine, elliptical trainer, treadmill; whirlpool bath, Jacuzzi <tm>, hot tub, spa; physical education, phys ed
2 **exercise,** motion, movement, maneuver; motor skill; program, routine, drill, workout; exercise systems; warm-up, stretching, warm-down; calisthenics, free exercise, daily dozen, constitutional; boot camp; parcourse exercise; gymnastic exercise, gymnastics; slimnastics; isometrics, isometric exercise, no-movement exercise; breather, wind sprint; aerobic exercise, aerobics, aquaerobics; aerobic dancing, aerobic dance; step aerobics, dancercise, dancercizing, fitaerobics, jazz ballet, Jazzercise; Callanetics; bodybuilding, weightlifting, weight training, pumping iron, resistance training strength training, resistance band exercise, free weights; running, jogging, roadwork, distance running; obligate running; cross-training, interval training, *fartlek* <Swedish>, circuit training; obstacle course, parkour; walking, fitness walking, healthwalking, aerobic walking, powerwalking, powerstriding; swimming, swimnastics, water exercise; yoga, pranayama, vinyasa, power yoga, yin yoga, ashtanga yoga; Pilates; situps, crunches, ab work
3 **physical fitness test;** stress test, treadmill test; cardiovascular text

VERBS 4 **exercise, work out,** warm up, aerobicize, stretch, lift weights, weight-lift, weight-train, pump iron, jog, run, bicycle, walk, fitness-walk, power-walk; practice

85 DISEASE

<illness>

NOUNS 1 **disease** <see list>, **illness,** sickness, malady, ailment, indisposition, disorder, complaint, morbidity, *morbus* <L>, affliction, affection, infirmity; disability, defect, handicap; deformity; birth defect, congenital defect; abnormality, condition, pathological condition; signs, symptoms, pathology, symptomatology, symptomology, syndrome; sickishness, malaise, seediness, rockiness, the pip, the crud, the creeping crud; complication, secondary disease, secondary condition; pre-existing condition; plant disease, blight
2 **fatal disease,** deadly disease, terminal disease, terminal illness, hopeless condition; **death,** clinical death, loss of vital signs; apparent death; brain death, local death, somatic death; sudden death, unexplained death; liver death; serum death; thymic death, mors thymica; cell death, molecular death; cot death, crib death, sudden infant death syndrome (SIDS)
3 **unhealthiness,** healthlessness; **ill health,** poor health, delicate health, shaky health, frail health, fragile health; sickliness, peakedness, feebleness, delicacy, weakliness, fragility, frailty; infirmity, unsoundness, debility, debilitation, enervation, exhaustion, decrepitude; wasting, languishing, languishment, cachexia, cachexy; chronic ill health, invalidity, invalidism; unwholesomeness, morbidity, morbidness; hypochondria, hypochondriasis, valetudinarianism, history of illness
4 **infection, contagion,** contamination, taint, virus, affliction; contagiousness, infectiousness, communicability; pestiferousness, epidemicity, inoculability; carrier, vector; epidemiology
5 **epidemic,** plague, pestilence, pest, pandemic, pandemia, scourge, bane; white plague, tuberculosis; pesthole, plague spot
6 **seizure, attack,** access, visitation; arrest; blockage, stoppage, occlusion, thrombosis, thromboembolism; stroke, ictus, apoplexy; spasm, throes, fit, paroxysm, convulsion, eclampsia, frenzy; epilepsy, falling sickness; tonic spasm, tetany, lockjaw, trismus, tetanus; laryngospasm, laryngismus; clonic spasm, clonus; cramp; vaginismus
7 **fever,** feverishness, febrility, febricity, pyrexia; hyperpyrexia, hyperthermia; heat, fire, fever heat;

flush, hectic flush; calenture; delirium, ague; chill, hypothermia, shivers, shakes

8 **collapse,** breakdown, crackup, prostration, exhaustion, burnout; nervous prostration, nervous breakdown, nervous exhaustion, neurasthenia; circulatory collapse

9 <disease symptoms> indication, **syndrome**; anemia; ankylosis; asphyxiation, anoxia, cyanosis; ataxia; bleeding, hemorrhage; colic; dizziness, vertigo; ague, chill, chills; hot flash, hot flush; dropsy, hydrops, edema; morning sickness; fainting; fatigue; headache, migraine; fever; constipation; diarrhea, flux, dysentery; indigestion, upset stomach, dyspepsia; inflammation; necrosis; insomnia; malaise; itching, pruritus; jaundice, icterus; backache, lumbago; vomiting, nausea; paralysis; skin eruption, rash; sore, abscess, discharge; hypertension, high blood pressure; hypotension, low blood pressure; tumor, growth; shock; convulsion, seizure, spasm; pain; fibrillation, tachycardia; shortness of breath, labored breathing, apnea, dyspnea, asthma; blennorhea; congestion, nasal discharge, rheum, sore throat, coughing, sneezing; wasting, cachexia, cachexy, tabes, marasmus, emaciation, atrophy; sclerosis

10 **inflammation,** inflammatory disease, -itis; muscle disease, muscular disease, muscular disorder, myopathy; collagen disease, connective-tissue disease

11 **deficiency disease** <see list>, nutritional disease, vitamin-deficiency disease, acquired immune deficiency syndrome (AIDS)

12 **genetic disease** <see list>, gene disease, gene-transmitted disease, hereditary disease, congenital disease

13 **infectious disease** <see list>, infection

14 **eye disease**, ophthalmic disease, disease of the eye, disease of vision; cataract; conjunctivitis, pinkeye; glaucoma; sty; eye defect, visual defect, defective vision

15 **ear disease,** otic disease, otic disorder; deafness; earache, otalgia; tympanitis; otosclerosis; vertigo, dizziness, loss of balance; Ménière's syndrome, Ménière's disease, apoplectical deafness

16 **respiratory disease**, upper respiratory disease; lung disease; cold, common cold, sinusitis; influenza, flu; bronchitis, pneumonia

17 **tuberculosis (TB),** white plague, phthisis, consumption

18 **venereal disease (VD)**, sexually transmitted disease (STD), social disease, Cupid's itch, Venus's curse, dose; chancre, chancroid; gonorrhea, clap, the clap, the claps; syphilis, syph, the syph, the pox; herpes, crabs; acquired immune deficiency syndrome (AIDS)

19 **cardiovascular disease;** heart disease, heart condition, heart trouble; vascular disease; hypertension, high blood pressure; angina, angina pectoris; cardiac infarction, myocardial infarction; cardiac arrest; congenital heart disease; congestive heart failure; coronary disease, ischemic heart disease; coronary thrombosis; heart attack, coronary, heart failure; tachycardia; heart surgery, bypass surgery, angioplasty

20 **blood disease,** hemic disease, hematic disease, hematopathology, anemia, leukemia, lymphoma, Hodgkin's disease; blood poisoning, toxemia, septicemia; hemophilia

21 **endocrine disease,** gland disease, glandular disease, endocrinism, endocrinopathy; diabetes, gestational diabetes, Type II diabetes; goiter; hyperglycemia, hypoglycemia; hyperthyroidism, hypothyroidism

22 **metabolic disease;** acidosis, alkalosis, ketosis; gout, podagra; galactosemia, lactose intolerance, fructose intolerance; phenylketonuria (PKU), maple syrup urine disease, congenital hypophosphatasia

23 **liver disease,** hepatic disease; gallbladder disease; jaundice, icterus

24 **kidney disease,** renal disease; nephritis

25 **neural disease,** nerve disease, **neurological disease**, neuropathy, motor neuron disease; brain disease; amyotrophic lateral sclerosis, Lou Gehrig's disease; palsy, cerebral palsy, Bell's palsy; chorea, St. Vitus's dance, the jerks; Huntington's chorea; headache, migraine; multiple sclerosis (MS); muscular dystrophy; Parkinson's disease, Parkinsonism; Alzheimer's disease; neuralgia; sciatica, sciatic neuritis; shingles, herpes zoster; spina bifida; meningitis; emotional trauma

26 **shock, trauma;** traumatism

27 **paralysis,** paralyzation, palsy, impairment of motor function; **stroke,** apoplexy; paresis; motor paralysis, sensory paralysis; hemiplegia, paraplegia, diplegia, quadriplegia; cataplexy, catalepsy; infantile paralysis, poliomyelitis, polio; atrophy, numbness

28 **heatstroke;** heat prostration, heat exhaustion; sunstroke, siriasis, insolation; calenture, thermic fever

29 **gastrointestinal disease,** disease of the digestive tract; stomach condition; colic; colitis; constipation, irregularity; diarrhea, dysentery, looseness of the bowels, flux, the trots, the shits*, the runs, Montezuma's revenge;

gastritis; gastroenteritis; indigestion, dyspepsia; stomachache, bellyache; cramps; heartburn, acid reflux, agita; stomach flu; ulcer, peptic ulcer, stomach cancer; food poisoning

30 **nausea,** nauseation, queasiness, squeamishness, qualmishness; qualm, pukes; motion sickness, travel sickness, **seasickness,** *mal de mer* <Fr>, airsickness, car sickness, motion discomfort; vomiting

31 **poisoning,** intoxication, venenation; septic poisoning, blood poisoning, sepsis, septicemia, toxemia, pyemia, septicopyemia; autointoxication; food poisoning, ptomaine poisoning, botulism, salmonellosis, listeriosis; milk sickness; ergotism, St. Anthony's fire; alcohol poisoning

32 **environmental disease, occupational disease** <see list>, disease of the workplace, environmental hazard, occupational hazard, biohazard; tropical disease; sick building syndrome

33 **vitamin deficiency disease,** avitaminosis; night blindness, xerophthalmia, beriberi, pellagra, pernicious anemia, scurvy, rickets, osteomalacia

34 **allergy,** allergic disorder; allergic rhinitis, hay fever, rose cold, pollinosis, spring allergy; asthma, bronchial asthma; hives, urticaria; eczema; conjunctivitis; cold sore; allergic gastritis; cosmetic dermatitis; Chinese restaurant syndrome, Kwok's disease; allergen; pollen count

35 **skin disease;** acne, sebaceous gland disorder; dermatitis; eczema; herpes; hives; itch; psoriasis; scabies; athlete's foot; melanoma, skin cancer

36 **skin eruption,** eruption, **rash,** efflorescence, breaking out, acne, pimple; diaper rash; drug rash, vaccine rash; prickly heat, heat rash; hives, urticaria, nettle rash; papular rash; rupia

37 **sore,** lesion; pustule, papule, papula, fester, pimple, hickey, zit; pock; ulcer, ulceration; bedsore; tubercle; blister, bleb, bulla, blain; whelk, wheal, welt, wale; boil, furuncle, furunculus; carbuncle; canker; canker sore; cold sore, fever blister; sty; abscess, gathering; gumboil, parulis; whitlow, felon, paronychia; bubo; chancre; soft chancre, chancroid; hemorrhoids, piles; bunion; chilblain, kibe; polyp; stigma, petechia; scab, eschar; fistula; suppuration, festering; swelling, rising

38 **trauma, wound, injury,** hurt, lesion; cut, incision, scratch, gash; puncture, stab, stab wound; flesh wound; laceration, mutilation; abrasion, scuff, scrape, chafe, gall; frazzle, fray; run, rip, rent, slash, tear; burn, scald, scorch, first-degree burn, second-degree burn, third-degree burn; flash burn; break, fracture, bone fracture, comminuted fracture, compound fracture, open fracture, greenstick fracture, spiral fracture, torsion fracture, stress fracture; rupture; crack, chip, craze, check, crackle; wrench; whiplash injury, whiplash; concussion; bruise, contusion, ecchymosis, black-and-blue mark; black eye, shiner, mouse; battering; battered child syndrome; sprain, strain, repetitive strain injury; paper cut

39 **growth,** neoplasm; **tumor,** intumescence; benign tumor, nonmalignant tumor, innocent tumor; malignant tumor, malignant growth, metastatic tumor, cancer, sarcoma, carcinoma; morbid growth; excrescence, outgrowth; proud flesh; exostosis; cyst, wen; fungus, fungosity; callus, callosity, corn, clavus; wart, verruca; mole, nevus

40 **gangrene,** mortification, necrosis, sphacelus, sphacelation; noma; moist gangrene, dry gangrene, gas gangrene, hospital gangrene; caries, cariosity, tooth decay; slough; necrotic tissue

41 <**animal disease**> anthrax, splenic fever, charbon, milzbrand, malignant pustule; malignant catarrh, malignant catarrhal fever; bighead; blackleg, black quarter, quarter evil, quarter ill; cattle plague, rinderpest; glanders; foot-and-mouth disease, hoof-and-mouth disease, aphthous fever; distemper; gapes; heaves, broken wind; hog cholera; mad cow disease; loco, loco disease, locoism; mange, scabies; pip; rot, liver rot, sheep rot; staggers, megrims, blind staggers, mad staggers; swine dysentery, bloody flux; stringhalt; Texas fever, blackwater; John's disease, paratuberculosis, pseudotuberculosis; rabies, hydrophobia; myxomatosis

42 **germ,** pathogen, contagium, bug, disease-causing agent, disease-producing microorganism; **microbe,** microorganism; **virus,** filterable virus, nonfilterable virus, adenovirus, echovirus, reovirus, rhinovirus, enterovirus, picornavirus, retrovirus, virion, bacteriophage, phage; human immunodeficiency virus (HIV), Ebola virus; rickettsia; bacterium, **bacteria,** coccus, streptococcus, staphylococcus, bacillus, spirillum, vibrio, spirochete, gram-positive bacteria, gram-negative bacteria, aerobe, aerobic bacteria, anaerobe, anaerobic bacteria; protozoon, amoeba, trypanosome; fungus, mold, spore; carcinogen, cancer-causing agent

43 **sick person,** ill person, sufferer, victim; valetudinarian, invalid, shut-in; incurable, terminal case; patient, case; inpatient, outpatient; apoplectic, bleeder, consumptive, dyspeptic, epileptic, rheumatic, arthritic, spastic; addict; the sick, the infirm; hypochondriac

44 **carrier,** vector, biological vector, mechanical vector; Typhoid Mary

45 **cripple,** defective, **handicapped person,** disabled person, physically challenged, incapable; amputee; paraplegic, quadriplegic, paralytic; deformity; the crippled, the handicapped

VERBS **46** **ail, suffer,** labor under, be affected with, complain of; feel ill, feel under the weather, feel awful, feel like hell, feel something terrible, not feel like anything, feel like the walking dead; look green about the gills

47 **take sick**, take ill, sicken; catch, contract, get, take, come down with, be stricken by, be seized by, fall a victim to; catch cold; take one's death; break out, break out with, break out in a rash, erupt; run a temperature, fever; be laid by the heels, be struck down, be brought down, be felled; drop in one's tracks, collapse; overdose (OD); go into shock, be traumatized

48 **fail, weaken,** sink, decline, run down, lose strength, lose one's grip, dwindle, droop, flag, wilt, wither, wither away, fade, **languish,** waste, waste away, pine, peak

49 **go lame,** founder

50 **afflict,** disorder, derange; sicken, indispose; weaken, enfeeble, enervate, reduce, debilitate, devitalize; invalid, incapacitate, **disable;** lay up, hospitalize

51 **infect,** disease, **contaminate,** taint, pollute; reinfect, superinfect

52 **poison,** empoison, envenom

ADJS **53** disease-causing, disease-producing, pathogenic; threatening, life-threatening; unhealthful

54 **unhealthy,** healthless, in poor health; infirm, unsound, unfit, invalid, valetudinary, valetudinarian, debilitated, cachectic, enervated, exhausted, drained; shut-in, housebound, homebound, wheelchair-bound; sickly, peaky, peaked; weakly, feeble, frail; weakened, decrepit, with low resistance, run-down, reduced, reduced in health; dying, terminal, moribund, languishing, failing; pale

55 **unwholesome, unhealthy,** unsound, morbid, diseased, pathological

56 **ill, ailing, sick, unwell,** indisposed, taken ill, down, bad, on the sick list; sickish, seedy, rocky, under the weather, out of sorts, all-overish, below par, white as a sheet, off-color, off one's feed; not quite right, not oneself; faint, faintish, feeling faint; feeling awful, feeling something terrible, feel crummy, feel shitty*; sick as a dog, laid low; in a bad way, critically ill, in danger, on the critical list, on the guarded list, in intensive care; terminal, inoperable, mortally ill, sick unto death, near death; far gone

57 **nauseated,** nauseous, queasy, squeamish, qualmish, qualmy; sick to one's stomach; pukish, puky, barfy; seasick, carsick, airsick, green around the gills

58 **feverish,** fevered, feverous, in a fever, febrile, pyretic; flushed, inflamed, hot, burning, fiery, hectic; hyperpyretic, hyperthermic; delirious

59 **laid up,** invalided, hospitalized, in hospital <Brit>; bedridden, bedfast, sick abed; down, prostrate, flat on one's back; in childbed, confined

60 **diseased,** morbid, pathological, bad, infected, contaminated, tainted, peccant, poisoned, septic; cankerous, cankered, ulcerous, ulcerated, ulcerative, gangrenous, gangrened, mortified, sphacelated; inflamed; congested; swollen, edematous

61 anemic, chlorotic; bilious; dyspeptic, liverish, colicky; dropsical, edematous, hydropic; gouty, podagric; neuritic, neuralgic; palsied, paralytic; pneumonic, pleuritic, tubercular, tuberculous, phthisic, consumptive; rheumatic, arthritic; rickety, rachitic; syphilitic, pocky, luetic; tabetic, tabid; allergic; allergenic; apoplectic; hypertensive; diabetic; encephalitic; epileptic; laryngitic; leprous; malarial; measly; nephritic; scabietic, scorbutic, scrofulous; variolous, variolar; tumorous; cancerous, malignant; carcinogenic, tumorigenic; HIV-positive

62 **contagious, infectious,** infective, catching, taking, spreading, communicable, zymotic, inoculable; pathogenic, germ-carrying; pestiferous, pestilent, pestilential, epidemic, epidemial, pandemic; epizootic, epiphytotic; endemic; sporadic; septic

63 **deficiency disease**

acquired immunodeficiency syndrome (AIDS)
anemia
anhidrosis
anoxemia
ariboflavinosis
beriberi
cachexia
chlorosis
cretinism
cytopenia
deficiency anemia
dermatitis
goiter
greensickness
hypoadenia
hypochromia
hypothyroidism
immunodeficiency
ischemia
Italian leprosy, Lombardy leprosy
keratomalacia
kwashiorkor
leukopenia, leucopenia
lymphopenia
maidism
malnutrition
night blindness
osteomalacia
osteoporosis
pellagra
pernicious anemia
protein deficiency
rickets, rachitis
scurvy
severe combined immune deficiency
struma

thrombocytopenia
undernutrition
vitamin deficiency
Wernicke-Korsakoff syndrome
xerophthalmia

64 disease

acute disease, acute condition
allergy, allergic disease
arthritis
atrophy
autoimmune disease
bacterial disease
blood disease
bone disease
cancer
cardiovascular disease
childhood disease, pediatric disease
chronic disease, chronic condition
chronic fatigue syndrome
circulatory disease
collagen disease
congenital disease
connective-tissue disease
contagious disease, infectious disease
deficiency disease
degenerative disease
digestive disease
endemic disease
endocrine disease
endocrine gland disease
epidemic disease
functional disease
fungus, fungal disease
gastric disease, stomach disease
gastroenterological disease
gastrointestinal disease
genetic disease
geriatric disease
glandular disease
hepatic disease, liver disease
hereditary disease
hypertrophy
iatrogenic disease
immunodeficiency disease
intestinal disease
joint disease
muscular disease
neurological disease
nutritional disease
occupational disease
ophthalmic disease
organic disease
pandemic disease
parasitic disease
protozoan disease
psychiatric disease
psychogenic disease, psychosomatic disease
pulmonary disease
radiation disease
renal disease, kidney disease
respiratory disease
rheumatoid arthritis
skin disease
sexually transmitted disease (STD), venereal disease
tropical disease
ulcer
urinogenital disease, urogenital disease
virus, viral disease
wasting disease
worm disease

65 environmental disease, occupational disease

aeroembolism, caisson disease, decompression sickness, tunnel disease, diver's palsy, the bends
alcohol poisoning
anoxemia
anoxia
anoxic anoxia
anthrax, pulmonary anthrax, woolsorter's disease
cadmium poisoning
carpal tunnel syndrome
chilblain
frostbite
housemaid's knee
immersion foot
jet lag
lead poisoning
mercury poisoning
Minamata disease
motion sickness
nature-deficit disorder
pneumoconiosis, black lung
radiation sickness
radionecrosis
reactive schizophrenia
red-out
repetitive stress injury, repetitive motion disorder
sick building syndrome
sunstroke
trench foot
writer's cramp, writer's palsy, writer's spasm

66 genetic disease

achromatic vision
adenosine deaminase deficiency, ADA deficiency
albinism
Christmas disease
color blindness
cystic fibrosis
dichromatic vision
Down syndrome, Down's syndrome
dysautonomia
Hartnup's disease
hemophilia
hip dysplasia
Huntington's chorea
ichthyosis
lipid histiocytosis
maple syrup urine disease
Milroy's disease
mucoviscidosis
muscular dystrophy
neurofibromatosis
Niemann-Pick disease
pancreatic fibrosis
sickle-cell anemia, sickle-cell disease
Tay-Sachs disease
thalassemia
Turner's syndrome
Werdnig-Hoffmann disease

67 infectious disease

acquired immune deficiency syndrome (AIDS)
acute articular rheumatism
African lethargy, encephalitis lethargica
ague
AIDS-related complex (ARC), pre-AIDS
alkali disease
amebiasis
amebic dysentery
anthrax, pulmonary anthrax, woolsorter's disease
Asian flu
bacillary dysentery
bastard measles
bird flu
black death
black fever
blackwater fever
breakbone fever
brucellosis
bubonic plague
cachectic fever
cerebral rheumatism
Chagas disease, American trypanosomiasis
Chagres fever
chicken pox, varicella
cholera, Asiatic cholera
cowpox
dandy fever
dengue, dengue fever
diphtheria
dumdum fever
dysentery
elephantiasis
enteric fever
erysipelas
famine fever
five-day fever
frambesia
German measles
glandular fever
grippe
Haverhill fever
hepatitis
herpangina
herpes
histoplasmosis
hookworm
infectious hepatitis
inflammatory rheumatism
influenza, flu, flu virus
jail fever
jungle rot
kala azar
Kew Gardens spotted fever
legionnaires' disease
lepra
leprosy, Hansen's disease
leptospirosis
loaiasis, loa loa
Lyme disease
lyssa
malaria, malarial fever

marsh fever
measles, rubeola
meningitis
milzbrand
mononucleosis, infectious mononucleosis, kissing disease, mono
mumps
ornithosis
osteomyelitis
paratyphoid fever
parotitis
pneumonia
poliomyelitis, infantile paralysis, polio
ponos
psittacosis, parrot fever
rabies, hydrophobia
rat-bite fever
relapsing fever
rheumatic fever
rickettsial pox
ringworm, tinea
Rocky Mountain spotted fever
rubella
scarlatina
scarlet fever
schistosomiasis
scrub typhus, tsutsugamushi disease
septic sore throat
shigellosis
sleeping sickness, sleepy sickness
smallpox, variola
snail fever
splenic fever
sporotrichosis
spotted fever
St. Anthony's fire
strep throat
streptococcus tonsilitis
swamp fever
syphilis
tetanus, lockjaw
thrush
tick-borne typhus
tick fever
toxic shock syndrome
tracheitis
trench fever
trench mouth, Vincent's infection, Vincent's angina
trypanosomiasis
tuberculosis
tularemia, deer fly fever, rabbit fever
typhoid fever, typhoid
typhus, typhus fever
undulant fever
urinary tract infection
vaccinia
venereal disease (VD)
viral dysentery
viral pneumonia
whooping cough, pertussis
yaws
yellow fever, yellow jack
zoster, shingles, zona

86 REMEDY

<relief of illness>

NOUNS 1 **remedy, cure,** corrective, alterative, remedial measure, sovereign remedy; relief, help, aid, assistance, succor; balm, balsam; healing agent; restorative, analeptic; healing quality, healing virtue; oil on troubled waters; specific, specific remedy; prescription, recipe, receipt; magic bullet

2 **nostrum,** patent medicine, quack remedy; snake oil

3 **panacea, cure-all,** universal remedy, theriac, catholicon, philosopher's stone; polychrest, broad-spectrum drug, broad-spectrum antibiotic; elixir, elixir of life, *elixir vitae* <L>

4 **medicine,** medicament, **medication,** medicinal, theraputant, pharmaceutical, **drug,** physic, preparation, mixture; herbs, medicinal herbs, simples, vegetable remedies; wonder drug, miracle drug; balsam, balm; tisane, ptisan; drops; powder; inhalant; electuary, elixir, syrup, lincture, linctus; officinal; specialized drug, orphan drug; prescription drug, ethical drug; over-the-counter drug, OTC drug, counter drug, nonprescription drug; proprietary medicine, proprietary drug, proprietary, patent medicine; proprietary name, generic name; materia medica; pharmacognosy; placebo, placebo effect; smart drug

5 **drug,** narcotic drug, controlled substance, designer drug, illegal drug, dope, banned substance

6 **dose,** dosage, draft, potion, portion, shot, injection; broken dose; booster, booster dose, recall dose, booster shot; drops; inhalant; megadose, microdose

7 **pill,** bolus, tablet, capsule, time-release capsule, lozenge, dragée, troche, pastille

8 **tonic,** bracer, cordial, restorative, analeptic, roborant, pick-me-up; shot in the arm; stimulant; vitamin shot, herb tea, ginseng, iron

9 **stimulant;** adrenalin, epinephrine; aloes; amphetamine sulphate, aromatic spirits of ammonia, caffeine, dextroamphetamine sulfate, Dexedrine, digitalin, digitalis, methamphetamine hydrochloride, methamphetamine, smelling salts, salts; pep pill

10 **palliative,** alleviative, alleviatory, lenitive, assuasive, assuager; soothing, abirritant

11 **balm,** lotion, salve, ointment, unguent, *unguentum* <L>, cream, cerate, unction, balsam, oil, emollient, demulcent; liniment, embrocation; vulnerary; collyrium, eyesalve, eyebath, eyewash; eardrops, eyedrops

12 **sedative,** sedative hypnotic, depressant, amobarbital, amobarbital sodium, Amytal <tm>, atropine, barbital, barbitone <Brit>, barbituric acid, belladonna, chloral hydrate, chloral, laudanum; meperidine, Demerol <tm>; morphine; pentobarbital, Nembutal <tm>; phenobarbital, Luminal <tm>; Quaalude <tm>, reserpine, scopolamine; secobarbital, Seconal <tm>; sleeping pill, sleeping tablet, sleeping potion; calmative, tranquilizer, chlorpromazine, Equanil <tm>, Librium <tm>, meprobamate, rauwolfia, Thorazine <tm>, Triavil <tm>, Valium <tm>; abirritant, soother, soothing syrup, quietener, pacifier; analgesic; acetaminophen, Tylenol <tm>; acetanilide, acetophenetidin; aspirin, acetylsalicylic acid, Bayer <tm>; buffered aspirin, Bufferin <tm>; headache powder; ibuprofen, Advil <tm>, Motrin <tm>, Nuprin <tm>; phenacetin; propoxyphene, Darvon <tm>; sodium salicylate; anodyne, paregoric; **pain killer**, pain pill; anti-inflammatory drug, nonsteroidal anti-inflammatory drug

(NSAID), anti-inflammatory; muscle relaxant; alcohol, liquor

13 **psychoactive drug, hallucinogen,** psychedelic, psychedelic drug, mind-altering drug, mind-bending drug

14 **antipyretic,** febrifuge, fever-reducer, fever pill

15 **anesthetic;** local anesthetic, topical anesthetic, general anesthetic; differential anesthetic; chloroform, ether, ethyl chloride, gas, laughing gas, nitrous oxide, novocaine, Novocain <tm>; sodium thiopental, Pentothal <tm>, truth serum

16 **cough medicine,** cough syrup, cough drops; horehound

17 **laxative,** cathartic, physic, purge, purgative, aperient, carminative, diuretic; stool softener; milk of magnesia, castor oil, Epsom salts; nauseant, emetic; douche, enema

18 **emetic,** vomitive, vomit, nauseant

19 **enema,** clyster, clysma, lavage, lavement

20 **prophylactic,** prophylaxis, preventive, preventative, protective

21 **antiseptic**, disinfectant, fumigant, fumigator, germicide, bactericide, microbicide; alcohol, carbolic acid, hydrogen peroxide; merbromin, Mercurochrome <tm>; tincture of iodine

22 **toothpaste,** tooth powder, dentifrice; mouthwash, gargle, fluoride, dental floss

23 **contraceptive,** birth control device, prophylactic, contraception; condom; rubber, skin, bag; oral contraceptive, birth control pill, the pill; Brompton, Brompton's mixture, Brompton's cocktail, morning-after pill, abortion pill, RU-486; diaphragm, pessary; spermicide, spermicidal jelly, contraceptive foam; intrauterine device (IUD), Dalkon shield <tm>, Lippes loop; abortion issue, anti-choice, pro-choice, pro-life, right-to-life

24 **vermifuge,** vermicide, worm medicine, anthelminthic

25 **antacid,** gastric antacid, alkalizer

26 **antidote,** countermeasure, counterpoison, counteraction, alexipharmic, antitoxin, counterirritant; theriaca, theriac

27 **antitoxin,** antitoxic serum; **antivenin;** serum, antiserum; interferon; antibody, antigen-antibody product, anaphylactic antibody, incomplete antibody, inhibiting antibody, sensitizing antibody; gamma globulin, serum gamma globulin, immune globulin, antitoxic globulin; lysin, precipitin, agglutinin, anaphylactin, bactericidin; antiantibody; antigen, Rh antigen, Rh factor; allergen; immunosuppressive drug

28 **vaccination,** inoculation; **vaccine**

29 **antibiotic,** ampicillin, bacitracin, erythromycin, gramicidin, neomycin, nystatin, penicillin, polymyxin, streptomycin; tetracycline, Terramycin <tm>; miracle drug, wonder drug, magic bullet; bacteriostat; sulfa drug, sulfa, sulfanilamide, sulfonamide, sulfathiazole

30 diaphoretic, sudorific

31 vesicant, vesicatory, epispastic

32 miscellaneous drugs, biopharmaceutical; anabolic steroid, muscle pill; antihistamine, antispasmodic, beta blocker, counterirritant, decongestant, expectorant, fertility drug, fertility pill, hormone, vasoconstrictor, vasodilator, azidothymidine (AZT), hormone replacement therapy

33 **dressing,** application, epithem; plaster, court plaster, mustard plaster, sinapism; poultice, cataplasm; formentation; compress, pledget; stupe; tent; tampon; **bandage,** bandaging, binder, cravat, triangular bandage, roller, roller bandage, four-tailed bandage; bandage compress, adhesive compress, adhesive bandage, Band-Aid <tm>; butterfly dressing; elastic bandage, Ace elastic bandage, Ace bandage <tm>, compression bandage; rubber bandage; plastic bandage; tourniquet; sling; splint, brace; cast, plaster cast; tape, adhesive tape, duct tape; lint, cotton, gauze, sponge; patch, nicotine patch

34 **pharmacology,** pharmacy, pharmaceutics; posology; materia medica

35 **pharmacist,** pharmaceutist, pharmacopolist, **druggist,** chemist <Brit>, apothecary, dispenser, gallipot; pharmacologist, pharmaceutical chemist, posologist; pill pusher, pill roller

36 **drugstore, pharmacy,** chemist, chemist's shop <Brit>, apothecary's shop, dispensary, dispensatory

37 **pharmacopoeia,** pharmacopedia, dispensatory

VERBS **38** **remedy**, help, relieve, cure; medicate; prescribe; treat; decongest

ADJS **39** **remedial,** curative, therapeutic, healing, medicating, corrective, disease-fighting, alterative, restorative, curing, analeptic, sanative, sanatory; salubrious, salutiferous; all-healing, panacean; adjuvant; **medicinal,** medicative, theriac, theriacal, iatric; anticancer; first-aid; self-medicating

40 **palliative,** lenitive, alleviative, assuasive, soothing, balmy, balsamic, demulcent, emollient, pain-relieving, analgesic, anodyne

41 **antidotal,** alexipharmic, counteractant; antitoxic; **antibiotic,** synthetic antibiotic, semisynthetic antibiotic, bacteriostatic, antimicrobial; antiluetic, antisyphilitic; antiscorbutic; antiperiodic; antipyretic, febrifugal; vermifugal, anthelmintic; antacid

42 **prophylactic**, preventive, protective

43 **antiseptic,** disinfectant, germicidal, bactericidal, **antibacterial**

44 **tonic**, stimulating, bracing, invigorating, stimulative, reviving, refreshing, restorative, analeptic, strengthening, roborant, corroborant

45 **sedative,** calmative, calmant, depressant, soothing, tranquilizing, quietening; narcotic, opiatic; analgesic, anodyne, paregoric; anti-inflammatory; muscle-relaxant; hypnotic, soporific, somniferous, somnifacient, sleep-inducing

46 psychochemical, psychoactive; ataractic; antidepressant, mood drug, mood elevation; hallucinogenic, **psychedelic,** mind-expanding, psychotomimetic

47 **anesthetic,** deadening, numbing

48 **cathartic,** laxative, purgative, aperient; carminative; diuretic

49 **emetic,** vomitive

87 SUBSTANCE ABUSE

<harmful drug intake>

NOUNS 1 **substance abuse, drug abuse,** narcotics abuse, drug use, glue-sniffing, solvent abuse; **addiction,** addictedness, drug addiction, narcotic addiction, opium addiction, opium habit, opiumism, morphine addiction, morphine habit, morphinism, heroin addiction, heroin habit, cocaine addiction, cocainism, coke habit, crack habit, barbiturate addiction, amphetamine addiction, meth addiction; habit, drug habit, jones, drug habituation, drug dependence, physical addiction, physical dependence, psychological addiction, psychological dependence, monkey on one's back, Mighty Joe Young; drug experience, drug intoxication, high, buzz, rush; frightening drug experience, bad trip, bum trip, bummer, drag; **alcoholism**, alcohol abuse, drinking habit, binge drinking, acute alcoholism, chronic alcoholism, dipsomania, hitting the bottle, Dutch courage, hard drinking, liquid lunch, barhopping; drunk driving; smoking, smoking habit, <number>-pack-a-day habit, nicotine addiction, chain-smoking, vaping; tolerance, acquired tolerance; withdrawal, withdrawal sickness, withdrawal syndrome, withdrawal symptoms, bogue, coming down, crash, abrupt withdrawal, cold turkey; detoxification, detox, drying out, taking the cure; Alcoholics Anonymous (AA); Narcotics Anonymous (NA); drug test; drug czar

2 <**drug use**> smoking, sniffing, injecting, snorting, freebasing, hitting up, shooting up, skin-popping, mainlining, pill-popping, banging, blowing, cocktailing; buzz, trip, acid trip, bad trip; drug pushing, drug trafficking, holding

3 **drug, narcotic,** dope, dangerous drug, controlled substance, abused substance, illegal drug, addictive drug, hard drug; soft drug, gateway drug; lifestyle drug; opiate; sedative, depressant, sedative hypnotic, antipsychotic tranquilizer, trank; hallucinogen, hallucinogenic drug, psychedelic, psychedelic drug, psychoactive drug, psychoactive chemical, psychochemical, psychotropic drug, psychotomimetic drug, mind-altering drug, mind-expanding drug, mind-blowing drug; designer drug; street drug; recreational drug; stimulant; antidepressant, Prozac <tm>; inhalant, volatile inhalant; drug of choice

4 <nonformal, **amphetamines**> meth, methamphetamine, bennies, benz, black mollies, brain ticklers, crank, crystal, dexies, diet pills, dolls, ecstasy, footballs, greenie, hearts, ice, jelly beans, lid poppers, pep pills, purple hearts, speed, uppers, ups, white crosses

5 <nonformal, **amyl nitrate**> amies, blue angels, blue devils, blue dolls, blue heavens, poppers, snappers; **barbiturates,** barbs, black beauties, candy, dolls, downers, downs, goofballs, gorilla pills, nebbies, nimbies, phennies, phenos, pink ladies, purple hearts, yellow jackets

6 <nonformal, **chloral hydrate**> joy juice, knockout drops, Mickey, Mickey Finn, peter

7 <nonformal, **cocaine**> basuco, bernice, C, big C, blow, charlie, coke, crack, crack cocaine, jumps, dust, flake, girl, gold dust, her, jay, joy powder, lady, lady snow, nose candy, Peruvian marching powder, rock, snow, stardust, toot, white, white girl, white lady, white stuff

8 <nonformal, **hashish**> black hash, black Russian, hash

9 <nonformal, **heroin**> big H, boy, brown, caballo, crap, doojee, flea powder, garbage, H, hard stuff, henry, him, his, horse, hombre, jones, junk, mojo, P-funk, scag, schmeck, smack, white stuff

10 <nonformal, **LSD**> acid, purple haze, big D, blotter, blue acid, blue cheer, blue heaven, California sunshine, cap, cubes, D, deeda, dots, electric Kool-Aid, haze, L, mellow yellows, orange cubes, pearly gates, pink owsley, strawberry fields, sugar, sunshine, tabs, yellow, yellow sunshine, orange sunshine

11 <nonformal, **marijuana**> Acapulco gold, aunt mary, bomb, boo, bush, doobie, gage, ganja, grass, grefa, hay, hemp, herb, Indian hay, J, jane, kif, mary, maryjane, mary warner, meserole, mighty mezz, moota, muggles, pod, pot, smoke, snop, tea, Texas tea, weed, yerba

12 <nonformal, **marijuana cigarette**> joint, joy stick, kick stick, reefer, roach, stick, twist

13 <nonformal, **mescaline**> beans, big chief, buttons, cactus, mesc

14 <nonformal, **morphine**> big M, emm, hocus, M, miss emma, miss morph, morph, moocah, white stuff

15 <nonformal, **pentobarbital**> nebbies, nemmies, nimby, yellow dolls, yellows

16 <nonformal, **opium**> black pills, brown stuff, hop, O, tar

17 <nonformal, **peyote**> bad seed, big chief, buttons, cactus, P, topi

18 <nonformal, **phencyclidine**> PCP, angel dust, animal trank, DOA, dust, elephant, hog, peace, rocket fuel, supergrass, superweed

19 <nonformal, **psilocybin**> magic mushroom, mushroom, shroom, STP

20 **dose,** hit, fix, toke, rock; **shot, injection,** bang, bhang; portion, packet, spliff, snort, blockbuster, blast, shoot-up, hype, bag, deck, dime bag; drug house, shooting gallery, needle park, crack house, opium den, balloon room, pot party, dope den

21 **addict,** drug addict, narcotics addict, user, drug user, drug abuser, junkie, head, druggy, doper, toker, fiend, freak, space cadet; cocaine user, cokie, coke head, crackhead, sniffer, snow drifter, flaky; opium user, opium addict, hophead, hopdog, tar distiller; heroin user, heroin addict, smackhead, smack-sack, schmecker; methedrine user, methhead; amphetamine user, pillhead, pill popper, speed freak; LSD user, acidhead, acid freak, tripper, cubehead; marijuana smoker, pothead; drug seller, drug dealer, pusher, contact, connection, mule; alcoholic, **alcohol abuser,** binge drinker; smoker, heavy smoker, chain-smoker, nicotine addict

VERBS **22** **use, be on,** get on; use occasionally, use irregularly, have a cotton habit, chip, chippy, joy pop; get a rush, go over the hump; sniff, snort, blow, toot, one and one; smoke marijuana, take on a number, blow a stick, toke, blast, weed out; smoke opium, blow a fill; freebase; inject, mainline, shoot, shoot up, jab, get down, get off, pop, skin pop, take pills, pop pills; withdraw, crash, come down, kick cold turkey, go cold turkey, go a la canona, hang tough, water out, detoxify, disintoxicate, detoxicate, dry out, kick, kick the habit; trip, blow one's mind, wig out; sell drugs, deal, push; buy drugs, score, make, connect; have drugs, be heeled, carry, hold, sizzle; drink, booze; smoke, smoke tobacco, puff, puff away, drag, chain-smoke, smoke like a chimney, vape

ADJS **23** **intoxicated,** under the influence, nodding, narcotized, poppied, far gone

24 <nonformal> **high,** bent, blasted, blind, bombed out, bonged out, buzzed, coked, coked out, flying, fried, geared, geared up, geezed, gonged, gorked, hopped-up, in a zone, junked, luded out, maxed, noddy, ripped, smashed, snowed, spaced, space out, spacey, stoned, strung out, switched-on, tanked, totaled, tranqued, tripping, trippy, wankered, wired, wrecked, zoned, zoned out, zonked, zonked out

25 **addicted,** hooked, zunked, on the needle; dependency-prone; supplied with drugs, holding, heeled, carrying, anywhere; using, on, behind acid

88 INTOXICATION, ALCOHOLIC DRINK

<harmful alcohol intake>

NOUNS **1** **intoxication,** inebriation, inebriety, insobriety, besottedness, sottedness, **drunkenness,** tipsiness, befuddlement, fuddle, fuddlement, fuddledness, tipsification, tiddliness; a high, soaking; Dutch courage, pot-valiance, pot-valiancy, pot-valor; hangover, katzenjammer, morning after

2 **bibulousness,** bibacity, bibaciousness, bibulosity, sottishness; serious drinking; crapulence, crapulousness; **intemperance**; bacchanalianism; Bacchus, Dionysus, fondness for the bottle

3 **alcoholism,** dipsomania, oenomania, alcoholic psychosis, alcoholic addiction, pathological drunkenness, problem drinking, heavy drinking, habitual drunkenness, ebriosity; delirium tremens; grog blossom, bottle nose; gin drinker's liver, cirrhosis of the liver

4 **drinking,** imbibing; social drinking; tippling, guzzling, gargling, bibing; winebibbing, winebibbery; toping; hard drinking, serious drinking; boozing, swilling, hitting the booze, hitting the bottle, hitting the sauce; alcoholism, Alcoholics Anonymous

5 **spree,** drinking bout, bout, celebration, potation, compotation, symposium, wassail, carouse, carousal, drunken carousal, drunken revelry, revel; bacchanal, bacchanalia, bacchanalian; debauch, orgy; driving under the influence (DUI)

6 <nonformal> **binge, drunk,** bust, tear, bender, toot, bat, pub crawl, jag, booze-up, brannigan, guzzle, randan, rip

7 **drink,** dram, potation, potion, libation, nip, draft, drop, spot, finger, two, sip, sup, suck, drench, guzzle, gargle, jigger; peg, swig, swill, pull; snort, jolt, shot, snifter, wet; quickie; round, round of drinks

8 **pick-me-up,** bracer, refresher, reviver, pickup, tonic, hair of the dog, hair of the dog that bit one

9 **drink, cocktail,** highball, long drink, mixed drink;

liquor, spirits; punch; eye-opener, nightcap, sundowner; chaser, *pousse-café* <Fr>, *apéritif* <Fr>; parting cup, stirrup cup, one for the road; hair of the dog; Mickey Finn, Mickey, knockout drops; mixer

10 **toast, pledge**, health

11 **drinker,** imbiber, social drinker, tippler, bibber; winebibber, oenophilist; drunkard, **drunk,** inebriate, sot, toper, guzzler, swiller, soaker, lovepot, tosspot, barfly, thirsty soul, serious drinker, devotee of Bacchus; swigger; hard drinker, heavy drinker, alcoholic, dipsomaniac, problem drinker, chronic alcoholic, chronic drunk, pathological drinker; carouser, reveler, wassailer; bacchanal, bacchanalian; pot companion

12 <nonformal> **drunk,** lush, lusher, soak, sponge, hooch hound, boozer, boozehound, booze fighter, booze freak, dipso, juicehead, loadie, ginhound, elbow bender, elbow crooker, shikker, bottle sucker, swillbelly, swillpot, swillbowl; souse, stew, bum, rummy, rumhound, stewbum; wino

13 **spirits, liquor,** intoxicating liquor, adult beverage, hard liquor, hard stuff, whiskey, firewater, snake juice, spiritus frumenti, schnapps, ardent spirits, strong waters, intoxicant, toxicant, inebriant, potable, potation, beverage, drink, strong drink, strong liquor, alcoholic drink, alcoholic beverage, alcohol, aqua vitae, water of life, brew, grog, social lubricant, nectar of the gods; booze; rum, the Demon Rum, John Barleycorn; the bottle, the cup, the cup that cheers, the ruddy cup, little brown jug; punch bowl, the flowing bowl

14 <nonformal> likker, hooch, juice, sauce, tiger milk, pig sweat, tiger sweat, sheepdip, moonshine, white lightning; medicine, snake medicine, corpse reviver; rotgut, poison, rat poison, formaldehyde, embalming fluid, shellac, panther piss

15 **liqueur, cordial;** brandy, flavored brandy

16 **beer,** brew, brewskie, suds, swipes; small beer; nonalcoholic beer, alcohol-free beer; draft beer, home brew, microbrew

17 **wine,** *vin* <Fr>, *vino* <Sp, Ital>; vintage wine, nonvintage wine; the grape; red wine, white wine, rosé wine, pink wine, blush wine; dry wine, sweet wine, heavy wine, light wine, full wine, thin wine, rough wine, smooth wine, still wine, sparkling wine; extra sec champagne, demi-sec champagne, sec champagne, brut champagne, bubbly; new wine, must; imported wine, domestic wine; fortified wine; wine of the country, *vin du campagne* <Fr>; jug wine, plonk <Brit>; Beaujolais wine

18 **bootleg liquor, moonshine**; hooch, shine, mountain dew, white lightning, white mule; bathtub gin; home brew

19 **liquor dealer,** liquor store owner; vintner, wine merchant; winegrower, winemaker, wine expert, oenologist; **bartender,** mixologist, barkeeper, barkeep, barman, tapster, publican <Brit>; barmaid, tapstress; brewer, brewmaster; distiller; bootlegger, moonshiner

20 **bar,** barroom, *bistro* <Fr>, cocktail lounge; taproom; **tavern, pub,** pothouse, alehouse, rumshop, grogshop, dramshop, groggery, gin mill, saloon, drinking saloon, beer joint, saloon bar <Brit>; lounge, piano bar, sports bar, dive bar; singles bar, gay bar; waterhole, watering hole; wine bar; public house; public, local; beer parlor, beer garden, rathskeller; nightclub, cabaret, dinner club, supper club; café, wine shop; barrel house, honky-tonk, dive; speakeasy, blind tiger, blind pig, after-hours joint; cash bar

21 **distillery,** still, distiller; **brewery,** brewhouse; winery, wine press; bottling works

VERBS **22** **intoxicate,** inebriate, addle, befuddle, bemuse, besot, go to one's head, make one see double, make one tiddly

23 <nonformal> **plaster,** pickle, swack, crock, stew, souse, stone, pollute, tipsify, booze up, boozify, fuddle, overtake

24 **tipple, drink,** dram <Brit>, nip; grog, guzzle, gargle; imbibe, have a drink, have a nip, have a dram, have a guzzle soak, bib, quaff, sip, sup, lap, lap up, take a drop, slake one's thirst, cheer the inner man, refresh the inner man, drown one's troubles, drown one's sorrows, commune with the spirits; down, toss off, tossdown, toss one's drink, knock back, throw one back, drink off, drink up, drain the cup, drink bottoms-up, drink deep; drink hard, drink like a fish, drink seriously, tope; take to drink, take to drinking, drink one's fill

25 <nonformal> **booze,** swig, swill, wet one's whistle; liquor, liquor up, lush, souse, tank up, hit the booze, hit the bottle, hit the sauce, exercise the elbow, bend the elbow, crook the elbow, raise the elbow, dip the beak, splice the main brace; chug-a-lug, chug

26 **get drunk,** be stricken drunk, get high, put on a high, take a drop too much; get plastered, get pickled, tie one on, get a bun on

27 **be drunk,** be intoxicated, have a drop too much, hungover, have more than one can hold, have a jag on, see double, be feeling no pain; stagger, reel; pass out

28 **go on a spree**; go on a binge, go on a bender, carouse, spree, revel, wassail, debauch; eat, drink, and be merry; paint the town red, pub-crawl, club-hop

29 **drink to, toast,** pledge, drink a toast to, drink to the health of, pledge the health of
30 **distill; brew;** bootleg, moonshine, moonlight
ADJS 31 **intoxicated,** inebriated, inebriate, inebrious, drunk, drunken, *shikker* <Yiddish>, tipsy, in liquor, in one's cups, under the influence, the worse for liquor, having had one too many; nappy, beery; tiddly, giddy, dizzy, muddled, addled, flustered, bemused, reeling, seeing double; mellow, merry, jolly, happy, gay, glorious; full; besotted, sotted, sodden, drenched, far-gone; drunk as a lord, drunk as a fiddler, drunk as a piper, drunk as a skunk, drunk as an owl; staggering drunk, drunk and disorderly; crapulent, crapulous; maudlin
32 **dead-drunk,** blind drunk, overcome, out, out cold, passed out, helpless, under the table
33 <nonformal> **fuddled,** muzzy, boozy, overtaken; swacked, plastered, shnockered, stewed, pickled, pissed, **soused,** soaked, boiled, fried, canned, tanked, potted, corned, bombed, ripped, smashed; bent, **crocked,** crocko, shellacked, sloshed, sozzled, zonked, tight, lushy, squiffy, afflicted, jug-bitten, oiled, lubricated, feeling no pain, polluted, raddled, organized, **high,** elevated, high as a kite, lit, lit up, lit to the gills, illuminated, loaded, stinko, tanked-up, stinking drunk, pie-eyed, pissy-eyed*, shitfaced*, cockeyed, cockeyed drunk, roaring drunk, rip-roaring drunk, skunk-drunk; half-seas over, three sheets to the wind, well-oiled, blotto, stiff, blind, paralyzed, stoned
34 full of Dutch courage, pot-valiant, pot-valorous
35 **bibulous,** bibacious, drunken, sottish, liquorish, given to drink, addicted to drink, liquor-loving, liquor-drinking, drinking, hard-drinking, swilling, toping, tippling, winebibbing
36 **intoxicating,** intoxicative, **inebriating,** inebriative, inebriant, heady, buzzy
37 **alcoholic,** spirituous, ardent, strong, hard, with a kick; winy, vinous
INTERJS 38 <toasts> skoal, prosit, prost, *à votre santé* <Fr>, *l'chaim* <Heb>, sláinte <Irl>, *salute* <Ital>, *na zdorovye* <Russ>, *salud* <Sp>, to your health, long life, to life, cheerio, cheers, to us, down the hatch, bottoms up, here's how, here's to you, here's looking at you, here's mud in your eye, here's good luck, here's to absent friends, confusion to our enemies

89 TOBACCO

<smoking substance>

NOUNS 1 **tobacco,** *tabac* <Fr>, nicotine; **the weed,** fragrant weed, filthy weed, pernicious weed; carcinogenic substance; smoke, tobacco smoke, cigarette smoke, cigar smoke, pipe smoke; secondary smoke, secondhand smoke; vaping
2 <tobaccos> flue-cured, bright, fire-cured, air-cured; Broadleaf, Burley, Cuban, Havana, Havana seed, Latakia, Turkish, Russian, Maryland, Virginia; plug tobacco, bird's-eye, canaster, leaf, lugs, seconds, shag; pipe tobacco
3 **smoking tobacco,** smokings, smoke, smokes
4 **cigar,** seegar; rope, stinker; cheroot, stogie, corona, belvedere, Havana, panatella, colorado, trichinopoly; cigarillo; box of cigars, cigar box, cigar case, humidor; cigar cutter
5 **cigarette;** butt, cig, fag, coffin nail, cancer stick; filter tip, high tar, low tar, methol; cigarette butt, stub; snipe; pack of cigarettes, carton of cigarettes, box of cigarettes, cigarette case, cigarette paper; electronic cigarette, e-cigarette
6 **pipe,** tobacco pipe; corncob, corncob pipe, Missouri meerschaum; briar pipe, briar; clay pipe, clay, churchwarden <Brit>; meerschaum; water pipe, hookah, nargileh, kalian, hubble-bubble; peace pipe, calumet; pipe rack, pipe cleaner, tobacco pouch
7 **chewing tobacco,** eating tobacco, oral tobacco; navy, navy plug, cavendish, twist, pigtail, plug, cut plug; quid, cud, fid, chew, chaw; tobacco juice
8 **snuff,** snoose; rappee; pinch of snuff; snuff bottle, snuffbox
9 **nicotine,** nicotia
10 **smoking,** smoking habit, habitual smoking; chain-smoking; smoke, puff, drag; **chewing;** tobacco addiction, nicotine addiction, tobaccoism, tabacosis, tabacism, tabagism, nicotinism; passive smoking
11 **tobacco user, smoker,** cigarette smoker, pipe smoker, cigar smoker, chewer, snuffer, snuff dipper, vaper
12 **tobacconist;** snuffman; tobacco store, tobaccoshop, cigar store, vape shop
13 **smoking room,** smoking car, smoker; smoke-free area, nonsmoking section
VERBS 14 <use tobacco> **smoke;** inhale, puff, draw, drag, pull; smoke like a furnace, smoke like a chimney; chain-smoke; chew, chaw; roll; take snuff, dip snuff, inhale snuff
ADJS 15 **tobacco**, tobaccoey, tobaccolike; **nicotinic;** smoking, chewing; snuffy; smoke-free, nonsmoking

90 HEALTH CARE

<physical and mental treatment>

NOUNS 1 **medicine, medical practice,** medical profession, medical care, **health care,** health-care industry, health-care delivery, primary care, primary treatment; **medical specialty or branch** <see list>; treatment, therapy; health insurance, Medicare, Medicaid; care, nursing care, home care, outpatient care, life care; family practice, general practice; preferred provider; animal testing, assisted dying, control group

2 **surgery** <see list>; operation; cosmetic surgery, plastic surgery, facelift, liposuction, nose job, tuck; operating theatre

3 **dentistry** <see list>, dental medicine, dental care

4 **doctor,** doc, **physician,** Doctor of Medicine, medical doctor (MD), medical practitioner, medical man, medico, croaker, sawbones; general practitioner (GP); family doctor; country doctor; intern; resident, house physician, resident physician; fellow; physician in ordinary; medical attendant, attending physician; specialist, board-certified physician, board-certified specialist; medical examiner, coroner; oculist, optometrist, radiologist, anesthesiologist; health maintenance organization (HMO)

5 **surgeon,** sawbones; operator, operative surgeon, plastic surgeon

6 **dentist,** tooth doctor; dental surgeon, oral surgeon, operative dentist; Doctor of Dental Surgery (DDS); Doctor of Dental Science (DDSc); Doctor of Dental Medicine (DMD); orthodondist, perdontist, exodontist, endodontist, prosthodontist

7 **veterinarian, vet**, veterinary, veterinary surgeon, horse doctor, animal doctor, horse whisperer

8 **health-care professional,** health-care provider, physician, nurse, midwife, therapist, therapeutist, practitioner; physical therapist, physiotherapist, speech therapist, occupational therapist

9 **healer,** nonmedical therapist; theotherapist; spiritual healer, divine healer, Christian healer; Christian Science practitioner; faith healer, witch doctor, shaman, alternative practitioner, osteopath, chiropractor, podiatrist, acupuncturist

10 **nurse,** sister, nursing sister <Brit>; probationer, probationist, probe; caregiver, hospice caregiver; practical nurse; registered nurse (RN), nurse practitioner

11 <hospital staff> paramedic, emergency medical technician (EMT); medevac; physician's assistant (PA); orderly, attendant, nurse's aide; audiologist; anesthetist; dietician, nutritionist; radiographer, X-ray technician; laboratory technician; radiotherapist; dietitian; hospital administrator; ambulance driver; custodian

12 **Hippocrates,** Galen; Aesculapius, Asclepius

13 **practice of medicine,** medical practice; general practice, restricted practice, limited practice; group practice; professional association (PA); family practice, private practice, health maintenance organization (HMO); orthodox medicine, conventional medicine, general medicine, preventive medicine, internal medicine, occupational medicine, public-health medicine, community medicine; unorthodox medicine, alternative medicine, acupuncture, faith healing, homeopathy, naturopathy, guided imagery, visualization, Ayurveda, shamanism, color therapy, art therapy

VERBS 14 **practice medicine,** doctor; examine, diagnose, screen; treat; prescribe, medicate, administer, inject; make a house call, be on call; intern; practice surgery, perform surgery, operate; practice dentistry; do a procedure

ADJS 15 **medical,** iatric, health, Hippocratic; surgical; chiropodic, pediatric, orthopedic, obstetric, obstetrical, neurological; dental; orthodontic, periodontic, prosthodontic, exodontic; osteopathic, chiropractic, naturopathic, hydropathic, allopathic, homeopathic; gynecological, internal, pathological, forensic; clinical; diagnostic; therapeutic; veterinary

16 **dentistry specialty**

endodontics, endodontia
exodontics, exodontia
family dentistry
general dentistry
gerodontics
implantology
operative dentistry
oral surgery, surgical dentistry
orthodontics, orthodontia
pedodontics, pedodontia
periodontics, periodontia
prosthetic dentistry, prosthodontics, prosthodontia
radiodontics, radiodontia

17 **medical specialty or branch**

adolescence medicine
anatomy
anesthesiology
audiology
aviation medicine
bacteriology
bariatrics
cardiography
cardiology
chemotherapy
chiropody
critical care medicine
dental surgery
dentistry
dermatology
diagnostics
dolorology
embryology
endocrinology
environmental medicine
epidemiology
etiology
family practice
fetology
fluoroscopy
folk medicine
functional medicine
general medicine
geriatrics, gerontology
gynecology
hematology
hygiene, feminine hygiene
immunochemistry
immunology
internal medicine
materia medica
mental hygiene
midwifery
mycology
neonatology
nephrology
neurology
neurosurgery

nosology
nutrition
obstetrics
oncology
ophthalmology
optometry
orthopedics
orthotics
osteopathy
otolaryngology
otology
parasitology
pathology
pediatrics
pharmacology
pharmacotherapy
physical medicine
physiopathology
physiotherapy
plastic surgery
podiatry
psychiatry
psychology
psychoneuroimmunology
pulmonology
radiology
rheumatology
serology
space medicine
speech therapy
surgery
surgical anatomy
symptomatology, semeiology
teratology
therapeutics
tocology
toxicology
traditional medicine
virology

18 **surgery**
apicectomy
appendectomy, appendicectomy
arterioplasty
autograft, autoplasty
cesarean section
chemosurgery
cholecystectomy
cholelithotomy
colostomy
cordotomy
craniotomy
cryosurgery
cystectomy
debridement
dermasurgery
dilatation and curettage (D & C)
electrosurgery
episiotomy
fenestration
gastrectomy
goniopuncture
hepatectomy
homograft, allograft, homoplasty
hysterectomy
ileostomy
iridectomy
keyhole surgery
labioplasty
laparotomy
laryngectomy
lobotomy, leukotomy
lithonephrotomy, nephrolithotomy
mastectomy
microsurgery
necrotomy
nephrectomy
neurotomy
oophorectomy, ovariectomy
orchidectomy, orchiectomy, testectomy
ostectomy
otoplasty
phlebotomy, venesection
pneumonectomy
rhinoplasty
rhizotomy
salpingectomy
thoracotomy
tracheostomy, tracheotomy
vasectomy

91 THERAPY, MEDICAL TREATMENT

<physical health care>

NOUNS 1 **therapy,** therapeutics, therapeusis, treatment, medical care, medical treatment, medication; noninvasive therapy, noninvasive treatment, nonsurgical therapy, nonsurgical treatment; disease-fighting, healing; healing arts; physical therapy, occupational therapy, psychotherapy; medicines

2 **nonmedical therapy;** theotherapy; **healing;** Christian healing, spiritual healing, divine healing; shamanism; faith healing

3 **hydrotherapy,** water therapy, hydrotherapeutics; hydropathy, water cure; cold-water cure; contrast bath, whirlpool bath

4 **heat therapy,** thermotherapy; heliotherapy, solar therapy; fangotherapy; hot bath, sweat bath, sunbath

5 **diathermy,** medical diathermy; electrotherapy, electrotherapeutics; radiothermy, high-frequency treatment; shortwave diathermy, ultrashortwave diathermy, microwave diathermy; ultrasonic diathermy; surgical diathermy, radiosurgery, electrosurgery, electrosection, electrocautery, electrocoagulation

6 **radiotherapy,** radiation therapy, radiotherapeutics; adjuvant therapy

7 **radiology,** radiography, radioscopy, radiation, fluoroscopy; diagnostic radiology, scanning, magnetic resonance imaging (MRI); thermal imaging

8 <**radiotherapeutic substance**> radium; cobalt; radioisotope, tracer, labeled element, tagged element, radioelement; radiocarbon, carbon, radiocalcium, radiopotassium, radiosodium, radioiodine; atomic cocktail

9 <diagnostic pictures and graphs> **X-ray,** scan, radiograph, radiogram, roentgenogram, roentgenograph; photofluorograph; X-ray movie; chest X-ray; pyelogram; orthodiagram; encephalograph, encephalogram; electroencephalograph, electroencephalogram (EEG); electrocorticogram; electrocardiogram (ECG, EKG); electromyogram; computer-assisted tomography (CAT), computerized axial tomography (CAT), computed tomography (CAT), computer-assisted tomography, computerized tomography (CAT), CAT scan; magnetic resonance imaging (MRI), MRI scan; positron emission tomography (PET), PET scan; ultrasound, ultrasonography; sonogram

10 case history, **medical history**, anamnesis; associative anamnesis; catamnesis, follow-up

11 **diagnostics,** prognostics; symptomatology, semeiology, semeiotics

12 **diagnosis**; **examination,** physical examination; study, test, workup; medical test, laboratory test, screening, diagnostic procedure; blood test, blood work, blood count, urinalysis, uroscopy; biopsy; Pap test, Pap smear; stress test; electrocardiography, electroencephalography,

electromyography; mammography; pregnancy test, amniocentesis, amnio, ultrasound; misdiagnosis

13 **prognosis,** prognostication; prognostic, symptom, sign

14 **treatment,** medical treatment, medical attention, medical care; **cure,** curative measures; medication, medicamentation; regimen, regime, protocol; first aid; hospitalization; physical therapy, acupressure, shiatsu

15 **immunization;** immunization therapy, immunotherapy; vaccine therapy, vaccinotherapy; toxin-antitoxin immunization; serum therapy, serotherapy, serotherapeutics; tuberculin test, scratch test, patch test; immunology, immunochemistry; immunity theory, side-chain theory; immunity; immunodeficiency

16 **vaccination,** inoculation; injection, hypodermic, hypodermic injection, shot, bing, hypospray, jet injection; booster, booster shot; antitoxin, vaccine

17 <methods of injection> cutaneous, percutaneous, subcutaneous, intradermal, intramuscular, intravenous, intramedullary, intracardiac, intrathecal, intraspinal

18 **transfusion,** blood transfusion; serum; blood bank, blood donor center, bloodmobile; blood donor

19 **surgery,** surgical treatment, **operation,** surgical operation, surgical intervention, surgical technique, surgical measure, the knife; instrument, device; respirator; unnecessary surgery, *cacoëthes operandi* <L>, tomomania; major surgery, minor surgery, laser surgery, plastic surgery

20 bloodletting, bleeding, venesection, phlebotomy; leeching; cupping

21 **hospital, clinic,** treatment center; general hospital, teaching hospital, university hospital, health center, base hospital; hospice, infirmary; nursing home, rest home, convalescent home, sanitarium, assisted living; sick bay, sick berth; trauma center; birthing center; wellness center; eldercare, extended care, managed care; aging in place

22 **pesthouse,** lazar house, lazaretto, lazaret

23 **health resort, spa,** watering place, baths; mineral spring, warm spring, hot spring; pump room, pump house; yoga retreat

VERBS **24** **treat,** doctor, minister to, care for, give care to, physic; **diagnose;** nurse; cure, remedy, heal; dress the wounds, bandage, poultice, plaster, strap, splint; bathe; massage, rub; operate on; purge, flux; **operate,** perform a procedure; transplant, replant

25 **medicate,** medicine, drug, dope, dose; salve, oil, anoint, embrocate

26 **irradiate,** radiumize, **X-ray,** roentgenize

27 bleed, let blood, leech, phlebotomize; cup; **transfuse,** give a transfusion; perfuse

28 **immunize,** inoculate, **vaccinate,** shoot

29 **undergo treatment,** take the cure, doctor, take medicine; go under the knife

92 PSYCHOLOGY, PSYCHOTHERAPY

<mental health care>

NOUNS **1** **psychology, psychology branch** <see list>, science of the mind, science of human behavior, mental philosophy; psychologism, pop psychology, psychobabble; mental states, mental processes

2 psychological school, school of psychology, system of psychology, psychological theory; Adlerian psychology; behaviorism, behavior psychology, behavioristic psychology, stimulus-response psychology; Freudian psychology, Freudianism; Gestalt psychology, configurationism; Horneyan psychology; Jungian psychology, analytical psychology; Pavlovian psychology; Reichian psychology, orgone theory; Skinnerian psychology; Sullivanian psychology

3 **psychiatry,** psychological medicine; neuropsychiatry; social psychiatry; prophylactic psychiatry

4 **psychosomatic medicine,** psychological medicine, medicopsychology; psychosocial medicine

5 **psychotherapy,** psychotherapeutics, mind cure, cognitive therapy

6 **psychoanalysis, analysis,** the couch, counseling, behavior therapy, behavior modification; psychoanalytic therapy, psychoanalytic method; depth psychology, psychology of depths; group analysis, group psychology, family therapy; play therapy; transactional analysis; psychognosis, psychognosy; dream analysis, interpretation of dreams, dream symbolism; psychological profile; depth interview; hypnotherapy; meditation, transcendental meditation (TM), insight meditation, vipassana, guided meditation, walking meditation, sitting meditation, sitting practice

7 **psychodiagnostics,** psychodiagnosis, psychological evaluation, psychiatric evaluation

8 **psychometrics,** psychometry, psychological measurement; **intelligence testing;** mental test, psychological screening; psychography; psychogram, psychograph, psychological profile; psychometer, IQ meter; lie detector, polygraph, psychogalvanometer, psychogalvanic skin response

9 **psychological test** <see list>, mental test; standardized test; developmental test, achievement test

10 **psychologist;** psychotherapist, **therapist,** psychotherapeutist; clinical psychologist; licensed psychologist, psychological practitioner; child psychologist; **psychiatrist,** alienist, somatist; neuropsychiatrist; psychopathist, psychopathologist; psychotechnologist, industrial psychologist; hypnotherapist; behavior therapist; psychobiologist, psychochemist, psychophysiologist, psychophysicist; psychographer; psychiatric social worker; psychoanalyst, analyst; **shrink**, headshrinker, shrinker; **counselor,** psychological counselor; counseling service

11 **personality tendency,** complexion, humor; somatotype; **introversion,** introvertedness, ingoingness; inner-directedness; **extroversion,** extrovertedness, outgoingness; other-directedness; syntony, ambiversion; schizothymia, schizothymic personality, schizoid personality; cyclothymia, cyclothymic personality, cycloid personality; mesomorphism, mesomorphy; endomorphism, endomorphy; ectomorphism, ectomorphy

12 <personality type> **introvert, extrovert,** syntone, ambivert; schizothyme, schizoid; cyclothymic, cyclothyme, cycloid; choleric, melancholic, sanguine, phlegmatic; endomorph, mesomorph, ectomorph; Type A; Type B

13 **pathological personality,** psychopathological personality, sick personality, psycho

14 **mental disorder,** emotional disorder, neurosis; psychonosema, psychopathyfunctional nervous disorder; reaction; emotional instability; maladjustment, social maladjustment; nervous breakdown, mental breakdown, crack-up; problems in living; brainstorm; insanity, **mental illness**; psychosis; schizophrenia; paranoia; manic-depressive psychosis, bipolar disorder; depression, melancholia; seasonal affective disorder (SAD), postpartum depression; endogenous depression; premenstrual syndrome (PMS); psychoneurosis, neuroticism, neurotic disorder, psychoneurotic disorder; brain disease, nervous disorder; cognitive disorder, eating disorder, sleep disorder, somatoform disorder, dissociative disorder, mood disorder, anxiety disorder, sexual disorder, impulse-control disorder, conversion disorder; battle fatigue

15 **personality disorder,** character disorder, moral insanity, sociopathy, psychopathy; psychopathic personality; sexual pathology, sexual psychopathy; compulsion, fixation, complex; obsessive-compulsive disorder; identity crisis, midlife crisis

16 **neurotic reaction,** neurosis, overreaction, disproportionate reaction, depression, mania

17 **psychological stress, stress;** frustration, external frustration, internal frustration; conflict, ambivalence, ambivalence of impulse; **trauma,** psychological trauma, emotional trauma, traumatism, mental shock, emotional shock, decompensation; rape trauma syndrome; post-traumatic stress disorder; shell shock

18 **psychosomatic symptom;** symptom of emotional disorder, emotional symptom, psychological symptom; thought disturbance, thought disorder, dissociative disorder, delirium, delusion, disorientation, hallucination; speech abnormality

19 **trance,** daze, stupor; catatonic stupor, catalepsy; cataplexy; dream state, reverie, daydreaming; somnambulism, sleepwalking; hypnotic trance; fugue, fugue state; amnesia; meditation; brown study

20 **dissociation,** mental dissociation, emotional dissociation, disconnection, dissociative disorder; dissociation of personality, personality disorganization, personality disintegration; schizoid personality; double personality, dual personality; multiple personality, split personality, alternating personality; schizoidism, schizothymia, schizophrenia; depersonalization; paranoid personality; paranoia

21 **fixation,** libido fixation, libido arrest, arrested development; infantile fixation, pregenital fixation, father fixation, Freudian fixation, mother fixation, parent fixation; regression, retreat to immaturity

22 **complex,** inferiority complex, superiority complex, parent complex, Oedipus complex, mother complex, Electra complex, father complex, Diana complex, persecution complex; castration complex; compulsion complex

23 **defense mechanism,** defense reaction; ego defense, psychotaxis; biological adjustive reactions, psychological adjustive reactions, sociological adjustive reactions; resistance; dissociation; negativism, alienation; escapism, escape mechanism, avoidance mechanism; escape, flight, withdrawal; isolation, emotional insulation; fantasy, fantasizing, escape into fantasy, dreamlike thinking, autistic thinking, dereistic thinking, idealization, wishful thinking, autism, dereism; wish-fulfillment, wish-fulfillment fantasy; sexual fantasy; compensation, overcompensation, decompensation; substitution; sublimation; regression, reversion; projection, identification, blame-shifting; displacement; intellectualization, rationalization

24 **suppression,** repression, inhibition, resistance, restraint, censorship, censor; block, psychological block, blockage, blocking; denial, negation, rejection; reaction formation; rigid control; suppressed desire

25 **catharsis,** purgation, abreaction, motor abreaction, psychocatharsis, emotional release, relief of tension, outlet; release therapy, acting-out, psychodrama; imaging

26 **conditioning,** classical conditioning, Pavlovian conditioning; instrumental conditioning; operant conditioning; psychagogy, reeducation, reorientation; conditioned reflex, conditioned stimulus, conditioned response; reinforcement, positive reinforcement, negative reinforcement; simple reflex, unconditioned reflex, startle reflex, **reflex**; **behavior**; suggestion

27 **adjustment,** adjustive reaction; readjustment, **rehabilitation;** psychosynthesis, integration of personality; fulfillment, self-fulfillment; self-actualization, peak experience; integrated personality, syntonic personality; stress management

28 **psyche,** psychic apparatus, **personality, self,** personhood; **mind,** pneuma, soul; preconscious, foreconscious, coconscious; **subconscious, unconscious,** stream of consciousness, subconscious mind, unconscious mind, submerged mind, subliminal, subliminal self; **libido,** psychic energy, libidinal energy, motive force, vital impulse, ego-libido, object libido; **id,** primitive self, pleasure principle, life instinct, death instinct; **ego,** conscious self; **superego,** ethical self, conscience; ego ideal; ego-id conflict; anima, animus, persona; collective unconscious, racial unconscious; hive mind; psychological me

29 **engram,** memory trace, traumatic trace, traumatic memory; unconscious memory; archetype, archetypal pattern, archetypal image, archetypal, symbol; imago, image, father image; race memory, racial memory; cultural memory; associative memory; **memory**

30 **symbol,** universal symbol, father symbol, mother symbol, phallic symbol, fertility symbol; figure eight; symbolism, symbolization

31 **surrogate,** substitute; father surrogate, father figure, father image; mother surrogate, mother figure, mother image

32 **gestalt,** pattern, figure, configuration, form, sensory pattern; figure-ground

33 **association,** association of ideas, chain of ideas, concatenation, mental linking; controlled association, free association, association by contiguity, association by similarity; association by sound, clang association; stream of consciousness; transference, identification, positive transference, negative transference; synesthesia

34 **cathexis,** cathection, desire concentration; charge, energy charge, cathectic energy; anticathexis, countercathexis, counterinvestment; hypercathexis, overcharge

35 **psychiatric treatment**, psychiatric care; psychosurgery, shock treatment, shock therapy, convulsive therapy, electroconvulsive therapy

VERBS **36** **psychologize,** psychoanalyze, analyze, counsel; abreact; fixate, obsess on; neuroticize

ADJS **37** **psychological; psychiatric,** neuropsychiatric; psychometric; **psychopathic,** psychopathological; psychosomatic, somatopsychic, psychophysical, psychophysiological, psychobiological; psychogenic, psychogenetic, functional; psychodynamic, psychoneurological, psychosexual, psychosocial, psychotechnical; psychotic

38 **psychotherapeutic;** psychiatric, psychoanalytic, psychoanalytical; psychodiagnostic; hypnotherapeutic

39 **neurotic,** psychoneurotic, disturbed, disordered; neurasthenic, psychasthenic; hysteric, hysterical, hypochondriac, phobic; deluded; dissociated; depressed, poopy; stressed; post-traumatic

40 **introverted,** introvert, introversive, subjective, ingoing, inner-directed; withdrawn, isolated; Type B

41 **extroverted,** extrovert, extroversive, outgoing, extrospective; other-directed; Type A

42 **subconscious, unconscious;** subliminal, extramarginal; preconscious, foreconscious, coconscious

43 **psychology branch**

abnormal psychology
academic psychology
ACT psychology
analytic psychology, introspective psychology
animal psychology
applied psychology
association psychology
behavioral psychology, behaviorism
biopsychology
child psychology
clinical psychology
cognitive psychology
comparative psychology
constitutional psychology
criminal psychology
depth psychology
developmental psychology
differential psychology
dynamic psychology, functional psychology
ecological psychology
educational psychology
ego psychology
empirical psychology
existential psychology
experimental psychology
faculty psychology
folk psychology, ethnic psychology
genetic psychology
Gestalt psychology, configurationism
group psychology
haptics

hedonics
holistic psychology
hormic psychology
individual psychology
industrial psychology
introspection psychology
Jungian psychology
mass psychology
medical psychology
morbid psychology
neuropsychology
objective psychology
ontogenetic psychology
parapsychology
phenomenological psychology
phylogenetic psychology
physiological psychology
polygenetic psychology
popular psychology
positive psychology
psychoacoustics
psychoasthenics
psychobiochemistry
psychobiology
psychochemistry
psychodiagnostics
psychodynamics
psychoendocrinology
psychogenetics
psychogeriatrics
psychographics
psychohistory
psycholinguistics
psychological medicine
psychological warfare
psychomathematics
psychometrics, psychometry
psychonomy, psychonomics
psychopathology
psychopharmacology
psychophysics
psychophysiology
psychosociology
psychosomatics
psychotechnics, psychotechnology
psychotherapy, psychotherapeutics
race psychology, racial psychology
rational psychology
reactology
reflexology
reverse psychology
self psychology
social psychology
sports psychology
structural psychology
transpersonal psychology
voluntaristic psychology

44 psychological test

alpha test
apperception test
aptitude test
association test
Babcock-Levy test
Bernreuter personality inventory
beta test
Binet test, Binet-Simon test
Brown personality inventory
Cattell's infant intelligence scale
CAVD test
controlled association test
free association test
frustration test
Gesell's development schedule
Goldstein-Sheerer test
inkblot test
intelligence quotient (IQ)
intelligence test
interest inventory
IQ test
Kent mental test
Minnesota Multiphasic Personality Inventory
Minnesota Preschool Scale
Oseretsky test
personality test
Rogers's process scale
Rorschach test
Rotter incomplete sentences blank
Stanford revision
Stanford scientific aptitude test
Stanford-Binet test
Szondi test
thematic apperception test (TAT)
Wechsler Adult Intelligence Scale
Wechsler-Bellevue intelligence scale
Wechsler Intelligence Scale for Children
word association test

93 FEELING

<emotional states>

NOUNS **1 feeling, emotion,** affect, sentiment, affection, affections, sympathies, beliefs; affective faculty, affectivity; emotional charge, cathexis; feelings, sensitiveness, sensibility, susceptibility, thin skin; bedside manner; emotional life; the logic of the heart; sense, deep sense, profound sense, gut sense, gut sensation; emotional intelligence, emotional quotient; sensation; impression, undercurrent, perception; hunch, intuition, feeling in one's bones, vibes, juju, presentiment; foreboding; reaction, response, gut reaction; instinct; emotional coloring, emotional shade, emotional nuance, tone; drama queen

2 passion, passionateness, strong feeling, powerful emotion; fervor, fervency, fervidness, impassionedness, ardor, ardency, warmth of feeling, warmth, heat, fire, verve, furor, fury, vehemence; heartiness, gusto, relish, savor; spirit, heart, soul; **liveliness**; **zeal**; **excitement**; **ecstasy**

3 heart, soul, spirit, *esprit* <Fr>, breast, bosom, inmost heart, inmost soul, heart of hearts, secret recesses of the heart, inner recesses of the heart, secret places, heart's core, heartstrings, cockles of the heart, bottom of the heart, being, innermost being, core of one's being; viscera, pit of one's stomach, **gut**, guts; bones

4 sensibility, sensitivity, sensitiveness, delicacy, fineness of feeling, tenderness, affectivity, susceptibility, impressionability; natural empathy, mirror neurons

5 sympathy, fellow feeling, sympathetic response, good feeling, responsiveness, relating, warmth, cordiality, **caring,** concern; response, echo, chord, sympathetic chord, vibrations, vibes; **empathy,** identification; involvement, sharing; pathos

6 tenderness, tender feeling, softness, gentleness, delicacy; tenderheartedness, softheartedness, warmheartedness, tender heart, sensitive heart, warm heart, soft place in one's heart, spot in one's heart; warmth, fondness, weakness

7 bad feeling, hard feelings; immediate dislike, disaffinity, personality conflict, bad vibes, bad juju, bad chemistry, bad blood, hostility, scunner, animosity; resentment, bitterness, ill will, intolerance, disappointment; hardheartedness

8 sentimentality, sentiment, sentimentalism, oversentimentality, oversentimentalism, bathos; nostalgia, nostomania; romanticism; sweetness and light, hearts-and-flowers; bleeding heart; mawkishness, cloyingness, maudlinness, namby-pamby, namby-pambyness, namby-pambyism; mushiness, sloppiness; mush, slush, slop, goo, schmaltz; sob story, tearjerker, soap opera

9 **emotionalism,** emotionality, lump in one's throat; emotionalizing, emotionalization; emotiveness, emotivity; visceralness; nonrationalness, unreasoningness; demonstrativeness, making scenes, excitability; theatrics, theatricality, histrionics, dramatics, hamminess, chewing up the scenery; sensationalism, melodrama, melodramatics, blood and thunder; yellow journalism; emotional appeal, human interest, love interest; overemotionalism, hyperthymia, excess of feeling, emotional instability

VERBS **10** **feel,** entertain a feeling, harbor a feeling, cherish a feeling, nurture a feeling; feel deeply, feel in one's viscera, feel in one's bones, feel in one's gut; experience; have a sensation, get an impression, receive an impression, **sense,** perceive; intuit, have a hunch

11 **respond, react,** be moved, be affected, be touched, be inspired, echo, catch the flame, catch the infection, be in tune; respond to, warm up to, take to heart, lay to heart, open one's heart to, be turned on to, nourish in one's bosom, feel in one's breast, cherish at the heart's core, treasure up in the heart; enter into the spirit of, be imbued with the spirit of; care about, feel for, sympathize with, empathize with, identify with, relate to emotionally, dig, be turned on by, be involved, share; color with emotion

12 **have deep feelings,** be all heart, have a tender heart, take to heart, be a person of heart, be a person of sentiment; have a soft place in one's heart, have a soft spot in one's heart; be a prey to one's feelings; love; hate

13 **emotionalize,** emote, give free play to the emotions, make a scene; be theatrical, theatricalize, ham it up, chew up the scenery; sentimentalize, gush, slobber over

14 **affect, touch, move,** stir; melt, soften, melt the heart, choke one up, give one a lump in the throat; penetrate, pierce, go through one, go deep; touch a chord, touch a sympathetic chord, touch one's heart, tug at the heart, tug at the heartstrings, go to one's heart, get under one's skin; come home to; touch to the quick, touch on the raw, flick one on the raw, smart, sting

15 **impress, affect,** strike, hit, smite, rock; make an impression, get to one; make a dent in, make an impact upon, sink in, strike home, come home to, hit the mark; tell, have a strong effect, traumatize, strike hard, impress forcibly

16 **impress upon,** bring home to, make it felt; stamp, stamp on, engrave, engrave on

ADJS **17** **emotional,** affective, emotive, affectional, **feeling,** sentient; soulful, of soul, of heart, of feeling, of sentiment; visceral, gut; glandular; emotiometabolic, emotiomotor, emotiomuscular, emotiovascular; demonstrative, overdemonstrative

18 **fervent,** fervid, **passionate,** impassioned, intense, ardent; hearty, cordial, enthusiastic, exuberant, unrestrained, vigorous; keen, breathless, **excited; lively**; zealous; warm, burning, heated, hot, volcanic, red-hot, fiery, flaming, glowing, ablaze, afire, on fire, boiling over, steaming, steamy; delirious, fevered, feverish, febrile, flushed; wired; intoxicated, drunk; obsessed

19 **emotionalistic,** emotive, overemotional, hysteric, hysterical, sensational, sensationalistic, melodramatic, theatric, theatrical, histrionic, dramatic, overdramatic, hammy, nonrational, unreasoning; hyperthymic

20 **sensitive,** sensible, emotionable, delicate; responsive, sympathetic, receptive; empathetic, caring; susceptible, impressionable; tender, soft, tenderhearted, softhearted, warmhearted

21 **sentimental,** sentimentalized, soft, mawkish, maudlin, cloying; sticky, gooey, schmaltzy, sappy, soppy, oversentimental, oversentimentalized, bathetic; mushy, sloppy, gushing, teary, beery, treacly; tearjerking; namby-pamby, romantic; nostalgic, nostomanic

22 **affecting, touching, moving,** emotive, pathetic; human-interest

23 **affected, moved, touched,** impressed; impressed with, impressed by, penetrated with, seized with, imbued with, devoured by, obsessed, obsessed with, obsessed by; wrought up by; stricken, wracked, racked, torn, agonized, tortured; worked up, all worked up, wired, excited

24 **deep-felt,** deepgoing, from the heart, heartfelt, homefelt; deep, profound; indelible; pervasive, pervading, absorbing; penetrating, penetrant, piercing; **poignant**, keen, sharp, acute

ADVS **25** **feelingly, emotionally,** affectively; affectingly, touchingly, movingly, with feeling, poignantly

26 fervently, fervidly, **passionately,** impassionedly, intensely, ardently, zealously; keenly, breathlessly, excitedly; warmly, heatedly, glowingly; heartily, cordially; enthusiastically, exuberantly, vigorously; kindly, heart and soul, with all one's heart, from the heart, from the bottom of one's heart

27 **sentimentally,** mawkishly, maudlinly, cloyingly; mushily, sloppily, gushingly

94 LACK OF FEELING

<unemotional states>

NOUNS 1 **unfeeling,** unfeelingness, affectlessness, lack of affect, lack of feeling, lack of feeling tone, emotional deadness, emotional numbness, emotional paralysis, anesthesia, **emotionlessness,** unemotionalism, unexcitability; dispassion, dispassionateness, unpassionateness, objectivity; passionlessness, spiritlessness, heartlessness, soullessness; coldness, coolness, frigidity, chill, chilliness, frostiness, iciness; coldheartedness, cold-bloodedness; cold heart, cold blood; cold fish; ice maiden; unresponsiveness, unsympatheticness; lack of touch, lack of contact, autism, self-absorption, withdrawal, catatonia; unimpressionableness, unimpressibility; insusceptibility, unsusceptibility; impassiveness, impassibility, impassivity; straight face, poker face, stone face, deadpan; immovability, untouchability; dullness, obtuseness; **inexcitability**

2 **insensibility,** insensibleness, unconsciousness, unawareness, obliviousness, oblivion; anesthesia, narcosis

3 **callousness, insensitivity,** insensitiveness, philistinism; coarseness, brutalization, hardness, hardenedness, hardheartedness, hardness of heart, hard heart, stonyheartedness, heart of stone, stoniness, marbleheartedness, flintheartedness, flintiness; obduracy, obdurateness, induration, inuredness; imperviousness, thick skin, rhinoceros hide, thick, hard-shell, armor, formidable defenses

4 **apathy, indifference, unconcern,** lack of caring, disinterest; withdrawnness, aloofness, detachment, ataraxy, ataraxia, dispassion; passiveness, passivity, supineness, insouciance, nonchalance; inappetence, lack of appetite; listlessness, spiritlessness, burnout, blah, blahs, heartlessness, plucklessness, spunklessness; lethargy, phlegm, lethargicalness, phlegmaticalness, phlegmaticness, hebetude, dullness, sluggishness, languor, languidness; soporifousness, sopor, coma, comatoseness, torpidness, torpor, torpidity, stupor, stupefaction, narcosis; acedia, sloth; resignation, resignedness, stoicism; numbness, benumbedness; hopelessness

VERBS 5 not be affected by, **remain unmoved**, not turn a hair, not care less; have a thick skin, have a heart of stone; be cold as ice, be a cold fish, be an icicle; not affect, leave one cold, leave one unmoved, unimpress, underwhelm

6 **callous, harden,** case-harden, harden one's heart, ossify, steel, indurate, inure; brutalize

7 **dull,** blunt, desensitize, obtund, hebetate

8 **numb,** benumb, paralyze, deaden, anesthetize, freeze, stun, stupefy, drug, narcotize

ADJS 9 **unfeeling, unemotional,** nonemotional, emotionless, affectless, emotionally dead, emotionally numb, emotionally paralyzed, anesthetized, drugged, narcotized; unpassionate, dispassionate, unimpassioned, objective; passionless, spiritless, heartless, soulless; lukewarm, Laodicean; cold, cool, frigid, frozen, chill, chilly, arctic, frosty, frosted, icy, coldhearted, cold-blooded, cold as charity; unaffectionate, unloving; unresponsive, unresponding, unsympathetic; out of touch, out of contact; in one's shell, in one's armor, behind one's defenses, behind a force field; autistic, self-absorbed, self-centered, egocentric, catatonic; unimpressionable, unimpressible, insusceptible, unsusceptible, unperturbed, imperturbable, undisturbed; impassive, impassible; immovable, untouchable; dull, obtuse, blunt; **inexcitable**

10 **insensible,** unconscious, unaware, **oblivious,** blind to, deaf to, dead to, lost to

11 **unaffected, unmoved, untouched,** dry-eyed, unimpressed, unshaken, unstruck, unstirred, unruffled, unanimated, uninspired

12 **callous,** calloused, insensitive, Philistine; thick-skinned, pachydermatous; hard, hardhearted, hardened, case-hardened, coarsened, brutalized, indurated, stony, stonyhearted, marblehearted, flinthearted, flinty, steely, impervious, inured, armored against, steeled against, proof against, as hard as nails

13 **apathetic, indifferent,** unconcerned, uncaring, disinterested, uninterested; withdrawn, aloof, detached, Olympian, above it all; passive, supine; stoic, stoical; insouciant, nonchalant, blasé, listless, spiritless, burned-out, blah, heartless, pluckless, spunkless; lethargic, phlegmatic, hebetudinous, dull, desensitized, sluggish, torpid, languid, slack, soporific, comatose, stupefied, in a stupor, numb, numbed, benumbed; resigned; hopeless

ADVS 14 **unfeelingly,** unemotionally, emotionlessly; with a straight face, poker face, deadpan; dispassionately, unpassionately; spiritlessly, heartlessly, coldly, coldheartedly, cold-bloodedly, in cold blood; with dry eyes

15 **apathetically,** indifferently, unconcernedly, disinterestedly, uninterestedly, uncaringly, impassively; listlessly, spiritlessly, heartlessly, plucklessly, spunklessly; lethargically, phlegmatically, dully, numbly

95 PLEASURE

<feeling satisfaction>

NOUNS 1 **pleasure, enjoyment;** quiet pleasure, euphoria, well-being, good feeling, comfort zone, contentment, content, ease, comfort; coziness, warmth; gratification, satisfaction, great satisfaction, hearty enjoyment, keen pleasure, keen satisfaction, pleasance; self-gratification, self-indulgence; instant gratification; luxury; relish, zest, gusto, *joie de vivre* <Fr>; sweetness of life; kicks, fun, entertainment, brain candy, amusement; beer and skittles <Brit>; intellectual pleasure, pleasures of the mind; strokes, stroking, ego massage; physical pleasure, creature comforts, bodily pleasure, sense pleasure, sensuous pleasure; sexual pleasure, voluptuousness, sensual pleasure, *volupté* <Fr>, animal pleasure, animal comfort, bodily comfort, fleshly delight, carnal delight, warm fuzzy; forepleasure, titillation, endpleasure, fruition; sensualism

2 **happiness,** felicity, gladness, delight, delectation; joy, joyfulness, joyance; cheer, cheerfulness, exhilaration, exuberance, high spirits, glee, sunshine; gaiety, overjoyfulness, overhappiness; intoxication; rapture, ravishment, bewitchment, enchantment, unalloyed happiness, double rainbow; elation, exaltation; ecstasy, ecstasies, transport; bliss, blissfulness; beatitude, beatification, blessedness; paradise, heaven, seventh heaven, cloud nine; smiley face, happy face; eudaimonia; joy-to-stuff ratio; happy camper

3 **treat,** regalement, regale; feast, banquet revelment, Lucullan feast; feast of the soul, banquet of the soul; round of pleasures, mad round; festivity, fete, fiesta, festive occasion, celebration, party, merrymaking, revel, revelry, jubilation, joyance; carnival, Mardi Gras; afterparty

4 **pleasure-loving**, pleasure principle, hedonism, hedonics; epicureanism, Cyrenaicism, eudaemonism, eudemonism; hedonic treadmill

5 <period of pleasure> **good time**, fun time, happy hour, bread and circuses, *la dolce vita* <Ital>, life of Riley, easy street, bed of roses, Elysium, Elysian fields, land of milk and honey

VERBS 6 **please,** pleasure, give pleasure, afford one pleasure, be to one's liking, sit well with one, meet one's wishes, strike one's fancy, feel good, feel right, strike one right; do one's heart good, warm the cockles of one's heart, tickle pink; suit

7 <nonformal> **hit the spot,** be just the ticket, be just what the doctor ordered, make a hit, go over big, go over with a bang

8 **gratify, satisfy,** sate, satiate; slake, appease, allay, assuage, quench; regale, feed, feast; do one's heart good, warm the cockles of the heart

9 **gladden,** make happy, happify; bless, beatify; cheer

10 **delight,** delectate, tickle, titillate, thrill, enrapture, enthrall, enchant, entrance, fascinate, captivate, bewitch, charm, becharm; enravish, ravish, imparadise; ecstasiate, transport, carry away

11 <nonformal> **give one a kick**, give a bang, give a charge, give a rush, knock out, knock off one's feet, knock one dead, knock one for a loop, knock one's socks off, thrill to death, thrill to pieces, tickle to death, tickle pink, wow, slay, send, freak out; stroke, massage one's ego

12 **be pleased, feel happy,** feel good, sing, purr, smile, laugh, be wreathed in smiles, beam; delight, joy, take great satisfaction; look like the cat that swallowed the canary; brim with joy, burst with joy, walk on air, tread on air, have stars in one's eyes, be in heaven, be in seventh heaven, be in paradise, be on cloud nine; fall into raptures, go into raptures; die with delight, die with pleasure

13 **enjoy,** pleasure in, be pleased with, receive pleasure from, derive pleasure from, take delight in, take pleasure in, get a kick out of, get a bang out of, get a charge out of, get a lift out of, get a rush out of; like, love, adore; delight in, rejoice in, indulge in, luxuriate in, revel in, riot in, bask in, wallow in, swim in; groove on, get high on; feast on; relish, appreciate, roll under the tongue, do justice to, savor, smack the lips; devour, eat up

14 **enjoy oneself,** have a good time, party, live it up, have the time of one's life, have a ball, have a blast; live large

ADJS 15 **pleased, delighted;** glad, gladsome; charmed, intrigued; thrilled; tickled, tickled to death, tickled pink, exhilarated; gratified, satisfied; pleased with, taken with, favorably impressed with, sold on, turned-on; pleased as Punch, pleased as a child with a new toy; euphoric, eupeptic; content, contented, easy, comfortable, cozy, in clover, snug as a bug in a rug; warm-and-fuzzy; well-received

16 **happy, glad,** joyful, joyous, flushed with joy, radiant, beaming, glowing, starry-eyed, sparkling, laughing, smiling, smirking, smirky, chirping, purring, singing, dancing, leaping, capering, cheerful, gay; blissful, blessed; beatified, beatific; thrice happy, happy as a lark, happy as a king, happy as the day is long, happy as a clam at high water, happy as a clam, happy as a pig in shit*, happy as a pig in poo

17 **overjoyed,** overjoyful, overhappy, brimming

with happiness, bursting with happiness, on top of the world; rapturous, raptured, enraptured, enchanted, entranced, enravished, ravished, rapt, possessed; sent, high, freaked-out, in raptures, transported, in a transport of delight, carried away, ravished away, beside oneself, beside oneself with joy, all over oneself; ecstatic, in ecstasies, ecstasiating; rhapsodic, rhapsodical; imparadised, in paradise, in heaven, in seventh heaven, on cloud nine; elated, elate, exalted, jubilant, exultant, flushed; blessed; blissed-out

18 **pleasure-loving,** pleasure-seeking, fun-loving, hedonic, hedonistic; Lucullan; epicurean, Cyrenaic, eudaemonic; carnivalesque; living large

ADVS 19 **happily, gladly,** joyfully, joyously, delightedly, with pleasure, to one's delight; blissfully, blessedly; ecstatically, rhapsodically, rapturously; elatedly, jubilantly, exultantly

20 **for fun,** for kicks, for the hell of it, for the heck of it, for the devil of it

INTERJS 21 **goody,** goody goody, goody gumdrops; whee, **wow,** umm, mmmm, oooo, oo-la-la; oh boy, boy oh boy, boy, man, hot damn, hotdog, hot ziggety, hot diggety, whoopee, wowie zowie, out of sight, outasight, groovy, keen-o, keen-o-peachy, peachy keen, hubba hubba, neato, awesome, awesomesauce, amazeballs, yowzer, ring-a-ding, woot

96 UNPLEASURE

<feeling dissatisfaction>

NOUNS 1 **unpleasure, unpleasantness**, lack of pleasure, joylessness, cheerlessness; unsatisfaction, nonsatisfaction, ungratification, nongratification; grimness; discontent; displeasure, dissatisfaction, discomfort, uncomfortableness, misease, malaise, painfulness; disquiet, inquietude, uneasiness, unease, discomposure, vexation of spirit, anxiety; angst, anguish, dread, nausea, existential woe, existential vacuum; the blahs; dullness, flatness, staleness, tastelessness, savorlessness; boredom, ennui, tedium, tediousness, spleen; emptiness, spiritual void, death of the heart, death of the soul; unhappiness; dislike

2 **annoyance, vexation,** bothersomeness, exasperation, aggravation; nuisance, pest, bother, botheration, public nuisance, trouble, problem, pain, difficulty, hot potato; trial; bed of nails; bore, crashing bore; drag, downer, royal pain; worry, worriment; downside, the bad news; stress, fear, pressure, anxiety, angst; headache; pain in the neck, pain in the ass; harassment, molestation, persecution, dogging, hounding, harrying; devilment, bedevilment; vexatiousness; bogey, bogy

3 **irritation, aggravation,** exacerbation, worsening, salt in the wound, twisting the knife in the wound, embitterment, provocation; fret, gall, chafe; irritant; pea in the shoe

4 **chagrin, distress;** embarrassment, abashment, discomfiture, egg on one's face, disconcertion, disconcertment, discountenance, discomposure, disturbance, confusion; humiliation, shame, shamefacedness, mortification, red face

5 **pain, distress,** grief, stress, stress of life, suffering, passion, dolor; ache, aching; pang, wrench, throes, cramp, spasm, twinge; wound, injury, hurt; sore, sore spot, soreness, tender spot, tenderness, lesion; strain, sprain; cut, stroke; shock, blow, hard blow, nasty blow; malady, illness, disease, plague; bane

6 **wretchedness, despair,** bitterness, infelicity, misery, anguish, agony, woe, woefulness, woesomeness, bale, balefulness; melancholy, melancholia, depression, sadness, disappointment, grief; heartache, aching heart, heavy heart, bleeding heart, broken heart, agony of mind, agony of spirit; suicidal despair, black night of the soul, despondency, gloom and doom, despond, slough of despond; desolation, prostration, crushing; extremity, depth of misery; sloth, acedia, mubblefubbles

7 **torment, torture,** cruciation, excruciation, crucifixion, passion, laceration, clawing, lancination, flaying, excoriation; the rack, the iron maiden, thumbscrews; persecution; martyrdom; purgatory, living death, hell, hell upon earth; holocaust; nightmare, horror; chamber of horrors

8 **affliction,** infliction; **curse, woe,** distress, grievance, sorrow, heart-sink, *tsures* <Yiddish>; trouble, peck of troubles, pack of troubles, sea of troubles; care, burden of care; burden, adversity, oppression, cross, cross to bear, cross to be borne, load, fardel, imposition, encumbrance, weight, albatross around one's neck, millstone around one's neck; thorn, thorn in the side, crown of thorns; white elephant; bitter pill, bitter draft, bitter cup, cup of bitterness; gall, gall and wormwood; Pandora's box

9 **trial, tribulation,** trials and tribulations; ordeal, fiery ordeal, the iron entering the soul, perfect storm

10 **tormentor,** torment; torturer; nuisance, pest, pesterer, pain, pain in the neck, pain in the ass, nag, nudzh, *nudnik* <Yiddish>, public nuisance; tease, teaser; annoyer, harasser, harrier, badgerer, heckler, plaguer, persecutor, sadist; molester, **bully**

11 **sufferer,** victim, prey; wretch, poor devil, object of compassion; martyr

VERBS **12** give no pleasure, give no joy, give no cheer, give no comfort, **disquiet,** discompose, leave unsatisfied; discontent; taste like ashes in the mouth; bore, be tedious, cheese off

13 **annoy,** irk, vex, nettle, provoke, pique, miff, peeve, distemper, ruffle, disturb, discompose, roil, rile, aggravate, make a nuisance of oneself, exasperate, exercise, try one's patience, try the patience of a saint; put one's back up, make one bristle; gripe; give one a pain; get, get one down, get one's goat, get under one's skin, get in one's hair, tread on one's toes; burn up, brown off; torment, molest, bother, pother; harass, harry, drive up the wall, hound, dog, nag, nobble, nudzh, persecute; heckle, pick at, prod at, rub it in, rub one's nose in it, badger, hector, bait, bullyrag, worry, worry at, nip at the heels of, chivy, hardly give one time to breathe, make one's life miserable, keep on at; bug, be on the back of, be at, ride, pester, tease, needle, devil, get after, get on, bedevil, pick on, tweak the nose, pluck the beard, give a bad time to; plague, beset, beleaguer; catch in the crossfire, catch in the middle; catch one off balance, trip one up; stalk

14 **irritate,** aggravate, exacerbate, worsen, rub salt in the wound, twist the knife in the wound, step on one's corns, barb the dart; touch a soft spot, touch a tender spot, touch a raw nerve, touch where it hurts; provoke, gall, chafe, fret, grate, grit, gravel, rasp; get on one's nerves, grate on, set on edge; set one's teeth on edge, go against the grain; rub one the wrong way, rub one's fur the wrong way

15 **chagrin,** embarrass, abash, discomfit, disconcert, discompose, confuse, throw into confusion, throw into a tizzy, throw into a hissy-fit, **upset,** confound, cast down, mortify, put out, put out of face, put out of countenance, put to the blush

16 **distress,** afflict, trouble, burden, give one a tough row to hoe, load with care, bother, disturb, perturb, disquiet, discomfort, agitate, upset, put to it; disappoint; worry, give one gray hair

17 **pain,** grieve, aggrieve, anguish; hurt, wound, bruise, hurt one's feelings; pierce, prick, stab, cut, sting; cut up, cut to the heart, cut to the quick, wound to the quick, hit one where one lives; be a thorn in one's side

18 **torture, torment,** agonize, harrow, savage, rack, scarify, crucify, impale, excruciate, lacerate, claw, rip, bloody, lancinate, macerate, convulse, wring; prolong the agony, kill by inches, make life miserable, make life not worth living; martyr, martyrize; tyrannize, push around; punish

19 **suffer,** hurt, ache, bleed; anguish, suffer anguish; agonize, writhe; go hard with, have a bad time of it, go through hell; quaff the bitter cup, drain the cup of misery to the dregs, be nailed to the cross

ADJS **20** **pleasureless,** joyless, cheerless, depressed, grim; sad, **unhappy**; unsatisfied, unfulfilled, ungratified; bored, cheesed-off; anguished, anxious, suffering angst, suffering dread, suffering nausea, uneasy, unquiet, prey to malaise; repelled, revolted, disgusted, sickened, nauseated, nauseous

21 **annoyed,** irritated, bugged; galled, chafed; bothered, troubled, disturbed, ruffled, roiled, riled; irked, vexed, piqued, nettled, provoked, peeved, miffed, griped, aggravated, exasperated; burnt-up, browned-off, cheesed-off, resentful, angry

22 **distressed,** afflicted, put-upon, beset, beleaguered; caught in the middle, caught in the crossfire; troubled, bothered, disturbed, perturbed, disquieted, discomforted, discomposed, agitated; hung up; uncomfortable, uneasy, ill at ease; chagrined, embarrassed, abashed, discomfited, disconcerted, upset, confused, mortified, put-out, out of countenance, cast down, chapfallen; weirded out

23 **pained,** grieved, aggrieved; wounded, hurt, injured, bruised, mauled; cut, cut to the quick; stung; anguished, aching, bleeding

24 **tormented,** plagued, harassed, harried, dogged, hounded, persecuted, beset; nipped at, worried, chivied, heckled, badgered, hectored, baited, bullyragged, ragged, pestered, teased, needled, deviled, bedeviled, picked on, bugged

25 **tortured,** harrowed, savaged, agonized, convulsed, wrung, racked, crucified, impaled, lacerated, excoriated, clawed, ripped, bloodied, lancinated; on the rack, under the harrow

26 **wretched,** miserable; woeful, woebegone, woesome; crushed, stricken, cut up, heartsick, heart-stricken, heart-struck; deep-troubled; desolate, disconsolate, suicidal

ADVS **27** to one's displeasure, to one's disgust

97 PLEASANTNESS

<feeling good>

NOUNS **1** **pleasantness,** pleasingness, pleasance, **pleasure**, pleasurefulness, pleasurableness, pleasurability, pleasantry, felicitousness, enjoyableness; bliss, blissfulness; sweetness, mellifluousness; mellowness; agreeableness, agreeability, complaisance, rapport, harmoniousness; compatibility; welcomeness; geniality, congeniality, cordiality, affability, amicability, amiability; amenity, graciousness; goodness, goodliness, niceness; **fun**; heaven

2 **delightfulness,** exquisiteness, loveliness; charm, winsomeness, grace, attractiveness, appeal, appealingness, winningness; sexiness; glamour; captivation, enchantment, entrancement, bewitchment, witchery, enravishment; charm offensive; **fascination**; invitingness, temptingness, tantalizingness; voluptuousness, sensuousness; luxury

3 **delectability,** delectableness, deliciousness, lusciousness; tastiness, flavorsomeness, savoriness; juiciness; succulence

4 **cheerfulness;** brightness, sunniness; sunny side, bright side; fair weather

VERBS 5 **make pleasant**, brighten, sweeten, gild, gild the lily; sentimentalize, saccharinize; please, gratify, satisfy; brighten one's day, make one's day

ADJS 6 **pleasant,** pleasing, pleasureful, pleasurable; fair, enjoyable, pleasure-giving; felicitous, felicific; likable, desirable, to one's liking, to one's taste, to one's fancy, after one's fancy, after one's own heart; agreeable, complaisant, harmonious, compatible; blissful; sweet, mellifluous, honeyed, dulcet; mellow; gratifying, satisfying, rewarding, heartwarming, grateful; welcome, welcome as the roses in May; genial, congenial, cordial, affable, amiable, amicable, gracious; good, goodly, nice, fine; cheerful

7 **delightful,** exquisite, lovely; thrilling, titillative; good-natured; charming, attractive, endearing, engaging, appealing, prepossessing, heartwarming, sexy, enchanting, bewitching, witching, entrancing, enthralling, intriguing, fascinating; captivating, irresistible, ravishing, enravishing; winning, winsome, taking, fetching, heart-robbing; inviting, tempting, tantalizing; voluptuous, zaftig, sensuous; luxurious, delicious

8 <nonformal> **fun,** kicky, chewy, dishy, drooly, sexy, toast, yummy

9 **blissful,** beatific, saintly, divine; sublime; heavenly, idyllic, paradisal, paradisiac, paradisiacal, paradisic, paradisical, empyreal, empyrean, Elysian; out of sight, out of this world

10 **delectable, delicious,** luscious; tasty, flavorsome, savory; juicy, succulent

11 **bright, sunny,** fair, mild, balmy; halcyon, Saturnian

ADVS 12 **pleasantly,** pleasingly, pleasurably, fair, enjoyably; blissfully; gratifyingly, satisfyingly; agreeably, genially, affably, cordially, amiably, amicably, graciously, kindly; cheerfully

13 **delightfully,** exquisitely; charmingly, engagingly, appealingly, enchantingly, bewitchingly, entrancingly, intriguingly, fascinatingly; ravishingly, enravishingly; winningly, winsomely; invitingly, temptingly, tantalizingly, voluptuously, sensuously; luxuriously

14 **delectably,** deliciously, lusciously, tastily, succulently, savorously

98 UNPLEASANTNESS

<feeling bad>

NOUNS 1 **unpleasantness,** unpleasingness, displeasingness, displeasure; disagreeableness, disagreeability; abrasiveness, woundingess, hostility, unfriendliness; undesirability, unappealingness, unattractiveness, unengagingness, uninvitingness, unprepossessingness; distastefulness, unsavoriness, unpalatability, nastiness, undelectability; ugliness; discomfort, pain, annoyance

2 **offensiveness,** objectionability, objectionableness, unacceptability; repugnance, contrariety, odiousness, repulsiveness, repellence, repellency, rebarbativeness, disgustingness, nauseousness, grossness, yuckiness, grunginess, scuzziness; loathsomeness, hatefulness, beastliness; vileness, foulness, putridness, putridity, rottenness, noxiousness; nastiness, fulsomeness, noisomeness, obnoxiousness, abominableness, heinousness; contemptibleness, contemptibility, despicability, despicableness, baseness, ignobleness, ignobility; unspeakableness; coarseness, crudeness, rudeness, obscenity

3 **dreadfulness,** horribleness, horridness, atrociousness, atrocity, hideousness, terribleness, awfulness; grimness, direness, banefulness

4 **harshness,** agony, agonizingness, excruciation, excruciatingness, torture, torturesomeness, torturousness, torment, tormentingness; desolation, desolateness; heartbreak, heartsickness

5 **distressfulness,** distress, grievousness, grief; painfulness, pain; harshness, bitterness, sharpness; lamentability, lamentableness, deplorability, deplorableness, pitiableness, pitifulness, pitiability, regrettableness; woe, sadness, sorrowfulness, mournfulness, lamentation, woefulness, woesomeness, woebegoneness, pathos, poignancy; comfortlessness, discomfort, misease; dreariness, cheerlessness, joylessness, dismalness, **depression,** bleakness, black cloud, dark cloud

6 **mortification,** humiliation, embarrassment, egg on one's face; disconcertedness, awkwardness, disappointment

7 **vexatiousness,** irksomeness, annoyance,

annoyingness, aggravation, exasperation, provocation, provokingness, tiresomeness, wearisomeness; troublesomeness, bothersomeness, harassment; worrisomeness, plaguesomeness, peskiness, pestiferousness

8 **harshness,** oppressiveness, burdensomeness, onerousness, weightiness, heaviness

9 **intolerability,** intolerableness, unbearableness, insupportableness, insufferableness, unendurability

VERBS 10 **be unpleasant; displease,** make unpleasant; be disagreeable, be undesirable, be distasteful, be abrasive

11 **offend,** give offense, repel, put off, turn off, revolt, disgust, nauseate, sicken, make one sick, make one sick to one's stomach, make one sick in the stomach, make one vomit, make one puke, make one retch, turn the stomach, gross out; stink in the nostrils; stick in one's throat, stick in one's crop, stick in one's craw, stick in one's gizzard; horrify, appall, shock; make the flesh creep, make the flesh crawl, make one shudder

12 **agonize,** excruciate, torture, torment, desolate

13 **mortify,** humiliate, embarrass, disconcert, disturb, chagrin, shame; bitch-slap*

14 **distress,** dismay, grieve, mourn, lament, sorrow, heart-sink; pain, discomfort, misease; get in one's hair, try one's patience, give one a hard time, give one a pain, give one a pain in the neck, give one a pain in the ass, give one a pain in the butt, disturb, put off

15 **vex,** irk, annoy, aggravate, exasperate, provoke, run afoul; trouble, worry, give one gray hair, plague, harass, bother, hassle; disappoint

16 **oppress,** burden, weigh upon, weight down, wear one down, be heavy on one, be the bane of one's existence, crush one; tire, exhaust, weary, wear out, wear upon one; prey on the mind, prey on, prey upon; haunt, haunt the memory, obsess; stalk

ADJS 17 **unpleasant,** unpleasing, unenjoyable; displeasing, disagreeable; unlikable, dislikable; abrasive, wounding, hostile, unfriendly; undesirable, unattractive, unappealing, unengaging, uninviting, unalluring; tacky, low-rent, low ride; unwelcome, thankless; distasteful, untasteful, unpalatable, unsavory, unappetizing, undelicious, undelectable; ugly; sour, bitter

18 **offensive,** objectionable, objectional, odious, repulsive, repellent, rebarbative, repugnant, revolting, forbidding; disgusting, sickening, loathsome, gross, yucky, grungy, scuzzy, beastly, vile, foul, nasty, nauseating; grody; fulsome, mephitic, miasmal, miasmic, malodorous, stinking, fetid, noisome, noxious; coarse, crude, rude, obscene; obnoxious, abhorrent, hateful, abominable, heinous, contemptible, despicable, detestable, execrable, beneath contempt, below contempt, base, ignoble, uncouth

19 **horrid,** horrible, horrific, horrifying, horrendous, unspeakable, beyond words; dreadful, atrocious, terrible, rotten, awful, beastly, hideous; tragic; dire, grim, baneful; appalling, shocking, disgusting

20 **distressing,** distressful, dismaying; from hell; afflicting, afflictive; painful, sore, harsh, bitter, sharp; grievous, dolorous, dolorific, dolorogenic; lamentable, deplorable, regrettable, pitiable, piteous, rueful, woeful, woesome, woebegone, sad, sorrowful, wretched, mournful, depressing, depressive, disappointing; pathetic, affecting, touching, moving, saddening, poignant; comfortless, discomforting, uncomfortable; desolate, dreary, cheerless, joyless, dismal, bleak; weaksauce

21 **mortifying,** humiliating, **embarrassing,** crushing, disconcerting, awkward, disturbing; toe-curling

22 **annoying, irritating,** galling, provoking, aggravating, exasperating; vexatious, vexing, irking, irksome, baneful, tiresome, wearisome; troublesome, bothersome, worrisome, bothering, troubling, disturbing, plaguing, plaguesome, plaguey, pestilent, pestilential, pesky, pesty, pestiferous; tormenting, harassing, worrying; pestering, teasing; importunate, importune; distasteful

23 **agonizing,** excruciating, harrowing, racking, rending, desolating, consuming; tormenting, torturous; heartbreaking, heartrending, heartsickening, heartwounding

24 **oppressive,** burdensome, crushing, trying, onerous, heavy, weighty; harsh, wearing, wearying, exhausting; overburdensome, tyrannous, grinding

25 **insufferable,** intolerable, insupportable, unendurable, unbearable, past bearing, not to be borne, not to be endured, for the birds, too much, a bit much, more than flesh and blood can bear, enough to drive one mad, enough to provoke a saint, enough to make a preacher swear, enough to try the patience of Job

ADVS 26 **unpleasantly,** distastefully unpleasingly; displeasingly, offensively, objectionably, odiously, repulsively, repellently, rebarbatively, repugnantly, revoltingly, disgustingly, sickeningly, loathsomely, vilely, foully, nastily, fulsomely, mephitically, malodorously, fetidly, noisomely, noxiously, obnoxiously, abhorrently, hatefully, abominably, contemptibly, despicably, detestably, execrably, nauseatingly

27 **horridly, horribly,** dreadfully, terribly, hideously; tragically; grimly, direly, banefully; appallingly, shockingly
28 **distressingly,** distressfully; painfully, sorely, grievously, lamentably, deplorably, pitiably, ruefully, woefully, woesomely, sadly, pathetically; agonizingly, excruciatingly, harrowingly, heartbreakingly
29 **annoyingly,** irritatingly, aggravatingly, provokingly, exasperatingly; vexatiously, irksomely, tiresomely, wearisomely; troublesomely, bothersomely, worrisomely, regrettably
30 **insufferably,** intolerably, unbearably, unendurably, insupportably
INTERJS 31 yuck, eeyuck, yuk, yeeuck, yeck, blech, phew, ugh; *feh* <Yiddish>; alas, alack, bah, tsk tsk

99 DISLIKE
<feeling aversion>

NOUNS 1 **dislike, distaste,** disrelish, scunner; disaffection, disfavor, disinclination; disaffinity; displeasure, disapproval, disapprobation; instant dislike; rejection
2 **hostility,** antagonism, **enmity**; **hatred, hate**; aversion, repugnance, repulsion, antipathy, allergy, grudge, abomination, abhorrence, horror, mortal horror; disgust, loathing; nausea; shuddering, cold sweat, creeping flesh
VERBS 3 **dislike,** mislike, disfavor, not like, have no liking for, be no love lost between, have no use for, not care for, have no time for, have a disaffinity for, have an aversion to, want nothing to do with, not think much of, take a dislike to, take a scunner to, not be able to bear, not be able to endure, not be able to abide, not give the time of day to, disapprove of; disrelish, have no taste for, not stomach, not have the stomach for, not be one's cup of tea; be hostile to, have it in for; hate, abhor, detest, loathe
4 **feel disgust,** be nauseated, sicken at, choke on, have a bellyful of; gag, retch, keck, heave, vomit, puke, chunder, hurl, upchuck, barf
5 **shudder at,** have one's flesh crawl at the thought of; shrink from, recoil, revolt at; grimace, make a face, make a wry face, turn up one's nose, look down one's nose, look askance, raise one's eyebrows, take a dim view of, show distaste for, disapprove of
6 **repel, disgust**, gross out; leave a bad taste in one's mouth, rub the wrong way, antagonize
ADJS 7 **unlikable,** distasteful, mislikable, dislikable, uncongenial, displeasing, unpleasant; not to one's taste, not one's sort, not one's cup of tea, counter to one's preferences, offering no delight, against the grain, uninviting; yucky, unlovable; abhorrent, odious; intolerable
8 **averse,** allergic, loath, reluctant, undelighted, out of sympathy, disaffected, disenchanted, disinclined, displeased, put off, not charmed, less than pleased; disapproving, censorious, judgmental, po-faced; unamiable, unfriendly, hostile; death on, down on
9 **disliked,** uncared-for, unvalued, unprized, misprized, undervalued; despised, detested, lowly, spat-upon, untouchable; unpopular, out of favor, gone begging; unappreciated, misunderstood; unsung, thankless; unwept, unlamented, unmourned, undeplored, unmissed, unregretted
10 **unloved,** unbeloved, uncherished, loveless; lovelorn, forsaken, rejected, jilted, thrown over, spurned, crossed in love
11 **unwanted,** unwished, undesired; unwelcome, undesirous, unasked, unbidden, uninvited, uncalled-for, unasked-for

100 DESIRE
<feeling attraction>

NOUNS 1 **desire, wish,** wanting, grasping, **want, need,** desideration; hope; fancy; will, mind, pleasure, will and pleasure; heart's desire; urge, drive, libido, pleasure principle; concupiscence; horme; wish fulfillment, fantasy; passion, ardor, sexual desire; curiosity, intellectual curiosity, thirst for knowledge, lust for learning; **eagerness**
2 **liking, love, fondness;** infatuation, crush; affection; relish, taste, gusto, gust; passion, weakness
3 **inclination, penchant,** partiality, fancy, favor, predilection, preference, propensity, proclivity, leaning, bent, turn, tilt, bias, affinity, tendency; mutual affinity, mutual attraction; sympathy, fascination
4 **wistfulness,** wishfulness, yearnfulness, **nostalgia;** wishful thinking; sheep's eyes, longing eye, wistful eye; daydream, daydreaming
5 **yearning, yen**; longing, desiderium, hankering, pining, honing, aching; languishment, languishing; nostalgia, homesickness; nostomania
6 **craving, coveting**, lust; hunger, thirst, appetite, appetition, appetency, appetence; aching void, hungry ghost; itch, itching, prurience, pruriency; lech, sexual desire; *cacoëthes* <L>, **mania**
7 **appetite,** stomach, relish, taste; **hunger,** hungriness; the munchies, peckishness; tapeworm, eyes bigger than one's stomach, wolf in one's stomach, canine appetite; empty stomach, emptiness, hollow hunger; **thirst,**

thirstiness, drought, dryness; polydipsia; torment of Tantalus; sweet tooth

8 **greed,** greediness, graspingness, avarice, cupidity, avidity, voracity, rapacity, lust, avariciousness; moneygrubbing; avidness, esurience, wolfishness; voraciousness, ravenousness, rapaciousness, sordidness, covetousness, acquisitiveness; itching palm; grasping; piggishness, hoggishness, swinishness; **gluttony**; inordinate desire, furor, craze, fury of desire, frenzy of desire, overgreediness; insatiable desire, insatiability; incontinence, intemperateness

9 **aspiration,** reaching high, upward looking; high goal, high aim, high purpose, dream, ideals, hope; **idealism**

10 **ambition,** ambitiousness, vaulting ambition; aim, target; climbing, status seeking, social climbing, careerism; opportunism; power-hunger; noble ambition, lofty ambition, magnanimity; American dream

11 <object of desire> **desire,** heart's desire, desideration, *desideratum* <L>; wish; **hope;** catch, quarry, prey, game, plum, prize, trophy, brass ring; status symbol; collectable, collectible; forbidden fruit, ideal, weakness, temptation; lodestone, magnet; golden vision, mecca, glimmering goal; land of heart's desire; something to be desired; dearest wish, ambition, the height of one's ambition; a sight for sore eyes, a welcome sight; the light at the end of the tunnel

12 **desirer,** wisher, wanter, hankerer, yearner, coveter; fancier, collector; moneygrubber; addict, freak, glutton, greedy pig, devotee, votary; aspirant, aspirer, solicitant, wannabee, wannabe, hopeful, would-be, candidate; lover, love interest, swain, suitor, toyboy, squeeze

13 **desirability; agreeability,** acceptability, unobjectionableness; attractiveness, attraction, magnetism, appeal, seductiveness, provocativeness, pleasingness; likability, lovability

VERBS 14 **desire,** desiderate, be desirous of, **wish,** lust after, bay after, kill for, give one's right arm for, die for, want, have a mind to, choose; would fain do, would fain have, would be glad of; like, have a taste for, acquire a taste for, fancy, take to, take a fancy to, take a shine to, have a fancy for; have an eye to, have one's eye on; lean toward, tilt toward, have a penchant for, have a weakness in one's heart for, have a soft spot in one's heart for; aim at, set one's cap for, have designs on; wish very much, wish to goodness; **love**; lust; prefer, favor

15 **want to,** wish to, like to, love to, dearly love to, choose to; itch to, burn to; ache to, long to

16 **wish for,** hope for, yearn for, yen for, have a yen for, itch for, lust for, pant for, long for, pine for, hone for, ache for, be hurting for, weary for, languish for, be dying for, thirst for, sigh for; cry for, clamor for; spoil for

17 **have one's heart set on,** want with all one's heart, want in the worst way; set one's heart on, give one's kingdom in hell for, give one's eyeteeth for

18 **crave, covet,** hunger after, thirst after, crave after, lust after, have a lech for, pant after, run mad after, hanker for, hanker after; crawl after; aspire after, be consumed with desire; have an itchy palm, have an itching palm, have sticky fingers

19 **hunger,** hunger for, feel hungry, be peckish; starve, be ravenous, raven; have a good appetite, be a good trencherman, have a tapeworm, have a wolf in one's stomach; eye hungrily, lick one's chops; **thirst,** thirst for; lick one's lips

20 **aspire, be ambitious;** aspire to, try to reach; aim high, keep one's eyes on the stars, raise one's sights, set one's sights, reach for the sky, dream of, hitch one's wagon to a star

ADJS 21 **desirous,** desiring, desireful, lickerish, wanting, wishing, needing, hoping; aspirational; dying to; tempted; appetitive, desiderative, optative, libidinous, libidinal; orectic; hormic; eager; lascivious, lustful

22 **desirous of,** keen on, set on, bent on; fond of, with a liking for, partial to; fain of, fain to; inclined toward, leaning toward; itching for, itching to, aching for, aching to, dying for, dying to; spoiling for; mad on, mad for, wild to, wild for, crazy to, crazy for

23 **wistful,** wishful; longing, yearning, yearnful, hankering, languishing, pining, honing; nostalgic, homesick

24 **craving,** coveting; hungering, hungry, thirsting, thirsty, athirst; itching, prurient; fervid; devoured by desire, in a frenzy of desire, fury of desire, mad with lust, consumed with desire

25 **hungry,** hungering, peckish; empty, unfilled; ravening, ravenous, voracious, sharp-set, wolfish, dog-hungry, hungry as a bear; hangry; starved, famished, starving, famishing, perishing with hunger, pinched with hunger; fasting, off food, unfed; keeping Lent, Lenten; underfed; half-starved, half-famished

26 **thirsty,** thirsting, athirst; dry, parched, droughty

27 **greedy,** avaricious, avid, voracious, rapacious, cupidinous, esurient, ravening, grasping, grabby, graspy, acquisitive, mercenary, sordid, overgreedy; ravenous, gobbling, devouring; miserly, money-hungry, moneygrubbing, money-mad, venal; covetous, coveting; piggish, hoggish, swinish, a hog for, greedy as a hog; **gluttonous**; omnivorous, all-devouring; insatiable, insatiate,

unsatisfied, unsated, unappeased, unappeasable, limitless, bottomless, unquenchable, quenchless, unslaked, unslakeable, slakeless; big-eyed; hangry

28 **aspiring, ambitious,** sky-aspiring, upward-looking, high-reaching; high-flying, social-climbing, careerist, careeristic, fast-track, fast-lane, on the make; power-hungry; would-be, wannabe

29 **desired, wanted,** coveted; wished-for, hoped-for, longed-for; sought-after, in demand, popular

30 **desirable,** sought-after, much sought-after, to be desired, to die for, much to be desired; enviable, worth having; likable, pleasing, after one's own heart; hot-selling; agreeable, acceptable, unobjectionable, cromulent; palatable; attractive, taking, winning, sexy, dishy, seductive, provocative, tantalizing, exciting; appetizing, tempting, toothsome, mouth-watering; lovable, adorable; buzzworthy

ADVS 31 **desirously,** wistfully, wishfully, longingly, yearningly, piningly, languishingly; cravingly, itchingly; hungrily, thirstily; aspiringly, ambitiously

32 **greedily,** avariciously, avidly, ravenously, raveningly, voraciously, rapaciously, covetously, graspingly, devouringly; wolfishly, piggishly, hoggishly, swinishly

101 EAGERNESS

<feeling interest>

NOUNS 1 **eagerness, enthusiasm,** avidity, avidness, keenness, forwardness, prothymia, readiness, promptness, quickness, alacrity, cheerful readiness, *empressement* <Fr>; keen desire, appetite; anxiousness, anxiety; zest, zestfulness, gusto, verve, liveliness, life, vitality, vivacity, élan, spirit, animation; impatience, breathless impatience; keen interest, fascination; craze

2 **zeal, ardor,** ardency, fervor, fervency, fervidness, spirit, warmth, fire, heat, heatedness, passion, passionateness, impassionedness, heartiness, intensity, abandon, vehemence; intentness, resolution; devotion, devoutness, devotedness, dedication, commitment, committedness; earnestness, seriousness, sincerity; loyalty, faithfulness, faith, fidelity; discipleship, followership

3 **overzealousness,** overeagerness, overanxiousness, overanxiety; unchecked enthusiasm, overenthusiasm, infatuation; overambitiousness; frenzy, fury; zealotry, zealotism; boosterism; mania, **fanaticism**

4 **enthusiast, zealot,** infatuate, energumen, rhapsodist; addict; faddist; pursuer; hobbyist, collector; fanatic, trainspotter; stalker; visionary; devotee, votary, aficionada, aficionado, fancier, admirer, follower; disciple, worshiper, idolizer, idolater; amateur, dilettante

5 <nonformal> **fan, buff, freak,** hound, fiend, demon, nut, bug, head, junkie, groupie, rooter, booster, great one for, sucker for; fan club, fanzine; eager beaver, -aholic

VERBS 6 **jump at,** catch, grab, grab at, go for, snatch, snatch at, fall all over oneself, get excited about, go at hammer and tongs, go at tooth and nail, go hog wild; go to great lengths, bend over backwards, fall over backwards; **desire**

7 **be enthusiastic,** rave, enthuse, be big for; get stars in one's eyes, rhapsodize, carry on over, rave on, make much of, make a fuss over, make an ado, make much ado about, make a to-do over, take on over, be over, be about, go on over, go on about, rave about, whoop it up about; go nuts, go gaga, go ape over; gush, gush over; effervesce, bubble over

ADJS 8 **eager, anxious,** agog, all agog; avid, keen, forward, prompt, quick, ready, ready and willing, alacritous, bursting to, dying to, raring to, gung ho; zestful, lively, full of life, vital, vivacious, vivid, spirited, animated; impatient; breathless, panting, champing at the bit; desirous

9 **zealous, ardent,** fervent, fervid, perfervid, spirited, intense, hearty, vehement, abandoned, passionate, impassioned, warm, heated, hot, hot-blooded, red-hot, fiery, white-hot, flaming, burning, afire, aflame, on fire, like a house afire; devout, devoted; dedicated, committed; earnest, sincere, serious, in earnest; loyal, faithful; intent, intent on, resolute

10 **enthusiastic,** enthused, big, **gung ho,** glowing, full of enthusiasm; enthusiastic about, infatuated with

11 <nonformal> **wild about,** crazy about, mad about, ape about, ape over, gone on, all in a dither over, gaga over, starry-eyed over, all hopped up about, hepped up over, hot about, hot for, hot on, steamed up about, turned-on, switched-on; hipped on, cracked on, bugs on, freaked-out, nuts on, nuts over, nuts about, keen on, keen about

12 **overzealous,** ultrazealous, overeager, over-anxious; overambitious; overdesirous; overenthusiastic, infatuated; feverish, perfervid, febrile, at fever pitch, at fevered pitch; hectic, frenetic, furious, frenzied, frumious, frantic, wild, hysteric, hysterical, delirious; insane; **fanatical**

ADVS 13 **eagerly,** anxiously; impatiently, breathlessly; avidly, promptly, quickly, keenly, readily; zestfully, vivaciously, animatedly; enthusiastically, with enthusiasm; with alacrity, with zest, with gusto, with relish, with open arms, avidiously

14 **zealously,** ardently, fervently, fervidly, perfervidly, heatedly, heartily, vehemently, passionately, impassionedly; intently, intensely; devoutly, devotedly; earnestly, sincerely, seriously

102 INDIFFERENCE

<feeling disinterest>

NOUNS 1 **indifference,** indifferentness; indifferentism; halfheartedness, zeallessness, perfunctoriness, fervorlessness; coolness, coldness, chilliness, chill, iciness, frostiness, stoicism; tepidness, lukewarmness, Laodiceanism; **neutrality,** neutralness; insipidity, vapidity; adiaphorism

2 **unconcern, disinterest,** detachment; disregard, dispassion, insouciance, carelessness, regardlessness; easygoingness; heedlessness, mindlessness, inattention; unmindfulness, incuriosity; insensitivity; disregardfulness, recklessness, negligence; unsolicitousness, unanxiousness; pococurantism; nonchalance, inexcitability, ataraxy, ataraxia, samadhi; indiscrimination, casualness; listlessness, lackadaisicalness, lack of feeling, lack of affect, **apathy**; sloth, acedia, phlegm, lethargy

3 **undesirousness,** desirelessness; nirvana; lovelessness, passionlessness; uneagerness, unambitiousness; lack of appetite, inappetence

VERBS 4 **not care, not mind,** not give a damn, not care a damn, not give a hoot, not give a shit*, not give a crap, not care less, not give two hoots, care nothing for, care nothing about, not care a straw about; shrug off, dismiss; take no interest in, have no desire for, not think twice about, have no taste for, have no relish for; hold no brief for; be halfhearted, temper one's zeal; lose interest

5 **not matter to,** be all one to, take it or leave it; make no difference, make no never-mind; sit on the fence, remain neutral

ADJS 6 **indifferent,** halfhearted, zealless, perfunctory, fervorless; cool, cold; tepid, lukewarm, Laodicean; neither hot nor cold, neither one thing nor the other; unmoved; blah, neuter, **neutral**

7 **unconcerned,** uninterested, **disinterested,** turned-off, dispassionate, insouciant, careless, regardless; easygoing; incurious; mindless, unmindful, heedless, inattentive, disregardful; devil-may-care, reckless, negligent; unsolicitous, unanxious; pococurante, nonchalant, inexcitable; ataractic; blasé, undiscriminating, casual; listless, lackadaisical, sluggish; bovine; numb, **apathetic**

8 **undesirous,** unattracted, desireless; loveless, passionless; inappetent; nirvanic; unenthusiastic, uneager; unambitious, unaspiring

ADVS 9 **indifferently,** with indifference, with utter indifference; coolly, coldly; lukewarmly, halfheartedly; perfunctorily; for all one cares

10 **unconcernedly,** uninterestedly, disinterestedly, dispassionately, insouciantly, carelessly, regardlessly; mindlessly; unmindfully, heedlessly, recklessly, negligently; nonchalantly; listlessly, lackadaisically; numbly, **apathetically**

PHRS 11 **who cares?,** I don't care, I couldn't care less; who gives a crap?; it's a matter of sublime indifference; never mind, what does it matter?, what's the difference?, what's the diff?, what are the odds?, what of it?, so what?, what the hell, it's all the same to me, it's no skin off one's nose; like it or lump it; forget it

12 **I should worry?,** I should fret?, that's your lookout, that's your problem, I feel for you but I can't reach you; that's your pigeon, that's your tough luck, tough titty*, tough shit*

103 HATE

<feeling extreme dislike>

NOUNS 1 **hate, hatred; dislike**; detestation, abhorrence, aversion, antipathy, repugnance, loathing, execration, abomination, odium; spite, spitefulness, despite, despitefulness, malice, malevolence, malignity; vials of hate, vials of wrath; rancor, venom; misanthropy, misanthropism; misandry, misogyny; misogamy; misopedia; anti-Semitism; race hatred, racism, racialism; bigotry; phobia, xenophobia; grudge; scorn, despising, **contempt**; hate crime

2 **enmity**; bitterness, **animosity**; hatefulness

3 **<hated thing>** anathema, abomination, detestation, aversion, abhorrence, antipathy, execration, hate; peeve, pet peeve; phobia; bugbear, bête noire, bane, bitter pill; fear; dislike

4 **hater**, man-hater, woman-hater, misanthropist, misanthrope, misogynist, anti-Semite, racist, racialist, white supremacist, bigot, redneck; phobic, Anglophobe, xenophobe; detester, loather

VERBS 5 **hate,** detest, loathe, abhor, execrate, abominate, hold in abomination, take an aversion to, shudder at, utterly detest, be death on, not stand, not stand the sight of, not stomach; scorn, spit on, **despise**; hate someone's guts

6 **dislike,** have it in for, feel aversion for, disrelish

ADJS 7 **hating,** abhorrent, loathing, despising, venomous, death on; averse to; disgusted; scornful, contemptuous; antagonistic; execrative

8 **hateful,** loathesome, accursed, aversive, odious, detestable; despiteful; unlikable; contemptible

COMBINING FORMS **9** mis-, miso-; -phobia, -phobiac, -phobe

104 LOVE

<feeling great affection>

NOUNS **1** **love, affection,** attachment, devotion, fondness, sentiment, warm feeling, soft spot in one's heart, weakness, like, liking, fancy, shine, amore <Ital>; partiality, predilection; intimacy; passion, tender feeling, tender passion, ardor, ardency, fervor, heart, flame, the real thing; physical love, Amor, Eros, bodily love, libido, sexual love, sex; desire, yearning; lasciviousness; charity, *caritas* <L>, brotherly love, Christian love, agape, loving concern, fellow feeling, caring; sentimental attachment; spiritual love, Platonic love; amour-propre; adoration, worship, hero worship; regard, admiration; idolization, idolism, idolatry, cult following; popular regard, popularity; faithful love, truelove; married love, conjugal love, uxoriousness; free love, free-lovism; lovemaking; self-love, narcissism, autophilia, egotism; patriotism, love of one's country; love-hate relationship

2 **amorousness,** amativeness, lovingness, meltingness, **affection,** affectionateness, demonstrativeness; mating instinct, reproductive drive, procreative drive, libido; carnality, sexiness, goatishness, hot pants, horniness; romantic love, romanticism, sentimentality, susceptibility; lovesickness, lovelornness; ecstasy, rapture; enchantment

3 **infatuation,** infatuatedness, passing fancy; crush, mash, pash, case; puppy love, young love, calf love; love at first sight, *coup de foudre* <Fr>; falling in love

4 **parental love, natural affection,** mother love, maternal love, father love, paternal love; filial love; parental instinct; unconditional love

5 **love affair,** affair, affair of the heart, amour, romance, *affaire d'amour* <Fr>, romantic tie, romantic bond, something between, thing, relationship, liaison, entanglement, involvement, intrigue, tryst; dalliance, amorous play, the love game, flirtation, hanky-panky, lollygagging; love triangle, triangle, eternal triangle; illicit love, unlawful love, forbidden love, unsanctified love, adulterous affair, adultery, unfaithfulness, infidelity, cuckoldry; hookup; friends with benefits; courtship, courting, wooing, pursuit, dating, dallying, betrothal, engagement, going together, going out with, going steady; speed-dating

6 **loveableness,** likeableness, lovability, likability, adoreableness, adorability, sweetness, loveliness, lovesomeness; cuddliness, cuddlesomeness; amiability, attractiveness, desirability, agreeability; charm, appeal, allurement; winsomeness, winning ways

7 Love, Cupid, Amor, Eros, Kama; Venus, Aphrodite, Astarte, Freya

8 <symbols> **cupid,** cupidon, amor, amourette, amoretto; love knot

9 **sweetheart,** loved one, love, beloved, darling, dear, dear one, dearly beloved, well-beloved, truelove, beloved object, object of one's affections, light of one's eye, light of one's life, light of love; sex object, prey, quarry, game; valentine; childhood sweetheart, college sweetheart

10 <nonformal> **sweetie, honey,** honeybunch, honey-bunny, honey bun, honeypie, hon, main squeeze, sweetie-pie, sweet patootie, tootsie, tootsie-pie, tootsy-wootsy, dearie, baby, dreamboat, heartthrob, poopsy, poopsy-woopsy, sugar, sugar-bun, sweets, cookie

11 **lover, admirer,** adorer, amorist; infatuate, paramour, suitor, wooer, pursuer, follower; flirt, coquette; vampire, vamp; conquest, catch; devotee; escort, companion, date, steady; significant other, soul mate, *bashert* <Yiddish>; squeeze; old flame, new flame; love interest; other woman

12 **beau,** inamorato, swain, suitor, escort, man, gallant, cavalier, squire, esquire, *caballero* <Sp>; *amoroso, cavaliere servente* <Ital>; sugar daddy; gigolo; **boyfriend**, fellow, young man, flame; old man; babe magnet; loverboy; seducer, lady-killer, ladies' man, sheik, philanderer, cocksman; Prince Charming, Lothario, Romeo; Casanova, Don Juan; boy toy; plus-one

13 **girlfriend, ladylove,** inamorata, *amorosa* <Ital>, lady, mistress, ladyfriend; lass, lassie, jo, gill, jill, Dulcinea; plus-one

14 <nonformal> **doll,** angel, baby, baby-doll, doll-baby, buttercup, ducks, ducky, pet, snookums, snooky, girl, sweetheart, best girl, dream girl

15 **favorite,** preference; darling, idol, jewel, apple of one's eye, fair-haired boy, man after one's own heart; pet, fondling, cosset, minion; spoiled child, lapdog; teacher's pet; matinee idol; tin god, little tin god

16 **fiancé, fiancée,** bride-to-be, husband-to-be, affianced, betrothed, future, intended, Mr. Right, Ms. Right

17 **loving couple,** soul mates, lovebirds, turtledoves, meaningful relationship, bill-and-cooers; newlyweds, honeymooners; star-crossed lovers; Romeo and Juliet, Anthony and Cleopatra, Tristan and Isolde, Abélard and Héloïse, Darby and Joan; item, bromance

VERBS 18 **love,** be fond of, be in love with, care for, like, fancy, have a fancy for, take an interest in, dote on, dote upon, be desperately in love, burn with love; be partial to, have a soft spot in one's heart for, have a weakness for, have a fondness for; court, woo, romance

19 <nonformal> **go for,** have an eye for, have eyes for, only have eyes for, be sweet on, have a crush on; have it bad, carry a torch for, have designs on

20 **cherish, hold dear,** hold in one's heart, hold in one's affections, think much of, think the world of, prize, treasure; admire, regard, esteem, revere; adore, idolize, worship, dearly love, think worlds of, love to distraction

21 **fall in love,** lose one's heart, become enamored, be smitten; take to, take a liking to, take a fancy to, take a shine to, fall for, become attached to, bestow one's affections on; fall head and ears in love, fall head over heels in love, be swept off one's feet; cotton to

22 **enamor**, endear; win one's heart, win the love of, win the affections of, take the fancy of, make a hit with; charm, becharm, infatuate, hold in thrall, command one's affection, fascinate, attract, allure, grow on, grow on one, strike one's fancy, tickle one's fancy, captivate, bewitch, enrapture, carry away, sweep off one's feet, turn one's head, inflame with love; seduce, vamp, draw on, tempt, tantalize

ADJS 23 **beloved, loved,** dear, darling, precious; pet, favorite; adored, admired, esteemed, revered; cherished, prized, treasured, held dear; well-liked, popular; well-beloved, dearly beloved, dear to one's heart, after one's heart, after one's own heart, dear as the apple of one's eye

24 **endearing, lovable,** likable, adorable, admirable, lovely, lovesome, sweet, winning, winsome; charming; angelic, seraphic; caressable, kissable; cuddlesome, cuddly

25 **amorous,** amatory, amative, erotic; **sexual**; loverly, loverlike; passionate, ardent, impassioned; desirous; lascivious

26 **loving,** lovesome, fond, adoring, devoted, affectionate, demonstrative, **romantic,** sentimental, tender, soft, melting; lovelorn, lovesick, languishing; wifely, husbandly, conjugal, uxorious, faithful; parental, paternal, maternal, filial; charitable, caritative; self-loving, narcissistic

27 **enamored,** charmed, becharmed, fascinated, captivated, bewitched, enraptured, enchanted; infatuated, infatuate; smitten, heartsmitten, heartstruck, lovestruck, besotted with

28 **in love,** head over heels in love, over head and ears in love

29 **fond of,** enamored of, partial to, **in love with,** attached to, wedded to, devoted to, wrapped up in; taken with, smitten with, struck with

30 <nonformal> **crazy about,** mad about, nuts about, nutty about, wild about, swacked on, sweet on, stuck on, gone on

ADVS 31 **lovingly,** fondly, affectionately, tenderly, dearly, adoringly, devotedly; amorously, ardently, passionately; with love, with affection, with all one's love

COMBINING FORMS 32 phil-, philo-, -phily; -phile; -philic, -philous

105 EXCITEMENT

<feeling eager interest>

NOUNS 1 **excitement,** emotion, excitedness, arousal, stimulation, exhilaration; a high, manic state, manic condition, heart-stopper

2 **thrill, sensation,** titillation; tingle, tingling; quiver, shiver, shudder, tremor, tremor of excitement, rush; flush, rush of emotion, surge of emotion

3 <nonformal> **kick, charge,** electricity, hullabaloo, boot, bang, belt, blast, flash, hit, jolt, large charge, rush, upper, lift; jollies

4 **agitation,** perturbation, ferment, turbulence, turmoil, tumult, embroilment, uproar, commotion, disturbance, ado, *brouhaha* <Fr>, to-do; pell-mell, flurry, ruffle, bustle, stir, swirl, swirling, whirl, vortex, eddy, hurry, hurry-scurry, hurly-burly; fermentation, yeastiness, effervescence, ebullience, ebullition; fume; agita

5 **trepidation,** trepidity; disquiet, disquietude, inquietude, unrest, restlessness, fidgetiness; fidgets, shakes, shivers, dithers, antsyness; quivering, quavering, quaking, heartquake, shaking, trembling; quiver, quaver, shiver, shudder, dread, didder, twitter, tremor, tremble, flutter; palpitation, pitapatation, pit-a-pat, pitter-patter; throb, throbbing; panting, heaving

6 **dither, tizzy**, swivet, foofaraw, pucker, twitter, twitteration, flutter, fluster, flusteration, flustration, fret, fuss, pother, bother, lather, stew, snit, flap; emotional crisis

7 **fever,** fever of excitement, fever pitch, heat, fever heat, fire; sexual excitement, rut

8 **fury, furor,** furore <Brit>, fire and fury; ecstasy, transport, rapture, ravishment; intoxication, abandon; passion, rage, raging passion, tearing passion, towering rage, towering passion; frenzy, orgy, orgasm; madness, craze, delirium, hysteria

9 **outburst,** outbreak, burst, flare-up, blaze, explosion, eruption, irruption, upheaval,

convulsion, spasm, seizure, fit, paroxysm; storm, superstorm, tornado, funnel cloud, whirlwind, cyclone, hurricane, gale, tempest, gust; steroid rage; road rage, air rage

10 **excitability,** excitableness, perturbability, agitability; emotional instability, explosiveness, explosivity, eruptiveness, inflammability, combustibility, tempestuousness, violence, latent violence; **irascibility**; irritability, edginess, touchiness, prickliness, **sensitivity**; skittishness, **nervousness**; excessive emotion, hyperthymia, **emotionalism**

11 **excitation**, excitement, arousal, arousing, stirring, stirring up, working up, working into a lather, lathering up, whipping up, steaming up, agitation, perturbation; stimulation, stimulus, exhilaration, animation; electrification, galvanization; provocation, irritation, aggravation, exasperation, exacerbation, fomentation, inflammation, infuriation, incitement

VERBS 12 **excite,** impassion, arouse, rouse, blow up, stir, stir up, set astir, stir the feelings, stir the blood, cause a stir, cause a commotion, play on the feelings; work up, work into, work up into a lather, lather up, whip up, key up, steam up; move; foment, incite; turn on; awaken, awake, wake, waken, wake up; call up, summon up, call forth; kindle, enkindle, light up, light the fuse, fire, inflame, heat, warm, set fire to, set on fire, warm the blood; fan, fan the fire, fan the flame, blow the coals, stir the embers, feed the fire, add fuel to the fire, pour oil on the fire; raise to a fever pitch, bring to the boiling point; overexcite; annoy, incense; enrage, infuriate; frenzy, madden

13 **stimulate**, whet, sharpen, pique, provoke, quicken, enliven, liven up, pick up, jazz up, animate, exhilarate, invigorate, galvanize, fillip, give a fillip to; infuse life into, give new life to, revive, renew, resuscitate

14 **agitate,** perturb, disturb, trouble, disquiet, discompose, discombobulate, unsettle, stir, ruffle, shake, shake up, shock, upset, make waves, jolt, jar, rock, stagger, electrify, pull one up short, give one a turn; fuss, flutter, flurry, rattle, disconcert, fluster

15 **thrill, tickle,** thrill to death, thrill to pieces, give a thrill, give one a kick, give one a charge, give one a lift; intoxicate, fascinate, titillate, take one's breath away

16 **be excitable,** excite easily; get excited, have a fit; catch the infection; explode, flare up, flash up, flame up, fire up, catch fire, take fire; fly into a passion, go into hysterics, have a tantrum, have a temper tantrum, come apart; ride off in all directions at once, run around like a chicken with its head cut off; rage, rave, rant, rant and rave, rave on, bellow, storm, ramp; be angry, smolder, seethe

17 <nonformal> **work oneself up,** work oneself into a sweat, work oneself into a lather, have a short fuse, get hot under the collar, run a temperature, race one's motor, get into a dither, get into a tizzy, get into a swivet, get into a stew; blow up, blow one's top, blow one's stack, blow one's cool, flip, flip out, flip one's lid, flip one's wig, freak out, pop one's cork, wig out, blow a gasket, fly off the handle, hit the ceiling, go ape, go hog wild, go bananas, lose one's cool, go off the deep end

18 **<be excited> thrill,** tingle, tingle with excitement, glow; swell, swell with emotion, be full of emotion; thrill to; turn on to, get high on, freak out on; heave, pant; throb, palpitate, go pit-a-pat; tremble, shiver, quiver, quaver, quake, flutter, twitter, shake, shake like an aspen leaf, have the shakes; fidget, have the fidgets, have ants in one's pants; toss and turn, toss, tumble, twist and turn, wriggle, wiggle, writhe, squirm; twitch, jerk

19 **change color,** turn color, go all colors; pale, whiten, blanch, turn pale; darken, look black; turn blue in the face; flush, blush, crimson, glow, mantle, color, redden, turn red, get red

ADJS 20 **excited,** impassioned; thrilled, agog, tingling, tingly, atingle, aquiver, atwitter; stimulated, exhilarated, high; manic; moved, stirred, stirred up, aroused, roused, switched-on, turned on, on one's mettle, fired, inflamed, wrought up, worked up, all worked up, worked up into a lather, lathered up, whipped up, steamed up, keyed up, hopped up; turned-on; carried away; bursting, ready to burst; effervescent, yeasty, ebullient

21 **in a tizzy,** in a dither, in a swivet, in a foofaraw, in a pucker, in a quiver, in a twitter, in a flutter, all aflutter, in a fluster, in a flurry, in a pother, in a bother, in a ferment, in a turmoil, in an uproar, in a stew, in a sweat, in a lather

22 **heated, passionate**, warm, hot, red-hot, flaming, burning, fiery, glowing, fervent, fervid; feverish, febrile, on fire, hectic, flushed; sexually excited, in rut; burning with excitement, het up, hot under the collar; seething, boiling, boiling over, steamy, steaming

23 **agitated,** perturbed, disturbed, troubled, disquieted, upset, antsy, unsettled, discomposed, flustered, ruffled, shaken

24 **turbulent,** tumultuous, tempestuous, boisterous, clamorous, uproarious

25 **frenzied,** frantic; ecstatic, transported, enraptured, ravished, in a transport, in ecstasy;

intoxicated, abandoned; orgiastic, orgasmic; raging, raving, roaring, bellowing, ramping, storming, howling, ranting, fulminating, frothing at the mouth, foaming at the mouth; freaked out; wild, hog-wild; violent, fierce, ferocious, feral, furious, ballistic; mad, madding, rabid, maniac, maniacal, demonic, demoniacal, possessed; carried away, distracted, delirious, beside oneself, out of one's wits; uncontrollable, running mad, amok, berserk; hysterical, in hysterics; wild-eyed, wild-looking, haggard; blue in the face

26 **overwrought,** overexcited, overstimulated, hyper; overcome, overwhelmed, overpowered, overmastered; hand-wringing; upset; theatrical; hyped, hyped up; snowed under

27 **restless,** restive, uneasy, unquiet, unsettled, unrestful, tense; fidgety, antsy, fussy, fluttery, hopping

28 **excitable,** emotional, highly emotional, overemotional, hyperthymic, perturbable, flappable, agitable; emotionally unstable; explosive, volcanic, eruptive, inflammable; irascible; irritable, edgy, touchy, wired, prickly, sensitive; skittish, startlish; high-strung, highly strung, on edge, high-spirited, mettlesome, high-mettled; nervous

29 **passionate,** fiery, vehement, hotheaded, impetuous, violent, volcanic, furious, fierce, wild; tempestuous, stormy, tornadic; simmering, to burst forth, to explode

30 **exciting,** thrilling, thrilly, stirring, moving, breathtaking, eye-popping; agitating, agitative, perturbing, disturbing, upsetting, troubling, gut-wrenching, disquieting, unsettling, distracting, jolting, jarring; heart-stirring, heart-thrilling, heart-swelling, heart-expanding, soul-stirring, spirit-stirring, deep-thrilling, mind-blowing; impressive, striking, telling; provocative, provoking, piquant, tantalizing; inflammatory; stimulating, stimulative, stimulatory; exhilarating, heady, intoxicating, maddening, ravishing; electric, galvanic, charged, overcharged; overwhelming, overpowering, overcoming, overmastering, more than flesh and blood can bear; suspensive, suspenseful, cliff-hanging, heart-stopping

31 **penetrating,** piercing, stabbing, cutting, stinging, biting, keen, brisk, sharp, caustic, astringent

32 **sensational,** lurid, yellow, melodramatic, Barnumesque; spine-chilling, eye-popping; blood-and-thunder, cloak-and-dagger; tabloid

ADVS 33 **excitedly,** agitatedly, perturbedly; aflutter; with beating heart, with leaping heart, with heart beating high, with heart going pitapat, with heart going pitter-patter, thrilling all over, with heart in mouth; with glistening eyes, all agog, all aquiver, all atingle; in a sweat, in a dither, in a tizzy

34 **heatedly, passionately,** warmly, hotly, glowingly, fervently, fervidly, feverishly

35 **frenziedly,** frantically, wildly, furiously, violently, fiercely, madly, rabidly, distractedly, deliriously, till one is blue in the face

36 **excitingly,** thrillingly, stirringly, movingly; provocatively, provokingly; stimulatingly, exhilaratingly

106 INEXCITABILITY

<feeling nothing>

NOUNS 1 **inexcitability,** inexcitableness, unexcitableness, imperturbability, imperturbableness, unflappability; steadiness, evenness; inirritability, unirritableness; dispassion, dispassionateness, unpassionateness, ataraxy, ataraxia; quietism; stoicism; even temper, steady temper, smooth temper, good temper, easy temper; unnervousness; patience; impassiveness, impassivity, stolidity; bovinity, dullness

2 **composure,** countenance; **calm,** calmness, grace under pressure, calm disposition, placidity, serenity, tranquility, soothingness, peacefulness; mental composure, peace of mind, calm of mind; calm mind, quiet mind, easy mind; resignation, resignedness, acceptance, fatalism, stoic calm; philosophicalness, philosophy, philosophic composure; quiet, quietness of mind, quietness of soul, quietude; decompression, imperturbation, indisturbance, unruffledness; coolness, coolheadedness, cool, sangfroid; icy calm; Oriental calm, Buddha-like composure, Buddha nature; shantih, the peace that passeth all understanding; anger management

3 **equanimity,** equilibrium, equability, balance; levelheadedness, level head, well-balanced mind, well-regulated mind; poise, aplomb, self-possession, self-control, self-command, self-restraint, restraint, possession, presence of mind; confidence, assurance, self-confidence, self-assurance, centered

4 **sedateness,** staidness, soberness, sobriety, sober-mindedness, seriousness, gravity, solemnity, sobersidedness; temperance, moderation; sobersides

5 **nonchalance,** casualness, offhandedness; easygoingness, lackadaisicalness; indifference, unconcern

VERBS 6 **be cool**, be composed, not turn a hair, not have a hair out of place, keep one's cool, look as if butter wouldn't melt in one's mouth; tranquilize, **calm**; set one's mind at ease, set one's mind at rest, make one easy

7 **compose oneself,** control oneself, restrain oneself,

collect oneself, get hold of oneself, get a grip on oneself, get a grip, get organized, master one's feelings, regain one's composure; calm down, cool off, cool down, sober down, hold one's temper, keep one's temper, simmer down, cool it; relax, decompress, unwind, take it easy, lay back, kick back; forget it, get it out of one's mind, get it out of one's head, drop it

8 <control one's feelings> **suppress, repress,** keep under, smother, stifle, choke back, hold back, fight down, fight back, inhibit; sublimate; get it together

9 **keep cool,** keep one's cool, **keep calm,** keep one's head, keep one's shirt on, hang loose, not turn a hair; take things as they come, roll with the punches; keep a stiff upper lip

ADJS 10 **inexcitable,** imperturbable, undisturbable, unflappable; unirritable, inirritable; dispassionate, unpassionate; steady; stoic, stoical; even-tempered; impassive, stolid; bovine, dull; unnervous; patient; long-suffering

11 **unexcited,** unperturbed, undisturbed, untroubled, unagitated, unruffled, unflustered, unstirred, unimpassioned

12 **calm, placid,** quiet, tranquil, serene, peaceful; cool, coolheaded, cool as a cucumber; philosophical

13 **composed, collected,** recollected, levelheaded; poised, together, in equipoise, equanimous, equilibrious, balanced, well-balanced; self-possessed, self-controlled, controlled, self-restrained; confident, assured, self-confident, self-assured; temperate, pacific

14 **sedate, staid,** sober, sober-minded, **serious,** grave, solemn, sobersided; temperate, moderate

15 **nonchalant, blasé,** indifferent, unconcerned; casual, offhand, relaxed, laid-back, throwaway; easygoing, easy, free and easy, devil-may-care, lackadaisical, *dégagé* <Fr>

ADVS 16 **inexcitably**, imperturbably, inirritably, dispassionately; steadily; stoically; calmly, placidly, quietly, tranquilly, serenely; coolly, composedly, levelheadedly; impassively, stolidly, stodgily, stuffily

17 **sedately,** staidly, soberly, seriously, sobersidedly

18 **nonchalantly,** casually, relaxedly, offhandedly, easygoingly, lackadaisically

107 CONTENTMENT

<feeling happiness, satisfaction>

NOUNS 1 **contentment,** content, contentedness, satisfiedness; satisfaction, entire satisfaction, fulfillment, gratification; ease, peace of mind, eupathy, composure; comfort; quality of life; well-being, euphoria; happiness; acceptance, resignation, reconcilement, reconciliation; acceptableness; clear conscience, clean conscience, dreamless sleep; serenity; satiety; halcyon days, white list

2 **complacency,** complacence; smugness, self-complacence, self-complacency, self-approval, self-approbation, self-satisfaction, self-content, self-contentedness, self-contentness; bovinity

3 **satisfactoriness,** adequacy, sufficiency; acceptability, admissibility, tolerability, agreeability, unobjectionability, unexceptionability, tenability, viability; competency

VERBS 4 **content, satisfy;** gratify; put at ease, set at ease, set one's mind at ease, set one's mind at rest, achieve inner harmony; indulge, satiate

5 **be content,** rest satisfied, rest easy, rest and be thankful, be of good cheer, be reconciled to, take the good the gods provide, accept one's lot, rest on one's laurels, let well enough alone, let sleeping dogs lie, take the bitter with the sweet; come to terms with oneself, learn to live in one's own skin; have no kick coming, not complain, not worry, have nothing to complain about, not sweat it, cool it, go with the flow; content oneself with, settle for; settle for less, take half a loaf, lower one's sights, cut one's losses; be pleased; have one's heart's desire

6 **be satisfactory,** do, suffice; suit, suit one down to the ground, serve, meet the needs of

ADJS 7 **content, contented,** satisfied; pleased; happy; easy, at ease, at one's ease, easygoing; composed; comfortable, of good comfort; fulfilled, gratified; euphoric, eupeptic; carefree, without care, *sans souci* <Fr>; accepting, resigned, reconciled; uncomplaining, unrepining

8 **untroubled,** unbothered, undisturbed, unperturbed, unworried, unvexed, unplagued, untormented, secure

9 **well-content,** well-pleased, well-contented, well-satisfied, highly satisfied, satiated, full, full-up

10 **complacent,** bovine; smug, self-complacent, self-satisfied, self-content, self-contented

11 **satisfactory,** satisfying; sufficient, sufficing, adequate, enough, commensurate, proportionate, proportionable, ample, equal to, competent

12 **acceptable,** admissible, agreeable, unobjectionable, unexceptionable, tenable, viable; okay (OK), all right, alright; passable, good enough, not bad, so-so; palatable

13 **tolerable,** bearable, endurable, supportable, sufferable

ADVS 14 **contentedly,** to one's heart's content; satisfiedly, with satisfaction; complacently,

smugly, self-complacently, self-satisfiedly, self-contentedly
15 **satisfactorily,** satisfyingly; acceptably, agreeably, admissibly; sufficiently, adequately, commensurately, amply, enough; tolerably, passably
16 **to one's satisfaction,** to one's delight, to one's great glee; to one's taste, to the king's taste, to the queen's taste

108 DISCONTENT

<feeling unhappiness, disapproval>

NOUNS 1 **discontent,** discontentment, discontentedness; **dissatisfaction,** unsatisfaction, dissatisfiedness, unfulfillment; resentment, envy; restlessness, restiveness, uneasiness, unease; malaise; rebelliousness; disappointment; unpleasure; unhappiness; ill humor; disgruntlement, sulkiness, sourness, petulance, peevishness, querulousness; vexation of spirit; cold comfort; divine discontent; Faustianism
2 **unsatisfactoriness,** dissatisfactoriness; inadequacy, insufficiency; unacceptability, inadmissibility, unsuitability, undesirability, objectionability, untenability, indefensibility; intolerability
3 **malcontent,** *frondeur* <Fr>; complainer, complainant, buzzkill, faultfinder, grumbler, growler, smellfungus, griper, grouser, croaker, carper, peevish person, petulant person, querulous person, whiner; reactionary, reactionist; rebel; spoilsport; tough customer, dissatisfied customer, tough cookie, angry young man
4 <nonformal> **grouch,** kvetch, kicker, griper, moaner, crank, crab, grump, beefer, bellyacher, bitcher, sorehead, picklepuss, sourpuss, churl

VERBS 5 **dissatisfy,** discontent, disgruntle, displease, fail to satisfy, be inadequate, not fill the bill, disappoint, leave much to be desired, leave a lot to be desired, dishearten, disillusion, put out; be discontented, complain
6 <nonformal> **beef,** bitch*, kvetch, bellyache, boo, hiss, carp, crab, gripe, grouch, grouse, grump, have an attitude, kick, moan, piss*, make a stink, squawk

ADJS 7 **discontented,** dissatisfied, disgruntled, unaccepting, unaccommodating, displeased, less than pleased, let down, disappointed; unsatisfied, ungratified, unfulfilled; resentful, dog-in-the-manger; envious; restless, restive, uneasy; rebellious; malcontent, malcontented, complaining, complaintful, critical of, pejorative, sour, faultfinding, grumbling, growling, murmuring, muttering, griping, croaking, peevish, petulant, sulky, brooding, querulous, querulant, whiny; unhappy; out of humor
8 <nonformal> **grouchy,** kvetchy, cranky, beefing, crabby, crabbing, grousing, griping, bellyaching, bitching; eye-rolling
9 **unsatisfactory,** dissatisfactory; unsatisfying, ungratifying, unfulfilling; displeasing; disappointing, disheartening, not up to expectation, not good enough, substandard; inadequate, incommensurate, insufficient; unpopular, not up to snuff
10 **unacceptable,** inadmissible, unsuitable, undesirable, objectionable, exceptionable, impossible, untenable, indefensible; intolerable; rejected

ADVS 11 **discontentedly,** dissatisfiedly
12 **unsatisfactorily,** dissatisfactorily; unsatisfyingly, ungratifyingly; inadequately, insufficiently; unacceptably, nowise, inadmissibly, unsuitably, undesirably, objectionably; intolerably

109 CHEERFULNESS

<feeling agreeableness>

NOUNS 1 **cheerfulness,** cheeriness, **good cheer,** cheer, cheery vein, cheery mood; blitheness, blithesomeness; gladness, felicity, gladsomeness; happiness; pleasantness, winsomeness, geniality, conviviality; brightness, radiance, sunniness; sanguineness, sanguinity, sanguine humor, euphoric mein, eupeptic mein; optimism, rosy expectation, hopefulness; irrepressibility, irrepressibleness; morale booster
2 **good humor,** good spirits, good cheer; high spirits, exhilaration, rare good humor; *joie de vivre* <Fr>
3 **lightheartedness,** lightsomeness, lightness, levity; buoyancy, buoyance, resilience, resiliency, bounce, springiness; springy step; jauntiness, perkiness, debonairness, carefreeness; breeziness, airiness, pertness, chirpiness, light heart
4 **gaiety,** gayness, *allégresse* <Fr>; liveliness, vivacity, vitality, life, animation, spiritedness, spirit, esprit, élan, sprightliness, high spirits, zestfulness, zest, vim, zip, vigor, verve, gusto, exuberance, heartiness; spirits, animal spirits; piss and vinegar; friskiness, skittishness, coltishness, rompishness, rollicksomeness, capersomeness; sportiveness, playfulness, frolicsomeness, gamesomeness, kittenishness
5 **merriment,** merriness; hilarity, hilariousness; joy, joyfulness, joyousness; glee, gleefulness, high glee; jollity, jolliness, joviality, jocularity, jocundity;

frivolity, levity; mirth, mirthfulness, amusement; fun, good time; **laughter**

VERBS 6 **smile,** exude cheerfulness, radiate cheer, not have a care in the world, beam, burst with cheer, brim with cheer, glow, radiate, sparkle, sing, lilt, whistle, chirp, chirrup, chirp like a cricket; walk on air, dance, skip, caper, frolic, gambol, romp, caracole; **laugh**; be a Pollyanna

7 **cheer,** gladden, brighten, put in good humor; encourage, hearten, pick up; inspire, inspirit, warm the spirits, raise the spirits, elevate one's mood, buoy up, boost, give a lift, put one on top of the world *and* on cloud nine; exhilarate, animate, invigorate, liven, enliven, vitalize; rejoice, rejoice the heart, do the heart good

8 **elate,** exalt, elevate, lift, uplift, flush

9 **cheer up,** take heart, drive dull care away; brighten up, light up, perk up; buck up; come out of it, snap out of it, revive

10 **be of good cheer,** bear up, keep one's spirits up, keep one's chin up, keep one's pecker up, keep a stiff upper lip, grin and bear it

ADJS 11 **cheerful,** cheery, of good cheer, in good spirits; in high spirits, exalted, elated, exhilarated, high; irrepressible; blithe, blithesome; glad, gladsome; happy, happy as a clam, happy as a lark, on top of the world, sitting on top of the world, sitting pretty, on cloud nine, over the moon; pleasant, genial, winsome; bright, sunny, bright and sunny, radiant, riant, sparkling, beaming, glowing, flushed, perky, rosy, smiling, laughing; sanguine, sanguineous, euphoric, eupeptic, ebullient, Pollyannaish; optimistic, hopeful; up

12 **lighthearted,** light, lightsome; buoyant, corky, resilient; jaunty, perky, debonair, carefree, free and easy; breezy, airy

13 **pert,** chirk, chirrupy, chirpy, chipper

14 **animated,** gay; spirited, sprightly, lively, vivacious, vital, zestful, zippy, exuberant, hearty; frisky, antic, skittish, coltish, rompish, capersome; full of beans *and* feeling one's oats, full of piss and vinegar; sportive, playful, playful as a kitten, kittenish, frolicsome, gamesome; rollicking, rollicky, rollicksome

15 **merry,** mirthful, hilarious; joyful, joyous, rejoicing; gleeful, gleesome; jolly, buxom; jovial, jocund, jocular; frivolous; laughter-loving, mirth-loving, risible; merry as a cricket, merry as the day is long; tickled to death, tickled pink, high as a kite

16 **cheering,** gladdening; encouraging, heartening, heartwarming, uplifting; inspiring, inspiriting; exhilarating, animating, enlivening, invigorating; cheerful, cheery, glad, joyful; morale-boosting

ADVS 17 **cheerfully,** cheerily, with good cheer, with a cheerful heart; irrepressibly; lightheartedly, lightly; jauntily, perkily, airily; pleasantly, genially, blithely; gladly, happily, joyfully, smilingly; optimistically, hopefully

18 **gaily,** exuberantly, heartily, spiritedly, animatedly, vivaciously, zestfully, with zest, with vim, with élan, with zip, with verve, with gusto

19 **merrily,** gleefully, hilariously; jovially, jocundly, jocularly; frivolously; mirthfully, laughingly

PHRS 20 cheer up, every cloud has a silver lining; don't let it get you down, don't let the bastards grind you down; chin up, buck up; it's always darkest before the dawn, banzai

110 ILL HUMOR

<feeling disagreeableness>

NOUNS 1 **ill humor,** bad humor, **bad temper,** rotten temper, ill temper, evil temper, ill nature, evil humor; sourness, biliousness, liverishness; choler, bile, gall, spleen; abrasiveness, causticity, corrosiveness, asperity; **anger**; discontent

2 **irascibility,** irritability, excitability, short temper, quick temper, short fuse; crossness, disagreeableness, disagreeability, gruffness, shortness, peevishness, querulousness, fretfulness, crabbedness, crankiness, testiness, crustiness, huffiness, huffishness, churlishness, bearishness, snappishness, waspishness; perversity, cross-grainedness, fractiousness

3 <nonformal> **crabbiness,** grouchiness, cantankerousness, crustiness, grumpiness, grumpishness, cussedness, huffiness, huffishness, meanness, orneriness, bitchiness, feistiness, ugliness, miffiness, saltiness, scrappiness, soreheadedness

4 **hot temper,** temper, quick temper, short temper, irritable temper, warm temper, fiery temper, fierce temper, short fuse, pepperiness, feistiness, spunkiness, hotheadedness, hot blood; sharp tongue

5 **touchiness,** tetchiness, ticklishness, prickliness, quickness to take offense, miffiness, sensitiveness, oversensitiveness, hypersensitiveness, sensitivity, oversensitivity, hypersensitivity, thin skin; temperamentalness, moodiness

6 **petulance,** petulancy, peevishness, pettishness, querulousness, fretfulness, resentfulness; shrewishness, vixenishness

7 **contentiousness,** quarrelsomeness; disputatiousness, argumentativeness, litigiousness; belligerence, truculence

8 **sullenness,** sulkiness, surliness, moroseness, glumness, grumness, grimness, mumpishness,

dumpishness, dourness; moodiness, moodishness; mopishness, mopiness; dejection, melancholy

9 scowl, frown, lower, glower, pout, moue, mow, grimace, wry face; sullen looks, black looks, hangdog look, long face

10 sulks, sullens, mopes, mumps, dumps, grumps, frumps, **blues,** blue devils, mulligrubs, pouts

11 <ill-humored person> sorehead, **grouch,** curmudgeon, grump, crank, crab, crosspatch, feist, fice, wasp, bear, grizzly bear, pit bull, junkyard dog; fury, Tartar, dragon, ugly customer; hothead, hotspur; fire-eater; sulker, churl, bellyacher, neurotic

12 bitch*, **shrew,** vixen, virago, termagant, brimstone, fury, witch, beldam, cat, tigress, she-wolf, she-devil, spitfire; fishwife; scold, common scold, harpy, nag, Xanthippe; old bag, old bat; battle-ax; biatch, ice maiden

VERBS **13 have a temper**, have a short fuse, have a devil in one, be possessed of the devil; be cross, get out on the wrong side of the bed

14 sulk, mope, mope around; grizzle, grump, grouch, bitch, fret; get oneself in a sulk; have the blues, be down in the dumps

15 look sullen, look black, look black as thunder, gloom, make a long face, have a long face; frown, scowl, knit the brow, lower, glower, pout, brood, make a moue, grimace, make a wry face, make a lip, hang one's lip, thrust out one's lower lip

16 sour, acerbate, exacerbate; embitter, bitter, envenom

ADJS **17 out of humor,** out of temper, out of sorts, in a bad humor, in a shocking humor, feeling evil; abrasive, caustic, corrosive, acid; angry; discontented

18 ill-humored, bad-tempered, ill-tempered, evil-humored, evil-tempered, ill-natured, ill-affected, ill-disposed

19 irascible, **irritable,** excitable, flappable; cross, cranky, testy; cankered, crabbed, spiteful, spleeny, splenetic, churlish, bearish, snappish, waspish; gruff, grumbly, grumbling, growling; disagreeable; perverse, fractious, cross-grained

20 <nonformal> **crabby, grouchy,** cantankerous, crusty, grumpy, grumpish, cussed, huffy, huffish, mean, mean as a junkyard dog, ornery, bitchy*, feisty, ugly, miffy, salty, scrappy, soreheaded

21 touchy, tetchy, miffy, ticklish, prickly, quick to take offense, thin-skinned, sensitive, oversensitive, hypersensitive, high-strung, highly strung, temperamental, prima-donnaish

22 peevish, petulant, pettish, querulous, fretful, resentful; catty; shrewish, vixenish, vixenly; nagging, naggy

23 sour, soured, sour-tempered, vinegarish; prune-faced; choleric, dyspeptic, bilious, liverish, jaundiced; bitter, embittered

24 sullen, sulky, surly, morose, dour, mumpish, dumpish, glum, grum, grim; moody, moodish; mopish, mopey, moping; glowering, lowering, scowling, frowning; dark, black; black-browed, beetle-browed; dejected, melancholy; somber

25 hot-tempered, hotheaded, passionate, hot, fiery, peppery, feisty, spunky, quick-tempered, short-tempered; hasty, quick, explosive, volcanic, combustible, vicious

26 contentious, quarrelsome; disputatious, controversial, litigious, polemic, polemical; argumentative, argumental; on the warpath, looking for trouble; scrappy; cat-and-doggish, cat-and-dog; bellicose, belligerent

ADVS **27 ill-humoredly,** ill-naturedly; irascibly, irritably, crossly, crankily, testily, huffily, cantankerously, crabbedly, sourly, churlishly, crustily, bearishly, snappily; perversely, fractiously, cross-grainedly

28 peevishly, petulantly, pettishly, querulously, fretfully

29 grouchily, crabbily, grumpily, grumblingly

30 sullenly, sulkily, surlily, morosely, mumpishly, glumly, grumly, grimly; moodily, mopingly; gloweringly, loweringly, scowlingly, frowningly

111 SOLEMNITY

<feeling seriousness>

NOUNS **1 solemnity,** solemness, dignity, soberness, sobriety, gravity, *gravitas* <L>, weightiness, somberness, grimness; sedateness, staidness; demureness, decorousness; seriousness, earnestness, thoughtfulness, sober-mindedness, sobersidedness; sobersides, humorlessness; long face, straight face; formality

VERBS **2 look serious,** honor the occasion, keep a straight face, compose one's features, wear an earnest frown; repress a smile, not crack a smile, wipe the smile off one's face, keep from laughing, make a long face

ADJS **3 solemn,** dignified, sober, grave, unsmiling, weighty, somber, frowning, grim; sedate, staid; demure, decorous; serious, earnest, thoughtful, pensive; sober-minded, sober-sided; in earnest; straight-faced, long-faced, grim-faced, grim-visaged, stone-faced, stony-faced; sober as a judge, grave as an undertaker; formal

ADVS **4 solemnly,** soberly, gravely, somberly, grimly; sedately, staidly, demurely, decorously; with dignity, seriously, earnestly, thoughtfully, sober-mindedly, sobersidedly; with a straight face; formally

112 SADNESS

<*feeling grief or disappointment*>

NOUNS 1 **sadness,** sadheartedness, weight of burden, burden of sorrow; heaviness, heavyheartedness, heavy heart, heaviness of heart; pathos, bathos

2 **unhappiness,** infelicity; displeasure; discontent; uncheerfulness, cheerlessness; joylessness, unjoyfulness; mirthlessness, unmirthfulness, humorlessness, infestivity; grimness; wretchedness, misery

3 **dejection, depression,** oppression, dejectedness, downheartedness, downcastness; discouragement, disheartenment, dispiritedness; *Schmerz, Weltschmerz* <Ger>; malaise; lowness, lowness of spirit, depression of spirit, oppression of spirit, downer, down trip; chill, chilling effect; low spirits, drooping spirits, sinking heart, funk; despondence, despondency, spiritlessness, heartlessness; black despondency, blank despondency, slough of despond; demotivation, hopelessness, despair, pessimism, gloom and doom, suicidal despair, death wish, self-destructive urge; weariness of life, *taedium vitae* <L>; sloth, acedia, noonday demon

4 **neurosis,** hypochondria, hypochondriasis, morbid anxiety

5 **melancholy,** melancholia, melancholiness, spleen; gentle melancholy, romantic melancholy; pensiveness, wistfulness, tristfulness; nostalgia, homesickness, nostalgy, *mal du pays* <Fr>

6 **blues,** blue devils, mulligrubs, mumps, dumps, doldrums, dismals, dolefuls, megrims, blahs, mopes, sulks, funks

7 **gloom,** gloominess, darkness, murk, murkiness, dismalness, bleakness, grimness, somberness, gravity, solemnity; dreariness, drearisomeness; wearifulness, wearisomeness

8 **glumness,** grumness, moroseness, sullenness, sulkiness, moodiness, mumpishness, dumpishness; mopishness, mopiness

9 **heartache,** aching heart, bleeding heart, grieving heart; heartsickness, heartsoreness; heartbreak, broken heart, brokenheartedness, heartbrokenness

10 **sorrow,** sorrowing, grief, care, carking care, woe; heartgrief, heartfelt grief; languishment, pining; anguish, misery, agony; prostrating grief, prostration; lamentation

11 **sorrowfulness,** mournfulness, ruefulness, woefulness, dolefulness, woesomeness, dolorousness, plaintiveness, plangency, grievousness, aggrievedness, lugubriousness, funerealness; weeping and wailing and gnashing of teeth; *lacrimae rerum* <L>, tearfulness

12 **disconsolateness,** disconsolation, inconsolability, inconsolableness, unconsolability, comfortlessness; desolation, desolateness; forlornness

13 **sourpuss,** picklepuss, gloomy Gus, moaning Minnie; mope, brooder; melancholic, melancholiac; depressive; Eeyore

14 **killjoy,** spoilsport, grinch, crepehanger, drag; damp, damper, **wet blanket,** party pooper; gloomster *and* doomster, doomsdayer, apocalypticist, apocalyptician, awfulizer, crapehanger; fussbudget, worrywart, skeleton at the feast; pessimist

VERBS 15 hang one's head, make a long face, look blue, sing the blues, get the blues, have the blues; drag one down; carry the weight of the world on one's shoulders; hang crape, apocalypticize, catastrophize, awfulize

16 **lose heart,** despond, give way, give oneself up to, give oneself over to; despondency; **despair,** sink into despair, throw up one's hands in despair, be suicidal, become suicidal, lose the will to live; **droop,** sink, languish, mope; reach the depths, plumb the depths, touch bottom, hit bottom, hit rock bottom

17 **grieve, sorrow;** weep, mourn; be dumb with grief; pine, pine away, pine over; brood over, mope, fret, take on; eat one's heart out, break one's heart over; agonize, ache, bleed

18 **sadden,** darken, cast a pall upon, cast a gloom upon, weigh upon, weigh heavy upon; deject, depress, oppress, crush, press down, hit one like a ton of bricks, cast down, lower, lower the spirits, get one down, take the wind out of one's sails, rains on one's parade, burst one's bubble, discourage, dishearten, take the heart out of, dispirit; damp, dampen, damp the spirits, dampen the spirits; dash, knock down, beat down; sink, sink one's soul, plunge one into despair

19 **sorrow,** aggrieve, oppress, grieve, plunge one into sorrow, embitter; draw tears, bring to tears; anguish, tear up, rip up, cut up, pierce the heart, lacerate the heart, rend the heart, pull at the heartstrings; be cut up; afflict, torment; break one's heart, make one's heart bleed; desolate, leave an aching void; prostrate, break down, crush, bear down, inundate, overwhelm

ADJS 20 **sad,** saddened; sadhearted, sad of heart; heavyhearted, heavy; oppressed, weighed upon, weighed down, weighted down, bearing the weight of the world, burdened with sorrow, laden with sorrow; sad-faced, long-faced; sad-eyed; sad-voiced

21 **unhappy,** uncheerful, uncheery, cheerless, joyless, unjoyful, unsmiling; mirthless, unmirthful, humorless, infestive; funny as a crutch; grim; out of humor, out of sorts, in bad humor, in bad spirits; sorry, sorryish; discontented; wretched, miserable; pleasureless

22 **dejected, depressed,** downhearted, down, downcast, cast down, bowed down, subdued; discouraged, disheartened, dispirited, dashed; low, feeling low, low-spirited, in low spirits; down in the mouth, in the doldrums, down in the dumps, in the dumps, in the doleful dumps, in the depths; despondent, desponding; despairing, weary of life, suicidal, world-weary; pessimistic; spiritless, heartless, woebegone; drooping, droopy, languishing, pining, haggard; hypochondriac, hypochondriacal

23 **melancholy,** melancholic, splenetic, blue, funky; atrabilious, atrabiliar; pensive, wistful, tristful; nostalgic, homesick

24 **gloomy, dismal,** murky, bleak, grim, somber, sombrous, solemn, grave; sad, funereal, funebrial, crepehanging, saturnine; dark, black, gray; dreary, drear, drearisome; weary, weariful, wearisome

25 **glum,** grum, morose, sullen, sulky, mumpish, dumpish, long-faced, crestfallen, chapfallen; moody, moodish, brooding, broody; mopish, mopey, moping

26 **sorrowful,** sorrowing, sorrowed, mournful, rueful, woeful, woesome, doleful, plaintive, plangent; anguished; dolorous, grievous, lamentable, lugubrious; tearful; careworn; grieved, grief-stricken, griefful, aggrieved, in grief, bereft, plunged in grief, dumb with grief, prostrated by grief, cut-up *and* torn-up, inconsolable

27 **sorrow-stricken,** sorrow-wounded, sorrow-struck, sorrow-torn, sorrow-worn, sorrow-wasted, sorrow-beaten, sorrow-blinded, sorrow-clouded, sorrow-shot, sorrow-burdened, sorrow-laden, sorrow-sighing, sorrow-sobbing, sorrow-sick, heartwrenching

28 **disconsolate,** inconsolable, unconsolable, comfortless, prostrate, prostrated, forlorn; desolate, *désolé* <Fr>; sick, sick at heart, heartsick, soul-sick, heartsore

29 **overcome,** crushed, borne-down, overwhelmed, inundated, spazzed-out, stricken, cut up, desolated, prostrate, prostrated, broken-down, undone; heart-stricken, heart-struck; brokenhearted, heartbroken

30 **depressing,** depressive, depressant, oppressive; discouraging, disheartening, dispiriting; morale-sapping, worst-case, downbeat, downer

ADVS **31** **sadly,** gloomily, dismally, drearily, heavily, bleakly, grimly, somberly, sombrously, solemnly, funereally, gravely, with a long face; depressingly

32 **unhappily,** uncheerfully, cheerlessly, joylessly, unjoyfully

33 **dejectedly,** downheartedly; discouragedly, dishearteningly, dispiritedly; despondently, despairingly, spiritlessly, heartlessly; disconsolately, inconsolably, unconsolably, forlornly

34 **melancholily,** pensively, wistfully, tristfully; nostalgically

35 **glumly,** grumly, morosely, sullenly; moodily, moodishly, broodingly, broodily; mopishly, mopily, mopingly

36 **sorrowfully,** mournfully, ruefully, woefully, woesomely, dolefully, dolorously, plaintively, grievously, grieffully, lugubriously; with a broken voice; heartbrokenly, brokenheartedly; tearfully, with tears in one's eyes

113 REGRET

<feeling very sorry>

NOUNS **1** **regret,** regrets, regretting, regretfulness, rue; **remorse,** remorsefulness, remorse of conscience; buyer's remorse; shame, shamefulness, shamefacedness, shamefastness; sorrow, grief, sorriness, repining; contrition, contriteness, attrition; bitterness; apologies; wistfulness

2 **compunction,** qualm, qualms, qualmishness, scruples, scrupulosity, scrupulousness, pang, pangs, pangs of conscience, throes, sting of conscience, twinge of conscience, twitch of conscience, touch of conscience, voice of conscience, pricking of heart, misgiving, better self

3 **self-reproach,** self-reproachfulness, self-accusation, self-condemnation, self-conviction, self-punishment, self-humiliation, self-debasement, self-hatred, self-flagellation; hair shirt; self-analysis, soul-searching, examination of conscience

4 **penitence,** repentance, change of heart; apology, humble apology, heartfelt apology, abject apology; better nature, good angel, guardian angel; reformation; deathbed repentance; mea culpa; penance; wearing a hairshirt, wearing a sackcloth, wearing a sackcloth and ashes, mortification of the flesh

5 **penitent,** confessor; prodigal son, prodigal returned; Magdalen

VERBS **6** **regret,** deplore, repine, be sorry for; rue, rue the day; bemoan, bewail; curse one's folly, reproach oneself, kick oneself, bite one's tongue, accuse oneself, condemn oneself, blame oneself, punish oneself, flagellate oneself, wear a hair shirt, make oneself miserable, debase oneself, hate oneself for one's actions, hide one's face in shame; examine one's conscience, search one's soul, consult one's better self, heed one's better self, analyze one's motives, search one's motives; cry over spilled milk, waste time in regret

7 **repent,** think better of, change one's mind, have second thoughts; laugh out of the other side of one's mouth; plead guilty, own oneself in the wrong, humble oneself, apologize, beg pardon, beg forgiveness, throw oneself on the mercy of the court; do penance; reform

ADJS 8 **regretful,** remorseful, full of remorse, ashamed, shameful, shamefaced, shamefast, sorry, rueful, repining, unhappy about; conscience-stricken, conscience-smitten; self-reproachful, self-reproaching, self-accusing, self-condemning, self-convicting, self-punishing, self-flagellating, self-humiliating, self-debasing, self-hating; wistful

9 **penitent, repentant**; penitential, penitentiary; contrite, abject, humble, humbled, sheepish, apologetic, touched, softened, melted; atoning

10 **regrettable,** much to be regretted; deplorable

ADVS 11 **regretfully,** remorsefully, sorrily, ruefully, unhappily

12 **penitently,** repentantly, penitentially; contritely, abjectly, humbly, sheepishly, apologetically

114 UNREGRETFULNESS

<feeling no regret>

NOUNS 1 **unregretfulness,** unremorsefulness, **unsorriness,** unruefulness; remorselessness, regretlessness, sorrowlessness; shamelessness, unashamedness

2 **impenitence,** impenitentness; nonrepentance, irrepentance, unrepentance; uncontriteness, unabjectness; seared conscience, heart of stone, callousness; hardness of heart, hardness, induration, obduracy; defiance; insolence; no regrets, no remorse

VERBS 3 **harden one's heart,** steel oneself; **have no regrets,** not look backward, not cry over spilled milk; have no shame, have no remorse, feel no remorse; feel nothing

ADJS 4 **unregretful,** unregretting, unremorseful, unsorry, unsorrowful, unrueful; **remorseless,** regretless, sorrowless, griefless; unsorrowing, ungrieving, unrepining; shameless, unashamed

5 **impenitent,** unrepentant, unrepenting, unrecanting; uncontrite, unabject; untouched, unsoftened, unmelted, callous; hard, hardened, obdurate; defiant; insolent

6 **unregretted,** unrepented, unatoned

ADVS 7 **unregretfully,** unremorsefully, unruefully; remorselessly, sorrowlessly, impenitently, shamelessly, unashamedly; without regret, without looking back, without remorse, without compunction, without any qualms, without scruples

115 LAMENTATION

<expressing deep sadness>

NOUNS 1 **lamentation,** lamenting, **mourning,** moaning, grieving, sorrowing, wailing, bewailing, bemoaning, keening, howling, ululation; **sorrow**; woe, misery; threnody

2 **weeping,** sobbing, crying, bawling; blubbering, whimpering, sniveling; tears, flood of tears, fit of crying; cry, good cry; tearfulness, weepiness, lachrymosity, melting mood; tearful eyes, swimming eyes, brimming eyes, overflowing eyes; tear, teardrop, lachryma; lacrimatory, tear bottle

3 **lament,** plaint; murmur, mutter; moan, groan; whine, whimper; wail, wail of woe; sob, *cri du coeur* <Fr>, cry, outcry, scream, howl, yowl, bawl, yawp, keen, ululation; jeremiad, tirade, dolorous tirade

4 **complaint,** grievance, peeve, pet peeve, groan; dissent, protest; hard luck story, sob story, sad story, tale of woe; complaining, scolding, groaning, faultfinding, sniping, destructive criticism, grumbling, murmuring; whining, petulance, peevishness, querulousness; backstabbing, trash talk

5 <nonformal> **beef,** kick, gripe, kvetch, grouse, bellyache, howl, holler, squawk, bitch*; beefing, grousing, kicking, griping, kvetching, bellyaching, squawking, bitching*, yapping

6 **dirge,** funeral song, death song, keen, elegy, epicedium, requiem, monody, threnody, threnode, coronach <Irl>, knell, death knell, passing bell, funeral march, dead march, muffled drums; eulogy, funeral oration, graveside oration

7 **<mourning garment>** mourning, weeds, widow's weeds, crape, black; deep mourning; sackcloth, sackcloth and ashes; cypress, cypress lawn, yew; mourning band; mourning ring

8 **lamenter,** griever, mourner; moaner, weeper, sniveler; complainer, faultfinder, smellfungus, malcontent

9 <nonformal> **grouch, kvetch,** kicker, griper, moaner, crank, crab, crybaby, blubberer, grouser, beefer, bellyacher, bitcher, sorehead, picklepuss, sourpuss, grumbler

VERBS 10 **lament,** mourn, moan, grieve, sorrow, keen, weep over, weep for, bewail, bemoan, deplore, repine, sigh, rue, give sorrow words; sing the blues, elegize, dirge, knell, toll the knell; pay one's last respects; wake, hold a wake, go to a funeral, sound the last post

11 wring one's hands, tear one's hair, gnash one's teeth, beat one's breast, sing the blues

12 **weep,** sob, cry, bawl, boo-hoo; blubber, ululate, whimper, snivel; shed tears, drop a tear; burst into tears, burst out crying, give way to tears, melt in tears, dissolve in tears, break down, break down and cry, turn on the waterworks; cry one's eyes out, cry oneself blind; cry before one is hurt

13 **wail,** ululate; moan, groan; howl, yowl, yawl; cry, squall, bawl, yawp, yell, scream, shriek; cry out, make an outcry; bay at the moon; tirade

14 **whine,** whimper, yammer, pule, grizzle

15 **complain,** groan; grumble, murmur, mutter, growl, clamor, croak, grunt, yelp; fret, fuss, make a fuss about, fret and fume; air a grievance, lodge a complaint, register a complaint; fault, find fault

16 <nonformal> **beef,** bitch*, kick, kvetch, bellyache, crab, gripe, grouch, grouse, grump, have an attitude, holler, howl, moan, piss*, piss and moan, make a stink, squawk, yap; raise a howl, put up a squawk, take on, yell bloody murder, scream bloody murder, give one a hard time, kick up a storm, kick up a row, kick up a fuss, raise a stink, put up a stink

17 **go into mourning;** put on mourning, wear mourning

ADJS 18 **lamenting,** grieving, mourning, moaning, sorrowing; wailing, bewailing, bemoaning; in mourning, in sackcloth and ashes; depressed, down

19 **plaintive,** plangent, **mournful,** moanful, wailful, lamentive, ululant; woebegone, disconsolate; sorrowful; howling, Jeremianic; whining, whiny, whimpering, puling; querulous, fretful, petulant, peevish; complaining, faultfinding

20 <nonformal> **grouchy, kvetchy,** cranky, beefing, crabby, crabbing, grousing, griping, bellyaching, bitching*

21 **tearful,** teary, weepy; lachrymal, lachrymose, lacrimatory; in the melting mood, on the edge of tears, ready to cry; weeping, sobbing, crying; blubbering, whimpering, sniveling; red-eyed; in tears, with tears in one's eyes, with tearful eyes, with watery eyes, with swimming eyes, with overflowing eyes, with eyes suffused in tears

22 **dirgelike**, knell-like, elegiac, elegiacal, epicedial, threnodic, plaintive, plangent

ADVS 23 **lamentingly,** plaintively, mournfully, moanfully, wailfully; sorrowfully; complainingly, groaningly, querulously, fretfully, petulantly, peevishly

116 REJOICING

<expressing extreme happiness>

NOUNS 1 **rejoicing,** jubilation, jubilance, jubilant display, jubilee, show of joy, raucous happiness; exultation, elation, triumph; the time of one's life, special day; whoopee, hoopla, festivity, merriment; celebration

2 **cheer,** hurrah, huzzah, hurray, hooray, yippee, rah, cowabunga; cry, shout, yell; hosanna, hallelujah, alleluia, paean, paean of cheers, chorus of cheers, three cheers; applause, fanfare, shout-out; high-five, fist bump, fist pump

3 **smile,** smiling; bright smile, gleaming smile, glowing smile, beam; silly smile, silly grin; grin, grinning; broad grin, ear-to-ear grin, toothful grin; stupid grin, idiotic grin; sardonic grin, smirk, simper

4 **laughter,** laughing, hilarity, risibility; laugh; boff, boffola, yuck; titter; giggle; chuckle, chortle; cackle, crow; snicker, snigger, snort, snirtle; ha-ha, hee-haw, hee-hee, ho-ho, tee-hee, yuk-yuk; guffaw, horselaugh; hearty laugh, belly laugh, Homeric laughter, cachinnation; shout, shriek, shout of laughter, burst of laughter, outburst of laughter, peal of laughter, roar of laughter, gales of laughter; fit of laughter, convulsion; heh heh

VERBS 5 **rejoice,** jubilate, **exult,** glory, joy, delight, bless one's stars, thank one's stars, bless one's lucky, thank one's lucky stars, congratulate oneself, hug oneself, rub one's hands, clap hands; dance for joy, skip for joy, jump for joy, dance, skip, frisk, rollick, revel, frolic, caper, gambol, caracole, romp; sing, carol, chirp, chirrup, chirp like a cricket, whistle, lilt; make merry

6 **cheer,** give a cheer, give three cheers, cry, shout, yell, cry for joy, yell oneself hoarse; huzzah, hurrah, hurray, hooray; shout hosanna, shout hallelujah; applaud; high-five

7 **smile,** crack a smile, break into a smile; beam, smile brightly; grin, grin like a Cheshire cat, grin like a chessy-cat; smirk, simper

8 **laugh,** burst out laughing, burst into laughter, burst out, laugh outright; laugh it up; titter; giggle; chuckle, chortle; cackle, crow; snicker, snigger, snort; ha-ha, hee-haw, hee-hee, ho-ho, tee-hee, har-de-har, yuk-yuk; guffaw, belly laugh, horselaugh; shout, shriek, give a shout of laughter, give a shriek of laughter; roar, cachinnate, roar with laughter; shake with laughter, shake like jelly; be convulsed with laughter, go into convulsions, fall about; burst with laughter, break up, crack up, split, split one's sides, split with laughter, bust a gut, pee in one's pants laughing, wet one's pants laughing, be in stitches, hold

one's sides, roll in the aisles; laugh oneself silly, die laughing, nearly die laughing; laugh in one's sleeve, laugh up one's sleeve, laugh in one's beard

9 **make laugh**, kill, slay, set the table on a roar, break one up, crack one up, get a laugh

ADJS 10 **rejoicing,** delighting, exulting; jubilant, exultant, elated, elate, flushed, euphoric, ecstatic

ADVS 11 **rejoicingly,** delightingly, exultingly; jubilantly, exultantly, elatedly

117 DULLNESS

<uninteresting state>

NOUNS 1 **dullness,** dryness, dustiness, uninterestingness; **stuffiness,** stodginess, woodenness, stiffness; barrenness, sterility, aridity, jejunity; insipidness, insipidity, vapidness, vapidity, inanity, hollowness, emptiness, superficiality, staleness, flatness, tastelessness; characterlessness, colorlessness, pointlessness; deadness, lifelessness, spiritlessness, bloodlessness, paleness, pallor, etiolation, effeteness; slowness, pokiness, dragginess, unliveliness; tediousness; dreariness, drearisomeness, dismalness; heaviness, leadenness, ponderousness; inexcitability; solemnity; lowness of spirit

2 **prosaicness,** prosiness; prosaism, prosaicism, prose, **plainness**; matter-of-factness, unimaginativeness; matter of fact; **simplicity**

3 **triteness,** corniness, squareness, banality, banalness, unoriginality, sameness, hackneyedness, commonplaceness, commonness, familiarness, platitudinousness; a familiar ring; redundancy, repetition, staleness, mustiness, fustiness; cliché

VERBS 4 **fall flat,** fall flat as a pancake; leave one cold, leave one unmoved, go over like a lead balloon, lay an egg, bomb, wear thin

5 prose, platitudinize, sing a familiar tune; pedestrianize; warm over; banalize

ADJS 6 **dull, dry,** dusty, dry as dust, mind-numbing; stuffy, stodgy, wooden, stiff; arid, barren, blank, sterile, jejune; insipid, vapid, inane, hollow, empty, superficial; ho-hum, blah, flat, tasteless; characterless, colorless, pointless; dead, lifeless, spiritless, bloodless, pale, pallid, etiolated, effete; cold; slow, poky, draggy, pedestrian, plodding, unlively; tedious; dreary, drearisome, dismal; heavy, leaden, ponderous, elephantine; dull as dish water; inexcitable; solemn; low-spirited

7 **uninteresting,** uneventful, unexciting; uninspiring; unentertaining, unenjoyable, unamusing, unfunny, unwitty

8 **prosaic,** prose, prosy, prosing, plain; **matter-of-fact,** unimaginative, unimpassioned

9 **trite;** corny, square, square-John, Clyde, hokey, fade, banal, unoriginal, platitudinous, stereotyped, stock, set, commonplace, common, truistic, twice-told, familiar, bromidic, old hat, back-number, bewhiskered, warmed-over, cut-and-dried; hackneyed, hackney; well-known; stale, musty, fusty; worn, timeworn, well-worn, moth-eaten, threadbare, worn thin

ADVS 10 **dully, dryly,** dustily, uninterestingly; stuffily, stodgily; aridly, barrenly, jejunely, insipidly, vapidly, inanely, hollowly, emptily, superficially, tastelessly, colorlessly, pointlessly; lifelessly, spiritlessly, bloodlessly, pallidly, effetely; slowly, draggily, ploddingly; tediously; drearily, drearisomely, dismally; heavily, ponderously

11 **tritely,** cornily, banally, commonplacely, commonly, familiarly, hackneyedly, unoriginally, truistically, stalely

118 TEDIUM

<boring state>

NOUNS 1 **tedium, monotony,** humdrum, irksomeness, irk; sameness, sameliness, samesomeness, wearisome sameness, more of the same, the same old thing, the same old story, the same damn thing; broken record, parrot; platitude, chestnut; undeviation, unvariation, invariability; the round, the daily round, the daily grind, the weary round, the treadmill, the squirrel cage, the rat race, the beaten track, the beaten path, drag; time on one's hands, time hanging heavily on one's hands; protraction, prolongation

2 **tediousness, monotonousness,** unrelievedness; humdrumness, humdrumminess; dullness; wearisomeness, wearifulness; tiresomeness, irksomeness, drearisomeness; boresomeness, boringness; prolixity, long-windedness; redundancy, repetition, repetitiveness, tick-tock; broken record

3 **weariness, tiredness,** wearifulness; jadedness, satiation, satiety; boredom, boredness; ennui, spleen, melancholy, life-weariness, *taedium vitae* <L>, world-weariness, *Weltschmerz* <Ger>; languor, listlessness, dispiritedness

4 **bore,** crashing bore, frightful bore; pest, nuisance; dryasdust; proser, twaddler, wet blanket; buttonholer; bromide; egoist

5 <nonformal> **drag,** drip, pill, flat tire, deadass, deadfanny, dull tool; headache, pain, pain in the neck, pain in the ass; broken record

VERBS 6 **be tedious, drag on,** go on forever; have a certain sameness, be infinitely repetitive, do the same old thing; weary, tire, irk, wear, wear on, wear upon, make one tired, fatigue, tire to death, jade; give one a pain in the ass, give one a bellyful, make one fed-up, pall, satiate, glut

7 **bore,** leave one cold, send to sleep; bore stiff, bore to tears, bore to death, bore to extinction, bore to distraction, bore out of one's life, bore out of all patience; buttonhole; wear out one's welcome, stay too long

8 **harp on,** harp upon, dwell on, dwell upon, harp upon one thing, harp on the same string, play the same old song, play the same old tune, sing the same old song, sing the same old tune, play the same broken record

ADJS 9 **tedious, monotonous,** humdrum, singsong, jog-trot, treadmill, unvarying, invariable, uneventful, broken-record, parrotlike, harping, everlasting, too much with us; blah, flat, dreary, drearisome, dry, dry-as-dust, dusty, dull; protracted, prolonged; prolix, long-winded; pedestrian, commonplace

10 **wearying,** wearing, **tiring;** wearisome, weariful, fatiguing, tiresome, irksome; boring, boresome, stupefyingly boring, stuporific, yawny; hamster-wheel

11 **weary,** weariful; **tired,** wearied, irked; good and tired, tired to death, weary unto death; sick, sick of, tired of, sick and tired of; jaded, satiated, palled, fed up, brassed off; blasé; splenetic, melancholy, melancholic, life-weary, world-weary, tired of living, half-dead; listless, dispirited

12 **bored,** uninterested; bored stiff, bored to death, bored to extinction, bored to tears, stupefied with boredom, stuporous with boredom; with eyes rolling

ADVS 13 **tediously, monotonously,** harpingly, everlastingly, unvaryingly, endlessly; long-windedly; boringly, boresomely; wearisomely, fatiguingly, wearyingly, tiresomely, irksomely, drearisomely; dully

14 on a treadmill, in a squirrel cage, on a hamster wheel, on the beaten track, on the same old round; without a change of menu, without a change of scenery, without a change of pace

PHRS 15 ho hum, heigh ho, what a life, que sera sera; the more things change, the more they stay the same; so what else is new?, go figure; mine eyes glaze over (MEGO)

119 AGGRAVATION

<annoyed state>

NOUNS 1 **aggravation,** worsening; exacerbation, embittering, embitterment, souring; deterioration; intensification, heightening, stepping-up, sharpening, deepening, increase, enhancement, amplification, enlargement, magnification, augmentation, exaggeration; exasperation, annoyance, irritation; hassle, aggro <Brit>; deliberate aggravation, provocation; contentiousness

VERBS 2 **aggravate, worsen,** make worse; **exacerbate,** embitter, sour; deteriorate; intensify, heighten, step up, sharpen, make acute, make more acute, bring to a head, deepen, increase, enhance, amplify, enlarge, magnify, build up, exaggerate; augment; rub salt in the wound, twist the knife, add insult to injury, inflame, pour oil on the fire, add fuel to the fire, heat up, hot up; increase pressure, increase tension, tighten, tighten up, tighten the screws, put the squeeze on; exasperate, annoy, irritate; rub it in; provoke, antagonize, hassle, be an *agent provocateur*

3 **worsen,** get worse, grow worse, take a turn for the worse, deteriorate, degenerate; go from push to shove, go from bad to worse; jump out of the frying pan and into the fire, avoid Scylla and fall into Charybdis

ADJS 4 **aggravated, worsened,** worse, worse and worse, exacerbated, embittered, soured, deteriorated; intensified, heightened, stepped-up, increased, deepened, enhanced, amplified, magnified, enlarged, augmented, heated up, hotted up; exasperated, irritated, annoyed; provoked, deliberately provoked; worse-off, out of the frying pan and into the fire

5 **aggravating,** aggravative; exasperating, exasperative; annoying, irritating; provocative; vexing, vexatious; contentious

ADVS 6 **from bad to worse**; aggravatingly, exasperatingly; annoyingly

120 RELIEF

<reduced pain state>

NOUNS 1 **relief,** easement, easing, ease; relaxation, relaxing, relaxation of tension, easing of tension, decompression, slackening, respite, let-up; reduction, diminishment, diminution, lessening, abatement, remission; remedy; alleviation, mitigation, palliation, softening, assuagement, allayment, defusing, appeasement, mollification, subduement; soothing, salving, anodyne; lulling; dulling, deadening, numbing, narcotizing, anesthesia, anesthetizing, analgesia; sedating, sedation; doping, doping up; comfort, solace, consolation; charity, benefaction

2 **release,** deliverance, freeing, removal; suspension, intermission, respite, surcease, reprieve; discharge; catharsis, purging, purgation,

purge, cleansing, cleansing away, emotional release

3 **lightening,** disburdening, unburdening, unweighting, unloading, disencumbrance, disembarrassment, easing of the load, a load off one's mind, something out of one's system

4 **sense of relief,** feeling of relief, sigh of relief

VERBS 5 **relieve,** give relief; **ease,** ease matters; relax, slacken; reduce, diminish, lessen, abate, remit, de-stress; alleviate, mitigate, palliate, soften, pad, cushion, assuage, allay, defuse, lay, appease, mollify, subdue, soothe; salve, pour balm into, pour oil on; poultice, foment, stupe; slake; lull; dull, deaden, dull the pain, deaden the pain, numb, benumb, anesthetize, tranquilize; sedate, narcotize, dope, dope up; temper the wind to the shorn lamb, lay the flattering unction to one's soul; take the sting out of; comfort, solace, pacify

6 **release,** free, deliver, reprieve, remove, free from, liberate; suspend, intermit, give respite, give surcease; relax, decompress, ease, destress; act as a cathartic, purge, purge away, cleanse, cleanse away; give release, cut loose

7 **lighten,** disburden, unburden, unweight, unload, unfreight, disencumber, disembarrass, ease one's load; set one's mind at ease, set one's mind at rest, set at ease, take a load off one's mind, smooth the ruffled brow of care; relieve oneself, let one's hair down, pour one's heart out, talk it out, let it all hang out, go public, get it off one's chest

8 **be relieved,** feel relief, feel better about, get something out of one's system, feel oneself again, be oneself again; get out from under; breathe easy, breathe easier, breathe more freely, breathe again, rest easier; heave a sigh of relief, draw a deep breath

ADJS 9 **relieving, easing,** alleviative, alleviating, alleviatory, ameliorating, mitigative, mitigating, palliative, assuaging, lenitive, assuasive, softening, subduing, soothing, demulcent, emollient, balmy, balsamic; remedial; dulling, deadening, numbing, benumbing, anesthetic, analgesic, anodyne, pain-killing, sedative, hypnotic; cathartic, purgative, cleansing; relaxing

10 **relieved,** breathing easy, breathing easier, breathing freely, able to breathe again, out from under, out of the woods; alleviated; decompressed; relaxed; calmed, restored

121 COMFORT

<relaxed pleasant state>

NOUNS 1 **comfort, ease,** well-being; contentment; clover, velvet, bed of roses; life of ease; solid comfort

2 **comfortableness,** easiness; restfulness, reposefulness, peace, peacefulness; softness, cushiness, cushioniness; coziness, snugness; friendliness, warmness; homelikeness, homeyness, homeliness; commodiousness, roominess, convenience; luxuriousness; hospitality

3 **creature comforts,** comforts, conveniences, excellent accommodations, amenities, good things of life, cakes and ale, egg in one's beer, all the comforts of home; all the heart can desire, luxuries, the best

4 **consolation,** solace, solacement, easement, heart's ease; encouragement, aid and comfort, assurance, reassurance, support, comfort, crumb of comfort, shred of comfort; condolence, sympathy; relief

5 **comforter,** consoler, solacer, encourager; the Holy Spirit, the Holy Ghost, the Comforter, the Paraclete

VERBS 6 **comfort,** console, solace, give comfort, bring comfort, bear up; condole with, sympathize with, extend sympathy; ease, put at ease, set at ease; bolster, support; relieve; assure, reassure; encourage, hearten, pat on the back; cheer; wipe away the tears

7 **be comforted, take comfort,** take heart; take hope, lift up one's heart, pull oneself together, pluck up one's spirits

8 **be at ease,** be easy, feel easy, stand easy; make oneself comfortable, make oneself at home, feel at home, put one's feet up, take a load off; relax, be relaxed; live a life of ease

9 **snug,** snug down, snug up; tuck in

10 **snuggle,** nestle, cuddle, cuddle up, curl up; nest; bundle; snuggle up to, snug together

ADJS 11 **comfortable,** comfy, hygge; contented; easy, easeful; restful, reposeful, peaceful, relaxing; soft, cushioned, cushy, cushiony; comfortable as an old shoe; cozy, snug, snug as a bug in a rug; friendly, warm; homelike, homey, down-home, homely, lived-in; commodious, roomy, convenient; low-maintenance, luxurious

12 **at ease,** at one's ease, easy, relaxed, laid-back; at rest, resting easy; at home, in one's element; unstressed

13 **comforting,** consoling, consolatory, of good comfort; condoling, condolent, condolatory, sympathetic; assuring, reassuring, supportive; encouraging, heartening; cheering; relieving; hospitable; warm-and-fuzzy

ADVS 14 **comfortably,** easily, with ease; restfully, reposefully, peacefully; cozily, snugly; commodiously, roomily, conveniently; luxuriously, voluptuously

15 **in comfort,** in ease, in clover, on velvet, in velvet, on a bed of roses, in a bed of roses; hygge

16 **comfortingly,** consolingly, assuringly, reassuringly, supportively, encouragingly, hearteningly; hospitably

122 WONDER

<*surprised state*>

NOUNS **1** **wonder,** wonderment, sense of wonder, marveling, marvel, astonishment, amazement, amaze, astoundment; dumbfoundment, stupefaction; surprise; awe, breathless wonder, breathless awe, sense of mystery, admiration; beguilement, fascination; bewilderment, puzzlement

2 **marvel,** wonder, prodigy, miracle, phenomenon, phenom; astonishment, amazement, marvelment, wonderment, wonderful thing, nine days' wonder, *annus mirabilis* <L>, amazing thing, astonishing thing, quite a thing, really something, sensation, rocker, stunner; one for the books, something to brag about, something to shout about, something to write home about, something else; rarity, nonesuch, nonpareil, exception, one in a thousand, one in a way, oner; curiosity, sight, spectacle, eye-popper; wonders of the world; masterpiece, chef d'oeuvre, masterstroke

3 **wonderfulness,** wondrousness, marvelousness, miraculousness, phenomenalness, prodigiousness, stupendousness, remarkableness, extraordinariness; beguilingness, fascination, enchantingness, enticingness, seductiveness, glamorousness; awesomeness, mysteriousness, mystery, numinousness; transcendence, transcendentness, surpassingness

4 inexpressibility, **ineffability,** ineffableness, inenarrability, noncommunicability, noncommunicableness, incommunicability, incommunicableness, indescribability, indefinableness, unutterability, unspeakability, unnameableness, innominability, unmentionability

VERBS **5** **wonder,** marvel, be astonished, be amazed, be astounded, be seized with wonder; gaze, gape, drop one's jaw, look aghast, stand aghast, look agog, gawk, stare, stare openmouthed, open one's eyes, rub one's eyes, hold one's breath; not know what to say, not know what to make of, not believe one's eyes, not believe one's senses, not believe one's ears

6 **astonish, amaze**, astound, surprise, startle, stagger, bewilder, perplex, flabbergast, confound, overwhelm, boggle, boggle the mind; awe, strike with wonder, strike with awe; dumbfound, strike dumb, strike dead; strike all of a heap, throw on one's beam ends, knock one's socks off, bowl over, dazzle, bedazzle, daze, bedaze; stun, stupefy, petrify, paralyze

7 take one's breath away, turn one's head, make one's head swim, make one's hair stand on end, make one's tongue cleave to the roof of one's mouth, make one stare, make one sit up, take notice, sweep off one's feet, carry off one's feet; blow one's mind

8 beggar description, baffle description, stagger belief

ADJS **9** wondering, rapt in wonder, marveling, **astonished, amazed,** surprised, astounded, flabbergasted, gobsmacked, bewildered, puzzled, confounded, dumbfounded, dumbstruck, staggered, overwhelmed, unable to believe one's senses, unable to believe one's eyes; aghast, agape, agog, all agog, gazing, gaping, at gaze staring, gauping, wide-eyed, popeyed, open-eyed, openmouthed, breathless; thunderstruck, wonder-struck, wonder-stricken, awestricken, awestruck, struck all of a heap; awed, in awe, in awe of; spellbound, fascinated, captivated, under a charm, beguiled, enthralled, enraptured, enravished, enchanted, entranced, bewitched, hypnotized, mesmerized, stupefied, lost in wonder, lost in amazement; transfixed, rooted to the spot

10 **wonderful,** wondrous, marvelous, awesome, miraculous, fantastic, fabulous, ace, cool, rad, wicked, phenomenal, brilliant, prodigious, stupendous, unheard-of, unprecedented, extraordinary, exceptional, rare, unique, singular, remarkable, striking, sensational, bar none; strange, passing strange, wondrous strange; beguiling, fascinating; incredible, inconceivable, outlandish, unimaginable, incomprehensible; bewildering, puzzling, enigmatic; *magnifique* <Fr>; supercalifragilisticexpialidocious, supercalifragilistic; must-see

11 **awesome,** awful, awing, awe-inspiring; transcendent, transcending, surpassing; mysterious, numinous; weird, eerie, uncanny, bizarre, bizarro; exotic; sweet

12 **astonishing, amazing**, surprising, startling, astounding, confounding, staggering, stunning, eye-opening, breathtaking, overwhelming, mind-boggling, mind–numbing, mind-blowing, jaw-dropping; spectacular, electrifying

13 **indescribable,** ineffable, inenarrable, inexpressible, unutterable, unspeakable, noncommunicable, incommunicable, indefinable, undefinable, unnameable, innominable, unwhisperable, unmentionable

ADVS 14 **wonderfully,** wondrously, marvelously, miraculously, fantastically, fabulously, phenomenally, prodigiously, stupendously, extraordinarily, exceptionally, remarkably, strikingly, sensationally; strangely, outlandishly, incredibly, inconceivably, unimaginably, incomprehensibly, bewilderingly, puzzlingly, enigmatically; beguilingly, fascinatingly

15 **awesomely,** awfully, awingly, awe-inspiringly; mysteriously, numinously, weirdly, eerily, uncannily, bizarrely; transcendently, surpassingly, surpassing, passing, passing fair

16 **astonishingly, amazingly**, astoundingly, staggeringly, confoundingly; surprisingly, startlingly, to one's surprise, to one's great surprise, to one's astonishment, to one's amazement; for a wonder, strange to say

17 **indescribably**, ineffably, inexpressibly, unutterably, unspeakably, inenarrably, indefinably, unnameably, unmentionably

18 in wonder, in astonishment, in amazement, in bewilderment, in awe, in admiration, with gaping mouth

INTERJS 19 <astonishment or surprise> my word, I declare, well I never, of all things, as I live and breathe, what, indeed, really, surely, how now, what on earth, what in the world, I'll be jiggered, holy moly, holy Christmas, holy cow, holy mackerel, holy Moses, holy guacamole, holy smoke, holy shit*, hush my mouth, shut my mouth, shut up, blow me down, strike me dead, shiver my timbers, *sacré bleu* <Fr>; what the fuck*, WTF

20 oh, O, ah, la, lo, lo and behold, hello, halloo, hey, whew, phew, wow, yipes, yike, drap

21 my; oh my; dear, dear me, goodness, gracious, goodness gracious, gee, my goodness, my stars, good gracious, good heavens, good lack, lackadaisy, blimey, my gosh, welladay, hoity-toity, zounds, gadzooks, gad so, bless my heart, God bless me, my oh my, heavens and earth, for crying out loud, jiminy

22 imagine, fancy, fancy that, just imagine, only think, well, I never, can you feature that, can you beat that, it beats the Dutch, do tell, pray tell, you don't say, the devil you say, I'll be, what do you know, what do you know about that, how about that, who would have thought it, did you ever, can it be, can such things be?, will wonders never cease, go on

23 **Seven Wonders of the Ancient World**

The Great Pyramids of Egypt at Giza
The Hanging Gardens of Babylon
The Statue of Zeus at Olympia
The Temple of Artemis (Diana) at Ephesus
The Mausoleum of King Mausolus at Halicarnassus
The Colossus of Rhodes
The Lighthouse of Alexandria

123 UNASTONISHMENT

<unsurprised state>

NOUNS 1 **unastonishment,** unamazement, unamazedness, nonastonishment, nonamazement, nonamazedness, nonwonder, nonwondering, nonmarveling, unsurprise, unsurprisedness, awelessness, wonderlessness; phlegmaticness, apathy, passivity, nonchalance; calm, calmness, coolness, **cool**, cool acceptance, calm acceptance, nodding acceptance, composure, composedness, sangfroid, inexcitability, expectation, unimpressibleness, refusal to be impressed, refusal to be awed, refusal to be amazed; poker face, straight face; predictability

VERBS 2 **accept, take for granted**, take as a matter of course, take in stride, take as it comes, treat as routine, show no amazement, refuse to be impressed, not blink an eye, not turn a hair, keep one's cool; see it coming

ADJS 3 **unastonished,** unsurprised, unamazed, unmarveling, unwondering, unastounded, undumbfounded, unbewildered; undazzled, undazed; unawed, aweless, wonderless, blasé; unimpressed, unmoved; calm, cool, cool as a cucumber, composed, nonchalant, inexcitable; expecting, expected; phlegmatic

124 HOPE

<anticipating good>

NOUNS 1 **hope, hopefulness,** hoping, hopes, fond hope, fervent hope, good hope, good cheer; aspiration, desire; prospect, expectation; sanguine expectation, happy expectation, cheerful expectation; trust, confidence, faith, assured faith, reliance, dependence; conviction, assurance, security, well-grounded hope; assumption, presumption; auspiciousness; promise, good prospect, bright prospect, fair prospect, good prognosis, hopeful prognosis, best case; great expectations, good prospects, high hopes; hoping against hope, prayerful hope; doomed hope, doomed hopes; greener pastures; plus side

2 **optimism,** optimisticalness, Pollyannaism, cheerful outlook, bright outlook, rosy outlook, rose-colored glasses; cheerfulness; bright side, silver lining; wishful thinking; philosophical optimism, Leibnizian optimism, Rousseauistic optimism, Pollyanna optimism, utopianism,

perfectionism, perfectibilism; millenarianism, chiliasm, millennialism

3 **ray of hope,** gleam of hope, glimmer of hope; faint hope, last hope; may the best man win

4 airy hope, unreal hope, **dream,** false hope, golden dream, pipe dream, bubble, chimera, fool's paradise, quixotic ideal, utopia; vision, castles in the air, air castle, cloud-cuckoo-land, lotus land; American dream

5 **optimist,** hoper, Pollyanna, ray of sunshine, irrepressible optimist, Dr Pangloss, idealist; hopemonger; Leibnizian optimist, philosophical optimist, utopian, perfectionist, perfectibilist, perfectibilitarian; millenarian, chiliast, millennialist, millennian; aspirer, aspirant, hopeful, dreamer, visionary

VERBS 6 **hope,** be in hopes, live in hopes, have reason to hope, entertain the hope, harbor the hope, cling to the hope, cherish the hope, foster the hope, nurture the hope; look for, prognosticate, expect; trust, confide, presume, feel confident, rest assured; pin one's hope upon, put one's trust in, hope in, rely on, count on, count upon, lean upon, bank on, set great store on; hope for, aspire to, desire; hope against hope, hope and pray, hope to God

7 **be hopeful,** get one's hopes up, keep one's spirits up, never say die, take heart, cheer up, buck up, be of good hope, be of good cheer, keep hoping, keep hope alive, keep the faith, keep smiling, cling to hope; hope for the best, knock on wood, touch wood, cross one's fingers, keep one's fingers crossed, allow oneself to hope; clutch at straws, catch at straws; wish

8 **be optimistic,** look on the bright side; look through rose-colored glasses, wear rose-colored glasses; call the glass half full, think positively, think affirmatively, be upbeat, think the best of, make the best of it, say that all is for the best, put a good face upon, put a bold face upon, put the best face upon; see the light at the end of the tunnel; count one's chickens before they are hatched, count one's bridges before they are crossed

9 **give hope,** raise hope, yield hope, afford hope, hold out hope, justify hope, inspire hope, raise one's hopes, raise expectations, lead one to expect; cheer; inspire, inspirit; assure, reassure, support; promise, hold out promise, augur well, bid fair, bid well, make fair promise, have good prospects

ADJS 10 **hopeful,** hoping, in hopes, full of hope, in good heart, of good hope, of good cheer; aspiring; expectant; sanguine, fond; confident, assured; undespairing

11 **optimistic,** upbeat, up, bright, sunny; bullish; cheerful; rosy, roseate, rose-colored, *couleur de rose* <Fr>; Pollyannaish, Leibnizian, Rousseauistic, Panglossian; utopian, idealistic, perfectionist, perfectibilitarian, millenarian, chiliastic, millennialistic, visionary

12 **promising,** of promise, full of promise, bright with promise, pregnant of good, best-case, favorable, looking up; aspiring, aspirant; auspicious, propitious; heartening; inspiring, inspiriting, encouraging, cheering, reassuring, supportive; on a wing and a prayer

ADVS 13 **hopefully,** hopingly; expectantly; optimistically; cheerfully; sanguinely, fondly; confidently

125 HOPELESSNESS

<anticipating bad>

NOUNS 1 **hopelessness,** unhopefulness, no hope, not a prayer, not a hope in hell, not the ghost of a chance; small hope, bleak outlook, bleak prospect, bleak prognosis, worst case, blank future, no future; losing battle; inexpectation; futility; impossibility

2 **despair, desperation,** desperateness, loss of hope; no way, no way out, no exit, despondency; disconsolateness; forlornness; letdown; cave of despair, cave of Trophonius; gloom and doom; acedia, sloth; apathy; downer

3 **irreclaimability,** irretrievability, irredeemability, irrecoverableness, unsalvageability, unsalvability; incorrigibility, irreformability; irrevocability, irreversibility; irreparability, incurability, irremediableness, curelessness, remedilessness, immedicableness; unrelievability, unmitigability

4 **forlorn hope,** vain expectation, doomed hope, foredoomed hope, fond hope, foolish hope, futility; counsel of perfection

5 dashed hopes, blighted hope, hope deferred; disappointment

6 **pessimism,** cynicism, malism, nihilism; uncheerfulness; gloominess, dismalness, gloomy outlook; negativism; defeatism; retreatism, Weltschmerz

7 **pessimist,** cynic, malist, nihilist; killjoy, gloomy Gus, calamity howler, worrywart, seek-sorrow, Job's comforter, prophet of doom, Cassandra, Eeyore; negativist; defeatist; retreatist; loser, born loser; drag

8 **lost cause,** fool's errand, wild-goose chase; hopeless case, hopeless situation; goner, gone goose, gone gosling, dead duck; terminal case

VERBS 9 **be hopeless,** have not a hope, have not a prayer, have no remedy, look bleak, look dark; be pessimistic, look on the dark side, be downbeat, think downbeat, think negatively, think the worst of, make the worst of, put the worst face upon, see the glass half empty; not hold one's breath

10 **despair,** despair of, despond, falter, lose hope, lose heart, abandon hope, give up hope, give up, give up all hope, give up all expectation, give way, give over, fall into despair, sink into despair, give oneself up, yield to despair, throw up one's hands in despair, turn one's face to the wall; curse God and die, write off

11 **shatter one's hopes,** dash one's hopes, crush one's hopes, burst one's bubble, bring crashing down around one's head, dash the cup from one's lips, disappoint, drive to despair, drive to desperation

ADJS 12 **hopeless,** unhopeful, without hope, affording no hope, worst-case, bleak, grim, dismal, cheerless, comfortless, down in the mouth; desperate, despairing, in despair; despondent; disconsolate; forlorn; apathetic

13 **futile,** vain; doomed, foredoomed, pointless

14 **impossible,** out of the question, not to be thought of, no-go, no-win, lose-lose

15 **past hope,** beyond recall, past praying for, beyond hope, abject; irretrievable, irrecoverable, irreclaimable, irredeemable, unsalvageable, unsalvable; incorrigible, irreformable; irrevocable, irreversible; irremediable, irreparable, inoperable, incurable, cureless, remediless, immedicable, beyond remedy, terminal; unrelievable, unmitigable; ruined, undone, kaput; lost, gone, gone to hell, gone to hell in a handbasket

16 **pessimistic,** pessimist, downbeat, cynical, nihilistic; uncheerful; gloomy, dismal, crepehanging, funereal, lugubrious; negative, negativistic; defeatist; Cassandran, Cassandrian, Cassandra-like

ADVS 17 **hopelessly,** desperately, forlornly; impossibly

18 **irreclaimably**, irretrievably, irrecoverably, irredeemably, unsalvageably, unsalvably; irrevocably, irreversibly; irremediably, incurably, irreparably

126 ANXIETY

<fear of future>

NOUNS 1 **anxiety, anxiousness**; apprehension, apprehensiveness, antsyness, misgiving, foreboding, forebodingness, suspense, strain, tension, stress, nervous strain, nervous tension; dread, fear; concern, concernment, anxious concern, solicitude, zeal; care, cankerworm of care; distress, trouble, vexation, unease; uneasiness, perturbation, disturbance, upset, agitation, disquiet, disquietude, inquietude, unquietness; nervousness; malaise, angst; pucker, yips, stew, all-overs, pins and needles, tenterhooks, shpilkes; overanxiety; anxious seat; anxiety neurosis, anxiety hysteria; performance anxiety

2 **worry,** worriment, worriedness; worries, worries and cares, troubles, concerns; worrying, fretting; harassment, torment

3 **worrier,** worrywart, nervous Nellie, fussbudget

VERBS 4 **concern,** give concern, trouble, bother, distress, disturb, upset, frazzle, disquiet, agitate; rob one of ease, rob one of sleep, rob one of rest, keep one on edge, keep one on tenterhooks, keep one on shpilkes, keep one on pins and needles

5 <**make anxious**> worry, upset, vex, fret, agitate, get to, harass, harry, torment, dog, hound, plague, persecute, haunt, beset

6 <**feel anxious**> worry, worry oneself, worry one's head about, worry oneself sick, trouble one's head, trouble oneself, be a prey to anxiety, lose sleep; have one's heart in one's mouth, have one's heart miss a beat, have one's heart skip a beat, have one's heart stand still, get butterflies in one's stomach; fret, fuss, chafe, stew, take on, fret and fume; tense up, bite one's nails, walk the floor, go up the wall, be on tenterhooks, be on shpilkes, be on pins and needles

ADJS 7 **anxious,** concerned, apprehensive, foreboding, misgiving, suspenseful, strained, tense, tensed up, nail-biting, white-knuckle; fearful; solicitous, zealous; troubled, bothered; uneasy, perturbed, disturbed, disquieted, agitated; nervous; on pins and needles, on tenterhooks, on shpilkes, on the anxious seat; all hot and bothered, in a pucker, in a stew; over-anxious, overapprehensive; trepidacious

8 **worried,** vexed, fretted; harassed, harried, tormented, dogged, hounded, persecuted, haunted, beset, plagued; worried sick, worried to a frazzle, worried stiff

9 **careworn,** heavy-laden, overburdened

10 **troublesome,** bothersome, distressing, distressful, disturbing, upsetting, disquieting; worrisome, worrying; fretting, chafing; harassing, tormenting, plaguing; annoying

ADVS 11 **anxiously,** concernedly, apprehensively, misgivingly, uneasily; worriedly; solicitously, zealously

127 FEAR, FEARFULNESS

<feeling or sensing danger>

NOUNS 1 **fear, fright,** affright; scare, alarm, consternation, dismay; dread, unholy dread, awe;

terror, horror, horrification, mortal fear, abject fear; **phobia** <see list>, funk, blue funk; panic, panic fear, panic terror, blind panic; stampede; cowardice

2 **fearfulness,** frighteningness, frightfulness, awfulness, scariness, fearsomeness, alarmingness, dismayingness, disquietingness, startlingness, disconcertingness, terribleness, dreadfulness, horror, horribleness, hideousness, appallingness, direness, ghastliness, grimness, grisliness, gruesomeness, ghoulishness; creepiness, spookiness, eeriness, weirdness, uncanniness

3 **fearfulness,** afraidness; timidity, timorousness, **shyness;** shrinkingness, bashfulness, diffidence, stage fright, mike fright, flop sweat; skittishness, startlishness, jumpiness, goosiness; shamefacedness

4 **apprehension,** apprehensiveness, misgiving, qualm, qualmishness, funny feeling; anxiety, angst; worry; doubt, mental reservation; foreboding

5 **trepidation,** trepidity, perturbation, fear and trembling; quaking, agitation; uneasiness, disquiet, disquietude, inquietude; nervousness; palpitation, heartquake; shivers, cold shivers, creeps, cold creeps, heebie-jeebies, chills of fear, chills of terror, icy fingers, icy clutch of dread, jimjams; horripilation, gooseflesh, goose bumps; sweat, cold sweat; thrill of fear, spasm of terror, quiver of terror; sinking stomach; blood running cold, knocking knees, chattering teeth

6 **frightening,** intimidation, bullying, browbeating, cowing, bulldozing, hectoring; demoralization, psychological warfare, war of nerves; cyberbullying, cyberharassment, cyberstalking, trolling; fat shaming

7 terrorization, **terrorizing,** horrification, scaremongering, panic-mongering, scare tactic, scare tactics; terrorism, terror tactics, terroristic tactics, rule by terror, reign of terror, sword of Damocles, war of nerves; agroterrorism, bioterrorism, cyberterrorism

8 **alarmist,** scaremonger, doomsayer, panic-monger; terrorist, bomber, assassin

9 **frightener,** scarer, hair-raiser; alarmist; scarebabe, bogey, bogeyman, bugaboo, bugbear; hobgoblin; scarecrow; horror, terror, holy terror; ogre, ogress, monster, vampire, werewolf, ghoul, bête noire, fee-faw-fum; incubus, succubus, nightmare; witch, goblin; ghost, specter, phantom, revenant; Frankenstein, Dracula, Wolf-man; mythical monsters

VERBS 10 **fear, be afraid;** apprehend, have qualms, misgive, eye askance; dread, stand in dread of, be in mortal dread of, be in mortal terror of, stand in awe of, stand aghast; be on pins and needles, sit upon thorns; have one's heart in one's mouth, have one's heart stand still, have one's heart skip a beat, miss a beat; quake in one's boots; sweat, break out in a cold sweat, sweat bullets

11 **take fright,** take alarm, push the panic button, press the panic button, hit the panic button; funk, go into a funk, get the wind up; lose courage; pale, grow pale, turn pale, change color, turn color; look as if one has seen a ghost; freeze, be paralyzed with fear, throw up one's hands in horror, jump out of one's skin; shit in one's pants*, shit green*

12 **start,** startle, jump, jump out of one's skin, jump a mile, leap like a startled gazelle; shy, fight shy, start aside, boggle, jib; panic, stampede, skedaddle

13 **flinch,** shrink, shy, shy away from, draw back, recoil, funk, quail, cringe, wince, blench, blink, say uncle, cry uncle; put one's tail between one's legs

14 **tremble,** shake, quake, shiver, quiver, quaver; tremble in one's boots, quake in one's boots, shake in one's boots, quake in one's shoes, tremble like an aspen leaf, quiver like a rabbit, shake all over

15 **frighten,** fright, affright, funk, frighten out of one's wits, frighten away, scare out of one's wits; scare, spook, scare one stiff, scare shitless*, scare spitless, scare the life out of, scare the pants off of, scare the hell out of, scare the shit out of*; scare one to death, scare the daylights out of, scare the living daylights out of; give one a fright, give one a scare, give one a turn; alarm, disquiet, raise apprehensions; shake, stagger; startle; unnerve, unman, unstring; give one goose-flesh, horripilate, give one the creeps, give one the willies, make one's flesh creep, chill one's spine, make one's nerves tingle, curl one's hair, make one's hair stand on end, make one's blood run cold, freeze the blood, curdle the blood, make one's teeth chatter, make one tremble, take one's breath away, make one shit one's pants*, make one shit green*

16 **put in fear,** put the fear of God into, throw a scare into; panic, stampede, send scuttling, throw blind fear into

17 **terrify,** awe, strike terror into; horrify, appall, shock, make one's flesh creep; frighten out of one's wits, frighten out of one's senses; strike dumb, stun, stupefy, paralyze, petrify, freeze

18 **daunt, deter,** shake, stop, stop in one's tracks, set back; discourage, dishearten; faze; awe, overawe

19 **dismay,** disconcert, appall, astound, confound, abash, discomfit, put out, take aback

20 **intimidate,** cow, browbeat, bulldoze, bludgeon, dragoon; bully, hector, harass, huff; bluster, bluster out of, bluster into; terrorize, put in bodily fear, use terror tactics, pursue a policy of *Schrecklichkeit,* systematically terrorize; threaten; demoralize

21 **frighten off, scare away,** bluff off, put to flight

ADJS 22 **afraid, scared,** scared to death, spooked; feared, afeared; fear-stricken, fear-struck; haunted with fear, phobic

23 **fearful,** fearing, fearsome, in fear; cowardly; timorous, timid, shy, rabbity, mousy, afraid of one's own shadow; shrinking, bashful, diffident; scary; skittish, skittery, startlish, gun-shy, jumpy, goosy; tremulous, trembling, trepidant, shaky, shivery; nervous; waiting for the bomb to drop

24 **apprehensive,** misgiving, antsy, qualmish, qualmy; anxious

25 **frightened,** frightened to death, affrighted, in a fright, frit, in a funk, in a blue funk; alarmed, disquieted; consternated, dismayed, daunted; startled; more frightened than hurt

26 **terrified,** terror-stricken, terror-struck, terror-smitten, terror-shaken, terror-troubled, terror-riven, terror-ridden, terror-driven, terror-crazed, terror-haunted; awestricken, awestruck; horrified, horror-stricken, horror-struck; appalled, astounded, aghast; frightened out of one's wits, frightened out of one's mind, scared to death, scared stiff, scared shitless*; unnerved, unstrung, unmanned, undone, cowed, awed, intimidated; stunned, petrified, stupefied, paralyzed, frozen; white as a sheet, pale as death, pale a ghost, deadly pale, ashen, blanched, pallid, gray with fear

27 **panicky,** panic-prone, panicked, in a panic, panic-stricken, panic-struck, terror-stricken, out of one's mind with fear, prey to blind fear

28 **frightening, frightful**; fearful, fearsome, fear-inspiring, nightmarish, hellish; scary, scaring, chilling, blood-tingling; alarming, startling, disquieting, dismaying, disconcerting; unnerving, daunting, deterring, deterrent, discouraging, disheartening, fazing, awing, overawing; stunning, stupefying, mind-boggling, mind–numbing, hair-raising

29 **terrifying,** terrorful, terror-striking, terror-inspiring, terror-bringing, terror-giving, terror-breeding, terror-breathing, terror-bearing, terror-fraught; bloodcurdling, hair-raising; petrifying, paralyzing, stunning, stupefying; terrorizing, terror, terroristic

30 **terrible,** terrific, tremendous; horrid, horrible, horrifying, horrific, horrendous; dreadful, dread, dreaded; awful; awesome, awe-inspiring; shocking, appalling, astounding; dire, direful, fell; formidable, redoubtable; hideous, ghastly, morbid, grim, grisly, gruesome, ghoulish, macabre

31 **creepy,** spooky, eerie, weird, uncanny

ADVS 32 **fearfully,** apprehensively, diffidently, for fear of; timorously, timidly, shyly, mousily, bashfully, shrinkingly; tremulously, tremblingly, quakingly, with fear and trembling; with heart in mouth, with bated breath

33 **in fear**, in terror, in awe, in alarm, in consternation; in mortal fear, in fear of one's life

34 **frightfully,** fearfully; alarmingly, startlingly, disquietingly, dismayingly, disconcertingly; shockingly, appallingly, astoundingly; terribly, terrifically, tremendously; dreadfully, awfully; horridly, horribly, horrifyingly, horrifically, horrendously

35 **phobia by name**

ablutophobia <washing, bathing>
acrophobia, altophobia, batophobia, hypsophobia <high places>
acrophobia <sharpness>
aerophobia <draft>
agoraphobia <open places>
agrizoophobia <wild animals>
agyrophobia <crossing a street>
ailurophobia, aelurophobia, galeophobia <cats>
alcoholophobia, dipsophobia <alcohol>
alektorophobia <chickens>
algophobia <pain>
allodoxaphobia <other people's opinions>
amaxophobia <being in vehicles>
ancraophobia <wind>
alliumphobia <garlic>
ambulophobia, basiphobia <walking>
androphobia <men>
anemophobia <anemia>
anginophobia <narrowness>
Anglophobia <English, England>
anthophobia <flowers>
anthropophobia <people>
antlophobia <floods>
apeirophobia <infinity>
apiphobia, melissophobia <bees>
arachibutyrophobia <peanut butter sticking in mouth>
arachnophobia <spiders>
arithmophobia, numerophobia <numbers>
asthenophobia <weakness>
astraphobia, astrapophobia <lightning>
ataxophobia, ataxiophobia <chaos, disorder>
atelophobia <imperfection>
atephobia <ruin, ruins>
aulophobia <flutes>
aurophobia <gold>
automysophobia <being dirty>
autophobia, monophobia, ermitophobia <being alone, loneliness>
aviatophobia <flying>
bacillophobia, microbiophobia <microbes>
bacteriophobia <bacteria>

ballistophobia <bullets>
barophobia <gravity>
bathophobia <depth>
batophobia <passing high buildings>
batrachophobia, herpetophobia <reptiles, frogs>
belonephobia <needles>
bibliophobia <books>
blennophobia, myxophobia <slime>
botanophobia <plants>
bromidrosiphobia, bromidrophobia <body odor>
brontophobia, tonitrophobia, keraunophobia <thunder>
cancerphobia, cancerophobia, carcinophobia <cancer>
cainophobia, cainotophobia <newness>
cardiophobia <heart disease>
carnophobia <meat>
chaetophobia, trichophobia <hair>
cheimaphobia, cheimatophobia, frigophobia <cold>
chionophobia <snow>
cholerophobia <cholera>
chrometophobia <money>
chromophobia <color>
chronophobia <duration, time>
cibophobia, sitophobia, sitiophobia <food>
claustrophobia <enclosed places>
climacophobia <stairs>
clinophobia <going to bed>
cnidophobia <insect stings>
coimetrophobia <cemeteries>
coitophobia <coitus, intercourse>
cometophobia <comets>
coprophobia <feces>
coprostasophobia <constipation>
cremnophobia <precipices>
cryophobia <ice>
crystallophobia, hyalophobia <crystals>
cyberphobia <computers>
cymophobia <waves>
cynophobia <dogs>
decidophobia <decisions>
demonophobia <demons>
demophobia <crowds>
dendrophobia <trees>
dentophobia <dentists>
dermatopathophobia <skin disease>
dermatosiophobia, dermatophobia <skin>
diabetophobia <diabetes>
didaskaleinophobia, scolionophobia <school>
dikephobia <justice>
diplopiaphobia <double vision>
doraphobia <fur>
dromophobia, kinetophobia, kinesophobia <motion>
dystychiphobia <accidents>
ecclesiophobia <church>
ecophobia, oecophobia, oikophobia, domatophobia <home>
eisoptrophobia <mirrors>
electrophobia <electricity>
eleutherophobia <freedom>
emetophobia <vomiting>
enetophobia <pins>
entomophobia <insects>
eosophobia <dawn>
eremikophobia <sand>
eremitophobia, eremophobia <stillness, solitude>
ergophobia <work>
erotophobia, genophobia <sex>
erythrophobia <blushing>
febriphobia <fever>
Francophobia, Gallophobia <French>
gametophobia <marriage>
gephyrophobia <crossing a bridge>
gerascophobia <growing old>
gerontophobia <old people, old age>
Germanophobia, Teutonophobia <Germans>
germophobia <germs>
geumatophobia <taste>
graphophobia <writing>
gymnophobia, nudophobia <nudity>
gynephobia <women>
hadephobia, stygiophobia <hell>
hagiophobia <saints>
hamartophobia, peccatiphobia <sin>
hamaxophobia, amaxophobia <riding in cars>
haptophobia, haphophobia, thixophobia <touch>
harpaxophobia <robbers>
hedonophobia <pleasure>
heliophobia <sun>
helminthophobia <worms>
hemaphobia, hematophobia, hemophobia <blood>
hierophobia <priests, holy people>
hippophobia <horses>
hodophobia <travel>
homichlophobia <fog>
homophobia <homosexuality>
hormephobia <shock>
hydrophobia <water>
hydrophobophobia <rabies>
hygrophobia <dampness>
hypegiaphobia <responsibility>
hypnophobia, noctiphobia <sleep>
iatrophobia <doctors, hospitals>
ichthyophobia <fish>
ideophobia <ideas>
isolophobia <solitude>
isopterophobia <termites>
Japanophobia <Japanese>
kakorraphiaphobia <failure>
katagelophobia <ridicule>
kenophobia <void>
kleptophobia <stealing>
koniophobia, coniophobia, amathophobia <dust>
kopophobia <fatigue>
lachanophobia <vegetables>
lalophobia, laliophobia, glossophobia, phonophobia <speech>
ligyrophobia <noise>
lilapsophobia <hurricanes>
limnophobia <lakes>
linonophobia <string>
logophobia <words>
lyssophobia, maniaphobia <insanity>
mastigophobia <beating>
mechanophobia <machinery>
meningitophobia <meningitis>
menophobia <menstruation>
metallophobia <metal>
microphobia <small things>
monophobia <one thing>
musicophobia <music>
musophobia <mice>
myrmecophobia <ants>
mysophobia <dirt>
necrophobia <corpses>
neophobia <new things>
nephophobia <clouds>

nephophobia, pathophobia <disease>
nomophobia <being without cellular service>
nosemaphobia, nosophobia <illness>
nosocomephobia <hospitals>
nucleomitophobia <nuclear weapons>
nyctophobia <night>
obesophobia, pocrescophobia <gaining weight>
ochlophobia <mobs>
ochophobia <vehicles>
odontophobia <teeth>
olfactophobia, osmophobia, ophresiophobia <smell>
ombrophobia <rain>
ommatophobia <eyes>
oneirophobia <dreams>
onomatophobia <names>
ophiciophobia, ophiophobia, snakephobia <snakes>
ornithophobia <birds>
panphobia, pantophobia <everything>
papaphobia <the Pope>
parasitophobia <parasites>
parthenophobia <young girls>
pathophobia <disease>
patroiophobia <heredity>
pediculophobia <lice, parasites>
pedophobia <children>
peniaphobia <poverty>
pentheraphobia <mother-in-law>
phagophobia <swallowing>
phalacrophobia <baldness>
pharmacophobia <drugs>
phasmophobia <ghosts>
phengophobia <daylight, sunlight>
philemaphobia, philematophobia <kissing>
philophobia <love>
philosophobia <philosophy>
phobophobia <fear>
photophobia <light>
phronemophobia <thinking>
pneumatophobia <spirits>
pnigophobia, pnigerophobia <smothering>
pogonophobia <beards>
poinephobia <punishment>
politicophobia <politics>
potamophobia <rivers>
potophobia <drink>
proteinphobia <protein>
pteronophobia <feathers>
pyrophobia <fire>
radiophobia <radiation>
rectophobia <rectum>
rhabdophobia <magic>
rhytiphobia <wrinkles>
Russophobia <Russians>
rypophobia <soiling>
samhainophobia <Halloween>
Satanophobia <Satan>
scabiophobia <scabies>
sciophobia <shadows>
selaphobia <light flashes>
selenophobia <moon>
sexophobia, heterophobia <opposite sex>
siderophobia <stars>
Sinophobia <Chinese>
sophophobia <learning>
spermophobia, spermatophobia <germs>
spheksophobia <wasps>
stasophobia <standing>
symmetrophobia <symmetry>
syngenesophobia <relatives>
syphilophobia <syphilis>
tachophobia <speed>
taphophobia <being buried alive>
taurophobia <bulls>
technophobia <technology>
telephonophobia <telephone>
teratophobia <monsters>
thaasophobia <being idle>
thalassophobia <sea>
thanatophobia <death>
theophobia <God>
thermophobia <heat>
tocophobia, maieusiophobia, maieuticophobia <childbirth>
tomophobia <surgery>
topophobia <certain places>
toxiphobia, toxophobia, toxicophobia <poison>
traumatophobia <wound, injury>
tredecaphobia, triskaidekaphobia <the number thirteen>
tremophobia <trembling>
trichinophobia <trichinosis>
trichopathophobia <hair disease>
trypanophobia, vaccinophobia <inoculation>
tuberculophobia, phthisiophobia <tuberculosis>
tyrannophobia <tyrants>
uranophobia, ouranophobia <heaven>
urophobia <urine>
ursaphobia <bears>
venereophobia <venereal disease>
vermiphobia, helminthophobia <worms>
xenophobia <foreigners>
xylophobia <forests>
zelophobia <jealousy>
zoophobia <animals>

36 phobia by subject

<accidents> dystychiphobia
<alcohol> alcoholophobia, dipsophobia
<anemia> anemophobia
<animals> zoophobia
<ants> myrmecophobia
<bacteria> bacteriophobia
<baldness> phalacrophobia
<beards> pogonophobia
<bears> ursaphobia
<bees> apiphobia, melissophobia
<being alone> autophobia, monophobia, eremiophobia, eremophobia
<being buried alive> taphophobia
<being dirty> automysophobia
<being idle> thaasophobia
<being in vehicles> amaxophobia
<being whipped> mastigophobia
<birds> ornithophobia
<blood> hemaphobia, hematophobia, hemophobia
<blushing> erythrophobia
<body odor> bromidrophobia, bromidrosiphobia
<books> bibliophobia
<bridges> gephyrophobia
<bullets> ballistophobia
<bulls> taurophobia
<cancer> cancerphobia, cancerophobia, carcinophobia
<cats> ailurophobia, aelurophobia, galeophobia
<cemeteries> coimetrophobia
<certain places> topophobia
<chaos, disorder> ataxophobia, ataxiophobia
<chickens> alektorophobia

<childbirth> ocophobia, maieusiophobia, maieuticophobia
<children> pedophobia
<Chinese> Sinophobia
<cholera> cholerophobia
<church> ecclesiophobia
<clouds> nephelophobia
<coitus, intercourse> coitophobia
<cold> cheimaphobia, cheimatophobia, frigophobia
<color> chromophobia, chromatophobia
<comets> cometophobia
<computers> cyberphobia
<constipation> coprostasophobia
<corpses> necrophobia
<crossing a bridge> gephyrophobia
<crossing a street> agyrophobia
<crowds> demophobia
<crystals> crystallophobia, hyalophobia
<dampness> hygrophobia
<dancing> chorophobia
<darkness> scotophobia, achluophobia, nyctophobia
<dawn> eosophobia
<daylight, sunlight> phengophobia
<death> thanatophobia
<decisions> decidophobia
<demons> demonophobia
<dentists> dentophobia
<depth> bathophobia
<diabetes> diabetophobia
<dirt> mysophobia
<disease> pathophobia
<doctors, hospitals> iatrophobia
<dogs> cynophobia
<double vision> diplopiaphobia
<draft> aerophobia
<dreams> oneirophobia
<drink> potophobia
<drugs> pharmacophobia
<duration, time> chronophobia
<dust> koniophobia, coniophobia, amathophobia
<electricity> electrophobia
<enclosed places> claustrophobia
<English, England> Anglophobia
<everything> panphobia, pantophobia
<eyes> ommatophobia
<failure> kakorraphiaphobia
<fatigue> kopophobia
<fear> phobophobia
<feathers> pteronophobia
<feces> coprophobia, scatophobia
<fever> febriphobia
<fire> pyrophobia
<fish> ichthyophobia
<floods> antlophobia
<flowers> anthophobia
<flutes> aulophobia
<flying> aviatophobia
<fog> homichlophobia
<food> cibophobia, sitophobia, sitiophobia
<foreigners> xenophobia
<forests> xylophobia
<freedom> eleutherophobia
<French> Francophobia, Gallophobia
<frogs, reptiles> batrachophobia
<fur> doraphobia
<gaining weight> obesophobia, pocrescophobia
<garlic> alliumphobia
<Germans> Germanophobia, Teutonophobia
<germs> spermophobia, spermatophobia, germophobia
<ghosts> phasmophobia
<God> theophobia
<going to bed> clinophobia
<gold> aurophobia
<gravity> barophobia
<growing old> gerascophobia
<hair> chaetophobia, trichophobia
<hair disease> trichopathophobia
<Halloween> samhainophobia
<heart disease> cardiophobia
<heat> thermophobia
<heaven> uranophobia, ouranophobia
<hell> hadephobia, stygiophobia
<heredity> patroiophobia
<high places> acrophobia, altophobia, batophobia, hypsophobia, hypsiphobia
<home> ecophobia, oecophobia, oikophobia, domatophobia
<homosexuality> homophobia
<horses> hippophobia
<hospitals> nosocomephobia
<hurricanes> lilapsophobia
<ice, frost> cryophobia
<ideas> ideophobia
<illness> nosemaphobia, nosophobia
<imperfection> atelophobia
<infinity> apeirophobia
<injury> traumatophobia
<inoculation> trypanophobia, vaccinophobia
<insanity> lyssophobia, maniaphobia
<insects> entomophobia
<insect stings> cnidophobia
<itching> acarophobia
<Japanese> Japanophobia
<jealousy> zelophobia
<justice> dikephobia
<kissing> philemaphobia, philematophobia
<lakes> limnophobia
<learning> sophophobia
<lice, parasites> pediculophobia, phthiriophobia
<light> photophobia
<light flashes> selaphobia
<lightning> astraphobia, astrapophobia
<loneliness> autophobia, monophobia, eremitophobia
<love> philophobia
<machinery> mechanophobia
<magic> rhabdophobia
<marriage> gametophobia, gamophobia
<meat> carnophobia
<men> androphobia
<meningitis> meningitophobia
<menstruation> menophobia
<metal> metallophobia
<mice> musophobia, murophobia
<microbes> bacillophobia, microbiophobia
<mirrors> eisoptrophobia, catoptrophobia
<mites> acarophobia
<mobs> ochlophobia
<money> chrometophobia
<monsters> teratophobia
<moon> selenophobia
<mother-in-law> pentheraphobia
<motion> dromophobia, kinetophobia, kinesophobia
<moving vehicles> ochophobia
<music> musicophobia
<names> onomatophobia
<narrowness> anginophobia
<needles> belonephobia
<newness> cainophobia, cainotophobia, centophobia
<new things> neophobia
<night> nyctophobia

<noise> ligyrophobia
<nuclear weapons> nucleomitophobia
<nudity> gymnophobia, nudophobia
<number 13> triskaidekaphobia
<numbers> arithmophobia, numerophobia
<old people, old age> gerontophobia
<one thing> monophobia
<open places> agoraphobia
<opposite sex> sexophobia, heterophobia
<other people's opinions> allodoxaphobia
<pain> algophobia, odynesphobia
<parasites> parasitophobia
<passing high buildings> batophobia
<peanut butter> arachibutyrophobia
<people> anthropophobia
<philosophy> philosophobia
<pins> enetophobia
<plants> botanophobia
<pleasure> hedonophobia
<poison> toxiphobia, toxophobia, toxicophobia
<politics> politicophobia
<the Pope> papaphobia
<poverty> peniaphobia
<precipices> cremnophobia
<priests, holy people> hierophobia
<protein> proteinphobia
<punishment> poinephobia
<rabies> hydrophobophobia
<radiation> radiophobia
<rain> ombrophobia
<rectum, rectal disease> rectophobia, proctophobia
<relatives> syngenesophobia
<reptiles> batrachophobia, herpetophobia
<responsibility> hypegiaphobia
<ridicule> katagelophobia
<riding in cars> hamaxophobia, amaxophobia
<rivers> potamophobia
<robbers> harpaxophobia
<ruin, ruins> atephobia
<Russians> Russophobia
<saints> hagiophobia
<sand> eremikophobia
<Satan> Satanophobia
<school> didaskaleinophobia, scolionophobia
<sea> thalassophobia
<sex> erotophobia, genophobia
<shadows> sciophobia, sciaphobia
<sharpness> acrophobia, aichurophobia
<shock> hormephobia
<sin> hamartophobia, peccatiphobia
<skin> dermatosiophobia, dermatophobia
<skin disease> dermatopathophobia
<sleep> hypnophobia, noctiphobia
<slime> blennophobia, myxophobia
<small things> microphobia
<smell> olfactophobia, osmophobia, ophresiophobia
<smothering> pnigophobia, pnigerophobia
<snakes> ophiciophobia, ophiophobia, snakephobia
<snow> chionophobia
<soiling> rypophobia
<solitude> isolophobia
<sound> acousticophobia
<sourness> acerophobia, acerbophobia
<speech> lalophobia, laliophobia, glossophobia, phonophobia
<speed> tachophobia
<spiders> arachnophobia
<spirits> pneumatophobia
<stairs> climacophobia
<standing> stasophobia
<stars> siderophobia
<stealing> kleptophobia
<stillness, solitude> eremitophobia, eremophobia
<string> linonophobia
<sun> heliophobia
<surgery> tomophobia
<swallowing> phagophobia
<symmetry> symmetrophobia
<syphilis> syphilophobia
<taste> geumatophobia
<technology> technophobia
<teeth> odontophobia
<telephone> telephonophobia
<termites> isopterophobia
<thinking> phronemophobia
<thirteen> tredecaphobia, triskaidekaphobia
<thunder> brontophobia, tonitrophobia, keraunophobia
<thunder and lightning> astraphobia, astrapophobia
<touch> haptophobia, haphophobia, thixophobia
<travel> hodophobia
<trees> dendrophobia
<trembling> tremophobia
<trichinosis> trichinophobia
<tuberculosis> tuberculophobia, phthisiophobia
<tyrants> tyrannophobia
<urine> urophobia
<vegetables> lachanophobia
<vehicles> ochophobia
<venereal disease> venereophobia, cypridophobia
<void> kenophobia
<vomiting> emetophobia
<walking> ambulophobia, basiphobia
<washing, bathing> ablutophobia
<wasps> spheksophobia
<water> hydrophobia, aquaphobia
<waves> cymophobia
<weakness> asthenophobia
<wild animals> agrizoophobia
<wind> ancraophobia
<without cellular service> nomophobia
<women> gynephobia, feminophobia
<words> logophobia
<work> ergophobia
<worms> vermiphobia, helminthophobia
<wound, injury> traumatophobia
<wrinkles> rhytiphobia
<writing> graphophobia
<young girls> parthenophobia

128 NERVOUSNESS

<feeling worry>

NOUNS 1 **nervousness, nerves,** nervosity, disquiet, uneasiness, apprehensiveness, disquietude, qualmishness, malaise, funny feeling, creeping feeling, creepy feeling, qualm, qualms, misgiving; undue excitability, morbid excitability, excessive irritability, state of nerves, case of nerves, spell of nerves, attack of nerves; agitation, trepidation; fear; panic; fidgets, fidgetiness, jitteriness, jumpiness; nail-biting; twitching, tic, vellication; stage fright, buck fever; nervous stomach, butterflies in one's stomach

2 <nonformal> **jitters,** willies, heebie-jeebies, jimjams, jumps, shakes, quivers, trembles, dithers, collywobbles, butterflies, shivers, cold shivers, creeps, sweat, cold sweat; antsyness, ants in one's pants, yips

3 **tension,** tenseness, tautness, strain, stress, stress and strain, mental strain, nervous tension, nervous strain, pressure

4 **frayed nerves**, frazzled nerves, jangled nerves, shattered nerves, raw nerves, raw nerve endings, twanging nerves, tingling nerves; neurosis; neurasthenia, nervous prostration, crackup, nervous breakdown

5 **nervous wreck,** wreck, a bundle of nerves

VERBS 6 **fidget,** have the fidgets; jitter, have the jitters; tense up; tremble

7 **fall apart,** lose self-control, go into hysterics; lose courage; go to pieces, have a nervous breakdown, fall to pieces, come apart, fall apart at the seams, come apart at the seams

8 <nonformal> **crack,** crack up, go haywire, blow one's cork, blow one's mind, blow one's stack, flip, flip one's lid, flip one's wig, wig out, freak out, spazz out, go out of one's skull; come unglued, come unstuck, come unhinged, go up the wall

9 **get on one's nerves,** jangle the nerves, grate on, jar on, put on edge, set one's teeth on edge, go against the grain, send one up the wall, drive one crazy; **irritate**

10 **unnerve,** unman, undo, unstring, unbrace, reduce to jelly, demoralize, shake, upset, psych out, dash, knock down, knock flat, crush, overcome, prostrate, freak someone out

ADJS 11 **nervous,** nervy; high-strung, overstrung, highly strung, all nerves; uneasy, apprehensive, qualmish, nail-biting, white-knuckle, frit; nervous as a cat; excitable; irritable, edgy, on edge, nerves on edge, on the ragged edge, unhinged, wired, panicky, fearful, frightened

12 **jittery, jumpy,** twittery, skittish, skittery, trigger-happy, gun-shy; shaky, shivery, quivery, in a quiver; tremulous, tremulant, trembly; jumpy as a cat on a hot tin roof; fidgety, fidgeting; fluttery, all of a flutter; twitchy; agitated; shaking, trembling, quivering, shivering; shook up, all shook up

13 **tense,** tensed-up, uptight, strained, stretched tight, taut, unrelaxed, under a strain

14 **unnerved,** unmanned, unstrung, undone, reduced to jelly, unglued, panicked, demoralized, shaken, upset, dashed, stricken, crushed; shot, shot to pieces; neurasthenic, prostrate, prostrated, overcome

15 **unnerving, nerve-racking,** nerve-rending, nerve-shaking, nerve-jangling, nerve-trying, nerve-stretching; jarring, grating

ADVS 16 **nervously,** shakily, shakingly, tremulously, tremblingly, quiveringly

129 UNNERVOUSNESS

<feeling calm>

NOUNS 1 **unnervousness, nervelessness;** sangfroid, **calmness**, inexcitability; unshakiness, untremulousness; steadiness, steady-handedness, steady nerves; no nerves, strong nerves, iron nerves, nerves of steel, icy nerves; cool head

ADJS 2 **unnervous,** nerveless, without a nerve in one's body; strong-nerved, iron-nerved, steel-nerved; coolheaded, calm, inexcitable; calm, cool, and collected; cool as a cucumber; steady, steady as a rock, rock-steady, steady-nerved, steady-handed; unshaky, unshaken, unquivering, untremulous, without a tremor; unflinching, unfaltering, unwavering, unshrinking, unblenching, unblinking; relaxed, unstrained, laid-back

130 EXPECTATION

<anticipating a happening>

NOUNS 1 **expectation,** expectance, expectancy, state of expectancy; predictability, predictableness; anticipation, prospect, thought; contemplation; likelihood, probability; confidence, presumption, reliance, overreliance; certainty; imminence; unastonishment

2 sanguine expectation, cheerful expectation, optimism, eager expectation, **hope**; the light at the end of the tunnel

3 **suspense,** state of suspense, cliff-hanging, limbo, nail-biting; waiting, expectant waiting, hushed expectancy; uncertainty, nervous expectation; anxiety, dread, pessimism, apprehension; what's happening, what's up

4 **expectations,** prospects, outlook, hopes, apparent destiny, apparent fate, future prospects; likelihoods, probabilities; prognosis; accountability, responsibility

VERBS 5 **expect,** be expectant, anticipate, have in mind, have in prospect, face, think, contemplate, have in contemplation, envision, envisage; hope; presume; dread; take for granted; not be surprised, not be a bit surprised; foresee

6 **look forward to,** reckon on, count on, predict,

foresee; look to, look for, watch for, look out for, watch out for, be on the watch for, be on the lookout for, keep a lookout for; be ready for; forestall

7 **be expected,** be one's probable fate, be one's probable destiny, be one's outlook, be one's prospect, be in store

8 **await,** wait, wait for, wait on, wait upon, stay for, tarry for; have an eye out for, keep an eye out for, lie in wait for, line up for; wait around, wait about, watch, watch and wait; bide one's time, bide, abide, mark time; cool one's heels; be in suspense, be on tenterhooks, be on pins and needles, hold one's breath, bite one's nails, sweat, sweat out, sweat it, sweat it out; wait up for, stay up for, sit up for; cross one's fingers; be on the waiting list; be on standby, be on call

9 **expect to,** intend, **plan on**

10 **be as expected,** be as one thought, be as one looked for, turn out that way, come as no surprise; be just like one, be one all over; expect it of, think that way about, not put it past; impend, be imminent; lead one to expect

ADJS 11 **expectant,** expecting, in expectation, in anticipation; anticipative, anticipant, anticipating, anticipatory; holding one's breath; waiting, awaiting, waiting for; forewarned, forearmed, forestalling, ready, prepared, on standby; looking forward to, looking for, watching for, on the watch for, on the lookout for; gaping, agape, agog, all agog, atiptoe, atingle, eager; sanguine, optimistic, hopeful; sure, confident; certain; unsurprised, not surprised

12 **in suspense,** on tenterhooks, on pins and needles, on tiptoe, on edge, with bated breath, tense, taut, in limbo, with muscles tense, quivering, keyed-up, biting one's nails; anxious, apprehensive; dreading; suspenseful, cliff-hanging

13 **expected,** anticipated, awaited, predicted, foreseen; taken for granted; presumed; probable; looked-for, hoped-for; due, promised; long-expected, long-awaited, overdue; in prospect, prospective; in the cards; in view, in one's eye, on the horizon; imminent

14 **to be expected,** as expected, up to expectations, according to expectation, just as one thought, just as predicted, on schedule, as one may have suspected, as one might think, as one might suppose; expected of, counted on, taken for granted; just like one, one all over, in character

ADVS 15 **expectantly,** expectingly; anticipatively, anticipatingly, anticipatorily; hopefully; with bated breath, in hushed expectancy, with breathless expectation; with ears pricked up, with eyes strained, with ears strained

131 INEXPECTATION

<anticipating nothing>

NOUNS 1 **inexpectation,** nonexpectation, inexpectance, inexpectancy, no expectation, **unanticipation; unexpectedness;** unforeseeableness, unpredictableness, unpredictability; unreadiness, unpreparedness; the unforeseen, the unlooked-for, the last thing one expects; improbability

2 **surprise,** surprisal, wonder; astonishment; surpriser, startler, shocker, blow, staggerer, eye-opener, revelation; bolt out of the blue, bolt from the blue, thunderbolt, thunderclap; bombshell, bomb; blockbuster, earthshaker; sudden turn, sudden development, switch; surprise ending, kicker, joker, catch; surprise package; surprise party; dawn raid; shock tactic

3 **start,** shock, jar, jolt, turn, fright

VERBS 4 **not expect,** hardly expect, not anticipate, not look for, not bargain for, not foresee, not think of, not see coming, have no thought of, have no expectation, think unlikely, think improbable

5 **be startled,** be taken by surprise, be taken aback, be given a start, be given a turn, be given a jolt; start, startle, jump, jump a mile, jump out of one's skin; shy, start aside, flinch

6 **be unexpected,** come unawares, come as a surprise, come as a shock, come out of left field, come out of nowhere, appear unexpectedly, turn up, pop up, bob up, drop from the clouds, appear like a bolt out of the blue, come like a burst, come like a thunderclap, come like a thunderbolt, burst upon one, flash upon one, come upon, fall upon, steal up on, creep up on

7 **surprise,** take by surprise, do the unexpected, spring a surprise, open one's eyes, give one a revelation; catch unawares, take unawares, catch short, take short, take aback, pull up short, raise some eyebrows, catch off-guard, cross one up; throw a curve, bowl over, come from behind, come from an unexpected quarter, come out of the blue, come upon unexpectedly, come upon without warning, spring upon, pounce upon; drop a bombshell, drop a brick; throw for a loop, knock for a loop; blindside, spring a mine under, ambush, bushwhack; drop in on; give a surprise party; astonish

8 **startle,** shock, electrify, jar, jolt, shake, stun, stagger, give one a turn, give the shock of one's life, make one jump out of his skin, take aback, take one's breath away, throw on one's beam ends, bowl down, bowl over, strike all of a heap; frighten

ADJS 9 inexpectant, nonexpectant, unexpecting;

unanticipative, unanticipating; **unsuspecting, unaware,** unguessing; uninformed, unwarned, unforewarned, unadvised, unadmonished; unready, unprepared, underprepared; off one's guard

10 **unexpected, unanticipated,** unlooked for, unhoped for, unprepared for, undivined, unguessed, unpredicted, unforeseen; unforeseeable, unpredictable, off-the-wall; improbable; contrary to expectation, beyond expectation, past expectation, on the contrary, au contraire <Fr>, out of one's reckoning, more than expected, more than one bargained for; out of the blue, dropped from the clouds, out of left field, from out in left field; without warning, unheralded, unannounced; sudden; out-of-the-way, extraordinary

11 **surprising, astonishing**; eye-opening, eye-popping; startling, shocking, amazing, electrifying, boggling, staggering, stunning, jarring, jolting

12 **surprised,** struck with surprise, openmouthed, amazed; **astonished**; taken by surprise, taken unawares, caught short; blindsided

13 **startled,** shocked, electrified, jarred, jolted, shaken, shook, staggered, given a turn, give a jolt, taken aback, bowled over, bowled down, struck all of a heap, able to be knocked down with a feather; speechless, flabbergasted

ADVS **14** **unexpectedly,** unanticipatedly, improbably, implausibly, unpredictably, unforseeably, by surprise, unawares, against all expectation, contrary to all expectation, on the contrary, when least expected, as no one would have predicted, without notice, without warning, in an unguarded moment, like a thief in the night; out of a clear sky, out of the blue, like a bolt from the blue; all of the sudden, suddenly

15 **surprisingly,** startlingly, to one's surprise, to one's great surprise; shockingly, staggeringly, stunningly, astonishingly

132 DISAPPOINTMENT

<unhoped-for outcome>

NOUNS **1** **disappointment,** sad disappointment, sore disappointment, bitter disappointment, cruel disappointment, failed expectation, blasted expectation, chagrin; dashed hope, blighted hope, betrayed hope, hope deferred, forlorn hope; dash, dash to one's hopes; blow, buffet; frustration, discomfiture, bafflement, defeat, balk, foiling; comedown, setback, letdown; failure, smackdown, fizzle, fiasco; disillusionment; tantalization, mirage, tease; dissatisfaction; fallen countenance; bad news, bummer

VERBS **2** **disappoint,** defeat expectation, defeat hope; dash, dash one's hope, crush one's hope; balk, bilk, thwart, frustrate, baffle, defeat, foil, cross; put one's nose out of joint; let down, cast down; disillusion; tantalize, tease; dissatisfy; leave in the lurch; burst someone's bubble; fail

3 **be disappointing,** let one down, not come up to expectation, come to nothing, not live up to expectation, not measure up to expectation, go wrong, turn sour, disappoint one's expectations, come short, fall short; peter out, fizzle, fizzle out, not make it, not hack it

4 **be disappointed,** have hoped for better, not realize one's expectations, fail of one's hopes, fail of one's ambitions, run into a stone wall, be let down; look blue, laugh on the wrong side of one's mouth; be crestfallen, be chapfallen be disenchanted

ADJS **5** **disappointed,** bitterly disappointed, sorely disappointed; let down, betrayed, ill-served, ill done-by; dashed, blighted, blasted, crushed; balked, bilked, thwarted, frustrated, baffled, crossed, dished <Brit>, defeated, foiled; caught in one's own trap; disillusioned; disenchanted, chagrined, crestfallen, chapfallen, out of countenance; soured; dissatisfied; regretful

6 **disappointing,** not up to expectation, falling short, out of the running, not up to one's hopes, second-best, third-best, runnerup; tantalizing, teasing; unsatisfactory, unsatisfying; disheartening

133 PREMONITION

<dreamed outcome>

NOUNS **1** **premonition,** presentiment, preapprehension, forefeeling, presage, presagement; **hunch**, feeling in one's bones; prediction

2 foreboding, boding; **apprehension,** misgiving, chill along the spine, creeping of the flesh, shudder of the flesh; wind of change

3 **omen, portent**; augury, auspice, soothsay, prognostic, prognostication; premonitory sign, premonitory symptom, premonitory shiver, premonitory chill, foretoken, foretokening, tokening, betokening, betokenment, foreshowing, prefiguration, presignifying, presignification, preindication, indicant, indication, sign, token, type, promise, sign of the times; foreshadowing, adumbration, foreshadow, shadow

4 **harbinger**, forerunner, precursor, messenger, herald, announcer; presager, premonitor, foreshadower, apparitor

5 **<omen>** bird of ill omen, owl, raven, stormy petrel, Mother Carey's chicken; gathering clouds, clouds on the horizon, dark clouds, black clouds, angry clouds, storm clouds, thundercloud, thunderhead; black cat; broken mirror; rainbow; ring around the moon; shooting star; halcyon bird; woolly bear, groundhog

6 **ominousness,** portentousness, portent, bodefulness, presagefulness, suggestiveness, significance, meaning, meaningfulness; fatefulness, fatality, doomfulness, sinisterness, banefulness, balefulness, direness

7 **inauspiciousness,** unpropitiousness, unfavorableness, unfortunateness, unluckiness, ill-fatedness, ill-omenedness; fatality

8 **auspiciousness,** propitiousness, favorableness; luckiness, fortunateness, prosperousness, beneficience, benignity, benignancy, benevolence; brightness, cheerfulness, cheeriness; good omen, good auspices

VERBS 9 **foreshadow, presage;** omen, be the omen of, auspicate; foreshow, adumbrate, shadow, shadow forth, cast their shadows before; predict; have an intimation, have a hunch, feel in one's bones, know in one's bones, feel the wind of change

10 **forebode,** bode, portend, croak; threaten, menace, lower, look black, spell trouble; warn, forewarn, raise a warning flag, give pause; have a premonition, have a presentiment, apprehend, preapprehend, fear for

11 **augur,** hint, divine; foretoken, preindicate, presignify, presign, presignal, pretypify, prefigure, betoken, token, typify, signify, mean, spell, indicate, point to, look like, be a sign of, show signs of

12 **promise,** suggest, hint, imply, give prospect of, make likely, give ground for expecting, raise expectation, lead one to expect, hold out hope, make fair promise, have a lot going for, have promise, show promise, bid fair, stand fair to

13 **herald, harbinger,** forerun, run before; speak of, announce, proclaim, preannounce; give notice, notify, talk about

ADJS 14 augured, **foreshadowed,** adumbrated, foreshown; indicated, signified; preindicated, prognosticated, foretokened, prefigured, pretypified, presignified, presigned; presignaled; presaged; promised, threatened; predicted

15 **premonitory, forewarning,** augural, monitory, warning, presageful, presaging, foretokening, preindicative, indicative, prognostic, prognosticative, presignificant, prefigurative; significant, meaningful, speaking; foreshowing, foreshadowing; pregnant with meaning, heavy with meaning; forerunning, precursory, precursive; intuitive; predictive

16 **ominous, portentous,** portending; foreboding, boding, bodeful; inauspicious, ill-omened, ill-boding, of ill omen, of fatal omen, of evil portent, loaded with doom, laden with doom, freighted with doom, fraught with doom, looming, looming over; fateful, doomful; presageful; apocalyptic; unpropitious, unpromising, unfavorable, unfortunate, unlucky; sinister, dark, black, gloomy, somber, dreary; threatening, menacing, lowering; bad, evil, ill, untoward; dire, baleful, baneful, ill-fated, ill-starred, evil-starred, star-crossed

17 **auspicious,** of good omen, of happy portent; propitious, favorable, favoring, fair, good; promising, of promise, full of promise; fortunate, lucky, prosperous; benign, benignant, bright, happy, golden, ripe

ADVS 18 **ominously,** portentously, bodefully, forebodingly; significantly, meaningly, meaningfully, speakingly, sinisterly; threateningly, menacingly, loweringly

19 **inauspiciously,** unpropitiously, unpromisingly, unfavorably, unfortunately, unluckily

20 **auspiciously,** propitiously, promisingly, favorably; fortunately, luckily, happily; brightly, fairly

134 PATIENCE

<calm state>

NOUNS 1 **patience,** patientness; **tolerance,** toleration, acceptance; indulgence, lenience, leniency; sweet reasonableness; forbearance, forbearing, forbearingness; sufferance, endurance; long-suffering, long-sufferance, longanimity; stoicism, fortitude, self-control; patience of Job; waiting game, waiting it out; adaptiveness, adaptivity; **perseverance**

2 **resignation,** meekness, humility, humbleness; obedience; amenability; submission, submissiveness; acquiescence, compliance, uncomplainingness; fatalism, submission to fate, submission to necessity, submission to the inevitable; quietude, quietism, passivity, passiveness; *zitzflaysh* <Yiddish>; passive resistance, nonviolent resistance, nonresistance; Quakerism

3 **stoic,** Spartan, man of iron; Job, Griselda

VERBS 4 **be patient,** forbear, bear with composure, **wait,** wait it out, play a waiting game, wait around, wait one's turn, watch for one's moment, keep one's shirt on, keep one's pants on, not hold one's breath; contain oneself, possess oneself, possess one's soul in patience; carry on, carry through

5 **endure,** bear, stand, support, sustain, suffer, tolerate, abide, bide, live with; persevere; bear

up under, bear the brunt, bear with, put up with, stand for, carry one's cross, bear one's cross, take what comes, take the bitter with the sweet, abide with, brook, brave, brave out, man up, hang in there, keep it up

6 <nonformal> **take it,** take it on the chin, take it like a man, not let it get one down, stand the gaff; bite the bullet; hold still for, stand still for, swallow, stick, hang in, hang in there, hang tough, tough it out, stick it out; lump it

7 **accept,** condone, countenance; overlook, not make an issue of, let go by, let pass; reconcile oneself to, resign oneself to, yield to, submit to, obey; accustom oneself to, adjust oneself to, sit through; accept one's fate, lay in the lap of the gods, take things as they come, roll with the punches; make the best of it, make the most of it, make the best of a bad bargain, make a virtue of necessity; submit with a good grace, grin and bear it, grin and abide, shrug, shrug it off, slough off, not let it bother one; take in good part, take in stride; rise above

8 **take,** pocket, swallow, down, stomach, eat, digest, disregard, turn a blind eye, ignore; swallow an insult, pocket the affront, turn the other cheek, take it lying down, turn aside provocation

ADJS 9 **patient,** armed with patience, with a soul possessed in patience, patient as Job, Job-like, Griselda-like; tolerant, tolerative, tolerating, accepting; understanding, indulgent, lenient; forbearing; philosophical; long-suffering, longanimous; enduring, endurant; stoic, stoical, Spartan; disciplined, self-controlled; persevering; impassive

10 **resigned,** reconciled; wait-and-see; **meek,** humble; obedient, amenable, submissive; acquiescent, compliant; accommodating, adjusting, adapting, adaptive; unresisting, passive; uncomplaining, long-suffering

ADVS 11 **patiently,** enduringly, stoically; tolerantly, indulgently, longanimously, leniently, forbearantly, forbearingly, philosophically, more in sorrow than in anger; perseveringly

12 **resignedly,** meekly, submissively, passively, acquiescently, compliantly, uncomplainingly

PHRS 13 Rome wasn't built in a day; all in good time; all things come to him who waits; don't hold your breath; time will tell

135 IMPATIENCE

<agitated state>

NOUNS 1 **impatience,** impatientness, unpatientness, breathless impatience; anxiety, anxiety attack, eagerness; tense readiness, restlessness, restiveness, ants in one's pants, prothymia; disquiet, disquietude, unquietness, uneasiness, nervousness; sweat, lather, stew, fretfulness, fretting, chafing; impetuousness; haste; excitement

2 **intolerance,** intoleration, unforbearance, nonendurance

3 **the last straw,** the straw that breaks the camel's back, the limit, the limit of one's patience, all one can bear, all one can stand

VERBS 4 **be impatient,** hardly wait; hasten; itch to, burn to; chomp at the bit, pull at the leash, not be able to sit down, not be able to stand still; chafe, fret, fuss, squirm; stew, sweat, sweat and stew, get into a dither, get into a stew, work oneself into a lather, work oneself into a sweat, get excited; wait impatiently, sweat it out, pace the floor; beat the gun, jump the gun, go off half-cocked, shoot from the hip

5 **have no patience with,** be out of all patience; lose patience, run out of patience, be exasperated, call a halt, have had it, blow the whistle

ADJS 6 **impatient,** unpatient; breathless; champing at the bit, rarin' to go; dying, anxious, eager; hopped-up, in a lather, in a sweat, in a stew, excited; edgy, on edge; restless, restive, unquiet, uneasy, on *shpilkes* <Yiddish>; fretful, fretting, chafing, antsy-pantsy, antsy, squirming, squirmy, about to pee one's pants, about to piss one's pants*; exasperated; impetuous; hasty

7 **intolerant,** unforbearing, unindulgent

ADVS 8 **impatiently,** breathlessly; anxiously; fretfully; restlessly, restively, uneasily; intolerantly; hastily

136 PRIDE

<self-respecting state>

NOUNS 1 **pride,** proudness, pridefulness; **self-esteem,** self-respect, self-confidence, self-reliance, self-consequence, face, independence, self-sufficiency; pardonable pride; obstinate pride, stiff-necked pride, stiff-neckedness; vanity, conceit; haughtiness, swell, arrogance, hubris; boastfulness; purse-pride

2 **proud bearing,** pride of bearing, military bearing, erect bearing, stiff backbone, straight backbone, **dignity,** dignifiedness, stateliness, courtliness, grandeur, loftiness; pride of place; nobility, lordliness, princeliness; majesty, regality, kingliness, queenliness; distinction, worthiness, augustness, venerability; sedateness, solemnity, gravity, *gravitas* <L>, sobriety

3 proudling; stiff neck; egoist; boaster, peacock; the proud

VERBS 4 **be proud,** hold up one's head, hold one's head high, stand up straight, hold oneself erect, never stoop; look one in the face, look one in the eye; stand on one's own two feet, pay one's own way; have one's pride

5 **take pride,** pride oneself, preen oneself, plume oneself on, pique oneself, congratulate oneself, hug oneself; be proud of, glory in, exult in, burst with pride

6 **make proud,** do one's heart good, do one proud, gratify, elate, flush, turn one's head

7 save face, save one's face, preserve one's dignity, guard one's honor, preserve one's honor, be jealous of one's repute, be jealous of one's good name, cover one's ass

ADJS 8 **proud, prideful,** proudful; self-esteeming, self-respecting; self-confident, self-reliant, independent, self-sufficient; proudhearted, proud-minded, proud-spirited, proud-blooded; proud-looking; proud as Punch, proud as Lucifer, proud as a peacock; erect, stiff-backed, stiff-necked; purse-proud, house-proud

9 **vain,** conceited; haughty, arrogant; boastful, egotistic

10 **puffed up,** swollen, bloated, swollen with pride, bloated with pride, puffed-up with pride; elated, flushed, flushed with pride; bigheaded, swellheaded; egotistical

11 **lofty, elevated,** triumphal, high, high-flown, highfalutin, highfaluting, high-toned; high-minded, lofty-minded; high-headed, high-nosed

12 **dignified,** stately, imposing, grand, courtly, magisterial, aristocratic; noble, ennobled, lordly, princely; majestic, regal, royal, kingly, queenly; worthy, august, venerable; statuesque; sedate, solemn, sober, grave

ADVS 13 **proudly,** pridefully, **with pride;** self-esteemingly, self-respectingly, self-confidently, self-reliantly, independently, self-sufficiently; erectly, with head erect, with head held high, with nose in air; stiff-neckedly; like a lord, *en grand seigneur* <Fr>

14 **dignifiedly, with dignity;** nobly, stately, imposingly, loftily, grandly, magisterially; majestically, regally, royally; worthily, augustly, venerably; sedately, solemnly, soberly, gravely

137 HUMILITY

<humble state>

NOUNS 1 **humility, humbleness**, meekness; lowliness, lowlihood, poorness, meanness, smallness, ingloriousness, undistinguishedness; unimportance; innocuousness; teachableness; submissiveness; modesty, unpretentiousness; plainness, simpleness, homeliness

2 **humiliation,** mortification, egg on one's face, chagrin, embarrassment; abasement, debasement, letdown, setdown, put-down, dump; comedown, descent, deflation, climb-down, wounded pride, injured pride; self-diminishment, self-abasement, self-abnegation; shame, disgrace; shamefacedness, shamefastness, hangdog look

3 **condescension,** condescendence, deigning, lowering oneself, stooping from one's high place

VERBS 4 **humiliate,** humble; mortify, embarrass; put out, put out of face, put out of countenance; shame, disgrace, put to shame, put to the blush, give one a red face; deflate, prick one's balloon; take it out of; marginalize; make one feel small, make one feel this high; do down; bitch-slap*

5 **abase, debase,** crush, abash, degrade, reduce, diminish, demean, lower, bring low, bring down, trip up, take down, set down, put in one's place, put down, diss, dump, dump on, knock one off his perch; take down a peg, take down a notch or two, make a fool of one, make a monkey of one, make an ass of one*

6 <nonformal> **cut one down to size,** knock one down to size, beat one down to size, take the shine out of, take the starch out of, take the wind out of one's sails; put one's nose out of joint, put a tuck in one's tail, make one sing small, take down a rung

7 **humble oneself,** demean oneself, abase oneself, climb down, get down from one's high horse; put one's pride in one's pocket; **eat humble pie,** eat crow, eat dirt, eat one's words, swallow one's pride, lick the dust, take shit*, eat shit*; come on bended knee, come hat in hand; go down on one's knees; pull in one's horns, draw in one's horns, sing small, lower one's tone, tuck one's tail; come down a peg, come down a peg or two; deprecate oneself, diminish oneself, discount oneself, belittle oneself; kiss one's ass

8 **condescend,** deign, vouchsafe; stoop, descend, lower oneself, demean oneself, trouble oneself, set one's dignity aside, set one's dignity to one side; patronize; be so good as to, so forget oneself, dirty one's hands, soil one's hands; talk down to, from high to low

9 **be humiliated,** be put out of countenance; be crushed, feel small, feel cheap, look foolish, look silly, be ready to sink through the floor; take shame, be ashamed, feel ashamed of oneself, be put to the blush, have a very red face; bite one's tongue; hang one's head, hide one's face, not dare to show one's face, not have a word to say for oneself; be taken down a rung

ADJS 10 **humble, lowly,** low, poor, mean, small, inglorious, undistinguished; unimportant; innocuous; biddable, teachable; modest, unpretentious, without airs; plain, simple, homely; humble-looking, humble-visaged; humblest, lowliest, lowest, least

11 humblehearted, humble-minded, humble-spirited, poor in spirit; **meek,** meekhearted, meek-minded, meek-spirited, lamblike, Christlike; abject, submissive

12 **self-abasing,** self-abnegating, self-deprecating, self-depreciating, self-doubting

13 **humbled,** reduced, diminished, lowered, brought down, bought low, set down, bowed down, in the dust, cut down to size; on one's knees, on one's marrowbones

14 **humiliated,** humbled, mortified, embarrassed, chagrined, abashed, crushed, out of countenance; blushing, ablush, red-faced, ashamed, shamed, ashamed of oneself, shamefaced, shamefast; crestfallen, chapfallen, hangdog; taken down a notch

15 **humiliating,** humiliative, humbling, chastening, mortifying, embarrassing, crushing

ADVS 16 **humbly,** meekly; modestly; with due deference, with bated breath; submissively; abjectly, on bended knee, on one's knees, on one's marrowbones, on all fours, with one's tail between one's legs, hat-in-hand

138 SERVILITY

<obedient state>

NOUNS 1 **servility,** slavishness, subservience, subserviency, menialness, abjectness, baseness, meanness; **submissiveness**; slavery, helotry, helotism, serfdom, peonage

2 **obsequiousness,** sycophancy, morigeration, fawningness, fawnery, toadyism, flunkyism; parasitism, sponging; ingratiation, insinuation; truckling, fawning, toadying, toadeating, groveling, cringing, bootlicking, back scratching, flattery; apple-polishing; ass-licking*, ass-kissing*, brown-nosing, sucking up; timeserving; obeisance, prostration; mealymouthedness

3 **sycophant, flatterer,** toady, toad, toadeater, lickspit, lickspittle, truckler, fawner, courtier, led captain, kowtower, groveler, cringer, spaniel; flunky, lackey, jackal; timeserver; creature, puppet, minion, lapdog, tool, cat's-paw, dupe, instrument, faithful servant, slave, helot, serf, peon; mealymouth

4 <nonformal> **apple-polisher,** ass-kisser*, brownnose, brownnoser, brownie, ass-licker*, ass-wiper*, suck-ass*; backslapper, backscratcher, clawback, back-patter; bootlicker, bootlick; handshaker; yes-man, stooge; doormat; Uncle Tom*

5 **parasite,** barnacle, leech; sponger, sponge, freeloader, gigolo, smell-feast; beat, deadbeat

6 **hanger-on, adherent,** dangler, appendage, dependent, satellite, follower, cohort, retainer, servant, man, shadow, tagtail, henchman, heeler

VERBS 7 **fawn,** truckle; **flatter**; toady, toadeat; bootlick, lickspittle, lick one's shoes, lick the feet of; grovel, crawl, creep, cower, cringe, crouch, stoop, kneel, bend the knee, fall on one's knees, prostrate oneself, throw oneself at the feet of, fall at one's feet, kiss one's ass, lick one's ass*, brown-nose, kiss one's feet, kiss the hem of one's garment, lick the dust, make a doormat of oneself; kowtow, bow, bow and scrape

8 **toady to,** truckle to, pander to, cater to; wait on, wait upon, wait on hand and foot, dance attendance, do service, fetch and carry, do the dirty work of, do the bidding of, jump at the bidding of, run after

9 **curry favor,** court, pay court to, make court to, run after, dance attendance on; suck up to, play up to; be a yes-man, agree to anything; fawn upon, fall over, fall all over; handshake, back-scratch, polish the apple

10 **ingratiate oneself,** insinuate oneself, worm oneself in, get into the good graces of, get in with, get next to, get on the good side of, get on the right side of, rub the right way

11 **attach oneself to,** pin oneself upon, fasten oneself upon, hang about, hang around, dangle, hang on the skirts of, hang on the sleeve of, become an appendage of, follow, follow at heel; follow the crowd, get on the bandwagon, go with the stream, hold with the hare and run with the hounds; latch onto, latch on

12 **sponge**, sponge on, sponge off of; feed on, fatten on, batten on, live off, live off of, use as a meal ticket; parasitize

ADJS 13 **servile**, slavish, subservient, menial, base, mean; **submissive**; under one's thumb

14 **obsequious, flattering,** sycophantic, sycophantical, morigerous, toadyish, fawning, truckling, ingratiating, smarmy, toadying, toadeating, bootlicking, back scratching, backslapping, ass-licking*, brownnosing, kiss-ass; groveling, sniveling, cringing, cowering, crouching, crawling; parasitic, leechlike, sponging; timeserving; abject, beggarly, hangdog; obeisant, prostrate, on one's knees, on one's marrowbones, on bended knee; mealymouthed; overattentive; sequacious

ADVS 15 **servilely,** slavishly, subserviently, menially, sequaciously; **submissively**
16 **obsequiously,** sycophantically, ingratiatingly, fawningly, trucklingly; hat-in-hand, cap-in-hand; abjectly, obeisantly, grovelingly, on one's knees; parasitically

139 MODESTY

<shy state>

NOUNS 1 **modesty, meekness;** humility; **unpretentiousness,** unassumingness, unpresumptuousness, unostentatiousness, unambitiousness, unobtrusiveness, unboastfulness
2 **self-effacement,** self-depreciation, self-deprecation, self-detraction, undervaluing of self, self-doubt, diffidence; hiding one's light under a bushel; low self-esteem, weak ego, lack of self-confidence, self-distrust; inferiority complex
3 **reserve, restraint,** constraint, backwardness, retiring disposition; low key, low visibility, low profile; reticence, reluctance, disinclination
4 **shyness, timidity,** timidness, timorousness, bashfulness, shamefacedness, shamefastness, pudicity, pudency, pudibundity, pudibundness, verecundity; coyness, demureness, demurity, skittishness, mousiness; self-consciousness, embarrassment; stammering, confusion; stagefright, mike fright, flop sweat
5 **blushing,** flushing, coloring, mantling, reddening, crimsoning; blush, flush, suffusion, red face
6 shrinking violet, modest violet, mouse

VERBS 7 **efface oneself,** deprecate oneself, doubt oneself, distrust oneself; have low self-esteem; reserve oneself, retire, shrink, retire into one's shell, keep in the background, not thrust oneself forward, keep a low profile, keep oneself to oneself, keep one's distance, remain in the shade, take a back seat, play second fiddle, know one's place, hide one's face, hide one's light under a bushel, avoid the limelight, eschew self-advertisement; disincline
8 **blush,** flush, mantle, color, change color, color up, redden, crimson, turn red, have a red face, get red in the face, blush up to the eyes; stammer; squirm; die of embarrassment

ADJS 9 **modest, meek;** humble; **unpretentious,** unpretending, unassuming, unpresuming, unpresumptuous, unostentatious, unobtrusive, unimposing, unboastful; unambitious, unaspiring
10 **self-effacing,** self-depreciative, self-depreciating, self-deprecating; diffident, deprecatory, deprecative, self-doubting, unself-confident, unself-reliant, unsure of oneself, self-distrustful, self-mistrustful; low in self-esteem
11 **reserved, restrained,** constrained; quiet; low-keyed, keeping low visibility, keeping a low profile; backward, retiring, shrinking
12 **shy, timid,** timorous, bashful, shamefaced, shamefast, pudibund, verecund, verecundious; coy, demure, skittish, mousy; reluctant, disinclined; self-conscious, conscious, confused; stammering, inarticulate
13 **blushing,** blushful; flushed, aflush, red, ruddy, red-faced, red in the face; sheepish; embarrassed

ADVS 14 **modestly, meekly;** humbly; unpretentiously, unpretendingly, unassumingly, unpresumptuously, unostentatiously, unobtrusively; quietly, without ceremony
15 **shyly, timidly,** timorously, bashfully, coyly, demurely, diffidently; shamefacedly, shamefastly, sheepishly, blushingly, with downcast eyes

140 VANITY

<vain state>

NOUNS 1 **vanity, vainness;** overproudness, overweening pride; self-importance, consequentiality, consequentialness, self-esteem, high self-esteem, high self-valuation, positive self-image, self-respect, self-assumption; self-admiration, self-delight, self-worship, self-endearment, self-love, *amour propre* <Fr>, self-infatuation, narcissism, narcism; autoeroticism, autoerotism, self-gratification; self-satisfaction, self-content, ego trip, self-approbation, self-congratulation, self-gratulation, self-complacency, smugness, complacency, self-sufficiency; vainglory, vaingloriousness; God's gift; bragging rights
2 **pride**; arrogance; **boastfulness**
3 **egotism, egoism,** egoisticalness, egotisticalness, ego, self-interest, individualism; egocentricity, egocentrism, self-centeredness, self-centerment, self-obsession; selfishness
4 **conceit, conceitedness,** self-conceit, self-conceitedness, immodesty, self-assertiveness; stuck-upness, chestiness, swelled-headedness, swelled head, swollen head, big head, large hat size; cockiness, pertness, perkiness; pomposity; obtrusiveness, bumptiousness; egomania, megalomania
5 **egotist, egoist,** egocentric, individualist; showoff, peacock; narcissist, narcist, Narcissus; swellhead, braggart, know-it-all, know-all, smart-ass, wiseass, smart aleck, smart alec, smart mouth, no modest violet, vaunter

VERBS 6 **be stuck on oneself,** be impressed with oneself, be overly impressed with oneself; ego-trip, be on an ego trip, go on an ego trip; think well of oneself, think one is it, think one's shit doesn't stink*, get too big for one's breeches, have a swelled head, know it all, have no false modesty, have no self-doubt, love the sound of one's own voice, be blinded by one's own glory, lay the flattering unction to one's soul; fish for compliments; toot one's own horn, **boast**; be vain as a peacock, give oneself airs

7 **puff up, inflate,** swell; go to one's head, turn one's head

ADJS 8 **vain,** vainglorious, bragging, braggadocious, overproud, overweening; self-important, self-esteeming, having high self-esteem, having high self-valuation, self-respecting, self-assuming, consequential; self-admiring, self-delighting, self-worshiping, self-loving, self-endeared, self-infatuated, narcissistic, narcistic; autoerotic, masturbatory; self-satisfied, self-content, self-contented, self-approving, self-gratulating, self-gratulatory, self-congratulating, self-congratulatory, self-complacent, smug, complacent, self-sufficient

9 **proud**; arrogant; boastful

10 **egotistic, egotistical,** egoistic, egoistical, self-interested; egocentric, egocentristic, self-centered, self-obsessed, narcissistic, narcistic; selfish; egomaniac; self-reflexive

11 **conceited,** self-conceited, immodest, self-opinionated; stuck-up, puffed up; swollen-headed, swelled-headed, big-headed, too big for one's britches, biggety, cocky, jumped-up; pert, perk, perky; peacockish, peacocky; know-all, know-it-all, smart-ass, wiseass, smarty, smart-alecky, overwise, wise in one's own conceit; aggressively self-confident, obtrusive, bumptious

12 **stuck on oneself**, impressed with oneself, pleased with oneself, full of oneself, all wrapped up in oneself

ADVS 13 **vainly,** self-importantly; egotistically, egoistically; conceitedly, self-conceitedly, immodestly; cockily, pertly, perkily

141 ARROGANCE

<overly vain state>

NOUNS 1 **arrogance,** arrogantness; overbearingness, bossiness, overbearing pride, overweening pride, stiff-necked pride, assumption of superiority, domineering, domineeringness; **pride,** proudness; superbia, sin of pride, chief of the deadly sins; haughtiness, hauteur; loftiness, Olympian loftiness, Olympian detachment; toploftiness, stuckupness, uppishness, uppityness, hoity-toitiness, hoity-toity; haughty airs; cornstarchy airs; high horse; condescension, condescendence, patronizing, patronization, patronizing attitude; purse-pride

2 **presumptuousness,** presumption, overweening, overweeningness, assumption, total self-assurance; hubris; **insolence**

3 **lordliness, imperiousness,** masterfulness, magisterialness, high-and-mightiness, aristocratic presumption; elitism

4 **aloofness, standoffishness,** offishness, chilliness, coolness, distantness, remoteness

5 **disdain,** disdainfulness, aristocratic disdain, contemptuousness, superciliousness, contumeliousness, cavalierness, you-be-damnedness

6 **snobbery,** snobbishness, snobbiness, snobbism; priggishness, priggery, priggism; snootiness, snottiness, sniffiness, high-hattedness, high-hattiness; tufthunting

7 **snob,** prig; elitist; highbrow, egghead, Brahmin, mandarin; name-dropper, snoot, cold fish

VERBS 8 **give oneself airs**; **condescend**, hold one's nose in the air, look down one's nose, toss the head, bridle; mount one's high horse, get on one's high horse, ride the high horse; patronize, deign, vouchsafe, stoop, descend, lower oneself, demean oneself, trouble oneself, set one's dignity aside, set one's dignity to one side, be so good as to, so forget oneself, dirty one's hands, soil one's hands; talk down to, talk *de haut en bas;* feel entitled

ADJS 9 **arrogant,** overbearing, superior, domineering, proud, haughty; lofty, top-lofty; high-flown, highfalutin, high-faluting; high-headed; high-nosed, stuck-up, uppish, uppity, upstage; hoity-toity, big, big as you please, six feet above contradiction; on one's high horse; condescending, patronizing; purse-proud

10 **presumptuous,** presuming, assuming, overweening, would-be, self-elect, self-elected, self-appointed, self-proclaimed, *soi-disant* <Fr>; insolent

11 **lordly, imperious,** aristocratic, totally self-assured, noble; hubristic; masterful, magisterial, magistral, high-and-mighty; elitist; U; dictatorial

12 **aloof,** standoffish, standoff, offish, chilly, cool, distant, remote, above all that; Olympian

13 **disdainful,** dismissive, **contemptuous,** supercilious, contumelious, cavalier, you-be-damned

14 **snobbish,** snobby, toffee-nosed, priggish, snippy; snooty, snotty, sniffy; high-hat, high-hatted, high-hatty

ADVS 15 **arrogantly,** haughtily, proudly, aloofly; condescendingly, patronizingly; loftily, toploftily; imperiously, magisterially; Olympianly; disdainfully, contemptuously, superciliously, contumeliously; with nose in air, with nose turned up, with head held high, with arms akimbo

16 **presumptuously,** overweeningly, aristocratically; hubristically; insolently

17 **snobbishly,** snobbily, priggishly; snootily, snottily

142 INSOLENCE

<disrespecting state>

NOUNS 1 **insolence; presumption,** presumptuousness; audacity, effrontery, boldness, assurance, hardihood, bumptiousness; hubris; overweening, overweeningness; contempt, contemptuousness, contumely; disdain, *sprezzatura* <Ital>; arrogance, uppishness, uppityness; obtrusiveness, pushiness; contempt of court

2 **impudence, impertinence,** flippancy, procacity, malapertness, pertness, sauciness, sassiness, cockiness, cheekiness, freshness, chutzpa, hutzpa, brazenness, brazenfacedness, brassiness, face of brass, shamelessness, rudeness, brashness, disrespect, disrespectfulness, derision, ridicule

3 <nonformal> **cheek,** face, brass, nerve, gall, chutzpah, crust, nads, stones

4 **sass,** sauce, lip, back talk, backchat, mouth

5 <impudent person> malapert; minx, hussy; whippersnapper, puppy, pup, upstart; boldface, brazenface; *chutzpadik* <Yiddish>; swaggerer

6 <nonformal> **smart aleck,** smarty, smart guy, smartmouth, smart-ass, wiseass, smarty-pants, ho-dad, wisenheimer, wiseguy, know-it-all, saucebox

VERBS 7 **have the audacity,** have the cheek; have the gall, have a nerve, have one's nerve; get fresh, get smart, forget one's place, dare, presume, take liberties, make bold, make free; hold in contempt, ridicule, taunt, deride

8 **sass,** sauce, **talk back,** answer back, lip, give one the lip, mouth off, provoke

ADJS 9 **insolent,** insulting; **presumptuous,** presuming, overpresumptuous, overweening; audacious, bold, assured, hardy, bumptious; contemptuous, contumelious; disdainful, arrogant, uppish, uppity; hubristic; forward, pushy, obtrusive, familiar; cool, cold

10 **impudent, impertinent,** pert, malapert, procacious, flip, flippant, cocky, cheeky, fresh, facy, crusty, nervy, *chutzpadik* <Yiddish>; uncalled-for, gratuitous, biggety; rude, disrespectful, derisive, brash, bluff; saucy, sassy; smart, smart-alecky, smart-ass, wiseass, snot-nosed

11 **brazen,** brazenfaced, boldfaced, barefaced, brassy, bold, bold as brass, unblushing, unabashed, aweless, **shameless,** dead to shame, lost to shame; swaggering

ADVS 12 **insolently, audaciously,** bumptiously, contumeliously; arrogantly; presumptuously, obtrusively, pushily; disdainfully

13 **impudently, impertinently,** pertly, procaciously, malapertly, flippantly, cockily, cheekily, saucily; rudely, brashly, disrespectfully, contemptuously, derisively, in a smart-alecky way, in a smart-ass fashion

14 **brazenly,** brazenfacedly, boldly, boldfacedly, **shamelessly,** unblushingly

143 KINDNESS, BENEVOLENCE

<kind, helpful state>

NOUNS 1 **kindness, kindliness,** kindly disposition; benignity, benignancy; goodness, decency, niceness; graciousness; kindheartedness, goodheartedness, warmheartedness, softheartedness, tenderheartedness, kindness of heart, goodness of heart, warmth of heart, softness of heart, tenderness of heart, affectionateness, warmth, loving-kindness, metta; soul of kindness, kind heart, heart of gold; brotherhood, fellow feeling, sympathy, fraternal feeling, feeling of kinship; pity, mercy, compassion; humaneness, humanity; charitableness

2 **good nature, good humor,** good disposition, grace, benevolent disposition, good temper, sweetness, sweet temper, sweet nature, good-naturedness, good-humoredness, good-temperedness, bonhomie; amiability, affability, geniality, cordiality; gentleness, mildness, lenity

3 **considerateness, consideration,** thoughtfulness, courteousness, mindfulness, heedfulness, regardfulness, attentiveness, solicitousness, solicitude, thought, regard, concern, delicacy, sensitivity, tact, tactfulness; indulgence, toleration, leniency; complaisance, accommodatingness, helpfulness, obligingness, agreeableness

4 **benevolence,** benevolentness, benevolent disposition, well-disposedness, **beneficence,** charity, charitableness, philanthropy; altruism, philanthropism, humanitarianism, welfarism, do-goodism; utilitarianism, Benthamism, greatest good of the greatest number; goodwill, grace, brotherly love, sisterly love, Christian charity, love, *caritas* <L>, love of mankind, love of man, love of humankind, good will toward man, *agape* <Gk>, flower power; brotherhood of man and fatherhood of God (BOMFOG); bigheartedness, largeheartedness, greatheartedness; hospitality; **generosity**; giving

5 **welfare;** welfare work, social service, social welfare, social work; child welfare; commonweal, public welfare, public works; welfare state, welfare statism, welfarism; relief, the dole, social security <Brit>

6 **good works,** good cause, benevolences, philanthropies, charities; works, public service, community service

7 **act of kindness,** kindness, favor, mercy, benefit, benefaction, benevolence, benignity, blessing, service, turn, break, good turn, good deed, kind deed, *mitzvah* <Heb>, office, good offices, kind offices, obligation, grace, act of grace, courtesy, kindly act, labor of love, good work; rescue, relief, largess, donation, alms

8 **philanthropist, altruist,** benevolist, humanitarian, man of good will, do-gooder, goo-goo, bleeding heart, well-doer, power for good; good Samaritan; well-wisher; welfare worker, social worker, caseworker; welfare statist; almsgiver, almoner; bodhisattva; Robin Hood, Lady Bountiful; Mr. Nice Guy

VERBS 9 **be kind,** be good, be nice, show kindness; treat well, do right by; favor, oblige, accommodate

10 **be considerate,** consider, respect, regard, think of, be thoughtful of, have consideration for, have regard for; remember; be mindful; be at one's service, fuss over one, spoil one

11 **be benevolent,** bear good will, wish well, give one's blessing, have one's heart in the right place, have a heart of gold; practice the golden rule, follow the golden rule, do as you would be done by, do unto others as you would have others do unto you; make love not war

12 **do a favor, do good,** do a kindness, do a good turn, do a good deed, do a kind deed, do good works, do a *mitzvah* <Heb>, do a solid, use one's good offices, render a service, confer a benefit; benefit, help; mean well

ADJS 13 **kind, kindly,** kindly-disposed; benign, benignant; good as gold, good, nice, decent; gracious; kindhearted, warm, warmhearted, softhearted, tenderhearted, goodhearted, tender, loving, affectionate, sweet; sympathetic, sympathizing, **compassionate**, tolerant, merciful; brotherly, fraternal, sisterly; humane, human; charitable, caritative; Christly, Christlike

14 **good-natured,** well-natured, good-humored, good-tempered, bonhomous, sweet, sweet-tempered; amiable, affable, genial, cordial, congenial; gentle, mild, mild-mannered; easy, easy-natured, easy to get along with, able to take a joke, **agreeable;** laid-back

15 **benevolent,** charitable, beneficent, philanthropic, altruistic, humanitarian; bighearted, largehearted, greathearted, freehearted; hospitable; generous; well-disposed; openhanded; almsgiving, eleemosynary; welfare, welfarist, welfaristic, welfare statist

16 **considerate,** thoughtful, mindful, heedful, regardful, solicitous, attentive, delicate, tactful, mindful of others; complaisant, accommodating, accommodative, at one's service, helpful, agreeable, obliging, indulgent, tolerant, lenient

17 **well-meaning,** well-meant, well-affected, well-disposed, well-intentioned; make-nice

ADVS 18 **kindly,** benignly, benignantly; good, nicely, well, favorably; kindheartedly, warmly, warmheartedly, softheartedly, tenderheartedly; humanely, humanly; brotherly

19 **good-naturedly,** good-humoredly, bonhomously; sweetly; amiably, affably, genially, cordially; graciously, in good part

20 **benevolently,** beneficently, charitably, philanthropically, altruistically, bigheartedly, with good will

21 **considerately,** thoughtfully, mindfully, heedfully, regardfully, tactfully, sensitively, solicitously, attentively; well-meaningly, well-disposedly; out of consideration, out of courtesy

144 UNKINDNESS, MALEVOLENCE

<unkind, harmful state>

NOUNS 1 **unkindness,** unkindliness; unbenignity, unbenignness; unamiability, uncordiality, ungraciousness, inhospitality, inhospitableness, ungeniality, unaffectionateness; unsympatheticness, uncompassionateness; disagreeableness

2 **unbenevolentness,** uncharitableness, ungenerousness

3 **inconsiderateness,** inconsideration, unthoughtfulness, unmindfulness, unheedfulness, thoughtlessness, heedlessness, respectlessness, disregardfulness, forgetfulness; unhelpfulness, unobligingness, unaccommodatingness; selfishness

4 **malevolence, ill will,** bad will, bad blood, bad temper, ill nature, ill-disposedness, ill disposition, evil disposition; evil eye, stink eye, whammy, blighting glance; bitch face, resting bitch face, trout pout

5 **malice, maliciousness,** maleficence; malignance, malignancy, malignity; meanness, orneriness, cussedness, bitchiness*, hatefulness, nastiness, invidiousness; wickedness, iniquitousness; deviltry, devilry, devilment; malice prepense, malice aforethought, evil intent; harmfulness, noxiousness

6 **spite,** despite; spitefulness, cattiness; gloating, unwholesome joy, unholy joy, *Schadenfreude* <Ger>

7 **rancor,** virulence, venomousness, venom, vitriol, gall, spleen, bile; sharp tongue; loathing

8 **causticity,** causticness, corrosiveness, mordancy, mordacity, bitingness; acrimony, asperity, acidity, acidness, acidulousness, acridity, acerbity, bitterness, tartness; sharpness, keenness, incisiveness, piercingness, stabbingness, trenchancy

9 **harshness,** roughness, ungentleness; severity, austerity, hardness, sternness, grimness, inclemency; stringency, astringency, asperity

10 **heartlessness, unfeeling,** unnaturalness, unresponsiveness, insensitivity, coldness, coldheartedness, cold-bloodedness; hardheartedness, hardness, hardness of heart, heart of stone; callousness, callosity; obduracy, induration; pitilessness, unmercifulness

11 **cruelty,** cruelness, sadistic cruelty, insensate cruelty, sadism, wanton cruelty; ruthlessness; inhumaneness, inhumanity, atrociousness; brutality, mindless brutality, senseless brutality, brutalness, brutishness, bestiality, animality, beastliness; barbarity, barbarousness, vandalism; savagery, viciousness, violence, fiendishness, heinousness; cheap shot; child abuse, spousal abuse; mental abuse, mental cruelty; truculence, fierceness, ferociousness, ferocity; excessive force, piling on; bloodthirst, bloodthirstiness, bloodlust, bloodiness, bloody-mindedness, sanguineousness; cannibalism; crime against humanity

12 **act of cruelty, atrocity,** cruelty, brutality, bestiality, barbarity, inhumanity; act of terrorism

13 **bad deed, disservice,** ill service, ill turn, bad turn

14 **beast,** beastess, animal, **brute,** monster, monster of cruelty, devil, devil incarnate; sadist, torturer, tormenter; Attila, Torquemada, the Marquis de Sade; malefactor, malfeasor, malfeasant, evildoer, miscreant

VERBS 15 **bear malice,** bear ill will, malign; do a bad turn; harshen, dehumanize, brutalize, bestialize; torture, torment; have a cruel streak, go for the jugular, have the killer instinct; have it in for

ADJS 16 **unkind,** unkindly, ill; unbenign, unbenignant; unamiable, disagreeable, uncordial, ungracious, inhospitable, ungenial, unaffectionate, unloving; unsympathetic, unsympathizing, uncompassionate, uncompassioned

17 **unbenevolent,** unbeneficient, uncharitable, unphilanthropic, unaltruistic, ungenerous

18 **inconsiderate,** unthoughtful, unmindful, unheedful, disregardful, thoughtless, heedless, respectless, mindless, unthinking, forgetful; tactless, insensitive; uncomplaisant; unhelpful, unaccommodating, unobliging, disobliging, uncooperative; selfish

19 **malevolent,** ill-disposed, evil-disposed, ill-natured, ill-affected, ill-conditioned, ill-intentioned, loathing

20 **malicious,** maleficent, malefic; malignant, malign; mean, ornery, cussed, bitchy*, hateful, nasty, baleful, baneful, invidious; wicked, iniquitous; harmful, noxious, toxic

21 **spiteful,** despiteful; catty, cattish, bitchy*; snide

22 **rancorous,** virulent, vitriolic; venomous, venenate, envenomed

23 **caustic,** mordant, mordacious, corrosive, corroding; **acrimonious,** acrid, acid, acidic, acidulous, acidulent, acerb, acerbate, acerbic, bitter, tart; sharp, sharpish, keen, incisive, trenchant, cutting, penetrating, piercing, biting, stinging, stabbing, scathing, scorching, withering, scurrilous, abusive, thersitical, foulmouthed, harsh-tongued

24 **harsh, rough,** rugged, ungentle; severe, austere, stringent, astringent, hard, stern, dour, grim, inclement, unsparing

25 **heartless, unfeeling,** unnatural, unresponsive, insensitive, cold, cold of heart, coldhearted, cold-blooded; hard, hardened, hard of heart, hardhearted, stonyhearted, marblehearted, flinthearted; callous, calloused; obdurate, indurated; unmerciful

26 **cruel,** cruelhearted, sadistic; **ruthless**; brutal, brutish, brute, bestial, beastly, animal, animalistic; abusive; mindless, soulless, insensate, senseless, subhuman, dehumanized, brutalized; sharkish, wolfish, slavering; barbarous, barbaric, uncivilized, unchristian; savage, ferocious, feral, mean, mean as a junkyard dog, vicious, fierce, atrocious, truculent, fell; inhuman, inhumane, unhuman; fiendish, fiendlike; demoniac, demoniacal, diabolic, diabolical, devilish, satanic, hellish, infernal; bloodthirsty, bloody-minded, bloody, sanguineous, sanguinary; cannibalistic, anthropophagous; murderous; Draconian, Tartarean

ADVS 27 **unkindly,** ill; unbenignly, unbenignantly; unamiably, disagreeably, uncordially, ungraciously, inhospitably, ungenially, unaffectionately, unlovingly; unsympathetically, uncompassionately

28 **unbenevolently,** unbeneficently, uncharitably, unphilanthropically, unaltruistically, ungenerously

29 **inconsiderately,** unthoughtfully, thoughtlessly, heedlessly, unthinkingly; unhelpfully, uncooperatively

30 **malevolently,** maliciously, maleficently,

malignantly; meanly, ornerily, cussedly, bitchily, cattily, hatefully, nastily, invidiously, balefully; wickedly, iniquitously; harmfully, noxiously, spitefully, in spite; with bad intent, with malice prepense, malice aforethought

31 **rancorously,** virulently, vitriolically; venomously, venenately

32 **caustically,** mordantly, mordaciously, corrosively, corrodingly; acrimoniously, acridly, acidly, acerbly, acerbically, bitterly, tartly; sharply, keenly, incisively, trenchantly, cuttingly, penetratingly, piercingly, bitingly, stingingly, stabbingly, scathingly, scorchingly, witheringly, thersitically, scurrilously, abusively

33 **harshly, roughly;** severely, austerely, stringently, sternly, grimly, inclemently, unsparingly

34 **heartlessly,** soullessly, unfeelingly, callously, coldheartedly; cold-bloodedly, in cold blood

35 **cruelly,** brutally, brutishly, bestially, animalistically, subhumanly, sharkishly, wolfishly, slaveringly; barbarously, savagely, ferociously, ferally, viciously, fiercely, atrociously, truculently, terroristically; ruthlessly; inhumanely, inhumanly, unhumanly; fiendishly, diabolically, devilishly

145 PITY

<feeling sympathy>

NOUNS **1** **pity, sympathy,** feeling, fellow feeling, commiseration, condolence, condolences; compassion, mercy, empathy, ruth, rue, humanity; sensitivity; clemency, quarter, reprieve, mitigation, relief, favor, grace; leniency, lenity, gentleness; forbearance; kindness, benevolence; pardon, forgiveness; self-pity; pathos

2 **compassionateness,** mercifulness, ruthfulness, ruefulness, softheartedness, tenderness, tenderheartedness, lenity, gentleness; bowels of compassion, bowls of mercy; bleeding heart, soft spot

VERBS **3** **pity, feel sorry for,** feel sorrow for, be sorry for; commiserate, compassionate; open one's heart; sympathize, sympathize with, feel for, weep for, lament for, bleed, bleed for, have one's heart bleed for, have one's heart go out to, condole with

4 **have pity,** have mercy upon, take pity on, take pity upon; melt, thaw; relent, forbear, relax, give quarter, spare, temper the wind to the shorn lamb, go easy on, let up on, ease up on, soften, mitigate, unsteel; reprieve, pardon, remit, forgive; put out of one's misery; be cruel to be kind; give a second chance, give a break

5 <excite pity> **move, touch,** affect, reach, soften, unsteel, melt, melt the heart, appeal to one's better feelings; move to tears, sadden, grieve

6 **beg for mercy,** ask for pity, cry for quarter, beg for one's life; fall on one's knees, throw oneself at the feet of, throw oneself at someone's mercy

ADJS **7** **pitying, sympathetic,** sympathizing, commiserative, condolent, understanding; compassionate, merciful, ruthful, rueful, clement, gentle, soft, melting, bleeding, tender, tenderhearted, softhearted, warmhearted; humane, human; lenient, forbearant; charitable

8 **pitiful, pitiable,** pathetic, piteous, touching, moving, affecting, heartrending, grievous, doleful, sad, heartbreaking, tearjerking; ruesome, rueful

9 **self-pitying,** self-pitiful, sorry for oneself

ADVS **10** **pitifully,** sympathetically; compassionately, mercifully, ruthfully, ruefully, clemently, humanely

146 PITILESSNESS

<feeling no sympathy>

NOUNS **1** **pitilessness, unmercifulness,** uncompassionateness, unsympatheticness, mercilessness, ruthlessness, unfeelingness, inclemency, relentlessness, inexorableness, unyieldingness, unforgivingness; heartlessness, heart of stone, hardness, steeliness, flintiness, harshness, induration, vindictiveness, cruelty; remorselessness, unremorsefulness; short shrift, tender mercies

VERBS **2** **show no mercy,** give no quarter, turn a deaf ear, be unmoved, claim one's pound of flesh, harden one's heart, steel one's heart, go by the rule book

ADJS **3** **pitiless,** unpitying, unpitiful; blind to pity, deaf to pity; **unsympathetic,** unsympathizing; uncompassionate, uncompassioned; merciless, unmerciful, without mercy, unruing, ruthless, dog-eat-dog, down-and-dirty, vindictive; unfeeling, bowelless, inclement, relentless, inexorable, unyielding, unforgiving; heartless, coldhearted, hard, hard as nails, callous, steely, flinty, harsh, savage, cruel; remorseless, unremorseful; out for oneself

ADVS **4** **pitilessly,** unsympathetically; mercilessly, **unmercifully,** ruthlessly, uncompassionately, inclemently, relentlessly, inexorably, unyieldingly, unforgivingly; heartlessly, harshly, savagely, cruelly; remorselessly, unremorsefully

147 CONDOLENCE

<expressing sympathy>

NOUNS **1** **condolence, condolences,** condolement, consolation, comfort, balm, soothing words, commiseration, **sympathy,** sharing of grief, sharing of sorrowsorrow

VERBS **2** **condole with,** commiserate, sympathize with, feel with, empathize with, express sympathy for, send one's condolences; pity; **console,** wipe away one's tears, comfort, speak soothing words, bring balm to one's sorrow; sorrow with, share in one's grief, help bear one's grief, grieve with, weep with, grieve for, weep for, share one's sorrow

ADJS **3** condoling, condolent, consolatory, comforting, commiserating, commiserative, **sympathetic,** empathic, empathetic; pitying

148 FORGIVENESS

<expressing no resentment>

NOUNS **1** **forgiveness,** forgivingness; unresentfulness, unrevengefulness; condoning, condonation, condonance, overlooking, disregard; patience; indulgence, forbearance, longanimity, long-suffering; kindness, benevolence; magnanimity; brooking, tolerance; peace talks

2 **pardon,** excuse, sparing, amnesty, indemnity, exemption, immunity, reprieve, grace; absolution, shrift, remission, remission of sin, forgiveness of sin; redemption, deliverance; letting go; exoneration, exculpation

VERBS **3** **forgive, pardon,** excuse, give forgiveness, grant forgiveness, spare; amnesty, grant amnesty to, grant immunity, grant exemption; hear confession, absolve, remit, acquit, give absolution, grant absolution, shrive, grant remission; exonerate, exculpate; blot out one's sins, wipe the slate clean, expunge from the record

4 **condone, overlook,** disregard, ignore, accept, take, swallow, let go, pass over, give one another chance, let one off this time, let one off easy, let something go, close one's eyes to, have in mind, shut one's eyes to, turn a blind eye to, blink at, wink at, connive at; show mercy; allow for, make allowances for; bear with, endure, regard with indulgence; pocket the affront, leave unavenged, turn the other cheek, bury one's head in the sand, hide one's head in the sand

5 **forget, forgive and forget,** dismiss from one's thoughts, think no more of, not give it another thought, not give it a second thought, let it go, let it pass, let bygones be bygones; write off, charge off, charge to experience; bury the hatchet; make peace, make up, shake hands

ADJS **6** **forgiving,** sparing, placable, conciliatory; kind, benevolent; magnanimous, generous; patient; forbearing, longanimous, long-suffering, stoic; unresentful, unrevengeful; tolerant, more in sorrow than in anger; exonerative

7 **forgiven, pardoned,** excused, spared, amnestied, reprieved, remitted; overlooked, disregarded, forgotten, not held against one, wiped away, removed from the record, blotted, canceled, condoned, indulged; absolved, shriven; redeemed, delivered; exonerated, exculpated, acquitted, not guilty, innocent, cleared, vindicated, off the hook; unresented; unavenged, unrevenged; uncondemned; swept clean

149 CONGRATULATION

<expressing pleasure for someone>

NOUNS **1** **congratulation,** congratulations, congrats, gratulation, felicitation, blessing, compliment, pat on the back; good wishes, best wishes; applause, **praise**, flattery

VERBS **2** **congratulate,** gratulate, felicitate, bless, compliment, tender one's congratulations, offer one's congratulations, offer felicitations, offer one's compliments; shake one's hand, pat one on the back; rejoice with one, wish one joy; applaud, praise, flatter

ADJS **3** **congratulatory,** congratulant, congratulational; gratulatory, gratulant; **complimentary**, flattering

INTERJS **4** **congratulations,** take a bow, nice going, **bravo, well done,** good show

5 <nonformal> **congrats, well done,** all right, awesome, right on, way to go, attaboy, attagirl, good deal, looking good, nice going, that's my boy, that's my girl, mazel tov

150 GRATITUDE

<expressing appreciation>

NOUNS **1** **gratitude, gratefulness,** thankfulness, appreciation, appreciativeness; obligation, sense of obligation, sense of indebtedness

2 **thanks,** thanksgiving, praise, laud, hymn, paean, benediction, eucharist; grace, prayer of thanks; thank you; sincere thanks; acknowledgment, cognizance, credit, crediting, recognition; bonus, gratuity, tip; thank offering, votary offering, meal offering; dana; hazard pay

VERBS **3** **be grateful,** be obliged, feel under an obligation, be under an obligation, lie under an obligation, be obligated, be indebted, be in the debt of, give credit, give due credit; be thankful, thank God, thank one's lucky stars, thank one's stars, bless one's stars; **appreciate,** be appreciative of; never forget; overflow with gratitude; not look a gift horse in the mouth

4 **thank,** extend gratitude, extend thanks, bless; give one's thanks, express one's appreciation; offer thanks, give thanks, tender thanks, render thanks, return thanks; acknowledge, make acknowledgments of, credit, recognize, give credit, give recognition, render credit, render recognition, give a big hand; fall all over one with gratitude; fall on one's knees; pay tribute

ADJS 5 **grateful, thankful; appreciative,** appreciatory, sensible; obliged, much obliged, beholden, indebted to, crediting, under obligation, acknowledging, cognizant of; bread-and-butter

INTERJS 6 **thanks, thank you,** I thank you, *merci* <Fr>, *gracias* <Sp>, *grazie* <Ital>, *danke, danke schön* <Ger>, gramercy, much obliged, many thanks, thank you kindly; thank you very much, *merci beaucoup* <Fr>; thanks a lot, thanks a bunch, thanks a heap, ta <Brit>; touché

151 INGRATITUDE

<lacking appreciation>

NOUNS 1 **ingratitude, ungratefulness,** unthankfulness, thanklessness, unappreciation, unappreciativeness; nonacknowledgment, nonrecognition, denial of due credit, denial of proper credit; benefits forgot; grudging thanks, halfhearted thanks

2 **ingrate,** ungrateful wretch, thankless wretch

VERBS 3 **be ungrateful,** feel no obligation, **not appreciate,** owe one no thanks; look a gift horse in the mouth; bite the hand that feeds one

ADJS 4 **ungrateful, unthankful,** unthanking, thankless, unappreciative, unappreciatory, unmindful, nonrecognitive, unrecognizing, ungracious, discourteous

5 unthanked, **unacknowledged**, unrecognized, nonrecognized, uncredited, denied due credit, denied proper credit, unrequited, unrewarded, forgotten, neglected, unduly neglected, unfairly neglected, ignored, blanked, cold-shouldered; ill-requited, ill-rewarded

152 RESENTMENT, ANGER

<upset, annoyed feeling>

NOUNS 1 **resentment,** resentfulness; **displeasure,** disapproval, disapprobation, dissatisfaction, discontent; vexation, irritation, annoyance, aggravation, exasperation; slow burn

2 **offense,** umbrage, pique; glower, scowl, angry look, dirty look, glare, frown

3 **bitterness,** bitter resentment, bitterness of spirit, heartburning; rancor, virulence, acrimony, acerbity, asperity; causticity; choler, gall, bile, spleen, acid, acidity, acidulousness; hard feelings, **animosity**; soreness, rankling, slow burn; gnashing of teeth

4 **indignation,** indignant displeasure, righteous indignation, grievance, grudge

5 **anger,** wrath, ire, mad; angriness, irateness, wrathfulness, soreness; infuriation, enragement; vials of wrath, grapes of wrath; heat, more heat than light; pugnacity, aggro, dancer

6 **temper,** dander, Irish, monkey; bad temper

7 **fume, huff**; dudgeon, high dudgeon; pique, pet, tiff, miff, stew, fret, ferment

8 **fit,** fit of anger, fit of temper, rage, wax, **tantrum,** temper tantrum; duck fit, cat fit, **conniption**, conniption fit, snit, paroxysm, convulsion; agriothymia; stamping one's foot

9 **outburst,** outburst of anger, burst, explosion, eruption, blowup, flare-up, access, blaze of temper; storm, scene, high words

10 **rage, passion;** fury, furor, frenzy; livid rage, living passion, towering rage, towering passion, blind rage, burning rage, raging passion, tearing passion, furious rage; vehemence, violence; the Furies, the Eumenides, the Erinyes; Nemesis; Alecto, Tisiphone, Megaera; steroid rage, roid rage

11 **provocation,** affront, offense; *casus belli* <L>, red rag, red rag to a bull, red flag, sore point, sore spot, tender spot, delicate subject, raw nerve, the quick, where one lives; slap in the face; last straw; incitement

VERBS 12 **resent,** be resentful, feel resentment, harbor resentment, nurse resentment, feel hurt, smart, feel sore, have one's nose out of joint; bear a grudge, hold a grudge, have a grudge, begrudge, bear malice

13 **take offense,** take umbrage; take amiss, take ill, take in bad part, take to heart, not take it as a joke, mind; get miffed, get huffy; be cut, be cut to the quick, get one's back up

14 <show resentment> redden, color, flush, mantle; **growl,** snarl, gnarl, snap, show one's teeth, spit; gnash one's teeth, grind one's teeth; glower, lower, scowl, glare, frown, give a dirty look, look daggers; stew, stew in one's own juice

15 <be angry> **burn, seethe,** simmer, sizzle, smoke, smolder, steam; be pissed*, be pissed off*, be browned off, be livid, be beside oneself, fume, stew, boil, fret, chafe; foam at the mouth; breathe fire and fury; rage, storm, rave, rant, bluster; take on, go on, carry on, rant and rave, kick up a row; raise Cain, raise hell, raise the devil, raise the roof, tear up the earth; throw a fit, have a conniption, have a conniption fit, have a duck fit, have a cat fit, go into a tantrum; stamp one's foot

16 **vent one's anger,** vent one's rancor, vent one's choler, vent one's spleen, pour out the vials of one's wrath; snap at, bite one's head off, take

one's head off, jump down one's throat; expend one's anger on, take it out on

17 **become angry**, anger, lose one's temper, become irate, forget oneself, let one's angry passions rise; get one's gorge up, get one's blood up, bridle, bridle up, bristle, bristle up, raise one's hackles, get one's back up; reach boiling point, boil over, climb the wall, go through the roof, hit the roof

18 <nonformal> **get mad,** get sore, get one's Irish up, get one's dander up, get one's hackles up, get one's monkey up <Brit>; see red, get hot under the collar, flip out, work oneself into a lather, work into a sweat, work into a stew, get oneself in a tizzy, do a slow burn, blow one's cool

19 **flare up,** blaze up, fire up, flame up, spunk up, ignite, kindle, take fire

20 **fly into a rage,** fly into a passion, fly into a temper, fly out, fly off at a tangent; fly off the handle, hit the ceiling, go into a tailspin, have a hemorrhage; explode, blow up; blow one's top, blow one's stack, blow a fuse, blow a gasket, flip one's lid, flip one's wig, wig out; kick up a fuss, kick up a row, kick up a storm; jump down someone's throat, take it out on someone

21 **offend,** give offense, give umbrage, affront, outrage; grieve, aggrieve; wound, hurt, cut, cut to the quick, hit one where one lives, sting, hurt one's feelings; step on one's toes

22 **anger, make angry,** make mad, raise one's gorge; make one's blood boil

23 <nonformal> **piss off***, tee off, tick off, piss*, get one's goat, get one's Irish up, get one's back up, get one's dander up, get one's hackles up, make sore, make one hot under the collar, put one's nose out of joint, burn one up, burn one's ass, burn one's butt, steam

24 **provoke,** incense, arouse, inflame, embitter; vex, irritate, annoy, aggravate, exasperate, nettle, fret, chafe; pique, peeve, miff, huff; ruffle, roil, rile, ruffle one's feathers, rankle; bristle, get one's back up, set up, put one's hair up, put one's fur up; stick in one's craw; stir up, work up, stir one's bile, stir the blood; wave the bloody shirt

25 **enrage,** infuriate, madden, drive one mad, frenzy, lash into fury, work up into a passion, make one's blood boil

ADJS 26 **resentful,** resenting; **bitter,** embittered, rancorous, virulent, acrimonious, acerb, acerbic, acerbate; caustic; choleric, splenetic, acid, acidic, acidulous, acidulent; sore, rankled, burning, stewing

27 **provoked,** vexed, piqued; peeved, miffed, huffy, riled, nettled, irritated, annoyed, aggravated, exasperated, put-out; huffed, in a snit

28 **angry,** angered, incensed, indignant, irate, ireful; livid, livid with rage, beside oneself, wroth, wrathful, wrathy, cross, wrought-up, worked up, riled up

29 **burning, seething,** simmering, smoldering, sizzling, boiling, steaming; flushed with anger

30 <nonformal> **mad, sore,** mad as a hornet, mad as a wet hen, mad as hell, sore as a boil; pissed*, pissed-off*, PO'd; teed off, TO'd; ticked, ticked off, browned-off, waxy, stroppy, hot, het up, hot under the collar, burned up, hot and bothered, boiling, boiling mad, hopping mad, fighting mad, roaring mad, fit to be tied, good and mad, steamed, hacked, bent out of shape, in a lather, red-assed

31 **in a temper,** in a huff, in a pet, in a snit, in a stew; in a wax, in high dudgeon

32 **infuriated,** infuriate, in a rage, in a passion, in a fury; furious, fierce, wild, savage; raving mad, rabid, foaming at the mouth, frothing at the mouth; fuming, in a fume; enraged, raging, raving, ranting, storming; ballistic

ADVS 33 **angrily,** indignantly, irately, wrathfully, infuriatedly, infuriately, furiously, heatedly; in anger, in hot blood, in the heat of passion

153 JEALOUSY

<resentment and feeling threatened>

NOUNS 1 **jealousy,** jealousness, heartburning, heartburn, jaundice, jaundiced eye, green in the eye, jaundice of the soul, green-eyed monster; Othello's flaw, horn-madness; **envy**; crime of passion

2 **suspiciousness,** suspicion, doubt, misdoubt, mistrust, distrust, untrust, distrustfulness, suspectitiousness

VERBS 3 **be jealous,** suffer pangs of jealousy, have green in the eye, be possessive, be overpossessive, view with a jaundiced eye; suspect, distrust, mistrust, doubt, misdoubt; be paranoid

4 make one jealous, put someone's nose out of joint

ADJS 5 **jealous,** jaundiced, jaundice-eyed, yellow-eyed, green-eyed, yellow, green, green with jealousy; horn-mad; invidious, **envious**; suspicious, distrustful

154 ENVY

<wanting what another has>

NOUNS 1 **envy,** enviousness, covetousness; emulousness; invidia, deadly sin of envy, invidiousness; grudging, grudgingness; resentment, resentfulness; jealousy; rivalry, competitiveness; meanness, meanspiritedness, ungenerousness; penis envy, class envy

VERBS 2 **envy,** be envious of, be covetous of, covet,

cast envious eyes, desire for oneself; resent; grudge, begrudge; turn green with envy, be jealous, eat one's heart out

ADJS 3 **envious,** envying, invidious, green with envy, green-eyed; jealous; covetous, desirous of; resentful; grudging, **begrudging;** mean, meanspirited, ungenerous; stink-eyed, squint-eyed

155 RESPECT

<feeling admiration and regard>

NOUNS 1 **respect, regard,** consideration, appreciation, favor; approbation, approval; esteem, estimation, prestige; reverence, veneration, awe; deference, deferential regard, reverential regard; honor, homage, duty; great respect, high regard, high opinion, admiration; adoration, breathless adoration, exaggerated respect, worship, hero worship, idolization; idolatry, deification, apotheosis; courtesy; well said

2 **obeisance,** reverence, homage; bow, nod, bob, bend, inclination, inclination of the head, curtsy, salaam, kowtow, scrape, bowing and scraping, making a leg; genuflection, kneeling, bending the knee; prostration; salute, salutation, namaste; presenting arms, dipping the colors, dipping the ensign, standing at attention; red carpet; submissiveness, submission; obsequiousness, servility

3 **respects,** regards; duties, attentions

VERBS 4 **respect,** entertain respect for, accord respect to, **regard,** esteem, hold in esteem, hold in consideration, favor, admire, think much of, think well of, think highly of, have a high opinion of, hold a high opinion of; appreciate, value, prize, treasure; revere, reverence, hold in reverence, venerate, honor, look up to, defer to, bow to, exalt, put on a pedestal, worship, hero-worship, deify, apotheosize, idolize, adore, worship the ground one walks on, stand in awe of; hold dear

5 **pay homage to,** do homage to, show respect for, demonstrate respect for, pay respect to, pay tribute to, do honor to, do the honors for; doff one's cap to, take off one's hat to; salute, present arms, dip the colors, dip the ensign, stand at attention; give the red-carpet treatment, roll out the red carpet; fire a salute

6 **bow,** make obeisance, salaam, kowtow, make one's bow, bow down, nod, incline the head, bow the head, bend the head, bend the neck, bob, bob down, curtsy, bob a curtsy, bend, make a leg, scrape, bow and scrape; genuflect, kneel, bend the knee, get down on one's knees, throw oneself on one's knees, fall on one's knees, fall down before, fall at the feet of, prostrate oneself, kiss the hem of one's garment

7 **command respect,** inspire respect, stand high, impress, have prestige, rank high, be widely reputed, be up there, be way up there; awe, overawe

ADJS 8 **respectful,** regardful, attentive; deferential, conscious of one's place, dutiful, honorific, ceremonious, appreciative, cap in hand; courteous

9 **reverent,** reverential; admiring, **adoring,** worshiping, worshipful, hero-worshiping, idolizing, idolatrous, deifying, apotheosizing; venerative, venerational, venerating; awestruck, awestricken, awed, in awe; on bended knee, God-fearing; solemn

10 **obeisant,** prostrate, on one's knees, on bended knee; submissive; obsequious; knowing one's place

11 **respected,** esteemed, revered, reverenced, adored, worshiped, venerated, honored, well-thought-of, admired, much-admired, appreciated, valued, prized, in high esteem, in high estimation, highly considered, well-considered, held in respect, held in regard, held in favor, held in consideration, time-honored, prestigious

12 **venerable,** reverend, estimable, honorable, worshipful, august, awe-inspiring, awesome, awful, dreadful; time-honored

ADVS 13 **respectfully,** regardfully, deferentially, reverentially; dutifully

ADVS, PREPS 14 in deference to, with due respect, with all respect, **with all due respect to,** with all due respect for, saving, excusing the liberty, saving your reverence, sir-reverence; out of respect for, out of consideration for, out of courtesy to

156 DISRESPECT

<lacking regard>

NOUNS 1 **disrespect, disrespectfulness,** lack of respect, low estimate, low esteem, disesteem, dishonor, irreverence; ridicule; disparagement; discourtesy; impudence, insolence; opprobrium; contempt

2 **indignity, affront**, offense, injury, humiliation; scurrility, contempt, contumely, despite, flout, flouting, mockery, jeering, jeer, mock, scoff, gibe, taunt, brickbat; insult, aspersion, uncomplimentary remark, snub, slight, slap in the face, kick in the face, left-handed compliment, backhanded compliment, damning with faint praise; cut, most unkindest cut of all; outrage, atrocity, enormity

3 <nonformal> **put-down,** dump, bringdown, brickbat, **dig,** dirty dig, ding, rank-out, rip, shot, slam, go-by

VERBS 4 **disrespect,** not respect, disesteem, hold a low opinion of, rate low, rank low, hold in low esteem, not care much for, pay a lefthanded compliment, pay a backhanded compliment, damn with faint praise, hold in contempt, have no time for; show disrespect for, show a lack of respect for, be disrespectful, treat with disrespect, turn one's back on, be overfamiliar with; trifle with, make bold with, make free with, take a liberty, take liberties with, play fast and loose with; ridicule; disparage

5 **offend, affront,** give offense to, snub, slight, disoblige, outrage, step on one's toes; dishonor, humiliate, treat with indignity; flout, mock, jeer at, scoff at, fleer at, gibe at, taunt, bitch-slap*; insult, call names, kick in the face, slap in the face, take by the beard; add insult to injury; give the cold shoulder, cut dead, spurn

6 <nonformal> **bad-mouth, put down,** trash, give the go-by, rubbish, dump on, dig at, dis, diss, rank out, rip, rip on, ride, roast, slam, hurl a brickbat

ADJS 7 **disrespectful,** irreverent, aweless; discourteous; insolent, impudent; flippant; ridiculing, derisive; disparaging

8 **insulting,** insolent, abusive, offensive, humiliating, degrading, pejorative, contemptuous, contumelious, calumnious; blasphemous; scurrilous, scurrile; backhand, backhanded, left-handed, cutting; contumacious, outrageous, atrocious, unspeakable

9 **unrespected,** disrespected, unregarded, unrevered, unvenerated, unhonored, unenvied; trivialized

157 CONTEMPT

<open disrespect>

NOUNS 1 **contempt, disdain, scorn,** contemptuousness, disdainfulness, superciliousness, snootiness, snottiness, sniffiness, toploftiness, scornfulness, despite, contumely, sovereign contempt; snobbishness; clannishness, cliquishness, exclusiveness, exclusivity; hauteur, airs, mock, arrogance; ridicule; insult; disparagement

2 **snub,** rebuff, repulse; slight, humiliation, spurning, spurn, disregard, the go-by; cut, cut direct, the cold shoulder; sneer, snort, sniff; contemptuous dismissal, dismissal, kiss-off; rejection

VERBS 3 **disdain, scorn,** despise, contemn, vilipend, disprize, misprize, rate low, rank low, be contemptuous of, feel contempt for, hold in contempt, hold cheap, look down upon, think little of, think nothing of, feel superior to, be above, hold beneath one, hold beneath contempt, look with scorn upon, view with a scornful eye, mock, give one the fish-eye, give one the beady eye, give one the stink eye, give one the hairy eyeball; put down, dump on; deride, ridicule; insult; disparage; thumb one's nose at, sniff at, sneeze at, snap one's fingers at, sneer at, snort at, curl one's lip at, shrug one's shoulders at; care nothing for, couldn't care less about, set at naught

4 **spurn,** scout, turn up one's nose at, scorn to receive, scorn to accept, not want any part of; spit upon

5 **snub,** rebuff, cut, cut dead, drop, repulse; high-hat, upstage; look down one's nose at, look coldly upon; cold-shoulder, turn a cold shoulder upon, give the cold shoulder, give the shoulder, turn the shoulder, give the go-by, give the kiss-off; turn one's back upon, turn away from, turn on one's heel, set one's face against, slam the door in one's face, show one his place, put one in his place, wave one aside; not be at home to, not receive

6 **slight,** ignore, pooh-pooh, make little of, dismiss, pretend not to see, disregard, overlook, neglect, pass by, pass up, give the go-by, leave out in the cold, take no note of, take no notice of, look right through, pay no attention, pay no regard to, refuse to acknowledge, refuse to recognize

7 **avoid,** avoid like the plague, go out of one's way to avoid, shun, dodge, steer clear of, have no truck with; keep one's distance, keep at a respectful distance, keep aloof, hold aloof, stand aloof; keep at a distance, hold at arm's length, keep at arm's length; be stuck-up, act holier than thou, give oneself airs

ADJS 8 **contemptuous, disdainful,** supercilious, snooty, snotty, sniffy, toplofty, toploftical, scornful, sneering, insulting, withering, contumelious; snobbish, snobby; clannish, cliquish, exclusive; stuck-up, conceited; haughty, arrogant

ADVS 9 **contemptuously,** scornfully, disdainfully; in contempt, with contempt, in disdain, in scorn; sneeringly, with a sneer, with curling lip

INTERJS 10 **bah,** pah, phooey, boo, phoo, pish, ecch, yeech, eeyuck, eeyuch, yeeuck, *feh* <Yiddish>, in your face

158 SPACE

<indefinite space>

NOUNS 1 **space, extent,** extension, spatial extension, uninterrupted extension, space continuum, continuum; expanse, expansion; spread, breadth;

depth, deeps; height, vertical space, air space; length; width; measure, volume; dimension, proportion, size; area, expanse tract, surface, surface extension, superficial extension; diameter, circumference; field, arena, sphere; capacity; acreage; void, empty space, emptiness, nothingness; infinite space, infinity, outer space, wastes of outer space, deep space, depths of outer space, interplanetary space, interstellar space, intergalactic space

2 **range, scope,** compass, reach, stretch, expanse; radius, sweep, carry, fetch, grasp; gamut, scale, register, diapason; spectrum, array; tract; range of motion

3 **room, latitude,** swing, play, way; spare room, room to spare, room to swing a cat, elbowroom, legroom; margin, leeway; breathing space; sea room; headroom, clearance; windage; amplitude; headway; living space; white space

4 **open space,** clear space; clearing, clearance, glade; open country, wide-open spaces, terrain, prairie, steppe, plain; field; wilderness, backcountry, boonies, boondocks, outback, desert, back o' beyond; back forty; distant prospect, distant perspective, empty view, far horizon; territory; living space; national territory, air space

5 **spaciousness,** roominess, size commodiousness, capacity, capaciousness, airiness, amplitude, extensiveness, extent, expanse; stowage, storage; seating capacity, seating

6 **fourth dimension, space-time,** time-space, space-time continuum, continuum, four-dimensional space; four-dimensional geometry, Minkowski world, Minkowski universe; spaceworld; other continuums; relativity, theory of relativity, Einstein theory, principle of relativity, principle of equivalence, general theory of relativity, special theory of relativity, restricted theory of relativity, continuum theory; time warp; cosmic constant

7 **inner space,** psychological space, the realm of the mind; personal space, room to be, individual space, private space, space; semantic space

8 intervening space; distance, interval, **gap**, remove; break, hiatus, lacuna, pause, interruption, intermission, lapse, blank; duration, period, span, spell, stretch, turn, while; commercial break

VERBS 9 **extend, reach,** stretch, expand, sweep, spread, run, go, go out, cover, carry, range, lie; reach out, stretch out, thrust out; span, straddle, take in, hold, enclose, encompass, surround, environ, contain; lengthen, widen, deepen, raise

ADJS 10 **spatial,** space, spacial; dimensional, proportional; two-dimensional, flat, surface, superficial, radial, three-dimensional (3-D), spherical, cubic, volumetric; galactic, intergalactic, interstellar; stereoscopic; fourth-dimensional; space-time, spatiotemporal

11 **spacious,** sizeable, roomy, commodious, capacious, ample; extensive, expansive, extended, wide-ranging; far-reaching, extending, spreading, vast, vasty, broad, wide, deep, high, voluminous, cavernous; airy, lofty; oversized; amplitudinous; widespread; infinite; areawide

ADVS 12 **extensively, widely,** broadly, vastly, abroad; far and wide, far and near; right and left, on all sides, on every side; infinitely

13 **everywhere,** everywheres, here, there, and everywhere; in every place, in every clime, in every region, in all places, in every quarter, in all quarters; all over, all round, all over hell, all over the map, all over the place, all over the ballpark, all over town, all over the world, the world over, on the face of the earth, under the sun, throughout the world, throughout the length and breadth of the land; from end to end, from pole to pole, from here to the back of beyond, from hell to breakfast; high and low, upstairs and downstairs, inside and out, in every nook and cranny, in every hole and corner; universally, in all creation; systemwide

14 **from everywhere,** everywhence, from the four corners of the earth, from all points of the compass, from every quarter, from all quarters; everywhere, everywhither, to the four winds, to the uttermost parts of the earth, to the ends of the earth, to hell and back

159 LOCATION

<definite place or position>

NOUNS 1 **location, situation, place, position,** *lieu* <Fr>, placement, emplacement, stead; whereabouts, whereabout, ubicity; area, district, region; locality, locale, locus; venue; abode; site, situs; spot, point, pinpoint, exact spot, exact point, very spot, very point, dot, X marks the spot; benchmark; bearings, coordinates, latitude and longitude, direction; setting, environs, environment; habitat, address; locavore; compass point

2 **station,** status, stand, standing, standpoint, pou sto; viewpoint, point of reference, reference point, angle, perspective, distance; coign of vantage; seat, post, base, footing, ground, venue; crime scene

3 **navigation,** guidance; dead reckoning, pilotage; coastal navigation; celestial guidance, astro-inertial guidance, celestial navigation, celo-navigation, astronavigation; consolan; loran; radar navigation; radio navigation; orienteering;

position, orientation, lay, lie, set, attitude, aspect, exposure, frontage, bearing, bearings, radio bearing, azimuth; position line, line of position; fix; remote sensing

4 **place,** stead, lieu

5 **map, chart;** hachure, contour line, isoline, layer tint; scale, graphic scale, representative fraction; legend; grid line, meridian, parallel, latitude, longitude; inset; index; projection, map projection, azimuthal equidistant projection, azimuthal projection, conic projection, Mercator projection; cartography, mapmaking; chorography, topography, photogrammetry, phototopography; cartographer, mapmaker, mapper; chorographer, topographer, photogrammetrist; political map, geological map

6 <act of placing> **placement, positioning,** emplacement, situation, location, siting, localization, locating, placing, putting; establishment, installation; allocation, collocation, disposition, assignment, deployment, posting, stationing, spotting; fixing, fixation, settling; deposition, reposition, deposit, disposal, dumping; stowage, storage, warehousing; loading, lading, packing; wayfinding

7 **establishment,** foundation, settlement, settling, colonization, population, peopling, plantation; lodgment, fixation; anchorage, mooring; installation, installment, inauguration, investiture, placing in office, initiation

8 **topography**, geography, topology; cartography, chorography; surveying, triangulation, navigation, geodesy; geodetic satellite, orbiting geophysical observatory (OGO); Global Positioning System (GPS); Geographic Information System (GIS)

VERBS 9 **have place,** be there; have its place, have its slot, **belong,** go, fit, fit in

10 **be located, be situated**, lie, be found, stand, rest, repose; lie in, have its seat in

11 **locate,** situate, site, place, position; emplace, spot, install, put in place; allocate, collocate, dispose, deploy, assign; localize, narrow down, pin down; map, chart, put on the map; put one's finger on, fix, assign to a place, consign to a place, relegate to a place; pinpoint, zero in on, home in on, find the spot; fix one's position, calculate one's position, triangulate, survey, find a line of position, get a fix on, get a navigational fix, get a bearing, navigate; turn up, track down

12 **place,** put, set, lay, pose, posit, site, seat, stick, station, post; billet, quarter; park, plump down; dump

13 <put violently> clap, slap, thrust, fling, hurl, throw, cast, chuck, toss; plump; plunk, plank, plop

14 **deposit,** repose, reposit, rest, lay, lodge; put down, set down, lay down

15 **load,** lade, freight, burden; fill; stow, store, put in storage, warehouse; pack, pack away; pile, dump, heap, heap up, stack, mass; bag, sack, pocket

16 **establish,** fix, plant, ensconce, site, pitch, seat, set, spot; found, base, ground, lay the foundation; build, put up, set up; build in; install, invest, vest, place in office, put in

17 **settle,** settle down, sit down, locate, park, ensconce, ensconce oneself; take up one's abode, take up one's quarters, make one's home, reside, inhabit; move, relocate, change address, establish residence, take up residence, take residence at, put up, live at, stay at, quarter at, billet at, move in, hang up one's hat; take root, strike root, put down roots, place oneself, plant oneself, get a footing, stand, take one's stand, take one's position; anchor, drop anchor, come to anchor, moor; squat; camp, bivouac; perch, roost, nest, hive, burrow; domesticate, set up housekeeping, keep house; colonize, populate, people; set up in business, go in business for oneself, set up shop, hang up one's shingle

ADJS 18 **located, placed,** sited, situated, situate, positioned, installed, emplaced, spotted, set, seated; stationed, posted, deployed, assigned, prepositioned, oriented; established, fixed, in place, settled, planted, ensconced, embosomed

19 **locational**, positional, situational, situal, directional; cartographic; topographic, geographic, chorographic, geodetic; geospatial; navigational; regional

ADVS 20 **in place,** in position, in situ, in loco

21 **where,** whereabouts, in what place, in which place; whither, to what place, to which place

22 **wherever,** where'er, wheresoever, wheresoe'er, wheresomever, whithersoever, wherever it may be; anywhere, anyplace

23 **here,** hereat, in this place, just here, on the spot; hereabouts, hereabout, in this vicinity, near here; somewhere about, somewhere near; aboard, on board, with us, among us; hither, hitherward, hitherwards, hereto, hereunto, hereinto, to this place

24 **there,** thereat, in that place, in those parts; thereabout, thereabouts, in that vicinity, in that neighborhood; thither, thitherward, thitherwards, to that place

25 **here and there**, in places, in various places, in spots, *passim* <L>

26 **somewhere,** someplace, in some place, someplace or other

PREPS 27 at, in, on, by; near, next to; with, among, in the midst of; to, toward; from

28 over, all over, here and there, on, in, at about, round about; through, all through, **throughout**

160 DISPLACEMENT

<removal from location>

NOUNS **1** **dislocation, displacement;** disjointing, disarticulation, unjointing, unhinging, luxation; heterotopia; shift, removal, forcible shift, forcible removal; knocking off course; eviction; uprooting, ripping out, deracination; rootlessness; disarrangement; incoherence; discontinuity; disruption; Doppler effect, red shift, violet shift; tongue twister

2 **dislodgment;** unplacement, unseating, upset, unsaddling, unhorsing, unsettling; deposal; relocation, translocation, transference, transshipment

3 **misplacement, mislaying,** misputting, mislocation, malposition, losing

4 displaced person (DP), stateless person, homeless person, bag person, Wandering Jew, man without a country, exile, drifter, vagabond, deportee, repatriate; displaced population, deported population; refugee, evacuee; outcast; waif, stray

VERBS **5** **dislocate, displace,** disjoint, disarticulate, unjoint, luxate, unhinge, put out of place, force out of place, push out of place, put out of joint, throw out of joint, throw out of gear, knock off course, throw off course, disrupt; disarrange

6 **dislodge,** unplace; evict; uproot, root up, root out, deracinate; relocate; depose, unseat, unsaddle, unsettle; unhorse, dismount; throw off, buck off

7 **misplace, mislay,** misput, lose, lose track of

ADJS **8** dislocatory, dislocating, heterotopic

9 **dislocated,** displaced; disjointed, unjointed, unhinged; dislodged; out, out of joint, out of gear; disarranged

10 unplaced, unestablished, **unsettled**; uprooted, deracinated; unhoused, evicted, unharbored, houseless, made homeless, homeless, stateless, exiled, outcast, expatriated; swinging in the wind

11 **misplaced, mislaid,** misput, gone missing, gone astray; **out of place,** out of one's element, like a fish out of water, in the wrong place, in the wrong box, in the wrong pew, in the right church but the wrong pew

12 **eccentric,** off-center, off-balance, unbalanced, uncentered

161 DIRECTION

<motion on course>

NOUNS **1** **direction,** directionality; line, direction line, line of direction, point, quarter, aim, way, track, range, bearing, azimuth, compass reading, heading, course; current, set; tendency, trend, inclination, bent, tenor, run, drift; orientation, lay, lie, lay of the land; steering, helmsmanship, piloting; navigation; line of march

2 <nautical and aviation terms> vector, tack; compass direction, azimuth, compass bearing, compass heading, magnetic bearing, magnetic heading, relative bearing, relative heading, true bearing, true heading, true course; lee side, weather side

3 **points of the compass,** cardinal points, cardinal directions, half points, quarter points, degrees, compass rose; compass card, lubber line; rhumb, loxodrome; magnetic north, true north, magnetic directions, compass directions, true directions; north, northward, nor'; south, southward; east, eastward, orient, sunrise; west, westward, occident, sunset; southeast, southwest, northeast, northwest; northing, southing, easting, westing

4 **orientation,** bearings; adaptation, adjustment, accommodation, alignment, collimation; disorientation; deviation

VERBS **5** **direct, point,** aim, turn, bend, train, fix, set, determine; point to, point at, hold on, fix on, sight on; take aim, aim at, turn upon, train upon; directionize, give a push in the right direction; locate; guide, signpost, indicate

6 **direct to,** give directions to, lead to, conduct to, point out to, show, show the way, point the way, steer, put on the track, put on the right track, set straight, set right, put right

7 <have a direction, take a direction> **bear, head,** turn, point, aim, take a heading, hold a heading, lead, go, steer, direct oneself, align oneself; incline, tend, trend, set, dispose, verge, tend to go, pilot, navigate

8 go west, wester, go east, easter, go north, go south

9 **head for,** bear for, go for, make for, hit for, hit out for, steer for, hold for, put for, set out for, set off for, strike out for, take off for, bend one's steps for, lay for, bear up for, bear up to, make up to, set in towards; set one's course for, set one's compass for, sail for; align one's march; break for, make a break for, run for, dash for, make a run for, make a dash for

10 **go directly,** go straight, follow one's nose, go straight on, head straight for, vector for, go straight to the point, steer a straight course, follow a course, keep one's course, hold one's course, hold steady for, arrow for, cleave to the line, keep pointed; **make a beeline,** go as the crow flies; take the airline, stay on the beam

11 **orient,** orientate, orient oneself, orient the map, orient the chart, take one's bearings, get one's bearings, get the lay of the land, get the lie of the land, see which way the land lies, see which way the wind blows; adapt, adjust, accommodate

ADJS 12 **directional,** azimuthal; direct, straight, arrow-straight, ruler-straight, straight-ahead, straightforward, straightaway, straightway; undeviating, unswerving, unveering; uninterrupted, unbroken; one-way, unidirectional, irreversible

13 **directable,** aimable, pointable, trainable; steerable, dirigible, guidable, leadable; directed, guided, aimed; well-aimed, well-directed, well-placed, on the mark, on the nose, on the money; **directional,** directive

14 northern, north, northernmost, northerly, northbound, arctic, boreal, hyperborean; southern, south, southernmost, southerly, southbound, meridional, antarctic, austral; eastern, east, easternmost, eastermost, easterly, eastbound, oriental; western, west, westernmost, westerly, westbound, occidental; northeastern, northeast, northeasterly; southeastern, southeast, southeasterly; southwestern, southwest, southwesterly; northwestern, northwest, northwesterly; cross-country, downwind, upwind; oblique, axial, parallel

ADVS 15 **north,** N, nor', northerly, northward, north'ard, norward, northwards, northwardly; north about

16 **south,** S, southerly, southward, south'ard, southwards, southwardly; south about

17 **east,** E, easterly, eastward, eastwards, eastwardly, where the sun rises; eastabout

18 **west,** W, westerly, westernly, westward, westwards, westwardly, where the sun sets; westabout

19 **northeast** (NE), nor'east, northeasterly, northeastward, northeastwards, northeastwardly; north-northeast (NNE); northeast by east (NE by E); northeast by north (NE by N)

20 **northwest** (NW), nor'west, northwesterly, northwestward, northwestwards, northwestwardly; north-northwest (NNW); northwest by west (NW by W); northwest by north (NW by N)

21 **southeast** (SE), southeasterly, southeastward, southeastwards, southeastwardly; south-southeast (SSE); southeast by east (SE by E); southeast by south (SE by S)

22 **southwest** (SW), southwesterly, southwestward, southwestwards, southwestwardly; south-southwest (SSW); southwest by south (SW by S)

23 **directly, direct,** straight, straightly, straightforward, straightforwards, undeviatingly, unswervingly, unveeringly; straight ahead, dead ahead; due, dead, due north; right, forthright; in a direct line, in a straight line, in line with, in a line for, in a beeline, as the crow flies, straight across; straight as an arrow

24 **clockwise,** rightward; **counterclockwise,** anticlockwise, widdershins, leftward; homeward; landward; seaward; earthward; heavenward; leeward, windward

25 **in every direction,** in all directions, in all manner of ways, every which way, everywhither, everyway, everywhere, at every turn, in all directions at once, in every quarter, on every side, all over the place, all over the ballpark, all over the map; around, all round, round about; forty ways from Sunday, six ways from Sunday; from every quarter, everywhence; from the four corners of the earth, to the four corners of the earth, from the four winds, to the four winds

PREPS 26 **toward,** towards, in the direction of, to, up, on, upon; upside; against, over against, versus; headed for, bound for, on the way to, on the road to, on high road to, in transit to, en route to, on route to, in passage to

27 **through,** by, passing by, passing through, by way of, by the way of, **via;** over, around, round about, here and there in, all through

162 PROGRESSION

<motion forwards>

NOUNS 1 **progression, progress,** going, going forward; ongoing, on-go, go-ahead, onward course, rolling, rolling on; advance, advancing, advancement, promotion, furtherance, furthering, preferment; forward motion, forwarding, forwardal; headway, way; leap, jump, forward leap, forward jump, quantum jump, quantum leap, leaps and bounds, spring, forward spring; progressiveness, progressivity; passage, course, march, career, full career; midpassage, midcourse, midcareer; travel; improvement

VERBS 2 **progress, advance,** proceed, go, go forward, move forward, step forward, go on, go ahead, go along, push ahead, press on, pass on, pass along, roll on; move, travel; go fast; make progress, come on, get along, come along, get ahead; further oneself; make headway, roll, gather head, gather way; make strides, make rapid strides, cover ground, get over the ground, make good time, make the best of one's way, leap forward, jump forward, spring forward, catapult oneself forward; make up for lost time, gain ground, make up leeway, make progress against, stem

3 **march on,** run on, rub on, jog on, roll on, flow on; drift along, go with the stream

4 **make one's way,** wend one's way, work one's way, weave one's way, worm one's way, thread one's way, inch forward, feel one's way, **muddle along,** muddle through, slog toward; go slow; carve one's way; push one's way, force one's way, fight one's way, go against the current, swim against the current, swim upstream; come a long way, move up in the world; move up, forge ahead, drive on, drive ahead, push on, push onward, press on, press onward, push forward, press forward, push, crowd; get somewhere, reach toward, raise one's sights

5 **advance,** further, promote, forward, hasten, contribute to, boost, foster, aid, facilitate, expedite, abet

ADJS **6** **progressive,** progressing, advancing, proceeding, ongoing, oncoming, onward, forward, forward-looking, go-ahead; moving; go-getting; face-first

ADVS **7** **in progress,** in mid-progress, in midcourse, in midcareer, in full career; going on; by leaps and bounds

8 **forward,** forwards, onward, onwards, forth, on, along, ahead; on the way to, on the road to, on the high road to, en route to, en route for

163 REGRESSION

<*motion backwards*>

NOUNS **1** **regression,** regress; recession; **retrogression,** retrocession, retroflexion, retroflection, reflux, refluence, retrogradation, retroaction, retrusion, reaction; return, reentry; setback, backset, throwback, rollback; backpedalling, backward motion, backward step; sternway; backsliding, lapse, relapse, recidivism, recidivation; arrested development

2 **retreat,** motion from, **withdrawal,** withdrawment, strategic withdrawal, exfiltration; retirement, fallback, pullout, pullback; advance to the rear; rout; disengagement; backing down, backing off, backing out; reneging, copping out, weaseling out, resigning, resignation

3 **reverse,** reversal, reversing, reversion, inversion; backing, backing up, backup, backflow; about-face, *volte-face* <Fr>, about-turn, right-about, right-about-face, turn to the right-about, U-turn, turnaround, turnabout, swingaround; backtrack, back trail; turn of the tide, reflux, refluence; role reversal

4 **countermotion,** countermovement, counteraction; recoil, rebound; countermarching

VERBS **5** **regress,** go backwards, recede, return, revert; retrogress, retrograde, retroflex, retrocede; pull back, jerk back, reach back, cock the arm, cock the fist; fall behind, get behind, go behind, fall astern, lose ground, slip back; backslide, lapse, relapse, recidivate; go down the tubes, go down the drain

6 **retreat,** sound a retreat, beat a retreat, beat a hasty retreat, withdraw, retire, pull out, pull back, backtrack, exfiltrate, advance to the rear, disengage; fall back, move back, go back, stand back; run back; draw back, draw off; back out, back out of, back off, back down, back away; defer, give ground, give place, take a back seat, play second fiddle; resign; crawfish, crawfish out, turn tail

7 **reverse,** go into reverse; back, back up, backpedal, back off, back away; backwater, make sternway; backtrack, backtrail, take the backtrack; countermarch; reverse one's field; take the reciprocal course; have second thoughts, think better of it, cut one's losses, go back to the drawing board

8 **turn back,** put back; double, double back, retrace one's steps; turn one's back upon; **return,** go back, come back, go home, come home

9 **turn around,** turn round, turn about, turn, make a U-turn, turn on a dime, turn tail, come about, go about, put about, fetch about; veer, veer around; swivel, pivot, pivot about, swing, round, swing round; wheel, wheel about, double wheel, whirl, spin; heel, turn upon one's heel; recoil, rebound, quail

10 **about-face,** *volte-face* <Fr>, right-about-face, do an about-face, do a right-about-face, do an about-turn, perform a *volte-face,* face about, face to the right-about, turn to the right-about

ADJS **11** **regressive,** recessive; retrogressive, retrocessive, retrograde, retral; retroactive; reactionary

12 **backward, reversed,** reflex, turned around, back; wrong-way, wrong-way around, counter, ass-backwards, bassackwards

ADVS **13** **backwards,** backward, retrally, hindwards, hindward, rearwards, rearward, arear, astern; back, away, fro; in reverse, ass-backwards; against the grain; counterclockwise, anticlockwise, widdershins; vice versa

COMBINING FORMS **14** an-, ana-, re-, retro-

164 DEVIATION

<*indirect course*>

NOUNS **1** **deviation,** deviance, deviancy, deviousness, departure, **digression,** diversion, divergence, divarication, branching off, divagation, declination, aberration, aberrancy, variation, indirection, exorbitation; tangent, parenthesis; detour, excursion, excursus, discursion; obliquity, bias, skew, slant; circuitousness; wandering, rambling, straying, errantry, pererration; drift, drifting, driftage; turning, shifting, swerving, swinging; turn, corner, bend, curve, dogleg, crook, hairpin, zigzag, twist, warp, swerve, veer, sheer, sweep; shift, double; tack, yaw; wandering course, twisting course, zigzag course, shifting course, wandering path, slalom course; long way around; margin of error

2 **deflection,** bending, deflexure, flection, flexure; torsion, distortion, contortion, torture, torturing, twisting, warping; skewness; refraction, diffraction, scatter, diffusion, dispersion; sidestep, crabwalk

VERBS 3 **deviate,** depart from, vary, diverge, divaricate, branch off, angle, angle off; digress, divagate, turn aside, go out of the way, detour, take a side road; swerve, veer, sheer, curve, shift, turn, trend, bend, heel, bear off; turn right, turn left, hang a right, hang a left; alter one's course, make a course correction, change the bearing; tack

4 **stray,** go astray, lose one's way, err; go off on a tangent; take a wrong turn; drift, go adrift; wander, wander off, ramble, rove, straggle, divagate, excurse, pererrate; meander, wind, twist, snake, twist and turn; lose one's bearings

5 **deflect,** deviate, divert, diverge, bend, curve, pull, crook, dogleg, hairpin, zigzag; warp, bias, twist, distort, contort, torture, skew; refract, diffract, scatter, diffuse, disperse; put rudder on

6 **avoid,** evade, dodge, duck, turn aside, turn to the side, draw aside, turn away, jib, shy, shy off; gee, haw; sidetrack, shove aside, shunt, switch; avert; head off, turn back; step aside, sidestep, move aside, move to the side, sidle; steer clear of, make way for, get out of the way of; go off, bear off, sheer off, veer off, ease off, edge off; fly off, go off at a tangent; glance, glance off

ADJS 7 **deviative,** deviatory, deviating, deviant, departing, aberrant, aberrational, aberrative, shifting, turning, swerving, veering; digressive, discursive, excursive, circuitous; devious, indirect, out-of-the-way; errant, erratic, zigzag, doglegged, wandering, rambling, roving, winding, twisting, meandering, snaky, serpentine, mazy, labyrinthine, vagrant, stray, desultory, planetary, undirected; out of sync; off-message

8 **deflective,** inflective, flectional, diffractive, refractive; refractile, refrangible; deflected, flexed, refracted, diffracted, scattered, diffuse, diffused, dispersed; distorted, skewed, skew; off-course, off-target, wide of the mark

9 **avertive,** evasive, dodging, dodgy, artful

165 LEADING
<going ahead>

NOUNS 1 **leading, heading,** foregoing; anteposition, the lead; preceding, precedence; priority; front, point, leading edge, cutting edge, forefront, front and center, vanguard, bleeding edge, van; herald, precursor

VERBS 2 **lead, head,** spearhead, stand at the head, stand first, be way ahead, head the line; take the lead, go in the lead, lead the way, break the trail, be the bellwether, lead the pack; be the point, be the point man; lead the dance; light the way, show the way, beacon, guide; get before, get ahead, get in front of, come to the front, come to the fore, lap, outstrip, pace, set the pace; not look back; get a head start, steal a march upon; precede, go before

ADJS 3 **leading, heading,** precessional, precedent, precursory, foregoing; first, foremost, headmost; preceding, antecedent; prior; chief; face-first

ADVS 4 **before,** in front, out in front, in the lead, outfront, foremost, headmost, in the van, in the forefront, in advance

166 FOLLOWING
<going behind>

NOUNS 1 **following,** heeling, **trailing,** tailing, shadowing; hounding, dogging, chasing, pursuit, pursual, pursuance; sequence; sequel; series

2 **follower,** successor; shadow, tail; pursuer, pursuivant; attendant, satellite, hanger-on, dangler, adherent, appendage, dependent, parasite, stooge, flunky; henchman, ward heeler, partisan, supporter, votary, sectary; camp follower, groupy; fan, buff; courtier; trainbearer; public; entourage, **following**; disciple, discipleship

VERBS 3 **follow,** go after, go behind, come after, come behind, move behind; pursue, shadow, tail, trail, trail after, follow in the trail of, camp on the trail of, heel, follow on the heels of, follow in the steps of, follow in the footsteps, tread close upon, breathe down the neck of, follow in the wake of, hang on the skirts of, stick like the shadow of, sit on the tail of, tailgate, go in the rear of, bring up the rear, eat the dust of, swallow one's dust; tag, tag after, tag along; string along; dog, bedog, hound, chase, chase after, get after, take out after, take off after; haunt

4 **lag,** lag behind, straggle, lag back, drag, trail, trail behind, hang back, hang behind, loiter, linger, loiter behind, linger behind, dawdle, get behind, fall behind, fall behindhand, let grass grow under one's feet

ADJS 5 **following,** trailing, on the track, on the trail; succeeding; back-to-back, consequent, consecutive

ADVS 6 **behind, after,** in the rear, in the train of, in the wake of; in back of

167 APPROACH

<motion towards>

NOUNS 1 **approach,** approaching, coming toward, going toward, coming near, going near, proximation, appropinquation, access, accession, nearing; advance, oncoming; advent, coming, forthcoming; flowing toward, afflux, affluxion; appulse; nearness; imminence; approximation; approach shot

2 **approachability,** accessibility, access, getatableness, come-at-ableness, attainability, openness

VERBS 3 **approach, near,** draw near, draw nigh, go near, come near, go toward, come toward, come closer, come nearer, come to close quarters; close, close in, close in on, close with; zoom in, zoom in on; accost, encounter, confront; proximate, appropinquate; advance, come, come forward, come on, come up, bear up, bear down, step up; ease up to, edge up to, sidle up to; bear down on, bear down upon, be on a collision course with; gain upon, narrow the gap; approximate

ADJS 4 **approaching, nearing,** advancing; attracted to, drawn to; coming, oncoming, forthcoming, upcoming, to come, provenient; approximate, proximate, approximative; prospective; near; imminent

5 **approachable, accessible,** getatable, come-at-able, attainable, open, easy to find, meet

168 RECESSION

<motion away from>

NOUNS 1 **recession,** recedence, receding, retrocedence, ceding; **retreat,** retirement, withdrawing, withdrawal; retraction, retractation, retractility; fleetingness, fugitiveness, fugitivity, evanescence; ebb

VERBS 2 **recede,** retrocede, cede; **retreat,** retire, withdraw; move off, move away, stand off stand, away, stand out from the shore; go, go away; die away, fade away, drift away; erode, wash away; diminish, decline, sink, shrink, dwindle, fade, ebb, wane; shy away, tail away, tail off; go out with the tide, fade into the distance; pull away, widen the distance

3 **retract,** withdraw, draw back, pull back, pull out, draw in, pull in; draw in one's claws, draw in one's horns; defer, take a back seat, play second fiddle, backpedal; shrink, wince, cringe, flinch, shy, fight shy, duck

ADJS 4 **recessive,** recessional, recessionary; recedent, retrocedent

5 **receding, retreating,** retiring, withdrawing; shy; diminishing, declining, sinking, shrinking, eroding, dwindling, ebbing, waning; fading, dying; fleeting, fugitive, evanescent

6 **retractile,** retractable, retrahent

169 CONVERGENCE

<coming together>

NOUNS 1 **convergence,** converging, confluence, concourse, conflux; mutual approach, approach; meeting, meet-up, congress, concurrence, coming together; concentration, concentralization, focalization, focus; meeting point, focal point, point of convergence, vanishing point; union, merger; crossing point, crossroads, crossing; collision course, narrowing gap; funnel, bottleneck; hub, spokes; asymptote; radius; tangent

VERBS 2 **converge, come together,** approach, run together, meet, unite, connect, merge; cross, intersect; fall in with, link up with; be on a collision course; go toward, narrow the gap, close with, close, close up, close in; funnel; taper, pinch, nip; centralize, center, come to a center; center on, center around, concentralize, concenter, concentrate, come to a point, tend to a point; come to a focus

ADJS 3 **converging,** convergent; **meeting,** uniting, merging; concurrent, confluent, mutually approaching, approaching; crossing, intersecting; connivent; focal, confocal, focusing, focused; centrolineal, centripetal; asymptotic, asymptotical; tangent, tangential, radial, radiating

170 CROSSING

<passing across>

NOUNS 1 **crossing,** intercrossing, intersecting, intersection; decussation, chiasma; traversal, transversion; cross-section, transection; cruciation; transit, transiting; crisscross; crosscourt

2 **crossing,** crossway, crosswalk, crossroad, pedestrian crosswalk, zebra, zebra crossing <Brit>; *carrefour* <Fr>; **intersection,** intercrossing; level crossing, grade crossing; crossover, overpass, flyover <Brit>, viaduct, undercrossing; traffic circle, rotary, roundabout; highway interchange, **interchange,** cloverleaf, spaghetti junction

3 **network,** webwork, weaving, meshwork, tissue, crossing over and under, interlacement, intertwinement, intertexture, texture, reticulum, reticulation; crossing-out, cancellation, scrubbing; net, netting; mesh, meshes; web, webbing; weave, weft; lace, lacery, lacing, lacework; screen, screening; sieve, riddle, raddle; wicker, wickerwork; basketwork, basketry; lattice, latticework; hachure, hatchure, hatching, cross-hatching; trellis, trelliswork, treillage; grate, grating; grille, grillwork; **grid,** gridiron; tracery, fretwork, fret, arabesque, filigree; plexus, plexure; reticle, reticule; wattle, wattle and daub

4 **cross,** crux, cruciform; crucifix, rood, rood tree; X, ex, exing, T, Y; swastika, gammadion, fylfot; crossbones; dagger

5 **crosspiece,** traverse, transverse, transversal, transept, transom, cross bitt; diagonal; crossbar, crossarm; swingletree, singletree, whiffletree, whippletree; doubletree

VERBS **6** **cross,** crisscross, cruciate; intersect, intercross, decussate; cut across, crosscut; traverse, transverse, lie across; bar, crossbar

7 net, web, mesh; lattice, trellis; grate, grid

ADJS **8** **cross, crossing,** crossed; crisscross, crisscrossed; intersecting, intersected, intersectional; crosscut, cut across; decussate, decussated; chiasmal, chiasmic, chiastic; secant

9 **transverse,** transversal, traverse; across, cross, crossway, crosswise, crossways, crosscourt, thwart, athwart, overthwart; oblique

10 **cruciform, crosslike,** cross-shaped, cruciate, X-shaped, cross, crossed; cruciferous

11 **netlike,** retiform, plexiform; reticulated, reticular, reticulate; cancellate, cancellated; netted, netty; meshed, meshy; laced, lacy, lacelike; filigreed; latticed, latticelike; grated, gridded; barred, crossbarred, mullioned; streaked, striped

12 **webbed,** webby, weblike, woven, interwoven, interlaced, intertwined; web-footed, palmiped

ADVS **13** **crosswise**, crossways, crossway, decussatively; cross, crisscross, across, thwart, thwartly, thwartways, athwart, athwartwise, overthwart; traverse, traversely; transverse, transversely, transversally; obliquely; sideways, sidewise; contrariwise, contrawise; crossgrained, across the grain, against the grain; athwartship, athwartships

171 DIVERGENCE

<taking different directions>

NOUNS **1** **divergence**, divergency, divarication; aberration, deviation; separation, division, decentralization; centrifugence; radial, radiating, radiating out, raying out, beaming out; spread, spreading, spreading out, splaying, fanning, fanning out, deployment; ripple effect

2 **radiation,** ray, sunray, radius, spoke; radiance, diffusion, scattering, dispersion, emanation; halo, aureole, glory, corona; ripple effect

3 **forking,** furcation, bifurcation, biforking, trifurcation, divarication, triforking; branching, branching off, branching out, ramification; arborescence, arborization

4 **fork, prong,** trident; Y, V; branch, ramification, stem, offshoot; crotch, crutch; fan, delta; groin, inguen; furcula, furculum, wishbone

VERBS **5** **diverge,** divaricate; aberrate; separate, divide, separate off, split off; spread, spread out, outspread, splay, fan out, deploy; go off, go away, fly off on a tangent, go off at a tangent; part company

6 **radiate,** radiate out, ray, ray out, beam out, diffuse, emanate, spread, disperse, scatter

7 **fork,** furcate, bifurcate, trifurcate, divaricate; **branch,** stem, ramify, branch off, branch out, spread-eagle

ADJS **8** **diverging,** divergent; divaricate, divaricating; palmate, palmated; fanlike, fan-shaped; deltoid, deltoidal, deltalike, delta-shaped; splayed; centrifugal

9 **radiating,** radial, radiate, radiated; rayed, spoked; radiative

10 **forked,** forking, furcate, biforked, bifurcate, bifurcated, forklike, trifurcate, trifurcated, tridentlike, pronged; crotched, Y-shaped, V-shaped; **branched,** branching; arborescent, arboreal, arboriform, treelike, tree-shaped, dendriform, dendritic; branchlike, ramous

172 MOTION

<process of moving>

NOUNS **1** **motion; movement,** moving, momentum; stir, unrest, restlessness; going, running, stirring; operation, operating, working, ticking; activity; kinesis, kinetics, kinematics; dynamics; kinesiatrics, kinesipathy, kinesitherapy, kinesiology; actuation, motivation; mobilization; motion detector, motion detection

2 **course,** career, set, midcareer, passage, progress, trend, advance, forward motion, going on, moving on, momentum; travel; flow, flux, flight, trajectory; stream, current, run, rush, onrush, ongoing; drift, driftage; backward motion, regression, retrogression, sternway, backing, going backwards, moving backwards; backflowing, reflowing, refluence, reflux, ebbing, subsiding, withdrawing; downward motion, descent, descending, sinking, plunging; upward motion, mounting, climbing, rising, ascent, ascending, soaring; oblique motion, crosswise motion; sideward motion, sidewise motion, sideways motion; radial motion, angular motion, axial motion; random motion, Brownian movement; perpetual motion

3 **mobility,** motivity, motility, movableness, movability; locomotion; motive power

4 **velocity**, rate, gait, pace, tread, step, stride, clip, lick

VERBS 5 **move,** budge, stir; go, run, flow, stream; progress, advance; wend, wend one's way; back, back up, regress, retrogress; ebb, subside, wane; descend, sink, plunge; ascend, mount, rise, climb, soar; go sideways, go crabwise; go round, go around, circle, rotate, gyrate, spin, whirl; travel; move over, get over; shift, change, change place; speed; hurry, do on the fly, do on the run

6 **set in motion, move,** actuate, motivate, push, shove, nudge, drive, impel, propel; mobilize; dispatch; muster

ADJS 7 **moving,** stirring, in motion; transitional; mobile, motive, motile, motor, motorial, motoric; motivational, impelling, propelling, propellant, driving, self-propelled; traveling; **active**; motion-detecting

8 **flowing,** fluent, passing, streaming, flying, running, going, progressive, rushing, onrushing; drifting; regressive, retrogressive, back, backward; back-flowing, refluent, reflowing; descending, sinking, plunging, downward, down-trending; ascending, mounting, rising, soaring, upward, up-trending; sideward, sidewise, sideways; rotary, rotatory, rotational, round-and-round; axial, gyrational, gyratory

ADVS 9 **underway,** under sail, on one's way, on the go, on the move, on the fly, on the run, on the march, **in motion,** astir; from pillar to post

COMBINING FORMS 10 moto-; -kinesia, kin-, kine-, kino-, kinesi-, kinesio-, kinet-, kineto-

173 QUIESCENCE

<absence of moving or action>

NOUNS 1 **quiescence,** quiescency, **stillness,** silence, quietness, quiet, quietude; calmness, restfulness, peacefulness, imperturbability, passiveness, passivity, placidness, placidity, tranquillity, serenity, peace, composure; quietism, contemplation, satori, nirvana, samadhi, ataraxy, ataraxia; rest, repose, silken repose, statuelike repose, marmoreal repose; sleep, slumber

2 **motionlessness,** immobility; **inactivity, inaction;** fixity, fixation

3 **standstill,** stand, stillstand; stop, halt, cessation; dead stop, dead stand, full stop; deadlock, lock, dead set; gridlock, stalemate, stoppage; freeze, strike; running down, dying down, subsidence, waning, ebbing, wane, ebb

4 **inertness, dormancy;** inertia; passiveness, passivity; suspense, abeyance, latency; torpor, apathy, indifference, indolence, lotus-eating, languor; stagnation, stagnancy, vegetation; estivation, hibernation; stasis; sloth; deathliness, deadliness; catalepsy, catatonia; entropy

5 **calm, lull,** calm before the storm; dead calm, flat calm, oily calm, windlessness, deathlike calm; doldrums, horse latitudes; anticyclone, eye of the hurricane

6 **stuffiness,** airlessness, closeness, oppressiveness, stirlessness, oppression

VERBS 7 **be still,** keep quiet, lie still; stop moving, cease motion, freeze up, seize up, come to a standstill; rest, repose; remain, stay, tarry; remain motionless, freeze; stand, stand still, be at a standstill; stand fast, stick fast, stick, stand firm, stay put; stand like a post; not stir, not stir a step, not move a muscle; not breathe, hold one's breath; bide, bide one's time, mark time, tread water, coast; rest on one's oars, put one's feet up, rest and be thankful

8 **quiet,** quieten, lull, soothe, quiesce, calm, calm down, tranquilize, pacify, passivize, assuage, pour oil on troubled waters; stop, halt, bring to a standstill; cease, wane, subside, ebb, run down, die down, die off, dwindle, molder

9 **stagnate, vegetate,** fust; estivate, hibernate; sleep, slumber; smolder, hang fire; **idle**

10 **sit,** set, sit down, be seated, remain seated, remain in situ; perch, roost

11 **becalm,** take the wind out of one's sails

ADJS 12 **quiescent, quiet,** still, stilly, stillish, hushed; quiet as a mouse; waning, subsiding, ebbing, dwindling, moldering; at rest, resting, reposing; restful, reposeful, relaxed, sedentary; cloistered, sequestered, sequestrated, isolated, secluded, sheltered; calm, tranquil, peaceful, peaceable, pacific, halcyon; placid, smooth; unruffled, untroubled, cool, undisturbed, unperturbed, unagitated, unmoved, unstirring, laid-back; stolid, stoic, stoical, impassive; even-tenored; calm as a mill pond; still as death

13 **motionless, unmoving,** unmoved, moveless, immobile, immotive; still, fixed, stationary, static, at a standstill; stock-still, dead-still; still as a statue, statuelike; still as a mouse; at anchor, riding at anchor; idle, unemployed; out of commission, down

14 **inert, inactive,** static, dormant, passive,

sedentary; latent, unaroused, suspended, abeyant, in suspense, in abeyance; sleeping, slumbering; estivating, hibernating; smoldering; stagnant, standing, foul; torpid, languorous, languid, apathetic, phlegmatic, sluggish, logy, dopey, groggy, heavy, leaden, dull, flat, slack, tame, dead, lifeless; catatonic, cataleptic

15 **untraveled,** stay-at-home, stick-in-the-mud, homekeeping

16 **stuffy,** airless, breathless, breezeless, windless; close, oppressive, stifling, suffocating; stirless, unstirring, not a breath of air, not a leaf stirring; ill-ventilated, unventilated, unvented

17 **becalmed,** in a dead calm

ADVS 18 quiescently, **quietly,** stilly, still; calmly, tranquilly, peacefully, serenely; placidly, smoothly, unperturbedly, coolly

19 **motionlessly,** movelessly, stationarily, fixedly

20 **inertly,** inactively, statically, dormantly, passively, latently; stagnantly; torpidly, languorously, languidly; like a bump on a log; sluggishly, heavily, dully, coldly, lifelessly, apathetically, phlegmatically; stoically, stolidly, impassively

174 SWIFTNESS

<fast moving>

NOUNS 1 **velocity, speed;** rapidity, celerity, swiftness, fastness, quickness, snappiness, speediness; haste, hurry, flurry, rush, precipitation; dispatch, expedition, promptness, promptitude, instantaneousness; flight, flit; lightning speed; fast rate, swift rate, smart pace, spanking pace, lively pace, snappy pace, round pace; relative velocity, angular velocity; airspeed, ground speed, speed over the bottom; miles per hour, knots; rpm; momentum

2 **speed of sound,** sonic speed, Mach, Mach number, Mach one, Mach two; subsonic speed; supersonic speed, ultrasonic speed, hypersonic speed, transsonic speed; transsonic barrier, sound barrier; escape velocity; speed of light, terminal velocity; warp speed, lightning speed; turbulent flow

3 **run, sprint**; dash, rush, plunge, headlong rush, headlong plunge, race, scurry, scamper, scud, scuttle, spurt, burst, burst of speed; canter, gallop, lope; high lope, hand gallop, full gallop; dead run; trot, extended trot, dogtrot, jog trot; full speed, open throttle, flat-out speed, wide-open speed, heavy right foot, maximum speed; fast-forward; fast track, fast lane; forced draft, flank speed <nautical>

4 **acceleration,** quickening; pickup, getaway; burst of speed; step-up, speedup; thrust, drive, impetus, kickstart; free fall; flying start; headlong plunge; overtaking; zip, zing

5 **speeder,** speedster, scorcher, hell-driver, sprinter, harrier; flier, goer, stepper; hummer, hustler, sizzler; speed demon, speed maniac; racer, **runner;** horse racer, turfman, jockey; Jehu; express messenger, courier, bicycle courier

6 <comparisons> lightning, greased lightning, thunderbolt, flash, streak of lightning, streak, blue streak, bat out of hell, light, electricity, thought, wind, shot, bullet, cannonball, rocket, arrow, dart, quicksilver, mercury, express train, jet plane, torrent, eagle, swallow, antelope, courser, gazelle, greyhound, hare, blue darter, striped snake, scared rabbit, New York minute

7 **speedometer,** accelerometer; cyclometer; tachometer; Mach meter; knotmeter, log, log line, patent log, taffrail log, harpoon log, ground log; windsock; wind gauge, anemometer

VERBS 8 **speed, go fast,** skim, fly, flit, fleet, wing one's way, outstrip the wind; zoom; make knots, foot; break the sound barrier, go at warp speed; go like the wind, go like a shot, go like a flash, go like lightning, go like a streak of lightning, go like greased lightning; rush, tear, dash, dart, shoot, hurtle, bolt, fling, scamper, scurry, scour, scud, scuttle, scramble, race, careen; hasten, haste, make haste, hurry, hie, post, kick-start; march in quick time, march in double-quick time; run, sprint, trip, spring, bound, leap; gallop, lope, canter; trot; make time, make good time, cover ground, get over the ground, make strides, make rapid strides, make the best of one's way

9 <nonformal> **barrel,** clip, tear, tear along, tear off, tear away, bowl along, thunder along, storm along, breeze, breeze along, tear up the track, tear up the road, eat up the track, eat up the road, scorch, sizzle, rip, zip, whiz, whisk, sweep, brush, nip, zing, fly low, highball, ball the jack, pour it on, boom, get the lead out, give it the gun, skedaddle, scoot, step on it, step on the gas, hump, hump it, stir one's stumps, hotfoot, hightail, make tracks, step lively, step, step along, carry the mail, hop, hop along, hop it, get, git, go like a bat out of hell, run like a scared rabbit, run like mad, go at full blast, go all out, go flat out, run wide open, go at full tilt, go at full steam, let her out, open her up, go hell-bent for leather, get a move on, give it the gas, go like blazes, go like blue blazes, floor it, let her rip, put the pedal to the metal, tool, cut along

10 **accelerate,** speed up, step up, hurry up, quicken; hasten; crack on, put on, put on steam, pour on the coal, put on more speed, open the throttle;

quicken one's pace; pick up speed, gain ground; race, rev

11 <nautical terms> put on sail, crack on sail, pack on sail, crowd sail, press her

12 **spurt,** make a spurt, make a dash, **dash** ahead, dart ahead, shoot ahead, rush ahead, put on speed, make a burst of speed; make one's move, plunge

13 **overtake,** outstrip, overhaul, catch up, catch up with, come up to, gain on, gain upon, pass, lap; outpace, outrun, outsail; leave behind, leave standing, leave looking, leave flatfooted; overwhelm

14 **keep up with,** keep pace with, run neck and neck

ADJS 15 **fast, swift,** speedy, rapid; quick, double-quick, express, fleet, hasty, expeditious, hustling, snappy, rushing, onrushing, dashing, flying, galloping, running, agile, nimble, lively, nimble-footed, fleet-footed, light-footed, light-legged, light of heel; winged, eagle-winged; mercurial; quick as lightning, quick as thought, swift as an arrow; breakneck, reckless, headlong, precipitate; quick as a wink, quick on the trigger, hair-trigger; prompt; rapid-response

16 **supersonic,** transonic, ultrasonic, hypersonic, faster than sound; warp; **high-speed,** high-velocity, high-geared

ADVS 17 **swiftly,** rapidly, quickly, snappily, speedily, with speed, fast, quick, apace, amain, on eagle's wings; at a great rate, at a good clip, with rapid strides, with giant strides, in seven-league boots, by leaps and bounds, trippingly; lickety-split, lickety-cut; hell-bent, hell-bent for election, hell-bent for leather; posthaste, post, hastily, expeditiously, promptly, with great haste, with all haste, whip and spur, hand over fist; double-quick, in double time, in double-quick time, on the double, on the double-quick; in high gear, in high; under press of sail, all sails set, under crowded sails, under press of sail and steam, under forced draft, at flank speed <all nautical>

18 <nonformal> **like a shot,** as if shot out of a cannon, like a flash, like a streak, like a blue streak, like a streak of lightning, like lightning, like greased lightning, like a bat out of hell, like a scared rabbit, like a house afire, like sixty, like mad, crazy, fury, like sin, to beat the band, to beat the devil

19 **in short order,** in no time, instantaneously, immediately if not sooner, in less than no time, in nothing flat; in a jiff, in a jiffy, before you can say Jack Robinson, in a flash, in a twink, in a twinkling, in the twinkling of an eye, *tout de suite* <Fr>, pronto; PDQ, pretty damn quick

20 **at full speed,** with all speed, at full throttle, at the top of one's bent, for all one is worth, hit the ground running, as fast as one's legs will carry one, as fast as one can lay feet to the ground; at full blast, at full drive, at full pelt; under full steam, in full sail; all out, flat out, wide open; full speed ahead

175 SLOWNESS

<slow moving>

NOUNS 1 **slowness, leisureliness,** pokiness, slackness, creeping, no hurry; sluggishness, sloth, torpor, laziness, idleness, indolence, sluggardy, languor, inertia, inertness; lentitude, lentor; deliberateness, deliberation, circumspection, tentativeness, cautiousness, reluctance, foot-dragging; drawl; gradualism; hesitation, slow start; slow lane

2 **slow motion,** leisurely gait, snail's pace, tortoise's pace; creep, crawl; walk, footpace, dragging pace, lumbering pace, trudge, waddle, saunter, stroll; slouch, shuffle, plod, shamble; limp, claudication, hobble; dogtrot, jog trot; jog, rack; mincing steps; slow march, dead march, funeral march, largo, andante

3 **dawdling,** lingering, loitering, tarrying, dalliance, dallying, dillydallying, shillyshallying, lollygagging, dilatoriness, delaying tactic, delayed action, procrastination, lag, lagging, goofing off; tardiness, unhurriedness

4 **slowing,** retardation, retardment, slackening, flagging, slowing down, slowing up; slowdown, slowup, letup, letdown, slack-up, slack-off, ease-off, ease-up; deceleration, negative acceleration, minus acceleration; delay, detention, setback, holdup, check, arrest, brake, obstruction; lag, drag

5 **slowpoke**, plodder, slow goer, slow-foot, **lingerer,** loiterer, dawdler, dawdle, laggard, procrastinator, foot-dragger, lollygagger, stick-in-the-mud, drone, slug, sluggard, lie-abed, sleepyhead, slow starter, goof-off, goldbrick; tortoise, snail; lardass; Sunday driver

VERBS 6 **go slowly,** go slow, go at a snail's pace, take it slow, get no place fast; drag, drag out; creep, crawl; laze, idle; go dead slow, get nowhere fast; inch, inch along; worm, worm along; poke, poke along; shuffle along, stagger along, toddle along, toddle off; drag along, drag one's feet, walk, traipse, mosey; saunter, stroll, amble, waddle, toddle; jogtrot, dogtrot; limp, hobble, claudicate

7 **plod,** plug, peg, shamble, trudge, tramp, stump, lumber; plod along, plug along, schlep; rub on, jog on, chug on

8 **dawdle,** linger, loiter, tarry, delay, dally, dillydally, shilly-shally, lollygag, waste time, take one's time, take one's own sweet time; goof off, goof around; lag, drag, trail; flag, falter, halt, not get started

9 **slow, slow down**, slow up, let down, let up, ease off, ease up, slack off, slack up, slacken, relax, moderate, taper off, lose speed, lose momentum; decelerate, retard, delay, detain, impede, obstruct, arrest, stay, check, curb, hold up, hold back, keep back, set back, hold in check; draw rein, rein in; throttle down, take one's foot off the gas; idle, barely tick over; brake, put on the brakes, put on the drag; reef, take in sail; backwater, backpedal; lose ground; clip the wings; regress; red-flag

ADJS 10 **slow, leisurely,** slack, moderate, gentle, easy, deliberate, go-slow, unhurried, relaxed, gradual, circumspect, tentative, cautious, reluctant, foot-dragging; creeping, crawling; poking, poky, slow-poky; tottering, staggering, toddling, trudging, lumbering, ambling, waddling, shuffling, sauntering, strolling; sluggish, languid, languorous, lazy, slothful, indolent, idle, slouchy; slow-going, slow-moving, slow-creeping, slow-crawling, slow-running, slow-sailing; slow-footed, slow-foot, slow-legged, slow-gaited, slow-paced, slow-stepped, easy-paced, slow-winged; snail-paced, snail-like, tortoiselike, turtlelike; limping, hobbling, hobbled; halting, claudicant; faltering, flagging; slow as slow, slow as molasses, slow as molasses in January, slow as death, slower than the seven-year itch

11 **dawdling,** lingering, loitering, tarrying, dallying, dillydallying, shilly-shallying, lollygagging, procrastinatory, procrastinative, dilatory, delaying, lagging, dragging

12 **delayed,** retarded, slowed-down, eased, slackened; detained, checked, arrested, impeded, set back, backward, behind; late, tardy

ADVS 13 **slowly,** slow, leisurely, unhurriedly, relaxedly, easily, moderately, gently; creepingly, crawlingly; pokingly, pokily; sluggishly, languidly, languorously, lazily, indolently, idly, deliberately, with deliberation, circumspectly, tentatively, cautiously, reluctantly; lingeringly, loiteringly, tarryingly, dilatorily; limpingly, haltingly, falteringly; in slow motion, at a funeral pace, with faltering steps, with halting steps; at a snail's pace, at a turtle's pace; in slow tempo, in march time; with agonizing slowness; in low gear; under easy sail

14 **gradually,** little by little, dribs and drabs

PHRS 15 **easy does it,** take it easy, go easy, slack off, slow down

176 TRANSFERAL, TRANSPORTATION

<moving to another place>

1 **transferal, transfer;** transmission, transference, transmittal, transmittance; transposition, transposal, transplacement; mutual transfer, interchange, metathesis; translocation, transplantation, translation; migration, transmigration; import, importation; export, exportation; deportation, extradition, expulsion, transit, transition, passage; communication, spread, spreading, dissemination, diffusion, contagion, ripple effect; metastasis; transmigration of souls, metempsychosis; passing over; osmosis, diapedesis; transduction, conduction, convection; transfusion, perfusion; transfer of property, transfer of right

2 **transferability**, conveyability; transmissibility, transmittability; movability, removability; **portability,** transportability; communicability, impartability; deliverability; carrying forward

3 **transportation,** conveyance, transport, carrying, bearing, packing, toting, lugging; carriage, carry, hauling, haulage, portage, porterage, waft, waftage; cartage, truckage, drayage, wagonage; ferriage, lighterage; telpherage; freightage, freight, expressage, railway express; airfreight, air express, airlift; package freight, package service; shipment, shipping, transshipment; containerization, cargo-handling; delivery; travel; public transportation, mass transit, rapid transit

4 **moving,** removal, movement, relocation, shift, removement, remotion; displacement, delocalization; fireman's carry

5 people mover, moving sidewalk, automated monorail; conveyor belt; **elevator**, lift <Brit>, escalator

6 **freight,** freightage; shipment, consignment, goods; cargo, payload; lading, load, pack; baggage, luggage, impedimenta

7 **carrier, conveyer;** transporter, hauler, carter, wagoner, drayman, shipper, trucker, common carrier, truck driver, driver; freighter; containerizer; stevedore, cargo handler; expressman, express, messenger, courier; importer, exporter; bearer, porter, redcap, skycap, bellboy; bus boy; coolie; litter-bearer, stretcher-bearer; caddie; shield-bearer, gun bearer; water carrier, water boy, *bheesty* <India>; the Water Bearer, Aquarius; letter carrier; cupbearer, Ganymede, Hebe; carrier pigeon, homing pigeon

8 **beast of burden;** pack animal, draft animal, packhorse, sumpter, sumpter horse, sumpter mule; horse, ass, mule; ox; camel, ship of the

desert, dromedary, llama; reindeer; elephant; sledge dog, husky, malamute, Siberian husky

9 <geological terms> **deposit,** sediment; drift, silt, loess, moraine, scree, sinter; alluvium, alluvion, diluvium; detritus, debris

VERBS 10 **transfer,** transmit, transpose, translocate, transplace, metathesize, switch; transplant, translate; pass, pass over, hand over, turn over, carry over, carry forward, make over, consign, assign; deliver; pass on, pass the buck, hand forward, hand on, relay; import, export; deport, extradite, expel; communicate, diffuse, disseminate, spread, impart; expedite; transfuse, perfuse, transfer property, transfer of right

11 **remove, move,** relocate, shift, send, shunt; displace, delocalize, dislodge; take away, cart off, cast away, carry off, carry away; manhandle; set aside, lay aside, put aside, put to one side, set to one side, side

12 **transport,** convey, freight, conduct, take; carry, bear, pack, tote, lug, manhandle; lift, waft, whisk, wing, fly; schlep

13 **haul,** cart, truck, bus; ship, barge, lighter, ferry; raft, float

14 **channel,** put through channels; pipe, tube, pipeline, flume, siphon, funnel, tap

15 **send,** send off, send away, send forth; dispatch, transmit, remit, consign, forward; expedite; ship, ship off, freight, airfreight, embark, containerize, transship, pass along, send on; express, air-express; express-mail; package-express; post, mail, airmail, drop a letter; messenger; export; email; drop-ship

16 **fetch,** bring, go get, go and get, go to get, go after, go fetch, go for, call for, pick up; get, obtain, procure, secure; bring back, retrieve; chase after, run after, shag, fetch and carry

17 ladle, dip, scoop; bail, bucket; dish, dish out, dish up; cup; shovel, spade, fork; spoon; **pour,** decant

ADJS 18 **transferable,** conveyable; transmittable, transmissible, transmissive, consignable, deliverable; movable, removable; portable, portative; transportable, transportative, transportive, carriageable; roadworthy, seaworthy, airworthy; importable, exportable; conductive, conductional; transposable, interchangeable; communicable, contagious, impartable; transfusable; metastatic, metastatical, metathetic, metathetical; mailable, expressable; assignable

ADVS 19 **by transfer**, from hand to hand, from door to door; by freight, by express, by rail, by trolley, by bus, by steamer, by airplane, by mail, by special delivery, by package express, by messenger, by hand; by email

20 **on the way,** along the way, on the road, on the high road, en route, in transit, on the wing, as one goes; in passing, *en passant* <Fr>; in mid-progress

177 TRAVEL

<journey to another place>

NOUNS 1 **travel,** traveling, going, journeying, touring, moving, movement, motion, locomotion, transit, progress, passage, course, crossing; commutation, straphanging; world travel, globe-trotting; junketing, jaunting; **tourism,** touristry; adventure travel, business tourism, heritage tourism, nature tourism

2 **travels,** journeys, journeyings, wanderings, voyagings, transits, peregrinations, peripatetics, migrations, transmigrations; odyssey

3 **wandering,** roving, roaming, rambling, gadding, traipsing, wayfaring, flitting, straying, drifting, gallivanting, peregrination, peregrinity, pilgrimage, errantry, divagation; roam, rove, ramble; itinerancy, itineracy; nomadism, nomadization, gypsydom; vagabonding, vagabondism, vagabondage; vagrancy, hoboism, waltzing Matilda <Austral>; bumming; the open road; wanderyear, *Wanderjahr* <Ger>; wanderlust

4 **migration,** transmigration, passage, trek; run <of fish>, flight <of birds and insects>; swarm, swarming <of bees>; **immigration,** in-migration; emigration, out-migration, expatriation; remigration; intermigration

5 **journey, trip,** *jornada* <Sp>, peregrination, sally, trek; road trip; progress, course, run; tour, grand tour; tourist season, low season, high season; tourist class; travel agency, travel bureau, holiday company <Brit>; conducted tour, package tour, package holiday; excursion, jaunt, junket, outing, pleasure trip; sightseeing trip, sightseeing tour, rubberneck tour; day trip; round trip, circuit, turn; cruise, package cruise, cruise to nowhere; expedition, campaign; safari, hunting expedition, hunting trip, stalk, shoot, photography safari; pilgrimage, hajj; business trip, voyage

6 **riding, driving**; motoring, automobiling; busing; motorcycling, bicycling, cycling, pedaling, biking; horseback riding, horse riding, equitation; horsemanship, manège; pony-trekking

7 **ride, drive;** spin, whirl; joyride; Sunday drive; airing; lift, pickup

8 **walking,** ambulation, perambulation, pedestrianism, shank's mare, shank's pony, going on foot, going afoot, footing, hoofing, footing it, hoofing it; strolling, sauntering, ambling, *flânerie*

<Fr>; tramping, marching, hiking, backpacking, trail hiking, footslogging, trudging, treading; lumbering, waddling; toddling, staggering, tottering; hitchhiking, hitching, thumbing, thumbing a ride; jaywalking

9 **nightwalking,** noctambulation, noctambulism; night-wandering, noctivagation; sleepwalking, somnambulation, somnambulism; sleepwalk

10 **walk,** ramble, amble, hike, tramp, traipse; slog, trudge, schlep; stroll, saunter; promenade; *passeggiata* <Ital>; jaunt, airing; constitutional, stretch; turn; peripatetic journey, peripatetic exercise, peripateticism; walking tour, walking excursion; march, forced march, route march; parade

11 **step,** pace, stride; footstep, footfall, tread; hoofbeat, clop; hop, jump; skip, hippety-hop

12 **gait, pace,** walk, step, stride, tread; saunter, stroll, strolling gait; shuffle, shamble, hobble, limp, hitch, waddle; totter, stagger, lurch; toddle, paddle; slouch, droop, drag; mince, mincing steps, scuttle, prance, flounce, stalk, strut, swagger; slink, slither, sidle; jog; swing, roll; amble, single-foot, rack, piaffer; trot, gallop; lock step; velocity; slowness

13 **march;** quick, quickstep march, quickstep, quick time; lockstep; double march, double-quick, double time; slow march, slow time; half step; goose step

14 **leg, limb,** shank; hind leg, foreleg; gamb, jamb <heraldry>; shin, cnemis; ankle, tarsus; hock, gambrel; calf; knee; thigh; popliteal space, ham, drumstick; gigot

15 <nonformal> gams, stems, trotters, hind legs, underpinnings, wheels, shanks, sticks, pins, stumps

16 **gliding,** sliding, slipping, slithering, coasting, sweeping, flowing, sailing; skating, in-line skating, skiing, tobogganing, sledding, boarding; glide, slide, slither, sweep, skim, flow

17 **creeping, crawling,** going on all fours; sneaking, stealing, slinking, sidling, gumshoeing, pussyfooting, walking on eggs, padding, prowling, nightwalking; worming, snaking; tiptoeing, tiptoe, tippytoe; creep, crawl, scramble, scrabble; all fours

VERBS 18 **travel,** go, move, pass, fare, wayfare, fare forth, fetch, flit, hie, sashay, cover ground; progress; move on, move along, go along; wend, wend one's way; betake oneself, direct one's course, bend one's steps, run, flow, stream; roll, roll on; commute, straphang

19 <go at a given speed> **go,** go at, reach, make, do, hit, clip off

20 **traverse,** cross, **travel over, travel through**, pass through, go over, pass over, cover, measure, transit, track, range, range over, range through, course, do, perambulate, peregrinate, overpass, go over the ground; patrol, reconnoiter, scout; sweep, make one's rounds, scour, scour the country; ply, voyage

21 **journey,** travel, make a journey, take a journey, go on a journey, take a trip, make a trip, fare, wayfare, gad around, gad about, get around, get about, navigate, trek, jaunt, peregrinate; junket, go on a junket; tour; hit the trail, take the road, go on the road; cruise, go on a cruise, voyage; go abroad, go to foreign places, go to foreign shores, range the world, globe-trot; travel light, live out of a suitcase; pilgrimage, pilgrim, go on a pilgrimage, make a pilgrimage; campaign, go overseas, go on an expedition, go on safari; go on a sightseeing trip, sightsee, rubberneck

22 **migrate,** transmigrate, trek; flit, take wing; run <of fish>, swarm <of bees>; emigrate, out-migrate, expatriate; **immigrate,** in-migrate; remigrate; intermigrate

23 **wander,** roam, rove, range, nomadize, gad, gad around, gad about, follow the seasons, wayfare, flit, traipse, gallivant, knock around, knock about, prowl, drift, stray, float around, straggle, meander, ramble, stroll, saunter, jaunt, peregrinate, pererrate, divagate, go about, run about, go the rounds; tramp, hobo, bum, go on the bum, vagabond, vagabondize, take to the road, travel the open road, beat one's way; hit the road, hit the trail, walk the tracks, count ties, pound the pavement

24 **go for an outing**, go for an airing, take the air, get some air; go for a walk; go for a ride; day-trip

25 **go to,** repair to, resort to, hie to, hie oneself to, arise and go to, direct one's course to, turn one's tracks to, make one's way to, set foot in, bend one's steps to, betake oneself to, visit, drop in, drop around, drop by, make the scene

26 **creep, crawl,** scramble, scrabble, grovel, go on hands and knees, go on all fours; worm, worm along, worm one's way, snake; inch, inch along; sneak, steal, steal along; pussyfoot, gumshoe, slink, sidle, pad, prowl, nightwalk; tiptoe, tippytoe, go on tiptoe

27 **walk,** ambulate, peripateticate, pedestrianize, traipse; step, tread, pace, stride, pad; foot, foot it; leg, leg it; hoof it, ankle, go on the heel and toe, ride shank's mare, ride the shank's pony, ride the shoeleather, ride the hobnail express, stump it; peg along, shuffle along; perambulate; circumambulate; jaywalk; power walk, exercise walk, speedwalk, racewalk

28 **<ways of walking>** stroll, saunter, *flâner* <Fr>;

shuffle, scuff, scuffle, straggle, shamble, slouch; stride, straddle; trudge, plod, peg, traipse, clump, stump, slog, footslog, drag, lumber, barge; stamp, stomp, tromp; swing, roll, lunge; hobble, halt, limp, hitch, lurch; totter, stagger; toddle, paddle; waddle, wobble, wamble, wiggle; link, slither, sidle; stalk; strut, swagger; mince, sashay, scuttle, prance, tittup, flounce, trip, skip, foot; hop, jump, hippety-hop; jog, jolt; bundle, bowl along; amble, pace; singlefoot, rack; piaffe, piaffer

29 **go for a walk,** perambulate, take a walk, take one's constitutional, take a stretch, stretch the legs; promenade, *passeggiare* <Ital>, parade

30 **march,** mush, footslog, tramp, hike, backpack, trail-hike; route-march; file, defile, file off; parade, go on parade; goose-step, do the goose step; do the lock step

31 **hitchhike**, hitch, beat one's way, thumb, thumb one's way, catch a ride; hitch a ride, hook a ride, bum a ride, cadge a ride, thumb a ride

32 **nightwalk,** noctambulate; **sleepwalk,** somnambulate, walk in one's sleep

33 **ride,** go for a ride, go for a drive; go for a spin, take a Sunday drive, go for a Sunday drive; **drive,** chauffeur; motor, taxi; bus; bike, cycle, wheel, pedal; motorcycle, bicycle, mountain bike; BMX, bicycle motocross; go by rail, entrain; joyride, take a joyride; catch a train, make a train

34 **go on horseback,** ride, horse-ride, pony-trek; ride bareback; mount, take horse; hack; ride hard, clap spurs to one's horse; trot, amble, pace, canter, gallop, tittup, lope; prance, frisk, curvet, piaffe, caracole

35 **glide,** coast, skim, sweep, flow; sail, fly, flit; slide, slip, skid, skitter, sideslip, slither, glissade, surf; skate, ice-skate, roller-skate, rollerblade, skateboard; ski; snowboard, board; toboggan, sled, sleigh; bellywhop

ADJS 36 **traveling,** going, moving, trekking, passing; progressing; itinerant, itinerary, circuit-riding; journeying, wayfaring, strolling; peripatetic; ambulant, ambulatory; ambulative; perambulating, perambulatory; peregrine, peregrinative, pilgrimlike; locomotive; walking, pedestrian, touring, on tour, globe-trotting, globe-girdling, mundivagant; touristic, touristical, touristy; expeditionary

37 **wandering,** roving, roaming, ranging, rambling, meandering, strolling, straying, straggling, shifting, flitting, landloping, errant, divagatory, discursive, circumforaneous; gadding, traipsing, gallivanting; nomad, nomadic, floating, drifting, gypsyish, gypsylike; transient, transitory, fugitive, peripatetic; vagrant, vagabond, vagabondish; footloose, footloose and fancy-free; migratory, migrational, transmigrant, transmigratory; viaggiatory

38 **nightwalking,** noctambulant, noctambulous; night-wandering, noctivagant; sleepwalking, somnambulant, somnambular

39 **creeping,** crawling, on hands and knees, on all fours; reptant, repent, reptile, reptatorial; on tiptoe, on tippytoe, atiptoe, tiptoeing, tiptoe, tippytoe

40 **traveled,** well-traveled, cosmopolitan

41 **wayworn,** way-weary, road-weary, leg-weary, travel-worn, travel-weary, travel-tired; travel-sated, travel-jaded; travel-soiled, travel-stained, dusty

ADVS 42 **on the move**, on the go, en route, in transit, on the wing, on the fly; on the run, on the jump, on the road, on the tramp, on the march; on the gad, on the bum

43 **on foot,** afoot, by foot, footback, on footback; on the heel and toe, by shank's mare, on shank's pony

44 **on horseback,** horseback, by horse, mounted, horse-drawn

178 TRAVELER

<one who journeys>

NOUNS 1 **traveler,** goer, viator, comer and goer, road warrior; wayfarer, journeyer, trekker; tourist, tourer; tripper, day-tripper; cicerone, travel guide, tourist guide; visitor, visiting fireman; excursionist, sightseer, rubberneck, rubbernecker, looky-loo; voyager, cruise-goer, cruiser, sailor, mariner; globe-trotter, globe-girdler, world traveler, cosmopolite; jet set, jet-setter; pilgrim, palmer, hajji; passenger, fare; commuter, straphanger; transient; passerby; adventurer, alpinist, climber, mountaineer, ecotourist, adventure traveler, adventure athlete; explorer, forty-niner, pioneer, pathfinder, voortrekker, trailblazer, trailbreaker; camper; fellow traveler; astronaut; reverse commuter

2 **wanderer,** rover, roamer, rambler, stroller, straggler, mover; gad, gadabout, runabout, go-about; itinerant, peripatetic, rolling stone, peregrine, peregrinator, bird of passage, migratory, visitant; drifter, floater; Wandering Jew, Ahasuerus, Ancient Mariner, Argonaut, Flying Dutchman, Oisin, Ossian, Gulliver, Ulysses, Odysseus; wandering scholar, Goliard; strolling player, wandering minstrel, troubadour

3 **vagabond,** vagrant, vag; bum, bummer, loafer, wastrel; tramp, turnpiker, piker, knight of the road, easy rider, hobo, bo, rounder, stiff, bindlestiff; landloper, sundowner, swagman,

swagsman; beggar; waif, homeless waif, bag person, dogie, stray, waifs and strays; ragamuffin, tatterdemalion; gamin, gamine, urchin, street urchin, dead-end kid, mudlark, guttersnipe; beachcomber, idler; ski bum, ski bunny, beach bum, beach bunny, surf bum, tennis bum; ragman, ragpicker

4 **nomad,** transient, Bedouin; gypsy, Bohemian

5 **migrant,** migrator, trekker; **immigrant,** in-migrant; migrant worker, migratory worker; emigrant, out-migrant, *émigré* <Fr>; expatriate; evacuee, *évacué* <Fr>; displaced person (DP), stateless person, exile; wetback

6 **pedestrian,** walker, walkist; foot traveler, foot passenger, hoofer, footbacker, ambulator, peripatetic; hiker, backpacker, trailsman, tramper; marcher, footslogger, foot soldier, infantryman, paddlefoot; hitchhiker; jaywalker; power walker, exercise walker, speedwalker, racewalker

7 **sleepwalker,** noctambulist, noctambule, nightwalker, somnambulist, somnambulator, somnambule

8 **rider,** equestrian, horseman, horserider, horseback rider, horsebacker, *caballero* <Sp>, cavalier, knight, chevalier; horse soldier, cavalryman, mounted policeman; horsewoman, equestrienne; cowboy, cowgirl, puncher, cowpuncher, cowpoke, *vaquero, gaucho* <Sp>; broncobuster, buckaroo; postilion, postboy; roughrider; jockey; steeplechaser; circus rider, trick rider

9 **driver,** reinsman, whip, Jehu, skinner; coachman, coachy, *cocher* <Fr>, *cochero* <Sp>, *voiturier* <Fr>; stage coachman; charioteer; harness racer; cabdriver, cabman, cabby, hackman, hack, hacky, jarvey; wagoner, wagonman, drayman, truckman; carter, cartman, carman; teamster; muleteer, mule skinner; bullwhacker; elephant driver, mahout; cameleer

10 driver, **motorist,** automobilist; chauffeur; taxidriver, cabdriver, cabby, hackman, hack, hacky, hackdriver, pilot; jitney driver; truck driver, teamster, truckman, trucker; bus driver, busman, bus jockey; speeder, road hog, Sunday driver, joyrider; hit-and-run driver; designated driver; backseat driver; new driver, learner

11 **cyclist**, cycler; bicyclist, bicycler, mountain biker, biker; motorcyclist, motorcycler

12 **engineer,** gearhead, motorhead, engineman, engine driver <Brit>; hogger, hoghead; Casey Jones; motorman; gripman

13 **trainman,** railroad man, railroader; conductor, guard <Brit>; brakeman, brakie; fireman, footplate man <Brit>, stoker; smoke agent, bakehead; switchman; yardman; yardmaster; trainmaster, dispatcher; stationmaster; lineman; baggage man, baggagesmasher; porter, redcap; trainboy, butcher; trainspotter

179 VEHICLE

<road transport machines>

NOUNS 1 **vehicle, conveyance,** carrier, means of carrying, means of transporting, means of transport, medium of transportation, carriage; public transportation; alternative fuel vehicle; watercraft, aircraft; car pool

2 **wagon,** waggon, wain; haywagon, milkwagon; dray, van, caravan; covered wagon, prairie schooner, Conestoga wagon, stagecoach

3 **cart,** two-wheeler; oxcart, horsecart, ponycart, dogcart; dumpcart; handcart, barrow, wheelbarrow, handbarrow; jinrikisha, ricksha; pushcart

4 **carriage,** four-wheeler; chaise, shay

5 **rig, equipage,** turnout, coach-and-four; team, pair, span; tandem, randem; spike, spike team, unicorn; three-in-hand, four-in-hand; three-up, four-up

6 **baby carriage,** baby buggy, perambulator, pram; go-cart; stroller, walker

7 **wheelchair,** Bath chair, push chair

8 **cycle,** wheel; bicycle, bike, mountain bike, all-terrain bike, touring bicycle, touring bike, racing bike, hybrid bike, velocipede; tandem bicycle; tricycle, three-wheeler, trike; BMX; motorcycle, motocycle, motorbike, iron; pig, chopper, motorscooter, minibike, moped, dirt bike, trail bike; pedicab; city bike; all-terrain vehicle

9 **automobile** <see list>, car, auto, motorcar, motocar, autocar, machine, motor, motor vehicle, motorized vehicle; all-terrain vehicle, four-wheel drive, all-wheel drive, lowrider; hot rod; off-road vehicle

10 <nonformal> **jalopy,** banger, bomber, beater, bus, buggy, wheels, tub, tuna wagon, heap, boat, short, crate, wreck, bomb, clunker, junker, junkheap, junkpile

11 **police car,** patrol car; prowl car, squad car, cruiser; police van, patrol wagon; wagon, paddy wagon, Black Maria, panda car <Brit>; foot patrol

12 **truck** <see list>, lorry <Brit>; trailer truck, truck trailer, tractor trailer, semitrailer, rig, semi; eighteen-wheeler; panel truck, van; armored vehicle; hook-and-ladder truck, cherry picker; fire truck, garbage truck

13 <public vehicles> **commercial vehicle;** bus, omnibus, chartered bus, autobus, motorbus, motor coach, articulated bus, jitney; express

bus, local bus; schoolbus; cab, taxicab, taxi, bicycle taxi, hack, gypsy cab; rental car; hired car, limousine, limo, stretch limo; public transportation; high-occupancy vehicle; city bike; people carrier

14 **train,** railroad train; choo-choo, choo-choo train; passenger train, Amtrak; aerotrain, bullet train; local, way train, milk train, accommodation train; shuttle train, shuttle; express train, express; lightning express, flier, cannonball express; local express; special, limited; parliamentary train, parliamentary <Brit>; freight train, goods train, freight, freighter, rattler; baggage train, luggage train; electric train; cable railroad; funicular; cog railroad, cog railway, rack-and-pinion railroad; subway, *métro* <Fr>, tube, underground <Brit>; elevated, el; monorail; streamliner; rolling stock

15 **railway car,** car, waggon; baggage car, boxcar, caboose, coach, gondola; diner, dining car, dining compartment; drawing room; freight car; hopper car; flatcar; parlor car; Pullman, Pullman car; refrigerator car, reefer; roomette, sleeper, sleeping car; smoker, smoking car, smoking compartment, non-smoking car; quiet car

16 **handcar,** go-devil; push car, trolley, truck car, rubble car

17 **streetcar,** trolley, trolley car, tram, tramcar; electric car, electric; trolley bus, trackless trolley; horsecar, horse box <Brit>; cable car, grip car

18 **tractor,** traction engine; Caterpillar <tm>, Cat, tracked vehicle; bulldozer, dozer

19 **trailer,** trail car; house trailer, mobile home; recreational vehicle, recreation vehicle (RV); truck trailer, semitrailer, highway trailer; camp trailer, camping trailer, caravan; camper, camping bus

20 **sled,** sleigh, sledge, dogsled, troika; snowmobile, weasel, skimobile, bombardier; runner, blade; toboggan, skiboggan

21 **skates,** ice skates, hockey skates, figure skates; roller skates, skateboard, bob skates; **skis, snowboard,** snowshoes

22 **Hovercraft** <tm>, hovercar, air-cushion vehicle (ACV), cushioncraft, ground-effect machine (GEM), captured-air vehicle (CAV), captured-air bubble (CAB), surface-effect ship

ADJS 23 **vehicular,** transportational; automotive, locomotive

24 **automobile**

brougham
cabriolet
commercial vehicle
compact car
convertible
coupe
estate car
four-door
hardtop
hatchback
hybrid
jeep
limousine, limo
luxury
mid-size
minibus
minicar
race car, racing car, racer, hot rod
roadster
runabout
saloon <Brit>
sedan
sedan limousine
sports car
sport-utility vehicle, SUV
station wagon
stock car
stretch limousine, stretch limo
tourer <Brit>
touring car, gran turismo
two-door
two-seater

25 **truck**

articulated vehicle
big rig
dump truck
flatbed truck
forklift truck, fork truck
four-by-four (4x4)
lorry <Brit>
minivan
monster truck
panel truck, panel van
pick-up truck, pickup
recreational vehicle (RV)
semitrailer, semi
six-by-six
tank truck
tow truck
tractor, tractor-trailer, tractor truck, truck tractor
van

180 SHIP, BOAT

<water transport machines>

NOUNS 1 **ship,** argosy, cargo ship, container ship, cruise ship, dredge, freighter, liner, merchant ship, merchantman, motorship, oceanographic research ship, paddleboat, paddle steamer, refrigeration ship, roll-on roll-off ship, ro-ro, side-wheeler, supertanker, tanker, trawler, (ULCC) ultra-large crude carrier, (VLCC) very large crude carrier, whaler, supercargo; **boat,** ark, canoe, gondola, kayak, lifeboat, motorboat, shell, skiff, whaleboat, workboat; vessel, craft, bottom, bark, hull, hulk, keel, watercraft; tub, bucket, rustbucket, hooker, packet; leviathan; party boat; mother ship

2 **steamboat,** steamer, steamship; motor ship

3 **sailboat,** sailing vessel, sailing boat, wind boat, ragboat, sailing yacht, sailing cruiser, sailing ship, tall ship, sail, sailer, windjammer, windship, windboat; galley; yacht, pleasure boat, pleasure craft

4 **motorboat,** powerboat, speedboat, stinkpot; launch, motor launch, steam launch, naphtha launch; cruiser, power cruiser, cabin cruiser, sedan cruiser, outboard cruiser

5 **liner,** ocean liner, ocean greyhound, passenger steamer, floating hotel, floating palace, luxury liner; cruise ship

6 **warship,** war vessel, naval vessel; man-of-war, man-o'-war, ship of war, armored vessel; United States Ship (USS); Her Majesty's Ship,

His Majesty's Ship (HMS); line-of-battle ship, ship of the line; aircraft carrier, flattop, assault transport, battle cruiser, battleship, coast guard cutter, communications ship, cruiser, destroyer, destroyer escort, guided missile cruiser, heavy cruiser; patrol boat, PT boat; gunboat, hospital ship, minelayer, mine ship, minesweeper; icebreaker

7 **battleship,** battlewagon, capital ship; cruiser, battlecruiser; destroyer, can, tin can

8 **carrier,** aircraft carrier, seaplane carrier, **flattop**

9 **submarine,** sub, submersible, underwater craft; U-boat, *U-boot, Unterseeboot* <Ger>, pigboat; nuclear submarine, nuclear-powered submarine; Polaris submarine; Trident submarine; hunter-killer submarine

10 **shipping,** ships, merchant marine, mercantile marine, merchant navy, merchant fleet, bottoms, tonnage; fleet, flotilla, argosy; line; fishing fleet, whaling fleet; navy

11 **float,** raft; balsa, balsa raft, Kon Tiki; life raft, Carling float; boom; pontoon; buoy, life buoy; life preserver; surfboard; cork; bob

12 **rigging,** rig, tackle, tackling, gear; ropework, roping; service, serving, whipping; standing rigging, running rigging; boatswain's stores; ship chandlery

13 **spar,** timber; **mast,** pole, stick, tree; bare pole

14 **sail,** canvas, muslin, cloth, rag; full sail, plain sail, press of sail, crowd of sail; reduced sail, reefed sail; square sail; fore-and-aft sail; luff, leech, foot, earing, reef point, boltrope, clew, cringle, head

15 **oar,** remi-; **paddle,** scull, sweep, pole; steering oar

16 **anchor,** mooring, hook, mudhook; anchorage, moorings; berth, slip; mooring buoy

ADJS 17 **rigged,** decked, trimmed; square-rigged, fore-and-aft rigged, Marconi-rigged, gaff-rigged, lateen-rigged

18 **seaworthy,** sea-kindly, fit for sea, snug, bold; watertight, waterproof; A1, A1 at Lloyd's; stiff, tender; weatherly; yare

19 **trim,** in trim; apoise, on an even keel

20 **shipshape,** Bristol fashion, shipshape and Bristol fashion, trim, trig, neat, tight, taut, ataunt, all ataunto, bungup and bilge-free

181 AIRCRAFT

<air transport machines>

NOUNS 1 **aircraft, airplane,** aeroplane <Brit>, plane, ship, fixed-wing aircraft, flying machine; aerodyne, heavier-than-air craft; kite; shuttle, space shuttle, lifting body; airplane part; flight instrument, aircraft instrument; aircraft engine; piston engine, radial engine, rotary engine, pancake engine; jet engine, fan-jet engine, rocket motor, turbofan, turbojet, turboprop, pulse jet, ramjet, reaction engine, reaction motor

2 **propeller plane,** single-prop; double-prop, twin-prop; multi-prop; piston plane; turbo-propeller plane, turboprop, prop-jet; puddle jumper

3 **jet plane, jet,** jet aircraft; turbojet, jump jet, ramjet, pulse-jet, blowtorch; single-jet, twin-jet, multi-jet; jet liner, business jet; deltaplanform jet, tailless jet, twin-tailboom jet; jumbo jet; subsonic jet; supersonic jet, supersonic transport (SST), Concorde

4 **rocket,** repulsor; rocket plane, rocket ship, spaceship

5 **rotor plane,** rotary-wing aircraft, rotocraft, rotodyne; gyroplane, gyro, **autogiro,** windmill; **helicopter,** copter, whirlybird, chopper, eggbeater

6 **ornithopter,** orthopter, wind flapper, mechanical bird

7 **flying platform,** flying ring, Hiller-CNR machine, flying bedstead; Hovercraft <tm>, air car, ground-effect machine, air-cushion vehicle, hovercar, cushioncraft; flying crow's nest, flying motorcycle, flying bathtub

8 **seaplane,** waterplane, hydroplane, aerohydroplane, aeroboat, floatplane, float seaplane; flying boat, clipper, boat seaplane; amphibian, amphibious aircraft, triphibian

9 **military aircraft,** warplane, battle plane, combat plane; carrier fighter, carrier-based plane, bomber, dive bomber, fighter, helicopter gunship, jet bomber, strategic bomber, jet fighter, jet tanker, night fighter, photo-reconnaissance plane, reconnaissance fighter, spy plane, airborne warning and control systems (AWACS) plane, Stealth Bomber, Stealth Fighter, tactical support bomber, torpedo bomber, troop carrier, troop transport; amphibian, flying boat; helicopter; suicide plane, kamikaze; bogey, bandit, enemy aircraft; air fleet, air armada; air force

10 **trainer;** Link trainer; flight simulator; dual-control trainer; basic trainer, primary trainer, intermediate trainer, advanced trainer; crew trainer, flying classroom; navigator-bombardier trainer, radio-navigational trainer

11 **light aircraft,** lighter-than-air craft; aerostat, airship, ship, dirigible balloon, blimp; rigid airship, semirigid airship; dirigible, zeppelin, Graf Zeppelin; gasbag, ballonet; hot-air balloon, balloon, *ballon* <Fr>

12 **glider,** gliding machine, hang glider; sailplane, soaring plane; rocket glider; student glider; air train, glider train

13 **parachute,** chute, umbrella, brolly; pilot chute, drogue chute; rip cord, safety loop, shroud lines,

harness, pack, vent; parachute jump, brolly-hop, base jump; skydive; brake parachute, braking parachute, deceleration parachute; parawing, paraglider, parafoil

14 **kite,** box kite, Eddy kite, Hargrave kite, cellular kite, tetrahedral kite

182 WATER TRAVEL

<journey by water>

NOUNS 1 **water travel**, travel by water, marine travel, ocean travel, sea travel, **navigation,** navigating, seafaring, sailing, steaming, passage-making, voyaging, cruising, coasting, gunkholing; inland navigation; boating, yachting, motorboating, canoeing, rowing, sculling; circumnavigation, periplus; navigability

2 <water travel methods> celestial navigation, astronavigation; radio navigation, radio beacon; loran; consolan, shoran; coastal navigation, coastwise navigation; dead reckoning; point-to-point navigation; pilotage; sonar, radar, sofar; plane sailing, traverse sailing, spherical sailing, parallel sailing, middle latitude sailing, Mercator sailing, rhumbline sailing; fix, line of position; sextant, chronometer, tables

3 **seamanship,** shipmanship; seamanliness, seamanlikeness; weather eye; sea legs

4 **pilotship,** pilotry, pilotage, helmsmanship; steerage; proper piloting

5 embarkation; disembarkation

6 **voyage,** ocean trip, sea trip, cruise, sail; course, run, passage; crossing; shakedown cruise; leg

7 **wake,** track; wash, backwash

8 <submarines> **surfacing,** breaking water; submergence, dive; stationary dive, running dive, crash dive

9 **way,** progress; headway, steerageway, sternway, leeway, driftway

10 **seaway, waterway,** fairway, road, channel, ocean lane, sea lane, ship route, steamer track, steamer lane; crossing; approaches; navigable water

11 aquatics, **swimming,** bathing, natation, balneation, aquacize; swim, bathe; crawl, freestyle, trudgen, Australian crawl, breaststroke, butterfly, sidestroke, dog paddle, doggie paddle, backstroke; treading water; floating; diving; wading; fin; flipper, flapper; fishtail; waterskiing, aquaplaning, surfboarding; surfing; windsurfing, boardsailing; free swimming

12 **swimmer,** bather, natator, merman, fish; bathing girl, mermaid; bathing beauty; frogman; diver

VERBS 13 **navigate,** sail, cruise, steam, run, seafare, voyage, ply, go on shipboard, go by ship, go on a voyage, take a voyage; go to sea, sail the sea, sail the ocean blue; boat, yacht, motorboat, canoe, row, scull; surf, windsurf, boardsail; steamboat; bear sail, carry sail; cross, traverse, make a passage, make a run; sail round, circumnavigate; coast

14 **pilot,** helm, coxswain, steer, guide, be at the helm, be at the tiller, direct, manage, handle, run, operate, conn, cond, be at the conn, have the conn; navigate, chart a course

15 **anchor,** come to anchor, lay anchor, cast anchor, let go the anchor, drop the hook; carry out the anchor; kedge, kedge off; dock, tie up; moor, pick up the mooring; run out a rope; lash, lash and tie; foul the anchor; disembark

16 **ride at anchor,** ride, lie, rest; ride easy; ride hawse full; lie athwart; set an anchor watch

17 **lay to, lie to,** lay by, lie by; lie near to the wind, head to wind, windward, be under the sea; lie ahull; lie off, lie off the land; lay up, lie up

18 **weigh anchor,** up-anchor, bring the anchor home, break out the anchor, cat the anchor, break ground, loose for sea; unmoor, drop the mooring, cast off, cast loose, cast away

19 **get underway,** have way upon, push off,shove off; hoist the blue Peter; put to sea, put out to sea, go to sea, head for blue water, go off soundings; sail, sail away; embark

20 **set sail,** hoist sail, unfurl sail, spread sail, heave out a sail, make sail, trim sail; square away, square the yards; crowd on sail, clap on sail, crack on sail, pack on sail, put on sail; clap on, crack on, pack on; give her beans

21 **make way,** gather way, make headway, make sternway; make knots, foot; go full speed ahead, go full speed astern; go at flank speed

22 run, **run with the wind,** sail before the wind, sail with the wind, sail down the wind, make a spinnaker run, sail off the wind, sail free, sail with the wind aft, sail with the wind abaft the beam; tack down wind; sail with the wind quartering

23 **bring off the wind,** pay off, bear off, bear away, put the helm to leeward, bear leeward, head to leeward, pay off the head

24 **sail against the wind,** sail on the wind, sail by the wind, sail to windward, bear to windward, head to windward; bring into the wind, bring by the wind, haul the wind, hail one's wind; uphelm, put the helm up; haul, haul off, haul up, haul to, bring to, heave to; sail into the wind's eye, sail into the teeth of the wind; sail to the windward of, weather

25 **sail near the wind,** sail close to the wind, lie close to the wind, sail full and by, hold a close wind, sail close-hauled, close-haul; work to to windward, go to windward, beat, ply; luff, luff up, sail closer

to the wind; sail too close to the wind, sail fine, touch the wind, pinch

26 **gain to windward of,** claw to windward of, eat the wind out of, have the wind of, be to windward of

27 **chart a course**, plot a course, lay out a course; shape a course, lay a course, lie a course

28 **follow a course**, keep the course, hold the course, hold on a course, stand on course, upon a course, stand on a straight course, maintain the heading, keep the heading, keep her steady, keep pointed, take a course

29 **drift off course, yaw,** yaw off, pay off, bear off, drift, sag; sag to leeward, bear to leeward, drive to leeward, make leeway, drive, fetch away; be set by the current, drift with the current, fall down

30 **change course,** change the heading, bear off, bear away, bear to starboard, bear to port; sheer, swerve; tack, cast, break, yaw, slew, shift, turn; cant, cant round, cant across; beat, ply; veer, wear, wear ship; jibe, jibe all standing, make a North River jibe; put about, come about, go about, bring about, fetch about, beat about, cast about, throw about; bring round, swing round, heave round, haul round; about ship, turn back, put back, turn on her heel, wind; swing the stern; box off; back and fill; stand off and on; double a point, round a point; miss stays; reroute

31 put the rudder hard left, put the rudder right, put the rudder hard over, put the helm hard over, put the rudder amidships, ease the rudder, ease the helm

32 **veer short,** wear short, bring by the lee, broach to, lie beam on to the seas

33 <come to a stop> fetch up, heave to, haul up, fetch up all standing

34 **backwater,** back, reverse, go astern; go full speed astern; make sternway

35 **sail for,** put away for, make for, make toward, make at, run for, stand for, head toward, steer toward, lay for, lay a course for, bear up for; bear up to, bear down on, run in with, close with; make, reach, fetch; heave alongside, go alongside; lay aboard, go aboard; lay in, lie in; put in, put into, put into port, approach anchorage

36 **sail away from,** head away from, steer away from, run from, stand from, lay away from; stand off, bear off, put off, shove off, haul off; stand off and on

37 **clear the land,** bear off the land, lay the land, settle the land, make sea room, get sea room

38 **make land,** reach land; close with the land, stand in for the land; sight land; smell land; make a landfall

39 **coast,** sail coastwise, stay in soundings, range the coast, skirt the shore, lie along the shore, hug the shore, hug the land, **hug the coast**

40 **weather the storm,** weather, ride, **ride out,** outride, ride a storm, ride out a storm; make heavy weather, make bad weather

41 **sail into,** run down, run in, ram; come afoul of, run afoul of, collide, fall aboard; nose into, head into, run prow on, run head-on, run end on, run head and head; run broadside on

42 **shipwreck,** wreck, pile up, cast away; go aground, run aground, ground, take the ground, beach, strand, run on the rocks; ground hard and fast

43 **careen**, list, heel, tip, cant, heave down, lay down, lie along; be on beam ends

44 **capsize,** upset, overset, overturn, turn over, turn turtle, upset the boat, keel, keel over, keel up; pitchpole, somersault; sink, founder, be lost, go down, go to the bottom, go to Davy Jones's locker; scuttle

45 **go overboard,** go by the board, go over the board, go over the side

46 **maneuver,** execute a maneuver; heave in together, keep in formation, maintain position, keep station, keep pointed, steam in line, steam in line of bearing; convoy

47 <submarines> **surface**, break water; **submerge,** dive, crash-dive, go below; rig for diving; flood the tanks, flood negative

48 <activities aboard ship> lay, lay aloft, lay forward; traverse a yard, brace a yard fore and aft; heave, haul; kedge; warp; boom; heave round, heave short, heave a peak; log, heave the log, stream the log; haul down, board; spar down; ratline down, clap on ratlines; batten down the hatches; unlash, cut loose, cast loose; clear hawse

49 **trim,** trim ship, trim up; trim by the head, trim by the stern, put in proper fore-and-aft trim, give greater draft fore and aft, put on an even keel; ballast, shift ballast, wing out ballast; break out ballast, break bulk, shoot ballast; clear the decks, clear for action, take action stations

50 **reduce sail,** shorten sail, take in sail, hand a sail, reef, reef one's sails; double-reef; lower sail, dowse sail; run under bare poles; snug down; furl, put on a harbor furl

51 **take bearings,** cast a traverse; correct distance and maintain the bearings; run down the latitude, take a sight, shoot the sun, bring down the sun; box the compass; take soundings

52 **signal,** make a signal, speak, hail and speak; dress ship; unfurl a banner, unfurl an ensign, break out a flag; hoist the blue Peter; show one's colors, exchange colors; salute, dip the ensign

53 **row,** paddle, ply the oar, pull, scull, punt; give way, row away; catch a crab, catch a lobster;

feather, feather an oar; sky an oar; row dry; pace, shoot; ship oars

54 **float,** ride, drift; sail, scud, run, shoot; skim, foot; ghost, glide, slip; ride the sea, plow the deep, walk the waters

55 **pitch,** toss, tumble, toss and tumble, pitch and toss, plunge, hobbyhorse, pound, rear, rock, roll, reel, swing, sway, lurch, yaw, heave, scend, flounder, welter, wallow; make heavy weather

56 **swim,** bathe, go swimming, go bathing; tread water; float, float on one's back, do the deadman's float, dog-paddle; wade, go wading; skinny-dip; aquacize; dive

ADJS 57 **nautical, marine,** maritime, naval, navigational; seafaring, seagoing, oceangoing, seaborne, water-borne; seamanly, seamanlike, salty; pelagic, oceanic

58 **aquatic,** water-dwelling, water-living, water-growing, water-loving; **swimming,** balneal, natant, natatory, natatorial; shore, seashore; tidal, estuarine, littoral, grallatorial; riverine; deep-sea

59 **navigable,** boatable

60 **floating,** afloat, awash; water-borne

61 **adrift,** afloat, unmoored, untied, loose, unanchored, aweigh; cast-off, started

ADVS 62 **on board,** on shipboard, on board ship, aboard, all aboard, afloat; on deck, topside; aloft; in sail; before the mast; athwart the hawse, athwarthawse

63 **underway,** making way, with steerageway, with way on; at sea, on the high seas, off soundings, in blue water; under sail, under canvas, with sails spread; under press of sail; under steam, under power; under bare poles; on the heading, off the heading, on course, off course; in soundings, homeward bound

64 **before the wind,** with the wind, down the wind, running free; off the wind, with the wind aft, with the wind abaft the beam, wing and wing, under the wind, under the lee; on a reach, on a beam, on a broad reach, with wind abeam

65 **against the wind,** on the wind, into the wind, up the wind, by the wind, head to wind; into the wind's eye, in the teeth of the wind

66 **near the wind,** close to the wind, close-hauled, on a beat, full and by

67 **coastward,** landward, to landward; coastwise, coastways, coast-to-coast

68 **leeward,** to leeward, alee, downwind; windward, to windward, weatherward, aweather, upwind

69 **aft,** abaft, baft, astern; fore and aft

70 **alongside,** board and board, yardarm to yardarm

71 **at anchor,** riding at anchor; lying to, hove to; lying ahull

72 **afoul,** foul, in collision; head and head, head-on, end on, prow on; broadside on

73 **aground,** on the rocks; hard and fast

74 **overboard,** over the board, over the side, by the board; aft the fantail

183 MARINER

<*water navigator*>

NOUNS 1 **mariner, seaman, sailor,** sailorman, navigator, seafarer, seafaring man, bluejacket, sea dog, water dog, Seabee, crewman, shipman, jack, jacky, jack afloat, jack-tar, tar, salt, gob, swabby, hearty, lobscouser, windsailor, windjammer; limey, limejuicer; common seaman, ordinary seaman (OD); able seaman, able-bodied seaman (AB); deep-sea man, saltwater sailer, bluewater sailer, deepwater sailor; fresh-water sailor; fair-weather sailor; whaler, fisherman, lobsterman; viking, sea rover, buccaneer, privateer, pirate; Jason, Argonaut, Ancient Mariner, Flying Dutchman; Neptune, Poseidon, Varuna, Dylan; yachtsman, yachtswoman, cruising sailor, racing sailor; submariner

2 <novice> **lubber,** landlubber; polliwog

3 <veteran> **old salt,** old sea dog, shellback, barnacle-back; master mariner

4 **navy serviceperson,** man-of-war's man, bluejacket; gob, swabbie, swabber; marine, leatherneck, gyrene, devil dog, jarhead, Royal Marine, jolly; horse marine; boot; midshipman, midshipmate, middy; cadet, naval cadet; coastguardsman, Naval Reservist, Seabee, frogman

5 **boatman,** boatsman, boat-handler, boater, waterman; oarsman, oar, rower, sculler, punter; galley slave; ferryman, ferrier; bargeman, barger, bargee <Brit>, bargemaster; lighterman, wherryman; gondolier, *gondoliere* <Ital>

6 hand, **deckhand,** deckie <Brit>, roustabout; stoker, fireman, bakehead; black gang; wiper, oiler, boilerman; cabin boy; yeoman, ship's writer; purser; ship's carpenter, chips; ship's cooper, bungs, Jimmy Bungs; ship's tailor, snip, snips; steward, stewardess, commissary steward, mess steward, hospital steward; commissary clerk; mail orderly; navigator; radio operator, sparks; landing signalman; gunner, gun loader, torpedoman; afterguard; complement; watch

7 <**ship's officer**> captain, shipmaster, master, skipper, commander, the Old Man; navigator, navigating officer, sailing master; deck officer, officer of the deck (OD); watch officer, officer of the watch; mate, first mate, chief mate, second mate, third mate, boatswain's mate; boatswain,

bos'n, pipes; quartermaster; sergeant-at-arms; chief engineer, engine-room officer; naval officer

8 **steersman,** helmsman, wheelman, wheelsman, boatsteerer; quartermaster; coxswain, cox; pilot, conner, sailing master; harbor pilot, docking pilot

9 **longshoreman,** wharf hand, dockhand, docker, dockworker, dock-walloper; stevedore, loader; roustabout, lumper

184 AVIATION

<journey by air>

NOUNS 1 **aviation, aeronautics;** airplaning, skyriding, **flying,** flight, winging; volation, volitation; aeronautism, aerodromics; powered flight, jet flight, subsonic flight, supersonic flight; cruising, cross-country flying; bush flying; gliding, sail-planing, soaring, sailing; volplaning; ballooning, balloonery, lighter-than-air aviation; barnstorming; high-altitude flying; blind flying, instrument flight, instrument flying, instrument flight rules (IFR); contact flying, visual flight, visual flying, visual flight rules (VFR), pilotage; skywriting; cloud-seeding; in-flight training, ground school; air traffic, airline traffic, air traffic control, air traffic controller; commercial aviation, general aviation, private aviation, private flying; astronautics; air show, flying circus; **atmospheric sciences** <see list>

2 air science, aeronautical science

3 **airmanship,** pilotship; **flight plan;** briefing, brief, rundown, debriefing; flight training, pilot training, flying lessons; washout

4 air-mindedness, aerophilia; air legs

5 airsickness; aerophobia, aeropathy

6 **navigation,** avigation, aerial navigation, air navigation; celestial navigation, astronavigation; electronic navigation, automatic electronic navigation, radio navigation, navar, radar, consolan, tacan, teleran, loran, shoran; omnidirectional range, omni-range, visual-aural range (VAR)

7 <**aeronautical organization**> Civil Aeronautics Administration (CAA); Federal Aviation Agency (FAA); Bureau of Aeronautics; National Advisory Committee for Aeronautics; Office of Naval Research (ONR); Civil Air Patrol; Caterpillar Club; Airline Pilots Association; Air Force

8 **takeoff,** liftoff, hopoff; rollout, climb; taxiing, takeoff run, takeoff power, rotation; daisy-clipping, grass-cutting; ground loop; level-off; jet-assisted takeoff (JATO), booster rocket, takeoff rocket; catapult, electropult

9 **flight,** trip, run; hop, jump; powered flight; solo flight, solo; inverted flight; supersonic flight; test flight, test hop; airlift; airdrop; scheduled flight; mercy flight; charter flight; connecting flight; nonstop flight; crop-dusting; skywriting; red-eye

10 **air travel,** air transport, air transportation; airfreight, air cargo; airline travel, airline, airline service, air service, feeder airline, commuter airline, scheduled airline, charter airline, nonscheduled airline, nonsked, short-hop airline; flying circus; shuttle, air shuttle, shuttle service; puddle-jumping; air taxi; frequent flier, frequent flyer

11 <**Air Force**> mission, flight operation; training mission; gunnery mission; combat rehearsal, dry run; transition mission; reconnaissance mission, reconnaissance, observation flight, search mission; milk run; box-top mission; combat flight; sortie, scramble; air raid; shuttle raid; bombing mission; bombing, strafing; air support, air cover, cover, umbrella, air umbrella

12 flight formation, formation flying, formation; close formation, loose formation, wing formation; V formation, echelon

13 <**flight maneuver**> acrobatic maneuvers, tactical maneuvers, acrobatics, tactical evolutions, aerobatics; stunting, stunt flying, rolling, crabbing, banking, porpoising, fishtailing, diving; dive, nosedive, power dive; zoom, chandelle; stall, whip stall; glide, volplane; spiral, split S, lazy eight, sideslip, pushdown, pull-up, pull-out; turn, vector in flight (VIF)

14 **roll,** barrel roll, aileron roll, outside roll, snap roll

15 **spin,** autorotation, tailspin, flat spin, inverted spin, normal spin, power spin, uncontrolled spin, falling leaf; whipstall

16 **loop,** spiral loop, ground loop, normal loop, outside loop, inverted normal loop, inverted outside loop, dead-stick loop, wingover, looping the loop; Immelmann turn, reverse turn, reversement; flipper turns

17 **buzzing,** flathatting, hedgehopping

18 **landing,** coming in, touching down, touchdown; arrival; landing run, landing pattern; approach, downwind leg, approach leg; holding pattern, stack up; ballooning in, parachute approach; blind landing, instrument landing, dead-stick landing, glide landing, stall landing, fishtail landing, sideslip landing, level landing, two-point landing, normal; landing three-point landing; tail-landing, high landing, low landing, thumped-in landing, pancake landing, belly landing, crash-landing, noseover, nose-up; overflight, overshoot, undershoot; practice landing, bounce drill

19 flying and landing guides marker, pylon; beacon; radio beacon, radio range station, radio marker; fan marker; radar beacon, racon; beam, radio

beam; beacon lights; runway lights, high-intensity runway approach lights, sequence flashers, flare path; wind indicator, wind cone, windsock, air sleeve; instrument landing system (ILS); touchdown rate of descent indicator (TRODI); ground-controlled approach (GCA); talking-down system, talking down

20 **crash,** crack-up, prang; crash-landing; collision, mid-air collision; near-miss, near collision

21 **blackout;** grayout; anoxia; useful consciousness; pressure suit, antiblackout suit

22 **airfield, airport**, airdrome, aerodrome <Brit>, drome, port, air harbor <Can>, aviation field, landing field, landing, field, airship station; air terminal, jetport; air base, air station, naval air station; airpark; heliport, helidrome; control tower, island; Air Route Traffic Control Center; baggage pickup, baggage carousel; airside, landside

23 **runway,** taxiway, strip, landing strip, airstrip, flight strip, takeoff strip; fairway, launching way; stopway; clearway; transition strip; apron; flight deck, landing deck; helipad; ramp

24 **hangar,** housing, dock, airdock, shed, airship shed; mooring mast

25 <**propulsion**> rocket propulsion, rocket power; jet propulsion, jet power; turbojet propulsion, pulse-jet propulsion, ram-jet propulsion, resojet propulsion; constant pressure, ram pressure, air ram; reaction propulsion, reaction, action and reaction; aeromotor, aircraft engine, power plant

26 **lift,** lift ratio, lift force, lift component, lift direction; aerostatic lift, dynamic lift, gross lift, useful lift, margin of lift

27 **drag,** resistance; drag ratio, drag force, drag component, induced drag, wing drag, parasite drag, parasitic drag, structural drag, profile drag, head resistance, drag direction, crosswind force

28 **drift,** drift angle; lateral drift, leeway

29 flow, **airflow**, air flow, laminar flow; turbulence, turbulent flow, burble, burble point, eddies

30 wash, **wake**, stream; downwash; backwash, slipstream, propeller race, propwash; exhaust, jet exhaust, blow wash; vapor trail, condensation trail, contrail, vortex

31 <**airspeed**> true air peed, operating speed, flying speed, cruising speed, knots, minimum flying speed, hump speed, peripheral speed, pitch speed, terminal speed, sinking speed, takeoff speed, landing speed, ground speed, speed over the ground; speed of sound; zone of no signal, Mach cone; sound barrier, sonic barrier, sonic wall; sonic boom, shock wave, Mach wave

32 <air, atmosphere> **airspace,** navigable airspace, international airspace; aerosphere; aerospace; space, empty space; weather, weather conditions; ceiling, ballonet ceiling, service ceiling, static ceiling, absolute ceiling; ceiling and visibility unlimited (CAVU); severe clear; cloud layer, cloud cover, ceiling zero; visibility, visibility zero; overcast, undercast; fog, soup; high-pressure area, low-pressure area; trough, trough line; front; air pocket, air hole, air bump, pocket, hole, bump; turbulence; clear-air turbulence (CAT); roughness; head wind, unfavorable wind; tailwind, favorable wind; crosswind; atmospheric tides; jetstream; wind shear

33 **airway,** air lane, airline, air route, skyway, corridor, flight path, lane, path

34 **course, heading,** vector; compass heading, compass course, compass direction, magnetic heading, true heading, true course

35 <**altitude**> altitude of flight, absolute altitude, critical altitude, density altitude, pressure altitude, sextant altitude; clearance; ground elevation

VERBS 36 **fly,** be airborne, wing, take wing, wing one's way, take a flight, make a flight, take to the air, take to the airways, take the air, volitate, be wafted; jet; aviate, airplane, aeroplane; travel by air, go by airline, travel by airline, go by plane, go by air, ride the skies; hop; soar, drift, hover; cruise; glide, sailplane, sail, volplane; hydroplane, seaplane; balloon; ferry; airlift; break the sound barrier; navigate, avigate

37 **pilot,** control, be at the controls, **fly,** manipulate, drive, fly left seat; copilot, fly right seat; solo; barnstorm; fly blind, fly by the seat of one's pants; follow the beam, ride the beam, fly on instruments; fly in formation, take position; peel off

38 **take off,** hop off, jump off, become airborne, get off the ground, leave the ground, take to the air, go aloft fly aloft, clear; rotate, power off; taxi

39 **ascend,** climb, gain altitude, mount; zoom, hoick, chandelle

40 <**maneuver**> stunt, perform aerobatics; crab, fishtail; spin, go into a tailspin; loop, loop the loop; roll, wingover, spiral, undulate, porpoise, feather, yaw, sideslip, skid, bank, dip, nose down, nose up, pull up, push down, pull out, plow, mush through

41 **dive,** nosedive, power-dive, go for the deck; lose altitude, dump altitude, settle

42 **buzz,** flathat, hedgehop

43 **land,** set her down, alight, light, touch down; descend, come down, dump altitude, fly down; come in, come in for a landing; level off, flatten out; upwind, downwind; overshoot, undershoot; make a dead-stick landing; pancake, thump in;

bellyland, settle down, balloon in; fishtail down; crash-land; ditch; nose up, nose over; talk down

44 **crash,** crack up, prang, spin in, fail to pull out

45 **stall,** lose power, conk out; flame out

46 **black out,** gray out

47 **parachute,** bail out, jump, make a parachute jump, hit the silk, make a brollyhop, skydive, base-jump

48 **brief,** give a briefing; debrief

ADJS 49 **aviation,** aeronautic, aeronautical, aerial; aviatorial, aviational, aviatic; aerodontic, aerospace, aerotechnical, aerostatic, aerostatical, aeromechanic, aeromechanical, aerodynamic, aerodynamical, avionic, aeronomic, aerophysical; aeromarine; aerobatic; airworthy, air-minded, air-conscious, aeromedical; airwise; airsick; air-traffic; subsonic, supersonic, hypersonic; propeller, prop, jet, turbojet

50 **flying,** airborne, winging, soaring; volant, volitant, volitational, hovering, fluttering; gliding; jet-propelled, rocket-propelled

ADVS 51 **in flight,** on the wing, on the fly, while airborne

52 **atmospheric sciences**

acronomy
aerial photography
aeroballistics
aerocartography
aerodontia
aerodynamics
aerogeography
aerogeology
aerognosy
aerography
aerology
aeromechanics
aerometry
aeronautical engineering
aeronautical meteorology
aerophotography
aerophysics
aeroscopy
aerospace research
aerostatics
aerostation
aerotechnics
aerothermodynamics
aircraft design
aircraft hydraulics
astroparticle physics
aviation medicine, aeromedicine
aviation technology
avionics
climatology
environmental science
hydrostatics
jet engineering
kinematics
kinetics
meteorology
micrometeorology
micrometry
photometry
pneumatics
rocket engineering
rocketry
supersonic aerodynamics
supersonics

185 AVIATOR

<air navigator>

NOUNS 1 **aviator,** airperson, airman, flier, **pilot,** air pilot, licensed pilot, private pilot, airline pilot, commercial pilot, aeronaut, flyboy, airplane driver, birdman; aircrew member; captain, chief pilot; copilot, second officer; flight engineer, third officer; jet pilot, jet jockey; instructor; test pilot; bush pilot; astronaut; cloud seeder, rainmaker; cropduster; barnstormer; stunt man, stunt flier

2 **aviatrix,** aviatress, airwoman, birdwoman; stuntwoman

3 **military pilot,** naval pilot, combat pilot; fighter pilot; bomber pilot; observer, reconnaissance pilot; radarman; aviation cadet, air cadet, flying cadet, pilot trainee; flyboy; ace; air force

4 **aircrew,** crew, flight crew; crewman, crewmate, crewmember, aircrewman; navigator, avigator; bombardier; gunner, machine gunner, belly gunner, tail gunner; crew chief; aerial photographer; meteorologist; flight attendant, steward, stewardess, hostess, air hostess, purser, stew

5 **ground crew,** landing crew, plane handlers; crew chief

6 **aircraft mechanic**, aircraftsman, aeromechanic, mechanic, grease monkey, ground engineer; rigger; aeronautical engineer, jet engineer, rocket engineer; ground tester, flight tester; air traffic controller

7 **balloonist,** ballooner, hot-air balloonist, aeronaut

8 **parachutist,** chutist, chuter, parachute jumper, sports parachutist; skydiver; paratrooper; paradoctor, paramedic; jumpmaster

9 <mythological fliers> Daedalus, Icarus

186 ARRIVAL

<coming to or reaching>

NOUNS 1 **arrival, coming,** advent, approach, appearance, reaching; attainment, accomplishment, achievement

2 **landing,** landfall; docking, mooring, tying up, dropping anchor; getting off, disembarkation, disembarkment, debarkation, deboarding, coming ashore, going ashore; deplaning, weighing anchor

3 **return,** homecoming, recursion; reentrance, reentry; remigration; prodigal's return

4 **welcome,** hero's welcome, greetings

5 **destination,** goal, bourn; port, haven, harbor, anchorage, journey's end; end of the line, terminus, terminal, terminal point, home plate; stop, stopping place, last stop; airport, air terminal, baggage claim

VERBS 6 **arrive,** arrive at, arrive in, come, come to, get to, approach, access, reach, hit; find, gain, attain, attain to, accomplish, achieve, make, make it, fetch, fetch up at, get there, reach one's destination, come to one's journey's end, end up; come to rest, settle, settle in; make an appearance, put in an appearance, show up, turn up, surface, pop up, bob up, make the scene; get in, come in, blow in, pull in, roll in; check in; clock in, punch in, ring in, time in, sign in; hit town; come to hand, be received

7 **arrive at,** come at, get at, reach, arrive upon, come upon, hit upon, strike upon, fall upon, light upon, pitch upon, stumble on, stumble upon

8 **land,** come to land, make a landfall, set foot on dry land; reach land, make land, make port; put in, put into port; dock, moor, tie up, anchor, drop anchor; go ashore, disembark, debark, unboat; detrain, debus, deplane, disemplane; alight

ADJS 9 **arriving,** approaching, entering, coming, incoming; inbound, inwardbound; homeward, homeward-bound; immigrant, second-generation

ADVS 10 **arriving,** on arrival, on arriving

187 RECEPTION

<welcoming or receiving>

NOUNS 1 **reception,** taking in, receipt, receiving; **welcome,** welcoming, cordial welcome, open arms, welcoming arms; hospitality; refuge

2 **admission,** admittance, acceptance; immission, intromission; installation, installment, instatement, inauguration, initiation; baptism, investiture, ordination; enlistment, enrollment, induction; baptism of fire; street credibility, street cred

3 **entree,** entrée, in, entry, entrance, access, opening, open door, open arms; a foot in the door, opening wedge

4 **ingestion;** eating; drinking, imbibing, imbibition; engorgement, ingurgitation, engulfment; swallowing, gulping; swallow, gulp, slurp

5 <drawing in> **suction,** suck, sucking; inhalation, inhalement, inspiration, aspiration; snuff, snuffle, sniff, sniffle

6 sorption, **absorption,** adsorption, chemisorption, chemosorption, engrossment, digestion, assimilation, infiltration; sponging, blotting; seepage, percolation; osmosis, endosmosis, exosmosis, electroosmosis; absorbency; absorbent, adsorbent, sponge, blotter, blotting paper

7 **<bringing in>** introduction; importing, import, importation, investiture, naturalization

8 readmission; reabsorption, resorbence

9 **receptivity, receptiveness,** welcoming, welcome, invitingness, openness, hospitality, cordiality, recipience, recipiency; receptibility, admissibility

VERBS 10 **receive,** take in; admit, let in, immit, intromit, give entrance, give admittance to; **welcome,** bid welcome, give a royal welcome, roll out the red carpet; give an entree, open the door to, give refuge to, give shelter to, give sanctuary to, throw open to; include

11 **ingest,** eat, tuck away, put away; imbibe, drink; swallow, devour, ingurgitate; engulf, engorge; gulp, gulp down, swill down, wolf down, gobble

12 **draw in,** suck, suckle, suck in, suck up, aspirate, pick up; inhale, inspire, breathe in; snuff, snuffle, sniff, sniffle, snuff in, snuff up, slurp

13 **absorb,** adsorb, chemisorb, chemosorb, assimilate, engross, digest, drink, imbibe, take up, take in, drink up, drink in, slurp up, swill up; blot, blot up, soak up, sponge; osmose; infiltrate, filter in; soak in, seep in, percolate in; internalize

14 **bring in,** introduce, import

15 readmit; reabsorb, resorb

ADJS 16 **receptive,** recipient; welcoming, open, hospitable, cordial, inviting, invitatory; introceptive; admissive, admissory; receivable, receptible, admissible; intromissive, intromittent; ingestive, imbibitory

17 sorbent, **absorbent,** adsorbent, chemisorptive, chemosorptive, assimilative, digestive; bibulous, imbibitory, thirsty, soaking, blotting; spongy, spongeous; osmotic, endosmotic, exosmotic; resorbent

18 **introductory,** introductive; initiatory, initiative, baptismal

188 DEPARTURE

<leaving>

NOUNS 1 **departure, leaving,** going, passing, parting; exit, walkout; egress; withdrawal, removal, retreat, retirement; evacuation, abandonment, desertion; decampment; escape, flight, getaway, elopement; exodus, hegira; migration, mass migration; defection, voting with one's feet; checkout

2 **start,** starting, start-off, setoff, setout, takeoff, getaway, liftoff; the starting gun, the starting pistol; break; the green light

3 **embarkation,** embarkment, boarding; entrainment; enplanement, emplanement

4 **leave-taking, leave,** parting, departure, conge; send-off, Godspeed; adieu, one's adieus, farewell, aloha, goodbye; valedictory address, valedictory, valediction, parting words; parting shot, Parthian shot; swan song; viaticum; stirrup cup, one for the road, one for luck, nightcap

5 **point of departure,** starting place, starting point, takeoff, start, base, baseline, basis; line of departure; starting line, starting post, starting gate, starting blocks, springboard, jumping-off point; stakeboat; port of embarkation

VERBS 6 **depart,** make off, begone, be off, take oneself off, take oneself away, take one's departure, take leave, take one's leave, leave, go, go away, go off, get away, get underway, come away, go one's way, get along, be getting along, go on, get on; move off, move away, move out, march off, march away; pull out; decamp; exit; break oneself away, tear oneself away, take wing, take flight

7 <nonformal> **beat it, split,** scram, amscray, up and go, trot, toddle, stagger along, mosey along, sashay along, buzz off, buzz along, bug out, bugger off <Brit>, beetle off, fuck off*, f off, get rolling, hightail it, pull up stakes, check out, clear out, cut out, haul ass, hit the road, hit the trail, piss off, get lost, flake off, get going, shove off, push along, push off, get out, get, git, get the hell out, make oneself scarce, vamoose, take off, skip, skip out, lam, take it on the lam, powder, take a powder, take a runout powder, skedaddle, absquatulate, clock off

8 **set out,** set forth, put forth, go forth, sally forth, sally, issue, issue forth, launch forth, set forward, set off, be off, be on one's way, outset, start, start out, start off, start on, strike out, get off, get away, get off the dime; get the green light, break; set sail

9 **quit, vacate**, evacuate, abandon, desert, turn one's back on, walk away from, leave to one's fate, leave flat, leave high and dry; leave a sinking ship, desert a sinking ship; withdraw, retreat, beat a retreat, retire, remove; walk away, abscond, disappear, vanish; bow out, make one's exit; jump ship

10 **hasten off,** hurry away; scamper off, dash off, whiz off, whip off, whip away, nip, nip off, tear off, tear out, light out, dig out, skin out, burn rubber, vamoose, leave quickly, skidoo

11 fling out, fling off, flounce out, flounce off

12 **run off, run away,** run along, flee, take to flight, fly, take to one's heels, cut and run, hightail, make tracks, absquatulate, scarper; run for one's life; beat a retreat, beat a hasty retreat; run away from

13 **check out;** clock, ring, punch out, sign out

14 **decamp,** break camp, strike camp, strike tent, pull up stakes

15 **embark,** go aboard, board, go on board; go on shipboard, take ship; hoist the blue Peter; entrain, enplane, emplane, embus; weigh anchor, up-anchor, put to sea

16 say goodbye, bid goodbye, say farewell, bid farewell, **take leave**, make one's adieus; bid Godspeed, give one a send-off, give one a big send-off, see off, see out; drink a stirrup cup, have one for the road

17 **leave home,** go from home; leave the country, emigrate, out-migrate, expatriate, defect; vote with one's feet; burn one's bridges; leave the nest

ADJS 18 **departing,** leaving; parting, last, final, farewell; valedictory; outward-bound

19 **departed,** left, gone, gone off, gone away

ADVS 20 **hence,** thence, whence; off, away, forth, out; therefrom, thereof

PREPS 21 **from,** away from; out, out of

INTERJS 22 **farewell, goodbye,** adieu, so long, see ya, I'm outa here, cheerio <Brit>, *au revoir* <Fr>, *adios* <Sp>, *hasta la vista* <Sp>, *hasta luego* <Sp>, *vaya con Dios* <Sp>, *auf Wiedersehen* <Ger>, *addio* <Ital>, *arrivederci, arrivederla* <Ital>, *ciao, do svidanye* <Russ>, *shalom* <Heb>, *sayonara* <Japanese>, *vale, vive valeque* <L>, aloha, until we meet again, until tomorrow, *à demain* <Fr>, see you later, see you, tata, toodleoo, I'll be seeing you, see you around, we'll see you, *à bientôt* <Fr>, *à toute a l'heure* <Fr>, *a domani* <Ital>; be good, keep in touch, come again; *bon voyage* <Fr>, pleasant journey, have a nice trip, *tsetchem leshalom* <Heb>, *glückliche Reise* <Ger>, happy landing; Godspeed, peace be with you, take care, *pax vobiscum* <L>; all good go with you, God bless you, toodles, peace out

23 **good night,** nighty-night, *bonne nuit* <Fr>, *gute Nacht* <Ger>, *buenas noches* <Sp>, *buona notte* <Ital>, lights out

189 ENTRANCE

<entering>

NOUNS 1 **entrance, entry,** access, entree, entrée; ingress, ingression; admission, reception; ingoing, incoming, income; importation, import, importing; input, intake; penetration, interpenetration, injection; infiltration, percolation, seepage, leakage; gatekeeping; insinuation; intrusion; introduction, **insertion**

2 **influx,** inflow, inflooding, incursion, indraft, indrawing, inpour, inrun, inrush; afflux

3 **immigration,** in-migration, incoming population, foreign influx; border-crossing

4 **incomer,** entrant, comer, arrival; new blood; new face; visitor, visitant; immigrant, in-migrant; newcomer, new girl, new boy, new kid; settler; trespasser, intruder

5 **entrance,** entry, gate, door, portal, entranceway, entryway; inlet, ingress, intake, adit, approach, access, means of access, in, way in; a foot in the door, an opening wedge, the camel's nose under the wall of the tent; opening; passageway, corridor, companionway, hall, hallway, passage, way; jetway, jet bridge; gangway, gangplank; vestibule; air lock

6 porch, propylaeum, portico, porte-cochere; portal, **threshold,** doorjamb, gatepost, doorpost, lintel; door, doorway, French door; gate, gateway; hatch, hatchway, scuttle; turnstile

VERBS 7 **enter,** go in, go into, access, cross the threshold, come in, find one's way into, put in, put into; be admitted, gain admission, gain admittance, have an entree, have an in; set foot in, step in, walk in; get in, jump in, leap in, hop in; drop in, look in, pop in, visit, drop by; breeze in, come breezing in; break in, burst in, burst into, bust in, come busting in; barge in, come barging in, wade in; thrust in, push in, press in, crowd in, jam in, wedge in, pack in, squeeze in; slip in, creep in, wriggle oneself into, worm oneself into, get one's foot in the door, edge in, work in, insinuate oneself, weigh in; irrupt, intrude; take in, admit; insert

8 **penetrate,** interpenetrate, pierce, pass through, go through, get through, get into, make way into, make an entrance, gain entree; crash, gatecrash

9 **flow in,** inpour, pour in, inrush, inflow

10 **filter in,** infiltrate, seep in, percolate into, leak in, soak in, perfuse, worm one's way into, insinuate

11 **immigrate,** in-migrate; cross the border

ADJS 12 **entering,** ingressive, incoming, ingoing; in, inward; inbound, inward-bound; inflowing, influent, inflooding, inpouring, inrushing; invasive, intrusive, irruptive; ingrowing

ADVS 13 **in,** inward, inwards, inwardly; thereinto

PREPS 14 **into, in,** to

190 EMERGENCE

<becoming known>

NOUNS 1 **emergence,** coming out, coming forth, coming into view, rising to the surface, surfacing, emerging; issuing, issuance, issue; extrusion; emission, emitting, giving forth, giving out; emanation; vent, venting, discharge; outbreak, breakout

2 **egress,** egression; **exit,** exodus; outgoing, outgo, going out; emersion; departure; evacuation; extraction; exfiltration

3 **outburst**, ejection

4 **outflow,** outflowing; discharge; outpouring, outpour; effluence, effusion, exhalation; efflux, effluxion, defluxion; exhaust; runoff, flowoff; outfall; drainage, drain; gush

5 **leakage,** leaking, weeping; leak; dripping, drippings, drip, dribble, drop, trickle; distillation

6 **exuding,** exudation, transudation; filtration, exfiltration, filtering; straining; percolation, percolating; leaching, lixiviation; effusion, extravasation; seepage, seep; perfusion; oozing, ooze; weeping, weep; excretion

7 **emigration,** out-migration, remigration; exile, expatriation, defection, deportation

8 **export,** exporting, exportation; outgoings

9 **outlet,** egress, exit, outgo, outcome, out, way out; loophole, escape; outfall, estuary; chute, flume, sluice, weir, floodgate; vent, ventage, venthole, port; safety valve; avenue, channel; spout, tap; opening, orifice; debouch; exhaust; door; outgate, sally port; vomitory; emunctory; pore; blowhole, spiracle; fire escape

10 **goer,** outgoer, leaver, departer; emigrant, émigré, out-migrant, migrant; colonist; expatriate, defector, refugee, remittance man, remittance woman; walk-off

VERBS 11 **emerge,** come out, issue, issue forth, come into view, extrude, come forth; surface, rise to the surface; sally, sally forth, come to the fore; emanate, effuse, arise, come; debouch, disembogue; jump out, leap out, hop out; bail out; burst forth, break forth, erupt; break cover, come out in the open; protrude

12 **exit,** make an exit, make one's exit; egress, go out, get out, walk out, march out, run out, pass out, bow out, include oneself out; walk out on, leave cold; escape; depart

13 **run out,** empty, find vent; exhaust, drain, drain out; flow out, outflow, outpour, pour out, sluice out, well out, gush out, spout out, spew, flow, pour, well, surge, gush, jet, spout, spurt, vomit forth, blow out, spew out

14 **leak,** leak out, drip, dribble, drop, trickle, trickle down, trill, distill

15 **exude,** exudate, transude, transpire, reek; emit, discharge, give off; filter, filtrate, exfiltrate; strain; percolate; leach, lixiviate; effuse, extravasate; seep, ooze; bleed; weep; excrete

16 **emigrate,** out-migrate, remigrate; exile, expatriate, defect; deport

17 **export,** send abroad

ADJS 18 **emerging,** emergent; issuing, arising, surfacing, coming, forthcoming; emanating, emanent, emanative, transeunt, transient

19 **outgoing,** outbound, outward-bound; outflowing, outpouring, effusive, effluent; effused, extravasated

20 exudative, exuding, transudative; percolative; porous, permeable, pervious, oozy, runny, weepy, leaky; excretory

ADVS 21 **forth**; out, outward, outwards, outwardly

PREPS 22 **out of,** ex; from; out, forth

191 INSERTION

<putting in>

NOUNS 1 **insertion, introduction,** insinuation, injection, infusion, perfusion, inoculation, intromission; entrance; penetration; interjection, interpolation; graft, grafting, engrafting, transplant, transplantation; infixing, implantation, embedment, tessellation, impactment, impaction; intercalation

2 **insert,** insertion; inset, inlay; gore, godet, gusset; graft, scion, cion; tessera; parentheses; filling, stuffing; inclusion, supplement; blow-in; tampon

VERBS 3 **insert,** introduce, insinuate, inject, infuse, perfuse, intromit; enter; penetrate; put in, stick in, set in, throw in, pop in, tuck in, whip in; slip in, ease in; interject; pot, hole; import; inoculate, vaccinate; intercalate

4 **install,** instate, inaugurate, initiate, invest, ordain; enlist, enroll, induct, sign up, sign on

5 **inset,** inlay; embed, bed, bed in; dovetail, mount

6 **graft,** engraft, ingraft, implant, imp; bud; inarch

7 **thrust in,** drive in, run in, plunge in, force in, push in, ram in, press in, stuff in, crowd in, squeeze in, cram in, jam in, tamp in, pound in, pack in, poke in, knock in, wedge in, blow in, impact; shoot

8 **implant,** transplant, bed out; infix; fit in, inlay; tessellate

192 EXTRACTION

<taking or drawing out>

NOUNS 1 **extraction, withdrawal,** removal; drawing, pulling, drawing out; ripping out, tearing out, wresting out, extracting; eradication, uprooting, unrooting, rooting out, deracination; squeezing out, pressing out, expressing, expression; avulsion, evulsion, cutting out, exsection, extirpation, excision, enucleation; extrication, evolvement, disentanglement, unravelment; excavation, mining, quarrying, drilling; dredging; exit strategy

2 **disinterment,** exhumation, disentombment, unearthing, uncovering, digging out; graverobbing

3 **drawing,** drafting, sucking, suction, aspiration, pipetting; pumping, siphoning, tapping, broaching; milking; drainage, draining, emptying; cupping; bloodletting, bleeding, phlebotomy, venesection

4 **evisceration,** gutting, **disembowelment,** shelling

5 **elicitation,** eduction, drawing out, drawing forth, bringing out, bringing forth; evocation, calling forth; arousal, derivation

6 **extortion,** exaction, claim, demand; wresting, wrenching, wringing, rending, tearing, ripping; wrest, wrench, wring; shakedown

7 <obtaining an extract> **squeezing,** pressing, expression; distillation; decoction; rendering, rendition; steeping, soaking, infusion, marinating; concentration

8 **extract,** extraction; essence, quintessence, spirit, elixir; decoction; distillate, distillation, sublimate; concentrate, concentration; infusion; refinement, purification

9 **extractor,** separator, excavator, digger, miner; siphon; aspirator, pipette; pump, vacuum pump; press, wringer; corkscrew; forceps, pliers, pincers, tweezers; crowbar; smelter; scoop

VERBS 10 **extract, take out,** get out, withdraw, remove; pull, draw; pull out, draw out, tear out, rip out, wrest out, pluck out, pick out, weed out, rake out; pry out, prize out, winkle out; pull up, pluck up; root up, root out, uproot, unroot, eradicate, deracinate, pull out by the roots, pull up by the roots; cut out, excise, exsect; enucleate; gouge out, avulse, evulse; extricate, evolve, disentangle, unravel; free, liberate; dig up, dig out, grub up, grub out, excavate, unearth, mine, quarry; dredge, dredge up, dredge out; smelt

11 **disinter,** exhume, disentomb, unbury, unsepulcher, dig up, excavate, uncover

12 **draw off,** draft off, draft, draw, draw from; suck, suck out, suck up, siphon off; pipette; vacuum; pump, pump out; tap, broach; let, let out; bleed, let blood, venesect, phlebotomize; milk; drain, decant; exhaust, empty

13 **eviscerate,** disembowel, gut, shell

14 **elicit,** educe, deduce, induce, derive, obtain, procure, secure; get from, get out of; evoke, call up, summon up, call forth, summon forth, call out; rouse, arouse, stimulate; draw out, draw forth, bring out, bring forth, pry out, winkle out, drag out, worm out, bring to light; wangle, wangle out of, worm out of

15 **extort,** exact, squeeze, claim, demand; wrest, wring from, wrench from, rend from, wrest from, tear from, force out, shake down

16 <obtain an extract> **squeeze out,** press out, express, wring, wring out, bleed; distill, distill out, elixirate; filter, filter out; decoct; render, melt down; refine; steep, soak, infuse; concentrate, essentialize

ADJS 17 **extractive,** eductive; educible; eradicative, uprooting; elicitory, evocative, arousing; exacting, exactive; extortionate, extortionary, extortive

18 **essential,** quintessential, pure

193 ASCENT

<motion upward>

NOUNS 1 **ascent,** ascension, levitation, **rise,** rising, uprising, uprise, uprisal; upgoing, upgo, uphill, upslope, upping; upcoming; taking off, leaving the ground, takeoff; soaring, zooming, gaining altitude, leaving the earth behind; spiraling up, gyring up; shooting up, rocketing up; defying gravity; jump, vault, spring, saltation, leap; mount, mounting; climb, climbing, upclimb, anabasis, clamber, escalade; surge, upsurge, upsurgence, upleap, upshoot, uprush; gush, jet, spurt, spout, fountain; updraft; upswing, upsweep, bounce; upgrowth; upgrade; uplift, elevation; uptick, increase; surfacing, breaking the surface

2 **upturn,** uptrend, upcast, upsweep, upbend, upcurve, upsurge

3 **stairs,** stairway, staircase, *escalier* <Fr>, escalator, flight of stairs, pair of stairs; steps, treads and risers; stepping-stones; spiral staircase, winding staircase, cockle stairs; companionway, companion; stile; backstairs; perron; fire escape; landing, landing stage; ramp, incline

4 **ladder,** scale; stepladder, folding ladder, rope ladder, fire ladder; hook ladder, extension ladder; Jacob's ladder, companion ladder, accommodation ladder, boarding ladder, loft ladder, side ladder, gangway ladder, quarter ladder, stern ladder, aerial ladder

5 **step,** stair, footstep, rest, footrest, stepping-stone; rung, round, rundle, spoke, stave, scale; doorstep; tread; riser; bridgeboard, string; step stool

6 **climber,** ascender, upclimber, soarer; mountain climber, mountaineer, alpinist, rock climber, rock-jock, cragsman; steeplejack; stegophilist

7 <comparisons> rocket, skyrocket; lark, skylark, eagle

VERBS 8 **ascend, rise,** mount, arise, up, uprise, levitate, upgo, go up, rise up, come up; go onwards and upwards; upsurge, surge, upstream, upheave; swarm up, upswarm, sweep up; upwind, upspin, spiral, spire, curl upwards; stand up, rear, rear up, tower, loom; upgrow, grow up

9 **shoot up,** spring up, jump up, leap up, vault up, start up, fly up, pop up, bob up; float up, surface, break water; gush, jet, spurt, fountain; upshoot, upstart, upspring, upleap, upspear, rocket, skyrocket

10 **take off,** leave the ground, leave the earth behind, gain altitude, claw skyward; become airborne; soar, zoom, fly, plane, kite, fly aloft; aspire; spire, spiral upward, gyre upward; hover, hang, poise, float, float in the air; rocket, skyrocket

11 **climb,** climb up, upclimb, mount, clamber, clamber up, scramble up, scrabble up, claw one's way up, struggle up, inch up, shin, shinny up, ramp, work one's way up, inch one's way up, climb the ladder; scale, escalade, scale the heights; climb over, surmount, go over the top

12 **mount,** get on, climb on, back; bestride, bestraddle; board, go aboard, go on board; get in, jump in, hop in, pile in; surmount, remount

13 **upturn,** turn up, cock up; trend upwards, slope up; upcast, upsweep, upbend, upcurve

ADJS 14 **ascending,** in the ascendant, mounting, rising, uprising, upgoing, upcoming; ascendant, ascensional, ascensive, anabatic; leaping, springing, saltatory; spiraling, skyrocketing; upward; uphill, uphillward, upgrade, upsloping, gradient; uparching, rearing, rampant; climbing, scandent, scansorial; gravity-defying

15 **upturned,** upcast, uplifted, turned-up, retroussé

ADVS 16 **up, upward,** upwards; skyward, heavenward; uplong, upalong; upstream, upstreamward; uphill; uphillward; upstairs; up attic, up steps; uptown; up north

INTERJS 17 alley-oop, **upsy-daisy;** excelsior, onward and upward

194 DESCENT

<motion downward>

NOUNS 1 **descent, descending,** descension, downcome, comedown, down; dropping, falling, plummeting, drop, fall, free-fall, downfall, debacle, collapse, crash; swoop, stoop, pounce, downrush, downflow, cascade, waterfall, cataract, downpour, defluxion; downturn, downcurve, downbend, downward trend, downtrend; declension, declination, inclination; gravitation; abseil, rappel; downgrade; down tick; decrease

2 **sinkage,** lowering, decline, slump, subsidence, submergence, lapse, decurrence, downgrade; cadence; droop, sag, swag; catenary; downer

3 **tumble, fall,** cropper, spill, flop; header; sprawl; pratfall; stumble, trip; dive, plunge, belly flop, nosedive; forced landing

4 **slide;** slip, slippage; glide, coast, glissade; glissando; slither; skid, sideslip; landslide, mudslide, landslip, subsidence; snowslide, snowslip <Brit>; avalanche

VERBS 5 **descend,** go down, come down, down, dip down, lose altitude, dump altitude; gravitate; fall, drop, precipitate, rain, rain down, pour down, fall down, drop down; collapse, crash; swoop, stoop, pounce; pitch, plunge, plummet; cascade, cataract; parachute; come down a peg; fall off, drop off; trend downward, down-tick, go downhill

6 **sink,** go down, sink down, submerge; set, settle, settle down; decline, lower, subside, give way, lapse, cave, cave in; droop, slouch, sag, swag; slump, slump down; flump, flump down; flop, flop down; plump, plop, plop down, plunk, plunk down; founder

7 **get down,** alight, touch down, light; land, settle, perch, come to rest; dismount, get off, uphorse; climb down; abseil, rappel

8 tumble, fall, fall down, come a cropper, take a fall, take a tumble, take a flop, take a spill, precipitate oneself; fall over, tumble over, trip over; sprawl, sprawl out, take a pratfall, spread-eagle, measure one's length; fall headlong, take a header, nosedive; fall prostrate, fall flat, fall on one's face, fall flat on one's ass; topple down, topple over; capsize, turn turtle; topple, lurch, pitch, stumble, stagger, totter, careen, list, tilt, trip, flounder

9 slide, slip, slidder, slip down, slide down; glide, skim, coast, glissade; slither; skid, sideslip; avalanche

10 light upon, alight upon, settle on; descend upon, come down on, fall on, drop on, hit upon, strike upon

ADJS **11 descending,** descendant, on the descendant; down, downward, declivitous; decurrent, deciduous; downgoing, downcoming; down-reaching; dropping, falling, plunging, plummeting, downfalling; sinking, downsinking, foundering, submerging, setting; declining, subsiding; collapsing, tumbledown, tottering; drooping, sagging; on the downgrade, downhill

12 downcast, **downturned;** hanging, down-hanging, collapsed

ADVS **13 down, downward,** downwards, from the top down; adown, below; downright; downhill, downgrade; downstreet; downline; downstream; downstairs; downtown; south, down south

195 CONTAINER

<objects for holding>

NOUNS **1 container, receptacle;** receiver, holder, vessel, utensil; repository, depository, reservoir, store; basin, pot, pan, drinking vessel, cup, glass, bottle, crockery, ladle; cask; box, case, crate, carton; bucket; can, pack, jar; kit; basket; luggage, suitcase, baggage, trunk, foot locker; cabinet, cupboard; shelf, drawer, locker; frame; compartment; packet; cart, truck; koozie; folder, Manila folder, file folder, accordion file; bento box; briefcase, attache case; glove compartment; toolbox; jewel case; jewelry box; lock box; safe-deposit box

2 bag, sack, sac, poke, bundle; **pocket,** fob; **balloon, bladder;** carryall, pouch; purse, handbag, tote, tote bag, duffle bag, satchel, hobo, pochette, baguette, bucket bag, clutch, drawstring bag, evening bag, lumbar pack, fanny pack, shopper, sling bag, wristlet; backpack, daypack; brown bag; barf bag; diplomatic pouch

196 CONTENTS

<objects held by container>

NOUNS **1 contents,** content, what is contained, what is included, what is comprised; insides, innards, guts, inner workings; components, constituents, ingredients, elements, items, parts, divisions, subdivisions; inventory, index, census, list; part; whole; composition; constitution, makeup, embodiment

2 load, lading, cargo, freight, charge, burden; payload; boatload, busload, carload, cartload, containerload, shipload, trailerload, trainload, truckload, vanload, wagonload; shipment, stowage, tonnage

3 lining, liner; interlining, interlineation; inlayer, inside layer, inlay, inlaying; filling, filler; packing, padding, wadding, stuffing; facing; doubling, doublure; bushing, bush; wainscot; insole; innards

4 <contents of a container> cup, cupful (etcetera)

5 <essential content> **substance,** sum and substance, stuff, material, matter, medium, building blocks, fabric; gist, heart, soul, meat, nub; the nitty-gritty, the bottom line, the name of the game, core, kernel, marrow, pith, sap, spirit, essence, quintessence, elixir, distillate, distillation, distilled essence, nucleus; sine qua non, irreducible content, indispensable content

6 enclosure, the enclosed, yard, corral, pen

VERBS **7 fill,** pack, load; line, interline, interlineate; inlay; face; wainscot, ceil; pad, wad, stuff; feather, fur; fill up, top up

197 ROOM

<compartment or part of space>

NOUNS **1 room,** chamber, *chambre* <Fr>, *salle* <Fr>, four walls

2 compartment, chamber, space, enclosed space; cavity, hollow, hole, concavity; cell, cellule; booth, stall, crib, manger; box, pew; crypt, vault

3 nook, corner, cranny, niche, recess, cove, bay, oriel, alcove; cubicle, roomlet, carrel, hole-in-the-wall, cubby, cubbyhole, snuggery, hidey-hole

4 hall; assembly hall, exhibition hall, convention hall; gallery; meetinghouse, meeting room; auditorium; concert hall; theater, music hall; stadium, dome, sports dome, arena, sportsplex; bandshell; lecture hall, lyceum, amphitheater; operating theater; dance hall; ballroom, grand ballroom; chapel

5 living room, great room; parlor, sitting room, morning room, drawing room, withdrawing room, front room, best room, foreroom, salon;

sun parlor, sunroom, lanai, lounge, sun lounge, sunporch, solarium, veranda, conservatory

6 **library,** stacks; **study,** studio, *atelier* <Fr>, workroom, den; **office,** workplace, cubicle, cube farm, home office; loft, sail loft

7 **bedroom,** boudoir, chamber, sleeping chamber, bedchamber, master bedroom, guest room, sleeping room, cubicle, cubiculum; nursery; dormitory room, dorm room

8 <private chamber> **sanctum,** sanctum sanctorum, holy of holies, adytum; den, retreat, closet, cabinet; cave, changing room

9 <ships> cabin, stateroom; saloon; house, deckhouse, trunk cabin, cuddy, shelter cabin

10 <trains> drawing room, stateroom, parlor car, Pullman car, roomette, bar car

11 **dining room,** *salle à manger* <Fr>, dinette; breakfast room, breakfast nook, dining hall, refectory, mess, messroom, mess hall, commons, canteen; dining car, diner; restaurant, cafeteria

12 **playroom,** recreation room, rec room, family room, game room, rumpus room; gymnasium

13 **utility room,** laundry room, sewing room, mudroom

14 **kitchen**, kitchenette, galley, pantry, larder, scullery; storeroom, smoking room

15 **closet,** clothes closet, wardrobe, cloakroom, walk-in closet; checkroom; linen closet; dressing room, fitting room, pantry

16 **attic,** attic room, garret, loft, sky parlor; cockloft, hayloft; storeroom, junk room, lumber room <Brit>

17 **basement; cellar,** cellarage; subbasement; wine cellar, potato cellar, storm cellar, cyclone cellar; coal bin, coal hole, hold, hole, bunker; glory hole; panic room, safe room; man cave

18 **corridor,** hall, hallway; passage, passageway; gallery, loggia; arcade, colonnade, pergola, cloister, peristyle; areaway; breezeway

19 **vestibule,** portal, portico, entry, entryway, entrance, entrance hall, entranceway, threshold; lobby, foyer; propylaeum, stoa; narthex, galilee

20 **waiting room;** anteroom, antechamber; side room, byroom; transit lounge, *salle d'attente* <Fr>; reception room, reception area, presence chamber, presence room, audience chamber; throne room; lounge, greenroom, wardroom; coat room, coat check

21 **porch,** stoop, veranda, deck, piazza, patio, lanai, gallery; sleeping porch

22 **balcony,** gallery, terrace, deck, observation deck

23 **floor, story,** level, flat; first floor, first story, ground floor, street floor, *rez-de-chaussée* <Fr>; mezzanine, mezzanine floor, *entresol* <Fr>; clerestory

24 **showroom,** display room, exhibition room, gallery

25 **hospital room;** ward, maternity ward, fever ward, charity ward, prison ward; private room, semi-private room; examining room, examination room, consulting room, consultation room, treatment room; operating room (OR), operating theater, surgery; labor room, delivery room; recovery room; emergency, emergency room; intensive care unit (ICU), intensive care, critical care; hospice care, palliative care; pharmacy, dispensary; clinic, nursery; laboratory, blood bank; nurses' station

26 **bathroom, restroom,** lavatory, washroom, water closet (WC), closet, privy, john, comfort station, toilet; little girls room, little boys room

27 <for vehicles> **garage,** parking garage, car park, parking lot; carport; coach house, carriage house; carbarn; roundhouse; hangar; boathouse; shed

198 TOP

<highest part>

NOUNS 1 **top,** topside, upper side, upside; surface; superstratum; topsides; upper story, top floor; clerestory; **roof,** ridgepole, roofpole; rooftop; ceiling

2 **summit,** top; tiptop, peak, pinnacle; crest, brow; ridge, edge; crown, cap, tip, point, spire, pitch; highest pitch, no place higher, apex, vertex, acme, *ne plus ultra* <Fr>, zenith, climax, apogee, pole; culmination; extremity, maximum, limit, upper extremity, highest point, very top, top of the world, extreme limit, utmost height, uppermost height; exosphere, sky, heaven, heavens, seventh heaven, cloud nine; meridian, noon, high noon; mountaintop; ninth degree

3 **topping,** icing, frosting; dressing, streusel

4 **<top part>** head, heading, headpiece, cap, *caput* <L>, capsheaf, crown, crest; topknot; pinhead, nailhead

5 **architectural topping**, head, crown, cap; bracket capital; cornice; cymatium, clerestory

6 **<capital style>** baroque, Byzantine, composite, Corinthian, Doric, Gothic, Greek, Greek Corinthian, Greek Ionic, Ionic, Moorish, Roman Corinthian, Roman Doric, Romanesque, Roman Ionic, Tuscan

7 **head,** headpiece, pate, poll, crown, sconce, noodle, noddle, noggin, bean, dome; brow, ridge

8 **skull,** cranium, pericranium, epicranium; brainpan, brain box, brain case

9 **phrenology,** craniology, metoposcopy, physiognomy; phrenologist, craniologist, metoposcopist, physiognomist

VERBS 10 **top,** top off, crown, cap, crest, head, tip, peak, surmount; overtop, outtop, have the top place, have the top spot, overarch; culminate, consummate, climax; ice, frost, dress; fill, top up

ADJS 11 **top,** topmost, uppermost, upmost, overmost, highest; tiptop, tip-crowning, maximum, maximal, ultimate; summital, apical, vertical, zenithal, climactic, climactical, consummate; acmic, acmatic; meridian, meridional; head, headmost, capital, chief, paramount, supreme, preeminent, uber; top-level, highest level, top-echelon, top-flight, top-ranking, top-drawer; peak, pitch, crowning

12 **topping,** crowning, capping, heading, surmounting, overtopping, outtopping, overarching; culminating, consummating, perfecting, climaxing

13 **topped,** headed, crowned, capped, crested, plumed, tipped, peaked, roofed

14 **topless,** headless, crownless

15 cranial; cephalic, encephalic

ADVS 16 **atop, on top,** at the top, on the top, topside; at the top of the tree, at the top of the ladder, on top of the roost, on top of the heap; on the crest, on the crest of the wave; at the head, at the peak, at the pinnacle, at the summit

PREPS 17 **atop,** on, upon, on top of, surmounting, topping; like white on rice

199 BOTTOM

<lowest part>

NOUNS 1 **bottom,** bottom side, underside, nether region, nether side, lower side, downside, underneath, fundament; belly, underbelly; buttocks, butt cheek, breech; rock bottom, bedrock, bed, hardpan; grassroots; substratum, underlayer, lowest level, lowest layer, lowest stratum, nethermost level, basecoat; nadir, the pits; depths, benthos

2 **base,** basement, foot, footing, sole, toe; foundation, core, underpinning, infrastructure; baseboard, mopboard, skirt; wainscot, dado; skeleton, bare bones, chassis, frame, undercarriage, underside; keel, keelson

3 ground covering, **ground,** earth, *terra firma* <L>; floor, flooring; parquet; deck; pavement, *pavé* <Fr>, paving, surfacing, asphalt, blacktop, macadam, concrete; cover, carpet, rug, area rug, floor covering; artificial turf, Astroturf <tm>

4 **bottom,** bed, floor, ground, basin, channel, coulee; nether region; riverbed, seabed, ocean bottom

5 **foot,** extremity, pes, pedes, *pied* <Fr>, trotter, pedal extremity, dog, tootsy; hoof, ungula; paw, pad, pug, *patte* <Fr>; forefoot, forepaw; harefoot, splay-foot, clubfoot; toe, digit; heel; sole, pedi, pedio; instep, arch; pastern; fetlock

VERBS 6 **base on,** found on, ground on, build on, bottom on, bed on, set on; root in; underlie, undergird; bottom, bottom out, hit bottom

ADJS 7 **bottom,** bottommost, undermost, nethermost, lowermost, deepest, lowest; rock-bottom, bedrock; ground, ground-level

8 **basic;** basal, basilar, base; **underlying, fundamental,** foundational, essential, elementary, elemental, primary, primal, primitive, rudimentary, original, grassroots; supporting; radical; nadiral

9 **pedal;** plantar; footed, hoofed, ungulate, clawed, taloned; toed

200 VERTICALNESS

<up-and-down>

NOUNS 1 **verticalness,** verticality, verticalism; erectness, uprightness; stiffness of posture, erectness of posture, position of attention, brace; straight up-and-downness, up-and-downness; steepness, sheerness, precipitousness, plungingness, **perpendicularity**, plumbness, aplomb; right-angledness, right-angularity, squareness, orthogonality; Y-axis

2 **vertical,** upright, **perpendicular,** plumb, normal; right angle, orthodiagonal; vertical circle, azimuth circle

3 **precipice,** cliff, sheer cliff, yawning cliff, sheer precipice, sheer drop, steep, bluff, wall, face, scar; crag; scarp, escarpment; palisade, palisades; brink

4 **erecting,** erection, elevation; rearing, raising; uprearing, upraising, lofting, uplifting, heaving up, heaving aloft; standing on end, standing upright, standing on its feet, standing on its base, standing at attention

5 **rising,** uprising, ascension, ascending, ascent; vertical height, vertical dimension; gradient, rise, uprise

6 <instruments> square, T square, try square, set square, carpenter's square; plumb, plumb line, plumb rule, plummet, bob, plumb bob, lead

VERBS 7 **stand,** stand erect, stand up, stand upright, stand up straight, be erect, be on one's feet; hold oneself straight, hold oneself stiff, stand ramrod-straight, have an upright carriage; stand at attention, brace, stand at parade rest

8 **rise,** arise, ascend, mount, uprise, rise up, get up, get to one's feet; stand up, stand on end; stick up, cock up; bristle; rear, ramp, uprear, rear up, rise

on the hind legs; upheave; sit up, sit bolt upright, straighten up; jump up, spring to one's feet

9 **erect,** elevate, rear, raise, pitch, set up, raise up, lift up, cast up; raise aloft, heave aloft, rear aloft; uprear, upraise, uplift, upheave; upright; upend, stand on end, stand upright; set on its feet, set on its base

10 **plumb,** plumb-line; square, square up

ADJS 11 **vertical, upright,** bolt upright, ramrod straight, erect, upstanding, standing up, stand-up; rearing, rampant; upended, upraised, upreared; downright; up-and-down

12 **perpendicular,** plumb, straight-up-and-down, straight-up, up-and-down; sheer, steep, precipitous, plunging; right-angled, right-angle, right-angular, orthogonal, orthodiagonal

ADVS 13 **vertically,** erectly, upstandingly, uprightly, upright, up, stark upright, bolt upright; on end, up on end, right on end, endwise, endways; on one's feet, on one's legs, on one's hind legs; at attention, braced, at parade rest <military>

14 **perpendicularly,** sheer, sheerly; up and down, straight up and down; plumb, *à plomb* <Fr>; at right angles, square

201 HORIZONTALNESS

<side-to-side>

NOUNS 1 **horizontalness,** horizontality; **levelness,** flatness, planeness, planarity, evenness, smoothness, flushness, alignment; unbrokenness, unrelievedness; transom

2 **recumbency,** recumbence, decumbency, decumbence, accumbency; accubation; **prostration,** proneness, procumbency; supineness, reclining, reclination; lying, lounging, **repose**; sprawl, loll; shavasana, savasana, corpse pose

3 **horizontal,** plane, level, flat, dead level, dead flat, homaloid; horizontal plane, level plane; horizontal line, level line; horizontal projection; horizontal surface, fascia; horizontal parallax; horizontal axis; horizontal fault; water level, sea level, mean sea level; ground, earth, steppe, plain, flatland, prairie, savanna, flats, sea of grass, bowling green, table, billiard table; floor, platform, ledge, terrace

4 **horizon,** skyline, rim of the horizon; sea line; apparent horizon, local horizon, visible horizon, sensible horizon, celestial horizon, rational horizon, geometrical horizon, true horizon, artificial horizon, false horizon; azimuth

VERBS 5 **lie,** lie down, lay, recline, repose, lounge, sprawl, loll, drape oneself, spread oneself, spread-eagle, splay, lie limply; lie flat, lie prostrate, lie prone, lie supine, lie on one's face, lie on one's back, lie on a level, hug the ground, hug the deck; grovel, crawl, kowtow

6 **level,** flatten, even, equalize, align, smooth, smoothen, level out, smooth out, flush; grade, roll, roll flat, steamroller, steamroll; lay, lay down, lay out; raze, rase, lay level, lay level with the ground; lay low, lay flat; fell; deck

ADJS 7 **horizontal,** level, flat, flattened; even, smooth, smoothened, smoothed out; tablelike, tabular; flush; homaloidal; plane, planar, plain; rolled, trodden, squashed, squashed flat, razed; flat as a pancake, flat as a board, flat as a table, flat as a billiard table, flat as a bowling green, flat as a tennis court, level as a plain

8 **recumbent,** accumbent, procumbent, decumbent; prostrate, prone, flat; supine, resupine; couchant, *couché* <Fr>; lying, reclining, reposing, flat on one's back; sprawling, lolling, lounging; corpselike; sprawled, spread, splay, splayed, draped; groveling, crawling, flat on one's belly, flat on one's face

ADVS 9 **horizontally,** flat, flatly, flatways, flatwise; evenly, flush; level, on a level; lengthwise, lengthways, at full length, on one's back, on one's nose

202 PENDENCY

<hanging down>

NOUNS 1 **pendency,** pendulousness, pendulosity, pensileness, pensility; **hanging,** suspension, dangling, danglement, suspense, dependence, dependency, swinging

2 **hang,** droop, dangle, swing, fall; sag, swag, bag

3 **overhang,** overhanging, impendence, impendency, projection, extension, protrusion, beetling, jutting; cantilever

4 **pendant,** hanger; hanging, drape; lobe, earlobe, lobule, lobus, lobation, lappet, wattle; lavalier, lavaliere; teardrop; uvula

5 **suspender,** hanger, supporter; suspenders, pair of suspenders, braces <Brit>, galluses

VERBS 6 **hang,** hang down, fall; depend, pend; dangle, swing, flap, flop; flow, drape, cascade; droop, lop; nod, weep; sag, swag, bag; trail, drag, draggle, drabble, daggle

7 **overhang,** hang over, hang out, impend, impend over, project, project over, beetle, jut, beetle over, jut over, thrust over, stick out over

8 **suspend,** hang, hang up, put up, fasten up; sling; oscillate, swing, sway, hover

ADJS 9 **pendent,** pendulous, pendulant, pendular, penduline, pensile; suspended, hung; hanging, pending, depending, dependent; falling; dangling, swinging, oscillating, falling loosely; weeping; flowing, cascading

10 **drooping,** droopy, limp, loose, nodding, floppy, loppy, lop; sagging, saggy, swag, sagging in folds; bagging, baggy, ballooning; lop-eared

11 **overhanging,** overhung, lowering, impending, impendent, pending; incumbent, superincumbent; projecting, jutting; beetling, beetle; beetle-browed; cantilevered

12 lobular, lobar, **lobed**, lobate, lobated

203 PARALLELISM

<lined up but not touching>

NOUNS 1 **parallelism,** coextension, nonconvergence, nondivergence, collaterality, concurrence, equidistance; collineation, collimation; alignment; parallelization; parallelotropism; analogy

2 **parallel,** paralleler; parallel line, parallel dash, parallel bar, parallel file, parallel series, parallel column, parallel trench, parallel vector; parallelogram, parallelepiped, parallelepipedon

3 <instruments> parallel rule, parallel ruler, parallelograph, parallelometer

VERBS 4 **parallel,** be parallel, coextend; run parallel, go alongside, go beside, run abreast, run side by side; match, equal

5 **parallelize,** place parallel to, equidistance; line up, align, realign; collineate, collimate; match; correspond, follow, equate

ADJS 6 **parallel,** paralleling, parallelistic; coextending, coextensive, nonconvergent, nondivergent, equidistant, equispaced, collateral, concurrent; lined up, aligned; equal, even; parallelogrammical, parallelogrammatical; parallelepipedal; parallelotropic; parallelodrome, parallelinervate; analogous

ADVS 7 **in parallel,** parallelwise, parallelly; side-by-side, alongside, abreast; equidistantly, nonconvergently, nondivergently; collaterally, coextensively

204 OBLIQUITY

<slanting>

NOUNS 1 **obliquity,** obliqueness; **deviation,** deviance, divergence, digression, divagation, vagary, excursion, skewness, aberration, squint, declination; deflection, deflexure; nonconformity; diagonality, crosswiseness, transverseness; indirection, indirectness, deviousness, circumlocution, circuitousness; indirect question

2 **inclination, leaning,** lean, angularity; slant, slaunch, rake, slope; tilt, tip, pitch, list, cant, swag, sway; leaning tower, tower of Pisa; bunny slope

3 **bias,** bend, bent, crook, warp, twist, turn, skew, slue, veer, sheer, swerve, lurch; deflection

4 **incline,** inclination, slope, grade, gradient, pitch, ramp, launching ramp, bank, talus, gentle slope, easy slope, bunny slope, glacis; rapid slope, steep slope, stiff climb, scarp, chute; helicline, inclined plane; faceplant; bevel, bezel, fleam; hillside, side; hanging gardens; shelving beach

5 **declivity,** descent, dip, drop, fall, falling-off, falling-away, decline; hang, hanging; downgrade, downhill

6 **acclivity,** ascent, climb, rise, rising, uprise, uprising, rising ground; upgrade, uphill, upgo, upclimb, uplift, steepness, precipitousness, abruptness, verticalness

7 **diagonal,** oblique, transverse, bias, bend <heraldry>, oblique line, slash, slant, virgule, scratch comma, serial comma, separatrix, solidus, cant; oblique angle, oblique figure, rhomboid, rhombus

8 **zigzag,** zig, zag; zigzaggery, flexuosity, crookedness, crankiness; switchback, hairpin, dogleg; chevron; traverse

VERBS 9 **oblique,** deviate, diverge, deflect, divagate, bear off, digress; angle, angle off, swerve, shoot off at an angle, veer, sheer, sway, slue, skew, twist, turn, bend, bias, dogleg; crook; circumlocute

10 **incline,** lean; slope, slant, camber, slaunch, rake, pitch, grade, bank, shelve; tilt, tip, list, cant, bevel, careen, keel, sidle, swag, sway; ascend, rise, uprise, climb, go uphill; descend, decline, dip, drop, fall, fall off, fall away, go downhill; retreat

11 cut, cut across, slant across, cut crosswise, cut transversely, cut diagonally, **catercorner,** diagonalize, slash, slash across

12 **zigzag,** zig, zag, stagger, crank, crankle, wind in and out; traverse

ADJS 13 **oblique,** obliquitous; devious, deviant, deviative, divergent, digressive, divagational, deflectional, excursive, off course; indirect, side, sidelong, roundabout; left-handed, sinister, sinistral; backhand, backhanded; circuitous

14 **askew, skew,** skewed; skew-jawed, skewgee, skew-whiff, askewgee, agee, agee-jawed; awry, wry; askance, askant, asquint, squinting, cockeyed; crooked; slaunchwise, slaunchways; wamperjawed, catawampous, yaw-ways, wonky, wonkish

15 **inclining,** inclined, inclinatory, inclinational; leaning, recumbent; sloping, sloped, aslope; raking, pitched; slanting, slanted, slant, aslant, slantways, slantwise; bias, biased; shelving, shelvy; tilting, tilted, atilt, tipped, tipping, tipsy,

listing, canting, careening; sideling, sidelong; out of square, out of plumb, bevel, beveled

16 <sloping downward> **downhill,** downgrade; descending, falling, dropping, dipping; declining, declined; declivous, declivitous, declivate

17 <sloping upward> **uphill,** upgrade; rising, uprising, ascending, climbing; acclivous, acclivitous, acclinate

18 **steep,** precipitous, bluff, plunging, abrupt, bold, sheer, sharp, rapid; headlong, breakneck; vertical

19 **transverse,** crosswise, crossways, thwart, athwart, across; diagonal, bendwise; catercorner, catercornered, cattycorner, cattycornered, kittycorner, kittycornered; slant, bias, biased; biaswise, biasways

20 **crooked,** zigzag, zigzagged, zigzaggy, zigzagwise, zigzagways, zigged, zagged, dogleg, doglegged; flexuous, twisty, hairpin, bendy, curvy, meandering; staggered, crankled; chevrony, chevronwise, chevronways

ADVS 21 **obliquely,** deviously, deviately, indirectly, circuitously; divergently, digressively, excursively, divagationally; sideways, sidewise, sidelong, sideling, on one side, to one side; at an angle

22 **askew,** awry; askance, askant, asquint, wonkily

23 **slantingly,** slopingly, aslant, aslope, atilt, rakingly, tipsily, slopewise, slopeways, slantwise, slantways, aslantwise, on a slant, at a slant; slaunchwise, slaunchways; off plumb, off the vertical; downhill, downgrade; uphill, upgrade

24 **transversely**, crosswise, crossways, athwart, across

25 **diagonally,** diagonalwise; on the bias, bias, biaswise; cornerwise, cornerways; catercornerways, **catercorner**, cattycorner, kittycorner

205 INVERSION

<opposite or upside-down>

NOUNS 1 **inversion,** turning over, turning upside down, the other way round, inverted order; eversion, turning inside out, invagination, intussusception; introversion, turning inward; reversing, reversal, turning front to back, side to side; reversion, turning back, turning backwards, retroversion, retroflexion, retroflection, revulsion; devolution, atavism; recidivism; transposition, transposal; topsy-turvydom, topsy-turviness; the world turned upside-down, upside-downness, the tail wagging the dog; pronation, supination, resupination

2 **overturn,** upset, overset, overthrow, upturn, turnover, spill; subversion; revolution; capsizing, capsize, capsizal, turning turtle; somersault, somerset, cartwheel, handspring; headstand, handstand; turning head over heels

3 <grammatical and rhetorical terms> metastasis, metathesis; anastrophe, chiasmus, hypallage, hyperbaton, hysteron proteron, palindrome, parenthesis, synchysis, tmesis

4 **inverse, reverse, converse, opposite**, other side of the coin, the flip side, B side; counter, contrary

VERBS 5 **invert,** inverse, turn over, turn upside down; introvert, turn in, turn inward; turn down; turn inside out, turn out, evert, invaginate, intussuscept; revert, recidivate, relapse, lapse, backslide; reverse, transpose, convert; put the cart before the horse, put in inverted order; turn into the opposite, turn about, flip-flop, turn the tables, turn the scale, tip the balance; rotate, revolve, pronate, supinate, resupinate

6 **overturn,** turn over, turn upside down, turn bottom side up, upturn, upset, overset, overthrow, subvert; go ass over elbows, turn ass over tincups, turn a somersault, go head over heels, turn head over heels; turn turtle, turn topsy-turvy, topsy-turvy, topsy-turvify, flip-flop; tip over, keel over, topple over; capsize; careen, set on its beam ends, set on its ears

ADJS 7 **inverted,** inversed, back-to-front, backwards, retroverted, reversed, transposed, backside forward, tail first; inside out, outside in, everted, invaginated, wrong side out; reverted, lapsed, recidivist, recidivistic; atavistic; devolutional; upside-down, topsy-turvy, ass over elbows, ass over tincups, arsy-varsy, bottom-up; capsized, head-over-heels; hyperbatic, chiastic, palindromic; resupinate; introverted; flipped, flip-flopped

ADVS 8 **inversely,** conversely, contrarily, contrariwise, vice versa, the other way around, backwards, turned around; upside down, over, topsy-turvy; bottom up, bottom side up; head over heels, heels over head

206 EXTERIORITY

<outside>

NOUNS 1 **exteriority,** externalness, externality, **outwardness,** outerness; appearance, outward appearance, seeming, mien, front, manner; window-dressing, cosmetics; openness; extrinsicality; superficiality, shallowness; extraterritoriality, foreignness; outdoorsman, outdoorswoman, nature boy, nature girl

2 **exterior,** external, **outside;** surface, superficies, covering, skin, outer skin, outer layer, epidermis, integument, envelope, crust, cortex, rind, shell; exoskeleton; cladding, plating; top, superstratum; periphery, fringe, circumference, outline,

lineaments, border; face, outer face, outer side, facade, front; facet; extrados, back; storefront, shopfront, shop window, street-front

3 **outdoors,** outside, the out-of-doors, the great out-of-doors, the open, the open air; outland, hinterland

4 **externalization,** exteriorization, bringing into the open, show, showing, display, displaying; projection; objectification, actualization, realization

VERBS 5 **externalize,** exteriorize, bring into the open, bring out, show, display, exhibit; objectify, actualize, project, realize; direct outward

6 **scratch the surface;** give a lick and a promise, do a cosmetic job, give a once-over-lightly, whitewash, give a nod

ADJS 7 **exterior, external;** extrinsic; outer, outside, out, outward, outward-facing, outlying, outstanding; outermost, outmost; front, facing; surface, superficial, epidermic, cortical, cuticular; exoskeletal; cosmetic, merely cosmetic; peripheral, fringe, roundabout; apparent, seeming; open, public; exomorphic

8 **outdoor,** out-of-door, out-of-doors, outside, without-doors; open-air, alfresco; out and about

9 extraterritorial, exterritorial; **extraterrestrial,** exterrestrial, extramundane; extragalactic, extralateral, extraliminal, extramural, extrapolar, extrasolar, extraprovincial, extratribal; foreign, outlandish, alien

ADVS 10 **externally,** outwardly, on the outside, exteriorly; without, outside, outwards, out; apparently, to all appearances; openly, publically, to judge by appearances; superficially, on the surface

11 **outdoors,** out of doors, outside, abroad, withoutdoors; in the open, in the open air, alfresco, *en plein air* <Fr>

COMBINING FORMS 12 e-, ec-, ect-, ecto-, ex-, ef-, epi-, eph-, extra-, hyper-, peripher-, periphero-, uber-

207 INTERIORITY

<inside>

NOUNS 1 interiority, internalness, internality, **inwardness,** innerness, inness; introversion, internalization; intrinsicality; depth

2 **interior, inside,** inner, inward, internal, intern; inner recess, recesses, innermost recesses, deepest recesses, penetralia, intimate places, secret places; bosom, secret heart, heart, heart of hearts, soul, vitals, vital center; inner self, inner life, inner landscape, inner man, interior man, inner nature; intrados; core, center

3 **inland,** inlands, interior, upcountry; midland, midlands; heartland; hinterland; Middle America

4 **insides,** innards, inwards, internals; inner mechanism, what makes it tick, works; guts, vitals, viscera, *kishkes* <Yiddish>, giblets; entrails, bowels, enteron; tripes, stuffings

VERBS 5 **internalize,** put in, keep within; introvert, bottle up; enclose, embed, surround, contain, comprise, include, enfold, take to heart, assimilate; introspect; retreat into

ADJS 6 **interior,** internal, inner, inside, inward; intestine; innermost, inmost, intimate, private; visceral, gut; intrinsic; deep; central; indoor; live-in

7 **inland,** interior, upcountry, up-river, landlocked; hinterland; midland, mediterranean; Middle American

8 intramarginal, intramural, intramundane, intramontane, intraterritorial, intracoastal, intragroupal; bicoastal

ADVS 9 **internally,** inwardly, interiorly, inly, intimately, deeply, profoundly, under the surface; intrinsically; centrally

10 **in,** inside, within; herein, therein, wherein

11 **inward,** inwards, inwardly, withinward, withinwards; inland, inshore

12 **indoors,** indoor, withindoors; nature-deprived

PREPS 13 **in, into;** within, at, inside, inside of, in the limits of; to the heart, to the core of

COMBINING FORMS 14 en-, em-, end-, endo-, ent-, ento-, eso-, infra-, in-, im-, il-, ir-, inter-, intra-, ob-

208 CENTRALITY

<centered or in the middle>

NOUNS 1 **centrality,** centralness, middleness, central position, middle position, mid position; equidistance; centricity, centricality; concentricity; centripetalism

2 **center,** centrum; **middle,** midpoint, heart, core, nucleus; core of one's being, where one lives; kernel; pith, marrow, medulla; nub, hub, nave, axis, pivot, fulcrum; navel, umbilicus, omphalos, bellybutton; bull's-eye; dead center; storm center, eye of the storm

3 <biological terms> central body, centriole, centrosome, centrosphere, nucleus; pressure point

4 **focus,** focal point, prime focus, point of convergence; center of interest, center of attention, focus of attention; center of consciousness; center of attraction, **centerpiece,** clou, mecca, cynosure; star, key figure; polestar, lodestar; magnet; center of gravity

5 **nerve center,** ganglion, center of activity, hub,

epicenter, hotbed, vital center; control center, guidance center

6 **headquarters** (HQ), central station, central office, main office, central administration, seat, base, base of operations, center of authority; general headquarters (GHQ), command post (CP), company headquarters; where the action is; home office; homeroom

7 **metropolis, capital;** art center, cultural center, medical center, shopping center, transportation center, trade center, manufacturing center, tourist center, community center, civic center; capital city; holy place, place of pilgrimage

8 **centralization,** centering; nucleation; focalization, focus, focusing; convergence; concentration, concentralization, pooling; centralism

VERBS 9 **centralize, center,** middle; center round, center on, center in, pivot on, revolve around

10 **focus,** focalize, come to a point, come to a focus, bring into focus; bring to a head, come to a head, get to the heart of the matter, home in on; zero in on, pinpoint; draw a bead on, get a handle on; concentrate, concenter, get it together; channel, direct, canalize, channelize; converge

ADJS 11 **central,** centric, middle; centermost, middlemost, midmost; equidistant; centralized, concentrated; umbilical, omphalic; axial, pivotal, key; centroidal; centrosymmetric; geocentric, epicentral; halfway

12 **nuclear,** nucleate, core

13 **focal,** confocal; converging; centrolineal, centripetal; cynosural; pivotal; attention-getting, attention-grabbing

14 **concentric;** homocentric, centric; coaxial, coaxal

ADVS 15 **centrally,** in the center, in the middle of, at the heart of

209 ENVIRONMENT

<conditions and influences>

NOUNS 1 **environment, surroundings, environs,** surround, ambience, entourage, circle, circumjacencies, circumambiencies, circumstances, environing circumstances; precincts, ambit, purlieus, milieu; neighborhood, vicinity, vicinage, area; suburbs, burbs, bedroom community, gated community; outskirts, outposts, borderlands; borders, boundaries, limits, periphery, perimeter, compass, circuit; context, situation; habitat; total environment, configuration, gestalt; 55+ community, active adult community

2 **setting, background,** backdrop, ground, surround, field, scene, arena, theater, locale, confines; back, rear, hinterland, distance; stage, stage setting, stage set, *mise-en-scène* <Fr>

3 <surrounding influence or condition> **milieu,** ambience, atmosphere, climate, air, aura, spirit, feeling, feel, quality, color, local color, sense, sense of place, note, tone, overtone, undertone, vibrations, vibes

4 <natural or suitable environment> **element,** medium; the environment

5 **surrounding,** encompassment, environment, circumambience, circumambiency, circumjacence, circumjacency; containment, enclosure; encirclement, cincture, encincture, circumcincture, circling, girdling, girding; envelopment, enfoldment, encompassing, compassing, embracement; circumposition; circumflexion; inclusion, involvement

VERBS 6 **surround,** environ, compass, encompass, enclose, close; go round, go around, compass about, outlie; envelop, enfold, lap, wrap, enwrap, embrace, enclasp, embosom, embay, involve, invest

7 **encircle,** circle, ensphere, belt, belt in, zone, cincture, encincture; girdle, gird, begird, engird; ring, band; loop; wreathe, twine around

ADJS 8 **environing,** surrounding, encompassing, enclosing; enveloping, wrapping, enwrapping, enfolding, embracing; encircling, circling; bordering, peripheral, perimetric; circumjacent, circumferential, circumambient, ambient; circumfluent, circumfluous; circumflex; roundabout, suburban, neighboring, neighbhorhood

9 **environmental,** environal; ecological; green

10 **surrounded,** environed, compassed, encompassed, enclosed, on all sides, hemmed-in; enveloped, wrapped, enfolded, lapped, wreathed

11 **encircled,** circled, ringed, cinctured, encinctured, belted, girdled, girt, begirt, zoned

ADVS 12 **around,** round, about, round about, in the neighborhood, in the vicinity; close, close about

13 **all round,** all about, on every side, on all sides, on all hands, right and left

COMBINING FORMS 14 amph-, amphi-, circum-, peri-

210 CIRCUMSCRIPTION

<range or restriction>

NOUNS 1 **circumscription, limiting,** circumscribing, bounding, demarcation, delimitation, definition, determination, specification; limit-setting, inclusion-exclusion, circling-in, circling-out, encincture, boundary-marking; containment

2 **limitation, limiting,** restriction, restricting, confinement, prescription, proscription, restraint, discipline, moderation, continence; qualification,

hedging; bounds, boundary, cap, limit; time limit, time constraint; quota; small space; proviso, condition; fish bowl; speed limit; visiting hours

3 **patent, copyright,** certificate of invention; **trademark, logo,** logotype, registered trademark, trade name, service mark; proprietary information

VERBS 4 **circumscribe,** bound; mark off, mark out, stake out, lay off, rope off; demarcate, delimit, delimitate, draw boundaries, mark boundaries, set boundaries, lay out boundaries, circle in, circle out, hedge in, set the limit, mark the periphery; define, determine, fix, specify; surround; enclose

5 **limit, restrict,** restrain, bound, confine, cap, ground; straiten, narrow, tighten; specialize; stint, scant; condition, qualify, hedge, hedge about; constrain; draw the line, set an end point, set a stopping place; set a quota; discipline, moderate, contain; restrain oneself, pull one's punches; patent, copyright, register

ADJS 6 **circumscribed,** circumscript; ringed, circled, hedged about; demarcated, delimited, defined, definite, determined, determinate, specific, stated, set, fixed; surrounded, encircled

7 **limited, restricted,** bound, bounded, finite; confined, prescribed, proscribed, cramped, strait, straitened, narrow; conditioned, qualified, hedged, capped; disciplined, moderated; deprived, in straitened circumstances, pinched, inhibiting, on short commons, on short rations, strapped; patented, registered, protected, copyrighted, proprietary

8 **restricted,** out of bounds, off-limits

9 **limiting, restricting,** defining, determining, determinative, confining; limitative, limitary, restrictive, definitive, exclusive, non-compete; frozen, rationed

10 **terminal,** limital; limitable, terminable

211 BOUNDS

<limiting line or area>

NOUNS 1 **bounds, limits,** boundaries, limitations, confines, pale, marches, bourns, verges, edges, outlines, outer markings, skirts, outskirts, fringes, metes, metes and bounds; periphery, perimeter; coordinates, parameters; compass, circumference, circumscription; statute of limitations

2 **outline, contour,** delineation, lines, lineaments, shapes, figure, figuration, configuration, gestalt; features, main features; profile, silhouette; relief; skeleton, framework, frame, armature

3 **boundary, bound, limit,** limitation, extremity; barrier, block, claustrum; delimitation, hedge, break point, breakoff point, cutoff, cutoff point, terminus; time limit, time frame, term, deadline, target date, terminal date, time allotment; finish, end, tail end; start, starting line, starting point, mark; limiting factor, determinant, limit condition, boundary condition; bracket, brackets, bookends; threshold, limen; upper limit, ceiling, apogee, high-water mark; price cap; lower limit, floor, low-water mark, nadir; confine, march, bourn, mete, compass, circumscription; boundary line, line, borderline, frontier, division line, interface, break, line of demarcation, line of circumvallation; county line

4 **border,** limbus, bordure <heraldry>, edge, limb, verge, brink, brow, brim, rim, margin, marge, skirt, fringe, hem, list, selvage, selvedge, side; forefront, cutting edge, front line, new guard, vanguard; sideline; shore, bank, coast; lip, labium, labrum, labellum; flange; ledge; frame, enframement, mat; featheredge; ragged edge

5 **frontier,** border, borderland, border ground, marchland, march, marches; outskirts, outpost, backwoods; frontier post, cow town; iron curtain, bamboo curtain, Berlin wall; Pillars of Hercules; three-mile limit, twelve-mile limit; last frontier

6 **curb,** kerb <Brit>, curbing; border stone, curbstone, kerbstone <Brit>, edgestone

7 **edging, bordering,** bordure <heraldry>, trimming, binding, skirting; fringe, fimbriation, fimbria; hem, selvage, list, welt; frill, frilling; beading, flounce, furbelow, galloon, motif, ruffle, valance

VERBS 8 **bound,** circumscribe, surround, limit, enclose, divide, separate

9 **outline,** contour; delineate; silhouette, profile, limn

10 **border,** edge, bound, rim, skirt, hem, hem in, ringe, befringe, lap, list, margin, marge, marginate, march, verge, line, side; adjoin; frame, enframe, set off; trim, bind; purl; purfle

ADJS 11 **bordering,** fringing, rimming, skirting; bounding, boundary, limiting, limit, determining, determinant, determinative; threshold, liminal, limbic; extreme, terminal; marginal, borderline, frontier; coastal, littoral, sea-bordering

12 **bordered,** edged; margined, marged, marginate, marginated; fringed, befringed, trimmed, skirted, fimbriate, fimbriated

13 lipped, labial, labiate

14 outlining, **delineated**, delineatory; peripheral, perimetric, perimetrical, circumferential; outlined, **in outline**

ADVS 15 on the verge, on the brink, on the borderline, on the point, **on the edge**, on the ragged edge, at the threshold, at the limit, at the bound; peripherally, marginally, at the periphery

16 **thus far,** so far, thus far and no farther

212 ENCLOSURE

<surrounding>

NOUNS 1 **enclosure; confinement,** containing, containment, circumscription, immurement, walling-in, hedging-in, hemming-in, boxing-in, fencing-in, circumvallation; imprisonment, incarceration, jailing, locking-up, lockdown; siege, besieging, beleaguerment, blockade, blockading, cordoning, quarantine, besetment; inclusion; envelopment

2 **packaging, packing,** package; boxing, crating, encasement; canning, tinning <Brit>; bottling; wrapping, enwrapment, bundling; shrink-wrapping

3 <enclosed place> **enclosure,** close, confine, precinct, enclave, pale, paling, list, cincture; jail, detention center; cloister; pen, coop, corral, fold; yard, park, court, courtyard, curtilage, toft; square, quadrangle, quad; field, delimited field, arena, theater, ground; reserve, sanctuary; container

4 **fence,** fencing, picket fence, wall, boundary, barrier; stone wall; paling, palisade; rail, railing; balustrade, balustrading; moat; arcade

VERBS 5 **enclose,** close in, bound, include, contain; compass, encompass; surround, encircle; shut in, pen in, coop in; fence in, wall in, wall up, rail in, rail off, screen off, curtain off; hem in, hedge in, box in, pocket; shut up, coop up, mew up; pen, coop, corral, cage, impound, mew; imprison, incarcerate, jail, lock up, lock down, lock away; besiege, beset, beleaguer, leaguer, cordon, cordon off, quarantine, blockade; yard, yard up; house in; chamber; stable, kennel, shrine, enshrine; wrap

6 **confine,** immure; quarantine; cramp, straiten, encase; cloister, closet, cabin, crib; bury, entomb, coffin, casket; bottle up, box up, box in

7 **fence, wall,** fence in, fence up; pale, rail, bar; pen up; hem, hem in, hedge, hedge in, hedge out; picket, palisade; bulkhead in

8 parenthesize, bracket, quote, air-quote, precede and follow, bookend

9 **package,** pack, parcel; box, box up, case, encase, crate, carton; can, tin <Brit>; bottle, jar, pot; barrel, cask, tank; sack, bag; basket, hamper; capsule, encyst; contain; wrap, enwrap, bundle; shrink-wrap; bandage

ADJS 10 **enclosed,** closed-in; confined, bound, immured, cloistered; imprisoned, incarcerated, jailed; caged, cramped, restrained, corralled; besieged, beleaguered, leaguered, beset, cordoned, cordoned off, quarantined, blockaded; shut-in, pent-up, penned, cooped, cooped up, mewed, walled-in, hedged-in, hemmed-in, boxed-in, fenced-in, fenced, walled, paled, railed, barred; hemmed, hedged

11 enclosing, confining, **cloistered,** cloisterlike, claustral, parietal, surrounding; limiting

12 **packed,** packaged, boxed, crated, canned, tinned <Brit>, parceled, cased, encased; bottled; capsuled, encapsuled; wrapped, enwrapped, bundled; shrink-wrapped; prepacked; vacuum-packed; bandaged, sheathed

213 INTERPOSITION

<putting or lying between>

NOUNS 1 **interposition, interposing,** interposal, interlocation, intermediacy, interjacence; intervention, intervenience, intercurrence, slipping-in, sandwiching; leafing-in, interleaving, interfoliation, tipping-in; intrusion; way station

2 **interjection** <see list>**,** interpolation, introduction, throwing-in, tossing-in, injection, insinuation; intercalation, interlineation; insertion; interlocution, remark, parenthetical remark, side remark, incidental remark, casual remark, *obiter dictum* <L>, aside, parenthesis; episode; infix, insert; comment

3 **interspersion,** interfusion, interlardment, interpenetration

4 **intermediary,** intermedium, mediary, medium; link, connecting link, tie, connection, go-between, liaison; middleman, middleperson, broker, agent, wholesaler, jobber, distributor; moderator, mediator

5 **partition,** dividing wall, division, separation; wall, barrier; median strip; panel; paries, parietes; brattice; bulkhead; diaphragm, midriff, midsection; septum, interseptum, septulum, dissepiment; border, dividing line, property line, party wall; buffer, bumper, mat, fender, cushion, pad, shock pad, collision mat; buffer state

VERBS 6 **interpose, interject,** interpolate, intercalate, interjaculate; mediate, go between, liaise; intervene; put between, sandwich; insert in, stick in, introduce in, insinuate in, sandwich in, slip in, inject in, implant in; leaf in, interleaf, tip in, interfoliate; foist in, fudge in, work in, drag in, lug in, drag in by the heels, worm in, squeeze in, smuggle in, throw in, run in, thrust in, edge in, wedge in; intrude

7 **intersperse,** interfuse, interlard, interpenetrate; intersow, intersprinkle

8 **partition,** set apart, separate, divide; wall off, fence off, screen off, curtain off

ADJS 9 interjectional, interpolative, intercalary; parenthetical, episodic

10 **intervening,** intervenient, interjacent, intercurrent; intermediate, intermediary, medial, mean, medium, mesne, median, middle

11 partitioned, **walled**; mural; septal, parietal

PREPS 12 **between,** betwixt, twixt, betwixt and between; among, amongst, 'mongst; amid, amidst, mid, midst; in the midst of, in the thick of

COMBINING FORMS 13 medi-, medio-, mes-, meso-; inter-, intra-

14 **interjection**

adios
ah
aha
ahem
ahoy
alack
alas
all hail
alleluia
aloha
amen
and how
attaboy
avast
aw
aw-shucks
aye
bah
banzai
bleep
boo
boy
bravo
by jingo
cheerio
cheers
chop-chop
ciao
crikey
criminy
cripes
dear
dear me
ditto
d'oh
duh
eek
egad, egads
eh
er
eureka
fiddlesticks
fie
fore
forsooth
gadzooks
gee
gee whillikers
gee whiz
geez
gesundheit
giddy-up
glory
golly
golly gee
golly whillikers
good golly
good gracious
goody
gosh
gracious
gracious me
ha
hallelujah
hark
heads up
hear ye, hear ye
heave-ho
heavens
heavens to Betsy
heigh-ho
hem
hep
hey
hi-hip
ho
ho-hum
holy cow
holy mackerel
holy moly
holy Toledo
hooray
hosanna
hotdog
howdy
hoy
huh
hup
hurrah
huzzah
jeepers
jeepers creepers
jeez
lackaday
lo
lo and behold
Lordy
mama
marry
mazel tov
my gracious
my my
my stars
my word
nah
nay
nerts
nope
nuts
oh
oh my god (OMG), ohmigosh
oh boy
oh dear
oh my
okay
okey-doke
okey-dokey
ole
oops
oopsy-daisy
ouch
ow
oy
oyez
peekaboo
phew
phooey
pish
pooh
presto
prithee
prosit
pshaw, psha
rah
rah-rah
rats
righto
roger
rot
salud
scram
shaddup
shalom
sheesh
shucks
shush
skoal
tallyho
ten-four
there, there
timber
touch, touché
tsk
tsk tsk
tush
tut-tut
ugh
uh-huh
uh-oh
uh-uh
um
viva
voila
wahoo
welcome
well
what
whatever
whee
whew
whoa
whoop-de-do
whoopee
whoops
why
wilco
woe is me
wow
wowie
wowie-zowie
yahoo
yea
yeah
yech
yeesh
yep
yikes
yippee
yo
yo mama
yoicks
yoo-hoo
yuck
yum, yum-yum
yup
zap
zooks
zounds
zowie, zowee
zut

214 INTRUSION

<infringing on>

NOUNS 1 **intrusion,** obtrusion, **interloping;** interposition, interposal, imposition, insinuation, interference, intervention, interventionism, interruption, injection, interjection; encroachment, entrenchment, trespass, trespassing, unlawful entry; impingement, infringement, invasion, incursion, inroad, influx, irruption, infiltration; entrance

2 **meddling,** intermeddling; butting-in, kibitzing, sticking one's nose in; meddlesomeness, intrusiveness, forwardness, obtrusiveness; officiousness, impertinence, presumption, presumptuousness; inquisitiveness

3 **intruder,** interloper, trespasser; crasher, gate-crasher, unwelcome guest, uninvited guest; invader, encroacher, infiltrator; wedding crasher, photo bomber

4 **meddler,** intermeddler; busybody, pry, Paul Pry, prier, Nosey Parker, snoop, snooper, *yenta* <Yiddish>, kibitzer, backseat driver

VERBS 5 **intrude,** obtrude, **interlope;** come between, interpose, insert oneself, intervene, interfere, insinuate, impose; encroach, infringe, impinge, trespass, trespass on, trespass upon, trench, entrench, invade, infiltrate; break in upon, break in, burst in, charge in, crash in, smash in, storm in; barge in, irrupt, cut in, thrust in, push in, press in, rush in, throng in, crowd in, squeeze in, elbow in, muscle in; butt in, horn in, chisel in; appoint oneself; crash, crash the gates; get in, get in on, creep in, steal in, sneak in, slink in, slip in; foist in, worm in, work in, edge in, shove in one's oar; foist oneself upon, thrust oneself upon; put on, put upon, impose on, impose upon, put one's two cents in

6 **interrupt,** put in, cut in, break in; jump in, chime in, chip in, put in one's two-cents worth, butt in

7 **meddle,** intermeddle, busybody, not mind one's business; meddle with, tamper with, mix oneself up with, inject oneself into, monkey with, fool with, mess with, fool around with, mess around with, jack with; pry, Paul-Pry, snoop, nose, stick one's nose in, poke one's nose in, stick one's long nose into; have a finger in, have a finger in the pie; kibitz

ADJS 8 **intrusive,** obtrusive, **interfering,** intervenient, invasive, interruptive

9 **meddlesome,** meddling; officious, overofficious, self-appointed, impertinent, presumptuous; busybody, busy; pushing, pushy, forward; prying, nosy, nosey, snoopy; inquisitive

PHRS 10 <nonformal> **none of your business;** what's it to you?, mind your own business, keep your nose out of this, butt out, go soak your head, go sit on a tack, go roll your hoop, go peddle your fish, go fly a kite, go chase yourself, go jump in the lake; too many cooks spoil the broth

215 CONTRAPOSITION

<placed over or against>

NOUNS 1 contraposition, anteposition, posing against, posing over against; **opposition,** opposing, opposure; antithesis, contrast, ironic juxtaposition, contrastive juxtaposition; confrontment, confrontation; polarity, polar opposition, polarization; contrariety; contention; hostility

2 **opposites,** antipodes, polar opposites, contraries; poles, opposite poles, antipoles, counterpoles, North Pole, South Pole; antipodal points, antipoints; contrapositives; night and day, black and white; antonyms

3 opposite side, other side, the other side of the picture, the other side of the coin, other face; reverse, inverse, obverse, converse; heads, tails <coin>; flip side, B-side

VERBS 4 contrapose, **oppose,** contrast, match, set over against, pose against, pose over against, put in opposition, set against one another, pit against one another; confront, face, front, stand opposite, lie opposite, stand opposed, vis-à-vis; be at loggerheads, be eyeball to eyeball, bump heads, meet head-on; counteract; contend; subtend; polarize; contraposit

ADJS 5 contrapositive, **opposite,** opposing, facing, confronting, confrontational, confrontive, eyeball-to-eyeball, one-on-one, face-to-face; opposed, on opposite sides, adversarial, at loggerheads, at daggers drawn, antithetic, antithetical; reverse, inverse, obverse, converse; antipodal; polar, polarized one-on-one, up against; love-hate

ADVS 6 **opposite**, poles apart, at opposite extremes; contrary, contrariwise, counter; just opposite, face-to-face, vis-à-vis, nose-to-nose, one-on-one, eyeball-to-eyeball, back-to-back

PREPS 7 **opposite to,** in opposition to, against, over against; versus, v, vs; facing, across, fronting, confronting, in front of; toward

COMBINING FORMS 8 ant-, anti-, anth-, cat-, cata-, cath-, kat-, kata-, co-, contra-, counter-, enantio-, ob-

216 FRONT

<forward part>

NOUNS 1 **front, fore,** forepart, forequarter, foreside, forefront, forehand; priority, anteriority; front office; frontier; foreland; foreground; proscenium; frontage; front page; frontispiece; preface, front matter, foreword; prefix; front view, full frontal, front elevation, front seat, front yard; head, heading; face, façade, frontal; fascia; false front, window dressing, display, persona; front man; bold front, brave front, brave face; facet; obverse <coin, medal>, head <coin>; lap; front burner

2 **vanguard,** van, point, point man; spearhead, advance guard, forefront, cutting edge, avant-garde, outguard; scout; pioneer, trailblazer; precursor; frontrunner, leader, first in line; front, battlefront, line, front line, forward line, battle line, line of departure, new guard; front rank, first line, first line of battle; outpost, farthest outpost; bridgehead, beachhead, airhead, railhead; advanced base

3 **prow, bow, stem,** rostrum, figurehead, nose, beak; bowsprit, jib boom; forecastle, forepeak; foredeck; foremast

4 **face,** facies, visage; physiognomy, phiz, dial; countenance, features, lineaments, favor; mug, mush, pan, kisser, map, puss

5 **forehead, brow,** lofty brow

6 **chin,** point of the chin, button

VERBS 7 be in front, stand in front, **lead, head,** head up; get ahead of, steal a march on, take the lead, come to the front, come to the fore, forge ahead; be the frontrunner, lead the pack, lead the field, be first; pioneer; front, front for, represent, speak for; spearhead; push the envelope; trailblaze

8 **confront, front**, affront, face, meet, encounter, breast, stem, brave, meet squarely, square up to, come to grips with, head into, wade into, meet face to face, meet eyeball to eyeball, meet one-on-one, come face to face with, look in the eye, stare in the face, stand up to, stand fast, hold one's ground, hang tough, tough it out, gut it out; call someone's bluff, call someone to account, bring someone to account; confront with, face with, bring face to face with, tell one to one's face, throw in one's face, present to, put before, bring before, set before, place before, lay before, lay it on the line; bring up, bring forward; put it to, put it up to; challenge, dare, defy, fly in the teeth of, throw down the gauntlet, ask for trouble, start something, do something about it

9 **front on,** face upon, face, look toward, look out upon, look over, overlook

ADJS 10 **front, frontal,** anterior; full-face, full-frontal, physiognomic; fore, forward, forehand; foremost, headmost; first, earliest, pioneering, trailblazing, advanced, front-running; leading, up-front, chief, head, prime, primary; confronting, confrontational, head-on, one-on-one, eyeball-to-eyeball; ahead, in front, one-up, one jump ahead, move ahead

11 **fronting, facing,** looking on, looking out on, opposite

ADVS 12 **before, ahead,** out ahead, up ahead, in front, in the front, in the lead, in the van, in advance, in the forefront, in the foreground; to the fore, to the front; foremost, headmost, first; before one's face, before one's eyes, under one's nose

13 **frontward,** frontwards, forward, forwards, vanward, headward, headwards, onward, onwards; facing

217 REAR

<part away from front>

NOUNS 1 **rear, rear end,** hind end, hind part, hinder part, afterpart, rearward, posterior, behind, breech, stern, tail, tail end; afterpiece, tailpiece, heelpiece, heel; back, backside, reverse <coin, medal>, tail <coin>; back door, postern, postern door; back seat, rumble seat; hindhead, occiput; wake, train; back burner

2 rear guard, **rear,** rear area, backyard

3 **back,** dorsum, ridge; dorsal region, lumbar region, backbone; hindquarter; loin

4 **buttocks, rump,** butt cheek, bottom, posterior, derrière; croup, crupper; podex; haunches; gluteal region; nates

5 <nonformal> **ass*,** arse, bum, behind, backside, buns, **butt**, can, cheeks, hind end, nether cheeks, stern, tail, rusty-dusty, fanny, prat, keister, popo, rear, rear end, tuchis, tushy, tush

6 **tail,** cauda, caudation, caudal appendage; tailpiece, scut <hare, rabbit, or deer>, brush <fox>, fantail <fowls>; rattail, rat's-tail; dock, stub; caudal fin; queue, cue, pigtail

7 **stern,** heel; poop, transom, counter, fantail; sternpost, rudderpost; after mast

VERBS 8 <be behind> **bring up the rear,** come last, **follow,** come after; trail, trail behind, lag behind, draggle, straggle; fall behind, fall back, fall astern; back up, back, go back, go backwards, regress, retrogress, get behind; revert

ADJS 9 **rear,** rearward, **back,** backward, retrograde, posterior, postern, tail; after, aft; hind, hinder; hindmost, hindermost, hindhand, posteriormost, aftermost, aftmost, rearmost; latter

10 <anatomy> posterial, dorsal, retral, tergal, lumbar, gluteal, sciatic, occipital

11 **tail,** caudal, caudate, caudated, tailed; taillike, caudiform

12 backswept, swept-back

ADVS **13** **behind,** in the rear, in back of; in the background; behind the scenes; behind one's back; back to back; tandem

14 **after;** aft, abaft, baft, astern; aback

15 **rearward,** rearwards, to the rear, hindward, hindwards, backward, backwards, posteriorly, retrad, tailward, tailwards

218 SIDE

<part away from center>

NOUNS **1** **side,** flank, hand; laterality, sidedness, handedness; unilaterality, unilateralism, bilaterality, bilateralism, multilaterality, many-sidedness; border; parallelism; bank, shore, coast; siding, planking; beam; broadside; quarter; hip, haunch; cheek, jowl, chop; temple; profile, side-view, half-face view; side entrance, side door; sideburns, burnsides

2 **lee side, lee,** leeward; lee shore; lee tide; lee wheel, lee helm, lee anchor, lee sheet, lee tack

3 **windward side, windward,** windwards, weather side, weather, weatherboard; weather wheel, weather helm, weather anchor, weather sheet, weather tack, weather rail, weather bow, weather deck; weather roll; windward tide, weather-going tide, windward ebb, windward flood

VERBS **4** **side, flank;** edge, skirt, border; stand side by side

5 **go sideways,** sidle, lateral, lateralize, edge, veer, angle, slant, skew, sidestep; go crabwise; sideslip, **skid;** make leeway

ADJS **6** **side,** lateral; flanking, skirting, facing, oblique; beside, to the side, off to one side; alongside, parallel; next-beside; sidelong, sideling, sidewise, sideway, sideways, sideward, sidewards, glancing; leeward, lee; windward, weather; side-by-side; peripheral

7 **sided, flanked,** handed; lateral; one-sided, unilateral, unilateralist, two-sided, bilateral, bilateralist; dihedral, bifacial; three-sided, trilateral, trihedral, triquetrous; four-sided, quadrilateral, tetrahedral; many-sided, multilateral, multifaceted, polyhedral; left-hand, sinistral, right-hand, dextral

ADVS **8** **laterally,** laterad; **sideways,** sideway, sidewise, sidewards, sideward, sideling, sidling, sidelong, aside, crabwise; side-to-side; edgeways, edgeway, edgewise; widthwise, widthways, thwartwise; askance, askant, asquint, glancingly; broadside, broadside on, on the beam; on its side, on its beam ends; on the other hand; right and left

9 **leeward,** to leeward, alee, downwind; **windward,** to windward, weatherward, aweather, upwind

10 **aside,** on one side, to one side, to the side, sidelong, on the side, on the one hand, on one hand, on the other hand; alongside, in parallel, side-by-side; nearby, in juxtaposition; away

PREPS **11** **beside,** alongside, abreast, abeam, by, on the flank of, along by, by the side of, along the side of

PHRS **12** **side by side,** cheek to cheek, cheek by cheek, cheek by jowl, shoulder to shoulder, yardarm to yardarm

219 RIGHT SIDE

<part toward the right>

NOUNS **1** **right side, right,** off side <horse or vehicle>, starboard; Epistle side, decanal side; recto <books>; right field; starboard tack; right wing; right-winger, conservative, reactionary

2 **rightness,** dextrality; dexterity, **right-handedness;** dextroversion, dextrocularity, dextroduction; dextrorotation, dextrogyration

3 right-hander; righty

ADJS **4** **right, right-hand,** dextral, dexter; off, starboard; rightmost; dextrorse; dextropedal; dextrocardial; dextrocerebral; dextrocular; clockwise, dextrorotary, dextrogyrate, dextrogyratory; right-wing, right-wingish, right-of-center, conservative, reactionary, dry

5 **right-handed,** dextromanual, dexterous

6 **ambidextrous,** ambidextral, ambidexter; dextrosinistral, sinistrodextral

ADVS **7** **rightward,** rightwards, rightwardly, right, to the right, dextrally, dextrad; on the right, dexter; starboard, astarboard

220 LEFT SIDE

<part toward the left>

NOUNS **1** **left side, left, left hand,** left-hand side, wrong side; near side, nigh side <horse or vehicle>, portside, port, larboard; Gospel side, cantorial side, verso <books>; left field; port tack; left wing, left-winger, radical, liberal, progressive

2 **leftness,** sinistrality, **left-handedness;** sinistration; levoversion, levoduction; levorotation, sinistrogyration

3 **left-hander, southpaw,** lefty, portsider

ADJS **4** **left, left-hand,** sinister, sinistral; near, nigh; larboard, port; sinistrorse; sinistrocerebral; sinistrocular; counterclockwise, levorotatory, sinistrogyrate; left-wing, left-wingish, left-of-center, radical, liberal, progressive, wet

5 **left-handed,** sinistromanual, sinistral, lefty, southpaw

ADVS 6 **leftward,** leftwards, leftwardly, left, to the left, sinistrally, sinister, sinistrad; on the left; larboard, port, aport

221 PRESENCE

<state of being present>

NOUNS 1 **presence,** being here, being there, hereness, thereness, physical presence, actual presence, spiritual presence, spirit guide, spirit animal; immanence, indwellingness, inherence; whereness, immediacy; ubiety; availability, accessibility; nearness; occurrence, existence; manifestness, materialness; presenteeism; present moment

2 **omnipresence,** all-presence, **ubiquity;** continuum, plenum; infinity; pluripresence

3 **permeation,** pervasion, penetration; suffusion, transfusion, perfusion, diffusion, imbuement; absorption; overrunning, overspreading, ripple effect, overswarming, whelming, overwhelming; saturation

4 **attendance,** frequenting, frequence; participation; number present; turnout, box office, draw

5 **attender,** visitor, churchgoer, moviegoer; patron; fan, buff, aficionado, supporter; frequenter, habitué, haunter; spectator; theatergoer; audience; regular customer, regular; zelig

VERBS 6 **be present,** be located, be situated, be there, be found, be met with; occur, exist; lie, stand, remain; fall in the way of; dwell in, indwell, inhere

7 **pervade,** permeate, penetrate; suffuse, inform, transfuse, perfuse, diffuse, leaven, imbue; fill, extend throughout, leave no void, occupy; overrun, overswarm, overspread, bespread, run through, meet one at every turn, whelm, overwhelm; creep with, crawl with, swarm with, be lousy with, teem with; honeycomb

8 **attend,** be at, be present at, find oneself at, go to, come to; appear, turn up, set foot in, show up, show one's face, make an appearance, put in an appearance, give the pleasure of one's company, make a personal appearance; materialize; visit, take in, do, catch; sit in, sit at; be on hand, be on deck; watch, see; witness, look on; participate, take part

9 **revisit,** return to, go back to, come again

10 **frequent, haunt,** resort to, hang, hang around, hang about, hang out

11 **present oneself,** report; report for duty

ADJS 12 **present,** attendant; on hand, on deck, on board, in attendance; immediate, immanent, indwelling, inherent, available, accessible, at hand, in view, within reach, within sight, in place; intrinsic

13 **omnipresent,** all-present, **ubiquitous,** everywhere; continuous, uninterrupted, infinite

14 **pervasive,** pervading, suffusive, perfusive, diffusive, suffusing

15 **permeated,** saturated, shot through, filled with, perfused, suffused, imbued; honeycombed; crawling, creeping, swarming, teeming, lousy with

ADVS 16 **here, there**

17 **in person,** personally, bodily, **in the flesh,** in one's own person

PREPS 18 **in the presence of,** in the face of, under the eyes, under the nose of, before

PHRS 19 all present and accounted for; standing room only (SRO)

222 ABSENCE

<state of not being present>

NOUNS 1 **absence,** nonpresence, awayness; nowhereness, **nonexistence**; want, lack, total lack, blank, deprivation; nonoccurrence, neverness; subtraction

2 **vacancy,** vacuity, voidness, **emptiness,** blankness, hollowness, inanition; bareness, barrenness, desolateness, bleakness, desertedness; nonoccupancy, nonoccupation, noninhabitance, nonresidence; job vacancy, opening, open place, open post, vacant post

3 **void, vacuum,** blank, emptiness, empty space, inanity, vacuity; nothingness; *tabula rasa* <L>, clean slate, blank slate; nothing

4 **absence,** nonattendance, absenting, leaving, taking leave, departure; running away, fleeing, decamping, bolting, skedaddling, absquatulating, absquatulation, abscondence, scarpering, desertion, defection; disappearance, escape; absentation, nonappearance, default, unauthorized absence, unexcused absence; truancy, hooky, French leave, cut; absence without leave (AWOL); absenteeism, truantism; leave, leave of absence, furlough; **vacation**, holiday, paid vacation, paid holiday, paid time off, time off, day off, comp time, compensation time, mental health day; authorized absence, excused absence, sick leave; sabbatical

5 **absentee, truant,** no-show, missing person

6 **nobody, no one,** no man, no woman, not one, not a single one, not a single person, not a soul, not a blessed soul, not a living soul, never a one, ne'er

a one, nary one, nobody on earth, nobody under the sun, nobody present; nonperson, unperson; nonentity

VERBS 7 **be absent,** stay away, keep away, keep out of the way, not come, not show up, not turn up, turn up missing, stay away in droves, fail to appear, default, sit out, include oneself out; phone it in

8 **absent oneself,** take leave, take a leave of absence, go on leave, go on furlough; **vacation,** go on vacation, go on holiday, take time off, take off from work; slip off, slip away, duck out, sneak out, slip out, make oneself scarce, leave the scene, bow out, exit, vacate, depart, disappear, escape; defect, desert

9 **play truant,** go AWOL, take French leave; play hooky, cut, skip, cut classes; jump ship

10 <nonformal> **split,** bugger off <Brit>, fuck off*, f off, make tracks, pull up stakes, push along, scarper <Brit>, push off, skedaddle, absquatulate, haul ass, bag ass, beat it, blow, boogie, bug out, cut, cut out, cut and run, peel out, bunk off, piss off*, scram, shove off, vamoose

ADJS 11 **absent,** not present, nonattendant, away, gone, departed, disappeared, vanished, absconded, out of sight; missing, among the missing, wanting, lacking, not found, nowhere to be found, omitted, taken away, subtracted, deleted; no longer present, no longer with us, no longer among us; long-lost; nonexistent; conspicuous by its absence

12 **nonresident,** not in residence, from home, **away from home,** on leave, on vacation, on holiday, on sabbatical leave; on tour, on the road; abroad, overseas; from away

13 **truant,** absent without leave **(AWOL)**

14 **vacant,** empty, hollow, inane, bare, vacuous, void, without content, with nothing inside, devoid, null, null and void; blank, clear, white, bleached; featureless, unrelieved, characterless, bland, insipid; barren

15 **available,** open, free, **unoccupied,** unfilled, uninhabited, unpopulated, unpeopled, untaken, untenanted, tenantless, untended, unmanned, unstaffed; deserted, abandoned, forsaken, godforsaken; untouristed

ADVS 16 **absently;** vacantly, emptily, hollowly, vacuously, blankly

17 **nowhere,** in no place, neither here nor there; nowhither

18 **away**, elsewhere, somewhere else, not here; elsewhither

PREPS 19 absent, lacking, sans; void of, empty of, free of, **without**

223 NEARNESS

<state of being close>

NOUNS 1 **nearness, closeness,** nighness, proximity, propinquity, intimacy, immediacy; approximation, approach, convergence; a rough idea; vicinity, vicinage, neighborhood, environs, surroundings, surround, setting, grounds, purlieus, confines, precinct; foreground, immediate foreground; convenience, handiness, accessibility

2 **short distance,** short way, little ways, step, short step, span, brief span, short piece, a little, intimate distance; shortcut; short range; close quarters, close range; middle distance; stone's throw, wurf, spitting distance, bowshot, gunshot, pistol shot; earshot, earreach, a whoop, a whoop and a holler, two whoops and a holler, ace, bit, hair, hairbreadth, hairsbreadth, finger's breadth, finger's width, an inch; inch, millimeter, centimeter; near miss

3 **juxtaposition,** apposition, adjacency; contiguity, contiguousness, conterminousness, coterminousness; butting, abuttal, abutment; adjunction, junction, connection, union; conjunction, conjugation, collocation; appulse, syzygy; perigee, perihelion

4 **meeting,** meeting up, joining, joining up, encounter; juncture; confrontation; rencontre; near-miss, collision course, near thing, narrow squeak, narrow brush, close call

5 **contact, touch,** touching, taction, tangency, contingence; gentle contact, tentative contact, caress, brush, glance, nudge, kiss, rub, graze; impingement, impingence; osculation

6 **neighbor,** neighborer, next-door neighbor, immediate neighbor; borderer; abutter, adjoiner; bystander, onlooker, looker-on; tangent; buffer state; ringside seat

VERBS 7 **near,** come near, nigh, draw near, draw nigh, approach, come within shouting distance; converge, shake hands; come within an inch

8 **be near**, be around, be in the vicinity, be in the neighborhood, approximate, approach, get warm, come near, have something at hand, have something at one's fingertips; give a rough idea, get a rough idea

9 **adjoin,** join, conjoin, connect, butt, abut, abut on, abut upon, be contiguous, be in contact; neighbor, border, border on, border upon, verge on, verge upon; lie by, stand by

10 **contact,** come in contact, touch, feel, impinge, bump up against, hit; osculate; graze, caress, kiss, nudge, rub, brush, glance, scrape, sideswipe, skim, skirt, shave; grope, feel up, cop a feel; have a near miss, brush by, graze by, squeak by

11 **meet, encounter**; come across, run across, meet up, fall across, cross the path of; come upon, run upon, fall upon, light upon, alight upon; come among, fall among; meet with, meet up with, come face to face with, confront, meet head-on, meet eyeball to eyeball; run into, bump into, run smack into, join up with, come up against, run up against, run, fall foul of; burst upon, bounce upon; be on a collision course; reconnect

12 **stay near,** keep close to; stand by, lie by; go with, march with, follow close upon, breathe down one's neck, stay on one's heels, stay on one's tail, tailgate; hang about, hang around, hang upon the skirts of, hover over; cling to, clasp, hug, huddle; hug the shore, hug the land, keep hold of the land, stay inshore

13 **juxtapose,** appose, join, adjoin, abut, butt against, neighbor; bring near, put with, place side by side, set side by side

ADJS **14** **near,** close, nigh, close-in, nearish, nighish, intimate, cheek-by-jowl, side-by-side, hand-in-hand, arm-in-arm, shoulder-to-shoulder, neck and neck; approaching, nearing, approximate, approximating, proximate, proximal, propinque; short-range; near the mark; warm, hot, burning

15 **nearby,** handy, convenient, neighboring, vicinal, propinquant, propinquous, ready at hand, easily reached, easily attained; accessible; one-stop; 24-hour

16 **adjacent, next,** immediate, contiguous, adjoining, abutting; neighboring, neighbor; in the neighborhood, in the vicinity; juxtaposed, juxtapositional, tangential; bordering, conterminous, coterminous, connecting; face-to-face; end-to-end, endways, endwise; joined

17 **in contact,** contacting, **touching,** meeting, contingent; impinging, impingent; tangent, tangential; osculatory; grazing, kissing, glancing, brushing, rubbing, nudging; interfacing, linking

18 **nearer,** nigher, **closer**

19 **nearest,** nighest, **closest,** nearmost, next, immediate

ADVS **20** **near, nigh,** close; hard, at close quarters; nearby, closeby, hard by, fast by, not far, not far off, in the vicinity, in the neighborhood of, at hand, at close range, near at hand, close at hand; thereabout, thereabouts, hereabout, hereabouts; nearabout, nearabouts, nigh about; about, around, close about, along toward; at no great distance, only a step; as near as no matter, as near as makes no difference; within reach, within range, within call, within hearing, within earshot, within earreach, within a whoop, within two whoops and a holler, within a stone's throw, a stone's throw away, in spitting distance, at one's elbow, at one's feet, at one's fingertips, under one's nose, at one's side, within one's grasp; just around the corner, just across the street, next-door, right next door, just next door

21 **in juxtaposition,** in conjunction, in apposition; beside

22 **nearly, near,** pretty near, close, closely; almost, all but, not quite, as good as, as near as makes no difference; well-nigh, just about; nigh, nigh hand

23 **approximately,** approximatively, practically, for practical purposes, for all practical purposes, at a first approximation, give or take a little, more or less; plus-minus; roughly, roundly, in round numbers; generally, generally speaking, roughly speaking, say; in the ballpark

PREPS **24** **near, nigh,** near to, close to, near upon, close upon, hard on, hard upon, bordering on, bordering upon, verging on, verging upon, on the confines of, at the threshold of, on the brink of, verge of, on the edge of, at next hand, at the point of, on the point of, on the skirts of; not far from; next door to, at one's door; nigh about, nigh on, nearabout

25 **against,** up against, on, upon, over against, opposite, nose to nose with, vis-à -vis, in contact with

26 **about, around,** just about; circa (c.), somewhere about, somewhere near, near upon, close upon, give or take, near enough to, upwards of, -ish, -something; in the neighborhood, in the vicinity of

224 INTERVAL

<space between>

NOUNS **1** **interval, gap,** space, intervening space, intermediate space, interspace, distance between, space between, interstice; clearance, margin, leeway, headroom, room; discontinuity, jump, leap, interruption; daylight; hiatus, caesura, lacuna, intermission; half space, single space, double space, em space, en space, hair space; time interval, interim

2 **crack, cleft,** cranny, chink, check, craze, chap, crevice, fissure, scissure, incision, notch, score, cut, gash, slit, split, rift, rent; hairline crack; opening, excavation, cavity, concavity, hole; gap, gape, abyss, abysm, gulf, chasm, void, canyon; breach, break, fracture, rupture; fault, flaw; slot, groove, furrow, moat, ditch, trench, dike, ha-ha; joint, seam; valley

VERBS **3** **interspace, space,** make a space, make room, set at intervals, dot, scatter, space out, separate, split off, part, dispart, set apart, keep apart

4 **cleave, crack,** check, incise, craze, cut, cut apart, gash, slit, split, rive, rent, rip open; open; gap, breach, break, fracture, rupture; slot, groove, furrow, ditch, trench

ADJS **5** intervallic, intervallary, interspatial, **interstitial**, discontinuous

6 **spaced,** interspaced, intervaled, spaced out, set at intervals, with intervals, with an interval, interspacial, interstitial; dotted, scattered, separated, parted, disparted, split-off

7 **cleft,** cut, cloven, cracked, sundered, rift, riven, rent, chinky, chapped, crazed; slit, **split;** gaping, gappy; hiatal, caesural, lacunar; fissured, fissural, fissile

225 HABITATION

<living in a place>

NOUNS **1** **habitation,** inhabiting, inhabitation, habitancy, inhabitancy, tenancy, occupancy, occupation, residence, residency, legal residence, residing, abiding, living, nesting, dwelling, commorancy <law>, lodging, staying, stopping, sojourning, staying over; squatting; cohabitation, living together, sharing quarters; day camp; living in sin; abode, **habitat**

2 **peopling,** peoplement, empeoplement, population, inhabiting; colonization, settlement, plantation

3 **housing,** domiciliation; lodgment, lodging, transient lodging, doss <Brit>, quartering, billeting, hospitality; living quarters; multifamily; housing development, subdivision, tract, public housing, housing project; housing problem, housing bill

4 **camping,** tenting, **encampment,** bivouacking; camp

5 **sojourn,** sojourning, sojournment, temporary stay; stay, stop; stopover, stopoff, stayover, layover

6 **habitability,** inhabitability, **livability**

VERBS **7** **inhabit, occupy,** tenant, move in, move into, take up one's abode, make one's home; rent, lease; reside, live, live in, dwell, lodge, stay, remain, abide, hang, hang out, stay in, domicile, domiciliate; room, bunk, crash, berth, doss down <Brit>; perch, roost, squat; nest; room together; cohabit, cohabitate, live together; live in sin

8 **sojourn,** stop, stay, **stop over,** stay over, lay over

9 **people,** empeople, populate, inhabit, denizen; colonize, settle, settle in, plant

10 **house,** domicile, domiciliate; provide with a roof, have as a guest, have as a lodger, shelter, harbor; lodge, quarter, put up, billet, room, bed, berth, bunk; stable

11 **camp,** encamp, tent; pitch, pitch camp, pitch one's tent, drive stakes; bivouac; go camping, camp out, sleep out, rough it

ADJS **12** **inhabited,** occupied, tenanted; peopled, empeopled, populated, colonized, settled; populous

13 **resident,** residentiary, in residence; residing, living, dwelling, commorant, lodging, staying, remaining, abiding, living in; cohabiting, live-in

14 **housed,** domiciled, domiciliated, lodged, quartered, billeted; stabled

15 **habitable,** inhabitable, occupiable, lodgeable, tenantable, livable, fit to live in, fit for occupation; homelike; multifamily

ADVS **16** **at home,** in the bosom of one's family, *chez soi* <Fr>; in one's element; back home, down home

226 NATIVENESS

<born in a place>

NOUNS **1** **nativeness,** nativity, native-bornness, indigenousness, indigenity, aboriginality, autochthonousness, **nationality;** nativism

2 **citizenship,** native-born citizenship, citizenship by birth, citizenhood, subjecthood; civism; dual citizenship

3 **naturalization,** naturalized citizenship, citizenship by naturalization, citizen by adoption, nationalization, adoption, admission, affiliation, assimilation, denization; indigenization; Americanization, Anglicization; acculturation, enculturation; papers, citizenship papers; culture shock

VERBS **4** naturalize, grant citizenship, confer citizenship, adopt, admit, affiliate, **assimilate**; Americanize, Anglicize; acculturate, acculturize; indigenize, go native

ADJS **5** **native,** natal, **indigenous,** endemic, autochthonous; mother, maternal, original, aboriginal, primitive; native-born, natural-born, home-grown, homebred, native to the soil, native to the place

6 **naturalized,** adopted, **assimilated**; indoctrinated, Americanized, Anglicized; acculturated, acculturized; indigenized

227 INHABITANT, NATIVE

<those born or living in place>

NOUNS **1** **population, inhabitants,** habitancy, dwellers, populace, people, whole people, people at large, citizenry, folk, souls, living souls, body, whole body, warm bodies; public, general public; community, society, nation, commonwealth, constituency, body politic, electorate; speech community, linguistic community, ethnic community, cultural community; colony, commune, neighborhood; nationality; census, head count; population statistics, demography, demographics

2 **inhabitant,** inhabiter, habitant; **occupant,** occupier, dweller, tenant, denizen, inmate; resident, residencer, residentiary, resider; townie; inpatient; resident maide, live-in maid; writer-in-residence, poet-in-residence, artist-in-residence, composer-in-residence; house detective; incumbent, *locum tenens* <L>; sojourner; addressee; indweller; au pair

3 **native,** indigene, autochthon, earliest inhabitant, first comer, primitive settler; primitive; **aborigine,** aboriginal; local, local yokel

4 **citizen,** national, subject; naturalized citizen, nonnative citizen, citizen by adoption, immigrant, metic; hyphenated American, hyphenate; cosmopolitan, cosmopolite, citizen of the world; active citizen; dual citizen

5 **fellow citizen,** fellow countryman, fellow countrywoman, compatriot, congener, countryman, countrywoman, *landsman* <Yiddish>, *paesano* <Ital>, *paisano* <Sp>; fellow townsman, home boy, home girl, hometowner

6 **townsperson,** townswoman, townsman, towny, towner, townie, local, villager, oppidan, city dweller, city person; big-city person, city slicker; metropolitan, urbanite; suburbanite; exurbanite; burgher, burgess, *bourgeois* <Fr>; townspeople, townfolks, townsfolk; locavore; micropolitan

7 **householder,** homeowner, house-owner, proprietor, freeholder, occupier, addressee; cottager, cotter, cottier, crofter; head of household

8 **lodger,** roomer, paying guest; boarder, board-and-roomer, transient, transient guest; renter, tenant, leaser, lessee, leaseholder, time-sharer, subleaser, sublessee; roommate, flatmate <Brit>; visitor, guest; boomerang child, boomerang kid

9 **settler,** habitant; colonist, colonizer, colonial, immigrant, incomer, planter; homesteader; squatter, nester; pioneer; sooner; precursor

10 wilderness settler, hinterlander; **frontiersman,** mountain man; backwoodsman, woodlander, woodsman, woodman, woodhick; mountaineer, hillbilly, ridge runner, brush ape, briar-hopper; cracker, redneck, desert rat, clamdigger, piny; country gentleman, country gentlewoman, ruralist, provincial, rustic, peasant, hayseed, hick, cottager

11 <regional inhabitants> Easterner, eastlander; Midwesterner; Westerner, westlander; Southerner, southlander; Northener, northlander, Yankee; Northman; New Englander, Down-Easter Yankee; Maritimer <Can>

228 ABODE, HABITAT

<place where animate object lives>

NOUNS 1 **abode, habitation,** place, dwelling, dwelling place, abiding place, place to live, where one lives, where one resides, where one is at home, roof, roof over one's head, residence, place of residence, domicile, *domus* <L>; lodging, lodgment, lodging place; seat, nest, living space, houseroom, sleeping place, place to rest one's head, crash pad; native heath, turf, home turf; address, permanent residence; housing; affordable housing, low-cost housing, low-and-middle-income housing, public housing, public-sector housing, scattersite housing; council house <Brit>; private housing, private-sector housing, market-rate housing

2 **home,** home sweet home; fireside, hearth, hearth and home, hearthstone, fireplace, chimney corner, ingle, ingleside, inglenook, chimenea; base, nest; household, ménage; homestead, home place, home roof, roof, rooftree, toft; place where one hangs one's hat; paternal roof, paternal domicile, family homestead, ancestral halls; hometown, birthplace, cradle; homeland, native land, motherland, fatherland; hominess, homeyness

3 **domesticity;** housewifery, **housekeeping, homemaking;** householding, householdry

4 **quarters,** living quarters; lodgings, lodging, lodgment; diggings, digs, pad, crib, room; rooms, berth, roost, accommodations; housing, shelter

5 **house,** dwelling, dwelling house, *casa* <Sp, Ital>; house and grounds, house and lot, homesite; building, structure, edifice, fabric, erection, hall; roof; lodge; manor house; townhouse, townhome, semidetached house, duplex, row house; country house, country seat, country estate; ranch house, raised ranch, farmhouse, farm; tiny house; prefabricated house, modular house, tract house, kit house; sod house, adobe house; lake dwelling; houseboat; cave dwelling, cliff dwelling; penthouse; split-level; parsonage, rectory, vicarage, deanery, manse; official residence, the White House, Number 10 Downing Street, the Kremlin; governor's mansion; presidential palace; embassy, consulate

6 **farmstead; ranch,** *rancho, hacienda* <Sp>, toft, steading <Brit>, grange, plantation

7 **estate; mansion,** palatial residence, stately home <Brit>, manor house; villa, château, *hôtel* <Fr>, resort, castle, tower; palace, *palais* <Fr>,

palazzo <Ital>, court, great house; ancestral hall, ancestral seat

8 **cottage,** cot, cote, bungalow, box; cabin, log cabin; second home, vacation home; chalet, lodge, snuggery; home away from home, *pied-à-terre* <Fr>, *casita* <Sp>

9 **hut,** hutch, **shack,** shanty, crib, hole-in-the-wall, shed; lean-to; booth, stall; tollbooth, tollhouse, sentry box, gatehouse, porter's lodge; outhouse, outbuilding; privy; pavilion, kiosk; Quonset hut, Nissen hut; hutment

10 <Native American houses> wigwam, tepee, tipi, hogan, wickiup, jacal, longhouse; tupik, igloo; ajouba

11 **hovel, dump**, rathole, hole, sty, pigsty, pigpen, tumbledown shack; squat

12 **outbuilding,** summerhouse, arbor, bower, gazebo, pergola, kiosk, alcove, retreat; conservatory, greenhouse, glasshouse <Brit>, lathhouse

13 **apartment,** flat, tenement, chambers <Brit>, room, rooms; studio apartment, flat <Brit>; bedsitter <Brit>, granny flat, flatlet; suite, suite of rooms, set of rooms; walkup, cold-water flat; penthouse; garden apartment; duplex apartment; railroad flat

14 **apartment building**, apartment house, flats, tenement; duplex, duplex house; tower block; apartment complex; cooperative, co-op, condominium, condo; high-rise apartment building, high-rise

15 **inn, hotel,** hostel, hostelry, tavern, *posada* <Sp>; tourist hotel, *parador* <Sp>, boutique hotel; resort; roadhouse, caravansary, caravanserai, guesthouse, bed and breakfast, B and B, B&B; youth hostel, hospice, elder hostel; lodging house, rooming house; boardinghouse, *pension* <Fr>, *pensione* <Ital>; dormitory, dorm, fraternity house, sorority house; bunkhouse; flophouse, fleabag, dosshouse; time-sharing

16 **motel,** motor court, motor inn, motor lodge, motor hotel, auto court; boatel

17 **trailer,** house trailer, camp trailer, **mobile home,** motor home, recreational vehicle (RV), camper, camper trailer, caravan; trailer court, trailer park, campground; tiny house

18 **habitat,** home, range, environment, surroundings, stamping grounds, stomping grounds, locality, native environment; microhabitat, ecosystem, terrain, purlieu

19 **zoo,** menagerie, zoological garden, zoological park, marine park, sea zoo, safari park; animal shelter

20 **barn,** stable, stall; cowbarn, cowhouse, cowshed, cowbyre, byre; mews; outbuilding

21 **kennel,** doghouse; pound, dog pound; cattery

22 **coop,** chicken house, chicken coop, henhouse, hencote, hencoop, hennery; brooder

23 **birdhouse, aviary,** birdcage; dovecote, pigeon house, pigeon loft, columbary; roost, perch, roosting place; rookery, heronry; eyrie

24 vivarium, terrarium, **aquarium**; fishpond

25 **nest,** nidus; beehive, apiary, hive, bee tree, hornet's nest, wasp's nest, vespiary

26 **lair,** den, cave, hole, covert, mew, form; burrow, tunnel, earth, run, couch, lodge

27 **haunt,** purlieu, **hangout**, stamping ground, stomping ground; gathering place, rallying point, meeting place, clubhouse, club; casino, gambling house; resort, health resort; spa, health spa, yoga retreat, baths, springs, watering place; meditation retreat

28 <disapproved place> **dive**, den, lair, den of thieves; hole, dump, joint; gyp joint, clip joint, strip club; whorehouse, cathouse, sporting house, brothel, bordello; stews, fleshpots

29 **camp, encampment**; bivouac; barrack, barracks, casern, cantonment, lines <Brit>; hobo jungle, hobo camp; detention camp, concentration camp; campground, campsite; homeless shelter

30 <deities of the household> lares and penates, Vesta, Hestia

VERBS 31 **keep house,** housekeep, practice domesticity, maintain a household, run a household; time-share, lease, rent, buy

ADJS 32 **residential,** residentiary, residing, in residence; domestic, domiciliary, domal; home, household, at home; mansional, manorial, palatial

33 **homelike,** homish, homey, homely; comfortable, friendly, cheerful, peaceful, cozy, snug, intimate; simple, plain, unpretending

34 **domesticated,** tame, tamed, broken; housebroken

229 FURNITURE

<large objects for rooms>

NOUNS 1 **furniture,** furnishings, movables, home furnishings, house furnishings, household effects, household goods, office furniture, school furniture, church furniture, library furniture, furnishments; cabinetmaking, cabinetwork, cabinetry; **furniture design, furniture style** <see list>; period furniture; piece of furniture, furniture piece, chair, beanbag chair, beanbag, easy chair, rocking chair, couch, sofa, sofa bed, sleep sofa, davenport, chaise lounge, chaise, coffee table, dining table, bed, bunk bed, air bed, water bed, table, desk, cabinet, chest of drawers, mirror, clock, screen; lamp, floor lamp, table lamp, desk lamp; suite, set of furniture, ensemble, decor; housewares

2 furniture style
Adam
Adapted Colonial
Adirondack
American Chippendale, Pilgrim
American Empire
American Jacobean
American Moderne
American Queen Anne
American Regency, Directory
American Restoration, Pillar and Scroll
Anglo-Dutch
Art Deco
Art Nouveau
Arts and Crafts
Baroque
Bauhaus
Biedermeier
Block-front
Boston Chippendale
boule, boulework
Byzantine
Chinese Chippendale
Chinoiserie
Chippendale
Colonial, Campaign
Contemporary
Cotswold School
Country Chippendale
Cromwellian, Commonwealth
Desornamentado
De Stijl
Directoire
Duncan Phyfe
Early American
Early Georgian
Eastlake
Egyptian
Elizabethan
Empire
Federal
French Provincial
French Renaissance
Georgian
Gothic
Gothic-Renaissance
Hepplewhite
International, International Gothic
Italian Renaissance
Jacobean
Japanese
Japonisme
Late Regency
Later Victorian
Louis XIII
Louis XIV
Louis XV
Louis XVI
Mannerist
Mission
Modern
Modernist
Morris
National Romanticism
Naturalistic
Neoclassical
Neo-Gothic, Cathédrale
Neo-Grec
Newport Chippendale
New York Chippendale
Palladian
Pennsylvania Dutch
Philadelphia Chippendale
Pop Art
Queen Anne
Regency
Renaissance Revival
Restoration, Carolean
Rococo
Rococo Revival, Louis Philippe, Louis XV Revival
Romano-Byzantine, Italo-Byzantine, Romanesque
Scandinavian Modern
Shaker
Sheraton
Spanish Renaissance
Stuart
Tudor
Turkish
Venetian
Victorian
Viking Revival, Dragonesque
William and Mary

230 TOWN, CITY

<geographic place where people live>

NOUNS **1 town,** township; **city, metropolis,** metro, metropolitan area, greater city, megalopolis, supercity, conurbation, big city, urban complex, spread city, urban sprawl, urban, spread, Standard Metropolitan Statistical Area (SMSA), urban corridor, strip city, municipality, *urbs* <L>, *polis* <Gk>, city government, municipal government; *ville* <Fr>, *Stadt* <Ger>; borough, burg, bourg, burgh <Scot>; suburb, suburbia, burbs, bedroom community, slurb, stockbroker belt, garden suburb <Brit>, commuter belt, outskirts, *faubourg* <Fr>, *banlieue* <Fr>; exurb, exurbia, bedroom town, streetcar suburb; market town <Brit>; small town; twin town; boom town, ghost town; industrial city; sister city; urbanization, citifying; clone town

2 village, hamlet; ham, thorp, wick; country town, crossroads

3 <nonformal> **one-horse town,** cowtown, jerkwater town, one-gas-station town, whistle-stop, jumping-off place; hick town, rube town, Podunk, Palookaville; wide place in the road

4 capital, capital city, **seat**, seat of government; county seat, county site, county town, shiretown <Brit>

5 town hall, town square, city hall, **municipal building;** courthouse; police headquarters, police station, station house, precinct house; firehouse, fire station; county building, county courthouse; community center; school; town green

6 <city districts> East Side, East End, West Side, West End; **downtown,** uptown, midtown; city center, main street, high street, city centre <Brit>, urban center, central city, center city, core, core city, inner city, suburbs, suburbia, burbs, outskirts, greenbelt, residential district, business district, business section, shopping center, financial district, residential area; Chinatown, Little Italy; asphalt jungle, concrete jungle, mean streets; slum, slums, the other side of the tracks, the wrong side of the tracks, blighted area, blighted neighborhood, blighted section, run-down neighborhood, tenement district, shantytown, hell's kitchen, half-acre; favela, tenderloin, red-light district, Bowery, skid row, skid road, tin pan alley; combat zone; enterprise zone; ghetto, urban ghetto, barrio

7 block, city block, square

8 square, plaza, *place* <Fr>, *piazza* <Ital>, *campo* <Ital>, marketplace, market, mart, rialto, forum, agora

9 circle, circus <Brit>; crescent

10 city planning, urban planning; urban studies, urbanology

ADJS **11 urban,** metropolitan, municipal, metro, burghal, civic, oppidan; main-street; citywide; city, town, village; citified; urbane; suburban;

interurban; downtown, uptown, midtown; inner-city, core, core-city, ghetto; small-town; boom-town

231 REGION

<part of country or world>

NOUNS 1 **region, area,** zone, belt, territory, terrain; place; space; country, land, ground, soil; territoriality; territorial waters, twelve-mile limit, three-mile limit, continental shelf, offshore rights; air space; heartland; hinterland; district, quarter, section, sector, department, division; salient, corridor; part, parts; neighborhood, vicinity, vicinage, neck of the woods, stamping ground, turf, backyard, purlieu, purlieus; premises, confines, precincts, environs, milieu; backcountry, last frontier

2 **sphere,** hemisphere, orb, **orbit,** ambit, circle; circuit, judicial circuit, beat, round, walk; realm, demesne, domain, dominion, jurisdiction, bailiwick, niche, forté; border, borderland, march; province, precinct, department; field, pale, arena

3 **zone;** climate, clime; **longitude,** longitude in arc, longitude in time; meridian, prime meridian; **latitude,** parallel; equator, the line; tropic, Tropic of Cancer, Tropic of Capricorn; tropics, subtropics, Torrid Zone; Temperate Zone, Variable Zone; Frigid Zone, Arctic Zone, Arctic Circle, Antarctic Zone, Antarctic Circle; horse latitudes, roaring forties; doldrums

4 **plot,** plot of ground, plot of land, parcel of land, plat, patch, tract, field, enclosure; lot; air space; block, square; section, forty <sixteenth of a section>, back forty; close, quadrangle, quad, enclave, pale, *clos* <Fr>, croft <Brit>, *kraal* <Africa>; real estate; allotment, holding, claim

5 **<territorial division>** state, territory, province, region, duchy, electorate, government, principality; county, shire, canton, *oblast, okrug* <Russ>, *département* <Fr>, *Kreis, Land* <Ger>; borough, ward, precinct, riding, *arrondissement* <Fr>; township, hundred, commune, wapentake; metropolis, metropolitan area, city, town; village, hamlet; district, congressional district, electoral district; magistracy, soke, bailiwick; shrievalty, sheriffalty, sheriffwick, constablewick <Brit>; archdiocese, archbishopric, stake; diocese, bishopric, parish; colony

6 **<regions of the world>** continent, landmass; Old World, the old country; New World, America; Northern Hemisphere, North America; Central America; Southern Hemisphere, South America; Latin America; Western Hemisphere, Occident, West; Eastern Hemisphere, Orient, Levant, East, eastland; Far East, Mideast, Middle East, Near East; Asia, Europe, Eurasia, Asia Major, Asia Minor, Africa; Antipodes, Australia, down under, Australasia, Oceania; Arctic, Antarctica; Third World; banana belt

7 **<regions of the US>** West, westland, wild West, West Coast, coast, left coast; Northwest, Pacific Northwest; Silicon Valley; Sierras; Rockies; Sunbelt; Southwest; Middle West, Midwest, Middle America, farm belt; Great Plains, heartlands, Plains states; North Central region; rust belt; East, eastland, East Coast, Eastern Seaboard; Middle Atlantic; Northeast, Southeast; North, northland, Snow Belt, Frost Belt; Appalachia; South, southland, Dixie, Dixieland; Deep South, Old South; Delta, bayous; Bible belt; borscht belt; Gulf Coast; New England, Down East, Yankeeland; lower forty-eight, forty-ninth parallel

ADJS 8 **regional,** territorial, geographical, areal, sectional, zonal, topographic, topographical

9 **local,** localized, of a place, geographically limited, topical, vernacular, parochial, provincial, insular, limited, confined

10 **U.S. state mottoes and nicknames**

Alabama "We dare defend our rights"; Heart of Dixie
Alaska "North to the future"; The Last Frontier
Arizona "God enriches"; Grand Canyon State
Arkansas "The people rule"; The Natural State
California "Eureka"; Golden State
Colorado "Nothing without providence"; Mile-High State, Centennial State
Connecticut "He who transplanted still sustains"; Constitution State
Delaware "Liberty and independence"; First State
District of Columbia "Justice for all"; Capital City
Florida "In God we trust"; Sunshine State
Georgia "Wisdom, justice, and moderation"; Peach State
Hawaii "The life of the land is perpetuated in righteousness"; Aloha State
Idaho "It is perpetual"; Gem State
Illinois "State sovereignty, national union"; Prairie State
Indiana "Crossroads of America"; Hoosier State
Iowa "Our liberties we prize and our rights we will maintain"; Hawkeye State
Kansas "To the stars through difficulties"; Sunflower State
Kentucky "United we stand, divided we shall fall"; Bluegrass State
Louisiana "Union, justice and confidence"; Pelican State
Maine "I direct"; Pine Tree State
Maryland "Strong deeds, gentle words"; Old Line State

Massachusetts "By the sword we seek peace, but peace only under liberty"; Bay State
Michigan "If you seek a pleasant peninsula, look about you"; Great Lakes State
Minnesota "The star of the north"; North Star State
Mississippi "By valor and arms"; Magnolia State
Missouri "The welfare of the people shall be the supreme law"; Show-Me State
Montana "Gold and silver"; Treasure State
Nebraska "Equality before the law"; Cornhusker State
Nevada "All for our country":; Silver State
New Hampshire "Live free or die"; Granite State
New Jersey "Liberty and prosperity"; Garden State
New Mexico "It grows as it goes"; Land of Enchantment
New York "Excelsior"; Empire State
North Carolina "To be rather than to seem"; Tar Heel State
North Dakota "Liberty and union, now and forever, one and inseparable"; Peace Garden State
Ohio "With God, all things are possible"; Buckeye State
Oklahoma "Labor conquers all things"; Sooner State
Oregon "She flies with her own wings"; Beaver State
Pennsylvania "Virtue, liberty and independence"; Keystone State
Rhode Island "Hope"; Little Rhody; Ocean State
South Carolina "Prepared in mind and resources"; Palmetto State
South Dakota "Under God, the people rule"; Mount Rushmore State
Tennessee "Agriculture and commerce"; Volunteer State
Texas "Friendship"; Lone Star State
Utah "Industry"; Beehive State
Vermont "Freedom and unity"; Green Mountain State
Virginia "Thus always to Tyrants"; Old Dominion
Washington "By and by"; Evergreen State
West Virginia "Mountaineers are always free"; Mountain State
Wisconsin "Forward"; Badger State
Wyoming "Equal rights"; Equality State

11 **U.S. Territories and Commonwealths**

American Samoa
Guam
Commonwealth of the Northern Mariana Islands
Commonwealth of Puerto Rico
United States Virgin Islands

12 **Canadian provinces and territories**

Alberta
British Columbia
Manitoba
New Brunswick
Newfoundland and Labrador
Northwest Territories
Nova Scotia
Nunavut
Ontario
Prince Edward Island
Quebec
Saskatchewan
Yukon Territory

232 COUNTRY

<political geographic place>

NOUNS 1 **country,** land; **nation,** nationality, **state,** nation-state, sovereign nation, sovereign state, self-governing state, polity, body politic; power, superpower, world power; microstate; republic, people's republic, commonwealth, commonweal; kingdom, sultanate; empire, empery; realm, dominion, domain; principality, principate; duchy, dukedom; grand duchy, archduchy, archdukedom, earldom, county, palatinate, seneschalty; chieftaincy, chieftainry; toparchy; city-state, *polis* <Gk>, free city; province, territory, possession; colony, settlement; protectorate, mandate, mandated territory, mandant, mandatee, mandatory; buffer state; ally, military ally, cobelligerent, treaty partner; satellite, puppet regime, puppet government; coalition government; free nation, free country, captive nation, iron-curtain country; nonaligned nation, unaligned nation, neutralist nation; developed nation, industrial nation, industrialized nation; underdeveloped nation, third-world nation, banana republic; federation, confederation, bloc, comity; United Nations

2 fatherland, *patria* <L>, land of our fathers, motherland, mother country, **native land,** native soil, one's native ground, one's native soil, the old country, country of origin, birthplace, cradle; home, homeland, home ground, God's country; the home front

3 **United States,** United States of America, US, USA, US of A, America, Columbia, the States, Yankeeland, Land of Liberty, the melting pot; stateside

4 **Britain,** Great Britain, United Kingdom, the UK, Britannia, Albion, Blighty, Limeyland, Tight Little Island, Land of the Rose, Sovereign of the Seas; British Empire, Commonwealth of Nations, British Commonwealth of Nations, the Commonwealth; perfidious Albion

5 <national personifications> Uncle Sam, Brother Jonathan; John Bull <Brit>

6 nationhood, peoplehood, **nationality;** statehood, nation-statehood, sovereignty, sovereign nationhood, sovereign statehood, independence, self-government, self-determination; internationality, internationalism; nationalism

7 **native**, countryman, countrywoman, citizen, national; nationalist, ultranationalist; patriot

233 THE COUNTRY

<area outside town, city>

NOUNS 1 **the country,** agricultural region, farm country, farmland, arable land, grazing region, grazing country, rural district, rustic region, province, provinces, countryside, woodland, grassland, woods and fields, meadows and pastures, the soil, grassroots; the sticks, the tall corn, yokeldom, hickdom; cotton belt, tobacco belt, black belt, farm belt, corn belt, fruit belt, wheat belt, citrus belt; dust bowl; highlands, moors, uplands, foothills; lowlands, veld, veldt, savanna, savannah, plains, prairies, steppes, wide-open spaces

2 **hinterland, backcountry,** outback <Austral>, upcountry, boonies, boondocks; the bush, bush country, bushveld, woods, woodlands, backwoods, forests, timbers, the big sticks, brush; wilderness, wilds, uninhabited region, virgin land, virgin territory; wasteland; frontier, borderland, outpost; wild West, cow country, cow town

3 **rusticity, ruralism,** inurbanity, agrarianism, bucolicism, provincialism, provinciality, simplicity, pastoral simplicity, unspoiledness; yokelism, hickishness, backwoodsiness; boorishness, churlishness, unrefinement, uncultivation; peasantry, gaucherie; agrarian society

4 ruralization, countrification, **rustication,** pastoralization

VERBS 5 **ruralize, countrify, rusticate,** pastoralize; farm; return to the soil

ADJS 6 **rustic, rural,** country, provincial, farm, pastoral, bucolic, Arcadian, agrarian, agrestic, agrestal, proto-industrial; agricultural; lowland, low-lying, upland, highland, prairie, plains

7 **countrified,** inurbane; country-born, country-bred, upcountry; farmerish, hobnailed, clodhopping, clodhopperish; boorish, clownish, loutish, lumpish, lumpen, cloddish, churlish; uncouth, unpolished, uncultivated, uncultured, unrefined; country-style, country-fashion

8 <nonformal> **rusticated,** hick, hicky, hickified, hicklike, from the sticks, rube, hayseed, yokel, yokelish, down-home, shit-kicking*, hillbilly, redneck

9 **hinterland,** back, back-country, upcountry, backroad, outback <Austral>, wild, wilderness, virgin; wild-West, cow-country; waste; backwood, backwoods, back of beyond, backwoodsy; woodland, sylvan

234 LAND

<area of ground>

NOUNS 1 **land, ground,** landmass, earth, glebe, sod, clod, soil, dirt, dust, clay, marl, mold; *terra* <L>, terra firma, terra incognita; terrain; dry land; arable land; marginal land; grassland, woodland; crust, earth's crust, lithosphere; regolith; topsoil, subsoil; alluvium, alluvion; eolian deposit, subaerial deposit; real estate, real property, landholdings, acres, territory, freehold; region; the country; earth science

2 **shore, coast,** *côte* <Fr>; strand, *playa* <Sp>, beach, beachfront, beachside shingle, plage, lido, riviera, sands, berm; waterside, waterfront; shoreline, coastline; foreshore; bank, embankment; riverside; lakefront, lakeshore; seashore, seacoast, seaside, seaboard, seabeach, seacliff, seabank, sea margin, oceanfront, oceanside, seafront, shorefront, tidewater, tideland, coastland, littoral, littoral zone; sand dune, sandbar, sandbank, tombolo; wetland, wetlands; bay, bayfront, bayside; drowned coast, submerged coast; rockbound coast, ironbound coast; loom of the land

3 **landsman,** landman, **landlubber**

ADJS 4 **terrestrial,** terrene, **earth,** earthly, telluric, tellurian; earthbound; sublunar, subastral; geophilous; terraqueous; fluvioterrestrial

5 earthy, **earthen,** soily, loamy, marly, gumbo; clayey, clayish; adobe; agrestal

6 **alluvial,** alluvious, estuarine, fluviomarine

7 **coastal,** littoral, seaside, **shore,** shoreside; shoreward; riparian, riparial, riparious; riverain, riverine; riverside; lakefront, lakeshore; oceanfront, oceanside; seafront, shorefront, shoreline; beachfront, beachside; bayfront, bayside; tideland, tidal, wetland

ADVS 8 **on land,** on dry land, on terra firma; onshore, ashore; alongshore; shoreward; by land, overland

9 **on earth,** on the face of the earth, in the world, in the wide world, in the whole wide world; under the sun, under the stars, beneath the sky, under heaven, below, here below

235 BODY OF LAND

<feature of the land>

NOUNS 1 **continent, mainland,** main, landform, continental landform, landmass; North America, South America, Africa, Europe, Asia, Eurasia, Eurasian landmass, Australia, Antarctica; subcontinent, India, Greenland; peninsula;

plate, tectonic plate, crustal plate, crustal segment, Pacific plate, American plate, African plate, Eurasian plate, Antarctic plate, Indian plate; continental divide, continental drift; plate tectonics; Gondwana, Laurasia, Pangaea

2 **island,** isle; islet, holm, ait; continental island; oceanic island; volcanic island; key, cay; sandbank, sandbar, bar; floating island; reef, coral reef, coral head; coral island, atoll; archipelago, island group, island chain; insularity; islandology

3 **continental,** mainlander; continentalist

4 **islander,** islandman, island-dweller, islesman, insular; islandologist

VERBS 5 insulate, isolate, island, enisle; island-hop

ADJS 6 **continental,** mainland

7 **insular,** insulated, isolated; island, islandy, islandish, islandlike; islanded, isleted, island-dotted; seagirt; archipelagic, archipelagian

236 PLAIN

<flat open land>

NOUNS 1 **plain, plains,** flat country, flatland, flats, flat, level; champaign, champaign country, open country, wide-open spaces; prairie, grassland, sea of grass, steppe, pampas, *pampa* <Sp>, savanna, tundra, vega, campo, llano, sebkha; veld, grass veld, bushveld, tree veld; wold, weald; moor, moorland, down, downs, lande, heath, fell <Brit>; lowland, lowlands, bottomland; basin, playa; sand plain, sand flat, strand flat; tidal flat, salt marsh; salt pan; salt flat, alkali flat; desert; plateau, upland, tableland, table, mesa, mesilla; peneplain; coastal plain, abyssal plain, tidal plain, alluvial plain, delta, delta plain, flood plain; mare, lunar mare

ADJS 2 champaign, **plain, flat,** open; campestral, campestrian

237 HIGHLANDS

<hilly or mountainous land>

NOUNS 1 **highlands, uplands,** highland, upland, high country, elevated land, dome, plateau, tableland, mesa, upland area, downs, downland, piedmont, moor, moorland, hills, heights, hill country, hilly country, wold, foothills, rolling country, mountains, mountain country, mountainous country, high terrain, peaks, range, *massif* <Fr>

2 **slope, declivity,** steep, versant, incline, rise, talus, brae <Scot>, mountainside, hillside, bank, gentle slope, easy slope, glacis, angle of repose, steep slope, rapid slope, fall line, bluff, cliff, headland, ness, *ben* <Scot, Ir>; precipice, wall, palisade, scar <Brit>, escarpment, scarp, fault scarp, rim, face; upper slopes, upper reaches; timberline, tree line

3 **plateau, tableland,** high plateau, table, mesa, table mountain, butte, moor, fell <Brit>, hammada

4 **hill,** down; brae; hillock, knob, butte, kopje, kame, monticle, monticule, monadnock, knoll, hummock, hammock, eminence, rise, mound, swell, barrow, tumulus, kop, tell, tel, jebel; dune, sand dune; moraine, drumlin; anthill, molehill; sandhill

5 **ridge,** ridgeline, *arête* <Fr>, chine, spine, horst, kame, comb <Brit>, esker, os, cuesta, serpent kame, Indian ridge, moraine, terminal moraine; saddle, hogback, hog's-back, saddleback, horseback, col, watershed; pass, gap, notch, wind gap, water gap

6 **mountain**, mount, alp, hump, tor, height, dizzying height, nunatak, dome; peak, pinnacle, summit, mountaintop, point, topmost point, crest, spine, pike <Brit>, *pic* <Fr>, *pico* <Sp>; crag, spur, cloud-topped peak, snowcapped peak, the roof of the world; needle, aiguille, pyramidal peak, horn; fold mountain, fold-belt mountain, alpine chain, fault-block mountain, basin and range; oceanic ridge, oceanic rise; volcano, volcanic mountain, volcanic spine, volcanic neck; seamount, submarine mountain, guyot; mountain range, range, massif; mountain system, chain, mountain chain, cordillera, sierra, cordilleran belt, fold belt; hill heaped upon hill; divide, Continental Divide; mountain-building, orogeny, orogenesis, epeirogeny, folding, faulting, block-faulting, volcanism; isostasy; orography, orology; acrophile

7 **valley,** vale, glen, dale, dell, hollow, holler, dip, flume, cleuch, corrie <Scot>, *cwm* <Welsh>; ravine, gorge, canyon, box canyon, *arroyo* <Sp>, barranca, bolson, coulee, gully, gulch, combe, comb, comb <Brit>, cirque, dingle, rift, rift valley, kloof, donga, graben, draw, wadi, basin, corrie, hanging valley; crevasse; chimney, ditch, chine, clough <Brit>, couloir; defile, pass, passage, col; crater, volcanic crater, caldera, meteorite crater, meteoritic crater

ADJS 8 **hilly,** rolling, undulating, upland; **mountainous,** montane, alpine, alpestrine, altitudinous; orogenic, orographic, orological, orometric

238 STREAM

<flowing body of water>

NOUNS 1 **stream, waterway,** watercourse, channel; meandering stream, flowing stream, lazy stream, racing stream, braided stream; spill stream;

adolescent stream; mountain stream; river; navigable river; underground river, subterranean river; moving road; dry stream, stream bed, stream channel, stream course, winterbourne, wadi, *arroyo* <Sp>; brook, branch; kill, bourn, bourne, run, creek, crick; rivulet, rill, rillet, streamlet, brooklet, runlet, runnel, rundle, rindle, beck <Brit>, gill <Brit>, burn <Scot>, sike; freshet, fresh; millstream, race; midstream, midchannel; drainage pattern, watershed; stream action, fluviation

2 **headwaters,** headstream, headwater, head, riverhead; source, fountainhead

3 **tributary,** feeder, branch, fork, prong, confluent, confluent stream, affluent, distributary; effluent, anabranch, branch feeder; bayou; billabong <Austral>

4 **flow,** flowing, flux, fluency, profluence, fluid motion, fluid movement; hydrodynamics; stream, current, set, trend, tide, water flow; drift, driftage; course, onward course, surge, gush, rush, onrush, spate, run, race; millrace, mill run; undercurrent, undertow; crosscurrent, crossflow; affluence, afflux, affluxion, confluence, convergence, concourse, conflux; downflow, downpour; defluxion; inflow; outflow

5 **torrent,** river, flood, flash flood, wall of water, waterflood, deluge; spate, pour, freshet, fresh

6 **overflow,** spillage, spill, spillover, overflowing, overrunning, alluvion, alluvium, inundation, flood, deluge, whelming, overwhelming, flush, washout, engulfment, submersion, cataclysm; the Flood, the Deluge

7 **trickle,** tricklet, dribble, drip, dripping, stillicide, drop, spurtle; percolation, leaching, lixiviation; distillation, condensation, sweating; seeping, seepage

8 **lap,** swash, wash, slosh, plash, splash; lapping, washing

9 **jet,** spout, spurt, spurtle, squirt, spit, spew, spray, spritz; rush, gush, flush; fountain, fount, font; geyser, spouter

10 **rapids,** rapid, white water, wild water, falls; ripple, riffle, riff; chute, shoot, sault

11 **waterfall,** cataract, fall, falls, Niagara, cascade, force <Brit>, linn <Scot>, sault; nappe; watershoot

12 **eddy,** back stream, gurge, swirl, twirl, whirl; whirlpool, vortex, gulf, maelstrom; Charybdis; countercurrent, counterflow, counterflux, backflow, reflux, refluence, regurgitation, ebb, backwash, backwater, snye <Can>

13 **tide,** tidal current, tidal stream, tidal flow, tidal flood, tide race; tidewater; tideway, tide gate; riptide, rip, tiderip, overfalls; direct tide, opposite tide; spring tide; high tide, high water, full tide; low tide, low water; neap tide, neap; lunar tide, solar tide; flood tide, ebb tide; rise of the tide, rising tide, flux, flow, flood; ebb, reflux, refluence; ebb and flow, flux and reflux; tidal amplitude, tidal range, intertidal zone, tidal flat, tidal pool; tideland; tide chart, tide table, tidal current chart; tide gauge, thalassometer

14 **wave,** billow, surge, swell, heave, undulation, lift, rise, send, scend; trough, peak; sea, heavy swell, ocean swell, ground swell; roller, roll; comber, comb; surf, breakers, spume; wavelet, ripple, riffle; tidal wave, tsunami, seismic sea wave, seiche, rogue wave; gravity wave, water wave; tide wave; bore, tidal bore, eagre, traveling wave; whitecap, white horse, white foam; rough sea, heavy sea, rough water, broken water, dirty water, dirty sea, choppy sea, chopping sea, popple, lop, chop, choppiness, overfall, angry sea; standing wave

15 water gauge, fluviograph, fluviometer; marigraph; Nilometer

VERBS 16 **flow,** stream, issue, pour, surge, run, course, rush, gush, flush, flood; empty into, flow into, join, join with, mingle waters; set, make, trend; flow in; flow out; flow back, surge back, ebb, regurgitate; meander

17 **overflow,** flow over, wash over, run over, well over, brim over, lap, lap at, lap over, overbrim, overrun, pour out, pour over, spill, slop, slosh, spill out, spill over; cataract, cascade; inundate, engulf, swamp, sweep, whelm, overwhelm, flood, deluge, submerge

18 **trickle,** dribble, dripple, drip, drop, spurtle; filter, percolate, leach, lixiviate; distill, condense, sweat; seep, weep; gurgle, murmur

19 **lap,** plash, splash, wash, swash, slosh

20 **jet,** spout, spurt, spurtle, squirt, spit, spew, spray, spritz, skoosh, play, gush, well, surge; vomit, vomit out, vomit forth

21 **eddy,** gurge, swirl, whirl, purl, reel, spin

22 **billow,** surge, swell, heave, lift, rise, send, scend, toss, popple, roll, wave, undulate; peak, draw to a peak, be poised; comb, break, dash, crash, smash; rise and fall, ebb and flow

ADJS 23 **streamy,** rivery, brooky, creeky; streamlike, riverine, riverlike; fluvial, fluviatile, fluviatic, fluviomarine

24 **flowing, streaming,** running, pouring, fluxive, fluxional, coursing, racing, gushing, rushing, onrushing, surging, surgy, torrential, rough, whitewater; fluent, profluent, affluent, defluent, decurrent, confluent, diffluent, refluent; tidal; gulfy, vortical; meandering, mazy, sluggish, serpentine

25 **flooded,** deluged, inundated, engulfed, swamped,

swept, whelmed, drowned, overwhelmed, afloat, awash; washed, water-washed; in flood, at flood, in spate

239 CHANNEL

<pathway for water>

NOUNS 1 **channel, conduit,** duct, canal, course; way, passage, passageway; trough, troughway, troughing; tunnel; ditch, trench; adit; ingress, entrance; egress, exit; stream; English Channel

2 **watercourse, waterway,** aqueduct, water channel, water gate, water carrier, culvert, canal; side-channel, intrariverine channel, snye <Can>; streamway, riverway; bed, stream bed, riverbed, creek bed, runnel; water gap; dry bed, *arroyo* <Sp>, wadi, winterbourne, gully, gullyhole, gulch; swash, swash channel; race, headrace, tailrace; flume; sluice; spillway; spillbox; irrigation ditch, water furrow; waterworks

3 **gutter,** trough, eaves trough; flume, chute, shoot; pentrough, penstock; guide

4 <metal founding> gate, ingate, runner, sprue, tedge

5 **drain,** sough, sluice, scupper; sink, sump; piscina; gutter, kennel; sewer, cloaca, headchute; cloaca maxima

6 **tube**; pipe; tubing, piping, tubulation; tubulure; nipple, pipette, tubulet, tubule; reed, stem, straw; hose, hosepipe <Brit>, garden hose, fire hose; sprinkler; pipeline; catheter; siphon; tap; efflux tube, adjutage; funnel; snorkel; siamese, siamese connection, siamese joint

7 **main,** water main, gas main, fire main

8 **spout,** beak, waterspout, downspout; gargoyle

9 **nozzle,** bib nozzle, pressure nozzle, spray nozzle, nose, snout; rose, rosehead; shower head, sprinkler head

10 **valve,** gate; faucet, spigot, tap; cock, petcock, draw cock, stopcock, sea cock, drain cock, ball cock; bunghole; needle valve; valvule, valvula

11 **floodgate,** flood-hatch, gate, head gate, penstock, water gate, sluice, sluice gate; tide gate, aboiteau <Can>; weir; lock, lock gate, dock gate; air lock

12 **hydrant,** fire hydrant, plug, water plug, fireplug

13 air passage, air duct, airway, air shaft, shaft, **air hole,** air tube; speaking tube; blowhole, breathing hole, spiracle; nostril; touchhole; spilehole, vent, venthole, ventage, ventiduct; ventilator, ventilating shaft; transom, louver, louverwork; wind tunnel

14 **chimney,** flue, flue pipe, funnel, stovepipe, stack, smokestack, smoke pipe, smokeshaft; Charley Noble; fumarole

VERBS 15 **channel,** channelize, canalize, conduct, convey, put through; pipe, funnel, siphon; trench; direct

ADJS 16 **tubular,** tubate, tubiform, tubelike, pipelike; cylindrical; tubed, piped; cannular; tubal

17 **valvular,** valval, valvelike; valved

240 SEA, OCEAN

<large body of salt water>

NOUNS 1 **ocean, sea,** ocean sea, great sea, main sea, main, ocean main, the bounding main, tide, salt sea, salt water, blue water, ocean blue, deep water, open sea, the brine, the briny, the big pond, the briny deep, the deep, the deep sea, the deep blue sea, drink, big drink, the herring pond; international water; high sea, high seas; the seven seas; hydrosphere; ocean depths, ocean deeps and trenches

2 **ocean** <see list>; **sea** <see list>, tributary sea, gulf, bay; big pond

3 spirit of the sea, the old man of the sea, sea devil, Davy, Davy Jones; sea god, Neptune, Poseidon, Oceanus, Triton, Nereus, Oceanid, Nereid, Thetis, Amphitrite, Calypso; Varuna, Dylan; mermaid, siren; merman, seaman, undine, sea nymph, water sprite, sea serpent

4 **<ocean zone>** pelagic zone, benthic zone, estuarine area, sublittoral, littoral, intertidal zone, splash zone, supralittoral

5 ocean floor, seabed, sea bottom, benthos, Davy Jones's locker; continental shelf, continental slope, submarine canyon, land bridge, abyssal plain, abyssal hill, midoceanic ridge, oceanic ridge, oceanic trench, volcanic island, seamount, guyot, atoll

6 **oceanography**, thalassography, hydrography, bathymetry; marine biology; aquaculture

7 oceanographer, thalassographer, hydrographer, marine biologist, deep-sea diver, underwater explorer

ADJS 8 **oceanic, marine, maritime,** pelagic, thalassic; ocean-going, sea-going, seafaring; undersea, underwater; nautical; oceanographic, oceanographical, hydrographic, hydrographical, bathymetric, bathymetrical, bathyorographical, thalassographic, thalassographical; terriginous; deep-sea

ADVS 9 **at sea,** on the high seas; afloat; by water, by sea

10 oversea, **overseas,** beyond seas, over the water, transmarine, across the sea, across the pond, coast-to-coast

11 **oceanward,** oceanwards, **seaward,** seawards, off; offshore, off soundings, out of soundings, in blue water

COMBINING FORMS **12** mari-, thalass-, thalasso-; oceano-; bathy-

13 ocean

Antarctic
Arctic
Indian
North Atlantic
South Atlantic
North Pacific
Pacific
South Pacific

14 sea

Adriatic Sea
Aegean Sea
Amundsen Sea
Andaman Sea
Arabian Sea
Arafura Sea
Aral Sea
Baffin Bay
Bali Sea
Baltic Sea
Banda Sea
Barents Sea
Bay of Bengal
Beaufort Sea
Bellingshausen Sea
Bering Sea
Black Sea
Caribbean Sea
Caspian Sea
Celebes Sea
Ceram Sea
China Sea
Chukchi Sea
Coral Sea
East China Sea
East Siberian Sea
Flores Sea
Great Australian Bight
Greenland Sea
Gulf of Alaska
Gulf of California
Gulf of Guinea
Gulf of Mexico
Gulf of Saint Lawrence
Hudson Bay
Inland Sea
Ionian Sea
Irish Sea
Kara Sea
Laptev Sea
Ligurian Sea
Macassar Strait
Mediterranean Sea
Molukka Sea
North Sea
Norwegian Sea
Persian Gulf
Philippine Sea
Red Sea
Ross Sea
Sargasso Sea
Savu Sea
Sea of Azov
Sea of Galilee
Sea of Japan
Sea of Marmara
Sea of Okhotsk
South China Sea
Sulu Sea
Tasman Sea
Timor Sea
Tyrrhenian Sea
Weddell Sea
White Sea
Yellow Sea

241 LAKE, POOL

<large body of fresh water>

NOUNS **1 lake,** landlocked water, loch <Scot>, lough <Irl>, *nyanza* <Africa>, mere, freshwater lake, natural lake; oxbow lake, bayou lake, glacial lake; volcanic lake; mountain lake; salt lake; tarn; inland sea; **pool,** lakelet, pond, pondlet, dew pond, linn <Scot>, dike, *étang* <Fr>; standing water, still water, stagnant water, dead water, bayou; watering hole, water pocket, swimming hole, aquascape; oasis; farm pond; fishpond; millpond, millpool; salt pond, salina, tidal pond, tidal pool; backwater; puddle, plash, sump; lagoon, *laguna* <Sp>; reservoir, artificial lake, manmade lake; dam; well, cistern, tank, artesian well, flowing well, spring

2 lake dweller, lakeside dweller, lacustrian, lacustrine dweller, pile dweller, pile builder; laker

3 lake dwelling, lacustrine dwelling, pile house, pile dwelling, stilt house, palafitte; crannog <Scot, Irl>; lake house, lakeside home; lakeside village

4 limnology, limnologist; limnimeter, limnograph

ADJS **5 lakish,** laky, lakelike; lacustrine, lacustral, lacustrian; pondy, pondlike, lacuscular; limnetic, limnologic, limnological, limnophilous; landlocked; poolside, lakeside, lake-dwelling

COMBINING FORMS **6** limn-, limno-, limni-, -limnion

7 major lakes

Aral Sea <Kazakhstan, Uzbekistan>
Athabaska <Can>
Baikal <Russia>
Bear <US>
Becharof <US>
Biwa <Japan>
Chad <Chad, Niger, Nigeria>
Champlain <US, Can>
Chapala <Mexico>
Derwent Water <Brit>
Erie <US, Can>
Eyre <Austral>
Finger Lakes <US>
Flathead <US>
Gairdner <Austral>
Garda <Italy>
George <US>
Great Bear <Can>
Great Salt <US>
Great Slave <Can>
Huron <US, Can>
Ladoga <Russ>
Lake of the Woods <Can>
Maggiore <It, Switz>
Manitoba <Can>
Manzala <Egypt>
Maracaibo <Venezuela>
Mead <US>
Michigan <US>
Moosehead <US>
Nettilling <Can>
Nipigon <Can>
Nyasa <Malawi, Mozambique, Tanzania>
Okeechobee <US>
Ontario <US, Can>
Pontchartrain <US>
Reindeer <Can>
St. Clair <US, Can>
Superior <US, Can>
Tahoe <US>
Tanganyika <Tanzania, Congo>
Texcoco <Mexico>
Titicaca <Bolivia, Peru>
Utah <US>
Victoria <Tanzania, Uganda>
Volta <Ghana>
Winnebago <US>
Winnipeg <Can>
Yellowstone <US>
Zurich <Switzerland>

242 INLET, GULF

<arm of larger or smaller body of water>

NOUNS **1 inlet, cove,** creek <Brit>, arm of the sea, arm, armlet, canal, reach, loch <Scot>, **bay, gulf,** sound; fjord, fiord, bight; estuary, firth, frith, bayou, mouth, outlet, *boca* <Sp>; harbor, natural harbor; road, roads, roadstead; strait, straits, kyle <Scot>, narrow, narrows, euripus, belt, gut, narrow seas

ADJS **2** gulfy, gulflike; gulfed, bayed, embayed; estuarine, fluviomarine, tidewater

3 major bays and gulfs

Baffin Bay <North America>
Bay of Bengal <Asia>
Bay of Biscay <Europe>
Bay of Campeche <North America>
Bay of Fundy <North America>
Bay of Naples <Europe>
Bay of Ob <Asia>
Bay of Quinte <North America>
Bay of Whales <Antarctica>
Botany Bay <Australia>
Buzzards Bay <North America>
Cape Cod Bay <North America>
Chesapeake Bay <North America>
Delaware Bay <North America>
Galveston Bay <North America>
Great Australian Bight <Australia>
Green Bay <North America>
Guanabara Bay <South America>
Gulf of Aden <Asia, Africa>
Gulf of Alaska <North America>
Gulf of Aqaba <Asia, Africa>
Gulf of Bothnia <Europe>
Gulf of California <North America>
Gulf of Carpentaria <Australia>
Gulf of Corinth <Europe>
Gulf of Guinea <Africa>
Gulf of Lions <Europe>
Gulf of Maine <North America>
Gulf of Mexico <North America>
Gulf of Oman <Asia>
Gulf of Panama <North America>
Gulf of Siam <Asia>
Gulf of Sidra <Africa>
Gulf of St. Lawrence <North America>
Gulf of Suez <Africa>
Gulf of Thailand <Asia>
Gulf of Tonkin <Asia>
Gulf of Venezuela <South America>
Gulf of Venice <Europe>
Hudson Bay <North America>
Humboldt Bay <North America>
James Bay <North America>
Massachusetts Bay <North America>
Montego Bay <North America>
Narragansett Bay <North America>
Penobscot Bay <North America>
San Diego Bay <North America>
San Francisco Bay <North America>
San Matias Gulf <South America>
Tampa Bay <North America>
Persian Gulf <Asia>
Table Bay <Africa>
Tasman Bay <Australia>

243 MARSH

<soft wet land>

NOUNS 1 **marsh,** marshland, **swamp,** swampland, wetland, fen, fenland, morass, mere, marish, *marais* <Fr>, bog, mire, quagmire, sump, wash, baygall; glade, everglade; slough, swale, wallow, hog wallow, buffalo wallow, sough <Brit>; bottom, bottoms, bottomland, slob land, holm <Brit>, water meadow, meadow; moor, moorland, peat bog; salt marsh; quicksand; taiga; mudflat, mud

VERBS 2 **mire,** bemire, sink in, bog, mire down, bog down, stick in the mud; stodge

ADJS 3 **marshy, swampy,** swampish, moory, moorish, fenny, wetland, marish, paludal, paludous; boggy, boggish, miry, mirish, quaggy, quagmiry, spouty, poachy; muddy; swamp-growing, uliginous

244 QUANTITY

<amount or number of>

NOUNS 1 **quantity,** quantum, amount, whole; mass, bulk, substance, matter, magnitude, amplitude, extent, sum; measure, measurement; strength, force, numbers; full price, full amount, full boat

2 **amount,** quantity, **indefinite quantity** <see list>, large amount, small amount, sum, number, count, group, total, reckoning, measure, parcel, passel, part, portion, clutch, ration, share, issue, allotment, lot, deal; batch, bunch, heap, pack, mess, gob, chunk, hunk, dose

3 **some,** somewhat, something; aught; any, anything

VERBS 4 **quantify,** quantize, count, number off, enumerate, number, rate, fix; parcel, apportion, mete out, issue, allot, divide; increase, decrease, reduce; quantitate, measure; set a quota; massify

ADJS 5 **quantitative,** quantitive, quantified, quantized, measured; some, certain, one; a, an; any

ADVS 6 **approximately,** nearly, some, about, circa; more or less, by and large, upwards of

PREPS 7 **to the amount of,** to the tune of; as much as, all of, no less than, upwards of

8 indefinite quantity

armful, armload
bag, bagful
bargeload
barrel, barrelful
basin, basinful
basket, basketful
bin, binful
bottle, bottleful
bowl, bowlful
box, boxful
bucket, bucketful
bundle
can, canful
cap, capful
carton, cartonful
case, caseful
crate, crateful
cup, cupful
flask, flaskful
glass, glassful
handful
jar, jarful
keg, kegful
kettle, kettleful
lapful
mouthful
mug, mugful
pail, pailful
pitcher, pitcherful
planeful, planeload
plate, plateful
pocketful
pot, potful
roomful
sack, sackful, sackload
scoop, scoopful
shovel, shovelful
spoon, spoonful
tablespoon, tablespoonful
tank, tankful
tankerload
teacup, teacupful

teaspoon, teaspoonful
thimble, thimbleful
truckload
tub, tubful

245 DEGREE

<amount or level measured>

NOUNS 1 **degree, grade,** step, *pas* <Fr>, leap; round, rung, tread, stair; point, mark, peg, tick; notch, cut; plane, level, plateau; period, space, interval; extent, measure, amount, ratio, proportion, stint, standard, height, pitch, reach, remove, compass, range, scale, scope, caliber; shade, shadow, nuance

2 **rank, standing,** level, footing, status, station; position, place, sphere, orbit, echelon; order, estate, precedence, condition; rate, rating; class, caste; hierarchy, power structure; drilldown

3 **gradation,** graduation, grading, staging, phasing, tapering, shading; gradualism

VERBS 4 graduate, **grade,** calibrate; phase in, phase out, taper off, shade off, scale; increase, decrease; change by degrees

ADJS 5 **gradual,** gradational, calibrated, graduated, phased, staged, tapered, scalar; regular, progressive; hierarchic, hierarchical; in scale; proportional

ADVS 6 **by degrees,** degreewise; **gradually,** gradatim; step by step, grade by grade, bit by bit, little by little, inch by inch, inchmeal, drop by drop; a little, fractionally; a little at a time, by slow degrees, by inches; slowly

7 **to a degree**, to some extent, in a way, in a measure, in some measure; somewhat, kind of, sort of, rather, pretty, quite, fairly; a little, a bit; slightly, scarcely, to a small degree; very, extremely, to a great degree

246 MEAN

<middle point between two things>

NOUNS 1 **mean, median,** middle; golden mean; medium, happy medium; middle of the road, middle course, *via media* <L>; middle state, middle ground, middle position, middle level, middle point, middle echelon, midpoint; macrolevel; average, balance, par, normal, norm, social norm, rule, run, generality; mediocrity, averageness, passableness, adequacy; averaging, mediocritization; checks and balances; center

VERBS 2 **average,** average out, split the difference, take the average, strike a balance, pair off, split down the middle; strike a happy medium, hit a happy medium; keep to the middle, avoid extremes; do, just do, pass, barely pass; mediocritize

ADJS 3 **medium,** mean, **intermediate,** intermediary, median, medial, mesial, mid-level, middle-echelon; average, normal, standard, par for the course; middle-of-the-road, moderate, fence-sitting, middle-ground; middling, ordinary, usual, routine, common, mediocre, merely adequate, passing, banal, so-so, vanilla, plain vanilla; central

ADVS 4 **mediumly,** medianly; medially, midway, intermediately, in the mean; centrally

5 **on the average,** in the long run, over the long haul; taking one thing with another, taking all things together, all in all, on the whole, all things considered, on balance; generally

COMBINING FORMS 6 medi-, mes-, mezzo-, semi-

247 GREATNESS

<large in importance or size>

NOUNS 1 **greatness, magnitude,** muchness; amplitude, ampleness, fullness, plenitude, great scope, great, compass, great reach; grandeur, grandness; immensity, enormousness, enormity, vastness, vastitude, tremendousness, expanse, boundlessness, infinity; stupendousness, formidableness, prodigiousness, humongousness; might, mightiness, strength, power, intensity; largeness, hugeness, gigantism, bulk; superiority

2 **glory,** eminence, preeminence, majesty, loftiness, prominence, distinction, outstandingness, consequence, notability, high standing, illustriousness; magnanimity, nobility, sublimity; fame, renown, celebrity; heroism; fifteen minutes of fame

3 **quantity, numerousness**; quantities, much, abundance, copiousness, superabundance, superfluity, profusion, plenty, plenitude; volume, mass, mountain, load; peck, bushel; bag, barrel, ton; world, acre, ocean, sea; flood, spate; multitude, countlessness

4 **lot, lots,** deal, no end of, good deal, great deal, considerable, sight, heap, pile, stack, loads, loadsa, raft, slew, whole slew, spate, wad, batch, mess, mint, peck, pack, pot, tidy sum, quite a little; oodles, gobs, scads, bags, masses, lashings

VERBS 5 **loom, bulk,** loom large, bulk large, stand out; tower, rear, soar, outsoar; tower above, rise above, overtop; exceed, transcend, outstrip; supersize; massify

ADJS 6 **great, grand,** considerable, consequential; mighty, powerful, strong, irresistible, intense; main, maximum, total, full, plenary, comprehensive, exhaustive; grave, serious, heavy, deep

7 **large, immense,** enormous, huge; gigantic,

mountainous, titanic, colossal, mammoth, Gargantuan, gigantesque, monster, monstrous, outsize, sizable, larger-than-life, overgrown, king-size, monumental; massive, massy, weighty, bulky, voluminous; vast, vasty, boundless, infinite, immeasurable, cosmic, astronomical, galactic; spacious, amplitudinous, extensive; tremendous, stupendous, awesome, prodigious, ginormous, humongous; supersized, supersize

8 **much, many,** beaucoup, ample, abundant, copious, generous, overflowing, superabundant, multitudinous, plentiful, numerous, countless

9 **eminent,** prominent, outstanding, standout, high, elevated, towering, soaring, overtopping, exalted, lofty, sublime, illustrious; august, majestic, noble, distinguished; magnificent, magnanimous, heroic, godlike, superb; famous, renowned, lauded, glorious

10 **remarkable,** outstanding, extraordinary, superior, marked, of mark, signal, conspicuous, striking; notable, much in evidence, noticeable, noteworthy; marvelous, wonderful, formidable, exceptional, uncommon, astonishing, appalling, humongous, fabulous, fantastic, incredible, brilliant, egregious

11 <nonformal> **terrific,** terrible, horrible, dreadful, awful, fearful, frightful, deadly; whacking, thumping, rousing, howling; awesome

12 downright, outright, out-and-out; absolute, utter, perfect, **consummate,** superlative, surpassing, the veriest, positive, definitive, classical, pronounced, decided, regular, proper, precious, profound, stark; thorough, thoroughgoing, complete, total; unmitigated, unqualified, unrelieved, unspoiled, undeniable, unquestionable, unequivocal; flagrant, arrant, shocking, shattering, egregious, intolerable, unbearable, unconscionable, glaring, stark-staring, rank, crass, gross

13 **extreme**, radical, out of this world, way-out, far out, too much; greatest, furthest, most, utmost, uttermost, the max; ultra, ultra-ultra; at the height, at the peak, at the limit, at the summit, at the zenith

14 **undiminished,** unabated, unreduced, unrestricted, unretarded, unmitigated

ADVS 15 **greatly, largely,** to a large extent, to a great extent, in great measure, on a large scale; much, muchly, pretty much, very much, mucho, jolly well, so, so very much, ever so much, ever so, never so; considerably, considerable; abundantly, plenty, no end of, no end, not a little, galore, a lot, a deal, a great deal, *beaucoup* <Fr>; highly, to the skies; like all creation, as all creation, like all get-out, as all get-out, in spades, with bells on, with bells on one's toes; undiminishedly, unabatedly, unreducedly, unrestrictedly, unretardedly, unmitigatedly

16 **vastly,** immensely, enormously, hugely, tremendously, gigantically, galactically, colossally, titanically, prodigiously, stupendously, humongously

17 **by far,** far and away, far, far and wide, by a long way, by a great deal, by a long shot, by a long chalk, out and away, by all odds

18 **very,** exceedingly, awfully, terribly, terrifically, quite, just, so, really, real, right, pretty, only too, mightily, mighty, almighty, powerfully, powerful

19 <in a positive degree> **positively**, decidedly, clearly, manifestly, unambiguously, patently, obviously, visibly, unmistakably, unquestionably, observably, noticeably, demonstrably, sensibly, quite; certainly, actually, really, truly, basically, verily, undeniably, indubitably, without doubt, assuredly, indeed, for a certainty, for real, seriously, in all conscience, posilutely

20 <in a marked degree> **intensely,** acutely, exquisitely, exceptionally, surpassingly, superlatively, eminently, preeminently; remarkably, markedly, notably, strikingly, signally, emphatically, pointedly, prominently, conspicuously, pronouncedly, impressively, famously, glaringly; particularly, singularly, peculiarly; uncommonly, extraordinarily, unusually; wonderfully, wondrous, amazingly, magically, surprisingly, astonishingly, marvelously, exuberantly, incredibly, awesomely; abundantly, richly, profusely, amply, generously, copiously; magnificently, splendidly, nobly, worthily, magnanimously

21 <in a distressing degree> **distressingly,** sadly, sorely, bitterly, piteously, grievously, miserably, cruelly, woefully, lamentably, balefully, dolorously, shockingly; terribly, awfully, dreadfully, frightfully, horribly, abominably, painfully, excruciatingly, torturously, agonizingly, deathly, deadly, something awful, something fierce, something terrible, in the worst way, within an inch of one's life; shatteringly, staggeringly; excessively, exorbitantly, extravagantly, inordinately, preposterously; unduly, improperly, intolerably, unbearably; inexcusably, unpardonably, unconscionably; flagrantly, blatantly, egregiously; unashamedly, unabashedly, baldly, nakedly, brashly, openly; **cursedly,** confoundedly, **damnably,** deucedly, infernally, hellishly

22 <in an extreme degree> **extremely,** utterly, totally, in the extreme, most; mondo; immeasurably, incalculably, indefinitely, infinitely; beyond compare, beyond comparison, beyond measure, beyond all bounds, all out, flat out, full-on;

perfectly, absolutely, essentially, fundamentally, radically; purely, completely, to the max; unconditionally, with no strings attached, unequivocally, downright, dead; with a vengeance

23 <in a violent degree> **violently,** furiously, hotly, fiercely, severely, desperately, madly, like mad; wildly, demonically, like one possessed, frantically, frenetically, fanatically, uncontrollably

COMBINING FORMS **24** meg-, mega-, multi-, super-, uber-

248 INSIGNIFICANCE

<small in importance or size>

NOUNS **1 insignificance,** inconsiderableness, unimportance, inconsequentialness, inconsequentiality, lowness, pettiness, meanness, triviality, nugacity, nugaciousness; smallness, tininess, diminutiveness, minuteness, exiguity, exiguousness; slightness, moderateness, scantiness, puniness, picayunishness, meagerness; daintiness, delicacy; littleness; fewness; insufficiency

2 modicum, minim; **minimum**; little, bit, little bit, wee bit, tiny bit, bite, particle, fragment, spot, speck, flyspeck, fleck, point, dot, jot, tittle, iota, ounce, dab, mote, mite; whit, ace, hair, scruple, groat, farthing, pittance, dole, trifling amount, smidgen, skosh, smitch, scooch, pinch, gobbet, dribble, driblet, dram, drop, drop in a bucket, drop in the ocean, tip of the iceberg; grain, granule, pebble; molecule, atom; thimbleful, spoonful, handful, nutshell; trivia, minutiae; dwarf

3 scrap, tatter, smithereen, patch, stitch, shred, tag; snip, snippet, snick, chip, nip; splinter, sliver, shiver; morsel, *morceau* <Fr>, crumb

4 hint, *soupçon* <Fr>, suspicion, suggestion, intimation; tip of the iceberg; trace, touch, dash, cast, smattering, sprinkling; tinge, tincture; taste, lick, smack, sip, sup, smell; look, thought, idea; shade, shadow; gleam, spark, scintilla

5 hardly anything, mere nothing, next to nothing, less than nothing, trifle, bagatelle, a drop in the bucket, a drop in the ocean; the shadow of a shade, the suspicion of a suspicion

ADJS **6 insignificant,** small, inconsiderable, inconsequential, negligible, no great shakes, footling, one-horse, pint-size, vest-pocket; unimportant, no skin off one's nose, trivial, trifling, nugacious, nugatory, petty, mean, niggling, piddling, picayune, picayunish, of no account, nickel-and-dime, penny-ante, Mickey Mouse; shallow, depthless, cursory, superficial, skin-deep; little, tiny, weeny, miniature, meager, few; short; low

7 dainty, delicate, gossamer, diaphanous; subtle, subtile, tenuous, thin, rarefied

8 mere, sheer, stark, bare, barebones, plain, simple, unadorned, unenhanced

ADVS **9** <in a small degree> **scarcely,** hardly, not hardly, barely, only just, by a hair, by an ace, by a jot, by a whit, by an iota, slightly, lightly, exiguously, fractionally, scantily, inconsequentially, insignificantly, negligibly, imperfectly, minimally, inappreciably, little; minutely, meagerly, triflingly, faintly, weakly, feebly; a little, a bit, just a bit, to a small extent, on a small scale; ever so little, as little as may be

10 <in a certain or limited degree> **to a degree,** to a certain extent, to some degree, in some measure, to such an extent; moderately, mildly, somewhat, detectably, just visibly, modestly, appreciably, visibly, fairly, tolerably, partially, partly, part, in part, partway, part of the way, incompletely, not exhaustively, not comprehensively; comparatively, relatively; merely, simply, purely, only; at least, at the least, leastwise, at worst, at any rate; at most, at the most, at best, at the outside; in a manner, in a manner of speaking, in a way, after a fashion; so far, thus far

11 <in no degree> **no way,** in your dreams, noways, nowise, in no wise, in no case, in no respect, by no means, by no manner of means, on no account, not on any account, not for anything in the world, for beans, under no circumstances, at no hand, nohow, not in the least, not much, not at all, never, not by a damn sight, not by a long shot; not nearly, nowhere near; not a bit, not a bit of it, not a whit, not a speck, not a jot, not an iota, jack squat

249 SUPERIORITY

<state of high quality>

NOUNS **1 superiority, preeminence,** greatness, lead, pride of place, transcendence, transcendency, ascendancy, ascendance, prestige, favor, prepotence, prepotency, preponderance; predominance, predominancy, hegemony; precedence, priority, prerogative, privilege, right-of-way; excellence, virtuosity, high caliber, inimitability, incomparability; seniority, deanship; clout, pull; success, accomplishment, skill

2 advantage, vantage, odds, leg up, inside track, pole position; **upper hand,** whip hand, trump hand; start, head start, flying start, running start; edge, bulge, jump, drop; card up one's sleeve, ace in the hole, something extra, something in reserve; vantage ground, vantage point, coign of vantage, high ground; one-upmanship

3 supremacy, primacy, paramountcy, first place, height, acme, zenith, be-all and end-all, summit, top spot; sovereignty, rule, hegemony, control; kingship, dominion, lordship, imperium, world power; command, sway; mastery, mastership; leadership, headship, presidency; authority, directorship, management, jurisdiction, power, say, last word; influence; effectiveness; maximum, highest, most, *ne plus ultra* <Fr, no more beyond>, the max; championship, crown, laurels, palms, first prize, blue ribbon, new high, record

4 superior, chief, head, boss, employer, honcho, commander, ruler, leader, dean, *primus inter pares* <L>, first among equals, master; higher-up, senior, principal, big shot; superman, genius; prodigy, nonpareil, paragon, virtuoso, ace, star, superstar, champion, winner, top dog, top banana, one in a thousand, one in a million, laureate, fugleman; Cadillac, Rolls-Royce, Mercedes-Benz, Ivy League; A1, A number 1, standout, moneymaker, record-breaker, the greatest, whizbang, world-beater, a tough act to follow; big fish in a small pond; alpha male, alpha female; supremist; equal opportunity employer

5 the best, the top of the line; the best people, nobility; aristocracy, barons, top people, elite, cream, crème de la crème, top of the milk, upper crust, upper class, one's betters; the brass, the VIP's, higher-ups, movers and shakers, lords of creation, ruling circles, establishment, power elite, power structure, ruling class, bigwigs, big boys, authorities, powers that be, officialdom; fast track; happy few, chosen few; limited edition

VERBS **6 excel,** surpass, exceed, transcend, get the ascendancy, have the ascendancy, get the edge, have the edge, have it all over, overcome, overpass, best, better, improve on, perfect, go one better; cap, trump; top, tower above, tower over, overtop; predominate, prevail, preponderate, carry the day; outweigh, overbalance, overbear

7 best, beat, beat out, defeat; beat all hollow, trounce, clobber, take to the cleaners, smoke, skin, skin alive, worst, whip, lick, have it all over, cut down to size; bear the palm, take the cake, bring home the bacon; triumph; **win**; pwn

8 overshadow, eclipse, throw into the shade, top, extinguish, take the shine out of; put to shame, show up, put one's nose out of joint, put down, fake out

9 outdo, outrival, outvie, outachieve, edge out, outclass, outshine, overmatch, outgun; outstrip, outgo, outrange, outreach, outpoint, outperform; outplay, overplay, outmaneuver, outwit; outrun, outstep, outpace, outmarch, run rings around, run circles around; outride, override; outjump, overjump; outleap, overleap

10 outdistance, distance; pass, surpass, overpass; get ahead, pull ahead, shoot ahead, walk away, walk off; leave behind, leave at the post, leave in the dust, leave in the lurch; come to the front, have a healthy lead, hold the field; steal a march

11 rule, command, lead, possess authority, have the authority, have the say, have the last word, have the whip hand, hold all the aces; take precedence, precede; come first, rank first, outrank, rank, rank out; come to the fore, come to the front; play first fiddle, star

ADJS **12 superior,** greater, better, finer; higher, upper, over, super, above; ascendant, in the ascendant, in ascendancy, coming; eminent, outstanding, rare, distinguished, marked, of choice, chosen; surpassing, exceeding, excellent, excelling, rivaling, eclipsing, capping, topping, transcending, transcendent, transcendental, bad; ahead, a cut above, a stroke above, one up on; more than a match for

13 superlative, supreme, greatest, best, highest, veriest, maximal, maximum, most, utmost, outstanding, stickout; top, topmost, uppermost, tiptop, top-level, top-echelon, topnotch, top-of-the-line, first-rate, first-class, jammin', top of the line, highest-quality, best-quality, far and away the best, the best by a long shot, the best by a long chalk, head and shoulders above, of the highest type, A1, A number 1, uber

14 chief, main, principal, paramount, foremost, headmost, leading, dominant, crowning, capital, cardinal; great, arch, banner, master, magisterial; central, focal, prime, primary, primal, first; preeminent, supereminent; predominant, preponderant, prevailing, hegemonic, hegemonical; ruling, overruling; sovereign; topflight, highest-ranking, ranking; star, superstar, stellar, world-class

15 peerless, matchless, champion; unmatched, unmatchable, unrivaled, unparagoned, unparalleled, immortal, unequaled, never-to-be-equaled, unpeered, unexampled, unapproached, unapproachable, unsurpassed, unexcelled; unsurpassable; inimitable, incomparable, beyond compare, beyond comparison, apples to oranges, unique; without equal, without parallel, *sans pareil* <Fr>; in a class by itself, *sui generis* <L>, easily first; second to none, *nulli secundus* <L>; unbeatable, invincible

ADVS **16 superlatively,** exceedingly, surpassingly; eminently, egregiously, prominently; supremely, paramountly, preeminently, the most, transcendently, to crown all, *par excellence* <Fr>;

inimitably, incomparably; to the highest degree, in the highest degree, far and away

17 **chiefly, mainly,** in the main, in chief; dominantly, predominantly; mostly, for the most part; principally, especially, particularly, peculiarly; primarily, in the first place, first of all, above all; indeed, even, yea, still more, more than ever, all the more, *a fortiori* <L>; ever so, never so, no end

18 **peerlessly,** matchlessly, unmatchably; unsurpassedly, unsurpassably; inimitably, incomparably; uniquely, second to none, *nulli secundus* <L>; unbeatably, invincibly

19 **advantageously,** to advantage, with advantage, favorably; melioratively, amelioratively, improvingly

COMBINING FORMS 20 preter-, super-, supra-, sur-, trans-, uber-, ultra-, arch-, prot-

250 INFERIORITY

<state of poor quality>

NOUNS 1 **inferiority, subordinacy,** subordination, secondariness; juniority, minority; subservience, subjection, servility, lowliness, humbleness, humility; back seat, second fiddle, second string, third string, second banana; insignificance

2 **inferior,** underling, understrapper <Brit>, subordinate, subaltern, **junior;** secondary, second fiddle, second stringer, third stringer, benchwarmer, low man on the totem pole, loser, nonstarter; lightweight, follower, pawn, cog, flunky, yes-man, creature; lower class, lower orders, lower ranks, lowlife, commonalty; infrastructure, commonality, hoi polloi, masses; satellite; B-list, C-list, D-list; trailer trash, white trash; Eurotrash

3 **inadequacy,** mediocrity, deficiency, imperfection, insufficiency; incompetence, incompetency, maladroitness, unskillfulness; failure; smallness; littleness; meanness, lowness, baseness, pettiness, triviality, shabbiness, vulgarity; fewness; subnormality

VERBS 4 **be inferior,** not come up to, not measure up, fall short, come up short, fail, not make it, not hack it, not cut the mustard, not make the cut, not make the grade; want, leave much to be desired, be found wanting; not compare, have nothing on, not hold a candle to, not approach, not come near; serve, subserve, rank under, rank beneath, follow, play second fiddle, take a back seat, sit on the bench

5 **bow to,** hand it to, tip the hat to, yield the palm; retire into the shade; give in, lose face; submit

ADJS 6 **inferior,** subordinate, subaltern, sub, small-scale, secondary; **junior, minor;** second string, third string, junior varsity; one-horse, penny-ante, dinky, second rank, third rank, second-rate, third-rate, low in the pecking order, low-rent, downscale, below the salt; subservient, subject, servile, low, lowly, humble, modest, scrub; lesser, less, lower, low-grade, B-list, C-list, D-list; in the shade, thrown into the shade; common, vulgar, ordinary; underprivileged, disadvantaged, nothing to write home about, crummy; beneath one's dignity, beneath one's station, infra dig, demeaning; half-assed, janky, jank

7 **inadequate, mediocre,** deficient, imperfect, insufficient; incompetent, unskillful, maladroit; small, small-time, little, mean, base, petty, trivial, shabby; not to be compared, not comparable, not a patch on; outclassed, outshone, not in it, not in the same league with, out of it, out of the picture, out of the running, left a mile behind

8 **least,** smallest, littlest, slightest, lowest, shortest; minimum, minimal, minim; few; minimalistic; small-batch, small-scale

ADVS 9 **poorly,** incompetently, **inadequately,** badly, maladroitly; least of all, at the bottom of the scale, at the nadir, at the bottom of the heap, in the gutter; beggarly; at a disadvantage

COMBINING FORMS 10 sub-, hyp-, hypo-

251 INCREASE

<become larger or greater>

NOUNS 1 **increase, gain,** augmentation, greatening, enlargement, amplification, growth, development, widening, spread, broadening, elevation, extension, aggrandizement, access, accession, increment, accretion; exponential growth; accretion rate; addition; expansion; inflation, swelling, ballooning, edema, fattening, tumescence, bloating, dilation; multiduplication, proliferation, productiveness; accruement, accrual, accumulation; advance, appreciation, ascent, mounting, crescendo, waxing, snowballing, rise, raise, boost, hike, up, upping, buildup; upturn, uptick, uptrend, upsurge, upswing; leap, jump; flood, surge, gush; ramp-up

2 **intensification, heightening,** deepening; tightening, turn of the screw; strengthening, beefing-up, enhancement, magnification, blowup, blowing up, exaggeration; aggravation, exacerbation, heating-up; concentration, condensation, consolidation; reinforcement, redoubling; pickup, step-up, acceleration, speedup, accelerando, escalation, upsurge; boom, explosion, baby boom, population explosion, information explosion

3 **gains,** winnings, cut, take, increase, profits

VERBS **4** **increase,** enlarge, aggrandize, amplify, amp, augment, extend, maximize, add to; expand, inflate; lengthen, broaden, fatten, fill out, thicken; raise, exalt, boost, hike, hike up, jack up, jump up, bump up, crank up, mark up, put up, up; build, build up; pyramid, parlay; progress

5 **intensify, heighten**, deepen, amplify, enhance, strengthen, beef up, aggravate, exacerbate; exaggerate, blow up, puff up, magnify; whet, sharpen; reinforce, double, redouble, triple; concentrate, condense, consolidate; complicate, ramify, make complex; give a boost to, step up, accelerate; key up, hop up, soup up, jazz up; add fuel to the fire, heat up, hot up; kick it up a notch, ramp up

6 **grow, increase,** advance, appreciate; spread, widen, broaden; gain, get ahead; wax, swell, balloon, bloat, mount, rise, go up, crescendo, snowball, skyrocket, mushroom; intensify, develop, gain strength, strengthen; accrue, accumulate; multiply, proliferate, breed, teem; run up, shoot up, boom, explode

ADJS **7** **increased, heightened,** raised, elevated, stepped-up; **intensified,** deepened, reinforced, strengthened, fortified, beefed-up, tightened, stiffened; enlarged, extended, augmented, aggrandized, amplified, enhanced, boosted, hiked; broadened, widened, spread; magnified, inflated, expanded, swollen, bloated; multiplied, proliferated; **accelerated,** hopped-up, jazzed-up, cranked up

8 **increasing, rising,** fast-rising, skyrocketing, meteoric; on the upswing, on the increase, on the rise; crescent, waxing, growing, fast-growing, flourishing, burgeoning, blossoming, swelling, lengthening, multiplying, proliferating; spreading, spreading like a cancer, spreading like wildfire, expanding; tightening, intensifying; incremental; crescendoing, snowballing, mushrooming, growing like a mushroom

ADVS **9** **increasingly,** growingly, more, more and more, on and on, greater and greater, evermore; in a crescendo

252 DECREASE

<become smaller>

NOUNS **1** **decrease,** decrescence, decrement, diminishment, diminution, **reduction,** lessening, lowering, waning, shrinking, shrinkage, withering, withering away, scaling down, scaledown, downsizing, build-down; miniaturization; downplaying, underplaying; depression, damping, dampening; letup, abatement, easing, easing off, slackening; de-escalation; alleviation, relaxation, mitigation; attenuation, extenuation, weakening, sagging, dying, dying off, dying away, trailing off, tailing off, tapering off, fade-out, languishment; depreciation, deflation; deduction; subtraction, abridgment; contraction; simplicity

2 **decline,** declension, subsidence, slump, lapse, drop, downtick; collapse, crash; dwindling, wane, ebb; downturn, downtrend, downward trend, downward curve, retreat, remission; fall, plunge, dive, decline and fall; decrescendo, diminuendo; catabasis, deceleration, slowdown; leveling off, bottoming out

3 decrement, waste, **loss,** dissipation, wear and tear, erosion, ablation, wearing away, depletion, corrosion, attrition, attrition rate, consumption, shrinkage, exhaustion; deliquescence, dissolution; extinction

4 **curtailment,** retrenchment, cut, cutback, drawdown, rollback, scaleback, pullback; moderation, restraint; abridgment; slash, slashing

5 **minimization,** minification, making light of, devaluing, undervaluing, belittling, belittlement, detraction; abridgment, miniaturization; qualification

VERBS **6** **decrease,** diminish, lessen; let up, bate, abate; decline, subside, shrink, wane, wither, ebb, ebb away, dwindle, languish, sink, sag, die down, die away, wind down, taper off, trail off, trail away, tail off; drop, drop off, dive, take a nosedive, plummet, plunge, fall, fall off, fall away, fall to a low ebb, run low; waste, wear, waste away, wear away, crumble, erode, ablate, corrode, consume, consume away, be eaten away; melt away, deliquesce; become extinct

7 **reduce,** decrease, diminish, lessen, take from; lower, depress, de-escalate, damp, dampen, step down, tune down, phase out, scale back, scale down, roll back; downgrade; depreciate, deflate; curtail, retrench; cut, cut down, cut back, cut down to size, trim away, chip away at, whittle away, whittle down, pare, pare down; deduct; shorten, abridge; compress, shrink, downsize; simplify

8 **abate,** bate, ease; **weaken,** dilute, water, water down, attenuate, extenuate; alleviate, mitigate, slacken, remit; enfeeble, debilitate; tail off, die off

9 **minimize,** minify, **belittle,** detract from; dwarf, bedwarf; play down, underplay, downplay, de-emphasize, tone down, moderate; hush

ADJS **10** **reduced, decreased,** diminished, lowered, dropped, fallen; bated, abated; deflated, contracted, shrunk, shrunken; simplified; back-to-basics, no-frills; dissipated, eroded, consumed, ablated, worn; curtailed, shorn, retrenched, cutback; weakened, attenuated, watered-down, diluted; scaled-down, miniaturized, abridged, pared-down; minimized, belittled, on a downer; lower, less, lesser, smaller, shorter; off-peak; downplayed, underplayed, toned down, de-emphasized

11 **decreasing,** diminishing, lessening, subsiding, declining, languishing, dwindling, waning, on the wane, on the slide, wasting; decrescent, reductive, deliquescent, contractive; diminuendo, decrescendo

ADVS **12** **decreasingly,** diminishingly, less, less and less, ever less; decrescendo, diminuendo; on a declining scale, at a declining rate

253 ADDITION

<process of adding>

NOUNS **1** **addition,** accession, annexation, affixation, suffixation, prefixation, agglutination, attachment, junction, joining, adjunction, uniting; **increase**; augmentation, supplementation, complementation, reinforcement; superaddition, admixture, superposition, superjunction, superfetation, suppletion; juxtaposition; adjunct, add-on, rider, extra, accessory

2 <math terms> plus sign, plus; addend; sum, summation, total, aggregate; subtotal

3 **adding,** totalizing, totalization, toting up, reckoning, computation, calculation, ringing up; adding machine, calculator

VERBS **4** **add,** add on, plus, put with, join with, unite with, bring together, affix, attach, annex, adjoin, append, conjoin, subjoin, prefix, suffix, infix, postfix, tag, tag on, tack on, slap on, hitch on, carry over; glue on, paste on, agglutinate; superpose, superadd; burden, encumber, saddle with; complicate, ornament, decorate

5 **add to,** augment, supplement, append; volumize; increase; reinforce, strengthen, fortify, beef up; recruit, swell the ranks of; superadd

6 **compute,** add up; sum, total, totalize, total up, tot, tot up, tote, tote up, tally, calculate

7 **be added,** advene, supervene

ADJS **8** **additive,** additional, additory; **cumulative,** accumulative; summative, summational; loaded

9 **added,** affixed, add-on, attached, annexed, appended, appendant; adjoined, adjunct, adjunctive, conjoined, subjoined; superadded, superposed, superjoined

10 **additional**, supplementary, supplemental; extra, plus, further, farther, fresh, more, new, other, another, ulterior; auxiliary, ancillary, supernumerary, contributory, accessory, collateral, supererogatory; surplus, spare, superfluous

ADVS **11** **additionally,** in addition, also, and then some, even more, more so, and also, and all, and so, as well, too, else, beside, besides, to boot, not to mention, let alone, into the bargain; on top of, over, above; beyond, plus; extra, on the side, for lagniappe; more, moreover, thereto, farther, further, furthermore, at the same time, then, again, yet; similarly, likewise, by the same token, by the same sign; item; therewith, withal; all included, altogether; among other things, *inter alia* <L>

PREPS **12** with, **plus, including,** inclusive of, along with, together with, coupled with, in conjunction with; as well as, to say nothing of, not to mention, let alone; over and above, in addition to, added to, linked to; with the addition of, attended by; kitchen-sink

CONJS **13** **and, also,** and also

PHRS **14** **et cetera,** and so forth, and so on, and so forth and so on; et al, *et alii* <L>, and all, and others, and other things; and everything else, and more of the same, and the rest, and the like; blah blah blah blah, dah-dah dah-dah dah-dah, and suchlike, and so on and so forth, and all that sort of thing, and all that, and all like that, and stuff like that, and all that jazz; yada yada, yadda yadda, yadda yadda yadda; and what not, and what have you, and I don't know what, and God knows what, and then some, you name it; and the following, *et sequens* <L>, et seq

COMBINING FORMS **15** super-, pleo-, pleio-

254 ADJUNCT

<something added>

NOUNS **1** **adjunct, addition,** increase, increment, augmentation, supplementation, complementation, *additum* <L>, additament, additory, addendum, addenda <pl>, accession, fixture; annex, annexation; appendage, appendant, pendant, appanage, tailpiece, coda; undergirding, reinforcement; appurtenance, appurtenant; accessory, attachment; supplement, complement, continuation, extrapolation, extension; offshoot, side issue, corollary, sidebar, side effect, spinoff, aftereffect; concomitant, accompaniment, additive, adjuvant; leftover, carryover

2 <written text> **postscript** (P.S.), **appendix;** rider, allonge, codicil; epilogue, envoi, coda, tail, afterword; back matter, front matter; note, marginalia, scholia, side note, commentary, annotation, footnote; interpolation, interlineation;

affix, prefix, suffix, infix; subscript, superscript; enclitic, proclitic

3 <building> wing, **addition,** annex, extension, ell, L, outhouse, outbuilding

4 **extra, bonus,** signing bonus, retention bonus, premium, hazard pay, something extra, extra dash, little extra, extra added attraction, lagniappe, something into the bargain, something for good measure, baker's dozen; peripheral; added value; padding, stuffing, filling; trimming, frill, flourish, filigree, decoration, ornament; bells and whistles; superaddition; fillip, wrinkle, twist; the works; benefit, perquisite, perk; freebie

255 SUBTRACTION

<process of taking away>

NOUNS **1** **subtraction, deduction,** subduction, removal, taking away; abstraction, ablation, sublation; erosion, abrasion, wearing, wearing away; refinement, purification; detraction

2 **reduction, diminution,** decrease, build-down, phasedown, drawdown, decrement, impairment, cut, cutting, curtailment, shortening, truncation; shrinkage, depletion, attrition, remission; depreciation, detraction, disparagement, derogation; retraction, retrenchment; extraction

3 **excision,** abscission, rescission, extirpation; elimination, exclusion, extinction, eradication, destruction, annihilation; cancellation, write-off, erasure; circumcision; amputation, mutilation

4 **castration,** gelding, emasculation, deballing, altering, fixing, spaying

5 <written text> **deletion,** erasure, cancellation, omission; editing, blue-penciling, striking, striking out; expurgation, bowdlerization, censoring, censorship; abridgment, abbreviation

6 <math terms> difference; subtrahend, minuend; negative; minus sign, minus

7 <thing subtracted> **deduction,** decrement, minus; refund, rebate

8 <result> **difference, remainder**, epact, discrepancy, net, balance, surplus, deficit, credit; contradistinction

VERBS **9** **subtract, deduct,** subduct, take away, take from, remove, withdraw, abstract, debit, dock; reduce, shorten, curtail, retrench, lessen, diminish, decrease, phase down, impair, bate, abate; depreciate, disparage, detract, derogate; erode, abrade, eat away, wear away, rub away, file away; extract, leach, drain, wash away; thin, thin out, weed; refine, purify

10 **excise,** cut out, cut, extirpate, enucleate; cancel, write off; eradicate, root out, wipe out, stamp out, eliminate, kill, kill off, liquidate, annihilate, knock off, destroy, extinguish; exclude, except, take out, cancel out, censor out, bleep out, rule out, bar, ban; set aside, set apart, isolate, pick out, cull; cut off, cut away, shear off, take off, strike off, lop off, truncate; minus; amputate, mutilate, abscind; prune, pare, peel, clip, crop, bob, dock, lop, nip, shear, shave, strip, strip off, strip away

11 **castrate,** geld, emasculate, eunuchize, neuter, spay, fix, alter, unsex, desex, deball; caponize; unman; sterilize

12 <written text> **delete,** erase, expunge, cancel, omit; **edit,** edit out, blue-pencil; strike, strike out, strike off, rub out, blot out, cross out, X out, cross off, kill, cut; void, rescind; censor, bowdlerize, expurgate; abridge, abbreviate

ADJS **13** **subtractive,** reductive, deductive, extirpative; ablative, erosive; censorial; removable, eradicable

PREPS **14** off, from; **minus,** less, without, excluding, except, excepting, with the exception of, save, leaving out, leaving aside, barring, exclusive of, not counting, exception taken of, discounting

256 REMAINDER

<something left over>

NOUNS **1** **remainder, remains, remnant,** relict, residue, residuum, residual, rest, balance; holdover; leavings, leftovers, oddments; refuse, odds and ends, scraps, rags, rubbish, waste, litter, orts, candle ends; scourings, offscourings; parings, sweepings, filings, shavings, sawdust; chaff, straw, stubble, husks; debris, detritus, ruins; end, fag end; stump, butt, butt end, stub, rump; survival, vestige, trace, hint, shadow, afterimage, afterglow; glut; fossil, relics

2 **dregs, grounds,** lees, dross, slag, draff, scoria, feces; sediment, settlings, deposit, deposits, deposition; precipitate, precipitation, sublimate; alluvium, alluvion, diluvium; overflow; silt, loess, moraine; scum, off-scum, froth; ash, ember, cinder, sinter, clinker; soot, smut

3 **survivor,** heir, successor, inheritor; widow, widower, relict, war widow, orphan; others, those left

4 **excess, surplus,** surplusage, overplus, overage; superfluity, redundancy, pleonasm; something for a rainy day; government surplus, military surplus

VERBS **5** **remain,** be left, be left over, survive, subsist, rest, stay

6 **leave,** leave over, leave behind, bequeath

ADJS **7** **remaining,** surviving, extant, vestigial, over, left, leftover, still around, remnant, remanent, odd, on the shelf; spare, to spare; unused, unconsumed, unutilized; surplus, superfluous; outstanding, unmet, unresolved; net; redundant

8 **residual,** residuary; sedimental, sedimentary

257 SIZE, LARGENESS

<great in size or amount>

NOUNS 1 **size, largeness, bigness,** greatness, vastness, vastitude, magnitude, order of magnitude, amplitude; mass, bulk, volume, body; dimensions, proportions, dimension, caliber, scantling, proportion; measure, measurement, gauge, scale; extent, extension, expansion, expanse, square footage, square yardage, scope, reach, range, ballpark, spread, coverage, area, circumference, ambit, girth, diameter, radius, boundary, border, periphery; linear measure, linear dimension, length, height, depth, procerity, breadth, width; wheelbase, wingspan

2 **capacity, volume,** content, holding capacity, cubic footage, cubic yardage, accommodation, room, space, measure, limit, burden; gallonage, tankage; poundage, tonnage, cordage; stowage; quantity

3 **full size,** full growth; lifesize

4 large size, extra extra large size, extra large size, economy size, family size, king size, California king size, queen size, giant size, plus size, 1X, 2X, 3X

5 **oversize,** outsize; overlargeness, overbigness; overgrowth, wild growth, uncontrolled growth, overdevelopment, sprawl; overweight, overheaviness; overstoutness, overfatness, overplumpness, bloat, bloatedness, obesity, chubbiness; gigantism, giantism, titanism; hyperplasia, hypertrophy, acromegalic gigantism, acromegaly, pituitary gigantism, normal gigantism

6 <large size> **sizableness,** largeness, bigness, greatness, grandness, grandeur, grandiosity; largishness, biggishness; voluminousness, capaciousness, generousness, copiousness, ampleness; tallness, toweringness; broadness, wideness; profundity; extensiveness, expansiveness, comprehensiveness; spaciousness; bagginess

7 <very large size> **hugeness,** vastness, vastitude; humongousness; enormousness, immenseness, enormity, immensity, tremendousness, prodigiousness, stupendousness, mountainousness; gigantism, giganticness, giantism, giantlikeness; monumentalism; monstrousness, monstrosity

8 **corpulence, obesity,** stoutness, largeness, bigness, *embonpoint* <Fr>; fatness, fattishness, adiposis, adiposity, endomorphy, fleshiness, beefiness, meatiness, heftiness, grossness; plumpness, buxomness, rotundity, fubsiness, tubbiness, roly-poliness; pudginess, podginess; chubbiness, chunkiness, stockiness, squattiness, squatness, dumpiness, portliness; paunchiness, bloatedness, puffiness, pursiness, blowziness; middle-age spread; weight problem; hippiness; steatopygia, steatopygy; bosominess, bustiness; double chin

9 **bulkiness, bulk,** hulkingness, hulkiness, massiveness, lumpishness, clumpishness; ponderousness, cumbrousness, cumbersomeness; clumsiness, awkwardness, unwieldiness, clunkiness

10 **lump,** clump, hunk, chunk, wodge; mass, piece, gob, glob, gobbet, dollop, cluster, gobs; batch, wad, heap, block, loaf; pat; clod; nugget; quantity

11 <something large> **whopper,** thumper, lunker, whale, jumbo; monster, hulk; large part, bulk, mass, lion's share, majority, better part

12 <corpulent person> **heavyweight,** pig, porker, heavy, human mountain; big person, large person; fat person, fatty, fatso, roly-poly, tub, tub of lard, tun, tun of flesh, whale, blimp, hippo, potbelly, gorbelly, swagbelly, dumpling, lardass

13 **giant** <see list>, giantess, amazon, colossus, titan, titaness, brute, hulk; long drink of water

14 **behemoth,** leviathan, monster; mammoth, mastodon; elephant, jumbo; whale; hippopotamus, hippo; dinosaur

VERBS 15 **size,** adjust, grade, group, range, rank, graduate, sort, match; gauge, measure, proportion; bulk; enlarge; fatten

ADJS 16 **large, sizable,** big, great, grand, tall, considerable, goodly, healthy, tidy, substantial, bumper; as big as all outdoors; numerous; largish, biggish; large-scale, larger than life; man-sized; large-size, large-sized, king-size, queen-size, plus-size; economy-size, family-size; good-sized, life-size, life-sized, jumbo, super-jumbo

17 **voluminous,** capacious, generous, ample, copious, broad, wide, extensive, expansive, comprehensive; spacious

18 **corpulent,** stout, fat, overweight, fattish, **obese,** adipose, gross, fleshy, beefy, meaty, hefty, porky, porcine; paunchy, paunched, bloated, puffy, blowzy, distended, swollen, pursy; abdominous, big-bellied, full-bellied, potbellied, gorbellied, swag-bellied, pot-gutted, pussle-gutted, plump, buxom, zaftig, pleasantly plump, full, huggy, rotund, fubsy, tubby, roly-poly; pudgy, podgy; thickbodied, thick-girthed, heavyset, thickset, chubby, chunky, stocky, squat, squatty, dumpy, square; pyknic, endomorphic; stalwart, brawny, burly; lusty, strapping; portly, imposing; full-figured; well-fed, corn-fed, grain-fed;

chubby-faced, round-faced, moonfaced; hippy, full-buttocked, steatopygic, steatopygous, fat-assed, lard-assed, broad in the beam, well-upholstered; bosomy, full-bosomed, chesty, busty, top-heavy; plump as a dumpling, plump as a partridge, fat as a quail, fat as a pig, fat as a hog, fat as bacon, XL, XXL

19 **bulky,** hulky, hulking, lumpish, lumpy, lumping, clumpish, lumbering, lubberly; massive, massy; elephantine, hippopotamic; ponderous, cumbrous, cumbersome; clumsy, awkward, unwieldy; clunky

20 **huge,** immense, vast, enormous, astronomic, astronomical, humongous, jumbo, king-size, queen-size, tremendous, prodigious, stupendous, macro, mega, giga; great big, larger than life, Homeric, mighty, titanic, colossal, monumental, heroic, heroical, epic, epical, towering, mountainous; profound, abysmal, deep as the ocean, deep as China; monster, monstrous; mammoth, mastodonic; gigantic, giant, giantlike, gigantesque, gigantean; cyclopean, brobdingnagian, gargantuan, herculean; elephantine; dinosaurian, dinotherian; infinite

21 <nonformal> **whopping,** walloping, whaling, whacking, spanking, slapping, lolloping, thumping, thundering, bumping, banging

22 **full-sized,** full-size, full-scale; full-grown, full-fledged, full-blown; full-formed, life-sized, large as life, larger than life; legal-sized

23 **oversize,** oversized; outsize, outsized, giant-size, king-size, queen-size, record-size, extra-large (XL), extra extra large (XXL), family-sized, overlarge, overbig, too big; overgrown, overdeveloped; overweight, overheavy; overfleshed, overstout, overfat, overplump, overfed, obese

24 this big, so big, yay big, this size, about this size, of that order

ADVS 25 largely, on a large scale, in a big way; in the large; as can be

COMBINING FORMS 26 hyper-, macr-, macro-, maxi-, meg-, mega-, megal-, megalo-, super-

27 **giant**

Abominable Snowman, yeti
Aegir
Alifanfaron
Amazon
Antaeus
Ascapart
Atlas
Balan
Bellerus
Big Foot, Sasquatch, Omah
Blunderbore
Briareüs
Brobdingnagian
Colossus
Cormoran
Cottus
Cyclops
Enceladus
Ephialtes
Ferragus
Galligantus
Gargantua
Godzilla
Gog
Goliath
Hercules, Heracles
Hymir
Jötunn
King Kong
Magog
Mimir
Og
Orion
Pantagruel
Patagonian
Paul Bunyan
Polyphemus
Titan
Tityus
Typhon
Ymir

258 LITTLENESS

<small in size or amount>

NOUNS 1 **littleness, smallness,** smallishness, diminutiveness, miniatureness, slightness, exiguity; puniness, pokiness, dinkiness; tininess, minuteness; undersize; petiteness; dwarfishness, stuntedness, runtiness, shrimpiness; shortness; scantiness; small scale; compactness, portability; miniaturization, microminiaturization, microscopy, micrography

2 **infinitesimalness;** undetectability, inappreciability, evanescence; intangibility, impalpability, tenuousness, imponderability; imperceptibility, invisibility

3 <small space> **tight spot**, corner, squeeze, pinch, not enough room to swing a cat; hole, pigeonhole; hole-in-the-wall; cubby, cubbyhole; dollhouse, playhouse, doghouse; no room to swing a cat

4 <small person or creature> **runt,** shrimp, wart, diminutive, wisp, chit, slip, snip, snippet, peanut, peewee, wee thing, pipsqueak, squirt, half pint, shorty, fingerling, small fry, dandiprat, tiddler; lightweight, featherweight; bantam, banty; pony; minnow, mini, minny; mouse, titmouse; nubbin, button

5 <creature small by species or birth> **dwarf,** dwarfling, midget, midge, pygmy, manikin, homunculus, atomy, micromorph, hop-o'-my-thumb; elf, gnome, brownie, hobbit, leprechaun; Lilliputian, Pigwiggen, Tom Thumb, Thumbelina, Alberich, Alviss, Andvari, Nibelung, Regin

6 **miniature,** mini; scaled-down version, miniaturized version; microcosm, microcosmos; baby; doll, puppet, toy; microvolume; Elzevir, Elzevir edition; duodecimo, twelvemo, pocket edition

7 <minute thing> **minutia**, **minutiae** <pl>, minim, drop, droplet, mite, point, vanishing point, mathematical point, point of a pin, pinpoint, pinhead, dot; mote, fleck, speck, flyspeck, jot, tittle, jot nor tittle, iota, trace, trace amount,

suspicion, *soupçon* <Fr>; particle, crumb, scrap, bite, snip, snippet; grain, grain of sand; barleycorn, millet seed, mustard seed; midge, gnat; microbe, microorganism, amoeba, bacillus, bacteria, diatom, germ, paramecium, protozoon, zoospore, animalcule, plankton, virus; cell; microchip; pixel

8 **atom,** atomy, monad; **molecule,** ion; nucleus; **electron,** proton, meson, neutrino, muon, quark, parton, subatomic particle, nuclear particle

VERBS **9** **make small,** contract; shorten; miniaturize, minify, minimize, scale down; reduce, scale back; digitize, pixelize

ADJS **10** **little,** small, smallish; slight, exiguous; puny, trifling, poky, piffling, pindling, piddling, piddly, paltry, picayune, dinky, negligible; cramped, limited; one-horse, two-by-four; pintsized, half-pint; knee-high, knee-high to a grasshopper; petite; short

11 **tiny;** teeny, teeny-weeny, eentsy-weentsy, wee, peewee, bitty, bitsy, little-bitty, little-bitsy, itsy-bitsy, itsy-witsy, dinky; minute, fine

12 **miniature, diminutive,** minuscule, minuscular, mini, micro, miniaturized, subminiature, minikin, small-scale, minimal; pony, bantam, banty; baby, baby-sized; bite-sized, child-sized; pocket, pocket-sized, pocket-size, vest-pocket; small-sized; fun-sized; toy; handy, compact, portable; duodecimo, twelvemo; nanosized, digitized, pixelated

13 **dwarf,** dwarfed, dwarfish, pygmy, midget, nanoid, elfin; Lilliputian, Tom Thumb; undersized, undersize, squat, dumpy; stunted, undergrown, runty, pint-size, pint-sized, sawed-off; shrunk, shrunken, wizened, shriveled; meager, scrubby, scraggy; rudimentary, rudimental

14 **infinitesimal, microscopic,** ultramicroscopic; evanescent, thin, tenuous; inappreciable; impalpable, imponderable, intangible; imperceptible, indiscernible, invisible, unseeable; atomic, subatomic; molecular; granular, corpuscular, microcosmic, microcosmical; embryonic, germinal

15 **microbic,** microbial, microorganic; animalcular, bacterial; microzoic; protozoan, microzoan; amoebic, amoeboid

ADVS **16** **small,** little, slightly, fractionally; on a small scale, in a small compass, in a small way, on a minuscule scale, on an infinitesimal scale; in miniature, in the small; in a nutshell

COMBINING FORMS **17** micr-, micro-, ultramicr-, ultramicro-; granul-, granulo-, granuli-, chondr-, chondro-; -cle, -ee, -een, -el, -ella, -illa, -et, -ette, -idium, -idion, -ie, -y, -ey, -ium, -kin, -let, -ling, -ock, -sy, -ula, -ule, -ulum, -ulus

259 EXPANSION, GROWTH

<increase in size>

NOUNS **1** **expansion, extension,** enlargement, increase, uptick, crescendo, upping, raising, hiking, magnification, aggrandizement, amplification, ampliation, broadening, widening; spread, spreading, sprawl, creeping, fanning out, dispersion, ripple effect; buildout; flare, splay, ramification; deployment; augmentation, addition; adjunct

2 **distension,** stretching; **inflation,** sufflation, blowing up; dilation, dilatation, dilating; diastole; swelling, swell; puffing, puff, puffiness, bloating, bloat, flatulence, flatulency, flatus, gassiness, windiness; turgidity, turgidness, turgescence; tumidness, tumidity, tumefaction; tumescence, intumescence; swollenness, bloatedness; dropsy, edema; tympanites, tympany, tympanism

3 **growth,** development; bodily development, maturation, maturing, coming of age, growing up, upgrowth; vegetation; reproduction, procreation, germination, pullulation; burgeoning, sprouting; budding, gemmation; outgrowth, excrescence; overgrowth

VERBS **4** <make larger> **enlarge,** expand, extend, widen, broaden, build, build up, aggrandize, amplify, crescendo, magnify, increase, augment, add to, add in, raise, up, scale up, hike, hike up; develop, bulk, bulk up; stretch, distend, dilate, swell, inflate, sufflate, blow up, puff up, huff, puff, bloat; pump, pump up; rarefy

5 <become larger> enlarge, **expand**, extend, increase, greaten, crescendo, develop, widen, broaden, bulk; stretch, distend, dilate, swell, swell up, swell out, puff up, puff out, pump up, bloat, tumefy, balloon, fill out; snowball

6 **spread,** spread out, outspread, outstretch; expand, extend, widen; open, open up, unfold; flare, flare out, broaden out, splay; spraddle, sprangle, sprawl; branch, branch out, ramify; fan, fan out, disperse, deploy; spread like wildfire; overrun, overgrow

7 **grow, develop**, wax, increase; gather, brew; grow up, mature, spring up, ripen, come of age, shoot up, sprout up, upshoot, upspring, upsprout, upspear, overtop, tower; burgeon, sprout, blossom, reproduce, procreate, grow out of, germinate, pullulate; vegetate; flourish, thrive, grow like a weed; mushroom; outgrow; overgrow, hypertrophy, overdevelop, grow uncontrollably

8 **fatten,** fat, plump, pinguefy, fill out; **gain weight,** gather flesh, take on weight, put on weight, become overweight; chub out; engross

ADJS 9 **expansive,** extensive; expansional, extensional; expansile, extensile, elastic, stretchy; expansible, inflatable, augmentative; distensive, dilatant; inflationary; developable

10 **expanded,** extended, enlarged, increased, upped, raised, hiked, amplified, ampliate, crescendoed, widened, broadened, built-up, beefed-up

11 **spread, spreading;** sprawling, sprawly; outspread, outstretched, spreadout, stretched-out, drawn-out; open, unfolded, gaping, patulous; widespread, wide-open; flared, spraddled, sprangled, splayed; flaring, flared-out, spraddling, sprangling, splaying; splay; fanned, fanning; fanlike, fan-shaped, fan-shape, flabelliform, deltoid

12 **grown,** full-grown, grown-up, mature, developed, well-developed, fully developed, full-fledged, of age; growing, sprouting, crescent, budding, flowering, florescent, flourishing, blossoming, blooming, burgeoning, fast-growing, thriving; overgrown, hypertrophied, overdeveloped

13 **distended,** dilated, inflated, sufflated, blown up, puffed up, **swollen,** swelled, bloated, turgid, tumid, plethoric, incrassate; puffy, pursy; flatulent, gassy, windy, ventose; tumefacient; dropsical, edematous; enchymatous; fat; puffed out, bouffant, bouffed up, bouffy, stuffed

260 CONTRACTION

<decrease in size>

NOUNS 1 **contraction** <see list>, contracture; systole, syneresis, synizesis, dwindling; **compression,** compressure, pressurizing, pressurization; compacting, compaction, compactedness; condensation, concentration, consolidation, solidification; circumscription, narrowing; reduction, diminuendo, lessening, waning; miniaturization; decrease; abbreviation, curtailment, shortening; constriction, stricture, striction, astriction, strangulation, stenosis, choking, choking off, coarctation; bottleneck, chokepoint, hourglass, hourglass figure, nipped waist, wasp waist; neck, cervix, isthmus, narrow place; astringency, constringency; puckering, pursing; knitting, wrinkling

2 **squeezing,** compression, clamping, clamping down, tightening; pressure, press, crush; pinch, squeeze, tweak, nip; scrunch

3 **shrinking,** shrinkage, atrophy; shriveling, withering; searing, parching, drying, drying up; attenuation, thinning; wasting, consumption, emaciation, emaceration; skin and bones; preshrinking, preshrinkage, Sanforizing <tm>

4 **collapse,** prostration, cave-in; implosion; **deflation**

5 **contractibility**, contractility, compactability, compressibility, condensability, reducibility; collapsibility; shrinkability

6 **contractor**, constrictor, clamp, compressor, compacter, condenser, vise, pincer, squeezer; thumbscrew; astringent, styptic; alum, astringent bitters, styptic pencil; tourniquet

VERBS 7 **contract, compress,** cramp, compact, condense, concentrate, consolidate, solidify; reduce, decrease; abbreviate, curtail, shorten; miniaturize; constrict, constringe, circumscribe, coarct, narrow, draw, draw in, draw together; strangle, strangulate, choke, choke off; pucker, pucker up, purse; knit, wrinkle

8 **squeeze,** compress, clamp, cramp, cramp up, tighten; roll up, wad up, roll up into a ball, scrunch, ensphere; press, pressurize, crush, appress; tense; pinch, tweak, nip

9 **shrink,** shrivel, wither, sear, parch, dry up; wizen, weazen; consume, waste, waste away, attenuate, thin, emaciate, macerate, emacerate; preshrink, Sanforize <tm>

10 **collapse, cave,** cave in, fall in; telescope; fold, fold up; implode; deflate, let the air out of, take the wind out of, flatten; puncture

ADJS 11 **contractive,** contractional, contractible, contractile, compactable; astringent, constringent, styptic; compressible, condensable, reducible; shrinkable; collapsible, foldable; deflationary; consumptive; circumscribable

12 **contracted,** compressed, cramped, compact, compacted, concentrated, condensed, consolidated, solidified, boiled-down; constricted, strangled, strangulated, choked, choked off, coarcted, squeezed, clamped, nipped, pinched, pinched-in, wasp-waisted; puckered, pursed; knitted, wrinkled; miniaturized; scaled-down; shortened, abbreviated

13 **shrunk,** shrunken; shriveled, shriveled up; withered, sear, parched, corky, dried-up; wasted, wasted away, consumed, emaciated, emacerated, thin, attenuated; wizened, wizen, weazened; preshrunk, Sanforized <tm>

14 **deflated,** punctured, flat, holed

15 **contraction**

ain't
aren't
can't
could've
didn't
doesn't
don't
hadn't
hasn't
haven't
he'd
he'll
he's
here's

I'd	they'd
I'll	they'll
I'm	they're
I've	they've
isn't	wasn't
it'll	we'd
it's	we'll
let's	we're
might've	we've
mightn't	weren't
mustn't	what's
oughtn't	who's
shan't	won't
she'd	would've
she'll	wouldn't
she's	you'd
should've	you'll
shouldn't	you're
that's	you've
there's	

261 DISTANCE, REMOTENESS

<space between or away from>

NOUNS 1 **distance, remoteness,** farness, far-offness, longinquity; separation, separatedness, divergence, clearance, margin, leeway; extent, length, space, reach, stretch, range, compass, span, stride, haul, a way, ways, piece; perspective, aesthetic distance, distancing; astronomical distance, interstellar distance, galactic distance, intergalactic distance, deep space, depths of space, infinity; mileage, light-years, parsecs; aloofness, standoffishness

2 **long way,** good ways, great distance, far cry, far piece; long step, tidy step, giant step, giant stride; long run, long haul, long road, long trail, day's march, miles away; marathon; long shot; long range; apogee, aphelion

3 the distance, **remote distance,** offing; horizon, the far horizon, where the earth meets the sky, vanishing point, background

4 **<remote region>** jumping-off place, godforsaken place, God knows where, the middle of nowhere, the back of beyond, nowheresville, the end of the rainbow, Thule, Ultima Thule, Timbuktu, Siberia, Darkest Africa, the South Seas, Pago Pago, the Great Divide, China, Outer Mongolia, pole, antipodes, end of the earth, North Pole, South Pole, Tierra del Fuego, Greenland, Yukon, Pillars of Hercules, remotest corner of the world, four corners of the earth; outpost, outskirts; hinterland; the sticks, the boondocks, the boonies; nowhere; frontier, outback; the moon; outer space

VERBS 5 **reach out,** stretch out, extend, extend out, go, go out, range out, carry out; outstretch, outlie, outdistance, outrange

6 **extend to,** stretch to, stretch away to, reach to, lead to, go to, get to, come to, run to, carry to

7 **keep one's distance, distance oneself,** remain at a distance, maintain distance, maintain clearance, keep at a respectful distance, separate oneself, keep away, stand off, stand away; keep away from, keep clear of, stand clear of, steer clear of, hold away from, give a wide berth to, keep a good leeway, keep a good margin, keep a good offing, keep out of the way of, keep at arm's length, keep a safe distance from, not touch with a ten-foot pole, stay aloof, stand aloof; maintain one's perspective, keep one's esthetic distance

ADJS 8 **distant,** distal, remote, removed, far, far-off, away, faraway, way-off, far-flung, at a distance, exotic, separated, apart, asunder; long-distance, long-range

9 **out-of-the-way,** godforsaken, back of beyond, outlying, upcountry; out of reach, inaccessible, ungetatable, unapproachable, untouchable, hyperborean, antipodean

10 thither, ulterior; yonder, yon; **farther, further,** remoter, more distant; outlying

11 transoceanic, transmarine, ultramarine, oversea, overseas; transatlantic, transpacific; tramontane, transmontane, ultramontane, transalpine; transarctic, transcontinental, transequatorial, transpolar, transpontine, transmundane, ultramundane; offshore

12 **farthest, furthest,** farthermost, farthest off, furthermost, ultimate, extreme, remotest, most distant, terminal

ADVS 13 yonder, yon; **in the distance,** in the remote distance; in the offing, on the horizon, in the background

14 **at a distance,** away, off, aloof, at arm's length; distantly, remotely

15 **far,** far off, far away, afar, afar off, a long way off, a good ways off, a long cry to, as far as the eye can see, out of sight; clear to hell and gone

16 **far and wide,** far and near, distantly and broadly, wide, widely, broadly, abroad; coast-to-coast

17 **apart,** away, aside, wide apart, wide away

18 **out of reach,** beyond reach, out of range, beyond the bounds, out-of-the-way, out of the sphere of; out of sight; out of hearing, out of earshot, out of earreach

19 **wide, clear;** wide of the mark, abroad, all abroad, astray, afield, far afield

PREPS **20** **as far as,** to, all the way to, the whole way to
21 **beyond,** past, over, across, the other side of, the far side of

262 FORM

<having shape>

NOUNS **1** **form, shape,** figure; figuration, configuration; formation, conformation; structure; build, make, frame; arrangement; makeup, format, layout; composition; cut, set, stamp, type, turn, cast, mold, impression, pattern, matrix, model, mode, modality; archetype, prototype, Platonic form, Platonic idea; style, fashion; aesthetic form, inner form, significant form; art form, genre
2 **contour;** broad lines, silhouette, profile, **outline**; organization
3 **appearance**, lineaments, features, physiognomy, cut of one's jib
4 <human form> **figure, form,** shape, frame, anatomy, **physique,** build, body-build, person; body
5 **forming,** shaping, molding, modeling, fashioning, making, making up, formulation; **formation,** conformation, figuration, configuration; sculpture; morphogeny, morphogenesis; creation
6 <grammatical terms> form, morph, allomorph, morpheme; morphology, morphemics
VERBS **7** **form,** formalize, shape, fashion, tailor, frame, figure, lick into shape; work, knead; set, fix; forge, drop-forge; mold, model, sculpt, sculpture; cast, found; thermoform; stamp, mint; carve, whittle, cut, chisel, hew, hew out; roughhew, roughcast, rough out, block out, lay out, sketch out; hammer out, knock out; whomp up, cobble up, cobble together; create; organize, systematize; format, reformat
8 <be formed> **form,** take form, shape, shape up, take shape; materialize
ADJS **9** **formative,** formal, formational, plastic, morphotic; formed, shaped, patterned, fashioned, tailored, framed, structured; forged, molded, modeled, sculpted; cast, founded; stamped, minted; carved, cut, whittled, chiseled, hewn; roughhewn, roughcast, roughed-out, blocked-out, laid-out, sketched-out; hammered-out, knocked-out, cobbled-up; **made, produced**
10 <biological terms> plasmatic, plasmic, protoplasmic, plastic, metabolic
11 <grammatical terms> morphologic, morphological, morphemic
COMBINING FORMS **12** morph-, morpho-, -morph, -morphism, -morphy, -form, -iform, -morphic, -morphous

263 FORMLESSNESS

<having no regular form>

NOUNS **1** **formlessness, shapelessness;** unformedness, amorphousness, amorphism; misshapenness; lack of definition; chaos, confusion, messiness, mess, muddle, orderlessness, untidiness; disorder; entropy; anarchy; indeterminateness, indefiniteness, indecisiveness, vagueness, mistiness, haziness, fuzziness, blurriness, unclearness, obscurity; lumpiness, lumpishness
2 unlicked cub, diamond in the rough, raw material
VERBS **3** **deform,** distort; misshape; unform, unshape; disorder, jumble, mess up, muddle, confuse; obfuscate, obscure, fog up, blur
ADJS **4** **formless, shapeless,** structureless, unstructured, featureless, characterless, nondescript, inchoate, lumpy, lumpish, blobby, baggy, inform; amorphous, amorphic, chaotic, orderless, disorderly, unordered, unorganized, confused, anarchic; kaleidoscopic; indeterminate, indefinite, undefined, indecisive, vague, misty, hazy, fuzzy, blurred, blurry, unclear, obscure; obfuscatory; unfinished, undeveloped
5 **unformed, unshaped,** unshapen, unfashioned, unlicked; unstructured; uncut, unhewn

264 SYMMETRY

<having equal parts or sides>

NOUNS **1** **symmetry,** symmetricalness, **proportion,** proportionality, balance, equilibrium; regularity, uniformity, evenness; equality; finish; harmony, congruity, consistency, conformity, correspondence, keeping; concord; eurythmy, eurythmics; dynamic symmetry; bilateral symmetry, trilateral symmetry, multilateral symmetry; parallelism, polarity; shapeliness
2 **symmetrization**, regularization, balancing, harmonization; evening, equalization; coordination, integration; compensation, playing off, playing off against, posing against, posing over against; counterbalance, balancing act
VERBS **3** symmetrize, regularize, **balance,** balance off, compensate; harmonize; **proportion,** proportionate; even, even up, equalize; coordinate, integrate; play off, play off against
ADJS **4** **symmetric, symmetrical,** balanced, balanced off, proportioned, eurythmic, harmonious, mirror-image; regular, uniform, even, even-steven, equal, equal on both sides, fifty-fifty, square, squared-

off; coequal, coordinate, equilateral, aligned; well-balanced, well-set, well-set-up; finished; enantiomorphic

5 shapely, well-shaped, **well-proportioned,** well-made, well-formed, well-favored; comely; trim, trig, neat, spruce, clean, clean-cut, clean-limbed

265 DISTORTION

<having changing shape>

NOUNS 1 **distortion,** torsion, twist, twistedness, **contortion,** crookedness, tortuosity; asymmetry, unsymmetry, disproportion, lopsidedness, imbalance, irregularity, skewness, deviation; **quirk**, turn, screw, wring, wrench, wrest; warp, buckle; knot, gnarl; anamorphosis; anamorphism

2 **perversion,** corruption, misdirection, misrepresentation, misinterpretation, misconstruction; falsification; twisting, false coloring, bending the truth, spin, spin control, slanting, straining, torturing; misuse; falsehood, travesty; debasement; crime wave

3 **deformity,** deformation, malformation, malconformation, monstrosity, teratology, freakishness, misproportion, misshapenness, misshape; disfigurement, defacement; mutilation, truncation; humpback, hunchback, crookback, camelback, kyphosis; swayback, lordosis; wryneck, torticollis; clubfoot, talipes, flatfoot, splayfoot; knock-knee; bowlegs; valgus; harelip; cleft palate; mutation

4 **grimace,** wry face, wry mouth, rictus, snarl; moue, mow, pout; scowl, frown; squint; tic

VERBS 5 **distort,** contort, turn awry; twist, turn, screw, wring, wrench, wrest; writhe; warp, buckle, crumple; knot, gnarl; crook, bend, spring; put out of kilter

6 **pervert, falsify,** twist, garble, put a false construction upon, give a spin, give a false coloring, color, varnish, slant, strain, torture; put words in someone's mouth; bias; misrepresent, misconstrue, misinterpret, misrender, misdirect; debase; misuse; send the wrong signal, send the wrong message, deliver the wrong signal, deliver the wrong message, lead up the garden path, lead down the garden path; exaggerate

7 **deform,** malform, misshape, twist, torture, disproportion; **disfigure,** deface; mutilate, truncate; blemish, mar

8 **grimace,** make a face, make a wry face, make a wry mouth, pull a face, screw up one's face, mug, mouth, make a mouth, mop, mow, mop and mow; pout

ADJS 9 distortive, contortive, contortional, torsional

10 **distorted,** contorted, warped, twisted, crooked; tortuous, labyrinthine, buckled, sprung, bent, bowed; cockeyed, crazy; crunched, crumpled; unsymmetric, unsymmetrical, asymmetric, asymmetrical, nonsymmetric, nonsymmetrical; irregular, deviative, anamorphous; one-sided, lopsided; awry, askew, off-center, left-of-center, right-of-center, off-target

11 **falsified, perverted,** twisted, garbled, slanted, doctored, biased, crooked; strained, tortured; misrepresented, misquoted; half-true, partially true, falsely colored; creative

12 **deformed, malformed,** misshapen, misbegotten, misproportioned, ill-proportioned, ill-made, ill-shaped, out of shape; dwarfed, stumpy; bloated; disfigured, defaced, blemished, marred; mutilated, truncated; grotesque, monstrous; sway-backed, round-shouldered; bowlegged, bandy-legged, bandy; knock-kneed; rickety, rachitic; clubfooted, talipedic; flatfooted, splayfooted, pigeon-toed; pug-nosed, snub-nosed, simous

13 **humpbacked,** hunchbacked, bunchbacked, crookbacked, crookedbacked, camelback, humped, gibbous, kyphotic

266 STRUCTURE

<having organized form>

NOUNS 1 **structure, construction,** architecture, tectonics, architectonics, frame, make, build, fabric, tissue, warp and woof, warp and weft, web, weave, texture, contexture, mold, shape, pattern, plan, fashion, arrangement, organization; organism, organic structure, constitution, composition; makeup, getup, setup; formation, conformation, format; configuration; making, building, creation, production, forging, fashioning, molding, fabrication, manufacture, shaping, structuring, patterning; anatomy, physique; form; morphology, science of structure; histology, zootomy

2 **structure, building,** edifice, construction, construct, erection, establishment, fabric; house; tower, pile, pyramid, skyscraper, ziggurat; prefabrication, prefab, packaged house; air structure, bubble, air hall <Brit>; superstructure, structural framework; flat-slab construction, post-and-beam construction, steel-cage construction, steel construction; complex; smart building, green building

3 **understructure,** understruction, underbuilding, undercroft, crypt; **substructure,** substruction; infrastructure, underpinning; spread foundation, footing; fill, backfill

4 **frame,** framing; braced framing; **framework,** skeleton, fabric, cadre, chassis, shell, armature;

lattice, latticework, scaffold; sash, casement, case, casing; window case, window casing, window frame, doorframe; picture frame

VERBS 5 **construct**, build; structure; organize; form; erect, raise, put up

ADJS 6 **structural,** formal, morphological, edificial, tectonic, textural; anatomic, anatomical, anatomically correct; organic, organismal, organismic; structured, patterned, shaped, formed; architectural, architectonic; constructional; superstructural, substructural, infrastructural; organizational

267 LENGTH

<longest dimension>

NOUNS 1 **length,** longness, lengthiness, overall length; wheelbase; extent, extension, measure, span, reach, stretch; distance; footage, yardage, mileage; infinity; perpetuity; long time; linear measures; oblongness; longitude

2 a length, **piece,** portion, part; coil, strip, bolt, roll; run

3 **line,** strip, bar, streak; stripe; string

4 **lengthening,** prolongation, elongation, production, protraction; prolixity, prolixness; extension, stretching, stretching out, stringing out, dragging out

VERBS 5 **be long, be lengthy,** extend, be prolonged, stretch, span; stretch out, extend out, reach out; stretch oneself, crane, crane one's neck, rubberneck; stand on tiptoes; outstretch, outreach; sprawl, straggle; last, endure

6 **lengthen, prolong,** prolongate, elongate, extend, expand, produce, protract, continue; make prolix; lengthen out, let out, draw out, drag out, stretch out, string out, spin out; stretch, draw, pull

ADJS 7 **long, lengthy;** longish, longsome; tall; extensive, far-reaching, fargoing, far-flung; sesquipedalian, sesquipedal; unabridged, full-length; as long as one's arm, a mile long; time-consuming, interminable, without end, no end of, no end to, infinite; long-lasting, enduring, long-range

8 **lengthened, prolonged,** prolongated, elongated, extended, protracted; prolix; long-winded; drawn-out, dragged out, long-drawn-out, stretched out, strung out, straggling; stretched, drawn, pulled

9 oblong, oblongated, oblongitudinal, **elongated;** rectangular; elliptical; lengthwise, lengthways, longitudinal

ADVS 10 **lengthily**, extensively, at length, *in extenso* <L>, *ad infinitum* <L>, ad nauseam

11 **lengthwise**, lengthways, longwise, longways, longitudinally, along, in length, at length; **endwise**, endways, endlong; *in extenso* <L>

268 SHORTNESS

<shortest dimension>

NOUNS 1 **shortness, briefness,** brevity; succinctness, curtness, terseness, summariness, compendiousness, compactness; conciseness; littleness; transience, short time, instantaneousness; banker's hours, French hours

2 **stubbiness,** stumpiness, stockiness, fatness, chubbiness, chunkiness, blockiness, squatness, squattiness, dumpiness; pudginess, podginess; snubbiness; lowness

3 **shortening,** abbreviation; reduction; abridgment, condensation, compression, conspectus, epitome, epitomization, summary, summation, summarization, précis, abstract, recapitulation, recap, wrapup, synopsis, encapsulation; curtailment, truncation, retrenchment; telescoping; elision, ellipsis, syncope, apocope; foreshortening; cutback; docking; contraction

4 **shortener**, cutter, abridger; abstracter, epitomizer, epitomist

5 **shortcut,** cut, cutoff; shortest way; beeline, one-touch

VERBS 6 **shorten, abbreviate,** cut; reduce; abridge, condense, compress, contract, boil down, abstract, sum up, summarize, recapitulate, recap, synopsize, epitomize, encapsulate, capsulize; curtail, truncate, retrench; bowdlerize; elide, cut short, cut down, cut off short, cut back, take in; dock, bob, shear, shave, trim, clip, snub, nip; hem; mow, reap, crop; prune, poll, pollard; stunt, check the growth of; telescope; foreshorten

7 **take a shortcut,** shortcut; cut across, cut through; cut a corner, cut corners; make a beeline, take the airline, go as the crow flies

ADJS 8 **short, brief,** abbreviated, abbreviatory, short and sweet; concise; curt, curtal, curtate, decurtate; succinct, summary, synoptic, synoptical, compendious, compact; one-touch; little; low; transient, instantaneous

9 **shortened, abbreviated; abridged,** compressed, zipped, condensed, epitomized, digested, abstracted, capsule, capsulized, encapsulated; bowdlerized; nutshell, vest-pocket; curtailed, cut short, shortcut, docked, bobbed, sheared, shaved, trimmed, clipped, snub, snubbed, nipped; mowed, mown, reaped, cropped; pruned, polled, pollarded; elided, elliptic, elliptical; foreshortened

10 **stubby,** stubbed, stumpy, undergrown, thickset, stocky, blocky, chunky, fat, chubby, tubby, dumpy;

squat, squatty, squattish; pudgy, podgy; pug, pugged; snub-nosed; turned-up, *retroussé* <Fr>

11 short-legged, breviped; short-winged, brevipennate

ADVS 12 **shortly,** briefly, summarily, in brief compass, economically, sparely, curtly, succinctly, in a nutshell, in two words, in a few words; abbreviatedly, for short; concisely, compendiously, synoptically

13 **short, abruptly,** suddenly, all of a sudden

269 BREADTH, THICKNESS

<large side-to-side dimension>

NOUNS 1 **breadth, width,** broadness, wideness, fullness, amplitude, latitude, distance across, distance crosswise, distance crossways, extent, span, expanse, spread; beam

2 **thickness,** the third dimension, hyperspace, distance through, depth; mass, bulk, body; corpulence, fatness, bodily size; coarseness, grossness

3 **diameter,** bore, caliber; **radius,** semidiameter; handbreadth, beam

VERBS 4 **broaden, widen,** deepen; expand, extend, extend to the side; spread, spread out, spread sidewise, spread sideways, outspread, outstretch; span

5 **thicken,** grow thick, thick; incrassate, inspissate; congeal, gel; fatten

ADJS 6 **broad, wide,** deep; broad-scale, wide-scale, wide-ranging, broad-based, exhaustive, comprehensive, in-depth, extensive; spread-out, expansive; spacious, roomy; ample, full; widespread

7 broad of beam, broad-beamed, broad-sterned, beamy, wide-set; wide-body, wide-bodied; wide-angle, widescreen; broad-ribbed, wide-ribbed, laticostate; broad-toothed, wide-toothed, latidentate; broad-gauge; broadloom

8 **thick,** three-dimensional; thickset, heavyset, thick-bodied, broad-bodied, thick-girthed; massive, bulky, corpulent; coarse, heavy, gross, crass, fat; full-bodied, full, viscous; dense; thicknecked, bullnecked

ADVS 9 breadthwise, breadthways, in breadth; widthwise, widthways; broadwise, broadways; broadside, broad side foremost; sidewise, sideways; through, depthwise, depth-ways, in depth

270 NARROWNESS, THINNESS

<small side-to-side dimension>

NOUNS 1 **narrowness, slenderness;** closeness, nearness; straitness, restriction, restrictedness, limitation, strictness, confinement, circumscription; crowdedness, incapaciousness, incommodiousness, crampedness; tightness, tight squeeze; hair, hairbreadth, hairsbreadth; finger's breadth, finger's width; narrow gauge

2 **narrowing, tapering,** taper; contraction, compression; stricture, constriction, strangulation, coarctation

3 **<narrow place>** narrow, narrows, strait; bottleneck, chokepoint; isthmus; channel, canal; pass, defile; neck, throat, craw; narrow gauge, single track

4 **thinness, slenderness,** slimness, frailty, slightness, gracility, lightness, airiness, delicacy, flimsiness, wispiness, laciness, paperiness, gauziness, gossameriness, diaphanousness, insubstantiality, ethereality, mistiness, vagueness; light texture, airy texture; fineness; tenuity, rarity, subtility, exility, exiguity; attenuation; dilution, dilutedness, wateriness, weakness

5 **leanness,** skinniness, fleshlessness, slightness, frailness, twigginess, spareness, meagerness, scrawniness, gauntness, gangliness, lankness, lankiness, gawkiness, boniness, skin and bones; haggardness, poorness, paperiness, peakedness, puniness, lean and hungry look; undernourishment, undernutrition, underweight; hatchet face, lantern jaw

6 **emaciation,** malnutrition, emaceration, attenuation, atrophy, tabes, marasmus, anorexia nervosa

7 <comparisons> paper, wafer, lath, slat, rail, rake, splinter, slip, shaving, streak, vein; gruel, soup; shadow, mere shadow; skeleton

8 **<thin person>** slim, lanky; twiggy, shadow, skeleton, stick, walking skeleton, corpse, barebones, bag of bones, stack of bones; rattlebones, spindleshanks, spindlelegs, gangleshanks, gammerstang, lathlegs, sticklegs, beanpole, beanstalk, broomstick, clothes pole, stilt; slip, sylph, ectomorph, long drink of water

9 **reducing, slenderizing,** slimming down; weight-watching, calorie-counting; fasting, dieting

10 **thinner,** solvent

VERBS 11 **narrow,** constrict, diminish, draw in, go in; restrict, limit, straiten, confine; **taper;** contract, compress, zip

12 **thin,** thin down, thin away, thin off, thin out, down; rarefy, subtilize, attenuate; dilute, water, water down, weaken; undernourish; emaciate, emacerate

13 **slenderize,** reduce, reduce weight, lose weight, take off weight, watch one's weight, lose flesh, weight-watch, count calories, diet, crash-diet; slim, slim down, thin down

ADJS 14 **narrow, slender;** narrowish, narrowy; close, near; tight, strait, isthmic, isthmian; close-fitting; restricted, limited, circumscribed, confined, constricted; cramped, cramp; incapacious, incommodious, crowded; meager, scant, scanty; narrow-gauge, narrow-gauged, single-track; angustifoliate, angustirostrate, angustiseptal, angustisellate; stenopeic

15 **tapered,** taper, tapering, cone-shaped, wedge-shaped, attenuated, fusiform, stenosed

16 **thin, slender,** slim, gracile; thin-bodied, thin-set, ectomorphic, narrow-waisted, wasp-waisted; svelte, slinky, sylphlike, willowy; girlish, boyish; thinnish, slenderish, slimmish; slight, slight-made; frail, delicate, light, airy, wispy, lacy, gauzy, papery, gossamer, diaphanous, insubstantial, ethereal, misty, vague, flimsy, wafer-thin, fine; finespun, thin-spun, fine-drawn, wiredrawn; threadlike, slender as a thread; tenuous, subtle, rare, rarefied; attenuated, attenuate, watery, weak, diluted, watered, watered-down, small

17 **lean,** lean-looking, **skinny**, fleshless, lean-fleshed, thin-fleshed, spare, meager, scrawny, scraggy, thin-bellied, gaunt, lank, lanky, wiry; gangling, gangly, gawky, spindling, spindly; flat-chested, flat; bony, rawboned, bareboned, rattleboned, skeletal, mere skin and bones, all skin and bones, nothing but skin and bones; twiggy; underweight, undersized, undernourished, spidery, thin as a rail, skinny as a rail; waifish

18 lean-limbed, thin-legged, lath-legged, stick-legged, spindle-legged, spindle-shanked, gangle-shanked, stilt-legged

19 **thin-faced**, lean-faced, horse-faced, thin-featured, hatchet-faced; wizen-faced, weazen-faced; lean-cheeked, thin-cheeked; lean-jawed, lantern-jawed

20 **haggard,** poor, puny, peaked, peaky, pinched; gaunt, drawn; shriveled, withered; wizened, weazeny; emaciated, emaciate, emacerated, wasted, attenuated, corpselike, skeletal, hollow-eyed, wraithlike, cadaverous; tabetic, tabid, marantic, marasmic; starved, anorexic, anorectic, starveling, starved-looking; undernourished, underfed, jejune; worn to a shadow

21 **slenderizing,** reducing, slimming

ADVS 22 **narrowly,** closely, nearly, barely, hardly, only just, by the skin of one's teeth

23 **thinly**, thin; meagerly, sparsely, sparingly, scantily

271 FILAMENT

<thin thread>

NOUNS 1 **filament; fiber;** thread; strand, suture; filature; hair; artificial fiber, natural fiber, animal fiber; fibril, fibrilla; cilium, ciliolum; tendril, cirrus; flagellum; web, cobweb, gossamer, spider web, spider's web; denier

2 **cord, line,** rope, wire, braided rope, twisted rope, flattened-strand rope, wire rope, locked-wire rope, cable, wire cable; yarn, spun yarn, skein, hank; string, twine; braid; ligament, ligature, ligation; tendon

3 **cordage,** cording, **ropework,** roping; tackle, tack, gear, rigging; ship's ropes

4 **strip, strap,** strop; lace, thong; band, bandage, fillet, fascia, taenia; belt, girdle; ribbon, ribband; tape, tapeline, tape measure; slat, lath, batten, spline, strake, plank; ligule, ligula

5 **spinner,** spinster; silkworm, spider; spinning wheel, spinning jenny, jenny, mule, mule-jenny; spinning frame, bobbin and fly frame; spinneret; rope walk

VERBS 6 <make threads> **spin**; braid, twist

ADJS 7 **threadlike,** thready; stringy, ropy, wiry; hairlike, hairy; filamentary, filamentous, filiform; fibrous, fibered, fibroid, fibrilliform; ligamental; capillary, capilliform; cirrose, cirrous; funicular, funiculate; flagelliform; taeniate, taeniform; ligulate, ligular; gossamer, gossamery, flossy, silky

272 HEIGHT

<bottom-to-top dimension>

NOUNS 1 **height,** heighth, vertical distance, perpendicular distance; **highness, tallness,** procerity; altitude, elevation, ceiling; loftiness, sublimity, exaltation; hauteur, toploftiness; eminence, prominence; stature

2 **height, elevation,** eminence, rise, raise, uprise, lift, rising ground, vantage point, vantage ground; heights, soaring heights, towering heights, Olympian heights, aerial heights, dizzying heights, higher ground; uppermost height, extreme height; sky, stratosphere, ether, heaven, heavens; zenith, apex, acme

3 **highlands**, highland, upland, uplands, moorland, moors, downs, wold, rolling country

4 **plateau,** tableland, table, mesa, table mountain, bench; **hill;** ridge; **mountain**, peak; mountain range; higher ground

5 watershed, water parting, **divide;** Great Divide, Continental Divide

6 **tower;** turret; campanile, bell tower, belfry; spire, church spire; lighthouse, light tower; cupola, lantern; dome; martello, martello tower; barbican; derrick, pole; windmill tower, observation tower, fire tower, watchtower, control tower; mast, radio mast, television mast, antenna tower, telephone tower, cell phone tower; water tower, standpipe; pinnacle; steeple, *flèche* <Fr>;

minaret; stupa, tope, pagoda; pyramid; pylon; shaft, pillar, column; pilaster; obelisk; monument; colossus; skyscraper

7 <**tall person**> longlegs, longshanks, highpockets, long drink of water; beanpole; giant; six-footer, seven-footer, grenadier <Brit>

8 **high tide,** high water, mean high water, flood tide, spring tide, flood; storm surge

9 <measurement of height> altimetry, hypsometry, hypsography; altimeter, hypsometer

VERBS 10 **tower,** soar, spire; rise, uprise, ascend, mount, rear; stand on tiptoe

11 **rise above,** tower above, tower over, clear, overtop, o'er top, outtop, top, surmount; overlook, look down upon, look down over; overhang, beetle; command, dominate, overarch, overshadow, command a view of; bestride, bestraddle

12 <become higher> **grow,** grow up, upgrow; uprise, rise up, **shoot up,** mount, sprout

13 **heighten,** elevate

ADJS 14 **high,** high-reaching, high-up, lofty, elevated, altitudinous, altitudinal, uplifted, upreared, uprearing, eminent, exalted, prominent, supernal, superlative, sublime; towering, towery, soaring, spiring, aspiring, mounting, ascending; towered, turreted, steepled; topping, outtopping, overtopping; overarching, overlooking, dominating; airy, aerial, ethereal; Olympian; monumental, colossal; high as a steeple; topless; high-set, high-pitched; high-rise, multistory; haughty, toplofty

15 skyscraping, **sky-high,** heaven-reaching, heaven-aspiring, heaven-high, heaven-kissing; cloud-touching, cloud-topped, cloud–capped, supernal; **mid-air**

16 giant, gigantic, colossal, statuesque, amazonian; **tall, lengthy,** long; rangy, lanky, lank, tall as a maypole; gangling, gangly; long-legged, long-limbed, leggy

17 **highland,** upland; hill-dwelling, mountain-dwelling

18 **hilly,** knobby, rolling; **mountainous,** mountained, alpine, alpen, alpestrine, alpigene; subalpine; monticuline, monticulous

19 **higher,** superior, greater; over, above; upper, upmost, uppermost, outtopping, overtopping, topmost; highest

20 altimetric, altimetrical, hypsometrical, hypsographic

ADVS 21 **on high,** high up, high; aloft, aloof; up, upward, upwards, straight up, to the zenith; above, over, o'er, overhead; above one's head, over head and ears; skyward, airward, in the air, in the clouds; on the peak, on the summit, on the crest, on the pinnacle; upstairs, abovestairs; tiptoe, on tiptoe; on stilts; on the shoulders of; supra, hereinabove, hereinbefore

273 SHAFT

<sticklike in shape>

NOUNS 1 **shaft, pole,** bar, rod, stick, scape, scapi-; stalk, stem; thill; tongue, wagon tongue; flagstaff; totem pole; Maypole; utility pole, telephone pole, telegraph pole; tent pole

2 **staff,** stave; **cane,** stick, walking stick, handstaff, shillelagh; Malacca cane; baton, marshal's baton, drum-major's baton, conductor's baton; swagger stick, swanking stick; pilgrim's staff, pastoral staff, shepherd's staff, crook; crosier, cross-staff, cross, paterissa; pikestaff, alpenstock; quarterstaff; lituus, thyrsus; crutch, crutch-stick

3 **beam, timber,** pole, spar

4 **post,** standard, **upright;** king post, queen post, crown post; newel; banister, baluster; balustrade, balustrading; gatepost, swinging post, hinging post, shutting post; doorpost, jamb, doorjamb; signpost, milepost; stile, mullion; stanchion; hitching post, snubbing post, Samson post

5 **pillar, column,** post, pier, pilaster; colonnette, columella; caryatid; atlas, atlantes <pl>; telamon, telamones; colonnade, arcade, pilastrade, portico, peristyle

6 **leg,** shank; **stake,** peg; pile, spile, stud; picket, pale, palisade

274 LOWNESS

<low in level>

NOUNS 1 **lowness, shortness,** squatness, squattiness, stumpiness, shallowness, stuntedness; prostration, supineness, proneness, recumbency, reclination, lying, lying down, reclining; depression, debasement; subjacency

2 **low tide,** low water, mean low water, dead low water, ebb tide, neap tide, neap, low ebb

3 lowland, **lowlands,** bottomland, swale; water meadow, piedmont, foothills, flats, depression

4 **base,** bottom, lowest point, nadir, depths; the lowest of the low; lowest level, underlying level, lower strata, substratum, bedrock

VERBS 5 **lie low, squat,** crouch, lay low, couch; crawl, grovel, lie prone, lie supine, lie prostrate, hug the earth, lie down; lie under, underlie

6 lower, debase, depress; flatten

ADJS 7 **low,** unelevated, flat, low-lying; short, squat, squatty, stumpy, runty; lowered, debased, depressed; demoted; reduced; prone, supine, prostrate, prostrated, couchant, crouched, stooped, recumbent, bowed; laid low, knocked flat, decked; low-set, low-hung; low-built, low-rise, low-sized, low-statured, low-bodied; low-level, low-leveled; neap, shallow, shoal; knee-high, knee-high to a grasshopper; low-necked, low-cut, décolleté

8 **lower,** inferior, under, nether, subjacent; down; less advanced; earlier; substrative, rock-bottom; lowest

ADVS 9 **low,** near the ground; at a low ebb

10 **below,** down below, **under;** infra, hereunder, hereinafter, hereinbelow; thereunder; belowstairs, downstairs, below deck; underfoot; below par, below the mark

PREPS 11 below, under, **underneath, beneath,** neath, at the foot of, at the base of

275 DEPTH

<deep in level>

NOUNS 1 **depth, deepness,** profoundness, profundity; deep-downness, extreme innerness, deep-seatedness, deep-rootedness; bottomlessness, plumblessness, fathomlessness; subterraneity, undergroundness; interiority; extensiveness, unfathomableness

2 **pit, deep, depth,** hole, hollow, cavity, shaft, well, gulf, chasm, abyss, abysm, yawning abyss; crater; crevasse; valley; underground, subterrane

3 **depths,** deeps, bowels, bowels of the earth, core; bottomless pit; infernal pit, hell, netherworld, underworld; dark depths, unknown depths, yawning depths, gaping depths, unfathomed deeps; outer space, deep space

4 **ocean depths,** the deep sea, the deep, trench, deep-sea trench, hadal zone, the deeps, the depths, bottomless depths, inner space, abyss; bottom waters; abyssal zone, Bassalia, Bassalian realm, bathyal zone, pelagic zone; seabed, seafloor, bottom of the sea, ocean bottom, ocean floor, ocean bed, ground, benthos, benthonic division, benthonic zone; Davy Jones's locker; Mariana Trench

5 <deep-sea trenches and deeps> Aleutian Trench, Bonin Trench, Cayman Trench, Diamantina Fracture, Eurasia Basin, Guatemala Trench, Ionian Basin, Japan Trench; Java, Sunda Trench; Kermandec Trench, Kuril Trench, Mariana Trench, Challenger Deep, North Ryukyu Trench; Peru-Chile, Atacama Trench; Philippine Trench, Puerto Rico Trench, Romanche Trench, Solomon Trench, South Sandwich Trench, Meteor Deep, Tonga Trench, Verna Trench, Yap Trench

6 **sounding**, soundings, fathoming, depth sounding, probing; echo sounding, echolocation; sonar; depth indicator; oceanography, bathometry, bathymetry; fathomage, depth of water

7 draft, submergence, **submersion**, sinkage, displacement

8 **deepening,** lowering, depression; sinking, sinkage, descent; excavation, digging, mining, tunneling; drilling, probing

VERBS 9 **deepen, lower,** depress, sink; founder; countersink; dig, excavate, tunnel, mine, drill; pierce to the depths; dive

10 **sound, take soundings,** make a sounding, heave the lead, cast the lead, sling the lead, **fathom, plumb,** plumb-line, plumb the depths, probe

ADJS 11 **deep, profound,** deep-down, penetrating; deepish, deepsome; deep-going, deep-lying, deep-reaching; deep-set, deep-laid; deep-sunk, deep-sunken, deep-sinking; deep-seated, deep-rooted, deep-fixed, deep-settled; deep-cut, deep-engraven; knee-deep, ankle-deep, waist-deep

12 **abysmal,** abyssal, yawning, cavernous, gaping, plunging; bottomless, without bottom, soundless, unsounded, plumbless, fathomless, unfathomed, unfathomable, rock-bottom; deep as a well, deep as the sea, deep as the ocean, deep as hell

13 **underground, subterranean,** subterraneous, hypogeal, buried, deep-buried

14 **underwater,** subaqueous; **submarine,** undersea; submerged, submersed, immersed, buried, engulfed, inundated, flooded, drowned, sunken

15 **deep-sea,** deep-water, blue-water; oceanographic, bathyal; benthic, benthal, benthonic; abyssal, Bassalian; bathyorographic, bathyorographical, bathymetric, bathymetrical; benthopelagic, bathypelagic

16 **deepest**, deepmost, profoundest; bedrock, rock-bottom

ADVS 17 **deep;** beyond one's depth, out of one's depth; over one's head, over head and ears; at bottom, at the core, at rock bottom

276 SHALLOWNESS

<having little depth>

NOUNS 1 **shallowness,** depthlessness; shoalness, shoaliness, no water, no depth; superficiality, exteriority, triviality, cursoriness, slightness; insufficiency; a lick and a promise, once-over-lightly; **surface,** superficies, skin, rind, epidermis; veneer, gloss; pinprick, scratch, mere scratch

2 **shoal, shallows,** shallow water, shoal water, flat, shelf; bank, bar, sandbank, sandbar, tombolo; reef, coral reef; ford; wetlands, tidal flats, flats, mudflat

VERBS 3 **shoal,** shallow; fill in, fill up, silt up

4 **scratch the surface, touch upon,** hardly touch, skim, skim over, skim the surface, graze the surface, hit the high spots, give a lick and a

promise, give it once over lightly, apply a Band-Aid; trivialize, trifle

ADJS 5 **shallow,** shoal, depthless, not deep, unprofound; **surface,** on the surface, near the surface, merely surface; superficial, cursory, slight, light, cosmetic, merely cosmetic, thin, jejune; skin-deep, epidermal; one-dimensional, trifling, trivial; ankle-deep, knee-deep; shallow-rooted, shallow-rooting; shallow-draft, shallow-bottomed, shallow-hulled

6 shoaly, shelfy; reefy; unnavigable; shallow-sea; neritic

277 STRAIGHTNESS

<having no curves, angles, bends>

NOUNS 1 **straightness,** directness, unswervingness, lineality, linearity, rectilinearity; verticalness; flatness, horizontalness; perpendicularity

2 **straight line,** straight, right line, direct line; straight course, straight stretch, straightaway; beeline, airline; shortcut; great-circle course; streamline; edge, side, diagonal, secant, transversal, chord, tangent, perpendicular, normal, segment, directrix, diameter, axis, radius, vector, radius vector; ray, plumb line, column

3 **straightedge, rule,** ruler; square, T square, triangle

VERBS 4 be straight, have no turns; arrow; go straight, make a beeline

5 **straighten,** set straight, put straight, rectify, make right, make good, square away; unbend, unkink, uncurl, unsnarl, disentangle; straighten up, square up; straighten out, extend; flatten, smooth, iron

ADJS 6 **straight;** straight-lined, dead straight, straight as an edge, straight as a ruler, ruler-straight, even, right, true, straight as an arrow, arrowlike; straightaway; rectilinear, rectilineal; **linear**, lineal, in a line; quasilinear; direct, undeviating, unswerving, unbending, undeflected; unbent, unbowed, unturned, uncurved, undistorted, uncurled; uninterrupted, unbroken; straight-side, straight-front, straight-cut; upright, vertical; flat, level, smooth, horizontal; plumb

ADVS 7 **straight,** straightly, on the straight, unswervingly, undeviatingly, directly; straight to the mark; down the alley, down the pipe, in the groove, on the beam, on the money

278 ANGULARITY

<having angles>

NOUNS 1 **angularity,** angularness, crookedness, hookedness; squareness, orthogonality, right-angledness, rectangularity; flection, flexure

2 **angle,** point, bight; vertex, apex; **corner,** quoin, coin, nook; crook, hook, crotchet; bend, curve, swerve, veer, inflection, deflection; ell, L; cant; furcation, bifurcation, fork; zigzag, zig, zag; chevron; elbow, knee, dogleg; crank; obtuse angle, oblique angle, acute angle, right angle, perpendicular

3 <angular measurement> goniometry; trigonometry; geometry

4 <angle measuring instruments> goniometer, radiogoniometer; pantometer, clinometer, graphometer, astrolabe; azimuth compass, azimuth circle; theodolite, transit theodolite, transit, transit instrument, transit circle; sextant, quadrant; bevel, bevel square, set square, T-square; protractor, bevel protractor; graduated cylinder

VERBS 5 **angle,** crook, hook, **bend,** elbow; crank; angle off, angle away, curve, swerve, veer, veer off, slant off, go off on a tangent; furcate, bifurcate, branch, fork; zigzag, zig, zag

ADJS 6 **angular;** cornered, crooked, hooked, bent, flexed, flexural; akimbo; knee-shaped, geniculate, geniculated, doglegged; crotched, Y-shaped, V-shaped; furcate, furcal, forked; sharp-cornered, sharp, pointed; zigzag, jagged, serrate, sawtooth, saw-toothed; mitered

7 **right-angled, rectangular**, right-angular, right-angle; orthogonal, orthodiagonal, orthometric; perpendicular, normal

8 **triangular,** trilateral, trigonal, oxygonal, deltoid; wedgeshaped, cuneiform, cuneate, cuneated

9 **quadrangular**, quadrilateral, quadrate, quadriform; rectangular, square; foursquare, orthogonal; tetragonal, tetrahedral; oblong; trapezoid, trapezoidal, rhombic, rhombal, rhomboid, rhomboidal; cubic, cubical, cubiform, cuboid, cube-shaped, cubed, diced; rhombohedral, trapezohedral

10 pentagonal, hexagonal, heptagonal, octagonal, decagonal, dodecagonal; pentahedral, hexahedral, octahedral, dodecahedral, icosahedral

11 multilateral, **multiangular**, polygonal; polyhedral, pyramidal, pyramidic; prismatic, prismoid; diamond

279 CURVATURE

<having curves>

NOUNS 1 **curvature,** curving, curvation, arcing; incurvature, incurvation; excurvature, excurvation; decurvature, decurvation; recurvature, recurvity, recurvation; rondure;

arching, vaulting, arcuation, concameration; aduncity, aquilinity, crookedness, hookedness; sinuosity, sinuousness, tortuosity, tortuousness; circularity; convolution; rotundity, roundness; convexity; concavity; curvaceousness

2 **curve,** sinus; bow, arc; crook, hook; parabola, hyperbola, witch of Agnesi; ellipse; caustic, catacaustic, diacaustic; catenary, festoon, swag; conchoid; lituus; tracery; circle; curl; coil, loop, spiral

3 **bend,** bending; bow, bowing, oxbow; Cupid's bow; turn, turning, sweep, meander, hairpin turn, S-curve, U-turn; flexure, flex, flection, conflexure, inflection, deflection; reflection; geanticline, geosyncline; detour

4 **arch,** span, vault, vaulting, concameration, camber; ogive; apse; dome, cupola, geodesic dome, igloo, concha; cove; arched roof, ceilinged roof; arcade, archway, arcature; voussoir, keystone, skewback

5 **crescent, semicircle,** scythe, sickle, meniscus; crescent moon, half-moon; lunula, lunule; horseshoe; rainbow

VERBS 6 **curve,** turn, arc, sweep; crook, hook, loop; incurve, incurvate; recurve, decurve, bend back, retroflex, detour; sag, swag; bend, flex; deflect, inflect; reflect, reflex; bow, embow; arch, vault; dome; hump, hunch; wind, curl; round

ADJS 7 **curved,** curve, curvate, curvated, **curving,** curvy, curvaceous, curvesome, curviform; curvilinear, curvilineal; wavy, undulant, billowy, billowing; sinuous, tortuous, serpentine, mazy, labyrinthine, meandering; bent, flexed, flexural, flexuous; incurved, incurving, incurvate, incurvated; recurved, recurving, recurvate, recurvated; geosynclinal, geanticlinal

8 **hooked,** crooked, aquiline, aduncous; hook-shaped, hooklike, uncinate, unciform; hamulate, hamate, hamiform; clawlike, unguiform, down-curving; hook-nosed, beak-nosed, parrot-nosed, aquiline-nosed, Roman-nosed, crooknosed, crookbilled; beaked, billed; beak-shaped, beaklike; bill-shaped, bill-like; rostrate, rostriform, rhamphoid

9 turned-up, **upcurving,** upsweeping, *retroussé* <Fr>

10 **bowed,** embowed, bandy; bowlike, bow-shaped, oxbow, Cupid's-bow; **convex, concave,** convexoconcave; arcuate, arcuated, arcual, arciform, arclike; arched, vaulted; humped, hunched, humpy, hunchy; gibbous, gibbose; humpbacked

11 **crescent-shaped,** crescentlike, crescent, crescentic, crescentiform; meniscoid, meniscoidal, menisciform; S-shaped, ess, S, sigmoid; **semicircular,** semilunar; horn-shaped, hornlike, horned, corniform; bicorn, two-horned; sickle-shaped, sicklelike, falcate, falciform; moon-shaped, moonlike, lunar, lunate, lunular, luniform

12 lens-shaped, lenticular, lentiform, lentoid

13 parabolic, parabolical, paraboloid, saucer-shaped; elliptic, elliptical, ellipsoid; bell-shaped, bell-like, campanular, campanulate, campaniform; hyperbolic, domical

14 pear-shaped, pearlike, pyriform, ovipyriform

15 heart-shaped, heartlike; cordate, cardioid, cordiform, obcordate

16 kidney-shaped, kidneylike, reniform, nephroid

17 turnip-shaped, turniplike, napiform

18 shell-shaped, shell-like; conchate, conchiform, conchoidal, cochleated

19 shield-shaped, shieldlike, peltate; scutate, scutiform; clypeate, clypeiform, aspidate

20 helmet-shaped, helmetlike, galeiform, cassideous, galeated

280 CIRCULARITY

<having circle shape>

NOUNS 1 **circularity, roundness,** ring-shape, ringliness, annularity; annulation

2 **circle,** circus, rondure, **ring,** annulus, O, full circle; circumference, radius; round, roundel, rondelle; cycle, circuit; orbit; closed circle; vicious circle, eternal return; magic circle, charmed circle, fairy ring; logical circle, circular reasoning, petitio principii; wheel; disk, discus, saucer; loop, looplet; noose, lasso; crown, diadem, coronet, corona; garland, chaplet, wreath; halo, glory, areola, aureole; annular muscle, sphincter

3 <thing encircling> **band,** belt, cincture, cingulum, girdle, girth, girt, zone, fascia, fillet; collar, collarband, neckband; necktie; necklace, bracelet, armlet, torque, wristlet, wristband, anklet; ring, earring, nose ring, finger ring; hoop; quoit; zodiac, ecliptic, equator, great circle; round trip

4 rim, felly; tire

5 circlet, **ringlet,** roundlet, annulet, eye, eyelet, grommet

6 **oval,** ovule, ovoid; ellipse

7 cycloid; epicycloid, epicycle; hypocycloid; lemniscate; cardioid; Lissajous figure

8 **semicircle,** half circle, hemicycle; crescent; quadrant, sextant, sector

9 <music and poetry> **round,** canon; rondo, rondino, rondeau, rondelet

VERBS 10 **circle,** round; orbit; encircle, surround, encompass, girdle; make a round trip, circumnavigate

ADJS 11 **circular, round,** rounded, circinate, annular, annulate, ring-shaped, ringlike; annulose; disklike, discoid; cyclic, cyclical, cycloid, cycloidal; epicyclic; planetary; coronal, crownlike; orbital; circulatory, circumferential

12 **oval,** ovate, ovoid, oviform, egg-shaped, obovate, ellipsoid, elliptic, prolate

281 CONVOLUTION

<having twists, complicated curves>

NOUNS 1 **convolution,** involution, circumvolution, **winding,** twisting, turning; meander, meandering; crinkle, crinkling; circuitousness, circumlocution, circumbendibus, circumambages, ambagiousness, ambages, convolutedness; Byzantinism; tortuousness, tortuosity; torsion, intorsion; sinuousness, sinuosity, sinuation, slinkiness; anfractuosity; snakiness; flexuousness, flexuosity; undulation, wave, waving; rivulation; complexity

2 **coil,** whorl, roll, curl, curlicue, ringlet, pigtail, spiral, helix, double helix, volute, volution, involute, evolute, gyre, scroll, turbination; kink, twist, twirl; screw, corkscrew, screw thread; tendril, cirrus; whirl, swirl, vortex; intricacy; squiggle; spheroid

3 curler, curling iron; curlpaper, papillote; crimper, crimping iron

VERBS 4 convolve, convolute, **wind,** twine, twirl, twist, turn, twist and turn, meander, crinkle; serpentine, snake, slink, worm; screw, corkscrew; whirl, swirl; whorl; scallop; wring; intort; contort; undulate, squiggle

5 **curl, coil;** crisp, kink, crimp, wave

ADJS 6 **convolutional,** convoluted, **winding,** twisting, twisty, turning; meandering, meandrous, mazy, labyrinthine; serpentine, snaky, anfractuous; roundabout, circuitous, ambagious, circumlocutory; Byzantine; sinuous, sinuose, sinuate; tortuous, torsional; tortile; flexular, flexuous, flexuose; involutional, involute, involuted; rivose, rivulose; sigmoidal; wreathy, wreathlike; ruffled, whorled, turbinate

7 **coiled,** tortile, snakelike, snaky, snake-shaped, serpentine, serpentlike, serpentiform; anguine, anguiform; eellike, eelshaped, anguilliform; wormlike, vermiform, lumbricoid, lumbricine, lumbriciform

8 **spiral,** spiroid, volute, voluted; **helical,** helicoid, helicoidal; anfractuous; screw-shaped, corkscrew, corkscrewy; verticillate, whorled, scrolled; cochlear, cochleate; turbinal, turbinate

9 **curly, curled;** kinky, kinked; frizzly, frizzy, frizzled, frizzed; crisp, crispy, crisped

10 **wavy,** undulant, undulatory, undulative, undulating, undulate, undulated; billowy, billowing, surgy, rolling

ADVS 11 **windingly,** twistingly, sinuously, tortuously, serpentinely, meanderingly, meandrously; in waves; wavily; in and out, round and round

282 SPHERICITY, ROTUNDITY

<having round or globular shape>

NOUNS 1 **sphericity, rotundity, roundness,** balllikeness, rotundness, orbicularness, orbicularity, orbiculation, orblikeness, sphericalness, sphericality, globularity, globularness, globosity, globoseness; spheroidity, spheroidicity; belly; cylindricality; convexity

2 **sphere; ball,** orb, orbit, **globe,** rondure; geoid; spheroid, globoid, ellipsoid, oblate spheroid, prolate spheroid; spherule, globule, globelet, orblet; glomerulus; pellet; boll; bulb, bulbil, bulbel, bulblet; knob, knot; gob, glob, blob, gobbet; pill, bolus; balloon, bladder, bubble; marble

3 **drop,** droplet; dewdrop, raindrop, teardrop; bead, pearl

4 **cylinder,** cylindroid, pillar, column; barrel, drum, cask; pipe, tube; roll, rouleau, roller, rolling pin; bole, trunk; rung

5 **cone,** conoid, conelet; complex cone, cone of a complex; funnel; ice-cream cone, cornet <Brit>; pinecone; cop; trumpet; top; traffic cone

VERBS 6 **round;** round out, fill out; cone

7 **ball,** snowball; sphere, spherify, globe, conglobulate; roll; bead; balloon, mushroom

ADJS 8 **rotund, round,** rounded, rounded out, round as a ball; bellied, bellylike; convex, bulging

9 **spherical,** sphereic, spheriform, spherelike, sphere-shaped; **globular,** global, globed, globose, globate, globelike, globe-shaped; orbicular, orbiculate, orbiculated, orbed, orb, orby, orblike; spheroid, spheroidal, globoid, ellipsoid, ellipsoidal; hemispheric, hemispherical; bulbous, bulblike, bulging; ovoid, obovoid

10 **beady,** beaded, bead-shaped, beadlike

11 **cylindric, cylindrical,** cylindroid, cylindroidal; columnar, columnal, columned, columelliform; tubular, tube-shaped; barrel-shaped, drum-shaped

12 **conical,** conic, coned, cone-shaped, conelike; conoid, conoidal; spheroconic; funnel-shaped, funnellike, funnelled, funnelform, infundibuliform, infundibular; bell-shaped

283 CONVEXITY, PROTUBERANCE

<curving or extending outward>

NOUNS 1 **convexity,** convexness, convexedness; excurvature, excurvation; camber; gibbousness, gibbosity; tuberousness, tuberosity; **bulging,** bulbousness, bellying, puffing, puffing out

2 **protuberance**, protuberancy, projection, protrusion, extrusion; prominence, eminence, salience, boldness, **bulging,** bellying; gibbousness, gibbosity; excrescence, excrescency; tuberousness, tuberosity, puffiness; salient; relief, high relief, *alto-rilievo* <Ital>, low relief, bas-relief, *basso-rilievo* <Ital>, embossment

3 **bulge,** bilge, bow, convex; bump; thank-you-ma'am, whoopdedoo, cahot <Can>; speed bump, Botts dots, silent policeman, sleeping policeman <Brit>, speed hump; hill, mountain; hump, hunch; lump, clump, bunch, blob; nubbin, nubble, nub; mole, nevus; wart, papilloma, verruca; knob, boss, bulla, button, bulb; stud, jog, joggle, peg, dowel; flange, lip; tab, ear, flap, loop, ring, handle; knot, knur, knurl, gnarl, burl, gall, ridge; rib, cost-, costo-, costi-; chine, spine, shoulder; welt, wale; blister, bleb, vesicle, blain; bubble; condyle; bubo; tubercle, tubercule; beer belly, beer gut, muffin top; bandha <Sanskrit>; dad bod

4 **swelling,** swollenness, edema; rising, lump, bump, pimple; pock, furuncle, boil, carbuncle; corn; pustule; dilation, dilatation; turgidity, turgescence, turgescency, tumescence, intumescence; tumor, tumidity, tumefaction; wen, cyst, sebaceous cyst; bunion; distension

5 **node,** nodule, nodulus, nodulation, nodosity

6 **breast,** bosom, bust, chest, crop, brisket; thorax; pigeon breast; breasts, dugs, teats; nipple, papilla, pap, mammilla, *mamelon, téton* <Fr>; mammillation, mamelonation; mammary gland, udder, bag; man breast

7 <offensive or nonformal> boobs, boobies, bubbies, tits*, titties*, jugs, headlights, knockers, knobs, bazooms, bags, bazongas, coconuts, hooter

8 **nose,** olfactory organ; snout, snoot, nozzle, muzzle; proboscis, antlia, trunk; beak, rostrum; bill, pecker; nib, neb; smeller, beezer, bugle, schnozzle, schnoz, schnozzola, conk; muffle, rhinarium; nostrils, noseholes, nares

9 <point of land> point, hook, spur, cape, tongue, bill; promontory, foreland, headland, head; naze, ness; peninsula, chersonese; delta; spit, sandspit; reef, coral reef; breakwater

VERBS 10 **protrude,** protuberate, project, extrude; stick out, jut out, poke out, stand out, shoot out; stick up, bristle up, start up, cock up, shoot up

11 **bulge,** bilge, bouge, belly, bag, balloon, pouch, pooch; pout; goggle, bug, pop; swell, swell up, dilate, distend, billow; swell out, belly out, round out

12 **emboss,** boss, chase, raise; ridge

ADJS 13 **convex,** convexed; excurved, excurvate, excurvated; bowed, bowed-out, out-bowed, arched; gibbous, gibbose; humped; rotund

14 **protruding,** protrusive, protrudent; protrusile, protrusible; protuberant, protuberating; projecting, extruding, jutting, outstanding; prominent, eminent, salient, bold; prognathous; excrescent, excrescential; emissile; sticking out

15 **bulging,** swelling, distended, bloated, potbellied, bellying, pouching; bagging, baggy; rounded, hillocky, hummocky, moutonnée; billowing, billowy, bosomy, ballooning, pneumatic; bumpy, bumped; bunchy, bunched; bulbous, bulbose; warty, verrucose, verrucated; meniscoid

16 **bulged,** bulgy, bugged-out; swollen, turgid, tumid, turgescent, tumescent, tumorous; bellied, ventricose; pouched, pooched; goggled, goggle; exophthalmic, bug-eyed, popeyed

17 studded, knobbed, knobby, **knoblike**, nubbled, nubby, nubbly, torose; knotty, knotted; gnarled, knurled, knurly, burled, gnarly; noded, nodal, nodiform; noduled, nodular; nodulated; bubonic; tuberculous, tubercular; tuberous, tuberose

18 **in relief,** in bold relief, in high relief, bold, raised, *repoussé* <Fr>; chased, bossed, embossed, bossy

19 **pectoral,** chest, thoracic; pigeon-breasted; mammary, mammillary, mammiform; mammalian, mammate; papillary, papillose, papulous; breasted, bosomed, chested; teated, titted, nippled; busty, bosomy, chesty

20 **peninsular;** deltaic, deltal

284 CONCAVITY

<curving or hollowed inward>

NOUNS 1 **concavity, hollowness;** incurvature, incurvation; depression, impression; emptiness

2 **cavity,** concavity, concave; **hollow,** hollow shell, shell; hole, pit, depression, dip, sink, fold; scoop, pocket, socket; basin, trough, bowl, punch bowl, cup, container; crater; antrum; lacuna; alveola, alveolus, alveolation; vug, vugg, vugh; crypt; armpit; funnel chest, funnel breast

3 **pothole, sinkhole,** pitchhole, chuckhole, mudhole, rut

4 **pit,** well, shaft, sump; chasm, gulf, abyss, abysm; excavation, dig, diggings, workings; mine, quarry

5 **cave, cavern,** cove, hole, grotto, grot, antre, subterrane; lair; tunnel, burrow, warren; subway; bunker, foxhole, dugout, *abri* <Fr>; sewer

6 **indentation,** indent, indention, indenture, dent, dint; gouge, furrow; sunken part, dimple; pit, pock, pockmark; impression, impress; imprint,

print; alveolus, alveolation; honeycomb, Swiss cheese; **notch**

7 recess, recession, niche, nook, inglenook, corner; cove, alcove; bay; pitchhole

8 <hollow in side of mountain> combe, *cwm* <Welsh>, cirque, corrie

9 valley, vale, dale, dell, dingle; glen, bottom, bottoms, bottom glade, intervale, strath <Scot>, gill <Brit>, *cwm* <Welsh>, wadi, grove; trench, trough, lunar rill; gap, pass, ravine

10 excavator, digger; archaeologist; sapper; miner; tunneler, sandhog, groundhog, burrower; gravedigger; dredger; quarryman; driller; steam shovel, navvy <Brit>; dredge

11 excavation, digging; mining; indentation, engraving

VERBS **12** <**be concave**> sink, dish, cup, bowl, hollow; retreat, retire; incurve, curve inward

13 hollow, hollow out, concave, dish, cup, bowl; cave, cave in

14 indent, dent, dint, depress, press in, stamp, tamp, punch, punch in, impress, imprint; pit; pock, pockmark; dimple; honeycomb; recess, set back; set in; notch; engrave

15 excavate, dig, dig out, scoop, scoop out, scoop up, gouge, gouge out, grub, shovel, spade, trowel, dike, delve, scrape, scratch, scrabble; dredge; trench, trough, furrow, groove; tunnel, burrow; drive, sink, lower; mine, sap; quarry; drill, bore

ADJS **16 concave,** concaved, incurved, incurving, incurvate; sunk, sunken; retreating, recessed, retiring; hollow, hollowed, empty; palm-shaped; dish-shaped, dished, dishing, dishlike, bowl-shaped; bowllike, crater-shaped, craterlike, saucer-shaped; spoonlike; cupped, cup-shaped, scyphate; funnel-shaped, infundibular, infundibuliform; funnel-chested, funnel-breasted; boat-shaped, boatlike, navicular, naviform, cymbiform, scaphoid; cavernous, cavelike

17 indented, dented, depressed; dimpled; pitted; cratered; pocked, pockmarked; honeycombed, alveolar, alveolate, faveolate; notched; engraved

285 SHARPNESS

<having edges or points>

NOUNS **1 sharpness, keenness,** edge; acuteness, acuity; pointedness, acumination; thorniness, prickliness, spinosity, spininess, bristliness; mucronation; denticulation, dentition; serration; cornification; acridity

2 sharp edge, **edge,** cutting edge, honed edge, knife-edge, razor-edge, saw-edge; jagged edge; featheredge, fine edge; edge tool; weapon

3 point, tip, cusp, vertex; acumination, mucro; nib, neb; needle; hypodermic needle, hypodermic syringe; drill, borer, auger, bit; prong, tine; prick, prickle; sting, acus, aculeus; tooth

4 <pointed projection> **projection,** spur, jag, snag, snaggle; horn, antler; cornicle; crag, peak, arête; spire, steeple, flèche; cog, sprocket, ratchet; sawtooth; harrow, rake; comb, pecten; nail, tack, pin; arrowhead; skewer, spit; tooth, snaggletooth, fang, denticle; barbed wire

5 thorn, bramble, brier, nettle, burr, awn, prickle, sticker; spike, spikelet, spicule, spiculum; spine; bristle; quill; **needle**, pine needle; thistle, catchweed, cleavers, goose grass, cactus; yucca, Adam's-needle, Spanish bayonet

VERBS **6** come to a point, taper to a point, end in a point, acuminate; prick, prickle, sting, stick, bite; be keen, have an edge, cut, needle; bristle with

7 sharpen, edge, acuminate, aculeate, spiculate, taper; **whet**, hone, oilstone, file, grind; strop, strap; set, reset; barb, spur, point, file to a point; spiralize

ADJS **8 sharp,** keen, edged, acute, fine, **cutting,** knifelike, cultrate; sharp-edged, keen-edged, razor-edged, knife-edged, sharp as broken glass; featheredged, fine-edged; acrid; two-edged, double-edged; sharp-set, sharp as a razor, sharp as a two-edged sword; sharpened, set

9 pointed, pointy, acuminate, acuate, aculeate, aculeated, acute, unbated; tapered, tapering; cusped, cuspate, cuspated, cuspidal, cuspidate, cuspidated; sharp-pointed; needlelike, needle-sharp, needle-pointed, needly, acicular, aciculate, aculeiform; mucronate, mucronated; toothed; spiked, spiky, spiculate; barbed, tined, pronged; horned, horny, cornuted, corniculate, cornified, ceratoid; spined, spiny, spinous, hispid, acanthoid, acanthous

10 prickly, pricky, muricate, echinate, acanaceous, acanthous, aculeolate; pricking, stinging; thorny, brambly, briery, thistly, nettly, burry; bristly

11 arrowlike, arrowy, arrowheaded; sagittal, sagittate, sagittiform

12 spearlike, hastate; lancelike, lanciform, lanceolate, lanceolar; spindle-shaped, fusiform

13 swordlike, gladiate, ensate, ensiform

14 toothlike, dentiform, dentoid, odontoid; toothed, toothy, fanged, tusked, corniculate, denticulate, cuspidate, muricate; snaggle-toothed, snaggled, jagged; emarginate

15 star-shaped, starlike, star-pointed, stellate, stellular

286 BLUNTNESS

<having dulled edges or points>

NOUNS 1 **bluntness, dullness,** unsharpness, obtuseness, obtundity; bluffness; abruptness; flatness, smoothness; toothlessness, lack of bite, lack of incisiveness

VERBS 2 **blunt, dull,** disedge, retund, obtund, take the edge off, take the sting out, take the bite out; turn, turn the edge of, turn the point of; weaken, repress; draw the teeth, draw the fangs; bate; flatten, smooth

ADJS 3 **blunt, dull,** obtuse, obtundent; bluntish, dullish; unsharp, unsharpened, unwhetted; unedged, edgeless; rounded, faired, smoothed, streamlined; unpointed, pointless; blunted, dulled; blunt-edged, dull-edged; blunt-pointed, dull-pointed, blunt-ended; bluff, abrupt; flat

4 **toothless,** teethless, edentate, edental, edentulous, biteless

287 SMOOTHNESS

<being flat and even>

NOUNS 1 **smoothness, flatness,** levelness, evenness, uniformity, regularity; sleekness, glossiness; slickness, slipperiness, lubricity, oiliness, greasiness, frictionlessness; silkiness, satininess, velvetiness; glabrousness, glabriety; downiness; suavity; peacefulness, dead calm

2 **polish,** gloss, glaze, burnish, varnish, wax, enamel, shine, luster, finish; patina

3 <**smooth surface**> smooth, plane, level, flat; tennis court, bowling alley, bowling green, billiard table, billiard ball; slide; glass, ice; marble, alabaster, ivory; silk, satin, velvet, a baby's ass; mahogany

4 **smoother;** roller, lawn-roller; sleeker, slicker; polish, burnish; abrasive, abrader, abradant; lubricant; flattener, iron; buffer, sander, burnisher

VERBS 5 **smooth,** flatten, plane, planish, level, even, equalize; dress, dub, dab; smooth down, smooth out, lay; plaster, plaster down; roll, roll smooth; harrow, drag; grade; mow, shave; lubricate, oil, grease

6 **press,** hot-press, iron, mangle, calender; roll

7 **polish,** shine, burnish, furbish, sleek, slick, slick down, gloss, glaze, glance, luster; rub, scour, buff; wax, varnish; finish

8 **grind, file**, sand, scrape, sandpaper, emery, pumice; levigate; abrade; sandblast

9 move smoothly; glide, skate, roll, ski, float, slip, slide, skid, coast

ADJS 10 **smooth;** smooth-textured, smooth-surfaced, even, level, plane, flat, regular, uniform, unbroken; peaceful, still; unrough, unroughened, unruffled, unwrinkled, unrumpled; glabrous, glabrate, glabrescent; downy, peachlike; silky, satiny, velvety, smooth as silk, smooth as satin, smooth as velvet, smooth as a billiard ball, smooth as a baby's ass; leiotrichous, lissotrichous; smooth-shaven; suave

11 **sleek,** slick, glossy, shiny, gleaming; silky, silken, satiny, velvety; **polished,** burnished, furbished; buffed, rubbed, finished; varnished, lacquered, shellacked, glazed, *glacé* <Fr>; glassy, smooth as glass

12 **slippery,** slippy, slick, slithery, sliddery, slippery as an eel; lubricous, lubric, oily, oleaginous, greasy, buttery, soaped, soapy; lubricated, oiled, greased

ADVS 13 **smoothly,** evenly, regularly, uniformly; like clockwork, on wheels

288 ROUGHNESS

<being uneven and broken>

NOUNS 1 **roughness, unsmoothness,** unevenness, irregularity, ununiformity, nonuniformity, inequality; bumpiness, pockedness, pockiness, holeyness, lumpiness, knobbliness; abrasiveness, abrasion, harshness, asperity; ruggedness, rugosity; jaggedness, raggedness, cragginess, scraggliness; joltiness; rough air, turbulence; choppiness; tooth; granulation; hispidity, bristliness, spininess, thorniness; nubbiness, nubbliness; scaliness, scabrousness

2 <**rough surface**> rough, broken ground; broken water, chop; corrugation, ripple, washboard; serration; gooseflesh, goose bumps, goose pimples, horripilation; tweed, corduroy, sackcloth; steel wool; sandpaper; potholed road, dirt road

3 **bristle,** barb, barbel, striga, setule, setula, seta; **stubble,** designer stubble; whiskers, five o'clock shadow

VERBS 4 **roughen,** rough, rough up, harshen; coarsen; granulate; gnarl, knob, stud, boss; pimple, horripilate; roughcast, rough-hew

5 **ruffle,** wrinkle, corrugate, crinkle, crumple, rumple; bristle; rub the wrong way, go against the grain, set on edge

ADJS 6 **rough, unsmooth;** uneven, ununiform, unlevel, inequal, broken, irregular, textured; jolty, bumpy, rutty, rutted, pitted, pocky, potholed; horripilant, pimply; corrugated, ripply, wimpled; choppy; ruffled, unkempt; shaggy, shagged; coarse, rank, unrefined; unpolished; rough-grained, coarse-grained, cross-grained; grainy, granulated; rough-hewn, rough-cast; homespun, linsey-woolsey; bouclé, tweed, tweedy, corduroy

7 **rugged,** ragged, harsh; rugose, rugous, wrinkled, crinkled, crumpled, corrugated; scratchy, abrasive, rough as a cob; jagged, jaggy; snaggy, snagged, snaggled; scraggy, scragged, scraggly; sawtooth, sawtoothed, serrate, serrated, toothed; craggy, cragged; rocky, gravelly, stony; rockbound, ironbound

8 **gnarled,** gnarly; knurled, knurly; knotted, knotty, knobbly, nodose, nodular, studded, lumpy

9 **bristly,** bristling, bristled, hispid, hirsute, whiskery; barbellate, whiskered, glochidiate, setaceous, setous, setose; strigal, strigose, strigate, studded; **stubbled,** stubbly; hairy

10 bristlelike, setiform, aristate, setarious

ADVS 11 **roughly,** rough, in the rough; unsmoothly, brokenly, unevenly, irregularly, raggedly, choppily, jaggedly; abrasively

12 cross-grained, **against the grain,** the wrong way

289 NOTCH

<small cut>

NOUNS 1 **notch, nick,** nock, cut, cleft, incision, gash, hack, blaze, scotch, score, kerf, crena, depression, jag; gouge; jog, joggle; **indentation**

2 **notching, serration,** serrulation, saw, sawtooth, sawteeth; denticulation, dentil, dentil band, dogtooth; crenation, crenelation, crenature, crenulation; scallop; rickrack; picot edge, Vandyke edge; deckle edge; cockscomb, crest; pinking shears

3 battlement, crenel, merlon, embrasure, castellation, machicolation; cog, zigzag

VERBS 4 **notch,** nick, cut, incise, gash, nock, slash, chop, crimp, scotch, score, blaze, jag, scarify, gouge; **indent**; scallop, crenelate, crenulate, machicolate; serrate, pink, mill, knurl, tooth, picot, Vandyke

ADJS 5 **notched,** nicked, incised, incisural, gashed, scotched, scored, chopped, blazed; **indented**; serrate, serrated, serrulated, saw-toothed, saw-edged, sawlike; crenate, crenated, crenulate, crenellated, battlemented, embrasured; scalloped; dentate, dentated, toothed, toothlike, tooth-shaped; lacerate, lacerated; jagged, jaggy; erose; serriform

290 FURROW

<large narrow cut>

NOUNS 1 **furrow, groove,** scratch, crack, fissure, cranny, chase, chink, score, **cut,** gash, striation, streak, stria, gouge, slit, incision; sulcus, sulcation; wrinkle, crinkle; rut, ruck, wheeltrack, well-worn groove; corrugation; flute, fluting; rifling; chamfer, bezel, rabbet, dado; microgroove; engraving

2 **trench, trough,** channel, ditch, dike, fosse, canal, cut, gutter, conduit, kennel <Brit>; moat; sunk fence, ha-ha; aqueduct; entrenchment; canalization; pleat, crimp, goffer

VERBS 3 **furrow, groove,** score, scratch, incise, cut, carve, chisel, gash, striate, streak, gouge, slit, crack; plow; rifle; channel, trough, flute, chamfer, rabbet, dado; trench, canal, canalize, ditch, gully, rut; corrugate, wrinkle, crinkle; pleat, crimp, goffer; engrave

ADJS 4 **furrowed, grooved,** scratched, scored, incised, cut, gashed, gouged, slit, striated, slotted; channeled, troughed, trenched, ditched, plowed; fluted, chamfered, rabbeted, dadoed; rifled; sulcate, sulcated; canaliculate, canaliculated; corrugated, corrugate; corduroy, corduroyed, rutted, rutty, rimose, wrinkly; wrinkled, pleated, crimped, goffered, crinkly; engraved; ribbed, costate

291 FOLD

<part bent over another part>

NOUNS 1 **fold,** double, fold on itself, doubling, doubling over, duplicature; ply; plication, plica, plicature; flection, flexure; **crease,** creasing; crimp; tuck, gather; ruffle, frill, ruche, ruching; flounce; lappet; lapel; buckling, geological fold, anticline, syncline; dog-ear

2 **pleat,** pleating, plait, plat; accordion pleat, box pleat, knife pleat, kick pleat

3 **wrinkle,** corrugation, ridge, furrow, crease, crimp, ruck, pucker, cockle; crinkle, crankle, rimple, ripple, wimple; crumple, rumple; crow's-feet

4 **folding, creasing,** infolding, infoldment, enfoldment, envelopment; plication, plicature; paper-folding, origami

VERBS 5 **fold,** fold on itself, fold up; double, ply, plicate; fold over, double over, double under, lap, turn under; **crease,** crimp; crisp; pleat, plait, plat; tuck, gather, tuck up, ruck, ruck up; ruffle, ruff, frill; flounce; twill, quill, flute; turn up, turn down, dog-ear; fold in, enfold, infold, wrap; interfold

6 **wrinkle, corrugate,** shirr, ridge, furrow, crease, crimp, crimple, cockle, cocker, pucker, purse; knit; ruck, ruckle; crumple, rumple; crinkle, rimple, ripple, wimple

ADJS 7 **folded,** doubled; plicate, plicated, plical; pleated, plaited; creased, crimped; tucked, gathered; flounced, ruffled; twilled, quilled, fluted; dog-eared; foldable, folding, flexural, flexible, flectional, pliable, pliant, willowy

8 wrinkled, wrinkly; corrugated, corrugate; creased, rucked, ruched, furrowed, ridged; cockled, cockly; puckered, puckery; pursed, pursy; knitted, knotted; rugged, rugose, rugous; crinkled, crinkly, cranklety, rimpled, rippled; crimped, crimpy; crumpled, rumpled

292 OPENING

<hole or empty space>

NOUNS **1 opening, aperture, hole,** hollow, **cavity,** orifice; slot, split, crack, check, leak, hairline crack; opening up, unstopping, uncorking, clearing, throwing open, laying open, broaching, cutting through; passageway; inlet; outlet; gap, gape, yawn, hiatus, lacuna, gat, space, interval; chasm, gulf; cleft; fontanel; foramen, fenestra; stoma; pore, porosity; fistula; disclosure; open space; window, window of opportunity

2 gaping, yawning, oscitation, oscitancy, dehiscence, pandiculation; gape, yawn; the gapes

3 hole, perforation, penetration, piercing, empiercement, puncture, goring, boring, puncturing, punching, pricking, lancing, broach, transforation, terebration; acupuncture, acupunctuation; trephining, trepanning; impalement, skewering, fixing, transfixion, transfixation; bore, borehole, drill hole; ear piercing, body piercing

4 mouth; maw, oral cavity, gob, gab; muzzle, jaw, lips, embouchure; bazoo, kisser, mug, mush, trap, yap; jaws, mandibles, chops, chaps, jowls; premaxilla

5 <**body orifice**> pore, sweat gland; aural cavity, nasal cavity, nostril; stoma; anus; asshole*, bumhole, bunghole; urethra; vagina

6 door, doorway; entrance, entry

7 window, casement; windowpane, window glass, pane, skylight; window frame, window ledge, windowsill, window bay

8 porousness, porosity; sievelikeness, cribriformity, cribrosity; screen, lattice, grate; sieve, strainer, colander; honeycomb; sponge; tea bag; filter, net

9 permeability, perviousness

10 opener; can opener; corkscrew, bottle screw, bottle opener, church key; **key,** clavis; latchkey; passkey, *passe-partout* <Fr>; master key, skeleton key; password, open sesame; keycard, swipe card, smart card; master switch

VERBS **11 open,** ope, open up; lay open, throw open; fly open, spring open, swing open; tap, broach; cut open, cut, cleave, split, slit, crack, chink, fissure, crevasse, incise; rift, rive; tear open, rent, tear, rip, rip open, part, dispart, separate, divide, divaricate; spread, spread out, open out, splay, splay out

12 unclose, unshut; unfold, unwrap, unroll; unstop, unclog, unblock, clear, unfoul, free, deobstruct; unplug, uncork, uncap; crack; unlock, unlatch, undo, unbolt; unseal, unclench, unclutch; uncover, uncase, unsheathe, unveil, undrape, uncurtain; disclose, expose, reveal, bare, take the lid off, manifest; gain access

13 make an opening, find an opening, make place, make space, make way, make room

14 breach, rupture; **break open,** force open, pry open, crack open, split open, rip open, tear open; break into, break through; break in, burst in, bust in, stave in, stove in, cave in; excavate, dig

15 perforate, pierce, empierce, penetrate, puncture, punch, hole, prick; tap, broach; stab, stick, pink, run through; transfix, transpierce, fix, impale, spit, skewer; gore, spear, lance, spike, needle; bore, drill, auger; ream, ream out, countersink, gouge, gouge out; trepan, trephine; punch full of holes, make look like Swiss cheese, make look like a sieve, riddle, honeycomb

16 gape, gap, yawn, oscitate, dehisce, hang open

ADJS **17 open,** unclosed, uncovered; unobstructed, unstopped, unclogged; clear, cleared, free; wide-open, unrestricted; disclosed; bare, exposed, unhidden, naked, bald; accessible

18 gaping, yawning, agape, oscitant, slack-jawed, openmouthed; dehiscent, ringent; ajar, half-open, cracked

19 apertured, slotted, holey; pierced, **perforated,** perforate, holed; honeycombed, like Swiss cheese, riddled, shot through, peppered; windowed, fenestrated; leaky

20 porous, porose; poriferous; like a sieve, sievelike, cribose, cribriform; spongy, spongelike; percolating, leachy

21 permeable, pervious, penetrable, openable, accessible

22 mouthlike, oral, orificial; mandibular, maxillary

INTERJS **23 open up,** open sesame, gangway, passageway, make way, make a hole, coming through, heads up, say ah

293 CLOSURE

<means of closing or enclosing>

NOUNS **1 closure, closing,** shutting, shutting up, occlusion; shutdown, shutting down, cloture; exclusion, shutting out, ruling out; blockade, embargo

2 imperviousness, impermeability, impenetrability, impassability; imperforation

3 obstruction, clog, block, blockade, sealing off,

blockage, strangulation, choking, choking off, stoppage, stop, bar, barrier, obstacle, impediment; occlusion; bottleneck, chokepoint; congestion, jam, traffic jam, gridlock, rush hour; gorge; constipation, obstipation, costiveness; infarct, infarction; embolism, embolus; blind alley, blank wall, deadend, cul-de-sac, dead-end street, impasse; cecum, blind gut; standstill, deadlock, stalemate

4 **stopper,** stop, stopple, stopgap; plug, cork, bung, spike, spill, spile, tap, faucet, spigot, valve, check valve, cock, sea cock, peg, pin; lid; tamper-resistant packaging

5 stopping, wadding, **stuffing,** padding, packing, pack, tampon; gland; gasket; bandage, tourniquet; wedge

VERBS 6 **close, shut,** occlude; close up, shut up, contract, constrict, strangle, strangulate, choke, choke off, squeeze, squeeze shut; exclude, shut out, squeeze out; rule out; fasten, secure; lock, lock up, lock out, key, padlock, latch, bolt, bar, barricade; seal, seal up, seal in, seal off, reseal; button, button up; snap; zipper, zip up; batten, batten down the hatches; put the lid on, slap the lid on, cover; contain; shut the door, slam, clap, bang

7 **stop, stop up;** obstruct, bar, stay; block, block up; clog, clog up, foul, silt up, choke off; choke, choke up; fill, fill up; stuff, pack, jam; congest, stuff up; plug, plug up; stopper, stopple, cork, bung, spile; cover; dam, dam up; stanch; chink; caulk; blockade, barricade, embargo; constipate, obstipate, bind; occlude

8 close shop, **close up**, close down, shut up, **shut down,** go out of business, fold, fold up, pull an el foldo, shutter, put up the shutters, discontinue; cease

ADJS 9 **closed, shut,** unopen, unopened; unvented, unventilated; fastened, secured; excluded, shut-out; ruled out, barred; contracted, constricted, choked, choked off, choked up, squeezed shut, strangulated, occluded; blank; blind, cecal, dead; dead-end, blind-alley, closed-end, closed-ended; exclusive, exclusionary, closed-door, in-camera, private, closed to the public; tamper-resistant; sealed, resealed, zippered, ziplocked

10 **unpierced,** pierceless, unperforated, imperforate, intact; untrodden, pathless, wayless, trackless

11 **stopped, stopped up;** obstructed, infarcted, blocked, blocked up; plugged, plugged up, bunged; clogged, clogged up; foul, fouled; choked, choked up, strangulated, strangled; full, stuffed, packed, jammed, bumper-to-bumper, jam-packed, like sardines; congested, stuffed up; constipated, obstipated, costive, bound; silted up

12 **close,** tight, compact, fast, shut fast, snug, staunch, firm; **sealed;** hermetic, hermetical, hermetically sealed; airtight, dusttight, dustproof, gastight, gasproof, lighttight, lightproof, oil-tight, oil-proof, raintight, rainproof, smoketight, smokeproof, stormtight, stormproof, watertight, waterproof, windtight, windproof; water-repellent, water-resistant; form-fitting

13 **impervious,** impenetrable, impermeable; impassable, unpassable; unpierceable, unperforable; punctureproof, nonpuncturable, holeproof

294 TEXTURE

<surface quality>

NOUNS 1 **texture,** surface texture; surface; finish, feel, touch; intertexture, contexture, constitution, consistency; grain, granular texture, fineness of grain, coarseness of grain; weave, woof, weftage, wale; nap, pile, shag, nub, knub, protuberance; pit, pock, indentation; structure

2 **roughness**; irregularity; bumpiness, lumpiness; coarseness, grossness, unrefinement, coarse-grainedness; cross-grainedness; graininess, granularity, granulation, grittiness, grit; pockiness; hardness

3 **smoothness**, fineness, refinement, fine-grainedness; delicacy, daintiness; filminess, gossameriness; down, downiness, fluff, fluffiness, velvet, velvetiness, fuzz, fuzziness, peach fuzz, peachiness; pubescence; satin, satininess; silk, silkiness; softness

VERBS 4 coarsen; grain, granulate; tooth, **roughen**; gnarl, knob; rumple, wrinkle; **smooth**, flatten

ADJS 5 **textural, textured,** -surfaced

6 **rough**, coarse, gross, unrefined, coarse-grained; cross-grained; grained, grainy, granular, granulated, gritty, gravelly, gravelish

7 **nappy,** pily, **shaggy,** hairy, hirsute; nubby, nubbly; bumpy, lumpy; studded, knobbed; pocked, pitted; woven, matted, ribbed, twilled, tweedy, woolly; fibrous; frizzly, frizzy

8 **smooth**; fine, refined, attenuate, attenuated, fine-grained; delicate, dainty; finespun, thin-spun, fine-drawn, wiredrawn; gauzy, filmy, gossamer, gossamery, downy, fluffy, velvety, velutinous, fuzzy, pubescent; satin, satiny, silky

295 COVERING

<concealing or on top of>

NOUNS 1 <act of covering> **covering,** coverage, obduction; **coating,** cloaking; screening, shielding, hiding, curtaining, veiling, clouding, obscuring, befogging, fogging, fuzzing, masking, mantling, shrouding, shadowing, blanketing; blocking, blotting out, eclipse, eclipsing, occultation; wrapping, enwrapping, enwrapment, sheathing, envelopment; overlaying, overspreading, laying on, laying over, superimposition, superposition; superincumbence; upholstering, upholstery; plasterwork, stuccowork, brickwork, cementwork, pargeting; incrustation; geocache, geocaching

2 **cover, covering,** coverage, covert, coverture, housing, hood, cowl, cowling, shelter; screen, shroud, shield, veil, pall, mantle, curtain, hanging, drape, drapery, window treatment; coat, cloak, mask, guise; vestment; camouflage

3 **skin,** dermis; cuticle; rind; flesh; bare skin, bare flesh, the buff; integument, tegument, tegmen, tegmentum, testa; scab; pelt, hide, coat, jacket, fell, fleece, fur, hair, vair <heraldry>; feathers, plumage; peel, peeling; epicarp; bark; cork, phellum; cortex, cortical tissue, epidermis; periderm, phelloderm; peridium; dermatogen; protective coloring

4 **overlayer,** overlay; appliqué, lap, overlap, overlapping, imbrication; flap, fly, tentfly; shutter

5 **cover,** lid, **top,** cap, screw-top; operculum; stopper

6 **roof,** roofing, roofage, top, housetop, rooftop; roof-deck, roof garden, penthouse; roofpole, ridgepole, rooftree; shingles, slates, tiles; eaves; ceiling, *plafond* <Fr>, overhead; skylight, lantern, cupola, dome; widow's walk, captain's walk; canopy, awning, marquee

7 **umbrella,** gamp, brolly, bumbershoot; sunshade, parasol, beach umbrella

8 **tent,** canvas; top, whitetop, round top, big top; tentage; tepee, wigwam, yurt

9 **rug, carpet,** floor cover, floor covering; carpeting, wall-to-wall carpet, wall-to-wall carpeting; mat; drop cloth, ground cloth, groundsheet; **flooring,** floorboards, duckboards; tiling; pavement, pavé; tarpaulin

10 **bedding,** blanket, coverlet, coverlid, blankie, security blanket, space blanket, cover, covers, spread, robe, buffalo robe, afghan, wrap, rug; lap robe; bedspread; bedcover; counterpane, counterpin; comfort, comforter, down comforter, duvet, continental quilt, quilt, feather bed, eiderdown; patchwork quilt; bedclothes, clothes; linen, bed linen; sheet, sheeting, bedsheet, fitted sheet, contour sheet, dust ruffle; pillowcase, pillow slip, case, slip, sham; electric blanket

11 horsecloth, horse blanket; caparison, housing; saddle blanket, saddlecloth

12 blanket, **coating,** coat; veneer, facing, veneering, revetment; pellicle, film, scum, skin, scale; slick, oil slick; varnish, enamel, lacquer, paint

13 **plating,** plate, cladding; nickel plate, silver plate, gold plate, copperplate, chromium plate, anodized aluminum; electroplate, electroplating, electrocoating

14 **crust,** incrustation, encrustation, shell; piecrust, pastry shell; lithosphere, stalactite, stalagmite; scale, scab, eschar

15 **shell,** seashell, lorication, lorica, conch; test, testa, episperm, pericarp, elytron, scute, scutum; operculum; exoskeleton; armor, mail, shield; carapace, plate, chitin, scale; protective covering, cortex, thick skin, thick hide, elephant skin

16 **hull,** shell, pod, capsule, case, husk, shuck; cornhusk, corn shuck; bark, jacket; chaff, bran, palea; seed coat; germ

17 **case,** casing, encasement; sheath, sheathing

18 **wrapper,** wrapping, gift wrapping, gift wrap, wrap; wrapping paper, tissue paper, waxed paper, aluminum foil, tin foil, plastic wrap, cling wrap, clingfilm, cellophane; binder, binding; bandage, bandaging; envelope, envelopment; jacket, jacketing; dust jacket, dust cover

VERBS 19 **cover,** cover up; apply to, put on, lay on; superimpose, superpose; lay over, overlay; spread over, overspread; clothe, cloak, mantle, muffle, blanket, canopy, cope, cowl, hood, veil, curtain, screen, shield, screen off, mask, cloud, obscure, fog, befog, fuzz; block, eclipse, occult; film, film over, scum

20 **wrap,** enwrap, wrap up, wrap about, wrap around; envelop, sheathe; surround, encompass, lap, smother, enfold, embrace, invest; shroud, enshroud; swathe, swaddle; box, case, encase, crate, pack, embox; containerize; package, encapsulate

21 **top, cap,** tip, crown; put the lid on, cork, stopper, plug; hood, hat, coif, bonnet; roof, roof in, roof over; ceil; dome, endome

22 **floor;** carpet; pave, causeway, cobblestone, flag, pebble; cement, concrete; surface, pave over, repave, resurface; blacktop, tar, asphalt, macadamize

23 **face,** veneer, revet; sheathe; board, plank, weatherboard, clapboard, lath; shingle, shake; tile, stone, brick, slate; thatch; glass, glaze, fiberglass; paper, wallpaper; wall in, wall up

24 **coat,** spread on, spread with; smear, smear on, besmear, slap on, dab, daub, bedaub, plaster, beplaster; flow on, pour on; lay on, lay it on thick, slather; undercoat, prime; paint, enamel, gild, gloss, lacquer; butter; tar; wallpaper

25 **plaster,** parget, stucco, cement, concrete, mastic,

grout, mortar; face, line; roughcast, pebble-dash, spatter-dash

26 **plate,** chromium-plate, copperplate, gold-plate, nickel-plate, silver-plate; electroplate, galvanize, anodize

27 **crust,** incrust, encrust; loricate; effloresce; scab, scab over

28 **upholster,** overstuff

29 **re-cover,** reupholster, recap

30 **overlie,** lie over; overlap, lap, lap over, override, imbricate, jut, shingle; extend over, span, bridge, bestride, bestraddle, arch over, overarch, hang over, overhang

ADJS **31** **covered,** covert, undercover; cloaked, mantled, blanketed, muffled, canopied, coped, cowled, hooded, shrouded, veiled, clouded, obscured, fogged, fogged in; eclipsed, occulted, curtained, screened, screened-in, screened-off; shielded, masked; housed; tented, under canvas; roofed, roofed-in, roofed-over, domed; walled, walled-in; wrapped, enwrapped, jacketed, enveloped, sheathed, swathed; boxed, cased, encased, encapsuled, encapsulated, packaged; coated, filmed, filmed-over, scummed; shelled, loricate, loricated; armored; ceiled; floored; paved, surfaced; plastered, stuccoed

32 **cutaneous,** cuticular; **skinlike,** skinny; skin-deep; epidermal, epidermic, dermal, dermic; ectodermal, ectodermic; endermic, endermatic; cortical; epicarpal; testaceous; hairy, furry; integumental, integumentary, tegumentary, tegumental, tegmental; vaginal; thecal

33 **plated,** chromium-plated, copperplated, gold-plated, nickel-plated, silver-plated; electroplated, galvanized, anodized

34 **upholstered,** overstuffed

35 **covering,** coating; cloaking, blanketing, shrouding, obscuring, veiling, screening, shielding, sheltering; wrapping, enveloping, sheathing

36 **overlying,** incumbent, superincumbent, superimposed; overlapping, lapping, shingled, equitant; imbricate, imbricated; spanning, bridging; overarched, overarching

PREPS **37** on, upon, over, o'er, above, on top of

296 LAYER

<covering over or under another>

NOUNS **1** **layer,** thickness; **level,** tier, stage, story, floor, gallery, step, ledge, deck, row, landing; stratum, strata, seam, *couche* <Fr>, vein, lode, belt, band, bed, course, measures; zone; shelf; overlayer, superstratum, overstory, topsoil, topcoat; underlayer, substratum, understratum, understory, underlay, undercoat; bedding; cultural layer, occupation layer, living floor

2 lamina, lamella; **sheet,** leaf, *feuille* <Fr>, foil; wafer, disk; plate, plating, cladding; covering, coat, coating, veneer, film, patina, scum, membrane, pellicle, sheathe, peel, skin, rind, hide; slick, oil slick; slice, cut, rasher, collop, sliver; slab, plank, deal, slat, tablet, table; panel, pane; fold, lap, flap, ply, plait; laminate; laminated glass, safety glass; laminated wood, plywood, layered fiberglass; liner

3 **flake,** flock, floccule, flocculus; scale, scurf, dandruff, squama; chip; shaving, paring, swarf

4 **stratification,** layering, **lamination,** lamellation, sequence; foliation; delamination, exfoliation; desquamation, furfuration; flakiness, scaliness

VERBS **5** **layer,** lay down, lay up, **stratify,** order, arrange in layers, arrange in levels, arrange in strata, arrange in tiers, **laminate;** shingle, sandwich; flake, scale; delaminate, desquamate, exfoliate; interface

ADJS **6** **layered,** in layers; **laminated,** laminate, laminous; lamellated, lamellate, lamellar, lamelliform; plated, coated; veneered, faced; two-ply, three-ply; two-level, bilevel, three-level, trilevel; one-story, single story, two-story, double-story; **stratified,** stratiform, straticulate; foliated, foliaceous, leaflike; terraced, multistage

7 **flaky,** flocculent, floccose; **scaly,** scurfy, squamous, lentiginous, furfuraceous, lepidote; scabby, scabious, scabrous

COMBINING FORMS **8** strati-, lamin-, lamino-, lamini-, lamell-, lamelli-

297 WEIGHT

<having heaviness>

NOUNS **1** **weight, heaviness,** weightiness, ponderousness, ponderosity, ponderability, leadenness, heftiness, heft; body weight, avoirdupois, fatness, beef, beefiness, chunk; poundage, tonnage; deadweight, live weight; gross weight, gr wt; net weight, neat weight, nt wt, net, nett; short-weight; underweight; overweight; overbalance, overweightage; solemnity, gravity

2 onerousness, **burdensomeness,** oppressiveness, deadweight, overburden, cumbersomeness, cumbrousness; massiveness, massiness, bulkiness, lumpishness, unwieldiness

3 <sports weights> bantamweight, featherweight, flyweight, heavyweight, light heavyweight, lightweight, middleweight, cruiser weight, welterweight; catchweight; fighting weight; jockey weight

4 **counterbalance**; makeweight; ballast, ballasting

5 <physics terms> **gravity,** gravitation, G, supergravity; specific gravity; gravitational field, gravisphere; gravitational pull; graviton; geotropism, positive geotropism, apogeotropism, negative geotropism; G suit, anti-G suit; **mass;** atomic weight, molecular weight, molar weight; quagma

6 **weight,** paperweight, letterweight; sinker, lead, plumb, plummet, bob; sash weight; sandbag

7 **burden,** burthen, pressure, oppression, deadweight; burdening, saddling, charging, taxing; overburden, overburdening, overtaxing, overweighting, weighing down, weighting down; charge, load, loading, lading, freight, cargo, bale, ballast; cumber, cumbrance, encumbrance; incubus; incumbency, superincumbency; handicap, drag, millstone; surcharge, overload

8 <systems of weight> avoirdupois weight, troy weight, apothecaries' weight; atomic weight, molecular weight; **unit of weight** <see list>

9 **weighing,** hefting, balancing; weighing-in, weigh-in, weighing-out, weigh-out; scale, weighing instrument

VERBS 10 **weigh,** weight; heft, balance, weigh in the balance, strike a balance, hold the scales, put on the scales, lay in the scales; counterbalance; weigh in, weigh out; be heavy, weigh heavy, lie heavy, have weight, carry weight; tip the scales, tilt the scales, tip the balance

11 **weigh on,** weigh upon, rest on, rest upon, bear on, bear upon, lie on, press, press down, press to the ground

12 **weight,** weigh down, weight down; hang like a millstone; ballast; lead, sandbag

13 **burden,** burthen, load, load down, load up, lade, cumber, encumber, charge, freight, tax, handicap, hamper, saddle; oppress, weigh one down, weigh on, weigh upon, weigh heavy on, bear hard upon, rest hard upon, lie hard upon, lie heavy upon, press hard upon, be an incubus to; overburden, overweight, overtax, overload

14 **outweigh,** overweigh, overweight, overbalance, outbalance, outpoise, overpoise

15 **gravitate,** descend, drop, plunge, precipitate, sink, settle, subside; tend, tend to go, incline, point, head, lead, lean

ADJS 16 **heavy,** ponderous, massive, massy, weighty, hefty, bulky, fat; leaden, heavy as lead; deadweight; heavyweight; overweight; solemn, grave

17 onerous, oppressive, **burdensome,** incumbent, superincumbent, cumbersome, cumbrous; massive; lumpish, unwieldy; ponderous

18 **weighted,** weighed down, weighted down; bogged down; burdened, oppressed, laden, cumbered, encumbered, charged, loaded, fraught, freighted, taxed, saddled, hampered; overburdened, overloaded, overladen, overcharged, overfreighted, overfraught, overweighted, overtaxed; borne-down, sinking, foundering

19 **weighable,** ponderable; appreciable, palpable, sensible

20 **gravitational,** mass

ADVS 21 **heavily,** heavy, weightily, leadenly; burdensomely, onerously, oppressively; ponderously, cumbersomely, cumbrously

22 **unit of weight**

assay ton
carat (c)
carat grain
centigram (cg)
dead-weight ton
decagram, decigram (dkg, dg)
displacement ton
dram, dram avoirdupois (dr)
dram apothecaries' (dr ap)
dyne
grain (gr)
gram (g)
gram equivalent, gram equivalent weight
gram molecule, gram-molecular weight
gross ton
hectogram (hg)
hundredweight (cwt)
international carat
kilogram, kilo (kg)
kiloton
long hundredweight
long ton (lt)
measurement ton
megaton
metric carat
metric ton (MT, t)
microgram (mcg)
milligram (mg)
mole, mol
myriagram (myg)
net ton
newton
ounce, ounce avoirdupois (oz, oz av)
ounce apothecaries' (oz ap)
ounce troy (oz t)
pearl grain
pennyweight (dwt, pwt)
pound, pound avoirdupois (lb, lb av)
poundal
pound apothecaries' (lb ap)
pound troy (lb t)
quintal
scruple
shipping ton
short hundredweight
short ton (st)
slug
sthene
stone (st)
ton (tn)

298 LIGHTNESS

<lack of heaviness>

NOUNS 1 **lightness,** levity, unheaviness, lack of weight; weightlessness; buoyancy, buoyance, floatability; levitation, ascent; volatility; airiness, ethereality; foaminess, frothiness, bubbliness, yeastiness; downiness, fluffiness, gossameriness; softness, gentleness, delicacy, daintiness, tenderness; light touch, gentle touch; frivolity

2 <comparisons> air, ether, feather, down, thistledown, flue, fluff, fuzz, sponge, gossamer,

cobweb, fairy, straw, chaff, dust, mote, cork, chip, bubble, froth, foam, spume
3 **lightening,** easing, easement, alleviation, relief; disburdening, disencumberment, unburdening, unloading, unlading, unsaddling, untaxing, unfreighting; unballasting
4 **leavening,** fermentation; leaven, ferment
5 <indeterminacy of weight> **imponderableness,** imponderability, unweighableness, unweighability; imponderables, imponderabilia
VERBS 6 **lighten,** make light, make lighter, reduce weight; unballast; ease, alleviate, relieve; disburden, disencumber, unburden, unload, unlade, off-load; be light, weigh lightly, have little weight, kick the beam; lose weight
7 **leaven,** raise, ferment
8 **buoy,** buoy up; float, float high, ride high, waft; sustain, hold up, bear up, uphold, upbear, uplift, upraise; refloat
9 **levitate,** rise, ascend; hover, float
ADJS 10 **light,** unheavy, imponderous, lightweight; weightless; airy, ethereal, aeriform; volatile; frothy, foamy, spumy, spumous, spumescent, bubbly, yeasty; downy, feathery, fluffy, gossamery; *soufflé* <Fr>, *mousse* <Fr>, *léger* <Fr>; light as air, light as a feather, light as gossamer; frivolous; insubstantial
11 **lightened,** eased, unburdened, disburdened, disencumbered, unencumbered, relieved, alleviated, out from under, breathing easier; mitigated
12 **light,** gentle, soft, delicate, dainty, tender, easy
13 **lightweight,** bantamweight, featherweight; underweight
14 **buoyant,** floaty, floatable; floating, supernatant
15 levitative, levitational
16 **lightening,** easing, alleviating, alleviative, alleviatory, relieving, disburdening, unburdening, disencumbering
17 **leavening,** raising, **fermenting,** fermentative, working; yeasty, barmy; enzymic, diastatic
18 **imponderable,** unweighable

299 RARITY

<lack of density, thickness>

NOUNS 1 **rarity,** rareness; thinness, tenuousness, tenuity; subtlety, subtility; fineness, slightness, flimsiness, unsubstantiality, insubstantiality; ethereality, airiness, immateriality, incorporeality, bodilessness, insolidity, low density; diffuseness, dispersedness, scatter, scatteredness; stuff that dreams are made of
2 **rarefaction,** attenuation, subtilization, etherealization; diffusion, dispersion, scattering; thinning, thinning-out, dilution, adulteration, watering, watering-down; decompression
VERBS 3 **rarefy, attenuate,** thin, thin out; dilute, adulterate, water, water down, cut; subtilize, etherealize; diffuse, disperse, scatter; expand; decompress
ADJS 4 **rare,** rarefied; subtle; thin, thinned, dilute, attenuated, attenuate; thinned-out, diluted, adulterated, watered, watered-down, cut; tenuous, fine, flimsy, slight, unsubstantial, insubstantial; airy, ethereal, vaporous, gaseous, windy; diffused, diffuse, dispersed, scattered; uncompact, uncompressed, decompressed
5 **rarefactive,** rarefactional

300 MEASUREMENT

<process determining amount or degree>

NOUNS 1 **measurement, measure;** mensuration, measuring, gauging; admeasurement; metage; estimation, estimate, rough measure, approximation, ballpark figure; quantification, quantitation, quantization; appraisal, appraisement, stocktaking, assay, assaying; assessment, determination, rating, valuation, evaluation; assizement, assize, sizing up, eyeballing; survey, surveying; triangulation; instrumentation; telemetry, telemetering; metric system; metrication; English system of measurement; calibration, recalibration, correction, computation, calculation
2 **measure,** measuring instrument, meter, instrument, gauge, barometer, rule, yardstick, measuring rod, measuring stick, standard, norm, canon, criterion, test, touchstone, check, benchmark; rule of thumb; pattern, model, type, prototype; scale, graduated scale, calibrated scale; meter-reading, reading, readout, value, degree, quantity; parameter
3 **extent,** quantity, degree, size, distance, length, breadth; weight
4 <**measure system**> U.S. liquid measure, British imperial liquid measure, U.S. dry measure, British imperial dry measure, apothecaries' measure, **linear measure** <see list>, square measure, circular measure, cubic measure, **volume measure** <see list>, **area measure** <see list>, surface measure, surveyor's measure, land measure, board measure
5 coordinates, Cartesian coordinates, rectangular coordinates, polar coordinates, cylindrical coordinates, spherical coordinates, equator coordinates; latitude, longitude; altitude, azimuth; declination, right ascension; ordinate, abscissa
6 **waterline;** watermark, tidemark, floodmark,

high-water mark; load waterline, load line mark, Plimsoll mark, Plimsoll line

7 **measurability,** mensurability, computability, determinability, quantifiability

8 science of measurement, **mensuration,** metrology

9 **measurer,** meter, gauger; geodesist, geodetic engineer; surveyor, land surveyor, quantity surveyor; topographer, cartographer, mapmaker, oceanographer, chorographer; appraiser, assessor; assayer; valuer, valuator, evaluator; estimator; quantifier, actuary; timekeeper

VERBS 10 **measure,** gauge, quantify, quantitate, quantize, mete, take the measure of, mensurate, triangulate, apply the yardstick to; estimate, make an approximation; assess, rate, appraise, valuate, value, evaluate, appreciate, prize; assay; size, size up, take the dimensions of; weigh, weigh up; survey; plumb, probe, sound, fathom; span, pace, step; calibrate, graduate, grade; divide; caliper; meter; read the meter, take a reading, check a parameter; compute, calculate, reckon; metrize

11 **measure off,** mark off, lay off, set off, rule off; step off, pace off, pace out; measure out, mark out, lay out; put at

ADJS 12 **measuring,** metric, metrical, mensural, mensurative, mensurational; valuative, valuational; quantitative, numerative; approximative, estimative; geodetic, geodetical, geodesic, geodesical, hypsographic, hypsographical, hypsometric, hypsometrical; topographic, topographical, chorographic, chorographical, cartographic, cartographical, oceanographic, oceanographical

13 **measured,** gauged, metered, quantified; quantitated, quantized; appraised, assessed, valuated, valued, rated, ranked; assayed; surveyed, plotted, mapped, admeasured, triangulated; known by measurement

14 **measurable,** mensurable, quantifiable, numerable, meterable, gaugeable, fathomable, determinable, computable, calculable; quantitatable, quantizable; estimable; assessable, appraisable, ratable; appreciable, perceptible, noticeable

ADVS 15 **measurably,** appreciably, perceptibly, noticeably

16 **area measure**

acre
are
arpent
centare
hectare (ha)
perch
pole
rood
section
square foot
square inch
kilometer
square mile
square meter

17 **linear measure**

absolute angstrom
Admiralty mile
angstrom, angstrom unit (a, å, A, Å)
arpent
astronomical unit
block
board foot (bd ft)
cable length
centimeter (cm)
chain, Gunter's chain
cubit
decameter
decimeter (dm)
ell
em
en
fathom (fthm)
fingerbreadth, finger
foot (ft)
footstep
furlong
hand
handbreadth, handsbreadth
hectometer (hm)
inch (in)
international angstrom
kilometer (km)
land mile
league
light-year
line
link
meter (m)
micron (μ)
mil
mile (mi)
millimeter (mm)
millimicron, micromillimeter
myriameter
nail
nautical mile (naut mi)
pace
palm
parsec
perch
pica
point (pt)
pole
rod
statute mile (stat mi)
step
stride
wavelength
yard (yd)

18 **volume measure**

barrel
bushel (bu)
centiliter
cord (cd)
cubic foot
cubic meter
cubic yard
cup
decaliter
decastere
deciliter (dl)
drop
dry pint
dry quart
fifth
finger
fluid ounce (fl oz)
fluidram
gallon (gal)
gill
hectoliter
hogshead
jeroboam
jigger
kiloliter
liquid pint
liquid quart
liter (l)
magnum
milliliter (ml)
minim
peck
pint (pt)
pony
quart (qt)
stere
tablespoon (tb, tbs)
teaspoon (tsp)

301 YOUTH

<*young time of life*>

NOUNS 1 **youth, youthfulness,** youngness, juvenility, juvenescence, tenderness, tender age, early years, school age, *jeunesse* <Fr>, jejuneness, prime of life, flower of life, salad days, springtime of life, springtide of life, seedtime of life, flowering time, bloom, florescence, budtime, younger days, school days, golden season of life, heyday of youth, heyday of the blood, young blood, early days; young fogey, young gun

2 **childhood**; boyhood; girlhood, maidenhood, maidenhead, puerility; puppyhood, calfhood; subteens, preteens; child-rearing

3 **immaturity,** undevelopment, inexperience, callowness, unripeness, greenness, rawness, naiveté, sappiness, freshness, juiciness, dewiness; minority, juniority, infancy, nonage; Peter Pan syndrome

4 **childishness,** childlikeness, puerility; boyishness, boylikeness; girlishness, girl-likeness, maidenliness

5 **infancy,** babyhood, the cradle, the crib, the nursery, incunabula; arsenic hour

6 **adolescence,** maturation, maturement, pubescence, **puberty;** nobility; preteen, tweenager

7 **teens,** teen years, teenage, teenagehood, tweenage, awkward age, growing pains

VERBS 8 make young, youthen, **rejuvenate,** reinvigorate; turn back the clock

ADJS 9 **young,** youngling, youngish, juvenile, juvenal, juvenescent, **youthful,** youthlike, in the flower of youth, in the bloom of youth, blooming, florescent, flowering, dewy, fresh-faced; young-looking, well-preserved

10 **immature,** unadult; inexperienced, unseasoned, unfledged, new-fledged, fledgling, callow, unripe, ripening, unmellowed, raw, green, vernal, primaveral, dewy, juicy, sappy, budding, tender, virginal, intact, innocent, naive, ingenuous, undeveloped, growing, unformed, unlicked, wet behind the ears, not dry behind the ears, unprepared; minor, underage, underaged

11 **childish,** childlike, kiddish, puerile; boyish, boylike, beardless; girlish, girl-like, maiden, maidenly; puppyish, puppylike, puplike, calflike, coltish, coltlike; knee-high

12 **infant,** infantile, infantine, babyish, baby; dollish, doll-like; kittenish, kittenlike; newborn, neonatal; in the cradle, in the crib, in the nursery, in swaddling clothes, in diapers, in nappies, in arms, at the breast, tied to mother's apron strings

13 **adolescent,** pubescent, nubile, preteen

14 **teenage,** teenaged, teenish, in one's teens; sweet sixteen

15 **junior,** Jr; younger, puisne

302 YOUNGSTER

<young person>

NOUNS 1 **youngster,** young person, **youth,** juvenile, rugrat, youngling, young'un, juvenal; stripling, slip, sprig, sapling; fledgling; hopeful, young hopeful; minor, infant; adolescent, pubescent; teenager, teener, teenybopper, preteen, tweenager, twenty-something, thirty-something, young adult; junior, younger, youngest, baby; millennial

2 **young people, youth,** young, younger generation, rising generation, new generation, baby boomers, boomers, Generation X, Generation Y, lost generation; millennials; young blood, young fry; children, tots, childkind; small fry, kids, little kids, little guys; boyhood, girlhood; babyhood

3 **child**; nipper, kid, kiddy, kiddo, kiddie, little one, little fellow, little guy, little bugger, shaver, little shaver, little squirt, tot, little tot, wee tot, pee-wee, tad, little tad, tyke, mite, chit, innocent, little innocent, moppet, poppet; darling, cherub, lamb, lambkin, kitten, offspring

4 **brat,** urchin; minx, imp, puck, elf, gamin, little monkey, whippersnapper, young whippersnapper, *enfant terrible* <Fr>, little terror, holy terror; spoiled brat; snotnose kid; juvenile delinquent (JD), punk, punk kid

5 **boy,** lad, laddie, youth, manchild, manling, young man, *garçon* <Fr>, *muchacho* <Sp>, schoolboy, schoolkid, fledgling, hobbledehoy; fellow; pup, puppy, whelp, cub, colt; master; sonny, sonny boy; bud, buddy; bub, bubba; buck, young buck; big guy

6 **girl,** girlie, maid, maiden, lass, girlchild, lassie, young thing, young creature, young lady, damsel in distress, damsel, damoiselle, demoiselle, *jeune fille* <Fr>, *mademoiselle* <Fr>, *muchacha* <Sp>, miss, missy, little missy, slip, wench, colleen <Irl>

7 <nonformal> **gal,** dame, chick, tomato, babe, baby, broad, doll, skirt, jill, chit, cutie, filly, heifer; teenybopper, weenybopper; frail

8 **schoolgirl,** schoolmaid, schoolmiss, junior miss, preteen; subdebutante; bobbysoxer, tomboy, hoyden, romp; piece, nymphet; virgin

9 **infant,** baby, babe, babe in arms, little darling, little angel, little doll, cherub, bouncing baby, puling infant, mewling infant, babykins, baby bunting; papoose, *bambino* <Ital>; toddler; suckling, nursling, fosterling, weanling; neonate; yearling, yearold; premature baby, preemie, incubator baby; preschooler; crumbcrusher, crumbcruncher, crumbgrinder, crumbsnatcher; rug rat, carpet rat, rug ape, carpet ape, curtain-climber; blue baby

10 **<young animal>** yearling, fledgling, birdling, nestling; chick, chicky, chickling; pullet, fry, fryer; duckling; gosling, cygnet; kitten, kit, catling; pup, puppy, whelp; cub; calf, dogie, weaner; colt, foal, filly; piglet, pigling, shoat; lamb, lambkin; kid,

yeanling; fawn; tadpole, polliwog; litter, nest, brood, clutch, spawn, farrow

11 <**young plant**> sprout, seedling, set; sucker, shoot, slip, offshoot; twig, sprig, scion, sapling

12 <**young insect**> larva, chrysalis, aurelia, cocoon, pupa, grub; nymph, nympha; wriggler, wiggler; caterpillar, maggot

303 AGE

<time of life>

NOUNS 1 **age,** years; time of life, stage of life; lifetime, lifespan, life expectancy, timespan, longevity; seven ages of man, infancy, childhood, youth, adolescence, adulthood, middle age, maturity, old age, declining years, senility

2 **maturity, adulthood,** majority, adultness, grown-upness, maturation, matureness, full growth, mature age, legal age, voting age, driving age, drinking age, *legalis homo* <L>; age of consent; ripeness, ripe age, riper years, full age, full bloom, flower of age, prime, prime of life, age of responsibility, age of discretion, years of discretion, age of matured powers; manhood, man's estate, virility, masculinity, maleness, manliness; womanhood, womanness, femininity, femaleness, womanliness; adult student; young fogey

3 **seniority,** eldership, deanship, primogeniture

4 **middle age,** middle life, meridian of life, the middle years, the wrong side of forty, the dangerous age, prime of life; change of life, perimenopause, menopause, climacteric, midlife crisis, middlescence; young at heart; club-sandwich generation

5 **old age,** oldness, eld, elderliness, senectitude, senescence, agedness, advanced age, advanced years; superannuation, pensionable age, retirement age, age of retirement; ripe old age, the golden years, senior citizenship, hoary age, hoariness, gray hairs, white hairs, grayness; decline of life, declining years, youth deficiency, the vale of years, threescore years and ten, the downward slope, the shady side; sunset of one's days, twilight of one's days, evening of one's days, winter of one's days; decrepitude, ricketiness, infirm old age, infirmity of age, infirmity, debility, caducity, feebleness; dotage, anecdotage, second childhood; senility, anility; longevity, long life, length of years, hale old age

6 **maturation,** development, growth, ripening, blooming, blossoming, flourishing; **mellowing,** seasoning, tempering; **aging,** senescence

7 **change of life,** perimenopause, menopause, climacteric, grand climacteric, midlife crisis, sea change

8 **geriatrics,** gerontology, geriatric medicine

VERBS 9 **mature, grow up,** grow, develop, ripen, flower, flourish, bloom, blossom; fledge, leave the nest, put up one's hair, not be in pigtails, put on long pants; come of age, come to maturity, attain majority, reach one's majority, reach twenty-one, reach voting age, reach the age of consent, reach manhood, reach womanhood, write oneself a man, come to man's estate, come into man's estate, assume the toga virilis, come into years of discretion, be in the prime of life, cut one's wisdom teeth, cut one's eyeteeth, have sown one's wild oats, settle down; mellow, season, temper

10 **age, grow old,** senesce, get on, get along, get on in years, get along in years, grow whiskers, have whiskers, be over the hill, turn gray, turn white; decline, wane, fade, fail, sink, waste away; dodder, totter, shake; wither, wrinkle, shrivel, wizen; live to a ripe old age, cheat the undertaker; be in one's dotage, be in one's second childhood

11 have had one's day, have seen one's day, have seen one's best days, have seen better days; show one's age, show marks of age, have one foot in the grave

ADJS 12 **adult, mature**, adults-only; of age, out of one's teens, big, grown, grown-up; old enough to know better; marriageable, of marriageable age, marriable, nubile

13 **mature,** ripe, ripened, of full age, of ripe age, developed, fully developed, well-developed, full-grown, full-fledged, fully fledged, full-blown, in full bloom, in one's prime; mellow, mellowed, seasoned, tempered, aged

14 **middle-aged,** midlife, fortyish, fiftiesh, matronly; perimenopausal, menopausal; middlescent

15 **past one's prime,** senescent, on the shady side, overblown, overripe, of a certain age, over the hill

16 **aged, elderly**, old, grown old in years, along in years, up in years, advanced in years, on in years, years old, advanced, advanced in life, at an advanced age, ancient, geriatric, gerontic; venerable, old as Methuselah, old as the hills; patriarchal; hoary, hoar, gray, white, gray-headed, white-headed, gray-haired, white-haired, gray-crowned, white-crowned, gray-bearded, white-bearded, gray with age, white with age; wrinkled, prune-faced; wrinkly, with crow's feet, marked with the crow's foot, late-life

17 **aging,** growing old, senescent, getting on, getting along, getting on in years, getting along in years, getting up in years, not as young as one used to be, long in the tooth; declining, sinking, waning, fading, wasting, doting

18 **really old,** stricken in years, decrepit, infirm, weak, debilitated, feeble, geriatric, timeworn,

the worse for wear, rusty, moth-eaten, mossbacked, fossilized, wracked with age, ravaged with age, run to seed; doddering, doddery, doddered, tottering, tottery, rickety, shaky, palsied; on one's last legs, with one foot in the grave; wizened, crabbed, withered, shriveled, like a prune, mummylike, papery-skinned; senile, anile

304 ADULT OR OLD PERSON

<older person>

NOUNS 1 **adult,** grownup, mature man, mature woman, grown man, grown woman, big boy, big girl; **man, woman;** major, *legalis homo* <L>; no chicken, no spring chicken; adult student

2 **old man,** elder, oldster; golden-ager, senior citizen, geriatric, patron; old chap, old party, old gentleman, old gent, codger, old codger, geezer, old geezer, gramps, gaffer, old duffer, old dog, old-timer, dotard, veteran, pantaloon, man of the world; patriarch, graybeard, reverend sir, venerable sir; grandfather, grandsire; Father Time, Methuselah, Nestor, Old Paar; sexagenarian, septuagenarian, octogenarian, nonagenarian, centenarian; curmudgeon; eld

3 **old woman,** old lady, little old lady, dowager, granny, old granny, dame, grandam, matron, matriarch, trot, old trot; old dame, hen, girl; old bag, bat, battleax; old maid; crone, hag, witch, beldam, frump, old wife; grandmother; woman of the world

4 <**old people**> the old, older generation, seniors, elds, retirees, over-the-hill gang; Darby and Joan, Baucis and Philemon

5 **senior,** Sr, *senex* <L>, elder, older; dean, *doyen* <Fr>, *doyenne* <Fr>; father, sire; firstling, first-born, eldest, oldest

VERBS 6 mature; **grow old**

ADJS 7 mature; middle-aged; aged, older

305 ORGANIC MATTER

<living nature>

NOUNS 1 **organic matter,** animate matter, living matter, all that lives, living nature, organic nature, organized matter; biology; flesh, tissue, fiber, brawn, plasm; flora and fauna, plant and animal life, animal and vegetable kingdom, biosphere, biota, ecosphere, noosphere; force of nature; DNA test

2 **organism,** organization, organic being, life-form, form of life, living being, living thing, being, animate being, creature, created being, individual, genetic individual, physiological individual, morphological individual; zoon, zooid; virus; aerobic organism, anaerobic organism; heterotrophic organism, autotrophic organism; microbe, microorganism

3 **biological classification,** taxonomy, biotaxy, kingdom, phylum; biome

4 **cell,** bioplast, cellule; procaryotic cell, eucaryotic cell; plant cell, animal cell; germ cell, somatic cell; corpuscle; unicellularity, multicellularity; germ layer, ectoderm, endoderm, mesoderm; **protoplasm,** energid; trophoplasm; chromatoplasm; germ plasm; cytoplasm; ectoplasm, endoplasm; cellular tissue, reticulum; plasmodium, coenocyte, syncytium

5 **organelle;** plastid; chromoplast, plastosome, chloroplast; mitochondrion; Golgi apparatus; ribosome; spherosome, microbody; vacuole; central apparatus, cytocentrum; centroplasm; central body, microcentrum; centrosome; centrosphere; centriole, basal body; pili, cilia, flagella, spindle fibers; aster; kinoplasm; plasmodesmata; cell membrane

6 **metaplasm;** cell wall, cell plate; structural polysaccharide; bast, phloem; xylem, xyl-, xylo-; cellulose, chitin

7 **nucleus,** cell nucleus; macronucleus, meganucleus; micronucleus; nucleolus; plasmosome; karyosome, chromatin strands; nuclear envelope; chromatin, karyotin; basichromatin, heterochromatin, oxychromatin

8 **chromosome;** allosome; heterochromosome, sex chromosome, idiochromosome; W chromosome; X chromosome, accessory chromosome, monosome; Y chromosome; Z chromosome; euchromosome, autosome; homologous chromosomes; univalent chromosome, chromatid; centromere; gene-string, chromonema; genome; chromosome complement; chromosome number, diploid number, haploid number; polyploidy; chromosome map

9 **genetic material, gene;** allele; operon; cistron, structural gene, regulator gene, operator gene; altered gene; deoxyribonucleic acid (DNA); DNA double helix, superhelix, supercoil; nucleotide, codon; ribonucleic acid (RNA); messenger RNA (mRNA); transfer RNA (tRNA); ribosomal RNA; anticodon; gene pool, gene complex, gene flow, genetic drift; genotype, biotype; hereditary character, heredity; genetic counseling; genetic screening; developmental genetics; recombinant DNA technology, gene mapping, gene splicing; gene transplantation, gene transfer, germline insertion; intronizing, intron, intervening sequence; exonizing, exon; genetic engineering, genetic fingerprinting, DNA fingerprinting, DNA

testing, genetic profile; designer gene; gene therapy; stem cell therapy

10 **gamete,** germ cell, reproductive cell; macrogamete, megagamete; microgamete; planogamete; genetoid; gamone; gametangium, gametophore; gametophyte; germ plasm, idioplasm

11 **sperm,** spermatozoa, seed, semen, jism*, gism*, come*, cum*, scum, spunk; seminal fluid, spermatic fluid, milt; sperm cell, male gamete; spermatozoon, spermatozoid, antherozoid; antheridium; spermatium, spermatiophore, spermatophore, spermagonium; pollen; spermatogonium; androcyte, spermatid, spermatocyte

12 **ovum,** egg, egg cell, female gamete, oösphere; oöcyte; oögonium; ovicell, oöecium; ovule; stirp; ovulation, ovulating; donor egg

13 **spore;** microspore; macrospore, megaspore; swarm spore, zoospore, planospore; spore mother cell, sporocyte; zygospore; sporocarp, cystocarp; basidium; sporangium, megasporangium, microsporangium; sporocyst; gonidangium; sporogonium, sporophyte; sporophore; sorus

14 **embryo,** zygote, oösperm, oöspore, blastula; *Anlage* <Ger>; fetus, germ, germen, rudiment; larva, nymph

15 **egg;** ovule; bird's egg; roe, fish eggs, caviar, spawn; yolk, yellow, vitellus; white, egg white, albumen, glair; eggshell

16 **cell division;** mitosis; amitosis; metamitosis, eumitosis; endomitosis, promitosis; haplomitosis, mesomitosis; karyomitosis; karyokinesis; interphase, prophase, metaphase, anaphase, telophase, diaster, cytokinesis; meiosis

ADJS 17 **organic,** organismic; organized; animate, living, vital, zoetic; biological, biotic; physiological

18 protoplasmic, plasmic, plasmatic; **genetic,** genic, hereditary

19 **cellular,** cellulous; unicellular, multicellular; corpuscular

20 **gametic**, gamic, sexual; **spermatic**, spermic, seminal, spermatozoal, spermatozoan, spermatozoic; sporal, sporous, sporoid; sporogenous

21 **nuclear,** nucleal, nucleary, nucleate; multinucleate; nucleolar, nucleolate, nucleolated; chromosomal; chromatinic; haploid, diploid, polyploid

22 **embryonic,** germinal, germinant, germinative, germinational; larval; fetal; in the bud; germiparous

23 **egglike,** ovicular, eggy; ovular; albuminous, albuminoid; yolked, yolky; oviparous

306 LIFE

<being alive>

NOUNS 1 **life, living,** vitality, being alive, having life, animation, animate existence; breath; liveliness, animal spirits, vivacity, spriteliness; long life, longevity; life expectancy, life span; viability; lifetime; immortality; birth; existence

2 **life force,** soul, spirit, indwelling spirit, force of life, living force, *vis vitae, vis vitalis* <L>, vital force, vital energy, animating force, animating power, animating principle, inspiriting force, archeus, élan vital, impulse of life, vital principle, vital spark, vital flame, spark of life, divine spark, life principle, vital spirit, vital fluid, anima, consciousness; breath, life breath, breath of life, breath of one's nostrils, divine breath, life essence, essence of life, pneuma; prana, atman, jivatma, jiva; blood, lifeblood, heartblood, heart's blood; heart, heartbeat, beating heart; seat of life; growth force, bathmism; life process; biorhythm, biological clock, internal clock; life cycle

3 **the living,** the living and breathing, all animate nature, the quick; the quick and the dead

4 **living being,** human being, living person, entity, living soul, living thing; life on earth; survivor; the quick

5 life cycle, **lifetime**, longevity, life expectancy

6 vivification, vitalization, animation, quickening

7 **biosphere**, ecosphere, noosphere; biochore, biotype, biocycle

VERBS 8 **live,** be alive, be animate, be vital, have life, exist, be, breathe, respire, live and breathe, fetch breath, draw breath, draw the breath of life, walk the earth, subsist

9 **come to life,** come into existence, come into being, come into the world, see the light, be incarnated, be born, be begotten, be conceived; quicken; revive, come to, come alive, come around, regain consciousness, show signs of life; awake, awaken; rise again, live again, rise from the grave, resurge, resurrect, resuscitate, reanimate, return to life

10 **vivify,** vitalize, energize, animate, quicken, inspirit, invigorate, enliven, imbue with life, endow with life, give birth to, give life to, put life into, put new life into, breathe life into, give a new lease on life, bring to life, bring into existence, bring into being, call into existence, call into being; conceive; give birth, reproduce

11 **keep alive,** feed, nourish, provide for, keep body and soul together, endure, survive, persist, last, last out, hang on, hang in, be spared, come through, continue, carry on, have nine lives; support life; cheat death

ADJS **12 living, alive,** having life, live, very much alive, alive and well, alive and kicking, conscious, breathing, quick, animate, animated, vital, viable, zoetic, instinct with life, imbued with life, endowed with life, vivified, enlivened, inspirited; in the flesh, among the living, in the land of the living, on this side of the grave, still with us, still breathing, above-ground, incarnate; existent; extant; long-lived, tenacious of life; capable of life, capable of survival

13 life-giving, animating, animative, quickening, vivifying, energizing

307 DEATH

<ending of life>

NOUNS **1 death, dying,** somatic death, clinical death, biological death, abiosis, decease, demise; brain death; perishing, release, passing away, passing, passing over, leaving life, making an end, departure, parting, going, going off, going away, exit, ending, end, end of life, cessation of life, end of the road, end of the line; loss of life, no life, ebb of life, expiration, expiry, dissolution, extinction, bane, annihilation, extinguishment, quietus; doom, crack of doom, summons of death, final summons, sentence of death, death knell, knell; sleep, rest, eternal rest, eternal sleep, last sleep, last rest; grave; reward, debt of nature, last debt; last muster, last roundup, curtains, big sleep; jaws of death, hand of death, finger of death, shadow of death, shades of death; rigor mortis; near-death experience (NDE); the beyond, the other side, the Great Divide

2 <personifications and symbols> **Death, Grim Reaper,** Reaper; pale horse, pale rider; angel of death, death's bright angel, Azrael; scythe of Death, sickle of Death; skull, death's-head, grinning skull, crossbones, skull and crossbones; *memento mori* <L>; white cross; great leveler, thief in the night, Last Summoner; shadow of death, dance of death

3 river of death, Styx, Stygian shore, Acheron; Jordan, Jordan's bank; valley of the shadow of death; Heaven; Hell

4 early death, early grave, untimely end, premature death; sudden death; stroke of death, death stroke; deathblow

5 violent death; killing; suffocation, smothering, smotheration; asphyxiation; choking, choke, strangulation, strangling; drowning, watery grave; fatal accident, accidental death; starvation; liver death, serum death; megadeath; suicide, assisted suicide; murder, assassination; capital punishment, execution

6 natural death; easy death, quiet death, peaceful death, easy end, quiet end, peaceful end, euthanasia, blessed release, welcome release; stillbirth

7 dying day, deathday; final hour, fatal hour, last hour, dying hour, running-out of the sands, deathtime

8 moribundity, extremity, last extremity, final extremity; **deathbed;** deathwatch; death struggle, agony, last agony, death agony, death throes, throes of death; last breath, last gasp, dying breath; death rattle, death groan; making an end, passing, passing away, crossing the Styx; extreme unction, last rites

9 swan song, *chant du cygne* <Fr>, death song, final words, last words

10 bereavement, bereavement counseling

11 deathliness, deathlikeness, deadliness; weirdness, eeriness, uncanniness, unearthliness; ghostliness, ghostlikeness; ghastliness, grisliness, gruesomeness, macabreness; paleness, haggardness, wanness, luridness, pallor; cadaverousness, corpselikeness; Hippocratic face, Hippocratic countenance, mask of death

12 death rate, death toll; **mortality,** mortalness, mortality rate; extinction, dissolution, abiosis, transience; mutability

13 obituary, obit, death notice, necrology, necrologue; register of deaths, roll of the dead, death roll, mortuary roll, bill of mortality; fatality list, casualty list; martyrology; death toll, body count

14 terminal case; **dying**

15 corpse, dead body, dead man, dead woman, dead person, cadaver, carcass, body; flatliner; *corpus delicti* <L>; stiff; the dead, the defunct, the deceased, the departed, the loved one; decedent, the late lamented; remains, mortal remains, organic remains, carrion, bones, skeleton, dry bones, relics, reliquiae; dust, ashes, earth, clay, tenement of clay; crowbait, food for worms; mummy, mummification; embalmed corpse; body bag

16 dead, the majority, the great majority; one's fathers, one's ancestors; the choir invisible

17 autopsy, postmortem, inquest, postmortem examination, ex post facto examination, necropsy, necroscopy; medical examiner, coroner, pathologist, mortality committee

VERBS **18 die, decease,** succumb, expire, perish, be taken by death, up and die, cease to be, cease to live, part, depart, quit this world, make one's exit, go, go the way of all flesh, go out, pass, pass on, pass away, meet one's death, meet one's end, meet one's fate, end one's life, end one's days, depart this life, put off mortality, shuffle off this mortal coil, lose one's life, fall, be lost, relinquish one's life, surrender one's life, resign one's life, resign one's being, give up the ghost, yield the ghost, yield the spirit, yield one's breath, take one's last breath, breathe one's last, stop breathing, fall asleep, close one's eyes, take one's last sleep, pay the debt of nature, pay the debt to nature, go out with the ebb, return to dust, return to the earth

19 <nonformal> **croak,** go west, kick the bucket, kick in, pop off, conk off, conk out, cop it, drop off, step off, go to the wall, go home feet first, knock off, pipe off, kick off, shove off, bow out, pass out, peg out, push up daisies, go for a burton <Brit>, belly up, go belly up, bite the dust, take the last count; flatline; check out, check in, cash in, cash in one's checks, cash in one's chips; turn up one's toes; slip one's cable; buy the farm, buy the ranch, have one's time, have it, buy it

20 **meet one's Maker,** go to glory, go to kingdom come, go to the happy hunting grounds, go to a better place, go to a better land, go to a better life, go to a better world, go to one's rest, go to one's reward, go home, go home feet first, go to one's last home, go to one's long account, go over to the majority, go over to the great majority, join the majority, join the great majority, reach a better place, be gathered to one's fathers, join one's ancestors, join the angels, join the choir invisible, die in the Lord, go to Abraham's bosom, pass over Jordan, walk through the valley of the shadow of death, cross the Stygian ferry, give an obolus to Charon; awake to life immortal

21 **drop dead,** fall dead, fall down dead; come to an untimely end; predecease

22 die in harness, die with one's boots on, make a good end, die fighting, die in the last ditch, die like a man

23 die a natural death; die a violent death, be killed; starve, famish; smother, suffocate; asphyxiate; choke, strangle; drown, go to a watery grave, go to Davy Jones's locker; catch one's death, catch one's death of cold

24 lay down one's life for one's country, give one's life for one's country, die for one's country, make the supreme sacrifice, do one's bit

25 be dying, be moribund, be terminal; die out, become extinct

26 **be dead**, be no more, sleep with the Lord, be asleep with the Lord, sleep with one's fathers, sleep with one's ancestors; lie in the grave, lie in Abraham's bosom

27 **bereave;** leave, leave behind; orphan, widow

ADJS 28 **deathly,** deathlike, deadly; weird, eerie, uncanny, unearthly; ghostly, ghostlike; ghastly, grisly, gruesome, macabre; pale, deathly pale, wan, lurid, blue, livid, haggard; cadaverous, corpselike; mortuary

29 **dead,** lifeless, breathless, without life, brain-dead, inanimate, exanimate, without vital functions; deceased, demised, defunct, croaked, departed, departed this life, destitute of life, gone, passed on, passed away, gone the way of all flesh, gone west, extinct, gone before, long gone, dead and gone, done for, dead and done for, no more, finished, taken off, taken away, released, fallen, bereft of life, gone for a burton; at rest, resting easy, still, out of one's misery; asleep, sleeping, reposing; asleep in Jesus, with the Lord, asleep in the Lord, dead in the Lord; called home, out of the world, gone to a better world, gone to a better place, gone to a better land, gone but not forgotten, launched into eternity, gone to glory, taken by God, called by God, at the Pearly Gates, in Abraham's bosom, joined the choir invisible, gone to kingdom come, with the saints, sainted, numbered with the dead; in the grave, deep-sixed, six feet under, pushing up daisies; carrion, food for worms; martyred; death-struck, death-stricken, smitten with death; stillborn, dead on arrival, DOA; late, late lamented

30 **stone-dead;** dead as a doornail, dead as a dodo, dead as a herring, dead as mutton; cold, stone-cold, stiff

31 **drowned,** in a watery grave, in Davy Jones's locker

32 **dying, terminal,** expiring, going, slipping, slipping away, sinking, sinking fast, fading, low, despaired of, given up, given up for dead, not long for this world, hopeless, bad, moribund, near death, deathlike, perishing, doomed, near one's end, at the end of one's rope, hanging by a thread, done for, at the point of death, at death's door, at the portals of death, *in articulo mortis* <L>, *in extremis* <L>, in the jaws of death, facing death, in the face of death; on one's last legs, half-dead, with one foot in the grave, tottering on the brink of the grave; on one's deathbed; at the last gasp; in critical condition, mortally ill; nonviable, unviable, incapable of life

33 **mortal,** perishable, subject to death, ephemeral, transient, mutable

34 **bereaved,** bereft, deprived; widowed; orphan, orphaned, parentless, fatherless, motherless

35 **postmortem,** postmortal, postmortuary, postmundane, post-obit, postobituary, **posthumous**

ADVS 36 **deathly, deadly;** to the death, *à la mort* <Fr>

PHRS 37 one's hour is come, one's days are

numbered, one's race is run, one's doom is sealed, life hangs by a thread, one's number is up, Death knocks at the door, Death stares one in the face, the sands of life are running out

308 KILLING

<causing a death>

NOUNS 1 **killing** <see list>, **slaying,** slaughter, dispatch, extermination, destruction, murder, destruction of life, taking of life, death-dealing, dealing of death, bane; kill; bloodshed, bloodletting, blood, gore, flow of blood; mercy killing, euthanasia, negative euthanasia, passive euthanasia; ritual murder, ritual killing, immolation, sacrifice, religious sacrifice, crucifixion; *auto-da-fé* <Sp>, act of faith; martyrdom, martyrization; lynching; stoning, lapidation; defenestration; braining; shooting, drive-by shooting; poisoning; execution; mass killing, biocide, ecocide, genocide; holocaust; mass murder

2 **homicide, manslaughter**; negligent homicide, unlawful killing; **murder,** bloody murder, first-degree murder, second-degree murder, capital murder; serial killing; hit, bump-off, bumping-off, rubbing out, blowing away, wasting, gangland-style execution, contract murder; kiss of death; foul play; assassination; terrorist killing; crime of passion; removal, elimination; liquidation, purge, purging; thuggery, thuggism, thuggee; justifiable homicide

3 **butchery,** butchering, slaughter, shambles, occision, slaughtering, hecatomb, holocaust

4 **carnage,** massacre, bloodbath, decimation, saturnalia of blood; mass murder, mass destruction, mass extermination, wholesale murder, pogrom, race-murder, genocide, race extermination, ethnic cleansing, the Holocaust, the final solution, Roman holiday

5 **suicide,** autocide, self-murder, self-homicide, self-destruction, self-slaughter, death by one's own hand, *felo-de-se* <L>, self-immolation, self-sacrifice; slashing one's wrists, disembowelment, ritual suicide, *hara-kiri, seppuku* <Japanese>, suttee, sutteeism, kamikaze; car of Juggernaut; mass suicide, race suicide, suicide pact; suicide bombing

6 **suffocation,** smothering, smotheration, asphyxiation, asphyxia; strangulation, strangling, burking, throttling, stifling, garrote, garroting; **choking,** choke; **drowning**

7 **execution,** capital punishment, death penalty, legalized killing, judicial murder, judicial execution

8 **fatality,** fatal accident, violent death, **casualty,** disaster, calamity; dead-on-arrival (DOA)

9 **deadliness,** lethality, mortality, fatality; malignance, malignancy, malignity, virulence, perniciousness, banefulness

10 **deathblow,** death stroke, final stroke, fatal blow, mortal blow, lethal blow, *coup de grâce* <Fr>

11 **killer,** slayer, slaughterer, butcher, bloodshedder; massacrer; manslayer, homicide, murderer, man-killer, bloodletter, man of blood, Cain; assassin, assassinator; cutthroat, thug, desperado, bravo, gorilla, apache, gunman; professional killer, contract killer, hired killer, hit man, button man, gun, trigger man, torpedo, gunsel; hatchet man; poisoner; strangler, hangman, garroter, burker; cannibal, maneater, anthropophagus; headhunter; mercy killer, euthanasiast; thrill killer, psychopath, homicidal maniac; serial killer; executioner; matador; exterminator, eradicator; death squad; terrorist, bomber; poison, pesticide; giant-killer

12 <place of slaughter> aceldama, field of blood, field of bloodshed; **slaughterhouse,** butchery, shambles, abattoir; bullring, arena, battleground, battlefield; stockyard; gas chamber, concentration camp, death camp, killing fields; Auschwitz, Belsen

VERBS 13 **kill,** slay, put to death, deprive of life, bereave of life, take life, take the life of, take one's life away, do away with, make away with, put out of the way, end, put an end to, end the life of, hasten someone's end, dispatch, do to death, do for, finish, finish off, kill off, take off, dispose of, exterminate, destroy, annihilate; liquidate, purge; carry off, carry away, remove from life; put down, put away, put to sleep, put one out of one's misery; launch into eternity, send to glory, send to kingdom come, send to one's last account, send to one's Maker; martyr, martyrize; immolate, sacrifice; lynch; cut off, cut down, nip in the bud; poison; chloroform; starve; euthanatize; execute

14 <nonformal> waste, zap, nuke, rub out, croak, snuff, bump off, knock off, bushwhack, lay out, polish off, blow away, blot out, erase, wipe out, blast, do in, off, hit, ice, gun down, pick off, put to bed with a shovel, scrag, take care of, take out, take for a ride, give the business, give the works, deep-six, get, fix, settle

15 **shed blood,** spill blood, let blood, bloody one's hands with, dye one's hands in blood, have blood on one's hands, pour out blood like water, wade knee-deep in blood

16 **murder,** commit murder; assassinate; remove, purge, liquidate, eliminate, get rid of

17 **slaughter,** butcher, massacre, decimate, mow

down, spare none, take no prisoners, wipe out, wipe off the face of the earth, annihilate, exterminate, liquidate, commit carnage, depopulate, slay en masse; purge, commit mass murder, commit mass destruction, murder wholesale, commit genocide, suicide-bomb

18 **strike dead,** fell, bring down, lay low; drop, drop in one's tracks, stop in one's tracks; shoot, shoot down, pistol, shotgun, machinegun, gun down, riddle, shoot to death; cut down, cut to pieces, cut to ribbons, put to the sword, stab to death, jugulate, cut the throat, slash the throat; deal a deathblow, give the quietus, *coup de grâce* <Fr>, silence; knock in the head, knock on the head; brain, blow one's brains out, poleax; stone, lapidate, stone to death; defenestrate; blow up, blow to bits, blow to pieces, blown to kingdom come, frag; disintegrate, vaporize; burn to death, incinerate, burn at the stake

19 **strangle,** garrote, throttle, choke, burke; suffocate, stifle, smother, asphyxiate, stop the breath; **drown**

20 **condemn to death,** sign one's death warrant, strike the death knell of, finger, give the kiss of death to

21 **be killed,** get killed, die a violent death, come to a violent end, meet with foul play; welter in one's own blood

22 **commit suicide,** take one's own life, kill oneself, die by one's own hand, do away with oneself, put an end to oneself; blow one's brains out; take an overdose, overdose, OD; commit hara-kiri, commit seppuku; sign one's own death warrant, doom oneself; jump overboard, do oneself in, off oneself

ADJS 23 **deadly, deathly,** deathful, killing, destructive, death-dealing, death-bringing, feral, fell; savage, brutal; internecine; fatal, mortal, lethal, malignant, malign, virulent, pernicious, baneful; life-threatening; capital; incurable, terminal, inoperable

24 **murderous,** slaughterous; cutthroat; redhanded; homicidal, man-killing, death-dealing; biocidal, genocidal; suicidal, self-destructive; soul-destroying; cruel; bloodthirsty, bloody-minded; bloody, gory, sanguinary; psychopathic, pathological

25 **killing** (types)

aborticide, feticide <fetus>
amicicide <friend>
avicide <birds>
biocide <chemical>
ceticide <whales>
deicide <god>
ecocide <large area>
elephanticide <elephants>
felicide <cats>
formicicide <ants>
fratricide <brother>
fungicide <fungi>
genocide <race or ethnic group>
giganticide <giant>
gynecide, femicide <woman>
herbicide <plants>
homicide <person>
infanticide <infant>
insecticide <insects>
mariticide <spouse, especially husband>
matricide <mother>
microbicide, germicide <germs>
ovicide <egg cell>
parenticide <parent>
parricide <kinsman>
patricide <father>
pesticide <pest>
phytocide <plants>
prolicide <own child>
regicide <king>
rodenticide <rodent>
senicide <old person>
sororicide <sister>
spermicide, spermaticide, spermatozoicide <spermatozoa>
suicide, autocide <self>
tauricide <bulls>
tickicide <ticks>
tyrannicide <tyrant>
uxoricide <wife>
vaticide <prophet>
vermicide, filaricide <worms>
vespacide <wasps>
viricide <viruses>

309 INTERMENT

<burying the dead>

NOUNS 1 **interment, burial,** burying, inhumation, sepulture, entombment; encoffinment, inurning, inurnment, urn burial; primary burial; secondary burial, reburial; disposal of the dead; burial customs, funeral customs, funerary customs; mass burial, burial at sea, military burial, full military rites

2 **cremation,** incineration, burning, reduction to ashes, pyre, scattering of the ashes

3 **embalmment,** embalming; mummification

4 last offices, last honors, **last rites,** funeral rites, last duty, last service, funeral service, funeral ceremony, burial service, graveside service, memorial service, exequies, obsequies; Office of the Dead, Memento of the Dead, requiem, requiem mass, dirge; extreme unction; viaticum; funeral oration, funeral sermon, eulogy; wake, deathwatch, Irish wake; lowering the body

5 **funeral, burial,** burying; funeral procession, cortege; dead march, muffled drum, last post, taps; dirge; burial at sea, deep six

6 **knell,** passing bell, death bell, funeral ring, tolling, tolling of the knell, funeral hymn, dirge

7 **mourner,** griever, lamenter, keener; mute, professional mourner; pallbearer, bearer; eulogist, eulogizer, elegist, epitaphist, obituarist

8 **undertaker,** mortician, funeral director; embalmer; gravedigger; sexton

9 **mortuary, morgue,** deadhouse, charnel house, lichhouse; ossuary, ossuarium; funeral home, funeral parlor, undertaker's establishment; crematorium, crematory, cinerarium; pyre, funeral pile; burning ghat

10 **hearse,** funeral car, funeral coach; catafalque
11 **coffin, casket,** burial case, box, kist <Scot>; wooden kimono, wooden overcoat; sarcophagus; mummy case
12 **urn,** cinerary urn, funerary vessel, funeral urn, funeral vessel, funerary urn, bone pot, ossuary, ossuarium, canopic jar, canopic vase
13 **bier,** litter
14 graveclothes, **shroud,** winding sheet, cerecloth, cerements; pall
15 **graveyard, cemetery,** burial ground, burial place, plot, family plot, burying place, burying ground, boneyard, bone orchard, burial yard, necropolis, polyandrium, memorial park, city of the dead, village of the dead; churchyard, God's acre, final resting place; garden of remembrance, garden of rest; potter's field; Golgotha, Calvary; urnfield; lych-gate; columbarium, cinerarium
16 **tomb,** sepulcher; **grave,** gravesite, burial, burial plot, plot, pit, deep six; resting place; last home, long home, narrow house, house of death, low house, low green tent; crypt, vault, burial chamber; ossuary, ossuarium; charnel house, bone house; mausoleum; catacombs; mastaba; cist grave, box grave, passage grave, shaft grave, beehive tomb; catafalque; shrine, reliquary, monstrance, tope, stupa; cenotaph; dokhma, tower of silence; pyramid, mummy chamber; burial mound, tumulus, barrow, cist, cromlech, dolmen, menhir, cairn; grave pit, common grave, mass grave, open grave
17 monument, gravestone
18 **epitaph,** inscription, *hic jacet* <L>, here lies, Rest in Peace (RIP); tombstone marking

VERBS **19** **inter,** inhume, **bury,** sepulture, inearth, lay to rest, consign to the grave, consign to earth, lower the body, lay in the grave, lay in the earth, lay under the sod, put six feet under; plant; tomb, entomb, ensepulcher, hearse; enshrine; inurn; encoffin, coffin; hold a funeral, conduct a funeral
20 **cremate,** incinerate, burn, reduce to ashes, burn on the pyre
21 lay out; **embalm;** mummify; lie in state

ADJS **22** **funereal,** funeral, funerary, funebrial, funebrous, funebrious, feral; burial, mortuary, exequial, obsequial; graveside; sepulchral, tomblike; cinerary; necrological, obituary, epitaphic; dismal; mournful; dirgelike; memorial, eulogistic, elegiac

ADVS **23** beneath the sod, underground, six feet under; at rest, resting in peace

PHRS **24** Rest in Peace **(RIP)**, *requiescat in pace* <L>, *requiescant in pace* <L pl>; *hic jacet* <L>, here lies; ashes to ashes and dust to dust

310 PLANTS

<plant kingdom>

NOUNS **1** **plants, vegetation; flora,** plant life, vegetable life; vegetable kingdom, plant kingdom; herbage, flowerage, verdure, greenery, greens, green plants; botany; vegetation spirit
2 **growth,** stand, crop; plantation, planting; clump, tuft, tussock, hassock; regrowth
3 **plant,** green plant**; vegetable; weed;** seedling; cutting; vascular plant, herbaceous plant; seed plant, spermatophyte; gymnosperm; angiosperm, flowering plant; monocotyledon, monocot, monocotyl; dicotyledon, dicot, dicotyl; polycotyledon, polycot, polycotyl; thallophyte, fungus; gametophyte, sporophyte; exotic, hothouse plant, greenhouse plant; ephemeral, annual, biennial, triennial, perennial; evergreen, deciduous plant; cosmopolite; aquatic plant, hydrophyte, amphibian; cultivated plant, garden plant, houseplant, pot plant; food plant, cereal, herb; medicinal plant; heirloom plant; companion plant
4 <varieties> legume, pulse, vetch, bean, pea, lentil; **herb** <see list>, potherb; succulent; **vine** <see list>, grapevine, creeper, ivy, climber, liana; **fern** <see list>, bracken; moss; wort, liverwort; algae; seaweed, kelp, sea moss, rockweed, gulfweed, sargasso, sargassum, sea lentil, wrack, sea wrack; fungus, mold, rust, smut, puffball, mushroom, toadstool; lichen; parasitic plant, parasite, saprophyte, perthophyte, heterophyte, autophyte; plant families, fruits and vegetables; **fruit** <see list>, apple, berry, bramble fruit, citrus fruit, grape, melon, peach, pear, pome fruit, stone fruit, **tropical fruit** <see list>; **vegetable** <see list>, bulb vegetable, leaf vegetable, stalk vegetable, root vegetable, seed vegetable, **tuber vegetable** <see list>
5 **grass,** gramineous plant, graminaceous plant, pasture grass, forage grass, lawn grass, ornamental grass; sea grass; aftergrass, fog; **cereal, cereal grass** <see list>, cereal plant, farinaceous plant, **grain,** corn <Brit>, whole grain, whole wheat; sedge; rush, reed, cane, bamboo
6 **turf,** sod, sward, greensward; divot
7 **green, lawn;** artificial turf, Astroturf <tm>; grassplot, greenyard; grounds; common, park, village green; golf course, links, fairway; bowling green, putting green; grass court
8 **grassland,** grass; parkland; meadow, meadow land, field, mead, swale, lea, ley, haugh, haughland, vega; crop circle; bottomland, water meadow; pasture, pastureland, pasturage, pasture

land, park; range, grazing, grazing land; prairie, savanna, savannah, steppe, steppeland, pampas, pampa, campo, llano, veld, veldt, grass veld, plain, champaign, campagna; herbage, verdure; moor, moorland, common, heath, downs, downland, wold

9 **shrubbery**; shrub, bush; scrub, bramble, brier, brier bush; topiary

10 **tree** <see list>, timber; shade tree, fruit tree, timber tree; **softwood tree** <see list>, **hardwood tree** <see list>; sapling, seedling, germling; conifer, coniferous tree, evergreen; pollard, pollarded tree, standard; deciduous tree, broad-leaved tree; ornamental tree; Christmas tree

11 <tree parts> trunk, bole, gnarl, knot, burl, burr, crown, limb, branch, bough, twig, switch, sprig, spur, leader, leaf, needle, cone, root; tree ring, annual ring, growth ring

12 <tree groupings> **forest**, tree line, tree zone, timberline, jungle, gallery forest, fringing forest, virgin forest, primeval forest, coniferous forest, deciduous forest; taiga, woodland, chaparral, plantation, stand, timberland, tree farm, tree nursery, orchard, orangery

13 **woodland,** wood, woods, timberland; timber, stand of timber, forest, forest land, forest cover, forest preserve, state forest, national forest; forestry, dendrology, silviculture; afforestation, reforestation; boondocks; wildwood, bush, scrub; bushveld, tree veld; shrubland, scrubland; pine barrens, palmetto barrens; hanger; **park,** parkland, chase <Brit>; park forest; arboretum; conservation land, nature preserve; primeval forest

14 **grove,** woodlet; holt, hurst, spinney, shaw, bosk; orchard; wood lot; coppice, copse; boscage

15 **thicket,** thickset, copse, coppice, copsewood, frith; bosket, bosquet, boscage; covert; motte; brake, canebrake; chaparral; chamisal; ceja

16 **brush,** scrub, bush, brushwood, shrubwood, scrubwood, shrub

17 **undergrowth,** underwood, underbrush, copsewood, undershrubs, boscage, frith; ground cover, tree litter, leaf litter, leaf mold, covert

18 **foliage,** leafage, leafiness, umbrage, foliation; frondage, frondescence; vernation; greenery

19 **leaf,** frond; leaflet, foliole; ligule; lamina, blade, leaf blade, spear, spire, pile, flag; needle, pine needle; floral leaf, petal, sepal; bract, bractlet, bracteole, spathe, involucre, involucrum, glume, lemma; cotyledon, seed leaf; stipule, stipula; scale leaf, modified leaf

20 **branch,** fork, limb, bough; deadwood; twig, sprig, switch; spray; shoot, offshoot, spear, frond; scion; sprout, sprit, slip, burgeon, thallus; sucker; runner, stolon, flagellum, sarmentum, sarment; bine; tendril; ramage; branchiness, branchedness, ramification

21 **stem**, stalk, stock, axis, *caulis* <L>; trunk, bole; spear, spire; straw; reed; cane; culm, haulm <Brit>; caudex; footstalk, pedicel, peduncle; leafstalk, petiole, petiolus, petiolule; seedstalk; caulicle; tigella; funicule, funiculus; stipe, anthrophore, carpophore, gynophore

22 **root,** radix, radicle; rootlet; taproot, tap; rhizome, rootstock; tuber, tubercle, tuberous root, root tuber; bulb, bulbil, corm, earthnut; lateral root, prop root, aerial root

23 **bud,** burgeon, gemma; leaf bud, foliage bud; apical bud, terminal bud, axillary bud, lateral bud, resting bud; gemmule, gemmula; plumule, acrospire; flower bud

24 **flower** <see list>, posy, blossom, bloom, blow; floweret, floret, floscule; wildflower; garden flower, pot plant, cut flowers; gardening, horticulture, floriculture; hortorium; community garden

25 **bouquet**, nosegay, posy, boughpot, flower arrangement; boutonniere, buttonhole; corsage; spray; wreath; festoon; garland, daisy chain, chaplet, lei; dried flower, pressed flower

26 **flowering,** florescence, efflorescence, flowerage, blossoming, blooming; inflorescence; blossom, bloom, blowing, blow, full blow; unfolding, unfoldment; anthesis, full bloom

27 <types of inflorescence> flower head; raceme, corymb, umbel, panicle, cyme, thyrse, thyrsus, verticillaster, spadix; head, capitulum; spike, spikelet; ament, catkin; strobile, cone, pinecone; ray flower, disk flower, cymose inflorescnce

28 <flower parts> petal, perianth, floral envelope; calyx, epicalyx, sepal; nectary; corolla, corolla tube, corona; androecium, anther, stamen, microsporophyll; pistil, gynoecium, ovary, ovule, micrypyle; style; stigma, carpel, megasporophyll; recewinptacle, torus; involucre, bract, whorl, spathe; pollen, pollen grain, pollen sac, pollen tube

29 **ear,** spike; auricle; ear of corn, mealie; **cob,** corncob

30 **seed vessel,** seedcase, seedbox, pericarp; hull, husk; capsule, pod, cod, seed pod, seed coat; pease cod, legume, legumen, boll, burr, follicle, silique

31 **seed; heirloom seed;** stone, pit, nut; pip; fruit; germling; grain, kernel, berry; flaxseed, linseed; hayseed; birdseed

32 **vegetation, growth;** germination, pullulation; burgeoning, sprouting; budding, luxuriation

33 <garden plants> seedling, cutting, bulb, corm,

rhizome, tuber; rock plant, alpine plant, bedding plant, creeper, ground cover, turf, climber, climbing plant, rambler; annual, biennial, perennial; herb, flower, woody plant, succulent

VERBS **34 vegetate, grow;** germinate, pullulate; root, take root, strike root; sprout up, shoot up, upsprout, upspear; burgeon, put forth, burst forth; sprout, shoot; bud, gemmate, put forth buds, put out buds; leaf, leave, leaf out, put out leaves, put forth leaves; flourish, luxuriate, riot, grow lush; overgrow, overrun; run to seed, dehisce; photosynthesize, change color

35 flower, be in flower, blossom, bloom, bud, be in bloom, blow, effloresce, floreate, burst into bloom, flourish, burgeon

ADJS **36 vegetable,** vegetal, vegetative, vegetational, vegetarian; **plantlike; herbaceous,** herbal, herbous, herbose, herby; leguminous, leguminose, leguminiform; cereal, farinaceous; weedy; fruity, fruitlike; tuberous, bulbous; rootlike, rhizoid, radicular, radicated, radiciform; botanic, botanical; green, grassy, leafy, verdant

37 algal, fucoid, confervoid; phytoplanktonic, diatomaceous; fungous, fungoid, fungiform

38 floral; flowery, florid; flowered, floreate, floriate, floriated; flowering, blossoming, blooming, abloom, bloomy, florescent, inflorescent, efflorescent, in flower, in bloom, in blossom; uniflorous, multiflorous; radiciflorous, rhizanthous; garden, horticultural, hortulan, floricultural; flowerlike

39 arboreal, arborical, arboresque, arboreous, arborary, arboraceous; **treelike,** arboriform, arborescent, dendroid, dendroidal, dendriform, dendritic; deciduous, nondeciduous; evergreen; softwood, hardwood; piny, piney; coniferous; citrous; palmate, palmaceous; bosky, bushy, shrubby, scrubby, scrubbly; bushlike, shrublike, scrublike

40 sylvan, silvan, sylvatic, **woodland, forest,** forestal; dendrologic, dendrological, silvicultural, afforestational, reforestational, reforested; tree-covered; wooded, timbered, forested, afforested, arboreous; woody, woodsy, bosky, bushy, shrubby, scrubby; copsy, braky; ligneous, ligniform

41 leafy, bowery, leavy; foliated, foliate, foliose, foliaged, leaved, multifoliate; **branched,** branchy, branching, ramified, ramate, ramous, ramose; twiggy

42 verdant, verdurous, verdured; mossy, moss-covered, moss-grown; grassy, grasslike, gramineous, graminaceous; turfy, swardy, turflike, caespitose, tufted; meadowy

43 luxuriant, flourishing, rank, lush, riotous, exuberant; dense, impenetrable, thick, heavy, gross; jungly, jungled; **overgrown,** overrun; weedy, unweeded, weed-choked, weed-ridden; gone to seed

44 perennial, ephemeral; hardy, half-hardy; deciduous, evergreen

45 apple

Anna
Arctic
Arkansas Black
Bailey Sweet
Baldwin
Belmont
Ben Davis
Blue Permain
Braeburn
Bramley
Buckingham
Collins
Cortland
Cox's Orange Pippin
Criterion
Delicious
Dorset Golden
Earliblaze
Early Harvest
Ein Shemer
Empire
English Sweet
Freedom
Gala
Gideon
Golden Delicious
Golden Harvest
Granny Smith
Gravenstein
Green Sweet
Grimes Golden
Hubbardston
Ingram
Jersey Black
Jerseymac
Jonared
Jonathan
Lady Sweet
Liberty
Lodi
Longfield
Macoun
McIntosh
McMahon
Missouri
Monroe
Mutsu
Newton Pippin
Northern Spy
Oldenburg
Ortley
Permain
Pippin
Porter
Prima
Priscilla
Rambo
Red Delicious
Redfree
Red Rome
Rhode Island Greening
Roman Stem
Rome
Rome Beauty
Roxbury Russet
Russet
Saint Lawrence
Sir Prize
Snowapple
Spartan
Starkrimson
Starr
Stayman
Twenty Ounce
Tydeman's Red
Virginia Beauty
Wealthy
Williams
Winesap
Winter Banana
Yellow Transparent
York Imperial

46 berry

bilberry
bearberry
blackberry
black raspberry
blueberry
boysenberry
buffalo berry
candleberry
checkerberry
cloudberry
cranberry
currant
dangleberry
dewberry
elderberry
gooseberry
huckleberry
Juneberry
lingonberry
loganberry

mulberry
partridgeberry
raspberry
sala berry
serviceberry
shadberry
strawberry
whortleberry

47 bramble fruit

blackberry
boysenberry
cloudberry
loganberry
raspberry
tayberry
wineberry

48 bulb vegetable, stalk vegetable

asparagus
broccoli
Brussels sprouts
cardoon
celery
chicory
chive
fennel
finocchio
garlic
globe artichoke
leek
onion
palm hearts
radish
rhubarb
rutabaga
scallion
sea kale
shallot
Swiss chard

49 cereal grass

barley
buckwheat
corn
maize
millet
oats
rice
rye
wheat

50 citrus fruit

citron
clementine
grapefruit
kumquat
lemon
lime
mandarin
naartje
orange
ortanique
pomelo
satsuma
shaddock
tangelo
tangerine

51 fern

adder's fern
air fern
asparagus fern
basket fern
beech fern
bladder fern
boulder fern
bracken
calamite
chain fern
Christmas fern
cliff brake
climbing fern
club moss
cycad
curly grass
grape fern
hart's tongue
holly fern
horsetail
interrupted fern
lady fern
lip fern
lycopod
maidenhair
marsh fern
moonwort
oak fern
osmunda
ostrich fern
polypody
rattlesnake fern
rock brake
seed fern
shield fern
silvery spleenwort
snuffbox fern
sword fern
tree fern
tropical fern
true fern
walking fern
wall fern
water clover
wood fern
woodsia

52 flower

acacia
acanthus
African violet
amaranthus
amaryllis
anemone, windflower
arbutus
arrowhead
asphodel
aster
autumn crocus
azalea
baby's breath
bachelor's button
begonia
belladonna
bitterroot
bittersweet
black-eyed Susan
bleeding heart
bluebell
bluet
bougainvillea
bridal wreath
broom
buttercup
cactus
calendula
calla lily
camellia
camomile
campanula
candytuft
carnation
cat's-paw
cattail
century plant
chamomile
Chinese lantern
Christmas cactus
Christmas rose
chrysanthemum
cineraria
clematis
clover
cockscomb
columbine
cornel
cornflower
cosmos
cowbell
cowslip
crocus
cyclamen
daffodil
dahlia
daisy
damask rose
dandelion
delphinium
dogtooth violet
Dutchman's-breeches
Easter lily
edelweiss
eglantine
elderflower
fireweed
flax
fleur-de-lis <Fr>
forget-me-not
forsythia
foxglove
foxtail
frangipani
freesia
fuchsia
gardenia
gentian
geranium
gladiolus
globeflower
goldenrod
groundsel
guelder rose
harebell
hawthorn
heather
hepatica
hibiscus
hollyhock
honeysuckle
horehound
hyacinth
hydrangea
hyssop
impatience, impatiens
Indian paintbrush
indigo
iris
jack-in-the-pulpit
japonica
jasmine
jonquil
kingcup
laburnum
lady's-slipper
larkspur
lavender
lilac
lily
lily of the valley
lobelia

lotus
love-lies-bleeding
lupine
magnolia
mallow
marguerite
marigold
marshmallow
marsh marigold
mayflower
meadow saffron
Michaelmas daisy
mignonette
milkwort
mimosa
moccasin flower
mock orange
monkshood
moonflower
morning glory
moss rose
motherwort
mullein
musk rose
myrtle
narcissus
nasturtium
oleander
opium poppy
orchid
oxalis
oxeye daisy
pansy
paper-white narcissus
passionflower
pennyroyal
peony
periwinkle
petunia
phlox
pink
plumbago
poinsettia
polyanthus
poppy
portulaca
pot marigold
primrose
primula
Queen Anne's lace
ragged robin
ragwort
rambler rose
ranunculus
resurrection plant
rhododendron
rose
safflower
shooting star
smilax
snapdragon
snowdrop
spiraea
St. John's wort
stock
strawflower
sunflower
sweet alyssum
sweetbrier
sweet pea
sweet william
tea rose
thistle
tiger lily
trailing arbutus
trillium
trumpet creeper
tulip
twinflower
umbrella plant
valerian
Venus's flytrap
verbena
veronica
viburnum
viola
violet
wake-robin
wallflower
water hyacinth
water lily
water milfoil
water pimpernel
wax flower
waxplant
white clover
wisteria
wolfsbane
wood anemone
wood hyacinth
woody nightshade
wood sorrel
yarrow
yellow water lily
yucca
zinnia

53 fruit

apple
apricot
atemoya
avocado
banana
berry
black currant
breadfruit
bullace plum
calmyrna
canistel
cantaloupe
carambola
cherimoya
cherry
citron
clementine
coconut
crabapple
currant
custard apple
damson
date
durian
fig
granadilla
grape
grapefruit
greengage
ground cherry
guava
haw
jackfruit
jujube
kiwi, kiwifruit
kumquat
lemon
lime
longan
loquat
mandarin orange
mango
May apple
medlar
melon
muskmelon
navel orange
nectarine
olive
orange
papaya
passion fruit
pawpaw
peach
pear
pepino
Persian melon
persimmon
pineapple
plantain
plum
pomegranate
pomelo
prickly pear
prune
quince
quinoa
raisin
rambutan
sapodilla
sapote
satsuma
sea grape
soursop
tamarillo
tamarind
tangelo
tangerine
tomato
watermelon

54 grape

Alicante
Almeria
Cabernet Sauvignon
cardinal
Champion
Chardonnay
Chenin Blanc
Concord
Delaware
Franconian
Hamburgh
Isabella
Italia
Labrusca
Lady Finger
Malaga
Martha
Merlot
Muscadet
Muscat
Pinot Blanc
Pinot Noir
Riesling
seedless
Superb
Thompson seedless
Tokay
White Corinth
Woodbury
zinfandel

55 hardwood tree

apple
ash
balsa
basswood
beech
birch
black walnut
blackwood
butternut
cherry
chestnut
cottonwood
ebony
elm

gopherwood
gum
hickory
holly
ironwood
lime
magnolia
mahogany
maple
oak
pear
poplar
rosewood
sycamore
walnut
willow
yellowwood
zebrawood

56 herb

angelica
anise
balm
basil
bay leaf
belladonna
bergamot
borage
bouquet garni
calendula
camomile
caraway
cardamom
catnip, catmint
chervil
chicory
chive
cilantro
clover
coriander
cumin, cummin
deadly nightshade
dill
fennel
feverroot
figwort
fraxinella,
gas plant
garlic
ginseng
hemp
henbane
horehound
hyssop
licorice
liverwort
mandrake
marjoram
mint
monkshood
mullein
mustard
oregano,
origanum
parsley
peppermint
rosemary
rue
sage
savory
sesame
sorrel
spearmint
sweet cicely
sweet woodruff
tansy
tarragon
thyme
wintergreen
yarrow

57 leaf vegetable

Brussels sprouts
cabbage
celery
chard
chicory
Chinese cabbage
corn salad
cress
dandelion
endive
grape leaf
green cabbage
kale
lettuce
mustard
rhubarb
Romaine
lettuce
sorrel
spinach
spinach beet
Swiss chard
watercress
white cabbage

58 melon

cantaloupe
casaba
Crenshaw
honeydew
muskmelon
Persian
watermelon
winter melon

59 peach

Clingstone
Elberta
Freestone
Greensboro
Heath
Late Crawford
Lovell
Mountain Rose
Muir
nectarine
Phillips
Susquehanna
Triumph
Yellow

60 pear

Anjou
Bartlett
Bosc
Clapp Favorite
Comice
Kieffer
Le Conte
Sheldon
Wilder Early
winter nellis

61 pome fruit

apple
chokeberry
crabapple
hawthorn
Japanese
plum
Juneberry
loquat
medlar
pear
quince
rose hip
rowan
service tree

62 root and tuber vegetable

beet
burdock
carrot
celeriac
chervil
Chinese artichoke
ginger
ginseng
gobo
horseradish
Jerusalem
artichoke
jicama
kohlrabi
lobok
parsley
parsnip
potato
radish
rutabaga
salsify
skirret
sweet potato
taro
turmeric
turnip
wasabi
water chestnut
yam
yuca

63 seed vegetable

baby corn
baked beans
bean
bean sprouts
black bean
broad bean
chick pea
corn
English pea
fava bean
flageolet
French bean
green bean
green pea
kidney bean
legume
lentil
lima bean
mung bean
navy bean
pea
peanut
pink bean
pinto bean
red bean
runner bean
snow pea
soybean
split green pea
split yellow pea
sugar snap pea
sweet corn
sweet pea
wax bean
yellow
snap bean

64 softwood tree

balsam
basswood
box elder
bristlecone fir
cedar
cypress
Douglas fir
hemlock
Japanese cedar
northern
white pine
ponderosa pine
poplar
redwood
spruce
sugar pine
tulipwood
tupelo
white fir
white pine
yellow
longleaf pine

65 stone fruit

apricot
cherry
date
mango
nectarine
olive
peach
plum
pluot

66 tree

abele
acacia
acajou
ailanthus, tree of heaven
alder
Aleppo pine
allspice
almond
apple
apricot
ash
aspen
avocado, alligator pear
bald cypress
balsa
balsam
banyan
basswood
bay
bayberry
bean
beech
betel palm
birch
bonsai
bo tree
boxwood
Brazil-nut
breadfruit
buckeye
buckthorn
butternut
buttonwood
cabbage tree
cacao
camphor tree
carnauba
carob
cashew
cassia
catalpa
cedar
cherimoya
cherry
chestnut
chinaberry trer,
China tree
chinquapin
Christmas tree
cinnamon
citron
clove
coconut, coco
cork oak
cottonwood
cypress
date palm
devilwood
dogwood
dwarf
ebony
elder
elm
eucalyptus
evergreen
ficus
fig
filbert
fir
flame tree
fruit
ginkgo
grapefruit
guava
gum
hardwood
hawthorn
hazel, hazelnut
hemlock
henna
hickory
holly
hoptree
hornbeam
horse chestnut
horseradish tree
inkwood
juniper
kola
kumquat
laburnum
lancewood
larch
laurel
lemon
lignum vitae
lime
linden
litchi, litchi nut
locust
logwood
loquat,
Japanese plum
macadamia
madroña, madrone
magnolia
mahogany
mango
mangrove
maple
medlar
mesquite
mimosa
monkey puzzle
mountain ash
mulberry
nutmeg
nux vomica
oak
olive
orange
osier
pagoda tree
palm
papaw
papaya
peach
pear
pecan
persimmon
pine
pistachio
pitch pine
plane
plum
poison sumac
pomegranate
pomelo
poplar
quince
raffia palm
rain tree
redwood
rice-paper tree
rosewood
rubber tree
sandalwood
sapodilla
sassafras
satinwood
senna
sequoia
serviceberry
shade tree
shortleaf pine
silver maple
sorrel tree
spruce
sugar maple
sycamore
tamarillo
tamarind
tamarugo
tangerine
teak
thorn tree
thuja
torchwood
tulip tree
tupelo
umbrella tree
upas
varnish tree
walnut
wandoo
wax palm
wax tree
wayfaring tree
weeping willow
western
hemlock
whitebeam
white birch
white cedar
white oak
white pine
white poplar
white spruce
whitethorn
wicopy
willow
witch hazel
woollybutt
wychelm

yellow poplar
yellowwood, gopher wood
yew
ylang-ylang
zebrawood

67 **tropical fruit**
akee
Asian pear
avocado
banana
breadfruit
camucamu
carambola
cherimoya
coconut
custard apple
durian
feijoya
fig
guarana
guava
horned melon
Indian fig
jaboticaba
jackfruit
Japanese persimmon
jujube
kiwi
litchi, lychee
longan
mamoncillo
mango
mangosteen
papaya
passion fruit
pepino
pineapple
plantain
pomegranate
prickly pear
rambutan
rose apple
salak
sapodilla
soursop
tamarillo
tamarind

68 **vegetable**
alfalfa sprout
artichoke
arugula
asparagus
bamboo sprout, bamboo shoot
bean
bean sprout
beet
bell pepper
black-eyed pea
Boston lettuce
broad bean
broccoli
Brussels sprout
butter bean
cabbage
cardoon
carrot
cassava
cauliflower
celery
chard
chayote
chickpea
chicory
Chinese cabbage
chive
collard greens
corn
cress
cucumber
dandelion
eggplant
endive
escarole
fennel
garbanzo bean
garlic
glasswort
globe artichoke
gourd
green bean
green pepper
iceberg lettuce
jalapeno pepper
kale
kidney bean
kohlrabi
leaf lettuce
leek
lentil
lettuce
lima bean
mung bean
mushroom
muskmelon
mustard
navy bean
New Zealand spinach
okra
olive
onion
parsley
parsnip
pea
pepper
petsai
pinto bean
plantain
pokeweed
potato
pumpkin
radiccio
radish
rampion
red bean
red cabbage
red pepper
rhubarb
rice
romaine
rutabaga
sauerkraut
scallion
sea kale
seaweed
shallot
snap bean
snow pea
sorrel
soybean
spinach
squash
string bean
succotash
sugar pea
summer squash
sweet corn
sweet potato
tomato
truffle
turnip
water chestnut
watercress
watermelon
wax bean
white bean
yam
yellow pepper
yellow squash
zucchini

69 **vine**
air potato
bittersweet
Boston ivy
cissus
clematis
cypress vine
English ivy
grape
greenbrier
honeysuckle
hop
ivy
jasmine
liana
morning glory
paradise flower
poison ivy
stephanotis
sword bean
traveler's-joy
trumpet creeper
trumpet flower
trumpet honeysuckle
velvet bean
Virginia creeper
virgins-bower
wisteria
woodbine

311 ANIMALS, INSECTS

<animal kingdom>

NOUNS 1 **animal life, animal kingdom,** brute creation, **fauna,** Animalia, animality; animal behavior; birds, beasts, and fish; the beasts of the field, the fowl of the air, and the fish of the sea; domestic animals, livestock, stock, cattle; wild animals, wild beasts, beasts of field, wildlife, denizens of the forest, denizens of the jungle, denizens of the wild, furry creatures; predators, beasts of prey; game, big game, small game; lower animal; animal rights; aggressive mimicry, alarm reaction, allogrooming

2 **animal,** creature, critter, living being, living thing, creeping thing; brute, beast, varmint, dumb animal, dumb creature, dumb friend, furry

friend, four-legged friend; pet, companion animal, animal companion

3 <**animal varieties**> vertebrate; invertebrate; biped, quadruped; mammal, mammalian, **primate** <see list>, warm-blooded animal; chordate; marsupial, marsupialian; canine; feline; rodent, gnawer; ungulate; ruminant; insectivore, herbivore, carnivore, omnivore; cannibal; **reptile**, **amphibian** <see list>; **fish** <see list>; aquatic; **bird** <see list>; cosmopolite; vermin, varmint; zooid, protist, protozoan; **worm** <see list>, **mollusk** <see list>, gastropod, arthropod, **insect** <see list>, arachnid; parasite, scavenger, predator, grazer; **fungi** <see list>

4 **pachyderm; elephant,** Jumbo, *hathi* <India>, heffalump; mammoth, woolly mammoth; mastodon; **rhinoceros,** rhino; **hippopotamus,** hippo, river horse; subungulate, proboscidean, Proboscidea

5 <**hoofed animal**> ungulate, ungulant; odd-toed ungulate, perissodactyl; even-toed ungulate, artiodactyl; deer, buck, doe, fawn; red deer, stag, hart, hind; roe deer, roe, roebuck; musk deer; fallow deer; hogdeer; white-tailed deer, Virginia deer; mule deer; elk, wapiti; moose; reindeer, caribou; deerlet; antelope; gazelle, kaama, wildebeest, gnu, hartebeest, springbok, reebok, dik-dik, eland, Cape elk, koodoo; camel, dromedary, ship of the desert; giraffe, camelopard, okapi; equine, equid, horse; pig, hog, swine; llama; goat, sheep; subungulate

6 **cattle** <see list>, kine, neat; beef cattle, beef, beeves <pl>; dairy cattle, dairy cows; bovine animal, bovine, critter; cow, moo-cow, bossy; milk cow, milker, milcher, dairy cow; bull, bullock, top cow; steer, stot, ox, oxen <pl>; calf, heifer, yearling, fatling, stirk; dogie, leppy; maverick; hornless cow, butthead, muley head, muley cow; zebu, Brahman; yak; musk ox; buffalo, water buffalo, Indian buffalo, carabao; bison, aurochs, wisent

7 **sheep** <see list>, jumbuck <Austral>; lamb, lambkin, yeanling; teg <Brit>; ewe, yow; ewe lamb; ram, tup <Brit>, wether; bellwether; mutton

8 **goat;** he-goat, buck, billy goat, billy; she-goat, doe, nanny goat, nanny; kid, doeling; mountain goat

9 **swine**, **pig** <see list>, hog, porker; shoat, piggy, piglet, pigling, micropig; suckling pig; gilt; boar, sow; barrow; wild boar, tusker, razorback; warthog, babirusa

10 **horse;** horseflesh, hoss, critter; equine, mount, nag; steed, prancer, dobbin; charger, courser, warhorse, destrier; colt, foal, filly; mare, brood mare; stallion, studhorse, stud, top horse, entire horse, entire; gelding, purebred horse, thoroughbred, blood horse; wild horse, Przewalsky's horse, tarpan; pony, Shetland pony, Shetland, shelty, Iceland pony, Galloway, cob; bronco, bronc, range horse, Indian pony, cayuse, mustang; bucking bronco, buckjumper, sunfisher, broomtail; cowcutting horse, stock horse, roping horse, cow pony, circus horse

11 <colored horse> appaloosa, bay, blood bay, bayard, chestnut, liver chestnut, gray, dapple-gray, black, grizzle, roan, sorrel, dun, buckskin, pinto, paint, piebald, skewbald, palomino, seal brown, strawberry roan, calico pony, painted pony

12 <inferior horse> nag, plug, hack, jade, crock, garron, crowbait, scalawag, rosinante; goat, stiff, dog; roarer, whistler; balky horse, balker, jughead; rogue; rackabones, scrag, stack of bones

13 **workhorse,** plow horse, beast of burden; hunter; stalking-horse; saddle horse, saddler, rouncy, steed, riding horse, rider, palfrey, mount; remount; polo pony; post-horse; cavalry horse; driving horse, road horse, roadster, carriage horse, coach horse, gigster; hack, hackney; draft horse, dray horse, cart horse, shaft horse, pole horse, thill horse, thiller, fill horse, filler; wheelhorse, wheeler, lead, leader; packhorse, jument, sumpter, sumpter horse; pit-pony; cow pony; warhorse

14 **racehorse;** show-horse, gaited horse, racer, galloper, trotter, pacer, sidewheeler; stepper, high-stepper, cob, prancer, turf horse, sprinter; ambler, padnag, pad; racker; single-footer; steeplechaser; bangtail

15 **ass,** donkey, burro, neddy, cuddy, moke, Rocky Mountain canary; jackass, jack, dickey; jenny, jenny ass, jennet; **mule,** sumpter mule, sumpter; hinny

16 **dog** <see list>, canine, pooch, bowwow; pup, puppy, puppy dog, whelp; man's best friend; bitch, gyp, slut; toy dog, lapdog; working dog; ratter; watchdog, bandog; sheep dog, shepherd, shepherd's dog; hound; rescue dog; Seeing Eye dog, hearing ear dog, guide dog; guard dog; police dog, sled dog; gazehound, sighthound; show dog, fancy dog; kennel, pack of dogs

17 sporting dog, hunting dog, hunter, field dog, scent hound, bird dog, gundog, water dog, hound, courser, setter, pointer, spaniel, retriever

18 cur, mongrel, lurcher, tyke, **mutt**; pariah dog

19 **fox,** reynard; **wolf,** timber wolf, lobo, **coyote,** brush wolf, prairie wolf, medicine wolf; dingo, jackal, **hyena;** Cape hunting dog, African hunting dog

20 **cat** <see list>, feline, pussy, puss, pussycat, domestic cat, house cat, tabby, grimalkin; kitten,

kitty, kitty-cat; kit, kitling; tomcat, tom; gib, gib-cat; mouser; ratter; Cheshire cat, Chessycat; silver cat, Chinchilla cat; blue cat, Maltese cat; tiger cat, tabby cat; tortoiseshell cat, calico cat; alley cat; Morris

21 <wild cats> big cat, jungle cat; lion, Leo, *simba* <Swahili>; tiger, Siberian tiger; leopard, panther, jaguar, cheetah; cougar, painter, puma, mountain lion, catamount, cat-a-mountain; lynx, ocelot; wildcat, bobcat, steppe cat, Pallas's cat

22 <**wild animal**> bear, bar; guinea pig, cavy; hedgehog, porcupine, quill pig; woodchuck, groundhog, whistle-pig; prairie dog, prairie squirrel; raccoon, coon; opossum, possum; weasel, mousehound <Brit>; wolverine, glutton; ferret, monk; skunk, polecat; zoril, stink cat <S Africa>, Cape polecat; foumart; primate, simian; ape; monkey, chimpanzee, chimp

23 **hare,** leveret, jackrabbit; **rabbit,** bunny, bunny rabbit, lapin; cottontail; Belgian hare, leporide; buck, doe

24 **reptile,** reptilian; **lizard;** saurian, dinosaur; crocodile, crocodilian, alligator, gator; tortoise, turtle, terrapin, sea turtle; cold-blooded animal, poikilotherm, Reptilia, Squamata, Rhynchocephalia, Crocodilia; reptilian brain

25 **serpent, snake,** ophidian; **viper,** pit viper; sea snake; boa constrictor

26 **amphibian,** batrachian, croaker, paddock; frog, rani-; tree toad, tree frog, bullfrog; toad, hoptoad, hoppytoad; newt, salamander; tadpole, polliwog; caecilian, apodan, urodele, caudate, salientian, anuran

27 **bird** <see list>, **fowl;** dicky-bird, birdy, birdie; fowls of the air, birdlife, avifauna, Aves, feathered friends; baby bird, chick, nestling, fledgling; wildfowl, game bird; waterfowl, water bird, wading bird, diving bird; sea bird; shorebird; migratory bird, migrant, bird of passage; songbird, oscine bird, warbler, passerine bird, perching bird; cage bird; flightless bird, ratite; seed-eating bird, insect-eating bird, fruit-eating bird, fish-eating bird; raptor, bird of prey; eagle, bird of Jove, eaglet; hawk, falcon; owl, bird of Minerva, bird of night; peafowl, peahen, peacock, bird of Juno; swan, cygnet; pigeon, dove, squab; stormy petrel, storm petrel, Mother Carey's chicken; fulmar, Mother Carey's goose

28 **poultry, fowl,** domestic fowl, barnyard fowl, barn-door fowl, dunghill fowl; **chicken** <see list>, chick, chicklet, chicky, chickabiddy; cock, rooster, chanticleer; hen, biddy, partlet; cockerel, pullet; setting hen, brooder, broody hen; capon, poulard; broiler, fryer, spring chicken; roaster, stewing chicken; Bantam, banty; game fowl; guinea fowl, guinea cock, guinea hen; goose, gander, gosling; duck, drake, duckling; turkey, gobbler, turkey gobbler; turkey-cock, tom, tom turkey; hen turkey; poult

29 **marine animal** <see list>, denizen of the deep; whale, cetacean; porpoise, dolphin, sea pig; sea serpent, sea snake, Loch Ness monster, sea monster, Leviathan; fish, game fish, tropical fish, panfish; shark, man-eating shark, man-eater; salmon, kipper, grilse, smolt, parr, alevin; minnow, minny, fry, fingerling; sponge; plankton, zooplankton, nekton, benthon, benthos, zoobenthos; **crustacean** <see list>, lobster, spiny lobster, crab, blueclaw, Dungeness crab, king crab, spider crab, land crab, stone crab, soft-shell crab; crayfish, crawfish, crawdaddy; mollusc, wentletrap, whelk, snail, cockle, mussel, clam, oyster, razor clam, quahog, steamer, toheroa, tridachna, giant clam

30 **fish** <see list>; saltwater fish, marine fish, freshwater fish; jawless fish, cyclostome, cartilaginous fish, elasmobranch, selachian, holocephalan, bony fish, lobe-finned fish, crossopterygian, dipnoan, ray-finned fish, teleost fish, flying fish, mouthbreeder, flatfish; food fish, game fish, aquarium fish, tropical fish, fossil fish; shoal, school

31 **invertebrate;** lower animal, protochordate, echinoderm, arthropod, arachnid, insect, **crustacean** <see list>, myriapod, mollusk, worm, coelenterate, sponge; protozoan, protozoon

32 **insect** <see list>, **bug;** beetle; arthropod; hexapod, myriapod; centipede, chilopod; millipede, diplopod; social insect; mite; arachnid, spider, tarantula, black widow spider, daddy longlegs, harvestman; scorpion; tick; larva, maggot, nymph, caterpillar; winged insect, fly, gnat, midge, mosquito, dragonfly, butterfly, moth, bee, wasp; creepy-crawly, pest

33 **ant,** emmet, pismire, pissant, antymire; red ant, black ant, fire ant, house ant, agricultural ant, carpenter ant, army ant; slave ant, slave-making ant; termite, white ant; queen, worker, soldier; ant farm

34 **bee,** honeybee, bumblebee, carpenter bee; queen, queen bee, worker, drone, Africanized bee; wasp; hornet, yellow jacket

35 **locust,** acridian; grasshopper, hopper, hoppergrass; cricket; cicada, cicala, dog-day cicada, seventeen-year locust; stick insect, mantis

36 **vermin;** parasite; **louse,** head louse, body louse, grayback, cootie; crab, crab louse; weevil; nit; flea, sand flea, dog flea, cat flea, chigoe, chigger, jigger, red bug, mite, harvest mite; roach, cockroach, *cucaracha* <Sp>; tick, mosquito

37 bloodsucker, parasite; **leech; tick,** wood tick, deer tick; **mosquito,** skeeter, culex; bedbug, housebug <Brit>

38 **worm** <see list>; earthworm, angleworm, fishworm, night crawler, nightwalker; measuring worm, inchworm; tapeworm, helminth; worm farm

ADJS 39 **animal,** animalian, animalic, animalistic, animal-like, theriomorphic, zoic, zooidal; zoologic, zoological; brutish, brutal, brute, brutelike; bestial, beastly, beastlike; wild, feral; subhuman, soulless; dumb; instinctual, instinctive, mindless, nonrational; half-animal, half-human, anthropomorphic, therianthropic

40 **vertebrate,** chordate, mammalian; viviparous; marsupial, cetacean

41 **canine,** doggish, doggy, doglike; vulpine, foxy, foxlike; lupine, wolfish, wolflike

42 **feline,** felid, cattish, catty, catlike; kittenish; leonine, lionlike; tigerish, tigerlike

43 ursine, bearish, bearlike

44 **rodent,** rodential; verminous; mousy, mouselike; ratty, ratlike

45 ungulate, hoofed, hooved; **equine,** hippic, horsy, horselike; **equestrian;** asinine, mulish; bovid, ruminant, cud-chewing; **bovine,** cowlike, cowish; bull-like, bullish, taurine; cervine, deerlike; caprine, caprid, hircine, goatish, goatlike; ovine, sheepish, sheeplike; porcine, swinish, piggish, hoggish

46 elephantlike, elephantine, pachydermous

47 reptile, **reptilian,** reptilelike, reptiloid, reptiliform, reptilian-brain; reptant, repent, creeping, crawling, slithering; lizardlike, saurian; crocodilian; serpentine, serpentile, serpentoid, serpentiform, serpentlike; snakish, snaky, snakelike, colubrine, ophidian, anguine; viperish, viperous, vipery, viperine, viperoid, viperiform, viperlike; amphibian, batrachian, froggy, toadish, salamandrian

48 **birdlike,** birdy; avian, avicular; gallinaceous, rasorial; oscine, passerine, perching; columbine, columbaceous, dovelike; psittacine; aquiline, hawklike; anserine, anserous, goosy; nidificant, nesting, nest-building; nidicolous, altricial; nidifugous, precocial

49 **fishlike,** fishy; piscine, pisciform; piscatorial, piscatory; eellike; selachian, sharklike, sharkish

50 **invertebrate,** invertebral; protozoan, protozoal, protozoic; crustaceous, crustacean; molluscan, molluscoid

51 insectile, **insectlike,** buggy; verminous; lepidopterous, lepidopteran; weevily

52 **wormlike,** vermicular, vermiform; wormy

53 planktonic, nektonic, benthonic, zooplanktonic, zoobenthoic

54 **animal collective names**

<antelopes> herd
<ants> colony
<apes> shrewdness
<asses> pace, herd, drove
<baboons> congress
<badgers> cete
<bass> shoal
<bears> sleuth, sloth
<beavers> colony
<bees> colony, grist, hive, hum, swarm
<birds> dissimulation, flight, volery
<bison> herd, troop
<boars> singular, sounder
<bovines> herd
<buffalo> herd
<camels> herd, flock
<caterpillars> army
<cats and dogs> rain
<cats> clowder, clutter
<cattle> herd, drove
<chickens> brood, clutch, flock, peep
<clams> bed
<colts> rag
<cows> flink, herd
<cranes> sedge, siege
<crickets> orchestra
<crows> murder
<deers> herd
<dogs> kennel, pack
<doves> dole, dule, flight
<ducks> brace, flock, gaggle, paddling, raft, team
<eagles> convocation
<eels> knot
<eggs> clutch
<elephants> herd, host, parade
<elks> gang, herd
<falcons> cast, passager
<ferrets> business
<finches> charm
<fishes> draught, school, shoal
<foxes> leash, skulk
<frogs> army, knot, colony
<geese> flock, gaggle, skein, wedge
<giraffes> herd
<gnats> cloud, horde
<goats> tribe, trip, herd
<goldfinches> charm
<gorillas> band
<grasshoppers> cluster
<grouses> covey
<hares> down, husk, leap
<hawks> cast, kettle
<hedgehogs> prickle
<hens> brood
<herons> siege
<hippopotami> huddle
<hogs> drift
<horses> harras, herd, pair, stable, team
<hounds> cry, mute, pack
<hummingbirds> hover
<jack rabbits> husk
<jays> band, party
<jellyfish> smack
<kangaroos> mob, troop
<kittens> kindle, kendle, litter
<lapwings> deceit
<larks> ascension, chattering, exaltation
<leopards> leap
<lions> pride
<locusts> host, plague
<magpies> tidings
<mallards> sord, sort
<mares> stud
<martens> richness
<mice> nest
<moles> labor, lobor
<monkeys> tribe, troop
<mules> barren, pack, rake, span
<nightingales> watch
<owls> parliament, wisdom
<oxen> team, yoke, drove, herd
<oysters> bed
<parrots> company
<partridges> covey
<peacocks> muster, ostentation
<penguins> colony
<pheasants> bouquet, covey, nest, nye, nide
<pigeons> flock
<pigs> drove, litter, herd
<plovers> congregation, wing

<polar bears> aurora
<ponies> string
<porpoises> school
<quails> bevy, covey
<rabbits> colony, nest
<racehorses> field
<ravens> conspiracy, unkindness
<reindeers> herd
<rhinoceroses> crash
<seals> pod, herd, school, trip, harem, rookery, spring
<sheep> drove, flock, herd
<skunks> stench
<slugs> cornucopia
<snakes> bed, slither
<sparrows> host
<squirrels> dray
<starlings> murmuration
<storks> mustering
<swallows> flight
<swans> ballet, bevy, wedge
<swines> drift, sounder
<teal> spring
<tigers> hide, streak
<toads> knot
<trout> hover
<turkeys> rafter
<turtledoves> pitying
<turtles> bale, bevy
<unicorns> blessing
<wasps> pail
<waterfowl> plump
<weasels> gam, sneak
<whales> gam, herd, pod, shoal, surfers
<wolves> pack, rout
<woodchucks> fall
<woodpeckers> descent
<worms> wriggle
<zebras> herd, stripe

55 animal young names

<antelope> calf
<bear> cub, whelp
<beaver> kit, kitten, pup
<bird> fledgling, nestling
<bison> calf
<bovine> calf
<cat> kit, kitten, kitty, puss, pussy
<cattle> calf, yearling
<chicken> chick, chicklet, pullet, cockerel
<cow> calf, heifer
<deer> fawn
<dog> pup, whelp
<duck> duckling
<eagle> eaglet, fledgling
<elephant> calf
<elk> calf
<falcon> cast
<fish> fingerling, fry
<fox> cub, kit, pup, whelp
<frog> polliwog, tadpole
<giraffe> cub, whelp
<goat> kid
<goose> gosling
<grouse> cheeper, poult
<hare> leveret
<hawk> eyas
<hen> chick, pullet
<hippopotamus> calf
<horse> colt, filly, filt, foal, yearling
<kangaroo> joey
<lion> cub, whelp
<monkey> baby
<moose> cub, calf
<owl> owlet
<oyster> spat
<partridge> cheeper
<pig> piglet, shoat, farrow, suckling
<pigeon> squab, squeaker
<quail> cheeper
<rabbit> bunny, kit, leveret
<reindeer> fawn
<rhinoceros> calf
<rooster> cockerel
<sea lion> pup
<seal> calf, pup
<shark> cub
<sheep> lamb, lambkin, cosset, hog, yearling
<swan> cygnet
<swine> piglet, shoat, farrow
<tiger> cub, whelp
<turkey> poult, chick
<whale> calf
<wolf> cub, whelp
<zebra> colt, foal

56 bird

albatross
auk
avocet
bald eagle
barn owl
bird of paradise
bittern
blackbird
blue jay
bluebill
bluebird
bowerbird
bufflehead
bullfinch
bunting
buzzard
canary
cardinal
cassowary
catbird
chaffinch
chickadee
chicken
chicken hawk
chimney swift
cockatoo
condor
coot
cormorant
cowbird
crake
crane
crow
curlew
dipper
diver
dove
duck
dunlin
eagle
egret
emu
falcon
finch
flamingo
flycatcher
frigate bird
frogmouth
fulmar
gannet
gnatcatcher
goldfinch
gooney bird
goose
goshawk
grackle
grebe
greenfinch
grey heron
grouse
guinea fowl
gull
harrier
hawk
heron
honeycreeper
hummingbird
ibis
jackdaw
jaeger
jay
kestrel
king eider
kingfisher
kite
kiwi
lapwing
lark
loon
lovebird
magpie
mallard
man-o-war bird
meadowlark
merlin
mockingbird
mud hen
myna
nighthawk
nightingale
notornis
oriole
osprey
ostrich
ouzel
owl
oystercatcher
parakeet
parrot
partridge
peacock
pelican
penguin
petrel
pewit
pheasant
pigeon
pipit
plover
pochard
prairie chicken
puffin
purple martin
quail
raptor
ratite
raven
razorbill
redpoll
redwing
rhea

roadrunner
robin
rook
sandpiper
sapsucker
scissortail
seabird
seagull
shag
shama
shelduck
shrike
skua
snipe
snowbird
sparrow
song thrush
spoonbill
starling
stork
sunbird
surfbird
swallow
swan
takahe
tern
thrasher
thrush
tit
towhee
turkey
vulture
wader
wagtail
warble
waterfowl
weaverbird
whippoorwill
whitethroat
wigeon
woodcock
woodpecker
wren
yellow finch
yellowbird
yellowhammer

57 cat

Abyssinian cat
American shorthair
Angora cat
Balinese
blue-point Siamese
Burmese
calico, tortoiseshell
chartreuse cat
Chinese
chocolate-point Siamese
Cornish rex
domestic shorthair cat
Egyptian cat, mau
exotic shorthair
Havana brown
Himalayan
Kashmir
Maine coon
Malayan cat
Maltese
Manx
marmalade cat
Oriental Shorthair
Persian
rex
Russian blue
seal-point Siamese
Siamese
Singapura
sphynx
tabby, tabby-cat
tortoiseshell cat
Turkish cat

58 cattle

Aberdeen Angus, Angus
Africander
Alderney
Andalusian
Ayrshire
Beefalo
Belted Galloway
Black Angus
Brahman
Brown Swiss
Cattalo
Charolais
Dairy Shorthorn
Devon
Dexter
Durham
Dutch Belted
Egyptian
French Canadian
Fribourg
Galloway
Guernsey
Hereford
Holstein, Holstein-Friesian
Icelandic
Jersey
Lincoln Red
Longhorn
Norwegian Red
Polled Hereford
Red Poll, Polled
Red Sindhi
Santa Gertrudis
Shetland
Shorthorn, Polled Durham
Sussex
Texas Longhorn
Welsh, Welsh Black
West Highland

59 chicken

Ameraucana
Ancona
Andalusian
Araucana
Australorp
Bantam
Barred Plymouth Rock
Brahma
Buckeye
Buttercup
Campine
Cochin
Cornish
Crevecoeur
Delaware
Dorking
Faverolle
Frizzle
Hamburg
Holland
Houdan
Ixworth
Jersey black giant
Langshan
Leghorn
Minorca
New Hampshire, New Hampshire red
Orpington
Plymouth Rock
Rhode Island red
Rhode Island white
Rock
Rock Cornish
Silkie
Spanish
Sultan
Sumatra
Sussex
Turken
white Leghorn
Wyandotte

60 crustacean

amphipod
barnacle
bass yabby
beach flea
branchiopod
brine shrimp
copepod
crab
crawdad
crawfish
crayfish
cumacean
daphnia
fiddler crab
hairy crab
hermit crab
horseshoe crab
isopod
king crab
krill
lobster
mantas shrimp
mussel shrimp
opossum shrimp
ostracod
pea crab
pebble crab
prawn
sailor shrimp
sand hopper
sand skater
sea centipede
sea flea
shellfish
shrimp
skeleton louse
soft-shell crab
spider crab
sponge crab
sponge shrimp
stenetrium
tadpole shrimp
water flea
weed shrimp

61 dog

affenpinscher
Afghan hound
Airedale, Airedale terrier
Akita
Alaskan malamute
Alsatian
American foxhound
American water spaniel
Australian cattle dog, Australian heeler, blue heeler
Australian terrier
Basenji
basset, basset hound
beagle
Bedlington terrier

Belgian sheepdog, Belgian shepherd
Bernese mountain dog
Bichon Frise
black Labrador
Blenheim spaniel
bloodhound, sleuth, sleuthhound
Border terrier
borzoi
Boston bull, Boston terrier
Bouvier des Flandres
boxer
Briard
Brittany spaniel
Brussels griffon
bulldog, bull
bull mastiff
bull terrier
cairn terrier
carriage, dog coach dog
Chesapeake Bay retriever
Chihuahua
chow, chow chow
clumber spaniel
Clydesdale terrier
cocker spaniel
collie
coonhound
corgi
dachshund, sausage dog, sausage hound
Dalmatian
Dandie Dinmont
deerhound
Doberman pinscher
elkhound
English bulldog
English cocker spaniel
English foxhound
English setter
English springer spaniel
English toy spaniel
Eskimo dog
field spaniel
foxhound
fox terrier
French bulldog
gazelle hound
German shepherd
German shorthaired pointer
German wirehaired pointer
giant schnauzer
golden retriever
Gordon setter
Great Dane
Great Pyrenees
greyhound
griffon
Groenendael
harrier
hound, hound dog
husky
Irish setter
Irish terrier
Irish water spaniel
Irish wolfhound
Italian greyhound
Jack Russell terrier
Japanese spaniel, Japanese Chin
keeshond
kelpie
Kerry blue terrier
King Charles spaniel
Komondor
kuvasz
Labrador retriever
Lakeland terrier
Lhasa apso
malamute
Malinois
Maltese
Manchester terrier
mastiff
Mexican hairless
miniature pinscher
miniature poodle
miniature schnauzer
Newfoundland
Norfolk spaniel
Norwegian elkhound
Norwich terrier
Old English sheepdog
otterhound
papillon
Pekingese
pit bull terrier
pointer
police dog
Pomeranian
poodle
pug, pug dog, mop dog, mops
puli
rat terrier
retriever
Rhodesian ridgeback
Rottweiler
Russian wolfhound
St. Bernard
Saluki
Samoyed
schipperke
schnauzer
Scottish deerhound
Scottish terrier
Sealyham terrier
setter
Shar-Pei
shepherd dog
Shetland sheepdog, Sheltie
Shih Tzu
Siberian husky
silky terrier
Skye terrier
spaniel
spitz
springer spaniel
Staffordshire bull terrier
Sussex spaniel
terrier
toy poodle
toy spaniel
toy terrier
Vizsla
water spaniel
Weimaraner
Welsh collie
Welsh corgi
Welsh springer spaniel
Welsh terrier
West Highland white terrier
whippet
wirehaired terrier
wolfhound
yellow Labrador
Yorkshire terrier

62 fish

albacore
alewife
alligator gar
amberjack
angelfish
arauana
archerfish
asp
balloonfish
barracuda
basking shark
bass
batfish
beluga
betta
blackfish
blindfish
blowfish
bluefish
bonefish
bowfin
boxfish
bream
brook trout
buffalofish
bullhead
butterfish
butterflyfish
candlefish
capelin
cardinalfish
carp
catfish
cavefish
char
chimaera
chub
cichlid
clingfish
clown anemone
clownfish
cod
codfish
cowfish
cutlassfish
damselfish
danios
darter
devilfish
devil ray
discus
doctorfish
dogfish
dolphin
dragonfish
eel
electric eel
electric ray
flatfish
flounder
flying fish
frogfish
garpike
giant bass
globefish
goatfish
goby
goldfish
gourami
grayling
grouper
gudgeon
guppy
haddock
hagfish
hake
halibut
hammerhead shark
hatchetfish
headstander

herring
hogfish
ide
kelpfish
killifish
kingfish
koi
lake trout
lanternfish
lionfish
loach
lumpfish
mackerel
manta
marlin
minnow
molly
mudfish
mudskipper
mullet
needlefish
northern pike
oarfish
oscar
paddlefish
paradise fish
parrotfish
perch
pickerel
pike
pikeperch
pipefish
piranha
platyfish
pollack
pompano
porgy
puffer
pupfish
rainbow trout
ray
redfin
redfish
red snapper
sailfish
salmon
salmon trout
sardine
sawfish
sea bass
sea horse
seaperch
sea trout
shad
shark
shiner
skate
smelt
snapper
snook
sole
spearfish
squawfish
stingray
striped bass
sturgeon
sucker
sunfish
surffish
swordfish
swordtail
tang
tarpon
tetra
tigerfish
tiger shark
triggerfish
trout
tuna
weakfish
whitefish
white shark
wimplefish
yellowtail
zander
zebrafish

63 fungi

agarics
ascomycetes
Ascomycota
aspergillus
basidiomycetes
Basidiomycota
bird's-nest fungus
black bread mold
black mold
blue mold
blue-green mold
boletus
bracket fungus
bread mold
brittlegill
cellular slime molds
chanterelle
club fungus
coral fungus
crumblecap
cup fungus
dead-man's fingers
deathcap
deuteromycetes
Deuteromycota
downy mildew
dung fungus
earth tongue
earthstar
Eumycota
false mildew
false morel
field mushroom
flask fungus
Fungi Imperfecti
gill fungus
green mold
groundwart
inky cap
jelly fungus
lorchel
Mastigomycotina
mildew
milkcap
mold
moniliales
morel
mushroom
mushroom pimple
myxomycetes
Myxomycota
oyster cap
penicillium
phycomycetes
pink gill
pore fungus
powdery mildew
puffball
read bread mold
ringstalk
ringworm fungus
roof mushroom
rust
sac fungus
scalecap
sheath mushroom
shell fungus
skin fungus
slime molds
slime mushroom
smoothcap
smut
stinkhorn
thrush fungus
toadstool
tooth fungus
tricholoma
truffle
verticillium
waxy cap
webcap
woodcrust
yeast
zygomycetes
Zygomycota

64 insect

acarid
acarine
ant
ant lion
aphid
apple maggot
arachnid
Arachnida
armyworm
bagworm
bark beetle
bedbug
bee
beetle
billbug
black fly
black widow
blackbeetle
bloodworm
boll weevil
bookworm
borer
bug
bumblebee
butterfly
carpet beetle
caterpillar
centipede
chafer
chigger
chinch bug
click beetle
cockroach
cootie
cricket
cutworm
daddy-longlegs
deer fly
doodlebug
dragonfly
drone
dung beetle
emperor butterfly
false scorpion
firefly
flea
fruit fly
gadfly
glowworm
gnat
grasshopper
grub
gypsy moth
harvestman
honeybee
hornet
horse fly
housefly
Japanese beetle
June bug

ladybug
leafhopper
locust
long-horned beetle
looper
louse
maggot
mayfly
mealworm
medfly
midge
mite
mosquito
moth
nit
nymph
opilionid
phalangid
pismire
praying mantis
pseudoscorpion
pupa
queen bee
roach
scale
scorpion
screwworm
silkworm
skipper
snapping beetle
soldier ant
spider
stag beetle
tarantula
tent fly
termite
tick
tiger beetle
tiger moth
wasp
water beetle
water bug
weevil
wireworm
woodworm
woolly bear
worker
yellow jacket

65 marine animal

cetacean
crustacean
dolphin
dugong
elephant seal
fur seal
harbor seal
manatee
octopus, octopod
phocid
pinniped
porpoise
sea calf
sea cow
sea dog
sea elephant
seal
sea lion
sea urchin
shellfish
sirenian
squid
walrus
whale

66 mollusk

amphineuran
bivalve
cephalopod
chambered nautilus
chiton
clam
conch
cone
cowry
cuttlefish
gastropod
lamellibranch
lampshell
limpet
murex
mussel
neopilina
octopod
octopus
oyster
rock shell
scallop
scaphopod
shellfish
slug
snail
spider conch
squid
tusk shell
volute

67 primate

angwantibo
anthropoid ape
ape
aye-aye
baboon
Barbary ape
Bengal
monkey
bush baby
capuchin
chacma
chimpanzee
colobus
drill
entellus
gibbon
gorilla
great ape
grivet
guenon
guereza
hanuman
howling monkey,
howler
king monkey
langur
lemur
loris
macaque, bonnet
monkey, lion-tailed
monkey
man
mandrill
marmoset
mountain gorilla
orangutan, orang
owl monkey
pongid
proboscis monkey
rhesus
saki
siamang
sloth monkey
spider monkey
squirrel monkey
tamarin
tarsier
vervet

68 reptile, amphibian

agama
alligator
anaconda
apodan
asp
auratus
basilisk
blindworm
boa
bog turtle
bullfrog
caecilian
caiman
chameleon
chelonid
chicken turtle
Chinese water dragon
cobra
congo snake
constrictor
cricket frog
crocodile
dinosaur
flying dragon
frog
galliwasp
gecko
Gila monster
glass snake
green frog
horned toad
iguana
Komodo dragon
lizard
loggerhead turtle
mamba
marine toad
monitor
mudpuppy
newt
pig frog
python
rainbow snake
rattlesnake
red-eyed tree frog
salamander
serpent
skink
slow worm
snake
snapping turtle
soft-shelled turtle
spring peeper
terrapin
toad
tortoise
tuatara
turtle
viper
waterdog

69 sheep

Abyssinian
American merino
American
Rambouillet
American Tunis
Berber
Black-faced Highland
Blackhead Persian
broadtail
Cheviot
Columbia
Corriedale
Corsican
Cotswold

Dorset Down
Hampshire
Karakul
Kerry Hill
Leicester
Lincoln
Merino
Mongolian
Oxford, Oxford Down
Panama
Rambouillet
Romanov
Romeldale
Romney
Romney Marsh
Ryeland
Scottish blackface
Shetland
Shropshire
Southdown
Suffolk
Tajik
Targhee
Tibetan
Welsh Mountain
Wensleydale

70 swine, pig

American Landrace
Berkshire
Cheshire
Chester White
Dorset
Duroc
Duroc Jersey
Hampshire
Hereford
Landrace
large black
large white
Mangalitsa
middle white
National Long White Lop-eared
Poland China
Romagna
Tamworth
Vietnamese Pot-bellied
Wessex saddleback
Yorkshire

71 worm

angleworm
annelid
armyworm
arrowworm
bearded worm
bloodworm
bollworm
bookworm
cankerworm
clamworm
composting worm
cottonworm
cutworm
dung worm
earthworm
earwom
eelworm
fecal worm
fireworm
fish worm
flatworm
fluke
glowworm
grey worm
hairworm
heligrammite
hookworm
hornworm
horsehair worm
inchworm
leech
looper
lugworm
manure worm
measuringworm
nematode
night crawler
pinworm
platyhelminth
polychaete
red hybrid
redworm
red wiggler
ribbon worm
rotifer
roundworm
sandworm
sea mouse
sea worm
silkworm
stink worm
striped worm
tapeworm
threadworm
tiger worm
tobacco hornworm
tomato hornworm
tubeworm
vinegar eel
vinegar worm
webworm
whipworm
wireworm
woodworm

312 HUMANKIND

<human race>

NOUNS 1 **humankind, mankind,** womankind, personkind, man, human species, human race, race of man, human family, the family of man, humanity, human beings, mortals, earthlings, mortality, flesh, mortal flesh, clay; generation of man, homo, genus Homo, Homo sapiens, Hominidae, hominids; archaic Homo; race, strain, stock, subrace, infrarace, subspecies; culture; ethnic group; ethnicity, ethnicism, roots; society, speech community; community, folk, persons, the people, the populace, world population; nationality, nation

2 **<races of humankind>** Caucasoid, Caucasian, white race; Nordic subrace, Alpine subrace, Mediterranean subrace; dolichocephalic people, brachycephalic people; xanthochroi, melanochroi; Archaic Caucasoid race, archaic white race, Australoid race; Polynesian race; Negroid, black race; Nilotic race, Melanesian race, Papuan race; Pygmoid race; Bushman race; Mongoloid, Mongolian, yellow race; Malayan, Malaysian, brown race; prehistoric races; majority, racial majority, ethnic majority; minority, racial minority, ethnic minority; persons of color

3 <* in some uses> Caucasian, white man, white woman, white person, paleface, ofay, the Man, Mister Charley, whitey, honky; Australian aborigine, Bushman; Negro, black man, black woman, black, colored person, person of color, darky, spade, nigger; African-American; negritude, Afroism, blackness; pygmy; Negrito, Negrillo; Native American, Indian, American Indian, Amerindian, Amerind, red man, red woman, injun, redskin; Latino; yellow man, yellow woman, Oriental, Asian, gook, slanteye; brown man, brown woman; mixed race, mulatto, quadroon, half-breed

4 **the people**, the populace, the population, the public, the world, everyone, everybody

5 **person, human,** human being, man, woman, child, member of the human race, member of the human family, Adamite, daughter of Eve; ethnic; mortal, life, soul, living soul; being, creature, fellow creature, clay, ordinary clay, flesh and blood, the naked ape, the noble animal; individual; personage, personality, personhood, individuality; body; somebody, one, someone; earthling, groundling, terran, worldling, tellurian; ordinary person; head, hand, nose; fellow; gal

6 **human nature,** humanity; frail humanity, fallen humanity, Adam, the generation of Adam, Adam's seed, Adam's offspring

7 God's image, lord of creation, God's creation; homo faber, symbol-using animal; reasoning animal, rational animal, animal capable of reason, naked ape

8 **humanness,** humanity, mortality; human nature, the way you are; frailty, human frailty, human fallibility, weakness, human weakness, weakness of the flesh, flesh, the weaknesses human flesh is heir to; human equation

9 humanization, **humanizing**; **anthropomorphism,** pathetic fallacy, anthropopathism, anthropomorphology

10 **anthropology,** science of man; social studies, cultural studies; cultural anthropology, physical anthropology, anthropogeny, anthropography, anthropogeography, cultural geography, human geography, demography, human ecology, anthropometry, craniometry, craniology, ethnology, ethnography, ethnoarchaeology, paleoanthropology, paleoethnology; material culture; behavioral science, sociology, social anthropology, social psychology, psychology; anatomy; anthropologist, ethnologist, ethnographer; sociologist; demographics, population study, population statistics; carbon dating

11 **humanism;** naturalistic humanism, scientific humanism, secular humanism; religious humanism; Christian humanism, integral humanism; new humanism; anthroposophy

VERBS 12 **humanize,** anthropomorphize, make human, civilize

ADJS 13 **human;** hominal; creaturely, creatural; Adamite, Adamitic; frail, weak, fleshly, finite, mortal; only human; earthborn, of the earth, earthy, tellurian, unangelic; humanistic; man-centered, homocentric, anthropocentric; anthropological, ethnographic, ethnological; demographic, epigraphic; social, societal, sociological; acultural

14 **manlike,** anthropoid, humanoid, hominid; anthropomorphic, anthropopathic, therioanthropic

15 **personal, individual,** private, peculiar, idiosyncratic; person-to-person, one-to-one, one-on-one, peer-to-peer, P2P

16 **public,** general, common; communal, societal, social; civic, civil; national, state; international, cosmopolitan, supernational, supranational

ADVS 17 **humanly,** mortally, after the manner of men

COMBINING FORMS 18 anthrop-, anthropo-, homin-, homini-

313 SEASON

<four periods of year>

NOUNS 1 **season,** time of year, season of the year, period, annual period; dry season, rainy season, cold season, monsoon; theatrical season, opera season, concert season; social season, the season; dead season, off-season; baseball season, football season, basketball season, hunting season, preseason; open season, closed season; seasonality, periodicity; **seasonableness**; seasonal affective disorder (SAD)

2 **spring,** springtide, springtime, seedtime, budtime, Maytime, Eastertide; *primavera* <Ital>, prime, prime of the year, vernal equinox

3 **summer,** summertide, summertime, good old summertime; growing season; midsummer; dog days, canicular days; the silly season, high summer; summer solstice; estivation

4 **autumn, fall,** fall of the year, fall of the leaf, harvest, harvest time, harvest home; autumnal equinox

5 **Indian summer,** St. Martin's summer, St. Luke's summer, little summer of St. Luke, St. Augustine's summer

6 **winter,** wintertide, wintertime; midwinter; Christmastime, Christmastide, Yule, Yuletide; winter solstice; hibernation

7 **equinox,** vernal equinox, autumnal equinox; **solstice,** summer solstice, winter solstice

VERBS 8 summer, winter, overwinter, pass the spring; hibernate, estivate

ADJS 9 **seasonal,** in season, out of season, off-season; early-season, mid-season, late-season; **spring,** springlike, vernal; **summer,** summery, summerly, summerlike, canicular, aestival; midsummer; **autumn,** autumnal, fall; **winter,** wintry, wintery, hibernal, hiemal, brumal, boreal, arctic, winterlike, snowy, icy; midwinter; equinoctial, solstitial, periodic

314 MORNING, NOON

<sunrise and midday>

NOUNS 1 **morning,** morn, morningtide, morning time, morntime, matins, morrow, waking time, reveille, get-up time, forenoon; *ante meridiem* (AM) <L>; this morning, this AM; early bird; breakfast time; lunchtime, lunch hour, lunch break; Aurora, Eos

2 **dawn,** the dawn of day, dawning, daybreak, dayspring, day-peep, sunrise, sunup, cockcrowing, cocklight, light, first light, daylight, aurora; break of day, peep of day, crack of dawn, prime, prime of the morning, first blush, flush

of the morning, brightening, first brightening; chanticleer, chantecler

3 **foredawn,** twilight, morning twilight, half-light, glow, dawnlight, first light, the dawn's early light, crepuscule, aurora; the small hours; alpenglow

4 **noon,** noonday, noontide, nooning, noontime, high noon, **midday,** midsun, meridian, *meridiem* <L>, twelve o'clock, 1200 hours, eight bells; noonlight, the blaze of noon; meridian devil, *daemonium meridianum* <L>; lunchtime; sext

ADJS 5 **morning,** matin, matinal, matutinal, antemeridian; auroral, dawn, dawning; forenoon

6 **noon,** noonday, noonish, midday, meridian, twelve-o'clock, high-noon; noonlit

ADVS 7 **in the morning,** before noon, mornings; at sunrise, at dawn, at dawn of day, at cockcrow, at first light, at the crack of dawn, at the break of dawn; with the sun, with the lark

8 **at noon**, at midday, at twelve-o'clock sharp

315 EVENING, NIGHT

<afternoon and night>

NOUNS 1 **afternoon,** *post meridiem* <L>; this afternoon, aft, PM; matinee; siesta

2 **evening,** eve, even, evensong time, evensong hour, eventide, vesper, crepuscle; close of day, decline of day, fall of day, shut of day, gray of the evening, grayness, evening's close, when day is done; nightfall, sunset, sundown, setting sun, going down of the sun, cockshut, cockshut time, cockshut light, retreat; shank of the afternoon, shank of the evening, the cool of the evening; cocktail hour, suppertime, dinnertime

3 **dusk,** dusking time, dusking-tide, dusk-dark, dust-dark, dusty-dark, twilight, evening twilight, crepuscule, crepuscular light, gloam, gloaming, glooming; duskiness, duskishness, brown of dusk, brownness, candlelight, candlelighting, owllight, owl's light, cocklight

4 **night, nighttime,** nighttide, lights-out, taps, bedtime, sleepy time, darkness, blackness; dark of night

5 eleventh hour, curfew

6 **midnight,** dead of night, hush of night, the witching hour; the witching time of night; midnight hours, small hours, wee small hours; late night; late-night snack, midnight snack, late-night supper, midnight supper

ADJS 7 **afternoon,** postmeridian

8 **evening,** evensong, vesper, vespertine, vespertinal, vesperal; twilight, twilighty, twilit, crepuscular; dusk, dusky, duskish

9 **nocturnal,** night, **nightly,** nighttime; nightlong, all-night; night-fallen; midnight; hypnic

10 **benighted,** night-overtaken

ADVS 11 **nightly,** nights, at night, by night; overnight, through the night, all through the night, nightlong, the whole night, all night

COMBINING FORMS 12 noc-, nocto-, nocti-, nyct-, nycto-, nycti-

316 RAIN

<water falling from sky>

NOUNS 1 **rain, rainfall,** fall, **precipitation,** precip, moisture, wet, rainwater, raininess; shower, sprinkle, flurry, patter, pitter-patter, splatter, intermittent rain, intermittent showers; streams of rain, sheet of rain, splash of rain, spurt of rain, fine rain, light rain, occasional rain, occasional showers, April showers, sun shower; drizzle, mizzle; mist, misty rain, Scotch mist; evening mist; fog drip; blood rain; raindrop, unfrozen hydrometeor; acid rain; weather system

2 **rainstorm,** brash, scud <Scot>; cloudburst, rainburst, burst of rain, torrent of rain, torrential rain, torrential downpour; waterspout, spout, rainspout, downpour, downflow, downfall, pour, pouring rain, pelting rain, teeming rain, drowning rain, spate <Scot>, plash, deluge, flood, heavy rain, driving rain, gushing rain, drenching rain, soaking rain, drencher, soaker, gullywasher, pluviosity, goosedrownder, lovely weather for ducks

3 **thunderstorm,** thundersquall, thundergust, thundershower; electric storm

4 **wet weather,** raininess, rainy weather, stormy weather, dirty weather, cat-and-dog weather, spell of rain, wet; rainy day; rains, rainy season, wet season, spring rains, monsoon; predominance of Aquarius, reign of St. Swithin; flood

5 **rainmaking,** seeding, cloud seeding, nucleation, artificial nucleation; rainmaker, rain doctor, cloud seeder; dry ice, silver iodide

6 Jupiter Pluvius, Zeus; Thor

7 **rain gauge,** pluviometer, pluvioscope, pluviograph; ombrometer, ombrograph; udometer, udomograph; hyetometer, hyetometrograph, hyetograph

8 **rainbow,** arc, double rainbow, primary rainbow, seconary rainbow, fogdog, fogbow, white rainbow, mistbow, seadog

9 <science of precipitation> hydrometeorology, hyetology, hyetography; pluviography, pluviometry, ombrology

VERBS 10 **rain, precipitate,** rain down, fall; weep; shower, shower down; sprinkle, spit, spritz, spatter, patter, pitter-patter, plash; drizzle, mizzle; pour, stream, stream down, pour with rain, pelt,

pelt down, drum, tattoo, come down in torrents, come down in sheets, come down in buckets, rain cats and dogs, rain tadpoles, rain bullfrogs, rain pitchforks, rain buckets, rain daggers; rainmake, seed clouds

ADJS 11 **rainy, showery;** pluvious, pluviose, pluvial; drizzly, drizzling, mizzly, drippy; misty, misty-moisty; torrential, pouring, streaming, pelting, drumming, driving, blinding, cat-and-doggish; wet

12 pluviometric, pluvioscopic, pluviographic, ombrometric, ombrographic, udometric, udographic, hyetometric, hyetographic, hyetometrographic; hydrometeorological, hyetological

317 AIR, WEATHER

<states of atmosphere>

NOUNS 1 **air;** ether; ozone; thin air, rarity

2 **atmosphere;** aerosphere, gaseous envelope, gaseous environment, gaseous medium, gaseousblanket, welkin, lift; biosphere, ecosphere, noosphere; air mass; atmospheric component, atmospheric gas; **atmospheric layer** <see list>, stratum, belt; sea air, ocean air

3 **weather, climate,** clime; the elements, forces of nature; microclimate, macroclimate, aerology; weather situation, weather pattern, weather conditions; fair weather, calm weather, good weather, halcyon days; stormy weather; rainy weather; windiness; heat wave, hot weather; cold wave, cold weather; weather system

4 <weather terms> weather map; isobar, isobaric line, isopiestic line; isotherm, isothermal line; isometric, isometric line; frontal system; high, high-pressure area, ridge; low, low-pressure area; front, wind-shift line, squall line; cold front, polar front, cold sector; warm front; occluded front, occlusion, stationary front; air mass; thermal, downdraft, updraft; cyclone, anticyclone; air pressure, air temperature, heat index, temperature-humidity index, dewpoint; humidity, relative humidity; precipitation; wind speed, wind strength, chill factor, windchill factor; ambient temperature; climate change, global warming; Alberta clipper

5 **meteorology,** weather science, aerology, aerography, air-mass analysis, weatherology, climatology, climatography, microclimatology, forecasting, long-range forecasting; barometry; pneumatics; anemology; nephology, anemometry, hyetography, micrometeorology, macrometeorology, mesometeorology, agricultural meteorology, aviation meteorology, maritime meteorology, hydrometeorology, mountain meteorology, planetary meteorology, atmospheric physics

6 **meteorologist,** weather scientist, aerologist, aerographer, weatherologist; climatologist, microclimatologist; weatherman, weather forecaster, weather prophet; weather report, weather forecast; weather bureau; weather ship; weather station; weather-reporting network

7 weather forecast, forecast, weather report, regional forecast, local forecast, general outlook, travel report, boating report, small craft advisory, long-term forecast, <number>-day forecast, storm watch, storm warning, tornado watch, tornado warning, hurricane watch, hurricane warning

8 **weather instrument**, meteorological instrument, aerological instrument; barometer, aneroid barometer, glass, weatherglass; barograph, barometrograph, recording barometer, mercury barometer; thermometer, thermograph; aneroidograph; vacuometer; hygrometer; wind gauge, anemometer, anemograph, windsock, wind cone, wind sleeve, drogue, weathercock; rain gauge, pluviometer, udometer; weather balloon, radiosonde; weather satellite, weather radar; hurricane-hunter aircraft; weather vane

9 **ventilation,** cross-ventilation, airing, aerage, perflation, refreshment; fanning, aeration; air conditioning, central air conditioning, air cooling; oxygenation, oxygenization

10 **ventilator**; aerator, blower; air conditioner, air filter, air cooler, ventilating system, cooling system; heat pump; air passage; fan

VERBS 11 **air,** air out, ventilate, cross-ventilate, wind, refresh, freshen; air-condition, air-cool; fan, winnow; aerate, airify, aerify; oxygenate, oxygenize

ADJS 12 **airy,** aery, aerial, aeriform, airlike, aeriferous, pneumatic, ethereal; exposed, roomy, light; airish, breezy; open-air, alfresco; atmospheric, tropospheric, stratospheric

13 climatal, **climatic**, climatical, climatographical, elemental; meteorological, meteorologic, aerologic, aerological, aerographic, aerographical, climatologic, climatological; macroclimatic, microclimatic, microclimatologic; barometric, barometrical, baric, barographic; isobaric, isopiestic, isometric; high-pressure, low-pressure; cyclonic, anti-cyclonic; seasonal

14 **atmospheric layer**

boundary layer
chemosphere
D layer, Dregion
E region, E layer, Heaviside layer, Kennelly-Heaviside layer

exosphere
F1 layer, F1 region
F2 layer, F2 region, Appleton layer
ionosphere
isothermal region
lower atmosphere
magnetosphere
mesosphere
outer atmosphere
ozone layer, ozonosphere
stratopause
stratosphere
substratosphere
thermosphere
tropopause
troposphere
upper atmosphere
Van Allen belt, Van Allen radiation belt

318 WIND

<movement of atmospheric air>

NOUNS **1** **wind,** current, **air current,** current of air, draft, movement of air, stream, stream of air, flow of air; updraft, uprush; downdraft, downrush, microburst; indraft, inflow, inrush; crosscurrent, crosswind, undercurrent; fall wind, gravity wind, katabatic wind, anabatic wind, headwind, tailwind, following wind; wind aloft; jet stream, upper-atmospheric wind, high-altitude wind, gradient wind, geostrophic wind, prevailing wind; surface wind, mountain wind, valley wind; wind shift, wind shear

2 <wind god; the wind personified> Aeolus, Boreas, Aquilo <north wind>; Eurus <east wind>; Zephyr, Zephyrus, Favonius <west wind>; Notus, Auster <south wind>; Caurus, Caecias <northwest wind>; Afer, Africus <southwest wind>; Argestes <northeast wind>

3 **puff,** puff of air, puff of wind, breath, breath of air, flatus, waft, capful of wind, whiff, whiffet, stir of air

4 **breeze,** light breeze, gentle breeze, light wind, gentle wind, softblowing wind, zephyr, air, light air, moderate breeze; fresh breeze, stiff breeze; cool breeze, cooling breeze; land breeze; sea breeze, onshore breeze, ocean breeze, cat's-paw

5 **gust,** wind gust, blast, blow, flaw, flurry, scud <Scot>, squall

6 **hot wind;** snow eater, thawer; chinook, chinook wind; simoom, samiel; foehn, föhn; khamsin; harmattan; sirocco, yugo; solano; Santa Ana; volcanic wind

7 **cold wind, wintry wind,** winter wind, raw wind, chilling wind, freezing wind, bone-chilling wind, sharp wind, piercing wind, icy wind, biting wind, the hawk, nipping wind, nippy wind, icy blasts; Arctic blast, boreal blast, hyperboreal blast, hyperborean blast; wind chill, wind chill factor

8 **north wind,** norther, mistral, bise, tramontane, Etesian winds, meltemi, vardarac, Papagayo wind; northeaster, nor'easter, Euroclydon, gregale, gregal, gregau, bura, Tehuantepec wind, Tehuantepecer; northwester, nor'wester; southeaster, sou'easter; southwester, sou'wester, kite-wind, libeccio; **east wind,** easter, easterly, levanter, sharav; **west wind,** wester, westerly; **south wind,** souther, southerly buster <Austral>; polar vortex

9 **prevailing wind**; polar easterlies; prevailing westerlies, prevailing southwesterlies, prevailing northwesterlies, antitrades; trade winds, trades; antitrade winds; doldrums, wind-equator; horse latitudes, roaring forties; intertropical convergence zone (ITCZ); equatorial low

10 <nautical terms> **headwind,** beam wind, **tailwind,** following wind, fair wind, favorable wind, apparent wind, relative wind, backing wind, veering wind, slant of wind; onshore wind, offshore wind, wind shear

11 **windstorm,** vortex, eddy, big wind, strong wind, great wind, high wind, dirty wind, ugly wind; storm, storm wind, stormy winds, tempest, tempestuous wind; williwaw; blow, violent blow, heavy blow; squall, thick squall, black squall, white squall; squall line, wind-shift line, line squall; line storm; equinoctial; gale, half a gale, whole gale; tropical cyclone, hurricane, typhoon, tropical storm, blizzard; thundersquall, thundergust; wind shear; bombogenesis, bomb cyclone

12 **dust storm, sandstorm,** shaitan, peesash, devil, khamsin, sirocco, simoom, samiel, harmattan

13 **whirlwind,** whirlblast, tourbillon, wind eddy; cyclone, tornado, twister, funnel cloud, rotary storm, typhoon, *baguio* <Sp>; sandspout, sand column, dust devil; waterspout, rainspout

14 **windiness,** gustiness; airiness, breeziness; draftiness

15 anemology, anemometry; **wind direction; wind force,** Beaufort scale, half-Beaufort scale, International scale; wind rose, barometric wind rose, humidity wind rose, hyetal wind, rain wind rose, temperature wind rose, dynamic wind rose; wind arrow, wind marker

16 **weather vane,** weathercock, vane, cock, wind vane, wind indicator, wind cone, wind sleeve, windsock, anemoscope; anemometer, wind-speed indicator, anemograph, anemometrograph

17 **blower,** bellows; blowpipe, blowtube, blowgun

18 **fan,** flabellum; punkah, thermantidote, electric fan, blower, window fan, attic fan, exhaust fan; ventilator; windsail, windscoop, windcatcher

VERBS **19** **blow,** waft; puff, huff, whiff; whiffle; breeze; breeze up, freshen; gather, brew, set in, blow up, pipe up, come up, blow up a storm; bluster, squall; storm, rage, blast, blow great guns, blow a hurricane; blow over

20 **sigh,** sough, whisper, mutter, murmur, sob, moan, groan, growl, snarl, wail, howl, scream, screech, shriek, roar, whistle, pipe, sing, sing in the shrouds

ADJS 21 **windy,** blowy; breezy, drafty, airy, airish; brisk, fresh; gusty, blasty, puffy, flawy; squally; prevailing; blustery, blustering, blusterous; aeolian, favonian, boreal; ventose

22 **stormy,** tempestuous, raging, storming, angry; turbulent; gale-force, storm-force, hurricane-force; dirty, foul; cyclonic, tornadic, typhonic, typhoonish; inclement; rainy; cloudy

23 **windblown,** blown; **windswept,** bleak, raw, exposed

24 anemological, anemographic, anemometric, anemometrical

319 CLOUD

<water condensation in sky>

NOUNS 1 **cloud,** high fog; fleecy cloud, cottony cloud, billowy cloud; **cloud bank,** cloud mass, cloud cover, cloud drift; cloud base; cloudling, cloudlet; cloudscape, cloud band; cloudland, Cloudcuckooland, Nephelococcygia; mackerel sky, buttermilk sky

2 <cloud types> ice cloud, water cloud, storm cloud, thunderhead, thunder cloud; cirrus, cirrocumulus, altostratus, cirrostratus, altocumulus, nimbostratus, stratocumulus, cumulostratus, stratus, cumulus, cumulonimbus, nimbus

3 **fog,** pea soup, peasouper, pea-soup fog; ground fog, coastal fog, fog drip, dense fog; London fog, London special, Scotch mist, brume; fog bank; **smog,** smoke-fog; smaze, smoke-haze; frost smoke; mist, drizzling mist, drisk; haze, gauze, film; vapor; wintry mix, snow showers

4 **cloudiness,** cloud cover, haziness, mistiness, fogginess, nebulosity, nubilation, nimbosity, overcast, heavy sky, dirty sky, lowering sky

5 nephology, nephelognosy; nephologist

6 nephelometer, nepheloscope

VERBS 7 **cloud,** becloud, encloud, cloud over, overcloud, cloud up, clabber up, overcast, overshadow, shadow, shade, darken, darken over, nubilate, obnubilate, obscure; smoke, oversmoke; fog, befog; fog in; smog; mist, mist over, mist up, bemist, enmist; haze

ADJS 8 **cloudy,** nebulous, nubilous, nimbose, nebulosus, nephological; clouded, overclouded, overcast; dirty, heavy, lowering, louring; dark; gloomy; cloud-flecked; cirrous, cirrose; cumulous, cumuliform, stratous, stratiform, cirrocumiliform, cirrocumuous, altocumuliform, altocumulous, altostratous, cirrostratous, nimbostratous, cumulonimbiform; lenticularis, mammatus, castellatus; thunderheaded, stormy, squally; mostly cloudy, partly cloudy

9 **cloud-covered,** cloud-laden, cloud-curtained, cloud-crammed, cloud-crossed, cloud-decked, cloud-hidden, cloud-wrapped, cloud-enveloped, cloud-surrounded, cloud-girt, cloud-flecked, cloud-eclipsed, cloud-capped, cloud-topped

10 **foggy,** soupy, pea-soupy, nubilous; fogbound, fogged-in; smoggy; hazy, misty; so foggy the seagulls are walking, so thick you can cut it with a knife

11 nephological

320 BUBBLE

<liquid ball of gas or air>

NOUNS 1 **bubble,** bleb, globule; vesicle, bulla, blister, blood blister, fever blister; balloon, bladder; air bubble, soap bubble

2 **foam, froth;** spume, sea foam, scud; spray, surf, breakers, whitewater, spoondrift, spindrift; suds, lather, soap suds; beer suds, head; scum, off-scum; collar; puff, mousse, soufflé, meringue

3 **bubbling,** bubbliness, effervescence, effervescency, sparkle, spumescence, frothiness, frothing, foaming; fizz, fizzle, carbonation; ebullience, ebulliency; ebullition, boiling; fermentation, ferment

VERBS 4 **bubble,** bubble up, burble; effervesce, fizz, fizzle; hiss, sparkle; ferment, work; foam, froth, froth up; have a head, foam over; boil, seethe, simmer; plop, blubber; guggle, gurgle; bubble over, boil over

5 **foam, froth,** spume, cream; lather, suds, sud; scum, mantle; aerate, whip, beat, whisk

ADJS 6 **bubbly,** burbly, **bubbling,** burbling; effervescent, spumescent, fizzy, sparkling, *mousseux* <Fr>, *spumante* <Ital>; carbonated; ebullient; puffed, soufflé, souffléed, beaten, whipped, chiffon; blistered, blistery, blebby, vesicated, vesicular; blistering, vesicant, vesicatory

7 **foamy,** foam-flecked, **frothy,** spumy, spumous, spumose; yeasty, barmy; sudsy, suddy, lathery, soapy, soapsudsy, soapsuddy; heady, with a head on, with a collar on

321 BEHAVIOR

<way of acting>

NOUNS 1 **behavior, conduct,** deportment, comportment, manner, manners, demeanor, mien, carriage, bearing, port, poise, posture, guise, air, address, presence; tone, style, lifestyle; way of life, habit of life, modus vivendi; way, way of acting, ways; trait behavior, behavior trait; methods, method, methodology; practice, praxis; procedure, proceeding; actions, acts, goings-on, doings, what one is up to, movements, moves, tactics; action, doing; activity; objective behavior, observable behavior; motions, gestures, gesticulation, hand-waving, air quotes; pose, affectation; pattern, behavior pattern; Type A behavior, Type B behavior; culture pattern, behavioral norm, folkway, custom

2 **good behavior,** sanctioned behavior; good citizenship; good manners, correct deportment, etiquette; courtesy; social behavior, sociability; bad behavior, poor behavior, **misbehavior**; discourtesy

3 **behaviorism,** behavioral science, behavior psychology, behavioristic psychology, Watsonian psychology, Skinnerian psychology; social science; behavior modification, behavior therapy ethology, animal behavior, human behavior, social behavior, ethology

VERBS 4 **behave**, act, do, go on; behave oneself, conduct oneself, manage oneself, handle oneself, guide oneself, comport oneself, deport oneself, demean oneself, bear oneself, carry oneself; acquit oneself, quit oneself; proceed, move, swing into action; **misbehave**

5 **behave oneself**, behave, act well, clean up one's act, act one's age, be good, be nice, do right, do what is right, do the right thing, do the proper thing, keep out of mischief, play the game, mind one's P's and Q's, be on one's good behavior, be on one's best behavior, play one's cards right, set a good example

6 **treat,** use, do by, deal by, act toward, behave toward, conduct oneself toward, act with regard to, conduct oneself vis-à-vis, conduct oneself in the face of; deal with, cope with, handle; respond to

ADJS 7 **behavioral;** behaviorist, behavioristic; ethological; **behaved,** behaviored, mannered, demeanored

322 MISBEHAVIOR

<behaving badly>

NOUNS 1 **misbehavior, misconduct,** misdemeanor; unsanctioned behavior, nonsanctioned behavior; frowned-upon behavior; naughtiness, badness; impropriety; venial sin; disorderly conduct, disorder, disorderliness, disruptiveness, disruption, rowdiness, rowdyism, riotousness, ruffianism, hooliganism, hoodlumism, aggro; vandalism, trashing; roughhouse, horseplay; discourtesy; vice; misfeasance, malfeasance, misdoing, delinquency, wrongdoing

2 **mischief,** mischievousness; devilment, deviltry, devilry; roguishness, roguery, scampishness; waggery, waggishness; impishness, devilishness, puckishness, elfishness; prankishness, pranksomeness; sportiveness, playfulness; high spirits, youthful spirits; foolishness

3 **mischief-maker,** mischief, rogue, devil, knave, rascal, rapscallion, scapegrace, scamp; wag; buffoon; funmaker, joker, jokester, practical joker, prankster, life of the party, cutup; rowdy, ruffian, hoodlum, hood, hooligan; imp, elf, puck, pixie, minx, bad boy, bugger, booger, little devil, little rascal, little monkey, *enfant terrible* <Fr>

VERBS 4 **misbehave**, misbehave oneself, misconduct oneself, misdemean, misdemean oneself, behave ill; get into mischief; act up, make waves, carry on, carry on something scandalous, sow one's wild oats; **cut up**, horse around, roughhouse, cut up rough; rock on; play the fool

ADJS 5 **misbehaving,** unbehaving; naughty, bad; improper, not respectable; out-of-order, off-base, out-of-line; disorderly, disruptive, rowdy, rowdyish, ruffianly

6 **mischievous,** mischief-loving, full of mischief, full of the devil, full of old nick; roguish, scampish, scapegrace, arch, knavish; devilish; impish, puckish, elfish, elvish; waggish, prankish, pranky, pranksome, trickish, tricksy; playful, sportive, high-spirited; foolish

ADVS 7 **mischievously,** roguishly, knavishly, scampishly, devilishly; impishly, puckishly, elfishly; waggishly; prankishly, playfully, sportively, in fun

323 WILL

<determination to do something>

NOUNS 1 **will, volition;** choice, determination, decision; wish, mind, fancy, discretion, pleasure, inclination, disposition, liking, appetence, appetency, desire; half a mind, half a notion, idle wish, velleity; appetite, passion, lust, sexual desire; animus, objective, intention; command; free choice, one's own will, one's own choice, one's own discretion, one's own initiative, free will, free hand; conation, conatus; will power, resolution; final will, final wishes

VERBS 2 **will, wish,** see, fit, think fit, think good, think proper, choose to, have a mind to; have half a mind to, have half a notion to; choose, determine, decide; resolve; command, decree; desire

3 have one's will, **have one's way, get one's way**, get one's wish, have one's druthers, write one's own ticket, have it all one's way, do as one pleases, please oneself; assert oneself, take the bit in one's teeth, take charge of one's destiny; stand on one's rights; take the law into one's own hands; have the last word, impose one's will; know one's own mind

ADJS 4 **volitional,** volitive; willing, voluntary; conative; *ex gratia* <L>; intentional

ADVS 5 **at will,** at choice, at pleasure, at one's pleasure, at one's will and pleasure, at one's own sweet will, at one's discretion, *à discrétion* <Fr>, *ad arbitrium* <L>; *ad libitum* <L>, ad lib; as one wishes, as it pleases oneself, as it suits oneself, in one's own way, in one's own sweet way, in one's own sweet time, as one thinks best, as it seems good, as it seems best, as far as one desires; of one's own free will, of one's own accord, on one's own; without coercion, unforced

324 WILLINGNESS

<cheerful compliance>

NOUNS 1 **willingness,** gameness, readiness; unreluctance, unloathness, ungrudgingness; agreeableness, agreeability, favorableness; acquiescence, consent; compliance, cooperativeness; receptivity, receptiveness, responsiveness, responsivity; amenability, tractableness, tractability, docility, biddability, biddableness, pliancy, pliability, malleability; eagerness, keenness, promptness, forwardness, alacrity, zeal, zealousness, ardor, enthusiasm, fervor; goodwill, cheerful consent; willing heart, willing mind, willing humor, favorable disposition, positive mood, right mood, receptive mood, willing ear; sacrificial lamb

2 **voluntariness,** volunteering; gratuitousness; spontaneity, spontaneousness, unforcedness; self-determination, self-activity, self-action, autonomy, autonomousness, independence, free will; volunteerism, voluntaryism, voluntarism; volunteer; labor of love

VERBS 3 **be willing**, be game, be ready; be of favorable disposition, take the trouble, find it in one's heart, find one's heart, have a willing heart; incline, lean; look kindly upon; be open to, bring oneself, agree, be agreeable to; acquiesce, consent; not hesitate to, would as lief, would as leave, would as lief as not, not care if one does, not mind if one does; play along, go along, do one's part, do one's bit, have a good mind to; be eager, be keen, be dying to, fall all over oneself, be spoiling for, be champing at the bit; be Johnny on the spot, step into the breach; enter with a will, lean over backward, bend over backward, go into heart and soul, go the extra mile, plunge into; cooperate, collaborate; lend a willing ear

4 **volunteer,** do voluntarily, do ex gratia, do of one's own accord, do of one's own volition, do of one's own free will; do independently; put forward, sacrifice oneself; offer

ADJS 5 **willing,** willinghearted, ready, game; disposed, inclined, minded, willed, fain, prone; well-disposed, well-inclined, favorably inclined, favorably disposed; predisposed; favorable, agreeable, cooperative; compliant, content, acquiescent, consenting; eager; keen, prompt, quick, alacritous, forward, ready and willing, zealous, ardent, enthusiastic; in the mood, in the humor, in a good mood; receptive, responsive; amenable, tractable, docile, pliant, in favor

6 **ungrudging,** ungrumbling, unreluctant, unloath, nothing loath, unaverse, unshrinking

7 **voluntary, volunteer**; *ex gratia* <L>, gratuitous; spontaneous, free, freewill; offered, proffered; discretionary, discretional, nonmandatory, optional, elective; arbitrary; self-determined, self-determining, autonomous, independent, self-active, self-acting; unsought, unbesought, unasked, unrequested, unsolicited, uninvited, unbidden, uncalled-for; unforced, uncoerced, unpressured, unrequired, uncompelled; unprompted, uninfluenced

ADVS 8 **willingly**, with a will, with good will, with right good will; eagerly, with zest, with relish, with open arms, without question, zealously, ardently, enthusiastically; readily, promptly, at the drop of a hat

9 **agreeably,** favorably, compliantly; lief, lieve, fain, as lief, as lief as not; ungrudgingly, ungrumblingly, unreluctantly, nothing loath, without reluctance, without demur, without hesitation, unstintingly, unreservedly

10 **voluntarily,** freely, gratuitously, spontaneously; optionally, electively, by choice; of one's own accord, of one's own free will, of one's own volition, without reservation, of one's own choice, at one's own discretion; without coercion, without pressure, without compulsion, without intimidation; independently

325 UNWILLINGNESS

<reluctance to act>

NOUNS 1 **refusal, unwillingness,** disinclination, nolition, indisposition, indisposedness, reluctance, renitency, renitence, grudgingness, grudging consent; unenthusiasm, lack of enthusiasm, lack of zeal, lack of eagerness, slowness, backwardness, dragging of the feet, foot-dragging, apathy, indifference; sullenness, sulk, sulks, sulkiness; cursoriness, perfunctoriness; recalcitrance, recalcitrancy, disobedience, refractoriness, fractiousness, intractableness, indocility, mutinousness; averseness, aversion, repugnance, antipathy, distaste, disrelish, no stomach for; obstinacy, stubbornness; opposition; resistance; disagreement, dissent

2 demur, demurral, scruple, **qualm,** qualm of conscience, reservation, compunction; hesitation, hesitancy, hesitance, pause, boggle, falter; qualmishness, scrupulousness, scrupulosity; stickling, boggling; faltering; shrinking; shyness, diffidence, modesty, bashfulness, retiring disposition, restraint; recoil; protest, objection

VERBS **3** **refuse, be unwilling,** would rather not, not care to, not feel like, not find it in one's heart to, not have the heart to, not have the stomach to; mind, object to, draw the line at, be dead set against, balk at; grudge, begrudge

4 **demur,** scruple, have qualms, have scruples; stickle, stick at, boggle, strain; falter, waver; hesitate, pause, be halfhearted, hang back, hang off, hold off; fight shy of, shy at, shy, crane, shrink, recoil, blench, flinch, wince, quail, pull back; make bones about, make bones of

ADJS **5** **unwilling, disinclined,** indisposed, not in the mood, averse, not feeling like; unconsenting; dead set against, opposed; resistant; disagreeing, differing, at odds; disobedient, recalcitrant, refractory, fractious, sullen, sulky, indocile, mutinous; cursory, perfunctory; involuntary, forced

6 **reluctant,** renitent, **grudging, loath;** backward, laggard, dilatory, slow, slow to, foot-dragging; unenthusiastic, unzealous, indifferent, apathetic, perfunctory; balky, balking, restive

7 **demurring,** qualmish, boggling, stickling, hedging, squeamish, scrupulous; diffident, shy, modest, bashful; hesitant, hesitating, faltering; shrinking

ADVS **8** **unwillingly,** involuntarily, against one's will; under compulsion, under coercion, under pressure; in spite of oneself

9 **reluctantly,** grudgingly, sullenly, sulkily; unenthusiastically, perfunctorily; with dragging feet, with a bad grace, with an ill grace, under protest; with a heavy heart, with no heart, with no stomach; over one's dead body, not on one's life

326 OBEDIENCE

<willingness to obey>

NOUNS **1** **obedience, obediency,** compliance; acquiescence, consent; deference, self-abnegation, submission, submissiveness; servility; eagerness to serve, readiness to serve, willingness to serve, dutifulness, duteousness; service, servitium, homage, fealty, allegiance, loyalty, faithfulness, faith, suit and service, suit service, observance, brand loyalty; doglike devotion, doglike obedience; conformity, lockstep; law-abidingness; obeisance, good behavior, best behavior

VERBS **2** **obey,** mind, heed, keep, observe, listen, hearken to; comply, conform, walk in lockstep; stay in line, not get out of line, not get off base, toe the line, toe the mark, come to heel, fall in, fall in line, obey the rules, follow the book, keep the law, behave, be on one's best behavior, do what one is told; do as one says, do the will of, defer to, do one's bidding, come at one's call, lie down and roll over for; take orders, attend to orders, do suit and service, follow the lead of; submit; serve at one's pleasure

ADJS **3** **obedient,** compliant, complying, allegiant; acquiescent, consenting, submissive, deferential, self-abnegating; willing, dutiful, duteous; under control; loyal, faithful, devoted; uncritical, unshakeable, doglike; conforming, in conformity; law-abiding

4 **at one's command,** at one's whim, at one's pleasure, at one's disposal, at one's nod, at one's call, at one's beck and call

5 **henpecked,** tied to one's apron strings, on a string, on a leash, in leading strings; wimpish; milk-toast, milquetoast, Caspar Milquetoast; under one's thumb; chicken-pecked

ADVS **6** **obediently,** compliantly; acquiescently, submissively; willingly, dutifully, duteously; loyally, faithfully, devotedly; in obedience to, in compliance with, in conformity with

7 at your service, at your command, at your orders, as you please, as you will, as thou wilt

327 DISOBEDIENCE

<unwillingness to obey>

NOUNS **1** **disobedience,** nonobedience, noncompliance; undutifulness, unduteousness; willful disobedience; insubordination, indiscipline; unsubmissiveness, intractability, indocility, recusancy; nonconformity; disrespect; lawlessness, waywardness, frowardness, naughtiness; violation, transgression, infraction, infringement, lawbreaking; civil disobedience, passive resistance; uncooperativeness, noncooperation; dereliction, deliberate negligence, default, delinquency, nonfeasance

2 **defiance,** refractoriness, recalcitrance, recalcitrancy, recalcitration, defiance of authority, contumacy, contumaciousness, obstreperousness, unruliness, restiveness, fractiousness, orneriness, feistiness; wildness; obstinacy, stubbornness

3 **rebelliousness,** mutinousness; riotousness; insurrectionism, insurgentism; factiousness, sedition, seditiousness; treasonableness, traitorousness, subversiveness, subversion; extremism

4 **revolt, rebellion,** revolution, mutiny, insurrection, insurgence, insurgency, uprising, rising, outbreak, general uprising, riot, civil disorder; peasant revolt; putsch, coup, coup d'état; strike, general strike; intifada; resistance movement, resistance; terrorism

5 **rebel,** revolter; insurgent, insurrectionary, insurrecto, insurrectionist; malcontent; insubordinate; mutineer, rioter, brawler; maverick, noncooperator, troublemaker, refusenik, agent provocateur; nonconformist; agitator; extremist; reactionary; revolutionary, revolutionist; traitor, subversive; freedom fighter; contra

VERBS 6 **disobey,** not mind, not heed, not keep, not observe, not listen, not hearken, pay no attention to, ignore, disregard, defy, set at defiance, fly in the face of, snap one's fingers at, scoff at, flout, go counter to, set at naught, set naught by, care naught for; be a law unto oneself, step out of line, get off-base, refuse to cooperate; not conform, hear a different drummer; violate, transgress; break the law; thumb one's nose at

7 **revolt, rebel,** kick over the traces, reluct, reluctate; rise up, rise, arise, rise up in arms, mount the barricades; mount a coup d'état; mutiny, mutineer; insurge, insurrect, riot, run riot; revolutionize, revolution, revolute, subvert, overthrow; call a general strike, strike; secede, break away

ADJS 8 **disobedient,** transgressive, uncomplying, violative, lawless, wayward, froward, naughty; recusant, nonconforming; undutiful, unduteous; self-willed, willful, obstinate; defiant; undisciplined, ill-disciplined, indisciplined

9 **insubordinate,** unsubmissive, indocile, uncompliant, uncooperative, noncooperative, noncooperating, intractable

10 **defiant,** refractory, recalcitrant, contumacious, obstreperous, unruly, restive, impatient of control, impatient of discipline; fractious, ornery, feisty; wild, untamed

11 **rebellious,** rebel, breakaway; mutinous, mutineering; insurgent, insurrectionary, riotous, turbulent; factious, seditious, seditionary; revolutionary, revolutional; traitorous, treasonable, subversive; extreme, extremistic

ADVS 12 **disobediently,** uncompliantly, against order and discipline, contrary to order and discipline; insubordinately, unsubmissively, indocilely, uncooperatively; unresignedly; disregardfully, floutingly, defiantly; intractably; obstreperously, contumaciously, restively, fractiously; rebelliously, mutinously; riotously

328 ACTION

<voluntary action>

NOUNS 1 **action, activity**, act, willed action, willed activity; acting, doing, activism, direct action, not words but action, happening; practice, actual practice, praxis; exercise, drill; operation, working, function, functioning; play; operations, affairs, workings; business, employment, work, occupation; behavior

2 **performance,** execution, carrying out, enactment; transaction; discharge, dispatch; conduct, handling, management, administration; achievement, accomplishment, effectuation, implementation; commission, perpetration, operationalization; completion

3 **act, action,** deed, doing, thing, thing done, overt act; turn; feat, stunt, trick; master stroke, *tour de force* <Fr>, exploit, adventure, enterprise, initiative, achievement, accomplishment, performance, production, track record; gesture; effort, endeavor, job, undertaking; transaction; dealing, deal; passage; operation, proceeding, process, step, measure, maneuver, move, movement; policy, tactics; *démarche* <Fr>, coup, stroke; blow, go; accomplished fact, *fait accompli* <Fr>, done deal; acta, *res gestae* <L>, doings, dealings, affairs; works; work, handiwork, hand

VERBS 4 **act,** serve, function; operate, work, move, practice, do one's thing; proceed; make, play, behave

5 **take action,** take steps, take measures; proceed, proceed with, go ahead with, go with, go through with; do something, go into action, swing into action, do something about, act on, act upon, take it on, run with it, get off the dime, get off one's ass, get off one's dead ass, get with it, get the picture; fish or cut bait, shit or get off the pot*, put up and shut up, put one's money where one's mouth is; go, have a go, take a whack, lift a finger, lend a hand; play a role, play a part in; stretch

forth one's hand, strike a blow; maneuver, make moves; get a life

6 **do,** effect, effectuate, make; bring about, bring to pass, bring off, produce, deliver, do the trick, put across, put through; swing, swing it, hack, hack it, cut it, cut the mustard; do one's part, carry one's weight, carry the ball, hold up one's end, hold up one's end of the bargain; tear off, achieve, accomplish, realize; render, pay; inflict, wreak, do to; commit, perpetrate; pull off; go and do, up and do, take and do

7 **carry out,** carry through, go through, fulfill, work out; bring off, carry off; put through, get through; implement; put into effect, put in practice, put into practice, carry into effect, execute, carry into execution, translate into action; suit the action to the word; rise to the occasion, come through

8 **practice,** put into practice, exercise, employ, use; carry on, conduct, prosecute, wage; follow, pursue; engage in, work at, devote oneself to, do, turn to, apply oneself to, employ oneself in; play at; take up, take to, undertake, tackle, take on, address oneself to, have a go at, turn one's hand to, go in for, go out for, make it one's business, follow as an occupation, set up shop; specialize in

9 **perform,** execute, enact; transact; discharge, dispatch; conduct, manage, handle; legislate, commission; dispose of, take care of, deal with, cope with; make, accomplish, complete

ADJS 10 **acting,** performing, practicing, serving, functioning, functional, operating, operative, operational, working, in harness; implementable; in action; behavioral

329 INACTION

<voluntary inaction>

NOUNS 1 **inaction,** passiveness, passivity, passivism; passive resistance, nonviolent resistance; passive-aggression; nonresistance, nonviolence; pacifism; neutrality, neutralness, neutralism, nonparticipation, noninvolvement; standpattism; do-nothingism, do-nothingness, do-nothing policy; laissez-faireism, *laissez-faire, laissez-aller* <Fr>; watching and waiting, watchful waiting, waiting game, a wait-and-see attitude, indecision; inertia, inertness, immobility, dormancy, stagnation, stagnancy, vegetation, stasis, paralysis, standstill; procrastination; idleness, indolence, torpor, torpidness, torpidity, sloth; stalemate, logjam; equilibrium, dead center; **inactivity**; quietude, serenity, quiescence; quietism, contemplation, meditation, passive self-annihilation; leisure; contemplative life; back burner

VERBS 2 **do nothing,** not stir, not budge, not lift a finger, not lift a hand, not move a foot, sit back, sit on one's hands, sit on one's ass, sit on one's butt, sit on one's duff, sit on one's dead ass, sit on the sidelines, be a sideliner, sit it out, take a rain-check, fold one's arms, twiddle one's thumbs; cool one's heels, cool one's jets; bide one's time, delay, watch and wait, wait and see, play a waiting game, lie low, tread water; hang fire, not go off half-cocked; lie back, rest upon one's oars, rest, put one's feet up, kick back, be still; repose on one's laurels; drift, coast; stagnate, vegetate, veg out, lie dormant, hibernate; lay down on the job, idle; freeze; back-burner

3 **refrain, abstain,** hold, spare, forbear, forgo, keep from; hold one's hand, stay one's hand, sit by, sit idly by, sit on one's hands

4 **let alone,** leave alone, leave well enough alone, let well enough alone; look the other way, not make waves, not look for trouble, not rock the boat; let be, leave be, let things take their course, let it have its way; leave things as they are; *laissez-faire* <Fr>, live and let live; take no part in, not get involved in, have nothing to do with, have no hand in, stand aloof, remain aloof, keep out of; tolerate, sit on the fence

5 **let go,** let pass, let slip, let slide, let ride; procrastinate, sit tight, defer

ADJS 6 **passive**; neutral, neuter; standpat, do-nothing; *laissez-faire, laissez-aller* <Fr>; inert, like a bump on a log, immobile, dormant, stagnant, stagnating, vegetative, vegetable, static, stationary, motionless, unmoving, paralyzed, paralytic; procrastinating; **inactive, idle**; quiescent; quietist, quietistic, contemplative, meditative; passive-aggressive

ADVS 7 **at a standstill,** at a halt; as a last resort

PHRS 8 if it ain't broke don't fix it, let sleeping dogs lie; *dolce far niente* <Ital>

330 ACTIVITY

<being active>

NOUNS 1 **activity, action,** activeness; movement, motion, stir; proceedings, doings, goings-on; activism, political activism, judicial activism; militancy; business

2 **liveliness,** animation, vivacity, vivaciousness, sprightliness, spiritedness, bubbliness, ebullience, effervescence, briskness, breeziness, peppiness; life, spirit, verve, energy, adrenalin; pep, moxie, oomph, pizzazz, piss and vinegar, vim

3 **quickness,** swiftness, speediness, alacrity, celerity, readiness, smartness, sharpness, briskness; promptness, promptitude; dispatch,

expeditiousness, expedition; agility, nimbleness, spryness, springiness

4 **bustle,** fuss, flurry, flutter, fluster, scramble, ferment, stew, sweat, whirl, swirl, vortex, maelstrom, stir, hubbub, hullabaloo, hoo-ha, foofaraw, flap, schemozzle, ado, to-do, bother, botheration, pother; fussiness, flutteriness; tumult, commotion, agitation; restlessness, unquiet, fidgetiness; spurt, burst, fit, spasm

5 **busyness, multtasking,** press of business, hive of activity; plenty to do, many irons in the fire, much on one's plate; the battle of life, rat race

6 **industry,** industriousness, assiduousness, assiduity, diligence, application, concentration, laboriousness, sedulity, sedulousness, unsparingness, relentlessness, zealousness, ardor, fervor, vehemence; **energy,** energeticalness, strenuousness, strenuosity, tirelessness, indefatigability

7 **enterprise,** enterprisingness, dynamism, **initiative,** aggression, microaggression, aggressiveness, killer instinct, force, forcefulness, pushfulness, pushingness, pushiness, push, drive, hustle, go, getup, get-up-and-get, get-up-and-go, go-ahead, go-getting, go-to-itiveness, up-and-comingness; adventurousness, venturousness, venturesomeness, adventuresomeness; spirit, gumption, spunk; ambitiousness

8 man of action, woman of action, **doer,** man of deeds; hustler, self-starter, bustler; go-getter, ball of fire, live wire, powerhouse, human dynamo, spitfire; workaholic, overachiever; beaver, busy bee, eager beaver, no slouch; operator, big-time operator, wheeler-dealer; winner; activist, political activist, militant; hacktivist; enthusiast; new broom, take-charge guy

9 **overactivity,** hyperactivity; hyperkinesia, hyperkinesis; franticness, frenziedness; overexertion, overextension; officiousness; a finger in every pie

VERBS **10** **be busy,** have one's hands full, have many irons in the fire, have a lot on one's plate; not have a moment to spare, not have a moment to call one's own, not be able to call one's time one's own; do it on the run; have other things to do, have other fish to fry; work, labor, drudge; busy oneself

11 **stir,** stir about, bestir oneself, stir one's stumps, get down to business, sink one's teeth into it, take hold, be up and doing

12 **bustle,** fuss, make a fuss, stir, stir about, rush around, rush about, tear around, hurry about, buzz about, whiz about, dart to and fro, run around, run around like a chicken with its head cut off, run around in circles

13 **hustle, drive,** drive oneself, push, scramble, go all out, make things hum, step lively, make the sparks fly, do one's damnedest; make up for lost time; press on, drive on; go ahead, forge ahead, shoot ahead, go full steam ahead

14 <nonformal> hump, get cutting, break one's neck, bear down on it, put one's back into it, get off the dime, get off one's ass, get off one's duff, get off one's dead ass, hit the ball, pour it on, lean on it, shake a leg, go to town, get the lead out, floor it, go wild, go gangbusters

15 **keep going,** keep on, keep on the go, keep on keeping on, keep on trucking, carry on, peg away, plug away, keep at it, keep moving, keep driving, keep the pot boiling, keep the ball rolling; keep busy, keep one's nose to the grindstone, stay on the treadmill, burn the candle at both ends

16 make the most of one's time, improve the shining hour, make hay while the sun shines, not let the grass grow under one's feet; get up early

ADJS **17** **active,** lively, animated, spirited, bubbly, ebullient, effervescent, vivacious, sprightly, chipper, perky, pert; spry, breezy, brisk, energetic, eager, keen, can-do; smacking, spanking; alive, live, full of life, full of pep, full of go, pizzazz, moxie, alive and kicking; peppy, snappy, zingy; frisky, bouncing, bouncy; mercurial, quicksilver; activist, activistic, militant

18 **quick,** swift, speedy, expeditious, snappy, celeritous, alacritous, dispatchful, prompt, ready, smart, sharp, quick on the draw, quick on the trigger, quick on the upswing; agile, nimble, spry, springy

19 **astir,** stirring, afoot, on foot; in full swing

20 **bustling,** fussing, fussy; fidgety, restless, fretful, jumpy, unquiet, unsettled; agitated, turbulent

21 **busy,** full of business; occupied, engaged, employed, working; at it; at work, on duty, on the job, in harness; involved, engagé; hard at work, hard at it; on the move, on the go, on the run, on the hop, on the jump, on the make; busy as a bee, busy as a beaver, busy-busy, busier than a one-armed paper hanger; up to one's elbows in, up to one's neck in, up to one's eyeballs in; tied up

22 **industrious,** assiduous, **diligent,** sedulous, laborious, hardworking, workaholic; hard, unremitting, unsparing, relentless, zealous, ardent, fervent, vehement; energetic, strenuous; never idle; unsleeping; tireless, unwearied, unflagging, indefatigable; stick-to-it-ive

23 **enterprising,** aggressive, dynamic, activist, proactive, driving, forceful, pushing, pushful, pushy, up-and-coming, go-ahead, hustling, go-getting; adventurous, venturous, venturesome, adventuresome; ambitious

24 **overactive,** hyperactive, hyper; hectic, frenzied, frantic, frenetic; hyperkinetic; intrusive, officious; full of beans

ADVS **25** **actively,** busily; lively, sprightly, briskly, breezily, energetically, animatedly, vivaciously, spiritedly, with life and spirit, with gusto; allegro, allegretto; full tilt, in full swing, all out; like a house afire

26 **quickly,** swiftly, expeditiously, with dispatch, readily, promptly; agilely, nimbly, spryly

27 **industriously,** assiduously, diligently, sedulously, laboriously; unsparingly, relentlessly, zealously, ardently, fervently, vehemently; energetically, strenuously, tirelessly, indefatigably

331 INACTIVITY

<not acting>

NOUNS **1** **inactivity, inaction**, inactiveness; lull, suspension; suspended animation; dormancy, hibernation; immobility, motionlessness, quiescence; inertia; underactivity; back burner

2 **idleness,** unemployment, underemployment, nothing to do, otiosity, inoccupation; **leisure,** leisureliness, unhurried ease; idle hands, idle hours, off hours, time on one's hands; **relaxation,** letting down, unwinding, putting one's feet up, slippered ease

3 **unemployment,** lack of work, joblessness, inoccupation, underemployment; layoff, furlough; normal unemployment, seasonal unemployment, technological unemployment, cyclical unemployment; unemployment insurance; shutdown, recession, depression

4 **idling, loafing,** lazing, *flânerie* <Fr>, goofing off, slacking, goldbricking; *dolce far niente* <Ital>; trifling; dallying, dillydallying, mopery, dawdling; loitering, tarrying, lingering; lounging, lolling

5 **indolence, laziness,** sloth, slothfulness, bone-laziness; laggardness, slowness, dilatoriness, remissness, do-nothingness, faineancy; inexertion, inertia; shiftlessness, do-lessness; hoboism, vagrancy; spring fever; ergophobia

6 **languor,** languidness, languorousness, languishment, lackadaisicalness, lotus-eating; listlessness, lifelessness, inanimation, enervation, slowness, lenitude, lentor, dullness, sluggishness, heaviness, dopiness, hebetude, supineness, lassitude, lethargy, loginess; kef, nodding; phlegm, apathy, indifference, passivity; torpidness, torpor, torpidity; stupor, stuporousness, stupefaction; sloth, slothfulness, acedia; sleepiness, somnolence, oscitancy, yawning, drowsiness; weariness, fatigue; jadedness, satedness; world-weariness, ennui, boredom

7 **lazybones,** lazyboots, lazylegs, indolent, lie-abed, slugabed

8 **idler,** loafer, lounger, loller, layabout, couch potato, lotus-eater, *flâneur, flâneuse* <Fr>, do-nothing, dolittle, *fainéant* <Fr>, goof-off, fuck-off*, goldbrick, goldbricker, clock watcher; sluggard, slug, slouch, sloucher, lubber, stick-in-the-mud, gentleman of leisure; time waster, time killer; dallier, dillydallier, mope, moper, doodler, diddler, dawdler, dawdle, laggard, loiterer, lingerer; waiter on Providence; trifler, putterer, potterer

9 **bum,** stiff, derelict, skid-row bum, Bowery bum; beachcomber; good-for-nothing, good-for-naught, ne'er-do-well, wastrel; drifter, vagrant, hobo, tramp; beggar

10 homeless person; street person; shopping-bag lady, bag person

11 **nonworker,** drone; cadger, bummer, moocher, sponger, freeloader, lounge lizard, social parasite, parasite, spiv <Brit>; beggar, mendicant, panhandler; the unemployed; the unemployable; the chronically unemployed, discouraged workers, lumpen proletariat; leisure class, rentiers, coupon-clippers, idle rich

VERBS **12** **idle,** do nothing, **laze,** lazy, take one's ease, take one's leisure, take one's time, **loaf,** lounge; lie around, lounge around, loll around, lollop about, moon, moon around, sit around, sit on one's ass, sit on one's butt, stand around, hang around, lie about, loiter about, loiter around, slouch, slouch around, bum around, mooch around; shirk, avoid work, goof off, lie down on the job; sleep at one's post; let the grass grow under one's feet; twiddle one's thumbs, fold one's arms; back-burner

13 **waste time,** consume time, kill time, idle away time, fritter away time, loiter away time, loiter out the time, beguile the time, while away the time, pass the time, lose time, waste the precious hours, burn daylight; trifle, dabble, fribble, footle, putter, potter, piddle, diddle, doodle

14 **dally, dillydally,** piddle, diddle, diddle-daddle, doodle, dawdle, loiter, lollygag, linger, lag, poke, take one's time, hang around, hang about, kick around

15 **take it easy,** take things as they come, drift, drift with the current, go with the flow, swim with the stream, coast, lead an easy life, live a life of ease, eat the bread of idleness, rest on one's oars; rest on one's laurels, lie back on one's record

16 **lie idle,** lie fallow; aestivate, hibernate, lie dormant; lay off, charge one's batteries, recharge one's batteries; lie up, lie on the shelf; ride at anchor, lay by, lie by, lay to, lie to; have nothing to do, have nothing on

ADJS 17 **inactive,** unactive; stationary, static, at a standstill; sedentary; quiescent, motionless; inanimate

18 **idle,** fallow, otiose; **unemployed,** unoccupied, disengaged, jobless, out of work, out of employ, out of a job, out of harness; free, available, at liberty, at leisure; at loose ends; unemployable, lumpen; leisure, leisured; off-duty, off-work, off; housebound, shut-in; back-burnered

19 **indolent, lazy,** bone-lazy, slothful, workshy, ergophobic; do-nothing, *fainéant* <Fr>, laggard, slow, dilatory, procrastinative, remiss, slack, slacking, lax; easy; shiftless, do-less; unenterprising, nonaggressive; good-for-nothing, ne'er-do-well; drony, dronish, spivvish, parasitic, cadging, sponging, scrounging

20 **languid,** languorous, listless, lifeless, inanimate, enervated, debilitated, pepless, lackadaisical, slow, wan, lethargic, logy, hebetudinous, supine, lymphatic, apathetic, sluggish, dopey, drugged, nodding, droopy, dull, heavy, leaden, lumpish, torpid, stultified, stuporous, inert, stagnant, stagnating, vegetative, vegetable, dormant; phlegmatic, numb, benumbed; moribund, dead, exanimate, dead to the world; sleepy, somnolent; pooped, weary; jaded, sated; blasé, world-weary, bored; out cold, comatose

332 ASSENT

<agreeing to do>

NOUNS 1 **assent, acquiescence**, concurrence, concurring, concurrency, compliance, agreement, acceptance, accession, agreeance; eager assent, hearty assent, warm assent, welcome; assentation; agreement in principle, general agreement; support; consent; oral agreement, written agreement; white list

2 **affirmative; yes,** yea, aye, amen, OK, yeah, booyah; nod, nod of assent; thumbs-up; affirmativeness, affirmative attitude, yea-saying; me-tooism; toadying, automatic agreement, knee-jerk assent, subservience, ass-licking*; yessir

3 **acknowledgment,** recognition, acceptance; appreciation; admission, confession, concession, allowance; avowal, profession, declaration; oath-taking, shout-out

4 **ratification, endorsement**, acceptance, approval, approbation, subscription, subscribership, signing-off, imprimatur, sanction, permission, the OK, the okay, the green light, the go-ahead, the nod, certification, confirmation, validation, authentication, authorization, warrant; affirmation, affirmance; stamp, rubber stamp, seal of approval, stamp of approval; seal, signet, sigil; signature, John Hancock; countersignature; electronic signature, e-signature; visa, *visé*; notarization; blood oath

5 **unanimity,** unanimousness, universal assent, univocal assent, unambiguous assent; like-mindedness, meeting of minds, one mind, same mind; total agreement; understanding, mutual understanding; concurrence, consent, general consent, common assent, common consent, consentaneity, accord, accordance, concord, concordance, agreement, general agreement; consensus, consensus of opinion; universal agreement, universal accord, agreement of all, shared sense, sense of the meeting; acclamation, general acclamation; unison, harmony, chorus, concert, one voice, single voice, one accord; general voice, vox pop, *vox populi* <L>

6 **assenter,** consenter, accepter, covenanter, covenantor; assentator, yea-sayer; yes-man, toady, creature, ass-licker*, ass-kisser*, brownnose, bootlicker, fellow traveler, supporter

7 **endorser,** subscriber, ratifier, approver, upholder, certifier, confirmer; signer, signatory, the undersigned; seconder; cosigner, cosignatory, party; underwriter, guarantor, insurer; notary, notary public

VERBS 8 **assent,** give assent, yield assent, **acquiesce,** consent, comply, accede, agree, agree to, agree with, have no problem with; find it in one's heart; take kindly to, hold with; accept, receive, buy, take one up on; subscribe to, acquiesce in, abide by; yes, say yes to; nod, nod assent, vote for, cast one's vote for, give one's voice for; welcome, hail, cheer, acclaim, applaud, accept in toto

9 **concur,** accord, coincide, agree, agree with, agree in opinion; enter into one's view, enter into the ideas of, enter into the feelings of, see eye to eye, be at one with, be of one mind with, go with, go along with, fall in with, chime in with, close with, meet, conform to, side with, join oneself with, identify oneself with; cast in one's lot, fall in line, fall into line, lend oneself to, play along, go along, take kindly to; echo, ditto, say "ditto" to, say "amen" to; join in the chorus, go along with the crowd, run with the pack, go with the current, swim with the stream; get on the bandwagon; rubber-stamp

10 **come to an agreement, agree,** concur on, settle on, agree with, agree on, agree upon, arrive at an agreement, come to an understanding, come to terms, reach an understanding, reach an agreement, reach an accord, strike a bargain, hammer out a bargain, covenant, get together;

shake hands on, shake on it, seal the deal; come around to

11 **acknowledge,** admit, own, confess, allow, avow, grant, warrant, concede, yield, defer; accept, recognize; agree in principle, express general agreement, go along with, not oppose, not deny, agree provisionally, agree for the sake of argument; bring oneself to agree, assent grudgingly, assent under protest; let the ayes have it; acknowledge the corn

12 **ratify, endorse,** sign off on, second, support, certify, confirm, validate, authenticate, accept, give the nod, give the OK, give the green light, give the go-ahead, give a nod of assent, give one's imprimatur, permit, give permission, approve; sanction, authorize, warrant, accredit; pass, pass on, pass upon, give thumbs up; amen, say amen to; visa; underwrite, subscribe to; sign, undersign, sign on the dotted line, put one's John Hancock on, initial, put one's mark on, put one's X on; autograph; cosign, countersign; seal, sign and seal, set one's seal, set one's hand and seal; affirm, swear and affirm, take one's oath, swear to; rubber stamp; notarize

ADJS 13 **assenting, agreeing,** acquiescing, acquiescent, compliant, consenting, consentient, consensual, submissive, unmurmuring, conceding, concessive, assentatious, agreed, content

14 **accepted, approved,** received; acknowledged, admitted, allowed, granted, conceded, recognized, professed, confessed, avowed, warranted; self-confessed; ratified, endorsed, certified, confirmed, validated, authenticated; certificatory, confirmatory, validating, warranting; signed, sealed, signed and sealed, countersigned, underwritten; stamped; sworn to, notarized, affirmed, sworn and affirmed; board certified

15 **unanimous,** solid, consentaneous, with one consent, with one voice; uncontradicted, unchallenged, uncontroverted, uncontested, unopposed; concurrent, concordant, of one accord; agreeing, in agreement, like-minded, of one mind, of the same mind; of a piece, at one, at one with, agreed on all hands, carried by acclamation

ADVS 16 **affirmatively,** assentingly, in the affirmative

17 **unanimously,** concurrently, consentaneously, by common consent, by general consent, with one consent, with one accord, with one voice, without contradiction, *nemine contradicente* <L>, nem con, without a dissenting voice, *nemine dissentiente* <L>, in chorus, in concert, in unison, in one voice, univocally, unambiguously, to a man, together, all together, all agreeing, as one, as one man, one and all, on all hands; by acclamation

INTERJS 18 **yes,** yea, aye, *oui* <Fr>, *sí* <Sp>, *da* <Russ>, *ja* <Ger>; yes sir, yes ma'am; why yes, *mais oui* <Fr>; indeed, yes indeed; surely, certainly, assuredly, most assuredly, right, right you are, exactly, precisely, just so, absolutely, positively, really, truly, rather <Brit>, quite, to be sure; all right, good, well and good, good enough, very well, *très bien* <Fr>; naturally, *naturellement* <Fr>; of course, as you say, by all means, by all manner of means; amen; hear hear <Brit>

19 <nonformal> **yeah,** yep, yup, uh-huh; yes sirree, same here, likewise, indeedy, yes indeedy, sure, sure thing, sure enough, surest thing you know; right on, righto; OK, okay, okey-dokey; Roger, Roger-dodger; fine; you bet, bet your ass, you can bet on it, you can say that again, you said it, you better believe it; capeesh?

PHRS 20 **so be it,** be it so, so mote it be, so shall it be, *amen* <Heb>; so it is, so is it; agreed, done, that's about the size of it; *c'est bien* <Fr>; that takes care of that, that's that, that's right; that makes two of us

333 DISSENT

<publicly disagreeing>

NOUNS 1 **dissent,** dissidence, dissentience; nonassent, nonconsent, nonconcurrence, nonagreement, agreement to disagree; minority opinion, minority report, minority position; disagreement, difference, variance, diversity, disparity; dissatisfaction, disapproval, disapprobation, red light, thumbs down; repudiation, rejection; refusal, opposition; dissension, disaccord; alienation, withdrawal, dropping out, secession; recusance, recusancy, nonconformity; apostasy; counterculture, underground, alternative; raspberry, Bronx cheer

2 **objection, protest**; kick, beef, bitch*, squawk, howl, protestation; remonstrance, remonstration, expostulation; challenge; demur, demurrer; reservation, scruple, compunction, qualm, twinge of conscience, qualm of conscience; complaint, grievance; exception; peaceful protest, nonviolent protest; demonstration, demo, protest demonstration, counterdemonstration, rally, march, sit-in, teach-in, boycott, strike, picketing, indignation meeting; pole-sitting; grievance committee; rebellion

3 **dissenter, dissident,** dissentient, recusant; objector, demurrer; minority voice, opposition voice; protester, protestant, detractor; separatist, schismatic; sectary, sectarian, opinionist;

nonconformist, odd man out; apostate; conscientious objector, passive resister; dissatisfied customer, bellyacher

VERBS 4 **dissent,** dissent from, be in dissent, say nay, disagree, discord with, differ, not agree, disagree with, agree to disagree, agree to differ; divide on, be at variance; take exception, withhold assent, take issue, beg to differ, raise an objection, rise to a point of order; be in opposition to, oppose, be at odds with; refuse to conform, kick against the pricks, march to a different drummer, hear a different drummer, swim against the tide, against the current, swim upstream; split off, withdraw, drop out, secede, separate oneself, disjoin oneself, schismatize

5 **object, protest**, kick, beef, put up a struggle, put up a fight; bitch*, squawk, howl, holler, put up a squawk, raise a howl; exclaim against, cry out against, make a stink about, raise a stink about; yell bloody murder; remonstrate, expostulate; raise objections, press objections, raise one's voice against, enter a protest; complain, exclaim at, state a grievance, air one's grievances; dispute, challenge, call in question; demur, scruple, boggle, dig in one's heels; demonstrate, demonstrate against, rally, march, sit-in, teach-in, boycott, strike, picket; rebel

ADJS 6 **dissenting,** dissident, dissentient, recusant; disagreeing, differing; opposing, in opposition; alienated; counterculture, antiestablishment, underground, alternative; breakaway; at variance with, at odds with; schismatic, schismatical, sectarian, sectary; heterodox; nonconforming; rebellious; resistant

7 **protesting,** protestant; **objecting,** expostulative, expostulatory, remonstrative, remonstrant; under protest

334 AFFIRMATION

<willing to validate>

NOUNS 1 **affirmation,** affirmance, assertion, assertation, asseveration, averment, declaration, vouch, allegation; avouchment, avowal; position, stand, stance; profession, statement, word, say, saying, say-so, positive declaration, positive statement, affirmative; manifesto, position paper; statement of principles, creed; pronouncement, proclamation, announcement, annunciation, enunciation; proposition, conclusion; predication, predicate; protest, protestation; utterance, dictum, *ipse dixit* <L>; emphasis, stress; admission, confession, disclosure; mission statement; booyah

2 **affirmativeness; assertiveness,** positiveness, absoluteness, speaking out, table-thumping; definiteness

3 **deposition,** sworn statement, affidavit, statement under oath, notarized statement, sworn testimony, affirmation; vouching, swearing; attestation; certification; **testimony;** authentication, validation, verification, vouch; substantiation, proof

4 **oath, vow,** avow, word, assurance, guarantee, warrant, promise, solemn oath, solemn affirmation, solemn word, solemn declaration, word of honor; pledge; Bible oath, ironclad oath; judicial oath, extrajudicial oath, Hippocratic oath; oath of office, official oath; oath of allegiance, loyalty oath, test oath; commitment; pledge of allegiance; blood oath

VERBS 5 **affirm, assert,** assever, asseverate, aver, state positively, protest, lay down, avouch, avow, declare, say, say loud and clear, say out loud, sound off, have one's say, speak, speak one's piece, speak one's mind, speak up, speak out, state, set down, express, put, put it, put in one's two-cents worth; allege, profess; stand on, stand for; predicate; issue a manifesto, manifesto, issue a position paper; announce, pronounce, annunciate, enunciate, proclaim; maintain, have, contend, argue, insist, hold, submit, maintain with one's last breath

6 **depose,** depone; **testify,** take the stand, witness; warrant, attest, certify, guarantee, assure; vouch, vouch for, swear, swear to, swear the truth, assert under oath; make an oath, take one's oath, vow; swear by bell, book, and candle; call heaven to witness, swear to God, swear on the Bible, kiss the book, swear to goodness, hope to die, cross one's heart, cross one's heart and hope to die; swear till one is blue in the face; corroborate, substantiate

7 administer an oath, place under oath, put under oath, put to one's oath, put upon oath; **swear,** swear in, adjure; charge

ADJS 8 **affirmative,** affirming, affirmatory, certifying, certificatory; assertive, assertative, assertional; annunciative, annunciatory; enunciative, enunciatory; declarative, declaratory; predicative, predicational; positive, absolute, emphatic, decided, table-thumping, unambiguously, unmistakably, loud and clear; attested, corroboratory, substantiating

9 **affirmed, asserted,** asseverated, avouched, avowed, averred, declared; alleged, professed; stated, pronounced, announced, annunciated, enunciated; predicated; manifestoed; deposed, warranted, attested, certified, vouched, vouched for, vowed, pledged, sworn, sworn to; strongly worded, emphatic, underscored; allegeable

ADVS 10 **affirmatively,** assertively, assertorily, declaratively, predicatively; **positively,** absolutely, decidedly, loudly, loud and clear, at the top of one's voice, at the top of one's lungs; emphatically, with emphasis, pointedly; without fear of contradiction; under oath, on one's honor, on one's word

335 NEGATION, DENIAL

<refusal to validate>

NOUNS 1 **negation,** negating, abnegation; negativeness, negativity, **negativism,** negative attitude, naysaying; obtusenss, perversity, orneriness, cross-grainedness; negative, no, nay, nix; defiance; refusal; unacceptance; pessimism, defeatism; deal breaker

2 **denial, disavowal,** disaffirmation, disaffirmance, disownment, disallowance; disclamation, disclaimer; renunciation, retraction, retractation, repudiation, recantation; revocation, nullification, annulment, abrogation; abjuration, abjurement, forswearing; contradiction, flat contradiction, absolute contradiction, contravention, contrary assertion, controversion, countering, crossing, gainsaying, impugnment; flat denial, emphatic denial, refutation, disproof; apostasy, defection; about-face, reversal

VERBS 3 **negate,** abnegate, negative; **say no,** no, naysay; shake one's head, wag the beard, waggle the beard, nix; refuse, reject

4 **deny,** not admit, not accept, refuse to admit, refuse to accept; disclaim, disown, disaffirm, disavow, disallow, abjure, forswear, renounce, retract, take back, recant; revoke, nullify, repudiate; contradict, fly in the face of, cross, assert the contrary, contravene, controvert, impugn, dispute, gainsay, oppose, counter, go counter to, go contra, contest, take issue with, join issue upon, run counter to; belie, give the lie to; deprecate; refute, disprove; reverse oneself, reverse gears; defect, apostatize

ADJS 5 **negative,** negatory, abnegative, negational; **denying,** disclaiming, disowning, disaffirming, disallowing, disavowing, renunciative, renunciatory, repudiative, recanting, abjuratory, revocative, revocatory; contradictory, contradicting, contradictive, opposing, contrary, contra, counter, opposite, naysaying, refuting, adversative, repugnant; obtuse, perverse, ornery, crossgrained, contrarious

ADVS 6 **negatively,** in the negative; in denial, in contradiction, in opposition; in no way

CONJS 7 **neither,** not either, **nor,** nor yet, or not, and not, also not

INTERJS 8 **no, nay,** negative, *non* <Fr>, *nein* <Ger>, *nyet* <Russ>; certainly not, absolutely no; no sir, no ma'am, no siree; not, not a bit, not a jot, I think not, not really; to the contrary, *au contraire* <Fr>, quite the contrary, far from it; no such thing, nothing of the kind, nothing of the sort, not so

9 **by no means,** by no manner of means; on no account, in no respect, in no case, under no circumstances, on no condition, no matter what; not at all, not in the least, never; in no wise, in no way, noways, noway, nohow, not even; out of the question, in your dreams; not for the world, not for anything in the world, not if one can help it, not if I know it, not at any price, not for love or money, not for the life of me, over one's dead body; a thousand times no; to the contrary, *au contraire* <Fr>, quite the contrary, far from it; God forbid

10 <nonformal> nope, nix, no dice, unhunh, no sirree; no way, no way José, not on your life, not by a long chalk, not by a long shot, not by a damn sight, not a bit of it, not much, not a chance, fat chance, nothing doing, forget it, that'll be the day, you've got to be kidding, you've got to be joking

336 IMITATION

<being a copy>

NOUNS 1 **imitation, copying,** counterfeiting, repetition; me-tooism, emulation, the sincerest form of flattery, following, mirroring, reflection, echo; copycat crime; simulation, modeling; fakery, forgery, plagiarism, plagiarizing, plagiary; imposture, impersonation, takeoff, hit-off, impression, burlesque, pastiche, *pasticcio* <Ital>; mimesis; parody, onomatopoeia

2 **mimicry, mockery,** apery, parrotry, mimetism; protective coloration, protective mimicry, aggressive mimicry, aposematic mimicry, synaposematic mimicry, cryptic mimicry, playing possum

3 **reproduction, duplication,** imitation, copy, dummy, mock-up, replica, facsimile, representation, paraphrase, approximation, model, version, knockoff, recording, cover version; transcript; computer model, computer simulation; parody, burlesque, pastiche, *pasticcio* <Ital>, travesty

4 **imitator,** simulator, me-tooer, impersonator, impostor, mimic, mimicker, mimer, mime, mocker; ventriloquist; mockingbird, cuckoo; parrot, polly, poll-parrot, polly-parrot, ape, aper, monkey; echo, echoer, echoist; copier, copyist, copycat; faker, imposter, counterfeiter, forger,

plagiarist; dissimulator, dissembler, deceiver, gay deceiver, hypocrite, phony, poseur; conformist, sheep, slave to fashion

VERBS 5 **imitate, copy,** repeat, ditto; do like, do, act like, go like, make like; mirror, reflect; echo, reecho, chorus; borrow, steal one's stuff, take a leaf out of one's book; assume, affect; simulate; counterfeit, fake, hoke, hoke up, forge, plagiarize, crib, lift; parody, pastiche, travesty; paraphrase, approximate

6 **mimic,** impersonate, mime, ape, parrot, copycat; do an impression; take off, hit off, hit off on, take off on, send up

7 **emulate,** follow, follow in the steps of, follow in the footsteps of, walk in the shoes of, put oneself in another's shoes, follow in the wake of, follow the example of, follow suit, follow like sheep, jump on the bandwagon, play follow the leader; copy after, model after, model on, pattern after, pattern on, shape after, take after, take a leaf out of one's book, take as a model

ADJS 8 **imitation,** mock, sham, copied, fake, phony, counterfeit, faux, dummy, forged, plagiarized, unoriginal, ungenuine; **pseudo,** synthetic, synthetical, artificial, manmade, ersatz, hokey, hoked-up, quasi

9 **imitative,** simulative, me-too, derivative; mimic, mimetic, apish, parrotlike; emulative; echoic, onomatopoetic, onomatopoeic

10 imitable, copiable, duplicable, replicable

ADVS 11 imitatively, apishly, apewise, parrotwise; onomatopoetically; synthetically; quasi

PREPS 12 **like, in imitation of,** after, in the semblance of, on the model of, *à la* <Fr>

COMBINING FORMS 13 quasi-, mim-, ne-, near-, semi-; -ish, -like; pseudo-

337 NONIMITATION

<being genuine>

NOUNS 1 **nonimitation, originality,** novelty, newness, innovation, freshness, uniqueness; authenticity; inventiveness, creativity, creativeness; idiosyncrasy; authentification; keeping it real

2 **original,** model, archetype, prototype, prototyping; master, pattern, mold, pilot model; innovation, new departure; original thought; precedent, invention

3 **autograph,** holograph, first edition; genuine article

VERBS 4 **originate,** invent; innovate; create; revolutionize; pioneer; authentificate

ADJS 5 **original,** novel, unprecedented; unique, *sui generis* <L>; new, fresh; underived, firsthand; authentic, imaginative, creative; avant-garde, revolutionary; pioneer, bellwether, trailblazing, first in the field; *nouvelle* <Fr>

6 **unimitated,** uncopied, unduplicated, unreproduced, unprecedented, unexampled; archetypal, archetypical, archetypic, seminal, prototypal; prime, primary, primal, primitive, pristine

338 COMPENSATION

<balancing of good for bad>

NOUNS 1 **compensation, recompense,** repayment, payback, recoup, indemnity, indemnification, measure for measure, rectification, restitution, reparation; amends, expiation, atonement, meed; damage control; redress, satisfaction, remedy; commutation, substitution; offsetting, balancing, counterbalancing, counteraction; payback time; retaliation, revenge

2 **offset,** setoff; **counterbalance,** counterpoise, equipoise, counterweight, makeweight; balance, ballast; trade-off, equivalent, consideration, something of value, *quid pro quo* <L>, something for something, tit for tat, give-and-take; retroaction

3 **counterclaim,** counterdemand

VERBS 4 **compensate,** make compensation, make good, set right, restitute, pay back, rectify, make up for; make amends, expiate, do penance, atone; recompense, repay, indemnify, cover; trade off, give and take; correct, retaliate; trade up, trade down

5 **offset**, set off, counteract, countervail, counterbalance, counterweigh, counterpoise, balance, play off against, set against, set over against, equiponderate; recoup, square, square up, settle the score

ADJS 6 **compensating, compensatory;** recompensive, amendatory, indemnificatory, reparative, rectifying, retributive; offsetting, counteracting, counteractive, countervailing, balancing, counterbalancing, zero-sum; expiatory, penitential; retaliatory

ADVS 7 **in compensation,** in return, back; in consideration, for a consideration

ADVS, CONJS 8 **notwithstanding,** but, all the same, still, yet, even; however, nevertheless, nonetheless; although, when, though; howbeit, albeit; at all events, in any event, in any case, at any rate; be that as it may, for all that, even so, on the other hand, rather, again, at the same time, just the same, that may be; after all, after all is said and done

ADVS, PREPS 9 **in spite of,** spite of, despite,

in despite of, with, even with; regardless of, regardless, irregardless, irrespective of, without respect to, without regard to; cost what it may, regardless of cost, at any cost, at all costs, whatever the cost

339 CAREFULNESS

<close or watchful attention>

NOUNS 1 **carefulness, care,** heed, concern, regard; attention; heedfulness, regardfulness, mindfulness, thoughtfulness; consideration, solicitude, caring, loving care, tender loving care (TLC), caregiving, compassion; circumspectness, circumspection; forethought, anticipation, preparedness; caution

2 **painstakingness,** painstaking, pains; diligence, assiduousness, assiduity, sedulousness, industriousness, industry; thoroughness, thoroughgoingness

3 **meticulousness,** exactingness, scrupulousness, scrupulosity, conscientiousness, punctiliousness, attention to detail, fine-tuning; particularness, particularity, circumstantiality; fussiness, criticalness, criticality; finicalness, finickingness, finickiness, finicality, persnicketiness; exactness, exactitude, accuracy, preciseness, precision, precisionism, precisianism, punctuality, correctness, prissiness; strictness, rigor, rigorousness, spit and polish; nicety, niceness, delicacy, detail, subtlety, refinement, minuteness, exquisiteness, elegance; fine-tooth comb

4 **vigilance,** wariness, prudence, watchfulness, watching, observance, surveillance; watch, vigil, lookout; *qui vive* <Fr>; invigilation, proctoring, monitoring; inspection; watch and ward; custody, custodianship, guardianship, stewardship; guard, guardedness, guard duty; sharp eye, weather eye, peeled eye, watchful eye, eagle eye, lidless eye, sleepless eye, unblinking eye, unwinking eye

5 **alertness, attentiveness; attention**; wakefulness, sleeplessness; readiness, promptness, promptitude, punctuality; quickness, agility, nimbleness; smartness, brightness, keenness, sharpness, acuteness, acuity

VERBS 6 **care,** mind, heed, reck, think, consider, regard, pay heed to, take heed of, take thought of; take an interest, be concerned; **pay attention**

7 **be careful,** take care, take good care, take heed, have a care, exercise care; be cautious; take pains, take trouble, be painstaking, go to great pains, go to great lengths, go out of one's way, go the extra mile, bend over backwards, use every trick in the book, not miss a trick; mind what one is doing, mind one's business, mind one's P's and Q's; watch one's step, pick one's steps, tread on eggs, tread warily, walk on eggshells, place one's feet carefully, feel one's way; treat gently, handle with gloves, handle with kid gloves

8 **be vigilant,** be watchful, never nod, never sleep, be on the watch, be on the lookout, be on the *qui vive* <Fr>, keep a sharp lookout, keep in sight, keep in view; keep watch, keep watch and ward, keep vigil; watch, look sharp, look about one, look with one's own eyes, be on one's guard, keep an eye out, sleep with one eye open, have all one's wits about one, keep one's eye on the ball, keep one's eyes open, keep a weather eye open, keep one's eyes peeled, keep the ear to the ground, keep a nose to the wind; keep alert, be on the alert; look out, watch out; look lively, look alive; stop, look, and listen

9 look after, nurture, foster, **tend, take care of**, care for, keep an eye on

ADJS 10 **careful,** heedful, regardful, mindful, thoughtful, considerate, caring, solicitous, loving, tender, curious; circumspect; attentive; cautious

11 **painstaking,** diligent, assiduous, sedulous, thorough, thoroughgoing, operose, industrious, elaborate; fine-toothed, fine-combed, fine-tuned

12 **meticulous,** exacting, scrupulous, conscientious, religious, punctilious, punctual, particular, fussy, critical, attentive, scrutinizing; thorough, thoroughgoing, thoroughpaced; finical, finicking, finicky, high-maintenance; exact, precise, precisionistic, precisianistic, persnickety, prissy, accurate, correct; close, narrow; strict, rigid, rigorous, spit-and-polish, exigent, demanding; nice, delicate, subtle, fine, refined, minute, detailed, exquisite

13 **vigilant,** wary, prudent, watchful, lidless, sleepless, observant, chary; on the watch, on the lookout; on guard, on one's guard, guarded; with open eyes, with one's eyes open, with one's eyes peeled, with a weather eye open; open-eyed, sharp-eyed, keen-eyed, Argus-eyed, eagle-eyed, hawk-eyed; all eyes, all ears, all eyes and ears; custodial

14 **alert,** on the alert, on the *qui vive* <Fr>, on one's toes, on top, on the job, on the ball, attentive; awake, wakeful, wide-awake, sleepless, unsleeping, unblinking, unwinking, unnodding, alive, ready, prompt, quick, agile, nimble, quick on the trigger, quick on the draw, quick on the uptake; smart, bright, keen, sharp

ADVS 15 **carefully,** heedfully, regardfully, mindfully, thoughtfully, considerately, solicitously, tenderly, lovingly; circumspectly; cautiously; with care, with great care; painstakingly, diligently, assiduously, industriously, sedulously, thoroughly, thoroughgoingly, nine ways to Sunday, to a T, to a turn, to a fare-thee-well

16 **meticulously,** exactingly, scrupulously, conscientiously, religiously, punctiliously, punctually, fussily; strictly, rigorously; exactly, accurately, precisely, with exactitude, with precision; nicely, with great nicety, refinedly, minutely, in detail, exquisitely

17 **vigilantly**, warily, prudently, watchfully, observantly; alertly, attentively; sleeplessly, unsleepingly, unwinkingly, unblinkingly, lidlessly, unnoddingly

340 NEGLECT

<inattention or failure to do>

NOUNS 1 **neglect,** neglectfulness, **negligence,** inadvertence, inadvertency, malperformance, dereliction, *culpa* <L>, culpable negligence, criminal negligence; remissness, laxity, laxness, slackness, looseness, laches; unrigorousness, permissiveness; noninterference, *laissez-faire* <Fr>, nonrestriction; disregard, airy disregard, slighting; inattention; oversight, overlooking; omission, nonfeasance, nonperformance, lapse, failure, default; poor stewardship, poor guardianship, poor custody; procrastination

2 **carelessness,** heedlessness, unheedfulness, disregardfulness, regardlessness, ignorance; unperceptiveness, impercipience, blindness, deliberate blindess; uncaring, unsolicitude, unsolicitousness, thoughtlessness, tactlessness, inconsiderateness, inconsideration; unthinkingness, unmindfulness, oblivion, forgetfulness; unpreparedness, unreadiness, lack of foresight, lack of forethought; recklessness; indifference; laziness; perfunctoriness; cursoriness, hastiness, offhandedness, casualness; easiness; nonconcern, insouciance; abandon, careless abandon, *sprezzatura* <Ital>

3 **slipshodness,** slipshoddiness, slovenliness, slovenry, sluttishness, untidiness, sloppiness, messiness; haphazardness; slapdash, slapdashness, a lick and a promise, loose ends; bad job, sad work, botch, slovenly performance; bungling; procrastination, avoidance

4 **unmeticulousness,** unexactingness, unscrupulousness, unrigorousness, unconscientiousness, unpunctiliousness, unpunctuality, unparticularness, unfussiness, unfinicalness, uncriticalness; inexactness, inexactitude, inaccuracy, imprecision, unpreciseness

5 **neglecter,** negligent, ignorer, disregarder; **procrastinator,** waiter on Providence, Micawber; slacker, shirker, malingerer, dodger, goof-off, goldbrick, idler; skimper; trifler; sloven, slob; bungler; slacktivist

VERBS 6 **neglect,** overlook, disregard, not heed, not attend to, take for granted, ignore; not care for, not take care of; pass over, gloss over; let slip, let slide, let the chance slip by, let go, let ride, let take its course; let the grass grow under one's feet; put off till tomorrow; not think, not consider, not give a thought to, take no thought of, take no account of, blind oneself to, turn a blind eye to, leave out of one's calculation; lose sight of, lose track of; be neglectful, be negligent, fail in one's duty, fail, lapse, default, let go by default; not get involved; nod, nod through, sleep through, sleep, be caught napping, be asleep at the switch

7 **leave undone,** leave, let go, leave half-done, pretermit, skip, jump, miss, omit, cut, blow off, let be, let alone, pass over, pass up, abandon; leave a loose thread, leave loose ends, let dangle, give a lick and a promise; slack, shirk, malinger, goof off, goldbrick; trifle; **procrastinate**

8 **slight;** turn one's back on, turn a cold shoulder to, get the cold shoulder, give the cold shoulder, get the go-by, give the go-by, cold-shoulder, leave out in the cold; not lift a finger, leave undone; scamp, skimp; slur, slur over, pass over, skate over, slubber over, skip over, dodge, waffle, fudge, blink, carefully ignore; skim, skim over, skim the surface, touch upon, touch upon lightly, touch in passing, pass over lightly, go once over lightly, hit the high spots, give a lick and a promise; cut corners, cut a corner

9 **do carelessly,** do by halves, do in a half-assed way, do in a slip-shod fashion, do anyhow, do in any old way; botch, bungle; trifle with, play at, play fast and loose with, mess around with, mess about with, muck around, muck about with, piss around with*, piss about with*; do offhand, dash off, knock off, throw off, toss off, toss out; roughhew, roughcast, rough out; knock out, hammer out, pound out, bat out; toss together, slap together, throw together, knock together, cobble up, patch together, patch, patch up, fudge up, fake up, whomp up, lash up, slap up; jury-rig

ADJS 10 **negligent, neglectful,** neglecting, derelict, culpably negligent; inadvertent, uncircumspec, ignorant; inattentive; unwary, unwatchful, asleep at the switch, off-guard, unguarded; **remiss,** slack, lax, relaxed, laid-back, loose, loosey-goosey, unrigorous, permissive, overly permissive; noninterfering, *laissez-faire* <Fr>, nonrestrictive; slighting; slurring, scamping, skimping; procrastinating

11 careless, heedless, unheeding, unheedful, disregardful, disregardant, regardless, unsolicitous, uncaring; tactless, respectless, thoughtless, unthinking, inconsiderate, untactful, undiplomatic, mindless of, unmindful, forgetful, oblivious; unprepared, unready; reckless; indifferent; lackadaisical; lazy, shirking; perfunctory, cursory, casual, cazh; offhand; easygoing, *dégagé* <Fr>, airy, flippant, insouciant, free and easy, free as a bird

12 slipshod, slipshoddy, slovenly, sloppy, messy, half-assed, lax, slapdash, shoddy, untidy; clumsy, bungling; haphazard, promiscuous, hit-or-miss, hit-and-miss; deficient, botched

13 unmeticulous, unexacting, unpainstaking, unscrupulous, unrigorous, unconscientious, unpunctilious, unpunctual, unparticular, unfussy, unfinical, uncritical; inexact, inaccurate, unprecise

14 neglected, unattended to, untended, unwatched, unchaperoned, uncared-for; disregarded, unconsidered, unregarded, overlooked, missed, omitted, passed by, passed over, passed up, gathering dust, ignored, slighted, blanked; unasked, unsolicited; half-done, undone, left undone; deserted, abandoned; in the cold, out in the cold; on the shelf, shelved, pigeonholed, on hold, on the back burner, put aside, laid aside, sidetracked, sidelined, shunted

15 unheeded, unobserved, unnoticed, unnoted, unperceived, unseen, undiscerned, undescried, unmarked, unremarked, unregarded, unminded, unconsidered, unthought-of, unmissed

16 unexamined, unstudied, unconsidered, unsearched, unscanned, unweighed, unsifted, unexplored, uninvestigated, unindagated, unconned

ADVS **17 negligently,** neglectfully, inadvertently; remissly, laxly, slackly, loosely; unrigorously, permissively; nonrestrictively; slightingly, lightly, slurringly; scampingly, skimpingly

18 carelessly, heedlessly, unheedingly, unheedfully, disregardfully, regardlessly, thoughtlessly, unthinkingly, unsolicitously, tactlessly, inconsiderately, unmindfully, forgetfully; inattentively, unwarily, unvigilantly, unguardedly, unwatchfully; recklessly; perfunctorily; once over lightly, cursorily; casually, offhand, offhandedly, airily; clumsily, bunglingly; sloppily, messily, sluttishly, shoddily, shabbily; haphazardly, promiscuously, hit or miss, hit and miss, helter-skelter, slapdash, anyhow, any old way, any which way

19 unmeticulously, unscrupulously, unconscientiously, unfussily, uncritically; inexactly, inaccurately, unprecisely, imprecisely, unrigorously, unpunctually

341 INTERPRETATION

<*understanding meaning*>

NOUNS **1 interpretation,** construction, reading, way of seeing, way of understanding, way of putting; constructionism, strict constructionism, loose constructionism; diagnosis; definition, description; **meaning**

2 rendering, rendition; text, edited text, diplomatic text, normalized text; version; reading, lection, variant, variant reading; edition, critical edition, scholarly edition; variorum edition, variorum; conflation, composite reading, composite text

3 translation, transcription, transliteration; Englishing; paraphrase, loose translation, free translation; decipherment, decoding, code cracking, unscrambling; amplification, restatement, rewording, simplification; metaphrase, literal translation, faithful translation, word-for-word translation; pony, trot, crib; interlinear, interlinear translation, bilingual text, bilingual edition; gloss, glossary; key; lipreading

4 explanation, explication, unfolding, elucidation, illumination, enlightenment, light, clarification, *éclaircissement* <Fr>, simplification; take; exposition, expounding, exegesis; illustration, demonstration, exemplification; reason, rationale; euhemerism, demythologization, allegorization; decipherment, decoding, cracking, unlocking, solution; editing, emendation; critical revision, rescension, diaskeuasis; mansplaining

5 <explanatory remark> **comment,** word of explanation, explanatory remark; annotation, notation, note, note of explanation, footnote, gloss, definition, scholium; exegesis; commentary, commentation; legend, appendix

6 interpretability, interpretableness, construability; definability, describability; translatability; explicability, explainableness, accountableness

7 interpreter, exegete, exegetist, exegesist, hermeneut; constructionist, strict constructionist, loose constructionist; commentator, annotator, scholiast; critic, textual critic, editor, diaskeuast, emender, emendator; cryptographer, cryptologist, decoder, decipherer, cryptanalyst, lipreader; **explainer,** lexicographer, definer, explicator, exponent, expositor, expounder, clarifier; demonstrator, euhemerist, demythologizer, allegorist; go-between; translator, metaphrast, paraphrast; oneirocritic; guide, *cicerone* <Ital>, dragoman

8 <science of interpretation> exegetics, hermeneutics; tropology; criticism, literary criticism, textual criticism; paleography, epigraphy; cryptology, cryptography, cryptanalysis; lexicography; diagnostics, symptomatology, semiology, semiotics; pathognomy; physiognomics, physiognomy; metoposcopy; oneirology, oneirocriticism

VERBS 9 **interpret,** diagnose; construe, put a construction on, take; understand, understand by, take to mean, take it that; read; read into, read between the lines; see in a special light, read in view of, take an approach to

10 **explain,** explicate, expound, make of, exposit; give the meaning, tell the meaning of, define, describe; spell out, unfold; account for, give reason for; clarify, elucidate, clear up, clear the air, cover, cover the waterfront, cover the territory, make clear, make plain; simplify, popularize; illuminate, enlighten, give insight, shed light upon, throw light upon; rationalize, euhemerize, demythologize, allegorize; tell how, show how, show the way, run by; demonstrate, show, illustrate, exemplify, represent; get to the bottom of, get to the heart of, make sense of, make head or tails of; decipher, crack, unlock, find the key to, unravel, demystify, read between the lines, read into, solve; explain oneself; explain away; overinterpret; mansplain

11 **comment upon,** commentate, remark upon; annotate, gloss; edit, make an edition

12 **translate,** render, transcribe, transliterate, put into, turn into, transfuse the sense of; construe; disambiguate

13 **paraphrase, rephrase,** reword, restate, rehash; give a loose translation

ADJS 14 **interpretative,** interpretive, interpretational, exegetic, exegetical, hermeneutic, hermeneutical; constructive, constructional; diagnostic; symptomatological, semeiological; tropological; definitional, descriptive

15 **explanatory,** explaining, exegetic, exegetical, explicative, explicatory, defining; expository, expositive; clarifying, elucidative, elucidatory; illuminating, illuminative, enlightening; demonstrative, illustrative, exemplificative; glossarial, annotative, critical, editorial, scholiastic; rationalizing, rationalistic, euhemeristic, demythologizing, allegorizing

16 **translational,** translative; paraphrastic, metaphrastic; literal, word-for-word, verbatim

17 **interpretable,** construable; definable, describable; translatable, renderable; Englishable; explainable, explicable, accountable, on book; diagnosable

ADVS 18 **by interpretation,** as here interpreted, as here defined, according to this reading; in explanation, to explain; that is, that is to say, as it were, *id est* <L>, i.e.; to wit, namely, *videlicet* <L>, viz, *scilicet* <L>, sc; in other words, in words to that effect

342 MISINTERPRETATION

<misunderstanding meaning>

NOUNS 1 **misinterpretation,** misunderstanding, misintelligence, misapprehension, misreading, misconstruction, mistaking, malobservation, misconception; misrendering, mistranslation, translator's error, eisegesis; misexplanation, misexplication, misexposition; misapplication; gloss; perversion, distortion, wrenching, twisting, contorting, torturing, squeezing, garbling; reversal; abuse of terms, misuse of words, catachresis; misquotation, miscitation; misjudgment; error; misrepresentation; sniglet

VERBS 2 **misinterpret, misunderstand,** misconceive, mistake, misapprehend; misread, misconstrue, put a false construction on, miss the point, take wrong, get wrong, get one wrong, take amiss, take the wrong way; get backwards, reverse, have the wrong way round, put the cart before the horse; misapply; misexplain, misexplicate, misexpound; misrender, mistranslate; quote out of context; misquote, miscite, give a false coloring, give a false impression, give a false idea, gloss; garble, pervert, distort, wrench, contort, torture, squeeze, twist the words, twist the meaning, stretch the meaning, strain the sense, misdeem, misjudge; bark up the wrong tree; misrepresent

ADJS 3 **misinterpreted, misunderstood,** mistaken, misapprehended, misread, eisegetical, misconceived, misconstrued; garbled, misquoted, misrepresented, perverted, distorted, catachrestic, catechrestical; backwards, reversed, ass-backwards

4 **misinterpretable, misunderstandable,** mistakable

343 COMMUNICATION

<giving information>

NOUNS 1 **communication,** communion, congress, commerce, intercourse; means of communication, speaking, speech, utterance, speech act, talking, linguistic intercourse, speech situation, speech circuit, converse, conversate, conversation; signalling; contact, touch, connection; interpersonal communication, intercommunication, intercommunion, grokking, interplay, interaction; exchange, interchange; answer, response, reply; one-way communication, two-way communication; dealings, dealing, traffic, truck; information; message; extrasensory perception (ESP), telepathy; writing; correspondence; social intercourse; media studies

2 **informing, telling,** imparting, impartation, impartment, conveyance, transmission, transmittal, transfer, transference, sharing, giving, sending, signaling, letting one in on; notification, alerting, announcement, publication, disclosure

3 **communicativeness,** talkativeness, sociability; unreserve, unreservedness, unreticence, unrestraint, unconstraint, unrestriction; unrepression, unsuppression; unsecretiveness, untaciturnity; candor, frankness; openness, plainness, freeness, outspokenness, plainspokenness; accessibility, approachability, conversableness; extroversion, outgoingness; baby talk

4 **communicability**, impartability, conveyability, transmittability, transmissibility, transferability; contagiousness

5 **communications,** electronic communications, communications industry, media, communications medium, communications media, mass communications, communications network; telecommunication, long-distance communication; radio communication, wire communication, broadcasting, satellite broadcasting, access provider, broadband, podcasting; communication theory, information theory; signaling; digital radio

VERBS 6 **communicate,** be in touch, be in contact, be in connection, hold communication; intercommunicate, interchange, commune with; grok; commerce with, deal with, traffic with, have dealings with, have truck with; speak, talk, be in a speech situation, converse, pass the time of day

7 communicate, **impart, tell,** lay on one, convey, transmit, transfer, send, send word, deliver a message, send a signal, send a message, disseminate, broadcast, pass, pass on, pass along, hand on; report, render, make known, get across, get over, let in on; give word, leave word; signal; share, share with; leak, let slip out, give

8 communicate with, get in touch, get in contact with, **contact**, make contact with, raise, reach, reach out, reach out to, get to, get through to, get hold of, make connection, establish connection, get in connection with; make advances, make overtures, approach, make up to; relate to; keep in touch, keep in contact with, maintain connection; answer, respond to, reply to, get back to; question, interrogate; correspond, drop a line; reconnect

ADJS 9 **communicational, communicating,** communional; transmissional; speech, verbal, linguistic, oral; on-message; conversational; intercommunicational, intercommunicative, intercommunional, interactional, interactive, interacting, interresponsive, responsive, answering; questioning, interrogative, interrogatory; telepathic

10 **communicative,** talkative, gossipy, newsy; sociable; unreserved, unreticent, unshrinking, unrestrained, unconstrained, unhampered, unrestricted; demonstrative, expansive, effusive; unrepressed, unsuppressed; unsecretive, unsilent, untaciturn; candid, frank; self-revealing, self-revelatory, soul-baring; open, free, outspoken, free-speaking, free-spoken, free-tongued; accessible, approachable, conversable, easy to speak to; extroverted, outgoing; well-said

11 **communicable,** impartable, conveyable, transmittable, transmissible, transferable; contagious; shareable

12 communicatively; verbally, talkatively, by word of mouth, orally, viva voce

344 UNCOMMUNICATIVENESS

<not giving information>

NOUNS 1 **uncommunicativenes,** closeness, indisposition to speak, disinclination to communicate; unconversableness, unsociability; nondisclosure, secretiveness; lack of message, lack of meaning, meaninglessness; miscommunication; digital detox

2 **taciturnity, untalkativeness,** unloquaciousness; silence; speechlessness, wordlessness, dumbness, muteness; quietness, quietude; laconicalness, laconism, curtness, shortness, terseness; brusqueness, briefness, brevity, conciseness, economy of words, sparingness of words, pauciloquy

3 **reticence**, reticency; **reserve,** reservedness, restraint, low key, constraint; guardedness, discreetness, discretion; suppression, repression; subduedness; backwardness, retirement, low profile; aloofness, standoffishness, distance, remoteness, detachment, withdrawal, withdrawnness, reclusiveness, solitariness; impersonality; coolness, coldness, frigidity, iciness, frostiness, chilliness; inaccessibility, unapproachability; undemonstrativeness, unexpansiveness, unaffability, uncongeniality; **introversion;** modesty, bashfulness, pudency; expressionlessness, blankness, impassiveness, impassivity; straight face, poker face, mask

4 prevarication, equivocation, tergiversation,

evasion, shuffle, fencing, dodging, parrying, waffling, tap dancing; weasel words

5 **man of few words,** clam, strong silent type, laconic; Spartan, Laconian; evader, weasel

VERBS 6 **keep to oneself,** keep one's own counsel; not open one's mouth, not say a word, not breathe a word, stand mute, hold one's tongue, clam up; bite one's tongue; have little to say, refuse comment, say neither yes nor no, waste no words, save one's breath; retire; keep one's distance, keep at a distance, keep oneself to oneself, stand aloof, hold oneself aloof; keep secret

7 **prevaricate,** equivocate, waffle, tergiversate, evade, dodge, sidestep, pussyfoot, say in a roundabout way, parry, duck, weasel, weasel out, palter; hum and haw, hem and haw, back and fill; mince words, mince the truth, euphemize

ADJS 8 **uncommunicative,** indisposed, disinclined to communicate; unconversational, unconversable; unsociable; secretive; meaningless

9 **taciturn, untalkative,** unloquacious, indisposed to talk; silent, speechless, wordless, mum; mute, dumb, quiet; close, closemouthed, close-tongued, snug, tight-lipped; close-lipped, tongue-tied, word-bound; laconic, curt, brief, terse, brusque, short, concise, sparing of words, economical of words, of few words

10 **reticent, reserved,** restrained, nonassertive, low-key, low-keyed, constrained; suppressed, repressed; subdued; guarded, discreet; backward, retiring, shrinking; aloof, standoffish, offish, standoff, distant, remote, removed, detached, Olympian, withdrawn; impersonal; cool, cold, frigid, icy, frosty, chilled, chilly; inaccessible, unapproachable, forbidding; undemonstrative, unexpansive, unaffable, uncongenial, ungenial; introverted; modest, verecund, verecundious, bashful; expressionless, blank, impassive

11 **prevaricating,** equivocal, tergiversating, tergiversant, waffling, evasive, weaselly, weasel-worded

345 SECRECY

<hiding something>

NOUNS 1 **secrecy,** secretness, airtight secrecy, close secrecy; crypticness; the dark; hiddenness, hiding, concealment; secretiveness, closeness; discreetness, discretion, uncommunicativeness; evasiveness, evasion, subterfuge; hugger-mugger, hugger-muggery; Area 51; back channel; down low, the down low

2 **privacy,** retirement, isolation, sequestration, seclusion; incognito, anonymity; **confidentialness,** confidentiality; closed meeting, closed session, executive session, private conference, secret meeting

3 **veil of secrecy,** veil, curtain, pall, wraps; iron curtain, bamboo curtain; wall of secrecy, barrier of secrecy, wall of silence; suppression, repression, stifling, smothering; censorship, blackout, hush-up, cover-up; seal of secrecy, official secrecy, classification, official classification; security, ironbound security; pledge of secrecy, oath of secrecy

4 **stealth,** stealthiness, furtiveness, clandestineness, clandestinity, clandestine behavior, surreptitiousness, covertness, slyness, shiftiness, sneakiness, slinkiness, underhandedness, underhand dealing, undercover activity, underground activity, covert activity, covert operation; prowl, prowling; stalking; hugger-mugger; counterintelligence; conspiracy, cabal, intrigue; funny business; secret service, intelligence agency

5 **secret,** confidence; private matter, personal matter, privity; trade secret; confidential information, privileged information, confidential communication, privileged communication; doctor-patient confidentiality, lawyer-client confidentiality; seal of the confessional, secret of the confessional; more than meets the eye; deep dark secret; solemn secret; guarded secret, hush-hush matter, classified information, eyes-only information, top-secret information, restricted information; confession; inside information, inside skinny; mystery, enigma; the arcane, arcanum, *arcanum arcanorum* <L>; esoterica, cabala, the occult, occultism, hermetism, hermeticism, hermetics; deep secret, profound secret, sealed book, mystery of mysteries; skeleton in the closet, skeleton in the cupboard, family secret; sealed orders, state secret

6 **cryptography,** cryptoanalysis, cryptoanalytics; **code, cipher;** secret language; code book, code word, code name; secret writing, coded message, cryptogram, cryptograph; secret ink, invisible ink, sympathetic ink; cryptographer

VERBS 7 **keep secret**, keep mum, veil, keep dark; keep it a deep, dark secret; secrete, conceal; keep to oneself, keep *in petto* <Ital>, bosom, keep close, keep snug, keep back, keep from, withhold, hold out on; not let it go further, keep within these walls, keep within the bosom of the lodge, keep between us; not tell, hold one's tongue, never let on, make no sign, not breathe a word, not whisper a word, clam up, be the soul of discretion; not give away, keep it under one's hat, keep under wraps, keep a lid on, keep buttoned up, keep one's own counsel; play one's cards close to the chest, play one's cards close to the vest; play dumb; not let the right hand know what the left is doing; keep in ignorance, keep in the dark, leave in the dark; classify; file and forget; have secret information, have confidential information, be in on the secret, know where the bodies are buried; anonymize

8 **cover up,** muffle up; hush up, hush, hush-hush, shush, hugger-mugger; suppress, repress, stifle, muffle, smother, squash, quash, squelch, kill, sit on, sit upon, put the lid on; censor, black out

9 **tell confidentially,** tell for one's ears only, mention privately, whisper, breathe, whisper in the ear; tell one a secret; take aside, see one alone, talk to in private, speak in privacy; say under one's breath

10 code, encode, encipher, cipher

ADJS **11** **secret,** close, closed, closet; cryptic, dark; unuttered, unrevealed, undivulged, undisclosed, unspoken, untold; hush-hush, top secret, supersecret, eyes-only, classified, restricted, under wraps, under security, under security restrictions; censored, suppressed, stifled, smothered, hushed-up, under the seal of secrecy, under the ban of secrecy; unrevealable, undivulgable, undisclosable, untellable, unwhisperable, unbreatheable, unutterable; latent, ulterior, concealed, hidden; arcane, esoteric, occult, cabalistic, hermetic; enigmatic, mysterious

12 **covert, clandestine,** quiet, unobtrusive, hugger-mugger, surreptitious, undercover, underground, under-the-counter, under-the-table, cloak-and-dagger, backdoor, hole-and-corner, underhand, underhanded; furtive, stealthy, privy, backstairs, sly, shifty, sneaky, sneaking, skulking, slinking, slinky, feline

13 **private,** privy, closed-door; intimate, inmost, innermost, interior, inward, personal; privileged, protected; secluded, sequestered, isolated, withdrawn, retired; incognito, anonymous

14 **confidential,** auricular, inside, esoteric; *in petto* <Ital>, close to one's chest, close to one's vest, under one's hat; off the record, not for the record, not to be minuted, within these four walls, in the bosom of the lodge, for no other ears, eyes-only, between us; not to be quoted, not for publication, not for release; not for attribution; unquotable, unpublishable, sealed; sensitive, privileged, under privilege

15 **secretive,** close-lipped, secret, close, dark; discreet; evasive, shifty; uncommunicative, close-mouthed

16 coded, encoded; ciphered, enciphered; cryptographic, cryptographical; hieroglyphic

ADVS **17** **secretly, in secret,** up one's sleeve, on the down-low; in the closet; with nobody the wiser; covertly, stownlins, in hidlings <Scot>, undercover, *à couvert* <Fr>, under the cloak of; behind the scenes, in the background, in a corner, in the dark, in darkness, behind the veil, behind the curtain, behind the veil of secrecy; *sub rosa* <L>, under the rose; underground; *sotto voce* <Ital>, under the breath, with bated breath, in a whisper; off the record

18 **surreptitiously, clandestinely,** secretively, furtively, stealthily, slyly, shiftily, sneakily, sneakingly, skulkingly, slinkingly, slinkily; by stealth, on the sly, on the quiet, on the qt, behind one's back, by a side door, like a thief in the night, underhand, underhandedly, under the table, under cloak of night, in holes and corners, in a hole-and-corner way

19 **privately,** privily, in private, in privacy, in privy; apart, aside; behind closed doors, *in camera* <L>, in chambers, in secret meeting, in closed meeting, in executive session, in private conference

20 **confidentially,** in confidence, in strict confidence, under the seal of secrecy, off the record; between ourselves, strictly between us, *entre nous* <Fr>, *inter nos* <L>, for your ears only, for your eyes only, between you and me, from me to you, between you and me and the bedpost

346 CONCEALMENT

<preventing disclosure>

NOUNS **1** **concealment, hiding,** secretion; burial, burying, interment, putting away; cover, covering, covering up, masking, screening; mystification, obscuration; darkening, obscurement, clouding; hiddenness, concealedness, covertness, occultation; eclipse; disappearance; secrecy; uncommunicativeness; invisibility; subterfuge, deception

2 **veil,** curtain, cover, screen, mask, camouflage; fig leaf; wraps; disguise

3 **ambush,** ambushment, ambuscade; surveillance, shadowing; lurking hole, lurking place; blind, stalking-horse; booby trap, trap

4 **hiding place,** hideaway, hideout, hidey-hole, hiding, concealment, cover, secret place; safe house; drop, accommodation address <Brit>; recess, corner, dark corner, nook, cranny, niche; hole, bolt-hole, foxhole, trench, dugout, lair, den; bomb shelter, storm shelter; asylum, sanctuary, retreat, refuge; covert, coverture, undercovert; cache, stash; safe-deposit box, bank vault, safe, lockbox; cubbyhole, cubby, pigeonhole; secret compartment; mother's skirts

5 **secret passage,** covert way, secret exit; back way, back door, side door; bolt-hole, escape route, escape hatch, escapeway; secret staircase, backstairs; underground, underground route, underground railroad

VERBS 6 **conceal, hide,** ensconce; cover, cover up, blind, screen, cloak, veil, screen off, curtain, blanket, shroud, enshroud, envelop; disguise, camouflage, mask, dissemble; plain-wrap, wrap in plain brown paper; whitewash; paper over, gloss over, varnish, slur over; distract attention from; obscure, obfuscate, cloud, becloud, befog, throw out a smoke screen, shade, throw into the shade; eclipse, occult; put out of sight, sweep under the rug, sweep under the carpet, keep undercover, keep under wraps; cover up one's tracks, lay a false scent, hide one's trail; hide one's light under a bushel

7 **secrete, hide away,** keep hidden, put away, store away, stow away, file and forget, bottle up, lock up, seal up, put out of sight; keep secret; cache, stash, deposit, plant; bury; bosom, embosom

8 <**hide oneself**> hide, conceal oneself, take cover, hide out, hide away, go into hiding, go to ground; stay in hiding, lie hid, lie hidden, lie low, lay low, lie perdue, lie snug, lie close, lie doggo, sit tight, burrow, hole up, go underground; play peekaboo, play hide and seek; keep out of sight, retire from sight, drop from sight, disappear, crawl into one's shell, retreat into one's shell, keep in the background, stay in the background, keep a low profile, stay in the shade; disguise oneself, masquerade, take an assumed name, assume a cover, change one's identity, go under an alias, remain anonymous, be incognito, sail under false colors, wear a mask; leave no address; reinvent oneself; stay in, keep to

9 **lurk,** couch; **lie in wait,** lay wait; sneak, skulk, slink, prowl, nightwalk, steal, creep, pussyfoot, gumshoe, tiptoe; stalk, shadow

10 **ambush,** ambuscade, waylay; lie in ambush, lay wait for, lie in wait for, lay for; stalk; set a trap for, still-hunt

ADJS 11 **concealed, hidden,** hid, occult, recondite, blind; covered; covert, undercover, under wraps; code-named; obscured, obfuscated, clouded, clouded over, wrapped in clouds, in a cloud, in a fog, in a mist, in a haze, beclouded, befogged; eclipsed, in eclipse, under an eclipse; in the wings; buried; underground; close, secluded, secluse, sequestered; in purdah, under house arrest, incommunicado; obscure, abstruse, mysterious; secret; unknown, latent

12 **unrevealed,** undisclosed, undivulged, unexposed; unapparent, invisible, unseen, unperceived, unspied, undetected; undiscovered, unexplored, untraced, untracked; unaccounted for, unexplained, unsolved

13 **disguised,** camouflaged, in disguise; masked, masquerading; incognito, incog, anonymous, unrecognizable; in plain wrapping, in plain brown paper; cryptic, coded, codified

14 **in hiding,** holed up, hidden out, undercover, in a dark corner, lying hid, doggo; in ambush, in ambuscade; waiting concealed, lying in wait; in the wings; lurking, skulking, prowling, sneaking, stealing; pussyfooted, pussyfoot, on tiptoe; stealthy, furtive, surreptitious

15 **concealing, hiding,** obscuring, obfuscatory; covering; unrevealing, nonrevealing, undisclosing

347 COMMUNICATIONS

<information via technology>

NOUNS 1 **communications,** signaling, telecommunication, comms, transmission; electronic communication, electrical communication; satellite communication; wire communication, wireless communication; communications engineering, communications technology; communications engineer; media, communications medium, communications media; communication theory, information theory; communication explosion, information explosion

2 **telegraph,** telegraph recorder, ticker; telegraphy, telegraphics, data transmission; teleprinter, telex, teletypewriter; teleprinter exchange; wire service; code; electricity; key, interrupter, transmitter, sender; receiver, sounder

3 **radio**, radiotelephony, radiotelegraphy, wireless <Brit>, wireless telephony, wireless telegraphy; line radio, wired radio, wired wireless <Brit>, wire wave communication; radiophotography; digital audio broadcasting (DAB); television; electronics

4 **telephone, phone**, horn, dog, telephone set, handset; telephony, telephonics, telephone mechanics, telephone engineering; high-frequency telephony; receiver, telephone receiver, earpiece; mouthpiece, transmitter; telephone extension, extension; wall telephone, desk telephone; dial telephone, rotary telephone, touch-tone telephone, push-button telephone, cordless phone; beeper; scrambler; telephone booth, telephone box, call box <Brit>, telephone kiosk, public telephone, coin telephone, pay station, pay phone; landline; car phone, digital phone, flip phone, mobile telephone, mobile phone, cellular phone, cellular telephone, cell phone, cell telephone; iPhone<tm>, smartphone;

SIM, SIM card; speakerphone, videophone; speed calling, call forwarding, call waiting, redial, caller ID service; phone card; facsimile transmission, fax; 3G, 4G, 5G, 800 number, 900 number; chat line; short message service, short message system; text messaging, messaging, texting; text-walking; sexting; caller ID; Do Not Call list

5 **radiophone**, radiotelephone, wireless telephone, wireless; headset, headphone

6 **intercom**, Interphone, intercommunication system

7 **telephone exchange,** telephone office, central office, central; automatic exchange, machine-switching office; step-by-step switching, panel switching, crossbar switching, electronic switching

8 **switchboard;** private branch exchange (PBX), business exchange, private exchange; in board, A board; out board, B board

9 **telephone operator, operator,** switchboard operator, telephonist, central; long distance; PBX operator

10 telephone mechanic; telephonic engineer; lineman, linewoman

11 **telephoner,** phoner, caller, party, calling party, subscriber

12 telephone number, **phone number**, unlisted number, fax number, cell phone number, cell; telephone book, phone book, telephone directory; telephone exchange, exchange; telephone area, area code; calling zone

13 telephone call, **phone call**, call, ring, buzz; local call, toll call, long-distance call; long distance, direct distance nondialing, direct distance dial, direct distance dialing (DDD); speed-dialing; trunk call; station-to-station call, person-to-person call; collect call; toll-free call; mobile call; dial tone, busy signal; crank call, nuisance call; conference call, video teleconference, teleconference; hot line; chat line, messagerie; voicemail, phonemail; electronic mail, email; telemarketing; direct marketing; multilevel marketing, multilevel sales; cold call; ringy-dingy, jingle, tinkle; flame mail; anytime minute

14 telegram, telegraph, wire, telex; cablegram, **cable**; radiogram, radiotelegram; day letter, night letter; fast telegram

15 telephoto, wirephoto, telecopier, facsimile, **fax**; telephotograph, radiophotograph

16 telegrapher, telegraphist, telegraph operator; sparks, brass pounder, dit-da artist; radiotelegrapher; wireman, wire chief

17 **line,** wire line, telegraph line, telephone line; private line, direct line; party line; hot line; trunk, trunk line; wide area telecommunications service (WATS), WATS line; cable, telegraph cable; transmission line, concentric cable, coaxial cable, co-ax, fiber cable, fiber-optic cable

18 computer networking, Internet, World Wide Web (WWW), electronic mail, **email**; modem; digital compression; broadband, access provider

VERBS 19 **telephone, phone**, call, call on the phone, put in a call, make a call, call up, ring, ring up, give a ring, give a buzz, give a call, give a jingle, give a buz; listen in; hold the phone, hold the wire; hang up, ring off; cold call; robocall

20 telegraph, telegram, flash, **wire**, send a wire, telex; **cable;** Teletype; radio; sign on, sign off

ADJS 21 **communicational,** telecommunicational, communications, communication, signal; telephonic, magnetotelephonic, microtelephonic, monotelephonic, thermotelephonic; telegraphic; Teletype; Wirephoto, facsimile, fax; phototelegraphic, telephotographic; radio, wireless <Brit>; radiotelegraphic; networkable

348 MANIFESTATION

<appearing or expressing>

NOUNS 1 **manifestation, appearance;** expression, evincement; indication, evidence, proof, proof positive; embodiment, incarnation, bodying forth, materialization; epiphany, theophany, pneumatophany, avatar; revelation, disclosure, showing forth; dissemination, publication; First Amendment

2 **display,** demonstration, show, showing, show-and-tell; presentation, showing forth, presentment, ostentation, exhibition, exhibit, exposition, expo, retrospective; production, performance, representation, enactment, projection; opening, unfolding, unfoldment; showcase, showcasing, unveiling, exposure, varnishing day

3 **manifestness,** apparentness, obviousness, plainness, clearness, crystal-clearness, perspicuity, distinctness, microscopical distinctness, patency, patentness, palpability, tangibility; evidentness, evidence, self-evidence; openness, openness to sight, overtness; visibility; unmistakableness, unquestionability

4 **conspicuousness, prominence,** salience, saliency, bold relief, high relief, strong relief, boldness, noticeability, pronouncedness, strikingness, demonstrativeness, outstandingness; highlighting, spotlighting, featuring; obtrusiveness; flagrance, flagrancy, arrantness, blatancy, notoriousness, notoriety; ostentation; dramatics, theatrics; cause celebre

VERBS 5 **manifest, show,** exhibit, demonstrate, display, breathe, unfold, develop; present, represent, evince, evidence; indicate, give sign, give token, token, betoken, mean; express, show forth, set forth; show off, showcase; make plain, make clear; produce, bring out, roll out, trot out, bring forth, bring forward, bring to the front, put forward, bring to notice, expose to view, bring to view, bring into view; reveal, divulge, disclose; illuminate, highlight, spotlight, feature, bring to the fore, place in the foreground, bring out in bold relief, bring out in strong relief, bring out in high relief; flaunt, dangle, wave, flourish, brandish, parade; affect, make a show of, make a great show of; perform, enact, dramatize; embody, incarnate, body forth, materialize

6 <**manifest oneself**> come out, come into the open, come out of the closet, come forth, surface; show one's colors, show one's true colors, wear one's heart upon one's sleeve; speak up, speak out, raise one's voice, assert oneself, let one's voice be heard, speak one's piece, speak one's mind, stand up and be counted, take a stand; open up, show one's mind, have no secrets; appear, materialize

7 **be manifest,** be there for all to see, make an appearance, be no secret, be no revelation, surface, lie on the surface, be seen with half an eye; need no explanation, speak for itself, tell its own story, tell its own tale; go without saying; leap to the eye, stare one in the face, hit one in the eye, strike the eye, glare, shout; come across, project; stand out, stick out, stick out a mile, stick out like a sore thumb, hang out

ADJS 8 **manifest, apparent,** evident, self-evident, axiomatic, indisputable, obvious, plain, clear, perspicuous, distinct, palpable, patent, tangible; visible, perceptible, perceivable, discernible, seeable, observable, noticeable, much in evidence; to be seen, easy to be seen, plain to be seen; plain as day, plain as the nose on one's face, plain as a pikestaff, big as life, big as life and twice as ugly; crystal clear, clear as crystal; express, explicit, unmistakable, not to be mistaken, open-and-shut; self-explanatory, self-explaining; **indubitable**

9 **manifesting,** manifestative, showing, displaying, showcasing, demonstrating, demonstrative, presentational, expository, expositional, exhibitive, exhibitional, expressive; evincive, evidential; indicative, indicatory; appearing, incarnating, incarnational, materializing; epiphanic, theophanic, angelophanic, Satanophanic, Christophanic, pneumatophanic; revelational, revelatory, disclosive; promulgatory; histrionic

10 open, overt, open to all, open as day, out of the closet; unclassified; **revealed, disclosed, exposed;** made public; bare, bald, naked

11 **unhidden, out,** unconcealed, unscreened, uncurtained, unshaded, veilless; unobscure, unobscured, undarkened, unclouded; undisguised, uncamouflaged

12 **conspicuous,** noticeable, notable, ostensible, prominent, bold, pronounced, salient, in relief, in bold relief, in high relief, in strong relief, striking, outstanding, in the foreground, sticking out, hanging out; highlighted, spotlighted, featured; obtrusive; flagrant, arrant, blatant, notorious; glaring, staring, stark-staring

13 **manifested,** demonstrated, exhibited, shown, displayed, showcased; manifestable, demonstrable, exhibitable, displayable

ADVS 14 **manifestly, apparently,** evidently, obviously, patently, plainly, clearly, distinctly, unmistakably, expressly, explicitly, palpably, tangibly; visibly, perceptibly, perceivably, discernibly, observably, noticeably

15 **openly,** overtly, before one, before one's eyes, before one's very eyes, under one's nose; to one's face, face-to-face; publicly, in public; in the open, out in the open, in open court, in plain sight, in broad daylight, in the face of day, in the light of day, for all to see, in public view, in plain view, in the marketplace; aboveboard, on the table

16 **conspicuously,** prominently, noticeably, ostensibly, notably, markedly, pronouncedly, saliently, strikingly, boldly, outstandingly; obtrusively; arrantly, flagrantly, blatantly, notoriously; glaringly, staringly

349 REPRESENTATION, DESCRIPTION

<giving true information>

NOUNS 1 **representation,** delineation, presentment, drawing, **portrayal**, portraiture, depiction, depictment, rendering, rendition, characterization, charactering, picturization, figuration, limning, imaging; prefigurement; illustration, exemplification, demonstration; projection, realization, manifestation; imagery, iconography; art; drama; conventional representation, plan, diagram, schema, schematization, blueprint, chart, map; clip art; conceptual model; sketch; mind map; visual; notation, mathematical notation, musical notation, score, tablature; dance notation, Laban dance notation system, labanotation, choreography; symbolization; writing, script, written word, text; writing system; alphabet, syllabary, Roman alphabet; alphabetic symbol, syllabic symbol, letter, ideogram, pictogram, logogram, logograph, hieroglyphic, hieroglyph, rune; printing; symbol

2 **description, portrayal,** portraiture, depiction, rendering, rendition, delineation, limning, representation; imagery; stream of consciousness; word painting, word picture, picture, portrait, image, photograph; evocation, impression; sketch, vignette, cameo; characterization, character, character sketch, profile; vivid description, exact description, realistic description, naturalistic description, slice of life, graphic account; specification, particularization, particulars, details, itemization, catalog, cataloging; narration; version; air quotes

3 **account,** recounting, statement, report, word, statement of fact; play-by-play description, blow-by-blow account, blow-by-blow description; case study, case history

4 **impersonation,** personation; mimicry, mimicking, mime, miming, pantomime, pantomiming, aping, dumb show; air guitar; mimesis, imitation; personification, embodiment, incarnation, realization; characterization, portrayal; acting, playing, dramatization, enacting, enactment, performing, performance; posing, masquerade

5 **image, likeness;** resemblance, semblance, similitude, simulacrum; effigy, icon, idol; copy, fair copy; picture; portrait; photograph; perfect likeness, exact likeness, duplicate, double, clone; replica, facsimile; match, fellow, mate, companion, twin; living image, very image, very picture, living picture, dead ringer, spitting image, spit and image, eidetic image; miniature, model; reflection, shadow, mirroring; trace, tracing; rubbing

6 **figure,** figurine; doll, dolly; teddy bear; puppet, marionette, *fantoche* <Fr>, *fantoccino, fantoccio* <Ital>, hand puppet, glove puppet; mannequin, manikin, model, dummy, working model, lay figure; wax figure, waxwork; scarecrow, corn dolly <Brit>, woman of straw, man of straw, snowman, snowwoman, gingerbread woman, gingerbread man; robot, automaton; sculpture, bust, statue, statuette, statuary, monument; portrait bust, portrait statue; death mask, life mask; carving, wood carving; figurehead

7 **representative,** representation, type, specimen, typification, embodiment, type specimen; cross-section; exponent; **example**, exemplar; exemplification, typicality, typicalness, representativeness; epitome, quintessence, figuration; mother of all

VERBS **8** **represent, delineate, depict,** render, characterize, hit off, character, portray, picture, picturize, limn, draw, paint; register, convey an impression of; catch a likeness, capture; notate, write, print, map, chart, diagram, schematize; trace, trace out, trace over; rub, take a rubbing; record, photograph, film, shoot, scan; symbolize

9 **describe, portray,** picture, render, depict, represent, delineate, limn, paint, draw; evoke, bring to life, make one see, define; outline, sketch; characterize, character; express, set forth, give words to; write

10 **go for**, go as, pass for, pass as, count for, count as, answer for, answer as, stand in the place of, be taken as, be regarded as, be the equivalent of; serve as, be accepted for

11 image, **mirror,** hold the mirror up to nature, reflect, figure; embody, body forth, incarnate, personify, personate, impersonate; illustrate, demonstrate, exemplify; project, realize; shadow, shadow forth; prefigure, pretypify, foreshadow, adumbrate

12 **impersonate,** personate; **mimic,** mime, pantomime, take off, do an impression of, give an impression of, mock; ape, copy; pose as, masquerade as, affect the manner of, affect the guise of, pass for, pretend to be, represent oneself to be; act, enact, perform, do; play, act as, act a part, play a part, act the part of, act out, role-play, portray

ADJS **13** **representational,** representative, depictive, delineatory, resemblant; illustrative, illustrational; pictorial, graphic, vivid; ideographic, pictographic, figurative; representing, portraying, limning, illustrating; typifying, symbolizing, symbolic, personifying, incarnating, embodying; imitative, mimetic, simulative, apish, mimish; echoic, onomatopoeic

14 **descriptive, depictive,** expositive, representative, representational, delineative; expressive, vivid, graphic, well-drawn, detailed, high-definition; realistic, naturalistic, true to life, lifelike, real-life, faithful; evocative

15 **typical,** typic, typal; exemplary, sample; **characteristic,** distinctive, distinguishing, quintessential; realistic, naturalistic; natural, normal, usual, regular, par for the course; true to type, true to form, the nature of the beast

ADVS **16** **descriptively,** representatively; expressively, vividly, graphically; faithfully, realistically, naturalistically

350 MISREPRESENTATION

<giving false information>

NOUNS **1** **misrepresentation, perversion,** distortion, deformation, garbling, twisting, slanting; inaccuracy; coloring, miscoloring, false coloring; false pretenses; falsification, **spin,** spin control, disinformation; misteaching; injustice, unjust representation; misdrawing, mispainting; misstatement, misreport, misquotation, misinformation; misdirection, misguidance; nonrepresentationalism, nonrealism, abstractionism, expressionism, calculated distortion; overstatement, exaggeration, hyperbole, overdrawing; understatement, litotes, conservative estimate; adulteration, forgery, counterfeiting; cover-up, whitewash

2 **bad likeness**, poor likeness, daub, botch; scribble, scratch, hen tracks, hen scratches; distortion, distorted image, false image, anamorphosis, astigmatism; travesty, parody, caricature, burlesque, gross exaggeration

VERBS 3 **misrepresent,** belie, give a wrong idea, pass off as, pawn off as, foist off as, fob off as, send the wrong message, deliver the wrong signal; put in a false light, pervert, distort, garble, twist, warp, deform, wrench, slant, put a spin on, twist the meaning of; color, miscolor, give a false coloring, put a false construction upon, put a false appearance upon, falsify; misteach; disguise, camouflage; misstate, misreport, misquote, put words into one's mouth, quote out of context; overstate, exaggerate, overdraw, blow up, blow out of all proportion, overemphasize; understate; travesty, parody, caricature, burlesque; misinform, disinform

4 **misdraw, mispaint;** overdraw, daub, botch, butcher, scribble, scratch

351 DISCLOSURE

<making something known>

NOUNS 1 **disclosure,** disclosing; **revelation,** revealment, revealing, making public, publicizing, broadcasting, announcement, breaking news; apocalypse; discovery, discovering; manifestation; unfolding, unfoldment, uncovering, unwrapping, uncloaking, taking the wraps off, taking from under wraps, removing the veil, unveiling, unmasking; exposure, exposition, exposé; baring, stripping, stripping bare, laying bare; outing; showing up

2 **divulgence, divulging,** divulgement, divulgation, evulgation, letting out, full report; betrayal, unwitting disclosure, indiscretion; leak, communication leak; giveaway, dead giveaway; telltale, telltale sign, obvious clue; blabbing, blabbering, babbling; tattling; state's evidence

3 **confession,** confessing, shrift, acknowledgment, admission, concession, avowal, self-admission, self-concession, self-avowal, owning, owning up, coming clean, unbosoming, unburdening oneself, getting a load off one's mind, fessing up, making a clean breast, baring one's breast; rite of confession

VERBS 4 **disclose, reveal,** let out, show, impart, discover, develop, leak, let slip out, let the cat out of the bag, spill the beans; manifest; unfold, unroll; open, open up, lay open, break the seal, bring into the open, get out in the open, bring out of the closet; expose, show up; bare, strip bare, lay bare, blow the lid off, blow wide open, rip open, crack wide open; bring to light, hold up to view; hold up the mirror to; unmask, dismask, tear off the mask, uncover, unveil, take the lid off, ventilate, take out from under wraps, take the wraps off, lift the veil, draw the veil, raise the curtain, let daylight in, shine some light on, unscreen, uncloak, undrape, unshroud, unfurl, unsheathe, unwrap, unpack, unkennel; put one wise, clue one in, bring one up to speed, put one in the picture, open one's eyes

5 **divulge,** divulgate, evulgate; **reveal,** make known, tell, breathe, utter, vent, ventilate, air, give vent to, give out, let out, let get around, out with, come out with; break it to, break the news; let in on, confide, confide to, let one's hair down, unbosom oneself, let into the secret; publish

6 **betray,** inform, inform on, talk, peach; rat, stool, sing, squeal, turn state's evidence; leak, spill, spill the beans; let the cat out of the bag, speak before one thinks, be unguarded, be indiscreet, kiss and tell, give away, give the show away, give the game away, betray a confidence, tell secrets, reveal a secret; have a big mouth, have a big bazoo, blab, blabber; babble, tattle, tell on, tattle on, tell tales, tell tales out of school; talk out of turn, let slip, let fall, let drop; blurt, blurt out

7 **confess,** break down and confess, **admit,** acknowledge, tell all, avow, concede, grant, own, own up, let on, implicate oneself, incriminate oneself, come clean; spill, spill it, spill one's guts; tell the truth, admit everything, let it all hang out, throw off all disguise; plead guilty, own oneself in the wrong, cop a plea; unbosom oneself, make a clean breast, get it off one's chest, get it out of one's system, unburden one's mind, unburden one's conscience, disburden one's heart, get a load off one's mind, fess up; out with it, spit it out, open up; throw oneself on the mercy of the court; reveal oneself, show one's colors, show one's true colors, come out of the closet, show one's hand, show one's cards, put one's cards on the table, lay one's cards on the table; acknowledge the corn

8 **be revealed,** become known, surface, come to light, appear, manifest itself, come to one's ears, transpire, leak out, get out, come out, out, come home to roost, come out in the wash, break forth,

show its face; show its colors, be seen in its true colors, stand revealed; blow one's cover

ADJS 9 **revealed,** disclosed

10 **disclosive, revealing,** revelatory, revelational, clueful; **disclosing,** showing, exposing, betraying; kiss-and-tell; eye-opening; talkative; admitted, confessed, self-confessed

11 confessional, admissive

352 PUBLICATION

<publicizing information>

NOUNS 1 **publication, publishing,** promulgation, evulgation, propagation, dissemination, diffusion, broadcast, broadcasting, spread, spreading, spreading abroad, divulgence, disclosure, circulation, ventilation, airing, noising, bandying, bruiting, bruiting about, spreading the word; self-publishing; display; issue, issuance; telecasting, videocasting, podcasting, blogging; printing; book, periodical; think piece

2 **announcement,** annunciation, enunciation; proclamation, pronouncement, pronunciamento; edict, decree; report, communiqué, declaration, statement; public declaration, public statement, program, programma, notice, notification, public notice; speech; circular, encyclical, encyclical letter; manifesto, position paper; broadside; rationale; white paper, white book; ukase; bulletin board, notice board

3 **press release,** release, handout, bulletin, official bulletin, notice, public service announcement

4 **publicity,** publicness, notoriety, fame, famousness, renown, notoriousness, infamy, notice, public notice, public recognition, celebrity, *réclame, éclat* <Fr>; limelight, spotlight, daylight, bright light, glare, public eye, public consciousness, exposure, currency, common knowledge, public knowledge, widest dissemination, maximum dissemination, public forum; ballyhoo, hoopla; report, public report; cry, hue and cry; public relations (PR), flackery; publicity story, press notice; propaganda; writeup, puff, plug, blurb, hype; photo opportunity, photo op, publicity stunt; name in bright lights; nanofamous

5 **promotion,** buildup, promo, flack, publicization, publicizing, promoting, advocating, advocacy, self-advocacy, bruiting, drumbeating, tub-thumping, press-agentry; **advertising,** salesmanship, Madison Avenue, hucksterism; advertising campaign; advertising agency; advertising medium, advertising media; advocacy group; product placement

6 **advertisement, ad,** advert, notice; **commercial,** message, important message, message from the sponsor, words from the sponsor; spot commercial, spot, network commercial; infomercial; reader, reading notice; display ad; want ad, classified ad; personal ad; spread, two-page spread, testimonial; advertorial; trailer; teaser; website ad, banner ad; Yellow Pages; bumper sticker; ad creep

7 **poster,** bill, placard, **sign,** show card, banner, *affiche* <Fr>; signboard, billboard, highway sign; sandwich board; marquee; bulletin board

8 **advertising matter,** promotional material, public relations handout, public relations release, literature; leaflet, leaf, folder, handbill, bill, flier, throwaway, handout, circular, pamphlet, brochure, broadside, broadsheet; insert, insertion, blow-in

9 **publicist,** publicizer, public relations person, public relations officer, PR person, image-maker, flack, pitchman, pitchperson, public relations specialist, publicity agent, press agent, agent, imagemaker; advertiser; adman, huckster; ad writer, copywriter, blurb writer; promoter, booster, plugger; ballyhooer, ballyhoo man; barker, spieler, skywriter; billposter; sign painter; sandwich person; spin doctor

VERBS 10 **publish,** promulgate, propagate, circulate, circularize, diffuse, disseminate, distribute, broadcast, televise, telecast, videocast, air, spread, spread around, spread far and wide, publish abroad, pass the word around, bruit, bruit about, advertise, repeat, retail, put about, bandy about, noise about, sound abroad, bruit abroad, set news afloat, spread a report; rumor, launch a rumor, voice, whisper, buzz, rumor about, whisper about, buzz about

11 **make public,** go public with; bring before the public, lay before the public, drag before the public, display, take one's case to the public, give out, put out, give to the world, make known; divulge; ventilate, air, give air to, bring into the open, get out in the open, open up, broach, give vent to

12 **announce,** annunciate, enunciate; declare, state, declare roundly, affirm, pronounce, give notice; say, make a statement, send a message, send a signal; report, make an announcement, make a report, issue a statement, publish a manifesto, issue a manifesto, present a position paper, issue a white paper, hold a press conference

13 **proclaim,** cry, cry out, promulgate, give voice to; herald, herald abroad; blazon, blaze, blaze abroad, blare, blare forth, thunder, declaim, shout, trumpet, trumpet forth, thunder forth, announce with flourish of trumpets, announce

with the beat of a drum; shout from the housetops, proclaim at the crossroads

14 **issue, bring out**, put out, get out, launch, get off, emit, put forth, give forth, send forth, offer to the public, pass out

15 **publicize,** give publicity; go public with; bring into the limelight, drag into the limelight, throw the spotlight on; advertise, promote, build up, cry up, sell, puff, boost, plug, ballyhoo; put on the map, make a household word of, establish; bark, spiel; make a pitch for, beat the drum for, thump the tub for; write up, give a write-up, press-agent; circularize; bulletin; bill; post bills, post, post up, placard; skywrite

16 <**be published**> come out, appear, break, hit the streets, issue, go forth, come forth, find vent, see the light, see the light of day, become public; circulate, spread, spread about, have currency, get around, get abroad, get afloat, get exposure, buzz about, go the rounds, pass from mouth to mouth, be on everyone's lips, go through the length and breadth of the land; spread like wildfire; blog

ADJS 17 **published,** public, made public, circulated, in circulation, promulgated, propagated, disseminated, issued, spread, diffused, distributed; in print; broadcast, telecast, televised; announced, proclaimed, declared, stated, affirmed; reported, brought to notice; common knowledge, common property, current; open, accessible, open to the public; hot off the press

18 publicational, promulgatory, propagatory; proclamatory, annunciatory, enunciative; declarative, declaratory; heraldic; promotional; on-message

ADVS 19 **publicly, in public; openly**; in the public eye, in the glare of publicity, in the limelight, in the spotlight, reportedly

353 MESSENGER

<delivering message>

NOUNS 1 **messenger,** message-bearer, dispatch-bearer, commissionaire <Brit>, nuncio, courier, diplomatic courier, carrier, runner, express, dispatch-rider, pony-express rider, post, postboy, postrider; bicycle messenger, motorcycle messenger; go-between; emissary; Mercury, Hermes, Iris, Pheidippides, Paul Revere; post office, courier service, package service, message service, message center; answering service

2 **herald, harbinger,** forerunner, vaunt-courier; evangel, evangelist, bearer of glad tidings; herald angel, Gabriel, buccinator

3 **announcer,** annunciator, enunciator; nunciate; proclaimer; crier, town crier, bellman

4 errand boy, office boy, messenger boy, copyboy; bellhop, bellboy, bellman, callboy, caller

5 **delivery person,** postman, mailman, mail carrier, letter carrier, rural route carrier; postmaster, postmistress; postal clerk

6 <other mail carriers> carrier pigeon, carrier, homing pigeon, homer; pigeon post; post-horse, poster; post coach, mail coach; post boat, packet boat, packet ship, mail boat, mail packet, mailer; mail train, mail car, post car, post-office car, railway mail car; mail truck; mailplane; electronic mail

354 FALSENESS

<untruthful action>

NOUNS 1 **falseness, falsehood,** falsity, inveracity, untruth, truthlessness, untrueness; fallaciousness, fallacy, erroneousness; false negative, false positive

2 spuriousness, **phoniness**, bogusness, ungenuineness, unauthenticity, unrealness, artificiality, factitiousness, syntheticness

3 **sham,** fakery, faking, falsity, feigning, pretending; fakeout, feint, pretext, pretense, hollow pretense, pretension, false pretense, false pretension; humbug, humbuggery; bluff, bluffing, four-flushing; speciousness, meretriciousness; cheating, fraud; imposture; deception, delusion; acting, playacting; representation, simulation, simulacrum; dissembling, dissemblance, dissimulation; seeming, semblance, appearance, face, ostentation, show, false show, outward show, false air; window dressing, front, false front, façade, gloss, varnish; gilt; color, coloring, false color; masquerade, facade, disguise; posture, pose, posing, attitudinizing; mannerism, affectation

4 **falseheartedness, falseness,** doubleheartedness, doubleness of heart, doubleness, duplicity, two-facedness, double-facedness, double-dealing, ambidexterity; double life; double standard; dishonesty, improbity, lack of integrity, Machiavellianism, bad faith; low cunning, cunning, artifice, wile; deceitfulness; faithlessness, treachery

5 **insincerity,** uncandidness, uncandor, unfrankness, disingenuousness, indirectness; emptiness, hollowness; mockery, hollow mockery; crossed fingers, tongue in cheek, unseriousness; halfheartedness; sophistry, jesuitry, jesuitism, casuistry

6 **hypocrisy,** hypocriticalness; Tartuffery, Tartuffism, Pecksniffery, pharisaism, sanctimony, sanctimoniousness, religiosity, false piety,

ostentatious devotion, pietism, Bible-thumping; mealymouthedness, unctuousness, oiliness, smarminess, smarm; cant, mummery, snuffling, mouthing; lip service; tokenism; token gesture, empty gesture; smooth tongue, smooth talk, sweet talk, soft soap; crocodile tears

7 **quackery,** chicanery, quackishness, quackism, mountebankery, charlatanry, charlatanism; imposture; humbug, humbuggery

8 **untruthfulness, dishonesty,** falsehood, unveracity, unveraciousness, truthlessness, mendaciousness, mendacity; credibility gap; lying, fibbing, fibbery, pseudology; pathological lying, habitual lying, mythomania

9 **deliberate falsehood, disinformation,** falsification, disinforming, falsifying; confabulation; perversion, distortion, straining, bending; misrepresentation, misconstruction, misstatement, coloring, false coloring, miscoloring, slanting, imparting a spin; tampering, cooking, fiddling; stretching, fictionalization, exaggeration; prevarication, equivocation; perjury, false swearing, oath breaking, false oath, false plea

10 **fabrication,** invention, concoction, disinformation; canard, base canard; forgery; fiction, figment, myth, legend, fable, story, romanticized version, extravaganza; old wives' tale, unfact

11 **lie, falsehood,** falsity, untruth, false statement, untruism, mendacity, prevarication, fib, taradiddle, tarradiddle, flimflam, flam, a crock, a crock of shit*; fiction, pious fiction, legal fiction; story, trumped-up story, farrago; yarn, tale, fairy tale, ghost story; far-fetched story, tall tale, tall story, cock-and-bull story, Cinderella story, fish story, flight of fancy; exaggeration; half-truth, stretching of the truth, slight stretching, white lie, little white lie; partial truth; propaganda, rumor, gossip, rumor mill, empty talk; a pack of lies

12 monstrous lie, consummate lie, deep-dyed falsehood, out-and-out lie, **whopper**, gross falsehood, flagrant falsehood, shameless falsehood, downright lie, barefaced lie, dirty lie, big lie; slander, libel; the big lie; bullshit*, load of crap

13 **fake,** fakement, put-up job, **phony**, rip-off, sham, mock, imitation, simulacrum, dummy; paste, tinsel, *clinquant* <Fr>, pinchbeck, shoddy, junk; counterfeit, forgery; frame-up, put-on; hoax, cheat, fraud, swindle; whited sepulcher, whitewash job; impostor

14 **bunk,** bunkum; humbug, humbuggery; hooey, hoke, hokum, bosh, bull, bullshit*, crap, baloney, flimflam, flam, smoke and mirrors, claptrap, moonshine, eyewash, hogwash, gammon, jiggery-pokery

VERBS 15 ring false, **not ring true**

16 **falsify,** belie, misrepresent, miscolor; misstate, misquote, misreport, miscite; overstate, understate; pervert, distort, strain, warp, slant, twist, stretch the truth, impart spin; garble; put a false appearance upon, give a false coloring, falsely color, give a color to, color, gild, gloss, gloss over, whitewash, varnish, paper over; fudge, dress up, titivate, embellish, embroider, trick out, prink out; deodorize, make smell like roses; disguise, camouflage, mask; propagandize, gossip

17 tamper with, manipulate, **fake,** juggle, sophisticate, doctor, cook, rig, cook the books, cook the accounts, juggle the books, juggle the accounts; pack, stack; adulterate; retouch; load; salt, plant, salt a mine

18 **fabricate, invent,** manufacture, trump up, make up, hatch, concoct, cook up, make out of whole cloth, fictionalize, mythologize, fudge, fake, hoke up; counterfeit, forge; fantasize, fantasize about

19 **lie,** tell a lie, falsify, speak falsely, speak with forked tongue, be untruthful, trifle with the truth, deviate from the truth, fib, story; stretch the truth, strain the truth, bend the truth; draw the longbow; exaggerate; lie flatly, lie in one's throat, lie through one's teeth, lie like a trooper, prevaricate, misstate, equivocate; deceive, fake out, mislead, tell a white lie; bullshit*

20 swear falsely, forswear oneself, perjure, **perjure oneself,** bear false witness

21 **sham, fake**, feign, counterfeit, simulate, put up, gammon; pretend, make a pretense, make believe, make a show of, make like, make as if, make as though; go through the motions; let on, let on like; affect, profess, assume, put on; dissimulate, dissemble, cover up; act, play, playact, put on an act, put on a charade, act a part, play a part; put up a front, put on a front, put on a false front; four-flush, bluff, put up a bluff; play possum, roll over and play dead

22 **pose as,** masquerade as, impersonate, pass for, assume the guise of, assume the identity of, set up for, act the part of, represent oneself to be, claim to be, pretend to be, make false pretenses, go under false pretenses, sail under false colors

23 **be hypocritical,** act the hypocrite, play the hypocrite; cant, be holier than the thou, reek of piety; shed crocodile tears, snuffle, snivel, mouth; give mouth honor, render lip service, give lip service; sweet-talk, soft-soap, blandish

24 play a double game, play a double role, **play both ends against the middle,** work both sides of the street, have it both ways at once, have one's cake

and eat it too, run with the hare and hunt with the hounds; two-time

ADJS **25 false, untrue,** truthless, not true, void of truth, devoid of truth, contrary to fact, in error, fallacious, erroneous; unfounded; disinformative

26 spurious, ungenuine, unauthentic, supposititious, bastard, pseudo, quasi, apocryphal, fake, phony, sham, mock, counterfeit, colorable, bogus, queer, dummy, make-believe, so-called, imitation; not what it's cracked up to be; falsified; dressed up, titivated, embellished, embroidered; garbled; twisted, distorted, warped, perverted, slanted; half-true, falsely colored; simulated, faked, feigned, colored, fictitious, fictive, counterfeited, pretended, affected, assumed, put-on; artificial, synthetic, ersatz; unreal; factitious, unnatural, manmade; illegitimate; *soi-disant* <Fr>, self-styled; pinchbeck, brummagem, tinsel, shoddy, tin, junky; mock-serious

27 specious, meretricious, gilded, tinsel, seeming, apparent, colored, colorable, plausible, ostensible

28 quack, quackish; charlatan, charlatanish, charlatanic

29 fabricated, invented, manufactured, concocted, hatched, trumped-up, made-up, put-up, cooked-up; forged; fictitious, fictional, fictionalized, figmental, mythical, fabulous, legendary; fantastic, fantasied, fancied

30 tampered with, manipulated, cooked, doctored, juggled, rigged, engineered; packed

31 falsehearted, false, false-principled, false-dealing; double, duplicitous, ambidextrous, double-dealing, doublehearted, double-minded, double-tongued, double-faced, two-faced, Janus-faced; Machiavellian, dishonest; crooked, deceitful; creative, artful, cunning, crafty; faithless, perfidious, treacherous

32 insincere, uncandid, unfrank, mealymouthed, unctuous, oily, disingenuous, ungenuine, pseudo, smarmy; dishonest; empty, hollow; tongue in cheek, unserious; sophistic, sophistical, jesuitic, jesuitical, casuistic

33 hypocritic, hypocritical, canting, Pecksniffian, pharisaic, pharisaical, pharisean, sanctimonious, goody-goody, goody two-shoes, holier-than-thou, simon-pure; artificial, dissembling, phony

34 untruthful, dishonest, unveracious, unveridical, truthless, lying, mendacious, untrue; perjured, forsworn; prevaricating, equivocal

ADVS **35 falsely,** untruly, truthlessly; erroneously; untruthfully, unveraciously; mendaciously; spuriously, ungenuinely; artificially, synthetically; unnaturally, factitiously; speciously, seemingly, apparently, plausibly, ostensibly; nominally, in name only

36 insincerely, uncandidly, unfrankly; emptily, hollowly; unseriously; ambiguously; **hypocritically,** mealy-mouthedly, unctuously

355 EXAGGERATION

<enlarged description>

NOUNS **1 exaggeration,** exaggerating; **overstatement,** big talk, tall talk, bullshit*, jive, hyperbole, hyperbolism; superlative; extravagance, profuseness, prodigality, overdoing it, going too far, overshooting; magnification, enlargement, amplification, dilation, dilatation, inflation, expansion, blowing up, puff, puffing up, aggrandizement, embellishment, elaboration, embroidery; stretching, heightening, enhancement; overemphasis, overstressing; overestimation; exaggerated lengths, extreme, extremism, stretch, exorbitance, inordinacy, overkill, excess; burlesque, travesty, caricature; crock, whopper, tall story; sensationalism, puffery, ballyhoo, touting, huckstering; grandiloquence; painting the lily, gilding the lily; to-do, hype, hoopla

2 overreaction, much ado about nothing, fuss, uproar, commotion, tempest in a teapot, making a mountain out of a molehill

VERBS **3 exaggerate,** hyperbolize; **overstate,** overspeak, overreach, overdraw, overcharge; overstress, overemphasize; overdo, carry too far, go to extremes; push to the extreme, indulge in overkill, overestimate; gild the lily; overpraise, oversell, tout, puff, ballyhoo, hype; stretch, stretch the truth, stretch the point, draw the longbow, embellish; magnify, inflate, amplify; aggrandize, build up; pile it on, lay it on thick, pour it on thick, spread it on thick, lay it on with a trowel; talk big, talk in superlatives, deal in the marvelous, make much of; **overreact**, make a federal case out of it, something out of nothing, make a mountain out of a molehill, create a tempest in a teapot, tempest in a teacup, make too much of, cry over spilt milk; caricature, travesty, burlesque, ham, ham it up

ADJS **4 exaggerated,** hyperbolical, magnified, amplified, inflated, aggrandized, stylized, embroidered, embellished, varnished; stretched, disproportionate, blown up out of all proportion, blown out of proportion, overblown; overpraised, oversold, overrated, touted, puff, puffed, ballyhooed, hyped; overemphasized, overemphatic, overstressed; overstated, overdrawn; overdone, overwrought, a bit thick; caricatural, melodramatic, far-fetched, too much, over the top; overestimated; overlarge, overgreat;

extreme, pushed to the extreme, exorbitant, inordinate, excessive; superlative, extravagant, profuse, prodigal; high-flown, grandiloquent; overexposed

5 **exaggerating, exaggerative,** hyperbolical

356 DECEPTION

<action of deceiving>

NOUNS 1 **deception,** calculated deception, **deceptiveness,** subterfuge, gimmickry, gimmickery, trickiness; falseness; fallaciousness, fallacy, intentional fallacy; self-deception, fond illusion, wishful thinking, willful misconception; vision, hallucination, phantasm, mirage, will-o'-the-wisp, delusion, delusiveness, illusion; deceiving, victimization, dupery; bamboozlement, hoodwinking; swindling, defrauding, conning, chizzling, flimflam, flimflammery; fooling, befooling, tricking, kidding, putting on; spoofing, spoofery; bluffing; circumvention, overreaching, outwitting; ensnarement, entrapment, enmeshment, entanglement; smoke and mirrors

2 **misleading,** misguidance, misdirection; bum steer; misinformation

3 **deceit, deceitfulness**, guile, falseness, insidiousness, underhandedness; shiftiness, furtiveness, surreptitiousness, indirection; hypocrisy; falseheartedness, duplicity; treacherousness; artfulness, craft, cunning; sneakiness; sneak attack; funny business

4 chicanery, chicane, skulduggery, knavery, **trickery,** dodgery, pettifogging, pettifoggery, artifice, sleight, machination; sharp practice, underhand dealing, foul play; connivery, connivance, collusion, conspiracy, covin <law>; fakery, charlatanism, mountebankery, quackery

5 juggling, jugglery, **trickery,** dirty pool, prestidigitation, conjuration, legerdemain, sleight of hand, smoke and mirrors; mumbo jumbo, hocus-pocus, hanky-panky, monkey business, hokey-pokey, nobbling, jiggery-pokery, shenanigans; juggling act

6 **trick,** artifice, device, ploy, gambit, stratagem, scheme, design, subterfuge, blind, ruse, wile, chouse, shift, dodge, artful dodge, sleight, pass, feint, fetch, chicanery; bluff; gimmick, joker, catch; curve, curveball, googly, bosey, wrong'un; dirty trick, dirty deal, fast deal, scurvy trick; sleight of hand, sleight-of-hand trick, hocus-pocus; juggle, juggler's trick; bag of tricks, tricks of the trade, wheelhouse, toolbox

7 **hoax,** deception, spoof, humbug, flam, fake, fakement, rip-off, sham; mare's nest; put-on

8 **fraud, fraudulence,** fraudulency, dishonesty; imposture; imposition, cheat, cheating, cozenage, swindle, dodge, fishy transaction, piece of sharp practice; customer-gouging, insider trading, short weight, chiseling; gyp joint; racket, illicit business; graft, grift; bunco; cardsharping; ballot-box stuffing, gerrymandering

9 <nonformal> **gyp,** diddle, diddling, scam, flimflam flam, ramp, snow job, snow, song and dance, number, bill of goods, burn, the business, dipsy-doodle, double cross, fiddle, hosing, the old army game, reaming, suckering, sting, con, ripoff

10 **confidence game,** con game, skin game, bunco game; confidence trick, shell game, thimblerig, thimblerigging; bucket shop, boiler room; goldbrick; bait-and-switch, the wire, the pay-off, the rag, pastposting; street entertainer, street performer; pyramid scheme

11 **cover, disguise,** camouflage, protective coloration; false colors, false front; incognito; smoke screen; masquerade, masque, mummery; mask, visor, vizard, false face, domino, domino mask; red herring, diversion

12 **trap,** gin; pitfall, trapfall, deadfall; flytrap, mousetrap, mole trap, rattrap, bear trap; deathtrap, firetrap; Venus's flytrap, Dionaea; Catch-22, zero-sum game; spring gun, set gun; baited trap; booby trap, mine; decoy; hidden danger

13 **snare,** springe; noose, lasso, lariat; bola; net, trawl, dragnet, seine, purse seine, pound net, gill net; cobweb; meshes, toils; fishhook, hook, sniggle; **bait**, ground bait; lure, fly, jig, squid, plug, wobbler, spinner; lime, birdlime

VERBS 14 **deceive,** beguile, trick, hoax, dupe, gammon, gull, pigeon, play one for a fool, play one for a sucker, bamboozle, snow, hornswoggle, diddle, scam, nobble, humbug, take in, put on, hocus-pocus, string along, put something over, put something across, slip one over on, pull a fast one on; play games; delude, mock; betray, let down, leave in the lurch, leave holding the bag, play one false, double-cross, cheat on; two-time; juggle, conjure; bluff; cajole, circumvent, get around, forestall; overreach, outreach, outwit, outmaneuver, outsmart

15 **fool,** befool, make a fool of, practice on one's credulity, pull one's leg, make an ass of; trick; spoof, kid, put one on; play a trick on, play a practical joke upon, send on a fool's errand; fake one out; sell one a bill of goods, give one a snow job

16 **mislead,** misguide, misdirect, lead astray, lead up the garden path, give a bum steer; fake someone out, feed one a line, throw off the scent, throw off

the track, throw off the trail, put on a false scent, draw a red herring across the trail; throw one a curve, throw one a curve ball; misinform

17 **hoodwink,** blindfold, blind, blind one's eyes, throw dust in one's eyes, pull the wool over one's eyes

18 **cheat,** victimize, gull, pigeon, fudge, swindle, defraud, practice fraud upon, euchre, con, finagle, fleece, mulct, fob, bilk, cozen, cog, chouse, cheat out of, chizzle, do out of, chouse out of, beguile out of, beguile of; obtain under false pretenses; live by one's wits; bunco, play a bunco game; sell gold bricks; shortchange, shortweight, skim off the top; stack the cards, stack deck, pack the deal, deal off the bottom of the deck, play with marked cards; cog the dice, load the dice; thimblerig; crib; throw a fight, throw a game, take a dive

19 <nonformal> **gyp,** clip, **scam,** rope in, hose, shave, beat, rook, flam, flimflam, diddle, dipsy-doodle, do a number on, hustle, fuck*, fuck with*, screw, have, pull something, pull a trick, pull a stunt, give the business, ramp, stick, sting, burn, gouge, chisel, hocus, hocus-pocus, play for a sucker, take for a sucker, make a patsy of, do, run a game on, slicker, take for a ride

20 **trap,** entrap, gin, catch, catch out, catch in a trap; catch unawares, ambush; **ensnare,** snare, hook, hook in, sniggle, noose; inveigle; net, mesh, enmesh, snarl, ensnarl, wind, tangle, entangle, entoil, enweb; trip, trip up; set a trap for, lay a trap for, bait the hook, spread the toils; lime, birdlime; lure, allure, decoy

ADJS **21** **deceptive, deceiving,** misleading, beguiling, false, fallacious, delusive, delusory; hallucinatory, illusive, illusory; tricky, trickish, tricksy, catchy; fishy, questionable, dubious, sketchy; delusional

22 **deceitful, false;** fraudulent, sharp, guileful, insidious, slick, slippery, slippery as an eel, shifty, tricky, trickish, cute, finagling, chiseling; underhand, underhanded, furtive, surreptitious, indirect; collusive, covinous; falsehearted, two-faced; treacherous; sneaky; cunning, artful, gimmicky, wily, crafty; calculating, scheming, double-dealing

ADVS **23** **deceptively,** beguilingly, falsely, fallaciously, delusively, trickily, misleadingly, with intent to deceive; under false colors, under cover of, under the garb of, in disguise

24 **deceitfully,** fraudulently, guilefully, insidiously, shiftily, trickily; underhandedly, furtively, surreptitiously, indirectly, like a thief in the night; **treacherously**

357 DECEIVER

<one who deceives>

NOUNS **1** **deceiver, deluder,** duper, misleader, beguiler, bamboozler; actor, playactor, role-player; dissembler, dissimulator; confidence man; double-dealer, Machiavelli, Machiavel, Machiavellian; dodger, Artful Dodger, counterfeiter, forger, faker; plagiarizer, plagiarist; entrancer, enchanter, charmer, befuddler, hypnotizer, mesmerizer; seducer, Don Juan, Casanova; tease, teaser; jilt, jilter; gay deceiver; fooler, joker, jokester, hoaxer, practical joker; spoofer, kidder, ragger, leg-puller

2 **trickster,** tricker; juggler, sleight-of-hand performer, **magician,** illusionist, conjurer, prestidigitator, manipulator

3 **cheat, cheater;** two-timer; swindler, defrauder, cozener, juggler, sharper, sharp, spieler, pitchman, pitchperson; confidence man, confidence trickster, horse trader; cardsharp, cardsharper; thimblerigger; shortchanger; shyster, pettifogger; land shark, land pirate, land grabber, mortgage shark; carpetbagger; crimp

4 <nonformal> **gyp,** gypper, gyp artist, flimflammer, flimflam man, blackleg, chiseler, bilker, fleecer, diddler, crook, sharpie, shark, jackleg, slicker, con man, con artist, bunco, bunco artist, bunco steerer, scammer, clip artist, smoothie, dipsy-doodle, hustler, hoser

5 **shill,** decoy, come-on man, plant, capper, stool pigeon, stoolie; *agent provocateur* <Fr>

6 **impostor,** ringer; impersonator; pretender; sham, shammer, humbug, *blagueur* <Fr>, fraud, fake, faker, phony, fourflusher, bluff, bluffer; charlatan, quack, quacksalver, quackster, mountebank, saltimbanco; wolf in sheep's clothing, ass in lion's skin, jackdaw in peacock's feathers; poser, poseur; malingerer

7 **masquerader,** masker; **impersonator,** personator; mummer, guisard; incognito, incognita

8 **hypocrite, phony,** sanctimonious fraud, pharisee, whited sepulcher, canter, snuffler, mealymouth, dissembler, dissimulator, pretender, poseur, poser; Tartuffe, Pecksniff, Uriah Heep, Joseph Surface; false friend, fair-weather friend; summer soldier; cupboard lover

9 **liar,** fibber, fibster, fabricator, fabulist, pseudologist; falsifier; prevaricator, equivocator, evader, mudger, waffler, palterer; storyteller; yarner, yarn spinner, spinner of yarns, double-talker; Ananias; Satan, Father of Lies; Baron Münchausen; Sir John Mandeville; consummate liar, liar of the first magnitude; dirty liar; pathological liar, mythomane, mythomaniac, pseudologue, confirmed liar, habitual liar;

perjurer, false witness; slanderer, libeler, libelant; bullshitter*, BSer

10 **traitor,** treasonist, **betrayer,** quisling, rat, serpent, snake, cockatrice, snake in the grass, double-crosser, double-dealer; double agent; trimmer, timeserver; turncoat; informer; archtraitor; Judas, Judas Iscariot, Benedict Arnold, Brutus; schemer, plotter, intriguer, conspirer, conspirator, conniver, machinator; pseud, two-timer

11 **subversive; saboteur,** fifth columnist, crypto; security risk; collaborationist, collaborator, fraternizer; fifth column, underground; Trojan horse; renegade

358 DUPE

<one who is fooled>

NOUNS **1** **dupe,** gull, gudgeon; **victim;** gullible person, dupable person, credulous person, trusting soul, simple soul, innocent, *naïf* <Fr>, babe, babe in the woods; greenhorn; toy, plaything; monkey; **fool**; stooge, cat's-paw

2 <nonformal> **sucker, patsy,** pigeon, chicken, fall guy, doormat, mug, fish, jay, easy mark, sitting duck, pushover, cinch, mark, vic, easy pickings, greeny, greener, chump, boob, *schlemiel* <Yiddish>, sap, saphead, prize sap, easy touch, soft touch, hornswoggler

359 RESOLUTION

<resolving something>

NOUNS **1** **resolution,** resolve, resolvedness, **determination,** decision, executive decision, fixed resolve, firm resolve, will, purpose; resoluteness, determinedness, determinateness, decisiveness, decidedness, purposefulness; definiteness; closure; earnestness, seriousness, sincerity, devotion, dedication, commitment, total commitment; the native hue of resolution; single-mindedness, relentlessness, persistence, tenacity, perseverance; self-will, obstinacy; control freak

2 **firmness,** firmness of mind, firmness of spirit, fixity of purpose, staunchness, settledness, steadiness, constancy, steadfastness, fixedness, unshakableness; stability; concentration; flintiness, steeliness; inflexibility, rigidity, unyieldingness; trueness, loyalty

3 **pluck, spunk, mettle,** backbone, grit, true grit, spirit, stamina, guts, moxie, pith, bottom, toughness; clenched teeth, gritted teeth; pluckiness, spunkiness, gameness, feistiness, mettlesomeness; courage

4 **willpower,** will, power, strong-mindedness, strength of mind, strength of purpose, fixity of purpose, strength, fortitude, moral fiber; iron will, will of iron, will of steel; a will of one's own, a mind of one's own, law unto oneself; the courage of one's convictions, moral courage

5 **self-control,** self-command, self-possession, strength of character, self-mastery, self-government, self-domination, self-restraint, self-conquest, self-discipline, self-denial; control, restraint, constraint, discipline; composure, possession, aplomb; independence

6 **self-assertion,** self-assertiveness, forwardness, **nerve,** pushiness, importunateness, importunacy; self-expression, self-expressiveness

VERBS **7** **resolve,** determine, decide, will, purpose, make up one's mind, make a resolution, make a point of; settle, settle on, fix, seal; conclude, come to a determination, come to a conclusion, come to a decision, determine once for all, boil down to

8 **be determined,** be resolved, attain closure; have a mind of one's own, have a will of one's own, know one's own mind; be in earnest, mean business, mean what one says; have blood in one's eyes, be out for blood, set one's mind upon, set one's heart upon; put one's heart into, devote oneself to, commit oneself, to dedicate oneself to, give oneself up to; buckle oneself, buckle down, buckle to; steel oneself, brace oneself, grit one's teeth, set one's teeth, set one's jaw; set one's shoulder to the wheel; take the bull by the horns, take the plunge, cross the Rubicon; nail one's colors to the mast, burn one's bridges, go for broke, shoot the works, kick down the ladder, throw away the scabbard; never say die, die hard, die fighting, die with one's boots on

9 **remain firm, stand fast**, stand firm, hold out, hold fast, get tough, take one's stand, set one's back against the wall, stand one's ground, hold one's ground, keep one's footing, hold one's own, hang in, hang in there, hang tough, dig in, dig one's heels in; stick to one's guns, stick, stick with it, stick fast, stick to one's colors, adhere to one's principles; not listen to the voice of the siren; take what comes, stand the gaff; put one's foot down, stand no nonsense

10 **not hesitate,** think nothing of, think little of, make no bones about, make no scruple of, stick at nothing, stop at nothing; not look back; go the whole hog, carry through, face out; go the whole nine yards

ADJS **11** **resolute, resolved,** determined, bound, bound and determined, decided, decisive, purposeful; definite; earnest, serious, sincere; devoted, dedicated, committed, wholehearted; single-minded, relentless, persistent, tenacious, persevering; obstinate

12 **firm, staunch,** standup, fixed, settled, steady, steadfast, constant, set, sot, flinty, steely; unshaken, not to be shaken, unflappable; undeflectable, unswerving, not to be deflected; immovable, unbending, inflexible, unyielding; true, committed, loyal

13 **unhesitating,** unhesitant, unfaltering, unflinching, unshrinking; stick-at-nothing

14 **plucky,** spunky, feisty, gutty, gutsy, gritty, mettlesome, dauntless, game, game to the last, game to the end; courageous

15 **strong-willed,** strong-minded, firm-minded; self-controlled, controlled, self-disciplined, self-restrained; self-possessed; self-assertive, self-asserting, forward, pushy, importunate; self-expressive; independent

16 **determined upon,** resolved upon, decided upon, intent upon, fixed upon, settled upon, set on, dead set on, sot on, bent on, hell-bent on; obsessed; clenched, verklempt

ADVS 17 **resolutely,** determinedly, decidedly, decisively, resolvedly, purposefully, with a will; firmly, steadfastly, steadily, fixedly, with constancy, staunchly; seriously, in all seriousness, earnestly, in earnest, in good earnest, sincerely; devotedly, with total dedication, committedly; hammer and tongs, tooth and nail; heart and soul, go-for-broke, with all one's heart, with all one's might, wholeheartedly; unswervingly; singlemindedly, relentlessly, persistently, tenaciously, like a bulldog, like a leech, perseveringly; obstinately, unyieldingly, inflexibly

18 **pluckily,** spunkily, feistily, gutsily, mettlesomely, gamely, dauntlessly, manfully, like a man; on one's mettle; courageously, heroically

19 **unhesitatingly,** unhesitantly, **unfalteringly,** unflinchingly, unshrinkingly

PHRS 20 **come what may,** cost what it may, whatever the cost, at any price, at any cost, at any sacrifice, at all risks, at all hazards, whatever may happen, though the heavens may fall, at all events, live or die, survive or perish, sink or swim, rain or shine, come hell or high water; in some way or other

360 PERSEVERANCE

<determinedly pursuing something>

NOUNS 1 **perseverance, persistence**, persistency, insistence, insistency, singleness of purpose; resolution; steadfastness, steadiness, stability; constancy, permanence; loyalty, fidelity; single-mindedness, concentration, undivided attention, unswerving attention, engrossment, preoccupation; endurance, stick-to-itiveness, staying power, bitterendism, pertinacity, pertinaciousness, tenacity, tenaciousness, doggedness, unremittingness, relentlessness, dogged perseverance, bulldog tenacity, unfailing grip, leechlike grip; plodding, plugging, slogging; bidding war; obstinacy, stubbornness; diligence, application, sedulousness, sedulity, industry, industriousness, hard work, heavy lifting, assiduousness, assiduity, unflagging efforts; tirelessness, indefatigability, stamina; patience, patience of Job; failure is not an option

VERBS 2 **persevere, persist,** carry on, go on, keep on, keep up, keep at, keep at it, keep going, keep driving, keep trying, try and try again, keep the ball rolling, keep the pot boiling, keep up the good work; not take "no" for an answer; not accept compromise, not accept defeat; endure, last, continue

3 keep doggedly at, **plod,** drudge, slog, slog away, soldier on, put one foot in front of the other, peg away at; plug, plug at, plug away, plug along; pound away, hammer away; keep one's nose to the grindstone

4 **stay with it,** hold on, hold fast, hang on, hang on like a bulldog, hang on like a leech, stick to one's guns; not give up, never say die, not give up the ship, not strike one's colors; come up fighting, come up for more; stay it out, stick out, hold out; hold up, last out, bear up, stand up; live with it, live through it; stay the distance, stay the course; sit tight, be unmoved, be unmoveable; brazen it out

5 prosecute to a conclusion, **go through with it,** carry through, follow through, see it through, see it out, follow up; go to the bitter end, go the distance, go all the way, go to any length, go to any lengths; leave no stone unturned, leave no avenue unexplored, overlook nothing, exhaust every move; move heaven and earth, go through fire and water

6 **die trying,** die in the last ditch, die in harness, die with one's boots on, die in one's boots, die at one's post, die in the attempt, die game, die hard, go down with flying colors

7 <nonformal> **stick,** stick to it, stick with it, stick it, stick it out, hang on for dear life, hang in, hang in there, hang tough, tough it out, keep on trucking, keep on keeping on; go the limit, go the whole hog, go the whole nine yards, go all out, shoot the works, go for broke, go through hell and high water; work one's ass off*, work one's butt off, work one's tail off

ADJS 8 **persevering,** perseverant, **persistent,** persisting, insistent; **enduring,** permanent, constant, lasting; continuing; stable, steady, steadfast; immutable, inalterable; resolute; diligent, assiduous, sedulous, industrious; dogged, plodding, slogging, plugging; pertinacious, tenacious, stick-to-itive; loyal, faithful; unswerving, unremitting, unabating, unintermitting, uninterrupted; single-minded, utterly attentive; rapt, preoccupied; unfaltering, unwavering, unflinching; relentless, unrelenting; obstinate, high-maintenance, stubborn; unrelaxing, unfailing, untiring, unwearying, unflagging, never-tiring, tireless, weariless, indefatigable, unwearied, unsleeping, undrooping, unnodding, unwinking, sleepless; undiscouraged, undaunted, indomitable, unconquerable, invincible, game to the last, game to the end, hanging in there; patient, patient as Job

ADVS 9 **perseveringly, persistently,** persistingly, insistently; resolutely; loyally, faithfully, devotedly; diligently, industriously, assiduously, sedulously; doggedly, sloggingly, ploddingly; pertinaciously, tenaciously; unremittingly, unabatingly, unintermittingly, uninterruptedly; unswervingly, unwaveringly, unfalteringly, unflinchingly; relentlessly, unrelentingly; indefatigably, tirelessly, wearilessly, untiringly, unwearyingly, unflaggingly, unrestingly, unsleepingly; patiently

10 **through thick and thin,** through fire and water, come hell or high water, through evil report and good report, rain or shine, fair or foul, in sickness and in health; come what may, all the way, down to the wire, to the bitter end

361 OBSTINACY

<*stubbornly adhering to something*>

NOUNS 1 **obstinacy,** obstinateness, pertinacity, restiveness, **stubbornness,** willfulness, self-will, hardheadedness, headstrongness, strongheadness; mind of one's own, will of one's own, set mind, fixed mind, inflexible will; perseverance, doggedness, determination, tenaciousness, tenacity, bitterendism; bullheadedness, pigheadedness, mulishness; obduracy, unregenerateness; stiff neck, stiff-neckedness; sullenness, sulkiness; balkiness; uncooperativeness; dogmatism, opinionatedness; overzealousness, fanaticism; intolerance, bigotry; bloody-mindedness <Brit>

2 **unyieldingness,** unbendingness, stiff temper, **inflexibility,** inelasticity, impliability, ungivingness, obduracy, toughness, firmness, stiffness, adamantness, rigorism, rigidity, straitlacedness, straightlacedness, stuffiness; hard line, hard-bittenness, hard-nosedness; fixity; unalterability, unchangeability, immutability, immovability; irreconcilability, uncompromisingness, intransigence, intransigency, intransigentism; implacability, inexorability, relentlessness, unrelentingness; sternness, grimness, dourness, flintiness, steeliness

3 **perversity,** perverseness, **contrariness,** wrongheadedness, waywardness, forwardness, difficultness, crossgrainedness, cantankerousness, feistiness, orneriness, cussedness; sullenness, sulkiness, dourness, stuffiness; irascibility

4 **ungovernability, unmanageability,** uncontrollability; indomitability, untamableness, intractability, refractoriness, shrewishness; incorrigibility; unsubmissiveness, unbiddability, indocility; irrepressibility, insuppressibility; unmalleability, unmoldableness; recidivism; recalcitrance, recalcitrancy, contumacy, contumaciousness; unruliness, obstreperousness, restiveness, fractiousness, wildness; defiance; resistance

5 **unpersuadableness,** deafness, blindness; closed-mindedness; positiveness, dogmatism

6 <obstinate person> **mule,** donkey, ass, perverse fool; bullethead, pighead; hardnose, hardhead, hammerhead, hard-liner; standpat, standpatter, stickler; intransigent, maverick; dogmatist, positivist, bigot, fanatic, purist; diehard, bitter-ender, last-ditcher; conservative; stick-in-the-mud

VERBS 7 balk, stickle; hold one's ground, not budge, dig one's heels in, **stand pat,** not yield an inch, stick to one's guns; hold out; stand firm; take no denial, not take "no" for an answer; take the bit in one's teeth; die hard; cut off one's nose to spite one's face; **persevere**; turn a deaf ear

ADJS 8 **obstinate, stubborn,** pertinacious, restive; willful, self-willed, strong-willed, hardheaded, headstrong, strongheaded; dogged, bulldogged, tenacious, perserving; bullheaded, bulletheaded, pigheaded, mulish, stubborn as a mule; set, set in one's ways, case-hardened, stiff-necked; sullen, sulky; balky, balking; unregenerate, uncooperative; bigoted, intolerant, overzealous, fanatic, fanatical; dogmatic, opinionated

9 **unyielding,** unbending, inflexible, hard, hard-line, inelastic, impliable, ungiving, firm, stiff, rigid, rigorous, stuffy; rock-ribbed, rock-hard, rocklike; adamant, adamantine; unmoved, unaffected; immovable, not to be moved; unalterable, unchangeable, immutable; uncompromising, intransigent, irreconcilable, hard-shell, hardcore; implacable, inexorable, relentless, unrelenting; stern, grim, dour; iron, cast-iron, flinty, steely

10 **obdurate,** tough, hard, hard-set, hard-mouthed, hard-bitten, hard-nosed, hard-boiled

11 **perverse,** contrary, wrongheaded, wayward, froward, difficult, cross-grained, cantankerous, feisty, ornery; sullen, sulky, stuffy; irascible

12 **ungovernable, unmanageable,** uncontrollable, indomitable, untamable, intractable, refractory; shrewish; incorrigible, unreconstructed; unsubmissive, unbiddable, indocile; irrepressible, insuppressible; unmalleable, unmoldable; recidivist, recidivistic; recalcitrant, contumacious; obstreperous, unruly, restive, wild, fractious, breachy; beyond control, out of hand; resistant, resisting; defiant; irascible; like a hog on ice

13 **unpersuadable,** deaf, blind; closed-minded; positive; dogmatic

ADVS **14** **obstinately, stubbornly,** pertinaciously; willfully, headstrongly; doggedly, tenaciously; bullheadedly, pigheadedly, mulishly; unregenerately; uncooperatively; with set jaw, with sullen mouth, with a stiff neck

15 **unyieldingly,** unbendingly, inflexibly, adamantly, obdurately, firmly, stiffly, rigidly, rigorously; unalterably, unchangeably, immutably, immovably, unregenerately; uncompromisingly, intransigently, irreconcilably; implacably, inexorably, relentlessly, unrelentingly; sternly, grimly, dourly

16 **perversely, contrarily,** contrariwise, waywardly, wrongheadedly, frowardly, crossgrainedly, cantankerously, feistily, sullenly, sulkily

17 **ungovernably,** unmanageably, uncontrollably, indomitably, untamably, intractably; shrewishly; incorrigibly; unsubmissively; irrepressibly, insuppressibly; contumaciously; unrulily, obstreperously, restively, fractiously

362 IRRESOLUTION

<uncertainty>

NOUNS **1** **irresolution, indecision,** unsettlement, unsettledness, irresoluteness, undeterminedness, indecisiveness, undecidedness, infirmity of purpose; mugwumpery, mugwumpism, fence-sitting, fence-straddling; double-mindedness, ambivalence, ambitendency; dubiety, dubiousness, uncertainty; instability, inconstancy, changeableness; capriciousness, mercuriality, fickleness; change of mind, second thoughts, tergiversation

2 **vacillation, fluctuation,** oscillation, pendulation, mood swing, **wavering,** wobbling, waffling, shilly-shally, shilly-shallying, blowing hot and cold; equivocation; second thoughts; backpedalling, reversal, about-face

3 **hesitation,** hesitance, **hesitancy,** hesitating, holding back, dragging one's feet; falter, faltering, shilly-shally, shilly-shallying; diffidence, tentativeness, caution, cautiousness

4 **weak will,** weak-mindedness; feeblemindedness, weakness, feebleness, faintness, faintheartedness, frailty, infirmity; wimpiness, wimpishness, spinelessness, invertebracy; abulia; fear; cowardice; pliability

5 **vacillator,** shillyshallyer, shilly-shally, **waverer,** wobbler, butterfly; mugwump, fence-sitter, fence-straddler; equivocator, tergiversator, prevaricator; ass between two bundles of hay; yo-yo, flip-flopper; wimp, weakling, jellyfish, milquetoast; quitter; don't know

VERBS **6** **not know one's own mind,** not know where one stands, be of two minds, have two minds, have mixed feelings, be in conflict, be conflicted; stagger, stumble, boggle

7 **hesitate,** pause, falter, hang back, hover; procrastinate; shilly-shally, hum and haw, hem and haw; wait to see how the cat jumps, wait to see how the wind blows, scruple, jib, demur, stick at, stickle, strain at; think twice about, stop to consider, ponder, wrinkle one's brow; debate, deliberate, see both sides of the question, balance, weigh one thing against another, consider both sides of the question, weigh the pros and cons; be divided, come down squarely in the middle, sit on the fence, straddle the fence, fall between two stools; yield, back down; retreat, withdraw, wimp out, chicken out, cop out; pull back, drag one's feet; flinch, shy away from, shy, back off; fear; not face up to, hide one's head in the sand

8 **vacillate, waver,** waffle, fluctuate, pendulate, oscillate, wobble, wobble about, teeter, totter, dither, swing from one thing to another, shilly-shally, back and fill, keep off and on, will and will not, keep hanging in midair, leave hanging in midair; blow hot and cold; equivocate, fudge and mudge; change one's mind, tergiversate; vary, alternate; shift, change horses in midstream, change

ADJS **9** irresolute, irresolved, unresolved; **undecided, indecisive,** undetermined, unsettled, infirm of purpose; dubious, uncertain; at loose ends, at a loose end; of two minds, in conflict, double-minded, ambivalent, ambitendent; changeable, mutable; capricious, mercurial, fickle; mugwumpian, mugwumpish, fence-sitting, fence-straddling

10 **vacillating,** vacillatory, waffling, oscillatory, wobbly, **wavering,** fluctuating, pendulating, oscillating, shilly-shallying, shilly-shally; inconsistent; mood-altering

11 **hesitant,** hesitating, pikerish; faltering;

shilly-shallying; diffident, tentative, timid, cautious; scrupling, jibbing, demurring, sticking, straining, stickling

12 **weak-willed,** weak-minded, feebleminded, weak-kneed, weak, wimpy, wimpish, feeble, fainthearted, frail, faint, infirm; spineless, invertebrate; without a will of one's own, unable to say "no"; abulic; afraid, chicken, chickenhearted, chicken-livered, cowardly; like putty, pliable

ADVS 13 **irresolutely,** irresolvedly, undecidedly, indecisively, undeterminedly; uncertainly; hesitantly, hesitatingly, falteringly; waveringly, vacillatingly, shilly-shally, shilly-shallyingly

363 CHANGING OF MIND

<change of decision or opinion>

NOUNS 1 **reverse, reversal,** flip, flip-flop, U-turn, turnabout, turnaround, **about-face,** about turn, *volte-face* <Fr>, right-about-face, right-about turn, right-about, a turn to the right-about; tergiversation, tergiversating; change of mind; second thoughts, better thoughts, afterthoughts, mature judgment; paradigm shift

2 **apostasy,** recreancy; treason, misprision of treason, betrayal, turning traitor, turning one's coat, changing one's stripes, ratting, going over, joining the opposition, going over to the opposition, siding with the enemy; defection; bolt, bolting, secession, breakaway; desertion; recidivism, recidivation, relapse, backsliding; faithlessness, disloyalty

3 **recantation,** withdrawal, disavowal, denial, reneging, unsaying, repudiation, palinode, palinody, retraction, retractation; disclaimer, disclamation, disownment, disowning, abjurement, abjuration, renunciation, renouncement, forswearing; expatriation, self-exile

4 **timeserver,** temporizer, opportunist, trimmer, weathercock; mugwump; chameleon, Vicar of Bray

5 **apostate,** turncoat, turnabout, recreant, renegade, renegado, renegate, defector, tergiversator, tergiversant; deserter, turntail, quisling, fifth columnist, collaborationist, collaborator, traitor; strikebreaker; bolter, seceder, secessionist, separatist, schismatic; backslider, recidivist; reversionist; convert, proselyte

VERBS 6 **change one's mind,** change one's song, change one's tune, sing a different tune, dance to another tune; come round, wheel, do an about-face, reverse oneself, do a flip-flop, do a U-turn, go over, change sides; swing from one thing to another; think better of it, have second thoughts, be of another mind; bite one's tongue

7 apostatize, apostacize, go over, change sides, **switch,** switch over, change one's allegiance, defect; turn one's coat, turn cloak; desert a sinking ship, leave a sinking ship; secede, break away, bolt, fall off, fall away; desert

8 **recant, retract,** repudiate, withdraw, take back, unswear, renege, welsh, abjure, disavow, disown; deny, disclaim, unsay, unspeak; renounce, forswear, eat one's words, eat one's hat, swallow, eat crow, eat humble pie; back down, back out, climb down, crawfish out, backwater, weasel

9 **be a timeserver,** trim, temporize, change with the times; sit on the fence, straddle the fence

ADJS 10 **timeserving,** trimming, temporizing; supple, neither fish nor fowl

11 **apostate,** recreant, renegade, tergiversating, tergiversant; treasonous, treasonable, traitorous, forsworn; collaborating; faithless, disloyal

12 **repudiative,** repudiatory; abjuratory, renunciative, renunciatory; schismatic; separatist, secessionist, breakaway; opportunistic, mugwumpian, mugwumpish, fence-straddling, fence-sitting

364 CAPRICE

<sudden change>

NOUNS 1 **caprice, whim,** humor, whimsy, freak, whim-wham; fancy, fantasy, conceit, notion, flimflam, toy, freakish inspiration, crazy idea, fantastic notion, fool notion, harebrained idea, brainstorm, vagary, megrim; fad, craze, passing fancy, next big thing; quirk, crotchet, crank, kink; maggot, maggot in the brain, bee in one's bonnet, flea in one's nose

2 **capriciousness,** caprice, whimsicalness, whimsy, whimsicality; humorsomeness, fancifulness, fantasticality, freakishness; crankiness, crotchetiness, quirkiness; moodiness, temperamentalness, prima-donnaism; petulance; arbitrariness, motivelessness

3 **fickleness, flightiness,** skittishness, inconstancy, lightness, levity; flakiness; volatility, mercurialness, mercuriality, erraticism; mood swing; faddishness, faddism; changeableness; unpredictability; unreliability, undependability; coquettishness; frivolousness; purposelessness, motivelessness

VERBS 4 **blow hot and cold,** keep off and on, have as many phases as the moon, chop and change, fluctuate, vacillate, flip-flop; act on impulse

ADJS 5 **capricious, whimsical,** freakish, humorsome, vagarious; fanciful, notional, fantasied, fantastic, fantastical, maggoty, crotchety, kinky, harebrained, cranky, flaky, quirky; wanton, wayward, vagrant; arbitrary, unreasonable, motiveless; moody, temperamental, prima-donnaish; petulant; unrestrained

6 **fickle, flighty,** skittish, light; coquettish, flirtatious, toying; versatile, inconstant, erratic, changeable; vacillating; volatile, mercurial, quicksilver; faddish; scatterbrained, unpredictable; impulsive; idiosyncratic; unreliable, undependable; polytropic

ADVS 7 **capriciously, whimsically,** fancifully, at one's own sweet will; flightily, lightly; arbitrarily, unreasonably, without rhyme or reason

365 IMPULSE

<sudden inclination to act>

NOUNS 1 **impulse;** natural impulse, blind impulse, irresistible impulse, **instinct,** urge, drive; vagrant impulse, fleeting impulse; involuntary impulse, reflex, knee jerk, automatic response; gut response, gut reaction, gut feeling; notion, fancy; sudden thought, flash, inspiration, brainstorm, brain wave, quick hunch; impulse buy

2 **impulsiveness,** impetuousness, impulsivity, impetuousity; hastiness, overhastiness, haste, quickness, suddenness; precipitateness, precipitance, precipitancy, precipitation; hair-trigger; recklessness, rashness; impatience

3 **thoughtlessness,** unthoughtfulness, heedlessness, carelessness, inconsideration, inconsiderateness; negligence, caprice

4 unpremeditation, indeliberation, undeliberateness, uncalculatedness, undesignedness, **spontaneity, spontaneousness,** unstudiedness; involuntariness; snap judgment, snap decision; snap shot, offhand shot

5 **improvisation, extemporization,** improvision, improvising, extempore, impromptu, ad-lib, ad-libbing, playing by ear, ad hoc measure, ad hoc solution, adhocracy, ad hockery, ad hocery, ad hocism; extemporaneousness, extemporariness; temporary measure, temporary arrangement, pro tempore measure, pro tempore arrangement, stopgap, makeshift, jury-rig; cannibalization; bricolage; jam session; thinking on one's feet

6 **improviser,** improvisor, improvisator, *improvvisatore,* **extemporizer,** ad-libber; cannibalizer; bricoleur; creature of impulse

VERBS 7 **act on the spur of the moment,** obey one's impulse, let oneself go; shoot from the hip, be too quick on the trigger, be too quick on the draw, be too quick on the uptake; blurt out, come out with, let slip out, say what comes uppermost, say the first thing that comes into one's mind, say the first thing that comes into one's head; be unable to help oneself; impulse-buy; reinvent oneself

8 **improvise, extemporize,** improvisate, improv, tapdance, talk off the top of one's head, speak off the cuff, think on one's feet, invent, make it up as one goes along, play it by ear, throw away the prepared text, depart from the prepared text, throw away the speech, scrap the plan, ad-lib, do offhand, wing it, vamp, fake, play by ear; dash off, strike off, knock off, throw off, toss off, toss out; make up, whip up, cook up, run up, rustle up, whomp up, slap up, slap together, throw together, lash up, cobble up; jury-rig; rise to the occasion; cannibalize

ADJS 9 **impulsive, impetuous,** hasty, overhasty, quick, sudden, snap; quick on the draw, quick on the trigger, quick on the uptake, hair-trigger; precipitate, headlong; reckless, rash; impatient

10 **unthinking,** unreasoning, unreflecting, uncalculating, unthoughtful, thoughtless, inadvertent, reasonless, heedless, careless, inconsiderate; unguarded; arbitrary, capricious

11 **unpremeditated,** unmeditated, uncalculated, undeliberated, spontaneous, undesigned, unstudied; unintentional, unintended, inadvertent, unwilled, indeliberate, undeliberate, collateral; involuntary, reflex, reflexive, knee-jerk, acting out, automatic, goose-step, lockstep; gut, unconscious; unconsidered, unadvised, snap, casual, offhand, throwaway; ill-considered, ill-advised, ill-devised; act-first-and-think-later

12 **extemporaneous,** extemporary, extempore, impromptu, unrehearsed, improvised, improvisatory, improvisatorial, improviso; ad-lib, *ad libitum* <L>; ad hoc, stopgap, makeshift, jury-rigged; offhand, off the top of one's head, off-the-cuff, spur-of-the-moment, quick and dirty; catch-as-catch-can; potluck

ADVS 13 **impulsively,** impetuously, hastily, suddenly, quickly, precipitately, headlong; recklessly, rashly

14 **on impulse,** on a sudden impulse, on the spur of the moment; without premeditation, unpremeditatedly, uncalculatedly, undesignedly; unthinkingly, unreflectingly, unreasoningly, unthoughtfully, thoughtlessly, heedlessly, carelessly, inconsiderately, unadvisedly; unintentionally, inadvertently, without willing, indeliberately, involuntarily

15 **extemporaneously**, extemporarily, extempore, impromptu, ad lib, offhand, out of hand; at sight, on sight; by ear, off the hip, off the top of one's head, off the cuff; at short notice

366 LEAP

<jumping or springing from>

NOUNS 1 **leap, jump, hop,** spring, skip, bound, bounce; pounce; upleap, upspring, jumpoff; hurdle; vault, pole vault; demivolt, curvet, capriole; jeté, grand jeté, tour jeté, saut de basque; jig, galliard, lavolta, Highland fling, morris; standing jump, running jump, flying jump; long jump, broad jump, standing broad jump, running broad jump; high jump, standing high jump, running high jump; leapfrog; jump shot; handspring; buck, buckjump; ski jump, jump turn, geländesprung, gelände jump; steeplechase; hippety-hop; jump-hop; hop, skip, and jump

2 **caper,** dido, gambol, frisk, curvet, cavort, capriole; **prance,** caracole; *gambade* <Fr>, gambado; falcade

3 **leaping, jumping,** bouncing, bounding, hopping, capering, cavorting, prancing, skipping, springing, saltation; vaulting, pole vaulting; hurdling, the hurdles, hurdle race, timber topping, steeplechase; leapfrogging; bungee-jumping

4 **jumper,** leaper, hopper; broad jumper, high jumper; vaulter, pole vaulter; hurdler, hurdle racer, timber topper; jumping jack; bucking bronco, buckjumper, sunfisher; jumping bean; kangaroo, gazelle, stag, jackrabbit, goat, frog, grasshopper, flea; salmon

VERBS 5 **leap, jump,** vault, spring, skip, hop, bound, bounce; upleap, upspring, updive; leap over, jump over; overleap, overjump, overskip, leapfrog; hurdle, clear, negotiate; curvet, capriole; buck, buckjump; ski jump; steeplechase; start, start up, start aside; pounce, pounce on, pounce upon; hippety-hop

6 **caper,** cut capers, cut a dido, curvet, cavort, capriole, gambol, gambado, frisk, flounce, trip, skip, bob, bounce, jump about; romp, ramp; **prance**; caracole

ADJS 7 **leaping, jumping,** springing, hopping, skipping, prancing, bouncing, bounding; saltant, saltatory, saltatorial

367 PLUNGE

<sudden falling or jumping>

NOUNS 1 **plunge, dive,** pitch, drop, fall; free-fall; header; swoop, pounce, stoop; swan dive, gainer, jackknife, cannonball; belly flop, belly buster, belly whopper; nosedive, power dive; parachute jump, skydive; bungee jump; crash dive, stationary dive, running dive

2 **submergence, submersion,** immersion, immergence, engulfment, inundation, burial; dipping, ducking, dousing, sousing, dunking, sinking; dip, duck, souse; baptism

3 **diving,** plunging; skydiving; bungee jumping; fancy diving, high diving; scuba diving, snorkeling, skin diving, pearl diving, deep-sea diving

4 **diver,** plunger; high diver; bungee jumper; parachute jumper, jumper, skydiver, sport jumper, paratrooper, smoke jumper, paramedic; skin diver, snorkel diver, scuba diver, free diver, pearl diver, deep-sea diver, frogman

5 <diving equipment> diving bell, diving chamber, bathysphere, bathyscaphe, benthoscope, aquascope; submarine; diving boat; scuba, self-contained underwater breathing apparatus, Aqua-Lung <tm>; diving goggles, diving mask, swim fins; wet suit; air cylinder; diving suit; diving helmet, diving hood; snorkel, periscope

VERBS 6 **plunge, dive,** pitch, plummet, drop, fall; skydive, parachute; bungee jump; free-fall; plump, plunk, plop; swoop, swoop down, stoop, pounce, pounce on, pounce upon; nose-dive, make a nosedive, take a nosedive; skin-dive; sound; take a header

7 **submerge,** submerse, immerse, immerge, merge, sink, bury, engulf, inundate, deluge, drown, overwhelm, whelm; dip, duck, dunk, douse, souse, plunge in water; baptize

8 **sink,** scuttle, send to the bottom, send to Davy Jones's locker; founder, go down, go to the bottom, sink like lead, go down like a stone; get out of one's depth

ADJS 9 **submersible,** submergible, immersible, sinkable; immersive

368 AVOIDANCE

<avoiding or withdrawing>

NOUNS 1 **avoidance, shunning;** forbearance, refraining; hands-off policy, nonintervention, noninvolvement, neutrality; **evasion**, elusion; side-stepping, getting around, circumvention; prevention, forestalling, forestallment; escape; evasive action, the runaround; zigzag, jink, juke, slip, dodge, duck, sidestep, shy; shunting off, sidetracking; bypassing; evasiveness, elusiveness; equivocation, waffle, fudging, fudge and mudge; avoiding reaction, defense mechanism, defense reaction; safe distance, wide berth; cold shoulder, snub; abstinence; shyness

2 **shirking, slacking,** goldbricking, cop-out, soldiering, goofing, goofing off, fucking off*;

clock-watching; malingering, skulking; passivity; dodging, ducking; welshing; truancy; tax evasion, tax dodging

3 **shirker,** shirk, **slacker,** eye-servant, eye-server, goof-off, soldier, old soldier, goldbricker, goldbrick; clock watcher; welsher; malingerer, skulker, skulk; truant; tax dodger, tax evader

4 **flight,** fugitation, exit, quick exit, making oneself scarce, getting the hell out, bolt, scarpering, disappearing act, hasty retreat; running away, decampment, bugging out; skedaddle, skedaddling, scramming, absquatulation; elopement; disappearance; French leave, absence without leave (AWOL); desertion; hegira; truancy, hooky, hookey

5 **fugitive,** fleer, person on the run, runaway, runagate, bolter, skedaddler; absconder, eloper; refugee, evacuee, boat person, *émigré* <Fr>; displaced person (DP), stateless person; escapee; illegal immigrant, wetback, day-crosser; draft dodger; truant, absentee; desserter

VERBS 6 **avoid,** shun, fight shy of, shy away from, keep from, keep away from, circumvent, keep clear of, avoid like the plague, steer clear of, give a miss to, skate around, keep out of the way of, get out of the way of, give a wide berth, keep remote from, stay detached from; make way for, give place to; keep one's distance, keep at a respectful distance, keep aloof, stand aloof, hold aloof; give the cold shoulder to, have nothing to do with, have no association with, not give the time of day, have no truck with; not meddle with, let alone, let well enough alone, keep hands off, not touch, not touch with a ten-foot pole, back off; turn away from, turn one's back upon, slam the door in one's face

7 **evade, elude,** beg, get out of, shuffle out of, skirt, get around, circumvent; take evasive action; give one the runaround; ditch, shake, shake off, get away from, give the runaround, give the slip; throw off the scent; play at hide and seek; lead one a chase, lead one on a merry chase, lead one a dance, lead one on a pretty dance; escape

8 **dodge, duck**; take evasive action, juke, jink, zigzag; throw off the track, throw off the trail; shy, shy away; swerve, sheer off; pull away, pull clear; pull back, shrink, recoil; sidestep, step aside; step back; parry, fence, ward off; have an out, have an escape hatch; shift, shift off, put off; hedge, pussyfoot, be on the fence, sit on the fence, beat around the bush, beat about the bush, hem and haw, beg the question, tapdance, dance around, equivocate, fudge and mudge

9 **shirk, slack,** lie on one's oars, rest upon one's oars, not pull fair, not pull one's weight; lie down on the job; soldier, duck duty, goof off, dog it, goldbrick; malinger, skulk; get out of, sneak out of, slip out of, slide out of, pass the buck, cop out, dodge, duck; welsh

10 **flee,** fly, take flight, take to flight, take wing, fugitate, run, cut and run, make a precipitate departure, run off, run away, run away from, bug out, decamp, pull up stakes, take to one's heels, make off, depart, do the disappearing act, make a quick exit, beat a retreat, beat a hasty retreat, turn tail, show the heels, show a clean pair of heels, show a light pair of heels; run for it, bolt, run for one's life; make a run for it; advance to the rear, make a strategic withdrawal; take French leave, go AWOL, slip the cable; desert; abscond, levant, elope, run away with; skip bail, jump bail; play hooky, play hookey

11 <nonformal> **beat it,** blow, scram, bug off, lam, book, air out, shemozzle, bugger off <Brit>, take it on the lam, take a powder, make tracks, cut ass, cut and run, peel out, split, skin out, skip, skip out, duck out, duck and run, dog it, vamoose, absquatulate, skedaddle, clear out, make oneself scarce, get the hell out, make a break for it, warp out

12 **slip away,** steal away, sneak off, shuffle off, slink off, slide off, slither off, skulk away, mooch off, duck out, slip out of

13 **not face up to,** hide one's head in the sand, not come to grips with, put off, procrastinate, temporize, waffle

ADJS 14 **avoidable, escapable,** eludible; evadable; preventable

15 **evasive,** elusive, elusory; shifty, slippery, slippery as an eel; cagey; shirking, malingering

16 **fugitive, runaway,** in flight, on the lam, hot; disappearing

369 ESCAPE

<getting free or away>

NOUNS 1 **escape; getaway**, break, breakout; deliverance; delivery, riddance, release, setting-free, freeing, freedom, liberation, extrication, rescue; emergence, issuance, issue, outlet, vent; leakage, leak; jailbreak, prisonbreak; evasion; flight; retreat; French leave; hooky; elopment; escapology; escapism

2 **narrow escape,** hairbreadth escape, close call, close shave, near miss, near go, near thing, near squeak, narrow squeak, close squeeze, tight squeeze, squeaker

3 <escape aid> bolt-hole, escape hatch, fire escape, life net, lifeboat, life raft, life buoy, lifeline, sally port, slide, inflatable slide, ejection seat, ejector

seat, emergency exit, escapeway, back door, trapdoor, secret passage

4 **loophole,** way out, way of escape, hole to creep out of, escape hatch, escape clause, saving clause, technicality; pretext; alternative, choice

5 **escapee,** escaper, evader; escape artist; escapologist; runaway, fugitive; escapist, Houdini

VERBS 6 **escape,** make one's escape, effect one's escape, make good one's escape; **get away,** make a getaway; free oneself, deliver oneself, gain one's liberty, get free, get clear of, bail out, get out, get out of, get well out of; break loose, cut loose, break away, break one's bonds, break one's chains, slip the collar, shake off the yoke; jump, skip; break jail, break prison, escape prison, fly the coop; leap over the wall; evade; flee; vamoose, take it on the lam

7 **get off,** go free, win freedom, go at liberty, go scot free, escape with a whole skin, escape without penalty, walk, beat the rap; get away with, get by, get by with, get off easy, get off lightly, get away with murder, get off cheap; cop a plea, cop out, get off on a technicality

8 scrape through, squeak through, squeak by, escape by the skin of one's teeth, have a close call, have a close shave

9 **slip away,** give one the slip, slip through one's hands, slip through one's fingers; slip through, sneak through; slip out of, slide out of, crawl out of, creep out of, sneak out of, wiggle out of, squirm out of, shuffle out of, wriggle out of, worm out of, find a loophole, elude

10 **find vent,** issue forth, come forth, exit, emerge, issue, debouch, erupt, break out, break through, come out, run out, leak out, ooze out

ADJS 11 **escaped,** loose, on the loose, disengaged, out of, well out of; fled, flown; fugitive, runaway; free as a bird, scot-free, at large, free

370 ABANDONMENT

<leaving or withdrawing support>

NOUNS 1 **abandonment, forsaking,** leaving, jilting; jettison, jettisoning, throwing overboard, throwing away, throwing aside, casting away, casting aside; withdrawal, evacuation, pulling out, absentation; cessation; disuse, desuetude

2 **desertion,** defection, ratting; dereliction, decampment; secession, bolt, breakaway, walkout; betrayal; schism, apostasy; deserter

3 <giving up> **relinquishment,** surrender, resignation, renouncement, renunciation, abdication, waiver, abjurement, abjuration, ceding, cession, handing over, standing down, stepping down, yielding, forswearing; withdrawing, dropping out

4 **derelict,** castoff; jetsam, flotsam, lagan, flotsam and jetsam; waifs and strays; rubbish, **junk,** trash, refuse, waste, waste product, solid waste; liquid waste, wastewater; dump, dump site, garbage dump, landfill, sanitary landfill, junkheap, junkpile, scrap heap, midden; abandonee, waif, throwaway, orphan, dogie; castaway; foundling; wastrel, reject, deselect, discard

VERBS 5 **abandon, desert, forsake**; quit, leave, leave behind, take leave of, depart from, absent oneself from, turn one's back upon, turn one's tail upon, say goodbye to, bid a long farewell to, walk away, walk out on, run out on, leave flat, leave high and dry, leave holding the bag, leave in the lurch, leave one to one's fate, throw to the wolves; withdraw, back out, drop out, pull out, stand down; go back on, go back on one's word; beg off, renege; vacate, evacuate; quit cold, toss aside; jilt, throw over; maroon; jettison; junk, deep-six, discard; let fall into disuse, let fall into desuetude

6 **defect,** secede, bolt, break away; pull out, withdraw one's support, decamp; sell out, sell down the river, betray; turn one's back on; apostatize

7 **give up, relinquish,** surrender, yield, yield up, waive, forgo, resign, renounce, throw up, abdicate, abjure, forswear, give up on, have done with, give up as a bad job, cede, hand over, lay down, wash one's hands of, write off, drop, drop all idea of, drop like a hot potato; cease, desist from, leave off, give over; hold one's hand, stay one's hand, cry quits, acknowledge defeat, throw in the towel, throw in the sponge

ADJS 8 **abandoned, forsaken,** deserted, left; untouristed; disused; derelict, castaway, jettisoned; marooned; junk, junked, discarded

371 CHOICE

<picking or choosing>

NOUNS 1 **choice, selection,** election, preference, decision, pick, choosing, free choice; alternativity; co-option, co-optation; will, volition, free will; preoption, first choice; designee; the pick

2 **option,** discretion, pleasure, will and pleasure; optionality; possible choice, alternative, alternate choice, possible action

3 **dilemma,** Scylla and Charybdis, quandary, fix, bind, the devil and the deep blue sea; *embarras de choix* <Fr>; choice of Hercules; Hobson's choice, **no choice,** only choice, zero option; limited choice, positive discrimination, affirmative action; lesser of two evils

4 **adoption, embracement,** acceptance, espousal; affiliation
5 **preference, predilection,** proclivity, bent, affinity, prepossession, predisposition, partiality, inclination, leaning, tilt, penchant, bias, tendency, taste, favoritism; favor, fancy, preferment; prejudice; personal choice, particular choice, druthers; chosen kind, chosen sort, style, one's cup of tea, type, bag, thing; way of life, lifestyle
6 **vote,** voting, suffrage, franchise, enfranchisement, voting right, right to vote; voice, say; representation; poll, polling, canvass, canvassing, counting heads, counting noses, counting hands, exit poll; ballot, balloting, secret ballot, absentee ballot; ballot box, voting machine; plebiscite, plebiscitum, referendum; yeas and nays, yea, aye, yes, nay, no; voice vote, *viva voce* vote; rising vote; hand vote, show of hands; absentee vote, proxy; casting vote, deciding vote; write-in vote, write-in; graveyard vote; single vote, plural vote; transferable vote, nontransferable vote; direct vote; Hare system, list system, cumulative voting, preferential voting, proportional representation; straw vote, straw poll; informal vote; record vote, snap vote
7 **selector,** chooser, optant, elector, balloter, **voter;** delegate, superdelegate; electorate; electoral college
8 **nomination,** designation, naming, proposal
9 **election,** appointment; political election; caucus; primary election, general election
10 **selectivity,** selectiveness, picking and choosing; choosiness; eclecticism; discretion, discrimination
11 **eligibility,** qualification, fitness, fittedness, suitability, acceptability, worthiness, desirability; competency
12 **elect,** elite, the chosen, the cream, crème de la crème; president-elect

VERBS 13 **choose, elect,** pick, go with, opt, opt for, co-opt, make one's choice, take one's choice, make choice of, have one's druthers, use one's option, take up one's option, exercise one's option, exercise one's discretion; shop around, pick and choose
14 **select,** make a selection; **pick,** handpick, pick out, single out, choose, like, choose out, smile on, give the nod, jump at, seize on; extract, excerpt; decide between, choose up sides, cull, glean, winnow, sift; side with; cherry-pick, separate the wheat from the chaff, separate the sheep from the goats
15 **adopt;** approve, ratify, pass, carry, endorse, sign off on; take up, go in for; accept, take on up on, embrace, advance, espouse; affiliate
16 **decide upon,** decide on, determine upon, settle upon, fix upon, resolve upon; make a decision, take a decision, make up one's mind
17 **prefer,** have preference, favor, like better, like best, wish, prefer to, set before, set above, regard before, honor before; rather, had rather, have rather, would rather, choose rather, had sooner, had as soon, would as soon; think proper, see fit, think fit, think best, please; tilt toward, incline toward, lean toward, tend toward, have a bias, have partiality, have a penchant
18 **vote,** cast one's vote, ballot, cast a ballot; go to the polls; have a say, have a voice; hold up one's hand, exercise one's suffrage, exercise one's franchise, stand up and be counted; plump, plump for; poll, canvass
19 **nominate,** name, designate; put up, propose, submit, name for office; run, run for office
20 **elect,** vote in, place in office; appoint
21 **put to choice,** offer, present, set before; put to vote, have a show of hands

ADJS 22 **elective;** volitional, voluntary, volitive; optional, discretional; alternative, disjunctive
23 **selective,** selecting, choosing; eclectic, eclectical; elective, electoral; appointing, appointive, constituent; adoptive; exclusive, discriminating; choosy, particular
24 **eligible, qualified,** fit, fitted, suitable, acceptable, admissible, worthy, desirable; with voice, with vote, with voice and vote, enfranchised
25 **preferable,** of choice, of preference, better, preferred, to be preferred, more desirable, favored; handpicked; preferential, preferring, favoring; not to be sniffed, not to be sneezed at
26 **chosen, selected,** picked; select, elect; handpicked, singled-out; adopted, accepted, embraced, espoused, approved, ratified, passed, carried; elected, unanimously elected, elected by acclamation; appointed; nominated, designated, named

ADVS 27 **at choice,** at will, at one's will and pleasure, at one's pleasure, electively, at one's discretion, at the option of, if one wishes; on approval; optionally; alternatively
28 **preferably,** by choice, by preference, in preference; by vote, by election, by suffrage; rather than, sooner than, first, sooner, rather, before

CONJS 29 or, either . . . or; and/or

PHRS 30 one man's meat is another man's poison, there's no accounting for taste

372 REJECTION

<refusing to accept or consider>

NOUNS 1 **rejection,** repudiation; abjurement, abjuration, renouncement, renunciation; disownment, disavowal, disclamation, recantation; exclusion, exception; disapproval, nonacceptance, zero tolerance, nonapproval, declining, declination, veto, line-item veto, refusal; contradiction, denial; passing by, passing up, ignoring, nonconsideration, discounting, dismissal, disregard; throwing out, throwing away, putting out, putting away, chucking, chucking out, heave-ho; discard; turning out, turning away, repulse, a flea in one's ear, rebuff; **spurning,** kiss-off, brush-off, cold shoulder, despising, despisal, contempt; scorn, disdain; bum's rush; excommunication; throwing shade

VERBS 2 **reject, repudiate,** abjure, forswear, renounce, disown, disclaim, recant; vote out; except, exclude, deselect, include out, close out, close the door on, leave out in the cold, cut out, blackball, blacklist; disapprove, decline, refuse; contradict, deny; pass by, pass up, waive, ignore, not hear of, wave aside, brush away, brush aside, brush off, refuse to consider, discount, dismiss, dismiss out of hand; disregard; throw out, throw away, chuck, chuck out, discard; turn out, turn away, shove away, push aside, repulse, repel, slap down, smack down, rebuff, send away with a flea in one's ear, show the door, send about one's business, send packing, excommunicate; turn one's back on; spurn, disdain, scorn, contemn, make a face at, turn up one's nose at, look down one's nose at, raise one's eyebrows at, despise

ADJS 3 **rejected,** repudiated; renounced, forsworn, disowned; denied, refused; excluded, excepted; disapproved, declined; ignored, blanked, discounted, not considered, dismissed, dismissed out of hand; discarded; repulsed, rebuffed; spurned, snubbed, disdained, scorned, contemned, despised; out of the question, not to be thought of, declined with thanks; excommunicated

4 rejective; renunciative, abjuratory; declinatory; dismissive; contemptuous, despising, **scornful,** disdainful; throwing shade

373 CUSTOM, HABIT

<common usage or practice>

NOUNS 1 **custom, convention,** use, usage, standard usage, standard behavior, wont, wonting, way, established way, time-honored practice, tradition, standing custom, folkway, manner, practice, praxis, prescription, observance, ritual, rite, consuetude, mores; institution; unwritten law; proper thing, what is done, social convention; bon ton, fashion; manners, protocol, etiquette; way of life, lifestyle; conformity; generalization, labeling, stereotyping

2 **culture,** society, civilization; trait, culture trait; key trait; complex, culture complex, trait-complex; culture area; culture center; shame culture, memory culture; folkways, mores, system of values, ethos, culture pattern; cultural change; cultural lag; culture conflict; acculturation, enculturation; cultural drift; ancient wisdom

3 **habit,** habitude, **custom,** second nature, matter of course; use, usage, trick, wont, way, practice, praxis; bad habit; stereotype; pattern, habit pattern; stereotyped behavior; force of habit; creature of habit; knee-jerk reaction, automatism; peculiarity, characteristic

4 **rule, norm,** procedure, **common practice,** the way things are done, form, prescribed form, set form; common run of things, ordinary run of things, matter of course, par for the course; standard operating procedure (SOP), standard procedure, drill; standing orders

5 **routine,** run, ritual, round, beat, track, beaten path, beaten track; pattern, custom; jog trot, rut, groove, well-worn groove; daily life, treadmill, squirrel cage, hamster wheel, hedonic treadmill; the working day, nine-to-five, the grind, the daily grind; red tape, redtapeism, bureaucracy, bureaucratism

6 **customariness,** accustomedness, wontedness, **habitualness;** inveteracy, inveterateness, confirmedness, settledness, fixedness; commonness, prevalence

7 **habituation,** accustoming; conditioning, seasoning, training; onboarding; familiarization, naturalization, breaking-in, orientation, adaptation; domestication, taming, breaking, housebreaking; acclimation, acclimatization; inurement, hardening, case-hardening, assuetude, assuefaction; adaption, adjustment, accommodation

8 **addiction**; **addict**

VERBS 9 **accustom, habituate,** wont; condition, season, train; familiarize, naturalize, break in, orient, orientate; domesticate, domesticize, tame, break, gentle, housebreak; put through the mill; acclimatize, acclimate; inure, harden, case-harden; adapt, adjust, accommodate; confirm, fix, establish; acculturate, enculturate

10 **become a habit,** take root, become fixed, grow on one, take hold of one, take one over

11 **be used to,** be wont, wont, make a practice of; get used to, get into the way of, get the knack of, get the hang of, take to, accustom oneself to; catch oneself doing; fall into a habit, addict oneself to

12 get in a rut, be in a rut, travel in a groove, travel in a rut, run on in a groove, follow the beaten path, follow the beaten track

ADJS 13 **customary,** wonted, consuetudinary; traditional, time-honored, immemorial; familiar, everyday, ordinary, usual; established, received, accepted, handed down; set, prescribed, prescriptive; normative, normal; standard, regular, stock, regulation; prevalent, prevailing, widespread, obtaining, generally accepted, popular, current; conventional, orthodox; inside the box; conformist, conformable

14 **habitual, regular,** frequent, constant, persistent; repetitive, recurring, recurrent; stereotyped; knee-jerk, goose-step, lockstep, automatic; **routine,** usual, nine-to-five, workaday, well-trodden, well-worn, beaten; trite, hackneyed; predictable

15 **accustomed,** wont, wonted, used to; conditioned, trained, seasoned; experienced, familiarized, naturalized, broken-in, run-in, oriented, orientated; acclimated, acclimatized; inured, hardened, case-hardened; adapted, adjusted, well-adjusted, accommodated; housebroken, potty-trained

16 **used to,** familiar with, conversant with, at home in, at home with, no stranger to, an old hand at, *au fait* <Fr>

17 **habituated,** *habitué* <Fr>; **in the habit of,** used to; never free from; in a rut

18 **confirmed,** inveterate, chronic, established, long-established, fixed, settled, rooted, thorough; incorrigible, irreversible; **deep-rooted,** deep-set, deep-settled, deep-seated, deep-fixed, deep-dyed; infixed, ingrained, fast, dyed-in-the-wool; implanted, inculcated, instilled; set, set in one's ways, settled in habit; addicted, given

ADVS 19 **customarily,** conventionally, accustomedly, wontedly; normatively, normally, usually; as is the custom; as is usual; as things go, as the world goes

20 **habitually, regularly,** routinely, frequently, persistently, repetitively, recurringly; inveterately, chronically; from habit, by force of habit, from force of habit, as is one's wont

374 UNACCUSTOMEDNESS

<uncommon experiences>

NOUNS 1 **unaccustomedness, newness,** unwontedness, disaccustomedness, unusedness, unhabituatedness; shakiness; **unfamiliarity,** unacquaintance, unconversance, unpracticedness, newness to; inexperience; ignorance

VERBS 2 **disaccustom,** cure, break off, stop, **wean**

3 **break the habit,** cure oneself of, disaccustom oneself, kick a habit, wean oneself from, break the pattern, break one's chains, break one's fetters; give up, leave off, abandon, drop, stop, discontinue, kick, shake, throw off, rid oneself of; get on the wagon, swear off

ADJS 4 **unaccustomed,** new, disaccustomed, unused, unwonted, unwont, wontless; uninured, unseasoned, untrained, unhardened; shaky, tyronic; unhabituated, not in the habit of; out of the habit of, rusty; unweaned; unused to, **unfamiliar with,** not used to, unacquainted with, unconversant with, unpracticed, new to, a stranger to; cub, greenhorn; inexperienced; ignorant

375 MOTIVATION, INDUCEMENT

<giving a reason for action>

NOUNS 1 **motive, reason, cause,** source, spring, mainspring; matter, score, consideration; ground, basis; sake; aim, goal, end, end in view, telos, final cause; ideal, principle, ambition, aspiration, inspiration, guiding light, guiding star, lodestar; impetus; calling, vocation; intention; ulterior motive, hidden agenda; rationale, rational motive, justification, driving force, group dynamic

2 **motivation,** moving, actuation, prompting, stimulation, animation, triggering, setting-off, setting in motion, getting underway; direction, inner-direction, other-direction; influence; hot button; carrot

3 **inducement,** enlistment, engagement, solicitation, persuasion, suasion; exhortation, hortation, preaching, preachment; selling, sales talk, salesmanship, hard sell, high pressure, hawking, huckstering, flogging; jawboning, arm-twisting; lobbying; coaxing, wheedling, working on, cajolery, cajolement, conning, snow job, smoke and mirrors, nobbling, blandishment, sweet talk, soft soap, soft sell; allurement; peer pressure

4 **incitement,** incitation, **instigation,** stimulation, arousal, excitement, agitation, inflammation, excitation, fomentation, eggement, firing, stirring, stirring-up, impassioning, whipping-up, rabble-rousing; waving the bloody shirt, rallying cry; provocation, irritation, exasperation; pep talk, pep rally

5 **urging, pressure,** pressing, pushing, entreaty, plea, advocacy; encouragement, abetment; insistence, instance; goading, prodding, exhortation, goosing, spurring, pricking, needling

6 **urge,** urgency; impulse, impulsion, compulsion; press, **pressure,** drive, push; sudden impulse, rash impulse; constraint, exigency, stress, pinch

7 **incentive,** inducement, encouragement, persuasive, invitation, provocation, incitement; stimulus, stimulation, stimulative, fillip, whet; carrot; reward, payment; profit; bait, lure; palm

oil, greased palm, bribe; sweetening, sweetener, flattery, interest, percentage, what's in it for one; offer one cannot refuse; payola, pork barrel; perk

8 **goad, spur, prod,** prick, sting, gadfly; oxgoad; rowel; whip, lash, gad, crack of the whip

9 **inspiration,** infusion, infection; vision quest; fire, firing, spark, sparking; animation, exhilaration, enlivenment; afflatus, divine afflatus; genius, animus, moving spirit, animating spirit, spirit guide, spirit animal; muse; the Muses; guiding light, angel; stroke of genius

10 **prompter, mover,** prime mover, motivator, impeller, energizer, galvanizer, inducer, actuator, animator, moving spirit, mover and shaker; encourager, abettor, inspirer, firer, spark, sparker, sparkplug; persuader, salesperson, brainwasher, spin doctor; stimulator, gadfly; tempter; coaxer, coax, wheedler, cajoler, pleader

11 **instigator,** inciter, exciter, urger, motivator; provoker, *provocateur* <Fr>, *agent provocateur* <Fr>, catalyst; agitator, fomenter, inflamer; agitprop; rabble-rouser, rouser, demagogue; firebrand, incendiary; seditionist, seditionary; lobbyist, activist; troublemaker, mischief-maker, ringleader; tactician, strategist; pressure group, special-interest group

VERBS 12 **motivate, move,** set in motion, actuate, move to action, impel, propel; stimulate, energize, galvanize, animate, spark; promote, foster; force, compel; ego-involve

13 **prompt,** provoke, evoke, elicit, call up, summon up, muster up, call forth, **inspire;** bring about, **cause**

14 **urge, press**, push, work on, twist one's arm; sell, flog; insist, insist upon, push for, not take no for an answer, importune, nag, pressure, high-pressure, browbeat, bring pressure to bear upon, throw one's weight around, throw one's weight into the scale, jawbone, build a fire under, talk around; grind in; lobby, pitch, hype; coax, wheedle, cajole, blandish, plead with, sweet-talk, soft-soap, exhort, call on, call upon, advocate, recommend, put in a good word, buck for

15 **goad, prod,** poke, nudge, prod at, goose, **spur**, spur on, encourage, prick, sting, needle; whip, lash; pick at, pick on, nibble at, nibble away at

16 **urge on**, urge along, egg on, hound on, hie on, hasten on, hurry on, speed on; goad on, spur on, drive on, whip on, whip along; cheer on, root on, root from the sidelines; aid and abet

17 **incite, instigate,** put up to; set on, sic on; foment, ferment, agitate, arouse, excite, stir up, work up, whip up, turn on; rally; inflame, incense, fire, heat, heat up, impassion; provoke, pique, whet, tickle; nettle; lash into a frenzy; wave the bloody shirt; pour oil on the fire, feed the fire, add fuel to the flame, fan, fan the flame, blow the coals, stir the embers

18 **kindle,** enkindle, fire, spark, spark off, trigger, trigger off, touch off, set off, light the fuse, enflame, set afire, set on fire, turn on

19 **rouse, arouse,** raise, raise up, waken, awaken, wake up, turn on, charge up, psych up, pump up, stir, stir up, set astir, **pique**

20 **inspire,** inspirit, spirit, spirit up; fire, fire one's imagination; animate, exhilarate, enliven; infuse, infect, inject, inoculate, imbue, inform; be the reason for, lie behind

21 **encourage,** hearten, embolden, give encouragement, pat on the back, clap on the back, stroke; invite, ask for; abet, aid and abet, countenance, keep in countenance; foster, nurture, nourish, feed

22 **induce, prompt,** move one to, influence, sway, incline, dispose, carry, bring, lead, lead one to; lure; tempt; determine, decide; enlist, procure, engage, interest in, get to do

23 **persuade, prevail on**, prevail upon, prevail with, sway, convince, lead to believe, bring round, bring to reason, bring to one's senses; win, win over, win around, bring over, draw over, gain, gain over; talk over, talk into, argue into, out-talk; wangle, wangle into; hook and hook in, con, do a snow job on, nobble, sell, sell one on, charm, captivate; wear down, overcome one's resistance, arm-twist, twist one's arm, put the screws to; bribe, grease one's palm, oil one's cross one's palm; brainwash

24 **persuade oneself,** make oneself easy about, make sure of, make up one's mind; follow one's conscience; be persuaded, rest easy, come around, buy

ADJS 25 **motivating, motivational,** motive, moving, animating, actuating, impelling, driving, impulsive, inducive, directive; urgent, pressing; compelling; causal, causative; goal-oriented

26 **inspiring, inspirational**, inspiriting; infusive; animating, exhilarating, enlivening

27 **provocative, provoking,** piquant, exciting, challenging, prompting, rousing, stirring, stimulating, stimulant, stimulative, stimulatory, energizing, electric, galvanizing, galvanic; encouraging, inviting, alluring; enticing; addictive; buzzworthy

28 **incitive,** inciting, incentive; instigative, instigating; agitative, agitational; inflammatory, incendiary, fomenting, rabble-rousing

29 **persuasive,** suasive, persuading; wheedling, cajoling; hortative, hortatory; exhortative, exhortatory; hard-selling

30 **moved, motivated,** prompted, impelled, actuated; stimulated, animated; minded, inclined, of a mind to, with half a mind to; inner-directed, other-directed; soft

31 **inspired,** fired, afire, on fire

376 PRETEXT

<hiding real reason for action>

NOUNS **1** **pretext, pretense, pretension,** lying pretension, show, ostensible motive, announced motive, public, motive, professed motive; front, facade, ruse, sham; excuse, apology, protestation, poor excuse, lame excuse; occasion, mere occasion; put-off; handle, peg to hang on, leg to stand on; subterfuge, refuge, device, stratagem, feint, dipsy-doodle, swiftie, trick; dust thrown in the eye, smoke screen, screen, cover, stalking-horse, blind; guise, semblance; mask, cloak, veil; cosmetics, mere cosmetics, gloss, varnish, color, coat of paint, whitewash; spit and polish; cover-up, cover story, alibi; Band-Aid

2 **claim,** profession, allegation

VERBS **3** pretext, make a pretext of, take as an excuse, take as a reason, urge as a motive, **pretend,** make a pretense of; put up a front, put up a false front; **allege, claim,** profess, purport, avow; protest too much

4 **hide under,** cover oneself with, shelter under, take cover under, wrap oneself in, cloak oneself with, mantle oneself with, take refuge in; conceal one's motive with; cover, cover up, gloss over, varnish over, apply a coat of paint, apply whitewash, stick on a Band-Aid

ADJS **5** **pretexted, pretended,** alleged, claimed, professed, purported, avowed; ostensible, hypocritical, specious; so-called, in name only

ADVS **6** **ostensibly, allegedly,** purportedly, professedly, avowedly; for the record, for public consumption; under the pretext of, as a pretext, as an excuse, as a cover, as a cover-up, as an alibi

377 ALLUREMENT

<enticing to action>

NOUNS **1** **allurement, allure,** enticement, inveiglement, invitation, come-hither, blandishment, cajolery; inducement; temptation, tantalization; seduction, seducement; beguilement, beguiling; fascination, captivation, enthrallment, entrapment, snaring; enchantment, witchery, bewitchery, bewitchment; attraction, interest, charm, glamour, appeal, magnetism; charisma; star quality; wooing; flirtation

2 **attractiveness, allure,** charmingness, bewitchingness, impressiveness, seductiveness, winsomeness, winning ways, winningness; sexiness, sex appeal

3 **lure,** charm, **come-on**, attention-getter, attention-grabber, attraction, draw, drawer, crowd-pleaser, headliner; clou, hook, gimmick, drawing card, drawcard; decoy, decoy duck; bait, ground bait, baited trap, baited hook; snare, trap; endearment; the song of the Sirens, the voice of the tempter, honeyed words; forbidden fruit

4 **tempter,** seducer, enticer, inveigler, charmer, enchanter, fascinator, tantalizer, teaser; coquette, flirt; Don Juan; Pied Piper of Hamelin; temptress, enchantress, seductress, siren; Siren, Circe, Lorelei, Parthenope; vampire, vamp, *femme fatale* <Fr>

VERBS **5** **lure,** allure, **entice, seduce,** inveigle, decoy, draw, draw on, lead on; come on to, give the come-on, give a come-hither look, bat the eyes at, make goo-goo eyes at, flirt with, flirt; woo; coax, cajole, blandish; ensnare; draw in, suck in, rope in; bait, offer bait to, bait the hook, angle with a silver hook

6 **attract, interest,** appeal, engage, impress, charismatize, fetch, catch one's eye, get one's eye, command one's attention, rivet one, attract one's interest, be attractive, tickle one's fancy; invite, summon, beckon; tempt, tantalize, titillate, tickle, tease, whet the appetite, make one's mouth water, dangle before one

7 **fascinate, captivate,** charm, becharm, spell, spellbind, cast a spell, put under a spell, beguile, intrigue, enthrall, infatuate, enrapture, transport, enravish, entrance, enchant, witch, bewitch, voodoo; carry away, sweep off one's feet, turn one's head, knock one's socks off; hypnotize, mesmerize; vamp; charismatize

ADJS **8** **alluring, fascinating,** captivating, riveting, charming, glamorous, glam, exotic, enchanting, spellful, spellbinding, entrancing, ravishing, enravishing, intriguing, enthralling, witching, bewitching; attractive, interesting, appealing, dishy, sexy, engaging, taking, eye-catching, catching, fetching, winning, winsome, prepossessing; exciting; charismatic; seductive, seducing, beguiling, enticing, inviting, come-hither; flirtatious, coquettish; coaxing, cajoling, blandishing; tempting, tantalizing, teasing, titillating, titillative, tickling; provocative; appetizing, mouth-watering, piquant; irresistible; siren, sirenic; ginchy; hypnotic, hypnic, mesmeric

ADVS **9** **alluringly, fascinatingly,** captivatingly, charmingly, enchantingly, entrancingly, enravishingly, intriguingly, beguilingly, glamorously, bewitchingly; attractively, appealingly, engagingly, winsomely; enticingly, seductively, with bedroom eyes; temptingly, provocatively; tantalizingly, teasingly; piquantly, appetizingly; irresistibly; hypnotically, mesmerically

378 BRIBERY

<offer of payment for action>

NOUNS 1 **bribery,** bribing, subornation, **corruption, graft,** bribery and corruption

2 **bribe,** bribe money, sop, sop to Cerberus, gratuity, payoff, boodle; hush money; payola; protection

VERBS 3 **bribe,** throw a sop to; grease, grease the palm, oil the palm, tickle the palm; purchase; buy, buy off, pay off; suborn, corrupt, tamper with; reach, get at, get to; approach, try to bribe; fix, take care of

ADJS 4 **bribable,** corruptible, purchasable, buyable; approachable; fixable; on the take, on the pad; venal, corrupt, bought and paid for, in one's pocket

379 DISSUASION

<advising against action>

NOUNS 1 **dissuasion,** talking out of, remonstrance, expostulation, admonition, monition, dehortation, warning, caveat, caution, cautioning; intimidation, **determent,** deterrence, scaring off, frightening off, turning around; contraindication

2 **deterrent,** determent; **discouragement,** disincentive, chilling effect, demotivation; deflection, roadblock, obstacle, red light, closed door; damp, damper, wet blanket, cold water, chill; alienation, disaffection

VERBS 3 **dissuade,** convince to the contrary, convince otherwise, talk out of; contraindicate; unconvince, unpersuade; remonstrate, expostulate, admonish, cry out against; warn, warn off, warn away, caution; enter a caveat; intimidate, scare off, frighten off, daunt, cow; turn around

4 **disincline,** indispose, disaffect, disinterest; **deter,** repel, turn from, turn away, turn aside; divert, deflect; distract, put off, turn off; wean from; discourage; pour cold water on, throw cold water on, throw a wet blanket on, lay a wet blanket on, be a wet blanket, damp, dampen, demotivate, cool, chill, quench, blunt; nip in the bud; take the starch out of, take the wind out of one's sails

ADJS 5 **dissuasive,** dissuading, disinclining, unwilling, **discouraging; deterrent,** off-putting, repellent, disenchanting; expostulatory, admonitory, monitory, cautionary; intimidating

380 INTENTION

<aim or purpose for action>

NOUNS 1 **intention, intent,** intendment, mindset, aim, effect, meaning, view, study, animus, point, purpose, function, set purpose, settled purpose, fixed purpose; sake; design, plan, project, idea, notion; quest, pursuit; proposal, prospectus, business plan; resolve, resolution, mind, will; motive; determination; desideratum, desideration, ambition, aspiration, desire; striving, nisus; work in progress

2 **objective,** object, aim, end, goal, destination, mark, object in mind, end in view, telos, final cause, ultimate aim, ultimate purpose, mission; end in itself; target, butt, bull's-eye, quintain; quarry, prey, game; reason for being, *raison d'être* <Fr>; by-purpose, by-end; the be-all and end-all; teleology

3 **intentionality,** deliberation, deliberateness, directedness; express intention, expressness, premeditation, predeliberation, preconsideration, calculation, calculatedness, predetermination, preresolution, forethought, aforethought, calculated risk

VERBS 4 **intend,** purpose, plan, purport, mean, think, propose; resolve, determine; project, design, destine; aim, aim at, take aim at, draw a bead on, set one's sights on, have designs on, go for, drive at, aspire to, be after, set before oneself, purpose to oneself, have every intention; harbor a design; desire

5 **contemplate,** meditate; envisage, envision, have in mind, have in view; have an eye to, have every intention, have a mind, have a notion, have half a mind, have half a notion, have a good notion

6 **plan, plan on,** figure on, plan for, plan out, count on, figure out, calculate, calculate on, reckon, do the math, reckon on, bargain on, bargain for, bank on, bank upon, make book on, expect, foresee

7 **premeditate,** calculate, preresolve, predetermine, predeliberate, preconsider, direct oneself, forethink, work out beforehand; plan; plot, scheme

ADJS 8 **intentional, intended,** proposed, purposed, telic, projected, designed, of design, aimed, aimed at, meant, purposeful, purposive, willful, voluntary, deliberate; deliberated; on-message; considered, studied, advised, calculated, contemplated, envisaged, envisioned, meditated, conscious, knowing, witting; planned; teleological

9 **premeditated,** predeliberated, preconsidered, predetermined, preresolved, prepense, aforethought, foremeant

ADVS 10 **intentionally, purposely,** purposefully, purposively, pointedly, on purpose, with purpose, prepensely, with a view, with an eye to, deliberately, designedly, willfully, voluntarily, of one's own accord, of one's own free will; wittingly, consciously, knowingly; advisedly, calculatedly, contemplatedly, meditatedly, premeditatedly, with premeditation, with intent, with full intent, by design, with one's eyes open; with malice aforethought, in cold blood

PREPS, CONJS 11 for, to; in order to, in order that, so, so that, so as to; **for the purpose of,** to the end that, with the intent that, with the view of, with a view to, with an eye to; in contemplation of, in consideration of; for the sake of

381 PLAN

<set of actions>

NOUNS 1 **plan, scheme,** design, method, program, device, contrivance, game, envisagement, conception, enterprise, idea, notion; organization, rationalization, systematization, schematization; charting, mapping, graphing, blueprinting; planning, calculation, figuring; planning function; long-range planning, long-range plan, long-term plan; master plan, the picture, the big picture; approach, attack, plan of attack; way, procedure; arrangement, prearrangement, system, disposition, layout, setup, lineup; schedule, timetable, time scheme, time frame; agenda, order of the day, dance card; deadline; plan of work; schema, schematism, scheme of arrangement; blueprint, guideline, guidelines, program of action; methodology; working plan, ground plan, tactical plan, strategic plan; tactics, strategy, game plan; mission statement; contingency plan; operations research; intention; forethought, foresight; back room; mise en place; Plan A, Plan B

2 **project,** projection, scheme; proposal, prospectus, proposition; scenario, game plan

3 **diagram, plot,** chart, blueprint, graph, bar graph, bar chart, pie graph, circle graph, pie chart, circle chart, area graph; flow diagram, flow chart; table; design, pattern, cartoon; sketch, draft, drawing, working drawing, rough; outline, delineation, skeleton, figure, profile; house plan, ground plan, ichnography; elevation, projection; map

4 **policy,** polity, principles, guiding principles; procedure, course, line, plan of action; creed; platform, party line; position paper; formula; rule

5 **intrigue,** web of intrigue, **plot, scheme,** deep-laid plot, deep-laid scheme, underplot, game, little game, secret plan, trick, stratagem, finesse, method; counterplot; conspiracy, confederacy, covin, complot, cabal; complicity, collusion, connivance; artifice; contrivance, contriving; scheming, schemery, plotting; finagling, machination, manipulation, maneuvering, engineering, rigging; frame-up; wire-pulling; inside job; expedient, last resort, eleventh-hour rescue; way out, loophole; search and rescue

6 **planner,** designer, deviser, contriver, framer, projector; enterpriser, entrepreneur; intrapreneur; organizer, promoter, developer, engineer; gearhead; expediter, facilitator, animator; policymaker, decision-maker; architect, tactician, strategist, strategian, mastermind, brains

7 **schemer,** plotter, counterplotter, finagler, Machiavelli; intriguer, cabalist; conspirer, conspirator, coconspirator, conniver; maneuverer, machinator, operator, opportunist, pot hunter, exploiter; wire-puller, wangler; treasure hunter, bounty hunter

VERBS 8 **plan, devise,** contrive, design, frame, shape, cast, concert, lay plans; organize, rationalize, systematize, schematize, methodize, configure, pull together, sort out; arrange, prearrange, make arrangements, set up, work up, work out; schedule; lay down a plan, shape a course, mark out a course; program; calculate, figure; project, cut out, make a projection, forecast, plan ahead; intend

9 **plot, scheme,** intrigue, be up to something; conspire, connive, collude, complot, cabal; hatch, hatch up, cook up, brew, concoct, hatch a plot, lay a plot; maneuver, machinate, finesse, operate, engineer, rig, wangle, angle, finagle; frame, frame up; counterplot, countermine

10 **plot;** map, chart, blueprint; diagram, graph; sketch, sketch in, sketch out, draw up a plan; map out, plot out, lay out, set out, mark out; lay off, mark off; design a prototype

11 **outline,** line, delineate, chalk out, brief; sketch, draft, trace; block in, block out; rough in, rough out

ADJS 12 **planned, devised,** designed, shaped, set, blueprinted, charted, mapped, contrived; plotted; premeditated; arranged; organized, rationalized, systematized, schematized, methodized, strategized; worked out, calculated, figured; projected; scheduled, on the agenda, in the works, in the pipeline, on the calendar, on the docket, on the anvil, on the carpet; tactical, strategic

13 **scheming, calculating,** designing, contriving, plotting, intriguing; resourceful; manipulatory, manipulative; opportunist, opportunistic; Machiavellian, Byzantine; conniving, connivent,

wangling, conspiring, conspiratorial, collusive; stratagemical

14 schematic, diagrammatic, configurable

382 PURSUIT

<following or chasing>

NOUNS 1 **pursuit,** pursuing, pursuance; **quest,** seeking, hunting, searching, all-points bulletin; following, follow, follow-up; tracking, trailing, tracking down, dogging, hounding, shadowing, stalking, tailing; chase, hot pursuit; hue and cry; all points bulletin (APB), dragnet, manhunt; wild-goose chase; trainspotting, aircraft spotting

2 **hunting,** gunning, shooting, venery, cynegetics, sport, sporting; **hunt, chase,** chevy, chivy <Brit>, coursing; blood sport; foxhunt, foxhunting; hawking, falconry; stalking, still hunt; scent trail

3 **fishing,** fishery; **angling,** piscatology, halieutics; fly-fishing, saltwater fishing, ice fishing, competitive fishing

4 **pursuer,** pursuant, **chaser,** follower; hunter, quester, seeker, tracker, trailer, tail

5 **hunter,** huntsman, sportsman, Nimrod; huntress, sportswoman; stalker; courser; trapper; big game hunter; jacklighter, jacker; gamekeeper; beater, whipper-in; falconer; gundog; poacher

6 **fisher,** fisherman, angler, *piscator* <L>, piscatorian, piscatorialist; Waltonian; dibber, dibbler, troller, trawler, trawlerman, dragger, jacker, jigger, bobber, guddler, tickler, drifter, drift netter, whaler, clamdigger, lobsterman

7 **quarry, game, prey,** venery, beasts of venery, victim, the hunted; kill; big game, small game

VERBS 8 **pursue, follow,** follow up, go after, take out after, take off after, bay after, run after, run in pursuit of, make after, go in pursuit of; raise the hunt, raise the hue and cry, hollo after; chase, give chase, chivy; hound, dog; quest, quest after, seek, seek out, hunt, search, send out a search party; trawl

9 **hunt,** go hunting, hunt down, chase, run, sport; engage in a blood sport; shoot, gun; course; ride to hounds, follow the hounds; track, trail; stalk, prowl after, still-hunt; poach; hound, dog; hawk, falcon; fowl; flush, start; drive, beat; jack, jacklight; trap, ensnare

10 **fish,** go fishing, angle; cast one's hook, cast one's net; bait the hook; shrimp, whale, clam, grig, still-fish, fly-fish, troll, bob, dap, dib, dibble, gig, jig; reel in

ADJS 11 **pursuing,** pursuant, following; questing, in quest of, seeking, searching; in pursuit, in hot pursuit, in full cry, tailing, chasing, trailing; hunting, cynegetic, fishing, piscatory, piscatorial, halieutic, halieutical

PREPS 12 after, **in pursuit of, in pursuance of,** in search of, on the lookout for, in the market for, out for; on the track of, on the trail of, on the scent of

INTERJS 13 <hunting cries> view halloo, yoicks; so-ho, tallyho, tallyho over, tallyho back

383 ROUTE, PATH

<way for traveling>

NOUNS 1 **route, path, way,** itinerary, **course,** track, run, line, road; trajectory, traject; direction; circuit, tour, orbit; walk, beat, round; trade route, traffic lane, sea lane, shipping lane, air lane, flight path; path of least resistance, primrose path, garden path; shortcut, detour; line of advance, line of retreat; scenic route

2 **path,** track, trail, pathway, footpath, footway, *piste* <Fr>; walkway, catwalk, skybridge, skywalk, flying bridge, flying walkway; sidewalk, walk, fastwalk, foot pavement <Brit>; boardwalk; nature trail, hiking trail; public walk, promenade, esplanade, alameda, parade, *prado* <Sp>, mall; towpath, towing path; bridle path, bridle trail; bicycle path, bicycle lane, bike lane, bike path; bus lane; berm; run, runway; beaten track, beaten path, rut, groove; garden path

3 **passageway,** pass, passage, defile; avenue, artery; corridor, aisle, aisleway, alley, lane, back alley; channel, conduit; ford, ferry, traject; opening, aperture; access, right of way, approach, inlet; exit, outlet; connection, communication; covered way, gallery, arcade, portico, colonnade, cloister, ambulatory; underpass, overpass, flyover <Brit>; tunnel, railroad tunnel, vehicular tunnel; junction, interchange, intersection

4 **byway,** bypath, byroad, bylane, bystreet, side road, side street; bypass, **detour,** roundabout way; bypaths and crooked ways, side path; back way, backstairs, back door, side door; back road, back street

5 **road, highway** <see list>, roadway, carriageway <Brit>, right-of-way; **street, alley** <see list>

6 **pavement,** paving; macadam, blacktop, bitumen, asphalt, tarmacadam, tarmac, tarvia, bituminous macadam; cement, concrete; tile, brick, paving brick; stone, paving stone, pavestone, flag, flagstone, flagging; cobblestone, cobble; gravel; washboard; curbstone, kerbstone <Brit>, edgestone; curb, kerb <Brit>, curbing; gutter, kennel <Brit>

7 **railway** <see list>, **railroad,** rail, line, track, trackage, railway line, railroad line, rail line; subway; junction; terminus, terminal, the end of

the line; roadway, roadbed, embankment; bridge, trestle

8 **cableway,** ropeway, wireway, wire ropeway, cable railway, rope railway, funicular, funicular railway; monorail; telpher, telpherway, telpher ropeway, telpher line; ski lift, chairlift, gondola, aerial tramway, tram

9 **bridge,** span, viaduct; cantilever bridge, clapper bridge, drawbridge, footbridge, pontoon bridge, rope bridge, skybridge, skywalk, flying bridge, flying walkway, suspension bridge, toll bridge, floating bridge, covered bridge, aqueduct; overpass, overcrossing, overbridge <Brit>, flyover <Brit>; stepping-stone, stepstone, catwalk; Bifrost

10 **railway**

cable railway
cog railway
electric railway
elevated railway, elevated, el, L
funicular railway
gravity-operated railway, gravity railroad
inclined railroad
light-rail rapid-transit system
mainline
métro <Fr>
monorail
rack railway, rack-and-pinion railway
scenic railroad
subway
tram, tramline, tramway, tramroad <Brit>
trolley, streetcar line
trunk, trunk line
underground, tube

11 **road, highway**

access road
arterial highway
artery
Autobahn <Ger>
autoroute <Fr>
autostrada <Ital>
beltway, circumferential, ring road, belt highway
busway
camino real <Sp>
causeway
country road
dirt road
divided highway, dual highway
expressway
fire road
freeway
highroad <Brit>
interstate highway
king's highway, queen's highway
limited access highway
main road, main drag
motorway <Brit>
parkway
pavé <Fr>
pike
post road
private road
shunpike
skyway
speedway
superhighway
switchback
throughway, thruway
toll road
trunk road
turnpike

12 **street, alley**

alley, alleyway
avenue
blind alley
boulevard
close <Brit>
court
crescent
cul-de-sac
dead-end street
drive
lane
mews
one-way street
place
row
thoroughfare
vennel <Scot>
wynd <Scot>

384 MANNER, MEANS

<way of acting>

NOUNS 1 **manner, way,** wise, **means,** mode, modality, form, fashion, style, tone, guise; method, methodology, system; algorithm; approach, attack, tack; technique, procedure, process, proceeding, measures, steps, course, practice; order; lines, line, line of action; *modus operandi* <L>, mode of operation (MO), manner of working, mode of procedure; routine; the way of, the how, the how-to, the drill

2 **means,** ways, **ways and means,** means to an end; wherewithal, wherewith; funds; resources, disposable resources, capital; bankroll; stock in trade, inventory, stock, supply; power, capacity, ability; power base, constituency, backing, support; recourses, resorts, devices; tools of the trade, tricks of the trade, bag of tricks

3 **instrumentality, agency;** machinery, mechanism, modality; gadgetry; mediation, going between, intermediation, service; expedient, recourse, resort, device

4 **instrument, tool,** implement, appliance, device; contrivance, makeshift, lever, mechanism; vehicle, organ; agent; medium, mediator, intermedium, intermediary, intermediate, interagent, liaison, go-between; expediter, facilitator, animator; midwife, servant, slave, handmaid, handmaiden; cat's-paw, puppet, dummy, pawn, creature, minion, stooge; stalking horse; toy, plaything; gadget, dupe

VERBS 5 **use, utilize,** adopt, effect; approach, attack; proceed, practice, go about; routinize

6 **find means, find a way,** have the wherewithal, develop a method; enable, facilitate; get by hook or by crook, obtain by fair means or foul; beg, borrow, or steal; think laterally; network

7 **be instrumental, serve,** subserve, serve one's purpose, come in handy, stand in good stead, fill the bill; minister to, act for, act in the interests of, promote, advance, forward, assist, facilitate; mediate, go between; liaise

ADJS 8 modal; **instrumental,** implemental; agential, agentive, agentival; effective, efficacious; **useful,** utile, handy, employable, serviceable; helpful, conducive, forwarding, favoring, promoting, assisting, facilitating; subservient, ministering, ministerial; mediating, mediatorial, intermediary

ADVS 9 how, **in what way**, in what manner, by what mode, by what means; to what extent; in what condition; by what name; at what price; after this fashion, in this way, in such wise, along these lines; thus, so, just so, thus and so; as, like, on the lines of

10 **anyhow,** anyway, anywise, anyroad, in any way, by any means, by any manner of means; in any event, at any rate, leastways, in any case; nevertheless, nonetheless, however, regardless, irregardless; at all, nohow

11 **somehow, in some way,** in some way or other, someway, by some means, somehow or other, somehow or another, in one way or another, in some such way, after a fashion; no matter how, by hook or by crook, by fair means or foul

12 herewith, therewith, wherewith, wherewithal; whereby, thereby, hereby

PREPS 13 **by means of,** by the agency of, through the agency of, by the good offices of, through the good offices of, through the instrumentality of, by the aid of, thanks to, by use of, by way of, by dint of, by the act of, through the medium of, by virtue of, at the hand of, at the hands of; with, through, by, per

PHRS 14 it isn't what you do, it's how you do it; there's more than one way to skin a cat

385 PROVISION, EQUIPMENT

<necessary supplies>

NOUNS 1 **provision,** providing; **equipment,** accouterment, fitting out, outfitting; supply, supplying, finding; furnishing, furnishment; chandlery, retailing, selling; logistics; procurement; investment, endowment, subvention, subsidy, subsidization; provisioning, victualing, purveyance, catering; armament; resupply, replenishment, reinforcement; supply line, line of supply; preparation

2 **provisions, supplies**; provender; merchandise; basics

3 **accommodations,** accommodation, facilities; lodgings; bed, board, full board; room and board, bed and board; subsistence, keep, fostering

4 **equipment,** matériel, equipage, munitions; furniture, furnishings, furnishments; fixtures, fittings, appointments, accouterments, appurtenances, trappings, installations, plumbing; appliances, utensils, conveniences; outfit, apparatus, rig, machinery, machine, moving part; stock-in-trade; plant, facility, facilities; paraphernalia, harness, things, gear, stuff, impedimenta <pl>, tackle; rigging; armament, munition; kit, duffel, effects, personal effects; government issue, military issue; industry standard

5 harness, caparison, trappings, **tack,** tackle

6 **provider, supplier,** furnisher; donor; patron; purveyor, provisioner, distributor, middleman; caterer, victualler, sutler; chandler, retailer, merchant; commissary, commissariat, quartermaster, shopkeeper, storekeeper, stock clerk, steward, manciple; grocer, vintner; procurer; megastore

VERBS 7 **provide, supply,** find, dish up, rustle up, offer up, furnish; accommodate; invest, endow, fund, subsidize; donate, give, afford, contribute, kick in, yield, present; make available; stock, store; provide for, make provision, make due provision for, plenish; prepare; support, maintain, keep; fill, fill up; replenish, restock, recruit

8 **equip, furnish, outfit,** gear, prepare, fit, fit up, fit out, fix up, rig, rig up, rig out, set up, turn out, appoint, accouter, clothe, dress; arm, heel, munition; man, staff

9 **provision,** provender, cater, victual, plenish, serve, cook for; provide a grubstake; **board,** feed; forage; fuel, gas, gas up, fill up, top off, coal, oil, bunker; purvey, sell

10 **accommodate,** furnish accommodations; house, lodge; put up, take in, board

11 **make a living,** earn a living, earn a livelihood, earn one's keep

12 **support oneself,** make one's way; make ends meet, keep body and soul together, keep the wolf from the door, keep one's head above water, hold one's head above water, keep afloat; survive, subsist, cope, eke out, make out, scrape along, manage, get by

ADJS 13 **provided, supplied, furnished,** provisioned, purveyed, catered; perquisited; invested, endowed; equipped, fitted, fitted out, outfitted, rigged, accoutered; armed, heeled; staffed, manned; readied, in place, prepared

14 **well-provided,** well-supplied, well-furnished, well-stocked, well-found; well-equipped, well-fitted, well-appointed; well-armed

386 STORE, SUPPLY

<source of supplies>

NOUNS 1 **store, hoard,** treasure, treasury; plenty, plenitude, abundance, cornucopia; heap, mass, stack, pile, dump, rick; collection, accumulation, cumulation, amassment, budget, stockpile; backlog; repertory, repertoire; stock-in-trade; inventory, stock, supply on hand; lock, stock, and barrel; stores, supplies, provisions, provisionment, rations; larder, commissariat, commissary; munitions; matériel; material, materials

2 **supply,** fund, **resource, resources**; means, assets, liquid assets, net asset; balance, pluses, black-ink items, financial resources, capital, capital goods, capitalization, available means, available resources, available funds, cash flow, stock in trade; venture capital; backing, support; grist, grist for the mill; holdings, property; labor resources

3 **reserve, reserves,** reservoir, resource; proved reserve, proven reserve; **stockpile, cache,** backup, reserve supply, store, standby, safeguard, something in reserve, something in hand, something to fall back on, reserve fund, emergency funds, nest egg, savings, petty cash, sinking fund; trust fund; proved reserves; backlog, unexpended balance; ace in the hole, a card up one's sleeve, an ace up one's sleeve; spare part, replacement part

4 **source of supply,** source, staple, resource; well, fountain, fount, font, spring, wellspring; mine, gold mine, bonanza, luau; quarry, lode, vein; oilfield, oil well, oil rig; cornucopia

5 **storage,** stowage; preservation, conservation, safekeeping, warehousing; cold storage, cold store, dry storage, dead storage; storage space, shelf-room; custody, guardianship; sequestration, escrow

6 **storehouse, storeroom,** stockroom, box room <Brit>, lumber room, store, storage, depository, repository, conservatory, reservoir, repertory, depot, supply depot, supply base, magazine, warehouse, megastore, big-box store, factory store, warehouse store, warehouse club, duty-free shop; bonded warehouse, entrepôt; dock; hold, cargo dock; attic, loft, cellar, basement, crawl space; closet, cupboard; wine cellar, larder; shed, stable, garage; treasury, treasure house, treasure room, exchequer, coffers; bank, vault, strongroom, strongbox; archives, library, stack room; armory, arsenal, dump; lumberyard; drawer, shelf; bin, bunker, bay, crib; rack, rick; vat, tank; elevator; crate, box; chest, locker, hutch; bookcase, stack; sail locker, chain locker, lazaret, lazaretto, glory hole

7 garner, **granary,** grain bin, elevator, grain elevator, **silo;** mow, haymow, hayloft, hayrick; crib, corncrib

8 **larder, pantry,** buttery; spence, stillroom <Brit>; root cellar; dairy, dairy bar

9 **museum; gallery,** art gallery, picture gallery, pinacotheca; science museum, natural history museum; salon; waxworks; museology, curatorship

VERBS **10** **store, stow,** lay in store; lay in, lay in a supply, lay in a store, store away, stow away, put away, lay away, put by, lay by, pack away, bundle away, lay down, stow down, salt down, salt away, sock away, squirrel away; deposit, reposit, lodge; cache, stash, bury away; bank, coffer, hutch; warehouse, reservoir; file, file away

11 **store up, stock up,** lay up, put up, save up, hoard up, treasure up, garner up, heap up, pile up, build up a stock, build up an inventory, provision; accumulate, cumulate, collect, amass, **stockpile;** backlog; garner, gather into barns; **hoard,** treasure, save, keep, hold, squirrel, squirrel away; hide, secrete

12 **reserve, save,** conserve, keep, retain, husband, husband one's resources, keep back, hold back, withhold; keep in reserve, keep in store, keep on hand, keep by one; sequester, put in escrow; preserve; set aside, put aside, set apart, put apart, put by, lay by, set by; save up, save to fall back upon, keep as a nest egg, save for a rainy day, provide for a rainy day

13 **have in store, have in reserve,** have to fall back upon, have something to draw on, have something laid by, have something laid by for a rainy day, have something up one's sleeve

ADJS **14** **stored, accumulated,** amassed, laid up, stocked; gathered, garnered, collected, heaped, piled; **stockpiled;** backlogged; **hoarded,** treasured; big-box

15 **reserved,** preserved, **saved,** conserved, put by, put aside, kept, retained, held, filed, withheld, held back, kept in reserve, held in reserve; in storage, warehoused, mothballed; bottled, pickled, canned, refrigerated, frozen; spare

ADVS **16** **in store,** in stock, in supply, on hand

17 **in reserve,** back, aside, by

387 USE

<using or utilizing>

NOUNS **1** **use, employment,** utilization, employ, usage; exercise, exertion, active use, wear; good use; ill use, wrong use, misuse; hard use, hard usage, rough usage; hard wear, heavy duty; application, appliance, deployment; expenditure, expending, using up, exhausting, dissipation, dissipating, consumption

2 **usage,** treatment, handling, management; way of dealing, means of dealing; stewardship, custodianship, guardianship, care

3 **utility, usefulness,** usability, use, utilizability, avail, good, advantage, benefit, added value, serviceability, service, helpfulness, functionality, profitability, applicability, availability, practicability, practicality, practical utility, operability, effectiveness, efficacy, efficiency;

readiness; instrumentality; ultimate purpose; bankability

4 **benefit, use,** service, avail, profit, advantage, point, percentage, mileage, what's in it for one, convenience; interest, behalf, behoof; value, worth, fruitfulness; commonweal, public good

5 **function, use,** purpose, role, part, point, end use, immediate purpose, ultimate purpose, operational purpose, operation; work, duty, office

6 **functionalism, utilitarianism;** pragmatism, pragmaticism; functional design, functional furniture, functional housing

7 <law terms> usufruct, imperfect usufruct, perfect usufruct, right of use, user, enjoyment of property; *jus primae noctis* <L>, *droit du seigneur* <Fr>; disposal; possession

8 **utilization,** using, making use of, making instrumental, using as a means, using as a tool; employment, employing; management, manipulation, handling, working, operation, exploitation, recruiting, recruitment, calling upon, calling into service; mobilization, mobilizing

9 **user,** employer; **consumer,** enjoyer, exploiter; customer, client; end user

VERBS 10 **use, utilize,** make use of, do with; employ, practice, ply, work, manage, handle, manipulate, operate, wield, play, exercise; have the use of, enjoy the use of; exert; reuse, repurpose, upcycle

11 **apply, put to use, put to good use,** carry out, put into execution, put into practice, put into operation, put in force, enforce; bring to bear upon, operationalize

12 **treat,** handle, manage, use, deal with, cope with, come to grips with, take on, tackle, contend with, do with; steward, care for

13 **spend,** consume, expend, pass, employ, put in; devote, bestow, give to, give over to, devote to, consecrate to, dedicate to; while, while away, wile; dissipate, **exhaust, use up**

14 **avail oneself of, make use of,** resort to, put to use, put to good use, have recourse to, turn to, look to, recur to, refer to, take to, betake oneself to; revert to, fall back on, fall back upon, rely on; convert to use, turn to use, put into requisition, press into service, enlist into service, lay under contribution, impress, call upon, call into play, bring into play, draw on, draw upon, recruit, muster; pick someone's brains

15 **take advantage of,** avail oneself of, make the most of, use to the full, make good use of, maximize, improve, turn to use, turn to profit, turn to account, turn to good account, turn to advantage, turn to good advantage, use to advantage, put to advantage, find one's account in, find one's advantage in; improve the occasion; profit by, benefit from, reap the benefit of; exploit, capitalize on, make capital of, make a good thing of, make hay, trade on, cash in on, play on, play off against; make the best of, make a virtue of necessity, make necessity a virtue

16 <take unfair advantage of> **exploit,** take advantage of, use, make use of, use for one's own ends; make a cat's-paw of, make a pawn of, sucker, play for a sucker; manipulate, work on, work upon, stroke, play on, play upon; play both ends against the middle; impose upon, presume upon; use ill, ill-use, abuse, misuse; batten on; milk, bleed, bleed white; drain, suck the blood from, suck dry; exploit one's position, feather one's nest, profiteer

17 **avail,** be of use, be of service, serve, suffice, do, answer, answer one's purpose, serve one's purpose, serve one's need, fill the bill, do the trick, suit one's purpose; bestead, stand one in good stead, be handy, come in handy, stand one in hand; advantage, be of advantage, be of service to; profit, benefit, pay, pay off, give good returns, yield a profit, bear fruit

ADJS 18 **useful,** employable, of use, of service, serviceable, commodious; good for; helpful, of help; advantageous, to one's advantage, to one's profit, profitable, remuneratory, bankable, beneficial; **practical,** banausic, pragmatical, **functional, utilitarian,** of general utility, of general application; fitting, proper, appropriate, expedient; well-used, well-thumbed; reusable, recyclable

19 **using, exploitive,** exploitative, manipulative, manipulatory

20 **handy, convenient;** available, accessible, ready, at hand, to hand, **on hand,** on tap, on deck, on call, at one's call, at one's beck and call, at one's elbow, at one's fingertips, just around the corner, at one's disposal; versatile, adaptable, all-around, of all work; crude but effective, quick and dirty; to the purpose; fast-food, convenience; one-stop

21 **effectual, effective,** active, efficient, efficacious, operative; instrumental; subsidiary, subservient

22 **valuable,** of value, all for the best, all to the good, profitable, bankable, yielding a return, well-spent, worthwhile, rewarding; gainful, remunerative, moneymaking, lucrative

23 **usable, utilizable**; applicable, appliable, employable, serviceable; practical, operable; reusable, recyclable; exploitable; manipulable, pliable, compliant; at one's service

24 **used,** employed, exercised, exerted, applied; previously owned, pre-owned, preloved, secondhand

25 **in use, in practice,** in force, in effect, in service, in operation, in commission

ADVS 26 **usefully,** to good use; profitably, advantageously, to advantage, to profit, to good effect; effectually, effectively, efficiently; serviceably, functionally, practically; handily, conveniently; by use of, by dint of

388 CONSUMPTION

<using up something>

NOUNS 1 **consumption, consuming,** using up, eating up; burning up; absorption, assimilation, digestion, ingestion, expenditure, expending, spending; squandering, wastefulness; finishing; depletion, drain, exhausting, exhaustion, impoverishment; waste, wastage, wasting away, erosion, ablation, wearing down, wearing away, attrition; throwing away

2 **consumable,** consumable item, consumable goods; nonrenewable resource, nonreusable item, nonrecyclable item, nonrecyclable resource; throwaway, throwaway item, disposable goods, disposable item; throwaway culture, throwaway psychology, instant obsolescence

VERBS 3 **consume,** spend, expend, **use up**; max out; absorb, assimilate, digest, ingest, eat, eat up, swallow, swallow up, gobble, gobble up; burn up; finish, finish off; exhaust, deplete, impoverish, drain, drain of resources; suck dry, bleed white, suck one's blood; wear away, erode, erode away, ablate; waste away; throw away, squander

4 **be consumed, be used up,** waste; run out, give out, peter out; run dry, dry up

ADJS 5 **used up, consumed,** eaten up, burnt up; finished, gone; unreclaimable, irreplaceable; nonrenewable, nonrecyclable, nonreusable; spent, exhausted, maxed-out, effete, dissipated, depleted, impoverished, drained, worn-out; worn away, eroded, ablated; out of, outta, wasted

6 **consumable, expendable,** spendable; exhaustible; replaceable; disposable, throwaway, no-deposit, no-deposit-no-return

389 MISUSE

<using incorrectly>

NOUNS 1 **misuse, misusage, abuse**, wrong use; misemployment, misapplication; mishandling, mismanagement, poor stewardship; corrupt administration, malversation, breach of public trust, maladministration; diversion, defalcation, misappropriation, conversion, embezzlement, peculation, pilfering, fraud; perversion, prostitution; profanation, violation, pollution, fouling, befoulment, desecration, defilement, debasement; malpractice, abuse of office, misconduct, malfeasance, misfeasance

2 **mistreatment**, ill-treatment, maltreatment, ill-use, ill-usage, abuse, verbal abuse; molesting, molestation, child abuse, child molestation; spousal abuse; self-abuse; violation, outrage, violence, injury, atrocity; cruel and unusual punishment; overuse

3 **persecution,** oppression, harrying, hounding, tormenting, bashing, harassment, nobbling, victimization, torture; witch-hunting, witch-hunt, red-baiting, McCarthyism; Spanish inquisition; open season, piling on

VERBS 4 **misuse,** misemploy, abuse, misapply; mishandle, mismanage, maladminister; divert, misappropriate, expropriate, convert, defalcate, embezzle, defraud, pilfer, peculate, feather one's nest; pervert, prostitute; profane, violate, pollute, foul, foul one's own nest, spoil, befoul, desecrate, defile, debase; verbally abuse, bad-mouth; misuse power, abuse power

5 **mistreat**, maltreat, ill-treat, ill-use, abuse, injure, molest; do wrong to, do wrong by; outrage, do violence to, do one's worst to; mishandle, manhandle; buffet, batter, bruise, savage, maul, knock about, rough, rough up; pollute; overuse, overwork, overtax

6 <offensive or nonformal> **screw,** screw over, shaft, kick around, stiff, give the short end of the stick, give the shitty end of the stick*, fuck*, fuck over*

7 **persecute,** oppress, torment, victimize, play cat and mouse with, harass, get after, keep after, get at, keep at, harry, hound, beset, nobble; pursue, hunt

ADVS 8 on one's back, on one's case, in one's face

390 DISUSE

<discontinuing use>

NOUNS 1 **disuse,** disusage, desuetude; **nonuse,** nonemployment; abstinence, abstention; neglect; inusitation; nonprevalence, unprevalence; **obsolescence,** obsoleteness, obsoletism, obsoletion, planned obsolescence; superannuation, retirement, pensioning off, early retirement; redundancy <Brit>

2 **discontinuance,** cessation, desisting, desistance; abdication, relinquishment, forebearance, resignation, renunciation, renouncement, abjurement, abjuration; waiver, nonexercise; abeyance, suspension, back burner, cold storage, limbo, bardo; phaseout, abandonment

3 **discard,** discarding, jettison, deep six,

disposal, dumping, waste disposal, solid waste disposal, burning, incineration, ocean burning, ocean incineration; compacting; scrapping, junking; removal, elimination; rejection; reject, throwaway, castaway, castoff, remains, rejectamenta <pl>; refuse

VERBS 4 **cease to use;** abdicate, relinquish; discontinue, disuse, quit, stop, drop, give up, give over, lay off, phase out, phase down, put behind one, let go, leave off, come off, cut out, desist, desist from, have done with; waive, resign, renounce, abjure, neglect; nol-pros, not pursue, not proceed with; decommission, put out of commission

5 **not use,** do without, dispense with, let alone, not touch, hold off; abstain, refrain, forgo, forbear, spare, waive; keep back, hold back, reserve, save, save up, sock away, squirrel away, tuck away, put under the mattress, hoard; keep in hand, have up one's sleeve; see the last of

6 **put away,** lay away, put aside, lay aside, set aside, push aside, sideline, put by, lay by, set by; stow, store; pigeonhole, shelve, put on the shelf, put in mothballs; table, lay on the table; table the motion, pass to the order of the day; put on hold, put on the back burner, postpone, delay

7 **discard,** reject, throw away, throw out, chuck, chuck away, shitcan*, eighty-six, cast, cast off, cast away, cast aside; get rid of, get quit of, get shut of, rid oneself of, shrug off, dispose of, slough, dump, ditch, jettison, throw overboard, heave overboard, toss overboard, deep-six, throw out the window, throw to the dogs, cast to the dogs, cast to the winds; sell off, sell out; throw over, jilt; part with, give away; throw to the wolves, write off, walk away from, abandon; remove, eliminate

8 **scrap, junk**, consign to the scrap heap, throw on the junk heap; superannuate, retire, pension off, put out to pasture, put out to grass

9 **obsolesce,** fall into disuse, go out, pass away; be superseded; superannuate

ADJS 10 **disused,** abandoned, deserted, discontinued, done with, derelict; out, out of use; old; relinquished, resigned, renounced, abjured; decommissioned, out of commission; outworn, worn-out, past use, not worth saving; **obsolete,** obsolescent, life-expired, superannuated, superannuate; superseded, outdated, out-of-date, outmoded, desuete; retired, pensioned off; on the shelf; written off; antique, antiquated, old-fashioned

11 **discarded,** rejected, castoff, castaway, scrapped, junked

12 **unused,** unutilized, unemployed, unapplied, unexercised; in abeyance, suspended; waived; unspent, unexpended, unconsumed; held back, held out, put by, put aside, saved, held in reserve, in hand, spare, to spare, extra, reserve; stored; untouched, unhandled; untapped; untrodden, unbeaten; new, brand-new, original, pristine, virgin, fresh, fresh off the assembly line, mint, in mint condition, factory-fresh; underused, underutilized

391 USELESSNESS

<not being useful>

NOUNS 1 **uselessness,** inutility; needlessness, unnecessity; unserviceability, **unusability,** unemployability, inoperativeness, inoperability, disrepair; unhelpfulness; inapplicability, unsuitability, unfitness; functionlessness; otioseness, otiosity; redundancy, tautology; superfluousness; excess baggage

2 **futility,** vanity, emptiness, hollowness; **fruitlessness,** bootlessness, unprofitableness, profitlessness, unprofitability, otiosity, worthlessness, valuelessness; triviality, nugacity, nugaciousness; unproductiveness; ineffectuality, ineffectiveness, inefficacy; impotence; effeteness; pointlessness, meaninglessness, purposelessness, aimlessness, fecklessness; the absurd, absurdity; inanity, fatuity; vicious circle, vicious cycle; rat race

3 **labor in vain,** labor lost, labor for naught; labor of Sisyphus, work of Penelope, Penelope's web; wild-goose chase, snipe hunt, bootless errand; waste of energy, waste of labor, waste of breath, waste of time, waste of effort, wasted effort, wasted breath, wasted labor; red herring; fool's errand; blind alley

4 **refuse, waste,** wastage, waste matter, waste stream, waste product, solid waste, liquid waste, wastewater, gray water, effluent, sewage, sludge; incinerator ash; industrial waste, hazardous waste, toxic waste, toxin, atomic waste, dumping; hazardous materials, HAZMAT; medical waste; offal; leavings, sweepings, dust, scraps, orts; garbage, gash, swill, pig-swill, slop, slops, hogwash; bilgewater; draff, lees, dregs; offscourings, scourings, rinsings, dishwater; parings, raspings, filings, shavings; scum; chaff, stubble, husks; weeds, tares; deadwood; rags, bones, wastepaper, shard, potsherd; scrap iron; slag, culm, slack

5 **rubbish,** rubble, trash, junk, shoddy, riffraff, raff, scrap, dust, **debris, litter,** lumber, truck

6 **trash pile,** rubbish heap, junkheap, junkpile, scrap heap, dustheap, dustbin, midden,

kitchen midden; wasteyard, junkyard, scrapyard, **dump,** dumpsite, garbage dump, landfill, sanitary landfill, toxic waste dump, dumping; garbology

7 wastepaper basket, wastebasket, shitcan*; litter basket, litter bin; garbage bag, garbage can, garbage pail, trash can, wastebin, dustbin <Brit>; Dumpster <tm>, skip <Brit>; garbage disposal, waste disposal unit, trash compactor, compactor, garbage grinder; compost, compost heap, compost pile, composter; circular file, file 13; recycling bin

VERBS 8 **be useless, be futile,** make no difference, cut no ice; die aborning; labor in vain, go on a wild-goose chase, run in circles, go around in circles, fall by the wayside, spin one's wheels, bang one's head against a brick wall, beat the air, lash the waves, tilt at windmills, sow the sand, bay at the moon, waste one's effort, waste one's breath, preach to the choir, speak to the winds, beat a dead horse, flog a dead horse, roll the stone of Sisyphus, carry coals to Newcastle, milk the ram, milk a he-goat into a sieve, pour water into a sieve, hold a farthing candle to the sun, look for a needle in a haystack, lock the barn door after the horse is stolen; attempt the impossible

ADJS 9 **useless,** of no use, no go; aimless, meaningless, purposeless, of no purpose, pointless, feckless; unavailing, of no avail, no avail, failed; ineffective, ineffectual; impotent; superfluous; frustaneous; dud

10 **needless,** unnecessary, unessential, nonessential, unneeded, uncalled-for, unrequired; unrecognized, neglected; tautological, tautologic, redundant

11 **worthless,** valueless, good-for-nothing, good-for-naught, no-good (NG), no-account, dear at any price, worthless as tits on a boar, not worth a dime, not worth a red cent, not worth a hill of beans, not worth shit*, not worth bubkes, not worth the paper it's written on, not worthwhile, not worth having, not worth mentioning, not worth speaking of, not worth a thought, not worth a damn, not worth the powder to blow it to hell, not worth the powder and shot, not worth the pains, not worth the trouble, of no earthly use, fit for the junkyard; trivial, penny-ante, nugatory, nugacious; junk, junky; cheap, shoddy, trashy, shabby

12 **fruitless,** gainless, profitless, bootless, otiose, **unprofitable,** unremunerative, nonremunerative; uncommercial; unrewarding, rewardless; abortive; barren, sterile, unproductive

13 **vain, futile,** hollow, empty, idle, unavailing; absurd; inane, fatuous, fatuitous

14 **unserviceable, unusable,** unemployable, inoperative, inoperable, unworkable; out of order, out of whack, on the blink, on the fritz, in disrepair; **unhelpful,** unconducive; inapplicable; unsuitable, unfit; functionless, nonfunctional, nonfunctioning, otiose, nonutilitarian; kaput

ADVS 15 **uselessly; needlessly,** unnecessarily; bootlessly, fruitlessly; futilely, vainly; purposelessly, to little purpose, to no purpose, aimlessly, pointlessly, fecklessly; tautologically

392 IMPROVEMENT

<making something better>

NOUNS 1 **improvement, betterment,** bettering, change for the better, turn for the better; melioration, amelioration; sea change; mend, mending, amendment; progress, progression, headway; breakthrough, quantum jump, quantum leap; advance, advancement; upward mobility; promotion, furtherance, preferment; rise, ascent, lift, uplift, uptick, upswing, uptrend, upbeat, edification; increase, upgrade, upping, boost, pickup; gentrification; enhancement, enrichment, good influence; euthenics, eugenics; restoration, revival, retro, recovery, comeback

2 **development,** refinement, elaboration, perfection; beautification, embellishment; maturation, coming-of-age, ripening, evolution, seasoning

3 **cultivation,** culture, refinement, polish, civility; cultivation of the mind; civilization; acculturation; enculturation, socialization; enlightenment, Age of Enlightenment, Age of Reason; education

4 **revision,** revise, revisal; revised edition; emendation, amendment, correction, corrigenda, rectification; editing, redaction, recension, revampment, blue-penciling; rewrite, rewriting, rescript, rescription; polishing, touching up, putting on the finishing touches, putting the gloss on, finishing, perfecting, tuning, fine-tuning; retrofitting; spell-checking

5 **reform,** reformation; regeneration; transformation; conversion; makeover; reformism, meliorism; gradualism, Fabianism, revisionism; utopianism; progressiveness, progressivism, progressism; radical reform, extremism, radicalism; revolution; quiet revolution; perestroika

6 **reformer,** reformist, meliorist; gradualist, Fabian, revisionist; utopian, utopist; progressive, progressivist, progressionist, progressist; resister, passive resister; radical, extremist; revolutionary; comeback kid

VERBS 7 <**get better**> **improve,** grow better, look better, show improvement, mend, amend, meliorate, ameliorate; look up, pick up, perk up; develop, shape up; advance, progress, make progress, make headway, gain, gain ground, go forward, get ahead, go ahead, come on, come along, come along nicely, get along; make strides, make rapid strides, take off, skyrocket, make up for lost time, turn around; straighten up and fly right; make the grade, graduate

8 **rally,** come about, come round, come back, take a favorable turn, get over, take a turn for the better, gain strength; come a long way; recuperate, recover

9 **improve, better,** change for the better, make an improvement; transform, transfigure; vet; improve upon, refine upon, mend, amend, emend; meliorate, ameliorate; advance, promote, foster, favor, nurture, forward, bring forward; lift, elevate, uplift, raise, boost; upgrade; gentrify; enhance, enrich, fatten, lard; make one's way, better oneself; be the making of; reform, put straight, set straight; reform oneself, turn over a new leaf, mend one's ways, straighten out, straighten oneself out, go straight; get it together, get one's ducks in a row; civilize, acculturate, socialize; enlighten, edify; educate

10 **develop,** elaborate; beautify, embellish; **cultivate;** come of age, come into its own, mature, ripen, evolve, season; gild the lily; formulate

11 **perfect, touch up,** finish, put on the finishing touches, polish, polish up, fine down, fine-tune, tone up, brush up, furbish, furbish up, spruce, spruce up, freshen, vamp, vamp up, rub up, brighten up, shine; retouch; revive, renovate; repair, fix; retrofit; streamline

12 **revise,** redact, recense, revamp, rewrite, redraft, rework, work over, retool; emend, amend, emendate, rectify, correct; edit, blue-pencil; straighten out; autocorrect; vet

ADJS 13 **improved, bettered;** changed for the better, advanced, ameliorated, enhanced, enriched, touched up; developed, perfected; beautified, embellished; upgraded; gentrified; reformed; transformed, transfigured, converted; cultivated, cultured, refined, polished, emended, civilized; educated

14 **better,** better off, better for, all the better for; before-and-after

15 **improving, bettering;** meliorative, ameliorative, amelioratory, medial; progressive, progressing, advancing, ongoing; mending, on the mend; on the lift, on the rise, on the upswing, on the upbeat, on the upgrade, looking up

16 **emendatory, corrective;** revisory, revisional; reformatory, reformative, reformational; reformist, reformistic, progressive, progressivist, melioristic; gradualistic, Fabian, revisionist; utopian; radical; revolutionary

17 **improvable,** ameliorable, corrigible, revisable, perfectible; emendable; curable

393 IMPAIRMENT

<making something worse>

NOUNS 1 **impairment, damage,** injury, harm, mischief, scathe, hurt, detriment, loss, weakening, sickening; worsening, disimprovement; disablement, incapacitation; collateral damage; encroachment, inroad, infringement; disrepair, dilapidation, ruinousness; breakage; breakdown, collapse, crash, crack-up; malfunction, glitch; bankruptcy; hurting, spoiling, ruination; sabotage, monkey-wrenching; mayhem, mutilation, crippling, hobbling, hamstringing, laming, maiming; destruction; the skids

2 **corruption**, pollution, contamination, vitiation, defilement, fouling, befouling; poisoning, envenoming; infection, festering, suppuration; perversion, prostitution, misuse; denaturing, adulteration

3 **deterioration,** decadence, decadency, degradation, debasement, derogation, deformation; degeneration, degeneracy, degenerateness, effeteness; etiolation, loss of tone, failure of nerve; depravation, depravedness; retrogression, retrogradation, retrocession, regression; devolution, involution; demotion; downward mobility; decline, declination, declension, worsening, comedown, descent, downtick, downtrend, downward trend, downturn, depreciation, decrease, drop, fall, plunge, free-fall, falling-off, lessening, slippage, slump, lapse, fading, dying, failing, failure, wane, ebb; loss of morale; shadow of one's former self

4 **waste,** wastage, consumption; withering, wasting, wasting away, atrophy, wilting, marcescence; emaciation

5 **wear,** use, hard wear; **wear and tear;** erosion, weathering, ablation, ravages of time, attrition

6 **decay,** decomposition, disintegration, dissolution, resolution, degradation, biodegradation, breakup, disorganization, corruption, spoilage, dilapidation; corrosion, oxidation, oxidization, rust; mildew, mold; degradability, biodegradability; radioactive decay

7 **rot, rottenness,** foulness, putridness, putridity, rancidness, rancidity, rankness, putrefaction, putrescence, spoilage, decay, decomposition, moldering; carrion; dry rot, wet rot

8 **wreck, ruins,** ruin, total loss; hulk, carcass,

skeleton; mere wreck, wreck of one's former self, perfect wreck; nervous wreck; rattletrap

VERBS 9 **impair, damage,** endamage, injure, harm, hurt, irritate; worsen, make worse, disimprove, deteriorate, put back, set back, aggravate, exacerbate, embitter; weaken; dilapidate; add insult to injury, rub salt in the wound

10 **spoil,** mar, botch, ruin, wreck, blight, play havoc with; destroy; pollute

11 <nonformal> **screw up,** foul up, fuck up*, bitch up*, blow, louse up, queer, snafu, snarl up, balls up, bugger, bugger up* <Brit>, gum up, ball up, bollix, bollix up, mess up, hash up, muck up; play hob with, play hell with, play merry hell with, play the devil with, rain on one's picnic, rain on one's parade; upset the apple cart, cook, sink, shoot down in flames; total; pulverize

12 **corrupt,** debase, degrade, degenerate, deprave, debauch, defile, violate, desecrate, profane, deflower, ravish, ravage, despoil; contaminate, confound, pollute, vitiate, poison, infect, taint; canker, ulcerate; pervert, warp, twist, distort; prostitute, misuse; denature; cheapen, devalue; coarsen, vulgarize, drag in the mud; adulterate, alloy, water, water down

13 <inflict an injury> **injure, hurt;** draw blood, wound; traumatize; stab, stick, pierce, puncture; cut, incise, slit, slash, gash, scratch; abrade, eat away at, scuff, scrape, chafe, fret, gall, bark, skin; break, fracture, rupture; crack, chip, craze, check; lacerate, claw, tear, rip, rend; run; frazzle, fray; burn, scorch, scald; mutilate, maim, rough up, make mincemeat of, maul, batter, savage; sprain, strain, wrench; bloody; blemish; bruise, contuse, bung, bung up; buffet, bash, pound, beat, beat black and blue; give a black eye; play havoc with

14 **cripple,** lame, maim; hamstring, hobble; wing; emasculate, castrate; incapacitate, disable

15 **undermine,** sap, mine, sap the foundations of, honeycomb; sabotage, monkey-wrench, throw a monkey-wrench in the works, toss a monkey-wrench in the works, subvert

16 **deteriorate,** sicken, worsen, get worse, grow worse, get no better fast, disimprove, degenerate; slip back, retrogress, retrograde, regress, relapse, fall back; jump the track; go to the bad; let oneself go, let down, slacken; be the worse for, be the worse for wear, have seen better days

17 **decline,** sink, fail, fall, slip, fade, die, wane, ebb, subside, lapse, run down, go down, go downhill, fall away, fall off, go off, slide, slump, hit a slump, take a nosedive, go into a tailspin, take a turn for the worse; hit the skids; reach the depths, hit bottom, touch bottom, hit rock bottom, have no lower to go

18 **languish,** pine, droop, flag, wilt; fade, fade away; wither, shrivel, shrink, diminish, wither on the vine, die on the vine, dry up, desiccate, wizen, wrinkle, sear; retrograde, retrogress

19 **waste, waste away,** wither away, atrophy, consume, consume away, erode away, emaciate, pine away; trickle away, dribble away; run to waste, run to seed

20 **wear, wear away,** wear down, wear off, wear out; abrade, fret, whittle away, rub off; fray, frazzle, tatter, wear ragged; weather, erode, ablate

21 **corrode, erode,** eat, gnaw, eat into, eat away, nibble away, gnaw at the root of; canker; oxidize, rust

22 **decay,** decompose, disintegrate; biodegrade; go into decay, fall into decay, go to pieces, fall to pieces, break up, crumble, crumble into dust; spoil, corrupt, canker, go bad; rot, putrefy, putresce; fester, suppurate, rankle; mortify, necrose, gangrene, sphacelate; mold, molder, molder away, rot away, rust away, mildew

23 **break,** break up, fracture, come apart, come unstuck, fall to pieces, fall apart, disintegrate; burst, rupture; crack, split, fissure; snap; break open, give way, give away, start, spring a leak, come apart at the seams

24 **break down,** founder, collapse; crash, cave in, fall in, come crashing down, come tumbling down, topple, topple down, topple over, totter to one's fall; totter, sway

25 get out of order, **malfunction,** get out of gear; get out of joint; go wrong

26 <nonformal> **get out of whack,** get out of kilter, get out of commission, go kaput, go on the blink, go on the fritz, go haywire, fritz out, go blooey, go kerflooey, give out, conk out, break down

ADJS 27 **impaired, damaged,** hurt, injured, harmed; deteriorated, worsened, cut to the quick, aggravated, exacerbated, irritated, embittered; weakened; worse, worse off, the worse for, all the worse for; imperfect; lacerated, mangled, cut, split, rent, torn, slit, slashed, mutilated, chewed-up; broken, shattered, smashed, in bits, in pieces, in shards, burst, busted, ruptured, sprung; cracked, chipped, crazed, checked; burned, scorched, scalded; damaging, injurious, traumatic, degenerative

28 **spoiled**, spoilt, marred, botched, blighted, **ruined,** wrecked; destroyed

29 <nonformal> **screwed up,** fouled up, fucked up*, loused up, snafued; buggered, buggered up <Brit>; gummed up, snarled up, balled up, bollixed up, messed up, hashed up, mucked up,

botched up; beat up, clapped-out <Brit>; totaled, kaput, finished, done for, done in, cooked, sunk, shot; queered

30 **crippled,** game, bad, handicapped, maimed; lame, halt, halting, hobbling, limping; knee-sprung; hamstrung; spavined; **disabled, incapacitated,** challenged; emasculated, castrated

31 **worn,** well-worn, deep-worn, worn-down, the worse for wear, dog-eared; timeworn; shopworn, shelfworn; worn to the stump, worn to the bone; worn ragged, worn to rags, worn to threads; threadbare, bare, sere

32 **shabby,** shoddy, seedy, scruffy, tacky, dowdy, tatty, ratty; holey, full of holes; raggedy, raggedy-ass, ragged, tattered, torn; patchy; frayed, frazzled; in rags, in tatters, in shreds; out at the elbows, out at the heels, down-at-heel, down-at-heels, down-at-the-heel, down-at-the-heels

33 **dilapidated, ramshackle,** decrepit, shacky, tottery, slummy, tumbledown, broken-down, run-down, in ruins, ruinous, ruined, derelict, gone to wrack and ruin, the worse for wear; battered, beaten-up, beat-up

34 **weatherworn,** weather-beaten, weather-battered, weathered, weather-wasted, weather-eaten, weather-bitten, weather-scarred; eroded; faded, washed-out, bleached, blanched, etiolated

35 **wasted,** atrophied, shrunken; withered, sere, shriveled, wilted, wizened, dried-up, desiccated; wrinkled, wrinkled like a prune; brittle, papery, parchmenty; emaciated; starved, worn to a shadow, reduced to a skeleton, skin and bones, worn to the bones

36 **worn-out,** used up, worn to a frazzle, frazzled, fit for the dust hole, fit for the wastepaper basket; exhausted, tired, fatigued, pooped, spent, effete, etiolated, played out, maxed-out, shotten, jaded, emptied, done, done up; run-down, dragged-out, laid low, at a low ebb, in a bad way, far-gone, on one's last legs

37 **in disrepair,** out of order, out of condition, out of service, malfunctioning, out of working order, inoperative; out of tune, out of gear; out of joint; broken

38 <nonformal> **out of whack**, out of kilter, out of kelter, out of sync, out of commission, on the fritz, fritzed, on the blink, blooey, kerflooey, haywire, wonky

39 **putrefactive,** putrefacient, rotting; septic; saprogenic, saprogenous; saprophilous, saprophytic, saprobic

40 **decayed,** decomposed; spoiled, corrupt, peccant, bad, gone bad; rotten, rotting, putrid, putrefied, foul; putrescent, mortified, necrosed, necrotic, sphacelated, gangrened, gangrenous; carious; cankered, ulcerated, festering, suppurating, suppurative; rotten to the core

41 **tainted, off,** blown, frowy; stale; sour, soured, turned; rank, rancid, strong, high, gamy

42 **blighted,** blasted, ravaged, despoiled; blown, flyblown, wormy, weevily, maggoty; moth-eaten, worm-eaten; moldy, moldering, mildewed, smutty, smutted; musty, fusty, frowzy, frowsy, frowsty

43 **corroded,** eroded, eaten; rusty, rust-eaten, rust-worn, rust-cankered

44 **corrupting,** corruptive; corrosive, corroding; erosive, eroding, damaging, injurious; pollutive

45 **deteriorating, worsening,** disintegrating, coming apart, coming unstuck, crumbling, cracking, fragmenting, going to pieces; decadent, degenerate, effete; retrogressive, retrograde, regressive, from better to worse; declining, sinking, failing, falling, waning, subsiding, slipping, sliding, slumping; languishing, pining, drooping, flagging, wilting; ebbing, draining, dwindling; wasting, fading, fading fast, withering, shriveling; tabetic, marcescent

46 **on the wane, on the decline,** on the downgrade, on the downward track, on the skids; tottering, nodding to its fall, on the way out

47 degradable, biodegradable, decomposable, putrefiable, putrescible

ADVS 48 out of the frying pan into the fire, from better to worse; for the worse

394 RELAPSE

<returning to worse condition>

NOUNS 1 **relapse, lapse,** falling back; reversion, regression; reverse, reversal, backward deviation, devolution, setback, backset; return, recurrence, renewal, recrudescence; throwback, atavism; recadency

2 **backsliding,** backslide; fall, fall from grace; lapsing, recidivism, recidivation; apostasy

3 **backslider,** recidivist, reversionist; apostate

VERBS 4 **relapse, lapse,** backslide, slide back, slip back, sink back, fall back, have a relapse, devolve, return to, revert to, recur to, yield again to, fall again into, recidivate; revert, regress; fall, fall from grace

ADJS 5 **relapsing, lapsing,** lapsarian, backsliding, recidivous; recadent; recrudescent; regressive; apostate

395 DESTRUCTION

<damaging something>

NOUNS 1 **destruction, ruin,** ruination, rack, rack and ruin, blue ruin; perdition, damnation, eternal damnation; universal ruin; wreck; devastation, ravage, havoc, holocaust, firestorm, hecatomb, carnage, shambles, slaughter, bloodbath, desolation; waste, consumption; decimation; dissolution, disintegration, breakup, disruption, disorganization, undoing, lysis; vandalism, depredation, spoliation, despoliation, despoilment; the road to ruin, the road to wrack and ruin; iconoclasm; disruptive technology

2 **end, fate, doom,** death, death knell, bane, deathblow, death warrant, *coup de grâce* <Fr>, final blow, quietus, cutoff, end of the world, extinction level event, eschaton, apocalypse

3 **fall, downfall,** prostration; overthrow, overturn, upset, upheaval; convulsion, subversion, sabotage, monkey-wrenching

4 **debacle, disaster,** cataclysm, catastrophe; breakup, breaking up; breakdown, collapse; crash, meltdown, smash, smashup, crack-up; wreck, wrack, shipwreck; cave-in, cave; washout; total loss, big one

5 **demolition,** demolishment; wrecking, wreckage, wrecking ball, leveling, razing, flattening, smashing, tearing down, bringing to the ground; dismantlement, disassembly, unmaking; hatchet job

6 **extinction,** extermination, elimination, eradication, extirpation; rooting out, deracination, uprooting, tearing up root and branch; annihilation, extinguishment, snuffing out; abolition, abolishment; annulment, nullification, voiding, negation; liquidation, purge; suppression; choking, choking off, suffocation, stifling, strangulation; silencing; nuclear winter

7 **obliteration,** erasure, effacement, deletion, expunction, blot, blotting, blotting out, wiping out; washing out, scrubbing, cancellation, cancel; annulment, abrogation; palimpsest, clean slate, tabula rasa

8 **destroyer,** ruiner, wrecker, bane, wiper-out, demolisher; vandal, hun; exterminator, annihilator; iconoclast, idoloclast; biblioclast; nihilist; terrorist, syndicalist; bomber, dynamiter, dynamitard; burner, arsonist; loose cannon

9 **eradicator,** expunger; eraser, rubber, India rubber, sponge; extinguisher

VERBS 10 **destroy,** deal destruction, unleash destruction, unleash the hurricane, nuke; **ruin,** ruinate, bring to ruin, lay in ruins, play hob with, raise hob with; throw into disorder, turn upside-down, upheave; wreck, wrack, shipwreck; damn, seal the doom of, condemn, confound; devastate, desolate, waste, lay waste, ravage, havoc, wreak havoc, despoil, depredate; vandalize; decimate; devour, consume, engorge, gobble, gobble up, swallow up; gut, gut with fire, incinerate, vaporize, ravage with fire and sword; dissolve, lyse

11 do for, fix, settle, **sink,** cook, cook one's goose, cut one down to size, cut one off at the knees, pull the plug on, pull the rug out from under, dish, scuttle, put the kibosh on, put the skids under, do in, undo, knock in the head, knock on the head, poleax, torpedo, knock out, clobber, KO, banjax, deal a knockout blow to, zap, shoot down, shoot down in flames; break the back of; make short work of, work off; hamstring; defeat

12 **put an end to,** make an end of, end, finish, finish off, put paid to, give the *coup de grâce* to, give the quietus to, deal a deathblow to, dispose of, get rid of, do in, do away with; cut off, take off, be the death of, sound the death knell of; put out of the way, put out of existence, slaughter, make away with, off, waste, blow away, kill off, strike down, kill; nip, nip in the bud; cut short; scrub

13 abolish, **nullify,** void, abrogate, annihilate, annul, tear up, repeal, revoke, negate, negative, invalidate, undo, cancel, cancel out, bring to naught, put to rest, lay to rest

14 **exterminate,** eliminate, eradicate, deracinate, extirpate, annihilate; wipe out; cut out, root up, root out, uproot, pull up by the roots, pluck up by the roots, cut up root and branch, strike at the root of, lay the ax to the root of; liquidate, vaporize, purge; remove, sweep away, wash away; wipe off the map, leave no trace

15 **extinguish,** quench, snuff out, put out, stamp out, trample out, trample underfoot; smother, choke, stifle, strangle, suffocate; silence; suppress, quash, squash, squelch, quell, put down

16 **obliterate,** expunge, efface, erase, raze, blot, sponge, wipe out, wipe off the map, rub out, blot out, sponge out, wash away; cancel, strike out, cross out, scratch, scratch out, rule out; blue-pencil; delete, dele, kill; leave on the cutting-room floor

17 **demolish, wreck,** total, rack up, undo, unbuild, unmake, dismantle, disassemble; take apart, tear apart, tear asunder, rend, take to pieces, pull to pieces, pick to pieces, tear to pieces, pull in pieces, tear to shreds, tear to tatters; sunder, cleave, split; disintegrate, fragment, break to pieces, make mincemeat of, reduce to rubble, atomize, pulverize, smash, shatter

18 **blow up,** blast, spring, explode, blow to pieces, blow to bits, blow to smithereens, blow to kingdom come, bomb, bombard, blitz; mine; self-destruct

19 **raze,** rase, fell, level, flatten, smash, prostrate,

raze to the ground, raze to dust; steamroller, bulldoze; pull down, tear down, take down, bring down, bring down about one's ears, bring tumbling down, bring crashing down, break down, throw down, cast down, beat down, knock down, knock over; cut down, chop down, mow down; blow down; burn down, incinerate

20 **overthrow,** overturn; upset, overset, upend, subvert, throw down, throw over; undermine, honeycomb, sap, sap the foundations, weaken

21 **overwhelm,** whelm, swamp, engulf; inundate

22 <**be destroyed**> **fall,** fall to the ground, tumble, come tumbling, come crashing down, topple, nod to its fall, bite the dust; break up, crumble, crumble to dust, disintegrate, go to pieces, fall to pieces; go by the board, go out the window, go up the spout, go down the tubes; self-destruct

23 **perish, expire,** succumb, die, cease, end, come to an end, go, pass, pass away, vanish, disappear, fade away, run out, peg out, conk out, come to nothing, come to naught, be no more, be done for; be all over with, be all up with

24 **go to ruin,** go to rack and ruin, go to the bad, go wrong, go to the dogs, go to pot, go to seed, run to seed, go to hell in a handbasket, go to the deuce, go to the devil, go to hell, go to the wall, go to perdition, go to glory; go up, go under; go to smash, go to shivers, go to smithereens

25 drive to ruin, drive to the bad, force to the wall, drive to the dogs, hound to destruction, harry to destruction

ADJS 26 **destructive,** destroying; **ruinous,** ruining; demolishing, demolitionary; disastrous, calamitous, cataclysmic, cataclysmal, catastrophic; fatal, fateful, doomful, baneful; bad news; deadly; consumptive, consuming, withering; devastating, desolating, ravaging, wasting, wasteful, spoliative, depredatory; vandalic, vandalish, vandalistic; subversive, subversionary; nihilist, nihilistic; suicidal, self-destructive; fratricidal, internecine, internecive

27 **exterminative,** exterminatory, annihilative, eradicative, extirpative, extirpatory; all-destroying, all-devouring, all-consuming

28 **ruined, destroyed,** wrecked, blasted, undone, down-and-out, broken, bankrupt; spoiled; irremediable; fallen, overthrown; devastated, desolated, ravaged, blighted, wasted; ruinous, in ruins, gutted; gone to rack and ruin; obliterated, annihilated, liquidated, vaporized; doomed, not long for this world

29 <nonformal> **shot,** done for, done in, finished, kaput; gone to pot, gone to the dogs, gone to hell in a handbasket, phut, belly up, blooey, kerflooey, dead in the water, washed up, all washed up, history, dead meat, down the tube, down the tubes, zapped, nuked, tapped out, wiped out, rubbed out, bust

396 RESTORATION

<returning something to original condition>

NOUNS 1 **restoration,** restoral, restitution, reestablishment, redintegration, reinstatement, reinstation, reformation, reinvestment, reinvestiture, instauration, reversion, reinstitution, reconstitution, recomposition; replacement; rehabilitation, redevelopment, reconversion, reactivation, reenactment; improvement; return to normal

2 **reclamation, recovery,** retrieval, salvage, salving; redemption, salvation

3 **revival,** revivification, revivescence, revivescency, **renewal,** resurrection, resuscitation, restimulation, reanimation, resurgence, recrudescence, comeback; retro; refreshment; second wind; renaissance, renascence, rebirth, new birth; rejuvenation, rejuvenescence, second youth, new lease on life; regeneration, regeneracy, regenerateness; regenesis, palingenesis, reincarnation; new hope, second chance; signs of life, vital signs

4 **renovation, renewal;** refreshment; redecorating; reconditioning, furbishment, refurbishment, refurbishing; retread, retreading; facelifting, facelift; slum clearance, urban renewal; remodeling; overhauling

5 **reconstruction,** re-creation, remaking, recomposition, remodeling, **rebuilding,** refabrication, refashioning; reassembling, reassembly; reformation; restructuring, perestroika

6 **reparation, repair,** repairing, fixing, mending, fix-up, making right, setting right, repairwork; servicing, maintenance; overhaul, overhauling; troubleshooting; rectification, correction, remedy; damage control; redress, amends, satisfaction, compensation, recompense; emendation

7 **cure,** curing, healing, remedy; therapy

8 **recovery,** rally, comeback, return, upturn; recuperation, convalescence

9 **restorability, reparability,** curability, recoverability, reversibility, remediability, retrievability, redeemability, salvageability, corrigibility

10 **mender,** fixer, doctor, restorer, renovator, repairer, repairman, repairwoman, handyman, maintenance man, maintenance woman, serviceman, servicewoman; trouble man, troubleshooter; Mr. Fixit, little Miss Fixit;

mechanic, mechanician; tinker, tinkerer; cobbler; salvor, salvager

VERBS 11 **restore,** put back, replace, return, place in *status quo ante;* reestablish, redintegrate, reform, reenact, reinstate, restitute; reinstall, reinvest, revest, reinstitute, reconstitute, recompose, recruit, rehabilitate, redevelop; reintegrate, reconvert, reactivate; make as good as new; refill, replenish; give back

12 **redeem, reclaim,** recover, retrieve; ransom; rescue; salvage, salve; recycle; win back, recoup

13 **remedy,** rectify, correct, right, patch up, emend, amend, redress, make good, make right, put right, set right, put to rights, set to rights, put straight, set straight, set up, heal up, knit up, make all square; pay reparations, give satisfaction, requite, restitute, recompense, compensate, remunerate

14 **repair, mend, fix,** fix up, do up, doctor, put in repair, put in shape, set to rights, put in order, put in condition; condition, recondition, commission, put in commission, ready; service, overhaul; patch, patch up; tinker, tinker up, fiddle, fiddle around; cobble; sew up, darn; recap, retread

15 **cure,** work a cure, **remedy, heal,** restore to health, heal up, knit up, bring round, bring around, pull round, pull around, give a new lease on life, give a fresh lease on life, make better, make well, fix up, pull through, set on one's feet, set on one's legs; snatch from the jaws of death

16 **revive,** revivify, renew, recruit; reanimate, reinspire, regenerate, rejuvenate, revitalize, breathe new life into, restimulate; refresh; resuscitate, bring to, bring round, bring around; recharge; resurrect, bring back, call back, recall to life, raise from the dead; rewarm, warm up, warm over; rekindle, relight, reheat the ashes, stir the embers; restore to health

17 **renovate, renew;** recondition, refit, revamp, furbish, refurbish; refresh, facelift; fix up, upgrade

18 **remake,** reconstruct, remodel, recompose, reconstitute, re-create, **rebuild,** refabricate, re-form, refashion, reassemble

19 **recuperate,** recruit, gain strength, recruit one's strength, renew one's strength, catch one's breath, get better; improve; rally, pick up, perk up, brace up, bounce back, take a new lease on life, take a fresh lease on life; take a favorable turn, turn the corner, be out of the woods, take a turn for the better; convalesce; sleep it off

20 **recover,** rally, revive, get well, get over, pull through, pull round, pull around, come round, come around, come back, make a comeback; get about, get back in shape, be oneself again, feel like a new person; survive, weather the storm, live through; come to, come to oneself, show signs of life; come up smiling, get one's second wind; come out of it, pull out of it, snap out of it

21 **heal,** heal over, close up, scab over, cicatrize, granulate; heal itself, right itself; knit, set

ADJS 22 **tonic, restorative,** restitutive, restitutory, restimulative; analeptic; reparative, reparatory; sanative; remedial, curative

23 **recuperative,** recuperatory; reviviscent; convalescent; buoyant, resilient, elastic

24 **renascent,** redivivus, redux, resurrected, renewed, revived, reborn, resurgent, recrudescent, reappearing, phoenixlike; like new; oneself again

25 **remediable, curable;** medicable, treatable; emendable, amendable, correctable, rectifiable, corrigible; improvable, ameliorable; reparable, repairable, mendable, fixable; restorable, recoverable, salvageable, retrievable, reversible, reclaimable, recyclable, redeemable; renewable; sustainable

397 PRESERVATION

<keeping something in good condition>

NOUNS 1 **preservation,** preserval, **conservation,** saving, salvation, salvage, keeping, safekeeping, maintenance, upkeep, support, service; custody, custodianship, guardianship, curatorship; protectiveness, protection; conservationism, environmental conservation, environmentalism, environmental activism; ecology, agroecology; nature conservation, nature conservancy, soil conservation, forest conservation, forest management, wildlife conservation, stream conservation, water conservation, wetlands conservation; self-preservation; sustainable energy, sustainable living; rewilding; carbon footprint

2 **food preservation;** storage, retention; curing, seasoning, salting, brining, pickling, marinating, corning; drying, dry-curing, jerking; dehydration, anhydration, evaporation, desiccation; smoking, fuming, smoke-curing, kippering; refrigeration, freezing, quick-freezing, blast-freezing, deep-freezing; freeze-drying, lyophilization; irradiation; canning, tinning <Brit>; bottling, processing, packaging; sterilization

3 **embalming,** mummification; taxidermy, stuffing; tanning

4 **preservative,** preservative medium; salt, brine, vinegar, formaldehyde, formalin, formol, embalming fluid, food additive; MSG, monosodium glutamate

5 **preserver,** saver, conservator, keeper, safekeeper; taxidermist; lifesaver, rescuer, deliverer, savior; **conservationist,** preservationist; National Wildlife

Service, Audubon Society, Sierra Club, Nature Conservancy; ranger, forest ranger, Smokey the Bear, fire warden, game warden

6 **life preserver,** life jacket, life vest, life belt, cork jacket, Mae West; life buoy, life ring, buoy, flotation device, floating cushion; man-overboard buoy; water wings; breeches buoy; lifeboat, life raft, rubber dinghy; life net; lifeline; safety belt; **parachute;** ejection seat, ejector seat, ejection capsule

7 **preserve,** reserve, reservation; park, paradise; national park, state park; national seashore; forest preserve, forest reserve, arboretum; national forest, state forest; wilderness preserve; Indian reservation; refuge, sanctuary, game preserve, game reserve, bird sanctuary, wildlife sanctuary; museum, library, archives, bank, store; protected area

VERBS 8 **preserve, conserve, sustain,** save, spare; keep, keep safe, keep inviolate, keep intact; patent, copyright, register; not endanger, not destroy; not use up, not waste, not expend; guard, protect; maintain, uphold, support, keep up, keep alive

9 **preserve, cure,** season, salt, brine, marinate, marinade, pickle, corn, dry, dry-cure, jerk, dry-salt; dehydrate, anhydrate, evaporate, desiccate; vacuum-pack; smoke, fume, smoke-cure, smoke-dry, kipper; refrigerate, freeze, quick-freeze, blast-freeze, keep on ice; freeze-dry, lyophilize; irradiate

10 **embalm,** mummify; stuff; tan

11 **put up,** put by, do up; **can,** tin <Brit>, bottle

ADJS 12 **preservative,** preservatory, conservative, conservatory; custodial, curatorial; **conservational,** conservationist; preserving, conserving, saving, salubrious, keeping, eco-friendly, environment-friendly; protective

13 **preserved,** conserved, kept, saved, spared; protected; untainted, unspoiled; intact, all in one piece, undamaged; well-preserved, well-conserved, well-kept, in a good state of preservation, none the worse for wear; embalmed, laid up in lavender, mummified, stuffed; carbon neutral

398 RESCUE

<saving from danger or harm>

NOUNS 1 **rescue,** deliverance, delivery, **saving;** lifesaving; extrication, release, freeing, liberation; bailout; salvation, salvage, redemption, ransom; recovery, retrieval; good riddance; 911

2 **rescuer,** lifesaver, lifeguard; coast guard, lifesaving service, air-sea rescue; emergency medical technician (EMT); savior; lifeboat; salvager, salvor; emancipator

VERBS 3 **rescue,** come to the rescue, deliver, **save,** be the saving of, save by the bell, redeem, ransom, salvage; recover, retrieve; free, set free, release, extricate, extract, liberate; snatch from the jaws of death; save one's bacon, save one's neck, save one's ass, bail one out

ADJS 4 **rescuable, savable;** redeemable; deliverable, extricable; salvageable; fit for release

399 WARNING

<telling of danger or trouble>

NOUNS 1 **warning, caution,** caveat, admonition, monition, admonishment; notice, notification; word to the wise, word of advice, enough said, nuff said; hint, broad hint, measured words, flea in one's ear, little birdy, kick under the table; tip-off; lesson, object lesson, example, deterrent example, warning piece; moral, moral of the story; alarm; code red; final warning, final notice, ultimatum; threat

2 **forewarning,** prewarning, premonition, precautioning; advance warning, advance notice, plenty of notice, prenotification; presentiment, hunch, funny feeling, foreboding; portent; evil portent

3 **warning sign,** premonitory sign, danger sign; preliminary sign, preliminary signal, preliminary token; symptom, early symptom, premonitory symptom, prodrome, prodroma, prodromata <pl>; precursor; omen; handwriting on the wall; straw in the wind; gathering clouds, clouds on the horizon; thundercloud, thunderhead; falling barometer, falling glass; storm petrel, stormy petrel, red light, red flag, Very lights; quarantine flag, yellow flag, yellow jack; death's-head, skull, crossbones; high sign, warning signal, alert, red alert; siren, klaxon, tocsin, alarm bell, burglar alarm, car horn, foghorn; tattoo; early warning system

4 **warner,** cautioner, admonisher, monitor; prophet of doom, messenger of doom, Cassandra, Jeremiah, Nostradamus, Ezekiel; lookout, lookout man; sentinel, sentry; signalman, signaler, flagman; lighthouse keeper

VERBS 5 **warn, caution,** advise, admonish; give warning, give fair warning, utter a caveat, address a warning to, put a flea in one's ear, drop a hint, have a word with one, say a word to the wise; tip, tip off; notify, put on notice, give notic, give advance notice, advance word; tell once and for all; issue an ultimatum; threaten; alert, warn against, put on one's guard, warn away, warn off;

give the high sign; put on alert, cry havoc, sound the alarm

6 **forewarn,** prewarn, precaution, premonish; prenotify, tell in advance, give advance notice; portend, forebode; give a head's up

ADJS 7 **warning,** cautioning, **cautionary;** monitory, monitorial, admonitory, admonishing, minatory; notifying, notificational; exemplary, deterrent

8 **forewarning,** premonitory; portentous, foreboding; precautionary, precautional; en garde; precursive, precursory, forerunning, prodromal, prodromic

400 ALARM

<warning signal>

NOUNS 1 **alarm,** alarum, alarm signal, **alert;** hue and cry; red light, danger signal, amber light, caution signal; alarm button, panic button, nurse's signal; beeper, buzzer; note of alarm; air-raid alarm; all clear; tocsin, alarm bell; signal of distress, SOS, Mayday, upside-down flag, flare; notice to mariners; storm warning, storm flag, storm, pennant, storm cone, hurricane watch, hurricane warning, hurricane, advisory, gale warning, small-craft warning, small-craft advisory, tornado watch, tornado warning, winter storm watch, winter storm advisory, winter weather advisory, severe thunderstorm watch, severe thunderstorm warning; fog signal, fog alarm, foghorn, fog bell; burglar alarm; car alarm; fire alarm, fire bell, fire flag, still alarm; siren, whistle, horn, klaxon, hooter; police whistle, watchman's rattle; alarm clock; five-minute gun, two-minute gun; lighthouse, beacon; blinking light, flashing light, occulting light

2 **false alarm,** cry of wolf; bugbear, bugaboo; bogy; flash in the pan, dud; false positive

VERBS 3 **alarm, alert,** arouse, put on the alert; warn; fly storm warnings; sound the alarm, give an alarm, raise an alarm, turn in an alarm, ring the tocsin, sound the tocsin, cry havoc, raise a hue and cry; give a false alarm, cry before one is hurt, cry wolf; frighten out of one's wits, scare out of one's wits, frighten to death, scare to death frighten, startle

ADJS 4 **alarmed,** aroused; alerted; frit, frightened to death, frightened out of one's wits, frightened; startled

401 HASTE

<rapidity of action>

NOUNS 1 **haste, hurry,** scurry, rush, race, speed, dash, drive, scuttle, scamper, scramble, hustle, bustle, flutter, flurry, hurry-scurry, helter-skelter; no time to be lost; shotgun approach; express lane

2 **hastiness, hurriedness,** quickness, swiftness, expeditiousness, alacrity, promptness; speed; furiousness, feverishness; precipitousness, precipitance, precipitancy, precipitation; rapidity; suddenness, abruptness; impetuousness, impetuosity, impulsiveness, rashness, impulsivity; eagerness, zealousness, overeagerness, overzealousness

3 **hastening, hurrying,** festination, speeding, forwarding, quickening, hotfooting, acceleration; forced march, double time, double-quick time, double-quick; fast-forward; skedaddle

VERBS 4 **hasten,** haste, **hurry,** accelerate, speed, speed up, hurry up, hustle up, rush, quicken, hustle, bustle, bundle, precipitate, forward; dispatch, expedite; whip, whip along, spur, urge; push, press; crowd, stampede; hurry on, hasten on, drive on, hie on, push on, press on; hurry along, lollop <Brit>, rush along, speed along, speed on its way; push through, railroad, steamroll

5 **make haste, hasten,** festinate, **hurry,** hurry up, race, run, post, rush, chase, tear, dash, spurt, leap, plunge, scurry, hurry-scurry, scamper, scramble, scuttle, hustle, bundle, bustle; bestir oneself, move quickly; make for, hurry on, dash on, press on, push on, crowd; double-time, go at the double; break one's neck, fall all over oneself; lose no time, not lose a moment; rush through, romp through, hurry through; dash off; make short work of, make fast work of, make the best of one's time, think on one's feet, make up for lost time; do on the run, do on the fly

6 <nonformal> **step on it,** snap to it, hop to it, hotfoot, bear down on it, shake it up, get moving, get going, get a move on, get cracking, get the lead out, shake the lead out, get the lead out of one's ass, get one's ass in gear, give it the gun, hump, hump it, hump oneself, tear ass, get a hustle on, get a wiggle on, stir one's stumps, not spare the horses, barrel along, tear off, make tracks

7 **rush into,** plunge into, dive into, plunge, plunge ahead, plunge headlong, cannonball; not stop to think, go off half-cocked, go off at half cock, leap before one looks, cross a bridge before one comes to it

8 **be in a hurry,** be under the gun, have no time to lose, have no time to spare, not have a moment to spare, hardly have time to breathe, work against time, work against the clock, work under pressure, have a deadline, do at the last moment

ADJS 9 **hasty, hurried,** festinate, quick, flying,

expeditious, prompt; quick-and-dirty, immediate, instant, on the spot, precipitant; onrushing, swift, speedy; urgent; furious, feverish; slap-bang, slapdash, cursory, passing, cosmetic, snap, superficial; spur-of-the-moment, last-minute, last-second, last-gasp

10 **precipitate,** precipitant, precipitous; **sudden,** abrupt; impetuous, impulsive, rash; headlong, breakneck; breathless, panting

11 **hurried, rushed,** pushed, pressed, railroaded, crowded, pressed for time, hard-pressed, hard-run; double-time, double-quick, on the double; fool-hasty

ADVS 12 **hastily, hurriedly,** quickly; expeditiously, promptly, with dispatch; all in one breath, in one word, in two words; apace, amain, hand over fist, immediately, instantly, in a second, in a split second, in a jiffy, at once, as soon as possible (ASAP); swiftly, speedily, on fast-forward; with haste, with great, with all haste, in a rush, in a mad rush, at fever pitch; furiously, feverishly, in a sweat, in a lather of haste, hotfoot; by forced marches; helter-skelter, hurry-scurry, pellmell; slapdash, cursorily, superficially, on the run, on the fly, in passing, on the spur of the moment

13 **posthaste,** in posthaste; post, express; by express, by airmail, by return mail, by express mail; by cable, by telegraph, by fax

14 **in a hurry, in haste,** in hot haste, in all haste; in short order; against time, against the clock

15 **precipitately,** precipitantly, precipitously, slap-bang; suddenly, abruptly; impetuously, impulsively, rashly; headlong, headfirst, headforemost, head over heels

INTERJS 16 **make haste,** make it quick, **hurry up;** now; at once, rush, immediate, urgent, instanter; step lively, look alive, on the double

17 <nonformal> **step on it,** snap to it, make it snappy, get a move on, get a wiggle on, chop-chop, shake a leg, stir your stumps, get the lead out, get moving, get going, get cracking, get with it, hop to it, move your tail, move your fanny, get on the ball, don't spare the horses

402 LEISURE

<cessation of action>

NOUNS 1 **leisure, ease,** convenience, freedom; retirement, semiretirement; rest, repose; free time, spare time, goof-off time, downtime, odd moments, idle hours; time to spare, time to burn, time to kill, time on one's hands, time at one's disposal, time at one's command, time to oneself; time, one's own sweet time; breathing room; all the time in the world; time off, holiday, vacation, furlough, sabbatical, leave; break, recess, breather, coffee break, lunch break; day of rest; letup; couch potato

2 **leisureliness, unhurriedness,** unhastiness, hastelessness, relaxedness; *dolce far niente* <Ital>; inactivity; slowness; otiosity; deliberateness, deliberation; contentment

VERBS 3 **have time,** have time enough, have time to spare, have plenty of time, have nothing but time, be in no hurry; lounge, loll

4 take one's leisure, take one's ease, **take one's time,** take one's own sweet time, do at one's leisure, do at one's convenience, do at one's pleasure; go slow; ride the gravy train, lead the life of Riley, take time to smell the flowers, take time to smell the roses; put one's feet up, be a couch potato

ADJS 5 **leisure, leisured;** idle, unoccupied, free, open, spare; retired, semiretired, unemployed, in retirement; otiose; on vacation, on holiday; after-dinner

6 **leisurely, unhurried,** laid-back, unhasty, hasteless, easy, relaxed; sluggish, lazy; deliberate; inactive; **slow**

ADVS 7 **at leisure,** at one's leisure, at one's convenience, at one's own sweet time, when one gets around to it, when it is handy, when one has the time, when one has a minute to spare, when one has a moment to call one's own

INTERJS 8 chill, easy does it, take it easy

403 ENDEAVOR

<trying to do>

NOUNS 1 **endeavor,** effort, striving, struggle, strain; all-out effort, best effort, college try, old college try, valiant effort; exertion; determination, resolution; enterprise; good move, good call, good decision

2 **attempt, trial,** effort, essay, assay, first attempt; endeavor, undertaking; approach, move; coup, stroke, step; gambit, offer, bid, strong bid; experiment, tentative; tentation, trial and error

3 <nonformal> **try,** whack, fling, shot, crack, bash, belt, go, stab, leap, lick, rip, ripple, cut, hack, smack; last shot, swan song

4 **one's best,** one's level best, one's utmost, one's damndest, one's darndest, one's best effort, one's best endeavor, the best one can, the best one knows how, all one can do, all one's got, all one's got in one, one's all, the top of one's bent, as much as in one lies

VERBS 5 **endeavor,** strive, struggle, strain, sweat, sweat blood, labor, get one's teeth into, come to grips with, take it on, make an all-out effort, move heaven and earth, exert oneself, apply oneself, use some elbow grease; spend oneself; seek, study, aim; resolve, be determined

6 **attempt, try**, essay, assay, offer; try one's hand, try it on, set about; undertake, approach, come to grips with, engage, take the bull by the horns; venture, venture on, venture upon, chance; make an attempt, make an effort, lift a finger, lift a hand

7 <nonformal> **tackle,** take on, make a try, give a try, have a go, take a shot, take a stab, take a crack, have a try, take a whack at; try on for size, go for it, go for the brass ring, have a fling at, have a go at, give a fling at, have a whirl, make a stab at, have a shot at, have a tabe at, have a crack at have a try at, have a whack at

8 **try to,** try and, **attempt to, endeavor to,** strive to, seek to, study to, aim to, venture to, dare to, pretend to

9 **try for, strive for,** strain for, struggle for, contend for, pull for, bid for, make a bid for, make a strong bid for, make a play for

10 **see what one can do,** see what can be done, see if one can do, do what one can, use one's endeavor; try anything once; **try one's hand,** try one's luck, tempt fate; make a cautious move, make a tentative move, experiment, feel one's way, test the waters, run it up the flagpole

11 **make a special effort,** go out of the way, go out of one's way, take special pains, put oneself out, put oneself out of the way, lay oneself out, fall over backward, bend over backward, lean over backward, fall all over oneself, trouble oneself, go to the trouble, take trouble, take pains, redouble one's efforts

12 **try hard,** push, make a bold push, put one's back into, put one's heart into, try until one is blue in the face, die trying, try and try; try, try again; exert oneself

13 **do one's best,** do one's level best, do one's utmost, try one's best, try one's utmost, do all one can, do everything one can, do the best one can, do the best one knows how, do all in one's power, do as much as in one lies, do what lies in one's power, do one's damnedest; put all one's strength into, put one's whole soul in, strain every nerve; give it one's all, go flat out; go for broke; be on one's mettle, die trying

14 <nonformal> **knock oneself out,** break one's neck, break one's balls, bust one's balls, bust a gut, bust one's ass, bust one's hump, rupture oneself, do it or know why not, break a leg, do one's damndest, try one's damndest, do one's darndest, try one's darndest, go all out, go the limit, go for broke, shoot the works, give it all one's got, give it one's best shot, go for it

15 **make every effort**, spare no effort, spare no pains, go all lengths, go to great lengths, go the whole length, go through fire and water, not rest, not relax, not slacken, move heaven and earth, leave no stone unturned, leave no avenue unexplored

ADJS 16 trial, tentative, experimental; venturesome, willing; determined, resolute; utmost, damndest

ADVS 17 out for, out to, **trying for**, on the make

18 at the top of one's bent, to one's utmost, as far as possible

404 UNDERTAKING

<*trying to do difficult thing*>

NOUNS 1 **undertaking,** enterprise, operation, work, venture, project, proposition, deal; matter at hand; program, plan; affair, business, matter, task, concern, interest; initiative, effort, attempt; action; engagement, contract, obligation, mission statement, commitment; *démarche* <Fr>

2 **adventure,** emprise, **mission;** quest, pilgrimage; expedition, exploration, escapade

VERBS 3 **undertake,** assume, accept, **take on,** take upon oneself, take in hand, take upon one's shoulders, take up, sign up, go with, tackle, attack; engage oneself, contract oneself, obligate oneself, commit oneself; put one's hand to, set one's hand to, engage in, devote oneself to, apply oneself to, address oneself to, give oneself up to; join oneself to, associate oneself with, come aboard; busy oneself with; move into, go into, go in for, go out for, enter on, enter upon, proceed to, embark in, embark upon, venture upon, go upon, launch, set forward, get going, get underway, initiate; set about, go about, lay about, go to do; go into action, swing into action, set to, turn to, buckle to, fall to; pitch into, plunge into, fall into, launch into, launch upon; go at, set at, have at, knuckle down to, buckle down to; put one's hand to the plow, put one's shoulder to the wheel; take the bull by the horns; endeavor, attempt; dare, take a shot at

4 **have in hand,** have one's hands in, have on one's hands, have on one's shoulders

5 **be in progress,** be in process, be on the anvil, be in the fire, be in the works, be in the hopper, be in the pipeline, be underway

6 **bite off more than one can chew**, take on too much, overextend oneself, overreach oneself, have too many irons in the fire, have too much on one's plate, stretch oneself too thin

ADJS 7 **undertaken,** assumed, accepted, taken on; ventured, attempted, chanced; in hand, on the anvil, in the fire, in progress, in process, on one's plate, in the works, in the hopper, in the pipeline, on the agenda, underway; contractual

8 **enterprising,** venturesome, adventurous, plucky, keen, eager; resourceful, ambitious; pioneering, groundbreaking; avant-garde

405 PREPARATION

<getting ready for something>

NOUNS 1 **preparation,** preparing, prep, prepping, **readying,** getting ready, making ready, makeready, taking measures; warm-up, getting in shape, getting in condition; mobilization; walk-up, run-up; prearrangement, lead time, advance notice, warning, advance warning, alerting; planning; trial, dry run, tryout; provision, arrangement; preparatory measure, preparatory step, preliminary act, preliminary measure, preliminary step; preliminary, preliminaries; clearing the decks; grounding, propaedeutic, preparatory study, preparatory instruction, preparatory school, prep school; basic training, familiarization, briefing, onboarding; prerequisite; processing, treatment, pretreatment; equipment; training; manufacture; spadework, groundwork, foundation; pioneering, trailblazing, pushing the envelope; all-nighter

2 **fitting,** checking the fit, fit, fitting out; **conditioning**; adaptation, adjustment, tuning; qualification, capacitation, enablement; equipment, furnishing

3 <a preparation> **concoction,** decoction, brew, confection; solution; composition, mixture, combination; emergency kit, go-bag, survival kit

4 **preparedness,** readiness; fitness, fittedness, suitedness, suitableness, suitability; condition, trim; qualification, qualifiedness, credentials, record, track record; competence, competency, ability, capability, proficiency, mastery; ripeness, maturity, seasoning, tempering; emergency preparedness; In Case of Emergency (ICE)

5 **preparer,** preparator, preparationist; trainer, coach, instructor, mentor, teacher, tutor; trailblazer, pathfinder; forerunner; paver of the way, pioneer

VERBS 6 **prepare,** make ready, get ready, prep, do the prep work, trim, ready, fix; arrange; make preparations, make arrangements, take measures, sound the note of preparation, clear the decks, clear for action, settle preliminaries, tee up; mobilize, marshal, deploy, marshal one's forces, deploy one's forces, deploy one's resources; prearrange; plan; try out; fix up, ready up, put in shape, put into shape; dress; treat, pretreat, process; cure, tan, taw; map out, sketch out, outline; get around to

7 make **up, get up, fix up,** rustle up; **concoct,** decoct, brew; compound, compose, put together, mix; make

8 **fit, condition,** adapt, adjust, suit, tune, attune, put in tune, put in trim, put in working order; customize; qualify, enable, capacitate; equip, fit out, supply, furnish

9 **prime,** load, charge, cock, set, precondition; wind, wind up; steam up, get up steam, warm up

10 **prepare to,** get ready to, get set for, fix to; be about to, be on the point of; ready oneself to, hold oneself in readiness

11 **prepare for,** provide for, arrange for, make arrangements for, make dispositions for, look to, look out for, see to, make provision, make due provision for; provide against, make sure against, forearm, provide for a rainy day, provide against a rainy day, prepare for the evil day; lay in provisions, lay up a store, keep as a nest egg, save to fall back upon, lay by, husband one's resources, salt something away, squirrel something away; set one's house in order, line up one's ducks

12 **prepare the way,** pave the way, smooth the path, smooth the road, clear the way, open the way, open the door to; build a bridge; break the ice; pioneer, go in advance, be the point, push the envelope, blaze the trail; prepare the ground, cultivate the soil, sow the seed; do the spadework, lay the groundwork, lay the foundation, lay the first stone, provide the basis; lead up to

13 **prepare oneself,** brace oneself, get ready, get set, put one's house in order, strip for action, get into shape, get into condition, roll up one's sleeves, spit on one's hands, limber up, warm up, flex one's muscles, gird up one's loins, buckle on one's armor, buckle up, get into harness, shoulder arms; sharpen one's tools, whet the knife, get one's sword; psych oneself up; do one's homework; get one's house in order; run up to, build up to, gear up, tool up, rev up

14 **be prepared, be ready,** stand by, stand ready, hold oneself in readiness

15 <be fitted> **qualify,** measure up, meet the requirements, check out, have the credentials, have the qualifications, have the prerequisites; be up to, be just the ticket, fill the bill

ADJS 16 **prepared, ready,** well-prepared, prepped, in readiness, in ready state, all ready, good and ready, prepared and ready; psyched up, pumped up, eager, keen, champing at the bit; alert, vigilant; revved up; ripe, mature; set, all set, on the mark, teed up; about to, fixing to;

prearranged; planned; primed, loaded, cocked, loaded for bear; familiarized, briefed, informed, put into the picture; groomed, coached; ready for anything; in the saddle, booted, spurred; armed and ready, in arms, up in arms, armed; in battle array, mobilized; provided, equipped; dressed; treated, pretreated, processed; cured, tanned, tawed; readied, available

17 **fitted, adapted,** adjusted, suited; qualified, fit, competent, able, capable, proficient; customized; checked out; well-adjusted, well-qualified, well-fitted, well-suited

18 **prepared for, ready for,** alert for, set for, all set for; loaded for, primed for; up for; equal to, up to

19 **ready-made,** ready-formed, ready-mixed, ready-furnished, ready-dressed; ready-built, prefabricated, prefab, preformed; ready-to-wear, ready-for-wear, off-the-rack; ready-cut, cut-and-dried; convenient, convenience, fast-food; ready-to-cook, precooked, oven-ready; instant

20 **preparatory,** preparative; propaedeutic; prerequisite; provident, provisional

ADJS, ADVS 21 **in readiness,** in store, in reserve; in anticipation

22 **in preparation,** in course of preparation, in progress, in process, underway, going on, in embryo, in production, on stream, under construction, in the works, in the hopper, in the pipeline, on the way, in the making, in hand, on the anvil, on the fire, in the oven; under revision; brewing, forthcoming

23 **afoot,** on foot, afloat, astir

PREPS 24 in preparation for, against, for; in order to; ready for, set for, fixing to

406 UNPREPAREDNESS

<unready for something>

NOUNS 1 **unpreparedness, unreadiness,** unprovidedness, nonpreparedness, nonpreparation, lack of preparation; vulnerability; extemporaneousness, improvisation, ad lib, planlessness, disorganization; unfitness, unfittedness, unsuitedness, unsuitableness, unsuitability, unqualifiedness, unqualification, lack of credentials, poor track record, disqualification, incompetence, incompetency, incapability; rustiness

2 **improvidence,** thriftlessness, unthriftiness, poor husbandry, lax stewardship; shiftlessness, fecklessness, thoughtlessness, heedlessness; happy-go-luckiness; hastiness; negligence

3 <raw or original condition> naturalness, inartificiality; **natural state,** nature, state of nature, nature in the raw; pristineness, intactness, virginity; defenselessness; natural man; artlessness

4 **undevelopment,** nondevelopment; immaturity, immatureness, callowness, unfledgedness, cubbishness, rawness, unripeness, greenness; unfinish, unfinishedness, unpolishedness, unrefinement, uncultivation; crudity, crudeness, rudeness, coarseness, roughness, the rough; oversimplification, oversimplicity, simplism, reductionism

5 **raw material;** crude, crude stuff; ore, rich ore, rich vein; unsorted mess, unanalyzed mass; rough diamond, diamond in the rough; unlicked cub; virgin soil, untilled ground; hot mess

VERBS 6 **be unprepared**, be unready, not be ready, lack preparation; go off half-cocked, go off at half cock; be taken unawares, be taken aback, be blindsided, be caught napping, be caught with one's pants down, be surprised, drop one's guard; extemporize, improvise, ad-lib, play by ear; have no plan, be innocent of forethought

7 **make no provision,** take no thought of tomorrow, take no thought of the morrow, seize the day, *carpe diem* <L>, let tomorrow take care of itself, live for the day, live like the grasshopper, live from hand to mouth; eat, drink, and be merry; make it up as one goes along

ADJS 8 **unprepared, unready,** unprimed; surprised, caught short, caught napping, caught with one's pants down, taken by surprise, taken aback, taken unawares, blindsided, caught off balance, caught off base, tripped up; unarranged, unorganized, haphazard; makeshift, rough-and-ready, extemporaneous, extemporized, improvised, ad-lib, off the top of one's head; spontaneous, ad hoc; impromptu, snap; unmade, unmanufactured, unconcocted, unhatched, uncontrived, undevised, unplanned, unpremeditated, undeliberated, unstudied; hasty, precipitate; unbegun

9 **unfitted**, unfit, ill-fitted, unsuited, unadapted, unqualified, disqualified, incompetent, incapable; unequipped, unfurnished, unarmed, ill-equipped, ill-furnished, unprovided, ill-provided

10 **raw,** crude; uncooked, unbaked, unboiled; underdone, undercooked, rare, red; half-baked

11 **immature, unripe,** underripe, unripened, impubic, raw, green, callow, wet behind the ears, cub, cubbish, unfledged, fledgling, unseasoned, unmellowed, vulnerable; ungrown, half-grown, adolescent, juvenile, puerile, boyish, girlish, inchoate; undigested, ill-digested; half-baked; half-cocked, at half cock

12 **undeveloped,** unfinished, unlicked, unformed; unfashioned, unwrought, unlabored, unworked, unprocessed, untreated; unblown; uncut,

unhewn; underdeveloped; backward, arrested, stunted; crude, rude, coarse, unpolished, unrefined; uncultivated, uncultured; rough, roughcast, roughhewn, in the rough; rudimentary, rudimental; embryonic, in embryo, fetal, *in ovo* <L>; oversimple, simplistic, reductive, reductionistic, unsophisticated; untrained; rusty, unpracticed; scratch

13 <in the raw or original state> **natural,** native, natural-looking, in a state of nature, in the raw; inartificial, artless; virgin, virginal, pristine, untouched, unsullied

14 **fallow,** untilled, uncultivated, unsown, unworked

15 **improvident,** prodigal, unproviding; thriftless, unthrifty, uneconomical; grasshopper; hand-to-mouth; shiftless, feckless, thoughtless, heedless; happy-go-lucky; negligent

407 ACCOMPLISHMENT

<successful completion of something>

NOUNS 1 **accomplishment, achievement,** fulfillment, performance, execution, effectuation, implementation, carrying out, carrying through, discharge, dispatch, consummation, **realization, attainment,** production, fruition; **success**; track record, track; *fait accompli* <Fr>, accomplished fact, done deal; mission accomplished

2 **completion,** completing, finish, finishing, conclusion, end, ending, termination, terminus, close, windup, rounding off, rounding out, topping off, wrapping up, wrap-up, finalization; perfection, culmination; ripeness, maturity, maturation, full development; tipping point, trigger point; next level; personal best

3 **finishing touch,** final touch, last touch, last stroke, final stroke, finishing stroke, finisher, craftsmanship, icing the cake, the icing on the cake; copestone, capstone, crown, crowning of the edifice; capper, climax

VERBS 4 **accomplish, achieve,** effect, effectuate, compass, consummate, do, execute, nail it, produce, deliver, make, enact, perform, discharge, fulfill, realize, attain, run with, hack, swing; work, work out; dispatch, dispose of, knock off, polish off, take care of, deal with, put away, make short work of; succeed, manage; come through, do the job, do the trick

5 **bring about,** bring to pass, bring to effect, bring to a happy issue; implement, carry out, carry through, carry into execution; bring off, carry off, pull off; put through, get through, put over, put across; come through with

6 **complete,** perfect, **finish,** finish off, conclude, terminate, end, bring to a close, carry to completion, prosecute to a conclusion; get through, get done; come off of, get through with, get it over, get it over with, finish up; clean up, wind up, button up, sew up, wrap up, mop up, close up, close out; put the lid on, call it a day; round off, round out, top off; top out, crown, cap; climax, culminate; give the finishing touches, give the finishing strokes, put the finishing touches on, lick in to shape, whip into shape, finalize, put the icing on the cake; autocomplete

7 **do to perfection,** do up brown, do to a turn, do to a T, do to a frazzle, do down to the ground, not do by halves, do oneself proud, use every trick in the book, leave no loose ends, leave nothing hanging; go all lengths, go to all lengths, go the whole length, go the whole way, go the limit, go whole hog, go all out, shoot the works, go for broke, nail it

8 **ripen,** ripe, **mature,** maturate; bloom, blow, blossom, flourish; come to fruition, bear fruit; mellow; grow up, reach maturity, reach its season; come to a head, draw to a head; bring to maturity, bring to a head

ADJS 9 **completing,** completive, completory, finishing, consummative, culminating, terminative, conclusive, concluding, fulfilling, finalizing, crowning; ultimate, last, final, terminal

10 **accomplished, achieved,** effected, effectuated, implemented, consummated, executed, discharged, fulfilled, realized, consummate, compassed, attained; dispatched, disposed of, set at rest; wrought, wrought out

11 **completed,** done, finished, concluded, done and done, terminated, ended, finished up; signed, sealed, and delivered; cleaned up, wound up, sewed up, sewn up, wrapped up, mopped up; washed up, through, done with; all over with, all said and done, all over but the shouting; perfective

12 **complete,** perfect, consummate, polished; exhaustive, thorough; fully realized

13 **ripe,** mature, matured, maturated, seasoned; blooming, abloom; mellow, full-grown, fully developed; late-blooming

ADVS 14 **to completion,** to the end, down-the-line, to the full, to the limit; to a turn, to a T, to a finish, to a frazzle

INTERJS 15 so much for that, that's that, *voilà* <Fr>

408 NONACCOMPLISHMENT

<not reaching goal>

NOUNS 1 **nonaccomplishment, nonachievement,** nonperformance, inexecution, nonexecution, nondischarging, noncompletion, nonconsummation, nonfulfillment, unfulfillment; nonfeasance, omission; neglect; loose ends, rough edges; endless task, work of Penelope, Sisyphean labor, Sisyphean toil, Sisyphean task; disappointment; failure

VERBS **2** neglect, leave undone, fail; be disappointed

ADJS **3** **unaccomplished, unachieved,** unperformed, unexecuted, undischarged, unfulfilled, unconsummated, unrealized, unattained; unfinished, uncompleted, undone; open-ended; neglected; disappointed

409 SUCCESS

<achieving planned result>

NOUNS **1** **success, successfulness,** fortunate outcome, prosperous issue, favorable termination; prosperity; accomplishment; victory; the big time

2 sure success, foregone conclusion, sure-fire proposition; **winner**, natural; shoo-in, sure thing, sure bet, cinch, lead-pipe cinch

3 **great success, triumph,** resounding triumph, brilliant success, striking success, meteoric success; flying colors; stardom; success story; bestseller; brief success, momentary success, nine days' wonder, flash in the pan, fad, next big thing

4 <nonformal> **smash**, hit, smash hit, gas, gasser, blast, boffo, showstopper, barnburner, howling success, roaring success, one for the book, wow, wowser, sensation, overnight sensation, sensaysh, phenom, sockeroo

5 **score,** hit, bull's-eye; goal, touchdown; slam, grand slam; strike; hole, hole in one; home run, homer

6 <successful person> **winner,** star, star in the firmament, success, superstar, megastar; prizewinner, lottery winner; phenom, comer, whiz kid, VIP; **victor**

VERBS **7** **succeed,** prevail, be successful, nail it, be crowned with success, meet with success, do very well, do famously, deliver, come through, make a go of it; go, come off, go off; prosper; fare well, work well, do wonders, work wonders, go to town, go great guns; make a hit, click, connect, catch on, take, catch fire, have legs; go over, go over big, go over with a bang; pass, graduate, qualify, win one's spurs, win one's wings, get one's credentials, be blooded; pass with flying colors

8 **achieve one's purpose**, gain one's end, secure one's object, attain one's objective, do what one set out to do, reach one's goal, bring it off, pull it off, hack it, swing it; make one's point; play it just right, handle it just right, not put a foot wrong, play it like a master

9 **score a success,** score, notch one up, hit it, hit the mark, ring the bell, turn up trumps, break the bank, make a killing, hit the jackpot

10 make good, **come through, achieve success,** make a success, have a good thing going, make it, get into the zone, wing, cruise, hit one's stride, make one's mark, give a good account of oneself, bear oneself with credit, do all right by oneself, do oneself proud, make out like a bandit; advance, progress, make one's way, make headway, get on, come on, get ahead; go places, go far; rise, rise in the world, work one's way up, step up, come up in the world, move up in the world, claw one's way up, scrabble one's way up, mount the ladder of success, pull oneself up by one's bootstraps; arrive, get there, make the scene; come out on top, come out on top of the heap; be a success, have it made, have it wrapped up, have the world at one's feet, eat high on the hog, live high on the hog; make a noise in the world, cut a swath, set the world on fire, set the river on fire; break through, score a breakthrough, make a breakthrough

11 **succeed with,** crown with success; make a go of it; accomplish, compass, achieve; bring off, carry off, pull off, do the trick, put through, bring through; put over, put across; get away with it, get by

12 manage, contrive, **succeed in;** make out, get on, get along, come on, come along, go on; scrape along, worry along, muddle through, get by, manage somehow; make it, make the grade, cut the mustard, hack it; clear, clear the hurdle; negotiate, engineer; swing, put over, put through

13 **win out,** win through, come through, rise to the occasion, beat the game, beat the system; triumph; weather out, weather the storm, live through, keep one's head above water; come up fighting, come up smiling, not know when one is beaten, persevere

ADJS **14** **successful,** succeeding, crowned with success; prosperous, fortunate; triumphant; ahead of the game, out in front, on top, sitting on top of the world, sitting pretty, on top of the heap; assured of success, surefire, made; coming, on the up-and-up, cooking with gas; nailed it

ADVS **15** **successfully,** swimmingly, well, to some purpose, to good purpose; beyond all expectation, beyond one's fondest dreams, from rags to riches, with flying colors

410 FAILURE

<lack of success>

NOUNS 1 **failure, unsuccessfulness,** unsuccess, successlessness, nonsuccess; no go; ill success; futility, uselessness; defeat; losing game, no-win situation; nonaccomplishment; bankruptcy

2 <nonformal> **flop,** flopperoo, megaflop, gigaflop, bust, frost, fizzle, lemon, clinker, dud, nonstarter, loser, washout, turkey, bomb, flat failure, dull thud, total loss, black mark; game over; the pits

3 **collapse,** crash, smash, comedown, breakdown, derailment, fall, pratfall, stumble, tumble, **downfall**, cropper; nosedive, tailspin; deflation, bursting of the bubble, letdown, disappointment

4 **miss,** near-miss; slip, slipup, slip 'twixt cup and lip; error, mistake

5 **abortion, miscarriage,** miscarrying, abortive attempt, vain attempt; wild-goose chase, merry chase; misfire, flash in the pan, wet squib, malfunction, glitch; dud; flunk, washout

6 **fiasco, botch,** botch-up, cock-up, balls-up, bungle, hash, mess, muddle, foozle, bollix, bitch-up*, screwup, fuck-up*

7 <unsuccessful person> **failure**, flash in the pan; bankrupt

8 <nonformal> **loser,** nonstarter, born loser, flop, washout, false alarm, dud, also-ran, bum, dull tool, bust, *schlemiel* <Yiddish>, turkey, hopeless case; underdog

VERBS 9 **fail,** be unsuccessful, fail of success, not work, not come off, come to grief, lose, not make the grade, go nowhere, be found wanting, not come up to the mark; not pass, flunk, flunk out; go to the wall, go on the rocks; labor in vain; come away empty-handed; tap out, go bankrupt

10 <nonformal> **lose out,** get left, not make it, not hack it, not get to first base, drop the ball; go for a burton, come a cropper <Brit>; flop, flummox, fall flat on one's ass, lay an egg, go over like a lead balloon, draw a blank, bomb, drop a bomb; fold, fold up; take it on the chin, take the count; crap out; strike out, fan, whiff

11 **sink,** founder, go down, go under, go south; slip, go downhill, be on the skids

12 **fall,** fall down, fall by the wayside, drop by the wayside, fall flat, fall flat on one's face; fall down on the job; fall short, fall through, fall to the ground; fall between two stools; fall dead; collapse, fall in; crash, go to smash

13 **come to nothing,** hang up, get nowhere; poop out, go phut; be all over, be all up with; fail miserably, fail ignominiously; fizz out, fizzle, fizzle out, peter out, misfire, flash in the pan, hang fire; blow up, blow up in one's face, explode, end up in smoke, go up in smoke, go up like a rocket and come down like a stick

14 **miss,** miss the mark, miss one's aim; slip, slip up; goof, blunder, foozle, err; botch, bungle; waste one's effort, run around in circles, spin one's wheels

15 **miscarry,** abort, be stillborn, die aborning; go amiss, go astray, go wrong, go on a wrong tack, take a wrong turn, derail, go off the rails

16 **stall,** stick, die, go dead, conk out, sputter, stop, run out of gas, out of steam, come to a shuddering halt, come to a dead stop

17 **flunk, flunk out**; **fail,** pluck, plough, bust, wash out, bomb, flush it

ADJS 18 **unsuccessful,** successless, failing; failed, manqué <Fr>; unfortunate; abortive, miscarrying, miscarried, stillborn, died aborning; fruitless, bootless, no-win, futile, useless; lame, ineffectual, ineffective, inefficacious, of no effect; malfunctioning, glitchy

ADVS 19 **unsuccessfully,** successlessly, without success; fruitlessly, bootlessly, ineffectually, ineffectively, inefficaciously, lamely; to little or no purpose, in vain

411 VICTORY

<winning competition>

NOUNS 1 **victory, triumph, conquest,** subduing, subdual; a feather in one's cap; total victory, grand slam; championship, crown, laurels, cup, trophy, belt, blue ribbon, first prize, flying colors; V-for-victory sign, V-sign, raised arms; victory lap; winning, win; knockout (KO); easy victory, walkover, walkaway, pushover, picnic; runaway victory, laugher, romp, shellacking; landslide victory, landslide; Pyrrhic victory, Cadmean victory; moral victory; winning streak; winning ways, triumphalism; success; ascendancy; mastery

2 **victor, winner,** victress, victrix, triumpher; conqueror, defeater, vanquisher, subduer, subjugator, *conquistador* <Sp>; top dog; master, master of the situation; hero, conquering hero; champion, champ, number one; easy winner, sure winner, shoo-in; pancratiast; runner-up

VERBS 3 **triumph,** prevail, be victorious, come out ahead, come out on top, clean up, chain victory to one's car; win, gain, capture, carry; win out, win through, carry it, carry off, carry away; win the day, carry the day, win the battle, come out first, finish in front, make a killing, remain in possession of the field; get the last laugh, have the last laugh; win the prize, win the laurels, bear the palm, take the cake, win one's spurs, win one's wings; fluke, win by a fluke; win by a nose, nose out, edge out; succeed; break the record, set a new mark

4 **win hands down**, win going away, win in a canter, walk, waltz, romp home, breeze home, waltz home, walk off with, waltz off with, walk away with, walk off with the game, walk over; have the game in one's own hands, have it all one's way; take by storm, carry by storm, sweep aside all obstacles, sweep, carry all before one, make short work of

5 defeat, **triumph over,** prevail over, best, beat, get the better, get the best of; surmount, overcome, outmatch, rise above

6 gain the ascendancy, come out on top, **get the advantage,** gain the upper hand, gain the whip hand, dominate the field, get the edge on, get the jump on, get the drop on, get a leg up on, get a stranglehold on

ADJS 7 **victorious, triumphant,** triumphal, **winning**, prevailing; conquering, vanquishing, defeating, overcoming; ahead of the game, ascendant, in the ascendant, in ascendancy, sitting on top of the world, sitting pretty, dominant; successful; flushed with success, flushed with victory; game-winning

8 **undefeated,** unbeaten, unvanquished, unconquered, unsubdued, unquelled, unbowed

ADVS 9 **triumphantly,** victoriously, in triumph; by a mile

412 DEFEAT

<failure to win competition>

NOUNS 1 **defeat; beating,** drubbing, thrashing; clobbering, hiding, lathering, whipping, lambasting, trimming, licking, trouncing; vanquishment, conquest, conquering, mastery, subjugation, subduing, subdual; overthrow, overturn, overcoming; fall, downfall, collapse, smash, crash, undoing, ruin, debacle, derailing, derailment; destruction; deathblow, quietus; Waterloo; concession, concession speech, failure

2 **discomfiture,** rout, repulse, rebuff; frustration, bafflement, confusion; checkmate, check, balk, foil; reverse, reversal, **setback**

3 **utter defeat,** total defeat, overwhelming defeat, crushing, defeat, smashing defeat, decisive defeat; no contest; smearing, pasting, creaming, clobbering, shellacking, whopping, whomping; whitewash, whitewashing, **shutout**

4 ignominious defeat, abject defeat, inglorious defeat, disastrous defeat, bitter defeat, stinging defeat, embarassing defeat, utter rout

5 **loser,** defeatee; the vanquished; good sport, good loser, game loser, sport; poor sport, poor loser; underdog, also-ran; booby, duck; stooge, fall guy; victim

VERBS 6 **defeat,** worst, best, get the better, get the best of, be too good for, be too much for, be more than a match for; outdo, outgeneral, outmaneuver, outclass, outshine, outpoint, outsail, outrun, outfight; triumph over; knock on the head, deal a deathblow to, put *hors de combat*; undo, ruin, destroy; beat by a nose, nose out, edge out

7 **overcome,** surmount; **overpower,** overmaster, overmatch; overthrow, overturn, overset; put the skids to; upset, trip, trip up, lay by the heels, send flying, send sprawling; silence, floor, deck, make bite the dust; overcome oneself, master oneself; kick the habit

8 **overwhelm,** whelm, snow under, overbear, defeat utterly, deal a crushing defeat, deal a smashing defeat; discomfit, rout, put to rout, put to flight, scatter, stampede, panic; confound; put out of court

9 <nonformal> **clobber,** trim, skin alive, beat, skunk, drub, massacre, marmelize <Brit>, lick, whip, thrash, knock off, hide, cut to pieces, run rings around, run circles around, throw for a loss, lather, trounce, lambaste; fix, settle, settle one's hash, make one say "uncle," do in, lick to a frazzle, beat all hollow, beat one's brains out, cook one's goose, make hamburger out of, make mincemeat out of, mop up the floor with, sandbag, banjax, bulldoze, steamroller, smear, paste, cream, shellac, whup, whop, whomp, shut out

10 **conquer,** vanquish, quell, suppress, put down, subdue, subjugate, put under the yoke, master; reduce, prostrate, fell, flatten, break, smash, crush, humble, bend, bring one to his knees; trample in the dust, tread underfoot, trample underfoot, trample down, ride roughshod over, run roughshod over, override; have one's way with

11 **thwart,** frustrate, dash, check, deal a check to, checkmate

12 **lose,** lose out, lose the day, come off second best, get the worst of it, meet one's Waterloo; fall, succumb, tumble, bow, go down, go under, bite the dust, lick the dust, take the count; snatch defeat from the jaws of victory; throw in the towel, say "uncle"; have enough

ADJS 13 **lost,** unwon

14 **defeated,** worsted, bested, outdone; beaten, discomfited, put to rout, routed, scattered, stampeded, panicked; confounded; overcome, overthrown, upset, overturned, overmatched,

overpowered, overwhelmed, whelmed, overmastered, overborne, overridden; fallen, down; floored, silenced; undone, done for, ruined, kaput, on the skids, *hors de combat* <Fr>; all up with; pwned

15 <nonformal> **beat,** clobbered, licked, whipped, trimmed, sandbagged, banjaxed, done in, lathered, creamed, shellacked, trounced, lambasted, settled, fixed; skinned alive; thrown for a loss

16 **shut out,** skunked, blanked, whitewashed, scoreless, not on the scoreboard

17 **conquered,** vanquished, quelled, suppressed, put down, subdued, subjugated, mastered; reduced, prostrate, prostrated, felled, flattened, smashed, crushed, broken; humbled, brought to one's knees

18 overpowering, overcoming, overwhelming, overmastering, overmatching, avalanchine

413 SKILL

<ability to do something well>

NOUNS 1 **skill,** skillfulness, **expertness, expertise,** proficiency, callidity, craft, moxie, cleverness; dexterity, dexterousness, dextrousness; adroitness, address, adeptness, deftness, handiness, hand, practical ability; coordination, timing; quickness, readiness; competence, capability, capacity, ability; efficiency; facility, prowess; grace, style, finesse; tact, tactfulness, diplomacy; *savoir-faire* <Fr>; artistry; artfulness; craftsmanship, workmanship, artisanship; know-how, savvy, bag of tricks; technical skill, technique, touch, technical brilliance, technical mastery, virtuosity, bravura, wizardry; brilliance; cunning; ingenuity, ingeniousness, resource, resourcefulness, wit; mastery, mastership, command, control, grip; steady hand; marksmanship, seamanship, airmanship, horsemanship

2 **agility,** nimbleness, spryness, lightness, featliness

3 **versatility**, ambidexterity, many-sidedness, all-roundedness, Renaissance versatility; adaptability, adjustability, flexibility; broad-gauge, many hats; Renaissance man, Renaissance woman

4 **talent,** flair, strong flair, gift, endowment, dowry, dower, natural gift, natural endowment, genius, instinct, faculty, bump; power, ability, capability, capacity, potential; caliber; forte, speciality, métier, long suit, strong point, strong suit, strength; equipment, qualification; talents, powers, parts; the goods, the stuff, the right stuff, what it takes, the makings

5 **aptitude,** inborn aptitude, innate aptitude, innate ability, genius, aptness, felicity, flair; bent, turn, propensity, leaning, inclination, tendency; turn for, capacity for, gift for, genius for; feeling for, good head for, an eye for, an ear for, a hand for, a way with

6 **knack,** art, hang, trick, way; touch, feel

7 art, science, craft; **skill;** technique, technic, technics, technology, technical knowledge, technical skill, technical know-how; mechanics, mechanism; method

8 accomplishment, acquirement, **attainment;** finish; coup, feat, clincher, classic; hit, smash hit

9 **experience, practice,** practical knowledge, practical skill, hands-on experience, fieldwork; background, past experience, seasoning, tempering; backstory, origin story; worldly wisdom, knowledge of the world, episteme, sophistication; sagacity

10 **masterpiece,** masterwork, *chef d'œuvre* <Fr>; master stroke, *coup de maître* <Fr>; **feat,** *tour de force* <Fr>, *pièce de résistance* <Fr>, magnum opus, classic, treasure, work of art, epic, crème de la crème, artistry

11 **expert, adept,** proficient, genius; artist, craftsman, artisan, skilled workman, journeyman; technician; seasoned hand, experienced hand; shark, sharp, sharpy, no slouch, tough act to follow; graduate; professional, pro; jack-of-all-trades, all-rounder, Renaissance man, Renaissance woman, handyman, handywoman; wordsmith; -smith, authority, authority figure, maven, know-it-all; professor; **consultant,** expert consultant, specialist, attaché, technical adviser; counselor, adviser, mentor; boffin, talking head, pundit, savant; diplomatist, diplomat; politician, statesman, statesperson, elder statesman; connoisseur, cognoscente; *cordon bleu* <Fr>; marksman, crack shot, dead shot; walking encyclopedia, illuminati

12 **talented person, talent,** man of parts, woman of parts, gifted person, prodigy, natural, **genius,** mental genius, intellectual genius, intellectual prodigy, mental giant; rocket scientist, brain surgeon; phenom; gifted child, child prodigy, wunderkind, whiz kid, boy wonder; polymath; one-trick pony

13 **master,** past master, grand master; master hand, world-class performer, champion, good hand, dab hand, skilled hand, practiced hand, practitioner, specialist; first chair; prodigy; wizard, magician; virtuoso; maestro; genius, man of genius, woman of genius, paragon; mastermind; master spirit, mahatma, sage

14 <nonformal> **ace, star,** superstar, crackerjack, dab, great, all-time great, topnotcher, first-rater, whiz, flash, hot stuff, pisser*, piss-cutter*, pistol, no slouch, world-beater, hot rock, the one who

wrote the book, right person for the job, smart cookie; geek, nerd

15 **champion,** champ, victor, titleholder, world champion; record holder, world-record holder; laureate; medal winner, Olympic medal winner, medalist, award winner, prizeman, prizetaker, prizewinner; most valuable player (MVP); hall of famer

16 **veteran,** vet, seasoned veteran, grizzled veteran, old pro; old hand, old-timer one of the old guard, old stager <Brit>; old campaigner, warhorse, old warhorse; salt, old salt, old sea dog, shellback

17 **sophisticate,** man of experience, man of the world; slicker, city slicker; man-about-town; cosmopolitan, cosmopolite, citizen of the world

VERBS 18 **excel in**, excel at, shine in, shine at, be master of; write the book, have a good command of, feel comfortable with, be at home in; have a gift for, have a flair for, have a talent for, have a bent for, have a faculty for, have a bump for, be a natural, be cut out to be, be born to be, have a good head for, have an ear for, have an eye for, be born for, show aptitude for, show talent for, have something to spare; have the knack, have the touch, have a way with, have the right touch, have the hang of it, have a lot going for one, be able to do it blindfolded, be able to do it standing on one's head; have something on the ball, have plenty on the ball

19 **know backwards and forwards,** know one's stuff, know one's onions, know the ropes, know all the ins and outs, know from A to Z, know from alpha to omega, know like the back of one's hand, know like a book, read like a book, know from the ground up, know all the tricks, know all the moves moves, know all the tricks of the trade, have game, know all the moves of the game; know what's what, know a thing or two, know what it's all about, know the score, know all the answers, know a hawk from a handsaw; have savvy; know one's way about, know the ways of the world, have been around, have been around the block, have been through the mill, have cut one's wisdom teeth, have cut one's eyeteeth, be long in the tooth, not be born yesterday; get around

20 **exercise skill,** handle oneself well, demonstrate one's ability, strut one's stuff, hotdog, grandstand, showboat, show expertise; cut one's coat according to one's cloth, play one's cards well

21 **be versatile,** double in brass, wear more than one hat

ADJS 22 **skillful,** good, goodish, excellent, expert, proficient; dexterous, good at, adroit, deft, adept, coordinated, well-coordinated, apt, no mean, handy; quick, ready; clever, cute, slick, slick as a whistle, neat, clean; fancy, graceful, stylish; every bit a; masterly, masterful; magistral, magisterial; authoritative, consummate, professional; the complete; crack, crackerjack, ace, first-rate, supreme; whiz-kid; virtuoso, bravura, technically superb; brilliant; cunning; tactful, diplomatic, politic, statesmanlike; ingenious, resourceful, daedal, Daedalian; artistic; workmanlike, well-done

23 **agile,** nimble, spry, sprightly, fleet, featly, peart, light, graceful, nimble-footed, light-footed, surefooted; nimble-fingered, neat-fingered, neat-handed

24 **competent,** capable, able, efficient, qualified, fit, fitted, suited, worthy; journeyman; fit for, fitted for; **equal to, up to;** up to snuff, up to the mark, *au fait* <Fr>; well-qualified, well-fitted, well-suited

25 **versatile,** ambidextrous, two-handed, all-around, broad-gauge, well-rounded, many-sided, generally capable; adaptable, adjustable, flexible, resourceful, supple, ready for anything; amphibious

26 **skilled, accomplished**; practiced; professional, career; trained, coached, prepared, primed, finished; at one's best, at concert pitch; initiated, initiate; technical; conversant

27 **skilled in,** proficient in, adept in, versed in, good at, expert at, handy at, a hand at, good hand at, master of, strong in, at home in; up on, well up on, well-versed

28 **experienced, practiced,** mature, matured, ripe, ripened, seasoned, tried, well-tried, tried and true, veteran, old, an old dog at; sagacious; worldly, worldly-wise, world-wise, wise in the ways of the world, knowing, shrewd, sophisticated, cosmopolitan, cosmopolite, blasé, dry behind the ears, not born yesterday, long in the tooth; been there done that

29 **talented, gifted, endowed,** with a flair; born for, made for, cut out for, with an eye for, with an ear for, with a bump for

30 well-laid, well-devised, well-contrived, **well-designed**, well-planned, well-worked-out; well-invented; well-weighed, well-reasoned, well-considered, well-thought-out, thought-out; cunning, clever

ADVS 31 **skillfully,** expertly, proficiently, excellently, well; cleverly, neatly, ingeniously, resourcefully; cunningly; dexterously, adroitly, deftly, adeptly, aptly, handily; agilely, nimbly, featly, spryly; competently, capably, ably, efficiently; masterfully; brilliantly, superbly, with genius, with a touch of genius; artistically, artfully; with skill, with consummate skill, with finesse

414 UNSKILLFULNESS

<lack of skill>

NOUNS **1 unskillfulness,** skill-lessness, inexpertness, unproficiency, uncleverness; unintelligence; inadeptness, undexterousness, indexterity, undeftness; inefficiency; incompetence, incompetency, inability, incapability, incapacity, inadequacy; ineffectiveness, ineffectuality; mediocrity, pedestrianism; **inaptitude**, inaptness, unaptness, ineptness, maladroitness; unfitness, unfittedness; untrainedness, unschooledness; thoughtlessness, inattentiveness; maladjustment; rustiness, nonuse

2 inexperience, unexperience, unexperiencedness, unpracticedness; rawness, greenness, unripeness, callowness, unfledgedness, unreadiness, immaturity; ignorance; unfamiliarity, unacquaintance, unacquaintedness, unaccustomedness; amateurishness, amateurism, unprofessionalness, unprofessionalism

3 clumsiness, awkwardness, bumblingness, maladroitness, unhandiness, left-handedness, heavy-handedness, fumblitis, ham-handedness, ham-fistedness; handful of thumbs; ungainliness, uncouthness, ungracefulness, gracelessness, inelegance; gawkiness, gawkishness; lubberliness, oafishness, loutishness, boorishness, clownishness, lumpishness; cumbersomeness, hulkiness, ponderousness; unwieldiness, unmanageability

4 bungling, blundering, boggling, fumbling, malperformance, muffing, botching, botchery, blunderheadedness; sloppiness, carelessness; too many cooks

5 bungle, blunder, botch, flub, boner, bonehead play, boggle, bobble, boo-boo, screwup, ball-up, fuck-up*, foul-up, foozle, bevue; fumble, muff, fluff, flop, miscue, misfire, mishit; slip, trip, stumble; *gaucherie* <Fr>; hash, mess; bad job, sad work, clumsy performance, poor show, poor performance; off day; error, mistake

6 mismanagement, mishandling, misdirection, misguidance, misconduct, misgovernment, misrule; misadministration, maladministration; malfeasance, malpractice, misfeasance, wrongdoing; nonfeasance, omission, negligence, neglect; bad policy, impolicy; inexpedience, inexpediency

7 incompetent, incapable; dull tool, mediocrity, duffer, hacker, no great shakes, no prize, no prize package, no brain surgeon, no rocket scientist; no conjuror; one who will not set the Thames on fire <Brit>; greenhorn

8 bungler, blunderer, blunderhead, boggler, slubberer, bumbler, hack, fumbler, botcher; bull in a china shop, ox; lubber, lobby, lout, oaf, gawk, boor, clown, slouch; clodhopper, clodknocker, bumpkin, yokel, geek; clod, dolt, sad sack, blockhead; awkward squad; blind leading the blind

9 <nonformal> **goof,** goofer, goofball, goofus, foul-up, fuck-up*, screwup, bobbler, bonehead, dub, jerk, bozo, foozler, clumsy, fumble-fist, klutz, butterfingers, muff, muffer, stumblebum, stumblebunny, duffer, lummox, slob, lump; gowk, rube, hick

VERBS **10** not know how, not have the knack, not have it in one; not be up to; not be versed; muddle along, pedestrianize; show one's ignorance, not have a clue

11 bungle, blunder, bumble, boggle, bobble, muff, muff one's cue, muff one's lines, fumble, be all thumbs, have a handful of thumbs; flounder, muddle, lumber; stumble, slip, trip, trip over one's own feet, get in one's own way, miss one's footing, miscue; commit a faux pas, commit a gaffe; blunder on, blunder into, blunder upon, blunder away, be not one's day; botch, mar, spoil, butcher, murder, make sad work of; play havoc with, play mischief with

12 <nonformal> **goof,** pull a boner, bobble, lay an egg, put one's foot in it, stick one's foot in it, stub one's toe, step on one's schvantz, step on one's pecker, drop the ball, drop a pop-up, drop a brick, bonehead into it; blow, blow it, bitch*, bitch up*, hash up, mess up, flub, flub the dub, make a mess of, make a hash of, make a faux pas, foul up, fuck up*, goof up, bollix up, screw up, louse up, gum up, gum up the works, bugger, bugger up <Brit>, play the devil with, play merry hell with; go at it ass-backwards; put one's foot in one's mouth; self-destruct

13 mismanage, mishandle, misconduct, misdirect, misguide, misgovern, misrule; misadminister, maladminister; be negligent

14 not know what one is about, not know one's interest, lose one's touch, make an ass of oneself, **make a fool of oneself,** lose face, stultify oneself, have egg on one's face, put oneself out of court, stand in one's own light, not know on which side one's bread is buttered, not know one's ass from one's elbow, not know one's ass from a hole in the ground, kill the goose that lays the golden egg, cut one's own throat, dig one's own grave, behave self-destructively, play with fire, burn one's fingers, jump out of the frying pan into the fire, lock the barn door after the horse is stolen, count one's chickens before they are hatched, buy a pig in a poke, aim at a pigeon and kill a crow, put the cart before the horse, put a square peg into a round hole, paint oneself into a corner, run before one can walk

ADJS 15 **unskillful,** skill-less, artless, inexpert, unproficient, unclever; inefficient; undexterous, undeft, inadept, unfacile; unapt, inapt, inept, hopeless, half-assed, lame-o, clunky, poor; mediocre, pedestrian; thoughtless, inattentive; unintelligent

16 **unskilled,** unaccomplished, untrained, untaught, unschooled, untutored, uncoached, unimproved, uninitiated, unprepared, unprimed, unfinished, unpolished; untalented, ungifted, unendowed; **amateurish,** unprofessional, unbusinesslike, semiskilled

17 **inexperienced,** unexperienced, unversed, unconversant, **unpracticed;** undeveloped, unseasoned; raw, green, green as grass, unripe, callow, unfledged, immature, unmatured, fresh, wet behind the ears, not dry behind the ears, in training, untried; unskilled in, unpracticed in, unversed in, unconversant with, unaccustomed to, unused to, unfamiliar with, unacquainted with, new to, uninitiated in, a stranger to, a novice at, a tyro at; ignorant; semiskilled

18 **out of practice,** out of training, out of form, soft, out of shape, out of condition, stiff, rusty; gone to seed, run to seed, over the hill, not what one used to be, losing one's touch, slipping, on the downgrade

19 **incompetent,** incapable, unable, inadequate, unequipped, unqualified, ill-qualified, out of one's depth, outmatched, unfit, unfitted, unadapted, not equal to, not up to, not cut out for; ineffective, ineffectual; unadjusted, maladjusted

20 **bungling,** blundering, blunderheaded, bumbling, fumbling, mistake-prone, accident-prone; clumsy, awkward, uncoordinated, maladroit, unhandy, left-hand, left-handed, heavy-handed, ham-handed, ham-fisted, cack-handed, clumsy-fisted, butterfingered, all thumbs, fingers all thumbs, with a handful of thumbs; stiff; ungainly, uncouth, ungraceful, graceless, inelegant, *gauche* <Fr>; gawky, gawkish; lubberly, loutish, oafish, boorish, clownish, lumpish, slobbish; sloppy, careless; ponderous, cumbersome, lumbering, hulking, hulky; unwieldy

21 **botched, bungled,** fumbled, muffed, spoiled, butchered, murdered; ill-managed, ill-done, ill-conducted, ill-devised, ill-contrived, ill-executed; mismanaged, misconducted, misdirected, misguided; impolitic, ill-considered, ill-advised; negligent

22 <nonformal> **goofed-up,** bobbled, bitched, bitched-up*, hashed-up, messed-up, fouled-up, fucked-up*, screwed-up, bollixed-up, loused-up, gummed-up; buggered, buggered-up <Brit>; snafued; clunky, half-assed; ass-backwards

ADVS 23 **unskillfully,** inexpertly, unproficiently, uncleverly; inefficiently; incompetently, incapably, inadequately, unfitly; undexterously, undeftly, inadeptly, unfacilely; unaptly, inaptly, ineptly, poorly

24 **clumsily,** awkwardly; bunglingly, blunderingly; maladroitly, unhandily; ungracefully, gracelessly, inelegantly, uncouthly; ponderously, cumbersomely, lumberingly, hulkingly, hulkily; ass-backwards

415 CUNNING

<cleverness in method>

NOUNS 1 **cunning,** cunningness, **craft, craftiness,** artfulness, art, artifice, wiliness, wiles, guile, slyness, insidiousness, foxiness, slipperiness, shiftiness, trickiness; low cunning, animal cunning; gamesmanship, one-upmanship; canniness, shrewdness, sharpness, acuteness, astuteness, cleverness; resourcefulness, ingeniousness, wit, inventiveness, readiness; subtlety, subtleness, Italian hand, fine Italian hand, finesse, restraint; cuteness, cutification; Jesuitism, Jesuitry, sophistry; satanic cunning, the cunning of the serpent; sneakiness, concealment, stealthiness, stealth; cageyness, wariness

2 **Machiavellianism,** Machiavellism; realpolitik; politics, diplomacy, diplomatics; jobbery, jobbing

3 **stratagem, artifice**, art, craft, wile, strategy, maneuver, device, wily device, contrivance, expedient, design, scheme, trick, cute trick, fetch, fakement, gimmick, ruse, red herring, shift, tactic, stroke, stroke of policy, master stroke, move, coup, gambit, ploy, dodge, artful dodge; game, little game, racket, grift; plot, conspiracy, intrigue; sleight, feint, jugglery; method in one's madness; subterfuge, blind, dust in the eyes; chicanery, knavery, deceit, trickery

4 **machination,** manipulation, wire-pulling; influence, political influence, behind-the-scenes influence; maneuvering, maneuvers, tactical maneuvers; tactics, devices, expedients, gimmickry; web of deceit

5 **circumvention,** getting round, getting around; evasion, elusion, the slip, pretext; the runaround, buck-passing, passing the buck; frustration, foiling, thwarting; outwitting, outsmarting, outguessing, outmaneuvering

6 slyboots, **sly dog**, fox, reynard, dodger, Artful

Dodger, crafty rascal, smooth citizen, slick citizen, smooth customer, cool customer, smooth operator, slickster, smoothy, smoothie, glib tongue, smooth talker, sweet talker, charmer; trickster, shyster, shady character, Philadelphia lawyer; horse trader, Yankee horse trader, wheeler-dealer; swindler

7 **strategist,** tactician; maneuverer, machinator, manipulator, wire-puller; calculator, schemer, intriguer

8 **Machiavellian,** Machiavel, Machiavellianist; diplomat, diplomatist, politician; political realist; influence peddler; powerbroker, kingmaker; power behind the throne, gray eminence, *éminence grise* <Fr>

VERBS 9 **live by one's wits,** fly by the seat of one's pants, play a deep game; use one's fine Italian hand, finesse; shift, dodge, twist and turn, zig and zag; have something up one's sleeve, hide one's hand, cover one's path, have an out, have a way out, have an escape hatch; trick, deceive

10 **maneuver,** manipulate, pull strings, pull wires; machinate, contrive, angle, jockey, engineer; play games; plot, scheme, intrigue; finagle, wangle; gerrymander; know a trick or two

11 **outwit, outfox,** outsmart, outguess, outfigure, outmaneuver, outgeneral, outflank, outplay, be one up on; get the better, get the best of, go one better, know a trick worth two of that; play one's trump card; overreach, outreach; circumvent, get round, get around, evade, stonewall, elude, frustrate, foil, give the slip, give the runaround; pass the buck; pull a fast one, steal a march on; make a fool of, make a sucker of, make a patsy of; be too much for, be too deep for; throw a curve, deceive, victimize

ADJS 12 **cunning, crafty, artful,** wily, guileful, sly, insidious, shifty, pawky, arch, smooth, slick, slick as a whistle, slippery, snaky, serpentine, foxy, vulpine, feline, no flies on; canny, shrewd, knowing, sharp, razor-sharp, cute, cutesy, cutesy-poo, acute, astute, clever; resourceful, ingenious, inventive, ready; subtle; Jesuitical, sophistical; tricky, trickish, sketchy, gimmicky; **Machiavellian,** Machiavellic, politic, diplomatic; strategic, tactical; deep, deep-laid; cunning as a fox, cunning as a serpent, crazy like a fox, slippery as an eel, too clever by half; sneaky, clandestine, stealthy; cagey, wary; scheming, designing; manipulative, manipulatory; deceitful

ADVS 13 **cunningly,** craftily, artfully, wilily, guilefully, insidiously, shiftily, foxily, trickily, smoothly, slick; slyly, on the sly; cannily, shrewdly, knowingly, astutely, cleverly; subtlely; cagily, warily; diplomatically

416 ARTLESSNESS

<simpleness in method>

NOUNS 1 **artlessness, ingenuousness,** guilelessness; simplicity, simpleness, plainness; simpleheartedness, simplemindedness; unsophistication, unsophisticatedness; *naïveté* <Fr>, naivety, naiveness, childlikeness; innocence; trustfulness, trustingness, unguardedness, unwariness, unsuspiciousness; openness, openheartedness, sincerity, candor; integrity, singleheartedness, single-mindedness, singleness of heart; directness, bluffness, bluntness, outspokenness

2 **naturalness,** naturalism, nature; state of nature; unspoiledness; unaffectedness, unaffectation, unassumingness, unpretendingness, unpretentiousness, undisguise; inartificiality, unartificialness, genuineness

3 **simple soul,** unsophisticate, naïf, ingenue, innocent, pure heart, child, mere child, infant, babe, baby, newborn babe, babe in the woods, lamb, dove; child of nature, noble savage; primitive; yokel, rube, hick; oaf, lout; dupe

VERBS 4 wear one's heart on one's sleeve, look one in the face, have no affectations

ADJS 5 **artless, simple,** plain, guideless; simplehearted, simpleminded; ingenuous, *ingénu* <Fr>; unsophisticated, naive; childlike, born yesterday; innocent, innocuous; trustful, trusting, unguarded, unwary, unreserved, confiding, unsuspicious, on the up and up; open, openhearted, sincere, candid, frank; singlehearted, single-minded; direct, bluff, blunt, outspoken

6 **natural,** naturelike, native; in the state of nature; primitive, primal, pristine, unspoiled, untainted, uncontaminated; **unaffected,** unassuming, unpretending, unpretentious, unfeigning, undisguising, undissimulating, undissembling, undesigning; genuine, inartificial, unartificial, unadorned, unvarnished, unembellished, uncontrived; homespun; pastoral, rural, arcadian, bucolic

ADVS 7 **artlessly,** ingenuously, guilelessly; simply, plainly; naturally, genuinely; naïvely; openly, openheartedly

417 AUTHORITY

<power to control>

NOUNS 1 **authority,** prerogative, right, **power,** faculty, competence, competency; mandate, popular authority, popular mandate, people's mandate, electoral mandate; regality, royal prerogative; constituted authority, vested authority; inherent authority; legal authority, lawful authority, rightful authority, legitimacy, law, eminent domain, divine right; derived authority, delegated authority, vicarious authority, indirect authority, invested authority; the say, the say-so; the man, Big Brother; rubber stamp; absolute power, absolutism

2 **authoritativeness, authority**, power, powerfulness, magisterialness, potency, potence, puissance, strength, might, mightiness, string pulling, wire pulling, clout, high places

3 **authoritativeness,** masterfulness, lordliness, magistrality, magisterialness; arbitrariness, peremptoriness, imperativeness, imperiousness, autocraticalness, high-handedness, dictatorialness, overbearingness, overbearance, overbearing, domineering, domineeringness, tyrannicalness, authoritarianism, bossism

4 **prestige, authority,** influence, influentialness; pressure, weight, weightiness, moment, consequence; eminence, stature, rank, seniority, preeminence, priority, precedence; greatness; importance, prominence

5 **governance, authority,** jurisdiction, control, command, power, rule, reign, regnancy, dominion, sovereignty, empire, empery, imperium, sway; government; administration, disposition; grip, claws, clutches, hand, hands, iron hand, talons

6 **dominance**, dominancy, **dominion,** domination; preeminence, supremacy, superiority; ascendance, ascendancy; upper hand, whip hand, sway; sovereignty, suzerainty, suzerainship, overlordship; primacy, principality, predominance, predominancy, predomination, prepotence, prepotency, hegemony; preponderance; balance of power; eminent domain

7 **mastership,** masterhood, masterdom, **mastery;** leadership, headship, lordship; hegemony; supervisorship, directorship; hierarchy, nobility, aristocracy, ruling class; chair, chairmanship; chieftainship, chieftaincy, chieftainry, chiefery; presidentship, presidency; premiership, prime-ministership, prime-ministry; governorship; princeship, princedom, principality; rectorship, rectorate; suzerainty, suzerainship; regency, regentship; prefectship, prefecture; proconsulship, proconsulate; provostship, provostry; protectorship, protectorate; seneschalship, seneschalsy; pashadom, pashalic; sheikhdom; emirate, viziership, vizierate; magistrateship, magistrature, magistracy; mayorship, mayoralty; sheriffdom, sheriffcy, sheriffalty, shrievalty; consulship, consulate; chancellorship, chancellery, chancellorate; seigniory; tribunate, aedileship; deanship, decanal authority, deanery; patriarchate, patriarchy; bishopric, episcopacy; archbishopric, archiepiscopacy, archiepiscopate; metropolitanship, metropolitanate; popedom, popeship, popehood, papacy, pontificate, pontificality; dictatorship, dictature; chess master, grand master, past master; self-governance

8 **sovereignty,** royalty, regnancy, majesty, empire, empery, imperialism, emperorship; kingship, kinghood; queenship, queenhood; kaisership, kaiserdom; czardom; rajaship; sultanship, sultanate; caliphate; the throne, the Crown, the purple; royal insignia; world leader

9 **scepter,** rod, staff, wand, staff of office, wand of office, baton, mace, truncheon, fasces; crosier, crook, cross-staff; caduceus; gavel; mantle; chain of office; portfolio

10 <**seat of authority**> saddle, helm, driver's seat; office of power, high office; seat, chair, bench; woolsack <Brit>; seat of state, seat of power; curule chair; dais; chairmanship, directorship, chieftainship, presidency, premiership, secretariat, governorship, mayoralty; consulate, proconsulate, prefecture, magistry; supremist

11 **throne,** royal seat; Peacock throne

12 <acquisition of authority> **accession; succession,** rightful succession, legitimate succession; usurpation, arrogation, assumption, taking over, seizure, seizure of power, takeover, coup d'etat, coup, revolution, overthrowing; anointment, anointing, consecration, coronation; selection, delegation, deputation, devolution, devolvement, assignment, nomination, appointment; election, mandate; authorization, empowerment, permission, grant, sanction, warrant, license, charter; consignation; job sharing

VERBS 13 possess authority, wield authority, have authority, **have power,** have the power, have in one's hands, have the right, have the say, have the say-so, have the whip hand, wear the crown, hold the prerogative, have the mandate; exercise sovereignty; be vested, be invested, carry authority, have clout, have what one says go, have one's own way; show one's authority, crack the whip, throw one's weight around, ride herd, have under one's thumb, wear the pants, have over a barrel; rule, control, govern; supervise

14 **take command, take charge**, take over, take the helm, take the reins of government, take the reins into one's hand, take office, gain authority, get the power into one's hands, gain the upper hand, get the upper hand, lead, take the lead; ascend to the

throne, mount the throne, succeed to the throne, accede to the throne, call the shots; assume command, assume, usurp, arrogate, seize; usurp the throne, seize the throne, usurp the crown, seize the mantle, usurp the prerogatives of the crown; seize power, execute a *coup d'état*

ADJS 15 **authoritative,** clothed with authority, vested with authority, invested with authority, commanding, imperative; governing, controlling, definitive, ruling; preeminent, supreme, administrative, managerial, bureaucratic, leading, superior; powerful, potent, puissant, mighty; dominant, ascendant, hegemonic, hegemonistic; influential, prestigious, weighty, momentous, consequential, eminent, substantial, considerable; great; important, prominent; ranking, senior; authorized, empowered, duly constituted, competent; official, *ex officio* <L>; authoritarian; absolute, autocratic, monocratic; totalitarian

16 **imperious,** imperial, **masterful,** authoritative, feudal, aristocratic, lordly, magistral, magisterial, commanding; arrogant; arbitrary, peremptory, imperative; absolute, absolutist, absolutistic; dictatorial, authoritarian; bossy, domineering, high-handed, overbearing, overruling; autocratic, monocratic, despotic, tyrannical; tyrannous, grinding, oppressive; repressive, suppressive; strict, severe

17 **sovereign; regal, royal,** majestic, purple; kinglike, kingly, every inch a king; imperial, imperious; imperatorial; monarchic, monarchical, monarchal, monarchial; tetrarchic; princely, princelike; queenly, queenlike; dynastic

ADVS 18 **authoritatively,** with authority, by virtue of office; commandingly, imperatively; definitively; powerfully, potently, puissantly, mightily; influentially, weightily, momentously, consequentially; officially, *ex cathedra* <L>

19 **imperiously, masterfully,** magisterially; arbitrarily, peremptorily; autocratically, dictatorially, high-handedly, domineeringly, overbearingly, despotically, tyrannically

20 **by authority of,** in the name of, by virtue of, by the power vested in

21 **in authority, in power,** in charge, in control, in command, at the reins, at the head, at the helm, at the wheel, in the saddle, in the driver's seat, on the throne

418 LAWLESSNESS

<absence of authority>

NOUNS 1 **lawlessness; licentiousness,** license, uncontrol, anything goes, unrestraint; indiscipline, insubordination, mutiny, disobedience; permissiveness; irresponsibility, unaccountability; willfulness, unchecked will, rampant will; interregnum, power vacuum; defiance of authority, lack of authority, breakdown of authority, breakdown of law and order; overthrow, coup, coup d'etat

2 **anarchy,** anarchism; disorderliness, unruliness, misrule, **disorder,** disruption, disorganization, confusion, arrogation, riot, turmoil, chaos, primal chaos, tohubohu; sturm and drang, storm and stress; antinomianism; nihilism; syndicalism, anarcho-syndicalism, criminal syndicalism, lynch law, mob rule, mob law, mobocracy, ochlocracy; law of the jungle; dog eat dog; subversion, sedition, unrestraint, insubordination, disobedience, revolution; rebellion

3 **anarchist,** anarch; antinomian; **nihilist,** syndicalist, anarcho-syndicalist; subversive, seditionary; revolutionist; mutineer, rebel

VERBS 4 **reject authority, defy authority,** usurp power, usurp authority, enthrone one's own will; take the law in one's own hands, act on one's own responsibility; do as one pleases, go as one pleases, indulge oneself; be a law unto oneself, answer to no man, undermine, arrogate; resist control; overthrow, depose, topple, disempower

ADJS 5 **lawless; licentious, ungoverned,** undisciplined, unrestrained; permissive; insubordinate, mutinous, disobedient; uncontrolled, uncurbed, unbridled, unchecked, rampant, untrammeled, unreined, reinless, anything goes; irresponsible, wildcat, unaccountable; selfwilled, willful, headstrong, heady, defiant; rebellious, riotous, seditious, insurgent

6 **anarchic, anarchical,** anarchial, anarchistic; unruly, disorderly, disorganized, chaotic; antinomian; **nihilistic**, syndicalistic, ochlocratic, mobocratic; every man for himself, ungovernable

ADVS 7 **lawlessly,** licentiously; anarchically, chaotically

419 PRECEPT

<rule for behavior>

NOUNS 1 **precept,** prescript, prescription, **teaching;** instruction, direction, charge, commission, injunction, dictate; order, command

2 **rule, law,** canon, maxim, dictum, moral, moralism; norm, standard; formula, form; rule of action, rule of conduct, moral precept; commandment, *mitzvah* <Heb>; sutra; tradition; ordinance, imperative, regulation, reg, *règlement* <Fr>; principle, principium, settled principle, general principle, general

truth, tenet, convention; guideline, ground rule, rubric, protocol, working rule, working principle, standard procedure; guiding principle, golden rule, caveat emptor; code; gold standard; executive order

3 **formula,** form, **recipe,** receipt; **prescription;** formulary

ADJS 4 **preceptive,** didactic, didactive, instructive, moralistic, **prescriptive;** prescript, prescribed, mandatory, non-discretionary, hard-and-fast, binding, dictated; formulary, standard, regulation, official, authoritative, canonical, statutory, rubric, rubrical, protocolary, protocolic; normative; conventional; traditional

420 COMMAND

<order for behavior>

NOUNS 1 **command, commandment,** order, direct order, command decision, bidding, behest, hest, imperative, dictate, dictation, will, pleasure, say-so, word, word of command; special order; authority

2 **injunction,** charge, commission, **mandate**

3 **direction, directive,** instruction, rule, regulation; prescript, prescription, precept; general order

4 **decree,** decreement, decretum, decretal, rescript, fiat, edict, *edictum* <L>; law; rule, ruling, dictum, ipse dixit; ordinance; proclamation, pronouncement, pronunciamento, declaration, ukase; bull, brevet; decree-law, senatus consult; diktat

5 **summons,** bidding, beck, call, calling, nod, beck and call, preconization; convocation, convoking; evocation, calling forth, invocation; requisition, indent <Brit>

6 **court order,** injunction, legal order, warrant, subpoena, citation; interdict, interdiction

7 process server, summoner

VERBS 8 **command, order,** dictate, direct, instruct, mandate, bid, enjoin, charge, commission, call on, call upon; issue a writ, issue an injunction; decree, rule, ordain, promulgate; give an order, give a direct order, issue a command, say the word, give the word, give the word of command; call the shots, call the signals, call the play; order about, order around; speak, proclaim, declare, pronounce

9 **prescribe,** require, demand, **dictate,** impose, lay down, set, fix, appoint, make obligatory, make mandatory; decide once and for all, carve in stone, set in concrete; authorize

10 **lay down the law,** put one's foot down, read the riot act, lower the boom, set the record straight

11 **summon, call,** demand, preconize; call for, send for, send out for, send after, bid come; cite, summons, subpoena, serve; page; convoke, convene, call together; call away; muster, invoke, conjure; order up, summon up, muster up, call up, conjure up, magic, magic up; evoke, call forth, summon forth, call out; recall, call back, call in; requisition, indent <Brit>

ADJS 12 **mandatory,** mandated, imperative, compulsory, prescript, prescriptive, obligatory, must; dictated, imposed, required, entailed, decretory; decisive, final, peremptory, absolute, eternal, written, hard-and-fast, carved in stone, set in concrete, ultimate, conclusive, binding, irrevocable, without appeal

13 **commanding,** imperious, imperative, jussive, peremptory, abrupt; directive, instructive; mandating, dictating, compelling, obligating, prescriptive, preceptive; decretory, decretive, decretal; authoritative

ADVS 14 **commandingly,** imperatively, peremptorily

15 **by order**, by command, at the word of command, as ordered, as required, to order; mandatorily, compulsorily, obligatorily

421 DEMAND

<requirement for behavior>

NOUNS 1 **demand, claim,** call; requisition, requirement, stated requirement, order, rush order, indent <Brit>; seller's market, land-office business; strong demand, heavy demand, draft, drain, levy, tax, taxing; imposition, impost, tribute, duty, dun, contribution; insistent demand, rush; exorbitant demand, extortionate demand, exaction, extortion, blackmail, emotional blackmail; **ultimatum,** nonnegotiable demand; notice, warning

2 **stipulation,** provision, proviso, condition; terms; exception, reservation; qualification

3 <nonformal> catch, Catch-22, zero-sum game, kicker, zinger, snag, joker; strings, strings attached; ifs, ands, and buts; whereases, howevers, howsomevers

4 **insistence,** exigence, importunity, importunateness, importunacy, demandingness, pertinaciousness, pertinacity; pressure, pressingness, urgency, exigency; persistence

VERBS 5 **demand,** ask, ask for, make a demand; call for, call on for, call upon one for, appeal to one for; call out for, cry for, cry out for, clamor for; claim, challenge, require; levy, impose, impose on one for; exact, extort, squeeze, screw; blackmail; requisition, put in requisition, dun, indent <Brit>, confiscate; order, put in an order, place an order, order up; deliver an ultimatum, issue an ultimatum; warn

6 **claim,** pretend to, lay claim to, stake a claim, put dibs on, have dibs on, assert a claim, vindicate a claim, assert a right to, assert a title to; have going for it, have going for one; challenge

7 **stipulate,** stipulate for, specifically provide, set conditions, set terms, make reservations; qualify

8 **insist,** insist on, insist upon, stick to, set one's heart on, set one's mind upon; take one's stand upon, stand on, stand upon, lay it on the line, make no bones about it; stand upon one's rights, put one's foot down; brook no denial, take no denial, not take no for an answer; maintain, contend, assert; urge, press; persist

ADJS 9 **demanding,** exacting, exigent; draining, taxing, exorbitant, extortionate, grasping; insistent, instant, importunate, urgent, pertinacious, pressing, loud, clamant, crying, clamorous; persistent

10 **claimed,** spoken for; requisitioned; requisitorial, requisitory

ADVS 11 **demandingly,** exactingly, exigently; exorbitantly, extortionately; insistently, importunately, urgently, pressingly, clamorously, loudly, clamantly

12 **on demand,** at demand, on call, upon presentation

422 ADVICE

<*suggestion for behavior*>

NOUNS 1 **advice, counsel,** recommendation, suggestion, rede; proposition, proposal; advising, advocacy; direction, instruction, guidance, briefing; exhortation, hortation, enjoinder, expostulation, remonstrance; sermons, sermonizing, preaching, preachiness; admonition, monition, monitory, monitory letter, caution, caveat, warning; idea, thought, opinion, precept; consultancy, consultantship, consultation, parley, advisement; council; counseling; guidance counseling, educational counseling, vocational guidance; mentorship; constructive criticism

2 piece of advice, **word of advice,** word to the wise, words of wisdom, pearls of wisdom, verb sap, verbum sap, word in the ear, maxim, hint, broad hint, flea in the ear, tip, one's two cents' worth, intimation, insinuation; earworm

3 **adviser, advisor,** counsel, counselor, consultant, professional consultant, expert, maven, boffin; instructor, guide, mentor, nestor, orienter, didact; confidant, confidante, personal adviser; admonisher, monitor, Dutch uncle; Polonius, preceptist; teacher; meddler, buttinsky, yenta, kibitzer, backseat driver; advocate; brain trust

4 **advisee,** counselee; client

VERBS 5 **advise, counsel,** recommend, suggest, advocate, propose, submit, propound; instruct, coach, guide, direct, brief; prescribe; weigh in with advice, give a piece of advice, give a hint, give a broad hint, hint at, intimate, insinuate, put a flea in one's ear, have a word with one, speak words of wisdom; meddle, kibitz; confer, consult with

6 **admonish, exhort,** expostulate, remonstrate, preach; enjoin, charge, call upon one to; caution, issue a caveat, wag one's finger; advise against, warn away, warn off, warn, dissuade; move, prompt, urge, incite, encourage, induce, persuade; implore

7 **take advice,** accept advice, follow advice, follow, follow implicitly, go along with, buy, buy into; consult, confer; solicit advice, desire guidance, implore counsel; be advised by; refer to, have at one's elbow, take one's cue from; seek a second opinion; put heads together, have a powwow with, huddle

ADJS 8 **advisory,** recommendatory; **consultative,** consultatory, consultive; directive, instructive; admonitory, monitory, monitorial, cautionary, warning; expostulative, expostulatory, remonstrative, remonstratory, remonstrant; exhortative, exhortatory, hortative, hortatory, preachy, didactic, moralistic, sententious

PHRS 9 too many cooks spoil the broth, another country heard from

423 COUNCIL

<*group making rules*>

NOUNS 1 **council,** conclave, *concilium* <L>, deliberative body, advisory body, assembly; deliberative assembly, consultative assembly; chamber, house; board, court, bench, panel; full assembly, plenum, plenary session; congress, diet, synod, senate, soviet; legislature; cabinet, divan, council of ministers, council of state, U.S. Cabinet, British Cabinet; kitchen cabinet, camarilla; staff; junta, directory; Sanhedrin; privy council; common council, county council, parish council, borough council, town council, city council, municipal council, village council; brain trust, brains trust, group of advisers, corps of advisers, body of advisers, inner circle; council of war; council fire; syndicate, association; conference; tribunal

2 **committee,** subcommittee, standing committee;

select committee, special committee, ad hoc committee; committee of one

3 **forum, conference,** discussion group, buzz session, roundtable, panel; open forum, colloquium, symposium; town meeting; board meeting; powwow; working lunch, power lunch, power breakfast; conference call, telemeeting

4 ecclesiastical council, chapter, classis, conclave, conference, caucus, congregation, consistory, convention, convocation, presbytery, session, synod, vestry; parochial council, parochial church council; diocesan conference, diocesan court; provincial court, plenary council; ecumenical council; Council of Nicaea, Council of Trent, Lateran Council, Vatican Council, Vatican Two; conciliarism

ADJS 5 **conciliar,** council, councilmanic, aldermanic; consultative, deliberative, advisory; synodal, synodic, synodical

ADVS 6 **in council,** in conference, in consultation, in a huddle, in conclave; in session, sitting

424 COMPULSION

<*forcing to do something*>

NOUNS 1 **compulsion,** obligation, obligement; command; necessity; inevitability; irresistibility, compulsiveness; forcing, enforcement; command performance; constraint, coaction; restraint; obsession; self-determination

2 **force**; **brute force,** naked force, rule of might, big battalions, main force, physical force; the right of the strong, the law of the jungle; tyranny; steamroller, irresistible force

3 **coercion,** coercing, intimidation, scare tactics, headbanging, arm-twisting, **duress**; the strong arm, strong-arm tactics, a gun to one's head, the sword, the mailed fist, the bludgeon, the boot in the face, the jackboot, the big stick, the club; terrorism; pressure, high pressure, high-pressure methods; violence; impressment

VERBS 4 **compel, force,** make; have, cause, cause to; constrain, bind, tie, tie one's hands; restrain; enforce, drive, impel; dragoon, use force upon, force one's hand, hold a gun to one's head; browbeat

5 **oblige,** necessitate, require, exact, demand, dictate, impose, call for; take no denial, brook no denial; leave no option, leave no escape, admit of no option

6 **press,** pressure; bring pressure to bear upon, put pressure on, bear down on, bear against, bear hard upon, put under duress

7 **coerce,** use violence, terrorize, ride roughshod, intimidate, bully, bludgeon, blackjack; hijack, shanghai, dragoon, carjack

8 <nonformal> **twist one's arm,** arm-twist, twist arms, knock heads, bang heads, knock heads together, bang heads together, strong-arm, steamroller, bulldoze, high-pressure, lean on, squeeze; put the screws on, put the screws to, get one over a barrel, get one under one's thumb, hold one's feet to the fire, turn on the heat; pull rank; ram down one's throat, cram down one's throat

9 **be compelled,** be coerced, have to; be stuck with, can't help but

ADJS 10 **compulsory,** compulsive, compulsatory, compelling; pressing, driving, imperative, imperious; constraining, coactive; restraining; irresistible

11 **obligatory, compulsory,** imperative, mandatory, required, dictated, binding; involuntary; necessary; inevitable

12 **coercive,** forcible; steamroller, bulldozer, sledgehammer, strong-arm; terroristic, violent

ADVS 13 **compulsively,** compulsorily, compellingly, imperatively, imperiously

14 **forcibly, by force,** by main force, by *force majeure*, by a strong arm; by force of arms, at gunpoint, with a gun to one's head, at the point of a gun, at the point of the sword, at bayonet point

15 **obligatorily**, compulsorily, mandatorily, by stress of, under press of; under the lash, under the gun; of necessity

425 STRICTNESS

<*strict control*>

NOUNS 1 **strictness,** severity, harshness, stringency, astringency, hard line; discipline, strict discipline, tight discipline, rigid discipline, regimentation, spit and polish; austerity, sternness, grimness, ruggedness, toughness; belt-tightening; Spartanism; authoritarianism; demandingness, exactingness; meticulousness

2 **firmness, rigor,** rigorousness, rigidness, rigidity, stiffness, hardness, obduracy, obdurateness, inflexibility, inexorability, unyieldingness, unbendingness, impliability, unrelentingness, relentlessness; uncompromisingness; stubbornness, obstinacy; purism; precisianism, puritanism, fundamentalism, orthodoxy

3 **firm hand, iron hand,** heavy hand, strong hand, tight hand, tight rein; tight ship, taut ship

VERBS 4 **keep a tight hand upon,** hold a tight hand upon, keep a firm hand on, keep a tight rein on, rule with an iron hand, rule with a rod of iron, knock heads together, bang heads together;

regiment, discipline; run a tight ship, run a taut ship, ride herd, keep one in line; maintain the highest standards, not spare oneself nor anyone else, go out of one's way, go the extra mile

5 **deal harshly with,** deal hard measure to, lay a heavy hand on, bear hard upon, take a hard line, not pull one's punches

ADJS 6 **strict, exacting,** exigent, demanding, not to be trifled with, stringent, astringent; disciplined, spit-and-polish; severe, harsh, dour, unsparing; stern, grim, austere, rugged, tough; Spartan, Spartanic; hard-line, authoritarian; meticulous

7 **firm, rigid,** rigorous, rigorist, rigoristic, stiff, hard, iron, steel, steely, hard-shell, obdurate, inflexible, ironhanded, inexorable, dour, unyielding, unbending, impliable, relentless, unrelenting, procrustean; uncompromising; stubborn, obstinate; purist, puristic; puritan, puritanic, puritanical, fundamentalist, orthodox; ironbound, rockbound, musclebound, ironclad; straitlaced, hidebound

ADVS 8 **strictly, severely, stringently,** harshly; sternly, grimly, austerely, ruggedly, toughly

9 **firmly, rigidly,** rigorously, stiffly, stiff, hardly, obdurately, inflexibly, impliably, inexorably, unyieldingly, unbendingly; uncompromisingly, relentlessly, unrelentingly; ironhandedly, with a firm hand, with a strong hand, with a heavy hand, with a tight hand, with an iron hand

426 LAXNESS

<free from control>

NOUNS 1 **laxness, laxity,** slackness, looseness, relaxedness; loosening, relaxation; imprecision, sloppiness, carelessness, remissness, negligence; indifference; weakness; impotence; unrestraint

2 **unstrictness,** nonstrictness, undemandingness, unsevereness, unharshness; leniency; **permissiveness,** overpermissiveness, overindulgence, softness; unsternness, unaustereness; easygoingness, easiness; flexibility, pliancy; latitude, lenience

VERBS 3 hold a loose rein, **give free rein to,** give the reins to, give one his head, give a free course to, give rope enough to; permit all, permit anything

ADJS 4 **lax, slack, loose,** relaxed; imprecise, sloppy, careless, slipshod; remiss, negligent; indifferent; weak; impotent; untrammeled, unrestrained; wifty

5 **unstrict,** undemanding, unexacting; unsevere, unharsh; unstern, unaustere; lenient; permissive, overpermissive, overindulgent, soft; easy, easygoing, laid-back, low-maintenance, concessory; flexible, pliant, yielding; all-access

427 LENIENCY

<allowing freedom>

NOUNS 1 **leniency,** lenience, lenientness, lenity; **clemency,** clementness, **mercifulness,** mercy, humaneness, humanity, pity, compassion; mildness, gentleness, tenderness, softness, moderateness; easiness, easygoingness; laxness; forebearance, forbearing, patience; acceptance, concession, tolerance; kid gloves, kid-glove treatment, light hand, light rein

2 **compliance,** complaisance, obligingness, accommodatingness, agreeableness; affability, graciosity, graciousness, generousness, decency, amiability; kindness, kindliness, benignity, benevolence

3 **indulgence, humoring,** obliging; favoring, gratification, pleasing; pampering, cosseting, coddling, mollycoddling, petting, spoiling; permissiveness, overpermissiveness, overindulgence, acquiescence; sparing the rod; laissez-faire

4 **spoiled child,** spoiled brat, pampered darling, mama's boy, mollycoddle, sissy; *enfant terrible* <Fr>, naughty child, holy terror

VERBS 5 **go easy on,** be easy on, ease up on, handle with kid gloves, handle with velvet gloves, use a light hand, use a light rein, slap one's wrist, spare the rod, let off the hook; **tolerate,** bear with

6 **indulge, humor,** oblige; favor, please, gratify, satisfy, cater to; give way to, yield to, let one have his own way; pamper, cosset, coddle, mollycoddle, pet, make a lapdog of, **spoil**; spare the rod; make few demands

ADJS 7 **lenient, mild,** gentle, mild-mannered, tender, humane, compassionate, clement, merciful; soft, moderate, easy, easygoing; lax; forgiving; forebearing, forbearant, patient; accepting, tolerant

8 **indulgent,** compliant, complaisant; obliging, accommodating, agreeable, amiable, gracious, generous, magnanimous, benignant, affable, decent, kind, kindly, benign, benevolent; hands-off, permissive, overpermissive, overindulgent, spoiling

9 **indulged,** pampered, coddled, **spoiled,** spoiled rotten

428 RESTRAINT

<limiting freedom>

NOUNS 1 **restraint, constraint;** inhibition; legal restraint, injunction, enjoining, enjoinder, interdict, veto; control, curb, check, rein, arrest, arrestation; retardation, deceleration, slowing down; cooling, cooling off, cooling down; retrenchment, curtailment; self-control; hindrance; rationing; thought control; restraint of trade, monopoly, protection, protectionism, protective tariff, tariff wall; clampdown, crackdown, proscription, prohibition; nondisclosure agreement, citizen's arrest; rap sheet

2 **suppression, repression**, oppression; subdual, quelling, putting down, shutting down, closing down, smashing, crushing; quashing, squashing, squelching; smothering, stifling, suffocating, strangling, throttling; extinguishment, quenching; censorship, censoring, bleeping, bleeping out, blue laws

3 **restriction, limitation,** confinement; Hobson's choice, no choice, zero option; circumscription; stint, cramping, cramp; qualification; speed limit

4 shackle, restraint, **restraints**, fetter, hamper, trammel, trammels, manacle, gyves, bond, bonds, irons, chains, ball and chain; stranglehold; handcuffs, cuffs, bracelets; stocks, bilbo, pillory; tether, spancel, leash, lead, leading string; rein; hobble, hopple; straitjacket, strait-waistcoat <Brit>, camisole; yoke, collar; bridle, halter; muzzle, gag; electronic ankle bracelet, offender's tag and monitor; iron rule, iron hand; search and seizure

5 **lock,** bolt, bar, padlock, catch, safety catch; barrier

6 restrictionist, protectionist, monopolist; censor; screw

VERBS 7 **restrain, constrain,** control, govern, guard, contain, keep under control, put under restraint, lay under restraint; inhibit; enjoin, clamp down on, crack down on, proscribe, prohibit; curb, check, arrest, bridle, get under control, rein, snub, snub in; retard, slow down, decelerate; cool, cool off, cool down; retrench, curtail; hold, hold in, keep, withhold, hold up, keep from; hinder; hold back, keep back, pull, set back; keep in, pull in, rein in; hold in check, keep in check, hold at bay, hold in leash, tie one down, tie one's hands; hold fast, keep a tight hand on; restrain oneself, not go too far, not go off the deep end

8 **suppress, repress**, stultify; keep down, hold down, keep under; close down, shut down; subdue, quell, put down, smash, crush; quash, squash, squelch; extinguish, quench, stanch, damp down, pour water on, pour cold water on, drown, kill; smother, stifle, suffocate, asphyxiate, strangle, throttle, choke off, muzzle, gag; censor, bleep, bleep out, silence; sit on, sit down on, slap down, smack down; jump on, crack down on, clamp down on, put the lid on, keep the lid on; bottle up, cork, cork up

9 **restrict, limit,** narrow, confine, tighten; ground, restrict to home, barracks, bedroom, quarters; circumscribe; keep in bounds, keep within bounds, keep from spreading, localize; cage in, hem, hem in, box, box in, box up; cramp, stint, cramp one's style; qualify

10 **bind, restrain**, tie, tie up, put the clamps on, strap, lash, leash, pinion, fasten, secure, make fast; hamper, trammel, entrammel; rope; chain, enchain; shackle, fetter, manacle, gyve, put in irons; handcuff, tie one's hands; tie hand and foot, hog-tie; straitjacket; hobble, hopple, put on a lead <Brit>, spancel; tether, picket, moor, anchor; tie down, pin down, peg down; get a stranglehold on, put a half nelson on; bridle; gag, muzzle

ADJS 11 **restraining,** constraining; inhibiting, inhibitive; suppressive, repressive, oppressive, stultifying; controlling, on top of, prohibitive

12 **restrictive,** limitative, restricting, narrowing, limiting, confining, cramping; censorial

13 **restrained, constrained,** inhibited, pent-up; guarded; controlled, curbed, bridled; under restraint, under control, in check, under discipline; grounded, out of circulation; slowed down, retarded, arrested, in remission; on leash, in leading strings

14 **suppressed, repressed; subdued,** quelled, put down, smashed, crushed; quashed, squashed, squelched; smothered, stifled, suffocated; censored

15 **restricted, limited, confined;** circumscribed, hemmed in, hedged in, boxed in; landlocked; shut-in, stormbound, weatherbound, windbound, icebound, snowbound; cramped, stinted; qualified; under arrest, up the river, doing time, in the big house

16 **bound, tied,** bound hand and foot, tied up, tied down, strapped, hampered, trammeled, shackled, handcuffed, fettered, manacled, tethered, leashed; in bonds, in irons, in chains, ironbound

429 CONFINEMENT

<limiting free movement>

NOUNS 1 **confinement,** locking-up, lockup, lockdown, caging, penning, putting behind barriers, impoundment, restraint, restriction; check, constraint

2 **quarantine, isolation,** cordoning off, segregation, separation, sequestration, seclusion; walling in, walling up, walling off; sanitary cordon, cordon; quarantine flag, yellow flag, yellow jack

3 **imprisonment, jailing,** incarceration, **internment,**

immurement, immuration; **detention, captivity,** detainment, duress, durance, durance vile; close arrest, house arrest; term of imprisonment; preventive detention; minimum-security imprisonment, minimum-security detention, maximum-security imprisonment, maximum-security detention; lockdown, solitary confinement

4 **commitment,** committal, consignment; recommitment, remand; mittimus <law>; institutionalization

5 **custody,** custodianship, keep, keeping, care, change, ward, guarding, hold, protective custody, preventive custody; protection, safekeeping; force field

6 **arrest,** arrestment, arrestation, pinch, bust, collar; **capture,** apprehension, seizure, netting; house arrest, protective custody, preventive custody

7 **place of confinement,** close quarters, not enough room to swing a cat; limbo, bardo, hell, purgatory; pound, pinfold, penfold; cage; enclosure, pen, coop

8 **prison,** prison house, correctional facility, correction facility, minimum-security facility, maximum-security facility, penitentiary, pen, keep, penal institution, bastille, state prison, federal prison; house of detention, detention center, detention home; jail, gaol <Brit>, jailhouse, lockup, bridewell <Brit>, county jail, city jail; maximum-security prison, minimum-security prison; military prison, guardhouse, stockade, brig; dungeon, oubliette, black hole; reformatory, house of correction, reform school, training school, industrial school; debtor's prison, sponging house; prison camp, internment camp, detention camp, labor camp, forced-labor camp, gulag, concentration camp; prisoner-of-war camp, prisoner-of-war stockade, POW camp, prison farm; cell; bullpen; solitary confinement, the hole, solitary; prison cell, jail cell; detention cell, holding cell; tank, drunk tank; cellblock, cellhouse; condemned cell, death cell, death house, death row; penal settlement, penal colony, Devil's Island, Alcatraz; halfway house

9 <nonformal> **slammer,** slam, jug, can, coop, cooler, hoosegow, stir, clink, pokey, poky, nick, quod, chokey <Brit>; **joint,** big house, big school, big cage, big joint, brig, tank, icebox

10 **jailer,** gaoler <Brit>, correctional officer, corrections officer; keeper, warder, prison guard, turnkey, bull, screw; warden, governor <Brit>, commandant, principal keeper; custodian, caretaker, guardian; guard

11 **prisoner, captive,** inmate, cageling; arrestee; convict, con; jailbird, gaolbird, stir bird, lifer, collar, yardbird, lag <Brit>, lagger <Brit>; detainee; internee; prisoner of war (POW); enemy prisoner of war (EPWS); political prisoner, prisoner of conscience, political detainee, terror suspect; trusty, trustee; condemned prisoner; parolee, ticket-of-leave man <Brit>, ticket-of-leaver <Brit>; ex-convict; chain-gang member, hostage

VERBS **12** **confine,** shut in, shut away, coop in, hem in, fence in, fence up, wall in, wall up, rail in; shut up, coop up, pen up, box up, mew up, bottle up, cork up, seal up, impound; pen, coop, pound, crib, mew, cloister, immure, cage, cage in, encage; enclose; hold, keep in, hold in custody, keep in custody, **detain,** keep in detention, constrain, ground, **restrain,** hold in restraint; check, inhibit; restrict; shackle

13 **quarantine, isolate,** segregate, separate, seclude; cordon, cordon off, seal off, rope off; wall off, set up barriers, put behind barriers

14 **imprison, incarcerate,** intern, immure; jail, gaol <Brit>, jug, put under security, put behind bars, put away, put into jail, throw into jail, throw under the jailhouse; throw in prison, cast in prison, clap up, clap in jail, clap in prison, send up the river, send to the big house; lock up, lock away, lock in, bolt in, put under lock and key, keep under lock and key; hold captive, hold prisoner, hold in captivity; hold under house arrest, throw in the tank, throw in the cooler

15 **arrest,** make an arrest, put under arrest, pick up; catch flat-footed; catch with one's pants down, catch with a hand in the till, catch one in the act, catch one red-handed, catch one in flagrante delicto, catch one dead to rights, have one dead to rights; run down, run to earth, take captive, take prisoner, apprehend, capture, seize, net, lay by the heels, take into custody, entrap

16 <nonformal> **bust,** pinch, make a pinch, nab, collar, nick, pull in, run in

17 **commit,** consign, commit to prison, send to jail, send up, send up the river; commit to an institution, institutionalize; recommit, remit, remand

18 **be imprisoned,** do time, **serve time**; pay one's debt to society, land in the cooler, lag <Brit>

ADJS **19** **confined,** in confinement, **shut-in,** pent, pent-up, penned in, kept in, under restraint, held, in detention; impounded; grounded, out of circulation; detained; restricted; cloistered, enclosed

20 **quarantined,** isolated, segregated, separated; cordoned, cordoned off, sealed off, roped off

21 **jailed,** jugged, imprisoned, incarcerated, interned, immured; in prison, in stir, in captivity, captive, behind bars, locked up, under lock and key, in durance vile, serving a sentence; doing time, on the inside, on ice, in the cooler, up the river, in the big house

22 **under arrest,** in custody, in hold, in charge <Brit>, under detention, in detention; under close arrest, under house arrest

430 FREEDOM

<ability to move freely>

NOUNS 1 **freedom, liberty;** license, loose; run, the run of; civil liberty; the Four Freedoms, freedom of speech and expression, free speech, freedom of speech; freedom of worship, freedom from want, freedom from fear; freedom of movement; constitutional freedom; lack of censorship; academic freedom; artistic license, poetic license; First Amendment

2 **right, rights, civil rights,** civil liberties, constitutional rights, legal rights; Bill of Rights, Petition of Right, Declaration of Right, Declaration of the Rights of Man, Magna Carta; unalienable rights, human rights, natural rights; life, liberty, and the pursuit of happiness; diplomatic immunity, executive privilege; grandfathered rights; habeas corpus

3 **unrestraint,** unconstraint, noncoercion, nonintimidation; unreserve, irrepressibleness, irrepressibility, uninhibitedness, exuberance; immoderacy, intemperance, incontinence, uncontrol, unruliness, indiscipline; abandon, abandonment, licentiousness, wantonness, riotousness, wildness; permissiveness, unstrictness, laxness; one's own way, one's own devices

4 **latitude, scope,** room, range, way, field, maneuvering space, maneuvering room, room to swing a cat; margin, clearance, space, open space, open field, elbowroom, breathing space, breathing room, leeway, sea room, wide berth; tolerance; free scope, full scope, ample scope, free hand, free play, free course; carte blanche, blank check; no holds barred; swing, play, full swing; rope, long rope, long tether, rope enough to hang oneself

5 **independence,** self-determination, self government, self-direction, autonomy, home rule; autarky, autarchy, self-containment, self-sufficiency; individualism, rugged individualism, individual freedom; self-reliance, self-dependence; inner-direction; no allegiance; singleness, bachelorhood; independent means; self-assessment; sense of direction

6 **free will,** free choice, **discretion,** option, choice, say, say-so, druthers, free decision; full consent; absolute free will, unconditioned free will, noncontingent free will

7 own free will, own account, own accord, own hook, own say-so, own discretion, own choice, own initiative, personal initiative, own responsibility, personal responsibility, individual responsibility, own volition, own authority, own power; own way, own sweet way; law unto oneself

8 **exemption,** exception, **immunity**; release, discharge; franchise, license, charter, patent, liberty; diplomatic immunity, congressional immunity, legislative immunity; special case, special privilege; grandfather clause, grandfathering; privilege; permission

9 **noninterference,** nonintervention; isolationism; laissez-faireism, let-alone principle, deregulation; *laissez-faire, laissez-aller* <Fr>; liberalism, free enterprise, free competition, self-regulating market; open market; capitalism; free trade; noninvolvement, nonalignment, neutrality

10 **liberalism,** libertarianism, latitudinarianism; broad-mindedness, open-mindedness, toleration, tolerance; unbigotedness; libertinism, freethinking, free thought; liberalization, liberation; nonconformity

11 **freeman,** freewoman; citizen, free citizen, burgess, bourgeois; franklin; emancipated slave, manumitted slave, freedman, freedwoman; dediticián

12 **free agent, independent,** freelance; individualist, rugged individualist; free spirit; liberal, libertarian, latitudinarian; libertine, freethinker; free trader; nonpartisan, neutral, undecided, mugwump; isolationist; nonaligned nation; third world, third force, developing world; indie; lone wolf, loner, nonconformist, one-man band

VERBS 13 liberalize, ease; **free, liberate**

14 **exempt,** free, release, discharge, let go, let off, set at liberty, spring; excuse, spare, except, grant immunity, make a special case of; grandfather; dispense, dispense from, give dispensation from; dispense with, save the necessity; remit, remise; absolve

15 give a free hand, let one have his head, give one his head; give the run of, give the freedom of; give one leeway, give full play; give one space, give one room; **give free rein to,** give the reins to, give rain to, give bridle to, give one line, give one rope; give one carte blanche, give one a blank check; let go one's own way, let one go at will

16 **not interfere,** leave alone, let alone, let be, leave well enough alone, let well enough alone, let

sleeping dogs lie; keep hands off, not tamper, not meddle, not involve oneself, not get involved, let it ride, let nature take its course; live and let live, leave one to oneself, leave one in peace; mind one's own business; tolerate; decontrol, deregulate

17 <nonformal> get off one's back, get off one's case, get off one's tail, get out of one's face, get out of one's hair, butt out, back off, leave be, call off the dogs, keep one's nose out, get lost, take a walk, not cramp someone's style

18 **be free,** feel free, feel free as a bird, feel at liberty; go at large, breathe free, breathe the air of freedom; have free scope, have one's druthers, have a free hand, have the run of; be at home, feel at home; be freed, be released; be exonerated, go scot-free, get off scot-free, walk

19 let oneself go, let go, let loose, cut loose, let one's hair down, give way to, open up, let it all hang out; go all out, go flat out, pull out all the stops; go unrestrained, run wild, have one's fling, sow one's wild oats

20 **stand on one's own two feet,** shift for oneself, fend for oneself, stand on one's own, strike out for oneself, trust one's good right arm, look out for number one; go it alone, be one's own man, pull a lone oar, play a lone hand, paddle one's own canoe; suffice to oneself, do for oneself, make one's own way, pay one's own way; ask no favors, ask no quarter; be one's own boss, call no man master, answer only to oneself, ask leave of no man; go one's own way, take one's own course; do on one's own, do one's own thing, do on one's own initiative, do on one's own hook, do on one's say-so, do in one's own sweet way; have a will of one's own, have one's own way, do what one likes, do what one wishes, do what one chooses, do as one pleases, go as one pleases, please oneself, suit oneself; have a free mind; freelance, be a free agent, you do you

ADJS **21** **free; at liberty,** at large, on the loose, loose, unengaged, disengaged, detached, unattached, uncommitted, uninvolved, clear, in the clear, go-as-you-please, easygoing, footloose, footloose and fancy-free, free and easy; free as air, free as a bird, free as the wind; scot-free; freeborn; freed, liberated, emancipated, manumitted, released, uncaged, sprung

22 **independent,** self-dependent; free-spirited, freeform, freewheeling, free-floating, freestanding; self-determined, self-directing, one's own man; freelance; inner-directed, individualistic; self-governed, self-governing, autonomous, sovereign; stand-alone, self-reliant, self-sufficient, self-subsistent, self-supporting, self-contained, autarkic, autarchic; nonpartisan, neutral, nonaligned; third-world, third-force

23 **free-acting,** free-going, free-moving, free-working; freehand, freehanded; free-spoken, outspoken, plainspoken, open, frank, direct, candid, blunt

24 **unrestrained,** unconstrained, unforced, uncompelled, uncoerced; unmeasured, uninhibited, unsuppressed, unrepressed, unreserved, go-go, exuberant; uncurbed, unchecked, unbridled, unmuzzled; unreined, reinless; uncontrolled, unmastered, unsubdued, ungoverned, unruly; out of control, out of hand, out of one's power; abandoned, intemperate, immoderate, incontinent, licentious, loose, wanton, rampant, riotous, wild; irrepressible; lax

25 **nonrestrictive,** unrestrictive; permissive, hands-off; indulgent; lax; liberal, libertarian, latitudinarian; broad-minded, open-minded, tolerant; unbigoted; libertine; freethinking

26 **unhampered,** untrammeled, unhandicapped, unimpeded, unhindered, unprevented, unclogged, unobstructed; clear, unencumbered, unburdened, unladen, unembarrassed, disembarrassed; free-ranging, free-range; anti-lock

27 **unrestricted,** unconfined, uncircumscribed, unbound, unbounded, unmeasured; unlimited, limitless, illimitable; unqualified, unconditioned, unconditional, without strings, no strings, no strings attached; absolute, perfect, unequivocal, full, plenary; open-ended, open, wide-open; permissive; decontrolled, deregulated

28 **unbound,** untied, **unfettered,** unshackled, unchained; unmuzzled, ungagged; uncensored; declassified

29 **unsubject,** ungoverned, unenslaved, unenthralled; unvanquished, unconquered, unsubdued, unquelled, untamed, unbroken, undomesticated, unreconstructed

30 **exempt, immune;** exempted, released, excused, excepted, let off, spared; grandfathered; privileged, licensed, favored, chartered; permitted; dispensed; unliable, unsubject, irresponsible, unaccountable, unanswerable

31 quit, clear, free, rid; free of, clear of, quit of, rid of, shut of, shed of

ADVS **32** **freely,** free; without restraint, without stint, unreservedly, with abandon; outright

33 **independently,** alone, by oneself, all by one's lonesome, under one's own power, under one's own steam, on one's own, on one's own hook, on one's own initiative; on one's own account, on one's own responsibility, on one's own say-so; of one's own free will, of one's own accord, of one's own volition, at one's own discretion

431 LIBERATION

<freeing from control>

NOUNS 1 **liberation, freeing,** setting free, setting at liberty; deliverance, delivery; rescue; emancipation, disenthrallment, manumission; enfranchisement, affranchisement; Emancipation Proclamation; Nineteenth Amendment; Equal Rights Amendment; women's liberation, women's lib; gay liberation, gay lib; men's lib

2 **release, freeing,** unhanding, loosing, unloosing; unbinding, untying, unbuckling, unshackling, unfettering, unlashing, unstrapping, untrussing, unmanacling, unleashing, unchaining, untethering, unhobbling, unharnessing, unyoking, unbridling; unmuzzling, ungagging; unlocking, unlatching, unbolting, unbarring; unpenning, uncaging; discharge, dismissal; parole, bail; convict release, springing; demobilization, separation from the service

3 **extrication,** freeing, releasing, clearing; **disengagement, disentanglement,** untangling, unsnarling, unraveling, disentwining, disinvolvement, unknotting, disembarrassment, disembroilment; dislodgment, breaking out, breaking loose, busting out, busting loose

VERBS 4 **liberate, free,** deliver, set free, set at liberty, set at large; emancipate, manumit, disenthrall; enfranchise, affranchise; rescue

5 **release, unhand, let go,** let loose, turn loose, cast loose, let out, let off, let go free, let off the hook; discharge, dismiss; let out on bail, grant bail to, go bail for; parole, put on parole; release from prison, spring; demobilize, separate from the service

6 **loose,** loosen, let loose, cut loose, cut free, unloose, unloosen; unbind, untie, unstrap, unbuckle, unlash, untruss; unfetter, unshackle, unmanacle, unchain, unhandcuff, untie one's hands; unleash, untether, unhobble; unharness, unyoke, unbridle; unmuzzle, ungag; unlock, unlatch, unbolt, unbar; unpen, uncage

7 **extricate,** free, release, clear, get out; disengage, disentangle, untangle, unsnarl, unravel, disentwine, disinvolve, unknot, detangle, disembarrass, disembroil; dislodge, break out, break loose, cut loose, tear loose

8 **free oneself from,** deliver oneself from, get free of, get quit of, get rid of, get clear of, get out of, get well out of, get around, extricate oneself, get out of a jam; throw off, shake off; break out, bust out, go over the wall, escape; wriggle out of

9 **go free,** go scot free, go at liberty, get off, get off scot-free, get out of, beat the rap, walk

ADJS 10 **liberated, freed, emancipated,** released; delivered, rescued, ransomed, redeemed; extricated, unbound, untied, unshackled; free; scot-free; on parole, out on bail; demobilized

432 SUBJECTION

<making others obey>

NOUNS 1 **subjection, subjugation;** domination; restraint, control; bondage, captivity; thrall, thralldom, enthrallment; slavery, enslavement, master-slave relationship; servitude, compulsory servitude, involuntary servitude, servility, bond service, indentureship; serfdom, serfhood, villenage, vassalage; helotry, helotism; debt slavery, peonage; feudalism, feudality; absolutism, tyranny; deprivation of freedom, disenfranchisement, disfranchisement; damaged goods; abusive relationship

2 **subservience,** subserviency, subjecthood, subordinacy, subordination, juniority, inferiority; lower status, subordinate role, satellite status; back seat, second fiddle, hind tit; service, servitorship

3 **dependence**, dependency, codependency, contingency, tutelage, chargeship, wardship; apprenticeship; clientship, clientage

4 **subdual, quelling,** conquest, crushing, trampling down, treading down, reduction, humbling, humiliation; breaking, taming, domestication, gentling; conquering; suppression

5 **subordinate,** junior, secondary, second-in-command, lieutenant, inferior; underling, understrapper, low man on the totem pole, errand boy, flunky, gofer, grunt; assistant, personal assistant, undersecretary, helper; strong right arm, right-hand man; servant, employee

6 **dependent, charge, ward,** client, protégé, encumbrance; pensioner, pensionary; public charge, ward of the state; child; foster child; dependency state, dependent state, client state, satellite, satellite state, puppet government, creature; hanger-on, parasite

7 **subject,** vassal, liege, liege man, liege subject, homager; captive; **slave,** servant, chattel, chattel slave, bondsman, bondman, bondslave, theow, thrall; indentured servant; laborer, esne; bondwoman, bondswoman, bondmaid; odalisque, concubine; galley slave; serf, helot, villein; churl; debt slave, peon; conscript

VERBS 8 **subjugate, subject,** subordinate; dominate; disfranchise, disenfranchise, divest of freedom, deprive of freedom; enslave, enthrall, hold in thrall, make a chattel of; take captive, lead into captivity; hold in subjection, hold in bondage, hold captive, hold in captivity; hold down, keep down, keep under; keep under one's thumb, have under one's thumb, have tied to one's apron strings, hold in leash, hold in leading strings, hold in swaddling clothes, keep at one's beck and call; vassalize, make dependent, make tributary; peonize

9 subdue, master, overmaster, quell, crush, reduce, beat down, break, break down, overwhelm; tread underfoot, trample on, trample down, trample underfoot, roll in the dust, trample in the dust, drag at one's chariot wheel; oppress, suppress; make one give in, make one say "uncle," conquer; kick around, tyrannize; unman; bring low, bring to terms, humble, humiliate, take down a notch, take down a peg, bend, bring one to his knees, bend to one's will

10 have subject, twist around one's little finger, make lie down and roll over, have eating out of one's hand, lead by the nose, make a puppet of, make putty of, make a sport of, make a plaything of; use as a doormat, treat like dirt under one's feet, walk all over

11 domesticate, tame, break, bust, gentle, break in, break to harness; housebreak

12 depend on, be at the mercy of, be the sport of, be the plaything of, be the puppet of, be putty in the hands of; not dare to say one's soul is one's own; eat out of one's hands; play second fiddle, suck hind tit, take a back seat; pay tribute

ADJS **13 subject, dependent,** tributary, client; subservient, subordinate, inferior; servile; liege, vassal, feudal, feudatory

14 subjugated, subjected, **enslaved,** enthralled, in thrall, captive, bond, unfree; disenfranchised, disfranchised, oppressed, suppressed; in subjection, in bondage, in captivity, in slavery, in bonds, in chains; under the lash, under the heel; in one's power, in one's control, in one's hands, in one's clutches, in one's pocket, under one's thumb, at one's mercy, under one's command, under one's orders, at one's beck and call, at one's feet, at one's pleasure; subordinated, playing second fiddle; at the bottom of the ladder, sucking hind tit

15 subdued, quelled, crushed, broken, reduced, mastered, overmastered, humbled, humiliated, brought to one's knees, brought low, made to grovel; **tamed, domesticated,** broken to harness, gentled; housebroken, housebroke

16 downtrodden, downtrod, kept down, kept under, ground down, overborne, trampled, oppressed; abused, misused, damaged; henpecked, browbeaten, led by the nose, in leading strings, tied to one's apron strings, ordered around, kicked around, regimented, tyrannized; slavish, servile, submissive; unmanned; treated like dirt under one's feet, treated like shit*

PREPS **17** under, below, beneath, underneath, **subordinate to**; at the feet of; under the heel of; at the beck and call of, at the whim of, at the pleasure of

433 SUBMISSION

<being obedient>

NOUNS **1 submission,** submittal, **yielding;** compliance, complaisance, acquiescence, acceptance; going along with, assent; consent; obedience; subjection; resignation, resignedness, stoicism, philosophical attitude; deference, homage, kneeling, obeisance; passivity, unassertiveness, passiveness, supineness, longanimity, long-suffering, nonresistance, nonopposition, nonopposal, quietness, nondissent, quietude, quietism; cowardice

2 surrender, capitulation; renunciation, giving over, abandonment, relinquishment, cession; giving up, giving in, backing off, backing down, retreat, recession, recedence, caving in, giving up the fort, the white flag, throwing in the towel

3 submissiveness, docility, tractability, prostration, biddability, yieldingness, compliableness, pliancy, pliability, flexibility, malleability, moldability, ductility, plasticity, facility; agreeableness, agreeability; subservience, servility

4 manageability, governability, controllability, manipulability, manipulatability, corrigibility, untroublesomeness; **tameness,** housebrokenness; tamableness, domesticability; milquetoast, Caspar Milquetoast

5 meekness, gentleness, tameness, mildness, mild-manneredness, peaceableness, lamblikeness, dovelikeness, spinelessness; self-abnegation, humility

VERBS **6 submit, comply,** take, accept, go along with, suffer, bear, brook, acquiesce, be agreeable, accede, assent; consent; relent, succumb, resign, resign oneself, give oneself up, not resist; take one's medicine, swallow the pill, face the music, face the facts; bite the bullet; knuckle down, knuckle under, knock under, take it, swallow it; jump through a hoop, dance to another's tune; take it lying down; put up with it, grin and bear it, make the best of it, take the bitter with the sweet, shrug, shrug off, live with it; obey

7 yield, cede, give way, give ground, back down, give up, give in, cave in, withdraw from the field, quit the field, break off combat, cease resistance, have no fight left

8 **surrender, give up,** capitulate, acknowledge defeat, cry quits, cry pax <Brit>, say "uncle," beg a truce, pray for quarter, implore mercy, throw in the towel, wave the white flag, lower the flag, lower the colors, haul down the flag, strike one's flag, throw down one's arms, lay down one's arms, deliver up one's arms, hand over one's sword, yield the palm, ask for mercy, pull in one's horns, come to terms; renounce, abandon, relinquish, cede, give over, hand over

9 **submit to, yield to, defer to,** bow to, give way to, knuckle under to, succumb to

10 **bow down,** bow, bend, stoop, crouch, bow one's head, bend the neck, bow submission; genuflect, curtsy; bow to, bend to, knuckle to, bend to one's will, bow to one's will, bend to one's yoke; kneel to, bend the knee to, fall on one's knees before, crouch before, fall at one's feet, throw oneself at the feet of, prostrate oneself before, truckle to, cringe to, cave in; kowtow, bow and scrape, grovel, do obeisance, do homage; kiss ass; take the line of least resistance

11 eat dirt, eat crow, eat humble pie, lick the dust, kiss the rod, take it on the chin

ADJS 12 **submissive, compliant,** compliable, complaisant, complying, acquiescent, consenting; assenting, accepting, agreeable; subservient, abject, obedient; servile; resigned, uncomplaining; unassertive; passive, supine, unresisting, nonresisting, unresistant, nonresistant, nonresistive, long-suffering, longanimous, nonopposing, nondissenting

13 **docile,** tractable, biddable, unmurmuring, yielding, pliant, pliable, flexible, malleable, moldable, ductile, plastic, facile, like putty in one's hands

14 **manageable, governable,** controllable, manipulable, manipulatable, handleable, corrigible, restrainable, untroublesome; domitable, tamable, domesticable; milktoast, milquetoast

15 **meek, gentle,** mild, mild-mannered, peaceable, pacific, quiet; subdued, chastened, tame, tamed, broken, housebroken, domesticated; lamblike, gentle as a lamb, dovelike; humble; spineless, soft, weak-kneed

16 **deferential, obeisant; subservient, obsequious,** servile; crouching, prostrate, prone, on one's belly, on one's knees, on one's marrowbones, on bended knee, bowed, bowing

ADVS 17 **submissively,** compliantly, complaisantly, acquiescently, agreeably; obediently; resignedly, uncomplainingly, with resignation; passively, supinely, unresistingly, unresistantly, nonresistively

18 **docilely,** tractably, biddably, yieldingly, pliantly, pliably, malleably, flexibly, plastically, facilely

19 **meekly, gently,** tamely, mildly, peaceably, pacifically, quietly, like a lamb

434 OBSERVANCE

<following rules, customs>

NOUNS 1 **observance,** observation, honoring; **keeping,** adherence, heeding; compliance, conformance, conformity, accordance; faith, faithfulness, fidelity; respect, deference; performance, practice, execution, discharge, carrying out, carrying through; dutifulness, acquittal, acquittance, fulfillment, satisfaction; heed, care; obeying the law; physical law; keeping the faith

VERBS 2 **observe, keep,** heed, follow, keep the faith; regard, defer to, respect, attend to, comply with, conform to; hold by, abide by, adhere to; live up to, act up to, practice what one preaches, be faithful to, keep faith with, do justice to, do the right thing by; fulfill, fill, meet, satisfy; make good, keep one's word, keep one's promise, make good one's word, make good one's promise, be as good as one's word, redeem one's pledge, stand to one's engagement; keep to the spirit of; obey the law

3 **perform, practice,** do, execute, discharge, carry out, carry through, carry into execution, do one's duty, do one's office, fulfill one's role, discharge one's function; honor one's obligations

ADJS 4 **observant,** respectful, regardful, mindful; **faithful,** devout, devoted, true, loyal, constant; semper fi; dutiful, duteous; as good as one's word; **practicing,** active; compliant, conforming; punctual, punctilious, scrupulous, meticulous, conscientious; obedient; Sabbatarian

435 NONOBSERVANCE

<not following rules, customs>

NOUNS 1 **nonobservance,** inobservance, unobservance, nonadherence; nonconformity, disconformity, **nonconformance,** noncompliance; apostasy; inattention, indifference, disregard; laxity; nonfulfillment, nonperformance, nonfeasance, failure, dereliction, delinquency, omission, default, slight, oversight; negligence; neglect, laches; abandonment; lack of ceremony

2 **violation,** infraction, breach, breaking; infringement, transgression, trespass, contravention; offense; breach of promise, breach of contract, breach of trust, breach of faith, bad faith, breach of privilege; breach of the peace

VERBS 3 **disregard,** lose sight of, pay no regard to; neglect; renege, **abandon**; defect; do one's own thing

4 **violate,** break, breach; infringe, transgress, trespass, contravene, trample on, trample upon, trample underfoot, do violence to, make a mockery of, outrage; defy, set at defiance, flout, set at naught, set naught by; take the law into one's own hands; break one's promise, break one's word

ADJS 5 **nonobservant,** inobservant, unobservant, nonadherent; nonconforming, unconforming, noncompliant, uncompliant; inattentive, disregardful; negligent; unfaithful, untrue, unloyal, inconstant, lapsed, renegade; contemptuous

436 PROMISE

<declaration of intent to do>

NOUNS 1 **promise, pledge,** solemn promise, troth, plight, faith, parole, word, word of honor, debt of honor, solemn declaration, solemn word; oath, vow; avouch, avouchment; assurance, guarantee, warranty, personal guarantee; entitlement

2 **obligation, commitment,** agreement, engagement, undertaking, recognizance, feasance; understanding, gentlemen's agreement, unwritten agreement, handshake; verbal agreement, nonformal agreement, pactum <law>; tacit agreement, unspoken agreement; contract, covenant, bond; designation, committal, earmarking; promissory note

3 **betrothal,** betrothment, intention, espousal, **engagement,** handfasting, affiance, troth, marriage contract, marriage vow, plighted troth, plighted faith, plighted love, exchange of vows; banns, banns of matrimony; prenuptial agreement, prenuptial contract, prenup; shotgun marriage

VERBS 4 **promise,** give a promise, make a promise, hold out an expectation; **pledge,** plight, troth, **vow;** give one's word, pledge one's word, pass ones word, give one's parole, give one's word of honor, plight one's troth, plight one's faith, pledge one's honor, plight one's honor; cross one's heart, cross one's heart and hope to die, swear; vouch, avouch, warrant, guarantee, assure; underwrite, countersign

5 **commit, engage,** undertake, obligate, bind, agree to, say yes, answer for, be answerable for, take on oneself, be responsible for, be security for, go bail for, accept obligation, accept responsibility, bind oneself to, put oneself down for; have an understanding; enter into a gentlemen's agreement; take the vows, take marriage vows; shake hands on, shake on it; contract, sign on the dotted line; designate, earmark

6 **be engaged,** affiance, betroth, troth, plight one's troth, say "I do"; contract, contract an engagement, pledge in marriage, promise in marriage; read the banns, publish the banns

ADJS 7 **promissory,** votive; under oath, upon oath, on one's word, on one's word of honor, on the Book, under hand and seal, avowed

8 **promised, pledged,** bound, committed, compromised, obligated; sworn, warranted, guaranteed, assured, underwritten, cosigned; contracted; engaged, plighted, affianced, betrothed, intended

ADVS 9 on one's honor, on one's word, on one's parole, on one's word of honor; solemnly

437 COMPACT

<agreement made>

NOUNS 1 **compact, pact, contract,** legal contract, valid contract, covenant, convention, transaction, accord, agreement, mutual agreement, agreement between parties, agreement among parties, signed agreement, written agreement, formal agreement, legal agreement, undertaking, stipulation; adjustment, accommodation; understanding, arrangement, bargain, dicker, deal, informal agreement; settlement, negotiated settlement; labor contract, union contract, wage contract, employment contract, collective agreement; deed; cartel, consortium; protocol; bond, binding agreement, ironclad agreement, covenant of salt; gentleman's agreement, gentlemen's agreement; prenuptial agreement; licensing agreement; nonverbal agreement, promise

2 **treaty,** international agreement, *entente, entente cordiale* <Fr>, concord, concordat, cartel, convention, consortium, protocol, paction, capitulation; alliance, league; nonaggression pact, mutual-defense treaty; arms treaty; trade agreement; arms control agreement; North Atlantic Treaty Organization (NATO); Southeast Asia Treaty Organization (SEATO); Warsaw Pact; gun control

3 signing, **signature**, sealing, closing, conclusion, solemnization; handshake

4 **execution,** completion; transaction; carrying out, discharge, fulfillment, prosecution, effectuation; enforcement; observance

VERBS 5 **contract,** compact, covenant, bargain, **agree,** engage, undertake, commit, mutually commit, make a deal, do a deal, stipulate, agree to, bargain for, contract for, contract out; preset, prearrange, promise; subcontract, outsource; cut a deal

6 treat with, **negotiate, bargain,** make terms, sit down with, sit down at the bargaining table

7 **sign, shake hands**, shake, affix one's John Hancock, seal, formalize, make legal and binding, solemnize; agree on terms, come to terms, come to an agreement; strike a bargain; plea-bargain

8 **arrange, settle**; adjust, fine-tune, accommodate, reshuffle, rejigger, compose, fix, make up, straighten out, put straight, set straight, work out, sort out, square away; conclude, close, close with, settle with

9 **execute,** complete, transact, promulgate, make; close a deal; make out, fill out; discharge, fulfill, render, administer; carry out, carry through, put through, prosecute; effect, effectuate, set in motion, implement; enforce, put in force; abide by, honor, live up to, adhere to, live by, observe

ADJS 10 contractual, covenantal, conventional, consensual

11 **contracted,** compacted, covenanted, agreed upon, bargained for, agreed, stipulated; engaged, undertaken; promised; arranged, settled; under hand and seal, signed, sealed, signed, sealed, and delivered; ratified

ADVS 12 **contractually, as agreed upon, as promised,** as contracted for, by the terms of the contract, according to the contract, according to the bargain, according to the agreement

438 SECURITY

<thing given as a pledge>

NOUNS 1 **security, surety,** indemnity, guaranty, guarantee, warranty, insurance, warrant, assurance, underwriting; obligation, full faith, credit; bond, tie; stocks and bonds; national security; Dow Jones

2 **pledge,** gage; undertaking; earnest, earnest money, God's penny, handsel; escrow; token payment; pawn, hock; bail, bond, vadimonium; replevin, replevy, recognizance; mainprise; hostage, surety

3 **collateral,** collateral security, collateral warranty; deposit, stake, forfeit; indemnity, IOU; caution money, caution; margin; cosigned promissory note; cosignage; seed money

4 **mortgage,** mortgage deed, deed of trust, lien, security agreement, real estate loan; bridge loan; vadium mortuum, mortuum vadium; dead pledge; vadium vivum, living pledge, antichresis; hypothec, hypothecation, bottomry, bottomry bond; adjustment mortgage, blanket mortgage, chattel mortgage, closed mortgage, participating mortgage, installment mortgage, leasehold mortgage, trust mortgage, reverse mortgage, jumbo mortgage; first mortgage, second mortgage, third mortgage; adjustable-rate mortgage (ARM), variable-rate mortgage (VRM), fixed-rate mortgage; equity loan, home equity loan; 30-year mortgage, 15-year mortgage; reverse equity; balloon mortgage

5 **lien,** general lien, particular lien; pignus legale, common-law lien, statutory lien, judgment lien, pignus judiciale, tax lien, mechanic's lien; mortgage bond

6 **guarantor,** warrantor, guaranty, guarantee; mortgagor; insurer, underwriter; sponsor, surety; godparent, godfather, godmother; bondsman, bailsman, mainpernor

7 **warrantee,** mortgagee; insuree, policyholder; godchild, godson, goddaughter

8 guarantorship, **sponsorship,** sponsion

VERBS 9 **secure, guarantee,** guaranty, warrant, assure, insure, ensure, bond, certify; countersecure; stand surety; sponsor, be sponsor for, sign for, sign one's note, back, stand behind of, stand back of, stand up for; endorse; indemnify, countersign; sign, cosign, underwrite, undersign, subscribe to; confirm, attest

10 **pledge,** impignorate, handsel, deposit, stake, post, put in escrow, put up, put up as collateral, lay out, lay down; pawn, put in pawn, hock, put in hock; mortgage, hypothecate, bottomry, bond; put up bail, bail out

ADJS 11 **secured,** covered, guaranteed, warranted, certified, insured, ensured, assured; certain, sure

12 **pledged,** staked, posted, deposited, in escrow, put up, put up as collateral; on deposit, at stake; asset-backed; as earnest; pawned, in pawn, in hock, hocked

13 **in trust,** held in trust, held in pledge, fiduciary; in escrow; mortgaged

439 OFFER

<presenting something for acceptance>

NOUNS 1 **offer,** offering, proffer, presentation, **bid,** submission; advance, overture, approach, invitation, come-on; hesitant approach, tentative approach, preliminary approach, feeling-out, feeler; asking price; counteroffer, counterproposal

2 **proposal,** proposition, suggestion, instance; motion, resolution; sexual advance, sexual approach, sexual invitation, sexual overture, indecent proposal, pass, improper suggestion; request

3 **ultimatum,** last word, final word, last offer,

final offer, firm bid, firm price, sticking point, ultimation

VERBS 4 **offer, proffer,** present, tender, offer up, put up, submit, extend, prefer, hold out, hold forth, place in one's way, lay at one's feet, put at one's disposal, place at one's disposal, put one in the way of

5 **propose, submit,** prefer; **suggest,** recommend, advance, commend to attention, propound, pose, put forward, bring forward, put forth, set forth, put it to, put before, set before, lay before, bring before, dish up, come out with, come up with; put a bee in one's bonnet, put ideas into one's head; bring up, broach, moot, introduce, open up, launch, start, kick off; move, make a motion, offer a resolution; postulate

6 **bid,** bid for, make a bid

7 make advances, approach, overture, make an overture, throw oneself at one, fling oneself at one; **solicit,** importune

8 <nonformal> **proposition,** come on to, hit on, put a move on, make a move on, jump one's bones*, make a pass, throw a pass, george, make a play for, play footsie with, pitch, mash

9 **urge upon,** press upon, ply upon, push upon, force upon, thrust upon; press, ply; insist

10 **volunteer,** come forward, step forward, offer oneself, proffer oneself, present oneself, be at one's service, not wait to be asked, not wait for an invitation, need no prodding, step into the breach, be Johnny-on-the-spot

440 REQUEST

<asking for something>

NOUNS 1 **request,** asking; the touch; desire, wish, expressed desire; petition, petitioning, impetration, address; application; requisition, indent <Brit>; demand; special request

2 **entreaty,** appeal, plea, bid, suit, call, cry, clamor, *cri du cœur* <Fr>, beseeching, impetration, obtestation; supplication, prayer, rogation, beseechment, imploring, imploration, obsecration, adjuration, imprecation; invocation, invocatory plea, invocatory prayer; act of contrition

3 importunity, importunateness, urgency, pressure, high pressure, hard sell; **urging,** pressing, plying; buttonholing; dunning; teasing, pestering, plaguing, nagging, nudging; coaxing, wheedling, cajolery, cajolement, blandishment, ragging

4 **invitation,** invite, bid, engraved invitation, bidding, biddance, call, calling, summons

5 **solicitation,** canvass, canvassing; suit, addresses; courting, wooing, speed-dating; fundraising; the touch

6 **beggary,** mendicancy, mendicity; **begging,** cadging, scrounging; mooching, bumming, panhandling

7 **petitioner,** supplicant, suppliant, suitor; solicitor; applicant, solicitant, claimant; aspirant, seeker, wannabee; candidate, postulant; bidder

8 **beggar,** mendicant, scrounger, cadger; bum, bummer, moocher, panhandler, sponger; *schnorrer* <Yiddish>; hobo, tramp; loafer; mendicant friar; mendicant order

VERBS 9 **request,** ask, make a request, beg leave, make bold to ask; desire, wish, wish for, express a wish for, crave; ask for, order, put in an order for, bespeak, call for, trouble one for; whistle for; **requisition,** make a requisition, put in a requisition, indent <Brit>; make application, apply for, file for, put in for; demand; pop the question

10 **petition,** present a petition, prefer a petition, sign a petition, circulate a petition; pray, sue; apply to, call on, call upon; memorialize

11 **entreat, implore, beseech,** beg, crave, plead, appeal, pray, supplicate, impetrate, obtest; adjure, conjure; invoke, imprecate, call on, call upon, cry upon, appeal to, cry to, run to; go hat in hand to; kneel to, go down on one's knees to, fall on one's knees to, go on bended knee to, throw oneself at the feet of, get down on one's marrow-bones; plead for, clamor for, cry for, cry out for; call for help

12 **importune, urge, press,** pressure, prod, prod at, apply pressure, exert pressure, push, ply; dun; beset, buttonhole, besiege, take by the lapels, grasp by the lapels; work on, tease, pester, plague, nag, nag at, make a pest of oneself, make a nuisance of oneself, try one's patience, bug, nudge; coax, wheedle, cajole, blandish, flatter, soft-soap

13 **invite, ask,** call, summon, call in, bid come, extend an invitation, issue an invitation, request the presence of, request the pleasure of one's company, send an engraved invitation

14 **solicit, canvass**; court, woo, address, sue, sue for, pop the question, propose; seek, bid for, look for; fish for, angle for; pass the hat

15 **beg**, scrounge, cadge; mooch, bum, panhandle; hit, hit up, touch, put the touch on, make a touch; pass the hat

ADJS 16 **supplicatory,** supplicative, suppliant, supplicant, supplicating, prayerful, precative; petitionary; **begging,** mendicant, cadging, scrounging, mooching; on one's knees, on bended knees, on one's marrow-bones; with joined hands, with folded hands

17 **imploring,** entreating, beseeching, begging, pleading, appealing, precatory, precative, adjuratory

18 **importunate;** teasing, pesty, pesky, pestering, plaguing, nagging, dunning; coaxing, wheedling, cajoling, flattering, soft-soaping; insistent, demanding, urgent

19 **invitational,** inviting, invitatory

INTERJS **20** **please,** prithee, pray, do, pray do, puhleez; be so good as to, be good enough, have the goodness; will you, may it please you; if you please, *s'il vous plaît* <Fr>; I beg you; for God's sake, for goodness sake, for heaven's sake, for mercy's sake; be my guest, feel free; gimme a break, cut me some slack

441 CONSENT

<agreeing to something>

NOUNS **1** **consent, assent,** agreement, accord, acceptance, approval, blessing, approbation, sanction, endorsement, ratification, backing; affirmation, affirmative, affirmative voice, affirmative vote, yea, aye, nod, okay, OK, okey-dokey, go-ahead, green light; leave, permission; willingness, readiness, promptness, promptitude, eagerness, unreluctance, unloathness, ungrudgingness, tacit consent, unspoken consent, silent consent, implicit consent, connivance; acquiescence, compliance; submission

VERBS **2** **consent, assent,** give consent, yield assent, be willing, be amenable, be persuaded, accede to, accord to, grant, say yes, say aye, say yea, vote affirmatively, vote aye, nod, nod assent; accept, play along, go along, agree to, sign off on, go along with; be in accord with, be in favor of, take kindly to, approve of, hold with; approve, give one's blessing to, okay (OK); sanction, endorse, ratify; consent to silently, consent to by implication; wink at, connive at; turn a willing ear; deign, condescend; have no objection, not refuse; permit

3 **acquiesce, comply, comply with,** fall in with, take one up on, be persuaded, come round, come around, come over, come to, see one's way clear to; **submit**

ADJS **4** **consenting, assenting,** affirmative, amenable, persuaded, approving, agreeing, favorable, accordant, consentient, consentual, consentant; sanctioning, endorsing, ratifying; acquiescent, compliant, compliable; submissive; willing, agreeable, content; ready, prompt, eager, unreluctant, unloath, nothing loath, unmurmuring, ungrudging, unrefusing; permissive

ADVS **5** **consentingly, assentingly,** affirmatively, approvingly, favorably, positively, agreeably, accordantly; acquiescently, compliantly; willingly; yes

442 REFUSAL

<denying something>

NOUNS **1** **refusal, rejection,** turndown, turning down; thumbs-down; nonconsent, nonacceptance, zero tolerance; declining, declination, declension, declinature; denial, disclamation, disclaimer, disallowance; decertification, disaccreditation; repudiation; disagreement, dissent; recantation; contradiction; negation, abnegation, negative, negative answer, nay, no, nix; unwillingness; disobedience; noncompliance, noncooperation, nonobservance; withholding, holding back, retention, deprivation

2 **repulse, rebuff,** peremptory refusal, flat refusal, point-blank refusal, summary negative; a flea in one's ear; kiss-off, slap in the face, kick in the teeth; short shrift

VERBS **3** **refuse, decline,** not consent, refuse consent, reject, turn down, decline to accept, not have, not buy; not hold with, not think of, not hear of; say no, say nay, vote nay, vote negatively, vote in the negative, side against, disagree, beg to disagree, dissent; shake one's head, negative, negate; vote down, turn thumbs down on; be unwilling; turn one's back on, turn a deaf ear to, set oneself against, set one's face against, be unmoved, harden one's heart, resist entreaty, resist persuasion; stand aloof, not lift a finger, have nothing to do with, wash one's hands of; hold out against; put one's foot down, set one's foot down, refuse point-blank, refuse summarily; decline politely, decline with thanks, beg off; repudiate, disallow, disclaim; decertify, disaccredit

4 **deny,** withhold, hold back; grudge, begrudge; close the hand, close the purse; deprive one of; renege

5 **repulse, rebuff,** repel, kiss one off, slap one in the face, kick one in the teeth, send one away with a flea in one's ear, give one short shrift, shut the door in one's face, slam the door in one's face, turn one away; slap one down, smack one down; deny oneself to, refuse to receive, not be at home to, cut, snub; not want anything to do with

ADJS **6** **unconsenting,** nonconsenting, negative; unwilling; uncompliant, uncomplying, uncomplaisant, inacquiescent, uncooperative; disobedient; rejective, declinatory; deaf to, not willing to hear of; dissenting

PHRS 7 I refuse, I won't, I will not, I will do no such thing; over my dead body, far be it from me, not if I can help it, not likely, not on your life, count me out, include me out, I'm not taking any, I won't buy it, it's no go, like hell I will, I'll be hanged if I will, try and make me, you have another guess coming, you should live so long, I'll see you in hell first, nothing doing; out of the question, not to be thought of, impossible; no, by no means, **no way,** no way José, there's no way; in a pig's eye, in a pig's ear, in a pig's ass, my eye, my ass; you've got to be kidding

443 PERMISSION

<formal consent>

NOUNS 1 **permission,** leave, allowance, vouchsafement; consent; permission to enter, admission, ticket, ticket of admission, boarding pass; implied consent, clearance; approbation, blessing; license, liberty; okay, OK, nod, go-ahead, green light, go sign, thumbs-up; special permission, charter, patent, dispensation, release, waiver; zoning variance, variance

2 sufferance, **tolerance,** toleration, **indulgence;** leniency; winking, overlooking, connivance; permissiveness; dispensation, exemption

3 **authorization, authority,** sanction, licensing, countenance, warrant, warranty, fiat; empowerment, enabling, entitlement, enfranchisement, certification; clearance, security clearance; ratification; legalization, legitimation, decriminalization

4 **carte blanche,** blank check, freedom, full authority, full power, free hand, open mandate

5 **grant, concession;** charter, franchise, liberty, diploma, patent, letters patent, brevet; royal grant

6 **permit,** license, warrant; building permit, learner's permit, work permit; driver's license, marriage license, hunting license, fishing license, gaming license; license plate, vanity plate; nihil obstat, imprimatur; credentials

7 **pass, passport,** safe-conduct, safeguard, protection; visa, entry visa, exit visa; green card; **clearance,** clearance papers; bill of health, clean bill of health, pratique, full pratique; ticket, ticketless; safe passage

8 **permissibility,** permissibleness, allowableness; admissibility, admissibleness; justifiableness, warrantableness, sanctionableness; validity, legitimacy, lawfulness, licitness, legality

VERBS 9 **permit, allow,** admit, let, leave, give permission, give leave, make possible; allow of, permit of; give room for, leave room for, open the door to; consent; grant, accord, vouchsafe; okay, OK, give the nod, give the go-ahead, give the green light, give the go sign, say the word, give the word; dispense, release, waive

10 suffer, countenance, have, **tolerate, condone,** brook, endure, stomach, bear, bear with, put up with, stand for, hear of, go along with; indulge; shut one's eyes to, wink at, blink at, overlook, connive at; leave the door open to, leave the way open to

11 **authorize, sanction,** warrant; give official sanction, legitimize, validate, legalize; empower, give power, enable, entitle; license; privilege; charter, patent, enfranchise, franchise; accredit, certificate, certify; ratify; legitimate, decriminalize

12 **give carte blanche,** give a blank check, give full power, give full authority, give an open mandate, give an open invitation, give free rein, give a free hand, leave alone, leave it to one; permit all, permit anything, open the floodgates, remove all restrictions, let someone get away with murder

13 may, can, have permission, be permitted, be allowed

ADJS 14 **permissive,** admissive, permitting, allowing; consenting; unprohibitive, nonprohibitive; tolerating, obliging, tolerant; suffering, indulgent, soft, liberal, lenient; hands-off; lax; easy come easy go

15 **permissible,** allowable, admissible; justifiable, warrantable, sanctionable; licit, lawful, legitimate, legal, legitimized, legalized, legitimated, decriminalized, legit

16 **permitted, allowed,** allowable, admitted; tolerated, on sufferance; unprohibited, unforbidden, unregulated, unchecked; unconditional, without strings

17 **authorized,** empowered, entitled; warranted, sanctioned; licensed, privileged; chartered, patented; franchised, enfranchised; accredited, certificated

ADVS 18 **permissively,** admissively; tolerantly, indulgently

19 **permissibly, allowably,** admissibly; with permission, by one's leave; licitly, lawfully, legitimately, legally

PHRS 20 by your leave, with your permission, if you please, with respect, may I?

444 PROHIBITION

<denying by authority>

NOUNS 1 **prohibition, forbidding,** forbiddance; ruling out, **disallowance,** denial, rejection; refusal; repression, suppression; ban, embargo, enjoinder, injunction, prohibitory injunction, proscription, inhibition, interdict, *interdictum*

<L>, interdiction; index; gag order; taboo; thou-shalt-not, don't, no-no; law, statute; preclusion, exclusion, prevention; forbidden fruit, contraband; sumptuary law, sumptuary ordinance; zoning, zoning law, restrictive convenant; forbidden ground, forbidden territory, no-man's-land, no-fly zone, no-go area; curfew; restriction, circumscription

2 **veto,** negative; absolute veto, qualified veto, limited veto, negative veto, countermand, suspensive veto, suspensory veto, item veto, line-item veto, pocket veto; thumbs-down, red light; blacklist

VERBS 3 **prohibit, forbid;** disallow, rule out, rule against, forfend; deny, reject; say no to, refuse; bar, debar, preclude, exclude, exclude from, shut out, shut the door on, close the door on, prevent; ban, put under the ban, outlaw, criminalize; repress, suppress; enjoin, put under an injunction, issue an injunction against, issue a prohibitory injunction; proscribe, inhibit, interdict, lay under an interdict, lay under an interdiction; put on the Index; embargo, put an embargo on; taboo

4 **not permit, not allow,** not have, not suffer, not tolerate, not endure, not stomach, not bear, not bear with, not countenance, not brook, brook no, not condone, not accept, not put up with, not go along with; not stand for, not hear of, put one's foot down on, set one's foot down on

5 **veto,** put one's veto upon, decide against, rule against, turn thumbs down on, negative, kill, nix

ADJS 6 **prohibitive,** prohibitory, prohibiting, forbidding; inhibitive, inhibitory, repressive, suppressive; proscriptive, interdictive, interdictory; preclusive, exclusive, preventive

7 **prohibited, forbidden,** forbade, forbid, *verboten* <Ger>, barred; vetoed; unpermissible, nonpermissible, not permitted, not allowed, unchartered, unallowed; disallowed, ruled out, contraindicated; beyond the pale, off limits, out of bounds; unauthorized, unsanctioned, unlicensed; banned, under the ban, outlawed, contraband; taboo, untouchable; illegal, unlawful, illicit

445 REPEAL

<revoking by authority>

NOUNS 1 **repeal, revocation,** revoke, revokement; reneging, renigging, going back on, welshing, **rescinding,** rescindment, rescission, reversal, striking down, abrogation, cassation; suspension; waiving, waiver, setting aside; countermand, counterorder; annulment, nullification, withdrawal, invalidation, voiding, voidance, vacation, vacatur, defeasance; cancellation, canceling, cancel, write-off; abolition, abolishment; recall, retraction, recantation

VERBS 2 **repeal, revoke, rescind,** reverse, strike down, abrogate; renege, renig, go back on, welsh; suspend; waive, set aside; countermand, counterorder; abolish, do away with; cancel, write off; annul, nullify, disannul, withdraw, invalidate, void, vacate, make void, declare null and void; overrule, override; recall, retract, recant; unwish

ADJS 3 **repealed, revoked, rescinded,** struck down, set aside; invalid, **void, null and void**

446 PROMOTION

<raising in position>

NOUNS 1 **promotion,** preferment, **advancement,** advance, step-up, upping, rise, elevation, upgrading, jump, step up, step up the ladder, furtherance; raise, boost; kicking upstairs, bumping upstairs; exaltation, aggrandizement; ennoblement, knighting; graduation, passing; pay raise

VERBS 2 **promote, advance,** prefer, up, boost, elevate, upgrade, jump; kick upstairs, bump upstairs, furthering; raise; exalt, aggrandize; ennoble, knight; pass, graduate; raise one's pay, up one's pay, boost one's pay

447 DEMOTION, DEPOSAL

<lowering in position>

NOUNS 1 **demotion,** degrading, degradation, disgrading, downgrading, debasement; abasement, humbling, humiliation, casting down; reduction, bump, bust; stripping of rank, depluming, despluming

2 **deposal, deposition, removal,** displacement, outplacement, supplanting, supplantation, replacement, deprivation, ousting, unseating; cashiering, firing, dismissal; pink slip, walking papers; reduction in forces (RIF); forced resignation; kicking upstairs; superannuation, pensioning off, putting out to pasture, retirement, the golden handshake, the golden parachute; suspension; impeachment; purge, liquidation; overthrow, overthrowal; dethronement, disenthronement, discrownment; disbarment, disbarring; unfrocking, defrocking, unchurching; deconsecration, expulsion, excommunication

VERBS 3 **demote,** degrade, disgrade, downgrade, debase, abase, humble, humiliate, lower, reduce, bump, bust; strip of rank, cut off one's spurs, deplume, displume; force out

4 **depose, remove from office,** send to the showers, give the gate, divest of office, deprive of office, strip of office, remove, displace, outplace, supplant, replace; oust; suspend; cashier, drum out, strip of rank, break, bust; give a pink slip, hand one's walking papers; dismiss; purge, liquidate; overthrow; retire, superannuate, pension, pension off, put out to pasture, give the golden handshake, give the golden parachute; kick upstairs; unseat, unsaddle; dethrone, disenthrone, unthrone, uncrown, discrown; disbar; unfrock, defrock, unchurch; strike off the roll, read out of; expel, excommunicate; deconsecrate

448 RESIGNATION, RETIREMENT

<withdrawal from position>

NOUNS 1 **resignation,** demission, withdrawal, **retirement,** pensioning, pensioning off, golden handshake, golden parachute, superannuation, emeritus status, retiracy; **abdication;** voluntary resignation; forced resignation, forced retirement, early retirement, deposal; relinquishment

VERBS 2 **resign,** demit, **quit,** leave, vacate, withdraw from; **retire,** superannuate, be superannuated, be pensioned, be pensioned off, be put out to pasture, get the golden handshake, get the golden parachute; relinquish, give up; retire from office, stand down, stand aside, step aside, give up one's post, hang up one's spurs; tender one's resignation, hand in one's resignation, send in one's papers, turn in one's badge, turn in one's uniform; **abdicate,** renounce the throne, give up the crown; pension off; be invalided out

ADJS 3 **retired,** in retirement, superannuated, on pension, pensioned, pensioned off, emeritus, emerita <feminine>

449 AID

<giving assistance>

NOUNS 1 **aid, help, assistance,** support, succor, relief, comfort, ease, remedy; mutual help, mutual assistance; service, benefit; ministry, ministration, office, offices, good offices; yeoman's service; therapy; protection; bailout, rescue; means to an end

2 **assist, helping hand,** hand, lift; boost, leg up; help in time of need; support group, self-help group, Alcoholics Anonymous (AA), Gamblers Anonymous, 12-step group; tough love, intervention; social assistance, counsel, guidance, moral support, constructive criticism, tender loving care (TLC); group effort; visual aid

3 **support,** maintenance, sustainment, sustentation, sustenance, subsistence, provision, total support, meal ticket; keep, upkeep; livelihood, living, meat, bread, daily bread; nurture, fostering, nurturance, nourishment, nutriture, mothering, parenting, rearing, family values, fosterage, foster care, care, caring, caregiving, tender loving care, TLC, co-parenting; manna, manna in the wilderness; economic support, price support, subsidy, subsidization, subvention, endowment, boost; support services, social services, welfare, relief, succor; technical support, tech support

4 **patronage,** fosterage, tutelage, sponsorship, **backing,** auspices, aegis, coattails, care, guidance, championing, championship, seconding; interest, advocacy, encouragement, abetment; countenance, favor, goodwill, charity, sympathy, handout

5 **furtherance,** helping along, advancement, advance, promotion, forwarding, facilitation, speeding, easing of the way, smoothing of the way, clearing of the track, greasing of the wheels, expedition, expediting, rushing; preferment, special treatment, preferential treatment; tailwind

6 **self-help,** self-helpfulness, self-support, self-sustainment, self-improvement; independence

7 helper, assistant; benefactor; facilitator, animator

8 reinforcements, **support, relief,** auxiliaries, reserves, reserve forces, staff

9 **facility,** accommodation, appliance, convenience, amenity, appurtenance; advantage; labor-saving device, time-saving device

10 **helpfulness,** aidfulness, cooperation, goodwill, charity; serviceability, utility, usefulness; advantageousness, profitability, favorableness, beneficialness

VERBS 11 **aid, help, assist,** comfort, abet, succor, relieve, ease, doctor, remedy; be of some help, put one's oar in; do good, do a world of good, benefit, avail; favor, befriend; give help, render assistance, offer aid, proffer aid, come to the aid of, rush to the assistance of, lend aid, give a hand, lend a hand, give a helping hand, lend a helping hand, stretch forth a helping hand, hold out a helping hand, boost, cater to, cater for; take by the hand, take in tow; give an assist, give a leg up, give a lift, give a boost, help a lame dog over a stile; save, redeem, bail out, rescue; protect; set up, put on one's feet; give new life to, resuscitate, rally, reclaim, revive, restore; be the making of, set one up in business; see one through

12 **support,** lend support, give support, furnish support, afford support; maintain, sustain, keep, upkeep; uphold, hold up, bear, upbear, bear up, bear out; reinforce, undergird, bolster, bolster

up, buttress, shore, shore up, prop, prop up, crutch; finance, fund, subsidize, subvention, subventionize; comp, pick up the tab, pick up the check, give new life to; other, maternize

13 **back, back up,** stand behind, stand back of, stand in back of, get behind, get in behind, get in back of; stand by, stick by, stick up for, champion; second, take the part of, take up the cause of, adopt the cause of, take under one's wing, go to bat for, take up the cudgels for, run interference for, side with, take sides with, associate oneself with, join oneself to, align oneself with, ally with, come down on the side of, range oneself on the side of, find time for

14 **abet, aid and abet,** encourage, hearten, embolden, comfort; advocate, hold a brief for, countenance, keep in countenance, endorse, lend oneself to, lend one's countenance to, lend one's support to, lend one's offices, put one's weight in the scale, plump for, thump the tub for, lend one's name to, give one's support to, give one's countenance to, give moral support to, hold one's hand, make one's cause one's own, weigh in for; subscribe, favor, go for, smile upon, shine upon

15 **patronize, sponsor,** take up, endow, finance

16 **foster, nurture,** nourish, mother, care for, lavish care on, feed, parent, rear, sustain, cultivate, cherish; pamper, coddle, cosset, fondle; nurse, suckle, cradle; dry-nurse, wet-nurse; spoon-feed; take in hand; co-parent

17 be useful, further, forward, advance, promote, stand in good stead, encourage, boost, favor, advantage, **facilitate,** set forward, put forward, push forward, give an impulse to; speed, expedite, quicken, hasten, lend wings to; conduce to, make for, contribute to

18 **serve,** lend oneself, give oneself, render service to, do service for, work for, labor in behalf of; minister to, cater to, do for; attend; pander to

19 oblige, **accommodate,** favor, do a favor, do a service

ADJS 20 **helping,** assisting, serving, promoting; **assistant, auxiliary,** adjuvant, subservient, subsidiary, ancillary, accessory; ministerial, ministering, ministrant; fostering, nurtural; care, caring, caregiving; instrumental

21 **helpful, useful,** utile, aidful; profitable, salutary, good for, beneficial; remedial, therapeutic; serviceable; contributory, contributing, conducive, **constructive**, positive, promotional, furthersome; at one's service, at one's command, at one's beck and call; right-hand; adjuvant

22 **favorable,** propitious; kind, kindly, kindly-disposed, all for, well-disposed, well-affected, well-intentioned, well-meant, well-meaning; benevolent, beneficent, benign, benignant; friendly, amicable, neighborly; cooperative

23 self-helpful, self-helping, self-improving; **self-supporting**, self-sustaining; self-supported, self-sustained; independent

ADVS 24 **helpfully,** helpingly; beneficially, favorably, profitably, advantageously, to advantage, to the good; serviceably, usefully

PREPS 25 helped by, with the help, with the assistance of, by the aid of; by means of

26 for, on behalf of, in behalf of, in aid of, in the name of, on account of, for the sake of, in the service of, in furtherance of, in favor of; remedial of

27 behind, back of, **supporting**, in support of

450 COOPERATION

<combined helpful action>

NOUNS 1 **cooperation, collaboration,** coaction, concurrence, synergy, synergism; support, backup; consensus, commonality; community, harmony, concordance, concord, fellowship, fellow feeling, solidarity, concert, united front, teamwork; pulling together, working together, communal activity, community activity, joining of forces, pooling, pooling of resources, joining of hands; bipartisanship, mutualism, mutuality, mutual assistance, coadjuvancy; reciprocity; back-scratching, give and take; joint effort, common effort, combined operation, joint operation, common enterprise, common endeavor, collective action, united action, mass action; job-sharing; coagency; coadministration, cochairmanship, codirectorship; duet, duumvirate; trio, triumvirate, troika; quartet, quintet, sextet, septet, octet; government by committee, coalition government; symbiosis, commensalism; cooperativeness, collaborativeness, team spirit, morale, esprit, *esprit de corps* <Fr>; communism, communalism, communitarianism, collectivism; quislingism; ecumenism, ecumenicism, ecumenicalism; collusion, complicity; networking; networker, team player

2 **affiliation, alliance,** allying, alignment, association, consociation, combination, union, unification, coalition, fusion, merger, coalescence, coadunation, amalgamation, league, federation, confederation, confederacy, consolidation, incorporation, inclusion, integration; hookup, tie-up, tie-in; partnership, copartnership, copartnery, cahoots; colleagueship, collegialism, collegiality; fraternity, confraternity, fraternization, fraternalism; sorority; fellowship, sodality; comradeship, camaraderie, freemasonry,

communalism, ecumenicism; adfiliation; reaffiliation

VERBS **3** **cooperate, collaborate,** do business, play ball, coact, concur; concert, harmonize, concord; join, band, league, associate, affiliate, ally, combine, unite, fuse, merge, coalesce, amalgamate, federate, confederate, consolidate; synergize; hook up, tie up, tie in; partner, be in league, go into partnership with, go partners, be in cahoots with; join together, club together, league together, band together; work together, get together, team up, buddy up, work as a team, job-share, act together, act in concert, pull together; hold together, hang together, keep together, stand together, stand shoulder to shoulder; put heads together; close ranks, make common cause, throw in together, unite efforts, join in, pitch in; network; reciprocate; conspire, collude, aid and abet, stonewall

4 **side with,** take sides with, unite with; join, join with, join up with, get together with, team up with, strike in with; throw in with, string along with, swing in with, go along with; line up with, align with, align oneself with, range with, range oneself with, stand up with, stand in with; join hands with, be hand in glove with, go hand in hand with; act with, take part with, go in with; cast in one's lot with, join one's fortunes with, stand shoulder to shoulder with, be cheek by jowl with, sink with, swim with, stand with, fall with; close ranks with, fall in with, make common cause with, pool one's interests with; enlist under the banner of, rally round, flock to

ADJS **5** **cooperative, cooperating,** cooperant, hand in glove; in cahoots; collaborative, coactive, coacting, coefficient, synergetic, synergic, synergical, synergistic, synergistical; fellow; concurrent, concurring, concerted, in concert; consensus, consensual, agreeing, in agreement, of like mind; harmonious, harmonized, concordant, common, communal, collective; mutual, reciprocal; joint, combined; coadjuvant, coadjutant; symbiotic, symbiotical, commensal; complicit, complicitous; uncompetitive, noncompetitive, communalist, communalistic, communist, communistic, communitarian, collectivist, collectivistic, ecumenic, ecumenical; conniving, collusive

ADVS **6** **cooperatively,** cooperatingly, coactively, coefficiently, concurrently; in consensus, consensually; **jointly,** combinedly, conjointly, concertedly, in concert with; harmoniously, concordantly; communally, collectively, together; as one, with one voice, unanimously, in chorus, in unison, as one man, en masse; side by side, hand in hand, hand in glove, shoulder to shoulder, back to back; all for one, one for all

7 **in cooperation,** in collaboration, in partnership, in cahoots, in collusion, in league

PREPS **8** with, **in cooperation with**

451 OPPOSITION

<contrary action>

NOUNS **1** **opposition,** opposing, opposure, crossing, oppugnancy, bucking, standing against; contraposition; resistance; **noncooperation;** contention; negation; rejection, refusal; counteraction, counterworking; contradiction, challenge, contravention, contraversion, rebutment, rebuttal, denial, impugnation, impugnment; countercurrent, head wind; crosscurrent, undercurrent, undertow; unfriendliness, stiff opposition; contest, pageant, beauty contest, beauty pageant; grudge match; line in the sand

2 **hostility, antagonism,** oppugnancy, oppugnance, oppugnation, antipathy, enmity, bad blood, inimicalness; contrariness, contrariety, orneriness, repugnance, repugnancy, perverseness, obstinacy; fractiousness, refractoriness, recalcitrance; uncooperativeness, noncooperation, negativeness, obstructionism, traversal, bloody-mindedness; friction, conflict, clashing, collision, cross-purposes, dissension, disaccord; latent hostility; rivalry, vying, competition; polarity

VERBS **3** **oppose, counter,** cross, go in opposition to, act in opposition to, go against, run against, strive against, run counter to, fly in the face of, fly in the teeth of, conflict with, butt heads; kick out against, make waves, protest; set oneself against, set one's heart against; be at cross-purposes, play at cross-purposes, obstruct, traverse, sabotage; take issue with, take one's stand against, lift a hand against, raise a hand against, declare oneself against, stand and be counted against, side against, vote against, vote nay, veto; make a stand against, make a dead set against; join the opposition; not put up with, not abide, not be content with; counteract, counterwork, countervail; resist, withstand

4 **contend against,** militate against, **contest,** combat, battle, clash with, clash, fight against, strive against, struggle against, labor against, take on, grapple with, join battle with, close with, come to close quarters with, go the the mat with, antagonize, fight, buck, counter; buffet, beat against, beat up against, breast, stem, stem the tide, stem the current, stem the flood, breast the wave, buffet the waves; rival, compete with, compete against, vie with, vie against; fight back, resist, offer resistance

5 **confront,** affront, front, go eyeball-to-eyeball with, go one-on-one with, take on, tackle, meet, face, meet head-on; encounter

6 **contradict,** cross, traverse, contravene, controvert, rebut, deny, gainsay; challenge, contest; oppugn, call into question; belie, be contrary to, come in conflict with, negate; reject

7 **be against,** be agin, reject; discountenance; not hold with, not have anything to do with; have a crow to pluck, have a bone to pick

ADJS 8 **oppositional,** opponent, opposing, opposed; anti, contra, confrontational, confrontive; at odds, at loggerheads; adverse, adversary, adversarial, adversative, oppugnant, antithetic, antithetical, repugnant, con, set against, dead set against; contrary, counter; negative; opposite, oppositive, death on; overthwart, cross; contradictory; unfavorable, unpropitious; hostile, antagonistic, unfriendly, enemy, inimical, alien, antipathetic, antipathetical, unsympathetic, averse; fractious, refractory, recalcitrant; uncooperative, noncooperative, obstructive, bloody-minded; ornery, perverse, obstinate; conflicting, clashing, dissentient, disaccordant; rival, competitive

ADVS 9 **in opposition,** in confrontation, eyeball-to-eyeball, one-on-one, head-on, at variance, at cross-purposes, at odds, at issue, at war with, up in arms, with crossed bayonets, at daggers drawn, at daggers, in hostile array, poised against one another; contra, contrariwise, counter, cross, athwart; against the tide, against the grain

PREPS 10 **opposed to,** adverse to, counter to, **in opposition to,** in conflict with, at cross-purposes with; against, agin, dead against, athwart; versus, vs; con, contra, face to face with, *vis-à-vis* <Fr>

452 OPPONENT

<one taking opposite position>

NOUNS 1 **opponent, adversary,** antagonist, assailant, foe, foeman, enemy, archenemy; adverse party, opposing party, opposite camp, opposite side, opposing side, the opposition, the loyal opposition, unfriendly; combatant

2 **competitor,** contestant, contender, corrival, vier, player, entrant; rival, archrival; emulator; the field; finalist, semifinalist; beauty contestant

3 **oppositionist,** opposer; obstructionist, obstructive, negativist, naysayer, wet noodle; contra; objector, protester, dissident, dissentient; resister; noncooperator; disputant, litigant, plaintiff, defendant; quarreler, irritable man, curmudgeon, scrapper, wrangler, brawler; diehard, bitter-ender, last-ditcher, intransigent, irreconcilable

453 RESISTANCE

<refusing to accept>

NOUNS 1 **resistance,** withstanding, countering, renitence, renitency, repellence, repellency; defiance; opposing, opposition; stand; repulsion, repulse, rebuff; objection, protest, remonstrance, dispute, challenge, demur; complaint; dissentience, dissent; reaction, hostile reaction, combative reaction, rebellion, counteraction; revolt; recalcitrance, recalcitrancy, recalcitration, fractiousness, refractoriness; reluctance; obstinacy; noncooperation; uncooperativeness, negativism; resistance movement, passive resistance, civil disobedience, mutiny, insurrection, insurgence

VERBS 2 **resist,** withstand; stand; endure; stand up, bear up, hold up, hold out; defy, tell one where to get off, throw down the gauntlet; be obstinate; be proof against, bear up against; repel, repulse, rebuff

3 **offer resistance,** fight back, bite back, not turn the other cheek, show fight, lift a hand, raise a hand, stand one's ground, hold one's ground, withstand, stand, take one's stand, make a stand, make a stand against, take one's stand against, square off, put up one's dukes, stand up to, stand up against, stand at bay; front, confront, meet head-on, fly in the teeth of, fly in the face of, face up to, face down, face out; object, protest, remonstrate, dispute, challenge, complain, complain loudly, exclaim at; dissent; revolt, mutiny; make waves; make a determined resistance; kick against, kick out against, recalcitrate; put up a fight, put up a struggle, not take lying down, hang tough, tough it out; oppose; contend with; strive against

4 **stand fast,** stand one's ground, hold one's ground, stand firm, make a resolute stand, hold one's own, remain firm, stick, stuck fast, stick to one's guns, stay it out, stick it out, stick around, hold out, not back down, not give up, not submit, never say die; fight to the last ditch, die hard, sell one's life dearly, go down with flying colors, refuse to bow down

ADJS 5 **resistant, resistive,** resisting, renitent, up against, withstanding, repellent; obstructive, retardant, retardative; unyielding, unsubmissive; hard-shell, hard-nosed; rebellious; proof against; objecting, protesting, disputing, disputatious, complaining, dissentient, dissenting; recalcitrant, fractious, obstinate, refractory; reluctant;

noncooperative, uncooperative; up in arms, on the barricades, not lying down; immune

454 DEFIANCE

<open resistance>

NOUNS 1 **defiance,** defying, defial; daring, daringness, audacity, boldness, bold front, brash bearing, brashness, brassiness, brazenness, bravado, insolence; bearding, beard-tweaking, nose-tweaking; arrogance; sauciness, sauce, cheekiness, cheek, rebelliousness, pertness, impudence, impertinence; bumptiousness, cockiness; contempt, contemptuousness, derision, disdain, disregard, despite; risk-taking, tightrope walking, funambulism; disobedience, insubordination; stare-down, staring contest

2 **challenge, dare,** double dare, threat, taunt; fighting words; defy; gauntlet, glove, chip on one's shoulder, slap of the glove, invitation to combat, bid to combat, call to arms; war cry, war whoop, battle cry, rebel yell; back talk, insult

VERBS 3 **defy,** bid defiance, hurl defiance, scream defiance; dare, double-dare, outdare; challenge, call out, throw the gauntlet, throw the glove, stand up to, knock the chip off one's shoulder, cross swords; oppose, protest; beard, beard the lion in his den, face, face out, look in the eye, stare down, stare out, confront, affront, front, say right to one's face, square up to, go eyeball-to-eyeball with, go one-on-one with; tweak the nose, pluck by the beard, slap one's face, shake one's fist at; give one the finger; ask for it, ask for trouble, look for trouble, make something of it, show fight, show one's teeth, bare one's fangs; dance the war dance; **brave**; be insubordinate

4 **flout,** disregard, slight, slight over, treat with contempt, set at defiance, fly in the teeth, fly in the face of, snap one's fingers at; thumb one's nose at, cock a snook at, bite the thumb at; disdain, despise, scorn; laugh at, laugh to scorn, laugh out of court, laugh in one's face; hold in derision, scout, scoff at, deride; give someone lip, sass

5 **put up a bold front,** show a bold front, bluster, throw out one's chest, strut, crow, look big, stand with arms akimbo, gasconade

6 **take a dare,** accept a challenge, take one up on, call one's bluff; start something, take up the gauntlet

ADJS 7 **defiant,** defying, challenging; daring, bold, brash, brassy, brazen, audacious, insolent; arrogant; saucy, cheeky, pert, impudent, impertinent; stubborn, obstinate; bumptious, cocky, sassy; contemptuous, disdainful, derisive, disregardful, greatly daring, regardless of consequences; obstreperous

ADVS 8 **in defiance of,** in the teeth of, in the face of, under one's very nose

455 ACCORD

<harmonious relationship>

NOUNS 1 **accord,** accordance, **concord,** concordance, harmony, symphony, sync; rapport; good vibrations, good vibes, good karma; amity; frictionlessness; *rapprochement* <Fr>; sympathy, empathy, identity, feeling of identity, fellow feeling, fellowship, kinship, togetherness, affinity; agreement, understanding, like-mindedness, congruence; congeniality, compatibility; oneness, unity, unison, union; community, communion, community of interests, meeting of the minds; solidarity, team spirit, esprit, *esprit de corps* <Fr>; mutuality, sharing, reciprocity, mutual supportiveness; bonds of harmony, ties of affection, cement of friendship; happy family; peace; love, *agape* <Gk>, charity, *caritas* <L>, brotherly love; correspondence

VERBS 2 **get along,** harmonize, agree with, agree, get along with, get on with, cotton to, hit it off with, harmonize with, be in harmony with, be in tune with, fall in with, chime in with, blend in with, go hand in hand with, be at one with; sing in chorus, be on the same wavelength, see eye to eye; sympathize, empathize, identify with, respond to, understand one another, enter into one's views, enter into the ideas of, enter into the feelings of; accord, correspond; reciprocate, interchange

ADJS 3 **in accord,** accordant, harmonious, in harmony, congruous, congruent, in tune, attuned, agreeing, in concert, in rapport, *en rapport* <Fr>, amicable; frictionless; sympathetic, simpatico, empathic, empathetic, understanding; like-minded, akin, of the same mind, of one mind, at one, united, together; concordant, corresponding; agreeable, congenial, compatible; peaceful

456 DISACCORD

<unharmonious relationship>

NOUNS 1 **disaccord, discord,** discordance, discordancy, asynchrony, unharmoniousness, inharmoniousness, disharmony, inharmony, incongruence, incongruency, disaffinity, incompatibility, incompatibleness; culture gap, generation gap, gender gap; noncooperation; conflict, open conflict, open war, friction, rub; jar, jarring, jangle, clash, clashing; touchiness, strained relations, tension; bad blood; unpleasantness; mischief; contention; enmity; Eris, Discordia; the Apple of Discord

2 **disagreement,** difficulty, misunderstanding, difference, difference of opinion, agreement to disagree, variance, division, dividedness; cross-purposes; polarity of opinion, polarization; credibility gap, disparity

3 **dissension, dissent,** dissidence, flak; bickering, infighting, faction, factiousness, partisanship, partisan spirit; divisiveness; quarrelsomeness; litigiousness; pugnacity, bellicosity, combativeness, aggressiveness, contentiousness, belligerence; feistiness, touchiness, irritability, shrewishness, irascibility

4 **falling-out,** breach of friendship, parting of the ways, bust-up; alienation, estrangement, disaffection, disfavor; breach, break, rupture, schism, split, rift, cleft, disunity, disunion, disruption, separation, cleavage, divergence, division, dividedness; division in the camp, house divided against itself; open rupture, breaking off of negotiations, recall of ambassadors

5 **quarrel,** open quarrel, dustup, **dispute, argument,** polemic, argy-bargy, slanging match, fliting, lovers' quarrel, controversy, altercation, fight, squabble, contention, strife, tussle, bicker, wrangle, snarl, tiff, spat, fuss; breach of the peace; fracas, donnybrook, donnybrook fair, brouhaha; dissent; broil, embroilment, imbroglio; words, sharp words, war of words, logomachy; feud, blood feud, vendetta; brawl; turf war

6 <nonformal> **row,** rumpus, row-de-dow, ruckus, ruction, brannigan, shindy, foofooraw, hoo-ha, barney, shemozzle, set-to, run-in, scrap, hassle, rhubarb; knock-down-and-drag-out, knock-down-and-drag-out fight; the dozens; handbags at dawn, handbag situation

7 **bone of contention,** apple of discord, sore point, tender spot, delicate issue, ticklish issue, rub, beef; bone to pick, crow to pluck; *casus belli* <L>, grounds for war

VERBS 8 **disagree,** differ, differ in opinion, hold opposite views, disaccord, be at variance, not get along, pull different ways, be at cross-purposes, have no measures with, misunderstand one another; conflict, clash, collide, jostle, jangle, jar; live like cat and dog, live a cat-and-dog life

9 **have a bone to pick with,** have a crow to pluck wit, have a beef with

10 **fall out,** have a falling-out, break with, split, separate, diverge, divide, agree to disagree, part company, come to a parting of the ways, reach a parting of the ways

11 **quarrel, dispute,** oppugn, flite, altercate, fight, squabble, tiff, spat, bicker, wrangle, spar, broil, have words, set to, join issue, make the fur fly; cross swords, feud, battle; brawl; be quarrelsome, be contentious, be thin-skinned, be touchy, be sensitive, get up on the wrong side of the bed; turf battle

12 <nonformal> **row,** scrap, hassle, kick up a row; mix it up, lock horns, bump heads

13 **pick a quarrel,** fasten a quarrel on, look for trouble, pick a bone with, pluck a crow with; have a chip on one's shoulder; add insult to injury

14 **sow dissension,** stir up trouble, make trouble, borrow trouble; **alienate,** estrange, separate, divide, disunite, disaffect, come between; irritate, provoke, aggravate; set at odds, set at variance; set against, pit against, sic on, sic at, set on, set by the ears, set at one's throat; add fuel to the fire, fan the flame, pour oil on the blaze, light the fuse, stir the pot

ADJS 15 **disaccordant,** unharmonious, inharmonious, disharmonious, out of tune, asynchronous, unsynchronized, out of sync, discordant, out of accord, dissident, dissentient, disagreeing, differing; conflicting, clashing, colliding; like cats and dogs; divided, faction-ridden, fragmented

16 **at odds,** at variance, at loggerheads, at square, at cross-purposes; at war, at strife, at feud, at swords' points, at daggers, at daggers drawn, up in arms

17 **partisan,** polarizing, **divisive,** factional, factious; **quarrelsome,** bickering, disputatious, wrangling, eristic, eristical, polemical; litigious, pugnacious, combative, aggressive, bellicose, belligerent; feisty, touchy, irritable, shrewish, **irascible**

457 CONTENTION

<heated disagreement>

NOUNS 1 **contention, contest**, contestation, combat, fighting, conflict, strife, war, struggle, blood on the floor, cut, thrust; fighting at close quarters, infighting; warfare; hostility, enmity; quarrel, altercation, controversy, dustup, polemic, debate, forensics, argument, dispute, disputation; litigation; words, war of words, paper war, logomachy; scrapping, hassling; quarreling, bickering, wrangling, squabbling; oppugnancy, contentiousness, disputatiousness, litigiousness, quarrelsomeness; cat-and-dog life; Kilkenny cats; competitiveness, vying, rivalrousness, competitorship; cold war; electronic warfare; bone of contention; bad call

2 **competition, rivalry,** trying conclusions, the issue, vying, emulation, jockeying; cutthroat

competition; run for one's money; sportsmanship, gamesmanship, lifemanship, one-upmanship, competitive advantage; rat race; feeding frenzy

3 **contest,** engagement, encounter, match, matching, meet, meeting, derby, pissing match*, pissing contest*, trial, test; *concours, rencontre* <Fr>; close contest, hard contest, closely fought contest, close one, tight one, horse race, crapshoot; fight, bout, go, tussle; joust, tilt; tournament, tourney; rally; game; games, adventure game, Olympic games, Olympics, gymkhana; cookoff, Bake-Off <tm>; spelling bee

4 **fight, battle,** fray, affray, combat, action, conflict, embroilment; gun battle; clash; brush, skirmish, scrimmage; tussle, scuffle, struggle, scramble, shoving match; exchange of blows, passage at, passage of arms, clash of arms; quarrel; pitched battle; battle royal; unarmed combat; fistfight, punch-out, duke-out, punch-up; hand-to-hand fight, hand-to-hand, stand-up fight, running fight, running engagement; tug-of-war; bullfight, tauromachy; dogfight, cockfight; street fight, rumble; air combat, aerial combat, sea combat naval combat, ground combat, armored combat, infantry combat, fire fight, hand-to-hand combat, house-to-house combat; internal struggle, intestine struggle, internecine struggle, internecine combat; rhubarb

5 **free-for-all,** knock-down-and-drag-out, brawl, broil, melee, scrimmage, fracas, riot

6 **death struggle,** life-and-death struggle, life-or-death struggle, struggle to the death, fight to the death, duel to the death, all-out war, total war, last-ditch fight, fight to the last ditch, fight with no quarter given

7 **duel,** single combat, monomachy, satisfaction, affair of honor

8 **fencing,** swordplay; swordsmanship, dueling

9 **boxing, fighting,** noble art of self-defense, manly art of self-defense, fisticuffs, pugilism, prizefighting, the fights, the ring; boxing match, prizefight, spar, bout; shadowboxing; close fighting, infighting, the clinches; Chinese boxing; savate

10 **wrestling,** rassling, grappling, *sumo* <Japanese>; **martial arts,** mixed martial arts; catch-as-catch-can; wrestling match, wrestling meet; Greco-Roman wrestling, Cornish wrestling, Westmorland wrestling, Cumberland wrestling; professional wrestling

11 **racing, track,** track sports; **horse racing**, the turf, the sport of kings; dog racing, automobile racing

12 **race,** contest of speed, contest of fleetness; derby; **horse race; automobile race**, off-road race; heat, lap, bell lap, victory lap; footrace, run, running event; torch race; match race, obstacle race, three-legged race, sack race, potato race; walk; ride, tie; endurance race, motorcycle race, bicycle race; boat race, yacht race, regatta; air race; dog race

VERBS 13 **contend, contest,** jostle; fight, battle, combat, war, declare war, go to war, take arms, take up arms, put up a fight, open hostilities, call to arms; wage war; strive, struggle, scramble, go for the brass ring; make the fur fly, feathers fly, tussle, scuffle; quarrel; clash, collide; wrestle, rassle, grapple, grapple with, go to the mat with; come to blows, close, try conclusions, mix it up, go toe-to-toe, exchange blows, exchange fisticuffs, box, spar, give and take, give one a knuckle sandwich; cut and thrust, cross swords, fence, thrust and parry; joust, tilt, tourney, run a tilt, run a tilt at, break a lance with; duel, fight a duel, give satisfaction; feud; skirmish; fight one's way; fight the good fight; brawl, broil; riot; do a job on

14 **raise one's hand against,** life one's hand against; make war on; draw the sword against, take up the cudgels, couch one's lance; square up, square off, come to the scratch; have at, jump; lay on, lay about one; pitch into, sail into, light into, lay into, rip into, strike the first blow, draw first blood; **attack**

15 **encounter, go up against,** come up against, run foul of, run afoul of; close with, come to close quarters, bring to bay, fight hand-to-hand

16 **engage, take on**, go against, go up against, close with, try conclusions with, enter the ring with, enter the arena with, put on the gloves with, match oneself against; join issue, join battle, do battle, give battle, engage in battle, engage in combat

17 **contend with,** engage with, cope with, fight with, strive with, struggle with, wrestle with, grapple with, bandy with, try conclusions with, measure swords with, tilt with, cross swords with; exchange shots, shoot it out with; lock horns, bump heads, fall to loggerheads, go to loggerheads; tangle with, mix it up with, have a brush with; have it out, fight it out, battle it out, settle it; fight hammer and tongs, fight tooth and nail, go at it hammer and tongs, go at it tooth and nail, duke it out, fight like devils, ask and give no quarter, make blood flow freely, battle *à outrance,* fight to the death, fight to the finish

18 **compete, contend,** vie, try conclusions, try the issue, jockey; compete with, compete against, vie with, challenge, cope, enter into competition with, give a run for one's money, meet; try one another, test one another; rival, emulate, outvie; keep up with the Joneses

19 **race,** race with, run a race; horse-race, boat-race
20 **contend for, strive for,** struggle for, fight for, vie for; stickle for, stipulate for, hold out for, make a point of
21 **dispute, contest,** oppugn, take issue with; fight over, quarrel over, wrangle over, squabble over, bicker over, strive about, contend about

ADJS 22 **contending,** contesting; contestant, disputant; striving, struggling; fighting, battling, warring; warlike; quarrelsome
23 **competitive,** competitory, competing, vying, rivaling, rival, rivalrous, emulous, in competition, in rivalry; cutthroat

458 WARFARE

<engaged conflict>

NOUNS 1 **war** <see list>, **warfare,** warring, warmaking, art of war, combat, fighting, *la guerre* <Fr>; armed conflict, armed combat, military operation, the sword, arbitrament of the sword, appeal to arms, appeal to the sword, resort to arms, force of arms, might of arms, bloodshed; state of war, hostilities, belligerence, belligerency, open war, open warfare, open hostilities; hot war, shooting war; total war, all-out war; wartime; battle; attack; war zone, theater of operations; trouble spot; warpath; localized war, major war, world war, atomic war, nuclear war, civil war, chemical war, biological war, bacteriological warfare, war of independence, naval war; offensive warfare, preventive warfare, psychological warfare; static warfare, trench warfare, guerrilla warfare; biowarfare, nuclear winter; limited war; rules of engagement; electronic warfare; germ warfare
2 **battle array,** order of battle, disposition, deployment, marshaling; open order; close formation; echelon
3 **campaign,** war, **drive,** expedition, battle plan, hostile expedition; crusade, holy war, jihad
4 **operation,** action; movement; **mission;** operations, military operations, land operations, naval operations, sea operations, air operations; combined operations, joint operations, coordinated operations; active operations, amphibious operations, airborne operations, fluid operations, major operations, minor operations, night operations, overseas operations; war plans, staff work; logistic; war game, dry run, kriegspiel, maneuver, maneuvers; strategy, tactics; battle; shock and awe, water torture, waterboarding; military base, airbase
5 **military science,** art of war, rules of war, science of war, rules of engagement, military affairs, military strategy, military tactics, military operations; siegecraft; warcraft, war, arms, profession of arms; generalship, soldiership; chivalry, knighthood, knightly skill
6 **declaration of war,** challenge; defiance
7 **call to arms,** call-up, call to the colors, rally; mobilization; muster, levy; conscription, recruitment; rallying cry, slogan, watchword, catchword, exhortation; battle cry, war cry, war whoop, rebel yell; banzai, gung ho, St. George, Montjoie, Geronimo, go for broke; bugle call, trumpet call, clarion, clarion call; remember the Maine, remember the Alamo, remember Pearl Harbor; battle orders, military orders
8 **service, military service;** active service, active duty; military duty, military obligation, compulsory service, conscription, draft, impressment; selective service, national service <Brit>; reserve status; recruiting, recruitment; enlisting, volunteering; embedded journalist
9 **militarization,** activation, mobilization; war footing, wartime footing, national emergency; war effort, war economy; martial law, suspension of civil rights; garrison state, military dictatorship; remilitarization, reactivation; arms race; war clouds, war scare
10 **warlikeness,** unpeacefulness, war spirit, warlike spirit, ferocity, fierceness; hard line; combativeness, contentiousness; hostility, antagonism; unfriendliness; aggression, aggressiveness; aggro; belligerence, belligerency, pugnacity, pugnaciousness, bellicosity, bellicoseness, truculence, fight; chip on one's shoulder; militancy, militarism, martialism, militaryism; saber rattling; chauvinism, jingoism, hawkishness, warmongering; waving of the bloody shirt; warpath; war fever; oppugnancy, quarrelsomeness
11 <rallying devices and themes> battle flag, banner, colors, gonfalon, bloody shirt, fiery cross, fiery crostarie, atrocity story, enemy atrocities; martial music, war song, battle hymn, national anthem, military band; national honor, face; foreign threat, totalitarian threat, Communist threat, colonialist threat, imperialist threat, Western imperialism, yellow peril; expansionism, manifest destiny; independence, self-determination
12 **war god**, Mars, Ares, Odin, Woden, Wotan, Tyr, Tiu, Tiw; war goddess, Athena, Minerva, Bellona, Enyo, Valkyrie

VERBS 13 **war, wage war,** make war, carry on war, carry on hostilities, engage in hostilities, engage in battle, wield the sword; battle, fight; spill blood, shed blood

14 **make war on,** levy war on; attack; declare war, challenge, combat, throw down the gauntlet, fling down the gauntlet; defy; open hostilities, plunge the world into war; launch a holy war on, go on a crusade against

15 **go to war,** break the peace, breach the peace, take up the gauntlet, go on the warpath, rise up in arms, take to arms, resort to arms, take arms, take up arms, take up the cudgels, take up the sword, appeal to the sword, unsheathe one's weapon, come to cold steel; take the offensive, take the field

16 **campaign,** undertake operations, open a campaign, make an expedition, go on a crusade

17 **serve,** do duty; fulfill one's military obligation, wear the uniform; soldier, see active duty, do active duty; **bear arms,** carry arms, shoulder arms, shoulder a gun, defend, protect; see action, see combat, hear shots fired in anger

18 **call to arms, call up,** call to the colors, rally; mobilize; muster, levy; conscript, recruit; sound the call to arms, give the battle cry, wave the bloody shirt, beat the drums, blow the bugle, blow the clarion

19 **militarize,** activate, mobilize, go on a wartime footing, put on a war footing, call to the colors, gird one's loins, gird up one's loins, muster one's resources; reactivate, remilitarize, take out of mothballs, retread

ADJS **20** **warlike, militant,** fighting, warring, battling; martial, **military,** soldierly, soldierlike; combative, contentious, gladiatorial; trigger-happy; belligerent, pugnacious, pugilistic, truculent, bellicose, scrappy, full of fight; aggressive, offensive; fierce, ferocious, savage, bloody, bloody-minded, bloodthirsty, sanguinary, sanguineous; unpeaceful, unpeaceable, unpacific; hostile, antagonistic, agonistic, enemy, inimical; unfriendly; quarrelsome; paramilitary, mercenary; don't ask don't tell

21 **militaristic, warmongering,** war-loving, warlike, saber-rattling, battle-hungry; chauvinistic, chauvinist, jingoistic, jingoist, jingoish, jingo, crusading; hard-line, hawkish, of the war party

22 **embattled,** battled, **engaged,** at grips, in combat, on the warpath, on the offensive; arrayed, deployed, ranged, in battle array, in the field; militarized; armed; war-ravaged, war-torn

ADVS **23** **at war,** up in arms; in the midst of battle, in the thick of the fray, thick of combat; in the cannon's mouth, at the point of the gun; at swords' points, at the point of the bayonet, at the point of the sword

24 **war**

American Civil War <1861–1865>
American Revolution, War of Independence, Revolutionary War <1775–1783>
Arab-Israeli War <1948–1949, 1956, 1967, 1973–1974, 1982>
Balkan Wars <1912–1913>
Boer Wars <1880–1881, 1899–1902>
Crimean War <1853–1856>
Crusades <11–13th centuries>
English Civil War <1642–1646>
Franco-Prussian War <1870–1871>
French and Indian War <1754–1763>
French Revolution <1789–1799>
Gallic War <58–50 BC>
Gaza War <2008–2009>
Greco-Persian Wars <492–449 BC>
Gulf War <1980–1988, 1990–1991>
Hundred Years' War <1337–1453>
Indian Wars <1622–1675, 1840–1880s>
Iran-Iraq War <1980–1990>
Iraq War, Operation Iraqi Freedom <2003–2011>
Italian Wars of Independence <1848–1849, 1859–1860>
Korean War <1950–1953>
Kosovo Crisis <1998–1999>
Mexican Civil War <1910–1920>
Mexican War <1846–1848>
Napoleonic Wars <1793–1815>
Norman Conquest <1066>
Opium Wars <1839–1842, 1856–1860>
Peloponnesian Wars <431–404 BC>
Persian Gulf War <1990–1991>
Punic Wars <264–241 BC, 218–201 BC>
Russian Revolution, Russian Civil War <1918–1920>
Russo-Finnish War, Winter War <1939–1940>
Russo-Japanese War <1904–1905>
Samnite Wars <343–341, 326–304, 298–290 BC>
Seven Weeks' War <1866>
Seven Years' War <1756–63>
Sino-Japanese Wars <1894–1895, 1937–1945>
Six-Day War <1967>
Spanish-American War <1898>
Spanish Civil War <1936–1939>
Taiping Rebellion <1850—1864>
Thirty Years' War <1618–1648>
Vietnam War, War in Southeast Asia <1955–1975>
War of 1812 <1812–1814>
War of the Austrian Succession <1740–1748>
War of the Polish Succession <1733–1738>
War of the Spanish Succession <1701–1714>
Wars of the Roses <1455–1485>
World War I, Great War, War of the Nations <1914–1918>
World War II <1939–1945>
Yom Kippur War <1973>

459 ATTACK

<*aggressive action*>

NOUNS **1** **attack, assault,** assailing, assailment; offense, **offensive; aggression**; onset, onslaught; strike; surgical strike, first strike, preventive war; descent on, descent upon; charge, rush, dead set at, run at, rush against; drive, push; sally, sortie; infiltration; *coup de main* <Fr>; frontal attack, frontal assault, head-on attack, flank attack; mass attack, kamikaze attack; banzai attack, banzai charge, suicide attack; hit-and-run attack; breakthrough; counterattack, counteroffensive; amphibious attack; gas attack; diversionary attack, diversion; assault and battery, simple assault, mugging, aggravated assault, aggravated battery, armed assault, unprovoked assault; preemptive strike; blitzkrieg, blitz, lightning attack, lightning war, panzer warfare, devastating attack, crippling attack, deep strike, shock tactics; atomic attack, thermonuclear attack, first-strike capacity, megadeath, overkill; nuclear winter; land attack, air attack, combined attack, terrorist attack, bioterror, biowarfare; personal attack; friendly fire

2 **surprise attack,** surprise, surprisal, unforeseen attack, sneak attack; Pearl Harbor; stab in the back; shock tactics

3 **thrust,** pass, lunge, swing, cut, stab, jab; feint; home thrust

4 **raid, strike,** foray, razzia; invasion, incursion, inroad, irruption; air raid, air strike, air attack, shuttle raid, fire raid, saturation raid; escalade, scaling, boarding, tank attack, armored attack, panzer attack

5 **siege,** besiegement, beleaguerment; encompassment, investment, encirclement, envelopment; blockading, blockade; cutting of supply lines; vertical envelopment; pincer movement

6 **storm,** storming, taking by storm, overrunning

7 **bombardment,** bombing, air bombing, strategic bombing, tactical bombing, saturation bombing; strafing; terrorist attack; suicide bombing; cluster bombing; direct hit

8 **gunfire,** fire, firing, musketry, shooting, fireworks, gunplay; gunfight, shootout; firepower, offensive capacity, bang

9 **volley,** salvo, burst, spray, strafe, fusillade, rapid fire; crossfire; drumfire, cannonade, cannonry, broadside, enfilade; **barrage**, artillery barrage; sharpshooting, sniping

10 **stabbing,** piercing, sticking; knifing, bayonetting; the sword; impalement, transfixion

11 **stoning,** lapidation

12 **assailant,** assailer, **attacker;** assaulter, mugger; **aggressor;** invader, raider; warrior; terrorist

13 **zero hour,** H-hour; D-day, target day

VERBS **14** **attack, assault,** assail, harry, assume the offensive, take the offensive; commit an assault upon; strike, hit, pound; go at, come at, have at, launch out against, make a dead set at; fall on, fall upon, set on, set upon, descend on, descend upon, come down on, swoop down on; pounce upon; lift a hand against, raise a hand against, draw the sword against, take up arms against, take the cudgels against; lay hands on, lay a hand on, bloody one's hands with; gang up on, attack in force; surprise, ambush; blitz, attack like lightning, hit like lightning

15 <nonformal> **pitch into,** light into, lambaste, pile into, sail into, wade into, lay into, plow into, tie into, rip into; let one have it, let one have it with both barrels, kick ass; land on, land on like a ton of bricks, climb all over, crack down on, lower the boom on, tee off on; mug, jump, bushwhack, sandbag, scrag; swipe at, lay at, go for, go at; blindside, blind-pop, sucker-punch; take a swing at, take a crack at, take a swipe at, take a poke at, take a shot at

16 **lash out at,** strike out at, hit out at, let drive at, let fly at; strike at, hit at, poke at, thrust at, swing at, swing on, make a thrust, lunge at, deal a blow at, flail at, flail away at, take a fling; cut and thrust; smite; feint

17 **launch an attack,** kick off an attack, mount an attack, push, thrust, mount an offensive, open an offensive, drive; advance against, advance upon, march upon, march against, bear down upon; infiltrate; strike; flank; press the attack, follow up the attack; counterattack, retaliate, take on

18 **charge,** rush, rush at, fly at, run at, dash at, make a dash at; tilt at, go full tilt at, run a tilt at, ride full tilt against; jump off, go over the top

19 **besiege,** lay siege to, encompass, surround, encircle, envelope, invest, hem in, set upon on all sides, get in a pincers, close the jaws of the pincers, close the jaws of the trap; blockade; beset, beleaguer, harry, harass, drive hard, press one hard; soften up

20 **raid,** foray, make a raid; **invade,** inroad, make an inroad, make an irruption into; escalade, scale, scale the walls, board; storm, take by storm, overwhelm, inundate

21 **pull a gun on,** draw a gun on; get the drop on, beat to the draw

22 **shoot at, shoot,** pull the trigger, fire upon, fire at, pop at, take a pop at, take a shot at, fire a shot at, blaze away at; open fire, commence firing, open up on; aim at, take aim at, level at, zero in on, take dead aim at, draw a bead on; snipe, snipe at; bombard, blast, strafe, shell, cannonade, mortar, barrage, blitz; pepper, fusillade, fire a volley; rake, enfilade; pour a broadside into; cannon; torpedo

23 **bomb,** drop a bomb, lay an egg; dive-bomb, glide-bomb, skip-bomb, pattern-bomb, suicide-bomb; atom-bomb, hydrogen-bomb; nuke, plaster

24 **mine,** plant a mine, trigger a mine

25 **stab,** stick, pierce, plunge in; run through, impale, spit, transfix, transpierce; spear, lance, poniard, bayonet, saber, sword, put to the sword; knife, dirk, dagger, stiletto; spike; cut down

26 **gore,** horn, tusk

27 **pelt, stone,** lapidate, pellet; brickbat, egg, chuck

28 **hurl at,** throw at, cast at, heave at, fling at, sling at, toss at, shy at, fire at, let fly at; hurl against, hurl at the head of

ADJS 29 **attacking,** assailing, assaulting, charging, driving, thrusting, advancing; **invading,** invasive, invasionary, incursive, incursionary, irruptive, storming; rapid-fire

30 **offensive,** combative, on the offensive, on the attack; aggressive; militant, hawkish, on the warpath; passive-aggressive

ADVS 31 **under attack,** under fire; under siege; counterattacking

INTERJS 32 **attack,** advance, charge, over the top, up and at 'em, have at them, give 'em hell, let 'em have it, fire, open fire; banzai, Geronimo

460 DEFENSE

<defending from an attack>

NOUNS 1 **defense,** defence <Brit>, **guard,** ward; protection; resistance; self-defense, self-protection, self-preservation; deterrent capacity; defense in depth; the defensive; covering one's ass, covering one's rear-end; defenses, psychological defenses, ego defenses, defense mechanism, escape mechanism, avoidance reaction, negative taxis, negative tropism; bunker atmosphere, bunker mentality; siege mentality; basic training; friendly fire

2 **military defense,** national defense, defense capability; Air Defense Command; civil defense; control of electromagnetic radiation for civil defense (CONELRAD); Emergency Broadcast System (EBS), Civil Defense Warning System; radar defenses, distant early warning (DEW) Line; antimissile missile, antiballistic-missile system (ABM); strategic defense initiative, Star Wars

3 **armor,** armature; armor plate; body armor, suit of armor, plate armor; panoply, harness; mail, chain mail, chain armor; bulletproof vest; battlegear; protective covering, cortex, thick skin, carapace, shell; spines, needles; human shield; army-navy surplus, army surplus

4 **fortification,** work, defense work, bulwark, rampart, fence, earthwork, stockade, barrier; enclosure

5 **entrenchment, trench,** ditch, fosse; moat; dugout, *abri* <Fr>; bunker; foxhole, slit trench; approach trench, communication trench, fire trench, gallery, parallel, coupure; tunnel, fortified tunnel; undermining, sap, single sap, double sap, flying sap; mine, countermine

6 **stronghold,** hold, safehold, fasthold, strong point, fastness, keep, ward, bastion, donjon, citadel, castle, tower, tower of strength; mote, motte; fort, fortress, post; bunker, pillbox, blockhouse, garrison, trenches, barricades; garrison house; acropolis; peel, peel tower; rath; martello tower, martello; bridgehead, beachhead; safeguard

7 **defender,** champion, advocate; upholder; guardian angel, angel; supporter; vindicator, apologist; protector; guard; henchman; paladin, knight, white knight; guard dog, attack dog, junkyard dog

VERBS 8 **defend, guard,** shield, screen, secure, guard against, ward; defend tooth and nail, defend to the death, defend to the last breath; safeguard, protect; stand by the side of, flank; advocate, champion; defend oneself, cover one's ass, cover one's rear-end, cover your ass (CYA)

9 **fortify,** embattle, battle; **arm;** armor, armor-plate; man; garrison, man the garrison, man the trenches, man the barricades; barricade, blockade; bulwark, wall, palisade, fence; castellate, crenellate; bank; entrench, dig in; mine; beef up

10 **fend off,** ward off, stave off, hold off, fight off, keep off, beat off, parry, fend, counter, turn aside; hold at bay, keep at bay, keep at arm's length; hold the fort, hold the line, stop, check, block, hinder, obstruct; repel, repulse, rebuff, drive back, push back; avert; go on the defensive, fight a holding action, delaying action, fall back to prepared positions

ADJS 11 **defensive,** defending, **guarding,** shielding, screening; protective; self-defensive, self-protective, self-preservative

12 **fortified,** battlemented, embattled, battled, entrenched; castellated, crenellated, casemated, machicolated; secured, protected

13 **armored,** armor-plated; in armor, panoplied, armed cap-a-pie, armed at all points, in harness; mailed, mailclad, ironclad; loricate, loricated

14 **armed,** heeled, carrying, gun-toting; accoutered, in arms, bearing arms, carrying arms, under

arms, sword in hand; well-armed, heavy-armed, full-armed, bristling with arms, armed to the teeth; light-armed; garrisoned, manned

15 **defensible,** defendable, tenable

ADVS 16 **defensively,** in defense, in self-defense; on the defensive, on guard; at bay, with one's back to the wall

461 COMBATANT

<entity in a war>

NOUNS 1 **combatant, fighter, battler,** scrapper; contestant, contender, competitor, rival, adversary, opponent, agonist; disputant, wrangler, squabbler, bickerer, quarreler; struggler, tussler, scuffler; brawler, rioter; feuder; belligerent, militant; gladiator; jouster, tilter; knight, belted knight; swordsman, blade, sword; fencer, foilsman, swordplayer; duelist, dueler; gamecock, fighting cock; tough, rough, rowdy, ruffian, thug, hoodlum, hood, hooligan, streetfighter, bully, bullyboy, bravo; gorilla, goon, plug-ugly, skinhead; hatchet man, enforcer, strong-arm man, strong arm, strong-armer; fire-eater, swaggerer, swashbuckler

2 **boxer,** pugilist, pug, palooka; street fighter, scrapper, pit bull

3 **wrestler,** rassler, grunt-and-groaner, grappler, scuffler, matman

4 **bullfighter,** toreador, *torero* <Sp>; banderillero, picador, matador

5 **militarist,** warmonger, war dog, war hound, war hawk, hawk; chauvinist, jingo, jingoist, hard-liner; conquistador, privateer, pirate, buccaneer; terrorist; special forces

6 **serviceperson, military man, military woman,** serviceman, servicewoman, navy man, navy woman; air serviceman, air servicewoman; soldier, warrior, brave, fighting man, foxhole buddy, legionary, hoplite, man-at-arms, rifleman, rifle; ninja; cannon fodder, food for powder, trooper, militiaman; warrioress, Amazon; spearman, pikeman, halberdier; military training, boot camp

7 <common soldiers> **GI,** GI Joe, dough, doughfoot, Joe Tentpeg, John Dogface, grunt, doughboy, Yank; Tommy Atkins, Tommy, Johnny, swaddy <Brit>; redcoat; weekend warrior

8 **enlisted man,** noncommissioned officer; common soldier, private, private soldier, buck private; private first class (pfc)

9 **infantryman,** foot soldier; light infantryman, chasseur, Zouave; rifleman, rifle, musketeer; fusileer, carabineer; sharpshooter, marksman, expert rifleman; sniper; grenadier

10 <offensive or nonformal> grunt, dogface, footslogger, paddlefoot, doughfoot, blisterfoot, crunchie, line doggie, groundpounder

11 **artilleryman,** artillerist, gunner, guns, cannoneer, machine gunner; bomber, bomb thrower, bombardier

12 **cavalryman,** mounted infantryman, trooper; dragoon, light dragoon, heavy dragoon; lancer, lance, uhlan, hussar; cuirassier; spahi; cossack

13 **tanker,** tank corpsman, tank crewman

14 **engineer,** combat engineer, pioneer, Seabee; sapper, miner

15 **elite troops,** shock troops, storm troops; rapid deployment force (RDF); commandos, rangers, special forces, special ops, Green Berets, marines, paratroops; guardsmen, guards, household troops; Life Guards, Horse Guards, Foot Guards, Grenadier Guards, Coldstream Guards, Scot Guards, Irish Guards; Swiss Guards; SWAT team, Navy Seals

16 **irregular,** casual; guerrilla, partisan, franctireur; bushfighter, bushwhacker; underground, resistance, maquis; Vietcong (VC), Charley; South West African People's Organization guerrilla; Shining Path Guerrilla; Contra; underground fighter, resistance fighter, freedom fighter; storm trooper; terrorist

17 **mercenary,** hireling, free lance, freelance, free companion, **soldier of fortune,** adventurer; gunman, gun, hired gun, hired killer, professional killer; terrorist

18 **recruit,** rookie, conscript, drafted man, draftee, inductee, selectee, enlistee, enrollee, trainee, boot; raw recruit, tenderfoot; awkward squad; draft, levy

19 **veteran, vet,** campaigner, old campaigner, old soldier, old trooper, warhorse, Veterans of Foreign Wars (VFW) member, American Legion member

20 **defense forces,** services, the service, armed forces, armed services, fighting machine; the military, the military establishment; professional forces, special forces, standing forces, regular forces, reserve forces, volunteer forces; combat troops, support troops; expeditionary force

21 branch, **branch of the service, corps**; service, arm of the service, Air Force, Army, Navy, Marine Corps, Coast Guard, Merchant Marine

22 <military units> unit, organization, tactical unit, outfit; army, field army, army group, corps, army corps, division, infantry division, armored division, airborne division, triangular division, pentomic division, Reorganization Objective Army Division (ROAD); regiment, battle group, battalion, garrison, company, troop, brigade,

legion, phalanx, cohort, platoon, section, battery, maniple; combat team, combat command; task force; commando unit; squad, squadron; detachment, detail, posse; kitchen police (KP); column, flying column; rank, file; train, field train; cadre

23 **army,** this man's army, soldiery, forces, armed forces, troops, host, array, legions; ranks, rank and file; standing army, regular army, active forces, regulars, professional soldiers, career soldiers; the line, troops of the line; line of defense, first line of defense, second line of defense; ground forces, ground troops; storm troops, assault troops; airborne troops, paratroops; ski troops, mountain troops; occupation force; elite troops; army base

24 **militia,** organized militia, national militia, mobile militia, boots on the ground, territorial militia, reserve militia, citizen's army; home reserve; National Guard, Air National Guard, state guard; home guard <Brit>; minutemen, trainband, yeomanry

25 **reserves,** auxiliaries, **second line of defense,** reinforcements, ready reserves, landwehr, army reserves, home reserves, territorial reserves, territorial army, home defense army <Brit>, supplementary reserves, organized reserves; U.S. Army Reserve, U.S. Naval Reserve, U.S. Marine Corps Reserve, U.S. Air Force Reserve, U.S. Coast Guard Reserve, National Guard; standby reserves, retired reserves

26 **volunteers, enlistees,** volunteer forces, volunteer army, volunteer militia, volunteer navy

27 **navy,** naval forces, first line of defense; fleet, flotilla, argosy, armada, squadron, escadrille, division, task force, task group; amphibious force; mosquito fleet; support fleet, destroyer fleet, auxiliary fleet, reserve fleet, mothball fleet; United States Navy (USN); Royal Navy (RN); marine, mercantile marine, merchant marine, merchant navy, merchant fleet; naval militia; naval reserve; coast guard; Seabees, Naval Construction Battalion; admiralty; gunboat diplomacy

28 **marines,** sea soldiers, Marine Corps, Royal Marines; leathernecks, devil dogs, gyrenes, jollies

29 **air force,** air corps, air service, air arm; U.S. Air Force (USAF); strategic air force, tactical air force; squadron, escadrille, flight, wing; airbase

30 **warhorse,** charger, courser, trooper

462 ARMS

<weapons and ammunition>

NOUNS 1 **arms, weapons,** deadly weapons, instruments of destruction, offensive weapons, military hardware, matériel, weaponry, armament, munitions, ordnance, munitions of war; musketry; missilery; small arms; sidearms; stand of arms; conventional weapons, nonnuclear weapons; nuclear weapons, atomic weapons, thermonuclear weapons, A-weapons, strategic nuclear weapon, tactical nuclear weapon; bacteriological weapon, biological weapon, chemical weapon; weapon of mass destruction (WMD); arms industry, arms maker, military-industrial complex; natural weapon; secret weapon; explosives

2 **armory, arsenal,** magazine, dump; ammunition depot, ammo dump, depot park, gun park, artillery park, park of artillery; atomic arsenal, thermonuclear arsenal, gun room, powder barrel, powder keg

3 **ballistics,** gunnery, musketry, artillery; rocketry, missilery; archery

4 **fist,** clenched fist; brass knuckles; knucks, knuckles, knuckle-dusters; club, bludgeon, blackjack, truncheon, billy, blunt instrument

5 **sword,** blade, cutlass, saber, rapier, foil, bayonet, machete; steel, cold steel; Excalibur; knife, switchblade, bowie knife, Swiss army knife, box cutter; dagger; axe

6 **arrow,** shaft, dart, reed, bolt; quarrel; chested arrow, footed arrow, bobtailed arrow; arrowhead, barb; flight, volley

7 **bow,** longbow, carriage bow; **bow and arrow;** crossbow, arbalest

8 **spear,** throwing spear, javelin, lance, harpoon, sharp weapon

9 **sling, slingshot;** throwing-stick, throw stick, spear-thrower, atlatl, wommera; **catapult,** arbalest, ballista, trebuchet

10 **gun, firearm;** shooting iron, gat, rod, heater, piece; shoulder weapon, shoulder gun; gun make; gun part; stun gun; automatic, BB gun, blunderbuss, Bren, Browning automatic rifle, burp gun, carbine, derringer, flintlock, forty-five, forty-four, Gatling gun, handgun, machine gun, musket, pistol, equalizer, semiautomatic, repeater, revolver, rifle, Saturday night special, sawed-off shotgun, shotgun, six-gun, six-shooter, submachine gun, thirty-eight, thirty-thirty, thirty-two, Thompson submachine, tommy gun, twenty-two, Uzi submachine gun, zip gun

11 **artillery, cannon,** guns, cannonry, ordnance, engines of war, Big Bertha, howitzer; field artillery; heavy artillery, heavy field artillery; self-propelled artillery; siege artillery, bombardment weapons; breakthrough weapons; siege engine, battering ram; mountain artillery, coast artillery, trench artillery, anti-aircraft artillery, flak; battery

12 **antiaircraft gun**, AA gun, ack-ack, pom-pom, skysweeper, Bofors, Oerlikon
13 **ammunition,** ammo, powder and shot, iron rations, round, live ammunition
14 **explosive,** high explosive; cellulose nitrate, cordite, dynamite, gelignite, guncotton, gunpowder, nitroglycerin, nitroglycerine, plastic explosive, plastique, powder, trinitrotoluene (TNT), trinitrotoluol (TNT), C4
15 **fuse,** detonator, exploder; cap, blasting cap, percussion cap, mercury fulminate, fulminating mercury; electric detonator, electric exploder; detonating powder; primer, priming; primacord
16 **charge,** load; blast; warhead, payload
17 **cartridge,** cartouche, shell; ball cartridge; clip, blank cartridge, dry ammunition
18 **missile, projectile,** bolt; brickbat, stone, rock, alley apple, Irish confetti; boomerang; bola; throwing-stick, throw stick, waddy; ballistic missile, cruise missile, Exocet missile, surface-to-air missile (SAM), surface-to-surface missile, Tomahawk missile; rocket; torpedo
19 **shot;** ball, cannonball, rifle ball, minié ball; **bullet,** slug, pellet; buckshot; dumdum bullet, expanding bullet, explosive bullet, manstopping bullet, manstopper, copkiller, Teflon bullet <tm>; tracer bullet, tracer; shell, high-explosive shell, shrapnel
20 **bomb,** bombshell, device; antipersonnel bomb, atomic bomb, atom bomb, A-bomb, atomic warhead, hydrogen bomb, H-bomb, nuclear bomb, blockbuster, depth charge, depth bomb, ash can, firebomb, incendiary bomb, incendiary, grenade, hand grenade, pineapple, letter bomb, Molotov cocktail, napalm bomb, neutron bomb, nuclear warhead, pipe bomb, plastic bomb, plastique bomb, plutonium bomb, smart bomb, stench bomb, stink bomb, time bomb; clean bomb, dirty bomb; mine, landmine; booby trap
21 **launcher,** projector, bazooka; rocket launcher, grenade launcher, hedgehog, minethrower, **mortar**
22 non-lethal weapon, riot control agent; stun gun, Taser <tm>, pepper spray, water cannon; rubber bullet, plastic bullet; minimal force, controlled force, soft kill, mission kill

463 ARENA
<place of conflict>

NOUNS 1 **arena,** scene of action, site, scene, setting, background, field, ground, terrain, sphere, place, locale, milieu, precinct, purlieu; course, range, walk; campus; theater, stage, stage set, scenery; platform; forum, agora, marketplace, open forum, public square; amphitheater, circus, hippodrome, coliseum, colosseum, stadium, bowl; hall, auditorium; gymnasium, gym, palaestra; lists, tiltyard, tilting ground; floor, pit, cockpit; bear garden; ring, prize ring, boxing ring, canvas, squared circle, wrestling ring, mat, bull ring; parade ground; athletic field, playing field; covered stadium, domed stadium; stamping ground, turf, bailiwick
2 **battlefield,** battleground, battle site, field, combat area, field of battle; field of slaughter, field of blood, field of bloodshed, aceldama, killing ground, killing field, shambles; battlefront, the front, front line, line, enemy line, firing line, battle line, line of battle; battle zone, war zone, combat zone; theater, theater of operations, theater of war, seat of war; beachhead, bridgehead; communications zone, zone of communications; no-man's-land; demilitarized zone (DMZ); jump area, jump zone, landing beach
3 **campground**, camp, campsite, camping ground, camping area, glamping, encampment, bivouac, tented field

464 PEACE
<state of no war>

NOUNS 1 **peace,** *pax* <L>; **peacetime,** state of peace, peaceable kingdom, the storm blown over; freedom from war, cessation of combat, exemption from hostilities, public tranquility, peace movement; harmony, concord, accord; universal peace, lasting peace, Pax Romana
2 **peacefulness,** tranquillity, serenity, calmness, quiet, peace and quiet, quietude, quietness, quiescence, quiet life, restfulness, rest, stillness, silence; order, orderliness, law and order, imposed peace; no hassle
3 **peace of mind,** peace of heart, peace of soul, peace of spirit, peace of God; ataraxia, shanti
4 **peaceableness,** unpugnaciousness, uncontentiousness, nonaggression; irenicism, dovelikeness, dovishness, pacifism, pacificism; peaceful coexistence; nonviolence, ahimsa; line of least resistance; meekness, lamblikeness
5 **noncombatant,** nonbelligerent, nonresistant, nonresister; civilian, citizen
6 **pacifist,** pacificist, peacenik, peace lover, dove, dove of peace; pacificator, peacemaker, bridgebuilder; peacemonger; conscientious objector, passive resister, conchie
7 **peace treaty**, peace agreement, nonaggression pact, disarmament treaty, arms reduction, arms

control; test ban; deescalation; amnesty, pardon, forgiveness, burying the hatchet

VERBS 8 **keep the peace,** remain at peace, wage peace; refuse to shed blood, keep one's sword in its sheath; forswear violence, beat one's swords into plowshares; pursue the arts of peace, pour oil on troubled waters; make love not war; defuse

ADJS 9 **pacific, peaceful,** peaceable; tranquil, serene; idyllic, pastoral; halcyon, soft, piping, calm, quiet, quiet as a lamb, quiescent, still, restful, untroubled, orderly, at peace; concordant; bloodless; peacetime; postwar, postbellum

10 **unbelligerent, peaceable,** pacific, peace-loving; unhostile, unbellicose, unpugnacious, uncontentious, unmilitant, unmilitary, nonaggressive, noncombative, nonmilitant; noncombatant, civilian; antiwar, dovelike; meek, passive, lamblike; pacifistic, pacifist, irenic; nonviolent; conciliatory

INTERJS 11 **peace,** peace be with you, peace be to you, *pax vobiscum, pax tecum* <L>; *shalom, shalom aleichem* <Heb>; go in peace, *vade in pace* <L>

465 PACIFICATION

<soothing conflict>

NOUNS 1 **pacification, peacemaking,** irenics, peacemongering, conciliation, propitiation, placation, appeasement, mollification, dulcification; calming, soothing, tranquilization; détente, relaxation of tension, easing of relations; mediation; placability; peacekeeping force, United Nations peacekeeping force

2 **peace offering,** peace offer, offer of parley, parley, peace overture; peace feelers; propitiatory gift; olive branch; white flag, truce flag, flag of truce; calumet, peace pipe, pipe of peace; downing of arms, hand of friendship, empty hands, outstretched hand; cooling off, cooling-off period; peace sign; compensation, reparation, atonement, restitution; amnesty, pardon, mercy, leniency, clemency; dove, lamb

3 **reconciliation,** reconcilement, rapprochement, reunion, shaking of hands, making up, kissing and making up

4 **adjustment,** accommodation, resolution, composition of differences, settlement of differences, compromise, arrangement, settlement, terms; consensus building, consensus seeking

5 **truce, armistice, peace**; pacification, treaty of peace, suspension of hostilities, end of hostilities, cease-fire, cessation, stand-down, breathing spell, cooling-off period, lull in hostilities; Truce of God, Peace of God, Pax Dei, Pax Romana; temporary truce, temporary arrangement, *modus vivendi* <L>; hollow truce; demilitarized zone, buffer zone, neutral territory; uneasy truce; peacekeeping mission

6 **disarmament,** reduction of armaments; unilateral disarmament; demilitarization, deactivation, disbanding, disbandment, demobilization, mustering out, reconversion, decommissioning; civilian life, mufti, civvy street <Brit>; defense cuts, arms reduction, arms control; test ban

VERBS 7 **pacify,** conciliate, placate, propitiate, appease, mollify, dulcify; calm, settle, soothe, tranquilize; smooth, smooth over, smooth out, smooth down, smooth one's feathers; allay, lay, lay the dust; pour oil on troubled waters, pour balm on, take the edge off of, take the sting out of; cool, defuse; clear the air

8 **reconcile,** bring to terms, bring together, reunite, heal the breach; bring about a détente; harmonize, restore harmony, put in tune; iron out, sort out, adjust, settle, compose, accommodate, arrange matters, settle differences, resolve, compromise; patch things up, make up, fix up, patch up a friendship, patch up a quarrel, smooth it over; weave peace between, mediate

9 **make peace,** cease hostilities, cease fire, stand down, raise a siege; cool it, chill out, bury the hatchet, smoke the peace pipe; negotiate a peace, dictate peace; make a peace offering, hold out the olive branch, hoist the white flag, wave the white flag; make the world a safer place, make the lion lie down with the lamb; turn the other cheek

10 **make up,** kiss and make up, make it up, make matters up, shake hands, come round, come together, come to an understanding, come to terms, let the wound heal, let bygones be bygones, forgive and forget, put it all behind one, settle one's differences, compose one's differences, meet halfway, compromise

11 **disarm,** lay down one's arms, unarm, turn in one's weapons, down one's arms, ground one's arms, put down one's gun, sheathe the sword, turn swords into plowshares; demilitarize, deactivate, demobilize, disband, reconvert, decommission

ADJS 12 **pacificatory,** pacific, irenic, conciliatory, reconciliatory, propitiatory, propitiative, placative, placatory, mollifying, appeasing; demobilized; pacifying, soothing, appeasable

13 **pacifiable,** placable, appeasable, propitiable

ADVS 14 **pacifically, peaceably;** with no hard feelings

466 MEDIATION

<intervening in conflict>

NOUNS 1 **mediation,** mediating, intermediation, **intercession; intervention,** interposition, putting oneself between, moderation, stepping in, declaring oneself in, involvement, interagency; interventionism; diplomacy, statesmanship; troubleshooting, good offices; peacekeeping mission

2 **arbitration,** arbitrament, compulsory arbitration, binding arbitration; nonbinding arbitration; umpirage, refereeship, mediatorship

3 **mediator,** intermediator, intermediate agent, intermediate, intermedium, **intermediary,** interagent, internuncio, mediatrix; medium; intercessor, interceder; ombudsman; intervener, intervenor; interventionist; go-between, liaison, middleman; connection; front, front man; deputy, agent; spokesman, spokeswoman, spokesperson, spokespeople; mouthpiece; negotiator, negotiant, negotiatress, negotiatrix; little Miss Fixit; troubleshooter; spin doctor; harmonizer

4 **arbitrator,** arbiter, impartial arbitrator, third party, unbiased observer; **moderator**, moderating influence; umpire, referee, judge; armchair quarterback; magistrate

5 **peacemaker,** make-peace, reconciler, smoother-over, peace negotiator, mediator; pacifier, pacificator, peace lover, pacifist; peacekeeper, United Nations peacekeeping force; conciliator, propitiator, appeaser; marriage counselor, family counselor; guidance counselor; camp counselor; patcher-up

VERBS 6 **mediate,** intermediate, **intercede,** go between; **intervene,** interpose, step in, step into the breach, declare oneself a party, involve oneself, put oneself between disputants, use one's good offices, act between; butt in, put one's nose in; represent; negotiate, bargain, treat with, make terms, meet halfway; arbitrate, moderate; umpire, referee, judge, officiate

7 **settle,** arrange, compose, patch up, adjust, straighten out, bring to terms, bring to an understanding; make peace; reconcile, conciliate

ADJS 8 **mediatory,** mediatorial, mediative, mediating, arbitral, going between, coming between; intermediatory, intermediary, intermedial, intermediate, middle, intervening, mesne, interlocutory; interventional, arbitrational, arbitrative; intercessory, intercessional; diplomatic; pacificatory

467 NEUTRALITY

<refusal to war>

NOUNS 1 **neutrality,** neutralism, strict neutrality; noncommitment, noninvolvement; independence, nonpartisanism, unalignment, nonalignment; anythingarianism, nothingarianism; mugwumpery, mugwumpism, fence-sitting, fence-straddling, fence, trimming; evasion, cop-out, abstention; impartiality, coexistence, avoidance; nonintervention, nonaggression

2 **indifference,** indifferentness, Laodiceanism; passiveness; apathy, phlegm, disinterest

3 **middle course, middle way,** *via media* <L>; middle ground, neutral ground, neutral territory, center, centerline; meeting ground, interface; gray area, penumbra, compromise; middle of the road, sitting on the fence, straddling the fence; medium, **happy medium;** mean, golden mean; moderation, moderateness; halfway measures, half measures, half-and-half measures; work-life balance

4 **neutral,** neuter; **independent,** nonpartisan; mugwump, fence-sitter, fence-straddler, trimmer; anythingarian, nothingarian; unaligned nation, nonaligned nation, third force, third world; game face

VERBS 5 **remain neutral,** stand neuter, hold no brief, keep in the middle of the road, straddle the fence, sit on the fence, sit out, sit on the sidelines, trim; evade, evade the issue, duck the issue, waffle, cop out, abstain

6 **steer a middle course,** hold a middle course, walk a middle path, follow the via media, strike a balance, preserve a balance, stay on an even keel, keep a happy medium, keep the golden mean, steer between, avoid Scylla and Charybdis; be moderate

ADJS 7 **neutral,** neuter; noncommitted, uncommitted, noninvolved, uninvolved; anythingarian, nothingarian; indifferent, Laodicean; tolerant; passive; apathetic; neither one thing nor the other, neither hot nor cold, inert; even, half-and-half, fifty-fifty; on the fence, on the sidelines, middle-of-the-road, centrist, center, moderate, midway; independent, nonpartisan; unaligned, nonaligned, third-force, third-world; impartial

468 COMPROMISE

<mutual concession>

NOUNS 1 **compromise,** composition, adjustment, accommodation, settlement, mutual concession, give-and-take; abatement of differences; bargain, deal, arrangement, understanding; concession, giving way, yielding; surrender, desertion of principle, evasion of responsibility, cop-out; middle ground, happy medium; meeting halfway; trade-off; face-saver

VERBS 2 **compromise,** make a compromise, reach a compromise, compound, compose, accommodate, adjust, settle, make an adjustment, make an arrangement, make a deal, do a deal, come to an understanding, strike a bargain, do something mutually beneficial; plea-bargain; strike a balance, take the mean, meet halfway, split the difference, go fifty-fifty, give and take; play politics; steer a middle course; make concessions, make trade-off, give way, yield, wimp out, chicken out; surrender, desert one's principles, evade responsibility, sidestep, duck responsibility, cop out, punt

PHRS 3 half a loaf is better than none; you can't win them all

469 POSSESSION

<control or owning>

NOUNS 1 **possession,** possessing, outright possession, free-and-clear possession; **owning,** having title to; seisin, nine points of the law, *de facto* possession, de jure possession, lawful possession, legal possession; property rights, proprietary rights; title, absolute title, free-and-clear title, original title; derivative title; adverse possession, squatting, squatterdom, squatter's right; claim, legal claim, lien; usucapion, usucaption, prescription; occupancy, occupation; hold, holding, tenure; tenancy, tenantry, lease, leasehold, sublease, underlease, undertenancy; gavelkind; villenage, villein socage, villeinhold; socage, free socage; burgage; frankalmoign, lay fee; tenure in chivalry, knight service; fiefdom, feud, feodum; freehold, alodium; fee simple, fee tail, fee simple absolute, fee simple conditional, fee simple defeasible, fee simple determinable; fee position; dependency, colony, mandate; prepossession, preoccupation, preoccupancy; chose in possession, bird in hand, nine tenths of the law; property

2 **ownership,** title, possessorship, *dominium* <L>, proprietorship, proprietary, property right; lordship, overlordship, seigniory; dominion, sovereignty; landownership, landowning, landholding, land tenure; nationalization, public domain, state ownership

3 **monopoly,** monopolization; corner, cornering, a corner on; exclusive possession; engrossment, forestallment

VERBS 4 **possess,** have, hold, have and hold, possess outright, possess free and clear, occupy, fill, enjoy, boast; be possessed of, have tenure of, have in hand, be seized of, have in one's grasp, have in one's possession, be enfeoffed of; command, have at one's command, at one's pleasure, at one's disposal, have going for one; claim, usucapt; squat, squat on, claim squatter's rights

5 **own,** have title to, have for one's own, have for one's very own, have to one's name, call one's own, have the deed for, hold in fee simple

6 **monopolize,** hog, grab all of, gobble up, call one's own, take it all, have all to oneself, have exclusive possession of, have exclusive rights to; engross, forestall, tie up; corner, get a corner on, corner the market

7 **belong to,** pertain to, appertain to; vest in

ADJS 8 **possessed, owned,** held; in seisin, in fee, in fee simple, free and clear; own, of one's own, in one's name; in one's possession, in hand, in one's grip, in one's grasp, at one's command, at one's disposal; on hand, by one, in stock, in store

9 **possessing,** having, holding, having and holding, occupying, owning; in possession of, possessed of, seized of, master of; tenured; enfeoffed; endowed with, blessed with; worth; propertied, property-owning, landed, landowning, landholding

10 **possessive,** possessory, **proprietary**

11 **monopolistic,** monopolist, monopolizing, hogging, hoggish; exclusive

ADVS 12 **free and clear, outright;** bag and baggage; by fee simple

470 POSSESSOR

<controller or owner>

NOUNS 1 **possessor,** holder, keeper, haver, enjoyer; a have

2 **proprietor,** proprietary, **owner;** titleholder, deedholder; proprietress, proprietrix; master, mistress, lord; landlord, landlady; lord of the manor, lady of the manor <Brit>, man of the house, lady of the house, mesne lord, mesne, feudatory, feoffee; squire, country gentleman, country gentlewoman; householder; beneficiary, cestui, cestui que trust, cestui que use

3 **landowner,** landholder, property owner, propertied person, landed person, man of property, freeholder; landed interests, landed gentry, slumlord, rent gouger; absentee landlord

4 **tenant, occupant,** occupier, incumbent, resident; lodger, roomer, boarder, paying guest; renter, hirer <Brit>, rent-payer, lessee, leaseholder; subtenant, sublessee, underlessee, undertenant;

tenant at sufferance, tenant at will; tenant from year to year, tenant for years, tenant for life; squatter; homesteader

5 **trustee,** fiduciary, holder of the legal estate; depository, depositary

471 PROPERTY

<things owned or controlled>

NOUNS 1 **property, properties, possessions,** holdings, havings, goods, chattels, effects, estate and effects, what one can call one's own, what one has to one's name, all one owns, all one has, all one can lay claim to, one's all; household possessions, household effects, lares and penates; hereditament, corporeal hereditament, incorporeal hereditament; acquest; acquisitions, receipts; inheritance; public property, common property; intellectual property

2 **belongings,** appurtenances, trappings, paraphernalia, appointments, accessories, perquisites, appendages, appanages, choses local; things, material things, mere things; consumer goods; choses, choses in possession, choses in action; personal effects, personal property, chattels personal, movables, choses transitory; what one can call one's own, what has to one's name

3 impedimenta, **luggage,** dunnage, **baggage,** bag and baggage, traps, tackle, apparatus, truck, gear, kit, outfit, duffel

4 **estate,** interest, equity, stake, part, percentage; right, title, claim, holding; use, trust, benefit; absolute interest, vested interest, contingent interest, beneficial interest, equitable interest; easement, right of common, common, right of entry; limitation; settlement, strict settlement; copyright, patent

5 freehold, estate of freehold; alodium, alod; frankalmoign, lay fee, tenure in, by free alms, appanage; mortmain, dead hand; leasehold

6 **real estate,** realty, real property, land, lands, buildings, chattels real, tenements; immoveables; *praedium* <L>, landed property, landed estate, property, grounds, acres; lot, lots, parcel, plot, plat, quadrat; demesne, domain; messuage, manor, honor, toft <Brit>

7 **assets, means, resources,** total assets, total resources; stock, stock-in-trade; worth, net worth, what one is worth; circumstances, funds; wealth; material assets, tangible assets, tangibles; intangible assets, intangibles; current assets, deferred assets, fixed assets, frozen assets, liquid assets, quick assets, assets and liabilities, net assets; assessed valuation

ADJS 8 **propertied,** proprietary; landed; copyrighted, patented

9 real, praedial; manorial, seignioral, seigneurial; feudal, feudatory, feodal; patrimonial

10 freehold, leasehold, copyhold; allodial

472 ACQUISITION

<attaining property>

NOUNS 1 **acquisition,** gaining, getting, getting hold of, coming by, **acquirement,** obtainment, obtention, attainment, securement, winning, realization; trover; accession; addition; procurement, procural, procurance, procuration; earnings, making, pulling down, dragging down, knocking down, moneymaking, breadwinning, moneygetting, moneygrubbing; treasure hunt

2 **collection, gathering,** gleaning, bringing together, assembling, putting together, piecing together, accumulation, cumulation, amassment, accretion, accretion rate, heaping up, grubbing

3 **gain, profit,** percentage, get, take, take-in, piece, slice, end, rakeoff, skimmings; gains, profits, earnings, winnings, return, returns, proceeds, bottom line, ettings, makings; income; receipts; fruits, pickings, gleanings; booty, spoils; pelf, lucre, filthy lucre; perquisite, perk, perks; pile, bundle, cleanup, killing, haul, mint; neat profit, clean profit, clear profit, net; gross profit, gross; paper profits; capital gains; interest, dividends; net profit, net revenue, revenue stream; getting ahead; hoard, store; wealth; next level

4 **profitableness,** profitability, profit margin, gainfulness, remunerativeness, rewardingness, bang for the buck

5 **yield, output,** make, production; proceeds, produce, product; crop, harvest, fruit, vintage, bearing; second crop, aftermath; bumper crop; gross domestic product

6 **find,** finding, **discovery;** trove; treasure trove, buried treasure, hidden treasure; Easter egg; windfall, windfall money, windfall profit, found money, easy money, money in the bank, bonus, gravy, bunce

7 **godsend, boon,** blessing; manna, manna from heaven, loaves and fishes, gift from on high; piece of luck

VERBS 8 **acquire,** get, gain, obtain, secure, procure; win, score; earn, make; reap, harvest; contract; take, catch, capture; net; come into possession of, enter into possession of, come into, come by, come in for, be seized of; draw, derive; walk into

9 <nonformal> **grab,** latch on to, glom on to, corral, bag, get hold of, lay hold of, rake in, rake up, rake off, skim, skim off, catch, collar, cop, dig

up, grub up, round up, drum up, get one's hands on, get one's mitts on, lay one's mitts on, get one's fingers on, get one's hooks into, snag, snaffle, scratch together, hook, land, throw together, nab, pick up, nail, scare up, scrape up; take home, pull down, drag down, knock down

10 **take possession,** appropriate, take up, take over, make one's own, move in, move in on, annex

11 **collect, gather**, glean, harvest, pick, pluck, cull, take up, pick up, get in, gather in, gather to oneself, bring together, get together, scrape together, scare up; heap up, amass, assemble, accumulate

12 **profit,** make profit, realize profit, reap profit, come out ahead, make money; rake it in, coin money, make a bundle, make a pile, make a killing, make a mint, clean up, laugh all the way to the bank; gain by, capitalize on, commercialize, make capital out of, cash in on, make a good thing of, turn to profit, turn to account, realize on, make money by, obtain a return, turn a penny, turn an honest penny; gross, net; realize, clear; kill two birds with one stone, turn to one's advantage; make a fast buck, make a quick buck; line one's pockets; earn out

13 **be profitable,** pay, repay, pay off, yield a profit, show a percentage, be worthwhile, be worth one's while, be a good investment, show a profit, pay interest; roll in

ADJS 14 **obtainable,** attainable, available, accessible, to be had

15 **acquisitive,** acquiring; grasping, hoggy, grabby; greedy

16 **gainful,** productive, **profitable,** remunerative, remuneratory, lucrative, fat, paying, well-paying, high-yield, high-yielding, bankable; advantageous, worthwhile, rewarding; banausic, moneymaking, breadwinning; high-paid, high-paying

ADVS 17 **profitably,** gainfully, remuneratively, lucratively, at a profit, in the black; for money; advantageously, to advantage, to profit, to the good

473 LOSS

<loss of property>

NOUNS 1 **loss, losing,** privation, getting away, losing hold of; deprivation, bereavement, taking away, stripping, dispossession, despoilment, despoliation, spoliation, robbery; setback, reversal; divestment, denudation; sacrifice, forfeit, forfeiture, giving up, giving over, denial; nonrestoration; expense, cost, debit; detriment, injury, damage; destruction, ruin, perdition, total loss, dead loss; collateral damage; losing streak; loser

2 **waste,** wastage, exhaustion, depletion, sapping, depreciation, dissipation, diffusion, wearing, wearing away, erosion, ablation, leaching away; molting, shedding, casting off, sloughing off; using, using up, consumption, expenditure, drain; stripping, clear-cutting; **impoverishment**, shrinkage; leakage, evaporation; decrement, decrease

3 **losses,** losings; red ink; net loss, bottom line; diminishing returns; going to the wall, going belly up

VERBS 4 **lose,** incur loss, suffer loss, undergo privation, undergo deprivation, be bereaved, be bereft of, have no more, meet with a loss; drop, kiss goodbye; let slip, let slip through one's fingers; forfeit, default; sacrifice; miss, wander from, go astray from; mislay, misplace; lose out; lose everything, go broke, lose one's shirt, take a bath, take to the cleaners, tap out, go to Tap City; have a setback, have a reversal

5 **waste, deplete,** depreciate, dissipate, wear, wear away, erode, ablate, consume, drain, shrink, dribble away; molt, shed, cast off, slough off; decrease; squander; labor in vain

6 **go to waste,** come to nothing, come to naught, go up in smoke, go down the drain; run to waste, go to pot, run to seed, go to seed, go down the tubes, go to the dogs; dissipate, leak, leak away, scatter to the winds

ADJS 7 **lost, gone;** forfeited, forfeit; by the board, out the window, down the drain, down the tube; **nonrenewable,** irreclaimable; long-lost; lost to; wasted, consumed, depleted, dissipated, diffused, expended; worn away, eroded, ablated, used, used up, shrunken; stripped, clear-cut; squandered; irretrievable; astray; the worse for wear

8 **bereft, bereaved,** divested, denuded, deprived of, shorn of, parted from, bereaved of, stripped of, dispossessed of, despoiled of, robbed of; out of, minus, wanting, lacking; cut off, cut off without a cent; out-of-pocket; penniless, destitute, broke, cleaned out, tapped out, wiped out, bust, belly up

ADVS 9 **at a loss,** unprofitably, to the bad; in the red; out, out-of-pocket

474 RETENTION

<retaining property>

NOUNS 1 **retention,** retainment, **keeping, holding,** maintenance, preservation; prehension; keeping in, holding in, bottling up, corking up, locking in, suppression, repression, inhibition, retentiveness, retentivity; tenacity; adhesion; tenaciousness; detention

2 **hold,** purchase, grasp, grip, clutch, clamp,

clinch, clench; seizure; bite, nip, toothhold; cling, clinging; toehold, foothold, footing; clasp, hug, embrace, bear hug, squeeze; grapple; handhold, firm hold, tight grip, iron grip, grip of iron, grip of steel, death grip, stranglehold

3 <**wrestling hold**> half nelson, full nelson, quarter nelson, three-quarter nelson, stranglehold, toehold, flying mare, body slam, lock, hammerlock, headlock, scissors, bear hug, pin, fall

4 **clutches,** claws, talons, pounces, unguals; nails, fingernails; pincers, nippers, chelae; tentacles; fingers, digits, hooks; hands, paws, meathooks, mitts; palm; prehensile tail; jaws, mandibles, maxillae; teeth, fangs

VERBS 5 **retain, keep,** save, save up, pocket, hip-pocket; maintain, preserve; keep in, hold in, bottle up, cork up, lock in, suppress, repress, inhibit, keep to oneself; persist in; hold one's own, hold one's ground; get a foothold

6 **hold, grip,** grasp, clutch, clip, clinch, clench; bite, nip; grapple; clasp, hug, embrace; cling, cling to, cleave to, stick to, adhere to, freeze to; hold on to, hold fast, hold tight, hang on to, keep a firm hold on, keep a tight hold on; hold on, hang on, hold on like a bulldog, stick like a leech, cling like a winkle, hang on for dear life; keep hold of, never let go, not part with; seize

7 **hold, keep,** harbor, bear, have, have and hold, hold on to; cherish, fondle, entertain, treasure, treasure up; foster, nurture, nurse; embrace, hug, clip, cling to; bosom, embosom, take to the bosom

ADJS 8 **retentive,** retaining, keeping, holding, gripping, grasping; tenacious, clinging; viselike; anal, anal-retentive

9 **prehensile,** raptorial; fingered, digitate, digitated, digital; clawed, taloned, jawed, toothed, dentate, fanged

ADVS 10 **for keeps**, to keep, **for good,** for good and all, for always; forever

475 RELINQUISHMENT

<giving up property>

NOUNS 1 **relinquishment, release,** giving up, letting go, dispensation; disposal, disposition, riddance, getting rid of, dumping; renunciation, forgoing, forswearing, swearing off, abstinence, resignation, abjuration, abandonment; recantation, retraction; surrender, cession, handover, turning over, yielding; sacrifice; abdication; derequisition

2 **waiver,** quitclaim, **disclaimer**, deed of release

VERBS 3 **relinquish,** give up, render up, surrender, yield, cede, hand over, turn over, cough up; take one's hands off, loose one's grip on; spare; resign, vacate; drop, waive, dispense with; forgo, do without, get along without, forswear, abjure, renounce, swear off; walk away from, abandon; recant, retract; disgorge, throw up; have done with, wash one's hands of, pack it in; part with, give away, dispose of, ditch, rid oneself of, get rid of, see the last of, dump; kiss goodbye, kiss off; sacrifice, make a sacrifice, forfeit; quitclaim; sell off

4 **release, let go,** leave go, let loose of, unhand, unclutch, unclasp, relax one's grip, relax one's hold

ADJS 5 **relinquished,** released, disposed of; waived, dispensed with; forgone, forsworn, renounced, abjured, abandoned; recanted, retracted; surrendered, ceded, yielded; sacrificed, forfeited

476 PARTICIPATION

<taking part in or having a share>

NOUNS 1 **participation, partaking,** sharing, having a part, having a share, having a voice, contribution, association; involvement, engagement; complicity; voting, suffrage; power-sharing; partnership, copartnership, copartnery, joint control, cochairmanship, joint chairmanship; joint tenancy, cotenancy; joint ownership, condominium, condo, cooperative, coop; communal ownership, commune

2 **communion,** community, communal effort, communal enterprise, cooperation, cooperative society, intercommunion; social life, socializing; collectivity, collectivism, collective enterprise, collective farm, kibbutz, kolkhoz; democracy, participatory democracy, town meeting, self-rule; collegiality; common ownership, public ownership, state ownership, communism, socialism; profit sharing; sharecropping

3 **communization,** communalization, **socialization,** nationalization, collectivization

4 **participator, participant**, partaker, player, playa, sharer; party, a party to, accomplice, accessory; partner, copartner; cotenant; shareholder

VERBS 5 **participate, take part, partake**, contribute, chip in, involve oneself, engage oneself, get involved; have a hand in, take a hand in, get in on, have a finger in, have a finger in the pie, have to do with, have a part in, be an accessory to, be implicated in, be a party to, be a player in; participate in, partake of, partake in, take part in, take an active part in, join, join in, figure in, make oneself part of, join oneself to, associate oneself with, play a part in, perform a part in, play a role in, get in the act; join up, sign on, enlist, volunteer, answer the call; climb on the bandwagon; have a voice in, help decide, be in on the decisions, vote, have suffrage, be enfranchised; enter into, go into; make the scene; sit in, sit on; bear a hand, pull an oar; come out of one's shell

6 **share, share in,** come in for a share, go shares, be partners in, have a stake in, have a percentage, have a piece of, partake in, divide with, divvy up with, halve, go halves, go halvsies, go halvers, go fifty-fifty, go even stephen, split the difference, share and share alike; do one's share, do one's part, pull one's weight; cooperate; apportion

7 **communize,** communalize, **socialize,** collectivize, nationalize

ADJS 8 **participating, participative,** participant, participatory; hands-on, involved, engaged, in, in on; implicated, accessory; partaking, sharing

9 **communal, common,** general, public, collective, popular, social, societal; mutual, commutual, reciprocal, associated, joint, conjoint, in common, share and share alike; cooperative; power-sharing, profit-sharing; collectivistic, communistic, socialistic

477 APPORTIONMENT

<dividing and sharing>

NOUNS 1 **apportionment, apportioning,** portioning, division, divvy, partition, repartition, partitionment, partitioning, parceling, budgeting, rationing, dividing, sharing, share-out, sharing out, splitting, cutting, slicing, cutting the pie, divvying up; reapportionment

2 **distribution,** dispersion, disposal, disposition; dole, doling, doling out, parceling out, giving out, passing around; **dispensation,** administration, issuance; disbursal, disbursement, paying out; redistribution; maldistribution; dealing, dispensing, divvying

3 **allotment,** assignment, appointment, setting aside, earmarking, tagging; underallotment, overallotment; appropriation; **allocation;** misallocation; reallocation

4 **dedication,** commitment, devoting, devotion, consecration

5 **portion, share,** interest, part, stake, stock, piece, bit, segment; bite, cut, slice, chunk, piece of the pie, piece of the action, lot, allotment, end, proportion, percentage, measure, quantum, quota, deal, dole, ratio, meed, moiety, mess, helping; contingent; dividend; commission, rake-off; equal share, half; lion's share, bigger half, big end; small share, modicum; allowance, ration, budget; load, work load; fate, destiny

VERBS 6 **apportion, portion,** parcel, partition, part, divide, share; share with, cut one in, deal one in, share and share alike, divide with, go fifty-fifty with, go halvsies with, go even stephen with; divide into shares, divide up, divvy, divvy up, divvy out, split, split up, carve, cut, slice, carve up, slice up, cut up, cut the pie, slice the melon; divide fifty-fifty, split fifty-fifty

7 **proportion,** proportionate, **prorate,** divide *pro rata,* appropriate

8 **parcel out,** portion out, measure out, serve out, spoon out, ladle out, dish out, deal out, dole out, hand out, mete out, ration, give out, hand around, pass around; mete, dole, deal; distribute, disperse; dispense, dispose, issue, administer; disburse, pay out

9 **allot,** lot, **assign,** appoint, set, detail; allocate, make assignments, make allocations, schedule; set apart, set aside, earmark, tag, mark out for; demarcate, set off, mark off, portion off; assign to, appropriate to, appropriate for; reserve, restrict to, restrict; ordain, destine, fate

10 **budget, ration;** allowance, put on an allowance; divvy; budget for

11 **dedicate,** commit, devote, consecrate, set apart

ADJS 12 **apportioned,** portioned out, parceled, allocated; **apportionable,** allocable, divisible, divvied, distributable, committable, appropriable, dispensable, donable, severable

13 **proportionate,** proportional; prorated, *pro rata* <L>; half; halvers, fifty-fifty, even stephen, half-and-half, equal; distributive, distributional; respective, particular, per head, per capita, several

ADVS 14 **proportionately, in proportion,** *pro rata* <L>; distributively; respectively, severally, each to each; share and share alike, in equal shares, half-and-half; fifty-fifty, even stephen

478 GIVING

<put into another's possession>

NOUNS 1 **giving, donation,** bestowal, bestowment; **endowment,** gifting, self-gifting; presentation, presentment; award, awarding; grant, granting; accordance, vouchsafement; conferment, conferral; investiture; delivery, deliverance, surrender; concession, communication, impartation, impartment; contribution, subscription; tithing; accommodation, supplying, furnishment, provision; offer; liberality

2 commitment, **consignment,** assignment, **delegation,** relegation, commendation, remanding, entrustment; enfeoffment, infeudation, infeodation; labor of love

3 **charity,** almsgiving; philanthropy
4 **gift, present,** presentation, offering, fairing <Brit>; tribute, award; free gift, freebie, gimme, gift horse; oblation; handsel; box <Brit>; Christmas present, Christmas gift, Christmas stocking, birthday present, birthday gift; peace offering; a little something; dowry; treat; goody bag; gift certificate, gift card; personal touch; doggy bag
5 **gratuity,** largess, bounty, liberality, donative, sportula; perquisite, perks; consideration, fee, **tip,** sweetener, inducement; grease, salve, palm oil; premium, bonus, something extra, gravy, bunce, lagniappe; baker's dozen; honorarium; incentive pay, time and a half, double time; bribe; slush fund
6 **donation,** donative; **contribution,** subscription; alms, pittance, charity, dole, handout, alms fee, widow's mite, pledge; Peter's pence; offering, offertory, votive offering, collection; tithe
7 **benefit,** benefaction, benevolence, blessing, favor, boon, grace; manna, manna from heaven
8 **subsidy,** subvention, subsidization, support, price support, depletion allowance, tax benefit, tax write-off; **grant,** grant-in-aid, bounty; **allowance,** stipend, allotment; aid, assistance, financial assistance, financial aid; help, pecuniary aid; scholarship, fellowship; honorarium; welfare, public welfare, public assistance, relief, relief payments, welfare payments, welfare aid, dole, aid to dependent children, bailout, food stamps, meal ticket; guaranteed annual income; alimony, palimony; annuity; pension, old-age insurance, retirement benefits, social security, remittance; unemployment insurance; golden handcuffs; handout
9 **endowment,** investment, **settlement,** foundation; fund; charitable foundation; dowry, portion, marriage portion, marriage money; dower, widow's dower; jointure, legal jointure, thirds; appanage; community chest; charity event, fundraiser, telethon
10 **bequest,** bequeathal, legacy, devise; inheritance; **will,** testament, last will and testament, living will, advance directive; probate, attested copy; codicil
11 **giver, donor,** donator, gifter, presenter, bestower, conferrer, grantor, awarder, imparter, vouchsafer; fairy godmother, Lady Bountiful, Santa Claus, Easter bunny, tooth fairy, Robin Hood, sugar daddy; cheerful giver; contributor, subscriber, supporter, backer, financer, funder, angel; subsidizer; patron, patroness, Maecenas; tither; almsgiver, almoner; philanthropist, humanitarian; assignor, consignor; settler; testate, testator, testatrix; feoffor; good neighbor, good Samaritan

VERBS 12 **give, present, donate,** slip, let have; bestow, confer, award, allot, render, bestow on; impart, let one know, communicate; grant, accord, allow, vouchsafe, yield, afford, make available; tender, proffer, offer, extend, come up with; issue, dispense, administer; serve, help to; distribute; deal, dole, mete; give out, deal out, dole out, mete out, hand out, dish out, shell out, fork out, fork over, fork up; make a present of, gift, gift with, give as a gift; give generously, give the shirt off one's back; be generous with, be liberal with, give freely; pour, shower, rain, snow, heap, lavish; give in addition, give as lagniappe, give into the bargain; regift
13 **deliver,** hand, **pass,** reach, forward, render, put into the hands of; transfer; hand over, give over, deliver over, fork over, pass over, turn over, come across with; hand out, give out, pass out, distribute, circulate; hand in, give in; surrender, resign
14 **contribute,** subscribe, chip in, kick in, pony up, pay up, give one's share, give one's fair share; put oneself down for, pledge; contribute to, give to, donate to, gift, gift with; put something in the pot, sweeten the kitty
15 **furnish,** supply, provide, afford, provide for; make available to, put one in the way of; accommodate with, favor with, indulge with; heap upon, pour on, shower down upon, lavish upon
16 commit, **consign,** assign, delegate, relegate, confide, commend, remit, remand, give in charge; entrust, trust, give in trust; enfeoff, infeudate
17 **endow,** invest, vest; endow with, favor with, bless with, grace with, vest with; settle on, settle upon; dower; philanthropize, aid, benefit, relieve
18 **bequeath, will,** will and bequeath, leave, devise, will to, hand down, hand on, pass on, transmit, provide for; make a will, draw up a will, execute a will, make a bequest, write one's last will and testament, write into one's will; add a codicil; entail
19 **subsidize, finance,** bankroll, greenback, fund; angel; aid, assist, support, help, pay the bills, pick up the check, pick up the tab, spring for, pop for; pension, pension off
20 **thrust upon,** force upon, press upon, push upon, obtrude on, ram down one's throat, cram down one's throat
21 **give away,** dispose of, part with, sacrifice, spare

ADJS 22 philanthropic, philanthropical, eleemosynary, **charitable**; giving, generous to a fault, liberal, generous; openhanded
23 **giveable,** presentable, bestowable; impartable, communicable; bequeathable, devisable; allowable; committable; fundable

24 **given,** allowed, accorded, granted, vouchsafed, bestowed; gratuitous; God-given, providential

25 donative, contributory; concessive; testate, testamentary; intestate

26 **endowed,** dowered, subsidized, invested; dower, dowry, dotal; subsidiary, stipendiary, pensionary

ADVS **27** as a gift, gratis, on one, on the house, free, all-expense-paid; to his heirs, to the heirs of his body, to his heirs and assigns, to his executors, to the administrators and assigns

479 RECEIVING

<getting or being given something>

NOUNS **1** **receiving,** receival, receipt, **getting,** taking; acquisition; derivation; assumption, acceptance; admission, admittance; reception

2 **inheritance,** heritance, heritage, patrimony, **birthright, legacy,** bequest, bequeathal; reversion; entail; heirship; succession, line of succession, mode of succession, law of succession; primogeniture, ultimogeniture, postremogeniture, borough-English, coheirship, coparcenary, gavelkind; hereditament, corporeal hereditament, incorporeal hereditament; heritable; heirloom

3 **recipient, receiver,** accepter, getter, taker, acquirer, obtainer, procurer, donee; payee, endorsee; addressee, consignee; holder, trustee; hearer, viewer, beholder, audience, auditor, listener, looker, spectator; the receiving end; charity case; receiver of stolen property, fence

4 **beneficiary,** allottee, donee, grantee, patentee; assignee, assign; devisee, legatee, legatary; trustee; feoffee; almsman, almswoman; stipendiary; pensioner, pensionary; annuitant

5 **heir,** heritor, inheritor; **heiress,** inheritress, inheritrix; coheir, joint heir, fellow heir, coparcener; heir expectant; heir apparent, apparent heir; heir presumptive, presumptive heir; statutory next of kin; legal heir, heir at law, heir general; heir by destination; heir of the body; heir in tail, heir of entail; fideicommissary heir, fiduciary heir; reversioner; remainderman; successor, next in line

VERBS **6** **receive, get,** gain, secure, have, come by, be in receipt of, be on the receiving end; obtain, acquire; admit, accept, take, take off one's hands; take in; assume, take on, take over; derive, draw, draw from, derive from; have an income of, drag down, pull down, rake in, have coming in, take home; accept stolen property, fence

7 **inherit,** be heir to, come into, come in for, come by, fall into, step into; step into the shoes of, succeed to

8 **be received,** come in, come to hand, pass into one's hands, fall into one's hands, go into one's pocket, come to one, fall to one, fall to one's share, fall to one's lot; accrue, accrue to

ADJS **9** **receiving,** on the receiving end; **receptive,** recipient

10 **received,** accepted, admitted, recognized, approved

480 TAKING

<taking possession>

NOUNS **1** **taking,** possession, taking possession, taking away; claiming, staking one's claim; acquisition; reception; theft; bumming, mooching; moonlight requisition; identity theft

2 **seizure, seizing,** grab, grabbing, snatching, snatch; kidnapping, abduction, forcible seizure; power grab, coup, coup d'état, seizure of power; hold; catch, catching; capture, collaring, nabbing; apprehension, prehension; arrest, arrestation, taking into custody; picking up, taking in, running in; dragnet

3 sexual possession, taking; sexual assault, ravishment, rape, violation, indecent assault, date rape, acquaintance rape, serial rape, gangbang; statutory rape; defloration, deflowerment, devirgination

4 **appropriation,** taking over, takeover, adoption, assumption, usurpation, arrogation; requisition, indent <Brit>; preoccupation, prepossession, preemption; conquest, occupation, subjugation, enslavement, colonization; infringement of copyright, plagiarism

5 **attachment,** annexation, annexure <Brit>; confiscation, sequestration; impoundment; **commandeering,** impressment; expropriation, nationalization, socialization, communalization, communization, collectivization; levy; distraint, distress; garnishment; execution; eminent domain, angary, right of eminent domain, right of angary

6 **deprivation, deprival,** privation, divestment, bereavement; relieving, disburdening, disburdenment; curtailment, abridgment; disentitlement

7 **dispossession,** disseisin, expropriation; reclaiming, repossessing, **repossession,** foreclosure; eviction; disendowment; disinheritance, disherison, disownment

8 **extortion,** shakedown, blackmail, bloodsucking, vampirism; protection racket; badger game

9 **rapacity,** rapaciousness, ravenousness, sharkishness, wolfishness, predaciousness, predacity; pillaging, looting

10 **take,** catch, bag, capture, seizure, haul; booty; hot property

11 **taker;** partaker; catcher, captor, capturer; appropriator, expropriator

12 **extortionist,** extortioner, **blackmailer,** racketeer, shakedown artist, bloodsucker, leech, vampire; predator, raptor, bird of prey, beast of prey; harpy; vulture, shark; profiteer; rack-renter; kidnapper, abductor

VERBS **13** **take,** possess, take possession; get, get into one's hold, get into one's possession; pocket, palm; draw off, drain off; skim, skim off, take up front; claim, stake one's claim, enforce one's claim; partake; acquire; receive; steal

14 **seize,** take hold of, get hold of, lay hold of, catch hold of, grab hold of, glom on to, latch on to, get hands on, lay hands on, clap hands on, put one's hands on, get into one's grasp, get into one's clutches; get one's fingers on, get one's hands on, get between one's finger and thumb; grab, grasp, grip, grapple, snatch, snatch up, nip, nail, clutch, claw, clinch, clench; clasp, hug, embrace; snap up, nip up, whip up, catch up; pillage, loot; take by assault, take by storm; kidnap, abduct, carry off; shanghai; take by the throat, throttle

15 **possess sexually,** take; rape, commit rape, commit date rape, commit acquaintance rape, ravish, violate, assault sexually, lay violent hands on, have one's will of; deflower, deflorate, devirginate

16 **seize on**, seize upon, fasten upon; spring upon, pounce upon, jump, swoop down upon; catch at, snatch at, snap at, jump at, make a grab for, scramble for

17 **catch, take,** catch flatfooted, land, nail, hook, snag, snare, sniggle, spear, harpoon; ensnare, enmesh, entangle, tangle, foul, tangle up with; net, mesh; bag, sack; trap, entrap; lasso, rope, noose

18 **capture,** apprehend, collar, run down, run to earth, nab, grab, lay by the heels, take prisoner; arrest, place under arrest, put under arrest, take into custody; pick up, take in, run in

19 **appropriate,** adopt, assume, usurp, arrogate, accroach; requisition, indent <Brit>; **take possession of,** possess oneself of, take for oneself, arrogate to oneself, take up, take over, help oneself to, make use of, make one's own, make free with, dip one's hands into; take it all, take all of, hog, monopolize, sit on; preoccupy, prepossess, preempt; jump a claim; conquer, overrun, occupy, subjugate, enslave, colonize; squat on; bum, mooch

20 **attach, annex;** confiscate, sequester, sequestrate, impound; commandeer, press, impress; expropriate, nationalize, socialize, communalize, communize, collectivize; exercise the right of eminent domain, exercise the right of angary; levy, distrain, replevy, replevin; garnishee, garnish

21 **take from,** take away from, **deprive of,** do out of, relieve of, disburden of, lighten of, ease of; deprive, bereave, divest; tap, milk, mine, drain, bleed, curtail, abridge; cut off; disentitle

22 wrest, wring, wrench, rend, rip; **extort**, exact, squeeze, screw, shake down, **blackmail**, levy blackmail, badger, play the badger game; force from, wrest from, wrench from, wring from, tear from, rip from, rend from, snatch from, pry loose from

23 **dispossess,** disseise, expropriate, foreclose; evict; disendow; disinherit, disherison, disown, cut out of one's will, cut off, cut off with a shilling, cut off without a cent

24 **strip,** strip bare, strip clean, fleece, shear, denude, skin, pluck, flay, despoil, divest, pick clean, pick the bones of; deplume, displume; milk; bleed, bleed white; exhaust, drain, dry, suck dry; impoverish, beggar; clean out, take to the cleaners; eat out of house and home

ADJS **25** **taking, catching;** private, deprivative; confiscatory, annexational, expropriatory; thievish; ripoff

26 **rapacious,** ravenous, ravening, vulturous, vulturine, sharkish, wolfish, lupine, predacious, predatory, raptorial; vampirish, bloodsucking, parasitic; extortionate; grasping, graspy, grabby, insatiable; all-devouring, all-engulfing

481 RESTITUTION

<returning something to owner>

NOUNS **1** **restitution,** restoration, restoring, giving back, sending back, remitting, remission, return, redress; reddition; extradition, rendition; repatriation; recommitment, remandment, remand; satisfaction

2 **reparation, recompense,** paying back, squaring, repayment, reimbursement, refund, remuneration, compensation, indemnification; retribution, atonement, redress, satisfaction, amends, making good, requital; conscience money; balloon payment

3 **recovery,** regaining; retrieval, retrieve; recuperation, recoup, recoupment; retake, retaking, recapture; repossession, repo, resumption, reoccupation; reclamation, reclaiming, take-back; redemption, ransom, salvage, trover; replevin, replevy; revival, restoration

VERBS **4** **restore, return, give back,** restitute, hand back, put back; take back, bring back; put the genie back into the bottle, put the toothpaste back into the tube; remit, send back; repatriate; extradite; recommit, remand; requite

5 **make restitution,** make reparation, **make amends,** make good, make up for, atone, give satisfaction, redress, recompense, pay back, square, repay, reimburse, refund, remunerate, compensate, requite, indemnify, make it up; pay damages, pay reparations; pay conscience money; overcompensate

6 **recover, regain,** retrieve, recuperate, recoup, get back, come by one's own; redeem, ransom; reclaim; repossess, resume, reoccupy; retake, recapture, take back; replevin, replevy; revive, renovate, restore

ADJS 7 **restitutive,** restitutory, **restorative;** compensatory, indemnificatory, retributive, reparative, reparatory; reversionary, reversional, revertible; redeeming, redemptive, redemptional; reimbursable

ADVS 8 **in restitution,** in reparation, in recompense, in compensation, to make up for, in return for, in retribution, in requital, in amends, in atonement, to atone for

482 THEFT

<taking without permission>

NOUNS 1 **theft, thievery,** stealage, **stealing,** thieving, purloining; swiping, lifting, snatching, snitching, pinching; conveyance, appropriation, conversion, liberation, annexation; pilfering, pilferage, filching, scrounging; abstraction; sneak thievery; shoplifting, boosting; poaching; graft; embezzlement; fraud, swindle

2 **larceny,** petit larceny, petty larceny, petty theft, grand larceny, grand theft, simple larceny, aggravated larceny, mixed larceny; automobile theft

3 **theft, robbery,** robbing; bank robbery; banditry, highway robbery; armed robbery, holdup, assault and robbery, mugging, push-in crime; purse snatching; pocket picking, pick-pocketing, jostling; hijacking, asportation; carjacking; cattle stealing, cattle rustling, cattle lifting; extortion; identity theft

4 <nonformal> **heist,** stickup, job, stickup job, bag job, boost, hustle, pinch, swipe, lift, burn, knockover, ripoff; sticky fingers

5 **burglary,** burglarizing, housebreaking, breaking and entering, break and entry, break-in, unlawful entry; second-story work; safebreaking, safecracking, safeblowing

6 **plundering, pillaging,** looting, sacking, freebooting, ransacking, rifling, spoiling, despoliation, despoilment, despoiling; rapine, spoliation, depredation, direption, raiding, ravage, ravaging, ravagement, rape, ravishment; pillage, plunder, sack; brigandage, brigandism, banditry; marauding, foraging; raid, foray, razzia; brain drain

7 **piracy,** buccaneering, privateering, freebooting; letters of marque, letters of marque and reprisal; air piracy, airplane hijacking, skyjacking; carjacking

8 **plagiarism,** plagiarizing, plagiary, piracy, literary piracy, appropriation, borrowing, cribbing; infringement; infringement of copyright; autoplagiarism; crib sheet, cheat sheet

9 **abduction,** kidnapping, snatching; shanghaiing, impressment, crimping

10 **grave-robbing,** body-snatching, resurrectionism

11 **booty,** spoil, **spoils,** loot, swag, ill-gotten gains, plunder, prize, haul, take, pickings, stealings, stolen goods, hot goods; boodle, squeeze, graft; perquisite, perks, pork barrel, spoils of office, public trough; till, public till; blackmail; hot property

12 **thievishness,** larcenousness, taking ways, light fingers, sticky fingers; kleptomania, bibliokleptomania

VERBS 13 **steal, thieve,** purloin, appropriate, take, snatch, palm, make off with, walk off with, run off, run away with, abstract, disregard the distinction between *meum* and *tuum*; have one's hand in the till; pilfer, filch; shoplift; poach; rustle; embezzle; defraud, swindle; extort

14 **rob,** commit robbery; pick pockets, jostle; hold up, stick someone up

15 **burglarize,** burgle, commit burglary, housebreak; crack a safe, blow a safe

16 <nonformal> **swipe,** pinch, bag, lift, hook, crib, cop, nip, snitch, snare, boost, annex, borrow, burn, clip, rip off, nick, nobble <Brit>; heist, knock off, knock over, tip over; stick up; mug; roll, jackroll; do a job; cook the books; case the joint

17 **plunder, pillage,** loot, sack, ransack, rifle, freeboot, spoil, spoliate, despoil, depredate, prey on, prey upon, raid, ravage, ravish, raven, sweep, gut; fleece; maraud, foray, forage

18 **pirate,** buccaneer, privateer, freeboot

19 **plagiarize,** pirate, borrow, crib, appropriate; pick one's brains; infringe a copyright

20 **abduct,** abduce, spirit away, carry off, carry away, magic away, run off with, run away with; kidnap, snatch, hold for ransom; skyjack, hijack, carjack; shanghai, crimp, impress

ADJS 21 **thievish,** thieving, larcenous, light-fingered, sticky-fingered; kleptomaniacal, burglarious; brigandish, piratical, piratelike; fraudulent

22 plunderous, **plundering, looting,** pillaging, ravaging, marauding, spoliatory; predatory, predacious

23 **stolen,** pilfered, purloined, ripped off; swiped, swipeable; pirated, plagiarized; hot

483 THIEF

<one taking without permission>

NOUNS **1** **thief, robber,** stealer, purloiner, lifter, *ganef* <Yiddish>, **crook**; larcenist, larcener; pilferer, filcher, petty thief, chicken thief; sneak thief, prowler; shoplifter, booster; poacher; grafter, petty grafter; jewel thief; swindler, con man; land pirate, land shark, land-grabber; grave robber, body snatcher, resurrectionist, ghoul; embezzler, peculator, white-collar thief; den of thieves

2 **pickpocket,** cutpurse, fingersmith, dip; purse snatcher; light-fingered gentry

3 **burglar,** yegg, cracksman; housebreaker, cat burglar, cat man, second-story thief, second-story man; safecracker, safebreaker, safeblower; pete blower, peterman

4 **bandit,** brigand, dacoit; gangster, mobster, goodfella; racketeer; thug, hoodlum

5 **robber,** holdup man, stickup man; highwayman, highway robber, footpad, road agent, bushranger <Austral>; mugger, sandbagger; train robber; bank robber, hijacker

6 **plunderer, pillager, looter,** marauder, rifler, sacker, spoiler, despoiler, spoliator, depredator, raider, moss-trooper, freebooter rapparee, forayer, forager, ravisher, ravager; wrecker

7 **pirate,** corsair, buccaneer, privateer, sea rover, rover, picaroon; viking, sea king; Blackbeard, Captain Kidd, Jean Lafitte, Henry Morgan; Captain Hook, Long John Silver; air pirate, airplane hijacker, skyjacker; hijacker, carjacker; record pirate, video pirate, bootlegger

8 cattle thief, abactor, rustler, **cattle rustler**; poacher

9 **plagiarist,** plagiarizer, cribber, pirate, literary pirate, copyright infringer

10 **abductor**, kidnapper; shanghaier, snatcher, baby-snatcher; crimp, crimper

484 PARSIMONY

<unwilling to spend money>

NOUNS **1** **parsimony,** parsimoniousness; frugality; stinting, pinching, scrimping, skimping, cheeseparing; economy, economy of means, economy of assumption, law of parsimony, Ockham's razor, elegance

2 **parsimoniousness**, niggardliness, penuriousness, meanness, minginess, shabbiness, sordidness; cost-consciousness

3 **stinginess,** ungenerosity, illiberality, cheapness, chintziness, tightness, narrowness, tight purse strings, nearness, closeness, closefistedness, closehandedness, tightfistedness, hardfistedness, miserliness, penny-pinching, hoarding, austerity; avarice

4 niggard, **tightwad**, cheapskate, miser, hard man with a buck, skinflint, scrooge, penny pincher, moneygrubber, pinchfist, pinchgut, churl, curmudgeon, muckworm, save-all, Silas Marner

VERBS **5** stint, **scrimp, skimp,** scamp, scant, screw, pinch, starve, famish; pinch pennies, rub the print off a dollar bill, rub the picture off a nickel; live upon nothing; grudge, begrudge

6 **withhold,** hold back, hold out on

ADJS **7** **parsimonious,** sparing, cheeseparing, stinting, scamping, scrimping, skimping; frugal; too frugal, overfrugal, frugal to excess; pennywise, penny-wise and pound-foolish; austere

8 niggardly, niggard, pinchpenny, **penurious**, grudging, mean, mingy, shabby, sordid

9 **stingy,** illiberal, ungenerous, chintzy, miserly, save-all, cheap, tight, narrow, near, close, closefisted, closehanded, tightfisted, pinchfisted, hardfisted; near as the bark on a tree; cost-conscious; pinching, penny-pinching; avaricious

ADVS **10** **parsimoniously,** stintingly, scrimpingly, skimpingly

11 niggardly, **stingily,** illiberally, ungenerously, closefistedly, tightfistedly; meanly, shabbily, sordidly

485 LIBERALITY

<willing to spend or be generous>

NOUNS **1** **liberality,** liberalness, freeness, freedom; generosity, generousness, largeness, unselfishness, munificence, largess, largesse, charity; bountifulness, bounteousness, bounty; hospitality, welcome, graciousness; openhandedness, freehandedness, open hand, free hand, easy purse strings; givingness; openheartedness, bigheartedness, largeheartedness, greatheartedness, freeheartedness; open heart, big heart, large heart, great heart, heart of gold; **magnanimity**

2 **cheerful giver,** free giver; contributor; Lady Bountiful; Santa Claus; philanthropist; almsgiver, altruist

VERBS **3** **give freely,** give cheerfully, give with an open hand, give with both hands, put one's hands in one's pockets, open the purse, loosen the purse strings, untie the purse strings; spare no expense, spare nothing, not count the cost, let money be no object; heap upon, lavish upon, shower down upon; give the coat off one's back, give the shirt off one's back, give more than one's share, give until it hurts; give of oneself, give of one's substance, not hold back, offer oneself; tip well; keep the change

ADJS 4 **liberal, free,** free with one's money, free-spending; generous, munificent, large, princely, handsome; unselfish, ungrudging; unsparing, unstinting, stintless, unstinted; bountiful, bounteous, lavish, profuse; hospitable, gracious; openhanded, freehanded, open; giving; openhearted, bighearted, largehearted, greathearted, freehearted; **magnanimous**

ADVS 5 **liberally, freely;** generously, munificently, handsomely; unselfishly, ungrudgingly; unsparingly, unstintingly; bountifully, bounteously, lavishly, profusely; hospitably, graciously; openhandedly, freehandedly; openheartedly, bigheartedly, largeheartedly, greatheartedly, freeheartedly; with open hands, with both hands, with an unsparing hand, without stint

486 PRODIGALITY

<excessive spending>

NOUNS 1 **prodigality, overliberality,** overgenerousness, overgenerosity; profligacy, extravagance, pound-foolishness, recklessness, reckless spending, reckless expenditure, overspending, frittering away; incontinence, intemperance; lavishness, profuseness, profusion; wastefulness, waste; dissipation, squandering, squandermania; *carpe diem* <L>; loose purse strings, leaking purse; conspicuous consumption conspicuous waste; splurge, spree

2 **prodigal,** wastrel, waster, squanderer; **spendthrift,** wastethrift, spender, spendall, big spender; Diamond Jim Brady; prodigal son; last of the big spenders

VERBS 3 **squander,** lavish, slather, blow, play ducks and drakes with; dissipate, scatter, sow broadcast, scatter to the winds, fritter away; run through, go through; throw away, throw one's money away, throw money around, spend money like water, hang the expense, let slip through one's fingers, let flow through one's fingers, spend as if money grew on trees, spend money as if it were going out of style, spend like a drunken sailor; gamble away; burn the candle at both ends; seize the day, live for the day, let tomorrow take care of itself

4 **waste, consume,** spend, expend, use up, exhaust; deplete, drain, suck dry, milk dry; misuse, abuse; lose; spill, pour down the drain; pour water into a sieve, cast pearls before swine, kill the goose that lays the golden egg, throw out the baby with the bath water; waste effort, labor in vain

5 **fritter away,** fool away, fribble away, dribble away, drivel away, trifle away, dally away, potter away, piss away*, muddle away, diddle away, squander in dribs and drabs; idle away, while away

6 **misspend,** misapply, throw good money after bad, throw the helve after the hatchet, throw out the baby with the bathwater, cast pearls before swine

7 **overspend,** spend more than one has, spend what one hasn't got, lavish; overdraw, overdraw one's account, live beyond one's means, have champagne tastes on a beer budget

ADJS 8 **prodigal, extravagant,** lavish, profuse, overliberal, overgenerous, overlavish, spendthrift, wasteful, profligate, dissipative; incontinent, intemperate; pound-foolish, penny-wise and pound-foolish; easy come, easy go

9 **wasted, squandered,** dissipated, consumed, spent, used, lost; gone to waste, run to seed, gone to seed; down the drain, down the spout, down the rathole; misspent

487 CELEBRATION

<special occasions>

NOUNS 1 **celebration,** celebrating; **observance,** formal observance, solemn observance, ritual observance, solemnization; marking the occasion, honoring the occasion; commemoration, memorialization, remembrance, memory; jubilee; red-letter day, **holiday; anniversary;** festivity; revel; rejoicing; ceremony, rite; religious rites; ovation, triumph; tribute; testimonial, testimonial banquet, testimonial dinner; toast; roast; salute; salvo; flourish of trumpets, fanfare, fanfaronade; dressing ship; high-five; binge, bender, blowout; ladies' night, hen night; party, afterparty; bachelor party, bachelorette party, stag party, stag night; wedding anniversary

VERBS 2 **celebrate, observe,** keep, mark, solemnly mark, honor; commemorate, memorialize; solemnize, signalize, hallow, mark with a red letter; party, party down, hold jubilee, jubilize, jubilate, maffick; make merry, make whoopie; binge; kill the fatted calf; sound a fanfare, blow the trumpet, beat the drum, fire a salute; dress ship; high-five

ADJS 3 **celebrative,** celebratory, celebrating, partying; **commemorative,** commemorating; memorial; solemn; festive, festal, gala

ADVS 4 **in honor of, in commemoration of,** in memory of, in remembrance of, to the memory of

5 anniversaries and holidays

Admission Day
Alaska Day
Advent
All Saints' Day
All Souls' Day
Allhallows
American Indian Day
Annunciation
Anzac Day
April Fools' Day, All Fools' Day
Arab League Day
Arbor Day
Armed Forces Day
Armistice Day
Ascension Day
Ash Wednesday
Assumption Day
Australia Day
autumnal equinox
Bairam
Baisakhi
Bastille Day
birthday
Bodhi Day
Bon
Boxing Day
Buddha's birthday
Canada Day
Candlemas
Carnival
Chinese New Year
Christmas Eve
Christmas, Xmas, Christmas Day
Chusuk
Cinco de Mayo
Citizenship Day
Columbus Day
Commonwealth Day
Confederate Memorial Day
Confucius's birthday
Constitution Day
Corpus Christi
Dasara
Day of the Dead, Día de los Muertos
Decoration Day
Dhammacakka
Discovery Day
Diwali
Dominion Day
Double Ten
Durga Puja, Navratri
Dusshera
Earth Day
Easter, Easter Sunday
Easter Monday
Eid
Eid ul-Adha
Eid ul-Fitr
Election Day
Emancipation Day
Emperor's birthday
Empire Day
engagement anniversary
Epiphany
Father's Day
feast day
Flag Day
Fourth of July
Good Friday
Grandparents' Day
Groundhog Day
Guru Gobind Singh's Birthday
Guru Nanak's Birthday
Guy Fawkes Day
Halloween
Hanukkah
High Holy Day
Holi
Holi Mohalla
Holy Innocents' Day
Human Rights Day
'Id al-Adha
Ides of March
Immaculate Conception
Inauguration Day
Independence Day
Islamic New Year's Day
Janmashtami
Karwa Chauth
Kenyatta Day
Kuhio Day
Kwanza, Kwanzaa
Labor Day
Lag b'Omer
Lailat ul-Bara'h
Lailat ul-Isra wal Mi'raj
Lailat ul-Qadr
Lammas
Lantern Festival
Lent
Lincoln's birthday
Lunar New Year
Mahashivaratri
Mardi Gras
Martin Luther King Jr. Day
Martinmas
Martyrdom of Guru Arjan
Martyrdom of Guru Tegh Bahadur
Maundy Thursday
May Day
Memorial Day
Mexican Independence Day
Michaelmas
Midsummer Day
Moharram
Mother's Day
Muhammad's birthday
Muhrarran
Nag Panchami
National Day
National Unity Day
Navaratri
New Year's Day, New Year's
New Year's Eve, first night
Noel
Oktoberfest
Omisoka
Pagan Sabbats
Palm Sunday
Pan American Day
Passover, Pesach
Pentecost
Posadas
President's Day
Purim
Queen's birthday
Queensland Day
Raksha Bandhan
Rama Naumi
Ramadan
Reformation Sunday
Remembrance Day
Republic Day
retirement, retirement anniversary
Rosh Hashanah
Sadie Hawkins Day
Saint Patrick's Day
Saint Valentine's Day
Santa Lucia Day
Shavuot, Shavuoth
Shrove Tuesday
Shrovetide
Spring Bank Holiday
Sukkoth, Sukkot, Succoth
summer solstice
Tet
Thanksgiving
Trinity Sunday
Twelfth Night
United Nations Day
V-E Day
vernal equinox
Vesak
Veterans' Day
Victoria Day
V-J Day
Walpurgis
Washington's birthday
wedding anniversary
Whitsunday
Whitsuntide
winter solstice
World Health Day
Yom Kippur, Day of Atonement

6 birthday flowers and birthstones

January: carnation, snowdrop; garnet
February: violet, primrose; amethyst
March: jonquil, violet; jasper, bloodstone, aquamarine
April: daisy, sweet pea; sapphire, diamond
May: hawthorn, lily of the valley; agate, emerald
June: rose, honeysuckle; emerald, pearl, moonstone, alexandrite
July: larkspur, water lily; onyx, ruby
August: gladiolus, poppy; carnelian, sardonyx, peridot
September: morning glory, aster; chrysolite, sapphire
October: calendula, cosmos; aquamarine, opal, tourmaline
November: chrysanthemum; topaz
December: narcissus, holly, poinsettia; ruby, turquoise, zircon

7 wedding anniversaries and gifts

1st: paper
2nd: cotton
3rd: leather
4th: linen, silk, fruit, flowers
5th: wood
6th: iron, sugar, candy
7th: wool, copper
8th: bronze, pottery
9th: pottery, willow
10th: tin, aluminum
11th: steel

12th: linen, silk	30th: pearl
13th: lace	35th: coral
14th: ivory	40th: ruby
15th: crystal	45th: sapphire
16th: tungsten	50th: gold
17th: turquoise	55th: emerald
18th: bismuth	60th: diamond
19th: bismuth, china	65th: star sapphire
20th: china	70th: platinum
25th: silver	75th: diamond

488 HUMOROUSNESS

<funniness>

NOUNS 1 **humorousness, funniness,** amusingness, laughableness, laughability, hilarity, hilariousness; wittiness; drollness, drollery; whimsicalness, quizzicalness; ludicrousness, ridiculousness, absurdity, absurdness, quaintness, eccentricity, incongruity, bizarreness, bizarrerie; richness, pricelessness; the funny side; barrel of laughs

2 **comicalness,** comicality, funiosity; farcicalness, farcicality, slapstick quality, broadness

3 bathos; anticlimax, comedown, shaggy dog story

ADJS 4 **humorous, funny,** amusing; witty; droll, whimsical, quizzical; laughable, risible, good for a laugh; ludicrous, ridiculous, hilarious, absurd, quaint, eccentric, incongruous, bizarre

5 <nonformal> **funny ha-ha,** priceless, too funny, too killing for words, hardy-har, hardy-har-har, har-har-har, rich, hysterical, ridic, ridonkulous

6 **comic, comical; farcical,** slapstick, broad; burlesque; tragicomic, tragico-comic, serio-comic, mock-heroic

ADVS 7 **humorously,** amusingly, funnily, laughably; wittily; drolly, whimsically, quizzically; comically, farcically, broadly; ludicrously, ridiculously, absurdly, quaintly, eccentrically, incongruously, bizarrely

489 WIT, HUMOR

<ability to be funny>

NOUNS 1 **wit, humor,** pleasantry, *esprit* <Fr>, salt, spice of wit, savor of wit; Attic wit, Attic salt, Atticism; ready wit, quick wit, nimble wit, agile wit, pretty wit; dry wit, dry humor, subtle wit; comedy; black humor, dark humor, sick humor, gallows humor; satire, sarcasm, irony; Varonnian satire, Menippean satire; parody, lampoon, lampoonery, travesty, caricature, burlesque, squib, takeoff, spoof; farce, mere farce; slapstick, slapstick humor, broad humor; visual humor, cartoon, comic strip, cartoon strip, the funnies; stand-up comedy; observational comedy; comedy club

2 **wittiness, humorousness,** funniness; facetiousness, pleasantry, jocularity, jocoseness, jocosity; joking, japery, joshing; smartness, cleverness, brilliance; pungency, saltiness; keenness, sharpness; keen-wittedness, quick-wittedness, nimble-wittedness

3 **drollery,** drollness; **whimsicality,** whimsicalness, humorsomeness, antic wit

4 waggishness, waggery; roguishness; **playfulness,** sportiveness, levity, frivolity, flippancy, merriment; prankishness, pranksomeness; trickery, trickiness, tricksiness, trickishness

5 **buffoonery,** buffoonism, clownery, clowning, clowning around, harlequinade; clownishness, buffoonishness; foolery, fooling, tomfoolery; horseplay; shenanigans, monkey tricks, monkeyshines, funny business; banter

6 **joke, jest,** gag, one-liner, wheeze, jape; fun, sport, play, kidding; story, yarn, funny story, good story; dirty story, dirty joke, blue story, blue joke, double entendre; shaggy-dog story; sick joke; ethnic joke; capital joke, good one, laugh, belly laugh, rib tickler, sidesplitter, thigh-slapper, howler, wow, hoot, scream, riot, panic; visual joke, sight gag; standing joke; point, punch line, gag line, tagline; cream of the jest; jest-book; knee-slapper

7 **witticism,** pleasantry; play of wit, *jeu d'esprit* <Fr>; crack, smart crack, wisecrack; quip, conceit, bright thought, happy thought, bright idea, brilliant idea; mot, bon mot, smart saying, stroke of wit, one-liner, zinger; epigram, turn of thought, aphorism, apothegm; flash of wit, scintillation; sound bite; sally, flight of wit; repartee, backchat, retort, riposte, snappy comeback; facetiousness, facetiae <pl>, quips, cranks; gibe, dirty crack, nasty crack; persiflage

8 **wordplay, play on words,** missaying, corruption, paronomasia, abuse of terms; **pun,** punning; equivoque, equivocality; anagram, logogram, logogriph, metagram; acrostic, double acrostic; amphiboly, amphibologism; palindrome; spoonerism; malapropism; Tom Swifty

9 **old joke,** old wheeze, old turkey, trite joke, hoary-headed joke, joke with whiskers; chestnut, corn, corny joke, oldie; Joe Miller, Joe Millerism; twice-told tale, retold story, warmed-over cabbage; knee-slapper

10 **prank,** trick, **practical joke,** waggish trick, antic, caper, frolic; monkeyshines, shenanigans, leg-pull

11 **sense of humor,** risibility, funny bone; comic genius

12 **humorist,** wit, funnyman, comic, *bel-esprit* <Fr>, life of the party; joker, jokester, gagman, jester, court jester, quipster, wisecracker, gagster; wag, wagwit; zany, madcap, cutup; prankster;

comedian, **comedienne**, stand-up comic, stand-up comedian, banana, straight man; clown; punster, punner; epigrammatist; satirist, ironist; burlesquer, caricaturist, cartoonist, parodist, lampooner; reparteeist; witling; gag writer, jokesmith

VERBS 13 **joke,** jest, wisecrack, crack wise, utter a mot, quip, jape, josh, fun, make fun, kid, kid around; make a funny; crack a joke, get off a joke, tell a good story; pun, play on words; scintillate, sparkle; make fun of, rag on, gibe at, fleer at, mock, scoff at, poke fun at, send up, take off, lampoon, make the butt of one's humor, be merry with; ridicule

14 **trick, play a practical joke,** play tricks, play pranks, play a joke on, play a trick on, make merry with; clown around, pull a stunt, pull a trick; pull one's leg, put one on

ADJS 15 **witty,** amusing; humorous, comic, comical, farcical; **funny**; jocular, joky, joking, jesting, jocose, tongue-in-cheek; facetious, joshing, whimsical, droll, humorsome; smart, clever, brilliant, scintillating, sparkling, sprightly; keen, sharp, rapierlike, pungent, pointed, biting, mordant; teasing; satiric, satirical, sarcastic, ironic, ironical; salty, salt, Attic; keen-witted, quick-witted, nimble-witted, dry-witted

16 **clownish,** buffoonish

17 waggish; roguish; **playful,** sportive; prankish, pranky, pranksome; tricky, trickish, tricksy

ADVS 18 **wittily,** humorously; jocularly, jocosely; facetiously; whimsically, drolly

19 in fun, in sport, in play, **in jest,** in joke, as a joke, jokingly, jestingly, with tongue in cheek; for fun, for sport

490 BANTER

<witty communication>

NOUNS 1 **banter,** badinage, persiflage, pleasantry, fooling, fooling around, **kidding**, kidding around, raillery, rallying, sport, good-natured banter, harmless teasing; ridicule; exchange, give-and-take; side-talk, byplay, asides; flyting, slanging, the dozens

2 **bantering,** twitting, chaffing, joking, jesting, japing, fooling, teasing, hazing; playing the dozens, backchat

3 <nonformal> **kidding,** joshing, jollying, jiving, fooling around; ribbing, ragging, razzing, roasting

4 **banterer,** chaffer, twitter; kidder, josher

VERBS 5 **banter,** twit, chaff, rally, joke, jest, jape, tease, haze; have a slanging match, play the dozens, backchat

6 <nonformal> **kid,** jolly, josh, fool around, jive, rub, put on; razz, roast, ride, needle

ADJS 7 **bantering,** chaffing, twitting; jollying, kidding, joshing, fooling, teasing, quizzical

491 COWARDICE

<lack of courage>

NOUNS 1 **cowardice, cowardliness;** fear; faintheartedness, faintheart, weakheartedness, chickenheartedness, henheartedness, pigeonheartedness; yellowness, white-liveredness, lily-liveredness, chicken-liveredness, weak-kneedness; weakness, softness; unmanliness, unmanfulness; timidness, timidity, timorousness, milksoppiness, milksoppishness, milksopism, cowardship

2 **uncourageousness,** unvaliantness, unvalorousness, unheroicness, ungallantness, unintrepidness; plucklessness, spunklessness, gritlessness, gutlessness, spiritlessness, heartlessness; defeatism

3 dastardliness, pusillanimousness, **pusillanimity**, poltroonery, poltroonishness, poltroonism, baseness, abjectness, cravenness; desertion under fire, bugout, skedaddling, lack of moral fiber

4 **cold feet**, weak knees, faintheart, chicken heart, yellow streak, white feather; gutlessness

5 **coward,** jellyfish, invertebrate, faintheart, weakling, weak sister, milksop, milquetoast, mouse, sissy, wimp, baby, big baby, chicken; namby-pamby; yellow-belly, white-liver, lily-liver, chicken-liver, white feather; fraid-cat, fraidy-cat, scaredy-cat; funk, funker

6 dastard, craven, poltroon, **recreant**, caitiff, arrant coward; sneak; deserter

VERBS 7 dare not; have a yellow streak, **have cold feet**, be unable to say "boo" to a goose

8 **lose one's nerve,** lose courage, get cold feet, show the white feather; falter, boggle, funk, chicken; put one's tail between one's legs, back out, funk out, wimp out, chicken out, have no stomach for; desert under fire, turn tail, bug out, skedaddle, run scared, scuttle, retreat

9 **cower,** quail, cringe, crouch, skulk, sneak, slink

ADJS 10 **cowardly,** coward; **afraid,** fearful; timid, timorous, overtimorous, overtimid, rabbity, mousy; fainthearted, weakhearted, chickenhearted, henhearted, pigeonhearted; white-livered, lily-livered, chicken-livered, milk-livered; yellow, yellow-bellied, with a yellow streak; weak-kneed, chicken, afraid of one's shadow; weak, soft; wimpy, wimpish, unmanly, unmanful, sissy, sissified; milksoppy, milksoppish;

panicky, panic-prone, funking, funky; daunted, dismayed, unmanned, cowed, intimidated

11 **uncourageous,** unvaliant, unvalorous, unheroic, ungallant, unintrepid, undaring, unable to say "boo" to a goose; unsoldierlike, unsoldierly; pluckless, spunkless, gritless, gutless, spiritless, heartless

12 dastardly, dastard; hit-and-run; poltroonish, poltroon; **pusillanimous,** base, craven, recreant, caitiff; dunghill, dunghilly

13 **cowering,** quailing, cringing; skulking, sneaking, slinking, sneaky, slinky

ADVS 14 cravenly, poltroonishly, like a coward, **cowardly, uncourageously,** unvaliantly, unvalorously, unheroically, ungallantly, unintrepidly, undaringly; plucklessly, spunklessly, gritlessly, spiritlessly, heartlessly; faintheartedly, weakheartedly, chickenheartedly; wimpishly

492 COURAGE

<mental or moral strength>

NOUNS 1 **courage,** courageousness, **nerve,** pluck, bravery, braveness, ballsiness, gutsiness, guttiness, boldness, nerves of steel, valor, valorousness, valiance, valiancy, gallantry, conspicuous gallantry, gallantry under fire, gallantry beyond the call of duty, gallantness, intrepidity, intrepidness, prowess, virtue; doughtiness, stalwartness, stoutness, stoutheartedness, lionheartedness, greatheartedness; heroism, heroicalness; chivalry, chivalrousness, knightliness; military spirit, martial spirit, fighting spirit, soldierly quality, soldierly virtues; manliness, manfulness, manhood, virility, machismo; Dutch courage, pot-valor, bold front, bravado

2 **fearlessness,** dauntlessness, undauntedness, unfearfulness, unfearingness, unafraidness, unapprehensiveness; confidence; untimidness, untimorousness, unshrinkingness, unshyness, unbashfulness

3 <nonformal> balls, **guts,** intestinal fortitude, spunk, brass balls, cojones, moxie, spizzerinctum, **backbone,** chutzpah

4 **daring,** derring-do, deeds of derring-do; **bravado,** bravura; **audacity,** audaciousness, overboldness; venturousness, venturesomeness, risk-taking, tightrope walking, funambulism; adventurousness, adventuresomeness, enterprise; foolhardiness

5 **fortitude, hardihood,** hardiness; pluckiness; spunkiness, grittiness, nerviness, mettlesomeness; gameness, gaminess; grit, stamina, toughness, pith, mettle, bottom; heart, spirit, stout heart, heart of oak; resolution, resoluteness, New Year's resolution; tenaciousness, tenacity, pertinaciousness, pertinacity, bulldog courage, true grit, stiff upper lip

6 **exploit,** feat, deed, enterprise, achievement, adventure, act of courage, gest, bold stroke, heroic act, heroic deed; prowess; heroics; aristeia

7 <brave person> **hero, heroine;** brave, stalwart, gallant, valiant, man of courage, woman of courage, person of mettle, valiant knight, good soldier, warrior, knight in shining armor; tragic hero, unsung hero; demigod, paladin; demigoddess; the brave; decorated hero; Hector, Achilles, Roland, David; lion, tiger, bulldog, fighting cock, gamecock; he-man; daredevil, stunt person

8 **encouragement,** heartening, inspiration, inspiriting, inspiritment, emboldening, assurance, reassurance, pat on the back, clap on the back, bucking up; self-talk

VERBS 9 **dare,** venture, make bold to, make so bold as to, take risks, walk the tightrope, have the nerve, have the guts, have the balls, have the courage of one's convictions, be a man; defy

10 **brave,** face, confront, affront, front, look one in the eye, say to one's face, face up to, meet, meet head-on, meet boldly, square up to, stand up to, stand up against, go eyeball-to-eyeball with, go one-on-one with; set at defiance; speak up, speak out, stand up and be counted; not flinch from, not shrink from, bite the bullet, look full in the face, put a bold face upon, show a bold front, present a bold front; head into, face up, come to grips with, grapple with; face the music; brazen, brazen out, brazen through; beard; put one's head in the lion's mouth, fly into the face of danger, take the bull by the horns, march up to the cannon's mouth, bell the cat, go through fire and water, court disaster, go in harm's way, throw caution to the wind, run the gauntlet, take one's life in one's hands, put one's ass on the line, put one's life on the line

11 **outbrave,** outdare; outface, face down, face out; outbrazen, brazen out; outlook, outstare, stare down, stare out <Brit>, stare out of countenance

12 steel oneself, **get up the nerve,** nerve oneself, muster courage, summon up courage, gather courage, pluck up heart, get up one's nerve, get up the courage, stiffen one's backbone

13 **take courage,** take heart, pluck up courage, take heart of grace; brace up, buck up

14 **keep up one's courage**, bear up, keep one's chin up, keep one's pecker up, keep a stiff upper lip,

hold up one's head, take what comes; hang in, hang in there, hang tough, stick it out, stick to one's guns, grin and bear it

15 **encourage,** hearten, embolden, nerve, pat on the back, clap on the back, assure, reassure, bolster, support, cheer on, root for; inspire, inspirit; incite, exhort; buck up; put upon one's mettle, make a man of; cheer

ADJS 16 **courageous,** plucky, brave, bold, valiant, valorous, gallant, intrepid, doughty, hardy, stalwart, stout, stouthearted, ironhearted, lionhearted, greathearted, bold-spirited, bold as a lion; heroic, herolike; chivalrous, chivalric, knightly, knightlike, soldierly, soldierlike; manly, manful, virile, macho

17 **resolute, tough, game;** spirited, spiritful, red-blooded, mettlesome; bulldoggish, tenacious, pertinacious

18 <nonformal> ballsy, **gutsy**, gutty, nervy, stand-up, dead game, gritty, spunky

19 **unafraid,** unfearing, unfearful; unapprehensive, undiffident; confident; fearless, dauntless, aweless, dreadless; unfrightened, unscared, unalarmed, unterrified; untimid, untimorous, unshy, unbashful

20 **undaunted,** undismayed, uncowed, unintimidated, unappalled, unabashed, unawed; unflinching, unshrinking, unquailing, unbowed, uncringing, unwincing, unblenching, unblinking

21 **daring,** audacious, overbold; adventurous, venturous, venturesome, adventuresome, enterprising; foolhardy

ADVS 22 **courageously,** bravely, boldly, heroically, valiantly, valorously, gallantly, intrepidly, doughtily, stoutly, hardily, stalwartly; pluckily, spunkily, gutsily, resolutely, gamely, tenaciously, pertinaciously, bulldoggishly, fearlessly, unfearingly, unfearfully; daringly, audaciously; chivalrously, knightly, yeomanly; like a man, like a soldier

493 RASHNESS

<undue hastiness>

NOUNS 1 **rashness,** brashness, brazen boldness, **incautiousness,** overboldness, imprudence, indiscretion, injudiciousness, improvidence; irresponsibility; unwariness, unchariness; overcarelessness; overconfidence, oversureness, overweeningness; impudence, insolence; gall, brass, cheek, chutzpah; hubris; temerity, temerariousness; heroics

2 **recklessness,** devil-may-careness; heedlessness, carelessness; impetuousness, impetuosity, hotheadedness; haste, hastiness, hurriedness, overeagerness, overzealousness, overenthusiasm; furiousness, desperateness, wantonness, wildness, wild oats; frivolity; precipitateness, precipitousness, precipitance, precipitancy, precipitation

3 **foolhardiness,** harebrainedness; **audacity,** audaciousness; more guts than brains; forwardness, boldness, presumption, presumptuousness; daring, daredeviltry, daredevilry, fire-eating; playing with fire, flirting with death, courting disaster, stretching one's luck, going for broke, brinkmanship, tightrope walking, funambulism; adventurousness

4 **daredevil,** devil, madcap, madbrain, wild man, hotspur, hellcat, rantipole, harumscarum, fire-eater; adventurer, adventuress, adventurist; brazen-face

VERBS 5 **be rash**, be reckless, carry too much sail, sail too near the wind, throw caution to the wind, go out of one's depth, go too far, go to sea in a sieve, take a leap in the dark, buy a pig in a poke, count one's chickens before they are hatched, catch at straws, lean on a broken reed, put all one's eggs in one basket, live in a glass house; go out on a limb, leave oneself wide open, drop one's guard, stick one's neck out, ask for it

6 **court danger,** ask for it, ask for trouble, defy danger, go in harm's way, thumb one's nose at the consequences, **tempt fate,** tempt the gods, tweak the devil's nose, bell the cat, play a desperate game, ride for a fall; play with fire, flirt with death, stretch one's luck, march up to the cannon's mouth, put one's head in a lion's mouth, beard the lion in his den, sit on a barrel of gunpowder, sleep on a volcano, play Russian roulette, playing with a loaded gun, working without a net; risk all, go for broke, shoot the works

ADJS 7 **rash,** brash, incautious, overbold, imprudent, indiscreet, injudicious, improvident; ill-considered; irresponsible; unwary, unchary; overcareless; overconfident, oversure, overweening, impudent, insolent, brazenfaced, brazen; hubristic; temerarious

8 **reckless,** devil-may-care; careless; impetuous, hotheaded; hasty, hurried, overeager, overzealous, overenthusiastic; furious, desperate, mad, wild, wanton, harum-scarum; precipitate, precipitous, precipitant; headlong, breakneck; slapdash, slap-bang; accident-prone; asking for it

9 **foolhardy,** harebrained, madcap, wild, wild-ass, madbrain, madbrained; audacious; forward, bold, presumptuous; daring, daredevil, risk-taking, fire-eating, death-defying; adventurous; frivolous, flippant

ADVS **10** **rashly,** brashly, incautiously, imprudently, indiscreetly, injudiciously, improvidently; unwarily, uncharily; overconfidently, overweeningly, impudently, insolently, brazenly, hubristically, temerariously

11 **recklessly,** happen what may; heedlessly, carelessly; impetuously, hotheadedly; hastily, hurriedly, overeagerly, overzealously, overenthusiastically; furiously, desperately, wildly, wantonly, madly, like mad, like crazy, like there was no tomorrow; precipitately, precipitously, precipitantly; headlong, headfirst, headforemost, head over heels, heels over head; slapdash, slam-bang; helter-skelter, ramble-scramble, hurry-scurry, holus-bolus

12 **foolhardily, daringly, audaciously,** presumptuously, harebrainedly

494 CAUTION

<*forethought to minimize risk*>

NOUNS **1** **caution, cautiousness;** slowness to act, slowness to commit oneself, slowness to make one's move; care, heed, solicitude; carefulness, heedfulness, mindfulness, regardfulness, thoroughness; paying mind, paying attention; guardedness; uncommunicativeness; gingerliness, tentativeness, hesitation, hesitancy, unprecipitateness; slow and careful steps, deliberate stages, wait-and-see attitude; prudence, prudentialness, circumspection, discretion, canniness; coolness, judiciousness; calculation, deliberateness, deliberation, careful consideration, prior consultation; safeness, safety first, no room for error; hedge, hedging, hedging one's bets, cutting one's losses; designated driver

2 **wariness,** chariness, cageyness, leeriness; suspicion, suspiciousness; distrust, distrustfulness, mistrust, mistrustfulness; reticence, skepticism, second thoughts, reservation

3 **precaution,** precautiousness; forethought, foresight, foresightedness, forehandedness, forethoughtfulness; providence, provision, nest egg, forearming; precautions, steps, measures, steps and measures, preventive measure, preventive step; safeguard, protection, safety net, safety valve, sheet anchor; insurance; rainy-day policy; lemon law; nightlight

4 **overcaution,** overcautiousness, overcarefulness, overwariness; unadventurousness

VERBS **5** **be cautious, be careful;** think twice, give it a second thought; make haste slowly, take it easy, take it slow; put the right foot forward, take one step at a time, pick one's steps, go step by step, feel one's way; pussyfoot, tiptoe, walk on tiptoe, walk on eggs, walk on eggshells, walk on thin ice; pull in one's horns, draw in one's horns; doubt, have second thoughts

6 **take precautions,** take steps, take measures, take steps and measures; prepare for, prepare against, provide for, provide against, forearm; guard against, make sure against, make sure; play safe, anticipate; keep on the safe side; leave no stone unturned, forget nothing, leave out nothing, overlook no possibility, leave no room for error, leave no margin for error, leave nothing to chance, consider every angle; look before one leaps; see how the land lies, see how the wind blows, see how the cat jumps; clear the decks, batten down the hatches, shorten sail, reef down, tuck in a reef, take in a reef, get out a sheet-anchor, have an anchor to windward; hedge, provide a hedge, hedge one's bets, cut one's losses; take out insurance; keep something for a rainy day

7 **beware, take care,** have a care, take heed, take heed at one's peril; keep at a respectful distance, keep out of harm's way; mind, mind one's business; be on one's guard, be on the watch, be on the lookout, be on the *qui vive*; look out, watch out; look sharp, keep one's eyes open, keep a weather eye out, keep a weather eye open, keep one's eye peeled, watch one's step, look about one, look over one's shoulder, keep tabs on; stop, look, and listen; not stick one's neck out, not go out on a limb, not expose oneself, not be too visible, keep a low profile, lie low, stay in the background, blend with the scenery; not blow one's cover; hold one's tongue

ADJS **8** **cautious, careful,** heedful, mindful, alert, regardful, thorough; prudent, circumspect, slow to act, slow to commit oneself, slow to make one's move, noncommittal, uncommitted; sly, crafty, scheming; discreet, politic, judicious, Polonian, Macchiavelian; unadventurous, no-risk, unenterprising, undaring; gingerly; guarded, on guard, on one's guard; uncommunicative; tentative, hesistant, unprecipitate, cool; deliberate; safe, on the safe side, leaving no stone unturned, forgetting nothing, leaving out nothing, overlooking no possibility, leaving no room for error, leaving no margin for error

9 **wary,** chary, cagey, leery, suspicious, suspecting, distrustful, mistrustful, shy; guarded, on guard; cautionary

10 **precautionary,** precautious, precautional; preventive, preemptive, prophylactic; forethoughtful, forethoughted, foresighted, foreseeing, forehanded; provident, provisional; anticipatory

11 **overcautious, overcareful,** overwary, unadventurous

ADVS 12 **cautiously, carefully,** heedfully, mindfully, regardfully; prudently, circumspectly, discreetly, judiciously; gingerly, guardedly, easy, with caution, with care

13 **warily,** charily, cagily; askance, askant, suspiciously, leerily, distrustfully

INTERJS 14 careful, be careful, **take care,** have a care, look out, watch out, watch your step, watch it, take heed, steady, look sharp, easy, take it easy, easy does it, go easy

495 FASTIDIOUSNESS

<excessive attention to detail>

NOUNS 1 **fastidiousness, particularity,** particularness; scrupulousness, scrupulosity; punctiliousness, punctilio, spit and polish; preciseness, precision; meticulousness, conscientiousness, criticalness; taste; sensitivity, discrimination, discriminatingness, discriminativeness; selectiveness, selectivity, pickiness, choosiness; strictness, perfectionism, precisianism, purism; puritanism, priggishness, prudishness, prissiness, propriety, straitlacedness, censoriousness, judgmentalness

2 **finicalness,** finickiness, finickingness, finicality; **fussiness,** pernicketiness, persnicketiness; squeamishness, queasiness

3 **nicety,** niceness, delicacy, delicateness, daintiness, exquisiteness, fineness, refinement, subtlety

4 overfastidiousness, **overscrupulousness,** overparticularity, overconscientiousness, overmeticulousness, overniceness, overnicety; overcriticalness, hypercriticism, slamming, hairsplitting; overrefinement, oversubtlety, supersubtlety; oversqueamishness, oversensitivity, hypersensitivity, morbid sensibility

5 **exclusiveness,** exclusivity, selectness, selectiveness, selectivity; cliquishness, clannishness; snobbishness, snobbery, snobbism; quiddity

6 **perfectionist,** precisian, precisianist, stickler, nitpicker, captious critic

7 **fussbudget,** fusspot, fuss, fusser, fuddy-duddy, granny, old woman, old maid; Mrs. Grundy

VERBS 8 **be hard to please,** want everything just so, **fuss,** fuss over; pick and choose; **turn up one's nose,** look down one's nose, look down on, disdain, scorn, spurn; not dirty one's hands, not soil one's hands

ADJS 9 **fastidious, particular,** scrupulous, meticulous, conscientious, exacting, precise, punctilious, spit-and-polish; sensitive, discriminating, discriminative; selective, picky, choosy, choicy; critical; strict, perfectionistic, precisianistic, puristic; puritanic, puritanical, priggish, prudish, prissy, proper, straitlaced, censorious, judgmental

10 **finical, finicky,** finicking, finikin; **fussy,** fussbudgety; squeamish, pernickety, persnickety, difficult, hard to please

11 **nice,** dainty, delicate, picture-perfect, fine, refined, exquisite, subtle

12 **overfastidious,** queasy, overparticular, overscrupulous, overconscientious, overmeticulous, overnice, overprecise; overcritical, hypercritical, ultracritical, hairsplitting; overrefined, oversubtle, supersubtle; oversqueamish, oversensitive, hypersensitive, morbidly sensitive; compulsive, anal, anal-compulsive

13 **exclusive,** selective, select, elect, elite; cliquish, clannish; snobbish, snobby; quiddative

ADVS 14 **fastidiously,** particularly, scrupulously, meticulously, conscientiously, critically, punctiliously; discriminatingly, discriminatively, selectively; finically, finickily, finickingly; fussily; squeamishly, queasily; refinedly, subtly

496 TASTE, TASTEFULNESS

<good judgment, taste>

NOUNS 1 **taste, good taste,** sound critical judgment, appreciation of excellence, discernment, preference for the best; **tastefulness,** quality, excellence, choiceness, elegance, grace, gracefulness, gracility, graciousness, graciosity, gracious living; propriety; refinement, finesse, polish, culture, cultivation, civilizedness, refined taste, cultivated taste, civilized taste, finish; niceness, nicety, delicacy, daintiness, subtlety, sophistication; discrimination, fastidiousness; acquired taste, connoisseurship; etiquette

2 **decorousness, decorum,** decency, properness, propriety, rightness, right thinking, seemliness, becomingness, fittingness, fitness, appropriateness, suitability, meetness, happiness, felicity; gentility, genteelness; civility, urbanity

3 **restraint,** restrainedness, **understatement,** unobtrusiveness, quietness, subduedness, quiet taste; simplicity; subtlety

4 **aesthetic taste,** artistic taste, virtuosity, virtu, expertise, expertism, connoisseurship; dilettantism; fine art of living; epicurism, epicureanism; gastronomy; aesthetics

5 **aesthete,** person of taste, lover of beauty

6 **connoisseur,** *cognoscente* <Ital>; judge, good judge, critic, expert, authority, maven, arbiter, arbiter of taste, tastemaker, trendsetter; epicure,

epicurean; gourmet, gourmand, *bon vivant* <Fr>, refined palate; oenophile, wine lover; virtuoso; dilettante, amateur; culture vulture; collector; gentleperson

ADJS 7 **tasteful, in good taste,** in the best taste; excellent, of quality, of the best, of the first water; **aesthetic,** artistic, pleasing, well-chosen, choice, of choice; pure, chaste; classic, classical, Attic, restrained, understated, unobtrusive, conservative, quiet, subdued, simple, low-key, unaffected

8 **elegant,** graceful, gracile, gracious; refined, polished, cultivated, civilized, cultured; nice, fine, delicate, dainty, subtle, sophisticated, discriminating, fastidious, sensitive

9 **decorous,** decent, proper, right, right-thinking, seemly, becoming, fitting, appropriate, suitable, meet, happy, felicitous; genteel; civil, urbane

ADVS 10 **tastefully, with taste,** in good taste, in the best taste; aesthetically, artistically; elegantly, gracefully; decorously, genteelly, decently, properly, seemly, becomingly; quietly, unobtrusively; simply

497 VULGARITY

<excessive embellishment>

NOUNS 1 **vulgarity,** vulgarness, vulgarism, commonness, meanness; **inelegance,** inelegancy, indelicacy, impropriety, indecency, indecorum, indecorousness, unseemliness, unbecomingness, unfittingness, inappropriateness, unsuitableness, unsuitability; ungentility; untastefulness, tastelessness, unaestheticness, unaestheticism, tackiness; bad taste, poor taste; vulgar taste, bourgeois taste, Babbittry, philistinism; popular taste, pop culture, pop; campiness, camp, high camp, low camp; baseness, kitsch

2 **coarseness,** grossness, rudeness, crudeness, crudity, crassness, rawness, roughness, earthiness; ribaldness, ribaldry; raunchiness, obscenity; meretriciousness, loudness, gaudiness

3 **unrefinement, uncouthness,** uncultivation, uncultivatedness, unculturedness; uncivilizedness, wildness; impoliteness, incivility, ill breeding; barbarism, barbarousness, barbarity, philistinism, Gothicism; savagery, savagism; brutality, brutishness, bestiality, animality, mindlessness; Neanderthalism, troglodytism; phubbing

4 **boorishness,** churlishness, carlishness, loutishness, lubberliness, lumpishness, cloddishness, clownishness, yokelism; ruffianism, rowdyism, hooliganism; parvenuism, arrivism, upstartness; roughness

5 commonness, commonplaceness, ordinariness, homeliness; **lowness,** baseness, meanness; ignobility, plebeianism

6 **vulgarian,** low-bred fellow, vulgar fellow, ill-bred fellow, mucker, guttersnipe; Babbitt, Philistine, bourgeois, Pooterish; *parvenu* and *arriviste, nouveau riche* <Fr>, upstart; bounder, cad, boor, churl, clown, lout, yahoo, redneck, looby, peasant, groundling, yokel; rough, ruffian, roughneck, rowdy, hooligan; vulgarist, ribald; guttermouth; rascal, rapscallion; vulgus, hoi polloi, rabble, riffraff, great unwashed, scum, huddled masses

7 **barbarian, savage,** Goth, animal, brute; Neanderthal, troglodyte

8 vulgarization, coarsening; popularization; dumbing down

VERBS 9 **vulgarize,** coarsen; popularize; dumb down; pander; commercialize

ADJS 10 **vulgar, inelegant,** indelicate, indecorous, indecent, improper, unseemly, unbeseeming, unbecoming, unfitting, inappropriate, unsuitable, ungenteel, undignified, discourteous; untasteful, tasteless, in bad taste, in poor taste, tacky, chintzy, Mickey Mouse, gauche, garish; offensive, offensive to gentle ears

11 **coarse,** gross, rude, crude, crass, raw, rough, earthy; ribald; raunchy, obscene; meretricious, loud, gaudy; cacological, solecistic

12 **unrefined,** unpolished, uncouth, unkempt, uncombed, unlicked; uncultivated, uncultured; uncivilized, noncivilized; impolite, uncivil, ill-bred; wild, untamed; barbarous, barbaric, barbarian, infra dig; outlandish, Gothic; primitive; savage, brutal, brutish, bestial, animal, mindless; Neanderthal, troglodytic; wild-and-woolly, rough-and-ready

13 **boorish,** churlish, carlish, loutish, redneck, lubberly, lumpish, cloddish, clownish, loobyish, yokelish; rowdy, rowdyish, ruffianly, roughneck, hooliganish, raffish, raised in a barn

14 **common,** commonplace, ordinary; plebeian; homely, homespun; general, public, popular, pop; vernacular; Babbittish, Philistine, bourgeois; campy, high-camp, low-camp, kitschy

15 **low, base,** mean, ignoble, vile, scurvy, sorry, scrubby, beggarly; low-minded, base-minded

ADVS 16 **vulgarly,** uncouthly, inelegantly, indelicately, indecorously, indecently, improperly, unseemly, untastefully, offensively; coarsely, grossly, rudely, crudely, crassly, roughly; ribaldly

498 ORNAMENTATION

<embellishment>

NOUNS 1 **ornamentation, ornament; decoration,** decor; adornment, embellishment, embroidery, elaboration; nonfunctional addition, nonfunctional adjunct; garnish, garnishment, garniture; trimming, trim; flourish; emblazonment, emblazonry; illumination; color, color scheme, color pattern, color compatibility, color design, color arrangement; arrangement, flower arrangement, floral decoration, furniture arrangement; table setting, table decoration; window dressing; interior decoration, interior decorating, room decoration, interior design; feng shui; redecoration, refurbishment, redoing

2 **ornateness,** elegance, **fanciness,** fineness, elaborateness; ostentation; richness, luxuriousness, luxuriance; floweriness, floridness, floridity; dizenment, bedizenment; gaudiness, flashiness; flamboyance, flamboyancy, chi-chi; overelegance, overelaborateness, overornamentation, busyness; clutteredness; baroqueness, baroque, rococo, arabesque, moresque, chinoiserie

3 **finery,** frippery, gaudery, gaiety, bravery, trumpery, folderol, trickery, chiffon, trappings, festoons, superfluity; frills, frills and furbelows, bells and whistles, gimmickry, Mickey Mouse, glitz, frillery, frilling, frilliness; foofaraw, fuss, froufrou; gingerbread; tinsel, clinquant, pinchbeck, paste; gilt, gilding

4 **trinket,** gewgaw, **knickknack**, nicknack, knack, gimcrack, kickshaw, doodad, whim-wham, bauble, fribble, bibelot, toy, gaud; bric-a-brac; sequin

5 **jewelry,** bijouterie, ice; costume jewelry, glass, paste, junk jewelry; bling, bling-bling; beads, worry beads, mala

6 **jewel,** bijou, **gem,** stone, precious stone, crown jewel; cultured pearl; rhinestone; pin, brooch, stickpin, breastpin, scatter pin, chatelaine; cuff link, tie clasp, tie clip, tie bar, tiepin, scarfpin, tie tack, tie tac; ring, band, wedding band, engagement ring, promise ring, mood ring, signet ring, school ring, class ring, circle, earring, nose ring; bracelet, wristlet, wristband, armlet, anklet; chain, necklace, torque; locket; beads, chaplet, wampum; bangle; charm; fob; crown, coronet, diadem, tiara; laurel

7 **motif,** ornamental motif, figure, detail, form, touch, repeated figure; pattern, theme, design, ornamental theme, ornamental composition, decorative composition; foreground detail, background detail; background, setting, foil, style, ornamental style, decorative style, national style, period style

VERBS 8 **ornament, decorate,** adorn, dress, trim, garnish, array, deck, bedeck, dizen, bedizen; prettify, beautify; redecorate, refurbish, redo; gimmick up, glitz up, sex up; embellish, furbish, embroider, enrich, grace, set off, set out, paint, color, blazon, emblazon, paint in glowing colors; dress up; spruce up, gussy up, doll up, fix up, primp up, prink up, prank up, trick up, trick out, deck out, bedight, fig out; primp, prink, prank, preen; smarten, smarten up, dandify, titivate, give a face lift

9 figure, filigree; **spangle,** bespangle; bead; tinsel; jewel, bejewel, gem, diamond; pavé; ribbon, beribbon; flounce; flower, garland, wreathe; feather, plume; flag; illuminate; paint; engrave

ADJS 10 **ornamental, decorative,** adorning, embellishing

11 **ornamented, adorned, decorated,** embellished, bedecked, decked out, tricked out, garnished, trimmed, dizened, bedizened; figured; flowered; festooned, befrilled, wreathed; spangled, bespangled, spangly; jeweled, bejeweled; beaded; studded; plumed, feathered; beribboned

12 **ornate, elegant, fancy,** fine, chichi, pretty-pretty; picturesque; elaborate, overornamented, overornate, overelegant, labored, high-wrought; ostentatious; glitzy, flashy; rich, luxurious, luxuriant; flowery, florid; flamboyant, fussy, frilly, frilled, flouncy, gingerbread, gingerbready; overelaborate, overlabored, overworked, overwrought, busy; cluttered; baroque, rococo, arabesque, moresque, gilded; gimmicked-up, glitzed-up, sexed-up; pimped-out

499 PLAINNESS

<undecoration>

NOUNS 1 **plainness,** simplicity, simpleness, ordinariness, commonness, commonplaceness, homeliness, prosaicness, prosiness, matter-of-factness; purity, chasteness, classic purity, classical purity, Attic simplicity

2 **naturalness,** inartificiality; **unaffectedness,** unassumingness, unpretentiousness; directness, straightforwardness; innocence, naïveté, chasteness

3 **unadornment,** unembellishment, unadornedness, unornamentation; **no frills,** no nonsense, back-to-basics; uncomplexity, uncomplication, uncomplicatedness, unsophistication, unadulteration; bareness, baldness, nakedness, nudity, starkness, undress, beauty unadorned

4 **inornateness, unelaborateness,** unfanciness, unfussiness; austerity, severity, starkness, Spartan simplicity; voluntary simplicity

VERBS 5 **simplify**

ADJS **6** **simple**, **plain**, ordinary, nondescript, common, commonplace, prosaic, prosy, matter-of-fact, homely, homespun, everyday, vanilla, conventional, workday, workaday, household, garden, common-variety, garden-variety; pure, pure and simple, chaste, classic, classical, Attic

7 **natural**, native; inartificial, unartificial; **unaffected**, unpretentious, unpretending, unassuming, unfeigning, direct, straightforward, honest, candid; innocent, naive

8 **unadorned**, **undecorated**, unornamented, unembellished, ungarnished, unfurbished, unvarnished, untrimmed; olde, olde-worlde; back-to-basics, no-frills, no-nonsense, vanilla, plain-vanilla, white-bread, white-bready; back-to-nature; uncomplex, uncomplicated, unsophisticated, unadulterated; undressed, undecked, unarrayed; bare, bald, blank, naked, nude, butt-naked

9 **inornate**, unornate, unelaborate, unfancy, unfussy; austere, monkish, cloistral, severe, stark, Spartan

ADVS **10** **plainly**, **simply**, ordinarily, commonly, commonplacely, prosaically, matter-of-factly

11 **unaffectedly**, naturally, unpretentiously, unassumingly, directly, straightforwardly

500 AFFECTATION

<pretense, unnaturalness>

NOUNS **1** **affectation**, **affectedness**; **pretension**, **pretense**, airs, pretentiousness, putting on airs, put-on; show, false show, mere show; front, false front, facade, mere facade, image, public image; feigned belief, hypocrisy; la-di-da, phoniness, sham; artificiality, unnaturalness, insincerity; prunes and prisms, graces; stylishness, mannerism

2 **mannerism**, *minauderie* <Fr>, trick of behavior, trick, **quirk**, habit, peculiarity, peculiar trait, idiosyncrasy, trademark

3 **posing**, pose, posturing, attitudinizing, attitudinarianism; peacockery, peacockishness; pompousness; putting on airs

4 **foppery**, foppishness, **dandyism**, coxcombry, puppyism, conceit

5 overniceness, overpreciseness, **overrefinement**, elegance, exquisiteness, preciousness, preciosity; goody-goodyism, goody-goodness; purism, formalism, formality, pedantry, precisionism, precisianism; euphuism; euphemism

6 prudery, **prudishness**, **prissiness**, priggishness, primness, smugness, stuffiness, old-maidishness, straitlacedness, stiff-neckedness, hidebound, narrowness, censoriousness, sanctimony, sanctimoniousness, puritanism, puritanicalness; false modesty, overmodesty, demureness

7 **phony**, **fake**, **fraud**; affecter; mannerist; pretender, actor, playactor, performer; paper tiger, hollow man, straw man, man of straw, empty suit

8 **poser**, **poseur**, striker of poses, posturer, posturist, posture maker, attitudinarian, attitudinizer, bluffer

9 **dandy**, **fop**, coxcomb, macaroni, gallant, dude, swell, sport, ponce, toff, exquisite, blood, fine gentleman, puppy, jackanapes, jack-a-dandy, fribble, clotheshorse, fashion plate; beau, Beau Brummel, spark, blade, ladies' man, lady-killer, masher, cocksman; man-about-town, boulevardier

10 fine lady, ***grande dame***, *précieuse* <Fr>; belle, toast

11 **prude**, prig, priss, puritan, bluenose, goody-goody, goody two-shoes, wowser, old maid; Victorian, mid-Victorian

VERBS **12** **affect**, assume, put on, assume airs, put on airs, wear, pretend, simulate, counterfeit, sham, fake, **feign**, make out like, make a show of, play, playact, act a part, play a part, play a scene, do a bit, put up a front, dramatize, histrionize, show off, play to the gallery, lay it on thick, overact, ham, ham it up, chew up the scenery, emote, tug at the heartstrings

13 **pose**, posture, attitudinize, peacock, strike a pose, strike an attitude, pose for effect

14 **mince**, mince it, prink; **simper**, smirk, bridle

ADJS **15** **affected**, **pretentious**, la-di-da, posy; mannered; artificial, unnatural, insincere; theatrical, stagy, histrionic; overdone, overacted, hammed up

16 **assumed**, put-on, pretended, simulated, phony, fake, **faked**, feigned, counterfeited; spurious, sham; deceptive, specious; hypocritical

17 **foppish**, **dandified**, dandy, coxcombical, conceited, chichi, pompous

18 <affectedly nice> overnice, overprecise, precious, exquisite, **overrefined**, elegant, mincing, simpering, namby-pamby; goody-goody, goody good-good; puristic, formalistic, pedantic, precisionistic, precisian, precisianistic, euphuistic, euphemistic

19 **prudish**, priggish, prim, prissy, smug, stuffy, old-maidish, overmodest, demure, straitlaced, stiff-necked, hidebound, narrow, censorious, po-faced <Brit>, sanctimonious, puritanical, Victorian, mid-Victorian

ADVS **20** **affectedly**, **pretentiously**; elegantly, mincingly; for effect, for show

21 **prudishly**, priggishly, primly, smugly, stuffily, straitlacedly, stiffneckedly, puritanically

501 OSTENTATION

<showiness>

NOUNS 1 **ostentation,** ostentatiousness, ostent; **pretentiousness,** pretension, pretense; loftiness, lofty affectations, triumphalism, grandstanding; bully pulpit

2 **pretensions,** vain pretensions; **airs,** lofty airs, graces, vaporing, highfalutin ways, highfaluting ways, side, swank, delusions of grandeur

3 **showiness,** flashiness, flamboyance, panache, dash, jazziness, jauntiness, sportiness, gaiety, glitter, glare, dazzle, dazzlingness; extravaganza; gaudiness, gaudery, glitz, gimmickry, razzmatazz, razzledazzle, tawdriness, meretriciousness; gorgeousness, colorfulness; loudness, blatancy, flagrancy, shamelessness, brazenness, luridness, extravagance, sensationalism, obtrusiveness, vulgarness, crudeness, extravagation

4 **display,** show, demonstration, manifestation, exhibition, parade; pageantry, pageant, spectacle, gala; vaunt, fanfaronade, blazon, flourish, flaunt, flaunting; daring, brilliancy, éclat, bravura, flair; dash, splash, splurge; figure; showmanship, exhibitionism, showing-off, fuss and feathers; theatrics, histrionics, dramatics, staginess, camp; false front, sham

5 **grandeur,** grandness, grandiosity, **magnificence,** gorgeousness, **splendor,** splendidness, splendiferousness, resplendence, brilliance, glory; nobility, proudness, state, stateliness, majesty; impressiveness, imposingness; sumptuousness, elegance, elaborateness, lavishness, luxuriousness; ritziness, poshness, plushness, swankiness; luxury, barbaric spendor, Babylonian splendor

6 **pomp,** circumstance, pride, state, solemnity, formality; pomp and circumstance; heraldry

7 **pompousness, pomposity,** pontification, pontificality, stuffiness, self-importance, inflation; grandiloquence, bombast, turgidity, orotundity

8 **swagger,** strut, swank, bounce, brave show; swaggering, strutting; swash, swashbucklery, swashbuckling, swashbucklering; peacockishness, peacockery

9 **stuffed shirt**, blimp, Colonel Blimp; bloated aristocrat

10 **strutter,** swaggerer, swanker <Brit>, swash, swasher, swashbuckler, peacock, miles gloriosus

11 **showoff**, exhibitionist, flaunter; grandstander, grandstand player, hotdog, hotshot, showboat

VERBS 12 **put oneself forward,** thrust oneself forward, come forward, step to the front, step to the fore, step into the limelight, take center stage, attract attention, make oneself conspicuous

13 cut a dash, **make a show**, put on a show, make one's mark, cut a swath, cut a figure; make a splash; splurge, splash; shine, glitter, glare, dazzle

14 give oneself airs, **put on airs,** put on, put on side, put on the dog, put up a front, put on the ritz, ritz it, look big, swank, swell, swell it, act the grand seigneur; pontificate, play the pontiff

15 **strut, swagger,** swank <Brit>, prance, stalk, peacock, swash, swashbuckle

16 **show off**, **grandstand**, hotdog, showboat, play to the gallery, please the crowd, ham it up; exhibit one's wares, parade one's wares, strut one's stuff, go through one's paces, show what one has

17 **flaunt,** vaunt, parade, display, demonstrate, manifest, make a great show of, exhibit, air, put forward, put forth, hold up, flash, sport; advertise; flourish, brandish, wave; dangle, dangle before the eyes; emblazon, blazon forth; trumpet, trumpet forth

ADJS 18 **ostentatious, pretentious,** posy; ambitious, vaunting, lofty, highfalutin, highfaluting, high-flown, high-flying; high-toned, tony, fancy, classy, glitzy, flossy; Gatsbyesque

19 **showy, flaunting,** flashy, snazzy, flashing, glittering, jazzy, glitzy, gimmicky, splashy, splurgy; camp; exhibitionistic, showoffy, bravura; gay, jaunty, rakish, dashing; gallant, brave, daring; sporty, dressy; frilly, flouncy, frothy, chichi

20 **gaudy, tawdry;** gorgeous, colorful; garish, loud, blatant, flagrant, shameless, brazen, brazenfaced, lurid, extravagant, sensational, spectacular, glaring, flaring, flaunting, screaming, obtrusive, vulgar, crude; meretricious, low-rent, low-ride, tacky

21 **grandiose,** grand, magnificent, splendid, splendiferous, splendacious, glorious, superb, fine, superfine, fancy, superfancy, swell; imposing, impressive, larger-than-life, awful, awe-inspiring, awesome; noble, proud, stately, majestic, princely; sumptuous, elegant, elaborate, luxurious, luxuriant, extravagant, deluxe; executive, plush, posh, ritzy, swank, swanky, Corinthian; palatial, Babylonian

22 **pompous**, stuffy, self-important, impressed with oneself, pontific, pontifical; inflated, swollen, bloated, tumid, turgid, flatulent, gassy, stilted; grandiloquent, bombastic; solemn, formal

23 **strutting, swaggering;** swashing, swashbuckling, swashbucklering; peacockish, peacocky; too big for one's britches

24 **theatrical,** theatric, stagy, dramatic, histrionic; spectacular

ADVS 25 **ostentatiously, pretentiously,** loftily; with flourish of trumpet, with beat of drum, with flying colors

26 **showily,** flauntingly, flashily, with a flair, glitteringly; gaily, jauntily, dashingly; gallantly, bravely, daringly
27 **gaudily,** tawdrily; gorgeously, colorfully; garishly, blatantly, flagrantly, shamelessly, brazenly, brazenfacedly, luridly, sensationally, spectacularly, glaringly, flaringly, obtrusively
28 **grandiosely,** grandly, magnificently, splendidly, splendiferously, splendaciously, gloriously, superbly; nobly, proudly, majestically; imposingly, impressively; sumptuously, elegantly, elaborately, luxuriously, extravagantly; palatially
29 **pompously,** pontifically, stuffily, self-importantly; stiltedly; bombastically

502 BOASTING

<prideful talk>

NOUNS **1** **boasting, bragging,** vaunting; boastfulness, braggadocio, braggartism; boast, brag, vaunt; side, bombast, bravado, vauntery, fanfaronade, blowing one's own horn, tooting one's own horn, gasconade, gasconism, rodomontade; bluster, swagger; vanity, conceit; jactation, jactitation; heroics
2 <nonformal> **big talk,** fine talk, fancy talk, tall talk, highfalutin, highfaluting, hot air, gas, bunk, bunkum, bullshit*; tall story, fish story; bragging rights
3 **self-approbation,** self-praise, self-laudation, self-gratulation, self-applause, self-boosting, self-puffery, self-vaunting, self-advertising, self-advertisement, self-adulation, self-glorification, self-dramatizing, self-dramatization, self-promoting, self-promotion; **vainglory,** vaingloriousness
4 **crowing,** exultation, elation, triumph, jubilation; **gloating**
5 **braggart, boaster,** brag, braggadocio, exaggerator, hector, fanfaron, Gascon, gasconader, miles gloriosus; **blowhard**, blower, big mouth, bullshitter*, bullshit artist*, hot-air artist, gasbag, windbag, big bag of wind, windjammer, windy; blusterer, panjandrum; Texan, Fourth-of-July orator; swashbuckler, rushbuckler

VERBS **6** **boast, brag,** make a boast of, vaunt, flourish, gasconade, vapor, puff, draw the longbow, advertise oneself, blow one's own trumpet, toot one's own horn, sing one's own praises, exaggerate one's own merits; bluster, swagger; speak for Buncombe
7 <nonformal> blow, blow off, mouth off, **blow hard,** talk big, sound off, toot one's own horn, blow one's own horn, bullshit*, shoot the shit*, spread oneself, lay it on thick, brag oneself up
8 **flatter oneself,** conceit oneself, congratulate oneself, hug oneself, shake hands with oneself, form a mutual admiration society with oneself, pat oneself on the back, take merit to oneself; think one's shit doesn't stink*
9 **exult,** triumph, glory, delight, joy, jubilate; **crow,** crow over, crow like a rooster; gloat, gloat over

ADJS **10** **boastful, boasting,** braggart, bragging, thrasonical, thrasonic, big-mouthed, vaunting, vaporing, gasconading, Gascon, fanfaronading, fanfaron; vain, pompous, conceited; vainglorious
11 **self-approving,** self-approbatory, self-praising, self-gratulating, self-boosting, self-puffing, self-adulating, self-adulatory, self-glorifying, self-glorying, self-glorious, self-lauding, self-laudatory, self-congratulatory, self-applauding, self-flattering, self-vaunting, self-advertising, self-dramatizing, self-promoting
12 **inflated,** swollen, windy, gassy, **bombastic,** high-swelling, high-flown, highfalutin, highfaluting, pretentious, extravagant, big, tall, hyped
13 **crowing,** exultant, exulting, elated, elate, jubilant, triumphant, flushed, cock-a-hoop, in high feather; **gloating**

ADVS **14** **boastfully,** boastingly, braggingly, vauntingly, vaingloriously; self-approvingly, self-praisingly
15 **exultantly,** exultingly, elatedly, jubilantly, triumphantly, triumphally, in triumph; **gloatingly**

503 BLUSTER

<threatening talk>

NOUNS **1** **bluster,** blustering, hectoring, bullying, **swagger,** swashbucklery, side; bravado, rant, rodomontade, fanfaronade; sputter, splutter; fuss, bustle, fluster, flurry; bluff; intimidation; boastfulness
2 **blusterer, swaggerer,** swasher, swashbuckler, fanfaron, bravo, bully, bullyboy, bucko, roisterer, cock of the walk, vaporer, blatherskite; ranter, raver, hectorer, hector, Herod; slanger <Brit>; bluff, bluffer; braggart

VERBS **3** **bluster,** hector; **swagger,** swashbuckle; bully; bounce, vapor, roister, rollick, gasconade, kick up a dust; sputter, splutter; rant, rage, rave, rave on, storm, out-Herod Herod; slang <Brit>; bluff, bluster and bluff, put up a bluff; intimidate; shoot off one's mouth, sound off, bogart, brag

ADJS **4** **blustering,** blustery, blusterous, hectoring, bullying, **swaggering,** swashing, swashbuckling, boisterous, roisterous, roistering, rollicking; ranting, raging, raving, storming; tumultuous; noisy, full of sound and fury

504 COURTESY

<respectful behavior>

NOUNS 1 **courtesy,** courteousness, common courtesy, **politeness,** civility, *politesse* <Fr>, amenity, agreeableness, urbanity, comity, affability; graciousness, gracefulness; complaisance; thoughtfulness, considerateness, tactfulness, tact, consideration, solicitousness, solicitude; respect, respectfulness, deference; civilization, quality of life

2 **gallantry,** gallantness, **chivalry,** chivalrousness, knightliness; courtliness, courtly behavior, courtly politeness; *noblesse oblige* <Fr>

3 **mannerliness, manners,** good manners, excellent manners, exquisite manners, good deportment, polite deportment, good behavior, polite behavior; *savoir-faire*; decency; correctness, correctitude, etiquette

4 **good breeding,** breeding; refinement, finish, polish, culture, cultivation; gentility, gentleness, genteelness, elegance; gentlemanliness, gentlemanlikeness, ladylikeness

5 **suavity, suaveness,** smoothness, smugness, blandness; unctuousness, oiliness, oleaginousness, smarm, smarminess; glibness, slickness, fulsomeness; sweet talk, fair words, soft words, soft tongue, sweet words, honeyed words, sweet tongue, incense; soft soap, butter

6 **courtesy, civility,** amenity, urbanity, attention, polite act, act of courtesy, act of politeness, graceful gesture, pleasantry; old-fashioned courtesy, old-fashioned civility, courtliness

7 amenities, **courtesies, civilities,** gentilities, graces, elegancies; dignities; formalities, ceremonies, rites, rituals, observances

8 **regards,** compliments, respects; best wishes, one's best, good wishes, best regards, kind regards, kindest regards, love, best love; greetings; remembrances, kind remembrances; compliments of the season

9 **gallant,** cavalier, chevalier, knight

VERBS 10 **mind one's manners,** mind one's P's and Q's; keep a civil tongue in one's head; mend one's manners; observe etiquette, observe protocol, follow protocol; be polite, be considerate

11 **extend courtesy,** do the honors, pay one's respects, make one's compliments, present oneself, pay attentions to, do service, wait on, wait upon

12 **give one's regards**, give one's compliments, give one's love, give one's best regards, give one's best, send one's regards, send one's compliments, send one's love; wish one joy, wish one luck, bid Godspeed

ADJS 13 **courteous, polite,** civil, urbane, gracious, graceful, agreeable, affable, fair; complaisant; obliging, accommodating; thoughtful, considerate, tactful, solicitous; respectful, deferential, attentive

14 **gallant, chivalrous,** chivalric, knightly; courtly; formal, ceremonious; old-fashioned, old-world

15 **mannerly, well-mannered,** good-mannered, well-behaved, well-spoken, fair-spoken; correct, correct in one's manners, correct in one's behavior; housebroken

16 **well-bred,** highbred, well-brought-up; cultivated, cultured, polished, refined, genteel, gentle; gentlemanly, gentlemanlike, ladylike

17 **suave, smooth,** smug, bland, glib, unctuous, oily, oleaginous, smarmy, soapy, buttery, fulsome, ingratiating, disarming; suave-spoken, fine-spoken, fair-spoken, soft-spoken, smooth-spoken, smooth-tongued, oily-tongued, honey-tongued, honey-mouthed, sweet-talking

ADVS 18 **courteously, politely,** civilly, urbanely, mannerly; gallantly, chivalrously, courtly, knightly; graciously, gracefully, with a good grace; complaisantly, complacently; out of consideration, out of courtesy; obligingly, accommodatingly; respectfully, attentively, deferentially

505 DISCOURTESY

<rude behavior>

NOUNS 1 **discourtesy,** discourteousness; **impoliteness,** unpoliteness; rudeness, incivility, inurbanity, gall, ungraciousness, ungallantness, uncourtesy, uncourtliness, ungentlemanliness, unmannerliness, mannerlessness, bad manners, ill manners, ill breeding, conduct unbecoming a gentleman, caddishness; inconsiderateness, inconsideration, unsolicitousness, unsolicitude, tactlessness, insensitivity; grossness, crassness, gross behavior, crass behavior, boorishness, vulgarity, coarseness, crudeness, offensiveness, loutishness, nastiness

2 **disrespect**, disrespectfulness; insolence; criminal contempt

3 **gruffness,** brusqueness, curtness, shortness, sharpness, abruptness, bluntness, brashness; harshness, roughness, severity; truculence, aggressiveness; surliness, crustiness, bearishness, beastliness, churlishness

ADJS 4 **discourteous,** uncourteous; **impolite,** unpolite, inurbane; rude, uncivil, ungracious, ungallant, uncourtly, inaffable, uncomplaisant, unaccommodating; disrespectful; insolent; impertinent

5 **unmanneryly,** unmannered, mannerless, ill-mannered, ill-behaved, ill-conditioned, bad-mannered

6 **ill-bred,** ungenteel, ungentle, caddish; ungentlemanly, ungentlemanlike; unladylike, unfeminine; vulgar, boorish, unrefined, inconsiderate, unsolicitous, tactless, insensitive; gross, offensive, crass, coarse, crude, loutish, nasty

7 **gruff,** brusque, curt, short, sharp, snippy, abrupt, blunt, bluff, brash, cavalier; harsh, rough, severe; truculent, aggressive; surly, crusty, bearish, beastly, churlish; vituperative; sharp-tongued

ADVS **8** **discourteously, impolitely, rudely,** uncivilly, ungraciously, ungallantly, ungenteelly, caddishly; inconsiderately, unsolicitously, tactlessly, insensitively

9 **gruffly,** brusquely, curtly, shortly, sharply, snippily, abruptly, bluntly, bluffly, brashly, cavalierly; harshly, crustily, bearishly, churlishly, boorishly, nastily

506 RETALIATION

<counterattack>

NOUNS **1** **retaliation, reciprocation,** exchange, interchange, give-and-take; retort, reply, return, comeback; counter, counterblow, counterstroke, counterblast, counterpunch, recoil, boomerang, backlash

2 **reprisal,** requital, retribution; recompense, compensation, reward, comeuppance, desert, deserts, **just deserts,** what is merited, what is due, what is condign, what's coming to one, a dose of one's own medicine; quittance, return of evil for evil; revenge; punishment

3 **tit for tat,** measure for measure, like for like, quid pro quo, something in return, blow for blow, a Roland for an Oliver, a game two can play, an eye for an eye, a tooth for a tooth, law of retaliation, law of equivalent retaliation, *lex talionis* <L>, talion; game at which two can play

VERBS **4** **retaliate,** retort, counter, strike back, hit back at, give in return; reciprocate, give in exchange, give and take; get back at, come back at, turn the tables upon; fight fire with fire, return the compliment

5 **requite,** quit, make requital, make reprisal, make retribution, get satisfaction, recompense, compensate, make restitution, indemnify, reward, redress, make amends, **repay,** pay, pay back, pay off, pay down, pay up; give one his comeuppance, give one his desserts, give one his just desserts, serve one right, give one what is coming to him

6 **give in kind,** cap, match, give as good as one gets, give as good as was sent; repay in kind, pay one in one's own currency, give one a dose of one's own medicine; return the like, return the compliment; return like for like, return evil for evil; return blow for blow, give one tit for tat, give a quid pro quo, give measure for measure, get an eye for an eye and a tooth for a tooth, observe the *lex talionis*

7 **get even with**, even the score, settle with, settle up with, settle accounts, square accounts, settle the score, fix, pay off old scores, pay back in full measure, be quits, make quits; fix one's wagon, take revenge; punish

ADJS **8** **retaliatory,** retaliative; **retributive,** retributory; reparative, compensatory, restitutive, recompensing, recompensive, reciprocal; punitive; recriminatory, like for like; revengeful, vindictive

ADVS **9** **in retaliation,** in exchange, in reciprocation; in return, in reply; in requital, in reprisal, in retribution, in reparation, in amends; in revenge

PHRS **10** what goes around comes around, one's chickens come home to roost; the shoe is on the other foot

507 REVENGE

<inflicting harm in retaliation>

NOUNS **1** **revenge, vengeance, avengement,** sweet revenge, getting even, evening of the score; wrath; revanche, revanchism; retaliation, reprisal; vendetta, feud, blood feud; the wrath of God

2 **revengefulness, vengefulness,** vindictiveness, rancor, grudgefulness, irreconcilableness, unappeasableness, implacableness, implacability

3 **avenger**, vindicator; revanchist, nemesis; the Furies, the Erinyes, the Eumenides

VERBS **4** **revenge, avenge,** take revenge, exact revenge, have one's revenge, wreak one's vengeance; retaliate, even the score, get even with; launch a vendetta

5 **harbor revenge,** breathe vengeance; have accounts to settle, have a crow to pick with; nurse one's revenge, brood over, dwell on, dwell upon, keep the wound open, wave the bloody shirt

6 **reap revenge,** reap vengeance; sow the wind and reap the whirlwind; live by the sword and die by the sword

ADJS **7** **revengeful, vengeful**, avenging; vindictive, vindicatory; revanchist; punitive, punitory; wrathful, rancorous, grudgeful, irreconcilable, unappeasable, implacable, unwilling to forgive and forget, unwilling to let bygones be bygones; retaliatory

508 RIDICULE

<contemptuous talk>

NOUNS 1 **ridicule, derision, mockery,** raillery, rallying, chaffing; panning, razzing, roasting, ragging, scoffing, jeering, sneering, snickering, sniggering, smirking, grinning, leering, fleering, snorting, levity, flippancy, smartness, smart-aleckiness, joshing, fooling, japery, twitting, taunting, booing, hooting, catcalling, hissing; **banter**

2 gibe, scoff, **jeer,** fleer, flout, mock, barracking <Brit>, **taunt,** twit, quip, jest, jape, put-on, leg-pull, foolery; insult; scurrility, caustic remark; cut, cutting remark, verbal thrust; gibing retort, rude reproach, short answer, back answer, comeback, parting shot, Parthian shot

3 **boo,** booing, hoot, catcall; Bronx cheer, raspberry, razz; hiss, hissing, the bird, the finger

4 scornful laugh, scornful smile, snicker, snigger, **smirk,** sardonic grin, leer, fleer, sneer, snort

5 **sarcasm,** irony, cynicism, satire, satiric wit, satiric humor, invective, innuendo; causticity

6 burlesque, **lampoon,** squib, parody, satire, farce, mockery, imitation, wicked imitation, wicked pastiche, takeoff, black humor, travesty, caricature

7 **laughingstock,** jestingstock, gazingstock, derision, mockery, figure of fun, byword, byword of reproach, jest, joke, butt, target, stock, goat, toy, game, fair game, victim, dupe, fool, everybody's fool, monkey, mug

VERBS 8 **ridicule, deride,** ride, make a laughingstock of, make a mockery of; roast, insult; make fun of, make game of, poke fun at, make merry with, put one on, pull one's leg; laugh at, laugh in one's face, grin at, smile at, snicker at, snigger at; laugh to scorn, hold in derision, laugh out of court, hoot down; point at, point the finger of scorn; pillory

9 **scoff, jeer,** gibe, barrack <Brit>, mock, revile, rail at, rally, chaff, twit, taunt, jape, flout, scout, have a fling at, cast in one's teeth; cut at; jab, jab at, dig at, take a dig at; pooh, pooh-pooh; sneer, sneer at, fleer, curl one's lip

10 **boo,** hiss, hoot, catcall, give the raspberry, give the Bronx cheer, razz, give the bird, whistle at

11 **burlesque,** lampoon, satirize, parody, caricature, travesty, take off on

ADJS 12 **ridiculing, derisive,** derisory; **mocking,** railing, rallying, chaffing; panning, razzing, roasting, ragging, scoffing, jeering, sneering, snickering, sniggering, smirky, smirking, grinning, leering, fleering, snorting, flippant, smart, smart-alecky, smart-ass, wiseass; joshing, jiving, fooling, japing, twitting, taunting, booing, hooting, catcalling, hissing, bantering, kidding, teasing, quizzical

13 satiric, **satirical; sarcastic,** ironic, ironical, sardonic, cynical, Rabelaisian, dry; caustic; laugh-out-loud (LOL)

14 **burlesque,** farcical, broad, slapstick; parodic, caricatural, macaronic, doggerel

ADVS 15 **derisively,** mockingly, scoffingly, jeeringly, sneeringly

509 APPROVAL

<positive feeling toward>

NOUNS 1 **approval,** approbation; sanction, acceptance, countenance, favor; admiration, esteem, respect; endorsement, support, backing, vote, favorable vote, yea vote, yea, voice, adherence, blessing, seal of approval, nod, nod of approval, wink, stamp of approval, OK, rubber stamp, green light, go-ahead, thumbs up

2 **applause,** plaudit, éclat, acclaim, acclamation; popularity; clap, handclap, clapping, handclapping, clapping of hands; cheer; burst of applause, thunder of applause; round of applause, hand, big hand; ovation, standing ovation; encore

3 **commendation,** good word, acknowledgment, recognition, appreciation; boost, buildup; puff, promotion; citation, accolade, kudos; rave review, good review; blurb, plug, promo, hype; honorable mention

4 **recommendation,** recommend, letter of recommendation; advocacy, advocating, advocation, patronage; reference, credential, letter of reference, voucher, testimonial; character reference, character, certificate of character, good character; letter of introduction

5 **praise,** bepraisement; laudation, laud; glorification, glory, exaltation, extolment, magnification, honor; eulogy, *éloge, hommage* <Fr>, eulogium; encomium, accolade, kudos, panegyric; paean; tribute, homage, meed of praise; congratulation; flattery; overpraise, excessive praise, idolizing, idolatry, deification, apotheosis, adulation, lionizing, hero worship, cult status

6 **compliment,** polite commendation, complimentary remark, flattering remark, flattery, pat on the back, stroke; bouquet, posy, trade-last

7 **praiseworthiness,** laudability, laudableness, commendableness, estimableness, meritoriousness, exemplariness, admirability

8 commender, eulogist, eulogizer; **praiser,** lauder, laudator, extoller, encomiast, panegyrist, booster, puffer, promoter, champion; plugger, tout, touter;

applauder; claque; rooter, fan, buff, adherent; admirer; appreciator; flatterer, fan club

VERBS **9 approve, approve of,** think well of, take kindly to; sanction, accept; admire, esteem, respect; endorse, bless, sign off on, OK; countenance, keep in countenance; hold with, uphold; favor, be in favor of, view with favor

10 applaud, acclaim, hail; clap, clap one's hands, give a hand, give a big hand, have a hand for, have a big hand for, hear a big hand for, hear it for; cheer; root for, cheer on; encore; applaud to the very echo; huzzah; raise the roof

11 commend, speak well of, speak highly of, speak in high terms of, speak warmly of, say a good word for; boost, give a boost to, puff, promote, cry up; plug, tout, hype; pour it on thick, spread it on thick, lay it on thick; recommend, advocate, put in a word, put in a good word for, support, back, lend one's name to, lend one's support to, lend one's backing to, make a pitch for; condone, bless

12 praise, bepraise, talk one up; **laud,** belaud; eulogize, panegyrize, pay tribute, salute, hand it to one; extol, glorify, magnify, exalt, bless; cry up, blow up, puff, puff up; boast of, brag about, make much of; celebrate, emblazon, sound the praises of, resound the praises of, ring one's praises, sing the praises of, trumpet, hype; praise to the skies; flatter; overpraise, praise to excess, idolize, deify, apotheosize, adulate, lionize, hero-worship; put on a pedestal

13 espouse, join oneself with, associate oneself with, take up, take for one's own; campaign for, crusade for, put on a drive for, take up the cudgels for, push for; carry the banner of, march under the banner of; beat the drum for, thump the tub for; lavish oneself on, fight the good fight for; devote oneself to, dedicate oneself to, give oneself for, sacrifice oneself for

14 compliment, pay a compliment, make one a compliment, give a bouquet, give a posy, say something nice about; hand it to, have to hand it to, pat on the back, take off one's hat to, doff one's cap to, congratulate

15 meet with approval, find favor with, **pass muster,** recommend itself, do credit to; redound to the honor of; ring with the praises of

ADJS **16** approbatory, approbative, **commendatory**, complimentary, laudatory, acclamatory, felicitous, eulogistic, panegyric, panegyrical, encomiastic, appreciative, appreciatory; admiring, regardful, respectful; flattering

17 approving, favorable, favoring, in favor of, pro, well-disposed, well-inclined, supporting, backing, advocating; promoting, promotional; touting, puffing, hyping; recommending

18 uncritical, uncriticizing, uncensorious, unreproachful; overpraising, overappreciative, unmeasured in one's praise, excessive in one's praise, idolatrous, adulatory, lionizing, hero-worshiping, fulsome; knee-jerk

19 approved, favored, backed, advocated, supported; favorite; accepted, received, admitted; recommended, bearing the seal of approval, highly touted, admired, applauded, well-thought-of, in good odor, acclaimed, cried up; popular; given a blessing

20 praiseworthy, worthy, commendable, estimable, **laudable,** admirable, meritorious, creditable; exemplary, model, unexceptionable; deserving, well-deserving; beyond all praise; good

PREPS **21 in favor of,** for, pro, all for

INTERJS **22 bravo,** bravissimo, well done, *iolé* <Sp>, *bene* <Ital>; hear, hear; aha; hurrah; good, fine, excellent, cool beans, dench, whizzo <Brit>, great, beautiful, swell, good for you, good enough, not bad, now you're talking; way to go, attaboy, attababy, attagirl, attagal, good boy, good girl; that's the idea, that's the ticket; encore, bis, take a bow, three cheers, one cheer more, congratulations

23 hail, all hail, *ave* <L>, *vive* <Fr>, *viva* <Ital>, *evviva* <Ital>, long life to, glory be to, honor be to

510 DISAPPROVAL

<negative feeling toward>

NOUNS **1 disapproval,** disapprobation, disfavor, disesteem, disrespect; dim view, poor opinion, low opinion, low estimation, adverse judgment; displeasure, distaste, dissatisfaction, discontent, discontentment, discontentedness, disgruntlement, indignation, unhappiness; doghouse; disillusion, disillusionment, disenchantment, disappointment; disagreement, opposition, opposure; rejection, thumbs-down, exclusion, ostracism, blackballing, blackball, ban; complaint, protest, objection, dissent

2 deprecation, discommendation, dispraise, denigration, disvaluation; ridicule; depreciation, disparagement; contempt

3 censure, reprehension, stricture, reprobation, blame, denunciation, denouncement, decrying, decrial, bashing, trashing, impeachment, arraignment, indictment, condemnation, damnation, fulmination, anathema; castigation, flaying, skinning alive, fustigation, excoriation; pillorying

4 criticism, adverse criticism, harsh criticism, hostile criticism, flak, bad notices, bad press, panning, brickbat, animadversion, imputation, reflection, aspersion, stricture, obloquy; knock, swipe, slam, rap, hit, roasting, home thrust; minor criticism, petty criticism, niggle, cavil, quibble, exception, nit; censoriousness, reproachfulness, priggishness; faultfinding, taking exception, carping, caviling, pettifogging, quibbling, captiousness, niggling, nitpicking, pestering, nagging; hypercriticism, hypercriticalness, overcriticalness, hairsplitting, trichoschistism

5 **reproof,** reproval, reprobation, a flea in one's ear; **rebuke,** reprimand, reproach, reprehension, scolding, chiding, rating, upbraiding, objurgation; admonishment, admonition; correction, castigation, chastisement, spanking, rap on the knuckles; lecture, lesson, sermon; disrecommendation, low rating, adverse report, wolf ticket

6 <nonformal> **piece of one's mind,** bit of one's mind, talking-to, speaking-to, roasting, raking-down, raking-over, raking over the coals, dressing, dressing-down, set-down; bawling-out, cussing-out, calling-down, jacking-up, going-over, chewing-out, chewing, reaming-out, reaming, ass-chewing, ass-reaming*, what-for, ticking-off

7 **berating,** rating, tongue-lashing; revilement, vilification, blackening, execration, abuse, vituperation, invective, contumely, hard words, cutting words, bitter words; tirade, diatribe, jeremiad, screed, philippic; attack, assault, onslaught, assailing; abusiveness; acrimony, telling off

8 **reproving look,** dirty look, nasty look, black look, frown, scowl, glare; hiss, boo; Bronx cheer, raspberry

9 **faultfinder,** disapprover, momus, basher, trasher, boo-bird; critic, criticizer, nitpicker, smellfungus, belittler, censor, censurer, castigator, carper, caviler, quibbler, pettifogger, detractor, cynic; scold, common scold; kvetch, complainer

VERBS 10 **disapprove,** disapprove of, not approve, raise an objection, go against, side against, go contra; disfavor, view with disfavor, raise one's eyebrows, frown at, frown on, frown upon, look black upon, look askance at, make a wry face at, grimace at, turn up one's nose at, shrug one's shoulders at; take a dim view of, not think much of, think ill of, think little of, have no respect for, have a low opinion of, not take kindly to, not hold with, hold no brief for, not sign off on; not hear of, not go for, not get all choked up over, be turned off by; not want any part of not have any part of, wash one's hands of, dissociate oneself from; object to, take exception to; oppose, set oneself against, set one's heart against; reject, categorically reject, disallow; turn thumbs down on, thumb down, vote down, veto, frown down, exclude, ostracize, blackball, ban; say no to, shake one's head at; dissent from, protest, object; turn over in one's grave

11 **discountenance,** not countenance, **not tolerate,** not brook, not condone, not suffer, not abide, not endure, not bear with, not put up with, not stand for

12 **deprecate,** discommend, dispraise, disvalue, not be able to say much for, denigrate, fault, faultfind, find fault with, put down, pick at, pick on, pick holes in, pick to pieces; ridicule; depreciate, disparage; hold in contempt, disdain, despise

13 **censure,** reprehend; **blame,** lay blame upon, cast blame upon; bash, trash, rubbish; reproach, impugn; condemn, damn, take out after; damn with faint praise; fulminate against, anathematize, anathemize, put on the Index; denounce, denunciate, accuse, decry, cry down, impeach, arraign, indict, call to account, exclaim against, declaim against, inveigh against, peg away at, cry out against, cry out upon, cry shame upon, raise one's voice against, raise a hue and cry against, shake up; reprobate, hold up to reprobation; animadvert upon, reflect upon, cast reflection upon, cast a reproach upon, cast a slur upon, complain against; throw a stone at, cast the first stone

14 **criticize;** pan, knock, slam, hit, rap, take a swipe at, snipe at, strike out at, tie into, tee off on, rip into, open up on, plow into; belittle

15 **find fault,** take exception, fault-find, pick holes, cut up, pick apart, pull apart, tear apart, pick to pieces, pull to pieces, tear to pieces; tear down, carp, cavil, quibble, nitpick, pick nits, pettifog, catch at straws

16 **nag,** niggle, carp at, fuss at, fret at, yap at, pick at, peck at, nibble at, pester, henpeck, pick on, bug, hassle

17 **reprove, rebuke,** reprimand, reprehend, put a flea in one's ear, scold, chide, rate, admonish, upbraid, objurgate, have words with, take a hard line with; lecture, read a lecture to; correct, rap on the knuckles, chastise, spank, turn over one's knees; take to task, call to account, bring to book, call on the carpet, read the riot act, give one a tongue-lashing, tonguelash; take down, set down, set straight, straighten out

18 <nonformal> **call down, dress down,** speak to, talk to, tell off, tell a thing or two, pin one's ears back, give a piece of one's mind, rake over the coals, haul over the coals, rake up one side and down the other, give it to, let one have it, let one

have it with both barrels, trim, come down on, come down hard on, jump on, jump all over, jump down one's throat; give one a hard time, give one what for; bawl out, give a bawling out, chew, chew out, chew ass, ream, ream out, ream ass, cuss out, jack up, sit on, sit upon, lambaste, give a going-over, tell where to get off; give the devil, give hell, give hail Columbia

19 **berate,** rate, betongue, jaw, clapper-claw, tongue-lash, rail at, rag, thunder against, fulminate against, rave against, yell at, bark at, yelp at; revile, vilify, blacken, execrate, abuse, vituperate, load with reproaches

20 <criticize severely> **attack,** assail; castigate, flay, skin alive, lash, slash, excoriate, fustigate, scarify, scathe, roast, scorch, blister, trounce; lay into

ADJS 21 **disapproving,** disapprobatory, unapproving, turned-off, displeased, dissatisfied, less than pleased, discontented, disgruntled, indignant, unhappy; disillusioned, disenchanted, disappointed; unfavorable, low, poor, opposed, opposing, con, against, agin, dead set against, death on, down on, dissenting; uncomplimentary; unappreciative

22 **condemnatory, censorious,** censorial, damnatory, denunciatory, reproachful, blameful, reprobative, objurgatory, po-faced <Brit>, priggish, judgmental; deprecative, deprecatory; derisive, ridiculing, scoffing; depreciative, disparaging; contemptuous; invective, inveighing; reviling, vilifying, blackening, execrating, execrative, execratory, abusive, vituperative

23 **critical, faultfinding,** carping, picky, nitpicky, caviling, quibbling, pettifogging, captious, cynical; nagging, niggling; hypercritical, ultracritical, overcritical, hairsplitting, trichoschistic; abusive

24 **unpraiseworthy,** illaudable; uncommendable, discommendable, not good enough; objectionable, exceptionable, unacceptable, not to be thought of, beyond the pale

25 **blameworthy,** blamable, to blame, at fault, much at fault; **reprehensible,** censurable, reproachable, reprovable, open to criticism, open to reproach; **culpable,** chargeable, impeachable, accusable, indictable, arraignable, imputable

ADVS 26 **disapprovingly,** askance, askant, **unfavorably;** censoriously, critically, reproachfully, rebukingly; captiously

INTERJS 27 God forbid, Heaven forbid, Heaven forfend, forbid it Heaven; by no means, not for the world, not on your life, over my dead body, not if I know it, nothing doing, no way, no way José, perish the thought, I'll be hanged if, I'll be damned if, shame, for shame, tuttut

511 FLATTERY

<*insincere praising talk*>

NOUNS 1 **flattery, adulation;** praise; blandishment, palaver, cajolery, cajolement, wheedling, inveiglement; blarney, bunkum, soft soap, soap salve, butter salve, oil, grease, eyewash; strokes, stroking, ego massage, sweet talk, fair words, sweet words, honeyed words, soft phrases, honeyed phrases, incense, pretty lies, sweet nothings; trade-last, compliment; ass-kissing*, ingratiation, fawning, sycophancy

2 **unction; unctuousness,** oiliness, sliminess; slobber, gush, smarm, smarminess; flattering tongue; insincerity

3 **overpraise,** overprizing, excessive praise, overcommendation, overlaudation, overestimation; idolatry

4 **flatterer,** adulator, courtier; cajoler, wheedler; backslapper, back scratcher, yes-man, bootlicker; blarneyer, soft-soaper; ass-kisser*, brownnoser, sycophant

VERBS 5 **flatter,** adulate, conceit; cajole, wheedle, blandish, palaver; slaver over, slobber over, beslobber, beslubber; oil the tongue, lay the flattering unction to one's soul, make fair weather; praise, compliment, praise to the skies; scratch one's back, kiss ass, fawn upon

6 <nonformal> **soft-soap,** butter, honey, **butter up,** soften up; stroke, massage the ego; blarney, jolly, pull one's leg; lay it on, pour it on thick, lay it on thick, lay it on with a trowel, overdo it, soap, oil; string along, kid along; play up to, get around; suck up to

7 **overpraise,** overprize, overcommend, overlaud; overesteem, overestimate, overdo it, protest too much; idolize, put on a pedestal; puff

ADJS 8 **flattering,** adulatory; complimentary; blandishing, cajoling, wheedling, blarneying, soft-soaping; fair-spoken, fine-spoken, smooth-spoken, smooth-tongued, mealymouthed, honey-mouthed, honey-tongued, honeyed, oily-tongued; fulsome, slimy, slobbery, gushing, protesting too much, smarmy, insinuating, oily, buttery, soapy, unctuous, smooth, bland; insincere, hypocritical, tongue-in-cheek; courtly, courtierly; fawning, sycophantic, obsequious

512 DISPARAGEMENT

<*slighting talk*>

NOUNS 1 **disparagement, faultfinding,** depreciation, detraction, deprecation, derogation, bad-mouthing, running down, knocking, putting down, belittling; sour grapes; slighting, minimizing, faint praise, lukewarm support, discrediting, decrying, decrial; disapproval; contempt; indignity, disgrace, comedown

2 **defamation,** malicious defamation, defamation of character, smear campaign, injury of one's reputation, injury to one's reputation; vilification, revilement, defilement, blackening, denigration; smear, character assassination, *ad hominem* <L>, personal attack, name-calling, smear word; muckraking, mudslinging

3 **slander,** scandal, **libel,** traducement; calumny, calumniation; backbiting, cattiness, bitchiness*

4 **aspersion,** slur, remark, reflection, imputation, insinuation, suggestion, sly suggestion, innuendo, whispering campaign; disparaging remark, uncomplimentary remark; poison-pen letter, hatchet job

5 lampoon, send-up, takeoff, pasquinade, **ridicule,** pasquin, pasquil, squib, lampoonery, satire, malicious parody, burlesque; caricature

6 **disparager,** depreciator, decrier, detractor, basher, trasher, boo-bird, belittler, debunker, deflater, slighter, derogator, knocker, hatchet man; slanderer, libeler, defamer, backbiter; calumniator, traducer; muckraker, mudslinger, social critic; cynic, railer, Thersites

7 **lampooner,** lampoonist, **satirist,** pasquinader; poison-pen writer

VERBS 8 **disparage,** depreciate, belittle, slight, minimize, make little of, degrade, debase, run down, knock down, put down, sell short; discredit, bring into discredit, reflect discredit upon, disgrace; detract from, derogate from, cut down to size; decry, cry down; speak ill of; speak slightingly of, not speak well of; disapprove of; hold in contempt; submit to indignity, submit to disgrace, bring down, bring low

9 **defame,** malign, bad-mouth, poor-mouth; asperse, cast aspersions on, cast reflections on, injure one's reputation, damage one's good name, give one a black eye; **slur,** cast a slur on, do a number on, do a job on, tear down

10 **vilify, revile,** defile, sully, soil, smear, smirch, besmirch, bespatter, tarnish, blacken, denigrate, blacken one's good name, give a black eye; call names, give a bad name, give a dog a bad name, stigmatize; muckrake, throw mud at, mudsling, heap dirt upon, drag through the mud, drag through the gutter; engage in personalities

11 **slander, libel;** slur, calumniate, traduce; stab in the back, backbite, speak ill of behind one's back

12 **lampoon,** ridicule, satirize, pasquinade; parody, send up, take off; dip the pen in gall, burlesque

ADJS 13 **disparaging, derogatory,** derogative, **deprecatory,** depreciative, slighting, belittling, minimizing, detractory, pejorative, backbiting, catty, bitchy*, contumelious, contemptuous, derisive, derisory, ridiculing; snide, insinuating; censorious; defamatory, vilifying, slanderous, scandalous, libelous; calumnious, calumniatory; abusive, scurrilous, scurrile

513 CURSE

<profane or obscene talk>

NOUNS 1 **curse,** malediction, malison, damnation, denunciation, commination, imprecation, execration; blasphemy; anathema, fulmination, thundering, excommunication; ban, proscription; hex, evil eye, jinx, whammy, double whammy; ill wishes

2 **vilification,** abuse, revilement, vituperation, invective, opprobrium, obloquy, contumely, calumny, scurrility, blackguardism; disparagement; slanging match

3 **cursing,** cussing, **swearing, profanity,** profane swearing, foul language, profane language, obscene language, blue language, bad language, strong language, indelicate language, vulgar language, vile language, colorful language, unrepeatable expressions, dysphemism, billingsgate, ribaldry, evil speaking, dirty language, dirty talk, obscenity, scatology, coprology, filthy language, filth; foul mouth, dirty mouth

4 **swear word,** oath, profane oath, curse; cuss, cuss word, dirty word, four-letter word, profanity, bad word, naughty word, no-no, foul invective, **expletive,** epithet, dirty name, dysphemism, obscenity, vulgarity; F-word

VERBS 5 **curse,** accurse, damn, darn, confound, blast, anathematize, fulminate against, thunder against, execrate, imprecate, proscribe; excommunicate; call down evil upon, call down curses on the head of; put a curse on; curse up hill and down dale; curse with bell, book, and candle; blaspheme; hex, give the evil eye, put a whammy on

6 **curse, swear, cuss,** execrate, rap out an oath, rip out an oath, take the Lord's name in vain; swear like a trooper, cuss like a sailor, make the air blue, swear till one is blue in the face; talk dirty, scatologize, coprologize, dysphemize, use strong language; blaspheme, profane

7 vilify, abuse, revile, vituperate, blackguard, call names, epithet, epithetize; **swear at,** damn, cuss out

ADJS 8 **cursing,** maledictory, imprecatory, damnatory, denunciatory, epithetic, epithetical;

abusive, vituperative, contumelious; calumnious, calumniatory; execratory, comminatory, fulminatory, excommunicative, excommunicatory; scurrilous, scurrile; blasphemous, profane, foul, foulmouthed, vile, thersitical, dirty, obscene, dysphemistic, scatologic, scatological, coprological, toilet, sewer, cloacal; ribald, Rabelaisian, raw, risqué

9 **cursed,** accursed, bloody, damned, damn, damnable, goddamned, goddamn, execrable

10 <euphemisms> **darned,** danged, confounded, deuced, blessed, blasted, dashed, blamed, goshdarn, doggone, doggoned, goldarned, goldanged, dadburned; blankety-blank; ruddy <Brit>

INTERJS 11 damn, damn it, God damn it, goddamn it, confound it, dagnabbit, hang it, devil take, a plague upon, a pox upon, go to hell

12 <euphemistic oaths> darn, dern, dang, dash, drat, blast, doggone, goldarn, goldang, gosh-darn, cripes, crikey, criminy, golly, gosh, heck, bugger all <Brit>, goodness, goodness gracious, jeepers, jeez, gee whillikers, gee whiz, oh snap, puh-leeze, sacre bleu, crap

514 THREAT

<warning of intention to harm>

NOUNS 1 **threat, menace,** threateningness, threatfulness, promise of harm, knife poised at one's throat, arrow aimed at one's heart, sword of Damocles; imminent threat, powder keg, timebomb, imminence; foreboding; warning; saber-rattling, muscle-flexing, woofing, bulldozing, scare tactics, intimidation, arm-twisting; denunciation, commination; veiled threat, implied threat, idle threat, hollow threat, empty threat; bomb threat

VERBS 2 **threaten, menace,** bludgeon, bulldoze, put the heat on, put the squeeze on, lean on; hold a pistol to one's head, terrorize, intimidate, twist one's arm, arm-twist; utter threats against, shake one's fist at; hold over one's head; denounce, comminate; lower, spell trouble, mean trouble, look threatening, loom, loom up; be imminent; forebode; warn

ADJS 3 **threatening, menacing,** threatful, minatory, minacious; lowering; imminent; ominous, foreboding; denunciatory, comminatory, abusive; fear-inspiring, intimidating, bludgeoning, muscle-flexing, saber-rattling, bulldozing, browbeating, bullying, hectoring, blustering, terrorizing, terroristic, stalking, trolling

ADVS 4 under duress, under threat, under the gun, at gunpoint, at knifepoint

515 FASTING

<abstaining from food>

NOUNS 1 **fasting,** abstinence from food; abstemiousness, starvation; punishment of Tantalus; religious fasting; hunger strike; anorexia nervosa, bulimia nervosa

2 **fast,** lack of food; spare diet, meager diet, Lenten diet, Lenten fare; prison fare; short commons, short rations, military rations, K rations; starvation diet, water diet, crash diet, bread and water, bare subsistence, bare cupboard; xerophagy, xerophagia; Barmecide feast, Barmecidal feast

3 **fast day**; Lent, Good Friday, Quadragesima; Yom Kippur' Tishah B'Av, Ninth of Av; Ramadan; meatless day, fish day, day of abstinence

VERBS 4 **fast,** not eat, go hungry, eat nothing, eat like a bird, dine with Duke Humphrey; eat sparingly, eat less, count calories

ADJS 5 **fasting,** uneating, unfed; abstinent, abstemious; keeping Lent, Lenten, quadragesimal; underfed

516 SOBRIETY

<abstaining from intoxicating substance>

NOUNS 1 **sobriety, soberness;** unintoxicatedness, uninebriatedness, undrunkenness; abstinence, abstemiousness; temperance; clear head; prohibition, temperance society; nondrinker, teetotaler

VERBS 2 **sober up,** sober off; sleep it off; bring one down, take off a high; dry out, clear one's head, detoxify; give up alcohol, go on the wagon

ADJS 3 **sober,** in one's sober senses, in one's right mind, in possession of one's faculties; clearheaded; **unintoxicated, uninebriated,** uninebriate, uninebrious, not drunk, undrunk, undrunken, untipsy, unfuddled; stone-cold sober, sober as a judge; able to walk the chalk, able to walk the chalk mark, able to walk the line; nondrinking, off the bottle, dry, straight, on the wagon, temperate, abstinent

4 **unintoxicating,** nonintoxicating, uninebriating; **nonalcoholic,** soft

517 SIGNS, INDICATORS

<symbol or signal>

NOUNS 1 **sign,** telltale sign, sure sign, tip-off, index, indicant, **indicator,** signal, measure; tip of the iceberg; symptom; note, keynote, mark, earmark, hallmark, badge, device, banner, stamp, signature, sigil, seal, trait, characteristic, character, peculiarity, idiosyncrasy, property, differentia; image, picture, representation, representative; insignia; notation; reference sign

2 **symbol, emblem, icon,** token, cipher, type; allegory; symbolism, symbology, iconology, iconography, charactery; conventional symbol; symbolic system; symbolization; semiotics, semiology; ideogram, logogram, pictogram; logo, logotype; totem, totem pole; love knot; symbol list

3 **indication,** signification, identification, differentiation, denotation, **designation,** denomination; characterization, highlighting; specification, naming, pointing, pointing out, pointing to, fingering, picking out, selection; symptomaticness, indicativeness; meaning; hint, suggestion; expression, manifestation; show, showing, disclosure

4 **pointer,** index, lead; direction, guide; fist, index finger, finger, arm; arrow; hand, hour hand, minute hand, gauge, needle, compass needle, lubber line; signpost, guidepost, finger post, direction post; milepost; blaze; guideboard, signboard

5 **mark, marking;** watermark; scratch, scratching, engraving, graving, score, scotch, cut, hack, gash, blaze; bar code; nick, notch; scar, cicatrix, scarification, cicatrization; brand, earmark; stigma; stain, discoloration; blemish, macula, spot, blotch, splotch, flick, patch, splash; mottle, dapple; dot, point; polka dot; tittle, jot; speck, speckle, fleck; tick, freckle, lentigo, mole; birthmark, strawberry mark, port-wine stain, vascular nevus, nevus, hemangioma; beauty mark, beauty spot; caste mark; check, checkmark; prick, puncture; tattoo, tattoo mark

6 **line,** score, stroke, slash, virgule, diagonal, dash, stripe, strip, streak, striation, striping, streaking, bar, band; squiggle; hairline; dotted line; lineation, delineation; sublineation, underline, underlining, underscore, underscoring; hatching, cross-hatching, hachure

7 **print, imprint,** impress, impression; dint, dent, indent, indentation, indention, concavity; sitzmark; stamp, seal, sigil, signet; colophon; fingerprint, finger mark, thumbprint, thumbmark, dactylogram, dactylograph; footprint, footmark, footstep, step, vestige; hoofprint, hoofmark; pad, paw print, pawmark, pug, pugmark; claw mark; fossil print, fossil footprint, ichnite, ichnolite; bump, boss, stud, pimple, lump, excrescence, convexity, embossment; ecological footprint

8 **track,** trail, path, course, *piste* <Fr>, line, wake; vapor trail, contrail, condensation trail; spoor, signs, traces, scent

9 **clue, cue, key,** tip-off, telltale, smoking gun, straw in the wind; trace, vestige, spoor, scent, whiff; lead, hot lead; catchword, cue word, keyword; evidence; hint, intimation, suggestion

10 **marker,** mark; bookmark; **landmark,** seamark; benchmark; milestone, milepost; cairn, menhir, catstone; lighthouse, lightship, tower, Texas tower; platform, watchtower, pharos; buoy, aid to navigation, navigation system, bell, gong, lighted buoy, nun, can, spar buoy, wreck buoy, junction buoy, special-purpose buoy; watermark, tidemark; monument

11 **identification,** identification mark; badge, identification badge, identification tag, dog tag, passport, personal identification number, PIN number (PIN); identification card, identity card, ID card (ID); Social Security number, driver's license number; card, business card, calling card, visiting card, press card, press pass; letter of introduction; signature, initials, monogram, calligram; credentials; serial number; countersign, countermark; theme, theme tune, theme song; criminal identification, forensic tool, DNA print, genetic fingerprint, voiceprint; fingerprint; dental record; place card

12 **password,** watchword, countersign; passcode; token; open sesame; secret grip; shibboleth

13 **label, tag;** ticket, docket <Brit>, tally; stamp, sticker; seal, sigil, signet; cachet; stub, counterfoil; token, check; brand, brand name, trade name, trademark name; trademark, registered trademark; government mark, government stamp, broad arrow <Brit>; hallmark, countermark; price tag; plate, bookplate, book stamp, colophon, *ex libris* <L>, logotype, logo; International Standard Book Number (ISBN); masthead, imprint, title page; letterhead, billhead; running head, running title

14 **gesture,** gesticulation; motion, movement; carriage, bearing, posture, poise, pose, stance, way of holding oneself; body language, kinesics; beck, beckon; shrug; charade, dumb show, pantomime; sign language, signing, gesture language; dactylology, deaf-and-dumb alphabet; hand signal, air quotes; chironomy

15 **signal,** sign; high sign, the wink, the nod; wink, flick of the eyelash, glance, leer; look in one's eyes, tone of one's voice; nod; nudge, elbow in the ribs, poke, kick, touch; alarm; beacon, signal beacon, marker beacon, radio beacon, lighthouse beacon; signal light, signal lamp, signal lantern; blinker; signal fire, beacon fire, watch fire, balefire, smoke signal; flare, parachute flare; rocket, signal rocket, Roman candle; signal gun, signal shot; signal siren, signal whistle, signal bell, bell, signal gong, police whistle, watchman's

rattle; fog signal, fog alarm, fog bell, foghorn, diaphone, fog whistle; traffic signal, traffic light, red light, stoplight, amber light, caution light, green light, go light; heliograph; signal flag; semaphore, semaphore telegraph, semaphore flag; wigwag, wigwag flag; international alphabet flag, international numeral pennant; red flag; white flag; yellow flag, quarantine flag; blue peter; pilot flag, pilot jack; signal post, signal mast, signal tower; telecommunications

16 **call, summons**; whistle; moose call, birdcall, duck call, hog call, goose call, crow call, hawk call, dog whistle; bugle call, trumpet call, fanfare, flourish; reveille, taps, last post; alarm, alarum; battle cry, war cry, war whoop, rebel yell, rallying cry; call to arms; Angelus, Angelus bell

VERBS **17** **signify,** betoken, stand for, identify, differentiate, note, speak of, talk, indicate, be indicative of, be an indication of, be significant of, connote, denominate, argue, bespeak, be symptomatic of, be diagnostic of, symptomize, characterize, mark, highlight, be the mark, be the sign of, give token, denote, mean; testify, give evidence, bear witness to; show, express, display, manifest, hint, suggest, reveal, disclose; entail, involve

18 **designate,** specify; denominate, name, denote; stigmatize; **symbolize,** stand for, typify, be taken as, symbol, emblematize, figure; point to, refer to, advert to, allude to, make an allusion to; pick out, select; point out, point at, put one's finger on, lay one's finger on, finger

19 **mark,** make a mark, put a mark on; pencil, chalk; mark out, demarcate, **delimit**, define; mark off, check, check off, tick, tick off, chalk up; punctuate, point; dot, spot, blotch, splotch, dash, speck, speckle, fleck, freckle; mottle, dapple; blemish; brand, stigmatize; stain, discolor; stamp, seal, punch, impress, imprint, print, engrave; score, scratch, gash, scotch, scar, scarify, cicatrize; nick, notch; blaze, blaze a trail; line, seam, trace, stripe, streak, striate; hatch; underline, underscore; prick, puncture, tattoo, riddle, pepper

20 **label, tag,** tab, ticket; stamp, seal; brand, earmark; hallmark; barcode

21 **gesture,** gesticulate; motion, motion to; use body language; beckon, wiggle the finger at; wave the arms, wig-wag, saw the air; shrug, shrug the shoulders; pantomime, mime, mimic, imitate, ape, take off

22 **signal,** signalize, sign, give a signal, make a sign; speak; flash; give the high sign, give the nod, give a high five, fist bump, fist pump; nod; nudge, poke, kick, dig one in the ribs, touch; wink, glance, raise one's eyebrows, leer; hold up the hand; wave, wave the hand, wave a flag, flag, flag down; unfurl a flag, hoist a banner, break out a flag; show one's colors, exchange colors; salute, dip; dip a flag, hail; half-mast; give an alarm, sound an alarm, raise a cry; beat the drum, sound the trumpet

ADJS **23** **indicative,** indicatory, signifying; connotative, indicating, signalizing; significant, significative, meaningful; symptomatic, symptomatologic, symptomatological, diagnostic, pathognomonic, pathognomonical; evidential, designative, denotative, denominative, naming; suggestive, implicative; expressive, demonstrative, exhibitive, telltale; representative; identifying, identificational; individual, peculiar, idiosyncratic; emblematic, symbolic, emblematical, symbolical; symbolistic, symbological, typical; figurative, figural, metaphorical; ideographic; semiotic, semantic; nominal, diagrammatic

24 **marked, designated,** flagged; signed, signposted; monogrammed, individualized, personal; own-brand, own-label; punctuated

25 **gestural,** gesticulative, gesticulatory; kinesic; pantomimic, in pantomime, in dumb show

518 MEANING

<sense of idea conveyed>

NOUNS **1** **meaning, significance, signification,** point, **sense,** idea, purport, import, where one is coming from; reference, referent; intension, extension; denotation; dictionary meaning, lexical meaning; emotive meaning, affective meaning, undertone, overtone, coloring; relevance, bearing, relation, pertinence, pertinency; substance, gist, pith, core, spirit, essence, gravamen, last word, name of the game, meat and potatoes, bottom line; drift, tenor; sum, sum and substance; literal meaning, true meaning, real meaning, unadorned meaning; secondary meaning, connotation; more than meets the eye, what is read between the lines; effect, force, impact, consequence, practical consequence, response; shifted meaning, displaced meaning, implied meaning, implication; Aesopian meaning, Aesopian language; totality of associations, value; syntactic meaning, structural meaning, grammatical meaning; symbolic meaning; metaphorical meaning, transferred meaning; semantic content, deep structure; semantic field, semantic domain, semantic cluster; range of meaning, span of meaning, scope; topic, subject matter; game changer

2 **intent, intention,** purpose, point, aim, object, end, design, plan; value, worth, use

3 **explanation, definition,** construction, sense-distinction, interpretation
4 acceptation, acception, accepted meaning, received meaning; **usage,** acceptance
5 **meaningfulness,** suggestiveness, expressiveness, pregnancy; significance, significancy, significantness; intelligibility, interpretability, readability; pithiness, meatiness, sententiousness; importance, import; game changer
6 <units> sign, symbol, significant, type, token, icon, verbal icon, lexeme, sememe, morpheme, glosseme, word, term, phrase, utterance, lexical form, lexical item, linguistic form, semantic unit, semiotic unit, semasiological unit; text; synonym, antonym, related word; derivation, etymology
7 **semantics,** semiotic, semiotics, significs, semasiology, semiology, linguistics; lexicology
VERBS **8** **mean, signify, denote, connote,** import, spell, have the sense of, be construed as, have the force of; be talking, be talking about; stand for, symbolize; imply, suggest, argue, breathe, bespeak, betoken, indicate; refer to; mean something, mean a lot, have impact, come home, hit one where one lives, hit one close to home; get across, convey
9 **intend,** have in mind, seek to communicate
ADJS **10** **meaningful,** meaning, significant, significative; literal, explicit; denotative, connotative, denotational, connotational, intensional, extensional, associational; referential; symbolic, metaphorical, figurative, allegorical, idiomatic; transferred, extended; intelligible, interpretable, definable, readable; suggestive, indicative, expressive; pregnant, full of meaning, loaded with meaning, laden with significance, fraught with meaning, freighted with significance, articulate; pithy, meaty, sententious, substantial, full of substance; pointed, full of point
11 **meant,** implied, **intended**
12 **semantic,** semantological, semiotic, semasiological, semiological; linguistic; lexological; symbolic, signific, iconic, lexemic, sememic, glossematic, morphemic, verbal, phrasal, lexical, philological; structural
ADVS **13** **meaningfully,** meaningly, significantly; suggestively, indicatively; expressively

519 LATENT MEANINGFULNESS

<implied or suggested meaning>

NOUNS **1** **latent meaningfulness, latency,** latentness, delitescence, latent content; **potentiality,** virtuality, possibility; dormancy
2 **implication, connotation,** import, latent meaning, underlying meaning, implied meaning, ironic suggestion, ironic implication, more than meets the eye, what is read between the lines; meaning; suggestion, allusion; coloration, tinge, undertone, overtone, undercurrent, something between the lines, intimation, touch, nuance, innuendo; code word, weasel word; hint; inference, supposition, presupposition, assumption, presumption; secondary sense, transferred sense, metaphorical sense; undermeaning, undermention, subsidiary sense, subsense, **subtext;** Aesopian meaning, cryptic meaning, hidden meaning, esoteric meaning, arcane meaning, occult meaning; symbolism, allegory
VERBS **3** be latent, underlie, lie under the surface, **lurk,** lie hid, lie low, lie beneath, hibernate, lie dormant, smolder; be read between the lines; make no sign, escape notice
4 **imply,** implicate, involve, import, connote, entail; mean; suggest, lead one to believe, bring to mind; hint, insinuate, infer, intimate; **allude to,** point to from afar, point indirectly to; write between the lines; allegorize; suppose, presuppose, assume, presume, take for granted; mean to say, mean to imply, mean to suggest
ADJS **5** **latent, lurking,** lying low, delitescent, hidden, obscured, obfuscated, veiled, muffled, covert, occult, mystic, cryptic; esoteric; underlying, under the surface, submerged; between the lines; hibernating, sleeping, dormant; potential, unmanifested, virtual, possible
6 **suggestive,** allusive, allusory, indicative, inferential; insinuating, insinuative, insinuatory; ironic; implicative, implicatory, implicational; referential
7 **implied,** implicated, inferred, involved; meant, indicated; suggested, intimated, insinuated, hinted; supposed, assumed, presumed, presupposed, reputative; hidden, arcane, esoteric, cryptic, Aesopian, Aesopic
8 **tacit, implicit,** implied, understood, taken for granted
9 **unexpressed,** unpronounced, unsaid, unspoken, unuttered, undeclared, unbreathed, unvoiced, wordless, silent; unmentioned, untalked-of, untold, unsung, unproclaimed, unpublished; unwritten, unrecorded; buttoned up
10 **symbolic,** symbolical, allegoric, allegorical, figural, figurative, tropological, **metaphoric,** metaphorical, anagogic, anagogical
ADVS **11** **latently,** underlyingly; potentially, virtually
12 **suggestively,** allusively, inferentially, insinuatingly; impliedly; by suggestion, by allusion
13 **tacitly, implicitly,** unspokenly, wordlessly, silently

520 MEANINGLESSNESS

<making no sense, having no meaning>

NOUNS 1 **meaninglessness,** unmeaningness, senselessness, nonsensicality; insignificance, unsignificancy, irrelevance; noise, mere noise, static, empty sound, talking to hear oneself talk, phatic communion, self-talk; inanity, emptiness, nullity; purposelessness, aimlessness, futility; dead letter; no bearing

2 **nonsense,** stuff and nonsense, pack of nonsense, folderol, balderdash, flummery, trumpery, rubbish, trash, *narrishkeit* <Yiddish>, vaporing, fudge; humbug, gammon, hocus-pocus; fandangle; rant, claptrap, fustian, rodomontade, bombast, absurdity; stultiloquence, twaddle, twiddle-twaddle, fiddle-faddle, fiddledeedee, fiddlesticks, blather, babble, babblement, bibble-babble, gabble, gibble-gabble, blabber, gibber, jabber, prate, prattle, palaver, rigmarole, rigamarole, galimatias, skimble-skamble, drivel, drool; gibberish, jargon, mumbo jumbo, double-talk, evasion, equivoke, ambiguity, amphigory, gobbledygook; glossolalia, speaking in tongues; logorrhea

3 <offensive or nonformal> **hogwash**, bullshit*, shit*, crap, crapola, horseshit*, horsefeathers, bull, poppycock, bosh, tosh <Brit>, applesauce, bunkum, bunk, garbage, guff, jive, bilge, piffle, moonshine, flapdoodle, a crock, a crock of shit*, claptrap, tommyrot, rot, malarkey, double Dutch, hokum, hooey, bushwa, balls, blah-blah-blah, baloney, blarney, tripe, hot air, gas, wind, waffle, yada yada, shizzle

VERBS 4 **be meaningless, mean nothing,** signify nothing, not mean a thing, not convey anything; not make sense, not figure, not compute; not register, not ring any bells

5 **talk nonsense,** twaddle, piffle, waffle, blather, blether, blabber, babble, gabble, gibble-gabble, jabber, gibber, prate, prattle, rattle, spiel; talk through one's hat; gas, bull, bullshit*, throw the bull, shoot off one's mouth, shoot the bull; drivel, vapor, drool, run off at the mouth; speak in tongues; not mean what one says

ADJS 6 **meaningless,** unmeaning, senseless, purportless, importless, nondenotative, nonconnotative; insignificant, unsignificant; empty, inane, null; phatic, garbled, scrambled; purposeless, aimless, designless, without rhyme or reason

7 **nonsensical,** silly, poppycockish; foolish, absurd; twaddling, twaddly; rubbishy, trashy; skimble-skamble; Pickwickian

ADVS 8 **meaninglessly,** unmeaningly, nondenotatively, nonconnotatively, senselessly, nonsensically; insignificantly, unsignificantly; purposelessly, aimlessly

521 INTELLIGIBILITY

<comprehensible meaning>

NOUNS 1 **intelligibility, comprehensibility,** apprehensibility, prehensibility, graspability, **understandability,** understandableness, knowability, cognizability, scrutability, penetrability, fathomableness, decipherability; recognizability, readability, interpretability; articulateness; open book

2 **clearness, clarity;** plainness, distinctness, microscopical distinctness, explicitness, clear-cutness, definition; lucidity, limpidity, pellucidity, crystal clarity, crystaline clarity, crystallinity, perspicuity, perspicuousness, transpicuity, transparency; simplicity, straightforwardness, directness, literalness; unmistakableness, unequivocalness, unambiguousness, unambiguity; coherence, connectedness, consistency, structure; plain language, plain style, plain English, plain speech, unadorned style; clear, plaintext, unencoded text; lowest common denominator

3 **legibility,** decipherability, **readability**

VERBS 4 **be understandable, make sense;** be plain, be clear, be obvious, be self-evident, be self-explanatory; speak for itself, tell its own tale, speak volumes, have no secrets, put up no barriers; read easily

5 <**be understood**> get over, go across, come through, register, penetrate, sink in, soak in; dawn on, be glimpsed; become apparent

6 **make clear,** make it clear, let it be understood, make crystal clear, make oneself understood, get over, put over, get across, put across; simplify, put in plain words, put in plain English, put in words of one syllable, spell out; elucidate, explain, define, demonstrate, explicate, clarify; illuminate, enlighten; put one in the picture; disambiguate; demystify, descramble; decode, decipher; make available to all, popularize, vulgarize

7 **understand, comprehend,** apprehend, have, know, conceive, realize, appreciate, have no problem with, ken, savvy, sense, make sense out of, make something of, make out, make heads or tails of; fathom, follow; grasp, seize, get hold of, grasp the meaning, seize the meaning, be seized of, take, take in, catch, catch on, get the meaning of, latch onto; master, learn; assimilate, absorb, digest

8 <nonformal> **read loud and clear,** read, read one, dig, get the idea, be with one, be with it, get the message, get the word, get the picture, get up to speed, get into one's head, get through one's head, get into one's thick head, get through one's thick head, get, get it, catch the drift, get the drift, have it taped, have it down pat, see where one is coming from, hear loud and clear, hear what one is saying, grok, have hold of, get the hang of, get a fix on, know like the back of one's hand, know inside out

9 **perceive,** see, discern, make out, descry; see the light, see daylight, wake up, wake up to, tumble to, come alive; see through, see to the bottom of, penetrate, see into, pierce, plumb; see at a glance, see with half an eye; have someone's number, read someone like a book

ADJS 10 **intelligible, comprehensible,** apprehensible, prehensible, graspable, knowable, cognizable, scrutable, fathomable, decipherable, plumbable, penetrable, interpretable; understandable, easily understood, easy to understand, exoteric; readable; articulate

11 **clear,** crystal clear, clear as crystal, clear as day, clear as the nose on one's face; plain, distinct, microscopically distinct, plain as pikestaffs; definite, defined, well-defined, clear-cut, clean-cut, crisp, obvious, made easy; direct, literal; simple, straightforward; explicit, express; unmistakable, unequivocal, univocal, unambiguous, unconfused; loud and clear; lucid, pellucid, limpid, crystalline, perspicuous, transpicuous, transparent, translucent, luminous; coherent, connected, consistent

12 **legible, decipherable, readable,** fair; uncoded, unenciphered, in the clear, clear, plaintext

ADVS 13 **intelligibly, understandably,** comprehensibly, apprehensibly; articulately; clearly, lucidly, limpidly, pellucidly, perspicuously, simply, plainly, distinctly, definitely; coherently; explicitly, expressly; unmistakably, unequivocally, unambiguously; in plain terms, in plain words, in plain English, in no uncertain terms, in words of one syllable

14 **legibly,** decipherably, readably, fairly

522 UNINTELLIGIBILITY

<incomprehensible meaning>

NOUNS 1 **unintelligibility, incomprehensibility,** inapprehensibility, ungraspability, unseizability, ununderstandability, inconceivability, unknowability, incognizability, inscrutability, impenetrability, unfathomableness, unsearchableness, numinousness; incoherence, unconnectedness, ramblingness; inarticulateness; ambiguity, equivocation

2 **abstruseness,** reconditeness; crabbedness, crampedness, knottiness; complexity, intricacy, complication; hardness, difficulty; profundity, profoundness, deepness; esotericism, esotery

3 **obscurity,** obscuration, obscurantism, obfuscation, mumbo jumbo, mystification; perplexity; unclearness, unclarity, unplainness, opacity; vagueness, indistinctness, indeterminateness, fuzziness, shapelessness, amorphousness; murkiness, murk, mistiness, mist, fogginess, fog, darkness, dark

4 **illegibility,** unreadability; undecipherability, indecipherability; invisibility; scribble, scrawl, hen track

5 **inexpressiveness,** unexpressiveness, expressionlessness, impassivity; uncommunicativeness; straight face, deadpan, poker face

6 **inexplicability,** unexplainableness, uninterpretability, indefinability, undefinability, unaccountableness; insolvability, inextricability; enigmaticalness, mysteriousness, mystery, strangeness, weirdness

7 <something unintelligible> Greek, Choctaw, double Dutch; gibberish, babble, jargon, garbage, gubbish, gobbledygook, noise, Babel; scramble, jumble, garble, muddle; purple prose; argot, cant, slang, secret language, Aesopian language, code, cipher, cryptogram; glossolalia, gift of tongues; enigma, riddle; double meaning

8 **enigma, mystery, puzzle,** puzzlement; Chinese puzzle, crossword puzzle, word game, jigsaw puzzle, Sudoku; problem, puzzling problem, baffling problem, why; question, question mark, vexed question, perplexed question, enigmatic question, sixty-four dollar question; perplexity; obscure point; knot, knotty point, crux, point to be solved; puzzler, poser, brain twister, brain teaser, sticker; mind-boggler, floorer, stumper; nut to crack, hard nut to crack, tough nut to crack; tough proposition

9 **riddle, conundrum,** paradox, charade, rebus; brainteaser, Chinese puzzle, tangram, acrostic, logogriph, anagram; riddle of the Sphinx, squaring of the circle; Sudoku, crossword

VERBS 10 **be incomprehensible, not make sense,** be too deep, go over one's head, defy comprehension, be beyond one, beat one, elude one, escape one, lose one, need explanation, need clarification, need translation, be Greek to, pass comprehension, pass understanding, not penetrate, make one's head swim; baffle, perplex, riddle, be sphinxlike, speak in riddles; speak in tongues; talk double Dutch, babble, gibber, ramble, drivel, mean nothing

11 **not understand,** be unable to comprehend, not have the first idea, not get, not get it, be unable to get through one's head, be unable to get into one's thick skull; be out of one's depth, be at sea, be lost; not know what to make of, make nothing of, not have the slightest idea, not be able to account for, not make head or tail of, not register; be unable to see, not see the wood for the trees; go over one's head, escape one; give up, pass; rack one's brains

12 **make unintelligible,** scramble, jumble, garble, mix up; encode, encipher; obscure, obfuscate, mystify, shadow; complicate

ADJS 13 **unintelligible, incomprehensible,** inapprehensible, ungraspable, unseizable, ununderstandable, unknowable, incognizable; unfathomable, inscrutable, impenetrable, unsearchable, numinous; ambiguous, equivocal; incoherent, unconnected, rambling; inarticulate; past comprehension, beyond one's comprehension, beyond understanding; Greek to one; ultracrepidarian

14 **hard to understand,** difficult, hard, tough, beyond one, **over one's head,** out of one's depth; knotty, cramp, crabbed; intricate, complex, overtechnical, perplexed, complicated; scrambled, jumbled, garbled; Johnsonian

15 **obscure,** obscured, obfuscated; vague, indistinct, indeterminate, undiscernible, fuzzy, shapeless, amorphous, amorphic, obfuscatory; unclear, unplain, opaque, muddy, clear as mud, clear as ditch water; dark, dim, blind, shadowy; murky, cloudy, foggy, fogbound, hazy, misty, nebulous

16 **recondite, abstruse,** abstract, transcendental; profound, deep; hidden; arcane, esoteric, occult; secret

17 **enigmatic,** enigmatical, cryptic, cryptical; sphinxlike; perplexing, **puzzling;** riddling; logogriphic, anagrammatic, mysterious

18 **inexplicable, unexplainable,** uninterpretable, undefinable, indefinable, funny, funny peculiar, unaccountable; insolvable, unsolvable, insoluble, inextricable; mysterious, mystic, mystical, shrouded in mystery, wrapped in mystery

19 **illegible, unreadable, unclear; undecipherable,** indecipherable

20 **inexpressive,** unexpressive, impassive, po-faced <Brit>; uncommunicative; expressionless; vacant, empty, blank; glassy, glazed, glazed-over, fishy, wooden; deadpan, poker-faced

ADVS 21 **unintelligibly, incomprehensibly,** inapprehensibly, ununderstandably

22 **obscurely,** vaguely, indistinctly, indeterminately; unclearly, unplainly; illegibly

23 reconditely, **abstrusely;** esoterically, occultly

24 inexplicably, unexplainably, undefinably, bafflingly, unaccountably, **enigmatically;** mysteriously, mystically

25 **expressionlessly,** vacantly, blankly, emptily, woodenly, glassily, fishily

PREPS 26 **beyond,** past, above; **too deep for**

PHRS 27 I don't understand, I can't see, I don't see how, I don't see why, it beats me, you've got me, it's beyond me, it's too deep for me, it has me guessing, I don't have the foggiest idea, it's Greek to me, I'm clueless; I give up, I pass

523 LANGUAGE

<*communication by word*>

NOUNS 1 **language**, speech, tongue, *lingua* <L>, modern language, spoken language, natural language; talk, parlance, locution, phraseology, idiom, lingo; dialect; idiolect, personal usage, individual speech habits, parole; system of oral communication, individual speech, competence, langue; usage, use of words; language type; language family, subfamily, language group; area language, regional language; world language, universal language; words, lexicon; foreign language; reversification; second language, nonnative speaker

2 **dead language,** ancient language, lost language; archaic language, archaism, archaic speech; parent language; classical language; living language, vernacular; sacred language, sacred tongue

3 **mother tongue,** native language, native tongue, natal tongue, native speech, vernacular, first language

4 **standard language,** standard dialect, prestige dialect, acrolect; national language, official language; educated speech, educated language; literary language, written language, formal written language, formal language; classical language; correct English, good English, Standard English, World English, Global English, the King's English, the Queen's English, Received Standard, Received Pronunciation; business English, bucreaucratese

5 **nonformal language**, nonformal speech, nonformal standard speech, informal language, spoken language, colloquial language, colloquial speech, vernacular language, vernacular speech, vernacular; **slang;** colloquialism, colloquial usage, conversationalism, vernacularism; ordinary language, ordinary speech; nonformal English,

conversational English, colloquial English, English as it is spoken; fuzzword

6 **substandard language,** nonstandard language, nonformal language; vernacular language, vernacular, demotic language, vulgate, vulgar tongue, common speech, low language; uneducated speech, illiterate speech; substandard usage; basilect; constructed language

7 **dialect,** idiom; class dialect; regional dialect, local dialect; idiolect; subdialect; folk speech, folk dialect, patois; provincialism, localism, regionalism, regional accent; Canadian French, French Canadian; Pennsylvania Dutch, Pennsylvania German; Yankee, New England dialect; Brooklynese; Southern dialect, Southern twang; Black English, Afro-Americanese; Cockney; Yorkshire; Midland, Midland dialect; Anglo-Indian; Australian English; Gullah; Acadian, Cajun; dialect atlas, linguistic atlas; isogloss, bundle of isoglosses; speech community; linguistic community; linguistic ambience; speech island, linguistic island, relic area; click language; upspeak

8 <**idioms**> Anglicism, Briticism, Englishism; Americanism, Yankeeism; Westernism, Southernism; Gallicism, Frenchism; Irishism, Hibernicism; Canadianism, Scotticism, Germanism, Russianism, Latinism

9 **jargon, lingo, slang,** cant, argot, patois, patter, vernacular; vocabulary, terminology, nomenclature, phraseology; gobbledygook, mumbo jumbo, gibberish; nonformal language; taboo language, vulgar language; obscene language, scatology; doublespeak, bizspeak, mediaspeak, policyspeak, technospeak, technobabble, ecobabble; shoptalk

10 <**jargons**> academese, cinemese, collegese, constablese, ecobabble, economese, sociologese, legalese, pedagese, societyese, stagese, telegraphese, Varietyese, Wall Streetese, journalese, newspaperese, newspeak, officialese, federalese, Pentagonese, Washingtonese, medical Greek, medicalese, businessese, businessspeak, computerese, technobabble, technospeak, psychobabble; Yinglish, Franglais, Spanglish; Eurojargon; man-talk, bloke-talk, woman-talk, hen-talk; shoptalk; pig Latin; glossolalia; lavender language

11 **lingua franca,** international language, jargon, **pidgin,** trade language; auxiliary language, interlanguage; creolized language, creole language, creole; koine; diplomatic language, business language, language universal, linguistic universal; pidgin English, talkee-talkee, Bêche-de-Mer, Beach-la-mar; Kitchen Kaffir; Chinook jargon, Oregon jargon; Sabir; Esperanto; artificial language, sign language, sign, American Sign Language (ASL), Ameslan; Morse code, cryptography, cryptanalysis; computer language; shorthand, stenography; constructed language

12 **language family;** Indo-European, Indo-Iranian, Anatolian, Hellenic, Tocharian, Italic, Celtic, Germanic, Baltic, Slavic; Finno-Ugric; Afroasiatic, Hamito-Semitic; Sino-Tibetan; Austronesian

13 **linguistics,** linguistic science, science of language; glottology, glossology; linguistic analysis; linguistic terminology, metalanguage; philology; paleography; speech origins, language origins, bowwow theory, dingdong theory, pooh-pooh theory; language study, foreign-language study, linguistic theory

14 **language element,** morpheme, phoneme, grapheme; letter, alphabet, word, phrase, sentence; grammar, syntax, part of speech, word class; context clue

15 **linguist,** linguistic scientist, linguistician, linguistic scholar; philologist, philologer, philologian; philologaster; grammarian, grammatist; grammaticaster; etymologist, etymologer; lexicologist; lexicographer, glossographer, glossarist; phoneticist, phonetician, phonemicist, phonologist, orthoepist; dialectician, dialectologist; semanticist, semasiologist; paleographer; logophile; morphologist, orthographer

16 **polyglot,** linguist, **bilingual,** diglot, trilingual, multilingual

17 **colloquializer;** jargonist, jargoneer, jargonizer; slangster; native speaker

VERBS 18 **speak, talk,** use language, communicate orally, communicate verbally; use nonformal speech, colloquialize, vernacularize; jargon, jargonize, cant; patter; utter, verbalize, articulate; reach out

ADJS 19 **linguistic,** lingual, glottological, glossological; descriptive, structural, glottochronological, lexicostatistical, psycholinguistic, sociolinguistic, metalinguistic; philological; lexicological, lexicographic, lexicographical; syntactic, syntactical, grammatical; grammatic, semantic; phonetic, phonemic, phonological; morphological; morphophonemic, graphemic, paleographic, paleographical

20 **vernacular, colloquial,** conversational, unliterary, nonformal, informal, demotic, spoken, vulgar, vulgate; unstudied, familiar, common, everyday; jargonistic; substandard, uneducated, low

21 **jargonish,** jargonal; **slang,** slangy, nonformal;

taboo, four-letter, obscene, vulgar; scatological; rhyming slang

22 **idiomatic; dialect,** dialectal, dialectological; provincial, regional, local

23 <language types> affixing, agglutinative, analytic, body, click; contact, pidgin; endangered, fusional, incorporative; inflectional, inflected, isolating, monosyllabic, polysyllabic, polysynthetic, polytonic, symbolic, synthetic; tonal, tone

COMBINING FORMS 24 lingu-, linguo-, lingui-, gloss-, glosso-, glott-, glotto-

524 SPEECH

<spoken word>

NOUNS 1 **speech, talk,** the power of speech, the faculty of speech, the verbal faculty, the oral faculty, talking, speaking, **discourse,** colloquy, oral communication, vocal communication, voice communication, viva-voce communication, communication, verbal intercourse; palaver, prattle, gab, jaw-jaw; rapping, yakking, yakkety-yak; words, accents; chatter; conversation; elocution; language; the mirror of the soul

2 **utterance, speaking,** spoken language, vocalization, locution, phonation, phonetics; speech act, linguistic act, linguistic behavior; string, utterance string, sequence of phonemes, expression; voice, tongue, vocalism, parlance; word of mouth, parol, the spoken word; elevator talk; vocable, word

3 **remark, statement,** earful, crack, one's two cents' worth, word, say, saying, utterance, observation, reflection, expression; note, thought, mention; assertion, averment, allegation, affirmation, pronouncement, position, dictum; declaration; interjection, exclamation; question; answer; address, greeting, apostrophe; sentence, phrase; subjoinder, Parthian shot; shoutout

4 **articulateness**, articulacy, oracy, readiness of speech, facility of speech; eloquence; way with words, word power

5 **articulation,** uttering, phonation, voicing, giving voice, vocalization; **pronunciation,** enunciation, utterance; delivery, attack

6 **intonation, inflection, modulation;** intonation pattern, intonation contour, intonation of foice, inflection of voice, speech tune, speech melody; suprasegmental, suprasegmental phoneme; tone, pitch; pitch accent, tonic accent

7 manner of speaking, way of saying, mode of expression, mode of speech; **tone of voice,** voice, *voce* <Ital>, tone; speaking voice, voice quality, vocal style, timbre; voice qualifier; paralinguistic communication

8 **accent,** regional accent, brogue, twang, burr, drawl, broad accent, trill, whine, nasality, stridor; **foreign accent;** guttural accent, clipped accent; broken English; speech impediment, speech defect; speech community, isogloss; speech therapy

9 **pause**, juncture, open juncture, close juncture; terminal, clause terminal, rising terminal, falling terminal; sandhi; word boundary, clause boundary

10 accent, accentuation, stress accent; **emphasis, stress,** word stress; ictus, beat, rhythmical stress; rhythm, rhythmic pattern, cadence; prosody, prosodics, metrics; stress pattern; level of stress; primary stress, secondary stress, tertiary stress, weak stress

11 vowel quantity, **quantity,** mora; long vowel, short vowel, full vowel, reduced vowel

12 **speech sound,** phone, vocable, phonetic unit, phonetic entity; puff of air, aspiration; stream of air, airstream, glottalic airstream; articulation, manner of articulation; stop, plosive, explosive, mute, check, occlusive, affricate, continuant, liquid, lateral, nasal; point of articulation, place of articulation; voice, voicing; sonority; palatalization, labialization, pharyngealization, glottalization; surd, voiceless sound; sonant, voiced sound; consonant; semivowel, glide, transition sound; velar, guttural, voiced consonant, frictionless continuant, labial, labiodental, labionasal, spirant, sibilant, aspirate, glottal stop, fricative, polyphone; vocalic, syllabic nucleus, syllabic peak, peak; vocoid; vowel; monophthong, diphthong, triphthong; syllable; phoneme, segmental phoneme, morphophoneme, digraph; modification, assimilation, dissimilation; allophone; parasitic vowel, epenthetic vowel, svarabhakti vowel, prothetic vowel; vowel gradation, vowel mutation; doubletalk

13 **phonetics,** articulatory phonetics, acoustic phonetics; phonology; morphophonemics, morphophonology; orthoepy; phonetic law; pronunciation; phonography; sound shift; umlaut, mutation, ablaut, gradation; rhotacism, betacism; Grimm's law, Verner's law, Grassmann's law

14 **phonetician,** phonetist, phoneticist; orthoepist

15 **ventriloquism,** ventriloquy; ventriloquist

16 talking machine, sonovox, voder, vocoder

17 **talker, speaker,** sayer, utterer, patterer; chatterbox; conversationalist

18 **speech organ,** vocal organ, articulator, voice, mouth; tongue, apex, tip, blade, dorsum, back; vocal cords, vocal bands, vocal processes, vocal folds; voice box, larynx, Adam's apple; syrinx; arytenoid cartilages; glottis, vocal chink,

epiglottis; lips, teeth, palate, hard palate, soft palate, velum, alveolus, teeth ridge, alveolar ridge, uvula; nasal cavity, oral cavity; pharynx, throat cavity, pharyngeal cavity

VERBS **19** **speak, talk;** patter the tongue, wag the tongue; mouth; chatter; converse; declaim

20 <nonformal> **yak,** yap, yakkety-yak, gab, spiel, chin, jaw, shoot off one's mouth, shoot the breeze, bat one's gums, bend one's ear, make chin music, rattle away, talk a blue streak, talk someone's ear off, flap one's jaw, natter, spout off, sound off

21 **speak up,** speak out, speak one's piece, speak one's mind, pipe up, open one's mouth, open one's lips, say out, say loud and clear, say out loud, sound off, lift one's voice, break silence, find one's tongue; take the floor; put in a word, get in a word edgewise; have one's say, put in one's two cents worth, relieve oneself, get a load off one's mind, give vent to, give voice to, pour one's heart out

22 **say,** utter, breathe, sound, voice, vocalize, phonate, articulate, enunciate, pronounce, lip, give voice, give tongue, give utterance; whisper; express, give expression, verbalize, put in words, find words to express; word, formulate, put into words, couch, phrase; present, deliver; emit, give, raise, let out, out with, come out with, give out with, put forth, set forth, pour forth; throw off, fling off; chorus, chime; tell, communicate; convey, impart, disclose; reach out, contact

23 **state,** declare, assert, aver, affirm, asserverate, allege; say, make a statement, send a message; announce, tell the world; relate, recite; quote; proclaim, nuncupate

24 **remark, comment,** observe, note; mention, speak, let drop, let fall, say by the way, make mention of; refer to, allude to, touch on, make reference to, call attention to; muse, reflect; opine; interject; blurt, blurt out, exclaim

25 <utter in a certain way> murmur, mutter, mumble, whisper, breathe, buzz, sigh; gasp, pant; exclaim, yell; sing, lilt, warble, chant, coo, chirp; pipe, flute; squeak; cackle, crow; bark, yelp, yap; growl, snap, snarl; hiss, sibilate; grunt, snort; roar, bellow, blare, trumpet, bray, blat, bawl, thunder, rumble, boom; scream, shriek, screech, squeal, squawk, yawp, squall; whine, wail, keen, blubber, sob; drawl, twang

26 **address, speak to,** talk to, bespeak, beg the ear of; appeal to, invoke; apostrophize; approach; buttonhole, take by the lapel; take aside, talk to in private, closet oneself with; accost, call to, hail, halloo, greet, salute, speak, speak fair

27 pass one's lips, escape one's lips, fall from the lips

28 inflect, modulate, intonate

ADJS **29** **speech; language, linguistic,** lingual; spoken, uttered, said, vocalized, voiced, verbalized, pronounced, sounded, articulated, enunciated; vocal, voiceful; oral, verbal, unwritten, *viva voce* <L>, nuncupative, parol

30 **phonetic,** phonic; articulatory, acoustic; intonated; pitched, pitch, tonal, tonic, oxytone, oxytonic, paroxytonic, barytone; **accented, stressed,** strong, heavy; unaccented, unstressed, weak, light, pretonic, atonic, posttonic; articulated; stopped, muted, checked, occlusive, nasal, nasalized, twangy, continuant, liquid, lateral, affricated; alveolabial, alveolar, alveolingual; low, high, mid, open, broad, close; front, back, central; wide, lax, tense, narrow; voiced, sonant, voiceless, surd; rounded, unrounded, flat; aspirated; labialized; palatalized, soft; unpalatalized, hard; pharyngealized, glottalized; velar, guttural; burring, frictionless, labial, spirant, sibilant, fricative, polyphonic, polyphonous, digraphic; consonant, consonantal, semivowel, glide, vowel; vowellike, vocoid, vocalic, syllabic; monophthongal, diphthongal, triphthongal; phonemic, allophonic; assimilated, dissimilated

31 **speaking, talking;** articulate, talkative; eloquent, well-spoken; true-speaking, clean-speaking, plain-speaking, plainspoken, outspoken, free-speaking, free-spoken, loud-speaking, loud-spoken, soft-speaking, soft-spoken; English-speaking

32 ventriloquial, ventriloquistic

ADVS **33** orally, **vocally,** verbally, by word of mouth, *viva voce* <L>; from the lips of, from his own mouth

525 IMPERFECT SPEECH

<speech disability>

NOUNS **1** **speech defect,** speech impediment, speech difficulty, impairment of speech, speech disability; dysarthria, dysphasia, dysphrasia; dyslalia, dyslogia; idioglossia, idiolalia; broken speech, cracked voice, broken voice, broken tones, broken accents; indistinct speech, blurred speech, muzzy speech; loss of voice, aphonia; nasalization, nasal tone, nasal accent, twang, nasal twang, talking through one's nose; falsetto, childish treble, artificial voice; shake, quaver, tremor; lisp, lisping; hiss, sibilation, lallation; croak, choked voice, hawking voice; crow; harshness, dysphonia, hoarseness; voicelessness; speech therapy

2 **inarticulateness,** inarticulacy, inarticulation; thickness of speech

3 **stammering, stuttering,** hesitation, faltering, traulism, dysphemia; palilalia; stammer, stutter

4 **mumbling, muttering,** maundering; unintelligible speech; droning, drone; mumble, mutter; jabber, jibber, gibber, gibbering, gabble; whispering, whisper, susurration; mouthing; murmuring

5 **mispronunciation,** misspeaking, cacology, cacoepy; lallation, lambdacism, paralambdacism; rhotacism, pararhotacism; gammacism; mytacism; corruption, language pollution

6 **aphasia, agraphia;** aphrasia, aphrasia paranoica; **aphonia,** loss of speech, aphonia clericorum, hysterical aphonia, stage fright, aphonia paralytica, aphonia paranoica, spastic aphonia, mutism, muteness; voiceless speech, sign language

VERBS 7 **speak poorly,** talk incoherently, be unable to put two words together; have an impediment in one's speech, have a bone in one's throat; speak thickly; croak; lisp; shake, quaver; drawl; mince, clip one's words; lose one's voice, get stage fright, clank, clank up, freeze, be struck dumb

8 **stammer, stutter,** stammer out; hesitate, falter, halt, mammer, stumble; hem, haw, hum, hum and haw, hem and haw

9 **mumble, mutter,** maunder; drone, drone on; swallow one's words, speak drunkenly, speak incoherently; jabber, gibber, gabble; splutter, sputter; blubber, sob; whisper, susurrate; murmur; babble; mouth

10 **nasalize,** whine, speak through one's nose, twang, snuffle

11 **mispronounce,** misspeak, missay, murder the King's English, murder the Queen's English

ADJS 12 <imperfectly spoken> inarticulate, indistinct, blurred, muzzy, unintelligible; **mispronounced;** shaky, shaking, quavering, breaking, cracked, tremulous, titubant; drawling, drawly; lisping; throaty, guttural, thick, velar; stifled, choked, choking, strangled; nasal, twangy, breathy, adenoidal, snuffling; croaking, hawking; harsh, dysphonic, hoarse

13 **stammering, stuttering,** halting, hesitating, faltering, stumbling, balbutient; aphasic; aphrasic; aphonic, dumb, mute

526 WORD

<terms, vocabulary>

NOUNS 1 **word,** free form, minimum free form, semanteme, **term,** keyword, name, expression, locution, linguistic form, lexeme; written unit; content word, function word; *logos* <Gk>, *verbum* <L>; verbalism, vocable, utterance, articulation; usage; syllable, polysyllable; homonym, homophone, homograph; monosyllable; synonym; related word; metonym; antonym; easy word, hard word; part of speech, word class; n-gram

2 **root,** etymon, primitive; eponym; derivative, derivation; cognate; doublet

3 **morphology,** morphemics; morphophonemics; morpheme; morph, allomorph; bound morpheme, bound form, free morpheme free form; difference of form, formal contrast; accidence; **inflection,** conjugation, declension; paradigm; derivation, word formation; formative; root, radical; theme, stem; word element, combining form; **affix, suffix, prefix,** infix; proclitic, enclitic; affixation, infixation, suffixation, prefixation; morphemic analysis, immediate constituent analysis, IC analysis, cutting; morphophonemic analysis

4 **word form,** formation, construction; back formation; clipped word; spoonerism; compound; endocentric compound, exocentric compound; acronym, acrostic; paronym, conjugate; proclitic, enclitic

5 **technical term,** technicality; jargon word; jargon

6 **barbarism, corruption,** vulgarism, impropriety, taboo word, dirty word, four-letter word, swear word, naughty word, bad word, obscenity, expletive; fuzzword; colloquialism, **slang,** localism; split infinitive

7 **loan word,** borrowing, borrowed word, paronym; loan translation, calque; foreignism

8 **neologism,** neology, neoterism, new word, new term, newfangled expression; **coinage;** new sense, new meaning; nonce word; ghost word

9 **catchword,** catch phrase, shibboleth, slogan, cry; pet expression, byword, cliché; **buzzword,** vogue word, fad word, in-word; euphemism, code word; commonplace, hackneyed expression

10 long word, **hard word**, jawbreaker, jawtwister, two-dollar word, five-dollar word, polysyllable; sesquipedalian, sesquipedalia <pl>; lexiphanicism, grandiloquence

11 hybrid word, hybrid; macaronicism, macaronic; hybridism, contamination; blendword, blend, portmanteau word, portmanteau, portmantologism, telescope word, counterword; ghost word

12 **archaism,** archaicism, antiquated word, antiquated expression; obsoletism, obsolete

13 **vocabulary,** lexis, words, word stock, wordhoard, stock of words; phraseology; thesaurus, Roget's; lexicon

14 **lexicology; lexicography,** lexigraphy, glossography; onomastics, toponymics; meaning, semantics, semasiology; denotation, connotation

15 **lexicographer,** lexicologist, linguist, philologist, glossographer, onomastician, semanticist, etymologist, grammarian, wordsmith, linguistic scientist

16 **etymology,** derivation, **word origin,** origin, word history, semantic history, etymon; historical linguistics, comparative linguistics; eponymy; folk etymology

17 echoic word, onomatopoeic word, onomatope; onomatopoeia; bowwow theory

18 **neologist,** word-coiner, neoterist; phraser, phrasemaker, phrasemonger; word nerd

ADJS **19** **verbal,** vocabular, vocabulary

20 **lexical**, lexicologic, lexicological; lexigraphic, lexigraphical, lexicographical, lexicographic; glossographic, glossographical; etymological, etymologic, derivational; onomastic, onomatologic; onomasiological; echoic, onomatopoeic; conjugate, paronymous, paronymic

21 neological, neoterical

22 **morphological,** morphemic; morphophonemic; inflective, inflectional, paradigmatic, derivational; affixal, prefixal, infixal, suffixal

COMBINING FORMS **23** log-, logo-, onomato-, -onym, -onymy

527 NOMENCLATURE

<*names, naming*>

NOUNS **1** **nomenclature,** terminology, orismology, glossology, vocabulary, lexicon; onomatology, onomastics; toponymics, toponymy, place-names, place-naming; antonomasia; polyonymy; taxonomy, classification, ontology, systematics, cladistics, biosystematics, cytotaxonomy, binomial nomenclature, binomialism, Linnaean method, trinomialism; kingdom, phylum, class, order, family, genus, species

2 **naming,** calling, **denomination,** appellation, designation, designating, styling, terming, definition, identification; christening, baptism; dubbing; nicknaming

3 **name,** appellation, appellative, denomination, common name, designation, style, heading, *nomen* <L>, cognomen, cognomination, full name; proper name, proper noun; moniker, handle; title, honorific; empty title, empty name; label, tag; epithet, byword; scientific name, trinomen, trinomial name, binomen, binomial name; hyponym; tautonym; typonym; middle name; eponym; namesake; secret name, cryptonym, euonym, password; professional title; title of respect, title of address; military title; place name, toponym; trade name, trademark; subject heading

4 **first name,** forename, Christian name, given name, baptismal name; **middle name**

5 **surname, last name,** family name, cognomen, second name, byname; maiden name; married name; patronym, matronym

6 <Latin terms> *praenomen, nomen, agnomen, cognomen*

7 **nickname,** sobriquet, byname, cognomen; epithet, agnomen; pet name, diminutive, hypocoristic, affectionate name

8 **alias, pseudonym,** anonym, assumed name, false name, fictitious name, *nom de guerre* <Fr>; pen name, nom de plume; stage name, *nom de théâtre* <Fr>, professional name; John Doe, Jane Doe, Richard Roe; screen name

9 **misnomer,** wrong name

10 **signature,** sign manual, **autograph,** hand, John Hancock; mark, mark of signature, cross, crisscross, X; initials; subscription; countersignature, countersign, countermark, counterstamp; endorsement; visa; monogram, cipher, device; seal, sigil, signet

VERBS **11** **name,** denominate, nominate, designate, call, term, style, dub, color; specify; define, identify; title, entitle; label, tag; **nickname;** christen, baptize

12 **misname,** misnomer, miscall, misterm, misdesignate

13 **be called,** be known by, be known as, go by, go as, go by the name of, go under the name of, pass under the name of, bear the name of, rejoice in the name of; go under an assumed name, go under a false name, have an alias

ADJS **14** **named, called,** yclept, styled, titled, denominated, monikered, denominate, **known as,** known by the name of, designated, termed, dubbed, identified as; christened, baptized; what one may well call; mononymous

15 **nominal,** cognominal; **titular,** in name only, nominative, formal; so-called, quasi; would-be, *soi-disant* <Fr>; self-called, self-styled, self-christened; honorific; agnominal, epithetic, epithetical; hypocoristic, diminutive; by name, by whatever name, under any other name; **alias,** also known as (aka)

16 denominative, nominative, appellative; eponymous, eponymic

17 **terminological,** nomenclatural, orismological; onomastic; toponymic, toponymous; taxonomic, classificatory, binomial, Linnaean, trinomial

COMBINING FORMS **18** onomato-, -onym, -onymy

528 ANONYMITY

<namelessness>

NOUNS 1 **anonymity, anonymousness,** namelessness; **incognito;** cover, cover name; code name; anonym; unknown quantity, no-name; Unknown Soldier; Anon.

2 what's-its-name, what's-his-name, whatshisname, what's-his-face, what's-her-name, what-you-may-call-it, whatchamacallit, what-you-may-call-'em, what-d'ye-call-'em, what-d'ye-call-it, whatzit; *je ne sais quoi* <Fr>, I don't know what; such-and-such; so-and-so, certain person, X, Mr. X; you-know-who

ADJS 3 **anonymous,** anon; nameless, unnamed, unidentified, undesignated, unspecified, innominate, without a name, unknown; undefined; unacknowledged; **incognito;** cryptonymous, cryptonymic; lesser-known

529 PHRASE

<multiword expression>

NOUNS 1 **phrase, expression,** locution, utterance, usage, term, verbalism; word-group, fixed expression, construction, endocentric construction, headed group, syntagm; syntactic structure; noun phrase, compound noun, verb phrase, verb complex, adverbial phrase, adjectival phrase, prepositional phrase; conditional phrase; phrasal verb; collocation; compound, multiword lexical unit (MLU), multiword expression (MWE); clause, coordinate clause, subordinate clause, independent clause; sentence, period, periodic sentence; paragraph; idiom, idiotism, phrasal idiom; turn of phrase, turn of expression, peculiar expression, manner of speaking, way of speaking; set phrase, set term; conventional phrase, common phrase, standard phrase; phraseogram, phraseograph; maxim, adage, moral, proverb, slogan, motto, quotation, quote, sound bite

2 **diction, phrasing;** phraseology, choice of words, wording

3 **phraser, phrasemaker,** phrasemonger, phraseman

ADJS 4 **phrasal,** phrase; phrasey

5 in set phrases, in set terms, in good set terms, in round terms

530 GRAMMAR

<language rules>

NOUNS 1 **grammar,** rules of language, linguistic structure, syntactic structure, sentence structure; grammaticalness, well-formedness, grammaticality, grammatical theory; traditional grammar, school grammar; descriptive grammar, structural grammar; case grammar; phrase-structure grammar; generative grammar, transformational grammar, transformational generative grammar; comparative grammar, relational grammar; tagmemic analysis; glossematics; stratificational grammar; parsing, construing, grammatical analysis; morphology; phonology, good grammar, good English, Standard English, correct grammar, business English; style guide, style sheet; controlled vocabulary, defining vocabulary; smart quotes

2 **syntax,** structure, syntactic structure, word order, word arrangement; syntactics, syntactic analysis; immediate constituent analysis, IC analysis, cutting; phrase structure; surface structure, shallow structure, deep structure, underlying structure; levels, ranks, strata; tagmeme, form-function unit, slot, filler, slot and filler; function, subject, predicate, complement, object, direct object, indirect object, modifier, qualifier, sentence modifier, construction modifier, appositive, attribute, attributive; inflection, diminuitive, intensive, formative; asyndeton, syndeton, apposition, hypotaxis, parataxis

3 **part of speech,** form class, major form class, function class; function word, empty word, form word; adjective, adjectival, attributive, attributive adjective, derived adjective, predicate adjective; adverb, adverbial, sentence adverb; **preposition** <see list>; verbal adjective, gerundive; participle, present participle, past participle, perfect participle; **conjunction** <see list>, subordinating conjunction, coordinating conjunction, conjunctive adverb, adversative conjunction, copula, copulative, copulative conjunction, correlative conjunction, disjunctive, disjunctive conjunction; interjection, exclamatory noun, exclamatory adjective; particle; adjective phrase, adverb phrase; linking word

4 **verb,** transitive, transitive verb, intransitive, intransitive verb, action verb, impersonal verb, neuter verb, deponent verb, defective verb, reflexive verb, irregular verb; predicate; finite verb; linking verb, copula; helping verb; verbal, verbid, nonfinite verb form; infinitive; auxiliary verb, auxiliary, modal auxiliary; verb phrase, phrasal verb; present participle, past participle, perfect participle

5 **noun; pronoun** <see list>, indefinite pronoun, personal pronoun, possessive pronoun, reflexive pronoun, relative pronoun; substantive, substantival, common noun, proper noun,

concrete noun, abstract noun, collective noun, quotation noun, compound noun, possessive noun, hypostasis, adherent noun, adverbial noun, attributive noun; verbal noun, gerund; nominal; noun phrase; mass noun, count noun, countable noun, uncount noun, uncountable noun; aptronym, contronym

6 **article,** definite article, indefinite article; determiner, noun determiner, determinative, post-determiner

7 **person;** first person; second person, proximate; third person; fourth person, obviative

8 number; singular, dual, trial, plural

9 **case;** common case, subject case, nominative; object case, objective case, accusative, dative, possessive case, genitive; local case, locative, essive, superessive, inessive, adessive, abessive, lative, allative, illative, sublative, elative, ablative, delative, terminative, approximative, prolative, perlative, translative; comitative, instrumental, prepositional, vocative; oblique case

10 **gender,** masculine, feminine, neuter, common gender; grammatical gender, natural gender; animate, inanimate

11 **mood,** mode; indicative, subjunctive, imperative, conditional, potential, obligative, permissive, optative, jussive

12 **tense;** present; historical present; past, preterit, preterite; aorist; imperfect; future; perfect, present perfect, future perfect; past perfect, pluperfect; progressive tense, durative; point tense

13 **aspect;** perfective, imperfective, inchoative, iterative, frequentative, desiderative

14 **voice;** active voice, active, passive voice, passive; middle voice, middle; medio-passive; reflexive

15 **punctuation, punctuation mark** <see list>; **diacritical mark or sign** <see list>, accent; **reference mark** <see list>, reference; point, tittle; stop, end stop

VERBS 16 grammaticize; parse, analyze; inflect, conjugate, decline; punctuate, mark, point; parenthesize, hyphenate, bracket; diagram, notate

ADJS 17 **grammatical, syntactical,** formal, structural; correct, well-formed; tagmemic, glossematic; functional; substantive, nominal, pronominal; verbal, transitive, intransitive; linking, copulative; attributive, adjectival, adverbal, participial; prepositional, post-positional; conjunctive

18 **conjunction**

according as
afore
after
against
albeit
also
although
an
and
and/or
as
as far as
as how
as if
as long as
as soon as
as though
as well as
because
before
being
both
but
'cause
considering
directly
either
ere
ergo
except
excepting
for
for and
forasmuch as
fore
gin
how
howbeit
however
if
immediately
in case
in order that
inasmuch as
insofar as
insomuch as
instantly
lest
let alone
like
much as
much less
nay
neither
never mind
nor
notwithstanding
now
once
once that
only
or
other than
otherwise
plus
provided
providing
rather than
save
saving
seeing
since
so
sobeit
so long as
so that
still
still less
supposing
syne
than
that
then
tho
though
till
unless
unlike
until
well
what
when
whence
whenever
whensoever
where
whereabout
whereabouts
whereas
whereat
whereby
wherefore
wherefrom
wherein
whereinto
whereof
whereon
whereso
wheresoever
wherethrough
whereto
whereunder
whereunto
whereupon
wherever
wherewith
whether
while
whilst
whither
why
without
yet

19 diacritical mark or sign

acute accent <´>
breve <˘>
cedilla <¸>
circumflex accent <ˆ>
diaeresis, umlaut <¨>
grave accent <`>
hacek, wedge, caron <ˇ>
krozek <°>
ligature <æ>
macron <¯>
schwa <ə>
tilde <~>

20 preposition

a
à la
abaft
aboard
about
above
absent
according to
across
adown
afore
after
against
agin
aloft
along
alongside
amid
amidst
among
amongst
an
anent
apart from
après
apropos
around
as
as of
as per
as regards
as to
as well as
aside
aside from
aslant
astraddle
astride
at
athwart
atop
bar
barring
batting
because
because of
before
behind
below
beneath
beside
besides
between
betwixt
beyond
but
but for
by
chez
circa
concerning
considering
contra
contrary to
cross
cum
despite
down
due to
during
ere
ex
except
except for
excepting
excluding
exclusive of
failing
following
for
forby, forbye
fore
forth
foul of
fro
from
given
hear
in
in between
in memoriam
in re
including
inclusive of
inside
inside of
instead of
into
irrespective of
less
like
maugre
mid
midst
minus
modulo
near
neath
next
next to
nigh
notwithstanding
o'
o'er
of
off
off of
on
onto
opposite
or
out
out of
outside
outside of
over
over against
over and above
owing to
pace
past
pending
per
plus
preparatory to
previous to
prior to
pro
pursuant to
qua
rather than
re
regarding
regardless of
relative to
respecting
round
sans
save
saving
since
subsequent to
than
thanks to
the
thorough
thro
throughout
thru
thwart
till
times
to
together with
touching
toward
tween, 'tween
twixt
under
underneath
unless
unlike
until
unto
up
up and down
up to
upon
upside
versus
via
vice
vis-à-vis
wanting
while
with
withal
within
without
worth

21 pronoun

all
another
any
anybody
anyone
anything
both
each
each other
either
few
he
her
hers
herself
him
himself
his
how
I
it
its
itself
many
me
mine
most
much

my
myself
neither
no one
nobody
none
nothing
one
one another
other
our
ours
ourselves
several
she
some
somebody
someone
something
that
their
theirs
them
themselves
these
they
this
those
us
we
what
whatever
when
where
which
whichever
who
whoever
whom
whomever
whose
why
you
your
yours
yourself

22 **punctuation mark**
ampersand <&>
angle brackets <<>>
apostrophe <’>
back slash <\>
braces <{}>
brackets, square brackets <[]>
colon <:>
comma <,>
decimal point <.>
ellipsis, suspension periods <...>, <***>
em dash <—>
en dash <–>
exclamation mark, exclamation point <!>
guillemets <<< >>>
hyphen <->, hard hyphen
interrobang <!?>
parentheses, parens <()>
period, full stop <Brit>, point, decimal point, dot <.>
question mark, interrogation mark <?>
quotation marks, quotes <“”>
semicolon <;>
single quotation marks, single quotes <‘’>
virgule, diagonal, solidus, slash mark, forward slash </>

23 **reference mark**
asterisk, star <*>
asterism <***>
bullet, centered dot <·>
caret <^>
dagger, obelisk <†>
ditto mark <">
double dagger, diesis <‡>
double prime <">
index, fist <☞>
leaders <......>
obelus <†>
paragraph <¶>
parallels <||>
prime <'>
section <§>
swung dash <~>

531 UNGRAMMATICALNESS

<not conforming to language rules>

NOUNS 1 **ungrammaticalness,** bad grammar, faulty grammar, faulty syntax; lack of concord, lack of agreement, incorrect usage, faulty reference, misplaced modifier, dangling modifier, shift of tense, shift of structure, anacoluthon, faulty subordination, faulty comparison, faulty coordination, faulty punctuation, lack of parallelism, sentence fragment, comma fault, comma splice; abuse of terms, corruption of speech, broken speech

2 **solecism,** ungrammaticism, **misusage,** missaying, misconstruction, barbarism, infelicity; corruption; antiphrasis, spoonerism, malapropism

VERBS 3 solecize, commit a solecism, use faulty grammar, use inappropriate grammar, ignore grammar, violate grammar, murder the King's English, murder the Queen's English

ADJS 4 **ungrammatic, ungrammatical,** solecistic, solecistical, **incorrect,** barbarous; faulty, erroneous; infelicitous, improper; careless, slovenly, slipshod; loose, imprecise

532 DICTION

<word choice and usage>

NOUNS 1 **diction,** words, wordage, verbiage, word-usage, usage, use of words, choice of words, formulation, way of putting, way of couching, word garment, word dressing; rhetoric, speech, talk; language, dialect, parlance, locution, expression, grammar; idiom; composition

2 **style;** mode, manner, strain, vein; fashion, way; rhetoric; manner of speaking, mode of expression, literary style, style of writing, command of language, command of idiom, form of speech, expression of ideas; feeling for words, feeling for language, way with words, sense of language, *Sprachgefühl* <Ger>; gift of gab, gift of the gab, blarney, the blarney; the power of expression, the grace of expression; linguistic tact, linguistic finesse; personal style; mannerism, trick, pecularity; affectation; editorial style; inflation, exaggeration, grandiloquence; the grand style, the sublime style, the sublime; the plain style; **stylistics,** stylistic analysis

3 stylist, master of style; rhetorician, rhetor, rhetorizer; mannerist; wordsmith; phrasemonger

VERBS 4 **phrase,** express, find a phrase for, give expression to, give words to, word, state, frame, conceive, style, couch, **put into words,** put in words, clothe in words, embody in words, couch in terms, express by words, express in words, find words to express, find words for; put, present, set out; formulate, formularize; paragraph; rhetorize

ADJS 5 **phrased,** expressed, worded, formulated, styled, put, presented, couched; stylistic, overdone

533 ELEGANCE

<stylish language>

NOUNS **1** **elegance,** elegancy; grace, gracefulness, gracility; taste, tastefulness, good taste; correctness, seemliness, comeliness, propriety, aptness, fittingness; refinement, precision, **exactitude**, lapidary quality, finish; discrimination, choice; restraint; polish, terseness, neatness; smoothness, flow, fluency; felicity, felicitousness, ease; clarity, clearness, lucidity, limpidity, pellucidity, perspicuity; distinction, dignity; purity, chastity, chasteness; plainness, straightforwardness, directness, simplicity, naturalness, unaffectedness, Atticism, unadorned simplicity, Attic quality; classicism, classicalism; well-rounded periods, well-turned periods, flowing periods; **the right word**, the right word in the right place, right word at the right time, *mot juste* <Fr>; appropriateness

2 harmony, proportion, symmetry, balance, equilibrium, order, orderedness, measure, measuredness, concinnity; rhythm; **euphony,** sweetness, beauty

3 <affected elegance> affectation, affectedness, studiedness, pretentiousness, mannerism, posiness <Brit>, manneredness, artifice, artfulness, artificiality, unnaturalness; euphuism, Gongorism, Marinism; preciousness, preciosity; euphemism; purism; overelegance, overelaboration, overniceness, overrefinement, hyperelegance

4 purist, classicist, Atticist, plain stylist

5 **euphuist**, Gongorist, Marinist, *précieux* <Fr>, *précieuse* <Fr>; phrasemaker, phrasemonger

ADJS **6** **elegant,** tasteful, graceful, polished, finished, round, terse; neat, trim, refined, exact, lapidary, lapidarian; restrained; clear, lucid, limpid, pellucid, perspicuous; simple, unaffected, natural, unlabored, fluent, flowing, easy; pure, chaste; plain, straightforward, direct, unadorned, gracile, no-frills, vanilla, plain vanilla; classic, classical; Attic, Ciceronian, Augustan

7 appropriate, fit, fitting, just, proper, correct, seemly, comely; felicitous, happy, apt, well-chosen; **well-put,** well-expressed, inspired

8 harmonious, balanced, symmetrical, orderly, ordered, measured, concinnate, concinnous; euphonious, **euphonic**, euphonical, sweet; smooth, tripping, smooth-sounding, fluent, flowing, fluid; classical

9 <affectedly elegant> affected, euphuistic, euphuistical; elaborate, elaborated; pretentious, mannered, artificial, unnatural, posy <Brit>, studied; precious, *précieux, précieuse* <Fr>, deluxe, overnice, overrefined, overelegant, overelaborate, hyperelegant; Gongoristic, Gongoresque, Marinistic

534 INELEGANCE

<simple language>

NOUNS **1** **inelegance,** inelegancy; inconcinnity, infelicity; clumsiness, cumbrousness, clunkiness, klutziness, leadenness, heavy-handedness, ham-handedness, ham-fistedness, heavy-footedness, heaviness, stiltedness, ponderousness, unwieldiness; sesquipedalianism, sesquipedality; turgidity, bombasticness, pompousness; gracelessness, ungracefulness; tastelessness, bad taste, impropriety, indecorousness, unseemliness; **incorrectness**, impurity; vulgarity, vulgarism, barbarism, barbarousness, coarseness, unrefinement, roughness, grossness, rudeness, crudeness, uncouthness; dysphemism; solecism; cacology, poor diction; cacophony, uneuphoniousness, harshness; loose construction, slipshod construction, ill-balanced sentences; lack of finish, lack of polish

ADJS **2** **inelegant,** clumsy, clunky, klutzy, heavy-handed, heavy-footed, ham-handed, ham-fisted, graceless, ungraceful, inconcinnate, inconcinnous, infelicitous, unfelicitous; tasteless, in bad taste, offensive to ears polite; **incorrect**, improper; indecorous, unseemly, uncourtly, undignified; unpolished, unrefined; impure, unclassical; vulgar, barbarous, barbaric, rude, crude, uncouth, Doric, outlandish; low, gross, coarse, dysphemistic, doggerel; cacologic, cacological, cacophonous, uneuphonious, harsh, ill-sounding; solecistic

3 stiff, **stilted, formal,** Latinate, labored, ponderous, elephantine, lumbering, cumbrous, leaden, heavy, unwieldy, sesquipedalian, inkhorn, turgid, bombastic, pompous; forced, awkward, cramped, halting; crabbed

535 PLAIN SPEECH

<clear language>

NOUNS **1** **plain speech,** plain speaking, plainspokenness, plain style, unadorned style, gracility, **plain English,** plain words, common speech, vernacular, household words, words of one syllable; plainness, simpleness, simplicity; more matter and less art; soberness, restrainedness; severity, austerity; spareness, leanness, baldness, bareness, starkness, unadornedness, naturalness, unaffectedness; directness, straightforwardness, calling a spade a spade, mincing no words, making no bones about it; unimaginativeness, prosaicness, matter-of-factness, prosiness, unpoeticalness; homespun, rustic style; candor, frankness, openness

VERBS 2 **speak plainly,** waste no words, call a spade a spade, come to the point, lay it on the line, not beat about the bush, mince no words, make no bones about it, talk turkey

ADJS 3 **plain-speaking,** simple-speaking; plain, common; plainspoken; simple, unadorned, unvarnished, pure, neat; sober, severe, austere, ascetic, spare, lean, bald, bare, stark, Spartan; natural, unaffected; direct, straightforward, woman-to-woman, man-to-man, one-on-one; commonplace, homely, homespun, rustic; candid, up-front, frank, straight-out, open; prosaic, prosing, prosy; unpoetical, unimaginative, dull, dry, matter-of-fact; point-blank

ADVS 4 **plainly,** simply, naturally, unaffectedly, matter-of-factly; in plain words, plainspokenly, **in plain English,** in words of one syllable; directly, point-blank, to the point; candidly, frankly

PHRS 5 read my lips, I'll spell it out

536 FIGURE OF SPEECH

<nonliteral language>

NOUNS 1 **figure of speech** <see list>, figure, image, trope, turn of expression, manner of speaking, way of speaking, ornament, literary device, device, flourish, flower; purple passage; imagery, nonliterality, nonliteralness, figurativeness, figurative language; figured style, florid style, flowery style, Gongorism, floridity, euphuism

VERBS 2 metaphorize, figure; similize; personify, personalize; symbolize

ADJS 3 **figurative,** tropologic, tropological; **metaphorical**, trolatitious; allusive, referential; mannered, figured, ornamented, flowery

ADVS 4 **figuratively,** tropologically; **metaphorically;** symbolically; figuratively speaking, so to say, so to speak, in a manner of speaking, as it were

5 **figure of speech**

adynaton
agnomination
alliteration
allusion
anacoluthon
anadiplosis
analogy
anaphora
anapodoton
anastrophe
antanaclasis
anthimeria
antimetabole
antiphrasis
antisthecon
antithesis
antonomasia
aphaersis
apocope
apophasis
aporia
aposiopesis
apostrophe
auxesis
catachresis
chiasmus
circumlocution
climax
congeries
conversion
correctio
ecphonesis
ellipsis
emphasis
enallage
epanalepsis
epanaphora
epanodos
epanorthosis
epenthesis
epidiplosis
epiphora
epistrophe
epizeuxis
eroteme
exclamation
gemination
gradatio
hendiadys
hypallage
hyperbaton
hyperbole
hypozeugma
hypozeuxis
hysteron proteron
inversion
irony
isocolon
kenning
litotes
malapropism
meiosis
metalepsis
metaphor
metathesis
metonymy
mixed metaphor
occupatio
onomatopoeia, onomatopy
oxymoron
paradiastole
paradox
paragoge
paralepsis
paregmenon
parenthesis
periphrasis
personification
pleonasm
ploce
polyptoton
polysyndeton
preterition
prolepsis
prosopopoeia
prosthesis
regression
repetition
rhetorical question
sarcasm
scesis onamaton
simile, similitude
spoonerism
syllepsis
symploce
syncope
synecdoche
tautology
Wellerism
zeugma

537 CONCISENESS

<economy in language>

NOUNS 1 **conciseness,** concision, briefness, brachylogy, **brevity,** the soul of wit; shortness, compactness; curtness, brusqueness, crispness, terseness, summariness; compression; taciturnity, reserve; pithiness, succinctness, pointedness, sententiousness; compendiousness; heart of the matter; one-pointedness

2 laconicness, laconism, laconicism, **economy of language**, economy of words; laconics; Atticism; commatism

3 aphorism, epigram; abridgment

4 **abbreviation,** shortening, clipping, cutting, pruning, truncation; ellipsis, aposiopesis, contraction, syncope, apocope, elision, crasis, syneresis

VERBS **5** **be brief,** come to the point, get to the bottom line, get to the nitty-gritty, make a long story short, cut the matter short, cut the shit*, be telegraphic, waste no words, put it in few words, give more matter and less art; shorten, condense, abbreviate

ADJS **6** **concise, brief,** short, short and sweet; condensed, compressed, tight, close, compact; compendious; curt, brusque, crisp, terse, summary; taciturn; reserved; pithy, succinct; laconic, Spartan; abridged, abbreviated, vest-pocket, synopsized, shortened, clipped, cut, pruned, contracted, truncated, docked; elliptic, syncopic, aposiopestic; telegraphic; sententious, epigrammatic, epigrammatical, gnomic, aphoristic, aphoristical, pointed, to the point; brachylogous; encapsuled

ADVS **7** **concisely, briefly,** shortly, standing on one leg; laconically; curtly, brusquely, crisply, tersely, summarily; pithily, succinctly, pointedly; sententiously, aphoristically, epigrammatically

8 **in brief,** in short, for short; in substance, in epitome, in outline; in a nutshell, in a capsule; in a word, in two words, in a few words, without wasting words, without mincing words; to be brief, to the point, to sum up, to come to the point, to cut the matter short, to make a long story short

538 DIFFUSENESS

<superfluity in language>

NOUNS **1** **diffuseness,** diffusiveness, diffusion; shapelessness, formlessness, amorphousness, blobbiness, unstructuredness; obscurity

2 **wordiness, verbosity,** verbiage, verbalism, verbality; prolixity, long-windedness, longiloquence, loquacity; flow of words, flux of words, cloud of words; profuseness, profusiveness, profusion; effusiveness, effusion, gush, gushing; outpour, tirade; logorrhea, verbal diarrhea, diarrhea of the mouth, talkativeness; copiousness, exuberance, rampancy, amplitude, extravagance, prodigality, fertility, fecundity, rankness, teemingness, prolificity, prolificacy, productivity, abundance, overflow, fluency; superfluity, superflux, superabundance, inundation; **redundancy,** pleonasm, repetitiveness, reiterativeness, reiteration, iteration, tautology, macrology, double-talk; repetition for effect, repetition for emphasis, palilogy

3 discursiveness, desultoriness, digressiveness, aimlessness; **rambling**, maundering, meandering, wandering, roving

4 **digression,** departure, deviation, discursion, excursion, excursus, sidetrack, side path, side road, byway, bypath; episode; rambling; segue

5 **circumlocution,** roundaboutness, circuitousness, ambages; deviousness, obliqueness, indirection; periphrase, periphrasis; ambagiousness

6 amplification, expatiation, enlargement, expansion, dilation, dilatation, dilating; **elaboration,** laboring; development, explication, unfolding, working-out, fleshing-out, detailing, filling in the empty places, filler, padding

VERBS **7** amplify, expatiate, dilate, expand, enlarge, enlarge upon, expand on, expand upon, **elaborate;** relate in extenso, rehearse in extenso; detail, particularize; develop, open out, fill in, flesh out, evolve, unfold; work out, explicate; descant, relate at large

8 **protract, extend,** spin out, string out, draw out, stretch out, go on about, be on about, drag out, run out, drive into the ground; pad, fill out; perorate; speak at length, spin a long yarn, never finish; verbify, chatter, talk one to death

9 **digress,** wander, get off the subject, wander from the subject, get sidetracked, excurse, ramble, maunder, stray, go astray; depart, **deviate,** turn aside, jump the track; go off on a tangent, go up blind alleys; segue

10 **circumlocute**, say in a roundabout way, talk in circles, go round about, go around and around, beat around the bush, beat about the bush, go round Robin Hood's barn; periphrase

ADJS **11** **diffuse,** diffusive; formless, unstructured; profuse, profusive; effusive, gushing, gushy; copious, exuberant, extravagant, prodigal, fecund, teeming, prolific, productive, abundant, superabundant, overflowing; redundant, pleonastic, repetitive, reiterative, iterative, tautologous, parrotlike

12 **wordy, verbose;** talkative; prolix, windy, long-winded, longiloquent; protracted, extended, lengthy, long, long-drawn-out, long-spun, spun-out, endless, unrelenting; padded, filled out

13 **discursive**, aimless, loose; rambling, maundering, wandering, peripatetic, roving, deviating; excursive, digressive, deviative, desultory, episodic; by the way, BTW; sidetracked

14 **circumlocutory,** circumlocutional, roundabout, circuitous, ambagious, oblique, indirect; periphrastic

15 expatiating, dilative, dilatative, enlarging, **amplifying**, expanding; developmental; garrulous

ADVS **16** **at length,** *ad nauseam* <L>, at large, in full, *in extenso* <L>, in detail, on and on

539 AMBIGUITY

<multiple meaning in language>

NOUNS 1 **ambiguity,** ambiguousness; equivocalness, equivocacy, equivocality; **double meaning,** amphibology, multivocality, polysemy, polysemousness; punning, paronomasia; double reference, double entendre; twilight zone, gray area; six of one and half dozen of the other; inexplicitness, uncertainty; irony, contradiction, oxymoron, enantiosis; levels of meaning, richness of meaning, complexity of meaning

2 <ambiguous word or expression> **ambiguity,** equivoque, equivocal, equivocality; equivocation, amphibology, double entendre; counterword, portmanteau word; polysemant; weasel word; squinting construction; pun

VERBS 3 **equivocate,** weasel; ironize; have mixed feelings, be uncertain

ADJS 4 **ambiguous, equivocal,** equivocatory, dilogical; multivocal, polysemous, polysemantic, amphibolous, amphibological; two-edged, two-sided, either-or, betwixt and between; bittersweet, mixed; inexplicit, uncertain; ironic; obscure, mysterious, funny, funny peculiar, enigmatic

540 TALKATIVENESS

<talking a lot>

NOUNS 1 **talkativeness,** loquacity, loquaciousness; overtalkativeness, loose tongue, runaway tongue, big mouth; gabbiness, windiness, gassiness; garrulousness, garrulity; **long-windedness,** prolixity, verbosity; multiloquence, multiloquy; volubility, fluency, glibness; fluent tongue, flowing tongue, gift of gab; openness, candor, frankness; effusion, gush, slush; gushiness, effusiveness, communicativeness; flow of words, flux of words, spate of words; gregariousness, sociability, conversableness

2 <**talking problem**> logomania, logorrhea, diarrhea of the mouth, verbal diarrhea, *cacoëthes loquendi,* blathering, gift of gab

3 **chatter,** jabber, gibber, babble, babblement, prate, prating, prattle, palaver, small talk, chat, natter, gabble, gab, jaw-jaw, blab, blabber, blather, blether, blethers, clatter, clack, cackle, talkee-talkee; *caquet, caqueterie, bavardage* <Fr>; twaddle, twattle, gibble-gabble, bibble-babble, chitter-chatter, prittle-prattle, tittle-tattle, mere talk, idle talk, idle chatter; guff, gas, hot air, blah-blah, yak, yakkety-yak, blah-blah-blah; watercooler moment; gossip; nonsense talk

4 **chatterer,** chatterbox, babbler, jabberer, prater, prattler, gabbler, gibble-gabbler, gabber, blabberer, blabber, blatherer, patterer, word-slinger, blab, rattle, bigmouth; magpie, jay, informer; windbag, gasbag, windjammer, hot-air artist, motormouth, ratchet-jaw, blabbermouth; idle chatterer, talkative person, big talker, great talker, nonstop talker, spendthrift of one's tongue

VERBS 5 **chatter,** chat, prate, prattle, patter, palaver, babble, gab, natter, gabble, gibble-gabble, tittle-tattle, jabber, gibber, blab, blabber, blather, blether, clatter, twaddle, twattle, rattle, clack, haver <Brit>, dither, spout, spout off, hold forth, pour forth, spin out, gush, have a big mouth, love the sound of one's own voice, talk to hear one's head rattle; jaw, gas, yak, yakkety-yak, run off at the mouth, beat one's gums, shoot off one's mouth; reel off; talk on, talk away, go on, run on, rattle on, run on like a mill race; ramble on; talk oneself hoarse, talk till one is blue in the face, talk oneself out of breath; talk too much; gossip; talk nonsense

6 <nonformal> talk one to death, talk one's head off, **talk one's ear off,** talk one deaf and dumb, talk one into a fever, talk the hind leg off a mule, like the sound of one's own voice, oil one's tongue, talk till one is blue in the face

7 **outtalk,** outspeak, talk down, outlast; filibuster

8 be loquacious, be garrulous, be a windbag, be a gasbag; have a big mouth, have a big bazoo

ADJS 9 **talkative,** loquacious, talky, big-mouthed, long-tongued, overtalkative, garrulous, running on, chatty; gossipy, newsy; gabby, windy, gassy, all jaw; multiloquent, multiloquious; longwinded, prolix, verbose; voluble, fluent; glib, flip, smooth; candid, frank; effusive, gushy; expansive, communicative; conversational; gregarious, sociable

10 **chattering,** prattling, prating, gabbling, jabbering, gibbering, babbling, blabbing, blabbering, blathering, babblative

ADVS 11 **talkatively,** loquaciously, garrulously; volubly, fluently, glibly; effusively, expansively, gushingly

541 CONVERSATION

<talking between two or more>

NOUNS 1 **conversation,** converse, conversing, rapping; interlocution, colloquy; exchange; verbal intercourse, conversational interchange, interchange of speech, give-and-take, cross-talk, repartee, backchat; discourse, colloquial discourse; communion, intercourse, social intercourse, communication

2 **talk,** palaver, speech, words; confabulation, confab, banter, repartee; chinfest, chinwag, talkfest, bull session; dialogue, duologue,

trialogue; interview, question-and-answer session, question-and-answer, Q and A; audience, audition, interlocution; interrogation, examination; talking shop

3 **chat,** cozy chat, friendly chat, friendly talk, little talk, coze, causerie, visit, *tête-à-tête* <Fr>, heart-to-heart talk, heart-to-heart; pillow talk, intimate discourse, backchat

4 **chitchat,** chitter-chatter, tittle-tattle, **small talk,** by-talk, cocktail-party chitchat, beauty-parlor chitchat, tea-table talk, table talk, idle chat, idle talk, gossip, backchat

5 **conference,** congress, convention, parley, palaver, confab, confabulation, conclave, powwow, huddle, consultation, colloquium, meeting; session, sitting, sit-down, séance; exchange of views, interchange of views; council, council of war; discussion; interview, audience; news conference, press conference; photo opportunity, photo op; high-level talk, conference at the summit, summit, summit conference; summitry; negotiations, bargaining, bargaining session; confrontation, eyeball-to-eyeball encounter; teleconference, telemeeting; council fire; conference table, negotiating table

6 **discussion,** debate, debating, deliberation, nonformalogue, exchange of views, canvassing, ventilation, airing, review, treatment, consideration, investigation, examination, study, analysis, logical analysis; logical discussion, dialectic; buzz session, rap, rap session; panel, panel discussion, open discussion, joint discussion, symposium, colloquium, conference, seminar; forum, open forum, town meeting; polemics; master class

7 **conversationalist,** converser, conversationist; talker, discourser, verbalist, confabulator; colloquist, colloquialist, collocutor; conversational partner; interlocutor, interlocutress, interlocutrice, interlocutrix; parleyer, palaverer; dialogist; Dr Johnson; interviewer, examiner, interrogator, cross-examiner; chatterer

VERBS 8 **converse,** talk together, talk with, speak with, converse with, strike up a conversation, visit with, discourse with, commune with, communicate with, take counsel with, commerce with, have a talk with, have a word with, chin, chew the fat, shoot the breeze, carry on, join in, engage in a conversation, exchange words; confabulate, confab, parley; colloque, colloquize; bandy words; communicate

9 **chat,** visit, gam, coze, pass the time of day, touch base with, have a friendly chat, have a cozy chat; have a little talk, have a heart-to-heart, let one's hair down; talk with one in private, talk tête-à-tête, be closeted with, make conversation, talk, engage in small talk; prattle, prittle-prattle, tittle-tattle; gossip

10 **confer,** hold a conference, parley, palaver, powwow, hold talks, hold a summit, sit down together, meet around the conference table, go into a huddle, deliberate, take counsel, counsel, put heads together; collogue; confer with, sit down with, consult with, advise with, discuss with, take up with, reason with; discuss, talk over; consult, refer to, call in; compare notes, exchange observations, exchange views; have conversations; negotiate, bargain

11 **discuss,** debate, reason, deliberate, deliberate upon, exchange views, exchange opinions, talk, talk over, hash over, hash out, talk of, talk about, rap, exchange ideas, colloquize, comment upon, reason about, discourse about, consider, treat, dissertate on, handle, deal with, take up, go into, examine, investigate, talk out, brainstorm, analyze, sift, study, canvass, review, pass under review, controvert, ventilate, air, thrash out, thresh out, hammer out, reason the point, consider the pros and cons; kick around, knock around; talk shop, talk turkey

ADJS 12 **conversational**, colloquial, confabulatory, interlocutory; communicative; chatty, chitchatty, cozy

ADVS 13 conversationally, colloquially; *tête-à-tête* <Fr>

542 SOLILOQUY

<talking to oneself>

NOUNS 1 **soliloquy,** monology, self-address; **monologue;** aside; solo; monodrama; monody; interior monologue, stream of consciousness, apostrophe; one-man show, one–woman show

2 **soliloquist,** soliloquizer, Hamlet; monodist, **monologist**

VERBS 3 **soliloquize,** monologize; **talk to oneself,** say to oneself, tell oneself, think out loud, think aloud; address the four walls, talk to the wall; have an audience of one; say aside, apostrophize; do all the talking, monopolize the conversation, hold forth without interruption

ADJS 4 soliloquizing, monologic, monological, self-addressing; apostrophic; soloistic; monodramatic; thinking aloud, talking to oneself

543 PUBLIC SPEAKING

<talking to public group>

NOUNS 1 **public speaking,** declamation, **speechmaking,** speaking, speechification, lecturing, speeching; after-dinner speaking; oratory, platform oratory, platform speaking; campaign oratory, stump speaking, the stump, the hustings <Brit>; the soap box; elocution; rhetoric, art of public speaking; eloquence; forensics, debating; speechcraft, wordcraft; preaching, pulpit oratory, Bible-thumping, the pulpit, homiletics; demagogism, demagogy, demagoguery, rabble-rousing; pyrotechnics

2 **speech,** speeching, speechification, **talk, oration, address,** declamation, harangue; public speech, public address, formal speech, set speech, prepared speech, prepared text; welcoming address, farewell address; curtain speech; campaign speech, stump speech, stump oratory; soapbox oratory, tub-thumping; say; tirade, screed, diatribe, jeremiad, philippic, invective; after-dinner speech; funeral oration, eulogy; allocution, exhortation, hortatory address, forensic, forensic address; recitation, recital, reading; salutatory, salutatory address; valediction, valedictory, valedictory address; inaugural address, inaugural; chalk talk; pep talk; pitch, sales talk; talkathon, filibuster; peroration; debate

3 **lecture, keynote,** keynote presentation; prelection, discourse; sermon, sermonette, homily, religious discourse, pulpit discourse, talk; preachment, preaching, preachification; evangelism, televison evangelism, TV evangelism; travel talk, travelogue

4 **speaker,** talker, public speaker, speechmaker, speecher, speechifier, spieler, jawsmith; after-dinner speaker, keynote speaker; spokesperson, spokesman, spokeswoman; demagogue, rabble-rouser; declaimer, ranter, tub-thumper, haranguer, spouter; valedictorian, salutatorian; panelist, debater

5 **lecturer,** praelector, discourser, reader, professor; preacher; sermonizer, sermonist, sermoner, homilist, pulpitarian, pulpiteer, Boanerges, hellfire preacher; evangelist, televison evangelist, TV evangelist, televangelist; expositor, expounder; chalk talker

6 **orator, public speaker,** platform orator, platform speaker; rhetorician, rhetor; silver-tongued orator, spellbinder; Demosthenes, Cicero, Franklin D Roosevelt, Winston Churchill, William Jennings Bryan, Martin Luther King; soapbox orator, soapboxer, stump orator

7 **elocutionist,** elocutioner; recitationist, reciter, diseur, diseuse; reader; improvisator; spokesperson

8 **rhetorician,** teacher of rhetoric, rhetor, elocutionist; speechwriter

VERBS 9 **make a speech**, give a talk, deliver an address, speechify, speak, talk, discourse; address; stump, go on the stump, take the stump; platform, soapbox; take the floor

10 declaim, hold forth, **orate,** elocute, spout, spiel, mouth; harangue, rant, out-Herod Herod, tub-thump, perorate, rodomontade; recite, read; debate; demagogue, rabble-rouse

11 **lecture,** prelect, read a lecture, deliver a lecture; preach, Bible-thump, preachify, sermonize, read a sermon

ADJS 12 declamatory, elocutionary, **oratorical,** rhetorical, forensic; eloquent; demagogic, demagogical

544 ELOQUENCE

<persuasive language>

NOUNS 1 **eloquence,** rhetoric, silver tongue, eloquent tongue, facundity; disertitude; articulateness; glibness, smoothness, slickness; felicitousness, felicity; oratory; expression, expressiveness, command of words, command of language, gift of gab, gift of the gab, gift of expression, vividness, graphicness; pleasing style, effective style; meaningfulness

2 **fluency,** flow; smoothness, facility, ease; grace, gracefulness, poetry; elegance

3 **vigor,** force, power, strength, vitality, drive, sinew, sinewiness, nervousness, nervosity, vigorousness, forcefulness, effectiveness, impressiveness, pizzazz, punch, clout; incisiveness, trenchancy, cuttingness, poignancy, bitingness, bite, mordancy; strong language

4 **spirit,** pep, liveliness, raciness, sparkle, vivacity, dash, verve, vividness; piquancy, poignancy, pungency

5 **vehemence,** passion, impassionedness, enthusiasm, ardor, ardency, fervor, fervency, fire, fieriness, glow, warmth, heat

6 **loftiness,** elevation, sublimity; grandeur, nobility, stateliness, majesty, gravity, *gravitas* <L>, solemnity, dignity

VERBS 7 **have the gift of gab**, have the gift of the gab, have a tongue in one's head; spellbind; shine

ADJS 8 **eloquent,** silver-tongued, silver; well-speaking, well-spoken, articulate, facund; glib, smooth, smooth-spoken, smooth-tongued, slick; felicitous; facile, slick as a whistle, spellbinding; Demosthenic, Demosthenian; Ciceronian

9 **fluent,** flowing, tripping; smooth, pleasing, facile, easy, graceful, elegant

10 **expressive,** graphic, vivid, suggestive, imaginative; well-turned; meaningful

11 **vigorous,** strong, powerful, imperative, forceful, forcible, vital, driving, sinewy, sinewed, punchy,

full of piss and vinegar, zappy, striking, telling, effective, impressive; incisive, trenchant, cutting, biting, piercing, poignant, penetrating, slashing, mordant, acid, corrosive; sensational

12 **spirited, lively,** peppy, gingery, racy, sparkling, vivacious; piquant, poignant, pungent

13 **vehement,** emphatic, **passionate, impassioned,** enthusiastic, ardent, fiery, fervent, burning, glowing, warm; urgent, stirring, exciting, stimulating, provoking

14 **lofty,** elevated, sublime, grand, majestic, noble, stately, grave, solemn, dignified; serious, weighty; moving, inspiring

ADVS 15 **eloquently; fluently,** smoothly, glibly, trippingly on the tongue; expressively, vividly, graphically; meaningfully; vigorously, powerfully, forcefully, spiritedly; tellingly, strikingly, effectively, impressively; vehemently, passionately, ardently, fervently, warmly, glowingly, in glowing terms

545 GRANDILOQUENCE

<colorful, lofty language>

NOUNS 1 **grandiloquence,** magniloquence, lexiphanicism, **pompousness,** pomposity, orotundity; rhetoric, mere rhetoric, rhetoricalness; high-flown diction, big talk, tall talk; grandioseness, grandiosity; loftiness, stiltedness; fulsomeness; pretentiousness, pretension, affectation; ostentation; flamboyancy, showiness, flashiness, gaudiness, meretriciousness, bedizenment, glitz, garishness; sensationalism, luridness, Barnumism; inflation, inflatedness, swollenness, turgidity, turgescence, flatulence, flatulency, tumidness, tumidity; sententiousness, pontification; swollen diction, swelling utterance; platitudinous ponderosity, polysyllabic profundity, pompous prolixity; Johnsonese; prose run mad; convolution, tortuosity, tortuousness, ostentatious complexity, ostentatious profundity

2 **bombast,** bombastry, pomposity, fustian, highfalutin, rant, rodomontade; **hot air**; balderdash, gobbledygook, purple prose, claptrap

3 high-sounding words, lexiphanicism, **hard words**; sesquipedalian word, big word, long word, two-dollar word, five-dollar word, jawbreaker, jawtwister, mouthful; antidisestablishmentarianism, honorificabilitudinitatibus, pneumonoultramicroscopicsilicovolcanoconiosis; polysyllabism, sesquipedalianism, sesquipedality; Latinate diction; academese, technical jargon; puff piece

4 **ornateness,** floweriness, floridness, floridity, lushness, luxuriance; flourish, flourish of rhetoric, flowers of speech, flowers of rhetoric, purple passages, beauties, fine writing; ornament, ornamentation, adornment, embellishment, elegant variation, embroidery, frill, colors, colors of rhetoric, figure, figure of speech

5 **phrasemonger,** rhetorician; phraseman, phrasemaker, fine writer, wordspinner; euphuist, Gongorist, Marinist; pedant

VERBS 6 **talk big**, talk highfalutin, phrasemake, **pontificate,** blow, vapor, Barnumize; inflate, bombast, lay it on, pile it on, lay it on thick, lay it on with a trowel; smell of the lamp

7 ornament, decorate, adorn, **embellish, embroider,** enrich; overcharge, overlay, overload, load with ornament, festoon, weight down with ornament, flourish; gild, gild the lily, trick out, varnish; paint in glowing colors, tell in glowing terms; to paint the lily; elaborate, convolute, involve

ADJS 8 **grandiloquent,** magniloquent, **pompous,** orotund; grandiose; fulsome; lofty, elevated, tall, stilted; pretentious, affected; overblown, overdone, overwrought; showy, flashy, ostentatious, gaudy, glitzy, meretricious, flamboyant, flaming, bedizened, flaunting, garish; lurid, sensational, sensationalistic; high-flown, highfalutin, high-flying; high-flowing, high-sounding, big-sounding, great-sounding, grandisonant, sonorous; rhetorical, declamatory; pedantic, inkhorn, lexiphanic; sententious, Johnsonian; convoluted, tortuous, labyrinthine, overelaborate, overinvolved; euphuistic, Gongoresque

9 **bombastic,** fustian, mouthy, inflated, swollen, swelling, turgid, turgescent, tumid, tumescent, flatulent, windy, gassy; overadorned, fulsome

10 sesquipedalian, sesquipedal, polysyllabic, jawbreaking, jawtwisting

11 **ornate,** purple, colored, fancy; adorned, embellished, embroidered, lavish, decorated, festooned, overcharged, overloaded, befrilled, flashy; flowery, florid, lush, luxuriant; figured, figurative

ADVS 12 **grandiloquently,** magniloquently, **pompously,** grandiosely, fulsomely, loftily, stiltedly, pretentiously; ostentatiously, showily; **bombastically,** turgidly, tumidly, flatulently, windily

13 **ornately,** fancily; flowerily, floridly

546 LETTER

<alphabetic unit>

NOUNS 1 **letter, written character, character,** sign, symbol, graph, digraph, grapheme, allograph, alphabetic character, alphabetic symbol, phonetic character, phonetic symbol; diacritic, diacritical mark, vowel point; logographic character, lexigraphic character; ideographic character, ideogrammic character, ideogrammatic character; initial; syllabic character, syllabic, syllabogram; pictographic symbol, ideophone; cipher, device; monogram; graphy; writing

2 <phonetic, ideographic symbols> phonogram; phonetic symbol; logogram, logograph, grammalogue; letter, word letter; ideogram, ideograph, phonetic, radical, determinative; pictograph, pictogram; hieroglyphic, hieroglyph, hieratic symbol, demotic character; rune, runic character; cuneiform, character; wedge, arrowhead, ogham; kana, hiragana, katakana; kanji; shorthand; hieroglyphics; capital letter, lowercase letter

3 **writing system, script,** letters; alphabet, letters of the alphabet, ABC's; phonetic alphabet, International Phonetic Alphabet (IPA); Initial Teaching Alphabet; phonemic alphabet; runic alphabet, futhark, futharc; alphabetism; syllabary; alphabetics, alphabetology, graphemics; paleography; speech sound

4 **spelling,** orthography; phonetic spelling, phonetic respelling, phonetics, phonography; normalization; spelling reform; spelling match, spelling bee, spelldown; bad spelling, cacography; spelling pronunciation; greengrocer's apostrophe, misspelling

5 **lettering,** initialing; inscription, epigraph, graffito, printing, calligraphy; handwriting; alphabetization; transliteration, romanization, pinyin, Wade-Giles system; transcription; phonetic transcription, phonography, lexigraphy

VERBS 6 **letter,** initial, inscribe, character, sign, mark; capitalize; alphabetize, alphabet; transliterate, transcribe

7 **spell,** orthographize; spell phonetically respell phonetically; spell out, write out, trace out; spell backward; outspell, spell down; syllabify, syllabize, syllable, syllabicate

ADJS 8 **literal, lettered; alphabetic, alphabetical;** abecedarian; graphemic, allographic; large-lettered, majuscule, majuscular, uncial; capital, capitalized, uppercase; small-lettered, minuscule, minuscular, lowercase, boldface, Roman, block capital, block letter; logographic, logogrammatic, lexigraphic, ideographic, ideogrammic, ideogrammatic, pictographic; transliterated, transcribed; orthographic, spelled; symbolical, phonogramic, phonographic, cuneiform, cuneal, hieroglyphic, hieroglyphical

547 WRITING

<written composition>

NOUNS 1 **writing,** scrivening, scrivenery, inscription, lettering; engrossment; pen, pen-and-ink; inkslinging, ink spilling, pen-pushing, pencil-pushing; typing, typewriting; macrography, micrography; stroke of the pen, dash of the pen, *coup de plume* <Fr>; secret writing, cryptography; alphabet, writing system; texting

2 **authorship, writing,** authorcraft, pencraft, wordsmanship, composition, the art of composition, inditing, inditement; one's pen; creative writing, literary art, verbal art, literary composition, literary production, verse-writing, short-story writing, novel-writing, playwriting, drama-writing; essay-writing; expository writing; technical writing; journalism, newspaper writing, investigative reporting, editorial writing, feature writing, rewriting, sports journalism; magazine writing; citizen journalism; blogging; content creation; songwriting, lyric-writing, libretto-writing; artistry, literary power, literary artistry, literary talent, literary flair, skill with words, skill with language, facility in writing, ready pen; writer's itch, graphomania, scribblemania, graphorrhea, *cacoëthes scribendi* <L>; automatic writing; writer's cramp, graphospasm

3 **handwriting,** hand, script, fist, chirography, calligraphy, autography; manuscript, scrive; autograph, holograph; **penmanship,** penscript, pencraft; stylography; graphology, graphanalysis, graphometry; paleography

4 **handwriting style**; printing, handprinting, block letter, lettering; stationery; writing materials, paper, foolscap, note paper, pad, papyrus, parchment, tracing paper, typing paper, vellum

5 **fine writing**, calligraphy, elegant penmanship, good hand, fine hand, good fist, fair hand, copybook hand

6 **bad writing**, cacography, bad hand, poor fist, cramped hand, crabbed hand, botched writing, childish scrawl, illegible handwriting, griffonage

7 **scribbling**, scribblement; scribble, scrabble, scrawl, scratch, *barbouillage* <Fr>; hen tracks, hen scratches, pothookery, pothooks, pothooks and hangers

8 **stenography, shorthand,** brachygraphy, tachygraphy; speedwriting; phonography, stenotype; contraction

9 **letter,** written character; alphabet, writing system; punctuation

10 <**written matter**> writing, the written word; piece; piece of writing, text, screed; copy, matter;

printed matter, printed word, literature, reading matter; nonfiction; fiction; composition, work, opus, production, literary production, literary artifact, lucubration, brainchild; essay, article; poem; play; letter; document; paper, parchment, scroll; script, scrip, scrive; penscript, typescript; manuscript (ms, mss), holograph, autograph; draft, first draft, second draft, recension, version; edited version, finished version, final draft; transcription, transcript, fair copy, engrossment; flimsy; original, author's copy; camera-ready copy; printout, computer printout, hard copy; gray literature; blog, post

11 **<ancient manuscript>** codex; scroll; palimpsest, *codex rescriptus* <L>; papyrus, parchment

12 **literature, writings,** letters, belles lettres, polite literature, humane letters, republic of letters, writing; work, literary work, text, literary text; works, complete works, oeuvre, canon, literary canon, author's canon; serious literature; classics, ancient literature; medieval literature, Renaissance literature; national literature, English literature, French literature; contemporary literature; underground literature; pseudonymous literature; folk literature, oral history; travel literature; wisdom literature; erotic literature, erotica; pornographic literature, pornography, porn, hard porn, soft porn, obscene literature, scatological literature; Weblog, blog, bulletin board; popular literature, pop literature; kitsch

13 **writer,** scribbler, penman, pen, penner; pen-driver, pencil-pusher, word-slinger, inkslinger, ink spiller, knight of the plume, knight of the quill; scribe, scrivener, amanuensis, secretary, recording secretary, clerk, administrative assistant; letterer; copyist, copier, transcriber; chirographer, calligrapher

14 **writing expert,** graphologist, handwriting expert, graphometrist; paleographer; handwriting recognition; character recognition

15 **author, writer,** scribe, composer, inditer; authoress, penwoman; creative writer, *littérateur* <Fr>, literary artist, literary craftsman, literary artisan, literary journeyman, belletrist, man of letters, literary man, literary lion; wordsmith, word painter; free lance, freelance writer; ghostwriter, ghost; collaborator, coauthor; prose writer, logographer; fiction writer, fictioneer; story writer, short story writer; storyteller; novelist; novelettist; diarist; newspaperman; annalist; poet; dramatist, humorist; scriptwriter, scenario writer, scenarist, script doctor; nonfiction writer; article writer, magazine writer; essayist; monographer; reviewer, critic, literary critic, music critic, art critic, drama critic, dance critic; columnist; pamphleteer; technical writer; copywriter, advertising writer; compiler, listmaker, encyclopedist, bibliographer; blogger

16 **hack writer,** hack, literary hack, Grub Street writer <Brit>, penny-a-liner, scribbler, potboiler; blogger

17 **stenographer,** brachygrapher, tachygrapher; phonographer, stenotypist

18 **typist,** keyboarder; texter; printer

VERBS 19 **write,** pen, pencil, push the pen, push the pencil; shed ink, spill ink, scribe, scrive; inscribe, scroll; superscribe; enface; take pen in hand; put in writing, put in black and white; draw up, draft, write out, make out; write down, record; take down in shorthand; type; transcribe, copy out, engross, make a fair copy, copy; trace; rewrite, revise, **edit,** recense, make a recension, make a critical revision; highlight

20 **scribble,** scrabble, scratch, scrawl, make hen tracks, make hen scratches, make chicken scratches, doodle

21 write, **author, compose,** indite, formulate, produce, prepare; dash off, knock off, knock out, throw on paper, pound out, crank out, grind, out, churn out; freelance; collaborate, coauthor; ghostwrite, ghost; novelize; scenarize; pamphleteer; editorialize; blog

ADJS 22 **written,** penned, penciled, lettered, literal, graphical, typed; inscribed; engrossed; in writing, in black and white, on paper; scriptural, scriptorial, graphic; calligraphic, chirographic, chirographical; stylographic, stylographical; manuscript, autograph, autographic, holograph, holographic, holographical, in one's own hand, under one's hand; longhand, in longhand, in script, handwritten; shorthand, in shorthand; italic, italicized; cursive, running, flowing; graphologic, graphological, graphometric, graphometrical; graphoanalytic, graphoanalytical; typewritten; printed

23 **scribbled,** scrabbled, scratched, scrawled; scribbly, scratchy, scrawly

24 **literary,** belletristic, lettered; classical

25 auctorial, authorial; polygraphic; graphomaniac, graphomaniacal, scribblemaniac, scribblemaniacal, scripturient

26 **alphabetic,** ideographic, etc

27 stenographic, stenographical; **shorthand,** in shorthand

28 **clerical, secretarial**

COMBINING FORMS 29 grapho-, -graphy, -graphia; -graph, -gram; -grapher

548 PRINTING

<*published composition*>

NOUNS **1 printing,** publishing, publication, photographic reproduction, photochemical process, phototypography, phototypy; photoengraving; letterpress, relief printing, typography, letterpress photoengraving; zincography, photozincography; line engraving, halftone engraving; stereotypy; wood-block printing, xylotypography, chromoxylography; intaglio printing, gravure; rotogravure, rotary photogravure; planographic printing, planography, lithography, typolithography, photolithography, lithogravure, lithophotogravure; offset printing, offset lithography, offset, dry offset, photo-offset; photogelatin process, albertype, collotype; electronography, electrostatic printing, onset, xerography, xeroprinting; stencil, mimeograph, silk-screen printing; color printing, chromotypography, chromotypy, two-color printing, three-color printing; book printing, job printing, sheetwork; history of printing, palaeotypography; photography; graphic arts, printmaking

2 composition, typesetting, setting, composing; hand composition, machine composition; hot-metal typesetting, cold-type typesetting, photosetting, photocomposition; imposition; justification; composing stick, galley chase, furniture, quoin; typesetting machine, phototypesetter, phototypesetting machine; computer composition, computerized typesetting; composition tape; line of type, slug; layout, dummy

3 print, imprint, stamp, impression, impress, letterpress; reprint, reissue; offprint; offcut; offset, setoff, mackle; duplicate, facsimile, carbon copy, repro

4 copy, printer's copy, manuscript, typescript; camera-ready copy; matter; composed matter, live matter, dead matter, standing matter

5 proof, proof sheet, pull <Brit>, trial impression; galley, galley proof, slip; page proof, foundry proof, plate proof, stone proof, press proof, cold-type proof, color proof, computer proof, engraver's proof, reproduction proof, repro proof, blueprint, blue, vandyke, progressive proof; author's proof; revise

6 type, key in, key, type in, type into, type up; print, stamp, letter; type size; type body, type shank, type stem, body, shank, stem, shoulder, belly, back, bevel, beard, feet, groove, nick, counter; ascender, descender, serif; lower case, minuscule; upper case, majuscule; capital, cap, small capital, small cap; ligature, logotype; bastard type, bottle-assed type, fat-faced type; pi; type lice; font; face, typeface; type class, roman, sans serif, script, italic, black letter; case, typecase; point, pica; en, em; typefounders, typefoundry

7 space, spacing, patent space, justifying space, justification space; spaceband, slug; quadrat, quad; em quad, en quad; em, en; three-em space, thick space; four-em space, five-em space, thin space; hair space

8 printing surface, plate, printing plate; typeform, locked-up page; duplicate plate, electrotype, stereotype, plastic plate, rubber plate; zincograph, zincotype; printing equipment

9 presswork, makeready; press, **printing press,** printing machine; platen press, flatbed cylinder press, cylinder press, rotary press, web press, rotogravure press; bed, platen, web

10 printed matter; reading matter, text, letterpress; advertising matter; advance sheets

11 press, printing office, print shop, printery, printers; publishers, publishing house, academic press; **pressroom,** composing room, proofroom

12 printer, printworker; compositor, typesetter, typographer, Linotyper; keyboarder; stoneman, makeup man; proofer; stereotyper, stereotypist, electrotyper; apprentice printer, devil, printer's devil; pressman

13 proofreader, reader, printer's reader <Brit>, copyholder; **copyreader,** copy editor

VERBS **14 print;** imprint, impress, stamp, enstamp; engrave; run, run off, strike; publish, issue, put in print, bring out, put out, get out; put to press, put to bed, see through the press; prove, proof, prove up, make a proof, pull a proof, pull; overprint; reprint, reissue; mimeograph, hectograph; multigraph

15 autotype, electrotype, Linotype <tm>, monotype, palaeotype, stereotype; keyboard

16 compose, set, set in print; make up, impose; justify, overrun; pi, pi a form

17 copy-edit; proofread, read, read copy, correct copy; vet

18 <be printed> go to press, come off press, come out, appear in print

ADJS **19 printed, in print;** typeset

20 typographic, typographical; phototypic, phototypographic; chromotypic, chromotypographic; stereotypic, palaeotypographical; boldface, boldfaced, blackface, black-faced, full-faced; lightface, light-faced; uppercase, lowercase; small caps

549 RECORD

<documented information>

NOUNS **1** **record, recording,** record-keeping, documentation, written word; chronicle, annals, history, story; roll, rolls, pipe roll <Brit>; account; register, registry, rota, roster, scroll, catalog, inventory, table, list, dossier, portfolio; letters, correspondence; vestige, trace, memorial, token, relic, remains; herstory; listmaking, glazomania; data entry, data mining, data management

2 **archive, archives**, public records, government archives, government papers, presidential papers, historical, historical records, memorabilia; clipping; cartulary; biographical records, biographical material, life records, papers, ana; parish rolls, parish register, parish records; paper trail

3 **registry**, registrar, registry office; archives, files; chancery; National Archives, Library of Congress; Somerset House <Brit>

4 **memorandum,** memo, memoir, *aide-mémoire* <Fr>, memorial; reminder; note, notation, annotation, jotting, docket, marginal note, marginalia, scholium, scholia, adversaria, footnote; jottings; entry, register, registry, item; minutes; inscription, personal note

5 **document,** official document, legal document, legal paper, legal instrument, instrument, writ, paper, parchment, scroll, roll, writing, script, scrip; holograph, chirograph; papers, ship's papers; docket, file, personal file, dossier; blank, form; deed, title deed, muniments; registration document, insurance papers; attachment; paper trail

6 **certificate,** certification, **ticket;** authority, authorization; credential, voucher, warrant, warranty, testimonial, charter; note; affidavit, sworn statement, notarized statement, deposition, witness, attestation; visa; passport; bill of health, clean bill of health; navicert <Brit>; diploma, sheepskin; certificate of proficiency, testamur <Brit>; birth certificate, death certificate, marriage certificate

7 **report,** bulletin, brief, statement, account, accounting; account rendered; minutes, the record, proceedings, transactions, acta; official report, annual report; report card, transcript; yearbook, annual; returns, census report, census returns, election returns, tally; case history; book report

8 <**official document**> state paper, white paper; blue book, green book, Red Book <Brit>, white book, yellow book; gazette, official journal, Congressional Record, Hansard

9 <**register**> genealogy, pedigree, studbook; Social Register, blue book; directory; Who's Who; Lloyd's Register

10 <**recording media**> bulletin board, notice board; scoresheet, scorecard, scoreboard; tape, magnetic tape, magnetic track, magnetic storage, cassette tape, videotape, ticker tape; computer disk, magnetic disk, diskette, floppy disL, floppy, hard disk, disk cartridge, CD-ROM drive, CD-ROM, laser disk, optical disk, zip drive, zip disk, zip file; memory; computer file, database; compact disk (CD), multimedia CD, DVD, DVD burner; phonograph record, disc, disk, platter; film, motion-picture film; slip, card, index card, filing card; library card, catalog card; microcard, microfiche, microdot, microfilm; file; recording instrument, photocopier, camera, videocamera, kiddie cam, camcorder, recorder, tape recorder, wiretap, bug, answering machine, videocassette recorder (VCR), personal stereo, flight recorder, black box; voice recognition, iris recognition

11 <**record book**> notebook, pocketbook, pocket notebook, blankbook; loose-leaf notebook, spiral notebook; memorandum book, memo book, commonplace book, adversaria; address book, directory; workbook; blotter, police blotter; docket, court calendar; calendar, desk calendar, appointment calendar, appointment schedule, engagement book, agenda, agenda book, Filofax <tm>, datebook; Moleskine <tm>; tablet, writing tablet; diptych, triptych; pad, scratch pad, notepad, legal pad; Post-it Note <tm>, sticky; scrapbook, memory book, album; diary, journal, daybook; log, ship's log, logbook; account book, ledger; cashbook, petty cashbook; checkbook; Domesday Book; catalog, classified catalog, index; yearbook, annual; guestbook, guest register, register, registry; cartulary, chartulary; art journal; blog, online journal; wish book, wish list

12 **monument,** monumental record, memorial record, **memorial;** necrology, obituary, memento, remembrance, testimonial; cup, trophy, prize, ribbon, plaque; marker; inscription; tablet, stone, hoarstone <Brit>, boundary stone, memorial stone; pillar, stele, stela, shaft, column, memorial column, rostral column, manubial column; cross; war memorial; arch, memorial arch, triumphal arch, victory arch; memorial statue, bust; monolith, obelisk, pyramid; tomb, grave; tomb of unknown soldier; gravestone, tombstone; memorial tablet, brass; headstone, footstone; mausoleum; cenotaph; cairn, mound, barrow, cromlech, dolmen, megalith, menhir, cyclolith, earthwork; shrine, reliquary, tope, stupa

13 recorder, registrar, blogger, listmaker

14 **registration, register, registry;** recording, record keeping, recordation; archiving; minuting, enrollment, matriculation, enlistment; impanelment; listing, tabulation, cataloging, inventorying, indexing; chronicling; entry, insertion, entering, posting; docketing, inscribing, inscription; booking, logging; recording instruments; preregistration

VERBS 15 **record,** put upon record, place upon record; inscribe, enscroll; register, enroll, matriculate, check in; impanel; poll; file, index, catalog, calendar, tabulate, list, docket; chronicle, document; minute, put in the minutes, put on the record, spread on the record; commit to an archive, preserve in an archive, archive; write, commit to writing, reduce to writing, put in writing, put in black and white, put on paper; write out; make out, fill out; write up, chalk, chalk up; write down, mark down, jot down, put down, set down, take down; note, note down, make a note, make a memorandum; post, post up; enter, make an entry, insert, write in, write into; book, log; cut, carve, grave, engrave, incise; put on tape, tape, tape-record; capture on film; videotape; keyboard, key; diarize

ADJS 16 **recording,** recordative, registrational; certificatory

17 **recorded,** registered; inscribed, written down, down; filed, indexed, enrolled, entered, logged, booked, posted; documented, chronicled; minuted; **on record,** on file, on the books; official, legal, of record; in black and white; duly noted; on-air, off-air

18 **documentary,** documentational, documental, archival, archived; epigraphic, inscriptional; necrological, obituary; testimonial

550 RECORDER

<documenter of information>

NOUNS 1 **recorder,** recordist, record keeper; **registrar,** register, prothonotary; archivist, documentalist; librarian, cybrarian; **clerk,** record clerk, penpusher, filing clerk; town clerk, municipal clerk, county clerk; bookkeeper, accountant, tax preparer; bean counter; scribe, scrivener; secretary, amanuensis; stenographer; notary, notary public; marker; scorekeeper, scorer, official scorer, timekeeper; engraver, stonecutter; reporter

2 **annalist,** genealogist, chronicler; cliometrician; historian

551 INFORMATION

<knowledge or facts conveyed>

NOUNS 1 **information,** info, gen, **facts, data,** metadataknowledge; fact of life; public knowledge, open secret, common knowledge; general information; news, factual information, hard information; evidence, proof; enlightenment, light; incidental information, sidelight; acquaintance, familiarization, briefing; instruction; intelligence, intel, actionable intelligence; the dope, the goods, the scoop, the skinny, the straight skinny, the inside skinny, the know, the gen; transmission, communication; report, word, message, presentation, account, statement, mention; white paper, white book, blue book; dispatch, bulletin, communiqué, handout, fact sheet, release; publicity, promotional material, broadside; notice, notification; notice board, bulletin board; announcement, publication; directory, guidebook; trivia; current events, current affairs; information processing; information overload; bullet points; big data

2 **inside information,** private information, confidential information; the lowdown, inside dope, inside wire, hot tip, dirt, poop; insider; pipeline; privileged information, classified information; insider trading; backchannel

3 **tip,** tip-off, pointer, clue, cue; steer; advice; whisper, passing word, word to the wise, word in the ear, bug in the ear, bee in the bonnet; warning, caution, monition, alerting, early warning; sound bite; aside

4 **hint,** gentle hint, intimation, indication, suggestion, mere suggestion, faint suggestion, suspicion, inkling, whisper, glimmer, glimmering; cue, clue, index, symptom, sign, spoor, track, scent, sniff, whiff, telltale, tip-off; implication, insinuation, innuendo; broad hint, gesture, signal, nod, wink, look, nudge, kick, prompt; disguised message, backward masking; rumor, leak, gossip

5 **informant, informer, source,** teller, interviewee, enlightener, deep throat; adviser, monitor; reporter, sports reporter, notifier, announcer, annunciator; spokesperson, spokespeople, spokeswoman, spokesman, press secretary, press officer, information officer, mouthpiece, messenger, correspondent; spin doctor; communicator, communicant, publisher; authority, witness, expert witness; tipster, tout; newsmonger, gossipmonger; information medium, information media, mass media, print media, electronic media, the press, radio, television; channel, the grapevine; information

network, network; information center; public relations officer; agent, handler; infopreneur

6 **informer,** betrayer, double-crosser, delator; fifth columnist; snitch, snitcher; whistleblower; tattler, tattletale, telltale, talebearer; blab, blabber, blabberer, blabbermouth; squealer, preacher, stool pigeon, stoolie, fink, rat, nark; spy; mole; grapevine, channel

7 information technology (IT), information theory, communication theory; data storage, data retrieval, information retrieval, electronic data processing (EDP), data processing, information processing; signal, noise; encoding, decoding; bit; redundancy, entropy; channel; information explosion, communication explosion, information superhighway

VERBS 8 **inform,** tell, speak on, speak for, apprise, advise, advertise, advertise of, give word, mention to, acquaint, enlighten, familiarize, brief, verse, give the facts, give an account of, give by way of information; instruct, educate; possess one of the facts; let know, have one to know, lead one to believe, lead one to understand; tell once and for all; notify, give notice, give notification, serve notice; communicate; send word, leave word; report; disclose; put in a new light, shed new light upon; announce, broadcast, convey, break the news

9 **post**, **keep posted**; wise up, clue in, fill in, bring up to speed, bring up to date, put in the picture

10 **hint,** intimate, suggest, insinuate, imply, indicate, adumbrate, lead one to gather, leave one to gather, justify one in supposing, give out a hint, give an inkling of, signal, hint at; **leak,** let slip out; allude to, make an allusion to, glance at; prompt, give the cue, put onto; put into one's head, put a bee in one's bonnet

11 **tip**, tip off, give one a tip, alert; give a pointer to; put hep, put hip, let in on, let in on the know; let next to, put next to, put on to, put on to something hot; confide, confide to, entrust with information, give confidential information, mention privately, mention confidentially, whisper, buzz, breathe, whisper in the ear, put a bug in one's ear

12 **inform on**, inform against, betray; tattle; turn informer; testify against, bear witness against; turn state's evidence, turn king's evidence, turn queen's evidence <Brit>

13 <nonformal> **sell one out, sell one down the river,** tell on, blab, snitch, squeal, peach, sell out, sing, rat, stool, fink, nark, finger, put the finger on, blow the whistle, shop, dime, drop a dime, spill one's guts, spill the beans, squawk, weasel, let the cat out of the bag, sell down the river

14 **learn**, come to know, be informed of, be apprised of, have it reported, get the facts, get wise to, get hep to, next to, on to, find out, get word; become conscious of, become aware of, become alive to, become awake to, awaken to, tumble to, open one's eyes to; realize, get wind of; overhear

15 **know**, be informed, be apprised, have the facts, be in the know, come to one's knowledge, come to one's ears, reach one's ears; be told, hear, overhear, hear tell of, hear say; get scent of, get wind of; know well; have inside information, know where the bodies are buried

16 **keep informed,** keep posted, stay briefed, keep up on, keep up-to-date, keep au courant, keep abreast of the times; keep track of, keep account of, keep watch on, keep tabs on, keep a check on, keep an eye on

ADJS 17 **informed**

18 **informative,** informing, informational, informatory; illuminating, instructive, enlightening; educative, educational; advisory, monitory; communicative

19 telltale, tattletale, kiss-and-tell

ADVS 20 from information received, according to reports, according to rumor, from notice given, as a matter of general information, by common report, from what one can gather, as far as anyone knows

552 NEWS

<report of events, new information>

NOUNS 1 **news,** tidings, intelligence, information, word, advice; happenings, current affairs, hard news; newsiness; newsworthiness; a nose for news; journalism, reportage, coverage, news coverage, news gathering; the press, the fourth estate, the press corps, print journalism, electronic journalism, investigative journalism, broadcast journalism, broadcast news, radio journalism, television journalism; news medium, news media, newspaper, newsletter, newsmagazine, radio, television, press association, news service, news agency, press agency, wire service, telegraph agency; press box, press gallery; yellow press, tabloid press, tabloid journalism, tabloidese; pack journalism; alternative press; newsserver, multimedia; new media; Internet forum, Internet cafe; squint media; contact person, point person; advice column, copywriting

2 **good news,** good word, glad tidings; gospel, evangel; fireside chat

3 **news item,** piece of news; **article, story,** piece, account; copy; scoop, beat, exclusive; interview; breaking story, newsbreak; feature story;

follow-up, sidebar; column, editorial; spot news; photo opportunity; outtake; sound bite; media hype, media circus; factoid, data point; gotcha question

4 **message, dispatch,** word, communication, communiqué, advice, press release, news release, release; press conference, news conference; embassy, embassage; letter; telegram; pneumatogram; text message, instant message

5 **bulletin,** news report, flash, brief, news brief, update, newsfeed

6 **report, rumor,** flying rumor, unverified report, unconfirmed report, hearsay, *on-dit* <Fr>, scuttlebutt, latrine rumor; talk, whisper, buzz, rumble, bruit, cry; idea afloat, news stirring; common talk, town talk, talk of the town, topic of the day, *cause célèbre* <Fr>; grapevine; canard, roorback

7 **gossip,** gossiping, gossipry, gossipmongering, newsmongering, mongering, back-fence gossip; talebearing, taletelling; tattle, tittle-tattle, chitchat, talk, idle talk, small talk, by-talk; piece of gossip, groundless rumor, tale, story

8 **scandal, dirt,** malicious gossip; juicy morsel, tidbit, choice bit of dirt; scandalmongering; gossip column; character assassination, slander; whispering campaign

9 **newsmonger, informant,** rumormonger, scandalmonger, gossip, gossipmonger, gossiper, *yenta* <Yiddish>, quidnunc, busybody, tabby; talebearer, taleteller, telltale, tattletale, tattler, tittle-tattler; gossip columnist, advice columnist; reporter, newspaperman, newsperson, journalist, cub reporter; sports reporter, sportswriter; fourth estate

10 <**secret news channel**> grapevine, grapevine telegraph, channel, back channel; pipeline; a little bird, a little birdie; informer, leak; insider information; contact

VERBS 11 **report,** give a report, give an account of, tell, relate; write up, make out a report, write up a report, publicize; editorialize; gather the news, newsgather; dig up, dig up dirt; bring word, tell the news, break the news, give tidings of; bring glad tidings, give the good word; announce; put around, spread, rumor; clue in, inform

12 **gossip,** talk over the back fence; tattle, tittle-tattle; talk; retail gossip, dish the dirt, tell idle tales

ADJS 13 **newsworthy,** front-page, with news value, newsy, informative; reportorial

14 **gossipy,** gossiping, newsy; talebearing, taletelling; tabloidesque

15 **reported, rumored,** whispered; rumored about, talked about, whispered about, bruited about, bandied about; in the news, in circulation, in the air, going around, going about, going the rounds, current, rife, afloat, in every one's mouth, on all tongues, on the street, all over the town, hot off the press; made public

ADVS 16 **reportedly,** allegedly, as they say, as it is said, as the story goes, as the fellow says, it is said

553 CORRESPONDENCE

<written communication of information>

NOUNS 1 **correspondence, letter writing,** written communication, exchange of letters, epistolary intercourse, epistolary communication; personal correspondence, business correspondence; mailing, mass mailing; electronic mail, email; text messaging, texting, instant messaging

2 **letter** <see list>, epistle, message, communication, dispatch, missive, favor; personal letter, business letter; note, line, chit, billet; reply, answer, acknowledgment, rescript

3 **card,** postcard, postal card, lettercard <Brit>; picture postcard; greeting card; e-card

4 **mail, post, postal services,** letter bag; post day <Brit>; domestic mail, general delivery, snail mail, airmail, surface mail, express mail, priority mail, special handling, special delivery, first-class mail, parcel post, registered mail, certified mail, insured mail, metered mail; mailing list; junk mail; direct mail, direct-mail advertising, direct-mail selling, mail-order selling; mail solicitation; fan mail; electronic mail, email; text message, instant message; Pony Express

5 **postage;** stamp, postage stamp; frank; postmark, cancellation; postage meter

6 **mailbox,** postbox, letter box, pillar box; letter drop, mail drop; mailing machine; mailbag, postbag; email box, voicemail box

7 **postal service,** postal system; post office (PO), general post office (GPO), sorting office, dead-letter office, sea post office, mailboat; postmaster, mailman, postman, mail carrier, letter carrier; mail clerk, post-office clerk, postal clerk; messenger, courier; postal union; electronic mail service

8 **correspondent,** letter writer, writer, communicator; pen pal; addressee

9 **address,** name and address, direction, **destination,** superscription; zone, zip code (ZIP), zip plus four (ZIP+4), postal code, postcode; letterhead, billhead; drop, accommodation address <Brit>; rural route; email address

VERBS 10 **correspond,** correspond with, communicate with, write, write to, write a letter, send a letter to, send a note, drop a line; use the mails; keep up a correspondence, exchange letters, write back

11 **reply, answer,** acknowledge, respond; reply by return mail

12 **mail, post,** dispatch, send, forward; airmail

13 **address,** direct, superscribe

ADJS **14** epistolary; **postal,** post; letter; mail-order, direct-mail; mail-in; mailable; send-in, sendable

PHRS **15** please reply, RSVP, *répondez s'il vous plaît* <Fr>

16 **letter**

aerogram
air letter
apostolic belief, papal brief
bull
chain letter
circular letter
cover letter
dead letter
Dear John
dimissory letter, dimissorial
drop letter
encyclical
encyclical letter
epistle
fan letter
form letter
invitation
letter credential
letter of condolence
letter of credence
letter of credit
letter of delegation
letter of intent
letter of introduction
letter of marque
letter of recommendation
letter of request
letter of resignation
letter overt
letter patent
letter rogatory
letter testamentary
love letter, *billet doux* <Fr>
market letter
memorandum, memo
monitory, monitory letter
newsletter
open letter
paschal letter
pastoral letter
pink slip
poison-pen letter
round robin

554 BOOK

<*published literary work*>

NOUNS **1** **book, volume, tome;** publication, writing, work, opus, production; title; opusculum, opuscule; trade book; textbook, schoolbook, coursebook, reader, grammar; reference book, playbook; songbook; notebook; storybook, novel; bestseller; coffee-table book; nonbook; children's book, board book, juvenile book, juvenile; picture book; coloring book, sketchbook; prayer book, psalter, psalmbook; classic, the book, the bible, magnum opus, great work, standard work, definitive work

2 **publisher,** book publisher; publishing house, press, small press, vanity press; editor, trade editor, reference editor, juvenile editor, textbook editor, dictionary editor, college editor, line editor; acquisitions editor, executive editor, managing editor, editor-in-chief; picture editor; packager; copy editor, copyeditor, fact checker, proofreader; production editor, permissions editor; printer, book printer, typesetter, compositor; bookbinder, bibliopegist; bookdealer, bookseller, book agent, book salesman; book packager; book manufacturer

3 **book, printed book,** bound book, bound volume, cased book, casebound book, clothbound book, clothback, leather-bound book; manufactured book, finished book; packaged book; hardcover, hardcover book, hardbound, hardbound book, hard book; paperback, paper-bound book; pocket book, soft-cover, soft-bound book, limp-cover book; trade paperback; self-published book; electronic book, **e-book**

4 **volume,** tome; folio; quarto, 4to; octavo, 8vo; twelvemo, 12mo; sextodecimo, sixteenmo, 16mo; octodecimoo, eighteenmo, 18mo; imperial, super, royal, medium, crown; trim size

5 **edition,** issue; volume, number; **printing,** impression, press order, print order, print run; copy; series, set, boxed set, collection, library; library edition; back number; trade edition, subscription edition, subscription book; school edition, text edition

6 **rare book,** early edition; first edition; signed edition; manuscript, scroll, codex; incunabulum, cradle book

7 **compilation,** omnibus; symposium; collection, collectanea, miscellany; collected works, selected works, complete works, corpus, *œuvres* <Fr>, canon; miscellanea, analects; ana; chrestomathy, delectus; compendium, **anthology,** composition, garland, florilegium; flowers, beauties; garden; *Festschrift* <Ger>; quotation book; album, photograph album; scrapbook; yearbook; display, exhibition; series, serialization

8 **handbook,** manual, enchiridion, vade mecum, gradus, how-to book; cookbook, cookery book; nature book, field guide; travel book, guidebook; sports book

9 **reference book** <see list>, work of reference; encyclopedia, cyclopedia; concordance; catalog; calendar; index; classified catalog, *catalogue raisonné* <Fr>, dictionary catalog; directory, city directory; telephone directory, telephone book, phone book; atlas, gazetteer; studbook; source book, casebook; record book; dictionary, lexicon, wordbook, Webster's; glossary, gloss, vocabulary, onomasticon, nomenclator; thesaurus, Roget's, storehouse of words, treasury of words, synonomicon; almanac

10 **textbook,** text, schoolbook, manual, manual of instruction; primer, alphabet book, abecedary, abecedarium; hornbook, battledore; gradus, exercise book, workbook; grammar, reader; spelling book, speller, casebook

11 **booklet,** pamphlet, brochure, chapbook, leaflet, folder, tract; circular; comic book

12 **makeup, design;** front matter, preliminaries, text, back matter; head, fore edge, back, tail; page, leaf, folio; type page; trim size; flyleaf, endpaper, endleaf, endsheet, signature; recto, verso, reverso; title page, half-title page; title, bastard title, binder's title, subtitle, running title; copyright page, imprint, printer's imprint, imprimatur, colophon; catchword, catch line; dedication, inscription; acknowledgments, preface, foreword, introduction; contents, contents page, table of contents; appendix, notes, glossary; errata; bibliography; index

13 **part, section,** book, volume; article; serial, installment; fascicle; passage, phrase, clause, verse, paragraph, chapter, column

14 **bookbinding,** bibliopegy; binding, cover, book cover, case, bookcase, hard binding, soft binding, mechanical binding, spiral binding, comb binding, plastic binding; library binding; headband, footband, tailband; jacket, book jacket, dust jacket, dust cover, wrapper; slipcase, slipcover; book cloth, binder's cloth, binder's board, binder board; folding, tipping, gathering, collating, sewing; signature; collating mark, niggerhead; Smyth sewing, side sewing, saddle stitching, wire stitching, stapling, perfect binding; smashing, gluing-off, trimming, rounding, backing, lining, lining-up; casemaking, stamping, casing-in

15 <bookbinding styles> Aldine, Arabesque, Byzantine, Canevari, cottage, dentelle, Etruscan, fanfare, Grolier, Harleian, Jansenist, Maioli, pointillé, Roxburgh

16 **bookstore,** bookshop, bookseller, book dealer; bookstall, bookstand; book club; bibliopole; online bookseller

17 **bookholder,** bookrest, book support, bookend; bookcase, revolving bookcase, revolving bookstand, bookrack, bookstand, bookshelf; stack, bookstack; book table, book tray, book truck; folder, folio; portfolio

18 **booklover,** philobiblist, bibliophile, bibliolater, book collector, bibliomane, bibliomaniac, bibliotaph; **bookworm,** bibliophage; book-stealer, biblioklept; word nerd

19 **bibliology,** bibliography; bookcraft, bookmaking, book printing, book production, book manufacturing, bibliogenesis, bibliogony; bookselling, bibliopolism

ADJS 20 **bibliological,** bibliographical; bibliothecal, bibliothecary; bibliopolic; bibliopegic

21 **reference book**

almanac
atlas
bilingual dictionary
biographical dictionary
children's dictionary
college dictionary
concordance
desk dictionary
dialect dictionary
dictionary of quotations
directory
encyclopedia
encyclopedic dictionary
etymological dictionary, etymologicon
foreign-language dictionary
geographical dictionary, gazetteer
glossary
guidebook
handbook
how-to book
idiom dictionary
index
lexicon
list book
manual
phrase book
reverse dictionary
rhyming dictionary
Roget's Thesaurus
school dictionary
specialized dictionary, special-subject dictionary
synonym dictionary
telephone directory, telephone book
thesaurus
unabridged dictionary
usage dictionary
vade mecum

555 PERIODICAL

<magazine published at regular intervals>

NOUNS 1 **periodical,** serial, **journal,** gazette; ephemeris; **magazine,** book, zine, webzine; pictorial; review; organ, house organ; trade journal, trade magazine; academic journal; daily, weekly, biweekly, bimonthly, fortnightly, monthly, quarterly, seasonal; annual, yearbook; newsletter; daybook, diary; back copy, back issue

2 **newspaper,** news, paper, sheet, rag, gazette, daily newspaper, daily, weekly newspaper, weekly, local paper, local rag, neighborhood newspaper, national newspaper; newspaper of record; tabloid, scandal sheet, extra, special, extra edition, special edition, Sunday paper, early edition, late edition; magazine section, comics, color supplement; online edition

3 **the press,** journalism, the public press, the fourth estate; print medium, the print media, print journalism, the print press, the public print; Fleet Street <Brit>; wire service, newswire; publishing, newspaper publishing, magazine publishing; the publishing industry, communications, mass media, the communications industry, public communication; satellite publishing; reportage, coverage, legwork

4 **journalist,** newspaperman, newspaperwoman, newsman, newswoman, journo, newsperson, newspeople, inkstained wretch, pressman, newswriter, gazetteer, representative of the press; reporter, newshawk, newshound; leg man;

interviewer; investigative reporter, investigative journalist; cub reporter; correspondent, foreign correspondent, war correspondent, special correspondent, stringer; publicist; rewriter, rewrite man; reviser, diaskeuast; editor, subeditor, managing editor, city editor, news editor, sports editor, woman's editor, feature editor, copy editor, copyman, copy chief, slotman; reader, copyreader; editorial writer, leader writer <Brit>; columnist, paragrapher, paragraphist; freelance reporter; photographer, news photographer, photojournalist; paparazzo; press baron; press corps

ADJS 5 **journalistic,** journalese; periodical, serial; magazinish, magaziny; newspaperish, newspapery; editorial; reportorial

556 TREATISE

<published research project>

NOUNS 1 **treatise,** piece, treatment, handling, tractate, tract; contribution; examination, survey, inquiry, discourse, discussion, disquisition, descant, exposition, screed; homily; memoir; dissertation, thesis; essay, theme; pandect; excursus; study, lucubration, étude; paper, research paper, term paper, position paper; sketch, outline, aperçu; causerie; monograph, research monograph; *morceau* <Fr>, paragraph, note; preliminary study, introductory study, first approach, prolegomenon; article, feature, special article; blue-sky research; think piece

2 **commentary,** commentation; comment, remark; criticism, critique, analysis; review, critical review, report, notice, write-up; editorial, leading article, leader <Brit>; gloss, running commentary, Op-Ed column

3 **discourser,** discusser, disquisitor, dissertator, doctoral candidate, expositor, descanter; symposiast, discussant; essayist; monographer, monographist; tractation, tractator; writer, author; scholar

4 **commentator,** commenter; expositor, expounder, exponent; annotator, scholiast; glossarist, glossographer; critic; reviewer, book reviewer; editor; editorial writer, editorialist, leader writer <Brit>; news analyst; publicist

VERBS 5 **write up,** touch upon, discuss, treat, treat of, deal with, take up, handle, go into, inquire into, survey; discourse, dissert, dissertate, descant, develop at thesis; **comment upon,** commentate, remark upon, annotate; expound; criticize, review

ADJS 6 dissertational, disquisitional, discoursive, discursive; expository, expositorial, expositive, exegetical; essayistic; monographic, commentative, commentatorial, annotative; critical, interpretive, interpretative; editorial

557 ABRIDGMENT

<shortened publication>

NOUNS 1 **abridgment,** compendium, compend, **condensation,** short version, shortened version, condensed version, potted version <Brit>, abbreviation, abbreviature, diminution, brief, digest, **abstract,** epitome, précis, capsule, nutshell, capsule version, capsulization, encapsulation, sketch, thumbnail sketch, synopsis, conspectus, syllabus, *aperçu* <Fr>, survey, review, overview, pandect, bird's-eye view; outline, skeleton, draft, blueprint, prospectus; topical outline; head, rubric; graphic abbreviation

2 **summary,** résumé, curriculum vitae (CV), recapitulation, recap, rundown, run-through; summation; review; sum, substance, sum and substance, wrapup; pith, meat, gist, drift, core, essence, main point

3 excerpt, extract, **selection**, extraction, excerption, snippet; passage, selected passage; clip, film clip, outtake, sound bite

4 **excerpts,** *excerpta* <L>, extracts, gleanings, cuttings, clippings, snippets, selections; flowers, florilegium, anthology; compendium, treasury; ephemera; fragments; analects; miscellany, miscellanea; collection, collectanea; ana

VERBS 5 **abridge,** shorten, **condense**, cut, clip; summarize, synopsize, wrap up; outline, sketch, sketch out, hit the high spots; capsule, capsulize, encapsulate; put in a nutshell

ADJS 6 **abridged,** condensed; shortened, clipped, abstracted, abbreviated, truncated, compressed; nutshell, compendious, brief; all but dissertation (ABD)

ADVS 7 in brief, in summary, in sum, to the point, laconically, in a nutshell

558 LIBRARY

<repository for publications>

NOUNS 1 **library,** book depository; learning center; media center, media resource center, information center; public library, town library, city library, municipal library, county library, state library; school library, community college library, college library, university library; special library, medical library, law library, art library; circulating library, lending library; rental library; book wagon, bookmobile; bookroom, bookery, *bibliothèque* <Fr>, *bibliotheca* <L>, athenaeum; reading room; national library, Bibliothèque Nationale, Bodleian Library, British Library, Library of Congress; carrel; interlibrary loan

2 **librarianship,** professional librarianship; **library science,** information science, library services, library and information services, library and information studies; cybrarianship

3 **librarian,** professional librarian, library professional; director, head librarian, chief librarian; head of service; library services director; cybrarian

4 **bibliography**, annotated bibliography; **index**; Books in Print, Paperbound Books in Print; publisher's catalog, publisher's list, backlist; National Union Catalog, Library of Congress Catalog, General Catalogue of Printed Books <Brit>, Union List of Serials; library catalog, computerized catalog, on-line catalog, integrated online system; CD-ROM workstation

559 RELATIONSHIP BY BLOOD

<persons related>

NOUNS 1 **blood relationship,** blood, ties of blood, consanguinity, common descent, common ancestry, biological relationship, genetic relationship, birth family, birth parent, **kinship,** kindred, relation, relationship, sibship; propinquity; cognation; agnation, enation; filiation, affiliation; alliance, connection, family connection, family tie; motherhood, maternity; fatherhood, paternity; patrocliny, matrocliny; patrilineage, matrilineage; patriliny, matriliny; patrisib, matrisib; brotherhood, brothership, fraternity; sisterhood, sistership; cousinhood, cousinship; parental unit; helicopter parent, tiger parent; underparent, free-range parent

2 **kinfolk**, kinfolks, kinsmen, kinsfolk, kindred, kinnery, kin, kith and kin, **family, relatives,** ancestry, relations, people, immediate family, folks, family member, connections; blood relation, blood relative, flesh, blood, flesh and blood, uterine kin, consanguinean; cognate; agnate, enate; kinsman, kinswoman, sib, sibling; german; near relation, distant relation; next of kin; collateral relative, collateral; distaff side, spindle side; sword side, spear side; tribesman, tribespeople, clansman, clanswoman; posterity

3 **father, mother; brother,** bub, bubba, bro, bud, buddy, frater; brethren; **sister,** sis, sissy; sistern; kid brother, kid sister; blood brother, blood sister, uterine brother, uterine sister, brother-german, sister-german; half brother, half sister, foster brother, foster sister, stepbrother, stepsister; **aunt,** auntie; **uncle,** unc, uncs, nunks, nunky, nuncle, **nephew, niece; cousin,** cousin-german; first cousin, second cousin; cousin once removed, cousin twice removed; country cousin; great-uncle, granduncle; great-granduncle; great-aunt, grandaunt; great-grandaunt; grandnephew, grandniece; **son, daughter**

4 **race**, people, folk, family, house, clan, tribe, nation; patriclan, matriclan, deme, sept, gens, phyle, phratry, totem; lineage, line, blood, strain, stock, stem, species, stirps, breed, brood, kind; plant kingdom, animal kingdom, class, order, etc; **ethnicity**; tribalism, clannishness, roots

5 **family,** fam, brood, nuclear family, binuclear family, extended family, one-parent family, single-parent family, single parent; house, household, hearth, hearthside, ménage, people, folk, homefolk, folks, homefolks; kin, relatives, relations; children, issue, descendants, progeny, offspring, litter, get, kids; legal guardian; co-parent

ADJS 6 **related,** kindred, akin; consanguineous, consanguinean, consanguineal, consanguine, of the blood; biological, genetic; natural, birth, by birth; cognate, uterine, agnate, enate; sib, sibling; allied, affiliated, congeneric; german, germane; collateral; foster, novercal; patrilineal, matrilineal; patroclinous, matroclinous; patrilateral, matrilateral; avuncular; intimately related, closely related, remotely related distantly related; family-friendly, family-style, family-sized

7 **racial, ethnic,** tribal, national, family, clannish, totemic, lineal; phyletic, phylogenetic, genetic; gentile, gentilic

COMBINING FORMS 8 adelpho-, phyl-

560 ANCESTRY

<line of descent>

NOUNS 1 **ancestry,** progenitorship; parentage, parenthood; grandparentage, grandfatherhood, grandmotherhood

2 **paternity, fatherhood,** fathership; natural fatherhood, birth fatherhood, biological fatherhood; fatherliness, paternalness; adoptive fatherhood

3 **maternity, motherhood,** mothership; natural motherhood, birth motherhood, biological motherhood; motherliness, maternalness; adoptive motherhood; surrogate motherhood

4 **lineage,** line, bloodline, descent, descendancy, line of descent, ancestral line, succession, extraction, derivation, birth, blood, breed, family, house, strain, sept, stock, race, stirps, seed; direct line, phylum; branch, stem; filiation, affiliation,

apparentation; side, father's side, mother's side; enate, agnate, cognate; male line, spear side, sword side; female line, distaff side, spindle side; consanguinity, common ancestry

5 **genealogy,** pedigree, stemma, genealogical tree, **family tree,** tree; genogram; descent, lineage, line, bloodline, ancestry

6 **heredity,** heritage, inheritance, birth; patrocliny, matrocliny; endowment, inborn capacity, inborn tendency, inborn susceptibility, inborn predisposition; diathesis; inheritability, heritability, hereditability; Mendel's law, Mendelism, Mendelianism; Weismann theory, Weismannism; Altmann theory, De Vries theory, Galtonian theory, Verworn theory, Wiesner theory; genetics, genetic engineering, genetic fingerprinting, pharmacogenetics, genesiology, eugenics; gene, factor, inheritance factor, determiner, determinant; character, dominant character, recessive character, allele, allelomorph; germ cell, germ plasm; chromosome; sex chromosome, X chromosome, Y chromosome; chromatin, chromatid; genetic code; DNA, RNA, replication

7 **ancestors,** antecedents, predecessors, ascendants, fathers, forefathers, forebears, progenitors, primogenitors; grandparents, grandparenthood; patriarchs, elders

8 **parent,** progenitor, ancestor, procreator, begetter; natural parent, birth parent, biological parent; grandparent; ancestress, progenitress, progenitrix; stepparent; adoptive parent; surrogate parent; empty-nester; co-parent

9 **father,** sire, genitor, paternal ancestor, pater, the old man, governor; patriarch, paterfamilias; stepfather; foster father, adoptive father; birth father

10 <nonformal> **papa,** pa, pap, pappy, pop, pops, dad, daddy, daddums, daddyo, big daddy, the old man, the governor, pater

11 **mother,** genetrix, dam, maternal ancestor, matriarch, materfamilias; stepmother; foster mother, adoptive mother; birth mother

12 <nonformal> **mama,** mater, the old woman, mammy, mam, ma, mom, mommy, mops, mummy, mumsy, mimsy, motherkin, motherkins

13 **grandfather,** grandsire; old man; great-grandfather

14 <nonformal> **grandpa,** grampa, gramper, gramp, gramps, grandpapa, grandpap, grandpappy, granddad, granddaddy, granddada, granfer, gramfer, granther, pop, grandpop

15 **grandmother,** grandam; great-grandmother, bubbie

16 <nonformal> **grandma,** granma, old woman; grandmamma, grandmammy, granny, grammy, gammy, grannam, gammer; nana

ADJS 17 **ancestral,** ancestorial, patriarchal; patrifocal; **parental,** parent; **paternal,** fatherly, fatherlike; **maternal,** motherly, motherlike; matrifocal; grandparental; grandmotherly, grandmaternal; grandfatherly, grandpaternal

18 **lineal,** family, familial, genealogical; kindred, akin; enate, enatic, agnate, agnatic, cognate, cognatic; direct, in a direct line; phyletic, phylogenetic; diphyletic

19 **hereditary,** patrimonial, inherited, innate; genetic, genic; patroclinous, matroclinous

20 **inheritable,** heritable, hereditable

561 POSTERITY

<future generations>

NOUNS 1 **posterity, progeny,** issue, offspring, fruit, seed, brood, breed, family; descent, succession; lineage, blood, bloodline; descendants, heirs, inheritors, sons, children, kids, little ones, little people, treasures, hostages to fortune, youngsters, younglings; grandchildren, great-grandchildren; new generation, young generation, rising generation

2 <of animals> **young,** brood, get, spawn, spat, fry; litter, farrow <of pigs>; clutch, hatch

3 **descendant; offspring,** child, scion; son, heir, a chip off the old block, sonny; daughter, heiress; grandchild, grandson, granddaughter; stepchild, stepson, stepdaughter; foster child; adopted child; daddy's boy, daddy's girl, mommy's boy, mommy's girl

4 <derived or collateral descendant> **offshoot,** offset, branch, sprout, shoot, filiation

5 **bastard,** illegitimate, illegitimate child, bastard child, whoreson, by-blow, child born out of wedlock, child born without benefit of clergy, child born on the wrong side of the blanket, natural child, love child, *nullius filius* <L>; illegitimacy, bastardy, bar sinister, bend sinister; hellspawn

6 sonship, sonhood; daughtership, daughterhood

ADJS 7 filial, sonly, sonlike; daughterly, daughterlike; multigenerational

562 LOVEMAKING, ENDEARMENT

<sexual activity>

NOUNS 1 **lovemaking,** dalliance, amorous dalliance, billing and cooing; fondling, caressing, hugging, kissing; cuddling, snuggling, nestling, nuzzling; bundling; sexual intercourse

2 <nonformal> **making love,** making out, necking,

petting, heavy petting, spooning, smooching, lollygagging, canoodling, playing kissy-face, playing kissy-kissy, playing kissy-poo, playing kissy-huggy, pitching woo, flinging woo, sucking face, swapping spit

3 embrace, **hug**, squeeze, fond embrace, embracement, clasp, enfoldment, bear hug, bro hug, group hug

4 **kiss,** buss, smack, smooch, osculation; French kiss, soul kiss; fish-kiss; air-kiss, mwah, cheek-kiss

5 **endearment; caress,** pat; sweet talk, soft words, honeyed words, terms of endearment, sweet nothings; line, blandishments, artful endearments; love call, mating call, wolf whistle

6 <**terms of endearment**> darling, dear, deary, sweetheart, sweetie, sweet, sweets, sweetkins, honey, hon, honeybun, honey-bunny, honeybunch, honey child, sugar, love, lover, precious, precious heart, pet, petkins, babe, baby, doll, baby-doll, cherub, angel, chick, chickabiddy, buttercup, duck, duckling, ducks, lamb, lambkin, snookums, poppet <Brit>

7 **courtship,** courting, wooing, dating; court, suit, suing, amorous pursuit, addresses; gallantry; serenade

8 **proposal,** marriage proposal, offer of marriage, popping of the question; engagement

9 **flirtation,** flirtiness, coquetry, dalliance; flirtatiousness, coquettishness, coyness; sheep's eyes, goo-goo eyes, puppy-dog eyes, amorous looks, coquettish glances, come-hither look; ogle, side-glance; bedroom eyes

10 **philandering,** philander, lady-killing; lechery, licentiousness, unchastity

11 **flirt,** coquette, gold digger, vamp; strumpet, whore

12 **philanderer,** philander, woman chaser, ladies' man, heartbreaker, rake, cad, man of the world; masher, lady-killer, wolf, skirt chaser, pantsman, man on the make, make-out artist; libertine, lecher, cocksman, seducer, gigolo, Casanova, Don Juan, Lothario; male prostitute, rent boy, stud; roving eye

13 **love letter,** billet-doux, mash note; valentine

VERBS 14 **make love,** bill and coo; dally, toy, trifle, wanton, make time; sweet-talk, whisper sweet nothings; go steady, keep company; copulate

15 <nonformal> **make out,** neck, pet, spoon, smooch, lollygag, canoodle, pitch woo, fling woo, play kissy-face, suck face, swap spit

16 **caress,** pet, pat; feel, feel up, fondle, dandle, coddle, cocker, cosset; pat on the head, chuck under the chin

17 **cuddle,** snuggle, nestle, nuzzle; lap; bundle

18 embrace, **hug**, clasp, press, squeeze, fold, enfold, bosom, embosom, put one's arms around, throw one's arms around, take to one's arms, take in one's arms, fold to the heart, press to the bosom

19 **kiss,** osculate, buss, smack, smooch; blow a kiss, nwah

20 **flirt,** coquet; philander, gallivant, play the field, play around, sow one's oats; make eyes at, ogle, eye, cast coquettish glances, cast sheep's eyes at, make goo-goo eyes at, look sweet upon; play hard to get

21 **court,** woo, date, press one's suit, pay court to, pay suit to, make suit to, cozy up to, eye up, chat up, pay one's court to, address, pay one's addresses to, pay attention to, lay siege to, fling oneself at, throw oneself at the head of; pursue, follow; chase; set one's cap at, set one's cap for; sue; serenade; spark, squire, esquire, beau, sweetheart, swain

22 **propose,** pop the question, ask for one's hand; become engaged

ADJS 23 amatory, amative; sexual; caressive; **flirtatious,** flirty; coquettish, coy, come-hither

563 MARRIAGE

<contractual relationship>

NOUNS 1 **marriage, matrimony,** wedlock, holy matrimony, holy wedlock, match, matching, matchup, splicing, union, matrimonial union, alliance, marriage sacrament, sacrament of matrimony, sacrament of marriage, bond of matrimony, state of matrimony, wedding knot, conjugal bond, conjugal knot, conjugality, nuptial bond, nuptial tie, one flesh; married state, married status, wedded state, wedded status, wedded bliss, conjugal bliss, weddedness, wifehood, husbandhood, spousehood; coverture, cohabitation; bed, marriage bed, bridal bed, bridebed; living as man and wife, common-law marriage; tying the knot, getting hitched, getting spliced; intermarriage, mixed marriage, interfaith marriage, interracial marriage; remarriage; arranged marriage; lesbian marriage, homosexual marriage, gay marriage, civil union; miscegenation; misalliance, *mésalliance* <Fr>

2 **marriageability,** marriageableness, nubility, ripeness; age of consent

3 **wedding, marriage,** marriage ceremony, wedding ceremony, nuptial mass; church wedding, civil wedding, civil ceremony, courthouse wedding; destination wedding; espousement, bridal; banns; wedding bells, nuptials, spousals, espousals, marriage vows, hymeneal rites, wedding service; commitment ceremony; *chuppah* <Heb>, wedding canopy; white wedding; wedding song,

marriage song, nuptial song, prothalamium, epithalamium, epithalamy, hymen, hymeneal; wedding veil; bridechamber, bridal suite, nuptial apartment; **honeymoon;** forced marriage, shotgun wedding; elopement

4 **wedding party;** wedding attendant, usher; best man, bridesman, groomsman; paranymph; bridesmaid, bridemaiden, maid of honor, matron of honor; attendant, flower girl, train bearer, ring bearer; wedding planner

5 **newlywed;** bridegroom, groom; bride, plighted bride, blushing bride; war bride, GI bride; honeymooner

6 **spouse,** espouser, espoused, **mate,** yokemate, partner, consort, better half, other half, one's promised, one's betrothed, soul mate, helpmate, helpmeet; old ball and chain

7 **husband,** married man, man, benedict, old man, hubby

8 **wife,** married woman, wedded wife, squaw, woman, lady, matron, old lady, old woman, little woman, ball and chain, feme, feme covert, better half, helpmate, helpmeet, rib, wife of one's bosom; wife in name only; wife in all but name, concubine, common-law wife; blushing bride, war bride, GI bride

9 **married couple,** wedded pair, bridal pair, happy couple, man and wife, husband and wife, man and woman, one flesh, Mr. and Mrs.; newlyweds, bride and groom, honeymooners, coupledom

10 **harem,** seraglio, serai, gynaeceum; zenana, purdah

11 **monogamist,** monogynist; **bigamist;** digamist, deuterogamist; trigamist; **polygamist,** polygynist, polyandrist; Bluebeard

12 **matchmaker,** marriage broker, matrimonial agent; matrimonial agency, marriage bureau; go-between; dating agency, dating service, lonely hearts club, computer dating

13 <god> Hymen; <goddesses> Hera, Teleia; Juno, Pronuba; Frigg

VERBS 14 **<join in marriage> marry,** wed, nuptial, join, unite, hitch, splice, couple, match, match up, make a match, arrange a match, join together, unite in marriage, join in holy matrimony, unite in holy wedlock, tie the knot, tie the nuptial knot, tie the wedding knot, celebrate a marriage, make one, pronounce man and wife; give away, give in marriage; marry off, find a mate for, find a husband for, find a wife for

15 **<get married> marry, wed,** contract matrimony, say "I do," mate, couple, espouse, wive, take to wife, take a wife, take a husband, get hitched, tie the knot, become one, be made one, pair off, give one's hand to, bestow one's hand upon, lead to the altar, take for better or for worse; make an honest man of, make an honest woman of; remarry, rewed; intermarry, interwed, miscegenate

16 **honeymoon,** go on a honeymoon, consummate one's marriage; second-honeymoon

17 **cohabit,** cohabitate, live together, live as man and wife, share one's bed and board; shack up

ADJS 18 **matrimonial, marital,** conjugal, connubial, nuptial, wedded, married, hymeneal; epithalamic; spousal; husbandly, uxorious; bridal, wifely, uxorial; premarital, concubinal, concubinary; engaged, affianced, promised, prenuptial

19 **monogamous,** monogynous, monandrous; **bigamous,** digamous; **polygamous,** polygynous, polyandrous; morganatic; miscegenetic

20 **marriageable,** nubile, eligible, ripe, of age, of marriageable age

21 **married, wedded,** newlywed, espoused, one, one bone and one flesh, mated, matched, coupled, partnered, paired, hitched, spliced, hooked

COMBINING FORMS 22 -gamy; -gamous

564 RELATIONSHIP BY MARRIAGE

<extended family>

NOUNS 1 **marriage relationship,** affinity, marital affinity; connection, family connection, marriage connection, matrimonial connection

2 **in-laws,** relatives-in-law; brother-in-law, sister-in-law, father-in-law, mother-in-law, son-in-law, daughter-in-law

3 stepfather, stepmother; stepbrother, stepsister; stepchild, stepson, stepdaughter

ADJS 4 **affinal,** affined, by marriage

565 CELIBACY

<abstention from sexual activity>

NOUNS 1 **celibacy,** singleness, singlehood, single blessedness, single state, unmarried state, unwed state; bachelorhood, bachelordom, bachelorism, bachelorship; spinsterhood, maidenhood, maidenhead, virginity, maiden state, virgin state, chastity, chasteness; monasticism, monachism, spiritual marriage, holy orders, the veil; misogamy, misogyny; self-restraint, self-denial; sexual abstinence, sexual abstention, continence

2 **celibate**; monk, monastic, lama, bhikkhu, priest, nun, cenobite, eremite; virgin, vestal; misogamist, misogynist; unmarried, single, lonely heart

3 **bachelor,** bach, old bach, single man, unmarried man, confirmed bachelor, unattached male; misogamist; Mr. Cool

4 **bachelorette,** unmarried woman, spinster,

spinstress, old maid, maid, maiden, bachelor girl, single girl, lone woman, maiden lady, feme sole, unattached female; virgin, virgo intacta, cherry; vestal, vestal virgin

VERBS 5 **be unmarried,** be single, live alone, enjoy single blessedness, bach, bach it, keep bachelor quarters, keep one's freedom, sit on the shelf; remain celibate, abstain

ADJS 6 **celibate**, celibatic; monastic, monachal, monkish, cenobitic, nunnish; misogamic, misogynous; sexually abstinent, sexually continent, abstinent, abstaining; self-restrained

7 **unmarried,** unwedded, unwed, single, sole, spouseless, wifeless, husbandless, unmated, mateless; bachelorly, bachelorlike; spinsterly, spinsterish, spinsterlike; old-maidish, old-maidenish; maiden, maidenly; virgin, virginal; independent, unattached, fancy-free; on the shelf

566 DIVORCE, WIDOWHOOD

<dissolution of marriage>

NOUNS 1 **divorce,** divorcement, grasswidowhood, civil divorce, **separation,** legal separation, conscious uncoupling, judicial separation, separate maintenance; interlocutory decree; dissolution of marriage; divorce decree, decree nisi, decree absolute; annulment, decree of nullity; nonconsummation of marriage, estrangement, living apart, desertion; broken marriage, broken home; breakup, split-up, split, marriage on the rocks, discordant couple

2 **divorcé,** divorced person, divorced man, divorced woman, free man, free woman; divorcer; grass widow, grass widower

3 **widowhood,** viduity; **widowerhood,** widowership; weeds, widow's weeds

4 **widow,** widow woman, relict; dowager, queen dowager, dowager queen, merry widow, war widow; **widower,** widowman

VERBS 5 **divorce, separate,** part, split, split up, split the sheets, unmarry, put away, obtain a divorce, dissolve one's marriage, come to a parting of the ways, untie the knot, sue for divorce, file for divorce; have one's marriage annulled; grant a divorce, grant a final decree; grant an annulment, grant a decree of nullity, annul a marriage, put asunder, regain one's freedom; break up, sunder; live apart, be estranged; desert, abandon, leave, walk out

6 **widow,** bereave, make a widow

ADJS 7 widowly, widowish, widowlike; **widowed,** widowered; **divorced;** separated, legally separated, split, estranged; on the rocks, uncoupled

567 SCHOOL

<place of teaching and learning>

NOUNS 1 **school** <see list>, **educational institution,** teaching institution, academic institution, scholastic institution, teaching and research institution, institute, academy, seminary, *Schule* <Ger>, *école* <Fr>, *escuela* <Sp>; alternative school; magnet school; certification program; seat of learning; special education

2 **preschool,** prekindergarten, pre-K, infant school <Brit>, nursery, nursery school; day nursery, daycare center, crèche; playschool; kindergarten

3 **elementary school,** grade school, graded school, the grades; primary school; junior school <Brit>; grammar school; folk school, home schooling

4 **secondary school,** academy, *Gymnasium* <Ger>; *lycée* <Fr>, lyceum; high school, high; junior high school, junior high, middle school, intermediate school; senior high school, senior high; preparatory school, prep school, public school <Brit>, seminary; grammar school <Brit>, Latin school; charter school

5 **college, university,** institution of higher education, institute of higher learning, degree-granting institution; tertiary school, graduate school, advanced degree, higher education, higher learning, postgraduate school, coeducational school; academe, academia, the groves of Academe, the campus, the halls of learning, the halls of ivy, ivied halls; alma mater; women's college; agricultural college; polytechnic, adult education, correspondence course; prerequisite, corequisite; course, class; path; distance learning, distance education, e-learning, online degree, virtual classroom; professional development; massive open online course (MOOC), nanodegree; acceptance letter; gap year; advanced placement; continuing education

6 **service school, service academy**, military academy, naval academy

7 **art school, performing arts school,** music school, conservatory, arts conservatory, school of the arts, dance school

8 **religious school** <see list>, parochial school, church-related school, church school; Sunday school

9 **reform school,** reformatory, correctional institution, industrial school, training school; borstal, borstal school, remand school <Brit>

10 **schoolhouse,** school building; little red schoolhouse; classroom building; portable classroom; hall; campus

11 **schoolroom, classroom;** recitation room; lecture room, lecture hall; auditorium, assembly hall; theater, amphitheater; gym, gymnasium, locker room

12 **governing board,** board; board of education, board of ed, school board; college board, board of regents, board of trustees, board of visitors

ADJS 13 **scholastic, academic,** institutional, school, classroom; collegiate; university; preschool; interscholastic, intercollegiate, extramural; intramural

14 **religious school**

Bible institute
Bible school
Catholic school
church school
convent school
denominational school
divinity school
Hebrew school, *heder* <Yiddish>
madrasah
mesivta
parish school
religious school, parochial school
Sabbath school
schola cantorum
scholasticate
seminary
Sunday school
Talmud Torah
theological seminary, theological school
vacation church school
yeshiva

15 **school**

academy
adult-education school
alternate school, alternative school
boarding school
business college, business school
charm school
community college
comprehensive school
conservatory
correspondence school
country day school
day school
distance learning institution
elementary school, grade school
extension school, extension program
field school
finishing school
graduate school
gymnasium
institute
junior college
junior high school, junior school, middle school, intermediate school
law school
lyceum, lycée
medical school
military school, military academy
night school
open-classroom school
polytechnic school, polytechnic <Brit>
preparatory school, prep school
preschool
primary school
private school
public school
reformatory school
religious school
school of continuing education, continuation school
secondary school, high school, senior high school
secretarial school
special needs school
state school
summer school
technical school, technical college, tech
university extension
vocational school, trade school
women's college

568 TEACHING
<instructing>

NOUNS 1 **teaching, instruction,** education, schooling, tuition; edification, enlightenment, illumination; tutelage, tutorage, tutorship; tutoring, coaching, direction, training, preparation, private teaching, teacher; spoon-feeding; guidance; pedagogy, pedagogics, didactics, didacticism; scholarship; catechization; computer-aided instruction, programmed instruction; home schooling; self-teaching, self-instruction; distance education; information; reeducation; school; **formal education,** coursework, schoolwork

2 **inculcation**, indoctrination, catechization, inoculation, implantation, infixation, infixion, impression, instillment, instillation, impregnation, infusion, imbuement; absorption, regurgitation; dictation; conditioning, brainwashing; reindoctrination

3 **training,** preparation, readying, conditioning, grooming, cultivation, development, improvement; discipline; breaking, housebreaking; upbringing, bringing-up, fetching-up, rearing, raising, breeding, nurture, nurturing, fostering; practice, rehearsal, exercise, drill, drilling; apprenticeship, in-service training, on-the-job training; work-study; military training, basic training, basic military training; manual training, sloyd; vocational training, vocational education; liberal arts, arithmetic, astronomy, geometry, grammar, logic, music, rhetoric; soap in the mouth, hotsaucing

4 preinstruction, pre-education; **priming,** cramming

5 **elementary education**, nursery school, preschool, primary education, home schooling; initiation, introduction, propaedeutic; rudiments, grounding, first steps, elements, ABC's, basics; reading, writing, and arithmetic, three R's; primer, hornbook, abecedarium, abecedary

6 **instructions,** directions, orders; briefing, final instructions; training manual

7 **lesson, teaching,** instruction, lecture, lecture-demonstration, harangue, discourse, disquisition, exposition, talk, homily, sermon, preachment; chalk talk; skull session; recitation, recital; assignment, exercise, task, set task, homework; moral, morality, moral compass, moralization, moral lesson; object lesson; grades, grading, grade point average

8 **study,** branch of learning, branch of knowledge; **discipline**, subdiscipline, subspecialty; field, specialty, academic specialty, area; course,

course of study, curriculum, syllabus, module, department; subject; major, minor; requirement, required course, elective course, core curriculum; refresher course; summer course, summer-session course, intersession course; crash course; gut course; correspondence course; distance-learning course; seminar, proseminar; professional development

9 physical education, phys ed, physical culture, gymnastics, calisthenics, eurythmics

VERBS 10 **teach, instruct,** give instruction, give lessons in, educate, school; edify, enlighten, civilize, illumine; direct, guide; get across, inform; show, show how, show the ropes, demonstrate; give an idea of; put in the right, set right; improve one's mind, enlarge the mind, broaden the mind; sharpen the wits, open the eyes, open the mind; teach a lesson, give a lesson to; ground, teach the rudiments, teach the basics; catechize; teach an old dog new tricks; reeducate

11 **tutor, coach**, mentor, direct; prime, cram, cram with facts, stuff with knowledge

12 **inculcate,** indoctrinate, catechize, inoculate, instill, infuse, imbue, impregnate, implant, infix, impress; impress upon the mind, impress upon the memory, urge on the mind, beat into, beat into one's head, knock into one's head, grind in, drill into, drum into one's head, drum into one's skull; condition, brainwash, program

13 **train;** drill, exercise; practice, rehearse; keep in practice, keep one's hand in; prepare, ready, condition, groom, fit, put in tune, form, lick into shape; rear, raise, bring up, fetch up, bring up by hand, breed; cultivate, develop, improve; nurture, foster, nurse; discipline, take in hand; put through the mill, put through the grind; break, break in, housebreak, house-train; put to school, send to school, apprentice

14 preinstruct, pre-educate; **initiate,** introduce

15 **give instructions,** give directions; **brief,** give a briefing

16 **expound,** exposit; explain; **lecture,** discourse, harangue, hold forth, give a lesson, read a lesson; preach, sermonize; moralize, point a moral

17 **assign,** give an assignment, make an assignment, give homework, set a task, set hurdles; lay out a course, make a syllabus

ADJS 18 **educational,** educative, educating, educatory, teaching, instructive, instructional, tuitional, tuitionary; cultural, edifying, enlightening, illuminating; informative, informational, boning up; didactic, preceptive; self instructional, self-teaching, autodidactic; lecturing, preaching, hortatory, exhortatory, homiletic, homiletical; initiatory, introductory, propaedeutic; disciplinary; coeducational; remedial

19 **scholastic, academic,** schoolish, pedantic, donnish; scholarly; pedagogical; collegiate, graduate, professional, doctoral, graduate-professional, postgraduate; interdisciplinary, cross-disciplinary, transdisciplinary; curricular, intramural, extramural, varsity

20 extracurricular, extraclassroom; nonscholastic, noncollegiate

569 MISTEACHING

<instructing wrongly or badly>

NOUNS 1 **misteaching,** misinstruction; **misguidance,** misdirection, misleading; sophistry; perversion, corruption; mystification, obscuration, obfuscation, obscurantism; misinformation, misknowledge; the blind leading the blind; college of Laputa

2 **propaganda;** propagandism, indoctrination; brainwashing; propagandist, agitprop; **disinformation;** war of nerves

VERBS 3 **misteach,** misinstruct, miseducate; **misinform;** misadvise, misguide, misdirect, mislead; pervert, corrupt; mystify, obscure, obfuscate

4 **propagandize,** carry on a propaganda; indoctrinate; **disinform,** brainwash

ADJS 5 **mistaught,** misinstructed; misinformed; misadvised, misguided, misdirected, misled

6 **misteaching**, misinstructive, miseducative, misinforming; misleading, misguiding, misdirecting; obscuring, mystifying, obfuscatory; propagandistic, indoctrinational; disinformational

570 LEARNING

<gaining knowledge, experience>

NOUNS 1 **learning,** intellectual acquirement, intellectual acquisition, intellectual attainment, stocking the mind, mental cultivation, mental culture, improving the mind, broadening the mind, acquisition of knowledge, scholarship; learning style; mastery, mastery of skills; self-education, self-instruction; knowledge, erudition; education; memorization; cultural literacy; professional student; study group, study hall

2 **absorption,** ingestion, imbibing, assimilation, taking-in, getting, getting hold of, getting the hang of, soaking-up, digestion; aha moment

3 **study, studying,** application, conning; reading, perusal; restudy, restudying, brushing up, boning up, review; contemplation; inspection; engrossment; brainwork, headwork, lucubration,

mental labor; exercise, practice, drill, flash card; grind, grinding, boning; cramming, cram, swotting; extensive study, wide reading; subject; college degree, associate degree, graduate degree

4 **studiousness, scholarliness,** scholarship; bookishness, diligence; learnedness, intellectuality, literacy, polymathy, erudition; binge learning

5 **teachableness, teachability,** teachable moment; **educability,** trainableness; aptness, aptitude, quickness, readiness; receptivity, mind like a blotter, ready grasp, quick mind, quick study; willingness, motivation, hunger for learning, thirst for learning, willingness to learn, curiosity, inquisitiveness; docility, malleability, moldability, pliability, facility, plasticity, impressionability, susceptibility, formability; brightness, cleverness, intelligence

VERBS 6 **learn,** get, get hold of, get into one's head, get through one's thick skull; gain knowledge, pick up information, gather knowledge, collect knowledge, glean knowledge; stock the mind, improve the mind, broaden the mind; stuff the mind, cram the mind; load the mind; find out, ascertain, discover, find, determine, figure out; become informed, gain knowledge of, gain understanding of, acquire information about, acquire intelligence about, research, become aware of, learn about, find out about, do the math; acquaint oneself with, make oneself acquainted with, become acquainted with; be informed

7 **absorb,** acquire, take in, ingest, imbibe, get by osmosis, assimilate, **digest**, soak up, drink in; soak in, seep in, percolate in

8 **memorize**, get by rote; fix in the mind

9 **master,** attain mastery of, make oneself master of, gain command of, become adept in, become familiar with, become conversant with, become versed in, become well-versed in, get up in, gain a good knowledge of, gain a thorough knowledge of, learn all about, get down pat, get down cold, get taped, get to the heart of; get the hang of, get the knack of; learn the ropes, learn the ins and outs; know well

10 **learn by experience,** learn by doing, live and learn, go through the school of hard knocks, learn the hard way; teach oneself, school oneself; learn a lesson, be taught a lesson

11 **be taught,** receive instruction, be tutored, be instructed, undergo schooling, pursue one's education, attend classes, go to school, attend school, take lessons, be mentored, matriculate, enroll, register; train, prepare oneself, ready oneself, go into training; serve an apprenticeship; apprentice, apprentice oneself to; study with, read with, sit at the feet of, learn from, have as one's master; monitor, audit

12 **study,** regard studiously, apply oneself to, con, crack a book, hit the books; read, peruse, go over, read up, read up on, have one's nose in a book; restudy, review; contemplate; examine; give the mind to; pore over, vet; be highly motivated, hunger for knowledge, thirst for knowledge; bury oneself in, wade through, plunge into, throw oneself into; dig, grind, bone, bone up on, swot; lucubrate, elucubrate, burn the midnight oil; make a study of; practice, drill

13 **browse, scan,** skim, dip into, thumb through, run over, run through, glance over, glance through, run the eye over, turn over the leaves, have a look at, hit the high spots, graze

14 **study up,** get up, study up on, read up on; review, brush up, polish up, **cram**, cram up, **bone up**; pull an all-nighter

15 study to be, study for, read for, read law; specialize in, go in for, make one's field; major in, minor in

ADJS 16 **educated**, learned; knowledgeable, erudite; literate, numerate; self-taught, self-instructed, autodidactic; well-aware, well-versed

17 **studious,** devoted to studies, **scholarly,** scholastic, academic, professorial, tweedy, donnish; owlish; rabbinic, mandarin; pedantic, dryasdust; bookish; diligent

18 **teachable, instructable, educable,** schoolable, trainable; apt, quick, ready, ripe for instruction; receptive, willing, motivated; hungry for knowledge, thirsty for knowledge; docile, malleable, moldable, pliable, facile, plastic, impressionable, susceptible, formable; bright, clever, intelligent

571 TEACHER

<one who instructs>

NOUNS 1 **teacher, instructor, educator,** preceptor, **mentor;** master, maestro; pedagogue, pedagogist, educationist, educationalist, tutor; schoolman; schoolteacher, schoolmaster, schoolkeeper; abecedarian, certified teacher, licensed teacher; professor, academic, member of academy; don, fellow; guide, docent; rabbi, pandit, pundit, guru; home tutor, private tutor

2 <**woman teacher**> instructress, educatress, preceptress, mistress; schoolmistress; schoolma'am, schoolmarm, dame, schooldame; governess, duenna

3 <**academic rank**> professor, associate professor, assistant professor, instructor, tutor, associate,

assistant, lecturer, reader <Brit>; visiting professor; emeritus, professor emeritus, retired professor

4 teaching fellow, teaching assistant (TA); paraeducator; teaching intern, fellow, intern; practice teacher, apprentice teacher, student teacher, pupil teacher; teacher's aide, paraprofessional; monitor, proctor, prefect, praepostor <Brit>; student assistant, graduate assistant

5 **tutor,** tutorer; substitute teacher, sub; coach, coacher; private instructor; crammer

6 **trainer,** handler, groomer; driller, drillmaster; **coach,** athletic coach

7 **lecturer,** lector, reader <Brit>, praelector, preacher, homilist

8 **principal, headmaster,** headmistress, vice-principal; president, chancellor, vice-chancellor, rector, provost, master; **dean,** academic dean, dean of the faculty, dean of women, dean of men; administrator, educational administrator; administration; department head, department chair

9 **faculty,** staff, faculty members, professorate, professoriate, professors, professordom, teaching staff

10 **instructorship, teachership,** preceptorship, schoolmastery; tutorship, tutorhood, tutorage, tutelage; professorship, professorhood, professorate, professoriate; chair, endowed chair; lectureship, readership <Brit>; fellowship, research fellowship; assistantship

ADJS 11 **pedagogic, pedagogical,** preceptorial, tutorial; teacherish, teachery, teacherlike, teachy, schoolteacherish, schoolteachery, schoolmasterish, schoolmasterly, schoolmastering, schoolmasterlike; schoolmistressy, schoolmarmish; professorial, professorlike, academic, tweedy, donnish; pedantic

572 STUDENT

<one who learns>

NOUNS 1 **student, pupil,** scholar, learner, studier, educatee, trainee; tutee; inquirer; mature student, adult-education student, continuing education student; self-taught person, autodidact; auditor; reader, reading enthusiast, great reader, printhead; bookworm, researcher; opsimath

2 **disciple,** follower, apostle; convert, proselyte; discipleship, disciplehood, pupilage, tutelage, studentship, followership

3 **schoolchild,** school kid, school-aged child; **schoolboy,** school lad; **schoolgirl;** day-pupil, day boy, day girl; preschool child, preschooler, nursery school child; kindergartner, grade schooler, primary schooler, intermediate schooler; secondary schooler, prep schooler, preppie, high schooler; schoolmate, schoolfellow, fellow student, classmate

4 **gifted student,** special student exceptional student; special education student, special ed student; learning disabled student (LD); learning impaired student; slow learner, underachiever; handicapped student; emotionally disturbed student; culturally disadvantaged student

5 **college student,** collegian, collegiate, university student, varsity student, college boy, college girl; coed; seminarian, seminarist

6 **undergraduate,** undergrad, cadet, midshipman; underclassman, freshman, freshie, plebe, sophomore, soph; upperclassman, junior, senior

7 <Brit terms> commoner, pensioner, sizar, servitor, exhibitioner, fellow commoner; sophister, questionist; wrangler, optime; passman; muggle

8 **graduate,** grad; **alumnus,** alumni, alumna, alumnae; old boy <Brit>; **graduate student,** grad student, master's degree candidate, doctoral candidate; **postgraduate,** postgrad; degrees; college graduate, college man, college woman, educated man, educated woman, educated class; meritocracy

9 **novice,** novitiate, noviciate, tyro, abecedarian, alphabetarian, beginner, entrant, neophyte, tenderfoot, greenhorn, freshman, fledgling; newbie; Bambi; catechumen, initiate, debutant; new boy <Brit>, newcomer; ignoramus; recruit, raw recruit, inductee, rookie, yardbird, boot; probationer, probationist, postulant; apprentice, articled clerk

10 **nerd,** egghead, grind, greasy grind, swotter, mugger; bookworm

11 **class,** form <Brit>, **grade;** track; year

ADJS 12 **studentlike,** schoolboyish, schoolgirlish; undergraduate, graduate, postgraduate; collegiate, college-bred; sophomoric; sophomorical; autodidactic; studious; learned, bookish; exceptional, gifted, special

13 probationary, probational, on probation; in detention

573 DIRECTION, MANAGEMENT

<guidance or supervision>

NOUNS 1 **direction, management, managing,** managery, handling, running, conduct; governance, command, control, chiefdom, government, controllership; authority; regulation, ordering, husbandry; manipulation, orchestration; guidance, lead, leading; steering, navigation; navigation system, Global Positioning System (GPS); pilotage, conning, the conn, the helm, the wheel; redirection

2 **supervision,** superintendence, intendance, intendancy, heading, heading up, bossing, running; surveillance, oversight, eye; charge, care, auspices, jurisdiction; responsibility, accountability

3 **administration,** executive function, executive role, command function, say-so, last word; decision-making; disposition, disposal, dispensation; officiation; lawmaking, legislation, regulation

4 **directorship, leadership,** managership, directorate, headship, governorship, chairmanship, convenership <Brit>, presidency, premiership, generalship, captainship; mastership; dictatorship, sovereignty; superintendence, superintendency, intendancy, foremanship, overseership, supervisorship; stewardship, custody, guardianship, shepherding, proctorship; personnel management; collective leadership

5 **helm,** conn, rudder, tiller, wheel, steering wheel; **reins;** joystick; remote control, remote

6 **domestic management,** housekeeping, homemaking, housewifery, ménage; domestic economy, home economics

7 **efficiency engineering,** scientific management, bean-counting, industrial engineering, management engineering, management consulting; management theory; efficiency expert, management consultant; time and motion study, time-motion study, time study; therblig

VERBS 8 **direct, manage,** regulate, conduct, carry on, handle, run, be in charge; control, command, head, govern, rule, boss, head up, pull the strings, mastermind, quarterback, call the signals; order, prescribe; organize; lay down the law, make the rules, call the shots; office, captain, skipper; lead, take the lead, lead on; manipulate, maneuver, engineer; take command; be responsible for; hold the purse strings; redirect

9 **guide,** steer, drive, run; herd, counsel, advise, shepherd; channel; pilot, take the helm, take the wheel, be at the helm, be at the tiller, hold the reins, be in the driver's seat; emcee

10 **supervise,** superintend, **boss,** oversee, overlook, ride herd on, crack the whip, stand over, keep an eye on, keep in order; cut work out for; straw-boss; take care of

11 **administer,** administrate; officiate; preside, preside over, preside at the board; chair, chairman, occupy the chair, take the chair

ADJS 12 **directing, directive,** directory, directorial; **managing, managerial;** commanding, controlling, governing; regulating, regulative, regulatory; head, chief; leading, guiding; redirecting

13 **supervising,** supervisory, overseeing, superintendent, boss; in charge, in the driver's seat, holding the reins

14 **administrative,** administrating; ministerial, executive; officiating, presiding

ADVS 15 in the charge of, in the hands of, in the care of; under the auspices of, under the aegis of; in one's charge, on one's hands, under one's care, under one's jurisdiction

574 DIRECTOR

<guide or supervisor>

NOUNS 1 **director,** director general, governor, rector, manager, administrator, intendant, conductor; person in charge, responsible person, key person, key player; ship's husband, supercargo; impresario, producer; deputy, agent

2 **superintendent; supervisor,** foreman, monitor, head, headman, overman, boss, chief, gaffer, ganger, taskmaster; overseer, overlooker; inspector, surveyor; proctor; subforeman, straw boss; slave driver; boatswain; floorman, floorwalker, floor manager; noncommissioned officer; controller, comptroller, auditor; department head; chief cook and bottle washer

3 **executive,** officer, official, pinstriper, employer, company official; suit; president, prexy, chief executive officer (CEO), chief executive, chief operating officer (COO), managing director, director; provost, prefect, warden, archon; policymaker, agenda-setter; magistrate; chairman of the board; chancellor, vice-chancellor; vice-president (VP), veep; secretary; treasurer; dean; executive officer, executive director, executive secretary; management, the administration; equal opportunity employer

4 **steward,** bailiff <Brit>, reeve, seneschal; majordomo, butler, housekeeper, *maître d'hôtel* <Fr>; master of ceremonies (MC), emcee, master of the revels; proctor, procurator, attorney; guardian, custodian, executor; curator, librarian; croupier; factor

5 **chairman,** chairwoman, **chair,** chairperson, convener <Brit>, speaker, presiding officer; co-chairman

6 **leader,** point person, conductor; file leader, fugleman; pacemaker, pacesetter, honcho; bellwether, bell mare, bell cow, Judas goat; standard-bearer, torchbearer; leader of men, born leader, charismatic leader, charismatic figure, inspired leader; messiah, Mahdi; führer, duce;

forerunner; ringleader; precentor, coryphaeus, choragus, symphonic conductor, choirmaster

7 **guide,** guider; shepherd, herd, herdsman, drover, cowherd, goatherd; tour guide, tour director, tour conductor, cicerone, mercury, courier, dragoman; pilot, river pilot, navigator, helmsman, timoneer, steerman, steerer, coxswain, boatsteerer, boatheader; automatic pilot, Gyropilot; pointer, fingerpost <Brit>, guidepost; leader, motivator, pacesetter, standard-bearer

8 **guiding star,** guiding light, cynosure, polestar, polar star, lodestar, Polaris, North Star

9 **compass,** magnetic compass, gyrocompass, gyroscopic compass, gyrostatic compass, Gyrosin compass, surveyor's compass, mariner's compass; needle, magnetic needle; direction finder, radio compass, radio direction finder (RDF)

10 **directory, guidebook,** handbook, Baedeker; city directory, business directory; telephone directory, telephone book, phone book, classified directory, Yellow Pages; bibliography; catalog, index, handlist, checklist, finding list; itinerary, road map, roadbook; gazetteer, reference book; relief map, contour map

11 **directorate,** directory, **management, the administration,** the brass, top brass, the people upstairs, the people in the front office, executive hierarchy; the executive, executive arm, executive branch; middle management; cabinet; board, governing board, governing body, board of directors, board of trustees, board of regents; steering committee, executive committee, interlocking directorate; cadre, executive council; infrastructure; council

575 MASTER

<one having authority over another>

NOUNS 1 **master, lord, lord and master,** overlord, seigneur, paramount, lord paramount, liege, liege lord, lord of the manor, *padrone* <Ital>, *patron*, *chef* <Fr>, patroon; **chief, boss,** *sahib* <India>, *bwana* <Swah>; employer; husband, man of the house, master of the house, paterfamilias; patriarch, elder; teacher, rabbi, guru, starets; church dignitary, ecclesiarch

2 **mistress,** governess, dame, madam; **matron,** housewife, homemaker, mistress of the house, lady of the house, chatelaine; housemistress, housemother; rectoress, abbess, mother superior; great lady, first lady; materfamilias, matriarch, dowager

3 **chief**, principal, headman; **master,** dean, doyen, doyenne; high priest, superior, senior; **leader**; important person, personage; owner, landowner

4 <nonformal> **top dog,** boss man, big boy, big daddy, big cheese, big hitter, big kahuna, biggie, kingpin, kingfish, el supremo, honcho, head honcho, top banana, big enchilada, bigwig, big gun, top gun, big shot, big wheel, very important person (VIP), himself, herself, man upstairs, woman upstairs, cock of the walk; queen bee, heavy momma, big momma, old man, quarterback, ringmaster, skipper, high priest

5 **figurehead,** nominal head, dummy, lay figure, front man, front, stooge, Charlie McCarthy, puppet, creature; straw man, lame duck

6 **governor, ruler;** captain, master, commander, commandant, commanding officer, intendant, castellan, chatelain, chatelaine; director, manager, executive

7 **head of state,** chief of state, leader; premier, prime minister, chancellor, grand vizier; doge; **president,** chief executive; President of the United States (POTUS), the man in the White House

8 potentate, **sovereign, monarch,** absolute monarch, ruler, prince, dynast, crowned head, emperor, king-emperor, **king**, anointed king, majesty, royalty, royal, royal personage; petty king, tetrarch, kinglet; grand duke; paramount, lord paramount, suzerain, overlord, overking, high king; chief, chieftain, high chief; prince consort; world leader

9 <ruler titles> caesar, kaiser, czar; Holy Roman Emperor; Dalai Lama, Pachen Lama; pharaoh; pendragon, rig, ardri; mikado, tenno; shogun, tycoon; khan, cham; shah, padishah; negus; bey; sheikh; sachem, sagamore; cacique; kaid; sultan, caliph, imam, hakim, nizam, nabab, emir; mogul

10 **queen,** princess; sovereign queen, sovereign princess, queen regent, queen regnant, empress, czarina; rani, maharani; grand duchess; queen consort

11 **regent,** protector, prince regent, queen regent

12 **<regional governors>** governor, governor-general, lieutenant governor; viceroy, vice-king, exarch, proconsul, khedive, stadtholder, vizier; nabob, nabab, subahdar; gauleiter; eparch; palatine; tetrarch; burgrave; collector; hospodar, vaivode; dey, bey, beg, beglerbeg, wali, vali, satrap; provincial; warlord; military governor

13 **tyrant, despot,** warlord; autocrat, autarch; oligarch; absolute ruler, absolute master, absolute monarch, omnipotent ruler, all-powerful ruler; dictator, duce, führer, commissar, pharaoh, caesar, czar; usurper, arrogator; oppressor, hard master, driver, slave driver; martinet, disciplinarian, stickler, tin god, petty tyrant

14 **the authorities, the powers that be,** ruling class, the lords of creation, the Establishment, the

interests, the power elite, the power structure; they, them; the inner circle; the ins, the in-group, those on the inside; management, the administration; higher echelons, top brass; higher-ups, the people upstairs, the people in the front office; **the top**, the corridors of power; prelacy, hierarchy; ministry; **bureaucracy,** officialdom; directorate; civil service; public office

15 **official,** officer, officiary, functionary, apparatchik; public official, public servant; officeholder, office-bearer, placeman <Brit>; government employee, public employee; civil servant; bureaucrat, politician, mandarin, red-tapist; petty tyrant, jack-in-office; The Man

16 <**public officials**> minister, secretary, secretary of state, undersecretary, cabinet minister, cabinet member, minister of state; chancellor; warden; archon; magistrate; syndic; commissioner; commissar; county commissioners; city manager, mayor, lord mayor, burgomaster; headman; councilman, councilwoman, councillor, city councilman, elder, city father, alderman, alderperson, selectman; supervisor, county supervisor; reeve, portreeve; legislator

17 **commissioned officer, officer,** military leader, military officer; top brass, the brass; commander-in-chief, generalissimo, captain general; hetman, sirdar, commanding officer, commandant; general of the army, general of the air force, five-star general, marshal, field marshal; general officer, general, four-star general; lieutenant general, three-star general; major general, two-star general, brigadier general, one-star general, brigadier; field officer; colonel, chicken colonel; lieutenant colonel; major; company officer; captain; lieutenant, first lieutenant; second lieutenant, shavetail, subaltern, sublieutenant; warrant officer, chief warrant officer; commander, the Old Man; commanding officer (CO); executive officer, exec; chief of staff; aide, aide-de-camp (ADC); officer of the day (OD), orderly officer; staff officer; senior officer, junior officer; brass hat; air marshal; petty officer

18 **army officer;** army noncommissioned officer, noncom (NCO); centurion; sergeant, sarge; sergeant major of the army, command sergeant major, sergeant major, first sergeant, top sergeant *and* topkick, first man, master sergeant, sergeant first class, technical sergeant, staff sergeant, specialist seven, platoon sergeant, mess sergeant, color sergeant, acting sergeant, lance sergeant; corporal, acting corporal, lance corporal, lance-jack; **Air Force noncommissioned officer,** chief master sergeant of the Air Force, chief master sergeant, senior master sergeant, airman first class

19 **naval officer,** navy officer; fleet admiral, navarch, admiral, vice admiral, rear admiral, commodore, captain, commander, lieutenant commander, lieutenant, lieutenant junior grade, ensign; warrant officer; naval noncommissioned officer, master chief petty officer of the Navy, master chief petty officer, senior chief petty officer, chief petty officer, petty officer first class, petty officer second class, petty officer third class; **Marine Corps noncommissioned officer,** sergeant major of the Marine Corps, sergeant major, master gunnery sergeant, first sergeant, master sergeant, gunnery sergeant, staff sergeant, sergeant, corporal, lance corporal

20 <**heraldic officials**> herald, king of arms, king at arms, earl marshal; Garter, Garter King of Arms, Clarenceux, Clarenceux King of Arms, Norroy and Ulster, Norroy and Ulster King of Arms, Norroy, Norroy King of Arms, Lyon, Lyon King of Arms; College of Arms

576 DEPUTY, AGENT

<one appointed to act for another>

NOUNS 1 **deputy, proxy, representative,** substitute, sub, vice, vicegerent, alternate, backup, stand-in, body double, alternative, alter ego, surrogate, procurator, secondary, understudy, pinch hitter, utility man, utility woman, scrub, reserve, the bench; assistant, right hand, second in command, number two, executive officer; exponent, advocate, pleader, paranymph, attorney, champion; lieutenant; aide; vicar, vicar general; locum tenens, locum; amicus curiae; puppet, dummy, creature, cat's-paw, figurehead; stuntman, stuntwoman; ghost writer

2 **delegate,** legate, appointee; commissioner, commissary, commissar; messenger, herald, emissary, envoy; minister, secretary

3 **agent, instrument,** implement, implementer, trustee, broker; expediter, facilitator; tool; steward; functionary; official; clerk, secretary; amanuensis; factor, consignee; puppet, cat's-paw; dupe

4 **go-between, middleman,** intermediary, medium, intermedium, intermediate, interagent, internuncio, broker; connection, contact; negotiator, negotiant; interpleader; arbitrator, mediator

5 **spokesperson,** spokesman, spokeswoman, spokespeople, official spokesman, official spokeswoman, official spokesperson, press officer, speaker, voice, mouthpiece; spin doctor; herald;

messenger; proloctor, prolocutress, prolocutrix; reporter, rapporteur

6 **diplomat,** diplomatist, diplomatic agent, diplomatic; emissary, envoy, legate, minister, foreign service officer; ambassador, ambassadress, ambassador-at-large; envoy extraordinary, plentipotentiary, minister plenipotentiary; nuncio, internuncio, apostolic delegate; vice-legate; resident, minister resident; chargé d'affaires, chargé, chargé d'affaires ad interim; secretary of legation, chancellor; attaché, commercial attaché, military attaché, consul, consul general, vice-consul, consular agent; career diplomat

7 **foreign office,** foreign service, diplomatic service; diplomatic mission, diplomatic staff, diplomatic corps; **embassy,** legation; consular service

8 **second in command**; vice-president, vice-chairman, vice-governor, vice-director, vice-master, vice-chancellor, vice-premier, vice-warden, vice-consul, vice-legate; vice-regent, viceroy, vicegerent, vice-king, vice-queen, vice-reine

9 **secret agent,** operative, cloak-and-dagger operative, undercover man, inside man; **spy,** espionage agent; counterspy, double agent; spotter; scout, reconnoiterer; intelligence agent, intelligence officer; military-intelligence man, naval-intelligence man; spymaster; spy-catcher, counterintelligence agent; agent provocateur; codetalker, windtalker; covert operative

10 **detective,** operative, investigator, sleuth, Sherlock Holmes; police detective, plainclothesman; private detective, private dick, private investigator (PI), inquiry agent; hotel detective, house detective, house dick, store detective; arson investigator; narcotics agent, narc; FBI agent, G-man; treasury agent, T-man; Federal, fed; Federal Bureau of Investigation (FBI); Secret Service

11 <nonformal> **dick,** gumshoe, gumshoe man, hawkshaw, sleuthhound, beagle, flatfoot, tec; eye, private eye; skip tracer, spotter

12 **secret service,** intelligence service, intelligence bureau, intelligence department; intelligence, military intelligence, naval intelligence; Central Intelligence Agency (CIA); **counterintelligence**

13 <group of delegates> **delegation,** deputation, commission, mission, legation; committee, subcommittee

VERBS 14 **represent, act for,** act on behalf of, substitute for, appear for, answer for, speak for, be the voice of, give voice to, be the mouthpiece of, hold the proxy of, hold a brief for, act in the place of, stand in the stead of, serve in one's stead, pinch-hit for; understudy, double for, stand in for, back up; front for; deputize, commission; ghostwrite, ghost

15 **deputize**, depute, authorize, empower, charge, designate, nominate

ADJS 16 **deputy,** deputative; **acting,** representative

17 **diplomatic,** ambassadorial, consular, ministerial, plenipotentiary

ADVS 18 by proxy, indirectly; in behalf of

577 SERVANT, EMPLOYEE

<one working for another>

NOUNS 1 **retainer,** dependent, follower; myrmidon, yeoman; vassal, liege, liege man, henchman, feudatory, homager; inferior, **underling, subordinate,** understrapper; **minion,** creature, hanger-on, lackey, flunky, stooge, drudge; peon, serf, bond servant, thrall, slave

2 **servant**, servitor, help, paid helper; **domestic,** domestic help, domestic servant, household servant; live-in help, day help; menial, drudge, slavey; scullion, turnspit; humble servant

3 **employee;** pensioner, hireling, mercenary, myrmidon; wage earner, staff member; hired man, hired hand, man Friday, girl Friday, right-hand man, go-to guy, point man, point person, assistant; worker, subordinate, subaltern; white-collar worker, nonmanual worker, skilled worker, semiskilled worker, unskilled worker, blue-collar worker, manual worker, laborer; part-time worker, freelance worker; hourly worker; officer worker, administrative assistant, secretary, clerk, messenger, runner, gofer

4 **right-hand man**, man, manservant, serving man, boy, *garçon* <Fr>, houseboy, houseman; butler; valet, gentleman, gentleman's gentleman; driver, chauffeur, coachman; gardener; handyman, odd-job man; lord-in-waiting, lord of the bedchamber, equerry; bodyguard, chaperon

5 **attendant,** tender, usher, server, squire, yeoman; errand boy, errand girl, gofer, office boy, office girl, copyboy; page, footboy; concierge; bellboy, bellman, bellhop; cabin boy, purser; porter, redcap; printer's devil; chore boy; caddie; bootblack, boots, shoeshine boy, shoeblack; trainbearer; cupbearer, Ganymede, Hebe; orderly; cabin attendant, flight attendant, steward, stewardess, hostess, airline stewardess, airline steward, airline host, airline hostess, stew, cabin crew, skycap; hat-check girl, cloakroom attendant; salesclerk, clerk, salesperson, sales associate, shop assistant

6 **lackey,** flunky, livery servant, liveried servant; footman

7 **waitperson,** waiter, waitress, waitron; carhop; counterman, soda jerk; busgirl, busboy; headwaiter, maître d', *maître d'hôtel* <Fr>; hostess; wine steward, sommelier; bartender, barkeeper, barkeep, barman, barmaid; barista

8 **maid,** maidservant, servitress, girl, servant girl, serving girl, wench, biddy, hired girl; lady-help <Brit>, au pair girl; live-in maid, live-out maid; handmaid, handmaiden; personal attendant; lady's maid, waiting maid, gentlewoman, abigail, soubrette; lady-in-waiting, maid-in-waiting, lady of the bedchamber; companion; chaperon; betweenmaid, tweeny <Brit>; duenna; parlormaid; kitchenmaid, scullery maid; cleaning person, cleaner, housekeeper; cook; housemaid, chambermaid, upstairs maid; nursemaid

9 **factotum,** do-all, general servant, man of all work; maid of all work, domestic drudge, slavey, Mister Fix-it, handyman, handyperson

10 **major-domo,** steward, house steward, butler, chamberlain, *maître d'hôtel* <Fr>, seneschal; housekeeper

11 **staff,** personnel, employees, help, hired help, occasional help, the help, crew, gang, men, women, force, servantry, retinue

12 **service,** servanthood, servitude, servitorship; **employment,** employ; ministry, ministration, attendance, tendance; serfdom, peonage, thralldom, slavery

VERBS **13** **serve, work for,** be in service, serve one's every need; minister to, administer to, pander to, do service; help; care for, do for, look after, wait on hand and foot, take care of; wait, wait on, attend, tend, attend on, dance attendance upon; make oneself useful; lackey, valet, maid, chore; drudge

ADJS **14** **serving,** servitorial, servitial, ministering, waiting, waiting on, attending, attendant; in the train of, in one's pay, in one's employ; helping; menial, servile

578 FASHION

<prevailing style, custom>

NOUNS **1** **fashion, style,** mode, vogue, trend, prevailing taste; proper thing, ton, bon ton; design; custom; convention; the swim, current of fashion, stream of fashion; height of fashion; the new look, the season's look; high fashion, *haute couture* <Fr>, designer label; flavor of the month, flavor of the week; personal style, signature

2 **fashionableness,** chic, ton, bon ton, fashionability, stylishness, modishness, voguishness; withitness; popularity, prevalence, currency; hit parade

3 **smartness, chic,** elegance; style-consciousness, clothes-consciousness; spruceness, nattiness, neatness, trimness, sleekness, dapperness, jauntiness; sharpness, spiffiness, classiness, niftiness; swankness, swankiness; foppery, foppishness, coxcombry, dandyism; hipness

4 the rage, the thing, the last word, *le dernier cri* <Fr>, **the latest thing,** the in thing, the latest wrinkle

5 **fad,** craze, rage, it; wrinkle; new take, next big thing, new new thing; novelty; faddishness, faddiness, faddism; **faddist;** the bandwagon, me-tooism

6 **society,** fashionable society, polite society, high society, high life, *beau monde, haut monde* <Fr>, good society; best people, people of fashion, right people; *monde* <Fr>, world of fashion, Vanity Fair; smart set; the Four Hundred, **upper crust**, upper cut; cream of society, *crème de la crème* <Fr>, cream of the crop, elite, carriage trade; café society, jet set, beautiful people, in-crowd, glitterati; drawing room, salon; social register; fast track

7 **clotheshorse**, fashion plate, fashionista; person of fashion, fashionable, man-about-town, man of the world, woman of the world, nob, *mondain, mondaine* <Fr>; arbiter of fashion, tastemaker, trendsetter, tonesetter; ten best-dressed, sharpy, snappy dresser; Beau Brummel, fop, dandy; **socialite**; clubwoman, clubman; salonist, salonnard; jetsetter; swinger; debutante, subdebutante, deb, subdeb, Sloane Ranger; rag trade

VERBS **8** **catch on,** become popular, **become the rage,** catch fire, take fire

9 **be fashionable,** be the style, be the rage, be the thing; have a run; cut a figure in society, give a tone to society, set the fashion, set the style, set the tone; dress to kill

10 **follow the fashion,** get in the swim, get on the bandwagon, climb on the bandwagon, jump on the bandwagon, join the parade, joint the club, follow the crowd, go with the stream, go with the tide, go with the current, go with the flow; keep in step, do as others do; keep up, keep up appearances, keep up with the Joneses

ADJS **11** **fashionable, in fashion,** smart, in style, in vogue; all the rage, all the thing; popular, prevalent, current; up-to-date, up-to-datish, up-to-the-minute, happening, switched-on, hip, with-it, in, trendy, newfashioned, modern, mod, new; in the swim; sought-after, much sought-after

12 **stylish,** modish, voguish, vogue; dressy; *soigné, soignée* <Fr>; *à la mode* <Fr>, in the mode

13 **chic, smart,** elegant; style-conscious, clothes-conscious; **well-dressed,** well-groomed, *soigné, soignée* <Fr>, dressed to advantage, all dressed up, dressed to kill, dressed to the teeth, dressed to the nines, well-turned-out; spruce, natty, neat, trim, sleek, smug, trig, tricksy, duded-up; dapper, dashing, jaunty; sharp, spiffy, classy, nifty, snazzy; swank, swanky, posh, ritzy, swell, nobby; genteel; exquisite, *recherché* <Fr>; cosmopolitan, sophisticated

14 **ultrafashionable,** ultrastylish, ultrasmart; chichi; foppish, dandified, dandyish, dandiacal

15 **trendy, faddish,** faddy, groovy

16 **socially prominent**, in society, high-society, elite; café-society, jet-set; lace-curtain, silk-stocking

ADVS 17 **fashionably,** stylishly, modishly, *à la mode* <Fr>, in the latest style, in the latest mode

18 **smartly,** dressily, chicly, elegantly, exquisitely; sprucely, nattily, neatly, trimly, sleekly; dapperly, jauntily, dashingly, swankly, swankily; foppishly, dandyishly

579 SOCIAL CONVENTION

<*prevailing social norms*>

NOUNS 1 **social convention,** convention, conventional usage, what is done, what one does, social usage, form, formality; custom; conformism, conformity; propriety, decorum, decorousness, correctness, decency, seemliness, civility, good form, etiquette; conventionalism, conventionality, Grundyism; Mrs. Grundy; class act

2 **the conventions,** the proprieties, the mores, the right things, accepted conduct, sanctioned conduct, what is done, civilized behavior; dictates of society, dictates of Mrs. Grundy

3 conventionalist, Grundy, Mrs. Grundy; conformist

VERBS 4 **conform,** observe the proprieties, play the game, follow the rules, fall in line, fall into line

ADJS 5 **conventional,** decorous, orthodox, correct, right, right-thinking, proper, decent, seemly, meet; accepted, recognized, acknowledged, received, admitted, approved, being done; *comme il faut, de rigueur* <Fr>; traditional, customary; formal; conformable

ADVS 6 **conventionally,** decorously, orthodoxly; customarily, traditionally; correctly, properly, as is proper, as it should be, *comme il faut* <Fr>; according to use, according to custom, according to the dictates of society, according to Mrs. Grundy

580 FORMALITY

<*conventional, formal behavior*>

NOUNS 1 **formality,** form, **formalness; ceremony,** ceremonial, ceremoniousness; the red carpet; ritual, rituality; extrinsicality, impersonality; formalization, stylization, conventionalization; stiffness, stiltedness, primness, prissiness, rigidness, starchiness, buckram, dignity, gravity, weight, *gravitas* <L>, weighty dignity, staidness, reverend seriousness, solemnity; pomp; pomposity

2 **formalism, ceremonialism, ritualism;** legalism; pedantry, pedantism, pedanticism; precisianism, preciseness, preciousness, preciosity, purism; punctiliousness, punctilio, scrupulousness; overrefinement

3 **etiquette,** social code, rules of conduct, code of conduct; formalities, social procedures, social conduct, social convention, what is done, what one does; **manners,** good manners, exquisite manners, quiet good manners, **politeness,** *politesse* <Fr>, natural politeness, comity, civility; amenities, decencies, civilities, elegancies, social graces, mores, proprieties; decorum, good form; courtliness, elegance; **protocol,** diplomatic code; punctilio, point of etiquette; convention, social usage; table manners

4 **<ceremonial function>** ceremony, ceremonial; rite, ritual, formality; solemnity, service, function, office, observance, performance; exercise, exercises; celebration, solemnization; liturgy, religious ceremony; rite of passage; convocation; commencement, commencement exercises; graduation, graduation exercises; baccalaureate service; inaugural, inauguration; initiation; formal, ball; wedding; funeral; set piece; empty formality, empty ceremony, mummery

VERBS 5 **formalize,** ritualize, solemnize, celebrate, dignify; observe; conventionalize, stylize

6 **stand on ceremony,** observe the formalities, follow protocol, do things by the book

ADJS 7 **formal,** formulary; formalist, formalistic; legalistic; pedantic, pedantical; official, stylized, conventionalized; extrinsic, outward, impersonal; surface, superficial, nominal

8 **ceremonious, ceremonial;** red-carpet; ritualistic, ritual; hieratic, hieratical, sacerdotal, liturgic; grave, solemn; pompous; stately; well-mannered; conventional, decorous

9 **stiff, stilted,** prim, prissy, rigid, starch, starchy, starched; buckram, in buckram

10 **punctilious,** scrupulous, precise, precisian, precisionist, precious, puristic; by-the-book; exact, meticulous; orderly, methodical

ADVS 11 **formally,** in due form, in set form; **ceremoniously,** ritually, ritualistically; solemnly; for form's sake, *pro forma* <L>, as a matter of form; by the book

12 stiffly, stiltedly, starchly, primly, rigidly

581 INFORMALITY

<casual, familiar behavior>

NOUNS 1 **informality, informalness,** unceremoniousness; casualness, offhandedness, ease, easiness, easygoingness; relaxedness; affability, graciousness, cordiality, sociability; Bohemianism, unconventionality; familiarity; naturalness, simplicity, plainness, homeliness, homeyness, folksiness, common touch, unaffectedness, unpretentiousness; unconstraint, unconstrainedness, looseness; irregularity; lack of convention, freedom, license; bad form

VERBS 2 **not stand on ceremony,** let one's hair down, be oneself, be at ease, feel at home, come as you are; relax

ADJS 3 **informal, unceremonious;** casual, offhand, offhanded, throwaway, unstudied, easy, easygoing, free and easy, loose, nonformal; *dégagé* <Fr>; relaxed; affable, gracious, cordial, sociable; Bohemian, unconventional, nonconformist; familiar; natural, simple, plain, homely, homey, down-home, folksy, *haymish* <Yiddish>; unaffected, unassuming; unconstrained; irregular; unofficial; cazh

ADVS 4 **informally, unceremoniously,** without ceremony; casually, offhand, offhandedly; relaxedly; familiarly; naturally, simply, plainly; unaffectedly, unassumingly; unconstrainedly, unofficially

582 SOCIABILITY

<tending toward companionship>

NOUNS 1 **sociability,** sociality, sociableness, fitness for society, fondness for society, socialmindedness, **gregariousness,** affability, companionability, compatibility, geniality, congeniality; hospitality; clubbability, clubbishness, clubbiness, clubbism; intimacy, familiarity; amiability, friendliness; communicativeness; social grace, civility, urbanity, courtesy

2 **camaraderie,** comradery, comradeship, **fellowship,** good-fellowship; male bonding; consorting, hobnobbing, hanging, hanging out

3 **conviviality, geniality,** joviality, jollity, gaiety, heartiness, cheer, good cheer, festivity, partying, merrymaking, merriment, revelry; social skill; people skills

4 **social life,** social intercourse, social activity, intercourse, communication, communion, intercommunion, fellowship, intercommunication, community, collegiality, commerce, congress, converse, conversation, social relations

5 **social circle,** social class, social set, one's crowd, one's set, clique, coterie, crowd, in-crowd; association

6 **association,** consociation, affiliation, bonding, social bonding, fellowship, kindred spirit, companionship, company, society; fraternity, fraternization; membership, participation, partaking, sharing, cooperation

7 **visit, social call,** call; formal visit, duty visit, required visit; exchange visit; flying visit, look-in; visiting, visitation; round of visits; social round, social whirl, mad round; play date

8 **appointment,** engagement, **date,** double date, blind date, fix-up; arrangement, interview, meeting, meet; engagement book, agenda book, personal digital assistant

9 **rendezvous,** tryst, assignation, booty call, meeting; blind date; trysting place, meeting place, place of assignation; assignation house; love nest

10 **social gathering,** social, sociable, social affair, social hour, hospitality hour, affair, gathering, get-together; function; reception, at home, salon, levee, soiree; matinee; reunion, family reunion; wake; last call; playgroup

11 **party** <see list>, **entertainment**, celebration, fete, bash, party time, festivity

12 <nonformal> **bash,** blast, clambake, wingding, hoodang, blowout, shindig, shindy, do, bean feast, knees-up, rave, rave-up

13 **tea,** afternoon tea, five-o'clock tea, high tea, cream tea

14 **bee,** quilting bee, raising bee, husking bee, cornhusking, corn shucking, husking

15 **debut,** coming out, presentation

16 <**sociable person**> joiner, mixer, good mixer, good company, pleasant company, excellent companion, life of the party, social butterfly, bon vivant; man-about-town, playboy, social lion, habitué; clubman, clubwoman; salonnard, salonist; party crasher, wedding crasher

VERBS 17 **associate with,** assort with, sort with, consort with, hobnob with, fall in with, socialize, interact, go around with, mingle with, mix with, touch elbows with, rub elbows with, touch shoulders with, rub shoulders with, eat off the same trencher; fraternize, fellowship, join in fellowship; keep company with, bear one's company, walk hand in hand with; join; flock together, herd together, club together

18 <nonformal> **hang with,** hang out with, hang around with, clique, clique with, gang up with, run with, with, chum, chum together, pal, pal with, pal up with, pal around with; take up with, plus-one; party-crash

19 **visit,** pay a visit, make a visit, call on, drop in,

stop in, look in, look one up, see, stop off, stop over, drop by, stop by, drop around; leave one's card; exchange visits

20 have a party, give a party, entertain

21 <nonformal> **throw a party**; party, have fun, live it up, have a ball, ball, boogie, jam, kick up one's heels, make whoopee, whoop it up, party down

ADJS 22 **sociable, social,** social-minded, fit for society, fond of society, gregarious, affable; companionable, companionate, compatible, genial, congenial; hospitable; neighborly; clubby, clubbable, clubbish; communicative; amiable, friendly; civil, urbane, courteous

23 **convivial,** boon, free and easy, hail-fellow-well-met; jovial, jolly, hearty, festive, gay

24 **intimate, familiar,** cozy, chatty, *tête-à-tête* <Fr>; man-to-man, woman-to-woman

ADVS 25 **sociably,** socially, gregariously, affably; friendlily, companionably, arm in arm, hand in hand, hand in glove

26 **party**

at-home
baby shower
ball
birthday party
block party, street party
cocktail party
coffee party, kaffee klatsch, coffee klatsch, coffeeklatch
costume party, costume ball
dinner party
fête champêtre <Fr>
garden party
hen party
housewarming
ice-cream social
ladies' night out, men's night out
masked ball
masquerade party, mask, masque, masquerade
open house
pajama party, slumber party
rave
shindig, shindy
shower
smoker
social
soiree
stag, stag party, stag weekend
surprise party
tailgate party
tea party
thé dansante <Fr>

583 UNSOCIABILITY

<tending toward solitude>

NOUNS 1 **unsociability,** insociability, unsociableness, dissociability, dissociableness; **ungregariousness,** uncompanionability; unclubbableness, unclubbability, ungeniality, uncongeniality; incompatibility, social incompatibility; unfriendliness; uncommunicativeness; sullenness, mopishness, moroseness; self-sufficiency, self-containment; autism, catatonia; bashfulness

2 **aloofness, standoffishness,** offishness, withdrawnness, remoteness, distance, detachment; coolness, coldness, frigidity, chill, chilliness, iciness, frostiness; cold shoulder; inaccessibility, unapproachability; private world

3 seclusiveness, **seclusion**; exclusiveness, exclusivity

VERBS 4 **keep to oneself,** keep oneself to oneself, not mix, not mingle, enjoy one's own company, prefer one's own company, stay at home, shun companionship, be a poor mixer, stand aloof, hold oneself aloof, keep one's distance, keep at a distance, keep in the background, retire, retire into the shade, creep into a corner, seclude oneself, stay in one's shell; have nothing to do with, be unfriendly, not give one the time of day; cocoon

ADJS 5 **unsociable,** insociable, dissociable, unsocial; ungregarious, nongregarious; uncompanionable, ungenial, uncongenial; incompatible, socially incompatible; unclubbable; unfriendly; uncommunicative; sullen, mopish, mopey, morose; close, snug; self-sufficient, self-contained; autistic, catatonic; bashful

6 **aloof, standoffish,** offish, standoff, distant, remote, withdrawn, removed, detached; cool, cold, cold-fish, frigid, chilly, icy, frosty; seclusive; exclusive; inaccessible, unapproachable; tight-assed

584 SECLUSION

<withdrawal from socializing>

NOUNS 1 **seclusion,** reclusion, retirement, **withdrawal, retreat,** recess; renunciation of the world, forsaking of the world; cocooning; sequestration, quarantine, separation, detachment, apartness; segregation, apartheid, Jim Crow; isolation; ivory tower, ivory-towerism, ivory-towerishness; privacy, privatism, secrecy; rustication; privatization; isolationism; opt-out

2 **hermitism,** hermitry, eremitism, anchoritism, anchoretism, cloistered monasticism, cocooning

3 **solitude,** solitariness, aloneness, loneness, singleness; loneliness, lonesomeness; separation anxiety; me time

4 forlornness, **desolation;** friendlessness, kithlessness, fatherlessness, motherlessness, homelessness, rootlessness; helplessness, defenselessness; abandonment, desertion; street people

5 **recluse, loner,** solitaire, solitary, solitudinarian; shut-in, invalid, bedridden invalid; cloistered monk, cloistered nun; **hermit,** eremite, anchorite, anchoret; marabout; hermitess, anchoress; ascetic; closet cynic; stylite, pillarist, pillar saint; Hieronymite, Hieronymian; Diogenes, Timon of Athens, St. Simeon Stylites, St. Anthony, desert saints, desert fathers; outcast, pariah; stay-at-

home, homebody; isolationist, seclusionist; ivory-towerist, ivory-towerite; one-man band

6 **retreat**, hideaway, cell, ivory tower, hidey-hole, lair, sanctum, sanctum sanctorum, inner sanctum

VERBS 7 **seclude oneself**, go into seclusion, retire, go into retirement, retire from the world, forsake the world, live in retirement, lead a retired life, lead a cloistered life, sequester oneself, be incommunicado, remain incommunicado, shut oneself up, live alone, live apart, retreat to one's ivory tower; stay at home; rusticate; take the veil; cop out, opt out of society, drop out of society

ADJS 8 **secluded,** seclusive, retired, withdrawn; isolated, shut off, insular, separate, separated, apart, detached, removed; segregated, quarantined; remote, out-of-the-way, upcountry, in a backwater, out-of-the-world, out-back, back of beyond; unfrequented, unvisited, off the beaten track; untraveled

9 **private,** privatistic, reclusive; ivory-towered, ivory-towerish

10 **recluse, reclusive,** sequestered, cloistered, sequestrated, shut up, shut in; hermitlike, hermitic, hermitical, eremitic, eremitical, hermitish; anchoritic, anchoritical; stay-at-home, domestic; homebound

11 **solitary,** alone; in solitude, by oneself, all alone; lonely, lonesome, lone; lonely-hearts

12 forlorn, lorn; abandoned, **forsaken, deserted, desolate,** godforsaken, friendless, unfriended, kithless, fatherless, motherless, homeless; helpless, defenseless; outcast

ADVS 13 **in seclusion,** in retirement, in retreat, in solitude; in privacy, in secrecy; far from the madding crowd

585 HOSPITALITY, WELCOME

<welcoming guests>

NOUNS 1 **hospitality,** hospitableness, receptiveness; honors of the house, freedom of the house; **cordiality,** amiability, graciousness, friendliness, neighborliness, geniality, heartiness, bonhomie, generosity, liberality, openheartedness, warmth, warmness, warmheartedness; open door; aloha spirit

2 **welcome,** welcoming, **reception**; cordial welcome, warm welcome, hearty welcome, pleasant reception, the glad hand, open arms; embrace, hug; welcome mat

3 **greetings** <see list>, salutations, salaams; regards, best wishes; **farewells** <see list>

4 **greeting, salutation,** salute, salaam; hail, hello, how-do-you-do; accost, address; nod, bow, bob; curtsy; wave; handshake, handclasp; namaste; open arms, embrace, hug, kiss; smile, nod of recognition

5 **host,** mine host; hostess, receptionist, greeter; landlord

6 **guest,** visitor, visitant; guest of honor; caller, company; invited guest, invitee; frequenter, habitué, haunter; uninvited guest, gate-crasher; moocher, freeloader; guest list

VERBS 7 **receive, admit,** accept, take in, let in, open the door to; be at home to, have the latchstring out, keep a light in the window, put out the welcome mat, keep the door open, keep an open house, keep the home fires burning

8 **entertain,** entertain guests, guest; host, preside, do the honors; give a party, throw a party; spread oneself

9 **welcome,** make welcome, bid one welcome, bid one feel at home, make one feel welcome, make one feel at home, make one feel like one of the family, do the honors of the house, give one the freedom of the house, hold out the hand, extend the right hand of friendship; glad hand, give the glad hand, glad eye; embrace, hug, welcome with open arms; give a warm reception to, kill the fatted calf, roll out the red carpet, give the red-carpet treatment, receive royally, make feel like a king, make feel like a queen

10 **greet,** hail, accost, address; salute, make one's salutations; bid hello, say hello, bid good day, bid good morning; exchange greetings, pass the time of day; give one's regards; shake hands, shake, give one some skin, give a high five, give a low five, press the flesh, press one's hand, squeeze one's hand; nod to, bow to; curtsy; tip the hat to, lift the hat, touch the hat, touch the cap; take one's hat off to, uncover; pull at the forelock; kiss, greet with a kiss, kiss hands, kiss cheeks

ADJS 11 **hospitable,** receptive, welcoming; cordial, amiable, gracious, friendly, neighborly, genial, hearty, open, openhearted, warm, warmhearted; generous, liberal

12 **welcome,** welcome as the roses in May, wanted, desired, wished-for; agreeable, desirable, acceptable; grateful, gratifying, pleasing

ADVS 13 **hospitably,** with open arms; friendlily

INTERJS 14 **welcome,** *soyez le bienvenu* <Fr>, *bien venido* <Sp>, *benvenuto* <Ital>, *willkommen* <Ger>; glad to see you

15 **greetings,** salutations, shoutout; hello, hullo, hail, hey, heigh, hi, aloha, *hola* <Sp>; how do you do?, how are you?, *comment allez-vous?*, *comment ça va?* <Fr>, *cómo está usted?* <Sp>, *come sta?* <Ital>, *wie geht's?* <Ger>; good morning, top of the morning, *guten Morgen* <Ger>; good day, *bon jour* <Fr>, *buenos días* <Sp>, *buon giorno*

<Ital>, *guten Tag* <Ger>; good afternoon, *buenas tardes* <Sp>; good evening, *bon soir* <Fr>, *buona sera* <Ital>, *guten Abend* <Ger>

16 <nonformal> **howdy,** howdy-do, how-de-do, how-do-ye-do, how-d'ye-do, how you doin'?, hi ya; how's things?, how's tricks?, how goes it?, how's every little thing?, how's the world treating you?, yo, ahoy, hey; long time no see

17 greetings and farewells

a bientot <Fr>
a demain <Fr>
a toute a l'heure <Fr>
adieu <Fr>
adios <Sp>
ahoy
all hail
aloha
arrivederci <Ital>
au revoir <Fr>
auf Wiedersehen <Ger>
ave
be good
be seeing you
bless you
bon matin <Fr>
bon soir <Fr>
bon voyage
bonjour <Fr>
bonne nuit <Fr>
buenas noches <Sp>
buenas tardes <Sp>
buenos dias <Sp>
buon giorno <Ital>
buona notte <Ital>
buona sera <Ital>
bye
bye-bye
catch you later
catch you on the flip side
check
cheerio
cheers
chin-chin
ciao <Ital>
come again
das vedanya <Russ>
enjoy
fare thee well
farewell
g'day
glad to see you
God be with you
God bless
Godspeed
good afternoon
good day
good evening
good luck
good morning
good night
good to see you
goodbye
greetings
gute Nacht <Ger>
guten Abend <Ger>
guten Morgen <Ger>
guten Tag <Ger>
hail
hallo
halloo
happy trails
hasta la vista <Sp>
hasta luego <Sp>
hasta mañana <Sp>
have a good one
have a nice day
hello
hello there
hey
hey-ho
hi
hi-de-hi
hi ya
hi, there
hola <Sp>
how are you?
how do you do?
how do?
how goes it?
how you be?
how you been?
how you doing?
howdy
howdy-do
howdy-doody
how's by you?
how's everything?
how's it going?
how's the world treating you?
how's things?
hullo
knoban wa <Japanese>
konichiwa <Japanese>
later
later on
mañana <Sp>
many happy returns
meh
namaste
over
over and out
pax <L>
peace
pip-pip
que pasa? <Sp>
regards
roger
salaam
salud <Sp>
salutations
sayonara <Japanese>
see ya
see you later
see you later, alligator
see you soon
shake
shalom <Jewish>
take care
take it easy
ten-four
toodleoo
toodles
welcome
what it is?
what's happening?
wie geht's? <Ger>
yo

586 INHOSPITALITY
<unfriendly to guests>

NOUNS **1 inhospitality,** inhospitableness, unhospitableness, unreceptiveness; **uncordialness,** ungraciousness, unfriendliness, unneighborliness; nonwelcome, nonwelcoming

2 unhabitability, uninhabitability, unlivability

3 ostracism, ostracization, thumbs down; banishment; proscription, ban; boycott, boycottage; **blackball,** blackballing, blacklist; rejection

4 outcast, social outcast, outcast of society, castaway, derelict, Ishmael; pariah, untouchable, leper; outcaste; *déclassé* <Fr>; outlaw; expellee, evictee; displaced person (DP); exile, expatriate, man without a country; undesirable; *persona non grata* <L>, unacceptable person

VERBS **5** have nothing to do with, have no truck with, refuse to associate with, steer clear of, **spurn,** turn one's back upon, not give one the time of day; deny oneself to, refuse to receive, not be at home to; shut the door upon; stay out

6 ostracize, turn thumbs down, disfellowship; reject, exile, banish; proscribe, ban, outlaw, put under the ban, criminalize; boycott, **blackball,** blacklist

ADJS **7 inhospitable,** unhospitable; unreceptive, closed; uncordial, ungracious, unfriendly, unneighborly

8 unhabitable, uninhabitable, nonhabitable, unoccupiable, untenantable, unlivable, unfit to live in, not fit for man or beast

9 unwelcome, unwanted; unagreeable, undesirable, unacceptable; **uninvited,** unasked, unbidden

10 outcast, cast-off, castaway, derelict; outlawed, outside the pale, outside the gates; rejected, disowned; abandoned, forsaken

587 FRIENDSHIP

<liking other people>

NOUNS 1 **friendship, friendliness**; amicability, amicableness, amity, peaceableness, unhostility; amiability, amiableness, congeniality, well-affectedness; neighborliness, neighborlikeness; sociability; affection, love; loving-kindness, kindness

2 **fellowship, companionship,** comradeship, colleagueship, chumship, palship, circle of friends, freemasonry, consortship, boon companionship; comradery, camaraderie, male bonding; brotherhood, fraternity, fraternalism, fraternization, sodality, confraternity; sisterhood, sorority; brotherliness, sisterliness; community of interest, *esprit de corps* <Fr>; chumminess

3 **good terms,** good understanding, good footing, friendly relations; harmony, compatibility, sympathy, fellow feeling, bonding, understanding, rapport, rapprochement; favor, goodwill, good graces, regard, respect, mutual regard, mutual respect, favorable regard, the good side of, the right side of, esprit de corps; an in; entente, entente cordiale, hands across the sea

4 **acquaintance,** acquaintedness, close acquaintance, acquaintanceship; introduction, presentation, knockdown

5 **familiarity, intimacy,** intimate acquaintance, closeness, nearness, face time, inseparableness, inseparability; affinity, special affinity, mutual affinity; chumminess, palliness, palsiness, palsy-walsiness, mateyness; togetherness; conversance

6 **cordiality, geniality,** heartiness, bonhomie, ardency, warmth, warmness, affability, warmheartedness; hospitality

7 **devotion, devotedness;** dedication, commitment; fastness, steadfastness, firmness, constancy, staunchness; triedness, trueness, true-blueness, tried-and-trueness

8 cordial friendship, warm friendship, ardent friendship, close friendship, passionate friendship, devoted friendship, bosom friendship, intimate friendship, familiar friendship, sincere friendship, beautiful friendship, fast friendship, firm friendship, staunch friendship, loyal friendship, lasting friendship, undying friendship, cross-sex friendship

VERBS 9 **be friends,** have the friendship of, have the ear of; be old friends, be friends of long standing, be long acquainted, go way back; know, be acquainted with; associate with; cotton to, hit it off, get on well with, hobnob with, fraternize with, keep company with, go around with; be close friends with, be best friends, be buddies, be inseparable; be on good terms, enjoy good relations with; keep on good terms, have an in with

10 **befriend,** make friends, win friends, gain the friendship of, strike up a friendship, get to know one another, take up with, shake hands with, get acquainted, make acquaintance with, pick up an acquaintance with; win friends and influence people; break the ice; warm to

11 <nonformal> **be buddy-buddy with,** be palsy-walsy with, click, have good chemistry, team up; get next to, get palsy with, get palsy-walsy with, get cozy with, cozy up to, snuggle up to, get close to, get chummy with, buddy up with, pal up with, play footsie with

12 **cultivate,** cultivate the friendship of, court, pay court to, pay addresses to, seek the company of, run after, shine up to, make up to, play up to, suck up to, extend the right of friendship, hold out the right of fellowship; make advances, approach, break the ice

13 **get on good terms with,** get into favor, win the regard of, get in the good graces of, get in good with, get in with, get on the in with, get next to, get on the good side of, get on the right side of; stay friends with, keep in with

14 introduce, present, **acquaint,** make acquainted, give an introduction, give a knockdown, do the honors

ADJS 15 **friendly,** friendlike; amicable, peaceable, unhostile; harmonious; amiable, congenial, *simpático* <Sp>, *simpatico* <Ital>, *sympathique* <Fr>, pleasant, agreeable, favorable, well-affected, well-disposed, well-intentioned, well-meaning, well-meant, well-intended; brotherly, fraternal, confraternal; sisterly; neighborly, neighborlike; sociable; kind

16 **cordial, genial,** gracious, courteous, hearty, ardent, warm, warmhearted, affable; compatible, cooperative; welcoming, receptive, hospitable

17 **friends with,** friendly with, at home with; **acquainted**

18 **on good terms,** on a good footing, on friendly terms, on speaking terms, on a first-name basis, on visiting terms; in good with, in with, on the in with, in, in favor, in one's good graces, in one's good books, on the good side of, on the right side of, regarded highly by, on a first-name basis with

19 **familiar, intimate,** close, near, inseparable, on familiar terms, on intimate terms, favorite, affectionate; just between the two, one-on-one, man-to-man, woman-to-woman; hand-in-hand, hand and glove, hand in glove; thick, thick as thieves; demonstrative, backslapping, effusive

20 **chummy**, matey; pally, palsy, palsy-walsy, buddy-buddy; companionable
21 **devoted**, dedicated, committed, fast, steadfast, supportive, constant, faithful, staunch, firm; tried, true, tried and true, true-blue, **loyal**, tested, trusty, trustful, trustworthy

ADVS 22 **amicably**, friendly, friendlily, friendliwise; amiably, congenially, pleasantly, agreeably, favorably; **cordially, genially**, heartily, ardently, warmly, with open arms; familiarly, intimately; arm in arm, hand in hand, hand in glove

588 FRIEND

<one who is liked>

NOUNS 1 **friend, acquaintance**, close acquaintance; confidant, confidante, repository; intimate, familiar, close friend, intimate friend, familiar friend; bosom friend, friend of one's bosom, inseparable friend, best friend; alter ego, other self, shadow; brother, fellow, fellowman, fellow creature, neighbor; mutual friend; sympathizer, well-wisher, partisan, advocate, favorer, backer, supporter; casual acquaintance; pickup; lover; girlfriend, boyfriend; live-in lover, person of opposite sex sharing living quarters (POSSLQ), significant other

2 **good friend, best friend** (BF), best friend forever (BFF), bestie, great friend, devoted friend, ardent friend, faithful friend, trusted friend, trusty friend, constant friend, staunch friend, fast friend; friend in need, friend indeed; kindred spirit; friend of <name>

3 **companion**, fellow, fellow companion, comrade, amigo, mate, comate, company, associate, peer, consociate, compeer, confrere, consort, colleague, **partner**, copartner, side partner, crony, old crony, gossip; girlfriend; roommate, chamberfellow; flatmate; bunkmate, bunkie; bedfellow, bedmate; schoolmate, schoolfellow, classmate, classfellow, school companion, school chum, fellow student; playmate, playfellow; teammate, yokefellow, yokemate; workmate, workfellow; kemo sabe, shipmate; messmate; confederate, comrade in arms; homeboy

4 <nonformal> **pal**, buddy, bud, buddy-boy, bosom buddy, asshole buddy*, main man, home boy, goombah*, landsman, paesan, paesano, pally, palsy-walsy, road dog, walkboy, cobber <Austral>, pardner, pard, sidekick, tillicum, chum, ace, mate, butty, my man, homeboy, homegirl

5 **boon companion**, boonfellow, booncoon; good fellow, jolly fellow, hearty, *bon vivant* <Fr>; pot companion

6 <famous friendships> Achilles and Patroclus, Castor and Pollux, Damon and Pythias, David and Jonathan, Diomedes and Sthenelus, Epaminondas and Pelopidas, Hercules and Iolaus, Nisus and Euryalus, Pylades and Orestes, Theseus and Pirithoüs, Christ and the beloved disciple; the Three Musketeers

589 ENMITY

<unfriendly feeling>

NOUNS 1 **enmity, unfriendliness**, inimicality; uncordiality, unamiability, ungeniality, disaffinity, incompatibility, incompatibleness; personal conflict, strain, tension; coolness, coldness, chilliness, chill, frost, frostiness, iciness, the freeze; inhospitality, unsociability

2 **disaccord**; ruffled feelings, ruffled feathers, strained relations, alienation, disaffection, estrangement

3 **hostility, antagonism**, repugnance, antipathy, spitefulness, spite, despitefulness, bellicosity, malice, malevolence, malignity, hatred, hate; dislike; conflict, contention, collision, clash, clashing, friction; quarrelsomeness; belligerence, intolerance; state of war

4 **animosity**, animus; **ill will**, ill feeling, bitter feeling, hard feelings, no love lost; bad blood, ill blood, feud, blood feud, vendetta; bitterness, sourness, soreness, rancor, resentment, acrimony, virulence, venom, vitriol

5 **grudge, spite**, crow to pick, bone to pick; peeve, pet peeve; peevishness

6 **enemy, foe**, foeman, adversary, antagonist, unfriendly; bitter enemy; sworn enemy; open enemy; secret enemy; public enemy, public enemy number one; archenemy, devil; the other side, the opposition, opponent, rival; bane, bête noire; no friend

VERBS 7 **antagonize**, set against, make enemies, set at odds, set at each other's throat, sick on each other; aggravate, exacerbate, heat up, provoke, envenom, embitter, infuriate, irritate, madden; divide, disunite, alienate, estrange; be alienated, be estranged, grow apart

8 **bear ill will**, bear malice, have it in for, hold it against, be down on; bear a grudge, harbor a grudge, nurse a grudge, owe a grudge, have a bone to pick with; no love is lost between; have a crow to pick; pick a quarrel; take offense, take umbrage; scorn, hate

ADJS 9 **unfriendly**, inimical, unamicable; uncordial, unamiable, ungenial, incompatible; strained, tense; discordant, unharmonious; cool, cold, chill, chilly, frosty, icy; inhospitable; unsociable

10 **hostile, antagonistic,** repugnant, antipathetic, set against, ill-disposed, acrimonious, snide, spiteful, despiteful, malicious, malevolent, malignant, hateful, full of hate, full of hatred; virulent, bitter, sore, sour, rancorous, acrid, caustic, venomous, vitriolic; conflicting, clashing, colliding; resentful, grudging, peevish; quarrelsome, contentious; provocative, off-putting; belligerent, bellicose

11 **alienated, estranged,** pffft, disaffected, separated, divided, disunited, torn, at variance; irreconcilable; distant; not on speaking terms

12 **on the outs**, at outs, at enmity, at variance, at odds, at loggerheads, at cross-purposes, at sixes and sevens, at each other's throats, at swords points, at daggers drawn, at war; on bad terms, in bad with

13 **on bad terms,** not on speaking terms, on the outs; in bad with, in bad odor with, in one's bad books, in one's black books, on one's shitlist*, on one's drop-dead list

ADVS **14** **unamicably,** inimically; uncordially, unamiably, ungenially; coolly, coldly, chillily, frostily; hostilely, antagonistically

590 MISANTHROPY

<dislike of other people>

NOUNS **1** **misanthropy,** misanthropism, people-hating, Timonism, cynicism, antisociality, antisocial attitudes; unsociability; **man-hating,** misandry; **woman-hating,** misogyny; **sexism,** sex discrimination, sexual stereotyping, male chauvinism, female chauvinism

2 **misanthrope,** misanthropist, people-hater, cynic, Timon, Timonist; **man-hater,** misandrist; **woman-hater,** misogynist; **sexist,** male chauvinist, female chauvinist, chauvinist

ADJS **3** **misanthropic,** people-hating, Timonist, Timonistic, cynical, antisocial; unsociable; **man-hating,** misandrist; **woman-hating,** misogynic, misogynistic, misogynous; **sexist,** male-chauvinistic, female-chauvinistic, chauvinistic

591 PUBLIC SPIRIT

<willingness to help public>

NOUNS **1** **public spirit,** social consciousness, social responsibility; citizenship, **good citizenship,** citizenism, civism; altruism, consciousness raising

2 **patriotism,** love of country; nationalism, nationality, ultranationalism, superpatriotism; Americanism, Anglicism, Briticism; blind patriotism, chauvinism, jingoism, overpatriotism; patriotics, flag-waving; saber-rattling

3 **patriot;** nationalist; ultranationalist; chauvinist, chauvin, jingo, jingoist; patrioteer, flag waver, superpatriot, hard hat, hundred-percenter, hundred-percent American; hawk

ADJS **4** **public-spirited,** civic; **patriotic;** nationalistic; ultranationalist, ultranationalistic; overpatriotic, superpatriotic, flagwaving, chauvinist, chauvinistic, jingoist, jingoistic; hawkish

592 BENEFACTOR

<one who helps cause or another person>

NOUNS **1** **benefactor,** benefactress, benefiter, succorer, befriender; ministrant, ministering angel; Samaritan, good Samaritan; helper, aider, assister, help, aid, **helping hand**; Johnny-on-the-spot, jack-at-a-pinch, fairy godmother; patron, backer, angel, cash cow; good person

2 **savior, redeemer,** deliverer, liberator, rescuer, freer, emancipator, manumitter

VERBS **3** **benefit, aid,** assist, succor; befriend, take under one's wing; back, support; save the day, save one's neck, save one's skin, save one's bacon

ADJS **4** **benefitting**, aiding, befriending, assisting; backing, supporting; saving, salving, salvational, redemptive, redeeming; liberating, freeing, emancipative, emancipating, manumitting

ADVS **5** by one's aid, by one's good offices, with one's support, on one's shoulders, on one's coattails

PREPS **6** with benefit of, by benefit of, with the aid of, by the aid of

593 EVILDOER

<one who does evil deed>

NOUNS **1** **evildoer, wrongdoer,** worker of ill, worker of evil, malefactor, malfeasant, malfeasor, misfeasor, malevolent, public enemy, sinner, villain, villainess, transgressor, delinquent, culprit; bad, bad guy, baddy, meany, wrongo, black hat, wrong'un; criminal, outlaw, felon, crook, lawbreaker, perpetrator, perp, gangster, mobster; racketeer, thief, robber, burglar, rapist, murderer, con; terrorist; **bad person**; deceiver

2 **troublemaker,** mischief-maker; holy terror; agitator

3 **thug, trouble,** repeat offender; ruffian, rough, bravo, rowdy, desperado, cutthroat, mad dog; gunman; bully, bullyboy, bucko; devil, hellcat, hell-raiser; gang member, gangster; killer, murderer

4 <nonformal> **hood,** roughneck, tough, bruiser, mug, mugger, bozo, ugly customer, hoodlum, hooligan, gorilla, ape, plug-ugly, strong-arm man, muscle man, goon; gun, gunsel, trigger man, rodman, torpedo, hatchet man; hellion, terror, holy terror, shtarker

5 **savage,** barbarian, brute, beast, animal, tiger, shark, hyena; wild man; cannibal, man-eater, anthropophagite; wrecker, vandal, nihilist, destroyer

6 **monster, fiend,** fiend from hell, demon, devil, devil incarnate, hellhound, hellkite; vampire, lamia, harpy, ghoul; werewolf, ape-man; ogre, ogress; Frankenstein's monster

7 **witch,** hag, vixen, hellhag, hellcat, she-devil, virago, brimstone, termagant, grimalkin, Jezebel, beldam, she-wolf, tigress, wildcat, bitch-kitty*, siren, fury

594 JURISDICTION

<administration of justice>

NOUNS 1 **jurisdiction,** legal authority, legal, power, legal right, legal sway, the confines of the law; original jurisdiction, appellate jurisdiction, exclusive jurisdiction, concurrent jurisdiction, civil jurisdiction, criminal jurisdiction, common-law jurisdiction, equitable jurisdiction, *in rem* jurisdiction, *in personam* jurisdiction, subject-matter jurisdiction, territorial jurisdiction; voluntary jurisdiction; mandate, cognizance

2 **judiciary,** judicial system, legal system, court system, judicature, judicatory, court, the courts, criminal justice system; criminal-justice system; justice, the wheels of justice, judicial process; judgment

3 magistracy, magistrature, magistrateship; **judgeship,** justiceship; mayoralty, mayorship

4 **bureau,** office, department; secretariat, ministry, commissariat; municipality, bailiwick; constabulary, constablery, sheriffry, sheriffalty, shrievalty; constablewick, sheriffwick

VERBS 5 **administer justice,** administer, administrate; preside, preside at the board; sit in judgment; judge

ADJS 6 **jurisdictional,** jurisdictive; judicatory, judicatorial, judicative, juridic, juridical; jural, jurisprudential, judicial, judiciary; magisterial; forensic

595 TRIBUNAL

<court of justice>

NOUNS 1 **tribunal, forum,** board, curia, Areopagus; judicature, judicatory, judiciary; council; inquisition, the Inquisition

2 **court,** law court, court of law, court of justice, court of arbitration, legal tribunal, judicature; **United States court** <see list>, federal court; **British court** <see list>, Crown court; high court, trial court, court of record, superior court, inferior court; criminal court, civil court, appeals court, appellate court, county court, district court, juvenile court, small claims court; kangaroo court, mock court

3 <**ecclesiastical court**> Papal Court, Curia, Rota, Sacra Romana Rota, Court of Arches, Court of Peculiars

4 **military court,** court-martial, general court-martial, special court-martial, summary court-martial, drumhead court-martial; naval court, captain's mast

5 **seat of justice,** judgment seat, mercy seat; bench; woolsack <Brit>

6 **courthouse,** court; county hall, city hall, town hall; **courtroom;** jury box; bench, bar; witness stand, witness box, dock

ADJS 7 **tribunal,** judicial, judiciary, court, curial; appellate

8 **British court**

Board of Green Cloth	Green Cloth
Council	High Court
Court of Admiralty	High Court of Appeal
Court of Appeal	High Court of Judicature, Supreme Court of Judicature
court of attachments	High Court of Justice
Court of Common	Judicial Committee of the Privy Council
Court of Common Bank	Lords Justices' Court
Court of Common Pleas	Palatine Court
Court of Criminal Appeal	Rolls Court
Court of Divorce and Matrimonial Causes	Stannary Court
Court of Exchequer	superior courts of Westminster
Court of Exchequer Chamber	Vice Chancellor's Court
court of piepoudre, court of dustyfoot	Wardmote, Wardmote Court
Court of Queen's Bench, Court of King's Bench	Woodmote
Court of the Duchy of Lancaster	

9 **United States court**

Court of Private Land Claims	Territorial court
Federal Court of Claims	United States Circuit Court of Appeals
Supreme Court, United States Supreme Court	United States District Court

596 JUDGE, JURY

<decider of court case>

NOUNS 1 **judge** <see list>, **magistrate,** justice, adjudicator, bencher, person on the bench, presiding officer, beak; justice of the peace (JP); arbiter, arbitrator, moderator; umpire, referee; his honor, her honor, your honor, his worship, her worship, his lordship; Mr. Justice; critic; special judge; judge and jury

2 <historical> tribune, praetor, ephor, archon, syndic, podesta; Areopagite; justiciar, justiciary; dempster, deemster, doomster, doomsman

3 Chief Justice, Associate Justice, Justice of the Supreme Court; Lord Chief Justice, Lord Justice, Lord Chancellor, Master of the Rolls, Baron of the Exchequer; Judge Advocate General

4 <Biblical> Pontius Pilate, Solomon, Minos, Rhadamanthus, Aeacus

5 **jury** <see list>, panel, jury of one's peers, country, twelve men in a box, twelve good men and true; inquest; jury panel, jury list, venire facias; hung jury, deadlocked jury; grand jury, petit jury, common jury; special jury, blue-ribbon jury, struck jury

6 **juror,** juryman, jurywoman, venire-man, venire-woman, talesman; foreman of the jury, foreman, foreperson; grand juror, grand juryman; petit-juror, petit-juryman; recognitor

7 **judge**

amicus curiae
assessor, legal assessor
associate justice
bankruptcy judge
barmaster <Brit>
chancellor
chief justice
circuit judge
district judge
hearing officer
judge advocate general (JAG)
judge, justice of assize
jurat
justice in eyre
justice of the peace
justiciar
lay judge
magistrate
master
military judge
ombudsman
ordinary, judge ordinary
police judge, police justice (PJ)
presiding judge, presiding officer
probate judge
puisne judge, puisne justice
recorder
tax judge
trial judge
vice-chancellor

8 **jury**

blue-ribbon jury, blue-ribbon panel
common jury
coroner's jury
elisor jury
grand jury
jury of inquest
jury of matrons, jury of women
jury of the vicinage
petit jury, petty jury, traverse jury
police jury
pyx jury
sheriff's jury
special jury
struck jury
trial jury

597 LAWYER

<one who assists others in legal matters>

NOUNS 1 **lawyer, attorney,** attorney-at-law, barrister, barrister-at-law, counselor, counselor-at-law, counsel, legal counsel, legal counselor, legal adviser, law officer, legal expert, solicitor, advocate, pleader; legal representation; member of the bar, legal practitioner, officer of the court; smart lawyer, pettifogger, Philadelphia lawyer; Juris Doctor (Jur.D.), proctor, procurator; friend at court, friend in court, amicus curiae; deputy, agent; intercessor; sea lawyer, latrine lawyer, guardhouse lawyer, self-styled lawyer, legalist; public prosecutor, public defender, defense lawyer, defense attorney, prosecuting attorney, trial lawyer, trial attorney; judge advocate, district attorney (DA), attorney general; bar association; sidebar comment; legal aid

2 legist, jurist, jurisprudent, jurisconsult; law member of a court-martial

3 <nonformal> **legal eagle,** shyster, mouthpiece, ambulance chaser, lip, fixer

4 **bar,** legal profession, members of the bar; representation, counsel, pleading, attorneyship; **practice,** legal practice, criminal practice, corporate practice; legal-aid practice, pro bono practice; **law firm,** legal firm, partnership; legal aid

VERBS 5 **practice law,** practice at the bar; be admitted to the bar; take silk <Brit>

ADJS 6 **lawyerly,** lawyerlike, barristerial; representing, of counsel

598 LEGAL ACTION

<judicial proceeding>

NOUNS 1 **lawsuit, suit,** suit in law, suit at law; countersuit; **litigation,** prosecution, action, legal action, proceedings, legal proceeding, legal process, legal procedure, due process, course of law; legal remedy; case, **court case,** cause, cause in court, legal case; judicial process; claim, counterclaim; test case; one's day in court; case file; class action

2 **summons, subpoena,** writ of summons; **writ, warrant**

3 **arraignment, indictment,** impeachment; complaint, charge; presentment; information; bill of indictment, true bill; bail

4 **jury selection,** impanelment, venire, venire facias, venire facias de novo, jury service, sequestration

5 **trial,** jury trial, trial by jury, trial at the bar, trial by law, hearing, inquiry, inquisition, inquest, assize; court-martial; examination, cross-examination; retrial; mistrial; change of venue; civil trial, criminal trial, bench trial

6 **pleadings,** arguments at the bar; **plea,** pleading, argument; defense, statement of defense; demurrer, general demurrer, special demurrer; refutation; rebuttal

7 **declaration,** statement, allegation, allegation of facts, statement of facts, procès-verbal; **deposition,** affidavit; claim; complaint; bill, bill of complaint; libel, narratio; nolle prosequi, nol pros; nonsuit

8 **testimony;** evidence; , cross-examination, direct examination; argument, presentation of the case; resting of the case; summing up, summation, summary, closing arguments, jury instructions, charge to the jury, charging of the jury

9 **judgment, decision,** landmark decision; **verdict,** directed verdict, special verdict, sealed verdict, **sentence**; acquittal; condemnation, penalty

10 **appeal,** appeal motion, application for retrial, appeal to a higher court; writ of error; certiorari, writ of certiorari

11 **litigant, litigator,** litigationist; **party,** party to a suit, suitor; injured party, aggrieved party, **plaintiff; defendant**; witness; accessory, accessory before the fact, accessory after the fact; panel, parties litigant

12 <legal terms> motion for summary judgment, search warrant, bench warrant, discovery, written interrogatories, witness list, plea bargaining, objection, perjury

VERBS 13 **sue, litigate, prosecute,** go into litigation, bring suit, put in suit, prosecute at law, go to law, seek in law, appeal to the law, seek justice, seek legal redress, implead, bring action against, bring legal action, start an action, prosecute a suit against, institute legal proceedings against; law, have the law in; take to court, bring into court, haul into court, drag into court, bring a case before the court, bring a case before the bar, bring before a jury, bring to justice, bring to trial, put on trial, bring to the bar, take before the judge; set down for hearing; seek legal protection

14 **summons,** issue a summons, subpoena

15 **arraign, indict,** impeach, cite, serve notice on, find an indictment against, present a true bill, claim, file a claim, pull up, bring up for investigation; press charges, prefer charges

16 **select a jury,** impanel a jury, impanel, panel

17 **call to witness,** bring forward, put on the stand; swear in; take oath; take the stand, testify

18 **try,** try a case, conduct a trial, bring to trial, put on trial, **hear,** give a hearing to, sit on; charge the jury, deliver one's charge to the jury; **judge,** sit in judgment

19 **plead,** enter a plea, enter a pleading, implead, conduct pleadings, argue at the bar; plead one's case, argue one's case, stand trial, present one's case, make a plea, tell it to the judge; hang the jury; rest, rest one's case; sum up one's case; throw oneself on the mercy of the court

20 **bring in a verdict,** judge, pass sentence, pronounce sentence; acquit; convict; penalize

ADJS 21 **litigious,** litigant, litigatory, litigating; causidical, lawyerly; litigable, actionable, justiciable, prosecutable; prosecutorial; moot, sub judice; unactionable, unprosecutable, unlitigable, frivolous, without merit

PHRS 22 **in litigation,** in court, in chancery, in jeopardy, at law, litigated, coram judice, brought before the court, brought before a judge, at bar, at the bar, on trial, up for investigation, up for hearing, before the court, before the bar, before the judge

599 ACCUSATION

<charge of wrongdoing>

NOUNS 1 **accusation,** accusal, finger-pointing, **charge,** complaint, plaint, count, blame, imputation, delation, reproach, taxing; accusing, bringing of charges, laying of charges, bringing to book; denunciation, denouncement; impeachment, arraignment, indictment, bill of indictment, true bill; allegation, allegement; ascription; insinuation, implication, innuendo, veiled accusation, unspoken accusation; information, information against, bill of particulars; charge sheet; specification; gravamen of a charge; prosecution, suit, lawsuit

2 **incrimination,** crimination, inculpation, implication, citation, involvement, impugnment; attack, assault; censure

3 **recrimination,** retort, countercharge

4 **trumped-up charge,** false witness; put-up job, frame-up, **frame**; false charge

5 **accuser,** accusant, accusatrix; incriminator, delator, allegator, impugner; informer; impeacher, indictor; **plaintiff, complainant,** claimant, appellant, petitioner, libelant, suitor, party, party to a suit, pursuer; prosecutor, the prosecution; hostile witness

6 **accused, defendant,** respondent, codefendant, corespondent, libelee, appellee, suspect, culprit, prisoner, prisoner before the court, accused person; prime suspect

VERBS 7 **accuse,** bring accusation; **charge, press charges**, prefer charges, bring charges, lay charges; complain, lodge a complaint, lodge a plaint; impeach, arraign, indict, bring in an indictment, hand up an indictment, return a true bill, article, cite, cite on several counts; book; denounce, denunciate; finger, point the finger at, lay the finger on, throw the book at, inform on, inform against; impute, ascribe; allege, insinuate, imply; bring to book; tax, task, take to task, take to account; reproach, twit, taunt with; report, put on report

8 **blame,** blame on, lay on, hold against, put the blame on, place the blame on, lay the blame on, place the blame for, fix the blame for, place responsibility for, fix responsibility for; fasten on, pin on, hang on

9 **accuse of, charge with,** tax with, task with, saddle with, lay to one's charge, place to one's account, lay at one's door, bring home to, throw in one's teeth, throw up to one, thrust in the face of; j'accuse <Fr>

10 **incriminate,** criminate, inculpate, implicate, involve; cry out against, cry upon, cry shame upon, raise one's voice against; attack, assail, impugn; censure; throw a stone at, cast the first stone, throw the first stone

11 **recriminate,** countercharge, retort an accusation

12 **trump up a charge,** bear false witness; **frame,** frame up, set up, put up a job on, plant evidence

ADJS 13 **accusing,** accusatory, accusatorial, accusative, pointing to; imputative, denunciatory; recriminatory; prosecutorial; condemnatory

14 **incriminating,** incriminatory, criminatory; delatorian; inculpative, inculpatory

15 **accused, charged,** blamed, tasked, taxed, reproached, denounced, impeached, indicted, arraigned; under a cloud, under a cloud of suspicion, under suspicion; incriminated, recriminated, inculpated, implicated, involved, in complicity; cited, impugned; under attack, under fire

600 JUSTIFICATION

<denial of wrongdoing>

NOUNS 1 **justification, vindication; clearing,** clearing of one's name, clearing of one's good name, clearance, purging, purgation, destigmatizing, destigmatization, exculpation; no bill, failure to indict; explanation, rationalization; reinstatement, restitution, restoration, rehabilitation

2 **defense, plea,** pleading; argument, statement of defense; answer, reply, counterstatement, response, riposte; grounds; refutation, rebuttal; demurrer, general demurrer, special demurrer; denial, objection, exception; special pleading; self-defense, plea of self-defense, Nuremberg defense, the devil-made-me-do-it defense, blame-the-victim defense

3 **apology,** apologia, apologetic; amende

4 **excuse,** cop-out, **alibi**, out; lame excuse, poor excuse, likely story, sob story; escape hatch, way out; credibility gap

5 **extenuation,** mitigation, palliation, softening; extenuative, palliative, saving grace; whitewash, whitewashing, decontamination; gilding, gloss, varnish, color, putting the best color on; qualification, allowance; extenuating circumstances, mitigating circumstances, diminished responsibility; five second rule; dichaeologia

6 warrant, reason, good reason, cause, call, right, basis, substantive basis, material basis, **ground, grounds,** foundation, substance

7 **justifiability, vindicability**, defensibility; explainability, explicability; excusability, pardonableness, forgivableness, remissibility, veniality; warrantableness, allowableness, admissibility, reasonableness, reasonability, legitimacy

8 **justifier, vindicator;** defender, pleader; advocate, successful advocate, proponent, champion; apologist, apologizer, apologetic, excuser; whitewasher

VERBS 9 **justify, vindicate,** do justice to, make justice prevail, make right prevail; fail to indict, no-bill; warrant, account for, show sufficient grounds for, give good reasons for; rationalize, explain; cry sour grapes, make a virtue of necessity; get off the hook, find an out, exculpate; clear, clear one's name, clear one's good name, purge, destigmatize, reinstate, restore, rehabilitate

10 **defend,** offer in defense, say in defense, allege in support, allege in vindication, support, uphold, sustain, maintain, assert, **stick up for**; answer, reply, respond, riposte, counter; refute, rebut; plead for, make a plea, offer as a plea, plead one's case, plead one's cause, put up a front, put up a brave front; advocate, champion, go to bat for, espouse, join oneself with, associate oneself with, stand up for, speak up for, contend for, speak for, argue for, urge reasons for, put in a good word for

11 **excuse, alibi**, offer excuse for, give as an excuse, cover with excuses, explain, offer an explanation; plead ignorance, plead insanity, plead diminished responsibility; apologize for, make apology for; alibi out of, crawl out of, worm out of, squirm out of, lie out of, have an out, have an alibi, have a story

12 **extenuate, mitigate,** palliate, soften, lessen, diminish, ease, mince; soft-pedal; slur over, ignore, pass by in silence, give the benefit of the doubt, not hold it against one, explain away, gloss over, smooth over, put a gloss upon, put a good face upon, varnish, whitewash, color, lend a color to, put the best face on, show in the best

colors, show to best advantage; allow for, make allowance for; give the devil his due

ADJS 13 **justifying,** justificatory; **vindicative,** vindicatory, rehabilitative; refuting; defensive; excusing, excusatory; apologetic, apologetical; extenuating, extenuative, palliative

14 **justifiable, vindicable,** defensible; excusable, pardonable, forgivable, expiable, remissible, exemptible, venial; condonable, dispensable; warrantable, allowable, admissible, reasonable, colorable, legitimate; innocuous, unobjectionable, inoffensive

601 ACQUITTAL

<setting free from charge of wrongdoing>

NOUNS 1 **acquittal,** acquittance, acquitment; **exculpation,** disculpation, verdict of acquittal, verdict of not guilty; **exoneration,** absolution, vindication, remission, compurgation, purgation, purging; clearing, clearance, destigmatizing, destigmatization, quietus; pardon, excuse, forgiveness, free pardon; discharge, release, dismissal, setting free; quashing of the charge; assoilment; grace

2 **exemption, immunity,** impunity, nonliability, dispensation, waiver; diplomatic immunity; **amnesty,** indemnity, nonprosecution, non prosequitur, nolle prosequi; stay; freedom

3 **reprieve,** respite, grace, remit

VERBS 4 **acquit, clear,** exculpate, **exonerate,** absolve, give absolution, grant absolution, bring in a verdict of not guilty, return a verdict of not guilty; vindicate, justify; pardon, excuse, forgive, show mercy; remit, grant remission, remit the penalty of; amnesty, grant amnesty, extend amnesty; discharge, release, dismiss, free, set free, let off, let go, let off scot-free, spare; quash the charge, quash the indictment, withdraw the charge; exempt, grant immunity, exempt from, dispense from; clear the skirts of, shrive, purge; blot out one's sins, wipe the slate clean; whitewash, decontaminate; destigmatize; non-pros; assoil

5 **reprieve,** respite, give a reprieve, grant a reprieve; stay

602 CONDEMNATION

<declaring guilty of wrongdoing>

NOUNS 1 **condemnation,** damnation, doom, **guilty verdict,** verdict of guilty; proscription, excommunication, anathematizing; denunciation, denouncement; censure; conviction; sentence, judgment, rap; capital punishment, corporal punishment, death penalty, death sentence, death warrant, burning at the stake; curse; three strikes; life sentence

2 attainder, attainture, attaintment; bill of attainder; civil death

VERBS 3 **condemn,** damn, doom; denounce, denunciate; censure; **convict,** find guilty, bring home to; proscribe, excommunicate, anathematize; blacklist, put on the Index; reprobate; pronounce judgment; sentence, pronounce sentence, pass sentence on; penalize; attaint; sign one's death warrant

4 **stand condemned,** be convicted, be found guilty

ADJS 5 **condemnatory,** damnatory, denunciatory, proscriptive; censorious

6 convicted, condemned, guilty, blameworthy, liable, sentenced

603 PENALTY

<payment for wrongdoing>

NOUNS 1 **penalty,** penalization, penance, penal retribution; sanctions, penal measures, punitive measures; **punishment**; reprisal, retaliation, compensation, price; the devil to pay

2 **handicap,** disability, **disadvantage**

3 **fine,** monetary penalty, financial penalty, mulct, amercement, sconce, **damages,** punitive damages, compensatory damages; distress, distraint; forfeit, forfeiture; escheat, escheatment

VERBS 4 **penalize,** put a penalty on, impose a penalty on, inflict a penalty on, impose sanctions on; **punish**; handicap, put at a disadvantage

5 **fine,** mulct, amerce, sconce, estreat, pillory; distrain, levy a distress; award damages

ADVS 6 on pain of, under pain of, upon pain of, **under penalty of**

604 PUNISHMENT

<suffering for wrongdoing>

NOUNS 1 **punishment,** punition, chastisement, chastening, correction, discipline, disciplinary measure, disciplinary action, castigation, infliction, scourge, ferule, what-for; pains, pains and punishments; pay, payment; crime fighting; retribution, retributive justice, nemesis; judicial punishment; punishment that fits the crime, condign punishment, well-deserved punishment; penalty, penal retribution; penalization; penology; cruel and unusual punishment; judgment; what's coming to one, just desserts, desserts; dukkha; three strikes

2 <**forms of punishment**> penal servitude, jailing, imprisonment, incarceration, confinement;

hard labor, rock pile, chain gang, labor camp; galleys; torture, torment, martyrdom; the gantlet, keelhauling, tar-and-feathering, railriding, picketing, the rack, impalement, dismemberment; walking the plank, perp walk; house arrest; exile

3 **light punishment, slap,** smack, whack, whomp, cuff, box, buffet, belt; blow; rap on the knuckles, box on the ear, slap in the face; slap on the wrist, token punishment

4 **corporal punishment,** whipping, beating, thrashing, spanking, flogging, paddling, flagellation, scourging, flailing, trouncing, basting, bastinado, drubbing, buffeting, belaboring; lashing, lacing, stripes; horsewhipping, strapping, belting, rawhiding, cowhiding; switching; clubbing, cudgeling, caning, truncheoning, fustigation; pistol-whipping; battery; dusting

5 <nonformal> licking, larruping, walloping, whaling, lathering, leathering, hiding, tanning, dressing-down, chewing out; paddling, swingeing; grounding

6 **capital punishment, execution;** legal murder, judicial murder, extreme penalty, death sentence, death penalty, death warrant; hanging, the gallows, the rope, the noose; summary execution; lynching, necktie party, vigilanteism, vigilante justice; the necklace; crucifixion, impalement; electrocution, the chair, the hot seat; gassing, the gas chamber; lethal injection; decapitation, decollation, beheading, the guillotine, the ax, the block; strangling, strangulation, garrote; shooting, fusillade, firing squad; burning, burning at the stake; poisoning, hemlock; stoning, lapidation; drowning; defenestration

7 **punisher,** discipliner, chastiser, chastener; executioner, executionist, Jack Ketch <Brit>; hangman; lyncher; electrocutioner; headsman, beheader, decapitator; strangler, garroter; sadist, torturer; hatchet man, hit man; lynch mob

8 penologist**; jailer**

VERBS 9 **punish,** chastise, chasten, discipline, correct, castigate, penalize, reprimand; take to task, bring to book, bring to account, call to account; deal with, settle with, settle accounts, square accounts, give one his desserts, give one his just desserts, serve one right; inflict upon, visit upon; teach one a lesson, give one a lesson, make an example of; pillory; masthead; reduce to the ranks

10 <nonformal> **let one have it**, attend to, do for, take care of, serve one out, give it to, have it out of; pay, pay out, fix, settle, fix one's wagon, settle one's hash, settle the score, give one his gruel, make it hot for one, give one his comeuppance; lower the boom, put one through the wringer, come down on, come down hard on, throw the book at, throw to the wolves; give what-for, give a going-over, climb one's frame, tell off, light into, lay into, land on, mop the floor with, wipe up the floor with, skin live, have one's hide

11 **slap,** smack, whack, thwack, whomp, cuff, box, buffet; strike; slap the face, box the ears, give a rap on the knuckles

12 **whip,** give a whipping, give a beating, give a thrashing, beat, thrash, spank, flog, scourge, flagellate, flay, flail, whale; smite, thump, trounce, baste, pummel, pommel, drub, buffet, belabor, lay on; lash, lace, cut, stripe; horsewhip; knout; strap, belt, rawhide, cowhide; switch, birch, give the stick; club, cudgel, cane, truncheon, fustigate, bastinado; pistol-whip

13 thrash soundly, **batter,** bruise

14 <nonformal> **beat up,** rough up, clobber, marmelize <Brit>, work over, lick, larrup, wallop, whop, swinge, beat one's brains out, whale, whale the tar out of, beat the shit out of*, kick the shit out of*, beat to a jelly, beat black and blue, knock one's lights out, nail, welt, trim, flax, lather, leather, hide, tan, tan one's hide, dress down, kick ass*, give a dressing-down, knock head, knock heads together; paddle; lambaste, dust one's jacket, take it out of one's hide, take it out of one's skin

15 **torture,** put to the question; rack, put on the rack; dismember, tear limb from limb; draw and quarter, break on the wheel, tar and feather, ride on a rail, picket, keelhaul, impale, grill, thumbscrew, persecute, work over

16 **execute,** put to death, inflict capital punishment; electrocute, burn, fry; send to the gas chamber; behead, decapitate, decollate, guillotine, bring to the block; crucify; shoot, execute by firing squad; burn at the stake; strangle, garrote, bowstring; stone, lapidate; defenestrate; send to the hot seat

17 **hang,** hang by the neck; string up, scrag, stretch; gibbet, noose, neck, bring to the gallows; **lynch;** draw, and quarter

18 **be hanged,** suffer hanging, swing, dance upon nothing, kick the air

19 **be punished,** suffer, suffer for, suffer the consequences, suffer the penalty, get it, catch it, get it in the neck, catch hell, catch the devil, take a licking, get a shellacking; get one's desserts, get one's just desserts; get it coming and going, be doubly punished, sow the wind and reap the whirlwind; get hurt, get one's fingers burned, get one's knuckles rapped

20 **take one's punishment,** bow one's neck, take the consequences, take one's medicine, take what is

coming to one, swallow the bitter pill, swallow one's medicine, pay the piper, face the music, stand up to it, make one's bed and lie on it, get what one is asking for; take the rap, take the fall

21 **deserve punishment,** have it coming, be for it, be in for it, be heading for a fall, be cruising for a bruising

ADJS 22 **punishing,** chastising, chastening, corrective, disciplinary, correctional; retributive; grueling; **penal, punitive,** punitory, inflictive; castigatory; baculine; penological; capital; corporal

605 INSTRUMENTS OF PUNISHMENT

<tool for punishing>

NOUNS 1 **whip, lash,** scourge, flagellum, strap, thong, rawhide, cowhide, blacksnake, kurbash, sjambok, belt, razor strap; knout; bullwhip, bullwhack; horsewhip; crop; quirt; rope's end; cat, cat-o'-nine-tails; whiplash; bastinado

2 **rod, stick,** switch; paddle, ruler, ferule, pandybat; birch, rattan; cane; club

3 <punishment devices> pillory, stocks, finger pillory; cucking stool, ducking stool, trebuchet; whipping post, branks, triangle, wooden horse, treadmill, crank

4 **<instruments of torture>** rack, wheel, Iron Maiden of Nuremberg; screw, thumbscrew; boot, iron heel, scarpines; Procrustean bed, bed of Procrustes

5 **<instruments of execution>** scaffold; block, guillotine, ax, maiden; stake; cross; gallows, gallows-tree, gibbet, tree, drop; hangman's rope, noose, rope, halter, hemp; electric chair, death chair, the chair, hot seat; gas chamber, lethal chamber, death chamber; the necklace, the needle

606 THE PEOPLE

<ordinary people>

NOUNS 1 **the people,** the populace, **the public,** the general public, people in general, everyone, everybody; the population, the citizenry, the whole people, the polity, the body politic; the community, the commonwealth, society, the society, the social order, the social fabric, the nation; the commonalty, the commonality, commonage, commoners, commons, *demos* <Gk>; the little people; common people, ordinary people, ordinary folk, persons, folk, folks, gentry; the common sort, plain folks, the common run, the rank and file, the boy next door, the girl next door, Brown, Jones and Robinson, John Q. Public, Joe Public, Joe Citizen, Middle America; Tom, Dick, and Harry; the salt of the earth, Everyman, Everywoman, the man in the street, the woman in the street, the common man, you and me, John Doe, Joe Sixpack, Joe Schmo, *vulgus* <L>, the third estate; the upper class; the middle class; the lower class, chav; demography, demographics; social anthropology

2 **the masses, the hoi polloi,** the many, the multitude, the crowd, the mob, the horde, the million, the booboisie, the majority, the mass of the people, the herd, the great unnumbered, the great unwashed, the vulgar masses, the common herd; *profanum vulgus, ignobile vulgus, mobile vulgus* <L>; audience, followers, sheeple

3 **rabble,** rabblement, scourge of the earth, bane, rout, ruck, common ruck, canaille, ragtag, ragtag and bobtail; rag, tag, and bobtail; riffraff, trash, raff, chaff, rubbish, dregs, sordes, offscourings, off-scum, scum, scum of the earth, dregs of society, swinish multitude, vermin, cattle; colluvies; black collar

4 **the underprivileged,** the disadvantaged, the poor, ghetto-dwellers, slum-dwellers, welfare cases, chronic poor, underclass, depressed class, poverty subculture, the wretched of the earth, outcasts, the homeless, the dispossessed, bag people, the powerless, the unemployable, lumpen, the lumpen proletariat, the lumpenprole, lower orders, second-class citizens, the have-nots, small potatoes, little folk

5 **common man,** commoner, little man, little fellow, average man, ordinary man, typical man, man in the street, one of the people, man of the people, regular guy, regular joe, Everyman, ham-and-egger; plebeian, pleb; proletarian, prole; ordinary Joe, average Joe, Joe Doakes, Joe Sixpack, John Doe, Jane Doe, John Smith, Mr. Brown, Mrs. Brown, Mr. Smith, Mrs. Smith, Joe Blow, John Q. Public, Mr. Nobody; nonentity; muggle; bourgeois

6 **peasant,** countryman, countrywoman, provincial, son of the soil, tiller of the soil; peon, hind, fellah, muzhik, serf, villein, churl; farmer, hick, yokel, rube, hayseed, shitkicker*, bumpkin, country bumpkin, rustic, clod, clodhopper, hillbilly, woodhick, boor, clown, lout, looby; townie

7 **upstart,** parvenu, adventurer, sprout; would-be gentleman; *nouveau riche, arriviste* <Fr>, newly rich, pig in clover; social climber, climber, name-dropper, tufthunter, status seeker

ADJS 8 **populational,** population; **demographic,** demographical; national, societal; popular, public, mass, grassroots, cultural, common, common as dirt, commonplace, communal, folk, tribal, plain, ordinary, lowly, low, mean, base; humble, homely; black-collar; rank-and-file, provincial, of the people; second-class, lowborn, lowbred, baseborn, earthborn, earthy, of humble birth, plebeian; third-estate; ungenteel, shabby-genteel, uncultured; vulgar, rude, coarse, below the salt; parvenu, upstart, risen from the ranks, jumped-up; newly rich, *nouveau-riche* <Fr>; non-U <Brit>

607 SOCIAL CLASS AND STATUS

<social and economic classes>

NOUNS 1 **class, social class, economic class,** social group, status group, accorded status, social category, order, grade, caste, estate, rank, ranking; status, social status, economic status, socioeconomic status, socioeconomic background, standing, footing, prestige, place, station, position, level, degree, stratum; social structure, hierarchy, pecking order, social stratification, social system, social gamut, social differentiation, social pyramid, class structure, class distinction, status system, power structure, stratification, social network, ordering, social scale, gradation, division, social inequality, inequality, haves and have-nots; social bias, class conflict, class identity, class difference, class prejudice, class struggle, class politics; ageism; mobility, social mobility, upward mobility, downward mobility, vertical mobility, horizontal mobility; social justice

2 **upper class, the one percent,** upper classes, first class, aristocracy, patriciate, second estate, ruling class, ruling circles, elite, elect, the privileged, the classes, the quality, the better sort, upper circles, upper cut, upper crust, crust, cream, upper-income group, higher-income group, higher tax bracket, the one-percent, gentlefolk, gentility, lords of creation; **high society,** high life, the Four Hundred, bon ton, *haut monde* <Fr>, First Families of Virginia (FFV); Social Register, Bluebook; nobility, gentry; status symbol; social ladder

3 **aristocracy,** aristocratic status, aristocraticalness, aristocraticness, high status, high rank, quality, high estate, gentility, social distinction, social prestige; birth, high birth, distinguished ancestry, distinguished heritage, blue blood, silk stocking

4 **aristocrat,** patrician, Brahmin, blue-blood, thoroughbred, member of the upper class, socialite, swell, upper-cruster, grandee, grand dame, dowager, magnifico, lord of creation; gentleman, lady, person of breeding; trophy wife; debutante

5 **middle class,** middle order, lower middle class, upper middle class, bourgeoisie, educated class, professional class, middle-income group, white-collar workers, salaried workers; suburbia; Middle America, silent majority; white bread; third estate; business class

6 **bourgeois,** member of the middle class, petit bourgeoisie, white-collar worker, salaried worker; pillar of society, solid citizen

7 **lower class,** lower classes, lower orders, plebeians, plebs, workers, working class, working people, proletariat, proles, rank and file, grassroots, laboring class, toilers, toiling class, the other half, low-income group, wage earners, hourly worker, blue-collar worker; bottom feeder, bottom rung; economy class

8 **the underclass, the underprivileged**

9 **worker**, workman, working person, working man, working woman, working girl, proletarian, laborer, laboring man, toiler, stiff, working stiff, artisan, mechanic, industrial worker, factory worker; grunt worker, grunt; child labor

ADJS 10 **upper-class,** aristocratic, patrician, upscale; gentle, genteel, of gentle blood; gentlemanly, gentlemanlike; ladylike, quite the lady; wellborn, well-bred, blue-blooded, of good breed; thoroughbred, purebred, pure-blooded, full-blooded; highborn, highbred; born to the purple, to the manner born, born with a silver spoon in one's mouth; high-society, socialite, hoity-toity, posh; **white collar; middle-class, bourgeois,** *petit-bourgeois* <Fr>, petty-bourgeois, suburban, white-bread; working class, **blue-collar,** proletarian, lower-class, born on the wrong side of the tracks; class-conscious; mobile, socially mobile, upwardly mobile, downwardly mobile, vertically mobile, horizontally mobile, déclassé

608 ARISTOCRACY, NOBILITY, GENTRY

<highest social class>

NOUNS 1 **aristocracy, nobility,** titled aristocracy, hereditary nobility, noblesse; royalty; elite, upper class, elect, the classes, upper circles, upper cut, upper crust, upper ten, upper ten thousand, the Four Hundred, Social Register, high society, high life, *haut monde* <Fr>; old nobility, *ancienne noblesse* <Fr>, *noblesse de robe, noblesse d'épée* <Fr>, *ancien régime* <Fr>; First Families of Virginia (FFV); peerage, baronage, lords temporal and spiritual; baronetage; knightage, chivalry; gentlefolk, beau monde, jet set

2 **nobility,** nobleness, aristocracy, aristocraticalness; gentility, genteelness; quality, rank, virtue, distinction; birth, high birth, noble birth, ancestry, high descent, honorable descent; lineage, pedigree; blood, **blue blood;** royalty

3 **gentry,** gentlefolk, gentlefolks, gentlepeople, better sort; lesser nobility, *petite noblesse* <Fr>; *samurai* <Japanese>; landed gentry, squirearchy

4 **nobleman,** noble, gentleman; peer; aristocrat, patrician, Brahman, blue blood, titled person, thoroughbred, silk stocking, lace curtain, swell, upper-cruster, life peer; grandee, magnifico, magnate, optimate; lord, laird, lordling; seignior, seigneur, *hidalgo* <Sp>; duke, grand duke, archduke, marquis, earl, count, viscount, baron, daimio, baronet; squire; esquire, armiger; palsgrave, waldgrave, margrave, landgrave; jet-setter

5 **knight,** cavalier, chevalier, *caballero* <Sp>; knight-errant, knight-adventurer; companion; bachelor, knight bachelor; baronet, knight baronet; banneret, knight banneret; Bayard, Gawain, Lancelot, Sidney, Sir Galahad, Don Quixote

6 **noblewoman,** peeress, gentlewoman; lady, dame, *doña* <Sp>, khanum; duchess, grand duchess, archduchess, marchioness, marquise, viscountess, countess, baroness, margravine

7 **prince,** prinz, knez, atheling, sheikh, sherif, mirza, khan, emir; princeling, princelet; crown prince, heir apparent; heir presumptive; prince consort; prince regent; **king;** princes of India; Muslim rulers

8 **princess,** *princesse* <Fr>, *infanta* <Sp>; crown princess; **queen**

9 <rank or office> lordship, ladyship; dukedom, marquisate, earldom, barony, baronetcy; viscountship, viscountcy, viscounty; knighthood, knight-errantship; seigniory, seigneury, seignioralty; pashaship, pashadom; peerage; princeship, princedom; kingship, queenship

ADJS 10 **noble,** ennobled, titled, of rank, high, exalted; **aristocratic,** patrician; gentle, genteel, of gentle blood; gentlemanly, gentlemanlike; ladylike, quite the lady; knightly, chivalrous; ducal, archducal; princely, princelike; regal, kingly, kinglike, every inch a king; queenly, queenlike

11 **wellborn,** well-bred, blue-blooded, well-connected, of good breed; thoroughbred, purebred, pure-blooded, full-blooded; highborn, highbred; born to the purple, high-caste, of good family; classy, U <Brit>

609 POLITICS

<government-related activity>

NOUNS 1 **politics,** polity, the art of the possible; practical politics, *Realpolitik* <Ger>; empirical politics; party politics, **partisan politics,** partisanism; politicization; reform politics; multiparty politics; power politics; machine politics, bossism, Tammany Hall, Tammanism; confrontation politics, confrontational politics; interest politics, single-issue politics, interest-group politics, pressure-group politics, (PAC) political action committee politics; consensus politics; fusion politics; career politics; petty politics, peanut politics; pork-barrel politics; kid-glove politics; silk-stocking politics; ward politics; electronic politics, technological politics; public affairs, civic affairs

2 **political science,** poli-sci, politics, government, civics; political philosophy, political theory; political behavior; political economy, comparative government, international relations, public administration; political geography, geopolitics; realpolitik; political scientist

3 **statesmanship,** statecraft, political leadership, governmental leadership, national leadership; transpartisan leadership, suprapartisan leadership; kingcraft, queencraft; senatorship

4 **policy,** polity, public policy; line, party line, party principle, party doctrine, party philosophy, position, bipartisan policy; noninterference, nonintervention, *laissez-faire* <Fr>, laissez-faireism; free enterprise; go-slow policy; government control, governmentalism; planned economy, managed currency, price supports, pump-priming; autarky, economic self-sufficiency; free trade; protection, protectionism; bimetallism; strict constructionism; localism, sectionalism, states' rights, nullification; political correctness

5 **foreign policy,** foreign affairs; world politics; diplomacy, diplomatic, diplomatics; shirt-sleeve diplomacy; shuttle diplomacy; dollar diplomacy, dollar imperialism; gunboat diplomacy; brinkmanship; nationalism, internationalism; expansionism, imperialism, manifest destiny, colonialism, neocolonialism; spheres of influence; balance of power; containment; deterrence; militarism, preparedness; tough policy, the big stick, twisting the lion's tail; brinksmanship; nonresistance, isolationism, neutralism, coexistence, peaceful coexistence; détente; compromise, appeasement; peace offensive; good-neighbor policy; open-door policy, open door; diplomatic doctrine; Monroe Doctrine; Truman Doctrine; Eisenhower Doctrine; Nixon Doctrine

6 **program,** historical program; Square Deal <Theodore Roosevelt>, New Deal <Franklin D Roosevelt>, Fair Deal <Harry S Truman>, New Frontier <John F Kennedy>, Great Society <Lyndon B Johnson>, Obamacare <Barack H Obama>; austerity program

7 **platform,** party platform, program, declaration of policy; **plank; issue;** keynote address, keynote speech; position paper

8 **political convention,** convention; conclave, powwow; national convention, quadrennial circus; state convention, county convention, preliminary convention, nominating convention; constitutional convention

9 **caucus,** legislative caucus, congressional caucus, packed caucus; secret caucus

10 **candidacy,** candidature, running, running for office, throwing one's hat in the ring, tossing one's hat in the ring, standing, standing for office

11 **nomination,** caucus nomination, direct nomination, petition nomination; acceptance speech

12 electioneering, **campaigning,** politicking, stumping, whistle-stopping; rally, clambake; campaign dinner, fund-raising dinner

13 **campaign,** political agenda, all-out campaign, hard-hitting campaign, hoopla campaign, hurrah campaign; canvass, solicitation; front-porch campaign; grassroots campaign; stump excursion, stumping tour, whistle-stop campaign; TV campaign, media campaign; campaign commitments, campaign promises; campaign fund, campaign contribution; campaign button

14 **smear campaign,** mudslinging campaign, negative campaign; whispering campaign; muckraking, mudslinging, dirty politics, dirty tricks, dirty pool, character assassination; political canard, roorback; last-minute lie

15 **election,** general election, by-election; congressional election, presidential election; partisan election, nonpartisan election; **primary,** primary election; direct primary, open primary, closed primary, nonpartisan primary, mandatory primary, optional primary, preference primary, presidential primary, presidential preference primary, runoff primary; caucus; runoff, runoff election; disputed election, contested election; referendum; close election, horse race, toss-up

16 **election district,** precinct, ward, borough; congressional district; safe district; swing district; close borough, pocket borough, rotten borough <Brit>; gerrymander, gerrymandered district, shoestring district; silk-stocking district; single-member district, single-member constituency; body politic

17 **right to vote,** suffrage, franchise, the vote; universal suffrage, male suffrage, female suffrage; suffragism, suffragettism; suffragist, woman-suffragist, suffragette; household franchise; one man one vote

18 **voting,** going to the polls, casting one's ballot; popular vote; red state, blue state, purple state; preferential voting, preferential system, alternative vote; proportional representation (PR), cumulative system, cumulative voting, Hare system, list system; single system, single transferrable vote; plural system; single-member district; absentee voting; proxy voting, card voting; voting machine; election fraud, colonization, floating, repeating, ballot-box stuffing; **vote**

19 **ballot, slate, ticket,** proxy; straight ticket, split ticket; Australian ballot; office-block ballot; Indiana ballot, party-column ballot; absentee ballot; long ballot, blanket ballot, jungle ballot; short ballot; nonpartisan ballot; sample ballot; party emblem

20 **polls,** poll, polling place, polling station, balloting place; voting booth, polling booth; ballot box; voting machine; pollbook

21 **returns,** election returns, poll, count, official count; recount; landslide, tidal wave; regime change

22 **electorate,** electors; **constituency,** constituents; electoral college; popular vote

23 **voter,** elector, balloter; registered voter; fraudulent voter, floater, repeater, ballot-box stuffer; proxy; slactivist

24 **political party,** party, major party, minor party, third party, splinter party; party in power, opposition party, loyal opposition; fraction, camp; machine, political machine, party machine, Tammany Hall; city hall; one-party system, two-party system, multiple party system, multiparty system; right, left, center; alt-right; new left; right-wing conspiracy, left-wing conspiracy; popular front; bloc, coalition; Citizens Party, Communist Party, Conservative Party, Constitution Party, Democratic Party, Federalist Party, Green Party, Labor Party, Labour Party, Liberal Party, Libertarian Party, People's Party, Populist Party, Progressive Party, Republican Party, Social Democratic Party, Socialist Party, Tea Party, Whig Party

25 **partisanism,** partisanship, party politics, partisanry

26 **nonpartisanism,** independence, neutralism; mugwumpery, mugwumpism

27 **partisan, party member,** party man, party woman; regular, stalwart, loyalist; wheelhorse, party wheelhorse; heeler, ward heeler, party hack; party faithful; right-winger, left-winger; Democrat, Republican

28 **nonpartisan, independent,** neutral, mugwump, undecided voter, uncommitted voter, centrist; swing vote; superdelegate

29 **political influence,** wire-pulling; social pressure, public opinion, special-interest pressure, group pressure; influence peddling; lobbying, lobbyism; logrolling, back scratching; political corruption; 527 group

30 wire-puller; influence peddler, four-percenter, **power broker,** fixer, five-percenter; logroller

31 **pressure group,** interest group, special-interest group, political action committee (PAC), single-issue group; special interest; vested interest; financial interests, farm interests, labor interests; minority interests, ethnic vote, black vote; Black Power, White Power, Polish Power

32 **lobby,** legislative lobby, special-interest lobby; **lobbyist,** registered lobbyist, lobbyer, parliamentary agent <Brit>

33 **front, movement,** coalition, political front; popular front, people's front, communist front; grassroots movement, ground swell, the silent majority; youth crusade, youth movement

34 <**political corruption**> graft, boodling, jobbery; pork-barrel legislation, pork-barreling; political intrigue

35 **spoils of office;** graft, boodle; slush fund; campaign fund, campaign contribution; public tit, public trough; spoils system; cronyism, nepotism

36 **political patronage,** patronage, favors of office, pork, pork barrel, plum, melon

37 **political jargon,** official jargon; officialese, federalese, Washingtonese, gobbledygook; bafflegab; political doubletalk, doublespeak, bunkum; pussyfooting; pointing with pride and viewing with alarm; new world order

VERBS **38** **politick,** politicize; look after one's fences, mend one's fences; caucus; gerrymander, lobby

39 **run for office,** run; throw one's hat in the ring, toss one's hat in the ring, go into politics, announce for, enter the lists, enter the arena, stand, stand for office; contest a seat; take the field

40 **campaign,** electioneer; stump, take the stump, take to the stump, stump the country, take to the hustings, hit the campaign trail, whistle-stop; canvass, go to the voters, go to the electorate, solicit votes, ring doorbells; shake hands and kiss babies

41 **support,** back, back up, come out for, endorse; go with the party, follow the party line; get on the bandwagon; nominate, **elect, vote**

42 **hold office,** hold a post, occupy a post, fill an office, be the incumbent, be in office, be elected, be voted in

ADJS **43** **political,** politic; governmental, civic; geopolitical; statesmanlike; diplomatic; suffragist; politico-commercial, politico-diplomatic, politico-ecclesiastical, politico-economic, politico-ethical, politico-geographical, politico-judicial, politico-military, politico-moral, politico-religious, politico-scientific, politico-social, politico-theological; politically correct (PC); politically incorrect, un-PC

44 **partisan,** party; bipartisan, biparty, two-party, government-issue

45 **nonpartisan, independent,** neutral, mugwumpian, mugwumpish, on the fence

610 POLITICIAN

<one active in government>

NOUNS **1** **politician,** politico, political leader, professional politician; party leader, party boss, party chieftain; machine politician, clubhouse politician, political hack; pol; old campaigner, warhorse; wheelhorse; reform politician, reformer, advocate; campaigner; White House, Oval Office; Downing Street

2 **statesman,** stateswoman, statesperson, solon, public man, public woman, national leader; elder statesman; ruler; governor, executive, administrator, leader; president, vice president; prime minister, premier

3 **legislator, lawmaker,** legislatrix, solon, lawgiver; congressman, congresswoman, Member of Congress; senator; representative; Speaker of the House; majority leader, minority leader; floor leader; whip, party whip; Member of Parliament (MP); state senator, assemblyman, assemblywoman, chosen, freeholder, councilman, alderman, alderperson, selectman, selectperson, city father

4 <**petty politician**> two-bit, politician, peanut politician, politicaster, statemonger, political dabbler; hack, political hack, party hack

5 <**corrupt politician**> dirty politician, crooked politician, jackleg politician; grafter, boodler; spoilsman, spoilsmonger; influence peddler

6 <**political intriguer**> strategist, machinator, gamesman, wheeler-dealer; operator, finagler, wire-puller; logroller, pork-barrel politician; Machiavellian; behind-the-scenes operator, gray eminence, *éminence grise* <Fr>, power behind the throne, kingmaker, powerbroker

7 <**political party leader**> boss, higher-up, man higher up, cacique, sachem; keynoter, policymaker; standard-bearer; ringleader; big shot

8 henchman, cohort, hanger-on, buddy, sidekick; heeler, ward heeler; hatchet man; partner in crime

9 **candidate,** aspirant, hopeful, political hopeful, wannabee, office seeker, baby kisser; running mate; leading candidate, head of the ticket, head of the slate; dark horse; stalking-horse; favorite son; presidential timber; defeated candidate, also-ran, dud

10 **campaigner,** electioneer, stumper, whistle-stopper, stump speaker, stump orator

11 **officeholder,** office-bearer, jack-in-office, elected official, public servant, public official, incumbent; holdover, lame duck; new broom; president-elect; ins, the powers that be

12 **political worker,** committeeman, committeewoman, precinct captain, precinct leader, district leader; party chairperson, state chairperson, national chairperson, chairperson of the national committee; speechwriter; political philosopher

VERBS **13** go into politics; **run,** get on the ticket, run for office; **campaign,** stump

ADJS **14** **statesmanlike,** statesmanly

611 POLITICO-ECONOMIC PRINCIPLES

<political beliefs>

NOUNS **1** **conservatism,** conservativeness, **right wing**, rightism; standpattism, unprogressiveness, backwardness; ultraconservatism, reaction, arch-conservative, reactionism, reactionarism, reactionaryism, reactionariness, die-hardism

2 **moderatism, moderateness**, middle-of-the-roadism; middle of the road, moderate position, via media, **center,** centrism; third force, nonalignment

3 **liberalism, progressivism,** leftism; left, **left wing,** progressiveness

4 **radicalism, extremism,** ultraism; radicalization; revolutionism; ultraconservatism; extreme left, extreme left wing, left-wing extremism, loony left; new left, old left; Jacobinism, sans-culottism, *sans-culotterie* <Fr>; **anarchism**, nihilism, syndicalism, anarcho-syndicalism, criminal syndicalism; extreme rightism, radical rightism, know-nothingism; extreme right, extreme right wing; social Darwinism; laissez-faireism; **royalism, monarchism**; Toryism, Bourbonism

5 **communism,** Bolshevism, Marxism, Marxism-Leninism, Leninism, Trotskyism, Stalinism, Maoism, Titoism, Castroism, revisionism; Marxian socialism; dialectical materialism; democratic centralism; dictatorship of the proletariat; Communist Party; Communist International, Comintern; Communist Information Bureau, Cominform; iron curtain

6 **socialism,** collective ownership, collectivization, public ownership; collectivism; creeping socialism; state socialism; guild socialism; Fabian socialism, Fabianism; utopian socialism; Marxian socialism, Marxism; phalansterism; Owenism; Saint-Simonianism, Saint-Simonism; nationalization

7 **welfarism,** welfare statism; womb-to-tomb security, cradle-to-grave security; social welfare; social security, social insurance; old-age and survivors insurance; unemployment compensation, unemployment insurance; workmen's compensation, workmen's compensation insurance; health insurance, Medicare, Medicaid, state medicine, socialized medicine; sickness insurance; public assistance, welfare, relief, welfare payments, aid to dependent children (ADC), old-age assistance, aid to the blind, aid to the permanently and totally disabled; guaranteed income, guaranteed annual income; welfare state; welfare capitalism

8 **capitalism,** capitalistic system, free enterprise, private enterprise, free-enterprise economy, free-enterprise system, free economy; finance capitalism; *laissez-faire* <Fr>, laissez-faireism; private sector; private ownership; state capitalism; individualism, rugged individualism; glocalization; localization

9 **conservative,** conservatist, rightist, right wing, right-winger, right; dry; standpat, standpatter; hard hat; social Darwinist; ultraconservative, arch-conservative, extreme right-winger, reactionary, reactionarist, reactionist, diehard; royalist, monarchist, Bourbon, Tory, imperialist; radical right

10 **moderate,** moderatist, moderationist, centrist, middle-of-the-roader; independent; center

11 **liberal,** liberalist, progressive, progressivist, left wing, leftist, left-winger, left; welfare stater; Lib-Lab; wet

12 **radical, extremist,** ultra, ultraist; **revolutionary,** revolutionist; subversive; extreme left-winger, left-wing extremist, red, Bolshevik; yippie; Jacobin, sansculotte; anarchist, nihilist; mild radical, parlor Bolshevik, pink, parlor pink, pinko; lunatic fringe

13 **Communist,** Bolshevist; Bolshevik, Red, commie, Bolshie; Marxist, Leninist, Marxist-Leninist, Trotskyite, Trotskyist, Stalinist, Maoist, Titoist, Castroite, revisionist; card-carrying Communist, avowed Communist; fellow traveler, Communist sympathizer, comsymp

14 **socialist,** collectivist; social democrat; state socialist; Fabian, Fabian socialist; Marxist; utopian socialist; Fourierist, phalansterian; Saint-Simonian; Owenite

15 **capitalist;** coupon-clipper; rich man
VERBS 16 **politicize;** democratize, republicanize, socialize, communize; nationalize; deregulate, privatize, denationalize; radicalize
ADJS 17 **conservative,** right-wing, right-of-center, dry; old-line, die-hard, unreconstructed, standpat, unprogressive, nonprogressive; ultraconservative, reactionary, reactionist
18 **moderate,** centrist, middle-of-the-road, independent
19 **liberal,** liberalistic, liberalist, wet, bleeding-heart; **progressive,** progressivistic; leftist, left-wing, on the left, left-of-center
20 **radical, extreme,** extremist, extremistic, ultraist, ultraistic; revolutionary, revolutionist; subversive; ultraconservative; extreme left-wing, red; anarchistic, nihilistic, syndicalist, anarcho-syndicalist; mildly radical, pink
21 **Communist,** communistic, Bolshevik, Bolshevist, commie, Bolshie, Red; Marxist, Leninist, Marxist-Leninist, Trotskyite, Trotskyist, Stalinist, Maoist, Titoist, Castroite; revisionist
22 **socialist,** socialistic, collectivistic; social-democratic; Fabian; Fourieristic, phalansterian; Saint-Simonian
23 **capitalist,** capitalistic, bourgeois, individualistic, nonsocialistic, free-enterprise, private-enterprise

612 GOVERNMENT

<*governing systems*>

NOUNS 1 **government,** governance, discipline, regulation; direction, management, administration, dispensation, disposition, oversight, supervision; regime, regimen; rule, sway, sovereignty, reign, regnancy, regency; empire, empery, dominion, dynasty; social order, civil government, political government, political system; form of government, system of government, political organization, polity, political party; local government, state government, national government, world government, international government
2 **control,** mastery, mastership, command, power, jurisdiction, dominion, domination; hold, grasp, grip, gripe; hand, hands, iron hand, clutches; talons, claws; helm, reins of government
3 **the government,** the authorities; the powers that be, national government, central government, the Establishment; the corridors of power, government circles; Uncle Sam, Washington; John Bull, the Crown, His Majesty's Government, Her Majesty's Government, Whitehall
4 <**kinds of government**> federal government, federation, federalism; constitutional government, majority rule; republic, commonwealth; democracy, representative government, representative democracy, direct democracy, pure democracy, town-meeting democracy; government of the people, by the people, for the people; parliamentary government; social democracy, welfare state; mob rule, tyranny of the majority, mobocracy, ochlocracy; minority government; pantisocracy; aristocracy, hierarchy, oligarchy, elitism, plutocracy, minority rule; feudal system; monarchy, monarchical government, absolute monarchy, constitutional monarchy, limited monarchy, kingship, queenship; dictatorship, tyranny, autocracy, autarchy; dyarchy, duarchy, duumvirate; triarchy, triumvirate; totalitarian government, totalitarian regime, totalitarianism, police state, canteen culture, despotism; fascism, communism; stratocracy, demagogy, military government, militarism, garrison state; martial law, rule of the sword; regency; hierocracy, theocracy, thearchy; patriarchy, patriarchate; gerontocracy; technocracy, meritocracy; autonomy, self-government, self-rule, self-determination, home rule; heteronomy, dominion rule, colonial government, colonialism, neocolonialism; provisional government; coalition government; tribalism, tribal system, clan system; isocracy, egalitarianism; caretaker government, interregnum; ideocracy
5 <**government by women**> matriarchy, matriarchate, gynarchy, gynocracy, gynecocracy; petticoat government
6 **world government;** supranational government, supergovernment, World Federalism; League of Nations, United Nations
7 <**principles of government**> democratism, power-sharing, republicanism; constitutionalism, rule of law, parliamentarism, parliamentarianism; monarchism, royalism; feudalism, feudality; imperialism; fascism, neofascism, Nazism, national socialism; statism, governmentalism; collectivism, communism, socialism; federalism; centralism; pluralism; political principles; glasnost
8 **dictatorship,** absolutism, despotism, tyranny, autocracy, autarchy, monarchy, absolute monarchy; authoritarianism; totalitarianism; one-man rule, one-party rule; Caesarism, Stalinism, kaiserism, czarism; benevolent despotism, paternalism
9 **despotism,** tyranny, fascism, domineering, domination, oppression; heavy hand, high hand, iron hand, iron heel, iron boot; big stick; terrorism, reign of terror; thought control

10 **bureaucracy,** officialism; beadledom, bumbledom; red-tapeism, red-tapery, red tape; federalese, official jargon

VERBS **11** **govern,** regulate; wield authority; command, officer, captain, head, lead, be master, be at the head of, preside over, chair; direct, manage, supervise, administer, administrate; discipline; stand over

12 **control,** hold in hand, have in one's power, be in power, have power, gain a hold upon; hold the reins, hold the helm, call the shots, be in the driver's seat; direct, have control of, have under control, have in hand, have well in hand; be master of the situation, have it all one's own way, have the game in one's own hands, hold all the aces; pull the strings

13 **rule,** sway, hold sway, reign, bear reign, have the sway, wield the scepter, wear the crown, sit on the throne; rule over, overrule

14 **dominate,** predominate, preponderate, prevail; have the ascendancy, have the upper hand, get under control; master, have the mastery of; bestride; dictate, lay down the law; rule the roost, wear the pants, crack the whip, ride herd; take the lead, play first fiddle; lead by the nose, twist around one's little finger; keep under one's thumb, bend to one's will

15 **domineer,** domineer over, lord it over; browbeat, order around, henpeck, intimidate, bully, cow, bulldoze, walk over, walk all over; castrate, unman; daunt, terrorize; tyrannize, tyrannize over, push around, kick around, despotize; grind, grind down, break, oppress, suppress, repress, weigh heavy on; keep under, keep down, beat down, clamp down on; overbear, overmaster, overawe; override, ride over, tread upon, trample down, trample underfoot, crush under an iron heel, ride roughshod over; keep a tight rein upon, rule with a rod of iron, rule with an iron fist; enslave, subjugate; compel, coerce

ADJS **16** **governmental,** gubernatorial; **political,** civil, civic; official, bureaucratic, administrative; democratic, republican, fascist, fascistic, oligarchal, oligarchic, oligarchical, aristocratic, aristocratical, theocratic, federal, federalist, federalistic, constitutional, parliamentary, parliamentarian; monarchic, monarchical, monarchial, monarchal; autocratic, monocratic, absolute; authoritarian; despotic, dictatorial; totalitarian; pluralistic; paternalistic, patriarchal, patriarchic, patriarchical; matriarchal, matriarchic, matriarchical; heteronomous; autonomous, self-governing, self-ruling, autarchic; executive, presidential; preponderous

17 **governing,** controlling, regulating, regulative, regulatory, commanding; ruling, reigning, sovereign, regnant, regnal, titular; master, chief, general, boss, head; dominant, predominant, predominate, preponderant, preponderate, prepotent, prepollent, prevalent, leading, paramount, supreme, number one, hegemonic, hegemonistic; ascendant, in the ascendant, in ascendancy; at the head, in chief; in charge

18 **executive,** administrative, ministerial; official, bureaucratic; supervisory, directing, managing

ADVS **19** **under control, in hand,** well in hand; **in one's power,** under one's control

COMBINING FORMS **20** -archy, -cracy, -ocracy

613 LEGISLATURE, GOVERNMENT ORGANIZATION

<lawmaking bodies>

NOUNS **1** **legislature**, legislative body; parliament, congress, assembly, general assembly, house of assembly, legislative assembly, national assembly, chamber of deputies, federal assembly, diet, soviet, court; unicameral legislature, bicameral legislature; legislative chamber, upper chamber, upper house, lower chamber, lower house; state legislature, state assembly; provincial legislature, provincial parliament; city council, city board, board of aldermen, common council, commission; representative town meeting, town meeting

2 **United States Government**, Federal Government; Cabinet, **U.S. Cabinet** <see list>; Executive Department, executive branch; government agency; legislature; Congress, Senate, Upper House, Senate committee; House of Representatives, House, Lower House, House of Representatives committee; Supreme Court

3 **cabinet,** ministry, council, advisory council, council of state, privy council, divan; shadow cabinet; kitchen cabinet, camarilla

4 **capitol,** statehouse; courthouse; city hall

5 **legislation,** lawmaking, legislature; enactment, enaction, constitution, passage, passing; resolution, concurrent resolution, joint resolution; act

6 **<legislative procedure>** introduction, first reading, committee consideration, tabling, filing, second reading, deliberation, debate, third reading, vote, division, roll call; filibustering, filibuster, talkathon; cloture; logrolling; steamroller methods; guillotine <Brit>

7 **veto,** executive veto, absolute veto, qualified veto, limited veto, suspensive veto, suspensory veto, item veto, pocket veto; veto power; veto message; senatorial courtesy

8 **referendum,** constitutional referendum, statutory

referendum, optional referendum, facultative referendum, compulsory referendum, mandatory referendum; mandate; plebiscite, plebiscitum; initiative, direct initiative, indirect initiative; recall

9 **bill,** omnibus bill, hold-up bill, companion bills amendment; clause, proviso; enacting clause, dragnet clause, escalator clause, saving clause; rider; joker; calendar, motion; question, previous question, privileged question

VERBS 10 **legislate,** make laws, enact laws, enact, pass, constitute, ordain, put in force; put through, jam through, railroad through, lobby through; table, pigeonhole; take the floor, get the floor, have the floor; yield the floor; filibuster; logroll, roll logs; veto, pocket, kill; decree

ADJS 11 **legislative,** legislatorial, lawmaking; deliberative; parliamentary, congressional; senatorial; bicameral, unicameral

12 **U.S. Cabinet**

Administrator of the Environmental Protection Agency
Administrator of the Small Business Administration
Ambassador to the United Nations
Attorney General
Director of the Central Intelligence Agency
Director of National Intelligence
Director of the Office of Management and Budget
Secretary of Agriculture
Secretary of Commerce
Secretary of Defense
Secretary of Education
Secretary of Energy
Secretary of Health and Human Services
Secretary of Homeland Security
Secretary of Housing and Urban Development
Secretary of Labor
Secretary of State
Secretary of the Interior
Secretary of the Treasury
Secretary of Transportation
Secretary of Veterans' Affairs
Trade Representative

614 UNITED NATIONS, INTERNATIONAL ORGANIZATIONS

<international relations>

NOUNS 1 **United Nations** (UN); League of Nations

2 <**United Nations organs**> Secretariat; General Assembly; Security Council; Trusteeship Council; International Court of Justice; **United Nations agency** <see list>, Economic and Social Council (ECOSOC), ECOSOC commission

3 international organization, non-UN international organization

4 **United Nations agency**

Food and Agricultural Organization (FAO)
International Civil Aviation Organization (ICAO)
International Fund for Agricultural Development (IFAD)
International Labor Organization (ILO)
International Maritime Organization (IMO)
International Monetary Fund (IMF)
International Telecommunication Union (ITU)
United Nations Anti-Terrorism Coalitions (UNATCO)
United Nations Educational, Scientific and Cultural Organization (UNESCO)
United Nations Industrial Development Organization (UNIDO)
Universal Postal Union (UPU)
World Bank Group (WBG)
World Health Organization (WHO)
World Intellectual Property Organization (WIPO)
World Meteorological Organization (WMO)
World Tourism Organization (UNWTO)

615 COMMISSION

<group seeking information>

NOUNS 1 **commission,** commissioning, delegation, devolution, devolvement, vesting, investing, investment, investiture; deputation; commitment, entrusting, entrustment, assignment, consignment, consignation; errand, task, office; care, cure, responsibility, purview, jurisdiction; mission, legation, embassy; authority; authorization, empowerment, power to act, full power, plenipotentiary power, vicarious authority, delegated authority; warrant, license, mandate, charge, trust, brevet, exequatur; agency, agentship, factorship; regency, regentship; lieutenancy; trusteeship, executorship; proxy, procuration, power of attorney

2 **appointment,** assignment, designation, nomination, naming, selection, tabbing; ordainment, ordination; posting, transferral

3 **installation,** installment, instatement, induction, placement, inauguration, investiture, taking office; accession, accedence; coronation, crowning, enthronement

4 **engagement,** employment, hiring, appointment, taking on, recruitment, recruiting; executive recruiting, executive search; retaining, retainment, briefing; preengagement, bespeaking; reservation, booking; exercise, function

5 executive search agency, executive search firm; executive recruiter, executive recruitment consultant, executive development specialist; **headhunter**, body snatcher, flesh peddler, talent scout

6 **rental,** rent; **lease,** let; hire, hiring; sublease, subrent; charter, bareboat charter; lend-lease
7 **enlistment,** enrollment; conscription, draft, drafting, induction, impressment, press; call, draft call, call-up, summons, call to the colors, letter from Uncle Sam; recruitment, recruiting; muster, mustering, mustering in, levy, levying; mobilization; selective service, compulsory military service
8 indenture, binding over; **apprenticeship**
9 **assignee, appointee,** selectee, nominee, candidate; licensee, licentiate; deputy, agent

VERBS **10** **commission, authorize,** empower, accredit; delegate, devolute, devolve, devolve upon, vest, invest; depute, deputize; assign, consign, commit, charge, entrust, give in charge; license, charter, warrant; detail, detach, post, transfer, send out, mission, send on a mission
11 **appoint, assign,** designate, nominate, name, select, tab, elect; ordain, ordinate
12 **install,** instate, induct, inaugurate, invest, put in, place, place in office; chair; crown, throne, enthrone, anoint
13 be instated, **take office,** accede; take the throne, mount the throne; attain to
14 **employ,** hire, give a job to, take into employment, take into one's service, take on, recruit, headhunt, engage, sign up, sign on; retain, brief <Brit>; bespeak, preengage; sign up for, reserve, book
15 **rent,** lease, let, hire, job, charter; sublease, sublet, underlet
16 **rent out,** rent; lease, lease out; let, let off, let out; hire out, hire; charter; sublease, sublet, underlet; lend-lease, lease-lend; lease-back; farm, farm out; job
17 **enlist,** list, enroll, sign up, sign on; conscript, draft, induct, press, impress, commandeer; detach, detach for service; summon, call up, call to the colors; mobilize, call to active duty; recruit, muster, levy, raise, muster in; join
18 indenture, article, bind, bind over; **apprentice**

ADJS **19** **commissioned,** authorized, accredited; delegated, deputized, appointed; devolutionary
20 **employed,** hired, hireling, paid, mercenary; rented, leased, let; sublet, underlet, subleased; chartered
21 indentured, articled, bound over; **apprenticed**

ADVS **22** **for hire,** for rent, to let, to lease

616 ASSOCIATE

<aid to someone in power>

NOUNS **1** **associate, confederate,** consociate, **colleague,** fellow member, companion, fellow, bedfellow, crony, consort, cohort, compeer, compatriot, confrere, brother, brother-in-arms, ally, adjunct, coadjutor; comrade in arms, comrade
2 **partner,** pardner, pard, copartner, side partner, buddy, sidekick, sidekicker; mate; business partner, nominal partner, ostensible partner, quasi partner, general partner, special partner, silent partner, secret partner, dormant partner, sleeping partner; plus-one
3 **accomplice,** cohort, confederate, fellow conspirator, coconspirator, partner in crime, accomplice in crime; accessory, accessory before the fact, accessory after the fact; abettor
4 **collaborator,** cooperator; coauthor; collaborationist; quisling, partner in crime
5 **coworker,** workfellow, workmate, fellow worker, work buddy, buddy; teammate, yokefellow, yokemate; benchfellow, shopmate; team player
6 **assistant,** helper, auxiliary, aider, aid, aide, paraprofessional; help, helpmate, helpmeet; deputy, agent; attendant, second, acolyte; best man, groomsman, paranymph; servant, employee; adjutant, aide-de-camp; lieutenant, executive officer; coadjutant, coadjutor; coadjutress, coadjutrix; sidesman <Brit>; supporting actor, supporting player; supporting instrumentalist, sideman; suffragan; special assistant
7 **right hand,** right-hand man, right-hand woman, strong right hand, man Friday, gal Friday, fidus Achates, second self, alter ego, confidant; Boswell
8 **follower, disciple,** adherent, votary; man, henchman, camp follower, hanger-on, devotee, satellite, creature, lackey, flunky, stooge, jackal, minion, myrmidon; yes-man, sycophant; goon, thug; puppet, cat's-paw; dummy, figurehead
9 **supporter,** upholder, maintainer, sustainer; support, mainstay, standby, stalwart, reliance, dependence; abettor, seconder, second; endorser, sponsor; backer, promoter, angel, rabbi; patron, Maecenas; friend at court, friend in court; champion, defender, apologist, advocate, exponent, protagonist; well-wisher, favorer, encourager, sympathizer; partisan, sider, sectary, votary; fan, buff, aficionado, admirer, lover

617 ASSOCIATION

<organized special-interest group>

NOUNS **1** **association,** society, body, organization; alliance, coalition, league, union; council; bloc, axis; partnership; federation, confederation, confederacy; grouping, assemblage; combination, combine; unholy alliance, gang, ring, mob; machine, political machine; economic community, common market, free trade area, customs union; credit union; cooperative, cooperative society, consumer cooperative, Rochdale cooperative; syndicate, guild; college, group, corps, band; labor union

2 **community, society,** commonwealth, social system; body; kinship group, clan, moiety, tribe, totemic group, phyle, phratry, phratria, gens, caste, subcaste, endogamous group; family, extended family, nuclear family, binuclear family; order, class, social class, economic class; colony, settlement; commune, ashram

3 **fellowship,** sodality; society, guild, order; brotherhood, fraternity, confraternity, confrerie, fraternal order, fraternal society; sisterhood, sorority; club, country club, lodge; peer group, peerage; secret society, cabal

4 **party,** interest, camp, **side;** interest group, lobby, pressure group, ethnic group; minority group, vocal minority; political action committee (PAC); silent majority; faction, division, sect, wing, caucus, splinter, splinter group, breakaway group, offshoot; political party; flash mob

5 **school, sect,** class, order; denomination, communion, confession, faith, church; persuasion, ism; disciples, followers, adherents

6 **clique,** coterie, set, circle, ring, junto, junta, cabal, camarilla, clan, group, grouping, cult; crew, mob, crowd, bunch, outfit; cell; cadre, cohort, inner circle; closed circle, charmed circle; ingroup, in-crowd, popular crowd, we-group; elite, elite group; leadership group; old-boy network; peer group, age group

7 **team,** outfit, squad, string, corps; eleven, nine, eight, five; **crew,** rowing crew; varsity, first team, first string; bench, reserves, second team, second string, third string; platoon, troupe; complement; **cast,** company

8 **organization,** establishment, foundation, institution, institute

9 **company,** firm, business firm, concern, house; business, industry, enterprise, business establishment, commercial enterprise; trust, syndicate, cartel, combine, pool, consortium, plunderbund; combination in restraint of trade; chamber of commerce, junior chamber of commerce; trade association

10 **branch,** organ, division, wing, arm, offshoot, affiliate; chapter, lodge, post; chapel; local; branch office; virtual office

11 **member,** affiliate, belonger, insider, initiate, one of us, cardholder, card-carrier, card-carrying member; enrollee, enlistee; associate, socius, fellow; brother, sister; comrade; honorary member; life member; member in good standing, dues-paying member; charter member; clubman, clubwoman, clubber; fraternity man, fraternity brother, frat brother, Greek, sorority woman; sorority sister, guildsman; committeeman; conventionist, conventioner, conventioneer; joiner; pledge; lifetime member

12 **membership,** members, associates, affiliates, body of affiliates, constituency

13 **partisanism,** partisanship, partiality; factionalism, sectionalism, faction; sectarianism, denominationalism; cliquism, cliquishness, cliqueyness; clannishness, clanship; exclusiveness, exclusivity; ethnocentricity; party spirit, *esprit de corps* <Fr>; the old college spirit

VERBS 14 **join,** join up, enter, go into, come into, get into, make oneself part of, swell the ranks of; enlist, enroll, affiliate, sign up, sign on, take up membership, take out membership; inscribe oneself, put oneself down; associate oneself with, affiliate with, league with, team, team up with; sneak in, creep in, insinuate oneself into; combine, associate

15 **belong,** hold membership, be a member, be on the rolls, be inscribed, subscribe, hold a card, carry a card, be in

ADJS 16 **associated,** corporate, incorporated; combined; nonprofit-making, nonprofit, not-for-profit

17 **associational,** social, society, communal; organizational; coalitional; sociable

18 **cliquish,** cliquey, clannish; ethnocentric; exclusive

19 **partisan,** party; partial, interested; factional, sectional, sectarian, sectary, denominational, dues-paying; peer-to-peer

ADVS 20 **in association,** conjointly

618 WEALTH

<having money, possessions>

NOUNS 1 **wealth, riches,** opulence, opulency, luxuriousness; richness, wealthiness; prosperity, prosperousness, affluence, comfortable circumstances, easy circumstances, independence; money, lucre, pelf, gold, mammon; substance, property, possessions, material wealth; **assets**; fortune, treasure, handsome fortune; fat purse, bulging purse, deep pockets; *embarras de richesses* <Fr>, money to burn; high income, six-figure income; high tax bracket, upper bracket; old money, new money

2 **large sum,** good sum, tidy sum, pretty penny, king's ransom; heaps of gold; thousands, millions, cool million, billion

3 <nonformal> **big bucks,** bundle, megabucks, gigabucks, big money, serious money, gobs, heaps, heavy lettuce, heavy jack, heavy money, important

money, pot, potful, power, mint, barrel, raft, load, loads, pile, wad, wads, nice hunk of change, packet <Brit>, long green, deep pockets

4 **<rich source>** mine, mine of wealth, gold mine, bonanza, luau, lode, rich lode, mother lode, pot of gold, Eldorado, Golconda, Seven Cities of Cibola; gravy train; rich uncle; golden goose; cash cow

5 **the golden touch,** Midas touch; philosopher's stone; Pactolus

6 **the rich, the wealthy,** the well-to-do, the well-off, the haves, privileged class; jet set, glitterati, country-club set, beau monde, affluential; plutocracy, timocracy

7 **rich person,** rich man, rich woman, wealthy man, wealthy woman, moneyed person, person of wealth, person of means, person of substance, fat cat, richling, deep pocket, moneybags, Mr. Moneybags, tycoon, magnate, baron, Daddy Warbucks, coupon-clipper, nabob; capitalist, plutocrat, bloated plutocrat; millionaire, multimillionaire, megamillionaire, millionairess, multibillionaire, multimillionairess, billionaire; parvenu; vulgarian; nouveau riche; yuppie

8 Croesus, Midas, Plutus, Timon of Athens; Rockefeller, Vanderbilt, Whitney, DuPont, Ford, Getty, Rothschild, Onassis, Hughes, Hunt, Trump; Jeff Bezos, Sergey Brin and Larry Page, Bill Gates, Warren Buffett

VERBS 9 **enrich,** richen; endow

10 **grow rich, get rich,** fill one's pockets, line one's pockets, feather one's nest, make money, coin money, have a gold mine, have the golden touch, make a fortune, make one's pile; strike it rich; come into money; make good, get on in the world, do all right by oneself, rake it in; hit the jackpot, clean up

11 **have money,** command money, be loaded, have deep pockets, have the wherewithal, have means, have independent means; afford, well afford

12 **live well,** live high, live high on the hog, live in clover, live the life of Riley, roll in it, wallow in wealth, live in the lap of luxury; have all the money in the world, have a mint, have money to burn; yuppify

13 worship mammon, worship the golden calf, worship the almighty dollar

ADJS 14 **wealthy, rich,** affluent, affluential, moneyed, monied, in funds, in cash, well-to-do, well-to-do in the world, well-off, well-situated, prosperous, comfortable, provided for, well provided for, fat, flush, flush with money, abounding in riches, worth a great deal, in clover, frightfully rich, rich as Croesus; independent, independently rich, independently wealthy; luxurious; opulent; privileged, born with a silver spoon in one's mouth; higher-income, upper-income, well-paid; rich and powerful, comfortably off

15 <nonformal> **loaded,** well-heeled, filthy rich, warm <Brit>, flush, in the money, in the chips, in the gravy, well-fixed, worth a bundle, made of money, rolling in money, rolling in it, wallowing in it, disgustingly rich, big-rich, rich-rich, oofy, lousy rich, upscale

619 POVERTY

<lacking money, possessions>

NOUNS 1 **poverty,** poorness, impecuniousness, impecuniosity; **straits,** dire straits, difficulties, hardship; financial distress, financial embarrassment, embarrassed circumstances, reduced circumstances, straitened circumstances, tight squeeze, hard pinch, crunch, cash crunch, credit crunch, budget crunch; cash-flow shortage; slender means, narrow means, insolvency, light purse; unprosperousness; broken fortune; genteel poverty; vows of poverty, voluntary poverty

2 **indigence,** penury, pennilessness, penuriousness, moneylessness; pauperism, pauperization, impoverishment, crushing poverty, chronic pauperism; subsistence level, poverty line; beggary, beggarliness, mendicancy; destitution, privation, deprivation; neediness, want, need, lack, pinch, gripe, necessity, dire necessity, disadvantagedness, necessitousness, homelessness; **hand-to-mouth existence**, bare subsistence, wolf at the door, bare cupboard, empty purse, empty pocket

3 **the poor, the needy,** the have-nots, the down-and-out, the disadvantaged, the underprivileged, the distressed, the underclass; the urban poor, ghetto-dwellers, barrio-dwellers; welfare rolls, welfare clients, welfare families; the homeless, the ranks of the homeless, bag people, street people; the other America; the forgotten man; depressed population, depressed area, chronic poverty area; underdeveloped nation, Third World, developing world; cardboard city

4 **poor person,** poorling, poor devil, down-and-out, down-and-outer, pauper, indigent, penniless man, hard case, starveling; homeless person, bag woman, bag lady, bag person, shopping-bag lady, shopping-cart woman, shopping-cart lady, street person, skell, slumdog; hobo, bum; beggar; welfare client; almsman, almswoman, charity case, casual; bankrupt

VERBS 5 **be poor,** be hard up, find it hard going, have seen better days, be on one's uppers, be pinched, be strapped, be in want, want, need, lack; starve, not know where one's next meal is coming from, live from hand to mouth, eke out a living, squeeze out a living; not have a penny, not have a sou, not have a penny to bless oneself with, not have one dollar to rub against another; sing for one's supper; go on welfare, use food stamps

6 **impoverish,** reduce, pauperize, beggar; eat out of house and home; cut off without a penny; bankrupt

ADJS 7 **poor,** ill off, badly off, poorly off, hard up, downscale, impecunious, unmoneyed; unprosperous; reduced, in reduced circumstances; straitened, in straitened circumstances, narrow, in narrow circumstances, feeling the pinch, strapped, financially embarrassed, financially distressed, pinched, squeezed, put to one's shifts, put to one's last shifts, at the end of one's rope, on the edge, on the ragged edge, down to bedrock, in Queer Street; short, short of money, short of funds, short of cash, out-of-pocket; unable to make ends meet, unable to keep the wolf from the door; poor as a church mouse; house-poor; land-poor

8 **indigent, poverty-stricken; needy,** necessitous, in need, in want, disadvantaged, deprived, underprivileged; beggared, beggarly, mendicant; impoverished, pauperized, starveling; ghettoized; bereft, bereaved; stripped, fleeced; down at heels, down at the heel, on one's uppers, down on one's uppers, out at the heels, out at elbows, in rags; on welfare, on relief, on the bread line, on the dole <Brit>

9 **destitute,** down-and-out, in the gutter; penniless, moneyless, fortuneless, out of funds, without a sou, without a penny to bless oneself with, without one dollar to rub against another; insolvent, in the red, bankrupt 625.11; homeless; propertyless, landless; need-based

10 <nonformal> **broke,** dead broke, bust, busted, dirt poor, needy, short on, flat, flat broke, flat on one's ass, flat-ass, down for the count, belly up, stone broke, stony, strapped, skint <Brit>, hurting, beat, oofless; down to one's last cent, cleaned out, tapped out, Tap City, wasted, wiped out, without a pot to piss in

620 LENDING

<loaning of money, objects>

NOUNS 1 **lending, loaning;** moneylending, lending at interest; advance, advancing, advancement; usury, loan-sharking, shylocking; pawnbroking, hocking; interest, interest rate, lending rate, the price of money; points, mortgage points

2 **loan,** the lend, **advance,** accommodation; lending on security; lend-lease

3 **lender, loaner;** loan officer; commercial banker; moneylender, moneymonger; money broker; banker; usurer, shylock, loan shark; pawnbroker; uncle; mortgagee, mortgage holder; creditor; financier

4 **lending institution,** savings and loan association, savings and loan, thrift, thrift institution, savings institution; savings and loan industry, thrift industry; building society <Brit>; finance company, financial corporation, loan office, mortgage company; commercial bank, bank; credit union; pawnshop, pawnbroker, pawnbrokery, hock shop, sign of the three balls; World Bank

VERBS 5 **lend, loan, advance,** accommodate with; loan-shark; float a loan, negotiate a loan; lend-lease, lease-lend; give credit

ADJS 6 **loaned, lent**, on loan, on credit

ADVS 7 **on loan,** on security; in advance

621 BORROWING

<temporarily using money, objects>

NOUNS 1 **borrowing,** money-raising; hitting up, hitting; financing, mortgaging; installment buying, installment plan, hire purchase <Brit>; debt, debtor; debt counseling; closing

2 **adoption, appropriation,** taking, deriving, derivation, assumption; imitation, simulation, copying, mocking; borrowed plumes; a leaf from someone else's book; adaptation; plagiarism, plagiary, pastiche, pasticcio; infringement, pirating; cribbing, lifting

VERBS 3 **borrow,** borrow the loan of, get on credit, get on tick, get on the cuff; get a loan, float a loan, negotiate a loan, go into the money market,.raise money; touch, hit up, hit one for, put the arm on, put the bite on; run into debt; pawn

4 **adopt, appropriate,** take, take on, take over, assume, make use of, take a leaf from someone's book, derive from; imitate, simulate, copy, mock, steal one's stuff; plagiarize, steal; pirate, infringe, crib, lift; adapt, parody

622 FINANCIAL CREDIT

<money loaned>

NOUNS 1 **credit, trust,** tick; borrowing power, borrowing capacity; commercial credit, cash credit, bank credit, book credit, tax credit, investment credit; credit line, line of credit; installment plan, installment credit, consumer credit, store credit, hire purchase plan <Brit>, never-never; credit standing, standing, **credit rating,** rating, Dun & Bradstreet rating, solvency;

credit squeeze, insolvency; credit risk; credit bureau, credit agency; credit insurance, credit life insurance; credit union, cooperative credit union

2 account, **credit account**, charge account; bank account, savings account, checking account; share account; bank balance; expense account; current account, open account; installment plan

3 **credit instrument;** paper credit; letter of credit, circular note; credit slip, credit memorandum, deposit slip, certificate of deposit; share certificate; negotiable instruments; **credit card,** plastic, plastic money, bank card, affinity card, custom credit card, gold card, platinum card, charge card, charge plate; debit card; smart card, supersmart card; phonecard; automated teller machine (ATM), cash machine, cash dispenser; credit history, credit limit; loyalty card

4 **creditor,** creditress; debtee; mortgagee, mortgage holder; noteholder; credit man; bill collector, collection agent; loan shark; pawnbroker; dunner, dun

VERBS **5** **credit,** credit with; credit to one's account, place to one's credit, place to one's account

6 **extend credit**, extend a line of credit, give credit, give a line of credit; sell on credit, trust, entrust; give tick; carry, carry on one's books

7 **receive credit,** take credit, charge, charge to one's account, keep an account with, go on tick, buy on credit, buy on the cuff, buy on the installment plan, buy on time, defer payment, put on layaway; go in hock for; have one's credit good for; close

ADJS **8** **credited,** of good credit, well-rated; cashless

ADVS **9** **to one's credit**, to one's account, to the credit of, to the account of, to the good

10 **on credit,** on account, on trust, on tick, on the cuff; on terms, on good terms, on easy terms, on budget terms, in installments, on time

623 DEBT

<money owed>

NOUNS **1** **debt, indebtedness,** indebtment, obligation, liability, financial commitment, due, dues, score, pledge, unfulfilled pledge, amount due, outstanding debt; bill, bills, chits, charges; floating debt; funded debt, unfunded debt; accounts receivable; accounts payable; borrowing; maturity; bad debts, uncollectibles, frozen assets; national debt, public debt; deficit, national deficit; megadebt; debt explosion

2 **arrears,** arrear, arrearage, back debts, back payments; the red; **deficit**, default, deferred payments; cash crunch, credit crunch; overdraft, bounced check, rubber check; dollar gap, unfavorable trade balance, unfavorable balance of payments; deficit financing

3 **interest,** premium, price, rate; **interest rate**, rate of interest, prime interest rate, prime rate, bank rate, lending rate, borrowing rate, the price of money; discount rate; annual percentage rate (APR); usury, excessive interest, exorbitant interest; points, mortgage points; simple interest, compound interest; net interest, gross interest; compensatory interest; lucrative interest; penal interest

4 **debtor,** borrower; mortgagor; insolvent

VERBS **5** **owe, be indebted,** be obliged, be obligated for, be financially committed, lie under an obligation, be bound to pay, owe money

6 **go in debt**, get into debt, run into debt, plunge into debt, incur a debt, contract a debt, go in hock, be overextended, run up a bill, run up a score, run up an account, run up a tab; run a deficit, show a deficit, operate at a loss; borrow; overspend, overdraw

7 mature, accrue, **fall due**

ADJS **8** **indebted, in debt,** plunged in debt, in difficulties, embarrassed, in embarrassed circumstances, in the hole, in hock, in the red, in dire straits, insolvent, encumbered, mortgaged, mortgaged to the hilt, tied up, involved; deep in debt, involved in debt, deeply involved in debt, burdened with debt, up to one's ears in debt; cash poor

9 **chargeable,** obligated, liable, pledged, responsible, answerable for

10 **due, owed,** owing, **payable,** receivable, redeemable, mature, **outstanding, unpaid,** in arrears, back

624 PAYMENT

<money paid>

NOUNS **1** **payment,** paying, paying off, paying up, payoff; defrayment, defrayal; paying out, doling out, disbursal; discharge, settlement, clearance, clearance sale, liquidation, amortization, amortizement, retirement, satisfaction; quittance; acquittance, acquitment, acquittal; debt service, interest payment, sinking-fund payment; remittance; installment, installment plan, layaway plan; hire purchase, hire purchase plan, never-never <Brit>; regular payments, monthly payments, weekly payments, quarterly payments; down payment, deposit, earnest, earnest money, binder; God's penny; the King's shilling <Brit>; cash, hard cash, spot cash, cash payment, cash on the nail, cash on the barrelhead; pay-as-you-go; prepayment; postponed payment, deferred payment, contango, carryover, continuation, backwardation <Brit>; payment in kind; accounts receivable, receivables

2 **reimbursement,** recoupment, recoup, return, restitution, settlement; payment in lieu; **refund,** refundment; kickback; payback, chargeback, **repayment**

3 **recompense, remuneration,** compensation; requital, requitement, quittance, retribution, reparation, redress, satisfaction, atonement, amends, return, restitution; blood money, wergild; indemnity, indemnification; price, consideration; reward, meed, guerdon; honorarium; workmen's compensation, workers' comp, solatium, damages, smart money; salvage

4 **pay, payment,** remuneration, compensation, total compensation, wages plus fringe benefits, side benefit, financial package, pay and allowances, financial remuneration; rate of pay; **paycheck,** salary, **wage**, wages, income, earnings, hire; real wages, purchasing power; payday, pay slip, pay stub, pay envelope, pay packet <Brit>; take-home pay, take-home income, wages after taxes, income after deductions, net income, net earnings, taxable income; gross income, adjusted gross income; living wage; minimum wage, base pay; portal-to-portal pay; severance pay, discontinuance wage, dismissal wage, golden parachute; wage scale; escalator plan, escalator clause, sliding scale; guaranteed income, guaranteed annual income, negative income tax; fixed income; wage freeze, wage rollback, wage reduction, wage control; guaranteed annual wage, guaranteed income plan; overtime pay; danger money, combat pay, flight pay; back pay; strike pay; **payroll;** golden handcuffs; royalty, advance; checkout, self-checkout

5 **fee,** stipend, allowance, emolument, tribute, honorarium; reckoning, account, bill; assessment, scot; initiation fee, footing; retainer, retaining fee; hush money, blackmail; blood money; mileage

6 <extra pay> **bonus, benefits**, premium, fringe benefit, extra allowance, bounty, perquisite, perquisites, perks, gravy, lagniappe, solatium; tip; overtime pay; bonus system; health insurance, life insurance, disability insurance; profit-sharing; holidays, vacation time, flextime, flexitime; pension program

7 **dividend; royalty; commission,** rake-off, cut

8 <the bearing of another's expense> **treat,** standing treat, picking up the check, picking up the tab; paying the bills, maintenance; child support, support; subsidy

9 **payer,** remunerator, compensator, recompenser; paymaster, purser, bursar, cashier, treasurer; defrayer; liquidator; taxpayer, ratepayer <Brit>

VERBS 10 **pay,** render, tender; recompense, remunerate, compensate, reward, guerdon, indemnify, satisfy; salary, fee; remit; prepay; pay in installments, pay on, pay in; make payments to, make payments towards, make payments on

11 **repay,** pay back, restitute, **reimburse,** recoup; requite, quit, atone, redress, make amends, make good, make up for, make up to, make restitution, make reparation; pay in kind, pay one in his own coin, give tit for tat; **refund,** kick back

12 **settle with,** reckon with, account with, pay out, settle accounts with, square oneself with, get square with, get even with, get quits with; even the score, clear off old scores, pay old debts, clear the board

13 **pay in full, pay off,** pay up, discharge, settle, settle up, square, clear, liquidate, amortize, retire, take up, lift, take up and pay off, honor, acquit oneself of; satisfy; meet one's obligations, meet one's commitments, redeem, redeem one's pledge, tear up one's mortgage, burn one's mortgage, have a mortgage-burning party, settle accounts, square accounts, make accounts square, strike a balance; pay the bill, pay the shot

14 **pay out,** fork out, fork over, shell out; expend

15 pay over, hand over; ante, **ante up,** put up; put down, lay down, lay one's money down, show the color of one's money

16 <nonformal> kick in, **fork over,** pony up, pay up, cough up, stump up <Brit>, come across, come through with, come across with, come down with, come down with the needful, plank down, plunk down, post, tickle the palm, grease the palm, cross one's palm with, lay on one; pay to the tune of

17 **pay cash,** make a cash payment, cash, pay spot cash, pay cash down, pay cash on the barrelhead, plunk down the money, put one's money on the line, pay at sight; pay in advance; pay as you go; pay cash on delivery, pay COD

18 **pay for,** pay the costs, bear the expense, pay the piper; finance, fund; defray, defray expenses; pay the bill, foot the bill, pick up the check, pick up the tab, spring for, pop for; honor a bill, acknowledge, redeem; pay one's way; pay one's share, chip in, go Dutch, Dutch-treat, go halvsies

19 **treat,** treat to, stand treat, go treat, stand to, pick up the check, pick up the tab, pay the bill, set up, blow to; stand drinks; maintain, support; subsidize

20 **be paid,** draw wages, be salaried, work for wages, be remunerated, collect for one's services, **earn,** get an income, pull down, drag down

ADJS **21** **paying,** remunerative, remuneratory; compensating, compensative, compensatory, disbursing; retributive, retributory; rewarding, rewardful; lucrative, moneymaking, profitable, gainful; repaying, satisfying, reparative; bankable

22 **paid,** paid-up, discharged, settled, liquidated, acquitted, paid in full, receipted, remitted; spent, expended; salaried, waged, hired; compensated; prepaid, postpaid; all-expense-paid

23 unindebted, unowing, **out of debt,** above water, out of the hole, out of the red, clear, all clear, free and clear, all straight; solvent

ADVS **24** **in compensation,** as compensation, in recompense, for services rendered, for professional services, in reward, in requital, in reparation, in retribution, in restitution, in exchange for, in amends, in atonement, to atone for

25 **cash,** cash on the barrelhead, strictly cash; cash down, money down, down; cash on delivery (COD); on demand, on call; pay-as-you-go

625 NONPAYMENT

<failure to pay>

NOUNS **1** **nonpayment, default, delinquency,** delinquence, nondischarge of debts, nonremittal, failure to pay; defection; protest, repudiation; dishonor, dishonoring; bad debt, uncollectible, dishonored bill, protested bill; tax evasion; creative accounting

2 **moratorium,** grace period; embargo, freeze; **write-off,** cancellation, obliteration

3 **insolvency, bankruptcy,** receivership, Chapter 11, failure; crash, collapse, bust, ruin; run on a bank; insufficient funds, overdraft, overdrawn account, not enough to cover, bounced check, bad check, kited check, rubber check; Chapter 7, Chapter 13

4 **insolvent,** insolvent debtor; **bankrupt,** failure; loser, heavy loser, lame duck

5 **defaulter,** delinquent, nonpayer; welsher, levanter; tax evader, tax dodger, tax cheat

VERBS **6** **not pay;** dishonor, repudiate, disallow, protest, stop payment, refuse to pay; **default,** welsh, levant; button up one's pockets, draw the purse strings; underpay; bounce a check, kite a check

7 **go bankrupt, go broke**, go into receivership, become insolvent, become bankrupt, fail, break, bust, crash, collapse, fold, fold up, belly up, go up, go belly up, go under, shut down, shut one's doors, go out of business, be ruined, go to ruin, go on the rocks, go to the wall, go to pot, go to the dogs, go bust; take a bath, be taken to the cleaners, be cleaned out, lose one's shirt, tap out

8 **bankrupt,** ruin, break, bust, wipe out; put out of business, drive to the wall, scuttle, sink; impoverish

9 declare a moratorium; **write off, forgive,** absolve, cancel, nullify, wipe the slate clean; wipe out, obliterate

ADJS **10** **defaulting,** nonpaying, **delinquent;** behindhand, in arrears, in hock, in the red

11 **insolvent, bankrupt,** in receivership, in the hands of receivers, belly-up, broken, broke, busted, ruined, failed, out of business, unable to pay one's creditors, unable to meet one's obligations, illiquid, on the rocks; destitute

12 **unpaid,** unremunerated, uncompensated, unrecompensed, unrewarded, unrequited; underpaid

13 **unpayable,** irredeemable, inconvertible

626 EXPENDITURE

<money spent>

NOUNS **1** **expenditure, spending,** expense, disbursal, disbursement; debit, debiting; budgeting, scheduling; costing, costing-out; payment; deficit spending; use; consumption

2 **spendings,** disbursements, payments, outgoings, outgo, outflow, **outlay,** money going out; capital outlay, capital expenditure; conspicuous consumption

3 **expenses, costs,** charges, disbursals, liabilities, damages; expense, cost, burden of expenditure; budget, budget item, budget line, line item; **overhead,** operating expense, operating costs, operating budget, general expenses; expense account, swindle sheet; business expenses, nonremunerated business expenses, out-of-pocket expenses; direct costs, indirect costs; distributed costs, undistributed costs; material costs; labor costs; carrying charge; unit cost; replacement cost; prime cost; cost of living, cost-of-living index, cost-of-living allowance (COLA), inflation

4 **spender,** expender, expenditor, disburser, buyer, purchaser; spend-all, spendthrift

VERBS **5** **spend, expend,** disburse, pay out, fork out, fork, over, shell out, lay out, outlay; go to the expense of; pay; put one's hands in one's pockets, open the purse, loosen the purse strings, throw money around, go on a spending spree, splurge, spend money like a drunken sailor, spend money as if it were going out of style, go through, run through, be out-of-pocket, squander; invest, sink money in, put out; throw money away; incur costs, incur expenses; budget, schedule, cost, cost out; use; consume

6 **be spent,** burn in one's pocket, burn a hole in one's pocket
7 **afford,** well afford, spare, spare the price, bear, stand, support, endure, undergo, meet the expense of, swing

627 RECEIPTS
<record of money spent>

NOUNS 1 **receipts,** receipt, **income, revenue,** profits, earnings, returns, proceeds, avails, take, takings, intake, take-in, get; credit, credits; gains; gate receipts, gate, box office; net receipts, net; gross receipts, gross; national income; net income, gross income, gross profit margin; earned income, take-home pay, unearned income; dividend, dividends, payout, payback; interest; royalties, commissions; receivables; disposable income; make, produce, yield, output, bang for the buck, fruits, first fruits; bonus, premium; legacy; winnings
2 <written acknowledgment> **receipt,** acknowledgment, voucher, warrant <Brit>; canceled check, bank statement; proof of purchase; receipt in full, receipt in full of all demands, release, acquittance, quittance, discharge
VERBS 3 **receive, pocket,** acquire; earn; accrue; acknowledge receipt of, receipt, mark paid
4 **yield, bring in,** afford, pay, pay off, return; gross, **net**

628 ACCOUNTS
<record of monetary transaction>

NOUNS 1 **accounts;** outstanding accounts, uncollected accounts, unpaid accounts; accounts receivable, receipts, assets; accounts payable, expenditures, liabilities; budget, budgeting; costing out
2 **account, reckoning,** tally, rendering-up, score; account current; account rendered, *compte rendu* <Fr>, account stated; balance, trial balance
3 **statement, bill,** itemized bill, bill of account, account, reckoning, check, score, tab; dun; **invoice,** manifest, bill of lading
4 **account book,** ledger, journal, daybook; register, registry, record book, books; inventory, catalog; log, logbook; cashbook; bankbook, passbook; balance sheet; cost sheet, cost card
5 entry, item, line item, minute, note, notation; single entry, double entry; **credit, debit**
6 **accounting,** accountancy, bookkeeping, double-entry bookkeeping, double-entry accounting, single-entry bookkeeping, single-entry accounting; comptrollership, controllership; business arithmetic; cost accounting, costing <Brit>, cost system, cost-accounting system; audit, auditing; stocktaking, inspection of books
7 **accountant,** bookkeeper; tax preparer; clerk, actuary, registrar, recorder, journalizer; calculator, reckoner; cost accountant, cost keeper; certified public accountant (CPA); chartered accountant (CA) <Brit>; auditor, bank examiner; bank accountant; accountant general; comptroller, controller; statistician; investment manager, money manager; financial advisor
VERBS 8 **keep accounts,** keep books, make up accounts, cast up accounts, render accounts; make an entry, enter, post, post up, journalize, book, docket, log, note, minute; credit, debit; charge off, write off; capitalize; carry, carry on one's books; carry over; balance, balance accounts, balance the books, strike a balance; close the books, close out
9 **take account of,** take stock, overhaul; inventory; audit, examine the books, inspect the books
10 **falsify accounts,** garble accounts, cook accounts, doctor accounts, cook the books, salt, fudge; surcharge
11 **bill,** send a statement; **invoice;** call, call in, demand payment, dun
ADJS 12 accounting, bookkeeping; budget, budgetary

629 TRANSFER OF PROPERTY OR RIGHT
<property delivered>

NOUNS 1 **transfer,** transference; **conveyance,** conveyancing; giving; delivery, deliverance; assignment, assignation; consignment, consignation; conferment, conferral, settling, settlement; vesting; bequeathal; sale; surrender, cession; transmission, transmittal; disposal, disposition, deaccession, deaccessioning; demise; alienation, abalienation; amortization, amortizement; enfeoffment; deeding; bargain and sale; lease and release; exchange, barter, trading; entailment
2 devolution, succession, reversion; shifting use, shifting trust
VERBS 3 **transfer, convey,** deliver, hand, pass, negotiate; give; hand over, turn over, pass over; assign, consign, confer, settle, settle on; cede, surrender; bequeath; entail; sell, sell off, deaccession; make over, sign over, sign away; transmit, hand down, hand on, pass on, devolve upon; demise; alienate, alien, abalienate, amortize; enfeoff; **deed,** deed over, give title to; exchange, barter, trade, trade away

4 change hands, change ownership; devolve, pass on, descend, succeed

ADJS **5 transferable, conveyable,** negotiable, alienable; assignable, consignable; devisable, bequeathable; heritable, inheritable

630 PRICE, FEE

<cost of property>

NOUNS **1 price, cost,** expense, expenditure, charge, damage, score, tab; rate, figure, amount; quotation, quoted price, price tag, ticket, sticker; price list, price range, prices current; stock market quotations; standard price, price point, asking price, list price, sale price, purchase price, selling price, retail price, sticker price, market price

2 worth, value, account, rate; face value, face; par value; market value; street value; fair value; net worth; conversion factor, conversion value; monetary value; money's worth, pennyworth, value received; bang for the buck; going rate; trade-in price

3 valuation, evaluation, value-setting, value-fixing, pricing, price determination, assessment, appraisal, appraisement, estimation, rating, bond rating; unit pricing, dual pricing

4 price index, business index; wholesale price index; consumer price index, retail price index; cost-of-living index; stock market index; price level; price ceiling, ceiling price, ceiling, top price; floor price, floor, bottom price; demand curve; rising prices, inflation, inflationary spiral

5 price controls, price-fixing, valorization; managed prices, fair-trading, fair trade, fair-trade agreement; price supports, rigid supports, flexible supports; price freeze; rent control; prix fixe

6 fee, dues, toll, charge, charges, demand, exaction, exactment, scot, shot, scot and lot; hire; fare, carfare; user fee; airport fee; license fee; entrance fee, entry fee, admission fee, admission; cover charge; portage, towage; wharfage, anchorage, dockage; pilotage; storage, cellarage; brokerage; salvage; service fee, service charge, access charge; commission, cut

7 freightage, freight, haulage, carriage, cartage, drayage, expressage, lighterage; poundage, tonnage

8 rent, rental; rent-roll; rent charge; rack rent, quitrent; ground rent, wayleave rent

9 tax, taxation, duty, tribute, taxes, rates <Brit>; income tax, property tax, inheritance tax, state tax, consumption tax, capital gains tax, gift tax, sales tax; contribution, assessment, revenue enhancement, cess <Brit>, levy, toll, impost, imposition; tax code, tax law; tithe; indirect taxation, direct taxation; tax burden, overtaxation, undertaxation; bracket creep, tax-bracket creep; progressive taxation, graduated taxation; regressive taxation; tax withholding; tax return, separate returns, joint return; tax evasion, tax avoidance; tax haven, tax shelter; tax deduction, deduction; tax write-off, write-off, tax relief; tax exemption, tax-exempt status; tax structure, tax base; taxable income, taxable goods, taxable property, ratables

10 tax collector, taxer, taxman, publican; collector of internal revenue, internal revenue agent, revenuer; tax farmer, farmer; assessor, tax assessor; exciseman <Brit>; Internal Revenue Service (IRS); Inland Revenue (IR) <Brit>; customs agent; customs, U.S. Customs Service, Bureau of Customs and Excise <Brit>; customhouse; taxpayer

VERBS **11 price,** set a price, name a price, fix the price of; place a value on, **value,** evaluate, valuate, appraise, assess, rate, prize, apprize; quote a price; set an arbitrary price on, control the price of, manage the price of, valorize; mark up, mark down, discount; fair-trade; reassess

12 charge, demand, ask, require; overcharge, undercharge; exact, assess, levy, impose; tax, assess a tax upon, slap a tax on, put a duty on, make dutiable, subject to a tax, subject to a fee, collect a tax on, collect a duty on; tithe; prorate, assess *pro rata;* charge for, stick for

13 cost, sell for, fetch, bring, bring in, stand one, set one back, knock one back; come to, run to, amount to, mount up to, come up to, total up to

ADJS **14 priced, valued,** evaluated, assessed, appraised, rated, prized; **worth,** valued at; good for; ad valorem, pro rata

15 chargeable, **taxable,** ratable <Brit>, assessable, dutiable, leviable, declarable; tithable

16 tax-free, nontaxable, nondutiable, tax-exempt; deductible, tax-deductible; duty-free

ADVS **17** at a price, for a consideration; to the amount of, to the tune of, in the neighborhood of

631 DISCOUNT

<lower cost>

NOUNS **1 discount,** cut, deduction, price reduction, slash, abatement, reduction, price-cutting, price cut, rollback; underselling; rebate, rebatement; bank discount, cash discount, chain discount, time discount, trade discount; write-off, charge-off; depreciation; allowance, concession; setoff; drawback, refund, kickback; premium, percentage, agio; trading stamp; bank rate

VERBS 2 **discount,** cut, deduct, bate, abate; take off, write off, charge off; knock down; depreciate, reduce; sell at a loss; allow, make allowance; rebate, refund, kick back; take a premium, take a percentage

ADVS 3 at a discount, at a reduction, at a reduced rate, below par, below cost, under cost; cost-efficient

632 EXPENSIVENESS

<higher cost>

NOUNS 1 **expensiveness, costliness,** dearness, high cost, great cost, highness, stiffness, steepness, priceyness; richness, sumptuousness, sumptuosity, luxuriousness; pretty penny

2 **preciousness,** dearness, value, high value, great value, worth, extraordinary worth, price, great price, valuableness; pricelessness, invaluableness

3 **high price,** high price tag, big price tag, big ticket, big sticker price, sticker shock, fancy price, good price, steep price, stiff price, luxury price, a pretty penny, an arm and a leg, exorbitant price, extortionate price; famine price, scarcity price; rack rent; bracket creep; inflationary prices, rising prices, spiraling prices, soaring costs; sellers' market; inflation, cost inflation, cost-push inflation, cost-push, demand-pull inflation, inflationary trend, hot economy, inflationary spiral, inflationary gap; reflation; stagflation, slumpflation

4 **exorbitance,** exorbitancy, extravagance, excess, excessiveness, inordinateness, immoderateness, immoderation, undueness, unreasonableness, outrageousness, preposterousness; unconscionableness, extortionateness

5 **overcharge,** surcharge, overassessment; gouging, price-gouging; extortion, extortionate price; holdup, armed robbery, highway robbery; profiteering, rack-rent; ripoff

VERBS 6 **cost much,** cost money, cost you, be dear, cost a pretty penny, cost an arm and a leg, cost a packet, run into money; be overpriced, price out of the market

7 **overprice,** set the price tag too high; **overcharge,** surcharge, overtax; hold up, soak, stick, sting, clip, make pay through the nose, gouge; commit highway robbery; victimize, rip off, swindle; exploit, skin, fleece, screw, put the screws to, bleed, bleed white; profiteer; rack, rack up the rents, rack rent; double-charge

8 **overpay,** overspend, pay too much, pay more than it's worth, pay dearly, pay exorbitantly, pay, pay through the nose, be had, be taken

9 **inflate,** heat the economy, heat up the economy; reflate

ADJS 10 **precious,** dear, valuable, worthy, rich, golden, of great price, worth a pretty penny, worth a king's ransom, worth its weight in gold, good as gold, precious as the apple of one's eye; priceless, invaluable, inestimable, without price, beyond price, not to be had for love or money, not for all the tea in China

11 **expensive,** dear, costly, of great cost, dear-bought, high, **high-priced,** premium, at a premium, top; big-ticket, fancy, stiff, steep, pricey, spendy; beyond one's means, not affordable, more than one can afford, sky-high; unpayable; upmarket, upscale rich, sumptuous, executive, posh, luxurious, gold-plated, high-rent; high-stakes

12 **overpriced,** grossly overpriced, exorbitant, excessive, extravagant, inordinate, immoderate, undue, unwarranted, unreasonable, fancy, unconscionable, outrageous, preposterous, out of bounds, out of sight, prohibitive; extortionate, cutthroat, gouging, usurious, exacting; inflationary, spiraling, skyrocketing, mounting; stagflationary, slumpflationary; reflationary

ADVS 13 **dear,** dearly; at a high price, at great cost, at a premium, at a great rate, at heavy cost, at great expense

14 **preciously,** valuably, worthily; pricelessly, invaluably, inestimably

15 **expensively,** richly, sumptuously, luxuriously

16 **exorbitantly,** excessively, grossly, extravagantly, inordinately, immoderately, unduly, unreasonably, unconscionably, outrageously, preposterously; extortionately, usuriously, gougingly

633 CHEAPNESS

<lowest cost>

NOUNS 1 **cheapness, inexpensiveness,** affordableness, affordability, reasonableness, modestness, moderateness, nominalness; glut on the market; shabbiness, shoddiness

2 **low price,** nominal price, reasonable price, modest price, manageable price, sensible price, moderate price; low charge, nominal charge, reasonable charge; bargain prices, budget prices, economy prices, easy terms, popular prices, rock-bottom prices; buyers' market; low price tag, small price tag, low sticker price, low tariff; reduced price, cut price, sale price; cheap rates, reduced rates; bargain rate, cut rate; economy of scale

3 **bargain,** advantageous purchase, buy, good buy, steal; money's worth, pennyworth, good pennyworth; special offer; loss leader

4 cheapening, **depreciation, devaluation,** reduction, lowering; deflation, deflationary spiral, cooling of the economy, cooling off of the economy; buyers' market; decline, plummet, plummeting, plunge, dive, nosedive, slump, sag, free fall; price fall, break; price cut, price reduction, cut, slash, **markdown;** oversupply

VERBS **5** **be cheap,** cost little, not cost anything, cost nothing, next to nothing; go dirt cheap, go for a song, go for nickels and dimes, go for peanuts, buy at a bargain, buy for a mere nothing; get one's money's worth, get a good pennyworth; buy at wholesale prices, buy at cost

6 cheapen, **depreciate,** devaluate, lower, reduce, devalue, **mark down,** cut prices, cut, slash, shave, trim, pare, underprice, knock the bottom out of, knock down; deflate, cool the economy, cool off the economy; beat down; come down, in price, fall in price; fall, decline, plummet, dive, nosedive, drop, crash, head for the bottom, plunge, sag, slump; break, give way; reach a new low; unload

ADJS **7** **cheap, inexpensive,** unexpensive, low, **low-priced,** bargain, frugal, reasonable, sensible, manageable, modest, moderate, affordable, to fit the pocketbook, budget, easy, economy, economic, economical; within means, within reach, within easy reach; nominal, token; austere; worth the money, well worth the money; cheap at half the price; shabby, shoddy, cheapo; deflationary

8 **dirt cheap,** cheap as dirt, dog-cheap, a dime a dozen, bargain-priced, bargain-basement, five-and-ten, dime-store

9 **reduced,** cut, cut-price, slashed, **marked down;** cut-rate; half-price; priced to go; giveaway, sacrificial; lowest, rock-bottom, bottom; deep-discount

ADVS **10** **cheaply,** cheap, on the cheap; inexpensively, reasonably, moderately, nominally; at a bargain, *à bon marché* <Fr>, for a song, for a mere song, for pennies, for nickels and dimes, for peanuts, at small cost, at a low price, at budget prices, at piggy-bank prices, at a sacrifice; at cost, at cost price, at prime cost, wholesale, at wholesale; at reduced rates

634 COSTLESSNESS

<absence of cost>

NOUNS **1** **costlessness,** gratuitousness, gratuity, freeness, expenselessness, complimentariness, no charge; free ride; freebie, gimme; labor of love; gift

2 **complimentary ticket,** pass, comp, free pass, free ticket, paper, free admission, guest pass, guest ticket, Annie Oakley; discount ticket, twofer; plus-one

3 **freeloader,** free rider, pass holder, deadhead, sponger

VERBS **4** **give, present,** comp; freeload, sponge

ADJS **5** **gratuitous, gratis, free,** free of charge, for free, for nothing, free for nothing, free for the asking, free gratis, free gratis for nothing, for love, free as air; freebie, freebee, freeby; costless, expenseless, untaxed, without charge, free of cost, free of expense, all-expense-paid; no charge; unbought, unpaid-for; **complimentary, on the house,** comp, given; giftlike; eleemosynary, charitable

ADVS **6** gratuitously, gratis, free, free of charge, for nothing, for the asking, at no charge, without charge, with the compliments of the management, as our guest, on the house

635 THRIFT

<money carefully spent>

NOUNS **1** **thrift, economy, thriftiness,** economicalness, savingness, sparingness, unwastefulness, **frugality,** frugalness; tight purse strings; parsimony, parsimoniousness; false economy; carefulness, care, chariness, canniness; prudence, providence, forehandedness; husbandry, management, good management, good stewardship, custodianship, prudent administration; austerity, austerity program, belt-tightening; economic planning; economy of means; thrift shop, thrift store, consignment store, donation store

2 **economizing,** economization, reduction of spending, reduction of government spending; cost-effectiveness; saving, scrimping, skimping, scraping, sparing, cheeseparing; retrenchment, curtailment, reduction of expenses, cutback, rollback, slowdown, cooling, cooling off, cooling down, low growth rate; reduction in forces (RIF); budget, spending plan

3 **economizer, saver,** string-saver, skimper

VERBS **4** **economize, save,** make economies; scrimp, skimp, scrape, scrape and save; manage, husband, husband one's resources, conserve; budget; live frugally, get along on a shoestring, get by on little; keep within compass, stay within one's means, keep within one's budget, balance income with outgo, live within one's income, make ends meet, cut one's coat according to one's cloth, stay ahead of the game; put something aside, save up, save for a rainy day, have a nest egg; supplement one's income, eke out one's income

5 **retrench, cut down,** cut down expenses, curtail expenses; cut corners, tighten one's belt, cut back, roll back, take a reef, slow down

ADJS **6** **economical, thrifty, frugal,** economic, unwasteful, conserving, saving, economizing, spare, sparing; Scotch; prudent, prudential, provident, forehanded; careful, chary, canny; scrimping, skimping, cheeseparing, austere; pennywise; parsimonious; cost-effective, cost-efficient; efficient, labor-saving, time-saving, money-saving

ADVS **7** **economically,** thriftily, frugally; cost-effectively, cost-efficiently; prudently, providently; carefully, charily, cannily; sparingly, with a sparing hand

636 ETHICS

<moral values and rules>

NOUNS **1** **ethics, principles,** standards, norms, principles of conduct, principles of behavior, principles of professional practice; morals, moral principles; code, ethical code, moral code, ethic, code of morals, code of ethics, ethical system, value system, values, axiology; norm, behavioral norm, normative system; moral climate, ethos, zeitgeist; Ten Commandments, decalogue; social ethics, professional ethics, bioethics, medical ethics, legal ethics, business ethics

2 ethical philosophy, moral philosophy, ethonomics, aretaics, eudaemonics, casuistry, deontology, empiricism, evolutionism, hedonism, ethical formalism, intuitionism, perfectionism, Stoicism, utilitarianism, categorical imperative, golden rule; egoistic ethics, altruistic ethics; Christian ethics; situation ethics; comparative ethics

3 **morality, morals,** morale; virtue; ethicality, ethicalness; scruples, good conscience, moral fiber, moral compass

4 **amorality,** unmorality; amoralism; moral delinquency, moral turpitude, moral bankruptcy; juvenile delinquency

5 **conscience,** grace, sense of right and wrong, moral sense; inward monitor, inner arbiter, moral censor, censor, ethical self, superego; voice of conscience, still small voice within, wee small voice, guardian angel; inner light, light within; tender conscience; clear conscience, clean conscience; social conscience; conscientiousness; twinge of conscience

ADJS **6** **ethical, moral,** moralistic; ethological; axiological

637 RIGHT

<the good>

NOUNS **1** **right,** rightfulness, rightness; what is right, what is proper, what should be, what ought to be, the seemly, the thing, the right thing, the proper thing, the right thing to do, the proper thing to do, what is done

2 **propriety, decorum,** decency, good behavior, good conduct, correctness, correctitude, rightness, properness, decorousness, goodness, goodliness, niceness, seemliness, cricket; fitness, fittingness, appropriateness, expediency, suitability; normativeness, normality; proprieties, decencies; rightmindedness, righteousness

ADJS **3** **right,** rightful; fit, suitable; proper, correct, **decorous**, good, nice, decent, seemly, due, appropriate, fitting, condign, right and proper, as it should be, as it ought to be, expedient, up to par, *comme il faut* <Fr>; kosher, according to Hoyle; in the right; normative, normal; rightminded, right-thinking, righteous; age-appropriate

ADVS **4** **rightly, rightfully,** right; by rights, by right, with good right, as is right, as is only right; properly, correctly, as is proper, as is fitting, duly, appropriately, fittingly, condignly, in justice, in equity; in reason, in all conscience

638 WRONG

<the bad>

NOUNS **1** **wrong,** wrongfulness, wrongness; **impropriety, indecorum;** incorrectness, improperness, indecorousness, unseemliness; unfitness, unfittingness, inappropriateness, unsuitableness, unsuitability; infraction, violation, delinquency, criminality, illegality, unlawfulness; abnormality, deviance, deviancy, aberrance, aberrancy; sinfulness, wickedness, unrighteousness; dysfunction, malfunction, out of order; maladaptation, maladjustment; malfeasance, malversation, malpractice; malformation; juvenile delinquency

2 **abomination,** horror, terrible thing; scandal, disgrace, shame, pity, atrocity, profanation, desecration, violation, sacrilege, infamy, ignominy

ADJS **3** **wrong, wrongful;** improper, incorrect, indecorous, undue, unseemly; unfit, unfitting, inappropriate, unsuitable; delinquent, criminal, illegal, unlawful; fraudulent, creative; abnormal, deviant, aberrant; dysfunctional, out of order; evil, sinful, wicked, unrighteous; not the thing, hardly the thing, not done, not cricket <Brit>; off-base, out-of-line, off-color, off the beam; abominable, terrible, scandalous, disgraceful, immoral, shameful, shameless, atrocious, sacrilegious, infamous, ignominious; maladapted, maladjusted, unjust

ADVS 4 **wrongly, wrongfully,** wrong; improperly, incorrectly, indecorously; unjustly

COMBINING FORMS 5 mis-, dis-; dys-, caco-

639 DUENESS

<obligation due>

NOUNS 1 **dueness, entitlement,** entitledness, deservingness, deservedness, meritedness, expectation, just expectation, justifiable expectation, expectations, outlook, prospect, prospects; justice

2 **due,** one's due, what one merits, what one is entitled to, what one has earned, what is owing, what one has coming, what is coming to one, acknowledgment, cognizance, recognition, credit, crediting; right

3 desserts, **just desserts**, deservings, merits, **dues**, due reward, due punishment, comeuppance, all that is coming to one, what's coming to one; the wrath of God; retaliation, vengeance

VERBS 4 **be due,** be one's due, **be entitled to,** have a right to, have a title to, have a rightful claim to, have a rightful claim upon, claim as one's right, have coming, come by honestly

5 **deserve,** merit, earn, rate, be in line for, be worthy of, be deserving, richly deserve

6 **get one's desserts,** get one's dues, get one's comeuppance, get his, get hers, get what is coming to one; get justice; serve one right, be rightly served; get for one's pains, reap the fruits of, get the benefit of, reap where one has sown, come into one's own

ADJS 7 **due, owed,** owing, payable, redeemable, coming, coming to

8 **rightful,** condign, appropriate, proper; fit, becoming; **fair, just**

9 warranted, justified, entitled, qualified, worthy; **deserved, merited,** richly deserved, earned

10 **due, entitled to,** with a right to; deserving, meriting, meritorious, worthy of; attributable, ascribable

ADVS 11 **duly,** rightfully, condignly, as is one's due, as is one's right

PHRS 12 what's sauce for the goose is sauce for the gander; give the devil his due; give credit where credit is due; he's made his bed let him lie in it; let the punishment fit the crime

640 UNDUENESS

<undeserved payment>

NOUNS 1 **undueness, undeservedness,** undeservingness, unentitledness, unentitlement, unmeritedness, unwarrantedness; disentitlement; lack of claim, lack of title, false claim, false title, invalid claim, invalid title, no claim, no title, empty claim; unearned increment; inappropriateness; impropriety; excess

2 **presumption,** assumption, imposition; license, licentiousness, undue liberty, liberties, familiarity, **presumptuousness,** freedom abused, liberty abused, hubris; lawlessness; injustice

3 **usurpation,** arrogation, seizure, unlawful seizure, **appropriation,** assumption, adoption, infringement, encroachment, invasion, trespass, trespassing; playing God

4 **usurper,** arrogator, pretender

VERBS 5 **not be entitled to,** have no right to, have no title to, have no claim upon, not have a leg to stand on

6 **presume, assume,** venture, hazard, dare, pretend, attempt, make bold, make so bold, make free, **take the liberty,** take upon oneself, go so far as to

7 presume on, impose on, encroach upon, obtrude upon; **take liberties,** take a liberty, overstep, overstep one's rights, overstep one's bounds, make free with, abuse one's rights, abuse a privilege, give an inch and take an ell; take for granted, presuppose; inconvenience, bother, trouble, cause to go out of one's way

8 <take to oneself unduly> **usurp,** arrogate, seize, grab, latch on to, **appropriate,** assume, adopt, take over, arrogate to oneself, accroach to oneself, pretend to, infringe, encroach, invade, trespass; play God

ADJS 9 **undue,** unowed, unowing, not coming, not outstanding; undeserved, unmerited, unearned; unwarranted, unjustified, unprovoked; unentitled, undeserving, unmeriting, nonmeritorious, unworthy; preposterous, outrageous

10 inappropriate; improper; excessive

11 **presumptuous,** presuming, licentious; hubristic

PHRS 12 give him an inch he'll take a mile; let a camel get his nose under the tent and he'll come in

641 DUTY

<moral obligation>

NOUNS 1 **duty, obligation,** charge, onus, burden, mission, devoir, must, ought, imperative, bounden duty, proper task, assigned task, what ought to be done, what one is responsible for, where the buck stops, deference, respect, fealty, allegiance, loyalty, homage; devotion, dedication, commitment; self-commitment, self-imposed duty; business, function, province, place; ethics; line of duty; call of duty; duties and responsibilities, assignment, workload; burden of proof; civic duty; mission creep

2 **responsibility,** incumbency; liability, accountability, accountableness, answerability, answerableness, amenability; product liability; responsibleness, dutifulness, duteousness, devotion to duty, dedication to duty, sense of duty, sense of obligation, code of honor, inner voice

VERBS 3 **should, ought to,** had best, had better, be expedient

4 **behoove,** become, befit, beseem, be bound, be obliged, be obligated, be under an obligation; owe it to, owe it to oneself; must

5 **be the duty of,** be incumbent on, be his to, be hers to, fall to, stand on, be a must, be an imperative for, duty calls one to

6 **be responsible for,** answer for, stand responsible for, be liable for, be answerable, be accountable for; be on the hook for, take the heat for, take the rap for

7 **be one's responsibility,** be one's office, be one's charge, be one's mission, be one's concern, rest with, lie upon, devolve upon, rest on the shoulders of, lie on one's door, fall to one, be on one's head

8 **incur a responsibility,** become bound to, become sponsor for

9 **take the responsibility,** accept the responsibility, take upon oneself, take upon one's shoulders, commit oneself; be where the buck stops; answer for, defer to one's duty; sponsor, be sponsor for, stand sponsor for; do at one's own risk, do at one's own peril; take the blame, be in the hot seat, be on the spot, take the heat for, take the rap for

10 **do one's duty,** perform one's duty, fulfill one's duty, discharge one's duty, do what one has to do, pay one's dues, do what is expected, do the needful, do the right thing, do justice to, do one's part, act one's part, play one's proper role; answer the call of duty, do one's bit; walk the walk

11 **meet an obligation,** satisfy one's obligations, stand to one's engagement, stand up to, acquit oneself, **make good,** redeem one's pledge

12 obligate, oblige, **require,** make incumbent, make imperative, tie, **bind,** pledge, commit, saddle with, put under an obligation; call to account, hold responsible, hold accountable, hold answerable

ADJS 13 **dutiful, duteous;** moral, ethical; conscientious, scrupulous, observant; obedient; deferential, respectful

14 **incumbent on,** chargeable to, behooving

15 **obligatory, binding,** imperative, imperious, peremptory, mandatory, compulsory, must, *de rigueur* <Fr>; necessary, required

16 **obliged,** obligated, obligate, under obligation; bound, duty-bound, in duty bound, tied, pledged, committed, saddled, beholden, bounden; obliged to, beholden to, bound to, indebted to

17 **responsible,** answerable; liable, **accountable,** incumbent, amenable, unexempt from, chargeable, on one's head, at one's doorstep, on the hook; responsible for, at the bottom of; to blame; on book

ADVS 18 **dutifully,** duteously, in the line of duty, as in duty bound; beyond the call of duty

642 PREROGATIVE

<right or privilege>

NOUNS 1 **prerogative, right,** due, droit; power, authority, prerogative of office; faculty, appurtenance; claim, proper claim, demand, interest, title, pretension, pretense, prescription; birthright; natural right, presumptive right, inalienable right, exclusive right; divine right; vested right, vested interest; property right; conjugal right; royal charter

2 **privilege, license,** liberty, freedom, immunity; franchise, patent, copyright, grant, warrant, blank check, carte blanche; favor, indulgence, special favor, dispensation; electronic rights

3 **human rights,** rights of man; constitutional rights, rights of citizenship, **civil rights,** civil liberties; rights of minorities, minority rights; gay rights; Bill of Rights

4 **women's rights,** rights of women; feminism, women's liberation, women's lib, womanism, women's movement, women's liberation movement, sisterhood

5 women's rightist, **feminist,** women's liberationist, women's liberation activist, womanist, women's libber, libber; suffragette, suffragist; bra burner

VERBS 6 have a right, have a claim, assert a claim, assert a right, exercise a right; defend a right

643 IMPOSITION

<excessive burden>

NOUNS 1 **imposition,** infliction, laying on, charging, taxing, tasking; burdening, weighting, weighting down, freighting, loading, loading down, heaping on, imposing an onus; exaction, demand; unwarranted demand, obtrusiveness, presumptuousness; inconvenience, trouble, bother, pain; inconsiderateness

2 administration, giving, bestowal; applying, application, dosing, dosage, meting out, prescribing; **forcing,** forcing on, enforcing; regimentation

3 charge, duty, tax, task; **burden,** weight, freight, cargo, load, onus

VERBS 4 **impose, impose on,** inflict on, put on, put upon, lay on, enjoin; put, place, set, lay, put down; levy, exact, demand; tax, task, charge, burden with, weight with, weight down with, yoke with, fasten upon, saddle with, stick with; subject to

5 **inflict,** wreak, do to, bring, bring upon, bring down upon, bring down on one's head, visit upon

6 administer, give, bestow; apply, put on, lay on, dose, dose with, dish out, mete out, prescribe, regiment; force, **force upon,** impose by force, strongarm, force down one's throat, enforce upon

7 **impose on,** impose upon, take advantage of; presume upon; deceive, play on, work on, out on, put over, put across; palm off on, fob off on, fob on, foist on; shift the blame, shift the responsibility, pass the buck

ADJS 8 **imposed, inflicted,** piled on, heaped on; burdened with, stuck with; self-inflicted; exacted, demanded

644 PROBITY

<honest behavior>

NOUNS 1 **probity,** truthfulness, assured probity, **honesty,** integrity, rectitude, uprightness, upstandingness, erectness, virtue, virtuousness, righteousness, goodness; cleanness, decency; honor, honorableness, worthiness, estimableness, reputability, nobility; unimpeachableness, unimpeachability, irreproachableness, irreproachability, blamelessness; immaculacy, unspottedness, stainlessness, pureness, purity; respectability; principles, high principles, high ideals, high-mindedness; character, good character, sterling character, moral strength, moral excellence; fairness, justness, justice; gentrification

2 **conscientiousness,** scrupulousness, scrupulosity, **scruples,** punctiliousness, meticulousness; scruple, point of honor, punctilio; qualm; twinge of conscience; overconscientiousness, overscrupulousness; fastidiousness

3 honesty, veracity, veraciousness, verity, **truthfulness,** truth, veridicality, truth-telling, truth-speaking; truth-loving; credibility, absolute credibility; objectivity

4 **candor,** candidness, frankness, plain dealing; sincerity, genuineness, authenticity; ingenuousness; artlessness; openness, openheartedness; freedom, freeness; unreserve, unrestraint, unconstraint; forthrightness, directness, straightforwardness; outspokenness, plainness, plainspokenness, plain speaking, plain speech, transparency, roundness, broadness; bluntness, bluffness, brusqueness

5 **undeceptiveness,** undeceitfulness, guilelessness

6 **trustworthiness,** faithworthiness, trustiness, trustability, reliability, dependability, dependableness, sureness; answerableness, responsibility; unfalseness, unperfidiousness, untreacherousness; incorruptibility, inviolability

7 **fidelity, faithfulness,** loyalty, faith; constancy, steadfastness, staunchness, firmness; trueness, troth, true blue; good faith, *bona fides* <L>, *bonne foi* <Fr>; allegiance, fealty, homage; bond, tie; attachment, adherence, adhesion; devotion, devotedness

8 **person of honor,** man of honor, woman of honor, man of his word, woman of her word; gentleman; honest man, good man; lady, real lady; honest woman, good woman; salt of the earth; square shooter, straight shooter, straight arrow; true blue, truepenny; trusty, faithful

VERBS 9 keep faith, not fail, **keep one's word**, keep one's promise, keep troth, show good faith, be as good as one's word, one's word is one's bond, redeem one's pledge, play by the rules, acquit oneself, make good; practice what one preaches

10 shoot straight, draw a straight furrow, put one's cards on the table, level with, play it straight, shoot from the hip

11 **tell the truth,** speak the truth, speak true, paint in its true colors, tell the truth and shame the devil; tell the truth, the whole truth, and nothing but the truth, stick to the facts

12 **be frank, be candid,** speak plainly, speak out, speak one's mind, say what one thinks, call a spade a spade, tell it like it is, make no bones about it, not mince words

ADJS 13 **honest, upright,** uprighteous, upstanding, erect, right, righteous, virtuous, good, clean, squeaky-clean, decent; honorable, full of integrity, reputable, estimable, creditable, worthy, noble, sterling, manly, yeomanly; Christian; unimpeachable, beyond reproach, irreproachable, blameless, immaculate, spotless, stainless, unstained, unspotted, unblemished, untarnished, unsullied, undefiled, pure; respectable, highly respectable; ethical, moral; principled, high-principled, high-minded, right-minded; uncorrupt, uncorrupted, inviolate; truehearted, true-blue, true-souled, true-spirited; true-dealing, true-disposing, true-devoted; law-abiding, law-loving, law-revering; fair, just

14 **straight, square**, foursquare, straight-arrow, honest and aboveboard, right as rain; fair and square; square-dealing, square-shooting, straight-shooting, up-and-up, on the up-and-up, on the level, on the square; aboveboard, open and aboveboard; bona fide, good-faith; authentic, all wool and a yard wide, veritable, genuine; singlehearted; honest as the day is long

15 **conscientious,** tender-conscienced; scrupulous, careful; punctilious, punctual, meticulous, religious, strict, nice; fastidious; overconscientious, overscrupulous

16 **honest,** veracious, **truthful,** true, true to one's word, veridical; truth-telling, truth-speaking, truth-declaring, truth-passing, truth-bearing, truth-loving, truth-seeking, truth-desiring, truth-guarding, truth-filled; true-speaking, true-meaning, true-tongued

17 **candid,** frank, sincere, genuine, ingenuous, frankhearted; open, openhearted, transparent, open-faced; artless; straightforward, direct, up-front, straight, forthright, downright, straight-out, straight-from-the-shoulder; plain, broad, round; unreserved, unrestrained, unconstrained, unchecked; unguarded, uncalculating; free; outspoken, plainspoken, free-spoken, free-speaking, free-tongued; explicit, unequivocal; blunt, bluff, brusque; heart-to-heart

18 **undeceptive,** undeceitful, undissembling, undissimulating, undeceiving, undesigning, uncalculating; guileless, unbeguiling, unbeguileful; unassuming, unpretending, unfeigning, undisguising, unflattering; undissimulated, undissembled; unassumed, unaffected, unpretended, unfeigned, undisguised, unvarnished, untrimmed

19 **trustworthy,** trusty, trustable, faithworthy, reliable, dependable, responsible, straight, sure, to be trusted, to be depended upon, to be relied upon, to be counted on, to be reckoned on, as good as one's word; tried, true, tried and true, tested, proven; unfalse, unperfidious, untreacherous; incorruptible, inviolable

20 **faithful,** loyal, devoted, allegiant; true, true-blue, true to one's colors; constant, steadfast, unswerving, steady, consistent, stable, unfailing, staunch, firm, solid

ADVS 21 **honestly,** uprightly, honorably, upstandingly, erectly, virtuously, righteously, decently, worthily, reputably, nobly; unimpeachably, irreproachably, blamelessly, immaculately, unspottedly, stainlessly, purely; high-mindedly, morally; conscientiously, scrupulously, punctiliously, meticulously, fastidiously

22 **truthfully,** truly, veraciously; to tell the truth, to speak truthfully; in truth, in sooth, of a truth, with truth, in good truth, in very truth; objectively

23 **candidly,** frankly, sincerely, genuinely, in all seriousness, in all soberness, from the heart, in all conscience; in plain words, in plain English, straight from the shoulder, not to mince the matter, not to mince words, without equivocation, with no nonsense, all joking aside; openly, openheartedly, unreservedly, unrestrainedly, unconstrainedly, forthrightly, directly, straightforwardly, outspokenly, plainly, plainspokenly, uninhibitedly, broadly, roundly, bluntly, bluffy, brusquely

24 **trustworthily,** trustily, reliably, dependably, responsibly; undeceptively, undeceitfully, guilelessly; incorruptibly, inviolably

25 **faithfully,** loyally, devotedly; constantly, steadfastly, steadily, responsibly, consistently, unfailingly, unswervingly, staunchly, firmly; in good faith, with good faith, *bona fide* <L>

645 IMPROBITY

<*dishonest behavior*>

NOUNS 1 **improbity,** untruthfulness, **dishonesty,** dishonor; unscrupulousness, unconscientiousness; corruption, corruptness, corruptedness; crookedness, criminality, feloniousness, fraudulence, fraudulency, underhandedness, unsavoriness, fishiness, shadiness, indirection, shiftiness, slipperiness, deviousness, evasiveness, unstraightforwardness, trickiness

2 **knavery,** roguery, rascality, rascalry, villainy, reprobacy, scoundrelism; chicanery; knavishness, roguishness, scampishness, villainousness, charlatanism; baseness, vileness, degradation, turpitude, moral turpitude

3 **deceitfulness;** falseness; perjury, forswearing, untruthfulness, credibility gap; inveracity; mendacity, mendaciousness; insincerity, unsincereness, uncandidness, uncandor, unfrankness, disingenuousness; hypocrisy; sharp practice; fraud; artfulness, craftiness; intrigue

4 **untrustworthiness,** unfaithworthiness, untrustiness, unreliability, undependability, irresponsibility

5 **infidelity, unfaithfulness,** unfaith, faithlessness, cheating, trothlessness; inconstancy, unsteadfastness, fickleness; disloyalty, unloyalty; falsity, falseness, untrueness; disaffection, recreancy, dereliction; bad faith, *mala fides* <L>, Punic faith; breach of promise, breach of trust,

breach of faith, barratry; breach of confidence, musical beds; dereliction of duty

6 **treachery,** treacherousness; **perfidy,** perfidiousness, falseheartedness, two-facedness, doubleness, sycophancy, false face; duplicity, double-dealing, foul play, dirty work, dirty pool, dirty trick, dirty game; broken promise, breach of promise, breach of faith

7 **treason,** petty treason, misprision of treason, high treason; lese majesty, sedition; quislingism, fifth-column activity; collaboration, fraternization; subversion, subversiveness, subversivism

8 **betrayal,** betrayment, letting down, **double cross**, sellout, Judas kiss, kiss of death, stab in the back

9 **corruptibility, venality,** bribability, purchasability

10 criminal, perpetrator, perp, scoundrel, traitor, deceiver

VERBS 11 <**be dishonest**> live by one's wits; shift, shift about, evade; deceive; cheat; falsify; lie; sail under false colors, put on a false face, pass oneself off as

12 **be unfaithful,** not keep faith, not keep troth, go back on, fail, break one's word, break one's promise, renege, go back on one's word, break faith, betray, perjure oneself, forswear oneself; forsake, desert; pass the buck; shift the responsibility, shift the blame; cheat, cheat on, two-time

13 play one false, prove false; stab one in the back, **backstab**, knife one; bite the hand that feeds one; play dirty pool; shift the goalposts, move the goalposts, change the rules; bamboozle

14 **betray, double-cross**, two-time, sell out, sell down the river, turn in; mislead, lead one down the garden path; let down; inform on

15 **act the traitor,** turn against, go over to the enemy, turn one's coat, sell oneself, sell out; collaborate, fraternize

ADJS 16 **dishonest,** dishonorable; unconscientious, unconscienced, conscienceless, unconscionable, shameless, without shame, without remorse, unscrupulous, unprincipled, unethical, immoral, amoral; corrupt, corrupted, rotten, bottom-dwelling; crooked, criminal, felonious, fraudulent, creative, underhand, underhanded; shady, up to no good, not kosher, unsavory, dark, sinister, insidious, indirect, slippery, devious, tricky, shifty, evasive, unstraightforward; fishy, questionable, suspicious, doubtful, dubious, hinky; ill-gotten, ill-got

17 **knavish,** roguish, scampish, rascally, scoundrelly, blackguardly, villainous, reprobate, recreant, base, vile, degraded; infamous, notorious

18 **deceitful;** falsehearted; perjured, forsworn, untruthful; insincere, unsincere, uncandid, unfrank, disingenuous; artful, crafty; calculating, scheming; tricky, cute, dodgy, slippery as an eel

19 **untrustworthy,** unfaithworthy, untrusty, trustless, unreliable, undependable, fly-by-night, irresponsible, unsure, not to be trusted, not to be depended, not to be relied upon

20 **unfaithful,** faithless, of bad faith, trothless; inconstant, unsteadfast, fickle; disloyal, unloyal; false, untrue, not true to; disaffected, recreant, derelict, barratrous; two-timing

21 **treacherous,** perfidious, falsehearted; shifty, slippery, tricky; **double-dealing,** double, ambidextrous; **two-faced**

22 **traitorous,** turncoat, double-crossing, two-timing, betraying; Judas-like, Iscariotic; treasonable, treasonous; quisling, quislingistic, fifth-column, Trojan-horse; subversive, seditious

23 **corruptible,** venal, bribable, purchasable, on the pad, mercenary, hireling

ADVS 24 **dishonestly,** dishonorably; unscrupulously, unconscientiously; crookedly, criminally, feloniously, fraudulently, underhandedly, like a thief in the night, insidiously, deviously, shiftily, evasively, fishily, suspiciously, dubiously, by fair means or foul; deceitfully; knavishly, roguishly, villainously; basely, vilely; infamously, notoriously

25 **perfidiously,** falseheartedly; unfaithfully, faithlessly; **treacherously;** traitorously, treasonably

646 HONOR

<token of esteem>

NOUNS 1 **honor,** great honor, distinction, glory, credit, ornament; A student, 4.0 GPA

2 **award,** reward, **prize;** first prize, second prize; blue ribbon; consolation prize; booby prize; Nobel Prize, Pulitzer Prize; sweepstakes; jackpot; Oscar, Academy Award, Emmy, Tony; gold medal, silver medal, bronze medal

3 **trophy,** laurel, **laurels,** bays, palm, palms, crown, chaplet, wreath, garland, feather in one's cap; civic crown; cup, loving cup, pot; America's Cup, Old Mug; belt, championship belt, black belt, brown belt; banner, flag

4 **citation,** eulogy, mention, honorable mention, kudos, accolade, tribute, praise

5 **decoration,** decoration of honor, order, ornament; ribbon, riband; blue ribbon, *cordon bleu* <Fr>; red ribbon, red ribbon of the Legion of Honor; cordon, grand cordon; garter; star, gold star

6 **medal, military honor**, order, medallion; military medal, service medal, war medal, soldier's medal; lifesaving medal, Carnegie hero's medal; police citation, departmental citation; spurs,

stripes, pips, star, gold star; badge of honor; Air Medal, Bronze Star Medal, Congressional Medal of Honor, Distinguished Conduct Medal, Distinguished Flying Cross, Distinguished Service Cross, Distinguished Service Medal, Distinguished Service Order, Distinguished Unit Citation, Medal of Honor, Military Cross, Navy Cross, Order of the Purple Heart, Silver Star Medal, Unit Citation

7 scholarship, fellowship; grant

VERBS 8 **honor**, do honor, pay regard to, pay honor to, recognize; cite; decorate, pin a medal on; crown, crown with laurel; hand it to one, take off one's hat to one, pay tribute, praise; give credit where credit is due; give one the red carpet treatment, roll out the red carpet

ADJS 9 **honored, distinguished;** laureate, crowned with laurel

10 **honorary, honorific, honorable**

ADVS 11 **with honor,** with distinction; *cum laude, magna cum laude, summa cum laude, insigne cum laude, honoris causa* <L>

647 INSIGNIA

<sign of rank, status>

NOUNS 1 **insignia, regalia,** ensign, **emblem, badge, symbol,** logo, marking, attribute; badge of office, mark of office, chain, chain of office, collar; wand, verge, *fasces* <L>, mace, staff, baton; livery, uniform, mantle, dress; tartan, tie, old school tie, regimental tie, club tie; ring, school ring, class ring; pin, button, lapel pin, lapel button; cap and gown, mortarboard; cockade; brassard; figurehead, eagle; cross, skull and crossbones, swastika, hammer and sickle, rose, thistle, shamrock, fleur-de-lis, caduceus; medal, decoration; heraldry, armory, blazonry, sigillography, sphragistics

2 <**heraldry insignia**> heraldic device, achievement, bearings, coat of arms, arms, armorial bearings, armory, blazonry, blazon; hatchment; shield, escutcheon, scutcheon, lozenge; charge, field; crest, torse, wreath, garland, bandeau, chaplet, mantling, helmet; crown, coronet; device, motto; pheon, broad arrow; animal charge, lion, unicorn, griffin, yale, cockatrice, falcon, alerion, eagle, spread eagle; marshaling, quartering, impaling, impalement, dimidiating, differencing, difference; ordinary, bar, bend, bar sinister, bend sinister, baton, chevron, chief, cross, fess, pale, paly, saltire; subordinary, billet, bordure, canton, flanch, fret, fusil, gyron, inescutcheon, mascle, orle, quarter, rustre, tressure; fess point, nombril point, honor point; cadency mark, file, label, crescent, mullet, martlet, annulet, fleur-de-lis, rose, cross moline, octofoil; tincture, gules, azure, vert, sable, purpure, tenne; metal, or, argent; fur, ermine, ermines, erminites, erminois, pean, vair; heraldic officials; Hershey bar, pip, hash mark

3 <**royal insignia**> regalia; scepter, rod, rod of empire; orb; armilla; purple, ermine, robe of state, robe of royalty, robes of office; purple pall; crown, royal crown, coronet, tiara, diadem; cap of maintenance, cap of dignity, cap of estate, triple plume, Prince of Wales's feathers; uraeus; seal, signet, great seal, privy seal; throne; badge of office

4 <**ecclesiastical insignia**> tiara, triple crown; ring, keys; miter, crosier, crook, pastoral staff; pallium; cardinal's hat, red hat

5 <**military insignia**> insignia of rank, grade insignia, chevron, stripe; star, bar, eagle, spread eagle, chicken, pip <Brit>, oak leaf; branch of service insignia, insignia of branch, insignia of arm; unit insignia, organization insignia, shoulder patch, patch; shoulder sleeve insignia, badge, aviation badge, aviation wings; parachute badge, submarine badge; service stripe, hash mark, overseas bar, Hershey bar; epaulet

6 <national insignia> American eagle, British lion and unicorn, Canadian maple leaf, English rose, French fleur-de-lis, Irish shamrock, Japanese rising sun, Nazi swastika, Roman eagle, Russian bear, Scottish thistle, Soviet hammer and sickle, Swiss cross, Welsh leek, Welsh daffodil

7 **flag,** banner, oriflamme, standard, gonfalon, gonfanon, guidon, *vexillum* <L>, *labarum* <L>; pennant, pennon, pennoncel, banneret, bannerette, banderole, swallowtail, burgee, ensign, streamer; bunting; coachwhip, long pennant; national flag, colors; royal standard; merchant flag, jack, Jolly Roger, black flag; house flag; Old Glory, Stars and Stripes, Star-Spangled Banner, red, white, and blue; Stars and Bars <Confederacy>; tricolor; Union Jack, Union Flag; yellow flag, white flag; vexillology; signal

648 TITLE

<named rank, status>

NOUNS 1 **title, honorific,** honor, title of honor; handle, handle to one's name; courtesy title

2 <**honorifics**> Excellency, Eminence, Reverence, Grace, Honor, Worship, Your Excellency; Lord, My Lord, milord, Lordship, Your Lordship; Lady, My Lady, milady, Ladyship, Your Ladyship; Highness, Royal Highness, Imperial Highness,

Serene Highness, Your Highness; Majesty, Royal Majesty, Imperial Majesty, Serene Majesty, Your Majesty; His Excellency, His Lordship, His Highness, His Majesty; Her Excellency, Her Ladyship, Her Highness, Her Majesty

3 Sir, sire, sirrah; Esquire; Master, Mister; mirza, effendi, sirdar, emir, khan, sahib

4 Mistress, Ms, madame

5 <ecclesiastical titles> Reverend, His Reverence, His Grace; Monsignor; Holiness, His Holiness; Dom, Brother, Sister, Father, Mother; Rabbi

6 **degree, academic degree** <see list>; bachelor, baccalaureate, bachelor's degree; master, master's degree; doctor, doctorate, doctor's degree, doctoral degree; terminal degree

ADJS 7 **titular,** titulary; honorific; honorary

8 the Noble, the Most Noble, the Most Excellent, the Most Worthy, the Most Worshipful; the Honorable, the Most Honorable, the Right Honorable; the Reverend, the Very Reverend, the Right Reverend, the Most Reverend

9 **academic degree**

(AA) Associate of Arts
(AAS) Associate in Applied Science
(AB) Bachelor of Arts <Artium Baccalaureus>
(ABLS) Bachelor of Arts in Library Science
(AdjA) Adjunct in Arts
(AM) Master of Arts <Artium Magister>
(AMusD) Doctor of Musical Arts
(AN) Associate in Nursing
(ArtsD) Doctor of Arts
(AS) Associate of Science
(BA) Bachelor of Arts
(BAE) Bachelor of Arts in Education
(BAN) Bachelor of Arts in Nursing
(BBA) Bachelor of Business Administration
(BCE) Bachelor of Chemical Engineering
(BCL) Bachelor of Civil Law
(BD) Bachelor of Divinity
(BFA) Bachelor of Fine Arts
(BLitt, Blit) Bachelor of Literature
(BMus) Bachelor of Music
(BNS) Bachelor of Naval Science
(BPhil) Bachelor of Philosophy
(BS) Bachelor of Science
(BSArch) Bachelor of Science in Architecture
(ChD) Doctor of Chemistry
(DD) Doctor of Divinity
(DDS) Doctor of Dental Surgery
(DEd) Doctor of Education
(DJ, Djur) Doctor of Jurisprudence
(DJS, D.Jur.Sc.) Doctor of Juridical Science
(DLit, Dlitt) Doctor of Letters
(DMD) Doctor of Dental Medicine
(DMin) Doctor of Ministry
(DMus) Doctor of Music
(DO) Doctor of Osteopathy
(DPH) Doctor of Public Health
(DPhil) Doctor of Philosophy <Brit>
(DS) Doctor of Science
(DSC) Doctor of Surgical Chiropody
(EdD) Doctor of Education
(EdS) Education Specialist
(JCD) Doctor of Canon Law
(JD) Doctor of Jurisprudence
(LittD) Doctor of Letters
(LLB) Bachelor of Laws
(LLD) Doctor of Laws
(LLM) Master of Laws
(MA) Master of Arts
(MALS) Master of Arts in Library Science
(MArch) Master of Architecture
(MAT) Master of Arts in Teaching
(MB) Bachelor of Medicine <Brit>
(MBA) Master in Business Administration
(MD) Doctor of Medicine
(MDiv) Master of Divinity
(Med) Master of Education
(MFA) Master of Fine Arts
(MLitt) Master of Literature
(MLS) Master of Library Science
(MPhil) Master of Philosophy
(MRE) Master of Religious Education
(MS) Master of Science
(MSW) Master of Social Work
(MusD) Doctor of Music
(OD) Doctor of Optometry
(PharD, PharmD) Doctor of Pharmacy
(PhD) Doctor of Philosophy
(SB) Bachelor of Science
(ScD, SD) Doctor of Science
(SM) Master of Science
(STD) Doctor of Sacred Theology
(ThB) Bachelor of Theology
(ThD) Doctor of Theology
(ThM) Master of Theology
(VMD) Doctor of Veterinary Medicine

649 JUSTICE

<fair and moral treatment>

NOUNS 1 **justice, justness;** equity, equitableness, level playing field; evenhandedness, measure for measure, give-and-take; balance, equality; right, rightness, rightfulness, meetness, properness, propriety, what is right; dueness; justification, justifiableness, justifiability, warrantedness, warrantability, defensibility; poetic justice; retributive justice, nemesis; summary justice, drumhead justice, rude justice; scales of justice; lawfulness, legality

2 **fairness,** fair-mindedness, candor; the fair thing, the right thing, the proper thing, the handsome thing; level playing field, square deal, fair shake; **fair play,** cricket; sportsmanship, good sportsmanship, sportsmanliness, sportsmanlikeness

3 **impartiality,** detachment, dispassion, loftiness, Olympian detachment, dispassionateness, disinterestedness, disinterest, unbias, unbiasedness, a fair field and no favor; neutrality; selflessness, unselfishness

4 <personifications> Justice, Justitia, blind Justice, blindfolded Justice; Rhadamanthus, Minos;

<deities> Jupiter Fidius, Deus Fidius; Fides, Fides publica Romani, Fides populi Romani; Nemesis, Dike, Themis; Astraea

VERBS 5 **be just, be fair,** do the fair thing, do the handsome thing, do right, be righteous, do it fair and square, do the right thing by; do justice to, see justice done, see one redressed, redress a wrong, redress an injustice, remedy an injustice, serve one right, shoot straight with, give a square deal, give a fair shake; give the devil his due; give and take; bend over backwards, lean over backwards, go out of one's way, go the extra mile

6 **play fair,** play the game, be a good sport, show a proper spirit; judge on its own merits, hold no brief

ADJS 7 **just, fair,** square, fair and square; equitable, balanced, level, even, evenhanded; right, rightful; justifiable, justified, warranted, warrantable, defensible; due, deserved, merited; meet, meet and right, right and proper, fit, proper, good, as it should be, as it ought to be; lawful, legal

8 **fair-minded**; sporting, sportsmanly, sportsmanlike; square-dealing, square-shooting

9 **impartial,** impersonal, evenhanded, equitable, dispassionate, disinterested, detached, objective, lofty, Olympian; unbiased, uninfluenced, unswayed; neutral; selfless, unselfish

ADVS 10 **justly, fairly,** fair, in a fair manner; rightfully, rightly, duly, deservedly, meetly, properly; equitably, equally, evenly, upon even terms; justifiedly, justifiably, warrantably, warrantedly; impartially, impersonally, dispassionately, disinterestedly, without distinction, without regard to persons, without respect to persons, without fear, without favor

11 in justice, in equity, in reason, in all conscience, in all fairness, to be fair, as is only fair, as is only right, as is right, as is just, as is fitting, as is proper

650 INJUSTICE

<unfair or immoral treatment>

NOUNS 1 **injustice, unjustness; inequity,** iniquity, inequitableness, iniquitousness; inequality, inequality of treatment, inequality of dealing; wrong, wrongness, wrongfulness, unmeetness, improperness, impropriety; undueness; what should not be, what ought not be, what must not be; unlawfulness, illegality

2 **unfairness;** unsportsmanliness, unsportsmanlikeness; foul play, foul, a hit below the belt, dirty pool

3 **partiality, onesidedness; bias,** leaning, inclination, tendentiousness; undispassionateness, undetachment, interest, involvement, partisanism, partisanship, *parti pris* <Fr>; unneutrality; slant, angle, spin; favoritism, preference, nepotism; unequal treatment, preferential treatment, discrimination, reverse discrimination, unjust legal disability, inequality

4 **injustice,** wrong, injury, grievance, disservice; raw deal, rotten deal, bad rap; imposition; mockery of justice, miscarriage of justice; great wrong, grave injustice, gross injustice; atrocity, outrage

5 unjustifiability, unwarrantability, indefensibility; inexcusability, unconscionableness, unpardonability, unforgivableness, inexpiableness, irremissibility

VERBS 6 not play fair, hit below the belt, give a raw deal, give a rotten deal, give a bad rap

7 do one an injustice, **wrong,** do wrong, do wrong by, do one a wrong, do a disservice; do a great wrong, do a grave injustice, do a gross injustice, commit an atrocity, commit an outrage

8 favor, prefer, show preference, **play favorites,** treat unequally, discriminate; slant, angle, put on spin

ADJS 9 **unjust, inequitable,** unequitable, iniquitous, unbalanced, discriminatory, uneven, unequal; wrong, wrongful, unrightful; undue, unmeet, undeserved, unmerited; unlawful, illegal

10 **unfair,** not fair; unsporting, unsportsmanly, **unsportsmanlike,** not done, not kosher, not cricket; dirty, foul, below the belt; sexist

11 **partial,** interested, involved, partisan, unneutral, one-sided, all on one side, way over to one side, undetached, unobjective, undispassionate, biased, tendentious, tendential, warped, influenced, swayed, slanted

12 **unjustifiable,** unwarrantable, unallowable, unreasonable, indefensible; inexcusable, unconscionable, unpardonable, unforgivable, inexpiable, irremissible

ADVS 13 **unjustly, unfairly;** wrongfully, wrongly, undeservedly; inequitably, iniquitously, unequally, unevenly; partially, interestedly, one-sidedly, undispassionately; unjustifiably, unwarrantably, unallowably, unreasonably, indefensibly; inexcusably, unconscionably, unpardonably, unforgivably, inexpiably, irremissibly

651 SELFISHNESS

<stinginess and disregard for others>

NOUNS 1 **selfishness,** selfism, **self-seeking,** self-serving, self-pleasing, self-indulgence, hedonism; self-advancement, self-promotion, self-advertisement; careerism, personal ambition; narcissism, self-love, self-devotion, self-jealousy, self-consideration, self-solicitude, self-sufficiency, self-absorption, ego trip, self-occupation; self-containment, self-isolation; autism, catatonia, remoteness; self-interest, self-concern, self-interestedness, interest; self-esteem, self-admiration; self-centeredness, self-obsession, egotism; avarice, greed, graspingness, grabbiness, acquisitiveness, possessiveness, covetousness; individualism, personalism, privatism, private desire, personal desires, private aims, personal aims; looking out for number one; me generation, entitlement generation

2 **ungenerousness,** unmagnanimousness, illiberality, meanness, smallness, littleness, paltriness, minginess, pettiness; niggardliness, stinginess

3 **self-seeker,** self-pleaser, self-advancer; member of the me generation, member of the entitlement generation; **narcissist,** egotist; timepleaser, timeserver, temporizer; fortune hunter, moneygrubber, tufthunter, name-dropper; self-server, careerist; opportunist; monopolist, hog, road hog; dog in the manger; individualist, loner, lone wolf

VERBS 4 **please oneself,** gratify oneself; ego-trip, be on an ego trip, go on an ego trip, be full of oneself; indulge oneself, pamper oneself, coddle oneself, consult one's own wishes, look after one's own interests, know which side one's bread is buttered on, take care of number one, look out for number one, take care of numero uno, look out for numero uno, think only of oneself; want everything, have one's cake and eat it; covet; monopolize, hog

ADJS 5 **selfish, self-seeking, self-serving,** self-advancing, self-promoting, self-advertising, careerist, opportunistic, ambitious for self, self-indulgent, self-pleasing, hedonistic, self-jealous, self-sufficient, self-interested, self-considerative, self-besot, self-devoted, self-occupied, self-absorbed, wrapped up in oneself, self-contained, autistic, remote; self-esteeming, self-admiring; self-centered, self-obsessed, narcissistic, egotistical; possessive; avaricious, greedy, covetous, grasping, graspy, grabby, acquisitive; individualistic, personalistic, privatistic

6 **ungenerous,** illiberal, unchivalrous, mean, small, little, paltry, mingy, petty; niggardly, stingy

ADVS 7 **selfishly, for oneself,** in one's own interest, from selfish movies, from self-interested motives, to gain some private ends

652 UNSELFISHNESS

<generosity and regard for others>

NOUNS 1 **unselfishness, selflessness;** self-subjection, self-subordination, self-suppression, self-abasement, self-effacement; humility; modesty; self-neglect, self-neglectfulness, self-forgetfulness; self-renunciation, self-renouncement; self-denial, self-abnegation; self-sacrifice, sacrifice, self-immolation, self-devotion, devotion, dedication, commitment, consecration; disinterest, disinterestedness; unpossessiveness, unacquisitiveness; **altruism**; martyrdom

2 **magnanimity,** magnanimousness, greatness of spirit, greatness of soul, **generosity,** generousness, openhandedness, liberality, liberalness; bigness, bigheartedness, greatheartedness, largeheartedness, big heart, great heart, greatness of heart; noble-mindedness, high-mindedness, idealism; benevolence; nobleness, nobility, princeliness, greatness, loftiness, elevation, exaltation, sublimity; chivalry, chivalrousness, knightliness, errantry, knight-errantry; heroism; consideration, considerateness, compassion

VERBS 3 not have a selfish bone in one's body, think only of others; be generous to a fault; put oneself out, go out of the way, lean over backwards; sacrifice, make a sacrifice; subject oneself, subordinate oneself, abase oneself; show compassion; take a backseat

4 observe the golden rule, do as one would be done by, do unto others as you would have others do unto you

ADJS 5 **unselfish, selfless;** self-unconscious, self-forgetful, self-abasing, self-effacing; **altruistic,** humble; unpretentious, modest; self-neglectful, self-neglecting; self-denying, self-renouncing, self-abnegating, self-abnegatory; self-sacrificing, self-immolating, sacrificing, self-devotional, self-devoted, devoted, dedicated, committed, consecrated, unsparing of self, disinterested; unpossessive, unacquisitive; ready to die for, martyred

6 **magnanimous,** great-souled, –great-spirited; **generous,** generous to a fault, openhanded, liberal; big, bighearted, greathearted, largehearted, great of heart, great of soul; noble-minded, high-minded, idealistic, public-spirited; benevolent, noble, princely, handsome, great, high, elevated, lofty, exalted, sublime; chivalrous, knightly; heroic

ADVS 7 **unselfishly, altruistically,** forgetful of self; for others

8 **magnanimously,** generously, openhandedly,

liberally; bigheartedly, greatheartedly, largeheartedly; nobly, handsomely; chivalrously, knightly

653 VIRTUE

<moral goodness>

NOUNS 1 **virtue, virtuousness, goodness,** righteousness, rectitude, right conduct, right, behavior, the straight and narrow, the right thing, integrity; probity; morality, moral fiber, moral rectitude, moral virtue, moral excellence, morale; saintliness, saintlikeness, angelicalness; godliness; aretaics

2 **purity,** immaculacy, immaculateness, spotlessness, unspottedness; upstandingness; uncorruptness, uncorruptedness, incorruptness; angel, saint, good egg; unsinfulness, sinlessness, unwickedness, uniniquitousness; undegenerateness, undepravedness, undissoluteness, undebauchedness; chastity; guiltlessness, innocence

3 **cardinal virtues,** natural virtues; prudence, justice, temperance, fortitude; theological virtues, supernatural virtues; faith, hope, charity, love

VERBS 4 **be good,** do no evil, do the right thing; keep in the right path, walk the straight path, follow the straight and narrow, keep on the straight and narrow path, fly right, resist temptation; fight the good fight

ADJS 5 **virtuous, good,** moral; upright, honest; righteous, just, straight, rightminded, right-thinking; angelic, seraphic; saintly, saintlike; godly; irreproachable; goody-goody

6 chaste, immaculate, spotless, **pure**; clean, squeaky-clean; guiltless, innocent; pure as the driven snow

7 **uncorrupt,** uncorrupted, incorrupt, incorrupted; unsinful, sinless; unwicked, uniniquitous, unerring, unfallen; undegenerate, undepraved, undemoralized, undissolute, undebauched

654 VICE

<moral badness>

NOUNS 1 **vice,** viciousness; criminality, **wrongdoing**; immorality, unmorality, evil; low road; amorality; unvirtuousness, ungoodness; unrighteousness, ungodliness, unsaintliness, unangelicalness; uncleanness, impurity, unchastity, fallenness, fallen state, lapsedness; waywardness, wantonness, prodigality; delinquency, moral delinquency; peccability; backsliding, recidivism; evil nature, carnality

2 **vice, weakness,** weakness of the flesh, flaw, moral flaw, moral blemish, frailty, infirmity; failing, failure; weak point, weak side, foible; bad habit, besetting sin; fault, imperfection; laxity, lack of principle

3 **iniquity, evil,** bad, wrong, error, obliquity, villainy, knavery, reprobacy, peccancy, abomination, atrocity, infamy, shame, disgrace, scandal, unforgivable sin, cardinal sin, mortal sin, sin; seven deadly sins, pride, covetousness, avarice, lust, anger, gluttony, envy, sloth

4 **wickedness, badness**, naughtiness, evilness, viciousness, sinfulness, iniquitousness, wicked ways; baseness, rankness, vileness, foulness, arrantness, nefariousness, heinousness, infamousness, villainousness, flagitiousness; fiendishness, hellishness; devilishness, devilry, deviltry; bad egg

5 turpitude, **moral turpitude; corruption,** corruptedness, corruptness, rottenness, moral pollution, moral pollutedness, absence of moral fiber; decadence, decadency, debasement, degradation, demoralization, abjection; degeneracy, degenerateness, degeneration, reprobacy, depravity, depravedness, depravation, perversion; dissoluteness, profligacy; abandonment, abandon; notoriety; low road

6 obduracy, hardheartedness, hardness, **callousness,** heartlessness, hardness of heart, heart of stone

7 **sewer,** gutter, pit, sink, sink of corruption, sinkhole; den of iniquity, den, fleshpot, hellhole; hole, joint, the pits; Sodom, Gomorrah, Babylon; brothel; road to hell

VERBS 8 **do wrong, sin**; misbehave, misdemean, misdo

9 **go wrong,** stray, go astray, err, deviate, deviate from the path of virtue, leave the straight and narrow, step out of line, go off base; fall, fall from grace, lapse, slip, trip; degenerate; go to the bad, go to the dogs; relapse, recidivate, backslide

10 **corrupt;** sully, soil, defile; demoralize, vitiate; mislead; seduce, tempt

ADJS 11 vice-prone, vice-laden, vicious, steeped in vice; **immoral**, unmoral; amoral, nonmoral; unethical

12 **unvirtuous,** virtueless, ungood; unrighteous, ungodly, unsaintly, unangelic; morally weak, lax; unclean, impure, spotted, flawed, blemished, maculate, unchaste; fleshly, carnal, wayward, wanton, prodigal; erring, fallen, lapsed, postlapsarian; frail, weak, infirm; Adamic; peccable; relapsing, backsliding, recidivist, recidivistic; of easy virtue

13 diabolic, diabolical, **devilish,** demonic, demoniac,

demoniacal, **satanic,** Mephistophelian; fiendish, fiendlike; hellish, hellborn, infernal

14 **corrupt,** corrupted, vice-corrupted, polluted, morally polluted, rotten, tainted, contaminated, vitiated; warped, perverted; decadent, debased, degraded, reprobate, depraved, debauched, debaucherous, dissolute, degenerate, profligate, abandoned, gone to the dogs, steeped in iniquity, rotten to the core, in the sewer, in the gutter

15 **evil-minded,** evilhearted, blackhearted; base-minded, low-minded; low-thoughted, dirty, dirty-minded; crooked

16 **wicked, evil,** vicious, bad, naughty, wrong, sinful, iniquitous, peccant, reprobate; dark, black; base, low, vile, foul, rank, flagrant, arrant, nefarious, heinous, villainous, criminal, up to no good, knavish, flagitious; abominable, atrocious, monstrous, unspeakable, execrable, damnable; shameful, disgraceful, scandalous, infamous, unpardonable, unforgivable; improper, reprehensible, blamable, blameworthy, unworthy

17 **hardened,** hard, case-hardened, obdurate, inured, indurated; **callous,** calloused, seared; hardhearted, heartless; shameless, lost to shame, blind to virtue, lost to all sense of honor, conscienceless, unblushing, brazen

18 irreclaimable, irredeemable, unredeemable, unregenerate, irreformable, incorrigible, past praying for; shriftless, graceless; lost

ADVS **19** **wickedly,** evilly, sinfully, iniquitously, peccantly, viciously; basely, vilely, foully, rankly, arrantly, flagrantly, flagitiously

655 WRONGDOING

<immoral or illegal behavior>

NOUNS **1** **wrongdoing, evildoing, wickedness,** misdoing, wrong conduct, misbehavior, misconduct, misdemeaning, misfeasance, malfeasance, malversation, malpractice, evil courses, machinations of the devil; sin; crime, criminality, lawbreaking, feloniousness, trespass, offense, transgression, infringement, infraction, breach, encroachment; criminal tendency; habitual criminality, criminosis; viciousness, vice; misprision, negative misprision, positive misprision, misprision of treason, misprision of felony; gang violence

2 **misdeed, misdemeanor,** misfeasance, malfeasance, malefaction, criminal act, **offense,** injustice, injury, **wrong,** iniquity, evil, peccancy, *malum* <L>; tort; error, fault, breach; impropriety, slight wrong, minor wrong, venial sin, indiscretion, peccadillo, misstep, trip, slip, lapse; transgression, trespass; sin; cardinal sin, deadly sin, mortal sin, grave sin, heavy sin, unutterable sin, unpardonable sin, unforgivable sin, inexpiable sin, original sin, capital sin, carnal sin; sin against the Holy Ghost; sin of commission; sin of omission, nonfeasance, omission, failure, dereliction, delinquency; crime, felony; capital crime; white-collar crime, execu-crime; computer crime; copycat crime; war crime, crime against humanity, genocide, terrorism; outrage, atrocity, enormity; car chase, gang violence

3 **original sin,** fall from grace, fall, fall of man, fall of Adam, Adam's fall, sin of Adam; **cardinal sins,** lust, gluttony, greed, sloth, wrath, envy, pride

VERBS **4** **do wrong,** do amiss, misdo, misdemean oneself, misbehave, err, offend; sin, commit sin; transgress, trespass

ADJS **5** **wrongdoing, evildoing,** malefactory, malfeasant; **wrong,** iniquitous, sinful, wicked; criminal, felonious, criminous; crime-infested, crime-ridden

656 GUILT

<sin or breach of law>

NOUNS **1** **guilt, guiltiness;** guilt complex; criminality, peccancy; guilty involvement, wrongful involvement, criminal involvement; culpability, reprehensibility, blame, blamability, blameworthiness; chargeability, answerability, much to answer for; censurability, censurableness, reproachability, reproachableness, reprovability, reprovableness, inculpation, implication, involvement, complicity, impeachability, impeachableness, indictability, indictableness, arraignability, arraignableness; bloodguilt, blood-guiltiness, red-handedness, dirty hands, red hands, bloody hands; ruth, ruefulness, remorse, guilty conscience, guilt feelings; onus, burden; blame game, blameshifting

VERBS **2** **be guilty**, look guilty, have no alibi, look like the cat that swallowed the canary, blush, stammer; have on one's hands, have to one's discredit, have much to answer for; have a red face; be caught in the act, be caught flatfooted, be caught redhanded, be caught with one's pants down, be caught with one's hand in the till, be caught with one's hand in the cookie jar; guilt someone

ADJS **3** **guilty,** guilty as hell, peccant, criminal, to blame, at fault, faulty, in the wrong, on one's head; culpable, reprehensible, censurable, reproachable, reprovable, inculpated, implicated, involved, impeachable, indictable, arraignable; red-handed, bloodguilty; caught in the act, caught flatfooted, caught red-handed, caught with one's pants down, caught with one's hand in the till, caught with one's hand in the cookie jar

ADVS 4 **red-handed,** red-hand, in the act, in the very act, *in flagrante delicto* <L>

5 **guilty,** shamefacedly, sheepishly, with a guilty conscience

657 INNOCENCE

<freedom from guilt or sin>

NOUNS 1 **innocence,** innocency, innocentness; unfallen state, unlapsed state, prelapsarian state, state of grace; unguiltiness, **guiltlessness,** faultlessness, blamelessness, reproachlessness, sinlessness, offenselessness; spotlessness, stainlessness, taintlessness, unblemishedness; purity, cleanness, cleanliness, whiteness, immaculateness, immaculacy, impeccability; clean hands, clean slate, clear conscience, nothing to hide

2 childlikeness; lamblikeness, dovelikeness, angelicness; unacquaintance with evil, uncorruptedness, incorruptness, pristineness, undefiledness; naiveté

3 **inculpability,** unblamability, unblamableness, unblameworthiness, irreproachability, irreproachableness, impeccability, impeccableness, unexceptionability, unexceptionableness, irreprehensibility, irreprehensibleness, uncensurability, uncensurableness, unimpeachability, unimpeachableness, unindictableness, unarraignableness

4 **innocent,** baby, babe, babe in arms, newborn babe, infant, babe in the woods, child, mere child, lamb, dove, angel; virgin

VERBS 5 know no wrong, have clean hands, have a clear conscience, look as if butter would not melt in one's mouth; have nothing to hide

ADJS 6 **innocent;** unfallen, unlapsed, prelapsarian; **unguilty,** not guilty, guiltless, faultless, blameless, reproachless, sinless, offenseless, with clean hands; clear, in the clear; without reproach; innocent as a lamb, lamblike, dovelike, angelic, childlike; unacquainted with evil, untouched by evil, uncorrupted, incorrupt, pristine, undefiled; innocuous

7 **spotless,** stainless, taintless, unblemished, unspotted, untainted, unsoiled, unsullied, **undefiled**, wemless; pure, clean, immaculate, impeccable, white, pure as driven snow, white as driven snow, squeaky-clean

8 **inculpable,** unblamable, unblameworthy, irreproachable, beyond reproach, irreprovable, irreprehensible, uncensurable, unimpeachable, unindictable, unarraignable, unobjectionable, unexceptionable, above suspicion, squeaky-clean, with clean hands

ADVS 9 **innocently, guiltlessly**, unguiltily, with a clear conscience; unknowingly, unconsciously, unawares

658 ATONEMENT

<repayment for offense>

NOUNS 1 **atonement, reparation, amends,** making amends, restitution, propitiation, expiation, redress, recompense, compensation, setting right, making right, making good, making up, squaring, redemption, reclamation, satisfaction, quittance; making it quits; indemnity, indemnification; compromise, composition; expiatory offering, expiatory sacrifice, piaculum, peace offering; eye for an eye, measure for measure; conciliation

2 **apology, excuse,** regrets; acknowledgment, penitence, contrition, breast-beating, *mea culpa* <L>, confession; abject apology

3 **penance,** penitence, repentance; penitential act, penitential exercise, mortification, maceration, flagellation, lustration; sacrifice, offering, peace offering; asceticism, fasting; purgation, purgatory; sackcloth and ashes; hair shirt; Lent; Day of Atonement, Yom Kippur

VERBS 4 **atone, atone for,** propitiate, expiate, compensate, restitute, recompense, redress, redeem, repair, satisfy, give satisfaction, **make amends**, make reparation, make compensation, make expiation, make restitution, make good, make right, rectify, set right, make up for, make matters up, square, square things, make it quits, pay the forfeit, pay the penalty, pay one's dues, pay back, wipe off old scores; wipe the slate clean; set one's house in order; live down, unlive; reconcile

5 **apologize,** beg pardon, **ask forgiveness,** beg indulgence, express regret; take back; fall down on one's knees, get down on one's marrowbones, come hat in hand; confess, admit

6 **do penance,** flagellate oneself, mortify oneself, mortify one's flesh, make oneself miserable, shrive oneself, purge oneself, cleanse oneself of guilt, stand in a white sheet, repent in sackcloth and ashes, wear a hair shirt, wear sackcloth, wear sackcloth and ashes; receive absolution; regret, show remorse, show compunction

ADJS 7 **atoning,** propitiatory, expiatory, piacular, reparative, reparatory, restitutive, restitutory, restitutional, redressing, recompensing, compensatory, compensational, righting, squaring, conciliatory; redemptive, redeeming, reclamatory, satisfactional; apologetic, apological; repentant, repenting; penitential, purgative, purgatorial; lustral, lustrative, lustrational, cleansing, purifying; ascetic

659 GOOD PERSON

<*moral person*>

NOUNS **1** **good person**, fine person, worthy, prince, nature's nobleman, noblewoman, person after one's own heart; *persona grata* <L>, acceptable person; good fellow, capital fellow, good sort, right sort, a decent sort of fellow, good lot, no end of a fellow; real person, mensch, cool cat; gentleman, perfect gentleman, a gentleman and a scholar; lady, perfect lady; gem, jewel, pearl, diamond; rough diamond, diamond in the rough; honest man

2 <nonformal> **good egg,** good guy, crackerjack, brick, trump, stout fellow, nice guy, Mr. Nice Guy, good Joe, likely lad, no slouch, doll, living doll, pussycat, sweetheart, sweetie

3 **good citizen,** respectable citizen, exemplary citizen, good neighbor, burgher, taxpayer, pillar of society, pillar of the church, salt of the earth; Christian, true Christian

4 **paragon, ideal,** beau ideal, nonpareil, person to look up to, **good example, role model,** shining example, gold standard; exemplar, epitome; model, pattern, standard, norm, mirror; *Übermensch* <Ger>; standout, one in a thousand, one in ten thousand, man of men, a man among men, woman of women, a woman among women

5 **hero,** god, demigod, phoenix; **heroine,** goddess, demigoddess; idol; fairy godmother

6 holy man; great soul, mahatma; guru, saint, angel

660 BAD PERSON

<*immoral person*>

NOUNS **1** **bad person**, unworthy person, disreputable person, unworthy, disreputable, undesirable, ***persona non grata*** <L>, unacceptable person, unwanted person, objectionable person, baddy, wrongo, bad news; bad egg, bad example

2 **bag egg,** wretch, miserable wretch, beggarly fellow, beggar, blighter, rotten apple; bum, bummer, lowlifer, lowlife, mucker, caitiff, pilgarlic; devil, poor devil, poor creature; sad case, sad sack, sad sack of shit*; good-for-nothing, good-for-naught, no-good, ne'er-do-well, wastrel, worthless fellow; derelict, skid-row bum, Bowery bum, tramp, hobo, beachcomber, drifter, drunkard, vagrant, vag, vagabond, truant, stiff, bindlestiff, swagman, sundowner <Austral>; human wreck; trailer trash, white trash

3 **rascal,** precious rascal, rogue, knave, **scoundrel,** villain, blackguard, scamp, scalawag, rapscallion, devil; shyster; sneak

4 **reprobate,** recreant, miscreant, bad lot, sorry lot, wrongo, wrong number, bad'un, wrong'un; scapegrace, black sheep; lost soul, lost sheep, backslider, recidivist, fallen angel; degenerate, pervert; profligate, lecher; trollop, whore; pimp

5 <offensive or nonformal> **jerk**, asshole*, prick, bastard*, son of a bitch* (SOB), horse's ass*, creep, motherfucker*, mother, dork, shit*, turd, birdturd, shithead*, shitface*, cunt*, cuntface*, dickhead*, fart, louse, meanie, heel, shitheel*, rat, rat bastard*, stinker, stinkard, pill, bugger, dirtbag, dweeb, twerp, sleaze, sleazoid, sleazebag, bad lot; slime, slimeball; jamoke, hood, hooligan

6 **beast**, animal; cur, dog, hound, whelp, mongrel; reptile, viper, serpent, snake; vermin, varmint, hyena; swine, pig; skunk, polecat; insect, worm

7 cad, bounder, rotter

8 **wrongdoer,** malefactor, sinner, transgressor, delinquent; malfeasor, misfeasor, nonfeasor; misdemeanant, misdemeanist; culprit, offender; evil person, evil man, evil woman, evil child, evildoer

9 **criminal,** felon, perpetrator, crook, perp, public enemy, lawbreaker, scofflaw; gangster, mobster, wiseguy, racketeer; swindler; thief; thug; desperado, desperate criminal; outlaw, fugitive, convict, con, jailbird, gaolbird <Brit>; gallows bird, ex-con; traitor, betrayer, quisling, Judas, double-dealer, two-timer, deceiver; stalker; gang member; most wanted

10 **the underworld,** gangland, gangdom, organized crime, organized crime family, the rackets, the mob, the syndicate, the Mafia, Cosa Nostra, Black Hand; gangsterism; gangster, ganglord, gangleader, caporegime, capo, button man, soldier

11 **the wicked,** the bad, the evil, the unrighteous, the reprobate; sons of men, sons of Belial, sons of the devil, children of the devil, limbs of Satan, children of darkness; scum of the earth, dregs of society

661 DISREPUTE

<*lack of good reputation*>

NOUNS **1** **disrepute, ill repute,** bad repute, bad reputation, poor reputation, evil repute, evil reputation, ill fame, shady reputation, unsavory reputation, bad name, bad odor, bad report, bad character; disesteem, dishonor, public dishonor, discredit; disfavor, ill-favor; disapprobation; bad rep

2 disreputability, disreputableness, **notoriety;** discreditableness, dishonorableness, unsavoriness, unrespectability; disgracefulness, shamefulness

3 **baseness, lowness,** meanness, crumminess, poorness, pettiness, paltriness, smallness, littleness, pokiness, cheesiness, beggarliness, shabbiness, shoddiness, squalor, scrubbiness, scumminess, scabbiness, scurviness, scruffiness, shittiness*; abjectness, wretchedness, miserableness, despicableness, contemptibleness, contemptibility, abominableness, execrableness, obnoxiousness; vulgarity, tastelessness, crudity, crudeness, tackiness, chintziness; vileness, foulness, rankness, fulsomeness, grossness, nefariousness, heinousness, atrociousness, monstrousness, enormity; degradation, debasement, depravity

4 **infamy,** infamousness; ignominy, ignominiousness; ingloriousness, ignobility, odium, obloquy, opprobrium; depluming, despluming, loss of honor, loss of name, loss of repute, loss of face; degradation, comedown, demotion

5 **disgrace,** scandal, humiliation; **shame,** dirty shame, low-down dirty shame, crying shame, burning shame; reproach, byword, byword of reproach, a disgrace to one's name

6 **stigma,** stigmatism, onus; brand, badge of infamy; slur, reproach, censure, reprimand, imputation, aspersion, reflection, stigmatization; pillorying; black eye, black mark; disparagement; stain, taint, attaint, tarnish, blur, smirch, smutch, smooch, smudge, smear, spot, blot, blot on one's escutcheon; bend sinister, bar sinister <heraldry>; baton, champain, point champain <heraldry>; mark of Cain; broad arrow <Brit>; shady past

VERBS 7 **disgrace oneself,** incur disgrace, incur dishonor, incur discredit, get a black eye, be shamed, earn a bad name, earn reproach, forfeit one's good opinion, fall into disrepute, seal one's infamy; lose one's good name, lose face, lose countenance, lose credit, lose caste; lower oneself, demean oneself, drag one's banner in the dust, degrade oneself, debase oneself, act beneath oneself, dirty one's hands, soil one's hands, get one's hands dirty, derogate, stoop, descend, ride to a fall, fall from one's high estate, fall from grace, fall from favor, foul one's own nest; scandalize, make oneself notorious, put one's good name in jeopardy; compromise oneself; raise eyebrows, cause eyebrows to raise, cause tongues to wag

8 **disgrace, dishonor, discredit,** reflect discredit upon, bring into discredit, reproach, cast reproach upon, be a reproach to; **shame,** put to shame, impute shame to, hold up to shame; hold up to public shame, hold up to public ridicule, pillory, bring shame upon, humiliate; degrade, debase, deplume, displume, defrock, unfrock, bring low

9 **stigmatize,** brand; stain, besmirch, smirch, tarnish, taint, attaint, blot, blacken, smear, bespatter, desecrate, sully, soil, defile, vilify, slur, cast a slur upon, blow upon; disapprove; disparage, defame; censure, reprimand, give a black eye, give a black mark, put in one's bad books; give a bad name, give a dog a bad name; expose, expose to infamy; pillory, gibbet; burn in effigy, hang in effigy; skewer, impale, crucify

ADJS 10 **disreputable,** discreditable, dishonorable, unsavory, shady, seamy, sordid; unrespectable, ignoble, ignominious, infamous, inglorious; notorious; unpraiseworthy; derogatory

11 **disgraceful, shameful,** pitiful, deplorable, opprobrious, sad, sorry, too bad; degrading, debasing, demeaning, beneath one, beneath one's dignity, *infra indignitatem* <L>, infra dig, unbecoming, unworthy of one; cheap, gutter; humiliating, humiliative; scandalous, shocking, outrageous, disheartening, soul-crushing

12 **base, low,** low-rent, low ride, low-down, cotton-picking, mean, crummy, poor, petty, paltry, small, little, shabby, shoddy, squalid, lumpen, scrubby, scummy, scabby, scurvy, scruffy, mangy, measly, cheesy, poky, beggarly, wretched, miserable, abject, despicable, contemptible, abominable, execrable, obnoxious, vulgar, tasteless, crude, tacky, chintzy; disgusting, odious, vile, foul, dirty, rank, fulsome, gross, flagrant, grave, arrant, nefarious, heinous, reptilian, atrocious, monstrous, unspeakable, unmentionable; degraded, debased, depraved

13 **in disrepute,** in bad repute, in bad odor; in disfavor, in discredit, in bad, in one's black books, out of favor, out of countenance, at a discount; in disgrace, in Dutch, in the doghouse, under a cloud; scandal-plagued, scandal-ridden; stripped of reputation, disgraced, discredited, dishonored, shamed, loaded with shame, unable to show one's face; in trouble

14 unrenowned, renownless, nameless, **inglorious,** unnotable, unnoted, unnoticed, unremarked, undistinguished, unfamed, uncelebrated, unsung, unhonored, unglorified, unpopular; no credit to; unknown, little known, obscure, unheard-of

ADVS 15 **disreputably,** discreditably, dishonorably, unrespectably, ignobly, ignominiously, infamously, ingloriously

16 **disgracefully,** scandalously, shockingly, deplorably, outrageously; **shamefully,** to one's shame, to one's shame be it spoken

17 **basely, meanly,** poorly, pettily, shabbily, shoddily, scurvily, wretchedly, miserably, abjectly, despicably, contemptibly, abominably, execrably, obnoxiously, odiously, vilely, foully, grossly, flagrantly, arrantly, nefariously, heinously, atrociously, monstrously

662 REPUTE

<good reputation>

NOUNS 1 **repute, reputation**; **name,** character, figure; **fame,** famousness, **renown**, kudos, report, glory; éclat, celebrity, popularity, recognition, a place in the sun; popular acceptance, popular favor, vogue; acclaim, public acclaim, réclame, publicity; notoriety, notoriousness, talk of the town; exposure; play, airplay; good rep

2 **reputability,** reputableness; good reputation, good name, good repute, high repute, good report, good track record, good odor, face, fair name, name to conjure with; good reference; good color

3 **esteem,** estimation, honor, regard, respect, approval, approbation, account, favor, consideration, credit, credibility, points, brownie point

4 **prestige,** honor; dignity; rank, standing, stature, high place, eminence, position, station, face, status

5 **distinction,** mark, note; importance, consequence, significance; notability, prominence, eminence, preeminence, greatness, conspicuousness, outstandingness; stardom; elevation, exaltation, exaltedness, loftiness, high and mightiness; nobility, grandeur, sublimity; excellence, supereminence

6 **illustriousness,** luster, brilliance, brilliancy, radiance, splendor, resplendence, resplendency, refulgence, refulgency, refulgentness, glory, blaze of glory, nimbus, halo, aura, envelope; charisma, mystique, glamour, numinousness, magic; cult of personality, personality cult; claim to fame; fifteen minutes of fame; hall of fame; all-American

7 **<posthumous fame>** memory, remembrance, blessed memory, sacred memory, legend, heroic legend, heroic myth; **immortality,** lasting fame, undying fame, niche in the hall of fame, secure place in history; immortal name

8 **glorification,** ennoblement, dignification, exaltation, elevation, enskying, enskyment, magnification, aggrandizement; enthronement; immortalization, enshrinement; beatification, canonization, sainting, sanctification; deification, apotheosis; lionization

9 **celebrity,** person of mark, person of note, person of consequence, notable, notability, luminary, great person, eminence, master spirit, worthy, name, big name, figure, public figure, somebody; important person, very important person (VIP), standout, personage, one in a hundred, one in a million; cynosure, model, very model, ideal type, idol, popular idol, tin god, little tin god; lion, social lion, pillar of the community; hero, heroine, popular hero, pop hero, folk hero, superhero; star, **superstar,** megastar, hot stuff; cult figure, cult hero; **immortal;** luminaries, galaxy, pleiad, constellation; celebutante; semicelebrity; favorite; honored guest, honoree

VERBS 10 **be somebody,** be something, impress, charismatize; figure, cut a figure, cut a dash, make a splash, make a noise in the world, make one's mark, leave one's mark; live, flourish; shine, glitter, gleam, glow

11 **gain recognition,** be recognized, get a reputation, **make a name**, make a name for oneself, make oneself known, come into one's own, come to the front, come to the fore, come into vogue; burst onto the scene, become an overnight celebrity, come onto the scene, come out of the woods, come out of nowhere, come out of left field; make points, make Brownie points

12 **honor,** confer honor upon, bestow honor upon; dignify, adorn, grace; distinguish, signalize, confer distinction on, give credit where credit is due

13 **glorify,** glamorize; exalt, elevate, ensky, raise, uplift, set up, ennoble, aggrandize, magnify, exalt to the skies; crown; throne, enthrone; immortalize, enshrine, hand one's name down to posterity, make legendary; beatify, canonize, saint, sanctify; deify, apotheosize, apotheose; lionize

14 **reflect honor,** lend credit, lend distinction, shed a luster, redound to one's honor, give one a reputation

ADJS 15 **reputable,** highly reputed, of repute, estimable, **esteemed,** much esteemed, highly esteemed, honorable, honored; meritorious, worth one's salt, noble, worthy, creditable; respected, respectable, highly respectable; revered, reverend, venerable, venerated, worshipful; well-thought-of, highly regarded, held in esteem, in good odor, in favor, in high favor; in one's good books; prestigious

16 **distinguished,** distingué; noted, notable, marked, of note, of mark; **famous,** famed, honored,

renowned, celebrated, popular, in favor, acclaimed, much acclaimed, sought-after, hot, world-class, notorious, well-known, best-known, in everyone's mouth, on everyone's tongue, on everyone's lips, talked-of, talked-about; far-famed, far-heard; fabled, legendary, mythical

17 **prominent,** conspicuous, outstanding, stickout, much in evidence, to the front, in the limelight; important, consequential, significant

18 **eminent,** high, exalted, elevated, enskyed, lofty, sublime, held in awe, awesome; immortal; great, big, grand; excellent, supereminent, mighty, high-and-mighty; glorified, ennobled, magnified, aggrandized; enthroned, throned; immortalized, shrined, enshrined; beatified, canonized, sainted, sanctified; idolized, godlike, deified, apotheosized

19 **illustrious,** lustrous, glorious, brilliant, radiant, splendid, splendorous, splendrous, splendent, resplendent, bright, shining; charismatic, glamorous, numinous, magic, magical

ADVS 20 **reputably,** estimably, honorably, nobly, respectably, worthily, creditably

21 **famously,** notably, notedly, notoriously, popularly, celebratedly; prominently, eminently, conspicuously, outstandingly; illustriously, gloriously

663 SENSUALITY

<sensual desire>

NOUNS 1 **sensuality,** sensualness, sensualism; appetitiveness, appetite; **voluptuousness,** luxuriousness, luxury; unchastity; pleasure-seeking; sybaritism; self-indulgence, hedonism, Cyrenaic hedonism, Cyrenaicism, ethical hedonism, psychological hedonism, hedonics, hedonic calculus; epicurism, epicureanism; pleasure principle; instant gratification; sensuousness

2 **carnality,** carnal-mindedness; fleshliness, flesh; animal nature, carnal nature, the flesh, the beast, Adam, the Old Adam, the offending Adam, fallen state, fallen nature, lapsed state, lapsed nature, postlapsarian nature; animality, animalism, bestiality, beastliness, brutishness, brutality; coarseness, grossness; swinishness; earthiness, unspirituality, nonspirituality, materialism; erotica

3 **sensualist,** voluptuary, pleasure-seeker, sybarite, Cyrenaic, Sardanapalus, Heliogabalus, **hedonist,** *bon vivant* <Fr>, carpet knight; epicure, epicurean; gourmet, gourmand; swine

VERBS 4 sensualize, carnalize, coarsen, brutify; *carpe diem* <L, seize the day>, live for the moment

ADJS 5 **sensual,** sensualist, sensualistic; appetitive; voluptuous, luxurious; **unchaste**, **hedonistic,** pleasure-seeking, pleasure-bent, bent on pleasure, luxury-loving, hedonic, epicurean, sybaritic; Cyrenaic; sensory, sensuous

6 **carnal,** carnal-minded, fleshly, bodily, physical; Adamic, fallen, lapsed, postlapsarian; animal, animalistic; brutish, brutal, brute; bestial, beastly, beastlike; Circean; coarse, gross; swinish; orgiastic; earthy, unspiritual, nonspiritual, material, materialistic

664 CHASTITY

<abstention from sexual intercourse>

NOUNS 1 **chastity,** virtue, virtuousness, honor; purity, cleanness, cleanliness; whiteness, snowiness; immaculacy, immaculateness, spotlessness, stainlessness, taintlessness, blotlessness, unspottedness, unstainedness, unblottedness, untaintedness, unblemishedness, unsoiledness, unsulliedness, **undefiledness**, untarnishedness; uncorruptness; sexual innocence, innocence

2 **decency,** seemliness, propriety, decorum, decorousness, elegance, delicacy; **modesty,** shame, pudicity, pudency

3 abstemiousness, abstaining, abstinence; celibacy; **virginity,** intactness, maidenhood, maidenhead; Platonic love; marital fidelity, marital faithfulness; continence, continency

ADJS 4 **chaste,** virgin, virtuous; pure, purehearted, pure in heart; clean, cleanly; immaculate, spotless, blotless, stainless, taintless, white, snowy, pure as driven snow, white as driven snow; unsoiled, unsullied, undefiled, untarnished, unstained, unspotted, untainted, unblemished, unblotted, uncorrupt; sexually innocent, innocent

5 decent, **modest**, decorous, delicate, elegant, proper, becoming, seemly

6 **virgin;** abstemious, abstinent; celibate; virginal, maidenly, vestal, intact; Platonic; continent

7 undefiled, undebauched, undissipated, undissolute, unwanton, unlicentious

665 UNCHASTITY

<partaking often in sexual intercourse>

NOUNS 1 **unchastity,** unchasteness; unvirtuousness; impurity, uncleanness, uncleanliness, taintedness, soiledness, sulliedness; indecency

2 incontinence, **uncontinence**; intemperance; unrestraint

3 **profligacy,** dissoluteness, licentiousness, license, unbridledness, wildness, fastness, rakishness, gallantry, libertinism, libertinage; dissipation,

debauchery, debauchment; venery, wenching, whoring, womanizing

4 wantonness, waywardness; looseness, laxity, lightness, loose morals, easy virtue, whorishness, chambering, **promiscuity,** sleeping around, swinging

5 **lasciviousness,** lechery, lecherousness, lewdness, bawdiness, **dirtiness**, salacity, salaciousness, carnality, animality, fleshliness, sexuality, sexiness, lust, lustfulness; obscenity; prurience, pruriency, sexual itch, concupiscence, lickerishness, libidinousness, randiness, horniness, lubricity, lubriciousness, sensuality, eroticism, goatishness; satyrism, satyriasis, gynecomania; nymphomania, hysteromania, uteromania, clitoromania; erotomania, eroticomania, aphrodisiomania

6 **seduction,** seducement, betrayal; feminine wile; violation, abuse; **debauchment, defilement,** ravishment, ravage, despoilment, fate worse than death; priapism; defloration, deflowering; rape, sexual assault, criminal assault; date rape, acquaintance rape

7 <illicit sexual intercourse> **adultery,** criminal conversation, criminal congress, criminal cohabitation, extramarital sex, premarital sex, extramarital relations, premarital relations, extracurricular sex, extracurricular relations, fornication; free love, free-lovism; incest; concubinage; cuckoldry

8 **prostitution,** harlotry, whoredom, street-walking; soliciting, solicitation; Mrs. Warren's profession; whoremonging, whoremastery, pimping, pandering

9 **brothel,** house of prostitution, house of assignation, house of joy, house of ill repute, whorehouse, bawdyhouse, massage parlor, sporting house, disorderly house, cathouse, bordello, bagnio, stew, dive, den of vice, den of iniquity, crib, joint; panel den; red-light district, tenderloin, stews, street of fallen women

10 libertine, swinger, profligate, rake, rakehell, rip, roué, wanton, **womanizer,** cocksman, walking phallus, debauchee, rounder, wolf, woman chaser, skirt chaser, gay dog, gay deceiver, gallant, philanderer, loverboy, lady-killer, Lothario, Don Juan, Casanova

11 **lecher,** satyr, goat, old goat, dirty old man; whorer, whoremonger, whoremaster, whorehound; Priapus; gynecomaniac; erotomaniac, eroticomaniac, aphrodisiomaniac

12 **seducer,** betrayer, deceiver; debaucher, ravisher, ravager, violator, despoiler, defiler; raper, rapist

13 **adulterer,** cheater, fornicator; **adulteress,** fornicatress, fornicatrix

14 <offensive or nonformal> trumpet, trollop, wench, hussy, slut, jade, baggage, *cocotte* <Fr>, grisette; tart, chippy, floozy, broad, bitch*, drab, trull, quean, harridan, Jezebel, harlot, wanton, whore, bad woman, loose woman, easy woman, easy lay, woman of easy virtue, frail sister; pickup; nymphomaniac, nymphet, nympho, hysteromaniac, uteromaniac, clitoromaniac; porn star

15 **seductress,** sex symbol, demimonde, demimondaine, demirep; courtesan, adventuress, femme fatale, blonde bombshell, fatal attraction, vampire, vamp, temptress; hetaera, houri, harem girl, odalisque; Jezebel, Messalina, Delilah, Thais, Phryne, Aspasia, Lais

16 **prostitute,** harlot, whore*, daughter of joy, lady of the evening, call girl, B-girl, scarlet woman, unfortunate woman, painted woman, fallen woman, erring sister, streetwalker, hustler, **hooker**, woman of the town, stew, meretrix, Cyprian, Paphian; white slave

17 **mistress,** woman, kept woman, kept mistress, paramour, concubine, doxy, playmate, spiritual wife, unofficial wife; live-in lover; other woman

18 procurer, **pimp,** pander, panderer, mack, mackman, ponce; bawd; **gigolo,** fancy man; procuress, **madam**; white slaver

VERBS 19 **be promiscuous,** sleep around, bedhop, swing; debauch, wanton, rake, chase women, womanize, whore, sow one's wild oats; philander; dissipate; fornicate, cheat, **commit adultery,** get a little on the side; grovel, wallow, wallow in the mire

20 **seduce,** betray, deceive, mislead, lead astray, lead down the garden path, lead down the primrose path; debauch, ravish, ravage, despoil, ruin; deflower, pop one's cherry; defile, soil, sully; violate, abuse; rape, force

21 **prostitute oneself,** sell one's ass*, streetwalk; pimp, procure, pander, whore

22 **cuckold;** wear horns, wear the horn

ADJS 23 **unchaste,** unvirtuous, unvirginal; impure, unclean; indecent; soiled, sullied, smirched, besmirched, defiled, tainted, maculate

24 **incontinent,** uncontinent; **orgiastic;** intemperate; unrestrained

25 **profligate,** licentious, unbridled, untrammeled, uninhibited, free; dissolute, dissipated, debauched, abandoned; **wild, fast,** gallant, gay, rakish; rakehell, rakehellish, rakehelly

26 **wanton,** wayward, Paphian; loose, lax, slack, loose-moraled, of loose morals, of easy virtue, easy, light, no better than she should be, whorish, chambering, **promiscuous**

27 freeloving; **adulterous,** illicit, extramarital, premarital; incestuous

28 **prostitute,** prostituted, whorish, harlot, scarlet, fallen, meretricious, streetwalking, hustling, on the town, on the streets, on the *pavé,* in the life, on the corner

29 **lascivious,** lecherous, sexy, salacious, carnal, animal, sexual, lustful, ithyphallic, hot, horny, sexed-up, hot to trot; prurient, itching, itchy; concupiscent, lickerish, libidinous, randy, lubricious; lewd, bawdy, adult, X-rated, hard, pornographic, porn, porno, dirty, obscene; erotic, sensual, fleshly; goatish, satyric, priapic, gynecomaniacal; nymphomaniacal, hysteromaniacal, uteromaniacal, clitoromaniacal; erotomaniacal, eroticomaniacal, aphrodisiomaniacal

666 INDECENCY

<offensive or shocking in nature>

NOUNS 1 **indecency,** indelicacy, inelegance, inelegancy, indecorousness, indecorum, **impropriety**, inappropriateness, unseemliness, indiscretion, indiscreetness; unchastity

2 **immodesty,** unmodestness, impudicity; exhibitionism; **shamelessness,** unembarrassedness; brazenness, brassiness, pertness, forwardness, boldness, procacity, bumptiousness; flagrancy, notoriousness, scandal, scandalousness

3 **vulgarity**, uncouthness, coarseness, crudeness, grossness, rankness, rawness, raunchiness; earthiness, frankness; spiciness, raciness, saltiness

4 **obscenity,** dirtiness, bawdry, raunch, ribaldry, **pornography,** porno, porn, hardcore pornography, soft porn, soft-core pornography, salacity, smut, dirt, filth; lewdness, bawdiness, salaciousness, smuttiness, foulness, filthiness, nastiness, vileness, offensiveness; scurrility, fescenninity; Rabelaisianism; erotic art, erotic literature, pornographic art, pornographic literature; sexploitation; blue movie, dirty movie, porno film, skin flick, adult movie, stag film, X-rated movie; pornographomania, erotographomania, iconolagny, erotology; dirty talk, scatology

ADJS 5 **indecent,** indelicate, inelegant, indecorous, improper, inappropriate, unseemly, unbecoming, indiscreet

6 **immodest,** unmodest; exhibitionistic; **shameless,** unashamed, unembarrassed, unabashed, unblushing, brazen, brazenfaced, brassy; forward, bold, pert, procacious, bumptious; flagrant, notorious, scandalous

7 **risqué,** risky, racy, salty, spicy, off-color, suggestive, scabrous

8 **vulgar,** uncouth, coarse, gross, rank, raw, broad, low, foul, gutter; earthy, frank, pulling no punches

9 **obscene,** lewd, adult, bawdy, ithyphallic, ribald, pornographic, salacious, sultry, lurid, dirty, smutty, raunchy, blue, smoking-room, impure, unchaste, unclean, foul, filthy, nasty, vile, fulsome, offensive, unprintable, unrepeatable, not fit for mixed company; scurrilous, scurrile, Fescennine; foulmouthed, foul-tongued, foul-spoken; Rabelaisian

667 ASCETICISM

<self-denial>

NOUNS 1 **asceticism,** ascetism, **austerity,** self-denial, self-abnegation, rigor; puritanism, eremitism, anchoritism, anchorite monasticism, anchoritic monasticism, monasticism, monachism; Sabbatarianism; Albigensianism, Waldensianism, Catharism; Yoga; mortification, self-mortification, maceration, flagellation; abstinence; belt-tightening, fasting; voluntary poverty, mendicantism, Franciscanism; Trappism

2 **ascetic, puritan,** Sabbatarian; Albigensian, Waldensian, Catharist; abstainer; anchorite, hermit; yogi, yogin; sannyasi, bhikshu, dervish, fakir, flagellant, Penitente; Buddha, bodhi; eremite; mendicant, Franciscan, barefooted Carmelite; Trappist

VERBS 3 deny oneself; abstain, tighten one's belt; flagellate oneself, wear a hair shirt, make oneself miserable

ADJS 4 **ascetic, austere,** self-denying, self-abnegating, rigorous, rigoristic; puritanical, eremitic, anchoritic, Sabbatarian; penitential; Albigensian, Waldensian, Catharist; abstinent; mendicant, discalced, barefoot, wedded to poverty, Franciscan; Trappist; flagellant; eremitical

668 TEMPERANCE

<moderation in action>

NOUNS 1 **temperance,** temperateness, **moderation,** moderateness, middle way, sophrosyne; golden mean, via media; nothing in excess, sobriety, soberness, frugality, forbearance, abnegation; renunciation, renouncement, forgoing; denial, self-denial; restraint, constraint, self-restraint; self-control, self-reining, self-mastery, discipline, self-discipline

2 **abstinence,** abstention, abstainment, abstemiousness, refraining, refrainment, avoidance, eschewal, denying oneself, refusing oneself, saying no to, passing up; total abstinence,

teetotalism, nephalism, Rechabitism; the pledge; Encratism, Shakerism; Pythagorism, Pythagoreanism; sexual abstinence, celibacy; chastity; gymnosophy; Stoicism; vegetarianism, veganism, fruitarianism, pescatarianism, flexitarianism; plain living, spare diet, simple diet; Spartan fare, Lenten fare; fish day, banyan day; fast; continence; asceticism; smokeout

3 prohibition, prohibitionism; Eighteenth Amendment, Volstead Act

4 abstainer, abstinent; **teetotaler,** teetotalist, sobersides; nephalist, Rechabite, hydropot, water-drinker; vegetarian, vegan, fruitarian, pescetarian, flexitarian, pescatarian; banian, banya; gymnosophist; Pythagorean, Pythagorist; Encratite, Apostolici, Shaker; ascetic; nonsmoker, nondrinker; moderationist

5 prohibitionist, dry; Anti-Saloon League; Women's Christian Temperance Union

VERBS **6 restrain oneself,** constrain oneself, curb oneself, hold back, avoid excess; limit oneself, restrict oneself; control oneself, control one's appetites, repress one's desires, inhibit one's desires, contain oneself, discipline oneself, master oneself, exercise self-control, exercise self-restraint, keep oneself under control, keep within bounds, keep within limits, know when one has had enough, deny oneself, refuse oneself, say no, just say no; live simply, live frugally; mortify oneself, mortify the flesh, control the fleshy lusts, control the carnal man, control the old Adam; eat to live, not live to eat; eat sparingly, diet; tighten one's belt

7 abstain, abstain from, refrain, **refrain from,** forbear, forgo, spare, withhold, hold back, avoid, shun, eschew, pass up, keep from, hold aloof from, have nothing to do with, take no part in, have no hand in, let alone, let well enough alone, let go by, deny oneself, do without, go without, make do without, not touch, never touch, keep hands off; fast

8 swear off, renounce, forswear, give up, abandon, stop, discontinue; take the pledge, get on the wagon, get on the water wagon, go on the wagon; kick, kick the habit, dry out

ADJS **9 temperate, moderate,** sober, frugal, restrained, sparing, stinting, measured

10 abstinent, abstentious, abstemious; teetotal, sworn off, on the wagon, on the water wagon; nephalistic, Rechabite; Encratic, Apostolic, Shaker; Pythagorean; sexually abstinent, celibate, chaste; Stoic; fasting; vegetarian, veganistic, vegan, fruitarian, uneaten, undevoured; Spartan, Lenten; maigre, meatless; continent; ascetic

11 prohibitionist, antisaloon, dry

ADVS **12 temperately,** moderately, sparingly, stintingly, frugally, in moderation, within compass, within bounds

669 INTEMPERANCE

<lack of moderation>

NOUNS **1 intemperance,** intemperateness, **indulgence,** self-indulgence, self-absorption; instant gratification; **overindulgence,** overdoing; unrestraint, unconstraint, indiscipline, uncontrol; immoderation, immoderacy, immoderateness; inordinacy, inordinateness; excess, excessiveness, too much, too-muchness; addiction; prodigality, extravagance; crapulence, crapulency, crapulousness; incontinence; swinishness, gluttony; drunkenness

2 dissipation, licentiousness; riotous living, free living, high living, fast pace, killing pace, fast lane, burning the candle at both ends; **debauchery,** debauchment; carousal, carousing, carouse; debauch, orgy, saturnalia; hedonism, sybaritism

3 dissipater, rounder, free liver, high liver; nighthawk, nightowl; debauchee; playboy, partyer, partygoer, party girl, **party animal**; pleasure-seeker

VERBS **4 indulge,** indulge oneself, indulge one's appetites, indulge in easy vices, deny oneself nothing, deny oneself not at all; give oneself up to, give free course to, give free rein to; live well, live high, live high on the hog, live it up, live off the fat of the land; indulge in, luxuriate in, wallow in; roll in; look out for number one

5 overindulge, overdo, carry to excess, carry too far, go the limit, go whole hog, know no limits, not know when to stop, bite off more than one can chew, spread oneself too thin; dine not wisely but too well; live above one's means, live beyond one's means; binge

6 dissipate, plunge into dissipation, debauch, wanton, carouse, run riot, live hard, live fast, squander one's money in riotous living, burn the candle at both ends, keep up a fast pace, keep up a killing pace, not know when to stop, sow one's wild oats, have one's fling, **party**; eat, drink, and be merry

ADJS **7 intemperate, indulgent,** self-indulgent; overindulgent, overindulging, unthrifty, unfrugal, immoderate, inordinate, excessive, too much, prodigal, extravagant, extreme, unmeasured, unlimited; crapulous, crapulent; undisciplined, uncontrolled, unbridled, unconstrained, uninhibited, unrestrained; incontinent; swinish, gluttonous; bibulous; party-hearty

8 **licentious, dissipated,** riotous, dissolute, debauched; free-living, high-living

9 orgiastic, saturnalian, corybantic

ADVS **10** **intemperately,** prodigally, **immoderately,** inordinately, excessively, in excess, to excess, to extremes, beyond all bounds, beyond all limits, without restraint; high, high on the hog

670 MODERATION

<avoidance of extreme action>

NOUNS **1** **moderation,** moderateness; restraint, constraint, control; judiciousness, prudence; steadiness, evenness, balance, equilibrium, stability; temperateness, temperance, sobriety; self-abnegation, self-restraint, self-control, self-denial; abstinence, continence, abnegation; mildness, lenity, gentleness; calmness, serenity, tranquillity, repose, calm, cool; unexcessiveness, unextremeness, unextravagance, nothing in excess; **happy medium,** golden mean, middle way, middle path, *via media* <L>, balancing act; moderationism, conservatism; nonviolence, pacifism, pacification, peace movement, ahimsa; impartiality, neutrality, dispassion; irenics, ecumenism

2 modulation, **abatement,** remission, **mitigation,** diminution, defusing, de-escalation, reduction, lessening, falling-off; relaxation, relaxing, slackening, easing, loosening, letup, letdown; alleviation, assuagement, allayment, palliation, leniency, relenting, lightening, tempering, softening, moderating, moderative, subdual; deadening, dulling, damping, blunting; drugging, narcotizing, sedating, sedation; pacification, tranquilization, tranquilizing, mollification, demulsion, dulcification, quieting, quietening, lulling, soothing, calming, hushing

3 **moderator, mitigator,** modulator, stabilizer, temperer, assuager; mediator, bridge-builder, calming hand, restraining hand, wiser head; alleviator, alleviative, palliative, lenitive; pacifier, soother, comforter, peacemaker, pacificator, dove of peace, mollifier; drug, anodyne, dolorifuge, soothing syrup, tranquilizer, calmative; sedative; balm, salve; cushion, shock absorber

4 **moderate,** moderatist, moderationist, middle-of-the-roader, centrist, neutral, compromiser; conservative

VERBS **5** **be moderate,** keep within bounds, keep within compass; practice self-control, practice self-denial, live within one's means, live temperately, do nothing in excess, **find balance,** strike a balance, keep a happy medium, seek the golden mean, steer an even course, keep to the middle way, be between Scylla and Charybdis; keep the peace, not resist, practice nonviolence, be pacifistic; not rock the boat, not make waves; cool it, keep one's cool, keep one's head, keep one's temper; sober down, settle down; remit, relent; take in sail; go out like a lamb; be conservative

6 **moderate, restrain,** constrain, control, keep within bounds; modulate, mitigate, defuse, abate, weaken, diminish, reduce, de-escalate, slacken, lessen, slow down; alleviate, assuage, allay, lay, lighten, palliate, extenuate, temper, attemper, lenify; soften, subdue, tame, hold in check, keep a tight rein, chasten, underplay, play down, downplay, de-emphasize, tone down; turn down the volume, lower the voice; drug, narcotize, sedate, tranquilize, deaden, dull, blunt, obtund, take the edge off, take the sting out, take the bite out; smother, suppress, stifle; damp, dampen, bank the fire, reduce the temperature, throw cold water on, throw a wet blanket on; sober, sober down, sober up; clear the air

7 **calm,** calm down, stabilize, tranquilize, pacify, mollify, appease, dulcify; quiet, hush, still, rest, compose, lull, soothe, gentle, rock, cradle, rock to sleep; cool, subdue, quell; ease, steady, smooth, smoothen, smooth over, smooth down, even out; keep the peace, be the dove of peace, pour oil on troubled waters, pour balm into

8 **cushion,** absorb the shock, **soften the blow,** break the fall, deaden, damp, dampen, soften, suppress, neutralize, offset; show pity, show mercy, show consideration, show sensitivity, temper the wind to the shorn lamb

9 **relax,** unbend; ease, **ease up,** ease off, let up, let down; abate, bate, remit, mitigate; slacken, slack, slake, slack off, slack up; loose, loosen; unbrace, unstrain, unstring

ADJS **10** **moderate, temperate,** sober; mild, soft, bland, gentle, tame; mild as milk, mild as mother's milk, mild as milk and water, gentle as a lamb; nonviolent, peaceable, peaceful, pacifistic; judicious, prudent

11 **restrained,** constrained, limited, controlled, stable, in control, in hand; tempered, softened, hushed, subdued, quelled, chastened

12 unexcessive, **balanced,** unextreme, unextravagant, conservative; reasonable

13 **equable,** even, low-key, low-keyed, cool, even-tempered, levelheaded, dispassionate; tranquil, reposeful, serene, calm

14 **mitigating,** assuaging, abating, diminishing, reducing, lessening, allaying, alleviating, relaxing, easing; tempering, **softening,** chastening, subduing; deadening, dulling, blunting, damping, dampening, cushioning; acid-neutralizing

15 **tranquilizing,** pacifying, mollifying, appeasing; cooling-off; **calming,** lulling, gentling, rocking, cradling, hushing, quietening, stilling; soothing, soothful, restful; dreamy, drowsy

16 **palliative,** alleviative, alleviatory, assuasive, lenitive, calmative, calmant, narcotic, sedative, demulcent, anodyne; antiorgastic, anaphrodisiac

ADVS **17** **moderately, in moderation,** restrainedly, subduedly, within reason, within bounds, within compass, in balance; temperately, soberly, prudently, judiciously, dispassionately; composedly, calmly, coolly, evenly, steadily, equably, tranquilly, serenely; soothingly, conservatively

671 VIOLENCE

<*physically harmful action*>

NOUNS **1** **violence,** vehemence, virulence, venom, furiousness, **force,** rigor, roughness, harshness, ungentleness, extremity, impetuosity, inclemency, severity, intensity, acuteness, sharpness; acrimony; fierceness, ferociousness, ferocity, viciousness, insensateness, savagery, destructiveness, destruction, vandalism; terrorism, barbarity, brutality, atrocity, inhumanity, bloodlust, killer instinct, murderousness, malignity, mercilessness, pitilessness, mindlessness, animality, brutishness; rage, raging, anger; domestic violence

2 **turbulence, turmoil,** chaos, upset, **fury,** furor, rage, frenzy, passion, fanaticism, zealousness, zeal, tempestuousness, storminess, wildness, tumultuousness, tumult, uproar, racket, cacophony, pandemonium, hubbub, commotion, disturbance, agitation, bluster, broil, brawl, embroilment, brouhaha, fuss, flap, row, rumpus, ruckus, foofaraw, ferment, fume, boil, boiling, seething, ebullition, fomentation; all hell let loose

3 **unruliness, disorderliness,** obstreperousness, Katy-bar-the-door; riot, rioting; looting, pillaging, plundering, rapine; wilding; laying waste, sowing with salt, sacking; scorched earth; attack, assault, onslaught, battering; criminal behavior, rape, violation, forcible seizure; killing, butchery, massacre, slaughter

4 **storm,** tempest, squall, line squall, tornado, cyclone, hurricane, tropical cyclone, typhoon, tsunami, storm center, tropical storm, eye of the storm, war of the elements; stormy weather, rough weather, foul weather, dirty weather; rainstorm; thunderstorm; windstorm; snowstorm; firestorm; bombogenesis, bomb cyclone

5 **upheaval,** convulsion, cataclysm, catastrophe, disaster; meltdown; fit, spasm, paroxysm, apoplexy, stroke; climax; earthquake, quake, temblor, diastrophism, epicenter, shock wave; tidal wave, tsunami

6 **outburst,** outbreak, eruption, debouchment, eructation, belch, spew; burst, dissilience, dissiliency; meltdown, atomic meltdown; torrent, rush, gush, spate, cascade, spurt, jet, rapids, volcano, volcan, burning mountain

7 **explosion, discharge,** blowout, blowup, detonation, fulmination, blast, burst, report; flash, flashpoint, flashing point, flare, flare-up, fulguration; bang, boom; backfire

8 **concussion, shock,** impact, crunch, smash; percussion, repercussion

9 <**violent person**> berserk, berserker; hothead, hotspur; devil, demon, fiend, brute, hellhound, hellcat, hellion, hell-raiser; beast, wild beast, tiger, dragon, mad dog, wolf, monster, mutant, savage; rapist, mugger, killer; Mafioso, hit man, contract killer, hired killer, hired gun; fury, virago, vixen, termagant, beldam, she-wolf, tigress, witch; firebrand, revolutionary, terrorist, incendiary, bomber, guerrilla, suicide bomber

10 <nonformal> **goon,** gorilla, ape, knuckle dragger, muscle man, plug-ugly, shtarker, cowboy, bozo, bruiser, hardnose, tough guy, tough, hoodlum, hood, meat-eater, gunsel, terror, holy terror, fire-eater, spitfire, tough customer, ugly customer

VERBS **11** **rage, storm,** rant, rave, roar; rampage, ramp, tear, tear around; carry on; come in like a lion; destroy, wreck, wreak havoc, ruin; sow chaos, sow disorder; terrorize, sow terror, vandalize, barbarize, brutalize; riot, loot, burn, pillage, sack, lay waste; slaughter, butcher; rape, violate; attack, assault, batter, savage, mug, maul, hammer; go for the jugular

12 **seethe, boil, fume,** foam, simmer, stew, ferment, stir, churn, see red

13 **erupt,** burst forth, burst out, break out, blow out, blow open, eruct, belch, vomit, spout, spew, disgorge, discharge, eject, throw forth, hurl forth

14 **explode,** blow up, burst, go off, go up, blow out, blast, bust; detonate, fulminate; touch off, trigger, trip, set off, let off; discharge, fire, shoot; backfire; melt down

15 **run amok,** go berserk, go on a rampage, cut loose, run riot, run wild

ADJS **16** **violent,** vehement, virulent, venomous, severe, rigorous, furious, fierce, intense, sharp, acute, keen, cutting, splitting, piercing; **destructive**; rough, bruising, contusive, tough; drastic, extreme, outrageous, excessive, exorbitant, unconscionable, intemperate, immoderate, extravagant; acrimonious; on the warpath

17 **unmitigated,** unsoftened, untempered, unallayed, unsubdued, unquelled; unquenched, unextinguished, unabated; unmixed, unalloyed; total

18 **turbulent,** tumultuous, raging, chaotic, hellish, anarchic, **storming,** stormy, tempestuous, troublous, frenzied, wild, wild-eyed, frantic, furious, infuriated, insensate, mad, demented, insane, enraged, ravening, raving, slavering; angry; blustering, blustery, blusterous; uproarious, rip-roaring; pandemoniac

19 **unruly, disorderly,** obstreperous; unbridled; riotous, wild, rampant; terroristic, anarchic, nihilistic, revolutionary

20 **boisterous, rampageous,** rambunctious, on the rampage, rumbustious, roisterous, wild, rollicking, rowdy, rough, hoody, harum-scarum; knockabout, rough-and-tumble, knock-down-and-drag-out

21 **savage, fierce, ferocious,** vicious, murderous, cruel, atrocious, mindless, brutal, brutish, bestial, insensate, monstrous, mutant, inhuman, pitiless, ruthless, merciless, bloody, sanguinary, kill-crazy; malign, malignant; feral, ferine; wild, untamed, tameless, undomesticated, ungentle; barbarous, barbaric; uncivilized, noncivilized

22 **fiery, heated,** inflamed, flaming, scorching, hot, red-hot, white-hot; fanatic, zealous, totally committed, hardcore, hard-line, ardent, passionate; hotheaded

23 **convulsive,** cataclysmic, disastrous, upheaving; seismic; spasmodic, paroxysmal, spastic, jerky, herky-jerky; orgasmic

24 **explosive,** bursting, detonating, explosible, explodable, fulminating, fulminant, fulminatory; cataclysmic; dissilient; volcanic, eruptive

ADVS 25 **violently, vehemently**, virulently, venomously, rigorously, severely, fiercely, drastically; furiously, wildly, madly, like mad, like fury, like blazes; all to pieces, with a vengeance

26 **turbulently,** tumultuously, riotously, uproariously, stormily, tempestuously, troublously, frenziedly, frantically, furiously, ragingly, enragedly, madly; angrily

27 **savagely, fiercely,** ferociously, atrociously, viciously, murderously, brutally, brutishly, mindlessly, bestially, barbarously, inhumanly, insensately, ruthlessly, pitilessly, mercilessly; tooth and nail, tooth and claw

672 GLUTTONY

<excessive eating, drinking>

NOUNS 1 **gluttony,** gluttonousness, **greed,** greediness, voraciousness, voracity, ravenousness, edacity, crapulence, crapulency, gulosity, rapacity, insatiability; omnivorousness; big appetite, piggishness, hoggishness, swinishness; overindulgence, overeating; eating disorder, polyphagia, hyperphagia, bulimia, bulimia nervosa, binge-purge syndrome, binging; intemperance

2 **epicureanism,** epicurism, gourmandise, gourmandism; gastronomy

3 **glutton,** greedy eater, big eater, hearty eater, good eater, trencherman, trencherwoman, belly-god, gobbler, greedygut, greedyguts, gorger, **gourmand,** gourmandizer, gormand, gormandizer, guttler, cormorant, bon vivant; animal, **hog, pig,** chow hound, khazer, wolf; omnivore; binger

VERBS 4 **gluttonize,** gormandize, indulge one's appetite, live to eat, love to eat; **gorge,** engorge, glut, cram, stuff, batten, guttle, guzzle, **devour,** raven, bolt, gobble, gulp, wolf, gobble down, gulp down, bolt down, wolf down, eat like a horse, tuck into, stuff oneself, hog it down, eat one's head off, fork it in, shovel it in, eat one out of house and home, wipe the plate clean

5 **overeat,** overgorge, overindulge, make a pig of oneself, make a hog of oneself, pig out, pork out, scarf; glut oneself, stuff oneself, blimp out

ADJS 6 **gluttonous, greedy,** voracious, ravenous, edacious, esurient, rapacious, insatiable, polyphagic, bulimic, hyperphagic, Apician; **piggish, hoggish,** swinish; crapulous, crapulent; intemperate; omnivorous, all-devouring; gorging, cramming, glutting, guttling, stuffing, guzzling, wolfing, bolting, gobbling, gulping, gluttonizing; binging

7 overfed, overgorged, overindulged

ADVS 8 **gluttonously,** greedily, voraciously, ravenously, edaciously; piggishly, hoggishly, swinishly

673 LEGALITY

<observance of law>

NOUNS 1 **legality, legitimacy,** lawfulness, legitimateness, licitness, rightfulness, validity, scope, applicability; jurisdiction; actionability, justiciability, constitutionality, constitutional validity; letter of the law; legal process, legal form, due process; legalism, constitutionalism; justice

2 **legalization,** legitimation, legitimatization, **decriminalization;** money-laundering; validation; authorization, sanction; legislation, enactment, authority, license, warrant

3 **law,** *lex, jus* <L>, statute, rubric, canon, institution; ordinance; act, enactment, measure, legislation; rule, ruling; prescript, prescription;

regulation, reg; dictate, dictation; form, formula, formulary, formality; standing order; bylaw; **edict**, decree; bill; manifesto, order, rescript, precept

4 the law, legal system, system of laws, legal branch, legal specialty

5 legal code, digest, pandect, capitulary, body of law, corpus juris, code, code of laws, digest of law; codification; civil code, penal code; Justinian Code; Napoleonic Code; lawbook, statute book, compilation; Blackstone; Uniform Code of Military Justice; written law, unwritten law, statute law, common law, private law, international law, military law, commercial law, contracts law, criminal law, civil law, labor law, constitutional law, case law; law of the land; canon, canon law

6 constitution, written constitution, unwritten constitution; law and equity; charter, codification, codified law; constitutional amendment; Bill of Rights, constitutional guarantees; constitutional interpretation

7 jurisprudence, law, legal science; nomology, nomography; **forensic science,** science of law, forensic medicine, legal medicine, medical jurisprudence, medico-legal medicine; forensic psychiatry; forensic chemistry, legal chemistry; criminology; constitutionalism, penology

8 <**codes of law**> Constitution of the U.S., Bill of Rights; Corpus Juris Civilis, Codex Juris Canonici, Pandects of Justinian; Law of Moses, Ten Commandments, Pentateuch, Torah, Koran, Qur'an, the Bible; Code of Hammurabi, Magna Carta, Napoleonic Code

VERBS **9 legalize, legitimize,** legitimatize, legitimate, make legal, declare lawful, **decriminalize;** launder money, wash money; validate; authorize, sanction, license, warrant; constitute, ordain, establish, put in force; prescribe, formulate; regulate, make a regulation, bring within the law; decree; legislate, enact; enforce; litigate, take legal action

10 codify, digest; compile, publish

ADJS **11 legal, legitimate,** legit, kosher, competent, by right, de jure, **licit, lawful,** rightful, according to law, within the law; actionable, litigable, justiciable, within the scope of the law; enforceable, legally binding; judicial, juridical; authorized, sanctioned, valid, applicable, warranted; constitutional; statutory, statutable; legalized, legitimized, decriminalized; legislative, lawmaking; lawlike; just

12 jurisprudent, jurisprudential; legalistic; **forensic;** nomistic, nomothetic; criminological

ADVS **13 legally,** legitimately, licitly, **lawfully,** by law, *de jure* <L>, in the eyes of the law, within the law

674 ILLEGALITY

<*disobeyance of law*>

NOUNS **1 illegality, unlawfulness,** illicitness, lawlessness, wrongfulness; unauthorization, impermissibility, unconstitutionality; legal flaw, technical flaw, legal irregularity; outlawry; anarchy, collapse of authority, breakdown of authority, paralysis of authority, anomie; illicit business

2 illegitimacy, illegitimateness, illegitimation; bastardy, bastardism; bend sinister, bar sinister, baton

3 lawbreaking, violation, breach of law, violation of law, infringement, contravention, infraction, transgression, trespass, trespassing, offense, breach, nonfeasance, encroachment; vice, fraud; crime, **criminality,** criminalism, habitual criminality, delinquency; flouting the law, making a mockery of the law

4 offense, wrong, illegality; violation; wrongdoing; much to answer for; **crime,** felony; misdemeanor; tort; delict, delictum

VERBS **5 break the law,** violate the law, breach the law, infringe, contravene, infract, violate, transgress, trespass, disobey the law, offend against the law, flout the law, make a mockery of the law, fly in the face of the law, set the law at defiance, snap one's fingers at the law, set the law at naught, circumvent the law, disregard the law, take the law into one's own hands, twist the law to one's own ends, torture the law to one's own purposes; commit a crime; have much to answer for; live outside the law

ADJS **6 illegal, unlawful,** illegitimate, illicit, nonlicit, nonlegal, lawless, wrongful, fraudulent, creative, against the law; unauthorized, unallowed, impermissible, unwarranted, unwarrantable, unofficial, unlicensed; unstatutory, instatutory, injudicial, extrajudicial; unconstitutional, nonconstitutional; flawed, irregular, contrary to law; actiónable, chargeable, justiciable, litigable; triable, punishable; **criminal,** felonious; outlaw, **outlawed**; contraband, bootleg, black-market; under-the-table, under-the-counter; unregulated, unchartered; anarchic, anarchistic, anomic

7 illegitimate, spurious, false; **bastard,** misbegot, misbegotten, miscreated, gotten on the wrong side of the blanket, baseborn, born out of wedlock, without benefit of clergy

ADVS **8 illegally,** unlawfully, illegitimately, illicitly; impermissibly; criminally, feloniously; contrary to law, in violation of law, against the law

675 RELIGIONS, CULTS, SECTS

<belief systems>

NOUNS 1 **religion** <see list>, religious belief, religious faith, **belief, faith,** teaching, doctrine, creed, credo, dogma, theology, orthodoxy; system of beliefs, belief system; persuasion, tradition

2 **cult,** ism; cultism; mystique, cult status

3 **sect** <see list>, sectarism, religious order, **denomination,** persuasion, faction, church, communion, community, group, fellowship, affiliation, order, school, party, society, body, organization; branch, variety, version, segment; offshoot; schism, division

4 **sectarianism,** sectarism, denominationalism, partisanism, the clash of creeds; schismatism; syncretism, eclecticism

5 **theism**; monotheism; polytheism, multitheism, myriotheism; ditheism, dyotheism, dualism; tritheism; tetratheism; pantheism, cosmotheism, theopantism, acosmism; physitheism, psychotheism, animotheism; physicomorphism; hylotheism; anthropotheism, anthropomorphism; anthropolatry; allotheism; monolatry, henotheism; autotheism; zootheism, theriotheism; deism

6 **animism,** animistic religion, animistic cult; voodooism, voodoo, hoodoo, wanga, juju, jujuism, obeah, obeahism; shamanism; fetishism, totemism; nature worship, naturism; primitive religion

7 **Christianity, Christian denomination** <see list>, Christianism, Christendom; Western Christianity, Latin Christianity, Roman Christianity; Eastern Christianity, Orthodox Christianity; Protestant Christianity; Judeo-Christian religion, Judeo-Christian belief; fundamentalism, Christian fundamentalism

8 **Catholicism,** Catholicity; Roman Catholicism, Romanism, Rome; papalism; popery, popeism, papism, papistry; ultramontanism; Catholic Church, Roman Catholic Church, Church of Rome; Eastern Rites, Uniate Rites, Uniatism, Alexandrian Rite, Antiochian Rite, Byzantine Rite

9 **Eastern Orthodoxy**, Orthodoxy; Eastern Orthodox Church, Holy Orthodox Catholic Apostolic Church, Greek Orthodox Church, Russian Orthodox Church; patriarchate of Constantinople, patriarchate of Antioch, patriarchate of Alexandria, patriarchate of Jerusalem

10 **Protestantism,** Reform, Reformationism; Evangelicalism; Zwinglianism; dissent; apostasy; new theology; Protestant ethic

11 **Anglicanism;** High-Churchism, Low-Churchism; Anglo-Catholicism; Church of England, Established Church; High Church, Low Church; Broad Church, Free Church

12 **Judaism;** Hebraism, Hebrewism; Israelitism; Orthodox Judaism, Conservative Judaism, Reform Judaism, Reconstructionism; Hasidism; rabbinism, Talmudism; Pharisaism; Sadduceeism; Karaism, Karaitism

13 **Islam,** Muslimism, Islamism, Moslemism, Muhammadanism, Mohammedanism; Sufism, Wahabiism, Sunnism, Shi'ism, Druzism; Black Muslimism; Muslim fundamentalism, militant Muslimism

14 **<other religions>** Buddhism, Zen Buddhism; Christian Science; Confucianism; Hinduism; Jainism; Mormonism; Rastafarianism; Shintoism; Sikhism; Zoroastrianism; Taoism; earth-based religion

15 **religionist,** religioner; zealot, iconoclast; **believer**; worshiper; cultist

16 **theist**; monotheist; polytheist, multitheist, myriotheist; ditheist, dualist; tritheist; tetratheist; pantheist, cosmotheist; psychotheist; physitheist; hylotheist; anthropotheist; anthropolater; allotheist; henotheist; autotheist; zootheist, theriotheist; deist

17 **Christian,** Nazarene, Nazarite; practicing Christian; Christian sectarian

18 **sectarian,** sectary, denominationalist, factionist, schismatic

19 **Catholic,** Roman Catholic (RC), Romanist, papist; ultramontane; Eastern-Rite Christian, Uniate

20 **Protestant,** non-Catholic, Reformed believer, Reformationist, Evangelical; Zwinglian; dissenter; apostate; Anglican, Episcopalian, Unitarian, born-again Christian

21 **Jew, Hebrew,** Judaist, Israelite; Orthodox Jew, Conservative Jew, Reform Jew, Reconstructionist; Hasid; Zionist; Essene; Rabbinist, Talmudist; Pharisee; Sadducee; Karaite

22 **Mormon,** Latter-day Saint, Josephite

23 **Muslim,** Muhammadan, Mohammedan, Mussulman, Moslem, Islamite; Shi'ite, Shia, Sectary; Motazilite, Sunni, Sunnite, Wahhabi, Sufi, Druze; dervish; abdal; Black Muslim; Muslim fundamentalist, Muslim militant

24 **Christian Scientist,** Christian Science practitioner; Buddhist, Zen Buddhist; Hindu; Sikh; Shintoist; Jainist; Rastafarian; Zoroastrian; Confucianist; Taoist

ADJS 25 **religious,** theistic; monotheistic; polytheistic, ditheistic, tritheistic; pantheistic, cosmotheistic; physicomorphic; anthropomorphic, anthropotheistic; deistic; theophoric

26 **sectarian,** sectary, denominational, schismatic, schismatical

27 **nonsectarian,** undenominational, **nondenominational;** interdenominational

28 **Protestant,** non-Catholic, Reformed, Reformationist, Evangelical; Lutheran, Calvinist, Calvinistic, Zwinglian; dissentient; apostate

29 **Catholic;** Roman Catholic (RC), Roman; Romish, popish, papish, papist, papistical; ultramontane

30 **Jewish,** Hebrew, Judaic, Judaical, Israelite, Israelitic, Israelitish; Orthodox, Conservative, Reform, Reconstructionist; Hasidic

31 **Muslim, Islamic,** Moslem, Islamitic, Islamistic, Muhammadan, Mohammedan; Shiite, Sunni, Sunnite

32 <Eastern religions> Buddhist, Buddhistic; Brahmanic, Brahmanistic; Vedic, Vedantic; Confucian, Confucianist; Taoist, Taoistic, Shintoist, Shintoistic; Zoroastrian, Zarathustrian, Parsee

33 **Christian denomination**

Adventism, Second Adventism
African Methodist Episcopal church
African Methodist Episcopal Zion church
Amish
Anabaptism
Anglicanism
Anglo-Catholicism
antinomianism
Arianism
Assemblies of God
Athanasianism
Baptist church
Boehmenism
Calvinism
Catholicism
Christadelphian
Christian Science, Church of Christ, Scientist
Churches of Christ
Churches of God
Churches of the Brethren
Churches of the Nazarene
Congregationalism
Coptic Church
Eastern Orthodox
Episcopalianism
Erastianism
Evangelicanism
Greek Orthodox
homoiousianism
homoousianism
Jansenism
Jehovah's Witness
latitudinarianism
Laudism, Laudianism
Liberal Catholicism
Lutheranism
Mennonitism
Methodism
Moral Rearmament
Mormonism
New Thought
Origenism
Orthodox Christianity
Oxford Movement
Pentecostal church
Practical Christianity
Presbyterianism
Puritanism
Puseyism
Quakerism, Society of Friends
quietism
Roman Catholicism
Rosicrucianism
Russian Orthodox
Sabellianism
Salvation Army
Seventh-day Adventist
Socinianism
Stundism
Swedenborgianism
Tractarianism
Trinitarianism
Ubiquitarianism
Uniatism
Unification church
Universalism
Wesleyanism, Wesleyism

34 **religion, sect**

anthroposophy
Babism, Babi
Baha'i, Bahaism
Brahmanism
Brahmoism
Buddhism
Ch'an Buddhism
Chen Yen Buddhism
Ching-t'u Buddhism
Christianity
Confucianism
Conservative Judaism
Dakshincharin Hinduism
Eleusinianism
Ethical Culture
Gnosticism
gymnosophy
Hare Krishna
Hasidism
Hinduism
Hinayana Buddhism
Islam
Jainism
Jodo Buddhism
Judaism
Lamaism
Lingayat Hinduism
Magianism
Mahayana Buddhism
Mandaeism
Mithraism
Nichiren Buddhism
Orphism
Orthodox Judaism
Parsiism, Parsism
Rastafarianism
Reconstructionism
Reform Judaism
reincarnationism
Rosicrucianism
Sabaeanism
Saivism
Shaivite Hinduism
Shamanism
Shiite Muslimism
Shin Buddhism
Shingon Buddhism
Shinto, Shintoism
Sikhism
Soka Gakkai Buddhism
Sufism
Sunni Muslimism
Taoism
Tendai Buddhism
Theosophy
Theravada Buddhism
T'ien-t'ai Buddhism
Unitarianism
Vaishnavite Hinduism
Vajrayana Buddhism
Vamacharin Hinduism
Vedanta, Vedantism
Wahabiism
Yoga, Yogism
Zen, Zen Buddhism
Zoroastrianism, Zoroastrism

676 THEOLOGY

<study of religion>

NOUNS **1** **theology, theology branch** <see list>, **religious study,** religion, divinity; theologism; doctrinism, doctrinalism; religious education

2 **doctrine, dogma**; **creed,** credo; credenda, articles of religion, articles of faith; Apostles' Creed, Nicene Creed, Athanasian Creed; Catechism

3 **theologian,** theologist, theologizer, theologer, theologician, theologue; divine; scholastic, schoolman; theological student, divinity student, theological; canonist

ADJS **4** **theological,** religious; divine; doctrinal, doctrinary, ecclesiological; canonic, canonical; physicotheological

5 **theology branch**

angelology
apologetics
Buddhist theology
canonics
Christian theology
Christology
covenant theology
crisis theology

demonology
doctrinal theology
dogmatics, dogmatic theology
eschatology
existential theology
feminist theology
fideism
hagiology
hierography, hagiography
hierology
Islamic theology
Judaism theology
liberation theology
Mercersburg theology
natural theology, rational theology
neo-orthodoxy, neo-orthodox theology
nonformalogical theology
patristics, patristic theology
phenomenological theology
philosophical theology
physicotheology
rationalism
sacerdotalism
school theology, scholastic theology
secularism
sophiology
soteriology, logos theology, logos Christology
systematics, systematic theology
theological hermeneutics

677 DEITY

<a god or worshipped being>

NOUNS 1 **deity, divinity,** divineness, supernatural being, immortal; godliness, godlikeness; godhood, godhead, godship, Fatherhood; heavenliness; divine essence; transcendence; god, goddess

2 **God;** Lord, Maker, Creator, Supreme Being, Almighty, King of Kings, Lord of Lords; Jehovah; *Yahweh, Adonai, Elohim* <all Heb>; Allah; the Great Spirit, Manitou, Prime Mover

3 <**Hinduism deity**> Brahma, the Supreme Soul, the Essence of the Universe; Atman, the Universal Ego, the Universal Self; Vishnu, the Preserver; Siva, the Destroyer, the Regenerator

4 <**Buddhism diety**> Buddha, the Blessed One, the Teacher, the Lord Buddha, bodhisattva, bodhi

5 <**Zoroastrianism**> Ahura Mazda, Ormazd, Mazda, the Lord of Wisdom, the Wise Lord, the Wise One, the King of Light, the Guardian of Mankind

6 <**Christian Science**> Mind, Divine Mind, Spirit, Soul Principle, Life, Truth, Love

7 **world spirit,** world soul, *anima mundi* <L>, universal life force, world principle, world-self, universal ego, universal self, infinite spirit, supreme soul, supreme principle, oversoul, nous, Logos, World Reason

8 Nature, **Mother Nature,** Dame Nature, Natura, Great Mother

9 Godhead, **Trinity;** Trimurti, Hindu trinity, Hindu triad

10 **Christ**, Jesus Christ, Jesus, Son of God, Emmanuel, Redeemer, Messiah; the Way, the Truth, and the Life; Light of the World

11 the Word, Logos, the Word Made Flesh, the Incarnation, God Incarnate, the Hypostatic Union

12 God the Holy Ghost, **the Holy Ghost, the Holy Spirit,** the Spirit of God, the Spirit of Truth, the Paraclete, the Comforter, the Intercessor, the Dove

13 <divine functions> creation, preservation, **dispensation**; providence, divine providence, dealings of providence, dispensations of providence, visitations of providence

14 <functions of Christ> salvation, redemption; atonement, propitiation; mediation, intercession; judgment

15 <functions of the Holy Ghost> inspiration, unction, regeneration, sanctification, comfort, consolation, grace, witness

ADJS 16 **divine,** heavenly, celestial, empyrean; godly, godlike; **transcendent,** superhuman, supernatural; self-existent; Christly, Christlike, redemptive, salvational, propitiative, propitiatory, mediative, mediatory, intercessive, intercessional; incarnate, incarnated, made flesh; messianic

17 **almighty, omnipotent,** all-powerful; creating, creative, making, shaping; **omniscient,** providential, all-wise, all-knowing, all-seeing; infinite, boundless, limitless, unbounded, unlimited, undefined, omnipresent, ubiquitous, zelig; perfect, sublime; eternal, everlasting, timeless, perpetual, immortal, permanent; one; immutable, unchanging, changeless, eternally the same; supreme, sovereign, highest; holy, hallowed, sacred, numinous; glorious, radiant, luminous; majestic; good, just, loving, merciful; triune, tripersonal, three-personed, three-in-one

678 MYTHICAL AND POLYTHEISTIC GODS AND SPIRITS

<gods, goddesses, spirits of mythology>

NOUNS 1 **the gods,** the immortals; the major deities, the greater gods; the minor deities, the lesser gods; pantheon; theogony; **spirits,** animistic spirit, animistic powers, manitou, huaca, nagual, mana, pokunt, tamanoas, wakan, zemi

2 **god,** *deus* <L>; deity, divinity, immortal, heathen god, pagan deity, pagan divinity; goddess, *dea* <L>; deva, devi, the shining ones; idol, false god, devil-god

3 godling, godlet, godkin; **demigod,** half-god, hero; cult figure; demigoddess, heroine

4 <**deity by religion**> **Celtic deity** <see list>, **Egyptian deity** <see list>, **Greek and Roman deity** <see list>, **Hindu deity** <see list>, **Norse and Germanic deity** <see list>, **specialized or tutelary deity** <see list>

5 **spirit,** intelligence, supernatural being; genius, daemon, demon; atua; specter; evil spirits

6 **elemental,** elemental spirit; sylph, spirit of the air; gnome, spirit of the earth, earth spirit; salamander, fire spirit; undine, water spirit, water-sprite

7 fairyfolk, elfenfolk, **the little people**, the little men, the good folk, denizens of the air; fairyland, faerie

8 **fairy,** sprite, fay, fairy man, fairy woman; elf, brownie, pixie, gremlin, ouphe, hob, cluricaune, puca, pooka, pwca, kobold, nisse, peri; imp, goblin; gnome, dwarf; garden gnome; sylph, sylphid; banshee; leprechaun; fairy queen; Ariel, Mab, Oberon, Puck, Titania, Béfind, Corrigan, Finnbeara; little green men

9 **nymph;** nymphet, nymphlin; dryad, hamadryad, wood nymph; vila, willi; tree nymph; oread, mountain nymph; limoniad, meadow nymph, flower nymph; Napaea, glen nymph; Hyades; Pleiades, Atlantides

10 **water spirit,** water god, water sprite, water nymph; undine, nix, nixie, kelpie; naiad, limniad, fresh-water nymph; Oceanid, Nereid, sea nymph, ocean nymph, mermaid, sea-maid, sea-maiden, siren; Thetis; merman, man fish; Neptune, the old man of the sea; Oceanus, Poseidon, Triton; Davy Jones, Davy

11 **forest spirit,** forest god, sylvan deity, vegetation spirit, vegetation daemon, field spirit, fertility god, corn spirit, faun, satyr, silenus, panisc, paniscus, panisca; Pan, Faunus; Cailleac; Priapus; Vitharr, Vidar, the goat god; Jack-in-the-green, Green Man, little green man

12 familiar spirit, familiar; genius, good genius, daemon, demon, *numen* <L>, totem; **guardian,** guardian spirit, guardian angel, angel, good angel, ministering angel, fairy godmother; guide, control, attendant godling, attendant spirit, invisible helper, special providence; tutelary god, tutelar god, tutelary genius, tutelary spirit; *genius tutelae, genius loci, genius domus, genius familiae* <all L>; household gods; penates, lares and penates; ancestral spirits; manes, pitris

13 **Santa Claus,** Santa, Saint Nicholas, Saint Nick, Kriss Kringle, Father Christmas

14 **mythology,** mythicism; legend, lore, folklore, mythical lore; fairy lore, fairyism; mythologist; urban legend, urban myth

ADJS 15 **mythic, mythical, mythological**; fabulous, legendary; folkloric

16 **divine,** godlike

17 fairy, faery, **fairylike,** fairyish, fay; sylphine, sylphish, sylphy, sylphidine, sylphlike; elfin, elfish, elflike; gnomish, gnomelike; pixieish

18 nymphic, nymphal, nymphean, nymphlike

19 **Celtic deity**

Aine
Amaethon
Angus Og
Arawn
Arianrhod
Blodenwedd
Bóann
Bodb
Bran
Brigit
Cernunnos
Dagda
Danu
Dewi
Dôn
Dylan
Epona
Fomorians
Goibniu
Gwydion
Lir
Llew Llaw Gyffes, Lleu
Lug, Lugh
Macha
Morrigan
Neman
Ogma
Ogmios
Rhiannon
Shannon
Teutates

20 **Egyptian deity**

Amon
Ammut
Anubis
Aten
Bast
Bastet
Bes
Buto
Geb
Hapi
Horus
Imhotep
Isis
Khem
Khensu
Ma'at
Min
Mut
Neph
Nephthys
Nut
Osiris
Ptah
Qebehsenuef
Ra, Amen-Ra, Amen-Re
Satet
Sekhmet
Selket
Seth, Set
Tefnut
Thoth

21 **Greek and Roman deity**

Aeolus
Apollo, Apollon, Phoebus, Phoebus Apollo
Athena, Minerva <Roman>
Bacchus, Dionysus
Chaos
Cupid, Amor, Eros <Gk>
Demeter, Ceres <Roman>
Diana, Artemis <Gk>
Erebus
Ge, Gaea, Gaia, Tellus <Roman>
Helios, Hyperion, Phaëthon
Hymen
Juno, Hera <Gk>
Lares and Penates
Mars, Ares <Gk>
Mercury, Hermes <Gk>
Mithras
Momus
Neptune, Poseidon <Gk>
Nike
Nyx
Olympic gods, Olympians
Persephone <Gk>, Proserpina, Proserpine
Pluto <Roman>, Hades, Dis, Orcus
Rhea, Ops
Saturn, Kronus <Gk>
Venus, Aphrodite <Gk>
Vesta, Hestia <Gk>
Vulcan, Hephaestus <Gk>
Zeus <Gk>, Jupiter <Roman>, Jove, Jupiter Fulgur, Fulminator, Jupiter Tonans, Jupiter Pluvius, Jupiter Optimus Maximus, Jupiter Fidius

22 **Hindu deity**
Aditi
Agni
Abhijit
Ardra
Aryaman
Asapurna
Asvins
Avalokita, Avalokitesvara
Bhaga
Bhairava
Bhairavi
Brahma
Bhudevi
Brihaspati
Candika
Candra
Chandi
Chitragupta
Daksha
Devaki
Devi
Dhara
Dharma
Dhatar
Dharti Mai
Didi Thakrun
Dipti
Durga
Dyaus
Ganesa, Ganesh, Ganesha, Ganapati
Garuda
Gauri
Hanuman
Hardaul
Himavat
Hiranyagarbha
Hotra
Indra, Indrani
Jaganmati
Ka
Kala
Kali
Kama
Kamsa
Karttikeya
Kaumudi
Krishna
Lakshmi
Malhal Mata
Manasa
Marut
Mitra
Narada
Parjanya
Parvati
Pushan, Pusan
Rahu
Rhibhus
Rudra
Sarasvati
Savitar
Siddhi
Sita
Siva, Shiva
Soma
Surya
Uma
Ushas
Vaja
Varuna
Varuni
Vayu
Vibhu
Vijaya
Vishnu
Vivasvan
Vrta
Yama

23 **Norse and Germanic deity**
Aesir
Asgard
Balder
Bor
Bori
Bragi
Forseti
Frey, Freyr
Freya, Freyja
Frigg, Frigga
Heimdall
Hel
Hermoder
Höder, Hödr
Hoenir
Ing
Ithunn, Idun
Loki
Nanna
Nerthus, Hertha
Njorth, Njord
Odin, Woden, Wotan
Reimthursen
Sif
Sigyn
Thor, Donar
Tyr, Tiu
Ull, Ullr
Vali
Vanir
Vitharr, Vidar
Völund
Wayland
Weland
Wyrd
Ymir

24 **specialized or tutelary deity**
agricultural deities
deities of fertility
deities of justice
deities of the household
deities of the netherworld
earth goddesses
Fates
forest gods
goddesses of discord
gods of commerce
gods of evil
gods of lightning
gods of marriage
love deities
moon goddesses
Muses
music Muses
poetry Muses
rain gods
sea gods
sun gods
thunder gods
war gods
water gods
wind gods

679 ANGEL, SAINT
<benevolent beings>

NOUNS 1 **angel,** celestial, celestial being, heavenly being; messenger of God; seraph, seraphim <pl>, angel of love; cherub, cherubim <pl>, angel of light; principality, archangel; recording angel; **saint,** beatified soul, canonized mortal; patron saint; martyr; redeemed soul, saved soul, soul in glory; guardian angel, divine messenger

2 **heavenly host,** host of heaven, choir invisible, angelic host, heavenly hierarchy, Sons of God, ministering spirits; Amesha Spentas

3 <**celestial hierarchy**> seraphim, cherubim, thrones; dominations, dominions, virtues, powers; principalities, archangels, angels; angelology

4 Azrael, **angel of death**, death's bright angel; Abdiel, Chamuel, Gabriel, Jophiel, Michael, Raphael, Uriel, Zadkiel

5 **the Madonna;** the Immaculate Conception; Mariology; Mariolatry

ADJS 6 **angelic,** angelical, seraphic, cherubic; heavenly, celestial; archangelic; **saintly, sainted,** full of grace, beatified, canonized; martyred; saved, redeemed, glorified, in glory

680 EVIL SPIRITS
<harmful presence>

NOUNS 1 **evil spirits, demons**, demonkind, powers of darkness, spirits of the air, host of hell, hellish host, hellspawn, denizens of hell, inhabitants of Pandemonium, souls in hell, damned spirits, lost souls, the lost, the damned

2 **devil,** *diable* <Fr>, *diablo* <Sp>, *diabolus* <L>, *diavolo* <Ital>

3 **Satan, Satan's designation** <see list>, Satanas

4 Beelzebub, Belial, Eblis, Azazel, Ahriman, Angra Mainyu; Mephistopheles, Mephisto; Shaitan,

Sammael, Asmodeus; Abaddon, Apollyon; Lilith; Aeshma, Pisacha, Putana, Ravana

5 <gods of evil> Set, Typhon, Loki; Nemesis; gods of the netherworld; Namtar, Azazel, Asmodeus, Baba Yaga

6 **demon,** fiend, fiend from hell, devil, Satan, daeva, rakshasa, dybbuk, shedu, bad spirit, evil spirit; hellion, hellhound, hellkite, she-devil; cacodemon, incubus, succubus; jinni, genie, genius, jinniyeh, afreet, afrit; evil genius; barghest; ghoul, lamia, Lilith, yogini, Baba Yaga, vampire, the undead

7 **imp,** pixie, sprite, elf, puck, kobold, tokoloshe, poltergeist, gremlin, Dingbelle, Fifinella, bad fairy, bad peri; little devil, young devil, devilkin, deviling; erlking; Puck, Robin Goodfellow, hobgoblin

8 **goblin, hobgoblin,** hob, ouphe

9 bugbear, bugaboo, **bogey,** bogle, boggart; bug, boogerman, bogeyman, boogeyman; bête noire, fee-faw-fum, Mumbo Jumbo

10 **Fury,** avenging spirit; the Furies, the Erinyes, the Eumenides, the Dirae; Alecto, Megaera, Tisiphone

11 **changeling,** elf child; shape-shifter, seachanger

12 **werefolk,** were-animals; werewolf, lycanthrope; werejaguar, jaguar-man, uturuncu; wereass, werebear, werecalf, werefox, werehyena, wereleopard, weretiger, werelion, wereboar, werecrocodile, werecat, werehare

13 **devilishness,** demonishness, fiendishness; devilship, devildom; horns, the cloven hoof, the Devil's pitchfork

14 **Satanism,** diabolism, devil-worship, **demonism,** devilry, diablerie, demonry; demonomy, demonianism; black magic; Black Mass; sorcery; demonolatry, demon worship, devil worship, chthonian worship; demonomancy; demonology, diabolology, diabology, demonography, devil lore

15 **Satanist,** Satan-worshiper, diabolist, devil-worshiper, demonist; demonomist, demoniast; demonologist, demonologer; demonolater, chthonian, demon worshiper; sorcerer

VERBS **16** **demonize,** devilize, diabolize; possess, obsess; bewitch, bedevil

ADJS **17** **demoniac, demoniacal,** demonic, demonical, demonish, demonlike; devilish, devil-like; satanic, diabolic, diabolical; hellish; fiendish, fiendlike; ghoulish, ogreish; foul, unclean, damned; inhuman

18 **impish,** puckish, elfish, elvish; mischievous

19 **Satan's designation**

Adversary
Angel of the bottomless pit
Angel of Darkness
Antichrist
Archfiend
Apollyon
Author of Evil, Father of Evil
Beelzebub
Common Enemy
Demon
Deuce
Devil Incarnate
Dickens
Eblis
Evil One
Evil Spirit
Father of Lies
Fiend
Foul Fiend
Haborym
His Satanic Majesty
Lord of the Flies
Lucifer
Mastema
Old Bendy
Old Enemy
Old Gentleman
Old Gooseberry
Old Harry
Old Ned
Old Nick
Old Clootie, Auld Clootie
Old Poker
Old Scratch
Old Serpent
O-Yama
Prince of Darkness
Prince of the Devils
Prince of the power of the air
Prince of this world
Shaitan
Tempter
Typhon
Wicked One

681 HEAVEN

<place where God or the good live>

NOUNS **1** **Heaven, Heaven's designation** <see list>

2 **the hereafter,** the afterworld, immortal life, life to come, immortality, eternal life, the afterlife, life after death

3 **Holy City,** Zion, New Jerusalem, Heavenly City, Celestial City, Kingdom of God, City Celestial, Heavenly City of God, City of God

4 Heaven of heavens, **seventh heaven,** the empyrean, throne of God, God's throne, celestial throne, the great white throne

5 <Christian Science> bliss, harmony, spirituality, the reign of Spirit, the atmosphere of Soul

6 <Mormon> celestial kingdom, terrestrial kingdom, telestial kingdom

7 <Muslim> Alfardaws, Assama, Assuma; Falak al Aflak

8 <Hindu, Buddhist, and Theosophical> nirvana; Buddha-field; devaloka, land of the gods; kamavachara, kamaloka; devachan; samadhi

9 <mythological> Olympus, Mount Olympus; Elysium, Elysian fields; fields of Aalu; Islands of the Blessed, Isles of the Blessed, Happy Isles, Fortunate Isles, Fortunate Islands; Avalon; garden of the Gods, abode of the Gods, garden of the Hesperides, Bower of Bliss; Tir-na-n'Og, Annwfn

10 <Norse> Valhalla, Asgard, Fensalir, Glathsheim, Vingolf, Valaskjalf, Hlithskjalf, Thruthvang, Thruthheim, Bilskirnir, Ydalir, Sökkvabekk, Breithablik, Folkvang, Sessrymnir, Noatun, Thrymheim, Glitnir, Himinbjorg, Vithi

11 **<removal to heaven>** apotheosis, resurrection, translation, gathering, ascension, the Ascension;

assumption, the Assumption; removal to Abraham's bosom

ADJS **12 heavenly,** heavenish; paradisal, paradisaic, paradisaical, paradisiac, paradisiacal, paradisic, paradisical; celestial, supernal, ethereal; empyrean, empyreal; unearthly, unworldly; otherworldly, extraterrestrial, extramundane, transmundane, transcendental; Elysian, Olympian; blessed, beatified, beatific, beatifical, glorified, in glory; from on high

ADVS **13 celestially,** paradisally, supernally, ethereally; in heaven, in Abraham's bosom, on high, among the blest, in glory

14 Heaven's designation

a better place
abode of the blessed
Abraham's bosom
better world
Beulah
Beulah Land
eternal home
eternity
Fiddler's Green
firmament
glory
God's kingdom
God's presence
happy hunting ground
heaven above
high heaven
inheritance of the saints in light
kingdom come
my Father's house
Olympus
Paradise
Svarga, Swarga, Swerga
the happy land
the heavenly kingdom
the kingdom of glory
the kingdom of God
the kingdom of heaven
the otherworld
the place up there
the presence of God
the Promised Land
the realm of light
the world above
Zion

682 HELL

<place where Satan or the bad live>

NOUNS **1 hell, Hades,** Sam Hill, Sheol, Gehenna, Tophet, Abaddon, Naraka, jahannan, avichi, perdition, Pandemonium, inferno, the pit, the bottomless pit, the abyss, **netherworld,** lower world, underworld, infernal regions, abode of the dead, world of the dead, abode of the damned, eternal damnation, place of torment, the grave, shades below; **purgatory**; limbo, bardo

2 hellfire, fire and brimstone, lake of fire and brimstone, everlasting fire, everlasting torment

3 <mythological> **Hades,** Orcus, Tartarus, Avernus, Acheron, pit of Acheron; Amenti, Aralu; Hel, Niflhel, Niflheim, Naströnd

4 <rivers of Hades> Styx, Stygian creek; Acheron, River of Woe; Cocytus, River of Wailing; Phlegethon, Pyriphlegethon, River of Fire; Lethe, River of Forgetfulness

5 <deities of the netherworld> Pluto, Orcus, Hades, Aides, Aidoneus, Dis, Dis pater, Rhadamanthus, Erebus, Charon, Cerberus, Minos; Osiris; Persephone, Proserpine, Proserpina, Persephassa, Despoina, Kore, Cora; Hel, Loki; Satan

VERBS **6 damn,** doom, send to hell, consign to hell, cast into hell, doom to perdition, condemn to hell, condemn to eternal punishment

7 go to hell, go to the devil, be damned, go the other way, go to the other place

ADJS **8 hellish, infernal,** sulfurous, brimstone, fire-and-brimstone; chthonic, chthonian; pandemonic, pandemoniac; devilish; Plutonic, Plutonian; Tartarean; Stygian; Lethean; Acherontic; purgatorial, hellborn

ADVS **9 hellishly, infernally,** in hell, in hellfire, below, in torment

683 SCRIPTURE

<holy writings>

NOUNS **1 scripture,** scriptures, **sacred writings, sacred texts, bible;** canonical writings, canonical books, sacred canon

2 Bible, Holy Bible, Scripture, the Scriptures, Holy Scripture, Holy Writ, the Book, the Good Book, the Book of Books, the Word, the Word of God; Vulgate, Septuagint, Douay Bible; Authorized Version, King James Version; Revised Version, American Revised Version; Revised Standard Version; Jerusalem Bible; Testament; canon

3 Old Testament, Tenach; Hexateuch, Octateuch; Pentateuch, Chumash, Five Books of Moses, **Torah,** the Law, the Jewish Law, the Mosaic Law, Law of Moses; the Prophets, Nebiim, Major Prophets, Minor Prophets; the Writings, Hagiographa, Ketubim; Apocrypha, noncanonical writings

4 New Testament; Gospels, Evangels, the Gospel, Good News, Good Tidings, Glad Tidings; Synoptic Gospels, Epistles, Pauline Epistles, Catholic Epistles, Johannine Epistles; Acts, Acts of the Apostles; Apocalypse, Revelation

5 <Jewish> Torah, **Talmud,** Targum, Mishnah, Gemara; Masorah, Bahir, Midrash

6 <Islamic> **Koran,** Qur'an, Hadith, Sunna

7 <other texts> sacred text, scripture, sacred writings, canonical writings, canon; Avesta, Zend-Avesta; Granth, Adigranth; Tao Té Ching; Analects of Confucius; the Eddas; Arcana Caelestia; Book of Mormon; Science and Health with Key to the Scriptures

8 <Hindu> **the Vedas, Veda,** Rig-Veda, Yajur-Veda, Sama-Veda, Atharva-Veda, sruti; Brahmana, Upanishad, Aranyaka; Samhita; shastra, Smriti, Purana, Tantra, Agama; Bhagavad-Gita

9 <Buddhist> Tripitaka; Vinaya Pitaka, Sutta

Pitaka, Abhidarma Pitaka; Dhammapada, Jataka; The Diamond Sutra, The Heart Sutra, The Lotus Sutra, Prajnaparamita Sutra

10 **revelation,** divine revelation; inspiration, afflatus, divine inspiration; theopneusty, theopneustia; theophany, theophania, epiphany; mysticism, direct communication, immediate intuition, mystical experience, mystical intuition, contemplation, ecstasy; **prophecy,** prophetic revelation, apocalypse

ADJS 11 **scriptural,** Biblical, Old-Testament, New-Testament, Gospel, Mosaic, Yahwist, Yahwistic, Elohist; revealed, revelational; prophetic, apocalyptic, apocalyptical; inspired, theopneustic; evangelic, evangelical, evangelistic, gospel; apostolic, apostolical; textual, textuary; canonical; Bible-thumping

12 Talmudic, Mishnaic, Gemaric, Masoretic; rabbinic

13 epiphanic, mystic, mystical

14 Koranic; Avestan; Eddic; Mormon

15 Vedic; tantrist

684 PROPHETS, RELIGIOUS FOUNDERS

<religious leaders>

NOUNS 1 **prophet**; Old Testament prophet, Abraham, Amos, Daniel, Ezekiel, Habakkuk, Haggai, Hosea, Isaac, Isaiah, Jacob, Jeremiah, Joel, Jonah, Joseph, Joshua, Malachi, Micah, Moses, Nahum, Obadiah, Samuel, Zechariah, Zephaniah; Minor Prophets

2 <Christian founders> **evangelist, apostle, disciple,** saint; Matthew, Mark, Luke, John; Paul; Peter; the Fathers, fathers of the church

3 Martin Luther, John Calvin, John Wycliffe, Jan Hus, John Wesley, John Knox, George Fox <Protestant reformers>; Emanuel Swedenborg <Church of the New Jerusalem>; Mary Baker Eddy <Christian Science>; Joseph Smith <Church of Jesus Christ of Latter-day Saints>

4 Buddha, Gautama Buddha <Buddhism>; Mahavira, Vardhamana, Jina <Jainism>; Mirza Ali Muhammad of Shiraz, the Bab <Babism>; Muhammad, Mohammed <Islam>; Confucius <Confucianism>; Lao-tzu <Taoism>; Zoroaster, Zarathustra <Zoroastrianism>; Nanak <Sikhism>

685 SANCTITY

<the sacred>

NOUNS 1 **sanctity,** sanctitude; **sacredness, holiness,** hallowedness, numinousness; sacrosanctness, sacrosanctity; heavenliness, transcendence, divinity, divineness; venerableness, venerability, blessedness; awesomeness, awfulness; inviolableness, inviolability; ineffability, unutterability, unspeakability, inexpressibility, inenarrableness; godliness; odor of sanctity

2 **the sacred,** the holy, the holy of holies, the numinous, the ineffable, the unutterable, the unspeakable, the inexpressible, the inenarrable, the transcendent

3 **sanctification,** hallowing; purification; beatitude, blessing; glorification, **exaltation**, enskying; consecration, dedication, devotion, setting apart; sainting, canonization, enshrinement; sainthood, beatification; blessedness; grace, state of grace; justification, justification by faith, justification by works

4 **redemption,** redeemedness, **salvation,** conversion, regeneration, new life, reformation, adoption; **rebirth,** new birth, second birth, **reincarnation,** spiritual rebirth; circumcision, spiritual purification, spiritual cleansing; spiritual awakening, metanoia

VERBS 5 **sanctify, hallow;** purify, cleanse, wash one's sins away; bless, beatify; glorify, exalt, ensky; consecrate, dedicate, devote, set apart; saint, canonize; enshrine

6 **redeem,** regenerate, reform, convert, **save,** give salvation

ADJS 7 **sacred, holy,** numinous, sacrosanct, religious, spiritual, heavenly, divine; faith-based; venerable, awesome, awful; inviolable, inviolate, untouchable; ineffable, unutterable, unspeakable, inexpressible, inenarrable

8 **sanctified, hallowed;** blessed, consecrated, devoted, dedicated, set apart; glorified, exalted, enskied; saintly, sainted, beatified, canonized

9 **redeemed, saved,** converted, regenerated, regenerate, justified, reborn, born-again, renewed; circumcised, spiritually purified, spiritually cleansed

COMBINING FORMS 10 sacr-, sacro-, hier-, hiero-, hagi-, hagio-

686 UNSANCTITY

<the profane>

NOUNS 1 **unsanctity,** unsanctitude; unsacredness, unholiness, unhallowedness, unblessedness; profanity, profaneness; unregenerateness, reprobation; **worldliness,** secularity, secularism; secular humanism

2 **the profane,** the unholy; the temporal, the secular, **the worldly,** the fleshly, the mundane; the world, the flesh, and the devil

ADJS 3 **unsacred,** nonsacred, unholy, unhallowed, unsanctified, unblessed; profane, **secular,** temporal, **worldly,** fleshly, mundane; unsaved, unredeemed, unregenerate, reprobate

687 ORTHODOXY

<accepted religious opinions, doctrines>

NOUNS **1** **orthodoxy,** orthodoxness, orthodoxism; soundness, soundness of doctrine, rightness, right belief, right doctrine; authoritativeness, authenticity, canonicalness, canonicity; traditionalism; the truth, religious truth, gospel truth

2 the faith, **true faith,** apostolic faith, primitive faith; old-time religion, faith of our fathers

3 the Church, **the true church,** Holy Church, Church of Christ, the Bride of the Lamb, body of Christ, temple of the Holy Ghost, body of Christians, members in Christ, disciples of Christ, followers of Christ; apostolic church; universal church, the church universal; church visible, church invisible; church militant, church triumphant

4 **true believer,** orthodox Christian; Sunni Muslim; Orthodox Jew; orthodox, orthodoxian, orthodoxist; textualist, textuary; canonist; fundamentalist; the orthodox

5 **strictness,** strict interpretation, scripturalism, evangelicalism; hyperorthodoxy, puritanism, puritanicalness, purism; staunchness; straitlacedness, stiff-neckedness, hideboundness; hard line; bigotry; dogmatism; fundamentalism, literalism, precisianism; bibliolatry; Sabbatarianism; sabbatism

6 **bigot**; **dogmatist**

ADJS **7** **orthodox,** orthodoxical; of the faith, of the true faith; sound, firm, faithful, true, true-blue, right-thinking; Christian; evangelical; scriptural, canonical; traditional, traditionalistic; literal, textual; standard, customary, conventional; authoritative, authentic, accepted, received, approved; correct, right, proper; textbook

8 **strict,** scripturalistic, evangelical; hyperorthodox, puritanical, purist, puristic, straitlaced; staunch; hidebound, hardline, creedbound; **bigoted; dogmatic; fundamentalist,** precisianist, precisianistic, literalist, literalistic; Sabbatarian

688 UNORTHODOXY

<unaccepted opinions, doctrines>

NOUNS **1** **unorthodoxy, heterodoxy;** unorthodoxness, unsoundness, un-Scripturality; unauthoritativeness, unauthenticity, uncanonicalness, uncanonicity; nonconformity

2 **heresy,** false doctrine, misbelief; fallacy, error

3 infidelity, infidelism; unchristianity; gentilism; **atheism,** unbelief

4 **paganism, heathenism;** paganry, heathenry; pagandom, heathendom; pagano-Christianism; allotheism; animism, animatism; idolatry

5 **heretic, misbeliever;** heresiarch; nonconformist; antinomian, Albigensian, Arian, Donatist

6 **gentile;** non-Christian; **non-Jew,** goy, goyim, non-Jewish man, *shegets* <Yiddish>, non-Jewish woman, *shiksa* <Yiddish>; non-Muslim, non-Moslem, non-Muhammadan, non-Mohammedan, kaffir; zendik, zendician, zendikite; non-Mormon; infidel; unbeliever

7 **pagan, heathen;** allotheist; animist; idolater

VERBS **8** **misbelieve,** err, stray, deviate, wander, go astray, stray from the path, step out of line, go wrong, fall into error; be wrong, be mistaken, be in error; serve Mammon

ADJS **9** **unorthodox,** nonorthodox, **heterodox, heretical**; unsound; unscriptural, uncanonical, apocryphal; unauthoritative, unauthentic, unaccepted, unreceived, unapproved; fallacious, erroneous; antinomian, Albigensian, Arian, Donatist

10 **infidel,** infidelic, misbelieving; **atheistic,** unbelieving; unchristian, non-Christian; gentile, non-Jewish, goyish, uncircumcised; non-Muslim, non-Muhammadan, non-Mohammedan, non-Moslem, non-Islamic; non-Mormon

11 **pagan,** paganish, paganistic; **heathen,** heathenish; pagano-Christian; allotheistic; animist, animistic; idolatrous

689 OCCULTISM

<belief in supernatural>

NOUNS **1** **occultism, esoterics,** esotericism, esoterica, esoterism, esotery; cabalism, cabala, kabala, kabballa; yoga, yogism, yogeeism; theosophy, anthroposophy; symbolics, symbolism; anagogics; anagoge; hermetics; shamanism, spiritism, animism; mystery, mystification; hocus-pocus, mumbo jumbo; mysticism

2 **supernaturalism,** supranaturalism, preternaturalism, transcendentalism; the supernatural, the supersensible, the paranormal; parallel universe; alien abduction

3 **metaphysics,** hyperphysics, transphysical science, the first philosophy, the first theology

4 **psychics,** psychism, psychicism; parapsychology, psychical research, psychic research; metapsychics, metapsychism, metapsychology; psychosophy; panpsychism; psychic monism, Enneagram

5 **spiritualism,** spiritism; mediumism; necromancy; séance, sitting; spirit

6 **psychic phenomena**, psyhical phenomena, spirit manifestation; materialization; spirit rapping, table tipping; poltergeistism, poltergeist; telekinesis, psychokinesis, power of mind over matter, telesthesia, teleportation; levitation; trance speaking, glossolalia; psychorrhagy; hallucination, déjà vu; séance; automatism, psychography, automatic writing, trance writing, spirit writing; Ouija board, Ouija; planchette; out-of-body experience; cosmic vibration, synchronicity; UFO sighting, alien encounter, alien life form

7 **ectoplasm,** exteriorized protoplasm; aura, emanation, effluvium; ectoplasy; bioplasma

8 **extrasensory perception** (ESP); **clairvoyance,** lucidity, second sight, insight, sixth sense, inner sense, third eye, the force; intuition; foresight; premonition; clairsentience, clairaudience, crystal vision, psychometry, metapsychosis, feyness

9 **telepathy,** mental telepathy, mind reading, thought transference, telepathic transmission; telergy, telesthesia; telepathic dream, telepathic hallucination, cosmic consciousness; lucid dreaming

10 **divination**; sorcery

11 **occultist,** esoteric, mystic, mystagogue, cabalist, supernaturalist, transcendentalist; adept, mahatma; yogi, yogin, yogist; theosophist, anthroposophist; fork bender, unspeller

12 **parapsychologist;** psychist, psychicist; metapsychist; panpsychist; metaphysician, metaphysicist

13 **psychic;** spiritualist, spiritist, **medium,** ecstatic, spirit rapper, automatist, psychographist; necromancer; empath

14 **clairvoyant;** clairaudient, clairsentient; seer, prophet; psychometer, psychometrist

15 **telepathist,** mental telepathist, **mentalist**, mind reader, thought reader

16 **diviner**; sorcerer

17 **astral body,** astral, linga sharira, design body, subtle body, vital body, etheric body, bliss body, Buddhic body, spiritual body, soul body; kamarupa, desire body, kamic body; causal body; mental body, mind body

18 <seven principles of man, theosophy> spirit, atman; mind, manas; soul, buddhi; life principle, vital force, prana; astral body, linga sharira; physical body, dense body, gross body, sthula sharira; principle of desire, kama

19 **spiritualization,** etherealization, idealization; dematerialization, immaterialization, unsubstantialization; disembodiment, disincarnation

VERBS **20** **spiritualize,** spiritize; etherealize; idealize; dematerialize, immaterialize, unsubstantialize; disembody, disincarnate; teleport

21 practice spiritualism, hold a séance, hold a sitting; call up spirits

22 telepathize, **read one's mind**

ADJS **23** **occult, esoteric,** esoterical, mysterious, mystic, mystical, recondite, obscure, arcane; anagogic, anagogical; metaphysic, metaphysical; cabalic, cabalistic; **paranormal, supernatural**; theosophical, theosophist, anthroposophical

24 **psychic,** psychical, spiritual; spiritualistic, spiritistic; mediumistic; clairvoyant, second-sighted, clairaudient, clairsentient, **telepathic;** **extrasensory,** psychosensory; supersensible, supersensual, pretersensual; telekinetic, psychokinetic; automatist; unconscious, subconscious; transphysical

690 SORCERY

<magic aided by evil spirits>

NOUNS **1** **sorcery,** necromancy, magic, sortilege, **wizardry,** theurgy, gramarye, rune, glamour; **witchcraft,** spellcraft, spellbinding, spellcasting; witchery, witchwork, bewitchery, enchantment; possession; voodooism, voodoo, hoodoo, wanga, juju, jujuism, obeah, obeahism; shamanism; magism, magianism; fetishism; totemism; vampirism; thaumaturgy, thaumaturgia, thaumaturgics, thaumaturgism; alchemy; white magic, natural magic; sympathetic magic, chaos magic; divination; spell, charm

2 **black magic,** the black art; diabolism, demonism, diablerie, demonology, Satanism

3 <**sorcery practices**> magic circle; ghost dance; Sabbath, coven, witches' Sabbath; ordeal, ordeal by fire; Halloween, trick or treat; Walpurgis Night, witching hour, Black Mass

4 **conjuration,** conjurement, evocation, invocation; **exorcism,** exorcisation; exsufflation; incantation

5 **sorcerer,** necromancer, **wizard,** wonder-worker, warlock, theurgist; male witch; thaumaturge, thaumaturgist, miracle-worker; alchemist; conjurer; diviner; dowser, water witch, water diviner; diabolist; Faust, Comus

6 **magician,** mage, magus; Merlin; prestidigitator, illusionist

7 **shaman,** shamanist; **voodoo,** voodooist, wangateur, **witch doctor,** obeah doctor, **medicine man,** mundunugu, isangoma; witch-hunter, witch-finder; exorcist, exorciser; unspeller

8 **sorceress,** shamaness; **witch,** witchwoman, hex, hag, lamia; witch of Endor; coven, witches' coven, Weird Sisters

9 **bewitcher,** enchanter, charmer, spellbinder; **enchantress**, siren, vampire; Circe; Medusa, Medea, Gorgon, Stheno, Euryale

VERBS 10 sorcerize, shamanize; make magic, work magic, wave a wand, rub the ring, rub the lamp; ride a broomstick; alchemize

11 **conjure,** conjure up, evoke, invoke, raise, summon, call up; **call up spirits,** conjure spirits, conjure up spirits, summon spirits, raise ghosts, evoke from the dead

12 **exorcise,** lay; lay ghosts, cast out devils; unspell

13 cast a spell, wave a wand, bewitch

ADJS 14 sorcerous, necromantic, **magic, magical,** magian, numinous, thaumaturgic, thaumaturgical, miraculous, wizardlike, wizardly; alchemical, alchemistic, alchemistical; shaman, shamanic, shamanist, shamanistic; witchlike, witchy, witch; voodoo, hoodoo, voodooistic; incantatory, incantational, spellbinding, hypnotic, hypnic, autohypnotic; talismanic, fetishistic

691 SPELL, CHARM

<magical words>

NOUNS 1 **spell,** magic spell, **charm,** glamour, wanga; hand of glory; evil eye, whammy; hex, jinx, curse; exorcism

2 **bewitchment,** witchery, bewitchery; enchantment, entrancement, fascination, captivation; illusion, maya; bedevilment; possession, obsession

3 **trance,** ecstasy, ecstasis, transport, mystic transport, seance; meditation, contemplation; rapture; yoga trance, dharana, dhyana, samadhi; hypnosis

4 **incantation,** conjuration, magic word, magic words, magic formula, invocation, evocation, chant; hocus-pocus, abracadabra, mumbo jumbo; open sesame, abraxas, paternoster, alakazam

5 **charm,** amulet, talisman, fetish, periapt, phylactery; voodoo, hoodoo, juju, obeah, mumbo jumbo; good-luck charm, good-luck piece, lucky piece, lucky charm, rabbit's foot, lucky bean, four-leaf clover, whammy; mascot; madstone; love charm, philter; scarab, scarabaeus, scarabee; veronica, sudarium; swastika, fylfot, gammadion; potion; bell, book, and candle

6 wish-bringer, wish-giver; wand, **magic wand**, Aaron's rod; Aladdin's lamp, magic ring, magic belt, magic spectacles, magic carpet, seven-league boots; wishing well, wishing stone, wishing cap, Fortunatus's cap; cap of darkness, Tarnkappe, Tarnhelm; fern seed; wishbone, wishing bone, merrythought <Brit>

VERBS 7 **cast a spell**, spell, spellbind; **entrance,** trance, put in a trance; **hypnotize,** mesmerize

8 **charm,** becharm, enchant, fascinate, captivate, glamour

9 **bewitch,** witch, hex, jinx; voodoo, hoodoo; possess, obsess; bedevil, diabolize, demonize; hagride; overlook, look on with the evil eye, cast the evil eye

10 **put a curse on,** put a hex on, put a juju on, put obeah on, give the evil eye, give the *malocchio,* give a whammy

ADJS 11 **bewitching,** witching; illusory, illusive, illusionary; charming, enchanting, entrancing, spellbinding, fascinating, glamorous, Circean

12 **enchanted, charmed,** becharmed, charmstruck, charm-bound; spellbound, spell-struck, spell-caught; fascinated, captivated; hypnotized, mesmerized; under a spell, in a trance

13 **bewitched,** witched, witch-charmed, witch-held, witch-struck; hag-ridden; **possessed,** taken over, obsessed

692 PIETY

<religious devotion>

NOUNS 1 **piety, piousness,** pietism; religion, faith; religiousness, religiosity, religionism, religious-mindedness; theism; love of God, adoration; devoutness, devotion, devotedness, worship, worshipfulness, prayerfulness, cultism; faithfulness, dutifulness, observance, churchgoing, conformity; sanctimony; reverence, veneration; discipleship, followership; daily communion; deism, mysticism, spirituality

2 **godliness,** godlikeness; fear of God; **sanctity,** sanctitude; odor of sanctity, beauty of holiness; righteousness, holiness, goodness; spirituality, spiritual-mindedness, holy-mindedness, heavenly-mindedness, godly-mindedness; purity, pureness, pureheartedness, pureness of heart; saintliness, saintlikeness; saintship, sainthood; angelicalness, seraphicalness; heavenliness; unworldliness, unearthliness, other-worldliness

3 **zeal,** zealousness, zealotry, zealotism; unction; evangelism, revival, evangelicalism, revivalism; pentecostalism, charismatic movement; charismatic renewal, baptism in the spirit; charismatic gift, gift of tongues, glossolalia; overreligiousness, religiosity, overpiousness, overrighteousness, overzealousness, overdevoutness; bibliolatry; fundamentalism, militance, fanaticism; sanctimony

4 **believer,** truster, accepter, receiver; God-fearing man, pietist, religionist, saint, theist; **devotee,** devotionalist, votary; **zealot,** zealotist, fundamentalist, militant; churchgoer, churchman, churchite; pillar of the church; communicant,

daily communicant; convert, proselyte, neophyte, catechumen; disciple, follower, servant, faithful servant; fanatic

5 **the believing, the faithful,** the righteous, the good; the elect, the chosen, the saved; the children of God, the children of light; Christendom, the Church

VERBS 6 **be pious,** be religious; have faith, trust in God, love God, fear God; witness, bear witness, affirm, believe; keep the faith, fight the good fight, let one's light shine, praise and glorify God, walk humbly with one's God; be observant, follow righteousness

7 **be converted, get religion**, receive Christ, accept Christ, stand up for Jesus, be washed in the blood of the Lamb; **be born again**, see the light, meet God, enter the church

ADJS 8 **pious,** pietistic; religious, religious-minded; theistic; **devout**, devoted, devotional, dedicated, worshipful, prayerful, cultish, cultist, cultistic; reverent, reverential, venerative, venerational, adoring, solemn; faithful, dutiful; orthodox; affirming, witnessing, believing; keeping the faith; observant, practicing

9 **godly, godlike; God-fearing**; righteous, holy, good; spiritual, spiritual-minded, holy-minded, godly-minded, heavenly-minded; pure, purehearted, pure in heart; saintly, saintlike; angelic, angelical, seraphic, seraphical; heavenly; unworldly, unearthly, otherwordly, not of the earth, not of this world

10 regenerate, regenerated, **converted, redeemed,** saved, God-fearing, theopathic, humble, prostrate; reborn, **born-again;** sanctified

11 **zealous,** zealotical; ardent, unctuous; overreligious, ultrareligious, overpious, overrighteous, overzealous, overdevout; holier-than-thou; crusading, missionary, Bible-thumping; fanatical; sanctimonious

693 SANCTIMONY

<hypocritical, affected religious devotion>

NOUNS 1 **sanctimony, sanctimoniousness;** pietism, piety, piousness, pietisticalness, false piety; religionism, religiosity; self-righteousness; goodiness, goody-goodiness; pharisaism, pharisaicalness; Tartuffery, Tartuffism; falseness, insincerity, hypocrisy; affectation; cant, mummery, snivel, snuffle; unction, unctuousness, oiliness, smarm, smarminesss, mealymouthedness

2 **lip service,** mouth honor, mouthing, lip praise; formalism, solemn mockery; brotherhood of man and fatherhood of God (BOMFOG)

3 **pietist,** religionist, **hypocrite,** religious hypocrite, canting hypocrite, pious fraud, religious humbug, spiritual humbug, whited sepulcher, pharisee, Holy Willie; bleeding heart; canter, ranter, snuffler, sniveler; dissembler, dissimulator; affecter, poser; **lip server,** lip worshiper, formalist; Pharisee, scribes and Pharisees; Tartuffe, Pecksniff, Mawworm, Joseph Surface

VERBS 4 be sanctimonious, **be hypocritical**; cant, snuffle, snivel; give mouth honor, pay lip service

ADJS 5 **sanctimonious,** sanctified, **pious,** pietistic, pietistical, self-righteous, pharisaic, pharisaical, holier-than-thou; goody, goody-goody, goo-goo; false, insincere, hypocritical; affected; Tartuffish, Tartuffian; canting, sniveling, unctuous, mealymouthed, smarmy

694 IMPIETY

<lack of religious devotion>

NOUNS 1 **impiety,** impiousness; ungodliness, godlessness; **irreverence,** undutifulness; desertion, renegadism, apostasy, recreancy; backsliding, recidivism, lapse, fall from grace; atheism, irreligion; unsanctity

2 **sacrilege, blasphemy,** blaspheming, impiety; profanity, profaneness; sacrilegiousness, blasphemousness; desecration, profanation; tainting, pollution, contamination

3 sacrilegist, **blasphemer,** Sabbath-breaker; deserter, renegade, apostate, recreant; backslider, recidivist; **atheist,** unbeliever

VERBS 4 **desecrate, profane,** dishonor, unhallow, commit sacrilege

5 **blaspheme;** vilify, abuse; curse, swear; take in vain; taint, pollute, contaminate

ADJS 6 **impious,** irreverent, undutiful; profane, profanatory; sacrilegious, blasphemous; renegade, apostate, recreant, backsliding, recidivist, recidivistic, lapsed, fallen, fallen from grace; atheistic, irreligious; unsacred

695 NONRELIGIOUSNESS

<not believing in religion>

NOUNS 1 **nonreligiousness, unreligiousness;** undevoutness; indevoutness, indevotion, undutifulness, nonobservance; adiaphorism, indifferentism, Laodiceanism, lukewarm piety; indifference; laicism, unconsecration; deconsecration, secularization, laicization, desacralization

2 **secularism,** worldliness, earthliness, earthiness, mundaneness; unspirituality, carnality; worldly-

mindedness, earthly-mindedness, carnal-mindedness; materialism, Philistinism
3 **ungodliness, godlessness**, unrighteousness, irreligion, unholiness, unsaintliness, unangelicalness; unchristianliness, un-Christliness; impiety; wickedness, sinfulness
4 **unregeneracy,** unredeemedness, **reprobacy,** gracelessness, shriftlessness
5 **unbelief,** disbelief; infidelity, infidelism, faithlessness; **atheism;** nullifidianism, minimifidianism
6 **agnosticism;** skepticism, doubt, incredulity, Pyrrhonism, Humism; scoffing
7 freethinking, free thought, latitudinarianism; humanism, secular humanism; areligious
8 **antireligion**; antichristianism, antichristianity; antiscripturism
9 **iconoclasm,** iconoclasticism, image breaking
10 **irreligionist;** worldling, earthling; materialist; iconoclast, idoloclast; anti-Christian, antichrist
11 **unbeliever,** disbeliever, nonbeliever; **atheist**, infidel, pagan, heathen, heretic; nullifidian, minimifidian; secularist; gentile
12 **agnostic;** skeptic, doubter, dubitante, doubting Thomas, scoffer, Pyrrhonist, Humist
13 **freethinker,** latitudinarian; humanist, secular humanist

VERBS 14 **disbelieve,** doubt; scoff; laicize, deconsecrate, secularize, desacralize

ADJS 15 **nonreligious,** unreligious, having no religious preference; undevout, indevout, indevotional, undutiful, nonobservant, nonpracticing; adiamorphic, indifferentist, indifferentistic, Laodicean, lukewarm, indifferent; unconsecrated, deconsecrated, secularized, laicized, desacralized
16 **secularist,** secularistic, worldly, earthly, earthy, terrestrial, mundane, temporal; unspiritual, profane, carnal, **secular;** humanistic, secular-humanistic; worldly minded, earthly minded, carnal-minded; materialistic, material, Philistine
17 ungodly, **godless**, irreligious, unrighteous, unholy, unsaintly, unangelic, unangelical; impious; wicked, sinful
18 **unregenerate,** unredeemed, unconverted, godless, reprobate, graceless, shriftless, lost, damned; lapsed, fallen, recidivist, recidivistic
19 **unbelieving,** disbelieving, faithless; infidel, infidelic; pagan, heathen; **atheistic,** atheist; nullifidian, minimifidian
20 **agnostic; skeptic,** skeptical, doubtful, dubious, incredulous, Humean, Pyrrhonic; Cartesian
21 **freethinking,** latitudinarian
22 **antireligious;** antichristian; antiscriptural; iconoclastic

696 WORSHIP
<reverence for deity>

NOUNS 1 **worship,** worshiping, adoration, devotion, homage, **veneration**, reverence, honor; adulation, esteem; cult, cultus, cultism; latria, dulia, hyperdulia; falling down and worshiping, prostration; co-worship; idolatry
2 **glorification,** glory, **praise,** extolment, laudation, laud, exaltation, magnification, dignification
3 **paean,** laud; hosanna, hallelujah, alleluia; **hymn,** hymn of praise, doxology, psalm, anthem, motet, canticle, chorale; **chant,** versicle; mantra, Vedic hymn, Vedic chant; plainsong, carol, gospel song; Introit, Miserere; Gloria, Gloria in Excelsis, Gloria Patri; Te Deum, Agnus Dei, Benedicite, Magnificat, Nunc Dimittis; response, responsory, report, answer; Trisagion; antiphon, antiphony; offertory, offertory hymn; hymnody, hymnology, hymnography, psalmody; hymnal
4 **prayer,** praying, supplication, invocation, imploration, impetration, entreaty, beseechment, appeal, petition, suit, aid prayer, bidding prayer, request, petitionary prayer, act of contrition, penitential prayer, orison, obsecration, obtestation, confession, rogation, devotions; genuflection, prostration; silent prayer, meditation, contemplation, communion; intercession prayer, intercessory prayer, suffrage; grace, thanks, thanksgiving; litany; breviary, canonical prayers; collect, collect of the Mass, collect of the Communion; Angelus; Paternoster, the Lord's Prayer; Hail Mary, Ave, Ave Maria; Kyrie Eleison; Pax; chaplet; rosary, beads, beadroll; Kaddish, Mourner's Kaddish; prayer wheel
5 **benediction, blessing,** benison, invocation, benedicite; sign of the cross; laying on of hands
6 **propitiation,** appeasement; atonement
7 oblation, **offering, sacrifice,** immolation, incense; libation, drink offering; scapegoating; burnt offering, holocaust; thank offering, votive offering, ex voto offering; heave offering, peace offering, sacramental offering, sin offering, piacular offering, whole offering; human sacrifice, mactation, infanticide, hecatomb; self-sacrifice, self-immolation; sutteeism; scapegoat, suttee; offertory, collection; penitence
8 divine service, **service,** public worship, liturgy, office, duty, exercises, devotions; meeting; church service, church, celebration; revival, revival meeting, camp meeting, tent meeting, praise meeting; watch meeting, watch-night service, watch night; prayer meeting, prayers, prayer, call to prayer; morning devotions, morning

services, morning prayers, matins, lauds; prime, prime song; tierce, undersong; sext; none, nones; novena; evening devotions, evening services, evening prayers, vesper, vespers, vigils, evensong; compline, night song, night prayer; bedtime prayer; Mass; pilgrimage, hajj

9 **worshiper,** adorer, venerator, votary, adulator, communicant, daily communicant, celebrant, churchgoer, chapelgoer, parishioner, follower; prayer, suppliant, supplicant, supplicator, petitioner; orans, orant; beadsman; revivalist, evangelist; idolater; flock, sheep, congregation, concourse, minyan <Heb>

10 <sacred object> cross, crucifix, chalice, relic, incense, holy water, thurible, censer, chrism, rosary beads, votive candle, vigil light; phylactery, tefillin, mezuzah, menorah; totem, talisman, charm, amulet

VERBS 11 **worship,** adore, reverence, **venerate**, revere, honor, respect, adulate, pay homage to, pay divine honors to, do service, lift up the heart, bow down and worship, humble oneself before, prostrate, genuflect; idolize

12 **glorify, praise,** laud, exalt, extol, magnify, bless, celebrate; praise God, praise the Lord, glorify the Lord, bless the Lord, praise God from whom all blessings flow; praise Father, Son, and Holy Ghost; give thanks; sing praises, sing the praises of, sound the praises of, resound the praises of; doxologize, hymn

13 **pray,** supplicate, invoke, petition, make supplication; implore, beseech, obtest; offer a prayer, send up a prayer, commune with God; say one's prayers; tell one's beads, recite the rosary; say grace, give thanks, return thanks; pray over

14 **bless,** give one's blessing, give benediction, confer a blessing upon, invoke benefits upon; cross, make the sign of the cross upon; lay hands on

15 propitiate, make propitiation; appease; **offer sacrifice,** sacrifice, make sacrifice to, immolate before, offer up an oblation

ADJS 16 **worshipful,** worshiping; adoring, adorant; devout, devotional; pious; reverent, reverential, dedicated; venerative, venerational; solemn; at the feet of; prayerful, praying, penitent, supplicatory, supplicant, suppliant; precatory, precative, imploring, honoring, on one's knees, on bended knee; prostrate before, in the dust; blessing, benedictory, benedictional; propitiatory; anthemic

INTERJS 17 **hallelujah,** alleluia, hosanna, praise God, praise the Lord, praise ye the Lord, amen, Heaven be praised, glory to God, glory be to God, glory be to God in the highest, bless the Lord, hallowed be Thy Name, praise God from whom all blessings flow; thanks be to God

18 O Lord, our Father which art in heaven; God grant, pray God that; God bless, God save, God forbid

697 IDOLATRY

<reverence for idol>

NOUNS 1 **idolatry,** idolatrousness, idolism, idolodulia, **idol worship;** heathenism, paganism; image worship, iconolatry, iconoduly; cult, cultism; totemism; fetishism, fetichism; demonism, demonolatry, demon worship, devil worship, Satanism; animal worship, snake worship, fire worship, pyrolatry, Parsiism, Zoroastrianism; sun worship, star worship, Sabaism; tree worship, plant worship, Druidism, nature worship; phallic worship, phallicism; hero worship; idolomancy

2 **idolization,** fetishization; deification, apotheosis

3 **idol; fetish,** totem, joss; graven image, golden calf, effigy; devil-god; Baal, Jaganatha, Juggernaut; sacred cow

4 **idolater,** idolatress, idolizer, idolatrizer, iconolater, cultist, idolist, idol worshiper, image-worshiper; **fetishist**, totemist; demon worshiper, devil worshiper, demonolater, chthonian; animal worshiper, zoolater, theriolater, therolater, snake worshiper, ophiolater; fire worshiper, pyrolater, Parsi, Zoroastrian; sun worshiper, heliolater; star worshiper, Sabaist; tree worshiper, arborolater, dendrolater, plant worshiper, Druid, nature worshiper; phallic worshiper; anthropolater, archaeolater; groupie, hero-worshiper

VERBS 5 **idolatrize,** idolize, idolify, idol; fetishize, fetish, totemize; make an idol of, deify, apotheosize; idealize, lionize, hero-worship, look up to

6 **worship idols,** worship the golden calf

ADJS 7 **idolatrous,** idolatric, idolatrical, idol worshiping; idolistic, idolizing, iconolatrous, cultish, **fetishistic**, totemistic; heathen, pagan; demonolatrous, chthonian; heliolatrous; bibliolatrous; zoolatrous; hero-worshiping, lionizing

698 THE MINISTRY

<one who ministers a church>

NOUNS 1 **the ministry, pastorate,** pastorage, pastoral care, care of souls, the Church, the cloth, the pulpit, the desk; **priesthood,** priestship; apostleship; call, vocation, sacred calling; holy orders; rabbinate

2 ecclesiasticalism, ecclesiology, priestcraft; <**ecclesiastical offices**> abbacy, archbishopric,

archiepiscopate, archiepiscopacy, archdeaconry; bishopric, bishopdom; canonry, canonicate; cardinalate, cardinalship; chaplaincy, chaplainship; curacy; deaconry, deaconship; deanery, deanship; episcopate, episcopacy; ministry; pastorate, pastorship, pastorage; pontificate, papacy, popedom; prebendaryship, prebend stall, prebendal stall; prelacy, prelature, prelateship, prelatehood; presbytery, presbyterate; primacy, primateship; rabbinate; rectorate, rectorship; vicariate, vicarship

3 **clericalism,** sacerdotalism; **priesthood**; priestism; episcopalianism; ultramontanism

4 **monasticism,** monachism, monkery, **monkhood,** friarhood; celibacy

5 ecclesiastical office, church office, dignity

6 **papacy,** papality, **pontificate,** popedom, the Vatican, Apostolic See, See of Rome, the Church

7 hierarchy, hierocracy; theocracy

8 **diocese, see,** archdiocese, bishopric, archbishopric; province; synod, conference; **parish**

9 **benefice,** living, **incumbency,** glebe, advowson; curacy, cure, charge, cure of souls, care of souls; prelacy, rectory, vicarage

10 **holy orders,** orders, major orders, apostolic orders, minor orders; calling, election, nomination, appointment, preferment, induction, institution, installation, investiture; conferment, presentation; ordination, ordainment, consecration, canonization, reading in <Brit>

VERBS 11 **be ordained,** take holy orders, take orders, take vows, read oneself in <Brit>; take the veil, wear the cloth

12 **ordain,** frock, canonize, consecrate; saint

ADJS 13 **ecclesiastic,** ecclesiastical, churchly; **ministerial, clerical,** sacerdotal, pastoral; **priestly,** priestish; prelatic, prelatical, prelatial; episcopal, episcopalian; archiepiscopal; primatal, primatial, primatical; canonical; capitular, capitulary; abbatical, abbatial; ultramontane; evangelistic; rabbinic, rabbinical; priest-ridden; parochial

14 **monastic,** monachal, monasterial, monkish; conventual

15 **papal,** pontific, pontifical, apostolic, apostolical; popish, papist, papistic, papistical, papish

16 **hierarchical,** hierarchal, hieratic; hierocratic; theocratic, theocratist

17 **ordained;** in orders, in holy orders, of the cloth

699 THE CLERGY

<church service leaders>

NOUNS 1 **clergy, ministry,** the cloth; clerical order, clericals; **priesthood;** priestery; presbytery; prelacy; Sacred College; rabbinate; hierocracy, pastorage; clerical venue; **religious order** <see list>

2 **clergyman,** clergywoman, clergyperson, man of the cloth, woman of the cloth, divine, ecclesiastic, churchman, cleric, clerical; clerk, clerk in holy orders, person in holy orders, tonsured cleric; minister, minister of the Gospel, parson, pastor, *abbé,* rector, curate, vicar, man of God, woman of God, servant of God, shepherd, sky pilot, Holy Joe, reverend; supply minister, supply preacher, supply clergy; chaplain; military chaplain, padre; the Reverend, the Very Reverend, Right Reverend; Doctor of Divinity (DD); elder

3 **preacher,** sermoner, sermonizer, sermonist, homilist; pulpiter, pulpiteer; predicant, predikant; preaching friar; circuit rider; televison preacher, TV preacher, telepreacher

4 **holy orders,** major orders, priest, presbyter, deacon, diaconus, subdeacon, subdiaconus; minor orders, acolyte, acolytus, exorcist, exorcista, reader, lector, doorkeeper, ostiarius; ordinand, candidate for holy orders

5 **priest, father,** father in Christ, padre, cassock, presbyter; curé, parish priest; confessor, father confessor, spiritual father, spiritual director, spiritual leader, holy father; penitentiary

6 **evangelist,** revivalist, evangel, evangelicalist; **missionary,** missioner; missionary apostolic, missionary rector, colporteur; television evangelist, TV evangelist, televangelist

7 benefice-holder, beneficiary, incumbent; resident, residentiary

8 church dignitary, ecclesiarch, ecclesiast, hierarch; lay officer

9 <Catholic> pope, pontiff; cardinal, dean, archbishop, bishop, provost, high priest, ecclesiarch, canon, monsignor

10 <Mormon> deacon, teacher, priest, elder, Seventy, high priest, bishop, patriarch, apostle; Aaronic priesthood, Melchizedek priesthood

11 <Jewish> rabbi, rebbe, rabbin; chief rabbi; *baal kore* <Yiddish>; cantor; priest, *kohen* <Heb>, high priest; maggid; Levite; scribe

12 <Muslim> imam, qadi, sheikh, mullah, murshid, mufti, hajji, muezzin, dervish, abdal, fakir, santon, ayatollah

13 <Hindu> Brahman, pujari, purohit, pundit, guru, bashara, vairagi, bairagi, Ramwat, Ramanandi; sannyasi; yogi, yogin; bhikshu, bhikhari

14 <Buddhist> bonze, bhikku, poonghie, talapoin, bodhisattva, guru; lama; Grand Lama, Dalai Lama, Panchen Lama

15 <pagan> Druid, Druidess; flamen; hierophant, hierodule, hieros, daduchus, mystes, epopt

16 **religious person**; monk, monastic, lama, bhikkhu; brother, lay brother; cenobite, conventual; caloyer, hieromonach; mendicant, friar; pilgrim, palmer; stylite, pillarist, pillar saint; beadsman; prior, claustral prior, conventual prior, grand prior, general prior; abbot; lay abbot, abbacomes; hermit; ascetic; celibate

17 <**clergywoman**> nun, sister, clergywoman, conventual; abbess, prioress; mother superior, lady superior, superioress, the reverend mother, holy mother; canoness, regular canoness, secular canoness; novice, postulant

18 **religious order**

Augustinian Friars, Austin Friars
Augustinian Hermit
Barnabite
Benedictine Monks, Black Monks
Bernardine
Bonhomme
Brigittine
Capuchin
Carmelite Friars, White Friars
Carthusian
Cistercian
Cluniac
Conventual
Crosier
Crutched Friars, Crossed Friars
Discalced Carmelite
Dominican Friars, Black Friars
Franciscan Friars, Gray Friars
Friars Minor
Friars Preacher
Gilbertine
Holy Cross
Hospitaler
Jesuit, Loyolite
Lorettine
Marist
Maryknoll
Maturine
Minorite
Observant
Oratorian
Pallottine Fathers and Brothers
preaching Friars, preaching brothers
Premonstratensian
Recollect, Recollet
Redemptorist
Salesian
Templar
Trappist

700 THE LAITY

<members of church>

NOUNS **1** **the laity, laypersons,** laymen, laywomen, nonclerics, nonordained persons, seculars, temporalty; brothers, sisters, brethren, sistren, people; flock, fold, sheep; **congregation,** parishioners, churchgoers, assembly; *minyan* <Heb>; **parish,** society; class; altar boy, altar girl

2 **layman,** layperson, laic, secular, churchman, **parishioner,** church member; brother, sister, lay brother, lay sister; laywoman, churchwoman; catchumen; communicant

ADJS **3** **lay,** laic, laical; **nonecclesiastical,** nonclerical, nonministerial, nonpastoral, nonordained; nonreligious; **secular,** secularist; secularistic; temporal, popular, civil; congregational

701 RELIGIOUS RITES

<church ceremonies>

NOUNS **1** **ritualism,** rituality, ritualization, **ceremonialism,** formalism, liturgism; symbolism, symbolics; cult, cultus, cultism; sacramentalism, sacramentarianism; sabbatism, Sabbatarianism; solemnization, solemn observance, **celebration;** liturgics, liturgiology

2 **ritualist,** ceremonialist, celebrant, liturgist, formalist, formulist, formularist; sacramentalist, sacramentarian; sabbatist, Sabbatarian; High-Churchman, High-Churchist; crucifer, thurifer, acolyte

3 **religious rite** <see list>, **ritual,** rituality, liturgy, holy rite; service, order of worship; ceremony, ceremonial; **observance**, ritual observance; formality, solemnity; form, formula, formulary, form of worship, form of service, mode of worship; prescribed form; function, duty, office, practice; sacrament, sacramental, mystery; ordinance; institution

4 **seven sacraments,** mysteries: baptism, confirmation, the Eucharist, penance, extreme unction, holy orders, matrimony

5 **unction,** sacred unction, sacramental anointment, chrism, chrisom, chrismation, chrismatory; extreme unction, **last rites,** viaticum; ointment; chrismal

6 **baptism,** baptizement; **christening;** immersion, total immersion; sprinkling, aspersion, aspergation; affusion, infusion; baptism for the dead; baptismal regeneration; baptismal gown, baptismal dress, baptismal robe, chrismal; baptistery, baptistry, font; confirmation, bar mitzvah, bas mitzvah <Jewish>

7 **Eucharist,** Lord's Supper, Last Supper, **Communion,** Holy Communion, the Sacrament, the Holy Sacrament; intinction; consubstantiation, impanation, subpanation, transubstantiation; real presence; elements, consecrated elements, bread and wine, body and blood of Christ; Host, wafer, loaf, bread, altar bread, consecrated bread; Sacrament Sunday

8 **Mass,** *Missa* <L>, Eucharistic rites; the Liturgy, the Divine Liturgy; parts of the Mass, High Mass, Low Mass

9 <**non-Christian rites**> initiation, rite of passage; circumcision; bar mitzvah, bas mitzvah <Jewish>; Kaddish, shivah; female circumcision; ritual cleaning, ritual bathing; fertility rite; sun dance, rain dance, war dance, ghost dance, potlatch; witches' Sabbath, Black Mass; hara-kiri

10 **sacred object,** sacred article; ritualistic manual, Book of Common Prayer, breviary, canon, haggadah <Jewish>, missal book, Mass book, book of hours, lectionary, prayer book; siddur, mahzor <Jewish>

11 psalter, **psalmbook;** Psalm Book, Book of Common Order; the Psalms, Book of Psalms, the Psalter, the Psaltery

12 **holy day,** hallowday, holytide, holiday; feast, fast, fast day; Sabbath; Sunday, Lord's day; saint's day; church calendar, ecclesiastical calendar; Advent calendar

13 **Christian holy days** <see list>; **Jewish holy days** <see list>

VERBS **14** **celebrate, observe, keep, solemnize;** ritualize; celebrate Mass; communicate, administer Communion; attend Communion, receive the Sacrament, partake of the Lord's Supper; attend Mass

15 **minister, officiate,** do duty, **perform a rite,** perform service, perform divine service; administer a sacrament, administer the Eucharist; anoint, chrism, bless; confirm, impose, lay hands on; make the sign of the cross

16 **baptize, christen;** dip, immerse; sprinkle, asperge; circumcise

17 **confess,** make confession, receive absolution; **shrive,** hear confession; **absolve,** administer absolution; administer extreme unction

ADJS **18** **ritualistic, ritual; ceremonial, ceremonious; formal,** formular, formulaic, formulary; liturgic, liturgical, **liturgistic, liturgistical;** solemn, consecrated; High-Church; **sacramental,** sacramentarian; eucharistic, eucharistical, baptismal; paschal; Passover; matrimonial, nuptial; funereal

19 **Christian holy days**

Advent <pre-Christmas>
All Saints' Day, Allhallows <Nov 1>
All Souls' Day <Nov 2>
Annunciation Day, Lady Day <Mar 25>
Ascension Day, Holy Thursday <40 days after Easter>
Ash Wednesday <start of Lent>
Assumption <Aug 15>
Candlemas, Candlemas Day, Presentation <Feb 2>
Christmas <Dec 25>
Circumcision, Holy Name Day <Jan 1>
Corpus Christi <Thurs after Trinity Sun>
Easter, Easter Sunday, Eastertide <1st Sunday after 1st full moon after vernal equinox>
Easter Even, Holy Saturday
Ember days <beginning of seasons>
Epiphany, Three Kings' Day <Jan 6>
Good Friday <Fri before Easter>
Hallowmas, Allhallowmas, Allhallowtide, Halloween, Allhallows, All Souls' Day <Oct 31>
Holy Thursday, Mauny Thursday <before Easter>
Holy Week, Passion Week <before Easter>
Lammas, Lammas Day, Lammastide, Feast of St. Peter's Chains <Aug 1>
Lent, Lententide <40 days before Easter>
Martinmas <Nov 11>
Michaelmas, Michaelmas Day, Michaelmastide <Sept 29>
Palm Sunday <Sun before Easter>
Pentecost, Whitsuntide, Whitsun, Whitsunday <7th Sun after Easter>
Quadragesima, Quadragesima Sunday
Septuagesima
Shrove Tuesday, Mardi Gras, Carnival, Pancake Day <Tues before Ash Wednesday>
Solemnity of Mary <Jan 1>
Trinity Sunday <Sun after Pentecost>
Twelfth-tide, Twelfth-night <night before Epiphany>
Whitweek, Whitmonday, Whit-Tuesday <after Pentecost>

20 **Jewish holy days**

Ninth of Av, Tishah b'Av
Hanukkah, Feast of the Dedication, Feast of Lights
High Holy Days <between Rosh Hashanah and Yom Kippur>
Lag b'Omer
Passover, Pesach
Purim
Rosh Hashanah, New Year
Rosh Hodesh, Rosh Chodesh
Shabuoth, Shavuoth, Pentecost, Feast of Weeks
Shemini Atzeres
Simhath Torah, Rejoicing over the Law
Sukkoth, Feast of Tabernacles
Yom Kippur, Day of Atonement

21 **religious rite**

ablution
absolution
anointing of the sick
aspersion, asperges
celebration
cleansing, purification
confession, auricular confession, the confessional, confessionary
confirmation
greater litany, lesser litany
high celebration
imposition, laying on of hands
invocation
invocation of saints
last rites
litany
love feast, agape
lustration
offertory
pax, kiss of peace
penitence, act of contrition
processional
reciting the rosary, telling one's beads
sign of the cross, signum crucis <L>, signing oneself, crossing oneself
sprinkling
Stations of the Cross
thurification, censing
viaticum

702 ECCLESIASTICAL ATTIRE

<religious clothing>

NOUNS **1** **canonicals,** clericals, robes, cloth; **vestments,** vesture; regalia; liturgical garments, ceremonial attire; pontificals, pontificalia, episcopal vestments; habit, veil

2 **robe,** frock, mantle, gown, cloak, surplice, scapular, cassock, cope, hood, clerical collar

3 **staff,** pastoral staff, crosier, cross, cross-staff, crook, paterissa

ADJS 4 vestmental, vestmentary

703 RELIGIOUS BUILDINGS

<place of worship>

NOUNS 1 **church,** bethel, meetinghouse, church house, house of God, place of worship, house of worship, house of prayer; conventicle; mission; basilica, major basilica, patriarchal basilica, minor basilica; **cathedral,** cathedral church; collegiate church

2 **temple,** fane; **tabernacle; synagogue,** *shul* <Yiddish>; **mosque,** masjid; dewal, girja; pagoda; kiack; pantheon; wat, ziggurat

3 **chapel,** chapel of ease, chapel royal, side chapel, school chapel, sacrament chapel, Lady chapel, oratory, oratorium; chantry; sacellum, sacrarium

4 **shrine,** holy place, dagoba, cella, naos; sacrarium, sanctum sanctorum, holy of holies, delubrum; tope, stupa; reliquary

5 **sanctuary,** holy of holies, sanctum, sanctum sanctorum, adytum, sacrarium

6 **cloister, monastery,** house, **abbey,** friary; priory, priorate; lamasery; **convent, nunnery;** ashram, hermitage, retreat

7 **parsonage,** pastorage, pastorate, manse, church house, clergy house; presbytery, **rectory,** vicarage, deanery; glebe; chapter house

8 bishop's palace; Vatican; Lambeth, Lambeth Palace

9 <church interior> vestry, sacristy, sacrarium, sanctuary, diaconicon, diaconicum; baptistery; aisle, ambry, apse, blindstory, chancel, choir, choir screen, cloisters, confessional, confessionary, crypt, Easter sepulcher, narthex, nave, porch, presbytery, rood loft, rood stair, rood tower, rood spire, rood steeple, transept, triforium; organ loft

10 <church furnishings> piscina; stoup, holy-water stoup, holy-water basin; baptismal font; patent; reredos; jube, rood screen, rood arch, chancel screen; altar cloth, cerecloth, chrismal; communion cloth, sacrament cloth, corporal, fanon, oblation cloth; rood cloth; baldachin; kneeling stool; prayer rug, prayer carpet, prayer mat

11 <church vessels> cruet; chalice; ciborium, pyx; chrismal, chrismatory; monstrance, ostensorium; reliquary; font, holy-water font

12 **altar,** scrobis; bomos, eschara, hestia; Lord's table, holy table, Communion table, chancel table, table of the Lord, God's board; rood altar; altar desk, missal stand; credence, prothesis, table of prothesis, altar of prothesis, predella; superaltar, retable, retablo, ancona, gradin; altarpiece, altar side, altar rail, altar carpet, altar stair; altar facing, altar front, frontal; altar slab, altar stone, mensal

13 **pulpit,** rostrum, ambo; lectern, desk, reading desk

14 <seats> **pew;** stall; mourners' bench, anxious bench, anxious seat, penitent form; amen corner; sedilia

ADJS 15 **churchly,** churchish, **ecclesiastical;** churchlike, templelike; cathedral-like, cathedralesque; tabernacular; synagogical, synagogal; pantheonic

16 claustral, cloistered; **monastic,** monachal, monasterial; coventual, conventical

704 SHOW BUSINESS, THEATER

<theatrical performance>

NOUNS 1 **show business,** show biz, the entertainment industry, performing arts; **the theater,** the footlights, **the stage,** the boards, the bright lights, Broadway, the Great White Way, the scenes, traffic of the stage; avant-garde theater, contemporary theater, experimental theater, total theater, epic theater, theater of the absurd, theater of cruelty, guerrilla theater, street theater; stagedom, theater world, stage world, stageland, playland; drama, legitimate stage, legitimate theater, legit, off Broadway, off-off-Broadway; music theater, musical theater, fringe theater; café theater, dinner theater; regional theater; repertory drama, repertory theater, stock; summer theater, summer stock, straw hat, straw hat circuit; vaudeville, variety; burlesque; circus, carnival; magic show; theatromania, theatrophobia

2 **dramatics; performance art;** dramatization, dramaticism, dramatism; **theatrics,** theatricism, theatricalism, theatricality, staginess; theatricals, amateur theatricals; histrionics, histrionism; dramatic art, histrionic art, Thespian art; dramatic stroke, *coup de théâtre* <Fr>; melodramatics, sensationalism; dramaturgy, dramatic structure, play construction, dramatic form; dramatic irony, tragic irony

3 **theatercraft, stagecraft,** stagery, scenecraft; showmanship

4 **stage show,** show; **play,** stage play, piece, vehicle, work; hit, hit show, gasser, success, critical success, audience success, word-of-mouth success, box-office hit, long run; short run, failure, flop, bomb, turkey

5 **tragedy,** tragic drama, melodrama; tragic flaw; buskin, cothurnus; tragic muse, Melpomene
6 **comedy;** comic relief; comic muse, Thalia; black comedy, black humor, satire, farce; sock, coxcomb, cap and bells, motley, bladder, slapstick, burlesque; historic comedy; bathroom humor
7 **act, scene**, number, turn, bit, shtick, routine; curtain raiser, curtain lifter; introduction; expository scene; monologue, soliloquy; prologue, epilogue; entr'acte, intermezzo, intermission, interlude, *divertissement* <Fr>, climax; finale, afterpiece; exodus, exode; chaser; curtain call, curtain; encore, ovation; hokum act; song and dance; burlesque act; stand-up comedy act, stand-up; open mike; **sketch, skit;** and scene
8 **acting,** playing, playacting, performing, performance, taking a role, taking a part, role-playing; representation, portrayal, characterization, interpretation, projection, enactment; impersonation, personation, miming, mimicking, mimicry, mimesis; pantomiming, mummery; Method acting; improvisation; ham, hammy acting, hamming, hamming up, camping it up, overacting, histrionics; stage presence; stage directions, business, stage business, acting device; stunt, gag; hokum, hoke; buffoonery, slapstick; patter; stand-up comedy; crossover
9 **repertoire,** repertory; stock
10 **role, part**, piece; cue, lines, side; cast; **character,** person, personage; lead, starring role, lead role, leading role, fat part, leading man, leading woman, leading lady, hero, heroine; antihero; title role, top billing, protagonist, principal character; supporting role, supporting character; ingenue, romantic lead; villain, heavy, bad guy, antagonist, deuteragonist; bit, bit part, minor role, speaking part; feed, feeder, straight part; walking part, walk-on, extra; double, stand-in, stunt person, stuntman, stuntwoman, understudy; top banana, second banana; chorus, Greek chorus; stock part, stock character; actor
11 **engagement,** playing engagement, booking; **run;** stand, one-night stand, one-nighter; circuit, barnstorming, vaudeville circuit, borscht circuit; tour, bus-and-truck, production tour; date, **gig**
12 **theatrical performance**, performance, show, presentation, presentment, production, entertainment, stage presentation, stage performance; bill; exhibit, exhibition; benefit performance, benefit; personal appearance; showcase, tryout, preview; premiere, premier performance, debut, opening night; farewell performance, swan song; command performance; matinee; sellout, full house
13 **production,** mounting, staging, putting on; stage management; direction, *mise-en-scène* <Fr>; blocking; rehearsal, dress rehearsal, walk-through, run-through, technical rehearsal, tech rehearsal, technical run, tech run, final dress, gypsy rehearsal, gypsy run-through, gypsy run
14 **theater, playhouse,** house, theatron, odeum; auditorium; opera house, opera; hall, music hall, concert hall; amphitheater; circle theater, arena, stadium, theater-in-the-round; vaudeville theater; burlesque theater; little theater, community theater; open-air theater, outdoor theater; Greek theater; children's theater; Elizabethan theater, Globe Theatre; showboat; dinner theater; cabaret, nightclub, club, night spot
15 **auditorium**, seating; parquet, orchestra, pit; orchestra circle, parquet circle, parterre; dress circle; fauteuil, theatre stall, stall <Brit>; box, box seat, loge; stage box; proscenium boxes, parterre boxes; balcony, gallery, mezzanine; peanut gallery, paradise; standing room; box office
16 **stage,** the boards; acting area, playing area, performing area; thrust stage, three-quarter-round stage, theater-in-the-round; apron, passerelle, apron stage, forestage; proscenium stage, proscenium arch, proscenium; bridge; revolving stage; orchestra, pit, orchestra pit; mosh pit; bandstand, shell, band shell; stage right, R; stage left, L; upstage, downstage, backstage, center stage; wings, coulisse; dressing room, greenroom; flies, fly gallery, fly floor; gridiron, grid; board, lightboard, switchboard; dock; prompter's box; curtain, grand drape, safety curtain, asbestos curtain, fire curtain; stage door
17 <stage requisites> **property, prop;** practical piece, handprop; costume; theatrical makeup, makeup, greasepaint, blackface, clown white; spirit gum
18 **stage lighting**, lights, instruments; footlights, foots, floats; floodlight, flood; bunch light; battens, houselights; limelight, follow spot, spotlight, spot, following spot, arc light, arc, klieg light, kleig light; color filter, color wheel, medium, gelatin, gel; projector, stroboscope, strobe, strobe light; lightboard; dimmer; marquee; light plot
19 setting, **stage setting,** stage set, set, *mise-en-scène* <Fr>; location, locale
20 **scenery,** decor; scene; screen, flat; cyclorama, cyc; batten; side scene, wing, coulisse; border; tormentor, teaser; wingcut, woodcut; transformation, transformation scene; flipper; counterweight; curtain, rag, hanging; drop, drop scene, drop curtain, scrim, cloth; backdrop, back cloth; act drop, act curtain; tab, tableau curtain
21 **playbook, script,** text, libretto; promptbook;

book, book of words; score; scenario, continuity, shooting script; scene plot; lines, actor's lines, cue, sides; stage direction; prompt book

22 **dramatist; playwright,** playwriter, dramaturge; doctor, play doctor, play fixer; dramatizer; scriptwriter, scenario writer, scenarist, scenarioist, **screenwriter;** gagman, gag writer, joke writer, jokesmith; librettist; tragedian, comedian; farcist, farcer; melodramatist; monodramatist; mimographer; choreographer

23 **theater person**, theatrician; showman, exhibitor, producer, impresario; director, auteur; stage director, stage manager; set designer, scenewright; costume designer, costumer, wardrobe master, wardrobe mistress; dresser; hair, wigmaker, designer; makeup artist, visagiste; propsmaster, propsmistress; prompter; callboy; playreader; master of ceremonies, (MC) emcee; box-office staff; ticket collector; usher, usherer, usherette, doorkeeper; ringmaster, equestrian director; barker, ballyhoo man, spieler

24 stage technician, **stagehand,** stage crew, machinist, sceneman, scene master, sceneshifter; flyman; carpenter; electrician; sound man, sound mixer, sound engineer; scene painter, scenic artist, scenewright

25 **agent,** actor's agent, playbroker, ten-percenter; booking agent; advance agent, advance man; press agent; publicity man, publicity agent; business manager, publicity manager

26 **patron,** patroness; **backer, angel**, promoter; Dionysus

27 **playgoer, theatergoer;** attender, spectator, audience, house; moviegoer, **motion-picture fan**; first-nighter; standee, groundling; *claqueur* <Fr>, hired applauder; pass holder, deadhead, stage-door Johnny; critic, reviewer, talent scout

VERBS 28 **dramatize, theatricalize**; melodramatize; scenarize; present, stage, produce, mount, put on, put on the stage, adapt for the stage; put on a show; try out, preview; give a performance; premiere; open, open a show, open a show cold; set the stage; ring up the curtain, ring down the curtain; star, feature, bill, headline, give top billing to; succeed, make a hit, be a hit, have legs, be a gas, be a gasser, run out of gas; fail, flop, bomb, bomb out; script

29 **act, perform, play,** playact, tread the boards, strut one's stuff; appear, appear on the stage; act like a trouper; register; emotionalize, emote; pantomime, mime; patter; sketch; troupe, barnstorm; improvise, ad-lib, wing it; steal the show, upstage, steal the spotlight; debut, make one's debut, make one's bow, come out, take the stage, make an entrance; act as foil, act as feeder, stooge, be straight man for; star, play the lead, get top billing, have one's name in lights, costar, understudy

30 **enact, act out**; represent, depict, portray; act a part, act a role, play a part, play a role, perform a part, perform a role, role-play, take a part, sustain a part, act the part of, play the part of; create a role; impersonate, personate; play opposite, support

31 **overact,** overdramatize, chew up the scenery, act all over the stage; ham, ham it up, camp it up; play to the gallery; mug, grimace; spout, rant, roar, declaim; milk a scene, milk it; **underact,** underplay, fluff, go blank, freeze, throw away

32 **rehearse,** practice, go through, walk through, run through, go over; block; go through one's part, read one's lines; learn one's lines, memorize, study one's part; be a fast study; interpret the part, get into character

ADJS 33 **dramatic,** dramatical, dramaturgic, dramaturgical; theatric, theatrical, histrionic, thespian; scenic; stagy; theaterlike, stagelike; rehearsed, staged, interpreted, improvised; spectacular; melodramatic; ham, hammy, campy; overacted, overplayed, milked; underacted, underplayed, thrown away; musical, choral; operatic; choreographic, terpsichorean; ballet, balletic; legitimate; stellar, all-star; stagestruck, starstruck; stageworthy, actor-proof; scenery-chewing

34 **tragic,** heavy; buskined, cothurned; tragicomic, tragicomical

35 **comic,** light; tragicomical, farcical, slapstick; camp, campy; burlesque

ADVS 36 **on the stage**, on the boards, before an audience, before the footlights; **in the limelight**, in the spotlight; onstage; downstage, upstage; backstage, offstage, behind the scenes; down left (DL); down right (DR); up left (UL); up right (UR)

705 DANCE

<movement performance>

NOUNS 1 **dancing** <see list>, terpsichore, dance; the light fantastic; **choreography;** dance drama, choreodrama; hoofing

2 **dance,** hop, **dancing party**, shindig, shindy; ball; masked ball, masque, mask, masquerade ball, masquerade, fancy-dress ball, cotillion, cotillon; promenade, prom, formal; country dance, square dance, barn dance, hoedown; mixer, stag dance; record hop; dinner-dance, tea dance, *thé dansant* <Fr>, dinner dance; dance-off

3 **dancer,** danseur, terpsichorean, hoofer, step dancer, tap dancer, clog dancer, go-go dancer,

foxtrotter; ballet dancer; ballerina, danseuse, coryphée; corps de ballet; twinkletoes; classical dancer; modern dancer; *corps de ballet* <Fr>; figurant, figurante; chorus girl, chorine, chorus boy; chorus line; geisha, geisha girl; nautch girl, bayadere; hula girl; taxi dancer; topless dancer; burlesque dancer, stripteaser, stripper, ecdysiast, bump-and-grinder; choreographer

4 **ballroom, dance hall,** dancery; dance palace; discotheque, disco; dance floor; nightclub, casino

VERBS 5 **dance,** trip the light fantastic, go dancing, trip, skip, hop, foot, prance, hoof, hoof it, clog, tap-dance, fold-dance; shake, shimmy, shuffle; waltz, one-step, two-step, foxtrot; choreograph; dance-off

ADJS 6 **dancing, dance,** terpsichorean; balletic; choreographic

7 **dancing (types)**

aerobic dancing	jazz tap
ballet	jitterbugging
ballroom dancing	lap dancing
belly dancing	line dancing
break dancing	marathon dancing
character dancing	modern ballet
choral dancing	modern dance
classical ballet	morris dancing
clog dancing	ritual dancing
comedy ballet	round dancing
country dancing	slam dancing
dirty dancing	social dancing
disco dancing	soft-shoe dancing
fan dancing	solo dancing
flamenco	square dancing
folklorico	step dancing
folk dancing	sword dancing
go-go dancing	tap dancing
interpretive dancing	taxi dancing
jazz dancing	trance dancing

706 MOTION PICTURES

<film performance>

NOUNS 1 **motion pictures, movies,** the movies, the pictures, moving pictures, films, the films, the cinema, the screen, the big screen, the silver screen, the flicks, the flickers, motion-picture industry, moviedom, filmmaking, filmdom, Hollywood; motion picture, movie, picture, film, flick, flicker, picture show, motion-picture show, moving-picture show, photoplay, photodrama; sound film, silent film, silent; cinéma vérité, direct cinema; vérité; magic realism; documentary film, docudrama, docutainment; feature, feature film, feature-length film, main attraction; theatrical film, big-screen film; motion-picture genre; TV movie, made-for-television movie, cable movie, miniseries; short, short movie, short subject; preview, sneak preview, spoiler alert; independent film, indie; B-movie, B-picture, Grade B movie, low-budget picture; educational film, training film, promotional film, trigger film; underground film, experimental film, avant-garde film, representational film, art film, surrealistic film; 3-D movie, 4-D movie; cartoon, animated cartoon, animation, cel animation, claymation, computer graphics; animatron, audioanimatron; video, rental movie, pay-per-view movie, video-on-demand; music video; rated movie, rating system, rating, (G) general audience, (PG) parental guidance suggested, (PG-13) parents strongly cautioned, (R) restricted, children under 17 require accompanying parent or guardian (NC-17), (X) no children under 17 admitted

2 **<movie type>** drama, comedy, musical, love story, mystery, thriller, adventure, actioner, romance, Western, spaghetti western, shoot-em-up, historical film, epic film, futuristic film, science fiction film, sci-fi film, space opera, foreign film, foreign language film, film noir, cult movie, girl flick, chick flick; date movie; art movie, buddy film, chopsocky, mumblecore

3 **script, screenplay,** motion-picture script, shooting script, storyboard, scenario, treatment, original screenplay, screen adaptation; plot, subplot, story; dialogue, book, lines; role, lead, romantic lead, stock character, ingenue, soubrette, cameo, bit, silent bit

4 motion-picture studio, **movie studio,** film studio, dream factory, animation studio, lot, back lot, sound stage, location; set, motion-picture set, film set, *mise-en-scène* <Fr>, properties, props, set dressing; motion-picture company, film company, production company; producer, filmmaker, moviemaker, director, auteur, screenwriter, scriptwriter, scenarist, editor, film editor, actor, actress, film actor, film actress, player, cinemactor, cinemactress, star, starlet, character actor, featured player, supporting actor, supporting actress, supporting player, bit player, extra; crew, film crew

5 **motion-picture photography,** photography, cinematography, camerawork, cinematics, camera angle, camera position, shot, take, footage, retake; screen test; rear-screen projection, mechanical effects, optical effects, process photography; special effects (FX); color photography, Technicolor, CinemaScope; black-and-white, color, colorization; cameraman, camerawoman, motion-picture camera person, cinematographer, director of photography (DP), first cameraman, lighting cameraman

6 motion-picture editing, **film editing,** editing, cutting, arranging, synchronizing; transition, fade, fade-out, fade-in, fade to black, dissolve, lap dissolve, overlap dissolve, out-focus-dissolve, match dissolve, cross-dissolve, mix; colorizing, colorization; freeze-frame; McGuffin; post production

7 motion-picture theater, **movie theater,** picture theater, picture house, film theater, cinema, movie house, movie palace, dream palace, art house, circuit theater, drive-in theater, drive-in, grind house, fleapit <Brit>, cineplex, multiplex; **screen,** movie screen, motion-picture screen, silver screen, aspect ratio, aspect format, screen proportion, widescreen; Cinerama, CinemaScope, VistaVision, Ultra-Panavision <tm>

VERBS **8** **film, shoot,** cinematize, filmmake; colorize

ADJS **9** motion-picture, **movie, film,** big-screen, cinema, cinematic, filmistic, filmic; colorized; black-and-white; animated; animatronic, audio-animatronic

707 ENTERTAINER

<performer>

NOUNS **1** **entertainer,** public entertainer, performer; artist, artiste; impersonator, female impersonator; vaudevillian, vaudevillist; dancer, hoofer; song and dance man; chorus girl, show girl, chorine; coryphée; chorus boy; burlesque queen, stripteaser, exotic dancer, ecdysiast; stripper, peeler, stripteuse, bump-and-grinder; dancing girl, nautch girl, belly dancer; go-go dancer; geisha, geisha girl; mountebank; magician, conjurer, prestidigitator, sleight-of-hand artist; circus performer, clown; mummer, guisard; singer, musician; performance artist

2 **actor, actress,** player, stage player, stage performer, playactor, histrion, histrio, thespian, Roscius, theatrical, trouper; child actor; mummer, pantomime, pantomimist; monologist, diseur, diseuse, reciter; dramatizer; mime, mimer, mimic; strolling player, stroller; barnstormer; character actor, character actress, character; villain, antagonist, bad guy, heavy, black hat, villainess; juvenile, ingenue; soubrette; foil, feeder, stooge, straight person; utility person; protean actor; featured actor, leading man, leading lady, lead actor, lead actress; Method actor; matinee idol, star of stage and screen; romantic lead; rising star

3 circus artist, **circus performer**; trapeze artist, aerialist, flier; high-wire artist, tightrope walker, slack-roper artist, equilibrist; **acrobat**, tumbler; bareback rider; juggler; lion tamer, sword swallower; snake charmer; clown; ringmaster, equestrian director; puppeteer

4 **movie actor,** motion-picture actor; movie star, film star; starlet; day player, under-five player, contract player

5 ham, ham actor; grimacer

6 **lead,** leading man, leading lady, leading actor, leading actress, principal, star, rising star, superstar, megastar, headliner, headline attraction, feature attraction; costar; hero, heroine, protagonist; juvenile lead; first tragedian, heavy lead; prima donna, diva, singer; prima ballerina

7 **supporting actor, supporting actress;** support, supporting cast; supernumerary, super, supe, spear-carrier, extra; bit player; walking gentleman, walking lady, walk-on, mute; figurant, figurante; understudy, stand-in, standby, substitute, swing

8 **tragedian,** tragedienne

9 **comedian,** comedienne, comic, funnyman; farcist, farcer; stand-up comic, stand-up comedian, light comedian, genteel comedian, low comedian, slapstick comedian, hokum comic, hoke comic

10 buffoon, *buffo* <Ital>, **clown,** fool, jester, zany, merry-andrew, jack-pudding, pickle-herring, motley fool, motley, wearer of the cap and bells; harlequin; Pierrot; Pantaloon, Pantalone; Punch, Punchinello, Pulcinella, Polichinelle; Punch and Judy; Hanswurst; Columbine; Harlequin; Scaramouch

11 **cast,** cast of characters, characters, persons of the drama, *dramatis personae* <L>; supporting cast; company, acting company, outfit, troupe; repertory company, stock company, touring company; ensemble, chorus, *corps de ballet* <Fr>; circus troupe

708 MUSIC

<musical performance>

NOUNS **1** **music, music variety** <see list>, harmonious sound, the universal tongue; music appreciation, music theory; catalog, discography, back catalog

2 **melody,** melodiousness, tunefulness, musicalness, musicality; **tune,** tone, musical sound, musical quality, tonality; sweetness, dulcetness, mellifluence, mellifluousness

3 **harmony,** concord, concordance, concert, consonance, consonancy, consort, accordance, accord, monochord, concentus, symphony, diapason; synchronism, synchronization; attunement, tune, attune; chime, chiming; unison, unisonance, homophony, monody; euphony; light harmony, heavy harmony; two-part harmony, three-part harmony; harmony of the spheres, music of the spheres; harmonics

4 air, aria, tune, **melody,** line, melodic line, refrain, note, song, solo, solo part, soprano part, treble, lay, descant, lilt, strain, measure; canto, cantus

5 **piece,** opus, **composition,** production, work; score; arrangement, adaptation, orchestration, harmonization, setting; form; transcription, accompaniment

6 **classical music,** classic; concert music, serious music, longhair music, symphonic music, chamber music, operatic music; semiclassic, semiclassical music

7 **popular music,** pop music, pop, light music, popular song, popular tune, ballad; hit, song hit, hit tune; Tin Pan Alley; karaoke; hip hop, rap music, gangsta rap; ambient music, mood music; chartbuster

8 **dance music**, ballroom music, dances; syncopated music, syncopation; ragtime, rag, doo-wop; modern dance music

9 **jazz;** hot jazz, Dixieland, Basin Street, New Orleans, Chicago, traditional jazz, trad; swing, jive; bebop, bop; mainstream jazz; avant-garde jazz, the new music, modern jazz, progressive jazz, third-stream jazz, cool jazz, acid jazz; boogie, boogie-woogie; rhythm-and-blues (R and B), blues; walking bass, stride, stride piano

10 **rock-and-roll, rock music,** rock 'n' roll, rock, hard rock, soft rock, acid rock, folk rock, country rock, rockabilly, hard core, full-tilt boogie, heavy metal, punk rock, New Wave, fusion, grunge, alternative rock, alt-rock

11 **folk music,** folk song, ethnic music, ethnomusicology; folk ballad, balladry; border ballads; country music, hillbilly music; country-and-western music, western swing; old-time country music, old-timey music; bluegrass; field holler; soul, reggae, ska

12 **march,** martial music, military music; military march, quick march, quickstep march; processional march, recessional march; funeral march, dead march; wedding march

13 **vocal music,** song; **singing,** caroling, warbling, lyricism, vocalism, vocalization; operatic singing, bel canto, coloratura, bravura; choral singing; folk singing; croon, crooning; yodel, yodeling; scat, scat singing; intonation; hum, humming; solmization, tonic sol-fa, solfeggio, solfège, sol-fa, sol-fa exercise; singalong

14 **song,** lay, *chanson* <Fr>, carol, ditty, canticle, lilt; ballad, ballade, *ballata* <Ital>; *canzone* <Ital>; canzonet, *canzonetta* <Ital>; aubade, serenade, lullaby, barcarole, glee, chantey, chanty, shantey, chant, plainsong, chorale, hymn, psalm, anthem; love song, torch song; A-side

15 **solo;** karaoke; aria; operatic aria

16 <Italian arias> arietta, arioso; aria buffa, aria da capo, aria d'agilità, aria da chiesa, aria d'imitazione, aria fugata, aria parlante; bravura, aria di bravura; coloratura, aria di coloratura; cantabile, aria cantabile; recitativo

17 **sacred music, church music,** liturgical music; hymn, hymn-tune, hymnody, hymnology; psalm, psalmody; chorale, choral fantasy, anthem; motet; oratorio; passion; mass; requiem mass, requiem, missa brevis, missa solemnis; offertory, offertory sentence, offertory hymn; cantata; doxology, introit, canticle, paean, prosodion; recessional

18 **part music,** polyphonic music, part song, part singing, ensemble music, ensemble singing; duet, duo, *duettino* <Ital>; trio, terzet, *terzetto* <Ital>; quartet, string quartet; quintet; sextet, sestet; septet, septuor; octet; cantata, lyric cantata; madrigal, *madrigaletto* <Ital>; chorus, chorale, glee club, choir; choral singing; four-part, soprano-alto-tenor-base (SATB); barbershop quartet

19 **round,** rondo, rondeau, roundelay, catch, troll; rondino, rondoletto; fugue, canon, fugato

20 **polyphony,** polyphonism; counterpoint, contrapunto; plainsong, Gregorian chant, Ambrosian chant; musica ficta, false music

21 **monody**, monophony, homophony

22 **part,** melody part, voice part, voice, line; descant, canto, cantus, cantus planus, cantus firmus, plainsong, plain chant; prick song, cantus figuratus; soprano, tenor, treble, alto, contralto, baritone, bass, bassus; undersong; accompaniment; continuo, basso continuo, figured bass, thorough bass; ground bass, basso ostinato; drone, drone bass, bourdon, burden

23 **response,** responsory report, answer; echo; antiphon, antiphony, antiphonal chanting, antiphonal singing

24 **passage,** phrase, musical phrase, strain, part, motive, motif, theme, subject, figure; leitmotiv; movement; introductory phrase, anacrusis; statement, exposition, development, variation; division; period, musical sentence; section; measure; **verse, stanza;** burden, bourdon; **chorus, refrain,** response; folderol, ornament, cadence, harmonic close, resolution; coda, tailpiece; ritornello; intermezzo, interlude; bass passage; tutti, tutti passage; bridge, bridge passage

25 <passages by speed> presto, prestissimo; allegro, allegretto; scherzo, scherzando; adagio, adagietto; andante, andantino; largo, larghetto, larghissimo; crescendo; diminuendo, decrescendo;

rallentando, ritardando; ritenuto; piano, pianissimo; forte, fortissimo; staccato, marcato, marcando; pizzicato; spiccato; legato; stretto

26 **overture, prelude,** introduction, operatic overture, dramatic overture, concert overture, voluntary, descant, vamp; curtain raiser

27 **impromptu, extempore,** improvisation, interpolation; cadenza; ornament, flourish, ruffles and flourishes, grace note, appoggiatura, mordent, upper mordent, inverted mordent; run, melisma; vamp; lick, hot lick, riff

28 **score,** musical score, musical copy, music, notation, musical notation, written music, copy, draft, transcript, transcription, version, edition, text, arrangement; part; full score, orchestral score, compressed score, short score, piano score, vocal score, instrumental score; tablature, lute tablature; opera score, opera; libretto; sheet music; songbook, songster; hymnbook, hymnal; music paper; music roll; piped-in music; background

29 **staff,** stave; line, ledger line; bar, bar line; space, degree; brace

30 **execution, performance;** rendering, rendition, music-making, touch, expression; fingering; pianism; intonation; repercussion; pizzicato, staccato, spiccato, parlando, legato, cantando, rubato, demilegato, mezzo staccato, slur; glissando

31 **musicianship;** musical talent, musical flair, musicality; virtuosity; pianism; musical ear, ear for music; musical sense, sense of rhythm; absolute pitch, perfect pitch; relative pitch

32 **musical occasion**; choral service, service of lessons and carols, service of song, sing, singing, community singing, community sing, singfest, songfest, sing-in; karaoke; folk-sing, hootenanny; festival, fest, music festival; opera festival; folk-music festival, jazz festival, rock festival; jam session; music video

33 **performance,** musical performance, program, musical program, program of music; concert, symphony concert, chamber concert; philharmonic concert, philharmonic; popular concert, pops, pop concert; promenade concert, prom; band concert; recital; service of music; concert performance; **medley,** potpourri; swan song, farewell performance; greatest hits

34 **musical theater,** music theater, lyric theater, musical stage, lyric stage; music drama, lyric drama; song-play; opera, grand opera, light opera, ballad opera; comic opera, *opéra bouffe* <Fr>, *opera buffa* <Ital>; operetta; musical comedy; musical; Broadway musical; musical drama; ballet, *opéra ballet* <Fr>, comedy ballet, *ballet d'action* <Fr>, *ballet divertissement* <Fr>; dance drama; chorus show; song-and-dance act; minstrel, minstrel show

VERBS 35 **harmonize,** be harmonious, be in tune, be in concert, chord, accord, symphonize, synchronize, chime, blend, blend in, segue; tune, attune, atone, sound together, sound in tune; assonate; melodize, musicalize

36 **tune, tune up,** attune, atone, chord, put in tune; voice, string; tone up, tone down

37 strike up, strike up a tune, strike up the band, break into music, pipe up, pipe up a song, yerk out, **burst into song**

38 **sing, vocalize,** rock out, carol, descant, lilt, troll, line out, belt out, tear off; warble, trill, tremolo, quaver, shake; chirp, chirrup, twit, twitter; sing along, pipe, whistle, tweedle, tweedledee; chant; intone, intonate; croon; hum; yodel; roulade; chorus, choir, sing in chorus; hymn, anthem, psalm; make a joyful noise unto the Lord; sing the praises of; minstrel; ballad; serenade; sol-fa, do-re-mi, solmizate

39 **play,** perform, execute, render, do; interpret; make music; concertize; symphonize; chord; accompany; play by ear; play at, pound out, saw away at

40 **strum,** thrum, pluck, plunk, pick, twang, sweep the strings

41 **fiddle**, play violin, play the violin; scrape, saw

42 **blow a horn,** sound the horn, sound, blow, wind, toot, tootle, pipe, tweedle; bugle, carillon, clarion, fife, flute, trumpet, whistle; bagpipe, doodle; lip, tongue, double-tongue, triple-tongue

43 **syncopate,** play jazz, swing, jive, rag, jam, riff

44 **beat time,** keep time, tap, tap out the rhythm, keep tempo; count, count the beats; beat the drum, **drum**, play drum, play the drums, thrum, beat, thump, pound; tomtom; ruffle; beat a tattoo, sound a tattoo

45 **conduct,** direct, lead, wield the baton

46 **compose,** write, arrange, score, set, set to music, put to music; musicalize, melodize, harmonize; orchestrate; instrument, instrumentate; adapt, make an adaptation; transcribe, transpose

ADJS 47 **musical,** musically inclined, musicianly, with an ear for music; virtuoso, virtuose, virtuosic; music-loving, music-mad, musicophile, philharmonic; absolute, aleatory, aleatoric

48 **melodious,** melodic; musical, musiclike; tuneful, tunable; fine-toned, tonal, pleasant-sounding, agreeable-sounding, pleasant, appealing, agreeable, catchy, singable; euphonious, euphonic, lyric, lyrical, melic; lilting, songful, songlike; sweet, dulcet, sweet-sounding, achingly sweet, sweet-flowing; honeyed, mellifluent,

mellifluous, mellisonant, music-flowing; rich, mellow; sonorous, canorous; golden, golden-toned; silvery, silver-toned; sweet-voiced, golden-voiced, silver-voiced, silver-tongued, golden-tongued, music-tongued; ariose, arioso, cantabile

49 **harmonious,** harmonic, symphonious; harmonizing, chiming, blending, well-blended, blended; concordant, consonant, accordant, according, in accord, in concord, in concert; synchronous, synchronized, in sync, symphonic, in tune, tuned, attuned; in unison, in chorus; unisonous, unisonant; homophonic, monophonic, monodic; assonant, assonantal; rhythmic

50 **vocal,** singing; choral, choric; four-part; operatic; hymnal; psalmic, psalmodic, psalmodial; sacred, liturgical; treble, soprano, tenor, alto, falsetto; coloratura, lyric, bravura, dramatic, heroic; baritone; bass

51 **instrumental,** orchestral, symphonic, concert; dramatico-musical; jazz, syncopated, jazzy, rock, swing

52 **polyphonic,** contrapuntal

ADJS, ADVS 53 <directions, style> legato; staccato; spiccato; pizzicato; forte, fortissimo; piano, pianissimo; sordo; crescendo, accrescendo; decrescendo, diminuendo, morendo; dolce; amabile; affettuoso, con affetto; amoroso, con amore lamentabile; agitato, con agitazione; leggiero; agilmente, con agilità; capriccioso, a capriccio; scherzando, scherzoso; appassionato, appassionatamente; abbandono; brillante; parlando; a cappella; trillando, tremolando, tremoloso; sotto voce; stretto

54 <slowly> largo, larghetto, allargando; adagio, adagietto; andante, andantino, andante moderato; calando; a poco; lento; ritardando, rallentando; downtempo

55 <fast> presto, prestissimo; veloce; accelerando; vivace, vivacissimo; desto, con anima, con brio; allegro, allegretto; affrettando, moderato

56 **music variety**

absolute music
acid rock
Afro-beat
aleatory music
art music
art rock
atonal music, atonalism
background music, mood music
ballet music
baroque music
beach music
big band
bluegrass
boy band
bubblegum
calypso
cathedral music
chamber music
church music
circus music
classical music
country-and-western music
country music
country rock
cowpunk
dance hall
dance music
deca-rock, glitter rock
Delta blues
disco
ear candy
easy listening music
electronic music, synthesized music
elevator music, Muzak <tm>
ensemble music
field music
folk music
folk rock
funk
fusion
girl band
gospel music
Gregorian chant
grunge
hard rock
heavy metal
heavy rock
hillbilly music
hiphop
house music, House
incidental music
inspirational music
instrumental music
jazz music, jazz
jazz rock
Latin rock
light music
loft jazz
martial music, military music
New Age, New Wave
operatic music
organ music
part music
piped music
plainsong
political rock
pomp rock
polyphonic music
pop-rock
popular music, pop music
program music
progressive rock
progressive soul
psychobilly
punkabilly
punk rock
raga-rock
ragtime music, ragtime
rap music
reggae
rhythm and blues, R and B, the blues
rock music, rock 'n' roll
rockabilly
rococo music
romantic music
sacred music
salon music
semiclassical music
shock rock
ska
soul music
swing music, swing
techno-pop, techno-music
thirdstream music
through-composed music
twelve-tone music, serialism
vocal music
wind music
Zopf music
zydeco

709 HARMONICS, MUSICAL ELEMENTS

<study of musical sound>

NOUNS 1 **harmonics,** harmony; melodics; rhythmics; musicality; music, **music theory,** theory; musicology; musicography

2 **harmonization; orchestration, instrumentation;** arrangement, setting, adaptation, transcription; accompaniment; harmonic progression, chordal progression; phrasing, modulation, intonation, preparation, suspension, solution, resolution; tone painting

3 **tone, tonality**

4 **pitch,** tuning, tune, tone, key, note, register, tonality; height, depth; pitch range, tessitura; classical pitch, high pitch, diapason pitch,

normal pitch, French pitch, international pitch, concert pitch, new philharmonic pitch, standard pitch, low pitch, Stuttgart pitch, Scheibler's pitch, philharmonic pitch, philosophical pitch; temperament, equal temperament; absolute pitch, perfect pitch

5 **voice,** *voce* <Ital>; *voce di petto* <Ital>, chest voice; *voce di testa* <Ital>, head voice; soprano, mezzo-soprano, dramatic soprano, soprano spinto, lyric soprano, coloratura soprano; alto; boy soprano; male soprano, castrato; contralto; tenor, lyric tenor, operatic tenor, heldentenor, heroic tenor, Wagnerian tenor; countertenor, male alto; baritone, light baritone, lyric baritone; bass, basso, basso profundo; basso cantante, lyric bass; basso buffo, comic bass; treble, falsetto

6 **scale,** gamut, register, compass, range, diapason; diatonic scale, chromatic scale, modal scale, enharmonic scale, major scale, minor scale, natural minor, harmonic minor, melodic minor, whole-tone scale; great scale; octave scale, twelve-tone scale, dodecuple scale, pentatonic scale; tetrachordal scale; tone block, tone row, tone cluster

7 **sol-fa,** tonic sol-fa, do-re-mi; Guidonian syllables, ut, re, mi, fa, sol, la; sol-fa syllables, do, re, mi, fa, sol, la, ti, do; solmization, solfeggio; fixed-do system, movable-do system; bobization

8 <diatonic series> tetrachord, chromatic tetrachord, enharmonic tetrachord, Dorian tetrachord; hexachord, hard hexachord, natural hexachord, soft hexachord; pentachord

9 **octave,** *ottava* <Ital>, eighth; *ottava alta* <Ital>, *ottava bassa* <Ital>; small octave, great octave; contraoctave, subcontraoctave, double contraoctave; one-line octave, two-line octave, four-line octave, two-foot octave, four-foot octave; tenor octave

10 **mode,** octave species; major mode, minor mode; Greek mode, Ionian mode, Dorian mode, Phrygian mode, Lydian mode, mixolydian mode, Aeolian mode, Locrian mode; hypoionian mode, hypodorian mode, hypophrygian mode, hypolydian mode, hypoaeolian mode, hypomixolydian mode, hypolocrian mode; Gregorian mode, ecclesiastical mode, church mode, medieval mode; plagal mode, authentic mode; Indian mode, Hindu mode, raga

11 **form,** arrangement, pattern, model, design; song form, lied form, primary form; sonata form, sonata allegro, ternary form, symphonic form, canon form, toccata form, fugue form, rondo form

12 **notation,** character, mark, symbol, signature, sign; proportional notation; chart, paper, dot; custos, direct; cancel; bar, measure; measure signature, time signature, key signature; tempo mark, metronome mark, metronomic mark; fermata, hold, pause; lead; slur, tie, ligature, vinculum, enharmonic tie; swell; accent, accent mark, expression mark; ledger, staff, stave, line, space, brace, rest, interval

13 **clef;** C clef, soprano clef; alto clef, viola clef; tenor clef; F clef, bass clef; G clef, treble clef

14 **note,** musical note, notes of a scale; tone; sharp, flat, natural; accidental; double whole note, breve; whole note, semibreve; half note, minim; quarter note, crotchet; eighth note, quaver; sixteenth note, semiquaver; thirty-second note, demisemiquaver; sixty-fourth note, hemidemisemiquaver; tercet, triplet; sustained note, dominant, dominant note; enharmonic, enharmonic note; separation, hammering, staccato, spiccato; connected, smooth, legato; responding note, report; shaped note, patent note

15 **key,** key signature, tonality, sharps and flats; keynote, tonic; tonic key; major, minor, major key, minor key, tonic major, tonic minor; supertonic, mediant, submediant, dominant, subdominant, subtonic; pedal point, organ point

16 **harmonic,** harmonic tone, overtone, upper partial tone; flageolet tone

17 **chord,** *concento* <Ital>, combination of tones, combination of notes; major chord, minor chord, primary chord, secondary chord, tonic chord, dominant chord; tertiary chord, third, fourth; interval, major interval, minor interval

18 **ornament,** grace, arabesque, embellishment; flourish, roulade, flight, run; passage, division; florid phrase, florid; coloratura; incidental, incidental note; grace note, appoggiatura, arpeggio, acciaccatura; rubato; mordent, single mordent, double mordent, long mordent; inverted mordent, pralltriller; turn, back turn, inverted turn; cadence, cadenza

19 **trill,** trillo; trillet, *trilleto* <Ital>; tremolo, tremolant, tremolando; quaver, quiver, tremble, tremor, flutter, falter, shake; vibrato

20 **interval,** degree, step, note, tone; second, third, fourth, fifth, sixth, seventh, octave; prime interval, unison interval, major interval, minor interval, harmonic intrval, melodic interval, enharmonic interval, diatonic interval; parallel intervals, consecutive intervals, parallel fifths, parallel octaves; whole step, major second; half step, halftone, semitone, minor second; augmented interval; diminished interval; diatonic semitone, chromatic semitone, less semitone, quarter semitone, tempered semitone, mean semitone; quarter step, enharmonic diesis; diatessaron,

diapason; Picardy third; augmented fourth, tritone

21 **rest,** pause; whole rest, breve rest, semibreve rest, half rest, minim, quarter rest, eighth rest, sixteenth rest, thirty-second rest, sixty-fourth rest

22 **rhythm,** beat, meter, measure, number, numbers, movement, lilt, swing; prosody, metrics; rhythmic pattern, rhythmic phrase

23 **cadence**, cadency, authentic cadence, plagal cadence, mixed cadence, perfect cadence, imperfect cadence, half cadence, deceptive cadence, false cadence, interrupted cadence, suspended cadence

24 **tempo,** time, beat, time pattern, timing; time signature; simple time, simple measure, compound time, compound measure; two-part time, duple time, three-part time, triple time, triplet, four-part time, quadruple time, five-part time, quintuple time, six-part time, sextuple time, seven-part time, septuple time, nine-part time, nonuple time; two-four time, six-eight time; tempo rubato, rubato; mixed times; syncopation, syncope; ragtime, rag; waltz time, three-four time, three-quarter time, andante tempo, march tempo; largo; presto

25 **accent**, accentuation, rhythmical accent, rhythmical accentuation, ictus, emphasis, stress arsis, thesis

26 **beat,** throb, pulse, pulsation; downbeat, upbeat, offbeat; bar beat

ADJS 27 **tonal,** tonic; chromatic, enharmonic; semitonic

28 **rhythmic,** rhythmical, cadent, cadenced, measured, metric, metrical; in rhythm, in numbers; beating, throbbing, pulsing, pulsating, pulsative, pulsatory

29 **syncopated;** ragtime, ragtimey; jazz; jazzy, jazzed, jazzed up, hot, swingy

ADVS 30 **in time,** in tempo, *a tempo* <Ital>

710 MUSICIAN

<musical performer>

NOUNS 1 **musician,** musico, music maker, professional musician; performer, executant, interpreter, tunester, artiste, artist, concert artist, player, virtuoso, virtuosa; maestro; recitalist; soloist, duettist; singer; street musician, busker

2 **popular musician**, pop musician; ragtime musician; jazz musician, jazzman; swing musician; big-band musician; rock musician, rock 'n' roll musician; blues rocker, soul man, soulster; shoegazer; stage-diver

3 **player, instrumentalist,** instrumental musician; bandman, bandsman, bandmate; orchestral musician; symphonist; concertist; accompanist, accompanyist

4 **wind player,** wind-instrumentalist, horn player; French-horn player, hornist; horner, piper, tooter; bassoonist, bugler, clarinetist, cornettist, fifer, oboist, piccoloist, saxophonist, trombonist; trumpeter, trumpet major; fluegelhornist; flutist, flautist

5 **string musician,** strummer, picker, thrummer, twanger; banjoist, banjo-picker, citharist, guitarist, guitar-picker, classical guitarist, folk guitarist, lute player, lutenist, lutist, lyrist, mandolinist, theorbist; violinist, fiddler; bass violinist, bassist, bass player, contrabassist; violoncellist, cellist, celloist; violist; harpist, harper; zitherist, psalterer

6 xylophonist, marimbaist, vibist, vibraphonist

7 **pianist,** pianiste, pianofortist, piano player, ivory tickler; keyboard player, keyboardist; harpsichordist, clavichordist, monochordist; accordionist, concertinist

8 **organist,** organ player

9 organ-grinder, hurdy-gurdist, hurdy-gurdyist, hurdy-gurdy man

10 **drummer, percussionist,** tympanist, timpanist, kettle-drummer; taborer

11 cymbalist, cymbaler; bell ringer, carilloneur, campanologist, campanist; triangle player

12 **orchestra, band,** chamber orchestra, symphony; ensemble, combo, group; strings, string section, woodwind, woodwinds, woodwind section, brass, brasses, brass section; desks; marching band; drum circle, drum corps; fife and drum corps; garage band; tribute band

13 **singer, vocalist,** vocalizer, voice, songster, songbird, warbler, lead singer, backup vocalist, caroler, melodist, minstrel, cantor; songstress, singstress, cantatrice, chanteuse, song stylist, canary; chanter, chantress; aria singer, lieder singer, opera singer, diva, prima donna; improvisator; rap singer; blues singer, torch singer; crooner, rock singer, rock-and-roll singer; yodeler; country singer, folk singer, folkie; psalm singer, hymner; singing voice

14 **minstrel,** ballad singer, balladeer, bard, rhapsode, rhapsodist; wandering minstrel, strolling minstrel, troubadour, trovatore, trouvère, minnesinger, scop, gleeman, fili, jongleur; street singer, wait; serenader; **folk singer,** folk-rock singer; country-and-western singer

15 **choral singer,** choir member, chorister, chorus singer, choralist; choirman, choirboy, choirgirl; chorus girl, chorine

16 **chorus,** chorale, **choir,** choral group, choral society, oratorio society, chamber chorus, men's

chorus, women's chorus, mixed chorus, ensemble, voices; **glee club**, singing club, singing society; *a cappella* choir; choral symphony

17 **conductor,** leader, maestro, symphonic conductor, music director, director; orchestra leader, band leader, bandmaster, band major, drum major

18 **choirmaster,** choral director, choral conductor, chorus master, song leader; choir chaplain, minister of music, precentor, cantor, chorister

19 **concertmaster,** concertmeister, first violinist; first chair

20 **composer,** scorer, arranger, musicographer; melodist, melodizer; harmonist, harmonizer; orchestrator; adapter; symphonist; tone poet; ballad maker, ballad writer, balladeer, balladist, balladmonger; madrigalist; lyrist; hymnist, hymnographer, hymnologist; contrapuntist; songwriter, songsmith, tunesmith; lyricist, librettist; musicologist, ethnomusicologist; music teacher

21 **music lover,** philharmonic person, music fan, music buff, musicophile; musicmonger; concertgoer, operagoer, opera lover; tonalist

22 <patrons> the Muses, the Nine, sacred Nine, tuneful Nine, Pierides; Apollo, Apollo Musagetes; Orpheus; Erato, Euterpe, Polymnia, Polyhymnia, Terpsichore, St. Cecilia

23 **songbird,** singing bird, **songster,** feathered songster, warbler; nightingale, Philomel; bulbul, canary, cuckoo, lark, mavis, mockingbird, oriole, ringdove, song sparrow, thrush

711 MUSICAL INSTRUMENTS

<music-producing devices>

1 **musical instrument,** instrument of music; electronic instrument, synthesizer, Mellotron <tm>, Moog synthesizer <tm>

2 **string instrument, stringed instrument,** chordophone; strings, string choir

3 **harp, lyre**

4 **plucked stringed instrument** <see list>

5 **viol and violin** <see list>, chest of viols; Stradivarius, Stradivari, Strad; Amati, Cremona, Guarnerius; bow, fiddlestick, fiddlebow; bridge, sound hole, soundboard, fingerboard, tuning peg, scroll; string, G string, D string, A string, E string

6 **wind instrument,** wind; aerophone; horn, pipe, tooter; mouthpiece, embouchure, lip, chops; valve, bell, reed, double reed, key, slide

7 brass, brass instrument, brass wind, **brass wind instrument** <see list>; brasses, brass choir

8 **woodwind** <see list>, wood instrument, woodwind instrument; woods, woodwind choir; reed instrument, reed; double-reed instrument, double reed; single-reed instrument, single reed

9 **bagpipe**, bagpipes, pipes, union pipes, war pipes, Irish pipes, doodlesack; cornemuse, musette; sordellina; chanter, drone; pipe bag

10 **harmonica,** mouth organ, mouth harp, harp, French harp, harmonicon; Jew's harp, mouth bow; kazoo

11 **accordion,** piano accordion; concertina; squeeze box; mellophone; bandonion

12 **keyboard instrument** <see list>, piano, harpsichord, clavichord, player piano; music roll, piano player roll

13 **organ,** pipe organ, keyboard wind instrument

14 **hurdy-gurdy,** vielle, barrel organ, hand organ, grind organ, street organ

15 **music box,** musical box; orchestrion, orchestrina

16 **percussion instrument, drum** <see list>, percussion, drum kit; drumstick, jazz stick, tymp stick

17 **keyboard,** fingerboard; console, keys, manual, claviature; piano keys, ivories, eighty-eight, organ manual, great, swell, choir, solo, echo; pedals

18 **carillon,** chimes, chime of bells; electronic carillon

19 **organ stop,** stop rank, register

20 string, chord, steel string, wound string, nylon string; fiddlestring, catgut; horsehair; music wire, piano wire

21 plectrum, plectron, pick

22 <aids> metronome, rhythmometer; tone measurer, monochord, sonometer; tuning fork, tuning bar, diapason; pitch pipe, tuning pipe; mute; music stand, music lyre; baton, conductor's baton, stick; MIDI

23 **brass wind instrument**

alpenhorn, alphorn
althorn, alto horn
ballad horn
baritone horn
bass horn
bombardon
buccina
bugle, bugle horn
clarion
cornet, cornet-à-pistons
cornopean
double-bell euphonium
E-flat horn
euphonium
F horn
flugelhorn
French horn
helicon
horn
hunting horn, *corno di caccia* <Ital>
key trumpet
lituus
lur
mellophone
nyas taranga
oliphant
ophicleide
orchestral horn
pocket trumpet
post horn
sackbut
saxcornet
saxhorn
saxophone
saxtuba
serpent

slide trombone, sliphorn
sousaphone
tenor tuba
tromba
trombone
trumpet
tuba
valve trombone
valve trumpet

24 keyboard instrument

baby grand
cembalo
clarichord
clavichord
clavicittern
clavicymbal, clavicembalo
clavicytherium
clavier
concert grand
console piano
cottage piano
couched harp
digital piano
dulcimer harpsichord
electronic keyboard
fortepiano
grand piano
hammer dulcimer
harmonichord
harpsichord
lyrichord
manichord
melodion
melopiano
monochord
pair of virginals
parlor grand
pianette
pianino
piano, pianoforte
piano-violin
Pianola <tm>
player piano, mechanical piano
sostinente pianoforte
spinet
square piano
street piano
upright, upright piano
violin piano
virginal

25 percussion instrument, drum

anvil
bass drum
bells
bones
bongo drum
carillon
castanets
celesta
chimes
clappers
conga
cowbell
crash cymbal
cymbals, potlids
drumhead
drumskin
finger cymbals
gamelan
glockenspiel
gong
handbells
highhat cymbal
kazoo
kettledrum, timbal, timpani
lithophone
lyra
maraca
marimba
mbira, kalimba
membranophone
metallophone
mirliton
musical glasses, glass harmonica
musical saw
nagara <India>
naker
orchestral bells
rattle
rattlebones
ride cymbal
side drum
sizzler
snappers
snare drum
spoons
tabor
tambourine
tam-tam
tenor drum
thumb piano
timbale
timbrel
tintinnabula
tom-tom
tonitruone
triangle
troll-drum
tubular bells
vibraphone, vibraharp, vibes
war drum
xylophone
xylorimba

26 plucked stringed instrument

acoustic guitar
angelica, angel lute
Appalachian dulcimer
Autoharp <tm>
archlute
balalaika
bandore
bandurria <Sp>
banjo
banjolin
banjorine
banjo-ukulele, banjuke, banjulele, banjo-uke
banjo-zither
bass guitar
bouzouki
centerhole guitar
chitarra
cittern
classical guitar
colascione
concert guitar
Dobro guitar <tm>
electric guitar
F-hole guitar
gittern
harp
Hawaiian guitar
lute
lyre
mando-bass
mando-cello
mandolin, mandola
mandolute
mandore
oud
pandora
psaltery
rhythm guitar
samisen
sitar
Spanish guitar
steel guitar
tamboura, tambura
theorbo
troubadour fiddle
ukulele, uke
vina
zither

27 viol and violin

alto viol, tenor viol
baritone viol, viola d'amore
baryton
basso da camera <Ital>
bass viol, viola da gamba
contrabass
crwth
descant viol
double bass, violone, bass viol, bass, doghouse, bass fiddle, bull fiddle
gusla, gusle
kit
kit violin
lira da braccio
lira da gamba
lyra viol
nyckelharpa
pocket fiddle, kit fiddle
rebab
rebec
treble viol
trumpet marine, tromba marina
vielle
viol da braccio, viola da braccio
viol da spalla, viola da spalla
viol di bordone, viola di bordone
viol di fagotto, viola di fagotto
viola, tenor
viola alta
viola bastarda
viola pomposa
violette
violin, fiddle
violinette
violino piccolo
violoncello, cello
violoncello piccolo
violotta

28 woodwind

aulos
bagpipe
bass oboe, basset oboe, heckelphone
bass clarinet
basset horn
bassoon
bombarde

bombardon
clarinet, licorice stick
contrabassoon,
  contrafagotto
double bassoon
English horn,
  cor anglais <Fr>
fife
fipple flute, fipple pipe
flageolet
flute
heckclarina
hornpipe
krummhorn, cromorne,
  cromorna, crumhorn
musette
nose-flute
oaten reed
oboe, hautboy, hautbois
oboe d'amore <Ital>
oboe da caccia <Ital>
ocarina, sweet potato
Pandean pipe
panpipe
pibgorn, pibcorn
piccolo
pipe
pommer
recorder
saxophone, sax
shakuhachi
shawm
sonorophone
syrinx, shepherd's pipe
tabor pipe
tenoroon
tin whistle, penny
  whistle
transverse flute
whistle

712 VISUAL ARTS

<*art making something to be viewed*>

NOUNS **1 visual arts;** art, artwork, the arts; fine art, fine arts, *beaux arts* <Fr>; minor arts; arts of design, design, designing; art form; abstract art, representative art; graphic arts; plastic art; **arts and crafts;** decorative arts; primitive art, cave art; folk art; process art; guerrilla art; calligraphy; commercial art, applied art, industrial art; modern art, contemporary art; sculpture; ceramics; photography; etching, acid etching, engraving; decoration; artist; artistic license

2 craft, manual art, industrial art, **handicraft,** arts and crafts, artisan work, artisanry, craftwork, artisanship; industrial design; woodcraft, woodwork, carpentry, woodworking, metalcraft, stonecraft; ceramics, glassmaking; fiber art; paper folding, origami, kirigami

3 painting, coloring; the brush; acrylic painting, oil painting, watercolor painthin, face painting; airbrushing

4 drawing, draftsmanship, sketching, delineation; black and white, charcoal; mechanical drawing, drafting; freehand drawing, life drawing, stick figure

5 scenography, ichnography, orthographic projection, orthogonal projection

6 artistry, art, talent, artistic skill, flair, artistic flair, artistic invention; artiness, arty-craftiness, artsy-craftsiness; artistic temperament, artistic taste; virtu, artistic quality

7 art style, style; lines; genre; **school, group, movement** <see list>; the grand style

8 treatment; technique, draftsmanship, brushwork, painterliness; composition, design, arrangement; grouping, balance; color, values; atmosphere, tone; shadow, shading; line; perspective

9 work of art, artwork; object of art, objet d'art, art object, artistic production, artistic creation, piece, work; study, design, composition; creation, brainchild; virtu, article of virtu; masterpiece, *chef d'œuvre* <Fr>, masterwork, master, old master, classic; museum piece; grotesque; statue; mobile, stabile; nude, still life; pastiche, *pasticcio* <Ital>; artware; bric-a-brac; kitsch

10 picture; image, likeness, representation, tableau; a poem without words; photograph; illustration, illumination; miniature; copy, reproduction; print, color print; engraving, stencil, block print; daub; abstraction, abstract; mural, fresco, wall painting; cyclorama, panorama; montage, collage, assemblage; still life, study in still life; tapestry, mosaic, stained glass, stained glass window, icon, altarpiece, diptych, triptych

11 scene, view, scape; landscape; waterscape, riverscape, seascape, seapiece; airscape, skyscape, cloudscape; snowscape; cityscape, townscape; farmscape; pastoral; treescape; diorama; exterior, interior

12 drawing; delineation; line drawing; sketch, draft; black and white, chiaroscuro; charcoal, crayon, pen-and-ink, pencil drawing, charcoal drawing, pastel, pastel painting, crayon drawing; silhouette; vignette; doodle; rough draft, rough outline, study, design; caricature; cartoon, sinopia; diagram, graph; mechanical drawing; silver-print drawing, tracing; graffito, scribble; clip art

13 painting, canvas, easel picture, silent poetry; oil painting, oil; watercolor, water, aquarelle, wash, wash drawing; acrylic painting; finger painting; tempera, egg tempera; gouache; sand painting; body painting, body art

14 portrait, portraiture, portrayal; head; profile; silhouette, shadow figure; nude; miniature

15 cartoon, caricature; comic strip; comic section, comics, funny paper, funnies; comic book; animated cartoon, animation

16 <visual arts> design specialty <see list>; animation, architecture, basketry, body decoration, bookbinding, calligraphy, caricature, clothing design, fashion design, decorative arts, crafts, drawing, enamelwork, floral decoration, furnishings design, furniture design, glass design, graphic arts, illustration, intaglio, interior design, jewelry design, lacquerwork, landscape design, lithography, metalwork, mixed media, mosaic, painting, photography, photo shoot; plastic art, pottery, printmaking, relief, engraving, screen printing, sculpture, light sculpture, serigraphy, tapestry, typography, woodcut

17 **studio,** *atelier* <Fr>; **gallery**

18 <art equipment> palette; easel; paintbox; art paper, drawing paper, watercolor paper, tracing paper; sketchbook, sketchpad; canvas, artists' canvas; canvas board; scratchboard; lay figure; camera obscura, camera lucida; maulstick; palette knife, spatula; brush, paintbrush; airbrush, spray gun; pencil, drawing pencil; pen, ink, marker, highlighter; crayon, charcoal, chalk, pastel; stump; painter's cream; ground; pigments, medium; siccative, drier; fixative, varnish; **paint**

VERBS 19 **portray, picture,** picturize, depict, limn, draw a picture, paint a picture; paint; brush, brush in; color, tint, colorize; lay on a color; daub; scumble; **draw, sketch,** delineate; draft; pencil, chalk, crayon, color in, charcoal; draw in, pencil in; dash off, scratch; doodle; design; diagram; cartoon; copy, trace; stencil; touch up; hatch, crosshatch, shade

ADJS 20 **artistic,** painterly; arty, arty-crafty, artsy-craftsy, artsy-fartsy; art-minded, art-conscious; imaginative, creative, stylized, aesthetic; tasteful; beautiful; decorative, ornamental; well-composed, well-grouped, well-arranged, well-varied; of consummate art; in the grand style

21 **pictorial,** pictural, **graphic,** picturesque; picturable; photographic; scenographic; painty, pastose; scumbled; monochrome, polychrome; freehand; nonverbal, extradictionary

22 **art school, group, movement**

abstract expressionism
action painting
Aesthetic Movement
American scene painting
Art Deco, Deco
Art Nouveau
Arts and Crafts movement
Ashcan school, the Eight
avant-garde
Barbizon school
baroque
Bauhaus
Biedermeier
Bolognese
British
classical abstraction
Cobra
cubism
Dada
De Stijl
Der Blaue Reiter
Die Brücke
Dutch
eclectic
expressionism
fauvism, Les Fauves
Flemish
Florentine
Fontainebleau
French
Glasgow
Gothic
Honfleur
Hudson River
impressionism
International Gothic, International
Italian
Jugendstil
L'Age d'or
letrist
Lombard
Madinensor
Madrid
Mannerist
Milanese
Modenese
modern art
modernism
Momentum
'N'
Neapolitan
neoclassicism
Neonism
New Objectivity
New York
op art
Origine
Paduan
Parisian
Phases
plein-air, pleinairism
pointillism
pre-Columbian
Pre-Raphaelite
Raphaelite
realism
Reflex
Restany
Rocky Mountain
rococo
Roman, Romanesque
romanticism
Scottish Colorists
Sienese
Spur
Suprematism
tachisme
tenebrists
The Ten
Tuscan
Umbrian
Unit One
Venetian
Wanderers
Washington

23 **design specialty**

accessory design
appearance design
architectural design
automotive design
book design
clothing design, fashion design
computer-aided design, computer-assisted design
costume design
ergonomics, human engineering, human factors engineering
environmental design
furniture design
garden design
graphic design
handbag design
immersive design
industrial design
information design
interior decorating
interior design
jewelry design
landscape architecture
lighting design
package design
pottery design
process design
product design
research design
stage design
systems design
textile design
typographic design
urban design

713 GRAPHIC ARTS

<2D visual art>

NOUNS 1 **graphic arts, graphics,** graphic design; printmaking; painting; drawing; relief-carving; photography; **printing**; computer graphics, digital art, graphic artist, graphic designer

2 **engraving** <see list>, engravement, graving, enchasing, tooling, chiseling, incising, incision, lining, scratching, slashing, scoring; inscription, inscript; type-cutting; marking, line, scratch, slash, score; hatching, cross-hatching; etchhing; stipple, stippling; tint, demitint, half tint; burr; photoengraving

3 **lithography,** planography, autolithography,

artist lithography; chromolithography; photolithography, offset lithography

4 stencil printing, stencil; silk-screen printing, serigraphy; monotype; glass printing, decal, decalcomania; cameography

5 **printmaking,** print, numbered print, imprint, impression, first impression, impress; negative; color print; etching; lithograph; autolithograph; chromolithograph; lithotype; crayon engraving, graphotype; block, block print, linoleum-block print, rubber-block print, wood engraving, woodprint, xylograph, cut, woodcut, woodblock; vignette

6 **plate,** steel plate, copperplate, chalcograph; zincograph; stone, lithographic stone; printing plate

7 **proof,** artist's proof, proof before letter, open-letter proof, remarque proof

8 **engraving tool,** graver, burin, tint tool, style; etching ball; etching ground, etching varnish; scorper; rocker; die, punch, stamp, intaglio, seal; hole punch

VERBS 9 **engrave,** grave, tool, enchase, incise, sculpture, inscribe, character, mark, line, crease, score, scratch, scrape, cut, carve, chisel; groove, furrow; stipple, cribble; hatch, crosshatch; lithograph, autolithograph; print

10 **etch,** eat, eat out, corrode, bite, bite in

ADJS 11 **engraved,** graven, graved, glypt-, glypto-; tooled, enchased, chased, inscribed, incised, marked, lined, creased, cut, carved, glyphic, sculptured, insculptured; grooved, furrowed; **printed**, imprinted, impressed, stamped, numbered

12 glyptic, glyptical, glyptographic, lapidary, lapidarian; xylographic, wood-block; lithographic, autolithographic, chromolithographic; aquatint, aquatinta, mezzotint

13 **engraving (types)**

acid-blast
aquatint
black-line engraving
cerography
chalcography
chalk engraving
chasing
copperplate engraving
crayon engraving
cribbling, *manière criblée* <Fr>
drypoint, draw-point engraving
eccentric engraving
electric engraving
etching
gem engraving
glass-cutting
glyptics, glyptography
intaglio
lignography
line cut
line engraving
linocut
lithograph
metal cut
metal engraving
mezzotint
photochemical engraving, photoetching
photoengraving
plate engraving
pyrography, pyrogravure, pokerwork
relief etching
relief method
soft-ground etching
steel engraving
stipple engraving
woodburning, xylopyrography
woodcut, wood engraving
xylography
zinc etching
zincography, zinc engraving

714 PHOTOGRAPHY

<art of taking photos>

NOUNS 1 **photography** <see list>, **picture-taking,** photo shoot; image capture; cinematography, motion-picture photography; color photography, black-and-white photography; photochromy, heliochromy; 3-D, three-dimensional photography; photofinishing; photogravure; radiography, X-ray photography; photogrammetry, phototopography; digital photography; point-and-click, point-and-shoot; 3D printing, 4-D

2 **photographer**, shutterbug, photojournalist, press photographer, paparazzo, lensman, shooter, photog; digital artist

3 **photograph, photo**, heliograph, picture, shot; snapshot, snap, image; black-and-white photograph; color photograph, color print, heliochrome; Polaroid <tm>; selfie; slide, slide show; diapositive, transparency; candid photograph; take; still, still photograph; photomural; montage, photomontage; aerial photograph, photomap; facsimile transmission, fax transmission; telephotograph, telephoto, wirephoto; photomicrograph, microphotograph; metallograph; microradiograph; electron micrograph; photochronograph, chronophotograph; radiograph, X-ray; portrait, closeup; action shot, action sequence; pinup, cheesecake, beefcake; police photograph, mug, mug shot; rogues' gallery; photobiography; faceprint; 3D printer

4 tintype, ferrotype, ambrotype, daguerreotype, calotype, talbotype, collotype, albertype, artotype, heliotype, photocollotype, autotype, vitrotype

5 **print,** photoprint, positive; glossy, matte, semi-matte; enlargement, blowup; photocopy, photostat, photostatic copy, stat, xerox, xerox copy; copy machine; microfilm, microfiche, microphotocopy, microprint, microcopy; blueprint, cyanotype; slide, transparency, lantern slide; contact printing, projection printing; photogravure; hologram; double exposure

6 shadowgraph, shadowgram, skiagraph, skiagram; radiograph, radiogram, scotograph; X-ray, X-ray photograph, roentgenograph, roentgenogram; photofluorogram; photogram

7 spectrograph, spectrogram; spectroheliogram

8 <motion pictures> **shot; take,** retake; close-up, long shot, medium shot, full shot, group shot, deuce shot, matte shot, process shot, boom shot, travel shot, trucking shot, follow-focus shot, pan shot, panoramic shot, rap shot, reverse shot, reverse-angle shot, wild shot, zoom shot; motion picture; kinescope

9 **exposure,** time exposure; shutter speed; f-stop, lens opening; film rating, film speed, film gauge, ASA number, *Deutsche Industrie Normen* (DIN), DX code; exposure meter, light meter

10 **film; negative;** printing paper, photographic paper; **plate;** dry plate; vehicle; motion-picture film, panchromatic film, monochromatic film, orthochromatic film, black-and-white film, color film, color negative film, color reversal film, Polaroid film <tm>; microfilm, bibliofilm; sound-on-film, sound film; sound track, soundstripe; Super-8, videotape, 35mm; roll, cartridge; pack, bipack, tripack; frame; emulsion, dope, backing

11 **camera,** Kodak, Polaroid <tm>; digital camera, digicam; camera phone, selfie stick; disposable camera; POV camera; photo booth; video camera, camcorder; TV camera, motion-picture camera, cinematograph; security camera; scanner

12 **projector;** motion-picture projector, cineprojector, cinematograph, vitascope; slide projector, magic lantern, stereopticon; slide viewer

13 **processing solution;** developer, soup; fixer, fixing bath; sodium thiosulfate, sodium hyposulfite, hypo; acid stop, stop bath, short-stop, short-stop bath; emulsion

VERBS 14 **photograph, shoot**, take a photograph, take a picture, take one's picture; snap, snapshot, snapshoot; film, capture on film; mug; daguerreotype, talbotype, calotype; photostat; xerox; microfilm; photomap; pan; X-ray, radiograph, roentgenograph; photobomb

15 **process; develop; print;** blueprint; blow up, enlarge

16 **project,** show, screen

ADJS 17 **photographic,** photo; photogenic, picturesome; photosensitive, photoactive; panchromatic; telephotographic, telephoto; tintype; three-dimensional (3-D)

18 **photography (types)**

acoustical holography
aerophotography, aerial photography, air photography
animation photography
architectural photography
astrophotography
available-light photography
candid photography
chronophotography
cinematography, motion-picture photography
cinephotomicrography
color photography
digital photography
documentary photography
electrophotography
fashion photography
flash photography
heliophotography
holography
infrared photography
integral photography
landscape photography
laser photography
macrophotography
microfilming
microphotography
miniature photography
phonophotography
photoheliography
photojournalism
photomacrography
photomicrography
photoreproduction
phototopography
portraiture
pyrophotography
radiation-field photography, Kirlian photography
radiography
reprography
schlieren photography
skiagraphy
spectroheliography
spectrophotography
sports photography
stereophotography
still-life photography
stroboscopic photography
studio photography
telephotography
thermography
time-lapse photography
underwater photography
uranophotography
wildlife photography
xerography
X-ray photography

715 SCULPTURE

<art of sculpting>

NOUNS 1 **sculpture, sculpturing;** plastic art, modeling; statuary; stonecutting; gem-cutting, masonry; carving, stone carving, bone-carving, cameo carving, scrimshaw, whittling, woodcarving, xyloglyphy; embossing, engraving, chasing, toreutics, founding, casting, molding, plaster casting, lost-wax process, *cire perdue* <Fr>; soft sculpture; ice sculpture; sculptor

2 <**sculptured piece**> sculpture; glyph; **statue;** marble, bronze, terra cotta, scrimshaw, woodcarving; mobile, stabile; cast; found object, *objet trouvé* <Fr>; collage, assemblage

3 **relief,** relievo; embossment, boss; half relief, *mezzo-rilievo* <Ital>; high relief, *alto-rilievo* <Ital>; low relief, bas-relief, *basso-rilievo* <Ital>, *rilievo stiacciato* <Ital>; sunk relief, *cavo-rilievo* <Ital>, coelanaglyphic sculpture, intaglio, *intaglio rilievo, intaglio rilevato* <Ital>; *repoussé* <Fr>; glyph, anaglyph; glyptograph; mask; plaquette; medallion; medal; cameo, cameo glass, sculptured glass; cut glass

4 <tools, materials> chisel, point, mallet, burin, modeling tool, spatula; cutting torch, welding torch, soldering iron; solder; modeling clay, Plasticine <tm>, sculptor's wax; plaster

VERBS 5 sculpture, **sculpt**, sculp, insculpture; carve, chisel, cut, grave, engrave, chase; weld, solder; assemble; model, mold; cast, found

ADJS 6 **sculptural,** sculpturesque, sculptitory; statuary; statuesque, statuelike; monumental, marmoreal; plastic

7 **sculptured,** sculpted; sculptile; molded, modeled, ceroplastic; carved, chiseled; graven, engraven, engraved, incised; in relief, in high relief, in low relief; glyphic, glyptic, anaglyphic, anaglyptic; anastatic; embossed, chased, hammered, toreutic; *repoussé* <Fr>; tactile

716 ARTIST

<maker of art>

NOUNS 1 **artist,** *artiste* <Fr>, creator, maker; fine artist, master, old master; dauber, daubster; copyist; **craftsman, artisan**; street artist

2 **illustrator**; limner, delineator, depicter, picturer, portrayer, imager; illuminator; calligrapher; commercial artist; drawer, renderer, doodler, scribbler; pastelist; jewelry maker

3 **draftsman,** draftswoman, sketcher, delineator; graphic artist; drawer, architectural draftsman; crayonist, charcoalist, pastelist; cartoonist, caricaturist, animator

4 **painter**; colorist; luminist, luminarist; oil painter, oil-colorist; watercolorist; acrylics painter; aquarellist; finger painter; monochromist, polychromist; genre painter, historical painter, landscape painter, landscapist, miniaturist, portrait painter, portraitist, marine painter, still-life painter, animal painter, religious painter; pavement artist; sign painter; scene painter, scenewright, scenographer

5 **photographer,** photographist, lensman, **cameraperson**, camerawoman, cameraman; cinematographer; snapshotter, snap shooter, shutterbug; daguerreotypist, calotypist, talbotypist; skiagrapher, shadowgraphist, radiographer, X-ray technician; digital artist

6 **sculptor,** sculptress, sculpturer; earth artist, environmental artist; statuary; figurer, figurist, modeler, molder, wax modeler, clay modeler; graver, chaser, carver; caster; stonecutter, mason, monumental mason, wood carver, xyloglyphic artist, whittler; ivory carver, bone carver, shell carver; gem carver, glyptic artist, glyptographic artist; engraver; lapidary

7 **ceramist,** ceramicist, **potter;** china decorator, china painter, tile painter, majolica painter; glassblower, glazer, glass decorator, pyroglazer, glass cutter; enamelist, enameler

8 **printmaker,** graphic artist; engraver, graver, burinist; inscriber, carver; etcher; line engraver; lithographer, autolithographer, chromolithographer; serigrapher, silk-screen artist; cerographer, cerographist; chalcographer; gem engraver, glyptographer, lapidary; wood engraver, xylographer; pyrographer, xylopyrographer; zincographer

9 **designer, stylist,** styler; costume designer, dress designer; *couturier, couturière* <Fr>; furniture designer, rug designer, textile designer

10 **architect,** civil architect; landscape architect, landscape gardener; city planner, urban planner, urbanist; functionalist

11 **decorator,** expert in decor, ornamentist, ornamentalist; interior decorator, interior designer, house decorator, room decorator, floral decorator, table decorator; window decorator, window dresser; confectionery decorator

717 ARCHITECTURE, DESIGN

<art of building and decoration>

NOUNS 1 **architecture,** architectural design, building design, the art and technique of building, inhabited sculpture, music in space; architectural science, architectural engineering, structural engineering, architectural technology, building science, building technology; architectonics, tectonics; **architectural style** <see list>; architectural specialty; landscape architecture, landscape gardening

2 **architectural element;** ornamentation, architectural ornamentation; column order, Doric, Ionic, Corinthian, Composite; type of construction, building type

3 **architect**, architectress, building designer; landscape architect, landscape gardener; architectural engineer; city planner, urban planner, urbanist, urbanologist

4 **design**, styling, patterning, planning, shaping

5 <**design specialties**> accessory design, appearance design, architectural design, automotive design, book design, clothing design, costume design, ergonomics, ergonomy, human engineering, human factors engineering, fashion design, jewlery design, furniture design, graphics design, industrial design, product design, interior design, landscape architecture, lighting design, package design, pottery design, reverse engineering, stage design, textile design, typographic design

6 **designer, stylist,** styler

ADJS 7 **architectural,** architectonic, tectonic; design, designer; ergonomically

8 **architectural style**

absolute
academic
action
additive
American colonial
American Georgian

Anglo-Saxon
Art Deco, Art Moderne
Art Nouveau
arts and crafts
baroque
Bauhaus
Beaux-Arts
brutalist
Byzantine
Carolingian
Chicago School
Chinese
churrigueresque, churrigueresco
cinquecento
Cistercian
classical
colonial
conceptual, invisible, imaginary, nowhere
Decorated
de Stijl
directed, programmed
Early American
Early English
Early Gothic
Early Renaissance
earthwork
eclectic
ecological
Edwardian
Egyptian
Elizabethan
Empire
endless
English decorated Gothic
English Georgian
English Renaissance
flamboyant Gothic
formalist
Francois Premier
French colonial
French Renaissance
functionalist
Georgian
German Renaissance
gingerbread
Gothic
Great West Road
Greco-Roman
Greek
Greek Revival
hard
High Gothic
High Renaissance
hi-tech
indeterminate
International, International Gothic
Islamic
Italianate
Italian Gothic
Italian Mannerism
Italian Renaissance
Jacobean
Japanese
Jesuit
kinetic
Louis XIV
Louis XV
mannerism
medieval
Mesopotamian
Mestizo
Mission
modern, modernism
Neo-Gothic
Neoclassical
New Brutalist
New England colonial
Norman
organicist
Palladian
perpendicular, rectilinear
Persian
pneumatic
postmodern
Prairie
Queen Anne
Regency
Renaissance
rococo
Roman
Romanesque
Romanesque Revival
Romantic
Shingle
Southern colonial
Spanish
Stuart
tensile
Tudor
Utopian, fantastic, visionary
vernacular
Victorian
Victorian Gothic

9 architectural specialties

church architecture, religious architecture
civic architecture
college architecture
commercial architecture
domestic architecture
governmental architecture
industrial architecture
institutional architecture
landscape architecture
library architecture
military architecture
museum architecture
recreational architecture

718 LITERATURE

<writings in prose or verse>

NOUNS **1 literature,** letters, belles lettres, polite literature, humane letters, republic of letters; work, **literary work,** text, literary text; works, complete works, oeuvre, canon, literary canon, author's canon; serious literature; classics, ancient literature; medieval literature, Renaissance literature; national literature, English literature, French literature; ethnic literature, black literature, Afro-American literature, Latino literature; contemporary literature; underground literature; pseudonymous literature; folk literature; travel literature; wisdom literature; erotic literature, erotica; pornographic literature, pornography, porn, hard porn, soft porn, obscene literature, scatological literature; popular literature, pop literature; chick lit; kitsch, fanfic, mash-up, must-read; Great American novel

2 authorship, writing, authorcraft, pencraft, wordsmanship, composition, the art of composition, inditing, inditement; one's pen; creative writing, literary art, verbal art, literary composition, literary production, verse-writing, short-story writing, novel writing, playwriting, drama-writing; essay-writing; expository writing; technical writing; journalism, newspaper writing, editorial writing, feature writing, rewriting; magazine writing; songwriting, lyric writing, libretto writing; artistry, literary power, literary artistry, literary talent, literary flair, skill with words, skill with language, facility in writing, ready pen; writer's itch, graphomania, scribblemania, graphorrhea, *cacoëthes scribendi* <L>; character development

3 writer, scribbler, penman, pen, penner; pen pusher, pencil driver, word-slinger, inkslinger, ink spiller, inkstained wretch, knight of the plume, knight of the quill

4 author, writer, scribe, composer, inditer, penman, wordsmith, compiler; authoress, penwoman; creative writer, *littérateur* <Fr>, literary artist, literary craftsman, literary journeyman, belletrist, man of letters, literary scholar; word painter; freelance, freelance writer; ghostwriter, ghost; collaborator, coauthor; prose writer, logographer; fiction writer, fictioneer; story writer, short story writer; storyteller, narrator; novelist; novelettist; diarist; chronicler, historian, historiographer; biographer; newspaperman; annalist; poet; dramatist, humorist; scriptwriter, scenario writer, scenarist; nonfiction writer; article writer, magazine writer; essayist; monographer; reviewer, critic, literary critic, music critic, art critic, drama critic, dance critic; cultural commentator; columnist; pamphleteer; technical writer; copywriter, advertising writer; encyclopedist, bibliographer

5 **hack writer,** hack, literary hack, Grub Street writer <Brit>, penny-a-liner, scribbler, potboiler

VERBS 6 **write,** author, pen, compose, indite, formulate, produce, prepare; dash off, knock off, knock out, throw on paper, pound out, crank out, grind out, churn out; freelance; compile; collaborate, coauthor; ghostwrite, ghost; novelize; scenarize; pamphleteer; editorialize

ADJS 7 **literary,** belletristic, lettered; classical

8 auctorial, **authorial**

719 HISTORY

<chronology of events>

NOUNS 1 **history,** the historical discipline, the investigation of the past, the record of the past, the story of mankind, study of the past; historical research; modern history; **annals, chronicles,** memorabilia, chronology; chronicle, record; historical method, historical approach, philosophy of history, historiography; cliometrics; documentation, recording; narrative history, oral history, oral record, survivors' accounts, witnesses' accounts; biography, memoir, memorial, life, story, life story, life history, adventures, fortunes, reminiscences, experiences; résumé, vita, curriculum vitae (CV); bio, biodata; life and letters, track record; legend, saint's legend, hagiology, hagiography; autobiography, memoirs, memorials, archive; journal, diary, confessions; profile, biographical sketch; obituary, necrology, martyrology; photobiography; case history; theory of history; epigraphy, archaeology; Clio, Muse of history; the past; herstory

2 **story,** tale, yarn, account, narrative, narration, chronicle, tradition, legend, folktale, folk history; anecdote, anecdotage; epic, epos, saga; minutes, notes; file, dossier; etymology

3 **historian,** cliometrician, historiographer; **chronicler,** annalist, recorder, archivist; **biographer,** memorialist, Boswell; autobiographer, autobiographist; diarist, Pepys; epigrapher, archaeologist

VERBS 4 **chronicle,** write history, historify; historicize; biograph, biography, biographize; immortalize; compile; document, report, record

5 **narrate,** tell, **relate, recount,** report, recite, rehearse, give an account of; commentate, voice over

ADJS 6 **historical, historic,** historied, historically accurate; fact-based; historicized; historiographical; cliometric; chronicled; chronologic, chronological; traditional, legendary; biographical, autobiographic, autobiographical; documentary, documented, archival; hagiographic, hagiographical, martyrologic, martyrological; necrologic, necrological; retro

7 **narrative,** narrational; fictional

ADVS 8 **historically,** historically speaking; as chronicled, as history tells us, according to accounts, by all accounts; as the record shows; retrospectively

720 POETRY

<writings in verse>

NOUNS 1 **poetry,** poesy, verse, song, rhyme; musical thought, music of the soul; lyric poetry

2 **poetics,** poetcraft, versecraft, versification, versemaking, *ars poetica* <L>; poetic language, poetic diction, poeticism; poetic license, poetic justice

3 **bad poetry,** doggerel, versemongering, poetastering, poetastery; poesy; crambo, crambo clink, crambo jingle, Hudibrastic verse; nonsense verse, amphigory; macaronics, macaronic verse; lame verses, limping meters, halting meters

4 **poem,** verse, rhyme; verselet, versicle; lyric poem, dramatic poem, narrative poem, alphabet poem

5 **book of verse,** garland, collection, anthology; poetic works, poesy, epos

6 **metrics,** prosody, versification; scansion, scanning; metrical pattern, metrical form, prosodic pattern, prosodic form, meter, numbers, measure; quantitative meter, syllabic meter, accentual meter, accentual-syllabic meter, duple meter, triple meter; free verse; alliterative meter

7 **meter, measure,** numbers; rhythm, cadence, movement, lilt, jingle, swing; sprung rhythm; accent, accentuation, metrical accent, stress, emphasis, ictus, beat; arsis, thesis; quantity, mora; metrical unit; foot, metrical foot; triseme, tetraseme; metrical group, metron, colon, period; dipody, syzygy, tripody, tetrapody, pentapody, hexapody, heptapody; monometer, dimeter, trimeter, tetrameter, pentameter, hexameter, heptameter, octameter; iambic pentameter, dactylic hexameter; Alexandrine; Saturnian meter; elegiac, elegiac couplet, elegiac distich, elegiac pentameter; heroic couplet; counterpoint;

caesura, diaeresis, masculine caesura, feminine caesura; catalexis; anacrusis

8 <**metrical feet**> amphibrach; amphimacer, cretic; anapest, antispast, bacchius; choriambus, choriamb; dactyl, dochmiac, epitrite; iamb, iambus, iambic; ionic, molossus, paeon, proceleusmatic; pyrrhic, dibrach; spondee, tribrach, trochee

9 **rhyme;** clink, crambo; consonance, assonance; alliteration; eye rhyme; male rhyme, masculine rhyme, single rhyme, female rhyme, feminine rhyme, double rhyme; initial rhyme, end rhyme; tail rhyme, rhyme royal; broken rhyme, half rhyme, near rhyme, pararhyme, slant rhyme; internal rhyme; terza rima, ottava rima; rime riche, identical rhyme; rhyme scheme; rhyming dictionary; unrhymed poetry, blank verse

10 <poetic divisions> **measure,** strain; syllable; line; verse; stanza, stave; strophe, antistrophe, epode; canto, book; refrain, chorus, burden; envoi; monostich, distich, tristich, tetrastich, pentastich, hexastich, heptastich, octastich; couplet; triplet, tercet; quatrain; sextet, sestet; septet; octave, octet; rhyme royal; Spenserian stanza

11 **muse;** the Muses, Pierides, *Camenae* <L>; Apollo, Apollo Musagetes; Calliope, Polyhymnia, Erato, Euterpe; Helicon, Parnassus; Castilian Spring, Pierian Spring, Hippocrene; Bragi; poetic genius, poesy, afflatus, fire of genius, creative imagination, inspiration

12 **poet,** poetess, poetress, maker; painter of the soul; ballad maker; bard, minstrel, scop, fili, baird, skald, jongleur, troubadour, *trovatore* <Ital>, trouveur, *trouvère* <Fr>, minnesinger; minor poet, major poet, arch-poet; laureate, poet laureate; occasional poet; lyric poet; epic poet; pastoral poet, pastoralist, idyllist, bucoliast; rhapsodist, rhapsode; vers-librist; elegist, librettist; lyricist, lyrist; odist; satirist; sonneteer; modernist, imagist, symbolist; Parnassian; beat poet

13 **bad poet;** rhymester, rhymer; metrist; versemaker, versesmith, versifier, verseman, versemonger; poetling, poetaster, poeticule; balladmonger

VERBS 14 **poetize,** versify, verse, write poetry, compose poetry, build the stately rime, sing deathless songs, make immortal verse; tune one's lyre, climb Parnassus, mount Pegasus; sing; elegize; poeticize

15 **rhyme,** assonate, alliterate; scan; jingle; cap verses, cap rhymes

ADJS 16 **poetic,** poetical, poetlike; lyrical, narrative, dramatic, lyrico-dramatic; bardic; runic, skaldic; epic, heroic; mock-heroic, Hudibrastic; pastoral, bucolic, eclogic, idyllic, Theocritean; didactic; elegiac, elegiacal; dithyrambic, rhapsodic, rhapsodical, Alcaic, Anacreontic, Homeric, Pindaric, sapphic; Castalian, Pierian; Parnassian, Sapphic; poetico-mythological; poetico-mystical, poetico-philosophic; comic, concrete, erotic, folk, metaphysical, nonsense, pattern, satirical, tragic

17 **metric, metrical,** prosodic, prosodical; **rhythmic,** rhythmical, measured, cadenced, scanning, scanned; accentual; iambic, dactylic, spondaic, pyrrhic, trochaic, anapestic, antispastic

18 **rhyming;** assonant, assonantal; alliterative, onomatopoeic; resonant; jingling; musical, lilting

ADVS 19 **poetically,** lyrically; metrically, rhythmically, in measure; musically

721 PROSE

<ordinary writing>

NOUNS 1 **prose**; prose fiction, nonfiction prose, expository prose; prose rhythm; prose style; poetic prose, polyphonic prose, prose poetry

2 **prosaism, prosaicism,** prosaicness, prosiness, pedestrianism, unpoeticalness; matter-of-factness, unromanticism, unidealism; unimaginativeness; plainness, commonness, commonplaceness, unembellishedness; insipidness, flatness, vapidity; dullness

VERBS 3 **prose,** write prose, write in prose; pedestrianize

ADJS 4 prose, in prose; unversified, **nonpoetic**, nonmetricalf

5 **prosaic,** prosy, prosing; unpoetical, poetryless; plain, common, commonplace, ordinary, unembellished, mundane; matter-of-fact, unromantic, unidealistic, unimpassioned; pedestrian, unimaginative; insipid, vapid, flat; humdrum, tiresome, dull

722 FICTION

<imagined stories>

NOUNS 1 **fiction,** narrative, narrative literature, imaginative narrative, prose fiction; narration, relation, relating, recital, rehearsal, telling, retelling, recounting, recountal, review, portrayal, graphic narration, description, delineation, presentation; **storytelling,** tale-telling, yarn-spinning, yarning; narrative poetry; operatic libretto; computer fiction, interactive fiction; pulp fiction

2 **narration, narrative**, relation, recital, rehearsal, telling, retelling, recounting, recountal, review; storytelling, tale-telling, yarn spinning, yarning

3 **story** <see list>, short story, tale, narrative, yarn,

account, narration, chronicle, relation, version; **novel** <see list>, *roman* <Fr>

4 <story elements> **plot,** fable, argument, story, line, storyline, subplot, secondary plot, mythos; structure, plan, architecture, architectonics, scheme, design; subject, topic, theme, motif; thematic development, development, continuity; action, movement; incident, episode; complication; rising action, turning point, climax, defining moment, falling action, *peripeteia* <Gk>, switch; *anagnorisis* <Gk>, recognition; denouement, catastrophe; *deus ex machina* <L>; catharsis; device, contrivance, gimmick; angle, slant, twist; character, characterization; speech, dialogue; tone, atmosphere, mood; setting, locale, world, milieu, background, backstory, region, local color

5 **narrator,** relator, reciter, recounter, *raconteur* <Fr>; anecdotist; **storyteller,** storier, taleteller, teller of tales, spinner of yarns, yarn spinner; word painter; persona, central consciousness, the I of the story; point-of-view; author, writer, short-story writer, novelist, novelettist, fictionist; fabulist, fableist, fabler, mythmaker, mythopoet; romancer, romancist; sagaman

6 <**narrative points of view**> documentary observer, camera-eye observer, fallible observer, first-person past narrator, first-person present narrator, omniscient observer; stream of consciousness, interior monologue; third-person past narrator, third-person present narrator

VERBS **7** **narrate,** tell, relate, recount, report, recite, rehearse, give an account of; tell a story, unfold a tale, a tale unfold, fable, fabulize; storify, fictionalize; romance; novelize; mythicize, mythify, mythologize, allegorize; retell

ADJS **8** **fictional,** fictionalized; novelistic, novelized, novelettish; mythical, mythological, legendary, fabulous; mythopoeic, mythopoetic, mythopoetical; allegorical, allegoric, parabolic, parabolical; romantic, romanticized; historical, historicized, fact-based

9 **narrative,** narrational; storied, storified; anecdotal, anecdotic; epic, epical

10 **novel (types)**

adventure novel
antinovel, anti-roman, nouveau roman
autobiographical novel
Bildungsroman <Ger>
bodice ripper
cliffhanger
collage novel
comic novel
detective novel
dime novel
dystopia, cacotopia, dystopian
entertainment
epic novel
epistolary novel
erotic novel
experimental novel
fantasy novel
fictional biography, fictionalized biography
Gothic novel
historical novel
historical romance, bodice-ripper
Kunstlerroman <Ger>
lyrical novel
naturalistic novel
novel of character
novel of ideas
novel of incident
novel of manners
novel of sensibility, sentimental novel
novel of the soil
novelette
novella
penny dreadful <Brit>
picaresque novel
political novel
pornographic novel
problem novel
proletarian novel
propaganda novel
psychological novel
psychological thriller
realistic novel
regional novel
roman à clef <Fr>
roman-fleuve <Fr>, river novel
romance novel
satirical novel
science fiction novel, sci-fi novel
social melodrama
sociological novel
stream-of-consciousness novel
surrealistic novel
techno-thriller
thesis novel
thriller
utopia, utopian novel
Victorian novel
Western

11 **story (types)**

adventure story
allegory
apologue
beast fable
bedtime story
chivalric romance
classical detective story
conte <Fr>
crime story
cyberpunk
detective story, whodunit
dime novel, penny dreadful
epic, epos
exemplum, didactic tale, moral tale
fable
fabliau
fairy tale, fairy story
fantasy
folktale, folk story
gest, geste
ghost story
hard-boiled detective story, tough-tec story
hero tale
historical fiction
horror story, chiller, chiller-diller
lai
legend
love story
Milesian tale
mystery, mystery story
myth, mythos
nursery tale, nursery rhyme
parable
romance
romantic adventure
saga
saint's legend
science fiction, sci-fi
short short story, short-short
short story
sketch
spy story
supernatural tale
suspense story
thriller, thriller-diller
vignette
Western, cowboy story

723 CRITICISM OF THE ARTS

<artistic judgment>

NOUNS **1** **criticism,** criticism of the arts, esthetic criticism, artistic criticism, artistic evaluation, artistic, analysis, artistic interpretation, critical commentary, **critique**, critical analysis, critical interpretation, critical evaluation, metacriticism, exegetics, hermeneutics; art criticism, formalist criticism, expressionist criticism, neoformalist criticism; music criticism; dramatic criticism; dance criticism; aesthetics

2 **review,** critical notice, commentary, critical treatment, critical treatise

3 **literary criticism,** Lit-Crit, literary analysis, literary evaluation, literary interpretation, literary exegetics, literary hermeneutics, poetics; critical approach; literary theory, theory of literature, critical theory, theory of criticism

4 **critic,** interpreter, exegete, analyst, explicator, theoretician, aesthetician; reviewer

VERBS 5 **criticize,** critique, evaluate, interpret, explicate, analyze, judge; theorize

ADJS 6 **critical,** evaluative, interpretive, exegetical, analytical, analytic, left-brain, explicative

724 OCCUPATION

<job or profession>

NOUNS 1 **occupation, work,** job, employment, business, employ, activity, function, enterprise, undertaking, affairs, labor; thing, bag; affair, matter, concern, concernment, interest, lookout; what one is doing, what one is about; silver ceiling, commerce

2 **task,** work, stint, job, labor, toil, industry, piece of work, **chore,** chare, odd job; **assignment,** charge, project, work in progress, errand, mission, commission, duty, service, exercise; things to do, matters in hand, irons in the fire, fish to fry; homework, take-home work; busywork, makework, benchwork

3 **function,** office, duty, job, province, place, role, part; capacity, character, **position**

4 <sphere of work or activity> **field,** sphere, profession, trade, province, bailiwick, turf, department, area, discipline, subdiscipline, orb, orbit, realm, arena, domain, walk; **specialty, niche,** speciality <Brit>, line of country; beat, round; shop; corporate culture; bricks and mortar, bricks and clicks; home front

5 **position,** job, employment, gainful employment, situation, office, post, place, station, berth, billet, appointment, engagement, gig; day job; desk job; incumbency, tenure; opening, vacancy; second job, moonlighting

6 **vocation, occupation,** business, work, line, line of work, line of business, line of endeavor, number, walk, walk of life, calling, mission, profession, practice, pursuit, specialty, specialization, *métier* <Fr>, trade, racket, game; career, lifework, life's work; career track, Mommy track; craft, art, handicraft; careerism, career building

7 **avocation, hobby,** hobbyhorse, sideline, byline, side interest, pastime, spare-time activity, outside interest; amateur pursuit, amateurism; unpaid work, volunteer work, sidelining

8 **professionalism,** professional standing, professional status

9 nonprofessionalism, **amateurism,** amateur standing, amateur status

VERBS 10 **occupy, engage,** busy, devote, spend, **employ,** occupy oneself, busy oneself, go about one's business, devote oneself; pass the time, spend the time; occupy one's time, take up one's time; attend to business, attend to one's work; mind one's business, mind the store, stick to one's knitting; telecommute, telework, work from home; reverse-commute

11 **busy oneself with,** do, occupy oneself with engage oneself with, employ oneself in, pass one's time in, spend one's time in; engage in, take up, devote oneself to, apply oneself to, address oneself to, have one's hands in, turn one's hand to; concern oneself with, make it one's business; be about, be doing, be occupied with, be engaged in, be employed in, be at work on; practice, follow as an occupation

12 **work, work at,** work for, have a job, be employed, ply one's trade, labor in one's vocation, do one's number, follow a trade, practice a profession, carry on a business, carry on a trade, keep up; do usiness, transact business, carry on business, conduct business; set up shop, set up in business, hang out one's shingle; stay employed, hold down a job; moonlight, consult; labor, toil

13 officiate, **function, serve;** perform as, act as, act one's part, play one's part, do duty, discharge the office of, perform the duties of, exercise the functions of, serve in the capacity of

14 **hold office,** fill an office, occupy a post

ADJS 15 **occupied, busy,** working; practical, realistic; banausic, moneymaking, breadwinning, utilitarian; materialistic; workaday, workday, prosaic; commercial

16 **occupational, vocational,** functional; **professional,** pro; official; technical, industrial; all in the day's work; field-based; home-based

17 **avocational, hobby**, amateur, nonprofessional

ADVS 18 **professionally,** vocationally; as a profession, as a vocation; in the course of business

725 EXERTION

<physical or mental effort>

NOUNS 1 **exertion, effort,** energy, elbow grease; endeavor; trouble, pains; great effort, mighty effort, might and main, muscle, one's back, nerve, and sinew, strong pull

2 **strain,** straining, **stress,** stressfulness, stress and strain, taxing, **tension,** stretch, rack; tug, pull, haul, heave; overexertion, overstrain, overtaxing, overextension, overstress

3 **struggle,** fight, battle, tussle, scuffle, wrestle, hassle

4 **work, labor,** employment, industry, toil, moil, travail, toil and trouble, sweat of one's brow; drudgery, sweat, slavery, spadework, shitwork*, rat race; treadmill; unskilled labor, hewing of wood, drawing of water; dirty work, grunt work, donkey work, scut work, thankless task; makework, tedious work, tiresome work, humdrum toil, grind, fag <Brit>; rubber room work, no-work job; manual labor, handwork, handiwork; forced labor; hand's turn, stroke of work, stroke; lick, lick of work, stitch of work; man-hour; **workload,** work schedule; task; fatigue

5 **hard work,** hard labor, backbreaking work, moil, warm work, uphill work, long haul, tough grind, the hard way, heavy lifting; hard job; labor of Hercules; laboriousness, toilsomeness, effortfulness, strenuousness, arduousness, operosity, operoseness; onerousness, oppressiveness, burdensomeness; troublesomeness

6 exercise, exercising; **practice,** drill, workout, preparation; yoga; constitutional, stretch; violent exercise; physical education

7 exerciser; horizontal bar, parallel bars, horse, side horse, long horse, rings; trapeze; trampoline; Indian club; medicine ball; punching bag; rowing machine; weight, dumbbell, barbell

VERBS 8 **exert,** exercise, ply, employ, use, put forth, put out, make with; practice

9 **exert oneself,** use some elbow grease, spread oneself, put forth one's strength, bend every effort, bend might and main, spare no effort, put on a full-court press, tax one's energies, break a sweat; put oneself out, lay oneself out, go all out; endeavor; do one's best; apply oneself, come to grips with; hump, hump it, hump oneself, buckle, knuckle, bear, lay to; lay to the oars, ply the oar

10 **strain,** tense, stress, stretch, tax, press, rack; pull, tug, haul, heave; strain the muscles, strain every nerve, strain every nerve and sinew; put one's back into it; sweat blood; overwork, work night and day, take on too much, spread oneself too thin, **overexert,** overstrain, overtax, overextend; drive oneself, whip oneself, flog oneself

11 **struggle, strive,** contend, fight, battle, buffet, scuffle, tussle, wrestle, hassle, fight one's way, agonize, huff and puff, grunt and sweat, sweat it, make heavy weather of it

12 **work, labor;** busy oneself; turn a hand, do a hand's turn, do a lick of work, earn one's keep; chore, do the chores, char, chare <Brit>

13 **work hard;** scratch, hustle, sweat, slave, sweat and slave, slave away, toil away, hammer at; hit the ball, bear down, pour it on; burn the candle at both ends; work one's head off, work one's fingers to the bone, break one's back, bust one's hump, bust one's ass; put one's heart and soul into it; beaver, beaver away, work like a beaver, work like a horse, work like a cart horse, work like a dog, work like a slave, work like a galley slave, work like a coal heaver, work like a Trojan; work overtime, be a workaholic, overwork, do double duty, work double hours, work day and night, work late, burn the midnight oil; persevere; lucubrate, elucubrate

14 **drudge,** grind, dig, fag <Brit>, grub, toil, moil, toil and moil, travail, plod, slog, peg, plug, hammer, peg away, plug away, hammer away, pound away, struggle along, struggle on, work away; keep one's nose to the grindstone; wade through

15 **set to work,** get rolling, get busy, get down to business, get down to work, roll up one's sleeves, spit on one's hands, gird up one's loins; fall to work, fall to, knuckle down to, turn to, set about, set one's hand to, start in, set up shop, enter on, launch into; get on the job, get going; go to it, get with it, get cracking, have at it, get one's teeth into it; hop to it; attack, set at, tackle; plunge into, dive into; pitch in; light into, wade into, tear into, sail into, put one's shoulder to the wheel, put one's hand to the plow; take on, undertake

16 **task, work, busy,** keep busy, fag <Brit>, sweat, drive, tax; overtask, overtax, overwork, overdrive; burden, oppress

ADJS 17 **laboring,** working; struggling, striving, straining; drudging, **toiling,** slaving, sweating, grinding, grubbing, plodding, slogging, pegging, plugging, persevering; hardworking; busy, industrious, hard at it

18 **laborious, toilsome, arduous,** strenuous, painful, effortful, operose, troublesome, onerous, oppressive, burdensome; wearisome, tiring, exhausting; heavy, hefty, tough, uphill, **backbreaking,** grueling, punishing, crushing,

killing, herculean; labored, forced, strained; straining, tensive, painstaking, intensive; hard-fought, hard-won, hard-earned

ADVS 19 **laboriously,** arduously, toilsomely, strenuously, operosely; effortfully, with effort, hard, by the sweat of one's brow; the hard way; with all one's might, for all one is worth, with a will, with might and main, with a strong hand, manfully; hammer and tongs, tooth and nail, *bec et ongles* <Fr>, heart and soul; industriously

726 WORKER, DOER

<one who works>

NOUNS 1 **doer,** agent, actor, performer, **worker,** practitioner, perpetrator; producer, maker, creator, fabricator, author, mover, prime mover; go-getter; architect; medium; executor, executant, executrix; operator, operative, operant, hand; subject; coworker, colleague; business associate; crowdsourcing, outsourcing

2 worker, **laborer, toiler,** moiler; member of the working class, proletarian, prole, blue-collar worker, lunch-bucket worker, laboring man, stiff, working stiff; workman, working man; workwoman, working woman; workfolk, workpeople; working girl, workgirl; factory worker, industrial worker; autoworker, steelworker; construction worker; commuter; home worker, telecommuter, teleworker; office worker, white-collar worker, desk jockey; career woman, career girl; jobholder, wageworker, wage earner, salaried worker; breadwinner; wage slave; employee, servant; hand, workhand, hourly worker; common laborer, unskilled laborer, navvy <Brit>, day laborer, dayworker, roustabout; casual, casual laborer; agricultural worker; migrant worker, migrant; menial, flunky; piece-worker, jobber; factotum, jack-of-all-trades; full-time worker, part-time worker; temporary employee, temporary, office temporary, temp; freelance worker, freelance, freelancer, self-employed person, independent contractor, consultant; volunteer; domestic worker, clerical worker, sales worker, service worker, repair worker, artistic worker, technical worker; labor force, work force, crew, shop floor, factory floor; personnel; labor market

3 **drudge,** grub, hack, fag, plodder, slave, galley slave, workhorse, beast of burden, slogger; grind, greasy grind, swot; slave labor, sweatshop labor; busy bee, beaver, ant

4 **professional,** member of a learned profession, professional practitioner; businessman, businesswoman, career woman; executive; pro, old pro, seasoned professional; gownsman; doctor, lawyer, member of the clergy, teacher, accountant; social worker; health-care professional, military professional; law-enforcement professional

5 **amateur,** nonprofessional, layman, member of the laity, laic

6 **skilled worker,** skilled laborer, journeyman, mechanic; craftsman, handicraftsman; craftswoman; craftsperson; craftspeople; artisan, artificer, artist; maker; wright; technician; apprentice; master, master craftsman, master workman, master carpenter

7 **engineer,** professional engineer; **technician,** technical worker, techie; data scientist, programmer, technologist

8 **smith;** farrier <Brit>, forger, forgeman, metalworker; Vulcan, Hephaestus, Wayland, Völund

727 UNIONISM, LABOR UNION

<workers' rights organization>

NOUNS 1 **unionism,** trade unionism, trades unionism <Brit>, labor unionism; **unionization;** collective bargaining; arbitration, nonbinding arbitration; industrial relations, labor relations, work relations; employee rights, employer rights; salary negotiations, labor negotiations, negotiated points, negotiation points, employee demands, management demands

2 **labor union,** trade union, trades union <Brit>; organized labor; collective bargaining; craft union, guild, horizontal union; industrial union, vertical union; local, union local, local union; company union

3 **union shop,** preferential shop, closed shop; open shop; nonunion shop; labor contract, union contract, sweetheart contract, yellow-dog contract; maintenance of membership

4 **unionist,** labor unionist, trade unionist, **union member,** trades unionist <Brit>, unionized worker, cardholder; shop steward, bargainer, negotiator; business agent; union officer; union organizer, labor organizer, organizer, labor union official; union contractor

5 **strike, walkout,** tie-up, industrial action <Brit>, job action; slowdown, rulebook slowdown, sick-in, sickout, blue flu; work stoppage, sit-down strike, sit-down; wildcat strike, outlaw strike; called strike, organized strike; sympathy strike; work-to-rule; general strike; boycott, boy-cottage, picketing, picket; buyers strike, consumers strike; lockout; revolt

6 **striker,** picket; sitdown striker; holdout

7 <strike enforcer> picket; goon, strong-arm man; flying squadron, flying squad, goon squad

8 **strikebreaker,** scab, rat, fink, scissorbill, goon, blackleg <Brit>

VERBS **9** organize, **unionize;** bargain, bargain collectively; arbitrate; submit to arbitration

10 strike, **go on strike,** go out, walk, walk out; hit the bricks, shut it down; slow down; sit down; boycott; picket; hold out; lock out; revolt

11 break a strike; scab, rat, fink, blackleg <Brit>

728 MONEY

<pay for goods, services>

NOUNS **1** **money, currency,** legal tender, medium of exchange, circulating medium, sterling <Brit>, cash, hard cash, cold cash; specie, coinage, mintage, coin of the realm, gold; silver; dollars; pounds, shillings, and pence; the wherewithal, the wherewith; lucre, filthy lucre, the almighty dollar, pelf, root of all evil, mammon; hard currency, soft currency; fractional currency; managed currency; necessity money, scrip, emergency money; monetary unit, monetary denomination; electronic money; burn rate, churn rate

2 <nonformal> **dough, bread,** jack, kale, bucks, scratch, change, mazuma, mopus, gelt, gilt, coin, spondulicks, oof, ooftish, wampum, possibles, moolah, boodle, blunt, dinero, do-re-mi, sugar, brass, tin, rocks, simoleons, shekels, berries, chips, green, green stuff, the needful, grease, ointment, palm oil, gravy, cabbage, lettuce, whip-out, the necessary, loot

3 **wampum,** wampumpeag, peag, sewan, roanoke, shell money; cowrie

4 specie, hard money; **coinage**; coin, piece, piece of money, piece of silver, piece of gold; roll of coins, rouleau; gold piece; ten-dollar gold piece, eagle; five-dollar gold piece, half eagle; twenty-dollar gold piece, double eagle; guinea, sovereign, pound sovereign, crown, half crown; doubloon; ducat; napoleon, louis d'or; moidore

5 **paper money;** cash; bill, dollar bill; note, negotiable note, negotiable instrument, legal-tender note; bank note, bill of exchange, Federal Reserve note; national bank note; government note, treasury note; silver certificate; gold certificate; scrip; fractional note, shinplaster; fiat money, assignat

6 <nonformal> folding money, **green stuff,** the long green, folding green, lean green, mint leaves, lettuce, greenbacks, frogskins, skins

7 <U.S. denominations> mill; cent, penny, copper, red cent; five cents, nickel; ten cents, dime; twenty-five cents, quarter, two bits; fifty cents, half-dollar, four bits; dollar, dollar bill; buck, smacker, frogskin, fish, skin; silver dollar, cartwheel, iron man; two-dollar bill, two-spot; five-dollar bill; fiver, five-spot, fin; ten-dollar bill; tenner, ten-spot, sawbuck; twenty-dollar bill, double sawbuck; fifty-dollar bill, half a C; hundred-dollar bill; C, C-note, century, bill; five hundred dollars, half grand, five-hundred-dollar bill, half G; thousand dollars, G, grand, thousand-dollar bill, G-note, yard, big one

8 <British denominations> mite; farthing; halfpenny, ha'penny, bawbee, mag, meg; penny; pence, p; new pence, np; two-pence, tuppence; threepence, thrippence, threepenny bit; fourpence, fourpenny, groat; sixpence, tanner, teston; shilling, bob; florin; half crown, half-dollar; crown, dollar; pound, quid; guinea; fiver, tenner, pony <£25>, monkey <£500>, plum <£100,000>, marigold <£1,000,000>

9 **foreign currency,** foreign money, foreign denominations; convertibility, foreign exchange; rate of exchange, exchange rate; parity of exchange; agio

10 **counterfeit,** counterfeit money, funny money, phony money, bogus money, false money, bad money, base coin, green goods; forgery, bad check, rubber check, bounced check, kite

11 **negotiable instrument,** negotiable paper, commercial paper, paper, bill; bill of exchange, bill of draft; certificate, certificate of deposit (CD); check, cheque <Brit>; blank check; bank check, teller's check; treasury check; cashier's check, certified check; traveler's check; banker's check; letter of credit, commercial letter of credit; money order (MO); postal order, post-office order <Brit>; draft, warrant, voucher, debenture; promissory note, note, IOU; note of hand; credit note; acceptance, acceptance bill, bank acceptance, trade acceptance; due bill; demand bill, sight bill, demand draft, sight draft; time bill, time draft; exchequer bill, treasury bill <Brit>; checkbook; electronic money

12 **token,** counter, slug; scrip, coupon; check, ticket, tag; hat check, baggage check

13 **sum,** amount of money; round sum, lump sum

14 **funds,** finances, moneys, exchequer, purse, budget, pocket; treasury, treasure, substance, assets, resources, total assets, worth, net worth, pecuniary resources, means, available means, available resources, available funds, cash flow, wherewithal, command of money; balance; pool, fund, kitty, petty cash; war chest; checking account, bank account; direct deposit; Swiss bank account, unnumbered bank account, unregistered bank account; reserves, cash reserves; savings,

savings account, nest egg; life savings, retirement fund, retirement plan, pension fund, pension plan; mattress money, contingency fund; bottom dollar; automated teller machine (ATM)

15 **capital,** fund; moneyed capital; principal, corpus; circulating capital, floating capital; fixed capital, working capital, equity capital, risk capital, venture capital; capital structure; capital gains distribution; capitalization; capital spending

16 **money market,** supply of short-term funds; tight money, cheap money; borrowing; lending; discounting, note discounting, note shaving, dealing in commercial paper

17 **bankroll;** roll, wad

18 **cash,** ready money, ready cash, the ready, available funds, money in hand, cash in hand, balance in hand, immediate resources, liquid assets, cash supply, cash flow; treasury

19 **petty cash,** pocket money, pin money, spending money, mad money, cheddar, change, small change, pocket change; nickels and dimes, chicken feed, peanuts, pittance; contingency fund

20 **precious metal**; gold, yellow stuff; nugget, gold nugget; silver, copper, nickel, coin gold, coin silver; bullion, ingot, bar

21 standard of value, gold standard, silver standard; monometallism, bimetallism; money of account

22 **numismatics,** numismatology; numismatist, numismatologist, science of coins

23 monetization; issuance, circulation; remonetization; demonetization; revaluation, devaluation

24 coining, coinage, **minting,** mintage, striking, stamping; counterfeiting, forgery; coin-clipping

25 **coiner, minter**, mintmaster, moneyer; counterfeiter, forger; coin-clipper

VERBS 26 monetize; **issue,** utter, **circulate;** remonetize, reissue; demonetize; revalue, devalue, devaluate

27 discount, discount notes, deal in commercial paper, shave; borrow, lend

28 **coin, mint;** print, stamp; counterfeit, forge; utter; pass a bad check, kite a check

29 **cash**, cash in, liquidate, convert into cash, realize

ADJS 30 **monetary,** pecuniary, nummary, nummular, financial, fiduciary; capital; fiscal; sumptuary; numismatic; sterling; moneywise

31 convertible, liquid, negotiable

729 FINANCE, INVESTMENT

<*money spent and invested*>

NOUNS 1 **finance, finances, money matters;** world of finance, financial world, financial industry, high finance, investment banking, international banking, Wall Street banking, Lombard Street; the gnomes of Zurich; economics; purse strings

2 **financing, funding,** backing, financial backing, sponsorship, patronization, support, financial support; stake, grubstake; subsidy; capitalizing, capitalization, provision of capital; deficit financing; crowdfunding

3 personal finance; bank account, savings account, checking account; telebanking; budget; pension, 401K, Individual Retirement Account (IRA), Keogh plan

4 **investment, venture, risk,** plunge, speculation; prime investment; ethical investment, conscience investment; money market, mutual fund, stock market, bond market; divestment, disinvestment; hedge fund

5 **banking,** money dealing, money changing; investment banking; banking industry

6 **financial condition,** state of the exchequer; **credit rating,** Dun & Bradstreet rating; capital spending

7 **solvency,** soundness, solidity; credit standing, creditworthiness; unindebtedness

8 **crisis,** financial crisis; dollar crisis, dollar gap

9 **financier,** moneyman, capitalist, finance capitalist; Wall Streeter; investor; financial expert, economist, authority on money and banking; international banker

10 **financer, backer,** funder, sponsor, patron, supporter, angel, Maecenas; cash cow, staker, grubstaker, moneymaker, money-spinner, meal ticket; **fundraiser**

11 **banker,** money dealer, moneymonger; money broker; discounter, note broker, bill broker <Brit>; moneylender; money changer, cambist; investment banker; bank president, bank manager, bank officer, loan officer, trust officer, banking executive; bank clerk, cashier, teller

12 **treasurer,** financial officer, bursar, purser, purse bearer, cashier, cashkeeper; accountant, auditor, controller, comptroller, bookkeeper; chamberlain, curator, steward, trustee; depositary, depository; receiver, liquidator; paymaster; Secretary of the Treasury, Chancellor of the Exchequer

13 **treasury,** treasure-house; subtreasury; depository, **repository**; storehouse; gold depository, Fort Knox; strongbox, safe, money chest, coffer, locker, chest; piggy bank, penny bank, bank; vault, strong room; safe-deposit box, safety-deposit box; cashbox, coin box, cash register, till; bursary; exchequer, fisc; public treasury, public funds, taxpayer funds, taxpayer money, pork barrel, public crib, public trough, public till; fixed asset; ka-ching

14 **bank,** banking house, lending institution, savings institution; automated teller machine (ATM), cash

machine, bank machine; central bank, Bank of England, the Old Lady of Threadneedle Street, Bank of France; Federal Reserve Bank, Federal Reserve System; World Bank, International Monetary Fund; clearing house; bank account, savings account, money market account, checking account, deposit, direct deposit, withdrawal

15 **purse, wallet,** pocketbook, bag, handbag, clutch, shoulder bag, porte-monnaie, billfold, change purse, money belt, money clip, poke, pocket; fanny pack; moneybag; purse strings; mattress money

VERBS **16** **finance, back,** fund, sponsor, patronize, support, provide for, capitalize, provide capital for, provide money for, pay for, bankroll, angel, put up the money, hold the purse strings; stake, grubstake; subsidize; set up, set up in business; refinance; upcharge

17 **invest,** place, put, sink; **risk, venture;** make an investment, lay out money, place out at interest, put out at interest; reinvest, roll over, plow back into; invest in, put money in, sink money in, pour money into, tie up one's money in; buy in, buy into, buy a piece of, buy a share of; financier; plunge, speculate; play the big board, play the stock exchange; day-trade

ADJS **18** **solvent,** sound, substantial, solid, good, sound as a dollar, creditworthy; able to pay, good for, unindebted, out of the hole, out of the red

19 **insolvent,** unsound, indebted

20 **financial**, monetary, fiscal, pecuniary, economic; bull, bear

730 BUSINESSMAN, MERCHANT

<one who works in or runs business>

NOUNS **1** businessman, businesswoman, **businessperson**, businesspeople, business associate; enterpriser, entrepreneur, man of commerce; small businessman; big businessman, magnate, tycoon, baron, king, top executive, business leader; director, manager; big boss; industrialist, captain of industry, industry leader; banker, financier; robber baron; intrapreneur; public company, private company; team effort

2 **merchant,** merchandiser, marketer, trader, trafficker, **dealer**, monger, chandler; tradesman, tradeswoman; storekeeper, shopkeeper; regrater; wholesaler, jobber, middleman; importer, exporter; distributor; retailer, retail merchant, retail dealer, retail seller, retail park; dealership, distributorship; franchise; concession, concession stand

3 salesman, seller, **salesperson**, salesclerk; saleswoman, saleslady, salesgirl; clerk, shop clerk, store clerk, shop assistant; floorwalker; agent, sales agent, selling agent; sales engineer; sales manager; salespeople, sales force, sales personnel; scalper, ticket scalper

4 **traveling salesman,** traveler, commercial traveler, traveling agent, traveling person, road warrior, knight of the road, bagman, drummer; detail man; door-to-door salesman, canvasser

5 **vendor,** peddler, huckster, hawker, higgler, cadger, colporteur, chapman; cheap-jack, cheap-john; coster, costermonger; sidewalk salesman

6 **solicitor,** canvasser

7 <nonformal> tout, touter, pitchperson, barker, spieler, ballyhooer, ballyhoo man

8 **auctioneer,** auction agent

9 **broker,** note broker, bill broker <Brit>, discount broker, cotton broker, hotel broker, insurance broker, mortgage broker, diamond broker, furniture broker, ship broker, grain broker; stockbroker; pawnbroker; money broker, money changer, cambist; land broker, real estate broker, realtor, real estate agent, estate agent <Brit>

10 ragman, old-clothesman, rag-and-bone man; **junkman,** junk dealer

11 **tradesmen,** tradespeople, tradesfolk, merchantry

ADJS **12** business, commercial, mercantile; entrepreneurial; auctionary

731 COMMERCE, ECONOMICS

<goods and services>

NOUNS **1** **commerce,** trade, traffic, truck, intercourse, dealing, **dealings;** business, business dealings, business affairs, business relations, commercial affairs, commercial relations; the business world, the world of trade, the world of commerce, the marketplace, marketspace; merchantry, mercantile business; **market,** freemarket, marketing, state of the market, buyers' market, sellers' market; industry; big business, Fortune 500; small business, medium business; fair trade, free trade, reciprocal trade, unilateral trade, multilateral trade; most favored nation; balance of trade; restraint of trade; market leader; market indicator; business administration; point of purchase, niche market, niche product; market share

2 **trade,** trading, doing business, trafficking; barter, bartering, exchange, interchange, swapping; give-and-take, horsetrading, dealing, deal-making, wheeling and dealing; buying and selling; wholesaling, jobbing; brokerage, agency; retailing, merchandising; commercial trade, export and import

3 **negotiation,** bargaining, haggling, higgling,

dickering, chaffering, chaffer, haggle; hacking out a deal, working out a deal, hammering out a deal, coming to terms; horsetrading; collective bargaining, package bargaining, pattern bargaining; bargaining chip

4 **transaction,** business transaction, commercial transaction, **deal,** business deal, negotiation, operation, turn; package deal

5 **bargain,** deal, dicker; agreement, contract; trade, swap; horse trade; trade-in; blind bargain, pig in a poke; hard bargain

6 custom, **customer**, clientele, client base, patronage, patrons, trade; goodwill, repute, good name; customer service, customer care, support service, technical support, tech support

7 **economy, economic system**, market, capitalist economy, capitalistic economy, free-enterprise economy, free-trade economy, private-enterprise economy, market economy, free-market economy, socialist economy, collectivized economy; overheated economy; healthy economy, sound economy, weak economy; gross national product (GNP); economic sector, public sector, private sector; economic self-sufficiency, autarky; economic policy, fiscal policy, monetary policy; microeconomics, macroeconomics; privatization, nationalization, denationalization, supply-side economics; economic theory; open market; behavioral economics, gig economy, Goldilocks economy, neuroeconomics, service economy, shadow economy; collaborative consumption

8 **standard of living,** standard of life, standard of comfort; real wages, take-home pay, take-home; **cost of living;** cost-of-living index, consumer price index; developed world; First World

9 economic indicator, econometrics; gross national product (GNP), price index, consumer price index, retail price index, cost-of-living index; unemployment rate, national debt, budget deficit

10 **business cycle, economic cycle,** business fluctuations; peak, peaking; low, bottoming out; prosperity, boom; boomlet, miniboom; crisis, **recession, depression,** economic depression, slowdown, cooling off, slump, bust, downturn, downtick; upturn, uptick, expanding economy, recovery; growth, economic growth, business growth, high growth rate, expansion, market expansion, economic expansion; trade cycle; trade deficit, trade gap, balance of payments; monetary cycle; inflation, deflation, stagflation; long tail

11 **economics,** eco, econ, economic science, the dismal science; political economy; dynamic economics; theoretical economics, plutology; classical economics; Keynesian economics, Keynesianism; supply-side economics; econometrics; economism, economic determinism; trickle-down economics

12 **economist,** economic expert, economic authority; political economist

13 **commercialism,** mercantilism; industrialism; mass marketing, guerrilla marketing

14 **commercialization;** industrialization

VERBS 15 **trade, deal,** traffic, truck, buy and sell, do business; barter; exchange, change, interchange, give in exchange, take in exchange, swap, switch; swap horses, horse-trade; trade off; trade in; trade sight unseen, make a blind bargain, sell a pig in a poke; marketize; ply one's trade

16 **deal in, trade in,** traffic in, handle, carry, be in; market, merchandise, **sell,** retail, wholesale, job

17 **trade with, deal with,** traffic with, traffic in, do business with, have dealings with, have truck with, transact business with; frequent as a customer, shop at, trade at, **patronize**, take one's business to; open an account with, have an account with; export, import; market, merchandise

18 **bargain**, drive a bargain, negotiate, haggle, higgle, chaffer, huckster, deal, dicker, barter, make a deal, do a deal, hack out a deal, work out a deal, hammer out a deal; bid, bid for, cheapen, beat down; underbid, outbid; drive a hard bargain; hold out for

19 **strike a bargain,** make a bargain, make a dicker, **make a deal,** get oneself a deal, put through a deal, shake hands, shake on it; bargain for, agree to; come to terms; be a bargain, be a go, be a deal, be on; network

20 put on a business basis, on a business footing, make businesslike; commercialize; industrialize

21 <adjust the economy> cool the economy, cool off the economy; heat the economy, heat up the economy

ADJS 22 **commercial,** business, trade, trading, mercantile, merchant; commercialistic, mercantilistic; industrial; wholesale, retail

23 **economic**, fiscal, monetary, pecuniary, financial, budgetary; inflationary, deflationary; socioeconomic, politico-economic, political-economical

732 ILLICIT BUSINESS

<illegal activity making money>

NOUNS 1 illicit business, illegitimate business, illegal operations, illegal commerce, illegal traffic, shady dealings, **racket**; the rackets, the syndicate, **organized crime**, Mafia, Cosa Nostra; **black market**, gray market; drug traffic, narcotics traffic; narcoterrorism; prostitution, streetwalking; pimping, traffic in women, white slavery; usury, loan-sharking, shylocking; protection racket; bootlegging, moon-shining; gambling; spam, computer virus, computer worm

2 **smuggling,** contrabandage, contraband; narcotics smuggling, dope smuggling, jewel smuggling, cigarette smuggling; gunrunning, rumrunning

3 **contraband,** smuggled goods; narcotics, drugs, dope, jewels, cigarettes; bootleg liquor; stolen goods, stolen property, hot goods, hot items

4 **racketeer;** Mafioso; black marketeer, gray marketeer; bootlegger, moonshiner; pusher, dealer, narcotics pusher, dope pusher, drug pusher; drug lord, drug-runner, drug mule; Medellin cartel

5 **smuggler,** contrabandist, runner; drug smuggler, mule; gunrunner, rumrunner

6 **fence,** receiver, receiver of stolen goods, swagman, swagsman, bagman, bagwoman

VERBS **7** <deal in illicit goods> push, shove; **sell under the counter;** black-market, black-marketeer; bootleg, moonshine; fence; spam

8 **smuggle,** run, sneak

733 PURCHASE

<buying something>

NOUNS **1** **purchase, buying, purchasing,** acquisition; **shopping**, marketing; shopping around, comparison shopping; window-shopping; impulse buying; shopping spree, retail therapy; repurchase, rebuying; mail-order buying, catalog shopping; online shopping, teleshopping, home shopping, e-commerce; installment buying, buying on credit, hire purchase <Brit>, layaway purchase; bulk buying, bulk purchasing; buying up, cornering, coemption; buying power, purchasing power; **consumerism**; consumer society, consumer sovereignty, consumer power, consumer confidence, acquisitive society; retail price index, consumer price index; wholesale price index; shopping list; Black Friday, Cyber Monday

2 **option,** first option, **first refusal,** refusal, preemption, right of preemption, prior right of purchase; call option

3 **market,** public, purchasing public, target audience; urban market, rural market, youth market, suburban market; **clientele, customers,** clientage, customer base, patronage, custom, trade; carriage trade; demand, consumer demand

4 **customer,** client; patron, patronizer, regular customer, regular buyer, regular; clientele; prospect; mark, sucker; credit history, credit limit, credit card

5 **buyer,** purchaser, emptor, **consumer,** vendee; **shopper,** marketer; shopaholic; bargain hunter; bidder; window-shopper, browser; purchasing agent, customer agent, personal shopper

6 by-bidder, decoy, come-on man, shill

VERBS **7** **purchase, buy,** procure, make a purchase, complete a purchase, make a buy, make a deal for, blow oneself to; buy up, regrate, corner, monopolize, engross, hoard; buy out; buy in, buy into, buy a piece of; repurchase, rebuy, buy back; buy on credit, buy on the installment plan, charge; buy sight unseen, buy blind; trade up

8 **shop,** market, go shopping, go marketing; shop around; window-shop, comparison-shop, **browse**, graze; impulse-buy; shop till one drops, hit the shops

9 **bid,** make a bid, offer, offer to buy, make an offer; give the asking price; by-bid, shill; bid up; bid in

ADJS **10** **purchasing, buying,** in the market; cliental; shoppable

11 **bought,** store-bought, boughten, store-boughten, purchased

734 SALE

<selling something>

NOUNS **1** **sale; wholesale, retail;** market, demand, outlet; buyers' market, sellers' market; mass market; conditional sale; tie-in sale, tie-in; turnover; bill of sale; cash sale, cash-and-carry

2 **selling,** merchandising, marketing; wholesaling, jobbing; retailing; direct selling; sell-through; telemarketing; mail-order selling, direct-mail selling, catalog selling, direct marketing; viral marketing; television selling, video selling; online selling, e-commerce; vending, peddling, hawking, huckstering; hucksterism; market research, marketing research, consumer research, consumer preference study, consumer survey, data warehousing; sales campaign, promotion, sales promotion; **salesmanship,** high-pressure salesmanship, hard sell, low-pressure salesmanship, soft sell; cold call; sellout; branding; trade-up

3 **sale,** sellout, closing-out sale, going-out-of-business sale, inventory-clearance sale, distress sale, fire sale; bazaar; rummage sale, white elephant sale, garage sale, tag sale, yard sale, flea market; tax sale

4 **auction,** auction sale, vendue, outcry, sale at auction, sale by auction, sale to the highest bidder; Dutch auction; auction block, block

5 **sales talk, sales pitch,** patter; **pitch**, spiel, ballyhoo

6 **sales resistance,** consumer resistance, buyer resistance

7 **salability,** salableness, commerciality, merchandisability, **marketability,** vendibility

VERBS **8** **sell,** merchandise, **market,** move, turn over, sell off, make a sale, effect a sale; convert into cash, turn into money; sell out, close out; sell up <Brit>; retail, sell retail, sell over the counter; wholesale, sell wholesale, job, be jobber for, be wholesaler for; dump, unload, flood the market with, get rid of; sacrifice, sell at a loss; remainder; resell, sell over; undersell, undercut, cut under; sell short; sell on consignment; telemarket

9 **vend,** dispense, **peddle,** hawk, huckster; tout; telemarket

10 **put up for sale,** put up, ask bids for, ask offers for, offer for sale, offer at a bargain

11 **auction,** auction off, auctioneer, sell at auction, sell by auction, put up for auction, put on the block, bring under the hammer; knock down, sell to the highest bidder

12 **be sold, sell,** bring, realize, sell for; change hands; sell like hotcakes, be in demand

ADJS **13** **sales,** selling, market, **marketing,** merchandising, retail, retailing, wholesale, wholesaling; vending

14 **salable, marketable,** retailable, merchandisable, merchantable, commercial, vendible; in demand; sold, sold out

15 **unsalable,** nonsalable, **unmarketable;** on one's hands, on the shelves, not moving, not turning over, unbought, unsold

ADVS **16** **for sale,** to sell, up for sale, in the market, on the market, in the marts of trade; at a bargain, marked down

17 **at auction,** at outcry, at public auction, by auction, on the block, under the hammer

735 MERCHANDISE

<goods>

NOUNS **1** **merchandise,** commodities, wares, **goods,** effects, vendibles; items, oddments; consumer goods, consumer items, retail goods, goods for sale; stock, stock-in-trade; staples; **inventory**; line, line of goods; sideline; job lot; mail-order goods, catalog goods; luxury goods, big-ticket items, upscale items

2 **commodity, ware,** vendible, **product,** article, item, article of commerce, article of merchandise; staple, staple item, standard article; special, feature, leader, lead item, loss leader; seconds; drug, drug on the market

3 **dry goods, soft goods;** textiles; yard goods, white goods, linens, napery; men's wear, ladies' wear, children's wear, infants' wear; sportswear, sporting goods; leatherware, leather goods

4 **hard goods, durables,** durable goods, consumer durable; fixtures, white goods, appliances; tools and machinery; hardware, ironmongery <Brit>; sporting goods, housewares, home furnishings, kitchenware; tableware, dinnerware, dinner service, place setting; flatware, hollow ware; metalware, brassware, copperware, silverware, ironware, tinware; woodenware; glassware; chinaware, earthenware, clayware, stoneware, graniteware; enamelware; ovenware

5 **furniture**, furnishings, home furnishings

6 **notions, sundries,** novelties, knickknacks, odds and ends; toilet goods, toiletries; cosmetics, makeup; giftware

7 **groceries,** grocery, food items, edibles, victuals, baked goods, packaged goods, canned goods, tinned goods; green goods, produce, truck

736 MARKET

<place for selling goods>

NOUNS **1** **market, mart, store, shop,** salon, boutique, wareroom, emporium, house, establishment; retail store; wholesale house, discount store, discount house, outlet store; warehouse; mail-order house; general store, country store; department store; warehouse store, superstore, megastore; co-op, cooperative; variety store, variety shop, dime store; ten-cent store, five-and-ten, five-and-dime, thrift store, thrift shop, swap shop, consignment shop, consignment store; convenience store, corner store, minimart, mom-and-pop store; chain store; concession; trading post, post; supermarket, grocery store, grocer; factory outlet, anchor store; army surplus store

2 **marketplace,** mart, market, open market, market overt, agora; **shopping center, shopping mall,** shopping plaza, plaza, mall, strip mall, arcade, shopping complex, commercial complex; factory outlet center, factory outlet; warehouse; emporium, rialto; staple; bazaar, fair, trade fair, show, auto show, boat show, exposition; flea market, flea fair, street market, farmers' market, fish market, meat market; trading post; home shopping, e-commerce, electronic commerce; pedestrian mall

3 **booth, stall, stand;** newsstand, kiosk, news kiosk; pushcart; roadside stand

4 **vending machine**, vendor, coin machine, coin-operated machine, slot machine, automat; reverse vending machine

5 **salesroom,** wareroom; showroom; auction room

6 **counter,** shopboard; notions counter; showcase; peddler's cart, pushcart

737 STOCK MARKET

<place for trading securities>

NOUNS 1 **stock market,** the market, **Wall Street;** securities market, commodity market; ticker market; open market, competitive market; steady market, strong market, hard market, stiff market; unsteady market, spotty market; weak market; long market; top-heavy market; market index, stock price index, Dow-Jones Industrial Average

2 **active market,** brisk market, lively market

3 **inactive market,** slow market, stagnant market, flat market, tired market, sick market; investors on the sidelines; aftermarket

4 **rising market,** booming market, buoyant market; **bull market,** bullish market, bullishness

5 **declining market,** sagging market, retreating market, off market, soft market; **bear market,** bearish market, bearishness; slump, sag; break, break in the market; profit-taking, selloff; crash, smash

6 **rigged market,** manipulated market, pegged market, put-up market; insider trading

7 **stock exchange,** exchange, Wall Street, change <Brit>, stock market, bourse, board; the Exchange, New York Stock Exchange, the Big Board; American Stock Exchange, Amex, curb, curb market, curb exchange; over-the-counter market, telephone market, outside market; third market; exchange floor; commodity exchange, pit, corn pit, wheat pit; quotation board; ticker, stock ticker; ticker tape

8 **financial district,** Wall Street, the Street; Lombard Street

9 **stock brokerage,** brokerage, brokerage house, brokerage office; wire house; bucket shop, boiler room

10 **stockbroker,** sharebroker <Brit>, **broker,** jobber, stockjobber, dealer, stock dealer; Wall Streeter; stock-exchange broker; floor broker, floor trader, floorman, specialist, market maker; pit man; curb broker; odd-lot dealer; two-dollar broker; day trader, night trader; broker's agent, customer's broker, registered representative; bond crowd

11 **speculator,** adventurer, operator; big operator, smart operator; plunger, gunslinger; scalper; stag <Brit>; lame duck; margin purchaser; arbitrager, arbitrageur, arb; inside trader

12 **bear,** short, short seller; shorts, short interest, short side; short account, bear account

13 **bull,** long, longs, long interest, long side; long account, bull account

14 **stockholder,** stockowner, **shareholder,** shareowner; bondholder, coupon-clipper; stockholder of record

15 **stock company,** joint-stock company; issuing company; stock insurance company; public company

16 **trust,** investment company; investment trust, holding company; closed-end investment company, closed-end fund; open-end fund, mutual fund, money-market fund; unit trust <Brit>; load fund, no-load fund, low-load fund, back-end fund; growth fund, income fund, dual purpose fund; trust fund; blind trust; shell company

17 **pool,** bear pool, bull pool, blind pool

18 **stockbroking,** brokerage, stockbrokerage, jobbing, stockjobbing, stockjobbery, stock dealing; bucketing, legal bucketing

19 **trading,** stock-market trading, market-trading; computer selling, programmed selling; playing the market; **speculation,** stockjobbing, stockjobbery; venture, flutter; flier, plunge; scalping; liquidation, profit taking; arbitrage, arbitraging; buying in, covering shorts; short sale; spot sale; round trade, round transaction, turn; risk capital, venture capital, equity capital; money-market trading, foreign-exchange trading, agiotage; buyout, takeover, hostile takeover, takeover bid; leveraged buyout; greenmail; leverage

20 **manipulation, rigging;** raid, bear raid, bull raid; corner, corner in, corner on the market, monopoly; washing, washed sale, wash sale

21 **option,** stock option, right, **put, call,** put and call, right of put and call; straddle, spread; strip; strap

22 **panic,** bear panic, rich man's panic

VERBS 23 **trade, speculate,** venture, operate, **play the market,** buy futures, sell futures, deal in futures; arbitrage; plunge, take a flier; scalp; bucket, bucketshop; stag, stag the market <Brit>; trade on margin; pyramid; be long, go long, be long of the market, be on the long side of the market; be short, be short of the market, be on the short side of the market; margin up, apply margin, deposit margin; wait out the market, hold on; be caught short, miss the market, overstay the market; scoop the market, make a killing, make a bundle

24 **sell,** convert, liquidate; throw on the market, dump, unload; sell short, go short, make a short sale; cover one's short, fulfill a short sale; make delivery, clear the trade; close out, sell out, terminate the account

25 manipulate the market, **rig the market;** bear, bear the market; bull, bull the market; raid the market; hold the market, peg the market; whipsaw; wash sales

26 corner, get a corner on, **corner the market;** monopolize, engross; buy up, absorb

738 SECURITIES
<instruments of investment>

NOUNS 1 **securities** <see list>, stocks and bonds, investment securities; arbitrage, program trading; day trading, day trade

2 **stock** <see list>, shares, equity, equity security, corporate stock; stock split, split; reverse split; stock list; stock ledger, share ledger; holdings, **portfolio,** investment portfolio; fund, **mutual fund** <see list>

3 **share, lot;** preference share; dummy share; holding, holdings, stockholding, stockholdings; block; round lot, full lot, even lot, board lot; odd lot, fractional lot

4 **stock certificate,** certificate of stock; street certificate; interim certificate; coupon

5 **bond** <see list>; nominal rate, coupon rate, current yield, yield to maturity

6 **issue,** issuance; flotation; stock issue, secondary issue; bond issue; poison pill

7 **dividend;** regular dividend; extra dividend, special dividend, plum, melon; payout ratio; cumulative dividend, accumulated dividends, accrued dividends; interim dividend; cash dividend; stock dividend; optional dividend; scrip dividend; liquidating dividend; phony dividend; interest; **return, yield,** return on investment, payout, payback

8 **assessment,** Irish dividend

9 **price, quotation;** bid-and-asked prices, bid price, asking price, offering price; actual price, delivery price, settling price, put price, call price; opening price, closing price; high, low; market price, quoted price, flash price; issue price; fixed price; parity; par, issue par; par value, nominal value, face value; stated value; book value; market value; bearish prices, bullish prices; swings, fluctuations; flurry, flutter; rally, decline

10 **margin;** thin margin, shoestring margin; exhaust price

11 <commodities> spots, spot grain; futures, future grain

VERBS 12 **issue, float,** put on the market; issue stock, go public; float a bond issue

13 **declare a dividend,** cut a melon

ADVS 14 dividend off, ex dividend; dividend on, cum dividend; coupon off, ex coupon; coupon on, cum coupon; warrants off, ex warrants; warrants on, cum warrants; when issued

15 **bond**

adjustment bond
annuity bond
appreciation bond
assented bond
asset-backed bond
assumed bond
baby bond
bearer bond
bearer certificate
bond anticipation note
callable bond
collateral trust bond
consolidated annuities, consols, bank annuities <Brit>
consolidated stock
convertible bond
convertible debenture
corporate bond
corporation stock <Brit>
coupon bond
current income bond
deep-discount bond
defense bond
deferred bond
definitive bond
discount bond
equipment bond
equipment note
equipment trust
equipment trust bond
equipment trust certificate
extended bond
Fannie Mae bond
Federal Agency bond
FICO bond
first mortgage bond, first
foreign bond
Freddie Mac bond
general mortgage bond
general obligation bond
gilt-edged bond
Ginnie Mae bond
government bond
guaranteed bond
high-grade bond
income bond
indenture
installment bond
interchangeable bond
interim bond
joint bond
junk bond, high-yield bond
Liberty bond
long-term bond
mortgage-backed bond
municipal bond
negotiable bond
noncallable bond
nonnegotiable bond
optional bond
par bond
participating bond
perpetual bond
premium bond
purchase money bond
redeemable bond
refunding bond
registered bond
registered certificate
revenue bond
savings bond
second mortgage bond, second
secured bond
serial bond
Series EE bond
Series HH bond
short-term bond
sinking-fund bond
small bond
state bond
subordinated bond
tax anticipation note
tax-exempt bond
tax-free bond
treasury bill
treasury bond
treasury note
trust indenture
trustee mortgage bond
turnpike bond
unsecured bond
voting bond
war bond
Z-bond, accrual bond, accretion bond
zero coupon bond

16 **mutual fund**

aggressive growth mutual fund
assets management mutual fund
balanced mutual fund
bond mutual fund
capital appreciation mutual fund
closed-end mutual fund
corporate bond mutual fund
double tax-exempt bond mutual fund
equity mutual fund
equity-income mutual fund
federal municipal bond mutual fund
federal municipal money market mutual fund
fixed-income mutual fund
global bond mutual fund
global mutual fund

government bond mutual fund
growth and income mutual fund
growth mutual fund
index mutual fund
international mutual fund
large-cap mutual fund
load mutual fund
mid-cap mutual fund
money market mutual fund
mutual funds of mutual fund
no-load mutual fund
small-cap mutual fund
speciality mutual fund, sector mutual fund
state municipal bond mutual fund
state municipal money market mutual fund
state tax-exempt income mutual fund
stock mutual fund
tax-exempt income mutual fund
tax-exempt market fund
triple tax-exempt bond mutual fund
U.S. Government money market fund

17 **securities**

active securities
American Depository Receipts (ADRs)
banker's acceptance
callable securities
certificate of accrual on treasury securities (CATS)
certificate of deposit (CD)
convertible securities, convertibles (CVs)
corporation securities
debenture of indebtedness, certificate of indebtedness
digested securities
fixed-income securities
foreign securities
futures contract
gilt-edged securities
government securities
international securities
junior securities
legal securities
liquid yield option notes (LYONs)
listed securities
margined securities
marketable securities
money-market certificate
mortgage-based securities
municipal securities
negotiable securities, negotiables
noncallable securities
note
obsolete securities
outside securities
outstanding securities
over-the-counter securities
pass-throughs, participation certificate
program trading
registered securities
senior securities
separate trading of registered interest and principal securities (STRIPS)
short-term note
speculative securities, cats and dogs
stamped securities
treasury bill
treasury bond
treasury certificate
treasury investment growth receipts (TIGRs)
treasury note
undigested securities
unlisted securities
unregistered securities
warrant

18 **stock**

active stock
assessable stock
authorized capital stock
blue chip stock, blue chip
borrowed stock
capital stock
common stock, ordinary shares <Brit>
convertible preferred stock
cumulative convertible preferred stock
cumulative preferred stock
cyclical stock
debenture stock
defensive stock
deferred stock
eighth stock
floating stock
growth stock
guaranteed stock
high-grade stock
hypothecated stock
inactive stock
income stock
industrials, rails, utilities
initial public offering
issued capital stock
letter stock
loaned stock
long stock
new issue
no-par stock
nonassessable stock
nonvoting stock
over-the-counter stock
pale blue chip
participating preferred stock
penny stock
preferred stock, preference stock <Brit>
protective stock
quality stock
quarter stock
seasoned stock
short stock
small cap stock
special situation stock
specialty stock
speculative stock
standard stock
ten-share unit stock
treasury stock
unissued capital stock
voting stock
voting-right certificate
watered stock

739 WORKPLACE

<place of employment, work>

NOUNS 1 **workplace,** worksite, **place of business;** workshop, shop; shop floor, workspace, working space, work area, loft; bench, workbench, worktable; counter, worktop; work station; desk, desktop; workroom; studio, *atelier* <Fr>, library; parlor, beauty parlor, funeral parlor; establishment, facility, installation; company, institution, house, firm, concern, agency, organization, corporation, privately held corporation, limited liability corporation; financial institution, stock exchange, bank; market, store, mall, shopping mall, megamall, retail park; food court, eating place; hotel, motel; gas station, truck stop; construction site, building site; dockyard, shipyard; farm, ranch, nursery; power station; government office; office building, office park, science park; virtual company, Internet startup

2 hive, hive of industry, beehive; factory town, mill town, manufacturing town; hub of industry, center of manufacture, industrial town

3 **plant, factory,** works, manufactory, manufacturing plant, installation, shop floor, job site; main plant, assembly plant, subassembly plant, feeder plant; foreign-owned plant, transplant; push-button plant, automated factory, cybernated factory, robot factory; assembly line, production line; defense plant, munitions plant, armory, arsenal; power plant; atomic

energy plant; machine shop; mill, sawmill, flour mill; yard, yards, railroad yard, brickyard, shipyard, dockyard, boatyard; ropewalk; mint; refinery, oil refinery, sugar refinery; distillery, brewery, winery; boilery; bindery, bookbindery; packinghouse; cannery; dairy, creamery; pottery; tannery; sweatshop; factory district, industrial zone, industrial area, industrial park, industrial estate <Brit>; factory belt, manufacturing quarter; enterprise zone

4 **foundry,** works, metalworks; steelworks, steelyard, steel mill; refinery, forge, furnace, bloomery, blast furnace; smelter; smithy, smithery, stithy, blacksmith's shop; brickworks; quarry, mine, colliery, coalmine; mint

5 **repair shop,** fix-it shop; garage; roundhouse; hangar

6 **laboratory,** lab; skunkworks; research laboratory, research installation, research facility, research center, research park

7 **office,** shop; home office, head office, main office, headquarters, executive office, corporate headquarters, company headquarters; office suite, executive suite, board room, conference room; chambers <Brit>; cubicle, closet, study, den, carrell; embassy, consulate, legation, chancery, chancellery; box office, ticket office; branch, branch office, local office, subsidiary office, bureau, business house; office park, executive park; shared workspace, coworking space; virtual office

8 <home workplace> **home office**, office, den, study; kitchen, laundry room, sewing room, workbench

740 WEAVING

<craft of creating fabric>

NOUNS 1 **weaving,** weave, warpage, weftage, warp and woof, warp and weft, texture, tissue; **fabric,** web, webbing; interweaving, interweavement, intertexture; interlacing, interlacement, interlacery; crisscross; intertwining, intertwinement; intertieing, interknitting, interthreading, intertwisting; lacing, enlacement; twining, entwining, entwinement; wreathing, knitting, twisting; **braiding,** plaiting, plashing

2 **braid,** plait, pigtail, **wreath,** wreathwork

3 **warp; woof, weft,** filling; shoot, pick

4 **weaver,** interlacer, webster, knitter, spinner; weaverbird, weaver finch, whirligig beetle

5 **loom,** weaver; hand loom; Navajo loom; knitting machine; spinning wheel; shuttle, distaff

VERBS 6 **weave,** loom, tissue; **interweave**, interlace, intertwine, interknit, interthread, intertissue, intertie, intertwist; inweave, intort; web, net; lace, enlace; twine, entwine; braid, plait, pleach, wreathe, raddle, knit, twist, mat, wattle; crisscross; twill, loop, noose; splice; felt, brush, nap; interconnect

ADJS 7 **woven,** loomed, textile; interwoven, interlaced, interthreaded, intertwined, interknit, intertissued, intertied, intertwisted; handwoven; laced, enlaced; wreathed, fretted, raddled, knit, knitted; twined, entwined; braided, plaited, platted, pleached; hooked; webbed

8 **weaving,** twining, entwining; intertwining, **interlacing,** interweaving, crosswise, crossways

741 SEWING

<craft of creating or repairing fabric goods>

NOUNS 1 **sewing, needlework,** stitchery, stitching; mending, basting, darning, hemming, quilting, embroidery, cross-stitching, cross stitch, needlepoint; **fancywork;** tailoring, garment-making; suture

2 **sewer, needleworker, seamstress,** sempstress, needlewoman; seamster, sempster, **tailor,** needleman, needler; embroiderer, embroideress; knitter; garmentmaker

3 **sewing machine**, sewer, embroidery hoop

VERBS 4 **sew, stitch,** needle; mend, baste; stitch up, sew up; **tailor**

742 CERAMICS

<art of creating things from clay>

NOUNS 1 **ceramics** <see list>, **pottery;** potting

2 **ceramic ware,** ceramics; pottery, crockery; china, porcelain; enamelware; refractory, cement; bisque, biscuit; pot, crock, vase, urn, jug, bowl; tile, tiling; brick, firebrick, refractory brick, adobe; glass; industrial ceramics; ceramist, ceramicist, potter

3 <materials> **clay**; potter's clay, potter's earth, fireclay, refractory clay; argil, adobe, terra cotta; porcelain clay, kaolin, china clay, china stone, marl, feldspar, petuntze, petuntse; flux; slip; glaze, overglaze, underglaze; crackle

4 **potter's wheel,** wheel; kick wheel, pedal wheel, hand-turned wheel, power wheel

5 **kiln,** oven, stove, furnace; acid kiln, brick kiln, cement kiln, enamel kiln, muffle kiln, limekiln, bottle kiln, beehive kiln, reverberatory, reverberatory kiln; pyrometer, pyrometric cone, Seger cone

VERBS 6 pot, shape, **throw,** throw a pot, turn a pot; cast, mold; **fire,** bake; glaze

ADJS 7 **ceramic,** earthen, clay, enamel, china, porcelain; fired, baked, glazed; refractory; hand-turned, hand-painted, thrown; industrial

8 **ceramics**

agateware
Albion ware
Allervale pottery
Arita ware
Arretine ware, terra sigillata
basalt, basaltes, basaltware
Belleek ware
Berlin ware
biscuit, bisque ware
blackware
blue and white ware
bone china
Castleford ware
Castor ware
champlevé, champlevé enamel
Chelsea porcelain
china, chinaware
Ch'ing porcelain
clayware
cloisonné, cloisonné enamel
Coalport
cottage china
crackle, crackleware
creamware
crockery
crouch ware
Crown Derby ware
Dedham pottery
delft, delftware
Derby porcelain
Doulton ware
Dresden china
earthenware
eggshell porcelain
enamel, enamelware
faience
glassware
glazed ware
gombroon
hard-paste porcelain
Hirado ware
Hizen porcelain
Imari ware
industrial ceramics
ironstone, ironstone china
istoriato ware
Jackfield ware
jasper, jasperware
Kakiemon ware
Kinkozan ware
lambrequin
Leeds pottery
Limoges, Limoges ware
Lowestoft ware
lusterware, luster pottery
majolica
Meissen ware
mezza-majolica
Nabeshima ware
Nanking ware
Old Worcester ware
ovenware
Palissy ware
Parian ware
Pennsylvania Dutch, German ware
porcelain
porcelain enamel
queensware
redware
refractory ware
Rockingham ware
Royal Copenhagen porcelain
Royal Doulton porcelain
Royal Worcester porcelain
salt-glazed ware
Samian ware
sanda ware
Satsuma ware
semiporcelain
Sèvres, Sèvres ware
Seto ware
slipware
soft-paste porcelain
Spode
spongeware
Staffordshire, Staffordshire ware
stoneware
Sung ware
T'ang ware
terra cotta
Tiffany glass
ting ware, ting yao
Toft ware
tulip ware
Wedgwood, Wedgwood ware
whiteware, white pottery
willowware
Worcester ware
yi-hsing ware, yi-hsing yao

743 AMUSEMENT

<entertaining activity>

NOUNS 1 **amusement,** entertainment, **diversion,** solace, divertisement, *divertissement* <Fr>, recreation, relaxation, regalement; pastime, *passe-temps* <Fr>; mirth; pleasure, enjoyment; clubbing

2 **fun,** action; funmaking, fun and games, **play,** sport, game; gaming, video gaming; good time, lovely time, pleasant time; big time, high time, high old time, picnic, laughs, lots of laughs, ball, great fun, time of one's life; a short life and a merry one; wild oats

3 **festivity,** merrymaking, merriment, gaiety, jollity, jollification, joviality, conviviality, whoopee, hoopla; larking, cavorting, skylarking, racketing, mafficking, holiday-making; **revelry,** revelment, reveling, revels; nightlife

4 **festival,** festivity, festive occasion, *fiesta* <Sp>, fete, gala, gala affair, blowout, jamboree; high jinks, do, great doings; *fête champêtre* <Fr>; feast, banquet; picnic; party; waygoose, wayzgoose; fair, state fair, county fair; carnival; kermis; Oktoberfest; Mardi Gras; Saturnalia; harvest festival, harvest home <Brit>; field day; gala day, feria

5 **frolic,** play, romp, rollick, frisk, gambol, caper, dido

6 revel, lark, escapade, ploy; celebration; party; **spree**, bout, fling, wingding, randan, randy; carouse, drinking bout

7 **round of pleasure,** mad round, whirl, merry-go-round, the rounds, the dizzy rounds

8 **sports;** athletics, agonistics; athleticism

9 **game;** card game; board game; parlor game, role-playing game, arcade game; children's game; computer game, video game, console game; gambling game; table game; word game; indoor game, outdoor game; play; scavenger hunt, contest; race; event, meet; bout, match, go; gambling

10 tournament, tourney, gymkhana, field day; rally; regatta

11 **playground,** playscape; **field**, athletic field, playing field; football field, gridiron; baseball field, diamond; infield, outfield; soccer field; archery ground, cricket ground, polo ground, croquet lawn, bowling green; bowling alley; links, golf links, golf course; fairway, putting green; gymnasium, gym; court, badminton court, basketball court, tennis court, racket court, squash court, pickleball court; billiard parlor, poolroom, pool hall; racecourse, track, course turf, oval; stretch; rink, glaciarium,

ice rink, skating rink; skateboard park; playroom

12 **swimming pool, pool,** swimming bath <Brit>, plunge, plunge bath, natatorium; swimming hole; wading pool, kiddy pool; lap pool; wave pool; infinity pool

13 **entertainment,** entertainment industry, show business, show biz; theater; dinner theatre; cabaret, tavern, roadhouse; café dansant, chantant; big dance; nightclub, night spot, nitery, hot spot; *boîte, boîte de nuit* <Fr>; juke joint, discothèque, disco; dance hall, dancing pavilion, ballroom, dance floor; casino; resort

14 **park,** public park, pleasure garden, pleasance, paradise, common, commons, playground; amusement park, Tivoli, fun fair, carnival; fairground; theme park, safari park

15 amusement ride, **ride**, merry-go-round, carousel, roundabout, whirligig, whip, flying horses; Ferris wheel; seesaw, teeter-totter; slide; swing; roller coaster; chutes, chute-the-chute; funhouse, arcade, funplex, video arcade; -drome

16 **toy, plaything,** sport; bauble, knickknack, gimcrack, gewgaw, kickshaw, whim-wham, trinket; doll, action figure, paper doll, stuffed animal, teddy bear, puppet, marionette, toy soldier, bobblehead; dollhouse; rocking horse; hoop, hula hoop, top, pinwheel, jack-in-the-box, jacks, pick-up sticks, blocks, checkers, chess, marbles, slingshot, ball; building blocks, plastic blocks; game, board game, card game, video game; trading card, sports card

17 **chess piece,** chessman, man, piece; bishop, knight, king, queen, pawn, rook, castle

18 **player,** frolicker, frisker, funmaker, funster, gamboler; pleasure-seeker, pleasurer, pleasurist, playboy; reveler, celebrant, merrymaker, rollicker, skylarker, carouser, cutup; contestant

19 **athlete,** jock, player, sportsman, sportswoman, contender, amateur athlete, professional athlete, competitor; letter man

20 **master of ceremonies, mistress of ceremonies,** emcee (MC), marshal; toastmaster; host, master of the revels, revel master; social director

VERBS 21 **amuse, entertain,** divert, regale, beguile, solace, recreate, refresh, enliven, exhilarate, put in good humor; relax, loosen up; delight, tickle, titillate, tickle pink, tickle to death, tickle the fancy; make one laugh, strike one as funny, raise a laugh, convulse, set the table on a roar, be the death of; wow, slay, knock dead, kill, break one up, crack one up, fracture one; have them rolling in the aisles; keep them in stitches

22 **amuse oneself,** pleasure oneself, take one's pleasure, give oneself over to pleasure; get one's kicks, get one's jollies; relax, let oneself go, loosen up; **have fun,** have a good time, have a ball, have lots of laughs, live it up, laugh it up; drown care, drive dull care away; beguile the time, kill time, while away the time; get away from it all

23 **play,** sport, disport; frolic, rollick, gambol, frisk, romp, caper, cut capers, lark about, antic, curvet, cavort, caracole, flounce, trip, skip, dance; cut up, cut a dido, horse around, fool around, futz around, carry on

24 **make merry, party**, revel, roister, jolly, lark, skylark, make whoopee, let oneself go, blow off steam, let off steam; cut loose, let loose, let go, let one's hair down, whoop it up, kick up one's heels; hell around, raise hell, blow off the lid; step out, go places and do things, go on the town, see life, paint the town red; go the dizzy rounds, go on the merry-go-round; celebrate; spree, go on a spree, go on a bender, go on a binge; carouse, jollify, wanton, debauch, pub-crawl, club-hop; sow one's wild oats, have one's fling

25 eat, drink, and be merry; feast, banquet

ADJS 26 **amused,** entertained; diverted, delighted, tickled, tickled pink, tickled to death, titillated

27 **amusing, entertaining,** diverting, beguiling; fun, funsome, more fun than a barrel of monkeys; recreative, recreational; delightful, frabjous, titillative, titillating; humorous

28 **festive,** festal; merry, gay, jolly, jovial, joyous, joyful, gladsome, convivial, gala, hilarious; merrymaking, on the loose; on the town, out on the town

29 **playful,** sportive, sportful; frolicsome, gamesome, rompish, larkish, capersome; waggish

30 **sporting,** sports; **athletic,** agonistic; gymnastic, palaestral; acrobatic

ADVS 31 **in fun,** for amusement, for fun, for the fun of it; for kicks, for laughs, for the heck of it, for the hell of it; just to be doing

744 SPORTS

<physical competitive activity>

NOUNS 1 **sport, sports, athletics,** athletic competition, game, **team game** <see list>, sports activity, play, contest, match; training camp; round, set, tournament; **aeronautical or air sport** <see list>; **animal sport** <see list>; **aquatic or water sport** <see list>; ball game; **court sport** <see list>; track and field; **gymnastics** <see list>; indoor sport; **outdoor sport** <see list>; **winter sport** <see list>; contact sport; combat sport, **martial art** <see list>; **target sport** <see list>; decathlon; triathlon, biathlon; bicycling, bicycle touring, cross-country cycling, cyclo-cross, bicycle motocross, road racing, off-road racing, track racing; motor sport, automobile racing, go-carting, jet-skiing, waterskiing, motorcycling, motocross, dirt-biking, snowmobiling, soapbox racing; in-line skating, in-line blading, Rollerblading, roller skating, roller hockey, skateboarding; target sport, archery, field archery, darts, marksmanship, target shooting, skeet shooting, trap shooting, clay pigeon; **throwing sport** <see list>; weightlifting, bodybuilding, iron-pumping, Olympic lifting, powerlifting, weight training; blood sport; extreme sport; sports science; dream team, game time, game-changer, hot-stove league; fantasy sport; sports psychology

VERBS 2 **play, compete;** practice, train, work out; try out, go out for; follow; smashmouth

3 **aeronautical or air sport**

aerial skiing
aerobatics
aeromodeling
aerotow
ballooning
bungee jumping
flying
freefalling
gliding
hang gliding
helicopter flying
hoverboard
hydroplane racing
kiting
microlighting
parachuting
paragliding
parasailing
skydiving
soaring
sports parachuting

4 **animal sport**

barrel racing
bronc riding, bronco busting
bullfighting
bull riding
calf roping
camel racing
carriage driving
cockfighting
cross-country riding
dog racing
dogsled racing
dressage
driving
endurance riding
equestrian sport
falconry
greyhound racing
harness racing
horseback riding
horsemanship
horse racing
pack riding
pigeon racing
point-to-point
polo
rodeo
show jumping
steeplechase
steer roping
steer wrestling
team penning
team roping
three-day event
trail riding
trotting
vaulting
Western riding

5 **aquatic or water sport**

bellyboarding, boogieboarding
birling
boating
body surfing, bodyboarding
canoeing
canoe polo
canoe slalom
canyoning
diving
dragon boat racing
fin swimming
fishing
inner tube water polo
Jet Skiing
kayaking
lifesaving
motorboat racing
offshore yacht racing
powerboat racing
rafting
rowing
sailing
sailplaning
scuba diving
sculling
skin diving
snorkeling
surfing, surfboarding
swimming
synchronized swimming
underwater diving
underwater hockey
underwaterball
water polo
waterskiing
whitewater canoeing
whitewater rafting
windsurfing, boardsailing, sailboarding
yachting

6 **combat sport, martial art**

aikido, aiki-jutsu
arm and wrist wrestling
arnis
bando
bersilat
bojutsu
boxing
capoeira
Cornish wrestling
dumog
escrima
fencing
freestyle wrestling
glimae
Greco-Roman wrestling
Greek boxing
haphido
hwarang-do
Iaido
Iaijutsu
Icelandic wrestling
jeet kune do
jobajutsu
jojutsu
jousting
judo
jujitsu, jujutsu
jukendo
kalari payat
karate
kendo
kenipo
kenjutsu
kiaijutsu
kickboxing
kobu jutsu
kung fu
kyujutsu
laido
lua
main tindju
mud wrestling
naginata jutsu
ninjutsu
pankation
pentjak-silat
pukulan
quigong
sambo wrestling
savate
self-defense
stick fighting
sumo wrestling
tae kwon do
t'ai chi
tang soo do
tegumi
Thai kickboxing
wrestling
wu shu, wushu

7 **court sport**

badminton
court tennis
handball
jai alai, pelota
pickleball
racquetball
squash
table tennis, Ping-Pong <tm>
tennis

8 **gymnastics**

balance beam
floor exercises
horizontal bar
mini-trampolining
parallel bars
pommel horse
rhythmic gymnastics
rings
trampolining
tumbling
uneven parallel bars
vaulting

9 **outdoor sport**
backpacking
bushwalking
camping, glamping
Frisbee <tm>
Frisbee golf
hiking
ice climbing
mountaineering, alpinism
orienteering
parkour
rock climbing
speleology, spelunking
superalpinism, Alpine climbing
wilderness survival

10 **target sport**
archery
boccie, bocci
bowling
Canadian 5-pin bowling
candlepins
carom billiards
clay pigeon shooting
croquet
curling
darts
duckpins
golf
green bowling
horseshoe pitching
pistol shooting
pool
rifle shooting
skittles <Brit>
sharpshooting
skeet, skeet shooting
snooker
tenpins
trapshooting

11 **team game**
arena football
Australian rules football
bandy
baseball
basketball
beach volleyball
Canadian football
cricket
curling
field hockey
football
Gaelic football
hurling
ice hockey
lacrosse
netball
roller hockey
rounders <Brit>
rugby
soccer, association football <Brit>
softball
speedball
team handball
volleyball, V-ball

12 **throwing sport**
boomeranging
discus throw
Frisbee <tm>
hammer throw
horseshoe pitching
javelin throw
shot put
ultimate Frisbee <tm>

13 **winter sport**
Alpine combined event
Alpine skiing
Alpine touring
bandy
biathlon
bobsledding
broomball
cross-country skiing, Nordic skiing, langlauf
curling
downhill skiing
figure skating
freestyle skiing, hotdogging
giant slalom
half-pipe
heli-skiing
hockey
ice boating
ice dancing
ice sailing
luge
mogul skiing
Nordic combined event
off-piste skiing
short-track speed skating
skating
skibob racing
skiing
skijoring
ski jumping
ski mountaineering
slalom
sledding
snowboarding
snowmobiling
snowshoeing
snow tubing
speed skating
super giant slalom
tobogganing
ultimate skate Frisbee <tm>

745 BASEBALL

<field game with bat and ball>

NOUNS 1 **baseball,** ball, the national pastime, hardball; organized baseball, league, loop, circuit, major league, big league, the majors, the big time, the bigs, professional baseball, the National League, the Senior Circuit, the American League, the Junior Circuit; minor league, triple-A, the minors, bush leagues, the bushes, college baseball; Little League baseball; division championship, playoff, League Championship Series, league championship, league pennant, World Series, All-Star Game; fantasy baseball; farm team, farm club, farm, farm system, bush league; rotisserie league; ballpark, ball field, field, park; stands, grandstand, boxes, lower deck, upper deck, outfield stands, bleachers; diamond; dugout; home plate, the plate, platter, dish; baseline, line, base path; base, bag, sack, first base, second base, third base, first, second, third, keystone, keystone sack, hot corner; infield, infield grass, infield turf; outfield, warning track, fences; foul line, foul pole; mound, pitcher's mound, hill; **baseball equipment or gear** <see list>

2 **baseball team,** team, nine, roster, squad, the boys of summer, club, ball club, personnel, crew; starting lineup, lineup batting order; **baseball player,** ball player; starter, regular; substitute, sub, utility player, benchwarmer, bench jockey, the bench; pitcher, hurler, motion, pitching motion, herky-jerky motion, right-hander, right-hand pitcher, righty, left-hander, left-hand pitcher, lefty, southpaw, portsider; starting pitcher, fifth starter, spot starter; starting rotation, rotation, pitching rotation; relief pitcher, reliever, fireman, closer, stopper, long reliever; middle reliever, inner reliever; short reliever, the bull pen; battery; catcher, backstop, receiver; fielder, glove man, outfielder, infielder, cover man, cut-off man, relay man; first baseman, first bagger; second baseman, keystone bagger; third baseman, hot-corner man; shortstop; left fielder, center fielder, right fielder; pinch hitter; designated hitter (DH), desi; batter, hitter, man at the plate, man in the box, man in the batter's box, stance, batting stance, pull hitter, power hitter, long-ball hitter, slugger, spray

hitter, contact hitter, banjo hitter, switch hitter, leadoff hitter, cleanup hitter; base runner, runner, designated runner; manager, pilot, coach, batting coach, pitching coach, bench coach, bullpen coach, first-base coach, third-base coach; official scorer; scout, talent scout

3 game, **ball game,** play, strategy; umpire, home-plate umpire, plate umpire, umpire in chief, umpire crew, first-base umpire, second-base umpire, third-base umpire; **pitch** <see list>, set, windup, kick, delivery, stuff, offering; strike zone, wheelhouse, kitchen; throwing arm, arm, cannon, soupbone; balk; count, balls and strikes, full count; at bat; hit, base hit, fly ball, tater, bingle, dinger, opposite-field hit; hard-hit ball, shot, bullet, scorcher; single, seeing-eye hit, excuse-me hit, banjo hit; extra-base hit; double, two-base hit, two-base shot, two-bagger; triple, three-base hit, three-bagger; home run, homer, four-bagger, long ball, round trip, round tripper, circuit clout, big salami, one you can hang the wash on, grand-slam home run, grand-slammer, cheap homer, Chinese homer; fly, pop fly, pop-up, can of corn, looper, blooper, bloop, Texas Leaguer, sacrifice fly, sac fly; line drive, liner, line shot, rope, clothesline; ground ball, grounder, wormburner, slow roller, roller, bunt, drag bunt, bleeder, squibbler, nubber, dying quail, come-backer, chopper; foul ball, foul; base on balls, walk, intentional pass, free ticket, free ride; error, passed ball, unearned run, earned run; out, strikeout, K, punchout, putout, foul-out, force-out, double play (DP), double killing, twin killing, triple play, assist; catch, shoestring catch, basket catch, circus catch; squeeze play, hit-and-run play, pickoff play, pickoff, pitch-out; base runner, baseburner, pinch-runner; run; complete game; inning, frame, top of the inning, bottom of the inning, extra innings; fireballing; ball boy, ball girl

4 **statistics,** averages, stats and numbers, percentages; batting average, earned-run average (ERA), slugging average, slugging percentage, fielding average, run batted in (RBI), ribby; the record book, the book

VERBS **5** play, **play ball**, take the field; umpire, call balls and strikes, officiate; pitch, throw, deliver, fire, sidearm, offer, offer up, bring it, burn it, throw smoke, blow it by, throw seeds; throw a bean ball, dust the batter off, back the batter off; relieve, put out the fire; bat, be up, step up to the plate, be in the batter's box; hit, belt, clout, connect, golf, chop, tomahawk; fly, hit a fly, sky it, pop, pop up; ground, bounce, lay it down, lay down a bunt; sacrifice, hit a sacrifice fly; get a base hit, put on one's hitting shoes; blast it, cream it, tear the cover off, hit it right on the screws, hit it right on the button, hit with the good wood, get good wood on it; hit a home run, homer, hit it out; single, double, triple; get aboard, be a base runner; walk, get a free ride, get a free pass; strike out, go downon strikes, out on strikes, go down swinging, fan, whiff, be called out on strikes, be caught looking; ground out, fly out, pop out; catch, haul in, grab, glove, flag down; misplay, make an error, bobble, boot; take a trip to the showers

6 **baseball equipment or gear**

bar mask
base
baseball, ball; pill, apple
baseball cap
bat, lumber, Louisville slugger; baseball doughnut
batting cage
batting glove
batting helmet
birdcage mask
catcher's mask
catcher's mitt
chest protector
cleats
glove
jockstrap; protective cup
pine-tar rag
rosin bag
shin pads, shin guards
uniform; sliding shorts

7 **baseball pitch**

back door
beanball, beaner
bender
breaking ball, breaker
brushback pitch, brush-off, brushing, dust-off
changeup, change-of-pace ball, circle changeup
curveball, curve, bende, Captain Hook, slurve
cut fastball, cutter
dime
duster
eefus ball
fadeaway
fastball, smoke, bullet, heater, hummer, four-seam fastball
floater
forkball
gopher ball
intentional walk, intentional pass
knuckleball, knuckler
knuckle curve
off-speed pitch
palmball
reverse curve
roundhouse curve
sailing fastball
screwball
screwgy
sinker
slider
slow ball
spitball, spitter
split-finger fastball, three-finger fastball
splitter
Uncle Charlie
wild pitch

746 FOOTBALL

<field game with spheroidal ball>

NOUNS **1** **football,** ball, footballing; American football; organized football, college football, NCAA football, conference, league; conference championship, post-season game, bowl invitation, Cotton Bowl, Gator Bowl, Orange Bowl, Rose Bowl, Sugar Bowl, Fiesta Bowl, national championship, mythical national championship; professional football, pro football, National

Football League (NFL); division championship, playoff, Super Bowl, Super Bowl championship, Pro Bowl; high school football; Pop Warner football, Pee Wee football; stadium, bowl, domed stadium, dome; field, gridiron; line, sideline, end line, endzone, goal line, goalpost, crossbar, yard line, midfield stripe, inbounds marker, hash mark, red zone; **football equipment or gear** <see list>, armament; official, zebra, sideline crew, chain gang; Canadian football; fantasy football; arena football

2 **football team,** eleven, team, squad, roster, personnel; first team, regulars, starting lineup, offensive team, offensive platoon, defensive team, defensive platoon, special team, kicking team; **football player;** substitute, sub, benchwarmer; ball, football, pigskin, oblate spheroid; line, linemen, forward wall, offensive linemen, front four, end, tackle, nose tackle, guard, noseguard, center, flanker, tight end; backfield, back, quarterback, signal-caller, field general, passer; halfback, fullback, kicker, punter, tailback, plunging back, slotback, flanker back, running back, wingback, blocking back, linebacker, defensive back, cornerback, safety, free safety, strong safety, weak safety; pass receiver, receiver, wide receiver, primary receiver

3 **football game,** game, strategy, game plan, ball control; **official** <see list>, zebra; kickoff, kick, coin toss, coin flip, placekick, squib kick, free kick, onside kick, runback, kickoff return; **play** <see list>, down, first down, second down, third down, fourth down; line, line of scrimmage, scrimmage line, flat; lineup, **formation** <see list>; pass from center, snap, hand-to-hand snap; live ball, ball in play, ball out of play, dead ball, play stopped, ball whistled dead; running play, passing play; ball carrier, ball handling, tuck, feint, handoff, pocket, straightarm; block, blocking, body block, brush block, chop block, cross block, lead block, screen block, shoulder block; tackle, neck tackle, shirt tackle, face-mask tackle, sack; yardage, gain, loss, long yardage, short yardage; forward pass, pass, **pass pattern** <see list>, pitchout, screen pass, quick release, bomb, incomplete pass, completed pass, pass completion; pass rush, blitz; possession, loss of possession, turnover, fumble, pass interception, interception; in bounds, out of bounds; **penalty** <see list>, infraction, foul, flag on the play; punt, quick kick, knuckler; punt return, fair catch; touchdown, conversion, field goal, safety; period, quarter, half, halftime, intermission, two-minute warning, thirty-second clock, sudden-death overtime; gun, final gun; smashmouth

4 **statistics,** averages, stats, numbers, average running yardage, average passing yardage, average punting yardage, average punt-return yardage

VERBS 5 **play football,** kick, kick off, run, scramble, pass, punt; complete a pass, catch a pass; block, tackle, double-team, blindside, sack, blitz, red-dog; lose possession, fumble, bobble, give up the ball; score, get on the scoreboard; officiate, blow the whistle, whistle the ball dead, drop a flag, call a penalty

6 **football equipment or gear**

cleats
face mask
football
gloves
helmet
jersey, shirt
kicking tee
mouth guard
numbers
pads (hip, knee, shoulder, thigh)
pants
shoes

7 **football formation**

2-5 defense
3-4 defense
4-3 defense, 4-4 defense
5-2 defense, 5-3 defense
6-1 defense, 6-2 defense
7-man line defense
dime formation defense
double coverage
double wing, wingback
empty backfield
flexbone, flex defense
goal line formation
huddle
I formation
man-to-man defense
nickel formation defense
Notre Dame box
option
overshift
power I
prevent defense
pro set
run-and-shoot offense
shotgun offense
short punt formation
single coverage
single wing, wingback; wildcat formation
slot
split end
split T
straight T
strong side
T formation
tackle spread
undershift
V formation
weak side
wedge, flying wedge
wing T
wishbone, wishbone T
zone blocking
zone defense

8 **football official**

back judge
field judge
head linesman, down judge
line judge
referee
side judge
umpire

9 **football pass pattern**

buttonhook
circle
comeback
crossing pattern
curl
down and out
flag pattern
flare, swing pass
flood
hook pattern
look-in pass
option pass
post pattern
screen pass
sideline pass
slant
spot pass
square-in

square-out
streak, fly
swing
up the middle, up the gut
zig in
zig out
Z pattern

10 football play

automatic, audible
blitz, red dog
bomb
bootleg
buck lateral
conversion
counter
cutback
dive
draw
drop kick
end-around
end run
fake procedure
fair catch
flare pass
flea-flicker
forward pass, pass
Hail Mary
halfback option
handoff
hook and lateral
inside run
keeper
lateral pass, lateral
man in motion
mousetrap
naked bootleg
naked reverse
off-tackle slant
onside kick
option
pitchout
play-action pass
plunge
power run
power sweep
quarterback sneak; quarterback scramble
quick kick
reverse
rollout
rush
scramble
screen pass
slant
squib kick
Statue of Liberty
sweep
trap
touchback
trap run
triple option
two-point conversion

11 football penalty

5-yard penalty
10-yard penalty
15-yard penalty
block in the back
chop block
clipping
crackback block
dead-ball foul
delay of game
encroachment
equipment violation
excessive timeouts
face mask
false start
grabbing the facemask
helmet-to-helmet collision
holding
horse-collar tackle
illegal batting
illegal blocking below the waist
illegal contact
illegal formation
illegal forward pass
illegal hands to the face
illegal kick, illegal kickoff
illegal motion
illegal participation
illegal position
illegal procedure
illegal shift
illegal touching of a forward pass, illegal touching of free kick, illegal touching of scrimmage kick
illegal use of hands
ineligible receiver downfield
intentional grounding
kick-catching interference
leaping
late hit
leverage
more than 11 players on the field
neutral zone infraction
offside
out-of-bounds kickoff
pass interference
personal foul
piling on
roughing the kicker
roughing the passer
roughing the snapper
running into the kicker
sideline infraction
spearing
substitution infraction, illegal substitution
tackling by the facemask
targeting
time count violation
tripping
unfair act
unnecessary roughness
unsportsmanlike conduct

747 BASKETBALL

<court game with ball>

NOUNS **1 basketball,** hoop, hoop sport, ball, b-ball, **hoops**; organized basketball, college basketball, National Collegiate Athletic Association (NCAA); professional basketball, pro basketball, National Basketball Association (NBA); tournament, competition, championship, Olympic Games, National Collegiate Athletic Association Tournament, NCAA Tournament, March Madness, Sweet 16, Final Four; National Invitational Tournament (NIT), National Association of Intercollegiate Athletics (NAIA), NAIA Tournament; basketball court, court, hardwood, pine, forecourt, midcourt, backcourt, baseline, sideline, basket, iron, backboard, glass, defensive board, offensive board, free-throw line, charity line, free-throw lane, foul lane, key, keyhole, foul line, the line; bracketology

2 basketball team, five, team, roster, squad, personnel; basketball player, hoopster, cager, hooper, center, right forward, left forward, corner man, right guard, left guard, point guard, shooting guard, point player, playmaker, swingman, trailer, backcourt man, disher-upper, gunner, sixth man

3 basketball game, game, play, strategy, **defense** <see list>, **offense** <see list>; official, referee, umpire, official scorekeeper, timer; foul, **violation** <see list>, infraction, foul trouble, fouling out; running game, fast break, passing game, draw and kick game; jump, center jump, jump ball, live ball; pass, passing, pass ball, assist, bounce pass, dish, feed; rebound; tactics, action, dribble, fake, handoff, ball control, ball handling, boxing out, sky shot, air ball, clear-out pass, outlet pass, basket hanging, freelancing, pivot, post, high post, low post, post-up, one-on-one, screening, pick, pick and roll, trap, turnover, steal, burn, pump fake, out-of-bounds, dead ball, throw-in, corner throw, buzzer play; flopping; restrictions, three-second rule, five-second rule, ten-second rule, twenty-four-second rule, thirty-second rule; **shot**

<see list>, score, basket, field goal, bucket, three-point play, three-pointer, free throw, foul shot; **quarter,** half, overtime period, overtime; courtside

VERBS 4 **play basketball,** play hoops, play ball, ride the pine, dribble, fake, pass, dish, work the ball around, take it coast to coast, give and go, sky it, clear the ball, hand off, guard, play tight, play loose, double-team, hand-check, block, screen, pick, press, set a pick, post up, steal, burn, freelance, shoot, score, sink one, can, swish, finger-roll, tip it in, use the backboard, dunk, slam dunk, make a free throw, shoot a brick, rebound, clear the board, freeze the ball, kill the clock; foul, commit a foul, commit a violation, foul out; flop; pump-fake

5 **basketball defense**

box-and-one defense
combination defense
man-to-man defense, man defense; full-court man to man, half-court man to man
matchup defense
multiple defense
pack-line defense
pressure defense, pressing defense
sagging defense, collapsing defense
set pattern
slough
stack defense
zone defense, zone; half-court zone, full-court pressure defense

6 **basketball foul**

backcourt violation
basket interference
blocking
carrying
charging
defensive three-second violation
disqualifying foul
double dribble
double foul
five-second rule
force-out
goaltending
hacking
held ball
intentional foul
kicking the ball
multiple foul
offensive foul
palming
personal foul, personal
pushing off
shot clock violation
stepping over the line
technical foul, technical; flagrant foul
ten-second backcourt violation
three-second lane violation
traveling, walking, running with the ball
tripping

7 **basketball offense**

ball-control offense
box play
clear out one side
continuity offense; flex, shuffle, swing
delay offense
fast-break offense
flip-flop offense
full-court press
full-court zone press
gap offense
give and go offense
half-court press
high post
inbounding play
low post
motion offense; 5 out motion, 3-2 motion, 4 out 1 motion, dribble drive, Princeton, triangle
press
press break
pressure offense
rotation offense
run and gun offense
running offense
stack offense
stall offense
zone offense; box and 1, 2-3, 3-2, 1-2-2, 1-3-1, 4-out, 5-out

8 **basketball shot**

bank shot
brick
charity shot
cripple
double clutch
dunk
finger-roll
free throw, foul shot, penalty shot
hook shot, hook
jump shot, jumper
layup, bunny
one-and-one
one-hand shot
pivot shot
penalty free throw
power stop, power drive
reverse layup
scoop shot
set shot
slam dunk
swish
teardrop
tip-in, putback
two-hand shot

748 TENNIS

<court game with racket and ball>

NOUNS 1 **tennis,** lawn tennis, indoor tennis, outdoor tennis, singles, doubles, mixed doubles, Canadian doubles, team tennis; court tennis, real tennis, royal tennis; table tennis, Ping-Pong <tm>; organized tennis, International Tennis Federation (ITF), United States Tennis Association (USTA); tournament, tennis competition, championship, crown, match, trophy; tennis ball, ball, tennis racket, racket, aluminum racket, Fiberglas racket, graphite racket, wooden racket, bat, sweet spot; tennis court, court, sideline, alley, doubles sideline, baseline, center mark, service line, half court line, backcourt, forecourt, midcourt, net, band; surface, slow surface, fast surface, grass surface, grass, grass court, hard court, clay court, competition court, all-weather court; squash, squash racquets, squash tennis, badminton

2 **tennis match,** game, strategy, serve-and-volley, power game; official, umpire, baseline umpire, linesman, line umpire, service-line umpire, net-court judge; ball boy, ball girl; play, coin toss, racket flip, grip, Eastern grip, Continental grip, Western grip, two-handed grip, **stroke** <see list>, shot, service, serve, return, spin, topspin, let ball, let, net-cord ball, rally, fault, double fault, foot fault; error, unforced error; score, point, service ace, ace, love, deuce, advantage, ad, game point, service break, break point, set point, match point, tiebreaker, lingering death; game, set, match; Van Alen Streamlined Scoring System (VASSS); fault line

VERBS 3 **play tennis,** play, serve, return, drive, volley, smash, lob, place the ball, serve and volley, play serve-and-volley tennis, fault, foot-fault, double-fault, make an unforced error; score a point, make a point, score, ace one's opponent, break service, break back

4 tennis stroke

approach shot	lob volley
backhand	overhead
backspin	passing shot
chop	reverse twist service
drive	serve, service
drop shot	slice
flat	smash, overhead smash
forehand	topspin
ground drive	tweener
groundstroke	twist service
half volley	two-handed backhand
lob	volley

749 HOCKEY

<*ice rink game with stick and puck*>

NOUNS **1 hockey, ice hockey**, Canadian national sport; professional hockey, National Hockey League (NHL), Clarence Campbell Conference, Smythe Division, Norris Division, Prince of Wales Conference, Patrick Division, Adams Division; amateur hockey, bantam hockey, midget hockey, pee-wee hockey, junior hockey, International Ice Hockey Federation; competition, series, championship, cup, Olympic Games, Stanley Cup, All-Star Game; rink, ice rink, hockey rink, boards, endzone, defensive zone, attacking zone, offensive zone, neutral zone, center ice, blue line, red line, goal line, crease, goal, net, cage, face-off spot, face-off circle, penalty box, penalty bench, players' bench; **hockey equipment or gear** <see list>; floor hockey

2 hockey team, team, skaters, squad, bench; line, forward line, center, forward, winger, right wingman, left wingman, linesman; defense, defender, right defenseman, left defenseman, goaltender, goalie, goalkeeper, goalminder; specialized player, playmaker, penalty killer, point, point man, enforcer

3 hockey game, hockey match; referee, linesman, goal judge, timekeepers, scorer; foul, **penalty** <see list>, infraction, offside, icing, icing the puck; play, skating, stick handling, puck handling, ragging, deking, checking, backchecking, forechecking, passing, shooting; pass, blind pass, drop pass, through-pass; check; offense, breakout, Montreal offense, headmanning, Toronto offense, play-off hockey, give-and-go, breakaway, peel-off, screening; shot, slap shot, wrist shot, backhand shot, flip, sweep shot; power play; score, point, finish off a play, feed, assist, hat trick; period, overtime, overtime period, sudden death overtime, shootout

4 field hockey, banty, bandy, hurley, hurling, shinty, shinny; International Hockey Board, *Fédération Internationale de Hockey* <Can>, International Federation of Women's Hockey Associations, United States Field Hockey Association, Field Hockey Association of America; hockey field, field, pitch, goal line, center line, center mark, bully circle, sideline, 7-yard line, alley, 25-yard line, striking circle, shooting circle, goalpost, goal, goal mouth; equipment, gear, stick, ball, shin pads

5 field hockey team, attack, outside left, inside left, center forward, inside right, outside right, defense, left halfback, center halfback, right halfback, left fullback, right fullback, wing half, goalkeeper

6 field hockey game, field hockey match; umpire, timekeeper; foul, infraction, advancing, obstructing, sticks, undercutting, penalty, free hit, corner hit, defense hit, penalty bully, penalty shot; play, bully, bully-off, pass-back, marking, pass, tackle, circular tackle, out-of-bounds, roll-in, push-in, hit-in; goal, point, score; period, half

VERBS **7 play hockey, skate,** pass, check, block, stick-handle, puck-handle, face off, rag, deke, give-and-go, headman, break out, shoot, score, clear, dig, freeze the puck, center, ice, ice the puck; tackle, mark; make a hat trick

8 hockey equipment or gear

abdominal protector	left-handed stick
	leg pads
catching glove, catch glove, trapper	mouthguard
	neck guard
chest protector	neutral stick
elbow pads	pants
face mask	puck
gloves	right-handed stick
goaltender's stick, goal stick	shin guards
	shoulder pads
helmet	skates
hip pads	socks
kneepads	stick
jersey	stick glove

9 hockey foul, penalty

abuse of officials	charging
aggressor penalty	checking from behind
attempt to injure	clipping
bench minor penalty	crosschecking
biting	delay of game
boarding, board-checking	diving
body-checking	ejection
butt-ending, stabbing	elbowing
broken stick	eye-gouging

falling on the puck
fighting
game misconduct penalty
goaltender interference
goaltender leaving the crease
gross misconduct penalty
handling the puck
head-butting
high-sticking
holding
holding the stick
hooking
icing
illegal equipment
instigator penalty
interference
joining a fight
kicking
kneeing
leaving a penalty bench
match penalty
major penalty, five-minute penalty
minor penalty, two-minute penalty
misconduct penalty
offsides
penalty shot
poke checking
roughing
slashing
slew footing
spearing
throwing the stick
too many men on the ice
tripping
unsportsmanlike conduct

750 BOWLING

<lane game with rolled ball>

NOUNS 1 **bowling,** kegling, kegeling, tenpin bowling, tenpins, candlepin bowling, candlepins, duckpin bowling, duckpins, fivepin bowling, rubber-band duckpin bowling, ninepins, skittles <Brit>; bowling organization, league, American Bowling Congress (ABC), Women's International Bowling Congress (WIBC), American Junior Bowling Congress; amateur bowling, league bowling; professional bowling, pro bowling, tour, Professional Bowlers Association (PBA), Professional Women's Bowling Association; tournament, competition, match-play tournament, round-robin tournament; alley, lane, gutter, foul line, rear cushion, bed, spot, pin spot, 1-3-strike pocket; equipment, pin, candlepin, duckpin, fivepin, rubber-band duckpin, tenpin; automatic pinsetter; bowling ball, ball, two-hole ball, three-hole ball, bowling shoes; bowling bag

2 **bowling game**, bowling string, frame; delivery, grip, two-finger grip, three-finger grip, conventional grip, semi-fingertip grip, full-fingertip grip, approach, three-step approach, three-step delivery, four-step approach, five-step approach, push-away, downswing, backswing, timing step, release, follow-through, straight ball, curve ball, backup, hook ball, gutter ball; pocket, Brooklyn side, Brooklyn hit, Jersey hit, crossover, strike, ten-strike, mark, double, turkey, foundation; spare, leave; spare leave, split, baby split, bed posts, goal posts, fenceposts, bucket, Christmas tree, Cincinnati, converted split, double pinochle, double wood, tandem, fence, fit-in split, Golden Gate, left fence, mother-in-law, right fence, washout, Woolworth; railroad, open frame; score, pinfall, miss, perfect game, 300 game, Dutch

3 **lawn bowling,** green bowling, lawn bowls, bowling on the green, bowls; American Lawn Bowling Association; **bowling green,** green, crown green, level green, rink, ditch; ball, bowl, jack, kitty, mat, footer; team, side, lead, leader, second player, third player, skip

751 GOLF

<course game with clubs and ball>

NOUNS 1 **golf**, golfing, the royal and ancient; professional golf, pro golf, tour, Professional Golfers Association of America (PGA), Ladies' Professional Golfers' Association (LPGA); pro-am, amateur golf, club, United States Golf Association (USGA); **tournament** <see list>, championship, title, championship cup; **golf course,** course, links, 9-hole course, 18-hole course, penal course, strategic course, green, tee, teeing ground, driving range; back marker, championship marker, middle marker, men's marker, front marker, womens' marker, hole, par-3 hole, par-4 hole, par-5 hole, front nine, back nine, water hole, fairway, dogleg, obstruction, rub of the green, casual water, rough, hazard, water hazard, bunker, sand hazard, sand trap, beach, collar, apron, fringe, putting green, grass green, sand green, out of bounds, pin, flagstick, flag, lip, cup; golf equipment, **golf clubs** <see list>, club cover, golf bag, golf ball, golf cart, golf glove; skins game; nineteenth hole; miniature golf, putt-putt; fore

2 **golfer,** player, scratch golfer, scratch player, handicapped golfer, dub, duffer, hacker, linksman, putter; team, twosome, threesome, foursome; caddie

3 **round,** 9 holes, 18 holes, 72 holes, match, stroke play, match play, medal play, four-ball match, three-ball match, best ball, mixed foursome, Scotch foursome; official, referee, official observer, marker; play, golfing grip, overlapping grip, Vardon grip, reverse overlap, interlocking grip, full-finger grip, address, stance, closed stance, square stance, open stance, waggle, swing, backswing, downswing, follow-through, pivot, body pivot, tee-off; stroke, **golf shot** <see list>, backspin, bite, distance, carry, run, lie, plugged lie, blind, stymie; score, scoring, strokes, eagle, double eagle, birdie, par, bogey, double bogey, penalty, hole-in-one, ace, halved hole, gross, handicap, net

VERBS **4 play golf,** shoot, tee up, tee off, drive, hit, sclaff, draw, fade, pull, push, hook, slice, top, sky, loft, dunk, putt, can, borrow, hole out, sink, shoot par, eagle, double eagle, birdie, par, bogey, double bogey, make a hole in one, ace; play through; concede, default; fore

5 golf clubs

1 iron, driving iron
2 iron, midiron
3 iron, mid mashie
4 iron, mashie iron
5 iron, mashie
6 iron, spade mashie
7 iron, mashie niblick
8 iron, pitching niblick
9 iron, niblick
ball, pill
chipper, chipping iron
hybrid
iron
lofter, lofting iron
long iron
middle iron
number 1 wood, driver
number 2 wood, brassie
number 3 wood, spoon
number 4 wood, cleek, short spoon
number 5 wood, baffy
pitching wedge
putter
sand iron
sand wedge
short iron
Texas wedge
track iron
utility iron
wedge
wood

6 golf shot

approach shot, approach
blast
bunker shot
chip shot, chip
chip-and-run
cut shot
draw
drive
dubbed shot
duck hook
duff
fade
fat shot
fairway wood shot
flop shot
full shot
gimme
hole in one
hole out
hook
lag
lob
lofted shot
long iron shot
Mulligan, Shapiro
pitch
pitch-and-run
pop-up
pull
punch, knock-down
push
putt
recovery shot
run-up
sand shot
sclaff
shank
slice
snake
tee shot
thin shot
top
water shot

752 SOCCER

<field game with round kicked ball>

NOUNS **1 soccer;** football, **association football** <Brit>, soccer football; league, college soccer, National Collegiate Athletic Association (NCAA), Federation of International Football Associations (FIFA); tournament, competition, championship, cup; professional soccer, pro soccer, North American Soccer League (NASL); soccer field, field, soccer pitch, pitch, goal line, touch line, halfway line, penalty area, penalty spot, penalty-kick mark, goal area, goal, goalpost, crossbar, 6-yard box, 18-yard box, corner area, corner flag, center mark, center circle; equipment, gear, ball, suit, uniform, shirt, shorts, kneesocks, shin guards, soccer shoes

2 soccer team, squad, side, soccer player, footballer <Brit>, forward, striker, outside right, inside right, center forward, lineman, midfielder, inside left, outside left, right half, center half, left half, defender, back, center back, right back, left back, winger, back four, sweeper; stopper, goalkeeper, goaltender, goalie

3 soccer game, match; official, referee, linesman; play, coin toss, coin flip, 3-3-4 offense, 5-2 offense, man-to-man offense, kickoff, **kick** <see list>, throw-in, goal kick, corner kick, corner, offside, ball control, pass, back-heel pass, outside-of-the-foot pass, push pass, back pass, tackle, sliding tackle, sliding block tackle, trap, chest trap, thigh trap, breakaway, header, head, shot, save; rule, law; **foul** <see list>; penalty, caution, red card, free kick, direct free kick, indirect free kick, penalty kick, yellow card; goal, score, point, tiebreaker, series of penalty kicks, shootout, bonus point; period, quarter, overtime period

VERBS **4 play soccer,** kick, kick off, trap, pass, dribble, screen, head, center, clear, mark, tackle, save

5 soccer foul

charging dangerously
charging from behind
charging the goalkeeper
continual breaking of rules
dangerous play
direct kick foul
dissenting from referee's decision
foul language, abusive language
handling the ball
impeding the progress of an opponent
indirect kick foul
jumping at an opponent
kicking an opponent
obstruction
offside
onside
pushing an opponent
spitting at an opponent
striking an opponent
tripping an opponent
ungentlemanly conduct

6 soccer kick

back heel
banana kick
bicycle kick
chip
corner kick
direct free kick
flick kick
free kick
goal kick
half-volley
instep kick, inside-of-the-foot kick
lofted kick
long pass
low drive
outside kick
overhead volley
penalty kick
punt
push kick
scissors kick
toe kick
volley, volley kick

753 SKIING

<gliding on snow skis>

NOUNS 1 **skiing**, snow-skiing, Alpine skiing, downhill skiing, Nordic skiing, cross-country skiing, langlauf, snowboarding, ski-jumping, jumping, freestyle skiing, hotdog skiing, hotdogging, ballet skiing, mogul skiing, skijoring, helicopter skiing, heli-skiing, off-trail skiing, mountain skiing, grass skiing, ski mountaineering; organized skiing, competitive skiing, *Fédération Internationale de Ski* <Fr> (FIS), International Freestyle Skiers Association; competition, championship, cup, race; slope, ski slope, ski run, nursery, beginner's slope, expert's slope, intermediate slope, expert's trail, marked trail, moguled trail, course, trail, mogul; ski lift, lift, ski tow, rope tow, J-bar, chairlift, T-bar, poma; racecourse, downhill course, slalom course, giant slalom course, super giant slalom course, parallel slalom course, dual slalom course; starting gate, fall line, drop, vertical drop, control gate, obligatory gate, flagstick, open gate, closed gate, blind gate, hairpin, flush, H, men's course, women's course, ski-jump, ramp, inrun, outrun, hill rating, 60-point hill, normal hill, big hill, cross-country course; **skiing equipment or gear** <see list>

2 **skier,** snow-skier, cross-country skier, ski-jumper, racer, downhill racer, slalom racer, giant slalom racer, mogul racer, snowboarder, freestyle skier, touring skier, forerunner, forejumper, skimeister

3 **ski race,** downhill race, slalom, giant slalom, super giant slalom, super G, slalom pole, rapid slalom pole, parallel slalom, dual slalom, Alpine race, cross-country race, biathlon; technique, style, Arlberg technique, Lilienfeld technique, wedeln, position, tuck, egg, Vorlage, sitting position, in run position, fish position, flight position; maneuver, **turn** <see list>

VERBS 4 **ski,** run, schuss, traverse, turn, check; hotdog, ski freestyle; snowboard

5 **skiing equipment or gear**

aluminum alloy pole
Alpine boots
Arlberg strap, safety strap
basket, snow basket
bent pole
crampons
cross-country binding
cross-country pole
cross-country ski
double boot
downhill pole
downhill ski
fiberglass pole
giant slalom ski
goggles
helmet
jumping ski
laminated wood ski
metal ski
molded boot
plastic ski
racing ski
release binding
short ski
ski boots
ski wax
slalom ski
snowboard
step-in binding
toe clamp

6 **skiing maneuver, turn**

aerial
carved turn, carve
check
Christiania, christie
climb
diagonal stride
double-pole stride
double-poling
edging
free-carving
freestyle
Gelðndesprung
herringbone
hockey stop
jet turn
jump turn
kick turn
parallel christie
parallel swing
parallel turn
pole plant
rotation turn
schuss
short swing
sideslip
sidestep
slalom
snap
snowplow, double stem, wedge
snowplow turn
stem turn
stem christie
step acceleration
step turn
Telemark
tempo
traverse
tuck
unweighting
uphill christie
wedeln

754 BOXING

<fighting with gloved hands>

NOUNS 1 **boxing, prizefighting,** fighting, pugilism, noble art of self-defense, the noble science, the sweet science, fisticuffs, the fistic sport, the fights, the fight game, the ring; amateur boxing, Olympic Games, International Amateur Boxing Association (IABA), Amateur Athletic Union (AAU), Golden Gloves; professional boxing, International Boxing Federation, World Boxing Council (WBC), World Boxing Association (WBA), European Boxing Union, club boxing, club fighting; Queensbury rules, Marquess of Queensbury rules; shadowboxing; boxing ring, ring, prize ring, square circle, square ring, canvas, corner, ropes, bell; boxing gloves, mitts, mittens, boxing shorts, tape, bandages, sparring helmet, mouthpiece; boxing purse

2 **boxer, fighter,** pugilist, prizefighter, pug, palooka, slugger, mauler; **weight** <see list>; division; manager; trainer; handler, second, sparring partner

3 **fight,** match, bout, prizefight, battle, duel, slugfest, haymaker; official, referee, ref, judge, timekeeper; strategy, fight plan, style, stance, footwork, offense, **punch** <see list>, blow, belt, biff, sock, sparring, jabbing, socking, pummeling; defense, blocking, ducking, parrying, slipping, feint, clinching; foul; win, knockout (KO),

technical knockout (TKO), decision, unanimous decision, split decision, win on points; round, canto, stanza

VERBS 4 **fight, box,** punch, spar, mix it up, prizefight, jab, sock, clinch, break, block, catch, slip a punch, duck, feint, parry, heel, thumb, knock down, knock out, slug, maul, land a rabbit punch, hit below the belt; go down, go down for the count, hit the canvas, shadow-box

5 **boxing punch**

backhand, backhander	Long Melford
backstroke	mishit, mislick
body blow, body slam	rabbit punch
bolo punch	right, right-hander
chop	round-arm blow
combination	roundhouse
corkscrew punch	short-arm blow
counterpunch	sideswipe
cross	sidewinder
flanker	sneak punch, sucker punch
follow-up	solar-plexus punch
haymaker	straight punch
hook	swing
jab	swipe
knockdown punch	the one-two, the old one-two
knockout punch	uppercut
left, left-hander, portsider	

6 **boxing weight**

bantamweight	light heavyweight
cruiserweight	light middleweight
featherweight	light welterweight
flyweight	lightweight
heavyweight	middleweight
junior featherweight	pinweight
junior lightweight	super bantamweight
junior middleweight	super heavyweight
light bantamweight	welterweight
light flyweight	

755 TRACK AND FIELD

<running, jumping, and throwing activities>

NOUNS 1 **track, track and field,** athletics <Brit>; governing organization, International Athletic Federation (IAAF), Amateur Athletic Union of the U.S. (AAU), National Federation of State High School Athletic Associations; games, competition, cup; stadium, arena, oval, armory, field house; lane, start line, starting block, finish line, infield; lap, lap of honor, victory lap; distance runner

2 **track meet, race,** meet, games, program; running event, run, running, heat, sprint racing, middle-distance running, long-distance running, relay racing, hurdles, hurdling; cross-country racing; **field event** <see list>; all-around event, **decathlon** <see list>, **heptathlon** <see list>, **pentathlon** <see list>; **triathlon** <see list>, **biathlon** <see list>; walking, racewalking, the walk, heel-and-toe racing

3 **biathlon**

cross-country skiing	rifle shooting

4 **decathlon**

100-meter run	high jump
110-meter hurdles	javelin
400-meter run	long jump
1500-meter run	pole vault
discus	shot put

5 **field event**

discus throw	multi-event contest
hammer throw	pole vault
high jump	shot put
javelin throw	triple jump
long jump, broad jump	

6 **heptathlon**

100-meter hurdles	javelin
200-meter run	long jump
800-meter run	shot put
high jump	

7 **pentathlon**

100-meter hurdles	javelin
200-meter run	long jump
high jump	

8 **triathlon**

100-meter dash	shot put
high jump	

756 AUTOMOBILE RACING

<racing automobiles>

NOUNS 1 **automobile racing, auto racing, car racing,** motor sport; Indy car racing, stock-car racing, drag racing, Formula car racing, midget-car racing, hot-rod racing, autocross, go-karting; racing association; race, competition, championship; track, speedway, Indianapolis Motor Speedway, the Brickyard, closed course, road course, road circuit, dirt track, grasstrack, super speedway; car, **racing car** <see list>, racer; racing engine; supercharger, turbocharger, blower, windmill; tires, racing tires, shoes, slicks; body, bodywork, spoiler, sidepod, roll bar, roll cage; wheel, wire wheel, wire, magnesium wheel, mag, alloy wheel; fuel, racing fuel, methanol, nitromethane, nitro, blend, pop, juice

2 **racing driver, driver,** fast driver, leadfoot, slow driver, balloon foot, novice driver, yellowtail; off-roading

3 **race,** driving, start, Le Mans start, flying start, paced start, grid start; position, qualifying, qualifying heat, starting grid, inside position,

pole, pole position, bubble; track, turn, curve, hairpin, hairpin curve, switchback, banked turn, corner, chicane, groove, shut-off, drift, straightaway, chute, pit, pit area; signal, black flag, white flag, checkered flag; lap, pace lap, victory lap, victory lane

VERBS 4 **drive, race,** start, jump, rev, accelerate, put the hammer down, slow down, back off, stroke it, draft, fishtail, nerf, shut the gate

ADVS 5 at top speed, flat-out, full-bore, ten-tenths ride the rail, spin, spin out, crash, t-bone

6 **racing car**

championship car
compact sprint car
dirt car
dragster
experimental car, X-car
Formula A
formula car
Formula F
Formula One
Formula SCCA
Formula Super Vee
Formula Vee
fuel dragster, slingshot, rail job
fueler
funny car
gas dragster
grand touring car (GT)
hobby car
Indy car
late-model sportsman
midget car
modified stock car
production car
prototype
quarter-midget car
sportsman
sports car
sprint car, big car
stock car
supercharger
touring car
turbine car
turbocharger

757 HORSE RACING

<racing horses>

NOUNS 1 **horse racing,** the turf, the sport of kings, the turf sport, the racing world, the racing establishment; flat racing; harness racing, trotting, pacing; steeplechase, hurdle race, point-to-point race; Jockey Club, Trotting Horse Club, Thoroughbred Racing Association (TRA), Thoroughbred Racing Protective Bureau (TRPB), state racing commission; General Stud Book, American Stud Book, Wallace's Trotting Register; Triple Crown, Kentucky Derby, Preakness Stakes, Belmont Stakes; Grand National, Derby, 2000 Guineas, Sty Leger, Gold Cup Race, Oaks; racetrack, track, racecourse, turf, oval, course, strip; rail, inside rail, infield, paddock, post; turf track, steeplejack course; gate, barrier; **track location or call** <see list>; track conditions, footing; racing equipment, tack; handicapping

2 **jockey,** jock, rider, race rider, pilot, bug boy, money rider; apprentice jockey, bug; breeder, owner; trainer; steward, racing secretary; railbird, turfman; **racehorse,** pony, thoroughbred, standardbred, mount, flyer, running horse, trotter, pacer, quarter horse, bangtail, daisycutter, filly, gee-gee; sire, dam, stallion, stud, stud horse, racing stud, mare, brood mare, gelding, ridgeling, rigling; horse, aged horse, three-year-old, sophomore, two-year-old, juvenile, colt, racing colt, baby, foal, tenderfoot, maiden, maiden horse, yearling, weanling; favorite, chalk, choice, odds-on favorite, public choice, top horse; runner, frontrunner, pacesetter; strong horse, router, stayer; winner, win horse, place horse, show horse, also-ran; nag, race-nag, beagle, beetle, hayburner, nine of hearts, palooka, pelter, pig, plater, selling plater; rogue, bad actor, cooler

3 **horse race,** race; race meeting, race card, scratch sheet; starters, field, weigh-in, weighing-in, post parade, post time, post position (PP); start, break, off; easy race, romp, shoo-in, armchair ride, hand ride; finish, dead heat, blanket finish, photo finish, Garrison finish; dishonest race, boat race, fixed race

4 statistics, records, condition book, chart, form, racing form, daily racing form, past performance, track record, tip sheet, par time, parallel-time chart; betting; pari-mutuel; horseracing bets

VERBS 5 **race, run**; start, break, be off; air, breeze; make a move, drive, extend, straighten out; fade, come back; screw in, screw through; ride out, run wide; win, romp in, breeze in; place, show, be in the money; be out of the money

ADJS 6 winning, in the money; losing, out of the money; on the chinstrap; out in front, on the Bill Daley

7 **track location or call**

backstretch
clubhouse turn
eighth pole, eighth post
far turn
five-eighths pole, five-eighths post
half-mile pole, half-mile post
mile pole, mile post
quarter pole, quarter post
sixteenth pole, sixteenth post
straightaway, home stretch, straight
winner's circle

758 CARDPLAYING

<games involving card decks>

NOUNS 1 **cardplaying,** card-playing, shuffling, cutting, cut, dealing, deal; **card game,** game; gambling, gambling games

2 **card, playing card,** board, pasteboard; **deck, pack; suit,** hearts, diamonds, spades, clubs, puppy-feet; hand; face card, blaze, coat card, coat, count card, court card, paint, paint-skin, picture card, redskin; king, figure, cowboy, sergeant from K Company, one-eyed king, king of hearts, suicide king; queen, bitch*, hen, lady, mop-squeezer, whore*, queen of spades, Black Maria, Maria,

slippery Anne; jack, knave, boy, j-bird, j-boy, john, one-eyed jack, jack of trumps, right bower, left bower; joker, bower, best bower; spot card, rank card, plain card; ace, bull, bullet, seed, spike, ace of diamonds, pig's eye, ace of clubs, puppyfoot; two, deuce, two-spot, duck, two of spades, curse of Mexico; three, trey, three-spot; four, four-spot, four of clubs, devil's bedposts; five, five-spot, fever; six, six-spot; seven, seven-spot, fishhook; eight, eight-spot; nine, nine-spot, nine of diamonds, curse of Scotland; ten, ten-spot; wild card

3 **bridge,** auction bridge, contract bridge, rubber bridge, duplicate bridge, tournament bridge; bridge player, partner, dummy, North and South, East and West, left hand opponent (LHO), bidder, responder, declarer, senior; suit, major suit, minor suit, trump suit, trumps, lay suit, plain suit, side suit; call, **bid** <see list>; pass; **hand** <see list>; play, lead, opening lead, trick, quick trick, honor trick, high-card trick, overtrick, odd trick, finesse, ruff, crossruff; score, adjusted score, grand slam, little slam, small slam, game, rubber, premium; honors, honors cards; yarborough, set, setback

4 **poker,** draw poker, stud poker, five-card stud, six-card stud, seven-card stud, eight-card stud, strip poker; poker hand, five of a kind, straight flush, royal flush, four of a kind, full house, full boat, flush, straight, three of a kind, two pairs, one pair; pot, jackpot, pool, ante, chip, stake, call, checking, raise

VERBS 5 **play cards, shuffle,** make up, make up the pack, fan, wash; cut; **deal,** serve, pitch

759 GAMBLING

<games of chance for money>

NOUNS 1 **gambling,** playing, **betting,** action, wagering, punting, hazarding, risking, staking, gaming, laying, taking odds, giving, odds, laying odds, sporting; speculation, play; drawing lots, casting lots, tossing a coin, flipping a coin, sortition

2 **gamble, chance, risk,** risky thing, hazard; gambler's chance, gambling chance, betting proposition, bet, matter of chance, sporting chance, luck of the draw, hazard of the die, roll of the dice, cast of the dice, throw of the dice, turn of the wheel, roll of the wheel, turn of the table, turn of the cards, fall of the cards, flip of a coin, toss of a coin, toss-up, toss; heads, tails, touch and go; blind bargain, pig in a poke; leap in the dark, shot in the dark; potshot, random shot, potluck; speculation, venture, flier, plunge; calculated risk; over-under; point spread; uncertainty; fortune, luck

3 **bet, wager, stake,** hazard, lay, play, chunk, shot; cinch bet, sure thing, mortal cinch, mortal lock, nuts; long shot; ante; parlay, double or nothing; dice bet, craps bet, sports bet, golf bet, horseracing bet, poker bet, roulette bet, telebet

4 **betting system;** pari-mutuel, off-track betting (OTB); perfecta, exacta, win, place, show, all-way bet, daily double

5 pot, jackpot, pool, **stakes,** kitty; bank; office pool

6 **gambling odds,** odds, price; even odds, square odds, even break; short odds, long odds, long shot; even chance, good chance, small chance, no chance; handicapper, odds maker, pricemaker; Murphy's Law

7 **gambling game** <see list>, game of chance, game, friendly game; card games

8 **dice,** bones, rolling bones, ivories, babies, cubes, devil's bones, devil's teeth, galloping dominoes, golf balls, marbles, Memphis dominoes, Mississippi marbles, Missouri marbles, craps, crap shooting, crap game, bank craps, casino craps, muscle craps, African dominoes, African golf, alley craps, army craps, blanket craps, army marbles, Harlem tennis, poor man's roulette, floating crap game, floating game, sawdust game; poker dice; false dice, crooked dice, loaded dice

9 <throw of dice> **throw,** cast, rattle, roll, shot, hazard of the die; dice point, **dice roll** <see list>

10 **poker,** draw poker, draw, five-card draw, open poker, stud poker, closed poker, stud, five-card stud, seven-card stud, up card, open card, down card, closed card; common card, community card, communal card; highball, high-low, lowball; straight poker, natural poker, wild-card poker; poker hand, duke, mitt, good hand, good cards, lock, cinch, cinch hand, ironclad hand, bad hand, iron duke, mortal cinch, nuts, immortals; bad cards, trash, rags; openers, progressive openers, bet, raise, kick, bump, pump, push, showdown

11 **blackjack, twenty-one,** vingt-et-un; deal, card count, stiff, hard seventeen, hard eighteen, soft count, soft hand, soft eighteen, hit, natural, snap, snapper, California blackjack; cut card, indicator card, sweat card; card-counting, ace-count, number count

12 **roulette,** American roulette, European roulette; wheel, American wheel, European wheel, wheel well, canoe, fret; layout, column, damnation alley, outside; zero, double zero, knotholes, house numbers

13 **cheating,** cheating scheme, cheating method, angle, con, grift, move, racket, scam, sting; deception

14 **lottery,** drawing, sweepstakes, sweepstake, sweep; draft lottery; **raffle**; state lottery, lotto,

Pick Six, Pick Four; tombola <Brit>; number lottery, numbers pool, numbers game, Chinese lottery; interest lottery, Dutch lottery, class lottery; tontine; grab bag, lottery money

15 **bingo,** slow death, beano, keno, lotto; bingo card, banker, counter

16 <gambling device> gambling wheel, wheel of fortune, big six wheel, Fortune's wheel, raffle wheel, paddle wheel; roulette wheel, American wheel, European wheel; cage, birdcage; goose, shaker, gooseneck; pinball machine; slot machine, slot, the slots, one-armed bandit; layout cloth, green cloth, gambling table, craps table, Philadelphia layout, roulette table; cheating device, gaff, gimmick, tool

17 pari-mutuel, pari-mutuel machine; totalizator, totalizer, tote, tote board, odds board

18 **chip,** check, counter, bean, fish

19 **casino, gambling house,** house, store, shop, gaming house, betting house, sporting house, betting parlor, gambling den, gambling hall; luxurious casino, carpet joint, rug joint; pit, pit boss; honest gambling house, right joint; disreputable gambling house, crib, dive, joint, sawdust joint, toilet; illegal gambling house, brace house, bust-out joint, clip joint, deadfall, flat joint, flat store, hell, juice joint, low den, nick joint, peek store, skinning house, snap house, sneak joint, steer joint, wire joint, wolf trap; handbook, book, sports book, bookie joint, racebook, horse parlor, horse room, off-track betting parlor, OTB

20 **bookmaker, bookie**, turf accountant; tout, turf consultant; numbers runner; bagman; pit boss

21 **gambler,** player, gamester, sportsman, sporting man, sport, hazarder; speculator, venturer, adventurer; bettor, wagerer, punter; high-stakes gambler, money player, high roller, plunger; petty gambler, low roller, piker, tinhorn, tinhorn gambler; professional gambler, pro, nutman; skillful gambler, sharp, shark, sharper, dean, professor, river gambler, dice gospeller, sharpie; cardsharp, cardshark, cardsharper; card counter, counter, caser, matrix player; crap shooter, boneshaker; compulsive gambler; spectator, kibitzer, lumber, sweater, wood

22 **cheater,** cheat, air bandit, bilk, bunco artist, dildock, grec, greek, grifter, hustler, mechanic, mover, rook, worker; deceiver; dupe, victim, coll, flat, john, lamb, lobster, mark, monkey, patsy, sucker

VERBS 23 **gamble,** game, sport, play, try one's luck, try one's fortune; speculate; run a game, bank a game; draw lots, draw straws, lot, cut lots, cast lots; cut the cards, cut the deck; match coins, toss, flip a coin, call, call heads or tails; shoot craps, play at dice, roll the bones; play the ponies; raffle off

24 **chance, risk, hazard,** set at hazard, venture, wager, take a flier; gamble on, take a gamble on; take a chance, take one's chance, take the chances of, try the chance, chance it; take the risk, run the risk, run a chance; take chances, tempt fortune; leave to luck, trust to chance, rely on fortune, take a leap in the dark; buy a pig in a poke; take potluck; raise the stakes, up the ante

25 **bet, wager,** gamble, hazard, stake, punt, lay, lay down, put up, make a bet, lay a wager, give odds, take odds, lay odds, make book, get a piece of the action; plunge; bet on, back; bet against, play against; play the ponies, follow the ponies; parlay; ante, ante up; cover, call, match a bet, meet a bet, see, fade; check, sandbag, pass, stand pat; betcha

26 **cheat,** pluck, skin, rook; load the dice, mark the cards

ADJS 27 speculative, uncertain; hazardous, risky, dicey; **lucky,** winning, hot, red-hot, on a roll; **unlucky**, losing, cold

28 **dice point, dice roll**

blanket roll, soft-pad roll
boxes, hard eight
craps
doublet
drop shot
dump over shot
eight, eighter, Ada from Decatur, Ada Ross, Ada Ross the stable hoss
English, ass English, body English, Jonah
even roll
fimps, hard ten
five, fee-bee, fever, phoebe, little Phoebe
four, little Dick Fisher, little Dick, little joe from Kokomo
Greek shot
little natural crap, slow crap
nine, Carolina, carolina nina, nina from caroliner
number
puppy feet
seven, natural, little natural, pass, skinny Dugan
six, captain hicks, Sister Hicks, Jimmy Hicks, sixie from Dixie, sixty days, sice
ten, big dick, big Joe from Boston
three, cockeyes
twelve, boxcars, high noon, Gary Cooper
two, snake eyes, Dolly Parton

29 **gambling game**

all fours
auction bridge
baccarat
bezique
bingo
blind poker
bridge
canasta
casino
crazy eights
chemin de fer
chuck-a-luck, birdcage
contract bridge, contract
craps
cribbage
draw poker
écarté
euchre
fan tan
faro
fish, go fish
gin
gin rummy
hazard

hearts
high, low, jack and the game
keno
loo
lottery
lotto
lowball poker
monte
numbers, policy
old maid
ombre
paddle wheel, raffle wheel
penny ante
picquet
pinball
pinochle
pitch and toss
poker
poker dice
quinze
rouge et noir
roulette
rum
rummy
seven-up
stud poker
three-card monte
trente-et-quarante
twenty-one, blackjack, vingt-et-un
war
wheel of fortune, big six wheel
whist

760 OTHER SPORTS

<competitive sporting activities>

NOUNS 1 **billiards**, pool, pocket billiards, snooker; billiard table, pool table, pocket, cue ball, cue stick, chalk; pool hall, billiards club

2 **boating**, sailing, canoeing, rowing, sculling, windsurfing, sailboarding, surfing, rafting, whitewater rafting; yachting, competitive sailing, day sailing; sailboat, canoe, catamaran, rowboat, kayak; regatta, America's Cup; sailor, yachtsman, yachtswoman, canoeist, rower, oarsman, oar, sculler, windsurfer, surfer, sailboarder; mariner, boater

3 **martial arts**; judo, the way of gentleness; karate, the way of the empty hand, sport karate, recreational karate, karate chop; tae kwon do, the way of the foot and fist; aikido, the way of harmony of the spirit, competition aikido; belt, grade, dan grade; dojo; tae bo, kickboxing, ultimate fighting

4 **fencing**; foil fencing, épée fencing, saber fencing; en garde, parry, riposte, thrust, feint, lunge

5 **gymnastics**; floor exercise, tumbling, vaulting, trampolining, balance beam, horizontal bar, uneven parallel bars, pommel horse, side horse, stationary rings

6 **mountain climbing**, mountaineering, rock climbing, bouldering, free climbing, clean climbing, aid climbing, big wall climbing, snow climbing, ice climbing, Alpine-style climbing, alpinism; climbing expedition, base camp, advance camp; rock face

7 **ice skating**, figure skating, free skating, pairs skating, ice dancing, speed skating; Olympic skating, professional skating; compulsory figure, loop, salchow, jump, axel jump, double axel, triple axel, toe jump, spin, camel spin, layback spin, sit spin

8 **swimming**, natation; synchronized swimming, diving, scuba, snorkeling, skinny-dipping, dog-paddling, Olympic swimming; crawl, American crawl, Australian crawl, back crawl, backstroke, breaststroke, butterfly stroke; flutter kick, scissors kick, back kick, wedge kick, frog kick, whip kick; lifeguarding, lifesaving; swimming pool, natatorium

761 EXISTENCE

<state of existing>

NOUNS 1 **existence, being;** subsistence, entity, essence, esse, isness, absolute essence, transcendental essence, pure being, thing-in-itself, noumenon; occurrence, presence, monadism; materiality, substantiality; life

2 **reality, actuality,** factuality, empirical existence, demonstrable existence, objective existence, the here and now; historicity; necessity; the real thing, the genuine article; facticity; truth; authenticity; sober reality, grim reality, hardball and the nitty-gritty, not a dream, more truth than poetry; thing, something, ens, entity, being, object, substance, phenomenon; reality check

3 **fact,** the case, fact of the matter, truth of the matter, not opinion, not guesswork, what's what, where it's at; matter of fact; bare fact, naked fact, bald fact, simple fact, sober fact, simple truth, sober truth; cold fact, hard fact, stubborn fact, brutal fact, painful fact, the nitty-gritty, the bottom line; actual fact, positive fact, absolute fact; self-evident fact, axiom, postulate, premise, accomplished fact, *fait accompli* <Fr>; accepted fact, conceded fact, admitted fact, fact of experience, well-known fact, established fact, inescapable fact, irreducible fact, indisputable fact, undeniable fact; demonstrable fact, provable fact; empirical fact; protocol, protocol statement; given fact, given, donné datum, circumstance; salient fact, significant fact; factlet, factoid, fact bite

4 **the facts,** the information, the particulars, the details, the specifics, the data; the dope, the scoop, the score, the skinny, the inside skinny; the picture, the gen, what's what; the facts of the matter, the truth of the matter, the facts of the case, the whole story; essentials, basic facts, essential facts, brass tacks, nitty-gritty; fact sheet

5 **self-existence,** uncreated being, noncontingent existence, aseity, innascibility

6 mere existence, **simple existence**, vegetable existence, vegetation, mere tropism; couch potato

7 <philosophy of being> ontology, metaphysics, existentialism

VERBS 8 **exist, be,** be in existence, be extant, have being; breathe, live; subsist, stand, obtain, hold, prevail, be the case; occur, be present, be there, be found, be true, be met with, happen to be

9 **live on,** continue to exist, persist, last, stand the test of time, abide, endure

10 **vegetate,** merely exist, just be, pass the time

11 **exist in,** consist in, subsist in, lie in, rest in, repose in, reside in, abide in, inhabit, dwell in, inhere in, be present in, be a quality of, be comprised in, be contained in, be constituted by, be coextensive with

12 **become,** come to be, go, get, get to be, turn out to be, materialize; be converted into, turn into; grow; be changed

ADJS 13 **existent, existing,** in existence, de facto; subsistent, subsisting; being, in being; living; present, extant, prevalent, current, in force, in effect, afoot, on foot, under the sun, on the face of the earth

14 **self-existent,** self-existing, innascible; uncreated, increate

15 **real, actual, factual** veritable, for real, de facto, simple, sober, hard; absolute, positive; self-evident, axiomatic; accepted, conceded, stipulated, given; admitted, well-known, established, inescapable, indisputable, undeniable; demonstrable, provable; empirical, objective, historical; true; honest-to-God, genuine, card-carrying, authentic; substantial

ADVS 16 **really, actually; factually;** genuinely, veritably, basically, truly; in reality, in actuality, in effect, in fact, de facto, in point of fact, as a matter of fact; positively, absolutely; no buts about it; no ifs, ands, or buts; obviously, manifestly

COMBINING FORMS 17 onto-

762 NONEXISTENCE

<state of not existing>

NOUNS 1 **nonexistence,** nonsubsistence; **nonbeing,** unbeing, not-being, nonentity; **nothingness,** nothing, nullity, nihility, invalidity; vacancy, deprivation, emptiness, inanity, vacuity; vacuum, void; nix; negativeness, negation, negativity; nonoccurrence, nonhappening; unreality, nonreality, unactuality; nonpresence, absence; negative space, white space

2 **nothing**, nil, *nihil* <L>, *nada* <Sp>, naught, aught; zero, 0, cipher; nothing whatever, nothing at all, nothing on earth, nothing under the sun, no such thing; thing of naught; bubkes

3 <nonformal> **zilch**, zip, zippo, nix, goose egg, Billy be damn, diddly, shit*, diddly shit*, squat, diddly squat, Sweet Fanny Adams <Brit>, bubkes, beans, a hill of beans, a hoot, a fart, a fuck*, fuck all*, bugger all <Brit>, jack-shit*, a rat's ass, chopped liver

4 **none,** not any, none at all, not a one, not a blessed one, never a one, ne'er a one, nary one; not a sausage <Brit>, not a bit, not a whit, not a speck, not an iota not a jot, not a shadow of a suspicion, neither hide nor hair

VERBS 5 **not exist,** not be in existence, not be met with, not occur, not be found, found nowhere, be absent, be lacking, be wanting, be null and void

6 **cease to exist**, cease to be, be annihilated, be destroyed, be wiped out, be extirpated, be eradicated; go, vanish, be no more, leave no trace; disappear, evaporate, fade, fade away, fade out, fly, flee, dissolve, melt away, die out, die away, pass, pass away, pass out of the picture, turn to nothing, turn to naught, peter out, come to an end, wind down, tail off, trail off, reach an all-time low; perish, expire, die

7 annihilate, exterminate, eradicate, extirpate, eliminate, liquidate, **wipe out,** stamp out, waste, take out, nuke, zap, put an end to

ADJS 8 **nonexistent,** unexistent, inexistent, nonsubsistent, unexisting, without being, nowhere to be found; minus, missing, lacking, wanting; **null, void,** devoid, empty, inane, vacuous; negative, less than nothing; absent

9 **unreal,** unrealistic, unactual, not real; merely nominal; immaterial; unsubstantial; imaginary, imagined, make-believe, fantastic, fanciful, fancied; illusory

10 **uncreated**, unmade, unborn, unbegotten, unconceived, unproduced

11 **no more, extinct, defunct, dead**, expired, passed away; vanished, gone glimmering; perished, obsolete, annihilated; gone, all gone; all over with, had it, finished, phut, pffft, kaput, down the tube, down the drain, up the spout, done for, dead and done for

ADVS 12 none, no, not at all, in no way, to no extent

COMBINING FORMS 13 nulli-

763 SUBSTANTIALITY

<having substance>

NOUNS 1 **substantiality,** substantialness; materiality; **substance,** body, mass; solidity, density, concreteness, **tangibility**, palpability, ponderability; sturdiness, stability, soundness, firmness, steadiness, stoutness, toughness, strength, durability

2 **substance, stuff,** fabric, material, matter, medium, the tangible; elements, constituent elements, constituents, ingredients, components, atoms, building blocks, parts

3 **something,** thing, an existence; being, entity, unit, individual, entelechy, monad; person, persona, personality, body, soul; creature, created being, contingent being; organism, life form, living thing, life; object

4 **embodiment,** incarnation, materialization, substantiation, concretization, hypostasis, reification

VERBS **5** **embody,** incarnate, materialize, concretize, body forth, lend substance to, reify, entify, hypostatize

ADJS **6** **substantial,** substantive; solid, concrete; **tangible**, sensible, appreciable, palpable, ponderable; material; real; created, creatural, organismic, organismal, contingent

7 **sturdy,** stable, **solid,** sound, firm, steady, tough, stout, strong, rugged; durable, lasting, enduring; hard, dense, unyielding, steely, adamantine; well-made, well-constructed, well-built, well-knit; well-founded, well-established, well-grounded; massive, bulky, heavy, chunky

ADVS **8** **substantially,** essentially, materially

COMBINING FORMS **9** stere-, ont-

764 UNSUBSTANTIALITY

<lacking substance>

NOUNS **1** **unsubstantiality,** insubstantiality, unsubstantialness; immateriality; bodilessness, incorporeality, unsolidity, unconcreteness; **intangibility,** impalpability, imponderability; thinness, tenuousness, attenuation, tenuity, evanescence, subtlety, subtility, fineness, airiness, mistiness, vagueness, ethereality; fragility, frailness; flimsiness; transience, ephemerality, ephemeralness, fleetingness, fugitiveness

2 thing of naught, nullity, zero; **nonentity, nobody**, nonstarter, nebbish, nonperson, unperson, cipher, man of straw, jackstraw, lay figure, puppet, dummy, hollow man; flash in the pan, dud; trifle; nothing

3 **spirit**, air, **thin air,** breath, mere breath, smoke, vapor, mist, ether, bubble, shadow, mere shadow; illusion; phantom

VERBS **4** spiritualize, **disembody,** dematerialize; etherealize, attenuate, subtilize, rarefy, fine, refine; weaken, enervate, sap

ADJS **5** **unsubstantial,** insubstantial, nonsubstantial, unsubstanced; **intangible**, impalpable, imponderable; immaterial; bodiless, incorporeal, unsolid, unconcrete; weightless; transient, ephemeral, fleeting, fugitive

6 **thin, tenuous,** subtile, subtle, evanescent, fine, overfine, refined, rarefied; ethereal, airy, windy, spirituous, vaporous, gaseous; air-built, cloud-built; chimerical, gossamer, gossamery, gauzy, shadowy, phantomlike; dreamlike, **illusory**, unreal; fatuous, fatuitous, inane; imaginary, fanciful

7 **fragile,** frail; flimsy, shaky, weak, papery, paper-thin, unsound, infirm

8 **baseless, groundless,** ungrounded, without foundation, unfounded, not well-founded, built on sand, written on water

COMBINING FORMS **9** pseudo-

765 STATE

<mode or condition of being>

NOUNS **1** **state,** mode, modality; **status,** situation, status quo, status in quo, position, standing, footing, location, bearings, walk of life; rank, estate, station, place, place on the ladder; condition, circumstance; case, lot; predicament, plight, pass, pickle, picklement, fix, jam, spot, bind

2 **the state of affairs,** the nature of things, the shape of things, the way it shapes up, the way of the world, how things stack up, **how things stand,** how things are, the way of things, the way it is, like it is, where it's at, **the way things are,** the way of it, the way things go, how it goes, the way the cookie crumbles, how it is, the status quo, status in quo, the size of it; how the land lies, the lay of the land; shape, phase, state of the art; state of mind, mindset

3 good condition, bad condition; adjustment, fettle, form, order, repair, shape, trim

4 **mode,** manner, way, tenor, vein, fashion, style, lifestyle, way of life, preference, thing, bag; form, shape, guise, complexion, makeup; role, capacity, character, part; modus vivendi, modus operandi

VERBS **5** be in a certain state, have a certain state, be such, be so, be thus, fare, go on, go along; enjoy a certain position, occupy a certain position; get on, come on; manage, contrive, make out, come through, get by; turn out, come out, stack up, shape up

ADJS **6** **conditional**, modal, formal, situational, statal

7 **in condition**, in order, in repair, in shape; out of order, out of commission, out of kilter, out of whack

766 CIRCUMSTANCE

<determining condition or factor>

NOUNS 1 **circumstance,** occurrence, occasion, event, incident; juncture, conjuncture, contingency, eventuality; condition

2 **circumstances,** total situation, existing conditions, existing situation, set of conditions, terms of reference, environment, environing circumstances, context, frame, setting, surround, surrounding conditions, parameters, status quo, status in quo, setup; state of affairs; the picture, the whole picture, full particulars, ins and outs, ball game, the score, how things stand, the way the cookie crumbles, the whole nine yards, lay of the land, layout, play-by-play description, blow-by-blow account

3 **particular,** instance, item, detail, point, count, case, fact, matter, article, datum, element, part, ingredient, factor, facet, aspect, thing; respect, regard, angle; minutia, minutiae <pl>, trifle, petty matter, trivial matter; incidental, minor detail

4 **circumstantiality,** particularity, specificity, thoroughness, minuteness of detail; accuracy

5 **circumstantiation,** itemization, particularization, specification, spelling-out, detailing, anatomization, atomization, analysis

VERBS 6 **itemize,** specify, circumstantiate, particularize, spell out, detail, go into detail, descend to particulars, give full particulars, put in context, atomize, anatomize; analyze; cite, instance, adduce, document, quote chapter and verse; substantiate

ADJS 7 **circumstantial,** conditional, provisional; incidental, occasional, contingent, adventitious, accidental, chance, fortuitous, casual, aleatory, aleatoric, unessential, inessential, nonessential; background

8 **environmental**, environing, surrounding, conjunctive, conjoined, contextual, attending, attendant, limiting, determining, parametric; grounded, based

9 **detailed,** minute, full, **particular**, meticulous, fussy, finicky, finicking, finical, persnickety, picayune, picky, nice, precise, exact, specific, special; age-specific

ADVS 10 thus, thusly, in such wise, thuswise, this way, this-a-way, thus and thus, thus and so, so, just so, like so *and* yea, like this, like that, just like that; similarly, precisely

11 accordingly, **in that case**, in that event, at that rate, that being the case, such being the case, that being so, under the circumstances, the condition being such, as it is, as matters stand, as the matter stands, therefore, consequently; as the case may be, as it may be, according to circumstances; as it may happen, as it may turn out, as things may fall; by the same token, equally

12 **circumstantially,** conditionally, provisionally; provided

13 fully, in full, in detail, minutely, specifically, particularly, in particular, wholly, *in toto* <L>, completely, at length, *in extenso* <L>, *ad nauseam* <L>

767 INTRINSICALITY

<essential nature of thing>

NOUNS 1 **intrinsicality,** internality, innerness, inwardness; inbeing, indwelling, immanence; innateness, inherence, indigenousness; essentiality, fundamentality; **subjectivity**, internal reality, nonobjectivity

2 **essence,** substance, stuff, very stuff, inner essence, essential nature, quiddity, esse; quintessence, epitome, embodiment, incarnation, model, pattern, purest type, typification, perfect example, elixir, flower; essential, principle, essential principle, fundamental, hypostasis, postulate, axiom; **gist**, gravamen, nub, nucleus, center, focus, kernel, core, pith, meat; heart, soul, heart and soul, spirit, sap, lifeblood, marrow, entelechy; model home

3 <nonformal> meat and potatoes, **nuts and bolts**, the nitty-gritty, the guts, the name of the game, the bottom line, where it's at, what it's all about, the ball game, the payoff, the score, where the rubber meets the road; back to basics; mother of all

4 **nature, character,** quality, suchness; constitution, crasis, composition, characteristics, makeup, constituents, building blocks; physique, physio; build, body-build, somatotype, frame, genetic makeup, system; complexion, humor, humors; temperament, temper, fiber, disposition, spirit, ethos, genius, dharma; way, habit, tenor, cast, hue, tone, grain, vein, streak, stripe, mold, brand, stamp; kind, sort, type, ilk; property, character trait, characteristic; tendency; the way of it, the nature of the beast

5 **inner nature,** inside, insides, internal reality, inner reality, esoteric reality, intrinsic reality, true being, essential nature, what makes one tick, center of life, vital principle, nerve center; spirit, indwelling spirit, soul, heart, heart and soul, breast, bosom, inner person, heart of hearts, insight, secret heart, inmost heart, inmost soul, innermost recesses of the heart, heart's core, bottom of the heart, cockles of the heart;

vitals, the quick, depths of one's being, guts, kishkes, where one lives; archeus, life force, *élan vital* <Fr>

VERBS 6 **inhere,** indwell, belong to nature, permeate by nature, makes one tick; run in the blood, run in the family, inherit, be born so, have it in the genes, be made that way, be built that way, be part and parcel of

ADJS 7 **intrinsic,** internal, inner, inward; **inherent,** resident, implicit, immanent, indwelling; inalienable, unalienable, uninfringeable, unquestionable, unchallengeable, irreducible, qualitative; ingrained, in the very grain; infixed, implanted, inwrought, deep-seated; subjective, esoteric, private, secret

8 **innate, inborn,** born, congenital; native, natural, natural to, connatural, native to, indigenous; constitutional, bodily, physical, temperamental, organic; inbred, genetic, hereditary, inherited, bred in the bone, in the blood, running in the blood, radical, rooted; connate, connatal, coeval; instinctive, instinctual, atavistic, primal

9 **essential,** of the essence, **fundamental;** primary, primitive, primal, elementary, elemental, simple, barebones, no-frills, bread-and-butter, original, *ab ovo* <L>, basic, gut, basal, underlying; substantive, substantial, material; constitutive, constituent; mandatory, compulsory; must-have

ADVS 10 **intrinsically, inherently,** innately; internally, inwardly, immanently; originally, primally, primitively; naturally, congenitally, genetically, by birth, by nature

11 **essentially,** fundamentally, primarily, basically; at bottom, *au fond* <Fr>, at heart; in essence, at the core, in substance, in the main; substantially, materially, most of all; per se, of itself, in itself, as such, qua

COMBINING FORMS 12 physi-, physic-

768 EXTRINSICALITY

<external influence on thing>

NOUNS 1 **extrinsicality,** externality, outwardness, extraneousness, otherness, discreteness; foreignness; **objectivity,** nonsubjectivity, impersonality; X factor

2 **nonessential,** inessential, unessential, nonvitalness, carrying coals to Newcastle, gilding the lily; accessory, extra, collateral; the other, not-self; appendage, appurtenance, auxiliary, supernumerary, **supplement**, addition, addendum, superaddition, adjunct; subsidiary, subordinate, secondary; contingency, contingent, incidental, accidental, accident, happenstance, mere chance; superfluity, superfluousness; fifth wheel, tits on a boar; triviality

ADJS 3 **extrinsic, external,** outward, outside, outlying; extraneous, foreign; **objective,** nonsubjective, impersonal, extraorganismic, extraorganismal; not of this world

4 **unessential,** inessential, nonessential, unnecessary, nonvital, superfluous; accessory, extra, collateral, auxiliary, supernumerary; adventitious, appurtenant, adscititious; additional, **supplementary,** supplemental, superadded, supervenient, make-weight; secondary, subsidiary, subordinate; incidental, circumstantial, contingent; trivial, throwaway; accidental, chance, fortuitous, casual, aleatory, aleatoric; indeterminate, unpredictable, capricious

769 ACCOMPANIMENT

<going with another>

NOUNS 1 **accompaniment,** concomitance, concomitancy, withness and togetherness; synchronism, simultaneity, simultaneousness; coincidence, co-occurrence, concurrence, concurrency, coexistence, symbiosis; parallelism; coagency

2 **company,** association, consociation, society, community; **companionship, fellowship,** consortship, partnership, face time; cohabitation

3 **attendant,** concomitant, corollary, **accessory,** appendage; adjunct

4 **accompanier,** accompanist; attendant, companion, fellow, mate, comate, consort, partner; companion piece

5 **escort,** conductor, usher, shepherd; guide, tourist guide, cicerone; squire, esquire, swain, cavalier; chaperon, duenna; bodyguard, guard, convoy, muscle; companion, sidekick, fellow traveler, travel companion, satellite, outrider; third wheel

6 **attendance, following,** cortege, retinue, entourage, suite, followers, followership, rout, train, body of retainers; **court,** cohort; parasite

VERBS 7 **accompany,** keep one company, keep company with, companion, hang with, go with, travel with, run with, go together, go along for the ride, go along with, attend, wait on; associate with, assort with, sort with, consort with, couple with, hang around with, hang out with, go hand in hand with; combine, **associate**, consociate, confederate, flock together, band together; go off with

8 **escort,** conduct, have in tow, marshal, usher, shepherd, guide, lead; convoy, guard; squire, esquire, attend, wait on, take out; chaperon; dance attendance on; bring with, bring along

ADJS 9 **accompanying,** attending, attendant, concomitant, accessory, collateral; combined, **associated**, coupled, paired; **fellow,** twin, joint, joined, conjoint, hand-in-hand, hand-in-glove, mutual; simultaneous, concurrent, coincident, synchronic, synchronized; correlative; parallel; complementary; joined at the hip; joined-up

ADVS 10 **hand in hand**, hand in glove, arm in arm, side by side, cheek by jowl, shoulder to shoulder; therewith, therewithal, herewith

11 **together,** collectively, mutually, jointly, unitedly, in conjunction, conjointly, *en masse* <Fr>, communally, corporately, in a body, all at once, *ensemble* <Fr>, in association, in company; simultaneously, coincidentally, concurrently, at once

PREPS 12 with, in company with, along with, **together with,** in association with, coupled with, paired with, partnered with, in conjunction with

COMBINING FORMS 13 co-, con-, col-, com-, cor-, meta-, syn-, sym-

770 ASSEMBLAGE

<gathering together>

NOUNS 1 **assemblage,** assembly, collection, gathering, ingathering, forgathering, congregation, assembling; concourse, concurrence, conflux, confluence, convergence; collocation, juxtaposition, junction; combination; mobilization, call-up, muster; roundup, rodeo, corralling, shepherding, marshaling; comparison; canvass, census, data-gathering, survey, inventory; arranging, arrangement

2 **assembly** <of persons>, **gathering,** forgathering, congregation, congress, conference, convocation, concourse, meeting, meet, get-together, turnout; convention, conventicle, synod, council, diet, conclave, levee; caucus; mass meeting, rally, sit-in, demonstration, demo; session, séance, sitting, sit-down; panel, forum, symposium, colloquium; committee, commission; *eisteddfod* <Welsh>; plenum, quorum; party, festivity, fete, at home, housewarming, soiree, reception, dance, ball, prom, do, shindig, brawl; rendezvous, date, assignation; flash mob

3 **company, group**, grouping, groupment, network, party, band, knot, gang, crew, complement, cast, outfit, pack, cohort, troop, troupe, tribe, body, corps, stable, bunch, mob, crowd; squad, platoon, battalion, regiment, brigade, division, fleet; team, string; covey, bevy; posse, detachment, contingent, detail; phalanx; faction, movement, wing, persuasion; in-group, old-boy network, out-group, peer group, age group; coterie, salon, clique, breakfast club, brat pack, set; junta, cabal

4 **throng,** multitude, horde, host, heap, army, panoply, legion; flock, cluster, galaxy; crowd, press, crush, flood, spate, deluge, mass, surge, storm, squeeze; mob, rabble, rout, ruck, ja, everybody and his uncle, everybody and his brother, all and then some

5 <animals> **flock,** bunch, pack, colony, host, troop, army, herd, drove, drive, drift, trip; pride <of lions>, sloth <of bears>, skulk <of foxes>, gang <of elk>, kennel <of dogs>, clowder <of cats>, pod <of seals>, gam <of whales>, school <of fish>, shoal <of fish>; <animal young> litter

6 <birds, insects> flock, flight, **swarm,** cloud; covey <of partridges>, bevy <of quail>, skein <of geese in flight>, gaggle <of geese on water>, watch <of nightingales>, charm <of finches>, murmuration <of starlings>, spring <of teal>; hive <of bees>, plague <of locusts>

7 **bunch,** group, grouping, groupment, crop, cluster, clump, knot, wad; grove, copse, thicket; batch, lot, slew, mess; tuft, wisp; tussock, hassock; shock, stook; arrangement, nosegay, posy, spray

8 **bundle,** bindle, pack, **package,** packet, deck, budget, parcel, fardel, sack, bag, poke, ragbag, bale, truss, roll, rouleau, bolt; fagot, fascine, fasces; quiver, sheaf; bouquet, nosegay, posy

9 **accumulation,** cumulation, gathering, amassment, congeries, acervation, collection, collecting, grouping; agglomeration, conglomeration, glomeration, conglomerate, agglomerate; aggregation, aggregate; conglobation; mass, lump, gob, chunk, hunk, wad; snowball; stockpile, stockpiling

10 **pile,** heap, stack, mass; mound, hill; molehill, anthill; bank, embankment, dune; haystack, hayrick, haymow, haycock, cock, mow, rick; drift, snowdrift; pyramid

11 **collection,** collector's items, collectibles, collectables; **holdings,** fund, treasure, hoard; corpus, corpora, body, data, raw data; compilation, collectanea; ana; anthology, florilegium, treasury, store, stockpile; *Festschrift* <Ger>; chrestomathy; museum, library, zoo, menagerie, aquarium

12 **set,** suit, suite, series, outfit, kit

13 **miscellany,** miscellanea, collectanea; **assortment,** medley, variety, mixture; mixed bag, hodgepodge, conglomerate, conglomeration, omnium-gatherum, potpourri, smorgasboard; sundries, oddments, odds and ends, bits and pieces; mixed tape

14 <a putting together> **assembly,** assemblage;

assembly line, production line; assembly-line production

15 **collector,** gatherer, accumulator, connoisseur, fancier, enthusiast, pack rat, magpie, hoarder; beachcomber; collection agent, bill collector, dunner; tax collector, tax man, exciseman <Brit>, customs agent

VERBS **16** **come together, assemble,** congregate, **collect,** come from far and wide; league, ally; **unite**; muster, meet, gather, forgather, gang up, mass, amass; merge, converge, flow together, fuse; group, flock, flock together; herd together; throng, crowd, swarm, teem, hive, surge, seethe, mill, stream, horde; be crowded, be mobbed, burst at the seams, be full to overflowing; cluster, bunch, bunch up, clot; gather around, gang around; rally, rally around; huddle, go into a huddle, close ranks; rendezvous, date; couple, copulate, link, link up

17 **convene, meet,** hold a meeting, hold a session, sit; convoke, summon, call together

18 <gather together> bring together, **assemble, gather;** drum up, muster, rally, mobilize; collect, collect up, fund-raise, take up a collection, raise, take up; accumulate, cumulate, amass, mass, bulk, batch; agglomerate, conglomerate, aggregate; combine, network, join, get together, gather together, draw together, bunch together, pack, pack in, cram, cram in; bunch, bunch up; cluster, clump; group, aggroup; gather in, get in, whip in; scrape together, scrape up, together, dredge up, dig up; round up, corral, drive together; put together, make up, compile, colligate; collocate, juxtapose, pair, match, partner; hold up together, compare

19 **pile,** pile on, heap, stack, heap up, pile up, stack up; mound, hill, bank, bank up; rick; pyramid; drift; stockpile, build up, ramp up

20 **bundle,** bundle up, **package,** parcel, parcel up, pack, bag, sack, truss, truss up; bale; wrap, wrap up, do up; roll up

ADJS **21** **assembled, collected, gathered;** congregate, congregated; meeting, in session; combined; joined; joint, leagued; accumulated, cumulate, massed, amassed; heaped, stacked, piled; glomerate, agglomerate, conglomerate, aggregate; clustered, bunched, lumped, clumped, knotted; bundled, packaged, wrapped up; fascicled, fasciculated; herded, shepherded, rounded up

22 **crowded,** packed, **crammed;** bumper-to-bumper, jam-packed, packed like sardines, chockablock; compact, firm, solid, dense, close, serried; teeming, swarming, crawling, seething, bristling, populous, milling, full

23 **cumulative,** accumulative, total, overall

771 DISPERSION

<breaking apart and distributing>

NOUNS **1** **dispersion, dispersal, scattering,** scatter, scatteration, diffraction; ripple effect; distribution, spreading, strewing, sowing, broadcasting, broadcast, spread, narrowcast, publication, dissemination, propagation, dispensation; radiation, divergence; expansion, splay; diffusion, circumfusion; dilution, attenuation, thinning, thinning-out, watering, watering-down, weakening; evaporation, volatilization, dissipation; fragmentation, shattering, pulverization; sprinkling, spattering; peppering, buckshot pattern, shotgun pattern; deployment; diaspora

2 **decentralization,** deconcentration

3 **disbandment,** dispersion, dispersal, diaspora, separation, parting; breakup, split-up; demobilization, deactivation, release, detachment; dismissal; dissolution, disorganization, disintegration; population drift, urban sprawl, sprawl

VERBS **4** **disperse, scatter,** diffract; **distribute,** broadcast, sow, narrowcast, disseminate, propagate, pass around, pass out, publish; diffuse, spread, dispread, circumfuse, strew, bestrew, dot; radiate, diverge; expand, splay, branch out, fan out, spread out; issue, deal out, dole out, retail, utter, dispense; sow broadcast, scatter to the winds; overscatter, overspread, oversow; sunder, hive off

5 **dissipate,** dispel, dissolve, attenuate, dilute, thin, thin out, water, water down, weaken; evaporate, volatilize; drive away, clear away, cast forth, blow off

6 **sprinkle,** besprinkle, asperge, spatter, splatter, splash; dot, spot, speck, speckle, freckle, stud; pepper, powder, dust; flour, crumb, bread, dredge

7 **decentralize,** deconcentrate

8 **disband, disperse, scatter,** separate, part, break up, split up; part company, go separate ways, bug out; demobilize, demob, deactivate, muster out, debrief, release, detach, discharge, let go; dismiss; dissolve, disorganize, disintegrate

ADJS **9** **dispersed, scattered, distributed,** dissipated, disseminated, strown, strewn, broadcast, spread, dispread; widespread, diffuse, discrete, sparse; diluted, thinned, thinned-out, watered, watered-down, weakened; sporadic; straggling, straggly; all over the place, few and far between, from hell to breakfast

10 **sprinkled,** spattered, splattered, asperged, splashed, peppered, spotted, dotted, powdered, dusted, specked, speckled, studded, freckled

11 dispersive, **scattering,** spreading, diffractive, diffractional, **distributive,** disseminative, diffusive, dissipative, attenuative

ADVS **12** **scatteringly,** dispersedly, diffusely, sparsely, **sporadically,** *passim* <L>, here and there; in places, in spots; at large, everywhere, throughout, wherever you look, wherever you turn, in all quarters

772 INCLUSION

<part of group>

NOUNS **1** **inclusion,** comprisal, comprehension, coverage, envisagement, embracement, encompassment, incorporation, embodiment, assimilation, reception; **membership,** participation, admission, admissibility, eligibility, legitimation, legitimization; power-sharing, enablement, enfranchisement; completeness, inclusiveness, comprehensiveness, exhaustiveness; whole; openness, toleration, tolerance; universality, generality; inclusivism

2 **entailment, involvement,** implication; assumption, presumption, presupposition, subsumption

VERBS **3** **include, comprise,** contain, comprehend, hold, take in; cover, cover a lot of ground, occupy, take up, fill; fill in, fill out, build into, complete; embrace, encompass, enclose, encircle, incorporate, assimilate, embody, constitute, admit, receive, envisage; legitimize, legitimatize; share power, enable, enfranchise, cut in, deal in, give a piece of the action; among, count in, work in; number among, take into account, take into consideration

4 <include as a necessary consequence> **entail, involve,** implicate, imply, assume, presume, presuppose, subsume, affect, take in, contain, comprise, call for, require, take, bring, lead to

ADJS **5** **included, comprised,** comprehended, envisaged, embraced, encompassed, added-in, covered, head-to-toe, subsumed; bound up with, forming a part of, making a part of, built-in, tucked-in, integrated; involved

6 **inclusive, including,** containing, comprising, covering, embracing, encompassing, enclosing, encircling, assimilating, incorporating, envisaging; counting, numbering; broad-brush, ballpark, all-in

7 **comprehensive,** sweeping, complete; whole; all-comprehensive, all-inclusive, non-exclusive; without omission, without exception, overall, universal, global, wall-to-wall, around-the-world, total, blanket, omnibus, umbrella, across-the-board; encyclopedic, compendious; synoptic; bird's-eye, panoramic

773 EXCLUSION

<left out of group>

NOUNS **1** **exclusion, barring,** debarring, debarment, preclusion, exception, omission, nonadmission, cutting-out, leaving-out; restriction, circumscription, narrowing, demarcation; rejection, repudiation; ban, bar, taboo, blackball, injunction; relegation; prohibition, embargo, blockade; boycott, lockout; inadmissibility, excludability, exclusivity

2 **elimination,** riddance, culling, culling out, winnowing-out, shakeout, eviction, chasing, bum's rush; severance; withdrawal, removal, detachment, disjunction; discard, eradication, clearance, ejection, expulsion, suspension; deportation, **exile,** expatriation, ostracism, outlawing, outlawry; disposal, disposition; liquidation, **purge**; obliteration

3 **exclusiveness,** narrowness, tightness; insularity, snobbishness, parochialism, ethnocentrism, ethnicity, xenophobia, know-nothingism; special case, exemption; **segregation,** separation, separationism, division; isolation, insulation, seclusion; quarantine; racial segregation, apartheid, color bar, Jim Crow, race hatred; out-group; outsider, non-member, stranger, the other, they; foreigner, alien, outcast, outlaw; *persona non grata* <L>; blacklist, blackball; monopoly; sexual discrimination; sizeism; cultural appropriation

VERBS **4** **exclude, bar,** debar, bar out, lock out, shut out, keep out, count out, close the door on, close out, cut out, cut off, preclude; reject, repudiate, blackball, turn thumbs down on, read out, drum out, ease out, freeze out, leave out in the cold, keep out in the cold, cold-shoulder, send to Coventry <Brit>, ostracize, wave off, wave aside; ignore, turn a blind eye, turn a deaf ear, filter out, tune out; ban, prohibit, proscribe, taboo, leave out, omit, pass over; relegate; blockade, embargo; tariff, trade barrier

5 **eliminate, get rid of,** rid oneself of, get quit of, get shut of, dispose of, remove, abstract, eject, expel, give the bum's rush, kick downstairs, cast out, chuck, throw overboard; deport, exile, outlaw, expatriate; clear, clear out, clear away, clear the decks; weed out, pick out; cut out, strike off, elide, censor; eradicate, root out; **purge,** liquidate

6 **segregate, separate,** separate out, divide, cordon, cordon off; isolate, insulate, seclude; set apart, keep apart; quarantine, put in isolation; put beyond the pale, ghettoize; set aside, lay aside, put aside, keep aside, box off, wall off, fence off; pick out, cull out, sift, screen, sieve, bolt, riddle, winnow, winnow out; thresh, thrash, gin

ADJS 7 **excluded, barred,** debarred, precluded, kept-out, shut-out, left-out, left out in the cold, passed-over; not included, not in it, not in the picture; excepted, excused; ignored; cold-shouldered; relegated; banned, prohibited, proscribed, tabooed; expelled, ejected, purged, liquidated; deported, exiled; blockaded, embargoed

8 **segregated, separated,** cordoned-off, divided; isolated, insulated, secluded; set apart, sequestered; quarantined; ghettoized, beyond the pale; peripheral

9 **exclusive, excluding,** exclusory; seclusive, preclusive, exceptional, inadmissible, prohibitive, preventive, prescriptive, restrictive; separative, segregative, closed-door; select, selective; narrow, insular, parochial, ethnocentric, xenophobic, snobbish; racist, sexist

PREP 10 **excluding, barring,** bar, exclusive of, precluding, omitting, without, absent, leaving out; excepting, except, except for, with the exception of, outside of, save, saving, save and except, let alone; besides, beside, aside from

774 EXTRANEOUSNESS

<outside normal existence>

NOUNS 1 **extraneousness, foreignness;** otherness, alienism, alienage, alienation; extrinsicality; exteriority; nonassimilation, nonconformity; intrusion

2 **intruder,** foreign body, foreign element, foreign intruder, foreign intrusion, interloper, encroacher; **impurity,** blemish; speck, spot, macula, blot, age spot; mote, splinter, sliver, weed, misfit; oddball; black sheep

3 **alien, stranger, foreigner, outsider,** non-member, not one of us, not our sort, not the right sort, the other, outlander, tramontane, ultramontane, barbarian; exile, outcast, outlaw, wanderer, refugee, émigré, displaced person (DP), asylum seeker; the Wandering Jew

4 **newcomer, new arrival**; *arriviste* <Fr>, Johnny-come-lately, new person, new kid; tenderfoot, greenhorn; settler, emigrant, immigrant; recruit, rookie; intruder, squatter, gate-crasher, stowaway; boat person

ADJS 5 **extraneous, foreign, alien,** strange, exotic, foreign-looking; unearthly, extraterrestrial; exterior, external; extrinsic; ulterior, outside, outland, outlandish; barbarian, barbarous, barbaric; foreign-born; intrusive

ADVS 6 abroad, in foreign parts; oversea, **overseas,** beyond seas; on one's travels

COMBINING FORMS 7 ep-, epi-, eph-, ex-, exo-, ef-, xen-, xeno-

775 RELATION

<connection to another>

NOUNS 1 **relation, relationship, connection;** relatedness, connectedness, association, affiliation, filiation, bond, union, alliance, tie, tie-in, link, linkage, linking, linkup, liaison, addition, adjunct, junction, combination, assemblage; deduction, disjunction, contrariety, disagreement, bad relation; positive relation, good relation, affinity, rapport, mutual attraction, sympathy, accord; closeness, propinquity, proximity, approximation, contiguity, nearness, intimacy; relations, dealings, affairs, business, transactions, doings, truck, intercourse; similarity, homology

2 relativity, dependence, contingency; relativism, indeterminacy, uncertainty, variability, variance; **interrelation,** correlation

3 **kinship,** common source, common stock, common descent, common ancestry, consanguinity, agnation, cognation, enation, relationship by blood; family relationship, affinity

4 **relevance,** pertinence, pertinency, cogency, relatedness, materiality, appositeness, germaneness; application, applicability, effect, appropriateness; connection, reference, bearing, concern, concernment, interest, respect, regard

VERBS 5 **relate to,** refer to, apply to, bear on, respect, regard, concern, involve, touch, affect, interest; pertain, pertain to, appertain, appertain to, belong to, fit; agree, agree with, answer to, correspond to, chime with; have to do with, have connection with, link with, link up with, connect, reconnect, put in context, tie in with, liaise with, deal with, treat of, touch upon

6 **relate, associate, connect,** interconnect, ally, link, link up, wed, marry, marry up, weld, bind, tie, couple, bracket, equate, identify; bring into relation with, bring to bear upon, apply; parallel, parallelize, draw a parallel; symmetrize; **interrelate,** relativize, correlate

ADJS 7 **relative,** comparative relational; relativistic, indeterminate, uncertain, variable; connective, linking, associative; **relating,** pertaining, appertaining, pertinent, referring, referable

8 **approximate,** approximating, approximative, proximate; near, close; comparable, relatable, commensurable; proportional, proportionate, proportionable; correlative; like, homologous, similar

9 **related, connected;** linked, tied, coupled, knotted, twinned, wedded, wed, married, married up, welded, conjugate, bracketed, bound, yoked, spliced, conjoined, conjoint, conjunct, joined; associated, affiliated, filiated, allied, associate, affiliate; interlocked, **interrelated,** interlinked, involved, implicated, overlapping, interpenetrating, relevant, correlated; in the same category, of that kind, of that sort, of that ilk, corresponding; parallel, collateral; congenial, sympathetic, compatible, affinitive

10 **kindred, akin,** related, of common descent, of common ancestry, agnate, cognate, enate, connate, connatural, congeneric, congenerous, consanguine, consanguineous, genetically related, related by blood, affinal

11 **relevant, pertinent,** appertaining, **germane, apposite,** cogent, material, admissible, applicable, applying, pertaining, belonging, involving, appropriate, **apropos,** to the purpose, to the point, in point, *ad rem* <L>

ADVS 12 **relatively,** comparatively, proportionately, not absolutely, to a degree, to an extent, to some extent; relevantly, pertinently, appositely, germanely

PREPS 13 **in relation to,** with relation to, with reference to, in reference to, with regard to, in regard to, with respect to, in respect to, in what concerns, relative to, relating to, pertaining to, pertinent to, appertaining to, referring to, in relation with, in connection with, apropos of, speaking of; as to, as for, as respects, as regards; in the matter of, on the subject of, in point of, on the score of; re, *in re* <L>; about, anent, of, on, upon, concerning, touching, respecting, regarding

776 UNRELATEDNESS

<lack of relation to another>

NOUNS 1 **unrelatedness,** irrelativeness, irrelation; **irrelevance,** irrelevancy, impertinence, inappositeness, uncogency, ungermaneness, immateriality, inapplicability; inconnection, disconnection, disconnect, inconsequence, independence; **unconnectedness,** separateness, delinkage, discreteness, dissociation, disassociation, disjuncture, disjunction

2 **misconnection,** misrelation, wrong linking, invalid linking, mismatch, mismatching, misalliance; misapplication, misapplicability, misreference

3 an irrelevance, **irrelevancy,** quite another thing, something else again, a whole nother thing, a whole different story, a whole different ball game

VERBS 4 **not concern,** not involve, not imply, not implicate, not entail, not relate to, not connect with, have nothing to do with, have no business with, cut no ice, make no never mind, have no bearing

5 foist, drag in; impose on

ADJS 6 **unrelated,** irrelative, unrelatable, unrelational, unconnected, unallied, unlinked, unassociated, unaffiliated, disaffiliated; disrelated, disconnected, dissociated, detached, discrete, disjunct, removed, separated, segregated, apart, other, independent, marked off, bracketed; isolated, insular; foreign, alien, strange, exotic, outlandish; incommensurable, incomparable; inconsistent, inconsonant; extraneous

7 **irrelevant,** irrelative; impertinent, inapposite, ungermane, uncogent, inconsequent, inapplicable, immaterial, inappropriate, inadmissible; wide of the point, away from the point, beside the point, beside the mark, wide of the mark, beside the question, off the subject, off-topic, not to the purpose, nothing to do with the case, not at issue, out-of-the-way; unessential, nonessential, extraneous, extrinsic; incidental, parenthetical

8 **far-fetched,** remote, distant, out-of-the-way, strained, forced, dragged in, neither here nor there, brought in from nowhere; imaginary; improbable

ADVS 9 **irrelevantly,** irrelatively, impertinently, inappositely, ungermanely, uncogently, amiss; without connection, without reference, without regard

777 CORRELATION

<mutual, reciprocal relation>

NOUNS 1 **correlation,** corelation; correlativity, correlativism; reciprocation, reciprocity, reciprocality, two-edged sword, relativity; **mutuality,** communion, community, commutuality, common ground; common denominator, common factor; proportionality, direct relationship, inverse relationship, direct ratio, inverse ratio, direct proportion, inverse proportion, covariation; equilibrium, balance, symmetry; correspondence, equivalence, equipollence, coequality

2 **interrelation,** interrelationship; interconnection, interlocking, interdigitation, intercoupling, interlinking, interlinkage, interalliance, interassociation, interaffiliation, interdependence, interdependency, codependency; dovetail

3 **interaction,** interworking, intercourse, intercommunication, interplay; alternation, seesaw; meshing, intermeshing, mesh, engagement; complementation, complementary

relation, complementary distribution; interweaving, interlacing, intertwining; interchange, tit for tat, trade-off, *quid pro quo* <L>; concurrence, coaction, cooperation, compromise; codependency

4 **correlate,** correlative; **correspondent,** analogue, counterpart; reciprocator, reciprocatist; each other, one another

VERBS 5 **correlate,** corelate; interrelate, interconnect, interassociate, interlink, intercouple, interlock, interdigitate, interally, intertie, interjoin, interdepend; interface; find common ground; dovetail

6 **interact,** interwork, **interplay;** mesh, intermesh, engage, fit, fit like a glove, dovetail, mortise; interweave, interlace, intertwine; interchange; coact, cooperate; codepend

7 **reciprocate,** correspond, correspond to, respond to, answer, answer to, go tit-for-tat; complement, coequal; cut both ways, cut two ways; counteract

ADJS 8 **correlative,** corelative, correlational, corelational; **correlated**, corelated; interrelated, interconnected, internetworked, interassociated, interallied, interaffiliated, interlinked, interlocked, intercoupled, intertied, interdependent; interchanged, converse

9 **interacting,** interactive, interworking, interplaying; in gear, in mesh; dovetailed, mortised; cooperative, cooperating

10 **reciprocal,** reciprocative, tit-for-tat, seesaw, seesawing; **corresponding,** correspondent, answering, analogous, homologous, equipollent, tantamount, equivalent, coequal; complementary, complemental

11 **mutual,** commutual, common, joint, communal, shared, sharing, conjoint; respective, two-way, cooperative

ADVS 12 **reciprocally,** back and forth, backward and forward, backwards and forwards, alternately, seesaw, to and fro; vice versa

13 **mutually, commonly,** communally, jointly; respectively, each to each; *entre nous* <Fr>

COMBINING FORMS 14 equi-

778 SAMENESS

<being the same as>

NOUNS 1 **sameness**, identity, identicalness, selfsameness, indistinguishability, undifferentiation, nondifferentiation, two peas in a pod; coincidence, correspondence, agreement, congruence; equivalence, equality, coequality; synonymousness, synonymity, synonymy; oneness, unity, homogeneity, consubstantiality; isogeny; homogeny; gender equality

2 **identification,** likening, unification, coalescence, combination, union, fusion, merger, blending, melding, synthesis

3 **the same,** selfsame, very same, one and the same, identical same, no other, none other, very thing, actual thing, a distinction without a difference, the same difference; equivalent; synonym; homonym, homograph, homophone; ditto, *idem* <L>; duplicate, double, clone, cookie-cutter copy, *Doppelgänger* <Ger>, twin, very image, look-alike, dead ringer, the image of, the picture of, spitting image, spit and image, exact counterpart, copy, replica, facsimile, carbon copy

VERBS 4 **coincide, correspond,** agree, chime with, match, tally, go hand in glove with, twin; complement

5 **identify,** make one, unify, unite, join, combine, coalesce, synthesize, merge, blend, meld, fuse

6 reproduce, **copy,** reduplicate, **duplicate,** ditto, clone

ADJS 7 **identical,** identic; **same,** selfsame, one, one and the same, all the same, all one, of the same kidney; indistinguishable, without distinction, without difference, undifferent, undifferentiated; cookie-cutter; alike, all alike, like, just alike, exactly alike, like two peas in a pod; duplicate, reduplicated, copied, twin; homogeneous, consubstantial; redundant, tautological

8 **coinciding,** coincident, coincidental; **corresponding,** correspondent, congruent; complementary; synonymous, equivalent, six of one and half a dozen of the other; equal, coequal, coextensive, coterminous; in parity, at parity

ADVS 9 **identically,** synonymously, alike; coincidentally, correspondently, correspondingly, congruently; equally, coequally, coextensively, coterminously; on the same footing, on all fours with; likewise, the same way, just the same, as is, ditto, same here; *ibid, ibidem* <L>

779 CONTRARIETY

<being opposite or incompatible>

NOUNS 1 **contrariety, oppositeness,** opposition; antithesis, contrast, contraposition, counterposition, contradiction, contraindication, contradistinction; antagonism, repugnance, oppugnance, oppugnancy, hostility, perversity, naysaying, negativeness, orneriness, inimicalness, antipathy, scunner; confrontation, showdown, standoff, Mexican standoff, clashing, collision, cross-purposes, conflict; polarity; discrepancy, inconsistency, disagreement; antonymy

2 **the opposite, the contrary,** the antithesis, the reverse, the other way around, the inverse, the

converse, the obverse, the counter; opposite sex; the other side, the mirror image, the reverse image, the other side of the coin, the flip side, the B side; the direct opposite, the polar opposite, the other extreme, the opposite extreme, other end of the spectrum; antipode, antipodes; countercheck, counterbalance, counterpoise, offset, setoff; opposite pole, antipole, counterpole, counterpoint; opposite number, vis-à-vis; antonym, opposite, opposite term, counterterm

3 <contrarieties when coexisting> self-contradiction, **paradox**, antinomy, oxymoron, ambivalence, irony, enantiosis, equivocation, ambiguity

VERBS 4 **go contrary to, run counter to,** counter, contradict, contravene, controvert, fly in the face of, be at cross-purposes, go against; oppose, be opposed to, run in opposition to, side against; conflict with, come in conflict with, oppugn, conflict, clash; contrast with, offset, set off, countercheck, counterbalance, countervail; counteract, counterwork; counterpose, contrapose, counterpoise, juxtapose in opposition

5 reverse, invert, obvert, transpose, flip

ADJS 6 **contrary;** contrarious, perverse, **opposite,** antithetic, antithetical, contradictory, counter, contrapositive, contrasted; converse, reverse, obverse, inverse; adverse, adversative, adversive, adversarial, opposing, opposed, oppositive, oppositional; anti, dead against; antagonistic, repugnant, oppugnant, ornery, naysaying, negative, hostile, combative, bellicose, belligerent, inimical, antipathetic, antipathetical, discordant; inconsistent, discrepant, conflicting, clashing, at cross-purposes, confronting, confrontational, confrontive, squared off, face to face, vis-à-vis, eyeball to eyeball, toe-to-toe, at loggerheads; contradistinct; antonymous; countervailing, counterpoised, balancing, counterbalancing, compensating

7 **diametric, diametrical, diametrically opposite,** diametrically opposed, at opposite poles, in polar opposition, antipodal, antipodean; retrograde; opposite as black and white, opposite as light and darkness, opposite as day and night, opposite as fire and water, opposite as the poles

8 self-contradictory, **paradoxical,** antinomic, oxymoronic, ambivalent, ironic; equivocal, ambiguous

ADVS 9 contrarily, contrariwise, **counter, conversely**, inversely, vice versa, topsy-turvy, upside down, arsy-varsy, on the other hand, on the contrary, to the contrary, at loggerheads, in flat opposition; rather, nay rather, quite the contrary, otherwise, just the other way, just the other way around, oppositely, just the opposite, just the reverse; by contraries, by way of opposition; against the grain; contrariously, perversely, ornerily

PREPS 10 **opposite,** over against, contra, in contrast with, contrary to, vis-à-vis

COMBINING FORMS 11 con-, contra-, counter-

780 DIFFERENCE

<being different>

NOUNS 1 **difference,** otherness, separateness, discreteness, distinctness, **distinction;** unlikeness, dissimilarity; variation, variance, variegation, variety, mixture, heterogeneity, diversity; deviation, divergence, divergency, departure; disparity, gap, inequality, odds; discrepancy, inconsistency, inconsonance, incongruity, discongruity, unconformity, nonconformity, disconformity, strangeness, unorthodoxy, incompatibility, irreconcilability; culture gap; disagreement, dissent, disaccord, disaccordance, inaccordance, discordance, dissonance, inharmoniousness, inharmony; contrast, opposition, contrariety; a far cry, a whale of a difference; difference of opinion; biodiversity, biological diversity; differentiatedness

2 **margin,** wide margin, narrow margin, **differential;** differentia, distinction, point of difference; nicety, subtlety, refinement, delicacy, fine distinction, subtle distinction, fine point; shade of difference, **nuance,** hairline; seeming difference, distinction without a difference

3 **a whole other thing**, a different thing, a different story, something else, something else again, another kettle of fish, another tune, different breed of cat, another can of worms, horse of a different color, bird of another feather; nothing of the kind, no such thing, quite another thing; other, another, tother, whole nother thing, different ball game, whole different ball game, special case, exception to the rule

4 **differentiation,** differencing, discrimination, distinguishing, distinction; demarcation, limiting, drawing the line; separation, separateness, discreteness, division, atomization, anatomization, analysis, disjunction, segregation, severance, severalization; modification, alteration, change, tweak, variation, diversification, disequalization; particularization, specification, individualization, individuation, personalization, specialization

VERBS 5 **differ, vary,** diverge, stand apart, be distinguished, be distinct; **deviate from,** diverge from, divaricate from, depart from; disagree with, disaccord with, conflict with, contrast with, stand over against, clash with, jar with; not be like, bear no resemblance to, not square with, not accord with, not go on all fours with; ring the changes

6 differentiate, difference; **distinguish,** make a distinction, discriminate, secern; separate, sever, severalize, segregate, divide; demarcate, mark, mark out, mark off, set off, set apart, draw a line, set limits; modify, vary, diversify, disequalize, change; particularize, individualize, individuate, personalize, specify, specialize; atomize, analyze, anatomize, disjoin; split hairs, sharpen a distinction, refine a distinction, chop logic

ADJS **7 different,** differing; unlike, not like, **dissimilar**; distinct, distinguished, differentiated, discriminated, discrete, separated, separate, disjoined, widely apart; various, variant, varying, varied, heterogeneous, multifarious, motley, assorted, variegated, diverse, divers, diversified; several, many; divergent, deviative, diverging, deviating, departing; disparate, unequal; discrepant, inconsistent, inconsonant, incongruous, incongruent, unconformable, incompatible, irreconcilable; disagreeing, in disagreement; at odds, at variance, clashing, inaccordant, disaccordant, discordant, dissonant, inharmonious, out of tune; contrasting, contrasted, poles apart, poles asunder, worlds apart; contrary; discriminable, separable, severable

8 other, another, whole nother, else, otherwise, other than, other from; not the same, not the type, not that sort, of another sort, of a sort, of sorts; **unique,** one-of-a-kind, rare, special, peculiar, *sui generis* <L, of its own kind>, in a class by itself

9 differentiative, differentiating, diacritic, diacritical, differential; **distinguishing,** discriminating, discriminative, discriminatory, characterizing, individualizing, individuating, personalizing, differencing, separative; diagnostic; **distinctive,** contrastive, characteristic, peculiar, idiosyncratic

ADVS **10 differently,** diversely, variously; in a different manner, in another way, with a difference; differentiatingly, distinguishingly

11 otherwise, in other ways, in other respects; elsewise, else; or else; than; other than; on the other hand; contrarily; alias

COMBINING FORMS **12** all-, de-, dis-, heter-, xen-

781 UNIFORMITY

<being unvarying, same as others>

NOUNS **1 uniformity,** evenness, equability; steadiness, stability, steadfastness, firmness, unbrokenness, seamlessness, constancy, unwaveringness, undeviatingness, persistence, perseverance, continuity, **consistency;** consonance, correspondence, accordance; unity, homogeneity, consubstantiality, monolithism; equanimity, equilibrium, unruffledness, serenity, tranquility, calm, calmness, cool

2 regularity, constancy, invariability, unvariation, undeviation, even tenor, smoothness, clockwork regularity; sameness, monotony, monotonousness, undifferentiation, the same old thing, the daily round, the daily routine, the treadmill; monotone, drone, dingdong, singsong, monologue

VERBS **3 persist,** prevail, persevere, run true to form, run true to type, continue the same; drag on, drag along; hum, drone

4 make uniform, uniformize; regulate, regularize, normalize, stabilize, damp; even, equalize, symmetrize, harmonize, balance, balance up, equilibrize; level, level out, level off, smooth, smooth out, even out, flatten; homogenize, assimilate, standardize, stereotype; clone

ADJS **5 uniform,** equable, equal, even; level, flat, smooth; regular, constant, steadfast, persistent, continuous; unvaried, unruffled, unbroken, seamless, undiversified, undifferentiated, unchanged; invariable, unchangeable, immutable; unvarying, undeviating, unchanging, steady, stable; cloned, clonish, cookie-cutter; ordered, balanced, measured; orderly, methodical, systematic, mechanical, faceless, robotlike, automatic; **consistent,** consonant, correspondent, accordant, homogeneous, alike, all alike, all of a piece, of a piece, consubstantial, monolithic; nonsexist, inclusive, nondiscriminatory

6 same, wall-to-wall, back-to-back; **monotonous,** humdrum, unrelieved, repetitive, drab, gray, ho-hum, samey, usual, as usual; tedious, boring

ADVS **7 uniformly,** equably, **evenly;** monotonously, in a rut, in a groove, dully, tediously, routinely, unrelievedly

8 regularly; constantly, steadily, continually; invariably, without exception, at every turn, every time one turns around, all the time, all year round, week in week out, year in year out, day in day out, around the clock, never otherwise; methodically, orderly, systematically; always; like clockwork

COMBINING FORMS **9** equi-, hol-, hom-, is-, mon-

782 NONUNIFORMITY

<being diverse>

NOUNS **1 nonuniformity,** unevenness, irregularity, raggedness, crazy-quilt, choppiness, jerkiness, disorder; difference; inequality; inconstancy,

inconsistency, variability, changeability, changeableness, mutability, capriciousness, mercuriality, wavering, instability, unsteadiness; variation, deviation, deviance, divergence, differentiation, divarication, ramification; versatility, diversity, diversification, nonformalization; nonconformity, nonconformism, unconformity, unconformism, unorthodoxy; pluralism, variegation, variety, variousness, motleyness, dappleness; multiculturalism, multiculturism, multiculti, rainbow

VERBS 2 **diversify, vary,** variegate, chop and change, waver, mutate; differentiate, divaricate, diverge, ramify; differ; dissent; disunify, break up, break down, fragment, partition, analyze

ADJS 3 **nonuniform,** ununiform, uneven, irregular, ragged, erose, choppy, jerky, jagged, rough, disorderly, unsystematic; different, unequal, unequable; inconstant, **inconsistent,** variable, varying, changeable, changing, mutable, capricious, impulsive, mercurial, erratic, spasmodic, sporadic, wavery, wavering, unstable, unsteady; deviating, deviative, deviatory, divergent, divaricate, ramified; diversified, variform, diversiform, nonformal; nonconformist, unorthodox; pluralistic, variegated, various, motley; multicultural, multiculti, multiracial, rainbow

ADVS 4 **nonuniformly,** ununiformly, unequally, unevenly, irregularly, inconstantly, **inconsistently,** unsteadily, erratically, spasmodically, by fits and starts, capriciously, impulsively, sporadically; unsystematically, chaotically, helter-skelter, higgledy-piggledy; in all manner of ways, every which way, all over the shop, all over the ballpark; here, there, and everywhere

COMBINING FORMS 5 diversi-, vari-, heter-

783 MULTIFORMITY

<having many forms>

NOUNS 1 **multiformity,** multifariousness, **variety,** nonuniformity, **diversity,** diversification, variation, variegation, variability, versatility, proteanism, manifoldness, multiplicity, heterogeneity; omniformity, omnifariousness; pluralism, multiculturalism; everything but the kitchen sink, all colors of the rainbow, polymorphism, heteromorphism; allotropy, allotropism; Proteus, shapeshifting, shapeshifter; infinite variety; reformatting

VERBS 2 **diversify, vary,** change form, change shape, shift shape, ring changes, cover the spectrum, variegate; branch out, spread one's wings; have many irons in the fire; format, reformat

ADJS 3 **multiform,** diversiform, variable, versatile; protean, proteiform; manifold, multifold, multiplex, multiple, multifarious, multiphase; polymorphous, polymorphic, heteromorphous, heteromorphic, metamorphic; omniform, omniformal, omnifarious, omnigenous; allotropic, allotropical

4 **diversified, varied, assorted,** heterogeneous, nonuniform; multipurpose; various, many and various, divers, diverse, sundry, several, many; of all sorts, of all kinds, of all descriptions, of all types; multiethnic, multicultural; multifunctional

ADVS 5 **variously,** severally, sundrily, multifariously, diversely, manifoldly

COMBINING FORMS 6 allo-, diversi-, heter-, multi-, omni-, parti-, party-, poecil-, poikil-, poly-, vari-

784 SIMILARITY

<having characteristics in common>

NOUNS 1 **similarity, likeness,** alikeness, **sameness,** similitude; resemblance, semblance; analogy, correspondence, conformity, accordance, agreement, comparability, commensurability, comparison, parallelism, parity, community, alliance, consimilarity; approximation, approach, closeness, nearness; assimilation, likening, simile, metaphor, parable, allegory; simulation, imitation, copying, aping, mimicking, taking-off, takeoff, burlesque, pastiche; identity; equivalence; synonymy

2 kinship, **affinity**, connection, family resemblance, family likeness, family favor, genetic resemblance; connaturality, connaturalness, connature, connateness, congeneracy; compatibility

3 likeness, like, the likes of, the like of, point of likeness, point in common; suchlike, such; analogue, parallel; cognate, congener; **counterpart, complement,** correspondent, pendant, similitude, tally; approximation, rough idea, sketch; coordinate, reciprocal, obverse, equivalent; correlate, correlative; close imitation, close reproduction, close copy, near duplicate, simulacrum; close match, matchup, fellow, mate; soul mate, kindred spirit, kindred soul, companion, twin, brother, sister, brother under the skin, sister under the skin; second self, alter ego; a chip off the old block; look-alike, the image of, the picture of, shadow, another edition; related form

4 **close resemblance**, striking resemblance, startling resemblance, marked resemblance, decided resemblance; close likeness, near likeness; faint resemblance, remote resemblance, mere hint, mere shadow

5 **set,** group, matching pair, matching set, his and hers, couple, pair, twins, look-alikes, two of a kind, birds of a feather, peas in a pod

6 <of words or sounds> assonance, alliteration, rhyme, slant rhyme, near rhyme, jingle, clink; pun, paronamasia

VERBS **7** **resemble,** be like, bear resemblance; put one in mind of, remind one of, bring to mind, be reminiscent of, suggest, evoke, call up, call to mind; **look like,** favor, mirror; take after, partake of, follow, appear like, seem like, sound like; smack of, be redolent of; have all the earmarks of, have every appearance of, have all the features of, have all the signs of, have every indication of; approximate, approach, near, come near, come close; compare with, stack up with; correspond, match, parallel, connect, relate; not tell apart, not tell one from the other; imitate, simulate, copy, ape, mimic, take off, counterfeit; nearly reproduce, nearly duplicate

8 **similarize,** approximate, assimilate, bring near; connaturalize

9 **assonate,** alliterate, rhyme, chime; pun

ADJS **10** **similar, like,** alike, something like, not unlike; resembling, resemblant, following, favoring, smacking of, suggestive of, on the order of; consimilar; simulated, imitated, imitation, copied, aped, mimicked, taken off, fake, phony, counterfeit, mock, synthetic, ersatz; nearly reproduced, nearly duplicated, nearly reduplicated; uniform with, homogeneous, identical

11 **analogous,** comparable; corresponding, correspondent, equivalent; parallel, paralleling; matching, cast in the same mold, of a kind, of a size, of a piece; duplicate, twin, of the same hue, of the same stripe; mix-and-match

12 **such as,** suchlike, so

13 **akin,** affinitive, related; connatural, connate, cognate, agnate, enate, conspecific, correlative; congenerous, congeneric, congenerical; brothers under the skin, sisters under the skin

14 **approximating,** approximative, approximate, approximable; near, close; much of a muchness, much the same, much at one, nearly the same, same but different; quasi, pseudo

15 **very like,** mighty like, powerful like, uncommonly like, remarkably like, extraordinarily like, strikingly like, ridiculously like, for all the world like, as like as can be; a lot alike, pretty much the same, the same difference, damned little difference; near-equal; as like as two peas in a pod; faintly like, remotely like

16 **lifelike,** speaking, faithful, living, breathing, to the life, true to life; realistic, natural

17 <of words or sounds> assonant, assonantal, alliterative, alliteral; **rhyming,** jingling, chiming, punning; soundalike

ADVS **18** **similarly,** correspondingly, like, likewise, either; in the same manner, in like manner, in kind; in that way, like that, like this; thus; so; by the same token, by the same sign; identically

19 so to speak, in a manner of speaking, as it were, in a manner, in a way; kind of, sort of

785 COPY

<imitating or reproducing>

NOUNS **1** **copy,** representation, **facsimile,** image, likeness, resemblance, semblance, similitude, picture, portrait, life mask, death mask, icon, simulacrum, twin; ectype; pastiche; fair copy, faithful copy; certified copy; imitation, counterfeit, forgery, fake, phony

2 reproduction, duplication, reduplication; reprography; transcription; tracing, rubbing; mimeography, xerography, hectography; model home

3 **duplicate, duplication,** dupe and ditto; double, cookie-cutter copy, clone; representation, reproduction, replica, repro, carbon copy, reduplication, facsimile, model, counterpart; a chip off the old block; triplicate, quadruplicate; repetition

4 **transcript,** transcription, apograph, tenor <law>; transfer, tracing, rubbing, carbon copy, carbon; manifold; microcopy, microform; microfiche, fiche; recording

5 **print,** offprint; impression, impress; **reprint,** proof, reproduction proof, repro proof, repro, second edition; photostatic copy, photostat, stat; mimeograph copy, ditto copy, hectograph copy, xerographic copy, xerox copy, xerox, carbon copy; **facsimile,** fax; photograph, positive, negative, enlargement, contact print, photocopy

6 **cast,** casting; **mold,** molding, die, stamp, seal

7 **reflection,** reflex; **shadow,** silhouette, outline; echo

VERBS **8** **copy, reproduce,** replicate, **duplicate,** dupe; clone; reduplicate; transcribe; trace; double; triplicate, quadruplicate; manifold, multigraph, mimeograph, mimeo, photostat, stat, facsimile, fax, hectograph, ditto, xerox, carbon-copy; microcopy, microfilm

ADVS **9** in duplicate, in triplicate

786 MODEL

<thing copied>

NOUNS **1** **model,** pattern, standard, criterion, classic example, rule, mirror, paradigm;

showpiece, showplace; original, urtext; type, **prototype,** antetype, archetype, genotype, biotype, type specimen, type species; **precedent**

2 **example,** exemplar; **representative,** type, symbol, emblem, exponent; exemplification, illustration, demonstration, explanation; instance, relevant instance, case, typical example, typical case, case in point, object lesson

3 **sample, specimen;** piece, taste, swatch; instance, for-instance

4 **ideal,** *beau ideal*, ego ideal, ideal type, acme, highest type; cynosure, apotheosis, idol; shining example, role-model, hero, superhero; model, the very model, mirror, paragon, epitome; cult figure; prime example, poster child

5 artist's model, dressmaker's model, photographer's model, mannequin; dummy, lay figure; clay model, wood model, pilot model, mock-up

6 **mold,** form, cast, template, matrix, negative; die, punch, hole punch, stamp, intaglio, seal, mint; last, shoe last

VERBS 7 **set an example,** set the pace, lead the way; **exemplify,** epitomize, fit the pattern; emulate, follow, hold up as a model, model oneself on

ADJS 8 **model, exemplary,** precedential, typical, paradigmatic, representative, standard, normative, classic; ideal

9 **prototypal**, prototypic, prototypical, archetypal, archetypic, archetypical, antitypic, antitypical

787 DISSIMILARITY

<being unlike>

NOUNS 1 **dissimilarity,** unsimilarity; dissimilitude, dissemblance, unresemblance; unlikeness, unsameness; **disparity,** diversity, divergence, gap, contrast, difference; nonuniformity; uncomparability, uncomparableness, incomparability, incomparableness, uncommensurableness, uncommensurability, incommensurableness, incommensurability, no resemblance, no common ground; culture gap; disguise, dissimilation, camouflage, camouflaging, masking; cosmetics; poor imitation, bad likeness, bad copy, botched copy, mere caricature, mere counterfeit

VERBS 2 **not resemble, bear no resemblance,** not look like, not compare with; differ; have little in common, have nothing in common; diverge, deviate

3 disguise, dissimilate, camouflage; do a cosmetic job on; vary

ADJS 4 **dissimilar,** unsimilar, unresembling, unresemblant; **unlike,** unalike, unidentical; disparate, diverse, divergent, contrasting, different; nonuniform; scarcely like, hardly like, a bit different, a mite different; off, a bit on the off side, offbeat; unmatched, odd, counter, out

5 **nothing like,** not a bit alike, not a bit of it, nothing of the sort, nothing of the kind, something else, something else again, different as night from day, quite another thing, cast in a different mold, not the same thing at all; not so you could tell it, not that you would know it, far from it; way off, away off, a mile off, way out, no such thing, no such a thing

6 **uncomparable,** not comparable, not to be compared, incomparable; incommensurable, uncommensurable, uncommensurate, incommensurate; unrelated, extraneous

ADVS 7 **dissimilarly,** differently, with a difference, disparately, contrastingly

788 AGREEMENT

<act of agreeing>

NOUNS 1 **agreement, accord**, accordance; concord, concordance; harmony, cooperation, peace, rapport, concert, consort, consonance, unisonance, unison, union, chorus, oneness; correspondence, coincidence, intersection, overlap, parallelism, symmetry, tally, equivalence; congeniality, compatibility, affinity; conformity, conformance, conformation, uniformity; congruity, congruence, congruency; consistency, self-consistency, coherence; synchronism, sync, timing; assent

2 **understanding,** entente; mutual understanding, cordial understanding, consortium; compact

3 <**general agreement**> consensus, consentaneity, consentaneousness, sense, unanimity; likemindedness, meeting of minds, intersection of minds, confluence of minds, sense of the meeting; family feeling; good vibrations

4 **adjustment, adaptation,** mutual adjustment, **compromise,** coaptation, arbitration, arbitrament; regulation, attunement, harmonization, coordination, accommodation, squaring, integration, assimilation; reconciliation, reconcilement, synchronization; consensus-building, consensus-seeking

5 fitness, **fittedness**, suitability, **appropriateness,** propriety, admissibility; aptness, aptitude, qualification; relevance, felicity, appositeness, applicability

VERBS 6 **agree, accord**, harmonize, concur, have no problem with, go along with, cooperate, correspond, conform, coincide, parallel, intersect, overlap, match, tally, hit, register, lock, interlock, check, square, dovetail, jibe; be consistent, cohere, stand together, hold together, hang together, fall in together, fit together, chime, chime with, chime in with; assent, come to an agreement, be of one mind, be of the same mind, be of like mind, subscribe to, see eye to eye, sing in chorus, have a meeting of the minds, climb on the bandwagon; go together, go with, conform with, be uniform with, square with, sort with, go on all fours with, consist with, register with, answer to, respond to

7 <**make agree**> harmonize, coordinate, bring into line, accord, make uniform, equalize, similarize, assimilate, homologize; pull together; adjust, set, regulate, accommodate, reconcile, synchronize, sync; adapt, fit, tailor, measure, proportion, adjust to, trim to, cut to, gear to, key to; fix, rectify, true, true up, right, set right, make plumb; tune, attune, put in tune

8 **suit, fit,** fit to a T, fit like a glove, qualify, do, serve, answer, be OK, do the job, do the trick, fill the bill, cut the mustard

ADJS 9 **agreeing, in agreement;** in accord, concurring, positive, affirmative, in rapport, in harmony, in accordance, in sync, at one, on all fours, of one mind, of the same mind, of like mind, like-minded, consentient, consentaneous, unanimous, unisonous, unisonant; harmonious, accordant, concordant, consonant; consistent, self-consistent; uniform, coherent, conformable, of a piece, equivalent, coinciding, coincident, corresponding, correspondent; answerable, reconcilable; commensurate, proportionate; congruous, congruent; agreeable, congenial, compatible, cooperating, cooperative, coexisting, coexistent, symbiotic; synchronized, synchronous, synchronic; empathetic

10 **apt,** apposite, appropriate, suitable; applicable, relevant, pertinent, likely, sortable, seasonable, opportune; **fitting,** befitting, suiting, becoming; fit, fitted, qualified, suited, adapted, geared, tailored, dovetailing, meshing; right, just right, well-chosen, pat, happy, felicitous, just what the doctor ordered; to the point, to the purpose, *ad rem* <L>, apropos, on the button, on the money, spot-on

ADVS 11 **in step,** in concert, in unison, in chorus, in line, in conformity, **in keeping,** hand in glove, just right; with it; unanimously, as one, with one voice, harmoniously, concordantly, consonantly, in synchronization, in sync, by consensus; agreeably, congenially, compatibly; fittingly

PREPS 12 **in agreement with**, together with, with, right with, in there with, right along there with; in line with, in keeping with; together on

PHRS 13 that's it, that's the thing, that's just the thing, that's the very thing, that's the idea, that's the ticket; right on; touché

789 DISAGREEMENT

<act of disagreeing>

NOUNS 1 **disagreement, discord,** discordance, discordancy; disaccord, disaccordance, inaccordance; disunity, disunion; disharmony, unharmoniousness; dissonance, dissidence; jarring, clashing; difference, variance, divergence, diversity; disparity, discrepancy, inequality; antagonism, opposition, conflict, controversy, faction, oppugnancy, repugnance, dissension, argumentation; dissent, negation, contradiction; parting of the ways

2 **inconsistency, incongruity,** asymmetry, inconsonance, incoherence; incompatibility, irreconcilability, incommensurability; disproportion, disproportionateness, nonconformity, unconformity, nonconformability, unconformability, heterogeneity, heterodoxy, unorthodoxy, heresy; self-contradiction, paradox, antinomy, oxymoron, ambiguity, ambivalence, equivocality, equivocalness, mixed message, mixed signal

3 **unfitness, inappropriateness,** unsuitability, impropriety; inaptness, inaptitude, inappositeness, irrelevance, irrelevancy, infelicity, uncongeniality, inapplicability, inadmissibility; abnormality, anomaly; maladjustment, misjoining, misjoinder; mismatch, mismatchment; misalliance

4 **misfit, nonconformist,** individualist, inner-directed person, oddball; **freak,** sport, anomaly; naysayer, crosspatch, dissenter; a fish out of water, a square peg in a round hole

VERBS 5 **disagree,** differ, vary, not see eye-to-eye, be at cross-purposes, tangle assholes*, disaccord, conflict, clash, jar, jangle, jostle, collide, square off, cross swords, break, break off; mismatch, mismate, mismarry, misally; part company, split up; dissent, agree to disagree, object, negate, contradict, counter; be out of step, march out of step, hear a different drummer

ADJS 6 **disagreeing,** differing, discordant, disaccordant; dissonant, dissident; inharmonious, unharmonious, disharmonious; discrepant, disproportionate; divergent, variant; at variance, at odds, at war, at daggers drawn, at opposite poles, at loggerheads, at cross-purposes; hostile, antipathetic, antagonistic, repugnant; inaccordant, out of accord, out of whack; jarring, clashing, grating, jangling; contradictory, contrary; disagreeable, cross, cranky, disputatious, ornery, negative, uncongenial, incompatible; immiscible

7 **inappropriate, inapt,** unapt, inapposite, misplaced, irrelevant, malapropos; unsuited, ill-suited; unfitted, ill-fitted; maladjusted, unadapted, ill-adapted; ill-sorted, ill-assorted, ill-chosen; ill-matched, ill-mated, mismatched, mismated, mismarried, misallied; unfit, inept, unqualified; unfitting, unbefitting; unsuitable, improper, unbecoming, unseemly; infelicitous, inapplicable, inadmissible; unseasonable, untimely, ill-timed; out of place, out of line, out of keeping, out of character, out of proportion, out of joint, out of tune, out of time, out of season, out of its element

8 inconsistent, **incongruous,** inconsonant, inconsequent, incoherent, incompatible, irreconcilable; incommensurable, incommensurate; disproportionate, out of proportion, self-contradictory, paradoxical, oxymoronic, absurd; abnormal, anomalous; misfiting; ambivalent, ambiguous

9 **nonconformist,** individualistic, inner-directed, perverse; **unorthodox,** heterodox, heretical

PREPS 10 **in disagreement with,** against, agin, counter to, clean counter to, contrary to, in defiance of, in contempt of, in opposition to; out of line with, not in keeping with

COMBINING FORMS 11 contra-, counter-, dis-, ill-, mal-, mis-

790 EQUALITY

<being equal>

NOUNS 1 **equality, parity,** par, equation, identity; equivalence, equivalency, convertibility, correspondence, parallelism, equipollence, coequality; likeness, levelness, evenness, coextension; balance, poise, equipoise, equilibrium, equiponderance; symmetry, proportion; level playing field; justice, equity, equal rights, gender equality; break-even point

2 **equating,** equation; equalizing, equilibration, evening, evening up; coordination, integration, accommodation, adjustment; even break, fair shake, affirmative action, equal opportunity

3 **the same**; **tie,** draw, standoff, Mexican standoff, wash, dead heat, stalemate, deadlock, impasse, neck-and-neck race, photo finish, even money; tied score, deuce; a distinction without a difference, six of one and half a dozen of the other, Tweedledum and Tweedledee

4 **equal, match,** mate, twin, fellow, like, equivalent, opposite number, counterpart, answer, vis à vis, equipollent, coequal, parallel, ditto; synonym; peer, compeer, colleague, peer group

VERBS 5 **equal, match,** rival, correspond, be even-steven, be tantamount to, be equal to; keep pace with, keep step with, run abreast; amount to, come to, come down to, run to, reach, touch; measure up to, come up to, stack up with, match up with; lie on a level with, balance, parallel, ditto; break even; tie, draw, knot; go shares, go halves, go Dutch

6 **equalize; equate**; even, equal out, equal, even up, even off, square, level, level out, level off, make both ends meet, synchronize; balance, strike a balance, poise, balance out, balance the accounts, balance the books; compensate, make up for, counterpoise; countervail, counterbalance, cancel; coordinate, integrate, proportion; fit, accommodate, adjust

ADJS 7 **equal, equalized,** like, alike, even, level, par, **on a par,** at par, at parity, au pair, commensurate, proportionate, flush; on the same level, on the same plane, on the same footing, on equal footing; on terms of equality, on even terms, on equal terms, on even ground; on a level, on a level playing field, on a footing, in the same boat; square, quits, zero-sum, even-steven; half-and-half, fifty-fifty; nip and tuck, drawn, tied, neck-and-neck, abreast, too close to call, deadlocked, stalemated, knotted

8 **equivalent,** tantamount, equiparant, equipollent, break-even, coequal, coordinate; identical; corresponding, correspondent; convertible, much the same, as broad as long, neither more nor less, all one, all the same, neither here nor there

9 **balanced, equanimous**, poised, apoise, on an even keel; equibalanced, equiponderant, equiponderous

10 **equisized,** equidimensional, equiproportional, equispaced; equiangular, isogonic, isometric; equilateral, equisided; coextensive

ADVS 11 **equally,** correspondingly, proportionately, equivalently, evenly; identically; without distinction, indifferently; to the same degree; as, so; as well; to all intents and purposes, all things being equal; as much as to say

12 to a standoff, to a tie, to a draw

COMBINING FORMS 13 co-, equi-, aequi-, homal-, is-, pari-

791 INEQUALITY

<being unequal>

NOUNS 1 **inequality, disparity,** unevenness, contrariety, difference; irregularity, nonuniformity, heterogeneity; disproportion, asymmetry; unbalance, imbalance, disequilibrium, overbalance, inclination of the balance, overcompensation, tippiness; inadequacy, insufficiency, shortcoming; odds, handicap; injustice, inequity, tilting of the scales, unfair discrimination, second-class citizenship, untouchability; unfair advantage, loaded dice

VERBS 2 **unequalize,** disproportion

3 **unbalance,** disbalance, disequilibrate, overbalance, overcompensate, **throw off balance,** upset, skew, destabilize

ADJS 4 **unequal,** disparate, uneven; irregular; disproportionate, **out of proportion,** skew, skewed, asymmetric, asymmetrical; mismatched, ill-matched, ill-sorted; inadequate, insufficient; at a disadvantage

5 **unbalanced,** ill-balanced, overbalanced, off-balance, tippy, listing, heeling, leaning, canting, top-heavy, off-center; lopsided, slaunchways, cockeyed, skewgee, skygodlin, skew-whiff; unstable, unsteady, tender

ADVS 6 **unequally,** disparately, disproportionately, variously, unevenly; nonuniformly

792 WHOLE

<complete amount, totality>

NOUNS 1 **whole, totality, entirety,** collectivity; complex; integration, embodiment; unity, integrity, wholeness; organic unity, oneness; integer

2 **total, sum,** sum total, sum and substance, **the amount,** whole amount, gross amount, grand total; entity

3 **all, the whole,** the entirety, everything, all the above all of the above, the aggregate, the assemblage, one and all, all and sundry, each and every, complete works; package, set, complement, package deal; the lot, the corpus, all she wrote, the ensemble; be-all, be-all and end-all, beginning and end, alpha and omega, A to Z, A to izzard, the whole range, the whole spectrum, length and breadth, sum and substance; everything from soup to nuts, everything but the kitchen sink; grand design, worldview, big picture

4 <nonformal> **whole bunch,** whole mess, whole caboodle, the kit and caboodle, whole kit and caboodle, whole kit and boodle, whole bit, whole shtick, whole megillah, whole shooting match, whole hog, whole animal, whole deal, whole schmear, **whole shebang,** whole works, the works, the full monty, whole ball of wax, whole show, whole nine yards; soup-to-nuts

5 **wholeness,** totality, completeness, unity, fullness, inclusiveness, exhaustiveness, comprehensiveness; holism, holistic approach, total approach; universality

6 **major part,** best part, better part, most; majority, generality, plurality; **bulk, mass,** body, main body; lion's share; substance, gist, meat, essence, thrust, gravamen

VERBS 7 form a whole, make a whole, constitute a whole; integrate, **unite**, form a unity

8 **total,** amount to, come to, run to, mount up to, add up to, tot, tot up to, tote, tote up to, reckon up to, aggregate to; aggregate, unitize; number, comprise, contain, encompass

ADJS 9 <not partial> **whole, total, entire,** aggregate, gross, all; integral, integrated; one, one and indivisible; inclusive, all-inclusive, exhaustive, comprehensive, omnibus, all-embracing, across-the-board, global; holistic; universal

10 intact, untouched, undamaged, all in one piece, unimpaired, virgin, pristine, unspoiled, pure

11 undivided, uncut, unsevered, unclipped, uncropped, unshorn; undiminished, unreduced, complete; 360-degree

12 **unabridged,** uncondensed, unexpurgated

ADVS 13 <not partially> **wholly, entirely,** all; **totally,** totes, *in toto* <L>, from start to finish, from soup to nuts, from A to Z, from A to izzard, across the board; altogether, all put together, in its entirety; in all, on all counts, in all respects, at large; as a whole, in the aggregate, in the lump, in the gross, in bulk, in the mass, *en masse* <Fr>; collectively, corporately, bodily, in a body, as a body; lock, stock, and barrel; hook, line, and sinker

14 **on the whole,** in the long run, over the long haul, all in all, to all intents and purposes, on balance, by and large, in the main, mainly, mostly, chiefly, substantially, essentially, effectually, for the most part, almost entirely, for all practical purposes, virtually; approximately, nearly, all but

COMBINING FORMS 15 pan-, pant-, panta-, coen-

793 PART

<portion or unit of whole>

NOUNS 1 **part, portion,** fraction; percentage; division; share, parcel, dole, quota, piece, piece of the action; cut, slice, vigorish; section, sector, segment; quarter, quadrant; item, detail, particular; installment; subdivision, subset, subgroup, subspecies; detachment, contingent; focus group; cross-section, sample, random sample, sampling; component, module, constituent, ingredient; adjunct; remainder; minority

2 **<part of writing>** section, front matter, back

matter, prologue, epilogue, foreword, preface, introduction, afterword, text, chapter, verse, article; sentence, clause, phrase, segment, string, constituent, paragraph, passage; number, book, fascicle; sheet, folio, page, signature, gathering

3 **piece, particle, bit,** scrap, bite, fragment, morsel, crumb, shard, potsherd, snatch, snack, snackette, appetizer; cut, cutting, clip, clipping, paring, shaving, rasher, snip, snippet, chip, slice, collop, dollop, scoop; tatter, shred, stitch; splinter, sliver; shiver, smithereen; lump, gob, gobbet, hunk, chunk; stump, butt, end, butt-end, fag-end, tail-end; modicum, moiety; bits and pieces, odds and ends; sound bite, sight bite, outtake

4 **member, organ;** appendage; limb; branch, imp, bough, twig, sprig, spray, switch; runner, tendril; offshoot, ramification, scion, spur; arm, leg, tail; hand; wing, pinion; lobe, lobule, hemisphere; facet, feature, integrant, integral part

5 **dose, portion;** slug, shot, nip, snort, dram; helping

VERBS 6 **separate, apportion**, share, share out, distribute, cut, cut up, rip up, tear up, slice, slice up, divide; analyze

ADJS 7 **partial,** part; **fractional,** sectional, componential, partitive; segmentary, segmental, modular; **fragmentary;** incomplete, open-ended

ADVS 8 **partly, partially,** part, **in part**

9 **piece by piece,** bit by bit, part by part, little by little, inch by inch, foot by foot, drop by drop; **piecemeal**, piecewise, bitwise, inchmeal, by inchmeal; by degrees, by inches; in snatches, in installments, in lots, in small doses, in driblets, in dribs and drabs; in detail

COMBINING FORMS 10 organo-; chir-; ali-, pter-, pterus-, pteryg-

794 COMPLETENESS

<having necessary parts>

NOUNS 1 **completeness, totality;** wholeness, entireness, entirety; unity, integrity, integrality, undividedness, intactness, untouchedness, unbrokenness; solidity, solidarity; thoroughness, exhaustiveness, unstintedness, inclusiveness, comprehensiveness, universality; pervasiveness, ubiquity, omnipresence; universe, cosmos, plenum

2 **fullness,** full; amplitude, plenitude; impletion, repletion, plethora; saturation, saturation point, satiety, congestion

3 **full measure, fill,** full house; max; load, capacity, complement, lading, charge; the whole bit; bumper, brimmer; bellyful, snootful, skinful, mouthful; crush, cram, jam-up

4 **completion,** fulfillment, **consummation**, culmination, perfection, realization, actualization, fruition, accomplishment, topping-off, closure

5 **limit,** end, extremity, extreme, acme, apogee, climax, **maximum**, max, ceiling, peak, summit, pinnacle, crown, top; utmost, uttermost, utmost extent, highest degree, nth degree, nth power, *ne plus ultra* <L>; all, the whole, the whole hog

VERBS 6 **<make whole> complete,** bring to completion, bring to fruition, mature; fill in, fill out, piece out, top off, eke, eke out, round out; make up, make good, replenish, refill; accomplish, fulfill

7 **fill,** charge, load, lade, freight, weight; stuff, wad, pad, pack, crowd, cram, jam, jam-pack, ram in, chock; **fill up,** fill to the brim, brim, top up, top off, fill to overflowing, fill the measure of; supercharge, saturate, satiate, congest; overfill, make burst at the seams, surfeit

8 **<be thorough>** go to all lengths, go all out, go the limit, go the whole way, go the whole hog, cover a lot of ground, make a federal case of, make a big deal of, do up brown, do with a vengeance, see it through, follow up, follow to a conclusion; leave nothing undone, not overlook a bet, use every trick in the book; move heaven and earth, leave no stone unturned; put the finishing touches to

ADJS 9 **complete, whole,** total, global, entire, intact, solid; full, full-fledged, full-dress, full-scale; full-grown, mature, matured, ripe, developed; uncut, unabbreviated, undiminished, unexpurgated

10 **thorough, thoroughgoing,** thorough-paced, exhaustive, intensive, broad-based, wall-to-wall, house-to-house, door-to-door, A-to-Z, comprehensive, all-embracing, all-encompassing, omnibus, radical, sweeping; pervasive, all-pervading, ubiquitous, omnipresent, universal; unmitigated, unqualified, unconditional, unrestricted, unreserved, all-out, balls-out, wholesale, whole-hog; out-and-out, through-and-through, outright, downright, straight; congenital, born, consummate, unalloyed, perfect, veritable, egregious, deep-dyed, dyed-in-the-wool; utter, absolute, total; sheer, clear, clean, pure, plumb, plain, regular

11 **full,** filled, **replete,** plenary, capacity, flush, round; brimful, brimming; chock-full, chock-a-block, chuck-full, cram-full, topful, no room to spar; jam-full, jam-packed, overcrowded; stuffed, overstuffed, packed, crammed; swollen, bulging, bursting, bursting at the seams, ready to burst, full to bursting, fit to bust; as full as a tick, packed like sardines; standing room only (SRO);

saturated, satiated, soaked; fully laden, coming out of one's ears; congested; overfull, surfeited

12 **fraught,** freighted, **laden,** loaded, charged, burdened; heavy-laden; full-laden, full-fraught, full-charged, supercharged

13 **completing,** fulfilling, filling; completive, completory, consummative, consummatory, culminative, perfective; complementary, complemental

ADVS **14** **completely, totally,** globally, entirely, wholly, fully, integrally, roundly, altogether, hundred percent, exhaustively, inclusively, comprehensively, bag and baggage, lock, stock, and barrel; unconditionally, unrestrictedly, unreservedly, with no strings attached; no ifs, ands, or buts; one and all; outright, *tout à fait* <Fr>; thoroughly, inside out; in full, in full measure; to the hilt

15 **absolutely,** perfectly, quite, right, stark, clean, sheer, plumb, plain; irretrievably, unrelievedly, irrevocably

16 **utterly, to the utmost,** all the way, all out, flat out, hammer and tongs and tooth and nail, to the full, to the limit, to the max, mondo, to the backbone, to the marrow, to the nth degree, to the nth power, to the skies, to the top of one's bent, to a fare-thee-well, to a fare-you-well, to beat the band, beat the Dutch, nine ways to Sunday, with a vengeance, all hollow

17 **throughout, all over**, overall, inside and out, through and through; through thick and thin, down to the ground, from the ground up, from the word "go," from the git-go; to the end, to the bitter end, to the death; at full length, *in extenso* <L>, *ad infinitum* <L>; every inch, every whit, every bit; root and branch, head and shoulders, heart and soul; to the brim, to the hilt, neck deep, up to the ears, up to the eyes; in every respect, in all respects, you name it; on all counts, at all points, for good and all

18 from beginning to end, **from start to finish**, from end to end, from first to last, from A to Z, from A to izzard, from soup to nuts, from hell to breakfast, from cover to cover; **from top to bottom**; from top to toe, from head to foot, cap-a-pie; from stem to stern, from clew to earing, fore and aft

COMBINING FORMS **19** hol-, integri-, pan-, per-, tel-, teleut-

795 INCOMPLETENESS

<lacking parts>

NOUNS **1** **incompleteness,** incompletion; deficiency, defectiveness, imperfection, inadequacy; underdevelopment, hypoplasia, immaturity, callowness, arrestment; sketchiness, scrappiness, patchiness; short measure, short weight; lick and a promise

2 <part lacking> **deficiency,** want, **lack,** need, deficit, defect, shortage, shortfall, underage; wantage, outage, ullage, slippage; defalcation, arrearage, default; omission, gap, hiatus, hole, vacuum, break, lacuna, discontinuity, interval

VERBS **3** **lack**, want, want for; fall short; be arrested, underdevelop, undergrow

ADJS **4** **incomplete, uncompleted, deficient**, defective, unfinished, imperfect, unperfected, inadequate; undeveloped, underdeveloped, undergrown, stunted, hypoplastic, immature, callow, infant, arrested, embryonic, wanting, lacking, needing, missing, partial, part, failing; in default, in arrears; in short supply, scanty; short, scant, shy; sketchy, patchy, scrappy; left hanging

5 mutilated, garbled, hashed, mangled, butchered, docked, hacked, lopped, truncated, castrated, **cut short**; abridged

ADVS **6** **incompletely, partially,** by halves, by half measures, in half measures, in installments, in bits and pieces; deficiently, imperfectly, inadequately

COMBINING FORMS **7** semi-, parti-

796 COMPOSITION

<arrangement of parts>

NOUNS **1** **composition,** constitution, **construction,** formation, fabrication, fashioning, shaping, organization; embodiment, incorporation, incarnation; make, makeup, getup, setup; building, buildup, structure, structuring, shaping-up, compiling; assembly, assemblage, putting together, piecing together; synthesis, syneresis; combination; compound; junction; mixture

2 **component, constituent, ingredient,** integrant, makings and fixings, element, factor, part, player, module, part and parcel; appurtenance, adjunct; feature, aspect, specialty, circumstance, detail, item

VERBS **3** **compose, constitute,** construct, fabricate; incorporate, embody, incarnate; form, organize, structure, shape, shape up; enter into, go into, go to make up; make, make up, build, build up, assemble, put together, piece together, compile; consist of, be a feature of, form a part of, combine in, unite in, merge in; consist, be made up of, be constituted of, contain; synthesize; combine; join; mix

ADJS **4** **composed of,** formed of, **made of,** made up of, made out of, compact of, consisting of; composing, comprising, constituting, including, inclusive of, containing, incarnating, embodying, subsuming; contained in, embodied in

5 **component,** constituent, modular, integrant, integral; **formative,** elementary

797 MIXTURE

<proportions of parts>

NOUNS **1** **mixture,** mixing, blending; **admixture,** composition, commixture, immixture, intermixture, mingling, minglement, commingling, comminglement, intermingling, interminglement, interlarding, interlardment; eclecticism, syncretism; pluralism, melting pot, multiculturism, multiculturalism, ethnic diversity, racial diversity, cultural diversity; cultural diffusion; fusion, interfusion, conflation; amalgamation, integration, alloyage, coalescence; merger, combination

2 **imbuement,** impregnation, **infusion,** suffusion, decoction, infiltration, instillment, instillation, permeation, pervasion, interpenetration, penetration; saturation, steeping, soaking, marination

3 **adulteration,** corruption, contamination, denaturalization, pollution, doctoring; fortifying, lacing, spiking; **dilution**, cutting, watering, watering down; debasement, bastardizing

4 **crossbreeding,** crossing, **interbreeding,** miscegenation; **hybridism,** hybridization, mongrelism, mongrelization; intermarriage

5 **compound, mixture, admixture,** intermixture, immixture, commixture, **composite, blend,** meld, composition, confection, concoction, combination, combo, ensemble, marriage; amalgam, alloy; paste, magma; cocktail

6 **hodgepodge,** hotchpotch, hotchpot; **medley, miscellany,** mélange, pastiche, conglomeration, assortment, assemblage, mixed bag, ragbag, grab bag, olio, *olla podrida* <Sp>, scramble, jumble, mingle-mangle, mix, mishmash, mess, can of worms, dog's breakfast, mare's nest, rat's nest, hurrah's nest, hash, patchwork, salad, gallimaufry, salmagundi, sundries, potpourri, stew, gumbo, sauce, slurry, omnium-gatherum, Noah's ark, odds and ends, oddments, all sorts, everything but the kitchen sink, all colors of the rainbow, broad spectrum, what you will

7 <slight admixture> **tinge,** tincture, touch, dash, smack, taint, tinct, tint, trace, vestige, hint, inkling, intimation, soupçon, suspicion, suggestion, whiff, modicum, thought, shade, tempering; sprinkling, seasoning, sauce, spice, infusion

8 **hybrid, crossbreed,** cross, mixed-blood, mixblood, half-breed, half-bred, half blood, half-caste; mongrel, cur; *ladino* <Sp>; mustee, mestee, *mestizo* <Sp>, *mestiza* <Sp feminine>, *métis* <Fr>, *métisse* <Fr feminine>; Eurasian; mulatto, quadroon, quintroon, octoroon; sambo; griffe; zebrule, zebrass, cattalo, mule, hinny, liger, tigon; tangelo, citrange, plumcot; alley cat; kitchen sink

9 **mixer, blender**, beater, agitator, food processor, shaker; cement mixer, eggbeater, churn; homogenizer, colloid mill, emulsifier; crucible, melting pot

VERBS **10** **mix**, admix, commix, immix, **intermix,** mingle, bemingle, commingle, immingle, intermingle, interlace, interweave, intertwine, interlard, intersperse, interleave; syncretize; blend, interblend, stir in; **amalgamate,** integrate, alloy, coalesce, fuse, merge, meld, compound, compose, conflate, concoct; combine; mix up, hash, stir up, scramble, conglomerate, shuffle, jumble, jumble up, mingle-mangle, throw together, toss together, entangle; knead, work; homogenize, emulsify

11 **imbue,** imbrue, **infuse,** suffuse, transfuse, breathe, instill, infiltrate, impregnate, permeate, pervade, penetrate, leaven; tinge, tincture, entincture, temper, color, dye, flavor, season, dredge, besprinkle; saturate, steep, decoct, brew

12 **adulterate,** corrupt, contaminate, debase, infect, denaturalize, pollute, denature, bastardize, tamper with, doctor, doctor up; fortify, spike, pep up, lace; **dilute,** cut, water, water down

13 **hybridize, crossbreed,** cross, interbreed, miscegenate, mongrelize

ADJS **14** **mixed**, mingled, blended, compounded, amalgamated; combined; composite, compound, complex, many-sided, multifaceted, intricate; conglomerate, pluralistic, multiracial, multicultural, multiethnic, multinational, heterogeneous, varied, miscellaneous, medley, motley, dappled, patchy, sundry, divers; promiscuous, indiscriminate, scrambled, jumbled, thrown together; half-and-half, fifty-fifty; amphibious; equivocal, ambiguous, ambivalent, ironic; syncretic, eclectic

15 **hybrid,** mongrel, interbred, crossbred, crossed, cross; half-breed, half-bred, half-blooded, half-caste; fusion, fusiony

16 miscible, mixable, assimilable, integrable

PREPS **17** among, amongst, 'mongst; amid, mid, amidst, midst, in the midst of, in the thick of; with, together with

798 SIMPLICITY

<without multiple, complicated parts>

NOUNS 1 **simplicity,** purity, simpleness, **plainness,** no frills, starkness, severity; unmixedness, monism; unadulteration, unsophistication, unspoiledness, intactness, fundamentality, elementarity, primitiveness, primitivity, primariness, naturalness; singleness, oneness, unity, integrity, homogeneity, uniformity; homeyness, unpretentiousness; unadornment; rusticity, voluntary simplicity

2 **simplification,** streamlining, refinement, purification, distillation; disentanglement, disinvolvement; uncluttering, decluttering, unscrambling, unsnarling, unknotting; stripping, stripping away, stripping down, paring down, narrowing, confining, bracketing; analysis; deconstruction

3 **oversimplification,** oversimplicity, oversimplifying; simplism, reductivism; intellectual childishness, intellectual immaturity, conceptual crudity

VERBS 4 **simplify,** streamline, **reduce,** reduce to essentials, factorize; purify, refine, distill; strip, strip down; narrow, confine, bracket, zero in, home in; oversimplify; analyze

5 **disinvolve,** disintricate, unmix, disembroil, **disentangle,** untangle, unscramble, unsnarl, unknot, untwist, unbraid, unweave, untwine, unwind, uncoil, unthread, unravel, ravel; **unclutter,** declutter, dejunk, clarify, clear up, disambiguate, sort out, get to the core, get to the essence

ADJS 6 **simple, plain,** bare, barebones, no-frills, mere; single, uniform, homogeneous, of a piece; pure, simon-pure, pure and simple; essential, elementary, indivisible, primary, primal, primitive, prime, pristine, irreducible, fundamental, basic, rustic; undifferentiable, undifferentiated, undifferenced, monolithic; austere, chaste, unadorned, uncluttered, spare, stark, severe; homely, homespun, grassroots, back-to-nature, bread-and-butter, down-home, vanilla, plain-vanilla, white-bread; beginning, entry-level; common, garden, everyday; unpretentious; natural

7 **unmixed,** unmingled, unblended, uncombined, uncompounded; unleavened; unadulterated, unspoiled, untouched, intact, virgin, uncorrupted, unsophisticated, unalloyed, untinged, undiluted, unfortified; clear, clarified, purified, refined, distilled, rectified; neat, straight, absolute, sheer, naked, bare

8 **uncomplicated,** uninvolved, incomplex, straightforward

9 **simplified,** streamlined, stripped down

10 **oversimplified,** oversimple; **simplistic,** reductive; intellectually childish, intellectually immature, conceptually crude

ADVS 11 **simply, plainly,** purely; merely, barely; singly, solely, only, alone, exclusively, just, simply and solely

COMBINING FORMS 12 hapl-

799 COMPLEXITY

<having complicated, interrelated parts>

NOUNS 1 **complexity,** complication, involvement, complexness, involution, convolution, tortuousness, Byzantinism, *chinoiserie* <Fr>, tanglement, entanglement, perplexity, **intricacy,** intricateness, ramification, crabbedness, technicality, subtlety

2 **complex,** perplex, tangle, tangled skein, mess, snafu, fuck-up*, ravel, snarl, snarl-up; knot, Gordian knot; maze, meander, Chinese puzzle, labyrinth; webwork, mesh; wilderness, jungle, morass, quagmire; Rube Goldberg contraption, Heath Robinson device <Brit>, wheels within wheels; mare's nest, rat's nest, hurrah's nest, can of worms, snake pit; hard nut to crack, riddle of the Sphinx, squaring the circle

VERBS 3 **complicate,** involve, perplex, ramify; confound, confuse, muddle, mix up, mess up, ball up, bollix up, screw up, foul up, fuck up*, snafu, muck up, louse up, implicate; tangle, entangle, embrangle, snarl, snarl up, ravel, knot, tie in knots

ADJS 4 **complex, complicated,** many-faceted, multifarious, ramified, perplexed, confused, confounded, involved, implicated, crabbed, **intricate,** elaborate, involuted, convoluted, multilayer, multilayered, multilevel; mixed up, balled up, bollixed up, screwed up, loused up, fouled up, fucked up*, snafued, mucked up, messed up; fucked up beyond all recognition*, FUBAR; tangled, entangled, tangly, embrangled, snarled, knotted, matted, twisted, raveled; mazy, daedal, labyrinthine, labyrinthian, meandering; devious, roundabout, deep-laid, Byzantine, subtle

5 **inextricable,** irreducible, unknottable, unsolvable

800 JOINING

<connecting>

NOUNS 1 **joining, junction,** joinder, jointure, connection, union, unification, bond, bonding, connectedness, connectivity, conjunction, conjoining, conjugation, liaison, marriage, hookup, splice, tie, tie-up, tie-in, knotting, entanglement, commerce; merger, merging; symbiosis; combination; conglomeration, aggregation, agglomeration, congeries; coupling, copulation, accouplement, coupledness, bracketing, yoking, pairing, splicing, wedding; linking, linkup, linkage, bridging, concatenation, chaining, articulation, agglutination; meeting, meeting place, meeting point, confluence, convergence, concurrence, concourse, gathering, massing, clustering; communication, intercommunication, intercourse

2 **interconnection,** interface, interjoinder, interlinking, interlocking, interdigitation; interassociation, interaffiliation

3 **fastening, attachment,** affixation, annexation; ligature, ligation, ligating; binding, bonding, gluing, sticking, tying, lashing, splicing, knotting, linking, trussing, girding, hooking, clasping, zipping, buckling, buttoning; **knot** <see list>; adhesive; splice, bond, fastener, Velcro

4 **joint,** join, joining, **juncture,** union, connection, link, connecting link, coupling, accouplement; clinch, embrace; articulation, symphysis; pivot, hinge; knee; elbow; wrist; ankle; knuckle; hip; shoulder; neck, cervix; ball-and-socket joint, pivot joint, hinged joint, gliding joint; toggle joint; connecting rod, tie rod; seam, suture, stitch, closure, mortise and tenon, miter, butt, scarf, dovetail, rabbet, weld; boundary, interface

VERBS 5 **put together, join,** conjoin, unite, unify, bond, connect, associate, league, band, merge, assemble, accumulate; join up, become a part of, associate oneself, enter into, come aboard; gather, mobilize, marshal, mass, amass, collect, conglobulate; combine; couple, pair, accouple, copulate, conjugate, marry, wed, tie the knot, link, link up, build bridges, yoke, knot, splice, tie, chain, bracket, ligate; concatenate, articulate, agglutinate; glue, tape, cement, solder, weld; fix together, lay together, piece together, clap together, tack together, stick together, lump together, roll into one; bridge over, bridge between, span; include, encompass, take in, cover, embrace, comprise

6 **interconnect,** interjoin, interface, mesh, intertie, interassociate, interaffiliate, interlink, interlock, interdigitate

7 **fasten, fix, attach,** affix, annex, put to, set to; graft, engraft; secure, anchor, moor; cement, knit, set, grapple, belay, make fast; clinch, clamp, cramp; tighten, trim, screw up; cinch, cinch up

8 **hook,** hitch; clasp, hasp, clip, snap; button, buckle, zipper; lock, latch; pin, skewer, peg, nail, nail up, tack, staple, toggle, screw, bolt, rivet; sew, stitch; wedge, jam, stick; rabbet, butt, scarf, mortise, miter, dovetail; batten, batten down; cleat; hinge, joint, articulate

9 **bind, tie,** brace, truss, lash, leash, rope, strap, lace, wire, chain; handcuff; splice, bend; gird, girt, belt, girth, girdle, band, cinch; tie up, bind up, do up, batten; wrap, wrap up, bundle; shrink-wrap; bandage, bandage up, swathe, swaddle

10 **yoke,** hitch up, hook up; harness, harness up; halter, bridle; saddle; tether, fetter

11 <**be joined**> **join,** connect, unite, meet, meet up, link up, merge, converge, come together; communicate, intercommunicate, network, interface; knit, grow together; cohere, adhere, hang together, hold together, clinch, embrace

ADJS 12 **joint,** combined, joined, **conjoint,** conjunct, conjugate, corporate, compact, cooperative, cooperating; concurrent, coincident; inclusive, comprehensive; coherent

13 **joined,** united, connected, copulate, coupled, linked, knit, bridged, tight-knit, knitted, bracketed, associated, conjoined, incorporated, integrated, merged, gathered, assembled, accumulated, collected; joined up, on board; allied, leagued, banded together; hand-in-hand, hand-in-glove, intimate, liaising; unseparated, undivided; wedded, matched, married, paired, yoked, mated; tied, bound, knotted, spliced, lashed; yogic

14 **fast, fastened,** fixed, secure, firm, close, tight, set, zipped up; bonded, glued, cemented, taped; jammed, wedged, stuck, frozen, seized, seized up

15 **inseparable,** impartible, indivisible, undividable, indissoluble, inalienable, inseverable, bound up in, bound up with

16 **joining, connecting,** meeting; communicating, intercommunicating; connective, connectional; conjunctive, combinative, combinatorial, copulative, linking, bridging, binding; yogic

17 jointed, articulate

ADVS 18 **jointly,** conjointly, corporately, together; in common, in partnership, mutually, in concord; all together, as one, in unison, in agreement, in harmony; concurrently, at once, in one fell swoop

19 securely, firmly, fast, tight; inseparably, indissolubly

20 **knot**

anchor knot
barrel knot, blood knot
becket knot
Blackwall hitch
bow
bowknot
bowline
bowline knot
builder's knot
butcher's knot
carrick bend
cat's-paw
clinch
clove hitch
constrictor knot
crossing knot
crown knot
cuckold's neck

diamond knot
double hitch
Englishman's tie
eye splice
figure-eight knot
figure-of-eight bend
fisherman's bend
fisherman's knot
flat knot
Flemish knot
French shroud knot
German knot
granny knot
half crown
half hitch
half-Windsor knot
hangman's knot
harness hitch
hawser bend
hawser fastening
heaving-line bend
inside clinch
lanyard knot
long splice
loop knot
magnus hitch
manrope knot
marlinespike hitch
marling hitch
masthead knot
Matthew Walker knot
mesh knot
midshipman's hitch
monkey's fist
netting knot
open hand knot
outside clinch
overhand knot
prolonge knot
reef knot
reeving-line bend
ring hitch, lark's head
ring knot
rolling hitch
rope-yarn knot
round seizing
round turn and half hitch
running bowline
running knot
sennit knot
sheepshank
Shelby knot
short splice
shroud knot
single knot
slide knot
slipknot, nooseknot
square knot
star knot
stevedore's knot
stopper's knot
studding-sail halyard bend
stunner hitch
surgeon's knot
sword knot
tack bend
timber knot, timber hitch
truckman's knot
truelove knot
Turk's-head
wall knot
weaver's knot, weaver's hitch
Windsor knot

801 ANALYSIS

<breaking down into parts>

NOUNS 1 **analysis,** analyzation, breakdown, breaking down, breakup, breaking up; anatomy, anatomizing, dissection; separation, division, subdivision, segmentation, reduction to elements, reduction to parts; chemical analysis, assay, assaying, resolution, titration, docimasy, qualitative analysis, quantitative analysis, volumetric analysis, gravimetric analysis; ultimate analysis, proximate analysis; microanalysis, semimicroanalysis; profiling; racial profiling; DNA profiling

2 **itemization,** enumeration, detailing, breakout, isolation; outlining, schematization, blocking, blocking out; resolution; scansion, parsing

3 **classification, categorization,** sorting, taxonomy, sorting out, sifting, sifting out, grouping, factoring, winnowing, shakeout, pigeonholing, categorizing; weighing, evaluation, gauging, assessment, appraisal, position statement, position paper, judgment; impact statement

4 **outline,** structural outline, **plan,** scheme, schema, chart, flow chart, graph; table, table of contents, index; diagram, block diagram, exploded view, blueprint; catalog, *catalogue raisonné* <Fr>; hierarchy, ontology, taxonomy, drilldown

5 **analyst, analyzer,** examiner; taxonomist

VERBS 6 **analyze, break down,** break up, anatomize, dissect, atomize, unitize; **divide, subdivide,** segment; assay, titrate; separate, make discrete, isolate, reduce, reduce to elements, resolve

7 **itemize,** enumerate, factorize, number, detail, break out; **outline,** schematize, block out, diagram, graph, chart; resolve; scan, parse

8 **classify,** class, **categorize,** catalog, sort, sort out, sift, group, factor, winnow, thrash out; weigh, weigh up, evaluate, judge, gauge, assess, appraise

ADJS 9 **analytical,** analytic; segmental; classificatory, enumerative; schematic

ADVS 10 **analytically,** by parts, by divisions, by sections; by categories, by types

802 SEPARATION

<disconnecting>

NOUNS 1 **separation, disjunction,** severalty, disjointure, disjointing, split-up, splitting-up, demerger, delinkage, disarticulation, disconnection, disconnectedness, discontinuity, incoherence, disengagement, disunion, nonunion, disassociation, segregation; parting, alienation, estrangement, removal, withdrawal, isolation, detachment, sequestration, abstraction; subtraction; divorce, divorcement; division, subdivision, partition, compartmentalization, segmentation, marking off; districting, zoning; dislocation, luxation; separability, partibility, dividableness, divisibility; separatism; separateness, discreteness, singleness, monism, unitariness

2 **severance,** disseverment, disseverance, sunderance, scission, fission, cleavage, dichotomy, parting; cutting, slitting, slashing, splitting, slicing; rending, tearing, ripping, laceration, hacking, chopping, butchering, mutilation; section, resection; surgery

3 **disruption, dissolution,** abruption, cataclasm; revolution; disintegration, breakup, crack-up, shattering, splintering, fragmentizing, fragmentation; bursting, dissilience, dissiliency;

scattering, dispersal, diffusion; stripping, scaling, exfoliation

4 **break,** breakage, breach, burst, rupture, fracture; crack, cleft, fissure, cut, **split,** slit; slash, slice; gap, rift, rent, rip, tear; chip, splinter, scale; dividing line, caesura, solidus

5 **dissection,** analysis, vivisection, resolution, breakdown, diaeresis; anatomy

6 **disassembly, dismantlement,** taking down, taking apart, dismemberment, dismounting; undoing, unbuilding; stripping, stripping down, divestiture, divestment, defoliation, deprivation; disrobing, unclothing, doffing

7 **separator,** sieve, centrifuge, ultracentrifuge; creamer, cream separator; breaker, stripper, mincer; slicer, cutter, microtome; analyzer

VERBS 8 **separate,** divide, disjoin, **disunite**, draw apart, dissociate, disassociate, grow apart, disjoint, disengage, disarticulate, disconnect; uncouple, unyoke; part, cut the knot, divorce, estrange; alienate, segregate, separate off, factor out, sequester, isolate, curtain off, shut off, set apart, set aside, split off, cut off, cut out, cut loose, cut adrift, chop off; withdraw, leave, depart, take one's leave, split; pull out, pull away, pull back, stand apart, stand aside, stand aloof, step aside; subtract; delete; expel, eject, throw off, throw out, cast off, cast out

9 **come apart,** spring apart, fly apart, come unstuck, come unglued, come undone, come apart at the seams, fall to pieces, disintegrate, come to pieces, go to pieces, fall apart, fall apart at the seams, plotz, atomize, unitize, fragmentize, pulverize, break up, bust up, unravel; come off, fall off, peel off, carry away; get loose, give way, start

10 **detach,** remove, disengage, take off, lift off, doff; unfasten, undo, unattach, unfix; free, release, liberate, loose, unloose, unleash, unfetter; unloosen, loosen; cast off, weigh anchor; **unhook,** unhitch, unclasp, unclinch, unbuckle, unbutton, unsnap, unscrew, unpin, unbolt; **untie,** unbind, unknit, unbandage, unlace, unzip, unstrap, unchain; unstick, unglue

11 **sever, dissever,** cut off, cut away, cut loose, shear off, hack through, hack off, ax, amputate; cleave, split, fissure; sunder, cut in two, dichotomize, halve, bisect; cut, incise, carve, slice, pare, prune, trim, trim away, resect, excise; slit, snip, lance, scissor; chop, hew, hack, slash; gash, whittle, butcher; saw, jigsaw; tear, rend, rive, rend asunder

12 break, burst, bust, breach; fracture, rupture; crack, **split**, check, craze, fissure; snap; chip, scale, exfoliate

13 shatter, splinter, shiver, break into pieces, **fragmentize**, break into smithereens; smash, crush, crunch, squash, squish; disrupt, demolish, break up, smash up; scatter, disperse, diffuse; fragment, fission, atomize; pulverize, grind, cut to pieces, mince, make mincemeat of, make hamburger of

14 **tear apart,** rip apart, take apart, pull apart, pick to pieces, rip to pieces, tear to pieces, tear to rags, tear to tatters, shred, rip to shreds; dismember, tear limb from limb, draw and quarter; mangle, lacerate, mutilate, maim; skin, flay, strip, peel, denude; defoliate

15 **disassemble,** take apart, take down, tear down; dismantle, demolish, dismount, unrig

16 **disjoint,** unjoint, unhinge, disarticulate, dislocate, luxate, throw out of joint, unseat

17 **dissect,** analyze, vivisect, anatomize, break down

18 apportion, portion, section, partition, compartmentalize, departmentalize, segment; divide, divide up, divvy, divvy up, parcel, parcel up, parcel out, **split,** split up, cut up, chop up, subdivide; district, zone

19 **part company,** part, **separate,** split up, dispel, disband, scatter, disperse, break up, break it up, go separate ways, diverge

ADJS 20 **separate, distinct,** discrete; unjoined, unconnected, unattached, unaccompanied, unattended, unassociated; apart, asunder, in two; discontinuous, noncontiguous, divergent; isolated, insular, detached, detachable, freestanding, free-floating, autonomous; independent, self-contained, stand-alone; noncohesive, noncohering, incoherent; bipartite, dichotomous, multipartite, multisegmental; subdivided, partitioned, curtained-off, marked-off, compartmentalized, departmentalized, siloed

21 **separated,** disjoined, disjoint, disjointed, disjunct, disconnected, disengaged, detached, disunited, divided, removed, divorced, alienated, estranged, distanced, segregated, sequestered, isolated, cloistered, shut off; scattered, dispersed, helter-skelter; disarticulated, dislocated, luxated, out of joint

22 **unfastened, unbound,** uncaught, unfixed, undone, loose, free, loosened, unloosened, clear; untied, unknit, unleashed, unfettered, unchained, unlaced, unbandaged, unhitched; unstuck, unglued; unclasped, unclinched, unbuckled, unbuttoned, unzipped, unsnapped; unscrewed, unpinned, unbolted; unanchored, adrift, afloat, floating, free-floating; loose-knit

23 **severed,** cut, cleaved, cleft, cloven, riven, hewn, sheared; splintered, shivered, cracked, split, slit, reft; rent, torn; tattered, shredded, in shreds; quartered, dismembered, in pieces

24 broken, busted, burst, ruptured, dissilient; sprung; shattered, broken up, broken to pieces, broken to bits, **fragmentized**, fragmentary, fragmented, in shards, in smithereens

25 **separating,** dividing, parting, distancing; separative, disjunctive

26 **separable,** severable, divisible, alienable, cleavable, partible; fissionable, fissile, scissile; dissoluble, dissolvable

ADVS **27** **separately,** severally, piecemeal, one by one; **apart,** adrift, asunder, in two, in twain; apart from, away from, aside from; abstractly, in the abstract, objectively, impersonally

28 **disjointedly,** unconnectedly, sporadically, spasmodically, discontinuously, by bits and pieces, by fits and starts

29 to pieces, all to pieces, to bits, to smithereens, to splinters, to shards, to tatters, to shreds

803 COHESION

<sticking together>

NOUNS **1** **cohesion,** cohesiveness, coherence, adherence, **adhesion**, sticking, sticking together, cling, clinging, binding, colligation, inseparability; cementation, conglutination, agglutination; concretion, condensation, accretion, solidification, set, congelation, congealment, clotting, coagulation, curdling; conglomeration, conglobation, compaction, agglomeration, consolidation; inspissation, incrassation; clustering, massing, bunching, nodality; colloidality, emulsification

2 consistency, connection, connectedness; junction; continuity, seriality, sequence, sequentialness, consecutiveness, orderliness

3 **tenacity,** tenaciousness, **adhesiveness,** cohesiveness, retention, adherence; tightness, snugness; stickiness, tackiness, gluiness, gumminess, viscidity, consistency, viscosity, glutinosity, mucilaginousness; gelatinousness, jellylikeness, gelatinity; pulpiness; persistence, persistency, stick-to-itiveness, toughness, stubbornness, obstinacy, bulldoggedness, bulldoggishness, bullheadedness

4 <something tenacious> **adhesive,** adherent, adherer; bulldog, barnacle, leech, limpet, remora; burr, cocklebur, clotbur, bramble, brier, prickle, thorn; sticker, bumper sticker, decalcomania, decal; glue, cement, gluten, mucilage, epoxy resin, paste, stickum, gunk; gum; resin, tar; plaster, adhesive plaster, court plaster; putty, size; syrup, molasses, honey; mucus; thickener; pulper; fixative; tape, Scotch tape <tm>, masking tape; Velcro <tm>; Band-Aid <tm>

5 **conglomeration,** consolidation, **conglomerate,** breccia, agglomerate, agglomeration, aggregate, congeries, cluster, bunch, mass, clot; concrete, concretion; compaction

VERBS **6** **cohere, adhere,** stick, cling, cleave, hold; persist, stay, stay put; cling to, freeze to; hang on, hold on; take hold of, clasp, grasp, hug, embrace, clinch; stick together, hang together, hold together; grow to, grow together; solidify, set, conglomerate, agglomerate, conglobate; congeal, coagulate, clabber, clot; cluster, mass, bunch

7 be consistent, connect, connect with, follow; join, link up

8 **hold fast,** stick close, stick like glue, stick like a wet T-shirt, stick like a second skin, hug the figure, mold to the figure; stick closer than a brother, stick like a barnacle, stick like a limpet, stick like a leech, cling like ivy, cling like a burr, hold on like a bulldog, factor in

9 **stick together**, cement, bind, colligate, paste, glue, agglutinate, conglutinate, gum; weld, fuse, solder, braze; gum up

ADJS **10** **cohesive,** cohering, coherent; adhering, sticking, clinging, inseparable, cleaving, holding together; cemented, stuck, agglutinative, agglutinated, agglutinate, conglutinate, conglutinated; concrete, condensed, solidified, set, congealed, clotted, coagulated; conglomerated, conglobate, compacted, consolidated, agglomerated; clustered, massed, bunched, nodal

11 consistent, connected; continuous, serial, uninterrupted, contiguous, sequential, sequent, consecutive; orderly, tight; joined

12 **adhesive,** adherent, stickable, self-adhesive, retentive; tenacious, clingy; sticky, tacky, gluey, gummy, gummous, glutenous, viscid, viscous, viscose, glutinous; inspissate, incrassate; colloidal; gooey, gunky; persistent, tough, stubborn, obstinate, bulldoggish, bulldogged, bulldoggy, bullheaded; stick–to-it-ive

804 NONCOHESION

<not staying together, loosening>

NOUNS **1** **noncohesion,** uncohesiveness, incoherence, inconsistency, discontinuity, **nonadhesion**, unadhesiveness, unadherence, untenacity, immiscibility; separateness, discreteness, aloofness, standoffishness; disjunction, unknitting, unraveling, dismemberment; dislocation; dissolution, chaos, anarchy, disorder, confusion, entropy; scattering, dispersion, dispersal; diffusion; mixum-gatherum

2 **looseness,** slackness, bagginess, **laxness,** laxity, relaxation, floppiness; sloppiness, shakiness, ricketiness

VERBS 3 **loosen, slacken**, relax; slack, slack off; ease, ease off, let up; loose, free, let go, unleash; disjoin, unknit, unravel, dismember, undo, unfasten, unpin; sow confusion, open Pandora's box; unstick, unglue; scatter, disperse, diffuse

ADJS 4 **incoherent,** uncoherent, noncoherent, inconsistent, **uncohesive, unadhesive,** nonadhesive, noncohesive, nonadherent, like grains of sand, untenacious, unconsolidated, tenuous; unjoined, disconnected, unconnected, unraveled, dismembered, gapped, open; disordered, chaotic, anarchic, anomic, confused; discontinuous, broken, detached, discrete, aloof, standoffish

5 **loose, slack,** lax, relaxed, easy, sloppy; shaky, rickety; flapping, streaming; loose-fitting, hanging, drooping, dangling; bagging, baggy

805 COMBINATION

<compounding>

NOUNS 1 **combination,** combine, combo, composition, compounding; **union,** unification, marriage, wedding, coupling, accouplement, linking, linkage, yoking; incorporation, aggregation, agglomeration, conglomeration, congeries; amalgamation, consolidation, assimilation, integration, solidification, encompassment, inclusion, ecumenism; junction; conjunction, conjugation; alliance, affiliation, reaffiliation, association, merger, league, hookup, tie-up; taking, buyout, takeover, leveraged buyout; federation, confederation, confederacy; collaboration; federalization, centralization, cartel; fusion, blend, blending, meld, melding; coalescence, coalition; synthesis, syncretism, syneresis, syncrasy; syndication; conspiracy, cabal, junta; package, package deal; collection; agreement; addition

2 **mixture, compound**

VERBS 3 **combine,** unite, unify, marry, wed, couple, link, yoke, yoke together; incorporate, amalgamate, consolidate, assimilate, integrate, solidify, coalesce, compound, put together, lump together, roll into one, come together, make one, unitize; connect, join; mix; add; merge, meld, blend, stir in, merge into, blend into, meld into, fuse, flux, melt into one, conflate; interfuse, interblend; encompass, include, comprise; take, take over, buy out; synthesize, syncretize; syndicate; reembody

4 **league, ally,** affiliate, associate, consociate; unionize, organize, cement a union; federate, confederate, federalize, centralize; join forces, join with, unite with, join together, come together, join up with, hook up with, tie in with, throw in with, stand up with, be in cahoots, pool one's interests, join fortunes with, stand together, close ranks, make common cause with; marry, wed, couple, yoke, yoke together, link; band together, club together, bunch, bunch up, gang up, gang, club; team with, **team up with**, pair, double up, buddy up, pair off, partner; go in partnership, go in partners; conspire, cabal, put heads together

ADJS 5 **combined, united,** amalgamated, incorporated, consolidated, integrated, assimilated, one, unitary, unitive, unitized, joined, joint, conjoint; conjunctive, combinative, combinatory, connective, conjugate; merged, blended, fused; mixed; synthesized, syncretized, syncretistic, eclectic

6 **leagued,** enleagued, **allied,** affiliated, affiliate, associated, associate, corporate; federated, confederated, federate, confederate; in league, in cahoots, in with; conspiratorial, cabalistic; partners with, in partnership; teamed, coupled, paired, married, wed, wedded, yoked, yoked together, linked, linked up

7 **combining, uniting,** unitive, unitizing, incorporating; merging, blending, fusing; combinative, combinatory; associative; federative, federal; corporative, incorporative, corporational; coalescent, symphystic

806 DISINTEGRATION

<breaking into small parts>

NOUNS 1 **disintegration, decomposition,** dissolution, decay, coming-apart, resolution, disorganization, degradation, breakup, breakdown, fragmentation, atomization; corruption; ruin, ruination, destruction; erosion, corrosion, crumbling, dilapidation, wear, wear and tear, waste, wasting, wasting away, ablation, ravagement, ravages of time; disjunction; incoherence; impairment

2 **dissociation**; electrolysis, catalysis, dialysis, hydrolysis, proteolysis, thermolysis, photolysis, catabolism; catalyst, hydrolyst, hydrolyte; **decay,** fission, splitting, atom smashing

VERBS 3 **disintegrate, decompose, decay,** biodegrade, dissolve, come apart, disorganize, break up, go to rack and ruin, crack up, disjoin, unknit, split, fission, atomize, fall to pieces; erode, corrode, ablate, consume, waste away, molder, molder away, crumble, crumble into dust

4 <chemical terms> dissociate; catalyze, dialyze,

hydrolyze, electrolyze, photolyze; split, fission, atomize

ADJS 5 **disintegrative,** decomposing, disintegrating, disruptive, disjunctive; destructive, ruinous; chaotic; erosive, corrosive, ablative; resolvent, solvent, separative; dilapidated, disintegrated, shacky, worn-out, worn, clapped-out, moldering, ravaged, wrecked, totaled; disintegrable, decomposable, degradable, biodegradable

6 <chemical terms> **dissociative**; catalytic, dialytic, hydrolytic, proteolytic, thermolytic, electrolytic, photolytic; catabolic

COMBINING FORMS 7 -lysis, lyso-, lysi-, -lyte

807 ORDER

<way something is organized>

NOUNS 1 **order, arrangement**; organization; disposition, disposal, deployment, marshaling; prioritization, putting in order; formation, structure, configuration, array, makeup, lineup, setup, layout; system, scheme, schedule; routine, even tenor, standard operating procedure; peace, quiet, quietude, tranquillity; regularity, uniformity; symmetry, proportion, concord, harmony, the music of the spheres, Tao, Dào; chronological order

2 continuity, logical order, serial order, reverse order, ascending order, descending order, alphabetical order, numerical order; degree; **hierarchy,** pecking order, gradation, subordination, superordination, rank, place, position, status; taxonomy, ontology; progression; sequence; category, class

3 **orderliness,** trimness, tidiness, neatness; good shape, good condition, fine fettle, good trim, apple-pie order, a place for everything and everything in its place; discipline, method, methodology, methodicalness, system, systematicness; anality, compulsiveness, compulsive neatness

VERBS 4 **order, arrange**

5 **form, take form,** get in position, take order, take shape, crystallize, shape up; arrange itself, place itself, take its place, fall in, fall into place, drop into place, fall into line, fall into order, fall into rank, take rank; come together, draw up, gather around, rally round; put to rights, whip into shape

ADJS 6 **orderly,** ordered, regular, well-regulated, **well-ordered**, methodical, formal, regular as clockwork, punctilious, uniform, systematic, symmetrical, harmonious; businesslike, routine, steady, normal, habitual, usual, en règle, in hand; arranged; scientific

7 **in order,** in trim, to rights, in apple-pie order; in condition, in good condition, in kilter, in shape, in good shape, in perfect order, in good form, in fine fettle, in good trim, in the pink, in the pink of condition; in repair, in commission, in adjustment, in working order, fixed; up to scratch, up to snuff; on form

8 **tidy,** trim, natty, neat, spruce, sleek, slick, slick as a whistle, smart, trig, dinky, snug, tight, shipshape, shipshape and Bristol fashion; well-kept, well-kempt, well-cared-for, well-groomed; neat as a button, neat as a pin, not a hair out of place

ADVS 9 **methodically, systematically,** regularly, through channels, uniformly, harmoniously, like clockwork

10 **in order,** in turn, in sequence, in succession, **hierarchically**, in series; step by step, by stages

808 ARRANGEMENT

<organizing things>

NOUNS 1 **arrangement, ordering,** structuring, shaping, forming, configurating, configuration, constitution; disposition, disposal, deployment, placement, marshaling, arraying; distribution, collation, collocation, allocation, allotment, apportionment; formation, formulation, form, array; regimentation; syntax; order

2 **organization,** methodization, ordering, planning, charting, codification, regulation, regularization, routinization, normalization, rationalization; adjustment, harmonization, tuning, fine-tuning, tuneup, tinkering; systematization, ordination, coordination

3 **grouping, classification**, categorization, taxonomy; gradation, subordination, superordination, ranking, placement; sorting, sorting out, assortment, sifting, screening, triage, culling, selection, shakeout; placement test

4 **table,** code, digest, index, inventory, census; table of organization; categorization, classification, hierarchy, ontology, taxonomy

5 **arranger, organizer,** coordinator, personal organizer; spreadsheet; sorter, sifter, sieve, riddle, screen, bolter, colander, grate, grating

6 <act of making neat> **cleanup,** red-up; tidy-up, trim-up, police-up

7 **rearrangement, reorganization,** reconstitution, reordering, restructuring, *perestroika* <Russ>, shakeup; redeployment, redisposition, realignment

VERBS 8 **arrange,** order, reduce to order, put in order, get in order, set in order, right, prioritize, put first things first, get one's ducks in a row; put to rights, set to rights, get it together, pull it

together, put in shape, whip into shape, sort out, unsnarl, make sense out of
9 dispose, distribute, fix, place, set out, collocate, allocate, compose, space, marshal, rally, array; align, line, **line up,** form up, range; regiment; allot, apportion, parcel out, deal, deal out
10 **organize,** methodize, systematize, rationalize, regularize, get one's house in order; harmonize, synchronize, tune, tune up; routinize, normalize, standardize; regulate, adjust, coordinate, fix, settle; plan, chart, codify
11 **classify, group,** categorize; grade, gradate, rank, subordinate; **sort,** sort out, assort; separate, divide; collate; sift, size, sieve, screen, bolt, riddle
12 tidy, **tidy up,** neaten, trim, put in trim, trim up, trig up <Brit>, **straighten up,** fix up, clean up, police, police up, groom, spruce, spruce up, clear up, clear the decks
13 **rearrange, reorganize,** reor, reconstitute, **reorder, restructure,** reshuffle, rejigger, tinker, tinker with, tune, tune up, fine-tune; shake up, shake out; redispose, redistribute, reallocate, realign

ADJS 14 **arranged, ordered,** disposed, configured, composed, constituted, fixed, placed, aligned, ranged, arrayed, marshaled, grouped, ranked, graded; organized, methodized, regularized, routinized, normalized, standardized, systematized; regulated, harmonized, synchronized; classified, categorized, sorted, assorted; orderly
15 organizational, formational, structural

COMBINING FORMS 16 tax-, taxi-, -taxia, -taxis

809 CLASSIFICATION

<categorizing things>

NOUNS 1 **classification, categorization,** classing, placement, ranging, pigeonholing, compartmentalizing, sorting, grouping; grading, stratification, ranking, rating; division, subdivision; cataloging, codification, tabulation, rationalization, indexing, filing; **taxonomy,** typology; hierarchy; analysis, arrangement
2 **class, category,** head, order, division, branch, set, group, grouping, bracket, pigeonhole; section, heading, rubric, label, title; subject heading; grade, rank, rating, status, estate, stratum, level, station, position; caste, clan, race, strain, blood, kin, sept; subdivision, subgroup, suborder, subclass, subcategory, subset; hyponym, hypernym, superordinate, subordinate
3 **kind,** sort, ilk, **type,** breed of cat, lot, variety, species, genus, genre, phylum, denomination, designation, description, style, strain, manner, nature, character, persuasion, the likes of; stamp, brand, feather, color, stripe, line, grain, kidney; make, mark, label, shape, cast, form, mold, model; tribe, clan, race, blood, kin, breed; league, realm, domain, sphere
4 **hierarchy,** class structure, power structure, pyramid, establishment, pecking order; natural hierarchy, order of being, chain of being, domain, realm, kingdom, animal kingdom, vegetable kingdom, mineral kingdom; the order of things
5 <**biological classifications**> kingdom; subkingdom, phylum, branch; superclass, class, subclass, superorder, order, suborder, superfamily, family, subfamily, tribe, subtribe, genus, subgenus, series, section, superspecies, species; subspecies, variety, subvariety, scion; biotype, genotype

VERBS 6 **classify,** class, assign, designate; **categorize,** type, put down as, pigeonhole, place, group, arrange, range; order, put in order, rank, rate, grade; sort, assort; distribute; divide, analyze, subdivide, break down; catalog, list, file, tabulate, rationalize, index, alphabetize, digest, codify

ADJS 7 **classificational,** classificatory; **categorical, taxonomic, taxonomical,** typologic, typological; ordinal; divisional, divisionary, subdivisional; typical, typal; special, specific, characteristic, particular, peculiar, denominative, differential, distinctive, defining, varietal
8 **classified,** classed, **cataloged,** pigeonholed, indexed, ordered, sorted, assorted, graded, grouped, ranked, rated, stratified, hierarchic, hierarchical, pyramidal; placed; filed, on file; tabular, indexical

ADVS 9 any kind, any sort, of any description, at all, whatever, whatevs, soever, whatsoever

COMBINING FORMS 10 speci-, specie-, gen-

810 DISORDER

<lack of order, organization>

NOUNS 1 **disorder, disorderliness,** disarrangement, derangement, disarticulation, disjunction, disorganization; discomposure, dishevelment, disarray, upset, disturbance, discomfiture, disconcertedness; irregularity, randomness, turbulence, perturbation, ununiformity, nonuniformity, unsymmetry, nonsymmetry, no rhyme or reason, disproportion, disharmony; indiscriminateness, promiscuity, promiscuousness, haphazardness; butterfly effect; randomicity, vagueness, trendlessness; entropy; disruption, destabilization; incoherence, unintelligibility; untogetherness; disintegration
2 **confusion, chaos,** anarchy, misrule, license, madhouse; Babel, cognitive dissonance;

muddle, morass, mix-up, foul-up, fuck-up*, snafu, screwup, ball-up, balls-up, hoo-ha, fine how-de-do, pretty kettle of fish, pretty piece of business, nice piece of work; kafuffle, kerfuffle

3 **jumble**, scramble, tumble, snarl-up, mess, bloody mess, holy mess, unholy mess, godawful mess, pickle, shemozzle, turmoil, welter, mishmash, hash, helter-skelter, farrago, crazy-quilt, higgledy-piggledy; shambles, tohubohu; clutter, litter, hodgepodge, rat's nest, mare's nest, hurrah's nest; topsy-turviness, arsy-varsiness, hysteron proteron

4 **commotion, hubbub**, Babel, tumult, turmoil, uproar, racket, riot, disturbance, rumpus, ruckus, ruction, disruption, fracas, hassle, shemozzle, shindy, hullabaloo, rampage; ado, to-do, trouble, bother, pother, dustup, stir, fuss, brouhaha, foofaraw, aggro <Brit>; row, brawl, free-for-all, donnybrook, donnybrook fair, broil, embroilment, melee, scramble; helter-skelter, pell-mell, roughhouse, rough-and-tumble

5 **pandemonium**, hell, bedlam, witches' Sabbath, Babel, confusion of tongues; cacophony, din, noise, static, racket

6 slovenliness, slipshodness, carelessness, negligence; untidiness, uneatness, looseness, **messiness**, sloppiness, dowdiness, seediness, shabbiness, tawdriness, chintziness, shoddiness, tackiness, grubbiness, frowziness, blowziness; slatternliness, frumpishness, sluttishness; squalor, squalidness, sordidness, sleaze factor; derangement

7 **slob**, slattern, sloven, frump, sloppy Joe, schlep, schlump; drab, trollop; pig, swine; litterbug

VERBS 8 lapse into disorder, fall into confusion, come apart, come apart at the seams, dissolve into chaos, slacken, come unstuck, come unglued, disintegrate, degenerate, detune, untune

9 **disorder**, disarrange, disorganize, dishevel; confuse, sow confusion, open Pandora's box, muddle, jumble, jumble up, mix up; discompose, upset, destabilize, unsettle, disturb, perturb

10 riot, roister, roil, carouse; create a disturbance, make a commotion, make trouble, cause a stir, cause a commotion, make a to-do, create a riot, cut loose, **run wild**, run riot, run amok, go on a rampage, go berserk

11 <nonformal> kick up a row, kick up a shindy, kick up a fuss, kick up a storm, piss up a storm*, raise the devil, raise the dickens, raise a rumpus, raise a ruckus, raise Cain, **raise hell**, raise sand, raise the roof, whoop it up, hell around, horse around, horse about; carry on, go on, maffick <Brit>; cut up, cut up rough, roughhouse

ADJS 12 **unordered, orderless, disordered**, unorganized, random, entropic, unarranged, ungraded, unsorted, unclassified; untogether; unmethodical, immethodical; unsystematic, systemless, nonsystematic; disjunct, unjoined; disarticulated, incoherent; discontinuous; formless, amorphous, inchoate, shapeless; ununiform, nonuniform, unsymmetrical, nonsymmetrical, disproportionate, misshapen; irregular, haphazard, desultory, erratic, sporadic, spasmodic, fitful, promiscuous, indiscriminate, casual, frivolous, capricious, hit-or-miss, vague, dispersed, wandering, planless, undirected, aimless, straggling, straggly; senseless, meaningless, gratuitous

13 **disorderly, in disorder**, disordered, **disorganized**, disarranged, discomposed, dislocated, deranged, convulsed; upset, disturbed, perturbed, unsettled, discomfited, disconcerted; turbulent, turbid, roily; out of order, out of place, misplaced, shuffled; out of kilter, out of whack, out of gear, out of joint, out of tune, on the fritz, haywire; cockeyed, skewgee, slaunchways, skygodlin, skew-whiff <Brit>, awry, amiss, askew, on the blink

14 disheveled, mussed up, **messed up**, slobby, rumpled, tumbled, ruffled, snarled, snaggy; tousled, tously; uncombed, shaggy, matted; windblown, schlumpy

15 slovenly, slipshod, careless, loose, slack, nonformal, negligent; untidy, unsightly, unneat, slobby, scuzzy, unkempt; **messy**, mussy, sloppy, mungy, gloppy, scraggly, poky, seedy, shabby, shoddy, schlocky, lumpen, chintzy, grubby, frowzy, blowzy, tacky; slatternly, sluttish, frumpish, frumpy, draggletailed, drabbletailed, draggled, bedraggled; down at the heel, out at the heels, out at the elbows, in rags, ragged, raggedy-ass, raggedy, tattered; squalid, sordid; dilapidated, ruinous, beat-up, shacky

16 confused, **chaotic**, anarchic, **muddled**, jumbled, scattered, scatterbrained, helter-skelter, higgledy-piggledy, hugger-mugger, skimble-skamble, in a mess; topsy-turvy, arsy-varsy, upside-down, ass-backwards; mixed up, balled up, bollixed up, screwed up, mucked up, fouled up, fucked up*, snafu; discomposed, discombobulated

ADVS 17 **in disorder, in disarray**, in confusion, Katy bar the door, in a jumble, in a tumble, in a muddle, in a mess; higgledy-piggledy, helter-skelter, hugger-mugger, skimble-skamble, harum-scarum, willy-nilly, all over, all over hell, all over the place, all over the shop

18 **haphazardly, unsystematically**, unmethodically, irregularly, desultorily, erratically, capriciously, promiscuously, indiscriminately, sloppily, carelessly, randomly, fitfully; at intervals, sporadically, spasmodically, by fits, by fits and

starts, in snatches, in spots; every now and then, every once in a while; at random, at haphazard, by chance, hit or miss

19 **chaotically,** anarchically, turbulently, riotously; confusedly, dispersedly, vaguely, wanderingly, aimlessly, planlessly, senselessly

811 DISARRANGEMENT

<bringing into disorder>

NOUNS 1 **disarrangement,** derangement, misarrangement, convulsion, dislocation; disorganization, shuffling; discomposure, disturbance, perturbation, disconcertedness; disorder; insanity

VERBS 2 **disarrange,** derange, misarrange; **disorder,** disorganize, disorient, throw out of order, put out of gear, dislocate, upset the apple-cart, disarray; dishevel, rumple, ruffle; tousle, muss, muss up, mess, mess up; litter, clutter, scatter

3 **confuse,** muddle, **jumble,** confound, garble, tumble, scramble, snarl, tie in knots, fumble, pi; shuffle, riffle; mix up, snarl up, ball up, bollix up, foul up, fuck up*, screw up, muck up, snafu; make a hash of, make a mess of, play hob with; disrupt

4 **discompose,** throw into confusion, upset, unsettle, disturb, trip up, perturb, trouble, distract, throw, throw into a tizzy, throw into a snit, agitate, convulse, embroil; psych, spook, bug; put out, inconvenience

ADJS 5 **disarranged**, confused, disordered

812 CONTINUITY

<uninterrupted order>

NOUNS 1 **continuity,** uninterruption, **uninterruptedness**, uninterrupted course, featurelessness, unrelievedness, monotony, unintermittedness, unbrokenness, uniformity, undifferentiation; fullness, plenitude; seamlessness, jointlessness, gaplessness, smoothness; consecutiveness, successiveness; continuousness, endlessness, ceaselessness, incessancy; constancy, continualness, constant flow; steadiness, steady state, equilibrium, stability

2 **series,** succession, run, **sequence,** consecution, progression, course, gradation; one thing after another; **continuum,** plenum; lineage, descent, filiation; connection, concatenation, catenation, catena, chain, chaining, linkup, articulation, reticulation, nexus; chain reaction, powder train; train, range, rank, file, line, string, thread, queue, row, bank, tier; windrow, swath; single file, Indian file; array; round, cycle, rotation, routine, the daily grind, daily life, recurrence, periodicity, flywheel effect, pendulum; endless chain, Mobius strip, endless round; gamut, spectrum, scale; drone, monotone, hum, buzz

3 **procession,** train, column, line, string, cortège; stream, steady stream; cavalcade, caravan, motorcade; parade, pomp; dress parade; promenade, review, march-past, flyover, flypast <Brit>, funeral; skimmington <Brit>; chain gang, coffel; mule train, pack train; queue, crocodile <Brit>

VERBS 4 **continue,** be **continuous,** not stop, connect, connect up, concatenate, continuate, catenate, join, link, chain, link up, follow up, string together, string, thread, form a series, run on, maintain continuity

5 **align,** line, line up, string out, rank, array, range, arrange, put in a row

6 **line up,** get in line, get on line, queue, queue up, enqueue, make a line, form a line, get in formation, fall in, fall in line, fall into rank, take rank, take one's place

7 **file,** file off; **parade,** go on parade, promenade, march past, fly over, fly past <Brit>

ADJS 8 **continuous,** continued, **continual,** continuing; **uninterrupted,** unintermittent, unintermitted, featureless, unrelieved, monotonous; connected, joined, linked, chained, concatenated, catenated, articulated; unbroken, serried, uniform, homogeneous, homogenized, cloned, clonish, cookie-cutter, undifferentiated, wall-to-wall, back-to-back, seamless, jointless, gapless, smooth, unstopped; unintermitting, unremitting; incessant, constant, steady, stable, ceaseless, unceasing, endless, unending, never-ending, interminable, perpetual, perennial; cyclical, repetitive, recurrent, periodic; straight, running, nonstop; round-the-clock, twenty-four-hour, all-hours; immediate, direct

9 **consecutive, successive,** successional, back-to-back, in order, running; progressive; serial, ordinal, seriate, catenary; sequent, **sequential;** linear, lineal, in-line; chronological

ADVS 10 **continuously,** continually; **uninterruptedly**, unintermittently; without cease, without stopping, with every other breath, without a break, back-to-back, wall-to-wall, unbrokenly, gaplessly, seamlessly, jointlessly, connectedly, together, cumulatively, on end; unceasingly, endlessly, *ad infinitum* <L>, perennially, interminably, again and again, repeatedly, time after time, time and again, time and time again, repetitively, cyclically, monotonously, unrelievedly, week in week out, year in year out, year-round, on and on, at a stretch, on a stretch; round the clock, **all day**, all day long, all the livelong day, twenty-four seven, 24/7, all-hours

11 **consecutively,** progressively, sequentially, successively, **in succession,** one after the other, back-to-back, in turn, turn about, turn and turn about; step by step; running, hand running; serially, in a series; in a line, in a row, in column, in file, in a chain, in single file, in Indian file

813 DISCONTINUITY

<interrupted order>

NOUNS **1** **discontinuity,** discontinuousness, discontinuation, discontinuance, noncontinuance; incoherence, disconnectedness, disconnection, delinkage, decoupling, discreteness, disjunction; nonuniformity; irregularity, **intermittence,** fitfulness; brokenness; nonseriality, nonlinearity, non sequitur; incompleteness; episode, parenthesis; time lag, time warp; broken thread, missing link; digression; breaking up, ghosting

2 **interruption,** suspension, break, fissure, breach, gap, hiatus, lacuna, caesura, crevasse; interval, **pause**, interim, lull, cessation, letup, **intermission**

VERBS **3** **discontinue,** interrupt, break, break off, break up, disjoin, disconnect, ghost; disarrange; intermit; pause; digress

ADJS **4** **discontinuous,** noncontinuous, unsuccessive, incoherent, nonserial, nonlinear, nonsequential, discontinued, disconnected, unconnected, unjoined, delinked, decoupled, broken; nonuniform, irregular; broken off, fragmentary, **interrupted,** suspended; disjunctive, discrete, discretive; intermittent, fitful, stop-and-go, on-again off-again; scrappy, snatchy, spotty, patchy, jagged; choppy, chopped-off, herky-jerky, jerky, spasmodic; episodic, parenthetic

ADVS **5** **discontinuously,** disconnectedly, brokenly, fragmentarily; at intervals; haphazardly, randomly, occasionally, infrequently, now and then, now and again, intermittently, fitfully, by fits and starts, by fits, by snatches, by catches, by jerks, spasmodically, episodically, by skips, skippingly; willy-nilly, here and there, in spots, sporadically, patchily

814 PRECEDENCE

<ordered by importance>

NOUNS **1** **precedence,** precedency, antecedence, antecedency, anteposition, anteriority, precession; the lead, front position, front seat, pole position, first chair; **priority,** preference, urgency; top priority, taking precedence, preemption; prefixation, prothesis; superiority; dominion; precursor; prelude; preliminaries, run-up, walk-up; preceding

VERBS **2** **precede,** antecede, **come first,** come before, go before, go ahead of, go in advance, stand first, stand at the head, head, head up, front, lead, take precedence, have priority, preempt; lead off, kick off, usher in; pilot, lead the way, blaze a trail, spearhead; head the table, sit on the dais; rank, outrank, rate; anticipate, foreshadow

3 <place before> **prefix, preface,** premise, prelude, prologize, preamble, introduce

ADJS **4** **preceding,** precedent, **prior,** antecedent, anterior, precessional, leading; preemptive; preliminary, precursory, prevenient, prefatory, exordial, prelusive, preludial, proemial, preparatory, initiatory, propaedeutic, inaugural; first, foremost, headmost, chief

5 **former,** foregoing, erstwhile, one-time, late, previous; aforesaid, aforementioned, beforementioned, abovementioned, aforenamed, forenamed, forementioned, said, named, same

ADVS **6** before; above, hereinbefore, hereinabove, *supra* <L>, *ante* <L>

815 SEQUENCE

<order for related things>

NOUNS **1** **sequence,** logical sequence, **succession,** successiveness, consecution, consecutiveness, following, coming after, accession; descent, lineage, line, family tree; series, serialization; order, order of succession; priority; progression, procession, rotation; continuity; continuation, prolongation, extension, posteriority; suffixation, subjunction, postposition; subsequence, sequel; cycle, process

VERBS **2** **succeed, follow,** ensue, come after, go after, come next; inherit, take the mantle of, step into the shoes of, step into the place of, take over; segue; tailgate, follow on the heels of, tail

3 <place after> suffix, append, subjoin

ADJS **4** **succeeding, successive,** following, ensuing, sequent, sequential, sequacious, posterior, subsequent, consequent; proximate, next; appendant, suffixed, postpositive, postpositional; serial; progressive; tailgating

816 PRECURSOR

<one that precedes>

NOUNS **1** **precursor, forerunner,** foregoer, vaunt-courier, avant-courier, frontrunner, lead-runner;

pioneer, frontiersman, bushwhacker; scout, pathfinder, explorer, point, point man, trailblazer, trailbreaker, guide; leader, leadoff man, leadoff woman, bellwether, fugleman; herald, announcer, messenger, harbinger, stormy petrel; predecessor, forebear, precedent, antecedent, ancestor; vanguard, avant-garde, avant-gardist, innovator, groundbreaker; prequel

2 curtain raiser, countdown, run-up, walk-up, lead-in, warm-up, kickoff, opening gun, opening shot; opening episode, first episode, prequel; **prelude,** preamble, preface, prologue, foreword, introduction, protasis, proem, proemium, prolegomenon, prolegomena, exordium; prefix, prefixture; frontispiece; **preliminary,** front matter; overture, voluntary, verse; premise, presupposition, postulate, prolepsis; **innovation,** breakthrough, leap

VERBS 3 **go before, pioneer,** blaze the trail, break the trail, trailblaze, break new ground, be in the vanguard; guide; lead, lead the way, show the way; precede; herald, count down, run up, lead in, forerun, usher in, introduce

ADJS 4 **preceding**; preliminary, exploratory, pioneering, trailblazing, path-breaking, door-opening, kickoff, inaugural; advanced, avant-garde, original

817 SEQUEL

<one that follows subsequently>

NOUNS 1 **sequel,** sequela, sequelae, sequelant, sequent, sequitur, consequence; continuation, continuance, **followup,** follow-through, perseverance; caboose; supplement, addendum, appendix, back matter; postfix, suffix; postscript (PS), subscript, postface; postlude, epilogue, conclusion, peroration, codicil; refrain, chorus, coda; envoi, colophon, tag; afterthought, second thought, double take, *arrière-pensée* <Fr>; parting shot, Parthian shot; last words, swan song, dying words, famous last words

2 **afterpart,** afterpiece; wake, trail, train, queue; tail, tailpiece, rear, rear end; tab, tag, trailer

3 **aftermath,** afterclap, afterglow, afterimage, aftereffect, side effect, byproduct, spinoff, aftertaste; aftergrowth, aftercrop; afterbirth, placenta, secundines; afterpain

4 **successor,** replacement, backup, backup man, backup woman, substitute, stand-in; descendant, posterity, heir, inheritor

VERBS 5 **succeed,** follow, come next, come after, come on the heels of; **follow up**, follow through, carry through, take the next step, drop the other shoe

818 BEGINNING

<first part>

NOUNS 1 **beginning,** commencement, **start,** running start, flying start, starting point, square one, outset, outbreak, onset, oncoming, get-go; dawn; creation, foundation, establishment, establishing, institution, origin, origination, setting-up, setting in motion; launching, launch, launch pad, launching pad; alpha, A; opening, rising of the curtain; day one; first crack out of the box, leadoff, kickoff, jumpoff, send-off, start-off, takeoff, blastoff, git-go, the word "go"; fresh start, new departure; opening wedge, leading edge, cutting edge, thin end of the wedge; entry level, bottom rung, bottom of the ladder, low place on the totem pole; daybreak; first home, starter home, first car, first job, first kiss, first date

2 **beginner,** neophyte, tyro; newcomer, new arrival, Johnny-come-lately; entry-level employee, low man on the totem pole; entrant, **novice**, novitiate, probationer, catechumen; recruit, raw recruit, rookie; apprentice, trainee, learner, student; baby, infant, newborn; nestling, fledging; freshman; tenderfoot, greenhorn, greeny, initiate; debutant, deb; **startup,** starter

3 **first,** first ever, prime, primal, primary, **initial,** alpha; initiation, initialization, first move, opening move, gambit, first step, baby step, openers, starters, first lap, first round, first inning, first stage, first leg; breaking-in, warming-up; first blush, first glance, first sight, first impression; early days

4 **origin,** origination, genesis, inception, incipience, incipiency, inchoation; divine creation, creationism, creation science; birth, birthing, bearing, parturition, pregnancy, nascency, nascence, nativity; infancy, babyhood, childhood, youth; freshman year; incunabula, beginnings, cradle; fountainhead, wellspring, source

5 **inauguration,** installation, installment, induction, **introduction,** initiation; inception; setting in motion; embarkation, embarkment, **launch,** launching, floating, flotation, unveiling; debut, first appearance, coming out; opener, preliminary, curtain raiser; maiden speech, inaugural address

6 **basics,** essentials, rudiments, elements, nuts and bolts; principles, principia, first principles, first steps, outlines, primer, hornbook, first reader, grammar, alphabet, ABC's, abecedarium; introduction, induction; groundwork, spacework

VERBS 7 **begin, commence, start;** start up, kick in, click in; start in, start off, start out, set out, set sail, set in, set to, set about, go into action, swing into action, get to, get down to, turn to, fall to, pitch in, dive in, plunge into, head into, go ahead, let her rip, fire off, blast away, take off, jump off, kick off, tee off, blast off, send off, get the show on the road, get the ball rolling, roll it, let it roll

8 **make a beginning,** make a move, **start up,** get going, get off, set forth, set out, launch forth, get off the ground, get underway, set up shop, get in there; set a course, get squared away; make an auspicious beginning, get off to a good start, make a dent; get in on the ground floor; break in, warm up, get one's feet wet, cut one's teeth

9 enter, enter on, enter upon, enter into, **embark on,** take up, go into, have a go at, take a crack at, take a whack at, take a shot at; **debut,** make one's debut

10 **initiate, originate,** create, invent; precede, take the initiative, take the first step, take the lead, pioneer; lead, lead off, lead the way; ahead, head up, stand at the head, stand first; break the ice, take the plunge, break ground, cut the first turf, lay the first stone, get one's feet wet

11 **start up,** inaugurate, institute, found, establish, set up; install, initiate, induct; introduce, broach, bring up, lift up, raise; **launch,** float; christen; usher in, ring in; set on foot, set abroach, set agoing, turn on, kick-start, jump-start, start going, start the ball rolling, get cracking

12 **open,** open up, breach, open the door to, cut the ribbon; open fire

13 **originate,** have origin, be born, take birth, get started, come into the world, become, come to be, get to be, see the light of day, rise, arise, take rise, take its rise, come forth, issue, issue forth, come out, spring up, crop up; burst forth, break out, erupt, irrupt; debut

14 engender, beget, procreate; **give birth to,** bear, birth, bring to birth, bring into the world; father, mother, sire

ADJS 15 **beginning,** initial, initiatory, initiative; incipient, inceptive, introductory, inchoative, inchoate; inaugural, inauguratory; prime, primal, primary, primitive, primeval; original, first, first ever, first of all; aboriginal, autochthonous; elementary, elemental, fundamental, foundational; rudimentary, rudimental, abecedarian; ancestral, primogenital, primogenitary; formative, creative, procreative, inventive; embryonic, in embryo, in the bud, budding, fetal, gestatory, parturient, pregnant, in its infancy; infant, infantile, incunabular; natal, nascent, prenatal, antenatal, neonatal; early; pregame; early-onset

16 **preliminary,** prefatory, preludial, proemial, precursory, preparatory; entry-level, door-opening; prepositive, prefixed

17 **first,** foremost, front, frontal, up-front, head, chief, principal, premier, leading, main, flagship; maiden

ADVS 18 first, firstly, **at first,** first off, first thing, for openers, for starters, as a gambit, up front, in the first place, first and foremost, before everything, *primo* <L>; principally, mainly, chiefly, most of all; primarily, initially; originally, in the beginning, at the start, at first glance, at first blush, at the outset, at the first go-off; from the ground up, from the foundations, from the beginning, from scratch, from the first, from the word "go," from the get-go, *ab origine* <L>, *ab initio* <L>; *ab ovo* <L>

COMBINING FORMS 19 acro-, arche-, eo-, ne-, neo-, proto-; *Ur-* <Ger>

819 MIDDLE

<intermediate part>

NOUNS 1 **middle,** median, midmost, midst; thick, thick of things; center, inside; heart, core, nucleus, kernel, heart of the matter; mean, midpoint; interior; midriff, diaphragm; waist, waistline, zone, girth, tummy, belly girt; equator; diameter; midday, midnight

2 **mid-distance,** middle distance; equidistance; **half,** moiety; **middle ground,** middle of the road, centrism; halfway point, midway, midcourse, midstream, halfway house; bisection; neutral ground, gray area, happy medium; middle way

VERBS 3 seek the middle, bisect, split down the middle; **center,** focus; average; double, fold, middle; straddle, compromise

ADJS 4 **middle,** medial, median, mesial, middling, mediocre, average, medium, mezzo, mean, mid; midmost, middlemost; central, core, nuclear; focal, pivotal; interior, inside, internal; intermediate, intermediary; equidistant, halfway, midway, equatorial, diametral, midfield, midcourse, midstream; midland, mediterranean; midships, amidships; centrist, moderate, middle-of-the-road; center-seeking, centripetal; mid-year

ADVS 5 **midway, halfway, in the middle,** betwixt and between, halfway in the middle; plump in the middle, smack in the middle, slap-dab in the middle, smack-dab in the middle; half-and-half, neither here nor there; medially, mediumly; in the mean; *in medias res* <L>; in the midst, in the thick of; midships, amidships

COMBINING FORMS 6 mid-, medi-, medio-, mes-, meso-, mesio-; intermedi-, intermedio-

820 END

<last part>

NOUNS 1 **end,** end point, **ending**, perfection, be-all and end-all, termination, terminus, terminal, terminating, term, period, expiration, expiry, phaseout, phasedown, discontinuation, closeout, cessation, ceasing, consummation, culmination, close, conclusion, finish, finis, finale, grand finale, the end, finishing, finalizing, finalization, a wrap, quietus, stoppage, windup, payoff, curtain, curtains, all she wrote, fall of the curtain, end of the road, end of the line; decease, taps, death; last, demise, last gasp, last breath, final twitch, last throe, last legs, last hurrah; omega, Ω, izzard, Z; goal, destination, stopping place, resting place, finish line, tape, wire, journey's end, last stop; denouement, catastrophe, apocalypse, final solution, resolution; last words, final words, peroration, swan song, dying words, envoi, coda, epilogue; fate, destiny, last things, eschatology, last trumpet, Gabriel's trumpet, crack of doom, doom; effect; end stage; happy ending, Hollywood ending, walking into the sunset

2 **extremity, extreme;** limit, ultimacy, definitiveness, boundary, farthest bound, jumping-off place, Thule, *Ultima Thule* <L>, pole; tip, point, nib; tail, tail end, butt end, tag, tag end, fag end; bitter end; stub, stump, butt; bottom dollar, bottom of the barrel; business end

3 **close,** closing, cessation; decline, lapse; homestretch, last lap, last round, last inning, ninth inning, last stage; beginning of the end; deadline, closing time; back nine; expiration date

4 **finishing stroke,** ender, **end-all,** quietus, stopper, deathblow, death stroke, *coup de grâce* <Fr>, kiss of death, mortal blow; finisher, clincher, equalizer, crusher, settler; knockout, knockout blow; sockdolager, kayo (KO), kayo punch; final stroke, finishing touch, crowning touch, last dab, last lick, last straw; closer

5 **<conclusions and complimentary closes>** affectionately, always, best, best regards, best wishes, cheers, cordially, cordially yours, ever, ever yours, faithfully, faithfully yours, love, lovingly, most sincerely, namaste, regards, respectfully, respectfully yours, sincerely, sincerely yours, with all good wishes, with all my love, with love, with peace, with regards, yours affectionately, yours faithfully, yours most sincerely, yours respectfully, yours sincerely, yours truly

VERBS 6 **end, terminate,** determine, close, close out, close the books on, phase out, phase down, finish, conclude, finish with, resolve, finish up, wind up; put an end to, put a period to, put paid to <Brit>, put to rest, lay to rest, make an end of, bring to an end, bring to a close, bring to a halt, end up; get it over, get over with, get through with, be done with; bring down the curtain, drop the curtain; put the lid on, fold up, wrap, wrap up, sew up; call off, call all bets off; dispose of, polish off; kibosh, put the kibosh on, put the skids under; stop, cease; perorate; abort; scrap, scratch; kill, extinguish, scrag, waste, take out, zap, give the quietus, put the finisher on, knock in the head, knock out, kayo (KO), shoot down, shoot down in flames, stop dead in one's tracks, wipe out; cancel, delete, expunge, censor, censor out, blank out, erase

7 **come to an end,** draw to a close, expire, die, come to rest, end up, land up; lapse, become void, become extinct, become defunct, run out, run its course, have its time, have it, pass, pass away, die away, wear off, wear away, go out, blow over, be all over, be no more; peter out, fizzle out

8 **complete**, perfect, finish, finish off, finish up, polish of, put the final touches on, put the finishing touches on, finalize

ADJS 9 **ended, at an end,** terminated, concluded, finished, complete, perfected, settled, decided, set at rest; over, all over, all up; all off, all bets off; done, done with, over with, through with, over and done with, through; washed up; all over but the shouting; dead, defunct, extinct; defeated, out of action, disabled; canceled, deleted, expunged, censored, blanked, bleeped, bleeped out; scrapped

10 <nonformal> belly-up, dead meat, **kaput**, shot, done for, shit out of luck* (SOL), scragged, shot down, shot down in flames, down in flames, wasted, zapped, pffft, phut, wiped out, washed up, down-and-out, down the tubes, totaled

11 **ending,** closing, concluding, finishing, culminating, culminative, consummative, consummatory, ultimate, definitive, perfecting, perfective, terminating, crowning, capping, conclusive

12 **final, terminal,** terminating, terminative, determinative, definitive, conclusive; last, last-ditch, last but not least, eventual, farthest, extreme, boundary, border, limbic, limiting, polar, endmost, ultimate; caudal, tail, tail-end; end-stage

ADVS 13 **finally,** in fine; **ultimately,** eventually, as a matter of course; lastly, last, at last, at the end, at the conclusion, at length, at long last; in conclusion, in sum; conclusively, once and for all

14 **to the end,** to the bitter end, all the way, to the last gasp, the last extremity, to a finish, till hell freezes over

PHRS 15 that's all for, that's final, that's that, that's

all she wrote, that buttons it up, that's the end of the matter, so much for that, nuff said, enough said; the subject is closed, the matter is ended, the deal is off

COMBINING FORMS **16** acr-, acro-, tel-, telo-, tele-

821 TIME

<measure of life>

NOUNS **1** **time, duration,** lastingness, continuity, term, while, tide, space; real time; psychological time; biological time; tense; period, time frame, timespan; time warp; cosmic time; kairotic time; quality time; space-time; the past, the present, the future; timebinding; chronology, chronometry, chronography, horology; tempo; time travel; recovery time; time management; time sink; brave new world

2 Time, **Father Time,** Cronus, Kronos

3 tract of time, corridors of time, whirligig of time, hourglass of time, sands of time, ravages of time, noiseless foot of time, scythe of time, time's winged chariot

4 **passage of time,** course of time, lapse of time, progress of time, process of time, succession of time, time flow, flow of time, flux of time, sweep of time, stream of time, tide of time, time and tide, march of time, step of time, flight of time, time's caravan; timeframe, life span

VERBS **5** **elapse,** lapse, **pass,** expire, run its course, run out, go by, pass by; flow, tick away, tick by, run, proceed, advance, roll on, press on, roll by, flit, fly, slip, slide, glide; drag on; continue, last, endure, run on, flow on

6 **spend time, pass time,** put in time, employ time, use time, fill time, occupy time, kill time, consume time, take time, take up time, while away the time; find time, look for time; race against time, buy time, work against time, run out of time, make time stand still; weekend, winter, summer; keep time, mark time, measure time

ADJS **7** **temporal, chronological,** timewise; chronometric, chronographic; durational, durative; lasting, continuous; temporary, pending

ADVS **8** **when,** at which time, what time, whenas, at which moment, at which instant, on which occasion, upon which, whereupon, at which, in which time, at what time, in what period, on what occasion, whenever

9 **at that time,** on that occasion, at the same time as, at the same time, at the moment that, then, concurrently, simultaneously, contemporaneously

10 **in the meantime**, meanwhile; during the time; for the duration; at a stretch

11 **then,** thereat, thereupon, at that time, at that moment, at that instant, in that case, in that instance, on that occasion; again, at another time, at some other time, anon

12 **whenever,** whene'er, whensoever, whensoe'er, at whatever time, at anytime, anytime, no matter when; if ever, once

13 in the year of our Lord, *anno Domini* <L> (AD); in the Common Era, in the Christian Era (CE); *ante Christum* <L> (AC), before Christ (BC); before the Common Era, before the Christian era (BCE); *anno urbis conditae* <L> (AUC); *anno regni* <L> (AR)

PREPS **14** **during,** pending; in the course of, in the process of, in the middle of; in the time of, at the time of, in the age of, in the era of; over, through, throughout, throughout the course of, for the period of; until the conclusion of

15 **until,** till, to, unto, up to, up to the time of

CONJS **16** **when, while,** whilst, the while; during the time, at the time that, at the same time that, at which time, during which time; whereas, as long as, as far as

PHRS **17** time flies, *tempus fugit* <L>, time runs out, time marches on

COMBINING FORMS **18** chron-, chrono-, -chronous

822 TIMELESSNESS

<lasting forever>

NOUNS **1** **timelessness,** neverness, datelessness, eternity; no time, no time at all, running out of time; time out of time, stopping time; everlasting moment; immortality

2 <a time that will never come> Greek calends, Greek kalends, when hell freezes over, the thirtieth of February

ADJS **3** timeless, dateless

ADVS **4** **never,** ne'er, not ever, at no time, on no occasion, not at all; **nevermore;** never in the world, never on earth; not in donkey's years, never in all one's born days, never in my life

5 without date, *sine die* <L>, open, openended

823 INFINITY

<unlimited time, space>

NOUNS **1** **infinity,** infiniteness, infinitude, the all, the be-all and end-all; boundlessness, limitlessness, endlessness; illimitability, interminability, termlessness; immeasurability, unmeasurability, immensity, incalculability, innumerability, incomprehensibility; measurelessness, countlessness, unreckonability, numberlessness; exhaustlessness, inexhaustibility; universality, world without end; all-inclusiveness, all-comprehensiveness; eternity, **perpetuity**, forever; eons; vastness; bottomless pit

VERBS 2 **have no limit**, have no bounds, have no end, know no limit, know no bounds, know no end, be without end, go on and on, go on forever, never cease, never end; last forever, perpetuate

ADJS 3 **infinite,** boundless, **endless,** limitless, termless, shoreless; unbounded, uncircumscribed, unlimited, illimited, infinitely continuous, infinitely extended, stretching everywhere, extending everywhere, without bound, without limit, without end, no end of, no end to to, bottomless; illimitable, interminable, interminate; immeasurable, incalculable, unreckonable, innumerable, incomprehensible, beyond comprehension, unfathomable; measureless, countless, sumless; unmeasured, unmeasurable, immense, unplumbed, untold, unnumbered, without measure, without number; exhaustless, inexhaustible; all-inclusive, all-comprehensive, universal; perpetual, eternal; mind-boggling

ADVS 4 **infinitely,** illimitably, boundlessly, limitlessly, interminably; immeasurably, measurelessly, immensely, incalculably, innumerably, incomprehensibly; endlessly, without end, without limit; *ad infinitum* <L>, **to infinity**; forever, eternally, in perpetuity

824 PERIOD

<portion of time>

NOUNS 1 **period, point,** juncture, stage; interval, lapse of time, time frame, space, span, timespan, stretch, time lag, time gap; time, while, moment, minute, instant, hour, day, season; psychological moment; pregnant moment, fateful moment, fated moment, kairos, moment of truth; spell; period piece

2 <**time periods**> moment, second, millisecond, microsecond, nanosecond; minute, New York minute; hour, man-hour; day, sun; weekday; week; workweek, office hours; fortnight; month, moon, lunation; calendar month, lunar month; quarter; semester, trimester, term, session, academic year, midyear; year, annum, twelvemonth; common year, regular year, intercalary year, leap year, bissextile year, defective year, perfect year, abundant year; solar year, lunar year, sidereal year; fiscal year; calendar year; century year; quinquennium, lustrum, luster; decade, decennium, decennary; century; millennium; academic calendar; business day, business cycle; daylight saving time; dog year; half day; run time, running time; **calendar** <see list>; **geological time period** <see list>

3 **term,** time, duration, **tenure;** spell; time slot

4 **age, generation,** time, day, date, cycle; eon, aeon; Platonic year, great year, *annus magnus, annus mirabilis* <L>

5 **era, epoch, age;** Common Era; Golden Age, Silver Age; Ice Age, glacial epoch; Stone Age, Bronze Age, Iron Age, steel Age; Middle Ages, Dark Ages; Era of Good Feeling; Jacksonian Age; Reconstruction Era, Gilded Age <1870s and 1880s>; Gay Nineties, Naughty Nineties, Mauve Decade, Gilded Age <1890s>; Roaring Twenties, Golden Twenties, Mad Decade, Age of the Red-Hot Mamas, Jazz Age, Flapper Era <1920s>; Depression Era; New Deal Era; Prohibition Era, industrial age

6 <modern age> Technological Age, Automobile Age, Air Age, Jet Age, Supersonic Age, Atomic Age, Electronic Age, Computer Age, Space Age, Age of Anxiety, Age of Aquarius

7 **calendars**

Abyssinian
Aztec
Babylonian
Buddhist
Chinese
church, ecclesiastical
Egyptian
Episcopalian liturgical
French Revolutionary, Revolutionary
Greek
Greek Orthodox
Gregorian
Hebrew
Hindu, Hinduist
Inca
Indian
Islamic, Moslem, Mohammedan
Jewish
Julian
lunar
lunisolar
Mayan
Mexican
Newgate
Orthodox Christian
perpetual
Roman
Roman Catholic
Runic
Sikhist, Sikh
solar
Western

8 **geological time periods**

Algonkian
Anthropocene
Archean
Archeozoic
Cambrian
Carboniferous
Cenozoic
Comanchean
Cretaceous
Devonian
Eocene
Glacial
Holocene, Recent Epoch
Jurassic
Lower Cretaceous
Lower Tertiary
Mesozoic
Miocene
Mississippian
Oligocene
Ordovician
Paleocene
Paleozoic
Pennsylvanian
Permian
Pleistocene
Pliocene
Precambrian
Proterozoic
Quaternary
Silurian
Tertiary
Triassic
Upper Cretaceous
Upper Tertiary

825 SPELL
<portion of time for job, duty>

NOUNS 1 **spell,** fit, stretch, go

2 **turn, bout,** round, inning, innings <Brit>, time, time at bat, place, say, whack, go; opportunity, chance; relief, spell; one's turn, one's move, one's say

3 **shift,** work shift, **tour,** tour of duty, stint, bit, watch, trick, time, turn, relay, spell of work, turn of work; day shift, night shift, late shift, swing shift, graveyard shift, dogwatch, anchor watch; lobster trick, lobster tour, sunrise watch; split shift, split schedule; flextime, flexitime; halftime, part-time, full-time; overtime; crime watch

4 **term,** time; **tenure,** continuous tenure, tenure in office; enlistment, hitch, tour; prison term, stretch; fiscal year; biorhythm, circadian rhythm, biological clock, body clock

VERBS 5 **take one's turn,** have a go; take turns, alternate, turn and turn about; time off, spell, spell off, relieve, cover, fill in for, take over for; put in one's time, work one's shift; stand one's watch, keep a watch; have one's innings <Brit>; do a stint; hold office, have tenure, have tenure of appointment; enlist, sign up; reenlist, re-up; do a hitch, do a tour, do a tour of duty; serve time, do time

826 INTERIM
<intermediate period>

NOUNS 1 **interim,** interval, interlude, intermission, pause, break, **timeout,** recess, coffee break, halftime, halftime intermission, interruption; lull, quiet spell, resting point, point of repose, plateau, letup, relief, vacation, holiday, time off, off-time; downtime; respite; interval <Brit>, entr'acte; *intermezzo* <Ital>; interregnum; armrest

2 **meantime, meanwhile,** while, the while

VERBS 3 **intervene,** interlude, interval; **pause,** break, recess, declare a recess; call a halt, call a break, call an intermission; call time, call timeout; take five, take ten, take a break

ADJS 4 **interim,** temporary, tentative, provisional, provisory

ADVS 5 **meanwhile, meantime,** in the meanwhile, in the meantime, in the interim, *ad interim* <L>; between acts, between halves, between periods, betweentimes, between now and then; till then, until then; in the intervening time, during the interval, at the same time, for the nonce, for a time, for a season

827 DURATION
<time something exists>

NOUNS 1 durability, endurance, **duration,** durableness, **lastingness,** perenniality, abidingness, long-lastingness, perdurability; continuance, perseverance, maintenance, steadfastness, constancy, stability, persistence, permanence, standing, long standing; longevity, long-livedness; antiquity, age; survival, survivability, viability, defiance of time, defeat of time; service life, serviceable life, useful life, shelf life, mean life; perpetuity

2 **protraction, prolongation,** continuation, extension, lengthening, drawing-out, stretching-out, dragging-out, spinning-out, lingering; perpetuation; procrastination

3 **length of time,** distance of time, vista of time, desert of time; corridor of time, tunnel of time; running time, run time

4 **long time,** long while, long; age, ages, aeon, century, eternity, years, years on end, time immemorial, coon's age, donkey's years, month of Sundays, right smart spell

5 **lifetime, life,** life's duration, life expectancy, lifespan, expectation of life, period of existence, all the days of one's life; **generation, age;** all one's born days, all one's natural life

VERBS 6 **endure, last,** last out, bide, abide, dwell, perdure, continue, run, extend, go on, carry on, hold on, keep on, stay on, run on, stay the course, go the distance, go through with, grind on, slog on, grind away, plug away; live, live on, continue to be, subsist, exist, tarry; keep one's head above water; persist, persevere; hang in, hang in there, hang tough; maintain, sustain, remain, stay, keep, hold, stand, prevail, last long, hold out; survive, defy time, defeat time; live to fight another day; perennate; live through; wear, wear well; stand the test of time

7 linger on, **linger,** tarry, go on, go on and on, wear on, crawl, creep, drag, **drag on,** drag along, drag its slow length along, drag a lengthening chain

8 **outlast, outstay,** last out, outwear, outlive, survive

9 **protract, prolong,** continue, extend, lengthen, lengthen out, draw out, spin out, drag out, stretch out; linger on, dwell on; dawdle, procrastinate, temporize, drag one's feet

ADJS 10 durable, perdurable, **lasting, enduring,** perduring, abiding, continuing, remaining, staying, stable, persisting, persistent, perennial; inveterate, agelong; steadfast, constant, intransient, immutable, unfading, evergreen, sempervirent, permanent, long-lasting, long-standing, of long duration, of long standing, diuturnal; long-term; long-lived, tough, hardy, vital, longevous, longeval; ancient, aged, antique; macrobiotic; chronic; perpetual

11 **protracted, prolonged**, extended, lengthened; long, overlong, time-consuming, interminable, marathon, lasting, lingering, languishing; long-continued, long-continuing, long-pending; drawn-out, stretched-out, dragged-out, spun-out, long-drawn, long-drawn-out; long-winded, prolix, verbose

12 daylong, nightlong, weeklong, monthlong, yearlong

13 lifelong, livelong, lifetime, for life

ADVS **14** **for a long time,** long, for long, interminably, unendingly, undyingly, persistently, protractedly, enduringly; for ever so long, for many a long day, for life, for a lifetime, for an age, for ages, for a coon's age, for a dog's age, for a month of Sundays, for donkey's years, forever and a day, forever and ever, for years on end, for days on end; all the year round, all the day long, the livelong day, as the day is long; morning, noon, and night; hour after hour, day after day, month after month, year after year; day in day out, month in month out, year in year out; till hell freezes over, till you're blue in the face, till the cows come home, till shrimps learn to whistle, till doomsday, from now till doomsday, from here to eternity, till the end of time; since time began, from way back, long ago, long since, time out of mind, time immemorial

828 TRANSIENCE

<short duration>

NOUNS **1** **transience,** transiency, transientness, impermanence, impermanency, **transitoriness**, changeableness, rootlessness, mutability, instability, temporariness, fleetingness, momentariness; finitude; ephemerality, ephemeralness, short duration; evanescence, volatility, fugacity, short-livedness; mortality, death, perishability, corruptibility, caducity; expedience, ad hoc, ad hockery, ad hocism, adhocracy; fugaciousness; one-hit wonder

2 **brevity, briefness,** shortness; swiftness, fleetness

3 **short time,** little while, little, instant, moment, mo, small space, span, spurt, short spell; no time, less than no time; bit, little bit, a breath, the wink of an eye, pair of winks; two shakes, two shakes of a lamb's tail, half a mo; just a second

4 **transient,** transient guest, boarder, temporary lodger; sojourner; passer, passerby; wanderer; **vagabond,** drifter, derelict, homeless person, bag person, tramp, hobo, bum; caller, guest, visitor

5 ephemeron, **ephemera**, ephemeral; ephemerid, ephemeris, ephemerides <pl>; mayfly; bubble, smoke; nine days' wonder, flash in the pan, passing fancy; snows of yesteryear; shooting star, meteor; ship that passes in the night

VERBS **6** **<be transient>** flit, fly, fleet; pass, pass away, vanish, evaporate, dissolve, evanesce, disappear, fade, melt, sink; fade like a shadow, vanish like a dream, vanish into thin air, burst like a bubble, go up in smoke, melt like snow

ADJS **7** **transient, transitory,** transitive; **fleeting;** temporary, temporal; **impermanent,** unenduring, undurable, nondurable, nonpermanent; frail, brittle, fragile, insubstantial; changeable, mutable, unstable, inconstant; capricious, fickle, impulsive, impetuous; short-lived, ephemeral, fly-by-night, evanescent, volatile, momentary; deciduous; passing, flitting, flying, fading, dying; fugitive, fugacious; perishable, mortal, corruptible; here today and gone tomorrow; expedient, ad hoc

8 **brief, short,** short-time, quick, brisk, swift, fleet, speedy, short and sweet; meteoric, cometary, flashing, flickering; short-term, short-termed, near-term

ADVS **9** **temporarily,** for the moment, for the time, *pro tempore* <L>, pro tem, for the nonce, for the time being, for a time, awhile

10 **transiently,** impermanently, evanescently, transitorily, changeably, mutably, ephemerally, **fleetingly**, flittingly, flickeringly, briefly, shortly, swiftly, quickly, for a little while, for a short time; momentarily, for a moment; trampy, in an instant

829 PERPETUITY

<endless duration>

NOUNS **1** **perpetuity,** perpetualness; **eternity,** eternalness, sempiternity, infinite duration; everness, foreverness, everlastingness, permanence, ever-duringness, duration, perdurability, indestructibility; constancy, stability, immutability, continuance, perseverance, continualness, perennialness, perenniality, ceaselessness, unceasingness, incessancy; timelessness; endlessness, never-endingness, interminability; infinity; coeternity

2 **forever**, an eternity, endless time, time without end

3 **immortality, eternal life**, deathlessness, imperishability, undyingness, incorruptibility, incorruption, athanasy, athanasia, life everlasting; eternal youth, fountain of youth

4 **perpetuation**, preservation, eternalization, immortalization; eternal re-creation, eternal return, eternal recurrence; steady-state universe

VERBS 5 **perpetuate,** preserve, preserve from oblivion, keep fresh, keep alive, perennialize, eternalize, eternize, **immortalize;** monumentalize; freeze, embalm

6 last forever, endure forever, **go on forever,** go on and on, live forever, have no end, have no limits, have no bounds, never cease, never end, never die, never pass

ADJS 7 **perpetual, everlasting,** everliving, ever-being, ever-abiding, ever-during, ever-durable, permanent, perdurable, indestructible; **eternal,** sempiternal, eterne, infinite, aeonian, eonian; dateless, ageless, timeless, immemorial; endless, unending, never-ending, without end, interminable, nonterminous, nonterminating; continual, continuous, steady, constant, ceaseless, nonstop, unceasing, never-ceasing, incessant, unremitting, unintermitting, uninterrupted; coeternal

8 **perennial,** indeciduous, **evergreen,** sempervirent, ever-new, ever-young; ever-blooming, ever-bearing

9 **immortal,** everlasting, deathless, undying, never-dying, imperishable, incorruptible, amaranthine; fadeless, unfading, never-fading, ever-fresh; frozen, embalmed

ADVS 10 **perpetually,** in perpetuity, everlastingly, eternally, permanently, perennially, perdurably, indestructibly, constantly, continually, steadily, ceaselessly, unceasingly, never-ceasingly, incessantly, never-endingly, **endlessly**, unendingly, interminably, without end, world without end, time without end; **infinitely,** *ad infinitum* <L>

11 **always,** all along, all the time, all the while, at all times; ever and always, invariably, without exception, never otherwise

12 **forever,** forevermore, for ever and ever, forever and aye; forever and a day, now and forever; ever, evermore, ever and anon, ever and again; aye, for aye; for good, for keeps, for good and all, for all time; throughout the ages, from age to age, in all ages; to the end of time, till time stops, till time runs out, to the crack of doom, to the last trumpet, till doomsday; till you're blue in the face, till hell freezes over, till the cows come home

13 **for life,** for all one's natural life, for the term of one's days, while life endures, while one draws breath, in all one's born days; from the cradle to the grave, from the womb to the tomb; **till death,** till death do us part

830 INSTANTANEOUSNESS

<extremely brief duration>

NOUNS 1 **instantaneousness, instantaneity,** momentariness, momentaneousness, immediateness, immediacy, near-simultaneity, near-simultaneousness; instant gratification; simultaneity

2 **suddenness,** abruptness, **precipitateness,** precipitance, precipitancy; unexpectedness, unanticipation, inexpectation

3 **instant, moment,** second, sec, split second, millisecond, microsecond, nanosecond, half a second, half a mo, minute, trice, twinkle, twinkling, twinkling of an eye, twinkle of an eye, twink, wink, bat of an eye, **flash,** crack, tick, stroke, coup, breath, twitch; two shakes of a lamb's tail, two shakes, shake, half a shake, **jiffy**, jiff, half a jiffy; one-touch

ADJS 4 **instantaneous,** instant, momentary, momentaneous, **immediate,** presto, quick as thought, quick as lightning; lightninglike, lightning-swift; nearly simultaneous; simultaneous; split-second; urgent, on-the-spot; fast-food, convenience-food; ready-to-wear, off-the-rack

5 **sudden, abrupt**, precipitant, **precipitate,** precipitous; hasty, headlong, impulsive, impetuous; speedy, swift, quick; unexpected, unanticipated, unpredicted, unforeseen, unlooked-for; surprising, startling, electrifying, shocking, nerve-shattering

ADVS 6 **instantly,** instanter, momentaneously, momentarily, momently, **instantaneously**, immediately, right off the bat; on the instant, on the dot, on the nail; one-touch

7 quickly, **in an instant**, in a trice, in a second, in a moment, in a mo, half a mo, in a bit, in a little bit, in a jiff, in a jiffy, in half a jiffy, in a flash, in a wink, in a twink, in a twinkling, in the twinkling of an eye, as quick as a wink, as quick as greased lightning, in two shakes, in a shake, in half a shake, in two shakes of a lamb's tail, before you can say Jack Robinson; in no time, in less than no time, in nothing flat, in short order; at the drop of a hat, like a shot, like a shot out of hell; with the speed of light

8 **at once,** at once and on the spot, then and there, now, right now, right away, right off, straightway, straightaway, forthwith, this minute, this very minute, without delay, without the least delay, in a hurry, *pronto* <Sp>, *subito* <Ital>; simultaneously, at the same instant, in the same breath; all at once, all together, at one time, at a stroke, at one stroke, at a blow, at one blow, at one swoop, at one fell swoop; at one jump

9 **suddenly,** sudden, of a sudden, on a sudden, all of a sudden, all at once; abruptly, sharp; **precipitously**, precipitately, precipitantly, impulsively, impetuously, hastily; dash; smack,

bang, slap, plop, plunk, plump, pop; unexpectedly, out of a clear blue sky, when least expected, before you know it; on short notice, without notice, without warning, without further ado, unawares, surprisingly, startlingly, like a thunderbolt, like a thunderclap, like a flash, like a bolt from the blue; no sooner said than done, bada-bing, bada bing bada boom

831 EVENT

<occasion or happening>

NOUNS 1 **event,** eventuality, eventuation, effect, issue, outcome, result, aftermath, consequence; realization, materialization, coming to be, coming to pass, incidence; contingency, contingent; accident

2 event, **occurrence, incident,** episode, experience, adventure, hap, **happening**, happenstance, phenomenon, fact, matter of fact, reality, particular, circumstance, occasion, turn of events; nonevent, pseudo-event, media event, media happening, photo opportunity; what's happening

3 **affair, concern,** matter, thing, concernment, interest, business, job, transaction, proceeding, doing; current affairs, current events; cause célèbre, matter of moment

4 **affairs, concerns, matters,** circumstances, relations, dealings, proceedings, doings, goings-on; course of events, run of events, run of things, the way of things, the way things go, what happens, current of events, march of events; the world, life, the times; order of the day; conditions, state of affairs, environing phenomena, ambient phenomena, state of things, condition of things

VERBS 5 **occur, happen**, hap, eventuate, **take place,** go down, go on, **transpire,** be realized, come, come off, come about, come true, come to pass, pass, pass off, go off, fall, befall, betide; be found, be met with

6 turn up, **show up**, **come along,** come one's way, cross one's path, come into being, come into existence, chance, crop up, spring up, pop up, arise, come forth, come on, draw on, appear, approach, materialize, present itself, be destined for one

7 turn out, result

8 **experience,** have, know, feel, taste; encounter, meet, meet with, meet up with, run up against; undergo, go through, pass through, be subjected to, come under, be exposed to, stand under, labor under, endure, suffer, sustain, pay, spend

ADJS 9 **happening, occurring,** current, actual, passing, taking place, on, going on, ongoing, prevalent, prevailing, that is, that applies, in the wind, afloat, afoot, underway, in hand, on foot, ado, doing; incidental, circumstantial, accompanying; accidental; occasional; resultant; eventuating

10 **eventful,** momentous, stirring, bustling, full of incident; phenomenal

11 eventual, **coming,** final, last, ultimate; contingent, collateral, secondary, indirect

ADVS 12 **eventually,** ultimately, finally, in the end, after all is said and done, in the long run, over the long haul; in the course of things, in the natural way of things, as things go, as times go, as the world goes, as the tree falls, the way the cookie crumbles, as things turn out, as it may be, as it may happen, as it may turn out, as luck will have it, as fate will have it

CONJS 13 in the event that, if, in case, if it should happen that, just in case, in any case, in either case, in the contingency that, in case that; provided

832 MEASUREMENT OF TIME

<time-keeping system>

NOUNS 1 **chronology,** timekeeping, timing, clocking, horology, **chronometry,** horometry, chronoscopy, chronography; watch-making, clock-making; scheduling, calendar-making; **dating,** carbon-14 dating, radiocarbon dating, absolute dating, dendrochronology

2 **time of day,** time, the time, the exact time; time of night; hour, minute; stroke of the hour, time signal, bell

3 standard time, civil time, zone time, slow time; mean time, solar time, mean solar time, sidereal time, apparent time, local time; military time, 24-hour clock, 12-hour clock; universal time, Greenwich time, Greenwich mean time (GMT); Eastern time, Eastern Standard Time (EST); Central Standard Time (CST); Mountain time, Mountain Standard Time (MST); Pacific time, Pacific Standard Time (PST); Atlantic time; Alaska time, Yukon time; daylight saving time (DST); fast time, summer time <Brit>; **time zone**

4 **date,** point of time, time, day; postdate, antedate; datemark; date line, International Date Line; calends, nones, ides; name day, saint's day; red-letter day, anniversary; Monday, Tuesday, Wednesday, hump day, Thursday, Friday, Saturday, Sunday

5 epact, annual epact, monthly epact, menstrual epact

6 **timepiece,** timekeeper, timer, chronometer, ship's watch; horologe, horologium; **clock,** Big Ben, ticker, **watch,** turnip; hourglass, sundial;

watch movement, clock movement, clockworks, watchworks; time stamp

7 **almanac,** The Old Farmer's Almanac, Nautical Almanac, Poor Richard's Almanac, World Almanac

8 **calendar,** calends; calendar stone, chronogram; almanac, astronomical calendar, ephemeris; perpetual calendar; Chinese calendar, church calendar, ecclesiastical calendar, Cotsworth calendar, Gregorian calendar, Hebrew calendar, Jewish calendar, Hindu calendar, international fixed calendar, Julian calendar, Muslim calendar, Revolutionary calendar, Roman calendar, ordo calendar

9 **chronicle,** chronology, register, registry, record; annals, journal, diary; time sheet, time book, log, daybook; timecard, time ticket, clock card, check sheet; datebook; date slip; **timetable,** schedule, timeline, time schedule, time chart; time scale; time study, motion study, time and motion study

10 **chronologist,** chronologer, chronographer, horologist, horologer; watchmaker, clockmaker; timekeeper, timer; chronicler, annalist, diarist, historian, historiographer; calendar maker, calendarist

VERBS 11 **time,** fix the time, set the time, mark the time; **keep time,** mark time, measure time, beat time; clock; watch the clock; set the alarm; synchronize

12 **punch the clock,** punch in, punch out, time in, time out; ring in, ring out; clock in, clock out; check in, check out; check off

13 **date,** be dated, date at, date from, date back, bear a date of, bear the date of, carry a date; fix the date, set the date, make a date; **predate,** backdate, antedate; **postdate**; update, bring up to date; datemark; date-stamp; dateline

14 chronologize, chronicle, calendar, intercalate

ADJS 15 **chronologic, chronological**, temporal, timekeeping; chronometric, chronometrical, chronoscopic, chronographic, chronographical, chronogrammatic, chronogrammatical, horologic, horological, horometric, horometrical, metronomic, metronomical, calendric, calendrical, intercalary, intercalated; dated, backdated; annalistic, diaristic; calendarial

ADVS 16 **o'clock,** of the clock, by the clock; half past, half, half after <Brit>; a quarter of, a quarter to, a quarter past, a quarter after

833 ANACHRONISM

<error in time placement>

NOUNS 1 **anachronism,** chronological error, historical error, **mistiming,** misdating, misdate, postdating, antedating; parachronism, metachronism, prochronism; prolepsis, anticipation; earliness, lateness, tardiness, unpunctuality; datedness

VERBS 2 **mistime, misdate;** antedate, foredate, postdate; lag

ADJS 3 **anachronous**, anachronistical, **anachronistic,** parachronistic, metachronistic, prochronistic, unhistorical, unchronological; **mistimed, misdated;** antedated, foredated, postdated; ahead of time, beforehand, early; behind time, behindhand, late, unpunctual, tardy; overdue, past due; unseasonable, out of season; dated, out-of-date

834 PREVIOUSNESS

<previous time>

NOUNS 1 **previousness,** earliness, **antecedence**, antecedency, priority, anteriority, precedence, precedency, precession; previous state, prior state, earlier state; preexistence; anticipation, predating, antedating; antedate; past time

2 **antecedent**, precedent, premise; forerunner, precursor, ancestor

VERBS 3 **be prior,** be before, be early, be earlier, come on the scene, appear earlier, precede, antecede, forerun, come before, go before, set a precedent; herald, usher in, proclaim, announce; anticipate, antedate, predate; **preexist**

ADJS 4 **previous, prior,** early, earlier, former, fore, prime, first, preceding, foregoing, above, anterior, anticipatory, antecedent; **preexistent;** older, elder, senior

5 prewar, antebellum, before the war; prerevolutionary; premundane, antemundane; prelapsarian, before the Fall; antediluvian, before the Flood; protohistoric, prehistoric; precultural; pre-Aryan; pre-Christian; premillenarian, premillennial; anteclassical, preclassical, pre-Roman, pre-Renaissance, pre-Romantic, pre-Victorian

ADVS 6 **previously,** priorly, hitherto, heretofore, thitherto, theretofore; before, early, earlier, ere, erenow, ere then; or ever; already, yet; before all; formerly

PREPS 7 **prior to, previous to, before,** in advance of, in anticipation of, in preparation for

COMBINING FORMS 8 ante-, anti-, fore-, pre-, pro-, prot-, proto-, proter-, protero-, supra-

835 SUBSEQUENCE

<later time>

NOUNS 1 **subsequence,** posteriority, succession, **ensuing,** following, sequence, coming after, supervenience, supervention; lateness; afterlife, next life; remainder, hangover; postdating; postdate; future time

2 sequel, followup, sequelae, aftermath; **consequence,** effect; posterity, offspring, descendant, heir, inheritor; successor; replacement, line, lineage, dynasty, family

VERBS 3 **come after,** follow after, go after, follow, follow on, follow upon, succeed, replace, take the place of, displace, overtake, supervene; ensue, issue, emanate, attend, result; follow up, trail, track, come close on, tread on the heels of, follow hard upon, dog the footsteps of; step into the shoes of, fill the shoes of, don the mantle of, assume the robe of

ADJS 4 **subsequent, after,** later, after-the-fact, *post factum, ex post facto* <L>, posterior, following, **succeeding,** successive, sequent, lineal, consecutive, ensuing, attendant; junior, cadet, puisne, younger

5 **posthumous,** after death; postprandial, postcibal, postcenal, after-dinner; postwar, *postbellum* <L>, after the war; postdiluvian, postdiluvial, after the flood, postlapsarian, after the Fall, post-industrial, postmodern, post-millennial

ADVS 6 **subsequently, after,** afterwards, after that, after all, later, next, since; thereafter, thereon, thereupon, therewith, then; in the process of time, in the course of time, as things worked out, in the sequel; at a subsequent time, at a later time, in the aftermath; *ex post facto* <L>; hard on the heels of, on the heels of

7 after which, on which, upon which, whereupon, whereon, whereat, whereto, whereunto, wherewith, wherefore, on, upon; hereinafter

PREPS 8 after, following, subsequent to, later than, past, beyond, behind; below, farther down, farther along

COMBINING FORMS 9 ante-, anti-, fore-, pre-, pro-, prot-, proto-, proter-, protero-, supra-; epi-, eph-, infra-, meta-, post-

836 SIMULTANEITY

<*occurring at the same time*>

NOUNS 1 **simultaneity, simultaneousness,** coincidence, co-occurrence, concurrence, concurrency, concomitance, concomitancy; **coexistence;** contemporaneousness, contemporaneity, coetaneousness, coetaneity, coevalness, coevalneity; unison; synchronism, synchronization, sync; isochronism; accompaniment, agreement

2 **contemporary,** coeval, concomitant, compeer; age group, peer group

3 **tie,** dead heat, draw, wash

VERBS 4 **coincide,** co-occur, concur; coexist; coextend; **synchronize,** isochronize, put in phase, be in phase, be in time, keep time, time; contemporize; accompany, agree, match, go along with, go hand in hand, keep pace with, keep in step; sync

ADJS 5 **simultaneous, concurrent,** co-occurring, coinstantaneous, concomitant; **tied,** neck-and-neck; coexistent, coexisting; **contemporaneous,** contemporary, coetaneous, coeval; coterminous, conterminous; unison, unisonous; photo-finish; isochronous, isochronal; coeternal; accompanying, collateral; agreeing

6 **synchronous,** synchronized, synchronic, synchronal, **in sync**, isochronal, isochronous; in time, in step, in tempo, in phase, with the beat, on the beat

ADVS 7 **simultaneously,** concurrently, coinstantaneously; together, all together, at the same time, at one and the same time, as one, as one man, in concert with, in chorus, with one voice, in unison, in a chorus, in the same breath; at one time, at a clip; synchronously, synchronically, isochronously, in phase, in sync, with the beat, on the beat, on the downbeat

837 THE PAST

<*earlier time*>

NOUNS 1 **the past,** past, foretime, former times, past times, times past, water under the bridge, days gone by, times gone by, bygone times, bygone days, bygones, yesterday, yesteryear; recent past, just yesterday, only yesterday; history, past history; dead past, dead hand of the past; the years that are past, the irrevocable past

2 **olden days,** old times, olden times, early times, old days, the olden time, times of old, days of old, days of yore, times of yore, yore, yoretime, foretime, eld, good old times, good old days, the way it was, glory days, lang syne, auld lang syne <Scot>, the long ago, time out of mind, days beyond recall; the old story, the same old story

3 **antiquity**, ancient times, time immemorial, ancient history, prehistory, protohistory, remote age, remote time, remote past, far past, dim pat, **distant past,** distance of time, past age, way back when; geological past, ice age; ancientness

4 memory, **remembrance,** recollection, reminiscence, fond remembrance, retrospection, retrospective, musing on the past, looking back, reprise; remembrance of things past; reliving, reexperiencing; revival; youth

5 <grammatical terms> past tense, preterit, perfect

tense, past perfect tense, pluperfect, historical present tense, past progressive tense, past participle; aorist; perfective aspect; preterition

VERBS **6** **pass, be past**, be a thing of the past, be history, elapse, lapse, slip by, slip away, be gone, fade, fade away, be dead and gone, be all over, have run its course, have run out, have had its day; pass into history; disappear; die

ADJS **7** **past,** gone, by, gone-by, **bygone,** gone glimmering, bypast, ago, over, departed, passed, passed away, elapsed, lapsed, vanished, faded, no more, lost forever, long gone, irrecoverable, never to return, not coming back; dead, dead as a dodo, expired, extinct, dead and buried, defunct, deceased; run out, blown over, finished, forgotten, wound up; passé, obsolete, has-been, dated, antique, antiquated

8 reminiscent, **retrospective, nostalgic,** remembered, recollected; relived, reexperienced; restored, revived; retro; diachronic

9 <grammatical terms> past, preterit, preteritive, pluperfect, past perfect; aorist, aoristic; perfective

10 **former,** past, fore, previous, late, recent, once, onetime, sometime, erstwhile, then, quondam; obsolescent; retired, emeritus, superannuated; prior; ancient, immemorial, early, primitive, primeval, prehistoric; old, **olden**

11 **foregoing,** aforegoing, preceding; last, latter

12 **back,** backward, into the past; early; retrospective, retro, retroactive, *ex post facto* <L>, *a priori* <L>

ADVS **13** **formerly,** previously, priorly; earlier, before, before now, erenow, erst, whilom, erewhile, hitherto, heretofore, thitherto, aforetime, beforetime, in the past, in times past; then; yesterday, only yesterday, recently; historically, prehistorically, in historic times, in prehistoric times

14 **once,** once upon a time, one day, one fine morning, time was

15 ago, since, gone by; back, back when; backward, into the past; **retrospectively,** reminiscently, retroactively

16 **long ago,** long since, a long while ago, a long time ago, some time ago, some time since, some time back, a way back, away back, ages ago, years ago, donkey's years ago; in times past, in times gone by, in the old days, in the good old days; anciently, of old, of yore, in ancient times, in olden times, in the olden times, in days of yore, early, in the memory of man, time out of mind

17 since, ever since, until now; since long ago, **long since,** from way back, since days of yore, ages ago, from time immemorial, from time out of mind, aeons ago, since the world was made, since the world was young, since time began, since the year one, since Hector was a pup, since God knows when

COMBINING FORMS **18** archae-, archaeo-, archeo-; pale-, paleo-, praeter-, preter-, retro-; -ed, y-

838 THE PRESENT

<now time>

NOUNS **1** **the present,** presentness, present time, the here and now; **now,** the present juncture, the present occasion, the present moment, the present hour, the present minute, this instant, this second, this moment, the present day, the time; the present age; today, this day, this day and age; this point, this stage, this hour, nowadays, the now, the way things are, the nonce, the time being; the times, our times, these days, modern times; contemporaneousness, contemporaneity, nowness, actuality, topicality; newness, modernity; the Now Generation, the me generation; historical present; present tense, present participle

ADJS **2** **present, immediate,** latest, current, running, extant, existent, existing, actual, topical, being, that is, as is, that be; present-day, present-time, present-age, modern, modern-day; contemporary, contemporaneous; up-to-date, plugged-in, up-to-the-minute, fresh, with it, new

ADVS **3** **now, at present,** at this point, at this juncture, at this stage, at this stage of the game, on the present occasion, at this time, at this moment, at this instant, at the present time; today, this day, in these days, in this day and age, in our time, nowadays; this night, tonight; here, hereat, here and now, even now, but now, just now, as of now, as things are; on the spot; for the nonce, for the time being; for this occasion; in the moment

4 until now, hitherto, till now, thitherto, hereunto, heretofore, until this time, by this time, **up to now,** up to the present, up to this time, to this day, to the present moment, to this very instant, **so far,** thus far, as yet, to date, yet, already, still, now as previously

COMBINING FORMS **5** ne-, neo-, nov-, novo-; cen-, ceno-, caen-, caeno-, -cene

839 THE FUTURE

<time to come>

NOUNS **1** **the future,** future, futurity, what is to come, imminence, subsequence, eventuality, hereafter, aftertime, afteryears, time to come, years to come; futurism, futuristics; **tomorrow,** the morrow, the morning after, *mañana* <Sp>;

immediate future, near future, time just ahead, immediate prospect, offing, next period; distant future, remote future, deep future, far future, long run, long term; by-and-by, the sweet by-and-by; time ahead, course ahead, prospect, outlook, anticipation, expectation, project, probability, prediction, extrapolation, forward look, foresight, prevision, prevenience, envisionment, envisagement, prophecy, divination, clairvoyance, crystal ball; determinism; future tense, future perfect; the womb of time

2 destiny, **fate,** doom, karma, kismet, what bodes, what looms, what is fated, what is destined, what is written, what is in the books; the Fates, the hereafter, the great hereafter, a better place, Paradise, Heaven, Elysian fields, Happy Isles, the Land of Youth, Valhalla; Hades, the Underworld, Hell, Gehenna; the afterworld, the otherworld, the next world, the world to come, life beyond the grave, world beyond the grave, the beyond, the great beyond, the unknown, the great unknown, the grave, abode of the dead, eternal home; **afterlife,** postexistence, future state, life to come, life after death

3 **doomsday,** doom, day of doom, day of reckoning, crack of doom, trumpet of doom; Judgment Day, Day of Judgment, the Judgment, second coming; eschatology, last things, last days

4 **futurity;** ultimateness, eventuality, finality

5 advent, coming, **approach of time,** time drawing on

VERBS 6 **come,** come on, approach, near, draw on, draw near; be to come; be fated, be destined, be doomed, be in the books, be in the cards; **loom,** threaten, await, stare one in the face, be imminent; lie ahead, lie in one's course, lie just around the corner; predict, foresee, envision, envisage, see ahead, previse, foretell, prophesy; anticipate, expect, hope, hope for, look for, look forward to, project, plot, plan, scheme, think ahead, extrapolate, take the long view

7 **live on,** postexist, survive, get by, get through, make it

ADJS 8 **future,** later, hereafter; coming, **forthcoming,** imminent, approaching, nearing, close at hand, waiting in the wings, nigh, prospective; eventual, ultimate, to-be, to come; projected, plotted, planned, looked-for, hoped-for, desired, emergent, predicted, prophesied, foreseen, anticipated, anticipatory, previsional, prevenient, envisioned, envisaged, probable, extrapolated; determined, fatal, fatidic, fated, destinal, destined, doomed; eschatological; futuristic; next-day

ADVS 9 **in the future,** in aftertime, afterward, afterwards, later, at a later time, after a time, after a while, anon; by and by, in the sweet by-and-by; tomorrow, *mañana* <Sp>, the day after tomorrow; *proximo* <L>, prox, in the near future, in the immediate future, just around the corner, imminently, soon, before long; probably, predictably, hopefully; fatally, by destiny, by necessity

10 in future, **hereafter,** hereinafter, thereafter, henceforth, henceforward, henceforwards, thence, thenceforth, thenceforward, thenceforwards, over the long haul, over the short haul, from this time forward, from this day on, from this day forward, from this point, from this time, from that time, from then on, from here on, from now on, from now on in, from here in, from here out, from this moment on

11 **in time,** in due time, in due season, in due course, all in good time, in the fullness of time, in God's good time, in the course of time, in the process of time, eventually, ultimately, **in the long run**

12 **sometime, someday,** some of these days, one of these days, some fine day, some fine morning, one fine day, one fine morning, some sweet day, sometime or other, somewhen, sooner or later, when all is said and done

PREPS 13 **about to,** at the point of, on the point of, on the eve of, on the brink of, on the edge of, on the verge of, near to, close upon, in the act of

840 IMMINENCE

<happening soon>

NOUNS 1 **imminence, imminency,** impendence, impendency, forthcomingness; **forthcoming,** coming, approach, loom; immediate future, near future; futurity

VERBS 2 **be imminent, impend**, overhang, hang over, lie over, **loom,** hang over one's head, hover, threaten, menace, lower; brew, gather; come on, draw on, draw near, draw nigh, rush up on one, forthcome, approach, loom up, near, be on the horizon, be in the offing, be just around the corner, await, face, confront, stare one in the face, be in store, breathe down one's neck, be about to be borning

ADJS 3 **imminent, impending,** impendent, next-day, overhanging, hanging over one's head, waiting, lurking, threatening, looming, lowering, menacing, lying in ambush; brewing, gathering, preparing; coming, forthcoming, upcoming, to come, about to be, about to happen, going to happen, approaching, nearing, looming up, looming in the distance; near, close, immediate, instant, soon to be, at hand, near at hand, close at hand; in the offing, on the horizon, in prospect, already in sight, just around the corner, in view, in one's eye, in store, in reserve, in the wind, in the womb of time; on the lap of the gods, in the cards; that will be, that is to be; future

ADVS 4 **imminently,** impendingly; anytime, anytime now, any moment, any second, any minute, any hour, any day; to be expected, as may be expected, as may be

CONJS 5 on the point of, **on the verge of,** on the eve of

841 NEWNESS

<coming into existence recently>

NOUNS 1 **newness,** freshness, maidenhood, dewiness, pristineness, mint condition, new-mintedness, newbornness, virginity, intactness, greenness, immaturity, rawness, callowness, brand-newness; presentness, nowness; **recentness,** recency, lateness; novelty, gloss of novelty, newfangledness, newfangleness; originality; uncommonness, unusualness, strangeness, unfamiliarity

2 **novelty, innovation,** neology, neologism, newfangled device, newfangled contraption, neoism, neonism, new wrinkle, latest wrinkle, the last word, the latest thing, *dernier cri* <Fr>; what's happening, what's in, the in thing, where it's at; new ball game; new look, latest fashion, latest fad; advance guard, vanguard, avant-garde; neophilia, neophiliac; startup

3 **modernity,** modernness; modernism; modernization, updating; state of the art; postmodernism, space age

4 **modern,** modern man; modernist; modernizer; neologist, neoterist, neology, neologism, neoterism, neoteric; modern generation, new generation; neonate, fledgling, stripling, neophyte, new man, upstart, *arriviste* <Fr>, *nouveau riche* <Fr>, parvenu; Young Turk, bright young man, comer; trendsetter; new kid on the block

VERBS 5 **innovate, invent,** make from scratch, make from the ground up, coin, new-mint, mint, inaugurate, neologize, neoterize; renew, renovate; give a new lease on life

6 **modernize,** streamline; update, bring up to date, keep current, stay current, move with the times

ADJS 7 **new,** young, fresh, fresh as a daisy, fresh as the morning dew; unused, firsthand, original; untried, untouched, unhandled, unhandseled, untrodden, unbeaten; virgin, virginal, intact, maiden, maidenly; green, vernal; dewy, pristine, ever-new, sempervirent, evergreen; immature, undeveloped, raw, callow, fledgling, unfledged, nestling; neological, neologistic, neophytic

8 **fresh,** additional, further, other, another; renewed

9 **brand-new,** new-made, new-built, new-wrought, new-shaped, new-mown, new-minted, new-coined, uncirculated, in mint condition, mint, new-begotten, new-grown, new-laid; newfound; newborn, neonatal, new-fledged; new-model, late-model, like new, factory-new, factory-fresh, oven-fresh, in its original carton

10 <nonformal> fire-new, brand-spanking new, spanking, spanking new; just out; hot, hottest, hot off the griddle, hot off the press; newfangled, newfangle, green

11 **novel, original,** unique, different; strange, unusual, uncommon; unfamiliar, unheard-of; first, first ever

12 **recent,** late, newly come, of yesterday; latter, later

13 **modern, contemporary,** present-day, present-time, twentieth-century, latter-day, space-age, neoteric, now, topical, newfashioned, fashionable, modish, mod, *à la mode* <Fr>, up-to-date, up-to-datish, up-to-the-minute, in, abreast of the times; advanced, progressive, forward-looking, modernizing, avant-garde; ultramodern, ultra-ultra, ahead of its time, far out, way-out, modernistic, modernized, streamlined; postmodern, trendy, faddish

14 state-of-the-art, **newest, latest,** the very latest, up-to-the-minute, last, most recent, newest of the new, new-fashioned; farthest out

ADVS 15 **newly,** freshly, new, anew, once more, from the ground up, from scratch, *ab ovo* <L>, afresh, again; as new

16 now, recently, **lately,** latterly, **of late,** not long ago, a short time ago, the other day, only yesterday; just now, right now; neoterically

842 OLDNESS

<existing a long time>

NOUNS 1 **oldness,** age, eld, hoary eld; elderliness, seniority, senior citizenship, senility, **old age**; ancientness, antiquity, dust of ages, cobwebs of antiquity; venerableness, eldership, primogeniture, great age, hoary age, the ancient and honorable; old order, old style, *ancien régime* <Fr>; primitiveness, primordialism, primordiality, aboriginality; atavism; old guard

2 **tradition, custom,** immemorial usage, immemorial wisdom; ancient wisdom, ways of the fathers; traditionalism, traditionality; oral tradition; myth, mythology, legend, lore, folklore, folktale, folk motif, folk history; racial memory, archetypal myth, archetypal image, archetype; collective unconscious; hive mind; *Spiritus Mundi* <L>; urban myth

3 **antiquation,** superannuation, staleness, disuse; **old-fashionedness**, unfashionableness, out-of-dateness; old-fogyishness, fogyishness, stuffiness, stodginess, fuddy-duddiness

4 **antiquarianism;** classicism, medievalism, Pre-Raphaelitism, nostalgia for the past, longing for the past; archaeology; Greek archaeology, Roman archaeology, Assyriology, Egyptology, Sumerology, Mayan archaeology, Aztec archaeology; archaeogeology, archaeoastronomy; crisis archeology, industrial archeology, underwater archeology, marine archeology, paleology, epigraphy, paleontology, human paleontology, paleethnology, paleonanthropology, paleoethnography; paleozoology, paleornithology, prehistoric anthropology; fossil hunting; dating method

5 **antiquarian,** antiquary; dryasdust; archaeologist; classicist, medievalist, Pre-Raphaelite; antique dealer, antique collector, antique-car collector; archaist; fossil hunter

6 **antiquity, antique,** archaism; relic, relic of the past; remains, survival, vestige, ruin, ruins; old thing, oldie, golden oldie; monument; fossil, index fossil, zone fossil, trace fossil, fossil record; petrification, petrified wood, petrified forest; artifact, artefact, eolith, mezzolith, microlith, neolith, paleolith, plateaulith; cave painting, petroglyph; ancient manuscript; museum piece

7 **ancient,** person of old, old Homo, **prehistoric man** <see list>, **prehistoric animal** <see list>; preadamite, antediluvian; anthropoid, humanoid, primate, fossil man, protohuman, prehuman, missing link, apeman, hominid; primitive, aboriginal, aborigine, bushman, autochthon; caveman, cave dweller, troglodyte; bog man, bog body, Lindow man; Stone Age man, Bronze Age man, Iron Age man

8 <**old person**> back number; pop, pops, dad, dodo, old dodo; fossil, antique, relic; mossback, longhair, square, mid-Victorian, antediluvian; old liner, old believer, conservative, hard-shell, traditionalist, reactionary; has-been; fogy, old fogy, regular old fogy, fud, fuddy-duddy, eld; granny, old woman, matriarch; old man, patriarch, elder, old-timer, Methuselah

VERBS **9** **age,** grow old, grow whiskers, have whiskers; **antiquate,** fossilize, date, superannuate, outdate; obsolesce, go out of use, go out of style, molder, fust, rust, fade, perish; lose currency, lose novelty; become obsolete, become extinct; belong to the past, be a thing of the past; deteriorate, crumble

ADJS **10** **old, age-old,** olden, old-time, old-timey; **ancient,** antique, archaic, venerable, hoary; of old, of yore; dateless, timeless, ageless; immemorial, old as Methuselah, old as Adam, old as God, old as history, old as time, old as the hills, out of the Ark; elderly

11 **primitive,** prime, primeval, primogenial, primordial, pristine; atavistic; aboriginal, autochthonous; ancestral, patriarchal; **prehistoric,** protohistoric, preglacial, preadamite, antepatriarchal; prehuman, protohuman, humanoid; archetypal

12 **traditional;** mythological, heroic; legendary, unwritten, oral, handed down; true-blue, tried and true; prescriptive, customary, conventional, understood, admitted, recognized, acknowledged, received; hallowed, time-honored, immemorial; venerable, hoary, worshipful; long-standing, of long standing, long-established, established, fixed, inveterate, rooted; folk, of the folk, folkloric

13 **antiquated,** grown old, superannuated, **antique,** old, age-encrusted, of other times, old-world; Victorian, mid-Victorian; historic, classical, medieval, Gothic; antediluvian; fossil, fossilized, petrified

14 **stale,** fusty, musty, rusty, dusty, moldy, mildewed; worn, **timeworn,** time-scarred; **moth-eaten,** moss-grown, crumbling, moldering, gone to seed, dilapidated, ruined, ruinous

15 **obsolete, passé, extinct,** gone out, gone-by, dead, past, run out, outworn

16 **old-fashioned,** old-fangled, old-timey, **dated,** out, out-of-date, **outdated,** so last year, outmoded, out of style, out of fashion, out of use, disused, out of season, unfashionable, styleless, behind the times, old school, old hat, back-number, has-been; <word1> is the new <word2>

17 **old-fogyish,** fogyish, old-fogy; fuddy-duddy, square, corny, cornball; stuffy, stodgy; aged, senile, ravaged with age

18 **secondhand, used,** worn, previously owned, unnew, not new, pawed-over; hand-me-down, reach-me-down

19 **older,** senior, Sr, major, elder, dean; **oldest,** eldest; first-born, firstling, primogenitary; former

20 archaeological, paleological; antiquarian; archaic; paleolithic, eolithic, neolithic, mezzolithic

ADVS **21** anciently

22 **prehistoric animal**

allosaurus
ammonite
anatosaurus
ankylosaurus
apatosaurus
archaeohippus
archaeopteryx
archaeornis
archaeotherium
archelon
archosaur
arthrodiran
atlantosaurus
aurochs
baryonyx Walker
basilosaurus
bothriolepis
brachiosaurus

brontops
brontosaurus
brontothere
camarasaurus
cantius trigonodus
ceratopsid
ceratosaurus
cetiosaurus
coccostean
coelacanth
coelodont
compsognathus
coryphodon
cotylosaur
creodont
crossopterygian
cynodictis
cynodont
deinonychus
denversaurus
diacodexis
diatryma
dimetrodon
dinichthyid
dinosaur
dinothere
diplodocus
dipnoan
diprotodon
dodo
duck-billed dinosaur
edaphosaurid
elasmosaurus
eohippus
eryopsid
eurypterid
eurypterus remipes
giant sloth
glyptodont
gorgosaurus
hadrosaurus
hesperornis
hoplophoneus
hyaenodon
hyracodont
hyracothere
ichthyornis
ichthyosaurus
iguanodon
imperial mammoth, imperial elephant
labyrinthodont
machairodont
mamenchisaurus
mammoth
mastodon
megalosaurus
megathere
merodus
merychippus
merycoidodon
merycopotamus
mesohippus
mesosaur
miacis
mosasaurus
nummulite
ornithomimid
ornithopod
ostracoderm
palaeodictyopteron
palaeomastodon
palaeoniscid
palaeophis
palaeosaur
palaeospondylus
pelycosaur
phytosaur
pinchosaurus
plesiosaurus
pliosaur
protoceratops
protohippus
protylopus
pteranodon
pteraspid
pterichthys
pterodactyl
pterosaur
quetzalcoatlus northropii
raptor
rhamphorhynchus
saber-toothed cat, saber-toothed tiger
sauropod
scelidosaurus
smilodon
stegocephalian
stegodon
stegosaurus
struthiomimus
teleoceras
therapsid
theriodont
theropod
thrinaxodon liorhinus
titanosaurus
titanothere
trachodon
triceratops
trilobite
tyrannosaurus, tyrannosaurus rex
uintathere
urus
woolly mammoth, northern mammoth

23 **prehistoric man**
Aurignacian man
Australanthropus
Australopithecus
Australopithecus afarensis
Australopithecus africanus
Australopithecus boisei
Australopithecus robustus
Bronze Age man
Brünn race
caveman, cave dweller
Cro-Magnon man
eolithic man
Florisbad man
Furfooz man, Grenelle man
Galley Hill man
Gigantopithecus
Grimaldi man
Heidelberg man
hominid
Homo erectus
Homo habilis
Iron Age man
Java man
Lucy
Meganthropus
Neanderthal, Neanderthal man
Neolithic man
Oreopithecus
Paleolithic man
Paranthropus
Peking man
Pithecanthropus
Plesianthropus
protohuman
Rhodesian man
Sinanthropus
Stone Age man
Swanscombe man
Zinjanthropus

843 TIMELINESS

<occurring at suitable time>

NOUNS 1 **timeliness, seasonableness,** opportuneness, convenience; expedience, expediency, meetness, fittingness, fitness, appropriateness, rightness, propriety, suitability; favorableness, propitiousness, auspiciousness, felicitousness; ripeness, pregnancy, cruciality, criticality, criticalness, expectancy, loadedness, chargedness

2 **opportunity,** chance, time, occasion; opening, room, scope, space, place, liberty; clear stage, fair field, level playing field, fair game, fair shake, even break; **opportunism;** equal opportunity, nondiscrimination, affirmative action, positive discrimination <Brit>; trump card; a leg up, stepping-stone, rung of the ladder; time's forelock; window of opportunity

3 **good opportunity, good chance,** favorable opportunity, golden opportunity, well-timed opportunity, the chance of a lifetime, a once-in-a-lifetime chance, happy coincidence, lucky break, lucky streak; suitable occasion, proper occasion, suitable time, proper time, good time, high time, due season; propitious moment, well-chosen moment; window of opportunity; Murphy's Law

4 crisis, critical point, crunch, crucial period, climax, climacteric; **turning point,** hinge, turn, turn of the tide, cusp, nexus; emergency, exigency, convergence of events, critical juncture, crossroads; pinch, clutch, rub, push, pass, strait,

extremity, spot; state of emergency, red alert, race against time

5 **crucial moment,** critical moment, loaded momen, charged moment, decisive moment, kairotic moment, kairos, pregnant moment, defining moment, turning point, climax, **moment of truth,** crunch, when push comes to shove, when the balloon goes up, point of no return, event horizon; psychological moment, right moment; nick of time, eleventh hour; zero hour, H-hour, D-day, A-day, target date, deadline; crisis management

VERBS 6 **be timely,** suit the time, befit the time, befit the season, befit the occasion, fall just right

7 **seize the opportunity,** take the opportunity, use the occasion, take the chance; take the bit in the teeth, leap into the breach, take the bull by the horns, bite the bullet, make one's move, cross the Rubicon; commit oneself, make an opening, drive an entering wedge

8 improve the occasion, turn to account, turn to good account, avail oneself of, **take advantage of,** put to advantage, profit by, cash in on, **capitalize on;** take time by the forelock, seize the opportunity, seize the present hour, *carpe diem* <L, seize the day>, make hay while the sun shines; strike while the iron is hot; not be caught flatfooted, not be behindhand, not be caught looking, don't let the chance slip by, get going, get off the dime

ADJS 9 **timely, well-timed,** seasonable, opportune, *in loco* <L>, convenient; expedient, meet, fit, fitting, befitting, suitable, sortable, appropriate; favorable, propitious, ripe, auspicious, lucky, providential, heaven-sent, fortunate, happy, felicitous

10 critical, **crucial**, pivotal, climactic, climacteric, climacterical, decisive; pregnant, kairotic, loaded, charged; exigent, emergent; eleventh-hour; time-critical, time-sensitive

11 **incidental,** occasional, casual, accidental; parenthetical, by-the-way

ADVS 12 **opportunely,** seasonably, propitiously, auspiciously, in proper time, in the proper season, in due time, in due course, in the fullness of time, in good time, all in good time; in the nick of time, just in time, at the eleventh hour; now or never

13 **incidentally,** by the way, by the by; while on the subject, speaking of, apropos, apropos of; in passing, *en passant* <Fr>; parenthetically, by way of parenthesis; for example

14 a bird in the hand is worth two in the bush, better late than never, every minute counts, every moment counts; live for the moment, you can't take it with you

844 UNTIMELINESS

<occurring at inconvenient time>

NOUNS 1 **untimeliness,** unseasonableness, inopportuneness, inopportunity, unripeness, inconvenience; inexpedience, irrelevance, irrelevancy; awkwardness, inappropriateness, impropriety, unfitness, unfittingness, wrongness, unsuitability; unfavorableness, unfortunateness, inauspiciousness, unpropitiousness, infelicity; intrusion, interruption; prematurity; lateness, afterthought, thinking too late; anachronism; staircase wit

2 **wrong time, bad time,** bad timing, poor timing, unsuitable time, unfortunate time; evil hour, unlucky day, unlucky hour, off-year, *contretemps* <Fr>; inopportune moment

VERBS 3 **ill-time, mistime,** miss the time; lack the time, not have time, have better things to do, be otherwise occupied, be engaged, be preoccupied, have other fish to fry

4 talk out of turn, speak inopportunely, interrupt, put one's foot in one's mouth, intrude, butt in, stick one's nose in, go off half-cocked, **open one's big mouth,** open one's big fat mouth; blow it, speak too late, speak too soon

5 **miss an opportunity,** miss the chance, miss out, miss the boat, miss one's turn, lose the opportunity, ignore opportunity's knock, lose the chance, blow the chance, throw away the opportunity, waste the opportunity, allow the occasion to go by, let slip through one's fingers, be left at the starting gate, be caught looking, oversleep, lock the barn door after the horse is stolen; fear of missing out (FOMO)

ADJS 6 **untimely,** unseasonable, inopportune, **ill-timed**, ill-seasoned, mistimed, unripe, unready, underprepared, ill-considered, too late, too soon, out of phase, out of sync; ill-starred; inconvenient, unhandy, discommodious; inappropriate, irrelevant, improper, unfit, wrong, out of line, off-base, unsuitable, inexpedient, unfitting, unbefitting, untoward, malapropos, intrusive; unfavorable, unfortunate, infelicitous, inauspicious, unpropitious, unhappy, unlucky, misfortuned; premature; not in time, late

ADVS 7 inopportunely, unseasonably, inconveniently, inexpediently; unpropitiously, inauspiciously, unfortunately, in an evil hour, at just the wrong time

845 EARLINESS

<being early>

NOUNS 1 **earliness,** early hour, time to spare; head start, running start, ground floor, first crack, early start, beginnings, first stage, early stage, very beginning, preliminaries; anticipation, foresight, prevision, prevenience; advance notice, lead time, a stitch in time, readiness, preparedness, preparation; first light; due course

2 prematurity, **prematureness**; untimeliness; precocity, precociousness, forwardness; precipitation, precipitancy, haste, hastiness, overhastiness, rush, impulse, impulsivity, impulsiveness

3 **promptness,** promptitude, **punctuality,** punctualness, readiness; instantaneousness, immediateness, immediacy, summariness, decisiveness, alacrity, quickness, speediness, swiftness, rapidity, expeditiousness, expedition, dispatch

4 **early bird**, early riser, early comer, first comer, first arrival, first on the scene; Johnny-on-the-spot; precursor

VERBS 5 **be early,** be ahead of time, take time by the forelock, be up and stirring, be beforehand, be ready and waiting, be off and running; gain time, draw on futurity, draw on the future; get there first; get a wiggle on, hop to it

6 **anticipate, foresee,** foreglimpse, previse, see the handwriting on the wall, foretaste, pave the way for; forestall, forerun, go before, **get ahead of,** win the start, break out ahead, get a head start, steal a march on, beat someone to the punch, beat someone to the draw; jump the gun, beat the gun, go off half-cocked; preempt; take the words out of one's mouth

ADJS 7 **early,** bright and early, with the birds, beforetime, in good time; forehand, forehanded; foresighted, anticipative, anticipatory, prevenient, previsional

8 **premature, too early,** too soon, oversoon; previous, a bit previous, prevenient; untimely; precipitate, hasty, overhasty, too soon off the mark, too quick on the draw, too quick on the uptake; unprepared, unripe, impulsive, rushed, unmatured; unpremeditated, unmeditated, ill-considered, half-cocked, half-baked, unjelled, uncrystallized, not firm; precocious, forward, advanced, far ahead, born before one's time

9 **prompt, punctual,** immediate, instant, instantaneous, quick, speedy, swift, expeditious, summary, decisive, apt, alert, ready, alacritous, Johnny-on-the-spot; as soon as possible (ASAP)

10 **earlier,** previous

ADVS 11 **early,** bright and early, beforehand, beforetime, early on, betimes, precociously, ahead of time, foresightedly, in advance, in anticipation, ahead, before, with time to spare

12 **in time, in good time,** soon enough, time enough, early enough; just in time, in the nick of time, with no time to spare, just under the wire, without a minute to spare

13 **prematurely,** too soon, oversoon, untimely, too early, before its time, before one's time; precipitately, impulsively, in a rush, hastily, overhastily; at half cock

14 **punctually, precisely,** exactly, sharp; on time, on the minute, to the minute, on the dot, spot on, bang on, at the gun, smack dab

15 **promptly,** without delay, without further delay, without further ado, directly, immediately, immediately if not sooner, instantly, instanter, on the instant, on the spot, at once, right off, right away, straightway, straightaway, forthwith, pronto, pretty damned quick (PDQ); quickly, swiftly, speedily, with all speed, summarily, decisively, smartly, expeditiously, apace, in no time, in less than no time; no sooner said than done

16 soon, **presently**, directly, shortly, in a short time, in a short while, before long, ere long, in no long time, in a while, in a little while, after a while, by and by, anon, betimes, *bientôt* <Fr>, in due time, in due course, at the first opportunity; in a moment, in a minute, *tout à l'heure* <Fr>

PHRS 17 the early bird gets the worm

846 LATENESS

<being late>

NOUNS 1 **lateness, tardiness, belatedness, unpunctuality;** late hour, small hours; eleventh hour, last minute, high time; unreadiness, unpreparedness; untimeliness

2 **delay,** stoppage, jam, logjam, obstruction, tie-up, bind, block, blockage, hang-up; delayed reaction, double take, afterthought; retardation, retardance, slow development, slowdown, slow-up, slowness, lag, time lag, lagging, dragging, dragging one's feet, foot-dragging, pigeonholing; detention, suspension, holdup, hindrance; delaying action, delaying tactic; wait, halt, stay, stop, pit stop, downtime, break, pause, interim, respite; reprieve, stay of execution; moratorium; red tape, red-tapery, red-tapeism, bureaucratic delay; delay of game

3 **waiting,** cooling one's heels, tarrying, tarriance; lingering, dawdling, dalliance, dallying, dillydallying; back burner; slow track

4 **postponement,** deferment, **deferral,** backburner, prorogation, putting-off, tabling, holding up, holding in suspension, carrying over; prolongation, protraction, continuation, extension of time; adjournment, adjournal, adjournment sine die

5 **procrastination,** cunctation, hesitation; temporization, a play for time, stall, tap dancing; the thief of time; Micawberism, Fabian policy; dilatoriness, slowness, backwardness, remissness, slackness, laxness; slow track

6 **latecomer,** late arrival, Johnny-come-lately; slow starter, dawdler, dallier, dillydallier; late bloomer, late developer; retardee; late riser, slug-abed; ten o'clock scholar

VERBS **7** **be late, not be on time,** be overdue, be behindhand, show up late, miss the boat; keep everyone waiting; stay late, stay up late, stay up into the small hours, burn the midnight oil, keep late hours; get up late, keep banker's hours; oversleep

8 **delay,** retard, detain, make late, slacken, lag, drag, drag one's feet, stonewall, dilly-dally, slow down, hold up, hold back, keep back, check, stay, stop, arrest, impede, block, hinder, obstruct, throw a monkey wrench in the works, confine; tie up with red tape

9 **postpone, delay,** defer, put off, give one a rain check, shift off, hold off, hold up, prorogue, put on hold, put on ice, put on the back burner, reserve, waive, suspend, hang up, stay, hang fire; protract, drag out, stretch out, prolong, extend, spin out, string out, continue, adjourn, recess, take a recess; hold over, lay over, stand over, let the matter stand, put aside, lay aside, set aside, push aside, lay by, set by, table, lay on the table, pigeonhole, shelve, put on the shelf; consult one's pillow about, sleep on

10 **be left behind,** be outrun, be outdistanced, make a slow start, be slow off the mark, be left at the post, be left at the starting gate; develop late

11 **procrastinate,** be dilatory, hesitate, let something slide, hang, hang back, hang fire; temporize, play for time, drag one's feet, hold off; stall, stall off, stall for time, tap-dance; talk against time, filibuster

12 **wait, delay,** stay, bide, abide, bide one's time; take one's time, take time, mark time; tarry, linger, loiter, dawdle, dally, dillydally; hang about, hold on, sit tight, hold one's breath; wait a second, wait up; hold everything, hold your horses, hold your water, keep your shirt on; stay up, sit up; wait and see, bide the issue, see which way the cat jumps, see how the cookie crumbles, see how the ball bounces, let sleeping dogs lie; wait for something to turn up; await

13 wait impatiently, tear one's hair, sweat it out, champ at the bit, chomp at the bit

14 be kept waiting, be stood up, be left; **cool one's heels**

15 **overstay,** overtarry

ADJS **16** **late, belated, tardy,** slow, slow on the draw, slow on the uptake, behindhand, never on time, backward, back, overdue, long-awaited, untimely; unpunctual, unready; latish; delayed, detained, held up, retarded, arrested, blocked, hung up, in a bind, obstructed, stopped, jammed, congested; weather-bound; postponed, in abeyance, put off, on hold, put on hold, on the back burner, put on the back burner; delayed-action; moratory

17 dilatory, **delaying,** Micawberish; slow off the mark; **procrastinating,** procrastinative, procrastinatory, go-slow; obstructive, obstructionist, obstructionistic, bloody-minded; lingering, loitering, lagging, dallying, dillydallying, slow, sluggish, laggard, foot-dragging, shuffling, backward; easygoing, lazy, lackadaisical; remiss, slack, work-shy, lax

18 later; last-minute, eleventh-hour, deathbed

ADVS **19** **late, behind,** behindhand, belatedly, backward, slow, behind time, after time; far on, deep into; late in the day, at the last minute, at the eleventh hour, none too soon, in the nick of time, under the wire

20 **tardily, slow, slowly,** deliberately, dilatorily, sluggishly, lackadaisically, leisurely, at one's leisure, lingeringly; until all hours, into the night

847 FREQUENCY

<occurring frequently>

NOUNS **1** **frequency,** frequence, **oftenness;** commonness, usualness, prevalence, common occurrence, routineness, habitualness; incidence, relative incidence; radio frequency

2 **constancy,** continualness, steadiness, sustainment, regularity, noninterruption, uninterruption, nonintermission, unintermission, incessancy, ceaselessness, constant flow, continuity; perpetuity; repetition; rapidity; rapid recurrence, rapid succession, rapid fire, quick fire, tattoo, staccato, chattering, stuttering; vibration, shuddering, juddering, pulsation, oscillation

VERBS **3** **be frequent**, occur often, have a high incidence, continue, recur; shudder, judder, vibrate, oscillate; frequent, hang out at

ADJS **4** **frequent,** oftentime, many, many times, **recurrent,** recurring, oft-repeated, thick-coming; common, of common occurrence, not rare, thick on the ground <Brit>, prevalent, usual, routine, habitual, ordinary, everyday; frequentative

5 **constant,** continual, perennial; steady, sustained, regular; periodic; incessant, ceaseless, unceasing, unintermitting, unintermittent, unintermitted, unremitting, relentless, unrelenting, unchanging, unvarying, uninterrupted, unstopped, unbroken;

perpetual; repeated; rapid, staccato, stuttering, chattering, machine gun; pulsating, juddering, vibrating, oscillating

ADVS 6 **frequently,** commonly, usually, ordinarily, routinely, habitually; often, oft, oftentimes, oft times; repeatedly, again and again, time after time; most often, most frequently, in many instances, many times, many a time, full many a time, many a time and oft, as often as can be, as often as not, more often than not; in quick succession, in rapid succession; often enough, not infrequently, not seldom, unseldom; as often as you wish, as often as you like, whenever you wish, whenever you like

7 **constantly,** continually, steadily, sustainedly, regularly, as regular as clockwork, with every other breath, every time one turns around, right along, unvaryingly, uninterruptedly, unintermittently, incessantly, unceasingly, ceaselessly, without cease, without ceasing, perennially, all the time, at all times, ever, ever and anon, on and on, without letup, without break, without intermission, without stopping; perpetually, always; rapidly; all year round, every day, every hour, every moment; daily, hourly, daily and hourly; night and day, day and night; morning, noon, and night; hour after hour, day after day, month after month, year after year; day in day out, month in month out, year in year out

848 INFREQUENCY

<occurring infrequently>

NOUNS 1 **infrequency,** infrequence, unfrequentness, seldomness; occasionalness; **rarity,** scarcity, scarceness, rareness, uncommonness, uniqueness, unusualness; sparsity; slowness; one-time offer

ADJS 2 **infrequent,** unfrequent, **rare,** scarce, scarce as hen's teeth, scarcer than hen's teeth, uncommon, unique, unusual, almost unheard-of, seldom met with, seldom seen, few and far between, sparse; one-time, one-shot, once in a lifetime; slow; like snow in August; unprecedented

3 **occasional,** casual, incidental; **odd,** sometime, extra, side, off, off-and-on, out-of-the-way, spare, sparetime, part-time

ADVS 4 **infrequently,** unfrequently, **seldom, rarely,** uncommonly, scarcely, hardly, scarcely ever, hardly ever, very seldom, not often, only now and then, at infrequent intervals, unoften, off-and-on; sparsely

5 **occasionally,** on occasion, sometimes, at times, at odd times, every so often, at various times, on divers occasions, now and then, every now and then, now and again, once in a while, every once in a while, every now and again, once and again, once or twice, betweentimes, betweenwhiles, at intervals, **from time to time;** only occasionally, only when the spirit moves, only when necessary, only now and then, at infrequent intervals, once in a blue moon, once in a coon's age; irregularly, sporadically

6 **once, one-time,** on one occasion, just once, only once, just this once, once and no more, once for all, once and for all

849 REPETITION

<repeated occurrence>

NOUNS 1 **repetition,** reproduction, duplication, reduplication, doubling, redoubling; **recurrence,** reoccurrence, cyclicality, return, reincarnation, rebirth, reappearance, renewal, resumption; resurfacing, reentry; echo, reecho, parroting; ditto; do-over; regurgitation, rehearsal, rote recitation; quotation; imitation; plagiarism; re-examination, second loo, another look

2 **iteration, reiteration,** recapitulation, recap, wrapup, retelling, recounting, recountal, recital, rehearsal, restatement, rehash; reissue, reprint; review, summary, précis, résumé, summing up, peroration; going over, going through, practicing; reassertion, reaffirmation; elaboration, dwelling upon; copy

3 **redundancy,** tautology, tautologism, pleonasm, macrology, battology; stammering, stuttering; padding, filling, filler, expletive

4 **repetitiousness,** repetitiveness, unnecessary repetition; harping; monotony, monotone, drone; tedium, daily grind, same old story; humdrum, dingdong, singsong, chime, jingle, jingle-jangle, trot, pitter-patter; rhyme, alliteration, assonance, slant rhyme, near rhyme; hamster wheel, treadmill; echolalia, repeated sounds

5 **repeat,** repetend, bis, ditto, echo; **refrain,** burden, chant, undersong, chorus, bob; bob wheel, bob and wheel; ritornel; rerun; rehash; reprint, reissue; remake; second helping

6 **encore,** repeat performance, repeat, **reprise;** replay, replaying, return match; repeat order

VERBS 7 **repeat, redo,** do again, do over, do a repeat, reproduce, relaunch, duplicate, reduplicate, double, redouble, ditto, echo, parrot, reecho; rattle off, reel off, regurgitate; renew, reincarnate, revive; come again, run it by again, say again, repeat oneself, quote, repeat word for word, repeat verbatim, repeat like a broken record; copy, imitate; plagiarize; reexamine, have a second look, take another look; start over

8 **iterate, reiterate,** rehearse, recapitulate, recount, rehash, recite, retell, retail, restate, reword, review, say again, run over, sum up, summarize, précis, resume, encapsulate; reissue, reprint; do over again, say over again, go over, practice, say over, go over the same ground, give an encore, quote oneself, go the same round, fight one's battles over again; tautologize, battologize, pad, fill; reaffirm, reassert

9 **dwell on,** insist upon, harp on, beat a dead horse, have on the brain, constantly revert to, labor, belabor, hammer away at, always trot out, sing the same old song, sing the same old tune, play the same old record, plug the same theme, never hear the last of; thrash over, thresh over, cover the same ground, go over again and again, go over and over

10 **din,** ding; drum, beat, hammer, pound; din in the ear, din into, drum into, say over and over

11 <be repeated> **repeat, recur,** reoccur, come again, come round again, go round again, come up again, resurface, reenter, return, reappear, resume; resound, reverberate, echo; revert, turn back, go back; keep coming, come again and again, happen over and over, run through like King Charles's head

ADJS 12 **repeated,** reproduced, doubled, redoubled; duplicated, reduplicated; regurgitated, recited by rote; echoed, reechoed, parroted; quoted, plagiarized; iterated, reiterated, reiterate; retold, twice-told; warmed up, warmed-over, *réchauffé* <Fr>

13 **recurrent,** recurring, returning, reappearing, revenant, ubiquitous, ever-recurring, cyclical, periodic, yearly, monthly, weekly, daily, circadian, thick-coming, frequent, incessant, continuous, year-to-year, month-to-month, week-to-week; haunting, thematic

14 **repetitious,** repetitive, repetitional, repetitionary, repeating, recursive; duplicative, reduplicative; imitative, parrotlike; echoing, reechoing, echoic; iterative, reiterative, reiterant; recapitulative, recapitulatory; battological, tautological, tautologous, **redundant;** hamster-wheel

15 **monotonous,** monotone; tedious; harping, labored, belabored, cliché-ridden; humdrum, singsong, chiming, chanting, dingdong, jog-trot, jingle-jangle; rhymed, rhyming, alliterative, alliterating, assonant

ADVS 16 **repeatedly,** often, frequently, recurrently, every time one turns around, with every other breath, like a tolling bell, again and again, over and over, over and over again, many times over, time and again, time after time, times without number, **ad nauseam;** year in year out, week in week out, year after year, day after day, day by day; many times, several times, a number of times, many a time, many a time and oft, full many a time and oft; every now and then, every once in a while; recursively

17 **again,** over, over again, once more, *encore,* two times, twice over, double-dipped, ditto; anew, *de novo* <L>, afresh; from the beginning, *da capo* <Ital>

INTERJS 18 **encore,** once more, again

850 REGULARITY OF RECURRENCE

<reoccurring regularly>

NOUNS 1 **regularity, regularness**, clockwork regularity, predictability, punctuality, smoothness, steadiness, evenness, unvariableness, methodicalness, systematicalness; repetition; uniformity; constancy; usual suspects

2 **periodicity,** periodicalness; cyclical motion, piston motion, pendulum motion, regular wave motion, undulation, pulsation; intermittence, intermittency, alternation; rhythm, meter, beat; oscillation; **recurrence,** go-round, reoccurrence, reappearance, return, the eternal return, cyclicalness, cyclicality, seasonality; resurfacing, reentry

3 **round,** revolution, rotation, **cycle,** circle, wheel, circuit; beat, upbeat, downbeat, thesis, arsis, pulse; systole, diastole; course, series, bout, turn, rota, spell

4 **anniversary**, **commemoration;** immovable feast, annual holiday; biennial, biennale, triennial, quadrennial, quinquennial, sextennial, septennial, octennial, nonennial, decennial, tricennial, jubilee, silver jubilee, golden jubilee, diamond jubilee; centennial, centenary; quasquicentennial; sesquicentennial; bicentennial, bicentenary; tercentennial, tercentenary, tricentenary; quincentennial, quincentenary; wedding anniversary, silver wedding anniversary, golden wedding anniversary; birthday, birthdate, date of birth, natal day, b-day; saint's day, name day; leap year, bissextile day; government holiday, bank holiday; religious holiday, holy day

VERBS 5 <occur periodically> **recur, reoccur**, return, repeat, reappear, come again, come up again, be here again, resurface, reenter, come round, come around, come round again, come in its turn; rotate, revolve, turn, circle, wheel, cycle, roll around, roll about, wheel around, go around, go round; intermit, alternate, come and go, ebb and flow; undulate; oscillate, pulse, pulsate; commute, shuttle

ADJS 6 **regular,** systematic, systematical,

methodical, ordered, orderly, **regular as clockwork**; everyday; uniform; constant

7 **periodic**, periodical, seasonal, epochal, cyclic, cyclical, serial, isochronal, metronomic; measured, steady, even, rhythmic, rhythmical; **recurrent**, recurring, reoccurring; intermittent, reciprocal, alternate, every other; circling, wheeling, rotary, rotational, wavelike, undulant, undulatory, oscillatory, pulsing, beating

8 momentary, momently, hourly; daily, diurnal, quotidian, circadian, nightly, tertian; biorhythmic; weekly, hebdomadal, hebdomadary; biweekly, semiweekly; fortnightly; monthly, menstrual, catamenial, estrous; bimonthly, semimonthly; quarterly; biannual, semiannual, semiyearly, half-yearly, semestral; yearly, annual; perennial; biennial, triennial, decennial; centennial, centenary; bissextile; secular

ADVS **9** **regularly,** systematically, methodically, **like clockwork**, at regular intervals, punctually, steadily; at stated times, at fixed periods, at established periods; intermittently, every so often, every now and then; uniformly; constantly

10 **periodically, recurrently,** seasonally, cyclically, epochally; rhythmically, on the beat, in time, synchronously, hourly, daily; every hour, every day; hour by hour, day by day; from hour to hour, from day to day

11 alternately, **by turns**, in turns, in rotation, turn about, turn and turn about, reciprocally, every other, one after the other; to and fro, up and down, from side to side; off and on, make and break, round and round

PHRS **12** what goes around comes around

851 IRREGULARITY OF RECURRENCE

<reoccurring irregularly>

NOUNS **1** **irregularity,** unmethodicalness, unsystematicness; **inconstancy,** unevenness, unsteadiness, uncertainty, desultoriness; variability, capriciousness, unpredictability, whimsicality, eccentricity; stagger, wobble, weaving, erraticness; roughness; fitfulness, sporadicity, sporadicalness, spasticity, jerkiness, fits and starts, patchiness, spottiness, choppiness, brokenness, disconnectedness, discontinuity; intermittence, fluctuation; nonuniformity; arrhythmia, fibrillation; assymetry; unusualness

VERBS **2** **intermit, fluctuate,** vary, lack regularity, go by fits and starts; break, disconnect

ADJS **3** **irregular**, unregular, unsystematic, unmethodical, immethodical; **inconstant,** unsteady, uneven, unrhythmical, unmetrical, rough, unequal, uncertain, unsettled; variable, deviative, heteroclite; capricious, erratic, off-again-on-again, eccentric; wobbly, wobbling, weaving, staggering, lurching, careening; fitful, spasmodic, spasmodical, spastic, spasmic, jerky, herky-jerky, halting; sporadic, patchy, spotty, scrappy, snatchy, catchy, choppy, broken, disconnected, discontinuous; nonuniform; intermittent, intermitting, desultory, fluctuating, wavering, wandering, rambling, veering; flickering, guttering; haphazard, disorderly

ADVS **4** **irregularly,** unsystematically, unmethodically; inconstantly, unsteadily, unevenly, unrhythmically, roughly, uncertainly; variably, capriciously, unpredictably, whimsically, eccentrically, wobblingly, lurchingly, erratically; **intermittently**, disconnectedly, discontinuously; nonuniformly; brokenly, desultorily, patchily, spottily, in spots, in snatches; by fits and starts, by fits, by jerks, by snatches, by catches; fitfully, sporadically, jerkily, spasmodically, haltingly; off and on, at irregular intervals, sometimes and sometimes not; when the mood strikes, when the spirit moves, at random

852 CHANGE

<becoming different>

NOUNS **1** **change,** alteration, modification; variation, variety, difference, diversity, diversification; **deviation,** diversion, aberrance, aberrancy, divergence; switch, switchover, changeover, turn, change of course, turnabout, about-face, U-turn, reversal, flip-flop; apostasy, defection, change of heart, change of mind; shift, transition, modulation, qualification; conversion, renewal, revival, revivification, retro; remaking, reshaping, re-creation, redesign, restructuring, *perestroika* <Russ>; role reversal; realignment, adaptation, adjustment, accommodation, fitting, tweaking, tweak; reform, reformation, improvement, amelioration, melioration, mitigation, constructive change, betterment, change for the better; take, new take; social mobility, vertical mobility, horizontal mobility, upward mobility, downward mobility; gradual change, progressive change, continuity; degeneration, deterioration, worsening, degenerative change, change for the worse, disorder, entropy; changeableness; rolling stone; change of scene

2 **revolution,** revolt, new order, break, break with the past, sudden change, radical change, revolutionary change, total change, catastrophic change, **upheaval,** overthrow, quantum jump, quantum leap, sea change; discontinuity

3 **transformation,** transmogrification; translation; metamorphosis, metamorphism; makeover; mutation, transmutation, permutation, vicissitude; mutant, mutated form, sport; transfiguration, transfigurement; metathesis, transposition, translocation, displacement, metastasis, heterotopia; transubstantiation, consubstantiation; transanimation, transmigration, reincarnation, metempsychosis avatar; metasomatism, metasomatosis; catalysis; metabolism, anabolism, catabolism; metagenesis; transformism; redecoration

4 **innovation,** introduction, discovery, invention, launching; neologism, neoterism, coinage; **breakthrough,** leap, quantum jump, quantum leap, new phase; novelty

5 transformer, transmogrifier, **innovator,** innovationist, introducer; precursor; alterant, alterer, alterative, agent, catalytic agent, catalyst; the winds of change; leaven, yeast, ferment; modifier, modificator; magician

VERBS **6** **be changed,** change, undergo a change, go through a change, dance to a different tune, be converted into, turn into; alter, mutate, modulate; transmutate; vary, checker, diversify; deviate, diverge, turn, take a turn, take a new turn, turn aside, turn the corner, shift, veer, jibe, tack, come about, come around, haul around, chop, chop and change, swerve, warp; change sides, change horses in midstream; revive, be renewed, feel like a new person; improve, ameliorate, meliorate, mitigate; degenerate, deteriorate, worsen; hit bottom, bottom out, reach the nadir, flop

7 **change, make a change**, alter, work a change, change someone's tune; mutate; modify; adapt; modulate, accommodate, adjust, fine-tune, fit, qualify; vary, diversify; convert, renew, recast, revamp, change over, exchange, revive; remake, reshape, re-create, redesign, rebuild, reconstruct, restructure; realign; refit; reform, improve, better, ameliorate, meliorate, mitigate; revolutionize, turn upside down, subvert, overthrow, break up; worsen, deform, denature; ring the changes; give a turn to, give a twist to, turn the tide, turn the tables, tip the balance; shift the scene; shuffle the cards; turn over a new leaf; about-face, do an about-face, do a 180, change direction, reverse oneself, turn one's coat, sing to a different tune, flip-flop, make a U-turn, change one's mind

8 **transform,** transfigure, transmute, transmogrify; translate; transubstantiate, metamorphose; metabolize; perform magic, conjure

9 **innovate,** make innovations, invent, discover, make a breakthrough, make a quantum jump, make a quantum leap, pioneer, revolutionize, introduce, introduce new blood; neologize, neoterize, coin

ADJS **10** **changed, altered,** modified, qualified, transformed, transmuted, metamorphosed; translated, metastasized; life-changing; deviant, aberrant, mutant; divergent; converted, renewed, revived, rebuilt, remodeled; reformed, improved, better, ameliorative, ameliatory; before-and-after; degenerate, worse, unmitigated; subversive, revolutionary; changeable; genetically modified

11 **innovational**, innovative, ameliorative

12 metamorphic, metabolic, anabolic, catabolic; metastatic, catalytic

13 presto, presto chango, hey presto <Brit>

PHRS **14** the shoe is on the other foot

853 PERMANENCE

<not changing>

NOUNS **1** **permanence**, permanency, immutability, **changelessness,** unchangingness, invariableness, invariability; **unchangeableness,** unchangeability, inalterability, inalterableness, inconvertibility, inconvertibleness; fixedness, constancy, steadfastness, firmness, solidity, immovableness, immovability, persistence, persistency, establishment, faithfulness, lastingness, abidingness, endurance, duration, continuance, perseverance, continuity, standing, long standing, inveteracy; durableness, durability; perpetualness; stability; immobility, stasis, frozenness, hardening, rigidity; quiescence, torpor, coma

2 **maintenance,** preservation, conservation

3 **conservatism,** conservativeness, opposition to change, resistance to change, unprogressiveness, fogyism, fuddy-duddyism, backwardness, old-fashionedness, standpattism; ultraconservatism, arch-conservatism; misocainea, misoneism; political conservatism, rightism; laissez-faireism; old school tie <Brit>

4 **conservative,** conservatist; conservationist; ultraconservative, arch-conservative, knee-jerk conservative, diehard, standpat, standpatter, old fogy, fogy, stick-in-the-mud, mossback, rightist, right-winger; old school

VERBS **5** **remain, maintain,** endure, last, stay, persist, bide, abide, stand, hold, subsist; be ever the same; take root, be here to stay; cast in stone

6 **be conservative,** save, preserve, oppose change, stand on ancient ways; stand pat, stand still; let things take their course, leave things as they are, let be, let alone, leave alone, stick with it, let it ride, follow a hands-off policy, let well enough alone, do nothing; stop the clock, turn back the clock

ADJS 7 **permanent, changeless,** unchanging, rock solid, immutable, unvarying, unshifting; unchanged, unchangeable, unvaried, unaltered, inalterable, inviolate, undestroyed, intact; constant, persistent, sustained, fixed, firm, solid, steadfast, like the Rock of Gibraltar, faithful; unchecked, unfailing, unfading; lasting, enduring, abiding, remaining, staying, continuing; durable, entrenched; perpetual; stable; immobile, static, stationary, frozen, rigid, rocklike; quiescent, torpid, comatose, vegetable, vegetative

8 **conservative,** preservative, old-line, diehard, standpat, opposed to change; backward, backward-looking, old-fashioned, unprogressive, nonprogressive, unreconstructed, status-quo, stuck-in-the-mud; ultraconservative, misoneistic, fogyish, old-fogyish; right-wing; *laissez-faire* <Fr>, hands-off; noninvasive, noninterventionist

ADVS 9 **permanently,** abidingly, lastingly, steadfastly, unwaveringly, changelessly, unchangingly; enduringly, perpetually, invariably, forever, always; statically, rigidly, inflexibly

10 *in status quo* <L>, as things are, as is, as usual, as per usual; at a standstill, without a shadow of turning

PHRS 11 the more it changes, the more it's the same thing; if it isn't broken don't fix it, let sleeping dogs lie

854 CHANGEABLENESS

<changing often or suddenly>

NOUNS 1 **changeableness,** changefulness, **changeability,** alterability, convertibility, modifiability; mutability, permutability, impermanence, transience, transitoriness; mobility, motility, movability; plasticity, malleability, workability, rubberiness, fluidity; resilience, adaptability, adjustability, flexibility, suppleness; nonuniformity

2 **inconstancy, instability,** changefulness, unstableness, unsteadiness, unsteadfastness, unfixedness, unsettledness, rootlessness; uncertainty, undependability, inconsistency, shiftiness, unreliability; variability, variation, variety, restlessness, deviability; unpredictability, irregularity; desultoriness, waywardness, wantonness; erraticism, eccentricity; freakishness, freakery; flightiness, impulsiveness, impulsivity, mercuriality, moodiness, whimsicality, capriciousness, caprice, fickleness

3 **changing, fluctuation,** vicissitude, variation, shiftingness; alternation, oscillation, vacillation, pendulation; mood swings; wavering, shifting, shuffling, teetering, tottering, seesawing, teeter-tottering; exchange, trading, musical chairs; bobbing and weaving

4 <comparisons> rollercoaster, Proteus, kaleidoscope, chameleon, shifting sands, rolling stone, April showers, cloud shapes, feather in the wind; water; wheel of fortune; whirligig; mercury, quicksilver; the weather, weathercock, weather vane; moon, phases of the moon; iridescence

VERBS 5 **change, fluctuate,** vary; shift; alternate, **vacillate,** tergiversate, oscillate, pendulate, waffle, blow hot and cold; ebb and flow, wax and wane; go through phases, waver, shuffle, swing, sway, wobble, wobble about, flounder, stagger, teeter, totter, seesaw, teeter-totter; back and fill, turn, ring the changes, have as many phases as the moon; exchange, trade, play musical chairs; metamorphose

ADJS 6 **changeable, alterable,** alterative, modifiable; mutable, permutable, impermanent, transient, transitory, rollercoaster; variable, checkered, ever-changing, many-sided, kaleidoscopic, variegated; movable, mobile, motile; plastic, malleable, rubbery, fluid; resilient, adaptable, adjustable, flexible, supple, able to adapt, able to roll with the punches, able to bend without breaking; protean, proteiform; metamorphic; nonuniform

7 **inconstant, changeable,** changeful, changing, shifting, uncertain, inconsistent, in a state of flux; shifty, unreliable, undependable; unstable, unfixed, infirm, restless, unsettled, unstaid, **unsteady**, wishy-washy, spineless, shapeless, amorphous, indecisive, irresolute, waffling, blowing hot and cold, like a feather in the wind, unsteadfast, unstable as water; variable, deviable, dodgy; unaccountable, unpredictable; vicissitudinous, vicissitudinary; whimsical, capricious, fickle, off-again-on-again; erratic, eccentric, freakish; volatile, giddy, dizzy, ditzy, scatterbrained, mercurial, moody, flighty, impulsive, impetuous; fluctuating, alternating, vacillating, wavering, wavery, wavy, mazy, flitting, flickering, guttering, fitful, shuffling; irregular, spasmodic; desultory, rambling, roving, vagrant, homeless, wanton, wayward, wandering, afloat, adrift; unrestrained, undisciplined, irresponsible, uncontrolled, fast and loose

ADVS 8 **changeably,** variably, inconstantly, shiftingly, shiftily, uncertainly, **unsteadily,** unsteadfastly, whimsically, capriciously, desultorily, erratically, waveringly; impulsively, impetuously, precipitately; back and forth, to and fro, in and out, off and on, on and off, round and round

855 STABILITY

<*uneasily changed*>

NOUNS 1 **stability,** firmness, soundness, substantiality, solidity; security, secureness, securement; **rootedness,** fastness; reliability; steadiness, steadfastness; constancy, invariability, undeflectability; imperturbability, unflappability, nerve, steady nerves, unshakable nerves, nerves of steel, unshakableness, unsusceptibility, unimpressionability, stolidness, stolidity, stoicism, cool, *sang-froid* <Fr>; iron will; equilibrium, balance, stable state, stable equilibrium, homeostasis; steady state; emotional stability, balanced personality; aplomb; uniformity

2 fixity, **fixedness**, fixture, fixation; infixion, implantation, embedment; establishment, stabilization, confirmation, entrenchment; inveteracy, deep-rootedness, deep-seatedness

3 **immobility,** immovability, unmovability, immovableness, irremovability, immotility; inextricability; firmness, solidity, unyieldingness, rigidity, inflexibility; inertia, inertness; immobilization

4 **unchangeableness,** unchangeability, unalterability, inalterability, unmodifiability, immutability, incommutability, inconvertibility; nontransferability; lastingness, permanence; irrevocability, indefeasibility, irreversibility; irretrievability, unreturnableness, unrestorableness; intransmutability

5 **indestructibility,** imperishability, incorruptibility, inextinguishability, immortality, deathlessness; invulnerability, invincibility, inexpugnability, impregnability; ineradicability, indelibility, ineffaceability, inerasableness

6 <comparisons> rock, Rock of Gibraltar, bedrock, pillar of strength, tower of strength, foundation; leopard's spots

VERBS 7 **stabilize,** stabilitate, stabilify; firm, firm up; steady, balance, counterbalance, ballast; immobilize, freeze, keep, retain; transfix, stick, hold, pin down, nail down; set in stone, cast in stone, write in stone

8 **secure,** make sure, make secure, firm up, tie, tie off, tie up, chain, tether; cleat, belay; wedge, jam, seize; make fast, fasten, fasten down; anchor, moor; batten, batten down; confirm, ratify

9 **fix,** define, set, settle; establish, found, ground, lodge, seat, entrench; root; infix, ingrain, set in, plant, implant, engraft, bed, embed; print, imprint, stamp, inscribe, engrave, impress; deep-dye, dye in the wool; stereotype

10 <become firmly fixed> **root, take root,** strike root, settle down; stick, stick fast; seize, seize up, freeze; catch, jam, lodge, foul

11 **stand fast, stand firm,** remain firm, stand pat, stay put, hold fast, not budge, not budge an inch, stand one's ground, hold one's ground, persist, persevere, hold one's own, dig in one's heels, take one's stand, stick to one's guns, put one's foot down; hold out, stick it out, tough it out, hang tough, stay the course; hold up; weather, weather the storm, ride it out, get home free; be imperturbable, be unflappable, not bat an eye, not bat an eyelash, keep one's cool

ADJS 12 **stable,** substantial, firm, solid, sound, stabile; firm as Gibraltar, solid as a rock, rocklike, built on bedrock; fast, secure; steady, unwavering, steadfast; balanced, in equilibrium, in a stable state; well-balanced; imperturbable, unflappable, unshakable, cool, unimpressionable, unsusceptible, impassive, stolid, stoic; without nerves, without a nerve in one's body, unflinching, iron-willed; reliable, predictable; fiducial

13 **established,** stabilized, **entrenched,** vested, firmly established; well-established, well-founded, **grounded,** well-grounded, on a rock, on bedrock, aground; old-line, long-established; confirmed, inveterate; settled, set; well-settled, well-set, in place; rooted, well-rooted; deep-rooted, deep-seated, deep-set, deep-settled, deep-fixed, deep-dyed, deep-engraven, deep-grounded, deep-laid; infixed, ingrained, implanted, engrafted, embedded, ingrown, inwrought; impressed, indelibly impressed, imprinted; engraved, graven, embossed; dyed-in-the-wool

14 **fixed,** fastened, anchored, riveted; **set,** settled, stated; staple

15 **immovable,** unmovable, immobile, immotile, unmoving, irremovable, stationary, frozen, not to be moved, at a standstill, on dead center; firm, unyielding, adamant, adamantine, rigid, inflexible; pat, standpat; at anchor

16 **stuck,** fast, stuck fast, fixed, transfixed, caught, fastened, tied, chained, tethered, anchored, moored, held, inextricable; jammed, impacted, congested, packed, wedged; seized, seized up, frozen; **rooted,** aground, grounded, stranded, high and dry

17 **unchangeable,** not to be changed, changeless, unchanged, unchanging, unvarying, unvariable, unalterable, unaltered, unalterative, immutable, incommutable, inconvertible, unmodifiable; insusceptible of change; constant, invariable, undeviating, undeflectable; lasting, unremitting, permanent; irrevocable, indefeasible, irreversible, nonreversible, reverseless; irretrievable,

unrestorable, unreturnable, nonreturnable; intransmutable, inert, noble

18 **indestructible,** undestroyable, **imperishable,** nonperishable, incorruptible; deathless, immortal, undying; invulnerable, invincible, inexpugnable, impregnable, indivisible; ineradicable, indelible, ineffaceable, inerasable; inextinguishable, unquenchable, quenchless, undampable

PHRS 19 stet, let it stand; what's done is done

856 CONTINUANCE

<continuing of action>

NOUNS 1 **continuance, continuation,** ceaselessness, unceasingness, uninterruptedness, unremittingness, continualness; prolongation, extension, protraction, perpetuation, lengthening, spinning out, stringing out; survival, holding out, hanging on, hanging in; maintenance, sustenance, sustained action, sustained activity; pursuance; run, way, straight course, uninterrupted course; progress, progression; persistence, perseverance; endurance, stamina, staying power; continuity; repetition

2 **resumption,** recommencement, rebeginning, reestablishment, revival, recrudescence, resuscitation, renewal, reopening, reentrance, reappearance; fresh start, new beginning; another try, another shot, another crack, another go

VERBS 3 **continue**, keep with it, stay with it, stay at it, carry on; remain, bide, abide, stay, tarry, linger; go on, go along, keep on, keep on keeping on, keep going, see it through, stay on, hold on, hold one's way, hold one's course, hold steady, run on, jog on, drag on, bash on, slog on, soldier on, plug away, grind on, stagger on, put one foot in front of the other; never cease, cease not; endure

4 **sustain,** protract, prolong, extend, perpetuate, lengthen, string out; maintain, keep, hold, retain, preserve; keep up, keep going, keep alive, survive

5 **persist, persevere,** keep at it, stick it out, stick to it, stick with it, never say die, see it through, hang in, hang tough, not know when one is licked; survive, make out, manage, get along, get on, eke out an existence, keep the even tenor of one's way; go on, go on with, go on with the show, press on; perseverate, iterate, reiterate, harp, go on about, chew one's ear off, run off at the mouth, beat a dead horse

6 **resume,** recommence, rebegin, renew, reestablish; revive, resuscitate, recrudesce; reenter, reopen, return to, go back to, begin again, take up again, make a new beginning, make a fresh start, start all over, have another try, have another shot, have another crack, have another go

ADJS 7 **continuing,** abiding; staying, remaining, sticking; continuous, ceaseless, unceasing, unending, endless, incessant, unremitting, steady, sustained, protracted, undying, indefatigable, persistent; repetitious, repetitive; resumed, recommenced, rebegun, renewed, reopened

857 CESSATION

<stopping of action>

NOUNS 1 **cessation, discontinuance,** discontinuation, phaseout, phasedown, scratching, scrubbing, breakoff; desistance, desinence, cease, surcease, ceasing, ending, halting, stopping, termination; close, closing, shutdown; sign-off; log-off; relinquishment, renunciation, abandonment, breakup

2 **stop,** stoppage, **halt,** stay, arrest, check, cutoff; stand, standstill; full stop, dead stop, screaming halt, grinding halt; strike, walkout, work stoppage, sit-down strike, lockout; sick-out, blue flu; end, ending, endgame, final whistle, gun, bell, checkmate; tie, stalemate, deadlock, wash, toss-up, standoff, Mexican standoff; terminal, end of the line, rest stop, stopping place, comfort break, terminus; closure

3 **pause, rest,** break, caesura, fermata, recess, intermission, interim, intermittence, interval, interlude, *intermezzo* <Ital>; respite, letup; interruption, suspension, timeout, break in the action, breathing spell, breathing space, cooling-off period; postponement, rainout; remission; abeyance, stay, drop, lull, lapse; truce, cease-fire, stand-down; vacation, holiday, time off, paid time off, day off, mental health day, playtime, leisure, leisure time; bus stop

4 <grammatical terms> pause, juncture, boundary, caesura; <punctuation> stop, point, period, comma, serial comma, Oxford comma, colon, semicolon

5 <legislatures> cloture; cloture by compartment, kangaroo cloture; guillotine; closure of debate

VERBS 6 **cease, discontinue,** end, stop, halt, end-stop, terminate, close the books on, close the books, put paid to, abort, cancel, scratch, scrub, hold, quit, stay, belay; desist, refrain, leave off, lay off, give over, have done with; cut it out, drop it, knock it off, relinquish, renounce, abandon; come to an end, draw to a close; hang up, ring off

7 **stop, come to a stop,** halt, come to a halt, stop in one's tracks, skid to a stop, stop dead, stall; bring up, pull up, pull in, pull into, head in, draw up, fetch up; stop short, come up short, bring up short, come to a screaming halt, come to a squealing halt, come to a grinding halt, stop on

a dime, come to a full stop, put on the brake, come to a standstill, grind to a halt, fetch up all standing; stick, jam, hang fire, seize, seize up, freeze; cease fire, stand down; run into a brick wall

8 <**stop work**> lay off, knock off, call it a day, call it quits; lay down one's tools, shut up shop, close shop, shut down, lock up, close down, secure; strike, walk out, call a strike, go on strike, go out on strike, stand down; work to rule

9 **pause, rest,** let up, take it easy, relax, rest on one's oars; recess, take a recess, call a recess; call timeout; take a break, break, take five, take ten; hang fire; catch one's breath, take a breather

10 **interrupt,** suspend, intermit, break, break off, take a break, cut off, break the thread, snap the thread

11 **put a stop to,** call a halt to, get it over with, blow the whistle on, put an end to, put paid to, call off the dogs; stop, stay, halt, arrest, check, flag down, wave down; block, brake, dam, stem, stem the tide, stem the current; pull up, draw rein, put on the brakes, hit the brake pedal; bring to a standstill, bring to a close, bring to a halt, freeze, bring to, bring up short, stop dead, stop dead in one's tracks, set one back on his heels, stop cold, stop short, cut short, check in full career; checkmate, stalemate, deadlock; thwart; do in

12 **turn off,** shut off, shut, shut down, close, power down; phase out, phase down, taper off, wind up, wind down; kill, cut, cut off short, switch off

INTERJS 13 **cease, stop, halt,** hold, freeze, stay, desist, quit it; let up, easy, take it easy, relax, get off it, leave off, stop it, forget it, no more, have done, hold everything, hold it, hold to, hold on, whoa, that's it, that's enough, that will do, enough, enough is enough, genug, all right already, *basta* <Ital>

14 <nonformal> cut it out, cool it, bag it, chill out, call it quits, can it, turn it off, chuck it, stow it, drop it, lay off, all right already, come off it, knock it off, break it off, break it up

858 CONVERSION

<change to something different>

NOUNS 1 **conversion,** reconversion, **changeover,** turning into, becoming; convertibility; change, sea change, transformation, transubstantiation, transmutation, metamorphosis; transition, transit, switch, switchover, passage, shift; reversal, about-face, flip-flop, role reversal, *volte-face* <Fr>; makeover, do-over, complete change, 360-degree change, 360; relapse, lapse, descent; breakthrough; growth, progress, development; transcendence; resolution; reduction, simplification; assimilation, naturalization, adoption, assumption; processing; alchemy

2 **new start, new beginning,** fresh start, clean slate, square one; reformation, reform, regeneration, revival, reclamation, redemption, amendment, improvement, renewal, recrudescence, **rebirth,** renascence, new birth, change of heart; change of mind, change of allegiance, change of conviction

3 apostasy, renunciation, **defection,** desertion, treason, crossing-over, abandonment; degeneration

4 **rehabilitation,** reconditioning, recovery, readjustment, reclamation, restoration; reeducation, reinstruction; **repatriation**

5 **indoctrination,** reindoctrination, counterindoctrination; **brainwashing,** menticide; subversion, alienation, corruption

6 **conversion,** proselytization, proselytism, evangelization, persuasion; indoctrination; spiritual rebirth

7 **convert,** proselyte, neophyte, catechumen, disciple, new man, new woman, new person, born-again person

8 apostate, **defector**, turncoat, traitor, deserter, renegade

9 **converter,** proselyter, proselytizer, missionary, apostle, evangelist, televangelist; reformer, rehabilitator

10 <instruments> philosopher's stone, melting pot, crucible, alembic, test tube, caldron, retort, mortar; potter's wheel, anvil, lathe; converter, transformer, transducer, engine, motor, machine

VERBS 11 **convert,** reconvert; **change over,** switch, switch over, shift, slide into; do over, redo, make over, rejigger; change, transform, transmute, metamorphose; change into, turn into, become, resolve into, assimilate to, bring to, reduce to, naturalize; make, render; reverse, do an about-face; change one's tune, sing a different tune, dance to another tune; turn back

12 **re-form,** remodel, reshape, **refashion,** recast; regroup, redeploy, rearrange; renew, new-model; be reborn, be born again, be a new person, feel like a new person; get it together, get one's act together, get one's shit together*, get one's ducks in a row; regenerate, reclaim, redeem, amend, set straight; reform, rehabilitate, set on the straight and narrow, make a new man of, restore self-respect; mend one's ways, change one's ways, turn over a new leaf, put on the new man, undergo a personality change

13 **defect,** renege, wimp out, chicken out, cop

out, turn one's coat, desert, apostatize, change one's colors, turn against, turn traitor; leave a sinking ship, desert a sinking ship; lapse, relapse; degenerate

14 **rehabilitate,** recondition, reclaim, recover, restore, readjust; reeducate, reinstruct; repatriate

15 **indoctrinate, brainwash,** reindoctrinate, counterindoctrinate; subvert, alienate, win away, corrupt

16 **convince,** persuade, wean, bring over, sweep off one's feet, win over; proselyte, proselytize, evangelize

17 **be converted into**, turn to, become, change into, alter into, pass into, slide into, grow into, ripen into, develop into, evolve into, merge into, shift into, lapse into, open into, resolve itself, settle into, come round to

ADJS **18** **convertible,** changeable, resolvable, transmutable, transformable, transitional, modifiable; reformable, reclaimable, renewable

19 **converted,** changed, transformed; naturalized, assimilated; reformed, regenerated, renewed, redeemed, reborn, born-again; liquidated; brainwashed

20 apostate, treasonable, traitorous, degenerate, renegade

859 REVERSION

<change to a former state>

NOUNS **1** **reversion,** reverting, retroversion, retrogradation, retrogression, retrocession, regress, relapse, **regression**, backsliding, lapse, slipping back, backing, recidivism, recidivation; reconversion; reverse, reversal, turnabout, about-face, right about-face, 180-degree shift, 180-degree change, flip-flop, turn; return, returning, retreat; disenchantment; reclamation, rehabilitation, redemption, return to the fold; reinstatement, restitution, restoration; retroaction; turn of the tide

2 **throwback,** atavism

3 **returnee, repeater;** prodigal son, lost lamb; reversioner, reversionist; recidivist, habitual criminal, habitual offender, two-time loser; backslider; lost-and-found

VERBS **4** **revert,** retrovert, **regress,** retrogress, retrograde, retrocede, reverse, return, return to the fold; backslide, slip back, recidivate, lapse, lapse back, relapse

5 **turn back,** change back, go back, hark back, cry back, break back, **turn,** turn around, turn about; make a round trip; do an about-face, flip-flop, do a flip-flop, hang a 180, ricochet; undo, turn back the clock, put the genie back into the bottle, put the toothpaste back into the tube; go back to go, go back to square one, go back to the drawing board

6 **revert to,** return to, recur to, go back to; hark back to, cry back to

ADJS **7** **reversionary,** reversional, **regressive,** recessive, retrogressive, retrograde; reactionary; recidivist, recidivistic, recidivous, lapsarian; retroverse, retrorse; retroactive; atavistic; revertible, returnable, reversible, recoverable

COMBINING FORMS **8** retro-

860 REVOLUTION

<sudden, extreme change>

NOUNS **1** **revolution,** radical change, total change, violent change, striking alteration, sweeping change; clean sweep, clean slate, square one, tabula rasa; transilience, quantum leap, quantum jump; **overthrow,** overturn, upset, convulsion, spasm, subversion, *coup d'*état; breakup, breakdown; **cataclysm,** catastrophe, debacle, *débâcle* <Fr>; revolutionary war, war of national liberation; bloodless revolution, palace revolution; technological revolution, electronic revolution, communications revolution, computer revolution, information revolution; green revolution; counterrevolution; revolt, reign of terror

2 **revolutionism,** revolutionariness, anarchism, syndicalism, terrorism; Bolshevism, Bolshevikism <Russia>; Jacobinism, sans-culottism <Fr>, Maoism <China>

3 **revolutionist, revolutionary,** revolutionizer; rebel; anarchist, anarch, syndicalist, criminal syndicalist, terrorist; subversive; red; sans-culottist <Fr>; Yankee, Yankee Doodle, Continental; Bolshevik, Bolshevist, Bolshie <Russ>, Marxist, Leninist, Communist, Commie, Red, Trotskyite, Trotskyist; Maoist; revolutionary junta

VERBS **4** **revolutionize,** make a radical change, make a clean sweep, break with the past; **overthrow, overturn,** throw the rascals out, let heads roll, upset; revolt

ADJS **5** **revolutionary;** revulsive, revulsionary; transilient; subversive, insurgent; cataclysmic, catastrophic; **radical,** sweeping; insurrectionary

6 revolutionist, **revolutionary,** anarchic, anarchical, syndicalist, terrorist, terroristic, agin the government; Bolshevistic, Bolshevik; sans-culottic, sans-culottish; Jacobinic, Jacobinical, Carbonarist, Fenian, Marxist, Leninist, Communist, Trotskyist, Trotskyite, Guevarist, Castroist, Castroite, Maoist, Vietcong, Mau-Mau

861 EVOLUTION

<gradual change>

NOUNS 1 **evolution, evolving,** evolvement; evolutionary change, gradual change, step-by-step change, peaceful change, nonviolent change; development, growth, rise, incremental change, developmental change, natural growth, natural development; flowering, blossoming; ripening, coming of age, maturation; accomplishment; advance, advancement, furtherance; progress, progression; elaboration, enlargement, amplification, expansion; devolution, degeneration; Petri dish

2 **unfolding,** unfoldment, unrolling, unfurling, unwinding; revelation, gradual revelation

3 <biological terms> genesis; phylogeny, phylogenesis; ontogeny, ontogenesis; physiogeny, physiogenesis; biological evolution, speciation, convergent evolution, parallel evolution; natural selection, adaptation; horotely, bradytely, tachytely; gradualism; microevolution, macroevolution; polygenesis, polygeny

4 **evolutionism,** theory of evolution; **Darwinism,** Darwinianism, punctuated equilibrium, Neo-Darwinism, organic evolution, survival of the fittest; Haeckelism, Lamarckism, Lamarckianism, Neo-Lamarckism, Lysenkoism, Weismannism, Spencerianism; social Darwinism, social evolution

VERBS 5 **evolve;** develop, grow, wax, change gradually, change step-by-step; progress, advance, come a long way; accomplish; ripen, mellow, mature, maturate; flower, bloom, blossom, bear fruit; degenerate

6 **elaborate, develop,** work out, enlarge, enlarge on, amplify, expand, expand on, detail, go into detail, go into, flesh out, pursue, spell out; complete

7 **unfold**, unroll, unfurl, unwind, unreel, uncoil, reveal, reveal gradually, expose gradually

ADJS 8 **evolutionary,** evolutional, evolutionist, evolutionistic; **evolving**, developing, unfolding; Darwinistic; maturing, maturational, maturative; progressing, advancing; devolutionary, degenerative; genetic, phylogenetic, ontogenetic, physiogenetic; horotelic, bradytelic, tachytelic

862 SUBSTITUTION

<change of one thing for another>

NOUNS 1 **substitution, exchange**, change, switch, switcheroo, swap, commutation, subrogation; surrogacy; vicariousness, representation, deputation, delegation; deputyship, agency, power of attorney; supplanting, supplantation, succession; replacement, displacement, shuffle; provision, provisionalness, provisionality, adhocracy, ad hockery, ad hocery, ad hocism; superseding, supersession, supersedure; tit for tat, *quid pro quo* <L>; job sharing; novation

2 **substitute,** sub, **substitution,** replacement, **backup**, second string, third string, secondary, utility player, succedaneum; change, exchange; ersatz, phony, fake, counterfeit, imitation, copy; surrogate; reserves, bench, backup personnel, spares; alternate, alternative, next best thing, lesser of two evils; successor, supplanter, superseder, capper; proxy, dummy, ghost; vicar, agent, representative; deputy; locum tenens, vice, vice-president, vice-regent; relief, fill-in, stand-in, understudy, pinch hitter, pinch runner; double; equivalent, equal; ringer; ghostwriter; analogy, comparison; metaphor, metonymy, euphemism, synecdoche; symbol, sign, token, icon; makeshift

3 **scapegoat,** goat, fall guy, can-carrier, patsy, catch dog, whipping boy, lamb to the slaughter

VERBS 4 **substitute, exchange,** change, ask in exchange, offer in exchange, switch, swap, ring in, put in the place of, change for, make way for, give place to; commute, redeem, compound for; pass off, pawn off, foist off, palm off, fob off; rob Peter to pay Paul; dub in; make do with, shift with, put up with; shuffle

5 **substitute for,** sub for, subrogate; act for, double for, double as, stand in for, sit in for, understudy for, fill in for, serve as proxy, don the mantle of, change places with, swap places with, stand in the stead of, step into the shoes of, fill the shoes of, pinch-hit, pinch-run; deputize; relieve, spell, spell off, cover for; ghost, ghostwrite; represent; supplant, supersede, succeed, replace, displace, **take the place of,** crowd out, cut out

6 <nonformal> cover up for, front for; take the rap for, take the fall for, carry the can, be the goat, be the patsy, be the fall guy

7 **delegate,** deputize, depute, commission, give the nod to, designate an agent, designate a proxy

ADJS 8 **substitute,** alternate, alternative, other, tother, equivalent, token, dummy, pinch, utility, backup, secondary; ad hoc, provisional; vicarious, ersatz, mock, phony, fake, bogus, counterfeit, imitation; proxy, deputy; makeshift, reserve, spare, stopgap, temporary, tentative; multiple-choice

9 **substitutional,** substitutionary, substitutive, provisional, supersessive; **substituted,** substituent

10 replaceable, **substitutable,** supersedable, expendable

ADVS 11 **instead**, rather; in its stead, in its place; in one's stead, in one's behalf, in one's place, in one's shoes; by proxy; as an alternative; *in loco parentis* <L>

PREPS **12** instead of, in the stead of, rather than, sooner than, in place of, in the place of, on behalf of, in lieu of; for, as proxy for, as a substitute for, as representing, in preference to, as an alternative to; replacing, as a replacement for, vice

COMBINING FORMS **13** pro-, vice-, quasi-, pseudo-

863 INTERCHANGE

<mutual change or exchange>

NOUNS **1** **interchange,** exchange, counterchange; transposition, transposal; mutual transfer, mutual replacement; mutual admiration, mutual support; cooperation; commutation, permutation, intermutation; alternation; interplay, **tradeoff,** compromise, reciprocation, reciprocality, reciprocity, mutuality, two-way traffic; *give-and-take,* something for something, *quid pro quo* <L>, measure for measure, tit for tat, an eye for an eye, a tooth for a tooth; retaliation, *lex talionis* <L>; crossfire; battledore and shuttlecock; repartee

2 **trading, swapping**; trade, swap, even trade, even-steven trade, switch; barter; logrolling, back scratching, pork barrel; pawning, castling

3 **interchangeability,** exchangeability, changeability, standardization; convertibility, commutability, permutability

VERBS **4** **interchange,** exchange, change, counterchange; alternate; transpose; convert, commute, permute; trade, **swap**, switch; bandy, bandy about, play at battledore and shuttlecock; reciprocate, trade off, compromise, settle, settle for, respond, keep a balance; give and take, give tit for tat, give as much as one takes, give as good as one gets, return the compliment, return the favor, pay back, compensate, requite, return; retaliate, get back at, get even with, be quits with; logroll, scratch each other's back, cooperate

ADJS **5** **interchangeable,** exchangeable, changeable, standard; equivalent; even, equal; returnable, convertible, commutable, permutable; commutative; retaliatory, equalizing; reciprocative, reciprocating, reciprocatory, reciprocal, traded-off, two-way; mutual, give-and-take; exchanged, transposed, switched, swapped, traded, **interchanged;** requited, reciprocated

ADVS **6** **interchangeably,** exchangeably; in exchange, in return; even, evenly, *au pair* <Fr>; reciprocally, mutually; in turn, each in its turn, every one in his turn, by turns, turn about, turn and turn about

PHRS **7** one good turn deserves another; you scratch my back I scratch yours

864 GENERALITY

<being general rather than specific>

NOUNS **1** **generality,** universality, cosmicality, inclusiveness; worldwideness, globality, globalism, ecumenicity, ecumenicalism; catholicity; internationalism, cosmopolitanism; **generalization,** universalization, globalization, ecumenization, internationalization; labeling, stereotyping

2 **ubiquity,** revalence, **commonness,** commonality, usualness, currency, occurrence; extensiveness, widespreadness, pervasiveness, sweepingness, rifeness, rampantness; normality, normalness, averageness, ordinariness, routineness, habitualness, standardness

3 **average,** ruck, run, ordinary run, run of the mill; any Tom, Dick, or Harry; Everyman; common man, average man, the man in the street, John Q Public, John Doe, Jane Doe, ordinary Joe, Joe Six-pack, Joe Blow, lowest common denominator; girl next door; everyman, everywoman

4 **all,** everyone, everybody, each and every one, one and all, all comers, all hands, every man Jack, every mother's son, every living soul, all the world, everyone and his brother, *tout le monde* <Fr>, the devil and all, whole, totality; everything, all kinds of things, all manner of things; you name it, what have you, all the above; Anytown, global village

5 **any,** anything, any one, aught, either; anybody, anyone

6 **whatever,** whate'er, whatsoever, whatsoe'er, what, whichever, anything soever which, no matter what, what have you, what you will

7 **whoever,** whoso, whosoever, whomever, whomso, whomsoever, anyone, no matter who, anybody

8 <idea or expression> **generalization,** general idea, abstraction, generalized proposition; glittering generality, sweeping statement, vague generalization; truism, platitude, conventional wisdom, commonplace; cliché, tired cliché, bromide, trite expression, hackneyed expression; labeling, stereotyping

VERBS **9** **generalize,** universalize, catholicize, ecumenicize, globalize, internationalize; broaden, widen, expand, extend, spread; make a generalization, deal in generalities, deal in abstractions; label, stereotype

10 **prevail,** predominate, obtain, dominate, reign, rule; be in force, be in effect; be the rule, be the fashion, be the rage, be the thing, have currency, be in; glocalize

ADJS **11** **general, generalized,** nonspecific, generic, indefinite, indeterminate, vague, abstract, nebulous, unspecified, undifferentiated, featureless, uncharacterized, bland, neutral

12 **prevalent, prevailing**, common, popular, current, running; regnant, reigning, ruling, predominant, predominating, dominant; rife, rampant, pandemic, epidemic, besetting; ordinary, normal, average, usual, routine, standard, par for the course, stereotyped, stereotypical; public, communal; glocal

13 **extensive,** broad, **wide,** liberal, diffuse, large-scale, broad-scale, broad-scope, broadly-based, wide-scale, sweeping; cross-disciplinary, interdisciplinary; widespread, far-spread, far-stretched, far-reaching, far-going, far-embracing, far-extending, far-spreading, far-flying, far-ranging, far-flung, wide-flung, wide-reaching, wide-extending, wide-extended, wide-ranging, wide-stretching; wholesale, indiscriminate; rife; panoramic, bird's-eye

14 universal, cosmic, cosmical, heavenwide, galactic, planetary, worldwide, transnational, planetwide, global, globalized; total, allover, holistic; catholic, all-inclusive, all-including, all-embracing, **all-encompassing**, comprehensive, all-comprehending, all-filling, all-pervading, all-covering, encyclopedic; nonsectarian, nondenominational, ecumenic, ecumenical; omnipresent, **ubiquitous**; cosmopolitan, international; national, nationwide, countrywide, statewide

15 every, **all**, any, whichever, whichsoever; each, each one; every one, each and every, each and all, one and all, all and sundry, all and some

16 trite, **commonplace,** hackneyed, platitudinous, truistic, overworked, quotidian; common, garden

ADVS 17 **generally, in general;** generally speaking, speaking generally, broadly, broadly speaking, roughly, roughly speaking, as an approximation; usually, as a rule, ordinarily, commonly, normally, routinely, as a matter of course, in the usual course; by and large, at large, altogether, overall, over the long haul, all things considered, taking one thing with another, taking all things together, on balance, all in all, taking all in all, taking it for all in all, on the whole, as a whole, in the long run, for the most part, for better or for worse; prevailingly, predominantly, mostly, chiefly, mainly

18 **universally, ubiquitously,** galactically, cosmically; everywhere, all over, the world over, all over the world, internationally; in every instance, without exception, invariably, always, never otherwise

COMBINING FORMS 19 glob-, globo-, omn-, omni-, pan-, pano-, pant-, panto-, panta-

865 PARTICULARITY

<being specific rather than general>

NOUNS 1 **particularity, individuality,** individualness, **singularity,** differentiation, differentness, distinctiveness, uniqueness; identity, individual identity, separate identity, concrete identity; personality, personship, personal identity; soul; selfness, selfhood, ipseity, egohood, self-identity; oneness, wholeness, integrity; personal equation, human factor; nonconformity; **individualism,** particularism; nominalism

2 **speciality, specialness,** specialty, specificality, **specificness,** definiteness; special case; specialty of the house, soup du jour, flavor of the month, today's special; limited edition

3 **the specific,** the special, **the particular,** the concrete, the individual, the unique

4 **characteristic, peculiarity, singularity,** particularity, specialty, individualism, character, property, nature, trait, quirk, point of character, bad point, good point, saving grace, redeeming feature, mannerism, keynote, trick, feature, distinctive feature, lineament; claim to fame, expertise, métier, forte, wheelhouse; mark, marking, earmark, hallmark, index, signature; badge, token; brand, cast, stamp, cachet, seal, mold, cut, figure, shape, configuration; impress, impression; differential, differentia; idiosyncrasy, idiocrasy, eccentricity; quality, **attribute;** savor, flavor, taste, gust, aroma, odor, smack, tang, taint

5 **self,** ego; oneself, I, myself, me, my humble self, number one, yours truly; yourself, himself, herself, itself; ourselves, yourselves; themselves; you; he, she; him, her; they, them; it; inner self, inner man; subliminal self, subconscious self; superego, better self, ethical self; other self, alter ego, alter; inner child, child within

6 **specification,** designation, stipulation, specifying, designating, stipulating, singling-out, featuring, highlighting, focusing on, denomination; allocation, attribution, fixing, selection, assignment, pinning down; specifications, particulars, minutiae, fine print

7 **particularization, specialization;** individualization, peculiarization, personalization; localization; itemization; special interest, pursuit, vocation, field

8 **characterization,** distinction, differentiation; definition, description

VERBS 9 **particularize, specialize; individualize,** peculiarize, personalize; descend to particulars, go into detail, get precise, get down to brass tacks, get down to cases, get down to the nitty-gritty, come to the point, lay it on the line, spell out; itemize, detail

10 **characterize,** distinguish, differentiate, define, describe; mark, earmark, mark off, mark out, demarcate, set apart, make special, make unique; keynote, sound the keynote, set the tone, set the mood, set the pace; be characteristic, be a feature of, be a trait of

11 **specify,** specialize, **designate,** stipulate, determine, single out, feature, highlight, focus on, mention, select, pick out, fix, set, assign, pin down; name, denominate, name names, state, mark, check, check off, indicate, signify, point out, put one's finger on, lay one's finger on; cite, quote, attribute

ADJS **12** **particular, special,** especial, specific, express, precise, concrete; singular, individual, individualist, individualistic, unique; personal, private, intimate, inner, solipsistic, esoteric; respective, several; fixed, definite, defined, distinct, different, different as night and day, determinate, certain, absolute; distinguished, noteworthy, exceptional, extraordinary; minute, detailed

13 **characteristic, peculiar, singular,** single, quintessential, intrinsic, unique, qualitative, **distinctive,** marked, distinguished, notable, nameable; appropriate, proper; idiosyncratic, idiocratic, in character, true to form, typical

14 this, this and no other, this one, this single; these; that, that one; those

ADVS **15** **particularly,** specially, especially, specifically, expressly, concretely, exactly, precisely, in particular, to be specific; definitely, distinctly; minutely, in detail, item by item, singly, separately

16 **personally,** privately, idiosyncratically, **individually;** in person, in the flesh; as for me, for all of me, for my part, as far as I am concerned

17 **characteristically,** peculiarly, singularly, intrinsically, uniquely, markedly, distinctively, in its own way, like no other

18 **namely,** nominally, that is to say, *videlicet* <L>, viz, *scilicet* <L>, scil, sc, to wit

19 each, apiece; severally, respectively, one by one, each to each; *per annum, per diem, per capita* <L>

PREPS **20** per, for each

COMBINING FORMS **21** -ness, -hood, -dom; aut-, auto-, idio-, self-; -acean, -aceous, -ey, -y, -ious, -ous, -ish, -ist, -istic, -istical, -itious, -itic, -ose, -some

866 SPECIALTY

<special knowledge, interest>

NOUNS **1** **specialty,** speciality, line, pursuit, mission, pet subject, business, line of business, line of country <Brit>, field, area, **main interest;** vocation; forte, métier, strong point, long suit; specialism, specialization; technicality; way, manner, style, type; lifestyle, way of life, preferences; cup of tea, bag, thing, thang, weakness

2 **special,** feature, main feature; leader, lead item, leading card

3 **specialist,** specializer, **expert,** authority, savant, scholar, connoisseur, maven; technical expert, technician, techie, nerd, digital native; pundit, critic; amateur, dilettante; fan, buff, freak, nut, aficionado; superuser; film buff, movie buff

VERBS **4** **specialize,** feature; narrow, restrict, limit, confine; specialize in, go in for, be into, have a weakness for, have a taste for, be strong in, follow, pursue, make one's business, make one's mission; major in, minor in; do one's thing

ADJS **5** **specialized,** specialist, specialistic; down one's alley, cut out for one, fits one like a glove; technical; restricted, limited, confined; featured, feature; expert, authoritative, knowledgeable

867 CONFORMITY

<behavior like most others>

NOUNS **1** **conformity; conformance,** conformation, other-directedness; compliance, acquiescence, goose step, lockstep, obedience, observance, subordination, traditionalism, orthodoxy; strictness; accordance, accord, correspondence, harmony, agreement, uniformity; consistency, congruity; accommodation, adaptation, adaption, pliancy, malleability, flexibility, adjustment; reconciliation, reconcilement; conventionality

2 **conformist,** conformer, sheep, trimmer, parrot, yes-man, organization man, company man, lackey; **conventionalist,** Mrs. Grundy, Babbitt, Philistine, middle-class type, button-down type, white-bread type, bourgeois, burgher, Middle American, plastic person, clone, square, three-piecer, yuppie, Barbie doll <tm>; model child; teenybopper; formalist, methodologist, perfectionist, precisianist, precisian, stick-in-the-mud; anal character, compulsive character; pedant

VERBS **3** **conform, comply,** correspond, accord, harmonize; adapt, adjust, accommodate, bend, meet, suit, fit, shape; comply with, agree with, tally with, fall in with, go by, be guided by, be regulated by, observe, follow, yield, take the shape of; adapt to, adjust to, gear to, assimilate to, accommodate to; reconcile, settle, compose; rub off corners; make conform, lick into shape, mold, force into a mold; straighten, rectify, correct, discipline

4 **follow the rules, toe the mark,** do it according to Hoyle, do it by the book, play the game; go through channels; fit in, follow the crowd, go with the crowd, follow the fashion, swim with the current, go with the tide, get on the bandwagon, trim one's sails to the breeze, follow the beaten path, do as others do, get in line, stay in line, fall in line, fall into line, fall in with; run true to form; keep in step, goose-step, walk in lockstep; keep up to standard, pass muster, come up to scratch

ADJS 5 **conformable**, adaptable, adaptive, adjustable; **compliant,** pliant, complaisant, malleable, flexible, plastic, acquiescent, unmurmuring, other-directed, submissive, tractable, obedient

6 **conformist,** conventional, bourgeois, plastic, square, straight, white-bread, white-bready, button-down, buttoned-down, cloned, clonish, cookie-cutter; orthodox, traditionalist, traditionalistic; kosher; formalistic, legalistic, precisianistic, anal, compulsive; pedantic, stuffy, hidebound, straitlaced, uptight; in accord, in keeping, in line, in step, in lockstep; corresponding, accordant, concordant, harmonious

ADVS 7 conformably, conformingly, in conformity, **obediently, pliantly**, flexibly, malleably, complaisantly, yieldingly, **compliantly,** submissively; conventionally, traditionally; anally, **compulsively;** pedantically

8 according to rule, according to regulations; according to Hoyle, **by the book**, by the numbers

PREPS 9 **conformable to, in conformity with**, in compliance with; according to, in accordance with, consistent with, in harmony with, in agreement with, in correspondence to; adapted to, adjusted to, accommodated to; proper to, suitable for, agreeable to, agreeably to; answerable to, in obedience to; congruent with, uniform with, in uniformity with; in line with, in step with, in lock-step with, in keeping with; after, by, per, as per

PHRS 10 don't rock the boat, don't make waves, get in line, shape up, shape up or ship out; when in Rome do as the Romans do

868 NONCONFORMITY

<behavior differing from most others>

NOUNS 1 **nonconformity,** unconformity, nonconformism, inconsistency, incongruity; inaccordance, disaccord, disaccordance; originality; **nonconformance,** disconformity; nonobservance, noncompliance, nonconcurrence, dissent, protest, rebellion, disagreement, contrariety, recalcitrance, refractoriness, recusance, recusancy; deviation, deviationism

2 **unconventionality,** unorthodoxy, revisionism, heterodoxy, heresy, originality, Bohemianism, beatnikism, hippiedom, counterculture, iconoclasm; eccentricity; alternative lifestyle, alternative society, alternative medicine

3 **nonconformist,** unconformist, **original,** eccentric, gonzo, deviant, deviationist, maverick, rebel, dropout, Bohemian, beatnik, free spirit, freethinker, independent, hippie, hipster, freak, flower child, New-Age Traveler; misfit, square peg in a round hole, fish out of water; *enfant terrible* <Fr>; dissenter; heretic; sectary, sectarian; nonjuror

VERBS 4 **not conform,** nonconform, not comply; get out of line, rock the boat, make waves, leave the beaten path, go out of bounds, upset the apple cart, break step, break bounds; drop out, opt out; dissent, swim against the current, swim against the tide, swim upstream, protest; hear a different drummer

ADJS 5 **nonconforming,** unconforming, nonconformable, unadaptable, unadjustable; **uncompliant,** unsubmissive; nonobservant; contrary, recalcitrant, refractory, recusant; deviant, deviationist, atypic, atypical, unusual; dissenting, dissident; antisocial

6 **unconventional,** unorthodox, eccentric, gonzo, heterodox, heretical; unfashionable, not done, not kosher, not cricket; offbeat, way-out, far out, kinky, out in left field, fringy, breakaway, out-of-the-way; **original,** maverick, Bohemian, beat, hippie, counterculture; nonformal, free and easy; outside the box

7 out of line, out of keeping, out of order, out of place, misplaced, out of step, out of turn, out of tune

869 NORMALITY

<expected condition, situation>

NOUNS 1 **normality, normalness**, typicality, normalcy, naturalness; health, wholesomeness, propriety, regularity; naturalism, naturism, realism; order

2 **usualness**, ordinariness, commonness, commonplaceness, averageness, mediocrity; generality, prevalence, currency
3 the normal, **the usual**, the ordinary, the common, the commonplace, the day-to-day, the way things are, the normal order of things; common variety, garden variety, the run of the mill
4 **rule**, law, principle, standard, criterion, canon, code, code of practice, maxim, prescription, guideline, rulebook, the book, regulation, reg, regs; norm, model, rule of behavior, ideal, ideal type, specimen type, exemplar; law of nature, natural law, universal law; form, formula, formulary, formality, prescribed form, set form; standing order, standard operating procedure; hard-and-fast rule, Procrustean law
5 **normalization**, standardization, regularization; codification, formalization

VERBS 6 **normalize**, standardize, regularize; codify, formalize
7 do the usual thing, make a practice of, carry on, carry on as usual, do business as usual

ADJS 8 **normal**, natural; general; typical, unexceptional; normative, prescribed, model, ideal, desired, white-bread, white-bready; naturalistic, naturistic, realistic; orderly
9 **usual**, regular; customary, habitual, accustomed, wonted, normative, prescriptive, standard, regulation, conventional; common, commonplace, ordinary, average, everyday, mediocre, familiar, household, vernacular, stock; prevailing, predominating, current, popular; universal

ADVS 10 **normally**, naturally; normatively, prescriptively, regularly; typically, usually, commonly, ordinarily, customarily, habitually, generally; mostly, chiefly, mainly, for the most part, most often, most frequently; as a rule, as a matter of course; as usual, as per usual; as may be expected, to be expected, as things go

COMBINING FORMS 11 norm-, normo-

870 ABNORMALITY

<unexpected condition, situation>

NOUNS 1 **abnormality,** abnormity; unnaturalness, unnaturalism, strangeness; **anomaly**, anomalousness, anomalism; aberration, aberrance, aberrancy; atypicality, atypicalness; irregularity, deviation, divergence, difference; eccentricity, erraticism, unpredictability, unpredictableness, randomness, chaos; monstrosity, teratism, amorphism, heteromorphism; subnormality; inferiority; superiority; derangement
2 **unusualness,** uncommonness, unordinariness, unwontedness, exceptionalness, exceptionality, extraordinariness; rarity, rareness, uniqueness; prodigiousness, marvelousness, wondrousness, fabulousness, mythicalness, remarkableness, stupendousness; incredibility, increditability, inconceivability, impossibility
3 **oddity,** queerness, curiousness, quaintness, peculiarity, absurdity, singularity; strangeness, outlandishness; bizarreness; fantasticality, anticness; freakishness, grotesqueness, grotesquerie, weirdness, gonzo, monstrousness, monstrosity, malformation, deformity, teratism
4 **<odd person>** oddity, character, type, case, natural, original, odd fellow, queer specimen; oddball, weirdo, odd fish, queer fish, odd duck, queer duck, rum one; rare bird, *rara avis* <L>; flake, eccentric; *meshuggenah* <Yiddish>; freak, screwball, crackpot, kook, nut, bird, gonzo; fanatic, crank, zealot; outsider, alien, foreigner; extraterrestrial, Martian, little green man, visitor from another planet; pariah, loner, lone wolf, solitary, hermit; hobo, tramp; maverick; outcast, outlaw, scapegoat; nonconformist
5 **<odd thing> oddity,** curiosity, wonder, funny thing, peculiar thing, strange thing; abnormality, **anomaly**; rarity, improbability, exception, one in a thousand, one in a million; prodigy, prodigiosity; curio, conversation piece; museum piece
6 monstrosity, **monster** <see list>, miscreation, abortion, teratism, abnormal birth, defective birth, abnormal fetus, defective fetus; **freak,** freak of nature
7 **supernaturalism,** supernaturalness, supernaturality, supranaturalism, supernormalness, preternaturalism, supersensibleness, superphysicalness, superhumanity; the paranormal; numinousness; unearthliness, unworldliness, otherworldliness, eeriness; transcendentalism; New Age; the supernatural, the occult, the supersensible; paranormality; supernature, supranature; mystery, mysteriousness, miraculousness, strangeness; faerie, witchery, elfdom
8 **miracle,** sign, signs and portents, prodigy, **wonder**, wonderwork; thaumatology, thaumaturgy; fantasy, enchantment

ADJS 9 **abnormal,** unnatural; **anomalous**, anomalistic; irregular, eccentric, erratic, deviative, divergent, different; aberrant, stray, straying, wandering; heteroclite, heteromorphic; formless, shapeless, amorphous; subnormal
10 **unusual,** unordinary, uncustomary, unwonted, uncommon, unfamiliar, atypic, atypical, unheard-of, *recherché* <Fr>; rare, unique,

sui generis <L, of its own kind>; out of the ordinary, out of this world, out-of-the-way, out of the common, out of the pale, off the beaten track, offbeat, breakaway; unexpected, not to be expected, unthought-of, undreamed-of

11 **odd,** queer, peculiar, absurd, singular, curious, oddball, **weird**, kooky, freaky, freaked-out, quaint, eccentric, gonzo, funny, rum; strange, outlandish, off-the-wall, surreal, not for real, passing strange, wondrous strange; flippy; unearthly; off, out

12 **fantastic,** fantastical, fanciful, antic, unbelievable, impossible, **incredible,** logic-defying, incomprehensible, unimaginable, unexpected, unaccountable, inconceivable

13 **freakish,** freak, freaky; **monstrous,** deformed, malformed, misshapen, misbegotten, teratogenic, teratoid; grotesque, bizarre, baroque, rococo

14 **extraordinary,** exceptional, remarkable, noteworthy, wonderful, marvelous, fabulous, mythical, legendary; stupendous, stupefying, prodigious, portentous, phenomenal; unprecedented, unexampled, unparalleled, not within the memory of man; indescribable, unspeakable, ineffable

15 **supernatural,** supranatural, preternatural; supernormal, hypernormal, preternormal, paranormal; superphysical, hyperphysical; numinous; supersensible, supersensual, pretersensual; superhuman, preterhuman, unhuman, nonhuman; supramundane, extramundane, transmundane, extraterrestrial; unearthly, unworldly, otherworldly, eerie; fey; psychical, spiritual, occult; transcendental; mysterious, arcane, esoteric

16 **miraculous, wondrous,** wonder-working, thaumaturgic, thaumaturgical, necromantic, prodigious; magical, enchanted, bewitched

ADVS 17 **unusually,** uncommonly, incredibly, unnaturally, abnormally, unordinarily, uncustomarily, unexpectedly; rarely, seldom, seldom if ever, once in a thousand years, hardly, hardly ever

18 **extraordinarily,** exceptionally, remarkably, wonderfully, marvelously, prodigiously, fabulously, unspeakably, ineffably, phenomenally, stupendously

19 **oddly,** queerly, peculiarly, singularly, curiously, quaintly, strangely, outlandishly, fantastically, fancifully; grotesquely, monstrously; eerily, mysteriously, supernaturally

COMBINING FORMS 20 terat-, terato-; medus-, medusi-, -pagus, anom-, anomo-, anomal-, anomalo-, anomali-, dys-, dis-, mal-, ne-, neo-, par-, para-, poly-, pseud-, pseudo-

21 **monster**

Abominable Snowman, yeti
Argus
basilisk
Bigfoot, Sasquatch
Briareus
bucentur
Cacus
Caliban
centaur
Cerberus
Ceto
Charybdis
chimera
cockatrice
Cyclops
dipsas
dragon
Echidna
Erebus
Frankenstein
Geryon
Gigantes
Gorgon
green-eyed monster
Grendel
griffin
Harpy
hippocampus
hippocentaur
hippocerf
hippogriff
hircocervus
Hydra
Jabberwock
Kraken
Ladon
Lamia
Leviathan
Loch Ness monster
manticore
Medusa
mermaid
merman
Midgard serpent
Minotaur
Mylodont
nixie
ogre
ogress
opinicus
Orthos, Orthros
Pegasus
Pongo
Python
roc
Sagittary
salamander
Sarsquatch
satyr
Scylla
sea horse
sea serpent
simurgh, simurg
siren
Sphinx
Talos
troll
Typhoeus
Typhon
unicorn
vampire
werewolf
windigo
wyvern
xiphopagus
yowie
zombie

871 LIST

<series of items>

NOUNS 1 **list, enumeration, itemization,** listing, shopping list, grocery list; laundry list; want list, wish list; hit list, drop-dead list, enemies list; blacklist; to-do list, bucket list; items, schedule, agenda; register, registry; inventory, repertory, tally; database, data base; spreadsheet, electronic spreadsheet; **checklist;** tally sheet; active list, civil list <Brit>, retired list, sick list; waiting list; short list; reading list; syllabus; A-list, B-list; shitlist*

2 **table,** contents, table of contents; computer listing, menu; chart

3 **catalog;** classified catalog, *catalogue raisonné* <Fr>; card catalog, bibliography, finding list,

handlist, reference list; filmography, discography; publisher's catalog, publisher's list; file, filing system, letter file, pigeonholes

4 **dictionary,** lexicon, glossary, **thesaurus,** Roget's, vocabulary, terminology, nomenclator; promptorium, gradus; gazetteer; almanac; telephone directory, address book; wordlist; book of lists

5 **bill,** statement, account, itemized account, invoice; ledger, books; bill of fare, **menu,** carte, wine list, dessert menu; bill of lading, manifest, waybill, docket

6 **roll, roster,** scroll, rota; roll call, muster, census, head count, poll, questionnaire, returns, census report; property roll, tax roll, cadastre; muster roll; checkroll, checklist; jury list; calendar, docket, agenda, order of business; daybook, journal, agenda book, diary; program, dramatis personae, credits, lineup; honor roll, dean's list; timetable, schedule, itinerary, prospectus

7 **index,** listing, tabulation; cataloging, itemization, filing, card file, card index, Rolodex <tm>, thumb index, indexing; registration, registry, enrollment

VERBS 8 **list, enumerate, itemize,** tabulate, catalog, tally; register, post, enter, enroll, book; impanel; file, pigeonhole, classify; index; inventory; calendar; score, keep score; schedule, program, put on the agenda; diarize; short-list

ADJS 9 **listed, enumerated,** entered, itemized, cataloged, tallied, inventoried; filed, indexed, tabulated; scheduled, programmed; put on the agenda; inventorial, glossarial, cadastral, classificatory, taxonomic; registered, recorded, noted

872 ONENESS

<state of being one or united into one>

NOUNS 1 **oneness,** unity, **singleness,** singularity, individuality, identity, selfsameness; particularity; uniqueness; intactness, inviolability, purity, simplicity, irreducibility, integrity, integrality; unification, uniting, integration, fusion, combination; solidification, solidity, solidarity, indivisibility, undividedness, wholeness; univocity, organic unity; uniformity; monocase, monotasking

2 **aloneness,** loneness, loneliness, lonesomeness, soleness, singleness; privacy, solitariness, **solitude**; separateness, aloofness, detachment, seclusion, sequestration, withdrawal, alienation, standing apart, keeping apart, isolation; celibacy, single blessedness

3 **one,** I, 1, unit, ace, atom; monad; one and only, none else, no other, nothing else, nought beside

4 **individual,** single, unit, integer, entity, singleton, item, article, point, module; person, wight, persona, soul, body, warm body; individuality, personhood; isolated case, single instance

VERBS 5 unify, reduce to unity, unitize, **make one**; integrate, unite

6 **stand alone,** stand apart, keep apart, keep oneself to oneself, withdraw, alienate oneself, sequester oneself, isolate oneself, feel out of place; individuate, become an individual; go solo, paddle one's own canoe, do one's own thing

ADJS 7 **one, single,** singular, individual, sole, unique, a certain, solitary, lone; exclusive; integral, indivisible, irreducible, monadic, monistic, unanalyzable, noncompound, atomic, unitary, unitive, unary, undivided, solid, wholecloth, seamless, uniform, simple, whole; an, any, any one, either

8 **alone, solitary,** solo; isolated, insular, apart, separate, separated, alienated, withdrawn, aloof, standoffish, detached, removed; **lone,** lonely, lonesome, lonely-hearts; private, reserved, reticent, reclusive, shy, nonpublic, ungregarious; friendless, kithless, homeless, rootless, companionless, unaccompanied, unescorted, unattended; unaided, unassisted, unabetted, unsupported, unseconded; single-handed, one-man, one-woman, one-person

9 **sole, unique,** singular, absolute, unrepeated, **alone,** lone, **only,** only-begotten, one and only, first and last; odd, impair, unpaired, azygous; celibate

10 unitary, integrated, integral, integrant; **unified,** united, rolled into one, composite

11 unipartite, unipart, **one-piece;** monadic, monadal; unilateral, **one-sided;** unilateralist, uniangulate, unibivalent, unibranchiate, unicameral, unicellular, unicuspid, unidentate, unidigitate; unidimensional, unidirectional; uniflorous, unifoliate, unifoliolate, unigenital, uniglobular, unilinear, uniliteral, unilobed, unilobular, unilocular, unimodular, unimolecular, uninuclear, uniocular, unisexual, unisex; unipolar, univalent, univocal; one-size; monolingual, monochromatic

12 **unifying,** uniting, unific; combining, combinative, combinatory; connective, connecting, connectional; conjunctive, conjunctival; coalescing, coalescent

ADVS 13 **singly,** individually, particularly, severally, one by one, one at a time; singularly, in the singular; alone, by itself, *per se* <L>; by oneself, by one's lonesome, on one's own, under one's own steam, single-handedly, solo, unaided; separately, apart; once

14 **solely,** exclusively, only, merely, purely, simply; entirely, wholly, totally; integrally, indivisibly, irreducibly, unanalyzably, undividedly

873 DOUBLENESS

<state of two combined>

NOUNS **1** **doubleness, duality,** dualism, duplexity, **twoness;** twofoldness, biformity; polarity; conjugation, pairing, coupling, yoking; doubling, duplication, twinning, bifurcation; dichotomy, bisection, halving, splitting down the middle, splitting fifty-fifty; duplicity, two-facedness, double-think, hypocrisy, Dr. Jekyll and Mr. Hyde; irony, enantiosis, ambiguity, equivocation, equivocality, ambivalence; Janus

2 **two,** 2, II, twain; **couple, pair,** matching pair, twosome, set of two, duo, duet, brace, team, span, yoke, double harness; match, matchup, mates; couplet, distich, double, doublet; duad, dyad; the two, both; Darby and Joan; tandem

3 **deuce;** pair, doubleton; craps, snake eyes

4 **twins,** pair of twins, identical twins, fraternal twins, exact mates, look-alikes, dead ringers, mirror image, carbon copy, Doppelganger, spit and image, spitting image; Tweedledum and Tweedledee, Siamese twins; Twin stars, Castor and Pollux, Gemini; pas de deux

VERBS **5** **double,** duplicate, replicate, dualize, twin; halve, split down the middle, split fifty fifty, bifurcate, dichotomize, bisect, transect; team, yoke, yoke together, span, double-team, double-harness; mate, match, couple, conjugate; **pair,** pair off, pair up, couple up, team up, match up, buddy up; talk out of both sides of one's mouth at once; square; copy, mirror, echo

ADJS **6** **two,** twain; **dual, double,** duple, duplex, doubled, twinned, duplicated, replicated, dualized; dualistic; dyadic; duadic; biform; bipartite, bipartisan, bilateral, either-or, two-sided, double-sided, binary; dichotomous; bifurcated, bisected, dichotomized, split down the middle, split fifty fifty; twin, identical, matched,; two-faced, duplicitous, hypocritical, double-faced, Janus-like; second, secondary; two-way, two-ply, dual-purpose, two-dimensional

7 **both,** the two, the pair; for two, tête-à-tête, *à deux* <Fr>

8 **coupled, paired,** yoked, yoked together, matched, matched up, mated, paired off, paired up, teamed up, buddied up; bracketed; conjugate, conjugated; biconjugate, bigeminate; bijugate

PHRS **9** it takes two to tango, it's not a one-way street

COMBINING FORMS **10** ambi-, amph-, amphi-, bi-, bin-, bis-, deut-, deuto-, deuter-, deutero-, di-, dis-, didym-, didymo-, duo-, dyo-, gem-, twi-, zyg-, zygo-

874 DUPLICATION

<two corresponding parts>

NOUNS **1** **duplication,** reduplication, replication, conduplication; reproduction, repro, **doubling;** twinning, gemination, ingemination; repetition, iteration, reiteration, echoing; imitation, parroting; copying; duplicate

2 **repeat,** encore, repeat performance; echo; do-over, retry

VERBS **3** **duplicate,** dupe, ditto; double, double up; multiply by two; twin, geminate, ingeminate; reduplicate, reproduce, replicate, redouble; repeat; copy, carbon-copy; double-dip

ADJS **4** **double, doubled, duplicate,** duplicated, reproduced, replicated, cloned, twinned, geminate, geminated, dualized

ADVS **5** **doubly;** twofold, as much again, twice as much; twice, two times, double-dip

6 **secondly,** second, secondarily, in the second place, in the second instance

7 again, another time, once more, once again, over again, yet again, *encore, bis* <Fr>; anew, afresh, new, freshly, newly

COMBINING FORMS **8** bi-, bis-, deuter-, deutero-, di-, dis-, diphy-, diphyo-, dipl-, diplo-, diss-, disso-, twi-

875 BISECTION

<divided into two equal parts>

NOUNS **1** **bisection,** bipartition, bifidity; **dichotomy, halving,** division, in half, by two, splitting in two, dividing in two, cutting in two, splitting fifty-fifty, dividing fifty-fifty; subdivision; bifurcation, forking, ramification, branching

2 **half,** moiety; halvsies; hemisphere, semisphere, semicircle, **fifty percent;** half-and-half, fifty-fifty

3 bisector, diameter, equator, halfway mark, divider, partition, line of demarcation, boundary

VERBS **4** **bisect, halve,** divide, divide in half, divide by two, transect, subdivide; cleave, fission, divide in two, split in two, cut in two, share and share alike, go halfers, go Dutch, dichotomize; bifurcate, fork, ramify, branch

ADJS **5** **half,** part, partly, partial, halfway

6 **halved, bisected,** divided; dichotomous; bifurcated, forked, forking, ramified, branched, branching; riven, split, cloven, cleft

7 **bipartite,** bifid, biform, bicuspid, biaxial, bicameral, binocular, binomial, binominal, biped, bipetalous, bipinnate, bisexual, bivalent, unibivalent

ADVS **8** **in half,** in halves, **in two,** in twain, by two,

down the middle; half-and-half, fifty-fifty; apart, asunder
COMBINING FORMS **9** bi-, demi-, dich-, dicho-, hemi-, semi-, sesqui-

876 THREE

<three units or members>

NOUNS **1** **three,** 3, III, **trio,** trey, threesome, trialogue, set of three, tierce, leash, troika; triad, trilogy, trine, trinity, triunity, ternary, ternion; triplet, tercet, terzetto; trefoil, shamrock, clover; tripod, trivet; triangle, tricorn, trihedron, trident, trisul, triennium, trimester, trinomial, trionym, triphthong, triptych, triplopy, trireme, triseme, triskelion, triumvirate; triple crown, triple threat; threespot, deuce-ace; triple-decker; menage a trois; hat trick
2 **threeness,** triplicity, triality, tripleness, trebleness, threefoldness; triunity, trinity
ADJS **3** **three, triple,** triplex, trinal, trine, trial; triadic, triadical; triune, three-in-one; triform; treble; triangular, deltoid, fan-shaped; triannual; trifold
COMBINING FORMS **4** tri-, ter-, ternati-

877 TRIPLICATION

<three corresponding parts>

NOUNS **1** **triplication,** triplicity, trebleness, **threefoldness;** triplicate
VERBS **2** **triplicate, triple,** treble, multiply by three, threefold; cube
ADJS **3** **triple,** triplicate, treble, threefold, trifold, triplex, trinal, trine, tern, ternary, ternal, ternate; three-ply; trilogic, trilocial
4 **third, tertiary**
ADVS **5** **triply,** trebly, trinely; threefold; **thrice,** three times, again and yet again
6 **thirdly,** in the third place
COMBINING FORMS **7** cub-, cubo-, cubi-; ter-; tert-, trit-, trito-

878 TRISECTION

<divided into three equal parts>

NOUNS **1** **trisection,** tripartition, trichotomy, trifurcation; triptych
2 **third,** tierce, third part, one-third; *tertium quid* <L, a third something>
VERBS **3** **trisect,** divide in thirds, divide in three, third, trichotomize; trifurcate
ADJS **4** **tripartite,** trisected, triparted, three-parted, trichotomous; three-sided, trihedral, trilateral; **three-dimensional;** three-forked, three-pronged, trifurcate; trident, tridental, tridentate, trifid; tricuspid; three-footed, tripodic, tripedal; trifoliate, trifloral, triflorate, triflorous, tripetalous, triadelphous, triarch; trimerous, 3-merous; three-cornered, tricornered, tricorn; trigonal, trigonoid; triquetrous, triquetral; trigrammatic, triliteral; *triangular,* triangulate, deltoid

879 FOUR

<four units or members>

NOUNS **1** **four,** 4, IV, tetrad, quatern, quaternion, quaternary, quaternity, **quartet,** quadruplet, **foursome;** quatre; Little Joe, little Joe from Kokomo, little Dick Fisher; quadrennium; tetralogy; tetrapody; tetraphony, four-part diaphony; quadrille, square dance; quatrefoil, quadrifoil, four-leaf clover; tetragram, tetragrammaton; quadrangle, quad, rectangle; tetrahedron; tetragon, square; biquadrate; quadrinomial; quadrature, squaring; quadrilateral
2 **fourness,** quaternity, quadruplicity, fourfoldness
VERBS **3** **square,** quadrate, form four, make four; form fours, form squares; cube, dice
ADJS **4** **four;** foursquare; quaternary, quartile, quartic, quadric, quadratic; tetrad, tetradic; quadrinomial, biquadratic; tetractinal, four-rayed, quadruped, four-legged; quadrivalent, tetravalent; quadrilateral
COMBINING FORMS **5** quadr-, quadri-, quadru-, tetr-, tetra-, tessar-, tessara-, tri-, trip-, tripl-, triplo-, tris-

880 QUADRUPLICATION

<four corresponding parts>

NOUNS **1** **quadruplication,** quadruplicature, quadruplicity, fourfoldness
VERBS **2** **quadruple,** quadruplicate, fourfold, form four, make four, multiply by four; quadrate, biquadrate, quadruplex
ADJS **3** **quadruplicate,** quadruple, quadraple, quadruplex, **fourfold,** four-ply, four-part, tetraploid, quadrigeminal, biquadratic
COMBINING FORMS **4** quadr-, quadri, quadru-, quater-, tetr-, tetra-, tetrakis-

881 QUADRISECTION

<divided into four equal parts>

NOUNS **1** **quadrisection,** quadripartition, **quartering**
2 **fourth,** one-fourth, **quarter,** one-quarter, fourth

part, twenty-five percent, twenty-five cents, two bits; quartern; quart; farthing; quarto, 4to, 4°

VERBS 3 **divide into four**, divide by four, quadrisect, quarter

ADJS 4 quadrisected, **quartered,** quarter-cut; quadripartite, quadrifid, quadriform; quadrifoliate, quadrigeminal, quadripinnate, quadriplanar, quadriserial, quadrivial, quadrifurcate; quadrumanal, quadrumanous

5 **fourth, quarter**

ADVS 6 **fourthly,** in the fourth place; quarterly, by quarters

882 FIVE AND OVER

<five or more units or members>

NOUNS 1 **five,** V, cinque, phoebe, little Phoebe, fever; quintet, fivesome, quintuplets, quints, cinquain, quincunx, pentad; fifth; five dollars, fiver, fin, finniff, five bucks; pentagon, pentahedron, pentagram; pentapody, pentameter, pentastich; pentarchy; Pentateuch; pentachord; pentathlon; five-pointed star, pentacle, pentalpha, mullet <heraldry>; five-spot; quinquennium

2 **six,** VI, sixie from Dixie, Sister Hicks, Jimmy Hicks, Captain Hicks, half a dozen, sextet, sestet, sextuplets, hexad; hexagon, hexahedron, hexagram, six-pointed star, estoile <heraldry>, Jewish star, star of David, *Magen David* <Heb>; hexameter, hexapody, hexastich; hexapod; hexarchy; Hexateuch; hexastyle; hexachord; six-shooter; sixth sense; six-pack

3 **seven**, VII, heptad, little natural; septet; heptagon, heptahedron; heptameter, heptastich; septemvir, heptarchy; Septuagint, Heptateuch; heptachord; week; seven deadly sins; seven seas; Seven Wonders of the World

4 **eight**, VIII, Ogdoad, eighter, Ada from Decatur, Ada Ross, Ada Ross the stable hoss; octad, octonary; octagon, octahedron; octastylos, oktostylos; octave, octavo, 8vo; octachord; octet, octal, octameter; Octateuch; piece of eight; Eightfold Path

5 **nine,** IX, niner, Nina from Carolina, Nina Ross the stable hoss, Nina Nina ocean liner; ennead; nonagon, enneagon, enneahedron; novena; enneastylos; nine days' wonder

6 **ten,** X, Big Dick, Big Dick from Battle Creek; decade; decagon, decahedron; decagram, decigram, decaliter, deciliter, decare, decameter, decimeter, decastere; decapod; decastylos; decasyllable; decemvir, decemvirate, decurion; decennium, decennary; Ten Commandments, Decalogue; tithe; decathlon

7 <**eleven** to ninety> eleven; twelve, dozen, boxcar, boxcars, duodecimo, twelvemo, 12mo; teens; thirteen, long dozen, baker's dozen; fourteen, two weeks, fortnight; fifteen, quindecima, quindene, quindecim, quindecennial; sixteen, sixteenmo, 16mo; twenty, score; twenty-four, four and twenty, two dozen, twenty-fourmo, 24mo; twenty-five, five and twenty, quarter of a century; thirty-two, thirty-twomo, 32mo; forty, twoscore, quadragenarian; fifty, L, half a hundred; sixty, sexagenary; Sexagesima; sexagenarian, threescore; sixty-four, sixty-fourmo, 64mo, sexagesimo-quarto; seventy, septuagenarian, threescore and ten; eighty, superager, octogenarian, fourscore; ninety, nonagenarian, four-score and ten

8 **hundred, century,** C, one C; centennium, centennial, centenary; centenarian; cental, centigram, centiliter, centimeter, centare, centistere; hundredweight (cwt); hecatomb; centipede; centumvir, centumvirate, centurion; great hundred, long hundred (120); gross (144), sesquicentennial, sesquicentenary (150); bicentenary, bicentennial (200); tercentenary, tercentennial (300)

9 **five hundred,** D, five centuries; five C's

10 **thousand,** M, chiliad; **millennium;** G, grand, thou, yard; chiliagon, chiliahedron, chiliaüdron; chiliarchia, chiliarch; millepede; milligram, milliliter, millimeter, kilogram, kilo, kiloliter, kilometer; kilocycle, kilohertz; kilobyte; gigabyte; ten thousand, myriad; one hundred thousand

11 **million;** ten million

12 **billion,** thousand million, milliard

13 trillion, quadrillion, quintillion, sextillion, septillion, octillion, nonillion, decillion, undecillion, duodecillion, tredecillion, quattuordecillion, quindecillion, sexdecillion, septendecillion, octodecillion, novemdecillion, vigintillion; googol, googolplex; zillion, jillion

14 <division into five or more parts> quinquesection, quinquepartition, sextipartition; decimation, decimalization; fifth, sixth; tenth, tithe, decima

VERBS 15 <divide by five> quinquesect; decimalize

16 <multiply by five or more> fivefold, sixfold; quintuple, quintuplicate; sextuple, sextuplicate; centuple, centuplicate

ADJS 17 **fifth,** quinary; fivefold, quintuple, quintuplicate; quinquennial; quinquepartite, pentadic, quinquefid; quincuncial, pentastyle; pentad, pentavalent, quinquevalent; pentagonal

18 **sixth,** senary; sixfold, sextuple; sexpartite, hexadic, sextipartite, hexapartite; hexagonal, hexahedral, hexangular; hexad, hexavalent; sextuplex, hexastyle; sexennial; hexatonic

19 **seventh,** septimal; sevenfold, septuple, septenary; septempartite, heptadic, septemfid; heptagonal, heptahedral, heptangular; heptamerous; hebdomal

20 **eighth,** octonary; eightfold, octuple; octadic; octal, octofid, octaploid; octagonal, octahedral, octan, octangular; octosyllabic; octastyle

21 **ninth,** novenary, nonary; ninefold, nonuple, enneadic; enneahedral, enneastyle, nonagonal

22 **tenth,** denary, decimal, tithe; tenfold, decuple; decagonal, decahedral; decasyllabic; decennial

23 **eleventh,** undecennial, undecennary

24 **twelfth,** duodenary, duodenal; duodecimal

25 thirteenth, fourteenth (etc.); eleventeenth, umpteenth; in one's teens

26 twentieth, vicenary, vicennial, vigesimal, vicesimal

27 sixtieth, sexagesimal, sexagenary

28 seventieth, septuagesimal, septuagenary

29 **hundredth,** centesimal, **centennial,** centenary, centurial; hundredfold, centuple, centuplicate; secular; centigrado

30 **thousandth,** millenary, **millennial;** thousandfold

31 millionth; billionth, quadrillionth, quintillionth

COMBINING FORMS **32** pent-, penta-, pen-, quinqu-, quinque-, quintquinti-; hex-, hexa-, sex-, sexi-, sexti-; hept-, hepta-, sept-, septi-; oct-, octa-, octo-; non-, nona-, ennea-; deca-, deka-, deci-; undec-, hendec-, hendeca-; dodec-, dodeca-; icos-, icosa-, icosi-, eicos-, eicosa-, cent-, centi-, hect-, hecto-, hecato-, hecaton; kilo-, milli-; meg-, mega-, micro-; giga-, nano-; pico-

883 PLURALITY

<large number or quantity>

NOUNS **1** **plurality,** pluralness; a greater number, a certain number; several, some, a few, more; plural number, the plural; compositeness, nonsingleness, nonuniqueness; pluralism, variety; numerousness

2 **majority,** plurality, more than half, the greater number, the greatest number, most, preponderance, preponderancy, greater part, better part, bulk, mass; lion's share

3 pluralization, plurification

4 **multiplication,** multiplying, proliferation, increase; duplication; multiple, multiplier, multiplicand, product, factor; factorization, exponentiation; multiplication table; lowest common multiple, least common multiple, greatest common divisor, highest common factor, greatest common factor; prime factor, submultiple, power, square, cube, fourth power, exponent, index, square root, cube root, surd, root mean square, factorial

VERBS **5** **pluralize,** plurify; raise to more than one, make more than one

6 **multiply,** proliferate, increase, duplicate

ADJS **7** **plural,** pluralized, more than one, more, several, severalfold; some, certain; not singular, composite, nonsingle, nonunique; plurative; pluralistic, various; many, beaucoup, numerous

8 **multiple,** multiplied, multifold, manifold; increased; multinomial, polynomial, preponderous

9 **majority,** most, the greatest number

ADVS **10** **in the majority;** and others, et al, et cetera; plurally

COMBINING FORMS **11** multi-; -fold

884 NUMEROUSNESS

<great number or quantity>

NOUNS **1** **numerousness, multiplicity,** manyness, manifoldness, multifoldness, multitudinousness, multifariousness, teemingness, swarmingness, rifeness, profuseness, profusion; plenty, abundance; countlessness, innumerability, infinitude, infinity

2 **<indefinite number>** a number, a certain number, one or two, two or three, a few, several, parcel, passel; eleventeen, umpteen; lots, lotsa

3 **<large number> multitude,** throng; a many, numbers, quantities, lots, flocks, scores, scads, oodles; an abundance of, all kinds of, all sorts of, no end of, quite a few, tidy sum; muchness, any number of, large amount; host, army, more than one can shake a stick at, fistful, slew, shitload*, shithouse full*, legion, rout, ruck, mob, jam, clutter; swarm, flock, flight, cloud, hail, bevy, covey, shoal, hive, nest, pack, litter, bunch; a world of, a mass of, worlds of, masses of; small fortune

4 **<immense number>** a myriad, a thousand, a thousand and one, a million, a billion, a quadrillion, a nonillion; umpteen, a zillion, jillion, gazillion, bazillion; googol, googolplex

VERBS **5** **teem with,** overflow with, **abound with,** burst with, bristle with, pullulate with, swarm with, throng with, creep with, crawl with, be alive with, have coming out of one's ears, have up the gazoo; clutter, crowd, jam, pack, overwhelm, overflow; multiply; outnumber; overcrowd

ADJS **6** **numerous,** many, manifold, not a few, no few; very many, full many, ever so many, considerable, quite some, quite a few; **multitudinous,** multitudinal, multifarious, multifold, multiple, **myriad,** thousand, million, billion; zillion, jillion; heaped-up; numerous as the stars, numerous as the sands, numerous as the hairs on the head

7 **several,** divers, sundry, various; fivish, sixish; some five or six; upwards of

8 **abundant,** copious, ample, plenteous, plentiful, thick on the ground <Brit>

9 **teeming,** swarming, crowding, thronging, overflowing, overcrowded, overwhelming, bursting, crawling, alive with, lousy with, populous, prolific, proliferating, crowded, packed, jammed, bumper-to-bumper, jam-packed, like sardines in a can, thronged, studded, bristling, rife, lavish, prodigal, superabundant, **profuse,** in profusion, thick, thick with, thick-coming, thick as hail, thick as flies

10 **innumerable,** numberless, unnumbered, countless, uncounted, uncountable, unquantifiable, unreckonable, untold, incalculable, immeasurable, unmeasured, measureless, inexhaustible, endless, infinite, without end, without limit, more than one can tell, more than you can shake a stick at, no end of, no end to; countless as the stars, countless as the sands; **astronomical,** galactic; millionfold, trillionfold

11 and many more, and what not, and heaven knows what

ADVS 12 **numerously,** multitudinously, profusely, swarmingly, teemingly, thickly, copiously, abundantly, prodigally; innumerably, countlessly, infinitely, incalculably, inexhaustibly, immeasurably; in throngs, in crowds, in swarms, in heaps; no end

COMBINING FORMS 13 multi-, myri-, myrio-, pluri-, poly-

885 FEWNESS

<very few in number or quantity>

NOUNS 1 **fewness,** infrequency, **sparsity,** sparseness, **scarcity,** paucity, scantiness, meagerness, miserliness, niggardliness, tightness, thinness, stringency, restrictedness; chintziness, chinchiness, stinginess, scrimpiness, skimpiness; rarity, exiguity; smallness; unsubstantiality, insubstantiality; skeleton staff

2 **a few,** too few, mere few, piddling few, piddly few, only a few, small number, limited number, not enough to count, not enough to matter, not enough to shake a stick at, **handful,** scattering, corporal's guard, sprinkling, trickle; low turnout, poor turnout, too few to mention

3 **minority,** least; the minority, the few; minority group; minimum; less

ADJS 4 **few, not many;** hardly any, scarcely any, precious little, precious few, of small number, to be counted on one's fingers, too few

5 **sparse,** scant, scanty, exiguous, infrequent, sporadic, scarce, scarce as hen's teeth, poor, piddling, piddly, thin, slim, meager, not much; miserly, niggardly, cheeseparing, tight; chintzy, chinchy, stingy, scrimpy, skimpy, skimping, scrimping; scattered, sprinkled, spotty, few and far between; rare, seldom met with, seldom seen, not thick on the ground <Brit>

6 **fewer, less,** smaller, not so much, not so many, reduced, minimal

7 **minority,** least

ADVS 8 **sparsely,** scantily, meagerly, exiguously, piddlingly; stingily, scrimpily, skimpily, thinly; scarcely, rarely, infrequently; scatteringly, scatterdly, spottily, in dribs and drabs, in bits and pieces, here and there, in places, in spots

886 CAUSE

<reason for action, condition>

NOUNS 1 **cause,** occasion, antecedents, grounds, ground, background, backstory, stimulus, base, basis, element, principle, factor; **determinant,** determinative; causation, causality, cause and effect, karma; etiology

2 **reason,** reason why, rationale, reason for, reason behind, underlying reason, rational ground, explanation, answer, the why, the wherefore, the whatfor, the whyfor, the why and wherefore, the idea, the big idea; stated cause, pretext, pretense, excuse

3 **immediate cause,** proximate cause, trigger, spark; domino effect, causal sequence, chain of cause and effect, nexus of cause and effect, ripple effect, slippery slope, contagion effect, knock-on, knock-on effect <Brit>; transient cause, occasional cause; formal cause; efficient cause; ultimate cause, immanent cause, remote cause, causing cause, first cause; final cause, end, end in view, teleology; provocation, last straw, straw that broke the camel's back, match in the powder barrel; butterfly effect, strange attraction, sensitive dependence on initial conditions; planetary influence, astrological influence

4 author, **agent**, originator, generator, begetter, engenderer, producer, maker, beginner, creator, mover, inventor; parent, mother, father, sire; **prime mover**; causer, effector; inspirer, instigator, catalyst, mobilizer; motivator, inspiration

5 **source, origin,** genesis, original, origination, derivation, rise, beginning, conception, inception, commencement, head; provenance, provenience,

background; root, radix, radical, taproot, grassroots; stem, stock

6 **fountainhead,** headwater, headstream, riverhead, springhead, headspring, mainspring, wellspring, wellhead, well, spring, fountain, fount, font; mine, quarry

7 **vital force,** vital principle, *élan vital* <Fr>, reproductive urge, a gleam in one's father's eye; egg, ovum, germ, spermatozoon, nucleus, seed; embryo; bud; loins; womb, matrix, uterus

8 **birthplace,** breeding place, breeding ground, birthsite, rookery, hatchery; hotbed, forcing bed; incubator, brooder; nest, nidus; cradle, nursery

9 <a principleor movement> **cause, mission,** principle, interest, issue, burning issue, commitment, faith, great cause, lifework; reason for being, *raison d'être* <Fr>; movement, mass movement, activity; drive, campaign, crusade; zeal, passion, fanaticism

VERBS 10 **cause,** be the cause of, lie at the root of; **bring about,** bring to pass, effectuate, effect, bring to effect, realize; impact, impact on, influence; occasion, make, create, engender, generate, produce, breed, work, do; originate, give origin to, give occasion to, give rise to, spark, spark off, set off, trigger, trigger off; give birth to, beget, bear, bring forth, labor, travail, author, father, sire, sow the seeds of; gestate, conceive, have the idea, have a bright idea; set up, set afloat, set on foot; found, establish, inaugurate, institute; engineer

11 **induce,** lead, procure, get, obtain, contrive, **effect,** bring, bring on, draw on, call forth, elicit, evoke, provoke, inspire, influence, instigate, egg on, motivate; draw down, open the door to; suborn; superinduce; incite, kindle

12 **determine,** decide, turn the scale, have the last word, tip the scale; necessitate, entail, require; contribute to, have a hand in, lead to, conduce to; advance, forward, influence, subserve; spin off, hive off <Brit>

ADJS 13 **causal,** causative; chicken-and-egg; occasional; originative, institutive, constitutive; at the bottom of, behind the scenes; formative, determinative, effectual, decisive, pivotal; etiological

14 **original, primary,** primal, primitive, pristine, primo, primeval, aboriginal, elementary, elemental, basic, basal, rudimentary, crucial, central, radical, fundamental; embryonic, in embryo, *in ovo* <L>, germinal, seminal, pregnant; generative, genetic, protogenic; effectual

COMBINING FORMS 15 uter-, utero-, metr-, metro-, -metrium, venter; etio-, aetio-, prot-, proto-; -facient, -factive, -fic, -ic, -ical, -etic

887 EFFECT

<something resulting from cause>

NOUNS 1 **effect, result,** resultant, **consequence,** consequent, sequent, sequence, sequel, sequela, sequelae; event, eventuality, eventuation, upshot, outcome, end state, logical outcome, possible outcome, scenario; outgrowth, spinoff, offshoot, offspring, issue, aftermath, legacy; side effect; product, precipitate, distillate, fruit, first fruits, crop, harvest, payoff; development, corollary; derivative, derivation, by-product; net result, end result; **cause-and-effect, karma**

2 **impact,** force, **repercussion,** reaction; backwash, backlash, reflex, recoil, response; mark, print, imprint, impress, impression; significance, import, meaning

3 **aftereffect,** aftermath, aftergrowth, aftercrop, afterclap, aftershock, afterimage, afterglow, aftertaste; wake, trail, track; domino effect

VERBS 4 **result,** ensue, issue, **follow,** attend, accompany; turn out, come out, fall out, redound, work out, pan out, fare; have a happy result, turn out well, come up roses; turn out to be, prove, prove to be; become of, come of, come about; develop, unfold; eventuate, terminate, end; end up, land up <Brit>, wind up

5 **result from,** be the effect of, be due to, originate in, originate from, **come from,** come out of, grow from, grow out of, follow from, follow on, proceed from, descend from, emerge from, issue from, ensue from, emanate from, flow from, derive from, accrue from, rise from, arise from, take its rise from, spring from, stem from, sprout from, bud from, germinate from; spin off; depend on, hinge on, pivot on, turn on, hang on, be contingent on; pay off, bear fruit

ADJS 6 **resultant, resulting,** following, ensuing; consequent, consequential, sequent, sequential, sequacious; necessitated, entailed, required; final; derivative, derivational

ADVS 7 **consequently, as a result,** as a consequence, in consequence, in the event, naturally, necessarily, of necessity, inevitably, of course, as a matter of course, and so, it follows that; therefore; accordingly; finally

CONJS 8 **resulting from,** coming from, arising from, deriving from, derivable from, consequent to, in consequence of; **owing to,** due to; attributed to, attributable to, dependent on, contingent on; caused by, occasioned by, at the bottom of; required by, entailed by, following from, following strictly from

PHRS 9 one thing leads to another, what goes up

must come down, what goes around comes around

888 ATTRIBUTION

<assignment of cause>

NOUNS 1 **attribution,** assignment, assignation, **ascription,** imputation, arrogation, placement, application, attachment, saddling, charge, blame; indictment; responsibility, answerability; credit, honor; accounting for, reference to, derivation from, connection with; guilt by association; etiology

2 **acknowledgment,** citation, tribute; confession; reference; trademark, signature; byline, credit line

VERBS 3 **attribute, assign,** ascribe, impute, give, place, put, apply, attach, refer

4 **attribute to, ascribe to,** impute to, assign to, lay to, put down to, set down to, apply to, refer to, point to; pin on, pinpoint, fix on, attach to, connect with, fasten upon, hang on, saddle on, place upon, father upon, settle upon, saddle with; blame, blame for, blame on, charge on, place the blame on, put the blame on, place the blame for, place the responsibility for, indict, fix the responsibility for, point to one, put the finger on, finger, fix the burden of, charge to, lay to one's charge, place to one's account, set to the account of, account for, lay at the door of, bring home to; acknowledge, confess; credit with, accredit with; put words in one's mouth

5 **trace to,** follow the trail to; **derive from,** trace the origin of, trace the derivation of; affiliate to, filiate to, father, fix the paternity of

ADJS 6 **attributable,** assignable, ascribable, imputable, traceable, referable, accountable, explicable; owing, due, assigned to, referred to, derivable from, derivative, derivational; charged, alleged, imputed, putative; credited, attributed

ADVS 7 **hence, therefore,** therefor, wherefore, wherefrom, whence, then, thence, *ergo* <L>, for which reason; consequently; accordingly; because of that, for that, by reason of that, for that reason, for the reason that, in consideration of something, from that cause, for that cause, on that account, on that ground, thereat; because of this, on this account, for this cause, on account of this, for this reason, hereat; thus, thusly, thuswise; on someone's head, on someone's doorstep, at someone's doorstep

8 **why,** whyever, whyfor, for why, how come, how is it that, wherefore, what for, for which, on what account, on account of what, on account of which, for what reason, for whatever reason, from what cause, *pourquoi* <Fr>

PREPS 9 **because of,** by reason of, as a result of, by virtue of, in virtue of, on account of, on the score of, for the sake of, owing to, due to, thanks to; considering, in consideration of, in view of; after

CONJS 10 **because,** since, as, for, cuz, whereas, inasmuch as, forasmuch as, insofar as, insomuch as, as things go; in that, for the cause that, for the reason that, in view of the fact that, taking into account that, seeing that, seeing as how, being as how; resulting from

889 OPERATION

<performance of practical work>

NOUNS 1 **operation, functioning,** action, performance, performing, working, work, workings, exercise, practice; agency; implementation; operations; management, direction, conduct, running, carrying-on, carrying-out, execution, seeing to, overseeing, oversight; handling, manipulation; responsibility; occupation; joint operation

2 **process, procedure,** proceeding, course; what makes it tick; act, step, measure, initiative, *démarche* <Fr>, move, maneuver, motion

3 **workability,** operability, operativeness, performability, negotiability, manageability, compassability, manipulatability, maneuverability; practicability, feasibility, viability

4 **operator,** operative, operant; handler, manipulator; manager, executive; functionary, agent; driver

VERBS 5 **operate, function,** run, work; manage, direct, conduct; carry on, carry out, carry through, make go, make work, carry the ball, perform; handle, manipulate, maneuver; deal with, see to, take care of; occupy oneself with; be responsible for

6 **operate on**, act on, act upon, work on, affect, influence, bear on, impact, impact on; have to do with, treat, focus on, concentrate on; bring to bear on

7 <**be operative**> operate, function, work, act, perform, go, run, be in action, be in operation, be in commission; percolate, perk, tick; be effective, go into effect, have effect, take effect, militate; be in force; have play, have free play

8 **function as,** work as, act as, act the part of, play the part of, have the function of, have the role of, have the job of, have the mission of; do one's thing

ADJS 9 **operative, operational,** go, functional,

practical, in working order; effective, effectual, efficient, efficacious; relevant, significant

10 **workable, operable,** operatable, performable, actable, doable, manageable, compassable, negotiable, manipulatable, maneuverable; practicable, feasible, practical, viable, useful

11 **operating, operational,** working, functioning, operant, functional, acting, active, running, going, going on, ongoing; in operation, in action, in practice, in force, in play, in exercise, at work, on foot; in process, in the works, on the fire, in the pipe, in the pipeline, in hand, up and going

12 **operational, functional**; managerial; agential, agentive, agentival; manipulational

COMBINING FORMS **13** -age, -al, -ance, -ence, -ation, -ing, -ion, -ism, -ization, -isation, -ment, -osis, -sis, -th, -ure

890 PRODUCTIVENESS

<operation yielding results>

NOUNS **1** **productiveness, productivity,** productive capacity; fruitfulness, fructification, procreativeness, progenitiveness, fertility, fecundity, fecundation, prolificness, prolificity, prolificacy; pregnancy; luxuriance, exuberance, generousness, bountifulness, plentifulness, plenteousness, richness, lushness, abundance, superabundance, copiousness, teemingness, swarmingness, uberty; teeming womb, teeming loins; sperm bank

2 proliferation, multiplication, fructification, pullulation, teeming; reproduction, production

3 **fertilization, enrichment,** fecundation; propagation, pollination; insemination; impregnation

4 **fertilizer,** dressing, top dressing, enricher, richener, procreator, propagator; organic fertilizer, manure, muck, mulch, night soil, dung, guano, compost, vermicompost, leaf litter, leaf mold, humus, peat moss, castor-bean meal, bone meal, fish meal; commercial fertilizer, inorganic fertilizer, chemical fertilizer, phosphate, superphosphate, ammonia, nitrogen, nitrate, potash, ammonium salts, sulfate, lime, marl

5 <goddesses> Demeter, Ceres, Isis, Astarte, Ashtoreth, Venus of Willenburg; <gods> Frey, Priapus, Dionysus, Pan, Baal; fertility cult

6 <comparisons> rabbit, Hydra, warren, seed plot, hotbed, rich soil, land flowing with milk and honey

VERBS **7** **produce, be productive,** proliferate, pullulate, fructify, be fruitful, multiply, procreate, propagate, generate, mushroom, spin off, hive off <Brit>, engender, beget, teem; reproduce

8 **fertilize, enrich,** make fertile, richen, fatten, feed; fructify, fecundate, fecundify, prolificate; inseminate, impregnate; pollinate, germinate, seed; cross-fertilize, cross-pollinate; dress, top-dress; manure, compost, mulch, marl

ADJS **9** **productive, fruitful,** fructiferous, fecund; fertile, pregnant, seminal, rich, flourishing, thriving, blooming; prolific, proliferous, uberous, teeming, swarming, bursting, bursting out, plenteous, plentiful, copious, generous, bountiful, abundant, luxuriant, exuberant, lush, superabundant; creative

10 **bearing, yielding,** producing; fruitbearing, fructiferous

11 **fertilizing,** enriching, richening, fattening, fecundatory, fructificative, **seminal,** germinal; compostable

891 UNPRODUCTIVENESS

<operation lacking results>

NOUNS **1** **unproductiveness,** unproductivity, ineffectualness; unfruitfulness, fruitlessness, barrenness, nonfruition, dryness, aridity, dearth, famine; sterileness, sterility, unfertileness, infertility, infecundity; wasted loins, withered loins, dry womb; birth control, contraception, family planning, planned parenthood; abortion; impotence, incapacity

2 **wasteland, waste,** desolation, barren, **barrens,** barren land; heath; **desert,** Sahara, sands, desert sands, badlands, dust bowl, salt flat, Death Valley, Arabia Deserta, lunar waste, lunar landscape; desert island; wilderness, howling wilderness, wild, wilds; treeless plain; bush, brush, outback; fallowness, aridness; desertification, desertization; sin city

VERBS **3** be unproductive, **come to nothing,** come to naught, prove infertile, hang fire, flash in the pan, fizzle out, peter out; **lie fallow;** stagnate, run to seed

ADJS **4** **unproductive,** nonproductive, nonproducing; **infertile, sterile,** unfertile, nonfertile, unfruitful, unfructuous, acarpous, infecund, unprolific, nonprolific; impotent, gelded; ineffectual; barren, desert, arid, dry, dried-up, sere, exhausted, drained, leached, sucked dry, **wasted,** gaunt, waste, desolate, jejune; childless, issueless, without issue; fallow, unplowed, unsown, untilled, uncultivated, unfecundated; celibate; virgin; menopausal

5 **uncreative,** noncreative, nonseminal, nongerminal, unfructified, unpregnant; uninventive, unoriginal, derivative

892 PRODUCTION

<process of making, creating>

NOUNS 1 **production, creation, making,** origination, invention, conception, innovation, originating, engenderment, engendering, genesis, beginning; devising, hatching, fabrication, concoction, coinage, mintage, contriving, contrivance; authorship; creative effort, generation; improvisation, making do; gross national product (GNP), net national product (NNP), national production of goods and services

2 production, **manufacture**, **manufacturing**, making, producing, devising, design, fashioning, framing, forming, formation, formulation; engineering, tooling-up; processing, conversion; casting, shaping, molding; machining, milling, finishing; assembly, composition, elaboration; workmanship, craftsmanship, skill; construction, building, erection, architecture; fabrication, prefabrication; handiwork, handwork, handicraft, crafting; mining, extraction, smelting, refining; growing, cultivation, raising, harvesting

3 industrial production, **industry, mass production,** volume production, assembly-line production; production line, assembly line; modular production, modular assembly, standardization; division of labor, industrialization; heavy industry; light industry; cottage industry; piecework, farmed-out work; badge engineering

4 **establishment,** foundation, constitution, institution, installation, formation, organization, inauguration, inception, setting-up, realization, materialization, effectuation; spinning-off, hiving-off <Brit>

5 **performance, execution,** doing, accomplishment, achievement, productive effort, productive effect, realization, bringing to fruition, fructification, effectuation, operation; overproduction, glut; underproduction, scarcity; productiveness, fructuousness

6 **bearing,** yielding, birthing; **fruition,** fruiting, fructification

7 **producer, maker,** craftsman, wright, smith; **manufacturer,** industrialist; creator, begetter, engenderer, author, mother, father, sire; ancestors; precursor; originator, initiator, establisher, inaugurator, introducer, institutor, beginner, mover, prime mover, motive force, instigator; founder, organizer, founding father, founding member, founder member, founding partner, cofounder; inventor, discoverer, deviser; developer; engineer; builder, constructor, artificer, architect, planner, conceiver, designer, shaper, master spirit, leading spirit; executor, executrix; facilitator, animator; grower, raiser, cultivator; effector, realizer; apprentice, journeyman, master, master craftsman, workman, artist, past master

VERBS 8 **produce, create,** make, **manufacture**, form, formulate, evolve, mature, elaborate, fashion, fabricate, prefabricate, cast, shape, configure, carve out, mold, extrude, frame; construct, build, erect, put up, set up, run up, raise, rear; make up, get up, prepare, compose, write, indite, devise, design, concoct, compound, churn out, crank out, pound out, hammer out, grind out, rustle up, gin up; put together, assemble, piece together, patch together, whomp up, fudge together, slap up, slap together, improvise; make to order, custom-make, custom-build, purpose-build <Brit>

9 **process,** convert; mill, machine; carve, chisel; mine, extract, pump, smelt, refine; raise, rear, grow, cultivate, harvest

10 **establish,** found, constitute, institute, install, form, set up, organize, equip, endow, inaugurate, realize, materialize, effect, effectuate

11 **perform,** do, work, act, execute, accomplish, achieve, deliver, come through with, realize, engineer, effectuate, bring about, bring to fruition, bring into being, cause; mass-produce, volume-produce, industrialize; overproduce; underproduce; be productive

12 **originate,** invent, conceive, discover, make up, devise, contrive, concoct, fabricate, coin, mint, frame, hatch, hatch up, cook up, strike out; improvise, make do with; think up, think out, dream up, design, plan, formulate, set one's wits to work; generate, develop, mature, evolve; breed, engender, beget, spawn; bring forth, give rise to, give being to, bring into being, call into being; procreate

13 **bear,** yield, produce, furnish; bring forth, usher into the world; fruit, **bear fruit,** fructify; spawn

ADJS 14 **productional,** creational, formational; executional; manufacturing, manufactural, fabricational, industrial, smokestack

15 **constructional,** structural, building, housing, edificial; architectural, architectonic

16 **creative,** originative, causative, productive, constructive, formative, fabricative, demiurgic; inventive; generative

17 **produced,** made, caused, brought about; effectuated, executed, performed, done; grown, raised

18 **made, manmade; manufactured**, created, crafted, formed, shaped, molded, cast, forged, machined, milled, fashioned, built, constructed, fabricated; mass-produced, volume-produced, assembly-line; well-made, well-built,

well-constructed; homemade, homestyle, homespun, handmade, handcrafted, handicrafted, self-made, do-it-yourself (DIY); machine-made; processed; assembled, put together; custom-made, custom-built, purpose-built <Brit>, custom, made to order, bespoke; ready-made, ready-formed, ready-prepared, ready-to-wear, ready-for-wear, off-the-shelf, off-the-rack; prefabricated, prefab; mined, extracted, smelted, refined; grown, raised, harvested, gathered

19 **invented,** originated, conceived, discovered, newfound; fabricated, coined, minted, new-minted; made-up, made out of whole cloth

20 **manufacturable,** producible, productible

ADVS **21** **in production;** in the works, in hand, on foot; under construction; in the pipeline; on-line

893 PRODUCT

<something made, created>

NOUNS **1** **product,** end product, production, manufacture, wares; work, oeuvre, **handiwork, artifact**; creation; creature; offspring, child, fruit, fruit of one's loins; result, effect, issue, outgrowth, outcome; invention, origination, coinage, mintage, new mintage, brainchild; concoction, composition; opus, opuscule; apprentice work; journeyman work; masterwork, masterpiece, *chef d'œuvre* <Fr>, work of an artist, work of a master, work of a past master, crowning achievement; piece of work; gross national product

2 **production,** produce, proceeds, net, **yield, output,** throughput; crop, harvest, take, return, bang

3 extract, distillation, essence; **byproduct,** secondary product, incidental product, spinoff, outgrowth, offshoot; residue, leavings, waste, waste product, industrial waste, solid waste, lees, dregs, ash, slag

4 <amount made> make, making; batch, lot, run, boiling

894 INFLUENCE

<act or power producing effect>

NOUNS **1** **influence,** influentiality; power, force, **clout**, potency, pressure, effect, indirect power, incidental power, say, the final say, the last word, say-so, a lot to do with, a lot to say about, veto power; prestige, favor, good feeling, credit, esteem, repute, personality, leadership, charisma, magnetism, charm, enchantment; weight, moment, consequence, importance, eminence; authority, control, domination, hold; sway, reign, rule; mastery, ascendancy, supremacy, dominance, predominance, preponderance; upper hand, whip hand, trump card; leverage, purchase; persuasion, suasion, suggestion, subtle influence, insinuation; halo effect; upselling

2 **favor,** special favor, interest; pull, drag, suction; connections, the right people, inside track; amicus curiae

3 **backstairs influence,** intrigues, deals, schemes, games, Machiavellian intrigues, Byzantine intrigues, ploys, sway; wires, strings, ropes; wire-pulling; influence peddling; lobby, lobbying, lobbyism; Big Brother

4 **sphere of influence,** orbit, ambit; bailiwick, vantage, stamping ground, footing, territory, turf, home turf, constituency, power base, niche

5 **influenceability,** swayableness, movability; persuadability, persuadableness, persuasibility, suasibility, openness, open-mindedness, get-at-ableness, perviousness, accessibility, receptiveness, responsiveness, amenableness; suggestibility, susceptibility, impressionability, malleability; weakness; putty in one's hands

6 <**influential person or thing**> **influence,** good influence; bad influence, sinister influence; person of influence, an influential, an affluential, a presence, a palpable presence, a mover and shaker, a person to be reckoned with, a player, a player on the scene, major player; heavyweight, big wheel, biggie, heavy hitter, big hitter, long-ball hitter, piledriver, big fish in a small pond, very important person (VIP), big shot, bigwig, big cheese, big kahuna; wheeler-dealer, influencer, wire-puller; powerbroker; power behind the throne, gray eminence, *éminence grise* <Fr>, hidden hand, manipulator, friend at court, friend in court, kingmaker; influence peddler, five-percenter, lobbyist; Svengali, Rasputin; pressure group, special-interest group, special interests, single-issue group, (PAC) political action committee; lobby; the Establishment, big government; ingroup, court, powers that be, superpower, lords of creation; key, key to the city, access, open sesame

VERBS **7** **influence,** make oneself felt, affect, weigh with, **sway,** bias, bend, incline, dispose, predispose, move, prompt, lead; color, tinge, tone, slant, impart spin; induce, persuade, jawbone, twist one's arm, hold one's feet to the fire, work, bend to one's will; lead by the nose, wear down, soften up; win friends and influence people, ingratiate oneself

8 <**exercise influence over**> govern, rule, control, order, regulate, direct, guide; determine, decide, dispose; have the say, have the say-so, have veto power over, have the last word, call the shots, be in the driver's seat, wear the pants; charismatize

9 exercise influence, exert influence, **use one's influence**, bring pressure to bear upon, **lean on**, act on, work on, bear upon, throw one's weight around, throw one's weight into the scale, say a few words to the right person, say a few words in the right quarter; charismatize; draw, draw on, lead on, magnetize; approach, go up to with hat in hand, make advances, make overtures, make up to, get cozy with; get at, get the ear of; pull strings, pull wires, pull ropes, wire-pull; lobby, lobby through; wheel and deal

10 have influence, **be influential**, carry weight, weigh, tell, count, cut ice, throw a lot of weight, have a lot to do with, have a lot to say about; be the decisive factor, be the one that counts, have pull, have suction, have drag, have leverage; have a way with one, have personality, have magnetism, have charisma, charm the birds out of the trees, charm the pants off one, be persuasive; have an in, have the inside track; have full play; have friends in high places

11 **have influence over**, have power over, have a hold over, have pull with, have clout with; lead by the nose, twist around one's little finger, have in one's pocket, keep under one's thumb, make sit up and beg, make lie down and roll over; hypnotize, mesmerize, dominate

12 **gain influence**, get in with, ingratiate oneself with, get cozy with; make peace, mend fences; gain a footing, take hold, move in, take root, strike root in, make a dent in; gain a hearing, make one's voice heard, make one sit up and take notice, be listened to, be recognized; get the mastery of, get control of, get the inside track, gain a hold upon; change the preponderance, turn the scale, turn the balance, turn the tables

ADJS 13 **influential,** powerful, affluential, potent, strong, to be reckoned with; effective, effectual, efficacious, telling; weighty, momentous, important, consequential, substantial, earth-shattering, prestigious, estimable, authoritative, reputable; **persuasive**, suasive, personable, winning, magnetic, charming, enchanting, charismatic

14 <in a position of influence> **well-connected,** favorably situated, near the seat of power; dominant, predominant, preponderant, prepotent, prepollent, regnant, ruling, swaying, prevailing, prevalent, on the throne, in the driver's seat; ascendant, in the ascendant, in ascendancy

15 **influenceable, swayable,** movable; persuadable, persuasible, suasible, open, open-minded, pervious, accessible, receptive, responsive, amenable; under one's thumb, in one's pocket, on one's payroll; coercible, bribable, compellable, vulnerable; plastic, pliant, pliable, malleable; suggestible, susceptible, impressionable, weak

895 ABSENCE OF INFLUENCE

<lack of power to create effect>

NOUNS 1 **lack of influence**, lack of power, lack of force, uninfluentiality, unauthoritativeness, **powerlessness**, forcelessness, impotence, impotency; ineffectiveness, inefficaciousness, inefficacy, ineffectuality; no say, no say-so, nothing to do with, nothing to say about; unpersuasiveness, lack of personality, lack of charm, lack of magnetism, lack of charisma; weakness, wimpiness, wimpishness

2 **uninfluenceability,** unswayableness, unmovability; unpersuadability, impersuadability, impersuasibility, unreceptiveness, imperviousness, unresponsiveness; unsuggestibility, unsusceptibility, unimpressionability; invulnerability; obstinacy

ADJS 3 **uninfluential, powerless,** forceless, impotent; weak, wimpy, wimpish; unauthoritative; ineffective, ineffectual, inefficacious; of no account, no-account, without any weight, featherweight, lightweight

4 **uninfluenceable,** unswayable, unmovable; unpliable, unyielding, inflexible; unpersuadable, impersuadable, impersuasible, unreceptive, unresponsive, vegged, unamenable; impervious, closed to; unsuggestible, unsusceptible, unimpressionable; invulnerable; obstinate

5 **uninfluenced, unmoved,** unaffected, unswayed

896 TENDENCY

<proneness to thought or action>

NOUNS 1 **tendency, inclination, leaning,** penchant, proneness, conatus, weakness, susceptibility; liability, readiness, willingness, eagerness, aptness, aptitude, disposition, proclivity, propensity, predisposition, predilection, a thing for, affinity, prejudice, liking, delight, soft spot; yen, lech, hunger, thirst; instinct for, feeling for, sensitivity to; bent, turn, bias, slant, tilt, spin, cast, warp, twist; probability; tropism

2 **trend,** drift, course, current, flow, stream, mainstream, main current, movement, glacial movement, motion, run, tenor, tone, set, set of the current, swing, bearing, line, direction, the general tendency, the general drift, the main course, the course of events, the way the wind blows, the way things go, sign of the times, spirit

of the age, spirit of the time, time spirit, zeitgeist; climate; the way it looks

VERBS 3 **tend,** have a tendency, incline, be disposed, lean, trend, have a penchant, set, go, head, lead, point, verge, turn, warp, tilt, bias, bend to, work toward, gravitate toward, set toward; show a tendency, show a direction, swing toward, point to, look to; conduce, contribute, serve, redound to; bode well

ADJS 4 **tending;** tendentious, tendential; leaning, inclining, inclinatory, inclinational; mainstream, main-current, mainline

PREPS 5 **tending to,** conducive to, leading to, inclined toward, inclining toward, heading toward, moving toward, swinging toward, working toward, pointing to

6 **inclined to,** leaning to, **prone to,** disposed to, drawn to, predisposed to, given to; apt to, likely to, liable to, calculated to, minded to, ready to, in a fair way to

897 LIABILITY

<likelihood of an action>

NOUNS 1 **liability, likelihood,** likeliness; probability, contingency, chance, eventuality; weakness, proneness; possibility; responsibility, legal responsibility; indebtedness, financial commitment, financial obligation, pecuniary obligation

2 **susceptibility, liability,** susceptivity, liableness, openness, exposure; vulnerability

VERBS 3 **be liable;** be subjected, be subjected to, be a pawn of, be a plaything of, be the prey of, lie under; expose oneself to, leave oneself open to, open the door to; gamble, stand to lose, stand to gain, stand a chance, **run the chance, run the risk,** let down one's guard, let down one's defenses; admit of, open the possibility of, be in the way of, bid fair to, stand fair to; owe, be in debt for, be indebted for

4 **incur,** contract, invite, welcome, run, **bring on**, bring down, bring upon, bring down upon, bring upon oneself, bring down upon oneself; be responsible for; fall into, fall in with; get, gain, acquire

ADJS 5 **liable, likely, prone**; probable; responsible, legally responsible, answerable; in debt, indebted, financially burdened, heavily committed, overextended; exposed, susceptible, at risk, overexposed, open, like a sitting duck, vulnerable

6 **liable to**, subject to, standing to, in a position to, incident to, dependent on; **susceptible prone to,** susceptive to, open to, vulnerable to, exposed to, naked to, in danger of, within range of, at the mercy of; capable of, ready for; likely to, apt to; obliged to, responsible for, answerable for

CONJS 7 lest, that, for fear that

898 INVOLVEMENT

<engagement in action>

NOUNS 1 **involvement,** involution, implication, **entanglement,** enmeshment, engagement, involuntary presence, involuntary cooperation, embarrassment; relation; inclusion; absorption

VERBS 2 **involve,** implicate, tangle, **entangle,** embarrass, enmesh, engage, draw in, drag into, suck into, catch up in, make a party to; interest, concern; absorb

3 **be involved,** be into, partake, participate, take an interest, interest oneself, have a role, have a part

ADJS 4 **involved,** implicated; interested, concerned, a party to; included

5 **involved in,** implicated in, tangled in, entangled in, enmeshed in, **caught up in**, tied up in, wrapped up in, all wound up in, dragged into, hooked into, sucked into; in deep, deeply involved, up to one's neck in, up to one's ears in, up to one's elbows in, up to one's ass in, head over heels in, absorbed in, immersed in, submerged in, far-gone

899 CONCURRENCE

<co-action with another>

NOUNS 1 **concurrence, collaboration,** coaction, **coworking,** collectivity, combined effort, combined operation, united action, concerted action, concert, synergy; cooperation; agreement; me-tooism; coincidence, simultaneity, synchronism; concomitance, accompaniment; union, junction, conjunction, combination, association, alliance, consociation; conspiracy, collusion, cahoots; concourse, confluence; accordance, concordance, correspondence, consilience; symbiosis, parasitism; saprophytism; meeting of the minds; conspiracy theory

VERBS 2 **concur, collaborate,** coact, co-work, synergize; cooperate; conspire, collude, connive, be in cahoots, go in together; combine, unite, associate, coadunate, join, conjoin; harmonize; coincide, synchronize, happen together; accord, correspond, agree

3 **go with, go along with**, go hand in hand with, be hand in glove with, team up with, join up with, buddy up with; keep pace with, run parallel to

ADJS 4 **concurrent,** concurring; coacting, coactive, collaborative, collective, coworking, cooperant, synergetic, synergic, synergistic; cooperative;

conspiratorial, collusive; united, joint, conjoint, combined, concerted, associated, associate, coadunate; coincident, synchronous, synchronic, in sync, coordinate; concomitant, accompanying; meeting, uniting, combining; accordant, agreeing, concordant, harmonious, consilient, at one with; symbiotic, parasitic, saprophytic

ADVS **5** **concurrently,** coactively, jointly, conjointly, concertedly, in concert, in harmony with, in unison with, synchronously, together; with one accord, with one voice, as one, as one man; **hand in hand, hand in glove**, shoulder to shoulder, cheek by jowl

900 COUNTERACTION

<opposite action>

NOUNS **1** **counteraction,** counterworking; opposition, opposure, counterposition, contraposition, confutation, contradiction; antagonism, repugnance, oppugnance, oppugnancy, antipathy, conflict, friction, interference, clashing, collision; reaction, repercussion, backlash, recoil, kick, backfire, boomerang effect; resistance, recalcitrance, dissent, revolt, perverseness, nonconformity, crankiness, crotchetiness, orneriness, renitency; going against the current, going against the tide, swimming upstream; contrariety

2 **neutralization,** nullification, annulment, cancellation, voiding, invalidation, vitiation, frustration, thwarting, undoing; offsetting, counterbalancing, countervailing, balancing; negation; equilibrium

3 **counteractant,** counteractive, **counteragent;** counterirritant; antidote, remedy, preventive, preventative, prophylactic, contraceptive; neutralizer, nullifier, offset; antacid, buffer

4 **counterforce,** countervailing force, counterinfluence, counterpressure; countercheck; counterpoise, counterbalance, counterweight; countercurrent, crosscurrent, undercurrent; counterblast; headwind, foul wind, crosswind; friction, drag

5 **countermeasure,** counterattack, counterstep; counterblow, counterstroke, countercoup, counterblast, counterfire; counterrevolution, counterinsurgency; counterterrorism; counterculture; retort, comeback; defense

VERBS **6** **counteract,** counter, counterwork, counterattack, countervail; counterpose, contrapose, oppose, antagonize, go in opposition to, go counter to, run counter to, go against, work against, go clean counter to, fly in the face of, run against, beat against, militate against; resist, fight back, bite back, lift a hand against, defend oneself; dissent, dissent from; cross, confute, contradict, contravene, oppugn, conflict, be antipathetic, be hostile, be inimical, interfere with, conflict with, come in conflict with, clash, collide, meet head-on, lock horns; go against the grain; swim upstream, swim against the tide; boomerang; countercheck

7 **neutralize, nullify,** annul, cancel, cancel out, negate, negative, negativate, invalidate, vitiate, void, frustrate, stultify, thwart, come to nothing, bring to nothing, undo; offset, counterbalance; buffer

ADJS **8** counteractive, counteractant, **counteracting,** counterworking, **counterproductive,** countervailing; opposing, oppositional; contradicting, contradictory; antagonistic, hostile, antipathetic, inimical, oppugnant, repugnant, conflicting, clashing; reactionary; resistant, recalcitrant, dissentient, dissident, revolutionary, breakaway, nonconformist, perverse, cranky, crotchety, ornery, renitent

9 **neutralizing, nullifying,** stultifying, annulling, canceling, negating, invalidating, vitiating, voiding; equalizing; balancing, balanced, counterbalanced, poised, in poise, offset, zero-sum; offsetting, counterbalancing, countervailing; antacid, buffering; antidotal

ADVS **10** counteractively, **antagonistically**, opposingly, in opposition to, counter to

COMBINING FORMS **11** ant-, anti-, anth-, contra-, counter-

901 SUPPORT

<assisting action>

NOUNS **1** **support, backing,** aid; upholding, upkeep, carrying, carriage, maintenance, sustaining, sustainment, sustenance, sustentation; reinforcement, backup; subsidy, subvention; support services, infrastructure; moral support; emotional support, psychological support, security blanket; reassurance; power base, constituency, party; supportive relationship, supportive therapy; strokes; approval; assent, concurrence; reliance; life-support, life-sustainment

2 **supporter, support;** upholder, bearer, carrier, sustainer, maintainer; staff, stave, cane, stick, walking stick, alpenstock, crook, crutch; advocate; stay, prop, fulcrum, bracket, brace, bracer, guy, guywire, guyline, shroud, rigging, standing rigging; ballast; bulwark, anchor; buttress, shoulder, arm, good right arm; mast, sprit, yard, yardarm; mainstay, backbone, spine, neck, cervix; athletic supporter, jock, jockstrap; brassiere, bra; G-string; bandeau, corset, girdle, foundation garment; reinforcement, stiffener; back, backing; rest, resting place

3 <mythology> Atlas, Hercules, Telamon; Chukwa, The Tortoise which Supports the Earth

4 **buttress,** buttressing; abutment, shoulder; bulwark, rampart; embankment, bank, retaining wall, bulkhead, bulkheading, plank buttress, piling; breakwater, seawall, mole, jetty, jutty, groin; pier, pier buttress, buttress pier; flying buttress, arch buttress; hanging buttress; beam

5 **footing,** foothold, toehold, hold, perch, purchase; standing, stand, stance, standing place, pou sto; footrest, footplate, footrail

6 **foundation,** firm foundation, base, basis, footing, basement, pavement, ground, grounds, groundwork, seat, sill, floor, flooring, fundament; bed, bedding; substructure, substruction, substratum; infrastructure; understructure, understruction, underbuilding, undergirding, undercarriage, underpinning, bearing wall; stereobate, stylobate; firm ground, solid ground, *terra firma* <L>; solid rock, solid bottom, rock bottom, bedrock; hardpan; riprap; fundamental, principle, premise; precedent; root, radical; rudiment

7 **foundation stone,** footstone; **cornerstone,** keystone, headstone, first stone, quoin; roadbed

8 **base, pedestal**; stand, standard; shaft, upright, column, pillar, post, jack, pole, staff, stanchion, pier, pile, piling, king-post, queen-post, pilaster, newel-post, banister, baluster, balustrade, colonnade, caryatid; dado, die; plinth, subbase; surbase; socle; trunk, stem, stalk, pedicel, peduncle, footstalk

9 **sill,** groundsel; mudsill; windowsill, window ledge; doorsill, threshold; doorstone

10 **frame,** underframe, infrastructure, chassis, skeleton; armature; mounting, mount, backing, setting; surround

11 **handle,** hold, grip, grasp, haft, helve

12 **scaffold,** scaffolding; stage, staging

13 **platform; stage,** estrade, dais, floor; rostrum, podium, pulpit, speaker's platform, speaker's stand, soapbox; hustings, stump; tribune, tribunal; emplacement; catafalque; landing stage, landing; heliport, landing pad; launching pad; terrace, step terrace, deck; balcony, gallery

14 **shelf, ledge,** shoulder, corbel, beam-end; mantel, mantelshelf, mantelpiece; retable, superaltar, gradin, predella; hob

15 **table,** board, stand; bench, workbench; counter, bar, buffet; **desk,** writing table, secretary, escritoire; lectern, reading stand, ambo, reading desk

16 **trestle,** horse; sawhorse, buck, sawbuck; clotheshorse; trestle board, trestle table, trestle and table; trestlework, trestling; A-frame

17 **seat, chair;** saddle, howdah

18 <saddle parts> pommel, horn; jockey; girth, girt, surcingle, bellyband; cinch, stirrup

19 sofa, **bed; couch;** the sack, the hay, kip, doss; futon; bedstead; litter, stretcher, gurney

20 **bedding,** underbed, underbedding; **mattress,** paillasse, pallet; air mattress, foam-rubber mattress, innerspring mattress; sleeping bag; pad, mat, rug; litter, bedstraw; pillow, cushion, bolster; springs, bedsprings, box springs; futon

VERBS 21 **support, bear,** carry, hold, sustain, maintain, bolster, reinforce, back, back up, shoulder, give support, furnish support, lend support; go to bat for; hold up, bear up, bolster up, keep up, buoy up, keep afloat; uphold, upbear, upkeep; brace, prop, crutch, buttress; shore, shore up; stay, mainstay; underbrace, undergird, underprop, underpin, underset; underlie, be at the bottom of, form the foundation of; cradle; cushion, pillow; subsidize; subvene; assent; concur; approve

22 **rest on, stand on,** lie on, recline on, repose on, bear on, lean on, abut on; sit on, perch, ride, piggyback on; straddle, bestraddle, stride, bestride; be based on, rely on

ADJS 23 **supporting, supportive,** bearing, carrying, burdened; holding, upholding, maintaining, sustaining, sustentative, suspensory; bracing, propping, shoring, bolstering, buttressing; life-sustaining; collaborative, corroborative, cooperative

24 **supported**, borne, upborne, held, buoyed-up, upheld, sustained, maintained; braced, guyed, stayed, propped, shored, shored up, bolstered, buttressed; based on, founded on, grounded on

ADVS 25 on, across, astride, astraddle, **straddled**, straddle-legged, straddleback, on the back of; horseback, on horseback; pickaback, piggyback

902 IMPULSE, IMPACT

<driving or striking force>

NOUNS 1 **impulse,** impulsion, impelling force, impellent; drive, **driving force**, driving power; motive power, power; force, irresistible force; clout; impetus; momentum; moment, moment of force; propulsion; incitement, incentive, compulsion

2 **thrust,** push, shove, boost; pressure; stress; press; prod, poke, punch, jab, dig, nudge; bump, jog, joggle, jolt; jostle, hustle; butt, bunt; head

3 **impact,** collision, clash, appulse, encounter,

meeting, impingement, bump, crash, crump, whomp; carom, carambole, cannon; sideswipe; smash, crunch; shock, brunt; concussion, percussion; thrusting, ramming, bulling, bulldozing, shouldering, muscling, steamrollering, railroading; hammering, smashing, mauling, sledgehammering; onslaught

4 **hit, blow,** stroke, knock, rap, pound, slam, bang, crack, whack, smack, thwack, smash, dash, swipe, swing, punch, poke, jab, dig, drub, thump, pelt, cut, chop, dint, slog; drubbing, drumming, drum roll, tattoo, fusillade; beating

5 <nonformal> **sock,** bang, bash, bat, belt, bonk, bust, clip, clout, duke, swat, yerk, plunk, larrup, paste, lick, biff, clump, clunk, clonk, wallop, whop, slam, slug, whomp, swack

6 **punch,** boxing punch, blow, belt, sock

7 **tap,** rap, pat, dab, chuck, touch, tip; love-tap; snap, flick, flip, fillip, flirt, whisk, brush; peck, pick

8 **slap,** smack, flap; box, cuff, buffet; spank; whip, lash, lash out, cut, stripe

9 **kick,** boot; punt, drop kick, placekick, kicking, calcitration

10 stamp, **stomp**, drub, clump, clop

VERBS 11 **impel**, give an impetus, set going, put in motion, set in motion, give momentum; **drive**, move, animate, actuate, forward; thrust, power; drive on, whip on; goad; propel; motivate, incite; compel

12 **thrust, push,** shove, boost; press, stress, bear, bear upon, bring pressure to bear upon; ram, ram down, tamp, pile drive, jam, crowd, cram; bull, bulldoze, muscle, steamroller, railroad; drive, force, run; prod, goad, poke, punch, jab, dig, nudge; bump, jog, joggle, jolt, shake, rattle; jostle, hustle, hurtle; elbow, shoulder; butt, bunt, buck, run against, bump against, butt against, bump up against, knock one's head against; assault

13 **collide,** come into collision, be on a collision course, **clash,** meet, encounter, confront each other, impinge; percuss, concuss; bump, hit, strike, knock, bang; run into, bump into, bang into, slam into, smack into, crash into, impact, smash into, dash into, carom into; rear-end; hit against, strike against, knock against; foul, fall foul of, fall afoul of, run afoul of; hurtle, hurt; carom, cannon, cannon into <Brit>; sideswipe; crash, smash, crump, whomp; smash up, crack up, crunch

14 **hit, strike,** knock, knock down, knock out, smite; land a blow, draw blood; poke, punch, jab, thwack, smack, clap, crack, swipe, whack; deal, fetch, swipe at, take a punch at, throw one at, deal a blow, hit a clip, let have it; thump, snap; strike at

15 <nonformal> **belt,** bat, clout, bang, slam, bash, biff, paste, wham, whop, clump, bonk, wallop, clip, cut, plunk, swat, soak, sock, slog, slug, yerk, clunk, clonk

16 **pound, beat,** hammer, maul, sledgehammer, knock, rap, bang, thump, drub, buffet, batter, pulverize, paste, patter, pommel, pummel, pelt, baste, lambaste; thresh, thrash; flail; spank, flap; whip

17 <nonformal> **clobber,** knock for a loop, marmelize <Brit>, knock cold, dust off, bash up, punch out, rough up, slap down, smack down, sandbag, work over, deck, coldcock, wallop, larrup

18 **tap,** rap, pat, dab, chuck, touch, tip; snap, flick, flip, fillip, tickle, flirt, whisk, graze, brush; bunt; peck, pick, beak

19 **slap,** smack, flap; box, cuff, buffet; spank; whip

20 **club,** cudgel, blackjack, sandbag, cosh <Brit>

21 **kick,** boot, kick about, kick around, calcitrate; kick downstairs; kick out; knee

22 **stamp, stomp,** trample, tread, drub, clump, clop

ADJS 23 **impelling,** impellent; impulsive, pulsive, moving, motive, animating, actuating, **driving;** thrusting

24 concussive, percussive, crashing, smashing; rocked

903 REACTION

<resisting or opposing force>

NOUNS 1 **reaction, response,** respondence, feedback; reply, answer, rise; **reflex,** reflection, reflex action; echo, bounce back, reverberation, resonance, sympathetic vibration; return; reflux, refluence; action and reaction; opposite response, negative response, retroaction, revulsion; predictable response, automatic reaction, autonomic reaction, knee-jerk, knee-jerk response, spontaneous response, unthinking response, spur-of-the-moment response; conditioned reflex

2 **recoil, rebound,** resilience, repercussion; bounce, bound, spring, bounce-back; repulse, rebuff; backlash, backlashing, kickback, kick, a kick like a mule, recalcitration; backfire, boomerang; ricochet, carom, cannon <Brit>

3 <a drawing back or aside> **retreat,** recoil, fallback, pullout, pullback, contingency plan, backup plan; evasion, avoidance, sidestepping; flinch, wince, cringe; sidestep, shy; dodge, duck

4 **reactionary,** reactionist, recalcitrant

VERBS 5 **react, respond,** reply, answer, riposte, snap back, come back at; rise to the fly, take the bait; go off half-cocked

6 **recoil, rebound,** resile; bounce, bound, spring; spring back, fly back, bounce back, snap back; repercuss, have repercussions; kick, kick back, kick like a mule, recalcitrate; backfire, boomerang; backlash, lash back; ricochet, carom, cannon, cannon off <Brit>

7 **pull back, draw back,** retreat, recoil, fade, fall back, reel back, hang back, start back, shrink back, give ground; shrink, flinch, wince, cringe, blink, blench, quail; shy, shy away, turn aside, evade, avoid, sidestep, weasel, weasel out, cop out; dodge, duck; jib, swerve, sheer off, give a wide berth

8 **get a reaction**, get a response, evoke a response, ring a bell, strike a responsive chord, strike fire, strike home, hit home, hit a nerve, get a rise out of

ADJS **9** **reactive,** reacting, merely reactive; **responsive,** respondent, responding, antiphonal; quick on the draw, quick on the uptake; reactionary; retroactionary, retroactive; revulsive; reflex, **reflexive**, knee-jerk; refluent

10 recoiling, rebounding, **resilient;** bouncing, bouncy, bounding, springing, springy; repercussive; recalcitrant

ADVS **11** **on the rebound,** on the return, on the bounce; on the spur of the moment, off the top of the head

904 PUSHING, THROWING

<pressing or hurling force>

NOUNS **1** **pushing, propulsion, propelling**; shoving, butting; drive, thrust, motive power, driving force, means of propulsion; push, shove; butt, bunt; shunt, impulsion

2 **throwing, projection,** jaculation, ejaculation, trajection, flinging, slinging, pitching, tossing, casting, hurling, lobbing, chucking, chunking, heaving, firing, burning, pegging; bowling, rolling; shooting, gunnery, gunning, musketry; trap shooting, skeet, skeet shooting; archery

3 **throw,** toss, fling, sling, cast, hurl, chuck, chunk, lob, heave, shy, pitch, peg; flip; put, shot put; pass, forward pass, lateral pass, lateral; serve, service; bowl

4 **shot,** discharge; ejection; detonation; gunfire; gun, cannon; bullet; salvo, **volley,** fusillade, tattoo, spray; bowshot, gunshot, stoneshot, potshot

5 **projectile;** ejecta, ejectamenta; missile; ball; discus, quoit

6 **propeller,** prop, airscrew, prop-fan; propellant, propulsor, driver; screw, wheel, screw propeller, twin screws; bow thruster; paddle wheel; turbine; fan, impeller, rotor; piston

7 **thrower,** pitcher, hurler, bowler, chucker, chunker, heaver, tosser, flinger, slinger, caster, jaculator; shot-putter; javelin thrower; discus thrower, discobolus

8 **shooter,** shot; gunner, gun, gunman; rifleman, musketeer, carabineer, pistoleer; cannoneer, artilleryman; Nimrod, hunter; trapshooter; archer, bowman, toxophilite; marksman, markswoman, targetshooter, sharpshooter, sniper; good shot, dead shot, deadeye, crack shot

VERBS **9** **push, propel,** impel, shove, thrust; drive, move, forward, advance, traject; sweep, sweep along; butt, bunt; shunt; pole, row; pedal, treadle; roll, troll, bowl, trundle

10 **throw,** fling, sling, pitch, toss, cast, hurl, heave, chuck, chunk, peg, lob, shy, fire, burn, pepper, launch, dash, let fly, let go, let rip, let loose; catapult; flip, snap, jerk; bowl; pass; serve; put, put the shot; bung; dart, lance, tilt; fork, pitchfork; pelt

11 **project,** jaculate, ejaculate

12 **shoot, fire,** fire off, let off, let fly, **discharge,** eject; detonate; gun, pistol; sharpshoot; shoot at, gun for; strike, hit, plug; shoot down, fell, drop, stop in one's tracks; riddle, pepper, pelt, pump full of lead; snipe, pick off; torpedo; pot; potshoot, potshot, take a potshot; load, prime, charge; cock

13 start, **start off**, start up, give a start, crank up, give a push, give a shove, jump-start, kick-start, put in motion, set in motion, set on foot, set going, start going; kick off, start the ball rolling; get off the ground, get off the mark, launch, float, set afloat; send, send off, send forth; bundle off

ADJS **14** **propulsive,** propulsory, **propellant,** propelling; motive; driving, pushing, shoving

15 **projectile,** trajectile, jaculatory, ejaculatory; ballistic, missile; ejective

16 jet-propelled, rocket-propelled, steam-propelled, gasoline-propelled, gas-propelled, diesel-propelled, wind-propelled, self-propelled

17 <means of propulsion> battery, diesel, diesel-electric, electric, gas, gasoline, gravity, jet, plasma-jet, prop-fan, pulse-jet, ram-jet, reaction, resojet, rocket, spring, steam, turbofan, turbojet, turbopropeller, turboprop, wind

905 PULLING

<force to draw towards>

NOUNS **1** **pulling, traction,** drawing, draft, dragging, heaving, tugging, towing; pulling power, tractive power, **pull;** tug-of-war; towage; towrope, towbar, towing cable, hawser; tow car, wrecker; hauling, haulage, drayage; man-hauling, man-haulage; attraction; extraction

2 **pull,** draw, heave, **haul,** tug, tow, lug, a long pull, a strong pull, strain, drag
3 **jerk,** yank, quick pull, sudden pull; twitch, tweak, pluck, hitch, wrench, snatch, start, bob; flip, flick, flirt, flounce; jig, jiggle; jog, joggle
VERBS 4 **pull,** draw, heave, **haul,** hale, lug, tug, **tow,** take in tow; trail, train; **drag,** man-haul, draggle, snake; troll, trawl
5 **jerk,** yerk, yank; twitch, tweak, pluck, snatch, hitch, wrench, snake; flip, flick, flirt, flounce; jiggle, jig, jigget, jigger; jog, joggle
ADJS 6 **pulling,** drawing, tractional, tractive, hauling, tugging, towing, towage; man-hauled

906 LEVERAGE
<increase force with machine>

NOUNS 1 **leverage,** fulcrumage; pry, prize
2 purchase, **hold,** advantage; **foothold,** toehold, footing; differential purchase; collier's purchase; traction
3 **fulcrum, axis, pivot,** bearing, rest, resting point; thole, tholepin, rowlock, oarlock
4 **lever;** pry, prize; bar, pinch bar, crowbar, crow, pinchbar, iron crow, wrecking bar, ripping bar, claw bar; cant hook, peavey; jimmy; handspike, marlinespike; boom, spar, beam, outrigger; pedal, treadle, crank; limb
5 **arm, strong-arm;** forearm; wrist; elbow; upper arm, biceps
6 **tackle,** purchase
7 windlass; capstan; **winch,** crab; reel; Chinese windlass, Spanish windlass
VERBS 8 get a purchase, get leverage, get a foothold; **pry,** prize, **lever,** wedge; pry out; jimmy, crowbar, pinchbar
9 reel in, wind in, bring in, draw in, pull in, crank in, trim, tighten, tauten, draw taut, take the strain; windlass, winch, crank, reel; tackle

907 ATTRACTION
<pulling toward>

NOUNS 1 **attraction,** traction, attractiveness, attractivity; mutual attraction; pulling power, **pull,** drag, draw, tug; magnetism; gravity, gravitation; centripetal force; capillarity, capillary attraction; adduction; **affinity,** sympathy; allurement; come-on
2 **attractor**, attractant, attrahent; adductor; cynosure, focus, center, center of attention, focal point; crowd-pleaser, charismatic figure; drawing card; sideshow; freak show; **lure**
3 **magnet,** artificial magnet, field magnet, bar magnet, horseshoe magnet, electromagnet, solenoid, paramagnet, permanent magnet, keeper, superconducting magnet, electromagnetic lifting magnet, magnetic needle; lodestone, magnetite; magnetic pole, magnetic north; lodestar, polestar; siderite
VERBS 4 **attract, pull,** draw, drag, tug, pull towards, draw towards, have an attraction; magnetize, magnet, be magnetic; lure; adduct
ADJS 5 attracting, drawing, pulling, dragging, tugging; eye-catching; **attractive, magnetic;** charismatic; magnetized, attrahent; sympathetic; alluring; adductive, adducent; associative
ADVS 6 attractionally, attractively; magnetically; charismatically

908 REPULSION
<pushing away>

NOUNS 1 **repulsion,** repellence, repellency, **repelling;** mutual repulsion, polarization; disaffinity; centrifugal force; magnetic repulsion, diamagnetism; antigravity; repulsive force; ejection
2 **repulse, rebuff;** dismissal, cold shoulder, snub, spurning, brush-off, cut; kiss-off; turnoff; rejection; refusal; discharge
VERBS 3 **repulse, repel,** rebuff, turn back, put back, beat back, force back, drive back, push back, thrust back; drive away, chase, chase off, chase away; send off, send away, send about one's business, send packing, pack off, dismiss; snub, cut, brush off, drop; kiss off, show someone the door; spurn, refuse; **ward off,** hold off, keep off, fend off, fight off, drive off, push off, keep at arm's length; stiff-arm; slap down, smack down; eject, discharge
ADJS 4 **repulsive,** repellent, **repelling;** diamagnetic, of opposite polarity, centrifugal, abducent, abductive; off-putting
ADVS 5 repulsively, repellently

909 EJECTION
<throwing out or away>

NOUNS 1 **ejection,** ejectment, throwing out, expulsion, **discharge,** extrusion, obtrusion, detrusion, ousting, ouster, removal, kicking out, booting out, chucking out; kicking downstairs; the boot, the bounce, the bum's rush, the old heave-ho, the chuck, the push; defenestration; rejection; jettison
2 **eviction,** ousting, dislodgment, dispossession, expropriation; **ouster,** throwing overboard
3 **depopulation,** dispeoplement, unpeopling; devastation, desolation

4 **banishment,** relegation, exclusion; **excommunication,** disfellowship; disbarment, unfrocking, defrocking; proscription; expatriation, exile, exilement; outlawing, outlawry, fugitation; **ostracism**, ostracization, thumbs-down, thumbing-down, blackballing, silent treatment, sending to Coventry, cold shoulder; deportation, transportation, extradition; rustication; degradation, demotion, stripping, depluming, displuming; deprivation

5 **dismissal, discharge,** forced separation; outplacement; **firing**, canning, cashiering, drumming out, dishonorable discharge, rogue's march; disemployment, layoff, removal, surplusing, displacing, furloughing; suspension; retirement, downshifting, silver ceiling; marching orders, the elbow, the bounce, the sack, the chuck, heave-ho; the boot, the gate, the ax; walking papers, pink slip; deposal

6 **evacuation,** voidance, voiding; elimination, removal; clearance, clearing, clearage; unfouling, freeing; scouring out, cleaning out, unclogging; exhaustion, exhausting, venting, emptying, depletion; unloading, **off-loading**, discharging cargo, discharging freight; draining, drainage; egress; excretion, defecation

7 **disgorgement,** disemboguement, expulsion, ejaculation, **discharge,** emission; eruption, eructation, extravasation, blowout, outburst; outpour, jet, spout, squirt, spurt

8 **vomiting,** vomition, disgorgement, regurgitation, egestion, emesis, the pukes, the heaves; retching, heaving, gagging; nausea; vomit, vomitus, puke, puking, barf, barfing, spew, egesta; the dry heaves; vomiturition

9 **belch, burp**, belching, wind, gas, eructation; **hiccup**

10 **fart**, **flatulence**, flatulency, flatuosity, flatus, breaking wind, passing gas, gas, wind

11 **ejector,** expeller, -fuge; ouster, evictor; **bouncer**, chucker, chucker-out

12 **dischargee,** expellee; ejectee; evictee

VERBS 13 **eject, expel, discharge,** extrude, obtrude, detrude, exclude, reject, cast, remove; oust, bounce, give the hook, put out, turn out, thrust out; throw out, run out, cast out, chuck out, give the chuck to, toss out, heave out, kick downstairs; kick out, boot out; give the bum's rush, give the old heave-ho, throw out on one's ear; defenestrate; jettison, throw overboard, discard, junk, throw away; be rid of, be shut of, see the last of

14 **drive out,** run out, chase out, chase away, run off, rout out; drum out, read out; freeze out, push out, force out, send packing, send about one's business; hunt out, harry out; smoke out, drive into the open; run out of town, ride on a rail

15 **evict, oust,** dislodge, dispossess, put out, turn out, turn out of doors, turn out of house and home, turn out bag and baggage, throw into the street; unhouse, unkennel

16 **depopulate,** dispeople, unpeople; devastate, desolate

17 **banish,** expel, cast out, thrust out, relegate, **ostracize,** disfellowship, exclude, send down, **blackball,** spurn, thumb down, turn thumbs down on, snub, cut, give the cold shoulder, send to Coventry, give the silent treatment; excommunicate; exile, expatriate, deport, transport, send away, extradite; outlaw, fugitate, ban, proscribe; rusticate

18 dismiss, **send off**, **send away,** turn away, bundle, bundle off, hustle out, pack off, send packing, send about one's business, send to the showers; bow out, show the door, show the gate; give the gate, give the air

19 **dismiss, discharge, expel**, cashier, drum out, disemploy, outplace, separate forcibly, lay off, suspend, surplus, furlough, turn off, make redundant, riff, turn out, release, fire, let go, let out, remove, displace, replace, strike off the rolls, give the pink slip; unfrock, defrock; degrade, demote, strip, deplume, displume, deprive; depose, disbar; break, bust; retire, put on the retired list; pension off, superannuate, put out to pasture; read out of; kick upstairs

20 <nonformal> **sack**, can, bump, bounce, kick, boot, give the ax, give the gate, give one the sack, give one the ax, give one the boot, give one's walking papers, send one to the showers, show one the door, show one the gate

21 **do away with,** exterminate, annihilate; purge, liquidate; shake off, shoo, dispel; throw off, fling off, cast off; eliminate, get rid of; throw away

22 **evacuate,** void; eliminate, remove; empty, empty out, deplete, exhaust, vent, drain; clear, **purge,** clean out, scour out, clear off, clear away, unfoul, unclog, flush out, blow, blow out, sweep out, make a clean sweep, clear the decks; defecate

23 **unload,** off-load, unlade, unpack, disburden, unburden, discharge, **dump;** unship, break bulk; pump out

24 **let out,** give vent to, give out, give off, throw off, blow off, emit, exhaust, evacuate, let go; exhale, expire, breathe out, let one's breath out, blow, puff; fume, steam, vapor, smoke, reek; open the floodgates, turn on the tap

25 **disgorge,** debouch, disembogue, **discharge**, exhaust, expel, ejaculate, throw out, cast forth, send out, send forth; erupt, eruct, blow out,

extravasate; pour out, pour forth, pour, outpour, decant; spew, jet, spout, squirt, spurt; cough up

26 **vomit,** spew, disgorge, regurgitate, egest, throw up, bring up, be sick, sick up, heave the gorge; retch, keck, heave, gag; reject; be seasick, feed the fish; spit up

27 <nonformal> **puke,** upchuck, chuck up, urp, oops, oops up, blow one's cookies, toss one's cookies, toss one's lunch, barf, ralph, ralph up, blow grits, cough up, retch

28 **belch, burp,** eruct, eructate; **hiccup**

29 <nonformal> **fart,** let a fart, cut a far, break wind, cut the cheese

ADJS 30 **ejective, expulsive,** ejaculative, emissive, extrusive; eliminant; vomitive, vomitory; eructative; flatulent, flatuous; rejected, rejective, spit-up

INTERJS 31 **go away,** begone, get you gone, go along, get along, run along, get along with you, away, away with you, off with you, off you go, on your way, go about your business, be off, get out of here, get out, clear out, leave, get a life, get out of town, **shoo,** scat, git, go hang yourself

32 <nonformal> **beat it, scram,** buzz off, bug off, shoo, skiddoo, skedaddle, vamoose, cheese it, make yourself scarce, get lost, take a walk, take a hike, go chase yourself, go play in the traffic, get the hell out, push off, shove off, take a powder, blow

910 OVERRUNNING

<going beyond or past>

NOUNS 1 **overrunning,** overgoing, overpassing; overrun, overpass; **overspreading,** overgrowth; inundation, whelming, overwhelming; burying, burial; seizure, taking; overflowing; exaggeration; surplus, excess; superiority

2 **infestation,** infestment; **invasion,** swarming, swarm, teeming, ravage, plague; overrunning, overswarming, overspreading; lousiness, pediculosis

3 **overstepping, transgression,** trespass, inroad, usurpation, incursion, intrusion, encroachment, infraction, **infringement**

VERBS 4 **overrun,** overgo, overpass, overreach, go beyond; overstep, overstride, overstep the mark, overstep the bounds; overleap, overjump; **overshoot,** overshoot the mark, overshoot the field; exaggerate; superabound, exceed, overdo

5 **overspread,** bespread, spread over, spill over; **overgrow,** grow over, run riot, cover, swarm over, teem over

6 **infest,** beset, invade, swarm, ravage, plague; **overrun,** overswarm, overspread; creep with, crawl with, swarm with; seize

7 **run over,** overrun; **ride over,** override, run down, ride down; trample, trample on, trample down, tread upon, step on, walk on, walk over, trample underfoot, ride roughshod over; hit-and-run; **inundate,** whelm, overwhelm; overflow; shout down

8 **pass,** go by, pass by, get ahead of, shoot ahead of; bypass; pass over, cross, go across, ford; step over, overstride, bestride, straddle

9 **overstep, transgress,** trespass, intrude, break bounds, overstep the bounds, go too far, know no bounds, encroach, infringe, invade, breach, irrupt, make inroads, make an incursion, advance upon; usurp

ADJS 10 **overrun, overspread,** overpassed, bespread; overgrown; inundated, whelmed, overwhelmed; buried

11 **infested,** beset, ravaged, teeming, lagued; lousy, pediculous, pedicular; wormy, grubby; ratty

911 SHORTCOMING

<action short of>

NOUNS 1 **shortcoming,** falling short, not measuring up, coming up short, **shortfall;** shortage, short measure, underage, deficit, limitation; inadequacy; insufficiency; delinquency; default, defalcation; arrear, arrears, arrearage; decline, slump; defectiveness, imperfection; inferiority; undercommitment; failure

VERBS 2 **fall short, come short,** run short, stop short, not make the course, not reach; not measure up, not hack it, not make the grade, not make the cut, not make it, not make out; want, want for, lack, not have it, be found wanting, not answer, not fill the bill, not suffice; not reach to, not stretch; decline, lag, lose ground, slump, collapse, fall away, run out of gas, run out of steam; lose out, fail

3 **fall through,** fall down, fall to the ground, fall flat, collapse, break down; get bogged down, get mired, get mired down, get hung up, come to nothing, come to naught, end up in smoke, go up in smoke; **fizzle out,** peter out, poop out; not make it; fall by the wayside, drop by the wayside, end; circle the drain

4 miss, **miscarry,** go amiss, go astray, miss the mark, miss by a mile; misfire; **miss out,** miss the boat, miss the bus; miss stays, miss one's mooring

ADJS 5 **short of,** short, fresh out of, clean out of, not all it is cracked up to be, not what it is cracked up to be; **deficient,** inadequate; insufficient; undercommitted; inferior; lacking, wanting, minus; unreached

ADVS 6 **behind,** behindhand, in arrears

7 **amiss,** astray, beside the mark, below the mark, beside the point, far from it, to no purpose, in vain, vainly, fruitlessly, bootlessly

912 ELEVATION

<*raising action*>

NOUNS 1 **elevation, raising,** lifting, upping, boosting, hiking; rearing, escalation, erection; uprearing, uplifting; upbuoying; uplift, upheaval, upthrow, upcast, upthrust; exaltation; apotheosis, deification; beatification, canonization; enshrinement, assumption; height; ascent; increase; antigravity; orogeny

2 **lift, boost, hike**, hoist, heave; a leg up; promotion

3 **lifter,** erector; crane, derrick, gantry crane, crab; jack, jackscrew; hoist, lift, hydraulic lift; forklift; hydraulic tailgate; lever; windlass; tackle; yeast, leaven

4 **elevator,** lift <Brit>; escalator, moving staircase, moving stairway, ski lift, chairlift; dumbwaiter; booster seat, booster cushion

VERBS 5 **elevate, raise,** rear, escalate, up, boost, hike; erect, heighten, lift, levitate, hoist, heist, heft, heave; raise up, rear up, lift up, hold up, set up; stick up, cock up, perk up; buoy up, upbuoy; upraise, uplift, uphold, uprear, uphoist; upheave, upthrow, upcast; throw up, cast up; jerk up; knock up, lob, loft; sky; ratchet up

6 **exalt,** elevate, ensky; deify, apotheosize; beatify, canonize; enshrine; put on a pedestal

7 **give a lift,** give a boost, give a leg up, help up, put on; mount, horse; enhance, upgrade

8 **pick up,** take up, pluck up, gather up; draw up, fish up, haul up, drag up; dredge, dredge up

ADJS 9 **raised, lifted, elevated**; upraised, uplifted, upcast; reared, upreared; rearing, rampant; upthrown, upflung; exalted, lofty; deified, apotheosized; canonized, sainted, beatified; enshrined, sublime; antigravitational; stilted, on stilts; erect, upright; high

10 elevating, elevatory, escalatory; lifting; **uplifting;** erective, erectile; levitative

913 DEPRESSION

<*lowering action*>

NOUNS 1 **depression, lowering; sinking;** ducking, submergence, pushing under, thrusting under, downthrust, downthrusting, detrusion, pushing down, pulling down, hauling down; reduction, de-escalation, diminution; demotion, debasement, degradation; concavity, hollowness; descent; decrease; deflation; sinkhole, crater

2 downthrow, **downcast**; overthrow, overturn; precipitation, fall, downfall; downpour, downpouring

3 **crouch, stoop,** bend, squat; bow, genuflection, kneeling, kowtow, kowtowing, salaam, reverence, obeisance, curtsy; bob, duck, nod; prostration, supination; crawling, groveling; abasement, self-abasement

VERBS 4 **depress, lower,** let down, take down, debase, de-escalate, **sink,** bring low, deflate, reduce, couch; pull down, haul down, take down a peg; bear down, downbear, squash; thrust down, press down, push down, detrude; indent

5 fell, **drop, bring down,** fetch down, down, take down, take down a peg, lay low, reduce to the ranks, cashier; raze, rase, raze to the ground; level, lay level; pull down, pull about one's ears; cut down, chop down, hew down, whack down, mow down; knock down, dash down, send headlong, floor, deck, lay out, lay by the heels, ground, bowl down, bowl over; trip, trip up, topple, tumble; prostrate, supinate; throw, throw down, cast down, precipitate; bulldog; spread-eagle, pin, pin down; blow over, blow down

6 **overthrow,** overturn; depose; demote

7 drop, let go of, let drop, let fall

8 **crouch,** duck, cringe, cower; stoop, bend, stoop down, squat, squat down, get down, hunker, hunker down, get down on one's haunches; hunch, hunch down, hunch over, scooch down, crouch down

9 **bow,** bend, kneel, genuflect, bend the knee, curtsy, make a low bow, make a leg, make a reverence, make an obeisance, salaam, bob, duck; **kowtow,** prostrate oneself; crawl, grovel; wallow, welter

10 **sit down,** seat oneself, park oneself, be seated

11 **lie down,** couch, drape oneself, recline; prostrate, supinate, prone; flatten oneself, prostrate oneself; hit the ground, hit the dirt

ADJS 12 **depressed, lowered,** debased, reduced, fallen, deflated; sunk, **sunken,** submerged; downcast, downthrown; prostrated, prostrate; low, at a low ebb; falling, precititous

914 CIRCUITOUSNESS

<*circular motion*>

NOUNS 1 **circuitousness,** circuity, circuition; **roundaboutness,** indirection, ambagiousness, meandering, deviance, deviancy, deviation; deviousness, digression, circumlocution; excursion, excursus; circling, wheeling, circulation, rounding, orbit, orbiting; spiraling, spiral, gyring, gyre; circumambulation, circumambience, circumambiency, circumflexion, circumnavigation, circummigration; turning, **turn**; circularity; convolution

2 **circuit, round,** revolution, **circle,** full circle, go-round, cycle, orbit, ambit; pass; round trip; beat, rounds, walk, tour, turn, lap, loop; round robin; traffic circle, roundabout, rotary; hex sign, dreamcatcher

3 detour, bypass, **roundabout way,** roundabout, ambages, circuit, circumbendibus, the long way around, digression, deviation, excursion

VERBS 4 **go in circles,** go roundabout, **meander,** deviate, go around Robin Hood's barn, take the long way around, go the long way around, twist and turn; detour, make a detour, go around, go round about, go out of one's way, bypass; digress; talk in circles, say in a roundabout way; equivocate, shilly-shally; dodge

5 **circle,** circuit, describe a circle, make a circuit, move in a circle, circulate; **go around,** go round, go about; wheel, orbit, go into orbit, round; make a pass; come full circle, close the circle, make a round trip, return to the starting point; cycle; spiral, gyre; go around in circles, chase one's tail, go round and round; revolve; compass, encompass, encircle, surround; skirt, flank; go the round, make the round of, make one's rounds, circuiteer; lap; circumambulate, circummigrate; circumnavigate, girdle, girdle the globe

6 **turn, go around,** round, turn a corner, round a corner, corner, round a bend, round a point

ADJS 7 **circuitous, roundabout,** out-of-the-way, devious, oblique, indirect, ambagious, meandering, backhanded; deviative, deviating, digressive, discursive, excursive; equivocatory; evasive; vacillating; circular, round, wheel-shaped, O-shaped; spiral, helical; orbital; rotary

8 circumambient, circumambulatory, circumforaneous, circumfluent, circumvolant, circumnavigatory, circumnavigable

ADVS 9 **circuitously,** deviously, obliquely, ambagiously, indirectly, round about, about it, about, round Robin Hood's barn, in a roundabout way, by a side door, by a side wind; circlewise, wheelwise

915 ROTATION

<rotating motion>

NOUNS 1 **rotation, revolution,** roll, gyration, spin, circulation; axial motion, rotational motion, angular motion, angular momentum, angular velocity; circumrotation, circumgyration, circumvolution, full circle; turning, whirling, swirling, spinning, wheeling, reeling, whir; spiraling, twisting upward, twisting downward, gyring, volution, turbination; centrifugation; swiveling, pivoting, swinging; rolling, trolling, trundling, bowling, volutation

2 **whirl,** wheel, reel, **spin,** turn, round; spiral, helix, helicoid, gyre; pirouette; swirl, twirl, eddy, gurge, surge; vortex, whirlpool, maelstrom, Charybdis; dizzy round, rat race; tourbillion, whirlwind, twister; rotary, roundabout, traffic circle

3 revolutions, revs; revolutions per minute (rpm)

4 **rotator, rotor;** roller, rundle; whirler, whirligig, top, whirlabout; merry-go-round, carousel, roundabout; **wheel,** disk; Ixion's wheel; rolling stone; revolving door; spit, rotisserie; whirling dervish

5 **axle, axis;** pivot, gudgeon, trunnion, **swivel,** spindle, arbor, pole, radiant; fulcrum; pin, pintle; hub, nave; axle shaft, axle spindle, axle bar, axle-tree; distaff; mandrel; gimbal; hinge, hingle; rowlock, oarlock

6 axle box, journal, journal box; hotbox; universal joint

7 **bearing,** ball bearing, journal bearing, saw bearing, tumbler bearing, main bearing, needle bearing, roller bearing, thrust bearing, bevel bearing, bushing; jewel; headstock

8 science of rotation, trochilics, gyrostatics

VERBS 9 **rotate, revolve, spin,** turn, round, go round, go around, turn round, turn around; spiral, gyrate, gyre, whirl like a dervish; circumrotate, circumvolute; circle, circulate; swivel, pivot, wheel, swing; pirouette, turn a pirouette; wind, twist, screw, crank; wamble

10 **roll,** trundle, troll, bowl; roll up, furl

11 **whirl,** whirligig, twirl, wheel, reel, spin, spin like a top, whirl like a dervish; centrifuge, centrifugate; swirl, gurge, surge, eddy, whirlpool

12 <move around in confusion> twist, twirl, seethe, mill, mill around, mill about, stir, roil, **moil,** be turbulent

13 <roll about in> **wallow,** welter, grovel, roll, flounder, tumble

ADJS 14 **rotating, revolving,** turning, gyrating; whirling, swirling, twirling, spinning, wheeling, reeling; rolling, trolling, bowling; antiroll

15 **rotary, rotational,** rotatory, rotative; trochilic, vertiginous; circumrotatory, circumvolutory, circumgyratory; spiral, spiralling, helical, gyral, gyratory, gyrational, gyroscopic, gyrostatic; whirly, swirly, gulfy; whirlabout, whirligig; vortical, cyclonic, tornadic, whirlwindy, whirlwindish

ADVS 16 **round, around,** round about, in a circle; round and round, in circles, like a horse in a mill; in a whirl, in a spin; head over heels, heels over head; clockwise, counterclockwise, anticlockwise, widdershins

916 OSCILLATION

<motion to and fro>

NOUNS 1 **oscillation,** vibration, vibrancy; to-and-fro motion; harmonic motion, simple harmonic motion; libration, nutation; pendulation; **fluctuation,** vacillation, wavering; electrical oscillation, mechanical oscillation, oscillating current; libration of the moon, libration in latitude, libration in longitude; vibratility; frequency, frequency band, frequency spectrum; resonance, resonant frequency, resonance frequency; periodicity

2 **waving,** wave motion, **undulation,** undulancy; brandishing, flourishing, flaunting, shaking, swaying; brandish, flaunt, flourish; wave

3 **pulsation, pulse, beat, throb;** beating, throbbing; systole, diastole; rat-a-tat, staccato, rataplan, drumming; rhythm, tempo; palpitation, flutter, arrhythmia, pitter-patter, pit-a-pat; fibrillation, ventricular fibrillation, tachycardia, ventricular tachycardia; heartbeat, heartthrob; pulse point; electrical shock, electric shock

4 **wave,** wave motion, ray; transverse wave, longitudinal wave; electromagnetic wave, continuous wave, electromagnetic radiation; light; radio wave; mechanical wave; acoustic wave, sound wave; seismic wave, shock wave; de Broglie wave; diffracted wave, guided wave; one-dimensional wave, two-dimensional wave, three-dimensional wave; periodic wave; standing wave, node, antinode; point break, sea wave, surface wave, tidal wave, tsunami, seismic sea wave; traveling wave; surge, storm surge; amplitude, crest, trough; scend; surf, roller, curler, comber, whitecap, white horse; tube; wavelength; frequency, frequency band, frequency spectrum; resonance, resonant frequency, resonance frequency; period; wave number; diffraction; reinforcement, interference; in phase, out of phase; wave equation, Schrödinger equation; Huygens' principle

5 **alternation, reciprocation;** regular play, rhythmic play, coming and going, to-and-fro, back-and-forth, ebb and flow, flux and reflux, systole and diastole, ups and downs, wax and wane; sine wave, Lissajous figure, Lissajous curve; seesawing, teetering, tottering, teeter-tottering; seesaw, teeter, teeter-totter, wigwag; zigzag, zigzagging, zig, zag

6 **swing,** swinging, sway, swag; rock, lurch, roll, reel, careen; wag, waggle; **wave,** waver; swing of the pendulum

7 seismicity, seismism; seismology, seismography, seismometry

8 <instruments> oscilloscope, oscillograph, oscillometer; wavemeter; harmonograph; vibroscope, vibrograph; kymograph; seismoscope, seismograph, seismometer; wave gauge

9 **oscillator,** vibrator; pendulum, pendulum wheel; metronome; swing; seesaw, teeter, teeter-totter, teeterboard, teetery-bender; rocker, rocking chair, cradle; rocking stone, logan stone, shuttle; shuttlecock

VERBS 10 **oscillate,** vibrate, librate, nutate; pendulate; **fluctuate,** vacillate, waver, wave; resonate; swing, sway, swag, dangle, reel, rock, lurch, roll, careen, toss, pitch; wag, waggle; wobble, wamble; bob, bobble; squeg; shake, flutter

11 **wave, undulate;** brandish, flourish, flaunt, shake, swing, wield; float, fly; flap, flutter; wag, wigwag

12 pulsate, **pulse, beat,** throb, not miss a beat; **palpitate,** go pit-a-pat; miss a beat; beat time, beat out, tick, ticktock; drum

13 **alternate,** reciprocate, swing, go to and fro, to-and-fro, come and go, pass and re-pass, ebb and flow, wax and wane, ride and tie, hitch and hike, back and fill; seesaw, teeter, teeter-totter; shuttle, shuttlecock, battledore and shuttlecock; wigwag, wibble-wabble; zigzag

14 <move up and down> **pump, shake,** bounce

ADJS 15 **oscillating,** oscillatory; vibrating, vibratory, harmonic; vibratile; librational, libratory; nutational; periodic, pendular, pendulous; **fluctuating,** fluctuational, fluctuant; wavering; vacillating, vacillatory; resonant

16 **waving, undulating,** undulatory, undulant; seismic

17 **swinging,** swaying, dangling, reeling, rocking, lurching, careening, rolling, tossing, pitching

18 pulsative, pulsatory, pulsatile; **pulsating,** pulsing, beating, throbbing, palpitating, palpitant, pit-a-pat, staccato; rhythmic

19 **alternate,** reciprocal, reciprocative; sine-wave; back-and-forth, to-and-fro, up-and-down, seesaw

20 seismatical, seismological, seismographic, seismometric; succussive, succussatory, sussultatory

ADVS 21 **to and fro, back and forth,** backward and forward, backwards and forwards, in and out, up and down, seesaw, shuttlewise, from side to side, from pillar to post, off and on, ride and tie, hitch and hike, round and round, like buckets in a well

917 AGITATION

<irregular motion>

NOUNS 1 **agitation, perturbation,** hecticness, conturbation; frenzy, excitement; trepidation, trepidity, fidgets, jitters, ants in the pants, antsiness, jitteriness, heebie-jeebies, jumpiness, nervousness, yips, nerviness <Brit>, nervosity, twitter, upset; unrest, malaise, unease, restlessness; fever, feverishness, febrility; disquiet, disquietude, inquietude, discomposure, hand-wringing; stir, churn, ferment, fermentation, foment; seethe, seething, ebullition, boil, boiling; embroilment, roil, turbidity, fume, disturbance, commotion, moil, turmoil, turbulence, swirl, tumult, tumultuation, hubbub, shemozzle, rout, fuss, row, to-do, bluster, fluster, flurry, flutteration, hoo-ha, flap, bustle, brouhaha, bobbery, hurly-burly; maelstrom; disorder

2 **shaking, quaking,** palsy, quivering, quavering, shivering, trembling, tremulousness, shuddering, vibration; juddering, succussion; jerkiness, fits and starts, spasms; jactation, jactitation; joltiness, bumpiness, the shakes, the shivers, the cold shivers, ague, chattering; chorea, rigor, St. Vitus's dance; delirium tremens, the DT's

3 **shake, quake,** quiver, quaver, falter, tremor, tremble, shiver, shudder, twitter, didder, dither; wobble; bob, bobble; jog, joggle; shock, jolt, jar, jostle; bounce, bump; jerk, twitch, tic, grimace, rictus, vellication; jig, jiggle; the shakes

4 **flutter,** flitter, flit, **flicker,** waver, dance; shake, quiver; sputter, splutter; flap, flop; beat, beating; palpitation, throb, pit-a-pat, pitter-patter

5 **twitching,** jerking, vellication; **fidgeting,** fidgets, fidgetiness; itchiness, formication, pruritus

6 **spasm,** convulsion, cramp, paroxysm, throes; orgasm, sexual climax; epitasis, eclampsia; seizure, grip, attack, fit, access, ictus; epilepsy, falling sickness; stroke, apoplexy

7 **wiggle,** wriggle; wag, waggle; writhe, squirm

8 **flounder,** flounce, stagger, totter, stumble, falter; wallow, welter; roll, rock, reel, lurch, careen, swing, sway; toss, tumble, pitch, plunge

9 <instruments> **agitator,** shaker, jiggler, vibrator; beater, stirrer, paddle, whisk, eggbeater; churn; blender

VERBS 10 **agitate, shake,** disturb, perturb, shake up, perturbate, disquiet, discompose, upset, trouble, unsettle, stir, swirl, flurry, flutter, flutter the dovecot, fret, roughen, ruffle, rumple, ripple, ferment, convulse; churn, whip, whisk, beat, paddle; excite; stir up, cause a stir, cause a commotion, muddy the waters, shake up a hornet's nest; work up, churn up, whip up, beat up; roil, rile; disarrange

11 **shake, quake,** vibrate, jactitate; tremble, quiver, quaver, falter, shudder, shiver, twitter, didder, chatter; shake in one's boots, shake like an aspen leaf, have the jitters, have the shakes, have ants in one's pants; have an ague; wobble; bob, bobble; jiggle, jog, joggle; shock, jolt, jar, jostle, hustle, jounce, bounce, jump, bump

12 **flutter,** flitter, flit, flick, flicker, gutter, bicker, wave, waver, dance; sputter, splutter; flap, flop, flip, beat, slat; palpitate, pulse, throb, pitter-patter, go pit-a-pat

13 **twitch,** jerk, vellicate; itch; jig, jiggle, jigger, jigget; **fidget,** have the fidgets

14 **wiggle,** wriggle; wag, waggle; writhe, squirm, twist and turn; have ants in one's pants

15 **flounder,** flounce, stagger, totter, stumble, falter, blunder, wallop; struggle, labor; wallow, welter; roll, rock, reel, lurch, careen, career, swing, sway; toss, tumble, thrash about, pitch, plunge, pitch and plunge, toss and tumble, toss and turn, be the sport of winds and waves; seethe

ADJS 16 **agitated,** disturbed, perturbed, disquieted, discomposed, troubled, upset, ruffled, flurried, flustered, unsettled; stirred up, **shaken,** shaken up, all worked up, all shook up; troublous, feverish, fidgety, jittery, antsy, jumpy, nervous, nervy <Brit>, restless, uneasy, unquiet, unpeaceful; all of a twitter, all of a flutter, giddy, in a spin; turbulent; excited

17 **shaking, vibrating,** chattering; quivering, quavering, quaking, shivering, shuddering, trembling, tremulous, palsied, aspen; succussive, succussatory; shaky, quivery, quavery, shivery, trembly; wobbly; juddering

18 **fluttering, flickering,** wavering, guttering, dancing; sputtering, spluttering, sputtery; fluttery, flickery, bickering, flicky, wavery, unsteady, desultory

19 **jerky,** herky-jerky, twitchy, twitchety, jerking, twitching, fidgety, jumpy, jiggety, vellicative; spastic, spasmodic, eclamptic, orgasmic, convulsive; fitful, saltatory

20 **jolting,** jolty, joggling, joggly, jogglety, jouncy, bouncy, bumpy, choppy, rough; **jarring,** bone-bruising

21 **wriggly,** wriggling, crawly, creepy-crawly; wiggly, wiggling; squirmy, squirming; writhy, writhing, antsy

ADVS 22 **agitatedly,** troublously, restlessly, uneasily, unquietly, unpeacefully, nervously, feverishly; excitedly

23 **shakily,** quiveringly, quaveringly, quakingly, tremblingly, shudderingly, tremulously; flutteringly, waveringly, unsteadily, desultorily; **jerkily,** spasmodically, fitfully, by jerks, by snatches, saltatorily, by fits and starts

918 SPECTATOR

<one who watches>

NOUNS 1 **spectator, observer;** looker, **onlooker,** looker-on, watcher, gazer, gazer-on, gaper, goggler, eyer, viewer, seer, beholder, perceiver, percipient; spectatress, spectatrix; witness, eyewitness; bystander, passerby; innocent bystander; sidewalk superintendent; kibitzer; girl-watcher, ogler, drugstore cowboy; birdwatcher; television viewer, televiewer, video-gazer, TV viewer, couch potato, armchair quarterback; Peeping Tom; binge-watcher

2 attender, **attendee**; theatergoer; audience, house, crowd, gate, fans, fan base

3 **sightseer,** excursionist, tourist, rubberneck, rubbernecker; slummer; tour group

4 **sightseeing,** rubbernecking, lionism; tour, walking tour, bus tour, sightseeing tour, sightseeing excursion, rubberneck tour; grand tour, globetrotting; guided tour; spectator sport; walkscore, walkability

VERBS 5 **spectate**, witness, see, look on, eye, ogle, gape; take in, look at, watch; attend

6 **sightsee,** see the sights, take in the sights, lionize, see the lions; **rubberneck**; go slumming; go on a tour, join a tour; take the grand tour, globe-trot

ADJS 7 spectating, spectatorial; onlooking; sightseeing, rubberneck; passing by, caught in the cross-fire, caught in the middle

919 INTELLECT

<mental capacity for knowledge>

NOUNS 1 **intellect,** mind; **mental faculty**, intellectual faculty, nous, reason, rationality, rational faculty, reasoning faculty, power of reason, ratio, discursive reason, intelligence, mentality, mental capacity, understanding, reasoning, intellection, conception; cognition, perception; brain, brains, brainpower, smarts, gray matter; thought; head, headpiece

2 **wits, senses,** faculties, parts, capacities, intellectual gifts, intellectual talents, mother wit; intellectuals; consciousness

3 **inmost mind,** inner recesses of the mind, mind's core, deepest mind, center of the mind; inner man; subconscious, subconscious mind; inmost heart

4 **psyche, spirit,** spiritus, **soul,** geist, heart, mind, inner mind, inner being, anima, animus; tabula rasa; shade, shadow, manes; breath, pneuma, breath of life, divine breath; *atman, purusha, buddhi, jiva, jivatma* <Sanskrit>; *ruach, nephesh* <Heb>; spiritual being, inner man; ego, the self, the I

5 **life principle,** vital principle, vital spirit, vital soul, *élan vital* <Fr>, vital force, *prana* <Hindu>; essence of life, substance of life, individual essence; divine spark, vital spark, vital flame; chi, qi, tao, ahimsa

6 brain, seat of thought, organ of thought; sensory, sensorium; encephalon; **gray matter**, head, cerebrum, pate, sconce, noddle; noodle, noggin, bean, upper story; sensation

ADJS 7 **mental, intellectual,** rational, reasoning, thinking, noetic, conceptive, conceptual, phrenic; intelligent; noological; endopsychic, psychic, psychical, psychologic, psychological, spiritual; cerebral; subjective, internal

920 INTELLIGENCE, WISDOM

<mental capacity to apply knowledge>

NOUNS 1 **intelligence,** understanding, comprehension, apprehension, mental grasp, intellectual grasp, prehensility of mind, intellectual power, **brainpower**, thinking power, power of mind, power of thought, critical thinking; ideation, conception; integrative power, esemplastic power; rationality, reasoning power, deductive power, ratiocination; sense, wit, mother wit, natural wit, native wit; intellect; intellectuality, intellectualism; capacity, mental capacity, mentality, caliber, reach of mind, compass of mind, scope of mind; intelligence quotient (IQ), mental ratio, mental age; sanity; knowledge; linear thinking

2 **smartness, braininess,** smarts, savvy, brightness, brilliance, cleverness, aptness, aptitude, native cleverness, mental alertness, nous, sharpness, keenness, acuity, acuteness; high IQ, mental ability, mental capability, gift, gifts, giftedness, talent, flair, genius; quickness, nimbleness, quickness of wit, nimbleness of wit, adroitness, dexterity; sharp-wittedness, keen-wittedness, quick-wittedness, nimble-wittedness; nimble mind, mercurial mind, quick parts, clear thinking, quick thinking; ready wit, quick wit, sprightly wit, *esprit* <Fr>

3 **shrewdness,** artfulness, cunning, cunningness, canniness, craft, craftiness, wiliness, guilefulness, slickness, slyness, pawkiness <Brit>, foxiness, animal cunning, low cunning; subtility, subtilty, subtlety; insinuation, insidiousness, deviousness

4 **sagacity,** sagaciousness, **astuteness,** acumen, longheadedness; foresight, foresightedness, providence; farsightedness, farseeingness,

longsightedness; discernment, insight, intuition, penetration, acuteness, acuity; perspicacity, perspicaciousness, perspicuity, perspicuousness; incisiveness, trenchancy, cogency; percipience, percipiency, perception, apperception; sensibility

5 **wisdom,** ripe wisdom, seasoned understanding, mellow wisdom, wiseness, sageness, sagacity, sapience, good understanding, sound understanding; erudition; profundity, profoundness, depth; logical necessity; broad-mindedness; conventional wisdom, received wisdom, prudential judgment

6 **sensibleness,** reasonableness, reason, rationality, sanity, saneness, soundness; practicality, practical wisdom, practical mind; sense, good sense, common sense, plain sense, horse sense; due sense of; level head, cool head, levelheadedness, balance, coolheadedness, coolness; soberness, sobriety, sober-mindedness; savvy, smarts

7 **judiciousness,** judgment, good judgment, sound judgment, cool judgment, soundness of judgment, discernment; **prudence,** prudentialism, providence, policy, polity; weighing, consideration, circumspection, circumspectness, reflection, reflectiveness, thoughtfulness; discretion, discreetness; discrimination

8 **genius,** spirit, soul; daimonion, demon, daemon; inspiration, afflatus, divine afflatus; Muse; fire of genius; **creativity;** talent; creative thought

9 <intelligent being> **intelligence, intellect,** head, brain, mentality, consciousness; wise man; Yoda; intellectual, thinker, academic, savant, scholar, walking encyclopedia; adept, maven

VERBS 10 **have all one's wits about one,** have all one's marbles, have smarts, have savvy, have a head on one's shoulders, have one's head screwed on right; have method in one's madness; use one's head, use one's wits, keep one's wits about one; know what's what, know the score, be wise as a serpent, be wise as an owl; be reasonable, listen to reason; be realistic, get real

11 be brilliant, scintillate, sparkle, coruscate

ADJS 12 **intelligent, intellectual**; ideational, conceptual, conceptive, discursive; sophic, noetic, phrenic; knowing, understanding, reasonable, rational, sensible, bright; sane; not so dumb, strong-minded; very smart, whip-smart

13 clear-witted, clearheaded, clear-eyed, clear-sighted; no-nonsense; awake, **wide-awake,** alive, **alert,** on the ball, focused

14 **smart,** brainy, bright, brilliant, scintillating; clever, apt, gifted, talented; sharp, keen; quick, nimble, adroit, astute, dexterous; sharp-witted, keen-witted, needle-witted, quick-witted, quick-thinking, steel-trap, nimble-witted, quick on the uptake; smart as a whip, sharp as a tack; nobody's fool, no dumbbell, not born yesterday, all there; nerdy, nerdish, nerdlike

15 **shrewd,** artful, cunning, knowing, crafty, wily, guileful, canny, slick, sly, pawky <Brit>, smart as a fox, foxy, crazy like a fox; subtle, subtile; insinuating, insidious, devious, Byzantine, calculating

16 **sagacious, astute,** longheaded, argute; understanding, discerning, penetrating, incisive, acute, trenchant, cogent, piercing; foresighted, foreseeing; forethoughted, forethoughtful, provident; farsighted, farseeing, longsighted; perspicacious, perspicuous; perceptive, percipient, apperceptive, appercipient

17 **wise,** sage, sapient, seasoned, **knowing,** knowledgeable; learned; profound, deep; wise as an owl, wise as a serpent, wise as Solomon; wise beyond one's years, in advance of one's age, wise in one's generation; broad-minded; Yoda-like

18 **sensible,** reasonable, reasoning, rational, logical; practical, pragmatic; philosophical; commonsense, commonsensical; **levelheaded,** balanced, coolheaded, cool, clearheaded, sound, sane, sober, sober-minded, well-balanced, lucid; realistic, ratiocinative; well thought-out; profound

19 **judicious,** judicial, judgmatic, judgmatical, **prudent,** prudential, politic, careful, provident, considerate, circumspect, sapient, thoughtful, reflective, reflecting; discreet; discriminative, discriminating; well-advised, well-judged, enlightened

ADVS 20 **intelligently,** understandingly, knowingly, discerningly; reasonably, rationally, sensibly; smartly, cleverly; shrewdly, artfully, cunningly; wisely, sagaciously, astutely; judiciously, prudently, discreetly, providently, considerately, circumspectly, thoughtfully

921 WISE PERSON

<person with wisdom>

NOUNS 1 **wise person,** wise man, wise woman, **sage,** sapient, person of wisdom; master, mistress, authority, mastermind, master spirit of the age, oracle; philosopher, thinker, lover of wisdom; rabbi; doctor; great soul, mahatma, guru, rishi; elder, wise old man, elder statesman; philosopher king; illuminate; seer; mentor; intellect, man of intellect; mandarin, intellectual; savant, scholar; logician, dialectician, sophist, syllogist, metaphysician; adept

2 <exemplars> Solomon, Socrates, Plato, Mentor, Nestor, Confucius, Buddha, Gandhi, Albert Schweitzer, Martin Luther King Jr

3 **the wise,** the intelligent, the sensible, the prudent, the knowing, the understanding

4 Seven Wise Men of Greece, Seven Sages, Seven Wise Masters; Solon, Chilon, Pittacus, Bias, Periander, Epimenides, Cleobulus, Thales

5 Magi, Three Wise Men, Wise Men of the East, Three Kings; Three Kings of Cologne; Gaspar, Caspar, Melchior, Balthasar

6 **wiseacre,** wisehead, wiseling, witling, wisenheimer, wiseguy, smart ass; wise fool; Gothamite, wise man of Gotham, wise man of Chelm; Buddha nature

922 UNINTELLIGENCE

<lacking mental capacity>

NOUNS 1 **unintelligence,** unintellectuality, unwisdom, unwiseness, intellectual weakness, mental weakness; senselessness, witlessness, mindlessness, brainlessness, primal stupidity, reasonlessness, lackwittedness, lackbrainedness, slackwittedness, slackmindedness; irrationality; ignorance; foolishness; incapacity, ineptitude; low IQ, low mental age

2 **unperceptiveness,** imperceptiveness, insensibility, impercipience, impercipiency, undiscerningness, unapprehendingness, incomprehension, nonunderstanding; blindness, mindblindness, purblindness; unawareness, lack of awareness, unconsciousness, lack of consciousness; shortsightedness, nearsightedness, dim-sightedness

3 **stupidity,** stupidness, **dumbness**, doltishness, boobishness, duncery, dullardism, blockishness, cloddishness, lumpishness, sottishness, asininity, ninnyism, simplemindedness, simpletonianism; oafishness, oafdom, yokelism, loutishness; density, denseness, opacity; grossness, crassness, crudeness, boorishness; dullness, dopiness, obtuseness, sluggishness, bovinity, cowishness, slowness, lethargy, stolidity, hebetude; dim-wittedness, dimness, dull-wittedness, slow-wittedness, beef-wittedness, dull-headedness, thick-wittedness, thick-headedness, unteachability, ineducability; wrongheadedness

4 <nonformal> **blockheadedness,** woodenheadedness, klutziness, dunderheadedness, goofiness, jolterheadedness <Brit>, joltheadedness <Brit>, chowderheadedness, chuckleheadedness, beetleheadedness, chumpiness, numskulledness, numskullery, cabbageheadedness, sapheadedness, muttonheadedness, meatheadedness, fatheadedness, boneheadedness, knuckleheadedness, blunderheadedness; dumb blond

5 **muddleheadedness,** addleheadedness, addlepatedness, puzzleheadedness

6 **empty-headedness,** empty-mindedness, absence of mind, airheadedness, bubbleheadedness; **vacuity,** vacuousness, vacancy, vacuum, emptiness, mental void, blankness, hollowness, inanity, vapidity, jejunity

7 **superficiality, shallowness,** unprofundity, lack of depth, unprofoundness, thinness; shallow-wittedness, shallow-mindedness; frivolousness, flightiness, lightness, fluffiness, frothiness, volatility, dizziness, ditziness

8 **feeblemindedness,** weak-mindedness; infirmity, weakness, feebleness, softness, mushiness

9 **mental deficiency,** mental retardation, amentia, mental handicap, subnormality, mental defectiveness; brain damage; arrested development, infantilism, retardation, retardment, backwardness; simplemindedness, simple-wittedness, simpleness, simplicity; idiocy, idiotism, profound idiocy, imbecility, half-wittedness, blithering idiocy; moronity, moronism, cretinism; mongolism, mongolianism, Down's syndrome; insanity; brain fade, brain fog, brain fart, mental lapse; brain freeze

10 **senility,** senilism, senile weakness, senile debility, caducity, decreptitude, senectitude, decline; childishness, second childhood, dotage, dotardism; anility; senile dementia, senile psychosis, **Alzheimer's**, Alzheimer's disease

11 puerility, puerilism, immaturity, **childishness;** infantilism, babyishness; Peter Pan syndrome

VERBS 12 **be stupid,** show ignorance, not have all one's marbles; drool, slobber, drivel, dither, blither, blather, maunder, dote, burble; not see an inch beyond one's nose, not have enough sense to come in out of the rain, not find one's way to first base; lose one's mind, lose one's marbles; not be all there; have a low IQ; dumb down

ADJS 13 **unintelligent,** unintellectual, unthinking, unreasoning, irrational, unwise, inept, not bright; ungifted, untalented; senseless, insensate; mindless, witless, reasonless, brainless, pin-brained, pea-brained, of little brain, headless, empty-headed; lackwitted, lackbrained, slackwitted, slackminded, lean-minded, lean-witted, short-witted; foolish; ignorant

14 **undiscerning,** unperceptive, imperceptive, impercipient, insensible, unapprehending, uncomprehending, nonunderstanding; shortsighted, myopic, nearsighted, dim-sighted; blind, purblind, mind-blind, blind as a bat; blinded, blindfold, blindfolded

15 **stupid, dumb,** dullard, doltish, blockish, klutzy, klutzish, duncish, duncical, cloddish, clottish

<Brit>, chumpish, lumpish, oafish, boobish, sottish, asinine, lamebrained, Boeotian; dense, thick, opaque, gross, crass, fat; bovine, cowish, beef-witted, beef-brained, beefheaded; unteachable, ineducable; wrongheaded

16 dull, dull of mind, dopey, obtuse, blunt, **dim**, wooden, heavy, sluggish, **slow**, slow-witted, hebetudinous, dim-witted, dull-witted, blunt-witted, dull-brained, dull-headed, dull-pated, thick-witted, thick-headed, thick-pated, thick-skulled, thick-brained, fat-witted, gross-witted, gross-headed

17 <nonformal> **blockheaded,** woodenheaded, stupidheaded, dumbheaded, dunderheaded, blunderheaded, clueless, jolterheaded, joltheaded, jingle-brained <Brit>, chowderheaded, chuckleheaded, beetleheaded, nitwitted, numskulled, cabbageheaded, pumpkin-headed, sapheaded, lunkheaded, muttonheaded, meatheaded, fatheaded, boneheaded, knuckleheaded, clodpated; dead from the neck up, dead between the ears, muscle-bound between the ears; featherheaded, airheaded, bubbleheaded, out to lunch, lunchy, dufus, dufus-assed, dickish, spastic, spazzy, three bricks shy of a load, without brain one, not playing with a full deck, not sixteen ounces to the pound, not all there, soft in the head

18 **muddleheaded,** fuddlebrained, scramblebrained, mixed-up, muddled, addled, addleheaded, addlepated, addlebrained, muddybrained, puzzleheaded, blear-witted; dizzy, muzzy, foggy

19 **empty-headed,** empty-minded, empty-noddled, empty-pated, empty-skulled; **vacuous,** vacant, empty, hollow, inane, vapid, jejune, blank, airheaded, bubbleheaded; rattlebrained, rattleheaded; scatterbrained

20 **superficial, shallow,** unprofound; shallow-witted, shallow-minded, shallow-brained, shallow-headed, shallow-pated; frivolous, dizzy, ditzy, flighty, light, volatile, frothy, fluffy, featherbrained, birdwitted, birdbrained

21 **feebleminded,** weak-minded, weak, feeble, infirm, soft, soft in the head, weak in the upper story

22 **mentally deficient,** mentally defective, mentally handicapped, retarded, mentally challenged, mentally retarded, backward, arrested, subnormal, not right in the head, not all there; simpleminded, simplewitted, simple, simpletonian; half-witted, half-baked; idiotic, moronic, imbecile, imbecilic, cretinous, cretinistic, mongoloid, spastic; crackbrained, cracked, crazy; babbling, driveling, slobbering, drooling, blithering, dithering, maundering, burbling; brain-damaged

23 **senile,** decrepit, doddering, doddery; childish, childlike, in one's second childhood, doting

24 puerile, immature, **childish;** childlike; infantile, infantine; babyish, babish

ADVS 25 **unintelligently, stupidly;** insensately, foolishly

923 FOOLISHNESS

<lacking good sense, judgment>

NOUNS 1 **foolishness, folly,** foolery, foolheadedness, stupidity, asininity; inanity, fatuity, fatuousness; ineptitude; silliness; frivolousness, frivolity, giddiness; triviality, triflingness, nugacity, desipience; nonsense, tomfoolery, poppycock; senselessness, insensateness, witlessness, **thoughtlessness**, brainlessness, mindlessness; idiocy, imbecility; craziness, madness, lunacy, insanity, daftness; eccentricity, queerness, crankiness, crackpottedness; weirdness; screwiness, nuttiness, wackiness, goofiness, daffiness, battiness, sappiness; zaniness, zanyism, clownishness, buffoonery, clowning, fooling around, horsing around, dicking around

2 **unwiseness,** unwisdom, **injudiciousness,** imprudence; indiscreetness, indiscretion, inconsideration, thoughtlessness, witlessness, inattention, unthoughtfulness, lack of sensitivity; unreasonableness, unsoundness, unsensibleness, senselessness, reasonlessness, irrationality, unreason, inadvisability; recklessness; childishness, immaturity, puerility, callowness; gullibility, bamboozlability; inexpedience; unintelligence; pompousness, stuffiness

3 absurdity, absurdness, **ridiculousness;** ludicrousness; **nonsense,** nonsensicality, stuff and nonsense, codswallop, horseshit*, bullshit*; preposterousness, fantasticalness, monstrousness, wildness, outrageousness

4 <foolish act> **folly, stupidity,** act of folly, absurdity, foolish thing, stupid thing, dumb thing to do; fool's trick, dumb trick; imprudence, indiscretion, unwise step; blunder, blooper, gaffe

5 stultification; infatuation; trivialization

VERBS 6 **be foolish;** be stupid; act the fool, play the fool; get funny, do the crazy act; fool, tomfool, trifle, frivol; fool around, horse around, dick around, clown, clown around; **make a fool of oneself**, make a monkey of oneself, stultify oneself, invite ridicule, put oneself out of court, play the buffoon; lose one's head, take leave of one's senses, go haywire; pass from the sublime to the ridiculous; strain at a gnat and swallow a camel; tilt at windmills; tempt fate, never learn

7 stultify, infatuate, turn one's head, befool; gull, **dupe**; make a fool of, make a monkey of, play for a sucker, **put on**

ADJS 8 **foolish,** fool, foolheaded, **stupid, dumb**, clueless, asinine; buffoonish; silly, apish, dizzy; fatuous, fatuitous, inept, inane; futile; senseless, witless, thoughtless, insensate, brainless; idiotic, moronic, imbecile, imbecilic, spastic; crazy, mad, daft, insane; infatuated, besotted, credulous, gulled, befooled, beguiled, fond, doting, gaga; sentimental, maudlin; dazed, fuddled

9 <nonformal> **screwy, nutty,** cockeyed, wacky, goofy, daffy, loony, batty, sappy, kooky, flaky, damn-fool, out of it, out to lunch, lunchy, dorky, dippy, birdbrained, spaced-out, doodle-brained, lame, ditzy, dizzy, loony-tune, dopey, fluffheaded, loopy, scatty, zerking

10 **unwise,** injudicious, **imprudent,** unpolitic, impolitic, contraindicated, counterproductive; indiscreet; inconsiderate, thoughtless, mindless, witless, unthoughtful, unthinking, unreflecting, unreflective; unreasonable, unsound, unsensible, senseless, insensate, reasonless, irrational, reckless, inadvisable, dickish; inexpedient; ill-advised, ill-considered, ill-gauged, ill-judged, ill-imagined, ill-contrived, ill-devised, on the wrong track, unconsidered; unadvised, misadvised, misguided; undiscerning; unforseeing, unseeing, shortsighted, myopic; suicidal, self-defeating

11 absurd, **nonsensical,** insensate, ridiculous, laughable, ludicrous; **foolish,** crazy; preposterous, cockamamie, fantastic, fantastical, grotesque, monstrous, wild, weird, outrageous, incredible, beyond belief, *outré* <Fr>, extravagant, bizarre; high-flown

12 foolable, befoolable, **gullible**, bamboozlable; naive, artless, guileless, inexperienced, impressionable; malleable, like putty; persuasible, biddable

ADVS 13 **foolishly, stupidly,** sillily, idiotically; unwisely, injudiciously, imprudently, indiscreetly, inconsiderately; myopically, blindly, senselessly, unreasonably, thoughtlessly, witlessly, imsensately, unthinkingly; absurdly, ridiculously

924 FOOL

<one lacking good sense>

NOUNS 1 **fool,** damn fool, tomfool, perfect fool, born fool; *schmuck* <Yiddish>; ass*, jackass*, stupid ass*, egregious ass*; zany, clown, buffoon, doodle; sop, milksop; mome, mooncalf, softhead; figure of fun; lunatic; ignoramus

2 **stupid person,** dolt, **dunce,** clod, Boeotian, dullard, donkey, yahoo, thickwit, dope, nitwit, dimwit, lackwit, half-wit, lamebrain, putz, lightweight, witling

3 <nonformal> **chump,** boob, booby, sap, prize sap, klutz, basket case, dingbat, dingdong, ding-a-ling, ninny, **ninnyhammer**, nincompoop, looby, noddy, saphead, mutt, jerk, jerkoff*, asshole*, goof, *schlemiel* <Yiddish>, galoot, gonzo, dumbo, dweeb, dropshop, dipshit*, nerd, twerp, yo-yo

4 <nonformal> **blockhead, airhead,** bubblehead, fluffhead, featherhead, woodenhead, dolthead, dumbhead, dummy, dum-dum, dumbo, dumb cluck, dodo head, doodoohead, dumbbell, dumb bunny, stupidhead, dullhead, bufflehead, bonehead, jughead, thickhead, thickskull, numskull, putz, lunkhead, chucklehead, knucklehead, chowderhead, headbanger, jolterhead <Brit>, muttonhead, beefhead, meathead, noodle, noodlehead, thimblewit, pinhead, pinbrain, peabrain, cabbagehead, pumpkin head, fathead, blubberhead, muddlehead, puzzlehead, addlebrain, addlehead, addlepate, tottyhead, puddinghead, stupe, mushhead, blunderhead, dunderhead, dunderpate, clodpate, clodhead, clodpoll, jobbernowl, gaby, gowk <Brit>, jive turkey, vegetable, dim-bulb, twit, sucker, dumb blond, mouthbreather, numbnuts, potato head

5 **oaf,** lout, boor, lubber, oik <Brit>, gawk, gawky, lummox, yokel, rube, hick, hayseed, bumpkin, clod, clodhopper, village idiot; yazzihamper

6 **silly,** silly Billy, silly ass*, goose

7 **scatterbrain,** scatterbrains, ditz, rattlebrain, rattlehead, rattlepate, harebrain, featherbrain, featherhead, giddybrain, giddyhead, giddypate, flibbertigibbet, lunatic, crank, wackadoodle

8 **idiot,** driveling idiot, blithering idiot; **imbecile, moron,** half-wit, natural, natural idiot, born fool, natural-born fool, mental defective, defective; cretin, basket case, spastic, spaz; simpleton, simp, juggins, jiggins, clot, berk, golem

9 dotard, senile; fogy, **old fogy,** fuddy-duddy, old fart, old fud

925 SANITY

<soundness of mind>

NOUNS 1 **sanity, saneness,** sanemindedness, soundness, soundness of mind, soundmindedness, sound mind, healthy mind, right mind, senses, reason, rationality, reasonableness, intelligibility, lucidity, coherence, stability, balance, wholesomeness; normalness, normality, normalcy; **mental health;** mental hygiene; mental balance, mental poise, mental equilibrium; sobriety, sober senses; a sound mind in a sound body, a healthy mind in a healthy body; contact with reality; lucid interval; knowing right from wrong; good sense, common sense, wits

VERBS 2 come to one's senses, sober up, recover one's sanity, recover one's balance, recover one's equilibrium, get things into proportion; see in perspective; **have all one's marbles**; have a good head on one's shoulder; have one's wits about one

3 bring to one's senses, bring to reason

ADJS 4 **sane,** sane-minded, not mad, rational, reasonable, sensible, lucid, normal, wholesome, clearheaded, clearminded, sober, balanced, sound, mentally sound, of sound mind, *compos mentis* <L>, sound-minded, healthy-minded, right, right in the head, **in one's right mind,** in possession of one's faculties, in possession of one's senses, together, all there; in touch with reality; with both oars in the water, playing with a full deck

926 INSANITY, MANIA

<unsoundness of mind>

NOUNS 1 **insanity,** insaneness, unsaneness, lunacy, **madness, craziness**, daftness, oddness, strangeness, queerness, abnormality; loss of touch with reality, loss of contact with reality, loss of mind, loss of reason; dementedness, dementia, athymia, brainsickness, mindsickness, mental sickness, sickness; criminal insanity, homicidal mania, hemothymia; mental illness, mental disease; brain damage; rabidness, mania, furor; alienation, aberration, mental disturbance, derangement, distraction, disorientation, mental derangement, mental disorder, unbalance, mental instability, unsoundness, unsoundness of mind; unbalanced mind, diseased mind, unsound mind, sick mind, disturbed mind, troubled mind, clouded mind, shattered mind, mind overthrown, mind unhinged, darkened mind, disordered mind, disordered reason; senselessness, witlessness, reasonlessness, irrationality; possession, pixilation; diminished capacity, mental deficiency

2 <nonformal> **nuttiness,** craziness, daffiness, battiness, screwiness, goofiness, kookiness, wackiness, dottiness, pottiness, *mishegas* <Yiddish>, looniness, lunchiness, balminess; bats in the belfry, a screw loose, one wheel in the sand, one sandwich short of a picnic; lame brains; stir-crazy, cabin fever

3 **psychosis,** psychopathy, psychopathology, psychopathic condition; certifiability; neurosis; psychopathia sexualis, sexual pathology; pathological drunkenness, pathological intoxication, dipsomania; pharmacopsychosis, drug addiction; moral insanity, psychopathic personality, abulia

4 schizophrenia, dementia praecox, mental dissociation, dissociation of personality; catatonic schizophrenia, catatonia, residual schizophrenia, hebephrenia, hebephrenic schizophrenia; schizothymia; schizophasia; thought disorder; schizoid personality, split personality, schizotypal personality; paranoia, paraphrenia, paranoiac psychosis, paranoid psychosis; paranoid schizophrenia; schizoaffective disorder

5 **depression,** melancholia, depressive psychosis, dysthymia, barythymia, lypothymia; melancholia hypochrondriaca; involutional melancholia, involutional psychosis; stuporous melancholia, melancholia attonita; flatuous melancholia; melancholia religiosa; postpartum depression; manic-depressive disorder, manic-depression, bipolar disorder; cyclothymia, poikilothymia, mood swings

6 **rabies,** hydrophobia, lyssa, canine madness; dumb rabies, sullen rabies, paralytic rabies; furious rabies

7 **frenzy,** furor, fury, maniacal excitement, fever, rage; seizure, attack, acute episode, **episode, fit,** paroxysm, spasm, convulsion; snit; amok, murderous insanity, murderous frenzy, homicidal mania, hemothymia; psychokinesia; furor epilepticus

8 **delirium,** deliriousness, brainstorm; calenture of the brain, afebrile delirium, lingual delirium, delirium mussitans; incoherence, wandering, raving, ranting; exhaustion delirium, exhaustion psychosis

9 delirium tremens (DTs), mania a potu, dementia a potu, delirium alcoholicum, delirium ebriositatis

10 <nonformal> the horrors, the shakes, the heebie-jeebies, the jimjams, the screaming meemies; blue Johnnies, blue devils, pink elephants, pink spiders, snakes, snakes in the boots, wigout

11 fanaticism, fanaticalness, **rabidness,** overzealousness, overenthusiasm, ultrazealousness, zealotry, zealotism, bigotry, perfervidness; extremism, extremeness, extravagance, excessiveness, overreaction; overreligiousness

12 **mania** <see lists>, craze, infatuation, enthusiasm, passion, fascination, crazy fancy, bug, rage, furor; manic psychosis; megalomania

13 **obsession,** prepossession, preoccupation, **hang-up, fixation,** tic, complex, fascination; hypercathexis; compulsion, morbid drive, obsessive compulsion, irresistible impulse; monomania, ruling passion, fixed idea, *idée fixe* <Fr>, one-track mind; possession

14 **mental institution**, insane asylum, asylum, lunatic asylum, madhouse, mental home, bedlam; bughouse, nuthouse, laughing academy, loony bin, booby hatch, funny farm; mental hospital, psychopathic hospital, psychopathic ward, psychiatric hospital, psychiatric ward; padded cell, rubber room

15 lunatic, **madperson**, madman, madwoman, dement, phrenetic, fanatic, *fou*, non compos; bedlamite, Tom o' Bedlam; demoniac, energumen; mental case, **maniac,** raving lunatic; homicidal maniac, psychopathic killer, berserk, berserker; borderline case; mental defective, idiot; hypochondriac; melancholic, depressive; neurotic; headcase

16 <nonformal> **nut,** nutso, nutter, nutball, nutbar, nutcase, loon, loony, loony tune, headcase, crazy, psycho, crackpot, screwball, weirdie, weirdo, kook, flake, crackbrain, *meshugana* <Yiddish>, fruitcake, schizo, wack, wacko, wigger, sickie, sicko, space cadet

17 psychotic, psycho, mental, **mental case**, certifiable case, psychopath, psychopathic case; psychopathic personality; paranoiac, paranoid; schizophrenic, schizophrene, schizoid; schiz, schizy, schizo; catatoniac; hebephreniac; manic-depressive; megalomaniac

18 **fanatic,** infatuate, bug, nut, buff, fan, freak, aficionado, devotee, **zealot**, enthusiast, energumen; monomaniac, crank; lunatic fringe

19 psychiatry, alienism, psychiatric care, psychotherapy, group therapy; psychiatrist, alienist, psychotherapist

VERBS **20** **be insane, be out of one's mind,** not be in one's right mind, not be right in the head, not be all there, have a demon, have devil; have bats in the belfry, have a screw loose, not have all one's marbles, not play with a full deck, not have both oars in the water; wander, ramble; rave, rage, rant, have a fit; dote, babble; drivel, drool, slobber, slaver; froth at the mouth, foam at the mouth, run mad, run amok, go berserk

21 **go mad,** take leave of one's senses, lose one's mind, lose one's senses, lose one's wits, crack up, go off one's head

22 <nonformal> **go crazy,** go bats, go cuckoo, go bughouse, go nuts, go nutso, go out of one's gourd, go out of one's skull, go out of one's tree, go off one's nut, go off one's rocker, go off the track, go off the deep end, blow one's top, blow one's stack, pop one's cork, flip one's lid, flip one's wig, wig out, go ape, go apeshit*, schiz out, go bananas, go crackers, go bonkers, go bonzo, blow one's mind, freak out, flip out, go hog wild, go round the bend, have a screw loose, have bats in one's belfry, have rocks in one's head, lose one's marbles

23 addle the wits, affect one's mind, go to one's head

24 **drive insane, drive crazy**, drive mad, madden, dement, craze, mad, make mad, send mad, unbalance, unhinge, undermine one's reason, derange, distract, frenzy, shatter, send out of one's mind, overthrow one's mind, drive up the wall

25 **obsess,** possess, beset, infatuate, preoccupy, be uppermost in one's thoughts, have a thing about; grip, hold, get a hold on, not let go; **fixate;** drive, compel, impel

ADJS **26** **insane,** unsane, mad, stark-mad, mad as a hatter, mad as a march hare, stark-staring mad, maddened, sick, crazed, lunatic, moonstruck, daft, non compos mentis, non compos, unsound, of unsound mind, **demented,** deranged, deluded, disoriented, unhinged, unbalanced, unsettled, distraught, wandering, mazed, crackbrained, brainsick, sick in the head, not right, not in one's right mind, touched, touched in the head, out of one's mind, out of one's senses, bereft of reason, reasonless, irrational, deprived of reason, senseless, witless; hallucinated; manic; queer, queer in the head, odd, strange, off, flighty; abnormal, mentally deficient

27 <nonformal> **crazy, nutty,** daffy, dotty, dippy, crazy as a loon, loony, loony-tune, goofy, wacky, wacked, balmy, barmy, flaky, kooky, potty, batty, ape, apeshit*, wiggy, wigged, lunchy, out to lunch, bonzo, bats, nuts, nutso, nutty as a fruitcake, fruity, fruitcakey, screwy, screwball, screwballs, crackers, bananas, bonkers, cray-cray, loopy, beany, buggy, bughouse, bugs, cuckoo, slaphappy, flipped, freaked-out, off-the-wall, gaga, haywire, off in the upper story, off one's nut, off one's rocker, off the track, off the hinges, round the bend, minus some buttons, nobody home, with bats in the belfry, just plain nuts, loco, mental, psycho, cracked, not right in the head, tetched, off one's head, out of one's head, out of one's gourd, out of one's skull, out of one's tree, not all there, *meshuga* <Yiddish>, *meshugga* <Yiddish>, not tightly wrapped, three bricks shy of a load, rowing with one oar in the water, up-the-wall, schizzy, schizoid, schizo

28 psychotic, psychopathic, psychoneurotic, **mentally ill,** mentally sick, certifiable; sociopathic; traumatized, deluded, disturbed, neurotic; schizophrenic, schizoid, schiz, schizy; hypochondriacal; dissociated, disconnected; depressed, depressive; manic; manic-depressive; maniacal; paranoiac, paranoid; catatonic; brain-damaged, brain-injured

29 **possessed,** possessed with a demon, possessed with the devil, pixilated, bedeviled, demonized, devil-ridden, demonic, demonical, demoniacal

30 **rabid, maniac, maniacal,** manic, raving mad, stark-raving mad, frenzied, frantic, frenetic; mad, madding, wild, furious, violent; desperate; hysterical, beside oneself, like one possessed, uncontrollable; raving, raging, ranting; frothing at the mouth, foaming at the mouth; amok, berserk, running wild; maenadic, corybantic, bacchic, Dionysiac

31 **delirious,** out of one's head, off one's head, off, deluded; giddy, dizzy, lightheaded; hallucinating, wandering, rambling, raving, ranting, babbling, incoherent, rootin'-tootin'

32 **fanatic, fanatical,** rabid; overzealous, ultrazealous, overenthusiastic, zealotic, bigoted, perfervid; extreme, extremist, extravagant, inordinate; unreasonable, irrational; wild-eyed, wild-looking, haggard; overreligious

33 **obsessed,** possessed, prepossessed, infatuated, preoccupied, fixated, hung up, besotted, gripped, held, fussy; monomaniac, monomaniacal; anal-retentive

34 **obsessive,** obsessional; **obsessing,** possessing, preoccupying, gripping, holding; driving, impelling, compulsive, compelling; anal-retentive

ADVS **35** madly, insanely, crazily; deliriously; fanatically, rabidly

36 **mania by name**

ablutomania <washing, bathing>
acromania <incurable insanity>
agoramania <open spaces>
agromania <living alone>
agyiomania <streets>
ailuromania <cats>
alcoholomania <alcohol>
amaxomania <being in vehicles>
amenomania <pleasing delusions>
Americamania <United States>
andromania <men>
Anglomania <England>
anthomania <flowers>
aphrodisiomania <sexual pleasure>
apimania <bees>
arithmomania <counting>
automania <solitude>
autophonomania <suicide>
ballistomania <bullets>
Beatlemania <the Beatles>
bibliomania <books>
bibliokleptomania <book theft>
bruxomania <grinding one's teeth>
cacodemonomania <demonic possession>
cheromania <gaiety>
Chinamania <China>
chionomania <snow>
choreomania <dancing>
chrematomania <money>
cleptomania <stealing>
clinomania <bed rest>
coprolalomania <foul speech>
cremnomania <cliffs>
cresomania <great wealth>
cynomania <dogs>
Dantomania <Dante>
demomania <crowds>
dipsomania <alcoholic beverages>
doramania <fur>
drapetomania <running away>
dromomania <traveling>
ecdemiomania <wandering>
edeomania <genitals>
egomania <one's self>
eleuthromania <freedom>
empleomania <public employment>
enomania <wine>
entheomania <religion>
entomomania <insects>
eremiomania <stillness>
ergasiomania <activity>
ergomania <work>
eroticomania <erotica>
erotographomania <erotic literature>
erotomania <sexual desire>
erythromania <blushing>
etheromania <ether>
ethnomania <ethnic or racial autonomy>
florimania <plants>
Francomania <France>
Gallomania <France>
gamomania <marriage>
gephyromania <crossing bridges>
glazomania <list making>
Germanomania <Germany>
Gorbymania <Mikhail S Gorbachev>
graphomania <writing>
Grecomania <Greece>
gymnomania <nakedness>
gynecomania <male lust>
hamartomania <sin>
hedonomania <pleasure>
heliomania <sun>
hieromania <priests>
hippomania <horses>
hodomania <travel>
homicidomania <murder>
hydrodipsomania <drinking water>
hydromania <water>
hylomania <woods>
hypermania <acute mania>
hypnomania <sleep>
hypomania <mild mania>
hysteromania <female lust>
ichthyomania <fish>
iconomania <icons>
idolomania <idols>
infomania <information>
Italomania <Italy>
kainomania <novelty>
kathisomania <sitting>
kinesomania <movement>
kleptomania <stealing>
lalomania <speech>
letheomania <narcotics>
litigiomania <legal disputes>
logomania <talking>
lycomania <lycanthropy>
lypemania <deep melancholy>
macromania <becoming larger>
megalomania <self-importance>
melomania <music>
mentulomania <penis>
mesmeromania <hypnosis>
metromania <writing>
micromania <becoming smaller>
monomania <one idea or subject>
musicomania <music>
musomania <mice>
mythomania <lying, exaggerations>
necromania <death; the dead>
nesomania <islands>
noctimania <night>
nosomania <imagined disease>
nostomania <homesickness>
nudomania <nudity>
nymphomania <female lust>

ochlomania <crowds>
oestromania <female lust>
oikomania <home>
oinomania <wine>
oligomania <several subjects>
oniomania <buying>
onomatomania <words, names>
ophidiomania <reptiles>
orchidomania <testicles>
ornithomania <birds>
paramania <complaints>
parousiamania <second coming of Christ>
pathomania <moral insanity>
phagomania <food; eating>
phaneromania <growths on one's body>
pharmacomania <medicines>
philopatridomania <homesickness>
phonomania <noise>
photomania <light>
phronemomania <thinking>
phthisiomania <tuberculosis>
plutomania <great wealth>
politicomania <politics>
poriomania <wanderlust>
pornographomania <pornography>
potomania <drinking; delirium tremens>
pseudomania <falsities>
pyromania <fire>
Russomania <Russia>
satyromania <male lust>
scribblemania <writing>
scribomania <writing>
siderodromomania <railroad travel>
sitomania <food>
sophomania <wisdom>
squandermania <spending>
submania <mild mania>
symmetromania <symmetry>
Teutonomania <Germany>
thalassomania <sea>
thanatomania <death>
theatromania <theater>
theomania <God>
timbromania <postage stamps>
tomomania <surgery>
trichomania <hair>
trichotillomania <pulling out one's hair>
tristimania <melancholia>
tromomania <delirium tremens>
Turkomania <Turkey>
typomania <writing for publication>
uteromania <female lust>
verbomania <words>
xenomania <foreigners>
zoomania <animals>

37 mania by subject

<activity> ergasiomania
<acute mania> hypermania
<alcohol> alcoholomania
<alcoholic beverages> dipsomania
<animals> zoomania
<bathing> ablutomania
<Beatles> Beatlemania
<becoming larger> macromania
<becoming smaller> micromania
<bed rest> clinomania
<bees> apimania
<being in vehicles> amaxomania
<birds> ornithomania
<blushing> erythromania
<book theft> bibliokleptomania
<books> bibliomania
<bullets> ballistomania
<buying> oniomania
<cats> ailuromania
<China> Chinamania
<cliffs> cremnomania
<complaints> paramania
<counting> arithmomania
<crossing bridges> gephyromania
<crowds> demomania, ochlomania
<dancing> choreomania
<Dante> Dantomania
<death; the dead> necromania
<death> thanatomania
<deep melancholy> lypemania
<delirium tremens> tromomania
<demonic possession> cacodemonomania
<dogs> cynomania
<drinking water> hydrodipsomania
<drinking> potomania
<England> Anglomania
<erotica> eroticomania
<erotic literature> erotographomania
<falsities> pseudomania
<female lust> hysteromania, nymphomania, oestromania, uteromania
<fires> pyromania
<fish> ichthyomania
<flowers> anthomania
<food; eating> phagomania
<food> sitomania
<foreigners> xenomania
<foul speech> coprolalomania
<France> Francomania, Gallomania
<freedom> eleuthromania
<fur> doramania
<gaiety> cheromania
<genitals> edeomania
<Germany> Germanomania, Teutonomania
<God> theomania
<great wealth> cresomania, plutomania
<Greece> Grecomania
<grinding one's teeth> bruxomania
<hair> trichomania
<home> oikomania
<homesickness> philopatridomania
<horses> hippomania
<hypnosis> mesmeromania
<icons> iconomania
<idols> idolomania
<imagined disease> nosomania
<incurable insanity> acromania
<information> infomania
<insects> entomomania
<Italy> Italomania
<lies; exaggerations> mythomania
<light> photomania
<lycanthropy> lycomania
<male lust> satyromania
<marriage> gamomania
<medicines> pharmacomania
<melancholia> tristimania
<men> andromania
<mice> musomania
<mild mania> hypomania, submania
<money> chrematomania
<moral insanity> pathomania
<movement> kinesomania
<murder> homicidomania
<music> melomania, musicomania
<nakedness> gymnomania
<narcotics> letheomania
<night> noctimania
<noise> phonomania
<novelty> kainomania
<nudity> nudomania
<one's own wisdom> sophomania
<one's self> egomania
<one subject> monomania
<open spaces> agoramania
<opium> opiomania
<own importance> megalomania
<penis> mentulomania
<picking at growths> phaneromania

<pinching off one's hair> trichorrhexomania
<plants> florimania
<pleasing delusions> amenomania
<pleasure> hedonomania
<politics> politicomania
<pornography> pornographomania
<postage stamps> timbromania
<priests> hieromania
<public employment> empleomania
<railroad travel> siderodromomania
<religion> entheomania
<reptiles> ophidiomania
<return home> nostomania
<running away> drapetomania
<Russia> Russomania
<satyriasis> gynecomania
<sea> thalassomania
<second coming of Christ> parousiamania
<several subjects> oligomania
<sexual pleasure> aphrodisiomania, erotomania
<sin> hamartomania
<sitting> kathisomania
<sleep> hypnomania
<snow> chionomania
<solitude> automania
<speech> lalomania
<spending> squandermania
<stealing> kleptomania
<stillness> eremiomania
<suicide> autophonomania
<sun> heliomania
<surgery> tomomania
<symmetry> symmetromania
<talking> logomania
<testicles> orchidomania
<theater> theatromania
<thinking> phronemomania
<travel> hodomania
<traveling> dromomania
<tuberculosis> phthisiomania
<United States> Americamania
<wandering> ecdemiomania
<wanderlust> poriomania
<washing> ablutomania
<water> hydromania
<wine> enomania, oinomania
<woods> hylomania
<words> verbomania
<work> ergomania
<writing for publication> typomania
<writing verse> metromania
<writing> graphomania, scribblemania, scribomania

927 ECCENTRICITY

<unusual behavior>

NOUNS 1 **eccentricity**, **idiosyncrasy**, idiocrasy, erraticism, erraticness, queerness, oddity, peculiarity, strangeness, singularity, freakishness, freakiness, quirkiness, crotchetiness, dottiness, crankiness, crankism, crackpotism; whimsy, whimsicality; abnormality, anomaly, unnaturalness, irregularity, deviation, deviancy, differentness, divergence, aberration; nonconformity, unconventionality

2 **quirk, idiosyncrasy**, twist, kink, crank, quip, trick, mannerism, crotchet, conceit, whim, maggot, maggot in the brain, bee in one's bonnet

3 **eccentric**, erratic, character; odd person; nonconformist, recluse

4 freak, **character**, crackpot, nut, screwball, weirdie, weirdo, kook, queer potato, oddball, flake, strange duck, odd fellow, crank, bird, goofus, wack, wacko

ADJS 5 **eccentric**, erratic, idiocratic, idiocratical, **idiosyncratic**, idiosyncratical, queer, queer in the head, odd, peculiar, strange, fey, singular, anomalous, freakish, funny; unnatural, abnormal, irregular, divergent, deviative, deviant, different, exceptional; unconventional; crotchety, quirky, dotty, maggoty <Brit>, cranky, crank, crankish, whimsical, twisted; solitary, reclusive, antisocial

6 <nonformal> kooky, goofy, birdy, funny, kinky, loopy, goofus, haywire, squirrelly, screwy, screwball, nutty, wacky, flaky, oddball, wacko, lunch, out to lunch, nobody home, weird

928 KNOWLEDGE

<information learned>

NOUNS 1 **knowledge,** knowing, knowingness, ken; command, reach; acquaintance, familiarity, intimacy; private knowledge, privity; information, data, database, datum, items, facts, factual base, corpus; certainty, certain knowledge; protocol, protocol statement, protocol sentence, protocol proposition; intelligence; practical knowledge, experience, **know-how**, expertise, métier; technic, technics, technique; self-knowledge

2 **cognizance; cognition**, noesis; recognition, realization; perception, insight, apperception, sudden insight, illumination, dawning, aha reaction, flashing; consciousness, awareness, mindfulness, note, notice; altered state of consciousness (ASC); sense, sensibility; appreciation, appreciativeness

3 **understanding, comprehension,** apprehension, intellection, prehension; conception, conceptualization, ideation; hipness, savvy; **grasp**, mental grasp, grip, command, mastery; precognition, familiarity, foreknowledge, clairvoyance; intelligence, wisdom; savoir-faire; street smarts

4 **learning,** enlightenment, education, schooling, instruction, edification, illumination; acquirements, acquisitions, attainments, accomplishments, skills; skill set, life skill, hard skill, soft skill, life hack; sophistication; store of knowledge; liberal education; acquisition of knowledge; science, technology, engineering, and mathematics (STEM)

5 **scholarship,** erudition, eruditeness, learnedness, reading, letters; intellectuality, intellectualism;

literacy; computer literacy, computeracy, numeracy; culture, literary culture, high culture, book learning, booklore; bookishness, bookiness, pedantry, pedantism, donnishness <Brit>; bluestockingism; bibliomania, book madness, bibliolatry, bibliophilism; classicism, classical scholarship, humanism, humanistic scholarship, accelerated learning

6 **profound knowledge,** deep knowledge, total command, total mastery; specialism, specialized knowledge, special knowledge; expertise, proficiency; wide knowledge, vast knowledge, extensive knowledge, generalism, general knowledge, interdisciplinary knowledge, cross-disciplinary knowledge; encyclopedic knowledge, polymathy, polyhistory, pansophy; **omniscience,** all-knowingness; information fatigue

7 slight knowledge, sneak preview

8 tree of knowledge, tree of knowledge of good and evil; forbidden fruit; bo tree, bodhi tree

9 lore, **body of knowledge,** corpus, body of learning, store of knowledge, system of knowledge, treasury of information; common knowledge; **canon;** literature, literature of the field, publications, materials; bibliography; encyclopedia, cyclopedia

10 **science, -ology** <see list>, **art**, study, discipline; research science; field, field of inquiry, concern, province, domain, area, arena, sphere, branch of study, field of study, branch of knowledge, department of knowledge, specialty, academic specialty, academic discipline; **technology,** technics, technicology, high technology, high-tech; **social science** <see list>, natural science; applied science, pure science, experimental science; exact science

11 **scientist,** man of science; **technologist;** practical scientist, experimental scientist, social scientist; boffin <Brit>; savant, scholar; authority, expert, maven; technocrat; intellectual; egghead; artist, artiste

VERBS 12 **know,** perceive, apprehend, prehend, cognize, recognize, discern, see, make out; conceive, conceptualize; realize, appreciate, **understand, comprehend,** fathom; dig, savvy; wot, wot of, ken; have, possess, grasp, seize, have hold of; have knowledge of, be informed, be apprised of, command, master, have a good command of, have information about, be acquainted with, be conversant with, be cognizant of, be conscious of, be aware of; know something by heart, know something by rote, know something from memory

13 **know well,** know full well, know damn well, know darn well, have a good knowledge of, have a thorough knowledge of, be well-informed, be learned in, be proficient in, be up on, be master of, command, be thoroughly grounded in, retain, have down pat, have down cold, have it taped, have at one's fingertips, have in one's head, know by heart, know by rote, know like a book, know like the back of one's hand, know backwards, know backwards and forwards, know inside out, know down to the ground, know one's stuff, know one's onions, know a thing or two, know one's way around; be expert in; know the ropes, know all the ins and outs, know the score, know all the answers; know what's what

14 learn <acquire knowledge>; come to one's knowledge

ADJS 15 **knowing,** knowledgeable, informed; **cognizant,** conscious, aware, mindful, sensible; intelligent; understanding, comprehending, apprehensive, apprehending; perceptive, insightful, apperceptive, percipient, perspicacious, appercipient, prehensile; shrewd, sagacious, wise; omniscient, all-knowing; multidisciplinary

16 cognizant of, **aware of,** conscious of, **mindful of,** sensible to, appreciative of, appreciatory of, no stranger to, seized of <Brit>; privy to, in the secret, let into, in the know, behind the scenes, behind the curtain; alive to, awake to; wise to, hep to, on to; streetwise, street-smart; apprised of, informed of; undeceived, undeluded

17 <nonformal> hep, **hip,** on the beam, go-go, **with it,** into, really into, groovy; chic, clued-up, clued in, in the know, trendy

18 **informed,** enlightened, instructed, versed, well-versed, educated, schooled, taught; posted, briefed, primed, trained; up on, up-to-date, abreast of, *au courant* <Fr>, *au fait* <Fr>, in the picture, wise to

19 **versed in,** informed in, read in, well-read in, up on, strong in, at home in, master of, expert in, authoritative in, proficient in, familiar with, at home with, **conversant with**, acquainted with, intimate with

20 **well-informed,** well-posted, well-educated, well-grounded, **well-versed,** well-read, widely read

21 **learned, erudite, educated,** cultured, cultivated, lettered, literate, civilized, scholarly, scholastic, studious; wise; profound, deep, abstruse; encyclopedic, pansophic, polymath, polymathic, polyhistoric

22 **book-learned,** book-read, literary, book-taught, book-fed, book-wise, book-smart, bookish, booky, book-minded; book-loving, bibliophilic, bibliophagic; pedantic, donnish <Brit>, scholastic, inkhorn; bluestocking

23 **intellectual,** intellectualistic; **highbrow,** highbrowed, highbrowish; elitist
24 **self-educated,** self-taught, autodidactic
25 **knowable,** cognizable, recognizable, **understandable,** comprehensible, apprehendable, apprehensible, prehensible, graspable, seizable, discernible, conceivable, appreciable, perceptible, distinguishable, ascertainable, discoverable
26 **known,** recognized, ascertained, conceived, grasped, apprehended, prehended, seized, perceived, discerned, appreciated, understood, **comprehended**, realized; pat, down pat
27 **well-known,** well-understood, well-recognized, **widely known**, commonly known, universally recognized, generally admitted, universally admitted; familiar, familiar as household words, household, common, current; proverbial; public, notorious; known by every schoolboy; talked-of, talked-about, in everyone's mouth, on everyone's tongue, on everyone's lips; commonplace, trite, hackneyed, platitudinous, truistic
28 scientific; technical, technological, technicological; high-tech; scholarly; disciplinary

ADVS 29 **knowingly,** consciously, wittingly, with forethought, understandingly, intelligently, studiously, learnedly, eruditely, as every schoolboy knows
30 to one's knowledge, to the best of one's knowledge, as far as one can see, as far as one can tell, as far as one knows, as well as can be said

31 **-ology by name**

abiology <inanimate things>
acarology <lice and ticks>
acrology <initial sounds>
adenology <glands>
aesthology <sensory organs>
agrology <soil>
alethology <truth>
algology, phycology <algae, seaweeds>
ambrology <amber>
anatripsology <friction>
andrology <male diseases>
angiology <blood vessels>
anorganology <inorganic things>
anthropology <mankind>
anthrozoology <interactions of mankind with other animals>
apiology, melittology <bees>
arachnology, araneology <spiders>
archeology, archaeology <ancient or historical artifacts>
archology <government>
areology <Mars>
argyrology <money boxes>
aristology <dining>
arthrology <joints>
asthenology <diseases of debility>
astrolithology <meteorites>
astrology <stellar and planetary influence>
atmology <water vapor>
audiology <hearing disorders>
auxology <growth>
axiology <values, ethics>
azoology <inanimate things>
bacteriology <bacteria>
balneology <therapeutic baths>
barology <weight>
batology <brambles>
bibliology <books>
bioecology <biological interrelationships>
biology <life, living things>
biometeorology <organic-atmospheric interrelationships>
bromatology <food>
brontology <thunder>
bryology, muscology <mosses>
Buddhology <Buddha, Buddhahood>
caliology <bird nests>
campanology <bells; bell-ringing>
carcinology <crustaceans>
cardiology <heart>
carpology, pomology <fruits>
cartology <maps>
cephalology <the head>
cetology <whales, dolphins>
cholology, choledology <bile>
choreology <dance notation>
chorology <geographical boundaries>
chrondrology <cartilage>
chronology <dates, time>
climatology <climate>
coleopterology <beetles>
conchology <shells>
cosmology <universe>
craniology <skull>
criminology <criminal behavior>
crustaceology <crustaceans>
cryology <snow and ice>
cryptology <codes and ciphers>
curiology <picture writing>
cyesiology <pregnancy>
cytology <cells>
cytopathology <cell pathology>
dactylology <fingers>
deltiology <picture postcards>
demology <human activities>
dendrochronology <tree-ring dating>
dendrology <trees, shrubs>
deontology <ethics>
dermatology <skin>
desmology <ligaments>
diabiology <the devil, devils>
dipteriology <flies>
dittology <double interpretation>
docimology <metal assaying>
dolorology <pain>
dosiology <dosage>
dysteleology <purposelessness>
ecclesiology <churches; church history>
ecology <environment>
edaphology <soils>
Egyptology <ancient Egypt>
eidology <mental imagery>
electrobiology <electricity in organisms>
electrology <electricity>
embryology <embryos>
endocrinology <endocrine glands>
enterology <internal organs>
entomology <insects>
epiphytology <plant diseases>
epistemology <human knowledge>
eremology <deserts>
ergology <work and its effects>
eschatology <last things, esp. final judgment>

ethnology <races and ethnic groups>
ethnozoology <animal lore>
ethology <animal behavior>
etiology <causes, esp. of disease>
etymology <derivation and history of words>
exobiology <life on other planets>
faunology <animal distribution>
fetology <fetus>
fluviology <watercourses, rivers>
garbology, garbageology <garbage, refuse>
gastrology <stomach>
gemology <gemstones>
geology <Earth's crust>
geomorphology <origin of geological features>
geratology <approaching extinction>
gerontology <old age>
glaciology <glaciers>
glossology <linguistics>
gnotobiology <germ-free biology>
grammatology <systems of writing>
graphology <handwriting>
gynecology <women's health>
hagiology <saints>
hamartiology <sin>
hedonology <pleasure>
helcology <ulcers>
heliology <Sun>
helminthology <worms, esp parasitic worms>
hematology <blood>
heortology <religious festivals>
hepatology <liver>
heresiology <heresies>
herpetology <reptiles>
hierology <sacred things>
hippology <horses>
hippopathology <diseases of the horse>
histology, histiology <tissues and organs>
historology <history>
horology <time, clocks>
hydrology <water>
hyetology <rainfall>
hygiology <health and hygiene>
hygrology <humidity>
hymenology <membranes>
hymenopterology <wasps, bees, ants>
hypnology <sleep; hypnotism>
hysterology <uterus>
iatrology <healing, medicine>
ichnolithology, ichnology <fossil footprints>
ichthyology, piscology <fish>
immunology <immunity to diseases>
irenology <peace>
journology <newspapers>
kalology <beauty>
kinesiology <bodily movement>
lalopathology <speech therapy>
laryngology <larynx>
lexicology <word forms and meanings>
lepidopterology <butterflies, moths>
limnology <lakes and ponds>
lithology, lithoidology <rock, stone>
loimology <infectious diseases>
malacology <mollusks>
malacostracology <crustaceology>
mantology <divination>
mastology <mammals>
meteorology <atmosphere and weather>
metrology <weights and measures>
microbiology <microorganisms>
micrology <tiny things>
microseismology <earthquake tremors>
morphology <form, shape>
muscology <mosses>
musicology <music>
mycology <fungi>
myology <muscles>
myrmecology <ants>
naology <church buildings>
nasology, rhinology <nose>
neonatology <newborns>
nephology <clouds>
nephrology <kidneys>
neurology <nervous system>
neuropathology <nervous system pathology>
neurypnology <hypnotism>
nomology <law>
noology <intuition>
nosology <classification of diseases>
nostology <old age, geriatrics>
numerology <numbers>
numismatology <coins>
odontology <the teeth>
oenology, enology <wine>
olfactology <smells>
ombrology <rain>
oncology <tumors>
oneirology <dreams>
onomasiology, onomatology <names, naming>
ontology <being, metaphysics>
oology <eggs, esp. birds'>
ophiology <snakes>
ophthalmology <eyes>
organology <body organs>
orismology <terminology>
ornithology <birds>
orology, oreology <mountains>
oryctology <fossils>
osmology <odors>
osteology <bones>
otolaryngology <ear, nose, throat>
otology <ear>
paleobiology <fossil life>
paleoethnology <prehistoric mankind>
paleoichtyology <fossil fishes>
paleontology <early history of life>
paleoornithology <fossil birds>
paleopedology <early soils>
paleoetiology <explanation of past phenomena>
paleozoology, zoogeolology <fossil animals>
palynology <pollen, spores>
parapsychology <beyond psychology>
parasitology <parasites>
paroemiology <proverbs>
pathology <diseases>
pedology <soil science>
penology <punishment>
petrology, stromatology <rocks>
pharmacology <drugs>
phenology <natural cycles>
philology <languages>
phitology <political economy>
phlebology <blood vessels>
phonology <vocal sounds>
photology <light and optics>
phrenology <skull shape>
phycology <algae>
physicotheology <natural theology>
physiology <living body>
phytology <plants>
phytopathology <plant diseases>
phytophysiology <plant physiology>
phytoserology <plant viruses>
piscatology <fishing>
pistology <religious faith>
planetology <planets>
pleology <running water>
pneumatology <spirit>
pomology <fruits>

ponerology <evil>
posology <drug administration>
potamology <rivers>
proctology <anus, rectum>
promorphology <fundamental shapes and forms>
psephology <election statistics>
psychology <the mind>
psychonosology <mental diseases>
psychopathology <insanity>
psychophysiology <body and mind>
pteridology <ferns>
pterology <insect wings>
pterylology <feathers>
ptochology <pauperism, unemployment>
pyretology <fever>
pyrgology <towers>
pyrology <fire and heat>
radiology, roentgenology <X-rays>
reflexology <reflexes and behavior>
rheology <flow and deformation of matter>
rhinology <nose>
roentgenology <medical X-rays>
runology <runes>
satanology <devil worship>
scatology <feces>
seismology <earthquakes>
selenology <the Moon>
semasiology <word meanings>
sematology, semeiology <symptoms>
semiology <signs, symbols>
serology <serums>
silphology <larval forms>
sinology <China>
siphonapterology <fleas>
sitology <diet, dietetics>
sociobiology <biology and behavior>
sociology <society>
somatology <organic bodies>
sophiology <ideas>
soteriology <salvation>
speciology <species>
spectrology <ghosts, phantoms>
speleology <caves>
spermatology <sperm>
sphygmoology <the pulse>
splanchnology <the viscera>
splenology <the spleen>
stereology <2- or 3-dimensional figures>
stoichiology <fundamental laws>
stomatology <mouth>
storiology <folklore>
suicidology <suicide>
symbology <symbols>
synchronology <comparative chronology>
synecology <plant, animal communities>
systematology <ordered arrangements>
taxology <scientific classification>
technology <mechanical and manufacturing arts>
tectology <structural morphology>
teleology <aims, determined ends>
teratology <tall tales; monsters>
terminology <system of names or terms>
thanatology <death>
thaumatology <miracles>
theology <divinity>
thermology, thermatology <heat>
therology <mammals>
thremmatology <plant or animal breeding>
threpsology <nutrition>
tidology <tides>
timbrology <stamps, stamp-collecting>
timology <values>
tocology <obstetrics>
tonology <tones, speech>
toxicology <poisons>
traumatology <wounds; shock>
tribology <friction; interacting surfaces>
trichology <hair>
typhology <blindness>
ufology <UFOs>
uranology <astronomy>
urbanology <cities>
urology <urogenital organs and diseases>
venereology <venereal disease>
vermiology <worms>
vexillology <flags>
victimology <victims>
virology <viruses>
vulcanology <volcanoes>
xyloology <the structure of wood>
zoology <animal life>
zoonosology <animal diseases>
zoophysiology <animal physiology>
zymology, zymotechnology <fermentation>

32 -ology by subject

<aims, determined ends> teleology
<ancient or historical artifacts> archeology
<animal behavior> ethology
<animal diseases> zoonosology
<animal distribution> faunology
<animal life> zoology
<animal physiology> zoophysiology
<ants> myrmecology
<anus, rectum> proctology
<astronomy> uranology
<atmosphere and weather> meteorology
<beauty> kalology
<bees> apiology, melittology
<beetles> coleopterology
<being, metaphysics> ontology
<bells; bell-ringing> campanology
<bile> chology, choledology
<biological interrelationships> bioecology
<bird nests> caliology
<birds> ornithology
<blindness> typhology
<blood vessels> angiology, phlebology
<blood> hematology
<body and mind> psychophysiology
<body organs> organology
<bones> osteology
<books> bibliology
<cartilage> chrondrology
<causes of disease> etiology
<caves> speleology
<cell pathology> cytopathology
<cells> cytology
<China> sinology
<church buildings> naology
<churches; church history> ecclesiology
<cities> urbanology
<classification of diseases> nosology
<clouds> nephology
<codes and ciphers> cryptology
<coins> numismatology
<comparative chronology> synchronology
<crustaceans> carcinology, crustaceology, malacostracology
<dance notation> choreology
<dates, dating> chronology
<death> thanatology
<derivation and history of words> etymology
<deserts> eremology
<devil worship> satanology
<didactic literature> gnomology
<diet> sitology
<dining> aristology

<diseases of debility> asthenology
<diseases> pathology
<divination> mantology
<divinity> theology
<dosage> dosiology, dosology, posology
<double interpretation> dittology
<dreams> oneirology
<drugs> pharmacology
<ear> otology
<early history of life> paleontology
<early soils> paleopedology
<Earth's crust> geology
<earthquake tremors> microseismology
<earthquakes> seismology
<eggs> oology
<election statistics> psephology
<electricity> electrology
<embryos> embryology
<endocrine glands> endocrinology
<environment> ecology, environmentology
<evil> ponerology
<explanation of past phenomena> paleoetiology
<extinction> geratology
<eyes> ophthalmology
<feathers> pterylology
<female health and disease> gynecology
<fermentation> zymology, zymotechnology
<ferns> pteridology
<fetus> fetology
<fever> pyretology
<fingers> dactylology
<fire and heat> pyrology
<fish> ichthyology, piscology
<fishing> piscatology
<flags> vexillology
<fleas> siphonapterology
<flies> dipteriology
<flow and deformation of matter> rheology
<folklore> storiology
<food> bromatology
<form, shape> morphology
<fossil animals> paleozoology, zoogeolology
<fossil birds> paleornithology
<fossil excrement> scatology
<fossil fishes> paleoichtyology
<fossil footprints> ichnolithology, ichnology
<fossil life> paleobiology
<fossils> oryctology
<friction> anatripsology
<fruits> carpology, pomology
<fundamental laws> stoichiology
<fundamental shapes and forms> promorphology
<fungi> mycology
<garbage, refuse> garbology, garbageology
<geographical boundaries> chorology
<germ-free biology> gnotobiology
<glands> adenology
<government> archology
<growth> auxology
<hair> trichology
<handwriting> graphology
<head> cephalology
<healing, medicine> iatrology
<health and hygiene> hygiology
<hearing disorders> audiology
<heart> cardiology
<heat> thermology, thermatology
<heresies> heresiology
<history> historology
<horses> hippology
<human activities> demology
<human knowledge> epistemology
<humidity> hygrology
<hypnotism> neurypnology
<ideas> sophiology
<immunity to diseases> immunology
<inanimate things> abiology, azoology
<infectious diseases> loimology
<initial sounds> acrology
<inorganic things> anorganology
<insanity> psychopathology
<insect wings> pterology
<insects> entomology
<interacting surfaces> tribology
<internal organs> enterology
<intuition> noology
<joints> arthrology
<lakes and ponds> limnology
<language meaning> semasiology
<languages> philology
<larval forms> silphology
<larynx> laryngology
<last things, esp. final judgment> eschatology
<law> nomology
<lice and ticks> acarology
<life on other planets> exobiology
<life, living things> biology
<ligaments> desmology
<light and optics> photology
<linguistics> glossology
<liver> hepatology
<living body> physiology
<male diseases> andrology
<mammals> mastology, therology
<mankind> anthropology
<maps> cartology
<Mars> areology
<mechanical and manufacturing arts> technology
<membranes> hymenology
<mental diseases> psychonosology
<mental imagery> eidology
<metal assaying> docimology
<meteorites> astrolithology
<microorganisms> microbiology
<miracles> thaumatology
<mollusks> mallacology
<monsters> teratology
<moral obligation> deontology
<mosses> bryology, muscology
<mountains> orology, oreology
<mouth diseases> stomatology
<muscles> myology
<names, naming> onomasiology, onomatology
<natural cycles> phenology
<natural theology> physicotheology
<nervous system> neurology
<newspapers> journology
<nose> nasology, rhinology
<nutrition> threpsology
<obstetrics> tocology
<odors> osmology
<old age, geriatrics> nostology
<old age> gerontology
<ordered arrangements> systematology
<organic bodies> somatology
<organic-atmospheric interrelationships> biometeorology
<pain> dolorology
<pathology of the nervous system> neuropathology
<peace> irenology
<physiology of the nervous system> neurophysiology
<picture postcards> deltiology
<picture writing> curiology

<plant diseases> epiphuytology, phytopathology
<plant or animal breeding> thremmatology
<plant physiology> phytophysiology
<plant viruses> phytoserology
<plants> phytology
<poisons> toxicology
<political economy> phitology
<pollen> palynology
<pregnancy> cyesiology
<prehistoric mankind> paleoethnology
<proverbs> paroemiology
<punishment of crime> penology
<purposelessness> dysteleology
<races and peoples> ethnology
<rain> ombrology
<rainfall> hyetology
<religious faith> pistology
<religious festivals> heortology
<reptiles> herpetology
<rivers> potamology
<rock, stone> lithology, lithoidology
<rocks> petrology, stromatology
<runes> runology
<running water> pleology
<sacred things> hierology
<saints> hagiology
<salvation> soteriology
<scientific classification> taxology
<seaweeds> algology, phycology
<sensory organs> aesthology
<serums> serology
<shells> conchology
<sin> hamartiology
<skin> dermatology
<skull shape> phrenology
<skull> craniology
<sleep> hypnology
<smells> olfactology
<snakes> ophiology
<society> sociology
<soils> edaphology, pedology
<species> speciology
<spectroscopic analysis> spectrology
<sperm> spermatology
<spiders> arachnology, araneology
<spirit> pneumatology
<spleen> splenology
<stamps, stamp-collecting> timbrology
<stellar and planetary influence> astrology
<stomach> gastrology
<structural morphology> tectology
<structure of wood> xyloology
<suicide> suicidology
<Sun> heliology
<symptoms> sematology, semeiology
<system of names or terms> terminology
<teeth> odontology
<terminology> orismology
<the devil, devils> diabiology
<the mind> psychology
<the Moon> selenology
<the pulse> sphygmoology
<therapeutic agents> acology
<therapeutic baths> balneology
<thunder> brontology
<tides> tidology
<time, clocks> horology
<tiny things> micrology
<tissues and organs> histology, histiology
<towers> pyrgology
<tree-ring dating> dendrochronology
<trees> dendrology
<truth> alethology
<tumors> oncology
<ulcers> helcology
<universe> cosmology
<urogenital organs and diseases> urology
<uterus> hysterology
<values> timology
<victims> victimology
<viscera> splanchnology
<vocal sounds> phonology
<volcanoes> vulcanology
<wasps, bees, ants> hymenopterology
<water vapor> atmology
<water> hydrology
<weight> barology
<weights and measures> metrology
<whales and dolphins> cetology
<wine> oenology, enology
<words and meanings> lexicology
<work and its effects> ergology
<worms, esp parasitic worms> helminthology
<worms> vermiology
<wounds, shock> traumatology
<X-rays> radiology, roentgenology

33 social science

anthropology
anthropometry
applied psychology
archaeology, archeology
cartography
cultural anthropology
domestic science
economics
ecopsychology
ethnography
ethnology
experimental psychology
genetics and growth studies
geography
history
human evolution
human geography
linguistic anthropology
linguistics
paleoanthropology
physical anthropology
physical geography
political science
primatology
psychology
social anthropology
social geography
social psychology
social statistics
sociology
sports psychology

929 INTELLECTUAL

<learned person>

NOUNS **1 intellectual, intellect,** intellectualist, literate, member of the intelligentsia, white-collar intellectual; brainworker, thinker; brain, rocket scientist, brain surgeon; pundit, Brahmin, mandarin, egghead, pointy-head; highbrow; wise man

2 intelligentsia, literati, illuminati; intellectual elite; clerisy

3 scholar, scholastic, clerk, learned clerk; a gentleman and a scholar; student; learned person, learned man, man of learning, giant of learning, colossus of knowledge, mastermind, savant, pundit; genius; polymath, polyhistor, polyhistorian, mine of information, walking encyclopedia; literary man, litterateur, man of letters; philologist, philologue; philomath, lover of learning; philosopher, philosophe; bookman; academician, academic, schoolman; classicist, classicalist, Latinist, humanist; Renaissance man, Renaissance woman; adult student, permanent student; special needs student

4 **bookworm,** bibliophage; grind, greasy grind; **booklover**, bibliophile, bibliophilist, philobiblist, bibliolater, bibliolatrist; bibliomaniac, bibliomane

5 **pedant;** formalist, precisionist, precisian, purist, bluestocking, *bas bleu* <Fr>; Dr Pangloss, Dryasdust

6 dilettante, half scholar, sciolist, **dabbler,** dabster, amateur, rank amateur, trifler, smatterer; grammaticaster, philologaster, criticaster, philosophaster, Latinitaster

930 IGNORANCE

<lack of knowledge>

NOUNS 1 **ignorance,** ignorantness, **unknowingness,** unknowing, nescience; lack of information, knowledge gap, hiatus of learning; empty-headedness, blankmindedness, vacuousness, vacuity, inanity; tabula rasa; unintelligence; unacquaintance, unfamiliarity; greenness, greenhornism, rawness, callowness, unripeness, green in the eye, inexperience; innocence, ingenuousness, simpleness, simplicity; gross ignorance, primal ignorance; ignorantism, know-nothingism, obscurantism; agnosticism

2 **incognizance, unawareness,** unconsciousness, insensibility, unwittingness, nonrecognition; deniability; nonrealization, incomprehension; unmindfulness; mindlessness; blindness, deafness

3 **unenlightenment,** benightedness, benightment, dark, darkness; savagery, barbarism, paganism, heathenism, Gothicism; age of ignorance, dark age; rural idiocy

4 **unlearnedness,** inerudition, ineducation, unschooledness, unletteredness; unscholarliness, unstudiousness; **illiteracy,** illiterateness, functional illiteracy, semiliteracy; unintellectuality, unintellectualism, Philistinism, bold ignorance

5 **slight knowledge,** vague notion, imperfect knowledge, a little learning, glimmering, glimpse, smattering, smattering of knowledge, smattering of ignorance, half-learning, semi-learning, semi-ignorance, sciolism; superficiality, shallowness, surface-scratching; **dilettantism,** dilettantship, amateurism

6 **the unknown,** the unknowable, the strange, the unfamiliar, the incalculable; matter of ignorance, sealed book, riddle, enigma, mystery, puzzle; *terra incognita* <L>, unexplored territory; frontier, frontiers of knowledge, unknown quantity, x, y, z, n; dark horse; guesswork, anybody's guess; complete blank; closed book; all Greek

7 **ignoramus, know-nothing;** no scholar, puddinghead, dunce, fool; simpleton; illiterate; aliterate; lowbrow; unintelligentsia, illiterati; greenhorn, greeny, beginner, tenderfoot, neophyte, novice, duffer; dilettante, dabbler; layperson; middlebrow

VERBS 8 **be ignorant,** be green, have everything to learn, **know nothing,** know from nothing; wallow in ignorance; not know any better; not know what's what, not know what it is all about, not know the score, not be with it, not know any of the answers; not know the time of day, not know what o'clock it is, not know beans, not know the first thing about, not know one's ass from one's elbow, not know the way home, not know enough to come in out of the rain, not know chalk from cheese, not know up from down, not know which way is up

9 **be in the dark,** be blind, labor in darkness, walk in darkness, be benighted, grope in the dark, have nothing to go on, have a lot to learn

10 **not know,** not rightly know, know not, know not what, know nothing of, wot not of, be innocent of, have no idea, have no conception, not have the first idea, **not have the slightest idea,** not have the least idea, not have the remotest idea, be clueless, not have a clue not have idea one, not have the foggiest, not pretend to say, not take upon oneself to say; be stumped; not know the half of it; not know from Adam, not know from the man in the moon; wonder, wonder whether; half-know, have a little learning, scratch the surface, know a little, smatter, dabble, toy with, coquet with; pass, give up

ADJS 11 **ignorant,** nescient, **unknowing,** uncomprehending, know-nothing; simple, dumb, empty, empty-headed, blank, blankminded, vacuous, inane, unintelligent; ill-informed, **uninformed**, unenlightened, unilluminated, unapprized, unposted, clueless, pig-ignorant; unacquainted, unconversant, unversed, uninitiated, unfamiliar, strange to; inexperienced; green, callow, innocent, ingenuous, gauche, awkward, naive, unripe, raw; groping, tentative, unsure

12 **unaware,** unconscious, insensible, unknowing, incognizant; mindless, witless; unprehensive, unrealizing, nonconceiving, unmindful, unwitting, unsuspecting; unperceiving, impercipient, unhearing, unseeing, uninsightful; unaware of, in ignorance of, unconscious of, **unmindful of,** insensible to, out of it, not with it; blind to, deaf to, dead to, a stranger to; asleep, napping, off one's guard, caught napping, caught tripping; tamasic, indifferent

13 **unlearned,** inerudite, unerudite, **uneducated,** unschooled, uninstructed, untutored, unbriefed,

untaught, unedified, unguided; ill-educated, misinstructed, misinformed, mistaught, led astray; hoodwinked, deceived; **illiterate,** functionally illiterate, unlettered, grammarless; unscholarly, unscholastic, unstudious; unliterary, unread, unbookish, unbook-learned, bookless, unbooked; uncultured, uncultivated, unrefined, rude, Philistine; barbarous, pagan, heathen; Gothic; nonintellectual, unintellectual; lowbrow, lowbrowed, lowbrowish; lesser-known

14 half-learned, **half-baked, half-cocked, half-assed**, half-ass, sciolistic; semiskilled; shallow, superficial; immature, sophomoric, sophomorical; dilettante, dilettantish, smattering, dabbling, amateur, amateurish, inexperienced; wise in one's own conceit

15 benighted, dark, in darkness, in the dark

16 **unknown,** unbeknown, unheard, **unheard-of,** unapprehended, unapparent, unperceived, unsuspected; unexplained, unascertained; uninvestigated, unexplored; unidentified, unclassified, uncharted, unfathomed, unplumbed, virgin, untouched; undisclosed, unrevealed, undivulged, undiscovered, unexposed, sealed; unfamiliar, strange; incalculable, unknowable, incognizable, undiscoverable; enigmatic, mysterious, puzzling

ADVS **17** **ignorantly,** unknowingly, unmindfully, unwittingly, witlessly, unsuspectingly, **unawares;** unconsciously, insensibly; for anything, for aught one knows, not that one knows

INTERJS **18** God knows, God only knows Lord knows, Heaven knows, nobody knows, damned if I know, search me, beats me, beats the hell out of me, beats the heck out of me, beats the shit out of me*, your guess is as good as mine, it has me guessing, it's Greek to me; you've got me, I give up, I pass, who knows?, how should I know?, I don't know what, dunno

931 THOUGHT

<process of thinking>

NOUNS **1** **thought, thinking, cogitation,** cerebration, ideation, noesis, mentation, intellection, intellectualization, ratiocination; using one's head, using one's noodle; workings of the mind; reasoning; brainwork, headwork, mental labor, mental effort, mental act, mental process, act of thought, mental exercise, intellectual exercise; deep-think; way of thinking, logic, habit of thought, habit of mind, thought pattern, line of thinking; heavy thinking, straight thinking; conception, conceit, conceptualization; abstract thought, imageless thought; excogitation, thinking out, thinking through; thinking aloud; idea; creative thought

2 **consideration, contemplation,** reflection, speculation, meditation, musing, rumination, deliberation, lucubration, brooding, study, pondering, weighing, revolving, turning over in the mind, looking at from all angles, noodling, noodling around; lateral thought, lateral thinking; advisement, counsel

3 **thoughtfulness,** contemplativeness, speculativeness, reflectiveness; pensiveness, wistfulness, reverie, musing, melancholy; preoccupation, absorption, engrossment, abstraction, brown study, intense thought, deep thought, profound thought; concentration, study, close study; one-pointedness; deep thinking

4 **thoughts,** burden of one's mind, mind's content; inmost thoughts, innermost thoughts, inmost mind, secret thoughts, mind's core, one's heart of hearts; **train of thought,** current of thought, flow of thought, flow of ideas, succession of thought, sequence of thought, chain of thought, sequence of ideas; stream of consciousness; association, association of ideas

5 mature thought, developed thought, ripe idea; **afterthought,** *arrière-pensée* <Fr>, *esprit d'escalier* <Fr>, second thought; **reconsideration,** reappraisal, revaluation, rethinking, re-examination, review, thinking over

6 **introspection,** self-communion, self-counsel, self-consultation, subjective inspection, subjective speculation, head trip; meditation

7 subject for thought, **food for thought**, something to chew on, something to get one's teeth into

VERBS **8** **think, cogitate,** cerebrate, put on one's thinking cap, intellectualize, ideate, conceive, conceptualize, form ideas, entertain ideas; reason; use one's head, use one's noodle, use one's noggin, use the mind, exercise the mind, set the brain to work, set the wits to work, bethink oneself, have something on one's mind, have a lot on one's mind

9 **think hard,** think one's head off, rack one's brains, ransack one's brains, crack one's brains, beat one's brains, cudgel one's brains, work one's head to the bone, do some heavy thinking, bend the mind, apply the mind, knit one's brow; sweat over, stew over, hammer, hammer away at; puzzle, puzzle over

10 **concentrate,** concentrate the mind, concentrate the thoughts, concentrate on, attend closely to, brood on, **focus on,** give the mind to, devote the mind to, glue the mind to, cleave to the thought of, fix the mind on, fix the thoughts upon, bend the mind upon, bring the mind to bear upon; get to the point; gather one's thoughts, collect one's thoughts, pull one's wits together, focus one's thoughts, fix one's thoughts, marshal one's ideas, arrange one's thoughts

11 **think about,** cogitate, apply the mind to, put one's mind to, apply oneself to, turn the mind to, turn the thoughts to, direct the mind upon, give thought to, trouble one's head about, occupy the mind with; think through, think out, puzzle out, sort out, reason out, excogitate, ratiocinate, work out, take stock of

12 **consider, contemplate,** speculate, reflect, wonder, study, ponder, perpend, weigh, deliberate, debate, meditate, muse, brood, ruminate, chew the cud, digest; introspect, be abstracted; wrinkle one's brow; fall into a brown study, retreat into one's mind, retreat into one's thoughts; toy with, play with, play around with, flirt with the idea

13 **think over,** ponder over, brood over, muse over, mull over, **reflect on,** reflect over, con over, deliberate over, run over, meditate over, ruminate over, chew over, digest, turn over, revolve, turn over in the mind, deliberate upon, meditate upon, muse on, bestow thought upon, bestow consideration upon, noodle, noodle around

14 **take under consideration,** entertain, take under advisement, take under active consideration, inquire into, **think it over,** have a look at, see about; sleep upon, consult with, advise with, take counsel of one's pillow

15 **reconsider,** re-examine, review; revise one's thoughts, reappraise, revaluate, rethink; view in a new light, have second thoughts, think better of

16 **think of,** bethink oneself of, seize on, flash on; tumble to; entertain the idea of, entertain thoughts of; conceive of; have an idea of, have thoughts about; have in mind, contemplate, consider, have under consideration; take it into one's head; bear in mind, keep in mind, hold the thought; harbor an idea, keep an idea, hold an idea, cherish an idea, foster an idea, nurse an idea, nurture an idea; ideate, premise, theorize, invent

17 <look upon mentally> **contemplate,** look upon, view, **regard,** see, view with the mind's eye, envisage, envision, visualize, imagine, image; meditate

18 **occur to,** occur to one's mind, occur, **come to mind,** rise to mind, rise in the mind, come into one's head, impinge on one's consciousness, claim one's thoughts, pass through one's head, pass through one's mind, dawn upon one, enter one's mind, cross one's mind, race through the mind, flash across the mind; strike, strike one, strike the mind, grab one, suggest itself, present itself, offer itself, present itself to the mind, give one pause

19 **impress,** make an impression, strike, grab, hit; catch the thoughts, arrest the thoughts, seize one's mind, sink into the mind, penetrate into the mind, embed itself in the mind, lodge in the mind, **sink in**

20 **occupy the mind**, occupy the thoughts, engage the thoughts, monopolize the thoughts, fasten itself on the mind, seize the mind, fill the mind, take up one's thoughts; **preoccupy,** occupy, absorb, engross, absorb the thoughts, engross the thoughts, obsess the mind, run in the head; foster in the mind; come uppermost, be uppermost in the mind; have in mind, have on one's mind, have on the brain, have constantly in one's thoughts

ADJS **21** **cognitive,** prehensive, thought, conceptive, conceptual, conceptualized, ideative, ideational, noetic, mental, cerebral; rational, logical, ratiocinative; thoughtful, cogitative, contemplative, reflective, speculative, deliberative, meditative, ruminative, ruminant, in a brown study, museful; pensive, wistful, musing; introspective; thinking, reflecting, contemplating, pondering, deliberating, excogitating, excogitative, meditating, ruminating; reasoned; studious, studying; sober, serious, deepthinking; concentrating, focused, on task, concentrative, concentrated, attentive

22 absorbed in thought, engrossed in thought, **absorbed, engrossed,** introspective, rapt, wrapped in thought, lost in thought, pensive, abstracted, immersed in thought, buried in thought, engaged in thought, occupied, **preoccupied**

ADVS **23** **thoughtfully,** contemplatively, reflectively, meditatively, ruminatively, musefully, cogitatively, introspectively; pensively, wistfully; on reconsideration, on second thought

24 on one's mind, on the brain, on one's chest, in the thoughts; in the heart, in one's inmost thoughts, in one's innermost thoughts

932 IDEA

<formulated thought>

NOUNS **1** **idea;** thought, mental object, intellectual object, **notion, concept,** conception, conceit, fancy; perception, sense, impression, mental impression, image, mental image, picture in the mind, mental picture, representation, recept, visualization; imago, ideatum, noumenon, essence; memory trace; sentiment, apprehension; reflection, observation; opinion; viewpoint, point of view; supposition, theory; plan, scheme

2 <philosophy> ideatum, ideate; noumenon;

universal, universal concept; idée-force; Platonic idea, Platonic form, archetype, prototype, subsistent form, eternal object, transcendent universal, eternal universal, pattern, model, exemplar, ideal, transcendent idea, transcendent essence, universal essence, innate idea; Aristotelian form, form-giving cause, formal cause; complex idea, simple idea; percept; construct of memory and association; Kantian idea, supreme principle of pure reason, regulative first principle, highest unitary principle of thought, transcendent nonempirical concept; Hegelian idea, highest category, the Absolute, the Absolute Idea, the Self-determined, the realized ideal; logical form, logical category; noosphere; history of ideas; idealism

3 **abstract idea,** abstraction, general idea, generality, abstract

4 **main idea,** intellectual basis, philosophical basis, leading idea, principal idea, fundamental idea, basic idea, guiding principle, crowning principle, big idea, precept, premise

5 **novel idea,** intellectual breakthrough, conceptual breakthrough, new wrinkle, latest wrinkle, new slant, new twist, new take

6 **good idea,** great idea, not a bad idea; bright thought, bright idea, brilliant idea, insight; brainchild, brainstorm, brain wave, inspiration; quantum leap

7 **absurd idea,** crazy idea, fool notion, brainstorm

8 **ideology,** system of ideas, body of ideas, system of theories; worldview; philosophy; ethos

ADJS 9 **ideational**, ideal, conceptual, conceptive, notional, fanciful, imaginative; intellectual; theoretical; ideological

10 ideaed, notioned, thoughted

933 ABSENCE OF THOUGHT

<unthinking>

NOUNS 1 **thoughtlessness,** thoughtfreeness; **vacuity,** vacancy, emptiness of mind, empty-headedness, blankness, mental blankness, blankmindedness; fatuity, inanity, foolishness; tranquillity, calm of mind, meditation; nirvana, ataraxia, tranquillity of mind; **oblivion,** forgetfulness, lack of memory, loss of memory, amnesia; mental block; quietism, passivity, apathy; blank mind, fallow mind, tabula rasa; unintelligence; ignorance; head in the clouds

VERBS 2 **not think,** make the mind a blank, let the mind lie fallow; not think of, not consider, be unmindful of; not enter one's mind, not enter one's head, be far from one's mind, be far from one's thoughts; pay no attention, pay no mind

3 get it off one's mind, get it off one's chest, **clear the mind**, relieve one's mind; put it out of one's thoughts, dismiss from the mind, push from one's thoughts, put away thought

ADJS 4 **thoughtless,** thoughtfree, incogitant, **unthinking,** unreasoning; unideaed; unintellectual; vacuous, vacant, blank, blankminded, relaxed, empty, empty-headed, fallow, fatuous, inane; unoccupied; calm, tranquil; nirvanic; oblivious, ignorant; quietistic, passive

5 **unthought-of,** undreamed-of, unconsidered, unconceived, unconceptualized; unimagined, unimaged; imageless

934 INTUITION, INSTINCT

<knowledge through feelings>

NOUNS 1 **intuition, intuitiveness, sixth sense;** intuitive reason, intuitive knowledge, direct perception, direct apprehension, immediate apprehension, immediate perception, unmediated perception, unmediated apprehension, subconscious perception, unconscious knowledge, subconscious knowledge, immediate cognition, knowledge without thought, knowledge without reason, flash of insight; intuitive understanding, tact, spontaneous sense; revelation, epiphany, moment of illumination; **insight,** inspiration, aperçu; precognition, anticipation, a priori knowledge; *satori, buddhi*; woman's intuition; second sight, second-sightedness, clairvoyance, extrasensory perception, presentiment; intuitionism, intuitivism; noology

2 **instinct,** natural instinct, unlearned capacity, innate proclivity, inborn proclivity, native tendency, natural tendency, impulse, blind impulse, unreasoning impulse, vital impulse; libido, id, primitive self; archetype, archetypal pattern, archetypal idea; unconscious urge, unconscious drive, subconscious urge, subconscious drive; collective unconscious, race memory; reflex, spontaneous reaction, unthinking response, knee-jerk, Pavlovian response, gut reaction

3 **hunch**, sense, presentiment, premonition, preapprehension, intimation, foreboding; suspicion, impression, intuition, intuitive impression, feeling, forefeeling, vague feeling, vague idea, funny feeling, feeling in one's bones, gut feeling, flash

VERBS 4 **intuit,** sense, feel, feel intuitively, feel in one's bones, know in one's bones, have a feeling, have a funny feeling, get the impression, have the impression, **have a hunch**, just know, know instinctively; grok; perceive, divine

ADJS 5 **intuitive,** intuitional, sensing, sensitive, perceptive, feeling; second-sighted, precognitive, telepathic, clairvoyant

6 **instinctive,** natural, inherent, innate, unlearned; unconscious, subliminal; involuntary, automatic, spontaneous, impulsive, reflex, knee-jerk; **instinctual,** libidinal

ADVS 7 **intuitively,** by intuition; instinctively, automatically, spontaneously, by instinct, instinctually

935 REASONING

<process of logical thinking>

NOUNS 1 **reasoning, reason,** logical thought, discursive reason, rationalizing, rationalization, ratiocination; the divine faculty; **rationalism, rationality,** discourse, discourse of reason; sweet reason, reasonableness; demonstration, proof; specious reasoning, sophistry; philosophy

2 **logic,** logics; **dialectics,** dialectic, dialecticism; art of reason, science of discursive thought; formal logic, material logic; doctrine of terms, doctrine of the judgment, doctrine of inference; traditional logic, Aristotelian logic; modern logic, epistemological logic; pragmatic logic, instrumental logic, experimental logic; psychological logic, psychologism; symbolic logic, mathematical logic, logistic; propositional calculus, calculus of individuals, functional calculus, combinatory logic, algebra of relations, algebra of classes, set theory, Boolean algebra; mereology

3 <methods> a priori reasoning, a fortiori reasoning, a posteriori reasoning; discursive reasoning; deduction, **deductive reasoning,** syllogism, syllogistic reasoning; hypothetico-deductive method; induction, **inductive reasoning,** epagoge; philosophical induction, inductive method, Baconian method; inference; generalization, particularization; synthesis, analysis; hypothesis and verification; closing argument

4 **argumentation,** argument, controversy, dispute, disagreement, disputation, polemic, debate, disceptation, eristic, art of dispute; contention, wrangling, bickering, hubbub, quibble, bicker, setto, rhubarb, hassle, passage of arms; war of words, verbal engagement, verbal contest, logomachy, flyting; paper war; adversarial procedure, confrontational occasion; academic disputation, defense of a thesis; defense, apology, apologia, apologetics; dialectics, dialecticism; pilpul, casuistry; polemics; litigation; examination, cross-examination

5 **argument**; case, plea, pleading, brief; special pleading; reason, consideration; refutation, elenchus, ignoratio elenchi; stance, position; grounds, evidence; pros, cons, pros and cons; talking point; dialogue, reasoning together, dialectic; formal argument; rationale, pretext, premise

6 **syllogism;** prosyllogism; mode; figure; mood; pseudosyllogism, paralogism; sorites, progressive sorites, Aristotelian sorites, regressive sorites, Goclenian sorites; categorical syllogism; enthymeme; dilemma; rule, rule of deduction, transformation rule; modus ponens, modus tollens

7 **premise,** proposition, position, assumed position, sumption, assumption, supposal, presupposition, hypothesis, thesis, theorem, lemma, statement, affirmation, categorical proposition, assertion, basis, ground, foundation; postulate, axiom, postulation, postulatum; data; major premise, minor premise; first principles; a priori principle, apriorism; philosophical proposition, philosopheme; hypothesis ad hoc; sentential function, propositional function, truth-function, truth table, truth-value

8 conclusion

9 **reasonableness,** reasonability, logicalness, logicality, rationality, sensibleness, soundness, justness, justifiability, admissibility, cogency; sense, common sense, sound sense, sweet reason, logic, reason; plausibility

10 **good reasoning,** right thinking, sound reasoning, ironclad reasoning, irrefutable logic; cogent argument, cogency; strong argument, knockdown argument; good case, good reason, sound evidence, strong point

11 **reasoner,** ratiocinator, thinker; **rationalist**; rationalizer; synthesizer; logician, logistician; logicaster; dialectician; syllogist, syllogizer; sophist; philosopher

12 **arguer,** controversialist, disputant, plaintiff, defendant, debater, eristic, argufier, devil's advocate, advocate, wrangler, proponent, litigator, mooter, lawyer, jurist, Philadelphia lawyer, guardhouse lawyer, latrine lawyer, disceptator, pilpulist, casuist; polemic, polemist, polemicist; logomacher, logomachist; apologist

13 **contentiousness,** litigiousness, quarrelsomeness, argumentativeness, disputatiousness, testiness, feistiness, combativeness; ill humor

14 **side,** interest; the affirmative, pro, yes, aye, yea; the negative, con, no, nay

VERBS 15 **reason;** logicalize, logicize; rationalize, provide a rationale; intellectualize; bring reason to bear, apply reason, use reason, put two and two together; construe, deduce, infer, generalize; synthesize, analyze, work out; theorize, hypothesize; premise; philosophize; syllogize; ratiocinate

16 **argue,** argufy, dispute, discept, dissent, disagree, logomachize, polemize, polemicize, moot, bandy words, chop logic, plead, pettifog, join issue, give and take, cut and thrust, try conclusions, cross swords, lock horns, contend, contest, spar, bicker, wrangle, hassle, have it out, have words; thrash out; take one's stand upon, put up an argument; take sides, take up a side; argue to no purpose; quibble, squabble, cavil; litigate

17 **be reasonable,** be logical, make sense, figure, **stand to reason,** be demonstrable, be irrefutable; hold good, hold water; have a leg to stand on; show wisdom

ADJS **18** **reasoning, rational,** ratiocinative, ratiocinatory; analytic, analytical; conceptive, conceptual; cerebral, noetic, phrenic

19 **argumentative,** argumental, dialectic, dialectical, controversial, disputatious, contentious, quarrelsome, dissenting, disputing, litigious, combative, factious, testy, feisty, petulant, ill-humored, eristic, eristical, polemic, polemical, logomachic, logomachical, pilpulistic, pro and con; diectic, apodeictic, aporetic; at cross-purposes, at odds

20 **logical, reasonable, rational**, cogent, sensible, sane, wise, sound, well-thought-out, legitimate, just, justifiable, admissible; credible; plausible; as it should be, as it ought to be; well-argued, well-founded, well-grounded

21 **reasoned,** advised, **considered,** calculated, meditated, contemplated, deliberated, studied, weighed, thought-out, well-reasoned

22 **dialectic**, dialectical, maieutic; syllogistic, syllogistical, enthymematic, enthymematical, soritical, epagogic, inductive, deductive, inferential, synthetic, synthetical, analytic, analytical, discursive, heuristic; a priori, a fortiori, a posteriori; categorical, hypothetical, propositional, postulated, conditional

23 **deducible,** derivable, **inferable;** sequential, following

ADVS **24** **reasonably, logically, rationally,** by the rules of logic, sensibly, sanely, soundly; syllogistically, analytically; realistically, pragmatically, plausibly; in reason, in all reason, within reason, within the bounds of reason, within the limits of reason, within reasonable limitations, within bounds, within the bounds of possibility, as far as possible, in all conscience

936 SOPHISTRY

<clever reasoning>

NOUNS **1** **sophistry,** sophistication, sophism, philosophism, **casuistry,** Jesuitry, Jesuitism, subtlety, oversubtlety; **false reasoning,** specious reasoning, rationalization, evasive reasoning, vicious reasoning, sophistical reasoning, special pleading; fallacy, fallaciousness; speciousness, speciosity, superficial soundness, apparent soundness, plausibleness, plausibility; insincerity, disingenuousness; equivocation, equivocalness; fudging, waffling, fudge and mudge; perversion, distortion, misapplication; vicious circle, circularity; mystification, obfuscation, obscurantism; reduction, trivialization

2 **illogicalness,** illogic, illogicality, unreasonableness, irrationality, reasonlessness, senselessness, unsoundness, unscientificness, junk science, invalidity, untenableness, inconclusiveness; inconsistency, incongruity, antilogy

3 <specious argument> **sophism,** sophistry, insincere argument, mere rhetoric, philosophism, solecism; paralogism, pseudosyllogism; claptrap, moonshine, empty words, doubletalk, doublespeak, sound and fury; bad case, weak point, flawed argument, **circular argument**; **fallacy,** logical fallacy, formal fallacy, material fallacy, verbal fallacy; crowd-pleasing argument, argument by analogy, begging the question, undistributed middle, *non sequitur* <L>, *hysteron proteron* <Gk>, paradox; contradition in terms

4 **quibble,** quiddity, quodlibet, quillet, Jesuitism, cavil; quip, quirk, shuffle, dodge

5 **quibbling, caviling,** boggling, captiousness, nitpicking, bickering; logic-chopping, choplogic, hairsplitting, trichoschistism; subterfuge, chicane, chicanery, pettifoggery; equivocation, tergiversation, prevarication, evasion, hedging, pussyfooting, sidestepping, dodging, shifting, shuffling, fencing, parrying, paltering, beating around the bush

6 **sophist,** sophister, philosophist, **casuist,** Jesuit; choplogic, logic-chopper; paralogist

7 **quibbler, caviler,** pettifogger, hairsplitter, captious critic, picayune critic, nitpicker; equivocator, Jesuit, mystifier, mystificator, obscurantist, prevaricator, palterer, tergiversator, shuffler, mudger; hedger; pussyfoot, pussyfooter, waffler

VERBS **8** reason speciously, reason ill, paralogize, reason in a circle, argue insincerely, pervert, distort, misapply; explain away, rationalize; prove that black is white and white black; not have a leg to stand on

9 **quibble, cavil,** bicker, boggle, chop logic, split hairs, nitpick, pick nits; Jesuitize; equivocate, mystify, obscure, prevaricate, tergiversate, doubletalk, doublespeak, tap-dance, misrepresent, misinform, fudge, palter, fence, parry, shift, shuffle, dodge, shy, evade, sidestep, hedge, skate around, pussyfoot, evade the issue; twist, slant; beat around the bush, avoid the issue, not come to the point, beg the question; pick holes in, pick to pieces; blow hot and cold; strain at a gnat and swallow a camel

ADJS **10** **sophistical,** sophistic, philosophistic, philosophistical, casuistic, casuistical, Jesuitic, Jesuitical, fallacious, specious, colorable, plausible, hollow, superficially sound, apparently sound; deceptive, illusive, empty; overrefined, oversubtle, insincere, disingenuous

11 **illogical, unreasonable,** irrational, reasonless, contrary to reason, senseless, without reason, without rhyme or reason; unscientific, nonscientific, unphilosophical; invalid, inauthentic, unauthentic, faulty, flawed, paralogical, fallacious; inconclusive, inconsequent, inconsequential, not following; inconsistent, incongruous, absonant, loose, unconnected; contradictory, self-contradictory, self-annulling, self-refuting, oxymoronic

12 **unsound,** unsubstantial, insubstantial, weak, feeble, poor, flimsy, unrigorous, inconclusive, unproved, unsustained, poorly argued

13 **baseless, groundless,** ungrounded, unfounded, ill-founded, unbased, unsupported, unsustained, invalid, without foundation, without basis, without sound basis; untenable, unsupportable, unsustainable; unwarranted, idle, empty, vain

14 **quibbling,** caviling, equivocatory, equivocal, captious, nitpicky, nitpicking, bickering; picayune, petty, trivial, trifling; paltering, shuffling, hedging, pussyfooting, evasive; **hairsplitting,** trichoschistic, logic-chopping, choplogic, choplogical

ADVS **15** **illogically,** unreasonably, irrationally, reasonlessly, senselessly; baselessly, groundlessly; untenably, unsupportably, unsustainably; out of all reason, out of all bounds

937 TOPIC

<subject thought and talked about>

NOUNS **1** **topic, subject,** subject of thought, matter, **subject matter,** what it is about, concern, focus of interest, focus of attention, watchlist, discrete matter, **category**; field, branch, discipline; theme, burden, text, motif, motive, angle, business at hand, case, matter in hand, question, problem, issue, bone of contention; point, point at issue, point in question, topic for discussion, main point, gist; plot; item on the agenda; head, heading, chapter, rubric; contents, substance, meat, essence, material part, basis; living issue, topic of the day; thesis

2 **caption, title, heading,** head, superscription, rubric; headline, banner headline; subject line, subject heading; overline; banner, banner head, streamer; scarehead, screamer; spread, spreadhead; drop head, dropline, hanger; running head, running title, jump head; subhead, subheading, subtitle; legend, motto, epigraph; title page; cutline; byline

VERBS **3** focus on, have regard to, distinguish, lift up, set forth, specify, zero in on, center on, be concerned with; include; caption, title, head, head up; **headline;** subtitle, subhead

ADJS **4** **topical, thematic**

938 INQUIRY

<request for information>

NOUNS **1** **inquiry,** inquiring, probing, inquest, inquirendo; inquisition; interpellation; inquiring mind; analysis; test drive

2 **examination,** school examination, examen, exam, test, quiz; oral examination, oral, doctor's oral, master's oral, viva voce examination, viva; catechesis, catchization; audition, hearing; multiple-choice test, multiple-guess test; written examination, written, blue book, test paper; course examination, midterm, midyear, midsemester; qualifying examination, preliminary examination, prelim; take-home examination; open-book test; unannounced examination, pop quiz, shotgun quiz, surprise quiz; final examination, final, comprehensive examination, comps; great go, greats; tripos, honors <Brit>

3 **examination,** inspection, scrutiny; survey, review, perusal, look-over, once over, look-see, perlustration, study, look-through, scan, run-through; visitation; overhaul, overhauling; quality control; confirmation, cross-check

4 **investigation,** indagation, **research,** legwork, inquiry into; data-gathering, gathering evidence, amassing evidence; perscrutation, **probe,** searching investigation, close inquiry, exhaustive study; police inquiry, police investigation, criminal investigation, detective work, detection, sleuthing; investigative bureau, investigative agency, bureau of investigation, department of investigation; legislative investigation, Congressional investigation, hearing; witch-hunt, fishing expedition, Inquisition

5 preliminary examination, tentative examination;

quick inspection, cursory inspection, glance, quick look, **first look**, once-over-lightly

6 **checkup,** check; spot check; physical examination, physical, physical checkup, health examination; self-examination; exploratory examination; testing, drug testing, alcohol testing, random testing; bench test

7 **re-examination,** reinquiry, recheck, **review,** reappraisal, revaluation, rethinking, revision, rebeholding, second look, further look

8 **reconnaissance;** recce, recco, recon; reconnoitering, reconnoiter, exploration, scouting; exploratory survey

9 **surveillance,** shadowing, following, trailing, tailing, 24-hour surveillance, observation, stakeout; spying, spycraft, espionage, espial, **intelligence**, intelligence-gathering, military intelligence, intelligence work, cloak-and-dagger work; intelligence agency, secret service, secret police; counterespionage, **counterintelligence**; wiretap, wiretapping, bugging, electronic surveillance, piggybacking; tagging

10 **question, query, inquiry,** demand, interrogation, interrogatory; interrogative; frequently asked question (FAQ); problem, issue, topic, case in question, point in question, bone of contention, controversial point, question before the house, debating point, controversy, question at issue, point at issue, moot point, moot case, question mark, *quodlibet* <L>; difficult question, knotty question, burning question; sixty-four-thousand-dollar question; leader, leading question; feeler, trial balloon, fishing question; trick question, poser, stumper, tough nut to crack, conundrum, enigma, mind-boggler; trivia question; cross-question, rhetorical question; cross-interrogatory; catechism, catechizing; easy question; gotcha question, honey trap; third rail

11 **interview,** press conference, press opportunity, photo opportunity, photo op

12 **questioning, interrogation**, querying, asking, seeking, pumping, probing, inquiring; quiz, quizzing, examination; challenge, dispute; interpellation, bringing into question; catechizing, catechization; catechetical method, Socratic method, Socratic induction

13 grilling, the grill, inquisition, pumping; police interrogation; **the third-degree**; direct examination, redirect examination, **cross-examination,** cross-interrogation, **cross-questioning**

14 **canvass, survey,** inquiry, questionnaire, questionary; exit poll; poll, public-opinion poll, opinion poll, opinion survey, statistical survey, opinion sampling, voter-preference survey; consumer-preference survey, market-research survey; consumer research, market research

15 **search,** searching, quest, hunt, hunting, stalk, stalking, still hunt, dragnet, posse, search party; search warrant; search-and-destroy mission; rummage, ransacking, turning over, turning upside down; forage; house-search, perquisition, domiciliary visit; exploration, probe; body search, frisk, toss, shake, shakedown, skin-search, body-shake, pat-down search; all-points bulletin

16 **inquirer,** asker, prober, querier, querist, questioner, questionist, interrogator; interviewer; interrogatrix; interpellator; quizzer, examiner, catechist; inquisitor, inquisitionist; cross-questioner, cross-interrogator, cross-examiner; interlocutor; pollster, poller, sampler, canvasser, opinion sampler; detective; secret agent; quizmaster

17 **examiner,** examinant, tester; inspector, scrutinizer, scrutator, scrutineer, quality-control inspector; monitor, reviewer; fact-checker; check-out pilot; observer; visitor, visitator; **investigator,** indagator; editor, copy editor, proofreader

18 seeker, hunter, searcher, perquisitor; rummager, ransacker; digger, delver; zetetic; **researcher,** fact finder, researchist, research worker, market researcher, consumer researcher; surveyor

19 **examinee,** examinant, examinate, questionee, quizzee; interviewee; informant, subject, witness; candidate; defendant, plaintiff, suspect

VERBS 20 **inquire, ask, question, query**; make inquiry, take up an inquiry, institute an inquiry, pursue an inquiry, follow up an inquiry, conduct an inquiry, carry on an inquiry, ask after, inquire after, ask about, ask questions, put queries; inquire of, require an answer, ask a question, put a question to, pose a question; bring into question, interpellate; demand, want to know; introspect

21 **interrogate, question,** query, quiz, test, examine; catechize; pump, pump for information, shoot questions at, pick the brains of, worm out of; interview; draw one out

22 grill, put on the grill, inquisition, pump, make inquisition; roast, put the pressure on, put the screws to, go over; **cross-examine,** cross-question, cross-interrogate, cross; third-degree, give the third degree; put to the question; extract information, pry out; put through the mill

23 **investigate,** indagate, sift, explore, look into, peer into, search into, go into, delve into, dig into, poke into, pry into; fact-find; probe, sound, plumb, fathom; check into, check on, check out, nose into, see into; poke about, root around, scratch around, cast about

24 **examine,** inspect, scrutinize, survey, canvass,

look at, peer at, eyeball, observe, scan, peruse, study; look over, give the once-over, run the eye over, pass the eyes over, scope out; go over, run over, pass over, pore over; overlook, overhaul; monitor, review, pass under review; set an examination, give an examination; take stock of, size, size up, take the measure; check, check out, check over, check through; check up on; autopsy, postmortem; soul-search; test-drive

25 make a close study of, **research,** scrutinize, examine thoroughly, vet, curate, go deep into, look closely at, probe; examine point by point, go over with a fine-tooth comb, go over step by step, subject to close scrutiny, try in all its phases, get down to nuts and bolts; perscrutate, perlustrate

26 **examine cursorily,** take a cursory view of, give a quick look, give a cursory look, give a once-over-lightly, give a dekko, **scan, skim,** skim over, skim through, glance at, give the once-over, pass over lightly, zip through, dip into, touch upon, touch upon lightly, touch upon in passing, hit the high spots; thumb through, flip through the pages, turn over the leaves, leaf through, page through, flick through

27 **re-examine,** recheck, reinquire, reconsider, reappraise, revaluate, rethink, **review,** revise, rebehold, take another loo, take a second look, take a further look; retrace, retrace one's steps, go back over; rejig, rejigger; take back to the old drawing board

28 **reconnoiter,** make a reconnaissance, case, scout, scout out, spy, spy out, play the spy, peep; watch, put under surveillance, stake out; bug; check up on, check up

29 **canvass,** survey, make a survey; poll, conduct a poll, sample, questionnaire

30 **seek, hunt,** look, quest, pursue, go in pursuit of, follow, go in search of, prowl after, see to, try to find; look up, hunt up; look for, look around for, look for high and low, look high and low, search out, search for, seek for, hunt for, cast about for; shop around for; fish for, angle for, bob for, dig for, delve for, go on a fishing expedition; ask for, inquire for; gun for, go gunning for; still-hunt

31 **search, hunt,** explore; research; read up on; hunt through, search through, look through, go through; dig, delve, burrow, root, pick over, poke, pry; look around, poke around, nose around, smell around; beat the bushes; forage; frisk

32 **grope,** grope for, feel for, fumble, grabble, scrabble, feel around, poke around, pry around, beat about, grope in the dark; feel one's way, pick one's way

33 **ransack, rummage,** rake, scour, comb; rifle; look everywhere, look into every hole and corner, look high and low, look upstairs and downstairs, look all over, look all over hell, search high heaven, turn upside down, turn inside out, leave no stone unturned; shake down, shake, toss

34 **search out,** hunt out, spy out, scout out, ferret out, fish out, pry out, winkle out, dig out, root out, grub up

35 **trace, stalk,** track, trail; follow, follow up, shadow, tail, dog the footsteps of, have an eye on, keep an eye on; nose, nose out, smell out, sniff out, follow the trail of, follow the scent of; follow a clue; trace down, hunt down, track down, run down, run to earth

ADJS **36** **inquiring, questioning,** querying, quizzing; quizzical, curious; interrogatory, interrogative, interrogational; inquisitorial, inquisitional; visitatorial, visitorial; catechistic, catechistical, catechetic, catechetical

37 **examining,** examinational; scrutatorial, examinatorial; testing, trying, tentative; groping, feeling; inspectional; inspectorial; interpellant; **investigative,** indagative; zetetic; heuristic, investigatory, investigational; exploratory, explorative, explorational; fact-finding; analytic, analytical; curious

38 **searching, probing,** prying, nosy; poking, digging, fishing, delving; in search of, in quest of, looking for, out for, on the lookout for, in the market for, loaded for bear, out for bear; all-searching; fact-finding, knowledge-seeking

ADVS **39** **in question,** at issue, in debate, in dispute, under consideration, under active consideration, under advisement, *subjudice* <L>, under examination, under investigation, under surveillance, up for discussion, open for discussion; before the house, on the docket, on the agenda, on the table, on the floor

939 ANSWER

<response to question>

NOUNS **1** **answer, reply, response,** responsion, replication; answering, respondence; riposte, uptake, retort, rejoinder, reaction, return, comeback, take, back answer, short answer, back talk, backchat; repartee, clever reply, ready reply, witty retort, snappy comeback, witty repartee; yes-and-no answer, evasive reply; acknowledgment, receipt, confirmation; rescript, rescription; antiphon; echo, reverberation

2 **rebuttal,** counterstatement, counterreply, counterclaim, counterblast, counteraccusation, countercharge, defense, contraremonstrance; rejoinder, replication, rebutter, surrebutter, surrebuttal, surrejoinder; confutation, refutation; last word, parting shot

3 **answerer,** replier, responder, **respondent,** responser; defendant

VERBS 4 **answer,** give answer, return answer, return for answer, offer, proffer, **reply, respond,** say, say in reply; retort, riposte, rejoin, return, throw back, flash back; come back, come back at, come right back at, answer back, talk back, shoot back, react; acknowledge, make acknowledgement, give acknowledgement; echo, reecho, reverberate

5 **rebut,** make a rebuttal; rejoin, surrebut, surrejoin; counterclaim, countercharge; confute, refute; have the last word, have the final say; fire the parting shot; lip off

ADJS 6 **answering, replying, responsive,** respondent, responding; rejoining, returning; antiphonal; echoing, echoic, reechoing; confutative, refutative; acknowledging, confirming

ADVS 7 in answer, in reply, in response, in return, in rebuttal

940 SOLUTION

<answer to a problem>

NOUNS 1 **solution,** resolution, answer, reason, explanation; finding, conclusion, determination, ascertainment, verdict, judgment; outcome, upshot, denouement, result, issue, end, end result, end state; accomplishment; **solving**, working, working-out, finding-out, resolving, clearing up, cracking; unriddling, riddling, unscrambling, unraveling, sorting out, untwisting, unspinning, unweaving, untangling, disentanglement; decipherment, deciphering, decoding, decryption; interpretation; happy ending, happy outcome, the answer to one's prayers, the light at the end of the tunnel; possible solution, scenario

VERBS 2 **solve, resolve,** find the solution, find the answer, problem-solve, clear up, get, get right, do, work, work out, find out, figure out, dope, dope out; straighten out, iron out, sort out, puzzle out; debug; psych, psych out; unriddle, riddle, unscramble, undo, untangle, disentangle, untwist, unspin, unweave, unravel, ravel, ravel out; decipher, decode, decrypt, crack, do the math; make out, interpret; answer, explain; unlock, pick the lock, open the lock; find the key of, find a clue to; get to the bottom of, get to the heart of, fathom, plumb, bottom; have it, hit it, hit upon a solution, hit the nail on the head, hit it on the nose; guess, divine, guess right; end happily, work out right, come up roses

ADJS 3 **solvable,** soluble, **resolvable,** open to solution, capable of solution, workable, doable, answerable; explainable, explicable, determinable, ascertainable; decipherable, decodable

941 DISCOVERY

<learning something for the first time>

NOUNS 1 **discovery, finding,** detection, spotting, catching, catching sight of, sighting, espial; recognition, determination, distinguishment; locating, location; disclosure, exposure, revelation, uncovering, unearthing, digging up, exhumation, excavation, bringing to light, bringing to view; find, trove, treasure trove, treasure chest, strike, lucky strike; accidental discovery, chance discovery, happening upon, stumbling upon, tripping over, casual discovery; serendipity; learning, **finding out,** determining, becoming conscious of, becoming cognizant of, becoming aware of; self-discovery; realization, enlightenment; rediscovery; invention; archaeology; happy accident

VERBS 2 **discover, find,** get; strike, hit; put one's hands on, lay one's hands on, lay one's fingers on, locate; hunt down, search out, trace down, track down, run down; trace; learn, **find out,** determine, become cognizant of, become conscious of, become aware of, get it; find out the hard way, discover to one's cost; discover oneself, find oneself; rediscover; invent

3 **come across,** run across, meet with, meet up with, fall in with, encounter, run into, come up against, bump into, run up against, come on, hit upon, strike on, light upon, alight upon, fall on, tumble on; **chance on**, happen on, happen upon, stumble on, stumble into, stumble across, stub one's toe on, trip over, bump up against, blunder upon, discover serendipitously

4 **uncover, unearth, dig up,** disinter, exhume, excavate; disclose, expose, reveal, blow the lid off, crack wide open, bring to light, lay bare; turn up, root up, rootle up <Brit>, fish up; worm out, ferret out, winkle out <Brit>, pry out

5 **detect,** spot, see, lay eyes on, catch sight of, catch a glimpse of, perceive, spy, espy, descry, sense, pick up, notice, discern, make out, recognize, distinguish, identify

6 **scent,** catch the scent of, sniff, smell, get a whiff of, get wind of; sniff out, nose out; be on the right scent, be near the truth, be warm, burn, have a fix on, place

7 **catch,** catch out; catch offside, catch off base; catch tripping, catch napping, catch off-guard, catch asleep at the switch; catch at, catch in the act, catch red-handed, catch in *flagrante delicto,*

catch with one's pants down, catch flat-footed, have the goods on, ensnare

8 <detect the hidden nature of> **see through,** detect, penetrate, see as it really is, see in its true colors, see the inside of, read between the lines, see the cloven hoof; open the eyes to, tumble to, catch on to, wise up to; be on to, be wise to, be hep to, have one's measure, have one's number, have dead to rights, read someone like a book

9 **turn up,** show up, be found; discover itself, expose itself, betray itself; hang out; materialize, come to light, come out; come along, come to hand; show one's true colors

ADJS **10** on the right scent, **on the right track,** on the trail of; hot, warm; discoverable, determinable, findable, detectable, spottable, disclosable, exposable, locatable, discernible; exploratory

INTERJS **11** eureka, I have it, at last, at long last, finally; ah hah

942 EXPERIMENT

<scientific test>

NOUNS **1** **experiment, experimentation;** experimental method; testing, trying, trying-out, trial; research and development, R and D; running it up the flagpole, trying it on, trying it out, exploration, bench test; **trial and error,** hit and miss, cut and try; empiricism, experimentalism, pragmatism, instrumentalism; rule of thumb; tentativeness, tentative method; control experiment, controlled experiment, control; experimental design; experimental proof, experimental verification; noble experiment; single-blind experiment, double-blind experiment; guesswork

2 **test, trial,** try; essay; check; docimasy, assay; determination, blank determination; proof, verification; touchstone, standard, criterion; crucial test; acid test, litmus test, litmus-paper test; ordeal, crucible; probation; feeling out, sounding out; test case; first draft, rough draft, rough sketch, mock-up; stab, crack, whack; trial balloon

3 **tryout,** workout, **rehearsal,** practice; pilot plan, pilot program; dry run, dummy run, practice run, practice game, exhibition game; road test; trial run, practical test, clinical trial; shakedown, shakedown cruise, bench test; flight test, test flight, test run; audition, hearing; cattle call; beta

4 **feeler,** probe, sound, sounder; trial balloon, pilot balloon, barometer; weather vane, weathercock; straw to show the wind, straw vote; sample, random sample, experimental sample

5 **laboratory,** lab, research laboratory, research center, research facility, experiment station, field station, research and development establishment, R and D establishment; proving ground; think tank, workshop

6 **experimenter,** experimentist, experimentalist, empiricist, bench scientist, researcher, research worker, R and D worker; experimental engineer; tester, tryer-out, test driver, test pilot; essayer; assayer; analyst, analyzer, investigator

7 **subject,** experimental subject, experimentee, testee, patient, sample; laboratory animal, experimental animal, test animal, **guinea pig,** lab rat

VERBS **8** **experiment,** experimentalize, research, make an experiment, **run an experiment,** run a sample, run a specimen; test, try, essay, cut and try, test out, try out, have a dry run, have a dummy run, have a test run, have a rehearsal, rehearse; run it up the flagpole and see who salutes; put to the test, put to the proof, prove, verify, validate, substantiate, confirm, put to trial, bring to test, make a trial of, give a trial to; give a try, have a go, give it a go, take a stab at, have a crack at, take a whack at; sample, taste; assay; play around with, fool around with; try out under controlled conditions; give a tryout, road-test, shake down; try one out, put one through his paces; experiment upon, practice upon; try it on; try on, try it for size; try one's strength, see what one can do; send up a trial balloon

9 **sound out, check out,** feel out, sound, get a sounding, get a reading, get a sense, probe, feel the pulse, read; put out a feeler, throw out a feeler, put out feelers, send up a trial balloon, fly a kite; see which way the wind blows, see how the land lies, test out, test the waters; take a straw vote, take a random sample, use an experimental sample

10 **stand the test,** stand up, hold up, hold up in the wash, pass, **pass muster,** get by, make it, hack it, cut the mustard, meet requirements, satisfy requirements

ADJS **11** **experimental,** test, trial; pilot; testing, proving, trying; probative, probatory, verificatory; probationary; tentative, provisional; empirical; trial-and-error, hit-or-miss, cut-and-try; heuristic

12 **tried,** well-tried, **tested,** proved, verified, confirmed, tried and true, field-tested

ADVS **13** **experimentally,** by rule of thumb, by trial and error, by hit and miss, hit or miss, by guess and by God

14 on trial, under examination, on probation, under probation, under suspicion, on approval

943 COMPARISON

<looking for differences, similarities>

NOUNS 1 **comparison,** compare, examining side by side, matching, matchup, holding up together, proportion, **comparative judgment**, comparative estimate; benchmarking; likening, comparing, analogy; parallelism; comparative relation; weighing, balancing; opposing, opposition, contrast; contrastiveness, distinctiveness, distinction; confrontment, confrontation; relation, relating, relativism; correlation; simile, similitude, metaphor, allegory, figure of comparison, trope of comparison; comparative degree; comparative method; comparative linguistics, comparative grammar, comparative literature, comparative anatomy

2 **collation,** comparative scrutiny, point-by-point comparison; verification, confirmation, checking; check, **cross-check**

3 **comparability,** comparableness, comparativeness; analogousness, equivalence, commensurability; proportionateness, proportionability; ratio, proportion, balance; similarity

VERBS 4 **compare, liken,** assimilate, similize, liken to, compare with; make a comparison, draw a comparison, run a comparison, do a comparative study, bring into comparison; analogize, bring into analogy; relate; metaphorize; draw a parallel, parallel; match, match up; examine side by side, view together, hold up together; weigh against, measure against; confront, bring into confrontation, contrast, oppose, set in opposition, set off against, set in contrast, put over against, set over against, set against, place against, counterpose; compare and contrast, note similarities and differences; weigh, balance

5 **collate,** scrutinize comparatively, compare point by point, painstakingly match; verify, confirm, check, **cross-check**

6 **compare notes,** exchange views, exchange observations, match data, match findings, put heads together

7 be comparable, compare, compare to, compare with, not compare with, admit of comparison, be commensurable, be of the same class, be worthy of comparison, be fit to be compared; **measure up to,** come up to, match up with, stack up with, hold a candle to; match, parallel; vie, vie with, rival; resemble

ADJS 8 **comparative,** relative, comparable, commensurate, commensurable, parallel, matchable, analogous; analogical; collatable; correlative; much at one, much of a muchness; similar; something of the sort, something to that effect

9 **incomparable,** incommensurable, not to be compared, of different orders; apples and oranges; unlike, dissimilar

ADVS 10 comparatively, relatively; **comparably**; dollar for dollar, pound for pound, ounce for ounce; on the one hand, on the other hand

PREPS 11 **compared to,** compared with, as compared with, by comparison with, in comparison with, beside, over against, taken with; than

944 DISCRIMINATION

<critical examination of differences>

NOUNS 1 **discrimination,** discriminateness, discriminatingness, discriminativeness; seeing distinctions, making distinctions, **appreciation of differences**; analytic power, analytic faculty; criticalness; finesse, refinement, delicacy; niceness of distinction, nicety, subtlety, refined discrimination, critical niceness; tact, tactfulness, feel, feeling, sense, sensitivity, sensibility; intuition, instinct; appreciation, appreciativeness; judiciousness; taste, discriminating taste, aesthetic judgment, artistic judgment; palate, refined palate, mouthfeel; ear, good ear, educated ear; eye, good eye; connoisseurship, savvy, selectiveness, fastidiousness

2 **discernment,** critical discernment, penetration, perception, perceptiveness, insight, perspicacity; flair; judgment, acumen; analysis

3 **distinction,** contradistinction, distinctiveness; **distinguishment,** differentiation, winnowing, shakeout, separation, separationism, division, segregation, segregationism, demarcation; subtle distinction, fine distinction, **nuance,** shade of difference, microscopic distinction; hairsplitting, trichoschistism

VERBS 4 **discriminate, distinguish,** draw distinctions, make distinctions, contradistinguish, compare and contrast, pick and choose, secern, distinguish in thought, separate, separate out, divide, analyze, subdivide, segregate, sever, severalize, differentiate, demark, demarcate, mark the interface, set off, set apart, grade, graduate, sift, sift out, sieve, sieve out, winnow, screen, screen out, sort, classify, sort out; pick out, select; separate the sheep from the goats, separate the men from the boys, separate the wheat from the chaff, winnow the chaff from the wheat; draw the line, set a limit; split hairs, draw a subtle distinction, make a fine distinction, subtilize

5 **be discriminating,** discriminate, exercise

discrimination, tell which is which; be tactful, exercise tact; be tasteful, use one's palate; shop around, pick and choose; use advisedly

6 **distinguish between**, make a distinction, draw a distinction, appreciate differences, see nuances, see shades of difference, see the difference, tell apart, tell one thing from another, know which is which, know what's what, not confound, not mix up; know a hawk from a handsaw, know one's ass from one's elbow

ADJS 7 **discriminating, discriminate,** discriminative, selective; discriminatory; tactful, sensitive; appreciative, appreciatory; critical; distinctive, distinguishing; differential; precise, accurate, exact; nice, fine, delicate, subtle, subtile, **nuanced,** refined; fastidious; contrastive

8 **discerning,** perceptive, perspicacious, insightful; astute, judicious; perfectionist, choosy

9 **discriminable, distinguishable,** separable, differentiable, contrastable, opposable

ADVS 10 **discriminatingly,** discriminatively, discriminately; with finesse; tactfully; tastefully

945 INDISCRIMINATION

<lack of discrimination>

NOUNS 1 **indiscrimination,** indiscriminateness, undiscriminatingness, undiscriminativeness, unselectiveness, **uncriticalness,** unparticularness; syncretism; unfastidiousness; lack of refinement, coarseness of intellect; casualness, promiscuousness, promiscuity; indiscretion, indiscreetness, imprudence; untactfulness, tactlessness, lack of feeling, insensitivity, insensibility, unmeticulousness, unpreciseness, inexactitude; generality, catholicity, catholic tastes; indifference; color blindness, tone-deafness; impartiality

2 **indistinction,** indistinctness, vagueness; indefiniteness; uniformity; facelessness, impersonality; indistinguishableness, undistinguishableness, indiscernibility; a distinction without a difference; randomness, generality, universality

VERBS 3 confound, confuse, mix, mix up, muddle, tumble, jumble, jumble together, blur, blur distinctions, **overlook distinctions; lump together**, take as one, roll into one

4 use loosely, use unadvisedly

ADJS 5 **undiscriminating, indiscriminate,** indiscriminative, undiscriminative, undifferentiating, unselective; wholesale, general, blanket; uncritical, uncriticizing, undemanding, nonjudgmental; unparticular, unfastidious; unsubtle; casual, promiscuous; undiscerning; unexacting, unmeticulous; indiscreet, undiscreet, imprudent; untactful, tactless, insensitive; catholic; indifferent; color-blind

6 **indistinguishable,** undistinguishable, undistinguished, indiscernible, **indistinct,** indistinctive, without distinction, not to be distinguished, undiscriminated, nondiscriminatory, inclusive, unindividual, unindividualized, undifferentiated, alike, six of one and half a dozen of the other; desultory; undefined, indefinite; faceless, impersonal; standard, interchangeable, stereotyped, uniform; random; miscellaneous, motley

946 JUDGMENT

<forming opinion by discerning>

NOUNS 1 **judgment, judging**, adjudgment, adjudication, judicature, deeming; judgment call; arbitrament, arbitration; resolution; good judgment; choice; discrimination; Last Judgment

2 **criticism;** censure; approval; **critique,** review, notice, critical notice, report, comment; book review, critical review, thumbnail review; literary criticism, art criticism, music criticism, critical journal, critical bibliography

3 **estimate, estimation**; view, opinion; assessment, assessing, **appraisal,** appraisement, appraising, appreciation, reckoning, stocktaking, valuation, valuing, evaluation, evaluating, value judgment, evaluative criticism, analyzing, weighing, weighing up, gauging, ranking, rank-ordering, rating; measurement; comparison; second opinion; public opinion

4 **conclusion,** deduction, inference, consequence, consequent, corollary; derivation, illation; induction; judgment day

5 **verdict, decision**, resolution, determination, **finding**, holding; diagnosis, prognosis; decree, ruling, consideration, order, pronouncement, deliverance; award, action, sentence; condemnation, doom; dictum; precedent; edict; execution of judgment

6 **judge,** judger, adjudicator, justice; arbiter; referee, umpire

7 **critic,** criticizer; connoisseur, cognoscente; literary critic, man of letters; textual critic; editor; social critic, muckraker; captious critic, smellfungus, caviler, carper, faultfinder; criticaster, criticule, critickin; censor, censurer; **reviewer,** commentator, commenter; scholiast, annotator

VERBS 8 **judge,** exercise judgment; **make a judgment call**; adjudge, adjudicate; be judicious, be judgmental; consider, regard, hold, deem, esteem, count, account, think of; allow, suppose, presume, opine, form an opinion, give an opinion, express an opinion, weigh in, put in one's two cents' worth

9 **estimate,** form an estimate, make an estimation; reckon, call, guess, figure; assess, appraise, give an appreciation, gauge, rate, rank, rank-order, put in rank order, class, mark, value, deem, evaluate, valuate, place a value on, set a value on, weigh, weigh up, prize, appreciate; size up, take one's measure, measure

10 **conclude,** draw a conclusion, be forced to conclude, come to a conclusion, arrive at a conclusion, come up with a conclusion, end up; find, hold; deduce, derive, take as proved, take as demonstrated, extract, gather, collect, glean, fetch; infer, draw an inference; induce; reason, reason that; put two and two together

11 **decide,** determine; find, hold, ascertain; resolve, settle, fix; make a decision, come to a decision, **make up one's mind**, settle one's mind, come down, settle the matter

12 **sit in judgment,** hold the scales, hold court; hear, give a hearing to; try; referee, umpire, officiate; arbitrate

13 **pass judgment,** pronounce judgment, utter a judgment, deliver judgment; agree on a verdict, return a verdict, hand down a verdict, bring in a verdict, find, find for, find against; pronounce on, act on, pronounce, report, rule, decree, order; **sentence,** pass sentence, hand down a sentence, doom, condemn; charge the jury

14 **criticize,** critique; censure, pick holes in, pick to pieces; approve; **review;** comment upon, annotate; moralize upon; pontificate; vet

15 **rank, rate,** count, be regarded, be thought of, be in one's estimation

ADJS 16 **judicial,** judiciary, judicative, judgmental; juridic, juridical, juristic, juristical; judicious; evaluative; critical; approbatory

ADVS 17 all things considered, on the whole, taking one thing with another, on balance, taking everything into consideration, taking everything into account; everything being equal, other things being equal, taking into account, considering, after all, this being so; therefore, wherefore; on the one hand, on the other hand, having said that; *sub judice* <L>, in court, before the bench, before the bar, before the court

947 PREJUDGMENT

<judging before examining>

NOUNS 1 **prejudgment,** prejudication, forejudgment; **preconception,** presumption, supposition, presupposition, presupposal, presurmise, preapprehension, prenotion, prepossession; predilection, predisposition; preconsideration, predetermination, predecision, preconclusion, premature judgment; ulterior motive, hidden agenda, *parti pris* <Fr>, an ax to grind, prejudice

VERBS 2 **prejudge,** forejudge; **preconceive,** presuppose, presume, presurmise; be predisposed; predecide, predetermine, preconclude, judge beforehand, judge prematurely, judge before the evidence is in, have one's mind made up; **jump to a conclusion,** go off half-cocked, beat the gun, jump the gun, shoot from the hip

ADJS 3 **prejudged,** forejudged, preconceived, preconceptual, presumed, presupposed, presurmised; predetermined, predecided, preconcluded, judged beforehand, judge prematurely; predisposed, predispositional; prejudicial, prejudging, prejudicative

948 MISJUDGMENT

<faulty judgment>

NOUNS 1 **misjudgment,** poor judgment, **error in judgment**, warped judgment, flawed judgment, skewed judgment; miscalculation, miscomputation, misreckoning, misestimation, misappreciation, misperception, misevaluation, misvaluation, misconjecture, wrong impression; misreading, wrong construction, misconstruction, misinterpretation; inaccuracy, error; unmeticulousness; injudiciousness; wrong end of the stick

VERBS 2 **misjudge,** judge amiss, miscalculate, misestimate, misreckon, misappreciate, misperceive, get a wrong impression, misevaluate, misvalue, miscompute, misdeem, misesteem, misthink, misconjecture; misread, misconstrue, put the wrong construction on things, get wrong, misread the situation; misinterpret; err; fly in the face of facts; get hold of the wrong end of the stick

949 OVERESTIMATION

<estimating too high>

NOUNS 1 **overestimation,** overestimate, overreckoning, overcalculation, **overrating,** overassessment, overvaluation, overappraisal; overreaction; overstatement, exaggeration, hype

VERBS 2 **overestimate,** overreckon, overcalculate, overcount, overmeasure, see more than is there; **overrate,** overassess, overappraise, overesteem, overvalue, overprize, overprice, make too much of, put on a pedestal, idealize, see only the good points of; overreact to; overstate, exaggerate; pump up, jump up, make a big deal, make a federal case of; hype

ADJS 3 **overestimated, overrated,** puffed up, pumped up, overvalued, on the high side; exaggerated

950 UNDERESTIMATION

<estimating too low>

NOUNS 1 **underestimation,** misestimation, underestimate, **underrating,** underreckoning, undervaluation, misprizing, misprizal, misprision; belittlement, depreciation, deprecation, minimization, disparagement; conservative estimate; negative outlook, pessimism

VERBS 2 **underestimate,** misestimate, **underrate,** underreckon, undervalue, underprize, misprize, underprice; make little of, set at little, set at naught, set little by, attach little importance to, not do justice to, sell short, think little of, make nothing of, think nothing of, see less than is there, miss on the low side, set no store by, make light of, shrug off, soft-pedal; depreciate, deprecate, minimize, belittle, bad-mouth, poor-mouth, put down, run down, take someone for an idiot, take someone for a fool; disparage; play down, understate

ADJS 3 **underestimated, underrated,** undervalued, on the low side; unvalued, unprized, misprized; underpriced, cheap

951 THEORY, SUPPOSITION

<principles to explain phenomena>

NOUNS 1 **theory,** theorization; theoretics, theoretic, theoric; **hypothesis,** hypothecation, hypothesizing; speculation, mere theory; doctrinairism, doctrinality, doctrinarity; analysis, explanation, abstraction; theoretical basis, theoretical justification; body of theory, theoretical structure, theoretical construct; unified theory

2 **theory,** explanation, proposed explanation, tentative explanation, rationalization, proposal, proposition, statement covering the facts, covering the evidence; **hypothesis,** working hypothesis

3 **supposition,** supposal, supposing; presupposition, presupposal; assumption, presumption, conjecture, inference, surmise, guesswork; postulate, postulation, set of postulates; proposition, **thesis,** concept, premise; axiom

4 **guess, conjecture,** unverified supposition, perhaps, speculation, guesswork, surmise, educated guess; guesstimate, hunch, shot, stab; rough guess, wild guess, blind guess, bold conjecture, shot in the dark, crude estimate

5 **<vague supposition>** suggestion, bare suggestion, suspicion, inkling, hint, clue, sense, feeling, feeling in one's bones, intuition, intimation, impression, notion, mere notion, hunch, sneaking suspicion, instinct, trace of an idea, half an idea, vague idea, hazy idea, idea

6 supposititiousness, presumptiveness, presumableness, theoreticalness, hypotheticalness, conjecturableness, speculativeness

7 **theorist,** theorizer, theoretic, theoretician, notionalist; speculator; hypothesist, hypothesizer; doctrinaire, doctrinarian; inquirer; synthesizer; armchair authority, armchair philosopher; thinker; researcher, experimenter

8 **supposer,** assumer, **surmiser,** conjecturer, guesser, guessworker, speculator, gambler

VERBS 9 **theorize, hypothesize,** hypothecate, form a hypothesis, speculate, postulate, have a theory, entertain a theory, espouse a theory, generalize

10 **suppose,** assume, presume, surmise, expect, suspect, infer, understand, gather, conclude, deduce, consider, reckon, reason, derive, divine, imagine, fancy, dream, conceive, believe, deem, repute, feel, think, be inclined to think, opine, say, daresay, be afraid; take, take it, take it into one's head, take for, take to be, take for granted, take as a precondition, presuppose, presurmise, prefigure; provisionally accept, provisonally agree to, take one up on, grant, stipulate, take it as given, let, let be, say for argument's sake, assume for argument's sake, say for the hell of it; draw a mental picture

11 **conjecture, guess,** guesstimate, give a guess, talk off the top of one's head, hazard a conjecture, venture a guess, risk assuming, risk stating, tentatively suggest, go out on a limb

12 **postulate,** predicate, posit, set forth, lay down, put forth, assert; pose, advance, propose, propound

ADJS 13 **theoretical, hypothetical,** hypothetic; postulatory, notional; speculative, **conjectural,** blue-sky; impressionistic, intuitive; general, generalized, abstract, ideal; unverified, merely theoretical, academic, moot; impractical, armchair, thought-provoking

14 **supposed,** suppositive, **assumed,** presumed, conjectured, inferred, understood, deemed, reputed, reputative, putative, alleged, accounted as; suppositional, supposititious; assumptive, presumptive; guessed; given, granted, taken as, taken for granted, agreed, stipulated; postulated,

postulational, premised; granted for the sake of argument

15 **supposable,** presumable, assumable, conjecturable, surmisable, imaginable, premissable

ADVS 16 **theoretically, hypothetically,** notionally, conceptually, ideally; **in theory,** in idea, in the ideal, in the abstract, on paper, in Never-Neverland

17 **supposedly,** supposably, presumably, presumedly, assumably, assumedly, presumptively, assumptively, reputedly, presumingly; suppositionally, supposititiously; seemingly, in seeming, quasi; as it were; on the assumption that

18 conjecturably, **conjecturally;** to guess, to make a guess, as a guess, as a rough guess, as an approximation, speculatively

CONJS 19 **supposing,** supposing that, **assuming that,** allowing that, if we assume that, let's say that, granted that, given that, on the assumption that, on the supposition that; if, as if, as though, by way of hypothesis

952 PHILOSOPHY

<pursuit of wisdom and truth>

NOUNS 1 **philosophy**; philosophical inquiry, philosophical investigation, philosophical speculation; investigation into first causes; branch of philosophy, **philosophy branch** <see list>, department of philosophy, division of philosophy; **school of philosophy** <see list>, philosophic system, school of thought; philosophic doctrine, philosophic theory; theory of knowledge; philosophastry, philosophastering; sophistry

2 **viewpoint**, point of view, outlook, attitude, opinion; feeling, sentiment, idea, thought, notion; tenet, dogma, doctrine, canon, principle; assertion, proposition, premise, assumption, precept, thesis, postulate, hypothesis, concept; supposition, presupposition, conjecture, speculation; maxim, axiom; rationalization, justification; conclusion, judgment; philosophical system, belief system, value system, set of beliefs, set of values, ethics, morals, school of thought, moral code, code of conduct, value judgment, standards, principles, ideology; honor system; acceptable face

3 <ancient philosophy> Platonic philosophy, Platonism, philosophy of the Academy; Aristotelian philosophy, Aristotelianism, philosophy of the Lyceum, Peripateticism, Peripatetic school; Stoic philosophy, Stoicism, philosophy of the Porch, philsophy of the Stoa; Epicureanism, philosophy of the Garden

4 materialism; idealism

5 monism, philosophical unitarianism, mind-stuff theory; pantheism, cosmotheism; hylozoism

6 pluralism; dualism, mind-matter theory

7 <political and economic philosophy> anarchism, capitalism, collectivism, communism, internationalism, isolationism, Marxism, monetarism, nationalism, socialism, utilitarianism, utopianism

8 **philosopher**, philosophizer, philosophe; philosophaster; **thinker**, speculator; casuist; metaphysician, cosmologist, logician, dialectician, syllogist; sophist; idealist, idealogue, visionary, dreamer

VERBS 9 **philosophize,** reason, probe

ADJS 10 **philosophical,** philosophic, sophistical; philosophicohistorical, philosophicolegal, philosophicojuristic, philosophicopsychological, philosophicoreligious, philosophicotheological; notional, abstract, esoteric, ideological, ideational, hypothetical, theoretical

11 absurdist, acosmistic, aesthetic, African, agnostic, Alexandrian, analytic, animalistic, animist, animistic, atomistic <for other ADJS, add -istic to a philosophy>

12 Aristotelian, Peripatetic; Augustinian, Averroist, Averroistic, Bergsonian, Berkeleian, Cartesian, Comtian, Hegelian, Neo-Hegelian, Heideggerian, Heraclitean, Humean, Husserlian, Kantian, Leibnizian, Parmenidean, Platonic, Neoplatonic, pre-Socratic, Pyrrhonic, Pyrrhonian, Pythagorean, Neo-Pythagorean, Sartrian, Schellingian, Schopenhauerian, Scotist, Socratic, Spencerian, Thomist, Thomistic, Viconian, Wittgensteinian

13 **philosophy branch**

aesthetics, theory of beauty, philosophy of art
analytic philosophy
axiology, value theory
casuistry
commonsense, naïve realism
cosmology
deontology
ethics, moral philosophy
logic, theory of argument
metaphysics, first philosophy, theory of existence
ontology, science of being
phenomenology
philosophy of biology
philosophy of education
philosophy of history
philosophy of language, philosophy of semantics
philosophy of law
philosophy of logic
philosophy of nature
philosophy of physics
philosophy of religion
philosophy of science
philosophy of signs, philosophy of semiotics
political philosophy
sentential calculus, propositional calculus
teleology
theology
theory of knowledge, epistemology, gnosiology

14 **school of philosophy**
analytic philosophy
Atomism
Averroism
British Empiricism
Classicism
Confucianism
continental philosopy
cosmotheism
criticism philosophy, critical philosophy
Cynicism
Cyrenaics, Cyrenaicism
deconstructionism
deism
deontological ethics
determinism
dialectical materialism
dualism
eclecticism
egoism
egoistic hedonism
Eleaticism, Eleatic school
empiricism
Epicureanism
Eretrian school
eristic school
essentialism
ethicism
ethics
eudaemonism
existentialism, existential philosophy
extremism
feminist philosophy
Frankfurt School
German idealism
Gnosticism
hedonism
Hegelianism
Hellenistic philosophy
historicism
holism
humanism
idealism
immaterialism
individualism
instrumentalism
intuitionism
Ionian school
Kantianism
Kyoto School
liberalism
linguistic and analytic philosophy
logical empiricism, logical positivism
logisism
Marxism
materialism
mechanism
Megarian School
mentalism
modernism
monism
mysticism
naturalism
Neohumanism
Neoplatonism
Neopositivism
Neo-Scholasticism
nominalism
Nyaya School
objectivism
pantheism
Peripatetic school
phenomenology
philosophy of organism
philosophy of signs
Platonism
Pluralist School
positivism
postmodernism
poststructuralism
pragmatism, pragmaticism
Praxis School
Pre-Socratic philosophy
process philosophy
Pythagoreanism
post-structuralism
rationalism
realism
reductionism
Romanticism
Scholasticism
secular humanism
semiotic, semiotics
skepticism
Socratism, Socratic philosophy
solipsism
Sophism, Sophists
speculative realism
spiritualism
Stoicism
structuralism
Sufi philosophy
Taoism
theism
theosophy
Thomism
Traditionalist School
transcendentalism, transcendental idealism
transhumanism
universalistic hedonism
utilitarianism
Vedanta
virtue ethics
vitalism
voluntarism
yogachara
zetetic philosophy

953 BELIEF

<something accepted or considered true>

NOUNS 1 **belief,** credence, credit, **believing,** faith, trust; hope; confidence, assuredness, convincedness, persuadedness, assurance; sureness, surety, certainty; reliance, dependence, reliance on, reliance in, dependence on, stock, store; acceptation, acception, acceptance; reception, acquiescence; blind faith, full faith and credit; suspension of disbelief; fideism; credulity

2 **belief, tenet, dogma,** precept, principle, principle of faith, article of faith, premise, canon, maxim, axiom; doctrine, teaching

3 **system of belief;** religion, faith, **belief system;** school, cult, ism, philosophy, ideology, worldview; political faith, political belief, political philosophy; creed, credo, credenda, dogma, canon; articles of religion, articles of faith, creedal statement, doctrinal statement, formulated belief, stated belief; gospel; catechism

4 **statement of belief**, statement of principles, manifesto, position paper; solemn declaration; deposition, affidavit, sworn statement; vote of confidence

5 **conviction,** persuasion, certainty; **firm belief,** moral certainty, implicit belief, staunch belief, settled judgment, mature judgment, mature belief, fixed opinion, unshaken confidence, steadfast faith, rooted belief, deep-rooted belief; leap of faith

6 **opinion,** sentiment, feeling, sense, impression, reaction, notion, idea, thought, mind, thinking, way of thinking, attitude, stance, posture, position, mindset, view, viewpoint, eye, sight, lights, observation, conception, concept, conceit, estimation, estimate, consideration, angle, theory, conjecture, supposition, assumption, presumption, conclusion, judgment, personal judgment; point of view; public opinion, public belief, general belief, prevailing belief, prevailing sentiment, common belief, community sentiment, popular belief, conventional wisdom, vox pop, *vox populi* <L>, climate of opinion; ethos; mystique; anecdotal evidence

7 profession, confession, declaration, profession of faith, profession of confession, **declaration of faith**

8 **believability,** persuasiveness, believableness, convincingness, **credibility,** credit,

trustworthiness, plausibility, tenability, acceptability, conceivability; reliability

9 **believer,** truster; religious believer; true believer; the assured, the faithful, the believing; fideist; ideologist, ideologue; conformist; innocent, naif

VERBS 10 **believe, credit,** trust, accept, receive, buy; give credit to, give credence to, give faith to, put faith in, take stock in, set store by, take to heart, attach weight to; be led to believe; accept implicitly, believe without reservation, rest assured, take for granted, take for gospel, accept for gospel, take as gospel truth, take on faith, accept on faith, take on trust, take on credit, pin one's faith on; take at face value; take one's word for, trust one's word, take at one's word; fall for; buy into, swallow; be certain

11 think, opine, **be of the opinion**, be persuaded, be convinced; be afraid, have the idea, have an idea, suppose, assume, presume, judge, guess, surmise, suspect, have a hunch, have an inkling, expect, have an impression, be under the impression, have a sense, have the sense, conceive, ween, trow, imagine, fancy, daresay; deem, esteem, hold, regard, consider, maintain, reckon, estimate; hold as, account as, set down as, set down for, view as, look upon as, take for, take, take it, get it into one's head

12 **state,** assert, swear, swear to God, declare, affirm, **vow**, avow, avouch, warrant, asseverate, confess, be under the impression, profess, express the belief, swear to a belief; depose, make an affidavit, make a sworn statement

13 **hold the belief,** have the opinion, entertain a belief, entertain an opinion, adopt a belief, embrace a belief, take as an article of faith; foster a belief, nurture a belief, cherish a belief, be wedded to, espouse a belief; get hold of an idea, get it into one's head, form a conviction

14 **be confident,** have confidence, be satisfied, be convinced, be certain, be easy in one's mind about, be secure in the belief, feel sure, rest assured, rest in confidence; doubt not, have no doubt, have no misgivings, have no diffidence, have no qualms, have no reservations, have no second thoughts

15 **believe in, have faith in,** pin one's faith to, confide in, have confidence in, place confidence in, repose confidence in, place reliance in, put oneself in the hands of, trust in, put trust in, have simple faith in, have childlike faith in, rest in, repose in, hope in; give the benefit of the doubt, get the benefit of the doubt

16 **rely on,** rely upon, depend on, depend upon, place reliance on, rest on, repose on, lean on, count on, calculate on, reckon on, bank on; trust to, swear by, take one's oath upon; bet on, gamble on, lay money on, bet one's bottom dollar on, make book on; take one's word for

17 **trust,** confide in, rely on, depend on, repose, place trust in, place confidence in, have confidence in, trust in, trust utterly, trust implicitly, deem trustworthy, think reliable, think dependable, take one's word, take at one's word; factor in, factor into

18 convince; **convert, win over,** lead one to believe, bring over, bring round, take in, talk over, talk through, bring to reason, bring to one's senses, persuade, lead to believe, give to understand; satisfy, assure; put one's mind at rest on; sell, sell one on; make one's point, drive home to; cram down one's throat, beat into one's head; be convincing, carry conviction; inspire belief, inspire confidence; evangelize, proselytize, propagandize, talk up

19 **convince oneself,** persuade oneself, sell oneself, make oneself easy about, make oneself easy on that score, satisfy oneself on that point, make sure of, make up one's mind

20 **find credence,** be believed, be accepted, be received; be swallowed, go down, pass current; carry conviction; have the ear of, gain the confidence of

ADJS 21 **believing,** of the belief, preceptive, principled; attitudinal; undoubting, undoubtful, doubtless; faithful, God-fearing, pious, pietistic, observant, devout; under the impression, impressed with; convinced, confident, positive, dogmatic, secure, persuaded, sold on, satisfied, assured; born-again; sure, certain; fideistic

22 **trusting,** trustful, trusty, confiding, unsuspecting, unsuspicious, without suspicion; childlike, innocent, guileless, naive; knee-jerk, credulous; relying, depending, reliant, dependent; gullible

23 **believed,** credited, held, trusted, accepted; received, of belief, authoritative, maintained; undoubted, unsuspected, unquestioned, undisputed, uncontested

24 **believable, credible,** creditable; tenable, conceivable, plausible, colorable, realistic; worthy of faith, trustworthy, trusty; fiduciary; reliable; unimpeachable, unexceptionable, unquestionable

25 fiducial, fiduciary; convictional

26 **convincing,** convictional, well-founded, persuasive, assuring, impressive, satisfying, satisfactory, confidence-building; decisive, absolute, conclusive, determinative; authoritative

27 **doctrinal, creedal,** preceptive, canonical, dogmatic, confessional, mandatory, of faith

ADVS 28 **believingly,** undoubtingly, undoubtfully, without doubt, without question, unquestioningly;

trustingly, trustfully, unsuspectingly, unsuspiciously; piously, devoutly; with faith; with confidence, on trust, on faith, on one's say-so

29 **in one's opinion,** to one's mind, in one's thinking, to one's way of thinking, the way one thinks, in one's estimation, according to one's lights, as one sees it, to the best of one's belief; in the opinion of, in the eyes of

954 CREDULITY

<willingness to believe>

NOUNS **1** **credulity, credulousness,** inclination to believe, disposition to believe, ease of belief, willingness to believe, wishful thinking; **blind faith,** unquestioning belief, knee-jerk response, knee-jerk agreement; uncritical acceptance, premature acceptation, unripe acceptation, hasty conviction, rash conviction; trustfulness, trustingness, unsuspiciousness, unsuspectingness; uncriticalness, unskepticalness; overcredulity, overcredulousness, overtrustfulness, overopenness to persuasion, gross credulity; infatuation, fondness, dotage; one's blind side

2 **gullibility, dupability,** bamboozlability, cullibility, deceivability, seduceability, persuadability, hoaxability; biddability; easiness, softness, weakness; simpleness, simplicity, ingenuousness, unsophistication; greenness, naïveness, **naivete,** naivety

3 **superstition,** superstitiousness; popular belief, old wives' tale; tradition, lore, folklore; charm, spell

4 trusting soul; dupe; **sucker**, patsy, easy mark, pushover

VERBS **5** **be credulous,** accept unquestioningly; not boggle at anything, **believe anything,** be easy of belief, be uncritical, believe at the drop of a hat, be a dupe, think the moon is made of green cheese, buy a pig in a poke

6 **fall for,** kid oneself, swallow, swallow anything, swallow whole, not choke on; swallow hook, line, and sinker; eat up, lap up, devour, gulp down, gobble up, buy, buy into, bite, nibble, rise to the fly, take the bait, swing at, go for, tumble for, be taken in, be suckered, be a sucker, be a patsy, be an easy mark

7 **be superstitious;** knock on wood, keep one's fingers crossed

ADJS **8** **credulous,** knee-jerk, easy of belief, ready to believe, inclined to believe, easily taken in; undoubting; trustful, trusting; unsuspicious, unsuspecting; unthinking, uncritical, unskeptical; overcredulous, overtrustful, overtrusting, overconfiding; fond, infatuated, doting; superstitious

9 **gullible,** dupable, bamboozlable, cullible, deceivable, foolable, deludable, exploitable, victimizable, seduceable, persuadable, hoaxable, humbugable, hoodwinkable; biddable; soft, easy, simple; ingenuous, unsophisticated, green, **naive**

955 UNBELIEF

<unwillingness to believe>

NOUNS **1** **unbelief, disbelief,** nonbelief, unbelievingness, discredit; refusal to believe, inability to believe; incredulity; unpersuadedness, unconvincedness, lack of conviction; denial, rejection; misbelief, heresy; infidelity, atheism, agnosticism; minimifidianism, nullifidianism

2 **doubt,** doubtfulness, dubiousness, dubiety; half-belief; reservation, question, question in one's mind; skepticism, skepticalness; total skepticism, Pyrrhonism; suspicion, suspiciousness, wariness, leeriness, **distrust,** mistrust, misdoubt, distrustfulness, mistrustfulness; misgiving, self-doubt, diffidence; qualm; scruple, scrupulousness; hesitation; apprehension; uncertainty; shadow of doubt, credibility gap; vote of no confidence

3 **unbelievability,** unbelievableness, incredibility, implausibility, impossibility, improbability, inconceivability, untenableness, untenability; unpersuasiveness, unconvincingness; **doubtfulness,** questionableness; credibility gap; unreliability

4 doubter, **doubting Thomas**; scoffer, skeptic, cynic, pooh-pooher, naysayer, disbeliever, nonbeliever, unbeliever

VERBS **5** **disbelieve,** unbelieve, misbelieve, **not believe,** find hard to believe, not admit, refuse to admit, not buy, take no stock in, set no store by; discredit, refuse to credit, refuse to give credence to, give no credence to; gag on, not swallow; negate, deny, naysay, say nay; scoff at, pooh-pooh; reject

6 **doubt,** be doubtful, be dubious, be skeptical, doubt the truth of, beg leave to doubt, have one's doubts, have doubts, harbor doubts, entertain doubts, have suspicions, half believe, have reservations, **take with a grain of salt,** be from Missouri, scruple, distrust, mistrust, misgive, cross one's fingers; be uncertain; suspect, smell a rat, see something funny; question, query, challenge, contest, dispute, cast doubt on, greet with skepticism, keep one's eye on, treat with reserve, call into question, raise a question, throw doubt upon, awake a doubt, awaken suspicion; doubt one's word, give one the lie; doubt oneself, be diffident

7 **be unbelievable,** be incredible, be hard to swallow, defy belief, pass belief, be hard to believe, strain one's credulity, stagger belief; shake one's faith, undermine one's faith; perplex, boggle the mind, stagger, fill with doubt

ADJS 8 **unbelieving,** disbelieving, nonbelieving; faithless, **without faith**; unconfident, unconvinced, unconverted; nullifidian, minimifidian, creedless; incredulous; repudiative; heretical; irreligious

9 **doubting, doubtful,** in doubt, dubious; questioning; **skeptical**, Pyrrhonic, from Missouri; distrustful, mistrustful, untrustful, mistrusting, untrusting; suspicious, suspecting, scrupulous, shy, wary, leery; agnostic; uncertain

10 **unbelievable, incredible,** unthinkable, **implausible,** unimaginable, inconceivable, not to be believed, hard to believe, hard of belief, beyond belief, unworthy of belief, not meriting belief, not deserving belief, tall; defying belief, staggering belief, passing belief; mind-boggling, preposterous, absurd, ridiculous, unearthly, ungodly; doubtful, dubious, doubtable, dubitable, questionable, problematic, problematical, unconvincing, open to doubt, open to suspicion; suspicious, suspect, funny; so-called, self-styled; thin, a bit thin; thick, a bit thick, a little too thick

11 under a cloud, unreliable

12 **doubted,** questioned, disputed, contested, moot; distrusted, mistrusted; suspect, suspected, under suspicion, under a cloud; discredited, exploded, rejected, disbelieved

ADVS 13 **unbelievingly,** doubtingly, doubtfully, dubiously, questioningly, skeptically, suspiciously; with a grain of salt, with reservations, with some allowance, with caution

14 **unbelievably,** incredibly, unthinkably, implausibly, inconceivably, unimaginably, staggeringly

956 INCREDULITY

<unwillingness to accept as true or real>

NOUNS 1 **incredulity, incredulousness,** uncredulousness, refusal to believe, disinclination to believe, resistance to belief, resistiveness to belief, tough-mindedness, hardheadedness, inconvincibility, unconvincibility, unpersuadability, unpersuasibility; suspiciousness, suspicion, wariness, leeriness, guardedness, cautiousness, caution; skepticism

2 ungullibility, uncullibility, undupability, undeceivability, unhoaxability, unseduceability; sophistication

VERBS 3 **refuse to believe,** resist believing, not allow oneself to believe, be slow to believe, be slow to accept; not kid oneself; disbelieve; be skeptical; not swallow, not be able to swallow, not go for, not fall for, not be taken in by; not accept, not buy, not buy into, reject

ADJS 4 **incredulous,** uncredulous, hard of belief, shy of belief, disposed to doubt, indisposed to believe, disinclined to believe, unwilling to accept; impervious to persuasion, inconvincible, unconvincible, unpersuadable, unpersuasible; suspicious, suspecting, wary, leery, cautious, guarded; skeptical

5 **ungullible,** uncullible, undupable, undeceivable, unfoolable, undeludable, unhoaxable, unseduceable, hoaxproof; sophisticated, wise, hardheaded, practical, realistic, tough-minded; nobody's fool, not born yesterday, nobody's sucker, nobody's patsy

957 EVIDENCE, PROOF

<something showing existence or truth>

NOUNS 1 **evidence, proof;** reason to believe, reason, grounds for belief; ground, **grounds,** material grounds, facts, data, information, record, premises, basis for belief; piece of evidence, item of evidence, fact, datum, relevant fact; indication, manifestation, sign, symptom, mark, token, mute witness; body of evidence, documentation; muniments, title deeds and papers; chain of evidence; clue; exhibit; intelligence; lowdown

2 **testimony,** attestation, attest, **witness;** testimonial, testimonium; statement, declaration, assertion, asseveration, affirmation, avouchment, avowal, averment, allegation, admission, disclosure, profession, word; confession; deposition, legal evidence, sworn evidence, sworn testimony; compurgation; affidavit, sworn statement; instrument in proof

3 **proof,** demonstration, ironclad proof, incontrovertible proof, proof positive, conclusive proof; determination, establishment, settlement; **conclusive evidence,** indisputable evidence, incontrovertible evidence, damning evidence, unmistakable sign, sure sign, absolute indication, smoking gun; open-and-shut case; burden of proof, onus; the proof of the pudding

4 **confirmation, substantiation,** proof, proving, proving out, bearing out, affirmation, attestation, authentication, validation, certification, ratification, verification; corroboration, support, supporting evidence, corroboratory evidence, fortification, buttressing, bolstering, backing, backing up, reinforcement, undergirding,

strengthening, circumstantiation, fact sheet; documentation; proof of purchase

5 **citation,** cite, reference, quotation; exemplification, instance, example, case, case in point, particular, item, illustration, demonstration; cross-reference

6 **witness, eyewitness,** spectator, earwitness; bystander, passerby; deponent, testifier, attestant, attester, attestator, voucher, swearer; informant, informer; character witness; cojuror, compurgator

7 **provability, demonstrability,** determinability; confirmability, supportability, verifiability

VERBS 8 **evidence,** evince, furnish evidence, show, go to show, mean, tend to show, witness to, testify to; **demonstrate,** illustrate, exhibit, manifest, display, express, set forth; approve; attest; indicate, signify, signalize, symptomatize, mark, denote, betoken, point to, give indication of, show signs of, bear on, touch on; connote, imply, suggest, involve; argue, breathe, tell, bespeak; speak for itself, speak volumes

9 **testify, attest,** give evidence, witness, witness to, bear witness; disclose; vouch, state one's case, depose, depone, warrant, swear, take one's oath, acknowledge, avow, affirm, avouch, aver, allege, asseverate, certify, give one's word; turn state's evidence, rat, squeal, sing; grass

10 **prove, demonstrate,** show, afford proof of, prove to be, prove true; establish, fix, determine, ascertain, make out, remove all doubt; settle, settle the matter; set at rest; clinch, cinch, nail down; prove one's point, make one's case, bring home to, make good, have a case; hold good, hold water; follow, follow from, follow as a matter of course

11 **confirm,** affirm, attest, warrant, uphold, **substantiate**, authenticate, validate, certify, ratify, verify; circumstantiate, corroborate, bear out, support, buttress, sustain, fortify, bolster, back, back up, reinforce, undergird, strengthen; document; probate, prove; double-check

12 **adduce,** produce, advance, present, bring to bear, offer, **proffer**, invoke, obtest, allege, plead, bring forward, bring on; rally, marshal, deploy, array; call to witness, call to the witness box, put in the witness box

13 **cite,** name, call to mind; instance, cite a particular, cite particulars, cite cases, cite a case in point, itemize, particularize, produce an instance, give a for-instance; exemplify, example, illustrate, demonstrate; document; **quote,** quote chapter and verse

14 **refer to,** direct attention to, appeal to, invoke; make reference to; cross-refer, make a cross-reference; reference, cross-reference

15 **have evidence, have proof,** have a case, possess incriminating evidence, have something on; have the goods on, have dead to rights, have bang to rights

ADJS 16 **evidential,** evidentiary, **factual,** symptomatic, significant, relevant, indicative, attestative, attestive, probative; founded on, grounded on, based on; implicit, suggestive; material, telling, convincing, weighty; overwhelming, damning; conclusive, determinative, decisive, final, incontrovertible, irresistible, indisputable, irrefutable, sure, certain, absolute; documented, documentary; valid, admissible; adducible; firsthand, authentic, reliable, empirical, eyewitness; hearsay, circumstantial, presumptive, nuncupative, cumulative, ex parte

17 **demonstrative,** demonstrating, demonstrational, telltale; evincive, apodictic

18 **confirming,** confirmatory, confirmative, certificatory; substantiating, verifying, verificative; **corroborating,** corroboratory, **corroborative,** supportive, **supporting**

19 **provable,** demonstrable, demonstratable, apodictic, evincible, attestable, confirmable, checkable, substantiatable, establishable, supportable, sustainable, verifiable, validatable, authenticatable

20 **proved,** proven, demonstrated, shown; established, fixed, settled, determined, nailed down, ascertained; evident, self-evident; confirmed, substantiated, attested, authenticated, certified, validated, verified; circumstantiated, corroborated, borne out; cross-checked, double-checked; collated; ostensible

21 **unrefuted,** unconfuted, unanswered, **uncontroverted**, uncontradicted, undenied; unrefutable

ADVS 22 **evidentially,** according to the evidence, on the evidence, as attested by, judging by; in confirmation, in corroboration of, in support of; at first hand, at second hand; dead to rights, bang to rights, with a smoking gun, with one's pants down

23 to illustrate, to prove the point, as an example, as a case in point, to name an instance, by way of example, **for example, for instance,** to cite an instance, as an instance; e.g., *exempli gratia* <L>; as, thus

24 which see, q.v., *quod vide* <L>; *loco citato* <L>, loc cit; *opere citato* <L>, op cit

PHRS 25 it is proven, there is nothing more to be said, it must follow; *quod erat demonstrandum* <L>, QED

958 DISPROOF

<evidence of falsity>

NOUNS 1 **disproof,** disproving, disproval, **invalidation,** disconfirmation, explosion, negation, redargution; exposure, exposé; circumstantial evidence, hearsay evidence, inadmissible evidence, incriminating evidence

2 **refutation, confutation,** confounding, refutal, rebuttal, answer, complete answer, crushing rejoinder, effective rejoinder, squelch, comeback; discrediting; overthrow, overthrowal, upset, upsetting, subversion, undermining, demolition; renunciation; contention; contradiction, controversion, denial

3 conclusive argument, elenchus, knockdown argument, floorer, sockdolager; **clincher,** crusher, settler, finisher, squelcher

VERBS 4 **disprove, invalidate,** disconfirm, discredit, prove the contrary, belie, give the lie to, redargue; **negate,** negative; expose, show up; explode, blow up, blow sky-high, puncture, deflate, shoot full of holes, poke full of holes, cut to pieces, cut the ground from under; knock the bottom out of, knock the props out from under, knock the chocks out from under, knock down, take the ground from under, undercut, cut the ground from under one's feet, not leave a leg to stand on, have the last word, leave nothing to say, put to rest, lay to rest

5 **refute, confute,** confound, rebut, parry, answer, answer conclusively, dismiss, dispose of; overthrow, overturn, overwhelm, upset, subvert, defeat, demolish, undermine; argue down, argue into a corner; show what's what; floor, finish, settle, squash, squelch, crush, smash all opposition; silence, reduce to silence, shut up, stop the mouth of; nonplus, take the wind out of one's sails; contradict, controvert, counter, run counter, deny

ADJS 6 **refuting, confuting,** confounding, confutative, refutative, refutatory, discomfirmatory; contradictory, contrary

7 **disproved,** disconfirmed, **invalidated,** negated, negatived, discredited, belied; exposed, shown up; punctured, deflated, exploded; refuted, confuted, confounded; upset, overthrown, overturned; contradicted, disputed, denied, impugned; dismissed, discarded, rejected

8 **unproved,** not proved, unproven, undemonstrated, unshown, not shown; untried, untested; unestablished, unfixed, unsettled, undetermined, unascertained; unconfirmed, unsubstantiated, unattested, unauthenticated, unvalidated, uncertified, unverified; uncorroborated, unsustained, unsupported, unsupported by evidence, groundless, without grounds, without basis, unfounded; inconclusive, indecisive; moot, sub judice; not following

9 **unprovable,** controvertible, undemonstrable, undemonstratable, unattestable, unsubstantiatable, unsupportable, unconfirmable, unsustainable, unverifiable

10 **refutable,** confutable, disprovable, defeasible

959 QUALIFICATION

<fitting quality or skill>

NOUNS 1 **qualification, limitation,** limiting, restriction, circumscription, modification, hedge, hedging; setting conditions, conditionality, provisionality, circumstantiality; specification; allowance, concession, cession, grant; grain of salt; reservation, exception, waiver, exemption; exclusion, ruling out, including out; specialness, special circumstance, special case, special treatment; mental reservation, salvo, *arrière-pensée* <Fr>, crossing one's fingers; extenuating circumstances

2 **condition,** provision, proviso, **stipulation,** whereas; definition; frame of reference; specification, parameter, given, *donnée* <Fr>, limitation, limiting condition, boundary condition, age limit; contingency, circumstance; catch, joker, kicker, string, a string to it; requisite, prerequisite, obligation; *sine qua non* <L>; clause, escape clause, escapeway, escape hatch, saving clause; escalator clause; terms, provisions; grounds; small print, fine print, fine print at the bottom; ultimatum

VERBS 3 **qualify, limit,** condition, hedge, hedge about, modify, restrict, restrain, circumscribe, delimit, set limits, set conditions, box in, narrow, set criteria; adjust to, regulate by; alter; temper, season, leaven, soften, modulate, moderate, assuage, mitigate, palliate, abate, reduce, diminish

4 **make conditional,** make contingent, condition; make it a condition, attach a condition, attach a proviso, **stipulate;** insist upon, make a point of; have a catch, have a kicker, have a joker in the deck, have a string attached; cross one's fingers behind one's back

5 **allow for,** make allowance for, make room for, provide for, open the door to, take account of, **take into account, take into consideration,** consider, consider the circumstances; allow, grant, concede, admit, admit exceptions, see the special circumstances; relax, relax the condition, waive, set aside, ease, lift temporarily, pull

one's punches; disregard, discount, leave out of account; consider the source, take with a grain of salt

6 **depend,** hang, rest, **hinge**; depend on, hang on, rest on, rest with, repose upon, lie on, lie with, stand on, be based on, be bounded by, be limited by, be dependent on, be predicated on, be contingent on, be conditional on; hinge on, turn on, revolve upon, have as a fulcrum

ADJS 7 **qualifying,** qualificative, qualificatory, modifying, modificatory, altering; **limiting,** limitational, restricting, limitative, restrictive, bounding; circumstantial, contingent; extenuating, extenuatory, mitigating, mitigative, mitigatory, modulatory, palliative, assuasive, lenitive, softening

8 **conditional, provisional,** provisory, stipulatory; parametric; specificative; specified, stipulated, defined, fixed, stated, given; temporary, expedient

9 **contingent, dependent,** depending; contingent on, dependent on, depending on, predicated on, based on, hanging on, hinging on, turning on, revolving on; depending on circumstances; circumscribed by, hedged by, hedged about by; boxed in; subject to, incidental to, incident to

10 **qualified,** modified, conditioned, **limited, restricted,** delimited, hedged, hedged about; tempered, seasoned, leavened, palliative, softened, moderated, mitigated, modulated

ADVS 11 **conditionally,** provisionally, with qualifications, with a string attached, with a catch to it; with a reservation, with an exception, with a grain of salt; temporarily, for the time being

CONJS 12 provided, provided that, provided always, providing, with this proviso, it being provided; **on condition,** on condition that, **with the stipulation,** with the understanding, according as, subject to

13 **granting, admitting,** allowing, admitting that, allowing that, copping to, seeing that; exempting, waiving

14 if, an, an', if and when, only if, if only, if and only if, if it be so, if it be true that, if it so happens, if it so turns out

15 so, just so, so that, so as, so long as, as long as

16 unless, unless that, if not, were it not, were it not that; except, excepting, except that, with the exception that, save, but; without, absent

960 NO QUALIFICATIONS

<lack of quality or skill>

NOUNS 1 **unqualifiedness,** unlimitedness, unconditionality, unrestrictedness, unreservedness, uncircumscribedness; categoricalness; absoluteness, definiteness, explicitness; decisiveness

ADJS 2 **unqualified, unconditional,** unconditioned, unrestricted, unhampered, unlimited, uncircumscribed, unmitigated, categorical, straight, unreserved, without reserve; unaltered, unadulterated, intact; implicit, unquestioning, undoubting, unhesitating; explicit, express, unequivocal, clear, unmistakable; peremptory, indisputable, inappealable; without exception, admitting no exception, unwaivable; positive, absolute, flat, definite, definitive, determinate, decided, decisive, fixed, final, conclusive; complete, entire, whole, total, global; utter, perfect, downright, outright, out-and-out, straight-out, all-out, flat-out

ADVS 3 <nonformal> **no ifs, ands, or buts; no strings attached,** no holds barred, no catch, no kicker, no joker in the deck, no small print, no fine print, no fine print at the bottom; downright, that's that, what you see is what you get

961 FORESIGHT

<ability to see what might happen>

NOUNS 1 **foresight,** foreseeing, looking ahead, prevision, divination, forecast; prediction; foreglimpse, foreglance, foregleam; preview, prepublication; prospect, prospection; anticipation, contemplation, envisionment, envisagement; **foresightedness;** farsightedness, longsightedness, farseeingness; sagacity, providence, discretion, preparation, provision, forehandedness, readiness, consideration, prudence

2 **forethought, premeditation,** predeliberation, preconsideration; caution; lead time, advance notice; run-up; plan, long-range plan, contingency plan; prospectus

3 **foreknowledge,** foreknowing, forewisdom, **precognition,** prescience, presage, presentiment, foreboding; clairvoyance; foreseeability; insight; premonition, expectation

4 **foretaste,** antepast, prelibation

VERBS 5 **foresee,** see beforehand, see ahead, foreglimpse, foretaste, anticipate, contemplate, envision, envisage, look forward to, look ahead, look beyond, look into the future, peep into the future; predict; think ahead, think beforehand; have an eye to the future

6 **foreknow,** know beforehand, precognize, know in advance, have prior knowledge; smell in the wind, scent from afar; have a presentiment, have a premonition; see the handwriting on the wall, have a hunch, feel in one's bones, just know, intuit

ADJS 7 **foreseeing,** foresighted; foreknowing, precognizant, precognitive, prescient; divinatory; forethoughted, forethoughtful; anticipant, anticipatory, expectant; **farseeing,** farsighted, longsighted; sagacious, provident, providential, forehanded, prepared, ready, prudent; intuitive; clairvoyant, telepathic

8 **foreseeable**; foreseen; predictable; intuitable

ADVS 9 foreseeingly, foreknowingly, with foresight; against the time when, for a rainy day

962 PREDICTION

<statement about what might happen>

NOUNS 1 **prediction,** foretelling, foreshowing, forecasting, prognosis, prognostication, presage, presaging; **prophecy,** prophesying, vaticination; soothsaying, soothsay; prefiguration, prefigurement, prefiguring; preshowing, presignifying, presigning; forecast, promise; apocalypse; prospectus; foresight; presentiment, foreboding; omen; guesswork, speculation, guestimation, hunch, feeling; probability, statistical prediction, actuarial prediction; improbability

2 **divination**, divining; augury, haruspication, haruspicy, pythonism, mantic, mantology; **fortunetelling** <see list>, crystal gazing, palm-reading, palmistry, tea-leaf reading, Tarot reading, I Ching; crystal ball; horoscopy, astrology; sorcery; clairvoyance, telepathy

3 **crystal ball**, Tarot cards; dowsing, witching, water witching; divining rod, divining stick, wand, witch stick, witching stick, dowsing rod, doodlebug; water diviner, dowser, water witch, water witcher; hydromancy

4 **predictor,** foreteller, prognosticator, seer, foreseer, forecaster, foreknower, presager, prefigurer; prophet, prophesier, soothsayer; diviner, divinator; augur; psychic; clairvoyant; prophetess, seeress, divineress, pythoness; Druid; **fortuneteller;** crystal gazer; palmist, palm reader; geomancer; haruspex, aruspex, astrologer; weather prophet; prophet of doom, calamity howler, Cassandra; religious prophets; speculator

5 <nonformal> dopester, tipster, tout, touter

6 **sibyl;** Pythia, Pythian, Delphic sibyl; Babylonian sibyl, Persian sibyl, Cimmerian sibyl, Cumaean sibyl, Erythraean sibyl, Hellespontine sibyl, Trojan sibyl, Libyan sibyl, Phrygian sibyl, Samian sibyl, Tiburtine sibyl

7 **oracle;** Delphic oracle, Delphian oracle, Python, Pythian oracle; Delphic tripod, tripod of the Pythia; Dodona, oracle of Dodona; sage

8 **predictability,** divinability, foretellableness, calculability, foreseeability, foreknowableness

VERBS 9 **predict,** make a prediction, **foretell,** soothsay, prefigure, forecast, prophesy, prognosticate, call, make a prophecy, make a prognosis, vaticinate, forebode, presage, see ahead, see the future, tell the future, read the future, see in the crystal ball; foresee; dope, dope out; call the turn, call one's shot; divine; dowse for water; tell fortunes, fortune-tell, cast one's fortune; read one's hand, read palms, read tea leaves, cast a horoscope; guess, speculate, guesstimate, make an educated guess; bet, bet on, gamble

10 **portend,** foretoken, foreshow, foreshadow

ADJS 11 **predictive,** predictory, predictional; **foretelling,** forewarning, forecasting; prefiguring, prefigurative, presignifying, presignificative; **prophetic,** prophetical, fatidic, fatidical, apocalyptic, apocalyptical; vatic, vaticinatory, vaticinal, mantic, sibyllic, sibylline; divinatory, oracular, auguring, augural; haruspical; foreseeing; presageful, presaging; prognostic, prognosticative, prognosticatory; fortunetelling; weather-wise

12 **ominous,** premonitory, foreboding, unfavorable, adverse

13 **predictable,** divinable, foretellable, calculable, anticipatable; foreseeable, foreknowable, precognizable; probable; improbable

14 **predicted,** prophesied, presaged, foretold, forecast, foreshown; foreseen, foreglimpsed, foreknown

15 **fortunetelling (methods)**

aptitude test
astrology <horoscopes, Zodiac>
belomancy
cartomancy
Chinese astrology
chirography
chirology
chiromancy
clairvoyance
crystal ball gazing
divination sticks
dream interpretation
face reading
fortune cookie
geloscopy
graphology, graptomancy <handwriting>
gyromancy
I Ching, I-Ching
ichthyomancy
intelligence quotient test, IQ test
knissomancy
lecanomancy
lithomancy
Magic 8-Ball <tm>
mantology
metopomancy
myomancy
necromancy
numerology
ololygmancy
oracle consultation
palmistry, palm reading
pegomancy
personality test
phrenology
retromancy
runes
séance
soothsaying
stercomancy
stone-casting
Tarot card reading
tea-leaf reading
xenomancy

963 NECESSITY

<something necessary>

NOUNS 1 **necessity,** necessariness, necessitude, necessitation, entailment; mandatoriness, mandatedness, obligatoriness, obligation, obligement; compulsoriness, compulsion, duress

2 **requirement,** requisite, requisition; **necessity, need,** want, occasion; need for, call for, demand, demand for; desideratum, desideration; prerequisite, prerequirement; must, must item; sine qua non; essential, indispensable, must-have; the necessary, the needful; necessities, necessaries, essentials, bare necessities, fundamentals

3 **needfulness,** requisiteness; essentiality, essentialness, vitalness; indispensability, indispensableness; irreplaceability; irreducibleness, irreducibility

4 **urgent need,** dire necessity; exigency, exigence, urgency, imperative, imperativeness, immediacy, pressingness, pressure; matter of necessity, case of need, case of emergency, **matter of life and death;** predicament

5 involuntariness, unwilledness, instinctiveness; compulsiveness; reflex action, Pavlovian reaction, conditioning, automatism; echolalia, echopraxia; automatic writing; **instinct,** impulse; blind impulse, blind instinct, knee-jerk reaction, sheer chemistry

6 **choicelessness,** no choice, no alternative, lack of choice, Hobson's choice, only choice, zero option, coercion; Catch-22; that or nothing; not a pin to choose, six of one and half a dozen of the other, distinction without a difference; indiscrimination

7 **inevitability,** inevitableness, unavoidableness, **necessity**, inescapableness, inevasibleness, unpreventability, undeflectability, ineluctability; irrevocability, indefeasibility; uncontrollability; relentlessness, inexorability, unyieldingness, inflexibility; fatedness, fatefulness, certainty, sureness; *force majeure* <Fr>, vis major, act of God, inevitable accident, unavoidable casualty; predetermination; God's will, will of Allah; doom, karma, one's lot, fate

VERBS 8 **necessitate,** oblige, dictate, constrain; coerce, impel, force, mandate; insist upon, compel

9 **require, need,** want, lack, must have, feel the want of, have occasion for, be in need of, be hurting for, stand in need of, not be able to dispense with, not be able to do without; **call for,** cry for, cry out for, clamor for; demand, ask, claim, exact; prerequire; need doing, want doing, take doing, be indicated

10 **be necessary,** lie under a necessity, be one's fate; be a must; can't be avoided, can't be helped; be under the necessity of, be in for; be obliged, must, needs must, have to, have got to, should, need, need to, have need to; not able to keep from, not able to help, cannot help but, cannot do otherwise; be forced, be driven

11 **have no choice**, have **no alternative,** have one's options reduced, have no option but, cannot choose but, be robbed of choice; be pushed to the wall, be driven into a corner; take it or leave it, like it or lump it, have that or nothing

ADJS 12 **necessary, obligatory,** compulsory, entailed, mandatory, fundamental; exigent, urgent, necessitous, importunate, imperative; choiceless, without choice, out of one's hands, out of one's control

13 **requisite, needful,** required, needed, necessary, wanted, called for, indicated, imperative; essential, vital, indispensable, unforgoable, irreplaceable; irreducible, irreductible; prerequisite

14 **involuntary, instinctive,** automatic, mechanical, reflex, reflexive, knee-jerk, autonomic, conditioned; unconscious, unthinking, blind; unwitting, unintentional, independent of one's will, unwilling, unwilled, against one's will, collateral; compulsory, compulsive; forced; impulsive

15 **inevitable, unavoidable,** ipso facto; necessary, inescapable, inevasible, unpreventable, undeflectable, ineluctable, irrevocable, indefeasible; uncontrollable, unstoppable; relentless, inexorable, unyielding, inflexible; irresistible, resistless; certain, fateful, sure, sure as fate, sure as death, sure as death and taxes; preordained, predestined, destined, fated; necessitarian, deterministic

ADVS 16 **necessarily,** needfully, requisitely; of necessity, from necessity, need, needs, perforce; without choice; willy-nilly, willing, unwilling, whether one will or not, whether or not, even though; come what may; compulsorily

17 if necessary, if need be, if worst comes to worst; for lack of something better

18 **involuntarily,** instinctively, automatically, mechanically, by reflex, reflexively; blindly, unconsciously, unthinkingly, without premeditation; unwittingly, unintentionally; compulsively; unwillingly

19 **inevitably,** unavoidably, necessarily, inescapably, come hell or high water, inevasibly, unpreventably, ineluctably; irrevocably, indefeasibly; uncontrollably; relentlessly,

inexorably, unyieldingly, inflexibly; fatefully, certainly, surely

PHRS **20** it is necessary, it must be, if need be, it needs must be, it must needs be, it will be, there's no two ways about it, it must have its way; it cannot be helped, there is no helping it, there is no help for it, that's the way the cookie crumbles, that's the way the ball bounces, what will be will be, it's God's will; the die is cast; it is fated

964 PREDETERMINATION

<determining in advance what will happen>

NOUNS **1** **predetermination,** predestination, foredestiny, **preordination,** foreordination, foreordainment; decree; foregone conclusion, par for the course, preconceived notion, preconceived opinion; necessity; foreknowledge, prescience

2 **fate,** fatality, **fortune,** lot, cup, portion, appointed lot, karma, kismet, weird, future; destiny, destination, end, final lot; doom, foredoom, God's will, will of Heaven; inevitability; the handwriting on the wall; book of fate; Fortune's wheel, wheel of fortune, wheel of chance; astral influences, stars, planets, constellation, astrology; unlucky day, Ides of March, Friday, Friday the thirteenth

3 **Fates,** Parcae, Clotho, Lachesis, Atropos; Nona, Decuma, Morta; Weird Sisters, Weirds; Norns; Urdur, Verthandi, Skuld; Fortuna, Lady Fortune, Dame Fortune; Providence, Heaven

4 **determinism, fatalism,** necessitarianism, necessarianism, predeterminism; predestinarianism, Calvinism, election

5 **determinist, fatalist,** necessitarian, necessarian; predestinationist, predestinarian, Calvinist

VERBS **6** **predetermine,** predecide, preestablish, preset; **predestine,** predestinate, **preordain,** foreordain; agree beforehand, preconcert

7 **destine, predestine,** necessitate, destinate, **ordain,** fate, mark, appoint, decree, intend; come with the territory; have in store for; **doom,** foredoom

ADJS **8** **determined,** predetermined, predecided, preestablished, **predestined,** predestinate, **preordained,** foreordained; foregone; open-and-shut; arranged

9 **destined, fated,** fateful, ordained, written, in the cards, marked, appointed, in store, cut-and-dried; doomed, foredoomed, devoted; untreatable; inevitable

10 deterministic, fatalistic, necessitarian, necessarian

PHRS **11** it is fated, it is written, it's in the cards; what will be will be, *che sarà sarà* <Ital>, *que será será* <Sp>; *c'est la vie, c'est la guerre* <Fr>

965 PREARRANGEMENT

<something arranged in advance>

NOUNS **1** **prearrangement,** preordering, preconcertedness; premeditation, plotting, planning, scheming; directed verdict; **reservation,** booking; overbooking

2 <nonformal> put-up job, packed jury, rigged game, rigged jury, packed deal, stacked deck, cold deck, boat race, tank job; frame-up, frame, setup

3 **schedule,** program, programma, bill, card, calendar, docket, slate; playbill; batting order, lineup, roster, rota; blueprint, budget; prospectus; schedule of operation, program of operation, order of the day, things to be done, **agenda,** list of agenda; protocol; laundry list, wish list; bill of fare, menu, *carte du jour* <Fr>

VERBS **4** **prearrange,** precontrive, predesign, preorder, preconcert; premeditate, plot, plan, scheme; **reserve,** book, overbook

5 <nonformal> fix, rig, pack, cook, cook up; **stack the deck,** stack the cards, cold-deck, pack the deal; put in the bag, sew up; frame, frame-up, set up; throw, tank, go in the tank, hold a boat race

6 **schedule,** line up, **slate, book,** book in, bill, program, calendar, docket, budget, put on the agenda

ADJS **7** **prearranged,** precontrived, predesigned, preordered, preconcerted, cut out; premeditated, plotted, planned, schemed; cut-and-dried, cut-and-dry

8 <nonformal> fixed, rigged, put-up, packed, stacked, cooked, cooked-up; in the bag, on ice, iced, cinched, sewed up; framed, framed-up, set-up

9 **scheduled,** slated, booked, billed, booked-in, to come

966 POSSIBILITY

<chance something might happen or be true>

NOUNS **1** **possibility,** possibleness, **the realm of possibility,** the domain of the possible, conceivableness, conceivability, thinkability, thinkableness, imaginability; probability, likelihood; what may be, what might be, what is possible, what one can do, what can be done, the possible, the attainable, the feasible; potential, potentiality, virtuality; contingency, eventuality; chance, prospect, odds; outside chance, off chance, remote possibility, ghost of a chance; hope, outside hope, small hope, slim odds; good possibility, good chance, safe bet, even chance; bare possibility, **24/7, 24/7/365**

2 **practicability,** practicality, **feasibility;** workability, operability, actability, performability, realizability, negotiability; viability, viableness; achievability, doability, compassability, attainability; surmountability, superability; realm of possibility

3 **accessibility,** access, approachability, openness, reachableness, come-at-ableness, get-at-ableness; penetrability, perviousness; obtainability, obtainableness, availability, donability, procurability, procurableness, securableness, getableness, acquirability; remote access

VERBS 4 **be possible,** could be, might be, have a chance, have a good chance, stand a chance, stand a good chance, bid fair to

5 **make possible, enable,** permit, permit of, clear the road for, clear the path for, smooth the way for, open the way for, open the door to, open up the possibility of, give a chance to

ADJS 6 **possible,** within the realm of possibility, within the range of possibility, in one's power, in one's hands, humanly possible; probable, likely; conceivable, conceivably possible, imaginable, thinkable, cogitable; plausible; potential, virtual; contingent; able, apt

7 **practicable,** practical, **feasible;** workable, actable, performable, effectible, realizable, compassable, operable, negotiable, doable, swingable, bridgeable; viable; achievable, attainable; surmountable, superable, overcomable

8 **accessible,** approachable, come-at-able, get-at-able, reachable, within reach; open, open to; penetrable, get-in-able, pervious; obtainable, attainable, available, procurable, securable, findable, easy to come by, getable, to be had, donable

ADVS 9 **possibly, conceivably,** imaginably, feasibly; within the realm of possibility; perhaps, perchance, haply; maybe, it may be, for all one knows

10 by any possibility, by any chance, by any means, by any manner of means; in any way, in any possible way, at any cost, at all, if at all, ever; on the bare possibility, on the off chance, by merest chance

11 if possible, if humanly possible, God willing, wind and weather permitting, Lord willing and the creek don't rise

967 IMPOSSIBILITY

<no change of happening or being true>

NOUNS 1 **impossibility,** impossibleness, the realm of the impossible, the domain of the impossible, **inconceivability,** unthinkability, unimaginability, what cannot be, what can never be, what cannot happen, hopelessness, Chinaman's chance, a snowball's chance in hell, no way in hell, no chance; self-contradiction, unreality, absurdity, paradox, oxymoron, logical impossibility; impossible, the impossible, impossibilism; no-no

2 **impracticability,** unpracticability, impracticality, unfeasibility; unworkability, inoperability, unperformability; unachievability, unattainability; unrealizability, uncompassability; insurmountability, insuperability

3 **inaccessibility,** unaccessibility; unapproachability, un-come-at-ableness, unreachableness; impenetrability, imperviousness; unobtainability, unobtainableness, unattainability, unavailability, unprocurableness, unsecurableness, ungettableness, unacquirability; undiscoverability, unascertainableness

VERBS 4 **be impossible,** be an impossibility, **not have a chance,** be a waste of time; contradict itself, be a logical impossibility, be a paradox; fly in the face of reason

5 **attempt the impossible,** try for a miracle, look for a needle in a haystack, try to be in two places at once, try to fetch water in a sieve, try to catch the wind in a net, try to weave a rope of sand, try to get figs from thistles, try to gather grapes from thorns, try to make bricks from straw, try to make cheese of chalk, try to make a silk purse out of a sow's ear, try to change the leopard's spots, try to get blood from a turnip; ask the impossible, cry for the moon; turn back time; walk on water

6 **make impossible,** rule out, disenable, disqualify, close out, bar, prohibit, put out of reach, leave no chance, make things difficult

ADJS 7 **impossible, not possible,** beyond the bounds of possibility, beyond the bounds of reason, contrary to reason, at variance with the facts; **inconceivable,** unimaginable, unthinkable, not to be thought of, out of the question; hopeless; absurd, ridiculous, preposterous; self-contradictory, paradoxical, oxymoronic, logically impossible; ruled-out, excluded, closed-out, barred, prohibited, forbidden; self-defeating

8 **impracticable,** impractical, unpragmatic, **unfeasible;** airy-fairy; unworkable, unviable, unperformable, inoperable, undoable, unnegotiable, unbridgeable; unachievable, unattainable, uneffectible; unrealizable, uncompassable; insurmountable, unsurmountable, insuperable, unovercomable; beyond one, beyond one's power, beyond one's control, out of one's depth, too much for

9 **inaccessible,** unaccessible; unapproachable, un-come-at-able; unreachable, beyond reach, out of reach; impenetrable, impervious; closed to, denied to, lost to, closed forever to; unobtainable, unattainable, unavailable, unprocurable,

unsecurable, ungettable, unacquirable; not to be had, not to be had for love or money; undiscoverable, unascertainable; back-ordered

ADVS **10 impossibly,** inconceivably, unimaginably, unthinkably; not at any price

PHRS **11** no can do, no way, no way José, yeah right

968 PROBABILITY

<chance that something will happen>

NOUNS **1 probability, likelihood,** likeliness, liability, aptitude, verisimilitude; **chance, odds;** expectation, outlook, prospect; favorable prospect, well-grounded hope, some hope, reasonable hope, fair expectation; good chance; presumption, presumptive evidence; tendency; probable cause, reasonable ground, reasonable presumption; leaning; probabilism; possibility

2 mathematical probability, statistical probability, statistics, predictability; probability theory, game theory, theory of games; operations research; probable error, standard deviation; stochastic independence, statistical independence, stochastic variable; probability curve, frequency curve, frequency polygon, frequency distribution, probability function, probability density function, probability distribution, cumulative distribution function; statistical mechanics, quantum mechanics, uncertainty principle, indeterminancy principle, Maxwell-Boltzmann distribution law, Bose-Einstein statistics, Fermi-Dirac statistics; mortality table, actuarial table, life table, combined experience table, Commissioners Standard Ordinary table; blip, hiccup

3 plausibility; reasonability; credibility; verisimilitude

VERBS **4 be probable, seem likely,** could be, offer a good prospect, offer the expectation, have a good chance, run a good chance, be in the running, come as no surprise; promise, be promising, make fair promise, bid fair to, stand fair to, show a tendency, be in the cards, have the makings of, have favorable odds, lead one to expect; make probable, probabilize, make more likely, smooth the way for; increase the chances

5 think likely, daresay, venture to say; anticipate; presume, suppose

ADJS **6 probable, likely,** liable, apt, verisimilar, in the cards, odds-on; promising, hopeful, fair, in a fair way; foreseeable, predictable; presumable, presumptive; statistical, actuarial; mathematically probable, statistically probable, predictable within limits; prone

7 plausible, colorable, apparent; reasonable; credible; conceivable

ADVS **8 probably,** in all probability, **in all likelihood,** likely, most likely, very likely; as likely as not, very like, like enough, like as not; doubtlessly, doubtless, no doubt, indubitably; presumably, presumptively; by all odds, ten to one, a hundred to one, dollars to doughnuts

PHRS **9** there is reason to believe, I am led to believe, it can be supposed, it would appear, it stands to reason, it might be thought, one can assume, appearances are in favor of, the chances are, the odds are, you can bank on it, you can make book on it, you can bet on it, you can bet your bottom dollar, you can just bet, you can't go wrong; I daresay, I venture to say

969 IMPROBABILITY

<unlikelihood that something will happen>

NOUNS **1 improbability, unlikelihood,** unlikeliness; doubtfulness, dubiousness, questionableness; implausibility, incredibility; little expectation, low order of probability, poor possibility, bare possibility, faint likelihood, poor prospect, poor outlook, a ghost of a chance, fat chance, chance in a million; long shot; small chance; Hollywood ending

VERBS **2 be improbable,** not be likely, be a stretch of the imagination, strain one's credulity, go beyond reason, go beyond belief, go far afield, go beyond the bounds of reason, be far-fetched, be fetched from afar, be a long shot

ADJS **3 improbable, unlikely,** unpromising, hardly possible, logic-defying, scarcely to be expected, scarcely to be anticipated; statistically improbable; doubtful, dubious, questionable, doubtable, dubitable, more than doubtful; far-fetched, implausible, incredible; unlooked-for, unexpected, unpredictable; back-ordered

PHRS **4** not likely, no fear, never fear, I ask you, you should live so long, don't hold your breath, don't bet on it, don't make book on it

970 CERTAINTY

<something that will definitely happen>

NOUNS **1 certainty, certitude,** certainness, sureness, surety, assurance, assuredness, certain knowledge; positiveness, absoluteness, definiteness, dead certainty, moral certainty, absolute certainty; unequivocalness, unmistakableness, unambiguity, nonambiguity, univocity, univocality; infallibility, infallibilism, inerrability, inerrancy; necessity, determinacy, determinateness, noncontingency, Hobson's choice, ineluctability, predetermination, predestination, inevitability; truth; proved fact, probatum

2 <nonformal> **sure thing,** dead certainty, dead cert, dead-sure thing, sure bet, sure card, aces wired, cinch, lead-pipe cinch, dead cinch, lock, mortal lock, shoo-in, open-and-shut case; rain check

3 **unquestionability,** undeniability, indubitability, indubitableness, indisputability, incontestability, incontrovertibility, irrefutability, unrefutability, unconfutability, irrefragability, unimpeachability; doubtlessness, questionlessness; demonstrability, provability, verifiability, confirmability; factuality, reality, actuality

4 **reliability, dependability,** dependableness, validity, trustworthiness, faithworthiness; unerringness; predictability, calculability; stability, substantiality, firmness, soundness, solidity, staunchness, steadiness, steadfastness; secureness, security; invincibility; authoritativeness, authenticity

5 **confidence,** confidentness, conviction, belief, fixed belief, settled belief, **sureness,** assurance, assuredness, surety, security, **certitude**; faith, subjective certainty; trust; positiveness, cocksureness; self-confidence, self-assurance, self-reliance; poise; courage; overconfidence, oversureness, overweening, overweeningness, hubris; pride, arrogance, pomposity, self-importance

6 **dogmatism,** dogmaticalness, pontification, positiveness, positivism, peremptoriness, opinionatedness, self-opinionatedness; bigotry; infallibilism

7 **dogmatist,** dogmatizer, opinionist, doctrinaire, bigot; positivist; infallibilist

8 **ensuring,** assurance; reassurance, reassurement; **certification;** ascertainment, determination, establishment; verification, corroboration, substantiation, validation, collation, check, cross-check, double-check, checking; independent witness, objective witness; confirmation

VERBS 9 **be certain**, be confident, feel sure, rest assured, have sewed up, have no doubt, doubt not; know, just know, know for certain; bet on, gamble on, bet one's bottom dollar on, bet the ranch on; admit of no doubt; go without saying, be axiomatic, be apodictic, bet one's life

10 **dogmatize,** lay down the law, pontificate, oracle, oraculate, proclaim, assert oneself

11 make sure, **make certain,** make sure of, make no doubt, make no mistake; remove all doubt, dismiss all doubt, erase all doubt; assure, ensure, insure, certify; ascertain, get a fix on, get a lock on; find out, get at, see to it, see that; determine, decide, establish, settle, fix, lock in, nail down, clinch, cinch, pin down, clear up, sort out, set at rest; assure onself, satisfy oneself; reassure

12 **verify, confirm,** test, prove, audit, collate, validate, check, check up, check on, check over, check through, double-check, triple-check, cross-check, recheck, check and doublecheck, check up and down, check over and through, check in and out, measure twice cut once

ADJS 13 **certain, sure,** sure-enough; well-founded; bound; positive, absolute, definite, perfectly sure, apodictic; decisive, conclusive; clear, clear as day, clear and distinct, unequivocal, unmistakable, unambiguous, nonambiguous, univocal; necessary, determinate, ineluctable, predetermined, predestined, inevitable; true

14 <nonformal> dead sure, sure as death, sure as death and taxes, sure as fate, sure as can be, sure as shooting, sure as God made little green apples, sure as hell, sure as the devil, shit-sure*, as sure as I live and breathe

15 **obvious,** patent, **unquestionable,** unexceptionable, undeniable, self-evident, axiomatic; indubitable, unarguable, indisputable, incontestable, irrefutable, unrefutable, unconfutable, incontrovertible, irrefragable, unanswerable, inappealable, unimpeachable, absolute; admitting no question, admitting no doubt; demonstrable, demonstratable, provable, verifiable, testable, confirmable; well-founded, well-established, well-grounded; factual, real, historical, actual

16 **undoubted,** not to be doubted, indubious, **unquestioned,** undisputed, uncontested, uncontradicted, unchallenged, uncontroverted, uncontroversial; doubtless, questionless, beyond a shadow of doubt, past dispute, beyond question

17 reliable, dependable, **sure,** surefire, trustworthy, trusty, faithworthy, to be depended upon, to be relied upon, to be counted on, to be reckoned on; predictable, calculable; secure, solid, sound, firm, fast, stable, substantial, staunch, steady, steadfast, faithful, **unfailing;** true to one's word; invincible

18 **authoritative,** authentic, magisterial, **official;** cathedral, ex cathedra; standard, approved, accepted, received, pontific; from the horse's mouth, straight from the horse's mouth

19 infallible, inerrable, inerrant, unerring

20 assured, made sure; determined, decided, **ascertained;** settled, established, fixed, cinched, iced, sewed up, taped, set, stated, determinate, secure; **certified,** attested, guaranteed, warranted, tested, tried, proved; wired, open-and-shut, nailed down, in the bag, on ice

21 **confident, sure,** secure, assured, reassured, decided, determined; convinced, persuaded,

positive, cocksure; unhesitating, unfaltering, unwavering; undoubting; self-confident, self-assured, self-reliant, sure of oneself; poised; unafraid; overconfident, oversure, overweening, hubristic; proud, arrogant, pompous, self-important

22 **dogmatic,** dogmatical, dogmatizing, pronunciative, didactic, positive, positivistic, peremptory, pontifical, oracular; opinionated, opinioned, opinionative, conceited; self-opinionated, self-opinioned; doctrinarian, doctrinaire; bigoted

ADVS 23 **certainly,** surely, assuredly, positively, absolutely, definitely, decidedly; without batting an eye; decisively, distinctly, clearly, unequivocally, unmistakably; **for certain,** for sure, for a fact, in truth, certes, forsooth, and no mistake; for a certainty, to a certainty; most certainly, most assuredly; indeed, indeedy; truly; of course, as a matter of course; by all means, by all manner of means; at any rate, at all events; nothing else but, no two ways about it, no buts about it; no ifs, ands, or buts; abso-bloody-lutely

24 **surely,** sure, to be sure, sure enough, for sure; sure thing, surest thing you know

25 **unquestionably,** without question, undoubtedly, **beyond the shadow of a doubt**, beyond a reasonable doubt, indubitably, admittedly, undeniably, unarguably, indisputably, incontestably, incontrovertibly, irrefutably, irrefragably; doubtlessly, doubtless, no doubt, without doubt, beyond doubt, beyond question, out of question

26 **without fail,** unfailingly, whatever may happen, come what may, come hell or high water; cost what it may; rain or shine, live or die, sink or swim

PHRS 27 it is certain, there is no question, there is not a shadow of doubt, that's for sure; that goes without saying, that is evident, that leaps to the eye

971 UNCERTAINTY

<something that is uncertain>

NOUNS 1 **uncertainty, incertitude, unsureness,** uncertainness; indemonstrability, unverifiability, unprovability, unconfirmability; unpredictability, unforeseeableness, incalculability, unaccountability; indetermination, indeterminacy, indeterminism; relativity, relativism, contingency, conditionality; controversiality; randomness, chance, chanciness, hit-or-missness, luck; entropy; indecision, indecisiveness, undecidedness, undeterminedness; hesitation, hesitancy; suspense, suspensefulness, agony of suspense, state of suspense; fickleness, capriciousness, whimsicality, erraticness, erraticism, changeableness; vacillation, irresolution; trendlessness; Heisenberg principle, indeterminacy principle, uncertainty principle; question mark; back order; mixed blessing; brain fade, brain fog

2 **doubtfulness,** dubiousness, doubt, dubiety, dubitancy, dubitation; questionableness, disputability, contestability, controvertibility, refutability, confutability, deniability; disbelief

3 **bewilderment,** disconcertion, disconcertedness, disconcert, disconcertment, embarrassment, confoundment, discomposure, unassuredness, confusion, cognitive dissonance; perplexity, puzzlement, baffle, bafflement, predicament, plight, quandary, dilemma, horns of a dilemma, nonplus; puzzle, problem, riddle, conundrum, mystery, enigma; fix, jam, pickle, scrape, stew; perturbation, disturbance, upset, bother, pother

4 **vagueness, indefiniteness,** indecisiveness, indeterminateness, indeterminableness, indefinableness, unclearness, indistinctness, haziness, fogginess, mistiness, murkiness, blurriness, fuzziness; obscurity, obscuration; looseness, laxity, inexactness, inaccuracy, imprecision; broadness, generality, sweepingness; ill-definedness, amorphousness, shapelessness, blobbiness; inchoateness, disorder, incoherence

5 **equivocalness,** equivocality, polysemousness, ambiguity

6 **unreliability,** undependability, untrustworthiness, unfaithworthiness, treacherousness, treachery; unsureness, insecurity, unsoundness, infirmity, insolidity, unsolidity, instability, insubstantiality, unsubstantiality, unsteadfastness, unsteadiness, desultoriness, shakiness; precariousness, hazard, danger, risk, riskiness, diceyness, dodginess, knife edge, moment of truth, tightrope walking, peril, perilousness, ticklishness, slipperiness, shiftiness, shiftingness; speculativeness; unauthoritativeness, unauthenticity

7 **fallibility,** errability, errancy, liability to error

8 <an uncertainty> **gamble, guess,** piece of guesswork, question mark, estimate, guesstimate, ball-park figure; chance, wager; toss-up, coin toss, touch and go; contingency, double contingency, possibility upon a possibility; question, open question; undecided issue, loose end; wild guess; gray area, twilight zone, borderline case; blind bargain, pig in a poke, sight-unseen transaction; leap in the dark; enigma; high wire

VERBS 9 **be uncertain, feel unsure; doubt**, have one's doubts, question, puzzle over, agonize over; wonder, wonder whether, wrinkle one's brow; not know what to make of, not be able to make head or tail of; be at sea, float in a sea of doubt; be at one's wit's end, not know which way to turn, be of two minds, be at sixes and sevens, not know where one stands, have mixed feelings, not know whether one stands on one's head or heels, be in a dilemma, be in a quandary, flounder, grope, beat about, thrash about, not know whether one is coming or going, go around in circles; go off in all directions at once

10 **hang in doubt,** hang over one's head, stop to consider, think twice; falter, dither, hesitate, vacillate

11 **depend,** all depend, be contingent on, be conditional on, hang upon; hang, hang in the balance, be touch and go, tremble in the balance, hang in suspense; hang by a thread, cliffhang, hang by a hair, hang by the eyelids

12 **bewilder,** disconcert, discompose, upset, perturb, disturb, dismay, tie one in knots; abash, embarrass, put out, pother, bother, moider, flummox, keep one on tenterhooks

13 **perplex, baffle,** confound, daze, amaze, maze, addle, fuddle, muddle, mystify, puzzle, nonplus, put to one's wit's end; keep one guessing, keep in suspense

14 <nonformal> **stump,** boggle, buffalo, bamboozle, stick, floor, throw, get, beat, beat the shit out of*, lick

15 **make uncertain,** obscure, muddle, muddy, fuzz, fog, confuse

ADJS 16 **uncertain, unsure;** doubting, agnostic, skeptical, unconvinced, unpersuaded; chancy, dicey, touch-and-go; unpredictable, unforeseeable, incalculable, uncountable, unreckonable, unaccountable, undivinable; indemonstrable, unverifiable, unprovable, unconfirmable; equivocal, polysemous, inexplicit, imprecise, ambiguous; fickle, capricious, whimsical, erratic, variable, wavering, irresponsible, changeable; hesitant, hesitating; indecisive, irresolute

17 **doubtful,** iffy; **in doubt**; dubitable, doubtable, **dubious**, questionable, problematic, problematical, speculative, conjectural, suppositional; debatable, moot, arguable, disputable, contestable, controvertible, controversial, refutable, confutable, deniable; mistakable; suspicious, suspect; open to question, open to doubt; in question, in dispute, at issue; loose-knit

18 **undecided,** undetermined, unsettled, unfixed, unestablished; untold, uncounted; pendent, dependent, pending, depending, contingent, conditional, conditioned; open, in question, at issue, in the balance, up in the air, up for grabs, in limbo, in suspense, in a state of suspense, suspenseful

19 **vague, indefinite,** indecisive, indeterminate, indeterminable, undetermined, unpredetermined, undestined; random, stochastic, entropic, chance, chancy, dicey, dodgy, aleatory, aleatoric, hit-or-miss; indefinable, undefined, ill-defined, unclear, unplain, indistinct, fuzzy, obscure, confused, hazy, shadowy, shadowed forth, misty, foggy, fogbound, murky, blurred, blurry, veiled; loose, lax, inexact, inaccurate, imprecise; nonspecific, unspecified; broad, general, sweeping; amorphous, shapeless, blobby; inchoate, disordered, orderless, chaotic, incoherent, fuzzyheaded

20 **unreliable,** undependable, untrustworthy, unfaithworthy, treacherous, unsure, not to be depended on, not to be relied on; insecure, unsound, infirm, unsolid, unstable, unsubstantial, insubstantial, unsteadfast, unsteady, desultory, shaky; **precarious,** hazardous, dangerous, perilous, risky, ticklish; shifty, shifting, slippery, slippery as an eel; provisional, tentative, temporary

21 unauthoritative, unauthentic, **unofficial,** nonofficial, apocryphal; **uncertified,** unverified, unchecked, unconfirmed, uncorroborated, unauthenticated, unvalidated, unattested, unwarranted; undemonstrated, unproved

22 **fallible,** errable, errant, liable to error, open to error, error-prone, wrongo

23 **unconfident, unsure,** unassured, insecure, unsure of oneself; unselfconfident, unselfassured, unselfreliant

24 **bewildered,** dismayed, distracted, distraught, abashed, disconcerted, embarrassed, discomposed, put-out, disturbed, upset, perturbed, bothered, all hot and bothered; confused; clueless, without a clue, guessing, mazed, in a maze; turned around, going around in circles, like a chicken with its head cut off; in a stew, in a pickle, in a jam, in a fix, in a scrape; lost, astray, abroad, adrift, at sea, off the track, out of one's reckoning, out of one's bearings, disoriented

25 **in a dilemma,** on the horns of a dilemma; perplexed, confounded, mystified, puzzled, **nonplussed, baffled,** bamboozled, buffaloed; at a loss, at one's wit's end, fuddled, addled, muddled, dazed; on tenterhooks, in suspense, in limbo; with bated breath

26 <nonformal> beat, licked, stuck, floored, stumped, thrown, buffaloed, boggled

27 **bewildering,** confusing, distracting, disconcerting, discomposing, dismaying, embarrassing, disturbing, upsetting, perturbing,

bothering; perplexing, baffling, mystifying, mysterious, puzzling, funny, funny peculiar, confounding; cringeworthy, cringe-inducing, cringe-making; **problematic**, problematical; intricate; enigmatic

ADVS **28** **uncertainly,** in an uncertain state, unsurely; **doubtfully**, dubiously; in suspense, at sea, on the horns of a dilemma, at sixes and sevens; perplexedly, disconcertedly, confusedly, dazedly, mazedly, in a daze, in a maze, around in circles

29 vaguely, **indefinitely,** indeterminably, indefinably, indistinctly, indecisively, obscurely; broadly, generally, in broad terms, in general terms

972 CHANCE

<something that happens unpredictably>

NOUNS **1** **chance, happenstance**, hap; luck; good luck, good fortune, **serendipity**, happy chance, dumb luck, rotten luck, tough luck; fortune, fate, destiny, whatever comes, lot; fortuity, randomness, randomicity, fortuitousness, adventitiousness, indeterminateness, indeterminacy, problematicness, uncertainty, flukiness, casualness, flip of a coin, crazy quilt, patternlessness, trendlessness, accidentality; break, the breaks, run of luck, the luck of the draw, the rub of the green, run of the cards, throw of the dice, the way things fall, the way the cards fall, how they fall, the way the cookie crumbles, the way the ball bounces; uncertainty principle, principle of indeterminacy, Heisenberg's principle; probability, stochastics, theory of probability, law of averages, statistical probability, actuarial calculation; random sample, risk, risk-taking, chancing, gamble, crapshoot; opportunity

2 Chance, Fortune, Lady Fortune, Dame Fortune, wheel of fortune, Fortuna, the fickle finger of fate; Luck, Lady Luck; blind chance

3 purposelessness, **causelessness,** randomness, dysteleology, unpredictability, designlessness, aimlessness; lack of motive, no attributable cause, nonintention

4 **haphazard,** chance-medley, **random;** random shot; potluck; spin of the wheel

5 **vicissitudes,** vicissitudes of fortune, ins and outs, **ups and downs,** ups and downs of life, chapter of accidents, feast and famine; chain of circumstances, concatenation of events, chain reaction, vicious circle, causal nexus, domino effect

6 <**chance event**> happening, hap, happenstance; fortuity, accident, casualty, adventure, hazard; contingent, contingency; fluke, freak, freak occurrence, freak accident, coincidence; crapshoot; chance hit, lucky shot, hot hand, long shot, one in a million, long odds

7 **even chance,** even break, fair shake, even odds, square odds, level playing field, touch and go, odds; half a chance, fifty-fifty; toss, toss-up, standoff

8 **good chance,** sporting chance, good opportunity, good possibility; odds-on, odds-on chance, likelihood, possibility, probability, favorable prospect, well-grounded hope; sure bet, sure thing, dollars to doughnuts; best bet, main chance, winning chance

9 **small chance,** little chance, dark horse, poor prospect, poor prognosis, poor lookout, little opportunity, poor possibility, unlikelihood, improbability, hardly a chance, not half a chance; off chance, outside chance, remote possibility, bare possibility, a ghost of a chance, slim chance, gambling chance, fighting chance; poor bet, long odds, long shot, hundred-to-one shot, one chance in a million; crapshoot

10 **no chance,** not a Chinaman's chance, not a snowball's chance in hell, not a prayer; impossibility, hopelessness

VERBS **11** **chance,** bechance, betide, come by chance, happen by chance, hap, hazard, happen, happen on, fall on, come, come along, happen along, bump into, turn up, pop up, befall; fall to one's lot, be one's fate

12 **risk, take a chance**, run a risk, push one's luck, press one's luck, lay one's ass on the line, put one's money where one's mouth is, gamble, bet; risk one's neck, shoot the works, go for broke; predict, prognosticate, make book; call someone's bluff

13 **have a chance,** have an opportunity, stand a chance, run a good chance, stand fair to, admit of; be in it, be in the running; have a chance at, have a fling at, have a shot at; have a small chance, have a slight chance, be a dark horse, barely have a chance

14 **not have a chance,** not stand a chance, have no chance, have no opportunity, not have a prayer, not have a Chinaman's chance, not stand a snowball's chance in hell; not be in it, be out of it, be out of the running

ADJS **15** **chance;** chancy, dicey, risky; fortuitous, accidental, aleatory, aleatoric; lucky, fortunate, blessed by fortune, serendipitous; casual, adventitious, incidental, contingent, iffy; causeless, uncaused; indeterminate, undetermined; unexpected, unpredictable, unforeseeable, unlooked-for, unforeseen; fluky; fatal, fatidic, destinal

16 purposeless, causeless, designless, aimless, driftless, undirected, objectless, unmotivated, mindless; **haphazard, random,** dysteleological, stochastic, stray, inexplicable, unaccountable, promiscuous, indiscriminate, casual, leaving much to chance

17 **unintentional,** unintended, unmeant, unplanned, undesigned, unpurposed, unthought-of; unpremeditated, unmeditated, unprompted, unguided, unguarded; unwitting, unthinking, unconscious, involuntary; collateral

18 impossible; improbable; certain; probable

ADVS **19** **by chance,** perchance, **by accident,** accidentally, casually, incidentally, by coincidence, unpredictably, fortuitously, out of a clear blue sky; by a piece of luck, by a fluke, by good fortune; as it chanced, as luck would have it, by hazard, as it may happen, as it may be, as the case may be, as it may chance, as it may turn out; somehow, in some way, in some way or other, somehow or other, for some reason

20 purposelessly, aimlessly; haphazardly, **randomly,** dysteleologically, stochastically, inexplicably, unaccountably, promiscuously, indiscriminately, casually, **at haphazard,** at random, at hazard

21 **unintentionally,** without design, **unwittingly,** unthinkingly, unexpectedly, unconsciously, involuntarily

INTERJS **22** break a leg, best of luck good luck

973 TRUTH

<real facts, things that are true>

NOUNS **1** **truth, trueness, verity,** veridicality, conformity to fact, conformity to reality, conformity to the evidence, conformity to the data, simple truth, unadorned truth, very truth, sooth, good sooth; more truth than poetry; unerroneousness, unfalseness, unfallaciousness; historical truth, objective truth, actuality, historicity, impersonality; fact, reality, the real world, things as they are; the true, ultimate truth; eternal verities; truthfulness, veracity

2 **a truth,** a self-evident truth, an axiomatic truth, **an axiom;** a premise, a given, a donnée, a donné; an accomplished fact, *fait accompli* <Fr>

3 **the truth,** the truth of the matter, the case; the home truth, the unvarnished truth, the simple truth, the basic truth, indisputable truth, the unadorned truth, the naked truth, the plain truth, the unqualified truth, the honest truth, the sober truth, the exact truth, the straight truth; the absolute truth, the intrinsic truth, the unalloyed truth, the cast-iron truth, the hard truth, the stern truth, gospel, gospel truth, Bible truth, revealed truth; the whole truth and nothing but the truth

4 <nonformal> **what's what,** how it is, how things are, like it is, where it's at, dinkum oil <Austral>, the straight of it, the straight scoop, the honest-to-God truth, God's truth, the real thing, the very model, the genuine article, the very thing, it, the article, the goods, the McCoy, the real McCoy, no imitation, chapter and verse, the gospel, the gospel truth, the lowdown, the skinny

5 **accuracy, correctness,** care for truth, attention to fact, right, subservience to the facts, rightness, **trueness,** rigor, rigorousness, exactness, exactitude; preciseness, precision; mathematical precision, pinpoint accuracy, scientific exactitude; factualness, factualism; faultlessness, perfection, absoluteness, flawlessness, impeccability, unimpeachability; faithfulness, fidelity; literalness, literality, literalism, textualism, textuality, the letter, literal truth; strictness, severity, rigidity; niceness, nicety, delicacy, subtlety, fineness, refinement; meticulousness; attention to detail; clockwork precision

6 **validity,** soundness, solidity, substantiality, justness; authority, authoritativeness; cogency, weight, force, persuasiveness

7 **genuineness, authenticity,** bona fides, bona fideness, legitimacy; realness, realism, photographic realism, absolute realism, realistic representation, naturalism, naturalness, truth to nature, lifelikeness, truth to life, slice of life, kitchen sink, true-to-lifeness, verisimilitude, faithful rendering, verism, verismo, faithfulness; absolute likeness, literalness, literality, literalism, truth to the letter; socialist realism; inartificiality, unsyntheticness; unspuriousness, unspeciousness, unfictitiousness, artlessness, unaffectedness; honesty, sincerity; unadulteration

VERBS **8** **be true,** be the case; conform to fact, square with the facts, square with the evidence; **prove true,** prove to be, prove out, be so in fact; hold true, hold good, hold water, hold together, stick together, hold up, hold up in the wash, wash, stand up, stand the test, be consistent, hold, remain valid; **be truthful**

9 seem true, **ring true, sound true**, carry conviction, convince, persuade, win over, have the ring of truth

10 **be right, be correct,** be just right, get it straight; be OK, add up; hit the nail on the head, hit it on the nose, be on the money, say a mouthful, hit the bull's-eye, score a bull's-eye

11 **be accurate,** dot one's i's and cross one's t's, cut it fine, be precise; make precise, precise, particularize; stick to the letter, go by the book

12 **come true,** come about, attain fulfillment, turn out, come to pass, come to be, happen as expected, become a reality

ADJS **13** **true, truthful;** unerroneous, not in error, in conformity with the facts, in conformity with the evidence, on the up-and-up, strictly on the up-and-up; gospel, hard, cast-iron; unfalse, unfallacious, unmistaken; real, veritable, **veracious**, sure-enough, objective, true to the facts, factual, actual, effectual, historical, documentary; objectively true; certain, undoubted, unquestionable; unrefuted, unconfuted, undenied; ascertained, proved, proven, verified, validated, certified, demonstrated, confirmed, determined, established, attested, substantiated, authenticated, corroborated; true as gospel; substantially true, categorically true

14 **valid, sound,** well-grounded, well-founded, conforming to reality, hard, solid, substantial; consistent, self-consistent, logical; good, just, sufficient; cogent, weighty, authoritative; legal, lawful, legitimate, binding

15 **genuine, authentic,** veridic, veridical, real, natural, all-natural, realistic, naturalistic, true to reality, true to nature, lifelike, true to life, verisimilar, veristic; literal, following the letter, letter-perfect, true to the letter; verbatim, verbal, word-perfect, word-for-word; true to the spirit; legitimate, rightful, lawful; bona fide, card-carrying, good, sure-enough, sincere, honest; candid, honest-to-God, dinkum; inartificial, unsynthetic; unspurious, unspecious, unsimulated, unfaked, unfeigned, undisguised, uncounterfeited, unpretended, unaffected, unassumed; unassuming, simple, unpretending, unfeigning, undisguising; unfictitious, unfanciful, unfabricated, unconcocted, uninvented, unimagined; unromantic; original, unimitated, uncopied; unexaggerated, undistorted; unflattering, unvarnished, uncolored, unqualified; unadulterated, honest-to-goodness; pure, simon-pure; sterling, twenty-four carat, all wool, a yard wide

16 **accurate, correct,** right, proper, just; all right, OK, okay, just right as rain, dead right, on target, on the money, on the nose, on the button, bang on, straight, straight-up-and-down; faultless, flawless, impeccable, unimpeachable, unexceptionable; absolute, perfect, letter-perfect; meticulous; factual, literal

17 **exact, precise,** express; even, square; absolutely right, positively right; faithful; direct; unerring, undeviating, constant; infallible, inerrant, inerrable; strict, close, severe, rigorous, rigid; mathematically exact, mathematical; mechanically precise, micrometrically precise; scientifically exact, scientific; religiously exact, religious; nice, delicate, subtle, fine, refined; pinpoint, microscopic

ADVS **18** **truly,** really, really-truly, **verily,** veritably, forsooth, in very sooth, **in truth,** in good truth, in very truth, actually, historically, objectively, impersonally, rigorously, strictly, strictly speaking, unquestionably, without question, in reality, in fact, factually, technically, in point of fact, as a matter of fact, for that matter, for the matter of that, to tell the truth, if you want to know the truth, to state the truth, of a truth, with truth; indeed, indeedy; certainly; indubitably, undoubtedly; no buts about it, nothing else but

19 **genuinely, authentically**, really, naturally, legitimately, honestly, veridically; warts and all; unaffectedly, unassumedly, from the heart, in one's heart of hearts, with all one's heart and soul

20 **accurately, correctly,** rightly, properly, straight; perfectly, faultlessly, flawlessly, impeccably, unimpeachably, unexceptionably; just right, just so; so, sic

21 **exactly,** precisely, to a T, expressly; just, dead, right, straight, even, square, plumb, directly, squarely, point-blank; unerringly, undeviatingly; literally, verbally, word-perfectly, verbatim, word for word, word by word, letter for letter, in the same words, to the letter, according to the letter; faithfully, strictly, rigorously, rigidly; definitely, positively, absolutely; in every respect, in all respects, for all the world, neither more nor less

22 to be exact, to be precise, strictly, technically, **strictly speaking**, not to mince the matter, by the book

23 to a nicety, to a T, to a tittle, to a turn, to a hair, within an inch

PHRS **24** right, that's right, **that is so**, amen, that's it, that's just it, just so, it is that; you are right, right you are, right as rain, it is for a fact, you speak truly, as you say; believe it or not; touché

25 <nonformal> **right on,** you better believe it, you've got something there, I'll say, I'll tell the world, I'll drink to that, righto, quite, rather, you got it, you said it, you said a mouthful, now you're talking, you can say that again, you're not kidding, that's for sure, ain't it the truth?, you're damn tootin', don't I know it, you're telling me, you're not just whistling Dixie, bet your ass, bet your sweet ass, bet your bippy, bet your boots, bet your life, fucking A*

974 WISE SAYING

<statement of rule or moral principle>

NOUNS **1** **maxim, aphorism,** apothegm, apophthegm, **epigram, dictum, adage, proverb,** gnome, words of wisdom, saw, saying, witticism, sentence, expression, phrase, catchword, catchphrase, word, byword, mot, motto, moral; precept, prescript, teaching, text, verse, sutra, distich, sloka; golden saying, proverbial saying; common saying, current saying, stock saying, pithy saying, wise saying, wise expression, oracle, sententious expression; **conventional wisdom,** common knowledge; ana, analects, proverbs, wisdom, wisdom literature, collected sayings

2 **axiom,** truth, a priori truth, postulate, truism, self-evident truth, general truth, universal truth, home truth, obvious truth, intrinsic truth; elephant in the room; theorem; proposition; brocard, principle, settled principle; formula; rule, law, dictate, dictum; golden rule

3 **platitude, cliché,** saw, old saw, commonplace, banality, bromide, chestnut, corn, triticism, tired phrase, trite saying, hackneyed saying, stock phrase, commonplace expression, familiar tune, familiar story, old song, old story, old song and dance, twice-told tale, retold story; reiteration; prosaicism, prosaism; prose; old joke

4 **motto, slogan,** watchword, catchword, catchphrase, tagline, tag, byword; device; epithet; inscription, epigraph

VERBS **5** aphorize, apothegmatize, epigrammatize, coin a phrase; proverb

ADJS **6** **aphoristic,** proverbial, epigrammatic, epigrammatical, axiomatical; sententious, pithy, gnomic, pungent, succinct, enigmatic, pointed; formulistic, formulaic; cliché, clichéd, banal, tired, stock, trite, tritical, platitudinous

ADVS **7** proverbially, to coin a phrase, in a nutshell, as the saying goes, as they say, as the fellow says, as it has been said, as it was said of old

975 ERROR

<mistake or failure>

NOUNS **1** **error, erroneousness;** untrueness, untruthfulness, untruth; wrongness, wrong; falseness, falsity; fallacy, fallaciousness, self-contradiction; fault, faultiness, defectiveness; sin, sinfulness, peccancy, flaw, flawedness, *hamartia* <Gk>; misdoing, misfeasance; errancy, aberrancy, aberration, deviancy, wrongdoing; heresy, unorthodoxy, heterodoxy; perversion, distortion; mistaking, misconstruction, misapplication, misprision; delusion, illusion; misjudgment; misinterpretation; faulty reasoning, flawed logic; fallibility, human error

2 **inaccuracy,** inaccurateness, **incorrectness,** uncorrectness, inexactness, unfactualness, inexactitude, unpreciseness, imprecision, unspecificity, looseness, laxity, unrigorousness; tolerance, allowance; negligence; approximation; deviation, standard deviation, probable error, predictable error, range of error; uncertainty

3 **mistake, error,** *erratum* <L>, *corrigendum* <L>; fault; gross error, bevue; human error; misconception, misapprehension, misunderstanding; misstatement, misquotation; misreport; misprint, typographical error, typo, printer's error, typist's error; clerical error; misidentification; misjudgment, miscalculation; misplay; misdeal; miscount; misuse; failure, miss, miscarriage; epic fail

4 slip, slipup, miscue; **lapse,** *lapsus* <L>, **oversight,** omission, balk, inadvertence, inadvertency, loose thread; misstep, trip, stumble, false step, wrong step, wrong move, bad move, false move; false note; slip of the tongue, *sus linguae, lapsus linguae* <L>; slip of the pen; Freudian slip

5 **blunder, faux pas,** gaffe, solecism; stupidity, indiscretion; botch, bungle

6 <nonformal> **goof,** boo-boo, muff, flub, foozle, bloomer, bloop, blooper, boot, bobble, boner, bonehead play, bonehead move, dumb trick, boob stunt, fool mistake; howler, clanger, screamer; fuck-up*, screwup, foul-up, snafu, muck-up, balls-up <Brit>, louse-up; pratfall, whoops

7 **grammatical error,** solecism, anacoluthon, anacoluthia, misusage, faulty syntax, missaying, mispronunciation; bull, Irish bull, fluff, malapropism, malaprop, Mrs. Malaprop; Pickwickian sense; spoonerism, marrow-sky; hypercorrection, hyperform; folk etymology; catachresis; misspelling; spell checking

VERBS **8** not hold water, not hold together, not stand up, not square, not figure, not add up, not hold up, not hold up in the wash, not wash

9 **err,** fall into error, go wrong, go amiss, go astray, get out of line, go awry, stray, get off-base, deviate, wander, transgress, sin; lapse, slip, **slip up,** trip, stumble; miscalculate

10 **be wrong,** mistake oneself, be mistaken, be in error, be at fault, be out of line, be off the track, be in the wrong, miss the truth, miss the point, miss by a mile, have another think coming; take wrong, receive a false impression, take the shadow for the substance, misconstrue, misinterpret, be misled, be misguided; deceive oneself, be deceived, delude oneself; labor under a false impression, get it wrong

11 bark up the wrong tree, back the wrong horse, count one's chickens before they are hatched

12 **misdo,** do amiss; misuse, misemploy, misapply; misconduct, mismanage; miscall, miscount, miscalculate, misdeal, misplay, misfield; misprint, miscite, misquote, misread, misreport, misspell

13 **mistake, make a mistake;** miscue, make a miscue; misidentify; misunderstand, misapprehend, misconceive, misinterpret; confuse, mix up, not distinguish

14 **blunder,** make a blunder, make a faux pas, blot one's copy book, make a colossal blunder, make a false step, make a wrong step, make a misstep; misspeak, misspeak oneself, trip over one's tongue; embarrass oneself, have egg on one's face; blunder into; botch, bungle

15 <nonformal> **make a boner**, pull a boner, make a boo-boo, make blooper; drop a brick <Brit>, goof, fluff, duff <Brit>, foozle, boot, bobble, blow, blow it, drop the ball; fuck up*, screw up, foul up, muck up, louse up; put one's foot in it, stick one's foot in it, put one's foot in one's mouth; muff one's cue, muff one's lines, blow one's lines, fall flat on one's face, fall flat on one's ass, step on one's dick, trip up, circle the drain

ADJS 16 **erroneous,** untrue, not true, not right; unfactual, factless, **wrong**, all wrong; peccant, perverse, corrupt; false, fallacious, self-contradictory; illogical; unproved; faulty, faultful, flawed, defective, at fault; out, off, all off, off the track, off the rails; wide, wide of the mark, beside the mark; amiss, awry, askew, deviant, deviative, deviational; erring, errant, aberrant; straying, astray, adrift; heretical, unorthodox, heterodox; abroad, all abroad; perverted, distorted; delusive, deceptive, illusory

17 **inaccurate, incorrect,** inexact, unfactual, unprecise, imprecise, unspecific, loose, lax, unrigorous; negligent; vague; approximate, approximative; out of line, out of plumb, out of true, out of square; off-base

18 **mistaken, in error,** erring, under an error, wrong, all wet, full of bull, full of shit*, full of hot air, full of it, full of prunes, full of crap, full of beans; off in one's reckoning; in the wrong box, in the right church but the wrong pew

19 unauthentic, inauthentic, unauthoritative, unreliable; misstated, misreported, miscited, misquoted, garbled; unfounded; spurious

ADVS 20 **erroneously,** falsely, by mistake, fallaciously; faultily, faultfully; untrue, untruly; wrong, wrongly; **mistakenly;** amiss, astray, on the wrong track

21 **inaccurately, incorrectly,** inexactly, unprecisely, by guess, by God, by golly

INTERJS 22 whoops, sorry about that

PHRS 23 you are wrong, you are mistaken, you're all wet, you're way off, you have another guess coming, don't kid yourself

976 ILLUSION

<false or wrong belief>

NOUNS 1 **illusion, delusion,** deluded belief; deception, **trick**; self-deception, self-deceit, self-delusion; dereism, autism; misconception, misbelief, false belief, wrong impression, warped conception, distorted conception; bubble, chimera, vapor; wishful thinking, *ignis fatuus* <L>, will-o'-the-wisp; dream, dream vision; dreamworld, dreamland, dreamscape; daydream; pipe dream, trip; fool's paradise, castle in the air, fond illusion; maya, confabulation; impossible dream

2 **illusoriness,** illusiveness, delusiveness; falseness, fallaciousness; unreality, unactuality; unsubstantiality, airiness, **immateriality**; idealization; seeming, semblance, simulacrum, appearance, false appearance, specious appearance, show, false show, false light; magic, sorcery, illusionism, sleight of hand, prestidigitation, magic show, magic act; magician, sorcerer, illusionist, Prospero; Mahamaya, magus, wizard, conjuror

3 fancy, imagination

4 phantom, phantasm, phantasma, wraith, specter; shadow, shade; phantasmagoria; **fantasy,** wildest dream; **figment of the imagination**, phantom of the mind; apparition, appearance; vision, waking dream, image; shape, form, figure, presence; eidolon, idolum; stuff that dreams are made of

5 **optical illusion,** trick of eyesight; afterimage, spectrum, ocular spectrum

6 **mirage,** fata morgana, will-o'-the-wisp, looming

7 **hallucination;** hallucinosis; tripping, mind-expansion; consciousness-expansion; delirium tremens; dream

VERBS 8 go on a trip, blow one's mind, freak out; **hallucinate;** expand one's consciousness; make magic, prestidigitate

ADJS 9 **illusory,** illusive; illusional, illusionary; Barmecide, Barmecidal; delusory, delusive; delusional, delusionary, deluding; dereistic, autistic; dreamy, dreamlike; visionary; imaginary; erroneous; deceptive; self-deceptive, self-deluding; chimeric, chimerical, fantastic; unreal, unactual, unsubstantial, airy; unfounded; false, fallacious, misleading; specious, seeming, apparent, ostensible, supposititious, all in the mind;

spectral, apparitional, phantom, phantasmal; phantasmagoric, surreal
10 **hallucinatory,** hallucinative, hallucinational; hallucinogenic, psychedelic, consciousness-expanding, mind-expanding, mind-blowing

977 DISILLUSIONMENT

<disenchanted by dashed belief>

NOUNS **1** **disillusionment,** disillusion, **disenchantment,** undeception, unspelling, return to reality, loss of one's illusions, loss of innocence, cold light of reality, enlightenment, bursting of the bubble; awakening, rude awakening, bringing back to earth; disappointment; debunking

VERBS **2** **disillusion,** disillude, disillusionize; **disenchant,** unspell, uncharm, break the spell, break the charm; disabuse, undeceive; correct, set right, set straight, put straight, tell the truth, enlighten, let in on, put one wise; clear the mind of; open one's eyes, awaken, wake up, unblindfold; disappoint; dispel one's illusions, dissipate one's illusions, rob one of one's illusions, strip one of one's illusions; bring one back to earth, let down easy; burst the bubble, puncture one's balloon; let the air out of, take the wind out of; knock the props out from under, take the ground from under; debunk; expose, show up

3 be disillusioned, be disenchanted, get back to earth, get one's feet on the ground, have one's eyes opened, return to reality, embrace reality; charge to experience; have another thing coming

ADJS **4** **disillusioning,** disillusive, disillusionary, **disenchanting,** disabusing, undeceiving, enlightening

5 disillusioned, disenchanted, unspelled, uncharmed, disabused, undeceived, stripped of illusion, robbed of illusion, enlightened, set right, put straight; with one's eyes open, sophisticated, blasé; disappointed

978 MENTAL ATTITUDE

<beliefs, feelings, and values held>

NOUNS **1** **attitude,** mental attitude; psychology; position, posture, stance; **way of thinking;** feeling, sentiment, the way one feels; feeling tone, affect, affectivity, emotion, emotivity; opinion

2 **outlook,** mental outlook; **point of view,** viewpoint, standpoint, perspective; position, stand, place, situation; side; footing, basis; where one is, where one sits, where one stands; view, sight, light, eye; respect, regard; angle, angle of vision, slant, way of looking at things, slant on things, where one is coming from; frame of reference, intellectual frame of reference, ideational frame of reference, framework, arena, world, universe, world of discourse, universe of discourse, system of discourse, reference system; phenomenology

3 **disposition,** character, nature, temper, **temperament,** mettle, constitution, complexion, humor, makeup, stamp, type, stripe, kidney, make, mold; turn of mind, inclination, mind, tendency, grain, vein, set, mental set, mindset, leaning, animus, propensity, proclivity, predilection, preference, predisposition; bent, turn, bias, slant, cast, warp, twist; idiosyncrasy, eccentricity, individualism; diathesis, aptitude; strain, streak

4 **mood,** humor, feeling, feelings, temper, frame of mind, state of mind, **mental state,** mindset, morale, cue, frame, tone, note, vein; mind, heart; spirit, spirits

5 <pervading attitudes> **climate,** mental climate, intellectual climate, spiritual climate, moral climate, mores, norms, climate of opinion, **ethos,** ideology, *Weltanschauung* <Ger>, worldview; zeitgeist, spirit of the time, spirit of the age

VERBS **6** **take the attitude,** feel about it, look at it, view, look at in the light of; be disposed to, tend toward, incline toward, prefer, lean toward, be bent on

ADJS **7** **attitudinal;** temperamental, dispositional, inclinational, constitutional; emotional, affective; mental, intellectual, ideational, ideological; spiritual; characteristic; innate

8 **disposed,** dispositioned, predisposed, prone, inclined, given, bent, bent on, apt, likely, minded, in the mood, in the humor

ADVS **9** **attitudinally; temperamentally,** dispositionally, constitutionally; emotionally; mentally, intellectually, ideationally, ideologically; morally, spiritually; by temperament, by disposition, by virtue of mindset, by the logic of character; from one's standpoint, from one's viewpoint, from one's angle, from where one stands, from where one sits, from where one is; within the frame of reference of discourse, within the framework, within the universe of discourse, within the reference system of discourse

979 BROAD-MINDEDNESS

<tolerant of varied views>

NOUNS **1** **broad-mindedness,** wide-mindedness, large-mindedness; breadth, broadness, broad gauge, **latitude**; unbigotedness, unhideboundness, unprovincialism, noninsularity, unparochialism, cosmopolitanism; ecumenicity, ecumenicism, ecumenicalism, ecumenism; broad mind, spacious mind

2 **liberalness**, liberality, catholicity, liberalmindedness; liberalism, libertarianism, latitudinarianism; freethinking, free thought
3 **open-mindedness,** openness, receptiveness, receptivity; persuadableness, persuadability, persuasibility; open mind
4 **tolerance,** toleration; indulgence, lenience, leniency, condonation, lenity; forbearance, patience, long-suffering; easiness, permissiveness; charitableness, charity, generousness, magnanimity; compassion, sympathy; sensitivity
5 **unprejudicedness, unbiasedness;** impartiality, evenhandedness, equitability, justice, fairness, justness, objectivity, detachment, dispassionateness, disinterestedness, impersonality; indifference, neutrality; unopinionatedness
6 **liberal,** liberalist; libertarian; freethinker, latitudinarian, ecumenist, ecumenicist; big person, broad-gauge person; bleeding heart, bleeding-heart liberal

VERBS 7 **keep an open mind,** be big, judge not, not write off, suspend judgment, listen to reason, open one's mind to, see both sides, judge on the merits; live and let live; lean over backwards, tolerate; accept, be easy with, view with indulgence, condone, brook, abide with, be content with; live with; shut one's eyes to, look the other way, wink at, blink at, overlook, disregard, ignore

ADJS 8 **broad-minded,** wide-minded, large-minded, broad, wide, wide-ranging, broad-gauged, catholic, spacious of mind; unbigoted, unfanatical, unhidebound, unprovincial, cosmopolitan, noninsular, unparochial; ecumenistic, ecumenical
9 **liberal, liberal-minded,** liberalistic; libertarian; freethinking, latitudinarian; bleeding-heart
10 **open-minded,** open, receptive, rational, admissive; persuadable, persuasible; unopinionated, unopinioned, unwedded to an opinion; unpositive, undogmatic; uninfatuated, unbesotted, unfanatical
11 **tolerant**, tolerating; indulgent, lenient, condoning; forbearing, forbearant, patient, long-suffering; charitable, generous, magnanimous; compassionate, sympathetic, sensitive
12 **unprejudiced, unbiased,** unprepossessed, unjaundiced; impartial, evenhanded, fair, just, equitable, objective, dispassionate, impersonal, detached, disinterested; indifferent, neutral; unswayed, uninfluenced, undazzled; non-sexist, inclusive
13 liberalizing, liberating, broadening, enlightening

980 NARROW-MINDEDNESS

<intolerant of varied views>

NOUNS 1 **narrow-mindedness,** narrowness, illiberality, uncatholicity; little-mindedness, **small-mindedness,** smallness, littleness, meanness, pettiness; close-mindedness; bigotry, bigotedness, fanaticism; insularity, insularism, provincialism, parochialism; hideboundness, straitlacedness, stuffiness; authoritarianism; shortsightedness, nearsightedness, purblindness; blind side, blind spot, tunnel vision, blinders; closed mind, mean mind, petty mind, shut mind; narrow views, narrow sympathies, cramped ideas; an ax to grind
2 **intolerance,** intoleration; **uncharitableness,** ungenerousness; unforbearance; noncompassion, insensitivity
3 **prejudice,** prejudgment, forejudgment, predilection, prepossession, preconception; **bias,** bent, leaning, inclination, twist; jaundice, jaundiced eye; partiality, partialism, partisanship, favoritism, onesidedness, undispassionateness, undetachment
4 **discrimination,** social discrimination, minority prejudice; xenophobia, know-nothingism; chauvinism, ultranationalism, superpatriotism; fascism; class consciousness, class prejudice, class distinction, class hatred, class war; anti-Semitism; redbaiting; racism, racialism, race hatred, race prejudice, race snobbery, racial discrimination; white supremacy, black supremacy, white power, black power, race relations; color line, color bar; social barrier, Jim Crow, Jim Crow law; segregation, apartheid; sex discrimination, sexism, manism, masculism, male chauvinism, feminism, womanism; ageism, age discrimination; social prejudice; glass ceiling, stained-glass ceiling
5 **bigot,** intolerant, illiberal, little person, Archie Bunker; **racist,** racialist, racial supremacist, white supremacist, black supremacist, pig; **chauvinist,** ultranationalist, jingo, superpatriot; **sexist,** male chauvinist, male chauvinist pig (MCP), manist, masculist, feminist, female chauvinist, womanist, dogmatist, doctrinaire; fanatic

VERBS 6 close one's mind, shut the eyes of one's mind, **take narrow views**, put on blinders, blind oneself, have a blind spot, have tunnel vision, constrict one's views; not see beyond one's nose, not see an inch beyond one's nose; view with a jaundiced eye, see but one side of the question, look only at one side of the shield
7 **prejudge,** forejudge, judge beforehand, precondemn, prejudicate, take one's opinions ready-made, accede to prejudice

8 **discriminate against**, draw the line, draw the color line; bait, bash; red-bait

9 **prejudice,** prejudice against, prejudice the issue, prepossess, jaundice, influence, sway, bias, bias one's judgment; warp, twist, bend, distort

ADJS **10** **narrow-minded,** narrow, narrow-gauged, closed, closed-minded, cramped, constricted, po-faced <Brit>, little-minded, small-minded, mean-minded, petty-minded, narrowhearted, narrow-souled, narrow-spirited, meanspirited, small-souled; small, little, mean, petty; uncharitable, ungenerous; bigot, bigoted, fanatical; illiberal, unliberal, uncatholic; provincial, insular, parochial; hidebound, creedbound, straitlaced, stuffy; authoritarian; shortsighted, nearsighted, purblind; deaf, deaf-minded, deaf to reason

11 **intolerant,** untolerating; unindulgent, uncondoning, unforbearing

12 **discriminatory; prejudiced,** prepossessed, **biased,** jaundiced, colored; partial, one-sided, partisan; influenced, swayed, warped, twisted; interested, nonobjective, undetached, undispassionate; xenophobic, know-nothing; chauvinistic, ultranationalist, superpatriotic; racist, racialist, anti-Negro, antiblack, antiwhite; anti-Semitic; sexist; dogmatic, doctrinaire, opinionated

981 CURIOSITY

<inquisitive interest>

NOUNS **1** **curiosity,** curiousness, **inquisitiveness;** interest, interestedness, lively interest; thirst for knowledge, desire for knowledge, lust for knowledge, itch for knowledge, mental acquisitiveness, inquiring mind, curious mind; attention; alertness, watchfulness, vigilance; nosiness, snoopiness, prying, snooping; eavesdropping; officiousness, meddlesomeness; morbid curiosity, ghoulishness; voyeurism, scopophilia, prurience, prurient interest; rubbernecking

2 inquisitive person, quidnunc; **inquirer,** questioner, querier, querist, inquisitor, inquisitress; detective; busybody, gossip, *yenta* <Yiddish>, pry, Paul Pry, **snoop,** snooper, nosy Parker; eavesdropper; sightseer; rubbernecker, rubberneck; watcher, Peeping Tom, voyeur, scopophiliac; Lot's wife; explorer

VERBS **3** **be curious, want to know,** take an interest in, take a lively interest, burn with curiosity; be alert, alert oneself, watch, be watchful, be vigilant; prick up one's ears, keep one's ear to the ground; eavesdrop; interrogate, quiz, question, inquire, query; keep one's eyes open, keep one's eye on, stare, gape, peer, gawk, rubber, rubberneck; seek, dig up, dig around for, nose out, nose around for; investigate

4 **pry, snoop,** peep, peek, spy, nose, nose into, have a long nose, poke one's nose in, stick one's nose in; meddle

ADJS **5** **curious, inquisitive,** inquisitorial, inquiring, interested, quizzical; alert, keen, tuned in, attentive; burning with curiosity, eaten up with curiosity, consumed with curiosity, curious as a cat; agape, agog, all agog, openmouthed, open-eyed; gossipy; overcurious, supercurious; morbidly curious, morbid, ghoulish; prurient, itchy, voyeuristic, scopophiliac; rubbernecking

6 **prying,** snooping, **nosy,** snoopy; meddlesome

982 INCURIOSITY

<lacking normal curiosity>

NOUNS **1** **incuriosity,** incuriousness, uninquisitiveness; boredom; inattention; uninterestedness, **disinterest**, disinterestedness, unconcern, uninvolvement, detachment, indifference, indifferentness, indifferentism, uncaring, apathy, passivity, passiveness, impassivity, impassiveness, listlessness, stolidity, lack of interest; carelessness, heedlessness, regardlessness, insouciance, unmindfulness; unperturbability; aloofness, withdrawal, reclusiveness; intellectual inertia; catatonia, autism; gullibility, credulity, blind faith; objectivity; attentional blink

VERBS **2** **take no interest in, not care;** mind one's own business, pursue the even tenor of one's way, glance neither to the right nor to the left, keep one's nose out, keep an open mind; be indifferent, not care less, lack emotion; disregard; take it or leave it; take on trust; live and let live

ADJS **3** **incurious, uninquisitive,** uninquiring; bored; inattentive; **uninterested,** unconcerned, disinterested, uninvolved, nonaligned, detached, indifferent, impersonal, apathetic, passive, impassive, stolid, phlegmatic, imperturbable, listless; careless, heedless, regardless, insouciant, mindless, unmindful; aloof, distant, withdrawn, reclusive, sequestered, eremitic; catatonic, autistic; not bothered; lackadaisical; unbiased, objective

983 ATTENTION

<applying the mind to something>

NOUNS **1** **attention, attentiveness, mindfulness**, regardfulness, heedfulness; attention span; heed, ear; consideration, thought, mind; **awareness**, consciousness, alertness; observation, observance, advertence, advertency, note, notice, remark, put one's finger on, regard, respect; intentness, intentiveness, concentration; diligence, assiduity, assiduousness, earnestness; care; curiosity

2 **interest,** concern, concernment; curiosity; enthusiasm, passion, ardor, zeal; cathexis; matter of interest, special interest; solicitude; watchlist

3 engrossment, **absorption,** intentness, single-mindedness, concentration, application, study, studiousness, preoccupation, engagement, involvement, **immersion**, submersion; obsession, monomania; rapt attention, absorbed attention, absorbed interest; deep study, deep thought, profound thought, contemplation, meditation

4 **close attention,** close study, scrutiny, fixed regard, rapt attention, fascinated attention, total attention, undivided attention; minute attention, meticulous attention, attention to detail, microscopic scrutiny, finicalness, finickiness; constant attention, unrelenting attention, close observance, harping, strict attention; special consideration

VERBS 5 **attend to,** look to, see to, advert to, be aware of; **pay attention to,** pay regard to, give mind to, pay mind to, not forget, spare a thought for, give heed to; bethink, bethink oneself; have a look at; turn to, give thought to, trouble one's head about; give one's mind to, direct one's attention to, set the mind to, turn the attention to; devote oneself to, devote the mind to, focus the mind on, fix the thoughts on, set one's thoughts on, apply the mind to, apply the attention to, apply oneself to, occupy oneself with, concern oneself with, give oneself up to, be absorbed in, be engrossed in, be into; sink one's teeth, take an interest in, take hold of; have a lot on one's mind, have a lot on one's plate; be preoccupied with; lose oneself in; hang on one's words, hang on the lips; drink in, drink in with rapt attention; be solicitous, suck up to, brown-nose

6 **heed, attend,** be heedful, tend, mind, be mindful, watch, observe, regard, look, see, view, mark, remark, animadvert, note, notice, take note, take notice, get a load of

7 hearken to, hark, **listen,** hear, give ear to, lend an ear to, bend an ear to, prick up the ears, strain one's ears, keep one's ears open, unstopper one's ears, keep an ear to the ground, listen with both ears, be all ears

8 **pay attention**, pay heed, take heed, give heed, look out, watch out, take care; look lively, look alive, look sharp, stay alert, be alert, sit up and take notice; be on the ball, keep one's eye on the ball, not miss a trick, not overlook a bet, keep a weather eye out; miss nothing; get after, seize on, keep one's eyes open; attend to business, mind one's business; pay close attention, pay strict attention, strain one's attention, not relax one's concern, give one's undivided attention, give special attention to, dance attendance on; keep in the center of one's attention, keep uppermost in one's thought; concentrate on, focus on, fix on; study, scrutinize, survey; be obsessed with; cathect

9 take cognizance of, **take notice of,** take note of, take heed of, take account of, take into consideration, take into account, bear in mind, keep in mind, hold in mind, reckon with, keep in sight, keep in view, not lose sight of, have in one's eye, have an eye to, have regard for

10 **call attention to,** direct attention to, bring under one's notice, bring to one's notice, hold up to notice, bring to attention, mention, mention in passing, touch on; **single out,** pick out, lift up, focus on, bring to notice, direct to the attention, feature, highlight, brightline; direct to, address to; specify, cite, refer to, allude to; alert one, call to one's attention, put one wise, put one on; point out, point to, point at, put one's finger on; excite attention, stimulate attention, drum up attention

11 meet with attention, fall under one's notice; **catch the attention,** strike one, impress one, draw the attention, hold the attention, focus the attention, catch the eye, meet the eye, catch one's ear, attract notice, attract attention, arrest attention, engage attention, fix one's attention, rivet one's attention, arrest the thoughts, awaken the mind, awaken the thoughts, excite notice, arouse notice, arrest one's notice, invite attention, solicit attention, claim attention, demand attention, act as a magnet

12 **interest,** concern, involve in, involve with, affect the interest, give pause; pique, titillate, tantalize, tickle, tickle one's fancy, attract, invite, fascinate, provoke, stimulate, arouse, excite, pique one's interest, excite interest, excite one's interest, whet one's interest, arouse one's passion, arouse one's enthusiasm, turn one on

13 **engross, absorb,** immerse, occupy, preoccupy, engage, involve, monopolize, exercise, take up; obsess; grip, hold, arrest, hold the interest, fascinate, enthrall, spellbind, hold spellbound, grab, charm, enchant, mesmerize, hypnotize, catch; absorb the attention, claim one's thoughts, engross the mind, engross the thoughts, engage the attention, involve the interest, occupy the attention, monopolize one's attention, engage the mind, engage the thoughts

14 **come to attention,** stand at attention

ADJS 15 **attentive,** heedful, **mindful,** regardful, advertent; intent, intentive, on top of, diligent, assiduous, intense, earnest, concentrated; careful, on guard, vigilant; observing, observant; watchful, aware, conscious, alert; curious; agog, openmouthed; open-eared, open-eyed, all eyes, all ears, all eyes and ears; on the job, on the ball, Johnny-on-the-spot; meticulous, sedulous, nice, finical, finicky, finicking, niggling

16 **interested,** concerned; alert to, sensitive to, on the watch; curious; tantalized, piqued, titillated, tickled, attracted, fascinated, excited, fired-up, turned-on; keen on, keen about, enthusiastic, passionate; fixating, cathectic

17 **engrossed, absorbed,** totally absorbed, single-minded, occupied, preoccupied, engaged, devoted, devoted to, intent, intent on, monopolized, obsessed, monomaniacal, swept up, taken up with, involved, caught up in, wrapped in, wrapped up in, engrossed in, absorbed in, absorbed with, absorbed by, lost in, immersed in, submerged in, buried in; over head and ears in, head over heels in, up to one's elbows in, up to one's ears in; contemplating, contemplative, studying, studious, meditative, meditating; solicitous, indulgent

18 **gripped,** held, **fascinated,** enthralled, rapt, spellbound, charmed, enchanted, mesmerized, hypnotized, fixed, caught, riveted, arrested, switched-on

19 **interesting,** stimulating, provocative, provoking, thought-provoking, thought-challenging, thought-inspiring; titillating, tickling, tantalizing, **inviting, exciting; piquant,** lively, racy, juicy, succulent, spicy, rich; readable

20 **engrossing, absorbing,** consuming, gripping, riveting, holding, arresting, engaging, attractive, fascinating, enthralling, spellbinding, enchanting, magnetic, hypnotic, mesmerizing, mesmeric; obsessive, obsessing

ADVS 21 **attentively,** with attention; heedfully, mindfully, regardfully, advertently; observingly, observantly; interestedly, with interest; raptly, with rapt attention; engrossedly, absorbedly, preoccupiedly; devotedly, intently, without distraction, with undivided attention

INTERJS 22 attention, look, see, look you, look here, looky, witness; tah-dah, presto, hey presto, voilà; lo, behold, lo and behold; **hark,** listen, listen up, hark ye, hear ye, oyez; *nota bene* (NB) <L, note well>; mark my words

23 hey, hail, ahoy, hello, hollo, hallo, halloo, halloa, ho, heigh, hi, hist; hello there, ahoy there, yo

984 INATTENTION

<failure to pay attention>

NOUNS 1 **inattention,** inattentiveness, **heedlessness,** unheedfulness, unmindfulness, thoughtlessness, attentional blink, continuous partial attention; inconsideration; incuriosity, indifference; inadvertence, inadvertency; unintentness, unintentiveness; disregard, disregardfulness, regardlessness, apathy; flightiness, giddiness, lightmindedness, dizziness, ditziness, scattiness; levity, frivolousness, flippancy; shallowness, superficiality; inobservance, unobservance, nonobservance; unalertness, unwariness, unwatchfulness; obliviousness, unconsciousness, unawareness; carelessness, negligence, oversight; distraction, absentmindedness, woolgathering, daydreaming, head in the clouds; attention deficit disorder (ADD), attention deficit hyperactivity disorder (ADHD)

VERBS 2 **be inattentive, pay no attention,** pay no mind, not attend, not notice, take no note of, take no notice of, take no account of, miss, not heed, give no heed, pay no regard to, not listen, hear nothing, not hear a word; disregard, overlook, ignore, pass over, pass by, have no time for, let pass, get by, get past; think little of, think nothing of, slight, make light of; close one's eyes to, shut one's eyes to, see nothing, be blind to, turn a blind eye, look the other way, blink at, wink at, connive at; bury one's head in the sand, hide one's head in the sand; turn a deaf ear to, stop one's ears, let come in one ear and go out the other, tune out; let well enough alone; not trouble oneself with, not trouble one's head about; be unwary, be off one's guard, be caught out

3 **wander, stray,** divagate, wander from the subject, ramble; have no attention span, have a short attention span, let one's attention wander, allow one's mind to wander, get off the track; fall asleep at the switch, woolgather, daydream

4 **dismiss,** dismiss from one's thoughts, drive from one's thoughts; **put out of mind,** put out of one's head, force one's thoughts from, think no more of, forget, forget it, forget about it, fuhgeddaboudit, let it go, let slip, not give it another thought, not give it a second thought, drop the subject, give it no more thought, obliviate; turn one's back upon, turn away from, turn one's attention from, walk away, abandon, leave out in the cold; put aside, set aside, lay aside, push aside, thrust aside, put to one side, thrust to one side, wave aside; put on the back burner, put on hold; turn up one's nose at, sneeze at; shrug off, brush off, brush aside, brush away, blow off, laugh off, laugh away,

dismiss with a laugh; slight, kiss off, slap down, smack down

5 escape notice, **escape attention**, escape one, get by, be missed, pass one by, not enter one's head, never occur to one, fall on deaf ears, not register, go over one's head

ADJS 6 **inattentive, unmindful,** inadvertent, thoughtless, incurious, indifferent; heedless, unheeding, unheedful, regardless, disregardful, disregardant; unobserving, inobservant, unobservant, unnoticing, unnoting, unremarking, unmarking; distracted; careless, negligent; scatterbrained, giddy, ditzy, scatty, flighty; absentminded, out to lunch

7 **oblivious,** unconscious, insensible, dead to the world, out of it, not with it; blind, deaf; preoccupied; in a world of one's own

8 **unalert,** unwary, unwatchful, unvigilant, uncautious, incautious; unprepared, unready; unguarded, off one's guard, off-guard; asleep, sleeping, nodding, napping, **asleep at the switch**, asleep on the job, not on the job, goofing off, looking out the window; daydreaming, woolgathering

985 DISTRACTION, CONFUSION

<mental confusion and disturbance>

NOUNS 1 **distraction,** distractedness, **diversion,** separation of attention, withdrawal of attention, divided attention, competing stimuli; too much on one's mind, too much on one's plate, cognitive dissonance, sensory overload; inattention

2 abstractedness, abstraction, **preoccupation,** absorption, engrossment, depth of thought, fit of abstraction; absentmindedness, absence of mind; bemusement, musing, musefulness; woolgathering, mooning, moonraking, stargazing, dreaming, **daydreaming**, fantasying, pipe-dreaming, castle-building; brown study, study, reverie, muse, dreamy abstraction, quiet ecstasy, muted ecstasy, trance; dream, daydream, fantasy, pipe dream; daydreamer, Walter Mitty

3 **confusion,** fluster, flummox, flutter, flurry, ruffle; disorientation, muddle, muddlement, fuddle, fuddlement, befuddlement, muddleheadedness, daze, maze; unsettlement, disorganization, disorder, chaos, mess, mix-up, screwup, shitshow*, snafu, balls-up, shemozzle, shuffle, jumble, discomfiture, discomposure, disconcertion, discombobulation, bewilderment, embarrassment, disturbance, perturbation, upset, frenzy, pother, bother, botheration, stew, pucker; tizzy, swivet, sweat; haze, fog, mist, cloud; perplexity

4 **dizziness, vertigo,** vertiginousness, spinning head, swimming, swimming of the head, giddiness, wooziness, lightheadedness; tiddliness, drunkenness

5 **flightiness,** giddiness, volatility, mercuriality; thoughtlessness, witlessness, brainlessness, empty-headedness, frivolity, frivolousness, dizziness, ditziness, scattiness, foolishness; scatterbrain, flibbertigibbet

VERBS 6 **distract, divert,** detract, distract the attention, divert attention, detract attention, divert the thoughts, draw off the attention, call away, take the mind off of, relieve the mind of, cause the mind to stray, cause the mind to wander, put off the track, derail, throw off the scent, lead the mind astray, beguile; throw off one's guard, catch off balance, put off one's stride, trip up

7 **confuse,** throw into confusion, throw into chaos, entangle, **mix up**, fluster; flummox, flutter, put into a flutter, flurry, rattle, ruffle, moider; muddle, fuddle, befuddle, addle, addle the wits, daze, maze, dazzle, bedazzle; upset, unsettle, raise hell, disorganize; throw into a tizzy; disconcert, discomfit, discompose, discombobulate, disorient, disorientate, bewilder, embarrass, put out, disturb, perturb, bother, pother, bug; fog, mist, cloud, becloud; perplex

8 **dizzy,** make one's head swim, cause vertigo, send one spinning, whirl the mind, swirl the senses, make one's head reel, make one's head spin, go to one's head; **intoxicate**

9 muse, moon, **dream, daydream,** pipe-dream, fantasy; abstract oneself, be lost in thought, let one's attention wander, let one's mind run on other things, dream of other things, muse on other things; wander, stray, ramble, divagate, let one's thoughts wander, let one's mind wander, give oneself up to reverie, woolgather, go woolgathering, let one's wits go bird's nesting, be in a brown study, be absent, be somewhere else, stargaze, be out of it, be not with it

ADJS 10 **distracted,** distraught; wandering, rambling; wild, frantic, beside oneself

11 abstracted, bemused, museful, musing, preoccupied, absorbed, engrossed, taken up; **absentminded, absent,** faraway, elsewhere, somewhere else, not there; pensive, meditative; lost, **lost in thought,** wrapped in thought; rapt, transported, ecstatic; dead to the world, unconscious, oblivious; dreaming, dreamy, drowsing, dozing, nodding, half-awake, betwixt sleep and waking, napping; daydreaming, daydreamy, pipe-dreaming; woolgathering, mooning, moony, moonraking, castle-building,

in the clouds, off in the clouds, stargazing, in a reverie

12 **confused, mixed-up,** crazy mixed-up; flustered, fluttered, ruffled, rattled, fussed; upset, unsettled, off-balance, off one's stride; disorganized, disordered, disoriented, disorientated, chaotic, jumbled, in a jumble, shuffled; shaken, shook, disconcerted, discomposed, discombobulated, embarrassed, put-out, disturbed, perturbed, bothered, all hot and bothered; in a stew, in a botheration, in a pucker; in a tizzy, in a pother; perplexed

13 **muddled,** in a muddle; fuddled, befuddled; muddleheaded, fuddlebrained; puzzleheaded, puzzlepated; addled, addleheaded, addlepated, addlebrained; adrift, at sea, foggy, fogged, in a fog, hazy, muzzy, misted, misty, cloudy, beclouded

14 **dazed,** mazed, dazzled, bedazzled, in a daze; silly, knocked silly, cockeyed; groggy, dopey, woozy; punch-drunk, punchy, slap-happy; shell-shocked

15 **dizzy,** giddy, vertiginous, spinning, swimming, turned around, going around in circles; lightheaded, tiddly, drunk, drunken

16 scatterbrained, rattlebrained, rattleheaded, rattlepated, scramblebrained, harebrain, **harebrained**, giddy, dizzy, ditzy, gaga, scatty, giddy-brained, giddy-headed, giddy-pated, giddy-witted, giddy as a goose, fluttery, frivolous, featherbrained, featherheaded; thoughtless, witless, brainless, empty-headed

17 **flighty,** volatile, mercurial

986 IMAGINATION

<ability to form original mental image>

NOUNS 1 **imagination,** imagining, imaginativeness, **fancy,** fantasy, conceit; mind's eye; flight of fancy, fumes of fancy; fantasticism

2 **creative thought,** conception; lateral thinking, association of ideas; creative imagination, creative power, creative ability, esemplastic imagination, esemplastic power, shaping imagination, poetic imagination, artistic imagination, blue-sky thinking; mythopoeia; mythification, mythicization; inspiration, stimulus, muse; Muses: Calliope <epic poetry>, Clio <history>, Erato <lyric and love poetry>, Euterpe <music>, Melpomene <tragedy>, Polyhymnia <sacred song>, Terpsichore <dancing and choral song>, Thalia <comedy>, Urania <astronomy>; genius; afflatus, divine afflatus; frenzy, ecstasy

3 **invention, inventiveness,** originality, creativity, fabrication, creativeness, ingenuity; productivity, prolificacy, fertility, fecundity; rich imagination, teeming imagination, fertile imagination, pregnant imagination, seminal imagination, germinal imagination, fertile mind; imagineering; fiction, fictionalization

4 **lively imagination,** active fancy, **vivid imagination,** colorful imagination, highly colored imagination, lurid imagination, ardent imagination, heated imagination, excited imagination, wild imagination; verve, vivacity of imagination

5 **figment of the imagination,** creature of the imagination, creation of the brain, coinage of the brain, fiction of the mind, whim, whimsy, figment, imagination, invention; caprice, vagary; brainchild; imagining, fancy, idle fancy, vapor, imagery; fantasy, make-believe; fabrication; phantom, vision, apparition, insubstantial image, eidolon, phantasm; fiction, myth, romance; wildest dreams, stretch of the imagination; chimera, bubble, illusion; hallucination, delirium, sick fancy; trip, drug trip

6 **visualization,** envisioning, envisaging, picturing, objectification, imaging, calling to the mind's eye, calling before the mind's eye, portraying in the mind, representing in the mind; depicting in the imagination, delineating in the imagination; conceptualization; picture, vision, image, mental image, mental picture, visual image, vivid image, lifelike image, eidetic image, concept, conception, mental representation, mental presentation; image-building, imagery, word-painting; poetic image, poetic imagery; imagery study; imagism, imagistic poetry

7 **idealism,** idealization; ideal, ideality; rose-colored glasses; visionariness, utopianism; flight of fancy, play of fancy, imaginative exercise; romanticism, romanticizing, romance; quixotism, quixotry; dreamery; impracticality, unpracticalness, unrealism, unreality; wishful thinking, wish fulfillment, wish-fulfillment fantasy, dream come true; autistic thinking, dereistic thinking, autism, dereism, autistic distortion

8 **dreaminess,** dreamfulness, musefulness, pensiveness; dreamlikeness; dreaming, musing; daydreaming, pipe-dreaming, dreamery, fantasying, castlebuilding

9 **dream;** reverie, daydream, pipe dream, wishful thinking; brown study; vision; nightmare, night terror, incubus, bad dream

10 air castle, castle in the air, castle in the sky, castle in Spain; Xanadu, Middle Earth, pleasure dome of Kubla Khan, pie in the sky, end of the rainbow

11 **utopia**, Utopia, **paradise**, Heaven, Heaven on earth; promised land; Holy Land; kingdom come; dreamland, dream world, lotus land,

land of dreams, land of enchantment, land of heart's desire, wonderland, cloudland, fairyland, land of faerie, faerie; Eden, Garden of Eden; the Promised Land, land of promise, land of plenty, land of milk and honey, Canaan, Goshen; Shangri-la, Atlantis, Arcadia, Agapemone, Camelot, Avalon, Happy Valley, land of Prester John, El Dorado, Emerald City, Treasure Island, Wonderland, Seven Cities of Cibola, Quivira; Laputa; Cockaigne, Big Rock-Candy Mountain, Fiddler's Green, never-never land, Neverland, Cloudcuckooland, Nephelococcygia, Erewhon, Land of Youth, Fountain of Youth; dystopia, kakotopia; Pandemonium; Middle Earth; millennium

12 **imaginer,** fancier, fantast; fantasist; mythmaker, mythopoet; mythifier, mythicizer; inventor; creative artist, composer, poet, creative writer; imagineer

13 **visionary, idealist**; prophet, seer; dreamer, daydreamer, dreamer of dreams, castle-builder, lotus-eater, wishful thinker; romantic, romanticist, romancer; Quixote, Don Quixote; utopian, utopianist, utopianizer; escapist, ostrich; enthusiast, rhapsodist

VERBS 14 **imagine,** fancy, conceive, conceit, **conceptualize,** ideate, figure to oneself; invent, create, originate, make, think up, dream up, shape, mold, coin, hatch, concoct, fabricate, produce; suppose; fantasize; fictionalize; use one's imagination; give free rein to the imagination, let one's imagination run riot, let one's imagination wild, allow one's imagination to run away with one; experience imaginatively, experience vicariously; imagineer

15 **visualize,** vision, **envision,** envisage, picture, image, objectify; picture in one's mind, picture to oneself, view with the mind's eye, contemplate in the imagination, form a mental picture of, represent, see, just see, have a picture of; call up, summon up, conjure up, call to mind, realize; have an inspiration

16 **idealize,** utopianize, quixotize, rhapsodize; romanticize, romance; paint pretty pictures of, paint in bright colors; see through rose-colored glasses; build castles in the air, build castles in Spain; live in a dream world

17 **dream;** dream of, dream on; daydream, pipe-dream, have stars in one's eyes, have one's head in the clouds, indulge in wish fulfillment; fantasy, conjure up a vision; blow one's mind, go on a trip, trip, freak out

ADJS 18 **imaginative,** conceptual, conceptive, ideational, ideative, notional; perceptive; **inventive,** original, innovative, originative, esemplastic, shaping, creative, ingenious, resourceful; productive, fertile, fecund, prolific, seminal, germinal, teeming, pregnant; inspired, visioned

19 **imaginary,** imaginational, notional; **imagined,** fancied; unreal, unrealistic, airy-fairy, unactual, nonexistent, never-never; visional, supposititious, all in the mind; illusory; not of this world

20 **fanciful,** notional, notiony, whimsical, maggoty <Brit>; airy-fairy; brain-born; fancy-bred, fancy-born, fancy-built, fancy-framed, fancy-woven, fancy-wrought; dream-born, dream-built, dream-created; **fantastic, fantastical,** fantasque, extravagant, preposterous, outlandish, wild, baroque, rococo, florid; Alice-in-Wonderland, bizarre, grotesque, Gothic

21 **fictitious, make-believe,** figmental, fictional, fictive, fabricated, fictionalized; nonhistorical, nonfactual, nonactual, nonrealistic; fabulous, mythic, **mythical,** mythological, legendary; mythified, mythicized

22 **chimeric,** chimerical, aerial, **ethereal,** phantasmal; vaporous, vapory; gossamer; air-built, cloud-built, cloud-born, cloud-woven

23 **ideal,** idealized; utopian, Arcadian, Edenic, paradisal; pie in the sky; heavenly, celestial; millennial

24 **visionary,** idealistic, quixotic; romantic, romanticized, romancing, romanticizing; poetic, poetical; storybook; impractical, unpractical, unrealistic; wish-fulfilling, autistic, dereistic; starry-eyed, dewy-eyed; in the clouds, with one's head in the clouds; airy, otherworldly, transmundane, transcendental

25 dreamy, dreamful; dreamy-eyed, dreamy-minded, dreamy-souled; dreamlike; day-dreamy, **dreaming,** daydreaming, pipe-dreaming, castle-building; entranced, tranced, in a trance, dream-stricken, enchanted, spellbound, spelled, charmed

26 **imaginable,** fanciable, conceivable, thinkable, cogitable; supposable

987 UNIMAGINATIVENESS

<lacking imagination>

NOUNS 1 **unimaginativeness,** unfancifulness; **prosaicness,** prosiness, prosaism, prosaicism, unpoeticalness; staidness, stuffiness; stolidity; dullness, dryness; aridness, aridity, barrenness, infertility, infecundity; unoriginality, uncreativeness, uninventiveness, dearth of ideas

2 <practical attitude> **realism,** realisticness, **practicalness,** practicality, practical-mindedness, sober-mindedness, sobersidedness, hardheadedness, matter-of-factness; down-to-

earthness, earthiness, worldliness, secularism; real world, the here and now; nuts and bolts, no nonsense, no frills; pragmatism, pragmaticism, positivism, scientism; unidealism, unromanticalness, unsentimentality; sensibleness, saneness, reasonableness, rationality; freedom from illusion, lack of sentimentality; lack of feelings

3 **realist,** pragmatist, positivist, practical person, hardhead

VERBS 4 **keep both feet on the ground,** stick to the facts, call a spade a spade; come down to earth, come down out of the clouds, know when the honeymoon is over

ADJS 5 **unimaginative,** unfanciful; unidealized, unromanticized; **prosaic**, prosy, prosing, unpoetic, unpoetical; literal, literal-minded; earthbound, mundane; staid, stuffy; stolid; dull, dry; arid, barren, infertile, infecund; unoriginal, uninspired; hedged, undaring, unaspiring, uninventive

6 **realistic,** realist, **practical**; pragmatic, pragmatical, scientific, scientistic, positivistic; unidealistic, unideal, unromantic, unsentimental, practical-minded, sober-minded, sobersided, hardheaded, straight-thinking, matter-of-fact, down-to-earth, with both feet on the ground; worldly, earthy, secular; sensible, sane, reasonable, rational, sound, sound-thinking; reductive, simplistic

988 SPECTER

<haunting thought>

NOUNS 1 **specter, ghost,** spectral ghost, spook, phantom, phantasm, phantasma, wraith, shade, shadow, fetch, apparition, appearance, presence, shape, form, eidolon, idolum, revenant, larva; **spirit;** sprite, shrouded spirit, disembodied spirit, departed spirit, restless spirit, wandering spirit, restless soul, soul of the dead, dybbuk; oni; Masan; astral spirit, astral; unsubstantiality, immateriality, incorporeal, incorporeity, incorporeal being, incorporeal entity; walking dead man, zombie; jinn, dijn, genie; duppy; vision, theophany; materialization; haunt, hant; banshee; poltergeist; control, guide; manes, lemures; grateful dead

2 White Lady, White Lady of Avenel, White Ladies of Normandy; Brocken specter; Wild Hunt; Flying Dutchman

3 **double,** etheric double, etheric self, co-walker, *Doppelgänger* <Ger>, doubleganger, fetch, wraith

4 eeriness, **ghostliness**, weirdness, uncanniness, spookiness

5 possession, spirit control; obsession

VERBS 6 **haunt,** hant, spook; possess, control; obsess

ADJS 7 **spectral,** specterlike; **ghostly,** ghostish, ghosty, ghostlike; spiritual, psychic, psychical; phantomlike, phantom, phantomic, phantomical, phantasmal, phantasmic, wraithlike, wraithy, shadowy; etheric, ectoplasmic, astral, ethereal; incorporeal; occult, supernatural

8 **disembodied,** bodiless, immaterial, discarnate, decarnate, decarnated

9 weird, eerie, eldritch, uncanny, unearthly, macabre; **spooky**, spookish, hairy

10 **haunted,** spooked, spooky, spirit-haunted, ghost-haunted, specter-haunted; possessed, ghost-ridden; obsessed

989 MEMORY

<something remembered, recalled>

NOUNS 1 **memory, remembrance, recollection,** mind; memory trace, engram; mind's eye, eye of the mind, mirror of the mind, tablets of the memory; corner of the memory, recess of the memory, inmost recesses of the memory; Mnemosyne, mother of the Muses; short-term memory, working memory; long-term memory, anterograde memory; computer memory, information storage; group memory, collective memory, mneme, racial memory; atavism; cover memory, screen memory, affect memory; eye memory, visual memory, kinesthetic memory; skill, verbal response, emotional response

2 **retention, retentiveness,** retentivity, memory span; good memory, retentive memory, retentive mind; total memory, eidetic memory, eidetic imagery, photographic memory, total recall; camera-eye; learning curve

3 **remembering, remembrance, recollection,** recollecting, exercise of memory, **recall,** recalling; reflection, reconsideration; retrospect, retrospection, hindsight, looking back, harking back; flashback, reminiscence, review, contemplation of the past, review of things past, nostalgia; memoir; memorization, memorizing, rote, rote memory, rote learning, learning by heart, commitment to memory; déjà vu

4 **recognition,** identification, reidentification, distinguishment; realization

5 **reminder,** remembrance, remembrancer; prompt, prompter, tickler; prompting, cue, hint; jogger, flapper; *aide-mémoire* <Fr>, memorandum

6 **memento,** remembrance, token, trophy, souvenir, **keepsake**, relic, favor, token of remembrance; commemoration, memorial; *memento mori* <L>; memories, memorabilia, memorials; history, memoirs

7 memorability, rememberability

8 **mnemonics**, memory training, mnemotechny, mnemotechnics, mnemonization; mnemonic device, *aide-mémoire* <Fr>

VERBS **9** **remember, recall,** recollect, flash on, mind; have a good memory, remember clearly, remember as if it were yesterday; have total recall, remember everything; reflect; think of, bethink oneself; call to mind, bring to mind, recall to mind, call up, summon up, conjure up, evoke, reevoke, revive, recapture, call back, bring back; think back, go back, look back, cast the eyes back, carry one's thoughts back, look back upon things past, use hindsight, retrospect, see in retrospect, go back over, hark back, retrace, reconstruct, review, turn back time; review in retrospect; write one's memoirs

10 **reminisce,** rake up the past, dig up the past

11 **recognize,** know, tell, distinguish, make out; identify, place, have; spot, nail, peg, cotton on, reidentify, know again, recover knowledge of, recall knowledge of, know by sight; realize

12 **keep in memory,** bear in mind, keep in mind, hold in mind, hold the memory of, retain the memory of, keep in view, have in mind, hold in one's thoughts, carry in one's thoughts, store in the mind, **retain,** keep; burden the memory, treasure, cherish, treasure up in the memory, enshrine in the memory, embalm in the memory, cherish the memory of; keep up the memory of, keep the memory alive, keep alive in one's thoughts; brood over, dwell on, dwell upon, fan the embers, let fester in the mind, let rankle in the breast

13 **be remembered,** sink in, penetrate, make an impression; live in one's memory, be easy to recall, remain in one's memory, be fresh in one's memory, stick in the mind, remain indelibly impressed on the memory, be stamped on one's memory, never be forgotten; haunt one's thoughts, obsess, run in the head, be in one's thoughts, be on one's mind; be burnt into one's memory, plague one; be like King Charles's head; rankle, rankle in the breast, fester in the mind

14 recur, recur to the mind, return to mind, come back, resurface, reenter

15 **come to mind,** pop into one's head, come to me, come into one's head, flash on the mind, pass in review

16 **memorize,** commit to memory, con; study; **learn by heart,** get by heart, learn by rote, get word-perfect, get letter-perfect, learn word for word, learn verbatim; know by heart, know from memory, have by heart, have by rote, have at one's fingertips; repeat by heart, give word for word, recite, repeat, parrot, repeat like a parrot, say one's lesson, rattle off, reel off; be a quick study; retain

17 **fix in the mind,** fix in the memory, instill, infix, inculcate, impress, imprint, stamp, inscribe, grave, engrave; impress on the mind, get into one's head, drive into one's head, hammer into one's head, get across, get into one's thick skull; burden the mind with, task the mind with, load the mind with, stuff the mind with, cram the mind with; inscribe in the memory, set in the tablets of memory, indelibly in the mind

18 **refresh the memory,** review, restudy, brush up, brush up on, rub up, polish up, bone up, get up on; cram, swot up

19 **remind, note to self,** put in mind, remember, put in remembrance, bring back, bring to recollection, refresh the memory of; remind one of, recall, suggest, put one in mind of; take one back, carry back, carry back in recollection; jog the memory, awaken the memory, arouse the memory, flap the memory, give a hint, give a suggestion, refresh one's memory; prompt, prompt the mind, give the cue, hold the promptbook; nudge, pull by the sleeve, nag; brush up; make a note

20 **try to recall,** think hard, rack one's brains, cudgel one's brains, crack one's brains; have on the tip of one's tongue, have on the edge of one's consciousness

ADJS **21** **recollective,** memoried; mnemonic; retentive; retrospective, in retrospect; reminiscent, nostalgic, mindful, remindful, suggestive, redolent, evocative

22 **remembered,** recollected, recalled; **retained,** pent-up in the memory, kept in remembrance, enduring, lasting, unforgotten; present to the mind, lodged in one's mind, stamped on the memory; vivid, eidetic, fresh, green, alive

23 **remembering,** mindful, keeping in mind, bearing in mind, holding in remembrance; unable to forget, haunted, plagued, obsessed, nagged, rankled

24 **memorable,** rememberable, recollectable; notable

25 **unforgettable,** never to be forgotten, never to be erased from the mind, indelible, indelibly impressed on the mind, fixed in the mind; haunting, persistent, recurrent, nagging, plaguing, rankling, festering; obsessing, obsessive

26 **memorial, commemorative**

ADVS **27** **by heart,** by rote, by memory, from memory, without book; memorably; rememberingly

28 **in memory of,** to the memory of, in remembrance, in commemoration, *in memoriam* <L>; in perpetual remembrance

990 FORGETFULNESS

<failure to remember>

NOUNS 1 **forgetfulness,** unmindfulness, absentmindedness, memorylessness; short memory, short memory span, little retentivity, little recall, mind like a sieve, memory like a sieve; loose memory, vague memory, fuzzy memory, dim recollection, hazy recollection; **lapse of memory,** decay of memory; obliviousness, oblivion, nirvana; obliteration; Lethe, Lethe water, waters of Lethe, waters of oblivion, river of oblivion; insensibility; trance; nepenthe; **forgetting;** heedlessness; forgiveness; senior moment, blonde moment, memory lapse

2 loss of memory, **memory loss, amnesia,** failure, blackout, memory gap; fugue; agnosia, unrecognition, body-image agnosia, ideational agnosia, astereognosis, astereocognosy; paramnesia, retrospective falsification, false memory, misremembrance, misattributed memory; amnesiac

3 block, blocking, **mental block,** memory obstruction; repression, suppression, defense mechanism, conversion, sublimation, symbolization

VERBS 4 **be forgetful,** suffer memory loss, be absentminded, have a short memory, have a mind like a sieve, have a short memory span, be unable to retain, have little recall, forget one's own name, be oblivious; misremember

5 **forget,** clean forget; **not remember,** disremember, disrecollect, fail to remember, forget to remember, have no remembrance of, have no recollection of, be unable to recollect, be unable to recall, draw a blank; lose, lose sight of, lose one's train of thought, lose track of what one was saying; have on the tip of the tongue; blow one's lines, go up in one's lines, fluff one's lines, forget one's lines, dry up; misremember, misrecollect

6 efface from the memory, erase from the memory, consign to oblivion, **unlearn**, obliterate, dismiss from one's thoughts; forgive

7 **be forgotten,** escape one, miss, slip one's mind, fade away from the memory, escape the memory, drop from one's thoughts; sink into oblivion, go in one ear and out the other

ADJS 8 **forgotten,** clean forgotten, **unremembered,** disremembered, disrecollected, unrecollected, unretained, unrecalled, past recollection, past recall, out of the mind, lost, erased, effaced, obliterated, gone out of one's head, beyond recall, consigned to oblivion, sunk in oblivion; out of sight out of mind; misremembered, misrecollected; half-remembered; on the tip of one's tongue

9 **forgetful, forgetting,** inclined to forget, memoryless, unremembering, unmindful, absentminded, oblivious, insensible to the past, with a mind like a sieve; blank, vacant, vacuous, empty-headed; suffering from amnesia, stricken with amnesia, amnesic, amnestic; blocked, repressed, suppressed, sublimated, converted; heedless; Lethean; in a trance, preoccupied, spaced-out, out to lunch

10 **forgettable,** unrememberable, unrecollectable; effaceable, eradicable, erasable

ADVS 11 **forgetfully,** forgettingly, unmindfully, absentmindedly, obliviously

991 SUFFICIENCY

<sufficient resources>

NOUNS 1 **sufficiency,** sufficientness, **adequacy,** adequateness, **enough,** a competence, a competency; satisfactoriness, satisfaction, satisfactory amount, enough to go around; good supply, adequate supply; exact measure, right amount, no more and no less; bare sufficiency, minimum, bare minimum, just enough, enough to get by on, enough to live on; self-sufficiency

2 **plenty,** plenitude, plentifulness, plenteousness, muchness; myriad, myriads, numerousness; amplitude, ampleness; substantiality, substantialness; abundance, copiousness; exuberance, riotousness; bountifulness, bounteousness, liberalness, liberality, generousness, generosity; lavishness, extravagance, prodigality; luxuriance, fertility, teemingness, productiveness; wealth, opulence, opulency, richness, affluence; more than enough; maximum; fullness, full measure, repletion, repleteness; overflow, outpouring, flood, inundation, flow, shower, spate, stream, gush, avalanche; landslide; prevalence, profuseness, profusion, riot; superabundance; overkill; no end of, great abundance, great plenty, quantities, much, as much as one could wish, one's fill, more than one can shake a stick at, lots, a fistful, scads; bumper crop, rich harvest, foison; rich vein, bonanza, oodles, luau; an ample sufficiency, enough and to spare, enough and then some; fat of the land

3 cornucopia, **horn of plenty**, horn of Amalthea, endless supply, bottomless well, bottomless pit; supply chain

VERBS 4 **suffice,** do, just do, serve, answer, quench; work, be equal to, avail; serve the purpose, do the trick, suit; qualify, meet, fulfill, satisfy, meet requirements; pass muster, make the grade, make the cut, hack it, cut the mustard, **fill the bill,** measure up to, prove acceptable; get by, scrape by, do it, do'er, do in a pinch, pass, pass in the dark; hold, stand, stand up, take it, bear; stretch, reach, go around; rise to the occasion

5 **abound, be plentiful**, exuberate, teem, teem with, creep with, crawl with, swarm with, be lousy with, bristle with; proliferate; overflow, run over, flood; flow, stream, rain, pour, shower, gush; flow with milk and honey, rain cats and dogs, stink of, roll in

ADJS 6 **sufficient,** sufficing; **enough, ample,** substantial, plenty, satisfactory, adequate, decent, due; competent, up to the mark, up to snuff; commensurate, proportionate, corresponding; suitable, fit; good, good enough, plenty good enough; sufficient for, up to, equal to; barely sufficient, minimal, minimum; hand-to-mouth

7 **plentiful,** plenty, **plenteous,** plenitudinous; galore, a gogo, up the kazoo, up to the ass in, in plenty, in quantity, aplenty; numerous; beaucoup, much, many; ample, all-sufficing; wholesale; well-stocked, well-provided, well-furnished, well-found; abundant, abounding, copious, exuberant, riotous; flush; bountiful, bounteous, lavish, generous, liberal, extravagant, prodigal; luxuriant, fertile, productive, rich, fat, wealthy, opulent, affluent; maximal; full, replete, well-filled, running over, overflowing; inexhaustible, exhaustless, bottomless; profuse, profusive, effuse, diffuse; prevalent, prevailing, rife, rampant, epidemic; lousy with, teeming; superabundant; a dime a dozen

ADVS 8 **sufficiently,** amply, substantially, satisfactorily, enough; competently, adequately; minimally

9 **plentifully,** plenteously, **aplenty**, in plenty, in quantity, in good supply; abundantly, in abundance, copiously, no end; superabundantly; bountifully, bounteously, lavishly, generously, liberally, extravagantly, prodigally; maximally; fully, in full measure, to the full, overflowingly; inexhaustibly, exhaustlessly, bottomlessly; exuberantly, luxuriantly, riotously; richly, opulently, affluently; profusely, diffusely, effusely; beyond one's wildest dreams, beyond the dreams of avarice

992 INSUFFICIENCY

<insufficient resources>

NOUNS 1 **insufficiency, inadequacy,** insufficientness, inadequateness; short supply, seller's market; none to spare; unsatisfactoriness, nonsatisfaction, nonfulfillment, coming short, falling short, falling shy, slippage, shortfall; money pit; undercommitment; disappointment, too little too late; a Band-Aid, a drop in the bucket, a drop in the ocean, a lick and a promise, a cosmetic measure; incompetence, incompetency, unqualification, unsuitability

2 **meagerness,** exiguousness, exiguity, scrimpiness, skimpiness, scantiness, spareness; meanness, miserliness, niggardliness, narrowness, stinginess, parsimony; smallness, slightness, puniness, paltriness; thinness, leanness, slimness, slim pickings, slenderness, scrawniness; jejuneness, jejunity; austerity; skeleton crew, corporal's guard

3 **scarcity,** scarceness; **sparsity,** sparseness; scantiness, scant sufficiency; dearth, paucity, poverty; rarity, rareness, uncommonness

4 **want, lack,** need, deficiency, deficit, shortage, shortfall, wantage, incompleteness, defectiveness, shortcoming, imperfection; absence, omission; destitution, impoverishment, beggary, deprivation; starvation, famine, drought, drying-up

5 **pittance,** dole, scrimption; drop in the bucket, drop in the ocean; mite, bit; short allowance, short commons, half rations, cheeseparings and candle ends; mere subsistence, starvation wages; widow's mite

6 **dietary deficiency,** vitamin deficiency; undernourishment, undernutrition, malnutrition, malnourishment, starvation diet, half rations, bread and water; Lenten fare, Spartan fare

VERBS 7 **want, lack,** need, require; miss, feel the want of, be sent away empty-handed; run short of

8 **be insufficient,** not qualify, be found wanting, leave a lot to be desired, kick the beam, not make it, not hack it, not make the cut, not cut it, not cut the mustard, be beyond one's depth, be in over one's head, **fall short,** fall shy, come short, not come up to; run short; want, want for, lack, fail, fail in; cramp one's style

ADJS 9 **insufficient,** unsufficing, **inadequate;** found wanting, defective, incomplete, imperfect, deficient, lacking, failing, wanting; too few, undersupplied, low on, light on; too little, not enough, precious little, a trickle, a mere trickle; unsatisfactory, unsatisfying; cosmetic, merely cosmetic, surface, superficial, symptomatic, merely symptomatic; incompetent, unequal to, unqualified, not up to it, not up to snuff, beyond one's depth, over one's head, outmatched; short-staffed, understaffed, shorthanded

10 **meager,** slight, scrimpy, skimp, skimpy, exiguous; scant, **scanty,** spare; miserly, niggardly, stingy, narrow, parsimonious, mean; hard to find, out of stock; austere, Lenten, Spartan, abstemious, ascetic; stinted, frugal, sparing; poor,

impoverished; small, puny, paltry; thin, lean, slim, slender, scrawny; dwarfish, dwarfed, stunted, undergrown; straitened, limited; jejune, watered, watery, unnourishing, unnutritious; subsistence, starvation

11 **scarce, sparse,** scanty; in short supply, at a premium; rare, uncommon, infrequent; scarcer than hen's teeth; not to be had, not to be had for love or money, not to be had at any price; out of print, out of stock, out of season, nonexistent; few and far between

12 **ill-provided,** ill-furnished, ill-equipped, ill-found, ill off; unprovided, unsupplied, unreplenished; bare-handed; unfed, underfed, undernourished; shorthanded, undermanned; **empty-handed,** poor, pauperized, impoverished, beggarly; hungry, starved, half-starved, on short commons, starving, starveling, famished, anorectic; hangry

13 **wanting, lacking,** needing, missing, in want of; for want of, in default of, in the absence of; short, short of, scant of; shy, shy of; out of, clean out of, fresh out of, destitute of, bare of, void of, empty of, devoid of, forlorn of, bereft of, deprived of, denuded of, unpossessed of, unblessed with, bankrupt in; out-of-pocket; at the end of one's rope, at the end of one's tether

ADVS 14 **insufficiently;** inadequately, unsubstantially, incompletely

15 **meagerly,** slightly, sparely, punily, scantily, poorly, frugally, sparingly

16 **scarcely,** sparsely, scantily, skimpily, scrimpily; rarely, uncommonly

PREPS 17 without, minus, less, sans, absent

COMBINING FORMS 18 hyp-, hypo-, under-, mal-, ill-, sub-

993 EXCESS

<more resources than necessary>

NOUNS 1 **excess, excessiveness,** inordinance, **inordinateness**, nimiety, immoderateness, immoderacy, immoderation, extravagance, extravagancy, intemperateness, incontinence, overindulgence, intemperance; unrestrainedness, abandon; gluttony; extreme, extremity, extremes; boundlessness; overlargeness, overgreatness, monstrousness, enormousness; overgrowth, overdevelopment, hypertrophy, gigantism, giantism, elephantiasis; overmuch, overmuchness, too much, too-muchness; exorbitance, exorbitancy, undueness, outrageousness, unconscionableness, unreasonableness; radicalism, extremism; egregiousness; fabulousness, hyperbole, exaggeration

2 **superabundance,** overabundance, superflux, **plethora,** redundancy, overprofusion, too many, too much, too much of a good thing, overplentifulness, overplenteousness, overplenty, oversupply, overstock, overaccumulation, oversufficiency, overmuchness, overcopiousness, overlavishness, overluxuriance, overbounteousness, overnumerousness; lavishness, extravagance, extravagancy, prodigality; plenty; more than enough, enough and to spare, enough in all conscience; overdose, overmeasure, one too many; egg in one's beer; more than one knows what to do with, drug on the market; spate, avalanche, landslide, deluge, flood, inundation; embarrassment of riches, money to burn; overpopulation; spare tire, fifth wheel; lagniappe

3 overfullness, plethora, **surfeit, glut;** satiety; engorgement, repletion, congestion; hyperemia; saturation, supersaturation; overload, overburden, overcharge, surcharge, overfreight, overweight; overflow, overbrimming, overspill; insatiability, insatiableness; all the market can bear

4 **superfluity,** superfluousness, fat; redundancy, redundance; unnecessariness, needlessness; fifth wheel, tits on a boar; featherbedding, payroll padding; duplication, duplication of effort, overlap; luxury, extravagance, frill, frills, bells and whistles, gimcrackery; frippery, froufrou, overadornment, bedizenment, gingerbread; ornamentation, embellishment; expletive, padding, filling; pleonasm, tautology; verbosity, prolixity; more than one really wants to know

5 **surplus,** surplusage, leftovers, doggy bag, plus, overplus, overstock, overage, overset, overrun, overmeasure, oversupply; margin; remainder, balance, **leftover**, extra, spare, something extra, something to spare; bonus, dividend; lagniappe; gratuity, tip, *pourboire* <Fr>; chad

6 **overdoing**, overcarrying, overreaching, supererogation; **overkill;** piling on, overimportance, overemphasis; overuse; overreaction; overwork, overexertion, overexercise, overexpenditure, overtaxing, overstrain, tax, strain; too much on one's plate, too many irons in the fire, too much at once; overachievement, overachieving

7 **overextension,** overdrawing, spreading too thin, overstretching, overstrain, overstraining, stretching, straining, stretch, strain, tension, extreme tension, breaking point; overexpansion; inflation, distension, overdistension, edema, turgidity, swelling, bloat, bloating

VERBS 8 **superabound,** overabound, know no bounds, swarm, pullulate, run riot, luxuriate,

teem; overflow, flood, overbrim, overspill, spill over, overrun, overspread, overswarm, overgrow, fill, saturate; meet one at every turn; hang heavy on one's hands, remain on one's hands; burst at the seams

9 **exceed,** surpass, pass, top, transcend, go beyond; overpass, overstep, overrun, **overreach,** overshoot, overshoot the mark

10 **overdo, go too far,** do twice over, do it to death, pass all bounds, know no bounds, overact, carry too far, overcarry, go to an extreme, go to extremes, go overboard, go off the deep end, jump off the deep end; run into the ground, drive into the ground; make a big deal of, make a federal case of; overemphasize, overstress; max out; overplay, overplay one's hand; overreact, protest too much; overreach oneself; overtax, overtask, overexert, overexercise, overstrain, overdrive, overspend, exhaust, overexpend, overuse; overtrain; overwork, overlabor; overelaborate, overdevelop, tell more than one wants to know; overstudy; burn the candle at both ends; spread oneself too thin, take on too much, have too much on one's plate, have too many irons in the fire, do too many things at once; exaggerate; overindulge

11 **pile it on,** lay it on, lay it on thick, lay it on with a trowel, talk too much, exaggerate

12 carry coals to Newcastle, teach fishes to swim, teach one's grandmother to suck eggs, kill the slain, beat a dead horse, flog a dead horse, labor the obvious, butter one's bread on both sides, preach to the converted, preach to the choir, paint the lily, gild the lily

13 **overextend,** overdraw, overstretch, overstrain, stretch, strain; reach the breaking point; overexpand, overdistend, overdevelop, inflate, swell

14 **oversupply,** overprovide, overlavish, overfurnish, overequip; overstock; overprovision, overprovender; overdose; flood the market, oversell; flood, deluge, inundate, engulf, swamp, whelm, overwhelm; lavish with, be prodigal with

15 **overload,** overlade, overburden, overweight, overcharge, surcharge; overfill, stuff, crowd, cram, jam, pack, jam-pack, congest, choke; overstuff, overfeed; gluttonize; surfeit, glut, gorge, satiate; **saturate,** soak, drench, supersaturate, supercharge

ADJS 16 **excessive, inordinate,** immoderate, overweening, hubristic, intemperate, extravagant, incontinent; unrestrained, unbridled, abandoned; gluttonous; extreme; overlarge, overgreat, overbig, larger than life, monstrous, enormous, jumbo, elephantine, gigantic; overgrown, overdeveloped, hypertrophied; overmuch, too much, a bit much, de trop; exorbitant, undue, outrageous, unconscionable, unreasonable; fancy, high, stiff, steep; out of bounds, out of all bounds, out of sight, out of this world, boundless; egregious; fabulous, hyperbolic, hyperbolical, exaggerated

17 **superfluous, redundant; excess,** in excess, duplicative; unnecessary, unessential, nonessential, needless, otiose, expendable, dispensable, unneeded, gratuitous, uncalled-for; expletive; pleonastic, tautologous, tautological; verbose, prolix; *de trop* <Fr>, supererogatory, supererogative; spare, to spare; on one's hands

18 **surplus,** overplus; remaining, unused, **leftover;** over, over and above; extra, spare, supernumerary, for lagniappe, as a bonus

19 **superabundant,** overabundant, plethoric, overplentiful, overplenteous, overplenty, oversufficient, overmuch; lavish, prodigal, overlavish, overbounteous, overgenerous, overliberal; overcopious, overluxuriant, riotous, overexuberant; overprolific, overnumerous; swarming, pullulating, teeming, overpopulated, overpopulous; plentiful

20 **overfull, overloaded,** overladen, overburdened, overfreighted, overfraught, overweighted, overcharged, surcharged, saturated, drenched, soaked, supersaturated, supercharged; surfeited, glutted, gorged, overfed, **bloated**, replete, **swollen**, satiated, stuffed, overstuffed, crowded, overcrowded, crammed, jammed, packed, jam-packed, like sardines in a can, bumper-to-bumper; choked, congested, stuffed up; overstocked, oversupplied; overflowing, in spate, running over, filled to overflowing; plethoric, hyperemic; bursting, ready to burst, bursting at the seams, at the bursting point, overblown, distended

21 **overdone,** overwrought; overdrawn, overstretched, overstrained; overwritten, overplayed, overacted

ADVS 22 **excessively, inordinately,** immoderately, intemperately, overweeningly, hubristically, overly, over, overmuch, too much; too, too-too; exorbitantly, unduly, unreasonably, unconscionably, outrageously

23 **in excess**, to excess, to extremes, to the extreme, all out, to the max, flat out, to a fault, too far, out of all proportion

24 superabundantly, overabundantly, lavishly, prodigally, **extravagantly;** more than enough, plentifully; without measure, out of measure, beyond measure

25 **superfluously,** redundantly, supererogatorily; tautologously; unnecessarily, needlessly, beyond need, beyond reason, to a fare-thee-well

PREPS **26** **in excess of,** over, beyond, past, above, **over and above,** above and beyond

COMBINING FORMS **27** arch-, hyper-, over-, super-, sur-, ultra-, extra-

994 SATIETY

<feeling of enough or too much>

NOUNS **1** **satiety, satiation, satisfaction,** fullness, surfeit, glut, repletion, engorgement; contentment; fill, bellyful, skinful; saturation, oversaturation, saturatedness, supersaturation; saturation point; more than enough, enough in all conscience, all one can stand, all one can take; too much of a good thing, much of a muchness

2 **satedness,** surfeitedness, cloyedness, jadedness; overfullness, fed-upness

3 cloyer, surfeiter, sickener; **overdose;** a diet of cake; warmed-over cabbage

VERBS **4** **satiate, sate, satisfy,** slake, allay; surfeit, glut, gorge, engorge; cloy, jade, pall; fill, fill up; saturate, oversaturate, supersaturate; stuff, overstuff, cram; overfill, overgorge, overdose, overfeed

5 **have enough,** have about enough of, have quite enough, **have one's fill;** have too much, have too much of a good thing, have a bellyful, have an overdose, be fed up, have all one can take, have all one can stand, have it up to here, up the kazoo, have had it

ADJS **6** **satiated, sated, satisfied,** slaked, allayed; surfeited, gorged, replete, engorged, glutted; cloyed, jaded; full, full of, with one's fill of, overfull, saturated, oversaturated, supersaturated; stuffed, overstuffed, crammed, overgorged, overfed; fed up, fed to the gills, fed to the teeth, stuffed to the gills; with a bellyful, with enough of; disgusted, sick of, tired of, sick and tired of

7 **satiating,** sating, **satisfying,** filling; surfeiting, overfilling; jading, cloying, cloysome

INTERJS **8** enough, *basta* <Ital>, *genug, genug shayn* <Yiddish>, all right already enough already

995 EXPEDIENCE

<well-suited and advisable>

NOUNS **1** **expedience, expediency,** advisability, politicness, desirability, recommendability; fitness, fittingness, appropriateness, **propriety,** decency, seemliness, suitability, rightness, feasibility, convenience; seasonableness, timeliness, opportuneness; usefulness; advantage, advantageousness, beneficialness, profit, profitability, percentage, mileage, worthwhileness, fruitfulness; wisdom, prudence; temporariness, provisionality

2 **expedient, means,** means to an end, provision, measure, step, action, effort, stroke, stroke of policy, coup, move, countermove, maneuver, demarche, course of action; tactic, device, contrivance, artifice, stratagem, shift; gimmick, dodge, trick; resort, resource; answer, solution; quick-and-dirty solution; working proposition, working hypothesis; temporary expedient, improvisation, ad hoc measure, ad hoc, ad hockery, ad hocism; fix, quick fix, jury-rigged expedient, makeshift, workaround, stopgap, shakeup, jury-rig; last expedient, last resort, last resource, *pis aller* <Fr>, last shift, trump

VERBS **3** **expedite one's affair,** work to one's advantage, not come amiss, come in handy, be just the thing, be just what the doctor ordered, fit to a T, fit like a glove, fit like a second skin; forward, advance, promote, profit, advantage, benefit; work, serve, answer, serve one's purpose, fill the bill, do the trick; suit the occasion, be fitting, fit, befit, be right

4 make shift, **make do,** make out, rub along <Brit>, cope, manage, manage with, get along on, get by on, do with; do as well as one can, do the best one can; use a last resort, scrape the bottom of the barrel

ADJS **5** **expedient, desirable,** to be desired, much to be desired, advisable, politic, recommendable; appropriate, meet, fit, fitting, befitting, right, proper, good, decent, becoming, seemly, likely, congruous, suitable, sortable, feasible, doable, swingable, convenient, happy, heaven-sent, felicitous; timely, seasonable, opportune, well-timed, in the nick of time; useful; advantageous, favorable; profitable, fructuous, worthwhile, worth one's while; wise

6 **practical,** practicable, pragmatic, pragmatical, banausic; feasible, workable, operable, realizable; efficient, effective, effectual

7 **makeshift,** makeshifty, **stopgap,** Band-Aid, improvised, improvisational, jury-rigged; last-ditch; ad hoc; quick and dirty; temporary, provisional, tentative

ADVS **8** **expediently,** fittingly, fitly, appropriately, suitably, sortably, congruously, rightly, properly, decently, feasibly, conveniently; practically; seasonably, opportunely; desirably, advisably; advantageously, to advantage, all to the good; as a last resort

PHRS **9** there's more than one way to skin a cat, where there's a will there's a way

996 INEXPEDIENCE

<unsuited and unwise>

NOUNS 1 **inexpedience**, inexpediency, undesirability, inadvisability, impoliticness, impoliticalness; unwiseness; unfitness, unfittingness, inappropriateness, unaptness, unsuitability, **counterproductiveness**, incongruity, unmeetness, wrongness, unseemliness; inconvenience, inconveniency, awkwardness; ineptitude, inaptitude; unseasonableness, untimeliness, inopportuneness; unfortunateness, infelicity; disadvantageousness, unprofitableness, unprofitability, worthlessness, futility, Barnum effect; uselessness

2 disadvantage, **drawback, liability;** detriment, impairment, prejudice, loss, damage, hurt, harm, mischief, injury; a step back, a step backward, a loss of ground; handicap, disability; drag, millstone around one's neck

3 **inconvenience,** discommodity, incommodity, disaccommodation, **trouble, bother;** inconvenientness, inconveniency, unhandiness, awkwardness, clumsiness, unwieldiness, troublesomeness, clunkiness; gaucheness, gaucherie

VERBS 4 **inconvenience,** put to inconvenience, **put out,** discommode, incommode, disaccommodate, disoblige, burden, embarrass; trouble, bother, put to trouble, put to the trouble of, impose upon; harm, disadvantage

ADJS 5 **inexpedient,** undesirable, inadvisable, **counterproductive,** impolitic, impolitical, unpolitic, not to be recommended, contraindicated; impractical, impracticable, dysfunctional, unworkable; ill-advised, ill-considered, unwise; unfit, unfitting, unbefitting, inappropriate, unsuitable, unmeet, inapt, inept, unseemly, improper, wrong, bad, out of place, out of order, incongruous, ill-suited; malapropos, inopportune, untimely, ill-timed, badly timed, unseasonable; infelicitous, unfortunate, unhappy; unprofitable; futile

6 **disadvantageous,** unadvantageous, unfavorable; unprofitable, profitless, unrewarding, worthless, useless; **detrimental,** deleterious, injurious, harmful, prejudicial, disserviceable

7 **inconvenient,** incommodious, discommodious; unhandy, awkward, clumsy, unwieldy, troublesome, onerous; gauche

ADVS 8 **inexpediently,** inadvisably, impoliticly, impolitically, undesirably; unfittingly, inappropriately, unsuitably, ineptly, inaptly, incongruously; inopportunely, unseasonably; infelicitously, unfortunately, unhappily

9 **disadvantageously,** unadvantageously, unprofitably, unrewardingly; uselessly; **inconveniently,** unhandily, with difficulty, ill

997 IMPORTANCE

<having worth or consequence>

NOUNS 1 **importance, significance, consequence,** consideration, **import,** note, mark, moment, weight, gravity; materiality; concern, concernment, interest; first order, high order, high rank; priority, primacy, precedence, preeminence, paramountcy, superiority, supremacy; value, worth, merit, excellence; self-importance; emphasis, oomph; front burner

2 notability, **noteworthiness,** remarkableness, salience, memorability; **prominence,** eminence, greatness, distinction, magnitude; prestige, esteem, repute, reputation, honor, glory, renown, dignity, fame; stardom, celebrity, celebrityhood, superstardom; semicelebrity, catbird seat

3 **gravity,** graveness, seriousness, solemnity, weightiness; *gravitas* <L>, grave affair; no joke, no laughing matter, nothing to sneeze at, hardball, matter of life and death, heavy scene

4 **urgency,** imperativeness, exigence, exigency; momentousness, crucialness, cruciality; consequentiality, consequentialness; press, pressure, high pressure, stress, tension, pinch; clutch, crunch; crisis, emergency; moment of truth, turning point, climax, defining moment

5 **matter of importance,** matter of consequence, thing of interest, point of interest, matter of concern, hot-button issue, object of note, one for the book, something to write home about, something special, no tea party, no picnic; not chicken feed; vital concern, vital interest; notabilia, memorabilia, great doings

6 **salient point,** cardinal point, high point, great point, key point; important thing, chief thing, the point, main point, main thing, essential matter, essence, the name of the game, the bottom line, what it's all about, where it's at, substance, gravamen, *sine qua non* <L>, issue, real issue, front-burner issue, prime issue; essential, fundamental, substantive point, material point; **gist,** nub, heart, meat, pith, kernel, core; **crux,** crucial point, pivotal point, critical point, pivot; turning point, climax, cusp, crisis; keystone, cornerstone; landmark, milestone, benchmark; linchpin; secret weapon, trump card

7 **feature, highlight,** high spot, main attraction, centerpiece, pièce de résistance; outstanding feature; best part, cream; selling point

8 personage, **important person,** person of importance, person of consequence, great man, great woman, person of mark, person of note, somebody, notable, notability, figure; celebrity, famous person, person of renown, personality; name, big name, megastar, nabob, mogul, captain of industry, panjandrum, person to be reckoned with, very important person, heavyweight; sachem; mover and shaker, lord of creation; worthy, pillar of society, salt of the earth, elder, father; dignitary, dignity; magnate; tycoon, baron; power; power elite, Establishment; interests; brass, top brass; top people, the great; ruling circle, lords of creation; the top, the summit

9 <nonformal> **big shot,** wheel, big wheel, big boy, big cat, big fish, biggie, big cheese, big noise, big-timer, big-time operator, bigwig, big man, big gun, high-muck-a-muck, high-muckety-muck, muckety-muck, kingpin, lion, something, very important person (VIP), brass hat, high man on the totem pole, suit; sacred cow, little tin god, tin god; big man on campus (BMOC); 800-pound gorilla; queen bee, heavy momma; first fiddle; mega-

10 **chief,** principal, chief executive, chief executive officer (CEO), paramount, lord of the manor, overlord, king, queen, monarch; leading light, luminary, master spirit, star, superstar, superman, superwoman, prima donna, lead

11 <nonformal> **boss,** honcho, big enchilada, biggest frog in the pond, big man, top man on the totem pole, high man on the totem pole, top dog, Mr. Big, head cheese, his nibs, himself, man upstairs

VERBS 12 **matter,** import, signify, count, tell, weigh, **carry weight,** cut ice, cut some ice, be prominent, stand out, mean much; be something, be somebody, amount to something; have a key to the executive washroom; be featured, star, get top billing, take the limelight

13 **value, esteem,** treasure, prize, appreciate, respect, rate highly, think highly of, think well of, think much of, set store by; attach importance to, ascribe importance to; make much of, make a fuss about, make a stir about, make an ado about, make much ado about; hold up as an example

14 **emphasize,** stress, lay emphasis on, lay stress upon, feature, highlight, brightline, place emphasis on, give emphasis to, accent, accentuate, punctuate, point up, bring to the fore, put in the foreground, put in bright lights; prioritize; spotlight; star, underline, underscore, italicize; overemphasize, overstress, overaccentuate, hammer home, rub in; harp on; dwell on, belabor; attach too much importance to, make a big deal of, make a federal case of, make a mountain out of a molehill; pull no punches

15 **feature,** headline; **star,** give top billing to

16 **dramatize,** play up, splash, make a production of; put on the map

ADJS 17 **important,** major, **consequential,** momentous, significant, game-changing, considerable, substantial, material, great, grand, big; superior, world-shaking, earthshaking; big-time, big-league, major-league, heavyweight; high-powered, double-barreled; bigwig, bigwigged; name, big-name, self-important; mega; A-1

18 **of importance,** of significance, of consequence, of note, of moment, of weight; of concern, of concernment, of interest, not to be overlooked, not hay, not chopped liver, not to be sneezed at; viable

19 **notable, noteworthy,** celebrated, remarkable, marked, standout, of mark, signal; memorable, rememberable, unforgettable, classic, historic, never to be forgotten; striking, telling, salient; eminent, prominent, conspicuous, noble, outstanding, distinguished; prestigious, esteemed, estimable, elevated, sublime, reputable; extraordinary, out of the ordinary, exceptional, special, rare; top-ten

20 **weighty,** heavy, grave, sober, sobering, solemn, **serious,** earnest; portentous, fateful, fatal; formidable, awe-inspiring, imposing, larger than life; world-shaking, earth-shattering

21 **emphatic,** decided, positive, forceful, forcible; emphasized, stressed, accented, accentuated, punctuated, pointed; underlined, underscored, starred, italicized, highlighted; red-letter, in red letters, in letters of fire

22 **urgent,** imperative, imperious, compelling, pressing, high-priority, high-pressure, crying, clamorous, insistent, instant, exigent; crucial, critical, pivotal, acute; fateful

23 **vital, all-important,** crucial, of vital importance, life-and-death, life-or-death; earth-shattering, epoch-making; essential, fundamental, indispensable, basic, substantive, bedrock, material; central, focal; bottom-line, meat-and-potatoes, gut; grassroots

24 **paramount, principal**, leading, foremost, main, chief, number one, numero uno, premier, prime, primary, preeminent, supreme, capital, cardinal; highest, uppermost, topmost, toprank, ranking, of the first rank, world-class, dominant, predominant, master, controlling, overruling, overriding, all-absorbing

ADVS 25 **importantly,** significantly, consequentially, materially, momentously, greatly, grandly;

eminently, prominently, conspicuously, outstandingly, saliently, signally, notably, markedly, remarkably

26 at the decisive moment, in the clutch, when the chips are down, when push comes to shove

998 UNIMPORTANCE

<*lacking worth or consequence*>

NOUNS 1 **unimportance, insignificance,** inconsequence, inconsequentiality, indifference, immateriality; inessentiality; ineffectuality; unnoteworthiness, unimpressiveness; inferiority, secondariness, low order of importance, low priority, dispensability, expendability, marginality; lack of substance; smallness, littleness, slightness, inconsiderableness, negligibility; irrelevancy, meaninglessness; pettiness, puniness, pokiness, picayune, picayunishness; marginalization; irrelevance

2 **paltriness,** poorness, meanness, sorriness, sadness, **pitifulness**, contemptibleness, pitiableness, despicableness, miserableness, wretchedness, vileness, crumminess, shabbiness, shoddiness, cheapness, cheesiness, beggarliness, worthlessness, uselessness, unworthiness, meritlessness; tawdriness, meretriciousness, gaudiness

3 **triviality,** trivialness, triflingness, nugacity, nugaciousness; superficiality, shallowness; slightness, slenderness, slimness, flimsiness; frivolity, frivolousness, lightness, levity; foolishness, silliness; inanity, emptiness, vacuity; triteness, vapidity; vanity, idleness, futility; much ado about nothing, tempest in a teapot, storm in a teacup, much cry and little wool, piss*; pettiness; snap of the fingers; no big deal, no biggie

4 **trivia,** triviata, trifles; trumpery, *nugae* <L>, gimcrackery, knickknackery, bric-a-brac; rubbish, trash, chaff; peanuts, chicken feed, chickenshit*, Mickey Mouse, small change; small beer; froth; minutiae, details, minor details; inessential, nonessential

5 **trifle, triviality,** oddment, bagatelle, fribble, gimcrack, gewgaw, frippery, froth, trinket, bibelot, curio, bauble, gaud, toy, knickknack, knickknackery, kickshaw, minikin, whim-wham, folderol; pin, button, hair, straw, rush, feather, fig, bean, hill of beans, molehill, sneeshing, pinch of snuff; bit, snap; a curse, a continental, a hoot, a damn, a darn, a shit*, a tinker's damn; picayune, rap, sou, halfpenny, farthing, brass farthing, cent, red cent, two cents, twopence <Brit>, tuppence <Brit>, penny, dime, plugged nickel; peppercorn; drop in the ocean, drop in the bucket; fleabite, pinprick; joke, jest, farce, mockery, child's play; small potatoes

6 an insignificancy, an inessential, a marginal matter, a marginal affair, a trivial affair, a small matter, a minor matter, no great matter; a little thing, hardly anything, scarcely anything, matter of no importance, matter of no consequence, matter of indifference; a nothing, a big nothing, a naught, a mere nothing, nothing in particular, nothing to signify, nothing to speak of, nothing worth speaking of, nothing to think twice about, nothing to boast of, nothing to write home about, thing of naught, nullity, nihility; technicality, **mere technicality**; red herring

7 **a nobody,** insignificancy, hollow man, jackstraw, **nonentity,** nonperson, empty suit, nebbish, an obscurity, a nothing, cipher, little man, nobody one knows; lightweight, mediocrity; whippersnapper, whiffet, pipsqueak, squirt, shrimp, scrub, runt; squit, punk; small potato, small potatoes; the little fellow, the little guy, the man in the street; common man; man of straw, dummy, figurehead; small fry, Mr. and Mrs. Nobody, John Doe and Richard Roe, John Doe and Mary Roe; Tom, Dick, and Harry; Brown, Jones, and Robinson

8 **trifling,** dallying, dalliance, flirtation, flirtiness, coquetry; toying, fiddling, playing, fooling, puttering, tinkering, pottering, piddling; dabbling, smattering; loitering, idling

9 <nonformal> monkeying, monkeying around, buggering around, diddling around, fiddling around, frigging around, fricking around, horsing around, fooling around, kidding around, messing around, pissing around*, playing around, screwing around, mucking around, farting around; jerking off

10 **trifler,** dallier, fribble; putterer, potterer, piddler, tinkerer, smatterer, dabbler; amateur, dilettante, Sunday painter; flirt, coquet; small fish

VERBS 11 **be unimportant,** be of no importance, not signify, **not matter,** not count, signify nothing, matter little, not make any difference; cut no ice, not amount to anything, make no never mind, not amount to a hill of beans, not amount to a damn; have no clout, have no pull

12 attach little importance to, give little weight to; make little of, underplay, de-emphasize, downplay, play down, minimize, marginalize, disregard, make light of, think little of, throw away, make nothing of, **think nothing of,** take no account of, set little by, set no store by, set at naught; snap one's fingers at; not care a straw about; not give a shit*, not give a hoot, not give two hoots for, not give a damn about, not

give a dime a dozen for; bad-mouth, deprecate, depreciate; **trivialize**

13 make much ado about nothing, make mountains out of molehills, have a storm in a teapot, have a tempest in a teacup

14 **trifle,** dally; flirt, coquet; toy, fribble, play, fool, play at, putter, potter, tinker, piddle; **dabble,** smatter; toy with, fiddle with, fool with, play with; idle, loiter; nibble, niggle, nickel-and-dime, nickel-dime

15 <nonformal> monkey, monkey around, fiddle, fiddle around, fiddle-faddle, frivol, horse around, fool around, play around, mess around, kid around, screw around, muck around, muck about, fart around, piss around*, bugger around <Brit>, diddle around, frig around; jerk off

ADJS **16** **unimportant, of no importance,** of little importance, of small importance, of no great importance, **of no account,** of no significance, of no concern, of no matter, of little or no consequence, no great shakes; no skin off one's nose; inferior, secondary, of a low order of importance, low-priority, expendable; marginal; one-dimensional, two-dimensional; not apropos, not related, irrelevant

17 **insignificant**, **inconsequential,** immaterial, of no consequence, insubstantial; nonessential, unessential, inessential, not vital, backburner, dispensable; unnoteworthy, unimpressive; inconsiderable, inappreciable, negligible; small, little, minute, footling, petit, minor, inferior; technical

18 <nonformal> **measly, small-time, two-bit,** Mickey Mouse, chickenshit*, nickel-and-dime, low-rent, piddly, pissy-ass*, dinky, poky, tinhorn, punk; not worth a dime, not worth a red cent, not worth beans, not worth a hill of beans, not worth bubkes, not worth shit*, not worth a second thought; one-horse, two-by-four, jerkwater

19 **trivial, trifling;** fribble, fribbling, nugacious, nugatory; catchpenny; slight, slender, flimsy; superficial, shallow; frivolous, light, windy, airy, frothy; idle, futile, vain, otiose; foolish, fatuous, asinine, silly; inane, empty, vacuous; trite, vapid; unworthy of serious consideration

20 petty, puny, **piddling,** piffling, niggling, pettifogging, technical, picayune, picayunish; small-beer

21 **paltry,** poor, common, mean, sorry, sad, pitiful, pitiable, pathetic, despicable, contemptible, beneath contempt, miserable, wretched, beggarly, vile, shabby, scrubby, scruffy, trampy, shoddy, scurvy, scuzzy, scummy, crummy, cheesy, trashy, rubbishy, garbagey, trumpery, gimcracky; tinpot; cheap, worthless, valueless, twopenny, twopenny-halfpenny <Brit>, two-for-a-cent, two-for-a-penny, dime-a-dozen; tawdry, meretricious, gaudy; Mickey Mouse, rinky-dink

22 unworthy, **worthless,** meritless, unworthy of regard, unworthy of consideration, beneath notice; no great shakes

ADVS **23** **unimportantly, insignificantly,** inconsequentially, immaterially, unessentially; pettily, paltrily; trivially, triflingly; superficially, shallowly; frivolously, lightly, idly

PHRS **24** it does not matter, it matters not, it does not signify, mox nix, it is of no consequence, it is of no importance, it makes no difference, it makes no never mind, it cannot be helped, it is all the same; it will all come out in the wash, it will be all the same a hundred years from now

25 **no matter, never mind,** think no more of it, do not give it another thought, do not give it a second thought, don't lose any sleep over it, let it pass, let it go, ignore it, forget it, skip it, drop it; fiddle-dee-dee

26 what does it matter?, what matter?, what's the difference?, what's the diff?, what do I care?, what of it?, what boots it?, what's the odds?, so what?, what else is new?; for aught one cares, big deal

999 GOODNESS

<good quality or effect>

NOUNS **1** **goodness,** excellence, quality, class; **virtue,** grace; **merit,** desert; value, worth; fineness, goodliness, fairness, niceness; superiority, first-rateness, skillfulness, proficiency; wholeness, soundness, healthiness; virtuousness; kindness, benevolence, benignity; beneficialness, helpfulness; favorableness, auspiciousness; expedience, advantageousness; usefulness; pleasantness, agreeableness; cogency, validity; profitableness, rewardingness; sattva

2 **superexcellence,** supereminence, preeminence, supremacy, primacy, paramountcy, peerlessness, unsurpassedness, matchlessness, superfineness; **superbness,** exquisiteness, magnificence, splendidness, splendiferousness, marvelousness, distinction, wow factor

3 tolerableness, tolerability, goodishness, passableness, fairishness, **adequateness**, satisfactoriness, acceptability, admissibility; sufficiency

4 **good, welfare,** well-being, benefit; public weal, common good; interest, advantage; behalf, behoof, edification; blessing, benison, boon; profit, avail, gain, betterment; world of good; favor; use, usefulness

5 **good thing,** a thing to be desired; treasure, gem, jewel, diamond, pearl; national treasure; boast, pride, pride and joy; prize, trophy, plum; winner, no slouch, nothing to sneeze at; catch, find; godsend, windfall; tour de force, chef d'oeuvre, masterpiece; bestseller; collector's item; hit

6 first-rater, topnotcher, world-beater; wonder, prodigy, genius, virtuoso, **star,** superstar; luminary, leading light, one in a thousand, one in a million; hard act to follow, tough act to follow; good egg; Boy Scout, Girl Scout

7 <nonformal> dandy, jim dandy, dilly, humdinger, pip, pippin, peach, **ace,** beaut, lulu, daisy, darb, doozy, honey, sweetheart, dream, lollapalooza, bitch, hot shit*, hot poo, pisser, pistol, corker, whiz, blinger, crackerjack, knockout, something else, something else again, barnburner, killer, killer-diller, smash, smash hit, the nuts, the cat's pajamas, the cat's meow, bitch-kitty*, whizbang, wow, wowser

8 **the best,** the very best, the best ever, the top of the heap, the top of the line, head of the class, tops; quintessence, essence, prime, optimum, superlative; choice, pick, select, elect, elite, chosen; cream, flower, fat; cream of the crop, pick of the crop, *crème de la crème* <Fr>, grade A, salt of the earth; *pièce de résistance* <Fr>; prize, champion, queen; nonesuch, paragon, nonpareil; gem of the first water

9 **harmlessness,** hurtlessness, uninjuriousness, **innocuousness,** benignity, benignancy; unobnoxiousness, inoffensiveness; innocence; heart of gold, kindness of heart, milk of human kindness

VERBS 10 **do good,** profit, avail; do a world of good; **benefit,** help, serve, be of service, advance, advantage, favor; be the making of, make a man of, make a woman of; do no harm, break no bones

11 **excel,** surpass, outdo, pass, do one better, go one better, transcend; do up brown, do in spades, do with a vengeance; be as good as, equal, emulate, rival, vie, vie with, challenge comparison, go one-on-one with; make the most of, optimize, exploit; cream off <Brit>, skim off the cream

ADJS 12 **good, excellent,** great; *bueno* <Sp>, *bon* <Fr>, bonny <Brit>, fine, nice, goodly, fair; splendid, capital, grand, elegant, famous, noble; royal, regal, fit for a king; very good, *très bon* <Fr>; boo-yah, boo-yaa; commendable, laudable, estimable; skillful; sound, healthy; virtuous; kind, benevolent; beneficial, helpful; profitable; favorable, auspicious; expedient, advantageous; useful; pleasant; cogent, valid

13 <nonformal> **swell,** dandy, bitchin'*, dope, jim dandy, neat, neato, cool, super, super-duper, bully, tough, mean, gnarly, heavy, bad, groovy, out of sight, fab, fantabulous, marvy, gear, something else, ducky, dynamite, keen, killer, hot, nifty, sexy, spiffy, spiffing, ripping, nobby, peachy, peachy-keen, delicious, scrumptious, scrumpdiddlyumptious, not too shabby, tits, out of this world, hunky-dory, crackerjack, boss, stunning, corking, smashing, solid, all wool and a yard wide; rum <Brit>, wizard <Brit>, bonzer <Austral>; bang-up, jam-up, slap-up, ace-high, fine and dandy, just dandy, but good, OK, okay, A-OK; copacetic, peachy keen; phat

14 **superior,** above par, head and shoulders above, crack; high-grade, high-class, high-quality, high-caliber, high-test, world-class, grade A; impressive; top-shelf

15 **superb,** super, superexcellent, supereminent, superfine, exquisite; magnificent, splendid, splendiferous, tremendous, immense, marvelous, wonderful, glorious, divine, heavenly, terrific, sensational; sterling, golden; gilt-edged, gilt-edge, blue-chip; of the highest type, of the best sort, of the first water, as good as good can be, as good as they come, as good as they make 'em, out of this world

16 **best,** very best, greatest, top-of-the-line, prime, optimum, optimal; choice, select, elect, elite, picked, handpicked; prize, champion; supreme, paramount, unsurpassed, surpassing, unparalleled, unmatched, unmatchable, matchless, makeless, peerless; quintessential; for the best, all for the best

17 **first-rate, first-class,** in a class by itself; of the first degree, highest degree; unmatched, matchless; champion, record-breaking

18 <nonformal> A-1, A number one, primo, first-chop, tiptop, topnotch, topflight, top-drawer, tops; topping <Brit>, top-hole <Brit>, cushty; wicked bad, wicked good

19 **up to par,** up to standard, **up to snuff**; up to the mark, up to the notch, up to scratch

20 **tolerable, goodish,** fair, fairish, moderate, tidy, decent, respectable, presentable, good enough, pretty good, not bad, not amiss, not half bad, not so bad, adequate, satisfactory, all right, OK, okay; better than nothing; acceptable, admissible, passable, unobjectionable, unexceptionable; workmanlike; sufficient

21 **harmless,** hurtless, unhurtful; well-meaning, well-meant; uninjurious, undamaging, innocuous, innoxious, innocent; unobnoxious, inoffensive; nonmalignant, benign; nonpoisonous, nontoxic, nonvirulent, nonvenomous, cruelty-free

ADVS 22 **excellently,** nicely, finely, capitally, splendidly, famously, royally; **well,** very well, fine, right, aright; one's best, at one's best, at the top of one's bent

23 **superbly,** exquisitely, magnificently, tremendously, immensely, terrifically, marvelously, wonderfully, gloriously, divinely; galactically

24 tolerably, fairly, fairishly, moderately, respectably, adequately, **satisfactorily,** passably, acceptably, unexceptionably, presentably, decently; fairly well, well enough, pretty well; rather, pretty

1000 BADNESS

<bad quality or effect>

NOUNS 1 **badness, evil,** evilness, viciousness, damnability, reprehensibility; moral badness, dereliction, peccancy, iniquity, sinfulness, wickedness; unwholesomeness, unhealthiness; inferiority; unskillfulness; unkindness, malevolence; inauspiciousness, unfavorableness; inexpedience; unpleasantness; invalidity; inaccuracy; improperness; deviltry

2 **terribleness, dreadfulness**, direness, awfulness, horribleness; atrociousness, outrageousness, heinousness, nefariousness; notoriousness, egregiousness, scandalousness, shamefulness, infamousness; abominableness, odiousness, loathsomeness, detestableness, despicableness, contemptibleness, hatefulness; offensiveness, grossness, obnoxiousness; squalor, squalidness, sordidness, wretchedness, filth, vileness, fulsomeness, nastiness, rankness, foulness, noisomeness; disgustingness, repulsiveness; uncleanness; beastliness, bestiality, brutality; rottenness, lousiness; the pits; shoddiness, shabbiness; scurviness, baseness; worthlessness

3 **evil, bad,** wrong, ill; harm, hurt, injury, damage, detriment; destruction; despoliation; mischief, havoc; outrage, atrocity; crime, foul play; abomination, grievance, vexation, woe, crying evil; poison; blight, venom, toxin, bane; corruption, pollution, infection, befoulment, defilement; environmental pollution, fly in the ointment, worm in the apple; skeleton in the closet; snake in the grass, Pandora's box; something rotten in the state of Denmark; ills the flesh is heir to; the worst; *annus horribilis* <L>

4 **bad influence,** malevolent influence, evil star, ill wind; evil genius, hoodoo, jinx, Jonah; curse, enchantment, whammy, double whammy, triple whammy, spell, hex, voodoo; evil eye; malediction; collateral damage

5 **harmfulness,** hurtfulness, injuriousness, banefulness, balefulness, detrimentalness, deleteriousness, perniciousness, mischievousness, noxiousness, venomousness, poisonousness, toxicity, virulence, noisomeness, malignance, malignancy, malignity, viciousness; unhealthiness; disease; deadliness, lethality; ominousness

VERBS 6 work evil, do ill; **harm, hurt; injure,** scathe, wound, damage; destroy; despoil, prejudice, disadvantage, impair, disserve, distress; wrong, do wrong, do wrong by, aggrieve, do evil, do a mischief, do an ill office to; molest, afflict; lay a hand on; get into trouble; abuse, bash, batter, outrage, violate, maltreat, mistreat; torment, harass, hassle, persecute, savage, crucify, torture; play mischief with, play havoc with, wreak havoc on, play hob with; corrupt, deprave, taint, pollute, infect, befoul, defile; poison, envenom, blight; curse, put a whammy on, give the evil eye, hex, jinx, bewitch; spell trouble, mean trouble, threaten, menace; doom; condemn

ADJS 7 **bad, evil**, ill, untoward, black, sinister; wicked, wrong, peccant, iniquitous, vicious; sinful; criminal; unhealthy; inferior; unskillful; unkind, malevolent; inauspicious, unfavorable; inexpedient; unpleasant; invalid; inaccurate; improper

8 <nonformal> **lousy,** punk, bum, badass, shitty*, crappy, cruddy, cheesy, dog-ass, gnarly, gross, raunchy, piss-poor, rat-ass*, **crummy,** grim, low-rent, low-ride, putrid, icky, skanky, yecchy, vomity, barfy, stinking, stinky, creepy, hairy, god-awful, gosh-awful

9 **terrible, dreadful,** awful, dire, horrible, horrid; atrocious, outrageous, heinous, villainous, nefarious; enormous, monstrous; deplorable, lamentable, regrettable, pitiful, pitiable, woeful, woesome, grievous, sad; flagrant, scandalous, shameful, shocking, infamous, notorious, arrant, egregious; unclean; shoddy, schlocky, shabby, scurvy, base; odious, obnoxious, offensive, gross, disgusting, repulsive, loathsome, abominable, detestable, despicable, contemptible, beneath contempt, hateful; blameworthy, reprehensible; rank, fetid, foul, filthy, vile, fulsome, noisome, nasty, squalid, sordid, wretched; beastly, brutal; as bad as they come, as bad as they make 'em, as bad as bad can be; worst; too bad; below par, subpar, not up to scratch, not up to snuff, not up to the mark, poor-quality, worthless

10 **execrable, damnable;** damned, accursed, cursed; infernal, hellish, devilish, fiendish, satanic, ghoulish, demoniac, demonic, demonical, diabolic, diabolical, unholy, ungodly

11 evil-fashioned, ill-fashioned, evil-shaped, ill-shaped, evil-qualitied, evil-looking, ill-looking, evil-favored, ill-favored, evil-hued, evil-faced, evil-minded, evil-eyed, ill-affected, evil-gotten, ill-gotten, ill-conceived

12 **harmful, hurtful,** scatheful, baneful, baleful, distressing, injurious, damaging, detrimental, deleterious, counterproductive, pernicious, mischievous; noxious, mephitic, venomous, venenate, poisonous, venenous, veneniferous, toxic, virulent, noisome; malignant, malign, malevolent, malefic, vicious; prejudicial, disadvantageous, disserviceable; corruptive, corrupting, corrosive, corroding; deadly, lethal; ominous

ADVS 13 **badly,** bad, ill, evil, evilly, wrong, wrongly, amiss; to one's cost

14 **terribly,** dreadfully, dreadful, horribly, horridly, awfully, atrociously, outrageously; flagrantly, scandalously, shamefully, shockingly, infamously, notoriously, egregiously, grossly, offensively, nauseatingly, fulsomely, odiously, **vilely,** obnoxiously, disgustingly, loathsomely; wretchedly, sordidly, shabbily, basely, abominably, detestably, despicably, contemptibly, foully, nastily; brutally, bestially, savagely, viciously; something fierce, something terrible

15 **harmfully,** hurtfully, banefully, balefully, injuriously, damagingly, detrimentally, deleteriously, counterproductively, perniciously, mischievously; noxiously, venomously, poisonously, toxically, virulently, noisomely; malignantly, malignly, malevolently, malefically, viciously; prejudicially, disadvantageously, disserviceably; corrosively, corrodingly

1001 BANE

<cause of trouble, annoyance>

NOUNS 1 **bane,** curse, affliction, infliction, visitation, plague, pestilence, pest, calamity, **scourge**, torment, open wound, running sore, grievance, woe, burden, crushing burden; disease; death; evil, harm; destruction; vexation; thorn, thorn in the side, pea in the shoe; bugbear, bête noire, bogy, bogeymen, nemesis, arch-nemesis

2 **blight,** blast; canker, cancer; mold, fungus, mildew, smut, must, rust; rot, dry rot; **pest;** worm, worm in the apple; moth

3 **poison,** venom, venin, virus, toxic, toxin, toxicant; eradicant, pesticide; insecticide, insect powder, bug bomb, diethyltoluamide (DEET); roach powder, roach paste; stomach poison, contact poison, systemic insecticide, systemic, fumigant, chemosterilant; chlorinated hydrocarbon insecticide, organic chlorine; organic phosphate insecticide; carbamate insecticide, sheepdip; termiticide, miticide, acaricide, vermicide, anthelminthic; rodenticide, ratsbane, rat poison; herbicide, defoliant, Agent Orange, nerve agent, paraquat, weed killer; fungicide; microbicide, germicide, antiseptic, disinfectant, antibiotic; toxicology; **pollutant**, toxic waste, environmental pollutant; hemlock, arsenic, cyanide; carcinogen

4 **bad air,** miasma, mephitis, malaria; effluvium, exhaust, exhaust gas; coal gas, chokedamp, blackdamp, firedamp; air pollution, atmospheric pollution, smoke, smog, exhaust fumes, carbon monoxide; secondhand smoke; acid rain; greenhouse gas

5 **animal poison,** sting, stinger, dart; fang, tang; beesting, snakebite

6 **poisonous plant**

aconite	laburnum
amanita	larkspur
angel's trumpet	locoweed
banewort	marijuana
bearded darnel	mayapple
belladonna	mescal bean
black henbane	monkshood
black nightshade	nightshade
bleeding heart	nux vomica
castor-oil plant	opium poppy
chinaberry	poinsettia
corn cackle	poison bean
cowbane	poisonberry
datura	poison bush
deadly nightshade	poison hemlock, poison parsley
death camas	poison ivy
death cup, death angel	poison oak
devil's trumpet	poison rye grass
elderberry	poison sumac
ergot	poison tobacco
fiddleneck	poisonweed
foxglove	pokeweed
gastrolobium	sheep laurel
hairy vetch	thornapple
hellebore	tobacco
hemlock	upas
henbane	water hemlock
horsetail	white snakeroot
jack-in-the-pulpit	wisteria
jimsonweed	wolfsbane

1002 PERFECTION

<excellence or excellent quality>

NOUNS 1 **perfection,** faultlessness, **flawlessness,** defectlessness, indefectibility, impeccability, absoluteness; infallibility; spotlessness, stainlessness, taintlessness, purity, immaculateness; sinlessness; chastity

2 **soundness, integrity,** intactness, wholeness, entireness, completeness; fullness, plenitude; finish; mint condition

3 acme of perfection, pink, **pink of perfection,**

culmination, perfection, height, top, acme, ultimate, summit, pinnacle, peak, highest pitch, climax, consummation, *ne plus ultra* <L>, the last word, a dream come true

4 standard of perfection, very model, quintessence; archetype, prototype, exemplar, mirror, **epitome;** *ne plus ultra* <L>, perfect specimen, highest type; classic, masterwork, masterpiece, *chef d'œuvre* <Fr>, crowning achievement, showpiece; ideal; role model; paragon; a 10

VERBS 5 **perfect,** develop, flesh out, ripen, **mature;** improve; crown, culminate, put on the finishing touch; lick into shape, whip into shape, fine-tune; complete; do to perfection

ADJS 6 **perfect, ideal,** faultless, flawless, unflawed, defectless, not to be improved, picture-perfect, impeccable, absolute; just right, just so; spotless, stainless, taintless, unblemished, untainted, unspotted, immaculate, pure, uncontaminated, unadulterated, unmixed; sinless; chaste; indefective, indefectible, trouble-free; infallible; beyond all praise, irreproachable, unfaultable, matchless, peerless; A-1, world-class, number-one

7 **sound, intact,** whole, entire, complete, integral; full; total, utter, unqualified

8 **undamaged, unharmed,** unhurt, uninjured, unscathed, unspoiled, virgin, inviolate, unimpaired; harmless, scatheless; unmarred, unmarked, unscarred, unscratched, undefaced, unbruised; unbroken, unshattered, untorn; undemolished, undestroyed; undeformed, unmutilated, unmangled, unmaimed; unfaded, unworn, unwithered, bright, fresh, untouched, pristine, mint; none the worse for wear, right as rain

9 **perfected, finished,** polished, refined; done to a T, to a turn; classic, classical, masterly, masterful, expert, proficient; ripened, ripe, matured, mature, developed, fully developed; thoroughgoing, thorough-paced; consummate, quintessential, archetypical, exemplary, model

ADVS 10 **perfectly,** ideally; faultlessly, **flawlessly,** impeccably; just right; spotlessly; immaculately, purely; infallibly; wholly, entirely, completely, fully, thoroughly, totally, absolutely

11 **to perfection,** to a turn, to a T, to a finish, to a nicety; to a fare-thee-well, to a fare-you-well, to a fare-ye-well; to beat the band

1003 IMPERFECTION

<lack of perfection or small flaw>

NOUNS 1 **imperfection,** imperfectness, room for improvement; **unperfectedness;** faultiness, defectiveness, defectibility; shortcoming, deficiency, lack, want, shortage, inadequacy, inadequateness; erroneousness, fallibility; inaccuracy, inexactness, inexactitude; unsoundness, incompleteness, patchiness, sketchiness, unevenness; impairment; mediocrity; immaturity, undevelopment; impurity, adulteration

2 **fault, defect,** deficiency, inadequacy, imperfection, kink, hangup; **flaw,** design flaw, hole, bug; something missing; catch, fly in the ointment, problem, little problem, curate's egg <Brit>, snag, drawback; crack, rift; weakness, frailty, infirmity, failure, failing, foible, shortcoming; weak point, Achilles' heel, vulnerable place, chink in one's armor, weak link, soft spot, underbelly; blemish, taint; malfunction, glitch

VERBS 3 **fall short,** come short, miss, miss out, miss the mark, miss by a mile, not qualify, fall down, **not measure up,** not come up to par, not come up to the mark, not come up to scratch, not come up to snuff, not pass muster, not bear inspection, not hack it, not make it, not cut it, not make the cut; not make the grade; fail

ADJS 4 **imperfect,** not perfect, less than perfect; good in parts; unperfected; defective, faulty, inadequate, deficient, short, not all it's cracked up to be, lacking, wanting, found wanting; off; erroneous, **fallible;** inaccurate, inexact, imprecise; unsound, incomplete, unfinished, partial, patchy, sketchy, uneven, unthorough; makeshift; damaged, impaired; mediocre; blemished; half-baked, immature, undeveloped; impure, adulterated, mixed

ADVS 5 **imperfectly,** inadequately, deficiently; incompletely, partially; faultily, defectively

1004 BLEMISH

<mark making imperfect>

NOUNS 1 **blemish,** disfigurement, disfiguration, defacement; **scar,** keloid, cicatrix; needle scar, track, crater; scratch; scab; blister, vesicle, bulla, bleb; weal, wale, welt, wen, sebaceous cyst; port-wine stain, port-wine mark, hemangioma, strawberry mark, macula; pock, pustule; pockmark, pit; nevus, birthmark, mole; freckle, lentigo; milium, whitehead, blackhead, comedo, pimple, zit, hickey, sty; crud; wart, verruca; crack, craze, check, rift, split; deformity, deformation, warp, twist, kink, distortion; flaw, defect, fault

2 **discoloration,** discolorment, discolor; bruise; foxing

3 **stain, taint,** tarnish; mark, brand, stigma; maculation, macule, macula; spot, blot, blur, blotch, patch, speck, speckle, fleck, flick, flyspeck;

daub, dab; smirch, smudge, smutch, smouch, smut, smear; splotch, splash, splatter, spatter; bloodstain; eyesore; caste mark, tattoo; stain remover, spot remover

VERBS 4 **blemish,** disfigure, deface, flaw, mar; scab; scar, cicatrize, scarify; crack, craze, check, split; deform, warp, twist, kink, distort

5 **spot,** bespot, **blot,** blotch, speck, speckle, bespeckle, maculate; freckle; flyspeck; spatter, splatter, splash, splotch

6 **stain,** bestain, **discolor,** smirch, besmirch, taint, attaint, tarnish; mark, stigmatize, brand; smear, besmear, daub, bedaub, slubber; blur, slur; darken, blacken; smoke, besmoke; scorch, singe, sear; dirty, soil

7 **bloodstain,** bloody, ensanguine

ADJS 8 **blemished,** disfigured, defaced, marred, **scarred**, keloidal, cicatrized, scarified, stigmatized, scabbed, scabby; pimpled, pimply; cracked, crazed, checked, split; deformed, warped, twisted, kinked, distorted; faulty, flawed, defective

9 **spotted,** spotty, maculate, maculated, macular, blotched, **blotchy,** splotched, splotchy; speckled, speckly, bespeckled; freckled, freckly, freckle-faced; spattered, splattered, splashed

10 **stained, discolored,** foxed, foxy, tainted, tarnished, smirched, besmirched; stigmatized, stigmatic, stigmatiferous; darkened, blackened, murky, smoky, inky; polluted, soiled

11 **bloodstained,** blood-spattered, bloody, sanguinary, gory, ensanguined

1005 MEDIOCRITY

<quality or state of not being very good>

NOUNS 1 **mediocrity,** mediocreness, fairishness, modestness, modesty, moderateness, middlingness, indifference; respectability, passableness, tolerableness; dullness, lackluster, tediousness

2 **ordinariness,** averageness, normalness, normality, commonness, **commonplaceness;** unexceptionality, unremarkableness, unnoteworthiness; conventionality

3 inferiority, inferiorness, poorness, lowliness, humbleness, **baseness,** meanness, commonness, coarseness, tackiness, tack; second-rateness, third-rateness, fourth-rateness

4 **low grade,** low class, low quality, poor quality; second best, next best

5 **mediocrity,** second-rater, third-rater, fourth-rater, nothing special, nobody special, no great shakes, no prize, no prize package, no brain surgeon, no rocket scientist, not much of a bargain, small potatoes, small beer; tinhorn; nobody, nonentity; middle class, bourgeoisie, burgherdom; suburbia, the burbs; Middle America, silent majority

6 irregular, second, third; schlock

ADJS 7 **mediocre, middling,** indifferent, fair, fairish, fair to middling, moderate, modest, medium, betwixt and between; respectable, passable, tolerable; so-so, *comme ci comme ça* <Fr>; of a kind, of a sort, of sorts; nothing to brag about, not much to boast of, nothing to write home about; bush-league; dull, lackluster, tedious; insipid, vapid, wishy-washy, namby-pamby

8 **ordinary, average,** normal, common, commonplace, garden, garden-variety, run-of-mill, run-of-the-mill, standard-issue, mundane, vanilla; unexceptional, unremarkable, unnoteworthy, unspectacular, nothing special, nobody special, no great shakes, no prize, no prize package, no brain surgeon, no rocket scientist; conventional; middle-class, bourgeois, plastic; suburban; usual, regular

9 inferior, poor, punk, **base, mean, common,** coarse, cheesy, tacky, tinny; shabby, seedy; cheap, Mickey Mouse, paltry; irregular; second-best; second-rate, third-rate, fourth-rate; second-class, third-class, fourth-class; low-grade, low-class, low-quality, low-test, low-rent, low-ride

10 below par, below standard, below the mark, substandard, **not up to scratch**, not up to snuff, not up to the mark, not up to standard, not up to specification, off

ADVS 11 **mediocrely,** middlingly, fairly, fairishly, middling well, fair to middling, moderately, modestly, indifferently, so-so; passably, tolerably

12 inferiorly, poorly, basely, meanly, commonly

1006 DANGER

<threat of harm, pain, loss>

NOUNS 1 **danger, peril, endangerment,** imperilment, jeopardy, hazard, risk, cause for alarm, menace, threat; crisis, emergency, hot spot, nasty spot, tricky spot, pass, pinch, strait, plight, predicament; powder keg, time bomb; dangerous person, unpredictable person, uncontrollable person, loose cannon; rocks ahead, breakers ahead, whitewater ahead, gathering clouds, storm clouds; dangerous ground, yawning chasm, gaping chasm, quicksand, thin ice; hornet's nest; house of cards, cardhouse; hardball, no tea party, no picnic; desperate situation; hazardous materials; double jeopardy

2 **dangerousness, hazardousness**, riskiness, treachery, precariousness, chanciness, dodginess, diceyness, perilousness; unsafeness,

unhealthiness; criticalness; ticklishness, slipperiness, touchiness, delicacy, ticklish business, shaky ground; insecurity, unsoundness, instability, unsteadiness, shakiness, totteriness, wonkiness; sword of Damocles; unreliability, undependability, untrustworthiness; unsureness, unpredictability, uncertainty, doubtfulness, dubiousness

3 exposure, openness, liability, nonimmunity, susceptibility; **unprotectedness, defenselessness,** nakedness, helplessness; lamb, sitting duck; roadkill; naiveté

4 **vulnerability,** pregnability, penetrability, assailability, vincibility; weakness; vulnerable point, weak link, weak point, soft spot, heel of Achilles, chink, chink in one's armor, the soft underbelly; tragic flaw, fatal flaw

5 <**hidden danger**> snags, rocks, reefs, ledges; coral heads; shallows, shoals; sandbank, sandbar, sands; quicksands; crevasses; rockbound coast, lee shore; undertow, undercurrent; **pitfall;** snake in the grass; trap, booby trap, springe, snare, tripwire; snarling dog, ticking package; cloud on the horizon

VERBS **6** **endanger,** imperil, peril; risk, hazard, gamble, gamble with; **jeopardize**, jeopard, jeopardy, compromise, put in danger, put in jeopardy, put on the spot, lay on the line; expose, lay open; incur danger, run into danger, encounter danger

7 **take chances,** take a chance, chance, risk, stake, gamble, hazard, press one's luck, push one's luck, run the chance, run the risk, run the hazard; risk one's neck, run a risk, go out on a limb, stick one's neck out, expose oneself, bare one's breast, lower one's guard, lay oneself open to, leave oneself wide open, open the door to, let oneself in for; drive recklessly; tempt Providence, **tempt fate**, forget the odds, defy danger, skate on thin ice, court destruction, dance on the razor's edge, go in harm's way, hang by a hair, hang by a thread, sleep on a volcano, sit on a barrel of gunpowder, build a house of cards, put one's head in the lion's mouth, march up to the cannon's mouth, play with fire, go through fire and water, go out of one's depth, go to sea in a sieve, carry too much sail, sail too near the wind; risk one's life, throw caution to the wind, take one's life in one's hand, dare, face up to, brave

8 **be in danger,** be in peril, be *in extremis,* be in a desperate case, have one's name on the danger list, have the chances against one, have the odds against one, have one's back to the wall, have something hanging over one's head; be despaired of; hang by a thread; tremble on the verge, totter on the brink, teeter on the edge; feel the ground sliding from under one; have to run for it; race against time, race against the clock; be threatened, be on the spot, be in a bind

ADJS **9** **dangerous,** dangersome, perilous, periculous, parlous, jeopardous, bad, ugly, serious, critical, explosive, beset with danger, fraught with danger; alarming, too close for comfort, menacing, threatening

10 **hazardous, risky,** chancy, dodgy, dicey, hairy, sketchy, aleatory, aleatoric, riskful, full of risk; adventurous, venturous, venturesome; speculative, wildcat

11 **unsafe,** unhealthy; unreliable, undependable, untrustworthy, treacherous, insecure, unsound, unstable, unsteady, shaky, tottery, wonky, rocky; unsure, uncertain, unpredictable, doubtful, dubious; on the brink, on the verge

12 **precarious,** ticklish, touchy, touch-and-go, critical, delicate; slippery, slippy; on thin ice, on slippery ground; hanging by a thread, trembling in the balance; nerve-racking

13 **in danger, in jeopardy,** in peril, at risk, in a bad way, bad off; endangered, imperiled, jeopardized, at the last extremity, *in extremis* <L>, in deadly peril, in desperate case; threatened, up against it, on-the-spot, on the hot seat, in the hot seat; sitting on a powder keg; between the hammer and the anvil, between Scylla and Charybdis, between two fires, between the devil and the deep blue sea, between a rock and a hard place; in a predicament; cornered

14 **unprotected,** unshielded, unsheltered, uncovered, unscreened, unguarded, undefended, unattended, unwatched, unfortified; armorless, unarmored, unarmed, bare-handed, weaponless; guardless, ungarrisoned, insecure, **defenseless,** helpless; unwarned, unsuspecting

15 **exposed,** open, out in the open, naked, bare; out on a limb; liable, susceptible, nonimmune

16 **vulnerable,** naïve, pregnable, penetrable, expugnable; assailable, attackable, surmountable; conquerable, beatable, vincible; weak

ADVS **17** **dangerously,** perilously, hazardously, riskily, critically, unsafely; precariously, ticklishly; at gun point

1007 SAFETY

<freedom from danger>

NOUNS **1** **safety,** safeness, **security,** surety, assurance; risklessness, immunity, clear sailing; **protection,** safeguard; harmlessness; airworthiness, crashworthiness, roadworthiness, seaworthiness; invulnerability; safety in numbers; wide berth, safe distance; safekeeping

VERBS 2 **be safe,** be on the safe side; **keep safe,** come through; weather, ride out, weather the storm; keep one's head above water, tide over; keep a safe distance; land on one's feet; save one's bacon, save one's neck; lead a charmed life, have nine lives

3 **play safe,** keep on the safe side, give danger a wide berth, watch oneself, watch out, take precautions, demand assurances; assure oneself, make sure, keep an eye out, keep a weather eye out, look before one leaps; save, protect

ADJS 4 **safe, secure,** safe and sound, not at risk; immune, immunized; insured; protected; firewalled; on the safe side; unthreatened, unmolested; unhurt, unharmed, unscathed, intact, untouched, with a whole skin, undamaged, whole

5 **unhazardous, nonhazardous, undangerous,** unperilous, unrisky, riskless, unprecarious; fail-safe, trouble-free; recession-proof; guaranteed, warranteed; dependable, reliable, trustworthy, sound, stable, steady, firm; as safe as houses; harmless; invulnerable; -proof

6 **in safety, out of danger,** past danger, in, home, out of the woods, over the hump, home free, free and dry, in the clear, out of harm's way; undercover, under lock and key; in shelter, in harbor, in port, at anchor, in the shadow of a rock; on sure ground, on solid ground, on *terra firma,* high and dry, above water; in safe keeping

7 snug, cozy, home free; crashworthy, roadworthy, airworthy, seaworthy, seakindly

ADVS 8 **safely, securely,** reliably, dependably; with safety, with impunity

INTERJS 9 all's well, all clear, all serene, A-OK; ally-ally out'n free

PHRS 10 the danger is past, the storm has blown over, the coast is clear

1008 PROTECTION

<being kept from danger>

NOUNS 1 **protection, guard,** shielding, **safekeeping;** policing, law enforcement; patrol, patroling, community policing, professional policing, bureaucratic policing; eye, protectiveness, watchfulness, vigilance, watchful eye, shepherding; house-sitting; protective custody; caretaking, safeguarding, security, security industry, public safety, safety; shelter, cover, shade, shadow, windbreak, lee; refuge; preservation; defense; protective coating, Teflon coating <tm>; police department, vice squad, SWAT team

2 **protectorship, guardianship,** stewardship, custodianship; **care,** charge, keeping, nurture, nurturing, nurturance, custody, fostering, fosterage, cocooning, fatherly eye, motherly eye; hands, safe hands, wing; auspices, patronage, tutelage, guidance; ward, wardship, wardenship, watch and ward; cure, pastorship, pastorage, pastorate; oversight, jurisdiction, management, ministry, administration, government, governance; child care, infant care, daycare, family service, aftercare; babysitting, baby-minding <Brit>; child-rearing; crime watch

3 **safeguard,** palladium, **guard,** preventive measure, precautionary steps, precaution; shield, screen, aegis; umbrella, protective umbrella; combination lock; patent, copyright; bulwark; backstop; fender, mudguard, bumper, buffer, cushion, pad, padding; seat belt, safety belt, air bag; protective clothing; shin guard, knuckle guard, knee guard, nose guard, hand guard, arm guard, ear guard, finger guard, foot guard; goggles, mask, face mask, welder's mask, fencer's mask; safety shoes; helmet, hard hat, crash helmet, sun helmet; cowcatcher, pilot; dashboard; windshield, windscreen <Brit>; dodger, cockpit dodger <Brit>; life preserver; lifeline, safety rail, guardrail, handrail; governor; safety, safety switch, interlock; safety valve, safety plug; fuse, circuit breaker; insulation; safety glass, laminated glass; lightning rod, lightning conductor; anchor, bower, sea anchor, sheet anchor, drogue; parachute; **safety net;** prophylactic, preventive; contraceptive

4 **insurance,** assurance <Brit>; annuity, variable annuity; social security; **nest egg,** savings account, provision; insurance company, stock company, mutual company; **insurance policy,** policy, certificate of insurance; deductible; insurance man, underwriter, insurance broker, insurance agent, insurance adjuster, actuary; lemon law

5 **protector,** keeper, protectress, safekeeper, minder; patron, patroness; tower, pillar, strong arm, tower of strength, rock; champion, defender

6 **guardian,** warden, governor; custodian, steward, keeper, **caretaker,** warder <Brit>, attendant; caregiver; next friend, prochein ami, guardian *ad litem;* curator, conservator; janitor; castellan; shepherd, herd, cowherd; game warden, gamekeeper; ranger, forest ranger, forester; lifeguard, lifesaver; air warden; guardian angel

7 chaperon, duenna; governess; escort

8 **nurse,** nursemaid, nurserymaid, nanny, amah, ayah, mammy; dry nurse, wet nurse; **babysitter,** baby-minder <Brit>, sitter

9 **guard,** guarder, guardsman, warder; outguard,

outpost; picket, outlying picket, inlying picket, outrider; advance guard, vanguard, van; rear guard; coast guard; armed guard, security guard; jailer; bank guard; railway guard, train guard; goalkeeper, goaltender, goalie; garrison; cordon

10 **watchman,** watch, watcher; watchkeeper; **lookout**, lookout man; sentinel, picket, sentry; scout, vedette; point, forward observer, spotter; patrol, patrolman, patroller, roundsman; night watchman, Charley; fireguard, fire patrolman, fire warden; airplane spotter; Argus

11 **watchdog,** bandog, guard dog, attack dog; sheep dog; Cerberus

12 **doorkeeper,** doorman, gatekeeper, Cerberus, warden, porter, janitor, concierge, ostiary, usher; receptionist

13 picket, picketer, demonstrator, picket line; counterdemonstrator

14 **bodyguard,** safeguard; convoy, escort; guards, praetorian guard; guardsman; yeoman, yeoman of the guard, beefeater, gentleman-at-arms, Life Guardsman

15 policeman, policewoman, constable, officer, **police officer**; peace officer, law enforcer, law enforcement agent, arm of the law; military policeman (MP); detective; police matron; patrolman, police constable <Brit>; trooper, mounted policeman, state police, state trooper; reeve, portreeve; sheriff, marshal; deputy sheriff, deputy, bound bailiff, catchpole, beagle, bombailiff; sergeant, police sergeant; roundsman; lieutenant, police lieutenant; captain, police captain; inspector, police inspector; superintendent, chief of police; commissioner, police commissioner; government man, federal, fed, G-man; narc; bailiff, tipstaff; mace-bearer, lictor, sergeant at arms; beadle; traffic officer, meter maid; dective

16 <nonformal> cop, copper, John Law, bluecoat, bull, flatfoot, gumshoe, gendarme, shamus, dick, pig*, flattie, bizzy, bobby, peeler <Brit>, Dogberry; blue; the cops, the law, the fuzz, feds, heat; New York's finest; tec, op

17 **police, police force,** law enforcement agency; the force, forces of law and order, long arm of the law; constabulary; state police, troopers, state troopers, highway patrol, county police, provincial police; security force; special police; tactical police, riot police; special weapons and tactics (SWAT), SWAT team, posse; vigilantes, vigilance committee; secret police, political police; Federal Bureau of Investigation (FBI); military police (MP); shore patrol (SP); Scotland Yard; Royal Canadian Mounted Police (RCMP), Mounties <Can>; Interpol, International Criminal Police Commission; neighborhood watch

VERBS 18 **protect, guard, safeguard,** secure, keep, bless, make safe, police, enforce the law; keep from harm; insure, underwrite; ensure, guarantee; patent, copyright, register; cushion; champion, go to bat for; ride shotgun, fend, defend; shelter, shield, screen, cover, cloak, shroud, temper the wind to the shorn lamb; harbor, haven; nestle; compass about, fence; arm, armor; put in a safe place, keep undercover

19 **care for,** take care of; preserve, conserve; provide for, support; take charge of, take under one's wing, make one a protégé; look after, see after, attend to, minister to, look to, see to, look out for, watch out for, have an eye on, keep an eye on, keep a sharp eye on, watch over, keep watch over, watch, mind, tend; keep tabs on; shepherd, ride herd on; chaperon, matronize; babysit; foster, nurture, cherish, nurse; mother, be a mother to, be a father to

20 **watch, keep watch,** keep guard, keep watch over, keep vigil, keep watch and ward; stand guard, stand sentinel; be on the lookout; mount guard; **police,** patrol, pound a beat, go on one's beat

ADJS 21 **protected, guarded,** safeguarded, defended; safe; patented, copyrighted; sheltered, shielded, screened, covered, cloaked; policed; armed; invulnerable

22 **under the protection of,** under the shield of, under the auspices of, under the aegis of, under one's wing, under the wing of, under the shadow of one's wing

23 **protective,** custodial, guardian, tutelary; curatorial; vigilant, watchful, on the watch, on top of; prophylactic, preventive; immunizing; protecting, guarding, safeguarding, sheltering, shielding, screening, covering; fostering, parental; defensive; Teflon-coated <tm>

1009 REFUGE

<shelter from danger>

NOUNS 1 **refuge, sanctuary,** safehold, asylum, haven, port, harborage, harbor; harbor of refuge, port in a storm, snug harbor, safe haven; game sanctuary, bird sanctuary, preserve, forest preserve, game preserve, rain forest; stronghold; political asylum; Rock of Gibraltar

2 **recourse,** resource, resort; last resort, last resource, *dernier ressort*, *pis aller* <Fr>; hope; expedient

3 **shelter,** cover, covert, coverture; concealment; dugout, cave, earth, funk hole, foxhole; bunker; trench; storm cellar, storm cave, cyclone cellar;

air-raid shelter, bomb shelter, bombproof, fallout shelter, safety zone, safety island; stockade, fort

4 **asylum,** home, retreat; poorhouse, almshouse, workhouse <Brit>, poor farm; orphanage; hospice, hospitium; old folks' home, rest home, nursing home, old soldiers' home, sailors' snug harbor; foster home; safe house; halfway house; retirement home, retirement village, retirement community, life-care home, continuing-care retirement community (CCRC)

5 **retreat,** recess, hiding place, **hideaway,** hideout, hidey-hole, priest hole; sanctum, inner sanctum, sanctum sanctorum, holy ground, holy of holies, adytum; private place, privacy, secret place; den, lair, mew; safe house; cloister, hermitage, ashram, cell; ivory tower; study, library; me time

6 **harbor,** haven, **port,** seaport, port of call, free port, treaty port, home port; hoverport; harborage, anchorage, anchorage ground, protected anchorage, moorage, moorings; roadstead, road, roads; berth, slip; dock, dockage, marina, basin; dry dock; shipyard, dockyard; wharf, pier, quay; harborside, dockside, pierside, quayside, landing, landing place, landing stage, jetty, jutty; breakwater, mole, groin; seawall, embankment, bulkhead

VERBS 7 **take refuge, take shelter,** seek refuge, claim sanctuary, claim refugee status, ask for political asylum, seek asylum; run into port; fly to, throw oneself into the arms of; bar the gate, lock the door, bolt the door, raise the drawbridge, let the portcullis down; take cover

8 **find refuge**, find sanctuary, make port, reach safety; seclude oneself, sequester oneself, dwell in an ivory tower, live in an ivory tower

1010 PROSPERITY

<thriving accompanied by money>

NOUNS 1 **prosperity, prosperousness**, thriving condition, flourishing condition; success; welfare, well-being, weal, happiness, felicity; quality of life; comfortable circumstances, easy circumstances, comfort, ease, security; life of ease, life of Riley, the good life; clover, velvet, bed of roses, luxury, lap of luxury, easy street, fat city, hog heaven; the affluent life, gracious life, gracious living; fat of the land; fleshpots, fleshpots of Egypt; milk and honey, loaves and fishes; a chicken in every pot, a car in every garage; fine linen; high standard of living; upward mobility; affluence, wealth

2 **good fortune,** good luck, happy fortune, fortune, luck, the breaks; **fortunateness,** luckiness, felicity; blessing, smiles of fortune, fortune's favor

3 **stroke of luck,** piece of good luck; blessing; fluke, lucky strike, scratch hit, break, good break, lucky break; run of luck, streak of luck; bonanza; Midas touch; high note, positive note; hot hand

4 **good times,** piping times, bright days, halcyon days, days of wine and roses, rosy era; heyday; prosperity, era of prosperity; fair weather, sunshine; golden era, golden age, golden time, golden days, high point, Saturnian age, reign of Saturn; honeymoon, second honeymoon; holiday; prime, youth; Age of Aquarius, millennium; utopia; heaven

5 roaring trade, land-office business, bullishness, bull market, bullish market, seller's market; **boom,** booming economy, expanding economy

6 **lucky dog**, lucky devil, fortune's favorite, favorite of the gods, fortune's child, destiny's darling

VERBS 7 **prosper,** enjoy prosperity, fare well, get on well, do well, have it made, have a good thing going, have everything going one's way, get on swimmingly, go great guns; turn out well, go well, take a favorable turn; succeed; come on, come a long way, get on; advance, progress, make progress, make headway, get ahead, move up in the world, pull oneself up by one's own boot-straps; live long and prosper

8 **thrive, flourish,** boom; blossom, bloom, flower; batten, fatten, grow fat; be fat, dumb, and happy

9 **be prosperous,** make good, make one's mark, rise in the world, get on in the world, make a noise in the world, do all right by oneself, make one's fortune; grow rich; drive a roaring trade, do a land-office business, rejoice in a seller's market

10 **live well,** live in clover, live on velvet, live a life of ease, live the life of Riley, lead the life of Riley, live high, **live high on the hog**, live off the fat of the land, ride the gravy train, piss on ice*, roll in the lap of luxury; bask in the sunshine, have one's place in the sun; have a good time of it, have a fine time of it

11 **be fortunate,** be lucky, be in luck, luck out, have all the luck, have one's moments, **lead a charmed life,** have a charmed life; fall into the shithouse and come up with a five-dollar gold piece*; get a break, get the breaks; hold aces, turn up roses; have a run of luck, hit a streak of luck; have it break good for one, have a stroke of luck; strike it lucky, make a lucky strike, strike oil, strike it rich, hit it big, strike a rich vein, come into money, drop into a good thing

ADJS 12 **prosperous,** in good case; successful, rags-to-riches; well-paid, high-income, higher-income, well-heeled, upscale; affluent, wealthy; comfortable, comfortably situated, easy; on easy street, in fat city, in hog heaven, **in clover**, on velvet, on a bed of roses, in luxury, high on the hog; up in the world, on top of the heap

13 **thriving,** flourishing, prospering, booming; vigorous, exuberant; in full swing, going strong; halcyon, palmy, balmy, rosy, piping, clear, fair; blooming, blossoming, flowering, fruiting; fat, sleek, in good case; dumb, and happy

14 **fortunate,** lucky, providential; in luck; **blessed,** blessed with luck, favored; born under a lucky star, born with a silver spoon in one's mouth, born on the sunny side of the hedge; out of the woods, over the hump; auspicious

ADVS 15 **prosperously,** thrivingly, flourishingly, boomingly, swimmingly

16 **fortunately,** luckily, providentially

1011 ADVERSITY

<*misfortune or tragedy*>

NOUNS 1 **adversity,** adverse circumstances, difficulties, hard knocks, rough going, **hardship,** trouble, troubles, sea of troubles, rigor, vicissitude, care, stress, pressure, stress of life; low point; hard case, hard plight, hard life, dog's life, vale of tears; wretched lot, miserable lot, hard lot, unhappy lot, tough row to hoe, hard row to hoe, ups and downs of life, things going against one; bitter cup, bitter pill; bummer, downer; the bad part, the downside; annoyance, irritation, aggravation; difficulty; trial, tribulation, cross, bane, curse, blight, affliction; plight, predicament; the pits, raw deal; turkey shoot

2 **misfortune,** mishap, ill hap, misadventure, mischance, *contretemps* <Fr>, grief; disaster, calamity, catastrophe, meltdown, cataclysm, tragedy; missed chance; shock, blow, hard blow, nasty blow, staggering blow; **accident,** casualty, collision, crash, plane crash, car crash; wreck, shipwreck; smash, smashup, crack-up, pileup; bad news; disaster area

3 reverse, **reversal,** reversal of fortune, **setback,** check, severe check, backset, throwback; comedown, descent, down

4 **unfortunateness, unluckiness,** lucklessness, ill success; unprosperousness; starcrossed life, ill-fated life; the slings and arrows of outrageous fortune; inauspiciousness

5 **bad luck,** bad break, ill luck, hard luck, hard lines <Brit>, tough luck, rotten luck, raw deal, tough break, rotten break, bad patch, devil's own luck; **ill fortune,** bad fortune, evil fortune, evil star, ill wind, evil dispensation; frowns of fortune

6 **hard times,** bad times, sad times; evil day, ill day; rainy day; stormy weather, heavy weather, storm clouds; depression, recession, slump, economic stagnation, bust; rough patch, bad spell; winter of discontent; bumpy ride

7 **unfortunate,** poor unfortunate, the plaything of fortune, the sport of fortune, fortune's fool; loser, sure loser, nonstarter, born loser; hard case, sad sack, hard-luck guy; *schlemiel* <Yiddish>, *schlimazel* <Yiddish>; odd man out; the underclass, the dispossessed, the homeless, the wretched of the earth; victim, victim of fate; martyr

VERBS 8 go hard with, go ill with; run one hard; oppress, weigh on, weigh heavy on, weigh down, **burden,** overburden, load, overload, bear hard upon, lie on, lie hard upon, lie heavy upon; try one, put one out

9 **have trouble;** be born to trouble, be born under an evil star; have a hard time of it, be up against it, make heavy weather of it, meet adversity, have a bad time, lead a dog's life, live a dog's life, have a tough row to hoe, hard row to hoe; bear the brunt, bear more than one's share; be put to one's wit's end, not know which way to turn; **be unlucky,** have bad luck, have rotten luck, be misfortuned, get the shortend of the stick, get the shitty end of the stick*, hit the skids

10 come to grief, have a mishap, **suffer misfortune,** fall, be stricken, be staggered, be shattered, be poleaxed, be felled, come a cropper, be clobbered; run aground, go on the rocks, go on the shoals, split upon a rock; sink, drown; founder

11 fall on evil days, come down in the world, go downhill, slip, be on the skids, come down, have a comedown, fall from one's high estate; deteriorate, degenerate, run to seed, go to seed, sink, decline; go to pot, go to the dogs, go belly up; reach the depths, touch bottom, **hit rock bottom**; have seen better days

12 **bring bad luck**; hoodoo, hex, jinx, Jonah, put the jinx on; put the evil eye on, whammy, put the whammy on, a double whammy on

ADJS 13 **adverse,** untoward, detrimental, **unfavorable;** sinister; hostile, antagonistic, inimical; contrary, counter, counteractive, conflicting, opposing, opposed, opposite, in opposition; difficult, troublesome, troublous, hard, trying, rigorous, stressful; wretched, miserable; not easy; harmful

14 **unfortunate, unlucky,** unprovidential, unblessed, unprosperous, sad, unhappy, hapless, fortuneless, misfortuned, luckless, donsie; out of luck, short of luck; **down on one's luck**, badly off, ill off, down in the world, in adverse circumstances; underprivileged, depressed; ill-starred, evil-starred, born under a bad sign, born under an evil star, planet-stricken, planet-struck, star-

crossed; fatal, dire, doomful, funest, ominous, inauspicious; in a jam, in a pickle, in a pretty pickle, in a tight spot, between a rock and a hard place, between the devil and the deep blue sea, caught in the crossfire, caught in the middle; up a tree, up the creek, up shit creek without a paddle*, up to one's ass in alligators

15 **disastrous, calamitous, catastrophic,** cataclysmic, cataclysmal, tragic, ruinous, wreckful, fatal, dire, black, woeful, sore, baneful, grievous; destructive; life-threatening, terminal

ADVS 16 **adversely,** untowardly, detrimentally, unfavorably; contrarily, conflictingly, opposingly, oppositely

17 **unfortunately, unluckily,** unprovidentially, sadly, unhappily, as ill luck would have it; by ill luck, by ill hap; in adverse circumstances, if worse comes to worse

18 **disastrously,** calamitously, catastrophically, cataclysmically, grievously, woefully, sorely, banefully, tragically, crushingly, shatteringly

INTERJS 19 **tough luck,** tough titty*, tough shit*, tough darts

1012 HINDRANCE

<something delaying or preventing progress>

NOUNS 1 **hindrance,** hindering, **hampering,** let; check, arrest, arrestment, arrestation; fixation; impediment, holdback; resistance, opposition; suppression, repression, restriction, restraint; obstruction, blocking, blockage, clogging, occlusion; bottleneck, traffic jam, gridlock; speed bump, sleeping policeman <Brit>; interruption, interference; retardation, retardment, detention, detainment, delay, holdup, setback; inhibition; constriction, squeeze, stricture, cramp, stranglehold; closure, closing up, closing off; obstructionism, bloody-mindedness <Brit>, negativism, foot-dragging; nuisance value; glass wall, glass ceiling, stained-glass ceiling

2 **prevention,** stop, stoppage, stopping, arrestation, estoppel; stay, staying, halt, halting; prohibition, forbiddance; debarment; **determent,** deterrence, discouragement; forestalling, preclusion, obviation, foreclosure

3 **frustration, thwarting**, balking, foiling; discomfiture, disconcertion, bafflement, confounding; defeat, upset; check, checkmate, balk, foil; derailing, derailment; vicious circle

4 **obstacle, obstruction,** obstructer; hang-up; block, blockade, cordon, curtain; difficulty, hurdle, hazard, bed of nails, nail-biter; deterrent, determent; drawback, objection; stumbling block, stumbling stone, stone in one's path; fly in the ointment, one small difficulty, hitch, catch, joker, a "but," a "however"; bureaucracy, red tape, regulations

5 **barrier,** bar; gate, portcullis; fence, wall, stone wall, **brick wall**, impenetrable wall; seawall, jetty, groin, mole, breakwater; bulwark, rampart, defense, buffer, bulkhead, parapet, breastwork, work, earthwork, mound; bank, embankment, levee, dike; ditch, moat; dam, weir, leaping weir, barrage, milldam, beaver dam, cofferdam, wicket dam, shutter dam, bear-trap dam, hydraulic-fill dam, rock-fill dam, arch dam, arch-gravity dam, gravity dam; boom, jam, logjam; roadblock; speed bump; backstop; iron curtain, bamboo curtain; glass ceiling

6 **impediment,** embarrassment, hamper; **encumbrance**, cumbrance; trouble, difficulty; handicap, disadvantage, inconvenience, penalty; white elephant; burden, burthen, imposition, onus, cross, weight, deadweight, ball and chain, millstone around one's neck; load, pack, cargo, freight, charge; impedimenta, lumber; technical difficulty, flat tire, gremlin, glitch, bug, hiccup

7 **curb, check,** countercheck, arrest, stay, stop, damper, holdback; brake, clog, drag, drogue, remora; chock, scotch, spoke, spoke in one's wheel; doorstop; check-rein, bearing rein, martingale; bit, snaffle, pelham, curb bit; shackle, chain, fetter, trammel; sea anchor, drift anchor, drift sail, drag sail, drag sheet; boot, Denver boot

8 **hinderer,** impeder, marplot, obstructer; frustrater, thwarter; obstructionist, negativist; filibuster, filibusterer

9 **spoilsport,** wet blanket, killjoy, grouch, grinch, sourpuss, malcontent, dog in the manger, party pooper

VERBS 10 **hinder, impede,** inhibit, arrest, check, countercheck, scotch, curb, snub; resist, oppose; stonewall, stall, stall off; suppress, repress; interrupt, intercept; intervene, interfere, intermeddle, meddle; damp, dampen, throw cold water; retard, slacken, delay, detain, hold back, keep back, set back, hold up; restrain; keep in check, bottle up, dam up

11 **hamper, impede,** cramp, embarrass; trammel, entrammel, enmesh, entangle, ensnarl, entrap, entwine, involve, entoil, toil, net, lime, tangle, snarl; fetter, shackle; handcuff, tie one's hands; encumber, cumber, burden, lumber, saddle with, weigh down, press down; hang like a millstone round one's neck; **handicap,** put at a disadvantage; lame, cripple, hobble, hamstring; cramp one's style, crab one's deal; gum up, gum up the works

12 **obstruct,** get in the way, stand in the way;

dog, **block**, block the way, put up a roadblock, blockade, block up, occlude; jam, crowd, pack; bar, barricade, bolt, lock; debar, shut out; shut off, close, close off, close up, close tight, shut tight; constrict, squeeze, squeeze shut, strangle, strangulate, stifle, suffocate, choke, choke off, chock; stop up

13 **stop, stay, halt,** bring to a stop, put a stop to, put an end to, bring to a shuddering halt, bring to a screeching halt; brake, slow down, put on the brakes, hit the brakes; block, stall, stymie, deadlock; nip in the bud

14 **prevent, prohibit**, forbid; bar, estop; save, help, keep from; deter, discourage, dishearten; avert, parry, keep off, ward off, stave off, fend off, fend, repel, deflect, turn aside; forestall, foreclose, preclude, exclude, debar, obviate, anticipate; rule out

15 **thwart, frustrate,** foil, cross, balk; spike, scotch, checkmate; counter, contravene, counteract, countermand, counterwork; stand in the way of, confront, brave, defy, challenge; defeat; discomfit, upset, disrupt, confound, flummox, discountenance, put out of countenance, disconcert, baffle, nonplus, perplex, stump; throw on one's beam ends, trip one up, throw one for a loss; circumvent, elude; sabotage, spoil, ruin, dish, dash, blast; destroy; throw a wrench in the machinery, throw a monkey wrench into the works; put a spoke in one's wheel, scotch one's wheel, spike one's guns, put one's nose out of joint, upset one's applecart; **derail;** take the wind out of one's sails, steal one's thunder, cut the ground from under one, knock the props from under one, knock the bottom out of; tie one's hands, clip one's wings

16 <nonformal> foul up, louse up, snafu, bollix, bollix up, gum, **gum up,** gum up the works; crimp, cramp, put a crimp in, cramp one's style; cook one's goose, cut one down to size; give one a hard time; queer, crab

ADJS 17 **hindering,** troublesome; **inhibitive,** inhibiting, suppressive, repressive; constrictive, strangling, stifling, choking; restrictive; obstructive, obstructing, occlusive, obstruent; cantankerous, bloody-minded <Brit>, contrary, crosswise; interruptive, interrupting; in the way

18 **hampering, impeding,** counterproductive, impedimental, impeditive; onerous, oppressive, burdensome, cumbersome, cumbrous, encumbering

19 **preventive,** preventative, avertive, prophylactic; **prohibitive**, forbidding; deterrent, deterring, discouraging; preclusive, forestalling; foot-dragging

20 **frustrating,** confounding, disconcerting, baffling, defeating

ADVS 21 under handicap, at a disadvantage, with everything against one

1013 DIFFICULTY

<something hard to do or deal with>

NOUNS 1 **difficulty,** difficultness; hardness, toughness, strain, the hard way, rigor, rigorousness, ruggedness; arduousness, laboriousness, strenuousness, toilsomeness, severity; troublesomeness, bothersomeness; onerousness, oppressiveness, burdensomeness; formidability, hairiness; complication, intricacy, complexity; abstruseness

2 tough proposition, tough one, toughie, large order, tall order; **hard job,** tough job, heavy lift, big undertaking, backbreaker, ballbuster, chore, man-sized job; brutal task, herculean task, Augean task; uphill work, rough go, heavy sledding, hard pull, dead lift; tough lineup to buck, hard road to travel; hard nut to crack, tough nut to crack, hard row to hoe, tough row to hoe, hard row of stumps; bitch*; handful, all one can manage, no easy task

3 **trouble,** the matter; headache, problem, besetment, inconvenience, disadvantage; the bad part, the downside; ado, great ado; peck of troubles, sea of troubles; hornet's nest, Pandora's box, can of worms; evil; bother, annoyance; anxiety, worry

4 **predicament, plight,** spot of trouble, strait, straits, parlous straits, tightrope, knife edge, thin edge; pinch, bind, pass, clutch, situation, emergency; pretty pass, nice predicament, pretty predicament, fine state of affairs, sorry plight; slough, quagmire, morass, swamp, quicksand; embarrassment, embarrassing position, embarrassing situation; complication, imbroglio; the devil to pay

5 <nonformal> **pickle,** crunch, hobble, pretty pickle, fine kettle of fish, how-do-you-do, fine how-do-you-do; spot, tight spot; squeeze, tight squeeze, ticklish spot, tricky spot, hot spot, hot seat, sticky wicket <Brit>; scrape, jam, hot water, tail in a gate, tit in the wringer; **mess**, holy mess, unholy mess, mix, stew; hell to pay; no-win situation

6 **impasse, corner**, box, hole, cleft stick; cul-de-sac, blind alley, deadend, deadend street, blank wall; extremity, end of one's rope, end of one's tether, wit's end, nowhere to turn; stalemate, deadlock; stand, standoff, standstill, logjam, halt, stop

7 **dilemma,** hot mess, horns of a dilemma, double

bind, damned-if-you-do-and-damned-if-you-don't, no-win situation, quandary, nonplus, conundrum; vexed question, thorny problem, knotty point, knot, crux, node, nodus, Gordian knot, hard nut to crack, can of worms, headache, poser, teaser, perplexity, puzzle, enigma; paradox, oxymoron; asses' bridge; bad hair day; trilemma, tetralemma

8 **crux, hitch,** pinch, rub, snag, hurdle, catch, joker, where the shoe pinches, complication

9 unwieldiness, unmanageability; unhandiness, inconvenience, impracticality; awkwardness, clumsiness; cumbersomeness, ponderousness, bulkiness, hulkiness; ham-handedness

VERBS 10 **be difficult,** present difficulties, pose problems, take some doing

11 **have difficulty, have trouble,** have a rough time, hit a snag, have a hard time of it, have one's hands full, have one's work cut out, get off to a bad start, get off on the wrong foot; be hard put, have much ado with; labor under difficulties, labor under a disadvantage, have the cards stacked against one, have two strikes against one; struggle, **flounder,** beat about, make heavy weather of it; have one's back to the wall, not know where to turn, come to a deadend, come to a standstill, not know whether one is coming or going, go around in circles, swim against the current; walk a tightrope, walk on eggshells, walk on hot coals, dance on a hot griddle

12 **get into trouble,** plunge into difficulties; let oneself in for, put one's foot in it; get in a jam, get in hot water, get in the soup, get into a scrape, get in a mess, get in a hole, get in a box, get in a bind; paint oneself into a corner, get one's ass in a bind, put oneself in a spot, put one's foot in one's mouth, strike a bad patch, be up a tree; have a tiger by the tail; burn one's fingers; get all tangled up, get all snarled up, get all balled up, get all bollixed up

13 **trouble, beset**; bother, pother, get one down, disturb, perturb, irk, plague, torment, drive one up the wall, give one gray hair, make one lose sleep; harass, vex, distress; inconvenience, put out, put out of the way, discommode; concern, worry; puzzle, perplex; put to it, give one trouble, complicate matters; give one a hard time, give one a bad time, make it tough for; be too much for; ail, be the matter; tree

14 **cause trouble,** bring trouble; ask for trouble, ask for it, bring down upon one, bring down upon one's head, bring down around one's ears; stir up a hornet's nest, kick up a fuss, kick up a storm; open Pandora's box, open a can of worms, put fire to tow; raise hell; raise merry hell, play hob, play hell, play the devil

15 put in a hole, put in a spot; embarrass; involve, enmesh, entangle

16 **corner,** run into a corner, drive into a corner, tree, chase up a tree, drive to the wall, push one to the wall, put one's back to the wall, have one on the ropes

ADJS 17 **difficult,** difficile; **not easy,** no picnic, hairy; hard, tough, rough, rugged, rigorous, brutal, severe; wicked, mean, formidable; arduous, strenuous, toilsome, laborious, operose, herculean; steep, uphill; hard-fought; hard-earned; jawbreaking; knotty, knotted; thorny, spiny, set with thorns; delicate, ticklish, tricky, sticky, critical, easier said than done, like pulling teeth; exacting, demanding; intricate, complex; abstruse; hard-ass

18 **troublesome,** besetting; bothersome, irksome, vexatious, painful, plaguey, problematic, annoying; burdensome, oppressive, onerous, heavy, hefty, crushing, backbreaking; **trying,** grueling

19 **unwieldy, unmanageable,** unhandy; inconvenient, impractical; awkward, clumsy, cumbersome, unmaneuverable; contrary, perverse, crosswise; ponderous, bulky, hulky, hulking, ungainly

20 **troubled,** trouble-plagued, beset, sore beset; bothered, vexed, irked, annoyed; plagued, harassed; distressed, perturbed; inconvenienced, embarrassed; put to it, hard put to it; worried, anxious; puzzled

21 **in trouble,** in deep trouble, in a predicament, in a sorry plight, in a pretty pass; in deep water, out of one's depth

22 <nonformal> in deep shit*, in deep doo-doo, in a jam, in a pickle, in a pretty pickle, in a spot, in a tight spot, in a fix, in a hole, in a bind, in a box; in a mess, in a scrape, in hot water, in the soup; up a tree, up to one's ass in alligators, up the creek, up shit creek without a paddle*, in Dutch, on-the-spot, behind the eight ball, out on a limb, on the hot seat

23 **in a dilemma,** dilemmatic, on the horns of a dilemma, **in a quandary;** between two stools; between Scylla and Charybdis, between the devil and the deep blue sea, between a rock and a hard place

24 at an impasse, at one's wit's end, at a loss, at a standstill, deadlocked; nonplussed, at a nonplus; baffled, perplexed, bewildered, mystified, stuck, stumped, stymied

25 **cornered,** in a corner, with one's back to the wall; **treed**, up a tree, up a stump; at bay

26 straitened, reduced to dire straits, in desperate straits, pinched, sorely pressed, **hard-pressed,**

hard up, up against it; driven from pillar to post; desperate, in extremities, *in extremis* <L>, at the end of one's rope, at the end of one's tether

27 **stranded,** grounded, aground, on the rocks, high and dry; **stuck,** stuck fast; foundered, swamped; castaway, marooned, wrecked, shipwrecked

ADVS **28** **with difficulty,** difficultly, with much ado; hardly, painfully; the hard way, arduously, strenuously, laboriously, toilsomely

29 **unwieldily,** unmanageably, unhandily, inconveniently; awkwardly, clumsily, cumbersomely; ponderously

1014 FACILITY

<something making action easier>

NOUNS **1** **facility, ease, easiness,** facileness, effortlessness; lack of hindrance, smoothness, freedom; clear coast, clear road, clear course; smooth road, royal road, highroad; easy going, plain sailing, smooth sailing, straight sailing; clarity, intelligibility; uncomplexity, uncomplicatedness, simplicity; low-hanging fruit

2 **handiness,** wieldiness, wieldableness, handleability, manageability, manageableness, maneuverability; **convenience,** practicality, practicableness, untroublesomeness; flexibility, pliancy, pliability, ductility, malleability; adaptability, feasibility

3 **easy thing,** mere child's play, simple matter, mere twist of the wrist; easy target, sitting duck; sinecure; open road

4 <nonformal> **cinch, snap,** pushover, breeze, waltz, duck soup, velvet, picnic, pie, cherry pie, apple pie, cakewalk, piece of cake, kid stuff, turkey shoot, no-brainer, setup, high road, walkover, no sweat

5 **facilitation, facilitating,** easing, smoothing, smoothing out, smoothing the way; speeding, expediting, expedition, quickening, hastening; streamlining; lubricating, greasing, oiling

6 disembarrassment, disentanglement, disencumbrance, disinvolvement, uncluttering, uncomplicating, unscrambling, unsnarling, disburdening, unburdening, unhampering; **extrication,** disengagement, **freeing,** clearing; deregulation; simplification

VERBS **7** **facilitate, ease;** grease the wheels; smooth, smooth the way, pave the way, ease the way, grease the ways, prepare the way, clear the way, make all clear for, make way for; run interference for, open the way, open the door to; not stand in the way of; open up, unclog, unblock, unjam, unbar, loose; lubricate, make frictionless, remove friction, grease, oil; speed, expedite, quicken, hasten; help along, help out, help on its way; aid; explain, make clear; simplify

8 **do easily,** make short work of, do with one's hands tied behind one's back, do with both eyes shut, do standing on one's head, do hands down, sail through, dance through, waltz through, wing it, take to like a duck to water

9 disembarrass, disencumber, unload, relieve, disburden, unhamper, get out from under; disentangle, disembroil, disinvolve, unclutter, unscramble, unsnarl; **extricate,** disengage, **free,** free up, clear; liberate

10 **go easily, run smoothly,** work well, work like a machine, go like clockwork, go like a sewing machine; present no difficulties, give no trouble, be painless, be effortless; flow, roll, glide, slide, coast, sweep, sail

11 **have it easy,** have it soft, have it all one's own way, have the game in one's hands, have it in the bag; win easily; breeze in, walk over the course, win in a walk, win hands down

12 **take it easy**, **go easy**, swim with the stream, drift with the current, go with the tide; cool it, not sweat it; take the line of least resistance; take it in one's stride, make little of, make light of, think nothing of

ADJS **13** **easy, facile,** effortless, smooth, painless; soft, cushy; plain, uncomplicated, straightforward, simple, Mickey Mouse, simple as ABC, easy as pie, easy as falling off a log, downhill all the way, like shooting fish in a barrel, like taking candy from a baby, no sooner said than done; clear; glib; light, unburdensome; nothing to it; casual, throwaway; on a plate; super-easy

14 **smooth-running,** frictionless, dissipationless, easy-running, easy-flowing; well-lubricated, well-oiled, well-greased

15 **handy,** wieldy, wieldable, handleable; tractable; flexible, pliant, yielding, malleable, ductile, pliable, manageable, maneuverable; **convenient,** foolproof, goofproof, practical, untroublesome, user-friendly; adaptable, feasible; child-friendly, toddler-friendly

ADVS **16** **easily,** facilely, **effortlessly**, readily, simply, lightly, swimmingly, without difficulty; no sweat, like nothing, slick as a whistle; hands down, unchallenging, with one hand tied behind one's back, with both eyes closed, standing on one's head; like a duck takes to water; **smoothly,** frictionlessly, like clockwork; on easy terms

1015 UGLINESS

<unpleasant to look at>

NOUNS 1 **ugliness, unsightliness, unattractiveness,** uncomeliness, unhandsomeness, unbeautifulness, unprettiness, unloveliness, unaestheticness, unpleasingness; unprepossessingness, ill-favoredness, inelegance; homeliness, plainness; unshapeliness, shapelessness; ungracefulness, gracelessness, clumsiness, ungainliness; uglification, uglifying, disfigurement, defacement; dysphemism; cacophony

2 **hideousness,** horridness, horribleness, frightfulness, dreadfulness, terribleness, awfulness; repulsiveness, repugnance, repugnancy, repellence, repellency, offensiveness, forbiddingness, loathsomeness; ghastliness, gruesomeness, grisliness; **deformity**, misshapenness

3 forbidding countenance, vinegar aspect, wry face, face that would stop a clock

4 **eyesore,** blot, blot on the landscape, blemish, sight, fright, horror, mess, no beauty, no beauty queen, ugly duckling; baboon; scarecrow, gargoyle, monster, monstrosity, teratism; witch, bag, dog, hag, harridan; something the cat dragged in, back end of a bus

VERBS 5 **offend,** offend the eye, offend one's aesthetic sensibilities, **look bad;** look something terrible, look like hell, look like the devil, look a sight, look a fright, look a mess, look like something the cat dragged in; uglify, disfigure, deface, blot, blemish, mar, scar, spoil; dysphemize

ADJS 6 **ugly, unsightly, unattractive,** unhandsome, unpretty, unlovely, uncomely, inelegant; unbeautiful, unbeauteous, beautiless, unaesthetic, unpleasing; homely, plain; not much to look at, not much for looks, short on looks, hard on the eyes; ugly as sin, ugly as the wrath of God, ugly as hell, homely as a mud fence, homely enough to sour milk, homely enough to stop a clock, not fit to be seen, grotty; uglified, disfigured, defaced, blotted, blemished, marred, spoiled; dysphemized, dysphemistic; cacophonous, cacophonic; butt-ugly

7 **unprepossessing,** ill-favored, hard-favored, evil-favored, ill-featured; ill-looking, evil-looking; hard-featured, hard-visaged; grim, grim-faced, grim-visaged; hatchet-faced, horse-faced

8 **unshapely,** shapeless, ill-shaped, ill-made, ill-proportioned; **deformed,** misshapen, misproportioned, malformed, misbegotten; grotesque, scarecrowish, gargoylish; monstrous, teratic, cacogenic

9 **ungraceful,** ungraced, graceless; clumsy, clunky, **ungainly**

10 inartistic, unartistic, **unaesthetic;** unornamental, undecorative

11 **hideous,** horrid, horrible, frightful, dreadful, terrible, awful; repulsive, repellent, repelling, rebarbative, repugnant, offensive, foul, forbidding, loathsome, loathly, revolting; ghastly, gruesome, grisly

ADVS 12 **uglily,** homelily, uncomelily, unattractively, unhandsomely, unbeautifully, unprettily

13 **hideously**, horridly, horribly, frightfully, dreadfully, terribly, awfully; repulsively, repugnantly, offensively, forbiddingly, loathsomely, revoltingly; gruesomely, ghastly

1016 BEAUTY

<pleasant to look at>

NOUNS 1 **beauty, beautifulness,** beauteousness, **prettiness, handsomeness,** attractiveness, loveliness, pulchritude, charm, grace, elegance, exquisiteness; bloom, glow; the beautiful; source of aesthetic pleasure, source of delight; beauty unadorned; eye candy

2 **comeliness,** fairness, sightliness, personableness, relatability, becomingness, pleasingness, goodliness, bonniness, agreeability, agreeableness; charisma

3 **good looks,** good appearance, good effect; good proportions, aesthetic proportions; **shapeliness,** good figure, good shape, nice body, lovely build, physical charm, bodily charm, curvaceousness, curves, pneumaticness, sexy body, sexiness; good bone structure; 10; bodily grace, gracefulness, gracility; good points, beauties, charms, delights, perfections, good features, delicate features

4 **daintiness,** delicacy, delicateness; **cuteness,** cunningness

5 **gorgeousness,** ravishingness; gloriousness, heavenliness, sublimity; splendor, splendidness, splendiferousness, splendorousness, splendrousness, sublimeness, resplendence; brilliance, brightness, radiance, luster; glamour

6 **thing of beauty,** vision, picture, poem, eyeful, **sight for sore eyes**, cynosure; masterpiece

7 **beauty,** charmer; beauty queen, beauty contest winner, beauty pageant winner, Miss America, Miss USA, Miss World, Miss Universe, bathing beauty; glamour girl, cover girl, model, arm candy; sex goddess; belle, reigning beauty, great beauty, lady fair; beau ideal, paragon; enchantress; the face that launch'd a thousand ships

8 <offensive or nonformal> **doll,** dish, **cutie,** angel,

angelface, babyface, beaut, honey, dream, **looker**, good-looker, stunner, dazzler; dreamboat, hunk, beauhunk; fetcher, bird, crumpet <Brit>, peach, knockout, raving beauty, centerfold, pinup girl, pinup, bunny, cutie pie, cute chick, slick chick, pussycat, sex kitten, ten; treasure; hottie, it girl, babe

9 <famous beauties> Venus, Venus de Milo; Aphrodite; Adonis, Hyperion, Narcissus; Astarte; Freya; Helen of Troy, Cleopatra; the Graces, houri, peri

10 **beautification,** prettification, cutification, **adornment;** decoration; **beauty care,** beauty treatment, cosmetology; facial; manicure, pedicure, mani-pedi; spray tan, tanning booth, fake tan; hairdressing; cosmetic surgery, plastic surgery

11 **makeup, cosmetics, beauty products,** beauty-care products; war paint, drugstore complexion; pancake makeup; powder, talcum, talcum powder; foundation, base; rouge, blush, blusher, paint; lip rouge, lipstick, lip color; nail polish; greasepaint, clown white; eye makeup, eyeliner, mascara, guyliner, eye shadow, kohl; cold cream, hand cream, hand lotion, vanishing cream, foundation cream; mudpack; eyebrow pencil; puff, powder puff; makeup brush; compact, vanity case; toiletries, shampoo, soap, body scrub, deodorant, perfume

12 **beautician,** beautifier, cosmetologist, makeup artist, cosmetician; hairdresser, *coiffeur* <Fr>, *coiffeuse* <Fr>, hairstylist; barber; manicurist, pedicurist

13 **beauty parlor**, beauty salon, beauty shop, hairdressing salon, hair salon; barbershop, barber

14 **hairdressing,** hair styling, hair coloring, barbering; shave, depilation, tweezing, electrolysis, waxing; hair replacement; hairstyle, hairdo; haircut, trim, permanent, perm; crop, bob, cut, ponytail, updo, plait, cornrows, braids, pigtails, bangs, chignon, bun, beehive, pompadour, pageboy, dreadlocks, sideburns, crewcut, buzzcut, number one buzz, number three buzz, flattop, ducktail, Mohawk, Afro, bowl haircut; comb-over; good hair, bedhead, hat head, hat hair

VERBS **15** **beautify, prettify,** cutify, pretty up, gussy up, doll up, grace, adorn; decorate; set off, set off to advantage, set off to good advantage, become one; glamorize; make up, paint, put on one's face, titivate, cosmetize, cosmeticize; primp

16 **look good;** look like a million, look fit to kill, knock dead, knock one's eyes out; take the breath away, beggar description; shine, beam, bloom, glow

ADJS **17** **beautiful, beauteous,** endowed with beauty; **pretty, handsome,** attractive, pulchritudinous, **lovely**, graceful, gracile; elegant; esthetic, aesthetically appealing; cute; pretty as a picture; tall dark and handsome; picturesque, scenic

18 **comely,** fair, **good-looking, nice-looking,** well-favored, personable, presentable, agreeable, becoming, pleasing, goodly, bonny, likely, sightly; pleasing to the eye, lovely to behold; shapely, well-built, built, well-shaped, well-proportioned, well-made, well-formed, stacked, well-stacked, curvaceous, curvy, pneumatic, amply endowed, built for comfort, built like a brick shithouse*, buxom, callipygian, callipygous; Junoesque, statuesque, goddesslike; slender; Adonis-like, hunky

19 **fine,** exquisite, flowerlike, dainty, delicate

20 **gorgeous,** ravishing; glorious, heavenly, divine, sublime; resplendent, splendorous, splendrous, splendiferous, splendid; brilliant, bright, radiant, shining, beaming, glowing, blooming, abloom, sparkling, dazzling; glamorous; babelicious

21 <nonformal> eye-filling, **easy on the eyes,** not hard to look at, drop-dead gorgeous, long on looks, looking fit to kill, dishy; cutesy, cutesy-poo; raving, devastating, **stunning,** killing

22 **beautifying,** cosmetic; decorative; cosmetized, cosmeticized, beautified, made-up, mascaraed, titivated

ADVS **23** **beautifully,** beauteously, prettily, handsomely, attractively, becomingly, comelily; elegantly, exquisitely; charmingly, enchantingly

24 daintily, delicately; **cutely**

25 **gorgeously,** ravishingly; ravingly, devastatingly, stunningly; gloriously, divinely, sublimely; resplendently, splendidly, splendorously, splendrously; brilliantly, brightly, radiantly, glowingly, dazzlingly

COMBINING FORMS **26** cal-, calo-, callo-, cali-, calli-

1017 MATHEMATICS

<science of numbers, quantities, shapes>

NOUNS **1** **mathematics** <see list>, **math**, maths, mathematic, **numbers, figures;** pure mathematics, abstract mathematics, applied mathematics, higher mathematics, elementary mathematics, classical mathematics, metamathematics, new mathematics, fuzzy math; algorithm, logarithm; **mathematical element** <see list>

2 <mathematical operations> notation, **addition, subtraction, multiplication, division,** numeracy, calculation, computation, reckoning, proportion, practice, equation, extraction of roots, inversion, reduction, involution, evolution, approximation, interpolation, extrapolation, transformation, differentiation, integration; arithmetic operation, algebraic operation, logical operation, associative operation, distributive operation

3 **number** <see list>, **numeral,** *número* <Sp>, no, n, digit, binary digit, binary bit, cipher, character, symbol, sign, notation, figure, base; decimal

4 <**number systems**> Arabic numerals, algorism, algorithm, Roman numerals; decimal system, binary system, binary code, octal system, duodecimal system, hexadecimal system; place-value notation, positional notation, fixed-point notation, floating-point notation

5 large number, astronomical number, boxcar number, zillion, jillion; googol, googolplex; infinity, infinite number, transfinite number, infinitude; billion, trillion

6 **sum,** summation, difference, product, number, count, x number, n number; account, cast, score, reckoning, tally, tale, the story, whole story, all she wrote, the bottom line, aggregate, amount, quantity; whole, total, running total; box score

7 **ratio,** rate, proportion; quota, quotum; **percentage,** percent; **fraction,** proper fraction, improper fraction, compound fraction, continued fraction, decimal fraction; common fraction, vulgar fraction; geometric ratio, geometric proportion, arithmetical proportion, harmonic proportion; rule of three; numerator, denominator; body mass index

8 series, progression; arithmetical progression, geometrical progression, harmonic progression; Fibonacci numbers

9 numeration, enumeration, **numbering, counting,** count, accounting, census, inventorying, telling, tally, tallying, scoring; page numbering, pagination, foliation; counting on the fingers, dactylonomy; measurement; quantification, quantifying, quantization; operational definition

10 **calculation,** computation, estimation, reckoning, figuring, number work, mental arithmetic, calculus; adding, footing, casting, ciphering, totaling, toting, totting; rounding up, rounding down, rounding off; algebraic expression

11 **summation,** summary, summing, summing up, recount, recounting, rehearsal, capitulation, recapitulation, recap, rehash, statement, reckoning, count, bean-counting, repertory, census, inventory, head count, nose count, body count; account, accounts; table, reckoner, ready reckoner

12 **division**; long division, short division, divisibility; quotient, ratio, proportion, percentage, fraction; reciprocal, inverse, dividend, divisor, aliquot part, remainder, residue; numerator, denominator, common denominator

13 account of, **count of,** a reckoning of, tab of, tally of, check of, track of

14 **figures, statistics,** indexes, indices; vital statistics

15 **calculator** <see list>, computer; estimator, figurer, reckoner, abacist, pollster; statistician, actuary; number-cruncher; accountant, bookkeeper

16 **mathematician,** arithmetician; geometer, geometrician; algebraist, trigonometrician, statistician, geodesist, mathematical physicist, topologist; analyst

VERBS 17 **number,** numerate, number off, **enumerate, count,** tell, tally, give a figure to, put a figure on, call off, name, call over, run over; count heads, call the roll; census, poll; page, paginate, foliate; measure; round, round out, round off, round down; quantify, quantitate, quantize

18 **calculate,** compute, estimate, reckon, figure, solve, reckon at, put at, cipher, cast, tally, score; figure out, do the math, work out, dope out, determine; take account of, figure in, figure on; arithmetize; **add,** add up, sum, **subtract,** take away, **multiply, divide,** multiply out, cross-multiply, times, algebraize, extract roots, raise to the power of, cube, square, decimalize; factor, factor out, factorize; **measure**

19 **tally**, sum up, sum, summate, say it all; aggregate, figure up, cipher up, reckon up, count up, add up, foot up, cast up, score up, tally up; total, total up, tote up, tot up; summarize, recapitulate, recap, rehash, recount, rehearse, recite, relate; detail, itemize, inventory; round up, round down, round off

20 **keep account of,** keep count of, keep track of, keep tabs, keep tally, keep a check on

21 check, verify, double-check, check on, check out; prove, demonstrate; balance, balance the books; audit, overhaul; take stock, inventory

ADJS 22 **mathematical,** numeric, numerical, numerary, arithmetic, arithmetical, algebraic, algebraical, geometric, geometrical, trigonometric, trigonometrical, analytic, analytical, combinatorial, topological, statistical

23 **numeric, numerical,** numeral, numerary, numerative; odd, impair, even, pair; arithmetical, algorismic, algorithmic; cardinal, ordinal; figural, figurate, figurative, digital; aliquot, submultiple, reciprocal, prime, fractional, decimal, exponential, logarithmic, logometric, differential, integral; positive, negative; rational, irrational, transcendental; surd, radical; real, imaginary; possible, impossible, finite, infinite, transfinite; whole; decenary, binary, ternary; signed, unsigned, nonnegative

24 **numerative,** enumerative; calculative, computative, estimative; calculating, computing, computational, estimating; statistical; quantifying, quantizing

25 **calculable,** computable, reckonable, estimable, countable, numberable, enumerable, numerable; measurable, mensurable, quantifiable; addable, subtractive, multipliable, dividable

26 **calculator**

abacus
adding machine
analog computer
arithmograph
arithmometer
calculating machine
cash register
compass
computer
counter
difference engine
digital computer
Napier's bones, Napier's rods
number-cruncher
online calculator
pari-mutuel machine
pocket calculator
programmable calculator
quipu
rule
scientific calculator
scorecard
slide rule, sliding scale
suan pan
tabulator
tally, tally stick
totalizator
Turing machine

27 **mathematical element**

addend
algorithm
aliquot
antilogarithm
argument
auxiliary equation
base
Bessel function
binomial
characteristic
characteristic equation
characteristic function
characteristic polynomial
characteristic root, characteristic value, eigenvalue, latent root, proper value
characteristic vector
coefficient
combination
common divisor, common measure
complement
congruence
constant
coordinate
cosecant
cosine
cotangent
cube
cube root
decimal
denominator
derivative
determinant
difference, remainder
differential
discriminate
dividend
division sign
divisor
e, belongs to
elliptical function
empty set, null set
equal sign
equation
exponent
exponential
expression
factor
factorial
formula
fraction
function
greatest common divisor (GCD)
haversine
hyperbolic
i
increment
index
integral
Laplace transform
least common denominator (LCD)
least common multiple (LCM)
logarithm, log
mantissa
matrix
minuend
minus sign
mixed decimal
modulus
monomial
multinomial
multiple
multiplicand
multiplication sign
multiplicator
multiplier
norm
numerator
parameter
part
permutation
pi
plus sign
polynomial
power
quadratic equation
quaternion
quotient
radical
radix
reciprocal
repeating decimal, circulating decimal
root
secant
sequence
series
set
simultaneous equations
sine
solution
square root
submultiple
subtrahend
summand
tangent
tensor
topological group
topological space
variable
vector
vector product
vector sum
versed sine, versine
vulgar fraction

28 **mathematics (branches)**

addition algebra
affine geometry
algebra
algebraic geometry
algebraic topology
analysis
analytic geometry
applied mathematics
arithmetic
associative algebra
binary arithmetic
Boolean algebra
calculus
calculus of differences
category theory
circle geometry
combinatorial mathematics, combinatorics
combinatorial topology
commutative algebra
complex algebra, double algebra
control theory
denumerative geometry
descriptive geometry
differential calculus
differential geometry
division algebra
elementary arithmetic
elementary algebra, ordinary algebra
equivalent algebras
Euclidean geometry
Fourier analysis
functional analysis
game theory
geodesic geometry
geodesy
geometry
Gödel's proof
graph theory
graphic algebra
group theory
harmonic analysis
higher algebra
higher arithmetic
homological algebra
hyperalgebra
hyperbolic geometry
infinitesimal calculus
integral calculus
intuitional geometry
invariant subalgebra
inverse geometry
Lagrangian function
Laplace's equation
linear algebra
line geometry
mathematical biology

mathematical biophysics
mathematical computing
mathematical ecology
mathematical geography
mathematical logic
mathematical physics
matrix algebra
measure theory
metageometry
modular arithmetic
multiple algebra
natural geometry
nilpotent algebra
noncommutative algebra
non-Euclidean geometry
n-tuple linear algebra
number theory
numerical analysis
operational calculus
operations research
plane geometry
plane trigonometry
point-set topology
political arithmetic
potential theory
probability theory
projective geometry
proper subalgebra
quadratics
quaternian algebra
reducible algebra
Riemannian geometry
semisimple algebra
set theory
simple algebra
solid geometry
speculative geometry
sphere geometry
spherical trigonometry
statistics
subalgebra
systems analysis, systems theory
topology
trigonometry, trig
universal algebra
universal geometry
vector algebra
zero algebra

29 **number (types)**

abundant number
algebraic number
Avogadro's
binary number
cardinal number, cardinal
complex integer, Gaussian integer
complex number
composite number, rectangular number
deficient number, defective number
directed number
even number, pair
Fermat number
figurate number
finite number
fraction
imaginary number, pure imaginary
infinity
integer
irrational number, irrational
Mersenne number
mixed number
natural number
negative number
nonnegative number
odd number, impair
ordinal number, ordinal
perfect number
polygonal number
positive number
prime number, rectilinear number, prime
pyramidal number
random number
rational number, rational
real number, real
round number, rounded number
serial number
signed number
surd, surd quantity
transcendental number
transfinite number
whole number

1018 PHYSICS

<science of matter and energy>

NOUNS 1 **physics;** natural science, physical science; **physics branch** <see list>, branch of physics; physical theory, quantum theory, relativity theory, special relativity theory, general relativity theory, unified field theory, grand unified theory (GUT); superunified theory, theory of everything (TOE), eightfold way, string theory, superstring theory, kinetic theory, wave theory, electromagnetic theory; philosophy, second philosophy, natural philosophy; physic

2 **physicist,** aerophysicist, astrophysicist, biophysicist

ADJS 3 **physical;** aerophysical, astrophysical, biophysical

4 **physics (branch)**

acoustics
aerodynamics
aerophysics
applied physics
astrophysics
basic conductor physics
biophysics
chaos theory, chaos dynamics, chaology
chemical physics, chemicophysics
classical physics, Newtonian physics
condensed-matter physics
cryogenics
crystallography
cytophysics
dynamics
electricity
electrodynamics
electromagnetism
electron optics
electronics, electron physics
electrophysics
fluid dynamics
fluid mechanics
geometric optics
geophysics
high-energy physics
hyperphysics
hypophysics
iatrophysics
kinematics
macrophysics
magnetism
mathematical physics
mechanics
medicophysics
microphysics
molecular physics
morphophysics
myophysics
Newtonian mechanics
nuclear physics
optics
organismic physics
physical chemistry, physicochemistry
physical optics
physicomathematics
plasma physics
psychophysics
quantum physics
radiation physics
radionics
solar physics
solid-state physics
statics
stereophysics
theoretical physics
thermodynamics
X-ray crystallography
zoophysics

1019 HEAT

<warm, hot temperature>

NOUNS 1 **heat, hotness,** heatedness; superheat, superheatedness; calidity, caloric; **warmth,** warmness; heat transfer; incalescence; radiant heat, thermal radiation, induction heat, convector heat, convected heat, coal heat, gas heat, oil heat, hot-air heat, steam heat, electric heat, solar heat, dielectric heat, ultraviolet heat, atomic heat, molecular heat; latent heat, specific heat; animal heat, body heat, blood heat, hypothermia;

fever heat, fever, pyrexia, feverishness, flush, calescence; heating, burning; smoke detector

2 <metaphors> ardor, ardency, fervor, fervency, fervidness, fervidity; eagerness; excitement; anger; sexual desire; love

3 **temperature,** temp; room temperature, comfortable temperature; comfort index, temperature-humidity index (THI); flashpoint; boiling point; melting point, freezing point; dew point; recalescence point; zero, absolute zero; thermometry, pyrometry

4 **lukewarmness,** tepidness, tepidity; tepidarium

5 **torridness,** torridity; extreme heat, intense heat, torrid heat, red heat, white heat, tropical heat, sweltering heat, African heat, Indian heat, Bengal heat, summer heat, oppressive heat; hot wind; incandescence, flashpoint

6 sultriness, stuffiness, closeness, oppressiveness; humidity, **humidness, mugginess,** stickiness, swelter, fug; tropical heat; overheating

7 **hot weather,** sunny weather, sunshiny weather; sultry weather, stuffy weather, humid weather, muggy weather, sticky weather, hot humid hazy (HHH); summer, midsummer, high summer; Indian summer, dog days, canicular days, canicule; heat wave, hot wave, hot spell, warm front, heat haze; broiling sun, midday sun; vertical rays; warm weather, fair weather; global warming, greenhouse effect

8 **hot day,** summer day; scorcher, roaster, broiler, sizzler, swelterer

9 **hot air,** superheated air; thermal; firestorm

10 **hot water,** boiling water; steam, vapor; volcanic water; hot spring, warm spring, thermal spring, thermae; geyser, Old Faithful; steaminess; boiling point

11 <**hot place**> oven, furnace, fiery furnace, inferno, hell; heater, warmer, burner; steam bath, sauna, solarium; tropics, subtropics, Torrid Zone, Sahara, Dearth Valley; equator; melting point

12 **glow,** incandescence, fieriness; **flush,** blush, bloom, redness, rubicundity, rosiness; whiteness; thermochromism; hectic, hectic flush; sunburn

13 **fire;** blaze, flame, ingle, devouring element; **combustion, ignition,** ignition temperature, ignition point, flashpoint, flashing point; conflagration; flicker, wavering flame, flickering flame; smoldering fire, sleeping fire; marshfire, ignis fatuus, will-o'-the-wisp; fox fire; witch fire, St. Elmo's fire, corposant; cheerful fire, cozy fire, crackling fire; roaring fire, blazing fire; raging fire, sheet of fire, sea of flames; bonfire, balefire; beacon fire, beacon, signal beacon, watch fire; towering inferno; alarm fire, two-alarm fire, three-alarm fire; wildfire, prairie fire, forest fire; backfire; brushfire; open fire; campfire; smudge fire; death fire, pyre, funeral pyre, crematory; burning ghat; fireball; first-degree burn, second-degree burn, third-degree burn

14 **flare,** flare-up, flash, flash fire, **blaze,** burst, outburst; deflagration

15 **spark,** sparkle; scintillation, scintilla; ignescence

16 **coal,** live coal, brand, firebrand, **ember,** burning ember; **cinder**

17 **fireworks** <see list>, **pyrotechnics,** pyrotechny

18 <perviousness to heat> transcalency; adiathermancy, athermancy

19 **thermal unit;** British thermal unit (BTU); Board of Trade unit (BOT); centigrade thermal unit; centigrade scale, Celsius scale, Fahrenheit scale; **calorie,** mean calorie, centuple calorie, rational calorie, small calorie, large calorie, great calorie, kilocalorie, kilogram-calorie; therm; joule

20 **thermometer,** thermal detector; mercury, glass; thermostat; calorimeter; thermograph

21 <**science of heat**> thermochemistry, thermology, thermotics, thermodynamics; volcanology; pyrology, pyrognostics; pyrotechnics, pyrotechny, ebulliometry; calorimetry

VERBS **22** <**be hot**> burn, scorch, parch, scald, swelter, roast, toast, cook, bake, fry, broil, sizzle, boil, seethe, simmer, stew; be in heat; shimmer with heat, give off waves of heat, radiate heat; blaze, combust, spark, catch fire, flame, flame up, flare, flare up; flicker; glow, incandesce, flush, blush, bloom; smolder; steam; sweat, schvitz; gasp, pant; suffocate, stifle, smother, choke; keep warm; run a temperature; sunbathe

23 **smoke,** fume, reek, smolder; smudge; carbonize

ADJS **24** **warm,** calid, thermal, thermic; toasty, warm as toast; sunny, sunshiny, sunbaked, partly sunny; fair, mild, genial; summery, aestival; **temperate,** warmish; balmy, **tropical,** equatorial, subtropical; semitropical; tepid, **lukewarm,** luke; room-temperature; blood-warm, blood-hot; unfrozen

25 **hot, heated, extremely hot,** five-alarm, three-alarm, torrid, thermal, thermic; sweltering, sweltry, canicular; burning, parching, scorching, searing, scalding, blistering, baking, roasting, toasting, broiling, grilling, chargrilling, simmering, sizzling; boiling, seething, ebullient; piping hot, scalding hot, burning hot, roasting hot, scorching hot, sizzling hot, smoking hot; red-hot, white-hot; ardent; flushed, sweating, sweaty, schvitzing, sudorific; overwarm, overhot, overheated; hot as fire, hot as a three-dollar pistol, hot as hell, hot as blazes, hot as the hinges of hell, hot enough to roast an ox, hot enough to fry an egg on, so hot you can fry eggs on the sidewalk, like a furnace, like an oven; feverish; hot and humid, HHH

26 **fiery,** igneous, firelike, pyric; combustive, conflagrative

27 **burning,** ignited, kindled, enkindled, blazing, ablaze, ardent, flaring, flaming, aflame, inflamed, alight, afire, **on fire,** in flames, in a blaze, flagrant; conflagrant, comburent; live, living; molten; glowing, aglow, in a glow, incandescent, candescent, candent; sparking, scintillating, scintillant, ignescent; flickering, aflicker, guttering; unquenched, unextinguished; slow-burning; smoldering; smoking, fuming, reeking

28 **sultry,** stifling, suffocating, stuffy, close, oppressive, steamy; humid, sticky, **muggy**

29 warm-blooded, hot-blooded

30 isothermal, isothermic; centigrade, Fahrenheit

31 diathermic, diathermal, transcalent; adiathermic, adiathermal, athermanous

32 pyrological, pyrognostic, pyrotechnic, pyrotechnical; pyrogenic, pyrogenous, pyrogenetic; thermochemical; thermodynamic, thermodynamical

COMBINING FORMS 33 igni-, pyr-, pyro-; therm-, thermo-, -thermous

34 **fireworks**

Bengali-light
bomb
candlebomb
cannon cracker
cap
Catherine wheel
chaser
cherry bomb
colored fire
cracker
cracker bonbon
firecracker
fizgig, fisgig
fizzer
flare
flowerpot
fountain
girandole
ladyfinger
mandarin cracker
maroon
pastille
peeoy
petard
pinwheel
rocket
Roman candle
serpent
six-inch salute
skyrocket
snake
sparkler
squib
tantrum
throwdown
torpedo
tourbillion
Vesuvius fountain
volcano
wheel
whiz-bang

1020 HEATING

<*creating warmth, heat*>

NOUNS 1 **heating, warming,** calefaction, torrefaction, increase of temperature, raising of temperature; superheating; pyrogenesis; decalescence, recalescence; preheating; **heating system** <see list>, heating method; solar radiation, insolation; dielectric heating; induction heating; heat exchange; cooking

2 **boiling,** seething, stewing, ebullition, ebullience, ebulliency, coction; decoction; **simmering;** boil; simmer

3 **melting,** fusion, liquefaction, liquefying, liquescence, running; **thawing,** thaw; liquation; fusibility; thermoplasticity

4 **ignition, lighting,** lighting up, kindling, firing; reaching flashpoint, reaching flashing point

5 **burning, combustion,** blazing, flaming; scorching, parching, singeing; searing, branding; blistering, vesication; cauterization, cautery; incineration; cremation; suttee, self-cremation, self-immolation; the stake, burning at the stake, *auto-da-fé*; scorification; carbonization; oxidation, oxidization; calcination; cupellation; deflagration; distilling, distillation; refining, smelting; pyrolysis; cracking, thermal cracking, destructive distillation; spontaneous combustion, thermogenesis

6 **burn,** scald, scorch, singe; sear; brand; sunburn, sunscald; windburn; mat burn; first-degree burn, second-degree burn, third-degree burn

7 incendiarism, **arson,** torch job, fire-raising <Brit>; pyromania; pyrophilia; pyrolatry, fire worship

8 incendiary, **arsonist,** torcher; pyromaniac, firebug; pyrophile, fire buff; pyrolater, fire worshiper

9 **flammability, inflammability,** combustibility; spontaneous combustion

10 **heater,** warmer; space heater; **stove, oven, furnace;** cooker, cookery; firebox; tuyere, tewel; burner, jet, gas jet, pilot light, pilot burner, element, heating element, Bunsen burner; heat lamp; heating pipe, steam pipe, hot-water pipe; heating duct, caliduct

11 **fireplace,** hearth, ingle; fireside, hearthside, ingleside, inglenook, chimney corner; firepit, chiminea; hearthstone; hob, hub; fireguard, fireboard, fire screen, fender; chimney, chimney piece, chimney-breast, chimney pot, chimney stack, flue, grate; smokehole; brazier, kiln, smelter, forge; pyre

12 **fireplace tool,** fire iron; andiron, firedog; tongs, pair of tongs, fire tongs, coal tongs; poker, stove poker, salamander, fire hook; lifter, stove lifter; pothook, crook, crane, chain; trivet, tripod; spit, turnspit; grate, grating; gridiron, grid, griddle, grill, griller; damper

13 **incinerator,** cinerator, burner; solid-waste incinerator, garbage incinerator; **crematory,** cremator, crematorium, burning ghat; calcinatory

14 **heating tool,** blowtorch, blowlamp <Brit>,

blast lamp, torch, alcohol torch, butane torch; soldering torch; blowpipe; burner; welder; acetylene torch, acetylene welder, cutting torch, cutting blowpipe, oxyacetylene torch, welding torch

15 cauterant, cauterizer, cauter, cautery, thermocautery, actual cautery; **hot iron**, branding iron, brand iron, brand; moxa; electrocautery; caustic, corrosive, mordant, escharotic, potential cautery; acid; lunar caustic; radium

16 <combustion products> scoria, sullage, slag, dross; ashes, ash; cinder, clinker, coal; coke, charcoal, brand, lava, carbon, calx; soot, smut, coom; smoke, smudge, fume, reek

VERBS 17 **heat**, raise the temperature, increase the temperature, heat up, hot, hot up, **warm**, fire, fire up, stoke up; chafe; take the chill off; tepefy; gas-heat, oil-heat, hot-air-heat, hot-water-heat, steam-heat, electric-heat, solar-heat; superheat; overheat; preheat; **reheat**, recook, warm over, warm up; mull; steam; foment; glow; cook, roast, toast, bake, braise, broil, fry

18 <metaphors> excite, inflame; incite, kindle, arouse; anger, enrage

19 insolate, sun-dry; **sun**, bask, bask in the sun, sun oneself, sunbathe, suntan, sun-worship, get a tan, tan

20 **boil**, stew, simmer, seethe; distill; scald, parboil, steam

21 **melt**, melt down, liquefy; run, colliquate, fuse, flux; refine, smelt; render; **thaw**, thaw out, unfreeze; defrost, de-ice

22 **ignite, set fire to**, fire, set on fire, set alight, kindle, enkindle, inflame, light, light up, strike a light, put a match to, put a torch to, torch, touch off, burn, conflagrate; build a fire; rekindle, relight, relume; feed, feed the fire, stoke, stoke the fire, add fuel to the flame; bank; poke the fire, stir the fire, blow up the fire, fan the flame; open the draft; reduce to ashes

23 **catch fire**, catch on fire, catch, take fire, burn, flame, combust, blaze, blaze up, burst into flames, go up in flames

24 **burn**, torrefy, scorch, parch, sear; singe, swinge; blister, vesicate; cauterize, brand, burn in; char, coal, carbonize; scorify; calcine; pyrolyze, crack; solder, weld, fuse, lag; vulcanize; cast, found; oxidize, oxidate; deflagrate; cupel; burn off; blaze, flame

25 **burn up**, incendiarize, **incinerate**, cremate, consume, burn to ashes, reduce to ashes, burn to a crisp, burn to a cinder; burn down, burn to the ground, go up in smoke; burn at the stake

ADJS 26 **heating, warming**, chafing, calorific; calefactory, calefactive, calefacient, calorifacient, calorigenic; fiery, burning; cauterant, cauterizing; calcinatory

27 **inflammatory**, inflammative, inflaming, kindling, enkindling, lighting; **incendiary**, incendive; arsonous

28 **flammable, inflammable, combustible**, burnable

29 **heated**, heated up, het, het up, hotted up, warmed, warmed up, centrally heated, gas-heated, oil-heated, kerosene-heated, hot-water-heated, hot-air-heated, steam-heated, solar-heated, electric-heated, baseboard-heated; superheated; overheated; preheated; reheated, recooked, warmed-over, *réchauffé* <Fr>; hot

30 **burned, burnt**, burned to the ground, incendiarized, torched, burned-out, burned-down, gutted; scorched, blistered, parched, singed, seared, charred, pyrographic, adust; sunburned; burnt-up, incinerated, cremated, consumed, consumed by fire; ashen, ashy, carbonized, pyrolyzed, pyrolytic

31 **molten, melted**, fused, liquefied; liquated; meltable, fusible; thermoplastic

32 **heating system**

baseboard heating	hot-water heating
central heating	hypocaust
convection heating	kerosene heating
electric heating	oil heating
furnace heating	panel heating
gas heating	radiant heating
heat pump	solar heating
heat ventilating and air conditioning (HVAC)	space heating
hot-air heating	steam heating
	stove heating

1021 FUEL

<material to create heat or power>

NOUNS 1 **fuel** <see list>, energy source; heat source, firing, combustible material, inflammable material, flammable material, burnable, combustible, inflammable, flammable; fossil fuel, nonrenewable energy, nonrenewable fuel source, nonrenewable resource; alternate energy source, alternative energy source, alternate energy, alternative energy, renewable energy, renewable fuel source; solar energy, solar radiation, insolation; wind energy; geothermal energy, geothermal heat, geothermal gradient; green energy; synthetic fuels, synfuels; solid fuel; fuel starter; fuel additive, dope, fuel dope; propellant; **oil**; gas

2 slack, coal dust, coom, comb, culm

3 **firewood**, stovewood, wood; woodpile; kindling, kindlings, kindling wood; brush, brushwood; fagot, bavin <Brit>; log, backlog, yule log

4 **lighter,** light, igniter, sparker; pocket lighter, cigar lighter, cigarette lighter, butane lighter; torch, flambeau, taper, spill; brand, firebrand; portfire; flint, flint and steel; detonator, fuse, sparkplug, ignition system

5 **match,** matchstick, lucifer; friction match, locofoco, vesuvian, vesta, fusee; safety match; matchbook

6 **tinder,** touchwood; punk, spunk, German tinder, amadou; tinder fungus; pyrotechnic sponge; tinderbox

7 renewable energy, soft energy; solar power, solar energy, alternate energy; photovoltaic cell, solar cell; wind power, wind farm; geothermal energy; water power, hydroelectric power; wave power, tidal power; biomass; solar collector

VERBS 8 **fuel,** fuel up; fill up, top off; refuel; coal, oil; stoke, feed, add fuel to the flame; detonate, explode

ADJS 9 **fuel,** energy, heat; fossil-fuel; alternative-energy, alternate-energy; oil-fired, coal-fired; gas-powered, oil-powered, wind-powered; water-driven, hydroelectric; wood-burning; coaly, carbonaceous, carboniferous; anthracite; clean-burning; bituminous; high-sulfur; lignitic; peaty; gas-guzzling

10 **fuel**

alcohol
alternative fuel
anthracite, hard coal
aviation fuel
benzine
bituminous coal, soft coal
blind coal
briquette, briquet
broken coal
buckwheat coal
butane
cannel, cannel coal
carbon
charcoal
chestnut coal
coal
coal gas
coke
crude oil
diesel fuel, diesel oil
egg coal
electricity
ethane
ethanol
ethyl gasoline
flaxseed coal
gas carbon
gasohol
gasoline, gas
glance coal
grate coal
heptane
hexane
high-octane gasoline
isooctane
jet fuel
kerosene, paraffin <Brit>
leaded gasoline
lignite, brown coal
liquid oxygen
lump coal
methane
methanol
motor fuel
mustard-seed coal
naphtha
natural gas
nuclear power, nuclear energy
nut coal
octane
oil, petroleum
pea coal
peat, turf
pentane
petrol <Brit>
premium gasoline, high-test gasoline
producer gas, air gas
propane
propellant
regular gasoline
renewable energy
rocket fuel
sea coal
solar power
steamboat coal
stove coal
unleaded gasoline, lead-free gasoline
water power
white gasoline
wind power
wood

1022 INCOMBUSTIBILITY

<material that cannot be burned>

NOUNS 1 **incombustibility,** uninflammability, noninflammability, **nonflammability;** unburnableness; fire resistance

2 **extinguishing,** extinguishment, extinction, quenching, dousing, **snuffing,** putting out; choking, damping, stifling, smothering, smotheration; controlling; fire fighting; going out, dying, burning out, flameout, burnout

3 **extinguisher,** fire extinguisher; fire apparatus, fire engine, hook-and-ladder, ladder truck; ladder pipe, snorkel, deluge set, deck gun; pumper, super-pumper; foam, carbon-dioxide foam, Foamite <tm>, foam extinguisher; drypowder extinguisher; carbon tetrachloride, carbon tet; water, soda, acid, wet blanket; sprinkler, automatic sprinkler, sprinkler system, sprinkler head; hydrant, fire hydrant, fireplug; fire hose

4 **firefighter,** fireman; pumpman; forest firefighter, fire warden, fire-chaser, smokechaser, smokejumper; volunteer fireman, vamp; fire-eater; fire department, fire brigade

5 **fireproofing;** fire prevention, fire resistance; fireproof material, fire-resistant material, fire-resisting material, fire-resistive material, fire-retardant material, fire retardant; asbestos; amianthus, earth flax, mountain flax; asbestos curtain, fire wall; fire break, fire line

VERBS 6 **fireproof,** flameproof

7 **fight fire; extinguish,** put out, quench, out, douse, snuff, snuff out, blow out, stamp out; stub out, dinch; choke, damp, smother, stifle, slack; bring under control, contain

8 **burn out,** go out, die, die out, die down, die away; fizzle, fizzle out; flame out

ADJS 9 incombustible, **noncombustible,** uninflammable, noninflammable, noncombustive, **nonflammable,** unburnable; asbestine, asbestous, asbestoid, asbestoidal; amianthine

10 **fireproof,** flameproof, fireproofed, fire-retarded, fire-resisting, fire-resistant, fire-resistive, fire-retardant

11 **extinguished,** quenched, snuffed, out; contained, under control

1023 COLD

<cool, cold temperature>

NOUNS **1** **cold, coldness; coolness,** coolth, freshness; low temperature, arctic temperature, drop in temperature, decrease in temperature, lack of heat; chilliness, nippiness, crispness, briskness, sharpness, bite; chill, nip, sharp air; frigidity, iciness, frostiness, extreme cold, intense cold, gelidity, algidity, algidness; rawness, bleakness, keenness, bitterness, severity, inclemency, rigor; freezing point; cryology; cryonics; cryogenics; absolute zero

2 <**cold sensation**> chill, chilliness, chilling; shivering, chills, shivers, cold shivers, shakes, didders, dithers, chattering of the teeth; creeps, cold creeps; gooseflesh, goose pimples, goosebumps, duck bumps, horripilation; frostbite, chilblains, kibe, cryopathy; ache, aching; ice-cream headache

3 **cold weather,** bleak weather, raw weather, bitter weather, wintry weather, arctic weather, freezing weather, zero weather, subzero weather; cold wave, snap, cold snap, cold spell, cold front; freeze, frost, hard frost, deep freeze, arctic frost, big freeze, hard freeze; winter, wintriness, depths of winter, hard winter, arctic conditions; wintry wind; coolness, chill, nip in the air, chilliness, nippiness; chill factor, windchill factor; ice age

4 <**cold place**> Siberia, Hell, Novaya Zemlya, Alaska, Iceland, the Hebrides, Greenland, the Yukon, Tierra del Fuego, Lower Slobbovia; North Pole, South Pole; Frigid Zones; the Arctic, Arctic Circle, Arctic Zone; Antarctica, the Antarctic; Antarctic Circle, Antarctic Zone; tundra; the freezer, the deep-freeze, igloo

5 **ice,** frozen water; ice needle, ice crystal; icicle, iceshockle; cryosphere; ice sheet, ice field, ice barrier, ice front; floe, ice floe, sea ice, ice island, ice raft, ice pack; ice foot, ice belt; shelf ice, sheet ice, pack ice, bay ice, berg ice, field ice; iceberg, berg, growler; calf; snowberg; icecap; ice pinnacle, serac, nieve penitente; glacier, glacieret, glaciation, ice dike; piedmont glacier; icefall; ice banner; ice cave; sleet, glaze, glazed frost, verglas; snow ice; névé, black ice, granular snow, firn; ground ice, anchor ice, frazil; lolly; sludge, slob, slob ice <Can>; ice cubes; crushed ice; Dry Ice <tm>, solid carbon dioxide; icequake; ice storm, freezing rain

6 **hail,** hailstone; soft hail, graupel, snow pellets, tapioca snow; hailstorm

7 **frost,** Jack Frost; hoarfrost, hoar, rime, rime frost, white frost; black frost; hard frost, sharp frost; killing frost; frost smoke; frost line; permafrost; silver frost; glaze frost; ground frost

8 **snow;** granular snow, corn snow, spring corn, spring snow, powder snow, wet snow, tapioca snow; snowfall; snowstorm, snow blast, snow squall, snow flurry, flurry, snow shower, blizzard, whiteout; snowflake, snow-crystal, flake, crystal; snow dust; snowdrift, snowbank, snow cover, snowscape, snow blanket, snow mantle, snow wreath, driven snow, drifting snow; snowcap; snow banner; snow bed, snowpack, snowfield, mantle of snow; snowland; snowshed; snow line; snowball, snowman; snowslide, snowslip, avalanche; snow slush, slush, slosh, snowmelt, melt, meltwater; snowbridge; snow fence; snowhouse, igloo; mogul

VERBS **9** **freeze, be cold,** grow cold, lose heat; **shiver,** quiver, shiver to death, quake, shake, tremble, shudder, didder, dither; chatter; chill, have a chill, have the cold shivers; freeze to death, freeze one's balls off, perish with the cold, horripilate, have goose pimples, have goosebumps, have duck bumps; have chilblains; get frostbite

10 **make cold,** freeze; **chill,** chill to the bone, chill to the marrow, make one shiver, make one's teeth chatter; nip, bite, cut, pierce, penetrate, penetrate to the bone, go through, go right through; freshen; air-condition; glaciate; freeze-dry; frost, frostbite; numb, benumb; refrigerate

11 hail, sleet, **snow**; snow in; snow under; frost, ice, ice up, ice over, glaze, glaze over, freeze over

ADJS **12** **cool,** coolish, temperate; chill, **chilly,** parky; fresh, brisk, crisp, bracing, sharpish, invigorating, stimulating

13 **unheated,** unwarmed; unmelted, unthawed

14 **cold, freezing,** freezing cold, crisp, brisk, nipping, nippy, snappy, raw, bleak, keen, sharp, bitter, biting, pinching, cutting, piercing, penetrating, perishing; inclement, severe, rigorous; snowcold; sleety; slushy; icy, icelike, ice-cold, glacial, ice-encrusted; cryospheric; supercooled, superchilled, extremely cold; frigid, bitter cold, bitterly cold, gelid, algid; below zero, subzero; numbing; wintry, wintery, winterlike, winterbound, hiemal, brumal, hibernal; arctic, Siberian, boreal, hyperborean; stone-cold, cold as death, cold as ice, cold as marble, cold as charity

15 <nonformal> **cold as hell,** cold as a welldigger's ass, cold as a witch's tit*, cold enough to freeze the tail off a grass monkey, cold enough to freeze the balls off a brass monkey, cold as a bastard, cold as a bitch*, colder than hell, colder than the devil

16 <**feeling cold**> cold, freezing; cool, chilly, nippy;

shivering, shivery, shaky, dithery; algid, aguish, aguey; chattering, with chattering teeth; frozen, half-frozen, frozen to death, chilled to the bone, blue with cold, so cold one could spit ice cubes

17 **frosty,** frostlike; frosted, frosted-over, frost-beaded, frost-covered, frost-checkered, rimed, hoary, hoar-frosted, rime-frosted; frost-riven, frost-rent; frosty-faced, frosty-whiskered; frostbound, frost-fettered

18 **snowy,** snowlike, niveous, nival; snow-blown, snow-drifted, snow-driven; snow-covered, snow-clad, snow-mantled, snow-robed, snow-blanketed, snow-sprinkled, snow-lined, snow-encircled, snow-laden, snow-loaded, snow-hung; snowcapped, snow-peaked, snow-crested, snow-crowned, snow-tipped, snow-topped; snow-bearded; snow-feathered; snow-still

19 frozen out, frozen in, **snowbound,** snowed-in, icebound

20 **cold-blooded,** hypothermic, heterothermic, poikilothermic; cryogenic; cryological

COMBINING FORMS 21 cryo-, kryo-; frigo-, psychro-; glacio-; chio-, chion-

1024 REFRIGERATION

<creating cold>

NOUNS 1 **refrigeration,** infrigidation, reduction of temperature; cooling, chilling; freezing, glacification, glaciation, congelation, congealment; refreezing, regelation; mechanical refrigeration, electric refrigeration, electronic refrigeration, gas refrigeration; food freezing, quick freezing, deep freezing, sharp freezing, blast freezing, dehydrofreezing; adiabatic expansion, adiabatic absorption, adiabatic demagnetization; cryogenics; super-cooling; air conditioning, **air cooling**; climate control

2 refrigeration anesthesia, crymoanesthesia, hypothermia, hypothermy; crymotherapy, cryo-aerotherapy; cold cautery, cryocautery; cryopathy

3 **cooler,** chiller; watercooler; air cooler, **air conditioner**; ventilator; fan; surface cooler; ice cube, ice pail, ice bucket, wine cooler; ice bag, ice pack, cold pack

4 **refrigerator,** refrigeratory, icebox, ice chest; Frigidaire <tm>, fridge, electric refrigerator, electronic refrigerator, gas refrigerator, refrigerator-freezer; refrigerator car, refrigerator truck, reefer; freezer ship; ice house

5 **freezer,** deep freeze, deep-freezer, quick-freezer, sharp-freezer; ice-cream freezer; ice machine, ice-cube machine, freezing machine, refrigerating machine; ice plant, icehouse, refrigerating plant

6 **cold storage;** frozen-food locker, locker, freezer locker, locker plant; coolhouse; coolerman; frigidarium; cooling tower

7 <cooling agent> **coolant; refrigerant;** cryogen; ice, Dry Ice <tm>, ice cubes; freezing mixture, liquid air, ammonia, carbon dioxide, Freon <tm>, ether; ethyl chloride; liquid oxygen, lox, liquid nitrogen, liquid helium

8 **antifreeze,** coolant, radiator coolant, alcohol, ethylene glycol

9 refrigerating engineering, refrigerating engineer

VERBS 10 **refrigerate; cool, chill;** refresh, freshen; ice, ice-cool; water-cool, air-cool; **air-condition;** ventilate

11 **freeze,** ice, glaciate, congeal; deep-freeze, quick-freeze, sharp-freeze, blast-freeze; freeze solid; freeze-dry; nip, blight, blast; refreeze, regelate

ADJS 12 **refrigerative,** refrigeratory, refrigerant, frigorific, algific; **cooling,** chilling; freezing, congealing; quick-freezing, deep-freezing, sharp-freezing, blast-freezing; freezable, glaciable

13 cooled, chilled; **air-conditioned;** iced, ice-cooled; air-cooled, water-cooled; super-cooled

14 **frozen,** frozen solid, glacial, gelid, congealed; icy, ice-cold, icy-cold, ice, icelike; deep-frozen, quick-frozen, sharp-frozen, blast-frozen; frostbitten, frostnipped

15 antifreeze, antifreezing

1025 LIGHT

<energy that makes things visible>

NOUNS 1 **light,** radiant energy, luminous energy, visible radiation, radiation in the visible spectrum, **illumination,** illuminance, radiation, radiance, radiancy, irradiance, irradiancy, irradiation, emanation; light wave; highlight; sidelight; photosensitivity; ambient light; light source; invisible light, black light, infrared light, ultraviolet light

2 **shine,** shininess, **luster, sheen,** gloss, glint, glister; glow, gleam, flush, sunset glow; light emission; lambency; incandescence, candescence; shining light; afterglow; skylight, air glow, night glow, day glow, twilight glow

3 **lightness, luminousness,** lightedness, luminosity, luminance; lucidity, lucence, lucency, translucence, translucency; backlight

4 **brightness,** brilliance, brilliancy, splendor, radiant splendor, glory, radiance, radiancy, resplendence, resplendency, vividness, luminance, contrast, flamboyance, flamboyancy; effulgence, refulgence, refulgency, fulgentness, fulgidity, fulgor; glare, blare, blaze; bright light, brilliant light, high beams, blazing light, glaring light, dazzling light, blinding light; TV lights, klieg light, footlights,

house lights; streaming light, flood of light, burst of light

5 **ray,** radiation, **beam,** gleam, stream, streak, pencil, patch, ray of light, beam of light; ribbon, ribbon of light, streamer, stream of light; electromagnetic radiation; violet ray, ultraviolet ray, infrared ray, X-ray, gamma ray, invisible radiation; actinic ray, actinic light, actinism; atomic beam, atomic ray; laser beam; solar rays; photon; visible spectrum; atomic clock, atomic time

6 **flash,** blaze, **flare,** flame, gleam, glint, glance; blaze of light, flash of light, gleam of light; green flash; solar flare, solar prominence, facula; Baily's beads

7 **glitter, glimmer,** shimmer, twinkle, blink; sparkle, spark; **scintillation,** scintilla; coruscation; glisten, glister, spangle, tinsel, glittering, glimmering, shimmering, twinkling; stroboscopic light, strobe light, blinking; firefly, glowworm

8 **flicker,** flutter, dance, quiver; flickering, fluttering, bickering, guttering, dancing, quivering, lambency; wavering light, flickering light, play, play of light, dancing light, glancing light; light show; candlelight

9 **reflection;** reflected light, incident light; reflectance, albedo; blink, iceblink, ice sky, snowblink, waterblink, water sky

10 **daylight,** dayshine, day glow, light of day; day, daytime, daytide; natural light; **sunlight, sunshine,** shine; noonlight, white light, midday sun, noonday light, noontide light, the blaze of noon; broad day, broad daylight, full sun; bright time; dusk, twilight; the break of dawn, the crack of dawn, cockcrow, dawn; sunburst, sunbreak; sunbeam, sun spark, ray of sunshine; green flash; solar energy; ambient light; visiting hours

11 **moonlight, moonshine,** moonglow; moonbeam, moonrise

12 **starlight,** starshine; earthshine

13 **luminescence;** luciferin, luciferase; phosphor, luminophor; ignis fatuus, will-o'-the-wisp, will-with-the-wisp, wisp, jack-o'-lantern, marshfire; friar's lantern; fata morgana; fox fire; St. Elmo's light, St. Elmo's fire, corona discharge, wild fire, witch fire, corposant; double corposant; bioluminescence, thermoluminescence, fluorescence, phosphorescence, radioluminescence

14 **celestial light,** halo, nimbus, aura, aureole, circle, ring, glory; rainbow, double rainbow, solar halo, lunar halo, ring around the sun, ring around the moon; white rainbow, fogbow; corona, solar corona, lunar corona; parhelion, parhelic circle, parhelic ring, mock sun, sun dog; anthelion, antisun, countersun; paraselene, mock moon, moon dog

15 <**nebulous light**> nebula; zodiacal light, gegenschein, counterglow, streamers

16 **polar lights**, aurora; northern lights, aurora borealis, merry dancers; southern lights, aurora australis; aurora polaris; aurora glory; streamer aurora, curtain aurora, arch aurora; polar ray

17 **lightning,** flash of lightning, stroke of lightning, fulguration, fulmination, bolt, lightning strike, bolt of lightning, streak, bolt from the blue, thunderbolt, thunderstroke, thunderball, fireball, firebolt, levin bolt, levin brand; fork lightning, forked lightning, chain lightning, globular lightning, ball lightning; summer lightning, heat lightning; sheet lightning, dark lightning; Jupiter Fulgur, Jupiter Fulminator; Thor

18 **iridescence,** opalescence, nacreousness, pearliness; **rainbow;** nacre, mother-of-pearl; nacreous clou, mother-of-pearl cloud

19 **lighting, illumination,** artificial light, artificial lighting; lamp light, arc light, calcium light, candlelight, electric light, fluorescent light, gaslight, incandescent light, full-spectrum light, mercury-vapor light, neon light, sodium light, strobe light, torchlight, streetlight, floodlight, spotlight; Christmas tree lights, safety light; tonality; light and shade, black and white, chiaroscuro, clairobscure, contrast, highlights; photoemission, light-emitting diode (LED), liquid-crystal display (LCD), light pen, headlamp; track lighting; tiki torch

20 **illuminant,** luminant; electricity; gas, illuminating gas; oil, petroleum, benzine; gasoline, petrol <Brit>; kerosene, paraffin <Brit>, coal oil; light source; fire, lantern

21 <measurement of light> **candlepower,** luminous intensity, luminous power, luminous flux, flux, intensity, light; quantum, light quantum, photon; unit of light, unit of flux; lux, candle-meter, lumen meter, lumeter, lumen, candle lumen; exposure meter, light meter, ASA scale, Scheiner scale

22 <**science of light**> photics, photology, photometry; optics, geometrical optics, physical optics; dioptrics, catoptrics, fiber optics; actinology, actinometry; heliology, heliometry, heliography

VERBS **23** **shine,** shine forth, burn, **give light,** incandesce; glow, beam, gleam, glint, luster, glance; flash, flare, blaze, flame, fulgurate; radiate, shoot, shoot out rays, send out rays; spread light, diffuse light; be bright, shine brightly, beacon; glare; daze, blind, dazzle, bedazzle

24 **glitter,** glimmer, shimmer, twinkle, blink, spangle, tinsel, coruscate; sparkle, spark, scintillate; glisten, glister, glisk

25 **flicker,** bicker, gutter, flutter, waver, dance, play, quiver

26 **luminesce,** phosphoresce, fluoresce; iridesce, opalesce

27 **grow light,** grow bright, light, **lighten,** brighten; dawn, break

28 **illuminate,** illumine, illume, luminate, light, light up, lighten, enlighten, brighten, brighten up, irradiate; bathe with light, flood with light; relumine, relume; shed light upon, cast light upon, throw light upon, shed luster on, shine upon, overshine; spotlight, highlight; floodlight; beacon

29 strike a light, light, **turn on the light,** switch on the light, open the light, make a light, shine a light

ADJS 30 **luminous,** luminant, luminative, luminificent, luminiferous, illuminant; **incandescent,** candescent; lustrous, orient; radiant, irradiative; shining, shiny, burning, lamping, streaming; beaming, beamy; gleaming, gleamy, glinting; glowing, aglow, suffused, blushing, flushing; rutilant, rutilous; **sunny,** sunshiny, bright and sunny, light as day, partly sunny; starry, starlike, starbright

31 **light,** lightish, lightsome; lucid, lucent, luculent, relucent; translucent, translucid, pellucid, diaphanous, transparent; clear, serene; cloudless, unclouded, unobscured

32 **bright,** brilliant, vivid, splendid, splendorous, splendent, resplendent, bright and shining; fulgid, fulgent, effulgent, refulgent; flamboyant, flaming; glaring, glary, garish; dazzling, bedazzling, blinding, pitiless; shadowless, shadeless

33 **shiny,** shining, lustrous, glossy, glassy, *glacé* <Fr>, bright as a new penny, sheeny, polished, burnished, shined

34 **flashing,** flashy, blazing, flaming, flaring, burning, fulgurant, fulgurating; aflame, ablaze; meteoric

35 **glittering,** glimmering, shimmering, twinkling, blinking, glistening, glistering; glittery, glimmery, glimmerous, shimmery, twinkly, blinky, spangly, tinselly; sparkling, scintillating, scintillant, scintillescent, coruscating, coruscant

36 **flickering,** bickering, fluttering, wavering, dancing, playing, quivering, lambent; flickery, flicky, aflicker, fluttery, wavery, quivery; blinking, flashing, stroboscopic

37 **iridescent,** opalescent, nacreous, pearly, pearl-like; rainbowlike

38 **luminescent,** photogenic; autoluminescent, bioluminescent

39 **illuminated,** luminous, **lightened,** enlightened, brightened, lighted, lit, lit up, well-lit, flooded with light, bathed with light, floodlit; irradiated, irradiate; alight, glowing, aglow, lambent, suffused with light; ablaze, blazing, in a blaze, fiery; lamplit, lanternlit, candlelit, torchlit, gaslit, firelit; sunlit, moonlit, starlit; spangled, bespangled, tinseled, studded; starry, starbright, star-spangled, star-studded

40 **illuminating,** illumining, lighting, lightening, brightening

41 **luminary,** photic; photologic, photological; photometric, photometrical; heliological, heliographic; actinic, photoactinic; catoptric, catoptrical; luminal

42 photosensitive; photophobic; phototropic

COMBINING FORMS 43 phot-, photo-, lumin-, lumino-, lumini-; fluoro-, fluori-; irido-; actino-, actini-

44 <**light units**> *bougie décimale* <Fr>, British candle, candle, candle-foot, candle-hour, decimal candle, foot-candle, Hefner candle, international candle, lamp-hour, lumen-hour

1026 LIGHT SOURCE

<device creating illumination>

NOUNS 1 **light source,** source of light, luminary, illuminator, luminant, illuminant, incandescent body, incandescent point, **light,** glim; **lamp,** light bulb, electric light bulb, lantern, candle, taper, torch, flame; match; fluorescent light, fluorescent tube, fluorescent lamp; starter, ballast; fire; sun, moon, stars

2 **candle,** taper; dip, farthing dip, tallow dip; tallow candle; wax candle, bougie; soy candle; rush candle, rushlight; corpse candle; votary candle

3 **torch,** flaming torch, flambeau, cresset, link; **flare,** signal flare, fusee; beacon

4 **traffic light,** stop-and-go light; stoplight, red light; go light, green light; caution light, amber light; pedestrian light

5 **firefly,** lightning bug, lampyrid, **glowworm,** fireworm; fire beetle; lantern fly, candle fly; luciferin, luciferase; phosphor, luminophor

6 **chandelier,** gasolier, electrolier, hanging fixture, ceiling fixture, luster; corona, corona lucis, crown, circlet; light holder, light fixture, candlestick; torchiere

7 **wick,** taper; candlewick, lampwick

1027 DARKNESS, DIMNESS

<lack of light>

NOUNS 1 **darkness, dark,** lightlessness; obscurity, obscure, tenebrosity, tenebrousness, leadenness; night, dead of night, deep night; sunlessness, moonlessness, starlessness; pitch-darkness, pitch-blackness, utter darkness, total darkness, intense darkness, velvet darkness, Cimmerian darkness, Stygian darkness, Egyptian darkness, Stygian gloom, Erebus; blackness, swarthiness; darkest hour

2 **darkishness,** darksomeness, **duskiness,** duskness; murkiness, murk; dimness, dim, dimming; semidarkness, semidark, partial darkness, bad light, dim light, half-light; gloaming, crepuscular light, dusk, twilight; romantic lighting, dimmed lights

3 **shadow,** shade, shadiness; umbra, umbrage, umbrageousness; thick shade, dark shade, gloom; mere shadow; penumbra; silhouette; skiagram, skiagraph

4 **gloom,** gloominess, somberness, sombrousness, somber; lowering, lower

5 **dullness,** flatness, lifelessness, drabness, deadness, somberness, lackluster, lusterlessness, lack of sparkle, lack of sheen; matte, matte finish

6 **darkening, dimming,** bedimming; obscuration, obscurement, obumbration, obfuscation; eclipsing, occulting, blocking the light; shadowing, shading, overshadowing, overshading, overshadowment, clouding, overclouding, obnubilation, gathering of the clouds, overcast; blackening; extinguishment; hatching, cross-hatching

7 **blackout,** dimout, brownout; fadeout

8 **eclipse,** occultation; total eclipse, partial eclipse, central eclipse, annular eclipse; solar eclipse, lunar eclipse

VERBS 9 **darken,** bedarken; obscure, obfuscate, obumbrate; eclipse, occult, occultate, block the light; black out, brown out; black, brown; blot out; overcast, darken over; shadow, shade, cast a shadow, spread a shadow over, spread shade over, encompass with shadow, overshadow; cloud, becloud, encloud, cloud over, overcloud, obnubilate; gloom, begloom, somber, cast a gloom over, murk; dim, bedim, dim out; mattify; blacken

10 **dull,** mat, deaden; tone down

11 turn off the light, switch off the light, close the light; extinguish

12 grow dark, **darken,** darkle, lower, lour; gloom, gloam; dusk; **dim,** grow dim; go out

ADJS 13 **dark, black,** darksome, darkling; lightless, beamless, rayless, unlighted, unilluminated, unlit; obscure, caliginous, obscured, obfuscated, eclipsed, occulted, clothed in darkness, shrouded in darkness, cloaked in darkness, mantled in darkness; tenebrous, tenebrific, tenebrious, tenebrose; Cimmerian, Stygian; **pitch-dark,** pitch-black, pitchy, dark as pitch, dark as the inside of a black cat; ebon, ebony; night-dark, night-black, dark as night, black as night; night-clad, night-cloaked, night-enshrouded, night-mantled, night-veiled, night-hid, night-filled; sunless, moonless, starless

14 **gloomy,** gloomful, glooming, dark and gloomy, Acheronian, Acherontic, somber, sombrous; lowering; funereal; stormy, cloudy, clouded, overcast; ill-lighted, ill-lit

15 **darkish,** darksome, semidark; **dusky,** dusk; fuscous, subfuscous, subfusc; murky, murksome, murk; dim, dimmed, bedimmed, dimmish, dimpsy, half-lit; dark-colored

16 **shadowy,** shady, shadowed, shaded, casting a shadow, tenebrous, darkling, umbral, umbrageous; overshadowed, overshaded, obumbrate, obumbrated; penumbral

17 lackluster, lusterless; dull, dead, deadened, lifeless, somber, drab, wan, flat, mat, murky

18 obscuring, obscurant

ADVS 19 **in the dark,** darkling, in darkness; in the night, in the dark of night, in the dead of night, at night, by night, all-night; dimly, wanly

1028 SHADE

<blocking of light>

NOUNS 1 **shade,** shader, **screen,** light shield, curtain, drape, drapery, blind, blinds, veil; awning, sunblind <Brit>; sunshade, parasol, umbrella, beach umbrella; cover; shadow; partial eclipse

2 eyeshade, eyeshield, visor, bill; goggles, colored spectacles, smoked glasses, dark glasses, **sunglasses,** shades

3 **lampshade;** moonshade; globe, light globe

4 **light filter,** filter, diffusing screen; smoked glass, frosted glass, ground glass; stained glass; butterfly; gelatin filter, celluloid filter; frosted lens; lens hood; sunscreen; sunroof; suncatcher

VERBS 5 **shade, screen,** veil, curtain, shutter, draw the curtains, put up the shutters, close the shutters; cover; shadow; cast a shadow

ADJS 6 **shading, screening,** veiling, curtaining; shadowing; covering

7 **shaded, screened,** veiled, curtained; sunproof; visored; shadowed, shady

1029 TRANSPARENCY

<allowing passage of light>

NOUNS 1 **transparency,** transparence, transpicuousness, **show-through,** transmission of light, admission of light; lucidity, pellucidity, clearness, clarity, limpidity;

nonopacity, uncloudedness; crystallinity, crystal-clearness; glassiness, glasslikeness, vitreousness, vitrescence; vitreosity, hyalescence; diaphanousness, diaphaneity, sheerness, thinness, gossameriness, filminess, gauziness; colorlessness

2 transparent substance, diaphane; **glass** <see list>, glassware, glasswork; vitrics; stemware; window, pane, windowpane, light, windowlight, shopwindow; vitrine; showcase, display case; watch crystal, watch glass; water, air

VERBS 3 **be transparent**, show through; pass light, transmit light; vitrify; reveal; crystallize

ADJS 4 **transparent,** transpicuous, light-pervious; show-through, see-through, peekaboo, revealing; lucid, lucent, pellucid, **clear,** limpid; nonopaque, colorless, unclouded, crystalline, crystal, crystal clear, clear as crystal; diaphanous, diaphane, sheer, thin; gossamer, gossamery, filmy, flimsy, gauzy, open-textured; insubstantial

5 **glass, glassy,** glasslike, clear as glass, vitric, vitreous, vitriform, hyaline, hyalescent; hyalinocrystalline

COMBINING FORMS 6 vitri-

7 **glass**

agate glass
antimony glass
arsenic glass
Baccarat glass
basalt glass
Bilbao glass
borax glass
blown glass
bone glass
bottle glass
bulletproof glass
camphor glass
carnival glass
Chevalier glass
coralene
cranberry glass
crown glass
cryolite glass
crystal, crystal glass
custard glass
cut glass
etched glass
Fiberglas <tm>
flashed glass
flat glass
flint glass
float glass
Fostoria <tm>
frosted glass
fused quartz
glass bead
glass brick
glass wool
ground glass
hobnail glass
ice glass
lace glass
Lalique glass
laminated glass, laminated safety glass
lead crystal
lead glass
milk glass
mirror
obsidian
opal glass
opaline
optical glass
ornamental glass
Orrefors glass
photosensitive glass
plastic glass
plate glass
porcelain glass
pressed glass
prism glass
Pyrex <tm>
quartz glass
reinforced glass
rhinestone
rock crystal
ruby glass
safety glass
Sandwich glass
satin glass
sheet glass
show glass
Silex glass <tm>
stained glass
Steuben glass
Swedish glass
Syracuse watch glass
tempered glass, tempered safety glass
uranium glass
uviol glass
Venetian glass
Vitaglass <tm>
vitreous silica
Waterford glass
window glass
wire glass, wired glass

1030 SEMITRANSPARENCY

<imperfectly transparent>

NOUNS 1 **semitransparency,** semipellucidity, semidiaphaneity; semiopacity

2 **translucence, translucency,** lucence, lucency, translucidity, pellucidity, lucidity; transmission of light, admission of light; milkiness, pearliness, opalescence

VERBS 3 **frost,** frost over

ADJS 4 **semitransparent,** semipellucid, semidiaphanous, semiopaque; frosty, frosted; milky, pearly, opalescent, opaline

5 **translucent,** lucent, translucid, lucid, pellucid; semitranslucent, semipellucid

1031 OPAQUENESS

<blocking passage of light>

NOUNS 1 **opaqueness, opacity,** intransparency, nontranslucency, imperviousness to light, adiaphanousness; roil, roiledness, turbidity, turbidness; cloudiness; blackness; darkness, obscurity, inscrutability, dimness

VERBS 2 opaque, **darken,** obscure; cloud, becloud; devitrify

ADJS 3 **opaque,** intransparent, nontransparent, nontranslucent, adiaphanous, impervious to light, impenetrable; **dark,** black, obscure, lightproof; cloudy, roiled, roily, grumly, turbid; covered; semiopaque

1032 ELECTRICITY, MAGNETISM

<form of energy creating current, power, metal attraction>

NOUNS 1 **electricity; electrical science** <see list>; electrical unit, electric unit, unit of measurement

2 **current, electric current** <see list>, current flow, amperage, electric stream, electric flow, juice; power source, power supply

3 **electrical field,** electric field, static field, electrostatic field, field of electrical force; tube of electric force, electrostatic tube of force; magnetic field, magnetic field of currents; electromagnetic field; variable field; static electricity, static cling

4 **circuit, electrical circuit,** path
5 **charge, electrical charge,** electric charge, positive charge, negative charge; live wire
6 **discharge,** arc, electric discharge; **shock,** electroshock, galvanic shock; energy vampire
7 **magnetism,** magnetic attraction; **electromagnetism;** magnetization; diamagnetism, paramagnetism, ferromagnetism; residual magnetism, magnetic remanence; magnetic memory, magnetic retentiveness; magnetic elements; magnetic dip, magnetic inclination, magnetic variation, magnetic declination; hysteresis, magnetic hysteresis, hysteresis curve, magnetic friction, magnetic lag, magnetic retardation, magnetic creeping; permeability, magnetic permeability, magnetic conductivity; magnetic circuit, magnetic curves, magnetic figures; magnetic flux, gilbert, weber, maxwell; magnetic moment; magnetic potential; magnetic viscosity; magnetics
8 **polarity,** polarization; **pole,** positive pole, anode, negative pole, cathode, magnetic pole, geomagnetic pole, magnetic axis; north pole, N pole; south pole, S pole
9 **magnetic force,** magnetic intensity, magnetic flux density, gauss, oersted; magnetomotive force; magnetomotivity; magnetic tube of force; line of force; magnetic field, electromagnetic field; geomagnetic storm
10 **electromagnetic radiation**, light, radio wave, microwave, infrared radiation, visible radiation, ultraviolent radiation (UV), UVA, UVB, X-rays, gamma rays; radar, radar gun; electromagnetic spectrum, visible spectrum, radio spectrum
11 electroaffinity, electric attraction; electric repulsion
12 **voltage,** volt, electromotive force (EMF), electromotivity, potential difference; potential, electric potential; tension, high tension, low tension
13 **resistance,** ohm, ohms, ohmage, ohmic resistance, electric resistance; surface resistance, skin effect, volume resistance; insulation resistance; reluctance, magnetic reluctance, magnetic resistance; specific reluctance, reluctivity; reactance, inductive reactance, capacitive reactance; impedance
14 **conduction,** electric conduction; conductance, conductivity, mho; superconductivity; gas conduction, ionic conduction, metallic conduction, liquid conduction, photoconduction; conductor, semiconductor, superconductor; nonconductor, dielectric, insulator
15 **induction;** electrostatic induction, magnetic induction, electromagnetic induction, electromagnetic induction of currents; self-induction, mutual induction; inductance, inductivity, henry
16 **capacitance,** capacity, farad; collector junction capacitance, emitter junction capacitance, resistance capacitance
17 **gain,** available gain, current gain, operational gain
18 **electric power, wattage,** watts; electric horsepower; hydroelectric power, hydroelectricity; power load
19 powerhouse, **power station, power plant,** central station; oil-fired power plant, coal-fired power plant; hydroelectric plant; nuclear power plant, atomic power plant; power grid, distribution system
20 **blackout, power failure,** power cut, power loss; brownout, voltage drop, voltage loss
21 **electrical device,** electrical appliance; **battery** <see list>, accumulator, storage battery, storage device; electric meter, meter; wire, cable, electric wire, electric cord, cord, power cord, power cable; Geiger counter
22 **electrician,** electrotechnician; radio technician; wireman; lineman, linesman; rigger; groundman; power worker
23 electrotechnologist, electrobiologist, electrochemist, electrometallurgist, electrophysicist, electrophysiologist, electrical engineer
24 **electrification,** electrifying, supplying electricity
25 **electrolysis;** ionization; galvanization, electrogalvanization; electrocoating, electroplating, electrogilding, electrograving, electroetching; ion, cation, anion; electrolyte, ionogen; nonelectrolyte

VERBS 26 **electrify,** galvanize, energize, charge; wire, wire up; shock; **generate,** step up, amplify, stiffen; step down; plug in, loop in; switch on, switch off, turn on, turn off, turn on the juice, turn off the juice, juice up, power down, power up; short-circuit, short
27 **magnetize;** electromagnetize; demagnetize, degauss
28 **electrolyze;** ionize; galvanize, electrogalvanize; electroplate, electrogild
29 **insulate,** isolate; **ground**

ADJS 30 **electric, electrical,** electrifying; on the grid; galvanic, voltaic; dynamoelectric, hydroelectric, photoelectric, piezoelectric; electrothermal, electrochemical, electromechanical, electropneumatic, electrodynamic, static, electrostatic; electromotive; electrokinetic; electroscopic, galvanoscopic; electrometric, galvanometric, voltametric; electrified, electric-powered, battery-powered, cordless; solar-powered

31 **magnetic,** electromagnetic; diamagnetic, paramagnetic, ferromagnetic; polar

32 electrolytic; hydrolytic; ionic, anionic, cationic; ionogenic

33 electrotechnical; electroballistic, electrobiological, electrochemical, electrometallurgical, electrophysiological

34 **charged, electrified, live,** hot; juiced up; high-tension, low-tension

35 **positive,** plus, electropositive; **negative,** minus, electronegative

36 nonconducting, nonconductive, insulating, dielectric; off the grid, off-grid

COMBINING FORMS **37** electr-, electro-; rheo-; magnet-, magneto-

38 **battery**

A battery
AA battery
AAA battery
acid cell
accumulator
air cell
alkaline battery, alkaline cell
atomic battery
B battery
C battery
cell
D battery
dry battery
dry cell
electronic battery
fuel cell
lead-acid battery
Leyden battery
Leyden jar
mercury cell
nickel-cadmium battery
nine-volt battery
primary battery
primary cell
secondary battery
secondary cell
solar battery
solar cell
storage battery
storage cell
voltaic battery
voltaic cell
voltaic pile
wet cell

39 **electric current**

absorption current
active current
alternating current (AC)
conduction current
convection current
delta current
dielectric displacement current
direct current (DC)
displacement current
eddy current
emission current
exciting current
free alternating current
galvanic current
high-frequency current
induced current
induction current
ionization current
juice
low-frequency current
magnetizing current
multiphase current
oscillating current
pulsating direct current
reactive current
rotary current
single-phase alternating current
stray current
supercurrent
thermionic current
thermoelectric current
three-phase alternating current
transient current
voltaic current
watt current
wattless current, idle current

40 **electrical science**

electrical engineering
electroacoustics
electroballistics
electrobiology
electrochemistry
electrodynamics
electrokinematics
electrokinetics
electromagnetics
electromechanics
electrometallurgy
electrometry
electronics
electro-optics
electrophotomicrography
electrophysics
electrophysiology
electrostatics
electrotechnology, electrotechnics
electrotherapeutics, electrotherapy
electrothermics
galvanism
hydroelectricity
magnetics
magnetometry
photoelectricity
pyroelectricity
thermionics
thermoelectricity
voltaism

1033 ELECTRONICS

<devices operating using electricity>

NOUNS **1** **electronics,** radionics, radioelectronics; electron physics, electrophysics, electron dynamics; electron optics; semiconductor physics, transistor physics; photoelectronics, photoelectricity; microelectronics; electronic engineering; avionics; electron microscopy; autolocation; nuclear physics; radio; television; radar; automation; digital detox

2 <electron theory> electron theory of atoms, electron theory of electricity, electron theory of solids, free electron theory of metals, band theory of solids

3 **electron** <see list>, negatron, cathode particle, beta particle; thermion; electron capture, electron transfer; electron spin; electron state, energy level; ground state, excited state; electron pair, lone pair, shared pair, electron-positron pair, duplet, octet; electron cloud; shells, electron layers, electron shells, valence shell, valence electrons, subvalent electrons; electron affinity, relative electron affinity

4 **electronic effect;** Edison effect, thermionic effect, photoelectric effect; feature fatigue

5 **electron emission;** thermionic emission; photoelectric emission, photoemission; collision emission, bombardment emission, secondary emission; field emission; grid emission, thermionic grid emission; electron ray, electron beam, cathode ray, anode ray, positive ray, canal ray; glow discharge, cathode glow, cathodoluminescence, cathodofluorescence; electron diffraction

6 electron flow, electron stream, **electronic current,** electron current; electric current; electron gas, electron cloud, space charge

7 electron volt; ionization potential; input voltage, output voltage; base signal voltage, collector signal voltage, emitter signal voltage; battery supply voltage; screen-grid voltage; inverse peak voltage; voltage saturation

8 **electronic circuit**, transistor circuit, semiconductor circuit; vacuum-tube circuit, thermionic tube circuit; printed circuit, microcircuit; chip, silicon chip, microchip; circuitry, circuit board; adapter card; hardwiring

9 **conductance,** electronic conductance; **resistance,** electronic resistance

10 **electron tube,** vacuum tube, tube, valve <Brit>, thermionic tube; radio tube, television tube; special-purpose tube; vacuum tube component

11 **photoelectric tube,** photoelectric cell, phototube, photocell; electron-ray tube, electric eye; photosensitivity, photosensitive devices

12 **transistor**, semiconductor device, solid-state device

13 **electronic device,** electronic meter, electronic measuring device; electronic tester, electronic testing device

14 electronics engineer, electronics physicist

ADJS **15** **electronic;** photoelectronic, photoelectric; autoelectronic; microelectronic; thermoelectronic; thermionic; anodic, cathodic; transistorized

16 **electron**

beta particle
bonding electron
bound electron
conduction electron
d-electron
delta ray
excess electron
extranuclear electron
f-electron
free electron
nuclear electron
orbital electron
p-electron
peripheral electron
photoelectron
planetary electron
positive electron
primary electron
recoil electron
secondary electron
s-electron
spinning electron
surface-bound electron
valence electron
wandering electron

1034 RADIO

<broadcast of sound using electric signals>

NOUNS **1** **radio,** wireless <Brit>; radiotelephony, radiotelegraphy; radio communications, telecommunication; digital radio

2 radiotechnology, radio engineering, communication engineering; radio electronics, radioacoustics; radiogoniometry

3 radio, **radio receiver** <see list>; radio telescope; radio set, receiver, receiving set, wireless, wireless set <Brit>, set; cabinet, console, housing; chassis; receiver part

4 **radio transmitter** <see list>, transmitter; transmitter part; microphone, radiomicrophone; **antenna,** aerial

5 radiomobile, mobile transmitter, remote-pickup unit

6 **radio station,** transmitting station, studio, studio plant; AM station, FM station, shortwave station, ultra-high-frequency station, clear-channel station; direction-finder station, RDF station; relay station, radio relay station, microwave relay station; amateur station, ham station, ham shack; pirate radio station, offshore station; Internet radio; satellite radio; drive time

7 **control room,** mixing room, monitor room, monitoring booth; control desk, console, master control desk, instrument panel, control panel, control board, jack field, mixer

8 **network,** net, radio links, hookup, communications net, circuit, network stations, network affiliations, affiliated stations; coaxial network, circuit network, coast-to-coast hookup, satellite network

9 **radio circuit,** radio-frequency circuit, audio-frequency circuit, superheterodyne circuit, amplifying circuit; electronic circuit

10 **radio signal,** radio-frequency signal, RF signal, direct signal, shortwave signal, AM signal, FM signal; reflected signal, bounce; unidirectional signal, beam; signal-noise ratio; radio-frequency amplifier, RF amplifier, radio-frequency stage, RF stage; radio silence

11 **radio wave,** electric wave, electromagnetic wave, Hertzian wave; shortwave, long wave, microwave, high-frequency wave, low-frequency wave, medium wave; ground wave, sky wave; carrier, carrier wave; wavelength

12 **frequency;** radio frequency (RF), intermediate frequency (IF), audio frequency (AF); high frequency (HF); very high frequency (VHF); ultra-high frequency (UHF); superhigh frequency (SHF); extremely high frequency (EHF); medium frequency (MF); low frequency (LF); very low frequency (VLF); upper frequencies, lower frequencies; carrier frequency; spark frequency; spectrum, frequency spectrum; cycles, cycles per second (CPS); hertz (Hz), kilohertz, kilocycles; megahertz, megacycles

13 **band,** frequency band, standard band, broadcast band, amateur band, citizens band (CB), police band, shortwave band, FM band; **channel,** radio channel, broadcast channel

14 **modulation;** amplitude modulation (AM); frequency modulation (FM); phase modulation (PM); sideband, side frequency, single sideband, double sideband

15 **amplification,** radio-frequency (RF), RF amplification, audio-frequency (AF), AF amplification, intermediate-frequency (IF), IF amplification, high-frequency amplification

16 **radio broadcasting,** broadcasting, the air waves, radiocasting; **airplay, airtime;** commercial radio, public radio, college radio, satellite radio, citizens band (CB), amateur radio, ham radio; AM broadcasting, FM broadcasting, shortwave broadcasting, public broadcasting; transmission, radio transmission; direction transmission, beam transmission, asymmetric transmission, vestigial transmission; multipath transmission, multiplex transmission; mixing, volume control, sound control, tone control, fade-in, fade-out; broadcasting regulation, Federal Communications Commission (FCC)

17 **pickup,** outside pickup, remote pickup, spot pickup

18 radiobroadcast, broadcast, radiocast, **radio program;** rebroadcast, rerun; simulcast; electronic journalism, broadcast journalism, broadcast news, newscast, newsbreak, newsflash; all-news radio, all-news format; sportscast; talk radio, talk show, audience-participation show, call-in show, phone-in show, interview show; network show; commercial program, commercial; sustaining program, sustainer; serial, soap opera; taped program, canned show, electrical transcription; sound effects

19 signature, **station identification,** call letters, call sign; theme song; station break, pause for station identification

20 **commercial,** commercial announcement, commercial message, message, spot announcement, spot, plug

21 **reception;** fading, fade-out; drift, creeping, crawling; **interference,** noise interference, station interference; **static,** atmospherics, noise; blasting, blaring; blind spot; jamming, deliberate interference

22 **radio listener,** listener, listener-in, tuner-inner; radio audience, audience, listenership

23 **broadcaster,** radiobroadcaster, radiocaster; newscaster, sportscaster; commentator, news commentator; anchor, news anchor, anchorman, anchorwoman; host, talk-show host, talk jockey; veejay (VJ); announcer, voiceover; disc jockey, disk jockey (DJ), deejay; shock jock; master of ceremonies (MC), emcee; program director, programmer; sound-effects man, sound man

24 **radioperson,** radio technician, radio engineer, sound engineer; radiotrician, radio electrician, radio repairman; radio operator; control engineer, volume engineer; mixer; amateur radio operator, ham, ham operator, radio amateur; Amateur Radio Relay League (ARRL); monitor; radiotelegrapher

VERBS **25** **broadcast,** radiobroadcast, radiocast, simulcast, radio, wireless <Brit>, radiate, transmit, send; narrowcast; shortwave; beam; newscast, sportscast, put on the air, go on the air, sign on; go off the air, sign off

26 monitor, check

27 listen in, **tune in;** tune up, tune down, tune out, tune off

ADJS **28** **radio,** wireless <Brit>; radiosonic; neutrodyne; heterodyne; superheterodyne; shortwave; radio-frequency, audio-frequency; high-frequency, low-frequency; radiogenic; WiFi

29 **radio receiver**

all-wave receiver
AM receiver
AM tuner
AM-FM receiver
AM-FM tuner
antenna
aviation radio
battery radio
boom box
car radio
citizens band radio (CB)
clock radio
communications receiver
crystal set
direction finder
facsimile receiver, fax
FM receiver
FM tuner
ghetto blaster, ghetto box, beat box
headband receiver
loudspeaker
mobile radio
multiplex receiver
pager, beeper
pocket radio
portable radio
radar receiver
radio direction finder (RDF)
radio-phonograph
radio-record player
radiophone
railroad radio
receiver
rechargeable-battery radio
regenerative receiver
relay receiver
scanner
ship-to-shore radio
shortwave receiver
single-signal receiver
six-band receiver
stereo receiver
superheterodyne
telephone receiver
three-way receiver
transceiver
transistor radio
transmitter-receiver
transponder
tuner
two-way radio
universal receiver
VHF-FM receiver
walkie-talkie
Walkman <tm>
weather radio
wireless

30 **radio transmitter**

AM transmitter
amateur transmitter, ham transmitter, rig
arc transmitter, spark transmitter
continuous-wave transmitter
Dictograph <tm>
facsimile transmitter, fax
fan marker
FM transmitter
link transmitter
locater beacon
microphone
picture transmitter
portable transmitter
pulse transmitter
radar gun
radio beacon

radio marker
radio range beacon
radiometeorograph
radiosonde
radiotelephone transmitter
relay transmitter
RT transmitter
shortwave transmitter
standby transmitter
tape transmitter
teleprinter
television transmitter
telex
transmitter receiver, transceiver
vacuum-tube transmitter
VHF-FM transmitter
walkie-talkie

1035 TELEVISION

<electronic broadcast of images and sound>

NOUNS **1 television, TV,** video, telly; the small screen, the tube, the boob tube, small screen; network television, public television, free television, local television; the dream factory; subscription television, pay television; cable television, cable TV, cable-television system, cable system, cable; closed-circuit television, closed circuit TV; public-access television, public-access TV; public broadcasting; satellite broadcasting, satellite television; digital television, digital TV, Internet television; high-definition TV, high-definition television (HDTV); ultra-high-definition television (UHDTV, UHD), sports broadcasting; celebreality, celebrity chef

2 television broadcast, telecast, television show, **TV show;** direct broadcast, live show; taped show, canned show; prime time, prime-time show; syndicated program; television drama, teleplay, made-for-television movie, made-for-TV movie; telefilm; series, dramatic series, miniseries; situation comedy, sitcom; romantic comedy, romcom, romedy; meet-cute; variety show; game show; serial, daytime serial, soap opera, soap; reality television, reality TV, reality show; quiz show; giveaway show; panel show; talk show; electronic journalism, broadcast journalism, broadcast news, newscast, news show; documentary, docudrama; telethon; public service announcement; edutainment, infotainment; film pickup; colorcast; simulcast; children's television, kidvid; television performer, TV performer, television personality, TV personality; news anchor, anchor, anchorman, anchorwoman, anchorperson; ratings, Nielsen rating, sweeps; people meter; multicasting; equal time; live action; jumping the shark; screen time; binge-watching

3 televising, telecasting; facsimile broadcasting; monitoring, mixing, shading, blanking, switching; scanning, parallel-line scanning, interlaced scanning; instant replay; screen grab

4 <**transmission**> photoemission, audioemission; television channel, TV band; video channel, picture channel, audio channel, sound channel, video frequency; picture carrier, sound carrier; beam, scanning beam, return beam; triggering pulse, voltage pulse, output pulse, timing pulse, equalizing pulse; synchronizing pulse, vertical synchronizing pulse, horizontal synchronizing pulse; audio signal, video signal; IF audio signal, IF video signal; synchronizing signal, blanking signal

5 <**reception**> picture, image; color television, dot-sequential television, field-sequential television, line-sequential television; black-and-white television; high-definition television (HDTV); definition, blacker than black synchronizing; shading, black spot, hard shadow; test pattern, scanning pattern, grid; vertical interference, rain; granulation, scintillation, snow, snowstorm; flare, bloom, woomp; picture shifts, blooping, rolling; double image, multiple image, ghost; video static, noise, picture noise; signal-to-noise ratio; fringe area

6 television studio, TV station, ident, identification

7 mobile unit, TV mobile; transmitter truck

8 transmitter, televisor; audio/video transmitter; transmitter part, adder, encoder; television mast, television tower; satellite transmitter

9 relay link, booster, booster amplifier, relay transmitter, booster station, relay station; microwave link; aeronautical relay, stratovision; communication satellite, satellite relay; Telstar, Intelsat, Syncom; Comsat

10 television camera, telecamera, pickup camera, pickup; camera tube, iconoscope, orthicon, vidicon; video camera, camcorder; mobile camera

11 television receiver, television set, TV set, **TV,** telly, televisor, boob tube, idiot box; picture tube, cathode-ray tube, kinescope, monoscope, projection tube; receiver part, amplifier, detector, convertor, electron tube, deflector, synchronizer, limiter, mixer; portable television; digital television; digital video recorder (DVR); screen, telescreen, videoscreen; raster; videocassette recorder (VCR), videorecorder, videotape recorder; videotape, videocassette; videophone, picturephone; projection television; satellite dish, dish; television recording

12 televiewer, viewer; television audience, viewing audience; viewership

13 television technician, television repairperson, television engineer; monitor, sound monitor, audio monitor, sound engineer, picture monitor, video monitor; pickup unit man, cameraman, camerawoman, sound man, sound woman;

broadcaster, media personality, host, **newscaster**, newsreader, commentator, announcer, talking head

VERBS **14** **televise,** telecast; colorcast; simulcast

15 teleview, watch television, watch TV; telerecord, record, tape; channel-surf, graze; zap

ADJS **16** **televisional,** televisual, televisionary, video; telegenic, videogenic; in synchronization, in sync, locked in

COMBINING FORMS **17** tele-, video-, TV-

1036 RADAR, RADIOLOCATORS

<use of reflecting radio waves for detection>

NOUNS **1** **radar,** radio detection, ranging; radar set, radiolocator; radar part; oscilloscope, radarscope; radar antenna; radar reflector; radiolocating, radiolocation

2 airborne radar, aviation radar; navar, navigation and ranging; teleran, television radar air navigation; radar bombsight, K-1 bombsight; radar dome, radome

3 **loran,** long range aid to navigation; **shoran,** short range aid to navigation; GEE navigation, consolan

4 **radiolocator;** direction finder, radio direction finder (RDF); radiogoniometer, high-frequency direction finder (HFDF), huff-duff; radio compass, wireless compass <Brit>

5 radar speed meter, electronic cop; radar highway patrol; **radar detector**, Fuzzbuster <tm>

6 **radar station,** control station; Combat Information Center (CIC); Air Route Traffic Control Center (ARTCC); beacon station, display station; fixed station, home station; portable field unit, mobile trailer unit; tracking station; direction-finder station, radio compass station; triangulation stations

7 **radar beacon,** racon; transponder; radar beacon buoy, marker buoy, radar marked beacon, ramark

8 <radar operations> data transmission, scanning, scan conversion, flector tuning, signal modulation, triggering signals; phase adjustment, locking signals; triangulation, three-pointing; mapping; range finding; tracking, automatic tracking, locking on; precision focusing, pinpointing; radar-telephone relay; radar navigation

9 <applications> detection, interception, ranging, ground control of aircraft, air traffic control, blind flying, blind landing, storm tracking; radar fence, radar screen; radar astronomy

10 pulse, radio-frequency pulse, RF pulse, high-frequency pulse, HF pulse, intermediate-frequency pulse, IF pulse, trigger pulse, echo pulse

11 signal, **radar signal**; transmitter signal, output signal; return signal, echo signal, video signal, reflection, picture, target image, display, signal display, trace, reading, return, echo, bounces, blips, pips; spot, CRT spot; 3-D display, double-dot display; deflection-modulated display, intensity-modulated display; radio-frequency echo, intermediate-frequency signal; beat signal, Doppler signal, local oscillator signal; beam, beavertail beam

12 **radar interference,** deflection, refraction, superrefraction; atmospheric attenuation, signal fades, blind spots, false echoes; clutter, ground clutter, sea clutter

13 <radar countermeasure> **jamming,** radar jamming; tinfoil, aluminum foil, chaff, window <Brit>

14 radar technician, radar engineer, radarman; air traffic controller; jammer

VERBS **15** transmit, send, radiate, beam; jam

16 reflect, return, echo, bounce back

17 receive, tune in, pick up, spot, home on; pinpoint; identify, trigger; lock on; sweep, scan; map

1037 RADIATION, RADIOACTIVITY

<powerful, dangerous form of energy>

NOUNS **1** **radiation,** radiant energy; ionizing radiation; **radioactivity,** activity, radioactive radiation, radioactive emanation, atomic radiation, nuclear radiation; natural radioactivity, artificial radioactivity; curiage; specific activity, high-specific activity; actinic radiation, ultraviolet radiation; radiotransparency, radiolucence, radiolucency; radiopacity; radiosensitivity, radiosensibility; half-life; radiocarbon dating; contamination, decontamination; saturation point; radioactivity detection identification and computation (radiac); fallout; China syndrome, nuclear winter

2 **radioluminescence,** autoluminescence; cathode luminescence; Cerenkov radiation, synchrotron radiation

3 **ray** <see list>, radiation, cosmic ray bombardment, electron shower; electron emission

4 **radioactive particle;** alpha particle, beta particle; heavy particle; high-energy particle; meson, mesotron; cosmic particle, solar particle, aurora particle, V-particle

5 **<radioactive substance>** radiator; alpha radiator, beta radiator, gamma radiator; fluorescent paint, radium paint; radium; fission products; radiocarbon, radiocopper, radioiodine, radiothorium; mesothorium; **radioactive element** <see list>, radioelement; radioisotope; tracer, tracer element, tracer atom; radioactive waste

6 <units of radioactivity> curie, dose equivalent, gray, half-life, megacurie, microcurie, millicurie, multicurie, rad, roentgen

7 **counter,** radioscope, radiodetector, atom-tagger; ionization chamber; ionizing event; X-ray spectrograph, X-ray spectrometer

8 **radiation physics,** radiological physics; radiobiology, radiochemistry, radiometallography, radiography, roentgenography, roentgenology, radiometry, spectroradiometry, radiotechnology, radiopathology; radiology; radiotherapy; radioscopy, curiescopy, roentgenoscopy, radiostereoscopy, fluoroscopy, photofluorography, orthodiagraphy; X-ray photometry, X-ray spectrometry, accelerator mass spectrometry; tracer investigation, atom-tagging; exposure, dose, absorbed dose

9 radiation physicist; radiobiologist, radiometallographer, radiochemist; radiologist

VERBS **10** radioactivate, activate, irradiate, charge; radiumize; **contaminate,** poison, infect

ADJS **11** **radioactive,** activated, radioactivated, irradiated, charged, hot; **contaminated,** infected, poisoned; exposed; radiferous; radioluminescent, autoluminescent

12 radiable; radiotransparent, radioparent, radiolucent; radiopaque, radium-proof; radiosensitive

13 **radiation ray**

actinic ray	extraordinary ray
alpha ray	gamma ray
anode ray	Grenz ray
Becquerel ray	infraroentgen ray
beta ray	Leonard ray
canal ray	nuclear radiation
cathode ray	ordinary ray
cosmic ray	positive ray
crepuscular ray	Roentgen ray
delta ray	X-ray, radiation

14 **radioactive element**

actinium	neptunium
americium	nobelium
astatine	plutonium
berkelium	polonium
californium	promethium
curium	protactinium
einsteinium	radium
fermium	radon emanation, radium emanation
francium	technetium
hahnium	thorium
lawrencium	uranium
mendelevium	

1038 NUCLEAR PHYSICS

<science of atomic nuclei and their energy>

NOUNS **1** **nuclear physics,** particle physics, nucleonics, atomics, atomistics, atomology, atomic science; quantum mechanics, wave mechanics; molecular physics; thermionics; mass spectrometry, mass spectrography; radiology

2 <**atomic theory**> quantum theory, Bohr theory, Dirac theory, Rutherford theory, Schrödinger theory, Lewis-Langmuir theory, octet theory, Thomson's hypothesis; law of conservation of mass, law of definite proportions, law of multiple proportions, law of Dulong and Petit, law of parity, correspondence principle; Standard Model; supersymmetry theory, unified field theory; atomism; quark model

3 atomic scientist, nuclear physicist, particle physicist; radiologist

4 **atom** <see list>; tracer, tracer atom, tagger atom; atomic model, nuclear atom; nuclide; **ion;** shell, subshell, planetary shell, valence shell; atomic unit; atomic constant; atomic mass, atomic weight, atomic number, proton number, mass number, nucleon number, neutron number

5 **isotope;** protium, deuterium, heavy hydrogen, tritium; radioactive isotope, **radioisotope;** carbon, strontium, uranium; artificial isotope; isotone; isobar, isomer, nuclear isomer

6 **elementary or subatomic particle** <see list>, fundamental particle, atomic particle, subnuclear particle, ultraelementary particle; atomic nucleus, nucleus; nuclear particle, nucleon; proton, **neutron** <see list>; deuteron, deuterium nucleus, triton nucleus, tritium nucleus, alpha particle, helium nucleus; nuclear force, weak force, strong force; weak interaction, strong interaction; fifth force; nucleosynthesis; nuclear resonance, Mössbauer effect, nuclear magnetic resonance (NMR); strangeness; charm

7 atomic cluster, molecule; radical, simple radical, compound radical, chain, straight chain, branched chain, side chain; ring, closed chain, cycle; homocycle, heterocycle; benzene ring, benzene nucleus, Kekulé formula; lattice, space lattice

8 **fission, nuclear fission,** fission reaction; **atom-smashing,** atom-chipping, splitting the atom; atomic reaction; atomic disintegration, atomic decay, alpha decay, beta decay, gamma decay; stimulation, dissociation, photodisintegration, ionization, nucleization, cleavage; neutron reaction, proton reaction; reversible reaction, nonreversible reaction; thermonuclear reaction; chain reaction; exchange reaction; breeding;

disintegration series; bombardment, atomization; bullet, target; proton gun

9 **fusion, nuclear fusion,** fusion reaction, thermonuclear reaction, thermonuclear fusion, laser-induced fusion, cold fusion

10 **fissionable material,** nuclear fuel; fertile material; critical mass, noncritical mass; parent element, daughter element; end product

11 **accelerator** <see list>, particle accelerator, atomic accelerator, atom smasher, atom cannon

12 mass spectrometer, mass spectrograph

13 **reactor** <see list>, **nuclear reactor**, pile, atomic pile, reactor pile, chain-reacting pile, chain reactor, furnace, atomic furnace, nuclear furnace, neutron factory; fast pile, intermediate pile, slow pile; lattice; bricks; rods; radioactive waste

14 atomic engine, atomic power plant, nuclear power plant, reactor engine

15 **nuclear power;** atomic energy, nuclear energy; thermonuclear power; activation energy, binding energy, mass energy; energy level; atomic research, atomic project; Atomic Energy Commission (AEC), Department of Energy (DoE)

16 **atomic explosion,** atom blast, A-blast; thermonuclear explosion, hydrogen blast, H-blast; ground zero; blast wave, Mach stem; Mach front; mushroom cloud; fallout, airborne radioactivity, fission particles, dust cloud, radioactive dust; flash burn; atom bomb atomic bomb, A-bomb, hydrogen bomb, thermonuclear bomb, nuke; fallout shelter

VERBS 17 **atomize,** nucleize; activate, accelerate; bombard, cross-bombard; cleave, fission, **split the atom**, smash the atom

ADJS 18 **atomic;** atomistic; atomiferous; monatomic, diatomic, triatomic, tetratomic, pentatomic, hexatomic, heptatomic; heteratomic, heteroatomic; subatomic, subnuclear, ultraelementary; dibasic, tribasic; cyclic, isocyclic, homocyclic, heterocyclic; isotopic, isobaric, isoteric

19 **nuclear, thermonuclear,** isonuclear, homonuclear, heteronuclear, extranuclear

20 fissionable, fissile, scissile

21 **accelerator**

atom smasher
betatron
bevatron
cascade transformer
charge-exchange accelerator
Cockcroft-Walton voltage multiplier
colliding-beam machine, collider
cosmotron
cyclotron
electron accelerator
electrostatic generator
induction accelerator
linear accelerator
microwave linear accelerator
particle accelerator
positive-ion accelerator
superconducting supercollider (SSC)
synchrocyclotron
synchrotron
tevatron
tokamak
Van de Graaff generator
wake-field accelerator

22 **atom**

acceptor atom
anion
antiatom
asymmetric carbon atom
Bohr atom
cation
diradical, biradical
discrete atom
excited atom
free radical
hot atom
impurity atom
isobar
isotere
isotopic isobar
labeled atom
neutral atom
normal atom
nuclear isomer
nuclide
radiation atom
recoil atom
stripped atom

23 **neutron**

delayed neutron
fast neutron
monoenergetic neutron
photoneutron
resonance neutron
slow neutron
thermal neutron

24 **reactor**

boiling water reactor
breeder reactor
Canada deuterium oxide-uranium reactor (CANDU)
gas-cooled reactor
fast-breeder reactor
fusion reactor
heterogeneous reactor
homogeneous reactor
nuclear reactor
plutonium reactor
power-breeder reactor
power reactor
pressurized-water reactor
stellarator
uranium reactor

25 **subatomic or elementary particle**

alpha particle
antibaryon
antielectron
antilepton
antimeson
antineutrino
antineutron
antiparticle
antiproton
antiquark
b quark, bottom quark
baryon
beta particle
B meson, B particle
boson
cascade particle
D meson, D particle
deuteron
electron
energy particle
fermion
flavor
gauge boson
gluino
gravitino
graviton
hadron
Higgs boson, God particle
hyperon
intermediate-vector boson
J particle, psi particle
kaon, K meson, K particle
lambda particle
lepton
magnetic monopole
matter particle
meson, mesotron
muon, mu-meson
neucleon
neutrino
neutron
omega particle, omega-zero particle, omega nought particle
phi-meson
photino
photon

pion, pi-meson
positron, positive electron
proton
quark
quark color
quark flavor
quarkonium
rho particle
s quark, strange quark
sigma particle
slepton
squark
strange particle
subnuclear particle
superstring
tachyon
tardyon
tau, tauon, tau lepton
tau meson
tau neutrin, tauonic neutrino
technifermion
t quark, top quark
triton
u quark, up quark
upsilon
virtual particle
weakon
weakly interactive massive particle (WIMP)
W particle
xi-particle
zino
Z particle
Z-zero particle

1039 MECHANICS

<science of force and motion>

NOUNS 1 **mechanics** <see list>; leverage; tools and machinery

2 **statics** <see list>

3 **dynamics** <see list>, kinetics, energetics

4 **hydraulics,** fluid dynamics, hydromechanics, hydrokinetics, fluidics, hydrodynamics, hydrostatics; hydrology, hydrography, hydrometry, fluviology

5 **pneumatics,** pneumatostatics; aeromechanics, aerophysics, aerology, aerometry, aerography, aerotechnics, aerodynamics, aerostatics

6 **engineering,** mechanical engineering, jet engineering; engineers

ADJS 7 **mechanical,** mechanistic, mechanized; locomotive, locomotor; motorized, power-driven; hydraulic, electronic; labor-saving; zoomechanical, biomechanical, aeromechanical, hydromechanical; souped-up

8 **static;** biostatic, electrostatic, geostatic

9 **dynamic,** dynamical, kinetic, kinetical, kinematic, kinematical; geodynamic, radiodynamic, electrodynamic

10 **pneumatic,** pneumatological; aeromechanical, aerophysical, aerologic, aerological, aerotechnical, aerodynamic, aerostatic, aerographic, aerographical

11 hydrologic, hydrometric, hydrometrical, hydromechanic, hydromechanical, hydrodynamic, hydrostatic, hydraulic

12 **dynamics (branches)**

aerodynamics
astrodynamics
barodynamics
biodynamics
cardiodynamics
chromodynamics
electrodynamics
fluid dynamics
geodynamics
gnathodynamics
hemodynamics, hematodynamics
hydrodynamics
kinesiology
magnetohydrodynamics, magnetofluid dynamics
megadynamics
myodynamics
pharmacodynamics
photodynamics
phytodynamics
pneodynamics, pneumatics
pneumodynamics
quantum chromodynamics
radiodynamics
thermodynamics
trophodynamics
zoodynamics

13 **mechanics (branches)**

aerodynamics
aeromechanics
animal mechanics
applied mechanics
atomechanics
auto mechanics
biomechanics, zoomechanics
celestial mechanics
classical mechanics
dynamics
electromechanics
fluid mechanics
hydromechanics, hydrodynamics
kinematics
kinetics
magnetohydrodynamics (MHD)
matrix mechanics
mechanical arts
Newtonian mechanics
micromechanics
practical mechanics
pure mechanics, abstract mechanics
quantum mechanics
rational mechanics
servomechanics
statistical mechanics
telemechanics
theoretical mechanics, analytical mechanics
wave mechanics

14 **statics (branches)**

aerostatics
biostatics
electrostatics
geostatics
gnathostatics
graphostatics
gyrostatics
hemastatics, hematostatics
hydrostatics
hygrostatics
magnetostatics
rheostatics
social statics
stereostatics
thermostatics

1040 TOOLS, MACHINERY

<apparatus and instruments for power>

NOUNS 1 **tool, instrument, implement,** utensil; apparatus, device, mechanical device, contrivance, contraption, gadget, gizmo, gimcrack, gimmick, means, mechanical means; gadgetry; **hand tool; power tool;** machine tool; speed tool; precision tool, precision instrument; garden tool, agricultural tool; mechanization, mechanizing; motorizing

2 **cutlery,** edge tool; **knife,** ax, dagger, sword, blade, cutter, whittle; steel, stainless steel, cold steel, naked steel; shiv, pigsticker, toad stabber, toad sticker; perforator, piercer, puncturer, point; sharpener; **saw;** trowel; shovel; plane; drill; valve

3 **machinery,** engineery; **machine,** mechanism, mechanical device; heavy machinery, earthmoving machinery, earthmover; farm machinery; mill; welder; pump; engine, motor; engine part; power plant, power source, drive, motive power, prime mover; **appliance,** convenience, facility, utility, public utility, home appliance, mechanical aid; fixture; labor-saving device

4 **mechanism,** machinery, movement, movements, moving parts, action, motion, works, workings, inner workings, what makes it work, innards, nuts and bolts, what makes it tick; drive train, power train; wheelwork, wheelworks, wheels, gear, wheels within wheels, epicyclic train; clockworks, watchworks, servomechanism; robot, automaton

5 **simple machine**; lever, wheel and axle, pulley, inclined plane; machine part, gear, gearwheel, shaft, crank, rod, hub, cam, coupling, bearing, ball bearing, roller bearing, journal, bush, differential

6 **machine tool**; drill, press drill, borer, lathe, mill, broaching machine, facing machine, threading machine, tapping machine, grinder, planer, shaper, saw

7 **hand tool**; hammer, screwdriver, drill, punch, awl, wrench, pliers, clamp, vise, chisel, wedge, ax, knife, saw, lever, crowbar, jack, pulley, wheel

8 **garden tool**; spade, shovel, trowel, fork, rake, hoe, tiller, plow, hedge trimmer, shears, lawn mower

9 **gear,** gearing, gear train; gearwheel, cogwheel, rack; gearshift; low, intermediate, high, neutral, reverse; differential, differential gear, differential gearing; transmission, gearbox; automatic transmission; selective transmission; standard transmission, stick shift, manual transmission, five-speed, five on the floor; synchronized shifting, synchromesh; spur gear, rack and pinion, helical gear, bevel gear, skew gear, worm gear, internal gear, external gear; gear tooth

10 **clutch,** cone clutch, plate clutch, dog clutch, disk clutch, multiple-disk clutch, rim clutch, friction clutch, cone friction clutch, slip friction clutch, spline clutch, rolling-key clutch

11 **tooling,** tooling up; retooling; instrumentation, industrial instrumentation; servo instrumentation

12 **mechanic,** mechanician; grease monkey; artisan, artificer; machinist, machiner; auto mechanic, aeromechanic

VERBS 13 **tool,** tool up, instrument; retool; **machine**, mill; mechanize, motorize; sharpen

ADJS 14 **mechanical;** machinelike; power, powered, power-driven, motor-driven, motorized; mechanized, mechanistic; electronic; labor-saving

15 **agricultural, gardening tool**

baler	pickax
billhook	pitchfork
binder	plow
blower	pruner
brush cutter	pruning saw
cant hook	rake
chisel plow	reaper
colter	ride-on lawn mower
combine	roller
crop duster	rototiller
cultivator	scuffle hoe
dibble, dibber	scythe
draw hoe	shears
edger	shovel
flail	shredder
grub hoe	sickle
harvester	spade
hayfork	spading fork
hay rake	sprinkler
hedge clipper	tiller
hoe	tractor
lawn mower, mower	trowel
mattock	weed trimmer
maul	wheelbarrow
pick	

16 **blacksmithing tool**

anvil	hoof tester
ball peen hammer	hot chisel
blower	mandrel
chisel	nipper
clinch cutter	post drill
clincher	post vise
clipping hammer	power hammer
cold chisel	pritchel
creaser	puncher
cross peen hammer	rasp
dipper	set hammer
drift	sledgehammer
drill	straight peen hammer
fileflatter	swage
floor mandrel	swage block
forge	swedge
fuller	swedge block
hammer	tongs
hardie	treadle hammer
hoof gauger	vise

17 **cutting, pointed, edged tool**

adz	cleaver
awl	clipper
ax	cold chisel
bill	drove, boaster
blade	firmer chisel
bodkin	gouge
bolster chisel	graver
burin	hardy
butcher knife	hatchet
carving knife	hook
chisel	jackknife

knife
machete
masonry chisel
paring chisel
pick
pinking shears
pipe cutter
punch
razor
router
scissors
scorper
scraper
scythe
shears
sickle
square-end chisel
wire cutter

18 drill

auger
bench drill
bit
bore
bow drill
breast drill
broach
cordless drill
corkscrew
countersink
diamond drill
drill press
eggbeater drill
electric drill
gimlet
hand drill
portable drill
power drill
push drill
reamer
rose reamer
seed drill
twist drill
wimble
woodborer

19 fastening, gripping tool

adjustable bar clamp
band clamp
bar clamp
bench dog
bench vise
bent-nose pliers
brace
C-clamp
channel-type pliers
chuck
clamp
claw
clip
corner clamp
cutting pliers
diagonal-cutting pliers
electric riveter
forceps
glue gun
grip
hand vise
holddown clamp
joint fastener
lineman's pliers
locking pliers
long-nose pliers
nail puller
needlenose pliers
pincers
pinchcock
pipe clamp
plate joiner
pliers
power nailer
pucellas
puller
riveter
screw clamp
slip-joint pliers
snap ring pliers
spring clamp
staple gun
stapler
toggle clamp
tongs
tweezers
vise
vise grip
web clamp

20 hammers, mallet

ball peen hammer
beetle
blacksmith's hammer
brick hammer
bushhammer
chipping hammer
claw hammer
cross peen hammer
demolition hammer
double-claw hammer
drywall hammer
electric hammer
engineer's hammer
framing hammer
fuller
joiner's mallet
long-handled hammer
machinist's hammer
maul
peen hammer
pile hammer
rip hammer
rubber mallet
scutch
shingler's hammer
shoemaker's hammer
sledgehammer
small anvil
soft-faced hammer
soft-faced mallet
stonemason's hammer
tack hammer
tilt hammer
triphammer
Warington hammer
wooden mallet

21 measuring, marking tool

bevel
butt gauge
caliper
carpenter's level
carpenter's pencil
carpenter's square
center punch
chalk liner
combination square
compass
depth gauge
dividers
electronic level
feeler gauge
folding rule
framing square
gauge
level
line level
marking gauge
mason's level
micrometer
miter box
miter square
mortise gage
plumb bob
plumb rule
protractor
rafter square
rule
ruler
scale
scratch awl
scriber
slide caliper
square
steel rule
straight edge
studfinder
tape measure
torpedo level
T square
turning caliper
wing divider

22 saw

backsaw
band saw
bench saw
bucksaw
butcher's saw
buzz saw
chain saw
circular saw
compass saw
coping saw
crosscut saw
crown saw
cutoff saw
diamond saw
dovetail saw
drywall saw
electric saw
flooring saw
flush cut saw
folding saw
frame saw
fretsaw
hacksaw
hand saw
jeweler's saw
jigsaw
keyhole saw
log saw
lumberman's saw
meat saw
one-man crosscut saw
pad saw
panel saw
pit saw
plumber's saw
portable circular saw
power saw
radial arm saw
reciprocating saw
ripsaw
saber saw
scroll saw
stationary circular saw
table saw
tree saw
two-handed saw
two-man crosscut saw
utility saw
vertical saw

23 screwdriver

auger screwdriver
cabinet-pattern screwdriver
clutch-head tip screwdriver
cordless screwdriver
electric screwdriver
flat-head screwdriver
impact driver
magnetic screwdriver
offset screwdriver
Phillips screwdriver
ratcheting screwdriver
screw gun
spiral ratchet screwdriver
stubby screwdriver
Yankee screwdriver

24 shaping, smoothing tool

adz
anvil
beading plane
belt sander
bench plane
block plane
brick trowel
buffer
bullnose plane
chamfering plane
circular file
corner trowel
die
disk sander
double cut file
drum sander
electric sander
emery wheel
file
finishing sander
flat file
flatter
float
fore plane
grinder
grinding wheel
grindstone
grooving plane
half-round file
hand sander
hone
jack plane
lathe
machine tool
multiplane
oilstone
plane
planer
power sander
putty knife
rasp
round file
router
router plane
sander
sandpaper
scraper
shaper
sharpener
shavehook
single cut file
slipstone
smoothing plane
spokeshave
stone
swage
swage block
tamper
thickness planer
trimming plane
trowel
trying plane
waterstone
whetstone

25 shovels, digger

bail
bar spade
bull tongue
coal shovel
cultivator
ditch spade
draw hoe
fire shovel
fork
garden spade
garden trowel
grub hoe
hoe
irrigating shovel
loy
mattock
peat spade
pitchfork
plow
posthole digger
power shovel
rake
scoop
scooper
spade
spatula
spud
trowel

26 wrench

adjustable wrench
Allen wrench
alligator wrench
bicycle wrench
box wrench
box-end wrench
crescent Wrench
crowfoot wrench
flare-nut wrench
gooseneck wrench
hexagonal wrench
lug wrench
monkey wrench
obstruction wrench
open-end wrench
pin wrench
pipe-gripping wrench
pipe wrench
ratcheting box-end wrench
socket wrench
spanner
sparkplug wrench
Stillson wrench
torque wrench
valve wrench

1041 AUTOMATION

<machines in production process>

NOUNS 1 **automation,** automatic control; **robotization**, cybernation; self-action, self-activity; self-movement, self-motion, self-propulsion; self-direction, self-determination, self-government, automatism, self-regulation; automaticity, automatization; servo instrumentation; computerization

2 autonetics, **automation technology**, automatic technology, automatic electronics, automatic engineering, automatic control engineering, servo engineering, servomechanics, system engineering, systems analysis, feedback system engineering; cybernetics; telemechanics; radiodynamics, radio control; systems planning, systems design; circuit analysis; bionics; communications theory, information theory; cleantech

3 **automatic control,** cruise control, cybernation, servo control, robot control, robotization; cybernetic control; electronic control, electronic-mechanical control; feedback control, digital feedback control, analog feedback control; cascade control, piggyback control; supervisory control; action, control action; derivative action, rate action, reset action; control agent; control means

4 semiautomatic control; **remote control,** push-button control, remote handling, tele-action; radio control; telemechanics; telemechanism; telemetry, telemeter, telemetering; transponder; bioinstrument, bioinstrumentation

5 control system, **automatic control system,** servo system, robot system; closed-loop system; open-sequence system; linear system, nonlinear system; carrier-current system; integrated system, complex control system; data system, data-handling system, data-reduction system, data-input system, data-interpreting system,

digital data reducing system; process-control system, annunciator system, flow-control system, motor-speed control system; automanual system; automatic telephone system; electrostatic spraying system; automated factory, automatic factory, robot factory, push-button plant; servo laboratory, servolab; electronic banking; electronic cottage

6 **feedback,** closed sequence, feedback loop, closed loop; multiple-feed closed loop; process loop, quality loop; feedback circuit, current-control circuit, direct-current circuit, alternating-current circuit, calibrating circuit, switching circuit, flip-flop circuit, peaking circuit; multiplier channels; open sequence, linear operation; positive feedback, negative feedback; reversed feedback, degeneration

7 <functions> accounting, analysis, automatic electronic navigation, automatic guidance, braking, comparison of variables, computation, coordination, corrective action, fact distribution, forecasts, impedance matching, inspection, linear calibration, nonlinear calibration, manipulation, measurement of variables, missile guidance, output measurement, processing, rate determination, record keeping, statistical communication, steering, system stabilization, ultrasonic flow detection, supersonic flow detection

8 **process control,** bit-weight control, color control, density control, dimension control, diverse control, end-point control, flavor control, flow control, fragrance control, hold control, humidity control, light-intensity control, limit control, liquid-level control, load control, pressure control, precision-production control, proportional control, quality control, quantity control, revolution control, temperature control, time control, weight control

9 **variable**, process variable; simple variable, complex variable; manipulated variable; steady state, transient state

10 values, target values; set point; differential gap; proportional band; dead band, dead zone; neutral zone

11 time constants; time lead, gain; time delay, dead time; lag, process lag, hysteresis, holdup, output lag; throughput

12 automatic device, automatic; semiautomatic; self-actor, self-mover; **robot, automaton**, mechanical man; cyborg; bionic man, bionic woman

13 **servomechanism,** servo; cybernion, automatic machine; servomotor; synchro, selsyn, autosyn; synchronous motor, synchronous machine

14 system component; control mechanism; **regulator,** control, controller, governor; servo control, servo regulator; control element

15 **automatic detector;** automatic analyzer; automatic indicator

16 **control panel,** console; coordinated panel, graphic panel; panelboard, set-up board

17 **computer,** computer science, electronic computer, electronic brain; electronic organizer; information machine, thinking machine; computer unit, hardware, computer hardware

18 <automatic devices> automatic pilot, autopilot, automaton, guided missile, robot, self-starter, speedometer

19 **control engineer**, servo engineer, **systems engineer**, systems analyst, automatic control system engineer, feedback system engineer, automatic technician, robot specialist; computer engineer, computer technologist, computer technician, computer programmer; cybernetic technologist, cyberneticist

VERBS 20 **automate,** automatize, robotize; robot-control, servo-control; program; computerize

21 self-govern, self-control, self-regulate, self-direct

ADJS 22 **automated,** cybernated, robotized; **automatic,** automatous, spontaneous; self-acting, self-active; self-operating, self-operative, self-working; self-regulating, self-regulative, self-governing, self-directing; self-regulated, self-controlled, self-governed, self-directed, self-steered; self-adjusting, self-closing, self-cocking, self-cooking, self-dumping, self-emptying, self-lighting, self-loading, self-opening, self-priming, self-rising, self-sealing, self-starting, self-winding, automanual; semiautomatic; computerized, computer-controlled

23 **self-propelled**, self-moved, horseless; self-propelling, self-moving, self-propellent; self-driven, self-drive; **automotive,** automobile, automechanical; locomotive, locomobile

24 **servomechanical,** servo-controlled; **cybernetic;** isotronic

25 **remote-control,** remote-controlled, telemechanic; telemetered, telemetric; by remote control

COMBINING FORMS 26 aut-, auto-, automat-, automato-, self-

1042 COMPUTER SCIENCE

<principles and use of computers>

NOUNS 1 **computer science** <see list>, computer systems, computer applications, computer hardware, computer software, computers, digital computers, computing, machine computation, number-crunching; cloud computing, fog computing; **computerization,** digitization**; data**

processing, electronic data processing (EDP), data storage and retrieval; data bank; **information science,** computer science, information processing, informatics; computer security; computer crime, computer fraud, computer virus, computer worm; hacking; handwriting recognition, voice recognition; virtual reality, virtual environment, artificial reality; geekdom, geekhood; third wave; Generation D

2 **computer,** electronic data processor, information processor, electronic brain, digital computer, general purpose computer, analog computer, hybrid computer, machine, **hardware,** computer hardware, gray goods, microelectronics device; processor, central processing unit (CPU), multiprocessor, microprocessor, coprocessor, mainframe computer, mainframe, dataflow computer, work station, minicomputer, microcomputer, personal computer (PC), home computer, desktop computer, laptop computer, laptop, notebook computer, briefcase computer, graphics tablet, tablet computer, tablet, phablet, pocket computer, handheld computer, wearable computer, personal organizer, personal digital assistant (PDA), minisupercomputer, superminicomputer, supermicrocomputer, supercomputer, graphoscope, array processor, neurocomputer, neural computer; multimedia computer; neural net, neural network, semantic net, semantic network; management information system (MIS); clone; abacus, calculator; fourth-generation computer, fifth-generation computer

3 **circuitry, circuit**, integrated circuit, logic circuit, **chip**, silicon chip, gallium arsenide chip, semiconductor chip, hybrid chip, wafer chip, superchip, microchip, neural network chip, transputer, board, printed circuit board (PCB), card, motherboard, sound card, video card; peripheral, peripheral device, peripheral unit, input device, output device; expansion slot; port, channel interface, serial interface, serial port, parallel port, parallel processing; read-write head; vacuum tube, transistor, bus, LED, network adapter, small computer systems interface (SCSI), register; accelerator board; hardwiring

4 **input device,** keyboard, keypad; reader, tape reader, card punch, scanner, optical scanner, optical character reader, optical character recognition (OCR), optical character recognition device, OCR device, data tablet, tablet, touchscreen, light pen, mouse, joystick, trackball, wand, point-and-click; docking station

5 **drive,** disk drive, floppy disk drive, hard disk drive, hard drive, tape drive, removable drive, USB drive, flash drive, external hard drive

6 **disk,** magnetic disk, floppy disk, floppy, diskette, minifloppy, microfloppy, hard disk, fixed disk, Winchester disk, removable disk, optical disk, disk pack; magnetic tape, mag tape, magnetic tape unit, magnetic drum; compact-disk read-only memory (CR-ROM), magneto-optical disk

7 **memory, storage,** memory bank, memory chip, firmware; main memory, main storage, cache memory, cache, random-access memory (RAM), read-only memory (ROM), programmable read-only memory (PROM), semiconductor memory, magnetic core memory, core, core storage, solid-state memory, auxiliary memory, secondary memory, disk pack, magnetic disk, primary storage, backing store, read/write memory, optical disk memory, bubble memory; memory card, memory stick; virtual memory, virtual storage

8 **retrieval, access,** random access, sequential access, direct access, data capture, capture; modem, router

9 **output device,** peripheral, terminal, workstation, video terminal, video display terminal (VDT), video display unit, visual display unit (VDU), flat-screen display, plasma display, plasma screen, graphics terminal, monitor, screen, display, cathode ray tube (CRT), monochrome monitor, color monitor, RGB monitor, active matrix display, window; printer, color printer, serial printer, character printer, impact printer, dot-matrix printer, daisy-wheel printer, printwheel printer, drum printer, line printer, line dot-matrix printer, chain printer, page printer, nonimpact printer, laser printer, electronic printer, graphics printer, color graphics printer, inkjet printer, thermal printer, bubble-jet printer, electrostatic printer; plotter; modem, modulator-demodulator; router

10 forms, computer forms, computer paper, continuous stationery; dialog box

11 **software, program,** computer program, source program, object program, binary file, binary program; program suite, suite of applications; bundle; software package, courseware, groupware, routine, subroutine, intelligent agent, agent, autonomous agent; application software; applet; authoring software; shareware, freeware; **word processor,** text editor, editor, print formatter, what-you-see-is-what-you-get (WYSIWYG), WYSIWYG word processor, post-formatted word processor; **spreadsheet**, electronic spreadsheet, spreadsheeting; desktop publishing program, database management system (DBMS), **database**; authoring tool, utility program, screen saver, computer game; bundled software; **computer application** <see list>, app, applications program, bootloader loader, bootstrap loader;

adbot, adware, botnet, computer virus, electronic virus, computer worm, phantom bug, malware, Trojan horse, logic bomb; grayware; developmental tool, presentation graphics; ad blocker; e-signature; firewall

12 systems program, **operating system** (OS), disk operating system (DOS), system software; Microsoft <tm> disk operating system (MS-DOS) <tm>; UNIX; control program monitor (CPM), application programming; cloud computing, fog computing

13 **language, programming language, scripting language** <see list>; formal language, assembler language, assembly language, command language, machine language, machine-readable language, conventional programming language, computer language, high-level language, fourth generation language, macrolanguage, preprocessor language, markup language, style sheet language, configuration language, construction language, query language, modeling language, hardware description language; compiler, interpreter, low-level language, application development language, assembly code, object code, job-control language (JCL), procedural language, problem-oriented language; source code, machine code; loader, parser, debugger, lookup table; scripting language, script; programming, scripting, coding, hacking, hackathon

14 **bit,** binary digit, infobit, kilobit, megabit, gigabit, terbit; **byte,** kilobyte, megabyte

15 **data, information,** big data; database, data capture, database management, data warehousing, data bank, input, input-output (I/O); **file,** data set, record, data record, data file, text file; data trail, data integrity

16 **network, computer network,** communications network, local area network (LAN), wireless network, WiFi; workgroup computing, mesh; neural network, neural net; online system, interactive system, online service; intranet; Internet; data highway

17 **programmer,** liveware, wetware; software engineer, computer engineer, computer scientist, data scientist, data wrangler; systems programmer, system software specialist, application programmer, systems analyst, systems engineer, system operator (sysop); computer designer, computer architect, operator, technician, key puncher, keyboarder; techie; hacker

18 <**computer terms**> access, address bar, archive, arrow key, authoring, auto-completion, auto-configure, autodial, back button, backup, bandwidth, batch file, batch processing, battery pack, baud rate, benchmark, beta test, binary tree, bit, bitmap, block, bookmark, boot, bootstrap, bug, byte, call to action, cgi, checkbox, click, clickthrough, clock rate, command, compatibility, computerate, computer-friendly, computer-literate, control character, controller, crash, cursor, cut-and-paste, data security, desktop, diagnostic, diff, digital, digital native, direct access, direct address, directory, display, domain name, dot-com, download, downtime, drag and drop, dropdown menu, email address, emoji, emulator, enter key, escape key, field, file, file folder, file format, file sharing, footprint, file transfer protocol (FTP), function key, geolocation, geotag, geotagging, gigabyte, gopher, graphics, grep, hacking, hashtag, helpdesk, home page, hot key, hotlist, icon, input, interactive, interface, job, key, kilobyte, login, logon, logoff, megabyte, meme, menu, message board, millennium bug, morphing, mouse pad, mouse potato, MP3, multimedia, navigation bar output, network card, network interface card, parity, password, plug-and-play, portal site, power user, pulldown, queue, random access, real time, record, save, scrollable, scroll bar, searchability, search engine, search engine optimization (SEO), sector, sentiment analysis, sequential access, signature, sleep mode, smiley, special character, spellchecker, subfolder, task bar, taskbar, toolbar, toolkit, turnkey operation, upload, uniform resource locator (URL), username, virus, wireframe, what you see is what you get (WYSIWYG), workaround

19 <**Internet terms**> the Net, World Wide Web (WWW), Web, dark web, deep web, Internet of things; cyberspace, information superhighway; Internet service provider (ISP), online service provider, service provider; communications protocol, push technology; DSL, cable, cable modem, high-speed Internet; electronic mail, email, mailbox, spam; intranet, Usenet; local area network (LAN), wide area network (WAN); website, site map, web page, home page; compression, encryption; file server, client-server; browser, gateway, search engine; content provider, e-business, click rate, clickthrough, clickbait, pageview, hits; bulletin board service (BBS), chat room, newsgroup, workgroup; netizen, surfer; wiki; Weblog, blog; captcha, meme, icon, favicon, netspeak; video calling, video chat, video conference, video conferencing, viral video; Tweeting, following, unfollowing, liking; rich media; hyperlink, hot link; screen name; Internet cafe; IP address; open source; social media

20 artificial intelligence, knowledge engineering,

knowledge representation, intelligent retrieval, natural language processing, expert systems, speech synthesis, robotics, hypertext, hypermedia, intelligent agent

VERBS 21 **computerize,** digitize; **program,** boot, boot up, initialize, log in, log out, run, load, download, upload, **compute,** crunch numbers; capture; **keyboard,** key in, input; browse, surf; search, google; cut and paste; export, import; bookmark; video-chat; virtualize

ADJS 22 **computerized;** wired; machine-usable, computer-usable; computer-aided, computer-assisted; computer-driven, computer-guided, computer-controlled, computer-governed; computer-literate, computerate; programmatic, programmable; flat-screen

23 **computer application**

authoring tool
batch processing
communications software
computer art
computer bulletin board
computer conferencing
computer games
computer graphics
computer typesetting
computer-aided design
computer-aided engineering
computer-aided manufacturing
computer-assisted instruction
database management system
desktop publishing (DTP)
electronic publishing
Internet access software, Internet service provider software
musical instrument digital interface (MIDI
office automation program
presentation software
screen saver, screensaver
simulation software
spell-checking, spellchecker
spreadsheet
time-sharing
Web design software
word processing

24 **computer science (branches)**

algorithms and data structures
artificial intelligence (AI)
automata theory
combinatorial processes
compiler design
computer-aided design (CAD)
computer-aided learning, computer-assisted learning (CAL)
computer-aided manufacturing (CAM)
computer-aided molecular desigd (CAMD)
computer-aided testing (CAT)
computer applications
computer architecture
computer-based learning
computer engineering
computer graphics and visualization
computer-integrated manufacture (CIM)
computer-managed instruction (CMI)
computer networks and systems
computer security and cryptography
concurrent, parallel, and distributed systems
cybernetics
databases
data processing
human-computer interaction
information retrieval (IR)
information storage and retrieval
information technology (IT)
language processing
logical design
machine organization
management information system (MIS)
mathematical foundations
natural language processing
neural networks
office automation
operating systems
optimization
programming
programming languages
robotics
scientific computing
simulation
software engineering
switching theory
symbol manipulation
systems analysis
theory of computation
theory of formal languages
utility programs

25 **programming, scripting language**

ADA
ALGOL, algorithmic-oriented language
APL, a programming language
APT, automatic programmed tools
BAL, basic assembly language
BASIC, beginners all-purpose symbolic instruction code
BCPL, Basic Combined Programming Language
C
C++
C#
COBOL, common business-oriented language
Cobra
COMIT, Computer On Module Interconnect Technology
COMPACT II
CPL
efl
eqn
FLOWMATIC
FORMAC
FORTH
FORTRAN, formula translator
Game Maker Language
GPSS
HTML, Hypertext Markup Language
IPL-V
Java
JavaScript
JOSS
JOVIAL
Lex
LISP, list processing
Logo
Objective-C
OCCAM
PASCAL
Perl
PHP
pic
PILOT, Programmed Instruction, Learning, or Teaching
PL/1
Postscript
Prolog
Python
Ratfor
Rexx
RPG II
Ruby
SGML, Standard Generalized Markup Language
S-Lang
SNOBOL, string-oriented symbolic language
SQL
Tcl
Visual Basic
yacc, yet another computer compiler

1043 ENGINEERING

<science of engines, machines, structures>

NOUNS 1 **engineering**, mechanical engineering, civil engineering, chemical engineering, electrical engineering, mining and metallurgy, industrial engineering; automotive engineering, aerospace engineering, aeronautical engineering, astronautical engineering, marine engineering, agricultural engineering; structural engineering, transportation engineering, hydraulic engineering, geotechnical engineering, construction engineering; material engineering, biochemical engineering, environmental engineering, sound engineering

2 **engineer,** registered engineer; mechanical engineer, civil engineer, chemical engineer, electrical engineer, mining engineer, metallurgical engineer, industrial engineer; automotive engineer, aerospace engineer, aeronautical engineer, astronautical engineer, marine engineer, agricultural engineer; structural engineer, transportation engineer, hydraulic engineer, construction engineer; material engineer, biochemical engineer, biomedical engineer, environmental engineer; electronics engineer; mechanic, technician

3 <**engine types**> internal combustion, external combustion; Wankel, reciprocating, fuel injection, steam, gasoline, diesel, jet, turboprop, turbojet, rocket, Stirling, locomotive; automotive, aircraft, marine, railroad

VERBS 4 **engineer**, construct, build, erect, survey, map, excavate, dig, grade, dredge, drill, tunnel, blast, pave; process, manufacture, measure; reverse-engineer

1044 FRICTION

<force slowing something it touches>

NOUNS 1 **friction, rubbing,** rub, frottage; frication, confrication, perfrication; **drag,** skin friction; **resistance,** frictional resistance; static friction, rolling friction, internal friction, sliding friction, slip friction

2 **abrasion,** attrition, **erosion,** wearing away, wear, detrition, ablation; rubbing against, rubbing together; ruboff; corrosion; erasure, erasing, rubbing away, rubbing off, rubbing out, obliteration; grinding, filing, rasping, limation; fretting; galling; chafing, chafe; levigation; scraping, grazing, scratching, scuffing; scrape, scratch, scuff; scrubbing, scrub; scouring, scour; polishing, burnishing, sanding, smoothing, dressing, buffing, shining; sandblasting; abrasive; brass-rubbing, heelball rubbing, graphite rubbing

3 **massage,** massaging, stroking, kneading; rubdown; backrub; massotherapy, massage therapy; whirlpool bath, Jacuzzi <tm>; vibrator; facial massage, facial

4 massager, masseur, masseuse, massage therapist; massotherapist

5 <mechanics> force of friction; force of viscosity; coefficient of friction; friction head; friction clutch, friction drive, friction gearing, friction pile, friction saw, friction welding

VERBS 6 rub, frictionize; massage, knead, rub down; caress, pet, stroke; pulverize; smooth, iron

7 **abrade,** abrase, gnaw, gnaw away; **erode,** erode away, ablate, wear, wear away, corrode; erase, rub away, rub off rub out, rub against; grind, rasp, file, grate; chafe, fret, gall; scrape, scratch, graze, scuff, bark, skin; fray, frazzle; scrub, scour

8 **buff,** burnish, polish, rub up, sandpaper, **sand,** smooth, dress, shine, furbish, sandblast; brush, curry

ADJS 9 **frictional,** friction; fricative; **rubbing**

10 **abrasive,** abradant, attritive, gnawing, erosive, ablative; scraping; **grinding, rasping;** chafing, fretting, galling

1045 DENSITY

<relationship between weight and size, closeness of parts>

NOUNS 1 **density,** denseness, **solidity, solidness,** firmness, compactness, closeness, spissitude; congestion, congestedness, crowdedness, jammedness; impenetrability, impermeability, imporosity; hardness; incompressibility; specific gravity, relative density; consistency, consistence, thick consistency, thickness; viscidity, viscosity, viscousness, gluiness, ropiness

2 **indivisibility, inseparability,** impartibility, infrangibility, indiscerptibility; indissolubility; cohesion, coherence; unity; insolubility, infusibility

3 **densification,** condensation, compression, **concentration,** inspissation, concretion, consolidation, conglobulation; hardening, solidification; agglutination, clumping, clustering

4 **thickening,** inspissation; congelation, **congealment, coagulation,** clotting, setting, concretion; gelatinization, gelatination, jellification, jellying, jelling, gelling; curdling, clabbering; distillation

5 **precipitation**, deposit, sedimentation; precipitate

6 **solid,** solid body, body, mass, bulk; lump, clump, cluster; block, cake; node, knot; concrete, concretion; conglomerate, conglomeration

7 **clot,** coagulum, coagulate; blood clot, grume, embolus, crassamentum; coagulant, coagulator, clotting factor, coagulase, coagulose, thromboplastin, coagulin; casein, caseinogen, paracasein, legumin; **curd,** clabber, loppered

milk, bonnyclabber, clotted cream, Devonshire cream

8 <instruments> densimeter, densitometer; aerometer, hydrometer, lactometer, urinometer, pycnometer

VERBS 9 **densify,** inspissate, densen; **condense,** compress, compact, consolidate, concentrate, come to a head; congest; squeeze, press, crowd, cram, jam, pack, ram down; steeve; pack in, jam in; solidify

10 **thicken,** thick; inspissate, incrassate; **congeal,** coagulate, clot, set, concrete; gelatinize, gelatinate, jelly, jellify, jell, gel; curdle, curd, clabber, lopper; cake, lump, clump, cluster, knot

11 **precipitate,** deposit, sediment, sedimentate

ADJS 12 **dense, compact,** close; close-textured, close-knit, close-woven, tight-knit; serried, thick, heavy, massy, thickset, thick-packed, thick-growing, thick-spread, thick-spreading; condensed, compressed, compacted, concrete, consolidated, concentrated; crowded, jammed, packed, jam-packed, packed in, jammed in, packed like sardines; congested, crammed, crammed full; **solid,** firm, substantial, massive; impenetrable, impermeable, imporous, nonporous; hard; incompressible; viscid, viscous, ropy, gluey; thick enough to be cut with a knife

13 **indivisible,** nondivisible, undividable, **inseparable,** impartible, infrangible, indiscerptible, indissoluble; cohesive, coherent; unified; insoluble, indissolvable, infusible

14 **thickened,** inspissate, inspissated, incrassate; **congealed, coagulated,** clotted, grumous; curdled, curded, clabbered; jellied, jelled, gelled, gelatinized; lumpy, lumpish; caked, cakey; coagulant, coagulating

ADVS 15 **densely,** compactly, close, closely, thick, thickly, heavily; solidly, firmly

1046 HARDNESS, RIGIDITY

<firm, solid, unbendable>

NOUNS 1 **hardness,** durity, **induration**; callousness, callosity; stoniness, rock-hardness, flintiness, steeliness; strength, toughness; solidity, impenetrability, density; restiveness, resistance; obduracy; hardness of heart

2 **rigidity, rigidness,** rigor; firmness, renitence, renitency, incompressibility; nonresilience, nonresiliency, inelasticity; tension, tensity, tenseness, tautness, tightness

3 **stiffness,** inflexibility, unpliability, unmalleability, intractability, unbendingness, unlimberness, starchiness; stubbornness, unyieldingness; unalterability, immutability; immovability; inelasticity, irresilience, irresiliency; inextensibility, unextensibility, unextendibility, inductility

4 **temper, tempering**; chisel temper, die temper, razor temper, saw file temper, set temper, spindle temper, tool temper; precipitation hardening, heat treating; hardness test, Brinell test; hardness scale, Brinell number, Brinell hardness number (Bhn); indenter; hardener, hardening, hardening agent

5 **hardening, toughening,** induration, firming; strengthening; tempering, case-hardening, steeling; seasoning; stiffening, rigidification, starching; solidification, setting, curing, caking, concretion; crystallization, granulation; callusing; sclerosis, arteriosclerosis, atherosclerosis, hardening of the arteries; lithification; lapidification; petrification, fossilization, ossification; glaciation; cornification, hornification; calcification; vitrification, vitrifaction

6 <comparisons> stone, rock, adamant, granite, flint, marble, diamond; steel, iron, nails; concrete, cement; brick; oak, heart of oak; bone; Mohs' scale

VERBS 7 **harden,** indurate, firm, toughen; callous; **temper,** anneal, oil-temper, heat-temper, case-harden, steel; season; **petrify,** lapidify, fossilize; lithify; vitrify; calcify; ossify; cornify, hornify

8 **solidify,** concrete, set, take a set, cure, cake; condense, thicken; crystallize, granulate, candy; hard-boil; anneal; freeze

9 **stiffen,** rigidify, starch; strengthen, toughen; back, brace, reinforce, shore up; tense, tighten, tense up, tension; trice up, screw up

ADJS 10 **hard, solid,** dure, lacking give, tough; resistive, resistant, steely, steellike, iron-hard, ironlike; **stony, rocky,** stonelike, rock-hard, rocklike, lapideous, lapidific, lapidifical, lithoid, lithoidal; diamondlike, adamant, adamantine; flinty, flintlike; marble, marblelike; granitic, granitelike; gritty; concrete, cement, cemental; horny; bony, osseous, ossific; petrifactive; vitreous; hard-boiled; hard as nails, hard as a rock; dense; obdurate; hardhearted

11 **rigid, stiff,** firm, renitent, incompressible; tense, taut, tight, unrelaxed; nonresilient, inelastic; rodlike, virgate; ramrod-stiff, ramrodlike, pokerlike; stiff as a poker, stiff as a board, stiff as buckram; starched, starchy

12 **inflexible,** unflexible, **unpliable,** unpliant, unmalleable, intractable, untractable, intractile, unbending, unlimber, unyielding, ungiving, stubborn, unalterable, immutable; immovable; adamant, adamantine; inelastic, nonelastic,

irresilient; inextensile, inextensible, unextensible, inextensional, unextendible, nonstretchable, inductile; intransigent

13 **hardened, toughened,** steeled, indurate, indurated, fortified; callous, calloused; solidified, set; crystallized, granulated; petrified, lapidified, fossilized; vitrified; sclerotic; ossified; cornified, hornified; calcified; crusted, crusty, incrusted; stiffened, strengthened, rigidified, backed, reinforced; frozen solid

14 **hardening, toughening,** indurative; petrifying, petrifactive

15 **tempered,** case-hardened, heat-treated, **annealed,** oil-tempered, heat-tempered, tempered in fire; seasoned; indurate, indurated

1047 SOFTNESS, PLIANCY

<not hard, firm, rigid>

NOUNS **1** **softness, give**, nonresistiveness, insolidity, unsolidity, nonrigidity; gentleness, easiness, delicacy, tenderness; lenity, leniency; mellowness; fluffiness, flossiness, downiness, featheriness; velvetiness, plushiness, satininess, silkiness; sponginess, pulpiness

2 **pliancy, pliability,** plasticity, flexibility, flexility, flexuousness, bendability, ductility, ductibility, tensileness, tensility, tractility, tractability, amenability, adaptability, facility, give, **suppleness**, willowiness, litheness, limberness; elasticity, resilience, springiness, resiliency, rubberiness; sponginess, pulpiness, doughiness, compressibility; malleability, moldability, fictility, sequacity; impressionability, susceptibility, responsiveness, receptiveness, sensibility, sensitiveness; formability, formativeness; extensibility, extendibility; agreeability; submissiveness

3 flaccidity, **flaccidness, flabbiness,** limpness, rubberiness, floppiness; looseness, laxness, laxity, laxation, relaxedness, relaxation

4 <comparisons> putty, clay, dough, blubber, rubber, wax, butter, soap, pudding; velvet, plush, satin, silk; wool, fleece; pillow, cushion; kapok; baby's bottom; puff; fluff, floss, flue; down, feathers, feather bed, eiderdown, swansdown, thistledown; breeze, zephyr; foam; snow

5 **softening,** softening-up; easing, padding, cushioning; mollifying, mollification; relaxation, laxation; mellowing; tenderizing

VERBS **6** **soften,** soften up; unsteel; ease, cushion; gentle, mollify, milden; subdue, tone down; mellow; tenderize; relax, laxate, loosen; limber, limber up, supple; massage, knead, plump, plump up, fluff, fluff up, shake up; mash, whip, smash, squash, pulp, pulverize; masticate, macerate; thaw, liquefy

7 **yield, give,** relent, relax, bend, unbend, give way; comply; mellow, loosen up, chill out; submit

ADJS **8** **soft,** nonresistive, nonrigid; mild, gentle, easy, delicate, tender; complaisant; mellow, mellowy; **softened,** mollified; whisper-soft, soft as putty, soft as clay, soft as dough, soft as a kiss, soft as a whisper, soft as a baby's bottom

9 pliant, **pliable, flexible**, flexile, flexuous, plastic, elastic, ductile, sequacious, facile, tractile, tractable, yielding, giving, bending; adaptable, malleable, moldable, shapable, fabricable, fictile; compliant, submissive; impressionable, impressible, susceptible, responsive, receptive, sensitive; formable, formative; bendable; **supple**, willowy, limber; lithe, lithesome, lissome, double-jointed, loose-limbed, whippy; resilient, springy; extensile, extensible, extendible; putty, waxy, doughy, pasty, puttylike

10 flaccid, **flabby,** limp, rubbery, flimsy, floppy; loose, lax, relaxed, slack, unstrung

11 **spongy,** pulpy, pithy, medullary; edematous; foamy; juicy

12 **pasty, doughy;** loamy, clayey, argillaceous

13 **squashy,** squishy, squushy, squelchy, mooshy

14 **fluffy,** flossy, **downy,** pubescent, feathery; fleecy, flocculent, woolly, lanate; furry

15 **velvety,** velvetlike, velutinous; plushy, plush; **satiny,** satinlike; cottony; **silky,** silken, silklike, sericeous, soft as silk

16 **softening,** easing; subduing, mollifying, emollient; demulcent; relaxing, loosening

ADVS **17** **softly,** gently, easily, delicately, tenderly; compliantly, submissively

1048 ELASTICITY

<flexible, returning to shape>

NOUNS **1** **elasticity,** resilience, resiliency, give; snap, bounce, bounciness; **stretch**, stretchiness, stretchability; extensibility; tone, tonus, tonicity; **spring,** springiness; rebound; flexibility; adaptability, responsiveness; buoyancy, buoyance; liveliness

2 **stretching;** extension; distension; **stretch,** tension, strain

3 **elastic;** elastomer; **rubber,** gum elastic; stretch fabric, latex, spandex; gum, chewing gum; whalebone, baleen; rubber band, elastic band; rubber ball, handball, tennis ball; sponge rubber, crepe rubber; spring; springboard; trampoline; racket, battledore; gutta-percha; neoprene; shock absorber

VERBS **4** **stretch;** extend; distend; flex

5 **give,** yield; bounce, spring, snap back, recoil, rebound, spring back
6 **elasticize;** rubberize, rubber; vulcanize, plasticize
ADJS 7 **elastic,** resilient, **springy,** bouncy; **stretchable, stretchy,** stretch; extensile; flexible; flexile; adaptable, adaptive, responsive; buoyant; lively; tensile
8 rubber, **rubbery,** rubberlike; rubberized

1049 TOUGHNESS

<strong, not easily damaged or broken>

NOUNS 1 **toughness,** resistance, **ruggedness;** strength, hardiness, vitality, stamina, sturdiness; stubbornness, stiffness; unbreakableness, unbreakability, infrangibility; cohesiveness, tenacity, viscidity; durability, lastingness; hardness; leatheriness, leatherlikeness; stringiness; staying power
2 <comparisons> leather; gristle, cartilage
VERBS 3 **toughen,** harden, stiffen, work-harden, temper, **strengthen**; season; be tough; endure, hang tough
ADJS 4 **tough, resistant;** shockproof, shock-resistant, impactproof, impact-resistant; tamper-proof, tamper-resistant, babyproof, childproof; stubborn, stiff; heavy-duty; hard as nails, tough as nails; strong, **hardy**, vigorous; cohesive, tenacious, viscid; durable, lasting; untiring; hard; chewy; leathery, leatherlike, coriaceous, tough as leather; sinewy, wiry; gristly, cartilaginous; stringy, fibrous; long-lasting
5 **unbreakable,** nonbreakable, infrangible, unshatterable, shatterproof, chip-proof, fractureproof; bulletproof, bombproof, fireproof; indestructible
6 **toughened,** hardened, tempered, annealed; seasoned; casehardened; vulcanized

1050 BRITTLENESS, FRAGILITY

<easily damaged or broken>

NOUNS 1 **brittleness, crispness,** crispiness; **fragility,** frailty, damageability, delicacy, flimsiness, breakability, breakableness, frangibility, fracturableness, crackability, crackableness, crunchability, crushability, crushableness; lacerability; fissility; friability, friableness, crumbliness, flakiness; vulnerableness, vulnerability; inelasticity
2 <comparisons> eggshell, old bone, piecrust, peanut brittle; matchwood, balsa, old paper, parchment, rice paper, dead leaf; glass, glass jaw, china, ice, icicle, glass house; house of cards; lamina, shale, slate, pottery
VERBS 3 **break,** shatter, fragment, fragmentize, fragmentate, **fall to pieces**, shard, fracture, chip off, flake, shiver, disintegrate
ADJS 4 **brittle, crisp,** crispy; **fragile,** frail, delicate, flimsy, breakable, frangible, crushable, crackable, crunchable, fracturable; lacerable; shatterable, shattery, shivery, splintery; friable, crumbly, flaky; fissile, scissile; brittle as glass; vulnerable; wafer-thin, papery; inelastic

1051 POWDERINESS, CRUMBLINESS

<easily crushed into tiny pieces>

NOUNS 1 **powderiness,** pulverulence, dustiness; chalkiness; **mealiness,** flouriness, branniness; efflorescence, bloom
2 **granularity, graininess,** granulation; sandiness, grittiness, gravelliness, sabulosity
3 **friability,** pulverableness, crispness, crumbliness, flakiness; brittleness
4 **pulverization,** comminution, trituration, attrition, detrition; levigation; reduction to powder, reductin to dust, pestling; fragmentation, sharding; brecciation; atomization, micronization; **powdering, crumbling,** flaking; abrasion; grinding, milling, grating, shredding; granulation, granulization; beating, pounding, shattering, flailing, mashing, smashing, crushing; disintegration, decomposition
5 **powder, dust,** chalk; dust ball, dust kitten, dust bunny, slut's wool, lint; efflorescence; **crumb**, crumble; meal, bran, flour, farina, grist; grits, groats; filings, raspings, sawdust; soot, smut; particle, particulate, particulates, airborne particles, air pollution; fallout; cosmic dust; dust cloud, dust devil; spore, pollen; pollen count
6 **grain,** granule, granulet; grit, sand; gravel, shingle; detritus, debris; breccia, collapse breccia; speck, mote, particle
7 **pulverizer,** comminutor, triturator, levigator; crusher; **mill; grinder;** granulator, pepper grinder, pepper mill; grater, cheese grater, nutmeg grater; shredder; pestle, mortar and pestle; masher; pounder; grindstone, millstone, quern, quernstone, muller; roller, steamroller; hammer; abrasive
8 koniology; konimeter
VERBS 9 **pulverize, powder,** comminute, triturate, contriturate, levigate, bray, pestle, disintegrate, reduce to powder, reduce to dust, grind to powder, grind to dust, grind up; fragment, shard, shatter; brecciate; atomize, micronize; **crumble**, crumb, chip, flake; granulate, granulize, grain; grind, grate, shred, abrade; mill, flour; beat,

pound, mash, smash, crush, crunch, flail, squash, scrunch, scrunch up; mince, kibble

10 <be reduced to powder> **powder**, come to dust, crumble, crumble to dust, disintegrate, fall to pieces, break up; effloresce; granulate, grain

ADJS 11 **powdery, dusty,** powder, pulverulent, pulverous, lutose; pulverized, pulverant, powdered, disintegrated, comminute, gone to dust, reduced to powder, dust-covered; particulate; ground, grated, pestled, milled, stone-ground, comminuted, triturated, levigated; sharded, crushed; fragmented; shredded; sifted; fine, impalpable; chalky, chalklike; mealy, floury, farinaceous; branny; furfuraceous, scaly, scurfy; flaky; detrited, detrital; scobiform, scobicular; efflorescent

12 **granular, grainy,** granulate, **granulated;** sandy, gritty, sabulous, arenarious, arenaceous, arenose; shingly, shingled, pebbled, pebbly; gravelly; breccial, brecciated; multigrain

13 pulverable, **pulverizable,** pulverulent, triturable; **friable,** crimp, crisp, **crumbly**

1052 MATERIALITY

<consisting of matter>

NOUNS 1 **materiality,** materialness; **corporeity,** corporality, corporeality, corporealness, bodiliness, embodiment, existence; substantiality, concreteness; **physicalness,** physicality; tangibility; palpability

2 **matter, material,** materiality, substance, stuff, hyle; raw material, organic matter; primal matter, initial substance, xylem; brute matter; element; chemical element; the four elements; earth, air, fire, water; elementary particle, fundamental particle; elementary unit, building block, unit of being, monad; constituent, component; atom; atomic particles; molecule; material world, physical world, real world, nature, natural world; hypostasis, substratum; plenum; antimatter

3 **body,** physical body, material body, corpus, anatomy, person, figure, **form,** frame, physique, carcass, bones, flesh, clay, clod, hulk; soma; torso, trunk; warm body

4 **object,** gadget, **article**, thing, material thing, affair, something, entity; whatsit, what's-its-name; something or other; artifact; inanimate object; animate being

5 <nonformal> **doodad**, thingum, thingamabob, thingumadad, thingy, thingumadoodle, thingamajig, thingumajig, thingumajigger, thingumaree, thingummy, dofunny, dojigger, dojiggy, domajig, domajigger, dohickey, doohickey, dowhacky, flumadiddle, gigamaree, gimmick, gizmo, dingus, hickey, jigger, hootmalalie, hootenanny, whatchy, widget, whatsis, whatsit, gismo, deely-bobber

6 **materialism,** physicism, epiphenomenalism, identity theory of mind, atomism, mechanism; physicalism, behaviorism, instrumentalism, pragmatism, pragmaticism; historical materialism, dialectical materialism, Marxism; positivism, logical positivism, positive philosophy, empiricism, naturalism; realism, natural realism, commonsense realism, commonsense philosophy, naïve realism, new realism, critical realism, representative realism, epistemological realism; substantialism; hylomorphism; hylotheism; hylozoism; worldliness, earthliness, animalism, secularism, temporality

7 **materialist,** physicist, atomist; historical materialist, dialectical materialist, Marxist; naturalist; realist, natural realist, commonsense realist, commonsense philosopher, epistemological realist; humanist, positivist; physical scientist

8 **materialization,** corporealization; substantialization, substantiation; **embodiment**, incorporation, personification, incarnation, manifestation; reincarnation, reembodiment, transmigration, metempsychosis

VERBS 9 **materialize**, corporalize; substantialize, substantify, substantiate; embody, body, incorporate, corporify, personify, incarnate; reincarnate, reembody, transmigrate; externalize

ADJS 10 **material,** materiate, hylic, substantial, tangible; corporeal, corporeous, corporal, **bodily; physical,** somatic, somatical, somatous; fleshly; worldly, earthly, here-and-now, secular, temporal, unspiritual, nonspiritual; empirical, spatiotemporal; objective, clinical

11 **embodied,** bodied, incorporated, incarnate

12 **materialist, materialistic,** atomistic, mechanist, mechanistic; Marxian, Marxist; naturalist, naturalistic, positivist, positivistic; commonsense, realist, realistic; hylotheistic; hylomorphous; hylozoic, hylozoistic

1053 IMMATERIALITY

<not consisting of matter>

NOUNS 1 **immateriality,** immaterialness; incorporeity, incorporeality, incorporealness, **bodilessness;** unsubstantiality, unsubstantialness; **intangibility**, impalpability, imponderability; inextension, nonextension; nonexteriority, nonexternality; unearthliness, unworldliness, ethereality, unreality; supernaturalism; spirituality, spiritualness, spirituousness, otherworldliness, ghostliness, shadowiness; occultism, the occult, occult phenomena; ghost-raising, ghost-hunting, ghostbusting; psychism, psychics, psychic research, psychical research, psychicism; spirit world, astral plane

2 incorporeal, incorporeity, immateriality, unsubstantiality

3 **immaterialism, idealism**, philosophical idealism, metaphysical idealism; objective idealism; absolute idealism; epistemological idealism; monistic idealism, pluralistic idealism; critical idealism; transcendental idealism; subjectivism; solipsism; subjective idealism; spiritualism; personalism; panpsychism, psychism, animism, hylozoism, animatism; Platonism, Platonic realism, Berkeleianism, Cambridge Platonism, Kantianism, Hegelianism, New England Transcendentalism; Neoplatonism; Platonic ideal, Platonic form, pure form, form, universal; transcendental object; transcendental

4 immaterialist, **idealist;** Berkeleian, Platonist, Hegelian, Kantian; Neoplatonist; spiritualist; psychist, panpsychist, animist; occultist; medium; ghost-raiser, ghost-hunter, ghostbuster

5 **dematerialization**; **disembodiment**, disincarnation; spiritualization

VERBS 6 **dematerialize**, immaterialize, unsubstantialize, insubstantialize, desubstantialize, **disembody,** disincarnate; spiritualize, spiritize; meditate

ADJS 7 **immaterial,** nonmaterial; unsubstantial, insubstantial, **intangible**, impalpable, imponderable; unextended, extensionless; incorporeal, incorporate, incorporeous; bodiless, unembodied, without body, asomatous; disembodied, disbodied, discarnate, decarnate, decarnated; metaphysical; unphysical, nonphysical; unfleshly; airy, ghostly, spectral, phantom, shadowy, ethereal; spiritual, astral, psychic, psychical; unearthly, unworldly, otherworldly, extramundane, transmundane; supernatural; occult; parapsychological

8 **idealist, idealistic,** immaterialist, immaterialistic; solipsistic; spiritualist, spiritualistic; panpsychist, panpsychistic; animist, animistic; Platonic, Platonistic, Berkeleian, Hegelian, Kantian; Neoplatonic, Neoplatonistic

1054 MATERIALS

<substance consisting of matter>

NOUNS 1 **materials,** substances, stuff, matter; **raw material,** staple, stock, grist, basic material; material resources, material means; store, supply; strategic materials; matériel; natural resource

2 <**building materials**> sticks and stones, lath and plaster, bricks and mortar, wattle and daub; roofing, roofage, tiles, shingles; walling, siding; flooring, pavement, paving material, paving, paving stone; masonry, stonework, flag, flagstone, ashlar, stone; covering materials; mortar, plasters; cement, concrete, cyclopean concrete, ferroconcrete, prestressed concrete, reinforced concrete, slag concrete, cinder concrete; brick, firebrick; cinder block, concrete block; clinker, adobe, clay; **tile,** tiling; glass, steel, slate, cobble, tar, asphalt, gravel

3 **wood** <see list>, lumber, timber, forest product; hardwood, softwood; stick, stick of wood, stave; billet; log, pole, post, beam, board, plank; deal; two-by-four, three-by-four; slab, puncheon; slat, splat, lath; boarding, timbering, timberwork, planking; lathing, lathwork; sheeting; paneling, panelboard, panelwork; plywood, plyboard; sheathing, sheathing board; siding, sideboard; weatherboard, clapboard; shingle, shake; driftwood; firewood, kindling, stovewood; cordwood; cord, cordage; brushwood; dead wood; pulpwood, sapwood, alburnum, heartwood, duramen; early wood, late wood, springwood, summerwood; drywall

4 cane, bamboo, rattan

5 **paper** <see list>, paper stock, stock; sheet, leaf, page; quire, ream, stationery; cardboard

6 **plastic** <see list>; thermoplastic; thermosetting plastic; resin plastic; cellulose plastic; protein plastic; cast plastic, molded plastic, extruded plastic; molding compounds; laminate; adhesive; plasticizer; **polymer** <see list>; **synthetic;** synthetic fabric, synthetic textile; synthetic rubber

VERBS 7 gather materials, procure materials; store, stock, stock up, lay in, restock; process, utilize

8 **paper**

bond paper
carbon paper
cardboard
computer paper
construction paper
crepe paper
fiberboard
foolscap
glossy paper
greaseproof paper
laminated paper
newsprint
onionskin
paper towel
posterboard
rag paper
rice paper
scratch paper
stationery
tissue paper
toilet paper (TP)
tracing paper
typing paper
watermarked paper
wax paper
wrapping paper
writing paper

9 **plastic**

acetate
acetate nitrate
acrylic
alkyd
aminoplast
Bakelite <tm>

casein plastic
cellophane
celluloid
cellulose acetate
cellulose ether
cellulose nitrate
cellulosic
coumarone-indene
epoxy
fluorocarbon plastic
Formica <tm>
furane
laminate
lignin
Lucite <tm>
melamine
multiresin
Mylar <tm>
neoprene
nitrate
nylon
phenolic
phenolic urea
Plexiglas <tm>
polyester
polyethylene
polymeric amide
polypropylene
polystyrene
polyurethane
polyvinyl chloride (PVC)
polyvinyl-formaldehyde
resinoid
silicone resin
Styrofoam <tm>
Teflon <tm>
terpene
tetrafluoroethylene
urea
urea formaldehyde
vinyl
Vinylite <tm>

10 **polymer**
addition polymer
atactic polymer
chloroprene rubber
condensation polymer
copolymer
epoxide resin
homopolymer
isoprene rubber
isotactic polymer
macromolecule
monomer
nylon
plasticizer
Plexiglas <tm>
polycarbonate
polyester
polyethylene, polyethene, polythene
polypropylene, polypropene
polystyrene
polyurethane
polyvinyl chloride (PVC)
resin
stereoregular polymer
syndiotactic polymer
Teflon <tm>
thermosetting plastic
vulcanite

11 **wood**
acacia
alder
applewood
ash
aspen
balsa
balsam
banyan
bass, basswood
beech, beechwood
betel palm
birch
boxwood
brierwood
burl
buttonwood
cacao
cedar, cedarwood
cherry
chestnut
citrus
coconut
cork
cottonwood
cypress
dogwood
ebony
elder
elm, elmwood
eucalyptus
fig
fir
fruit wood
gum, gumwood
hawthorn
hazel, hazelwood
hemlock
hickory
ironwood
juniper
knotty pine
lancewood
larch
laurel
lignum vitae
linden
loblolly pine
locust
logwood
magnolia
mahogany
maple
mesquite
monkeypod
myrtle
oak
olive
palm
pear
pecan
pine
poplar
redwood
rosewood
rubber
sandalwood
satinwood
sequoia
sisal
sour gum
spruce
sugar maple
sumac
sycamore
teak, teakwood
tulipwood
tupelo
walnut
willow
yew
zebrawood

1055 INORGANIC MATTER

<substance not consisting of living matter>

NOUNS 1 **inorganic matter,** nonorganic matter; inanimate matter, lifeless matter, **nonliving matter,** unorganized matter, inert matter, dead matter, brute matter; mineral kingdom, mineral world; matter, mere matter

2 **inanimateness,** inanimation, **lifelessness,** inertness; insensibility, insentience, insensateness, senselessness, unconsciousness, unfeelingness

3 inorganic chemistry; chemicals

ADJS 4 **inorganic,** unorganic, nonorganic; mineral, nonbiological; nonbiodegradable; unorganized, inorganized; material

5 **inanimate,** inanimated, unanimated, exanimate, azoic, nonliving, dead, lifeless, soulless; inert; insentient, unconscious, nonconscious, insensible, insensate, senseless, unfeeling; dumb, mute

1056 OILS, LUBRICANTS

<liquid, combustible substances>

NOUNS 1 **oil; fat,** lipid, grease; sebum, tallow, vegetable oil, animal oil; ester, glyceryl ester; fixed oil, fatty oil, nonvolatile oil, volatile oil, essential oil; saturated fat, hydrogenated fat, unsaturated fat, polyunsaturated fat; drying oil, semidrying oil, nondrying oil; glycerol, wax

2 **lubricant,** lubricator, lubricating oil, lubricating agent, antifriction; graphite, plumbago, black lead; silicone; glycerin, glycerine; wax, cerate; mucilage, mucus, synovia; spit, spittle, saliva; Vaseline <tm>, petroleum jelly, K-Y <tm>; soap, lather

3 **ointment, balm,** salve, lotion, cream, unguent, unguentum, inunction, inunctum, unction, chrism, chrisom; soothing syrup, lenitive, embrocation, demulcent, emollient, liniment; spikenard, nard; balsam; pomade, pomatum, brilliantine; styling mousse, styling gel; cold cream, hand lotion, face cream, lanolin; eyewash, collyrium; sunblock, suntan lotion, tanning cream

4 **petroleum,** rock oil, fossil oil, shale oil, coal oil; **fuel;** fuel oil; mineral oil; crude oil, crude; motor oil; gasoline, gas; kerosene, paraffin

5 **oiliness, greasiness,** unctuousness, unctiousness, unctuosity; fattiness, fatness, pinguidity; richness; sebaceousness; adiposis, adiposity; soapiness, saponacity, saponaceousness; smoothness, slickness, sleekness, slipperiness, **lubricity**; waxiness; creaminess

6 **lubrication,** lubricating, oiling, greasing, lubrification; nonfriction; lubricity, lube, grease job, lube job; anointment, unction, inunction; chrismatory, chrismation

7 lubritorium, lubritory; grease rack, grease pit; lubricator, oilcan, grease gun

VERBS 8 **oil,** grease; **lubricate,** lubrify; anoint, salve, unguent, embrocate, dress, pour oil on, pour balm upon; smear, daub; slick, slick on; pomade; lard; glycerolate, glycerinate, glycerinize; wax, beeswax; smooth the way, soap the way, grease the wheels; soap, lather

ADJS 9 **oily, greasy;** unctuous, unctional; unguinous; **oleaginous,** oleic; unguentary, **unguent,** unguentous; chrismal, chrismatory; fat, **fatty,** adipose; pinguid, pinguedinous, pinguescent; rich; sebaceous; blubbery, tallowy, suety; lardy, lardaceous; buttery, butyraceous; soapy, saponaceous; paraffinic; mucoid; smooth, slick, sleek, slippery; creamy; waxy, waxen, cereous, cerated

10 **lubricant,** lubricating, **lubricative,** lubricatory, lubricational; lenitive, unguentary, emollient, soothing, moisturizing

COMBINING FORMS 11 ole-, oleo-, oli-; lip-, lipo-, lipar-, liparo-; cer-, cero-; sebo-, sebi-; steat-, steato-; petr-, petro-, petri-

1057 RESINS, GUMS

<semisolid sticky substances>

NOUNS 1 **resin; gum,** gum resin; oleoresin; hard resin, varnish resin, vegetable resin; synthetic resin, plastic, resinoid; resene; **rosin,** colophony, colophonium, colophonone, resinate

VERBS 2 resin, resinize, resinate; rosin

ADJS 3 **resinous,** resinic, resiny; resinoid; rosiny; **gummy,** gummous, gumlike; pitchy

1058 MINERALS, METALS

<substance formed under ground>

NOUNS 1 **mineral** <see list>; inorganic substance; extracted matter, extracted material; mineral world, mineral kingdom; mineral resources; mineraloid, gel mineral, mineral aggregate; mineralization; crystalline element, crystalline compound; inorganic mineral, natural mineral, silicate, carbonate, oxide, sulfide, sulfate

2 **ore** <see list>, mineral; mineral-bearing material; unrefined mineral, untreated mineral; natural mineral, native mineral

3 **metal, metallic element** <see list>; metallic; native metal, alkali metal, earth metal, alkaline-earth metal, noble metal, precious metal, base metal, rare metal, rare-earth metal, rare-earth element; metalloid, semimetal, nonmetal; gold bullion, silver bullion; gold dust; leaf metal, metal leaf, metal foil; metalwork, metalware; metallicity, metalleity

4 **alloy,** alloyage, fusion, compound; amalgam; shape-memory alloy

5 **cast,** casting; ingot, bullion; pig, sow; sheet metal; button, gate, regulus; wrought iron

6 **mine,** pit; **quarry;** diggings, workings; open cut, opencast; bank; shaft; coalmine, colliery; strip mine; gold mine, silver mine

7 **deposit,** mineral deposit, pay dirt; **vein, lode,** seam, dike, ore bed; shoot, chute, ore chute; chimney; stock; placer, placer deposit, placer gravel; country rock; lodestuff, gangue, matrix, veinstone

8 **mining;** coal mining, gold mining; long-wall mining; room-and-pillar mining; strip mining; placer mining; hydraulic mining; prospecting; mining claim, lode claim, placer claim; gold fever; gold rush

9 **miner,** mineworker, pitman; coalminer, collier <Brit>; gold miner, gold digger; gold panner; placer miner; quarry miner; prospector, desert rat, sourdough; wildcatter; forty-niner; hand miner, rockman, powderman, driller, draw man; butty

10 **mineralogy;** mineralogical chemistry; crystallography; petrology, petrography, micropetrography; geology; mining geology, mining engineering; geoengineering

11 **metallurgy;** metallography, metallurgical chemistry, metallurgical engineering, physical metallurgy, powder metallurgy, electrometallurgy, hydrometallurgy, pyrometallurgy, production metallurgy, extractive metallurgy

12 **mineralogist; metallurgist,** electrometallurgist,

metallurgical engineer; petrologist, petrographer; geologist; mining engineer

VERBS 13 mineralize; petrify

14 **mine;** quarry; pan, pan for gold; prospect; hit pay dirt; mine out

ADJS 15 **mineral;** inorganic; mineralized, petrified; asbestine, carbonous, graphitic, micaceous, alabastrine, quartzose, silicic; sulfurous, sulfuric; ore-bearing, ore-forming

16 **metal, metallic,** metallike, metalline, metalloid, metalloidal, metalliform; semimetallic; nonmetallic; metallo-organic, metallorganic, organometallic; bimetallic, trimetallic; metalliferous, metalbearing

17 **metal-like**; brass, brassy, brazen; bronze, bronzy; copper, coppery, cuprous, cupreous; gold, golden, gilt, aureate; nickel, nickelic, nickelous, nickeline; silver, silvery; iron, ironlike, ferric, ferrous, ferruginous; steel, steely; tin, tinny; lead, leaden; pewter, pewtery; mercurial, mercurous, quicksilver; gold-filled, gold-plated, silver-plated

18 **mineralogical, metallurgical,** petrological, crystallographic

19 **metallic element**

actinium
aluminum
americium
antimony
barium
beryllium
bismuth
cadmium
cerium
cesium
chromium
cobalt
copper
dysprosium
erbium
europium
gadolinium
gallium
germanium
gold
hafnium
holmium
indium
iridium
iron
lanthanum
lawrencium
lead
lithium
lutetium
magnesium
manganese
mercury
molybdenum
neodymium
nickel
niobium
osmium
palladium
phosphorus
platinum
polonium
potassium
praseodymium
promethium
protactinium
quicksilver
radium
rhenium
rhodium
rubidium
ruthenium
samarium
scandium
silver
sodium
strontium
tantalum
technetium
terbium
thallium
thorium
thulium
tin
titanium
tungsten
uranium
vanadium
ytterbium
yttrium
zinc
zirconium

20 **mineral**

alabaster
amphibole
anhydrite
antimony
apatite
argillite
arsenic
asbestos
asphalt
augite
azurite
barite
bauxite
bitumen
boron
brimstone
bromine
brookite
brucite
calcite
carbon
carnelian
chalcedony
chert
chlorite
chromite
clay
coal
coke
corundum
cryolite
diamond
diatomite
dolomite
elaterite
emery
epidote
epsomite
feldspar
flint
fluorite
fluorspar
fool's gold
garnet
glauconite
graphite
gypsum
holosiderite
hornblende
ilmenite
iolite
iron pyrites
jet
kaolinite
kyanite
lazurite
lignite
lime
magnesite
malachite
maltha
marcasite
marl
meerschaum
mica
microlite
microlith
mineral charcoal
mineral coal
mineral oil
mineral salt
mineral tallow
mineral tar
mineral wax
molybdenite
monazite
moonstone
obsidian
olivine
orthoclase
ozokerite
peat
peridot
perlite
phosphate rock
phosphorus
pitchblende
pumice
pumicite
pyrite
pyroxene
quartz
realgar
red clay
rhodonite
rock salt
serpentine
siderite
silica
silicate
silicon
sodalite
spar
spinel
sulfur
talc
tellurium
topaz

tourmaline
tripoli
umber
vermiculite
wollastonite
wulfenite
zeolite
zircon

21 ore

amblygonite
argentite
arsenopyrite, mispickel
azurite
barite
bauxite
beryl
bornite
calaverite
carnotite
cassiterite
celestite
cerussite
chalcocite
chalcopyrite
chromite
cinnabar
cuprite
galena
garnierite
goethite
hematite
hemimorphite
hydrozincite
ilmenite
iron ore
ironstone
limonite
lodestone
magnetite
malachite
molybdenite
monazite
niobite
pitchblende
pyrargyrite
pyrite
scheelite
siderite
smithsonite
sphalerite
stibnite
sylvanite
tetrahedrite
tinstone
turgite
uranitite
wolframite
zincite

1059 ROCK

<hard substances on earth's surface>

NOUNS 1 **rock, stone** <see list>; living rock, rock formation; **igneous rock,** plutonic rock, abyssal rock, hypabyssal rock, magmatic rock, acid rock, mafic rock, felsic rock, ultrabasic rock, ultramafic rock; volcanic rock, extrusive rock, effusive rock, scoria; magma, intrusive rock; granite, basalt, porphyry, lava, aa, pahoehoe <Hawaii>; **sedimentary rock,** lithified sediment, stratified rock, clastic rock, nonclastic rock; limestone, sandstone; **metamorphic rock,** schist, gneiss; conglomerate, pudding stone, breccia, rubble, rubblestone, scree, talus, tuff, tufa, brash; sarsen, sarsen stone, druid stone; monolith; crag, craig; bedrock; mantlerock, regolith; saprolite, geest, laterite; building stone

2 **sand;** grain of sand; sands of the sea; sand pile, sand dune, sand hill; sand reef, sandbar

3 **gravel,** shingle, chesil <Brit>

4 **pebble,** pebblestone, gravelstone; jackstone, checkstone; fingerstone; slingstone; drakestone; spall

5 **boulder,** river boulder, shore boulder, glacial boulder

6 **sediment,** geological sediment, organic sediment, inorganic sediment, oceanic sediment, alluvial deposit, lake sediment, glacial deposit, eolian deposit; mud, sand, silt, clay, loess; rock, boulder, stone, gravel, granule, pebble

7 **precious stone, gem, gemstone** <see list>; stone: crystal, crystal lattice, crystal system; semiprecious stone; gem of the first water; birthstone

8 petrification, petrifaction, lithification, crystallization; **rock cycle**, sedimentation, deposition, consolidation, cementation, compaction, magmatism, metamorphosis, recrystallization, foliation

9 **geology**, geoscience, petrology, crystallography; petrochemistry; petrogenesis; fracking

VERBS 10 petrify, lithify, crystallize, turn to stone; harden

ADJS 11 **stone, rock,** lithic; petrified; petrogenic, petrescent; adamant, adamantine; flinty, flintlike; marbly, marblelike; granitic, granitelike; slaty, slatelike

12 **stony, rocky,** lapideous; stonelike, rocklike, lithoid, lithoidal; sandy, gritty; gravelly, shingly, shingled; pebbly, pebbled; porphyritic, trachytic; crystal, crystalline; bouldery, rock-strewn, boulder-strewn, rock-studded, rock-ribbed; craggy; monolithic

COMBINING FORMS 13 petr-, petro-, petri-, saxi-, lith-, litho-, -lith; grano-; blast-, blasto-, -blast, orth-, ortho-, par-; para-; -clast; -lithic, litic; -clastic; crystall-, crystallo-

14 gemstone

achroite
agate
alexandrite
amethyst
aquamarine
beryl
black opal
bloodstone
brilliant
carbuncle
carnelian
cat's-eye
chalcedony
chrysoberyl
chrysolite
chrysoprase
citrine
coral
demantoid, Uralian emerald
diamond
emerald
fire opal
garnet
girasol
harlequin opal
heliotrope
hyacinth
jacinth
jade, jadestone
jargoon
jasper
kunzite
lapis lazuli
moonstone
morganite
onyx
opal
pearl
peridot
plasma
rhodolite
rose quartz
ruby
sapphire
sard

sardonyx
siberite
spinel, spinel ruby
sunstone
tanzanite
tiger's eye
topaz
tourmaline
turquoise
water sapphire
white sapphire
zircon

15 **rock, stone**
anthraconite
aplite
basalt
beetlestone
boulder
brimstone
brownstone
buhr, buhrstone
cairngorm
chalk
clinkstone
dendrite
diabase
diorite
dolerite
dolmen
dolomite
dripstone
eaglestone
emery
fieldstone
flag, flagstone
flint
floatstone
freestone
geode
gneiss
goldstone
granite
granulite
graywacke
greenstone
grit
gritrock, gritstone
hairstone
hoarstone
ironstone
lava
limestone
lodestone
Lydian stone
marble
megalith
menhir
milkstone
monolith
mudstone
obsidian
omphalos
pitchstone
porphyry
pumice
quarrystone
quartz
quartzite
rance
rottenstone
sandstone
serpentine
shale
slab
slate
stone
smokestone
snakestone
soapstone
stalactite
stalagmite
starstone
steatite
stinkstone
tinstone
touchstone
trap, traprock
tufa
wacke
whitestone

1060 CHEMISTRY, CHEMICALS

<science of substances and their makeup>

NOUNS 1 **chemistry,** chemical science, science of substances, science of matter; **chemistry (branches)** <see list>

2 **chemical element** <see list>, element; chemical symbol; table of elements, periodic table, periodic table of elements; radical group; free radical, diradical; ion, anion, cation; atom; molecule, macromolecule; trace element, microelement, micronutrient, minor element; chemical, **chemical compound;** organic chemical, biochemical, inorganic chemical; fine chemicals, heavy chemicals; agent, reagent; metal, nonmetal, semimetal, metalloid, heavy metal, alkali metal, noble metal; alkaline-earth element, transition element, noble gas, rare-earth element, lanthanide, actinide, transuranic element, supertransuranic element, superheavy element; inert gas, rare gas; period, short period, long period; family, group; s-block, p-block, d-block, f-block; chemical equation

3 **acid;** hydracid, oxyacid, sulfacid; acidity; **base,** alkali, nonacid; pH; neutralizer, antacid; alkalinity

4 **valence,** valency, positive valence, negative valence; monovalence, univalence, bivalence, trivalence, tervalence, quadrivalence, tetravalence, multivalence, polyvalence; covalence, electrovalence

5 **atomic weight,** atomic mass, atomic volume, mass number; **molecular weight,** molecular mass, molecular volume; atomic number, valence number

6 chemicalization, **chemical process** <see list>, chemical action, chemism; chemical apparatus, beaker, Bunsen burner, burette, centrifuge, condenser, crucible, graduated cylinder, pipette, test tube

7 chemist, chemical scientist; agricultural chemist, analytical chemist, astrochemist, biochemist, inorganic chemist, organic chemist, physical chemist, physiochemist, theoretical chemist

VERBS 8 **chemicalize,** chemical; alkalize, alkalinize, alkalify; acidify, acidulate, acetify; borate, carbonate, chlorinate, hydrate, hydrogenate, hydroxylate, nitrate, oxidize, reduce, pepsinate, peroxidize, phosphatize, sulfate, sulfatize, sulfonate; calcify, carburize, deuterate, esterify, fluorinate, fluoridate, halogenate, tritrate; isomerize, metamerize, polymerize, copolymerize, homopolymerize; ferment, work; catalyze; electrolyze; bond, intercalate, invert, neutralize, ionize

ADJS 9 **chemical;** astrochemical, biochemical, chemicobiologic; physicochemical, physiochemical, chemicophysical, chemicobiological, chemicophysiologic, chemicophysiological, chemicodynamic, chemicoengineering, chemicomechanical, chemicomineralogical, chemicopharmaceutical, chemurgic, electrochemical, iatrochemical, chemotherapeutic, chemotherapeutical, chemophysiologic, chemophysiological, macrochemical, microchemical, phytochemical, photochemical, radiochemical, thermochemical, zoochemical; organic, inorganic; elemental, elementary; acid; alkaline, alkali, nonacid, basic; isomeric, isomerous, metameric, metamerous, heteromerous, polymeric, polymerous, copolymeric, copolymerous, monomeric, monomerous, dimeric, dimerous

10 valent; univalent, monovalent, monatomic, bivalent, trivalent, tervalent, quadrivalent, tetravalent, multivalent, polyvalent; covalent, electrovalent

COMBINING FORMS 11 chem-, chemo-, chemi-, chemic-, chemico-; -mer, -merous, -meric; -valent

12 **chemical element**

actinium (Ac)
aluminum (Al)
americium (Am)
antimony (Sb)
argon (Ar, A)
arsenic (As)
astatine (At)
barium (Ba)
berkelium (Bk)
beryllium (Be)
bismuth (Bi)
boron (B)
bromine (Br)
cadmium (Cd)
calcium (Ca)
californium (Cf)
carbon (C)
cerium (Ce)
cesium (Cs)
chlorine (Cl)
chromium (Cr)
cobalt (Co)
copper (Cu)
curium (Cm)
dysprosium (Dy)
einsteinium (Es, E)
erbium (Er)
europium (Eu)
fermium (Fm)
fluorine (F)
francium (Fr)
gadolinium (Gd)
gallium (Ga)
germanium (Ge)
gold (Au)
hafnium (Hf)
helium (He)
holmium (Ho)
hydrogen (H)
indium (In)
iodine (I)
iridium (Ir)
iron (Fe)
krypton (Kr)
lanthanum (La)
lawrencium (Lw)
lead (Pb)
lithium (Li)
lutetium (Lu)
magnesium (Mg)
manganese (Mn)
mendelevium (Md, Mv)
mercury (Hg)
molybdenum (Mo)
neodymium (Nd)
neon (Ne)
neptunium (Np)
nickel (Ni)
niobium (Nb)
nitrogen (N)
nobelium (No)
osmium (Os)
oxygen (O)
palladium (Pd)
phosphorus (P)
platinum (Pt)
plutonium (Pu)
polonium (Po)
potassium (K)
praseodymium (Pr)
promethium (Pm)
protactinium (Pa)
radium (Ra)
radon (Rn)
rhenium (Re)
rhodium (Rh)
rubidium (Rb)
ruthenium (Ru)
samarium (Sm)
scandium (Sc)
selenium (Se)
silicon (Si)
silver (Ag)
sodium (Na)
strontium (Sr)
sulfur (S)
tantalum (Ta)
technetium (Tc)
tellurium (Te)
terbium (Tb)
thallium (Tl)
thorium (Th)
thulium (Tm)
tin (Sn)
titanium (Ti)
tungsten, wolfram (W)
unnihexium (Unh)
unnilpentium, hahnium (Unp)
unnilquadrium, rutherfordium (Unq)
uranium (U)
vanadium (V)
xenon (Xe)
ytterbium (Yb)
yttrium (Y)
zinc (Zn)
zirconium (Zr)

13 **chemical process**

acetification
acidification, acidulation
alkalization, alkalinization
aromatization
carbonation
catalysis
chain reaction
chlorination
condensation
copolymerization
cyclization
electrolysis
electrophilic reaction
fermentation, ferment
geometric isomerization
heterolysis
heterolytic fission
homolysis
homolytic fission
homopolymerization
hydration
hydrogenation
hydroxylation
ionization
isomerization
isotope effect
metamerization
neutralization
nitration
nucleophilic reaction
optical isomerization
oxidation
oxidization
phosphatization
photochemical reaction
polymerization
position isomerization
pyrolysis
radiochemical reaction
reduction
ring opening
saturization
sulfation
sulfatization
sulfonation
synthesis
tautoisomerization

14 **chemistry (branches)**

actinochemistry
agricultural chemistry
alchemy, alchemistry
analytical chemistry
applied chemistry
astrochemistry
atomic chemistry
biochemistry
biogeochemistry
business chemistry
capillary chemistry
catalysis
chemiatry
chemical dynamics
chemical engineering
chemical physics
chemicobiology
chemicoengineering
chemophysiology
chemurgy
colloid chemistry
colorimetry, colorimetric analysis
crystallography
cytochemistry
electrochemistry
engineering chemistry
galactochemistry
galvanochemistry
geochemistry
histochemistry
hydrochemistry
iatrochemistry
immunochemistry
industrial chemistry
inorganic chemistry
lithochemistry
macrochemistry
magnetochemistry
metachemistry
metallurgy
microchemistry
mineralogical chemistry

natural product chemistry
neurochemistry
nuclear chemistry
organic chemistry
pathological chemistry, pathochemistry
petrochemistry
pharmaceutical chemistry
phonochemistry
photochemistry
physical chemistry, physiochemistry, physiological chemistry
phytochemistry
piezochemistry
pneumatochemistry
polymer chemistry
psychobiochemistry, psychochemistry
pure chemistry
quantum chemistry
radiochemistry
soil chemistry
spectrochemistry
stereochemistry
structural chemistry
surface chemistry
synthetic chemistry
technochemistry
theoretical chemistry
thermochemistry
topochemistry
ultramicrochemistry
zoochemistry, zoochemy
zyochemistry, zymurgy

1061 LIQUIDITY
<being liquid>

NOUNS 1 **liquidity, fluidity,** fluidness, liquidness, liquefaction; wateriness; rheuminess, runniness; juiciness, sappiness, succulence; milkiness, lactescence; lactation; chylifaction, chylification; serosity; suppuration; moisture, wetness; fluency, flow, flowage, flux, fluxion, fluxility; circulation; turbulence, turbidity, turbulent flow; streamline flow; hemorrhage; secretion; liquid state; solubleness; fluid mechanics, hydrology

2 **fluid, liquid;** liquor, drink, beverage; liquid extract, fluid extract, condensation; juice, sap, latex, extract; milk, whey, buttermilk, ghee; water; body fluid, blood; stock, meat juice, gravy, sauce, soup; semiliquid; fluid mechanics, hydraulics; solvent, liquefier, liquefacient; solution, infusion, decoction

3 flowmeter, fluidmeter, hydrometer, sphygmomanometer

ADJS 4 **fluid,** fluidal, fluidic, fluent, **flowing,** fluxible, fluxile, fluxional, fluxionary, runny; circulatory, circulation, turbid; **liquid,** liquidy; watery; juicy, sappy, succulent, moist; wet; uncongealed, unclotted; rheumy; bloody; liquefied, liquefying, liquefiable

5 **milky,** lacteal, lacteous, lactic; lactescent, lactiferous; milk, milch

1062 SEMILIQUIDITY
<somewhat liquid>

NOUNS 1 **semiliquidity,** semifluidity; butteriness, creaminess; pulpiness

2 **viscosity,** viscidity, viscousness, slabbiness, lentor; thickness, spissitude, heaviness, stodginess; **stickiness,** tackiness, glutinousness, glutinosity, toughness, tenaciousness, tenacity, adhesiveness, clinginess, clingingness, gumminess, gauminess, gumlikeness; ropiness, stringiness; clamminess, sliminess, mucilaginousness; gooeyness, gunkiness; gluiness, gluelikeness; syrupiness, treacliness <Brit>; gelatinousness, jellylikeness, gelatinity, gelation; colloidality; doughiness, pastiness; thickening, curdling, clotting, coagulation, incrassation, inspissation, clabbering, loppering, lobbering, jellification

3 **mucosity,** mucidness, mucousness, pituitousness, snottiness; **sliminess**

4 **muddiness,** muckiness, miriness, slushiness, sloshiness, sludginess, sloppiness, slobbiness, slabbiness, squashiness, squelchiness, ooziness; **turbidity,** turbidness, dirtiness

5 **semiliquid,** semifluid; goo, goop, gook, gunk, glop, sticky mess, gaum; paste, pap, pudding, putty, butter, cream; pulp; jelly, gelatin, gelatine, jell, gel, jam, agar, isinglass; glue; size; gluten; mucilage; mucus; dough, batter; mousse, syrup, molasses, treacle <Brit>, honey; egg white, albumen, glair; starch, cornstarch; curd, clabber, bonnyclabber; gruel, porridge, loblolly; soup, gumbo, gravy, puréepulp; yogurt

6 gum, chewing gum, bubblegum; chicle, chicle gum; ABC gum

7 **emulsion,** emulsoid; emulsification; emulsifier; **colloid,** colloider

8 **mud, muck,** mire, slush, slosh, sludge, slob <Irl>, squash, swill, slime; slop, ooze; clay, slip; gumbo; gook, gunk, glop, guck

9 mud puddle, puddle, loblolly, slop; mudhole, slough, muckhole, chuckhole, chughole; hog wallow

VERBS 10 **emulsify,** emulsionize; colloid, colloidize; cream; churn, whip, beat up; thicken, inspissate, incrassate, curdle, clot, coagulate, congeal, clabber, lopper; jell, jelly, jellify, gel

ADJS 11 **semiliquid,** semifluid, semifluidic; buttery; creamy; emulsive, colloidal; pulpy; half-frozen, half-melted

12 **viscous, viscid,** viscose, slabby; thick, heavy, stodgy, soupy, thickened, inspissated, incrassated; curdled, clotted, grumous, coagulated, clabbered, loppered; **sticky, tacky,** tenacious, adhesive, clingy, clinging, tough; gluey, gluelike, glutinous, glutenous, glutinose; gumbo, gumbolike; gummy, gaumy, gummous, gumlike, syrupy; treacly <Brit>; ropy, stringy; mucilaginous, clammy, slimy, slithery; gooey, gunky, gloppy, goopy, gooky; gelatinous, jellylike, jellied, jelled; tremelloid,

tremellose; glairy; doughy, pasty; starchy, amylaceous; pulpy, soft, mushy

13 **mucous,** muculent, mucoid, mucinous, pituitous, phlegmy, snotty; mucific, muciferous

14 **slimy; muddy,** miry, mucky, slushy, sloshy, sludgy, sloppy, slobby, slabby, splashy, squashy, squishy, squelchy, oozy, sloughy, plashy, sposhy; **turbid,** dirty

1063 PULPINESS

<pulverized or mixed with water>

NOUNS 1 **pulpiness,** pulpousness; softness; flabbiness; **mushiness,** mashiness, squashiness, creaminess; pastiness, doughiness; sponginess, pithiness; fleshiness, overripeness, succulence

2 **pulp, paste, mash,** mush, smash, squash, crush; pudding, porridge, sponge; sauce, butter; poultice, cataplasm, plaster; pith; paper pulp, wood pulp, sulfate pulp, sulfite pulp, rag pulp; pulpwood; pulp lead, white lead; dental pulp, tooth pulp

3 **pulping,** pulpification, pulpefaction; blending, steeping; digestion; **maceration,** mastication

4 **pulper,** pulpifier, macerator, pulp machine, digester; **masher,** smasher, potato masher, ricer, beetle; blender, food processor, food mill

VERBS 5 **pulp,** pulpify; **macerate,** masticate, chew; regurgitate; mash, smash, squash, crush

ADJS 6 **pulpy,** pulpous, pulpal, pulpar, pulplike, pulped; **pasty,** doughy; pultaceous; mushy; macerated, masticated, chewed; regurgitated; squashy, squelchy, squishy; soft, flabby; fleshy, succulent; spongy, pithy

1064 LIQUEFACTION

<making or becoming liquid>

NOUNS 1 **liquefaction, liquefying,** liquidizing, liquidization, fluidification, fluidization; liquescence, liquescency, deliquescence, deliquiation, deliquium; solution, dissolution, dissolving; infusion, soaking, steeping, brewing; melting, thawing, running, fusing, fusion; decoagulation, unclotting; solubilization; colliquation; lixiviation, percolation, leaching

2 **solubility,** solubleness, dissolvability, dissolvableness, dissolubility, dissolubleness; meltability, fusibility

3 **solution;** decoction, infusion, mixture; chemical solution; lixivium, leach, leachate; suspension, colloidal suspension; emulsion, gel, aerosol

4 **solvent** <see list>, dissolvent, dissolver, dissolving agent, resolvent, resolutive, **thinner,** diluent; anticoagulant; liquefier, liquefacient; menstruum; universal solvent, alkahest; flux

VERBS 5 **liquefy, liquidize,** liquesce, fluidify, fluidize; melt, run, thaw, colliquate; melt down; fuse, flux; deliquesce; dissolve, solve; thin, cut; solubilize; hold in solution; unclot, decoagulate; leach, lixiviate, percolate; infuse, decoct, steep, soak, brew

ADJS 6 **liquefied,** melted, molten, thawed; unclotted, decoagulated; in solution, in suspension, liquescent, deliquescent; colloidal

7 **liquefying,** liquefactive; colliquative, melting, fusing, thawing; **dissolving,** dissolutive, dissolutional

8 **solvent,** dissolvent, resolvent, resolutive, thinning, cutting, diluent; alkahestic

9 liquefiable; **meltable,** fusible, thawable; **soluble,** dissolvable, dissoluble; water-soluble

10 **solvent**

acetone	gasoline
alcohol	glycerol
alkahest	glycol
amyl alcohol	kerosene
benzene, benzol	methyl alcohol
carbolic acid	naphtha
carbon disulfide	pentane
carbon tetrachloride	phenol
chloroform	propylene glycol
denatured alcohol	pyridine
ether	toluene
ethyl acetate	turpentine
ethyl chloride	urethane
furfural	xylene, xylol

1065 MOISTURE

<water or liquid in or on something>

NOUNS 1 **moisture,** damp, wet; **dampness, moistness,** moistiness, **wetness,** wettedness, wettishness, wateriness, humectation; soddenness, soppiness, soppingness, sogginess; swampiness, bogginess, marshiness; dewiness; mistiness, fogginess; raininess, pluviosity, showeriness; rainfall; exudation; secretion

2 **humidity,** humidness, dankness, dankishness, **mugginess,** closeness, stickiness, sweatiness; absolute humidity, relative humidity; dew point, saturation, saturation point; humidification

3 **water,** *aqua* <L>, *agua* <Sp>, *eau* <Fr>; Adam's ale, H2O; hydrol; hard water, soft water; heavy water; water supply, water system, waterworks; drinking water, tap water; rain water, rain; snowmelt, meltwater; groundwater, underground water, subsurface water, subterranean water; water table, aquifer, artesian basin, artesian spring, sinkhole; spring water, well water; seawater, salt water; limewater; fresh water; standing water; mineral water; soda water,

carbonated water; steam, water vapor; hydrosphere; hydrometeor; head, hydrostatic head; hydrothermal water; distilled water; wetting agent, wetting-out agent, liquidizer, moisturizer; humidifier; bottled water, commercially bottled water, designer water; water cycle, hydrological cycle, evaporation, transpiration, precipitation, runoff, percolation

4 **dew,** dewdrops, morning dew, night dew, evening damp; fog drip, false dew; guttation; haze, mist, fog, cloud

5 **sprinkle, spray,** sparge, shower; spindrift, spume, froth, foam; splash, plash, swash, slosh; splatter, spatter

6 **wetting, moistening,** dampening, damping; humidification; dewing, bedewing; watering, **irrigation;** hosing, wetting down, hosing down; sprinkling, spraying, spritzing, sparging, aspersion, aspergation; splashing, swashing, splattering, spattering; affusion, baptism; bath, bathing, rinsing, laving; **flooding**, drowning, inundation, deluge; immersion, submersion

7 **soaking,** soakage, soaking through, sopping, **drenching,** imbruement, sousing; ducking, dunking; soak, drench, souse; **saturation,** permeation; waterlogging; steeping, maceration, seething, infusion, brewing, imbuement; injection, impregnation; infiltration, percolation, leaching, lixiviation; pulping

8 **sprinkler,** sparger, sparge, sprayer, speed sprayer, concentrate sprayer, mist concentrate sprayer, spray, spray can, atomizer, aerosol; nozzle; aspergil, aspergillum; **shower,** shower bath, shower head, needle bath; syringe, fountain syringe, douche, enema, clyster; watering can; water pistol, water gun, squirt gun; lawn sprinkler; sprinkling system, sprinkler head; hydrant, irrigator

9 <water sciences> hygrology, hygrometry, psychrometry, hydrography, hydrology; hydraulics; hydrotherapy, hydrotherapeutics, taking the waters

10 <water instruments> hygrometer, hair hygrometer, hygrograph, hygrodeik, hygroscope, hygrothermograph; psychrometer, sling psychrometer; hydrostat; rain gauge, pluviometer; hydrograph; humidor; hygrostat

VERBS **11** **be damp**, not have a dry thread; drip, weep; seep, ooze, percolate; exude; sweat; secrete

12 **moisten, dampen,** moisturize, damp, **wet,** wet down; humidify, humect, humectate; **water, irrigate**; dew, bedew; sprinkle, besprinkle, spray, spritz, sparge, asperge; bepiss; splash, dash, swash, slosh, splatter, spatter, bespatter; dabble, paddle; slop, slobber; hose, hose down; syringe, douche; sponge; dilute, adulterate

13 **soak, drench,** imbrue, souse, sop, sodden; saturate, permeate; bathe, lave, wash, rinse, douche, flush; water-soak, waterlog; steep, seethe, macerate, infuse, imbue, brew, impregnate, inject, injest; infiltrate, percolate, leach, lixiviate

14 **flood,** float, **inundate, deluge,** turn to a lake, turn to a sea, swamp, whelm, overwhelm, drown; duck, dip, dunk; submerge; sluice, pour on, flow on; rain

ADJS **15** **moist,** moisty; **damp,** dampish; wet, wettish; undried, tacky; humid, dank, muggy, sticky; dewy, bedewed, roric, roriferous; rainy; marshy, swampy, fenny, boggy

16 **watery,** waterish, aqueous, aquatic; liquid; splashy, plashy, sloppy, swashy <Brit>; hydrous, hydrated; hydraulic; moist; hydrodynamic

17 **soaked,** drenched, soused, bathed, steeped, macerated; saturated, permeated; watersoaked, waterlogged; soaking, sopping; wringing wet, soaking wet, sopping wet, wet to the skin, like a drowned rat; sodden, soppy, **soggy,** soaky; dripping, dripping wet; dribbling, seeping, weeping, oozing; flooded, overflowed, whelmed, swamped, engulfed, inundated, deluged, drowned, submerged, submersed, immersed, dipped, dunked; awash, weltering

18 wetting, dampening, moistening, **watering**, humectant; drenching, soaking, sopping; **irrigational,** irriguous

19 hygric, hygrometric, hygroscopic, hygrophilous, hygrothermal

COMBINING FORMS **20** hydr-, hydro-, hydrat-, hydrato-, aqui-, aqua-; hygr-, hygro-

1066 DRYNESS

<lack of liquid or water>

NOUNS **1** **dryness, aridness,** aridity, waterlessness, siccity; **drought;** juicelessness, saplessness; thirst, thirstiness, dehydration, xerostomia; corkiness; watertightness, watertight integrity; parchedness

2 <comparisons> desert, dust, bone, parchment, stick, mummy, biscuit, cracker

3 **drying, desiccation,** drying up, exsiccation; **dehydration,** anhydration; evaporation; air-drying; blow-drying; freeze-drying; insolation, sunning; drainage; withering, mummification; dehumidification; blotting

4 **dryer, drier,** desiccator, desiccative, siccative, exsiccative, exsiccator, dehydrator, dehydrant; dehumidifier; evaporator; hairdryer, blow-dryer; clothes dryer; tumble dryer; absorbent; clothesline

VERBS **5** thirst; drink up, soak up, sponge up; parch

6 **dry, desiccate,** exsiccate, dry up, **dehydrate,** anhydrate; evaporate; dehumidify; air-dry; drip-dry; dry off; insolate, sun, sun-dry; hang out to dry, air; spin-dry, tumbler-dry; blow-dry; freeze-dry; smoke, smoke-dry; cure; torrefy, burn, fire, kiln, bake, parch, scorch, sear; wither, shrivel; wizen, weazen; mummify; sponge, blot, soak up; wipe, rub, swab, brush; towel; drain

ADJS **7** **dry, arid;** waterless, unwatered, undamped, anhydrous; bone-dry, dry as dust, dry as a bone; like parchment, parched; droughty; juiceless, sapless; moistureless; **thirsty,** thirsting, athirst; high and dry; sandy, dusty; desert, Saharan; drought-stricken

8 rainless, fine, fair, bright and fair, pleasant

9 **dried, dehydrated,** desiccated, dried-up, exsiccated; evaporated; squeezed dry; parched, baked, sunbaked, burnt, scorched, seared, sere, sun-dried, adust; wind-dried, air-dried; drip-dried; blow-dried; freeze-dried; withered, shriveled, wizened, weazened; corky; mummified

10 **drying,** dehydrating, desiccative, desiccant, exsiccative, exsiccant, siccative, siccant; evaporative

11 **watertight, waterproof,** moistureproof, dampproof, leakproof, seepproof, dripproof, stormproof, stormtight, rainproof, raintight, showerproof, floodproof; dry-shod

1067 VAPOR, GAS

<substances of particles mixed with air>

NOUNS **1** **vapor,** volatile; **fume,** reek, exhalation, breath, effluvium, expiration; fluid; miasma, mephitis, fetid air, fumes; smoke, smudge; smog; wisp of smoke, plume of smoke, puff of smoke; damp, chokedamp, blackdamp, firedamp, afterdamp; steam, water vapor; **cloud**

2 **gas** <see list>; rare gas, noble gas, inert gas, halogen gas; fluid, compressible fluid; atmosphere, air; pneumatics, aerodynamics

3 **vaporousness,** vaporiness; vapor pressure, vapor tension; aeriness; ethereality, etherialism; **gaseousness,** gaseous state, gassiness, gaseity; gas, stomach gas, flatulence, flatus, wind, windiness, farting, flatuosity; burping; fluidity

4 **volatility,** vaporability, vaporizability, evaporability

5 **vaporization, evaporation,** volatilization, gasification; sublimation; distillation, fractionation; etherification; aeration, aerification; fluidization; atomization; exhalation; fumigation; smoking; steaming; etherealization

6 vaporizer, evaporator; atomizer, aerosol, spray; propellant; condenser; still, retort

7 vaporimeter, manometer, pressure gauge; gas meter, gasometer; pneumatometer, spirometer; aerometer, airometer; eudiometer

VERBS **8** **vaporize, evaporate,** volatilize, **gasify;** sublimate, sublime; distill, fractionate; etherify; aerate, aerify; carbonate, oxygenate, hydrogenate, chlorinate, halogenate; atomize, spray; fluidize; reek, fume; exhale, give off, emit, send out; smoke; steam; fumigate, perfume; etherize

ADJS **9** **vaporous,** vaporish, vapory, vaporlike; **airy,** aerial, ethereal, atmospheric; **gaseous,** in the gaseous state, gasified, gassy, gaslike, gasiform, fizzy, carbonated; vaporing; reeking, reeky; miasmic, miasmal, miasmatic, mephitic, fetid, effluvial; fuming, fumy; smoky, smoking, smoggy; steamy, steaming; ozonic; oxygenous; oxyacetylene; pneumatic, aerostatic, aerodynamic

10 volatile, volatilizable; **vaporable,** vaporizable, vaporescent, vaporific; **evaporative,** evaporable

COMBINING FORMS **11** vapo-, vapori-, atm-, atmo-; aer-, aero-, mano-, pneum-, pneumo-, pneumat-, pneumato-

12 **gas**

acetylene, ethyne
air gas, producer gas
ammonia
argon
avgas
biogas
blister gas
bottled gas
butane
carbon dioxide
carbon monoxide
carbonic-acid gas
carbureted-hydrogen gas
chlorine
chlorofluorocarbon
coal gas
damp
ethane
ether, ethyl ether
ethyl chloride
ethylene, ethene, olefiant gas
ethylene oxide
fluorocarbon
fluorine
formaldehyde
Freon <tm>
helium
hydrogen
hydrogen bromide
hydrogen chloride
hydrogen cyanide
hydrogen fluoride
hydrogen iodide
hydrogen sulfide
ideal gas, perfect gas
illuminating gas
inert gas
ketene
krypton
lewisite
liquid oxygen
marsh gas, swamp gas
mephitis
methane
mustard gas
natural gas
neon
nerve gas
nitric oxide
nitrogen
nitrogen dioxide
nitrous oxide, laughing gas
noble gas
oil gas
oxygen
ozone
phosgene, carbon oxychloride
phosphine
Pintsch gas
poison gas
propane
propylene
radon gas
refrigerator gas
sewer gas

sneeze gas
synthesis gas
tear gas, lachrymatory gas
vesicatory gas
vinyl chloride
water gas, blue gas
xenon

1068 BIOLOGY

<science of living things>

NOUNS 1 **biology** <see list>, biological science, life science, the science of life, the study of living things; **botany** <see list>, plant biology, phytobiology, phytology, plant science; **plant kingdom,** vegetable kingdom; plants, flora, plantlife; **zoology** <see list>, animal biology, animal science; **animal kingdom,** kingdom Animalia, phylum, class, order, family, genus, species; animals, fauna, animal life; endangered species

2 **biologist,** naturalist, life scientist; botanist, plant scientist, plant biologist, phytobiologist, phytologist; zoologist, animal biologist, animal scientist <for other NOUNS add -ist or -er to names of branches listed>

3 **life science**; natural history, biological science; anatomy, biochemistry, biology, biophysics, botany, cell biology, embryology, ethnobiology, microbiology, paleontology, pathology, physiology, zoology; taxonomy, systematics; nanoscience; intelligent design

ADJS 4 **biological,** biologic, microbiological; **botanical,** botanic, plant, phytological, phytologic, phytobiological; **zoological,** zoologic, faunal <for other ADJS add -ic or -ical to the names of branches listed>

5 **biology (branches)**

aerobiology
agrobiology
anatomy
aquatic biology
aquatic microbiology
autoecology
bacteriology
biobehavioral science
biochemical genetics
biochemistry
biodynamics
biogeography
biometry, biometrics, biostatistics
bionics
biophysics
biotechnology, biotech
biothermodynamics
botany
cell biology
cell physiology
chronobiology
conservation biology
cryobiochemistry
cryobiology
cytogenetics
cytology
cytotaxonomy
developmental biology
ecology, bioecology, bionomics
electrobiology
electrophysiology
embryology
enzymology
ethnobiology
eugenics
evolution
exobiology, astrobiology, bioastronautics, space biology, space bioscience, xenobiology
genetics
gnotobiosis
histology
human ecology
hydrobiology
hydrology, hydrogeology, geohydrology
limnology
marine biology
mathematical biology
medicine
microbiology
molecular biology
morphology
natural classification
natural history
neurobiology
neurochemistry
neuroendocrinology
neurogenetics
neuroscience
organology
paleontology
palynology
parasitology
phylogenetic classification, phyletic classification, phyletics
physiology
population biology
population genetics
proteomics
radiobiology
sociobiology
somatology
synecology
taxonomy, systematics
virology
zoogeography, animal geography
zoology

6 **botany (branches)**

agriculture
agrobiology
agronomy
algology
applied botany
aquiculture
bacteriology
botanical histochemistry
bryology
dendrology
economic botany
ethnobotany
evolution
floriculture
forestry
fungology
genetics
geobotany
gnotobiology
histology
horticulture
hydroponics
mycology
olericulture
paleobotany
palynology
phycology
physiology
phytobiology
phytochemistry, plant biochemistry
phytoecology, plant ecology
phytogeography, plant geography
phytography
phytology
phytosociology
phytotomy, plant anatomy
plant breeding
plant cytology
plant morphology
plant pathology, phytopathology, vegetable pathology
plant physiology, vegetable physiology
plant taxonomy
pomology
pteridology
research botany
seed biology
silviculture
systematic botany, systematic taxonomy

7 **zoology (branches)**

anatomy
animal behavior
animal chemistry, zoochemistry
animal pathology, zoopathology
animal physiology, zoonomy
animal psychology
apiculture
applied zoology
arachnology
behavioral ecology
biochemistry
biometrics
biophysics

comparative anatomy, zootomy
comparative embryology
comparative psychology
conchology
cytogenetics
cytology
ecology
embryology
endocrinology
entomology
ethology
evolution
genetics
helminthology
herpetology
histology
ichthyology
invertebrate zoology
malacology
mammalogy
marine biology
morphology
ophiology
ornithology
paleontology
parasitology
physiological chemistry
physiology
protozoology
research zoology
sociobiology
systematic zoology, systematics, taxonomy
vertebrate zoology
veterinary medicine
wildlife management
zoogeography
zoography

1069 AGRICULTURE

<*science of farming*>

NOUNS 1 **agriculture, farming** <see list>, husbandry; cultivation, culture, geoponics, tillage, tilth; green revolution; agrology, agronomy, agronomics, agrotechnology, agricultural science, agroscience, agriscience; thremmatology; agroecosystem; agrogeology, agricultural geology; agrochemistry; agricultural engineering; agricultural economics; rural economy, rural economics, farm economy, farm economics, agrarian economy, agrarian economics, agrarianism, agrarian society; agribusiness, agrobusiness, agribiz, agroindustry; sharecropping; intensive farming, factory farming, mixed farming, crop farming, organic farming, subsistence farming; cereology

2 **horticulture, gardening;** landscape gardening, landscape architecture, groundskeeping; truck gardening, market gardening, olericulture; flower gardening, flower-growing, floriculture; viniculture, viticulture; orcharding, fruit-growing, pomiculture, citriculture; arboriculture, silviculture; indoor gardening; heirloom plant, heirloom seed

3 **forestry,** arboriculture, tree farming, silviculture, forest management; Christmas tree farming; forestation, afforestation, reforestation; lumbering, logging; deforestation; woodcraft

4 <agricultural deities> vegetation spirit, fertility god, year-daemon, forest god, green man, corn god, Ceres, Demeter, Gaea, Triptolemus, Dionysus, Persephone, Kore, Flora, Aristaeus, Pomona, Frey

5 **agriculturist,** agriculturalist; agrologist, agronomist; **farmer,** granger, husbandman, yeoman, cultivator, tiller, sodbuster, tiller of the soil; rural economist, agrotechnician; boutique farmer, contour farmer, crop-farmer, dirt farmer, truck farmer; gentleman-farmer; peasant, countryman, rustic; grower, raiser; planter, tea-planter, coffee-planter; peasant holder; tenant farmer, crofter <Brit>, peasant farmer; sharecropper, cropper, collective farm worker; agricultural worker, farm worker, farmhand, farm laborer, migrant worker, migratory worker, migratory laborer, bracero, picker; plowman, plowboy; farmboy, farmgirl; sower; reaper, harvester, harvestman; haymaker; agriscientist

6 **horticulturist,** nurseryman, **gardener,** grower, green thumb, propagator; landscape gardener, landscapist, landscape architect; truck gardener, market gardener, olericulturist; **florist,** floriculturist; vinegrower, viniculturist, viticulturist, vintager; vinedresser; orchardist, orchardman, fruitgrower

7 **forester;** arboriculturist, arborist, silviculturist, dendrologist, verderer, tree farmer, topiarist; conservationist; **ranger,** forest ranger, forest manager; woodsman, woodman, woodcraftsman, woodlander; logger, lumberman, timberman, lumberjack, lumberer; woodcutter, wood chopper; tapper; tree surgeon

8 **farm,** farmplace, farmstead, farmhold, farmery, farmlet; grange, location <Austral>; boutique farm, crop farm, dirt farm, tree farm; plantation, cotton plantation, *hacienda* <Sp>; aquafarm, aquaponics; croft, homecroft <Brit>; homestead, steading; toft <Brit>; mains; demesne, homefarm, demesne farm, manor farm; barnyard, farmyard, barton; collective farm, *kibbutz* <Heb>; farmland, cropland, arable land, plowland, fallow; grassland, pasture; forest, deciduous forest, evergreen forest

9 **field, tract,** plat, plot, patch, piece of land, parcel of land; cultivated land; clearing; hayfield, cornfield, wheat field; paddy, paddy field, rice paddy

10 **garden** <see list>; bed, flower bed, border, ornamental border; paradise; garden spot; vineyard, vinery, grapery, grape ranch; herbarium; botanical garden; compost pile, compost heap, seed tray; English garden

11 **nursery;** conservatory, **greenhouse,** glasshouse <Brit>, forcing house, summerhouse, lathhouse, hothouse, coolhouse; potting shed; force bed, forcing bed, forcing pit, hotbed, cold frame; seedbed; cloche; pinery, orangery

12 **growing,** raising, rearing, cultivation; **green thumb**

13 **cultivation,** cultivating, culture, tilling, dressing, working; harrowing, plowing, contour plowing, furrowing, listing, fallowing, weeding, hoeing, pruning, thinning; overcropping, overcultivation; irrigation, overirrigation

14 **planting,** setting; **sowing,** seeding, semination, insemination; breeding, hydridizing; dissemination, broadcast, broadcasting; transplantation, resetting; retimbering, reforestation; agrarian society

15 **harvest,** harvesting, reaping, gleaning, gathering, cutting; wildcraft; nutting; cash crop, root crop, crop; industrial crop

VERBS **16** **farm, ranch,** work the land; **grow, raise,** rear; crop; dryfarm; sharecrop; **garden;** have a green thumb

17 **cultivate,** culture, dress, work, till, till the soil, dig, delve, spade; mulch; plow, plow in, plow under, plow up, list, fallow, backset, double-dig, rototill, fork; take cuttings, graft; irrigate; harrow, rake; weed, weed out, hoe, cut, prune, thin, thin out; force; overcrop, overcultivate; slash and burn; top-dress, compost, fertilize

18 **plant,** implant, set, put in; sow, seed, seed down, seminate, inseminate; disseminate, broadcast, sow broadcast, scatter seed; drill; bed; dibble; transplant, reset, pot; vernalize; forest, afforest; deforest; retimber, reforest; factory-farm

19 **harvest**, reap, crop, glean, gather, gather in, bring in, get in the harvest, reap and carry; pick, pluck; dig, grabble; mow, cut; hay; nut; crop herbs

ADJS **20** **agricultural, agrarian,** agrestal, agro-; geoponic, geoponical, agronomic, agronomical; farm, farming; arable; rustic, bucolic, rural

21 **horticultural;** olericultural; vinicultural, viticultural; arboricultural, silvicultural

22 **farming (types)**

boutique farming
contour farming
crop farming
dirt farming
dry farming
dryland farming
factory farming
fruit farming
grain farming
hydroponics, tank farming
intensive farming
livestock farming
mixed farming
organic farming
sharecropping
share farming
slash-and-burn
strip farming
stubble-mulch farming, trash farming
subsistence farming
tree farming
truck farming

23 **garden (types)**

allotment
alpine garden
antique garden
apiary
arboretum
beer garden
border garden
botanical garden, botanic garden
bottle garden
conservatory
cottage garden
cutting garden
dish garden
dry garden
English garden
flower bed
flower garden
formal garden
fragrance garden
French formal garden
greenhouse
hanging garden
heirloom garden
herb garden
herbarium
home garden
hotbed
hothouse
hydroponics
indoor garden
Italian garden
Japanese garden
kitchen garden
knot garden
market garden
maze garden
nursery
orchard
organic garden
ornamental garden
peace garden
physic garden
potager
rock garden, rockery
roof garden
rose garden
sunken garden
tea garden
terraced garden
terrarium
truck garden
vegetable garden
victory garden
walled garden
water garden
winter garden
xeriscape
Zen garden

1070 ANIMAL HUSBANDRY

<breeding and caring for animals>

NOUNS **1** **animal husbandry,** animal rearing, animal raising, animal culture, stock raising, **ranching;** zooculture, zootechnics, zootechny; thremmatology; gnotobiotics; herding, grazing, keeping flocks and herds, running livestock, livestock farming; transhumance; breeding, stockbreeding, stirpiculture; line breeding, selective breeding; horse training, dressage, manege; horsemanship; pisciculture, fish culture; apiculture, bee culture, beekeeping; cattle raising; sheepherding; stock farming, fur farming; factory farming; pig-keeping; dairy farming, chicken farming, pig farming; cattle ranching; worm farming

2 **stockman,** stock raiser, stockkeeper <Austral>; breeder, stockbreeder; sheepman; cattleman, cow keeper, cowman, grazier <Brit>; **rancher,** ranchman, ranchero; ranchhand; dairyman, dairy farmer; milkmaid; stableman, stableboy, groom, hostler, equerry; trainer, breaker, tamer; broncobuster, buckaroo; blacksmith, horseshoer, farrier

3 **herder,** drover, herdsman, herdboy; shepherd, shepherdess, sheepherder, sheepman; goatherd; swineherd, pigman, pigherd, hogherd; gooseherd, gooseboy, goosegirl; swanherd; cowherd, neatherd <Brit>; cowboy, cowgirl, cowhand, puncher, cowpuncher, cowpoke, waddy, cowman, cattleman, *vaquero* <Sp>, gaucho; horseherd, wrangler, horse wrangler

4 **apiarist,** apiculturist, **beekeeper,** beeherd

5 **farm,** stock farm, animal farm; **ranch,** rancho, rancheria; station <Austral>; horse farm, stable, stud farm; cattle ranch; dude ranch; pig farm, piggery; chicken farm, turkey farm, duck farm, poultry farm; sheep farm; fur farm, mink farm; dairy farm; factory farm; animal enclosure; stockfeed

VERBS 6 **raise, breed,** rear, grow, hatch, feed, nurture, fatten; keep, run; ranch, farm; culture; back-breed

7 **tend; groom,** rub down, brush, curry, currycomb; water, drench, feed, fodder; bed, bed down, litter; milk; harness, saddle, hitch, bridle, yoke; gentle, handle, manage; tame, train, break; deworm; ear-tag

8 drive, **herd,** drove <Brit>, herd up, punch cattle, **shepherd,** ride herd on; spur, goad, prick, lash, whip; wrangle, round up; corral, cage

1071 EARTH SCIENCE

<sciences of the earth and its parts>

NOUNS 1 earth science, **earth sciences** <see list>; geoscience; geography, geology, rock hunting, rock hounding, geological science, oceanography, oceanographic science, meteorology, atmospheric science, planetary science, space science; geological record; geolocation, geocaching; geographical information system (GIS), Global Positioning System (GPS)

2 **earth scientist,** geoscientist; **geologist,** rock hound, rock hunter, geographer, oceanographer, astronomer, stargazer, meteorologist, weather man <for other NOUNS, add -ist or -er to names of branches listed below>

3 **earth sciences**

aerology
aeronomy
astrogeology
bathymetry
biogeography
biostratigraphy
chronostratigraphy
climatology
crystallography
economic geology
engineering geology
environmental geology
environmental science
environmental studies
geoarchaeology, archaeological geology
geobotanical prospecting
geobotany
geochemistry
geochronology
geochronometry
geocosmogony
geodesy
geodynamics
geography
geological cartography
geology, geologic science
geomagnetism
geomorphology
geophysics
geopolitics
geoscience
glacial geology
glaciology
gravimetry
historical geology
hydrography
igneous petrology
invertebrate paleontology
hydrology, geohydrology, hydrogeology
lithostratigraphy
macrogeography
magnetostratigraphy
marine geology
marine science
metamorphic petrology
meteorology
micropaleontology
mineralogy
mining geology
oceanography
oceanology
paleobiogeography
paleobotany
paleoclimatology
paleogeography
paleogeophysics
paleolimnology
paleomagnetism
paleontology
paleopedology
palynology
pedology, soil science
petrochemistry
petrogenesis
petrography
petroleum geology
petrology, lithology
physical climatology
physical geography, physiography
physical geology
physical oceanography
planetology
plate tectonics
radiometric dating
sedimentary petrology
sedimentology
seismography
seismology
stratigraphy
structural geology
submarine geology
tectonic geology, geotectonic geology
tectonics
tectonophysics
thalassography
topography
urban geology
vertebrate paleontology
volcanology, vulcanology

1072 THE ENVIRONMENT

<sciences of the ecosystem>

NOUNS 1 **the environment,** the natural world, the ecology, global ecology, ecosystem, global ecosystem, the biosphere, the ecosphere, the balance of nature, macroecology, microecology; **ecology,** bioregion; environmental protection, environmental policy; environmental control, environmental management; environmental assessment, environmental auditing, environmental monitoring, environmental impact analysis; environmentally friendly, environmentally conscious; emission control; **environmental science** <see list>, environmentology; biome

2 **environmental destruction,** ecocide, ecocatastrophe; environmental pollution, pollution, contamination; **air pollution,** atmospheric pollution, air quality; **water pollution,** stream pollution, lake pollution, ocean pollution, groundwater pollution, pollution of the aquifer; **environmental pollutant** <see list>; eutrophication; biodegradation, biodeterioration, microbial degradation; light pollution

3 **environmentalist,** environmental activist,

conservationist, preservationist, nature-lover, doomwatcher <Brit>, duck-squeezer, ecofreak, tree-hugger, eagle freak; Green Panther; ecocentric

4 **environmental pollutant**

acid rain
aerosol sprays
aircraft noise
asbestos
automobile exhaust
azo compounds
benzene
beryllium
calcium carbonates
carbon dioxide
carbon monoxide
carbon tetrachloride
carcinogens
chemical waste
chlordane
chlorine
chlorobenzenes
chloroethanes
chlorofluorocarbons (CFCs)
chlorohydrocarbons
chloromethane
chlorophenol
chloropropanones
chlorpropham
chromium
coal smoke
dibromochloropropane (DBCP)
dichlorides
dichloroacetate
dichlorobenzenes
dichlorodiphenyltrichloroethane (DDT)
dichloroethanes
dichlorophenol
dichloropropane
dioxins
endosulfan
endrin
ethanes
ethylene
ethylene dibromide (EDB)
ethylene glycol
ethylene oxide
exhaust fumes
fenoxaprop ethyl
fluorenes
fluorocarbons
fluorohydrocarbons
formaldehyde
fungicides
gasoline
halon
heptachlor
herbicides
hexachlorethane
hexone
hydrocarbons
hydrochlorofluorocarbon (HCFC)
industrial particulate matter
isocyanuric acid
kepone
lead
lead paint
leaded gasoline
leptophos
malathion
mercury
metalaxyl
methyl ethyl ketone
methyl parathion
mining waste
mirex
nabam
naphthalene
nitro compounds
nitrogen oxides
nitroso compounds
noise
nuclear waste
paraquat dichloride
parathion
pentachloraphenol (PCP)
pesticides
phosphate
polybrominated biphenyls (PBBs)
polychlorinated biphenyls (PCBs)
radon
radionuclides
secondhand smoke
sewage
smog
smoke
solid waste
sulfur oxides
sulfuric acid
tobacco smoke
toxaphene
toxic waste
trichloroacetic acid
trichlorobenzene
trichloroethylene (TCE)
trimethylbenzenes
triphenyltin hydroxide, DuTer <tm>
ultraviolet radiation
vinyl chloride

5 **environmental science**

autecology
bioecology, bionomics
ecology
environmental archaeology
environmental biology
environmental chemistry
environmental design
environmental engineering
environmental geology
environmental health
environmental horticulture
environmental management
environmental toxicology
human ecology
land management
synecology
wildlife management
zoo-ecology

1073 THE UNIVERSE, ASTRONOMY

<science of matter outside earth's atmosphere>

NOUNS 1 **universe, world, cosmos,** cosmological model; creation, created universe, created nature, all, all creation, all tarnation, all that is, everything that is, all being, totality, totality of being, sum of things; omneity, allness; nature, system; wide world, whole wide world, world without end; plenum; macrocosm, macrocosmos, megacosm; metagalaxy; open universe, closed universe, inflationary universe, flat universe, oscillating universe, steady-state universe, expanding universe, pulsating universe; Einsteinian universe, Newtonian universe, Friedmann universe; Ptolemaic universe, Copernican universe; sidereal universe; observable universe

2 **the heavens,** heaven, **sky,** firmament; empyrean, welkin, lift, lifts; the blue, blue sky, azure, cerulean, the blue serene; ether, **air,** hyaline; vault, cope, canopy, vault of heaven, canopy of heaven, starry sphere, celestial sphere, starry heaven; Caelus

3 **space, outer space,** cosmic space, deep space, empty space, ether space, pressureless space, celestial spaces, interplanetary space, interstellar space, intergalactic space, intercosmic space, metagalactic space, the void, the void above, ocean of emptiness; chaos; outermost reaches of space; astronomical unit, light-year, parsec; interstellar medium; close encounter

4 **celestial phenomenon,** the stars, fixed stars, starry host; music of the spheres, harmony of the spheres; orb, sphere; heavenly body, celestial body, celestial sphere; comet; comet cloud; morning star, daystar, Lucifer, Phosphor, Phosphorus; evening star, Vesper, Hesper, Hesperus, Venus; North Star, polestar, polar star,

lodestar, Polaris; Dog Star, Sirius, Canicula; Bull's Eye, Aldebaran

5 **constellation** <see list>, configuration, asterism, stellar group, stellar population; zodiacal constellation; cluster, star cluster, galactic cluster, open cluster, globular cluster, stellar association, supercluster; Magellanic clouds

6 **galaxy,** island universe, galactic nebula; spiral galaxy, spiral nebula, spiral; barred spiral galaxy, barred spiral; elliptical galaxy, spheroidal galaxy; disk galaxy; irregular galaxy; radio galaxy; lenticular galaxy; active galaxy; Seyfert galaxy, starburst galaxy; the Local Group; the Galaxy, the Milky Way, the galactic circle; galactic cluster, supergalaxy; great attractor; chaotic attractor; continent of galaxies, great wall of galaxies, sheet of galaxies; galactic coordinates, galactic pole, galactic latitude, galactic longitude; galactic noise, cosmic noise; galactic nucleus, active galactic nucleus; cosmic string; Hubble classification

7 **nebula,** nebulosity; gaseous nebula; hydrogen cloud; dark nebula; dust cloud; dark matter, cold dark matter; interstellar cloud; planetary nebula; whirlpool nebula; cirronebula; ring nebula; diffuse nebula; emission nebula; reflection nebula; absorption nebula; galactic nebula; anagalactic nebula; bright diffuse nebula; dark cloud, coalsack; Nebula of Lyra, Nebula of Orion, Crab Nebula, the Coalsack, Black Magellanic Cloud; nebulous stars; nebular hypothesis

8 **star** <see list>; quasar, quasi-stellar radio source; pulsar, pulsating star, eclipsing binary X-ray pulsar; luminary; Nemesis, the Death Star; Hawking radiation; magnitude, stellar magnitude, visual magnitude; relative magnitude, absolute magnitude, apparent nebula; star populations, stellar populations; mass-luminosity law; spectrum-luminosity diagram, Hertzsprung-Russell diagram; star catalog, star atlas, star chart, sky atlas, sky survey, Messier catalog, Dreyer's New General Catalog (NGC); star cloud, star cluster, globular cluster, open cluster; Pleiades, Seven Sisters, Hyades, Beehive; stellar evolution, stellar birth, protostar, molecular cloud, main sequence, gravitational collapse, dying star, red giant, white dwarf; nova, supernova, supernova remnant, neutron star, black hole, giant black hole, mini-black hole, starving black hole, supermassive black hole, frozen black hole, event horizon, singularity, white hole, active galactic nucleus

9 **planet,** wanderer, wandering star, terrestrial planet, inferior planet, superior planet, secondary planet, major planet, inner planet, outer planet; minor planet, planetoid, asteroid; asteroid belt; Earth; Jupiter; Mars, the Red Planet; Mercury; Neptune; Pluto; Saturn; Uranus; Venus; solar system; syzygy

10 **Earth,** planet Earth, third planet, the world, *terra* <L>; globe, terrestrial globe, Spaceship Earth, the blue planet; geosphere, biosphere, magnetosphere; vale, vale of tears; Mother Earth, Ge, Gaea, Gaia, Tellus, Terra; whole wide world, four corners of the earth, the length and breadth of the land

11 **moon, satellite,** natural satellite; orb of night, queen of heaven, queen of night; silvery moon; new moon, wet moon; crescent moon, crescent, increscent moon, increscent, waxing moon, waxing crescent moon, first quarter, last quarter; decrescent moon, decrescent, waning moon, waning crescent moon; gibbous moon; half-moon, demilune; full moon, harvest moon, hunter's moon; horned moon; eclipse, lunar eclipse, eclipse of the moon; artificial satellite

12 <moon goddess> Diana, Phoebe, Cynthia, Artemis, Hecate, Selene, Luna, Astarte, Ashtoreth; man in the moon

13 **sun;** orb of day, daystar; sunshine, solar radiation, sunlight; solar disk; photosphere, chromosphere, corona; sunspot; sunspot cycle; solar flare, solar prominence; solar wind; eclipse, eclipse of the sun, solar eclipse, total eclipse, partial eclipse, central eclipse, annular eclipse; solar corona, Baily's beads

14 <sun god, goddess> Sol, Helios, Hyperion, Titan, Phaëthon, Phoebus, Phoebus Apollo, Apollo, Ra, Amen-Ra, Shamash, Surya, Savitar, Amaterasu

15 **meteor;** falling star, shooting star, meteoroid, fireball, bolide; **meteorite,** meteorolite; micrometeoroid, micrometeorite; aerolite; chondrite; siderite; siderolite; tektite; meteor dust, cosmic dust; meteor trail, meteor train; meteor swarm; meteor shower, meteoric shower; radiant, radiant point; meteor crater

16 **orbit,** circle, **trajectory;** circle of the sphere, great circle, small circle; ecliptic; zodiac; zone; meridian, celestial meridian; colures, equinoctial colure, solstitial colure; equator, celestial equator, equinoctial, equinoctial circle, equinoctial line; equinox, vernal equinox, autumnal equinox; longitude, celestial longitude, geocentric longitude, heliocentric longitude, galactic longitude, astronomical longitude, geographic longitude, geodetic longitude; apogee, perigee; aphelion, perihelion; period; revolution, eccentric inclination, rotation, rotational axis, rotational period; parabolic orbit, hyperbolic orbit

17 **observatory,** astronomical observatory;

radio observatory, orbiting astronomical observatory (OAO), orbiting solar observatory (OSO); ground-based observatory, optical observatory, infrared observatory; **planetarium;** orrery; telescope, astronomical telescope; planisphere, astrolabe, flux collector; reflector, refractor, Newtonian telescope, Cassegrainian telescope; radio telescope, radar telescope; spectroscope, spectrograph; spectrohelioscope, spectroheliograph; coronagraph; heliostat, coelostat; observation; seeing, bright time, dark time

18 **cosmology,** cosmography, **cosmogony;** stellar cosmogeny, astrogony; cosmism, cosmic philosophy, cosmic evolution; nebular hypothesis; big bang theory, expanding universe theory; oscillating universe theory, pulsating universe theory; steady state theory, continuous creation theory; plasma theory; creationism, creation science

19 **astronomy, stargazing,** uranology, starwatching, astrognosy, astrography, uranography, uranometry; astrophotography, stellar photometry; spectrography, spectroscopy, radio astronomy, radar astronomy, X-ray astronomy; **astrophysics,** solar physics; celestial mechanics, gravitational astronomy; astrolithology; meteoritics; astrogeology; stellar statistics; astrochemistry, cosmochemistry; optical astronomy, observational astronomy; infrared astronomy, ultraviolet astronomy; exobiology, astrobotany

20 **astrology,** astromancy, horoscopy; astrodiagnosis; natural astrology; judicial astrology, mundane astrology; genethliacism, genethlialogy, genethliacs, genethliac astrology; horoscope, nativity; **zodiac, zodiac signs** <see list>; house, mansion; house of life, mundane house, planetary house; aspect

21 **cosmologist;** cosmogenist, cosmogener; cosmographer, cosmographist; cosmic philosopher, cosmist

22 **astronomer,** stargazer, observer, uranologist, uranometrist, uranographer, uranographist, astrographer, astrophotographer; radio astronomer, radar astronomer; **astrophysicist,** solar physicist; astrogeologist; cosmochemist

23 **astrologer,** astrologian, astromancer, stargazer, Chaldean, astroalchemist, horoscoper, horoscopist, genethliac

ADJS **24** **cosmic,** cosmical, **universal;** cosmologic, cosmological, cosmogonal, cosmogonic, cosmogonical; cosmographic, cosmographical

25 **celestial, heavenly,** empyrean, empyreal; uranic; astral, starry, stellar, stellary, sphery; star-spangled, star-studded; cometary; galactic, intergalactic, extragalactic, anagalactic; sideral, sidereal; zodiacal; equinoctial; **astronomic, astronomical**, astrophysical, astrologic, astrological, astrologistic, astrologous; planetary, planetarian, planetal, circumplanetary; planetoidal, planetesimal, asteroidal; solar, heliacal; terrestrial; lunar, lunular, lunate, lunulate, lunary, cislunar, translunar, Cynthian; semilunar; meteoric, meteoritic; nebular, nebulous, nebulose; interstellar, intersidereal; interplanetary; intercosmic

26 **extraterrestrial,** exterrestrial, extraterrene, extramundane, alien, space; transmundane, otherworldly, transcendental; extrasolar

ADVS **27** universally, everywhere

28 **constellation**

Air Pump, Pump
Andromeda, the Chained Lady
Antlia, Antlia Pneumatica, the Air Pump
Apus, the Bird of Paradise
Aquarius, the Water Bearer
Aquila, the Eagle
Ara, the Altar
Argo, Argo Navis, the Ship Argo
Aries, the Ram
Auriga, the Charioteer
Bootes, the Herdsman
Caelum, Caela Sculptoris, the Sculptor's Tool, Chisel
Camelopardalis, Camelopardus, the Giraffe
Cancer, the Crab
Canes Venatici, the Hunting Dogs
Canis Major the Larger Dog, Orion's Hound
Canis Minor, the Lesser Dog
Capricorn, the Goat
Carina, the Keel
Cassiopeia, the Lady in the Chair
Centaurus, the Centaur
Cepheus, the Monarch
Cetus, the Whale
Chamaeleon, the Chameleon
Circinus, the Compasses
Columba, Columba Noae, Noah's Dove
Coma Berenices, Berenice's Hair
Corona Australis, the Wreath, the Southern Crown
Corona Borealis, the Northern Crown
Corvus, the Crow
Crater, the Cup
Crux, the Southern Cross
Cygnus, the Swan
Delphinus, the Dolphin
Dorado, Swordfish
Draco, the Dragon
Equuleus, the Foal
Eridanus, the River
Fornax, the Furnace
Gemini, the Twins
Grus, the Crane
Hercules
Horologium, the Clock
Hydra, the Sea Serpent
Hydrus, the Water Snake
Indus, the Indian
Lacerta, the Lizard
Leo, the Lion
Leo Minor, the Lesser Lion
Lepus, the Hare
Libra, the Balance
Lupus, the Wolf
Lynx, the Lynx
Lyra, the Lyre
Malus, the Mast
Mensa, the Table
Microscopium, the Microscope
Monoceros, the Unicorn

Musca, the Fly
Norma, the Rule
Northern Cross
Octans, the Octant
Ophiuchus, the Serpent Bearer
Orion, the Giant Hunter
Orion's Belt
Orion's Sword
Pavo, the Peacock
Pegasus, the Winged Horse
Perseus
Phoenix
Pictor, the Painter
Pisces, the Fishes
Piscis Australis, the Southern Fish
Puppis, the Stern
Pyxis, Mariner's Compass
Reticulum, the Net
Sagitta, the Arrow
Sagittarius, the Archer
Scorpio, Scorpius, the Scorpion
Sculptor
Scutum, the Shield
Serpens, the Serpent
Sextans, the Sextant
Southern Cross
Taurus, the Bull
Telescopium, the Telescope
Triangulum, the Triangle
Triangulum Australe, the Southern Triangle
Tucana, the Toucan
Ursa Major, the Great Bear, the Big Dipper
Ursa Minor, the Lesser Bear, the Little Dipper
Vela, the Sails
Virgo, the Virgin, Maiden
Volans, Piscis Volans, the Flying Fish
Vulpecula, the Little Fox

29 **star (types)**

A star
alpha
astral body
B star
beta
binary star
black dwarf
blaze star
blue-white giant
brown dwarf
C star, carbon star
Cepheid, Cepheid variable
circumpolar star
close binary star
comparison star
dark star
delta
double star
dwarf star
early-type star
eclipsing binary
eclipsing variable
eruptive variable
evening star
F star
fixed star
flare star
gamma
giant star
gravity star
Greenwich star
G star
hydrogen star
intrinsic variable
irregular star
K star
late-type star
long-period variable
M star
main sequence star
morning star
multiple star
N star
nautical star
nebulous star
neutron star
nova
O-type star
quasar
quasi-stellar radio source
R star
radio star
red dwarf
red giant
red supergiant
RR Lyrae star
runaway star
semiregular variable
silicon star
solar star, sun star
spectroscopic binary
standard star
supermassive star
supernova
variable star
visible binary, visual binary
white dwarf
X-ray binary star
X-ray star
yellow dwarf
yellow giant
zenith star

30 **zodiac signs**

Capricorn the Goat <Dec 23–Jan 19>
Aquarius the Water Carrier <Jan 20–Feb 19>
Pisces the Fishes <Feb 20–Mar 21>
Aries the Ram <Mar 22–Apr 20>
Taurus the Bull <Apr 21–May 21>
Gemini the Twins <May 22–June 22>
Cancer the Crab <June 23–July 23>
Leo the Lion <July 24–Aug 23>
Virgo the Virgin <Aug 24–Sept 23>
Libra the Scales <Sept 24–Oct 23>
Scorpio the Scorpion <Oct 24–Nov 22>
Sagittarius the Archer <Nov 23–Dec 22>

1074 ROCKETRY, MISSILERY

<use of rockets, missiles>

NOUNS 1 **rocketry,** rocket science, rocket engineering, rocket research, rocket technology; **missilery,** missile science, missile engineering; rocket testing, missile testing; ground test, firing test, static firing; rocket program, missile program; instrumentation; telemetry

2 **rocket** <see list>, rocket engine, rocket motor, reaction engine, reaction motor; rocket thruster, thruster; retrorocket; rocket exhaust; plasma jet, plasma engine; ion engine; jetavator

3 **missile** <see list>, ballistic missile, guided missile; torpedo; rocket, projectile rocket, ordnance rocket, combat rocket, military rocket; bird; payload; warhead, nuclear warhead, thermonuclear warhead, atomic warhead; multiple warhead, multiple-missile warhead

4 **rocket bomb**, flying bomb, torpedo, cruising missile; robot bomb, robomb, V-weapon, P-plane; buzzbomb, bumblebomb, doodlebug

5 **multistage rocket,** step rocket; two-stage rocket, three-stage rocket; single-stage rocket, single-step rocket, one-step rocket; booster, booster unit, booster rocket, takeoff booster, takeoff rocket; piggyback rocket

6 **test rocket,** research rocket, high-altitude research rocket, registering rocket, instrument rocket, instrument carrier, test instrument vehicle, rocket laboratory; probe

7 **proving ground,** testing ground; firing area; impact area; control center, mission control, bunker; radar tracking station, tracking station, visual tracking station; meteorological tower

8 **rocket propulsion,** reaction propulsion, jet propulsion, blast propulsion; fuel, propellant, solid fuel, liquid fuel, hydrazine, liquid oxygen, lox; charge, propelling charge, propulsion charge,

powder charge, powder grain, high-explosive charge; thrust, constant thrust; exhaust, jet blast, backflash

9 **rocket launching**, rocket firing, ignition, launch, shot, shoot; countdown; liftoff, blastoff; guided control, automatic control, programming; flight, trajectory; burn; burnout, end of burning; velocity peak; altitude peak, ceiling; descent; airburst; impact

10 **rocket launcher,** projector; launching pad, launch pad, launching platform, firing table; silo; takeoff ramp; tower projector, launching tower; launching mortar, launching tube, projector tube, firing tube; rocket gun, bazooka, antitank rocket; superbazooka; multiple projector, calliope, Stalin organ, Katusha; antisubmarine projector, Mark 10, hedgehog; Minnie Mouse launcher, mousetrap; Meilewagon

11 rocket scientist, rocket technician, rocketeer, rocketer, rocket engineer, missile engineer

VERBS **12** rocket, skyrocket

13 **launch**, project, shoot, fire, blast off; abort

14 **rocket, missile**

AA target rocket
ABM, antiballistic missile
airborne rocket
anchor rocket
antiaircraft rocket
antimine rocket
antimissile
antiradar rocket, window rocket
antisubmarine rocket, antisub rocket
antitank rocket
ASM, air-to-surface missile
ATA missile, air-to-air missile (AAM)
ATG rocket, air-to-ground rocket
atom-rocket
ATS, air-to-ship
AUM, air-to-underwater missile
barrage rocket
bat bomb
bazooka rocket
bombardment rocket
booster
chemical rocket
combat high-explosive rocket
Congreve rocket
countermissile
demolition rocket
fin-stabilized rocket
fireworks rocket
flare rocket
flying tank
GAPA, ground-to-air pilotless aircraft
glide bomb
GTA rocket, ground-to-air rocket
GTG rocket, ground-to-ground rocket
guided missile
harpoon rocket
high-altitude rocket
homing rocket
HVAR, high velocity aircraft rocket
IBM, intercontinental ballistic missile
incendiary antiaircraft rocket
incendiary rocket
ion rocket
IRBM, intermediate range ballistic missile
launch vehicle, launcher
line-throwing rocket
liquid-fuel rocket
long-range rocket
MIRV, multiple independently targetable re-entry vehicle
MRV, multiple re-entry vehicle
multistage rocket
ram rocket
retro-float light
retrorocket
rockoon
SAM, surface-to-air missile
scud
signal rocket
skyrocket
smart rocket
smokeless powder rocket
smoke rocket
snake, antimine
solid-fuel rocket
SRB, solid rocket booster
space rocket
spinner
spin-stabilized rocket
SSM, surface-to-surface missile
STS rocket, ship-to-shore rocket
submarine killer
supersonic rocket
target missile
torpedo rocket
training rocket, training missile
trajectory missile
transoceanic rocket
ullage rocket
Vernier, vernier rocket
winged rocket
XAAM, experimental air-to-air missile
XASM, experimental air-to-surface missile
XAUM, experimental air-to-underwater missile
XSAM, experimental surface-to-air missile
XSSM, experimental surface-to-surface missile

1075 SPACE TRAVEL

<exploration of outer space>

NOUNS **1** **space travel, astronautics**, cosmonautics, **space flight,** navigation of empty space; interplanetary travel, space exploration; manned flight; spacewalk; space navigation, astrogation; space science, space technology, space engineering; aerospace science, aerospace technology, aerospace engineering; space research, aerospace research; space medicine, aerospace medicine, bioastronautics; astrionics; escape velocity; rocketry; multistage flight, step flight, shuttle flights; trip to the moon, trip to Mars, grand tour; space terminal, target planet; space age; space tourism, astrotourism

2 **spacecraft** <see list>, spaceship, space rocket, rocket ship, manned rocket, interplanetary rocket; mother ship; rocket; orbiter; shuttle, space shuttle; capsule, space capsule, ballistic capsule; nose cone, heat shield, heat barrier, thermal barrier; module, command module, lunar excursion module (LEM), lunar module (LM); moon ship, Mars ship; deep-space ship; exploratory ship, reconnaissance rocket; ferry rocket, tender rocket, tanker ship, fuel ship; multistage rocket, shuttle rocket, retrorocket, rocket thruster, thruster, attitude-control rocket, main rocket; burn; space docking, docking, docking maneuver; orbit, parking orbit, geostationary orbit; earth orbit, apogee, perigee; lunar orbit, moon orbit, apolune, perilune, apocynthion, pericynthion; guidance system, terrestrial guidance; soft landing, hard landing; injection, insertion, lunar insertion, Earth insertion; reentry, splashdown

3 flying saucer, unidentified flying object **(UFO);** foo fighter

4 rocket engine; atomic power plant; solar battery; power cell

5 **space station,** astro station, space island, island base, cosmic stepping-stone, halfway station, advance base; manned station; inner station, outer station, transit station, space airport, spaceport, spaceport station, space platform, space dock, launching base, research station, space laboratory, space observatory; tracking station, radar tracking station; radar station; radio relay station, radio mirror; space mirror, solar mirror; moon station, moon base, lunar base, lunar city, observatory on the moon

6 **artificial satellite** <see list>, **satellite,** space satellite, robot satellite, unmanned satellite; communications satellite, active communications satellite, communications relay satellite, weather satellite, earth satellite, astronomical satellite, meteorological satellite, geostationary satellite, geosynchronous satellite, spy satellite, orbiting observatory, space observatory, geophysical satellite, navigational satellite, geodetic satellite, research satellite, interplanetary monitoring satellite, automated satellite; **probe, space probe** <see list>, geo probe, interplanetary explorer, planetary probe; orbiter, lander

7 <satellite telemetered recorders> micro-instrumentation; aurora particle counter, cosmic ray counter, gamma ray counter, heavy particle counter, impulse recorder, magnetometer, solar ultraviolet detector, solar X-ray detector, telecamera

8 **astronaut,** astronavigator, cosmonaut, spaceman, spacewoman, space crew member, shuttle crew member, space traveler, rocketeer, rocket pilot; space doctor; space crew; planetary colony, lunar colony; extraterrestrial visitor, alien, saucerman, man from Mars, Martian, little green man; close encounter

9 rocketry, rocket propulsion; burn, thrust, escape velocity, orbit, parking orbit, transfer orbit, insertion, injection, trajectory, flyby, rendezvous, docking, reentry, splashdown, soft landing, hard landing; launch vehicle, multistage rocket, payload, retrorocket, solid rocket booster, engine, booster, propellant, liquid fuel, solid fuel; rocket society, American Rocket Society, American Interplanetary Society, British Interplanetary Society

10 <space hazards> cosmic particles, intergalactic matter, aurora particles, radiation, cosmic ray bombardment; rocket debris, satellite debris, space junk; meteors, meteorites; asteroids; meteor dust impacts, meteoric particles, space bullets; extreme temperatures; the bends, blackout, weightlessness

11 **spacesuit,** pressure suit, G suit, anti-G suit; space helmet

VERBS 12 **travel in space**, go into outer space; launch, lift off, blast off, enter orbit, orbit the earth, **go into orbit**; navigate in space, astrogate; escape earth, break free, leave the atmosphere, shoot into space; rocket to the moon, park in space, hang in space, float in space, space-walk

ADJS 13 **astronautical,** cosmonautical, spacetraveling, spacefaring; astrogational; rocketborne, spaceborne; extravehicular

14 **spacecraft, artificial satellite, space probe**

A-1
Alouette
Anik
Anna
Apollo
Ariane
Ariel
Astro
ATDA
Atlas-Score
ATS
Aurora 7 <Mercury>
Biosatellite
Cassini
communications satellite, comsats
Comsat
Copernicus
cosmic background explorer (COBE)
Cosmos
Courier
D1-C
D2-D
Deep Space
Diapason
Discoverer
Early Bird
Echo
Einstein
Elektron
ERS
(ESSA) environmental survey satellite
Explorer
Explorer 760
Faith 7 <Mercury>
FR-1
Freedom 7 <Mercury>
Friendship 7 <Mercury>
Galileo
GATV
Gemini
Geostationary Operational Environmental Satellite
Greb
Hubble Space Telescope
International Space Shuttle
Intelsat
killersat
Lageos, laser geodynamic satellite
Lani Bird
Liberty Bell 7 <Mercury>
Lofti
Luna
Lunar Orbiter
Lunar Prospector
Lunik
Mariner
Mars Global Surveyor
Mars Pathfinder
Mars Sojourner
Mars Surveyor
Mercury
Midas
MIR
Molniya
Nimbus
(OAO) orbiting astronomical observatory

(OGO) orbiting geophysical observatory
orbiter
(OSO) orbiting solar observatory
OV1
OV3
Pageos
Pegasus
Pioneer
Polyot
probe
Proton
Ranger
Relay
ROSAT
Samos
San Marco
Secor
Sigma 7 <Mercury>
Skylab
Solar Max
Soyuz
Spacelab
space shuttle, shuttle
space station
Spartan
Sputnik
Stardust
Surveyor
Syncom
Tardis
Telstar
(TIROS) television and infrared observation satellite
Transit
Ulysses
Vanguard
Venera
Viking
Voskhod
Vostok
WRESAT
Zondd

Index

How to Use This Index

Numbers after index entries refer to categories and paragraphs in the main section of this book. They do not refer to page numbers.

The part of the number before the decimal point refers to the category in which you will find synonyms and related words for the term you are looking up. The part of the number after the decimal point refers to the paragraph or paragraphs within the category. For example, **abdomen** 2.18 tells you that you can find words related to **abdomen** in paragraph 18 of category 2.

In the index, the determiners **a**, **an**, and **the** have been removed from the beginning of some phrases. This allows these phrases to appear alphabetically by the main word of the phrase.

Words, of course, frequently have more than one meaning. Each of those meanings may have synonyms or related words. In many cases, words are spelled the same even if they are multiple parts of speech and different meanings. The word **abandon**, for example, is used as a noun and a verb.

All instances of the Nouns, Verbs, and Adjectives are indexed here by category and paragraph. The other parts of speech can be found by using the words in the Nouns, Verbs, and Adjectives paragraphs. For example, looking up a word in its Adjective form will get you to the Adverb forms in the book.

In the eighth edition of this "conceptual" thesaurus (as opposed to an "alphabetical" thesaurus), you will combine referral to the index with referral to the list of categories. Familiarity with the category scheme will greatly aid you in finding synonyms and related words.

A 818.1
a 244.5
aa 1059.1
AA gun 462.12
Aaronic priesthood 699.10
Aaron's rod 691.6
abacist 1017.15
abactor 483.8
abacus 1042.2
Abaddon 680.4, 682.1
abalienate 629.3
abalienation 629.1
abandon (n) 101.2, 105.8, 340.2, 430.3, 654.5, 993.1 (v) 188.9, 340.7, 370.5, 374.3, 390.7, 433.8, 435.3, 475.3, 566.5, 668.8, 857.6, 984.4
abandoned 101.9, 105.25, 222.15, 340.14, 370.8, 390.10, 430.24, 475.5, 584.12, 586.10, 654.14, 665.25, 993.16
abandonee 370.4
abandon hope 125.10
abandonment 188.1, 370.1, 390.2, 430.3, 433.2, 435.1, 475.1, 584.4, 654.5, 857.1, 858.3
abase 137.5, 447.3
abasement 137.2, 447.1, 913.3
abase oneself 137.7, 652.3
abash 96.15, 127.19, 137.5, 971.12
abashed 96.22, 137.14, 971.24
abashment 96.4
abate 16.10, 120.5, 252.6, 252.8, 255.9, 631.2, 670.6, 670.9, 959.3
abated 252.10
abatement 16.5, 120.1, 252.1, 631.1, 670.2
abatement of differences 468.1
abating 670.14
abattis 10.20
abattoir 308.12
abbacomes 699.16
abbacy 698.2
abbandono 708.53
abbatial 698.13
abbatical 698.13
abbé 699.2
abbess 575.2, 699.17
abbey 703.6
abbot 699.16
abbreviate 255.12, 260.7, 268.6, 537.5
abbreviated 260.12, 268.8, 268.9, 537.6, 557.6
abbreviation 255.5, 260.1, 268.3, 537.4, 557.1
abbreviatory 268.8
abbreviature 557.1
ABC gum 1062.6
ABC's 546.3, 568.5, 818.6
abdal 675.23, 699.12
abdicate 370.7, 390.4, 448.2
abdication 370.3, 390.2, 448.1, 475.1
Abdiel 679.4
abdomen 2.18
abdominal 2.31
abdominal viscera 2.16
abdominous 257.18
abduce 482.20
abducent 908.4
abduct 480.14, 482.20
abduction 480.2, 482.9
abductive 908.4
abductor 480.12, 483.10
abecedarian (n) 571.1, 572.9 (a) 546.8, 818.15
abecedarium 554.10, 568.5, 818.6
abecedary 554.10, 568.5
Abélard and Héloïse 104.17
aberrance 638.1, 852.1, 870.1
aberrancy 164.1, 638.1, 852.1, 870.1, 975.1
aberrant 164.7, 638.3, 852.10, 870.9, 975.16
aberrate 171.5
aberration 164.1, 171.1, 204.1, 870.1, 926.1, 927.1, 975.1
aberrational 164.7
aberrative 164.7
abessive 530.9
abet 162.5, 375.21, 449.11, 449.14
abetment 375.5, 449.4
abettor 375.10, 616.3, 616.9
abeyance 173.4, 390.2, 857.3
abeyant 173.14
Abhidarma Pitaka 683.9
abhor 99.3, 103.5
abhorrence 99.2, 103.1, 103.3
abhorrent 98.18, 99.7, 103.7
abide 130.8, 134.5, 225.7, 761.9, 827.6, 846.12, 853.5, 856.3
abide by 332.8, 434.2, 437.9
abide in 761.11
abide with 134.5, 979.7
abiding (n) 225.1 (a) 225.13, 827.10, 853.7, 856.7
abidingness 827.1, 853.1
abiding place 228.1
abigail 577.8
ability 18.2, 384.2, 405.4, 413.1, 413.4
abiogenesis 78.6
abiogenetic 78.16
abiosis 307.1, 307.12
abirritant 86.10, 86.12
abject 113.9, 125.15, 137.11, 138.14, 433.12, 661.12
abject apology 113.4, 658.2
abject defeat 412.4
abject fear 127.1
abjection 654.5
abjectness 138.1, 491.3, 661.3
abjuration 335.2, 363.3, 370.3, 372.1, 390.2, 475.1
abjuratory 335.5, 363.12, 372.4
abjure 335.4, 363.8, 370.7, 372.2, 390.4, 475.3
abjured 390.10, 475.5
abjurement 335.2, 363.3, 370.3, 372.1, 390.2
A-blast 1038.16
ablate 252.6, 388.3, 393.20, 473.5, 806.3, 1044.7
ablated 252.10, 388.5, 473.7
ablation 252.3, 255.1, 388.1, 393.5, 473.2, 806.1, 1044.2
ablative (n) 530.9 (a) 255.13, 806.5, 1044.10
ablaut 524.13
ablaze 93.18, 1019.27, 1025.34, 1025.39
able 18.14, 405.17, 413.24, 966.6
able-bodied 15.16
able-bodied seaman 183.1
ablepsia 30.1
ableptical 30.9
able seaman 183.1
able to adapt 854.6
able to be knocked down with a feather 131.13
able to bend without breaking 854.6
able to breathe again 120.10
able to pay 729.18
able to roll with the punches 854.6
able to take a joke 143.14
able to walk the chalk 516.3
able to walk the chalk mark 516.3
able to walk the line 516.3
abloom 310.38, 407.13, 1016.20
ablush 137.14
ablution 79.5
ablutionary 79.28
abnegate 335.3
abnegation 335.1, 442.1, 668.1, 670.1
abnegative 335.5
abnormal 638.3, 789.8, 870.9, 926.26, 927.5
abnormal birth 870.6
abnormal fetus 870.6
abnormality 85.1, 638.1, 789.3, 870.1, 870.5, 926.1, 927.1
abnormity 870.1
A board 347.8
abode 159.1, 225.1, 228.1
abode of the damned 682.1
abode of the dead 682.1, 839.2
abode of the Gods 681.9
aboiteau 239.11
abolish 395.13, 445.2
abolishment 395.6, 445.1
abolition 395.6, 445.1
A-bomb 462.20, 1038.16
abominable 98.18, 638.3, 654.16, 661.12, 1000.9
abominableness 98.2, 661.3, 1000.2
abominate 103.5
abomination 80.4, 99.2, 103.1, 103.3, 638.2, 654.3, 1000.3
aboriginal (n) 227.3, 842.7 (a) 226.5, 818.15, 842.11, 886.14
aboriginality 226.1, 842.1
aborigine 227.3, 842.7
abort 410.15, 820.6, 857.6, 1074.13
abortion 410.5, 870.6, 891.1
abortion issue 86.23
abortion pill 86.23
abortive 391.12, 410.18
abortive attempt 410.5
abound 991.5
abounding 991.7
abounding in riches 618.14
abound with 884.5
about-face (n) 163.3, 335.2, 362.2, 363.1, 852.1, 858.1, 859.1 (v) 163.10, 852.7
about ship 182.30
about this size 257.24
about to 405.16
about to be 840.3
about to happen 840.3
about to pee one's pants 135.6
about turn 363.1
about-turn 163.3
above 249.12, 272.19, 834.4
above all that 141.12
aboveboard 644.14
above-ground 306.12
above it all 94.13
abovementioned 814.5
above par 999.14
above suspicion 657.8
above water 624.23, 1007.6
ab ovo 767.9
abracadabra 691.4
abradant (n) 287.4 (a) 1044.10
abrade 255.9, 287.8, 393.13, 393.20, 1044.7, 1051.9
abrader 287.4
Abraham 684.1
abrase 1044.7
abrasion 85.38, 255.1, 288.1, 1044.2, 1051.4
abrasive (n) 79.17, 287.4, 1044.2, 1051.7 (a) 58.16, 98.17, 110.17, 288.7, 1044.10
abrasiveness 98.1, 110.1, 288.1
abraxas 691.4
abreact 92.36
abreaction 92.25
abreast 790.7
abreast of 928.18
abreast of the times 841.13
abri 284.5, 460.5
abridge 252.7, 255.12, 268.6, 480.21, 557.5
abridged 252.10, 268.9, 537.6, 557.6, 795.5
abridger 268.4
abridgment 252.1, 252.4, 252.5, 255.5, 268.3, 480.6, 537.3, 557.1
abroad 222.12, 971.24, 975.16
abrogate 395.13, 445.2
abrogation 335.2, 395.7, 445.1
abrupt 204.18, 286.3, 401.10, 420.13, 505.7, 830.5
abruption 802.3
abruptness 204.6, 286.1, 401.2, 505.3, 830.2
abrupt withdrawal 87.1
abscess 85.9, 85.37
abscind 255.10
abscissa 300.5
abscission 255.3
abscond 188.9, 368.10
absconded 222.11
abscondence 222.4
absconder 368.5
abseil (n) 194.1 (v) 194.7
absence 222.1, 222.4, 762.1, 992.4
absence of color 36.1
absence of mind 922.6, 985.2
absence of moral fiber 654.5

A
C

absence without leave 222.4, 368.4
absent 222.11, 762.8, 985.11
absentation 222.4, 370.1
absentee 222.5, 368.5
absentee ballot 371.6, 609.19
absenteeism 222.4
absentee landlord 470.3
absentee vote 371.6
absentee voting 609.18
absenting 222.4
absentminded 984.6, 985.11, 990.9
absentmindedness 984.1, 985.2, 990.1
absent oneself 222.8
absent oneself from 370.5
absent without leave 222.13
absolute 18.13, 247.12, 334.8, 417.15, 417.16, 420.12, 430.27, 612.16, 708.47, 761.15, 794.10, 798.7, 865.12, 872.9, 953.26, 957.16, 960.2, 970.13, 970.15, 973.16, 1002.6
Absolute, the 932.2
absolute altitude 184.35
absolute ceiling 184.32
absolute certainty 970.1
absolute contradiction 335.2
absolute credibility 644.3
absolute dating 832.1
absolute essence 761.1
absolute fact 761.3
absolute free will 430.6
absolute humidity 1065.2
Absolute Idea, the 932.2
absolute idealism 1053.3
absolute indication 957.3
absolute interest 471.4
absolute likeness 973.7
absolutely right 973.17
absolute magnitude 1073.8
absolute master 575.13
absolute monarch 575.8, 575.13
absolute monarchy 612.4, 612.8
absoluteness 334.2, 960.1, 970.1, 973.5, 1002.1
absolute pitch 708.31, 709.4
absolute power 417.1
absolute realism 973.7
absolute ruler 575.13
absolute title 469.1
absolute truth, the 973.3
absolute veto 444.2, 613.7
absolute zero 1019.3, 1023.1
absolution 148.2, 601.1
absolutism 417.1, 432.1, 612.8
absolutist 417.16
absolutistic 417.16
absolve 148.3, 430.14, 601.4, 625.9, 701.17
absolved 148.7
absonant 61.4, 936.11
absorb 7.18, 187.13, 388.3, 521.7, 570.7, 737.26, 898.2, 931.20, 983.13
absorbed 931.22, 983.17, 985.11
absorbed attention 983.3
absorbed by 983.17
absorbed dose 1037.8
absorbed in 898.5, 983.17
absorbed interest 983.3
absorbed in thought 931.22
absorbed with 983.17
absorbency 187.6
absorbent (n) 187.6, 1066.4 (a) 187.17
absorbing 93.24, 983.20
absorb the attention 983.13
absorb the shock 670.8
absorb the thoughts 931.20
absorption 2.17, 7.8, 187.6, 221.3, 388.1, 568.2, 570.2, 898.1, 931.3, 983.3, 985.2
absorption nebula 1073.7
absquatulate 188.7, 188.12, 222.10, 368.11
absquatulating 222.4
absquatulation 222.4, 368.4
abstain 329.3, 390.5, 467.5, 565.5, 667.3, 668.7
abstainer 667.2, 668.4
abstain from 668.7
abstaining (n) 664.3 (a) 565.6
abstainment 668.2
abstemious 515.5, 664.6, 668.10, 992.10
abstemiousness 515.1, 516.1, 664.3, 668.2
abstention 390.1, 467.1, 668.2
abstentious 668.10
abstergent (n) 79.17 (a) 79.28
abstersion 79.2
abstersive 79.28
abstinence 368.1, 390.1, 475.1, 516.1, 664.3, 667.1, 668.2, 670.1
abstinence from food 515.1
abstinent (n) 668.4 (a) 515.5, 516.3, 565.6, 664.6, 667.4, 668.10
abstract (n) 268.3, 557.1, 712.10, 932.3 (v) 255.9, 268.6, 482.13, 773.5 (a) 522.16, 864.11, 951.13, 952.10
abstract art 712.1
abstracted 268.9, 557.6, 931.22, 985.11
abstractedness 985.2
abstracter 268.4
abstract idea 932.3
abstraction 255.1, 482.1, 712.10, 802.1, 864.8, 931.3, 932.3, 951.1, 985.2
abstractionism 350.1
abstract mathematics 1017.1
abstract noun 530.5
abstract oneself 985.9
abstract thought 931.1
abstruse 346.11, 522.16, 928.21, 1013.17
abstruseness 522.2, 1013.1
absurd 391.13, 488.4, 520.7, 789.8, 870.11, 923.11, 955.10, 967.7
absurd, the 391.2
absurd idea 932.7
absurdist 952.11
absurdity 391.2, 488.1, 520.2, 870.3, 923.3, 923.4, 967.1
absurdness 488.1, 923.3
abulia 362.4, 926.3
abulic 362.12
abundance 247.3, 386.1, 538.2, 884.1, 890.1, 991.2
abundance of, an 884.3
abundant 247.8, 538.11, 884.8, 890.9, 991.7
abundant year 824.2
abuse (n) 389.1, 389.2, 510.7, 513.2, 665.6 (v) 387.16, 389.4, 389.5, 486.4, 510.19, 513.7, 665.20, 694.5, 1000.6
abuse a privilege 640.7
abused 432.16
abused substance 87.3
abuse of office 389.1
abuse of terms 342.1, 489.8, 531.1
abuse oneself 75.22
abuse one's rights 640.7
abuse power 389.4
abusive 144.23, 144.26, 156.8, 510.22, 510.23, 512.13, 513.8, 514.3
abusiveness 510.7
abusive relationship 432.1
abut 223.9, 223.13
abutment 223.3, 901.4
abut on 223.9, 901.22
abuttal 223.3
abutter 223.6
abutting 223.16
abut upon 223.9
ab work 84.2
abysm 224.2, 275.2, 284.4
abysmal 257.20, 275.12
abyss 224.2, 275.2, 275.4, 284.4
abyss, the 682.1
abyssal 275.12, 275.15
abyssal hill 240.5
abyssal plain 236.1, 240.5
abyssal rock 1059.1
abyssal zone 275.4
academe 567.5
academese 523.10, 545.3
academia 567.5
academic (n) 571.1, 920.9, 929.3 (a) 567.13, 568.19, 570.17, 571.11, 951.13
academic calendar 824.2
academic dean 571.8
academic degree 648.6
academic discipline 928.10
academic disputation 935.4
academic freedom 430.1
academician 929.3
academic institution 567.1
academic journal 555.1
academic press 548.11
academic specialty 568.8, 928.10
academic year 824.2
academy 567.1, 567.4
Academy Award 646.2
Acadian 523.7
acanaceous 285.10
acanthoid 285.9
acanthous 285.9, 285.10
a cappella 708.53
a cappella choir 710.16
a capriccio 708.53
Acapulco gold 87.11
acaricide 1001.3
acarpous 891.4
accede 332.8, 433.6, 615.13
accedence 615.3
accede to 441.2
accede to prejudice 980.7
accede to the throne 417.14
accelerando (n) 251.2 (a) 708.55
accelerate 174.10, 251.5, 401.4, 756.4, 1038.17
accelerated 251.7
accelerated learning 928.5
acceleration 174.4, 251.2, 401.3
accelerator 1038.11
accelerator board 1042.3
accelerator mass spectrometry 1037.8
accelerometer 174.7
accent (n) 524.8, 524.10, 530.15, 709.12, 709.25, 720.7 (v) 997.14
accented 524.30, 997.21
accent mark 709.12
accents 524.1
accentual 720.17
accentual meter 720.6
accentual-syllabic meter 720.6
accentuate 997.14
accentuated 997.21
accentuation 524.10, 709.25, 720.7
accept 123.2, 134.7, 148.4, 332.8, 332.11, 332.12, 371.15, 404.3, 433.6, 441.2, 479.6, 509.9, 585.7, 953.10, 979.7
acceptability 100.13, 107.3, 371.11, 953.8, 999.3
acceptable 100.30, 107.12, 371.24, 585.12, 999.20
acceptable face 952.2
acceptableness 107.1
acceptable person 659.1
accept a challenge 454.6
accept advice 422.7
acceptance 106.2, 107.1, 134.1, 187.2, 332.1, 332.3, 332.4, 371.4, 427.1, 433.1, 441.1, 479.1, 509.1, 518.4, 728.11, 953.1
acceptance bill 728.11
acceptance letter 567.5
acceptance speech 609.11
acceptation 518.4, 953.1
accept Christ 692.7
accepted 332.14, 371.26, 373.13, 404.7, 479.10, 509.19, 579.5, 687.7, 761.15, 953.23, 970.18
accepted conduct 579.2
accepted fact 761.3
accepted meaning 518.4
accepter 332.6, 479.3, 692.4
accept for gospel 953.10
accept implicitly 953.10
accepting 107.7, 134.9, 427.7, 433.12
accept in toto 332.8
acception 518.4, 953.1
accept obligation 436.5
accept one's fate 134.7
accept one's lot 107.5
accept on faith 953.10
accept responsibility 436.5
accept stolen property 479.6
accept the responsibility 641.9
accept unquestioningly 954.5

access (n) 85.6, 152.9, 167.1, 167.2, 187.3, 189.1, 189.5, 251.1, 383.3, 894.6, 917.6, 966.3, 1042.8, 1042.18 (v) 186.6, 189.7
access charge 630.6
accessibility 167.2, 221.1, 223.1, 343.3, 894.5, 966.3
accessible 167.5, 221.12, 223.15, 292.17, 292.21, 343.10, 352.17, 387.20, 472.14, 894.15, 966.8
accession 167.1, 251.1, 253.1, 254.1, 332.1, 417.12, 472.1, 615.3, 815.1
accessories 471.2
accessory (n) 5.31, 253.1, 254.1, 476.4, 598.11, 616.3, 768.2, 769.3 (a) 253.10, 449.20, 476.8, 768.4, 769.9
accessory after the fact 598.11, 616.3
accessory before the fact 598.11, 616.3
accessory chromosome 305.8
accessory design 717.5
access provider 343.5, 347.18
acciaccatura 709.18
accidence 526.3
accident 768.2, 831.1, 972.6, 1011.2
accidental (n) 709.14, 768.2 (a) 766.7, 768.4, 831.9, 843.11, 972.15
accidental death 307.5
accidental discovery 941.1
accidentality 972.1
accident-prone 414.20, 493.8
acclaim (n) 509.2, 662.1 (v) 332.8, 509.10
acclaimed 509.19, 662.16
acclamation 332.5, 509.2
acclamatory 509.16
acclimate 373.9
acclimated 373.15
acclimation 373.7
acclimatization 373.7
acclimatize 373.9
acclimatized 373.15
acclinate 204.17
acclivitous 204.17
acclivity 204.6
acclivous 204.17
accolade 509.3, 509.5, 646.4
accommodate 143.9, 161.11, 373.9, 385.7, 385.10, 437.8, 449.19, 465.8, 468.2, 788.7, 790.6, 852.7, 867.3
accommodated 373.15
accommodate to 867.3
accommodate with 478.15, 620.5
accommodating 134.10, 143.16, 427.8, 504.13
accommodatingness 143.3, 427.2
accommodation 161.4, 257.2, 373.7, 385.3, 437.1, 449.9, 465.4, 468.1, 478.1, 620.2, 788.4, 790.2, 852.1, 867.1
accommodation address 346.4, 553.9
accommodation ladder 193.4
accommodations 228.4, 385.3
accommodation train 179.14
accommodative 143.16
accompanier 769.4
accompaniment 254.1, 708.5, 708.22, 709.2, 769.1, 836.1, 899.1
accompanist 710.3, 769.4
accompany 708.39, 769.7, 836.4, 887.4
accompanying 769.9, 831.9, 836.5, 899.4
accompanyist 710.3
accomplice 476.4, 616.3
accomplice in crime 616.3
accomplish 186.6, 328.6, 328.9, 407.4, 409.11, 794.6, 861.5, 892.11
accomplished 407.10, 413.26
accomplished fact 328.3, 407.1, 761.3
accomplished fact, an 973.2
accomplishment 186.1, 249.1, 328.2, 328.3, 407.1, 409.1, 413.8, 794.4, 861.1, 892.5, 940.1
accomplishments 928.4
accord (n) 332.5, 437.1, 441.1, 455.1, 464.1, 708.3, 775.1, 788.1, 867.1 (v) 332.9, 443.9, 455.2, 478.12, 708.35, 788.6, 788.7, 867.3, 899.2
accordance 332.5, 434.1, 455.1, 478.1, 708.3, 781.1, 784.1, 788.1, 867.1, 899.1
accordant 441.4, 455.3, 708.49, 781.5, 788.9, 867.6, 899.4
accorded 478.24
accorded status 607.1
according 708.49
according to expectation 130.14
according to Hoyle 637.3
according to law 673.11
accordion 711.11
accordion file 195.1
accordionist 710.7
accordion pleat 291.2
accord respect to 155.4
accord to 441.2
accost (n) 585.4 (v) 167.3, 524.26, 585.10
accouchement 1.1
account (n) 349.3, 549.1, 549.7, 551.1, 552.3, 622.2, 624.5, 628.2, 628.3, 630.2, 662.3, 719.2, 722.3, 871.5, 1017.6, 1017.11 (v) 946.8
accountability 130.4, 573.2, 641.2
accountable 341.17, 641.17, 888.6
accountableness 341.6, 641.2
accountancy 628.6
accountant 550.1, 628.7, 726.4, 729.12, 1017.15
accountant general 628.7
account as 953.11
account book 549.11, 628.4
account current 628.2
accounted as 951.14
account for 341.10, 600.9, 888.4
accounting (n) 549.7, 628.6, 1017.9, 1041.7 (a) 628.12
accounting for 888.1
account of 1017.13
account rendered 549.7, 628.2
accounts 628.1, 1017.11
accounts payable 623.1, 628.1
accounts receivable 623.1, 624.1, 628.1
account stated 628.2
account with 624.12
accouple 800.5
accouplement 800.1, 800.4, 805.1
accouter 5.41, 385.8
accoutered 385.13, 460.14
accouterment 385.1
accouterments 5.2, 385.4
accredit 332.12, 443.11, 615.10
accredited 443.17, 615.19
accredit with 888.4
accrescendo 708.53
accretion 251.1, 472.2, 803.1
accretion rate 251.1, 472.2
accroach 480.19
accroach to oneself 640.8
accrual 251.1
accrue 251.6, 479.8, 623.7, 627.3
accrued dividends 738.7
accrue from 887.5
accruement 251.1
accrue to 479.8
accubation 201.2
acculturate 226.4, 373.9, 392.9
acculturated 226.6
acculturation 226.3, 373.2, 392.3
acculturize 226.4
acculturized 226.6
accumbency 201.2
accumbent 201.8
accumulate 251.6, 386.11, 472.11, 770.18, 800.5
accumulated 386.14, 770.21, 800.13
accumulated dividends 738.7
accumulation 251.1, 386.1, 472.2, 770.9
accumulative 253.8, 770.23
accumulator 770.15, 1032.21
accuracy 339.3, 766.4, 973.5
accurate 339.12, 944.7, 973.16
accurse 513.5
accursed 103.8, 513.9, 1000.10
accusable 510.25
accusal 599.1
accusant 599.5
accusation 599.1
accusative (n) 530.9 (a) 599.13
accusatorial 599.13
accusatory 599.13
accusatrix 599.5
accuse 510.13, 599.7
accused (n) 599.6 (a) 599.15
accused person 599.6
accuse of 599.9
accuse oneself 113.6
accuser 599.5
accusing (n) 599.1 (a) 599.13
accustom 373.9
accustomed 373.15, 869.9
accustomedness 373.6
accustoming 373.7
accustom oneself to 134.7, 373.11
AC-DC 75.30
ace (n) 185.3, 223.2, 248.2, 249.4, 413.14, 588.4, 748.2, 751.3, 758.2, 872.3, 999.7 (v) 751.4 (a) 122.10, 413.22
Ace bandage 86.33
ace-count 759.11
acedia 94.4, 96.6, 102.2, 112.3, 125.2, 331.6
Ace elastic bandage 86.33
ace-high 999.13
ace in the hole 249.2, 386.3
aceldama 308.12, 463.2
ace of clubs 758.2
ace of diamonds 758.2
ace one's opponent 748.3
acerb 64.6, 67.5, 144.23, 152.26
acerbate (v) 110.16 (a) 67.5, 144.23, 152.26
acerbic 17.14, 64.6, 67.5, 68.6, 144.23, 152.26
acerbity 17.5, 64.2, 67.1, 68.1, 144.8, 152.3
acervation 770.9
acescence 67.3
acescency 67.1
acescent 67.5
aces wired 970.2
acetaminophen 86.12
acetanilide 86.12
acetic 67.5, 67.6
acetification 67.3
acetify 67.4, 1060.8
acetophenetidin 86.12
acetose 67.6
acetous 67.6
acetylene torch 1020.14
acetylene welder 1020.14
acetylsalicylic acid 86.12
an ace up one's sleeve 386.3
ache (n) 26.5, 96.5, 1023.2 (v) 26.8, 96.19, 112.17
ache for 100.16
Acheron 307.3, 682.3, 682.4
Acheronian 1027.14
Acherontic 682.8, 1027.14
aches and pains 26.1
ache to 100.15
achievability 966.2
achievable 966.7
achieve 186.6, 328.6, 407.4, 409.11, 892.11
achieved 407.10
achieve inner harmony 107.4
achievement 186.1, 328.2, 328.3, 407.1, 492.6, 647.2, 892.5
achievement test 92.9
achieve one's purpose 409.8
achieve orgasm 75.24
achieve satisfaction 75.24
achieve success 409.10
Achilles 492.7
Achilles and Patroclus 588.6
Achilles' heel 16.4, 1003.2
achiness 26.5
aching (n) 26.5, 96.5, 100.5, 1023.2 (a) 26.12, 96.23
aching for 100.22
aching heart 96.6, 112.9

achingly sweet 708.48
aching to 100.22
aching void 100.6
achoo (n) 57.1 (v) 57.2
achroma 37.1
achromasia 37.1
achromatic 36.7, 37.7, 38.8, 38.9
achromatic color 35.6
achromaticity 36.1
achromatism 35.1, 36.1
achromatization 36.3
achromatize 36.5
achromatized 36.8
achromatizer 36.4
achromatopsia 30.3
achromatosis 37.1
achromatous 36.7
achromic 36.7
achy 26.12
acicular 285.9
aciculate 285.9
acid (n) 67.2, 87.10, 152.3, 1020.15, 1022.3, 1060.3 (a) 17.14, 67.6, 68.6, 110.17, 144.23, 152.26, 544.11, 1060.9
acid-base metabolism 2.20, 7.12
acid bath 79.9
acid etching 712.1
acid freak 87.21
acidhead 87.21
acidic 144.23, 152.26
acidification 67.3
acidify 67.4, 1060.8
acidity 17.5, 67.1, 68.1, 144.8, 152.3, 1060.3
acid jazz 708.9
acid kiln 742.5
acidness 144.8
acid-neutralizing 670.14
acidosis 85.22
acid rain 316.1, 1001.4
acid reflux 26.5, 85.29
acid rock 708.10, 1059.1
acid stop 714.13
acid taste 62.1
acid test 942.2
acid trip 87.2
acidulant 67.2
acidulate 67.4, 1060.8
acidulated 67.6
acidulation 67.3
acidulent 67.6, 144.23, 152.26
acidulous 17.14, 67.6, 144.23, 152.26
acidulousness 67.1, 68.1, 144.8, 152.3
acier 39.4
ack-ack 462.12
acknowledge 150.4, 332.11, 351.7, 553.11, 624.18, 888.4, 939.4, 957.9
acknowledged 332.14, 579.5, 842.12
acknowledge defeat 370.7, 433.8
acknowledge receipt of 627.3
acknowledge the corn 332.11, 351.7
acknowledging 150.5, 939.6
acknowledgment 150.2, 332.3, 351.3, 509.3, 553.2, 627.2, 639.2, 658.2, 888.2, 939.1
acknowledgments 554.12
acmatic 198.11
acme 198.2, 249.3, 272.2, 786.4, 794.5, 1002.3
acme of perfection 1002.3
acmic 198.11
acne 85.35, 85.36
acolyte 616.6, 699.4, 701.2
acolytus 699.4
acomia 6.4
acomous 6.17
acosmism 675.5
acosmistic 952.11
acoustic (n) 50.1 (a) 48.13, 50.17, 524.30
acoustical 48.13, 50.17
acoustical engineer 50.5
acoustical network 50.8
acoustical phenomenon 50.1
acoustician 50.5
acoustic meatus 2.10
acoustic nerve 2.10
acoustic phenomenon 50.1
acoustic phonetics 48.9, 524.13
acoustics 50.5
acoustic theory 50.5
acoustic tile 51.4
acoustic wave 916.4
acousto-optic 29.9
acousto-optical 29.9
acquaint 551.8, 587.14
acquaintance 551.1, 587.4, 588.1, 928.1
acquaintance rape 480.3, 665.6
acquaintanceship 587.4
acquainted 587.17
acquaintedness 587.4
acquainted with 928.19
acquaint oneself with 570.6
acquest 471.1
acquiesce 324.3, 332.8, 433.6, 441.3
acquiesce in 332.8
acquiescence 134.2, 324.1, 326.1, 332.1, 427.3, 433.1, 441.1, 867.1, 953.1
acquiescent 134.10, 324.5, 326.3, 332.13, 433.12, 441.4, 867.5
acquiescing 332.13
acquirability 966.3
acquire 472.8, 479.6, 480.13, 570.7, 627.3, 897.4
acquire a taste for 100.14
acquired immune deficiency syndrome 85.11, 85.18
acquired taste 496.1
acquired tolerance 87.1
acquire information about 570.6
acquire intelligence about 570.6
acquirement 413.8, 472.1
acquirements 928.4
acquirer 479.3
acquiring 472.15
acquisition 472.1, 479.1, 480.1, 733.1
acquisition of knowledge 570.1, 928.4
acquisitions 471.1, 928.4
acquisitions editor 554.2
acquisitive 100.27, 472.15, 651.5
acquisitiveness 100.8, 651.1
acquisitive society 733.1
acquit 148.3, 598.20, 601.4
acquitment 601.1, 624.1
acquit oneself 321.4, 641.11, 644.9
acquit oneself of 624.13
acquittal 434.1, 598.9, 601.1, 624.1
acquittance 434.1, 601.1, 624.1, 627.2
acquitted 148.7, 624.22
acre 247.3
acreage 158.1
acres 234.1, 471.6
acrid 17.14, 64.6, 67.5, 68.6, 144.23, 285.8, 589.10
acridian 311.35
acridity 17.5, 64.2, 68.1, 144.8, 285.1
acridness 64.2
acrimonious 17.14, 144.23, 152.26, 589.10, 671.16
acrimony 17.5, 144.8, 152.3, 510.7, 589.4, 671.1
acrobat 707.3
acrobatic 743.30
acrobatic maneuvers 184.13
acrobatics 184.13
acrolect 523.4
acromegalic gigantism 257.5
acromegaly 257.5
acronym 526.4
acrophile 237.6
acropolis 460.6
acrospire 310.23
across 170.9, 204.19
across-the-board 772.7, 792.9
acrostic 489.8, 522.9, 526.4
acrylic paint 35.8
acrylic painting 712.3, 712.13
acrylics painter 716.4
act (n) 328.1, 328.3, 613.5, 673.3, 704.7, 889.2 (v) 321.4, 328.4, 349.12, 354.21, 704.29, 889.7, 892.11
acta 328.3, 549.7
actability 966.2
actable 889.10, 966.7
act all over the stage 704.31
act a part 349.12, 354.21, 500.12, 704.30
act a role 704.30
act as 349.12, 724.13, 889.8
act as a cathartic 120.6
act as a magnet 983.11
act as feeder 704.29
act as foil 704.29
act beneath oneself 661.7
act between 466.6
act curtain 704.20
act drop 704.20
act-first-and-think-later 365.11
act for 384.7, 576.14, 862.5
act holier than thou 157.7
act in concert 450.3
acting (n) 328.1, 349.4, 354.3, 704.8 (a) 328.10, 576.16, 889.11
acting area 704.16
acting company 707.11
acting corporal 575.18
acting device 704.8
acting out 365.11
acting-out 92.25
acting sergeant 575.18
actinic 1025.41
actinic light 1025.5
actinic radiation 1037.1
actinic ray 1025.5
actinide 1060.2
actinism 1025.5
actinology 1025.22
actinometry 1025.22
act in opposition to 451.3
act in the interests of 384.7
act in the place of 576.14
action 321.1, 328.1, 328.3, 330.1, 404.1, 457.4, 458.4, 598.1, 722.4, 743.2, 747.3, 759.1, 889.1, 946.5, 995.2, 1040.4, 1041.3
actionability 673.1
actionable 598.21, 673.11, 674.6
actionable intelligence 551.1
action and reaction 184.25, 903.1
actioner 706.2
action figure 743.16
actions 321.1
action sequence 714.3
action shot 714.3
action verb 530.4
activate 17.12, 458.19, 1037.10, 1038.17
activated 1037.11
activating 17.15
activation 17.9, 458.9
activation energy 1038.15
activator 17.6
active (n) 530.14 (a) 17.13, 172.7, 330.17, 387.21, 434.4, 889.11
active adult community 209.1
active algolagnia 75.11
active birth 1.1
active citizen 227.4
active communications satellite 1075.6
active duty 458.8
active fancy 986.4
active forces 461.23
active galactic nucleus 1073.6, 1073.8
active galaxy 1073.6
active list 871.1
active market 737.2
active matrix display 1042.9
activeness 330.1
active operations 458.4
active service 458.8
active use 387.1
active voice 530.14
activewear 5.20
activism 328.1, 330.1
activist (n) 330.8, 375.11 (a) 17.13, 330.17, 330.23
activistic 330.17
activity 17.4, 172.1, 321.1, 328.1, 330.1, 724.1, 886.9, 1037.1
act like 336.5
act like a tonic 17.10
act like a trouper 704.29
act of contrition 440.2, 696.4
act of courage 492.6

act of courtesy 504.6
act of cruelty 144.12
act of faith 308.1
act of folly 923.4
act of God 963.7
act of grace 143.7
act of kindness 143.7
act of love 75.7
act of politeness 504.6
act of terrorism 144.12
act of thought 931.1
act on 328.5, 889.6, 894.9, 946.13
act on behalf of 576.14
act one's age 321.5
act one's part 641.10, 724.13
act on impulse 364.4
act on one's own responsibility 418.4
act on the spur of the moment 365.7
actor 357.1, 500.7, 704.10, 706.4, 707.2, 726.1
actor-proof 704.33
actor's agent 704.25
actor's lines 704.21
act out 349.12, 704.30
actress 706.4, 707.2
Acts 683.4
acts 321.1
Acts of the Apostles 683.4
act the fool 923.6
act the grand seigneur 501.14
act the hypocrite 354.23
act the part of 349.12, 354.22, 704.30, 889.8
act the traitor 645.15
act together 450.3
act toward 321.6
actual 761.15, 831.9, 838.2, 970.15, 973.13
actual cautery 1020.15
actual energy 17.1
actual fact 761.3
actuality 761.2, 838.1, 970.3, 973.1
actualization 206.4, 794.4
actualize 206.5
actual practice 328.1
actual presence 221.1
actual price 738.9
actual thing 778.3
actuarial 968.6
actuarial calculation 972.1
actuarial prediction 962.1
actuarial table 968.2
actuary 300.9, 628.7, 1008.4, 1017.15
actuate 172.6, 375.12, 902.11
actuated 375.30
actuating 375.25, 902.23
actuation 172.1, 375.2
actuator 375.10
act up 322.4
act upon 328.5, 889.6
act up to 434.2
act well 321.5
act with 450.4
act with regard to 321.6
acuate 285.9
acuity 285.1, 339.5, 920.2, 920.4
aculeate (v) 285.7 (a) 285.9
aculeated 285.9
aculeiform 285.9
aculeolate 285.10
aculeus 285.3
acultural 312.13
acumen 920.4, 944.2
acuminate (v) 285.6, 285.7 (a) 285.9
acumination 285.1, 285.3
acupoint 2.4
acupressure 91.14
acupunctuation 292.3
acupuncture 25.3, 90.13, 292.3
acupuncture point 2.4
acupuncturist 90.9
acus 285.3
acute 17.13, 24.13, 26.10, 58.14, 93.24, 285.8, 285.9, 415.12, 671.16, 920.16, 997.22
acute alcoholism 87.1
acute angle 278.2
acute episode 926.7
acuteness 58.1, 285.1, 339.5, 415.1, 671.1, 920.2, 920.4
acute pain 26.2
acute sense of hearing 48.3
acute sight 27.1
ad 352.6, 748.2
Ada from Decatur 882.4
adage 529.1, 974.1
adagietto (n) 708.25 (a) 708.54
adagio (n) 708.25 (a) 708.54
Adam 76.5, 312.6, 663.2
adamant (n) 1046.6 (a) 361.9, 855.15, 1046.10, 1046.12, 1059.11
adamantine 361.9, 763.7, 855.15, 1046.10, 1046.12, 1059.11
adamantness 361.2
Adamic 654.12, 663.6
Adamite (n) 312.5 (a) 312.13
Adamitic 312.13
Adam's ale 1065.3
Adam's apple 524.18
Adams Division 749.1
Adam's fall 655.3
Adam's-needle 285.5
Adam's offspring 312.6
Adam's rib 77.5
Adam's seed 312.6
adapt 161.11, 373.9, 405.8, 621.4, 708.46, 788.7, 852.7, 867.3
adaptability 413.3, 854.1, 1014.2, 1047.2, 1048.1
adaptable 387.20, 413.25, 854.6, 867.5, 1014.15, 1047.9, 1048.7
adaptation 161.4, 373.7, 405.2, 621.2, 708.5, 709.2, 788.4, 852.1, 861.3, 867.1
adapted 373.15, 405.17, 788.10
adapter 710.20
adapter card 1033.8
adapt for the stage 704.28
adapting 134.10
adaption 373.7, 867.1
adaptive 134.10, 867.5, 1048.7
adaptiveness 134.1
adaptivity 134.1
adapt to 867.3
Ada Ross 882.4
Ada Ross the stable hoss 882.4
A-day 843.5
ad blocker 1042.11
adbot 1042.11
ad creep 352.6
add 253.4, 805.3, 1017.18
addable 1017.25
add a codicil 478.18
added 253.9
added-in 772.5
added value 254.4, 387.3
addend 253.2
addenda 254.1
addendum 254.1, 768.2, 817.1
adder 1035.8
add fuel to the fire 105.12, 119.2, 251.5, 456.14
add fuel to the flame 375.17, 1020.22, 1021.8
addict 85.43, 87.21, 100.12, 101.4, 373.8
addicted 87.25, 373.18
addictedness 87.1
addicted to drink 88.35
addiction 87.1, 373.8, 669.1
addictive 375.27
addictive drug 87.3
addict oneself to 373.11
add in 259.4
adding 253.3, 1017.10
adding machine 253.3
add insult to injury 119.2, 156.5, 393.9, 456.13
additament 254.1
addition 251.1, 253.1, 254.1, 254.3, 259.1, 472.1, 768.2, 775.1, 805.1, 1017.2
additional 253.8, 253.10, 768.4, 841.8
additive (n) 254.1 (a) 253.8
additive color 35.8
additory (n) 254.1 (a) 253.8
additum 254.1
addle 88.22, 971.13, 985.7
addlebrain 924.4
addlebrained 922.18, 985.13
addled 88.31, 922.18, 971.25, 985.13
addlehead 924.4
addleheaded 922.18, 985.13
addleheadedness 922.5
addlepate 924.4
addlepated 922.18, 985.13
addlepatedness 922.5
addle the wits 926.23, 985.7
add on 253.4
add-on (n) 253.1 (a) 253.9
address (n) 159.1, 228.1, 321.1, 413.1, 440.1, 524.3, 543.2, 553.9, 585.4, 751.3 (v) 440.14, 524.26, 543.9, 553.13, 562.21, 585.10
address a warning to 399.5
address bar 1042.18
address book 549.11, 871.4
addressee 227.2, 227.7, 479.3, 553.8
addresses 440.5, 562.7
address oneself to 328.8, 404.3, 724.11
address the four walls 542.3
address to 983.10
add to 251.4, 253.5, 259.4
adduce 766.6, 957.12
adducent 907.5
adducible 957.16
adduct 907.4
adduction 907.1
adductive 907.5
adductor 907.2
add up 253.6, 973.10, 1017.18, 1017.19
add up to 792.8
ade 10.49
adenoidal 525.12
adenovirus 85.42
adept (n) 413.11, 689.11, 920.9, 921.1 (a) 413.22
adept in 413.27
adeptness 413.1
adequacy 18.2, 107.3, 246.1, 991.1
adequate 18.14, 107.11, 991.6, 999.20
adequateness 991.1, 999.3
adequate supply 991.1
adessive 530.9
à deux 873.7
adfiliation 450.2
adhere 800.11, 803.6
adherence 434.1, 509.1, 644.7, 803.1, 803.3
adherent (n) 138.6, 166.2, 509.8, 616.8, 803.4 (a) 803.12
adherent noun 530.5
adherents 617.5
adherer 803.4
adhere to 434.2, 437.9, 474.6
adhere to one's principles 359.9
adhering 803.10
adhesion 474.1, 644.7, 803.1
adhesive (n) 800.3, 803.4, 1054.6 (a) 803.12, 1062.12
adhesive bandage 86.33
adhesive compress 86.33
adhesiveness 803.3, 1062.2
adhesive plaster 803.4
adhesive tape 86.33
ad hoc (n) 828.1, 995.2 (a) 365.12, 406.8, 828.7, 862.8, 995.7
ad hoc committee 423.2
ad hocery 365.5, 862.1
ad hocism 365.5, 828.1, 862.1, 995.2
ad hockery 365.5, 828.1, 862.1, 995.2
ad hoc measure 365.5, 995.2
adhocracy 365.5, 828.1, 862.1
ad hoc solution 365.5
ad hominem 512.2
adiabatic absorption 1024.1
adiabatic demagnetization 1024.1
adiabatic expansion 1024.1
adiamorphic 695.15
adiaphanous 1031.3
adiaphanousness 1031.1
adiaphorism 102.1, 695.1
adiathermal 1019.31
adiathermancy 1019.18
adiathermic 1019.31
adieu 188.4
Adigranth 683.7

adipose 257.18, 1056.9
adiposis 257.8, 1056.5
adiposity 257.8, 1056.5
adit 189.5, 239.1
adjacency 223.3
adjacent 223.16
adjectival (n) 530.3 (a) 530.17
adjectival phrase 529.1
adjective 530.3
adjective phrase 530.3
adjoin 211.10, 223.9, 223.13, 253.4
adjoined 253.9
adjoiner 223.6
adjoining 223.16
adjourn 846.9
adjournal 846.4
adjournment 846.4
adjournment sine die 846.4
adjudge 946.8
adjudgment 946.1
adjudicate 946.8
adjudication 946.1
adjudicator 596.1, 946.6
adjunct (n) 253.1, 254.1, 259.1, 616.1, 768.2, 769.3, 775.1, 793.1, 796.2 (a) 253.9
adjunction 223.3, 253.1
adjunctive 253.9
adjuration 440.2
adjuratory 440.17
adjure 334.7, 440.11
adjust 161.11, 257.15, 373.9, 405.8, 437.8, 465.8, 466.7, 468.2, 788.7, 790.6, 808.10, 852.7, 867.3
adjustability 413.3, 854.1
adjustable 413.25, 854.6, 867.5
adjustable-rate mortgage 438.4
adjusted 373.15, 405.17
adjusted gross income 624.4
adjusted score 758.3
adjusting 134.10
adjustive reaction 92.27
adjustment 92.27, 161.4, 373.7, 405.2, 437.1, 465.4, 468.1, 765.3, 788.4, 790.2, 808.2, 852.1, 867.1
adjustment mortgage 438.4
adjust oneself to 134.7
adjust to 788.7, 867.3, 959.3
adjutage 239.6
adjutant 616.6
adjuvant (n) 254.1 (a) 86.39, 449.20, 449.21
adjuvant therapy 91.6
Adlerian psychology 92.2
ad lib 406.1
ad-lib (n) 365.5 (v) 365.8, 406.6, 704.29 (a) 365.12, 406.8
ad-libber 365.6
ad-libbing 365.5
ad libitum 365.12
adman 352.9
admeasured 300.13
admeasurement 300.1
administer 90.14, 437.9, 477.8, 478.12, 573.11, 594.5, 612.11, 643.6
administer absolution 701.17
administer an oath 334.7
administer a sacrament 701.15
administer Communion 701.14
administer extreme unction 701.17
administer justice 594.5
administer the Eucharist 701.15
administer to 577.13
administrate 573.11, 594.5, 612.11
administrating 573.14
administration 328.2, 417.5, 477.2, 571.8, 573.3, 612.1, 643.2, 1008.2
administration, the 574.3, 574.11, 575.14
administrative 417.15, 573.14, 612.16, 612.18
administrative assistant 547.13, 577.3
administrator 571.8, 574.1, 610.2
admirability 509.7
admirable 104.24, 509.20
admiral 575.19
admiralty 461.27
admiration 104.1, 122.1, 155.1, 509.1
admire 104.20, 155.4, 509.9
admired 104.23, 155.11, 509.19
admirer 101.4, 104.11, 509.8, 616.9
admiring 155.9, 509.16
admissibility 107.3, 187.9, 443.8, 600.7, 772.1, 788.5, 935.9, 999.3
admissible 107.12, 187.16, 371.24, 443.15, 600.14, 775.11, 935.20, 957.16, 999.20
admissibleness 443.8
admission 187.2, 189.1, 226.3, 332.3, 334.1, 351.3, 443.1, 479.1, 630.6, 772.1, 957.2
admission fee 630.6
admission of light 1029.1, 1030.2
admissive 187.16, 351.11, 443.14, 979.10
admissory 187.16
admit 187.10, 189.7, 226.4, 332.11, 351.7, 443.9, 479.6, 585.7, 658.5, 772.3, 959.5
admit everything 351.7
admit exceptions 959.5
admit of 897.3, 972.13
admit of comparison 943.7
admit of no doubt 970.9
admit of no option 424.5
admittance 187.2, 479.1
admitted 332.14, 351.10, 443.16, 479.10, 509.19, 579.5, 761.15, 842.12
admitted fact 761.3
admitting no doubt 970.15
admitting no exception 960.2
admitting no question 970.15
admix 797.10
admixture 253.1, 797.1, 797.5
admonish 379.3, 399.5, 422.6, 510.17
admonisher 399.4, 422.3
admonishing 399.7
admonishment 399.1, 510.5
admonition 379.1, 399.1, 422.1, 510.5
admonitory 379.5, 399.7, 422.8
ado (n) 105.4, 330.4, 810.4, 1013.3 (a) 831.9
adobe (n) 742.2, 742.3, 1054.2 (a) 234.5
adobe house 228.5
adolescence 301.6, 303.1
adolescent (n) 302.1 (a) 14.3, 301.13, 406.11
adolescent beard 3.8
adolescent stream 238.1
Adonai 677.2
Adonis 1016.9
Adonis-like 1016.18
a donné 973.2
a donnée 973.2
adopt 226.4, 371.15, 384.5, 480.19, 621.4, 640.8
adopt a belief 953.13
adopted 226.6, 371.26
adopted child 561.3
adoption 226.3, 371.4, 480.4, 621.2, 640.3, 685.4, 858.1
adoptive 371.23
adoptive father 560.9
adoptive fatherhood 560.2
adoptive mother 560.11
adoptive motherhood 560.3
adoptive parent 560.8
adopt the cause of 449.13
adorability 104.6
adorable 100.30, 104.24
adorant 696.16
adoration 104.1, 155.1, 692.1, 696.1
adore 95.13, 104.20, 155.4, 696.11
adoreableness 104.6
adored 104.23, 155.11
adorer 104.11, 696.9
adoring 104.26, 155.9, 692.8, 696.16
adorn 5.43, 498.8, 545.7, 662.12, 1016.15
adorned 498.11, 545.11
adorning 498.10
adornment 498.1, 545.4, 1016.10
ad rem 775.11, 788.10
adrenal 13.8
adrenalin 17.2, 86.9, 330.2
adrenaline-charged 17.13
adrenaline rush 17.3
adrift 182.61, 802.22, 854.7, 971.24, 975.16, 985.13
adroit 413.22, 920.14
adroitness 413.1, 920.2
adscititious 768.4
adsorb 187.13
adsorbent (n) 187.6 (a) 187.17
adsorption 187.6
adulate 509.12, 511.5, 696.11
adulation 509.5, 511.1, 696.1
adulator 511.4, 696.9
adulatory 509.18, 511.8
adult (n) 304.1 (a) 14.3, 303.12, 665.29, 666.9
adult beverage 88.13
adult education 567.5
adult-education student 572.1
adulterate 16.11, 299.3, 354.17, 393.12, 797.12, 1065.12
adulterated 16.19, 299.4, 1003.4
adulteration 65.1, 299.2, 350.1, 393.2, 797.3, 1003.1
adulterer 665.13
adulteress 665.13
adulterous 665.27
adulterous affair 104.5
adultery 75.7, 104.5, 665.7
adulthood 14.1, 303.1, 303.2
adult movie 666.4
adultness 303.2
adults-only 303.12
adult student 303.2, 304.1, 929.3
adumbrate 133.9, 349.11, 551.10
adumbrated 133.14
adumbration 133.3
auncity 279.1
auncous 279.8
adust 40.4, 1020.30, 1066.9
ad valorem 630.14
advance (n) 162.1, 167.1, 172.2, 251.1, 392.1, 439.1, 446.1, 449.5, 620.1, 620.2, 624.4, 861.1 (v) 162.2, 162.5, 167.3, 172.5, 251.6, 371.15, 384.7, 392.7, 392.9, 409.10, 439.5, 446.2, 449.17, 620.5, 821.5, 861.5, 886.12, 904.9, 951.12, 957.12, 995.3, 999.10, 1010.7
advance against 459.17
advance agent 704.25
advance base 1075.5
advance camp 760.6
advanced 216.10, 303.16, 392.13, 816.4, 841.13, 845.8
advanced age 303.5
advanced base 216.2
advanced degree 567.5
advanced in life 303.16
advanced in years 303.16
advance directive 478.10
advanced placement 567.5
advanced trainer 181.10
advanced years 303.5
advance guard 216.2, 841.2, 1008.9
advance man 704.25
advancement 162.1, 392.1, 446.1, 449.5, 620.1, 861.1
advance notice 399.2, 405.1, 845.1, 961.2
advance sheets 548.10
advance to the rear (n) 163.2 (v) 163.6, 368.10
advance upon 459.17, 910.9
advance warning 399.2, 405.1
advance word 399.5
advancing (n) 162.1, 620.1, 749.6 (a) 162.6, 167.4, 392.15, 459.29, 861.8
advantage (n) 249.2, 387.3, 387.4, 449.9, 748.2, 906.2, 995.1, 999.4 (v) 387.17, 449.17, 995.3, 999.10
advantageous 387.18, 472.16, 995.5, 999.12
advantageousness 449.10, 995.1, 999.1

advantageous purchase 633.3
advene 253.7
advent 167.1, 186.1, 839.5
Advent calendar 701.12
adventitious 766.7, 768.4, 972.15
adventitiousness 972.1
adventure 328.3, 404.2, 492.6, 706.2, 831.2, 972.6
adventure athlete 178.1
adventure game 457.3
adventurer 178.1, 461.17, 493.4, 606.7, 737.11, 759.21
adventures 719.1
adventuresome 330.23, 492.21
adventuresomeness 330.7, 492.4
adventuress 493.4, 665.15
adventure travel 177.1
adventure traveler 178.1
adventurist 493.4
adventurous 330.23, 404.8, 492.21, 493.9, 1006.10
adventurousness 330.7, 492.4, 493.3
adverb 530.3
adverbal 530.17
adverbial 530.3
adverbial noun 530.5
adverbial phrase 529.1
adverb phrase 530.3
adversaria 549.4, 549.11
adversarial 215.5, 451.8, 779.6
adversarial procedure 935.4
adversary (n) 452.1, 461.1, 589.6 (a) 451.8
adversative 335.5, 451.8, 779.6
adversative conjunction 530.3
adverse 451.8, 779.6, 962.12, 1011.13
adverse circumstances 1011.1
adverse criticism 510.4
adverse judgment 510.1
adverse party 452.1
adverse possession 469.1
adverse report 510.5
adversity 96.8, 1011.1
adversive 779.6
advert 352.6
advertence 983.1
advertency 983.1
advertent 983.15
advertise 352.10, 352.15, 501.17, 551.8
advertisement 352.6
advertise of 551.8
advertise oneself 502.6
advertiser 352.9
advertising 352.5
advertising agency 352.5
advertising campaign 352.5
advertising matter 352.8, 548.10
advertising media 352.5
advertising medium 352.5
advertising writer 547.15, 718.4
advertorial 352.6
advert to 517.18, 983.5
advice 422.1, 551.3, 552.1, 552.4
advice column 552.1
advice columnist 552.9
Advil 86.12
advisability 995.1
advisable 995.5
advise 399.5, 422.5, 551.8, 573.9
advise against 422.6
advised 380.8, 935.21
advisee 422.4
advisement 422.1, 931.2
adviser 413.11, 422.3, 551.5
advise with 541.10, 931.14
advising 422.1
advisor 422.3
advisory (n) 400.1 (a) 422.8, 423.5, 551.18
advisory body 423.1
advisory council 613.3
advocacy 352.5, 375.5, 422.1, 449.4, 509.4
advocacy group 352.5
advocate (n) 422.3, 460.7, 576.1, 588.1, 597.1, 600.8, 610.1, 616.9, 901.2, 935.12 (v) 375.14, 422.5, 449.14, 460.8, 509.11, 600.10
advocated 509.19
advocating (n) 352.5, 509.4 (a) 509.17
advocation 509.4
advowson 698.9
adware 1042.11
ad writer 352.9
adynamia 16.1
adytum 197.8, 703.5, 1009.5
Aeacus 596.4
aedileship 417.7
aegis 449.4, 1008.3
aeolian 318.21
Aeolian mode 709.10
Aeolus 318.2
aeon 824.4, 827.4
aeonian 829.7
aerage 317.9
aerate 317.11, 320.5, 1067.8
aeration 317.9, 1067.5
aerator 317.10
aerial (n) 1034.4 (a) 184.49, 272.14, 317.12, 986.22, 1067.9
aerial combat 457.4
aerial heights 272.2
aerialist 707.3
aerial ladder 193.4
aerial navigation 184.6
aerial photograph 714.3
aerial photographer 185.4
aerial root 310.22
aerial tramway 383.8
aeriferous 317.12
aerification 1067.5
aeriform 298.10, 317.12
aerify 317.11, 1067.8
aeriness 1067.3
aerobatic 184.49
aerobatics 184.13
aerobe 85.42
aerobic bacteria 85.42
aerobic dance 84.2
aerobic dancing 84.2
aerobic exercise 84.2
aerobic fitness 84.1
aerobicize 84.4
aerobic organism 305.2
aerobics 84.2
aerobic walking 84.2
aeroboat 181.8
aerodontic 184.49
aerodrome 184.22
aerodromics 184.1
aerodynamic 184.49, 1039.10, 1067.9
aerodynamical 184.49
aerodynamics 1039.5, 1067.2
aerodyne 181.1
aerographer 317.6
aerographic 317.13, 1039.10
aerographical 317.13, 1039.10
aerography 317.5, 1039.5
aerohydroplane 181.8
aerolite 1073.15
aerologic 317.13, 1039.10
aerological 317.13, 1039.10
aerological instrument 317.8
aerologist 317.6
aerology 317.3, 317.5, 1039.5
aeromarine 184.49
aeromechanic (n) 185.6, 1040.12 (a) 184.49
aeromechanical 184.49, 1039.7, 1039.10
aeromechanics 1039.5
aeromedical 184.49
aerometer 1045.8, 1067.7
aerometry 1039.5
aeromotor 184.25
aeronaut 185.1, 185.7
aeronautic 184.49
aeronautical 184.49
aeronautical engineer 185.6, 1043.2
aeronautical engineering 1043.1
aeronautical or air sport 744.1
aeronautical relay 1035.9
aeronautical science 184.2
aeronautics 184.1
aeronautism 184.1
aeronomic 184.49
aeropathy 184.5
aerophilia 184.4
aerophobia 184.5
aerophone 711.6
aerophysical 184.49, 1018.3, 1039.10
aerophysicist 1018.2
aerophysics 1039.5
aeroplane (n) 181.1 (v) 184.36
aerosol 1064.3, 1065.8, 1067.6
aerospace (n) 184.32 (a) 184.49
aerospace engineer 1043.2
aerospace engineering 1043.1, 1075.1
aerospace medicine 1075.1
aerospace research 1075.1
aerospace science 1075.1
aerospace technology 1075.1
aerosphere 184.32, 317.2
aerostat 181.11
aerostatic 184.49, 1039.10, 1067.9
aerostatical 184.49
aerostatic lift 184.26
aerostatics 1039.5
aerotechnical 184.49, 1039.10
aerotechnics 1039.5
aerotrain 179.14
aeruginous 44.5
aerugo 44.2
aery 317.12
Aesculapius 90.12
Aeshma 680.4
Aesopian 519.7
Aesopian language 518.1, 522.7
Aesopian meaning 518.1, 519.2
Aesopic 519.7
aesthesia 24.2
aesthete 496.5
aesthetic 496.7, 712.20, 952.11
aesthetically appealing 1016.17
aesthetic distance 261.1
aesthetic form 262.1
aesthetician 723.4
aesthetic judgment 944.1
aesthetic proportions 1016.3
aesthetics 496.4, 723.1
aesthetic taste 496.4
aestival 44.4, 313.9, 1019.24
aestivate 22.15, 331.16
aestivating 22.2
aestivation 22.2
AF amplification 1034.15
afeared 127.22
afebrile delirium 926.8
Afer 318.2
affability 97.1, 143.2, 427.2, 504.1, 581.1, 582.1, 587.6
affable 97.6, 143.14, 427.8, 504.13, 581.3, 582.22, 587.16
affair 104.5, 404.1, 582.10, 724.1, 831.3, 1052.4
affaire d'amour 104.5
affair of honor 457.7
affair of the heart 104.5
affairs 328.1, 328.3, 724.1, 775.1, 831.4
affect (n) 93.1, 978.1 (v) 5.44, 93.14, 93.15, 145.5, 336.5, 348.5, 354.21, 500.12, 772.4, 775.5, 889.6, 894.7
affectation 321.1, 354.3, 500.1, 532.2, 533.3, 545.1, 693.1
affected 93.23, 354.26, 500.15, 533.9, 545.8, 693.5
affectedness 500.1, 533.3
affecter 500.7, 693.3
affectibility 24.2
affecting 93.22, 98.20, 145.8
affection 85.1, 93.1, 100.2, 104.1, 104.2, 587.1
affectional 93.17
affectionate 104.26, 143.13, 587.19
affectionately 820.5
affectionate name 527.7
affectionateness 104.2, 143.1
affections 93.1
affective 93.17, 978.7
affective faculty 93.1
affective meaning 518.1
affectivity 93.1, 93.4, 978.1
affectless 25.6, 94.9
affectlessness 25.1, 94.1
affect memory 989.1
affect one's mind 926.23
affect the guise of 349.12
affect the interest 983.12
affect the manner of 349.12
afferent neuron 2.14
affettuoso 708.53
affiance (n) 436.3 (v) 436.6

affianced (n) 104.16 (a) 436.8, 563.18
affiche 352.7
affidavit 334.3, 549.6, 598.7, 953.4, 957.2
affiliate (n) 617.10, 617.11 (v) 226.4, 371.15, 450.3, 617.14, 805.4 (a) 775.9, 805.6
affiliated 559.6, 775.9, 805.6
affiliated stations 1034.8
affiliates 617.12
affiliate to 888.5
affiliate with 617.14
affiliation 226.3, 371.4, 450.2, 559.1, 560.4, 582.6, 675.3, 775.1, 805.1
affinal 564.4, 775.10
affined 564.4
affinitive 775.9, 784.13
affinity 100.3, 371.5, 455.1, 564.1, 587.5, 775.1, 775.3, 784.2, 788.1, 896.1, 907.1
affinity card 622.3
affirm 332.12, 334.5, 352.12, 524.23, 692.6, 953.12, 957.9, 957.11
affirmance 332.4, 334.1
affirmation 332.4, 334.1, 334.3, 441.1, 524.3, 935.7, 957.2, 957.4
affirmative (n) 332.2, 334.1, 441.1 (a) 334.8, 441.4, 788.9
affirmative, the 935.14
affirmative action 371.3, 790.2, 843.2
affirmative attitude 332.2
affirmativeness 332.2, 334.2
affirmative voice 441.1
affirmative vote 441.1
affirmatory 334.8
affirmed 332.14, 334.9, 352.17
affirming 334.8, 692.8
affix (n) 254.2, 526.3 (v) 253.4, 800.7
affixal 526.22
affixation 253.1, 526.3, 800.3
affixed 253.9
affixing 523.23
affix one's John Hancock 437.7
afflatus 375.9, 683.10, 720.11, 920.8, 986.2
afflict 26.7, 85.50, 96.16, 112.19, 1000.6
afflicted 26.9, 88.33, 96.22
afflicting 98.20
affliction 85.1, 85.4, 96.8, 1001.1, 1011.1
afflictive 26.10, 98.20
affluence 238.4, 618.1, 991.2, 1010.1
affluent (n) 238.3 (a) 238.24, 618.14, 991.7, 1010.12
affluential (n) 618.6 (a) 618.14, 894.13
affluential, an 894.6
affluent life, the 1010.1
afflux 167.1, 189.2, 238.4
affluxion 167.1, 238.4
afford 385.7, 478.12, 478.15, 618.11, 626.7, 627.4
affordability 633.1
affordable 633.7
affordable housing 228.1
affordableness 633.1
afford hope 124.9
affording no hope 125.12
afford one pleasure 95.6
afford proof of 957.10
afford support 449.12
afforest 1069.18
afforestation 310.13, 1069.3
afforestational 310.40
afforested 310.40
affranchise 431.4
affranchisement 431.1
affray 457.4
affrettando 708.55
affricate 524.12
affricated 524.30
affright (n) 127.1 (v) 127.15
affrighted 127.25
affront (n) 152.11, 156.2 (v) 152.21, 156.5, 216.8, 451.5, 454.3, 492.10
affusion 701.6, 1065.6
afghan 295.10
aficionada 101.4
aficionado 101.4, 221.5, 616.9, 866.3, 926.18
afire 93.18, 101.9, 375.31, 1019.27
aflame 101.9, 1019.27, 1025.34
aflicker 1019.27, 1025.36
afloat 182.60, 182.61, 238.25, 405.23, 552.15, 802.22, 831.9, 854.7
aflush 139.13
afoot 330.19, 405.23, 761.13, 831.9
aforegoing 837.11
aforementioned 814.5
aforenamed 814.5
aforesaid 814.5
aforethought (n) 380.3 (a) 380.9
a fortiori 935.22
afraid 127.22, 362.12, 491.10
afraidness 127.3
afraid of one's own shadow 127.23
afraid of one's shadow 491.10
A-frame 901.16
afreet 680.6
Africa 231.6, 235.1
African 952.11
African-American 312.3
African dominoes 759.8
African golf 759.8
African heat 1019.5
African hunting dog 311.19
Africanized bee 311.34
African plate 235.1
Africus 318.2
afrit 680.6
Afro 1016.14
Afro-Americanese 523.7
Afro-American literature 718.1
Afroasiatic 523.12
aft (n) 315.1 (a) 217.9
after 217.9, 835.4
afterbirth 817.3
aftercare 1008.2
afterclap 817.3, 887.3
aftercrop 817.3, 887.3
afterdamp 1067.1
after death 835.5
after-dinner 11.6, 402.5, 835.5
after-dinner speaker 543.4
after-dinner speaking 543.1
after-dinner speech 543.2
aftereffect 254.1, 817.3, 887.3
afterglow 256.1, 817.3, 887.3, 1025.2
aftergrass 310.5
aftergrowth 817.3, 887.3
afterguard 183.6
after-hours joint 88.20
afterimage 256.1, 817.3, 887.3, 976.5
afterlife 835.1, 839.2
afterlife, the 681.2
aftermarket 737.3
after mast 217.7
aftermath 472.5, 817.3, 831.1, 835.2, 887.1, 887.3
aftermost 217.9
afternoon (n) 315.1 (a) 315.7
afternoon tea 8.6, 582.13
after one's fancy 97.6
after one's heart 104.23
after one's own heart 97.6, 100.30, 104.23
afterpain 817.3
afterpart 217.1, 817.2
afterparty 95.3, 487.1
afterpiece 217.1, 704.7, 817.2
after-shave lotion 70.3
aftershock 887.3
aftertaste 62.1, 817.3, 887.3
after-the-fact 835.4
after the Fall 835.5
after the flood 835.5
after the war 835.5
afterthought 817.1, 844.1, 846.2, 931.5
afterthoughts 363.1
aftertime 839.1
afterword 254.2, 793.2
afterworld, the 681.2, 839.2
afteryears 839.1
aftmost 217.9
against 510.21
against one's will 963.14
against the current 333.4
against the grain 99.7
against the law 674.6
agalloch 70.4
Agama 683.8
agape (n) 104.1, 143.4, 455.1 (a) 122.9, 130.11, 292.18, 981.5
Agapemone 986.11
agar 1062.5
agasp 21.12
agave juice 66.3
agave nectar 66.3
agave sap 66.3
agave syrup 66.3
age (n) 303.1, 824.4, 824.5, 827.1, 827.4, 827.5, 842.1 (v) 303.10, 842.9
age-appropriate 637.3
aged 303.13, 303.16, 304.7, 827.10, 842.17
aged horse 757.2
age discrimination 980.4
agedness 303.5
agee 204.14
agee-jawed 204.14
age-encrusted 842.13
age group 617.6, 770.3, 836.2
ageism 607.1, 980.4
ageless 829.7, 842.10
age limit 959.2
agelong 827.10
agency 384.3, 615.1, 731.2, 739.1, 862.1, 889.1
agenda 381.1, 549.11, 871.1, 871.6, 965.3
agenda book 549.11, 582.8, 871.6
agenda-setter 574.3
agent 213.4, 352.9, 384.4, 466.3, 551.5, 574.1, 576.3, 597.1, 615.9, 616.6, 704.25, 726.1, 730.3, 852.5, 862.2, 886.4, 889.4, 1042.11, 1060.2
agential 384.8, 889.12
agentival 384.8, 889.12
agentive 384.8, 889.12
Agent Orange 1001.3
agent provocateur 327.5, 357.5, 375.11, 576.9
agentship 615.1
Age of Anxiety 824.6
Age of Aquarius 824.6, 1010.4
age of consent 303.2, 563.2
age of discretion 303.2
Age of Enlightenment 392.3
age of ignorance 930.3
age of matured powers 303.2
Age of Reason 392.3
age of responsibility 303.2
age of retirement 303.5
Age of the Red-Hot Mamas 824.5
age-old 842.10
ages 827.4
age-specific 766.9
age spot 2.4, 774.2
agglomerate (n) 770.9, 803.5 (v) 770.18, 803.6 (a) 770.21
agglomerated 803.10
agglomeration 770.9, 800.1, 803.1, 803.5, 805.1
agglutinate (v) 253.4, 800.5, 803.9 (a) 803.10
agglutinated 803.10
agglutination 253.1, 800.1, 803.1, 1045.3
agglutinative 523.23, 803.10
agglutinin 86.27
aggrandize 251.4, 259.4, 355.3, 446.2, 662.13
aggrandized 251.7, 355.4, 662.18
aggrandizement 251.1, 259.1, 355.1, 446.1, 662.8
aggravate 96.13, 96.14, 98.15, 119.2, 152.24, 251.5, 393.9, 456.14, 589.7
aggravated 96.21, 119.4, 152.27, 393.27
aggravated assault 459.1
aggravated battery 459.1
aggravated larceny 482.2
aggravating 98.22, 119.5
aggravation 96.2, 96.3, 98.7, 105.11, 119.1, 152.1, 251.2, 1011.1

aggravative 119.5
aggregate (n) 253.2, 770.9, 803.5, 1017.6 (v) 770.18, 792.8, 1017.19 (a) 770.21, 792.9
aggregate, the 792.3
aggregate fruit 10.38
aggregate to 792.8
aggregation 770.9, 800.1, 805.1
aggression 330.7, 458.10, 459.1
aggressive 17.13, 330.23, 456.17, 458.20, 459.30, 505.7
aggressively self-confident 140.11
aggressive mimicry 311.1, 336.2
aggressiveness 17.2, 330.7, 456.3, 458.10, 505.3
aggressor 459.12
aggrieve 96.17, 112.19, 152.21, 1000.6
aggrieved 96.23, 112.26
aggrievedness 112.11
aggrieved party 598.11
aggro 119.1, 152.5, 322.1, 458.10, 810.4
aggroup 770.18
aghast 122.9, 127.26
agile 174.15, 330.18, 339.14, 413.23
agile wit 489.1
agility 330.3, 339.5, 413.2
agilmente 708.53
agin 510.21
aging (n) 303.6 (a) 303.17
aging in place 91.21
agin the government 860.6
agio 631.1, 728.9
agiotage 737.19
agita 24.4, 26.5, 85.29, 105.4
agitability 105.10
agitable 105.28
agitate 96.16, 105.14, 126.4, 126.5, 375.17, 811.4, 917.10
agitated 96.22, 105.23, 126.7, 128.12, 330.20, 917.16
agitating 105.30
agitation 24.4, 105.4, 105.11, 126.1, 127.5, 128.1, 330.4, 375.4, 671.2, 917.1
agitational 375.28
agitative 105.30, 375.28
agitato 708.53
agitator 327.5, 375.11, 593.2, 797.9, 917.9
agitprop 375.11, 569.2
aglow 1019.27, 1025.30, 1025.39
agnate (n) 559.2, 560.4 (a) 559.6, 560.18, 775.10, 784.13
agnatic 560.18
agnation 559.1, 775.3
agneau 10.16
agnomen 527.6, 527.7
agnominal 527.15
agnosia 990.2
agnostic (n) 695.12 (a) 695.20, 952.11, 955.9, 971.16
agnosticism 695.6, 930.1, 955.1
Agnus Dei 696.3
ago 837.7
agog 101.8, 105.20, 122.9, 130.11, 981.5, 983.15
a gogo 991.7
agonist 461.1
agonistic 458.20, 743.30
agonistics 743.8
agonize 26.7, 26.8, 96.18, 96.19, 98.12, 112.17, 725.11
agonized 26.9, 93.23, 96.25
agonize over 971.9
agonizing 26.10, 98.23
agonizingness 98.4
agonizing pain 26.6
agony 26.6, 96.6, 98.4, 112.10, 307.8
agony of mind 96.6
agony of spirit 96.6
agony of suspense 971.1
agora 230.8, 463.1, 736.2
agraphia 525.6
agrarian 233.6, 1069.20
agrarian economics 1069.1
agrarian economy 1069.1
agrarianism 233.3, 1069.1
agrarian society 233.3, 1069.1, 1069.14
agree 324.3, 332.8, 332.9, 332.10, 437.5, 455.2, 775.5, 778.4, 788.6, 836.4, 899.2
agreeability 97.1, 100.13, 104.6, 107.3, 324.1, 433.3, 1016.2, 1047.2
agreeable 63.8, 97.6, 100.30, 107.12, 143.14, 143.16, 324.5, 427.8, 433.12, 441.4, 455.3, 504.13, 585.12, 587.15, 708.48, 788.9, 1016.18
agreeableness 97.1, 143.3, 324.1, 427.2, 433.3, 504.1, 999.1, 1016.2
agreeable-sounding 708.48
agreeance 332.1
agree beforehand 964.6
agreed 332.13, 437.11, 951.14
agreed on all hands 332.15
agreed upon 437.11
agree for the sake of argument 332.11
agreeing 332.13, 332.15, 441.4, 450.5, 455.3, 788.9, 836.5, 899.4
agree in opinion 332.9
agree in principle 332.11
agreement 332.1, 332.5, 436.2, 437.1, 441.1, 455.1, 731.5, 778.1, 784.1, 788.1, 805.1, 836.1, 867.1, 899.1
agreement among parties 437.1
agreement between parties 437.1
agreement in principle 332.1
agreement of all 332.5
agreement to disagree 333.1, 456.2
agree on 332.10
agree on a verdict 946.13
agree on terms 437.7
agree provisionally 332.11
agree to 332.8, 436.5, 437.5, 441.2, 731.19
agree to anything 138.9
agree to differ 333.4
agree to disagree 333.4, 456.10, 789.5
agree upon 332.10
agree with 81.4, 332.8, 332.9, 332.10, 455.2, 775.5, 867.3
agrestal 233.6, 234.5, 1069.20
agrestic 233.6
agribiz 1069.1
agribusiness 1069.1
agricultural 233.6, 1069.20
agricultural ant 311.33
agricultural chemist 1060.7
agricultural college 567.5
agricultural economics 1069.1
agricultural engineer 1043.2
agricultural engineering 1043.1, 1069.1
agricultural geology 1069.1
agriculturalist 1069.5
agricultural meteorology 317.5
agricultural region 233.1
agricultural science 1069.1
agricultural tool 1040.1
agricultural worker 726.2, 1069.5
agriculture 1069.1
agriculturist 1069.5
agriothymia 152.8
agriscience 1069.1
agriscientist 1069.5
agro- 1069.20
agrobusiness 1069.1
agrochemistry 1069.1
agroecology 397.1
agroecosystem 1069.1
agrogeology 1069.1
agroindustry 1069.1
agrologist 1069.5
agrology 1069.1
agronomic 1069.20
agronomical 1069.20
agronomics 1069.1
agronomist 1069.5
agronomy 1069.1
agroscience 1069.1
agrotechnician 1069.5
agrotechnology 1069.1
agroterrorism 127.7
aground 855.13, 855.16, 1013.27
agua 1065.3
ague 85.7, 85.9, 917.2
aguey 1023.16
aguish 1023.16
aha moment 570.2
aha reaction 928.2
Ahasuerus 178.2
ahead (v) 818.10 (a) 216.10, 249.12
ahead of its time 841.13
ahead of the game 409.14, 411.7
ahead of time 833.3
ahimsa 464.4, 670.1, 919.5
-aholic 101.5
Ahriman 680.4
Ahura Mazda 677.5
aid (n) 86.1, 449.1, 478.8, 592.1, 616.6, 901.1 (v) 162.5, 449.11, 478.17, 478.19, 592.3, 1014.7
aid and abet 375.16, 375.21, 449.14, 450.3
aid and comfort 121.4
aid climbing 760.6
aide 575.17, 576.1, 616.6
aide-de-camp 575.17, 616.6
aide-mémoire 549.4, 989.5, 989.8
aider 592.1, 616.6
Aides 682.5
aidful 449.21
aidfulness 449.10
aiding 592.4
aidless 19.18
Aidoneus 682.5
aid prayer 696.4
aid to dependent children 478.8, 611.7
aid to navigation 517.10
aid to the blind 611.7
aid to the permanently and totally disabled 611.7
aiguille 237.6
aikido 760.3
ail 26.8, 85.46, 1013.13
aileron roll 184.14
ailing 85.56
ailment 85.1
aim (n) 100.10, 161.1, 375.1, 380.1, 380.2, 518.2 (v) 161.5, 161.7, 380.4, 403.5
aimable 161.13
aim at 100.14, 161.5, 380.4, 459.22
aim at a pigeon and kill a crow 414.14
aimed 161.13, 380.8
aimed at 380.8
aim high 100.20
aimless 391.9, 520.6, 538.13, 810.12, 972.16
aimlessness 391.2, 520.1, 538.3, 972.3
aim to 403.8
air (n) 33.4, 209.3, 298.2, 317.1, 318.4, 321.1, 708.4, 764.3, 1029.2, 1052.2, 1067.2, 1073.2 (v) 317.11, 351.5, 352.10, 352.11, 501.17, 541.11, 757.5, 1066.6
Air Age 824.6
air a grievance 115.15
air arm 461.29
air armada 181.9
air attack 459.1, 459.4
air bag 1008.3
air ball 747.3
air bandit 759.22
air base 184.22
airbase 458.4, 461.29
air bed 229.1
air bombing 459.7
airborne 184.50
airborne division 461.22
airborne operations 458.4
airborne particles 1051.5
airborne radar 1036.2
airborne radioactivity 1038.16
airborne troops 461.23
airborne warning and control systems plane 181.9
airbrush 712.18
airbrushing 712.3
air bubble 320.1
air-built 764.6, 986.22
air bump 184.32
airburst 1074.9
air cadet 185.3

air car 181.7
air cargo 184.10
air castle 124.4, 986.10
air combat 457.4
air-condition 317.11, 1023.10, 1024.10
air-conditioned 1024.13
air conditioner 317.10, 1024.3
air conditioning 317.9, 1024.1
air-conscious 184.49
air-cool 317.11, 1024.10
air-cooled 1024.13
air cooler 317.10, 1024.3
air cooling 317.9, 1024.1
air corps 461.29
air cover 184.11
aircraft 179.1, 181.1, 1043.3
aircraft carrier 180.6, 180.8
aircraft engine 181.1, 184.25
aircraft instrument 181.1
aircraft mechanic 185.6
aircraftsman 185.6
aircraft spotting 382.1
aircrew 185.4
aircrewman 185.4
aircrew member 185.1
air-cured 89.2
air current 318.1
air-cushion vehicle 179.22, 181.7
air cylinder 367.5
Air Defense Command 460.2
airdock 184.24
air-dried 1066.9
airdrome 184.22
airdrop 184.9
air-dry 1066.6
air-drying 1066.3
air duct 239.13
air-express 176.15
airfield 184.22
air filter 72.3, 317.10
air fleet 181.9
air flow 184.29
airflow 184.29
Air Force 184.7, 461.21
air force 181.9, 185.3, 461.29
Air Force noncommissioned officer 575.18
airfreight (n) 184.10 (v) 176.15
air freshener 72.3
air glow 1025.2
air guitar 349.4
air gun 53.6
air hall 266.2
air harbor 184.22
airhead 216.2, 924.4
airheaded 922.17, 922.19
airheadedness 922.6
air hole 184.32, 239.13
air hostess 185.4
airify 317.11
airiness 109.3, 158.5, 270.4, 298.1, 299.1, 318.14, 764.1, 976.2
airing 177.7, 177.10, 317.9, 352.1, 541.6
airish 317.12, 318.21
air-kiss 562.4
air lane 184.33, 383.1
air legs 184.4
airless 173.16
airlessness 173.6
airlift (n) 184.9 (v) 184.36
airlike 317.12
airline 184.10, 184.33, 277.2
airline host 577.5
airline hostess 577.5
airline pilot 185.1
Airline Pilots Association 184.7
airline service 184.10
airline steward 577.5
airline stewardess 577.5
airline traffic 184.1
airline travel 184.10
air lock 189.5, 239.11
airmail (n) 553.4 (v) 176.15, 553.12
airman 185.1
airman first class 575.18
airmanship 184.3, 413.1
air marshal 575.17
air mass 317.2, 317.4
air-mass analysis 317.5
air mattress 901.20
Air Medal 646.6
air-minded 184.49
air-mindedness 184.4
Air National Guard 461.24
air navigation 184.6
airometer 1067.7
air one's grievances 333.5
air operations 458.4
air out 317.11, 368.11
airpark 184.22
air passage 239.13, 317.10
airperson 185.1
air pilot 185.1
air piracy 482.7
air pirate 483.7
airplane (n) 181.1 (v) 184.36
airplane driver 185.1
airplane hijacker 483.7
airplane hijacking 482.7
airplane part 181.1
airplane spotter 1008.10
airplaning 184.1
airplay 662.1, 1034.16
air pocket 184.32
air pollution 82.1, 1001.4, 1051.5, 1072.2
airport 184.22, 186.5
airport fee 630.6
air pressure 317.4
air purifier 72.3
air quality 1072.2
air-quote 212.8
air quotes 321.1, 349.2, 517.14
air race 457.12
air rage 105.9
air raid 184.11, 459.4
air-raid alarm 400.1
air-raid shelter 1009.3
air ram 184.25
air route 184.33
Air Route Traffic Control Center 184.22, 1036.6
airs 157.1, 500.1, 501.2
airscape 33.6, 712.11
air science 184.2
airscrew 904.6
air-sea rescue 398.2
air service 184.10, 461.29
air serviceman 461.6
air servicewoman 461.6
air shaft 239.13
airship 181.11
airship shed 184.24
airship station 184.22
air show 184.1
air shuttle 184.10
airsick 85.57, 184.49
airsickness 85.30, 184.5
airside 184.22
air sleeve 184.19
air space 158.1, 158.4, 231.1, 231.4
airspace 184.32
airspeed 174.1
air station 184.22
airstream 524.12
air strike 459.4
airstrip 184.23
air structure 266.2
air support 184.11
air taxi 184.10
air temperature 317.4
air terminal 184.22, 186.5
airtight 15.20, 293.12
airtight secrecy 345.1
airtime 1034.16
air traffic 184.1
air-traffic 184.49
air traffic control 184.1, 1036.9
air traffic controller 184.1, 185.6, 1036.14
air train 181.12
air transport 184.10
air transportation 184.10
air travel 184.10
air tube 239.13
air umbrella 184.11
air warden 1008.6
air waves, the 1034.16
airway 184.33, 239.13
airwise 184.49
airwoman 185.2
airworthiness 1007.1
airworthy 176.18, 184.49, 1007.7
airy 109.12, 158.11, 270.16, 272.14, 298.10, 299.4, 317.12, 318.21, 340.11, 764.6, 976.9, 986.24, 998.19, 1053.7, 1067.9
airy disregard 340.1
airy-fairy 967.8, 986.19, 986.20
airy hope 124.4
airy texture 270.4
aisle 383.3, 703.9
aisleway 383.3
ait 235.2
ajar 61.5, 292.18
ajouba 228.10
akimbo 278.6
akin 455.3, 559.6, 560.18, 775.10, 784.13
alabaster (n) 37.2, 287.3 (a) 37.8
alabastrine 37.8, 1058.15
a la carte (n) 8.14 (a) 11.6
à la carte 8.11
alacritous 101.8, 324.5, 330.18, 845.9
alacrity 101.1, 324.1, 330.3, 401.2, 845.3
Aladdin's lamp 691.6
alakazam 691.4
a la king 10.12
alameda 383.2
a la mode 11.6
à la mode 578.12, 841.13
alarm (n) 127.1, 399.1, 400.1, 517.15, 517.16 (v) 127.15, 400.3
alarm bell 399.3, 400.1
alarm button 400.1
alarm clock 400.1
alarmed 127.25, 400.4
alarm fire 1019.13
alarming 127.28, 1006.9
alarmingness 127.2
alarmist 127.8, 127.9
alarm reaction 311.1
alarm signal 400.1
alarum 400.1, 517.16
Alaska 1023.4
Alaska time 832.3
albatross around one's neck 96.8
albedo 1025.9
Alberich 258.5
Alberta clipper 317.4
Albert Schweitzer 921.2
albertype 548.1, 714.4
albescence 37.1
albescent 37.7, 37.8
albification 37.3
Albigensian (n) 667.2, 688.5 (a) 667.4, 688.9
Albigensianism 667.1
albinal 37.10
albinic 37.10
albinism 28.1, 36.3, 37.1
albinistic 37.10
albino (n) 37.1 (a) 37.10
Albion 232.4
album 549.11, 554.7
albumen 305.15, 1062.5
albuminoid 305.23
albuminous 305.23
alburnum 1054.3
Alcaic 720.16
Alcatraz 429.8
alchemical 690.14
alchemist 690.5
alchemistic 690.14
alchemistical 690.14
alchemize 690.10
alchemy 690.1, 858.1
alcohol 86.12, 86.21, 88.13, 1024.8
alcohol abuse 87.1
alcohol abuser 87.21
alcohol flush syndrome 41.3
alcohol-free beer 88.16
alcoholic (n) 87.21, 88.11 (a) 88.37
alcoholic addiction 88.3
alcoholic beverage 88.13
alcoholic drink 10.49, 88.13
alcoholic psychosis 88.3
Alcoholics Anonymous 87.1, 88.4, 449.2
alcoholism 87.1, 88.3, 88.4
alcohol poisoning 85.31
alcohol testing 938.6
alcohol torch 1020.14
alcopop 10.49
alcove 197.3, 228.12, 284.7
Aldebaran 1073.4

al dente 11.9
alderman 575.16, 610.3
aldermanic 423.5
alderperson 575.16, 610.3
Aldine 554.15
aleatoric 708.47, 766.7, 768.4, 971.19, 972.15, 1006.10
aleatory 708.47, 766.7, 768.4, 971.19, 972.15, 1006.10
Alecto 152.10, 680.10
alehouse 88.20
alembic 858.10
alerion 647.2
alert (n) 399.3, 400.1 (v) 399.5, 400.3, 551.11 (a) 23.8, 339.14, 405.16, 494.8, 845.9, 920.13, 981.5, 983.15
alerted 400.4
alert for 405.18
alerting 343.2, 405.1, 551.3
alertness 23.1, 339.5, 981.1, 983.1
alert one 983.10
alert oneself 981.3
alert to 983.16
Aleutian Trench 275.5
alevin 311.29
Alexandrian 952.11
Alexandrian Rite 675.8
Alexandrine 720.7
alexipharmic (n) 86.26 (a) 86.41
Alfardaws 681.7
Alfredo 10.12
alfresco 206.8, 317.12
alfresco meal 8.6
algae 310.4
algal 310.37
algebraic 1017.22
algebraical 1017.22
algebraic expression 1017.10
algebraic operation 1017.2
algebraist 1017.16
algebraize 1017.18
algebra of classes 935.2
algebra of relations 935.2
algesia 26.4
algetic 26.11
algid 1023.14, 1023.16
algidity 1023.1
algidness 1023.1
algific 1024.12
algolagnia 75.11
algolagniac 75.16
algolagny 75.11
algorism 1017.4
algorismic 1017.23
algorithm 384.1, 1017.1, 1017.4
algorithmic 1017.23
alias (n) 527.8 (a) 527.15
alibi (n) 376.1, 600.4 (v) 600.11
alibi out of 600.11
Alice-in-Wonderland 986.20
alien (n) 773.3, 774.3, 870.4, 1075.8 (v) 629.3 (a) 206.9, 451.8, 774.5, 776.6, 1073.26
alien abduction 689.2
alienable 629.5, 802.26
alienage 774.1
alienate 456.14, 589.7, 629.3, 802.8, 858.15
alienated 333.6, 589.11, 802.21, 872.8
alienate oneself 872.6
alienation 92.23, 333.1, 379.2, 456.4, 589.2, 629.1, 774.1, 802.1, 858.5, 872.2, 926.1
alien encounter 689.6
alienism 774.1, 926.19
alienist 92.10, 926.19
alien life form 689.6
alight (v) 184.43, 186.8, 194.7 (a) 1019.27, 1025.39
alight upon 194.10, 223.11, 941.3
align 201.6, 203.5, 808.9, 812.5
aligned 203.6, 264.4, 808.14
alignment 161.4, 201.1, 203.1, 450.2
align oneself 161.7
align oneself with 449.13, 450.4
align one's march 161.9
align with 450.4
alike 778.7, 781.5, 784.10, 790.7, 945.6
alikeness 784.1
aliment (n) 10.3 (v) 7.17, 8.19
alimental 7.21
alimentary 7.21
alimentary canal 2.17, 7.8
alimentation 7.1, 10.3
alimentive 7.21
alimony 478.8
aliquot 1017.23
aliquot part 1017.12
A-list 871.1
aliterate 930.7
alive 306.12, 330.17, 339.14, 920.13, 989.22
alive and kicking 83.9, 306.12, 330.17
alive and well 83.10, 306.12
alive to 24.11, 928.16
alive with 884.9
alkahest 1064.4
alkahestic 1064.8
alkali (n) 1060.3 (a) 1060.9
alkali flat 236.1
alkalify 1060.8
alkali metal 1058.3, 1060.2
alkaline 1060.9
alkaline-earth element 1060.2
alkaline-earth metal 1058.3
alkalinity 1060.3
alkalinize 1060.8
alkalize 1060.8
alkalizer 86.25
alkalosis 85.22
all (n) 792.3, 794.5, 864.4, 1073.1 (a) 792.9, 864.15
all, the 823.1
all abroad 975.16
all-absorbing 997.24
all-access 426.5
all aflutter 105.21
all agog 101.8, 122.9, 130.11, 981.5
Allah 677.2
all alike 778.7, 781.5
all alone 584.11
all-American 662.6
all and some 864.15
all and sundry (n) 792.3 (a) 864.15
all and then some 770.4
all animate nature 306.3
allantoic membrane 2.6
allargando 708.54
all-around 387.20, 413.25
all-around event 755.2
all ataunto 180.20
allative 530.9
allay 95.8, 120.5, 465.7, 670.6, 994.4
allayed 994.6
allaying 670.14
allayment 120.1, 670.2
all being 1073.1
all bets off 820.9
all but dissertation 557.6
all clear (n) 400.1 (a) 624.23
all colors of the rainbow 783.1, 797.6
all comers 864.4
all-comprehending 864.14
all-comprehensive 772.7, 823.3
all-comprehensiveness 823.1
all-consuming 395.27
all-covering 864.14
all creation 1073.1
all depend 971.11
all-destroying 395.27
all-devouring 100.27, 395.27, 480.26, 672.6
all dressed up 578.13
all ears 48.14, 339.13, 983.15
allegation 334.1, 376.2, 524.3, 598.7, 599.1, 957.2
allegation of facts 598.7
allegator 599.5
allege 334.5, 376.3, 524.23, 599.7, 957.9, 957.12
allegeable 334.9
alleged 334.9, 376.5, 888.6, 951.14
allege in support 600.10
allege in vindication 600.10
allegement 599.1
allegiance 326.1, 641.1, 644.7
allegiant 326.3, 644.20
allegoric 519.10, 722.8
allegorical 518.10, 519.10, 722.8
allegorist 341.7
allegorization 341.4
allegorize 341.10, 519.4, 722.7
allegorizing 341.15
allegory 517.2, 519.2, 784.1, 943.1
allégresse 109.4
allegretto (n) 708.25 (a) 708.55
allegro (n) 708.25 (a) 708.55
allele 305.9, 560.6
allelomorph 560.6
alleluia 116.2, 696.3
all-embracing 792.9, 794.10, 864.14
all-encompassing 794.10, 864.14
all-engulfing 480.26
allergen 85.34, 86.27
allergenic 85.61
allergic 24.12, 85.61, 99.8
allergic disorder 85.34
allergic gastritis 85.34
allergic rhinitis 85.34
allergy 24.3, 85.34, 99.2
allergy diet 7.13
alleviate 120.5, 252.8, 298.6, 670.6
alleviated 120.10, 298.11
alleviating 120.9, 298.16, 670.14
alleviation 120.1, 252.1, 298.3, 670.2
alleviative (n) 86.10, 670.3 (a) 86.40, 120.9, 298.16, 670.16
alleviator 670.3
alleviatory (n) 86.10 (a) 120.9, 298.16, 670.16
all-expense-paid 624.22, 634.5
alley 383.3, 383.5, 748.1, 749.4, 750.1
alley apple 462.18
alley cat 311.20, 797.8
alley craps 759.8
all eyes 339.13, 983.15
all eyes and ears 339.13, 983.15
all-female 77.13
all-filling 864.14
all for 449.22
all for the best 387.22, 999.16
all fours 177.17
all girl 77.13
all gone 762.11
all Greek 930.6
all hands 864.4
all-healing 86.39
all hell let loose 671.2
all hopped up about 101.11
all hot and bothered 126.7, 971.24, 985.12
all-hours 812.8
alliance 437.2, 450.2, 559.1, 563.1, 617.1, 775.1, 784.1, 805.1, 899.1
allied 559.6, 775.9, 800.13, 805.6
allied health care 83.5
alligator 311.24
all-important 997.23
all in 21.8
all-in 772.6
all in a dither over 101.11
all-including 864.14
all-inclusive 772.7, 792.9, 823.3, 864.14
all-inclusiveness 823.1
all in one piece 397.13, 792.10
all in the day's work 724.16
all in the mind 976.9, 986.19
alliteral 784.17
alliterate 720.15, 784.9
alliterating 849.15
alliteration 720.9, 784.6, 849.4
alliterative 720.18, 784.17, 849.15
alliterative meter 720.6
all jaw 540.9
all kinds of 884.3
all kinds of things 864.4
all-knowing 677.17, 928.15
all-knowingness 928.6
all manner of things 864.4
all muscle 15.16
all-natural 973.15
all nerves 128.11
allness 1073.1
all-news format 1034.18
all-news radio 1034.18
all-night 315.9

all-nighter 405.1
all-night vigil 23.1
allocable 477.12
allocate 159.11, 477.9, 808.9
allocated 477.12
allocation 159.6, 477.3, 808.1, 865.6
allocution 543.2
allodial 471.10
all of a flutter 128.12, 917.16
all of a piece 781.5
all of a twitter 917.16
all off 820.9, 975.16
allograph 546.1
allographic 546.8
allogrooming 311.1
allomorph 262.6, 526.3
all one 778.7, 790.8
all one can bear 135.3
all one can do 403.4
all one can lay claim to 471.1
all one can manage 1013.2
all one can stand 135.3, 994.1
all one can take 994.1
all one has 471.1
all one owns 471.1
all one's born days 827.5
all one's got 403.4
all one's got in one 403.4
all one's natural life 827.5
allonge 254.2
all on one side 650.11
allopathic 90.15
allophone 524.12
allophonic 524.30
allosome 305.8
allot 244.4, 477.9, 478.12, 808.9
allotheism 675.5, 688.4
allotheist 675.16, 688.7
allotheistic 688.11
allotment 10.6, 231.4, 244.2, 477.3, 477.5, 478.8, 808.1
allotropic 783.3
allotropical 783.3
allotropism 783.1
allotropy 783.1
allottee 479.4
all-out 794.10, 960.2
all-out campaign 609.13
all-out effort 403.1
all-out war 457.6, 458.1
all over 820.9
allover 864.14
all over but the shouting 407.11, 820.9
all-overish 85.56
all over oneself 95.17
all-overs 126.1
all over the place 771.9
all over the town 552.15
all over with 407.11, 762.11
allow 332.11, 443.9, 478.12, 631.2, 946.8, 959.5
allowable 443.15, 443.16, 478.23, 600.14
allowableness 443.8, 600.7
allowance (n) 10.6, 332.3, 443.1, 477.5, 478.8, 600.5, 624.5, 631.1, 959.1, 975.2 (v) 477.10
allowed 332.14, 443.16, 478.24
allow for 148.4, 600.12, 959.5
allowing 443.14
allow of 443.9
allow oneself to hope 124.7
allow one's imagination to run away with one 986.14
allow one's mind to wander 984.3
allow the occasion to go by 844.5
alloy (n) 797.5, 1058.4 (v) 393.12, 797.10
alloyage 797.1, 1058.4
alloy wheel 756.1
all-pervading 794.10, 864.14
all points bulletin 382.1
all-points bulletin 382.1, 938.15
all-powerful 18.13, 677.17
all-powerfulness 18.3
all-powerful ruler 575.13
all-presence 221.2
all-present 221.13
all-purpose flour 10.34
all ready 405.16
all right 83.10, 107.12, 973.16, 999.20
all-roundedness 413.3
all-rounder 413.11
all said and done 407.11
all-searching 938.38
all-seeing 677.17
all set 405.16
all set for 405.18
all she wrote 792.3, 820.1, 1017.6
all shook up 128.12, 917.16
all skin and bones 270.17
all sorts 797.6
all sorts of 884.3
all-star 704.33
All-Star Game 745.1, 749.1
all straight 624.23
all-sufficing 991.7
all talk and no action 19.15
all tarnation 1073.1
all-terrain bike 179.8
all-terrain vehicle 179.8, 179.9
all that is 1073.1
all that is coming to one 639.3
all that lives 305.1
all the above 864.4
all the above all of the above 792.3
all the better for 392.14
all the comforts of home 121.3
all the days of one's life 827.5
all the heart can desire 121.3
all the market can bear 993.3
all the rage 578.11
all there 920.14, 925.4
all the same 778.7, 790.8
all the thing 578.11
all the time in the world 402.1
all the world 864.4
all the worse for 393.27
all thumbs 414.20
all-time great 413.14
all to the good 387.22
allude to 517.18, 519.4, 524.24, 551.10, 983.10
all up 820.9
all up with 412.14
allure (n) 377.1, 377.2 (v) 104.22, 356.20, 377.5
allurement 104.6, 375.3, 377.1, 907.1
alluring 375.27, 377.8, 907.5
allusion 519.2
allusive 519.6, 536.3
allusory 519.6
alluvial 234.6
alluvial deposit 1059.6
alluvial plain 236.1
alluvion 234.1, 238.6, 256.2
alluvious 234.6
alluvium 234.1, 238.6, 256.2
all washed up 395.29
all-way bet 759.4
all-weather court 748.1
all wet 975.18
all-wheel drive 179.9
all wind 19.15
all-wise 677.17
all wool 973.15
all wool and a yard wide 644.14, 999.13
all worked up 93.23, 105.20, 917.16
all wound up in 898.5
all wrapped up in oneself 140.12
all wrong 975.16
ally (n) 232.1, 616.1 (v) 450.3, 770.16, 775.6, 805.4
allying 450.2
ally with 449.13
alma mater 567.5
almanac 554.9, 832.7, 832.8, 871.4
almightiness 18.3
Almighty 677.2
almighty 18.13, 677.17
almighty dollar, the 728.1
almoner 143.8, 478.11
almost unheard-of 848.2
alms 143.7, 478.6
alms fee 478.6
almsgiver 143.8, 478.11, 485.2
almsgiving (n) 478.3 (a) 143.15
almshouse 1009.4
almsman 479.4, 619.4
almswoman 479.4, 619.4
alod 471.5
alodium 469.1, 471.5
aloe 67.2
aloes 86.9
aloeswood 70.4
aloha 188.4
aloha spirit 585.1
alone 584.11, 872.8, 872.9
aloneness 584.3, 872.2
along in years 303.16
alongside 218.6
aloof 94.13, 141.12, 344.10, 583.6, 804.4, 872.8, 982.3
aloofness 94.4, 141.4, 261.1, 344.3, 583.2, 804.1, 872.2, 982.1
alopecia 6.4
alp 237.6
alpen 272.18
alpenglow 314.3
alpenstock 273.2, 901.2
alpestrine 237.8, 272.18
alpha 818.1, 818.3
alpha and omega 792.3
alphabet (n) 349.1, 523.14, 546.3, 547.1, 547.9, 818.6 (v) 546.6
alphabetarian 572.9
alphabet book 554.10
alphabetic 546.8, 547.26
alphabetical 546.8
alphabetical order 807.2
alphabetic character 546.1
alphabetics 546.3
alphabetic symbol 349.1, 546.1
alphabetism 546.3
alphabetization 546.5
alphabetize 546.6, 809.6
alphabetology 546.3
alphabet poem 720.4
alphabet soup 10.10
alpha decay 1038.8
alpha female 249.4
alpha girl 77.5
alpha male 249.4
alpha mom 77.7
alpha particle 1037.4, 1038.6
alpha radiator 1037.5
alpigene 272.18
alpine 237.8, 272.18
alpine chain 237.6
alpine plant 310.33
Alpine race 753.3
Alpine skiing 753.1
Alpine-style climbing 760.6
Alpine subrace 312.2
alpinism 760.6
alpinist 178.1, 193.6
already in sight 840.3
alright 107.12
also known as 527.15
also-ran 410.8, 412.5, 610.9, 757.2
Alston's Glasgow type 30.6
altar 703.12
altar boy 700.1
altar bread 701.7
altar carpet 703.12
altar cloth 703.10
altar desk 703.12
altar facing 703.12
altar front 703.12
altar girl 700.1
altar of prothesis 703.12
altarpiece 703.12, 712.10
altar rail 703.12
altar side 703.12
altar slab 703.12
altar stair 703.12
altar stone 703.12
alter (n) 865.5 (v) 255.11, 852.6, 852.7, 959.3
alterability 854.1
alterable 854.6
alterant 852.5
alteration 780.4, 852.1
alterative (n) 86.1, 852.5 (a) 86.39, 854.6
altercate 456.11
altercation 456.5, 457.1
altered 852.10
altered gene 305.9
altered state of consciousness 928.2
alter ego 576.1, 588.1, 616.7, 784.3, 865.5

alterer 852.5
altering (n) 255.4 (a) 959.7
alter into 858.17
alternate (n) 576.1, 862.2 (v) 362.8, 825.5, 850.5, 854.5, 863.4, 916.13 (a) 850.7, 862.8, 916.19
alternate choice 371.2
alternate energy 17.1, 1021.1, 1021.7
alternate-energy 1021.9
alternate energy source 1021.1
alternating 854.7
alternating-current circuit 1041.6
alternating personality 92.20
alternation 777.3, 850.2, 854.3, 863.1, 916.5
alternative (n) 333.1, 369.4, 371.2, 576.1, 862.2 (a) 333.6, 371.22, 862.8
alternative birth 1.1
alternative energy 17.1, 1021.1
alternative-energy 1021.9
alternative energy source 1021.1
alternative fuel vehicle 179.1
alternative lifestyle 75.10, 868.2
alternative medicine 90.13, 868.2
alternative practitioner 90.9
alternative press 552.1
alternative rock 708.10
alternative school 567.1
alternative society 868.2
alternative vote 609.18
alternativity 371.1
alter one's course 164.3
altimeter 272.9
altimetric 272.20
altimetrical 272.20
altimetry 272.9
altitude 272.1, 300.5
altitude of flight 184.35
altitude peak 1074.9
altitudinal 272.14
altitudinous 237.8, 272.14
Altmann theory 560.6
alto (n) 58.6, 708.22, 709.5 (a) 58.13, 708.50
alto clef 709.13
altocumuliform 319.8
altocumulous 319.8
altocumulus 319.2
altogether, the 6.3
alto-rilievo 283.2, 715.3
altostratous 319.8
altostratus 319.2
altricial 311.48
alt-right 609.24
alt-rock 708.10
altruism 143.4, 591.1, 652.1
altruist 143.8, 485.2
altruistic 143.15, 652.5
altruistic ethics 636.2
alum 260.6
aluminum foil 295.18, 1036.13
aluminum racket 748.1
alumna 572.8
alumnae 572.8
alumni 572.8
alumnus 572.8
alveola 284.2
alveolabial 524.30
alveolar 284.17, 524.30
alveolar ridge 2.8, 524.18
alveolate 284.17
alveolation 284.2, 284.6
alveolingual 524.30
alveolus 2.8, 284.2, 284.6, 524.18
Alviss 258.5
always 820.5
always trot out 849.9
Alzheimer's 922.10
Alzheimer's disease 85.25, 922.10
amabile 708.53
amadou 1021.6
amah 1008.8
amalgam 797.5, 1058.4
amalgamate 450.3, 797.10, 805.3
amalgamated 797.14, 805.5
amalgamation 450.2, 797.1, 805.1
amanuensis 547.13, 550.1, 576.3
amaranthine 829.9
amaroidal 64.6
amass 386.11, 472.11, 770.16, 770.18, 800.5
amassed 386.14, 770.21
amassing evidence 938.4
amassment 386.1, 472.2, 770.9
Amaterasu 1073.14
amateur (n) 101.4, 496.6, 726.5, 866.3, 929.6, 998.10 (a) 724.17, 930.14
amateur athlete 743.19
Amateur Athletic Union 754.1
Amateur Athletic Union of the U.S. 755.1
amateur band 1034.13
amateur bowling 750.1
amateur boxing 754.1
amateur golf 751.1
amateur hockey 749.1
amateurish 414.16, 930.14
amateurishness 414.2
amateurism 414.2, 724.7, 724.9, 930.5
amateur pursuit 724.7
amateur radio 1034.16
amateur radio operator 1034.24
Amateur Radio Relay League 1034.24
amateur standing 724.9
amateur station 1034.6
amateur status 724.9
amateur theatricals 704.2
Amati 711.5
amative 104.25, 562.23
amativeness 104.2
amatory 104.25, 562.23
amaurosis 30.1
amaurotic 30.9
amaze (n) 122.1 (v) 122.6, 971.13
amazed 122.9, 131.12
amazement 122.1, 122.2
amazing 122.12, 131.11
amazing thing 122.2
Amazon 461.6
amazon 76.9, 257.13
amazonian 15.17, 272.16
ambages 281.1, 538.5, 914.3
ambagious 281.6, 538.14, 914.7
ambagiousness 281.1, 538.5, 914.1
ambassador 576.6
ambassador-at-large 576.6
ambassadorial 576.17
ambassadress 576.6
ambergris 70.2, 70.4
amber light 400.1, 517.15, 1026.4
ambidexter 219.6
ambidexterity 354.4, 413.3
ambidextral 219.6
ambidextrous 219.6, 354.31, 413.25, 645.21
ambience 209.1, 209.3
ambient 209.8
ambient food 10.2, 10.3
ambient light 1025.1, 1025.10
ambient music 708.7
ambient phenomena 831.4
ambient snacking 8.1
ambient temperature 317.4
ambiguity 520.2, 522.1, 539.1, 539.2, 779.3, 789.2, 873.1, 971.5
ambiguous 522.13, 539.4, 779.8, 789.8, 797.14, 971.16
ambiguousness 539.1
ambisextrous 75.30
ambisextrousness 75.10
ambisexual 75.30
ambisexuality 75.2, 75.10
ambit 209.1, 231.2, 257.1, 894.4, 914.2
ambitendency 362.1
ambitendent 362.9
ambition 100.10, 100.11, 375.1, 380.1
ambitious 100.28, 330.23, 404.8, 501.18
ambitious for self 651.5
ambitiousness 100.10, 330.7
ambivalence 92.17, 362.1, 779.3, 789.2, 873.1
ambivalence of impulse 92.17
ambivalent 362.9, 779.8, 789.8, 797.14
ambiversion 92.11
ambivert 92.12
amble (n) 177.10, 177.12 (v) 175.6, 177.28, 177.34
ambler 311.14
ambling (n) 177.8 (a) 175.10
amblyopia 28.2
ambo 703.13, 901.15
AM broadcasting 1034.16
ambrosia 10.8, 66.2, 70.2
ambrosial 63.8, 66.5, 70.9
Ambrosian chant 708.20
ambrotype 714.4
ambry 703.9
ambulance chaser 597.3
ambulance driver 90.11
ambulant 177.36
ambulate 177.27
ambulation 177.8
ambulative 177.36
ambulator 178.6
ambulatory (n) 383.3 (a) 177.36
ambulatory care 83.5
ambuscade (n) 346.3 (v) 346.10
ambush (n) 346.3 (v) 131.7, 346.10, 356.20, 459.14
ambushment 346.3
ameliatory 852.10
ameliorable 392.17, 396.25
ameliorate 392.7, 392.9, 852.6, 852.7
ameliorated 392.13
ameliorating 120.9
amelioration 392.1, 852.1
ameliorative 392.15, 852.10, 852.11
amelioratory 392.15
amen (n) 332.2 (v) 332.12
amenability 134.2, 324.1, 641.2, 1047.2
amenable 134.10, 324.5, 441.4, 641.17, 894.15
amenableness 894.5
amen corner 703.14
amend 392.7, 392.9, 392.12, 396.13, 858.12
amendable 396.25
amendatory 338.6
amende 600.3
amendment 392.1, 392.4, 858.2
amends 338.1, 396.6, 481.2, 624.3, 658.1
amenities 121.3, 504.7, 580.3
amenity 97.1, 449.9, 504.1, 504.6
Amen-Ra 1073.14
ament 310.27
Amenti 682.3
amentia 922.9
amerce 603.5
amercement 603.3
America 231.6, 232.3
American Bowling Congress 750.1
American breakfast 8.6
American crawl 760.8
American dream 100.10, 124.4
American eagle 647.6
American football 746.1
American Indian 312.3
American Interplanetary Society 1075.9
Americanism 523.8, 591.2
Americanization 226.3
Americanize 226.4
Americanized 226.6
American Junior Bowling Congress 750.1
American Lawn Bowling Association 750.3
American League, the 745.1
American Legion member 461.19
American plan 8.11
American plate 235.1
American Revised Version 683.2
American Rocket Society 1075.9
American roulette 759.12
American Sign Language 49.3, 523.11
American Stock Exchange 737.7

American Stud Book 757.1
American wheel 759.12, 759.16
America's Cup 646.3, 760.2
Amerind 312.3
Amerindian 312.3
Amesha Spentas 679.2
Ameslan 523.11
amethyst 46.1
amethystine 46.3
Amex 737.7
amiability 97.1, 104.6, 143.2, 427.2, 582.1, 585.1, 587.1
amiable 97.6, 143.14, 427.8, 582.22, 585.11, 587.15
amiableness 587.1
amianthine 1022.9
amianthus 1022.5
amicability 97.1, 587.1
amicable 97.6, 449.22, 455.3, 587.15
amicableness 587.1
amicus curiae 576.1, 597.1, 894.2
amidships 819.4
amies 87.5
amigo 588.3
amino acid 7.6
amiss 810.13, 975.16
amitosis 305.16
amity 455.1, 587.1
ammo 462.13
ammo dump 462.2
ammonia 890.4, 1024.7
ammonium salts 890.4
ammunition 462.13
ammunition depot 462.2
amnesia 92.19, 933.1, 990.2
amnesiac 990.2
amnesic 990.9
amnestic 990.9
amnestied 148.7
amnesty (n) 148.2, 464.7, 465.2, 601.2 (v) 148.3, 601.4
amnio 91.12
amniocentesis 91.12
amnion 2.6
amniotic sac 2.6
amobarbital 86.12
amobarbital sodium 86.12
amoeba 85.42, 258.7
amoebic 258.15
amoeboid 258.15
amok (n) 926.7 (a) 105.25, 926.30
among 772.3
among the living 306.12
among the missing 222.11
Amor 104.1, 104.7
amor 104.8
amoral 645.16, 654.11
amoralism 636.4
amorality 636.4, 654.1
amore 104.1
amoretto 104.8
amorist 104.11
amorosa 104.13
amoroso (n) 104.12 (a) 708.53
amorous 75.25, 104.25
amorous dalliance 562.1
amorous looks 562.9
amorousness 104.2
amorous play 104.5
amorous pursuit 562.7
amorphic 263.4, 522.15
amorphism 263.1, 870.1
amorphous 263.4, 522.15, 810.12, 854.7, 870.9, 971.19
amorphousness 263.1, 522.3, 538.1, 971.4
amortization 624.1, 629.1
amortize 624.13, 629.3
amortizement 624.1, 629.1
Amos 684.1
amount 244.1, 244.2, 245.1, 630.1, 1017.6
amount, the 792.2
amount due 623.1
amount of money 728.13
amount to 630.13, 790.5, 792.8
amount to something 997.12
amour 104.5
amourette 104.8
amour propre 140.1
amour-propre 104.1
amp (n) 50.10 (v) 251.4
amperage 18.1, 1032.2
amphetamine addiction 87.1
amphetamine sulphate 86.9
amphetamine user 87.21
amphibian (n) 181.8, 181.9, 310.3, 311.3, 311.26 (a) 311.47
amphibious 413.25, 797.14
amphibious aircraft 181.8
amphibious attack 459.1
amphibious force 461.27
amphibious operations 458.4
amphibological 539.4
amphibologism 489.8
amphibology 539.1, 539.2
amphibolous 539.4
amphiboly 489.8
amphibrach 720.8
amphierotic 75.30
amphierotism 75.10
amphigory 520.2, 720.3
amphimacer 720.8
amphitheater 197.4, 463.1, 567.11, 704.14
Amphitrite 240.3
ampicillin 86.29
ample 107.11, 158.11, 247.8, 257.17, 269.6, 884.8, 991.6, 991.7
ampleness 247.1, 257.6, 991.2
ample scope 430.4
ample sufficiency, an 991.2
ampliate 259.10
ampliation 259.1
amplification 119.1, 251.1, 259.1, 341.3, 355.1, 538.6, 861.1, 1034.15
amplified 119.4, 251.7, 259.10, 355.4
amplifier 48.8, 50.10, 1035.11
amplify 50.14, 119.2, 251.4, 251.5, 259.4, 355.3, 538.7, 861.6, 1032.26
amplifying 538.15
amplifying circuit 1034.9
amplitude 50.1, 53.1, 158.3, 158.5, 244.1, 247.1, 257.1, 269.1, 538.2, 794.2, 916.4, 991.2
amplitude modulation 1034.14
amplitudinous 158.11, 247.7
amply endowed 1016.18
amputate 255.10, 802.11
amputation 255.3
amputee 85.45
amscray 188.7
AM signal 1034.10
AM station 1034.6
Amtrak 179.14
amulet 691.5, 696.10
amuse 743.21
amuse-bouche 8.2
amused 743.26
amuse-gueule 10.8
amusement 95.1, 109.5, 743.1
amusement park 743.14
amusement ride 743.15
amuse oneself 743.22
amusing 488.4, 489.15, 743.27
amusingness 488.1
amylaceous 1062.12
amylase 7.10
amyotrophic lateral sclerosis 85.25
Amytal 86.12
an 244.5, 872.7
ana 549.2, 554.7, 557.4, 770.11, 974.1
anabasis 193.1
anabatic 193.14
anabatic wind 318.1
anabolic 2.31, 852.12
anabolic steroid 86.32
anabolism 2.20, 7.12, 852.3
anabranch 238.3
anachronism 833.1, 844.1
anachronistic 833.3
anachronistical 833.3
anachronous 833.3
anacoluthia 975.7
anacoluthon 531.1, 975.7
Anacreontic 720.16
anacrusis 708.24, 720.7
anaerobe 85.42
anaerobic bacteria 85.42
anaerobic fitness 84.1
anaerobic organism 305.2
anaerobic respiration 2.21
anagalactic 1073.25
anagalactic nebula 1073.7
anaglyph 715.3
anaglyphic 715.7
anaglyptic 715.7
anagnorisis 722.4
anagoge 689.1
anagogic 519.10, 689.23
anagogical 519.10, 689.23
anagogics 689.1
anagram 489.8, 522.9
anagrammatic 522.17
anal 474.8, 495.12, 867.6
anal character 867.2
anal-compulsive 495.12
analects 554.7, 557.4, 974.1
Analects of Confucius 683.7
analeptic (n) 86.1, 86.8 (a) 9.3, 86.39, 86.44, 396.22
analgesia 25.1, 120.1
analgesic (n) 25.3, 86.12 (a) 25.9, 86.40, 86.45, 120.9
anal intercourse 75.7
anality 807.3
analog computer 1042.2
analog feedback control 1041.3
analogical 943.8
analogize 943.4
analogous 203.6, 777.10, 784.11, 943.8
analogousness 943.3
analogue 777.4, 784.3
analogy 203.1, 784.1, 862.2, 943.1
anal-retentive 474.8, 926.33, 926.34
anal sex 75.7
analysis 92.6, 541.6, 556.2, 723.1, 766.5, 780.4, 798.2, 801.1, 802.5, 809.1, 935.3, 938.1, 944.2, 951.1, 1041.7
analyst 92.10, 723.4, 801.5, 942.6, 1017.16
analytic 523.23, 723.6, 801.9, 935.18, 935.22, 938.37, 952.11, 1017.22
analytical 723.6, 801.9, 935.18, 935.22, 938.37, 1017.22
analytical chemist 1060.7
analytical psychology 92.2
analytic faculty 944.1
analytic power 944.1
analyzation 801.1
analyze 92.36, 530.16, 541.11, 723.5, 766.6, 780.6, 782.2, 793.6, 798.4, 801.6, 802.17, 809.6, 935.15, 944.4
analyze one's motives 113.6
analyzer 801.5, 802.7, 942.6
analyzing 946.3
anamnesis 91.10
anamorphism 265.1
anamorphosis 265.1, 350.2
anamorphous 265.10
Ananias 357.9
anapest 720.8
anapestic 720.17
anaphase 305.16
anaphrodisiac 670.16
anaphylactic 24.12
anaphylactic antibody 86.27
anaphylactin 86.27
anaphylaxis 24.3
anarch 418.3, 860.3
anarchial 418.6
anarchic 263.4, 418.6, 671.18, 671.19, 674.6, 804.4, 810.16, 860.6
anarchical 418.6, 860.6
anarchism 418.2, 611.4, 860.2, 952.7
anarchist 418.3, 611.12, 860.3
anarchistic 418.6, 611.20, 674.6
anarcho-syndicalism 418.2, 611.4
anarcho-syndicalist (n) 418.3 (a) 611.20
anarchy 263.1, 418.2, 674.1, 804.1, 810.2
anastatic 715.7
anastrophe 205.3
anathema 103.3, 510.3, 513.1
anathematize 510.13, 513.5, 602.3
anathematizing 602.1
anathemize 510.13

Anatolian 523.12
anatomic 266.6
anatomical 266.6
anatomically correct 266.6
anatomization 766.5, 780.4
anatomize 766.6, 780.6, 801.6, 802.17
anatomizing 801.1
anatomy 2.1, 262.4, 266.1, 312.10, 801.1, 802.5, 1052.3, 1068.3
anaudia 51.2
anaudic 51.12
ancestor 560.8, 816.1, 834.2
ancestorial 560.17
ancestors 560.7, 892.7
ancestral 560.17, 818.15, 842.11
ancestral hall 228.7
ancestral halls 228.2
ancestral line 560.4
ancestral seat 228.7
ancestral spirits 678.12
ancestress 560.8
ancestry 559.2, 560.1, 560.5, 608.2
anchor (n) 180.16, 901.2, 1008.3, 1034.23, 1035.2 (v) 159.17, 182.15, 186.8, 428.10, 800.7, 855.8
anchorage 159.7, 180.16, 186.5, 630.6, 1009.6
anchorage ground 1009.6
anchored 855.14, 855.16
anchoress 584.5
anchoret 584.5
anchoretism 584.2
anchor ice 1023.5
anchorite 584.5, 667.2
anchorite monasticism 667.1
anchoritic 584.10, 667.4
anchoritical 584.10
anchoritic monasticism 667.1
anchoritism 584.2, 667.1
anchorman 1034.23, 1035.2
anchorperson 1035.2
anchor store 736.1
anchor watch 825.3
anchorwoman 1034.23, 1035.2
ancienne noblesse 608.1
ancien régime 608.1, 842.1
ancient (n) 842.7 (a) 303.16, 827.10, 837.10, 842.10
ancient and honorable, the 842.1
ancient grain 10.4
ancient history 837.3
ancient language 523.2
ancient literature 547.12, 718.1
ancient manuscript 842.6
Ancient Mariner 178.2, 183.1
ancientness 837.3, 842.1
ancient times 837.3
ancient wisdom 373.2, 842.2
ancillary 253.10, 449.20
ancona 703.12
andante (n) 175.2, 708.25 (a) 708.54
andante moderato 708.54
andante tempo 709.24
andantino (n) 708.25 (a) 708.54
and buts 421.3
and happy 1010.13
and heaven knows what 884.11
andiron 1020.12
and many more 884.11
and mathematics 928.4
and quarter 604.17
andric 76.12
androcyte 305.11
androecium 310.28
androgynal 75.31
androgyne 75.17, 76.9
androgynism 75.12
androgynous 75.31
androgyny 75.12, 77.2
andromania 75.5
ands 421.3
and scene 704.7
and the pursuit of happiness 430.2
Andvari 258.5
and what not 884.11
anecdotage 303.5, 719.2
anecdotal 722.9
anecdotal evidence 953.6
anecdote 719.2
anecdotic 722.9
anecdotist 722.5
anemia 16.1, 36.2, 85.9, 85.20
anemic 16.12, 36.7, 85.61
anemograph 317.8, 318.16
anemographic 318.24
anemological 318.24
anemology 317.5, 318.15
anemometer 174.7, 317.8, 318.16
anemometric 318.24
anemometrical 318.24
anemometrograph 318.16
anemometry 317.5, 318.15
anemoscope 318.16
aneroid barometer 317.8
aneroidograph 317.8
anesthesia 25.1, 94.1, 94.2, 120.1
anesthesiologist 90.4
anesthetic (n) 22.10, 25.3, 86.15 (a) 25.9, 86.47, 120.9
anesthetist 90.11
anesthetize 22.20, 25.4, 94.8, 120.5
anesthetized 22.21, 25.6, 94.9
anesthetizing (n) 120.1 (a) 25.9
anfractuosity 281.1
anfractuous 281.6, 281.8
angary 480.5
angel (n) 104.14, 375.9, 460.7, 478.11, 562.6, 592.1, 616.9, 653.2, 657.4, 659.6, 678.12, 679.1, 704.26, 729.10, 1016.8 (v) 478.19, 729.16
angel dust 87.18
angelface 1016.8
angelic 104.24, 653.5, 657.6, 679.6, 692.9
angelical 679.6, 692.9
angelicalness 653.1, 692.2
angelic host 679.2
angelicness 657.2
angel of death 307.2, 679.4
angel of light 679.1
angel of love 679.1
angelology 679.3
angelophanic 348.9
angels 679.3
Angelus 517.16, 696.4
Angelus bell 517.16
anger (n) 38.2, 110.1, 152.5, 654.3, 671.1, 1019.2 (v) 152.17, 152.22, 1020.18
angered 152.28
anger management 106.2
angina 26.5, 85.19
angina pectoris 85.19
angioplasty 85.19
angiosperm 310.3
angle (n) 27.7, 33.3, 159.2, 278.2, 650.3, 722.4, 759.13, 766.3, 937.1, 953.6, 978.2 (v) 164.3, 204.9, 218.5, 278.5, 381.9, 382.10, 415.10, 650.8
angle away 278.5
angle for 440.14, 938.30
angle off 164.3, 204.9, 278.5
angle of repose 237.2
angle of vision 27.7, 978.2
angler 382.6
angle with a silver hook 377.5
angleworm 311.38
Anglican 675.20
Anglicanism 675.11
Anglicism 523.8, 591.2
Anglicization 226.3
Anglicize 226.4
Anglicized 226.6
angling 382.3
Anglo-Catholicism 675.11
Anglo-Indian 523.7
Anglophobe 103.4
Angra Mainyu 680.4
angriness 152.5
angry 26.11, 38.9, 96.21, 110.17, 152.28, 318.22, 671.18
angry clouds 133.5
angry look 152.2
angry sea 238.14
angry young man 108.3
angst 96.1, 96.2, 126.1, 127.4
anguiform 281.7
anguille 10.24
anguilliform 281.7
anguine 281.7, 311.47
anguish (n) 26.6, 96.1, 96.6, 112.10 (v) 26.8, 96.17, 96.19, 112.19
anguished 26.9, 96.20, 96.23, 112.26
angular 278.6
angularity 204.2, 278.1
angular momentum 915.1
angular motion 172.2, 915.1
angularness 278.1
angular velocity 174.1, 915.1
angustifoliate 270.14
angustirostrate 270.14
angustisellate 270.14
angustiseptal 270.14
anhydrate 397.9, 1066.6
anhydration 397.2, 1066.3
anhydrous 1066.7
anile 303.18
anility 303.5, 922.10
anima 92.28, 306.2, 919.4
animadversion 510.4
animadvert 983.6
animadvert upon 510.13
animal (n) 144.14, 311.2, 497.7, 593.5, 660.6, 672.3 (a) 144.26, 311.39, 497.12, 663.6, 665.29
animal and vegetable kingdom 305.1
animal behavior 311.1, 321.3
animal biologist 1068.2
animal biology 1068.1
animal capable of reason 312.7
animal cell 305.4
animal charge 647.2
animal comfort 95.1
animal companion 311.2
animal cracker 10.30
animalcular 258.15
animalcule 258.7
animal culture 1070.1
animal cunning 415.1, 920.3
animal doctor 90.7
animal enclosure 1070.5
animal farm 1070.5
animal fiber 271.1
animal food 10.4
animal heat 1019.1
animal husbandry 1070.1
animal hypnosis 22.7
Animalia 311.1
animalian 311.39
animalic 311.39
animalism 663.2, 1052.6
animalistic 144.26, 311.39, 663.6, 952.11
animality 144.11, 311.1, 497.3, 663.2, 665.5, 671.1
animal kingdom 311.1, 559.4, 809.4, 1068.1
animal life 311.1, 1068.1
animal-like 311.39
animal magnetism 22.8, 75.3
animal nature 663.2
animal noise 60.1
animal oil 1056.1
animal painter 716.4
animal pleasure 95.1
animal poison 1001.5
animal raising 1070.1
animal rearing 1070.1
animal rights 311.1
animals 1068.1
animal science 1068.1
animal scientist 1068.2
animal shelter 228.19
animal spirits 109.4, 306.1
animal sport 744.1
animal testing 90.1
animal trank 87.18
animal worship 697.1
animal worshiper 697.4
anima mundi 677.7
animate (n) 530.10 (v) 9.2, 17.10, 105.13, 109.7, 306.10, 375.12, 375.20, 902.11 (a) 305.17, 306.12
animate being 305.2, 1052.4
animated 9.4, 17.13, 101.8, 109.14, 306.12, 330.17, 375.30, 706.9
animated cartoon 706.1, 712.15
animate existence 306.1
animate matter 305.1
animating 17.15, 109.16, 306.13, 375.25, 375.26, 902.23

animating force 306.2
animating power 306.2
animating principle 306.2
animating spirit 375.9
animation 17.4, 17.8, 101.1, 105.11, 109.4, 306.1, 306.6, 330.2, 375.2, 375.9, 706.1, 712.15, 712.16
animation studio 706.4
animatism 688.4, 1053.3
animative 17.15, 306.13
animator 17.6, 375.10, 381.6, 384.4, 449.7, 716.3, 892.7
animatron 706.1
animatronic 706.9
animism 675.6, 688.4, 689.1, 1053.3
animist (n) 688.7, 1053.4 (a) 688.11, 952.11, 1053.8
animistic 688.11, 952.11, 1053.8
animistic cult 675.6
animistic powers 678.1
animistic religion 675.6
animistic spirit 678.1
animosity 17.5, 93.7, 103.2, 152.3, 589.4
animotheism 675.5
animus 92.28, 323.1, 375.9, 380.1, 589.4, 919.4, 978.3
anion 1032.25, 1060.2
anionic 1032.32
ankle (n) 2.7, 177.14, 800.4 (v) 177.27
ankle-deep 275.11, 276.5
anklet 280.3, 498.6
ankylosis 85.9
Anlage 305.14
annalist 547.15, 550.2, 718.4, 719.3, 832.10
annalistic 832.15
annals 549.1, 719.1, 832.9
anneal 15.13, 1046.7, 1046.8
annealed 1046.15, 1049.6
annex (n) 254.1, 254.3 (v) 253.4, 472.10, 480.20, 482.16, 800.7
annexation 253.1, 254.1, 480.5, 482.1, 800.3
annexational 480.25
annexed 253.9
annexure 480.5
Annie Oakley 634.2
annihilate 255.10, 308.13, 308.17, 395.13, 395.14, 762.7, 909.21
annihilated 395.28, 762.11
annihilation 255.3, 307.1, 395.6
annihilative 395.27
annihilator 395.8
anniversary 487.1, 832.4, 850.4
annotate 341.11, 556.5, 946.14
annotated bibliography 558.4
annotation 254.2, 341.5, 549.4
annotative 341.15, 556.6
annotator 341.7, 556.4, 946.7
announce 133.13, 334.5, 352.12, 524.23, 551.8, 552.11, 834.3
announced 334.9, 352.17
announced motive 376.1
announce for 609.39
announcement 334.1, 343.2, 351.1, 352.2, 551.1
announcer 133.4, 353.3, 551.5, 816.1, 1034.23, 1035.13
announce with flourish of trumpets 352.13
announce with the beat of a drum 352.13
annoy 96.13, 98.15, 105.12, 119.2, 152.24
annoyance 96.2, 98.1, 98.7, 119.1, 152.1, 1011.1, 1013.3
annoyed 96.21, 119.4, 152.27, 1013.20
annoyer 96.10
annoying 98.22, 119.5, 126.10, 1013.18
annoyingness 98.7
annual (n) 310.3, 310.33, 549.7, 549.11, 555.1 (a) 850.8
annual epact 832.5
annual holiday 850.4
annual percentage rate 623.3
annual period 313.1
annual report 549.7
annual ring 310.11
annuitant 479.4
annuity 478.8, 1008.4
annul 395.13, 445.2, 900.7
annul a marriage 566.5
annular 280.11
annular eclipse 1027.8, 1073.13
annularity 280.1
annular muscle 280.2
annulary 73.5
annulate 280.11
annulation 280.1
annulet 280.5, 647.2
annulling 900.9
annulment 335.2, 395.6, 395.7, 445.1, 566.1, 900.2
annulose 280.11
annulus 280.2
annum 824.2
annunciate 334.5, 352.12
annunciated 334.9
annunciation 334.1, 352.2
annunciative 334.8
annunciator 353.3, 551.5
annunciator system 1041.5
annunciatory 334.8, 352.18
annus horribilis 1000.3
annus magnus 824.4
annus mirabilis 122.2, 824.4
Annwfn 681.9
anode 1032.8
anode ray 1033.5
anodic 1033.15
anodize 295.26
anodized 295.33
anodized aluminum 295.13
anodyne (n) 25.3, 86.12, 120.1, 670.3 (a) 86.40, 86.45, 120.9, 670.16
anoint 91.25, 615.12, 701.15, 1056.8
anointed king 575.8
anointing 417.12
anointment 417.12, 1056.6
anomalism 870.1
anomalistic 870.9
anomalous 789.8, 870.9, 927.5
anomalousness 870.1
anomaly 789.3, 789.4, 870.1, 870.5, 927.1
anomic 674.6, 804.4
anomie 674.1
Anon. 528.1
anon 528.3
anonym 527.8, 528.1
anonymity 345.2, 528.1
anonymize 345.7
anonymous 345.13, 346.13, 528.3
anonymousness 528.1
anoöpsia 28.5
anorectic 270.20, 992.12
anorexia 7.13
anorexia nervosa 7.13, 270.6, 515.1
anorexic 270.20
anosmia 72.1
another (n) 780.3 (a) 253.10, 780.8, 841.8
another can of worms 780.3
another crack 856.2
another edition 784.3
another go 856.2
another kettle of fish 780.3
another look 849.1
another shot 856.2
another try 856.2
another tune 780.3
anoxia 85.9, 184.21
anserine 311.48
anserous 311.48
answer (n) 343.1, 524.3, 553.2, 600.2, 696.3, 708.23, 790.4, 886.2, 903.1, 939.1, 940.1, 958.2, 995.2 (v) 343.8, 387.17, 553.11, 600.10, 777.7, 788.8, 903.5, 939.4, 940.2, 958.5, 991.4, 995.3
answerability 641.2, 656.1, 888.1
answerable 641.17, 788.9, 897.5, 940.3
answerable for 623.9, 897.6
answerableness 641.2, 644.6
answer as 349.10
answer back 142.8, 939.4
answer conclusively 958.5
answerer 939.3
answer for 349.10, 436.5, 576.14, 641.6, 641.9
answering (n) 939.1 (a) 343.9, 777.10, 939.6
answering machine 549.10
answering service 353.1
answer one's purpose 387.17
answer only to oneself 430.20
answer the call 476.5
answer the call of duty 641.10
answer the call of nature 12.12
answer to 775.5, 777.7, 788.6
answer to no man 418.4
answer to one's prayers, the 940.1
ant 311.33, 726.3
antacid (n) 86.25, 900.3, 1060.3 (a) 86.41, 900.9
Antaean 15.17
Antaeus 15.6
antagonism 99.2, 451.2, 458.10, 589.3, 779.1, 789.1, 900.1
antagonist 452.1, 589.6, 704.10, 707.2
antagonistic 103.7, 451.8, 458.20, 589.10, 779.6, 789.6, 900.8, 1011.13
antagonize 99.6, 119.2, 451.4, 589.7, 900.6
antarctic 161.14
Antarctic, the 1023.4
Antarctica 231.6, 235.1, 1023.4
Antarctic Circle 231.3, 1023.4
Antarctic plate 235.1
Antarctic Zone 231.3, 1023.4
ante (n) 758.4, 759.3 (v) 624.15, 759.25
antebellum 834.5
antecede 814.2, 834.3
antecedence 814.1, 834.1
antecedency 814.1, 834.1
antecedent (n) 816.1, 834.2 (a) 165.3, 814.4, 834.4
antecedents 560.7, 886.1
antechamber 197.20
anteclassical 834.5
antedate (n) 832.4, 834.1 (v) 832.13, 833.2, 834.3
antedated 833.3
antedating 833.1, 834.1
antediluvian (n) 842.7, 842.8 (a) 834.5, 842.13
antelope 174.6, 311.5
antemeridian 314.5
ante meridiem 314.1
antemundane 834.5
antenatal 818.15
antenna 3.10, 73.4, 1034.4
antenna tower 272.6
antepast 8.10, 10.9, 961.4
antepatriarchal 842.11
anteposition 165.1, 215.1, 814.1
anterior 216.10, 814.4, 834.4
anteriority 216.1, 814.1, 834.1
anterograde memory 989.1
anteroom 197.20
antetype 786.1
ante up 624.15, 759.25
ant farm 311.33
anthelion 1025.14
anthelminthic 86.24, 1001.3
anthelmintic 86.41
anthem (n) 696.3, 708.14, 708.17 (v) 708.38
anthemic 696.16
anther 310.28
antheridium 305.11
antherozoid 305.11
anthesis 310.26
anthill 237.4, 770.10
anthology 554.7, 557.4, 720.5, 770.11
Anthony and Cleopatra 104.17
anthracite 1021.9
anthrax 85.41
anthrophore 310.21
anthropocentric 312.13
anthropogeny 312.10
anthropogeography 312.10
anthropography 312.10
anthropoid (n) 842.7 (a) 312.14
anthropolater 675.16, 697.4
anthropolatry 675.5
anthropological 312.13

anthropologist 312.10
anthropology 312.10
anthropometry 312.10
anthropomorphic 311.39, 312.14, 675.25
anthropomorphism 312.9, 675.5
anthropomorphize 312.12
anthropomorphology 312.9
anthropopathic 312.14
anthropopathism 312.9
anthropophagite 593.5
anthropophagous 144.26
anthropophagus 308.11
anthropophagy 8.1
anthroposophical 689.23
anthroposophist 689.11
anthroposophy 312.11, 689.1
anthropotheism 675.5
anthropotheist 675.16
anthropotheistic 675.25
anti 451.8, 779.6
anti-aircraft artillery 462.11
antiaircraft gun 462.12
antiantibody 86.27
antibacterial 79.28, 86.43
antiballistic-missile system 460.2
antibiotic (n) 86.29, 1001.3 (a) 86.41
antiblack 980.12
antiblackout suit 184.21
antibody 2.25, 83.4, 86.27
antic (n) 489.10 (v) 743.23 (a) 109.14, 870.12
anticancer 86.39
anticathexis 92.34
anti-choice 86.23
antichresis 438.4
antichrist 695.10
anti-Christian 695.10
antichristian 695.22
antichristianism 695.8
antichristianity 695.8
anticipant 130.11, 961.7
anticipatable 962.13
anticipate 130.5, 494.6, 814.2, 834.3, 839.6, 845.6, 961.5, 968.5, 1012.14
anticipate a blessed event 78.12
anticipated 130.13, 839.8
anticipating 78.18, 130.11
anticipating a blessed event 78.18
anticipation 130.1, 339.1, 833.1, 834.1, 839.1, 845.1, 934.1, 961.1
anticipative 130.11, 845.7
anticipatory 130.11, 494.10, 834.4, 839.8, 845.7, 961.7
anticlimax 488.3
anticline 291.1
anticness 870.3
anticoagulant 1064.4
anticodon 305.9
antic wit 489.3
anticyclone 173.5, 317.4
anti-cyclonic 317.13
antidepressant (n) 87.3 (a) 86.46
antidisestablishmentarianism 545.3
antidotal 86.41, 900.9
antidote 86.26, 900.3
antiestablishment 333.6
antifreeze (n) 1024.8 (a) 1024.15
antifreezing 1024.15
antifriction 1056.2
antigen 2.25, 83.4, 86.27
antigen-antibody product 86.27
antigravitational 912.9
antigravity 908.1, 912.1
anti-G suit 297.5, 1075.11
antihero 704.10
antihistamine 86.32
anti-inflammatory (n) 86.12 (a) 86.45
anti-inflammatory drug 86.12
antiknock 51.4
anti-lock 430.26
antilogy 936.2
antiluetic 86.41
antimatter 1052.2
antimicrobial 86.41
antimissile missile 460.2
anti-Negro 980.12
antinode 916.4
antinomian (n) 418.3, 688.5 (a) 418.6, 688.9
antinomianism 418.2
antinomic 779.8
antinomy 779.3, 789.2
Antiochian Rite 675.8
antiodontalgic 25.3
antiorgastic 670.16
antipasto 10.9
antipathetic 451.8, 589.10, 779.6, 789.6, 900.8
antipathetical 451.8, 779.6
antipathy 99.2, 103.1, 103.3, 325.1, 451.2, 589.3, 779.1, 900.1
antiperiodic 86.41
antipersonnel bomb 462.20
antiperspirant 72.3
antiphon 696.3, 708.23, 939.1
antiphonal 903.9, 939.6
antiphonal chanting 708.23
antiphonal singing 708.23
antiphony 696.3, 708.23
antiphrasis 531.2
antipodal 215.5, 779.7
antipodal points 215.2
antipode 779.2
antipodean 261.9, 779.7
Antipodes 231.6
antipodes 215.2
antipodes 261.4, 779.2
antipoints 215.2
antipole 779.2
antipoles 215.2
antipsychotic tranquilizer 87.3
antipyretic (n) 86.14 (a) 86.41
antiquarian (n) 842.5 (a) 842.20
antiquarianism 842.4
antiquary 842.5
antiquate 842.9
antiquated 390.10, 837.7, 842.13
antiquated expression 526.12
antiquated word 526.12
antiquation 842.3
antique (n) 842.6, 842.8 (a) 390.10, 827.10, 837.7, 842.10, 842.13
antique-car collector 842.5
antique collector 842.5
antique dealer 842.5
antiquity 827.1, 837.3, 842.1, 842.6
antireligion 695.8
antireligious 695.22
antiroll 915.14
antisaloon 668.11
Anti-Saloon League 668.5
antiscorbutic 86.41
antiscriptural 695.22
antiscripturism 695.8
anti-Semite 103.4
anti-Semitic 980.12
anti-Semitism 103.1, 980.4
antisepsis 79.3
antiseptic (n) 79.17, 86.21, 1001.3 (a) 79.27, 86.43
antisepticize 79.24
antiserum 86.27
antisocial 590.3, 868.5, 927.5
antisocial attitudes 590.1
antisociality 590.1
antispasmodic 86.32
antispast 720.8
antispastic 720.17
antistrophe 720.10
antisubmarine projector 1074.10
antisun 1025.14
antisyphilitic 86.41
antitank rocket 1074.10
antithesis 215.1, 779.1
antithesis, the 779.2
antithetic 215.5, 451.8, 779.6
antithetical 215.5, 451.8, 779.6
antitoxic 86.41
antitoxic globulin 86.27
antitoxic serum 86.27
antitoxin 86.26, 86.27, 91.16
antitrades 318.9
antitrade winds 318.9
antitypic 786.9
antitypical 786.9
antivenin 86.27
antiwar 464.10
antiwhite 980.12
antler 285.4
antlia 283.8
antonomasia 527.1
antonym 518.6, 526.1, 779.2
antonymous 779.6
antonyms 215.2
antonymy 779.1
antre 284.5
antrum 284.2
antsiness 917.1
ants in one's pants 128.2, 135.1
ants in the pants 917.1
antsy 105.23, 105.27, 127.24, 135.6, 917.16, 917.21
antsyness 105.5, 126.1, 128.2
antsy-pantsy 135.6
antymire 311.33
A number 1 (n) 249.4 (a) 249.13
A number one 999.18
anuran 311.26
anus 2.18, 292.5
anvil 2.10, 858.10
anxiety 96.1, 96.2, 101.1, 126.1, 127.4, 130.3, 135.1, 1013.3
anxiety attack 135.1
anxiety disorder 92.14
anxiety hysteria 126.1
anxiety neurosis 126.1
anxious 96.20, 101.8, 126.7, 127.24, 130.12, 135.6, 1013.20
anxious bench 703.14
anxious concern 126.1
anxiousness 101.1, 126.1
anxious seat 126.1, 703.14
any (n) 244.3, 864.5 (a) 244.5, 864.15, 872.7
anybody 864.5, 864.7
anybody's guess 930.6
any number of 884.3
any one (n) 864.5 (a) 872.7
anyone 864.5, 864.7
anything 244.3, 864.5
anythingarian (n) 467.4 (a) 467.7
anythingarianism 467.1
anything goes (n) 418.1 (a) 418.5
anything soever which 864.6
anytime minute 347.13
any Tom, Dick, or Harry 864.3
Anytown 864.4
anywhere 87.25
A-OK 999.13
A-1 997.17, 999.18, 1002.6
A1 (n) 249.4 (a) 180.18, 249.13
A1 at Lloyd's 180.18
aorist (n) 530.12, 837.5 (a) 837.9
aoristic 837.9
aorta 2.16, 2.23
aortic 2.33
apache 308.11
apart 261.8, 584.8, 776.6, 802.20, 872.8
apartheid 584.1, 773.3, 980.4
apartment 228.13
apartment building 228.14
apartment complex 228.14
apartment house 228.14
apartness 584.1
apathetic 25.6, 94.13, 102.7, 125.12, 173.14, 325.6, 331.20, 467.7, 982.3
apathy 25.1, 94.4, 102.2, 123.1, 125.2, 173.4, 325.1, 331.6, 467.2, 933.1, 982.1, 984.1
ape (n) 15.7, 311.22, 336.4, 593.4, 671.10 (v) 336.6, 349.12, 517.21, 784.7 (a) 926.27
ape about 101.11
aped 784.10
ape-man 593.6
apeman 842.7
ape over 101.11
aper 336.4
aperçu 556.1, 557.1, 934.1
aperient (n) 86.17 (a) 86.48
aperitif 62.4
apéritif 10.9, 88.9
aperture 292.1, 383.3
apertured 292.19
apery 336.2
apex 198.2, 272.2, 278.2, 524.18
aphasia 51.2, 525.6
aphasic 51.12, 525.13
aphelion 261.2, 1073.16
aphonia 51.2, 525.1, 525.6
aphonia clericorum 525.6
aphonia paralytica 525.6
aphonia paranoica 525.6

aphonic 51.12, 525.13
aphorism 489.7, 537.3, 974.1
aphoristic 537.6, 974.6
aphoristical 537.6
aphorize 974.5
aphrasia 525.6
aphrasia paranoica 525.6
aphrasic 525.13
aphrodisia 75.5, 75.7
aphrodisiac (n) 75.6 (a) 75.26
aphrodisiomania 665.5
aphrodisiomaniac 665.11
aphrodisiomaniacal 665.29
Aphrodite 104.7, 1016.9
aphroditous 75.26
aphthous fever 85.41
apiarist 1070.4
apiary 228.25
apical 198.11
apical bud 310.23
Apician 672.6
apiculture 1070.1
apiculturist 1070.4
aping 349.4, 784.1
apish 336.9, 349.13, 923.8
aplenty 991.7
aplomb 106.3, 200.1, 359.5, 855.1
apnea 85.9
Apocalypse 683.4
apocalypse 351.1, 395.2
apocalypse 683.10, 820.1, 962.1
apocalyptic 133.16, 683.11, 962.11
apocalyptical 683.11, 962.11
apocalyptician 112.14
apocalypticist 112.14
apocalypticize 112.15
a poco 708.54
apocope 268.3, 537.4
apocrine 13.8
Apocrypha 683.3
apocryphal 354.26, 688.9, 971.21
apocynthion 1075.2
apodan 311.26
apodeictic 935.19
apodictic 957.17, 957.19, 970.13
apoenzyme 7.10
apogee 198.2, 211.3, 261.2, 794.5, 1073.16, 1075.2
apogeotropism 297.5
apograph 785.4
apoise 180.19, 790.9
Apollo 710.22, 720.11, 1073.14
Apollo Musagetes 710.22, 720.11
Apollyon 680.4
apologetic (n) 600.3, 600.8 (a) 113.9, 600.13, 658.7
apologetical 600.13, 658.7
apologetics 935.4
apologia 600.3, 935.4
apologies 113.1
apologist 460.7, 600.8, 616.9, 935.12
apologize 113.7, 658.5
apologize for 600.11
apologizer 600.8
apology 113.4, 376.1, 600.3, 658.2, 935.4
apolune 1075.2
apophthegm 974.1
apoplectic (n) 85.43 (a) 85.61
apoplectical deafness 85.15
apoplexy 85.6, 85.27, 671.5, 917.6
aporetic 935.19
aposematic mimicry 336.2
aposiopesis 537.4
aposiopestic 537.6
apostacize 363.7
apostasy 333.1, 335.2, 363.2, 370.2, 394.2, 435.1, 675.10, 694.1, 852.1, 858.3
apostate (n) 333.3, 363.5, 394.3, 675.20, 694.3, 858.8 (a) 363.11, 394.5, 675.28, 694.6, 858.20
apostatize 335.4, 363.7, 370.6, 858.13
a posteriori 935.22
a posteriori reasoning 935.3
apostle 572.2, 684.2, 699.10, 858.9
Apostles' Creed 676.2
apostleship 698.1
Apostolic 668.10
apostolic 683.11, 698.15
apostolical 683.11, 698.15
apostolic church 687.3
apostolic delegate 576.6
apostolic faith 687.2
Apostolici 668.4
apostolic orders 698.10
Apostolic See 698.6
apostrophe 524.3, 542.1
apostrophic 542.4
apostrophize 524.26, 542.3
apothecaries' measure 300.4
apothecaries' weight 297.8
apothecary 86.35
apothecary's shop 86.36
apothegm 489.7, 974.1
apothegmatize 974.5
apotheose 662.13
apotheosis 155.1, 509.5, 662.8, 681.11, 697.2, 786.4, 912.1
apotheosize 155.4, 509.12, 662.13, 697.5, 912.6
apotheosized 662.18, 912.9
apotheosizing 155.9
app 1042.11
Appalachia 231.7
appall 98.11, 127.17, 127.19
appalled 127.26
appalling 98.19, 127.30, 247.10
appallingness 127.2
appaloosa 311.11
appanage 254.1, 471.5, 478.9
appanages 471.2
apparatchik 575.15
apparatus 385.4, 471.3, 1040.1
apparel (n) 5.1 (v) 5.39
appareled 5.45
apparent 31.6, 31.7, 33.11, 206.7, 348.8, 354.27, 968.7, 976.9
apparentation 560.4
apparent character 33.2
apparent death 85.2
apparent destiny 130.4
apparent fate 130.4
apparent heir 479.5
apparent horizon 201.4
apparently sound 936.10
apparent nebula 1073.8
apparentness 348.3
apparent soundness 936.1
apparent time 832.3
apparent wind 318.10
apparition 33.1, 33.5, 976.4, 986.5, 988.1
apparitional 976.9
apparitor 133.4
appassionatamente 708.53
appassionato 708.53
appeal (n) 97.2, 100.13, 104.6, 377.1, 440.2, 598.10, 696.4 (v) 377.6, 440.11
appealing 75.25, 97.7, 377.8, 440.17, 708.48
appealingness 97.2
appeal motion 598.10
appeals court 595.2
appeal to 440.11, 524.26, 957.14
appeal to a higher court 598.10
appeal to arms 458.1
appeal to one for 421.5
appeal to one's better feelings 145.5
appeal to the law 598.13
appeal to the sword (n) 458.1 (v) 458.15
appear 31.4, 33.8, 33.10, 221.8, 348.6, 351.8, 352.16, 704.29, 831.6
appearance 33.1, 33.2, 33.5, 186.1, 206.1, 262.3, 348.1, 354.3, 976.2, 976.4, 988.1
appearance design 717.5
appear earlier 834.3
appear for 576.14
appearing (n) 33.1 (a) 33.11, 348.9
appear in print 548.18
appear like 33.10, 784.7
appear like a bolt out of the blue 131.6
appear on the horizon 33.8
appear on the scene 33.8
appear on the stage 704.29
appear to be 33.10
appear to one's eyes 33.8, 33.10
appear unexpectedly 131.6
appeasable 465.12, 465.13
appease 95.8, 120.5, 465.7, 670.7, 696.15
appeasement 120.1, 465.1, 609.5, 696.6
appeaser 466.5
appeasing 465.12, 670.15
appellant 599.5
appellate 595.7
appellate court 595.2
appellate jurisdiction 594.1
appellation 527.2, 527.3
appellative (n) 527.3 (a) 527.16
appellee 599.6
append 253.4, 253.5, 815.3
appendage 2.7, 138.6, 166.2, 254.1, 768.2, 769.3, 793.4
appendages 471.2
appendant (n) 254.1 (a) 253.9, 815.4
appended 253.9
appendicular skeleton 2.2
appendix 2.18, 254.2, 341.5, 554.12, 817.1
apperceive 24.6
apperception 24.1, 920.4, 928.2
apperceptive 920.16, 928.15
appercipient 920.16, 928.15
appertain 775.5
appertaining 775.7, 775.11
appertain to 469.7, 775.5
appetence 100.6, 323.1
appetency 100.6, 323.1
appetite 8.1, 100.6, 100.7, 101.1, 323.1, 663.1
appetition 100.6
appetitive 100.21, 663.5
appetitiveness 663.1
appetizer 8.2, 10.7, 10.9, 62.4, 793.3
appetizing 63.10, 100.30, 377.8
applaud 116.6, 149.2, 332.8, 509.10
applauded 509.19
applauder 509.8
applaud to the very echo 509.10
applause 116.2, 149.1, 509.2
apple 310.4
apple-cheeked 41.9, 83.13
apple fritter 10.44
apple of discord 456.7
Apple of Discord, the 456.1
apple of one's eye 104.15
apple pie 1014.4
apple-pie order 807.3
apple-polisher 138.4
apple-polishing 138.2
apples and oranges 943.9
applesauce 10.12, 520.3
apples to oranges 249.15
applet 1042.11
appliable 387.23
appliance 384.4, 387.1, 449.9, 1040.3
appliances 385.4, 735.4
applicability 387.3, 673.1, 775.4, 788.5
applicable 387.23, 673.11, 775.11, 788.10
applicant 440.7
application 86.33, 330.6, 360.1, 387.1, 440.1, 570.3, 643.2, 775.4, 888.1, 983.3
application development language 1042.13
application for retrial 598.10
application programmer 1042.17
application programming 1042.12
application software 1042.11
applications program 1042.11
applied 387.24
applied art 712.1
applied mathematics 1017.1
applied science 928.10
appliqué 295.4
apply 387.11, 643.6, 775.6, 888.3
apply a Band-Aid 276.4
apply a coat of paint 376.4
apply for 440.9
applying (n) 643.2 (a) 775.11
apply margin 737.23
apply oneself 403.5, 725.9

apply oneself to 328.8, 404.3, 570.12, 724.11, 931.11, 983.5
apply paint 35.14
apply pressure 440.12
apply reason 935.15
apply the attention to 983.5
apply the mind 931.9
apply the mind to 931.11, 983.5
apply the yardstick to 300.10
apply to 295.19, 440.10, 775.5, 888.4
apply whitewash 376.4
appoggiatura 708.27, 709.18
appoint 371.20, 385.8, 420.9, 477.9, 615.11, 964.7
appointed 371.26, 615.19, 964.9
appointed lot 964.2
appointee 576.2, 615.9
appointing 371.23
appointive 371.23
appointment 371.9, 417.12, 477.3, 582.8, 615.2, 615.4, 698.10, 724.5
appointment calendar 549.11
appointments 385.4, 471.2
appointment schedule 549.11
appoint oneself 214.5
apportion 244.4, 476.6, 477.6, 793.6, 802.18, 808.9
apportionable 477.12
apportioned 477.12
apportioning 477.1
apportionment 477.1, 808.1
appose 223.13
apposite 775.11, 788.10
appositeness 775.4, 788.5
apposition 223.3, 530.2
appositive 530.2
appraisable 300.14
appraisal 300.1, 630.3, 801.3, 946.3
appraise 300.10, 630.11, 801.8, 946.9
appraised 300.13, 630.14
appraisement 300.1, 630.3, 946.3
appraiser 300.9
appraising 946.3
appreciable 297.19, 300.14, 763.6, 928.25
appreciate 63.5, 95.13, 150.3, 155.4, 251.6, 300.10, 521.7, 928.12, 946.9, 997.13
appreciated 155.11, 928.26
appreciate differences 944.6
appreciation 150.1, 155.1, 251.1, 332.3, 509.3, 928.2, 944.1, 946.3
appreciation of differences 944.1
appreciation of excellence 496.1
appreciative 150.5, 155.8, 509.16, 944.7
appreciativeness 150.1, 928.2, 944.1
appreciative of 928.16
appreciator 509.8
appreciatory 150.5, 509.16, 944.7
appreciatory of 928.16
apprehend 24.6, 127.10, 133.10, 429.15, 480.18, 521.7, 928.12
apprehendable 928.25
apprehended 928.26
apprehending 928.15
apprehensibility 521.1
apprehensible 521.10, 928.25
apprehension 126.1, 127.4, 130.3, 133.2, 429.6, 480.2, 920.1, 928.3, 932.1, 955.2
apprehensive 126.7, 127.24, 128.11, 130.12, 928.15
apprehensiveness 126.1, 127.4, 128.1
apprentice (n) 572.9, 726.6, 818.2, 892.7 (v) 568.13, 570.11, 615.18
apprentice chef 11.3
apprenticed 615.21
apprentice jockey 757.2
apprentice oneself to 570.11
apprentice printer 548.12
apprenticeship 432.3, 568.3, 615.8
apprentice teacher 571.4
apprentice work 893.1
appress 260.8
apprise 551.8
apprised of 928.16
apprize 630.11
approach (n) 167.1, 169.1, 184.18, 186.1, 189.5, 223.1, 381.1, 383.3, 384.1, 403.2, 439.1, 750.2, 784.1, 840.1 (v) 167.3, 169.2, 186.6, 223.7, 223.8, 343.8, 378.3, 384.5, 403.6, 439.7, 524.26, 587.12, 784.7, 831.6, 839.6, 840.2, 894.9
approachability 167.2, 343.3, 966.3
approachable 167.5, 343.10, 378.4, 966.8
approach anchorage 182.35
approaches 182.10
approaching (n) 167.1 (a) 167.4, 169.3, 186.9, 223.14, 839.8, 840.3
approach leg 184.18
approach of time 839.5
approach shot 167.1
approach trench 460.5
approbation 155.1, 332.4, 441.1, 443.1, 509.1, 662.3
approbative 509.16
approbatory 509.16, 946.16
appropinquate 167.3
appropinquation 167.1
appropriable 477.12
appropriate (v) 472.10, 477.7, 480.19, 482.13, 482.19, 621.4, 640.8 (a) 387.18, 496.9, 533.7, 637.3, 639.8, 775.11, 788.10, 843.9, 865.13, 995.5
appropriate for 477.9
appropriateness 496.2, 533.1, 637.2, 775.4, 788.5, 843.1, 995.1
appropriate to 477.9
appropriation 477.3, 480.4, 482.1, 482.8, 621.2, 640.3
appropriator 480.11
approval 155.1, 332.4, 441.1, 509.1, 662.3, 901.1, 946.2
approve 332.12, 371.15, 441.2, 509.9, 901.21, 946.14, 957.8
approved 332.14, 371.26, 479.10, 509.19, 579.5, 687.7, 970.18
approve of 441.2, 509.9
approver 332.7
approving 441.4, 509.17
approximable 784.14
approximate (v) 167.3, 223.8, 336.5, 784.7, 784.8 (a) 167.4, 223.14, 775.8, 784.14, 975.17
approximating 223.14, 775.8, 784.14
approximation 167.1, 223.1, 300.1, 336.3, 775.1, 784.1, 784.3, 975.2, 1017.2
approximative (n) 530.9 (a) 167.4, 300.12, 775.8, 784.14, 975.17
appulse 167.1, 223.3, 902.3
appurtenance 254.1, 449.9, 642.1, 768.2, 796.2
appurtenances 385.4, 471.2
appurtenant (n) 254.1 (a) 768.4
apricot 42.2
April showers 316.1, 854.4
a priori 837.12, 935.22
a priori knowledge 934.1
a priori principle 935.7
a priori reasoning 935.3
apriorism 935.7
a priori truth 974.2
apron 5.17, 184.23, 704.16, 751.1
apron stage 704.16
apropos 775.11, 788.10
apse 279.4, 703.9
apt 413.22, 533.7, 570.18, 788.10, 845.9, 920.14, 966.6, 968.6, 978.8
aptitude 413.5, 570.5, 788.5, 896.1, 920.2, 968.1, 978.3
aptness 413.5, 533.1, 570.5, 788.5, 896.1, 920.2
aptronym 530.5
apt to 897.6
aqua 1065.3
aquacize (n) 182.11 (v) 182.56
aquaculture 240.6
aquaerobics 84.2
aquafarm 1069.8
Aqua-Lung 367.5
aquamanile 79.12
aquamarine 45.3
aquaplaning 182.11
aquaponics 1069.8
aquarelle 712.13
aquarellist 716.4
aquarium 228.24, 770.11
aquarium fish 311.30
aquascape 241.1
aquascope 367.5
aquatic (n) 311.3 (a) 182.58, 1065.16
aquatic or water sport 744.1
aquatic plant 310.3
aquatics 182.11
aquatint 713.12
aquatinta 713.12
aqua vitae 88.13
aqueduct 239.2, 290.2, 383.9
aqueous 1065.16
aqueous humor 2.9
aquifer 1065.3
aquiline 279.8, 311.48
aquiline-nosed 279.8
aquilinity 279.1
Aquilo 318.2
aquiver 105.20
Arabesque 554.15
arabesque (n) 170.3, 498.2 (a) 498.12
arabesque 709.18
Arabia Deserta 891.2
Arabic numerals 1017.4
arable 1069.20
arable land 233.1, 234.1, 1069.8
arachnid 311.3, 311.31, 311.32
arachnoid membrane 2.6
Aralu 682.3
Aranyaka 683.8
arb 737.11
arbalest 462.7, 462.9
arbiter 466.4, 496.6, 596.1, 946.6
arbiter of fashion 578.7
arbiter of taste 496.6
arbitrage (n) 737.19, 738.1 (v) 737.23
arbitrager 737.11
arbitrageur 737.11
arbitraging 737.19
arbitral 466.8
arbitrament 466.2, 788.4, 946.1
arbitrament of the sword 458.1
arbitrariness 364.2, 417.3
arbitrary 324.7, 364.5, 365.10, 417.16
arbitrate 466.6, 727.9, 946.12
arbitration 466.2, 727.1, 788.4, 946.1
arbitrational 466.8
arbitrative 466.8
arbitrator 466.4, 576.4, 596.1
arbor 228.12, 915.5
arboraceous 310.39
arborary 310.39
arboreal 171.10, 310.39
arboreous 310.39, 310.40
arborescence 171.3
arborescent 171.10, 310.39
arboresque 310.39
arboretum 310.13, 397.7
arborical 310.39
arboricultural 1069.21
arboriculture 1069.2, 1069.3
arboriculturist 1069.7
arboriform 171.10, 310.39
Arborio rice 10.36
arborist 1069.7
arborization 171.3
arborolater 697.4
arc (n) 279.2, 316.8, 704.18, 1032.6 (v) 279.6
arcade 197.18, 212.4, 273.5, 279.4, 383.3, 736.2, 743.15
arcade game 743.9
Arcadia 986.11
Arcadian 233.6
Arcadian 986.23
arcadian 416.6
Arcana Caelestia 683.7

arcane 345.11, 519.7, 522.16, 689.23, 870.15
arcane, the 345.5
arcane meaning 519.2
arcanum 345.5
arcanum arcanorum 345.5
arcature 279.4
arch (n) 199.5, 279.4, 549.12 (v) 279.6 (a) 249.14, 322.6, 415.12
archaeoastronomy 842.4
archaeogeology 842.4
archaeolater 697.4
archaeological 842.20
archaeologist 284.10, 719.3, 842.5
archaeology 719.1, 842.4, 941.1
archaic 842.10, 842.20
Archaic Caucasoid race 312.2
archaic Homo 312.1
archaicism 526.12
archaic language 523.2
archaic speech 523.2
archaic white race 312.2
archaism 523.2, 526.12, 842.6
archaist 842.5
archangel 679.1
archangelic 679.6
archangels 679.3
arch aurora 1025.16
archbishop 699.9
archbishopric 231.5, 417.7, 698.2, 698.8
arch buttress 901.4
arch-conservatism 853.3
arch-conservative 611.1, 611.9, 853.4
arch dam 1012.5
archdeaconry 698.2
archdiocese 231.5, 698.8
archducal 608.10
archduchess 608.6
archduchy 232.1
archduke 608.4
archdukedom 232.1
arched 279.10, 283.13
arched roof 279.4
archenemy 452.1, 589.6
archer 904.8
archery 462.3, 744.1, 904.2
archery ground 743.11
archetypal (n) 92.29 (a) 337.6, 786.9, 842.11
archetypal idea 934.2
archetypal image 92.29, 842.2
archetypal myth 842.2
archetypal pattern 92.29, 934.2
archetype 92.29, 262.1, 337.2, 786.1, 842.2, 932.2, 934.2, 1002.4
archetypic 337.6, 786.9
archetypical 337.6, 786.9, 1002.9
archeus 306.2, 767.5
arch-gravity dam 1012.5
Archie Bunker 980.5
archiepiscopacy 417.7, 698.2
archiepiscopal 698.13
archiepiscopate 417.7, 698.2
archigenesis 78.6
arching 279.1
archipelagian 235.7
archipelagic 235.7
archipelago 235.2
architect 381.6, 716.10, 717.3, 726.1, 892.7
architectonic 266.6, 717.7, 892.15
architectonics 266.1, 717.1, 722.4
architectress 717.3
architectural 266.6, 717.7, 892.15
architectural design 717.1, 717.5
architectural draftsman 716.3
architectural element 717.2
architectural engineer 717.3
architectural engineering 717.1
architectural ornamentation 717.2
architectural science 717.1
architectural specialty 717.1
architectural style 717.1
architectural technology 717.1
architectural topping 198.5
architecture 266.1, 712.16, 717.1, 722.4, 892.2
archival 549.18, 719.6
archive (n) 549.2, 719.1, 1042.18 (v) 549.15
archived 549.18
archives 386.6, 397.7, 549.2, 549.3
archiving 549.14
archivist 550.1, 719.3
arch-nemesis 1001.1
archon 574.3, 575.16, 596.2
arch over 295.30
arch-poet 720.12
archrival 452.2
archtraitor 357.10
archway 279.4
arciform 279.10
arcing 279.1
arc light 704.18, 1025.19
arclike 279.10
Arctic 231.6
arctic 313.9, 1023.14
arctic 94.9, 161.14
Arctic, the 1023.4
Arctic blast 318.7
Arctic Circle 231.3, 1023.4
arctic conditions 1023.3
arctic frost 1023.3
arctic temperature 1023.1
arctic weather 1023.3
Arctic Zone 231.3, 1023.4
arcual 279.10
arcuate 279.10
arcuated 279.10
arcuation 279.1
ardency 93.2, 101.2, 104.1, 544.5, 587.6, 1019.2
ardent 88.37, 93.18, 101.9, 104.25, 324.5, 330.22, 544.13, 587.16, 671.22, 692.11, 1019.25, 1019.27
ardent friend 588.2
ardent friendship 587.8
ardent imagination 986.4
ardent spirits 88.13
ardor 17.4, 93.2, 100.1, 101.2, 104.1, 324.1, 330.6, 544.5, 983.2, 1019.2
ardri 575.9
arduous 725.18, 1013.17
arduousness 725.5, 1013.1
area 158.1, 159.1, 209.1, 231.1, 257.1, 568.8, 724.4, 866.1, 928.10
area code 347.12
Area 51 345.1
area graph 381.3
areal 231.8
area language 523.1
area measure 300.4
area rug 199.3
areaway 197.18
areawide 158.11
areligious 695.7
arena 158.1, 197.4, 209.2, 212.3, 231.2, 308.12, 463.1, 704.14, 724.4, 755.1, 928.10, 978.2
arenaceous 1051.12
arena football 746.1
arenarious 1051.12
arenose 1051.12
areola 280.2
Areopagite 596.2
Areopagus 595.1
Ares 458.12
aretaics 636.2, 653.1
arête 237.5, 285.4
argent (n) 647.2 (a) 37.7
argentine 37.7
Argestes 318.2
argil 742.3
argillaceous 1047.12
Argonaut 178.2, 183.1
argosy 180.1, 180.10, 461.27
argot 522.7, 523.9
arguable 971.17
argue 334.5, 517.17, 518.8, 935.16, 957.8
argue at the bar 598.19
argue down 958.5
argue for 600.10
argue insincerely 936.8
argue into 375.23
argue into a corner 958.5
argue one's case 598.19
arguer 935.12
argue to no purpose 935.16
argufier 935.12
argufy 935.16
argument 456.5, 457.1, 598.6, 598.8, 600.2, 722.4, 935.4, 935.5
argumental 110.26, 935.19
argumentation 789.1, 935.4
argumentative 110.26, 935.19
argumentativeness 110.7, 935.13
argument by analogy 936.3
arguments at the bar 598.6
Argus 27.11, 1008.10
Argus-eyed 27.21, 339.13
argute 58.14, 920.16
arguteness 58.1
argy-bargy 456.5
aria 708.4, 708.15
aria buffa 708.16
aria cantabile 708.16
aria da capo 708.16
aria da chiesa 708.16
aria d'agilità 708.16
aria di bravura 708.16
aria di coloratura 708.16
aria d'imitazione 708.16
aria fugata 708.16
Arian (n) 688.5 (a) 688.9
aria parlante 708.16
aria singer 710.13
arid 117.6, 891.4, 987.5, 1066.7
aridity 117.1, 891.1, 987.1, 1066.1
aridness 891.2, 987.1, 1066.1
Ariel 678.8
arietta 708.16
ariose 708.48
arioso (n) 708.16 (a) 708.48
arise 23.6, 33.8, 190.11, 193.8, 200.8, 327.7, 818.13, 831.6
arise and go to 177.25
arise from 887.5
arising (n) 33.1 (a) 190.18
arista 3.9
Aristaeus 1069.4
aristate 288.10
aristeia 492.6
aristocracy 249.5, 417.7, 607.2, 607.3, 608.1, 608.2, 612.4
aristocrat 607.4, 608.4
aristocratic 136.12, 141.11, 417.16, 607.10, 608.10, 612.16
aristocratical 612.16
aristocraticalness 607.3, 608.2
aristocratic disdain 141.5
aristocraticness 607.3
aristocratic presumption 141.3
aristocratic status 607.3
Aristotelian 952.12
Aristotelian form 932.2
Aristotelianism 952.3
Aristotelian logic 935.2
Aristotelian philosophy 952.3
Aristotelian sorites 935.6
arithmetic (n) 568.3 (a) 1017.22
arithmetical 1017.22, 1017.23
arithmetical progression 1017.8
arithmetical proportion 1017.7
arithmetician 1017.16
arithmetic operation 1017.2
arithmetize 1017.18
ark 180.1
Arlberg technique 753.3
arm (n) 2.7, 242.1, 517.4, 617.10, 745.3, 793.4, 901.2, 906.5 (v) 18.10, 385.8, 460.9, 1008.18
armada 461.27
armament 385.1, 385.4, 462.1, 746.1
an arm and a leg 632.3
armature 211.2, 266.4, 460.3, 901.10
arm candy 1016.7
armchair 951.13
armchair authority 951.7
armchair philosopher 951.7
armchair quarterback 466.4, 918.1
armchair ride 757.3
armed 385.13, 405.16, 458.22, 460.14, 1008.21
armed and ready 405.16
armed assault 459.1
armed at all points 460.13
armed cap-a-pie 460.13

armed combat 458.1
armed conflict 458.1
armed forces 461.20, 461.23
armed guard 1008.9
armed robbery 482.3, 632.5
armed services 461.20
armed to the teeth 460.14
armed with patience 134.9
arm guard 1008.3
armiger 608.4
armilla 647.3
arm-in-arm 223.14
armipotent 18.12
armistice 465.5
armlet 242.1, 280.3, 498.6
arm of the law 1008.15
arm of the sea 242.1
arm of the service 461.21
armor (n) 94.3, 295.15, 460.3 (v) 460.9, 1008.18
armored 295.31, 460.13
armored against 94.12
armored attack 459.4
armored combat 457.4
armored division 461.22
armored vehicle 179.12
armored vessel 180.6
armorial bearings 647.2
armorless 1006.14
armor plate 460.3
armor-plate 460.9
armor-plated 460.13
armory 386.6, 462.2, 647.1, 647.2, 739.3, 755.1
armpit 284.2
armrest 826.1
arms 458.5, 462.1, 647.2
arms control 464.7, 465.6
arms control agreement 437.2
arms industry 462.1
arms maker 462.1
arms of Morpheus, the 22.2
arms race 458.9
arms reduction 464.7, 465.6
arms treaty 437.2
arm-twist 375.23, 424.8, 514.2
arm-twisting 375.3, 424.3, 514.1
Army 461.21
army 461.22, 461.23, 770.4, 770.5, 884.3
army ant 311.33
army base 461.23
army corps 461.22
army craps 759.8
army fatigues 5.7
army group 461.22
army marbles 759.8
army-navy surplus 460.3
army noncommissioned officer 575.18
army officer 575.18
army reserves 461.25
army surplus 460.3
army surplus store 736.1
army uniform 5.7
aroma 68.1, 69.1, 70.1, 865.4
aromatherapeutic 70.9
aromatherapy 69.2, 70.1
aromatic (n) 70.2 (a) 68.6, 69.9, 70.9
aromatic gum 70.2
aromatic rice 10.36
aromatic spirits of ammonia 86.9
aromatic water 70.2
aromatize 69.7, 70.8
around-the-world 772.7
arousal 23.2, 105.1, 105.11, 192.5, 375.4
arouse 17.10, 23.5, 105.12, 152.24, 192.14, 375.17, 375.19, 400.3, 983.12, 1020.18
aroused 75.27, 105.20, 400.4
arouse notice 983.11
arouse one's enthusiasm 983.12
arouse one's passion 983.12
arouser 17.6
arouse the memory 989.19
arousing (n) 105.11 (a) 75.26, 192.17
arpeggio 709.18
arraign 510.13, 598.15, 599.7
arraignability 656.1
arraignable 510.25, 656.3
arraignableness 656.1
arraigned 599.15
arraignment 510.3, 598.3, 599.1
arrange 381.8, 405.6, 437.8, 466.7, 708.46, 807.4, 808.8, 809.6, 812.5
arrange a match 563.14
arranged 381.12, 437.11, 807.6, 808.14, 964.8
arranged marriage 563.1
arrange for 405.11
arrange in layers 296.5
arrange in levels 296.5
arrange in strata 296.5
arrange in tiers 296.5
arrange itself 807.5
arrange matters 465.8
arrangement 262.1, 266.1, 381.1, 405.1, 437.1, 465.4, 468.1, 498.1, 582.8, 708.5, 708.28, 709.2, 709.11, 712.8, 770.1, 770.7, 807.1, 808.1, 809.1
arrange one's thoughts 931.10
arranger 710.20, 808.5
arranging 706.6, 770.1
arrant 247.12, 348.12, 654.16, 661.12, 1000.9
arrant coward 491.6
arrantness 348.4, 654.4
array (n) 5.1, 158.2, 461.23, 807.1, 808.1, 812.2 (v) 5.39, 498.8, 808.9, 812.5, 957.12
arrayed 5.45, 458.22, 808.14
arraying 808.1
array processor 1042.2
arrear 623.2, 911.1
arrearage 623.2, 795.2, 911.1
arrears 623.2, 911.1
arrest (n) 85.6, 175.4, 428.1, 429.6, 480.2, 857.2, 1012.1, 1012.7 (v) 175.9, 428.7, 429.15, 480.18, 846.8, 857.11, 983.13, 1012.10
arrestation 428.1, 429.6, 480.2, 1012.1, 1012.2
arrest attention 983.11
arrested 175.12, 406.12, 428.13, 795.4, 846.16, 922.22, 983.18
arrested development 92.21, 163.1, 922.9
arrestee 429.11
arresting 983.20
arrestment 429.6, 795.1, 1012.1
arrest one's notice 983.11
arrest the thoughts 931.19, 983.11
arrhythmia 851.1, 916.3
arrière-pensée 817.1, 931.5, 959.1
arrival 33.1, 184.18, 186.1, 189.4
arrive 33.8, 186.6, 409.10
arrive at 186.6, 186.7
arrive at a conclusion 946.10
arrive at an agreement 332.10
arrive in 186.6
arrive upon 186.7
arriving 186.9
arrivism 497.4
arriviste 606.7, 774.4, 841.4
arrogance 136.1, 140.2, 141.1, 142.1, 157.1, 454.1, 970.5
arrogant 136.9, 140.9, 141.9, 142.9, 157.8, 417.16, 454.7, 970.21
arrogantness 141.1
arrogate 417.14, 418.4, 480.19, 640.8
arrogate to oneself 480.19, 640.8
arrogation 417.12, 418.2, 480.4, 640.3, 888.1
arrogator 575.13, 640.4
arrondissement 231.5
arrow (n) 174.6, 462.6, 517.4 (v) 277.4
arrow aimed at one's heart 514.1
arrow for 161.10
arrowhead 285.4, 462.6, 546.2
arrowheaded 285.11
arrow key 1042.18
arrowlike 277.6, 285.11
arrow-straight 161.12
arrowy 285.11
arroyo 237.7, 238.1, 239.2
arse 217.5
arsenal 386.6, 462.2, 739.3
arsenic 1001.3
arsenic hour 301.5
arsis 720.7, 850.3
arson 1020.7
arson investigator 576.10
arsonist 395.8, 1020.8
arsonous 1020.27
ars poetica 720.2
arsy-varsiness 810.3
arsy-varsy 205.7, 810.16
art 349.1, 413.6, 413.7, 415.1, 415.3, 712.1, 712.6, 724.6, 928.10
art and technique of building, the 717.1
art center 208.7
art-conscious 712.20
art critic 547.15, 718.4
art criticism 723.1, 946.2
artefact 842.6
Artemis 1073.12
arterial 2.33
arterial blood 2.25
arteriole 2.23
arteriosclerosis 1046.5
artery 2.23, 383.3
artesian basin 1065.3
artesian spring 1065.3
artesian well 241.1
art film 706.1
art form 262.1, 712.1
artful 164.9, 354.31, 356.22, 415.12, 645.18, 920.15
artful dodge 356.6, 415.3
Artful Dodger 357.1, 415.6
artful endearments 562.5
artfulness 356.3, 413.1, 415.1, 533.3, 645.3, 920.3
art gallery 386.9
art house 706.7
arthritic (n) 85.43 (a) 85.61
arthropod 311.3, 311.31, 311.32
article (n) 530.6, 547.10, 552.3, 554.13, 556.1, 735.2, 766.3, 793.2, 872.4, 1052.4 (v) 599.7, 615.18
article, the 973.4
articled 615.21
articled clerk 572.9
article of commerce 735.2
article of faith 953.2
article of merchandise 735.2
article of virtu 712.9
articles of faith 676.2, 953.3
articles of religion 676.2, 953.3
article writer 547.15, 718.4
articulacy 524.4
articulate (v) 523.18, 524.22, 800.5, 800.8 (a) 50.16, 518.10, 521.10, 524.31, 544.8, 800.17
articulated 524.29, 524.30, 812.8
articulated bus 179.13
articulateness 521.1, 524.4, 544.1
articulation 524.5, 524.12, 526.1, 800.1, 800.4, 812.2
articulator 524.18
articulatory 524.30
articulatory phonetics 524.13
artifact 842.6, 893.1, 1052.4
artifice 354.4, 356.4, 356.6, 381.5, 415.1, 415.3, 533.3, 995.2
artificer 726.6, 892.7, 1040.12
artificial 336.8, 354.26, 354.33, 500.15, 533.9
artificial blond 37.9
artificial coloring 35.8
artificial fiber 271.1
artificial flavoring 63.3
artificial horizon 201.4
artificial insemination 78.3
artificial intelligence 1042.20
artificial isotope 1038.5
artificiality 354.2, 500.1, 533.3
artificial lake 241.1
artificial language 523.11
artificial light 1025.19
artificial lighting 1025.19
artificial magnet 907.3
artificial nucleation 316.5
artificial radioactivity 1037.1
artificial reality 1042.1

artificial respiration 2.21
artificial satellite 1073.11, 1075.6
artificial sweetener 7.5, 66.2
artificial turf 199.3, 310.7
artificial voice 525.1
artillerist 461.11
artillery 462.3, 462.11
artillery barrage 459.9
artilleryman 461.11, 904.8
artillery park 462.2
artiness 712.6
artiodactyl 311.5
artisan 413.11, 607.9, 716.1, 726.6, 1040.12
artisanry 712.2
artisanship 413.1, 712.2
artisan work 712.2
artist 413.11, 707.1, 710.1, 712.1, 716.1, 726.6, 892.7, 928.11
artiste 707.1, 710.1, 716.1, 928.11
artistic (n) 723.1 (a) 413.22, 496.7, 712.20
artistic creation 712.9
artistic criticism 723.1
artistic evaluation 723.1
artistic flair 712.6
artistic imagination 986.2
artistic interpretation 723.1
artistic invention 712.6
artistic judgment 944.1
artistic license 430.1, 712.1
artistic production 712.9
artistic quality 712.6
artistic skill 712.6
artistic taste 496.4, 712.6
artistic temperament 712.6
artistic worker 726.2
artist-in-residence 227.2
artist lithography 713.3
artistry 413.1, 413.10, 547.2, 712.6, 718.2
artists' canvas 712.18
artist's colors 35.8
artist's model 786.5
artist's proof 713.7
art journal 549.11
artless 406.13, 414.15, 416.5, 644.17, 923.12
artlessness 406.3, 416.1, 644.4, 973.7
art library 558.1
art-minded 712.20
art movie 706.2
art object 712.9
art of composition, the 547.2, 718.2
art of dispute 935.4
art of public speaking 543.1
art of reason 935.2
art of the possible, the 609.1
art of war 458.1, 458.5
artotype 714.4
art paper 712.18
arts, the 712.1
arts and crafts 712.1, 712.2
art school 567.7
arts conservatory 567.7
arts of design 712.1
art style 712.7
artsy-craftsiness 712.6
artsy-craftsy 712.20
artsy-fartsy 712.20
art therapy 90.13
artware 712.9
artwork 712.1, 712.9
arty 712.20
arty-craftiness 712.6
arty-crafty 712.20
aruspex 962.4
arytenoid cartilages 524.18
as a bonus 993.18
ASA number 714.9
ASA scale 1025.21
as bad as bad can be 1000.9
as bad as they come 1000.9
as bad as they make 'em 1000.9
asbestine 1022.9, 1058.15
asbestoid 1022.9
asbestoidal 1022.9
asbestos 1022.5
asbestos curtain 704.16, 1022.5
asbestous 1022.9
as big as all outdoors 257.16
as broad as long 790.8
ascend 172.5, 184.39, 193.8, 200.8, 204.10, 272.10, 298.9
ascendance 249.1, 417.6
ascendancy 249.1, 411.1, 417.6, 894.1
ascendant 193.14, 249.12, 411.7, 417.15, 612.17, 894.14
ascendants 560.7
ascender 193.6, 548.6
ascending (n) 172.2, 200.5 (a) 172.8, 193.14, 204.17, 272.14
ascending order 807.2
ascend to the throne 417.14
ascension 193.1, 200.5, 681.11
Ascension, the 681.11
ascensional 193.14
ascensive 193.14
ascent 172.2, 193.1, 200.5, 204.6, 251.1, 298.1, 392.1, 912.1
ascertain 570.6, 946.11, 957.10, 970.11
ascertainable 928.25, 940.3
ascertained 928.26, 957.20, 970.20, 973.13
ascertainment 940.1, 970.8
ascetic (n) 584.5, 667.2, 668.4, 699.16 (a) 535.3, 658.7, 667.4, 668.10, 992.10
asceticism 658.3, 667.1, 668.2
ascetism 667.1
Asclepius 90.12
ascribable 639.10, 888.6
ascribe 599.7, 888.3
ascribe importance to 997.13
ascribe to 888.4
ascription 599.1, 888.1
as earnest 438.12
aseity 761.5
asepsis 79.1, 79.3
aseptic 79.27
as expected 130.14
asexual 75.29
asexuality 75.9
as full as a tick 794.11
Asgard 681.10
as good as good can be 999.15
as good as one's word 434.4, 644.19
as good as they come 999.15
as good as they make 'em 999.15
ash 256.2, 893.3, 1020.16
ashamed 113.8, 137.14
ashamed of oneself 137.14
as hard as nails 94.12
ash blond 35.9
ash-blond 37.9
ash cake 10.29
ash can 462.20
ashen 36.7, 39.4, 127.26, 1020.30
ashen-hued 36.7
ashes 307.15, 1020.16
ash-gray 39.4
ashiness 36.2, 39.1
ashlar 1054.2
ash pone 10.29
ashram 617.2, 703.6, 1009.5
ashtanga yoga 84.2
Ashtoreth 890.5, 1073.12
ashy 36.7, 39.4, 1020.30
Asia 231.6, 235.1
Asia Major 231.6
Asia Minor 231.6
Asian 312.3
A-side 708.14
aside 213.2, 542.1, 551.3
asides 490.1
asinine 311.45, 922.15, 923.8, 998.19
asininity 922.3, 923.1
as is 838.2
as it ought to be 637.3, 649.7, 935.20
as it should be 637.3, 649.7, 935.20
ask 421.5, 440.9, 440.13, 630.12, 938.20, 963.9
ask about 938.20
ask after 938.20
askance 204.14
ask and give no quarter 457.17
askant 204.14
ask a question 938.20
ask bids for 734.10
asker 938.16
askew 204.14, 265.10, 810.13, 975.16
askewgee 204.14
ask for 375.21, 421.5, 440.9, 938.30
ask forgiveness 658.5
ask for it 454.3, 493.5, 493.6, 1013.14
ask for mercy 433.8
ask for one's hand 562.22
ask for pity 145.6
ask for political asylum 1009.7
ask for trouble 216.8, 454.3, 493.6, 1013.14
ask in exchange 862.4
asking 440.1, 938.12
asking for it 493.8
asking price 439.1, 630.1, 738.9
ask leave of no man 430.20
ask no favors 430.20
ask no quarter 430.20
ask offers for 734.10
ask questions 938.20
ask the impossible 967.5
aslant 204.15
asleep 22.22, 25.6, 25.8, 307.29, 930.12, 984.8
asleep at the switch 340.10, 984.8
asleep in Jesus 307.29
asleep in the Lord 307.29
asleep on one's feet 22.21
asleep on the job 984.8
as like as can be 784.15
as like as two peas in a pod 784.15
as long as one's arm 267.7
aslope 204.15
Asmodeus 680.4, 680.5
as much as in one lies 403.4
as much as one could wish 991.2
asomatous 1053.7
as one may have suspected 130.14
as one might suppose 130.14
as one might think 130.14
asonia 49.1
aspartame 66.2
Aspasia 665.15
aspect 33.3, 159.3, 530.13, 766.3, 796.2, 1073.20
aspect format 706.7
aspect ratio 706.7
aspen 917.17
aspergation 701.6, 1065.6
asperge 701.16, 771.6, 1065.12
asperged 771.10
aspergil 1065.8
aspergillum 1065.8
asperity 68.1, 110.1, 144.8, 144.9, 152.3, 288.1
asperous 68.6
asperse 512.9
aspersion 156.2, 510.4, 512.4, 661.6, 701.6, 1065.6
asphalt (n) 199.3, 383.6, 1054.2 (v) 295.22
asphalt jungle 80.11, 230.6
asphyxia 308.6
asphyxiate 307.23, 308.19, 428.8
asphyxiating 71.5
asphyxiation 85.9, 307.5, 308.6
aspic 10.13
aspidate 279.19
aspirant (n) 100.12, 124.5, 440.7, 610.9 (a) 124.12
aspirate (n) 524.12 (v) 52.10, 187.12
aspirated 524.30
aspiration 2.21, 52.4, 100.9, 124.1, 187.5, 192.3, 375.1, 380.1, 524.12
aspirational 100.21
aspirator 192.9
aspire 100.20, 193.10
aspire after 100.18
aspirer 100.12, 124.5
aspire to 100.20, 124.6, 380.4
aspirin 86.12
aspiring 100.28, 124.10, 124.12, 272.14
asportation 482.3
asquint 28.11, 204.14

ass 311.15, 361.6
as safe as houses 1007.5
assail 459.14, 510.20, 599.10
assailability 1006.4
assailable 1006.16
assailant 452.1, 459.12
assailer 459.12
assailing (n) 459.1, 510.7 (a) 459.29
assailment 459.1
assail the ear 48.12
assail the nostrils 71.4
Assama 681.7
assassin 127.8, 308.11
assassinate 308.16
assassination 307.5, 308.2
assassinator 308.11
assault (n) 459.1, 510.7, 599.2, 671.3 (v) 459.14, 671.11, 902.12
assault and battery 459.1
assault and robbery 482.3
assaulter 459.12
assaulting 459.29
assault sexually 480.15
assault the ear 48.12
assault transport 180.6
assault troops 461.23
assay (n) 300.1, 403.2, 801.1, 942.2 (v) 300.10, 403.6, 801.6, 942.8
assayed 300.13
assayer 300.9, 942.6
assaying 300.1, 801.1
ass between two bundles of hay 362.5
assemblage 617.1, 712.10, 715.2, 770.1, 770.14, 775.1, 796.1, 797.6
assemblage, the 792.3
assemble 472.11, 715.5, 770.16, 770.18, 796.3, 800.5, 892.8
assembled 770.21, 800.13, 892.18
assembler language 1042.13
assembling 472.2, 770.1
assembly 423.1, 613.1, 700.1, 770.1, 770.2, 770.14, 796.1, 892.2
assembly code 1042.13
assembly hall 197.4, 567.11
assembly language 1042.13
assembly line 739.3, 770.14, 892.3
assembly-line 892.18
assembly-line production 770.14, 892.3
assemblyman 610.3
assembly plant 739.3
assemblywoman 610.3
assent (n) 332.1, 433.1, 441.1, 788.1, 901.1 (v) 332.8, 433.6, 441.2, 788.6, 901.21
assentation 332.1
assentatious 332.13
assentator 332.6
assenter 332.6
assent grudgingly 332.11
assenting 332.13, 433.12, 441.4
assent under protest 332.11
assert 334.5, 421.8, 524.23, 600.10, 951.12, 953.12
assert a claim 421.6, 642.6
assert a right 642.6
assert a right to 421.6
assertation 334.1
assert a title to 421.6
assertative 334.8
asserted 334.9
assertion 334.1, 524.3, 935.7, 952.2, 957.2
assertional 334.8
assertive 334.8
assertiveness 334.2
assert oneself 323.3, 348.6, 970.10
assert the contrary 335.4
assert under oath 334.6
asserverate 524.23
asses' bridge 1013.7
assess 300.10, 630.11, 630.12, 801.8, 946.9
assessable 300.14, 630.15
assess a tax upon 630.12
assessed 300.13, 630.14
assessed valuation 471.7
assessing 946.3
assessment 300.1, 624.5, 630.3, 630.9, 738.8, 801.3, 946.3
assessor 300.9, 630.10
assess pro rata 630.12
asset-backed 438.12
assets 386.2, 471.7, 618.1, 628.1, 728.14
assets and liabilities 471.7
assever 334.5
asseverate 334.5, 953.12, 957.9
asseverated 334.9
asseveration 334.1, 957.2
assibilate 57.2
assibilation 57.1
assiduity 330.6, 339.2, 360.1, 983.1
assiduous 330.22, 339.11, 360.8, 983.15
assiduousness 330.6, 339.2, 360.1, 983.1
assign (n) 479.4 (v) 159.11, 176.10, 477.9, 478.16, 568.17, 615.10, 615.11, 629.3, 809.6, 865.11, 888.3
assignable 176.18, 629.5, 888.6
assignat 728.5
assignation 582.9, 629.1, 770.2, 888.1
assignation house 582.9
assigned 159.18
assigned task 641.1
assigned to 888.6
assignee 479.4, 615.9
assignment 159.6, 417.12, 477.3, 478.2, 568.7, 615.1, 615.2, 629.1, 641.1, 724.2, 865.6, 888.1
assignor 478.11
assign to 477.9, 888.4
assign to a place 159.11
assimilability 7.2
assimilable 7.21, 797.16
assimilate 7.18, 187.13, 207.5, 226.4, 388.3, 521.7, 570.7, 772.3, 781.4, 784.8, 788.7, 805.3, 943.4
assimilated 226.6, 524.30, 805.5, 858.19
assimilate to 858.11, 867.3
assimilating 772.6
assimilation 2.17, 2.20, 7.8, 7.12, 187.6, 226.3, 388.1, 524.12, 570.2, 772.1, 784.1, 788.4, 805.1, 858.1
assimilative 2.31, 7.22, 187.17
ass in lion's skin 357.6
assist (n) 449.2, 745.3, 747.3, 749.3 (v) 384.7, 449.11, 478.19, 592.3
assistance 86.1, 449.1, 478.8
assistant (n) 432.5, 449.7, 571.3, 576.1, 577.3, 616.6 (a) 449.20
assistant professor 571.3
assistantship 571.10
assisted dying 90.1
assisted living 91.21
assisted suicide 307.5
assister 592.1
assisting 384.8, 449.20, 592.4
assize 300.1, 598.5
assizement 300.1
associate (n) 571.3, 588.3, 616.1, 617.11 (v) 450.3, 617.14, 769.7, 775.6, 800.5, 805.4, 899.2 (a) 775.9, 805.6, 899.4
associated 476.9, 617.16, 769.9, 775.9, 800.13, 805.6, 899.4
associate degree 570.3
Associate Justice 596.3
associate oneself 800.5
associate oneself with 404.3, 449.13, 476.5, 509.13, 600.10, 617.14
associate professor 571.3
associates 617.12
associate with 582.17, 587.9, 769.7
association 92.33, 423.1, 450.2, 476.1, 582.5, 582.6, 617.1, 769.2, 775.1, 805.1, 899.1, 931.4
associational 518.10, 617.17
association by contiguity 92.33
association by similarity 92.33
association by sound 92.33
association football 752.1
association neuron 2.14
association of ideas 92.33, 931.4, 986.2
associative 775.7, 805.7, 907.5
associative anamnesis 91.10
associative memory 92.29
associative operation 1017.2
assoil 601.4
assoilment 601.1
assonance 720.9, 784.6, 849.4
assonant 708.49, 720.18, 784.17, 849.15
assonantal 708.49, 720.18, 784.17
assonate 708.35, 720.15, 784.9
as soon as possible 845.9
assort 808.11, 809.6
assorted 780.7, 783.4, 808.14, 809.8
assortment 770.13, 797.6, 808.3
assort with 582.17, 769.7
ass over elbows 205.7
ass over tincups 205.7
assuage 95.8, 120.5, 173.8, 670.6, 959.3
assuagement 120.1, 670.2
assuager 86.10, 670.3
assuaging 120.9, 670.14
assuasive (n) 86.10 (a) 86.40, 120.9, 670.16, 959.7
assuefaction 373.7
assuetude 373.7
Assuma 681.7
assumable 951.15
assume 5.43, 336.5, 354.21, 404.3, 417.14, 479.6, 480.19, 500.12, 519.4, 621.4, 640.6, 640.8, 772.4, 951.10, 953.11
assume a cover 346.8
assume airs 500.12
assume command 417.14
assumed 354.26, 404.7, 500.16, 519.7, 951.14
assumed name 527.8
assumed position 935.7
assume for argument's sake 951.10
assumer 951.8
assume the guise of 33.10, 354.22
assume the identity of 354.22
assume the offensive 459.14
assume the robe of 835.3
assume the toga virilis 303.9
assuming 141.10
assumption 124.1, 141.2, 417.12, 479.1, 480.4, 519.2, 621.2, 640.2, 640.3, 681.11, 772.2, 858.1, 912.1, 935.7, 951.3, 952.2, 953.6
Assumption, the 681.11
assumption of superiority 141.1
assumptive 951.14
assurance 106.3, 121.4, 124.1, 142.1, 334.4, 436.1, 438.1, 492.8, 953.1, 970.1, 970.5, 970.8, 1007.1, 1008.4
assure 121.6, 124.9, 334.6, 436.4, 438.9, 492.15, 953.18, 970.11
as sure as I live and breathe 970.14
assured 106.13, 124.10, 142.9, 436.8, 438.11, 953.21, 970.20, 970.21
assured, the 953.9
assured faith 124.1
assuredness 953.1, 970.1, 970.5
assured of success 409.14
assured probity 644.1
assure oneself 1007.3
assure onself 970.11
assuring 121.13, 953.26
assymetry 851.1
Assyriology 842.4
Astarte 104.7, 890.5, 1016.9, 1073.12
aster 305.5
astereocognosy 990.2
astereognosis 990.2
asterism 1073.5
asteroid 1073.9
asteroidal 1073.25
asteroid belt 1073.9
asteroids 1075.10

asthenia 16.1
asthenic 16.12
asthma 85.9, 85.34
asthmatic 2.32
asthmatic wheeze 2.21
astigmatic 28.11
astigmatical 28.11
astigmatism 27.1, 28.1, 350.2
astigmia 28.1
astir 330.19, 405.23
astonied 25.7
astonish 122.6, 131.7
astonished 122.9, 131.12
astonishing 122.12, 131.11, 247.10
astonishing thing 122.2
astonishment 122.1, 122.2, 131.2
astound 122.6, 127.19
astounded 122.9, 127.26
astounding 122.12, 127.30
astoundment 122.1
Astraea 649.4
astral (n) 689.17, 988.1 (a) 988.7, 1053.7, 1073.25
astral body 689.17, 689.18
astral influences 964.2
astral plane 1053.1
astral spirit 988.1
astray 473.7, 971.24, 975.16
astriction 260.1
A string 711.5
astringence 64.2
astringency 17.5, 64.2, 67.1, 68.1, 144.9, 260.1, 425.1
astringent (n) 260.6 (a) 17.14, 64.6, 68.6, 105.31, 144.24, 260.11, 425.6
astringent bitters 260.6
astrionics 1075.1
astroalchemist 1073.23
astrobotany 1073.19
astrochemical 1060.9
astrochemist 1060.7
astrochemistry 1073.19
astrodiagnosis 1073.20
astrogate 1075.12
astrogation 1075.1
astrogational 1075.13
astrogeologist 1073.22
astrogeology 1073.19
astrognosy 1073.19
astrogony 1073.18
astrographer 1073.22
astrography 1073.19
astro-inertial guidance 159.3
astrolabe 278.4, 1073.17
astrolithology 1073.19
astrologer 962.4, 1073.23
astrologian 1073.23
astrologic 1073.25
astrological 1073.25
astrological influence 886.3
astrologistic 1073.25
astrologous 1073.25
astrology 962.2, 964.2, 1073.20
astromancer 1073.23
astromancy 1073.20
astronaut 178.1, 185.1, 1075.8
astronautical 1075.13
astronautical engineer 1043.2
astronautical engineering 1043.1
astronautics 184.1, 1075.1
astronavigation 159.3, 182.2, 184.6
astronavigator 1075.8
a strong pull 905.2
astronomer 1071.2, 1073.22
astronomic 257.20, 1073.25
astronomical 247.7, 257.20, 884.10, 1073.25
astronomical calendar 832.8
astronomical distance 261.1
astronomical longitude 1073.16
astronomical number 1017.5
astronomical observatory 1073.17
astronomical satellite 1075.6
astronomical telescope 1073.17
astronomical unit 1073.3
astronomy 568.3, 1073.19
astrophotographer 1073.22
astrophotography 1073.19
astrophysical 1018.3, 1073.25
astrophysicist 1018.2, 1073.22
astrophysics 1073.19
astro station 1075.5
astrotourism 1075.1
Astroturf 199.3, 310.7
A student 646.1
astute 415.12, 920.14, 920.16, 944.8
astuteness 415.1, 920.4
asunder 261.8, 802.20
as usual 781.6
asylum 346.4, 926.14, 1009.1, 1009.4
asylum seeker 774.3
asymmetric 265.10, 791.4
asymmetrical 265.10, 791.4
asymmetric transmission 1034.16
asymmetry 265.1, 789.2, 791.1
asymptote 169.1
asymptotic 169.3
asymptotical 169.3
asynchronous 456.15
asynchrony 456.1
asyndeton 530.2
Atacama Trench 275.5
at a disadvantage 791.4
at a discount 661.13
at a distance 261.8
at a loose end 362.9
at a loss 971.25, 1013.24
at a loss for words 51.12
at a low ebb 393.36, 913.12
at an advanced age 303.16
at anchor 173.13, 855.15, 1007.6
at an end 820.9
at an impasse 1013.24
at a nonplus 1013.24
at a premium 632.11, 992.11
ataractic 86.46, 102.7
ataraxia 94.4, 102.2, 106.1, 173.1, 464.3, 933.1
ataraxy 94.4, 102.2, 106.1, 173.1
at a standstill 173.13, 331.17, 855.15, 1013.24
ataunt 180.20
atavism 205.1, 394.1, 842.1, 859.2, 989.1
atavistic 205.7, 767.8, 842.11, 859.7
ataxia 85.9
at bat 745.3
at bay 1013.25
at concert pitch 413.26
at cross-purposes 456.16, 589.12, 779.6, 789.6, 935.19
at daggers 456.16
at daggers drawn 215.5, 456.16, 589.12, 789.6
at death's door 307.32
at each other's throats 589.12
at ease 107.7, 121.12
atelier 197.6, 712.17, 739.1
at enmity 589.12
at fault 510.25, 656.3, 975.16
at feud 456.16
at fevered pitch 101.12
at fever pitch 101.12
at flood 238.25
at gaze staring 122.9
at grips 458.22
at half cock 406.11
athanasia 829.3
Athanasian Creed 676.2
athanasy 829.3
at hand 221.12, 387.20, 840.3
Atharva-Veda 683.8
atheism 688.3, 694.1, 695.5, 955.1
atheist (n) 694.3, 695.11 (a) 695.19
atheistic 688.10, 694.6, 695.19
atheling 608.7
Athena 458.12
athenaeum 558.1
athermancy 1019.18
athermanous 1019.31
atherosclerosis 1046.5
athirst 100.24, 100.26, 1066.7
athlete 743.19
athlete's foot 85.35
athletic 15.16, 743.30
athletic coach 571.6
athletic competition 744.1
athletic field 463.1, 743.11
athleticism 743.8
athletics 743.8, 744.1, 755.1
athletic shoes 5.27
athletic supporter 901.2
athletic team uniform 5.7
at home (n) 582.10, 770.2 (a) 121.12, 228.32
at home in 373.16, 413.27, 928.19
at home with 373.16, 587.17, 928.19
athwart 170.9, 204.19
athymia 25.2, 926.1
atilt 204.15
atingle 74.8, 105.20, 130.11
atiptoe 130.11, 177.39
at issue 971.17, 971.18
at it 330.21
Atlantean 15.17
atlantes 273.5
Atlantic time 832.3
Atlantides 678.9
Atlantis 986.11
at large 369.11, 430.21
Atlas 15.6
Atlas 901.3
atlas 273.5, 554.9
atlatl 462.9
at leisure 331.18
at liberty 331.18, 430.21
at loggerheads 215.5, 451.8, 456.16, 589.12, 779.6, 789.6
at loose ends 331.18, 362.9
Atman 677.3
atman 306.2
atman 689.18, 919.4
atmosphere 209.3, 317.2, 712.8, 722.4, 1067.2
atmosphere of Soul, the 681.5
atmospheric 317.12, 1067.9
atmospheric attenuation 1036.12
atmospheric component 317.2
atmospheric gas 317.2
atmospheric layer 317.2
atmospheric physics 317.5
atmospheric pollution 1001.4, 1072.2
atmospherics 1034.21
atmospheric science 1071.1
atmospheric sciences 184.1
atmospheric tides 184.32
atmospheric visibility 31.2
at odds 325.5, 451.8, 456.16, 589.12, 780.7, 789.6, 935.19
at odds with 333.6
A to izzard 792.3
atoll 235.2, 240.5
atom 248.2, 258.8, 872.3, 1038.4, 1052.2, 1060.2
atom blast 1038.16
atom bomb 462.20
atom-bomb 459.23
atom bomb atomic bomb 1038.16
atom cannon 1038.11
atom-chipping 1038.8
atomerg 17.7
atomic 258.14, 872.7, 1038.18
atomic accelerator 1038.11
Atomic Age 824.6
atomic arsenal 462.2
atomic attack 459.1
atomic beam 1025.5
atomic bomb 462.20
atomic clock 1025.5
atomic cluster 1038.7
atomic cocktail 91.8
atomic constant 1038.4
atomic decay 1038.8
atomic disintegration 1038.8
atomic energy 1038.15
Atomic Energy Commission 1038.15
atomic energy plant 739.3
atomic engine 1038.14
atomic explosion 1038.16
atomic furnace 1038.13
atomic heat 1019.1
atomic mass 1038.4, 1060.5
atomic meltdown 671.6
atomic model 1038.4
atomic nucleus 1038.6
atomic number 1038.4, 1060.5
atomic particle 1038.6
atomic particles 1052.2
atomic pile 1038.13

atomic power 18.4
atomic power plant 1032.19, 1038.14, 1075.4
atomic project 1038.15
atomic radiation 1037.1
atomic ray 1025.5
atomic reaction 1038.8
atomic research 1038.15
atomics 1038.1
atomic science 1038.1
atomic scientist 1038.3
atomic time 1025.5
atomic unit 1038.4
atomic volume 1060.5
atomic war 458.1
atomic warhead 462.20, 1074.3
atomic waste 391.4
atomic weapons 462.1
atomic weight 297.5, 297.8, 1038.4, 1060.5
atomiferous 1038.18
atomism 1038.2, 1052.6
atomist 1052.7
atomistic 952.11, 1038.18, 1052.12
atomistics 1038.1
atomization 766.5, 780.4, 806.1, 1038.8, 1051.4, 1067.5
atomize 395.17, 766.6, 780.6, 801.6, 802.9, 802.13, 806.3, 806.4, 1038.17, 1051.9, 1067.8
atomizer 70.6, 1065.8, 1067.6
atomology 1038.1
atoms 763.2
atom smasher 1038.11
atom smashing 806.2
atom-smashing 1038.8
atom-tagger 1037.7
atom-tagging 1037.8
atomy 258.5, 258.8
atonal 61.4
atonalism 61.1
atonality 61.1
at one 332.15, 455.3, 788.9
atone 338.4, 481.5, 624.11, 658.4, 708.35, 708.36
atone for 658.4
atonement 338.1, 465.2, 481.2, 624.3, 658.1, 677.14, 696.6
at one's beck and call 326.4, 387.20, 432.14, 449.21
at one's best 413.26
at one's call 326.4, 387.20
at one's command 326.4, 449.21, 469.8
at one's disposal (v) 469.4 (a) 326.4, 387.20, 469.8
at one's doorstep 641.17
at one's ease 107.7, 121.12
at one's elbow 387.20
at one's feet 432.14
at one's fingertips 387.20
at one's mercy 432.14
at one's nod 326.4
at one's pleasure (v) 469.4 (a) 326.4, 432.14
at one's service 143.16, 387.23, 449.21
at one's whim 326.4
at one's wit's end 971.25, 1013.24
at one with 332.15, 899.4
atonic 524.30
atoning 113.9, 658.7
atony 16.1
at opposite poles 779.7, 789.6
at outs 589.12
A to Z 792.3
A-to-Z 794.10
at par 790.7
at parity 778.8, 790.7
at peace 464.9
atrabiliar 112.23
atrabilious 112.23
atramentous 38.8
at rest 121.12, 173.12, 307.29
atria 2.16
at risk 897.5, 1006.13
atrocious 26.10, 98.19, 144.26, 156.8, 638.3, 654.16, 661.12, 671.21, 1000.9
atrociousness 98.3, 144.11, 661.3, 1000.2
atrocious pain 26.6
atrocity 98.3, 144.12, 156.2, 389.2, 638.2, 650.4, 654.3, 655.2, 671.1, 1000.3
atrocity story 458.11
atrophied 393.35
atrophy (n) 85.9, 85.27, 260.3, 270.6, 393.4 (v) 393.19
atropine 86.12
Atropos 964.3
at sea 971.24, 985.13
at sixes and sevens 589.12
at square 456.16
at stake 438.12
at strife 456.16
at swords points 589.12
at swords' points 456.16
attach 253.4, 480.20, 800.7, 888.3
attach a condition 959.4
attach a proviso 959.4
attaché 413.11, 576.6
attache case 195.1
attached 253.9
attached to 104.29
attach importance to 997.13
attach little importance to 950.2, 998.12
attachment 104.1, 253.1, 254.1, 480.5, 549.5, 644.7, 800.3, 888.1
attach oneself to 138.11
attach to 888.4
attach too much importance to 997.14
attach weight to 953.10
attack (n) 85.6, 381.1, 384.1, 458.1, 459.1, 510.7, 524.5, 599.2, 671.3, 749.5, 917.6, 926.7 (v) 384.5, 404.3, 457.14, 458.14, 459.14, 510.20, 599.10, 671.11, 725.15
attackable 1006.16
attack dog 460.7, 1008.11
attacker 459.12
attack in force 459.14
attacking 459.29
attacking zone 749.1
attack like lightning 459.14
attack of nerves 128.1
attain 186.6, 407.4
attainability 167.2, 966.2
attainable 167.5, 472.14, 966.7, 966.8
attainable, the 966.1
attain closure 359.8
attainder 602.2
attained 407.10
attain fulfillment 973.12
attain majority 303.9
attain mastery of 570.9
attainment 186.1, 407.1, 413.8, 472.1
attainments 928.4
attain one's objective 409.8
attaint (n) 661.6 (v) 602.3, 661.9, 1004.6
attaintment 602.2
attain to 186.6, 615.13
attainture 602.2
attar 70.2, 70.4
attar of roses 70.2
attemper 670.6
attempt (n) 403.2, 404.1 (v) 403.6, 404.3, 640.6
attempted 404.7
attempt the impossible 391.8, 967.5
attempt to 403.8
attend 48.10, 221.8, 449.18, 577.13, 769.7, 769.8, 835.3, 887.4, 918.5, 983.6
attendance 221.4, 577.12, 769.6
attendant (n) 90.11, 166.2, 563.4, 577.5, 616.6, 769.3, 769.4, 1008.6 (a) 221.12, 577.14, 766.8, 769.9, 835.4
attendant godling 678.12
attendant spirit 678.12
attend classes 570.11
attend closely to 931.10
attend Communion 701.14
attendee 918.2
attender 221.5, 704.27, 918.2
attending 577.14, 766.8, 769.9
attending physician 90.4
attend Mass 701.14
attend on 577.13
attend school 570.11
attend to 48.10, 434.2, 604.10, 983.5, 1008.19
attend to business 724.10, 983.8
attend to one's work 724.10
attend to orders 326.2
attention 48.1, 48.2, 339.1, 339.5, 504.6, 981.1, 983.1
attentional blink 982.1, 984.1
attention deficit disorder 984.1
attention deficit hyperactivity disorder 984.1
attention-getter 377.3
attention-getting 208.13
attention-grabber 377.3
attention-grabbing 208.13
attentions 155.3
attention span 983.1
attention to detail 339.3, 973.5, 983.4
attention to fact 973.5
attentive 48.14, 143.16, 155.8, 339.10, 339.12, 339.14, 504.13, 931.21, 981.5, 983.15
attentiveness 143.3, 339.5, 983.1
attenuate (v) 16.10, 16.11, 252.8, 260.9, 270.12, 299.3, 764.4, 771.5 (a) 270.16, 294.8, 299.4
attenuated 16.19, 252.10, 260.13, 270.15, 270.16, 270.20, 294.8, 299.4
attenuation 16.5, 252.1, 260.3, 270.4, 270.6, 299.2, 764.1, 771.1
attenuative 771.11
attest (n) 957.2 (v) 334.6, 438.9, 957.8, 957.9, 957.11
attestable 957.19
attestant 957.6
attestation 334.3, 549.6, 957.2, 957.4
attestative 957.16
attestator 957.6
attested 334.8, 334.9, 957.20, 970.20, 973.13
attested copy 478.10
attester 957.6
attestive 957.16
at the bottom of 641.17, 886.13
at the bottom of the ladder 432.14
at the breast 301.12
at the bursting point 993.20
at the end of one's rope 307.32, 619.7, 992.13, 1013.26
at the end of one's tether 992.13, 1013.26
at the feet of 696.16
at the head 612.17
at the height 247.13
at the last extremity 1006.13
at the last gasp 307.32
at the limit 247.13
at the mercy of 897.6
at the peak 247.13
at the Pearly Gates 307.29
at the point of death 307.32
at the portals of death 307.32
at the summit 247.13
at the zenith 247.13
Attic 489.15, 496.7, 499.6, 533.6
attic 197.16, 386.6
attic fan 318.18
Atticism 489.1, 533.1, 537.2
Atticist 533.4
Attic quality 533.1
attic room 197.16
Attic salt 489.1
Attic simplicity 499.1
Attic wit 489.1
Attila 144.14
attire (n) 5.1 (v) 5.39
attired 5.45
attitude 159.3, 952.2, 953.6, 978.1
attitude-control rocket 1075.2
attitudinal 953.21, 978.7
attitudinarian 500.8
attitudinarianism 500.3
attitudinize 500.13
attitudinizer 500.8
attitudinizing 354.3, 500.3
attorney 574.4, 576.1, 597.1
attorney-at-law 597.1
attorney general 597.1
attorneyship 597.4

attract 104.22, 377.6, 907.4, 983.12
attractant 907.2
attract attention 501.12, 983.11
attracted 983.16
attracted to 167.4
attracting 907.5
attraction 100.13, 377.1, 377.3, 905.1, 907.1
attractive 97.7, 100.30, 377.8, 907.5, 983.20, 1016.17
attractiveness 97.2, 100.13, 104.6, 377.2, 907.1, 1016.1
attractivity 907.1
attract notice 983.11
attract one's interest 377.6
attractor 907.2
attrahent (n) 907.2 (a) 907.5
attributable 639.10, 888.6
attribute (n) 530.2, 647.1, 865.4 (v) 865.11, 888.3
attributed 888.6
attribute to 888.4
attribution 865.6, 888.1
attributive (n) 530.2, 530.3 (a) 530.17
attributive adjective 530.3
attributive noun 530.5
attrition 16.5, 113.1, 252.3, 255.2, 388.1, 393.5, 1044.2, 1051.4
attrition rate 252.3
attritive 1044.10
attune (n) 708.3 (v) 405.8, 708.35, 708.36, 788.7
attuned 455.3, 708.49
attunement 708.3, 788.4
atua 678.5
at variance 456.16, 589.11, 589.12, 780.7, 789.6
at variance with 333.6
at variance with the facts 967.7
at war 456.16, 589.12, 789.6
atwitter 105.20
at work 330.21, 889.11
atypic 868.5, 870.10
atypical 868.5, 870.10
atypicality 870.1
atypicalness 870.1
aubade 708.14
aubergine (n) 10.35 (a) 46.3
auburn 40.4, 41.10
auburn-haired 40.5
au contraire 131.10
au courant 928.18
auction (n) 734.4 (v) 734.11
auction agent 730.8
auctionary 730.12
auction block 734.4
auction bridge 758.3
auctioneer (n) 730.8 (v) 734.11
auction off 734.11
auction room 736.5
auction sale 734.4
auctorial 547.25, 718.8
audacious 142.9, 454.7, 492.21, 493.9
audaciousness 492.4, 493.3
audacity 142.1, 454.1, 492.4, 493.3
audial 48.13
audibility 48.1
audible 24.14, 48.13, 50.16
audience 48.2, 48.6, 221.5, 479.3, 541.2, 541.5, 606.2, 704.27, 918.2, 1034.22
audience chamber 197.20
audience-participation show 1034.18
audience success 704.4
audient 48.5
audile 48.13
audio 48.13
audio amplifier 50.10
audioanimatron 706.1
audio-animatronic 706.9
audiocassette player 50.11
audiocassette recorder 50.11
audio channel 1035.4
audio distortion 50.13
audioemission 1035.4
audio frequency 50.2, 1034.12
audio-frequency (n) 1034.15 (a) 1034.28
audio-frequency circuit 1034.9
audiologist 90.11
audiology 48.9
audiometer 48.9
audiometry 48.9
audio monitor 1035.13
audiophile 50.11
audio signal 1035.4
audio sound system 50.11
audiotape 50.12
audio/video transmitter 1035.8
audio-visual 48.13
audit (n) 628.6 (v) 570.11, 628.9, 970.12, 1017.21
auditing 628.6
audition 48.1, 48.2, 541.2, 938.2, 942.3
auditioner 48.5
auditive 48.13
auditor 48.5, 479.3, 572.1, 574.2, 628.7, 729.12
auditorial 48.13
auditorium 197.4, 463.1, 567.11, 704.14, 704.15
auditory (n) 48.6 (a) 48.13
auditory apparatus 2.10, 48.7
auditory canal 2.10
auditory effect 50.1
auditory impairment 49.1
auditory meatus 2.10
auditory nerve 2.10
auditory ossicles 2.10
auditory phenomenon 50.1
auditory range 48.4
auditory sensation 48.1
auditory sense 48.1
auditory stimulus 50.1
auditory tube 2.10
Audubon Society 397.5
au fait 373.16, 413.24, 928.18
Augean stables 80.11
Augean task 1013.2
auger (n) 285.3 (v) 292.15
aught 244.3, 762.2, 864.5
augment 119.2, 251.4, 253.5, 259.4
augmentation 119.1, 251.1, 253.1, 254.1, 259.1
augmentative 259.9
augmented 119.4, 251.7
augmented fourth 709.20
augmented interval 709.20
augur (n) 962.4 (v) 133.11
augural 133.15, 962.11
augured 133.14
auguring 962.11
augur well 124.9
augury 133.3, 962.2
august 136.12, 155.12, 247.9
Augustan 533.6
Augustinian 952.12
augustness 136.2
auld lang syne 837.2
au naturel 11.6
aunt 77.7, 559.3
Aunt Flow 12.9
auntie 75.15, 559.3
aunt mary 87.11
au pair (n) 227.2 (a) 790.7
au pair girl 577.8
aura 209.3, 662.6, 689.7, 1025.14
aural 2.28, 48.13
aural cavity 292.5
aural examination 48.1
aural sense 48.1
aureate 43.4, 1058.17
aureateness 43.1
aurelia 302.12
aureole 171.2, 280.2, 1025.14
auric 43.4
auricle 2.10, 310.29
auricomous 43.5
auricular 48.13, 345.14
auriculate 48.15
auriform 48.15
aurify 43.3
auriscope 48.9
auriscopy 48.9
aurochs 311.6
Aurora 314.1
aurora 314.2, 314.3, 1025.16
aurora australis 1025.16
aurora borealis 1025.16
aurora glory 1025.16
auroral 314.5
aurora particle 1037.4
aurora particle counter 1075.7
aurora particles 1075.10
aurora polaris 1025.16
Auschwitz 308.12
auscultate 48.10
auscultation 48.1
auscultator 48.9
auspicate 133.9
auspice 133.3
auspices 449.4, 573.2, 1008.2
auspicious 124.12, 133.17, 843.9, 999.12, 1010.14
auspiciousness 124.1, 133.8, 843.1, 999.1
Auster 318.2
austere 144.24, 425.6, 484.7, 499.9, 535.3, 633.7, 635.6, 667.4, 798.6, 992.10
austerity 144.9, 425.1, 484.3, 499.4, 535.1, 635.1, 667.1, 992.2
austerity program 609.6, 635.1
austral 161.14
Australasia 231.6
Australia 231.6, 235.1
Australian aborigine 312.3
Australian ballot 609.19
Australian crawl 182.11, 760.8
Australian English 523.7
Australoid race 312.2
Austronesian 523.12
autacoid 13.2
autarch 575.13
autarchic 430.22, 612.16
autarchy 430.5, 612.4, 612.8
autarkic 430.22
autarky 430.5, 609.4, 731.7
auteur 704.23, 706.4
authentic 337.5, 644.14, 687.7, 761.15, 957.16, 970.18, 973.15
authenticatable 957.19
authenticate 332.12, 957.11
authenticated 332.14, 957.20, 973.13
authentication 332.4, 334.3, 957.4
authentic cadence 709.23
authenticity 337.1, 644.4, 687.1, 761.2, 970.4, 973.7
authentic mode 709.10
authentificate 337.4
authentification 337.1
author (n) 547.15, 556.3, 718.4, 722.5, 726.1, 886.4, 892.7 (v) 547.21, 718.6, 886.10
authorcraft 547.2, 718.2
authoress 547.15, 718.4
authorial 547.25, 718.8
authoring 1042.18
authoring software 1042.11
authoring tool 1042.11
authoritarian 417.15, 417.16, 425.6, 612.16, 980.10
authoritarianism 417.3, 425.1, 612.8, 980.1
authoritative 18.12, 413.22, 417.15, 417.16, 419.4, 420.13, 687.7, 866.5, 894.13, 953.23, 953.26, 970.18, 973.14
authoritative in 928.19
authoritativeness 417.2, 417.3, 687.1, 970.4, 973.6
authorities 249.5
authorities, the 575.14, 612.3
authority 18.1, 249.3, 413.11, 417.1, 417.2, 417.4, 417.5, 420.1, 443.3, 496.6, 549.6, 551.5, 573.1, 615.1, 642.1, 673.2, 866.3, 894.1, 921.1, 928.11, 973.6
authority figure 413.11
authority on money and banking 729.9
authorization 332.4, 417.12, 443.3, 549.6, 615.1, 673.2
authorize 18.10, 332.12, 420.9, 443.11, 576.15, 615.10, 673.9
authorized 417.15, 443.17, 615.19, 673.11
authorized absence 222.4
Authorized Version 683.2
author's canon 547.12, 718.1
author's copy 547.10
authorship 547.2, 718.2, 892.1
author's proof 548.5
autism 92.23, 94.1, 583.1, 651.1, 976.1, 982.1, 986.7

autistic 94.9, 583.5, 651.5, 976.9, 982.3, 986.24
autistic distortion 986.7
autistic thinking 92.23, 986.7
auto 179.9
autobiographer 719.3
autobiographic 719.6
autobiographical 719.6
autobiographist 719.3
autobiography 719.1
autobus 179.13
autocar 179.9
autochthon 227.3, 842.7
autochthonous 226.5, 818.15, 842.11
autochthonousness 226.1
autocide 308.5
autoclave 79.24
autoclaved 79.27
autocomplete 407.6
auto-completion 1042.18
auto-configure 1042.18
autocorrect 392.12
auto court 228.16
autocracy 612.4, 612.8
autocrat 575.13
autocratic 417.15, 417.16, 612.16
autocraticalness 417.3
autocross 756.1
auto-da-fé 308.1, 1020.5
autodial 1042.18
autodidact 572.1
autodidactic 568.18, 570.16, 572.12, 928.24
autoelectronic 1033.15
autoerotic 75.30, 140.8
autoeroticism 75.8, 75.10, 140.1
autoerotism 140.1
autogiro 181.5
autograph (n) 337.3, 527.10, 547.3, 547.10 (v) 332.12 (a) 547.22
autographic 547.22
autography 547.3
autohypnosis 22.7
autohypnotic 690.14
autointoxication 85.31
autolithograph (n) 713.5 (v) 713.9
autolithographer 716.8
autolithographic 713.12
autolithography 713.3
autolocation 1033.1
autoluminescence 1037.2
autoluminescent 1025.38, 1037.11
automanual 1041.22
automanual system 1041.5
automat 8.17, 736.4
automate 1041.20
automated 1041.22
automated factory 739.3, 1041.5
automated satellite 1075.6
automated teller machine 622.3, 728.14, 729.14
automatic (n) 462.10, 1041.12 (a) 365.11, 373.14, 781.5, 934.6, 963.14, 1041.22
automatic agreement 332.2
automatic analyzer 1041.15
automatic control 1041.1, 1041.3, 1074.9
automatic control engineering 1041.2
automatic control system 1041.5
automatic control system engineer 1041.19
automatic detector 1041.15
automatic device 1041.12
automatic electronic navigation 184.6, 1041.7
automatic electronics 1041.2
automatic engineering 1041.2
automatic exchange 347.7
automatic factory 1041.5
automatic guidance 1041.7
automatic indicator 1041.15
automaticity 1041.1
automatic laundry 79.11
automatic machine 1041.13
automatic pilot 574.7, 1041.18
automatic pinsetter 750.1
automatic reaction 903.1
automatic response 365.1
automatic sprinkler 1022.3
automatic technician 1041.19
automatic technology 1041.2
automatic telephone system 1041.5
automatic tracking 1036.8
automatic transmission 1040.9
automatic writing 547.2, 689.6, 963.5
automation 1033.1, 1041.1
automation technology 1041.2
automatism 373.3, 689.6, 963.5, 1041.1
automatist (n) 689.13 (a) 689.24
automatization 1041.1
automatize 1041.20
automaton 349.6, 1040.4, 1041.12, 1041.18
automatous 1041.22
auto mechanic 1040.12
automechanical 1041.23
automobile (n) 179.9 (a) 1041.23
Automobile Age 824.6
automobile race 457.12
automobile racing 457.11, 744.1, 756.1
automobile theft 482.2
automobiling 177.6
automobilist 178.10
automotive (n) 1043.3 (a) 179.23, 1041.23
automotive design 717.5
automotive engineer 1043.2
automotive engineering 1043.1
autonetics 1041.2
autonomic 963.14
autonomic nervous system 2.14
autonomic reaction 903.1
autonomous 324.7, 430.22, 612.16, 802.20
autonomous agent 1042.11
autonomousness 324.2
autonomy 324.2, 430.5, 612.4
autophilia 104.1
autophyte 310.4
autopilot 1041.18
autoplagiarism 482.8
autopsy (n) 307.17 (v) 938.24
auto racing 756.1
autorotation 184.15
auto show 736.2
autosome 305.8
autosuggestion 22.8
autosyn 1041.13
autotheism 675.5
autotheist 675.16
autotrophic organism 305.2
autotype (n) 714.4 (v) 548.15
autoworker 726.2
autumn (n) 313.4 (a) 313.9
autumnal 313.9
autumnal equinox 313.4, 313.7, 1073.16
auxiliaries 449.8, 461.25
auxiliary (n) 530.4, 616.6, 768.2 (a) 253.10, 449.20, 768.4
auxiliary fleet 461.27
auxiliary language 523.11
auxiliary memory 1042.7
auxiliary verb 530.4
avail (n) 387.3, 387.4, 999.4 (v) 387.17, 449.11, 991.4, 999.10
availability 221.1, 387.3, 966.3
available 221.12, 222.15, 331.18, 387.20, 405.16, 472.14, 966.8
available funds 386.2, 728.14, 728.18
available gain 1032.17
available means 386.2, 728.14
available resources 386.2, 728.14
avail nothing 19.7
avail oneself of 387.14, 387.15, 843.8
avails 627.1
avalanche (n) 194.4, 991.2, 993.2, 1023.8 (v) 194.9
avalanchine 15.19, 18.12, 412.18
Avalon 681.9, 986.11
avant-courier 816.1
avant-garde (n) 216.2, 816.1, 841.2 (a) 337.5, 404.8, 816.4, 841.13
avant-garde film 706.1
avant-garde jazz 708.9
avant-garde theater 704.1
avant-gardist 816.1
avarice 100.8, 484.3, 651.1, 654.3
avaricious 100.27, 484.9, 651.5
avariciousness 100.8
avatar 33.1, 348.1
Ave 696.4
Ave Maria 696.4
avenge 507.4
avengement 507.1
avenger 507.3
avenging 507.7
avenging spirit 680.10
avenue 190.9, 383.3
aver 334.5, 524.23, 957.9
average (n) 246.1, 864.3 (v) 246.2, 819.3 (a) 246.3, 819.4, 864.12, 869.9, 1005.8
average Joe 606.5
average man 606.5, 864.3
averageness 246.1, 864.2, 869.2, 1005.2
average out 246.2
average passing yardage 746.4
average punting yardage 746.4
average punt-return yardage 746.4
average running yardage 746.4
averages 745.4, 746.4
averaging 246.1
averment 334.1, 524.3, 957.2
Avernus 682.3
averred 334.9
Averroist 952.12
Averroistic 952.12
averse 99.8, 325.5, 451.8
averseness 325.1
averse to 103.7
aversion 99.2, 103.1, 103.3, 325.1
aversive 103.8
avert 164.6, 460.10, 1012.14
avertive 164.9, 1012.19
avert one's eyes 30.8
avert the eyes 27.19
Aves 311.27
Avesta 683.7
Avestan 683.14
avgolemono 10.10
avian 311.48
aviary 228.23
aviate 184.36
aviatic 184.49
aviation (n) 184.1 (a) 184.49
aviational 184.49
aviation badge 647.5
aviation cadet 185.3
aviation field 184.22
aviation meteorology 317.5
aviation radar 1036.2
aviation wings 647.5
aviator 185.1
aviatorial 184.49
aviatress 185.2
aviatrix 185.2
avichi 682.1
avicular 311.48
avid 100.27, 101.8
avidity 100.8, 101.1
avidness 100.8, 101.1
avifauna 311.27
avigate 184.36
avigation 184.6
avigator 185.4
avionic 184.49
avionics 1033.1
avitaminosis 85.33
avocado 44.4
avocation 724.7
avocational 724.17
avoid 157.7, 164.6, 368.6, 668.7, 903.7
avoidable 368.14
avoidance 340.3, 368.1, 467.1, 668.2, 903.3
avoidance mechanism 92.23
avoidance reaction 460.1
avoid excess 668.6
avoid extremes 246.2
avoiding reaction 368.1
avoid like the plague 157.7, 368.6
avoid one's gaze 27.19

avoid Scylla and Charybdis 467.6
avoid Scylla and fall into Charybdis 119.3
avoid the issue 936.9
avoid the limelight 139.7
avoid work 331.12
avoirdupois 297.1
avoirdupois weight 297.8
avouch (n) 436.1 (v) 334.5, 436.4, 953.12, 957.9
avouched 334.9
avouchment 334.1, 436.1, 957.2
avow (n) 334.4 (v) 332.11, 334.5, 351.7, 376.3, 953.12, 957.9
avowal 332.3, 334.1, 351.3, 957.2
avowed 332.14, 334.9, 376.5, 436.7
avowed Communist 611.13
avulse 192.10
avulsion 192.1
avuncular 559.6
await 130.8, 839.6, 840.2, 846.12
awaited 130.13
awaiting 130.11
awake (v) 23.4, 23.5, 105.12, 306.9 (a) 23.8, 339.14, 920.13
awake a doubt 955.6
awaken 23.4, 23.5, 105.12, 306.9, 375.19, 977.2
awakening 23.2, 977.1
awaken suspicion 955.6
awaken the memory 989.19
awaken the mind 983.11
awaken the thoughts 983.11
awaken to 551.14
awake the dead 53.7
awake the echoes 53.7
awake to 928.16
awake to life immortal 307.20
award (n) 478.1, 478.4, 646.2, 946.5 (v) 478.12
award damages 603.5
awarder 478.11
awarding 478.1
award winner 413.15
aware 24.11, 27.21, 928.15, 983.15
awareness 24.1, 928.2, 983.1
awareness ribbon 5.31
aware of 928.16
awash 182.60, 238.25, 1065.17
away (v) 168.2 (a) 34.4, 222.11, 261.8
away from home 222.12
away from the point 776.7
awayness 222.1
away off 787.5
awe (n) 122.1, 127.1, 155.1 (v) 122.6, 127.17, 127.18, 155.7
A-weapons 462.1
awed 122.9, 127.26, 155.9
aweigh 182.61
awe-inspiring 122.11, 127.30, 155.12, 501.21, 997.20
aweless 123.3, 142.11, 156.7, 492.19
awelessness 123.1
awesome 122.10, 122.11, 127.30, 155.12, 247.7, 247.11, 501.21, 662.18, 685.7
awesomeness 122.3, 685.1
awestricken 122.9, 127.26, 155.9
awestruck 122.9, 127.26, 155.9
awful 98.19, 122.11, 127.30, 155.12, 247.11, 501.21, 685.7, 1000.9, 1015.11
awfulize 112.15
awfulizer 112.14
awfulness 98.3, 127.2, 685.1, 1000.2, 1015.2
awful silence 51.1
awing 122.11, 127.28
awkward 98.21, 257.19, 414.20, 534.3, 930.11, 996.7, 1013.19
awkward age 301.7
awkwardness 98.6, 257.9, 414.3, 844.1, 996.1, 996.3, 1013.9
awkward squad 414.8, 461.18
awl 1040.7
awn 3.9, 285.5
awned 3.25
awning 295.6, 1028.1
awny 3.25
awry 204.14, 265.10, 810.13, 975.16
ax (n) 605.5, 1040.2, 1040.7 (v) 802.11
ax, the 604.6, 909.5
axe 462.5
axel jump 760.7
axial 161.14, 172.8, 208.11
axial motion 172.2, 915.1
axial skeleton 2.2
axillary bud 310.23
axiological 636.6
axiology 636.1
axiom, an 973.2
axiom 761.3, 767.2, 935.7, 951.3, 952.2, 953.2, 974.2
axiomatic 348.8, 761.15, 970.15
axiomatical 974.6
axiomatic truth, an 973.2
axis 208.2, 277.2, 310.21, 617.1, 906.3, 915.5
axle 915.5
axle bar 915.5
axle box 915.6
axle shaft 915.5
axle spindle 915.5
axle-tree 915.5
axon 2.14
ax to grind, an 947.1, 980.1
ayah 1008.8
ayatollah 699.12
aye 332.2, 371.6, 441.1, 935.14
Ayurveda 90.13
Azazel 680.4, 680.5
azidothymidine 86.32
azimuth 159.3, 161.1, 161.2, 201.4, 300.5
azimuthal 161.12
azimuthal equidistant projection 159.5
azimuthal projection 159.5
azimuth circle 200.2, 278.4
azimuth compass 278.4
azoic 1055.5
Azrael 307.2, 679.4
Aztec archaeology 842.4
Aztec two-step 12.2
azure (n) 45.1, 647.2, 1073.2 (v) 45.2 (a) 45.3
azurean 45.3
azure-blue 45.3
azure-colored 45.3
azured 45.3
azureness 45.1
azureous 45.3
azure-tinted 45.3
azurine 45.3
azygous 872.9
Baal 697.3, 890.5
baal kore 699.11
Bab, the 684.4
Baba Yaga 680.5, 680.6
Babbitt 497.6, 867.2
Babbittish 497.14
Babbittry 497.1
babblative 540.10
babble (n) 520.2, 522.7, 540.3 (v) 52.11, 351.6, 520.5, 522.10, 525.9, 540.5, 926.20
babblement 520.2, 540.3
babbler 540.4
babbling (n) 351.2 (a) 52.19, 540.10, 922.22, 926.31
babe 77.6, 302.7, 302.9, 358.1, 416.3, 562.6, 657.4, 1016.8
babe in arms 302.9, 657.4
babe in the woods 358.1, 416.3, 657.4
Babel 61.2, 522.7, 810.2, 810.4, 810.5
babelicious 1016.20
babe magnet 104.12
babies 759.8
babirusa 311.9
babish 922.24
baboon 1015.4
baby (n) 16.6, 104.10, 104.14, 258.6, 302.1, 302.7, 302.9, 416.3, 491.5, 562.6, 657.4, 757.2, 818.2 (a) 258.12, 301.12
baby back ribs 10.17
baby bird 311.27
baby blues 27.9
baby boom 78.1, 251.2
baby boomers 302.2
baby boomlet 78.1
baby buggy 179.6
baby bunting 302.9
baby carriage 179.6
baby clothes 5.30
baby-doll 104.14, 562.6
babyface 1016.8
babyhood 301.5, 302.2, 818.4
babyish 301.12, 922.24
babyishness 922.11
babykins 302.9
baby kisser 610.9
baby linen 5.30
Babylon 654.7
Babylonian 501.21
Babylonian sibyl 962.6
Babylonian splendor 501.5
baby-minder 1008.8
baby-minding 1008.2
babymoon 20.3
babyproof (v) 15.14 (a) 1049.4
baby's bottom 1047.4
babysit 1008.19
babysitter 1008.8
babysitting 1008.2
baby-sized 258.12
baby-snatcher 483.10
baby split 750.2
baby step 818.3
baby talk 343.3
baby tooth 2.8
baccalaureate 648.6
baccalaureate service 580.4
bacchanal 88.5, 88.11
bacchanalia 8.9, 88.5
bacchanalian 88.5, 88.11
bacchanalianism 88.2
bacchic 926.30
bacchius 720.8
Bacchus 88.2
bach (n) 565.3 (v) 565.5
bachelor 565.3, 608.5, 648.6
bachelordom 565.1
bachelorette 565.4
bachelorette party 487.1
bachelor girl 77.5, 565.4
bachelorhood 430.5, 565.1
bachelorism 565.1
bachelorlike 565.7
bachelorly 565.7
bachelor party 487.1
bachelor's degree 648.6
bachelorship 565.1
bach it 565.5
bacillus 85.42, 258.7
bacitracin 86.29
back (n) 206.2, 209.2, 217.1, 217.3, 524.18, 548.6, 554.12, 746.2, 752.2, 901.2 (v) 163.7, 172.5, 182.34, 193.12, 217.8, 438.9, 449.13, 509.11, 592.3, 609.41, 729.16, 759.25, 901.21, 957.11, 1046.9 (a) 163.12, 172.8, 217.9, 233.9, 524.30, 623.10, 837.12, 846.16
backache 26.5, 85.9
backachy 26.12
back alley 383.3
back and fill 182.30, 344.7, 362.8, 854.5, 916.13
back-and-forth (n) 916.5 (a) 916.19
back answer 508.2, 939.1
back away 163.6, 163.7
backbite 512.11
backbiter 512.6
backbiting (n) 512.3 (a) 512.13
backboard 747.1
backbone 217.3, 359.3, 492.3, 901.2
backbreaker 1013.2
backbreaking 725.18, 1013.18
backbreaking work 725.5
back-breed 1070.6
back burner 217.1, 329.1, 331.1, 390.2, 846.3
back-burner 329.2, 331.12
backburner (n) 846.4 (a) 998.17
back-burnered 331.18
back button 1042.18
back catalog 708.1
back channel 345.1, 552.10
backchannel 551.2
backchat (n) 142.4, 489.7, 490.2, 541.1, 541.3, 541.4, 939.1 (v) 490.5
backchecking 749.3
back cloth 704.20

back copy 555.1
back-country 233.9
backcountry 158.4, 231.1, 233.2
backcourt 747.1, 748.1
backcourt man 747.2
back crawl 760.8
backdate 832.13
backdated 832.15
back debts 623.2
back door 217.1, 346.5, 369.3, 383.4
backdoor 345.12
back down 163.6, 362.7, 363.8, 433.7
backdrop 209.2, 704.20
backed 509.19, 1046.13
back-end fund 737.16
back end of a bus 1015.4
backer 478.11, 588.1, 592.1, 616.9, 704.26, 729.10
back-fence gossip 552.7
backfield 746.2
backfill 266.3
backfire (n) 56.3, 671.7, 900.1, 903.2, 1019.13 (v) 671.14, 903.6
backflash 1074.8
backflow 163.3, 238.12
back-flowing 172.8
backflowing 172.2
back formation 526.4
back forty 158.4, 231.4
back four 752.2
background (n) 209.2, 261.3, 413.9, 463.1, 498.7, 708.28, 722.4, 886.1, 886.5 (a) 766.7
background detail 498.7
backhand 156.8, 204.13
backhanded 156.8, 204.13, 914.7
backhanded compliment 156.2
backhand shot 749.3
back-heel pass 752.3
backhouse 12.10
backing (n) 163.3, 172.2, 384.2, 386.2, 441.1, 449.4, 509.1, 554.14, 714.10, 729.2, 859.1, 901.1, 901.2, 901.10, 957.4 (a) 509.17, 592.4
backing down 163.2, 433.2
backing off 163.2, 433.2
backing out 163.2
backing store 1042.7
backing up 163.3, 957.4
backing wind 318.10
back issue 555.1
back kick 760.8
backlash (n) 506.1, 887.2, 900.1, 903.2 (v) 903.6
backlashing 903.2
backlight 1025.3
backlist 558.4
backlog (n) 386.1, 386.3, 1021.3 (v) 386.11
backlogged 386.14
back lot 706.4
back marker 751.1
back matter 254.2, 554.12, 793.2, 817.1
back nine 751.1, 820.3
back number 554.5, 842.8
back-number 117.9, 842.16
back o' beyond 158.4
back of beyond 233.9, 261.9, 584.8
back of beyond, the 261.4
back off 163.6, 163.7, 362.7, 368.6, 430.17, 756.4
back of the house 11.4
back order 971.1
back-ordered 967.9, 969.3
back out 163.6, 363.8, 370.5, 491.8
back out of 163.6
backpack (n) 195.2 (v) 177.30
backpacker 178.6
backpacking 177.8
back pass 752.3
back-patter 138.4
back pay 624.4
back payments 623.2
backpedal 163.7, 168.3, 175.9
backpedalling 163.1, 362.2
back road 383.4
backroad 233.9
back room 381.1
backrub 1044.3
back-scratch 138.9
back scratcher 511.4
backscratcher 138.4
back scratching (n) 138.2, 609.29, 863.2 (a) 138.14
back-scratching 450.1
back seat 217.1, 250.1, 432.2
backseat driver 178.10, 214.4, 422.3
backset (n) 163.1, 394.1, 1011.3 (v) 1069.17
backside 217.1, 217.5
backside forward 205.7
backslapper 138.4, 511.4
backslapping 138.14, 587.19
backslide (n) 394.2 (v) 163.5, 205.5, 394.4, 654.9, 859.4
backslider 363.5, 394.3, 660.4, 694.3, 859.3
backsliding (n) 163.1, 363.2, 394.2, 654.1, 694.1, 859.1 (a) 394.5, 654.12, 694.6
backspin 751.3
backstab 645.13
backstabbing 17.5, 115.4
backstage 704.16
backstairs (n) 193.3, 346.5, 383.4 (a) 345.12
backstairs influence 894.3
backstop 745.2, 1008.3, 1012.5
backstory 413.9, 722.4, 886.1
back stream 238.12
back street 383.4
backstroke 182.11, 760.8
backswept 217.12
backswing 750.2, 751.3
back talk 142.4, 454.2, 939.1
back the batter off 745.5
back the wrong horse 975.11
back-to-back 166.5, 781.6, 812.8, 812.9
back to basics 767.3
back-to-basics (n) 499.3 (a) 252.10, 499.8
back-to-front 205.7
back-to-nature 499.8, 798.6
backtrack (n) 163.3 (v) 163.6, 163.7
back trail 163.3
backtrail 163.7
back turn 709.18
back up 163.7, 172.5, 217.8, 449.13, 576.14, 609.41, 901.21, 957.11
backup (n) 163.3, 386.3, 450.1, 576.1, 750.2, 817.4, 862.2, 901.1, 1042.18 (a) 862.8
backup man 817.4
backup personnel 862.2
backup plan 903.3
backup vocalist 710.13
backup woman 817.4
backward 139.11, 163.12, 172.8, 175.12, 217.9, 325.6, 344.10, 406.12, 837.12, 846.16, 846.17, 853.8, 922.22
backwardation 624.1
backward deviation 394.1
backward-looking 853.8
backward masking 551.4
backward motion 163.1, 172.2
backwardness 139.3, 325.1, 344.3, 611.1, 846.5, 853.3, 922.9
backwards 205.7, 342.3
backward step 163.1
backwash 182.7, 184.30, 238.12, 887.2
backwater (n) 238.12, 241.1 (v) 163.7, 175.9, 182.34, 363.8
back way 346.5, 383.4
backwood 233.9
backwoods (n) 211.5, 233.2 (a) 233.9
backwoodsiness 233.3
backwoodsman 227.10
backwoodsy 233.9
backyard 217.2, 231.1
Baconian method 935.3
bacteria 85.42, 258.7
bacterial 258.15
bactericidal 86.43
bactericide 86.21
bactericidin 86.27
bacteriological warfare 458.1
bacteriological weapon 462.1
bacteriophage 85.42
bacteriostat 86.29
bacteriostatic 86.41
bacterium 85.42
baculine 604.22
bad (n) 593.1, 654.3, 1000.3 (a) 64.7, 71.5, 82.5, 85.56, 85.60, 133.16, 249.12, 307.32, 322.5, 393.30, 393.40, 654.16, 996.5, 999.13, 1000.7, 1006.9
bad, the 660.11
bad actor 757.2
bad air 1001.4
badass 1000.8
bad behavior 321.2
bad blood 93.7, 144.4, 451.2, 456.1, 589.4
bad boy 322.3
bad break 1011.5
bad breath 71.1
bad call 457.1
bad cards 759.10
bad case 936.3
bad character 661.1
bad check 625.3, 728.10
bad chemistry 93.7
bad condition 765.3
bad copy 787.1
baddable 75.25
bad debt 625.1
bad debts 623.1
bad deed 144.13
bad dream 986.9
baddy 593.1, 660.1
bad ear 48.3
bad egg 654.4, 660.1
bad example 660.1
bad eyesight 28.1
bad fairy 680.7
bad faith 354.4, 435.2, 645.5
bad feeling 93.7
bad for 82.5
bad form 581.1
bad fortune 1011.5
badge 517.1, 517.11, 647.1, 647.5, 865.4
badge engineering 892.3
badge of honor 646.6
badge of infamy 661.6
badge of office 647.1, 647.3
badger 96.13, 480.22
badgered 96.24
badgerer 96.10
badger game 480.8
bad grammar 531.1
bad guy 593.1, 704.10, 707.2
bad habit 373.3, 654.2
bad hair day 1013.7
bad hand 547.6, 759.10
bad humor 110.1
badinage 490.1
bad influence 894.6, 1000.4
bad job 340.3, 414.5
bad juju 93.7
badlands 891.2
bad language 513.3
bad light 1027.2
bad likeness 350.2, 787.1
bad lot 660.4, 660.5
bad luck 1011.5
badly off 619.7, 1011.14
badly timed 996.5
bad-mannered 505.5
bad manners 505.1
badminton 748.1
badminton court 743.11
bad money 728.10
bad-mouth 156.6, 389.4, 512.9, 950.2, 998.12
bad-mouthing 512.1
bad move 975.4
bad name 661.1
badness 82.1, 322.1, 654.4, 1000.1
bad news (n) 132.1, 660.1, 1011.2 (a) 395.26
bad news, the 96.2
bad notices 510.4
bad odor 71.1, 661.1
bad off 1006.13
bad part, the 1011.1, 1013.3
bad patch 1011.5
bad peri 680.7
bad person 593.1, 660.1
bad poet 720.13
bad poetry 720.3

bad point 865.4
bad policy 414.6
bad press 510.4
bad rap 650.4
bad relation 775.1
bad rep 661.1
bad report 661.1
bad reputation 661.1
bad repute 661.1
bad seed 87.17
bad smell 71.1
bad-smelling 71.5
bad spell 1011.6
bad spelling 546.4
bad spirit 680.6
bad taste 64.1, 497.1, 534.1
bad taste in the mouth 64.1
bad temper 110.1, 144.4, 152.6
bad-tempered 110.18
bad time 844.2
bad times 1011.6
bad timing 844.2
bad trip 87.1, 87.2
bad turn 144.13
bad'un 660.4
bad vibes 93.7
bad will 144.4
bad woman 665.14
bad word 513.4, 526.6
bad writing 547.6
Baedeker 574.10
baffle (n) 51.4, 971.3 (v) 51.9, 132.2, 522.10, 971.13, 1012.15
baffled 132.5, 971.25, 1013.24
baffle description 122.8
bafflegab 609.37
bafflement 132.1, 412.2, 971.3, 1012.3
baffler 51.4
baffling 971.27, 1012.20
baffling problem 522.8
bag (n) 2.13, 86.23, 87.20, 195.2, 202.2, 247.3, 283.6, 371.5, 480.10, 724.1, 729.15, 745.1, 765.4, 770.8, 866.1, 1015.4 (v) 159.15, 202.6, 212.9, 283.11, 472.9, 480.17, 482.16, 770.20
bag and baggage 471.3
bag ass 222.10
bagatelle 248.5, 998.5
bag egg 660.2
bagel 10.31
baggage 195.1, 471.3, 665.14
baggage car 179.15
baggage carousel 184.22
baggage check 728.12
baggage claim 186.5
baggage man 178.13
baggage pickup 184.22
baggagesmasher 178.13
baggage train 179.14
bagged 21.8
bagginess 257.6, 804.2
bagging 202.10, 283.15, 804.5
baggy 5.47, 202.10, 263.4, 283.15, 804.5
bag job 482.4
bag lady 619.4
bagman 730.4, 732.6, 759.20
bagnio 79.10, 665.9
bag of bones 2.2, 270.8
bag of tricks 356.6, 384.2, 413.1
bag people 606.4, 619.3
bag person 160.4, 178.3, 331.10, 619.4, 828.4
bagpipe (n) 711.9 (v) 708.42
bagpipes 711.9
bags 247.4, 283.7
baguette 195.2
baguio 318.13
bag woman 619.4
bagwoman 732.6
Bahir 683.5
bail (n) 431.2, 438.2, 598.3 (v) 176.17
bailiff 574.4, 1008.15
bailiwick 231.2, 231.5, 463.1, 594.4, 724.4, 894.4
bail one out 398.3
bail out 184.47, 190.11, 369.6, 438.10, 449.11
bailout 398.1, 449.1, 478.8
bailsman 438.6
Baily's beads 1025.6, 1073.13
bairagi 699.13
baird 720.12
bait (n) 356.13, 375.7, 377.3 (v) 96.13, 377.5, 980.8
bait-and-switch 356.10
baited 96.24
baited hook 377.3
baited trap 356.12, 377.3
bait the hook 356.20, 377.5, 382.10
bake 11.5, 742.6, 1019.22, 1020.17, 1066.6
baked 11.7, 742.7, 1066.9
baked goods 735.7
baked potato 10.35
bakehead 178.13, 183.6
bakehouse 11.4
Bake-Off 457.3
baker 11.3
baker's dozen 254.4, 478.5, 882.7
bakery 11.4, 66.1
baking (n) 11.2 (a) 1019.25
baklava 10.41
balance (n) 106.3, 246.1, 255.8, 256.1, 264.1, 338.2, 386.2, 533.2, 628.2, 649.1, 670.1, 712.8, 728.14, 777.1, 790.1, 855.1, 920.6, 925.1, 943.3, 993.5 (v) 264.3, 297.10, 338.5, 362.7, 628.8, 781.4, 790.5, 790.6, 855.7, 943.4, 1017.21
balance accounts 628.8
balance beam 760.5
balanced 106.13, 264.4, 533.8, 649.7, 670.12, 781.5, 790.9, 855.12, 900.9, 920.18, 925.4
balanced diet 7.13
balanced off 264.4
balanced personality 855.1
balance income with outgo 635.4
balance in hand 728.18
balance off 264.3
balance of nature, the 1072.1
balance of payments 731.10
balance of power 417.6, 609.5
balance of trade 731.1
balance out 790.6
balance sheet 628.4
balance the accounts 790.6
balance the books 628.8, 790.6, 1017.21
balance up 781.4
balancing (n) 264.2, 297.9, 338.1, 900.2, 943.1 (a) 338.6, 779.6, 900.9
balancing act 264.2, 670.1
balbutient 525.13
balcony 197.22, 704.15, 901.13
bald 6.17, 292.17, 348.10, 499.8, 535.3
baldachin 703.10
bald as a coot 6.17
bald as an egg 6.17
balderdash 520.2, 545.2
bald fact 761.3
baldhead 6.4
baldheaded 6.17
baldheadedness 6.4
baldness 6.4, 499.3, 535.1
baldpate 6.4
bald-pated 6.17
bald-patedness 6.4
baldy 6.4
bale (n) 96.6, 297.7, 770.8 (v) 770.20
baleen 1048.3
balefire 517.15, 1019.13
baleful 133.16, 144.20, 1000.12
balefulness 96.6, 133.6, 1000.5
balk (n) 132.1, 412.2, 745.3, 975.4, 1012.3 (v) 132.2, 361.7, 1012.15
balk at 325.3
balked 132.5
balker 311.12
balkiness 361.1
balking (n) 1012.3 (a) 325.6, 361.8
balky 325.6, 361.8
balky horse 311.12
ball (n) 282.2, 462.19, 580.4, 705.2, 743.2, 743.16, 745.1, 746.1, 746.2, 747.1, 748.1, 749.4, 750.1, 750.3, 752.1, 770.2, 904.5 (v) 75.21, 282.7, 582.21
ballad (n) 708.7, 708.14 (v) 708.38
ballade 708.14
balladeer 710.14, 710.20
balladist 710.20
ballad maker 710.20, 720.12
balladmonger 710.20, 720.13
ballad opera 708.34
balladry 708.11
ballad singer 710.14
ballad writer 710.20
ball and chain 428.4, 563.8, 1012.6
ball-and-socket joint 800.4
ballast (n) 297.4, 297.7, 338.2, 901.2, 1026.1 (v) 182.49, 297.12, 855.7
ballasting 297.4
ballata 708.14
ball bearing 915.7, 1040.5
ball boy 745.3, 748.2
ballbreaker 77.6
ballbuster 1013.2
ball carrier 746.3
ball cartridge 462.17
ball club 745.2
ball cock 239.10
ball control 746.3, 747.3, 752.3
ball dress 5.11
balled up 393.29, 799.4, 810.16
ballerina 705.3
ballet (n) 708.34 (a) 704.33
ballet d'action 708.34
ballet dancer 705.3
ballet divertissement 708.34
balletic 704.33, 705.6
ballet skiing 753.1
ballet skirt 5.9
ball field 745.1
ball game 744.1, 745.3, 766.2
ball game, the 767.3
ball girl 745.3, 748.2
ball handling 746.3, 747.3
balling 75.7
ball in play 746.3
ballista 462.9
ballistic 105.25, 152.32, 904.15
ballistic capsule 1075.2
ballistic missile 462.18, 1074.3
ballistics 462.3
ball lightning 1025.17
ball-likeness 282.1
ballocks 2.13
ball of fire 17.6, 330.8
ballon 181.11
ballonet 181.11
ballonet ceiling 184.32
balloon (n) 181.11, 195.2, 282.2, 320.1 (v) 14.2, 184.36, 251.6, 259.5, 282.7, 283.11
ballooner 185.7
balloonery 184.1
balloon foot 756.2
balloon in 184.43
ballooning (n) 184.1, 251.1 (a) 202.10, 283.15
ballooning in 184.18
balloonist 185.7
balloon mortgage 438.4
balloon payment 481.2
balloon room 87.20
ballot (n) 371.6, 609.19 (v) 371.18
ballot box 371.6, 609.20
ballot-box stuffer 609.23
ballot-box stuffing 356.8, 609.18
balloter 371.7, 609.23
balloting 371.6
balloting place 609.20
ball out of play 746.3
ballpark (n) 257.1, 745.1 (a) 772.6
ball-park figure 971.8
ballpark figure 300.1
ball player 745.2
ballproof 15.20
ballroom 197.4, 705.4, 743.13
ballroom music 708.8
balls 17.3, 492.3, 520.3
balls and strikes 745.3
ballsiness 492.1
balls-out 794.10
balls up 393.11
balls-up 410.6, 810.2, 975.6, 985.3
ballsy 492.18

ball the jack 174.9
ball up 393.11, 799.3, 811.3
ball-up 414.5, 810.2
ball whistled dead 746.3
ballyhoo (n) 352.4, 355.1, 734.5 (v) 352.15, 355.3
ballyhooed 355.4
ballyhooer 352.9, 730.7
ballyhoo man 352.9, 704.23, 730.7
balm 25.3, 70.2, 86.1, 86.4, 86.11, 147.1, 670.3, 1056.3
balminess 70.1, 926.2
balmy 70.9, 86.40, 97.11, 120.9, 926.27, 1010.13, 1019.24
balmy sleep 22.4
balneae 79.10
balneal 79.28, 182.58
balneation 79.7, 182.11
balneum 79.10
baloney 354.14, 520.3
balsa 180.11, 1050.2
balsam 70.2, 86.1, 86.4, 86.11, 1056.3
balsamic 86.40, 120.9
balsamic vinaigrette 10.12
balsamic vinegar 10.12
balsa raft 180.11
Balthasar 921.5
Baltic 523.12
baluster 273.4, 901.8
balustrade 212.4, 273.4, 901.8
balustrading 212.4, 273.4
Bambi 572.9
bambino 302.9
bamboo 310.5, 1054.4
bamboo curtain 211.5, 345.3, 1012.5
bamboozlability 923.2, 954.2
bamboozlable 923.12, 954.9
bamboozle 356.14, 645.13, 971.14
bamboozled 971.25
bamboozlement 356.1
bamboozler 357.1
ban (n) 444.1, 510.1, 513.1, 586.3, 773.1 (v) 255.10, 444.3, 510.10, 586.6, 773.4, 909.17
banal 117.9, 246.3, 974.6
banality 117.3, 974.3
banalize 117.5
banalness 117.3
banana (n) 489.12 (a) 43.4
banana belt 231.6
banana republic 232.1
bananas 926.27
banana split 10.47
banausic 387.18, 472.16, 724.15, 995.6
band (n) 47.5, 271.4, 280.3, 296.1, 498.6, 517.6, 617.1, 710.12, 748.1, 770.3, 1034.13 (v) 47.7, 209.7, 450.3, 800.5, 800.9
bandage (n) 86.33, 271.4, 293.5, 295.18 (v) 30.7, 91.24, 212.9, 800.9
bandage compress 86.33
bandaged 212.12
bandages 754.1
bandage up 800.9
bandaging 86.33, 295.18
Band-Aid (n) 86.33, 376.1, 803.4 (a) 995.7
Band-Aid, a 992.1
bandanna 5.25
B and B 228.15
band concert 708.33
bandeau 5.24, 647.2, 901.2
banded 47.15
banded together 800.13
banderillero 461.4
banderole 647.7
bandha 283.3
bandied about 552.15
bandit 181.9, 483.4
banditry 482.3, 482.6
band leader 710.17
band major 710.17
bandman 710.3
bandmaster 710.17
bandmate 710.3
bandog 311.16, 1008.11
bandonion 711.11
band shell 704.16
bandshell 197.4
bandsman 710.3
bandstand 704.16
band theory of solids 1033.2
band together 450.3, 769.7, 805.4
bandwagon, the 578.5
bandwidth 1042.18
bandy (n) 749.4 (v) 863.4 (a) 265.12, 279.10
bandy about 352.10, 863.4
bandying 352.1
bandy-legged 265.12
bandy with 457.17
bandy words 541.8, 935.16
bane 85.5, 96.5, 103.3, 307.1, 308.1, 395.2, 395.8, 589.6, 606.3, 1000.3, 1001.1, 1011.1
baneful 82.5, 98.19, 98.22, 133.16, 144.20, 308.23, 395.26, 1000.12, 1011.15
banefulness 98.3, 133.6, 308.9, 1000.5
bang (n) 3.6, 17.3, 18.1, 53.3, 56.1, 56.3, 87.20, 105.3, 459.8, 671.7, 893.2, 902.4, 902.5 (v) 53.7, 56.6, 56.8, 293.6, 902.13, 902.15, 902.16
banger 10.21, 179.10
bang for the buck 472.4, 627.1, 630.2
bang heads 424.8
bang heads together 424.8, 425.4
banging (n) 87.2 (a) 56.11, 257.21
bang into 902.13
bangle 498.6
bang on 973.16
bang one's head against a brick wall 19.7, 391.8
bangs 3.6, 1016.14
bangtail 311.14, 757.2
bang-up 999.13
banian 668.4
banish 586.6, 909.17
banishment 586.3, 909.4
banister 273.4, 901.8
banjax 395.11, 412.9
banjaxed 412.15
banjo eyes 2.9, 27.9
banjo hit 745.3
banjo hitter 745.2
banjoist 710.5
banjo-picker 710.5
bank (n) 204.4, 211.4, 218.1, 234.2, 237.2, 276.2, 386.6, 397.7, 620.4, 729.13, 729.14, 739.1, 759.5, 770.10, 812.2, 901.4, 1012.5, 1058.6 (v) 184.40, 204.10, 386.10, 460.9, 770.19, 1020.22
bankability 387.3
bankable 387.18, 387.22, 472.16, 624.21
bank acceptance 728.11
bank account 622.2, 728.14, 729.3, 729.14
bank accountant 628.7
bank a game 759.23
bank balance 622.2
bankbook 628.4
bank card 622.3
bank check 728.11
bank clerk 729.11
bank craps 759.8
bank credit 622.1
bank discount 631.1
banked turn 756.3
banker 620.3, 729.11, 730.1, 759.15
banker's check 728.11
banker's hours 268.1
bank examiner 628.7
bank guard 1008.9
bank holiday 20.4, 850.4
banking 184.13, 729.5
banking executive 729.11
banking house 729.14
banking industry 729.5
bank machine 729.14
bank manager 729.11
bank note 728.5
Bank of England 729.14
bank officer 729.11
Bank of France 729.14
bank on 124.6, 380.6, 953.16
bank president 729.11
bank rate 623.3, 631.1
bank robber 483.5
bank robbery 482.3
bankroll (n) 384.2, 728.17 (v) 478.19, 729.16
bankrupt (n) 410.7, 619.4, 625.4 (v) 619.6, 625.8 (a) 395.28, 625.11
bankrupt 625.11 619.9
bankruptcy 393.1, 410.1, 625.3
bankrupt in 992.13
bank statement 627.2
bank the fire 670.6
bank up 770.19
bank upon 380.6
bank vault 346.4
banlieue 230.1
banned 444.7, 773.7
banned substance 86.5
banner (n) 352.7, 458.11, 517.1, 646.3, 647.7, 937.2 (a) 249.14
banner ad 352.6
banneret 608.5, 647.7
bannerette 647.7
banner head 937.2
banner headline 937.2
banns 436.3, 563.3
banns of matrimony 436.3
banquet (n) 8.6, 8.9, 743.4 (v) 8.24, 743.25
banquet of the soul 95.3
banquet revelment 95.3
banshee 678.8, 988.1
Bantam 311.28
bantam (n) 258.4 (a) 258.12
bantam hockey 749.1
bantamweight (n) 297.3 (a) 298.13
banter (n) 489.5, 490.1, 508.1, 541.2 (v) 490.5
banterer 490.4
bantering (n) 490.2 (a) 490.7, 508.12
banty (n) 258.4, 311.28, 749.4 (a) 258.12
banya 668.4
banyan day 668.2
banzai 458.7
banzai attack 459.1
banzai charge 459.1
baptism 187.2, 367.2, 527.2, 701.6, 1065.6
baptismal 187.18, 701.18
baptismal dress 701.6
baptismal font 703.10
baptismal gown 701.6
baptismal name 527.4
baptismal regeneration 701.6
baptismal robe 701.6
baptism for the dead 701.6
baptism in the spirit 692.3
baptism of fire 187.2
baptistery 701.6, 703.9
baptistry 701.6
baptize 16.11, 79.19, 367.7, 527.11, 701.16
baptized 527.14
baptizement 701.6
bar (n) 47.5, 88.20, 235.2, 267.3, 273.1, 276.2, 293.3, 311.22, 428.5, 517.6, 595.6, 597.4, 647.2, 647.5, 708.29, 709.12, 728.20, 773.1, 901.15, 906.4, 1012.5 (v) 47.7, 170.6, 212.7, 255.10, 293.6, 293.7, 444.3, 773.4, 967.6, 1012.12, 1012.14
bar association 597.1
barb (n) 3.10, 3.17, 288.3, 462.6 (v) 285.7
barbarian (n) 497.7, 593.5, 774.3 (a) 497.12, 774.5
barbaric 144.26, 497.12, 534.2, 671.21, 774.5
barbaric spendor 501.5
barbarism 497.3, 526.6, 531.2, 534.1, 930.3
barbarity 144.11, 144.12, 497.3, 671.1
barbarize 671.11
barbarous 144.26, 497.12, 531.4, 534.2, 671.21, 774.5, 930.13
barbarousness 144.11, 497.3, 534.1
barbate 3.25
bar beat 709.26

barbecue (n) 8.6, 10.13, 11.4 (v) 11.5
barbecued 11.7
barbecue sauce 10.12
barbecuing 11.2
barbed 285.9
barbed wire 285.4
barbel 3.10, 73.4, 288.3
barbell 84.1, 725.7
barbellate 288.9
barber (n) 1016.12, 1016.13 (v) 3.22
barbering 1016.14
barber pole 47.5, 47.6
barbershop 1016.13
barbershop quartet 708.18
barbican 272.6
barbicel 3.17
Barbie doll 867.2
barbigerous 3.24, 3.25
barbital 86.12
barbitone 86.12
barbiturate addiction 87.1
barbiturates 87.5
barbituric acid 86.12
barbouillage 547.7
barbs 87.5
barb the dart 96.14
barbule 3.10, 3.17, 73.4
bar car 197.10
barcarole 708.14
bar chart 381.3
bar code 47.6, 517.5
barcode 517.20
bar cookie 10.43
bard 710.14, 720.12
bardic 720.16
bardo 390.2, 429.7, 682.1
bare (v) 6.5, 292.12, 351.4 (a) 6.14, 222.14, 248.8, 292.17, 348.10, 393.31, 499.8, 535.3, 798.6, 798.7, 1006.15
bare-ankled 6.16
bare-armed 6.16
bare-ass 6.14
bare as the back of one's hand 6.14
bare-backed 6.16
bareback rider 707.3
bareboat charter 615.6
bareboned 270.17
bare bones 199.2
barebones (n) 270.8 (a) 248.8, 767.9, 798.6
bare-bottomed 6.14
bare-breasted 6.14, 6.16
bare-chested 6.16
bare cupboard 515.2, 619.2
bared 6.12
barefaced 6.16, 142.11
barefaced lie 354.12
bare fact 761.3
bare flesh 295.3
barefoot 6.15, 667.4
barefooted 6.15
barefooted Carmelite 667.2
bare-handed 6.16, 992.12, 1006.14
bareheaded 6.16
bare-kneed 6.16
barelegged 6.16
barely audible 52.16
barely have a chance 972.13
barely heard 52.16
barely pass 246.2
barely see 28.8
barely sufficient 991.6
barely tick over 175.9
barely touching 73.12
bare minimum 991.1
bare necessities 963.2
bare-necked 6.16
bareness 6.3, 222.2, 499.3, 535.1
bare of 992.13
bare one's breast 1006.7
bare one's fangs 454.3
bare pole 180.13
bare possibility 966.1, 969.1, 972.9
bare skin 295.3
bare subsistence 515.2, 619.2
bare sufficiency 991.1
bare suggestion 951.5
bare-throated 6.16
barf (n) 909.8 (v) 99.4, 909.27
barf bag 195.2
barfing 909.8
barfly 88.11
barfy 64.7, 80.23, 85.57, 1000.8
bargain (n) 437.1, 468.1, 633.3, 731.5 (v) 437.5, 437.6, 466.6, 541.10, 727.9, 731.18 (a) 633.7
bargain and sale 629.1
bargain-basement 633.8
bargain collectively 727.9
bargained for 437.11
bargainer 727.4
bargain for 380.6, 437.5, 731.19
bargain hunter 733.5
bargaining 541.5, 731.3
bargaining chip 731.3
bargaining session 541.5
bargain on 380.6
bargain-priced 633.8
bargain prices 633.2
bargain rate 633.2
barge 176.13, 177.28
bargee 183.5
barge in 189.7, 214.5
bargeman 183.5
bargemaster 183.5
barger 183.5
barghest 680.6
bar graph 381.3
bar-hop 8.29
barhopping 8.3, 87.1
baric 317.13
baring 6.1, 351.1
baring one's breast 351.3
barista 577.7
baritone (n) 708.22, 709.5 (v) 54.9 (a) 54.11, 708.50
bark (n) 56.3, 59.1, 60.1, 180.1, 295.3, 295.16 (v) 6.8, 56.8, 59.6, 60.2, 352.15, 393.13, 524.25, 1044.7
bark at 510.19
barkeep 88.19, 577.7
barkeeper 88.19, 577.7
barker 352.9, 704.23, 730.7
barking (n) 60.1 (a) 60.6
bark up the wrong tree 342.2, 975.11
barley 10.4
barleycorn 258.7
bar line 708.29
bar magnet 907.3
barmaid 88.19, 577.7
barman 88.19, 577.7
Barmecidal 976.9
Barmecidal feast 515.2
Barmecide 976.9
Barmecide feast 515.2
bar mitzvah 701.6, 701.9
barmy 298.17, 320.7, 926.27
barn 228.20
barnacle 138.5, 803.4
barnacle-back 183.3
barnacles 29.3
barnburner 409.4, 999.7
barn dance 705.2
barn-door fowl 311.28
barney 456.6
bar none 122.10
barnstorm 184.37, 704.29
barnstormer 185.1, 707.2
barnstorming 184.1, 704.11
Barnum effect 996.1
Barnumesque 105.32
Barnumism 545.1
Barnumize 545.6
barnyard 1069.8
barnyard fowl 311.28
barograph 317.8
barographic 317.13
barometer 300.2, 317.8, 942.4
barometric 317.13
barometrical 317.13
barometric wind rose 318.15
barometrograph 317.8
barometry 317.5
baron 608.4, 618.7, 730.1, 997.8
baronage 608.1
baroness 608.6
baronet 608.4, 608.5
baronetage 608.1
baronetcy 608.9
Baron Münchausen 357.9
Baron of the Exchequer 596.3
barons 249.5
barony 608.9
baroque (n) 198.6, 498.2 (a) 498.12, 870.13, 986.20
baroqueness 498.2
bar out 773.4
barrack (n) 228.29 (v) 508.9
barracking 508.2
barracks (n) 228.29 (v) 428.9
barrage (n) 55.1, 459.9, 1012.5 (v) 459.22
barranca 237.7
barratrous 645.20
barratry 645.5
barred 47.15, 170.11, 212.10, 293.9, 444.7, 773.7, 967.7
barred spiral 1073.6
barred spiral galaxy 1073.6
barrel (n) 3.17, 247.3, 282.4, 618.3 (v) 174.9, 212.9
barrel along 401.6
barrel-chested 15.16
barrel house 88.20
barrel of laughs 488.1
barrel organ 711.14
barrel roll 184.14
barrel-shaped 282.11
barren (n) 891.2 (a) 19.15, 117.6, 222.14, 391.12, 891.4, 987.5
barren land 891.2
barrenness 117.1, 222.2, 891.1, 987.1
barrens 891.2
barricade 293.6, 293.7, 460.9, 1012.12
barricades 460.6
barrier 211.3, 212.4, 213.5, 293.3, 428.5, 460.4, 757.1, 1012.5
barrier of secrecy 345.3
barring 773.1
barrio 230.6
barrio-dwellers 619.3
barrister 597.1
barrister-at-law 597.1
barristerial 597.6
barroom 88.20
barrow 179.3, 237.4, 309.16, 311.9, 549.12
bar sinister 561.5, 647.2, 661.6, 674.2
bartender 88.19, 577.7
barter (n) 629.1, 731.2, 863.2 (v) 629.3, 731.15, 731.18
bartering 731.2
bar the gate 1009.7
barton 1069.8
barythymia 926.5
barytone 524.30
basal 199.8, 767.9, 886.14
basal body 305.5
basal metabolic 2.31
basal metabolism 2.20, 7.12
basalt 1059.1
bas bleu 929.5
base (n) 159.2, 188.5, 199.2, 208.6, 228.2, 274.4, 745.1, 886.1, 901.6, 901.8, 1016.11, 1017.3, 1060.3 (v) 159.16 (a) 98.18, 138.13, 199.8, 250.7, 491.12, 497.15, 606.8, 645.17, 654.16, 661.12, 1000.9, 1005.9
baseball 745.1
baseball cap 5.25
baseball equipment or gear 745.1
baseball field 743.11
baseball player 745.2
baseball season 313.1
baseball team 745.2
baseball uniform 5.7
baseboard 199.2
baseboard-heated 1020.29
baseborn 606.8, 674.7
baseburner 745.3
base camp 760.6
base canard 354.10
basecoat 199.1
base coin 728.10
based 766.8
based on 901.24, 957.16, 959.9
base hit 745.3
base hospital 91.21
base jump 181.13
base-jump 184.47
baseless 764.8, 936.13
baseline 188.5, 745.1, 747.1, 748.1
baseline umpire 748.2

basement 12.10, 197.17, 199.2, 386.6, 901.6
basement membrane 2.6
base metal 1058.3
base-minded 497.15, 654.15
baseness 98.2, 138.1, 250.3, 491.3, 497.1, 497.5, 645.2, 654.4, 661.3, 1000.2, 1005.3
base of operations 208.6
base on 199.6
base on balls 745.3
base path 745.1
base pay 624.4
base runner 745.2, 745.3
base signal voltage 1033.7
bash (n) 403.3, 582.11, 582.12, 902.5 (v) 393.13, 510.13, 902.15, 980.8, 1000.6
bashara 699.13
basher 510.9, 512.6
bashert 104.11
bashful 127.23, 139.12, 325.7, 344.10, 583.5
bashfulness 127.3, 139.4, 325.2, 344.3, 583.1
bashing 389.3, 510.3
bash on 856.3
bash up 902.17
basic 199.8, 767.9, 798.6, 886.14, 997.23, 1060.9
basic facts 761.4
basichromatin 305.7
basic idea 932.4
basic material 1054.1
basic military training 568.3
basics 385.2, 568.5, 818.6
basic trainer 181.10
basic training 405.1, 460.1, 568.3
basic truth, the 973.3
basidium 305.13
basilar 199.8
basilar membrane 2.10
basilect 523.6
basilica 703.1
basin 79.12, 195.1, 199.4, 236.1, 237.7, 284.2, 1009.6
basin and ewer 79.12
basin and pitcher 79.12
basin and range 237.6
Basin Street 708.9
basis 188.5, 375.1, 600.6, 886.1, 901.6, 935.7, 937.1, 978.2
basis for belief 957.1
bask 1020.19
basket (n) 2.13, 195.1, 747.1, 747.3 (v) 212.9
basketball 747.1
basketball court 743.11, 747.1
basketball game 747.3
basketball player 747.2
basketball season 313.1
basketball team 747.2
basket case 924.3, 924.8
basket catch 745.3
basket hanging 747.3
basketry 170.3, 712.16
basketwork 170.3
bask in 95.13
bask in the sun 1020.19
bask in the sunshine 1010.10
bas mitzvah 701.6, 701.9
bas-relief 283.2, 715.3
bass (n) 708.22, 709.5 (v) 54.9 (a) 54.11, 708.50
bassackwards 163.12
Bassalia 275.4
Bassalian 275.15
Bassalian realm 275.4
bass-baritone 54.9
bass clef 709.13
bassist 710.5
bassness 54.1
basso (n) 709.5 (v) 54.9
basso buffo 709.5
basso cantante 709.5
basso continuo 708.22
bassoonist 710.4
basso ostinato 708.22
basso profundo (n) 709.5 (v) 54.9
basso-rilievo 283.2, 715.3
bass passage 708.24
bass player 710.5
bassus 708.22
bass violinist 710.5
bast 305.6
bastard (n) 76.5, 561.5 (a) 354.26, 674.7
bastard child 561.5
bastardism 674.2
bastardize 797.12
bastardizing 797.3
bastard title 554.12
bastard type 548.6
bastardy 561.5, 674.2
baste 11.5, 604.12, 741.4, 902.16
bastille 429.8
bastinado (n) 604.4, 605.1 (v) 604.12
basting 11.2, 604.4, 741.1
bastion 460.6
basuco 87.7
bat (n) 30.4, 88.6, 304.3, 748.1, 902.5 (v) 745.5, 902.15
batch (n) 244.2, 247.4, 257.10, 770.7, 893.4 (v) 770.18
batch file 1042.18
batch processing 1042.18
bate 252.6, 252.8, 255.9, 286.2, 631.2, 670.9
bat ear 48.7
bated 52.17, 252.10
bated breath 52.4
bath (n) 79.8, 79.9, 79.10, 79.12, 1065.6 (v) 79.19
Bath chair 179.7
bathe (n) 79.8, 182.11 (v) 79.19, 91.24, 182.56, 1065.13
bathed 1065.17
bathed in sweat 12.22
bathed with light 1025.39
bather 182.12
bathetic 93.21
bathe with light 1025.28
bathhouse 79.10
bathing 79.7, 182.11, 1065.6
bathing beauty 182.12, 1016.7
bathing girl 182.12
bathing place 79.10
bathing suit 5.29
bathing trunks 5.29
bathmism 306.2
bathometry 275.6
bathos 93.8, 112.1, 488.3
bathroom 12.10, 79.10, 197.26
bathroom humor 704.6
baths 79.10, 91.23, 228.27
bathtub 79.12
bathtub gin 88.18
bath water 79.10
bathyal 275.15
bathyal zone 275.4
bathymetric 240.8, 275.15
bathymetrical 240.8, 275.15
bathymetry 240.6, 275.6
bathyorographic 275.15
bathyorographical 240.8, 275.15
bathypelagic 275.15
bathyscaphe 367.5
bathysphere 367.5
bat of an eye 830.3
baton 273.2, 417.9, 647.1, 647.2, 661.6, 674.2, 711.22
bat one's gums 524.20
bat out 340.9
bat out of hell 174.6
batrachian (n) 311.26 (a) 311.47
bats 926.27
bats in the belfry 926.2
battalion 461.22, 770.3
batten (n) 271.4, 704.20 (v) 15.13, 293.6, 672.4, 800.8, 800.9, 855.8, 1010.8
batten down 800.8, 855.8
batten down the hatches 182.48, 293.6, 494.6
batten on 138.12, 387.16
battens 704.18
batten upon 8.28
batter (n) 745.2, 1062.5 (v) 389.5, 393.13, 604.13, 671.11, 902.16, 1000.6
battercake 10.45
battered 393.33
battered child syndrome 85.38
batterie de cuisine 11.4
battering 85.38, 671.3
battering ram 462.11
battery (n) 461.22, 462.11, 604.4, 745.2, 1032.21 (a) 904.17
battery pack 1042.18
battery-powered 1032.30
battery supply voltage 1033.7
bat the eyes 28.10
bat the eyes at 377.5
battiness 923.1, 926.2
batting average 745.4
batting coach 745.2
batting order 965.3
batting stance 745.2
battle (n) 457.4, 458.1, 458.4, 725.3, 754.3 (v) 451.4, 456.11, 457.13, 458.13, 460.9, 725.11
battle à outrance 457.17
battle array 458.2
battle-ax 110.12
battleax 304.3
battle cruiser 180.6
battlecruiser 180.7
battle cry 59.1, 454.2, 458.7, 517.16
battled 458.22, 460.12
battledore 554.10, 1048.3
battledore and shuttlecock (n) 863.1 (v) 916.13
battle fatigue 92.14
battlefield 308.12, 463.2
battle flag 458.11
battlefront 216.2, 463.2
battlegear 460.3
battleground 308.12, 463.2
battle group 461.22
battle-hungry 458.21
battle hymn 458.11
battle it out 457.17
battle line 216.2, 463.2
battlement 289.3
battlemented 289.5, 460.12
battle of life, the 330.5
battle orders 458.7
battle plan 458.3
battle plane 181.9
battler 461.1
battle royal 457.4
battleship 180.6, 180.7
battle site 463.2
battlewagon 180.7
battle zone 463.2
battling 457.22, 458.20
battological 849.14
battologize 849.8
battology 849.3
batty 923.9, 926.27
bauble 498.4, 743.16, 998.5
Baucis and Philemon 304.4
baud rate 1042.18
bavardage 540.3
bavin 1021.3
bawbee 728.8
bawd 665.18
bawdiness 665.5, 666.4
bawdry 666.4
bawdy 665.29, 666.9
bawdyhouse 665.9
bawl (n) 59.1, 115.3 (v) 59.6, 60.2, 115.12, 115.13, 524.25
bawling (n) 115.2 (a) 59.10, 60.6
bawling-out 510.6
bawl out 510.18
bay (n) 53.5, 197.3, 234.2, 240.2, 242.1, 284.7, 311.11, 386.6 (v) 53.10, 60.2 (a) 40.4
bayadere 705.3
bay after 100.14, 382.8
Bayard 608.5
bayard (n) 311.11 (a) 40.4
bay at the moon 60.2, 115.13, 391.8
bay-colored 40.4
bayed 242.2
Bayer 86.12
bayfront (n) 234.2 (a) 234.7
baygall 243.1
bay ice 1023.5
bay oil 70.2
bayonet (n) 462.5 (v) 459.25
bayonetting 459.10
bayou 238.3, 241.1, 242.1
bayou lake 241.1
bayous 231.7
bay rum 70.3
bays 646.3
bayside (n) 234.2 (a) 234.7
bay window 2.19
bazaar 734.3, 736.2
bazillion 884.4
bazoo 292.4

bazooka 462.21, 1074.10
B&B 228.15
b-ball 747.1
BB gun 462.10
B board 347.8
b-day 850.4
be 306.8, 761.8
be a bargain 731.19
be a base runner 745.5
be able 18.11
be able to do it blindfolded 413.18
be able to do it standing on one's head 413.18
be about 101.7, 724.11
be about to 405.10
be about to be borning 840.2
be above 157.3
be abrasive 98.10
be absent 222.7, 762.5, 985.9
be absentminded 990.4
be absorbed in 983.5
be abstracted 931.12
be accepted 953.20
be accepted for 349.10
be accountable for 641.6
be accurate 973.11
beach (n) 234.2, 751.1 (v) 182.42
beach bum 178.3
beach bunny 178.3
beachcomber 79.16, 178.3, 331.9, 660.2, 770.15
beachcombing 79.4
beachfront (n) 234.2 (a) 234.7
beachhead 216.2, 460.6, 463.2
Beach-la-mar 523.11
beachside 234.7
beachside shingle 234.2
beach umbrella 295.7, 1028.1
be a cold fish 94.5
beacon (n) 27.8, 184.19, 400.1, 517.15, 1019.13, 1026.3 (v) 165.2, 1025.23, 1025.28
beacon fire 517.15, 1019.13
beacon lights 184.19
beacon station 1036.6
be a couch potato 402.4
be acquainted with 587.9, 928.12
bead (n) 282.3 (v) 282.7, 498.9
be a dark horse 972.13
be added 253.7
be a deal 731.19
beaded 282.10, 498.11
beaded brow 12.7
beaded with sweat 12.22
beading 211.7
beadle 1008.15
beadledom 612.10
beadlike 282.10
be admitted 189.7
be admitted to the bar 597.5
beadroll 696.4
beads 498.5, 498.6, 696.4
bead-shaped 282.10
beadsman 696.9, 699.16
beads of sweat 12.7
be a dupe 954.5
be advised by 422.7
beady 282.10
be a fast study 704.32
be a father to 1008.19
be a feature of 796.3, 865.10
be affected 93.11
be affected with 85.46
be afflicted 26.8
be afraid 127.10, 951.10, 953.11
be a free agent 430.20
be after 380.4
be against 451.7
be a gas 704.28
be a gasbag 540.8
be a gasser 704.28
be agin 451.7
beagle 576.11, 757.2, 1008.15
be a go 731.19
be a good investment 472.13
be a good sport 649.6
be a good trencherman 100.19
be agreeable 433.6
be agreeable to 324.3
be ahead of time 845.5
be a hit 704.28
be airborne 184.36
beak (n) 2.11, 216.3, 239.8, 283.8, 596.1 (v) 902.18
beaked 279.8
beaker 1060.6
beaklike 279.8
beak-nosed 279.8
beak-shaped 279.8
be a law unto oneself 327.6, 418.4
be alert 981.3, 983.8
be alienated 589.7
be alive 306.8
be alive with 884.5
be-all 792.3
be-all and end-all 249.3, 792.3, 820.1
be-all and end-all, the 380.2, 823.1
be all ears 48.10, 983.7
be all heart 93.12
be all one to 102.5
be all over 410.13, 820.7, 837.6
be all over with 395.23
be allowed 443.13
be all thumbs 414.11
be all up with 395.23, 410.13
be a logical impossibility 967.4
be a long shot 969.2
beam (n) 116.3, 184.19, 218.1, 269.1, 269.3, 273.3, 901.4, 906.4, 1025.5, 1034.10, 1035.4, 1036.11, 1054.3 (v) 95.12, 109.6, 116.7, 1016.16, 1025.23, 1034.25, 1036.15
be a man 492.9
be amazed 122.5
be ambitious 100.20
be a member 617.15
be amenable 441.2
beam-end 901.14
beaming 95.16, 109.11, 1016.20, 1025.30
beaming out 171.1
beamless 1027.13
beam of light 1025.5
be a mother to 1008.19
beam out 171.6
beam transmission 1034.16
be a must 641.5, 963.10
beam wind 318.10
beamy 269.7, 1025.30
bean 198.7, 310.4, 759.18, 919.6, 998.5
be an accessory to 476.5
be an agent provocateur 119.2
be a natural 413.18
beanbag 229.1
beanbag chair 229.1
bean counter 550.1
bean-counting 573.7, 1017.11
bean curd 10.13, 10.48
be an easy mark 954.6
beanery 8.17
be a new person 858.12
bean feast 8.9, 582.12
be angry 105.16
be an icicle 94.5
be animate 306.8
be an imperative for 641.5
be an impossibility 967.4
be an incubus to 297.13
be an indication of 517.17
be annihilated 762.6
beano 759.15
beanpole 270.8, 272.7
beans 10.35, 87.13, 762.3
beanstalk 270.8
be answerable 641.6
be answerable for 436.5
be antipathetic 900.6
beany 926.27
be a paradox 967.4
be a party to 476.5
be a patsy 954.6
be a pawn of 897.3
be a person of heart 93.12
be a person of sentiment 93.12
be a player in 476.5
be a plaything of 897.3
be apodictic 970.9
be a Pollyanna 109.6
be a poor mixer 583.4
be appreciative of 150.3
be apprised 551.15
be apprised of 551.14, 928.12
be a prey to anxiety 126.6
be a prey to one's feelings 93.12
be a quality of 761.11
be a quick study 989.16
bear (n) 110.11, 311.22, 737.12 (v) 1.3, 134.5, 161.7, 176.12, 433.6, 443.10, 449.12, 474.7, 626.7, 725.9, 737.25, 818.14, 886.10, 892.13, 901.21, 902.12, 991.4 (a) 729.20
bearable 107.13
bear account 737.12
bear a child 1.3
bear a date of 832.13
bear against 424.6
bear a grudge 152.12, 589.8
bear a hand 476.5
bear arms 458.17
bear away 182.23, 182.30
beard (n) 2.13, 3.8, 548.6 (v) 454.3, 492.10
bearded 3.25
bearding 454.1
beardless 6.17, 301.11
beardlessness 6.4
bear down 112.19, 167.3, 725.13, 913.4
bear down on 167.3, 182.35, 424.6
bear down on it 330.14, 401.6
bear down upon 167.3, 459.17
beard the lion in his den 454.3, 493.6
beard-tweaking 454.1
be a reproach to 661.8
bearer 309.7, 901.2
bearer of glad tidings 353.2
bear false witness 354.20, 599.12
bear for 161.9
bear fruit 387.17, 407.8, 861.5, 887.5, 892.13
bear garden 463.1
bear good will 143.11
bear hard upon 297.13, 424.6, 425.5, 1011.8
bear hug 474.2, 474.3, 562.3
bear ill will 144.15, 589.8
bearing (n) 33.4, 159.3, 161.1, 321.1, 472.5, 517.14, 518.1, 775.4, 818.4, 892.6, 896.2, 906.3, 915.7, 1040.5 (a) 1.4, 890.10, 901.23
bearing arms 460.14
bearing in mind 989.23
bearing out 957.4
bearing rein 1012.7
bearings 159.1, 159.3, 161.4, 647.2, 765.1
bearing the seal of approval 509.19
bearing the weight of the world 112.20
bearing wall 901.6
bear in mind 931.16, 983.9, 989.12
bearish 110.19, 311.43, 505.7
bearish market 737.5
bearishness 110.2, 505.3, 737.5
bearish prices 738.9
bear leeward 182.23
bearlike 311.43
bear malice 144.15, 152.12, 589.8
bear market 737.5
bear more than one's share 1011.9
Bearnaise 10.12
bear no resemblance 787.2
bear no resemblance to 780.5
bear off 164.3, 164.6, 182.23, 182.29, 182.30, 182.36, 204.9
bear off the land 182.37
be aromatic 69.6
bear on 297.11, 775.5, 889.6, 901.22, 957.8
bear one's company 582.17
bear one's cross 134.5
bear oneself 321.4
bear oneself with credit 409.10
be around 223.8
bear out 449.12, 957.11
bear panic 737.22
bear pool 737.17
bear raid 737.20
bear reign 612.13
bear resemblance 784.7
be arrested 795.3
bear sail 182.13

bear the brunt 134.5, 1011.9
bear the date of 832.13
bear the expense 624.18
bear the market 737.25
bear the name of 527.13
bear the palm 249.7, 411.3
bear to leeward 182.29
bear to port 182.30
bear to starboard 182.30
bear to windward 182.24
bear trap 356.12
bear-trap dam 1012.5
bear up 15.10, 109.10, 121.6, 167.3, 298.8, 360.4, 449.12, 453.2, 492.14, 901.21
bear up against 453.2
bear up for 161.9, 182.35
bear upon 297.11, 894.9, 902.12
bear up to 161.9, 182.35
bear up under 134.5
bear with 134.5, 148.4, 427.5, 443.10
bear with composure 134.4
bear witness 692.6, 957.9
bear witness against 551.12
bear witness to 517.17
bear young 1.3
be as expected 130.10
be as good as 999.11
be as good as one's word 434.2, 644.9
be ashamed 137.9
be a shot in the arm 17.10
be a sideliner 329.2
be a sign of 133.11
be asleep at the switch 340.6
be asleep with the Lord 307.26
be as one looked for 130.10
be as one thought 130.10
beast 144.14, 311.2, 593.5, 660.6, 671.9
beast, the 663.2
beastess 144.14
beastlike 311.39, 663.6
beastliness 80.2, 98.2, 144.11, 505.3, 663.2, 1000.2
beastly 80.24, 98.18, 98.19, 144.26, 311.39, 505.7, 663.6, 1000.9
beast of burden 311.13, 726.3
beast of prey 480.12
be astonished 122.5
be astounded 122.5
be a stretch of the imagination 969.2
beasts of field 311.1
beasts of prey 311.1
beasts of the field, the fowl of the air, and the fish of the sea, the 311.1
beasts of venery 382.7
be a success 409.10
be a sucker 954.6
be at 96.13, 221.8
beat (n) 55.1, 138.5, 231.2, 373.5, 383.1, 524.10, 552.3, 709.22, 709.24, 709.26, 720.7, 724.4, 850.2, 850.3, 914.2, 916.3, 917.4 (v) 21.6, 55.4, 182.25, 182.30, 249.7, 320.5, 356.19, 382.9, 393.13, 411.5, 412.9, 604.12, 708.44, 849.10, 902.16, 916.12, 917.10, 917.12, 971.14, 1051.9 (a) 21.8, 412.15, 619.10, 868.6, 971.26
beatable 1006.16
beat about 182.30, 938.32, 971.9, 1013.11
beat about the bush 368.8, 538.10
beat a dead horse 391.8, 849.9, 856.5, 993.12
beat a devil's tattoo 55.4
beat against 451.4, 900.6
beat a hasty retreat 163.6, 188.12, 368.10
beat all hollow 249.7, 412.9
beat a retreat 163.6, 188.9, 188.12, 368.10
beat around the bush 368.8, 538.10, 936.9
beat a ruffle 55.4
be at a standstill 173.7
beat a tattoo 55.4, 708.44
beat back 908.3
beat black and blue 393.13, 604.14
beat by a nose 412.6
be at cross-purposes 451.3, 456.8, 779.4, 789.5
beat down 112.18, 395.19, 432.9, 612.15, 633.6, 731.18
be at ease 121.8, 581.2
beaten 21.10, 320.6, 373.14, 412.14
beaten path 373.5, 383.2
beaten path, the 118.1
beaten track 373.5, 383.2
beaten track, the 118.1
beaten-up 393.33
beater 179.10, 382.5, 797.9, 917.9
be at fault 975.10
be a thing of the past 837.6, 842.9
be at home 430.18
be at home in 413.18
be at home to 585.7
be a thorn in one's side 96.17
beatific 95.16, 97.9, 681.12
beatifical 681.12
beatification 95.2, 662.8, 685.3, 912.1
beatified 95.16, 662.18, 679.6, 681.12, 685.8, 912.9
beatified soul 679.1
beatify 95.9, 662.13, 685.5, 912.6
be a timeserver 363.9
beating (n) 55.1, 412.1, 604.4, 902.4, 916.3, 917.4, 1051.4 (a) 55.7, 709.28, 850.7, 916.18
beating around the bush 936.5
beating heart 306.2
beat into 568.12
beat into one's head 568.12, 953.18
beat it 188.7, 222.10, 368.11
beatitude 95.2, 685.3
be at loggerheads 215.4
beatnik 868.3
beatnikism 868.2
be at odds with 333.4
beat off 460.10
beat one 522.10
beat one down to size 137.6
beat one's brains 931.9
beat one's brains out 412.9, 604.14
beat one's breast 115.11
beat one's gums 540.5
be at one's service 143.10, 439.10
beat one's swords into plowshares 464.8
beat one's way 177.23, 177.31
be at one's wit's end 971.9
be at one with 332.9, 455.2
beat out 249.7, 916.12
beat poet 720.12
be a trait of 865.10
be at sea 522.11, 971.9
beat signal 1036.11
be at sixes and sevens 971.9
beat someone to the draw 845.6
beat someone to the punch 845.6
beat the air 391.8
be at the bottom of 901.21
beat the bushes 938.31
be at the conn 182.14
be at the controls 184.37
beat the drum 487.2, 517.22, 708.44
beat the drum for 352.15, 509.13
beat the drums 458.18
beat the game 409.13
beat the gun 135.4, 845.6, 947.2
be at the head of 612.11
be at the helm 182.14, 573.9
be at the mercy of 432.12
beat the rap 369.7, 431.9
beat the system 409.13
be at the tiller 182.14, 573.9
beat time 708.44, 832.11, 916.12
beat to a jelly 604.14
beat to the draw 459.21
be attractive 377.6
beat up (v) 604.14, 917.10, 1062.10 (a) 21.8, 393.29
beat-up 393.33, 810.15
beat up against 451.4
be at variance 333.4, 456.8
be at work on 724.11
beau (n) 104.12, 500.9 (v) 562.21
Beau Brummel 500.9, 578.7
beaucoup 247.8, 883.7, 991.7
Beaufort scale 318.15
beauhunk 1016.8
beau ideal 659.4, 786.4, 1016.7
Beaujolais wine 88.17
beau monde 578.6, 608.1, 618.6
beaut 999.7, 1016.8
beauteous 1016.17
beauteousness 1016.1
beautician 1016.12
beauties 545.4, 554.7, 1016.3
beautification 392.2, 1016.10
beautified 392.13, 1016.22
beautifier 1016.12
beautiful 712.20, 1016.17
beautiful, the 1016.1
beautiful friendship 587.8
beautifulness 1016.1
beautiful people 578.6
beautify 392.10, 498.8, 1016.15
beautifying 1016.22
beautiless 1015.6
beauty 533.2, 1016.1, 1016.7
beauty care 1016.10
beauty-care products 1016.11
beauty contest 451.1
beauty contestant 452.2
beauty contest winner 1016.7
beauty mark 517.5
beauty of holiness 692.2
beauty pageant 451.1
beauty pageant winner 1016.7
beauty parlor 739.1, 1016.13
beauty-parlor chitchat 541.4
beauty products 1016.11
beauty queen 1016.7
beauty salon 1016.13
beauty shop 1016.13
beauty sleep 22.2
beauty spot 517.5
beauty treatment 1016.10
beauty unadorned 499.3, 1016.1
beaux arts 712.1
beaver (n) 330.8, 726.3 (v) 725.13
beaver away 725.13
beaver dam 1012.5
beavertail beam 1036.11
be aware of 24.6, 928.12, 983.5
be a waste of time 967.4
be a wet blanket 379.4
be a windbag 540.8
be a workaholic 725.13
be axiomatic 970.9
be a yes-man 138.9
be based on 901.22, 959.6
be before 834.3
be beforehand 845.5
be begotten 306.9
be behindhand 846.7
be believed 953.20
be benevolent 143.11
be benighted 930.9
be bent on 978.6
be bereaved 473.4
be bereft of 473.4
be beside oneself 152.15
be best friends 587.9
be between Scylla and Charybdis 670.5
be beyond one 522.10
be beyond one's depth 992.8
be big 979.7
be big for 101.7
be blessed-eventing 78.12
be blind 30.8, 930.9
be blinded by one's own glory 140.6
be blindsided 406.6
be blind to 30.8, 984.2
be blooded 409.7
bebop 708.9
be born 1.2, 306.9, 818.13
be born again 692.7, 858.12
be born for 413.18
be born on the wrong side of the blanket 1.2
be born out of wedlock 1.2
be born so 767.6
be born to be 413.18
be born to trouble 1011.9

be born under an evil star 1011.9
be bound 641.4
be bounded by 959.6
be bound to pay 623.5
be brief 537.5
be bright 1025.23
be brilliant 920.11
be brought down 85.47
be browned off 152.15
be buddies 587.9
be buddy-buddy with 587.11
be built that way 767.6
be burnt into one's memory 989.13
be busy 330.10
be called 527.13
be called out on strikes 745.5
becalm 173.11
becalmed 173.17
be candid 644.12
be careful 339.7, 494.5
be caught flatfooted 656.2
be caught in the act 656.2
be caught looking 745.5, 844.5
be caught napping 340.6, 406.6
be caught out 984.2
be caught redhanded 656.2
be caught short 737.23
be caught with one's hand in the cookie jar 656.2
be caught with one's hand in the till 656.2
be caught with one's pants down 406.6, 656.2
be cautious 339.7, 494.5
be certain 953.10, 953.14, 970.9
bechamel 10.12
be champing at the bit 324.3
bechance 972.11
be changed 761.12, 852.6
be chapfallen be disenchanted 132.4
be characteristic 865.10
becharm 95.10, 104.22, 377.7, 691.8
becharmed 104.27, 691.12
be cheap 633.5
Bêche-de-Mer 523.11
be cheek by jowl with 450.4
beck 238.1, 420.5, 517.14
beck and call 420.5
beckon (n) 517.14 (v) 377.6, 517.21
be cleaned out 625.7
be clear 521.4
be clobbered 1011.10
be close friends with 587.9
be closeted with 541.9
becloud 319.7, 346.6, 985.7, 1027.9, 1031.2
beclouded 346.11, 985.13
be clueless 930.10
be coerced 424.9
be coextensive with 761.11
be cognizant of 928.12
be cold 1023.9
be cold as ice 94.5
become 641.4, 761.12, 818.13, 858.11, 858.17
become acquainted with 570.6
become adept in 570.9
become a habit 373.10
become airborne 184.38, 193.10
become alive to 551.14
become an appendage of 138.11
become angry 152.17
become an individual 872.6
become an overnight celebrity 662.11
become a part of 800.5
become apparent 521.5
become a reality 973.12
become attached to 104.21
become awake to 551.14
become aware of 551.14, 570.6, 941.2
become bankrupt 625.7
become bound to 641.8
become cognizant of 941.2
become conscious of 551.14, 941.2
become conversant with 570.9
become defunct 820.7
become enamored 104.21
become engaged 562.22
become extinct 252.6, 307.25, 820.7, 842.9
become familiar with 570.9
become fixed 373.10
become informed 570.6
become insolvent 625.7
become irate 152.17
become known 351.8
become lost to sight 34.2
become manifest 33.8
become obsolete 34.2, 842.9
become of 887.4
become one 563.15, 1016.15
become overweight 259.8
become popular 578.8
become public 352.16
become sponsor for 641.8
become suicidal 112.16
become the rage 578.8
become versed in 570.9
become visible 33.8
become void 820.7
become well-versed in 570.9
be comforted 121.7
becoming (n) 858.1 (a) 496.9, 639.8, 664.5, 788.10, 995.5, 1016.18
becoming aware of 941.1
becoming cognizant of 941.1
becoming conscious of 941.1
becomingness 496.2, 1016.2
be commensurable 943.7
be comparable 943.7
be compelled 424.9
be composed 106.6
be comprised in 761.11
be conceived 306.9
be concerned 339.6
be concerned with 937.3
be conditional on 959.6, 971.11
be confident 953.14, 970.9
be confined 1.3
be conflicted 362.6
be conscious of 24.6, 928.12
be conservative 670.5, 853.6
be considerate 143.10, 504.10
be consistent 788.6, 803.7, 973.8
be conspicuous 31.5
be constituted by 761.11
be constituted of 796.3
be construed as 518.8
be consumed 34.2, 388.4
be consumed with desire 100.18
be contained in 761.11
be contemptuous of 157.3
be content 107.5
be contentious 456.11
be content with 979.7
be contiguous 223.9
be contingent on 887.5, 959.6, 971.11
be continuous 812.4
be contrary to 451.6
be conversant with 928.12
be converted 692.7
be converted into 761.12, 852.6, 858.17
be convicted 602.4
be convinced 953.11, 953.14
be convincing 953.18
be convulsed with laughter 116.8
be cool 106.6
be correct 973.10
be covetous of 154.2
be credulous 954.5
be crestfallen 132.4
be cross 110.13
be crowded 770.16
be crowned with success 409.7
be cruel to be kind 145.4
be cruising for a bruising 604.21
be crushed 137.9
be curious 981.3
be cut 152.13
be cut out to be 413.18
be cut to the quick 152.13
be cut up 112.19
bed (n) 199.1, 199.4, 229.1, 239.2, 296.1, 385.3, 548.9, 563.1, 750.1, 901.6, 901.19, 1069.10 (v) 20.6, 22.17, 22.19, 191.5, 225.10, 855.9, 1069.18, 1070.7
bedabble 80.18
be damned 682.7
be damp 1065.11
bed and board 385.3
bed and breakfast 228.15
bedarken 38.7, 1027.9
be dated 832.13
bedaub 80.16, 295.24, 1004.6
bedaze 25.4, 122.6
bedazed 25.7
bedazzle 30.7, 122.6, 985.7, 1025.23
bedazzled 30.10, 985.14
bedazzling 30.11, 1025.32
bedbug 311.37
bedchamber 197.7
bedclothes 295.10
bedcover 295.10
bedding 295.10, 296.1, 901.6, 901.20
bedding plant 310.33
bed down 20.6, 22.17, 1070.7
beddy-bye 22.2
be dead 307.26
be dead and gone 837.6
be dead set against 325.3
be deaf 49.4
be dear 632.6
be death on 103.5
be deceived 975.10
bedeck 5.39, 5.42, 498.8
bedecked 5.45, 498.11
be demonstrable 935.17
be dependent on 959.6
be deserving 639.5
be desirous of 100.14
be despaired of 1006.8
be desperately in love 104.18
be destined 839.6
be destined for one 831.6
be destroyed 762.6
be determined 359.8, 403.5
bedevil 96.13, 680.16, 691.9
bedeviled 96.24, 926.29
bedevilment 96.2, 691.2
bedew 1065.12
bedewed 1065.15
bedewing 1065.6
bedfast 85.59
bedfellow 588.3, 616.1
bedhead 1016.14
bedhop 665.19
be diagnostic of 517.17
be difficult 1013.10
be diffident 955.6
bedight 498.8
be dilatory 846.11
bedim 1027.9
bedimmed 1027.15
bedimming 32.2, 36.3, 1027.6
bed in 191.5
be disagreeable 98.10
be disappointed 132.4, 408.2
be disappointing 132.3
be discontented 108.5
be discriminating 944.5
be disenchanted 977.3
be disillusioned 977.3
be disposed 896.3
be disposed to 978.6
be disrespectful 156.4
be distasteful 98.10
be distinct 780.5
be distinguished 780.5
be divided 362.7
bedizen 5.42, 35.14, 498.8
bedizened 498.11, 545.8
bedizenment 5.1, 498.2, 545.1, 993.4
bed jacket 5.21
bedlam 53.3, 810.5, 926.14
bedlamite 926.15
bedlam let loose 53.3
bed linen 295.10
bedmate 588.3
bed of nails 96.2, 1012.4
bed of Procrustes 605.4
bed of roses 95.5, 121.1, 1010.1
bedog 166.3
be doing 724.11
bed on 199.6
be done for 395.23
be done with 820.6
be doomed 839.6
be doubly punished 604.19
be doubtful 955.6
Bedouin 178.4

bed out 191.8
be downbeat 125.9
be down in the dumps 110.14
be down on 589.8
bedpan 12.11
bed posts 750.2
bedrabble 80.19
bedraggle 80.19
bedraggled 80.21, 810.15
bedrape 5.39
be dressed in 5.44
bedridden 85.59
bedridden invalid 584.5
be driven 963.10
be driven into a corner 963.11
bedrock (n) 199.1, 274.4, 855.6, 901.6, 1059.1 (a) 199.7, 275.16, 997.23
bedroom (n) 197.7 (v) 428.9
bedroom community 209.1, 230.1
bedroom eyes 27.5, 562.9
bedroom town 230.1
be drunk 88.27
bedsheet 295.10
bedside manner 93.1
bedsitter 228.13
bedsore 85.37
bedspread 295.10
bedsprings 901.20
bedstead 901.19
bedstraw 901.20
bedtime 22.2, 315.4
bedtime prayer 696.8
be dubious 955.6
be due 639.4
be due to 887.5
be dumb with grief 112.17
bedwarf 252.9
be dying 307.25
be dying for 100.16
be dying to 324.3
bee 311.32, 311.34, 582.14
be eager 324.3
be earless 49.4
be earlier 834.3
be early 834.3, 845.5
be easy 121.8
be easy in one's mind about 953.14
be easy of belief 954.5
be easy on 427.5
be easy to recall 989.13
be easy with 979.7
be eaten away 252.6
bee culture 1070.1
beef (n) 10.14, 15.2, 18.1, 115.5, 297.1, 311.6, 333.2, 456.7 (v) 108.6, 115.16, 333.5
beef-brained 922.15
beef bread 10.20
beefcake 75.4, 76.6, 714.3
beef cattle 311.6
beefeater 1008.14
beefed-up 251.7, 259.10
beefer 108.4, 115.9
beef extract 10.14
be effective 889.7
be effortless 1014.10
beefhead 924.4
beefheaded 922.15
beefiness 15.2, 257.8, 297.1
beefing (n) 115.5 (a) 108.8, 115.20
beefing-up 251.2
beefsteak 10.14, 10.18
beef tea 10.49
beef up 15.13, 251.5, 253.5, 460.9
beef-witted 922.15
beef-wittedness 922.3
beefy 15.15, 257.18
beeherd 1070.4
Beehive 1073.8
beehive 228.25, 739.2, 1016.14
beehive kiln 742.5
beehive tomb 309.16
bee in one's bonnet 364.1, 927.2
bee in the bonnet 551.3
beekeeper 1070.4
beekeeping 1070.1
be elected 609.42
beeline 268.5, 277.2
Beelzebub 680.4
be employed 724.12
be employed in 724.11
be energetic 17.11
be enfeoffed of 469.4
be enfranchised 476.5
be engaged 436.6, 844.3
be engaged in 724.11
be engrossed in 983.5
been there done that 413.28
be enthusiastic 101.7
be entitled to 639.4
be envious of 154.2
beep (n) 53.5 (v) 53.10
beeper 347.4, 400.1
be equal to 790.5, 991.4
beer 10.49, 88.16
be eradicated 762.6
beer and skittles 95.1
beer-bellied 2.31
beer belly 2.18, 283.3
beerbelly 2.19
be erect 200.7
beer garden 88.20
beer gut 283.3
beer joint 88.20
beer parlor 88.20
beer suds 320.2
beery 88.31, 93.21
beesting 1001.5
be estranged 566.5, 589.7
beeswax 1056.8
beetle (n) 311.32, 757.2, 1063.4 (v) 202.7, 272.11 (a) 202.11
beetle-browed 110.24, 202.11
beetleheaded 922.17
beetleheadedness 922.4
beetle off 188.7
beetle over 202.7
beetling (n) 202.3 (a) 202.11
beet-red 41.6
bee tree 228.25
beet sugar 66.2, 66.3
be even-steven 790.5
be ever the same 853.5
beeves 311.6
be evident 31.4
be exasperated 135.5
be excitable 105.16
be exonerated 430.18
be expectant 130.5
be expected 130.7
be expecting 78.12
be expedient 641.3
be expert in 928.13
be exposed 31.5
be exposed to 831.8
be extant 761.8
be extirpated 762.6
be eyeball to eyeball 215.4
beezer 283.8
be fair 649.5
be faithful to 434.2
befall 831.5, 972.11
be far-fetched 969.2
be far from one's mind 933.2
be far from one's thoughts 933.2
be fashionable 578.9
be fat, dumb, and happy 1010.8
be fated 839.6
be featured 997.12
be fed up 994.5
be feeling no pain 88.27
be felled 85.47, 1011.10
be fetched from afar 969.2
be financially committed 623.5
Béfind 678.8
be first 216.7
befit 641.4, 995.3
befit the occasion 843.6
befit the season 843.6
befit the time 843.6
be fitting 995.3
befitting 788.10, 843.9, 995.5
be fit to be compared 943.7
befog 295.19, 319.7, 346.6
befogged 346.11
befogging 295.1
be fond of 63.5, 104.18
befool 356.15, 923.7
befoolable 923.12
befooled 923.8
befooling 356.1
be foolish 923.6
be forced 963.10
be forced to conclude 946.10
before-and-after 392.14, 852.10
beforehand 833.3
beforementioned 814.5
before one's eyes 31.6
before the Fall 834.5
before the Flood 834.5
before the war 834.5
beforetime 845.7
be forgetful 990.4
be forgotten 990.7
be for it 604.21
be fortunate 1010.11
befoul 80.17, 389.4, 1000.6
befouled 80.21
befouling 393.2
befoulment 80.4, 389.1, 1000.3
be found 159.10, 221.6, 761.8, 831.5, 941.9
be found guilty 602.4
be found wanting 250.4, 410.9, 911.2, 992.8
be fragrant 70.7
be frank 644.12
be free 430.18
be freed 430.18
be frequent 847.3
be fresh in one's memory 989.13
befriend 449.11, 587.10, 592.3
befriender 592.1
befriending 592.4
be friends 587.9
be friends of long standing 587.9
befrilled 498.11, 545.11
befringe 211.10
befringed 211.12
be from Missouri 955.6
be fruitful 890.7
befuddle 88.22, 985.7
befuddled 985.13
befuddlement 88.1, 985.3
befuddler 357.1
be full of beans 17.11
be full of emotion 105.18
be full of ginger 17.11
be full of oneself 651.4
be full of pep 17.11, 83.6
be full of piss and vinegar 17.11
be full of zip 17.11
be full to overflowing 770.16
be futile 391.8
beg (n) 575.12 (v) 368.7, 384.6, 440.11, 440.15
be game 324.3
be garrulous 540.8
be gathered to one's fathers 307.20
beg a truce 433.8
be generous to a fault 652.3
be generous with 478.12
beget 78.8, 818.14, 886.10, 890.7, 892.12
begetter 560.8, 886.4, 892.7
begetting 78.2, 78.3
be getting along 188.6
beg forgiveness 113.7
beg for mercy 145.6
beg for one's life 145.6
beggar (n) 178.3, 331.9, 331.11, 440.8, 619.4, 660.2 (v) 480.24, 619.6
beggar description 122.8, 1016.16
beggared 619.8
beggarliness 619.2, 661.3, 998.2
beggarly 138.14, 497.15, 619.8, 661.12, 992.12, 998.21
beggarly fellow 660.2
beggary 440.6, 619.2, 992.4
begging (n) 440.6 (a) 440.16, 440.17
begging the question 936.3
begild 35.14, 43.3
begin 818.7
begin again 856.6
beg indulgence 658.5
beginner 572.9, 818.2, 886.4, 892.7, 930.7
beginner's slope 753.1
beginning (n) 818.1, 886.5, 892.1 (a) 798.6, 818.15
beginning and end 792.3
beginning of the end 820.3
beginnings 818.4, 845.1
begird 209.7
begirt 209.11
be given a jolt 131.5

be given a start 131.5
be given a turn 131.5
beg leave 440.9
beg leave to doubt 955.6
beglerbeg 575.12
be glimpsed 521.5
begloom 1027.9
beg off 370.5, 442.3
be gone 34.2, 837.6
begone 188.6
be good 143.9, 321.5, 653.4
be good for 81.4
begotten 1.4
beg pardon 113.7, 658.5
be grateful 150.3
be gravid 78.12
be great with child 78.12
be Greek to 522.10
be green 930.8
begrime 80.15
begrudge 152.12, 154.2, 325.3, 442.4, 484.5
begrudging 154.3
beg the ear of 524.26
beg the question 368.8, 936.9
beg to differ 333.4
beg to disagree 442.3
be guided by 867.3
beguile 356.14, 377.7, 743.21, 985.6
beguiled 122.9, 923.8
beguilement 122.1, 377.1
beguile of 356.18
beguile out of 356.18
beguiler 357.1
beguile the time 331.13, 743.22
beguiling (n) 377.1 (a) 122.10, 356.21, 377.8, 743.27
beguilingness 122.3
be guilty 656.2
be had 632.8
behalf 387.4, 999.4
be half-blind 28.8
be halfhearted 102.4, 325.4
be hand in glove with 450.4, 899.3
be handy 387.17
be hanged 604.18
be hard put 1013.11
be hard to believe 955.7
be hard to please 495.8
be hard to swallow 955.7
be hard up 619.5
be harmonious 708.35
behave 321.4, 321.5, 326.2, 328.4
behaved 321.7
behave ill 322.4
behave oneself 321.4, 321.5
behave self-destructively 414.14
behave toward 321.6
behavior 92.26, 321.1, 328.1, 653.1
behavioral 321.7, 328.10
behavioral economics 731.7
behavioral norm 321.1, 636.1
behavioral science 312.10, 321.3
behaviored 321.7
behaviorism 92.2, 321.3, 1052.6
behaviorist 321.7
behavioristic 321.7
behavioristic psychology 92.2, 321.3
behavior modification 92.6, 321.3
behavior pattern 321.1
behavior psychology 92.2, 321.3
behavior therapist 92.10
behavior therapy 92.6
behavior therapy ethology 321.3
behavior trait 321.1
behead 604.16
beheader 604.7
beheading 604.6
be heading for a fall 604.21
be heard 48.12
be heavy 297.10
be heavy on one 98.16
be heedful 983.6
be heeled 87.22
be heir to 479.7
behemoth 257.14
be hep to 941.8
be here again 850.5
be here to stay 853.5
be hers to 641.5
behest 420.1
be highly motivated 570.12
behind (n) 217.1, 217.5 (a) 175.12
behind acid 87.25
behind a force field 94.9
behind bars 429.21
behindhand 625.10, 833.3, 846.16
behind one's defenses 94.9
behind the curtain 32.5, 928.16
behind the eight ball 1013.22
behind the scenes 32.5, 886.13, 928.16
behind-the-scenes influence 415.4
behind-the-scenes operator 610.6
behind the times 842.16
behind time 833.3
be his to 641.5
be history 837.6
behold 27.12
beholdable 31.6
beholden 150.5, 641.16
beholden to 641.16
beholder 479.3, 918.1
be holier than the thou 354.23
behoof 387.4, 999.4
behoove 641.4
behooving 641.14
be hopeful 124.7
be hopeless 125.9
be hostile 900.6
be hostile to 99.3
be humiliated 137.9
be hurting for 100.16, 963.9
be hypocritical 354.23, 693.4
beige 40.3
beignet 10.44
be ignorant 930.8
be illegitimate 1.2
be imbued with the spirit of 93.11
be imminent 130.10, 514.2, 839.6, 840.2
be impatient 135.4
be imperturbable 855.11
be implicated in 476.5
be impossible 967.4
be impotent 19.7
be impressed with oneself 140.6
be imprisoned 429.18
be improbable 969.2
be in 617.15, 731.16, 864.10
be in a bind 1006.8
be in a brown study 985.9
be in accord with 441.2
be in a certain state 765.5
be in action 889.7
be inadequate 108.5
be in a desperate case 1006.8
be in a dilemma 971.9
be in a hurry 401.8
be in a quandary 971.9
be in a rut 373.12
be in a speech situation 343.6
be inattentive 984.2
be in bloom 310.35
be in cahoots 805.4, 899.2
be in cahoots with 450.3
be incarnated 306.9
be in charge 573.8
be inclined to think 951.10
be incognito 346.8
be in commission 889.7
be incommunicado 584.7
be incomprehensible 522.10
be in concert 708.35
be in conflict 362.6
be in connection 343.6
be in contact 223.9, 343.6
be incredible 955.7
be incumbent on 641.5
be in danger 1006.8
be indebted 150.3, 623.5
be indebted for 897.3
be in debt for 897.3
be in demand 734.12
be indicated 963.9
be indicative of 517.17
be indifferent 982.2
be indiscreet 351.6
be in dissent 333.4
be in earnest 359.8
be in effect 864.10
be ineffective 19.7
be in error 688.8, 975.10
be in existence 761.8
be in extremis 1006.8
be infanticipating 78.12
be in favor of 441.2, 509.9
be inferior 250.4
be infinitely repetitive 118.6
be in flower 310.35
be influential 894.10
be in for 963.10
be in force 864.10, 889.7
be in for it 604.21
be informed 551.15, 570.6, 928.12
be informed of 551.14
be in front 216.7
being (n) 93.3, 305.2, 312.5, 761.1, 761.2, 763.3 (a) 761.13, 838.2
being alive 306.1
being brought to bed 1.1
being done 579.5
being here 221.1
being there 221.1
be in harmony with 455.2
be in heat 75.20, 1019.22
be in heaven 95.12
be in hopes 124.6
be inimical 900.6
be in it 972.13
be in league 450.3
be in line for 639.5
be in love with 104.18
be in luck 1010.11
be in mortal dread of 127.10
be in mortal terror of 127.10
be in need of 963.9
be innocent of 930.10
be innocent of forethought 406.6
be in no hurry 402.3
be in office 609.42
be in one's dotage 303.10
be in one's estimation 946.15
be in one's second childhood 303.10
be in one's thoughts 989.13
be in on the decisions 476.5
be in on the secret 345.7
be in operation 889.7
be in opposition to 333.4
be in over one's head 992.8
be in paradise 95.12
be in peril 1006.8
be in phase 836.4
be in power 612.12
be in process 404.5
be in progress 404.5
be in receipt of 479.6
be in rut 75.20
be insane 926.20
be inscribed 617.15
be inseparable 587.9
be in service 577.13
be in seventh heaven 95.12
be inspired 93.11
be instated 615.13
be in stitches 116.8
be in store 130.7, 840.2
be instructed 570.11
be instrumental 384.7
be insubordinate 454.3
be insufficient 992.8
be in suspense 130.8
be in the batter's box 745.5
be in the best of health 83.6
be in the books 839.6
be in the cards 839.6, 968.4
be in the dark 930.9
be in the debt of 150.3
be in the driver's seat 573.9, 612.12, 894.8
be in the family way 78.12
be in the fire 404.5
be in the hopper 404.5
be in the hot seat 641.9
be in the know 551.15
be in the money 757.5
be in the neighborhood 223.8
be in the offing 840.2
be in the pink 83.6
be in the pipeline 404.5
be in the prime of life 303.9

be in the running 968.4, 972.13
be in the vanguard 816.3
be in the vicinity 223.8
be in the way of 897.3
be in the works 404.5
be in the wrong 975.10
be intimate 75.21
be in time 836.4
be into 866.4, 898.3, 983.5
be in touch 343.6
be intoxicated 88.27
be in tune 93.11, 708.35
be in tune with 455.2
be invalided out 448.2
be invested 417.13
be invisible 32.3
be involved 93.11, 898.3
be in want 619.5
be irrefutable 935.17
be jealous 153.3, 154.2
be jealous of one's good name 136.7
be jealous of one's repute 136.7
bejewel 498.9
bejeweled 498.11
be jobber for 734.8
be Johnny on the spot 324.3
be Johnny-on-the-spot 439.10
be judgmental 946.8
be judicious 946.8
be just 649.5
be just around the corner 840.2
be just like one 130.10
be just right 973.10
be just the thing 995.3
be just the ticket 95.7, 405.15
be just what the doctor ordered 95.7, 995.3
be keen 285.6, 324.3
be kept waiting 846.14
be killed 307.23, 308.21
be kind 143.9
be knocked up 78.12
be known as 527.13
be known by 527.13
bel 50.7
belabor 604.12, 849.9, 997.14
belabored 849.15
belaboring 604.4
be lacking 762.5
be laid by the heels 85.47
be late 846.7
belated 846.16
belatedness 846.1
be latent 519.3
belaud 509.12
belay 800.7, 855.8, 857.6
bel canto 708.13
belch (n) 58.3, 671.6, 909.9 (v) 58.9, 671.13, 909.28
belching 909.9
beldam 110.12, 304.3, 593.7, 671.9
beleaguer 96.13, 212.5, 459.19
beleaguered 96.22, 212.10
beleaguerment 212.1, 459.5
be learned in 928.13
be led to believe 953.10
be left 256.5, 846.14
be left at the post 846.10
be left at the starting gate 844.5, 846.10
be left behind 846.10
be left over 256.5
be lengthy 267.5
bel-esprit 489.12
be let down 132.4
belfry 272.6
Belgian hare 311.23
be liable 897.3
be liable for 641.6
Belial 680.4
be liberal with 478.12
belie 335.4, 350.3, 354.16, 451.6, 958.4
belied 958.7
belief 675.1, 953.1, 953.2, 970.5
beliefs 93.1
belief system 675.1, 952.2, 953.3
believability 953.8
believable 953.24
believableness 953.8
believe 692.6, 951.10, 953.10
believe anything 954.5
believe at the drop of a hat 954.5
believed 953.23
believe in 953.15
believer 675.15, 692.4, 953.9
believe without reservation 953.10
believing (n) 953.1 (a) 692.8, 953.21
believing, the 692.5, 953.9
be light 298.6
be like 784.7
be like King Charles's head 989.13
be limited by 959.6
be listened to 894.12
belittle 252.9, 510.14, 512.8, 950.2
belittled 252.10
belittlement 252.5, 950.1
belittle oneself 137.7
belittler 510.9, 512.6
belittling (n) 252.5, 512.1 (a) 512.13
be livid 152.15
bell (n) 54.4, 517.10, 517.15, 711.6, 754.1, 832.2, 857.2 (v) 53.10, 60.2
belladonna 86.12
bell, book, and candle 691.5
bellbottoms 5.18
bellboy 353.4, 577.5
bell cow 574.6
belle 500.10, 1016.7
belles lettres 547.12, 718.1
belletrist 547.15, 718.4
belletristic 547.24, 718.7
bellhop 353.4, 577.5
bellicose 110.26, 456.17, 458.20, 589.10, 779.6
bellicoseness 458.10
bellicosity 456.3, 458.10, 589.3
bellied 282.8, 283.16
belligerence 110.7, 456.3, 458.1, 458.10, 589.3
belligerency 458.1, 458.10
belligerent (n) 461.1 (a) 110.26, 456.17, 458.20, 589.10, 779.6
belling 54.13
bell lap 457.12
bell-like 279.13
bellman 353.3, 353.4, 577.5
bell mare 574.6
Bellona 458.12
bellow (n) 59.1 (v) 59.6, 60.2, 105.16, 524.25
bellowing 105.25
bellow like a bull 59.6
bellow out 59.8
bellows 2.22, 318.17
bell ringer 710.11
bell ringing 54.3
bells and whistles 254.4, 498.3, 993.4
bell-shaped 279.13, 282.12
Bell's palsy 85.25
bell the cat 492.10, 493.6
bell tower 272.6
bellwether (n) 311.7, 574.6, 816.1 (a) 337.5
belly (n) 2.18, 199.1, 282.1, 548.6 (v) 283.11
bellyache (n) 26.5, 85.29, 115.5 (v) 108.6, 115.16
bellyacher 108.4, 110.11, 115.9, 333.3
bellyaching (n) 115.5 (a) 108.8, 115.20
bellyband 901.18
belly buster 367.1
bellybutton 208.2
belly dancer 707.1
belly flop 194.3, 367.1
bellyful 794.3, 994.1
belly girt 819.1
belly-god 672.3
belly gunner 185.4
bellying (n) 283.1, 283.2 (a) 283.15
bellyland 184.43
belly landing 184.18
belly laugh (n) 116.4, 489.6 (v) 116.8
bellylike 282.8
belly out 283.11
belly up (v) 307.19, 625.7 (a) 395.29, 473.8, 619.10
belly-up 625.11, 820.10
bellywhop 177.35
belly whopper 367.1
Belmont Stakes 757.1
be loaded 618.11
be located 159.10, 221.6
be logical 935.17
be long 267.5, 737.23
belong 159.9, 617.15
be long acquainted 587.9
belonger 617.11
belonging 775.11
belongings 471.2
be long in the tooth 413.19
be long of the market 737.23
belong to 469.7, 775.5
belong to nature 767.6
belong to the past 842.9
be loquacious 540.8
be lost 182.44, 307.18, 522.11
be lost in thought 985.9
be lousy with 221.7, 991.5
beloved (n) 104.9 (a) 104.23
beloved object 104.9
below contempt 98.18
below par 85.56, 1000.9, 1005.10
below standard 1005.10
below the belt 650.10
below the limen of hearing 51.10
below the mark 1005.10
below the salt 250.6, 606.8
below the threshold of hearing 51.10
below zero 1023.14
Belsen 308.12
belt (n) 5.19, 5.31, 47.5, 105.3, 231.1, 242.1, 271.4, 280.3, 296.1, 317.2, 403.3, 411.1, 604.3, 605.1, 646.3, 754.3, 760.3, 902.5, 902.6 (v) 209.7, 604.12, 745.5, 800.9, 902.15
belted 209.11
belted knight 461.1
belt in 209.7
belting 604.4
belt out 708.38
belt-tightening 425.1, 635.1, 667.1
be lucky 1010.11
belvedere 27.8, 89.4
be made one 563.15
be made that way 767.6
be made up of 796.3
be magnetic 907.4
be manifest 348.7
be master 612.11
be master of 413.18, 928.13
be master of the situation 612.12
be meaningless 520.4
be mentored 570.11
be merry with 489.13
be met with 221.6, 761.8, 831.5
be mindful 143.10, 983.6
bemingle 797.10
bemire 80.15, 243.2
be misfortuned 1011.9
be misguided 975.10
be misled 975.10
be missed 984.5
bemist 319.7
be mistaken 688.8, 975.10
bemoan 113.6, 115.10
bemoaning (n) 115.1 (a) 115.18
be mobbed 770.16
be moderate 467.6, 670.5
be more than a match for 412.6
be moribund 307.25
be moved 93.11
bemud 80.15
bemuse 88.22
bemused 88.31, 985.11
bemusement 985.2
be mute 51.5
ben 237.2
be nailed to the cross 96.19
be nauseated 99.4
bench 84.1, 272.4, 417.10, 423.1, 595.5, 595.6, 617.7, 739.1, 749.2, 862.2, 901.15
bench, the 576.1, 745.2
bench coach 745.2
bencher 596.1
benchfellow 616.5
bench jockey 745.2

benchmark 159.1, 300.2, 517.10, 997.6, 1042.18
benchmarking 943.1
bench scientist 942.6
bench test 938.6, 942.1, 942.3
bench trial 598.5
benchwarmer 250.2, 745.2, 746.2
bench warrant 598.12
benchwork 724.2
bend (n) 155.2, 164.1, 204.3, 204.7, 278.2, 279.3, 647.2, 913.3 (v) 155.6, 161.5, 164.3, 164.5, 204.9, 265.5, 278.5, 279.6, 412.10, 432.9, 433.10, 800.9, 867.3, 894.7, 913.8, 913.9, 980.9, 1047.7
bendability 1047.2
bendable 1047.9
bend an ear 48.10
bend an ear to 983.7
bend back 279.6
bender 88.6, 487.1
bend every effort 725.9
bending (n) 164.2, 279.3, 354.9 (a) 1047.9
bending the knee 155.2
bending the truth 265.2
bend might and main 725.9
bend one's ear 524.20
bend one's steps course 177.18
bend one's steps for 161.9
bend one's steps to 177.25
bend over backward 324.3, 403.11
bend over backwards 101.6, 339.7, 649.5
bends, the 1075.10
bend sinister 561.5, 647.2, 661.6, 674.2
bend the elbow 88.25
bend the eyes 27.13
bend the head 155.6
bend the knee 138.7, 155.6, 913.9
bend the knee to 433.10
bend the mind 931.9
bend the mind upon 931.10
bend the neck 155.6, 433.10
bend the truth 354.19
bend to 433.10, 896.3
bend to one's will 432.9, 433.10, 612.14, 894.7
bend to one's yoke 433.10
bendwise 204.19
bendy 204.20
be near 223.8
be near the truth 941.6
beneath contempt 98.18, 998.21, 1000.9
beneath notice 998.22
beneath one 661.11
beneath one's dignity 250.6, 661.11
beneath one's station 250.6
be necessary 963.10
Benedicite 696.3
benedicite 696.5
benedict 563.7
Benedict Arnold 357.10
benediction 150.2, 696.5
benedictional 696.16
benedictory 696.16
benefaction 120.1, 143.7, 478.7
benefactor 449.7, 592.1
benefactress 592.1
benefice 698.9
benefice-holder 699.7
beneficence 143.4
beneficent 143.15, 449.22
beneficial 81.5, 387.18, 449.21, 999.12
beneficial interest 471.4
beneficialness 81.1, 449.10, 995.1, 999.1
beneficiary 470.2, 479.4, 699.7
beneficience 133.8
benefit (n) 143.7, 254.4, 387.3, 387.4, 449.1, 471.4, 478.7, 704.12, 999.4 (v) 143.12, 387.17, 449.11, 478.17, 592.3, 995.3, 999.10
benefiter 592.1
benefit from 387.15
benefit performance 704.12
benefits 624.6
benefits forgot 151.1
benefitting 592.4
be neglectful 340.6
be negligent 340.6, 414.13
benevolence 133.8, 143.4, 143.7, 145.1, 148.1, 427.2, 478.7, 652.2, 999.1
benevolences 143.6
benevolent 143.15, 148.6, 427.8, 449.22, 652.6, 999.12
benevolent despotism 612.8
benevolent disposition 143.2, 143.4
benevolentness 143.4
benevolist 143.8
Bengal heat 1019.5
be nice 143.9, 321.5
benight 30.7
benighted 30.9, 315.10, 930.15
benightedness 30.1, 930.3
benightment 930.3
benign 81.5, 133.17, 143.13, 427.8, 449.22, 999.21
benignancy 133.8, 143.1, 999.9
benignant 133.17, 143.13, 427.8, 449.22
benignity 133.8, 143.1, 143.7, 427.2, 999.1, 999.9
benign tumor 85.39
benison 696.5, 999.4
bennies 87.4
be noisy 53.9
be no love lost between 99.3
be no more 307.26, 395.23, 762.6, 820.7
be no revelation 348.7
be no secret 348.7
be noticeable 31.4
be not one's day 414.11
be not with it 985.9
bent (n) 100.3, 161.1, 204.3, 371.5, 413.5, 896.1, 978.3, 980.3 (a) 87.24, 88.33, 265.10, 278.6, 279.7, 978.8
benthal 275.15
Benthamism 143.4
benthic 275.15
benthic zone 240.4
benthon 311.29
benthonic 275.15, 311.53
benthonic division 275.4
benthonic zone 275.4
benthopelagic 275.15
benthos 199.1, 240.5, 275.4, 311.29
benthoscope 367.5
bento box 195.1
bent on 100.22, 359.16, 978.8
bent on pleasure 663.5
bent out of shape 152.30
be null and void 762.5
benumb 25.4, 94.8, 120.5, 1023.10
benumbed 25.6, 94.13, 331.20
benumbedness 94.4
benumbing 120.9
benz 87.4
benzene nucleus 1038.7
benzene ring 1038.7
benzine 1025.20
be obligated 150.3, 641.4
be obligated for 623.5
be obliged 150.3, 623.5, 641.4, 963.10
be oblivious 990.4
be observant 27.13, 692.6
be obsessed with 983.8
be obstinate 453.2
be obvious 31.4, 521.4
be occupied with 724.11
be of advantage 387.17
be of another mind 363.6
be off 188.6, 188.8, 757.5
be off and running 845.5
be of favorable disposition 324.3
be off one's guard 984.2
be off the track 975.10
be of good cheer 107.5, 109.10, 124.7
be of good hope 124.7
be of like mind 788.6
be of no importance 998.11
be of one mind 788.6
be of one mind with 332.9
be of service 387.17, 999.10
be of service to 387.17
be of some help 449.11
be of the opinion 953.11
be of the same class 943.7
be of the same mind 788.6
be of two minds 362.6, 971.9
be of use 387.17
be OK 788.8, 973.10
be old friends 587.9
be on 87.22, 731.19
be on about 538.8
be on a collision course 169.2, 223.11, 902.13
be on a collision course with 167.3
be on an ego trip 140.6, 651.4
be on beam ends 182.43
be on call 90.14, 130.8
be on cloud nine 95.12
be on deck 221.8
be one all over 130.10
be one's charge 641.7
be one's concern 641.7
be one's due 639.4
be oneself 581.2
be oneself again 83.7, 120.8, 396.20
be one's fate 963.10, 972.11
be one's mission 641.7
be one's office 641.7
be one's outlook 130.7
be one's own boss 430.20
be one's own man 430.20
be one's probable destiny 130.7
be one's probable fate 130.7
be one's prospect 130.7
be one's responsibility 641.7
be one up on 415.11
be on everyone's lips 352.16
be on good terms 587.9
be on hand 221.8
be on one's best behavior 321.5, 326.2
be on one's feet 200.7
be on one's good behavior 321.5
be on one's guard 339.8, 494.7
be on one's head 641.7
be on one's last leg 16.8
be on one's mettle 403.13
be on one's mind 989.13
be on one's uppers 619.5
be on one's way 188.8
be on pins and needles 126.6, 127.10, 130.8
be on shpilkes 126.6
be on standby 130.8
be on tenterhooks 126.6, 130.8
be on the alert 339.8
be on the anvil 404.5
be on the back of 96.13
be on the ball 983.8
be on the fence 368.8
be on the hook for 641.6
be on the horizon 840.2
be on the long side of the market 737.23
be on the lookout 339.8, 494.7, 1008.20
be on the lookout for 130.6
be on the money 973.10
be on the point of 405.10
be on the qui vive 339.8, 494.7
be on the rag 12.18
be on the receiving end 479.6
be on the right scent 941.6
be on the rolls 617.15
be on the safe side 1007.2
be on the same wavelength 455.2
be on the short side of the market 737.23
be on the skids 410.11, 1011.11
be on the spot 641.9, 1006.8
be on the waiting list 130.8
be on the watch 339.8, 494.7
be on the watch for 130.6
be on to 941.8
be open to 324.3
be opposed to 779.4
be optimistic 124.8
be ordained 698.11
be otherwise occupied 844.3
be outdistanced 846.10
be out for blood 359.8
be out of all patience 135.5
be out of it 972.14, 985.9

be out of line 975.10
be out of one's depth 522.11
be out of one's mind 926.20
be out-of-pocket 626.5
be out of step 789.5
be out of the money 757.5
be out of the running 972.14
be out of the woods 396.19
be outrun 846.10
be over 101.7
be overdue 846.7
be overextended 623.6
be overfamiliar with 156.4
be overly impressed with oneself 140.6
be overpossessive 153.3
be overpriced 632.6
be over the hill 303.10
be pacifistic 670.5
be paid 624.20
be painless 1014.10
be painstaking 339.7
be palsy-walsy with 587.11
be parallel 203.4
be paralyzed with fear 127.11
be paranoid 153.3
be part and parcel of 767.6
be partial to 63.5, 104.18
be partners in 476.6
be past 837.6
be patient 134.4
be peckish 100.19
be pensioned 448.2
be pensioned off 448.2
be permitted 443.13
be persuaded 375.24, 441.2, 441.3, 953.11
be persuasive 894.10
be pessimistic 125.9
be pinched 619.5
be pious 692.6
bepiss 1065.12
be plain 521.4
beplaster 295.24
be pleased 95.12, 107.5
be pleased with 95.13
be plentiful 991.5
be poised 238.22
be poleaxed 1011.10
be polite 504.10
be poor 619.5
be possessed of 469.4
be possessed of the devil 110.13
be possessive 153.3
be possible 966.4
bepraise 509.12
bepraisement 509.5
be precise 973.11
be predicated on 959.6
be predisposed 947.2
be pregnant 78.12
be preoccupied 844.3
be preoccupied with 983.5
be prepared 405.14
be present 221.6, 761.8
be present at 221.8
be present in 761.11
be prior 834.3
be probable 968.4
be prodigal with 993.14
be productive 890.7, 892.11
be proficient in 928.13
be profitable 472.13
be prolonged 267.5
be prominent 997.12
be promiscuous 665.19
be promising 968.4
be proof against 453.2
be prosperous 1010.9
be proud 136.4
be proud of 136.5
be punished 604.19
be pushed to the wall 963.11
be put out of countenance 137.9
be put out to pasture 448.2
be put to one's wit's end 1011.9
be put to the blush 137.9
be putty in the hands of 432.12
be quarrelsome 456.11
bequeath 256.6, 478.18, 629.3
bequeathable 478.23, 629.5
bequeathal 478.10, 479.2, 629.1
bequest 478.10, 479.2
be quits 506.7
be quits with 863.4
be rash 493.5
berate 510.19
berating 510.7
be ravenous 100.19
be read between the lines 519.3
be ready 324.3, 405.14
be ready and waiting 845.5
be ready for 130.6
be ready to sink through the floor 137.9
be realistic 920.10
be realized 831.5
be reasonable 920.10, 935.17
bereave 307.27, 480.21, 566.6
bereaved 307.34, 473.8, 619.8
bereaved of 473.8
bereavement 307.10, 473.1, 480.6
bereavement counseling 307.10
bereave of life 308.13
be reborn 858.12
be received 186.6, 479.8, 953.20
be reckless 493.5
be recognized 662.11, 894.12
be reconciled to 107.5
be redolent of 69.6, 784.7
be reflected 54.7
bereft 112.26, 307.34, 473.8, 619.8
bereft of 992.13
bereft of life 307.29
bereft of light 30.9
bereft of reason 926.26
be regarded 946.15
be regarded as 349.10
be regulated by 867.3
be relaxed 121.8
be released 430.18
be relieved 120.8
be religious 692.6
be remembered 989.13
be reminiscent of 784.7
be remunerated 624.20
be renewed 852.6
be resentful 152.12
be resolved 359.8
be responsible for 436.5, 573.8, 641.6, 889.5, 897.4
be revealed 31.4, 351.8
berg 1023.5
bergamot oil 70.2
berg ice 1023.5
Bergsonian 952.12
beribbon 498.9
beribboned 498.11
beriberi 85.33
be rid of 909.13
be right 973.10, 995.3
be righteous 649.5
be rightly served 639.6
berk 924.8
Berkeleian (n) 1053.4 (a) 952.12, 1053.8
Berkeleianism 1053.3
Berlin wall 211.5
berm 234.2, 383.2
Bermuda shorts 5.18
bernice 87.7
be robbed of choice 963.11
berries 728.2
berry 10.38, 310.4, 310.31
berry-brown 40.3
berserk (n) 671.9, 926.15 (a) 105.25, 926.30
berserker 671.9, 926.15
berth (n) 180.16, 228.4, 724.5, 1009.6 (v) 225.7, 225.10
be ruined 625.7
beryl-blue 45.3
beryl-green 44.4
berylline 44.4, 45.3
be safe 1007.2
be salaried 624.20
be sanctimonious 693.4
be satisfactory 107.6
be satisfied 953.14
be seasick 909.26
be seated 173.10, 913.10
be secure in the belief 953.14
be security for 436.5
beseech 440.11, 696.13
beseeching (n) 440.2 (a) 440.17
beseechment 440.2, 696.4
beseem 641.4
be seen 31.4
be seen in its true colors 351.8
be seen no more 34.2
be seen with half an eye 348.7
be seized by 85.47
be seized of 469.4, 472.8, 521.7
be seized with wonder 122.5
be self-evident 521.4
be self-explanatory 521.4
be sensible of 24.6
be sensitive 456.11
be sensitive to 24.6
be sent away empty-handed 992.7
be sent back 54.7
beset (v) 96.13, 126.5, 212.5, 389.7, 440.12, 459.19, 910.6, 926.25, 1013.13 (a) 96.22, 96.24, 126.8, 212.10, 910.11, 1013.20
be set by the current 182.29
besetment 212.1, 1013.3
besetting 864.12, 1013.18
besetting sin 654.2
beset with danger 1006.9
be shamed 661.7
be shattered 1011.10
be short 737.23
be short of the market 737.23
be shut of 909.13
be sick 909.26
beside 218.6
beside oneself 95.17, 105.25, 152.28, 926.30, 985.10
beside oneself with joy 95.17
beside the mark 776.7, 975.16
beside the point 776.7
beside the question 776.7
besiege 212.5, 440.12, 459.19
besieged 212.10
besiegement 459.5
besieging 212.1
be significant of 517.17
be silent 51.5
be single 565.5
be situated 159.10, 221.6
be skeptical 955.6, 956.3
beslobber 511.5
be slow off the mark 846.10
be slow to accept 956.3
be slow to believe 956.3
beslubber 511.5
besmear 35.14, 80.16, 295.24, 1004.6
besmirch 38.7, 80.16, 512.10, 661.9, 1004.6
besmirched 38.11, 80.21, 665.23, 1004.10
besmirchment 80.4
be smitten 104.21
besmoke 80.15, 1004.6
besmutch 80.16
besnow 37.5
be so 765.5
be so good as to 137.8, 141.8
besoil 80.16
be so in fact 973.8
be sold 734.12
be solicitous 983.5
be somebody 662.10, 997.12
be something 662.10, 997.12
be somewhere else 985.9
be sorry for 113.6, 145.3
besot 25.4, 88.22
besotted 88.31, 923.8, 926.33
besottedness 88.1
besotted with 104.27
bespangle 47.7, 498.9
bespangled 47.13, 498.11, 1025.39
be spared 306.11
bespatter 80.18, 512.10, 661.9, 1065.12
bespeak 440.9, 517.17, 518.8, 524.26, 615.14, 957.8
bespeaking 615.4
bespeckle 47.7, 1004.5
bespeckled 1004.9
bespectacled 29.11
be spent 626.6
be sphinxlike 522.10
be spoiling for 324.3
bespoke 5.48, 892.18
be sponsor for 438.9, 641.9
bespot 47.7, 1004.5
bespread (v) 221.7, 910.5 (a) 910.10
besprinkle 771.6, 797.11, 1065.12

best (n) 820.5 (v) 249.6, 249.7, 411.5, 412.6 (a) 249.13, 999.16
best, the 121.3, 249.5, 999.8
be staggered 1011.10
bestain 1004.6
be stamped on one's memory 989.13
be startled 131.5
best ball 751.3
best-before date 10.50
best behavior 326.1
best bet 972.8
best bib and tucker 5.10
best bower 758.2
best by a long chalk, the 249.13
best by a long shot, the 249.13
best case 124.1
best-case 124.12
best clothes 5.10
bestead 387.17
bested 412.14
best effort 403.1
best ever, the 999.8
best friend 588.1, 588.2
best friend forever 588.2
best girl 104.14
bestial 144.26, 311.39, 497.12, 663.6, 671.21
bestiality 75.11, 144.11, 144.12, 497.3, 663.2, 1000.2
bestialize 144.15
bestie 588.2
be still 173.7, 329.2
be stillborn 410.15
bestir oneself 330.11, 401.5
best-known 662.16
best love 504.8
best man 563.4, 616.6
best one can, the 403.4
best one knows how, the 403.4
be stood up 846.14
bestow 387.13, 478.12, 643.6
bestowable 478.23
bestowal 478.1, 643.2
bestow consideration upon 931.13
bestowed 478.24
bestower 478.11
bestow honor upon 662.12
bestowment 478.1
bestow on 478.12
bestow one's affections on 104.21
bestow one's hand upon 563.15
bestow thought upon 931.13
best part 792.6, 997.7
best people 578.6
best people, the 249.5
best-quality 249.13
bestraddle 193.12, 272.11, 295.30, 901.22
be straight 277.4
be straight man for 704.29
be strapped 619.5
best regards 504.8, 820.5
bestrew 771.4
be stricken 1011.10
be stricken by 85.47
be stricken drunk 88.26
bestride 193.12, 272.11, 295.30, 612.14, 901.22, 910.8
be strong 15.9
be strong in 866.4
best room 197.5
be struck down 85.47
be struck dumb 525.7
best seat in the house 33.6
bestseller 409.3, 554.1, 999.5
be stuck on oneself 140.6
be stuck-up 157.7
be stuck with 424.9
be stumped 930.10
be stupid 922.12, 923.6
best wishes 149.1, 504.8, 585.3, 820.5
be subjected 897.3
be subjected to 831.8, 897.3
be successful 409.7
be such 765.5
be suckered 954.6
be suicidal 112.16
be superannuated 448.2
be superseded 390.9
be superstitious 954.7
be surprised 406.6
be swallowed 953.20
be sweet on 104.19
be swept off one's feet 104.21
be symptomatic of 517.17
bet (n) 759.2, 759.3, 759.10 (v) 759.25, 962.9, 972.12
beta 942.3
beta blocker 86.32
betacism 524.13
be taciturn 51.5
be tactful 944.5
beta decay 1038.8
bet against 759.25
be taken 632.8
be taken aback 131.5, 406.6
be taken as 349.10, 517.18
be taken by death 307.18
be taken by surprise 131.5
be taken down a rung 137.9
be taken in 954.6
be taken to the cleaners 625.7
be taken unawares 406.6
betake oneself 177.18
betake oneself to 177.25, 387.14
be talking 518.8
be talking about 518.8
be tantmount to 790.5
beta particle 1033.3, 1037.4
beta radiator 1037.5
be tasteful 944.5
beta test 1042.18
be taught 570.11
be taught a lesson 570.10
betcha 759.25
be tedious 96.12, 118.6
be telegraphic 537.5
bête noire 103.3, 127.9, 589.6, 680.9, 1001.1
be terminal 307.25
be thankful 150.3
be theatrical 93.13
be the bane of one's existence 98.16
be the bellwether 165.2
be the case 761.8, 973.8
be the cause of 886.10
be the death of 395.12, 743.21
be the decisive factor 894.10
be the dove of peace 670.7
be the duty of 641.5
be the effect of 887.5
be the equivalent of 349.10
be the fall guy 862.6
be the fashion 864.10
be the frontrunner 216.7
be the goat 862.6
be the incumbent 609.42
bethel 703.1
be the making of 392.9, 449.11, 999.10
be the mark 517.17
be the matter 1013.13
be the mouthpiece of 576.14
be the omen of 133.9
be the one that counts 894.10
be the patsy 862.6
be the plaything of 432.12
be the point 165.2, 405.12
be the point man 165.2
be the prey of 897.3
be the puppet of 432.12
be the rage 578.9, 864.10
be there 159.9, 221.6, 761.8
be the reason for 375.20
be there for all to see 348.7
be the rule 864.10
be the saving of 398.3
be the sign of 517.17
be the soul of discretion 345.7
be the sport of 432.12
be the sport of winds and waves 917.15
be the style 578.9
be the thing 578.9, 864.10
be the voice of 576.14
be the worse for 393.16
be the worse for wear 393.16
bethink 983.5
bethink oneself 931.8, 983.5, 989.9
bethink oneself of 931.16
be thin-skinned 456.11
be thoroughly grounded in 928.13
be thoughtful of 143.10
be thought of 946.15
be threatened 1006.8
be thus 765.5
betide 831.5, 972.11
be timely 843.6
be to come 839.6
betoken 133.11, 348.5, 517.17, 518.8, 957.8
betokening 133.3
betokenment 133.3
be told 551.15
bet on 759.25, 953.16, 962.9, 970.9
bet one's bottom dollar on 953.16, 970.9
bet one's life 970.9
betongue 510.19
be too deep 522.10
be too deep for 415.11
be too good for 412.6
be too much for 412.6, 415.11, 1013.13
be to one's liking 95.6
be too quick on the draw 365.7
be too quick on the trigger 365.7
be too quick on the uptake 365.7
be touch and go 971.11
be touched 93.11
be touchy 456.11
be tough 1049.3
be to windward of 182.26
be transparent 1029.3
be traumatized 85.47
betray 351.6, 356.14, 370.6, 551.12, 645.12, 645.14, 665.20
betray a confidence 351.6
betrayal 351.2, 363.2, 370.2, 645.8, 665.6
betrayed 132.5
betrayed hope 132.1
betrayer 357.10, 551.6, 660.9, 665.12
betraying 351.10, 645.22
betray itself 941.9
betrayment 645.8
betray oneself 33.8
betroth 436.6
betrothal 104.5, 436.3
betrothed (n) 104.16 (a) 436.8
betrothment 436.3
be true 761.8, 973.8
be truthful 973.8
better (v) 249.6, 392.9, 852.7 (a) 249.12, 371.25, 392.14, 852.10
bettered 392.13
better for 392.14
better half 563.6, 563.8
bettering (n) 392.1 (a) 392.15
betterment 392.1, 852.1, 999.4
better nature 113.4
better off 392.14
better oneself 392.9
better part 257.11, 792.6, 883.2
better place, a 839.2
better self 113.2, 865.5
better sort 608.3
better sort, the 607.2
better than nothing 999.20
better thoughts 363.1
bet the ranch on 970.9
betting 757.4, 759.1
betting house 759.19
betting parlor 759.19
betting proposition 759.2
betting system 759.4
bettor 759.21
be turbulent 915.12
be turned off by 510.10
be turned on by 93.11
be turned on to 93.11
be tutored 570.11
between a rock and a hard place 1006.13, 1011.14, 1013.23
betweenmaid 577.8
between Scylla and Charybdis 1006.13, 1013.23
between the devil and the deep blue sea 1006.13, 1011.14, 1013.23
between the hammer and the anvil 1006.13
between the lines 519.5
between two fires 1006.13
between two stools 1013.23
between us 345.14

betwixt and between 539.4, 1005.7
betwixt sleep and waking 985.11
be unable 19.8
be unable to comprehend 522.11
be unable to get into one's thick skull 522.11
be unable to get through one's head 522.11
be unable to help oneself 365.7
be unable to put two words together 525.7
be unable to recall 990.5
be unable to recollect 990.5
be unable to retain 990.4
be unable to say "boo" to a goose 491.7
be unable to see 522.11
be unbelievable 955.7
be uncertain 539.3, 955.6, 971.9
be uncritical 954.5
be under an obligation 150.3, 641.4
be understandable 521.4
be under the gun 401.8
be under the impression 953.11, 953.12
be under the necessity of 963.10
be under the sea 182.17
be underway 404.5
be undesirable 98.10
be unexpected 131.6
be unfaithful 645.12
be unflappable 855.11
be unfriendly 583.4
be ungrateful 151.3
be unguarded 351.6
be uniform with 788.6
be unimportant 998.11
be unlucky 1011.9
be unmarried 565.5
be unmindful of 933.2
be unmoveable 360.4
be unmoved 146.2, 360.4, 442.3
be unpleasant 98.10
be unprepared 406.6
be unproductive 891.3
be unready 406.6
be unseen 32.3
be unsuccessful 410.9
be untruthful 354.19
be unwary 984.2
be unwilling 325.3, 442.3
be up 745.5
be up against it 1011.9
be up and doing 17.11, 330.11
be up and stirring 845.5
be up a tree 1013.12
be upbeat 124.8
be up on 928.13
be uppermost in one's thoughts 926.25
be uppermost in the mind 931.20
be up there 155.7
be up to 18.11, 405.15
be up to something 381.9
be used to 373.11
be used up 388.4
be useful 449.17
be useless 391.8
be vain as a peacock 140.6
bevel (n) 204.4, 278.4, 548.6 (v) 204.10 (a) 204.15
bevel bearing 915.7
beveled 204.15
bevel gear 1040.9
bevel protractor 278.4
bevel square 278.4
beverage 8.4, 10.49, 88.13, 1061.2
be versatile 413.21
be vested 417.13
be victorious 411.3
be vigilant 23.3, 27.13, 339.8, 981.3
be vigorous 17.11
be visible 31.4
be vital 306.8
be voted in 609.42
bevue 414.5, 975.3
bevy 770.3, 770.6, 884.3
be wafted 184.36
bewail 113.6, 115.10
bewailing (n) 115.1 (a) 115.18
be wanting 762.5
beware 494.7
be warm 941.6
be washed in the blood of the Lamb 692.7
be watchful 27.13, 339.8, 981.3
be way ahead 165.2
be way up there 155.7
be wedded to 953.13
be well-informed 928.13
be well-preserved 83.6
be where the buck stops 641.9
bewhisker 3.20
bewhiskered 3.25, 117.9
be wholesaler for 734.8
be widely reputed 155.7
bewilder 122.6, 971.12, 985.7
bewildered 122.9, 971.24, 1013.24
bewildering 122.10, 971.27
bewilderment 122.1, 971.3, 985.3
be willing 324.3, 441.2
be wiped out 762.6
be wise as an owl 920.10
be wise as a serpent 920.10
be wise to 941.8
bewitch 95.10, 104.22, 377.7, 680.16, 690.13, 691.9, 1000.6
bewitched 104.27, 122.9, 691.13, 870.16
bewitcher 690.9
bewitchery 377.1, 690.1, 691.2
bewitching 97.7, 377.8, 691.11
bewitchingness 377.2
bewitchment 95.2, 97.2, 377.1, 691.2
be with child 78.12
be with it 521.8
be with one 521.8
be without end 823.2
be with young 78.12
be wont 373.11
be worth one's while 472.13
be worthwhile 472.13
be worthy of 639.5
be worthy of comparison 943.7
be wreathed in smiles 95.12
be wrong 688.8, 975.10
bey 575.9, 575.12
beyond, the 307.1, 839.2
beyond all praise 509.20, 1002.6
beyond a shadow of doubt 970.16
beyond belief 923.11, 955.10
beyond compare 249.15
beyond comparison 249.15
beyond comprehension 823.3
beyond control 361.12
beyond expectation 131.10
beyond hope 125.15
beyond one 522.14, 967.8
beyond one's comprehension 522.13
beyond one's control 967.8
beyond one's depth 992.9
beyond one's means 632.11
beyond one's power 967.8
beyond price 632.10
beyond question 970.16
beyond reach 967.9
beyond recall 125.15, 990.8
beyond remedy 125.15
beyond reproach 644.13, 657.8
beyond the bounds of possibility 967.7
beyond the bounds of reason 967.7
beyond the pale 444.7, 510.24, 773.8
beyond understanding 522.13
beyond words 98.19
bezel 204.4, 290.1
B-girl 665.16
Bhagavad-Gita 683.8
bhang 87.20
bhikhari 699.13
bhikkhu 565.2, 699.16
bhikku 699.14
bhikshu 667.2, 699.13
bialy 10.31
bialystoker 10.31
biannual 850.8
Bias 921.4
bias (n) 100.3, 164.1, 204.3, 204.7, 371.5, 650.3, 896.1 (v) 164.5, 204.9, 265.6, 894.7, 896.3 (a) 204.15, 204.19
bias (n) 978.3, 980.3 (v) 980.9
biased 204.15, 204.19, 265.11, 650.11, 980.12
bias one's judgment 980.9
biasways 204.19
biaswise 204.19
biatch 110.12
biathlon 744.1, 753.3, 755.2
biaxial 875.7
bib (n) 5.17 (v) 8.29, 88.24
bibacious 88.35
bibaciousness 88.2
bibacity 88.2
bib and tucker 5.6
bibber 88.11
bibble-babble 520.2, 540.3
bibelot 498.4, 998.5
bibing 88.4
Bible 683.2
bible 683.1
Bible, the 673.8
bible, the 554.1
Bible belt 231.7
Bible oath 334.4
Bible-thump 543.11
Bible-thumping (n) 354.6, 543.1 (a) 683.11, 692.11
Bible truth 973.3
Biblical 683.11
biblioclast 395.8
bibliofilm 714.10
bibliogenesis 554.19
bibliogony 554.19
bibliographer 547.15, 718.4
bibliographical 554.20
bibliography 554.12, 554.19, 558.4, 574.10, 871.3, 928.9
biblioklept 554.18
bibliokleptomania 482.12
bibliolater 554.18, 929.4
bibliolatrist 929.4
bibliolatrous 697.7
bibliolatry 687.5, 692.3, 928.5
bibliological 554.20
bibliology 554.19
bibliomane 554.18, 929.4
bibliomania 928.5
bibliomaniac 554.18, 929.4
bibliopegic 554.20
bibliopegist 554.2
bibliopegy 554.14
bibliophage 554.18, 929.4
bibliophagic 928.22
bibliophile 554.18, 929.4
bibliophilic 928.22
bibliophilism 928.5
bibliophilist 929.4
bibliopole 554.16
bibliopolic 554.20
bibliopolism 554.19
bibliotaph 554.18
bibliotheca 558.1
bibliothecal 554.20
bibliothecary 554.20
bibliothèque 558.1
Bibliothèque Nationale 558.1
bib nozzle 239.9
bibulosity 88.2
bibulous 88.35, 187.17, 669.7
bibulousness 88.2
bicameral 613.11, 875.7
bicameral legislature 613.1
bicentenary 850.4, 882.8
bicentennial 850.4, 882.8
biceps 2.7, 906.5
bicker (n) 456.5, 935.4 (v) 456.11, 917.12, 935.16, 936.9, 1025.25
bickerer 461.1
bickering (n) 456.3, 457.1, 935.4, 936.5, 1025.8 (a) 456.17, 917.18, 936.14, 1025.36
bicker over 457.21
bicoastal 207.8
bicolor 47.9
bicolored 47.9
biconjugate 873.8
bicorn 279.11
bicuspid (n) 2.8 (a) 875.7
bicycle (n) 179.8 (v) 84.4, 177.33
bicycle courier 174.5
bicycle lane 383.2
bicycle messenger 353.1

bicycle motocross (n) 744.1 (v) 177.33
bicycle path 383.2
bicycler 178.11
bicycle race 457.12
bicycle taxi 179.13
bicycle touring 744.1
bicycling 177.6, 744.1
bicyclist 178.11
bid (n) 403.2, 439.1, 440.2, 440.4, 758.3 (v) 420.8, 439.6, 731.18, 733.9
bid a long farewell to 370.5
bid-and-asked prices 738.9
bid come 420.11, 440.13
biddability 324.1, 433.3, 954.2
biddable 137.10, 433.13, 923.12, 954.9
biddableness 324.1
biddance 440.4
bid defiance 454.3
bidder 440.7, 733.5, 758.3
bidding 420.1, 420.5, 440.4
bidding prayer 696.4
bidding war 360.1
biddy 77.6, 77.9, 311.28, 577.8
bide 130.8, 134.5, 173.7, 827.6, 846.12, 853.5, 856.3
bide one's time 130.8, 173.7, 329.2, 846.12
bidet 79.12
bide the issue 846.12
bid fair 124.9, 133.12
bid fair to 897.3, 966.4, 968.4
bid farewell 188.16
bid for 403.9, 439.6, 440.14, 731.18
bid Godspeed 188.16, 504.12
bid goodbye 188.16
bid good day 585.10
bid good morning 585.10
bid hello 585.10
bid in 733.9
bid one feel at home 585.9
bid one welcome 585.9
bid price 738.9
bid to combat 454.2
bid up 733.9
bid welcome 187.10
bid well 124.9
bien cuit 11.8
biennale 850.4
biennial (n) 310.3, 310.33, 850.4 (a) 850.8
bier 309.13
bifacial 218.7
biff (n) 17.3, 754.3, 902.5 (v) 902.15
bifid 875.7
bifidity 875.1
bifocal lens 29.2
bifocals 29.3
biforked 171.10
biforking 171.3
biform 873.6, 875.7
biformity 873.1
Bifrost 383.9
bifteck 10.18
bifurcate (v) 171.7, 278.5, 873.5, 875.4 (a) 171.10
bifurcated 171.10, 873.6, 875.6
bifurcation 171.3, 278.2, 873.1, 875.1
big 101.10, 141.9, 257.16, 303.12, 502.12, 652.6, 662.18, 997.17
bigamist 563.11
bigamous 563.19
big appetite 672.1
big as life 31.7, 348.8
big as life and twice as ugly 348.8
big as you please 141.9
big baby 16.6, 491.5
big bag of wind 502.5
big-band musician 710.2
big bang theory 1073.18
big battalions 424.2
big battalions, the 18.9
big-bellied 2.31, 257.18
Big Ben 832.6
Big Bertha 462.11
Big Board, the 737.7
big boss 730.1
big-box 386.14
big-box store 386.6
big boy 304.1, 575.4, 997.9
big boys 249.5
Big Brother 417.1, 894.3
big bruiser 15.7
big bucks 618.3
big business 731.1
big businessman 730.1
big C 87.7
big cage 429.9
big cat 311.21, 997.9
big cheese 575.4, 894.6, 997.9
big chief 87.13, 87.17
big city 230.1
big-city person 227.6
big D 87.10
big daddy 560.10, 575.4
big dance 743.13
big data 551.1, 1042.15
Big Dick 882.6
Big Dick from Battle Creek 882.6
big drink 240.1
big-eared 48.15
big eater 8.16, 672.3
bigeminate 873.8
big enchilada 575.4, 997.11
big end 477.5
big-eyed 100.27
big fish 997.9
big fish in a small pond 249.4, 894.6
big freeze 1023.3
big game 311.1, 382.7
big game hunter 382.5
bigger half 477.5
biggest frog in the pond 997.11
biggety 140.11, 142.10
biggie 575.4, 894.6, 997.9
big girl 304.1
biggish 257.16
biggishness 257.6
big government 894.6
big gun 575.4, 997.9
big guy 302.5
big H 87.9
big hand 509.2
big head 140.4
bighead 85.41
big-headed 140.11
bigheaded 136.10
big heart 485.1, 652.2
bighearted 143.15, 485.4, 652.6
bigheartedness 143.4, 485.1, 652.2
big hill 753.1
big hitter 575.4, 894.6
big house 429.9
bight 242.1, 278.2
big idea 932.4
big idea, the 886.2
big joint 429.9
big kahuna 575.4, 894.6
big-laden 78.18
big league 745.1
big-league 997.17
big lie 354.12
big lie, the 354.12
big M 87.14
big man 997.9, 997.11
big man on campus 997.9
big momma 575.4
big money 618.3
big mouth 502.5, 540.1
bigmouth 540.4
big-mouthed 502.10, 540.9
big name 662.9, 997.8
big-name 997.17
bigness 78.5, 257.1, 257.6, 257.8, 652.2
big noise 997.9
big nothing, a 998.6
big one 395.4, 728.7
big operator 737.11
bigot (n) 103.4, 361.6, 687.6, 970.7, 980.5 (a) 980.10
bigoted 361.8, 687.8, 926.32, 970.22, 980.10
bigotedness 980.1
bigotry 103.1, 361.1, 687.5, 926.11, 970.6, 980.1
big person 257.12, 979.6
big picture 792.3
big picture, the 381.1
big pond 240.2
big pond, the 240.1
big price tag 632.3
big-rich 618.15
Big Rock-Candy Mountain 986.11
bigs, the 745.1
big salami 745.3
big school 429.9
big-screen 706.9
big screen, the 706.1
big-screen film 706.1
big shot 249.4, 575.4, 610.7, 894.6, 997.9
big six wheel 759.16
big sleep 307.1
big-sounding 545.8
big spender 486.2
big stick 612.9
big stick, the 424.3, 609.5
big sticker price 632.3
big sticks, the 233.2
big talk 355.1, 502.2, 545.1
big talker 540.4
big ticket 632.3
big-ticket 632.11
big-ticket items 735.1
big time 743.2
big-time 997.17
big time, the 409.1, 745.1
big-time operator 330.8, 997.9
big-timer 997.9
big toe 2.7
big top 295.8
big undertaking 1013.2
bi-guy 75.14
big-voiced 53.12
big wall climbing 760.6
big wheel 575.4, 894.6, 997.9
bigwig (n) 575.4, 894.6, 997.9 (a) 997.17
bigwigged 997.17
bigwigs 249.5
big wind 318.11
big with child 78.18
big with young 78.18
big word 545.3
bijou 498.6
bijouterie 498.5
bijugate 873.8
bike (n) 179.8 (v) 177.33
bike lane 383.2
bike path 383.2
biker 178.11
biking 177.6
bikini 5.29
bikini briefs 5.22
bilateral 218.7, 873.6
bilateralism 218.1
bilateralist 218.7
bilaterality 218.1
bilateral symmetry 264.1
bilbo 428.4
bile 2.17, 7.8, 13.2, 110.1, 144.7, 152.3
bilevel 296.6
bilge (n) 80.9, 80.12, 283.3, 520.3 (v) 283.11
bilges 80.12
bilgewater 80.9, 391.4
bilingual 523.16
bilingual edition 341.3
bilingual text 341.3
bilious 43.6, 85.61, 110.23
biliousness 43.2, 110.1
bilk (n) 759.22 (v) 132.2, 356.18
bilked 132.5
bilker 357.4
bill (n) 283.8, 283.9, 352.7, 352.8, 598.7, 613.9, 623.1, 624.5, 628.3, 673.3, 704.12, 728.5, 728.7, 728.11, 871.5, 965.3, 1028.2 (v) 352.15, 628.11, 704.28, 965.6
billabong 238.3
bill and coo 562.14
bill-and-cooers 104.17
billboard 352.7
bill broker 729.11, 730.9
bill collector 622.4, 770.15
billed 279.8, 965.9
billet (n) 553.2, 647.2, 724.5, 1054.3 (v) 159.12, 225.10
billet at 159.17
billet-doux 562.13
billeted 225.14
billeting 225.3
billfold 729.15

Bill Gates 618.8
billhead 517.13, 553.9
billiard ball 287.3
billiard parlor 743.11
billiards 760.1
billiards club 760.1
billiard table 201.3, 287.3, 760.1
billing and cooing 562.1
billingsgate 513.3
billion, a 884.4
billion (n) 618.2, 882.12, 1017.5 (a) 884.6
billionaire 618.7
billionth 882.31
bill-like 279.8
bill of account 628.3
bill of attainder 602.2
bill of complaint 598.7
bill of draft 728.11
bill of exchange 728.5, 728.11
bill of fare 8.14, 871.5, 965.3
bill of goods 356.9
bill of health 443.7, 549.6
bill of indictment 598.3, 599.1
bill of lading 628.3, 871.5
bill of mortality 307.13
bill of particulars 599.1
Bill of Rights 430.2, 642.3, 673.6, 673.8
bill of sale 734.1
billow (n) 238.14 (v) 238.22, 283.11
billowing 279.7, 281.10, 283.15
billowy 279.7, 281.10, 283.15
billowy cloud 319.1
billposter 352.9
bills 623.1
bill-shaped 279.8
billy 76.8, 311.8, 462.4
Billy be damn 762.3
billy goat 76.8, 311.8
Bilskirnir 681.10
bimetallic 1058.16
bimetallism 609.4, 728.21
bimonthly (n) 555.1 (a) 850.8
bin 386.6
binary 873.6, 1017.23
binary bit 1017.3
binary code 1017.4
binary digit 1017.3, 1042.14
binary file 1042.11
binary program 1042.11
binary system 1017.4
binary tree 1042.18
binaural system 50.11
bind (n) 371.3, 765.1, 846.2, 1013.4 (v) 211.10, 293.7, 424.4, 428.10, 436.5, 615.18, 641.12, 775.6, 800.9, 803.9
binder 86.33, 295.18, 624.1
binder board 554.14
binder's board 554.14
binder's cloth 554.14
binder's title 554.12
bindery 739.3
binding (n) 211.7, 295.18, 554.14, 800.3, 803.1 (a) 419.4, 420.12, 424.11, 641.15, 800.16, 973.14
binding agreement 437.1
binding arbitration 466.2
binding energy 1038.15
binding over 615.8
bindle 770.8
bindlestiff 178.3, 660.2
bind oneself to 436.5
bind over 615.18
bind up 800.9
bine 310.20
bing 91.16
binge (n) 88.6, 487.1 (v) 8.25, 487.2, 669.5
binge drinker 87.21
binge drinking 87.1
binge learning 570.4
binge-purge syndrome 672.1
binger 672.3
binge-watcher 918.1
binge-watching 1035.2
binging (n) 672.1 (a) 672.6
bingle 745.3
bingo 759.15
bingo card 759.15
binocs 29.4
binocular 29.9, 875.7
binoculars 29.4
binomen 527.3
binomial 527.17, 875.7
binomialism 527.1
binomial name 527.3
binomial nomenclature 527.1
binominal 875.7
binuclear family 559.5, 617.2
bio 719.1
bioastronautics 1075.1
biochemical (n) 1060.2 (a) 1060.9
biochemical engineer 1043.2
biochemical engineering 1043.1
biochemist 1060.7
biochemistry 1068.3
biochore 306.7
biocidal 308.24
biocide 308.1
biocycle 306.7
biodad 76.10
biodata 719.1
biodegradability 393.6
biodegradable 393.47, 806.5
biodegradation 393.6, 1072.2
biodegrade 393.22, 806.3
biodeterioration 1072.2
biodiversity 780.1
bioethics 636.1
biogenesis 1.1, 78.6
biogenetic 78.16
biograph 719.4
biographer 718.4, 719.3
biographical 719.6
biographical material 549.2
biographical records 549.2
biographical sketch 719.1
biographize 719.4
biography (n) 719.1 (v) 719.4
biohazard 85.32
bioinstrument 1041.4
bioinstrumentation 1041.4
biologic 1068.4
biological 305.17, 559.6, 1068.4
biological adjustive reactions 92.23
biological classification 305.3
biological clock 306.2, 825.4
biological death 307.1
biological diversity 780.1
biological evolution 861.3
biological fatherhood 560.2
biological motherhood 560.3
biological parent 560.8
biological relationship 559.1
biological science 1068.1, 1068.3
biological time 821.1
biological urge 75.5
biological vector 85.44
biological war 458.1
biological weapon 462.1
biologist 1068.2
biology 305.1, 1068.1, 1068.3
bioluminescence 1025.13
bioluminescent 1025.38
biomass 1021.7
biome 305.3, 1072.1
biomechanical 1039.7
biomedical engineer 1043.2
biomom 77.7
bionic 15.15, 18.12, 83.12
bionic man 1041.12
bionics 1041.2
bionic woman 1041.12
biopharmaceutical 86.32
biophysical 1018.3
biophysicist 1018.2
biophysics 1068.3
bioplasma 689.7
bioplast 305.4
biopsy 91.12
bioregion 1072.1
biorhythm 306.2, 825.4
biorhythmic 850.8
biosphere 305.1, 306.7, 317.2, 1073.10
biosphere, the 1072.1
biostatic 1039.8
biosystematics 527.1
biota 305.1
biotaxy 305.3
bioterror 459.1
bioterrorism 127.7
biotic 305.17
biotype 305.9, 306.7, 786.1, 809.5
biowarfare 458.1, 459.1
bipack 714.10
bipartisan 609.44, 873.6
bipartisan policy 609.4
bipartisanship 450.1
bipartite 802.20, 873.6, 875.7
bipartition 875.1
biparty 609.44
biped (n) 311.3 (a) 875.7
bipetalous 875.7
bipinnate 875.7
bipolar disorder 92.14, 926.5
biquadrate (n) 879.1 (v) 880.2
biquadratic 879.4, 880.3
birch (n) 605.2 (v) 604.12
bird 10.22, 77.6, 311.3, 311.27, 870.4, 927.4, 1016.8, 1074.3
bird, the 508.3
birdbrained 922.20, 923.9
birdcage 228.23, 759.16
birdcall 60.1, 517.16
bird dog 311.17
birdhouse 228.23
birdie (n) 311.27, 751.3 (v) 751.4
birdies 50.13
bird in hand 469.1
birdlife 311.27
birdlike 311.48
birdlime (n) 356.13 (v) 356.20
birdling 302.10
birdman 185.1
bird of another feather 780.3
bird of ill omen 133.5
bird of Jove 311.27
bird of Juno 311.27
bird of Minerva 311.27
bird of night 311.27
bird of passage 178.2, 311.27
bird of prey 311.27, 480.12
bird sanctuary 397.7, 1009.1
birds and the bees 75.2
birds, beasts, and fish 311.1
birdseed 10.4, 310.31
bird's egg 305.15
bird's-eye (n) 89.2 (a) 772.7, 864.13
bird's-eye view 27.7, 33.6, 557.1
birds of a feather 784.5
birdsong 60.1
birdwatcher 918.1
birdwitted 922.20
birdwoman 185.2
birdy (n) 311.27 (a) 311.48, 927.6
birr 52.13
birth (n) 1.1, 78.6, 306.1, 560.4, 560.6, 607.3, 608.2, 818.4 (v) 818.14 (a) 559.6
birth certificate 549.6
birth control 891.1
birth control device 86.23
birth control pill 86.23
birthdate 850.4
birthday 850.4
birthday gift 478.4
birthday present 478.4
birthday suit 6.3
birth defect 85.1
birth family 559.1
birth father 560.9
birth fatherhood 560.2
birthing 1.1, 818.4, 892.6
birthing center 91.21
birthmark 517.5, 1004.1
birth mother 560.11
birth motherhood 560.3
birth pangs 1.1
birth parent 559.1, 560.8
birthplace 228.2, 232.2, 886.8
birth rate 78.1
birthright 479.2, 642.1
birthsite 886.8
birthstone 1059.7
birth throes 1.1
bis 849.5
biscotti 10.30, 10.43
biscotto 10.30
biscuit (n) 10.30, 10.43, 742.2, 1066.2 (a) 40.3
bise 318.8
bisect 802.11, 819.3, 873.5, 875.4
bisected 873.6, 875.6
bisection 819.2, 873.1, 875.1
bisector 875.3
bisexed 75.30

bisexual (n) 75.14 (a) 75.30, 875.7
bisexualism 75.10
bisexuality 75.2, 75.10
bishop 699.9, 699.10, 743.17
bishopdom 698.2
bishopric 231.5, 417.7, 698.2, 698.8
bishop's palace 703.8
bismarck 10.44
bison 311.6
bisque 10.10, 742.2
bissextile 850.8
bissextile day 850.4
bissextile year 824.2
bistecca 10.18
bistro 8.17, 88.20
bit 223.2, 248.2, 285.3, 477.5, 551.7, 704.7, 704.10, 706.3, 793.3, 825.3, 828.3, 992.5, 998.5, 1012.7, 1042.14, 1042.18
bitch 77.9, 311.16, 999.7
bit different, a 787.4
bite (n) 8.2, 8.7, 17.5, 26.2, 62.2, 68.2, 248.2, 258.7, 474.2, 477.5, 544.3, 751.3, 793.3, 1023.1 (v) 8.27, 26.7, 68.5, 285.6, 474.6, 713.10, 954.6, 1023.10
bite back 453.3, 900.6
bite in 713.10
bite into 8.27
biteless 286.4
bite off more than one can chew 404.6, 669.5
bite one's head off 152.16
bite one's nails 126.6, 130.8
bite one's tongue 51.5, 113.6, 137.9, 344.6, 363.6
bite-sized 258.12
bite the bullet 134.6, 433.6, 492.10, 843.7
bite the dust 307.19, 395.22, 412.12
bite the hand that feeds one 151.3, 645.13
bite the thumb at 454.4
bite the tongue 68.5
bite to eat 8.7
biting 17.14, 24.13, 26.10, 68.6, 105.31, 144.23, 489.15, 544.11, 1023.14
bitingness 68.1, 144.8, 544.3
biting one's nails 130.12
biting wind 318.7
bitmap 1042.18
bit much, a 98.25, 993.16
bit of one's mind 510.6
bit on the off side, a 787.4
bit part 704.10
bit player 706.4, 707.7
bit previous, a 845.8
bits and pieces 770.13, 793.3
bitsy 258.11
bitter (v) 110.16 (a) 17.14, 62.9, 64.6, 68.6, 98.17, 98.20, 110.23, 144.23, 152.26, 589.10, 1023.14
bitter as gall 64.6
bitter as wormwood 64.6
bitter cold 1023.14
bitter cup 96.8, 1011.1
bitter defeat 412.4
bitter disappointment 132.1
bitter draft 96.8
bitter end 820.2
bitter-ender 361.6, 452.3
bitterendism 360.1, 361.1
bitter enemy 589.6
bitter feeling 589.4
bitterly cold 1023.14
bitterly disappointed 132.5
bitterness 17.5, 62.1, 64.2, 67.1, 68.1, 93.7, 96.6, 98.5, 103.2, 113.1, 144.8, 152.3, 589.4, 1023.1
bitterness of spirit 152.3
bitter pill 64.2, 96.8, 103.3, 1011.1
bitter resentment 152.3
bitters 67.2
bittersweet 62.9, 66.5, 539.4
bittersweetness 62.1
bitter taste 62.1, 64.2
bitter weather 1023.3
bitter words 510.7
bit thick, a 355.4, 955.10
bit thin, a 955.10
bitty 258.11
bitumen 383.6
bituminous 1021.9
bituminous macadam 383.6
bit-weight control 1041.8
bivalence 1060.4
bivalent 875.7, 1060.10
bivouac (n) 228.29, 463.3 (v) 159.17, 225.11
bivouacking 225.4
biweekly (n) 555.1 (a) 850.8
bizarre 122.11, 488.4, 870.13, 923.11, 986.20
bizarreness 488.1, 870.3
bizarrerie 488.1
bizarro 122.11
bizspeak 523.9
bizzy 1008.16
blab (n) 540.3, 540.4, 551.6 (v) 351.6, 540.5, 551.13
blabber (n) 520.2, 540.3, 540.4, 551.6 (v) 351.6, 520.5, 540.5
blabberer 540.4, 551.6
blabbering (n) 351.2 (a) 540.10
blabbermouth 540.4, 551.6
blabbing (n) 351.2 (a) 540.10
black (n) 38.1, 115.7, 311.11, 312.3 (v) 38.7, 80.16, 1027.9 (a) 38.8, 38.10, 110.24, 112.24, 133.16, 654.16, 1000.7, 1011.15, 1027.13, 1031.3
black-and-blue 26.11, 38.12
black-and-blue mark 85.38
black and white 215.2, 712.4, 712.12, 1025.19
black-and-white (n) 706.5 (a) 706.9
black-and-white film 714.10
black-and-white photograph 714.3
black-and-white photography 714.1
black-and-white television 1035.5
black ant 311.33
black art, the 690.2
black as a crow 38.8
black as coal 38.8
black as ink 38.8
black as midnight 38.8
black as night 38.8, 1027.13
black as pitch 38.8
black as tar 38.8
blackball (n) 510.1, 586.3, 773.1, 773.3 (v) 372.2, 510.10, 586.6, 773.4, 909.17
blackballing 510.1, 586.3, 909.4
Blackbeard 483.7
black beauties 87.5
black belt 233.1, 646.3
black bile 2.24
black box 549.10
black-browed 110.24
black cat 133.5
black cloud 98.5
black clouds 133.5
black collar 606.3
black-collar 606.8
black comedy 704.6
blackdamp 1001.4, 1067.1
black despondency 112.3
blacken 11.5, 38.7, 80.16, 510.19, 512.10, 661.9, 1004.6, 1027.9
blackened 11.7, 38.11, 1004.10
Black English 523.7
blackening (n) 11.2, 38.5, 38.6, 510.7, 512.2, 1027.6 (a) 510.22
blackening agent 38.6
blacken one's good name 512.10
blacken one's name 38.7
blacken one's reputation 38.7
blacker than black synchronizing 1035.5
black eye 85.38, 661.6
blackface (n) 704.17 (a) 548.20
black-faced 548.20
black flag 647.7, 756.3
Black Friday 733.1
black frost 1023.7
black gang 183.6
blackguard (n) 660.3 (v) 513.7
blackguardism 513.2
blackguardly 645.17
black-haired 38.13
Black Hand 660.10
black hash 87.8
black hat 593.1, 707.2
blackhead 1004.1
blackhearted 654.15
black hole 429.8, 1073.8
black humor 489.1, 508.6, 704.6
black ice 1023.5
blacking 38.6
black ink 38.6
black-ink items 386.2
blackish 38.9
blackishness 38.2
blackjack (n) 462.4, 759.11 (v) 424.7, 902.20
black lead 1056.2
blackleg (n) 85.41, 357.4, 727.8 (v) 727.11
black letter 548.6
black light 1025.1
blacklist (n) 444.2, 586.3, 773.3, 871.1 (v) 372.2, 586.6, 602.3
black literature 718.1
black-locked 38.13
black look 27.5, 510.8
black looks 38.2, 110.9
Black Magellanic Cloud 1073.7
Black magic 680.14, 690.2
blackmail (n) 421.1, 480.8, 482.11, 624.5 (v) 421.5, 480.22
blackmailer 480.12
black man 312.3
Black Maria 179.11, 758.2
black mark 410.2, 661.6
black market 732.1
black-market (v) 732.7 (a) 674.6
black marketeer 732.4
black-marketeer 732.7
Black Mass 680.14, 690.3, 701.9
black mollies 87.4
black mood 38.2
Black Muslim 675.23
Black Muslimism 675.13
blackness 38.1, 312.3, 315.4, 1027.1, 1031.1
black night of the soul 96.6
black out 25.5, 30.8, 32.3, 184.46, 345.8, 1027.9
blackout 21.2, 25.2, 32.2, 34.1, 184.21, 345.3, 990.2, 1027.7, 1032.20, 1075.10
black pills 87.16
Black Power 609.31
black power 980.4
black quarter 85.41
black race 38.1, 312.2
black Russian 87.8
black sheep 660.4, 774.2
black-skinned 38.10
blacksmith 1070.2
blacksmith's shop 739.4
blacksnake 605.1
black spot 1035.5
black squall 318.11
Blackstone 673.5
blackstrap 66.2
black supremacist 980.5
black supremacy 980.4
black tie 5.11
blacktop (n) 199.3, 383.6 (v) 295.22
black vote 609.31
blackwash (n) 38.6 (v) 38.7
blackwater 85.41
black widow spider 311.32
black woman 312.3
black words 38.2
bladder 195.2, 282.2, 320.1, 704.6
blade 76.5, 179.20, 310.19, 461.1, 462.5, 500.9, 524.18, 1040.2
blagueur 357.6
blah (n) 94.4 (a) 94.13, 102.6, 117.6, 118.9
blah-blah 540.3
blah-blah-blah 520.3, 540.3
blah feeling 16.1
blahs 94.4, 112.6
blahs, the 96.1
blain 85.37, 283.3
blamability 656.1
blamable 510.25, 654.16
blame (n) 510.3, 599.1, 656.1, 888.1 (v) 510.13, 599.8, 888.4
blamed 513.10, 599.15

blame for 888.4
blameful 510.22
blame game 656.1
blameless 644.13, 657.6
blamelessness 644.1, 657.1
blame on 599.8, 888.4
blame oneself 113.6
blame-shifting 92.23
blameshifting 656.1
blame-the-victim defense 600.2
blameworthiness 656.1
blameworthy 510.25, 602.6, 654.16, 1000.9
blanch 11.5, 26.8, 36.5, 36.6, 37.5, 105.19
blanched 11.7, 36.8, 37.7, 127.26, 393.34
blanching 11.2, 36.3, 37.3
bland 16.17, 65.2, 222.14, 504.17, 511.8, 670.10, 864.11
bland diet 7.13
bland food 7.13
blandish 354.23, 375.14, 377.5, 440.12, 511.5
blandishing 377.8, 511.8
blandishment 375.3, 377.1, 440.3, 511.1
blandishments 562.5
blandness 65.1, 504.5
blank (n) 158.8, 222.1, 222.3, 549.5 (a) 117.6, 222.14, 293.9, 344.10, 499.8, 522.20, 922.19, 930.11, 933.4, 990.9
blankbook 549.11
blank cartridge 19.6, 462.17
blank check 430.4, 443.4, 642.2, 728.11
blank despondency 112.3
blank determination 942.2
blanked 151.5, 340.14, 372.3, 412.16, 820.9
blanket (n) 295.10, 295.12 (v) 295.19, 346.6 (a) 772.7, 945.5
blanket ballot 609.19
blanket craps 759.8
blanket drill 22.2, 22.3
blanketed 295.31
blanket finish 757.3
blanketing (n) 295.1 (a) 295.35
blanket mortgage 438.4
blankety-blank 513.10
blank future 125.1
blankie 295.10
blanking 1035.3
blanking signal 1035.4
blank mind 933.1
blankminded 930.11, 933.4
blankmindedness 930.1, 933.1
blankness 222.2, 344.3, 922.6, 933.1
blank out 820.6
blank slate 222.3
blank verse 720.9
blank wall 293.3, 1013.6
blare (n) 53.5, 58.3, 1025.4 (v) 53.10, 58.9, 60.2, 352.13, 524.25
blare forth 352.13
blaring (n) 1034.21 (a) 53.13
blarney (n) 511.1, 520.3, 532.2 (v) 511.6
blarney, the 532.2
blarneyer 511.4
blarneying 511.8
blasé 94.13, 102.7, 106.15, 118.11, 123.3, 331.20, 413.28, 977.5
blaspheme 513.5, 513.6, 694.5
blasphemer 694.3
blaspheming 694.2
blasphemous 156.8, 513.8, 694.6
blasphemousness 694.2
blasphemy 513.1, 694.2
blast (n) 53.3, 53.5, 56.3, 87.20, 105.3, 318.5, 409.4, 462.16, 582.12, 671.7, 1001.2 (v) 53.7, 53.10, 56.8, 87.22, 308.14, 318.19, 395.18, 459.22, 513.5, 671.14, 1012.15, 1024.11, 1043.4
blast away 818.7
blasted 87.24, 132.5, 393.42, 395.28, 513.10
blasted expectation 132.1
blast-freeze 397.9, 1024.11
blast freezing 1024.1
blast-freezing (n) 397.2 (a) 1024.12
blast-frozen 1024.14
blast furnace 739.4
blasting (n) 1034.21 (a) 56.11
blasting cap 462.15
blast it 745.5
blast lamp 1020.14
blastoderm 2.4
blast off 818.7, 1074.13, 1075.12
blastoff 818.1, 1074.9
blastogenesis 78.6
blastogenetic 78.16
blast propulsion 1074.8
blast the ear 53.7
blastula 305.14
blast wave 1038.16
blasty 318.21
blat (n) 53.5, 58.3 (v) 53.10, 58.9, 60.2, 524.25
blatancy 59.5, 348.4, 501.3
blatant 53.13, 59.10, 60.6, 348.12, 501.20
blate 60.2
blather (n) 520.2, 540.3 (v) 520.5, 540.5, 922.12
blatherer 540.4
blathering (n) 540.2 (a) 540.10
blatherskite 503.2
blatting 53.13
blaze (n) 105.9, 289.1, 517.4, 517.5, 758.2, 1019.13, 1019.14, 1025.4, 1025.6 (v) 289.4, 352.13, 517.19, 1019.22, 1020.23, 1020.24, 1025.23
blaze abroad 352.13
blaze a trail 517.19, 814.2
blaze away at 459.22
blazed 289.5
blaze of glory 662.6
blaze of light 1025.6
blaze of noon, the 314.4, 1025.10
blaze of temper 152.9
blaze the trail 405.12, 816.3
blaze up 152.19, 1020.23
blazing (n) 1020.5 (a) 1019.27, 1025.34, 1025.39
blazing fire 1019.13
blazing light 1025.4
blazon (n) 501.4, 647.2 (v) 352.13, 498.8
blazon forth 501.17
blazonry 647.1, 647.2
bleach (n) 36.4, 37.4 (v) 36.5, 36.6, 37.5, 79.18
bleached 36.8, 37.7, 79.25, 222.14, 393.34
bleached blond 35.9
bleached-blond 37.9
bleached out 36.8
bleached white 36.8
bleachers 27.8, 745.1
bleaching 36.4, 37.3
bleaching agent 36.4
bleaching substance 36.4
bleach out 36.6
bleak 98.20, 112.24, 125.12, 318.23, 1023.14
bleakness 98.5, 112.7, 222.2, 1023.1
bleak outlook 125.1
bleak prognosis 125.1
bleak prospect 125.1
bleak weather 1023.3
blear 32.6
bleared 32.6
blearedness 28.2
blear-eyed 28.13
bleariness 28.2, 32.2
blear-witted 922.18
bleary 32.6
bleary-eyed 28.13
bleat 60.2
bleb 85.37, 283.3, 320.1, 1004.1
blebby 320.6
bled white 36.7
bleed 12.17, 12.18, 91.27, 96.19, 112.17, 145.3, 190.15, 192.12, 192.16, 387.16, 480.21, 480.24, 632.7
bleeder 85.43, 745.3
bleed for 145.3
bleeding (n) 12.8, 36.3, 85.9, 91.20, 192.3 (a) 12.23, 96.23, 145.7
bleeding edge 165.1
bleeding heart 93.8, 96.6, 112.9, 143.8, 145.2, 693.3, 979.6
bleeding-heart 611.19, 979.9
bleeding-heart liberal 979.6
bleeding white 36.3
bleed white 387.16, 388.3, 480.24, 632.7
bleep (n) 58.4 (v) 428.8
bleeped 820.9
bleeped out 820.9
bleeping 428.2
bleeping out 428.2
bleep out 255.10, 428.8
blemish (n) 517.5, 774.2, 1003.2, 1004.1, 1015.4 (v) 265.7, 393.13, 517.19, 1004.4, 1015.5
blemished 265.12, 654.12, 1003.4, 1004.8, 1015.6
blench 37.5, 127.13, 325.4, 903.7
blend (n) 526.11, 756.1, 797.5, 805.1 (v) 708.35, 778.5, 797.10, 805.3
blended 708.49, 797.14, 805.5
blender 797.9, 917.9, 1063.4
blend in 708.35
blending (n) 778.2, 797.1, 805.1, 1063.3 (a) 708.49, 805.7
blend into 805.3
blend into the background 34.2
blend in with 455.2
blend with the scenery 494.7
blendword 526.11
blennorhea 85.9
bless 95.9, 149.2, 150.4, 509.9, 509.11, 509.12, 685.5, 696.12, 696.14, 701.15, 1008.18
blessed 95.16, 95.17, 513.10, 681.12, 685.8, 1010.14
blessed by fortune 972.15
blessed event 1.1
blessed memory 662.7
blessedness 95.2, 685.1, 685.3
Blessed One, the 677.4
blessed release 307.6
blessed with 469.9
blessed with luck 1010.14
blessing (n) 143.7, 149.1, 441.1, 443.1, 472.7, 478.7, 509.1, 685.3, 696.5, 999.4, 1010.2, 1010.3 (a) 696.16
bless one's lucky 116.5
bless one's stars 116.5, 150.3
bless the Lord 696.12
bless with 478.17
blether (n) 540.3 (v) 520.5, 540.5
blethers 540.3
blight (n) 85.1, 1000.3, 1001.2, 1011.1 (v) 393.10, 1000.6, 1024.11
blighted 132.5, 393.28, 393.42, 395.28
blighted area 230.6
blighted hope 125.5, 132.1
blighted neighborhood 230.6
blighted section 230.6
blighter 660.2
blighting glance 144.4
Blighty 232.4
blimp 181.11, 257.12, 501.9
blimp out 672.5
blind (n) 346.3, 356.6, 376.1, 415.3, 751.3, 1028.1 (v) 30.7, 346.6, 356.17, 1025.23 (a) 25.6, 28.11, 30.9, 87.24, 88.33, 293.9, 346.11, 361.13, 522.15, 922.14, 963.14, 984.7
blind, the 30.4
blind alley 293.3, 391.3, 1013.6
blind-alley 293.9
blind as a bat 30.9, 922.14
blind as a mole 30.9
blind as an owl 30.9
blind baking 11.2
blind bargain 731.5, 759.2, 971.8
blind chance 972.2
blind date 582.8, 582.9
blind drunk 88.32
blinded 30.10, 922.14
blinders 30.5, 980.1
blind faith 953.1, 954.1, 982.1
blind flighy 184.1
blind flying 1036.9
blindfold (n) 30.5 (v) 30.7, 356.17 (a) 30.10, 922.14

blindfolded 30.10, 922.14
blindfolded Justice 649.4
blindfolding 30.1
blind gate 753.1
blind guess 951.4
blind gut 2.18, 293.3
blind impulse 365.1, 934.2, 963.5
blinding (n) 30.1 (a) 30.11, 35.20, 316.11, 1025.32
blinding light 1025.4
blind instinct 963.5
blind Justice 649.4
blind landing 184.18, 1036.9
blind leading the blind 30.4, 414.8
blind leading the blind, the 569.1
blind man 30.4
blindness 25.1, 28.1, 30.1, 340.2, 361.5, 922.2, 930.2
blind oneself 980.6
blind oneself to 30.8, 340.6
blind one's eyes 356.17
blind panic 127.1
blind pass 749.3
blind patriotism 591.2
blind pig 88.20
blind pool 737.17
blind-pop 459.15
blind rage 152.10
blinds 30.5, 1028.1
blind side 30.1, 980.1
blindside 131.7, 459.15, 746.5
blindsided 131.12, 406.8
blind spot 30.1, 980.1, 1034.21
blind spots 1036.12
blind staggers 85.41
blindstory 703.9
blind the eyes 30.7
blind tiger 88.20
blind to 94.10, 930.12
blind to pity 146.3
blind to virtue 654.17
blind trust 737.16
bling 498.5
bling-bling 498.5
blinger 999.7
blink (n) 27.4, 1025.7, 1025.9 (v) 28.10, 127.13, 340.8, 903.7, 1025.24
blinkard 28.7
blink at 30.8, 148.4, 443.10, 979.7, 984.2
blinker (n) 517.15 (v) 30.7
blinkered 28.11, 30.10
blinkering 30.1
blinkers 29.3, 30.5
blink-eyed 28.11
blinking (n) 28.7, 1025.7 (a) 28.11, 1025.35, 1025.36
blinking light 400.1
blinky 28.11, 1025.35
blintz 10.45
blip 968.2
blips 1036.11
bliss 95.2, 97.1, 681.5
bliss body 689.17
blissed-out 95.17
blissful 95.16, 97.6, 97.9
blissfulness 95.2, 97.1
B-list (n) 250.2, 871.1 (a) 250.6
blister (n) 85.37, 283.3, 320.1, 1004.1 (v) 510.20, 1020.24
blister beetle 75.6
blistered 320.6, 1020.30
blisterfoot 461.10
blistering (n) 1020.5 (a) 320.6, 1019.25
blistery 320.6
blithe 109.11
blitheness 109.1
blither 922.12
blithering 922.22
blithering idiocy 922.9
blithering idiot 924.8
blithesome 109.11
blithesomeness 109.1
blitz (n) 459.1, 746.3 (v) 395.18, 459.14, 459.22, 746.5
blitzkrieg 459.1
blizzard 318.11, 1023.8
bloat (n) 257.5, 259.2, 993.7 (v) 251.6, 259.4, 259.5
bloated 136.10, 251.7, 257.18, 259.13, 265.12, 283.15, 501.22, 993.20
bloated aristocrat 501.9
bloatedness 257.5, 257.8, 259.2
bloated plutocrat 618.7
bloated with pride 136.10
bloating 251.1, 259.2, 993.7
blob 282.2, 283.3
blobbiness 538.1, 971.4
blobby 263.4, 971.19
bloc 232.1, 609.24, 617.1
block (n) 92.24, 211.3, 230.7, 231.4, 257.10, 293.3, 605.5, 713.5, 734.4, 738.3, 746.3, 846.2, 990.3, 1012.4, 1042.18, 1045.6 (v) 293.7, 295.19, 460.10, 704.32, 746.5, 747.4, 749.7, 754.4, 846.8, 857.11, 1012.12, 1012.13
block, the 604.6
blockade (n) 212.1, 293.1, 293.3, 459.5, 773.1, 1012.4 (v) 212.5, 293.7, 459.19, 460.9, 773.4, 1012.12
blockaded 212.10, 773.7
blockading 212.1, 459.5
blockage 85.6, 92.24, 293.3, 846.2, 1012.1
blockbuster 87.20, 131.2, 462.20
block capital 546.8
block diagram 801.4
blocked 293.11, 846.16, 990.9
blocked-out 262.9
blocked up 293.11
block-faulting 237.6
blockhead 414.8, 924.4
blockheaded 922.17
blockheadedness 922.4
blockhouse 460.6
block in 381.11
blockiness 268.2
blocking 34.1, 92.24, 295.1, 704.13, 746.3, 754.3, 801.2, 990.3, 1012.1
blocking back 746.2
blocking out 801.2
blocking the light 1027.6
blockish 922.15
blockishness 922.3
block letter (n) 547.4 (a) 546.8
block out 262.7, 381.11, 801.7
block print 712.10, 713.5
blocks 743.16
block the light 1027.9
block the way 1012.12
block up 293.7, 1012.12
blocky 268.10
blog (n) 547.10, 547.12, 549.11, 1042.19 (v) 352.16, 547.21
blogger 547.15, 547.16, 549.13
blogging 352.1, 547.2
bloke 76.5
bloke-talk 523.10
blond (n) 35.9 (a) 37.9, 43.5
blonde (n) 35.9 (a) 37.9, 43.5
blonde bombshell 665.15
blonde moment 990.1
blond-haired 37.9
blond-headed 37.9
blondness 37.1
blood (n) 2.25, 306.2, 308.1, 500.9, 559.1, 559.2, 559.4, 560.4, 561.1, 608.2, 809.2, 809.3, 1061.2 (a) 2.33
blood alcohol 2.25
blood and thunder 93.9
blood-and-thunder 105.32
blood bank 91.18, 197.25
bloodbath 308.4, 395.1
blood bay 311.11
blood blister 320.1
blood-borne 12.23
blood brother 559.3
blood cell 2.25
blood clot 1045.7
blood-colored 41.7
blood corpuscle 2.25
blood count 2.25, 91.12
bloodcurdling 127.29
blood disease 85.20
blood donor 91.18
blood donor center 91.18
blood feud 456.5, 507.1, 589.4
blood group 2.25
blood grouping 2.25
bloodguilt 656.1
blood-guiltiness 656.1
bloodguilty 656.3
blood heat 1019.1
blood horse 311.10
blood-hot 1019.24
bloodied 96.25
bloodiness 144.11
bloodless 16.12, 36.7, 117.6, 464.9
bloodlessness 16.1, 36.2, 117.1
bloodless revolution 860.1
bloodletter 308.11
bloodletting 91.20, 192.3, 308.1
bloodline 560.4, 560.5, 561.1
bloodlust 144.11, 671.1
bloodmobile 91.18
blood money 624.3, 624.5
blood oath 332.4, 334.4
blood on the floor 457.1
blood platelet 2.25
blood poisoning 85.20, 85.31
blood pressure 2.25
blood rain 316.1
blood-red 41.7
blood relation 559.2
blood relationship 559.1
blood relative 559.2
blood running cold 127.5
blood serum 2.25
bloodshed 308.1, 458.1
bloodshedder 308.11
bloodshot 28.13
bloodshot eyes 28.2
blood sister 559.3
blood-spattered 1004.11
blood sport 382.2, 744.1
bloodstain (n) 1004.3 (v) 1004.7
bloodstained 1004.11
bloodstream 2.25
blood substitute 2.25
bloodsucker 311.37, 480.12
bloodsucking (n) 480.8 (a) 480.26
blood test 91.12
bloodthirst 144.11
bloodthirstiness 144.11
bloodthirsty 144.26, 308.24, 458.20
blood-tingling 127.28
blood transfusion 91.18
blood type 2.25
blood vessel 2.23
blood-warm 1019.24
blood work 91.12
bloody (v) 12.17, 96.18, 393.13, 1004.7 (a) 2.33, 12.23, 41.7, 144.26, 308.24, 458.20, 513.9, 671.21, 1004.11, 1061.4
bloody flux 12.2, 85.41
bloody hands 656.1
bloody mess 810.3
bloody-minded 144.26, 308.24, 451.8, 458.20, 846.17, 1012.17
bloody-mindedness 144.11, 361.1, 451.2, 1012.1
bloody murder 308.2
bloody one's hands with 308.15, 459.14
bloody-red 41.7
bloody shirt 458.11
blooey 393.38, 395.29
bloom (n) 41.3, 83.1, 301.1, 310.24, 310.26, 1016.1, 1019.12, 1035.5, 1051.1 (v) 83.6, 303.9, 310.35, 407.8, 861.5, 1010.8, 1016.16, 1019.22
bloomer 975.6
bloomery 739.4
blooming (n) 303.6, 310.26 (a) 14.3, 41.9, 83.13, 259.12, 301.9, 310.38, 407.13, 890.9, 1010.13, 1016.20
bloomy 310.38
bloop 745.3, 975.6
blooper 745.3, 923.4, 975.6
blooping 50.13, 1035.5
blossom (n) 310.24, 310.26 (v) 14.2, 259.7, 303.9, 310.35, 407.8, 861.5, 1010.8
blossoming (n) 303.6, 310.26, 861.1 (a) 14.3, 251.8, 259.12, 310.38, 1010.13
blot (n) 80.5, 395.7, 661.6, 774.2, 1004.3, 1015.4 (v) 38.7, 47.7, 187.13, 395.16, 661.9, 1004.5, 1015.5, 1066.6

blotch (n) 47.3, 80.5, 517.5, 1004.3 (v) 38.7, 47.7, 517.19, 1004.5
blotched 47.13, 1004.9
blotchiness 38.3
blotchy 38.11, 47.13, 1004.9
blotless 664.4
blotlessness 664.1
blot one's copy book 975.14
blot on one's escutcheon 661.6
blot on the landscape 1015.4
blot out 255.12, 308.14, 395.16, 1027.9
blot out one's sins 148.3, 601.4
blotted 148.7, 1015.6
blotter 87.10, 187.6, 549.11
blotting (n) 187.6, 395.7, 1066.3 (a) 187.17
blotting out 295.1, 395.7
blotting paper 187.6
blotto 88.33
blot up 187.13
blouse 5.15
blow (n) 8.9, 87.7, 96.5, 131.2, 132.1, 310.24, 310.26, 318.5, 318.11, 328.3, 604.3, 754.3, 902.4, 902.6, 1011.2 (v) 21.5, 53.10, 87.22, 222.10, 310.35, 318.19, 368.11, 393.11, 407.8, 414.12, 486.3, 502.7, 545.6, 708.42, 909.22, 909.24, 975.15
blow a fill 87.22
blow a fuse 152.20
blow a gasket 105.17, 152.20
blow a horn 708.42
blow a hurricane 318.19
blow a kiss 562.19
blow a safe 482.15
blow a stick 87.22
blow away 308.14, 395.12
blow-by-blow account 349.3, 766.2
blow-by-blow description 349.3
blow down 395.19, 913.5
blow-dried 1066.9
blow-dry 1066.6
blow-dryer 1066.4
blow-drying 3.15, 1066.3
blower 317.10, 318.17, 318.18, 502.5, 756.1
blow for blow 506.3
blow great guns 318.19
blow grits 909.27
blowgun 318.17
blow hard 502.7
blowhard 502.5
blowhole 190.9, 239.13
blow hot and cold 362.8, 364.4, 854.5, 936.9
blow in 186.6, 191.7
blow-in 191.2, 352.8
blowing 87.2, 310.26
blowing away 308.2
blowing hot and cold (n) 362.2 (a) 854.7
blowing one's own horn 502.1
blowing up 251.2, 259.2, 355.1
blow it 414.12, 844.4, 975.15
blow it by 745.5
blow job 75.7
blowlamp 1020.14
blown 318.23, 393.41, 393.42
blown out of proportion 355.4
blown over 837.7
blown to kingdom come 308.18
blown up 259.13
blown up out of all proportion 355.4
blow off 340.7, 502.7, 771.5, 909.24, 984.4
blow off steam 743.24
blow off the lid 743.24
blow one's brains out 308.18, 308.22
blow one's cookies 909.27
blow one's cool 105.17, 152.18
blow one's cork 128.8
blow one's cover 351.8
blow oneself to 733.7
blow one's lines 975.15, 990.5
blow one's mind 87.22, 122.7, 128.8, 926.22, 976.8, 986.17
blow one's own horn 502.7
blow one's own trumpet 502.6
blow one's stack 105.17, 128.8, 152.20, 926.22
blow one's top 105.17, 152.20, 926.22
blow open 671.13
blow out 190.13, 671.13, 671.14, 909.22, 909.25, 1022.7
blowout 8.9, 487.1, 582.12, 671.7, 743.4, 909.7
blow out of all proportion 350.3
blow out the cobwebs 9.2
blow over 318.19, 820.7, 913.5
blowpipe 318.17, 1020.14
blow sky-high 958.4
blow the bugle 458.18
blow the chance 844.5
blow the clarion 458.18
blow the coals 105.12, 375.17
blow the horn 53.10
blow the lid off 351.4, 941.4
blow the trumpet 487.2
blow the whistle 135.5, 551.13, 746.5
blow the whistle on 857.11
blow to 624.19
blow to bits 308.18, 395.18
blow to kingdom come 395.18
blow to pieces 308.18, 395.18
blowtorch 181.3, 1020.14
blow to smithereens 395.18
blowtube 318.17
blow up 105.12, 105.17, 152.20, 251.5, 259.4, 308.18, 318.19, 350.3, 395.18, 410.13, 509.12, 671.14, 714.15, 958.4
blowup 152.9, 251.2, 671.7, 714.5
blow up a storm 318.19
blow up in one's face 410.13
blow upon 661.9
blow up the fire 1020.22
blow wash 184.30
blow wide open 351.4
blowy 318.21
blowzed 41.9
blowziness 257.8, 810.6
blowzy 41.9, 257.18, 810.15
blubber (n) 1047.4 (v) 115.12, 320.4, 524.25, 525.9
blubberer 115.9
blubberhead 924.4
blubbering (n) 115.2 (a) 115.21
blubbery 1056.9
bludgeon (n) 462.4 (v) 127.20, 424.7, 514.2
bludgeon, the 424.3
bludgeoning 514.3
blue (n) 35.13, 45.1, 548.5, 1008.16 (v) 45.2 (a) 45.3, 112.23, 307.28, 666.9
blue, the 1073.2
blue acid 87.10
blue angels 87.5
blue around the gills 36.7
blue baby 302.9
Bluebeard 563.11
blue-black 38.8
blue blood 607.3, 608.2, 608.4
blue-blood 607.4
blue-blooded 607.10, 608.11
Bluebook 607.2
blue book 549.8, 549.9, 551.1, 938.2
blue cat 311.20
blue cheer 87.10
blue-chip 999.15
blueclaw 311.29
bluecoat 1008.16
blue-collar 607.10
blue-collar worker 577.3, 607.7, 726.2
blue darter 174.6
blue devils 87.5, 110.10, 112.6, 926.10
blue dolls 87.5
blue flu 727.5, 857.2
blue funk 127.1
bluegrass 708.11
blue-green 44.4
blue heaven 87.10
blue heavens 87.5
blue in the face 105.25
bluejacket 183.1, 183.4
blue jeans 5.18
blue Johnnies 926.10
blue joke 489.6
blue language 513.3
blue laws 428.2
blue line 749.1
blue movie 666.4
blueness 45.1
bluenose 500.11
blue-pencil 255.12, 392.12, 395.16
blue-penciling 255.5, 392.4
blue peter 517.15
blue planet, the 1073.10
blue-plate special 8.6, 8.17
blueprint (n) 349.1, 381.1, 381.3, 548.5, 557.1, 714.5, 801.4, 965.3 (v) 381.10, 714.15
blueprinted 381.12
blueprinting 381.1
blue ribbon 249.3, 411.1, 646.2, 646.5
blue-ribbon jury 596.5
blue ruin 395.1
blues 110.10, 112.6, 708.9
blue serene, the 1073.2
blue sky 1073.2
blue-sky 951.13
blue-sky research 556.1
blue-sky thinking 986.2
blues rocker 710.2
blues singer 710.13
blue state 609.18
bluestocking (n) 929.5 (a) 928.22
bluestockingism 928.5
blue story 489.6
blue streak 174.6
blue water 240.1
blue-water 275.15
bluewater sailer 183.1
blue with cold 1023.16
blue-yellow blindness 30.3
bluff (n) 200.3, 237.2, 354.3, 356.6, 357.6, 503.1, 503.2 (v) 354.21, 356.14, 503.3 (a) 142.10, 204.18, 286.3, 416.5, 505.7, 644.17
bluffer 357.6, 500.8, 503.2
bluffing 354.3, 356.1
bluffness 286.1, 416.1, 644.4
bluff off 127.21
bluish 45.3
bluish-green 44.4
bluishness 45.1
blunder (n) 414.5, 923.4, 975.5 (v) 410.14, 414.11, 917.15, 975.14
blunder away 414.11
blunderbuss 462.10
blunderer 414.8
blunderhead 414.8, 924.4
blunderheaded 414.20, 922.17
blunderheadedness 414.4, 922.4
blundering (n) 414.4 (a) 414.20
blunder into 414.11, 975.14
blunder on 414.11
blunder upon 414.11, 941.3
blunt (n) 728.2 (v) 16.10, 25.4, 94.7, 286.2, 379.4, 670.6 (a) 94.9, 286.3, 416.5, 430.23, 505.7, 644.17, 922.16
blunted 286.3
blunt-edged 286.3
blunt-ended 286.3
blunting (n) 16.5, 670.2 (a) 670.14
blunt instrument 462.4
bluntish 286.3
bluntness 286.1, 416.1, 505.3, 644.4
blunt-pointed 286.3
blunt-witted 922.16
blur (n) 32.2, 661.6, 1004.3 (v) 32.4, 263.3, 945.3, 1004.6
Blu-ray 50.12
blurb 352.4, 509.3
blurb writer 352.9
blur distinctions 945.3
blurping 50.13
blurred 32.6, 263.4, 525.12, 971.19
blurredness 28.2
blurred speech 525.1
blurred vision 28.1
blurriness 32.2, 263.1, 971.4
blurring the eyes 30.1
blurry 32.6, 263.4, 971.19
blurt (n) 59.2 (v) 59.7, 351.6, 524.24

blurting 59.11
blurt out 59.7, 351.6, 365.7, 524.24
blush (n) 35.2, 41.3, 139.5, 1016.11, 1019.12 (v) 41.4, 41.5, 105.19, 139.8, 656.2, 1019.22
blusher 1016.11
blushful 139.13
blushing (n) 41.1, 41.3, 139.5 (a) 41.9, 41.11, 137.14, 139.13, 1025.30
blushing bride 563.5, 563.8
blush unseen 32.3
blush up to the eyes 139.8
blush wine 88.17
bluster (n) 502.1, 503.1, 671.2, 917.1 (v) 127.20, 152.15, 318.19, 454.5, 502.6, 503.3
bluster and bluff 503.3
blusterer 502.5, 503.2
blustering (n) 503.1 (a) 53.13, 318.21, 503.4, 514.3, 671.18
bluster into 127.20
blusterous 318.21, 503.4, 671.18
bluster out of 127.20
blustery 318.21, 503.4, 671.18
B-movie 706.1
BMX (n) 179.8 (v) 177.33
bo 178.3
boa constrictor 311.25
Boanergean 59.10
Boanerges 543.5
boar 76.8, 311.9
board (n) 8.5, 10.1, 10.6, 385.3, 423.1, 567.12, 574.11, 595.1, 704.16, 737.7, 758.2, 901.15, 1042.3, 1054.3 (v) 8.18, 8.21, 177.35, 182.48, 188.15, 193.12, 295.23, 385.9, 385.10, 459.20
board-and-roomer 8.16, 227.8
board book 554.1
board certified 332.14
board-certified physician 90.4
board-certified specialist 90.4
boarder 8.16, 227.8, 470.4, 828.4
board game 743.9, 743.16
boarding 177.16, 188.3, 459.4, 1054.3
boardinghouse 228.15
boarding ladder 193.4
boarding pass 443.1
board lot 738.3
board measure 300.4
board meeting 423.3
board of aldermen 613.1
board of directors 574.11
board of ed 567.12
board of education 567.12
board of regents 567.12, 574.11
Board of Trade unit 1019.19
board of trustees 567.12; 574.11
board of visitors 567.12
board room 739.7
boards 749.1
boards, the 704.1, 704.16
boardsail 182.13
boardsailing 182.11
board shorts 5.18
boardwalk 383.2
boast (n) 502.1, 999.5 (v) 140.6, 469.4, 502.6
boaster 136.3, 502.5
boastful 136.9, 140.9, 502.10
boastfulness 136.1, 140.2, 502.1, 503.1
boasting (n) 502.1 (a) 502.10
boast of 509.12
boat (n) 179.10, 180.1 (v) 182.13
boatable 182.59
boatel 228.16
boater 183.5, 760.2
boat-handler 183.5
boatheader 574.7
boathouse 197.27
boating 182.1, 760.2
boating report 317.7
boatlike 284.16
boatload 196.2
boatman 183.5
boat person 368.5, 774.4
boat race 457.12, 757.3, 965.2
boat-race 457.19
boat seaplane 181.8
boat-shaped 284.16
boat shoes 5.27
boat show 736.2
boatsman 183.5
boatsteerer 183.8, 574.7
boatswain 183.7, 574.2
boatswain's mate 183.7
boatswain's stores 180.12
boatyard 739.3
bob (n) 155.2, 180.11, 200.6, 297.6, 585.4, 728.8, 849.5, 905.3, 913.3, 917.3, 1016.14 (v) 3.22, 155.6, 255.10, 268.6, 366.6, 382.10, 913.9, 916.10, 917.11
bob a curtsy 155.6
bob and wheel 849.5
bobbed 268.9
bobber 382.6
bobbery 917.1
bobbin and fly frame 271.5
bobbing and weaving 854.3
bobble (n) 414.5, 917.3, 975.6 (v) 414.11, 414.12, 745.5, 746.5, 916.10, 917.11, 975.15
bobbled 414.22
bobblehead 743.16
bobbler 414.9
bobby 1008.16
bobbysoxer 302.8
bobcat 311.21
bob down 155.6
bob for 938.30
bobization 709.7
bob skates 179.21
bobtailed arrow 462.6
bob up 33.9, 131.6, 186.6, 193.9
bob wheel 849.5
boca 242.1
bod 2.1, 76.5
bode 133.10
bodeful 133.16
bodefulness 133.6
bode well 896.3
bodhi 667.2, 677.4
bodhisattva 143.8, 677.4, 699.14
bodhi tree 928.8
bodice 5.15
bodied 1052.11
bodiless 764.5, 988.8, 1053.7
bodilessness 299.1, 764.1, 1053.1
bodiliness 1052.1
bodily 663.6, 767.8, 1052.10
bodily appetite 75.5
bodily charm 1016.3
bodily comfort 95.1
bodily development 14.1, 259.3
bodily entity 2.1
bodily fluid 2.24
bodily function 12.1
bodily grace 1016.3
bodily love 104.1
bodily pleasure 95.1
bodily size 269.2
bodily structure 2.1
boding (n) 133.2 (a) 133.16
Bodleian Library 558.1
body (n) 2.1, 76.5, 227.1, 257.1, 262.4, 269.2, 307.15, 312.5, 548.6, 617.1, 617.2, 675.3, 756.1, 763.1, 763.3, 770.3, 770.11, 792.6, 872.4, 1045.6, 1052.3 (v) 1052.9 (a) 523.23
body and blood of Christ 701.7
body armor 460.3
body art 712.13
body bag 307.15
body block 746.3
body-build 262.4, 767.4
bodybuilding 84.2, 744.1
body clock 825.4
body clothes 5.22
body count 307.13, 1017.11
body decoration 712.16
body double 576.1
body fluid 2.24, 1061.2
body forth 348.5, 349.11, 763.5
bodyguard 577.4, 769.5, 1008.14
body heat 1019.1
body-image agnosia 990.2
bodying forth 348.1
body language 517.14
body louse 311.36
body mass index 1017.7
body odor 12.7, 71.1
body of advisers 423.1
body of affiliates 617.12
body of Christ 687.3
body of Christians 687.3
body of evidence 957.1
body of ideas 932.8
body of knowledge 928.9
body of law 673.5
body of learning 928.9
body of retainers 769.6
body of theory 951.1
body painting 712.13
body piercing 292.3
body pivot 751.3
body politic 227.1, 232.1, 609.16
body politic, the 606.1
body scrub 1016.11
body search 938.15
body-shake 938.15
body slam 474.3
body snatcher 483.1, 615.5
body-snatching 482.10
bodysuit 5.9
bodywash 79.17
bodywear 5.22
body weight 297.1
bodywork 756.1
Boeotian (n) 924.2 (a) 922.15
bœuf 10.14
boff 116.4
boffin 413.11, 422.3, 928.11
boffo 409.4
boffola 116.4
Bofors 462.12
bog (n) 12.10, 80.12, 243.1 (v) 243.2
bogart 503.3
bog body 842.7
bog down 243.2
bogey (n) 96.2, 127.9, 181.9, 680.9, 751.3 (v) 751.4
bogeyman 127.9, 680.9
bogeymen 1001.1
boggart 680.9
bogged down 297.18
bogginess 1065.1
boggish 243.3
boggle (n) 325.2, 414.5 (v) 122.6, 127.12, 325.4, 333.5, 362.6, 414.11, 491.8, 936.9, 971.14
boggled 971.26
boggler 414.8
boggle the mind 122.6, 955.7
boggling (n) 325.2, 414.4, 936.5 (a) 131.11, 325.7
boggy 243.3, 1065.15
bogle 680.9
bog man 842.7
bogue 87.1
bogus 354.26, 862.8
bogus money 728.10
bogusness 354.2
bogy 96.2, 400.2, 1001.1
Bohemian (n) 178.4, 868.3 (a) 581.3, 868.6
Bohemianism 581.1, 868.2
Bohr theory 1038.2
boil (n) 10.7, 85.37, 283.4, 671.2, 917.1, 1020.2 (v) 11.5, 79.24, 152.15, 320.4, 671.12, 1019.22, 1020.20
boil down 268.6
boil down to 359.7
boiled 11.7, 79.27, 88.33
boiled-down 260.12
boiled fish 10.24
boiled meat 10.13
boiler factory 53.6
boilerman 183.6
boiler room 53.6, 356.10, 737.9
boilery 739.3
boiling (n) 11.2, 320.3, 671.2, 893.4, 917.1, 1020.2 (a) 105.22, 152.29, 152.30, 1019.25
boiling mad 152.30
boiling over 93.18, 105.22
boiling point 1019.3, 1019.10
boiling water 1019.10
boil over 152.17, 320.4
boil up 11.5
boisterous 53.13, 105.24, 503.4, 671.20
boisterousness 53.2
boîte 743.13
boîte de nuit 743.13
bola 356.13, 462.18
bold 142.9, 142.11, 180.18, 204.18, 283.14, 283.18, 348.12, 454.7, 492.16, 493.9, 666.6
bold as a lion 492.16

bold as brass 142.11
bold conjecture 951.4
boldface (n) 142.5 (a) 546.8, 548.20
boldfaced 142.11, 548.20
bold front 216.1, 454.1, 492.1
bold ignorance 930.4
boldness 142.1, 283.2, 348.4, 454.1, 492.1, 493.3, 666.2
bold relief 348.4
bold-spirited 492.16
bold stroke 492.6
bole 282.4, 310.11, 310.21
bolide 1073.15
boll 282.2, 310.30
bollix (n) 410.6 (v) 393.11, 1012.16
bollixed up 393.29, 799.4, 810.16
bollixed-up 414.22
bollix up 393.11, 414.12, 799.3, 811.3, 1012.16
Bolshevik (n) 611.12, 611.13, 860.3 (a) 611.21, 860.6
Bolshevikism 860.2
Bolshevism 611.5, 860.2
Bolshevist (n) 611.13, 860.3 (a) 611.21
Bolshevistic 860.6
Bolshie (n) 611.13, 860.3 (a) 611.21
bolson 237.7
bolster (n) 901.20 (v) 121.6, 449.12, 492.15, 901.21, 957.11
bolstered 901.24
bolstering (n) 957.4 (a) 901.23
bolster up 449.12, 901.21
bolt (n) 267.2, 363.2, 368.4, 370.2, 428.5, 462.6, 462.18, 770.8, 1025.17 (v) 8.23, 79.22, 174.8, 293.6, 363.7, 368.10, 370.6, 672.4, 773.6, 800.8, 808.11, 1012.12
bolt down 8.23, 672.4
bolter 363.5, 368.5, 808.5
bolt from the blue 131.2, 1025.17
bolt-hole 346.4, 346.5, 369.3
bolt in 429.14
bolting (n) 79.4, 222.4, 363.2 (a) 672.6
bolt of lightning 1025.17
bolt out of the blue 131.2
boltrope 180.14
bolt the door 1009.7
bolt upright 200.11
bolus 8.2, 86.7, 282.2
bomb (n) 87.11, 131.2, 179.10, 410.2, 462.20, 704.4, 746.3 (v) 117.4, 395.18, 410.10, 410.17, 459.23, 704.28
bombailiff 1008.15
bombard 395.18, 459.22, 1038.17
bombardier 179.20, 185.4, 461.11
bombardment 53.3, 459.7, 1038.8
bombardment emission 1033.5
bombardment weapons 462.11
bombast (n) 501.7, 502.1, 520.2, 545.2 (v) 545.6
bombastic 501.22, 502.12, 534.3, 545.9
bombasticness 534.1
bombastry 545.2
bomb cyclone 318.11, 671.4
bombe 10.47
bombed 88.33
bombed out 87.24
bomber 127.8, 179.10, 181.9, 308.11, 395.8, 461.11, 671.9
bomber pilot 185.3
bombilate 52.13
bombilation 52.7
bombinate 52.13
bombinating 52.20
bombination 52.7
bombing 184.11, 459.7
bombing mission 184.11
bombogenesis 318.11, 671.4
bomb out 704.28
bombproof (n) 1009.3 (a) 15.20, 1049.5
bombshell 131.2, 462.20
bomb shelter 346.4, 1009.3
bombsight 29.5
bomb threat 514.1
bomb thrower 461.11
bomos 703.12
bon 999.12
bona fide 644.14, 973.15
bona fideness 973.7
bona fides 644.7, 973.7
bonanza 386.4, 618.4, 991.2, 1010.3
bonbon 10.40
bond (n) 428.4, 436.2, 437.1, 438.1, 438.2, 644.7, 738.5, 775.1, 800.1, 800.3 (v) 438.9, 438.10, 800.5, 1060.8 (a) 432.14
bondage 432.1
bond crowd 737.10
bonded 800.14
bonded warehouse 386.6
bondholder 737.14
bonding 582.6, 587.3, 800.1, 800.3
bond issue 738.6
bondmaid 432.7
bondman 432.7
bond market 729.4
bond of matrimony 563.1
bond rating 630.3
bonds 428.4
bond servant 577.1
bond service 432.1
bondslave 432.7
bondsman 432.7, 438.6
bonds of harmony 455.1
bondswoman 432.7
bondwoman 432.7
bone (n) 37.2, 1046.6, 1066.2 (v) 570.12 (a) 2.26
bone-bruising 917.20
bone carver 716.6
bone-carving 715.1
bone-chilling wind 318.7
bone-dry 1066.7
bone fracture 85.38
bonehead 414.9, 924.4
boneheaded 922.17
boneheadedness 922.4
bonehead into it 414.12
bonehead move 975.6
bonehead play 414.5, 975.6
bone house 309.16
bone-laziness 331.5
bone-lazy 331.19
boneless rump 10.14
bone meal 890.4
bone of contention 456.7, 457.1, 937.1, 938.10
bone orchard 309.15
bone pot 309.12
boner 414.5, 975.6
bones 2.2, 93.3, 307.15, 391.4, 759.8, 1052.3
bones, the 2.2
boneshaker 759.21
bone-tired 21.10
bone to pick 456.7, 589.5
bone up 570.14, 989.18
bone up on 570.12
bone-weary 21.10
boneyard 309.15
bonfire 1019.13
bonged out 87.24
bonhomie 143.2, 585.1, 587.6
bonhomous 143.14
boniness 270.5
boning 570.3
boning up (n) 570.3 (a) 568.18
Bonin Trench 275.5
bonk (n) 902.5 (v) 75.21, 902.15
bonkers 926.27
bon mot 489.7
bonne bouche 10.8
bonne foi 644.7
bonnet (n) 5.25 (v) 5.40, 295.21
bonneted 5.45
bonniness 1016.2
bonny 999.12, 1016.18
bonnyclabber 1045.7, 1062.5
bon ton 373.1, 578.1, 578.2, 607.2
bonus 150.2, 254.4, 472.6, 478.5, 624.6, 627.1, 993.5
bonus point 752.3
bonus system 624.6
bon vivant 8.16, 496.6, 582.16, 588.5, 663.3, 672.3
bony 2.26, 270.17, 1046.10
bony fish 311.30
bony framework 2.2
bony labyrinth 2.10
bonze 699.14
bonzer 999.13
bonzo 926.27
boo (n) 59.1, 87.11, 508.3, 510.8 (v) 108.6, 508.10
boob 358.2, 924.3
boo-bird 48.6, 510.9, 512.6
boobish 922.15
boobishness 922.3
booboisie, the 606.2
boo-boo 414.5, 975.6
boob stunt 975.6
boob tube 1035.11
boob tube, the 1035.1
booby 412.5, 924.3
booby hatch 926.14
booby prize 646.2
booby trap 346.3, 356.12, 462.20, 1006.5
boodle 378.2, 482.11, 609.35, 728.2
boodler 610.5
boodling 609.34
booger 322.3
boogerman 680.9
boogeyman 680.9
boogie (n) 708.9 (v) 222.10, 582.21
boogie-woogie 708.9
boo-hoo 115.12
booing (n) 508.1, 508.3 (a) 508.12
book (n) 352.1, 554.1, 554.3, 554.13, 555.1, 704.21, 706.3, 720.10, 759.19, 793.2 (v) 368.11, 549.15, 599.7, 615.14, 628.8, 871.8, 965.4, 965.6
Book, the 683.2
book, the 554.1, 745.4, 869.4
book agent 554.2
bookbinder 554.2
bookbindery 739.3
bookbinding 554.14, 712.16
bookcase 386.6, 554.14, 554.17
book cloth 554.14
book club 554.16
book collector 554.18
book cover 554.14
bookcraft 554.19
book credit 622.1
book dealer 554.16
bookdealer 554.2
book depository 558.1
book design 717.5
booked 549.17, 965.9
booked-in 965.9
bookend (n) 554.17 (v) 212.8
bookends 211.3
bookery 558.1
book-fed 928.22
bookholder 554.17
bookie 759.20
bookie joint 759.19
book in 965.6
bookiness 928.5
booking 549.14, 615.4, 704.11, 965.1
booking agent 704.25
bookish 570.17, 572.12, 928.22
bookishness 570.4, 928.5
book jacket 554.14
bookkeeper 550.1, 628.7, 729.12, 1017.15
bookkeeping (n) 628.6 (a) 628.12
book-learned 928.22
book learning 928.5
bookless 930.13
booklet 554.11
booklore 928.5
booklover 554.18, 929.4
book-loving 928.22
book madness 928.5
bookmaker 759.20
bookmaking 554.19
bookman 929.3
book manufacturer 554.2
book manufacturing 554.19
bookmark (n) 517.10, 1042.18 (v) 1042.21
book-minded 928.22
bookmobile 558.1

Book of Books, the 683.2
Book of Common Order 701.11
Book of Common Prayer 701.10
book of fate 964.2
book of hours 701.10
book of lists 871.4
Book of Mormon 683.7
Book of Psalms 701.11
book of verse 720.5
book of words 704.21
book packager 554.2
bookplate 517.13
book printer 554.2
book printing 548.1, 554.19
book production 554.19
book publisher 554.2
bookrack 554.17
book-read 928.22
book report 549.7
bookrest 554.17
book review 946.2
book reviewer 556.4
bookroom 558.1
books 628.4, 871.5
book salesman 554.2
bookseller 554.2, 554.16
bookselling 554.19
bookshelf 554.17
bookshop 554.16
Books in Print 558.4
book-smart 928.22
bookstack 554.17
bookstall 554.16
book stamp 517.13
bookstand 554.16, 554.17
book-stealer 554.18
bookstore 554.16
book support 554.17
book table 554.17
book-taught 928.22
book tray 554.17
book truck 554.17
book value 738.9
book wagon 558.1
book-wise 928.22
bookworm 554.18, 572.1, 572.10, 929.4
booky 928.22
Boolean algebra 935.2
boom (n) 53.3, 54.2, 56.4, 180.11, 251.2, 671.7, 731.10, 906.4, 1010.5, 1012.5 (v) 52.13, 53.7, 54.7, 56.9, 174.9, 182.48, 251.6, 524.25, 1010.8
boom box 50.11
boomerang (n) 462.18, 506.1, 903.2 (v) 900.6, 903.6
boomerang child 227.8
boomerang effect 900.1
boomerang kid 227.8
boomers 302.2
booming (n) 52.7, 54.2, 56.4 (a) 52.20, 53.11, 53.12, 54.12, 56.12, 59.10, 1010.13
booming economy 1010.5
booming market 737.4
boomlet 731.10
boom shot 714.8
boom town 230.1
boom-town 230.11
boon (n) 472.7, 478.7, 999.4 (a) 582.23
boon companion 588.5
boon companionship 587.2
booncoon 588.5
boondagger 75.15
boondocks 158.4, 233.2, 310.13
boondocks, the 261.4
boonfellow 588.5
boonies 158.4, 233.2
boonies, the 261.4
boor 414.8, 497.6, 606.6, 924.5
boorish 25.6, 233.7, 414.20, 497.13, 505.6
boorishness 25.1, 233.3, 414.3, 497.4, 505.1, 922.3
boost (n) 251.1, 392.1, 446.1, 449.2, 449.3, 482.4, 509.3, 902.2, 912.2 (v) 109.7, 162.5, 251.4, 352.15, 392.9, 446.2, 449.11, 449.17, 482.16, 509.11, 902.12, 912.5
boosted 251.7
booster 86.6, 91.16, 101.5, 352.9, 483.1, 509.8, 1035.9, 1074.5, 1075.9
booster amplifier 1035.9
booster cushion 912.4
booster dose 86.6
boosterism 101.3
booster rocket 184.8, 1074.5
booster seat 912.4
booster shot 86.6, 91.16
booster station 1035.9
booster unit 1074.5
boosting 482.1, 912.1
boost one's pay 446.2
boot (n) 105.3, 183.4, 461.18, 572.9, 605.4, 902.9, 975.6, 1012.7, 1042.18 (v) 5.40, 745.5, 902.21, 909.20, 975.15, 1042.21
boot, the 909.1, 909.5
bootblack 79.14, 577.5
boot camp 84.2, 461.6
booted 5.45, 405.16
booter 5.38
booth 197.2, 228.9, 736.3
booting out 909.1
boot in the face, the 424.3
bootleg (v) 88.30, 732.7 (a) 674.6
bootlegger 88.19, 483.7, 732.4
bootlegging 732.1
bootleg liquor 88.18, 732.3
bootless 19.15, 391.12, 410.18
bootless errand 391.3
bootlessness 19.3, 391.2
bootlick (n) 138.4 (v) 138.7
bootlicker 138.4, 332.6, 511.4
bootlicking (n) 138.2 (a) 138.14
bootloader loader 1042.11
bootmaker 5.38
bootmaking 5.32
boot out 909.13
boots 5.27, 577.5
boots on the ground 461.24
bootstrap 1042.18
bootstrap loader 1042.11
boot up 1042.21
booty 472.3, 480.10, 482.11
booty call 582.9
boo-yaa 999.12
boo-yah 999.12
booyah 332.2, 334.1
booze (n) 88.13 (v) 8.29, 87.22, 88.25
booze fighter 88.12
booze freak 88.12
boozehound 88.12
boozer 88.12
booze up 88.23
booze-up 88.6
boozify 88.23
boozing 88.4
boozy 88.33
bop 708.9
borate 1060.8
Bordelaise 10.12
bordello 228.28, 665.9
border (n) 206.2, 211.4, 211.5, 213.5, 218.1, 231.2, 257.1, 704.20, 1069.10 (v) 211.10, 218.4, 223.9 (a) 820.12
border ballads 708.11
border-crossing 189.3
bordered 211.12
borderer 223.6
border ground 211.5
bordering (n) 211.7 (a) 209.8, 211.11, 223.16
borderland 211.5, 231.2, 233.2
borderlands 209.1
borderline (n) 211.3 (a) 211.11
borderline case 926.15, 971.8
border on 223.9
borders 209.1
border stone 211.6
border upon 223.9
bordure 211.4, 211.7, 647.2
bore (n) 96.2, 118.4, 238.14, 269.3, 292.3 (v) 96.12, 118.7, 284.15, 292.15
boreal 161.14, 313.9, 318.21, 1023.14
boreal blast 318.7
Boreas 318.2
bored 96.20, 118.12, 331.20, 982.3
boredness 118.3
boredom 96.1, 118.3, 331.6, 982.1
bored stiff 118.12
bored to death 118.12
bored to extinction 118.12
bored to tears 118.12
borehole 292.3
bore out of all patience 118.7
bore out of one's life 118.7
borer 285.3, 1040.6
boresome 118.10
boresomeness 118.2
bore stiff 118.7
bore to death 118.7
bore to distraction 118.7
bore to extinction 118.7
bore to tears 118.7
boring (n) 292.3 (a) 26.13, 118.10, 781.6
boringness 118.2
boring pain 26.2
born 1.4, 767.8, 794.10
born-again 685.9, 692.10, 858.19, 953.21
born-again Christian 675.20
born-again person 858.7
born before one's time 845.8
borne 901.24
borne-down 112.29, 297.18
borne out 957.20
born fool 924.1, 924.8
born for 413.29
born leader 574.6
born loser 125.7, 410.8, 1011.7
born on the sunny side of the hedge 1010.14
born on the wrong side of the tracks 607.10
born out of wedlock 674.7
born to the purple 607.10, 608.11
born under a bad sign 1011.14
born under a lucky star 1010.14
born under an evil star 1011.14
born with a silver spoon in one's mouth 607.10, 618.14, 1010.14
born yesterday 416.5
borough 230.1, 231.5, 609.16
borough council 423.1
borough-English 479.2
borrow 336.5, 384.6, 482.16, 482.19, 621.3, 623.6, 728.27, 751.4
borrowed plumes 621.2
borrowed word 526.7
borrower 623.4
borrowing 482.8, 526.7, 621.1, 623.1, 728.16
borrowing capacity 622.1
borrowing power 622.1
borrowing rate 623.3
borrow the loan of 621.3
borrow trouble 456.14
borscht 10.10
borscht belt 231.7
borscht circuit 704.11
borstal 567.9
borstal school 567.9
boscage 310.14, 310.15, 310.17
Bose-Einstein statistics 968.2
bosey 356.6
bosh 354.14, 520.3
bosk 310.14
bosket 310.15
bosky 310.39, 310.40
bos'n 183.7
bosom (n) 93.3, 207.2, 283.6, 767.5 (v) 345.7, 346.7, 474.7, 562.18
bosom buddy 588.4
bosomed 283.19
bosom friend 588.1
bosom friendship 587.8
bosominess 257.8
bosomy 257.18, 283.15, 283.19
bosquet 310.15
boss (n) 249.4, 283.3, 517.7, 574.2, 575.1, 610.7, 715.3, 997.11 (v) 283.12, 288.4, 573.8, 573.10 (a) 573.13, 612.17, 999.13
bossed 283.18
bossiness 141.1
bossing 573.2
bossism 417.3, 609.1
boss man 575.4

bossy (n) 77.9, 311.6 (a) 283.18, 417.16
Boston type 30.6
Boswell 616.7, 719.3
botanic 310.36, 1068.4
botanical 310.36, 1068.4
botanical garden 1069.10
botanist 1068.2
botany 310.1, 1068.1, 1068.3
botch (n) 340.3, 350.2, 410.6, 414.5, 975.5 (v) 340.9, 350.4, 393.10, 410.14, 414.11, 975.14
botched 340.12, 393.28, 414.21
botched copy 787.1
botched up 393.29
botched writing 547.6
botcher 414.8
botchery 414.4
botching 414.4
botch-up 410.6
both (n) 873.2 (a) 873.7
bother (n) 96.2, 105.6, 330.4, 643.1, 810.4, 971.3, 985.3, 996.3, 1013.3 (v) 96.13, 96.16, 98.15, 126.4, 640.7, 971.12, 985.7, 996.4, 1013.13
botheration 96.2, 330.4, 985.3
bothered 26.9, 96.21, 96.22, 126.7, 971.24, 985.12, 1013.20
bothering 98.22, 971.27
bothersome 26.13, 98.22, 126.10, 1013.18
bothersomeness 96.2, 98.7, 1013.1
botnet 1042.11
bo tree 928.8
bottle (n) 195.1 (v) 212.9, 397.11
bottle, the 88.13
bottle-assed type 548.6
bottled 212.12, 386.15
bottled water 1065.3
bottle-green 44.4
bottle kiln 742.5
bottleneck 169.1, 260.1, 270.3, 293.3, 1012.1
bottle nose 88.3
bottle opener 292.10
bottle screw 292.10
bottle sucker 88.12
bottle up 207.5, 212.6, 346.7, 428.8, 429.12, 474.5, 1012.10
bottling 212.2, 397.2
bottling up 474.1
bottling works 88.21
bottom (n) 180.1, 199.1, 199.4, 217.4, 243.1, 274.4, 284.9, 359.3, 492.5 (v) 199.6, 940.2 (a) 199.7, 633.9
bottom dollar 728.14, 820.2
bottom-dwelling 645.16
bottom feeder 607.7
bottom glade 284.9
bottoming out 252.2, 731.10
bottomland 236.1, 243.1, 274.3, 310.8
bottomless 6.14, 100.27, 275.12, 823.3, 991.7
bottomless depths 275.4
bottomlessness 275.1
bottomless pit 275.3, 823.1, 991.3
bottomless pit, the 682.1
bottomless well 991.3
bottom line 472.3, 473.3, 518.1
bottom-line 997.23
bottom line, the 196.5, 761.3, 767.3, 997.6, 1017.6
bottommost 199.7
bottom of the barrel 820.2
bottom of the heart 93.3, 767.5
bottom of the inning 745.3
bottom of the ladder 818.1
bottom of the sea 275.4
bottom on 199.6
bottom out 199.6, 852.6
bottom price 630.4
bottom rung 607.7, 818.1
bottomry (n) 438.4 (v) 438.10
bottomry bond 438.4
bottoms 180.10, 243.1, 284.9
bottom side 199.1
bottom-up 205.7
bottom waters 275.4
Botts dots 283.3
botulism 85.31
bouclé 288.6
boudoir 197.7
bouffant 259.13
bouffed up 259.13
bouffy 259.13
bouge 283.11
bough 310.11, 310.20, 793.4
boughpot 310.25
bought 733.11
bought and paid for 378.4
boughten 733.11
bought low 137.13
bougie 1026.2
bouillabaisse 10.10, 10.11
bouilli 10.13
bouillon 10.10, 10.14
boulanger 11.3
boulder 1059.5, 1059.6
bouldering 760.6
boulder-strewn 1059.12
bouldery 1059.12
boulevardier 500.9
bounce (n) 109.3, 193.1, 366.1, 501.8, 903.2, 917.3, 1034.10, 1048.1 (v) 366.5, 366.6, 503.3, 745.5, 903.6, 909.13, 909.20, 916.14, 917.11, 1048.5
bounce, the 909.1, 909.5
bounce a check 625.6
bounce back (n) 903.1 (v) 54.7, 83.7, 396.19, 903.6, 1036.16
bounce-back 903.2
bounced check 623.2, 625.3, 728.10
bounce drill 184.18
bounce pass 747.3
bouncer 15.6, 909.11
bounces 1036.11
bounce upon 223.11
bounciness 1048.1
bouncing (n) 366.3 (a) 15.15, 83.12, 330.17, 366.7, 903.10
bouncing baby 302.9
bouncy 330.17, 903.10, 917.20, 1048.7
bound (n) 211.3, 366.1, 903.2 (v) 174.8, 210.4, 210.5, 211.8, 211.10, 212.5, 366.5, 903.6 (a) 210.7, 212.10, 293.11, 359.11, 428.16, 436.8, 641.16, 775.9, 800.13, 970.13
bound and determined 359.11
boundaries 209.1, 211.1
boundary (n) 210.2, 211.3, 212.4, 257.1, 800.4, 820.2, 857.4, 875.3 (a) 211.11, 820.12
boundary condition 211.3, 959.2
boundary line 211.3
boundary-marking 210.1
boundary stone 549.12
bound bailiff 1008.15
bound book 554.3
bounded 210.7
bounden 641.16
bounden duty 641.1
bounder 497.6, 660.7
bound form 526.3
bound hand and foot 428.16
bounding (n) 210.1, 366.3 (a) 211.11, 366.7, 903.10, 959.7
bounding main, the 240.1
boundless 247.7, 677.17, 823.3, 993.16
boundlessness 247.1, 823.1, 993.1
bound morpheme 526.3
bound over 615.21
bounds 210.2, 211.1
bound to 641.16
bound up in 800.15
bound up with 772.5, 800.15
bound volume 554.3
bounteous 485.4, 991.7
bounteousness 485.1, 991.2
bountiful 485.4, 890.9, 991.7
bountifulness 485.1, 890.1, 991.2
bounty 478.5, 478.8, 485.1, 624.6
bounty hunter 381.7
bouquet 70.1, 310.25, 509.6, 770.8
Bourbon 611.9
Bourbonism 611.4
bourdon 708.22, 708.24
bourg 230.1
bourgeois (n) 227.6, 430.11, 497.6, 606.5, 607.6, 867.2 (a) 497.14, 607.10, 611.23, 867.6, 1005.8
bourgeoisie 607.5, 1005.5
bourgeois taste 497.1
bourn 186.5, 211.3, 238.1
bourne 238.1
bourns 211.1
bourse 737.7
bout 88.5, 457.3, 457.9, 743.6, 743.9, 754.3, 825.2, 850.3
boutique 736.1
boutique farm 1069.8
boutique farmer 1069.5
boutique hotel 228.15
boutonniere 310.25
bovid 311.45
bovine (n) 311.6 (a) 102.7, 106.10, 107.10, 311.45, 922.15
bovine animal 311.6
bovinity 106.1, 107.2, 922.3
bow (n) 155.2, 216.3, 279.2, 279.3, 283.3, 462.7, 585.4, 711.5, 913.3 (v) 138.7, 155.6, 279.6, 412.12, 433.10, 913.9
bow and arrow 462.7
bow and scrape 138.7, 155.6, 433.10
bowdlerization 79.2, 255.5
bowdlerize 79.18, 255.12, 268.6
bowdlerized 79.26, 268.9
bow down 155.6, 433.10
bow down and worship 696.11
bowed 265.10, 274.7, 279.10, 283.13, 433.16
bowed down 112.22, 137.13
bowed-out 283.13
bowelless 146.3
bowel movement 12.2, 12.4
bowels 2.18, 207.4, 275.3
bowels of compassion 145.2
bowels of the earth 275.3
bower 228.12, 758.2, 1008.3
Bower of Bliss 681.9
Bowery 230.6
bowery 310.41
Bowery bum 331.9, 660.2
bowie knife 462.5
bowing (n) 279.3 (a) 433.16
bowing and scraping 155.2
bowl (n) 8.12, 284.2, 463.1, 742.2, 746.1, 750.3, 904.3 (v) 284.12, 284.13, 904.9, 904.10, 915.10
bowl along 174.9, 177.28
bowl down 131.8, 913.5
bowled down 131.13
bowled over 131.13
bowlegged 265.12
bowlegs 265.3
bowler 904.7
bowl haircut 1016.14
bowlike 279.10
bowling (n) 750.1, 904.2, 915.1 (a) 915.14
bowling alley 287.3, 743.11
bowling bag 750.1
bowling ball 750.1
bowling game 750.2
bowling green 201.3, 287.3, 310.7, 743.11, 750.3
bowling on the green 750.3
bowling organization 750.1
bowling shoes 750.1
bowling string 750.2
bowl invitation 746.1
bowllike 284.16
bowl over 122.6, 131.7, 131.8, 913.5
bowls 8.12, 750.3
bowl-shaped 284.16
bowls of mercy 145.2
bowman 904.8
bow one's head 433.10
bow one's neck 604.20
bow out 188.9, 190.12, 222.8, 307.19, 909.18
bow-shaped 279.10
bowshot 223.2, 904.4
bowsprit 216.3
bowstring 604.16
bow submission 433.10
bow the head 155.6
bow thruster 904.6
bow tie 5.11

bow to 155.4, 250.5, 433.9, 433.10, 585.10
bow to one's will 433.10
bowwow 311.16
bowwow theory 523.13, 526.17
box (n) 195.1, 197.2, 228.8, 309.11, 386.6, 478.4, 604.3, 704.15, 902.8, 1013.6 (v) 212.9, 295.20, 428.9, 457.13, 604.11, 754.4, 902.19
box canyon 237.7
boxcar 179.15, 882.7
boxcar number 1017.5
boxcars 882.7
box cutter 462.5
boxed 212.12, 295.31
boxed in 428.15, 959.9
boxed-in 212.10
boxed set 554.5
boxer 461.2, 754.2
boxer briefs 5.22
boxers 5.22
boxes 745.1
box grave 309.16
box in 212.5, 212.6, 428.9, 959.3
boxing 212.2, 457.9, 754.1
boxing gloves 754.1
boxing-in 212.1
boxing match 457.9
boxing out 747.3
boxing punch 902.6
boxing purse 754.1
boxing ring 463.1, 754.1
boxing shorts 754.1
box kite 181.14
box lunch 8.6
box of cigarettes 89.5
box of cigars 89.4
box off 182.30, 773.6
box office 221.4, 627.1, 704.15, 739.7
box-office hit 704.4
box-office staff 704.23
box on the ear 604.3
box pleat 291.2
box room 386.6
box score 1017.6
box seat 704.15
box springs 901.20
box the compass 182.51
box the ears 604.11
box-top mission 184.11
box up 212.6, 212.9, 428.9, 429.12
boy 87.9, 302.5, 577.4, 758.2
boycott (n) 333.2, 586.3, 727.5, 773.1 (v) 333.5, 586.6, 727.10
boy-cottage 727.5
boycottage 586.3
boyfriend 104.12, 588.1
boyhood 301.2, 302.2
boyish 270.16, 301.11, 406.11
boyishness 76.1, 301.4
boylike 301.11
boylikeness 301.4
boy next door, the 606.1
Boy Scout 999.6
boys of summer, the 745.2
boy soprano 709.5
boys' room 12.10
boy toy 104.12
boy wonder 413.12
bozo 15.7, 414.9, 593.4, 671.10
B-picture 706.1
bra 5.24, 901.2
bra burner 642.5
brace (n) 86.33, 200.1, 708.29, 709.12, 873.2, 901.2 (v) 9.2, 15.13, 200.7, 800.9, 901.21, 1046.9
brace a yard fore and aft 182.48
braced 15.18, 901.24
braced framing 266.4
brace house 759.19
bracelet 280.3, 498.6
bracelets 428.4
brace oneself 359.8, 405.13
bracer 9.1, 86.8, 88.8, 901.2
bracero 1069.5
braces 202.5
brace up 9.2, 15.13, 396.19, 492.13
brachycephalic people 312.2
brachygrapher 547.17
brachygraphy 547.8
brachylogous 537.6
brachylogy 537.1
bracing (n) 9.1 (a) 9.3, 17.15, 81.5, 86.44, 901.23, 1023.12
bracken 310.4
bracket (n) 211.3, 809.2, 901.2 (v) 212.8, 530.16, 775.6, 798.4, 800.5
bracket capital 198.5
bracket creep 630.9, 632.3
bracketed 775.9, 776.6, 800.13, 873.8
bracketing 798.2, 800.1
bracketology 747.1
brackets 211.3
brackish 64.7, 68.9
brackishness 68.4
bract 310.19, 310.28
bracteole 310.19
bractlet 310.19
bradytelic 861.8
bradytely 861.3
brae 237.2, 237.4
brag (n) 502.1, 502.5 (v) 502.6, 503.3
brag about 509.12
braggadocio 502.1, 502.5
braggadocious 140.8
braggart (n) 140.5, 502.5, 503.2 (a) 502.10
braggartism 502.1
bragging (n) 502.1 (a) 140.8, 502.10
bragging rights 140.1, 502.2
Bragi 720.11
brag oneself up 502.7
Brahma 677.3
Brahman 311.6, 608.4, 699.13
Brahmana 683.8
Brahmanic 675.32
Brahmanistic 675.32
Brahmin 141.7, 607.4, 929.1
braid (n) 3.7, 271.2, 740.2 (v) 271.6, 740.6
braided 740.7
braided rope 271.2
braided stream 238.1
braiding 740.1
braids 1016.14
Braille 30.6
brain (n) 2.15, 919.1, 919.6, 920.9, 929.1 (v) 25.4, 308.18 (a) 2.30
brain-born 986.20
brain box 198.8
brain candy 95.1
brain case 198.8
brainchild 547.10, 712.9, 893.1, 932.6, 986.5
brain damage 922.9, 926.1
brain-damaged 922.22, 926.28
brain-dead 307.29
brain death 85.2, 307.1
brain disease 85.25, 92.14
brain drain 482.6
brain fade 922.9, 971.1
brain fag 21.1
brain fart 922.9
brain fog 922.9, 971.1
brain food 10.3
brain freeze 922.9
braininess 920.2
braining 308.1
brain-injured 926.28
brainless 922.13, 923.8, 985.16
brainlessness 922.1, 923.1, 985.5
brainpan 198.8
brainpower 919.1, 920.1
brains 10.20, 381.6, 919.1
brainsick 926.26
brainsickness 926.1
brainstorm (n) 92.14, 364.1, 365.1, 926.8, 932.6, 932.7 (v) 541.11
brains trust 423.1
brain surgeon 413.12, 929.1
brain teaser 522.8
brainteaser 522.9
brain ticklers 87.4
brain trust 422.3, 423.1
brain twister 522.8
brainwash 375.23, 568.12, 569.4, 858.15
brainwashed 858.19
brainwasher 375.10
brainwashing 568.2, 569.2, 858.5
brain wave 365.1, 932.6
brainwork 570.3, 931.1
brainworker 929.1
brainy 920.14
braise 11.5, 40.2, 1020.17
braised 11.7
braising 11.2
brake (n) 175.4, 310.15, 1012.7 (v) 175.9, 857.11, 1012.13
brake horsepower 18.4
brakeman 178.13
brake parachute 181.13
brakie 178.13
braking 1041.7
braking parachute 181.13
braky 310.40
bramble 285.5, 310.9, 803.4
bramble fruit 310.4
brambly 285.10
bran 10.4, 295.16, 1051.5
branch (n) 171.4, 238.1, 238.3, 310.11, 310.20, 461.21, 560.4, 561.4, 617.10, 675.3, 739.7, 793.4, 809.2, 809.5, 937.1 (v) 171.7, 259.6, 278.5, 875.4
branched 171.10, 310.41, 875.6
branched chain 1038.7
branchedness 310.20
branch feeder 238.3
branchiness 310.20
branching (n) 171.3, 875.1 (a) 171.10, 310.41, 875.6
branching off 164.1, 171.3
branching out 171.3
branchlike 171.10
branch of chemistry 1060.1
branch off 164.3, 171.7
branch office 617.10, 739.7
branch of knowledge 568.8, 928.10
branch of learning 568.8
branch of philosophy 952.1
branch of physics 1018.1
branch of service insignia 647.5
branch of study 928.10
branch of the service 461.21
branch out 171.7, 259.6, 771.4, 783.2
branchy 310.41
brand (n) 517.5, 517.13, 661.6, 767.4, 809.3, 865.4, 1004.3, 1019.16, 1020.6, 1020.15, 1020.16, 1021.4 (v) 517.19, 517.20, 661.9, 1004.6, 1020.24
branding 734.2, 1020.5
branding iron 1020.15
brand iron 1020.15
brandish (n) 916.2 (v) 348.5, 501.17, 916.11
brandishing 916.2
brand loyalty 326.1
brand name 517.13
brand-new 390.12, 841.9
brand-newness 841.1
brand-spanking new 841.10
brandy 88.15
branks 605.3
brannigan 53.4, 88.6, 456.6
branniness 1051.1
branny 1051.11
brash (n) 316.2, 1059.1 (a) 142.10, 454.7, 493.7, 505.7
brash bearing 454.1
brashness 142.2, 454.1, 493.1, 505.3
brass (n) 142.3, 493.1, 549.12, 710.12, 711.7, 728.2, 997.8 (a) 1058.17
brass, the 249.5, 574.11, 575.17
brassard 647.1
brass choir 711.7
brassed off 118.11
brasserie 8.17
brasses 710.12, 711.7
brass farthing 998.5
brass hat 575.17, 997.9
brassiere 5.24, 901.2
brassiness 58.1, 142.2, 454.1, 666.2
brass instrument 711.7
brass knuckles 462.4
brass pounder 347.16
brass ring 100.11
brass-rubbing 1044.2
brass section 710.12

brass tacks 761.4
brassware 735.4
brass wind 711.7
brass wind instrument 711.7
brassy 53.13, 58.15, 142.11, 454.7, 666.6, 1058.17
brat 302.4
brat pack 770.3
brattice 213.5
brattle (n) 55.3 (v) 55.6
bravado 454.1, 492.1, 492.4, 502.1, 503.1
brave (n) 461.6, 492.7 (v) 134.5, 216.8, 454.3, 492.10, 1006.7, 1012.15 (a) 492.16, 501.19
brave, the 492.7
brave face 216.1
brave front 216.1
braveness 492.1
brave new world 821.1
brave out 134.5
bravery 492.1, 498.3
brave show 501.8
bravo 308.11, 461.1, 503.2, 593.3
bravura (n) 413.1, 492.4, 501.4, 708.13, 708.16 (a) 413.22, 501.19, 708.50
brawl (n) 53.3, 456.5, 457.5, 671.2, 770.2, 810.4 (v) 53.9, 456.11, 457.13
brawler 327.5, 452.3, 461.1
brawling 53.13, 59.10
brawn 15.2, 305.1
brawniness 15.2
brawny 15.16, 257.18
bray (n) 53.5, 58.3 (v) 53.10, 58.9, 60.2, 524.25, 1051.9
braze 803.9
brazen (v) 492.10 (a) 40.4, 53.13, 58.15, 142.11, 454.7, 493.7, 501.20, 654.17, 666.6, 1058.17
brazen boldness 493.1
brazen-face 493.4
brazenface 142.5
brazenfaced 142.11, 493.7, 501.20, 666.6
brazenfacedness 142.2
brazen it out 360.4
brazen-mouthed 53.12
brazenness 142.2, 454.1, 501.3, 666.2
brazen out 492.10, 492.11
brazen through 492.10
brazier 1020.11
breach (n) 224.2, 435.2, 456.4, 655.1, 655.2, 674.3, 802.4, 813.2 (v) 224.4, 292.14, 435.4, 802.12, 818.12, 910.9
breach of confidence 645.5
breach of contract 435.2
breach of faith 435.2, 645.5, 645.6
breach of friendship 456.4
breach of law 674.3
breach of privilege 435.2
breach of promise 435.2, 645.5, 645.6
breach of public trust 389.1
breach of the peace 435.2, 456.5
breach of trust 435.2, 645.5
breach the law 674.5
breach the peace 458.15
breachy 361.12
bread (n) 10.1, 10.28, 449.3, 701.7, 728.2 (v) 8.18, 771.6
bread and butter 10.1
bread-and-butter 150.5, 767.9, 798.6
bread-and-butter pickle 67.2
bread and circuses 95.5
bread and water 515.2, 992.6
bread and wine 701.7
breadbasket 2.19
breadcrust 10.28
bread pudding 10.41
breadstuff 10.28
breadth 158.1, 257.1, 269.1, 300.3, 979.1
breadwinner 726.2
breadwinning (n) 472.1 (a) 472.16, 724.15
break (n) 20.2, 85.38, 143.7, 158.8, 188.2, 211.3, 224.2, 369.1, 402.1, 456.4, 633.4, 737.5, 757.3, 795.2, 802.4, 813.2, 826.1, 846.2, 852.2, 857.3, 972.1, 1010.3 (v) 16.9, 20.8, 182.30, 188.8, 224.4, 238.22, 352.16, 373.9, 393.13, 393.23, 412.10, 432.9, 432.11, 435.4, 447.4, 568.13, 612.15, 625.7, 625.8, 633.6, 754.4, 757.5, 789.5, 802.12, 813.3, 826.3, 851.2, 857.9, 857.10, 909.19, 1025.27, 1050.3, 1070.7
breakability 1050.1
breakable 16.14, 1050.4
breakableness 16.2, 1050.1
breakage 393.1, 802.4
break a lance with 457.13
break a leg 403.14
break and entry 482.5
break a strike 727.11
break a sweat 725.9
break away 327.7, 363.7, 369.6, 370.6
breakaway (n) 363.2, 370.2, 749.3, 752.3 (a) 327.11, 333.6, 363.12, 868.6, 870.10, 900.8
breakaway group 617.4
break back 748.3, 859.5
break bounds 868.4, 910.9
break bread 8.20
break bread with 8.21
break bulk 182.49, 909.23
break camp 188.14
break cover 190.11
break down 21.5, 112.19, 115.12, 393.24, 393.26, 395.19, 432.9, 782.2, 801.6, 802.17, 809.6, 911.3
breakdown 21.2, 85.8, 393.1, 395.4, 410.3, 801.1, 802.5, 806.1, 860.1
break down and confess 351.7
break down and cry 115.12
breakdown of authority 418.1, 674.1
breakdown of law and order 418.1
breaker 802.7, 1070.2
breakers 238.14, 320.2
breakers ahead 1006.1
break even 790.5
break-even 790.8
break-even point 790.1
break faith 645.12
breakfast (n) 8.6 (v) 8.21
breakfast club 770.3
breakfast food 10.34
breakfast nook 8.17, 197.11
breakfast restaurant 8.17
breakfast room 197.11
breakfast table 8.6
breakfast time 314.1
break for 161.9
break forth 33.9, 190.11, 351.8
break free 1075.12
break ground 182.18, 818.10
break in 189.7, 214.5, 214.6, 292.14, 373.9, 432.11, 568.13, 818.8
break-in 482.5
breaking (n) 373.7, 432.4, 435.2, 568.3 (a) 525.12
breaking and entering 482.5
breaking down 801.1
breaking-in 373.7, 818.3
breaking loose 431.3
breaking news 351.1
breaking off of negotiations 456.4
breaking out 85.36, 431.3
breaking point 993.7
breaking story 552.3
breaking the surface 193.1
breaking up 395.4, 801.1, 813.1
breaking water 182.8
breaking wind 909.10
break in the action 857.3
break in the market 737.5
break into 292.14
break into a smile 116.7
break into music 708.37
break into pieces 802.13
break into smithereens 802.13
break in upon 214.5
break it to 351.5
break it up 802.19
break jail 369.6
break loose 369.6, 431.7
breakneck 174.15, 204.18, 401.10, 493.8
break new ground 816.3
break no bones 999.10
break of dawn, the 1025.10
break of day 314.2
break off 374.2, 789.5, 813.3, 857.10
breakoff 857.1
break off combat 433.7
breakoff point 211.3
break one's back 725.13
break one's bonds 369.6
break one's chains 369.6, 374.3
break oneself away 188.6
break one's eyes away 27.19
break one's fast 8.20
break one's fetters 374.3
break one's heart 112.19
break one's heart over 112.17
break one's neck 330.14, 401.5, 403.14
break one's promise 435.4, 645.12
break one's word 435.4, 645.12
break one up 116.9, 743.21
break on the wheel 604.15
break open 292.14, 393.23
break out 85.47, 369.10, 431.7, 431.8, 671.13, 749.7, 801.7, 818.13
breakout 190.1, 369.1, 749.3, 801.2
break out a flag 182.52, 517.22
break out ahead 845.6
break out ballast 182.49
break out in a cold sweat 127.10
break out in a rash 85.47
break out in a sweat 12.16
break out the anchor 182.18
break out with 85.47
break point 211.3, 748.2
break prison 369.6
breakroom 8.17
breaks, the 972.1, 1010.2
break service 748.3
break silence 524.21
break step 868.4
break the back of 19.10, 395.11
break the bank 409.9
break the charm 977.2
break the fall 670.8
break the habit 374.3
break the ice 405.12, 587.10, 587.12, 818.10
break the law 327.6, 674.5
break the neck of 19.10
break the news 351.5, 551.8, 552.11
break the pattern 374.3
break the peace 458.15
break the record 411.3
break the seal 351.4
break the sound barrier 174.8, 184.36
break the spell 977.2
break the thread 857.10
break the trail 165.2, 816.3
break through 292.14, 369.10, 409.10
breakthrough 392.1, 459.1, 816.2, 852.4, 858.1
breakthrough weapons 462.11
break to harness 432.11
break to pieces 395.17
break up 116.8, 393.22, 393.23, 395.22, 566.5, 771.8, 782.2, 801.6, 802.9, 802.13, 802.19, 806.3, 813.3, 852.7, 1051.10
breakup 393.6, 395.1, 395.4, 566.1, 771.3, 801.1, 802.3, 806.1, 857.1, 860.1
break water 182.47, 193.9
breakwater 283.9, 901.4, 1009.6, 1012.5
break wind 909.29
break with 456.10
break with the past (n) 852.2 (v) 860.4
breast (n) 10.15, 10.23, 93.3, 283.6, 767.5 (v) 216.8, 451.4
breast-beating 658.2
breasted 283.19
breast feathers 3.18
breastfeed 8.19

breast of lamb 10.16
breastpin 498.6
breasts 2.13, 283.6
breaststroke 182.11, 760.8
breast the wave 451.4
breastwork 1012.5
breath, a 828.3
breath 2.21, 20.2, 52.4, 69.1, 73.1, 306.1, 306.2, 318.3, 764.3, 830.3, 919.4, 1067.1
breathable 2.32, 70.9
breathe 20.8, 52.10, 69.6, 69.8, 306.8, 345.9, 348.5, 351.5, 518.8, 524.22, 524.25, 551.11, 761.8, 797.11, 957.8
breathe again 120.8
breathe down one's neck 223.12, 840.2
breathe down the neck of 166.3
breathe easier 120.8
breathe easy 120.8
breathe fire and fury 152.15
breathe free 430.18
breathe in 69.8, 187.12
breathe life into 306.10
breathe more freely 120.8
breathe new life into 9.2, 396.16
breathe one's last 307.18
breathe out 909.24
breather 20.2, 84.2, 402.1
breather the air of freedom 430.18
breathe vengeance 507.5
breath freshener 72.3
breathing (n) 2.21 (a) 2.32, 306.12, 784.16
breathing easier 120.10, 298.11
breathing easy 120.10
breathing freely 120.10
breathing hole 239.13
breathing place 20.2
breathing room 402.1, 430.4
breathing space 20.2, 158.3, 430.4, 857.3
breathing spell 20.2, 465.5, 857.3
breathing time 20.2
breathless 21.12, 51.12, 93.18, 101.8, 122.9, 135.6, 173.16, 307.29, 401.10
breathless adoration 155.1
breathless awe 122.1
breathless impatience 101.1, 135.1
breathlessness 21.3
breathless wonder 122.1
breath of air 2.21, 318.3
breath of fresh air 9.1
breath of life 306.2, 919.4
breath of one's nostrils 306.2
breathtaking 105.30, 122.12
breathy 525.12
breathy voice 52.4
breccia 803.5, 1051.6, 1059.1
breccial 1051.12
brecciate 1051.9
brecciated 1051.12
brecciation 1051.4
bred 1.4, 78.17
bred in the bone 767.8
breech (n) 199.1, 217.1 (v) 5.40
breech birth 1.1
breechcloth 5.19
breechclout 5.19
breeched 5.45
breeches 5.18
breeches buoy 397.6
breed (n) 559.4, 560.4, 561.1, 809.3 (v) 78.8, 78.12, 251.6, 568.13, 886.10, 892.12, 1070.6
breeder 75.13, 757.2, 1070.2
breed in and in 78.8
breeding (n) 78.2, 504.4, 568.3, 1038.8, 1069.14, 1070.1 (a) 78.18
breeding ground 886.8
breeding place 886.8
breed of cat 809.3
breed true 78.8
breeze (n) 318.4, 1014.4, 1047.4 (v) 174.9, 318.19, 757.5
breeze along 174.9
breeze home 411.4
breeze in 189.7, 757.5, 1014.11
breezeless 173.16
breeze up 318.19
breezeway 197.18
breeziness 109.3, 318.14, 330.2
breezy 109.12, 317.12, 318.21, 330.17
Breithablik 681.10
Bren 462.10
brethren 559.3, 700.1
breve 709.14
breve rest 709.21
brevet 420.4, 443.5, 615.1
breviary 696.4, 701.10
breviped 268.11
brevipennate 268.11
brevity 268.1, 344.2, 537.1, 828.2
brew (n) 10.49, 88.13, 88.16, 405.3 (v) 11.5, 14.2, 88.30, 259.7, 318.19, 381.9, 405.7, 797.11, 840.2, 1064.5, 1065.13
brewer 88.19
brewery 88.21, 739.3
brewhouse 88.21
brewing (n) 11.2, 1064.1, 1065.7 (a) 405.22, 840.3
brewmaster 88.19
brewpub 8.17
brewski 10.49
brewskie 88.16
briar 89.6
Briarean 15.17
Briareus 15.6
briar-hopper 227.10
briar pipe 89.6
bribability 645.9
bribable 378.4, 645.23, 894.15
bribe (n) 375.7, 378.2, 478.5 (v) 375.23, 378.3
bribe money 378.2
bribery 378.1
bribery and corruption 378.1
bribing 378.1
bric-a-brac 498.4, 712.9, 998.4
brick (n) 383.6, 659.2, 742.2, 1046.6, 1054.2 (v) 295.23
brickbat (n) 156.2, 156.3, 462.18, 510.4 (v) 459.27
brick kiln 742.5
brick-red 41.6
bricks 1038.13
bricks and clicks 724.4
bricks and mortar 724.4, 1054.2
brick wall 1012.5
brickwork 295.1
brickworks 739.4
bricky 41.6
brickyard 739.3
Brickyard, the 756.1
bricolage 365.5
bricoleur 365.6
bridal (n) 563.3 (a) 563.18
bridal bed 563.1
bridal outfit 5.2
bridal pair 563.9
bridal suite 563.3
bride 563.5
bride and groom 563.9
bridebed 563.1
bridechamber 563.3
bridegroom 563.5
bridemaiden 563.4
Bride of the Lamb, the 687.3
bridesmaid 563.4
bridesman 563.4
bride-to-be 104.16
bridewell 429.8
bridge (n) 27.8, 383.7, 383.9, 704.16, 708.24, 711.5, 758.3 (v) 295.30
bridgeable 966.7
bridge between 800.5
bridgeboard 193.5
bridge-builder 670.3
bridgebuilder 464.6
bridged 800.13
bridgehead 216.2, 460.6, 463.2
bridge loan 438.4
bridge mix 10.9
bridge over 800.5
bridge passage 708.24
bridge player 758.3
bridging (n) 800.1 (a) 295.36, 800.16
bridle (n) 428.4 (v) 141.8, 152.17, 428.7, 428.10, 500.14, 800.10, 1070.7
bridled 428.13
bridle path 383.2
bridle trail 383.2
bridle up 152.17
brief (n) 184.3, 549.7, 552.5, 557.1, 935.5 (v) 184.48, 381.11, 422.5, 551.8, 568.15, 615.14 (a) 268.8, 344.9, 537.6, 557.6, 828.8
briefcase 195.1
briefcase computer 1042.2
briefed 405.16, 928.18
briefing 184.3, 405.1, 422.1, 551.1, 568.6, 615.4
briefness 268.1, 344.2, 537.1, 828.2
briefs 5.22
brief span 223.2
brief success 409.3
brier 285.5, 310.9, 803.4
brier bush 310.9
briery 285.10
brig 429.8, 429.9
brigade 461.22, 770.3
brigadier 575.17
brigadier general 575.17
brigand 483.4
brigandage 482.6
brigandish 482.21
brigandism 482.6
bright (n) 89.2 (a) 35.19, 79.25, 97.11, 109.11, 124.11, 133.17, 339.14, 570.18, 662.19, 920.12, 920.14, 1002.8, 1016.20, 1025.32
bright and early 845.7
bright and fair 1066.8
bright and shining 1025.32
bright and sunny 109.11, 1025.30
bright as a new penny 1025.33
bright color 35.4
bright-colored 35.19
bright days 1010.4
bright diffuse nebula 1073.7
brighten 97.5, 109.7, 1025.27, 1025.28
brightened 1025.39
brightening (n) 314.2 (a) 1025.40
brighten one's day 97.5
brighten up 109.9, 392.11, 1025.28
bright-eyed 17.13
bright-eyed and bushy-tailed 17.13, 83.9
bright eyes 2.9, 27.9
bright-hued 35.19
bright idea 489.7, 932.6
bright light 352.4, 1025.4
bright lights, the 704.1
brightline 983.10, 997.14
brightness 35.4, 35.6, 97.4, 109.1, 133.8, 339.5, 570.5, 920.2, 1016.5, 1025.4
bright outlook 124.2
bright prospect 124.1
bright-red 41.6
bright side 97.4, 124.2
bright smile 116.3
bright thought 489.7, 932.6
bright time 1025.10, 1073.17
bright with promise 124.12
bright young man 841.4
brillante 708.53
brilliance 35.4, 413.1, 489.2, 501.5, 662.6, 920.2, 1016.5, 1025.4
brilliancy 501.4, 662.6, 1025.4
brilliant 35.19, 122.10, 247.10, 413.22, 489.15, 662.19, 920.14, 1016.20, 1025.32
brilliant idea 489.7, 932.6
brilliantine 1056.3
brilliant light 1025.4
brilliant success 409.3
brim (n) 211.4 (v) 794.7
brimful 794.11
brimmer 794.3
brimming 794.11
brimming eyes 115.2
brimming with happiness 95.17
brim over 238.17
brimstone (n) 110.12, 593.7 (a) 682.8
brim with cheer 109.6
brim with joy 95.12

brinded 47.15
brindle (n) 47.3 (a) 47.15
brindled 47.15
brine (n) 68.4, 397.4 (v) 397.9
brine, the 240.1
Brinell hardness number 1046.4
Brinell number 1046.4
Brinell test 1046.4
bring 176.16, 375.22, 630.13, 643.5, 734.12, 772.4, 886.11
bring about 182.30, 328.6, 375.13, 407.5, 886.10, 892.11
bring about a détente 465.8
bring a case before the bar 598.13
bring a case before the court 598.13
bring accusation 599.7
bring action against 598.13
bring along 769.8
bring around 396.15, 396.16
bring back 176.16, 396.16, 481.4, 989.9, 989.19
bring bad luck 1011.12
bring balm to one's sorrow 147.2
bring before 216.8, 439.5
bring before a jury 598.13
bring before the public 352.11
bring by the lee 182.32
bring by the wind 182.24
bring charges 599.7
bring comfort 121.6
bring crashing down 395.19
bring crashing down around one's head 125.11
bring down 137.5, 308.18, 395.19, 512.8, 897.4, 913.5
bringdown 156.3
bring down about one's ears 395.19
bring down around one's ears 1013.14
bring down on one's head 643.5
bring down the curtain 820.6
bring down the sun 182.51
bring down upon 643.5, 897.4
bring down upon one 1013.14
bring down upon oneself 897.4
bring down upon one's head 1013.14
bring face to face with 216.8
bring forth 192.14, 348.5, 886.10, 892.12, 892.13
bring forward 216.8, 348.5, 392.9, 439.5, 598.17, 957.12
bring glad tidings 552.11
bring home the bacon 249.7
bring home to 93.16, 599.9, 602.3, 888.4, 957.10
bring in 187.14, 627.4, 630.13, 906.9, 1069.19
bring in an indictment 599.7
bring in a verdict 598.20, 946.13
bring in a verdict of not guilty 601.4
bringing back to earth 977.1
bringing forth 192.5
bringing into question 938.12
bringing into the open 206.4
bringing of charges 599.1
bringing out 192.5
bringing to book 599.1
bringing to fruition 892.5
bringing together 472.2
bringing to light 941.1
bringing to the ground 395.5
bringing to view 941.1
bringing-up 568.3
bring into analogy 943.4
bring into being 306.10, 892.11, 892.12
bring into comparison 943.4
bring into confrontation 943.4
bring into court 598.13
bring into discredit 512.8, 661.8
bring into existence 306.10
bring into focus 208.10
bring into line 788.7
bring into play 387.14
bring into question 938.20
bring into relation with 775.6
bring into the limelight 352.15
bring into the open 206.5, 351.4, 352.11
bring into the wind 182.24
bring into the world 818.14
bring into view 348.5
bring it 745.5
bring it off 409.8
bring legal action 598.13
bring low 137.5, 432.9, 512.8, 661.8, 913.4
bring near 223.13, 784.8
bring off 328.6, 328.7, 407.5, 409.11
bring off the wind 182.23
bring on 886.11, 897.4, 957.12
bring one back to earth 977.2
bring one down 516.2
bring oneself 324.3
bring oneself to agree 332.11
bring one to his knees 412.10, 432.9
bring one up to speed 351.4
bring out 192.14, 206.5, 348.5, 352.14, 548.14
bring out in bold relief 348.5
bring out in high relief 348.5
bring out in strong relief 348.5
bring out of the closet 351.4
bring over 375.23, 858.16, 953.18
bring pressure to bear upon 375.14, 424.6, 894.9, 902.12
bring reason to bear 935.15
bring round 182.30, 375.23, 396.15, 396.16, 953.18
bring shame upon 661.8
bring someone to account 216.8
bring suit 598.13
bring the anchor home 182.18
bring the mind to bear upon 931.10
bring through 409.11
bring to 182.24, 396.16, 857.11, 858.11
bring to account 604.9
bring to a close 407.6, 820.6, 857.11
bring to a halt 820.6, 857.11
bring to a happy issue 407.5
bring to a head 119.2, 208.10, 407.8
bring to an end 820.6
bring to an understanding 466.7
bring to a screeching halt 1012.13
bring to a shuddering halt 1012.13
bring to a standstill 173.8, 857.11
bring to a stop 1012.13
bring to attention 983.10
bring to bay 457.15
bring to bear 957.12
bring to bear on 889.6
bring to bear upon 387.11, 775.6
bring to birth 818.14
bring to book 510.17, 599.7, 604.9
bring to completion 794.6
bring to effect 407.5, 886.10
bring to fruition 794.6, 892.11
bring together 253.4, 465.8, 472.11, 770.18
bring to justice 598.13
bring to life 306.10, 349.9
bring to light 192.14, 351.4, 941.4
bring to maturity 407.8
bring to mind 519.4, 784.7, 989.9
bring to naught 395.13
bring to nothing 900.7
bring to notice 348.5, 983.10
bring to one's notice 983.10
bring to one's senses 375.23, 925.3, 953.18
bring to pass 328.6, 407.5, 886.10
bring to reason 375.23, 925.3, 953.18
bring to recollection 989.19
bring to ruin 395.10
bring to tears 112.19
bring to terms 432.9, 465.8, 466.7
bring to test 942.8
bring to the bar 598.13
bring to the block 604.16
bring to the boiling point 105.12
bring to the fore 348.5, 997.14
bring to the front 348.5
bring to the gallows 604.17
bring to trial 598.13, 598.18
bring to view 348.5
bring trouble 1013.14
bring tumbling down 395.19
bring under control 1022.7
bring under one's notice 983.10
bring under the hammer 734.11
bring up 216.8, 439.5, 568.13, 818.11, 857.7, 909.26
bring up by hand 568.13
bring up for investigation 598.15
bring upon 643.5, 897.4
bring upon oneself 897.4
bring up short 857.7, 857.11
bring up the rear 166.3, 217.8
bring up to date 551.9, 832.13, 841.6
bring up to speed 551.9
bring with 769.8
bring within the law 673.9
bring word 552.11
brininess 68.4
brining 397.2
brink 200.3, 211.4
brinkmanship 493.3, 609.5
brinksmanship 609.5
briny 68.9
briny, the 240.1
briny deep, the 240.1
brio 17.4
brioche 10.31, 10.41
brisk (v) 9.2 (a) 9.3, 17.13, 68.7, 105.31, 318.21, 330.17, 828.8, 1023.12, 1023.14
brisken 9.2
brisket 10.14, 283.6
brisk market 737.2
briskness 17.4, 68.2, 330.2, 330.3, 1023.1
bristle (n) 3.2, 285.5, 288.3 (v) 152.17, 152.24, 200.8, 288.5
bristled 288.9
bristlelike 3.23, 288.10
bristles 3.8
bristle up 152.17, 283.10
bristle with 285.6, 884.5, 991.5
bristliness 3.1, 285.1, 288.1
bristling 288.9, 770.22, 884.9
bristling with arms 460.14
bristly 3.24, 3.25, 285.10, 288.9
Bristol fashion 180.20
Britain 232.4
Britannia 232.4
britches 5.18
Briticism 523.8, 591.2
British Cabinet 423.1
British Commonwealth of Nations 232.4
British court 595.2
British Empire 232.4
British imperial dry measure 300.4
British imperial liquid measure 300.4
British Interplanetary Society 1075.9
British Library 558.1
British lion and unicorn 647.6
British thermal unit 1019.19
brittle 16.14, 393.35, 828.7, 1050.4
brittle as glass 1050.4
brittleness 16.2, 1050.1, 1051.3
bro 559.3
broach (n) 292.3 (v) 192.12, 292.11, 292.15, 352.11, 439.5, 818.11
broaching 192.3, 292.1
broaching machine 1040.6
broach to 182.32
broad (n) 77.6, 302.7, 665.14 (a) 158.11, 257.17, 269.6, 488.6, 508.14, 524.30, 644.17, 666.8, 864.13, 971.19, 979.8
broad accent 524.8
broad arrow 517.13, 647.2, 661.6

broad awake 23.8
broadband 343.5, 347.18
broad-based 269.6, 794.10
broad-beamed 269.7
broad-bodied 269.8
broad-brush 772.6
broadcast (n) 352.1, 771.1, 1034.18, 1069.14 (v) 50.14, 343.7, 352.10, 551.8, 771.4, 1034.25, 1069.18 (a) 352.17, 771.9
broadcast band 1034.13
broadcast channel 1034.13
broadcaster 1034.23, 1035.13
broadcasting 343.5, 351.1, 352.1, 771.1, 1034.16, 1069.14
broadcasting regulation 1034.16
broadcast journalism 552.1, 1034.18, 1035.2
broadcast news 552.1, 1034.18, 1035.2
Broad Church 675.11
broad day 1025.10
broad daylight 1025.10
broaden 251.4, 251.6, 259.4, 259.5, 269.4, 864.9
broadened 251.7, 259.10
broadening (n) 251.1, 259.1 (a) 979.13
broadening the mind 570.1
broaden out 259.6
broaden the mind 568.10, 570.6
broad gauge 979.1
broad-gauge (n) 413.3 (a) 269.7, 413.25
broad-gauged 979.8
broad-gauge person 979.6
broad grin 116.3
broad hint 399.1, 422.2, 551.4
broad humor 489.1
broad in the beam 257.18
broad jump 366.1
broad jumper 366.4
Broadleaf 89.2
broad-leaved tree 310.10
broad lines 262.2
broadloom 269.7
broadly-based 864.13
broad mind 979.1
broad-minded 430.25, 920.17, 979.8
broad-mindedness 430.10, 920.5, 979.1
broadness 257.6, 269.1, 488.2, 644.4, 971.4, 979.1
broad of beam 269.7
broad-ribbed 269.7
broad-scale 269.6, 864.13
broad-scope 864.13
broadsheet 352.8
broad-shouldered 15.16, 76.13
broadside 218.1, 352.2, 352.8, 459.9, 551.1
broad spectrum 797.6
broad-spectrum antibiotic 86.3
broad-spectrum drug 86.3
broad-sterned 269.7
broad-toothed 269.7
Broadway 704.1
Broadway musical 708.34
Brobdingnagian 15.6
brobdingnagian 15.17, 257.20
brocard 974.2
brochure 352.8, 554.11
Brocken specter 988.2
brogue 524.8
bro hug 562.3
broil (n) 10.7, 456.5, 457.5, 671.2, 810.4 (v) 11.5, 456.11, 457.13, 1019.22, 1020.17
broiled 11.7
broiled fish 10.24
broiler 311.28, 1019.8
broiling (n) 11.2 (a) 1019.25
broiling sun 1019.7
broke 473.8, 619.10, 625.11
broken 228.34, 288.6, 393.27, 393.37, 395.28, 412.17, 432.15, 433.15, 625.11, 802.24, 804.4, 813.4, 851.3
broken accents 525.1
broken dose 86.6
broken-down 112.29, 393.33
broken English 524.8
broken fortune 619.1
broken ground 288.2
broken heart 96.6, 112.9
brokenhearted 112.29
brokenheartedness 112.9
broken home 566.1
broken-in 373.15
broken marriage 566.1
broken mirror 133.5
brokenness 813.1, 851.1
broken off 813.4
broken promise 645.6
broken record 118.1, 118.2, 118.5
broken-record 118.9
broken rhyme 720.9
broken speech 525.1, 531.1
broken thread 813.1
broken to bits 802.24
broken to harness 432.15
broken tones 525.1
broken to pieces 802.24
broken up 802.24
broken voice 525.1
broken water 238.14, 288.2
broken wind 2.21, 85.41
broker 213.4, 576.3, 576.4, 730.9, 737.10
brokerage 630.6, 731.2, 737.9, 737.18
brokerage house 737.9
brokerage office 737.9
broker's agent 737.10
brolly 181.13, 295.7
brolly-hop 181.13
bromance 104.17
bromide 118.4, 864.8, 974.3
bromidic 117.9
Brompton 86.23
Brompton's cocktail 86.23
Brompton's mixture 86.23
bronc 311.10
bronchi 2.22
bronchial 2.32
bronchial asthma 85.34
bronchial tube 2.22
bronchitis 85.16
bronchus 2.22
bronco 311.10
broncobuster 178.8, 1070.2
Bronx cheer 59.1, 333.1, 508.3, 510.8
bronze (n) 715.2 (v) 40.2 (a) 40.4, 1058.17
Bronze Age 824.5
Bronze Age man 842.7
bronze-brown 40.4
bronze-colored 40.4
bronzed 40.4
bronze medal 646.2
Bronze Star Medal 646.6
bronzy 1058.17
brooch 498.6
brood (n) 302.10, 559.4, 559.5, 561.1, 561.2 (v) 78.12, 110.15, 931.12
brooder 112.13, 228.22, 311.28, 886.8
brooding (n) 78.5, 931.2 (a) 108.7, 112.25
brood mare 77.9, 311.10, 757.2
brood on 931.10
brood over 112.17, 507.5, 931.13, 989.12
broody 112.25
broody hen 311.28
brook (n) 238.1 (v) 134.5, 433.6, 443.10, 979.7
brooking 148.1
brooklet 238.1
Brooklynese 523.7
Brooklyn hit 750.2
Brooklyn side 750.2
brook no 444.4
brook no denial 421.8, 424.5
brooky 238.23
broom 79.23
broomstick 270.8
broomtail 311.10
broth 10.10
brothel 228.28, 654.7, 665.9
Brother 648.5
brother 699.16, 700.2, 784.3
brother 76.10, 559.3, 588.1, 616.1, 617.11
brother-german 559.3
brotherhood 143.1, 559.1, 587.2, 617.3
brotherhood of man and fatherhood of God 143.4, 693.2
brother-in-arms 616.1
brother-in-law 564.2
Brother Jonathan 232.5
brotherliness 587.2
brotherly 143.13, 587.15
brotherly love 104.1, 143.4, 455.1
brothers 700.1
brothership 559.1
brothers under the skin 784.13
brother under the skin 784.3
brought about 892.17
brought down 137.13
brought in from nowhere 776.8
brought low 432.15
brought to notice 352.17
brought to one's knees 412.17, 432.15
brouhaha 53.3, 59.4, 105.4, 456.5, 671.2, 810.4, 917.1
brow 33.4, 198.2, 198.7, 211.4, 216.5
browbeat 127.20, 375.14, 424.4, 612.15
browbeaten 432.16
browbeating (n) 127.6 (a) 514.3
brown (n) 40.1, 87.9 (v) 11.5, 40.2, 1027.9 (a) 40.3
brown as a berry 40.3
brown bag 10.2, 195.2
brown-bag 8.21
brown-bagging 8.6, 10.2
brown-bag lunch 8.6
brown belt 646.3
brown-black 38.8
browned 11.7
browned-off 96.21, 152.30
brown-haired 40.5
Brownian movement 172.2
brownie 10.42, 138.4, 258.5, 678.8
brownie point 662.3
browning 40.1
Browning automatic rifle 462.10
brownish 40.3
brownish-gray 40.3
brownishness 40.1
brownish-red 40.4
brownish-yellow 40.3
Brown, Jones and Robinson 606.1
Brown, Jones, and Robinson 998.7
brownness 40.1, 315.3
brown-nose 138.7, 983.5
brownnose 138.4, 332.6
brownnoser 138.4, 511.4
brown-nosing 138.2
brownnosing 138.14
brown of dusk 315.3
brown off 96.13
brown out 1027.9
brownout 32.2, 1027.7, 1032.20
brown race 40.1, 312.2
brown rice 10.36
brown rice syrup 66.3
brown sauce 10.12
brown study 92.19, 931.3, 985.2, 986.9
brown stuff 87.16
brown sugar 66.2, 66.3
brows 3.12
browse 8.18, 8.28, 570.13, 733.8, 1042.21
browser 733.5, 1042.19
browsing 8.1
bruise (n) 46.1, 85.38, 1004.2 (v) 96.17, 389.5, 393.13, 604.13
bruised 96.23
bruiser 15.7, 593.4, 671.10
bruising 671.16
bruit (n) 552.6 (v) 352.10
bruit about 352.10
bruit abroad 352.10
bruited about 552.15
bruiting 352.1, 352.5
bruiting about 352.1
brumal 313.9, 1023.14
brume 319.3
brummagem 354.26
brunch 8.6

brune 40.3
brunet (n) 35.9 (a) 38.13, 40.3, 40.5
brunette (n) 35.9 (a) 38.13, 40.3, 40.5
brunt 902.3
brush (n) 3.9, 73.1, 217.6, 223.5, 233.2, 310.16, 457.4, 712.18, 891.2, 902.7, 1021.3 (v) 73.7, 79.23, 174.9, 223.10, 712.19, 740.6, 902.18, 1044.8, 1066.6, 1070.7
brush, the 712.3
brush ape 227.10
brush aside 372.2, 984.4
brush away 372.2, 984.4
brush block 746.3
brush by 73.7, 223.10
brushfire 1019.13
brush in 712.19
brushing 223.17
brushing up 570.3
brush off 79.23, 372.2, 908.3, 984.4
brush-off 372.1, 908.2
brush on paint 35.14
brush up 79.20, 392.11, 570.14, 989.18, 989.19
brush up on 989.18
brush wolf 311.19
brushwood 310.16, 1021.3, 1054.3
brushwork 712.8
brusque 344.9, 505.7, 537.6, 644.17
brusqueness 344.2, 505.3, 537.1, 644.4
Brussels biscuit 10.30
brutal 144.26, 308.23, 311.39, 497.12, 663.6, 671.21, 1000.9, 1013.17
brutal fact 761.3
brutality 144.11, 144.12, 497.3, 663.2, 671.1, 1000.2
brutalization 94.3
brutalize 94.6, 144.15, 671.11
brutalized 94.12, 144.26
brutalness 144.11
brutal task 1013.2
brut champagne 88.17
brute (n) 144.14, 257.13, 311.2, 497.7, 593.5, 671.9 (a) 144.26, 311.39, 663.6
brute creation 311.1
brute force 18.1, 424.2
brutelike 311.39
brute matter 1052.2, 1055.1
brute strength 15.2, 18.1
brutify 663.4
brutish 144.26, 311.39, 497.12, 663.6, 671.21
brutishness 144.11, 497.3, 663.2, 671.1
Brutus 357.10
BSer 357.9
B side 205.4
B-side 215.3
B side, the 779.2
BTW 538.13
bub 302.5, 559.3
bubba 302.5, 559.3
bubbie 560.15
bubble (n) 124.4, 266.2, 282.2, 283.3, 298.2, 320.1, 756.3, 764.3, 828.5, 976.1, 986.5 (v) 52.11, 320.4
bubble bath 79.17
bubblegum 1062.6
bubblehead 924.4
bubbleheaded 922.17, 922.19
bubbleheadedness 922.6
bubble-jet printer 1042.9
bubble memory 1042.7
bubble over 101.7, 320.4
bubble up 320.4
bubbliness 298.1, 320.3, 330.2
bubbling (n) 320.3 (a) 52.19, 320.6
bubbly (n) 88.17 (a) 298.10, 320.6, 330.17
bubkes 762.2, 762.3
bubo 85.37, 283.3
bubonic 283.17
buccaneer (n) 183.1, 461.5, 483.7 (v) 482.18
buccaneering 482.7
buccinator 353.2
buck (n) 76.8, 302.5, 311.5, 311.8, 311.23, 366.1, 728.7, 901.16 (v) 366.5, 451.4, 902.12
buckaroo 178.8, 1070.2
bucket (n) 180.1, 195.1, 747.3, 750.2 (v) 176.17, 737.23
bucket bag 195.2
bucketing 737.18
bucket list 871.1
bucket shop 356.10, 737.9
bucketshop 737.23
buck fever 128.1
buck for 375.14
bucking 451.1
bucking bronco 311.10, 366.4
bucking up 492.8
buckjump (n) 366.1 (v) 366.5
buckjumper 311.10, 366.4
buckle (n) 265.1 (v) 265.5, 725.9, 800.8
buckled 265.10
buckle down 359.8
buckle down to 404.3
buckle oneself 359.8
buckle on one's armor 405.13
buckle to 359.8, 404.3
buckle up 405.13
buckling 291.1, 800.3
buck naked 6.14
bucko 76.6, 503.2, 593.3
buck off 160.6
buck-passing 415.5
buck private 461.8
buckram (n) 580.1 (a) 580.9
bucks 728.2
buckshot 462.19
buckshot pattern 771.1
buckskin 311.11
bucktooth 2.8
buck up 9.2, 109.9, 124.7, 492.13, 492.15
buckwheat cake 10.45
bucoliast 720.12
bucolic 233.6, 416.6, 720.16, 1069.20
bucolicism 233.3
bucreaucratese 523.4
bud (n) 76.5, 302.5, 310.23, 559.3, 588.4, 886.7 (v) 191.6, 310.34, 310.35
Buddha 667.2, 677.4, 684.4, 921.2
Buddha-field 681.8
Buddha-like composure 106.2
Buddha nature 106.2, 921.6
buddhi 689.18, 919.4, 934.1
Buddhic body 689.17
Buddhism 675.14
Buddhist (n) 675.24 (a) 675.32
Buddhistic 675.32
buddied up 873.8
budding (n) 14.1, 259.3, 310.32 (a) 14.3, 259.12, 301.10, 818.15
buddy 302.5, 559.3, 588.4, 610.8, 616.2, 616.5
buddy-boy 588.4
buddy-buddy 587.20
buddy film 706.2
buddy up 450.3, 805.4, 873.5
buddy up with 587.11, 899.3
bud from 887.5
budge 172.5
budget (n) 386.1, 477.5, 626.3, 628.1, 635.2, 728.14, 729.3, 770.8, 965.3 (v) 477.10, 626.5, 635.4, 965.6 (a) 628.12, 633.7
budgetary 628.12, 731.23
budget crunch 619.1
budget deficit 731.9
budget for 477.10
budgeting 477.1, 626.1, 628.1
budget item 626.3
budget line 626.3
budget prices 633.2
budtime 301.1, 313.2
bueno 999.12
buff (n) 101.5, 166.2, 221.5, 509.8, 616.9, 866.3, 926.18 (v) 287.7, 1044.8 (a) 15.16, 40.3, 43.4
buff, the 6.3, 295.3
buffalo (n) 311.6 (v) 971.14
buffalo chips 12.4
buffaloed 971.25, 971.26
buffalo robe 295.10
buffalo wallow 243.1
Buffalo wing 10.23
buff-colored 43.4
buffed 15.16, 15.18, 287.11
buffer (n) 213.5, 287.4, 900.3, 1008.3, 1012.5 (v) 900.7
buffered aspirin 86.12
Bufferin 86.12
buffering 900.9
buffer state 213.5, 223.6, 232.1
buffer zone 465.5
buffet (n) 8.9, 8.17, 132.1, 604.3, 901.15, 902.8 (v) 389.5, 393.13, 451.4, 604.11, 604.12, 725.11, 902.16, 902.19
buffeting 604.4
buffet lunch 8.6
buffet supper 8.6
buffet the waves 451.4
buffing 1044.2
bufflehead 924.4
buffo 707.10
buffoon 322.3, 707.10, 924.1
buffoonery 489.5, 704.8, 923.1
buffoonish 489.16, 923.8
buffoonishness 489.5
buffoonism 489.5
buff-yellow 43.4
bug (n) 50.9, 85.42, 101.5, 311.32, 549.10, 680.9, 757.2, 926.12, 926.18, 1003.2, 1012.6, 1042.18 (v) 48.10, 96.13, 283.11, 440.12, 510.16, 811.4, 938.28, 985.7
bugaboo 127.9, 400.2, 680.9
bugbear 103.3, 127.9, 400.2, 680.9, 1001.1
bug bomb 1001.3
bug boy 757.2
bug-eyed 28.12, 283.16
bugeyes 28.6
bugged 96.21, 96.24
bugged-out 283.16
bugger (n) 76.5, 322.3, 660.5 (v) 19.9, 393.11, 414.12
bugger all 762.3
bugger around 998.15
buggered 393.29, 414.22
buggered up 393.29
buggered-up 414.22
buggering around 998.9
bugger off 188.7, 222.10, 368.11
bugger up 19.9, 414.12
bugging 48.2, 938.9
bugging out 368.4
buggy (n) 179.10 (a) 311.51, 926.27
bughouse (n) 926.14 (a) 926.27
bug in the ear 551.3
bugle (n) 283.8 (v) 53.10, 708.42
bugle call 458.7, 517.16
bugler 710.4
bug off 368.11
bug out 188.7, 222.10, 368.10, 491.8, 771.8
bugout 491.3
bugs 926.27
bugs on 101.11
build (n) 15.2, 262.1, 262.4, 266.1, 767.4 (v) 159.16, 251.4, 259.4, 266.5, 796.3, 892.8, 1043.4
build a bridge 405.12
build a fire 1020.22
build a fire under 17.10, 375.14
build a house of cards 1006.7
build bridges 800.5
build castles in Spain 986.16
build castles in the air 986.16
build-down 252.1, 255.2
builder 892.7
build in 159.16
building (n) 228.5, 266.1, 266.2, 796.1, 892.2 (a) 892.15
building block 1052.2
building blocks 196.5, 743.16, 763.2, 767.4
building design 717.1
building designer 717.3
building permit 443.6
buildings 471.6
building science 717.1
building site 739.1
building society 620.4
building stone 1059.1
building technology 717.1

building type 717.2
build into 772.3
build on 199.6
buildout 259.1
build the stately rime 720.14
build up 119.2, 251.4, 259.4, 352.15, 355.3, 770.19, 796.3
buildup 251.1, 352.5, 509.3, 796.1
build up an inventory 386.11
build up a stock 386.11
build up to 405.13
built 892.18, 1016.18
built for comfort 1016.18
built-in 772.5
built on bedrock 855.12
built on sand 764.8
built-up 259.10
bulb 282.2, 283.3, 310.22, 310.33
bulbel 282.2
bulbil 282.2, 310.22
bulblet 282.2
bulblike 282.9
bulbose 283.15
bulbous 282.9, 283.15, 310.36
bulbousness 283.1
bulbul 710.23
bulb vegetable 310.4
bulge (n) 2.19, 249.2, 283.3 (v) 283.11
bulged 283.16
bulging (n) 283.1, 283.2 (a) 282.8, 282.9, 283.15, 794.11
bulging purse 618.1
bulgy 283.16
bulimia 7.13, 672.1
bulimia nervosa 515.1, 672.1
bulimic 672.6
bulk (n) 244.1, 247.1, 257.1, 257.9, 257.11, 269.2, 792.6, 883.2, 1045.6 (v) 247.5, 257.15, 259.4, 259.5, 770.18
bulk buying 733.1
bulkhead 213.5, 901.4, 1009.6, 1012.5
bulkhead in 212.7
bulkheading 901.4
bulkiness 257.9, 297.2, 1013.9
bulk large 247.5
bulk purchasing 733.1
bulk up 259.4
bulky 247.7, 257.19, 269.8, 297.16, 763.7, 1013.19
bull (n) 76.8, 311.6, 354.14, 420.4, 429.10, 520.3, 737.13, 758.2, 975.7, 1008.16 (v) 520.5, 737.25, 902.12 (a) 76.12, 729.20
bulla 85.37, 283.3, 320.1, 1004.1
bull account 737.13
bulldog (n) 492.7, 803.4 (v) 913.5
bulldog courage 492.5
bulldogged 361.8, 803.12
bulldoggedness 803.3
bulldoggish 492.17, 803.12
bulldoggishness 803.3
bulldoggy 803.12
bulldog tenacity 360.1
bulldoze 127.20, 395.19, 412.9, 424.8, 514.2, 612.15, 902.12
bulldozer (n) 15.6, 179.18 (a) 424.12
bulldozing (n) 127.6, 514.1, 902.3 (a) 514.3
bullet 174.6, 462.19, 745.3, 758.2, 904.4, 1038.8
bullethead 361.6
bulletheaded 361.8
bulletin (n) 352.3, 549.7, 551.1, 552.5 (v) 352.15
bulletin board 352.2, 352.7, 547.12, 549.10, 551.1
bulletin board service 1042.19
bullet point 47.3
bullet points 551.1
bulletproof 15.20, 1049.5
bulletproof vest 460.3
bullet train 179.14
bullfight 457.4
bullfighter 461.4
bullfrog 311.26
bullheaded 361.8, 803.12
bullheadedness 361.1, 803.3
bullhorn 50.11, 53.6
bull in a china shop 414.8
bulling 902.3
bullion 728.20, 1058.5
bullish 124.11, 311.45
bullish market 737.4, 1010.5
bullishness 737.4, 1010.5
bullish prices 738.9
bull-like 311.45
bull market 737.4, 1010.5
bullnecked 269.8
bullock 76.8, 311.6
bullpen 429.8
bull pen, the 745.2
bullpen coach 745.2
bull pool 737.17
bull raid 737.20
bull ring 463.1
bullring 308.12
bull-roarer 53.6
bull session 541.2
Bull's Eye 1073.4
bull's-eye 208.2, 380.2, 409.5
bull the market 737.25
bullwhack 605.1
bullwhacker 178.9
bullwhip 605.1
bully (n) 15.7, 96.10, 461.1, 503.2, 593.3, 749.6 (v) 127.20, 424.7, 503.3, 612.15 (a) 999.13
bullyboy 15.7, 461.1, 503.2, 593.3
bully circle 749.4
bullying (n) 127.6, 503.1 (a) 503.4, 514.3
bully-off 749.6
bully pulpit 501.1
bullyrag 96.13
bullyragged 96.24
bulwark (n) 460.4, 901.2, 901.4, 1008.3, 1012.5 (v) 460.9
bum (n) 88.12, 178.3, 217.5, 331.9, 410.8, 440.8, 619.4, 660.2, 828.4 (v) 52.13, 177.23, 440.15, 480.19 (a) 1000.8
bum a ride 177.31
bum around 331.12
bumbershoot 295.7
bumble 414.11
bumblebee 311.34
bumblebomb 1074.4
bumbledom 612.10
bumbler 414.8
bumbling 414.20
bumblingness 414.3
bumhole 292.5
bummer 87.1, 132.1, 178.3, 331.11, 440.8, 660.2, 1011.1
bumming 177.3, 440.6, 480.1
bump (n) 52.3, 56.1, 184.32, 283.3, 283.4, 413.4, 447.1, 517.7, 759.10, 902.2, 902.3, 917.3 (v) 56.6, 447.3, 902.12, 902.13, 909.20, 917.11
bump against 902.12
bump-and-grinder 705.3, 707.1
bumped 283.15
bumper (n) 8.4, 213.5, 794.3, 1008.3 (a) 257.16
bumper crop 472.5, 991.2
bumper sticker 352.6, 803.4
bumper-to-bumper 293.11, 770.22, 884.9, 993.20
bump heads 215.4, 456.12, 457.17
bumpiness 288.1, 294.2, 917.2
bumping 257.21
bumping-off 308.2
bumping upstairs 446.1
bump into 223.11, 902.13, 941.3, 972.11
bumpkin 414.8, 606.6, 924.5
bump off 308.14
bump-off 308.2
bumptious 140.11, 142.9, 454.7, 666.6
bumptiousness 140.4, 142.1, 454.1, 666.2
bump up 251.4
bump up against 223.10, 902.12, 941.3
bump upstairs 446.2
bumpy 283.15, 288.6, 294.7, 917.20
bumpy ride 1011.6
bum's rush 372.1, 773.2
bum's rush, the 909.1
bum steer 356.2
bum trip 87.1
bun 3.7, 10.31, 1016.14
bunce 472.6, 478.5
bunch (n) 244.2, 283.3, 617.6, 770.3, 770.5, 770.7, 803.5, 884.3 (v) 770.16, 770.18, 803.6, 805.4
bunchbacked 265.13
bunched 283.15, 770.21, 803.10
bunches 3.7
bunching 803.1
bunch light 704.18
bunch together 770.18
bunch up 770.16, 770.18, 805.4
bunchy 283.15
bunco (n) 356.8, 357.4 (v) 356.18
bunco artist 357.4, 759.22
bunco game 356.10
bunco steerer 357.4
bundle (n) 195.2, 472.3, 618.3, 770.8, 1042.11 (v) 121.10, 177.28, 212.9, 401.4, 401.5, 562.17, 770.20, 800.9, 909.18
bundle away 386.10
bundled 212.12, 770.21
bundled software 1042.11
bundle off 904.13, 909.18
bundle of isoglosses 523.7
bundle of nerves,a 128.5
bundle up 5.39, 770.20
bundling 212.2, 562.1
Bundt cake 10.42
bung (n) 293.4 (v) 293.7, 393.13, 904.10
bungalow 228.8
bunged 293.11
bungee jump (n) 367.1 (v) 367.6
bungee jumper 367.4
bungee jumping 367.3
bungee-jumping 366.3
bunghole 239.10, 292.5
bungle (n) 410.6, 414.5, 975.5 (v) 340.9, 410.14, 414.11, 975.14
bungled 414.21
bungler 340.5, 414.8
bungling (n) 340.3, 414.4 (a) 340.12, 414.20
bungs 183.6
bung up 393.13
bungup and bilge-free 180.20
bunion 85.37, 283.4
bunk (n) 354.14, 502.2, 520.3 (v) 225.7, 225.10
bunk bed 229.1
bunker (n) 197.17, 284.5, 386.6, 460.5, 460.6, 751.1, 1009.3, 1074.7 (v) 385.9
bunker atmosphere 460.1
bunker mentality 460.1
bunkhouse 228.15
bunkie 588.3
bunkmate 588.3
bunk off 222.10
bunkum 354.14, 502.2, 511.1, 520.3, 609.37
bunny 311.23, 1016.8
bunny rabbit 311.23
bunny slope 204.2, 204.4
buns 217.5
Bunsen burner 1020.10, 1060.6
bunt (n) 745.3, 902.2, 904.1 (v) 902.12, 902.18, 904.9
bunting 647.7
buoy (n) 180.11, 397.6, 517.10 (v) 298.8
buoyance 109.3, 298.1, 1048.1
buoyancy 109.3, 298.1, 1048.1
buoyant 109.12, 298.14, 396.23, 1048.7
buoyant market 737.4
buoyed-up 901.24
buoy up 109.7, 298.8, 901.21, 912.5
bura 318.8
burble (n) 184.29 (v) 52.11, 320.4, 922.12
burble point 184.29
burbling 52.19, 320.6, 922.22
burbly 320.6
burbs 209.1, 230.1, 230.6
burbs, the 1005.5
burden (n) 96.8, 196.2, 257.2, 297.7, 641.1, 643.3, 656.1, 708.22, 708.24, 720.10, 849.5,

937.1, 1001.1, 1012.6 (v) 96.16, 98.16, 159.15, 253.4, 297.13, 725.16, 996.4, 1011.8, 1012.11
burdened 297.18, 794.12, 901.23
burdened with 643.8
burdened with debt 623.8
burdened with sorrow 112.20
burdening 297.7, 643.1
burden of care 96.8
burden of expenditure 626.3
burden of one's mind 931.4
burden of proof 641.1, 957.3
burden of sorrow 112.1
burdensome 98.24, 297.17, 725.18, 1012.18, 1013.18
burdensomeness 98.8, 297.2, 725.5, 1013.1
burden the memory 989.12
burden the mind with 989.17
burden with 643.4
bureau 594.4, 739.7
bureaucracy 373.5, 575.14, 612.10, 1012.4
bureaucrat 575.15
bureaucratic 417.15, 612.16, 612.18
bureaucratic delay 846.2
bureaucratic policing 1008.1
bureaucratism 373.5
Bureau of Aeronautics 184.7
Bureau of Customs and Excise 630.10
bureau of investigation 938.4
burelage 47.2
burelé (n) 47.2 (a) 47.10
burette 1060.6
burg 230.1
burgage 469.1
burgee 647.7
burgeon (n) 310.20, 310.23 (v) 14.2, 259.7, 310.34, 310.35
burgeoning (n) 14.1, 259.3, 310.32 (a) 14.3, 251.8, 259.12
burger 10.32
burgess 227.6, 430.11
burgh 230.1
burghal 230.11
burgher 227.6, 659.3, 867.2
burgherdom 1005.5
burglar 483.3, 593.1
burglar alarm 399.3, 400.1
burglarious 482.21
burglarize 482.15
burglarizing 482.5
burglarproof 15.20
burglary 482.5
burgle 482.15
burgomaster 575.16
burgoo 10.11
burgrave 575.12
burial (n) 309.1, 309.5, 309.16, 346.1, 367.2, 910.1 (a) 309.22
burial at sea 309.1, 309.5
burial case 309.11
burial chamber 309.16
burial customs 309.1
burial ground 309.15
burial mound 309.16
burial place 309.15
burial plot 309.16
burial service 309.4
burial yard 309.15
buried 275.13, 275.14, 346.11, 910.10
buried in 983.17
buried in thought 931.22
buried treasure 472.6
burin 713.8, 715.4
burinist 716.8
burke 308.19
burker 308.11
burking 308.6
burl 283.3, 310.11
burled 283.17
burlesque (n) 336.1, 336.3, 350.2, 355.1, 489.1, 508.6, 512.5, 704.1, 704.6, 784.1 (v) 350.3, 355.3, 508.11, 512.12 (a) 488.6, 508.14, 704.35
burlesque act 704.7
burlesque dancer 705.3
burlesque queen 707.1
burlesquer 489.12
burlesque theater 704.14
Burley 89.2
burliness 15.2
burly 15.16, 257.18
burn (n) 26.3, 85.38, 238.1, 356.9, 482.4, 747.3, 1020.6, 1074.9, 1075.2, 1075.9 (v) 26.7, 40.2, 152.15, 309.20, 356.19, 393.13, 482.16, 604.16, 671.11, 747.4, 904.10, 941.6, 1019.22, 1020.22, 1020.23, 1020.24, 1025.23, 1066.6
burnable (n) 1021.1 (a) 1020.28
burn a hole in one's pocket 626.6
burn at the stake 308.18, 604.16, 1020.25
burn daylight 331.13
burn down 395.19, 1020.25
burned 11.8, 393.27, 1020.30
burned-down 1020.30
burned-out 16.18, 21.10, 94.13, 1020.30
burned to the ground 1020.30
burned up 152.30
burner 395.8, 1019.11, 1020.10, 1020.13, 1020.14
burn in 1020.24
burn in effigy 661.9
burning (n) 26.3, 309.2, 390.3, 604.6, 904.2, 1019.1, 1020.5 (a) 26.10, 26.11, 35.19, 68.7, 75.28, 85.58, 93.18, 101.9, 105.22, 152.26, 152.29, 223.14, 544.13, 1019.25, 1019.27, 1020.26, 1025.30, 1025.34
burning at the stake 602.1, 604.6, 1020.5
burning ember 1019.16
burning ghat 309.9, 1019.13, 1020.13
burning hot 1019.25
burning issue 886.9
burning mountain 671.6
burning out 1022.2
burning pain 26.3
burning question 938.10
burning rage 152.10
burning shame 661.5
burning the candle at both ends 669.2
burning up 388.1
burning with curiosity 981.5
burning with excitement 105.22
burn in one's pocket 626.6
burnish (n) 287.2, 287.4 (v) 287.7, 1044.8
burnished 287.11, 1025.33
burnisher 287.4
burnishing 1044.2
burn it 745.5
burn off 1020.24
burn one's bridges 188.17, 359.8
burn one's butt 152.23
burn one's fingers 414.14, 1013.12
burn one's mortgage 624.13
burn one up 152.23
burn on the pyre 309.20
burn out 21.4, 21.5, 1022.8
burnout 16.1, 21.1, 21.2, 85.8, 94.4, 1022.2, 1074.9
burn rate 728.1
burn rubber 188.10
burnsides 3.8, 218.1
burnt 41.9, 1020.30, 1066.9
burnt cork 38.6
burn the candle at both ends 330.15, 486.3, 669.6, 725.13, 993.10
burn the midnight oil 570.12, 725.13, 846.7
burn to 100.15, 135.4
burn to a cinder 1020.25
burn to a crisp 1020.25
burn to ashes 1020.25
burn to death 308.18
burnt offering 696.7
burn to the ground 1020.25
burnt-out 21.10
burnt sienna 40.1
burnt umber 40.1
burnt up 388.5
burnt-up 96.21, 1020.30
burn up 96.13, 388.3, 1020.25
burn with curiosity 981.3
burn with love 104.18
burp (n) 909.9 (v) 909.28
burp gun 462.10
burping 1067.3
burr (n) 58.3, 285.5, 310.11, 310.30, 524.8, 713.2, 803.4 (v) 52.13, 58.9
burrheaded 3.24
burrheadedness 3.1
burring 52.20, 524.30
burro 311.15
burrow (n) 228.26, 284.5 (v) 159.17, 284.15, 346.8, 938.31
burrower 284.10
burry 285.10
bursar 624.9, 729.12
bursary 729.13
burst (n) 56.1, 56.3, 105.9, 152.9, 174.3, 330.4, 459.9, 671.6, 671.7, 802.4, 1019.14 (v) 56.8, 393.23, 671.14, 802.12 (a) 393.27, 802.24
burst at the seams 770.16, 993.8
burst forth 33.9, 190.11, 310.34, 671.13, 818.13
burst in 189.7, 214.5, 292.14
bursting (n) 802.3 (a) 56.11, 105.20, 671.24, 794.11, 884.9, 890.9, 993.20
bursting at the seams 794.11, 993.20
bursting of the bubble 410.3, 977.1
bursting out 890.9
bursting to 101.8
bursting with happiness 95.17
bursting with health 83.8
burst into 189.7
burst into bloom 310.35
burst into flames 1020.23
burst into laughter 116.8
burst into song 708.37
burst into tears 115.12
burst like a bubble 828.6
burst of applause 509.2
burst of laughter 116.4
burst of light 1025.4
burst of rain 316.2
burst of speed 174.3, 174.4
burst one's bubble 112.18, 125.11
burst on the ear 56.8
burst onto the scene 662.11
burst out 59.7, 116.8, 671.13
burst out crying 115.12
burst out laughing 116.8
burst someone's bubble 132.2
burst the bubble 977.2
burst upon 223.11
burst upon one 131.6
burst upon the view 33.9
burst with 884.5
burst with cheer 109.6
burst with energy 17.11
burst with health 83.6
burst with joy 95.12
burst with laughter 116.8
burst with pride 136.5
burthen (n) 297.7, 1012.6 (v) 297.13
bury 212.6, 309.19, 346.7, 367.7
bury away 386.10
burying 309.1, 309.5, 346.1, 910.1
burying ground 309.15
burying place 309.15
burying the hatchet 464.7
bury oneself in 570.12
bury one's head in the sand 148.4, 984.2
bury the hatchet 148.5, 465.9
bus (n) 179.10, 179.13, 1042.3 (v) 176.13, 177.33
bus-and-truck 704.11
busboy 577.7
bus driver 178.10
busgirl 577.7
bush 87.11, 196.3, 310.9, 310.13, 310.16, 891.2, 1040.5
bush, the 233.2
bush country 233.2
bushed 21.8
bushel 247.3
busheler 5.35
bushelman 5.35
bushes, the 745.1
bushfighter 461.16
bush flying 184.1

bushing 196.3, 915.7
bush league 745.1
bush-league 1005.7
bush leagues 745.1
bushlike 310.39
Bushman 312.3
bushman 842.7
Bushman race 312.2
bush pilot 185.1
bushranger 483.5
bushveld 233.2, 236.1, 310.13
bushwa 520.3
bushwhack 131.7, 308.14, 459.15
bushwhacker 461.16, 816.1
bushy 3.24, 310.39, 310.40
busier than a one-armed paper hanger 330.21
business (n) 328.1, 330.1, 404.1, 617.9, 641.1, 704.8, 724.1, 724.6, 731.1, 775.1, 831.3, 866.1 (a) 730.12, 731.22
business, the 356.9
business administration 731.1
business affairs 731.1
business agent 727.4
business arithmetic 628.6
business associate 726.1, 730.1
business at hand 937.1
business card 517.11
business casual 5.20
business class 607.5
business correspondence 553.1
business cycle 731.10, 824.2
business day 824.2
business deal 731.4
business dealings 731.1
business directory 574.10
business district 230.6
business end 820.2
business English 523.4, 530.1
businessese 523.10
business establishment 617.9
business ethics 636.1
business exchange 347.8
business expenses 626.3
business firm 617.9
business fluctuations 731.10
business growth 731.10
business house 739.7
business index 630.4
business jet 181.3
business language 523.11
business leader 730.1
business letter 553.2
businesslike 807.6
businessman 726.4, 730.1
business manager 704.25
business partner 616.2
businesspeople 730.1
businessperson 730.1
business plan 380.1
business relations 731.1
business section 230.6
businessspeak 523.10
business tourism 177.1
business transaction 731.4
business trip 177.5
businesswoman 77.5, 726.4, 730.1
business world, the 731.1
busing 177.6
bus jockey 178.10
busker 710.1
buskin 5.9, 704.5
buskined 704.34
bus lane 383.2
busload 196.2
busman 178.10
busman's holiday 20.3
buss (n) 562.4 (v) 562.19
bus stop 857.3
bust (n) 88.6, 283.6, 349.6, 410.2, 410.8, 429.6, 447.1, 549.12, 625.3, 731.10, 902.5, 1011.6 (v) 410.17, 429.16, 432.11, 447.3, 447.4, 625.7, 625.8, 671.14, 802.12, 909.19 (a) 395.29, 473.8, 619.10
bust a gut 116.8, 403.14
busted 393.27, 619.10, 625.11, 802.24
bust in 189.7, 292.14
bustiness 257.8
busting loose 431.3
busting out 431.3
bustle (n) 105.4, 330.4, 401.1, 503.1, 917.1 (v) 330.12, 401.4, 401.5
bustler 330.8
bustling 330.20, 831.10
bus tour 918.4
bust out 431.8
bust-out joint 759.19
bust up 802.9
bust-up 456.4
busty 257.18, 283.19
busy (v) 724.10, 725.16 (a) 214.9, 330.21, 498.12, 724.15, 725.17
busy as a beaver 330.21
busy as a bee 330.21
busy bee 330.8, 726.3
busybody (n) 214.4, 552.9, 981.2 (v) 214.7 (a) 214.9
busy-busy 330.21
busyness 330.5, 498.2
busy oneself 330.10, 724.10, 725.12
busy oneself with 404.3, 724.11
busy signal 347.13
busywork 724.2
but, a 1012.4
butane lighter 1021.4
butane torch 1020.14
butch (n) 76.9 (a) 75.30
butcher (n) 178.13, 308.11 (v) 308.17, 350.4, 414.11, 671.11, 802.11
butchered 414.21, 795.5
butchering 308.3, 802.2
butcher's meat 10.13
butchery 308.3, 308.12, 671.3
but good 999.13
butler 574.4, 577.4, 577.10
butt (n) 89.5, 217.5, 256.1, 380.2, 508.7, 793.3, 800.4, 820.2, 902.2, 904.1 (v) 223.9, 800.8, 902.12, 904.9
butt against 223.13, 902.12
butt cheek 199.1, 217.4
butte 237.3, 237.4
butt end 256.1, 820.2
butt-end 793.3
butter (n) 10.48, 504.5, 1047.4, 1062.5, 1063.2 (v) 295.24, 511.6
butter cracker 10.30
buttercup 104.14, 562.6
buttered eggs 10.26
butterfingered 414.20
butterfingers 414.9
butterflies 128.2
butterflies in one's stomach 128.1
butterfly 47.6, 182.11, 311.32, 362.5, 1028.4
butterfly dressing 86.33
butterfly effect 810.1, 886.3
butterfly stroke 760.8
butteriness 1062.1
butter knife 8.12
buttermilk 10.49, 1061.2
buttermilk sky 319.1
butter one's bread on both sides 993.12
butter salve 511.1
butterscotch 10.40
butter up 511.6
buttery (n) 386.8 (a) 287.12, 504.17, 511.8, 1056.9, 1062.11
butthead 311.6
butt heads 451.3
butt in 214.5, 214.6, 466.6, 844.4
butting 223.3, 904.1
butting-in 214.2
buttinsky 422.3
butt-naked 499.8
buttocks 199.1, 217.4
button (n) 216.6, 258.4, 283.3, 647.1, 998.5, 1058.5 (v) 293.6, 800.8
button-down 867.6
button-down type 867.2
buttoned-down 867.6
buttoned up 519.9
buttonhole (n) 310.25 (v) 118.7, 440.12, 524.26
buttonholer 118.4
buttonholing 440.3
buttoning 800.3
button man 308.11, 660.10
button one's lip 51.6
buttons 87.13, 87.17
button up 51.6, 293.6, 407.6
button up one's pockets 625.6
butt out 430.17
buttress (n) 901.2, 901.4 (v) 15.13, 449.12, 901.21, 957.11
buttressed 15.18, 901.24
buttressing (n) 901.4, 957.4 (a) 901.23
buttress pier 901.4
butt-ugly 1015.6
butty 588.4, 1058.9
butyraceous 1056.9
buvette 8.17
buxom 109.15, 257.18, 1016.18
buxomness 257.8
buy (n) 633.3 (v) 228.31, 332.8, 375.24, 378.3, 422.7, 733.7, 953.10, 954.6
buyable 378.4
buy and sell 731.15
buy a piece of 729.17, 733.7
buy a pig in a poke 414.14, 493.5, 759.24, 954.5
buy a share of 729.17
buy at a bargain 633.5
buy at cost 633.5
buy at wholesale prices 633.5
buy back 733.7
buy blind 733.7
buy drugs 87.22
buyer 626.4, 733.5
buyer resistance 734.6
buyers' market 633.2, 633.4, 731.1, 734.1
buyer's remorse 113.1
buyers strike 727.5
buy for a mere nothing 633.5
buy futures 737.23
buy in 729.17, 733.7
buying (n) 733.1 (a) 733.10
buying and selling 731.2
buying in 737.19
buying on credit 733.1
buying power 733.1
buying up 733.1
buy into 422.7, 729.17, 733.7, 953.10, 954.6
buy it 307.19
buy off 378.3
buy on credit 622.7, 733.7
buy on the cuff 622.7
buy on the installment plan 622.7, 733.7
buy on time 622.7
buy out 733.7, 805.3
buyout 737.19, 805.1
buy sight unseen 733.7
buy the farm 307.19
buy the ranch 307.19
buy time 821.6
buy up 733.7, 737.26
buzz (n) 57.1, 58.3, 74.1, 87.1, 87.2, 347.13, 552.6, 812.2 (v) 52.13, 57.2, 58.9, 184.42, 352.10, 524.25, 551.11
buzz about 330.12, 352.10, 352.16
buzz along 188.7
buzzbomb 1074.4
buzzcut 1016.14
buzzed 87.24
buzzer 400.1
buzzer play 747.3
buzzing (n) 52.7, 184.17 (a) 52.20
buzzkill 108.3
buzz off 188.7
buzz session 423.3, 541.6
buzzword 526.9
buzzworthy 100.30, 375.27
buzzy 88.36
BVD 5.22
bwana 575.1
by 837.7
by-and-by 839.1
by-bid 733.9
by-bidder 733.6
by birth 559.6
by-blow 561.5
by-election 609.15
by-end 380.2
by free alms 471.5
bygone 837.7

bygone days 837.1
bygones 837.1
bygone times 837.1
bylane 383.4
bylaw 673.3
byline 724.7, 888.2, 937.2
by marriage 564.4
by name 527.15
byname 527.5, 527.7
by one 469.8
by oneself 584.11
bypass (n) 383.4, 914.3 (v) 910.8, 914.4
bypassing 368.1
bypass surgery 85.19
bypast 837.7
bypath 383.4, 538.4
bypaths and crooked ways 383.4
byplay 490.1
by-product 817.3, 887.1, 893.3
by-purpose 380.2
byre 228.20
by remote control 1041.25
by right 673.11
byroad 383.4
byroom 197.20
bystander 223.6, 918.1, 957.6
bystreet 383.4
by-talk 541.4, 552.7
byte 1042.14, 1042.18
by the board 473.7
by-the-book 580.10
by the people 612.4
by the way 538.13
by-the-way 843.11
by two 875.1
byway 383.4, 538.4
by whatever name 527.15
byword 508.7, 526.9, 527.3, 661.5, 974.1, 974.4
by word of mouth 343.12
byword of reproach 508.7, 661.5
Byzantine (n) 198.6, 554.15 (a) 281.6, 381.13, 799.4, 920.15
Byzantine intrigues 894.3
Byzantine Rite 675.8
Byzantinism 281.1, 799.1
C 87.7, 728.7, 882.8
cab 179.13
cabal (n) 345.4, 381.5, 617.3, 617.6, 770.3, 805.1 (v) 381.9, 805.4
cabala 345.5, 689.1
cabalic 689.23
cabalism 689.1
cabalist 381.7, 689.11
cabalistic 345.11, 689.23, 805.6
caballero 104.12, 178.8, 608.5
caballo 87.9
cabaret 88.20, 704.14, 743.13
cabbage 10.35, 728.2
cabbagehead 924.4
cabbageheaded 922.17
cabbageheadedness 922.4
cabby 178.9, 178.10
cabdriver 178.9, 178.10
cabin (n) 197.9, 228.8 (v) 212.6
cabin attendant 577.5
cabin boy 183.6, 577.5
cabin crew 577.5
cabin cruiser 180.4
Cabinet 613.2
cabinet 195.1, 197.8, 229.1, 423.1, 574.11
cabinet 613.3, 1034.3
cabinetmaking 229.1
cabinet member 575.16
cabinet minister 575.16
cabinetry 229.1
cabinetwork 229.1
cabin fever 926.2
cable (n) 271.2, 347.14, 347.17, 1032.21, 1035.1, 1042.19 (v) 347.20
cable car 179.17
cablegram 347.14
cable modem 1042.19
cable movie 706.1
cable railroad 179.14
cable railway 383.8
cable system 1035.1
cable television 1035.1
cable-television system 1035.1
cable TV 1035.1
cableway 383.8
cabman 178.9
caboose 179.15, 817.1
ca-ca (n) 12.4 (v) 12.13
cache (n) 346.4, 386.3, 1042.7 (v) 346.7, 386.10
cachectic 85.54
cache memory 1042.7
cachet 517.13, 865.4
cachexia 16.1, 85.3, 85.9
cachexy 16.1, 85.3, 85.9
cachinnate 116.8
cachinnation 53.3, 59.1, 116.4
cacique 575.9, 610.7
cack-handed 414.20
cackle (n) 58.3, 116.4, 540.3 (v) 58.9, 60.5, 116.8, 524.25
cacodemon 680.6
cacoepy 525.5
cacoëthes 100.6
cacoëthes loquendi 540.2
cacoëthes operandi 91.19
cacoëthes scribendi 547.2, 718.2
cacogenic 1015.8
cacography 546.4, 547.6
cacologic 534.2
cacological 497.11, 534.2
cacology 525.5, 534.1
cacophonic 1015.6
cacophonous 61.4, 534.2, 1015.6
cacophony 58.2, 61.1, 534.1, 671.2, 810.5, 1015.1
cacount on 130.6
cactus 87.13, 87.17, 285.5
cad 497.6, 562.12, 660.7
cadastral 871.9
cadastre 871.6
cadaver 307.15
cadaverous 21.9, 36.7, 270.20, 307.28
cadaverousness 36.2, 307.11
caddie 577.5, 751.2
caddish 505.6
caddishness 505.1
cadence 194.2, 524.10, 708.24, 709.18, 709.23, 720.7
cadenced 709.28, 720.17
cadency 709.23
cadency mark 647.2
cadent 709.28
cadenza 708.27, 709.18
cadet (n) 183.4, 572.6 (a) 835.4
cadge 440.15
cadge a ride 177.31
cadger 331.11, 440.8, 730.5
cadging (n) 440.6 (a) 331.19, 440.16
Cadillac 249.4
Cadmean victory 411.1
cadmium lemon 43.1
cadmium orange 42.1
cadmium yellow 43.1
cadre 266.4, 461.22, 574.11, 617.6
caduceus 417.9, 647.1
caducity 16.3, 303.5, 828.1, 922.10
Caecias 318.2
caecilian 311.26
Caelus 1073.2
caesar 575.9, 575.13
Caesarism 612.8
Caesar salad 10.37
caespitose 310.42
caesura 224.1, 720.7, 802.4, 813.2, 857.3, 857.4
caesural 224.7
café 8.17, 88.20
café dansant 743.13
café society 578.6
café-society 578.16
cafeteria 8.17, 197.11
café theater 704.1
caffè 8.17
caffeine 86.9
caftan 5.21
cage (n) 429.7, 749.1, 759.16 (v) 212.5, 429.12, 1070.8
cage bird 311.27
caged 212.10
cage in 428.9, 429.12
cageling 429.11
cager 747.2
cagey 368.15, 415.12, 494.9
cageyness 415.1, 494.2
caging 429.1
cahoots 450.2, 899.1
cahot 283.3
Cailleac 678.11
Cain 308.11
cairn 309.16, 517.10, 549.12
caitiff (n) 491.6, 660.2 (a) 491.12
cajole 356.14, 375.14, 377.5, 440.12, 511.5
cajolement 375.3, 440.3, 511.1
cajoler 375.10, 511.4
cajolery 375.3, 377.1, 440.3, 511.1
cajoling 375.29, 377.8, 440.18, 511.8
Cajun 523.7
cake (n) 10.42, 1045.6 (v) 1045.10, 1046.8
caked 1045.14
cakes and ale 121.3
cakewalk 1014.4
cakey 1045.14
caking 1046.5
calamari 10.24
calambac 70.4
calamitous 395.26, 1011.15
calamity 308.8, 1001.1, 1011.2
calamity howler 125.7, 962.4
calamus 3.17
calando 708.54
calcification 1046.5
calcified 1046.13
calcify 1046.7, 1060.8
calcimine (n) 37.4 (v) 35.14, 37.6
calcimining 35.12
calcination 1020.5
calcinatory (n) 1020.13 (a) 1020.26
calcine 1020.24
calcitrate 902.21
calcitration 902.9
calcium 7.11
calcium cyclamate 66.2
calcium light 1025.19
calculability 962.8, 970.4
calculable 300.14, 962.13, 970.17, 1017.25
calculate 253.6, 300.10, 380.6, 380.7, 381.8, 1017.18
calculated 380.8, 381.12, 935.21
calculated deception 356.1
calculated distortion 350.1
calculatedness 380.3
calculated risk 380.3, 759.2
calculate on 380.6, 953.16
calculate one's position 159.11
calculating 356.22, 381.13, 645.18, 920.15, 1017.24
calculation 253.3, 300.1, 380.3, 381.1, 494.1, 1017.2, 1017.10
calculative 1017.24
calculator 253.3, 415.7, 628.7, 1017.15, 1042.2
calculus 1017.10
calculus of individuals 935.2
caldarium 79.10
caldera 237.7
caldron 858.10
calefacient 1020.26
calefaction 1020.1
calefactive 1020.26
calefactory 1020.26
calendar (n) 549.11, 554.9, 613.9, 832.8, 871.6, 965.3 (v) 549.15, 832.14, 871.8, 965.6
calendarial 832.15
calendarist 832.10
calendar maker 832.10
calendar-making 832.1
calendar month 824.2
calendar stone 832.8
calendar year 824.2
calender 287.6
calendric 832.15
calendrical 832.15
calends 832.4, 832.8
calenture 85.7, 85.28
calenture of the brain 926.8
calescence 1019.1
calf 2.7, 177.14, 302.10, 311.6, 1023.5
calfhood 301.2
calflike 301.11
calf love 104.3
calf's brains 10.15
calf's head 10.15
calf's liver 10.15

caliber 18.2, 245.1, 257.1, 269.3, 413.4, 920.1
calibrate 245.4, 300.10
calibrated 245.5
calibrated scale 300.2
calibrating circuit 1041.6
calibration 300.1
calico 47.12
calico cat 47.6, 311.20
calico pony 311.11
calid 1019.24
calidity 1019.1
caliduct 1020.10
California blackjack 759.11
California king size 257.4
California sunshine 87.10
caliginous 1027.13
caliper 300.10
caliph 575.9
caliphate 417.8
calisthenics 84.2, 568.9
call (n) 48.2, 59.1, 60.1, 347.13, 420.5, 421.1, 440.2, 440.4, 517.16, 582.7, 600.6, 615.7, 698.1, 737.21, 758.3, 758.4 (v) 59.6, 60.2, 60.5, 347.19, 420.11, 440.13, 527.11, 628.11, 759.23, 759.25, 946.9, 962.9
call a break 826.3
call a general strike 327.7
call a halt 135.5, 826.3
call a halt to 857.11
call all bets off 820.6
Callanetics 84.2
call an intermission 826.3
call a penalty 746.5
call a recess 857.9
call a spade a spade 535.2, 644.12, 987.4
call a strike 857.8
call attention to 524.24, 983.10
call away 420.11, 985.6
call back 396.16, 420.11, 989.9
call balls and strikes 745.5
call box 347.4
callboy 353.4, 704.23
call down 510.18
call down curses on the head of 513.5
call down evil upon 513.5
called 527.14
called by God 307.29
called for 963.13
called home 307.29
called strike 727.5
caller 347.11, 353.4, 585.6, 828.4
caller ID 347.4
caller ID service 347.4
call for (n) 963.2 (v) 176.16, 420.11, 421.5, 424.5, 440.9, 772.4, 963.9
call for help 440.11
call forth 105.12, 192.14, 375.13, 420.11, 886.11
call forwarding 347.4
call girl 665.16
call heads or tails 759.23
call heaven to witness 334.6
callidity 413.1
calligram 517.11
calligrapher 547.13, 716.2
calligraphic 547.22
calligraphy 546.5, 547.3, 547.5, 712.1, 712.16
call in 420.11, 440.13, 541.10, 628.11
calling 375.1, 420.5, 440.4, 527.2, 698.10, 724.6
calling a spade a spade 535.1
calling before the mind's eye 986.6
calling card 517.11
calling-down 510.6
calling forth 192.5, 420.5
calling into service 387.8
calling party 347.11
calling to the mind's eye 986.6
calling upon 387.8
calling zone 347.12
call in question 333.5
call-in show 1034.18
call into being 306.10, 892.12
call into existence 306.10
call into play 387.14
call into question 451.6, 955.6
Calliope 720.11
calliope 1074.10
callipygian 1016.18
callipygous 1016.18
call it a day 20.8, 407.6, 857.8
call it quits 857.8
call letters 1034.19
call names 156.5, 512.10, 513.7
call no man master 430.20
call of duty 641.1
call off 820.6, 1017.17
call off the dogs 430.17, 857.11
call of nature 12.1
call on 375.14, 420.8, 440.10, 440.11, 582.19
call one's bluff 454.6
call one's own 469.5, 469.6
call one's shot 962.9
call on for 421.5
call on the carpet 510.17
call on the phone 347.19
call option 733.2
callosity 85.39, 144.10, 1046.1
callous (v) 94.6, 1046.7 (a) 25.6, 94.12, 114.5, 144.25, 146.3, 654.17, 1046.13
calloused 94.12, 144.25, 654.17, 1046.13
callousness 25.1, 94.3, 114.2, 144.10, 654.6, 1046.1
call out 59.8, 192.14, 420.11, 454.3
call out for 421.5
call over 1017.17
callow 301.10, 406.11, 414.17, 795.4, 841.7, 930.11
callowness 301.3, 406.4, 414.2, 795.1, 841.1, 923.2, 930.1
call price 738.9
call sign 1034.19
call someone's bluff 216.8, 972.12
call someone to account 216.8
call the glass half full 124.8
call the play 420.8
call the roll 1017.17
call the shots 417.14, 420.8, 573.8, 612.12, 894.8
call the signals 420.8, 573.8
call the turn 962.9
call time 826.3
call timeout 826.3, 857.9
call to 524.26
call to account 510.13, 510.17, 604.9, 641.12
call to action 1042.18
call to active duty 615.17
call to arms (n) 454.2, 458.7, 517.16 (v) 457.13, 458.18
call together 420.11, 770.17
call to mind 784.7, 957.13, 986.15, 989.9
call to one's attention 983.10
call to prayer 696.8
call to the colors (n) 458.7, 615.7 (v) 458.18, 458.19, 615.17
call to the witness box 957.12
call to witness 598.17, 957.12
call up 105.12, 192.14, 347.19, 375.13, 420.11, 458.18, 615.17, 690.11, 784.7, 986.15, 989.9
call-up 458.7, 615.7, 770.1
call upon 375.14, 387.14, 420.8, 440.10, 440.11
call upon one for 421.5
call upon one to 422.6
call up spirits 689.21, 690.11
callus 85.39
callusing 1046.5
call waiting 347.4
calm (n) 51.1, 106.2, 123.1, 173.5, 670.1, 781.1 (v) 106.6, 173.8, 465.7, 670.7 (a) 106.12, 123.3, 129.2, 173.12, 464.9, 670.13, 933.4
calm acceptance 123.1
calmant 86.45, 670.16
calm as a mill pond 173.12
calmative (n) 86.12, 670.3 (a) 86.45, 670.16
calm before the storm 173.5
calm, cool, and collected 129.2
calm disposition 106.2
calm down 106.7, 173.8, 670.7
calmed 120.10
calming (n) 465.1, 670.2 (a) 670.15
calming hand 670.3
calm mind 106.2
calmness 106.2, 123.1, 129.1, 173.1, 464.2, 670.1, 781.1
calm of mind 106.2, 933.1
calm weather 317.3
caloric 1019.1
calorie 17.7, 1019.19
calorie-counting 7.13, 270.9
calorifacient 1020.26
calorific 8.33, 1020.26
calorigenic 1020.26
calorimeter 1019.20
calorimetry 1019.21
calotype (n) 714.4 (v) 714.14
calotypist 716.5
caloyer 699.16
calque 526.7
calumet 89.6, 465.2
calumniate 512.11
calumniation 512.3
calumniator 512.6
calumniatory 512.13, 513.8
calumnious 156.8, 512.13, 513.8
calumny 512.3, 513.2
Calvary 309.15
calve 1.3
calved 1.4
Calvinism 964.4
Calvinist (n) 964.5 (a) 675.28
Calvinistic 675.28
calvities 6.4
calx 1020.16
Calypso 240.3
calyx 310.28
cam 1040.5
camaraderie 450.2, 582.2, 587.2
camarilla 423.1, 613.3, 617.6
camber (n) 279.4, 283.1 (v) 204.10
cambist 729.11, 730.9
cambric tea 16.7
Cambridge Platonism 1053.3
camcorder 549.10, 714.11, 1035.10
camel 311.5
camelback (n) 265.3 (a) 265.13
cameleer 178.9
camelopard 311.5
Camelot 986.11
camel's hair 3.2
camel's nose under the wall of the tent, the 189.5
camel spin 760.7
Camenae 720.11
cameo 349.2, 706.3, 715.3
cameo carving 715.1
cameo glass 715.3
cameography 713.4
camera 29.2, 549.10, 714.11
camera angle 706.5
camera-eye 989.2
camera-eye observer 722.6
camera lucida 712.18
cameraman 706.5, 716.5, 1035.13
camera obscura 712.18
cameraperson 716.5
camera phone 714.11
camera position 706.5
camera-ready copy 547.10, 548.4
camera tube 1035.10
camerawoman 706.5, 716.5, 1035.13
camerawork 706.5
camisole 428.4
camouflage (n) 295.2, 346.2, 356.11, 787.1 (v) 346.6, 350.3, 354.16, 787.3
camouflaged 32.5, 346.13
camouflaging 787.1
camp (n) 225.4, 228.29, 463.3, 497.1, 501.4, 609.24, 617.4 (v) 159.17, 225.11 (a) 501.19, 704.35
campagna 310.8
campaign (n) 177.5, 458.3, 609.13, 886.9 (v) 177.21, 458.16, 609.40, 610.13
campaign button 609.13
campaign commitments 609.13
campaign contribution 609.13, 609.35

campaign dinner 609.12
campaigner 461.19, 610.1, 610.10
campaign for 509.13
campaign fund 609.13, 609.35
campaigning 609.12
campaign oratory 543.1
campaign promises 609.13
campaign speech 543.2
campaniform 279.13
campanile 272.6
campanist 710.11
campanological 54.13
campanologist 710.11
campanology 54.3
campanular 279.13
campanulate 279.13
camp counselor 466.5
camper 178.1, 179.19, 228.17
camper trailer 228.17
campestral 236.2
campestrian 236.2
campfire 1019.13
camp follower 166.2, 616.8
campground 228.17, 228.29, 463.3
campiness 497.1
camping 225.4
camping area 463.3
camping bus 179.19
camping ground 463.3
camping it up 704.8
camping trailer 179.19
camp it up 704.31
camp meeting 696.8
campo 230.8, 236.1, 310.8
camp on the trail of 166.3
camp out 225.11
campsite 228.29, 463.3
camp trailer 179.19, 228.17
campus 463.1, 567.10
campus, the 567.5
campy 497.14, 704.33, 704.35
can (n) 12.10, 12.11, 180.7, 195.1, 217.5, 429.9, 517.10 (v) 18.11, 212.9, 397.11, 443.13, 747.4, 751.4, 909.20
Canaan 986.11
Canadian doubles 748.1
Canadian football 746.1
Canadian French 523.7
Canadianism 523.8
Canadian maple leaf 647.6
Canadian national sport 749.1
canaille 606.3
canal (n) 2.23, 239.1, 239.2, 242.1, 270.3, 290.2 (v) 290.3
canaliculate 290.4
canaliculated 290.4
canalization 290.2
canalize 208.10, 239.15, 290.3
canal ray 1033.5
canape 62.4
canapé 10.32
canard 354.10, 552.6
canary (n) 710.13, 710.23 (a) 43.4
canary-yellow 43.4
canaster 89.2
can-carrier 862.3
cancel (n) 395.7, 445.1, 709.12 (v) 255.10, 255.12, 395.13, 395.16, 445.2, 625.9, 790.6, 820.6, 857.6, 900.7
canceled 148.7, 820.9
canceled check 627.2
canceling (n) 445.1 (a) 900.9
cancellate 170.11
cancellated 170.11
cancellation 170.3, 255.3, 255.5, 395.7, 445.1, 553.5, 625.2, 900.2
cancel out 255.10, 395.13, 900.7
cancer 85.39, 1001.2
cancer-causing agent 85.42
cancerous 85.61
cancer stick 89.5
candent 1019.27
candescence 1025.2
candescent 1019.27, 1025.30
candid 343.10, 416.5, 430.23, 499.7, 535.3, 540.9, 644.17, 973.15
candidacy 609.10
candidate 100.12, 440.7, 610.9, 615.9, 938.19
candidate for holy orders 699.4
candidature 609.10
candidness 644.4
candid photograph 714.3
candied 66.5
candle 1026.1, 1026.2
candle ends 256.1
candle fly 1026.5
candlelight 315.3, 1025.8, 1025.19
candlelighting 315.3
candlelit 1025.39
candle lumen 1025.21
candle-meter 1025.21
candlepin 750.1
candlepin bowling 750.1
candlepins 750.1
candlepower 1025.21
candlestick 1026.6
candlewick 1026.7
can do 18.11
can-do 17.13, 18.14, 330.17
candor 343.3, 416.1, 535.1, 540.1, 644.4, 649.2
candy (n) 10.40, 66.2, 87.5 (v) 66.4, 1046.8
candy bar 10.40
candy cane 47.6
candy store 66.1
candy-stripe (n) 47.5 (a) 47.15
cane (n) 30.6, 273.2, 310.5, 310.21, 605.2, 901.2, 1054.4 (v) 604.12
canebrake 310.15
cane juice 66.3
canescence 37.1, 39.1
canescent 37.7, 39.4
cane sugar 66.2, 66.3
cane syrup 66.2, 66.3
Canevari 554.15
Canicula 1073.4
canicular 313.9, 1019.25
canicular days 313.3, 1019.7
canicule 1019.7
canine (n) 2.8, 311.3, 311.16 (a) 311.41
canine appetite 100.7
canine madness 926.6
canine tooth 2.8
caning 604.4
can it 51.6
canker (n) 85.37, 1001.2 (v) 393.12, 393.21, 393.22
cankered 85.60, 110.19, 393.40
cankerous 85.60
canker sore 85.37
cankerworm of care 126.1
canned 88.33, 212.12, 386.15
canned foods 10.5
canned goods 735.7
canned show 1034.18, 1035.2
cannery 739.3
cannibal (n) 8.16, 308.11, 311.3, 593.5 (a) 8.31
cannibalism 8.1, 144.11
cannibalistic 8.31, 144.26
cannibalization 365.5
cannibalize 365.8
cannibalizer 365.6
canniness 415.1, 494.1, 635.1, 920.3
canning 11.2, 212.2, 397.2, 909.5
cannoli 10.41
cannon (n) 462.11, 745.3, 902.3, 903.2, 904.4 (v) 459.22, 902.13, 903.6
cannonade (n) 56.4, 459.9 (v) 459.22
cannonading 56.12
cannonball (n) 174.6, 367.1, 462.19 (v) 401.7
cannonball express 179.14
cannoneer 461.11, 904.8
cannon fodder 461.6
cannon into 902.13
cannon off 903.6
cannonry 459.9, 462.11
cannot 19.8
cannot choose but 963.11
cannot do otherwise 963.10
cannot help but 963.10
cannular 239.16
canny 415.12, 635.6, 920.15
canoe (n) 180.1, 759.12, 760.2 (v) 182.13
canoeing 182.1, 760.2
canoeist 760.2
can of corn 745.3
can of worms 797.6, 799.2, 1013.3, 1013.7
canon 280.9, 300.2, 419.2, 547.12, 554.7, 673.3, 673.5, 683.2, 683.7, 699.9, 701.10, 708.19, 718.1, 869.4, 928.9, 952.2, 953.2, 953.3
canoness 699.17
canon form 709.11
canonic 676.4
canonical 419.4, 676.4, 683.11, 687.7, 698.13, 953.27
canonical books 683.1
canonicalness 687.1
canonical prayers 696.4
canonicals 5.1, 702.1
canonical writings 683.1, 683.7
canonicate 698.2
canonicity 687.1
canonist 676.3, 687.4
canonization 662.8, 685.3, 698.10, 912.1
canonize 662.13, 685.5, 698.12, 912.6
canonized 662.18, 679.6, 685.8, 912.9
canonized mortal 679.1
canon law 673.5
canonry 698.2
canoodle 562.15
canoodling 562.2
can opener 292.10
canopic jar 309.12
canopic vase 309.12
canopied 295.31
canopy (n) 295.6, 1073.2 (v) 295.19
canopy of heaven 1073.2
canorous 708.48
cant (n) 204.2, 204.7, 278.2, 354.6, 522.7, 523.9, 693.1 (v) 182.30, 182.43, 204.10, 354.23, 523.18, 693.4
cantabile (n) 708.16 (a) 708.48
cant across 182.30
cantaloupe 42.2
cantando 708.30
cantankerous 110.20, 361.11, 1012.17
cantankerousness 110.3, 361.3
cantata 708.17, 708.18
cantatrice 710.13
can't be avoided 963.10
can't be helped 963.10
canteen 8.17, 197.11
canteen culture 612.4
canter (n) 174.3, 357.8, 693.3 (v) 174.8, 177.34
cantharis 75.6
can't help but 424.9
cant hook 906.4
canticle 696.3, 708.14, 708.17
cantilever 202.3
cantilever bridge 383.9
cantilevered 202.11
cantina 8.17
canting 204.15, 354.33, 693.5, 791.5
canting hypocrite 693.3
canto 708.4, 708.22, 720.10, 754.3
canton 231.5, 647.2
cantonment 228.29
cantor 699.11, 710.13, 710.18
cantorial side 220.1
cant round 182.30
cantus 708.4, 708.22
cantus figuratus 708.22
cantus firmus 708.22
cantus planus 708.22
canvas 180.14, 295.8, 463.1, 712.13, 712.18, 754.1
canvas board 712.18
canvass (n) 371.6, 440.5, 609.13, 770.1, 938.14 (v) 371.18, 440.14, 541.11, 609.40, 938.24, 938.29
canvasser 730.4, 730.6, 938.16
canvassing 371.6, 440.5, 541.6
canyon 224.2, 237.7
canzone 708.14
canzonet 708.14

canzonetta 708.14
cap (n) 5.25, 87.10, 198.2, 198.4, 198.5, 210.2, 295.5, 462.15, 548.6 (v) 5.40, 198.10, 210.5, 249.6, 295.21, 407.6, 506.6
capability 18.2, 405.4, 413.1, 413.4
capability of feeling 24.3
capable 18.14, 405.17, 413.24
capable of 897.6
capable of life 306.12
capable of solution 940.3
capable of survival 306.12
capacious 158.11, 257.17
capaciousness 158.5, 257.6
capacitance 1032.16
capacitate 405.8
capacitation 405.2
capacities 919.2
capacitive reactance 1032.13
capacity (n) 18.2, 158.1, 158.5, 257.2, 384.2, 413.1, 413.4, 724.3, 765.4, 794.3, 920.1, 1032.16 (a) 794.11
capacity for 413.5
cap and bells 5.9, 704.6
cap and gown 647.1
caparison (n) 5.2, 5.10, 295.11, 385.5 (v) 5.41
cape 283.9
Cape elk 311.5
Cape hunting dog 311.19
Cape polecat 311.22
caper (n) 366.2, 489.10, 743.5 (v) 109.6, 116.5, 366.6, 743.23
capering (n) 366.3 (a) 95.16
capersome 109.14, 743.29
capersomeness 109.4
capful of wind 318.3
capillament 3.2
capillarity 907.1
capillary (n) 2.23 (a) 2.33, 3.23, 271.7
capillary attraction 907.1
capilliform 271.7
cap in hand 155.8
capital (n) 208.7, 230.4, 384.2, 386.2, 548.6, 728.15 (a) 198.11, 249.14, 308.23, 546.8, 604.22, 728.30, 997.24, 999.12
capital city 208.7, 230.4
capital crime 655.2
capital expenditure 626.2
capital fellow 659.1
capital gains 472.3
capital gains distribution 728.15
capital gains tax 630.9
capital goods 386.2
capitalism 430.9, 611.8, 952.7
capitalist (n) 611.15, 618.7, 729.9 (a) 611.23
capitalist economy 731.7
capitalistic 611.23
capitalistic economy 731.7
capitalistic system 611.8
capitalization 386.2, 728.15, 729.2
capitalize 546.6, 628.8, 729.16
capitalized 546.8
capitalize on 387.15, 472.12, 843.8
capitalizing 729.2
capital joke 489.6
capital letter 546.2
capital murder 308.2
capital outlay 626.2
capital punishment 307.5, 308.7, 602.1, 604.6
capital ship 180.7
capital sin 655.2
capital spending 728.15, 729.6
capital structure 728.15
capitol 613.4
capitular 698.13
capitulary (n) 673.5 (a) 698.13
capitulate 433.8
capitulation 433.2, 437.2, 1017.11
capitulum 310.27
capo 660.10
cap of darkness 691.6
cap of dignity 647.3
cap of estate 647.3
cap of maintenance 647.3
capon 311.28
caponize 255.11
caporegime 660.10
capped 5.45, 198.13, 210.7
capper 357.5, 407.3, 862.2
capping 198.12, 249.12, 820.11
cap rhymes 720.15
capriccioso 708.53
caprice 364.1, 364.2, 365.3, 854.2, 986.5
capricious 362.9, 364.5, 365.10, 768.4, 782.3, 810.12, 828.7, 851.3, 854.7, 971.16
capriciousness 362.1, 364.2, 782.1, 851.1, 854.2, 971.1
caprid 311.45
caprine 311.45
capriole (n) 366.1, 366.2 (v) 366.5, 366.6
Capri pants 5.18
Capris 5.18
capsheaf 198.4
capsizal 205.2
capsize (n) 205.2 (v) 182.44, 194.8, 205.6
capsized 205.7
capsizing 205.2
capstan 906.7
capstone 407.3
capsule (n) 86.7, 295.16, 310.30, 557.1, 1075.2 (v) 212.9, 557.5 (a) 268.9
capsuled 212.12
capsule version 557.1
capsulization 557.1
capsulize 268.6, 557.5
capsulized 268.9
captain (n) 183.7, 185.1, 575.6, 575.17, 575.19, 1008.15 (v) 573.8, 612.11
captain general 575.17
Captain Hicks 882.2
Captain Hook 483.7
Captain Kidd 483.7
captain of industry 730.1, 997.8
captainship 573.4
captain's mast 595.4
captain's walk 295.6
captcha 1042.19
caption (n) 937.2 (v) 937.3
captious 510.23, 936.14
captious critic 495.6, 936.7, 946.7
captiousness 510.4, 936.5
captivate 95.10, 104.22, 375.23, 377.7, 691.8
captivated 104.27, 122.9, 691.12
captivating 97.7, 377.8
captivation 97.2, 377.1, 691.2
captive (n) 429.11, 432.7 (a) 429.21, 432.14
captive audience 48.6
captive nation 232.1
captivity 429.3, 432.1
captor 480.11
capture (n) 429.6, 480.2, 480.10, 1042.8 (v) 349.8, 411.3, 429.15, 472.8, 480.18, 1042.21
captured-air bubble 179.22
captured-air vehicle 179.22
capture on film 549.15, 714.14
capturer 480.11
caput 198.4
cap verses 720.15
caquet 540.3
caqueterie 540.3
car 179.9, 179.15, 756.1
carabao 311.6
carabineer 461.9, 904.8
caracole (n) 366.2 (v) 109.6, 116.5, 177.34, 366.6, 743.23
car alarm 400.1
carambole 902.3
caramel 10.40, 40.1
caramelize 40.2, 66.4
carapace 295.15, 460.3
caravan 179.2, 179.19, 228.17, 812.3
caravansary 228.15
caravanserai 228.15
carbamate insecticide 1001.3
carbarn 197.27
carbine 462.10
carbo 7.5
carbohydrate 7.5
carbolic acid 86.21
carbon 7.11, 91.8, 785.4, 1020.16, 1038.5
carbonaceous 1021.9
Carbonarist 860.6
carbonate (n) 1058.1 (v) 1060.8, 1067.8
carbonated 320.6, 1067.9
carbonated water 10.49, 1065.3
carbonation 320.3
carbon black 38.6
carbon copy 548.3, 778.3, 785.3, 785.4, 785.5, 873.4
carbon-copy 785.8, 874.3
carbon dating 312.10
carbon dioxide 1024.7
carbon-dioxide foam 1022.3
carbon footprint 397.1
carbon-14 dating 832.1
carboniferous 1021.9
carbonization 1020.5
carbonize 1019.23, 1020.24
carbonized 1020.30
carbon monoxide 1001.4
carbon neutral 397.13
carbonous 1058.15
carbon tet 1022.3
carbon tetrachloride 1022.3
carbs 7.5
carbuncle 85.37, 283.4
carburize 1060.8
carcass 2.1, 307.15, 393.8, 1052.3
car chase 655.2
carcinogen 85.42, 1001.3
carcinogenic 85.61
carcinogenic substance 89.1
carcinoma 85.39
car crash 1011.2
card (n) 517.11, 549.10, 553.3, 758.2, 965.3, 1042.3 (v) 79.21
cardboard 1054.5
cardboard city 619.3
card-carrier 617.11
card-carrying 761.15, 973.15
card-carrying Communist 611.13
card-carrying member 617.11
card catalog 871.3
card count 759.11
card counter 759.21
card-counting 759.11
card file 871.7
card game 743.9, 743.16, 758.1
card games 759.7
cardholder 617.11, 727.4
cardhouse 1006.1
cardiac arrest 85.19
cardiac infarction 85.19
cardinal (n) 699.9 (a) 41.6, 249.14, 997.24, 1017.23
cardinalate 698.2
cardinal directions 161.3
cardinal point 997.6
cardinal points 161.3
cardinal-red 41.6
cardina's hat 647.4
cardinalship 698.2
cardinal sin 654.3, 655.2
cardinal sins 655.3
cardinal virtues 653.3
card index 871.7
cardio 84.1
cardioid (n) 280.7 (a) 279.15
cardiorespiratory fitness 84.1
cardiovascular disease 85.19
cardiovascular fitness 84.1
cardiovascular text 84.3
card-playing 758.1
cardplaying 758.1
card punch 1042.4
cardshark 759.21
cardsharp 357.3, 759.21
cardsharper 357.3, 759.21
cardsharping 356.8
card up one's sleeve, a 386.3
card up one's sleeve 249.2
card voting 609.18
care (n) 90.1, 96.8, 112.10, 126.1, 339.1, 387.2, 429.5, 434.1, 449.3, 449.4, 494.1, 573.2, 615.1, 635.1, 983.1, 1008.2, 1011.1 (v) 339.6 (a) 449.20
care about 93.11
careen (n) 916.6, 917.8 (v) 174.8, 182.43, 194.8, 204.10, 205.6, 916.10, 917.15

careening 204.15, 851.3, 916.17
career (n) 162.1, 172.2, 724.6 (v) 917.15 (a) 413.26
career building 724.6
career diplomat 576.6
career girl 726.2
careerism 100.10, 651.1, 724.6
careerist (n) 651.3 (a) 100.28, 651.5
careeristic 100.28
career politics 609.1
career soldiers 461.23
career track 724.6
career woman 77.5, 726.2, 726.4
care for 91.24, 104.18, 339.9, 387.12, 449.16, 577.13, 1008.19
care for truth 973.5
carefree 107.7, 109.12
carefreeness 109.3
careful 339.10, 494.8, 635.6, 644.15, 920.19, 983.15
careful consideration 494.1
carefully ignore 340.8
carefulness 339.1, 494.1, 635.1
caregiver 90.10, 1008.6
caregiving (n) 339.1, 449.3 (a) 449.20
careless 102.7, 340.11, 365.10, 414.20, 426.4, 493.8, 531.4, 810.15, 982.3, 984.6
careless abandon 340.2
carelessness 102.2, 340.2, 365.3, 414.4, 426.1, 493.2, 810.6, 982.1, 984.1
care naught for 327.6
care nothing about 102.4
care nothing for 102.4, 157.3
care of souls 698.1, 698.9
caress (n) 73.1, 223.5, 562.5 (v) 73.8, 223.10, 562.16, 1044.6
caressable 104.24
caressing 73.2, 562.1
caressive 562.23
caress the ear 48.12
caretaker 429.10, 1008.6
caretaker government 612.4
caretaking 1008.1
careworn 112.26, 126.9
carfare 630.6
cargo 196.2, 297.7, 643.3, 1012.6
cargo dock 386.6
cargo pants 5.18
cargo ship 180.1
carhop 577.7
car horn 399.3
caribou 311.5
caricatural 355.4, 508.14
caricature (n) 350.2, 355.1, 489.1, 508.6, 512.5, 712.12, 712.15, 712.16 (v) 350.3, 355.3, 508.11
caricaturist 489.12, 716.3
caries 85.40
carillon (n) 54.4, 711.18 (v) 708.42
carilloneur 710.11
car in every garage, a 1010.1
caring (n) 93.5, 104.1, 339.1, 449.3 (a) 93.20, 339.10, 449.20
cariosity 85.40
carious 393.40
caritas 104.1, 143.4, 455.1
caritative 104.26, 143.13
carjack 424.7, 482.20
carjacker 483.7
carjacking 482.3, 482.7
carking care 112.10
Carling float 180.11
carlish 497.13
carlishness 497.4
carload 196.2
carman 178.9
carmelized 66.5
carminative (n) 86.17 (a) 86.48
carmine (n) 41.1 (v) 41.4 (a) 41.6
carnage 308.4, 395.1
carnal 75.25, 654.12, 663.6, 665.29, 695.16
carnal abuse 75.11
carnal delight 95.1
carnal desire 75.5
carnality 75.2, 104.2, 654.1, 663.2, 665.5, 695.2
carnalize 663.4
carnal knowledge 75.7
carnal-minded 663.6, 695.16
carnal-mindedness 663.2, 695.2
carnal nature 663.2
carnal passion 75.5
carnal sin 655.2
carnassial 2.8
carnation 41.6, 41.8
carnation-red 41.6
Carnegie heros medal 646.6
carnelian 41.6
carnival 95.3, 704.1, 743.4, 743.14
carnivalesque 95.18
carnivore 8.16, 311.3
carnivorism 8.1
carnivority 8.1
carnivorous 8.31
carnivorousness 8.1
car of Juggernaut 308.5
carol (n) 696.3, 708.14 (v) 60.5, 116.5, 708.38
caroler 710.13
caroling 708.13
carom (n) 902.3, 903.2 (v) 902.13, 903.6
carom into 902.13
carotene 42.1
carotid 2.23
carotid artery 2.23
carousal 88.5, 669.2
carouse (n) 88.5, 669.2, 743.6 (v) 88.28, 669.6, 743.24, 810.10
carousel 743.15, 915.4
carouser 88.11, 743.18
carousing 669.2
carp 108.6, 510.15
car park 197.27
carp at 510.16
carpe diem (n) 486.1 (v) 406.7, 663.4, 843.8
carpel 310.28
carpenter 704.24
carpenter ant 311.33
carpenter bee 311.34
carpenter pants 5.18
carpenter's square 200.6
carpentry 712.2
carper 108.3, 510.9, 946.7
carpet (n) 199.3, 295.9 (v) 295.22
carpet ape 302.9
carpetbagger 357.3
carpeting 295.9
carpet joint 759.19
carpet knight 663.3
carpet rat 302.9
car phone 347.4
carping (n) 510.4 (a) 510.23
car pool 179.1
carpophore 310.21
carport 197.27
car racing 756.1
carrefour 170.2
carrel 197.3, 558.1
carrell 739.7
carriage 33.4, 179.1, 179.4, 321.1, 517.14, 630.7, 901.1
carriageable 176.18
carriage bow 462.7
carriage horse 311.13
carriage house 197.27
carriage trade 578.6, 733.3
carriageway 383.5
carried 371.26
carried away 95.17, 105.20, 105.25
carried by acclamation 332.15
carrier 85.4, 85.44, 179.1, 180.8, 353.1, 353.6, 901.2, 1034.11
carrier-based plane 181.9
carrier-current system 1041.5
carrier fighter 181.9
carrier frequency 1034.12
carrier pigeon 353.6
carrier wave 1034.11
carrion (n) 80.7, 80.9, 307.15, 393.7 (a) 307.29
carrot 375.2, 375.7
carrot-colored 42.2
carrot-top 35.9
carrot-topped 41.10
carroty 41.10, 42.2
carry (n) 158.2, 751.3 (v) 48.12, 78.12, 87.22, 158.9, 176.12, 371.15, 375.22, 411.3, 622.6, 628.8, 731.16, 901.21
carry a card 617.15
carry a date 832.13
carryall 195.2
carry all before one 411.4
carry arms 458.17
carry a torch for 104.19
carry authority 417.13
carry away 95.10, 104.22, 176.11, 308.13, 377.7, 411.3, 482.20, 802.9
carry back 989.19
carry back in recollection 989.19
carry by storm 411.4
carry coals to Newcastle 391.8, 993.12
carry conviction 953.18, 953.20, 973.9
carry forward 176.10
carrying (n) 901.1 (a) 78.18, 87.25, 460.14, 901.23
carrying a fetus 78.18
carrying an embryo 78.18
carrying arms 460.14
carrying charge 626.3
carrying coals to Newcastle 768.2
carrying distance 48.4
carrying-on 889.1
carrying out 328.2, 407.1, 434.1, 437.4
carrying-out 889.1
carrying over 846.4
carrying through 407.1, 434.1
carry in one's thoughts 989.12
carry into effect 328.7
carry into execution 328.7, 407.5, 434.3
carry it 411.3
carry off 176.11, 308.13, 328.7, 407.5, 409.11, 411.3, 480.14, 482.20
carry off one's feet 122.7
carry on 134.4, 152.15, 306.11, 322.4, 328.8, 330.15, 360.2, 541.8, 573.8, 671.11, 743.23, 810.11, 827.6, 856.3, 869.7, 889.5
carry on a business 724.12
carry on an inquiry 938.20
carry on a propaganda 569.4
carry on as usual 869.7
carry on a trade 724.12
carry on business 724.12
carry one's cross 134.5
carry oneself 321.4
carry one's thoughts back 989.9
carry one's weight 328.6
carry on hostilities 458.13
carry on one's books 622.6, 628.8
carry on over 101.7
carry on something scandalous 322.4
carry on war 458.13
carry out 261.5, 328.7, 387.11, 407.5, 434.3, 437.9, 889.5
carryout 8.6
carry out the anchor 182.15
carry over 176.10, 253.4, 628.8
carryover 254.1, 624.1
carry sail 182.13
carry the ball 328.6, 889.5
carry the banner of 509.13
carry the can 862.6
carry the day 249.6, 411.3
carry the mail 174.9
carry the weight of the world on one's shoulders 112.15
carry through 134.4, 328.7, 359.10, 360.5, 407.5, 434.3, 437.9, 817.5, 889.5
carry to 261.6
carry to completion 407.6
carry to excess 669.5
carry too far 355.3, 669.5, 993.10
carry too much sail 493.5, 1006.7
carry weight 297.10, 894.10, 997.12
carry young 78.12
carsick 85.57
car sickness 85.30
cart (n) 179.3, 195.1 (v) 176.13
cartage 630.7

carte 8.14, 871.5
carte blanche 430.4, 443.4, 642.2
carte du jour 965.3
cartel 437.1, 437.2, 617.9, 805.1
carter 178.9
Cartesian 695.20, 952.12
Cartesian coordinates 300.5
cart horse 311.13
cartilage (n) 2.2, 2.3, 1049.2 (a) 2.26
cartilaginous 2.26, 1049.4
cartilaginous fish 311.30
cartload 196.2
cartman 178.9
cart off 176.11
cartographer 159.5, 300.9
cartographic 159.19, 300.12
cartographical 300.12
cartography 159.5, 159.8
carton (n) 195.1 (v) 212.9
carton of cigarettes 89.5
cartoon (n) 381.3, 489.1, 706.1, 712.12, 712.15 (v) 712.19
cartoonist 489.12, 716.3
cartoon strip 489.1
cartouche 462.17
cartridge 50.11, 50.12, 462.17, 714.10
cartulary 549.2, 549.11
cartwheel 205.2, 728.7
carve 262.7, 290.3, 477.6, 549.15, 713.9, 715.5, 802.11, 892.9
carved 262.9, 713.11, 715.7
carved in stone 420.12
carve in stone 420.9
carve one's way 162.4
carve out 892.8
carver 716.6, 716.8
carvery 8.17
carve up 477.6
carving 349.6, 715.1
carving knife 8.12
car wash 79.11
caryatid 273.5, 901.8
casa 228.5
Casanova 104.12, 357.1, 562.12, 665.10
cascade (n) 194.1, 238.11, 671.6 (v) 194.5, 202.6, 238.17
cascade control 1041.3
cascading 202.9
case (n) 85.43, 104.3, 195.1, 266.4, 295.10, 295.16, 295.17, 530.9, 548.6, 554.14, 598.1, 765.1, 766.3, 786.2, 870.4, 935.5, 937.1, 957.5 (v) 212.9, 295.20, 938.28
case, the 761.3, 973.3
casebook 554.9, 554.10
casebound book 554.3
cased 212.12, 295.31
cased book 554.3
case file 598.1
case grammar 530.1
case-harden 15.13, 94.6, 373.9, 1046.7
case-hardened 94.12, 361.8, 373.15, 654.17, 1046.15
casehardened 1049.6
case-hardening 15.5, 373.7, 1046.5
case history 91.10, 349.3, 549.7, 719.1
casein 1045.7
caseinogen 1045.7
case in point 786.2, 957.5
case in question 938.10
case law 673.5
casemaking 554.14
casemated 460.12
casement 266.4, 292.7
case of emergency 963.4
case of need 963.4
case of nerves 128.1
caser 759.21
casern 228.29
case study 349.3
case the joint 482.16
caseworker 143.8
Casey Jones 178.12
cash (n) 624.1, 728.1, 728.5, 728.18 (v) 624.17, 728.29
cash-and-carry 734.1
cash bar 88.20
cashbook 549.11, 628.4
cashbox 729.13
cash cow 592.1, 618.4, 729.10
cash credit 622.1
cash crop 1069.15
cash crunch 619.1, 623.2
cash discount 631.1
cash dispenser 622.3
cash dividend 738.7
cash flow 386.2, 728.14, 728.18
cash-flow shortage 619.1
cashier (n) 624.9, 729.11, 729.12 (v) 447.4, 909.19, 913.5
cashiering 447.2, 909.5
cashier's check 728.11
cash in 307.19, 728.29
cash in hand 728.18
cash in on 387.15, 472.12, 843.8
cash in one's checks 307.19
cash in one's chips 307.19
cashkeeper 729.12
cashless 622.8
cash machine 622.3, 729.14
cash on the barrelhead 624.1
cash on the nail 624.1
cash payment 624.1
cash poor 623.8
cash register 729.13
cash reserves 728.14
cash sale 734.1
cash supply 728.18
casing 266.4, 295.17
casing-in 554.14
casino 228.27, 705.4, 743.13, 759.19
casino craps 759.8
casita 228.8
cask (n) 195.1, 282.4 (v) 212.9
casket (n) 309.11 (v) 212.6
Caspar 921.5
Caspar Milquetoast (n) 433.4 (a) 326.5
Cassandra 125.7, 399.4, 962.4
Cassandra-like 125.16
Cassandran 125.16
Cassandrian 125.16
cassation 445.1
casse-croûte 8.7
Cassegrainian telescope 1073.17
casserole 10.7, 10.11
cassette 50.12
cassette player 50.11
cassette recorder 50.11
cassette tape 549.10
cassideous 279.20
cassock 699.5, 702.2
cast (n) 2.5, 27.4, 28.5, 33.4, 35.1, 86.33, 248.4, 262.1, 617.7, 704.10, 707.11, 715.2, 759.9, 767.4, 770.3, 785.6, 786.6, 809.3, 865.4, 896.1, 904.3, 978.3, 1017.6, 1058.5 (v) 1.3, 6.10, 159.13, 182.30, 262.7, 381.8, 390.7, 715.5, 742.6, 892.8, 904.10, 909.13, 1017.18, 1020.24 (a) 1.4, 262.9, 892.18
cast a ballot 371.18
cast about 182.30, 938.23
cast about for 938.30
cast a glance 27.17
cast a gloom over 1027.9
cast a gloom upon 112.18
cast a horoscope 962.9
Castalian 720.16
cast anchor 182.15
castaneous 40.4
cast a pall upon 112.18
cast a reproach upon 510.13
cast a shadow 1027.9, 1028.5
cast aside 390.7
cast a slur on 512.9
cast a slur upon 510.13, 661.9
cast a spell 377.7, 690.13, 691.7
cast aspersions on 512.9
cast at 459.28
cast a traverse 182.51
cast away 176.11, 182.18, 182.42, 390.7
castaway (n) 370.4, 390.3, 586.4 (a) 370.8, 390.11, 586.10, 1013.27
cast blame upon 510.13
cast coquettish glances 562.20
cast doubt on 955.6
cast down (v) 96.15, 112.18, 132.2, 395.19, 913.5 (a) 96.22, 112.22
caste 245.2, 607.1, 617.2, 809.2
castellan 575.6, 1008.6
castellate 460.9
castellated 460.12
castellation 289.3
castellatus 319.8
caste mark 517.5, 1004.3
cast envious eyes 154.2
caster 716.6, 904.7
caster sugar 66.2
cast forth 771.5, 909.25
castigate 510.20, 604.9
castigation 510.3, 510.5, 604.1
castigator 510.9
castigatory 604.22
Castilian Spring 720.11
cast in a different mold 787.5
casting 715.1, 785.6, 892.2, 904.2, 1017.10, 1058.5
casting a shadow 1027.16
casting aside 370.1
casting away 370.1
casting down 447.1
casting lots 759.1
casting off 473.2
casting one's ballot 609.18
casting vote 371.6
cast in one's lot 332.9
cast in one's lot with 450.4
cast in one's teeth 508.9
cast in prison 429.14
cast in stone 853.5, 855.7
cast in the eye 28.5
cast in the same mold 784.11
cast into hell 682.6
cast-iron 15.15, 361.9, 973.13
cast-iron truth, the 973.3
castle 228.7, 460.6, 743.17
castle-builder 986.13
castle-building (n) 985.2 (a) 985.11, 986.25
castlebuilding 986.8
castle in Spain 986.10
castle in the air 976.1, 986.10
castle in the sky 986.10
castles in the air 124.4
cast light upon 1025.28
castling 863.2
cast loose 182.18, 182.48, 431.5
cast lots 759.23
cast of characters 707.11
cast of countenance 33.4
cast off 6.6, 182.18, 390.7, 473.5, 802.8, 802.10, 909.21
cast-off 182.61, 586.10
castoff (n) 370.4, 390.3 (a) 390.11
castoff clothes 5.5
castoffs 5.5
castoff skin 2.5
cast of the dice 759.2
cast one's eye 27.13
cast one's eyes down 27.19
cast one's fortune 962.9
cast one's hook 382.10
cast one's net 382.10
cast one's vote 371.18
cast one's vote for 332.8
Castor and Pollux 588.6, 873.4
castor-bean meal 890.4
castor oil 86.17
cast out 773.5, 802.8, 909.13, 909.17
cast out devils 690.12
cast pearls before swine 486.4, 486.6
cast plastic 1054.6
castrate 19.12, 77.12, 255.11, 393.14, 612.15
castrated 19.19, 75.29, 393.30, 795.5
castration 19.5, 255.4
castration complex 92.22
castrato 19.6, 75.9, 709.5
cast reflections on 512.9
cast reflection upon 510.13
cast reproach upon 661.8
Castroism 611.5
Castroist 860.6
Castroite (n) 611.13 (a) 611.21, 860.6
cast sheep's eyes at 562.20
cast the evil eye 691.9

cast the eyes back 989.9
cast the eyes on 27.12
cast the eyes upon 27.12
cast the first stone 510.13, 599.10
cast their shadows before 133.9
cast the lead 275.10
cast to the dogs 390.7
cast to the winds 390.7
cast up 200.9, 912.5, 1017.19
cast up accounts 628.8
casual (n) 461.16, 619.4, 726.2 (a) 5.47, 102.7, 106.15, 340.11, 365.11, 581.3, 766.7, 768.4, 810.12, 843.11, 848.3, 945.5, 972.15, 972.16, 1014.13
casual acquaintance 588.1
casual clothes 5.20
casual day 5.20
casual discovery 941.1
casual dress 5.20
Casual Friday 5.20
casual glance 27.4
casual laborer 726.2
casualness 102.2, 106.5, 340.2, 581.1, 945.1, 972.1
casual remark 213.2
casual sex 75.7
casualty 308.8, 972.6, 1011.2
casualty list 307.13
casual water 751.1
casual wear 5.20
casuist 935.12, 936.6, 952.8
casuistic 354.32, 936.10
casuistical 936.10
casuistry 354.5, 636.2, 935.4, 936.1
casus belli 152.11, 456.7
Cat 179.18
cat 27.11, 76.5, 110.12
cat 311.20, 605.1
catabasis 252.2
catabolic 2.31, 806.6, 852.12
catabolism 2.20, 7.12, 806.2, 852.3
catacaustic 279.2
catachresis 342.1, 975.7
catachrestic 342.3
cataclasm 802.3
cataclysm 238.6, 395.4, 671.5, 860.1, 1011.2
cataclysmal 395.26, 1011.15
cataclysmic 395.26, 671.23, 671.24, 860.5, 1011.15
catacombs 309.16
catadioptric system 29.2
catafalque 309.10, 309.16, 901.13
catalepsy 22.6, 25.2, 85.27, 92.19, 173.4
cataleptic 22.21, 25.8, 173.14
cataleptic hypnosis 22.7
catalexis 720.7
catalog (n) 349.2, 549.1, 549.11, 554.9, 574.10, 628.4, 708.1, 801.4, 871.3 (v) 549.15, 801.8, 809.6, 871.8
catalog card 549.10
cataloged 809.8, 871.9
catalog goods 735.1
cataloging 349.2, 549.14, 809.1, 871.7
catalog selling 734.2
catalog shopping 733.1
catalogue raisonné 554.9, 801.4, 871.3
catalysis 806.2, 852.3
catalyst 375.11, 806.2, 852.5, 886.4
catalytic 806.6, 852.12
catalytic agent 852.5
catalyze 806.4, 1060.8
catamaran 760.2
catamenia 12.9
catamenial 12.24, 850.8
catamenial discharge 12.9
catamite 75.14
catamnesis 91.10
catamount 311.21
cat-a-mountain 311.21
cat-and-dog 110.26
cat-and-doggish 110.26, 316.11
cat-and-dog life 457.1
cat-and-dog weather 316.4
cataphor 22.5
cataplasm 86.33, 1063.2
cataplexy 85.27, 92.19
catapult (n) 184.8, 462.9 (v) 904.10
catapult oneself forward 162.2
cataract (n) 30.1, 85.14, 194.1, 238.11 (v) 194.5, 238.17
catastrophe 395.4, 671.5, 722.4, 820.1, 860.1, 1011.2
catastrophic 395.26, 860.5, 1011.15
catastrophic change 852.2
catastrophize 112.15
catatonia 25.2, 94.1, 173.4, 583.1, 651.1, 926.4, 982.1
catatoniac 926.17
catatonic 25.8, 94.9, 173.14, 583.5, 926.28, 982.3
catatonic schizophrenia 926.4
catatonic stupor 92.19
catatony 25.2
catawampous 204.14
catbird seat 997.2
cat burglar 483.3
catcall (n) 53.6, 508.3 (v) 508.10
catcalling (n) 508.1 (a) 508.12
catch (n) 100.11, 104.11, 131.2, 356.6, 421.3, 428.5, 480.2, 480.10, 708.19, 745.3, 959.2, 999.5, 1003.2, 1012.4, 1013.8 (v) 48.11, 85.47, 101.6, 221.8, 356.20, 472.8, 472.9, 480.17, 521.7, 745.5, 754.4, 855.10, 941.7, 983.13, 1020.23
catch a crab 182.53
catch a glimpse of 27.12, 941.5
catch a likeness 349.8
catch a lobster 182.53
catch a pass 746.5
catch a ride 177.31
catch-as-catch-can (n) 457.10 (a) 365.12
catch asleep at the switch 941.7
catch a smell of 69.8
catch at 480.16, 941.7
catch a train 177.33
catch at straws 124.7, 493.5, 510.15
catch a wink 22.13
catchbasin 80.12
catch cold 85.47
catch dog 862.3
catcher 480.11, 745.2
catch fire 105.16, 409.7, 578.8, 1019.22, 1020.23
catch flat-footed 429.15, 941.7
catch flatfooted 480.17
catch forty winks 22.14
catch hell 604.19
catch hold of 480.14
catch in a trap 356.20
catch in flagrante delicto 941.7
catching (n) 480.2, 941.1 (a) 82.7, 85.62, 377.8, 480.25
catching sight of 941.1
catch in the act 941.7
catch in the crossfire 96.13
catch in the middle 96.13
catch it 604.19
catchization 938.2
catch line 554.12
catch napping 941.7
catch off balance 985.6
catch off base 941.7
catch off-guard 131.7, 941.7
catch offside 941.7
catch on 409.7, 521.7, 578.8
catch one dead to rights 429.15
catch one in flagrante delicto 429.15
catch one in the act 429.15
catch one off balance 96.13
catch one red-handed 429.15
catch one's breath 20.8, 396.19, 857.9
catch one's death 307.23
catch one's death of cold 307.23
catch one's ear 983.11
catch oneself doing 373.11
catch one's eye 377.6
catch on fire 1020.23
catch on to 941.8
catch out 356.20, 941.7
catchpenny 998.19
catch phrase 526.9
catchphrase 974.1, 974.4
catchpole 1008.15
catch red-handed 941.7
catch short 131.7
catch sight of 27.12, 941.5
catch some Z's 20.8, 22.14
catch the attention 983.11
catch the devil 604.19
catch the drift 521.8
catch the ear 48.12
catch the eye 31.4, 33.8, 983.11
catch the flame 93.11
catch the infection 93.11, 105.16
catch the scent of 941.6
catch the thoughts 931.19
catch tripping 941.7
Catch-22 356.12, 421.3, 963.6
catchumen 700.2
catch unawares 131.7, 356.20
catch up 174.13, 480.14
catch up in 898.2
catch up with 174.13
catchweed 285.5
catchweight 297.3
catch with a hand in the till 429.15
catch with one's pants down 429.15, 941.7
catchword 458.7, 517.9, 526.9, 554.12, 974.1, 974.4
catchy 356.21, 708.48, 851.3
cate 10.8
catechesis 938.2
catechetic 938.36
catechetical 938.36
catechetical method 938.12
Catechism 676.2
catechism 938.10, 953.3
catechist 938.16
catechistic 938.36
catechistical 938.36
catechization 568.1, 568.2, 938.12
catechize 568.10, 568.12, 938.21
catechizing 938.10, 938.12
catechrestical 342.3
catechumen 572.9, 692.4, 818.2, 858.7
categorical 809.7, 935.22, 960.2
categorical imperative 636.2
categorically reject 510.10
categorically true 973.13
categoricalness 960.1
categorical proposition 935.7
categorical syllogism 935.6
categorization 801.3, 808.3, 808.4, 809.1
categorize 801.8, 808.11, 809.6
categorized 808.14
categorizing 801.3
category 807.2, 809.2, 937.1
catena 812.2
catenary (n) 194.2, 279.2 (a) 812.9
catenate 812.4
catenated 812.8
catenation 812.2
cater 385.9
catercorner (v) 204.11 (a) 204.19
catercornered 204.19
catered 385.13
caterer 11.3, 385.6
cater for 449.11
catering 11.1, 385.1
Caterpillar 179.18
caterpillar 302.12, 311.32
Caterpillar Club 184.7
cater to 138.8, 427.6, 449.11, 449.18
caterwaul (n) 58.4, 59.1, 60.1 (v) 58.8, 59.6, 60.2
cat-eyed 27.21
cat fit 152.8
cat flea 311.36
cat food 10.4
catgut 711.20
Catharism 667.1
Catharist (n) 667.2 (a) 667.4
catharsis 12.2, 79.2, 92.25, 120.2, 722.4
cathartic (n) 79.17, 86.17 (a) 79.28, 86.48, 120.9
cathect 983.8
cathectic 983.16
cathectic energy 92.34
cathection 92.34

cathedral (n) 703.1 (a) 970.18
cathedral church 703.1
cathedralesque 703.15
cathedral-like 703.15
catheter 239.6
cathexis 92.34, 93.1, 983.2
cathode 1032.8
cathode glow 1033.5
cathode luminescence 1037.2
cathode particle 1033.3
cathode ray 1033.5
cathode ray tube 1042.9
cathode-ray tube 1035.11
cathodic 1033.15
cathodofluorescence 1033.5
cathodoluminescence 1033.5
Catholic (n) 675.19 (a) 675.29
catholic 864.14, 945.5, 979.8
Catholic Church 675.8
Catholic Epistles 683.4
Catholicism 675.8
Catholicity 675.8
catholicity 864.1, 945.1, 979.2
catholicize 864.9
catholicon 86.3
catholic tastes 945.1
cathouse 228.28, 665.9
cation 1032.25, 1060.2
cationic 1032.32
catkin 310.27
catlike 311.42
catling 302.10
cat man 483.3
catnap (n) 22.3 (v) 22.13
cat-o'-nine-tails 605.1
catoptric 1025.41
catoptrical 1025.41
catoptrics 1025.22
CAT scan 91.9
cat's meow, the 999.7
cat's pajamas, the 999.7
cat's-paw 138.3, 318.4, 358.1, 384.4, 576.1, 576.3, 616.8
catstone 517.10
catsup 10.12
cattalo 797.8
cattery 228.21
cat the anchor 182.18
cattiness 144.6, 512.3
cattish 144.21, 311.42
cattle 311.1, 311.6, 606.3
cattle call 942.3
cattle lifting 482.3
cattleman 1070.2, 1070.3
cattle plague 85.41
cattle raising 1070.1
cattle ranch 1070.5
cattle ranching 1070.1
cattle rustler 483.8
cattle rustling 482.3
cattle stealing 482.3
cattle thief 483.8
catty 110.22, 144.21, 311.42, 512.13
cattycorner 204.19
cattycornered 204.19
catwalk 383.2, 383.9
cat whisker 3.10, 73.4
Caucasian 312.2, 312.3
Caucasoid 312.2
caucus (n) 371.9, 423.4, 609.9, 609.15, 617.4, 770.2 (v) 609.38
caucus nomination 609.11
cauda 217.6
caudal 217.11, 820.12
caudal appendage 217.6
caudal fin 217.6
caudate (n) 311.26 (a) 217.11
caudated 217.11
caudation 217.6
caudex 310.21
caudiform 217.11
caught 855.16, 983.18
caught flatfooted 656.3
caught in one's own trap 132.5
caught in the act 656.3
caught in the cross-fire 918.7
caught in the crossfire 96.22, 1011.14
caught in the middle 96.22, 918.7, 1011.14
caught napping 406.8, 930.12
caught off balance 406.8
caught off base 406.8
caught red-handed 656.3
caught short 131.12, 406.8
caught tripping 930.12
caught up in 898.5, 983.17
caught with one's hand in cookie jar, the 656.3
caught with one's hand in the till 656.3
caught with one's pants down 406.8, 656.3
caulicle 310.21
cauliflower ear 2.10, 48.7
cauliflower-eared 48.15
caulis 310.21
caulk 293.7
Caurus 318.2
causal 375.25, 886.13
causal body 689.17
causality 886.1
causal nexus 972.5
causal sequence 886.3
causation 886.1
causative 375.25, 886.13, 892.16
cause (n) 375.1, 598.1, 600.6, 886.1, 886.9 (v) 375.13, 424.4, 886.10, 892.11
cause a commotion 105.12, 810.10, 917.10
cause and effect 886.1
cause-and-effect 887.1
cause a stir 105.12, 810.10, 917.10
cause celebre 348.4
cause célèbre 552.6, 831.3
caused 892.17
cause eyebrows to raise 661.7
cause for alarm 1006.1
cause in court 598.1
causeless 972.15, 972.16
causelessness 972.3
causer 886.4
causerie 541.3, 556.1
cause the mind to stray 985.6
cause the mind to wander 985.6
cause to 424.4
cause to go out of one's way 640.7
cause tongues to wag 661.7
cause trouble 1013.14
cause vertigo 985.8
causeway 295.22
causidical 598.21
causing cause 886.3
caustic (n) 279.2, 1020.15 (a) 17.14, 64.6, 68.6, 105.31, 110.17, 144.23, 152.26, 508.13, 589.10
causticity 17.5, 64.2, 68.1, 110.1, 144.8, 152.3, 508.5
causticness 144.8
caustic remark 508.2
cauter 1020.15
cauterant (n) 1020.15 (a) 1020.26
cauterization 1020.5
cauterize 1020.24
cauterizer 1020.15
cauterizing 1020.26
cautery 1020.5, 1020.15
caution (n) 339.1, 362.3, 379.1, 399.1, 422.1, 438.3, 494.1, 551.3, 752.3, 956.1, 961.2 (v) 379.3, 399.5, 422.6
cautionary 379.5, 399.7, 422.8, 494.9
cautioner 399.4
cautioning (n) 379.1 (a) 399.7
caution light 517.15, 1026.4
caution money 438.3
caution signal 400.1
cautious 175.10, 339.10, 362.11, 494.8, 956.4
cautiousness 175.1, 362.3, 494.1, 956.1
cavalcade 812.3
cavalier (n) 104.12, 178.8, 504.9, 608.5, 769.5 (a) 141.13, 505.7
cavaliere servente 104.12
cavalierness 141.5
cavalry horse 311.13
cavalryman 178.8, 461.12
cave (n) 197.8, 228.26, 284.5, 395.4, 1009.3 (v) 194.6, 260.10, 284.13
cave art 712.1
caveat 379.1, 399.1, 422.1
caveat emptor 419.2
cave dweller 842.7
cave dwelling 228.5
cave in 16.9, 194.6, 260.10, 284.13, 292.14, 393.24, 433.7, 433.10
cave-in 260.4, 395.4
cavelike 284.16
caveman 76.6, 842.7
cavendish 89.7
cave of despair 125.2
cave of Trophonius 125.2
cave painting 842.6
cavern 284.5
cavernous 158.11, 275.12, 284.16
caviar 10.24, 305.15
cavil (n) 510.4, 936.4 (v) 510.15, 935.16, 936.9
caviler 510.9, 936.7, 946.7
caviling (n) 510.4, 936.5 (a) 510.23, 936.14
caving in 433.2
cavity 197.2, 224.2, 275.2, 284.2, 292.1
cavo-rilievo 715.3
cavort (n) 366.2 (v) 366.6, 743.23
cavorting 366.3, 743.3
cavy 311.22
caw (n) 58.3 (v) 58.9, 60.5
cay 235.2
Cayman Trench 275.5
cayuse 311.10
cazh 340.11, 581.3
C clef 709.13
CD player 50.11
CD-ROM 549.10
CD-ROM drive 549.10
CD-ROM workstation 558.4
cease (n) 857.1 (v) 34.2, 173.8, 293.8, 370.7, 395.23, 820.6, 857.6
cease fire 465.9, 857.7
cease-fire 465.5, 857.3
cease hostilities 465.9
ceaseless 812.8, 829.7, 847.5, 856.7
ceaselessness 812.1, 829.1, 847.2, 856.1
cease motion 173.7
cease not 856.3
cease publication 34.2
cease resistance 433.7
cease to be 34.2, 307.18, 762.6
cease to exist 34.2, 762.6
cease to live 307.18
cease to use 390.4
ceasing 820.1, 857.1
cecal 293.9
cecity 30.1
cecum 2.18, 293.3
cede 168.2, 370.7, 433.7, 433.8, 475.3, 629.3
ceded 475.5
ceding 168.1, 370.3
ceil 196.7, 295.21
ceiled 295.31
ceiling 31.2, 184.32, 198.1, 211.3, 272.1, 295.6, 630.4, 794.5, 1074.9
ceiling and visibility unlimited 31.2, 184.32
ceilinged roof 279.4
ceiling fixture 1026.6
ceiling price 630.4
ceiling unlimited 31.2
ceiling zero 184.32
ceja 310.15
cel animation 706.1
celebrant 696.9, 701.2, 743.18
celebrate 487.2, 509.12, 580.5, 696.12, 701.14, 743.24
celebrate a marriage 563.14
celebrated 662.16, 997.19
celebrate Mass 701.14
celebrating (n) 487.1 (a) 487.3
celebration 88.5, 95.3, 116.1, 487.1, 580.4, 582.11, 696.8, 701.1, 743.6
celebrative 487.3
celebratory 487.3
celebreality 1035.1
celebrity 247.2, 352.4, 662.1, 662.9, 997.2, 997.8
celebrity chef 1035.1
celebrityhood 997.2
celebutante 662.9
celeritous 330.18

celerity 174.1, 330.3
celestial (n) 679.1 (a) 677.16, 679.6, 681.12, 986.23, 1073.25
celestial being 679.1
celestial body 1073.4
Celestial City 681.3
celestial equator 1073.16
celestial guidance 159.3
celestial horizon 201.4
celestial kingdom 681.6
celestial light 1025.14
celestial longitude 1073.16
celestial mechanics 1073.19
celestial meridian 1073.16
celestial navigation 159.3, 182.2, 184.6
celestial phenomenon 1073.4
celestial spaces 1073.3
celestial sphere 1073.2, 1073.4
celestial throne 681.4
celiac 2.31
celibacy 565.1, 664.3, 668.2, 698.4, 872.2
celibate (n) 565.2, 699.16 (a) 565.6, 664.6, 668.10, 872.9, 891.4
celibatic 565.6
cell 197.2, 258.7, 305.4, 347.12, 429.8, 584.6, 617.6, 1009.5
cella 703.4
cellar 197.17, 386.6
cellarage 197.17, 630.6
cell biology 1068.3
cellblock 429.8
cell death 85.2
cell division 305.16
cellhouse 429.8
cellist 710.5
cell membrane 305.5
cell nucleus 305.7
celloist 710.5
cellophane 295.18
cell phone 347.4
cell phone number 347.12
cell phone tower 272.6
cell plate 305.6
cell telephone 347.4
cellular 305.19
cellular kite 181.14
cellular phone 347.4
cellular telephone 347.4
cellular tissue 305.4
cellule 197.2, 305.4
celluloid filter 1028.4
cellulose 7.5, 305.6
cellulose nitrate 462.14
cellulose plastic 1054.6
cellulous 305.19
cell wall 305.6
cell yell 50.13
celo-navigation 159.3
Celsius scale 1019.19
Celtic 523.12
Celtic deities 678.4
cement (n) 383.6, 742.2, 803.4, 1046.6, 1054.2 (v) 295.22, 295.25, 800.5, 800.7, 803.9 (a) 1046.10
cemental 1046.10
cementation 803.1, 1059.8
cement a union 805.4
cemented 800.14, 803.10
cement kiln 742.5
cement mixer 797.9
cement of friendship 455.1
cementwork 295.1
cemetery 309.15
cenobite 565.2, 699.16
cenobitic 565.6
cenotaph 309.16, 549.12
cense 70.8
censer 70.5, 70.6, 696.10
censer bearer 70.5
censing 70.5
censor (n) 92.24, 428.6, 510.9, 636.5, 946.7 (v) 255.12, 345.8, 428.8, 773.5, 820.6
censored 345.11, 428.14, 820.9
censorial 255.13, 428.12, 510.22
censoring 255.5, 428.2
censorious 99.8, 495.9, 500.19, 510.22, 512.13, 602.5
censoriousness 495.1, 500.6, 510.4
censor out 255.10, 820.6
censorship 92.24, 255.5, 345.3, 428.2
censurability 656.1
censurable 510.25, 656.3
censurableness 656.1
censure (n) 510.3, 599.2, 602.1, 661.6, 946.2 (v) 510.13, 599.10, 602.3, 661.9, 946.14
censurer 510.9, 946.7
census (n) 196.1, 227.1, 770.1, 808.4, 871.6, 1017.9, 1017.11 (v) 1017.17
census report 549.7, 871.6
census returns 549.7
cent 728.7, 998.5
cental 882.8
centare 882.8
centenarian 304.2, 882.8
centenary (n) 850.4, 882.8 (a) 850.8, 882.29
centennial (n) 850.4, 882.8 (a) 850.8, 882.29
centennium 882.8
center (n) 207.2, 208.2, 246.1, 467.3, 609.24, 611.2, 611.10, 746.2, 747.2, 749.2, 767.2, 819.1, 907.2 (v) 169.2, 208.9, 749.7, 752.4, 819.3 (a) 467.7
center around 169.2
center back 752.2
center circle 752.1
center city 230.6
centered 106.3
center fielder 745.2
centerfold 1016.8
center forward 749.5, 752.2
center half 752.2
center halfback 749.5
center ice 749.1
center in 208.9
centering 208.8
center jump 747.3
center line 749.4
centerline 467.3
center mark 748.1, 749.4, 752.1
centermost 208.11
center of activity 208.5
center of attention 208.4, 907.2
center of attraction 208.4
center of authority 208.6
center of consciousness 208.4
center of gravity 208.4
center of interest 208.4
center of life 767.5
center of manufacture 739.2
center of the mind 919.3
center on 169.2, 208.9, 937.3
centerpiece 208.4, 997.7
center round 208.9
center-seeking 819.4
center stage 704.16
centesimal 882.29
centigrade 1019.30
centigrade scale 1019.19
centigrade thermal unit 1019.19
centigrado 882.29
centigram 882.8
centiliter 882.8
centimeter 223.2, 882.8
centipede 311.32, 882.8
centistere 882.8
central (n) 347.7, 347.9 (a) 207.6, 208.11, 246.3, 249.14, 524.30, 819.4, 886.14, 997.23
central administration 208.6
central air conditioning 317.9
Central America 231.6
central apparatus 305.5
central bank 729.14
central body 208.3, 305.5
central city 230.6
central consciousness 722.5
central eclipse 1027.8, 1073.13
central government 612.3
Central Intelligence Agency 576.12
centralism 208.8, 612.7
centrality 208.1
centralization 208.8, 805.1
centralize 169.2, 208.9, 805.4
centralized 208.11
centrally heated 1020.29
central nervous system 2.14
centralness 208.1
central office 208.6, 347.7
central position 208.1
central processing unit 1042.2
central station 208.6, 1032.19
Central Standard Time 832.3
centric 208.11, 208.14
centricality 208.1
centricity 208.1
centrifugal 171.8, 908.4
centrifugal action 18.6
centrifugal force 18.6, 908.1
centrifugate 915.11
centrifugation 915.1
centrifuge (n) 802.7, 1060.6 (v) 915.11
centrifugence 171.1
centriole 208.3, 305.5
centripetal 24.9, 169.3, 208.13, 819.4
centripetal action 18.6
centripetal force 18.6, 907.1
centripetalism 208.1
centrism 611.2, 819.2
centrist (n) 609.28, 611.10, 670.4 (a) 467.7, 611.18, 819.4
centroidal 208.11
centrolineal 169.3, 208.13
centromere 305.8
centroplasm 305.5
centrosome 208.3, 305.5
centrosphere 208.3, 305.5
centrosymmetric 208.11
centrum 208.2
centumvir 882.8
centumvirate 882.8
centuple (v) 882.16 (a) 882.29
centuple calorie 1019.19
centuplicate (v) 882.16 (a) 882.29
centurial 882.29
centurion 575.18, 882.8
century 728.7, 824.2, 827.4, 882.8
century year 824.2
cephalalgia 26.5
cephalic 198.15
cephalin-cholesterol 7.7
ceramic 742.7
ceramic cartridge 50.11
ceramicist 716.7, 742.2
ceramic pickup 50.11
ceramics 712.1, 712.2, 742.1, 742.2
ceramic ware 742.2
ceramist 716.7, 742.2
cerate 86.11, 1056.2
cerated 1056.9
ceratoid 285.9
Cerberus 682.5, 1008.11, 1008.12
cereal (n) 10.34, 310.3, 310.5 (a) 310.36
cereal bar 10.43
cereal bowl 8.12
cereal grain 10.4
cereal grass 310.5
cereal plant 310.5
cerebellar 2.30
cerebellum 2.15
cerebral 2.30, 919.7, 931.21, 935.18
cerebral matter 2.15
cerebral palsy 85.25
cerebrate 931.8
cerebration 931.1
cerebrum 2.15, 919.6
cerecloth 309.14, 703.10
cerements 309.14
ceremonial (n) 580.1, 580.4, 701.3 (a) 580.8, 701.18
ceremonial attire 702.1
ceremonialism 580.2, 701.1
ceremonialist 701.2
ceremonies 504.7
ceremonious 155.8, 504.14, 580.8, 701.18
ceremoniousness 580.1
ceremony 487.1, 580.1, 580.4, 701.3
Cerenkov radiation 1037.2
cereology 1069.1
cereous 1056.9
Ceres 890.5, 1069.4
cerise (n) 41.1 (a) 41.6
cerographer 716.8
cerographist 716.8
ceroplastic 715.7
certain, a 872.7

certain 130.11, 244.5, 438.11, 865.12, 883.7, 953.21, 957.16, 963.15, 970.13, 972.18, 973.13
certain knowledge 928.1, 970.1
certainness 970.1
certain number, a 883.1, 884.2
certain person 528.2
certainty 130.1, 928.1, 953.1, 953.5, 963.7, 970.1
certifiability 926.3
certifiable 926.28
certifiable case 926.17
certificate (n) 549.6, 728.11 (v) 443.11
certificated 443.17
certificate of character 509.4
certificate of deposit 622.3, 728.11
certificate of insurance 1008.4
certificate of invention 210.3
certificate of proficiency 549.6
certificate of stock 738.4
certification 332.4, 334.3, 443.3, 549.6, 957.4, 970.8
certification program 567.1
certificatory 332.14, 334.8, 549.16, 957.18
certified 332.14, 334.9, 438.11, 957.20, 970.20, 973.13
certified check 728.11
certified copy 785.1
certified mail 553.4
certified public accountant 628.7
certified teacher 571.1
certifier 332.7
certify 332.12, 334.6, 438.9, 443.11, 957.9, 957.11, 970.11
certifying 334.8
certiorari 598.10
certitude 970.1, 970.5
cerulean (n) 1073.2 (a) 45.3
ceruleous 45.3
cerulescent 45.3
cerumen 2.24
cervical 2.29
cervine 311.45
cervix 2.13, 260.1, 800.4, 901.2
cess 630.9
cessation 173.3, 370.1, 390.2, 465.5, 813.2, 820.1, 820.3, 857.1
cessation of combat 464.1
cessation of life 307.1
cession 370.3, 433.2, 475.1, 629.1, 959.1
cesspit 80.12
cesspool 71.3, 80.12
cestui 470.2
cestui que trust 470.2
cestui que use 470.2
cetacean (n) 311.29 (a) 311.40
ceviche 10.24
C4 462.14
cgi 1042.18
chad 993.5
chador 5.26
chafe (n) 85.38, 96.3, 1044.2 (v) 26.7, 96.14, 126.6, 135.4, 152.15, 152.24, 393.13, 1020.17, 1044.7
chafed 26.11, 96.21
chaff (n) 256.1, 295.16, 298.2, 391.4, 606.3, 998.4, 1036.13 (v) 490.5, 508.9
chaffer (n) 490.4, 731.3 (v) 731.18
chaffering 731.3
chaffing (n) 490.2, 508.1 (a) 490.7, 508.12
chafing (n) 135.1, 1044.2 (a) 26.13, 126.10, 135.6, 1020.26, 1044.10
chagrin (n) 96.4, 132.1, 137.2 (v) 96.15, 98.13
chagrined 96.22, 132.5, 137.14
chain (n) 237.6, 498.6, 647.1, 812.2, 1012.7, 1020.12, 1038.7 (v) 428.10, 800.5, 800.9, 812.4, 855.8
chain armor 460.3
chain discount 631.1
chained 812.8, 855.16
chain gang 604.2, 746.1, 812.3
chain-gang member 429.11
chaining 800.1, 812.2
chain lightning 1025.17
chain locker 386.6
chain mail 460.3
chain of being 809.4
chain of cause and effect 886.3
chain of circumstances 972.5
chain of evidence 957.1
chain of ideas 92.33
chain of office 417.9, 647.1
chain of thought 931.4
chain printer 1042.9
chain-reacting pile 1038.13
chain reaction 812.2, 972.5, 1038.8
chain reactor 1038.13
chain restaurant 8.17
chains 428.4
chain-smoke 87.22, 89.14
chain-smoker 87.21
chain-smoking 87.1, 89.10
chain store 736.1
chain victory to one's car 411.3
chair (n) 229.1, 417.7, 417.10, 571.10, 574.5, 901.17 (v) 573.11, 612.11, 615.12
chair, the 604.6, 605.5
chairlift 383.8, 753.1, 912.4
chairman (n) 574.5 (v) 573.11
chairman of the board 574.3
chairmanship 417.7, 417.10, 573.4
chairperson 574.5
chairperson of the national committee 610.12
chairwoman 574.5
chaise 179.4, 229.1
chaise lounge 229.1
chalcograph 713.6
chalcographer 716.8
Chaldean 1073.23
chalet 228.8
chalice 696.10, 703.11
chalk (n) 35.8, 37.2, 712.18, 757.2, 760.1, 1051.5 (v) 37.5, 517.19, 549.15, 712.19
chalkiness 37.1, 1051.1
chalklike 1051.11
chalk out 381.11
chalk talk 543.2, 568.7
chalk talker 543.5
chalk up 517.19, 549.15
chalky 37.7, 1051.11
challenge (n) 333.2, 451.1, 453.1, 454.2, 458.6, 938.12 (v) 216.8, 333.5, 421.5, 421.6, 451.6, 453.3, 454.3, 457.18, 458.14, 955.6, 1012.15
challenge comparison 999.11
challenged 16.18, 19.16, 393.30
Challenger Deep 275.5
challenging 375.27, 454.7
chalone 13.2
cham 575.9
chamber (n) 12.11, 197.1, 197.2, 197.7, 423.1 (v) 212.5
chamber chorus 710.16
chamber concert 708.33
chamberfellow 588.3
chambering (n) 665.4 (a) 665.26
chamberlain 577.10, 729.12
chambermaid 577.8
chamber music 708.6
chamber of commerce 617.9
chamber of deputies 613.1
chamber of horrors 96.7
chamber orchestra 710.12
chamber pot 12.11
chambers 228.13, 739.7
chambre 197.1
chameleon 47.6, 363.4, 854.4
chameleonic 47.11
chameleonlike 47.11
chamfer (n) 290.1 (v) 290.3
chamfered 290.4
chamisal 310.15
champ (n) 8.2, 411.2, 413.15 (v) 8.27
champaca oil 70.2
champaign (n) 236.1, 310.8 (a) 236.2
champaign country 236.1
champain 661.6
champ at the bit 17.11, 135.4, 846.13
champing at the bit 101.8, 135.6, 405.16
champion (n) 249.4, 411.2, 413.13, 413.15, 460.7, 509.8, 576.1, 600.8, 616.9, 999.8, 1008.5 (v) 449.13, 460.8, 600.10, 1008.18 (a) 249.15, 999.16, 999.17
championing 449.4
championship 249.3, 411.1, 449.4, 747.1, 748.1, 749.1, 751.1, 752.1, 753.1, 756.1
championship belt 646.3
championship cup 751.1
championship marker 751.1
Chamuel 679.4
Chance 972.2
chance (n) 759.2, 825.2, 843.2, 897.1, 966.1, 968.1, 971.1, 971.8, 972.1 (v) 403.6, 759.24, 831.6 (a) 766.7, 768.4, 971.19
chance (v) 972.11, 1006.7 (a) 972.15
chanced 404.7
chance discovery 941.1
chance hit 972.6
chance in a million 969.1
chance it 759.24
chancel 703.9
chancellery 417.7, 739.7
chancellor 571.8, 574.3, 575.7, 575.16, 576.6
chancellorate 417.7
Chancellor of the Exchequer 729.12
chancellorship 417.7
chancel screen 703.10
chancel table 703.12
chance-medley 972.4
chance of a lifetime, the 843.3
chance on 941.3
chancery 549.3, 739.7
chanciness 971.1, 1006.2
chancing 972.1
chancre 85.18, 85.37
chancroid 85.18, 85.37
chancy 971.16, 971.19, 972.15, 1006.10
chandelier 1026.6
chandelle (n) 184.13 (v) 184.39
chandler 385.6, 730.2
chandlery 385.1
change (n) 429.5, 728.2, 728.19, 737.7, 780.4, 852.1, 858.1, 862.1, 862.2 (v) 5.43, 172.5, 362.8, 731.15, 780.6, 852.6, 852.7, 854.5, 858.11, 862.4, 863.4
changeability 782.1, 854.1, 863.3
changeable 16.17, 47.11, 362.9, 364.6, 782.3, 828.7, 852.10, 854.6, 854.7, 858.18, 863.5, 971.16
changeableness 16.2, 362.1, 364.3, 782.1, 828.1, 852.1, 854.1, 971.1
change address 159.17
change back 859.5
change by degrees 245.4
change color 36.6, 105.19, 127.11, 139.8, 310.34
change countenance 36.6
change course 182.30
changed 852.10, 858.19
changed for the better 392.13
change direction 852.7
change for 862.4
change form 783.2
change for the better (n) 392.1, 852.1 (v) 392.9
change for the worse 852.1
changeful 854.7
changefulness 854.1, 854.2
change gradually 861.5
change hands 629.4, 734.12
change horses in midstream 362.8, 852.6
change into 5.44, 858.11, 858.17
changeless 677.17, 853.7, 855.17
changelessness 853.1
changeling 680.11
change of allegiance 858.2
change of conviction 858.2
change of course 852.1
change of heart 113.4, 852.1, 858.2
change of life 303.4, 303.7

change of mind 362.1, 363.1, 852.1, 858.2
change of scene 852.1
change of venue 598.5
change one's allegiance 363.7
change one's colors 858.13
change one's identity 346.8
change one's mind 113.7, 362.8, 363.6, 852.7
change one's song 363.6
change one's tune 363.6, 858.11
change one's ways 858.12
change over 852.7, 858.11
changeover 852.1, 858.1
change ownership 629.4
change place 172.5
change places with 862.5
change purse 729.15
changer 50.11
change ringing 54.3
change shape 783.2
change sides 363.6, 363.7, 852.6
change someone's tune 852.7
change step-by-step 861.5
change the bearing 164.3
change the heading 182.30
change the preponderance 894.12
change the rules 645.13
change with the times 363.9
changing (n) 854.3 (a) 782.3, 854.7
changing one's stripes 363.2
changing room 197.8
channel (n) 182.10, 190.9, 199.4, 238.1, 239.1, 270.3, 290.2, 383.3, 551.5, 551.6, 551.7, 552.10, 1034.13 (v) 176.14, 208.10, 239.15, 290.3, 573.9
channeled 290.4
channel interface 1042.3
channelize 208.10, 239.15
channel-surf 1035.15
chanson 708.14
chant (n) 691.4, 696.3, 708.14, 849.5 (v) 524.25, 708.38
chantant 743.13
chant du cygne 307.9
chantecler 314.2
chanter 710.13, 711.9
chanteuse 710.13
chantey 708.14
chanticleer 76.8, 311.28, 314.2
chanting 849.15
chantress 710.13
chantry 703.3
chanty 708.14
chaos 263.1, 418.2, 671.2, 804.1, 810.2, 870.1, 985.3, 1073.3
chaos magic 690.1
chaotic 263.4, 418.6, 671.18, 804.4, 806.5, 810.16, 971.19, 985.12
chaotic attractor 1073.6
chap 76.5, 224.2
chaparral 310.12, 310.15
chapatty 10.45
chapbook 554.11
chapeau 5.25
chapel 197.4, 617.10, 703.3
chapelgoer 696.9
chapel of ease 703.3
chapel royal 703.3
chaperon (n) 577.4, 577.8, 769.5, 1008.7 (v) 769.8, 1008.19
chapfallen 96.22, 112.25, 132.5, 137.14
chaplain 699.2
chaplaincy 698.2
chaplainship 698.2
chaplet 280.2, 310.25, 498.6, 646.3, 647.2, 696.4
chapman 730.5
chapped 224.7
chappie 76.5
chaps 292.4
chapter 423.4, 554.13, 617.10, 793.2, 937.1
chapter and verse 973.4
Chapter 11 625.3
chapter house 703.7
chapter of accidents 972.5
Chapter 7 625.3
Chapter 13 625.3
char (n) 79.14 (v) 38.7, 725.12, 1020.24
character (n) 349.2, 509.4, 517.1, 546.1, 546.2, 560.6, 644.1, 662.1, 704.10, 707.2, 709.12, 722.4, 724.3, 765.4, 767.4, 809.3, 865.4, 870.4, 927.3, 927.4, 978.3, 1017.3 (v) 349.8, 349.9, 546.6, 713.9
character actor 706.4, 707.2
character actress 707.2
character assassination 512.2, 552.8, 609.14
character development 718.2
character disorder 92.15
character dress 5.9
charactering 349.1
characteristic (n) 373.3, 517.1, 767.4, 865.4 (a) 349.15, 780.9, 809.7, 865.13, 978.7
characteristics 767.4
characterization 349.1, 349.2, 349.4, 517.3, 704.8, 722.4, 865.8
characterize 349.8, 349.9, 517.17, 865.10
characterizing 780.9
characterless 65.2, 117.6, 222.14, 263.4
characterlessness 117.1
character printer 1042.9
character recognition 547.14
character reference 509.4
characters 707.11
character sketch 349.2
character trait 767.4
character witness 957.6
charactery 517.2
charade 517.14, 522.9
charbon 85.41
charbroiling 11.2
charcoal (n) 38.4, 38.6, 712.4, 712.12, 712.18, 1020.16 (v) 38.7, 712.19
charcoal drawing 712.12
charcoal-gray 39.4
charcoalist 716.3
chare (n) 724.2 (v) 725.12
charge (n) 18.1, 92.34, 105.3, 196.2, 297.7, 419.1, 420.2, 432.6, 459.1, 462.16, 573.2, 598.3, 599.1, 615.1, 630.1, 630.6, 641.1, 643.3, 647.2, 698.9, 724.2, 794.3, 888.1, 1008.2, 1012.6, 1032.5, 1074.8 (v) 17.10, 297.13, 334.7, 405.9, 420.8, 422.6, 459.18, 576.15, 599.7, 615.10, 622.7, 630.12, 643.4, 733.7, 794.7, 904.12, 1032.26, 1037.10
chargé 576.6
chargeability 656.1
chargeable 510.25, 623.9, 630.15, 641.17, 674.6
chargeable to 641.14
charge account 622.2
chargeback 624.2
charge card 622.3
charged 105.30, 297.18, 599.15, 794.12, 843.10, 888.6, 1032.34, 1037.11
chargé d'affaires 576.6
chargé d'affaires ad interim 576.6
charged moment 843.5
chargedness 843.1
charged up 17.13
charge for 630.12
charge in 214.5
charge off 148.5, 628.8, 631.2
charge-off 631.1
charge on 888.4
charge one's batteries 9.2, 331.16
charge plate 622.3
charger 311.10, 461.30
charges 623.1, 626.3, 630.6
charge sheet 599.1
chargeship 432.3
charge the jury 598.18, 946.13
charge to 888.4
charge to experience 148.5, 977.3
charge to one's account 622.7
charge to the jury 598.8
charge up 17.10, 375.19
charge with 599.9
charging (n) 297.7, 643.1 (a) 459.29
charging of the jury 598.8
chargrilling (n) 11.2 (a) 1019.25
chariness 494.2, 635.1
charioteer 178.9
charisma 18.1, 377.1, 662.6, 894.1, 1016.2
charismatic 377.8, 662.19, 894.13, 907.5
charismatic figure 574.6, 907.2
charismatic gift 692.3
charismatic leader 574.6
charismatic movement 692.3
charismatic renewal 692.3
charismatize 18.11, 377.6, 377.7, 662.10, 894.8, 894.9
charitable 104.26, 143.13, 143.15, 145.7, 478.22, 634.5, 979.11
charitable foundation 478.9
charitableness 143.1, 143.4, 979.4
charities 143.6
charity 104.1, 120.1, 143.4, 449.4, 449.10, 455.1, 478.3, 478.6, 485.1, 653.3, 979.4
charity case 479.3, 619.4
charity event 478.9
charity line 747.1
charity ward 197.25
charivari 53.3
charlatan (n) 357.6 (a) 354.28
charlatanic 354.28
charlatanish 354.28
charlatanism 354.7, 356.4, 645.2
charlatanry 354.7
Charles Atlas 15.6
Charley 461.16, 1008.10
charley horse 26.2
Charley Noble 239.14
charlie 87.7
Charlie McCarthy 575.5
charm (n) 97.2, 104.6, 377.1, 377.3, 498.6, 690.1, 691.1, 691.5, 696.10, 770.6, 894.1, 954.3, 1016.1, 1038.6 (v) 95.10, 104.22, 375.23, 377.7, 691.8, 983.13
charm-bound 691.12
charmed 95.15, 104.27, 691.12, 983.18, 986.25
charmed circle 280.2, 617.6
charmer 357.1, 377.4, 415.6, 690.9, 1016.7
charming 97.7, 104.24, 377.8, 691.11, 894.13
charmingness 377.2
charm offensive 97.2
charms 1016.3
charmstruck 691.12
charm the birds out of the trees 894.10
charm the pants off one 894.10
charnel house 309.9, 309.16
Charon 682.5
charqui 10.14
charred 38.11, 1020.30
chart (n) 159.5, 349.1, 381.3, 709.12, 757.4, 801.4, 871.2 (v) 159.11, 349.8, 381.10, 801.7, 808.10
chart a course 182.14, 182.27
chartbuster 708.7
charted 381.12
charter (n) 417.12, 430.8, 443.1, 443.5, 549.6, 615.6, 673.6 (v) 443.11, 615.10, 615.15, 615.16
charter airline 184.10
chartered 430.30, 443.17, 615.20
chartered accountant 628.7
chartered bus 179.13
charter flight 184.9
charter member 617.11
charter school 567.4
charting 381.1, 808.2
chartreuse (n) 35.5 (a) 43.4, 44.4
chartulary 549.11
charwoman 79.14
chary 339.13, 494.9, 635.6
Charybdis 238.12, 915.2
chase (n) 290.1, 310.13, 382.1, 382.2 (v) 166.3, 283.12, 382.8, 382.9, 401.5, 562.21, 715.5, 908.3
chase after 166.3, 176.16

chase away 908.3, 909.14
chased 283.18, 713.11, 715.7
chase off 908.3
chase one's tail 914.5
chase out 909.14
chaser 88.9, 382.4, 704.7, 716.6
chase up a tree 1013.16
chase women 665.19
chasing (n) 166.1, 715.1, 773.2 (a) 382.11
chasm 224.2, 275.2, 284.4, 292.1
chasseur 461.9
chassis 199.2, 266.4, 901.10, 1034.3
chaste 496.7, 499.6, 533.6, 653.6, 664.4, 668.10, 798.6, 1002.6
chasten 604.9, 670.6
chastened 433.15, 670.11
chastener 604.7
chasteness 499.1, 499.2, 533.1, 565.1
chastening (n) 604.1 (a) 137.15, 604.22, 670.14
chastise 510.17, 604.9
chastisement 510.5, 604.1
chastiser 604.7
chastising 604.22
chastity 533.1, 565.1, 653.2, 664.1, 668.2, 1002.1
chat (n) 540.3, 541.3 (v) 540.5, 541.9
château 228.7
chatelain 575.6
chatelaine 498.6, 575.2, 575.6
chat line 347.4, 347.13
chatoyancy 47.2
chatoyant 47.10
chat room 1042.19
chattel 432.7
chattel mortgage 438.4
chattels 471.1
chattel slave 432.7
chattels personal 471.2
chattels real 471.6
chatter (n) 55.3, 524.1, 540.3 (v) 55.6, 60.5, 524.19, 538.8, 540.5, 917.11, 1023.9
chatterbox 524.17, 540.4
chatterer 540.4, 541.7
chattering (n) 847.2, 917.2 (a) 55.8, 540.10, 847.5, 917.17, 1023.16
chattering of the teeth 1023.2
chattering teeth 127.5
chatty 540.9, 541.12, 582.24
chat up 562.21
chauffeur (n) 178.10, 577.4 (v) 177.33
chaussé 5.45
chaussure 5.27
chauvin 591.3
chauvinism 458.10, 591.2, 980.4
chauvinist (n) 461.5, 590.2, 591.3, 980.5 (a) 458.21, 591.4
chauvinistic 458.21, 590.3, 591.4, 980.12
chav 606.1
chaw (n) 8.2, 89.7 (v) 8.27, 89.14
cheap 391.11, 484.9, 633.7, 661.11, 950.3, 998.21, 1005.9
cheap as dirt 633.8
cheap at half the price 633.7
cheapen 393.12, 633.6, 731.18
cheapening 633.4
cheap homer 745.3
cheap-jack (n) 730.5 (a) 16.14
cheap-john 730.5
cheap money 728.16
cheapness 484.3, 633.1, 998.2
cheapo 633.7
cheap rates 633.2
cheap shot 17.5, 144.11
cheapskate 484.4
cheat (n) 354.13, 356.8, 357.3, 759.22 (v) 356.18, 645.11, 645.12, 665.19, 759.26
cheat death 306.11
cheater 357.3, 665.13, 759.22
cheaters 29.3
cheating 354.3, 356.8, 645.5, 759.13
cheating device 759.16
cheating method 759.13
cheating scheme 759.13
cheat on 356.14, 645.12
cheat out of 356.18
cheat sheet 482.8
cheat the undertaker 303.10
check (n) 47.4, 85.38, 175.4, 224.2, 292.1, 300.2, 412.2, 428.1, 429.1, 517.5, 517.13, 524.12, 628.3, 728.11, 728.12, 749.3, 759.18, 857.2, 938.6, 942.2, 943.2, 970.8, 1004.1, 1011.3, 1012.1, 1012.3, 1012.7 (v) 27.13, 47.7, 175.9, 224.4, 393.13, 412.11, 428.7, 429.12, 460.10, 517.19, 749.7, 753.4, 759.25, 788.6, 802.12, 846.8, 857.11, 865.11, 938.24, 943.5, 970.12, 1004.4, 1012.10, 1017.21, 1034.26 (a) 47.14
checkable 957.19
check and doublecheck 970.12
check a parameter 300.10
checkbook 549.11, 728.11
checkbox 1042.18
checked 47.14, 175.12, 393.27, 524.30, 1004.8
checked out 405.17
checkedy 47.14
checker (n) 47.4 (v) 47.7, 852.6
checkerboard 47.4, 47.6
checkered 47.14, 854.6
checkered flag 756.3
checkers 743.16
checker-work 47.4
check in 186.6, 307.19, 549.15, 832.12
check in and out 970.12
check in full career 857.11
checking 47.4, 749.3, 758.4, 943.2, 970.8
checking account 622.2, 728.14, 729.3, 729.14
checking the fit 405.2
check into 938.23
checklist 574.10, 871.1, 871.6
checkmark 517.5
checkmate (n) 412.2, 857.2, 1012.3 (v) 412.11, 857.11, 1012.15
check of 1017.13
check off 517.19, 832.12, 865.11
check on 938.23, 970.12, 1017.21
check one's speech 51.7
check out 27.13, 188.7, 188.13, 307.19, 405.15, 832.12, 938.23, 938.24, 942.9, 1017.21
checkout 188.1, 624.4
check-out pilot 938.17
check over 938.24, 970.12
check over and through 970.12
check-rein 1012.7
checkroll 871.6
checkroom 197.15
checks 47.4
checks and balances 246.1
check sheet 832.9
checkstone 1059.4
check the growth of 268.6
check through 938.24, 970.12
check up 938.28, 970.12
checkup 938.6
check up and down 970.12
check up on 938.24, 938.28
check valve 293.4
cheddar 728.19
cheek 142.3, 218.1, 454.1, 493.1
cheek-by-jowl 223.14
cheekiness 142.2, 454.1
cheek-kiss 562.4
cheeks 217.5
cheeky 142.10, 454.7
cheep 60.5
cheer (n) 10.1, 59.1, 95.2, 109.1, 116.2, 509.2, 582.3 (v) 9.2, 59.6, 95.9, 109.7, 116.6, 121.6, 124.9, 332.8, 492.15, 509.10
cheerful 95.16, 97.6, 109.11, 109.16, 124.11, 228.33
cheerful consent 324.1
cheerful expectation 124.1, 130.2
cheerful fire 1019.13
cheerful giver 478.11, 485.2
cheerfulness 95.2, 97.4, 109.1, 124.2, 133.8
cheerful outlook 124.2
cheerful readiness 101.1
cheeriness 109.1, 133.8
cheering (n) 59.1 (a) 9.3, 109.16, 121.13, 124.12
cheerlead 59.9
cheerleading 59.1
cheerless 96.20, 98.20, 112.21, 125.12
cheerlessness 96.1, 98.5, 112.2
cheer on 375.16, 492.15, 509.10
cheers 820.5
cheer the inner man 88.24
cheer up 109.9, 124.7
cheery 109.11, 109.16
cheery mood 109.1
cheery vein 109.1
cheese 10.48
cheese blintz 10.45
cheesecake 10.42, 714.3
cheese dip 10.9
cheesed-off 96.20, 96.21
cheese grater 1051.7
cheese off 96.12
cheeseparing (n) 484.1, 635.2 (a) 484.7, 635.6, 885.5
cheeseparings and candle ends 992.5
cheese sauce 10.12
cheesiness 661.3, 998.2
cheesy 661.12, 998.21, 1000.8, 1005.9
cheetah 47.6, 311.21
chef (n) 11.3, 575.1 (v) 7.17
chef de cuisine 11.3
chef d'oeuvre 122.2, 999.5
chef d'œuvre 413.10, 712.9, 893.1, 1002.4
chef's salad 10.37
chelae 474.4
chemical (n) 1060.2 (v) 1060.8 (a) 1060.9
chemical action 1060.6
chemical analysis 801.1
chemical apparatus 1060.6
chemical closet 12.11
chemical compound 1060.2
chemical element 1052.2, 1060.2
chemical engineer 1043.2
chemical engineering 1043.1
chemical equation 1060.2
chemical fertilizer 890.4
chemicalization 1060.6
chemicalize 1060.8
chemical process 1060.6
chemicals 1055.3
chemical science 1060.1
chemical scientist 1060.7
chemical solution 1064.3
chemical symbol 1060.2
chemical toilet 12.11
chemical war 458.1
chemical weapon 462.1
chemicobiologic 1060.9
chemicobiological 1060.9
chemicodynamic 1060.9
chemicoengineering 1060.9
chemicomechanical 1060.9
chemicomineralogical 1060.9
chemicopharmaceutical 1060.9
chemicophysical 1060.9
chemicophysiologic 1060.9
chemicophysiological 1060.9
chemism 1060.6
chemisorb 187.13
chemisorption 187.6
chemisorptive 187.17
chemist 86.35, 86.36, 1060.7
chemistry 75.5, 1060.1
chemist's shop 86.36
chemophysiologic 1060.9
chemophysiological 1060.9
chemosorb 187.13
chemosorption 187.6
chemosorptive 187.17
chemosterilant 1001.3
chemotherapeutic 1060.9
chemotherapeutical 1060.9
chemurgic 1060.9
cheque 728.11
cherish 104.20, 449.16, 474.7, 989.12, 1008.19
cherish a belief 953.13
cherish a feeling 93.10
cherish an idea 931.16
cherish at the heart's core 93.11
cherished 104.23

cherish the hope 124.6
cherish the memory of 989.12
cheroot 89.4
cherry (n) 41.1, 565.4 (a) 41.6
cherry bomb 53.6
cherry-colored 41.6
cherry-pick 371.14
cherry picker 179.12
cherry pie 1014.4
cherry-red 41.6
chersonese 283.9
cherub 302.3, 302.9, 562.6, 679.1
cherubic 679.6
cherubim 679.1, 679.3
Cheshire cat 311.20
chesil 1059.3
chess 743.16
chessboard 47.4
chessman 743.17
chess master 417.7
chess piece 743.17
Chessycat 311.20
chest (n) 283.6, 386.6, 729.13 (a) 283.19
chested 283.19
chested arrow 462.6
chestiness 140.4
chestnut (n) 118.1, 311.11, 489.9, 974.3 (a) 40.4, 41.10
chestnut-brown 40.4
chest of drawers 229.1
chest of viols 711.5
chest trap 752.3
chest voice 709.5
chest X-ray 91.9
chesty 257.18, 283.19
cheval glass 29.6
chevalier 178.8, 504.9, 608.5
chevron 204.8, 278.2, 647.2, 647.5
chevronways 204.20
chevronwise 204.20
chevrony 204.20
chevy 382.2
chew (n) 8.2, 89.7 (v) 8.27, 89.14, 510.18, 1063.5
chew ass 510.18
chewed 1063.6
chewed-up 393.27
chewer 89.11
chewing (n) 8.1, 89.10, 510.6 (a) 8.32, 89.15
chewing gum 1048.3, 1062.6
chewing out 604.5
chewing-out 510.6
chewing tobacco 89.7
chewing up the scenery 93.9
chew one's ear off 856.5
chew out 510.18
chew over 931.13
chew the cud 8.27, 931.12
chew the fat 541.8
chew up 8.27
chew up the scenery 93.13, 500.12, 704.31
chewy 97.8, 1049.4
chi 919.5
chiaroscuro 712.12, 1025.19
chiasma 170.1
chiasmal 170.8
chiasmic 170.8
chiasmus 205.3
chiastic 170.8, 205.7
chic (n) 578.2, 578.3 (a) 5.46, 578.13, 928.17
Chicago 708.9
chicane 356.4, 756.3, 936.5
chicanery 354.7, 356.4, 356.6, 415.3, 645.2, 936.5
chi-chi 498.2
chichi 498.12, 500.17, 501.19, 578.14
chick 77.6, 302.7, 302.10, 311.27, 311.28, 562.6
chickabiddy 311.28, 562.6
chicken (n) 10.22, 16.6, 77.10, 311.28, 358.2, 491.5, 647.5 (v) 491.8 (a) 16.12, 77.14, 362.12, 491.10
chicken-and-egg 886.13
chicken colonel 575.17
chicken coop 228.22
chicken farm 1070.5
chicken farming 1070.1
chicken feed 10.4, 728.19, 998.4
chicken heart 491.4
chickenhearted 362.12, 491.10
chickenheartedness 491.1
chicken house 228.22
chicken in every pot, a 1010.1
chicken-liver 491.5
chicken-livered 362.12, 491.10
chicken-liveredness 491.1
chicken out 362.7, 468.2, 491.8, 858.13
chicken-pecked 326.5
chicken thief 483.1
chicken wing 10.23
chick flick 706.2
chicklet 311.28
chickling 302.10
chick lit 718.1
chicky 302.10, 311.28
chicle 1062.6
chicle gum 1062.6
chide 510.17
chiding 510.5
chief (n) 249.4, 574.2, 575.1, 575.3, 575.8, 647.2, 997.10 (a) 165.3, 198.11, 216.10, 249.14, 573.12, 612.17, 814.4, 818.17, 997.24
chief cook 11.3
chief cook and bottle washer 574.2
chiefdom 573.1
chief engineer 183.7
chiefery 417.7
chief executive 574.3, 575.7, 997.10
chief executive officer 574.3, 997.10
Chief Justice 596.3
chief librarian 558.3
chief master sergeant 575.18
chief master sergeant of the Air Force 575.18
chief mate 183.7
chief of police 1008.15
chief of staff 575.17
chief of state 575.7
chief of the deadly sins 141.1
chief operating officer 574.3
chief petty officer 575.19
chief pilot 185.1
chief rabbi 699.11
chieftain 575.8
chieftaincy 232.1, 417.7
chieftainry 232.1, 417.7
chieftainship 417.7, 417.10
chief thing 997.6
chief warrant officer 575.17
chiffon (n) 498.3 (a) 320.6
chigger 311.36
chignon 3.7, 3.13, 1016.14
chigoe 311.36
chilblain 85.37
chilblains 1023.2
child 302.3, 312.5, 416.3, 432.6, 561.3, 657.4, 893.1
child abuse 144.11, 389.2
child actor 707.2
childbearing 1.1
childbed 1.1
childbirth 1.1
child born on the wrong side of the blanket 561.5
child born out of wedlock 561.5
child born without benefit of clergy 561.5
child care 1008.2
child-friendly 1014.15
childhood 301.2, 303.1, 818.4
childhood sweetheart 104.9
childish 301.11, 922.23, 922.24
childishness 301.4, 922.10, 922.11, 923.2
childish scrawl 547.6
childish treble 525.1
childkind 302.2
child labor 607.9
childless 891.4
childlike 301.11, 416.5, 657.6, 922.23, 922.24, 953.22
childlikeness 301.4, 416.1, 657.2
child molestation 389.2
child of nature 416.3
child prodigy 413.12
childproof (v) 15.14 (a) 1049.4
child psychologist 92.10
child-rearing 301.2, 1008.2
children 302.2, 559.5, 561.1
children of darkness 660.11
children of God, the 692.5
children of light, the 692.5
children of the devil 660.11
children's book 554.1
children's game 743.9
children's television 1035.2
children's theater 704.14
children's wear 5.30, 735.3
children under 17 require accompanying parent or guardian 706.1
child-sized 258.12
child's play 998.5
child support 624.8
child welfare 143.5
child within 865.5
chiliad 882.10
chiliagon 882.10
chiliahedron 882.10
chiliarch 882.10
chiliarchia 882.10
chiliasm 124.2
chiliast 124.5
chiliastic 124.11
chiliaüdron 882.10
chill (n) 85.7, 85.9, 94.1, 102.1, 112.3, 379.2, 583.2, 589.1, 1023.1, 1023.2, 1023.3 (v) 20.7, 379.4, 1023.9, 1023.10, 1024.10 (a) 20.10, 94.9, 589.9, 1023.12
chill along the spine 133.2
chillax 20.7
chilled 344.10, 1024.13
chilled to the bone 1023.16
chiller 1024.3
chill factor 317.4, 1023.3
chilliness 94.1, 102.1, 141.4, 344.3, 583.2, 589.1, 1023.1, 1023.2, 1023.3
chilling (n) 1023.2, 1024.1 (a) 127.28, 1024.12
chilling effect 112.3, 379.2
chilling wind 318.7
chill one's spine 127.15
chill out 465.9, 1047.7
chill-out 20.10
chillout 20.2
chills 85.9, 1023.2
chills of fear 127.5
chills of terror 127.5
chill to the bone 1023.10
chill to the marrow 1023.10
chilly 94.9, 141.12, 344.10, 583.6, 589.9, 1023.12, 1023.16
chilly look 27.5
Chilon 921.4
chilopod 311.32
chime (n) 54.3, 708.3, 849.4 (v) 54.8, 524.22, 708.35, 784.9, 788.6
chime in 214.6
chime in with 332.9, 455.2, 788.6
chimenea 228.2
chime of bells 711.18
chimera 124.4, 976.1, 986.5
chimeric 976.9, 986.22
chimerical 764.6, 976.9, 986.22
chimes 54.4, 711.18
chime with 775.5, 778.4, 788.6
chiminea 1020.11
chiming (n) 54.3, 708.3 (a) 54.13, 708.49, 784.17, 849.15
chimney 237.7, 239.14, 1020.11, 1058.7
chimney-breast 1020.11
chimney corner 228.2, 1020.11
chimney piece 1020.11
chimney pot 1020.11
chimney stack 1020.11
chimney sweep 79.16
chimney sweeper 79.16
chimp 311.22
chimpanzee 311.22
chin (n) 216.6 (v) 524.20, 541.8
China 261.4
china (n) 742.2, 1050.2 (a) 742.7
china 8.12
china clay 742.3
china decorator 716.7
Chinaman's chance 967.1
china painter 716.7
china stone 742.3
China syndrome 1037.1

Chinatown 230.6
chinaware 735.4
Chinchilla cat 311.20
chinchiness 885.1
chinchy 885.5
chine 237.5, 237.7, 283.3
Chinese boxing 457.9
Chinese calendar 832.8
Chinese homer 745.3
Chinese lottery 759.14
Chinese puzzle 522.8, 522.9, 799.2
Chinese restaurant syndrome 85.34
Chinese windlass 906.7
chinfest 541.2
chink (n) 52.3, 54.3, 224.2, 290.1, 1006.4 (v) 52.15, 54.8, 292.11, 293.7
chink in one's armor 16.4, 1003.2, 1006.4
chinky 224.7
chinoiserie 498.2, 799.1
chinook 318.6
Chinook jargon 523.11
chinook wind 318.6
chinos 5.18
chintziness 484.3, 661.3, 810.6, 885.1
chintzy 484.9, 497.10, 661.12, 810.15, 885.5
chinwag 541.2
chin whiskers 3.8
chip (n) 85.38, 248.3, 296.3, 298.2, 758.4, 759.18, 793.3, 802.4, 1033.8, 1042.3 (v) 87.22, 393.13, 802.12, 1051.9
chip away at 252.7
chip in 214.6, 476.5, 478.14, 624.18
chip off 1050.3
chip off the old block, a 561.3, 784.3, 785.3
chip on one's shoulder 454.2, 458.10
chipped 393.27
chipped beef 10.14
chipper 83.9, 109.13, 330.17
chip-proof 1049.5
chippy 87.22
chips 183.6, 728.2
chirk (n) 58.5 (v) 58.7, 60.5 (a) 109.13
chirking 58.5
chirk up 9.2
chirograph 549.5
chirographer 547.13
chirographic 547.22
chirographical 547.22
chirography 547.3
chironomy 517.14
chiropodic 90.15
chiropractic (n) 73.2 (a) 90.15
chiropractor 90.9
chirp (n) 58.5 (v) 58.7, 60.5, 109.6, 116.5, 524.25, 708.38
chirpiness 109.3
chirping (n) 58.5 (a) 95.16
chirp like a cricket 109.6, 116.5
chirpy 109.13
chirr (n) 58.3 (v) 58.9, 60.5
chirrup (n) 58.5 (v) 58.7, 60.5, 109.6, 116.5, 708.38
chirrupy 109.13
chisel (n) 715.4, 1040.7 (v) 262.7, 290.3, 356.19, 713.9, 715.5, 892.9
chiseled 262.9, 715.7
chiseler 357.4
chisel in 214.5
chiseling (n) 356.8, 713.2 (a) 356.22
chisel temper 1046.4
chit 258.4, 302.3, 302.7, 553.2
chitchat 541.4, 552.7
chitchatty 541.12
chitin 295.15, 305.6
chitlins 10.20
chits 623.1
chitter 60.5
chitter-chatter 540.3, 541.4
chitterlings 10.20
chivalric 492.16, 504.14
chivalrous 492.16, 504.14, 608.10, 652.6
chivalrousness 492.1, 504.2, 652.2
chivalry 458.5, 492.1, 504.2, 608.1, 652.2
chivied 96.24
chivy (n) 382.2 (v) 96.13, 382.8
chizzle 356.18
chizzling 356.1
chloral 86.12
chloral hydrate 86.12
chloranemia 36.2, 44.1
chloranemic 36.7, 44.4
chloremia 44.1
chloremic 44.4
chlorinate 79.24, 1060.8, 1067.8
chlorinated hydrocarbon insecticide 1001.3
chlorination 79.3
chlorine 7.11
chloroform (n) 86.15 (v) 25.4, 308.13
chlorophyll 44.1
chloroplast 305.5
chlorosis 44.1
chlorotic 44.4, 85.61
chlorpromazine 86.12
chock (n) 1012.7 (v) 794.7, 1012.12
chock-a-block 794.11
chockablock 770.22
chock-full 794.11
chocolate (n) 10.40, 40.1 (a) 40.3
chocolate-brown 40.3
chocolate-colored 40.3
Choctaw 522.7
choice (n) 323.1, 369.4, 371.1, 430.6, 533.1, 757.2, 946.1, 999.8 (a) 496.7, 999.16
choice bit of dirt 552.8
choiceless 963.12
choicelessness 963.6
choice morsel 10.8
choiceness 496.1
choice of Hercules 371.3
choice of words 529.2, 532.1
choicy 495.9
choir (n) 703.9, 708.18, 710.16, 711.17 (v) 708.38
choirboy 710.15
choir chaplain 710.18
choirgirl 710.15
choir invisible 679.2
choir invisible, the 307.16
choirman 710.15
choirmaster 574.6, 710.18
choir member 710.15
choir screen 703.9
choke (n) 307.5, 308.6 (v) 51.8, 260.7, 293.6, 293.7, 307.23, 308.19, 395.15, 993.15, 1012.12, 1019.22, 1022.7
choke back 106.8
choked 58.15, 260.12, 293.9, 293.11, 525.12, 993.20
chokedamp 1001.4, 1067.1
choked off 260.12, 293.9
choked up 51.12, 293.9, 293.11
choked voice 525.1
choke off 51.8, 260.7, 293.6, 293.7, 428.8, 1012.12
choke on 99.4
choke one up 93.14
chokepoint 260.1, 270.3, 293.3
choke up 51.5, 293.7
chokey 429.9
choking (n) 260.1, 293.3, 307.5, 308.6, 395.6, 1022.2 (a) 525.12, 1012.17
choking off 260.1, 293.3, 395.6
choler 2.24, 110.1, 152.3
choleric (n) 92.12 (a) 110.23, 152.26
cholesterol 7.7
chomp (n) 8.2 (v) 8.27
chomp at the bit 846.13
chondrite 1073.15
choo-choo 179.14
choo-choo train 179.14
choose 100.14, 323.2, 371.13, 371.14
choose out 371.14
chooser 371.7
choose rather 371.17
choose to 100.15, 323.2
choose up sides 371.14
choosiness 371.10, 495.1
choosing (n) 371.1 (a) 371.23
choosy 371.23, 495.9, 944.8
chop (n) 10.4, 10.13, 10.19, 218.1, 238.14, 288.2, 902.4 (v) 289.4, 745.5, 802.11, 852.6
chop and change 364.4, 782.2, 852.6
chop block 746.3
chop down 395.19, 913.5
chophouse 8.17
chop logic 780.6, 935.16, 936.9
choplogic (n) 936.5, 936.6 (a) 936.14
choplogical 936.14
chop off 802.8
chopped 289.5
chopped liver 762.3
chopped-off 813.4
chopper 179.8, 181.5, 745.3
choppers 2.8
choppiness 238.14, 288.1, 782.1, 851.1
chopping 802.2
chopping sea 238.14
choppy 288.6, 782.3, 813.4, 851.3, 917.20
choppy sea 238.14
chops 10.15, 292.4, 711.6
chopsocky 706.2
chopsticks 8.12
chop up 802.18
choragus 574.6
choral 704.33, 708.50
choral conductor 710.18
choral director 710.18
chorale 696.3, 708.14, 708.17, 708.18, 710.16
choral fantasy 708.17
choral group 710.16
choralist 710.15
choral service 708.32
choral singer 710.15
choral singing 708.13, 708.18
choral society 710.16
choral symphony 710.16
chord (n) 93.5, 277.2, 709.17, 711.20 (v) 708.35, 708.36, 708.39
chordal progression 709.2
chordate (n) 311.3 (a) 311.40
chordophone 711.2
chore (n) 724.2, 1013.2 (v) 577.13, 725.12
chorea 85.25, 917.2
chore boy 577.5
choreodrama 705.1
choreograph 705.5
choreographer 704.22, 705.3
choreographic 704.33, 705.6
choreography 349.1, 705.1
choriamb 720.8
choriambus 720.8
choric 708.50
chorine 705.3, 707.1, 710.15
chorion 2.6
chorister 710.15, 710.18
chorographer 159.5, 300.9
chorographic 159.19, 300.12
chorographical 300.12
chorography 159.5, 159.8
choroid coat 2.9
chortle (n) 116.4 (v) 116.8
chorus (n) 332.5, 704.10, 707.11, 708.18, 708.24, 710.16, 720.10, 788.1, 817.1, 849.5 (v) 336.5, 524.22, 708.38
chorus boy 705.3, 707.1
chorus girl 705.3, 707.1, 710.15
chorus line 705.3
chorus master 710.18
chorus of cheers 116.2
chorus show 708.34
chorus singer 710.15
chose in possession 469.1
chosen (n) 610.3, 999.8 (a) 249.12, 371.26
chosen, the 371.12, 692.5
chosen few 249.5
chosen kind 371.5
chosen sort 371.5
choses 471.2
choses in action 471.2
choses in possession 471.2
choses local 471.2
choses transitory 471.2
chouse (n) 356.6 (v) 356.18

chouse out of 356.18
chow 10.2
chowder 10.10
chowderhead 924.4
chowderheaded 922.17
chowderheadedness 922.4
chow down 8.22
chow hound 672.3
chowhound 8.16
chrestomathy 554.7, 770.11
chrism (n) 696.10, 701.5, 1056.3 (v) 701.15
chrismal (n) 701.5, 701.6, 703.10, 703.11 (a) 1056.9
chrismation 701.5, 1056.6
chrismatory (n) 701.5, 703.11, 1056.6 (a) 1056.9
chrisom 701.5, 1056.3
Christ 677.10
Christ and the beloved disciple 588.6
christen 527.11, 701.16, 818.11
Christendom 675.7, 692.5
christened 527.14
christening 527.2, 701.6
Christian (n) 659.3, 675.17 (a) 644.13, 687.7
Christian charity 143.4
Christian denomination 675.7
Christian ethics 636.2
Christian fundamentalism 675.7
Christian healer 90.9
Christian healing 91.2
Christian holy days 701.13
Christian humanism 312.11
Christianism 675.7
Christianity 675.7
Christian love 104.1
Christian name 527.4
Christian Science 675.14
Christian Science practitioner 90.9, 675.24
Christian Scientist 675.24
Christian sectarian 675.17
Christlike 137.11, 143.13, 677.16
Christly 143.13, 677.16
Christmas 20.9
Christmas gift 478.4
Christmas present 478.4
Christmas stocking 478.4
Christmastide 313.6
Christmastime 313.6
Christmas tree 310.10, 750.2
Christmas tree farming 1069.3
Christmas tree lights 1025.19
Christophanic 348.9
chroma 35.6
chromatic 35.16, 709.27
chromatic aberration 35.7
chromatic circle 35.7
chromatic color 35.6
chromaticism 35.1
chromaticity 35.6
chromaticity coordinate 35.7
chromaticity diagram 35.7
chromaticness 35.6
chromatics 35.10
chromatic scale 709.6
chromatic semitone 709.20
chromatic spectrum 35.7
chromatic tetrachord 709.8
chromatid 305.8, 560.6
chromatin 305.7, 560.6
chromatinic 305.21
chromatin strands 305.7
chromatism 35.1
chromatography 35.10
chromatology 35.10
chromatoplasm 305.4
chromatoscopy 35.10
chromesthesia 24.5
chromism 35.1
chromium 7.11
chromium plate 295.13
chromium-plate 295.26
chromium-plated 295.33
chromogen 35.8
chromolithograph 713.5
chromolithographer 716.8
chromolithographic 713.12
chromolithography 713.3
chromonema 305.8
chromoplast 305.5
chromosomal 305.21
chromosome 305.8, 560.6
chromosome complement 305.8
chromosome map 305.8
chromosome number 305.8
chromosphere 1073.13
chromotypic 548.20
chromotypographic 548.20
chromotypography 548.1
chromotypy 548.1
chromoxylography 548.1
chronic 373.18, 827.10
chronic alcoholic 88.11
chronic alcoholism 87.1
chronically unemployed, the 331.11
chronic drunk 88.11
chronic fatigue syndrome 21.1
chronic ill health 82.1, 85.3
chronicle (n) 549.1, 719.1, 719.2, 722.3, 832.9 (v) 549.15, 719.4, 832.14
chronicled 549.17, 719.6
chronicler 550.2, 718.4, 719.3, 832.10
chronicles 719.1
chronicling 549.14
chronic pauperism 619.2
chronic poor 606.4
chronic poverty area 619.3
chronogram 832.8
chronogrammatic 832.15
chronogrammatical 832.15
chronographer 832.10
chronographic 821.7, 832.15
chronographical 832.15
chronography 821.1, 832.1
chronologer 832.10
chronologic 719.6, 832.15
chronological 719.6, 812.9, 821.7, 832.15
chronological error 833.1
chronological order 807.1
chronologist 832.10
chronologize 832.14
chronology 719.1, 821.1, 832.1, 832.9
chronometer 182.2, 832.6
chronometric 821.7, 832.15
chronometrical 832.15
chronometry 821.1, 832.1
chronophotograph 714.3
chronoscopic 832.15
chronoscopy 832.1
chronotype 2.1
chrysalis 302.12
chthonian (n) 680.15, 697.4 (a) 682.8, 697.7
chthonian worship 680.14
chthonic 682.8
chubbiness 257.5, 257.8, 268.2
chubby 257.18, 268.10
chubby-faced 257.18
chub out 259.8
chuck (n) 10.2, 10.14, 902.7, 904.3 (v) 60.5, 159.13, 372.2, 390.7, 459.27, 773.5, 902.18, 904.10
chuck, the 909.1, 909.5
chuck away 390.7
chucker 904.7, 909.11
chucker-out 909.11
chuck-full 794.11
chuckhole 284.3, 1062.9
chucking 372.1, 904.2
chucking out 372.1, 909.1
chuckle (n) 52.5, 116.4 (v) 116.8
chucklehead 924.4
chuckleheaded 922.17
chuckleheadedness 922.4
chuck out 372.2, 909.13
chuck under the chin 562.16
chuck up 909.27
chuck wagon 8.17
chug 88.25
chug-a-lug 88.25
chughole 1062.9
chug on 175.7
Chukwa 901.3
chum (n) 588.4 (v) 582.18
Chumash 683.3
chumminess 587.2, 587.5
chummy 587.20
chump 358.2, 924.3
chumpiness 922.4
chumpish 922.15
chumship 587.2
chum together 582.18
chunder 99.4
chunk (n) 244.2, 257.10, 297.1, 477.5, 759.3, 770.9, 793.3, 904.3 (v) 904.10
chunker 904.7
chunkiness 257.8, 268.2
chunking 904.2
chunky 257.18, 268.10, 763.7
chuppah 563.3
church 617.5, 675.3, 696.8, 703.1
Church, the 687.3, 692.5, 698.1, 698.6
church calendar 701.12, 832.8
church dignitary 575.1, 699.8
church feast 20.4
church furniture 229.1
churchgoer 221.5, 692.4, 696.9
churchgoers 700.1
churchgoing 692.1
church house 703.1, 703.7
church invisible 687.3
churchish 703.15
churchite 692.4
church key 292.10
churchlike 703.15
churchly 698.13, 703.15
churchman 692.4, 699.2, 700.2
church member 700.2
church militant 687.3
church mode 709.10
church music 708.17
Church of Christ 687.3
Church of England 675.11
church office 698.5
Church of Rome 675.8
church-related school 567.8
church school 567.8
church service 696.8
church spire 272.6
church triumphant 687.3
church universal, the 687.3
church visible 687.3
churchwarden 89.6
church wedding 563.3
churchwoman 700.2
churchyard 309.15
churl 108.4, 110.11, 432.7, 484.4, 497.6, 606.6
churlish 110.19, 233.7, 497.13, 505.7
churlishness 110.2, 233.3, 497.4, 505.3
churn (n) 797.9, 917.1, 917.9 (v) 671.12, 917.10, 1062.10
churn out 547.21, 718.6, 892.8
churn rate 728.1
churn up 917.10
chute 181.13, 190.9, 204.4, 238.10, 239.3, 756.3, 1058.7
chuter 185.8
chutes 743.15
chute-the-chute 743.15
chutist 185.8
chutzpa 142.2
chutzpadik (n) 142.5 (a) 142.10
chutzpah 142.3, 492.3, 493.1
chyle 2.24
chylifaction 1061.1
chylifactive 2.33
chylifactory 2.33
chylific 2.33
chylification 1061.1
ciabatta 10.28
ciborium 703.11
cicada 311.35
cicala 311.35
cicatrix 517.5, 1004.1
cicatrization 517.5
cicatrize 396.21, 517.19, 1004.4
cicatrized 1004.8
Cicero 543.6
cicerone 178.1, 341.7, 574.7, 769.5
Ciceronian 533.6, 544.8
cig 89.5
cigar 89.4
cigar box 89.4
cigar case 89.4
cigar cutter 89.4
cigarette 89.5
cigarette break 20.2
cigarette butt 89.5
cigarette case 89.5

cigarette lighter 1021.4
cigarette paper 89.5
cigarettes 732.3
cigarette smoke 89.1
cigarette smoker 89.11
cigarette smuggling 732.2
cigarillo 89.4
cigar lighter 1021.4
cigar smoke 89.1
cigar smoker 89.11
cigar store 89.12
cilia 3.12, 305.5
ciliate 3.24
ciliolum 3.2, 271.1
cilium 3.2, 3.17, 271.1
Cimmerian 1027.13
Cimmerian darkness 1027.1
Cimmerian sibyl 962.6
cinch (n) 358.2, 409.2, 759.10, 901.18, 970.2, 1014.4 (v) 800.7, 800.9, 957.10, 970.11
cinch bet 759.3
cinched 965.8, 970.20
cinch hand 759.10
cinch up 800.7
Cincinnati 750.2
cincture (n) 209.5, 212.3, 280.3 (v) 209.7
cinctured 209.11
cinder 256.2, 1019.16, 1020.16
cinder block 1054.2
cinder concrete 1054.2
Cinderella story 354.11
cinema (n) 706.7 (a) 706.9
cinema, the 706.1
cinemactor 706.4
cinemactress 706.4
CinemaScope 706.5, 706.7
cinematic 706.9
cinematics 706.5
cinematize 706.8
cinematograph 714.11, 714.12
cinematographer 706.5, 716.5
cinematography 706.5, 714.1
cinéma vérité 706.1
cinemese 523.10
cineplex 706.7
cineprojector 714.12
Cinerama 706.7
cinerarium 309.9, 309.15
cinerary 309.22
cinerary urn 309.12
cinerator 1020.13
cinereal 39.4
cinereous 36.7, 39.4
cineritious 36.7, 39.4
cinerous 39.4
cingulum 280.3
cinnamon 40.3
cinquain 882.1
cinque 882.1
cion 191.2
cipher (n) 61.1, 345.6, 517.2, 522.7, 527.10, 546.1, 762.2, 764.2, 998.7, 1017.3 (v) 345.10, 1017.18
ciphered 345.16
ciphering 1017.10
cipher up 1017.19
circadian 849.13, 850.8
circadian rhythm 825.4
Circe 377.4, 690.9
Circean 663.6, 691.11
circinate 280.11
circle (n) 209.1, 230.9, 231.2, 279.2, 280.2, 498.6, 617.6, 850.3, 914.2, 1025.14, 1073.16 (v) 172.5, 209.7, 280.10, 850.5, 914.5, 915.9
circle chart 381.3
circled 209.11, 210.6
circle graph 381.3
circle in 210.4
circle of friends 587.2
circle of the sphere 1073.16
circle out 210.4
circlet 280.5, 1026.6
circle theater 704.14
circle the drain 911.3, 975.15
circling (n) 209.5, 914.1 (a) 209.8, 850.7
circling-in 210.1
circling-out 210.1
circuit (n) 177.5, 209.1, 231.2, 280.2, 383.1, 704.11, 745.1, 850.3, 914.2, 914.3, 1032.4, 1034.8, 1042.3 (v) 914.5
circuit analysis 1041.2
circuit board 1033.8
circuit breaker 1008.3
circuit clout 745.3
circuiteer 914.5
circuition 914.1
circuit network 1034.8
circuitous 164.7, 204.13, 281.6, 538.14, 914.7
circuitousness 164.1, 204.1, 281.1, 538.5, 914.1
circuit rider 699.3
circuit-riding 177.36
circuitry 1033.8, 1042.3
circuit theater 706.7
circuit training 84.2
circuity 914.1
circular (n) 352.2, 352.8, 554.11 (a) 280.11, 914.7
circular argument 936.3
circular file 391.7
circularity 279.1, 280.1, 914.1, 936.1
circularize 352.10, 352.15
circular measure 300.4
circular note 622.3
circular reasoning 280.2
circular tackle 749.6
circulate 352.10, 352.16, 478.13, 728.26, 914.5, 915.9
circulate a petition 440.10
circulated 352.17
circulating 2.33
circulating capital 728.15
circulating library 558.1
circulating medium 728.1
circulation (n) 2.25, 352.1, 728.23, 914.1, 915.1, 1061.1 (a) 1061.4
circulatory 2.33, 280.11, 1061.4
circulatory collapse 85.8
circumambages 281.1
circumambience 209.5, 914.1
circumambiencies 209.1
circumambiency 209.5, 914.1
circumambient 209.8, 914.8
circumambulate 177.27, 914.5
circumambulation 914.1
circumambulatory 914.8
circumbendibus 281.1, 914.3
circumcincture 209.5
circumcise 701.16
circumcised 685.9
circumcision 255.3, 685.4, 701.9
circumference 158.1, 206.2, 211.1, 257.1, 280.2
circumferential 209.8, 211.14, 280.11
circumflex 209.8
circumflexion 209.5, 914.1
circumfluent 209.8, 914.8
circumfluous 209.8
circumforaneous 177.37, 914.8
circumfuse 771.4
circumfusion 771.1
circumgyration 915.1
circumgyratory 915.15
circumjacence 209.5
circumjacencies 209.1
circumjacency 209.5
circumjacent 209.8
circumlocute 204.9, 538.10
circumlocution 204.1, 281.1, 538.5, 914.1
circumlocutional 538.14
circumlocutory 281.6, 538.14
circummigrate 914.5
circummigration 914.1
circumnavigable 914.8
circumnavigate 182.13, 280.10, 914.5
circumnavigation 182.1, 914.1
circumnavigatory 914.8
circumplanetary 1073.25
circumposition 209.5
circumrotate 915.9
circumrotation 915.1
circumrotatory 915.15
circumscribable 260.11
circumscribe 210.4, 211.8, 260.7, 428.9, 959.3
circumscribed 210.6, 270.14, 428.15
circumscribed by 959.9
circumscribing 210.1
circumscript 210.6
circumscription 210.1, 211.1, 211.3, 212.1, 260.1, 270.1, 428.3, 444.1, 773.1, 959.1
circumspect 175.10, 339.10, 494.8, 920.19
circumspection 175.1, 339.1, 494.1, 920.7
circumspectness 339.1, 920.7
circumstance 501.6, 761.3, 765.1, 766.1, 796.2, 831.2, 959.2
circumstances 209.1, 471.7, 766.2, 831.4
circumstantial 766.7, 768.4, 831.9, 957.16, 959.7
circumstantial evidence 958.1
circumstantiality 339.3, 766.4, 959.1
circumstantiate 766.6, 957.11
circumstantiated 957.20
circumstantiation 766.5, 957.4
circumvallation 212.1
circumvent 356.14, 368.6, 368.7, 415.11, 1012.15
circumvention 356.1, 368.1, 415.5
circumvent the law 674.5
circumvolant 914.8
circumvolute 915.9
circumvolution 281.1, 915.1
circumvolutory 915.15
circus 230.9, 280.2, 463.1, 704.1
circus artist 707.3
circus catch 745.3
circus horse 311.10
circus performer 707.1, 707.3
circus rider 178.8
circus troupe 707.11
cire perdue 715.1
cirque 237.7, 284.8
cirrhosis of the liver 88.3
cirrocumiliform 319.8
cirrocumulus 319.2
cirrocumuous 319.8
cirronebula 1073.7
cirrose 3.24, 271.7, 319.8
cirrostratous 319.8
cirrostratus 319.2
cirrous 271.7, 319.8
cirrus 271.1, 281.2, 319.2
cisgender 75.13
cisgendered 75.2
cislunar 1073.25
cist 309.16
cistern 241.1
cist grave 309.16
cistron 305.9
citadel 460.6
citation 420.6, 509.3, 599.2, 646.4, 888.2, 957.5
cite (n) 957.5 (v) 420.11, 598.15, 599.7, 646.8, 766.6, 865.11, 957.13, 983.10
cite a case in point 957.13
cite a particular 957.13
cite cases 957.13
cited 599.15
cite on several counts 599.7
cite particulars 957.13
citharist 710.5
citified 230.11
citifying 230.1
citizen 227.4, 232.7, 430.11, 464.5
citizen by adoption 226.3, 227.4
citizenhood 226.2
citizenism 591.1
citizen journalism 547.2
citizen of the world 227.4, 413.17
citizenry 227.1
citizenry, the 606.1
citizen's army 461.24
citizen's arrest 428.1
citizens band 1034.13, 1034.16
citizenship 226.2, 591.1
citizenship by birth 226.2
citizenship by naturalization 226.3
citizenship papers 226.3
Citizens Party 609.24
citrange 797.8
citreous 43.4
citriculture 1069.2

citrine 44.4
citrinous 44.4
citron 43.4
citron-yellow 43.4
citrous 310.39
citrus belt 233.1
citrus fruit 10.38, 310.4
cits 5.8
city (n) 230.1, 231.5 (a) 230.11
city bike 179.8, 179.13
city block 230.7
city board 613.1
City Celestial 681.3
city center 230.6
city centre 230.6
city council 423.1, 613.1
city councilman 575.16
city directory 554.9, 574.10
city dweller 227.6
city editor 555.4
city father 575.16, 610.3
city government 230.1
city hall 230.5, 595.6, 609.24, 613.4
city jail 429.8
city library 558.1
city manager 575.16
City of God 681.3
city of the dead 309.15
city person 227.6
city planner 716.10, 717.3
city planning 230.10
cityscape 33.6, 712.11
city slicker 227.6, 413.17
city-state 232.1
citywide 230.11
civet 10.13, 70.2
civic 230.11, 312.16, 591.4, 609.43, 612.16
civic affairs 609.1
civic center 208.7
civic crown 646.3
civic duty 641.1
civics 609.2
civil 312.16, 496.9, 504.13, 582.22, 612.16, 700.3
Civil Aeronautics Administration 184.7
Civil Air Patrol 184.7
civil architect 716.10
civil ceremony 563.3
civil code 673.5
civil court 595.2
civil death 602.2
civil defense 460.2
Civil Defense Warning System 460.2
civil disobedience 327.1, 453.1
civil disorder 327.4
civil divorce 566.1
civil engineer 1043.2
civil engineering 1043.1
civil government 612.1
civilian (n) 464.5 (a) 464.10
civilian clothes 5.8
civilian dress 5.8
civilian life 465.6
civilities 504.7, 580.3
civility 392.3, 496.2, 504.1, 504.6, 579.1, 580.3, 582.1
civilization 373.2, 392.3, 504.1
civilize 312.12, 392.9, 568.10
civilized 392.13, 496.8, 928.21
civilized behavior 579.2
civilizedness 496.1
civilized taste 496.1
civil jurisdiction 594.1
civil law 673.5
civil liberties 430.2, 642.3
civil liberty 430.1
civil list 871.1
civil rights 430.2, 642.3
civil servant 575.15
civil service 575.14
civil time 832.3
civil trial 598.5
civil union 563.1
civil war 458.1
civil wedding 563.3
civism 226.2, 591.1
civvies 5.8
civvy street 465.6
clabber (n) 1045.7, 1062.5 (v) 803.6, 1045.10, 1062.10
clabbered 1045.14, 1062.12
clabbering 1045.4, 1062.2
clabber up 319.7
clack (n) 53.6, 55.3, 56.2, 540.3 (v) 55.6, 56.7, 60.5, 540.5
clacker 53.6
clacket 55.3
clad 5.45
cladding 206.2, 295.13, 296.2
cladistics 527.1
claim (n) 192.6, 231.4, 376.2, 421.1, 469.1, 471.4, 598.1, 598.7, 642.1 (v) 192.15, 376.3, 421.5, 421.6, 469.4, 480.13, 598.15, 963.9
claimant 440.7, 599.5
claim as one's right 639.4
claim attention 983.11
claimed 376.5, 421.10
claiming 480.1
claim one's pound of flesh 146.2
claim one's thoughts 931.18, 983.13
claim refugee status 1009.7
claim sanctuary 1009.7
claim squatter's rights 469.4
claim to be 354.22
claim to fame 662.6, 865.4
clairaudience 689.8
clairaudient (n) 689.14 (a) 689.24
clairobscure 1025.19
clairsentience 689.8
clairsentient (n) 689.14 (a) 689.24
clairvoyance 689.8, 839.1, 928.3, 934.1, 961.3, 962.2
clairvoyant (n) 689.14, 962.4 (a) 689.24, 934.5, 961.7
clam (n) 61.1, 311.29, 344.5 (v) 382.10
clamant 53.13, 421.9
clambake 8.6, 582.12, 609.12
clamber (n) 193.1 (v) 193.11
clamber up 193.11
clamdigger 227.10, 382.6
clammed up 51.10
clamminess 1062.2
clammy 12.22, 1062.12
clamor (n) 53.3, 59.4, 61.2, 440.2 (v) 53.9, 59.8, 115.15
clamor for 100.16, 421.5, 440.11, 963.9
clamorous 53.13, 59.10, 105.24, 421.9, 997.22
clamorousness 53.2, 59.5
clamoursome 53.13, 59.10
clamoursomeness 59.5
clamp (n) 260.6, 474.2, 1040.7 (v) 260.8, 800.7
clampdown 428.1
clamp down on 428.7, 428.8, 612.15
clamped 260.12
clamping 260.2
clamping down 260.2
clam up 51.6, 344.6, 345.7
clan 559.4, 617.2, 617.6, 809.2, 809.3
clandestine 345.12, 415.12
clandestine behavior 345.4
clandestineness 345.4
clandestinity 345.4
clang (n) 53.3, 54.3, 58.3, 60.1 (v) 54.8, 58.9
clang association 92.33
clang color 50.3
clanger 975.6
clanging (n) 54.3 (a) 53.13
clangor (n) 53.3, 54.3, 58.3 (v) 53.9, 54.8, 58.9
clangorous 53.13
clangorousness 53.2
clang tint 50.3
clank (n) 54.3, 58.3 (v) 54.8, 58.9, 525.7
clanking 54.3
clank up 525.7
clannish 157.8, 495.13, 559.7, 617.18
clannishness 157.1, 495.5, 559.4, 617.13
clanship 617.13
clansman 559.2
clanswoman 559.2
clan system 612.4
clap (n) 53.3, 56.1, 85.18, 509.2 (v) 56.6, 159.13, 293.6, 509.10, 902.14
clap, the 85.18
clapboard (n) 1054.3 (v) 295.23
clap eyes on 27.12
clap hands 116.5
clap hands on 480.14
clap in jail 429.14
clap in prison 429.14
clap of thunder 56.5
clap on 182.20
clap one's hands 509.10
clap on ratlines 182.48
clap on sail 182.20
clap on the back (n) 492.8 (v) 375.21, 492.15
clapped-out 393.29, 806.5
clapper 53.6, 54.4
clapper bridge 383.9
clapper-claw 510.19
clapping 509.2
clapping of hands 509.2
claps, the 85.18
clap spurs to one's horse 177.34
clap together 800.5
claptrap 354.14, 520.2, 520.3, 545.2, 936.3
clap up 429.14
claque 509.8
claqueur 704.27
Clarence Campbell Conference 749.1
Clarenceux 575.20
Clarenceux King of Arms 575.20
clarification 79.4, 341.4
clarified 798.7
clarifier 79.13, 341.7
clarify 79.22, 341.10, 521.6, 798.5
clarifying 341.15
clarinetist 710.4
clarion (n) 458.7 (v) 53.10, 708.42
clarion call 53.5, 458.7
clarion-voiced 53.12
clarity 31.2, 521.2, 533.1, 1014.1, 1029.1
clash (n) 56.1, 58.3, 61.2, 456.1, 457.4, 589.3, 902.3 (v) 35.15, 56.6, 58.9, 61.3, 451.4, 456.8, 457.13, 779.4, 789.5, 900.6, 902.13
clashing (n) 451.2, 456.1, 589.3, 779.1, 789.1, 900.1 (a) 35.21, 61.5, 451.8, 456.15, 589.10, 779.6, 780.7, 789.6, 900.8
clashing colors 35.5
clash of arms 457.4
clash of creeds, the 675.4
clash with 451.4, 780.5
clasp (n) 474.2, 562.3 (v) 223.12, 474.6, 480.14, 562.18, 800.8, 803.6
clasping 800.3
class (n) 245.2, 527.1, 559.4, 567.5, 572.11, 607.1, 617.2, 617.5, 700.1, 807.2, 809.2, 809.5, 999.1, 1068.1 (v) 801.8, 809.6, 946.9
class act 579.1
class action 598.1
class conflict 607.1
class-conscious 607.10
class consciousness 980.4
class dialect 523.7
class difference 607.1
class distinction 607.1, 980.4
classed 809.8
class envy 154.1
classes, the 607.2, 608.1
classfellow 588.3
class hatred 980.4
classic (n) 413.8, 413.10, 554.1, 708.6, 712.9, 1002.4 (a) 496.7, 499.6, 533.6, 786.8, 997.19, 1002.9
classical 247.12, 496.7, 499.6, 533.6, 533.8, 547.24, 718.7, 842.13, 1002.9
classical conditioning 92.26
classical dancer 705.3
classical economics 731.11
classical guitarist 710.5
classicalism 533.1
classicalist 929.3

classical language 523.2, 523.4
classical mathematics 1017.1
classical music 708.6
classical pitch 709.4
classical purity 499.1
classical scholarship 928.5
classic example 786.1
classicism 533.1, 842.4, 928.5
classicist 533.4, 842.5, 929.3
classic purity 499.1
classics 547.12, 718.1
class identity 607.1
classification 345.3, 527.1, 801.3, 808.3, 808.4, 809.1
classificational 809.7
classificatory 527.17, 801.9, 809.7, 871.9
classified 345.11, 808.14, 809.8
classified ad 352.6
classified catalog 549.11, 554.9, 871.3
classified directory 574.10
classified information 345.5, 551.2
classify 345.7, 801.8, 808.11, 809.6, 871.8, 944.4
classiness 578.3
classing 809.1
classis 423.4
class lottery 759.14
classmate 572.3, 588.3
class politics 607.1
class prejudice 607.1, 980.4
class ring 498.6, 647.1
classroom (n) 567.11 (a) 567.13
classroom building 567.10
class structure 607.1, 809.4
class struggle 607.1
class war 980.4
classy 501.18, 578.13, 608.11
clastic rock 1059.1
clatter (n) 53.3, 55.3, 540.3 (v) 55.6, 540.5
clatter about 55.6
clattering 55.8
clattery 53.13, 55.8
claudicant 175.10
claudicate 175.6
claudication 175.2
clause 529.1, 554.13, 613.9, 793.2, 959.2
clause boundary 524.9
clause terminal 524.9
claustral 212.11, 703.16
claustral prior 699.16
claustrum 211.3
claviature 711.17
clavichord 711.12
clavichordist 710.7
clavis 292.10
clavus 85.39
claw 96.18, 393.13, 480.14
clawback 138.4
claw bar 906.4
clawed 96.25, 199.9, 474.9
clawing 96.7
clawlike 279.8
claw mark 517.7
claw one's way up 193.11, 409.10
claws 417.5, 474.4, 612.2
claw skyward 193.10
claw to windward of 182.26
clay (n) 89.6, 234.1, 307.15, 312.1, 312.5, 742.3, 1047.4, 1052.3, 1054.2, 1059.6, 1062.8 (a) 742.7
clay court 748.1
clayey 234.5, 1047.12
clayish 234.5
claymation 706.1
clay model 786.5
clay modeler 716.6
clay pigeon 744.1
clay pipe 89.6
clayware 735.4
clean (v) 37.6, 79.18 (a) 79.25, 264.5, 413.22, 644.13, 653.6, 657.7, 664.4, 794.10
clean as a hound's tooth 79.25
clean as a new penny 79.25
clean as a whistle 79.25
clean bill of health 83.2, 443.7, 549.6
clean bomb 462.20
clean-burning 1021.9
clean climbing 760.6
clean conscience 107.1, 636.5
clean-cut 31.7, 264.5, 521.11
cleaned 79.26
cleaned out 79.26, 473.8, 619.10
cleaned up 79.26, 407.11
cleaner 79.14, 79.17, 577.8
cleaner-off 79.14
cleaner-out 79.14
cleaner-up 79.14
clean forget 990.5
clean forgotten 990.8
clean hands 657.1
clean house 79.18
cleaning (n) 79.2 (a) 79.28
cleaning agent 79.17
cleaning cloth 79.17
cleaning device 79.17
cleaning lady 79.14
cleaning man 79.14
cleaning out 79.2, 79.5, 909.6
cleaning person 577.8
cleaning solvent 79.17
cleaning tool 79.17
cleaning up 79.2, 79.5
cleaning woman 79.14
clean-limbed 264.5
cleanliness 79.1, 81.2, 657.1, 664.1
cleanly 79.25, 664.4
cleanly habits 79.1
cleanness 79.1, 644.1, 657.1, 664.1
clean one's plate 8.24
clean out 79.18, 480.24, 909.22
cleanout 79.2
clean out of 911.5, 992.13
clean profit 472.3
cleanse 72.4, 79.18, 120.6, 685.5
cleanse away 120.6
cleansed 79.26
cleanse oneself of guilt 658.6
cleanser 79.16, 79.17
clean-shaven 6.17
cleansing (n) 79.2, 120.2 (a) 79.28, 120.9, 658.7
cleansing away 120.2
cleansing cream 79.17
clean slate 222.3, 395.7, 657.1, 858.2, 860.1
clean-speaking 524.31
clean sweep 860.1
cleantech 1041.2
clean up 79.18, 407.6, 411.3, 472.12, 618.10, 808.12
cleanup 79.2, 472.3, 808.6
clean up after 79.18
cleanup hitter 745.2
clean up one's act 321.5
clear (n) 521.2 (v) 79.22, 184.38, 272.11, 292.12, 366.5, 409.12, 431.7, 472.12, 600.9, 601.4, 624.13, 749.7, 752.4, 773.5, 909.22, 1014.9 (a) 31.7, 50.16, 222.14, 292.17, 348.8, 430.21, 430.26, 430.31, 521.11, 521.12, 533.6, 624.23, 657.6, 794.10, 798.7, 802.22, 960.2, 970.13, 1010.13, 1014.13, 1025.31, 1029.4
clearage 909.6
clear-air turbulence 184.32
clearance 158.3, 158.4, 184.35, 224.1, 261.1, 430.4, 443.1, 443.3, 443.7, 600.1, 601.1, 624.1, 773.2, 909.6
clearance papers 443.7
clearance sale 624.1
clear and distinct 970.13
clear as crystal 31.7, 348.8, 521.11, 1029.4
clear as day 31.7, 521.11, 970.13
clear as ditch water 522.15
clear as glass 1029.5
clear as mud 522.15
clear as the nose on one's face 521.11
clear away 771.5, 773.5, 909.22
clear-channel station 1034.6
clear coast 1014.1
clear conscience 107.1, 636.5, 657.1
clear course 1014.1
clear-cut 31.7, 473.7, 521.11
clear-cutness 521.2
clear-cutting 473.2
cleared 148.7, 292.17
clear-eyed 27.21, 920.13
clear eyes 2.9, 27.9
clear for action 182.49, 405.6
clear hawse 182.48
clear head 516.1
clearheaded 516.3, 920.13, 920.18, 925.4
clearing 158.4, 292.1, 431.3, 600.1, 601.1, 909.6, 1014.6, 1069.9
clearing house 729.14
clearing of one's good name 600.1
clearing of one's name 600.1
clearing of the track 449.5
clearing the decks 405.1
clearing up 940.1
clearminded 925.4
clearness 31.2, 348.3, 521.2, 533.1, 1029.1
clear of 430.31
clear off 909.22
clear off old scores 624.12
clear one's good name 600.9
clear one's head 516.2
clear one's name 600.9
clear out 34.2, 79.18, 188.7, 368.11, 773.5
clear-out pass 747.3
clear profit 472.3
clear road 1014.1
clear sailing 1007.1
clear sight 27.1
clear-sighted 27.21, 920.13
clear soup 10.10
clear space 158.4
clear stage 843.2
clear the air 341.10, 465.7, 670.6
clear the ball 747.4
clear the board 624.12, 747.4
clear the decks 182.49, 405.6, 494.6, 773.5, 808.12, 909.22
clear the hurdle 409.12
clear the land 182.37
clear the mind 933.3
clear the mind of 977.2
clear the path for 966.5
clear the road for 966.5
clear the skirts of 601.4
clear the throat 13.6
clear the trade 737.24
clear the way 405.12, 1014.7
clear thinking 920.2
clear up 341.10, 798.5, 808.12, 940.2, 970.11
clearway 184.23
clear-witted 920.13
cleat 800.8, 855.8
cleavable 802.26
cleavage 456.4, 802.2, 1038.8
cleave 224.4, 292.11, 395.17, 802.11, 803.6, 875.4, 1038.17
cleaved 802.23
cleavers 285.5
cleave to 474.6
cleave to the line 161.10
cleave to the thought of 931.10
cleaving 803.10
clef 709.13
cleft (n) 224.2, 289.1, 292.1, 456.4, 802.4 (a) 224.7, 802.23, 875.6
cleft palate 265.3
cleft stick 1013.6
clemency 145.1, 427.1, 465.2
clement 145.7, 427.7
clementness 427.1
clench (n) 474.2 (v) 474.6, 480.14
clenched 359.16
clenched fist 462.4
clenched teeth 359.3
Cleobulus 921.4
Cleopatra 1016.9
clerestory 197.23, 198.1, 198.5
clergy 699.1
clergy house 703.7
clergyman 699.2
clergyperson 699.2
clergywoman 699.2, 699.17
cleric 699.2
clerical (n) 699.2 (a) 547.28, 698.13
clerical collar 702.2

clerical error 975.3
clericalism 698.3
clerical order 699.1
clericals 699.1, 702.1
clerical venue 699.1
clerical worker 726.2
clerisy 929.2
clerk 547.13, 550.1, 576.3, 577.3, 577.5, 628.7, 699.2, 730.3, 929.3
clerk in holy orders 699.2
cleuch 237.7
clever 413.22, 413.30, 415.12, 489.15, 570.18, 920.14
cleverness 413.1, 415.1, 489.2, 570.5, 920.2
clever reply 939.1
clew 180.14
cliché (n) 117.3, 526.9, 864.8, 974.3 (a) 974.6
clichéd 974.6
cliché-ridden 849.15
click (n) 52.3, 56.2, 1042.18 (v) 52.15, 56.7, 409.7, 587.11 (a) 523.23
clickbait 1042.19
click in 818.7
clicking (n) 55.2 (a) 55.7
click language 523.7
click rate 1042.19
clickthrough 1042.18, 1042.19
client (n) 387.9, 422.4, 432.6, 733.4 (a) 432.13
clientage 432.3, 733.3
cliental 733.10
client base 731.6
clientele 731.6, 733.3, 733.4
client-server 1042.19
clientship 432.3
client state 432.6
cliff 200.3, 237.2
cliff dwelling 228.5
cliffhang 971.11
cliff-hanging (n) 130.3 (a) 105.30, 130.12
climacteric (n) 303.4, 303.7, 843.4 (a) 843.10
climacterical 843.10
climactic 198.11, 843.10
climactical 198.11
climatal 317.13
climate 209.3, 231.3, 317.3, 896.2, 978.5
climate change 317.4
climate control 1024.1
climate of opinion 953.6, 978.5
climatic 317.13
climatical 317.13
climatographical 317.13
climatography 317.5
climatologic 317.13
climatological 317.13
climatologist 317.6
climatology 317.5
climax (n) 75.7, 198.2, 407.3, 671.5, 704.7, 722.4, 794.5, 843.4, 843.5, 997.4, 997.6, 1002.3 (v) 75.24, 198.10, 407.6
climaxing 198.12
climb (n) 184.8, 193.1, 204.6 (v) 172.5, 184.39, 193.11, 204.10
climb all over 459.15
climb down 137.7, 194.7, 363.8
climb-down 137.2
climber 178.1, 193.6, 310.4, 310.33, 606.7
climbing (n) 100.10, 172.2, 193.1 (a) 193.14, 204.17
climbing expedition 760.6
climbing plant 310.33
climb on 193.12
climb one's frame 604.10
climb on the bandwagon 476.5, 578.10, 788.6
climb over 193.11
climb Parnassus 720.14
climb the ladder 193.11
climb the wall 152.17
climb up 193.11
clime 231.3, 317.3
clinch (n) 474.2, 800.4 (v) 474.6, 480.14, 754.4, 800.7, 800.11, 803.6, 957.10, 970.11
clincher 413.8, 820.4, 958.3
clinches, the 457.9
clinching 754.3
cling (n) 474.2, 803.1 (v) 474.6, 803.6
clingfilm 295.18
clinginess 1062.2
clinging (n) 474.2, 803.1 (a) 474.8, 803.10, 1062.12
clingingness 1062.2
cling like a burr 803.8
cling like a winkle 474.6
cling like ivy 803.8
cling to 223.12, 474.6, 474.7, 803.6
cling to hope 124.7
cling to the hope 124.6
cling wrap 295.18
clingy 803.12, 1062.12
clinic 91.21, 197.25
clinical 90.15, 1052.10
clinical death 85.2, 307.1
clinical dextran 2.25
clinical psychologist 92.10
clinical trial 942.3
clink (n) 52.3, 54.3, 429.9, 720.9, 784.6 (v) 52.15, 54.8
clinker 61.1, 256.2, 410.2, 1020.16, 1054.2
clinometer 278.4
clinquant 354.13, 498.3
Clio 719.1, 986.2
cliometric 719.6
cliometrician 550.2, 719.3
cliometrics 719.1
clip (n) 172.4, 462.17, 557.3, 793.3, 902.5 (v) 174.9, 255.10, 268.6, 356.19, 474.6, 474.7, 482.16, 557.5, 632.7, 800.8, 902.15
clip art 349.1, 712.12
clip artist 357.4
clip joint 228.28, 759.19
clip off 177.19
clip one's wings 1012.15
clip one's words 525.7
clipped 268.9, 537.6, 557.6
clipped accent 524.8
clipped word 526.4
clipper 181.8
clipping 537.4, 549.2, 793.3
clippings 557.4
clip the wings 175.9
clip the wings of 19.9
clique (n) 582.5, 617.6, 770.3 (v) 582.18
clique with 582.18
cliquey 617.18
cliqueyness 617.13
cliquish 157.8, 495.13, 617.18
cliquishness 157.1, 495.5, 617.13
cliquism 617.13
C-list (n) 250.2 (a) 250.6
clitoral 2.29
clitoris 2.13
clitter (n) 55.3 (v) 55.6
clitterclatter 55.3
cloaca 80.12, 239.5
cloacal 513.8
cloaca maxima 80.12, 239.5
cloak (n) 5.12, 295.2, 376.1, 702.2 (v) 5.40, 295.19, 346.6, 1008.18
cloak-and-dagger 105.32, 345.12
cloak-and-dagger operative 576.9
cloak-and-dagger work 938.9
cloaked 5.45, 295.31, 1008.21
cloaked in darkness 1027.13
cloaking (n) 295.1 (a) 295.35
cloakmaker 5.35
cloak oneself with 376.4
cloakroom 197.15
cloakroom attendant 577.5
clobber 249.7, 395.11, 412.9, 604.14, 902.17
clobbered 412.15
clobbering 412.1, 412.3
cloche 1069.11
clock (n) 229.1, 832.6 (v) 188.13, 832.11
clock card 832.9
clock chimes 54.4
clock in 186.6, 832.12
clocking 832.1
clockmaker 832.10
clock-making 832.1
clock movement 832.6
clock off 188.7
clock out 832.12
clock rate 1042.18
clock watcher 331.8, 368.3
clock-watching 368.2
clockwise 219.4
clockwork precision 973.5
clockwork regularity 781.2, 850.1
clockworks 832.6, 1040.4
clod 234.1, 257.10, 414.8, 606.6, 924.2, 924.5, 1052.3
cloddish 233.7, 497.13, 922.15
cloddishness 497.4, 922.3
clodhead 924.4
clodhopper 414.8, 606.6, 924.5
clodhopperish 233.7
clodhoppers 5.27
clodhopping 233.7
clodknocker 414.8
clodpate 924.4
clodpated 922.17
clodpoll 924.4
clog (n) 293.3, 1012.7 (v) 293.7, 705.5
clog dancer 705.3
clogged 293.11
clogged up 293.11
clogging 1012.1
clogs 5.27
clog up 293.7
cloister (n) 197.18, 212.3, 383.3, 703.6, 1009.5 (v) 212.6, 429.12
cloistered 173.12, 212.10, 212.11, 429.19, 584.10, 703.16, 802.21
cloistered monasticism 584.2
cloistered monk 584.5
cloistered nun 584.5
cloisterlike 212.11
cloisters 703.9
cloistral 499.9
clone (n) 349.5, 778.3, 785.3, 867.2, 1042.2 (v) 778.6, 781.4, 785.8
cloned 781.5, 812.8, 867.6, 874.4
clone town 230.1
clonic spasm 85.6
clonish 781.5, 812.8, 867.6
clonk (n) 902.5 (v) 902.15
clonus 85.6
clop (n) 52.3, 177.11, 902.10 (v) 52.15, 902.22
clop-clop 55.1
clos 231.4
close (n) 212.3, 231.4, 407.2, 820.1, 820.3, 857.1 (v) 167.3, 169.2, 209.6, 293.6, 437.8, 457.13, 622.7, 820.6, 857.12, 1012.12 (a) 173.16, 223.14, 270.14, 293.12, 339.12, 344.9, 345.11, 345.15, 346.11, 484.9, 524.30, 537.6, 583.5, 587.19, 770.22, 775.8, 784.14, 800.14, 840.3, 973.17, 1019.28, 1045.12
close acquaintance 587.4, 588.1
close a deal 437.9
close arrest 429.3
close at hand 839.8, 840.3
close attention 983.4
close borough 609.16
close call 223.4, 369.2
close contest 457.3
close copy 784.3
closed 293.9, 345.11, 586.7, 980.10
closed book 930.6
closed card 759.10
closed chain 1038.7
closed circle 280.2, 617.6
closed-circuit television 1035.1
closed circuit TV 1035.1
closed course 756.1
closed door 379.2
closed-door 293.9, 345.13, 773.9
closed-end 293.9
closed-ended 293.9
closed-end fund 737.16
closed-end investment company 737.16
closed forever to 967.9
closed gate 753.1
closed-in 212.10
closed loop 1041.6
closed-loop system 1041.5

closed meeting 345.2
closed mind 980.1
closed-minded 361.13, 980.10
closed-mindedness 361.5
closed mortgage 438.4
closed-out 967.7
close down 34.2, 293.8, 428.8, 857.8
closed poker 759.10
closed primary 609.15
closed season 313.1
closed sequence 1041.6
closed session 345.2
closed shop 727.3
closed stance 751.3
closed to 895.4, 967.9
closed to the public 293.9
closed universe 1073.1
close election 609.15
close encounter 1073.3, 1075.8
close fighting 457.9
closefisted 484.9
closefistedness 484.3
close-fitting 270.14
close formation 184.12, 458.2
close friend 588.1
close friendship 587.8
closehanded 484.9
closehandedness 484.3
close-haul 182.25
close imitation 784.3
close in 167.3, 169.2, 212.5
close-in 223.14
close in on 167.3
close inquiry 938.4
close juncture 524.9
close-knit 1045.12
close likeness 784.4
close-lipped 344.9, 345.15
closely fought contest 457.3
closely related 559.6
close match 784.3
close-mindedness 980.1
close-mouthed 345.15
closemouthed 344.9
closeness 173.6, 223.1, 270.1, 344.1, 345.1, 484.3, 587.5, 775.1, 784.1, 1019.6, 1045.1, 1065.2
close observance 983.4
close of day 315.2
close off 1012.12
close one 457.3
close one's ears 49.4
close one's eyes 22.16, 307.18
close one's eyes to 30.8, 148.4, 984.2
close one's mind 980.6
close one's mouth 51.5
close out 372.2, 407.6, 628.8, 734.8, 737.24, 773.4, 820.6, 967.6
closeout 820.1
close quarters 223.2, 429.7
closer (n) 745.2, 820.4 (a) 223.18
close range 223.2
close ranks 450.3, 770.16, 805.4
close ranks with 450.4
close reproduction 784.3
close resemblance 784.4
close secrecy 345.1
close shave 369.2
close shop 293.8, 857.8
close squeeze 369.2
closest 223.19
close study 931.3, 983.4
closet (n) 12.10, 197.8, 197.15, 197.26, 386.6, 739.7 (v) 212.6 (a) 345.11
closet cynic 584.5
close-textured 1045.12
close the books 628.8, 857.6
close the books on 820.6, 857.6
close the circle 914.5
close the door on 372.2, 444.3, 773.4
close the hand 442.4
close the jaws of the pincers 459.19
close the jaws of the trap 459.19
close the light 1027.11
close the purse 442.4
close the shutters 1028.5
close tight 1012.12
closet oneself with 524.26
close-tongued 344.9
close to one's chest 345.14
close to one's vest 345.14
closetstool 12.11
close up 169.2, 293.6, 293.8, 396.21, 407.6, 1012.12
close-up 714.8
closeup 714.3
close up like a clam 51.6
close with 167.3, 169.2, 182.35, 332.9, 437.8, 451.4, 457.15, 457.16
close with the land 182.38
close-woven 1045.12
closing (n) 293.1, 437.3, 621.1, 820.3, 857.1 (a) 820.11
closing argument 935.3
closing arguments 598.8
closing down 428.2
closing off 1012.1
closing-out sale 734.3
closing price 738.9
closing time 820.3
closing up 1012.1
closure 293.1, 359.1, 794.4, 800.4, 857.2, 1012.1
closure of debate 857.5
clot (n) 803.5, 924.8, 1045.7 (v) 770.16, 803.6, 1045.10, 1062.10
clotbur 803.4
cloth 4.1, 180.14, 702.1, 704.20
cloth, the 698.1, 699.1
clothback 554.3
clothbound book 554.3
clothe 5.39, 18.10, 295.19, 385.8
clothed 5.45
clothed in darkness 1027.13
clothed with authority 417.15
clothe in words 532.4
clothes 5.1, 295.10
clothes closet 197.15
clothes-conscious 578.13
clothes-consciousness 578.3
clothes dryer 1066.4
clotheshorse 500.9, 578.7, 901.16
clothesless 6.13
clothesline 745.3, 1066.4
clothes pole 270.8
clothe with power 18.10
clothier 5.33
clothing (n) 5.1 (a) 5.45
clothing accessory 5.31
clothing design 712.16, 717.5
Clotho 964.3
clotted 803.10, 1045.14, 1062.12
clotted cream 1045.7
clotting 803.1, 1045.4, 1062.2
clotting factor 1045.7
clottish 922.15
cloture 293.1, 613.6, 857.5
cloture by compartment 857.5
clou 208.4, 377.3
cloud (n) 319.1, 770.6, 884.3, 985.3, 1065.4, 1067.1 (v) 295.19, 319.7, 346.6, 985.7, 1027.9, 1031.2
cloud band 319.1
cloud bank 319.1
cloud base 319.1
cloud-born 986.22
cloud-built 764.6, 986.22
cloudburst 316.2
cloud-capped 272.15, 319.9
cloud computing 1042.1, 1042.12
cloud cover 184.32, 319.1, 319.4
cloud-covered 319.9
cloud-crammed 319.9
cloud-crossed 319.9
Cloudcuckooland 319.1, 986.11
cloud-cuckoo-land 124.4
cloud-curtained 319.9
cloud-decked 319.9
cloud drift 319.1
cloud-eclipsed 319.9
clouded 47.12, 295.31, 319.8, 346.11, 1027.14
clouded mind 926.1
clouded over 346.11
cloud-enveloped 319.9
cloud-flecked 319.8, 319.9
cloud-girt 319.9
cloud-hidden 319.9
cloudiness 319.4, 1031.1
clouding 295.1, 346.1, 1027.6
cloud-laden 319.9
cloudland 319.1, 986.11
cloud layer 184.32
cloudless 1025.31
cloudlet 319.1
cloudling 319.1
cloud mass 319.1
cloud nine 95.2, 198.2
cloud of words 538.2
cloud on the horizon 1006.5
cloud over 319.7, 1027.9
cloudscape 33.6, 319.1, 712.11
cloud seeder 185.1, 316.5
cloud seeding 316.5
cloud-seeding 184.1
cloud shapes 854.4
clouds on the horizon 133.5, 399.3
cloud-surrounded 319.9
cloud-topped 272.15, 319.9
cloud-topped peak 237.6
cloud-touching 272.15
cloud up 319.7
cloud-woven 986.22
cloud-wrapped 319.9
cloudy 318.22, 319.8, 522.15, 985.13, 1027.14, 1031.3
clough 237.7
clout (n) 18.1, 249.1, 417.2, 544.3, 894.1, 902.1, 902.5 (v) 745.5, 902.15
cloven 224.7, 802.23, 875.6
cloven hoof, the 680.13
clover 10.4, 121.1, 876.1, 1010.1
clover honey 66.2
cloverleaf 170.2
clowder 770.5
clown (n) 414.8, 489.12, 497.6, 606.6, 707.1, 707.3, 707.10, 924.1 (v) 923.6
clown around 489.14, 923.6
clownery 489.5
clowning 489.5, 923.1
clowning around 489.5
clownish 233.7, 414.20, 489.16, 497.13
clownishness 414.3, 489.5, 497.4, 923.1
clown white 704.17, 1016.11
cloy 994.4
cloyed 994.6
cloyedness 994.2
cloyer 994.3
cloying 64.7, 66.6, 93.21, 994.7
cloyingness 66.1, 93.8
cloysome 994.7
club (n) 228.27, 462.4, 605.2, 617.3, 704.14, 745.2, 751.1 (v) 604.12, 805.4, 902.20
club, the 424.3
clubbability 582.1
clubbable 582.22
clubber 617.11
clubbiness 582.1
clubbing 604.4, 743.1
clubbish 582.22
clubbishness 582.1
clubbism 582.1
club boxing 754.1
clubby 582.22
club cover 751.1
club fighting 754.1
clubfoot 199.5, 265.3
clubfooted 265.12
club-hop 88.28, 743.24
clubhouse 228.27
clubhouse politician 610.1
clubman 578.7, 582.16, 617.11
clubs 758.2
club sandwich 10.32
club-sandwich generation 303.4
club soda 10.49
club tie 647.1
club together 450.3, 582.17, 805.4
clubwoman 578.7, 582.16, 617.11
cluck 60.5
clue 517.9, 551.3, 551.4, 951.5, 957.1
clued in 24.11, 928.17
clued-up 928.17
clueful 351.10
clue in 551.9, 552.11
clueless 922.17, 923.8, 930.11, 971.24

clue one in 351.4
clump (n) 52.3, 257.10, 283.3, 310.2, 770.7, 902.5, 902.10, 1045.6 (v) 52.15, 177.28, 770.18, 902.15, 902.22, 1045.10
clumped 770.21
clumping 1045.3
clumpish 257.19
clumpishness 257.9
clumsiness 257.9, 414.3, 534.1, 996.3, 1013.9, 1015.1
clumsy (n) 414.9 (a) 257.19, 340.12, 414.20, 534.2, 996.7, 1013.19, 1015.9
clumsy-fisted 414.20
clumsy performance 414.5
clunk (n) 52.3, 902.5 (v) 52.15, 902.15
clunker 179.10
clunkiness 257.9, 534.1, 996.3
clunky 257.19, 414.15, 414.22, 534.2, 1015.9
clunter 55.3
cluricaune 678.8
cluster (n) 257.10, 770.4, 770.7, 803.5, 1045.6, 1073.5 (v) 770.16, 770.18, 803.6, 1045.10
cluster bombing 459.7
clustered 770.21, 803.10
clustering 800.1, 803.1, 1045.3
clutch (n) 195.2, 244.2, 302.10, 474.2, 561.2, 729.15, 843.4, 997.4, 1013.4, 1040.10 (v) 474.6, 480.14
clutch at straws 124.7
clutches 417.5, 474.4, 612.2
clutter (n) 810.3, 884.3, 1036.12 (v) 811.2, 884.5
cluttered 498.12
clutteredness 498.2
Clyde 117.9
clypeate 279.19
clypeiform 279.19
clysma 86.19
clyster 86.19, 1065.8
cnemis 2.7, 177.14
C-note 728.7
coach (n) 179.15, 405.5, 571.5, 571.6, 745.2 (v) 422.5, 568.11
coach-and-four 179.5
coached 405.16, 413.26
coacher 571.5
coach horse 311.13
coach house 197.27
coaching 568.1
coachman 178.9, 577.4
coachwhip 647.7
coachy 178.9
coact 450.3, 777.6, 899.2
coacting 450.5, 899.4
coaction 424.1, 450.1, 777.3, 899.1
coactive 424.10, 450.5, 899.4
coadjutant (n) 616.6 (a) 450.5
coadjutor 616.1, 616.6
coadjutress 616.6
coadjutrix 616.6
coadjuvancy 450.1
coadjuvant 450.5
coadministration 450.1
coadunate (v) 899.2 (a) 899.4
coadunation 450.2
coagency 450.1, 769.1
coagulant (n) 1045.7 (a) 1045.14
coagulase 1045.7
coagulate (n) 1045.7 (v) 803.6, 1045.10, 1062.10
coagulated 803.10, 1045.14, 1062.12
coagulating 1045.14
coagulation 803.1, 1045.4, 1062.2
coagulator 1045.7
coagulin 1045.7
coagulose 1045.7
coagulum 1045.7
coal (n) 38.4, 1019.16, 1020.16 (v) 385.9, 1020.24, 1021.8
coal bin 197.17
coal-black 38.8
coal dust 1021.2
coalesce 450.3, 778.5, 797.10, 805.3
coalescence 450.2, 778.2, 797.1, 805.1
coalescent 805.7, 872.12
coalescing 872.12
coal-fired 1021.9
coal-fired power plant 1032.19
coal gas 1001.4
coal heat 1019.1
coal hole 197.17
coalition 450.2, 609.24, 609.33, 617.1, 805.1
coalitional 617.17
coalition government 232.1, 450.1, 612.4
coalmine 739.4, 1058.6
coalminer 1058.9
coal mining 1058.8
coal oil 1025.20, 1056.4
coalsack 1073.7
Coalsack, the 1073.7
coal tongs 1020.12
coaly 38.8, 1021.9
coaptation 788.4
coarct 260.7
coarctation 260.1, 270.2
coarcted 260.12
coarse 58.15, 64.6, 98.18, 269.8, 288.6, 294.6, 406.12, 497.11, 505.6, 534.2, 606.8, 663.6, 666.8, 1005.9
coarse-grained 288.6, 294.6
coarse-grainedness 294.2
coarsen 288.4, 294.4, 393.12, 497.9, 663.4
coarsened 94.12
coarseness 58.2, 94.3, 98.2, 269.2, 294.2, 406.4, 497.2, 505.1, 534.1, 663.2, 666.3, 1005.3
coarseness of grain 294.1
coarseness of intellect 945.1
coarsening 497.8
coast (n) 194.4, 211.4, 218.1, 231.7, 234.2 (v) 173.7, 177.35, 182.13, 182.39, 194.9, 287.9, 329.2, 331.15, 1014.10
coastal 211.11, 234.7
coastal fog 319.3
coastal navigation 159.3, 182.2
coastal plain 236.1
coast artillery 462.11
Coast Guard 461.21
coast guard 398.2
coast guard 461.27, 1008.9
coast guard cutter 180.6
coastguardsman 183.4
coasting 177.16, 182.1
coastland 234.2
coastline 234.2
coast-to-coast hookup 1034.8
coastwise navigation 182.2
coat (n) 3.2, 4.2, 5.13, 35.8, 295.2, 295.3, 295.12, 296.2, 758.2 (v) 5.40, 35.14, 295.24
coat card 758.2
coat check 197.20
coated 295.31, 296.6
coating (n) 35.8, 35.12, 295.1, 295.12, 296.2 (a) 295.35
coat of arms 647.2
coat of paint 35.8, 376.1
coat room 197.20
coattails 449.4
coauthor (n) 547.15, 616.4, 718.4 (v) 547.21, 718.6
co-ax 347.17
coax (n) 375.10 (v) 375.14, 377.5, 440.12
coaxal 208.14
coaxer 375.10
coaxial 208.14
coaxial cable 347.17
coaxial network 1034.8
coaxing (n) 375.3, 440.3 (a) 377.8, 440.18
cob 310.29, 311.10, 311.14
cobalt 7.11, 91.8
cobber 588.4
cobble (n) 383.6, 1054.2 (v) 396.14
cobbled-up 262.9
cobbler 5.38, 10.41, 396.10
cobblestone (n) 383.6 (v) 295.22
cobble together 262.7
cobble up 262.7, 340.9, 365.8
cobbling 5.32
Cobb salad 10.37
cobelligerent 232.1
cobweb 16.7, 271.1, 298.2, 356.13
cobwebby 16.14
cobwebs of antiquity 842.1
cocaine addiction 87.1
cocaine user 87.21
cocainism 87.1
coccus 85.42
co-chairman 574.5
cochairmanship 450.1, 476.1
cocher 178.9
cochero 178.9
cochlea 2.10
cochlear 281.8
cochleate 281.8
cochleated 279.18
cock (n) 76.8, 239.10, 293.4, 311.28, 318.16, 770.10 (v) 405.9, 904.12
cockade 647.1
cock-a-doodle-doo 60.5
cock-a-hoop 502.13
Cockaigne 986.11
cockamamie 923.11
cock-and-bull story 354.11
cock a snook at 454.4
cockatrice 357.10, 647.2
cockcrow 1025.10
cockcrowing 314.2
cocked 405.16
cocker 291.6, 562.16
cockerel 76.8, 311.28
cockeyed 28.12, 88.33, 204.14, 265.10, 791.5, 810.13, 923.9, 985.14
cockeyed drunk 88.33
cockeyes 28.6
cockfight 457.4
cockiness 140.4, 142.2, 454.1
cockle (n) 291.3, 311.29 (v) 291.6
cocklebur 803.4
cockled 291.8
cockles of the heart 93.3, 767.5
cockle stairs 193.3
cocklight 314.2, 315.3
cockloft 197.16
cockly 291.8
Cockney 523.7
cock of the walk 503.2, 575.4
cockpit 463.1
cockpit dodger 1008.3
cockroach 311.36
cockscomb 10.20, 289.2
cockshut 315.2
cockshut light 315.2
cockshut time 315.2
cocksman 104.12, 500.9, 562.12, 665.10
cocksure 970.21
cocksureness 970.5
cocktail 8.4, 10.49, 88.9, 797.5
cocktail hour 20.2, 315.2
cocktailing 87.2
cocktail lounge 88.20
cocktail-party chitchat 541.4
cock the arm 163.5
cock the ears 48.10
cock the eye 27.18
cock the fist 163.5
cock up 193.13, 200.8, 283.10, 912.5
cock-up 410.6
cocky 140.11, 142.10, 454.7
cocoa (n) 10.49 (a) 40.3
cocoa-brown 40.3
cocoa-colored 40.3
coconscious (n) 92.28 (a) 92.42
coconspirator 381.7, 616.3
cocoon (n) 302.12 (v) 583.4
cocooning 584.1, 584.2, 1008.2
cocotte 665.14
coction 1020.2
Cocytus 682.4
cod 310.30
coda 254.1, 254.2, 708.24, 817.1, 820.1
coddle 11.5, 427.6, 449.16, 562.16
coddled 11.7, 427.9
coddled eggs 10.26
coddle oneself 651.4
coddling 427.3
code (n) 345.6, 347.2, 419.2, 522.7, 636.1, 673.5, 808.4, 869.4 (v) 345.10
code book 345.6
code cracking 341.3

coded 345.16, 346.13
coded message 345.6
codefendant 599.6
code name 345.6, 528.1
code-named 346.11
code of conduct 580.3, 952.2
code of ethics 636.1
Code of Hammurabi 673.8
code of honor 641.2
code of laws 673.5
code of morals 636.1
code of practice 869.4
code of silence, the 51.2
codepend 777.6
codependency 432.3, 777.2, 777.3
code red 399.1
codetalker 576.9
code word 345.6, 519.2, 526.9
codex 547.11, 554.6
Codex Juris Canonici 673.8
codex rescriptus 547.11
codger 304.2
codicil 254.2, 478.10, 817.1
codification 673.5, 673.6, 808.2, 809.1, 869.5
codified 346.13
codified law 673.6
codify 673.10, 808.10, 809.6, 869.6
coding 1042.13
codirectorship 450.1
codon 305.9
codswallop 923.3
coed 572.5
coeducational 568.18
coeducational school 567.5
coefficient 450.5
coefficient of friction 1044.5
coelanaglyphic sculpture 715.3
coelenterate 311.31
coelostat 1073.17
coemption 733.1
coenocyte 305.4
coenzyme 7.10
coequal (n) 790.4 (v) 777.7 (a) 264.4, 777.10, 778.8, 790.8
coequality 777.1, 778.1, 790.1
coerce 424.7, 612.15, 963.8
coercible 894.15
coercing 424.3
coercion 424.3, 963.6
coercive 424.12
coetaneity 836.1
coetaneous 836.5
coetaneousness 836.1
coeternal 829.7, 836.5
coeternity 829.1
coeval (n) 836.2 (a) 767.8, 836.5
coevalneity 836.1
coevalness 836.1
coexist 836.4
coexistence 467.1, 609.5, 769.1, 836.1
coexistent 788.9, 836.5
coexisting 788.9, 836.5
coextend 203.4, 836.4
coextending 203.6
coextension 203.1, 790.1
coextensive 203.6, 778.8, 790.10
coffee (n) 10.49, 40.1 (a) 40.3
coffee bar 8.17
coffee break 8.7, 20.2, 402.1, 826.1
coffee-brown 40.3
coffee-colored 40.3
coffeehouse 8.17
coffee-planter 1069.5
coffeeroom 8.17
coffee shop 8.17
coffee spoon 8.12
coffee table 229.1
coffee-table book 554.1
coffel 812.3
coffer (n) 729.13 (v) 386.10
cofferdam 1012.5
coffers 386.6
coffin (n) 309.11 (v) 212.6, 309.19
coffin nail 89.5
cofounder 892.7
cog (n) 250.2, 285.4, 289.3 (v) 356.18
cogence 18.1
cogency 18.1, 775.4, 920.4, 935.9, 935.10, 973.6, 999.1
cogent 18.12, 775.11, 920.16, 935.20, 973.14, 999.12
cogent argument 935.10
cogitable 966.6, 986.26
cogitate 931.8, 931.11
cogitation 931.1
cogitative 931.21
cognate (n) 526.2, 559.2, 560.4, 784.3 (a) 559.6, 560.18, 775.10, 784.13
cognatic 560.18
cognation 559.1, 775.3
cognition 919.1, 928.2
cognitive 931.21
cognitive disorder 92.14
cognitive dissonance 810.2, 971.3, 985.1
cognitive therapy 92.5
cognizability 521.1
cognizable 521.10, 928.25
cognizance 150.2, 594.1, 639.2, 928.2
cognizant 24.11, 928.15
cognizant of 150.5, 928.16
cognize 928.12
cognomen 527.3, 527.5, 527.6, 527.7
cognominal 527.15
cognomination 527.3
cognoscente 413.11, 496.6, 946.7
cog railroad 179.14
cog railway 179.14
cog the dice 356.18
cogwheel 1040.9
cohabit 75.21, 225.7, 563.17
cohabitate 75.21, 225.7, 563.17
cohabitation 75.7, 225.1, 563.1, 769.2
cohabiting 225.13
coheir 479.5
coheirship 479.2
cohere 788.6, 800.11, 803.6
coherence 521.2, 788.1, 803.1, 925.1, 1045.2
coherent 521.11, 788.9, 800.12, 803.10, 1045.13
cohering 803.10
cohesion 803.1, 1045.2
cohesive 803.10, 1045.13, 1049.4
cohesiveness 803.1, 803.3, 1049.1
cohort 138.6, 461.22, 610.8, 616.1, 616.3, 617.6, 769.6, 770.3
coif (n) 3.15 (v) 3.22, 5.40, 295.21
coifed 5.45
coiffeur 1016.12
coiffeuse 1016.12
coiffure (n) 3.15 (v) 3.22
coign of vantage 27.7, 159.2, 249.2
coil (n) 3.7, 267.2, 279.2, 281.2 (v) 281.5
coiled 281.7
coin (n) 278.2, 728.2, 728.4 (v) 728.28, 841.5, 852.9, 892.12, 986.14
coinage 526.8, 728.1, 728.4, 728.24, 852.4, 892.1, 893.1
coinage of the brain 986.5
coin a phrase 974.5
coin box 729.13
coincide 332.9, 778.4, 788.6, 836.4, 899.2
coincidence 769.1, 778.1, 788.1, 836.1, 899.1, 972.6
coincident 769.9, 778.8, 788.9, 800.12, 899.4
coincidental 778.8
coinciding 778.8, 788.9
coin-clipper 728.25
coin-clipping 728.24
coined 892.19
coiner 728.25
coin flip 746.3, 752.3
coin gold 728.20
coining 728.24
coin laundry 79.11
coin machine 736.4
coin money 472.12, 618.10
coin of the realm 728.1
coin-operated laundry 79.11
coin-operated machine 736.4
coin silver 728.20
coinstantaneous 836.5
coin telephone 347.4
coin toss 746.3, 748.2, 752.3, 971.8
coital 75.25
coition 75.7
coitus 75.7
coitus interruptus 75.7
cojones 492.3
cojuror 957.6
coke 87.7, 1020.16
Coke-bottle glasses 29.3
coked 87.24
coked out 87.24
coke habit 87.1
coke head 87.21
cokie 87.21
col 237.5, 237.7
colander 79.13, 292.8, 808.5
colature 79.4
cold (n) 85.16, 1023.1 (a) 25.8, 35.16, 75.29, 94.9, 102.6, 117.6, 142.9, 144.25, 307.30, 344.10, 583.6, 589.9, 759.27, 1023.14, 1023.16
cold as charity 94.9, 1023.14
cold as death 1023.14
cold as hell 1023.15
cold as ice 1023.14
cold as marble 1023.14
cold blood 94.1
cold-blooded 25.6, 94.9, 144.25, 1023.20
cold-blooded animal 311.24
cold-bloodedness 94.1, 144.10
cold call (n) 347.13, 734.2 (v) 347.19
cold cash 728.1
cold cautery 1024.2
coldcock 25.4, 902.17
cold comfort 108.1
cold cream 79.17, 1016.11, 1056.3
cold creeps 74.4, 127.5, 1023.2
cold cuts 10.13
cold dark matter 1073.7
cold deck 965.2
cold-deck 965.5
cold drink 10.49
cold enough to freeze the tail off a grass monkey 1023.15
colder than hell 1023.15
colder than the devil 1023.15
cold fact 761.3
cold feet 491.4
cold fish 94.1, 141.7
cold-fish 583.6
cold frame 1069.11
cold front 317.4, 1023.3
cold fusion 1038.9
cold heart 94.1
coldhearted 94.9, 144.25, 146.3
coldheartedness 94.1, 144.10
cold light of reality 977.1
coldness 75.2, 94.1, 102.1, 144.10, 344.3, 583.2, 589.1, 1023.1
cold of heart 144.25
cold pack 1024.3
cold season 313.1
cold sector 317.4
cold shivers 74.4, 127.5, 128.2, 1023.2
cold shivers, the 917.2
cold shoulder 368.1, 372.1, 583.2, 908.2, 909.4
cold-shoulder 157.5, 340.8, 773.4
cold shoulder, the 157.2
cold-shouldered 151.5, 773.7
cold shower 79.8
cold snap 1023.3
cold sore 85.34, 85.37
cold spell 1023.3
cold steel 462.5, 1040.2
cold storage 386.5, 390.2, 1024.6
cold store 386.5
Coldstream Guards 461.15
cold sweat 12.7, 99.2, 127.5, 128.2
cold turkey 87.1
cold-type proof 548.5
cold-type typesetting 548.2
cold war 457.1

cold water 379.2
cold-water cure 91.3
cold-water flat 228.13
cold wave 3.15, 317.3, 1023.3
cold weather 317.3, 1023.3
cold wind 318.7
coleslaw 10.37
colic 26.5, 85.9, 85.29
colicky 26.12, 85.61
coliseum 463.1
colitis 85.29
coll 759.22
collaborate 324.3, 450.3, 547.21, 645.15, 718.6, 899.2
collaborating 363.11
collaboration 450.1, 645.7, 805.1, 899.1
collaborationist 357.11, 363.5, 616.4
collaborative 450.5, 899.4, 901.23
collaborative consumption 731.7
collaborativeness 450.1
collaborator 357.11, 363.5, 547.15, 616.4, 718.4
collage 712.10, 715.2
collagen 7.6
collagen disease 85.10
collapse (n) 16.1, 21.2, 85.8, 194.1, 252.2, 260.4, 393.1, 395.4, 410.3, 412.1, 625.3 (v) 16.9, 21.5, 85.47, 194.5, 260.10, 393.24, 410.12, 625.7, 911.2, 911.3
collapse breccia 1051.6
collapsed 194.12
collapse of authority 674.1
collapsibility 260.5
collapsible 260.11
collapsing 194.11
collar (n) 5.31, 280.3, 320.2, 428.4, 429.6, 429.11, 647.1, 751.1 (v) 429.16, 472.9, 480.18
collarband 280.3
collaring 480.2
collatable 943.8
collate 808.11, 943.5, 970.12
collated 957.20
collateral (n) 438.3, 559.2, 768.2 (a) 203.6, 253.10, 365.11, 559.6, 768.4, 769.9, 775.9, 831.11, 836.5, 963.14, 972.17
collateral damage 393.1, 473.1, 1000.4
collaterality 203.1
collateral relative 559.2
collateral security 438.3
collateral warranty 438.3
collating 554.14
collating mark 554.14
collation 8.5, 8.7, 808.1, 943.2, 970.8
colleague 588.3, 616.1, 726.1, 790.4
colleagueship 450.2, 587.2
collect (n) 696.4 (v) 386.11, 472.11, 770.16, 770.18, 800.5, 946.10
collectable 100.11
collectables 770.11
collect a duty on 630.12
collectanea 554.7, 557.4, 770.11, 770.13
collect a tax on 630.12
collect call 347.13
collected 106.13, 386.14, 770.21, 800.13
collected sayings 974.1
collected works 554.7
collect for one's services 624.20
collectible 100.11
collectibles 770.11
collecting 770.9
collection 386.1, 472.2, 478.6, 554.5, 554.7, 557.4, 696.7, 720.5, 770.1, 770.9, 770.11, 805.1
collection agent 622.4, 770.15
collective 450.5, 476.9, 899.4
collective action 450.1
collective agreement 437.1
collective bargaining 727.1, 727.2, 731.3
collective enterprise 476.2
collective farm 476.2, 1069.8
collective farm worker 1069.5
collective leadership 573.4
collective memory 989.1
collective noun 530.5
collective ownership 611.6
collective unconscious 92.28, 842.2, 934.2
collectivism 450.1, 476.2, 611.6, 612.7, 952.7
collectivist (n) 611.14 (a) 450.5
collectivistic 450.5, 476.9, 611.22
collectivity 476.2, 792.1, 899.1
collectivization 476.3, 480.5, 611.6
collectivize 476.7, 480.20
collectivized economy 731.7
collect knowledge 570.6
collect of the Communion 696.4
collect of the Mass 696.4
collect oneself 106.7
collect one's thoughts 931.10
collector 100.12, 101.4, 496.6, 575.12, 770.15
collector junction capacitance 1032.16
collector of internal revenue 630.10
collector signal voltage 1033.7
collector's item 999.5
collector's items 770.11
collect up 770.18
colleen 302.6
college 567.5, 617.1
college baseball 745.1
college basketball 747.1
college board 567.12
college boy 572.5
college-bred 572.12
college degree 570.3
college editor 554.2
college football 746.1
college girl 572.5
college graduate 572.8
college library 558.1
college man 572.8
College of Arms 575.20
college of Laputa 569.1
college radio 1034.16
collegese 523.10
college soccer 752.1
college student 572.5
college sweetheart 104.9
college try 403.1
college woman 572.8
collegialism 450.2
collegiality 450.2, 476.2, 582.4
collegian 572.5
collegiate (n) 572.5 (a) 567.13, 568.19, 572.12
collegiate church 703.1
collide 35.15, 182.41, 456.8, 457.13, 789.5, 900.6, 902.13
colliding 35.21, 456.15, 589.10
collier 1058.9
collier's purchase 906.2
colliery 739.4, 1058.6
colligate 770.18, 803.9
colligation 803.1
collimate 203.5
collimation 161.4, 203.1
collineate 203.5
collineation 203.1
colliquate 1020.21, 1064.5
colliquation 1064.1
colliquative 1064.7
collision 184.20, 451.2, 589.3, 779.1, 900.1, 902.3, 1011.2
collision course 169.1, 223.4
collision emission 1033.5
collision mat 213.5
collocate 159.11, 770.18, 808.9
collocation 159.6, 223.3, 529.1, 770.1, 808.1
collocutor 541.7
collogue 541.10
colloid (n) 1062.7 (v) 1062.10
colloidal 803.12, 1062.11, 1064.6
colloidality 803.1, 1062.2
colloidal suspension 1064.3
colloider 1062.7
colloidize 1062.10
colloid mill 797.9
collop 296.2, 793.3
colloque 541.8
colloquial 523.20, 541.12
colloquial discourse 541.1
colloquial English 523.5
colloquialism 523.5, 526.6
colloquialist 541.7
colloquialize 523.18
colloquializer 523.17
colloquial language 523.5
colloquial speech 523.5
colloquial usage 523.5
colloquist 541.7
colloquium 423.3, 541.5, 541.6, 770.2
colloquize 541.8, 541.11
colloquy 524.1, 541.1
collotype 548.1, 714.4
collude 381.9, 450.3, 899.2
collusion 356.4, 381.5, 450.1, 899.1
collusive 356.22, 381.13, 450.5, 899.4
colluvies 80.10, 606.3
collyrium 86.11, 1056.3
collywobbles 26.5, 128.2
cologne 70.3
cologne water 70.3
colon 2.18, 720.7, 857.4
colonel 575.17
Colonel Blimp 501.9
colonial 227.9
colonial government 612.4
colonialism 609.5, 612.4
colonialist threat 458.11
colonist 190.10, 227.9
colonization 159.7, 225.2, 480.4, 609.18
colonize 159.17, 225.9, 480.19
colonized 225.12
colonizer 227.9
colonnade 197.18, 273.5, 383.3, 901.8
colonnette 273.5
colony 227.1, 231.5, 232.1, 469.1, 617.2, 770.5
colophon 517.7, 517.13, 554.12, 817.1
colophonium 1057.1
colophonone 1057.1
colophony 1057.1
color (n) 33.4, 35.1, 35.4, 35.8, 41.1, 50.3, 209.3, 354.3, 376.1, 498.1, 600.5, 706.5, 712.8, 809.3 (v) 35.14, 41.5, 105.19, 139.8, 152.14, 265.6, 350.3, 354.16, 498.8, 527.11, 600.12, 712.19, 797.11, 894.7
colorable 354.26, 354.27, 600.14, 936.10, 953.24, 968.7
colorado 89.4
colorant 35.8
color arrangement 498.1
coloration 35.1, 35.11, 519.2
colorational 35.16
colorative 35.16
coloratura (n) 708.13, 708.16, 709.18 (a) 708.50
coloratura soprano 709.5
color balance 35.1
color bar 773.3, 980.4
color-blind 30.9, 945.5
colorblind 28.11
color blindness 30.3, 35.1, 945.1
colorcast (n) 1035.2 (v) 1035.14
color chart 35.7
color circle 35.7
color clash 35.5
color-code 35.14
color compatibility 498.1
color control 1041.8
color coordination 35.4
color cycle 35.7
color design 498.1
color disk 35.7
colored 35.17, 354.26, 354.27, 545.11, 980.12
colored glasses 29.3
colored pencils 35.8
colored spectacles 1028.2
colorfast 35.18
color film 714.10
color filter 35.8, 704.18
colorful 35.19, 47.9, 501.20
colorful imagination 986.4
colorful language 513.3
colorfulness 35.4, 501.3
color gamut 35.7

color gelatin 35.8
color graphics printer 1042.9
color harmony 35.1
color hearing 24.5
colorific 35.16
colorimetric quality 35.6
colorimetry 35.10
color in 712.19
color index 35.7
coloring (n) 35.1, 35.8, 35.11, 41.3, 50.3, 139.5, 350.1, 354.3, 354.9, 518.1, 712.3 (a) 35.16, 41.11
coloring book 554.1
colorist 716.4
colorization 706.5, 706.6
colorize 35.14, 706.8, 712.19
colorized 35.17, 706.9
colorizing 706.6
colorless 36.7, 117.6, 1029.4
colorlessness 36.1, 117.1, 1029.1
color line 980.4
color mixture curve 35.7
color mixture function 35.7
color monitor 1042.9
color negative film 714.10
color pattern 498.1
color perception 35.1
color photograph 714.3
color photography 706.5, 714.1
color print 712.10, 713.5, 714.3
color printer 1042.9
color printing 35.11, 548.1
color proof 548.5
color quality 35.6
color remover 36.4
color reversal film 714.10
colors 458.11, 545.4, 647.7
color scheme 35.1, 35.4, 498.1
color sergeant 575.18
colors in patches 47.4
colors of rhetoric 545.4
color solid 35.7
color spectrum 35.7
color supplement 555.2
color system 35.7
color television 1035.5
color theory 35.10
color therapy 90.13
color triangle 35.7
color up 41.5, 139.8
color vision 27.1, 35.1
colorwash 35.8
color wheel 35.7, 704.18
color with emotion 93.11
colory 35.19, 47.9
colossal 247.7, 257.20, 272.14, 272.16
colosseum 463.1
colossus 15.6, 257.13, 272.6
colossus of knowledge 929.3
colostrum 2.24, 13.2
colporteur 699.6, 730.5
colt 76.8, 302.5, 302.10, 311.10, 757.2
coltish 109.14, 301.11
coltishness 109.4
coltlike 301.11
colubrine 311.47
columbaceous 311.48
columbarium 309.15
columbary 228.23
Columbia 232.3
Columbine 707.10
columbine 311.48
columella 273.5
columelliform 282.11
column 272.6, 273.5, 277.2, 282.4, 461.22, 549.12, 552.3, 554.13, 759.12, 812.3, 901.8
columnal 282.11
columnar 282.11
columned 282.11
columnist 547.15, 555.4, 718.4
column order 717.2
colures 1073.16
coma 22.6, 25.2, 94.4, 853.1
comate 588.3, 769.4
comatose 22.21, 22.22, 25.8, 94.13, 331.20, 853.7
comatoseness 94.4
comb (n) 237.5, 237.7, 237.7, 238.14, 285.4, 1021.2 (v) 79.21, 238.22, 938.33
combat (n) 457.1, 457.4, 458.1 (v) 451.4, 457.13, 458.14
combatant 452.1, 461.1
combat area 463.2
combat command 461.22
combat engineer 461.14
combat fatigue 21.1
combat flight 184.11
Combat Information Center 1036.6
combative 456.17, 458.20, 459.30, 779.6, 935.19
combativeness 456.3, 458.10, 935.13
combative reaction 453.1
combat pay 624.4
combat pilot 185.3
combat plane 181.9
combat rehearsal 184.11
combat rocket 1074.3
combat sport 744.1
combat team 461.22
combat troops 461.20
combat zone 230.6, 463.2
comb binding 554.14
combe 237.7, 284.8
comber 238.14, 916.4
comb honey 66.2
combination 405.3, 450.2, 617.1, 770.1, 775.1, 778.2, 796.1, 797.1, 797.5, 800.1, 805.1, 872.1, 899.1
combination in restraint of trade 617.9
combination lock 1008.3
combination of notes 709.17
combination of tones 709.17
combinative 800.16, 805.5, 805.7, 872.12
combinatorial 800.16, 1017.22
combinatory 805.5, 805.7, 872.12
combinatory logic 935.2
combine (n) 617.1, 617.9, 805.1 (v) 450.3, 617.14, 769.7, 770.18, 778.5, 796.3, 797.10, 800.5, 805.3, 899.2
combined 450.5, 617.16, 769.9, 770.21, 797.14, 800.12, 805.5, 899.4
combined attack 459.1
combined effort 899.1
combined experience table 968.2
combined operation 450.1, 899.1
combined operations 458.4
combine in 796.3
combining 805.7, 872.12, 899.4
combining form 526.3
combo 710.12, 797.5, 805.1
comb-over 1016.14
comburent 1019.27
combust 1019.22, 1020.23
combustibility 105.10, 1020.9
combustible (n) 1021.1 (a) 110.25, 1020.28
combustible material 1021.1
combustion 1019.13, 1020.5
combustive 1019.26
come 33.8, 167.3, 186.6, 190.11, 831.5, 839.6, 972.11
come aboard 404.3, 800.5
come about 163.9, 182.30, 392.8, 831.5, 852.6, 887.4, 973.12
come a cropper 194.8, 410.10, 1011.10
come across 223.11, 348.7, 624.16, 941.3
come across with 478.13, 624.16
come afoul of 182.41
come after 166.3, 217.8, 815.2, 817.5, 835.3
come again 221.9, 849.7, 849.11, 850.5
come again and again 849.11
come alive 23.4, 306.9, 521.9
come along 162.2, 392.7, 409.12, 831.6, 941.9, 972.11
come along nicely 392.7
come a long way 162.4, 392.8, 861.5, 1010.7
come among 223.11
come and go 850.5, 916.13
come apart 16.9, 105.16, 128.7, 393.23, 802.9, 806.3, 810.8
come apart at the seams 16.9, 128.7, 393.23, 802.9, 810.8
come around 12.18, 306.9, 375.24, 396.20, 441.3, 850.5, 852.6
come around to 332.10
come as a shock 131.6
come as a surprise 131.6
come as no surprise 130.10, 968.4
come as you are 581.2
come at 186.7, 459.14
come-at-able 167.5, 966.8
come-at-ableness 167.2, 966.3
come at one's call 326.2
come away 188.6
come away empty-handed 410.9
come back 163.8, 392.8, 396.20, 757.5, 939.4, 989.14
comeback 392.1, 396.3, 396.8, 506.1, 508.2, 900.5, 939.1, 958.2
come back at 506.4, 903.5, 939.4
come-backer 745.3
comeback kid 392.6
come barging in 189.7
come before 814.2, 834.3
come behind 166.3
come between 214.5, 456.14
come breezing in 189.7
come busting in 189.7
come by 472.8, 479.6, 479.7
come by chance 972.11
come by honestly 639.4
come by one's own 481.6
come clean 351.7
come close 784.7
come close on 835.3
come closer 167.3
come crashing down 393.24, 395.22
comedian 489.12, 704.22, 707.9
comedienne 489.12, 707.9
comedo 1004.1
come down 87.22, 184.43, 194.5, 633.6, 946.11, 1011.11
comedown 132.1, 137.2, 194.1, 393.3, 410.3, 488.3, 512.1, 661.4, 1011.3
come down a peg 137.7, 194.5
come down a peg or two 137.7
come down hard on 510.18, 604.10
come down in buckets 316.10
come down in sheets 316.10
come down in the world 1011.11
come down in torrents 316.10
come down on 194.10, 459.14, 510.18, 604.10
come down on the side of 449.13
come down out of the clouds 987.4
come down squarely in the middle 362.7
come down to 790.5
come down to earth 987.4
come down with 85.47, 624.16
come down with the needful 624.16
comedy 489.1, 704.6, 706.2
comedy ballet 708.34
comedy club 489.1
come face to face with 216.8, 223.11
come first 249.11, 814.2
come forth 1.2, 33.8, 190.11, 348.6, 352.16, 369.10, 818.13, 831.6
come forward 33.8, 167.3, 439.10, 501.12
come from 887.5
come from an unexpected quarter 131.7
come from behind 131.7
come from far and wide 770.16
come full circle 914.5
come hat in hand 137.7, 658.5
come-hither (n) 377.1 (a) 377.8, 562.23
come-hither look 27.5, 562.9
come home 163.8, 518.8
come home to 93.14, 93.15
come home to roost 351.8
come in 75.20, 184.43, 186.6, 189.7, 479.8

come in conflict with 451.6, 779.4, 900.6
come in contact 73.6, 223.10
come in for 472.8, 479.7
come in for a landing 184.43
come in for a share 476.6
come in handy 384.7, 387.17, 995.3
come in its turn 850.5
come in like a lion 671.11
come in sight 33.8
come in through a side door 1.2
come into 472.8, 479.7, 617.14
come into being 306.9, 831.6
come into collision 902.13
come into existence 306.9, 831.6
come into its own 392.10
come into man's estate 303.9
come into money 618.10, 1010.11
come into one's head 931.18, 989.15
come into one's own 639.6, 662.11
come into possession of 472.8
come into the open 348.6
come into the picture 33.8
come into the world 1.2, 306.9, 818.13
come into view 31.4, 33.8, 190.11
come into vogue 662.11
come into years of discretion 303.9
come last 217.8
come like a burst 131.6
come like a thunderbolt 131.6
come like a thunderclap 131.6
comeliness 533.1, 1016.2
comely 264.5, 533.7, 1016.18
come near 167.3, 223.7, 223.8, 784.7
come nearer 167.3
come next 815.2, 817.5
come of 887.4
come of age 14.2, 259.7, 303.9, 392.10
come off 390.4, 409.7, 802.9, 831.5
come off of 407.6
come off press 548.18
come off second best 412.12
come on 162.2, 167.3, 392.7, 409.10, 409.12, 765.5, 831.6, 839.6, 840.2, 941.3, 1010.7
come-on 377.3, 439.1, 907.1
come on as 33.10
come on bended knee 137.7
come one's way 33.8, 831.6
come on like gangbusters 17.11
come-on man 357.5, 733.6
come on the heels of 817.5
come on the scene 834.3
come on to 377.5, 439.8
come onto the scene 662.11
come out 33.8, 190.11, 348.6, 351.8, 352.16, 369.10, 548.18, 704.29, 765.5, 818.13, 887.4, 941.9
come out ahead 411.3, 472.12
come out first 411.3
come out for 609.41
come out in the open 190.11
come out in the wash 36.6, 351.8
come out of 887.5
come out of it 109.9, 396.20
come out of left field 131.6, 662.11
come out of nowhere 131.6, 662.11
come out of one's shell 476.5
come out of the blue 131.7
come out of the closet 348.6, 351.7
come out of the woods 662.11
come out on top 409.10, 411.3, 411.6
come out on top of the heap 409.10
come out with 351.5, 365.7, 439.5, 524.22
come over 441.3
comer 189.4, 409.6, 841.4
comer and goer 178.1
come right back at 939.4
come round 363.6, 392.8, 396.20, 441.3, 465.10, 850.5
come round again 849.11, 850.5
come round to 858.17
come short 132.3, 911.2, 992.8, 1003.3
come sick 12.18
comestible 8.33
comestibles 10.1
comet 1073.4
cometary 828.8, 1073.25
comet cloud 1073.4
come through 306.11, 328.7, 407.4, 409.7, 409.10, 409.13, 521.5, 765.5, 1007.2
come through with 407.5, 624.16, 892.11
come to 186.6, 221.8, 261.6, 306.9, 396.20, 441.3, 630.13, 790.5, 792.8
come to a center 169.2
come to a conclusion 359.7, 946.10
come to a deadend 1013.11
come to a dead stop 410.16
come to a decision 359.7, 946.11
come to a determination 359.7
come to a focus 169.2, 208.10
come to a full stop 857.7
come to a grinding halt 857.7
come to a halt 857.7
come to a head 12.15, 208.10, 407.8, 1045.9
come to an agreement 332.10, 437.7, 788.6
come to anchor 159.17, 182.15
come to an end 395.23, 762.6, 820.7, 857.6
come to an understanding 332.10, 465.10, 468.2
come to an untimely end 307.21
come to a parting of the ways 456.10, 566.5
come to a point 169.2, 208.10, 285.6
come to a screaming halt 857.7
come to a shuddering halt 410.16
come to a squealing halt 857.7
come to a standstill 173.7, 857.7, 1013.11
come to a stop 857.7
come to attention 983.14
come to a violent end 308.21
come to be 761.12, 818.13, 973.12
come to blows 457.13
come to close quarters 167.3, 457.15
come to close quarters with 451.4
come to cold steel 458.15
come to dust 1051.10
come to fruition 407.8
come together 75.21, 169.2, 465.10, 770.16, 800.11, 805.3, 805.4, 807.5
come to grief 410.9, 1011.10
come to grips with 216.8, 387.12, 403.5, 403.6, 492.10, 725.9
come to hand 33.8, 186.6, 479.8, 941.9
come to heel 326.2
come to know 551.14
come to land 186.8
come to life 306.9
come to light 33.8, 351.8, 941.9
come to man's estate 303.9
come to maturity 303.9
come to me 989.15
come to mind 931.18, 989.15
come to naught 395.23, 473.6, 891.3, 911.3
come to nothing 132.3, 395.23, 410.13, 473.6, 891.3, 900.7, 911.3
come to one 479.8
come to one's ear 48.12
come to one's ears 351.8, 551.15
come to oneself 396.20
come to one's journey's end 186.6
come to one's knowledge 551.15, 928.14
come to one's senses 925.2
come to pass 831.5, 973.12
come to pieces 802.9
come to rest 186.6, 194.7, 820.7
come to terms 332.10, 433.8, 437.7, 465.10, 731.19
come to terms with oneself 107.5
come to the aid of 449.11
come to the fore 33.8, 165.2, 190.11, 216.7, 249.11, 662.11
come to the front 165.2, 216.7, 249.10, 249.11, 662.11
come to the point 535.2, 537.5, 865.9
come to the rescue 398.3
come to the scratch 457.14
come to the surface 33.8
come toward 167.3
come true 831.5, 973.12
come tumbling 395.22
come tumbling down 393.24
come unawares 131.6
come under 831.8
come undone 802.9
come unglued 16.9, 128.8, 802.9, 810.8
come unhinged 128.8
come unstuck 16.9, 128.8, 393.23, 802.9, 810.8
come up 167.3, 193.8, 318.19
come up again 849.11, 850.5
come up against 223.11, 457.15, 941.3
come up fighting 360.4, 409.13
come up for more 360.4
come up in the world 409.10
come upon 131.6, 186.7, 223.11
come upon the stage 33.8
come upon unexpectedly 131.7
come upon without warning 131.7
comeuppance 506.2, 639.3
come uppermost 931.20
come up roses 887.4, 940.2
come up short 250.4, 857.7
come up smiling 396.20, 409.13
come up to 174.13, 630.13, 790.5, 943.7
come up to scratch 867.4
come up with 439.5, 478.12
come up with a conclusion 946.10
come within an inch 223.7
come within earshot 48.12
come within shouting distance 223.7
come with the territory 964.7
comfit 10.40
comfort (n) 20.1, 95.1, 107.1, 120.1, 121.1, 121.4, 147.1, 295.10, 449.1, 677.15, 1010.1 (v) 120.5, 121.6, 147.2, 449.11, 449.14
comfortable 20.10, 95.15, 107.7, 121.11, 228.33, 618.14, 1010.12
comfortable as an old shoe 121.11
comfortable circumstances 618.1, 1010.1
comfortableness 121.2
comfortable temperature 1019.3
comfortably off 618.14
comfortably situated 1010.12
comfort break 857.2
comforter 121.5, 295.10, 670.3
Comforter , the 121.5, 677.12
comfort food 8.8
comfort index 1019.3
comforting 121.13, 147.3
comfortless 98.20, 112.28, 125.12
comfortlessness 98.5, 112.12
comfort room 12.10
comforts 121.3
comfort station 12.10, 197.26
comfort zone 20.1, 95.1
comfy 121.11
comic (n) 489.12, 707.9 (a) 488.6, 489.15, 704.35, 720.16
comical 488.6, 489.15
comicality 488.2
comicalness 488.2
comic bass 709.5

comic book 554.11, 712.15
comic genius 489.11
comic muse 704.6
comic opera 708.34
comic relief 704.6
comics 555.2, 712.15
comic section 712.15
comic strip 489.1, 712.15
Cominform 611.5
coming (n) 33.1, 167.1, 186.1, 839.5, 840.1 (a) 167.4, 186.9, 190.18, 249.12, 409.14, 639.7, 831.11, 839.8, 840.3
coming after 815.1, 835.1
coming and going 916.5
coming apart 393.45
coming-apart 806.1
coming ashore 186.2
coming between 466.8
coming by 472.1
coming clean 351.3
coming down 87.1
coming forth 33.1, 190.1
coming in 184.18
coming into being 33.1
coming into view 190.1
coming near 167.1
coming of age 14.1, 259.3, 861.1
coming-of-age 392.2
coming on the scene 33.1
coming out 190.1, 582.15, 818.5
coming out of one's ears 794.11
coming out of the closet 75.10
comings and goings 33.1
coming short 992.1
coming to 639.7
coming to be 831.1
coming together 169.1
coming to pass 831.1
coming to terms 731.3
coming toward 167.1
coming unstuck 393.45
coming up short 911.1
Comintern 611.5
comitative 530.9
comity 232.1, 504.1, 580.3
comma 857.4
comma fault 531.1
command (n) 31.3, 249.3, 323.1, 413.1, 417.5, 419.1, 420.1, 424.1, 573.1, 612.2, 928.1, 928.3, 1042.18 (v) 249.11, 272.11, 323.2, 420.8, 469.4, 573.8, 612.11, 928.12, 928.13
commandant 429.10, 575.6, 575.17
command a view of 272.11
command decision 420.1
commandeer 480.20, 615.17
commandeering 480.5
commander 183.7, 249.4, 575.6, 575.17, 575.19
commander-in-chief 575.17
command function 573.3
commanding 417.15, 417.16, 420.13, 573.12, 612.17
commanding officer 575.6, 575.17, 575.17
command language 1042.13
commandment 419.2, 420.1
command module 1075.2
command money 618.11
command of idiom 532.2
command of language 532.2, 544.1
command of money 728.14
command of words 544.1
command one's affection 104.22
command one's attention 377.6
commandos 461.15
commando unit 461.22
command performance 424.1, 704.12
command post 208.6
command respect 155.7
command sergeant major 575.18
comma splice 531.1
commatism 537.2
comme ci comme ça 1005.7
comme il faut 579.5, 637.3
commemorate 487.2
commemorating 487.3
commemoration 487.1, 850.4, 989.6
commemorative 487.3, 989.26
commence 818.7
commence firing 459.22
commencement 580.4, 818.1, 886.5
commencement exercises 580.4
commend 478.16, 509.11
commendable 509.20, 999.12
commendableness 509.7
commendation 478.2, 509.3
commendatory 509.16
commender 509.8
commend to attention 439.5
commensal 8.31, 450.5
commensalism 450.1
commensurability 784.1, 943.3
commensurable 775.8, 943.8
commensurate 107.11, 788.9, 790.7, 943.8, 991.6
comment (n) 213.2, 341.5, 556.2, 946.2 (v) 524.24
commentary 254.2, 341.5, 556.2, 723.2
commentate 341.11, 556.5, 719.5
commentation 341.5, 556.2
commentative 556.6
commentator 341.7, 556.4, 946.7, 1034.23, 1035.13
commentatorial 556.6
commenter 556.4, 946.7
comment upon 341.11, 541.11, 556.5, 946.14
commerce 75.7, 343.1, 582.4, 724.1, 731.1, 800.1
commerce with 343.6, 541.8
commercial (n) 352.6, 1034.18, 1034.20 (a) 724.15, 730.12, 731.22, 734.14
commercial affairs 731.1
commercial announcement 1034.20
commercial art 712.1
commercial artist 716.2
commercial attaché 576.6
commercial aviation 184.1
commercial bank 620.4
commercial banker 620.3
commercial break 158.8
commercial complex 736.2
commercial credit 622.1
commercial enterprise 617.9
commercial fertilizer 890.4
commercialism 731.13
commercialistic 731.22
commerciality 734.7
commercialization 731.14
commercialize 472.12, 497.9, 731.20
commercial law 673.5
commercial letter of credit 728.11
commercially bottled water 1065.3
commercial message 1034.20
commercial paper 728.11
commercial pilot 185.1
commercial program 1034.18
commercial radio 1034.16
commercial relations 731.1
commercial trade 731.2
commercial transaction 731.4
commercial traveler 730.4
commercial vehicle 179.13
Commie 860.3
commie (n) 611.13 (a) 611.21
comminate 514.2
commination 513.1, 514.1
comminatory 513.8, 514.3
commingle 797.10
comminglement 797.1
commingling 797.1
comminute (v) 1051.9 (a) 1051.11
comminuted 1051.11
comminuted fracture 85.38
comminution 1051.4
comminutor 1051.7
commiserate 145.3, 147.2
commiserating 147.3
commiseration 145.1, 147.1
commiserative 145.7, 147.3
commissar 575.13, 575.16, 576.2
commissariat 10.5, 385.6, 386.1, 594.4
commissary 10.5, 385.6, 386.1, 576.2
commissary clerk 183.6
commissary steward 183.6
commission (n) 328.2, 419.1, 420.2, 477.5, 576.13, 613.1, 615.1, 624.7, 630.6, 724.2, 770.2 (v) 18.10, 328.9, 396.14, 420.8, 576.14, 615.10, 862.7
commissionaire 353.1
commissioned 615.19
commissioned officer 575.17
commissioner 575.16, 576.2, 1008.15
Commissioners Standard Ordinary table 968.2
commissioning 615.1
commissions 627.1
commit 328.6, 429.17, 436.5, 437.5, 477.11, 478.16, 615.10, 641.12
commit acquaintance rape 480.15
commit a crime 674.5
commit adultery 75.21, 665.19
commit a faux pas 414.11
commit a foul 747.4
commit a gaffe 414.11
commit an assault upon 459.14
commit an atrocity 650.7
commit an outrage 650.7
commit a solecism 531.3
commit a violation 747.4
commit burglary 482.15
commit carnage 308.17
commit date rape 480.15
commit genocide 308.17
commit hara-kiri 308.22
commit highway robbery 632.7
commit mass destruction 308.17
commit mass murder 308.17
commitment 101.2, 334.4, 359.1, 404.1, 429.4, 436.2, 477.4, 478.2, 587.7, 615.1, 641.1, 652.1, 886.9
commitment ceremony 563.3
commitment to memory 989.3
commit murder 308.16
commit oneself 359.8, 404.3, 641.9, 843.7
commit rape 480.15
commit robbery 482.14
commit sacrilege 694.4
commit seppuku 308.22
commit sin 655.4
commit suicide 308.22
committable 477.12, 478.23
committal 429.4, 436.2
committed 101.9, 359.11, 359.12, 436.8, 587.21, 641.16, 652.5
committedness 101.2
committee 423.2, 576.13, 770.2
committee consideration 613.6
committeeman 610.12, 617.11
committee of one 423.2
committeewoman 610.12
commit to an archive 549.15
commit to an institution 429.17
commit to memory 989.16
commit to prison 429.17
commit to writing 549.15
commix 797.10
commixture 797.1, 797.5
commode 12.10, 12.11
commodious 121.11, 158.11, 387.18
commodiousness 121.2
commodities 735.1
commodity 735.2
commodity exchange 737.7
commodity market 737.1
commodore 575.19
common (n) 310.7, 310.8, 471.4, 743.14 (a) 117.9, 246.3, 250.6, 312.16, 450.5, 476.9, 497.14, 499.6, 523.20, 535.3, 606.8, 721.5, 777.11, 798.6, 847.4, 864.12, 864.16, 869.9, 928.27, 998.21, 1005.8, 1005.9
common, the 869.3
commonage 606.1
commonality 250.2, 450.1, 864.2
commonality, the 606.1
commonalty 250.2

commonalty, the 606.1
common ancestry 559.1, 560.4, 775.3
common as dirt 606.8
common assent 332.5
common belief 953.6
common card 759.10
common case 530.9
common cold 85.16
common consent 332.5
common council 423.1, 613.1
common courtesy 504.1
common denominator 777.1, 1017.12
common descent 559.1, 775.3
common effort 450.1
common endeavor 450.1
common enterprise 450.1
commoner 572.7, 606.5
Common Era 824.5
commoners 606.1
common factor 777.1
common fraction 1017.7
common gender 530.10
common good 999.4
common grave 309.16
common ground 777.1
common herd, the 606.2
common jury 596.5
common knowledge (n) 352.4, 551.1, 928.9, 974.1 (a) 352.17
common laborer 726.2
common law 673.5
common-law jurisdiction 594.1
common-law lien 438.5
common-law marriage 563.1
common-law wife 563.8
commonly known 928.27
common man 606.5, 864.3, 998.7
common man, the 606.1
common market 617.1
common name 527.3
commonness 117.3, 373.6, 497.1, 497.5, 499.1, 721.2, 847.1, 864.2, 869.2, 1005.2, 1005.3
common noun 530.5
common occurrence 847.1
common ownership 476.2
common people 606.1
common phrase 529.1
commonplace (n) 526.9, 864.8, 974.3 (a) 117.9, 118.9, 497.14, 499.6, 535.3, 606.8, 721.5, 864.16, 869.9, 928.27, 1005.8
commonplace, the 869.3
commonplace book 549.11
commonplace expression 974.3
commonplaceness 117.3, 497.5, 499.1, 721.2, 869.2, 1005.2
common practice 373.4
common property (n) 471.1 (a) 352.17
common ruck 606.3
common run, the 606.1
common run of things 373.4
commons 10.6, 197.11, 606.1, 743.14
common saying 974.1
common scold 110.12, 510.9
common seaman 183.1
common sense 920.6, 925.1, 935.9
commonsense 920.18, 1052.12
commonsense philosopher 1052.7
commonsense philosophy 1052.6
commonsense realism 1052.6
commonsense realist 1052.7
commonsensical 920.18
common soldier 461.8
common sort, the 606.1
common source 775.3
common speech 523.6, 535.1
common stock 775.3
common talk 552.6
common touch 581.1
common variety 869.3
common-variety 499.6
commonweal 143.5, 232.1, 387.4
commonwealth 227.1, 232.1, 612.4, 617.2
Commonwealth, the 232.4
commonwealth, the 606.1
Commonwealth of Nations 232.4
common year 824.2
commorancy 225.1
commorant 225.13
commotion 53.3, 105.4, 330.4, 355.2, 671.2, 810.4, 917.1
comms 347.1
communal 312.16, 450.5, 476.9, 606.8, 617.17, 777.11, 864.12
communal activity 450.1
communal card 759.10
communal effort 476.2
communal enterprise 476.2
communalism 450.1, 450.2
communalist 450.5
communalistic 450.5
communalization 476.3, 480.5
communalize 476.7, 480.20
communal ownership 476.1
commune 227.1, 231.5, 476.1, 617.2
commune with 343.6, 541.8
commune with God 696.13
commune with the spirits 88.24
communicability 82.3, 85.4, 343.4
communicable 82.7, 85.62, 176.18, 343.11, 478.23
communicant 551.5, 692.4, 696.9, 700.2
communicate 176.10, 343.6, 343.7, 478.12, 524.22, 541.8, 551.8, 701.14, 800.11
communicate orally 523.18
communicate verbally 523.18
communicate with 343.8, 541.8, 553.10
communicating 343.9, 800.16
communication (n) 343.1, 383.3, 478.1, 524.1, 541.1, 551.1, 552.4, 553.2, 582.4, 800.1 (a) 347.21
communicational 343.9, 347.21
communication engineering 1034.2
communication explosion 347.1, 551.7
communication leak 351.2
communications (n) 343.5, 347.1, 555.3 (a) 347.21
communication satellite 1035.9
communications engineer 347.1
communications engineering 347.1
communications industry 343.5
communications industry, the 555.3
communications media 343.5, 347.1
communications medium 343.5, 347.1
communications net 1034.8
communications network 343.5, 1042.16
communications protocol 1042.19
communications relay satellite 1075.6
communications revolution 860.1
communications satellite 1075.6
communications ship 180.6
communications technology 347.1
communications theory 1041.2
communications zone 463.2
communication theory 343.5, 347.1, 551.7
communication trench 460.5
communicative 343.10, 540.9, 541.12, 551.18, 582.22
communicatively 343.12
communicativeness 343.3, 540.1, 582.1
communicator 551.5, 553.8
Communion 701.7
communion 343.1, 455.1, 476.2, 541.1, 582.4, 617.5, 675.3, 696.4
communion 777.1
communional 343.9
communion cloth 703.10
Communion table 703.12
communiqué 352.2, 551.1, 552.4
communism 450.1, 476.2, 611.5, 612.4, 612.7, 952.7
Communist (n) 611.13, 860.3 (a) 611.21, 860.6
communist 450.5
communist front 609.33
communistic 450.5, 476.9, 611.21
Communist Information Bureau 611.5
Communist International 611.5
Communist Party 609.24, 611.5
Communist sympathizer 611.13
Communist threat 458.11
communitarian 450.5
communitarianism 450.1
community 227.1, 312.1, 450.1, 455.1, 476.2, 582.4, 617.2, 675.3, 769.2, 777.1, 784.1
community, the 606.1
community activity 450.1
community card 759.10
community center 208.7, 230.5
community chest 478.9
community college library 558.1
community garden 310.24
community medicine 90.13
community of interest 587.2
community of interests 455.1
community policing 1008.1
community sentiment 953.6
community service 143.6
community sing 708.32
community singing 708.32
community theater 704.14
communization 476.3, 480.5
communize 476.7, 480.20, 611.16
commutability 863.3
commutable 863.5
commutation 177.1, 338.1, 862.1, 863.1
commutative 863.5
commute 177.18, 850.5, 862.4, 863.4
commuter 178.1, 726.2
commuter airline 184.10
commuter belt 230.1
commutual 476.9, 777.11
commutuality 777.1
comp (n) 634.2 (v) 449.12, 634.4 (a) 634.5
compact (n) 437.1, 788.2, 1016.11 (v) 260.7, 437.5, 1045.9 (a) 258.12, 260.12, 268.8, 293.12, 537.6, 770.22, 800.12, 1045.12
compactability 260.5
compactable 260.11
compact disc 50.12
compact disk 549.10
compact disk player 50.11
compact-disk read-only memory 1042.6
compacted 260.12, 437.11, 803.10, 1045.12
compactedness 260.1
compacter 260.6
compacting 260.1, 390.3
compaction 260.1, 803.1, 803.5, 1059.8
compactness 258.1, 268.1, 537.1, 1045.1
compact of 796.4
compactor 391.7
companion (n) 104.11, 193.3, 349.5, 577.8, 588.3, 608.5, 616.1, 769.4, 769.5, 784.3 (v) 769.7
companionability 582.1
companionable 582.22, 587.20
companion animal 311.2
companionate 582.22
companion bills amendment 613.9
companion ladder 193.4
companionless 872.8
companion piece 769.4
companion plant 310.3
companionship 582.6, 587.2, 769.2
companionway 189.5, 193.3

company 461.22, 582.6, 585.6, 588.3, 617.7, 617.9, 707.11, 739.1, 769.2, 770.3
company headquarters 208.6, 739.7
company man 867.2
company officer 575.17
company official 574.3
company union 727.2
comparability 784.1, 943.3
comparable 775.8, 784.11, 943.8
comparableness 943.3
comparative 943.8
comparative anatomy 943.1
comparative degree 943.1
comparative estimate 943.1
comparative ethics 636.2
comparative government 609.2
comparative grammar 530.1, 943.1
comparative judgment 943.1
comparative linguistics 526.16, 943.1
comparative literature 943.1
comparative method 943.1
comparativeness 943.3
comparative relation 943.1
comparative relational 775.7
comparative scrutiny 943.2
compare (n) 943.1 (v) 770.18, 943.4, 943.7
compare and contrast 943.4, 944.4
compare notes 541.10, 943.6
compare point by point 943.5
compare to 943.7
compare with 784.7, 943.4, 943.7
comparing 943.1
comparison 770.1, 784.1, 862.2, 943.1, 946.3
comparison of variables 1041.7
comparison-shop 733.8
comparison shopping 733.1
compartment 195.1, 197.2
compartmentalization 802.1
compartmentalize 802.18
compartmentalized 802.20
compartmentalizing 809.1
compass (n) 158.2, 209.1, 211.1, 211.3, 245.1, 247.1, 261.1, 574.9, 709.6 (v) 209.6, 212.5, 407.4, 409.11, 914.5
compassability 889.3, 966.2
compassable 889.10, 966.7
compass about 209.6, 1008.18
compass bearing 161.2
compass card 161.3
compass course 184.34
compass direction 161.2, 184.34
compass directions 161.3
compassed 209.10, 407.10
compass heading 161.2, 184.34
compassing 209.5
compassion 24.3, 143.1, 145.1, 339.1, 427.1, 652.2, 979.4
compassionate (v) 145.3 (a) 24.12, 143.13, 145.7, 427.7, 979.11
compassionateness 145.2
compass needle 517.4
compass of mind 920.1
compass point 159.1
compass reading 161.1
compass rose 161.3
compatibility 97.1, 455.1, 582.1, 587.3, 784.2, 788.1, 1042.18
compatible 97.6, 455.3, 582.22, 587.16, 775.9, 788.9
compatriot 227.5, 616.1
compeer 588.3, 616.1, 790.4, 836.2
compel 375.12, 424.4, 612.15, 902.11, 926.25, 963.8
compellable 894.15
compelling 375.25, 420.13, 424.10, 926.34, 997.22
compend 557.1
compendious 268.8, 537.6, 557.6, 772.7
compendiousness 268.1, 537.1
compendium 554.7, 557.1, 557.4
compensate 264.3, 338.4, 396.13, 481.5, 506.5, 624.10, 658.4, 790.6, 863.4
compensated 624.22
compensating 338.6, 624.21, 779.6
compensation 92.23, 264.2, 338.1, 396.6, 465.2, 481.2, 506.2, 603.1, 624.3, 624.4, 658.1
compensational 658.7
compensation time 222.4
compensative 624.21
compensator 624.9
compensatory 338.6, 481.7, 506.8, 624.21, 658.7
compensatory damages 603.3
compensatory interest 623.3
compete 457.18, 744.2
compete against 451.4, 457.18
competence, a 991.1
competence 18.1, 18.2, 405.4, 413.1, 417.1, 523.1
competency, a 991.1
competency 18.1, 18.2, 107.3, 371.11, 405.4, 417.1
competent 18.14, 107.11, 405.17, 413.24, 417.15, 673.11, 991.6
compete with 451.4, 457.18
competing 457.23
competing stimuli 985.1
competition 451.2, 457.2, 747.1, 749.1, 750.1, 752.1, 753.1, 755.1, 756.1
competition aikido 760.3
competition court 748.1
competitive 451.8, 457.23
competitive advantage 457.2
competitive fishing 382.3
competitive market 737.1
competitiveness 154.1, 457.1
competitive sailing 760.2
competitive skiing 753.1
competitor 452.2, 461.1, 743.19
competitorship 457.1
competitory 457.23
compilation 554.7, 673.5, 770.11
compile 673.10, 718.6, 719.4, 770.18, 796.3
compiler 547.15, 718.4, 1042.13
compiling 796.1
complacence 107.2
complacency 107.2, 140.1
complacent 107.10, 140.8
complain 108.5, 115.15, 333.5, 453.3, 599.7
complain against 510.13
complainant 108.3, 599.5
complainer 108.3, 115.8, 510.9
complaining (n) 115.4 (a) 108.7, 115.19, 453.5
complain loudly 453.3
complain of 85.46
complaint 85.1, 115.4, 333.2, 453.1, 510.1, 598.3, 598.7, 599.1
complaintful 108.7
complaisance 97.1, 143.3, 427.2, 433.1, 504.1
complaisant 97.6, 143.16, 427.8, 433.12, 504.13, 867.5, 1047.8
complected 35.17
complement (n) 183.6, 254.1, 530.2, 617.7, 770.3, 784.3, 792.3, 794.3 (v) 777.7, 778.4
complemental 777.10, 794.13
complementary 769.9, 777.10, 778.8, 794.13
complementary color 35.7
complementary distribution 777.3
complementary relation 777.3
complementation 253.1, 254.1, 777.3
complete (v) 328.9, 407.6, 437.9, 772.3, 794.6, 820.8, 861.6, 1002.5 (a) 247.12, 407.12, 772.7, 792.11, 794.9, 820.9, 960.2, 1002.7
complete, the 413.22
complete answer 958.2
complete a pass 746.5
complete a purchase 733.7
complete blank 930.6
complete change 858.1
completed 407.11
completed pass 746.3
complete game 745.3
completeness 772.1, 792.5, 794.1, 1002.2
complete works 547.12, 554.7, 718.1, 792.3
completing (n) 407.2 (a) 407.9, 794.13
completion 328.2, 407.2, 437.4, 794.4
completive 407.9, 794.13
completory 407.9, 794.13
complex (n) 92.15, 92.22, 266.2, 373.2, 792.1, 799.2, 926.13 (a) 522.14, 797.14, 799.4, 1013.17
complex carbohydrate 7.5
complex cone 282.5
complex control system 1041.5
complex idea 932.2
complexion (n) 33.4, 35.1, 92.11, 765.4, 767.4, 978.3 (v) 35.14
complexioned 35.17
complexity 281.1, 522.2, 799.1, 1013.1
complexity of meaning 539.1
complexness 799.1
complex variable 1041.9
compliable 433.12, 441.4
compliableness 433.3
compliance 134.2, 324.1, 326.1, 332.1, 427.2, 433.1, 434.1, 441.1, 867.1
compliant 134.10, 324.5, 326.3, 332.13, 387.23, 427.8, 433.12, 434.4, 441.4, 867.5, 1047.9
complicate 251.5, 253.4, 522.12, 799.3
complicated 522.14, 799.4
complicate matters 1013.13
complication 85.1, 522.2, 722.4, 799.1, 1013.1, 1013.4, 1013.8
complicit 450.5
complicitous 450.5
complicity 381.5, 450.1, 476.1, 656.1
compliment (n) 149.1, 509.6, 511.1 (v) 149.2, 509.14, 511.5
complimentariness 634.1
complimentary 149.3, 509.16, 511.8, 634.5
complimentary remark 509.6
complimentary ticket 634.2
compliments 504.8
compliments of the season 504.8
compline 696.8
complot (n) 381.5 (v) 381.9
comply 326.2, 332.8, 433.6, 441.3, 867.3, 1047.7
complying 326.3, 433.12
comply with 434.2, 441.3, 867.3
component (n) 793.1, 796.2, 1052.2 (a) 796.5
componential 793.7
components 196.1, 763.2
comportment 321.1
comport oneself 321.4
compose 405.7, 437.8, 465.8, 466.7, 468.2, 547.21, 548.16, 670.7, 708.46, 718.6, 796.3, 797.10, 808.9, 867.3, 892.8
composed 106.13, 107.7, 123.3, 808.14
composed matter 548.4
composedness 123.1
composed of 796.4
composed salad 10.37
compose one's differences 465.10
compose oneself 106.7
compose one's features 111.2
compose poetry 720.14
composer 547.15, 710.20, 718.4, 986.12
composer-in-residence 227.2
composing (n) 548.2 (a) 796.4
composing room 548.11
composing stick 548.2
Composite 717.2
composite (n) 797.5 (a) 797.14, 872.10, 883.7
composite 198.6
composite fruit 10.38
compositeness 883.1
composite reading 341.2
composite text 341.2
composition 196.1, 262.1, 266.1, 405.3, 468.1, 532.1, 547.2, 547.10, 548.2, 554.7, 658.1,

708.5, 712.8, 712.9, 718.2, 767.4, 796.1, 797.1, 797.5, 805.1, 892.2, 893.1
composition of differences 465.4
composition tape 548.2
compositor 548.12, 554.2
compos mentis 925.4
compost (n) 391.7, 890.4 (v) 890.8, 1069.17
compostable 890.11
composter 391.7
compost heap 80.10, 391.7, 1069.10
compost pile 391.7, 1069.10
composure 106.2, 107.1, 123.1, 173.1, 359.5
compotation 8.3, 88.5
compote 10.40
compound (n) 526.4, 529.1, 796.1, 797.5, 805.2, 1058.4 (v) 405.7, 468.2, 797.10, 805.3, 892.8 (a) 797.14
compounded 797.14
compound for 862.4
compound fraction 1017.7
compound fracture 85.38
compounding 805.1
compound interest 623.3
compound measure 709.24
compound noun 529.1, 530.5
compound radical 1038.7
compound time 709.24
comprehend 521.7, 772.3, 928.12
comprehended 772.5, 928.26
comprehending 928.15
comprehensibility 521.1
comprehensible 521.10, 928.25
comprehension 772.1, 920.1, 928.3
comprehensive 247.6, 257.17, 269.6, 772.7, 792.9, 794.10, 800.12, 864.14
comprehensive examination 938.2
comprehensiveness 257.6, 772.1, 792.5, 794.1
compress (n) 86.33 (v) 252.7, 260.7, 260.8, 268.6, 270.11, 1045.9
compressed 260.12, 268.9, 537.6, 557.6, 1045.12
compressed score 708.28
compressibility 260.5, 1047.2
compressible 260.11
compressible fluid 1067.2
compression 260.1, 260.2, 268.3, 270.2, 537.1, 1042.19, 1045.3
compression bandage 86.33
compressor 260.6
compressure 260.1
comprisal 772.1
comprise 207.5, 772.3, 772.4, 792.8, 800.5, 805.3
comprised 772.5
comprising 772.6, 796.4
compromise (n) 465.4, 467.3, 468.1, 609.5, 658.1, 777.3, 788.4, 863.1 (v) 465.8, 465.10, 468.2, 819.3, 863.4, 1006.6
compromised 436.8
compromise oneself 661.7
compromiser 670.4
comps 938.2
compte rendu 628.2
comp time 222.4
comptroller 574.2, 628.7, 729.12
comptrollership 628.6
compulsatory 424.10
compulsion 18.1, 92.15, 375.6, 424.1, 902.1, 926.13, 963.1
compulsion complex 92.22
compulsive 424.10, 495.12, 867.6, 926.34, 963.14
compulsive character 867.2
compulsive gambler 759.21
compulsive neatness 807.3
compulsiveness 424.1, 807.3, 963.5
compulsoriness 963.1
compulsory 420.12, 424.10, 424.11, 641.15, 767.9, 963.12, 963.14
compulsory arbitration 466.2
compulsory figure 760.7
compulsory military service 615.7
compulsory referendum 613.8
compulsory service 458.8
compulsory servitude 432.1
compunction 113.2, 325.2, 333.2
compurgation 601.1, 957.2
compurgator 957.6
computability 300.7
computable 300.14, 1017.25
computation 253.3, 300.1, 1017.2, 1017.10, 1041.7
computational 1017.24
computative 1017.24
compute 253.6, 300.10, 1017.18, 1042.21
computed tomography 91.9
computer 1017.15, 1041.17, 1042.2
computeracy 928.5
Computer Age 824.6
computer-aided 1042.22
computer-aided instruction 568.1
computer application 1042.11
computer applications 1042.1
computer architect 1042.17
computer-assisted 1042.22
computer-assisted tomography 91.9, 91.9
computerate (n) 1042.18 (a) 1042.22
computer composition 548.2
computer-controlled 1041.22, 1042.22
computer crime 655.2, 1042.1
computer dating 563.12
computer designer 1042.17
computer disk 549.10
computer-driven 1042.22
computer engineer 1041.19, 1042.17
computerese 523.10
computer fiction 722.1
computer file 549.10
computer forms 1042.10
computer fraud 1042.1
computer-friendly 1042.18
computer game 743.9, 1042.11
computer-governed 1042.22
computer graphics 706.1, 713.1
computer-guided 1042.22
computer hardware 1041.17, 1042.1, 1042.2
computerization 1041.1, 1042.1
computerize 1041.20, 1042.21
computerized 1041.22, 1042.22
computerized axial tomography 91.9
computerized catalog 558.4
computerized tomography 91.9
computerized typesetting 548.2
computer language 523.11, 1042.13
computer listing 871.2
computer literacy 928.5
computer-literate (n) 1042.18 (a) 1042.22
computer memory 989.1
computer model 336.3
computer network 1042.16
computer networking 347.18
computer paper 1042.10
computer printout 547.10
computer program 1042.11
computer programmer 1041.19
computer proof 548.5
computer revolution 860.1
computers 1042.1
computer science 1041.17, 1042.1, 1042.1
computer scientist 1042.17
computer security 1042.1
computer selling 737.19
computer simulation 336.3
computer software 1042.1
computer systems 1042.1
computer technician 1041.19
computer technologist 1041.19
computer unit 1041.17
computer-usable 1042.22
computer virus 732.1, 1042.1, 1042.11
computer worm 732.1, 1042.1, 1042.11
computing (n) 1042.1 (a) 1017.24
comrade 588.3, 616.1, 617.11
comrade in arms 588.3, 616.1
comradery 582.2, 587.2
comradeship 450.2, 582.2, 587.2
Comsat 1035.9
comsymp 611.13
Comtian 952.12
Comus 690.5
con (n) 356.9, 429.11, 593.1, 660.9, 759.13, 935.14 (v) 356.18, 375.23, 570.12, 989.16 (a) 451.8, 510.21
con affetto 708.53
con agilità 708.53
con agitazione 708.53
con amore lamentabile 708.53
con anima 708.55
con artist 357.4
conation 323.1
conative 323.4
conatus 323.1, 896.1
con brio 708.55
concameration 279.1, 279.4
concatenate 800.5, 812.4
concatenated 812.8
concatenation 92.33, 800.1, 812.2
concatenation of events 972.5
concave (n) 284.2 (v) 284.13 (a) 279.10, 284.16
concaved 284.16
concave mirror 29.6
concavity 197.2, 224.2, 279.1, 284.1, 284.2, 517.7, 913.1
conceal 345.7, 346.6
concealed 32.5, 345.11, 346.11
concealed microphone 50.9
concealedness 346.1
concealing 346.15
concealment 32.1, 345.1, 346.1, 346.4, 415.1, 1009.3
conceal oneself 346.8
conceal one's motive with 376.4
concede 332.11, 351.7, 751.4, 959.5
conceded 332.14, 761.15
conceded fact 761.3
conceding 332.13
conceit (n) 136.1, 140.4, 364.1, 489.7, 500.4, 502.1, 927.2, 931.1, 932.1, 953.6, 986.1 (v) 511.5, 986.14
conceited 136.9, 140.11, 157.8, 500.17, 502.10, 970.22
conceitedness 140.4
conceit oneself 502.8
conceivability 953.8, 966.1
conceivable 928.25, 953.24, 966.6, 968.7, 986.26
conceivableness 966.1
conceivably possible 966.6
conceive 78.11, 306.10, 521.7, 532.4, 886.10, 892.12, 928.12, 931.8, 951.10, 953.11, 986.14
conceived 892.19, 928.26
conceive of 931.16
conceiver 892.7
conceiving 78.4
concenter 169.2, 208.10
concento 709.17
concentralization 169.1, 208.8
concentralize 169.2
concentrate (n) 192.8 (v) 169.2, 192.16, 208.10, 251.5, 260.7, 931.10, 1045.9
concentrated 208.11, 260.12, 931.21, 983.15, 1045.12
concentrate on 889.6, 931.10, 983.8
concentrate sprayer 1065.8
concentrate the mind 931.10
concentrate the thoughts 931.10
concentrating 931.21
concentration 169.1, 192.7, 192.8, 208.8, 251.2, 260.1, 330.6, 359.2, 360.1, 931.3, 983.1, 983.3, 1045.3
concentration camp 228.29, 308.12, 429.8
concentrative 931.21
concentric 208.14
concentric cable 347.17
concentricity 208.1
concentus 708.3

concept 932.1, 951.3, 952.2, 953.6, 986.6
conception 78.4, 381.1, 886.5, 892.1, 919.1, 920.1, 928.3, 931.1, 932.1, 953.6, 986.2, 986.6
conceptive 919.7, 920.12, 931.21, 932.9, 935.18, 986.18
conceptual 919.7, 920.12, 931.21, 932.9, 935.18, 986.18
conceptual breakthrough 932.5
conceptual crudity 798.3
conceptualization 928.3, 931.1, 986.6
conceptualize 928.12, 931.8, 986.14
conceptualized 931.21
conceptually crude 798.10
conceptual model 349.1
concern (n) 24.3, 93.5, 126.1, 143.3, 339.1, 404.1, 617.9, 724.1, 739.1, 775.4, 831.3, 928.10, 937.1, 983.2, 997.1 (v) 126.4, 775.5, 898.2, 983.12, 1013.13
concerned 126.7, 898.4, 983.16
concernment 126.1, 724.1, 775.4, 831.3, 983.2, 997.1
concern oneself with 724.11, 983.5
concerns 126.2, 831.4
concert (n) 332.5, 450.1, 708.3, 708.33, 788.1, 899.1 (v) 381.8, 450.3 (a) 708.51
concert artist 710.1
concerted 450.5, 899.4
concerted action 899.1
concertgoer 710.21
concert hall 197.4, 704.14
concertina 711.11
concertinist 710.7
concertist 710.3
concertize 708.39
concertmaster 710.19
concertmeister 710.19
concert music 708.6
concert overture 708.26
concert performance 708.33
concert pitch 709.4
concert season 313.1
concession 332.3, 351.3, 412.1, 427.1, 443.5, 468.1, 478.1, 631.1, 730.2, 736.1, 959.1
concession speech 412.1
concession stand 730.2
concessive 332.13, 478.25
concessory 426.5
conch 2.10, 295.15
concha 2.10, 279.4
conchate 279.18
conchie 464.6
conchiform 279.18
conchoid 279.2
conchoidal 279.18
concierge 577.5, 1008.12
conciliar 423.5
conciliarism 423.4
conciliate 465.7, 466.7
conciliation 465.1, 658.1
conciliator 466.5
conciliatory 148.6, 464.10, 465.12, 658.7
concilium 423.1
concinnate 533.8
concinnity 533.2
concinnous 533.8
concise 268.8, 344.9, 537.6
conciseness 268.1, 344.2, 537.1
concision 537.1
conclave 423.1, 423.4, 541.5, 609.8, 770.2
conclude 359.7, 407.6, 437.8, 820.6, 946.10, 951.10
concluded 407.11, 820.9
concluding 407.9, 820.11
conclusion 334.1, 407.2, 437.3, 817.1, 820.1, 935.8, 940.1, 946.4, 952.2, 953.6
conclusive 407.9, 420.12, 820.11, 820.12, 953.26, 957.16, 960.2, 970.13
conclusive argument 958.3
conclusive evidence 957.3
conclusive proof 957.3
concoct 354.18, 381.9, 405.7, 797.10, 892.8, 892.12, 986.14
concocted 354.29
concoction 354.10, 405.3, 797.5, 892.1, 893.1
concomitance 769.1, 836.1, 899.1
concomitancy 769.1, 836.1
concomitant (n) 254.1, 769.3, 836.2 (a) 769.9, 836.5, 899.4
concord (n) 264.1, 332.5, 437.2, 450.1, 455.1, 464.1, 708.3, 788.1, 807.1 (v) 450.3
concordance 332.5, 450.1, 455.1, 554.9, 708.3, 788.1, 899.1
concordant 332.15, 450.5, 455.3, 464.9, 708.49, 788.9, 867.6, 899.4
concordat 437.2
Concorde 181.3
concours 457.3
concourse 169.1, 238.4, 696.9, 770.1, 770.2, 800.1, 899.1
concrete (n) 199.3, 383.6, 803.5, 1045.6, 1046.6, 1054.2 (v) 295.22, 295.25, 1045.10, 1046.8 (a) 720.16, 763.6, 803.10, 865.12, 1045.12, 1046.10
concrete, the 865.3
concrete block 1054.2
concrete identity 865.1
concrete jungle 80.11, 230.6
concreteness 763.1, 1052.1
concrete noun 530.5
concretion 803.1, 803.5, 1045.3, 1045.4, 1045.6, 1046.5
concretization 763.4
concretize 763.5
concubinage 665.7
concubinal 563.18
concubinary 563.18
concubine 432.7, 563.8, 665.17
concupiscence 75.5, 100.1, 665.5
concupiscent 75.27, 665.29
concur 332.9, 450.3, 788.6, 836.4, 899.2, 901.21
concur on 332.10
concurrence 169.1, 203.1, 332.1, 332.5, 450.1, 769.1, 770.1, 777.3, 800.1, 836.1, 899.1, 901.1
concurrency 332.1, 769.1, 836.1
concurrent 169.3, 203.6, 332.15, 450.5, 769.9, 800.12, 836.5, 899.4
concurrent jurisdiction 594.1
concurrent resolution 613.5
concurring (n) 332.1 (a) 450.5, 788.9, 899.4
concuss 25.4, 902.13
concussed 25.8
concussion 85.38, 671.8, 902.3
concussive 902.24
cond 182.14
condemn 395.10, 510.13, 602.3, 946.13, 1000.6
condemnation 510.3, 598.9, 602.1, 946.5
condemnatory 510.22, 599.13, 602.5
condemned 602.6
condemned cell 429.8
condemned prisoner 429.11
condemn oneself 113.6
condemn to death 308.20
condemn to eternal punishment 682.6
condemn to hell 682.6
condensability 260.5
condensable 260.11
condensation 238.7, 251.2, 260.1, 268.3, 557.1, 803.1, 1045.3, 1061.2
condensation trail 184.30, 517.8
condense 238.18, 251.5, 260.7, 268.6, 537.5, 557.5, 1045.9, 1046.8
condensed 260.12, 268.9, 537.6, 557.6, 803.10, 1045.12
condensed version 557.1
condenser 29.2, 260.6, 1060.6, 1067.6
condescend 137.8, 141.8, 441.2
condescendence 137.3, 141.1
condescending 141.9
condescension 137.3, 141.1
condign 637.3, 639.8
condign punishment 604.1
condiment 10.12, 63.3
condition (n) 84.1, 85.1, 210.2, 245.2, 405.4, 421.2, 765.1, 766.1, 959.2 (v) 210.5, 373.9, 396.14, 405.8, 568.12, 568.13, 959.3, 959.4
conditional (n) 530.11 (a) 765.6, 766.7, 935.22, 959.8, 971.18
conditionality 959.1, 971.1
conditional phrase 529.1
conditional sale 734.1
condition book 757.4
conditioned 210.7, 373.15, 959.10, 963.14, 971.18
conditioned reflex 92.26, 903.1
conditioned response 92.26
conditioned stimulus 92.26
conditioning (n) 92.26, 373.7, 405.2, 568.2, 568.3, 963.5 (a) 81.5
condition of things 831.4
conditions 831.4
condo 228.14, 476.1
condolatory 121.13
condolement 147.1
condolence 121.4, 145.1, 147.1
condolences 145.1, 147.1
condolent 121.13, 145.7, 147.3
condole with 121.6, 145.3, 147.2
condoling 121.13, 147.3
condom 86.23
condominium 228.14, 476.1
condonable 600.14
condonance 148.1
condonation 148.1, 979.4
condone 134.7, 148.4, 443.10, 509.11, 979.7
condoned 148.7
condoning (n) 148.1 (a) 979.11
conduce 896.3
conduce to 449.17, 886.12
conduce to health 81.4
conducive 384.8, 449.21
conduct (n) 321.1, 328.2, 573.1, 889.1 (v) 176.12, 239.15, 328.8, 328.9, 573.8, 708.45, 769.8, 889.5
conduct a funeral 309.19
conductance 1032.14, 1033.9
conduct an inquiry 938.20
conduct a poll 938.29
conduct a trial 598.18
conduct business 724.12
conducted tour 177.5
conduction 1032.14
conductional 176.18
conductive 176.18
conductivity 1032.14
conduct oneself 321.4
conduct oneself in the face of 321.6
conduct oneself toward 321.6
conduct oneself vis-à-vis 321.6
conductor 178.13, 574.1, 574.6, 710.17, 769.5, 1032.14
conductor's baton 273.2, 711.22
conduct pleadings 598.19
conduct to 161.6
conduct unbecoming a gentleman 505.1
conduit 239.1, 290.2, 383.3
conduplication 874.1
condyle 283.3
cone (n) 50.8, 282.5, 310.11, 310.27 (v) 282.6
cone clutch 1040.10
coned 282.12
cone friction clutch 1040.10
conelet 282.5
conelike 282.12
cone of a complex 282.5
cone-shaped 270.15, 282.12
Conestoga wagon 179.2
cone vision 27.1
confab (n) 541.2, 541.5 (v) 541.8
confabulate 541.8
confabulation 354.9, 541.2, 541.5, 976.1
confabulator 541.7
confabulatory 541.12
confection 10.40, 405.3, 797.5
confectioners powdered sugar 66.3
confectioners sugar 66.3
confectionery 10.40, 66.1

confectionery decorator 716.11
confederacy 381.5, 450.2, 617.1, 805.1
confederate (n) 588.3, 616.1, 616.3 (v) 450.3, 769.7, 805.4 (a) 805.6
confederated 805.6
confederation 232.1, 450.2, 617.1, 805.1
confer 422.5, 422.7, 478.12, 541.10, 629.3
confer a benefit 143.12
confer a blessing upon 696.14
confer citizenship 226.4
confer distinction on 662.12
conference 48.2, 423.1, 423.3, 423.4, 541.5, 541.6, 698.8, 746.1, 770.2
conference at the summit 541.5
conference call 347.13, 423.3
conference championship 746.1
conference room 739.7
conference table 541.5
confer honor upon 662.12
conferment 478.1, 629.1, 698.10
conferral 478.1, 629.1
conferrer 478.11
confervoid 310.37
confer with 541.10
confess 332.11, 351.7, 658.5, 701.17, 888.4, 953.12
confessed 332.14, 351.10
confessing 351.3
confession 332.3, 334.1, 345.5, 351.3, 617.5, 658.2, 696.4, 888.2, 953.7, 957.2
confessional (n) 703.9 (a) 351.11, 953.27
confessionary 703.9
confessions 719.1
confessor 113.5, 699.5
confetti 47.6
confidant 422.3, 588.1, 616.7
confidante 422.3, 588.1
confide 124.6, 351.5, 478.16, 551.11
confide in 953.15, 953.17
confidence 106.3, 124.1, 130.1, 345.5, 492.2, 953.1, 970.5
confidence-building 953.26
confidence game 356.10
confidence man 357.1, 357.3
confidence trick 356.10
confidence trickster 357.3
confident 106.13, 124.10, 130.11, 492.19, 953.21, 970.21
confidential 345.14
confidential communication 345.5
confidential information 345.5, 551.2
confidentiality 345.2
confidentialness 345.2
confidentness 970.5
confide to 351.5, 551.11
confiding 416.5, 953.22
configurable 381.14
configurating 808.1
configuration 33.3, 92.32, 209.1, 211.2, 262.1, 262.5, 266.1, 807.1, 808.1, 865.4, 1073.5
configurationism 92.2
configuration language 1042.13
configure 381.8, 892.8
configured 808.14
confine (n) 211.3, 212.3 (v) 210.5, 212.6, 270.11, 428.9, 429.12, 798.4, 846.8, 866.4
confined 85.59, 210.7, 212.10, 231.9, 270.14, 428.15, 429.19, 866.5
confinement 1.1, 210.2, 212.1, 270.1, 428.3, 429.1, 604.2
confines 209.2, 211.1, 223.1, 231.1
confines of the law, the 594.1
confining (n) 798.2 (a) 210.9, 212.11, 428.12
confirm 15.13, 332.12, 373.9, 438.9, 701.15, 855.8, 942.8, 943.5, 957.11, 970.12
confirmability 957.7, 970.3
confirmable 957.19, 970.15
confirmation 332.4, 701.4, 701.6, 855.2, 938.3, 939.1, 943.2, 957.4, 970.8
confirmative 957.18
confirmatory 332.14, 957.18
confirmed 332.14, 373.18, 855.13, 942.12, 957.20, 973.13
confirmed bachelor 565.3
confirmed liar 357.9
confirmedness 373.6
confirmer 332.7
confirming 939.6, 957.18
confiscate 421.5, 480.20
confiscation 480.5
confiscatory 480.25
confiture 10.40
conflagrant 1019.27
conflagrate 1020.22
conflagration 1019.13
conflagrative 1019.26
conflate 797.10, 805.3
conflation 341.2, 797.1
conflexure 279.3
conflict (n) 92.17, 451.2, 456.1, 457.1, 457.4, 589.3, 779.1, 789.1, 900.1 (v) 35.15, 61.3, 456.8, 779.4, 789.5, 900.6
conflicting 35.21, 61.5, 451.8, 456.15, 589.10, 779.6, 900.8, 1011.13
conflict of sounds 61.2
conflict with 451.3, 779.4, 780.5, 900.6
confluence 169.1, 238.4, 770.1, 800.1, 899.1
confluence of minds 788.3
confluent (n) 238.3 (a) 169.3, 238.24
confluent stream 238.3
conflux 169.1, 238.4, 770.1
confocal 169.3, 208.13
conform 326.2, 579.4, 788.6, 867.3
conformable 373.13, 579.5, 788.9, 867.5
conformance 434.1, 788.1, 867.1
conformation 262.1, 262.5, 266.1, 788.1, 867.1
conformer 867.2
conforming 326.3, 434.4
conforming to reality 973.14
conformism 579.1
conformist (n) 336.4, 579.3, 867.2, 953.9 (a) 373.13, 867.6
conformity 264.1, 326.1, 373.1, 434.1, 579.1, 692.1, 784.1, 788.1, 867.1
conformity to fact 973.1
conformity to reality 973.1
conformity to the data 973.1
conformity to the evidence 973.1
conform to 332.9, 434.2
conform to fact 973.8
conform with 788.6
confound 96.15, 122.6, 127.19, 393.12, 395.10, 412.8, 513.5, 799.3, 811.3, 945.3, 958.5, 971.13, 1012.15
confounded 122.9, 412.14, 513.10, 799.4, 958.7, 971.25
confounding (n) 958.2, 1012.3 (a) 122.12, 958.6, 971.27, 1012.20
confoundment 971.3
confraternal 587.15
confraternity 450.2, 587.2, 617.3
confrere 588.3, 616.1
confrerie 617.3
confrication 1044.1
confront 167.3, 215.4, 216.8, 223.11, 451.5, 453.3, 454.3, 492.10, 840.2, 943.4, 1012.15
confrontation 215.1, 223.4, 541.5, 779.1, 943.1
confrontational 215.5, 216.10, 451.8, 779.6
confrontational occasion 935.4
confrontational politics 609.1
confrontation politics 609.1
confront each other 902.13
confronting 215.5, 216.10, 779.6
confrontive 215.5, 451.8, 779.6
confrontment 215.1, 943.1
confront with 216.8
Confucian 675.32
Confucianism 675.14
Confucianist (n) 675.24 (a) 675.32
Confucius 684.4, 921.2
confuse 96.15, 263.3, 799.3, 810.9, 811.3, 945.3, 971.15, 975.13, 985.7
confused 32.6, 61.5, 96.22, 139.12, 263.4, 799.4, 804.4, 810.16, 811.5, 971.19, 971.24, 985.12
confusing 971.27
confusion 96.4, 139.4, 263.1, 412.2, 418.2, 804.1, 810.2, 971.3, 985.3
confusion of sounds 61.2
confusion of tongues 810.5
confutability 971.2
confutable 958.10, 971.17
confutation 900.1, 939.2, 958.2
confutative 939.6, 958.6
confute 900.6, 939.5, 958.5
confuted 958.7
confuting 958.6
con game 356.10
conge 188.4
congeal 269.5, 803.6, 1024.11, 1045.10, 1062.10
congealed 803.10, 1024.14, 1045.14
congealing 1024.12
congealment 803.1, 1024.1, 1045.4
congelation 803.1, 1024.1, 1045.4
congener 227.5, 784.3
congeneracy 784.2
congeneric 559.6, 775.10, 784.13
congenerical 784.13
congenerous 775.10, 784.13
congenial 97.6, 143.14, 455.3, 582.22, 587.15, 775.9, 788.9
congeniality 97.1, 455.1, 582.1, 587.1, 788.1
congenital 767.8, 794.10
congenital defect 85.1
congenital disease 85.12
congenital heart disease 85.19
congenital hypophosphatasia 85.22
congeries 770.9, 800.1, 803.5, 805.1
congest 293.7, 794.7, 993.15, 1045.9
congested 85.60, 293.11, 794.11, 846.16, 855.16, 993.20, 1045.12
congestedness 1045.1
congestion 85.9, 293.3, 794.2, 993.3, 1045.1
congestive heart failure 85.19
conglobate (v) 803.6 (a) 803.10
conglobation 770.9, 803.1
conglobulate 282.7, 800.5
conglobulation 1045.3
conglomerate (n) 770.9, 770.13, 803.5, 1045.6, 1059.1 (v) 770.18, 797.10, 803.6 (a) 770.21, 797.14
conglomerated 803.10
conglomeration 770.9, 770.13, 797.6, 800.1, 803.1, 803.5, 805.1, 1045.6
conglutinate (v) 803.9 (a) 803.10
conglutinated 803.10
conglutination 803.1
congrats 149.1
congratulant 149.3
congratulate 149.2, 509.14
congratulate oneself 116.5, 136.5, 502.8
congratulation 149.1, 509.5
congratulational 149.3
congratulations 149.1
congratulatory 149.3
congregate (v) 770.16 (a) 770.21
congregated 770.21
congregation 48.6, 423.4, 696.9, 700.1, 770.1, 770.2
congregational 700.3
Congress 613.2
congress 75.7, 169.1, 343.1, 423.1, 541.5, 582.4, 613.1
congress 770.2
congressional 613.11
congressional caucus 609.9
congressional district 231.5, 609.16

congressional election 609.15
congressional immunity 430.8
Congressional investigation 938.4
Congressional Medal of Honor 646.6
Congressional Record 549.8
congressman 610.3
congresswoman 610.3
congruence 455.1, 778.1, 788.1
congruency 788.1
congruent 455.3, 778.8, 788.9
congruity 264.1, 788.1, 867.1
congruous 455.3, 788.9, 995.5
conic 282.12
conical 282.12
conic projection 159.5
conifer 310.10
coniferous 310.39
coniferous forest 310.12
coniferous tree 310.10
conjecturable 951.15
conjecturableness 951.6
conjectural 951.13, 971.17
conjecture (n) 951.3, 951.4, 952.2, 953.6 (v) 951.11
conjectured 951.14
conjecturer 951.8
conjoin 223.9, 253.4, 800.5, 899.2
conjoined 253.9, 766.8, 775.9, 800.13
conjoining 800.1
conjoint 476.9, 769.9, 775.9, 777.11, 800.12, 805.5, 899.4
conjugal 104.26, 563.18
conjugal bliss 563.1
conjugal bond 563.1
conjugality 563.1
conjugal knot 563.1
conjugal love 104.1
conjugal right 642.1
conjugate (n) 526.4 (v) 530.16, 800.5, 873.5 (a) 526.20, 775.9, 800.12, 805.5, 873.8
conjugated 873.8
conjugated protein 7.6
conjugation 78.3, 223.3, 526.3, 800.1, 805.1, 873.1
conjunct 775.9, 800.12
conjunction 223.3, 530.3, 800.1, 805.1, 899.1
conjunctiva 2.6
conjunctival 872.12
conjunctive 530.17, 766.8, 800.16, 805.5, 872.12
conjunctive adverb 530.3
conjunctivitis 85.14, 85.34
conjuncture 766.1
conjuration 356.5, 690.4, 691.4
conjure 356.14, 420.11, 440.11, 690.11, 852.8
conjurement 690.4
conjurer 357.2, 690.5, 707.1
conjure spirits 690.11
conjure up 420.11, 690.11, 986.15, 989.9
conjure up a vision 986.17
conjure up spirits 690.11
conjuror 976.2
conk (n) 283.8 (v) 3.22
conk off 307.19
conk out 16.9, 184.45, 307.19, 393.26, 395.23, 410.16
con man 357.4, 483.1
conn (n) 573.5 (v) 182.14
conn, the 573.1
connatal 767.8
connate 767.8, 775.10, 784.13
connateness 784.2
connatural 767.8, 775.10, 784.13
connaturality 784.2
connaturalize 784.8
connaturalness 784.2
connature 784.2
connect 87.22, 169.2, 223.9, 409.7, 745.5, 775.5, 775.6, 784.7, 800.5, 800.11, 803.7, 805.3, 812.4
connected (n) 709.14 (a) 521.11, 775.9, 800.13, 803.11, 812.8
connectedness 521.2, 775.1, 800.1, 803.2
connecting 223.16, 800.16, 872.12
connecting flight 184.9
connecting link 213.4, 800.4
connecting rod 800.4
connection 75.7, 87.21, 213.4, 223.3, 343.1, 383.3, 466.3, 559.1, 564.1, 576.4, 775.1, 775.4, 784.2, 800.1, 800.4, 803.2, 812.2
connectional 800.16, 872.12
connections 559.2, 894.2
connection with 888.1
connective 775.7, 800.16, 805.5, 872.12
connective tissue 2.3, 2.4
connective-tissue disease 85.10
connectivity 800.1
connectivum 2.3
connect up 812.4
connect with 803.7, 888.4
conner 183.8
conning 356.1, 375.3, 570.3, 573.1
conning tower 27.8
conniption 152.8
conniption fit 152.8
connivance 356.4, 381.5, 441.1, 443.2
connive 381.9, 899.2
connive at 148.4, 441.2, 443.10, 984.2
connivent 169.3, 381.13
conniver 357.10, 381.7
connivery 356.4
conniving 381.13, 450.5
connoisseur 413.11, 496.6, 770.15, 866.3, 946.7
connoisseur of food 8.16
connoisseurship 496.1, 496.4, 944.1
connotation 518.1, 519.2, 526.14
connotational 518.10
connotative 517.23, 518.10
connote 517.17, 518.8, 519.4, 957.8
connubial 563.18
conoid (n) 282.5 (a) 282.12
conoidal 282.12
con over 931.13
conquer 412.10, 432.9, 480.19
conquerable 1006.16
conquered 412.17
conquering (n) 412.1, 432.4 (a) 411.7
conquering hero 411.2
conqueror 411.2
conquest 104.11, 411.1, 412.1, 432.4, 480.4
conquistador 411.2, 461.5
cons 935.5
consanguine 559.6, 775.10
consanguineal 559.6
consanguinean (n) 559.2 (a) 559.6
consanguineous 559.6, 775.10
consanguinity 559.1, 560.4, 775.3
conscience 92.28, 636.5
conscience investment 729.4
conscienceless 645.16, 654.17
conscience money 481.2
conscience-smitten 113.8
conscience-stricken 113.8
conscientious 339.12, 434.4, 495.9, 641.13, 644.15
conscientiousness 339.3, 495.1, 636.5, 644.2
conscientious objector 333.3, 464.6
conscious 23.8, 24.11, 139.12, 306.12, 380.8, 928.15, 983.15
consciousness 23.1, 24.1, 306.2, 919.2, 920.9, 928.2, 983.1
consciousness-expanding 976.10
consciousness-expansion 976.7
consciousness raising 591.1
conscious of 928.16
conscious of one's place 155.8
conscious self 92.28
conscious uncoupling 566.1
conscript (n) 432.7, 461.18 (v) 458.18, 615.17
conscription 458.7, 458.8, 615.7
consecrate 477.11, 685.5, 698.12
consecrated 652.5, 685.8, 701.18
consecrated bread 701.7
consecrated elements 701.7
consecrate to 387.13
consecration 417.12, 477.4, 652.1, 685.3, 698.10
consecution 812.2, 815.1
consecutive 166.5, 803.11, 812.9, 835.4
consecutive intervals 709.20
consecutiveness 803.2, 812.1, 815.1
consensual 332.13, 437.10, 450.5
consensus (n) 332.5, 450.1, 788.3 (a) 450.5
consensus building 465.4
consensus-building 788.4
consensus of opinion 332.5
consensus politics 609.1
consensus seeking 465.4
consensus-seeking 788.4
consent (n) 324.1, 326.1, 332.1, 332.5, 433.1, 441.1, 443.1 (v) 324.3, 332.8, 433.6, 441.2, 443.9
consentaneity 332.5, 788.3
consentaneous 332.15, 788.9
consentaneousness 788.3
consentant 441.4
consenter 332.6
consentient 332.13, 441.4, 788.9
consenting 324.5, 326.3, 332.13, 433.12, 441.4, 443.14
consenting adult 75.7
consent to by implication 441.2
consent to silently 441.2
consentual 441.4
consequence 247.2, 417.4, 518.1, 662.5, 817.1, 831.1, 835.2, 887.1, 894.1, 946.4, 997.1
consequent (n) 887.1, 946.4 (a) 166.5, 815.4, 887.6
consequential 140.8, 247.6, 417.15, 662.17, 887.6, 894.13, 997.17
consequentiality 140.1, 997.4
consequentialness 140.1, 997.4
conservation 386.5, 397.1, 853.2
conservational 397.12
conservationism 397.1
conservationist (n) 397.5, 853.4, 1069.7, 1072.3 (a) 397.12
conservation land 310.13
conservatism 611.1, 670.1, 853.3
conservatist 611.9, 853.4
Conservative 675.30
conservative (n) 219.1, 361.6, 611.9, 670.4 (a) 219.4, 397.12, 496.7, 611.17, 670.12
conservative (n) 842.8, 853.4 (a) 853.8
conservative estimate 350.1, 950.1
Conservative Jew 675.21
Conservative Judaism 675.12
conservativeness 611.1, 853.3
Conservative Party 609.24
conservator 397.5, 1008.6
conservatory (n) 197.5, 228.12, 386.6, 567.7, 1069.11 (a) 397.12
conserve (n) 10.40 (v) 386.12, 397.8, 635.4, 1008.19
conserved 386.15, 397.13
conserving 397.12, 635.6
consider 143.10, 339.6, 541.11, 931.12, 931.16, 946.8, 951.10, 953.11, 959.5
considerable (n) 247.4 (a) 247.6, 257.16, 417.15, 884.6, 997.17
considerate 24.12, 143.16, 339.10, 504.13, 920.19
considerateness 24.3, 143.3, 504.1, 652.2
consideration 143.3, 155.1, 338.2, 339.1, 375.1, 478.5, 504.1, 541.6, 624.3, 652.2, 662.3, 920.7, 931.2, 935.5, 946.5, 953.6, 961.1, 983.1, 997.1
consider both sides of the question 362.7
considered 380.8, 935.21
consider every angle 494.6

consider the circumstances 959.5
consider the pros and cons 541.11
consider the source 959.5
consign 176.10, 176.15, 429.17, 478.16, 615.10, 629.3
consignable 176.18, 629.5
consignation 417.12, 615.1, 629.1
consigned to oblivion 990.8
consignee 479.3, 576.3
consignment 429.4, 478.2, 615.1, 629.1
consignment clothes 5.5
consignment shop 736.1
consignment store 635.1, 736.1
consignor 478.11
consign to a place 159.11
consign to earth 309.19
consign to hell 682.6
consign to oblivion 990.6
consign to the grave 309.19
consign to the scrap heap 390.8
consilience 899.1
consilient 899.4
consimilar 784.10
consimilarity 784.1
consist 796.3
consistence 1045.1
consistency 264.1, 294.1, 521.2, 781.1, 788.1, 803.2, 803.3, 867.1, 1045.1
consistent 521.11, 644.20, 781.5, 788.9, 803.11, 973.14
consist in 761.11
consisting of 796.4
consist of 796.3
consistory 423.4
consist with 788.6
consociate (n) 588.3, 616.1 (v) 769.7, 805.4
consociation 450.2, 582.6, 769.2, 899.1
consolan 159.3, 182.2, 184.6, 1036.3
consolation 120.1, 121.4, 147.1, 677.15
consolation prize 646.2
consolatory 121.13, 147.3
console (n) 711.17, 1034.3, 1034.7, 1041.16 (v) 121.6, 147.2
console game 743.9
consoler 121.5
consolidate 251.5, 260.7, 450.3, 805.3, 1045.9
consolidated 260.12, 803.10, 805.5, 1045.12
consolidation 251.2, 260.1, 450.2, 803.1, 803.5, 805.1, 1045.3, 1059.8
consoling 121.13
consomme 10.10
consonance 708.3, 720.9, 781.1, 788.1
consonancy 708.3
consonant (n) 524.12 (a) 524.30, 708.49, 781.5, 788.9
consonantal 524.30
consort 563.6, 588.3, 616.1, 708.3, 769.4, 788.1
consorting 582.2
consortium 437.1, 437.2, 617.9, 788.2
consortship 587.2, 769.2
consort with 582.17, 769.7
conspecific 784.13
conspectus 268.3, 557.1
conspicuity 31.2
conspicuous 31.7, 247.10, 348.12, 662.17, 997.19
conspicuous by its absence 222.11
conspicuous consumption 626.2
conspicuous consumption conspicuous waste 486.1
conspicuous gallantry 492.1
conspicuousness 31.2, 348.4, 662.5
conspiracy 345.4, 356.4, 381.5, 415.3, 805.1, 899.1
conspiracy theory 899.1
conspirator 357.10, 381.7
conspiratorial 381.13, 805.6, 899.4
conspire 381.9, 450.3, 805.4, 899.2
conspirer 357.10, 381.7
conspiring 381.13
constable 1008.15
constablery 594.4
constablese 523.10
constablewick 231.5, 594.4
constabulary 594.4, 1008.17
constancy 359.2, 360.1, 587.7, 644.7, 781.1, 781.2, 812.1, 827.1, 829.1, 847.2, 850.1, 853.1, 855.1
constant 35.18, 359.12, 360.8, 373.14, 434.4, 587.21, 644.20, 781.5, 812.8, 827.10, 829.7, 847.5, 850.6, 853.7, 855.17, 973.17
constant attention 983.4
constant flow 812.1, 847.2
constant friend 588.2
constantly revert to 849.9
constant pressure 184.25
constant thrust 1074.8
constellation 662.9, 964.2, 1073.5
consternated 127.25
consternation 127.1
constipate 293.7
constipated 293.11
constipation 85.9, 85.29, 293.3
constituency 227.1, 384.2, 609.22, 617.12, 894.4, 901.1
constituent (n) 793.1, 793.2, 796.2, 1052.2 (a) 371.23, 767.9, 796.5
constituent elements 763.2
constituents 196.1, 609.22, 763.2, 767.4
constitute 613.10, 673.9, 772.3, 796.3, 892.10
constitute a whole 792.7
constituted 808.14
constituted authority 417.1
constituting 796.4
constitution 196.1, 266.1, 294.1, 613.5, 673.6, 767.4, 796.1, 808.1, 892.4, 978.3
constitutional (n) 84.2, 177.10, 725.6 (a) 81.5, 612.16, 673.11, 767.8, 978.7
constitutional amendment 673.6
constitutional convention 609.8
constitutional freedom 430.1
constitutional government 612.4
constitutional guarantees 673.6
constitutional interpretation 673.6
constitutionalism 612.7, 673.1, 673.7
constitutionality 673.1
constitutional law 673.5
constitutional monarchy 612.4
constitutional referendum 613.8
constitutional rights 430.2, 642.3
constitutional validity 673.1
Constitution of the U.S. 673.8
Constitution Party 609.24
constitutive 767.9, 886.13
constrain 210.5, 424.4, 428.7, 429.12, 670.6, 963.8
constrained 139.11, 344.10, 428.13, 670.11
constraining 424.10, 428.11
constrain oneself 668.6
constraint 139.3, 344.3, 359.5, 375.6, 424.1, 428.1, 429.1, 668.1, 670.1
constrict 260.7, 270.11, 293.6, 1012.12
constricted 260.12, 270.14, 293.9, 980.10
constriction 260.1, 270.2, 1012.1
constrictive 1012.17
constrict one's views 980.6
constrictor 260.6
constringe 260.7
constringency 260.1
constringent 260.11
construability 341.6
construable 341.17
construct (n) 266.2 (v) 266.5, 796.3, 892.8, 1043.4
constructed 892.18
constructed language 523.6, 523.11
construction 266.1, 266.2, 341.1, 518.3, 526.4, 529.1, 796.1, 892.2
constructional 266.6, 341.14, 892.15
construction engineer 1043.2
construction engineering 1043.1
constructionism 341.1
constructionist 341.7
construction language 1042.13
construction modifier 530.2
construction site 739.1
construction worker 726.2
constructive 341.14, 449.21, 892.16
constructive change 852.1
constructive criticism 422.1, 449.2
constructive metabolism 2.20
construct of memory and association 932.2
constructor 892.7
construe 341.9, 341.12, 935.15
construing 530.1
consubstantial 778.7, 781.5
consubstantiality 778.1, 781.1
consubstantiation 701.7, 852.3
consuetude 373.1
consuetudinary 373.13
consul 576.6
consular 576.17
consular agent 576.6
consular service 576.7
consulate 228.5, 417.7, 417.10, 739.7
consul general 576.6
consulship 417.7
consult 422.7, 541.10, 724.12
consultancy 422.1
consultant 413.11, 422.3, 726.2
consultantship 422.1
consultation 422.1, 541.5
consultation room 197.25
consultative 422.8, 423.5
consultative assembly 423.1
consultatory 422.8
consulting room 197.25
consultive 422.8
consult one's better self 113.6
consult one's own wishes 651.4
consult one's pillow about 846.9
consult with 422.5, 541.10, 931.14
consumable (n) 388.2 (a) 8.33, 388.6
consumable goods 388.2
consumable item 388.2
consume 8.22, 252.6, 260.9, 387.13, 388.3, 393.19, 395.10, 473.5, 486.4, 626.5, 806.3, 1020.25
consume away 252.6, 393.19
consumed 252.10, 260.13, 388.5, 473.7, 486.9, 1020.30
consumed by fire 1020.30
consumed with curiosity 981.5
consumed with desire 100.24
consumer 8.16, 387.9, 733.5
consumer confidence 733.1
consumer cooperative 617.1
consumer credit 622.1
consumer demand 733.3
consumer durable 735.4
consumer goods 471.2, 735.1
consumerism 733.1
consumer items 735.1
consumer power 733.1
consumer preference study 734.2
consumer-preference survey 938.14
consumer price index 630.4, 731.8, 731.9, 733.1
consumer research 734.2, 938.14
consumer researcher 938.18
consumer resistance 734.6
consumer society 733.1
consumer sovereignty 733.1

consumers strike 727.5
consumer survey 734.2
consume time 331.13, 821.6
consuming (n) 8.1, 388.1 (a) 98.23, 395.26, 983.20
consummate (v) 198.10, 407.4 (a) 198.11, 247.12, 407.10, 407.12, 413.22, 794.10, 1002.9
consummated 407.10
consummate liar 357.9
consummate lie 354.12
consummate one's marriage 563.16
consummating 198.12
consummation 75.7, 407.1, 794.4, 820.1, 1002.3
consummative 407.9, 794.13, 820.11
consummatory 794.13, 820.11
consumption 8.1, 85.17, 252.3, 260.3, 387.1, 388.1, 393.4, 395.1, 473.2, 626.1
consumption tax 630.9
consumptive (n) 85.43 (a) 85.61, 260.11, 395.26
contact (n) 73.1, 87.21, 223.5, 343.1, 552.10, 576.4 (v) 48.12, 223.10, 343.8, 524.22 (a) 523.23
contact flying 184.1
contact hitter 745.2
contacting 223.17
contact lens 29.3
contact lenses 29.3
contact person 552.1
contact poison 1001.3
contact print 785.5
contact printing 714.5
contacts 29.3
contact sport 744.1
contact with reality 925.1
contagion 85.4
contagion effect 886.3
contagious 82.7, 85.62, 176.18, 343.11
contagiousness 82.3, 85.4, 343.4
contagium 85.42
contain 158.9, 207.5, 210.5, 212.5, 212.9, 293.6, 428.7, 772.3, 772.4, 792.8, 796.3, 1022.7
contained 1022.11
contained in 796.4
container 195.1, 212.3, 284.2
containerize 176.15, 295.20
containerload 196.2
container ship 180.1
containing (n) 212.1 (a) 772.6, 796.4
containment 209.5, 210.1, 212.1, 609.5
contain oneself 134.4, 668.6
contaminate 80.17, 85.51, 393.12, 694.5, 797.12, 1037.10
contaminated 80.20, 82.5, 85.60, 654.14, 1037.11
contamination 80.4, 82.1, 85.4, 393.2, 526.11, 694.2, 797.3, 1037.1, 1072.2
contango 624.1
contemn 157.3, 372.2
contemned 372.3
contemplate 27.14, 130.5, 380.5, 570.12, 931.12, 931.16, 931.17, 961.5
contemplated 380.8, 935.21
contemplate in the imagination 986.15
contemplating 931.21, 983.17
contemplation 27.6, 130.1, 173.1, 329.1, 570.3, 683.10, 691.3, 696.4, 931.2, 961.1, 983.3
contemplation of the past 989.3
contemplative 329.6, 931.21, 983.17
contemplative life 329.1
contemplativeness 931.3
contemporaneity 836.1, 838.1
contemporaneous 836.5, 838.2
contemporaneousness 836.1, 838.1
contemporary (n) 836.2 (a) 836.5, 838.2, 841.13
contemporary art 712.1
contemporary literature 547.12, 718.1
contemporary theater 704.1
contemporize 836.4
contempt 103.1, 142.1, 156.1, 156.2, 157.1, 372.1, 454.1, 510.2, 512.1
contemptibility 98.2, 661.3
contemptible 98.18, 103.8, 661.12, 998.21, 1000.9
contemptibleness 98.2, 661.3, 998.2, 1000.2
contempt of court 142.1
contemptuous 103.7, 141.13, 142.9, 156.8, 157.8, 372.4, 435.5, 454.7, 510.22, 512.13
contemptuous dismissal 157.2
contemptuousness 141.5, 142.1, 157.1, 454.1
contend 215.4, 334.5, 421.8, 457.13, 457.18, 725.11, 935.16
contend about 457.21
contend against 451.4
contender 452.2, 461.1, 743.19
contend for 403.9, 457.20, 600.10
contending 457.22
contend with 387.12, 453.3, 457.17
content (n) 95.1, 107.1, 196.1, 257.2 (v) 107.4 (a) 95.15, 107.7, 324.5, 332.13, 441.4
content creation 547.2
contented 95.15, 107.7, 121.11
contentedness 107.1
contention 215.1, 451.1, 456.1, 456.5, 457.1, 589.3, 935.4, 958.2
contentious 110.26, 119.5, 458.20, 589.10, 935.19
contentiousness 110.7, 119.1, 456.3, 457.1, 458.10, 935.13
contentment 95.1, 107.1, 121.1, 402.2, 994.1
content oneself with 107.5
content provider 1042.19
contents 196.1, 554.12, 871.2, 937.1
contents page 554.12
content word 526.1
conterminous 223.16, 836.5
conterminousness 223.3
contest (n) 451.1, 457.1, 457.3, 743.9, 744.1 (v) 335.4, 451.4, 451.6, 457.13, 457.21, 935.16, 955.6
contestability 971.2
contestable 971.17
contestant (n) 452.2, 461.1, 743.18 (a) 457.22
contest a seat 609.39
contestation 457.1
contested 955.12
contested election 609.15
contesting 457.22
contest of fleetness 457.12
contest of speed 457.12
context 209.1, 766.2
context clue 523.14
contextual 766.8
contexture 266.1, 294.1
contiguity 223.3, 775.1
contiguous 223.16, 803.11
contiguousness 223.3
continence 210.2, 565.1, 664.3, 668.2, 670.1
continency 664.3
continent (n) 231.6, 235.1 (a) 664.6, 668.10
Continental 860.3
continental, a 998.5
continental (n) 235.3 (a) 235.6
continental breakfast 8.6
Continental Divide 237.6, 272.5
continental divide 235.1
continental drift 235.1
Continental grip 748.2
continental island 235.2
continentalist 235.3
continental landform 235.1
continental quilt 295.10
continental shelf 231.1, 240.5
continental slope 240.5
continent of galaxies 1073.6
contingence 223.5
contingency 432.3, 766.1, 768.2, 775.2, 831.1, 897.1, 959.2, 966.1, 971.1, 971.8, 972.6
contingency fund 728.14, 728.19
contingency plan 381.1, 903.3, 961.2
contingent (n) 477.5, 768.2, 770.3, 793.1, 831.1, 972.6 (a) 223.17, 763.6, 766.7, 768.4, 831.11, 959.7, 959.9, 966.6, 971.18, 972.15
contingent being 763.3
contingent interest 471.4
contingent on 959.9
continual 812.8, 829.7, 847.5
continualness 812.1, 829.1, 847.2, 856.1
continuance 817.1, 827.1, 829.1, 853.1, 856.1
continuant (n) 524.12 (a) 524.30
continuate 812.4
continuation 254.1, 624.1, 815.1, 817.1, 827.2, 846.4, 856.1
continue 267.6, 306.11, 360.2, 812.4, 821.5, 827.6, 827.9, 846.9, 847.3, 856.3
continued 812.8
continued fraction 1017.7
continue the same 781.3
continue to be 827.6
continue to exist 761.9
continuing 360.8, 812.8, 827.10, 853.7, 856.7
continuing-care retirement community 1009.4
continuing education 567.5
continuing education student 572.1
continuity 704.21, 722.4, 781.1, 803.2, 807.2, 812.1, 815.1, 821.1, 847.2, 852.1, 853.1, 856.1
continuo 708.22
continuous 221.13, 781.5, 803.11, 812.8, 821.7, 829.7, 849.13, 856.7
continuous creation theory 1073.18
continuousness 812.1
continuous partial attention 984.1
continuous stationery 1042.10
continuous tenure 825.4
continuous wave 916.4
continuum 158.1, 158.6, 221.2, 812.2
continuum theory 158.6
contorse 26.7
contort 164.5, 265.5, 281.4, 342.2
contorted 265.10
contorting 342.1
contortion 164.2, 265.1
contortional 265.9
contortive 265.9
contour (n) 211.2, 262.2 (v) 211.9
contour farmer 1069.5
contour feather 3.16
contour feathers 3.18
contour line 159.5
contour map 574.10
contour plowing 1069.13
contour sheet 295.10
Contra 461.16
contra (n) 327.5, 452.3 (a) 335.5, 451.8
contraband (n) 444.1, 732.2, 732.3 (a) 444.7, 674.6
contrabandage 732.2
contrabandist 732.5
contrabassist 710.5
contraception 86.23, 891.1
contraceptive 86.23, 900.3, 1008.3
contraceptive foam 86.23
contract (n) 404.1, 436.2, 437.1, 731.5 (v) 85.47, 258.9, 260.7, 268.6, 270.11, 293.6, 436.5, 436.6, 437.5, 472.8, 897.4
contract a debt 623.6
contract an engagement 436.6
contract bridge 758.3
contracted 252.10, 260.12, 293.9, 436.8, 437.11, 537.6

contract for 437.5
contractibility 260.5
contractible 260.11
contractile 260.11
contractility 260.5
contraction 252.1, 260.1, 268.3, 270.2, 537.4, 547.8
contractional 260.11
contractive 252.11, 260.11
contract killer 308.11, 671.9
contract matrimony 563.15
contract murder 308.2
contract oneself 404.3
contractor 260.6
contract out 437.5
contract player 707.4
contracts law 673.5
contractual 404.7, 437.10
contracture 260.1
contradict 335.4, 372.2, 451.6, 779.4, 789.5, 900.6, 958.5
contradicted 958.7
contradicting 335.5, 900.8
contradiction 335.2, 372.1, 442.1, 451.1, 539.1, 779.1, 789.1, 900.1, 958.2
contradict itself 967.4
contradictive 335.5
contradictory 335.5, 451.8, 779.6, 789.6, 900.8, 936.11, 958.6
contradistinct 779.6
contradistinction 255.8, 779.1, 944.3
contradistinguish 944.4
contradition in terms 936.3
contrail 184.30, 517.8
contraindicate 379.3
contraindicated 444.7, 923.10, 996.5
contraindication 379.1, 779.1
contralto (n) 708.22, 709.5 (v) 54.9 (a) 54.11
contraoctave 709.9
contrapose 215.4, 779.4, 900.6
contraposit 215.4
contraposition 215.1, 451.1, 779.1, 900.1
contrapositive 215.5, 779.6
contrapositives 215.2
contraption 1040.1
contrapuntal 708.52
contrapuntist 710.20
contrapunto 708.20
contraremonstrance 939.2
contraries 215.2
contrariety 98.2, 215.1, 451.2, 775.1, 779.1, 780.1, 791.1, 868.1, 900.1
contrariness 361.3, 451.2
contrarious 335.5, 779.6
contrary (n) 205.4 (a) 335.5, 361.11, 451.8, 779.6, 780.7, 789.6, 868.5, 958.6, 1011.13, 1012.17, 1013.19
contrary, the 779.2
contrary assertion 335.2
contrary to expectation 131.10
contrary to fact 354.25
contrary to law 674.6
contrary to reason 936.11, 967.7
contrast (n) 215.1, 779.1, 780.1, 787.1, 943.1, 1025.4, 1025.19 (v) 215.4, 943.4
contrastable 944.9
contrast bath 91.3
contrasted 779.6, 780.7
contrasting 780.7, 787.4
contrastive 50.16, 780.9, 944.7
contrastive juxtaposition 215.1
contrastiveness 943.1
contrast with 779.4, 780.5
contravene 335.4, 435.4, 451.6, 674.5, 779.4, 900.6, 1012.15
contravention 335.2, 435.2, 451.1, 674.3
contraversion 451.1
contretemps 844.2, 1011.2
contribute 385.7, 476.5, 478.14, 896.3
contribute to 162.5, 449.17, 478.14, 886.12
contributing 449.21
contribution 421.1, 476.1, 478.1, 478.6, 556.1, 630.9
contributor 478.11, 485.2
contributory 253.10, 449.21, 478.25
contrite 113.9
contriteness 113.1
contrition 113.1, 658.2
contriturate 1051.9
contrivance 381.1, 381.5, 384.4, 415.3, 722.4, 892.1, 995.2, 1040.1
contrive 381.8, 409.12, 415.10, 765.5, 886.11, 892.12
contrived 381.12
contriver 381.6
contriving (n) 381.5, 892.1 (a) 381.13
control (n) 249.3, 359.5, 413.1, 417.5, 428.1, 432.1, 573.1, 612.2, 670.1, 678.12, 894.1, 942.1, 988.1, 1041.14 (v) 184.37, 417.13, 428.7, 573.8, 612.12, 670.6, 894.8, 988.6
control action 1041.3
control agent 1041.3
control board 1034.7
control center 208.5, 1074.7
control character 1042.18
control desk 1034.7
control element 1041.14
control engineer 1034.24, 1041.19
control experiment 942.1
control freak 359.1
control gate 753.1
control group 90.1
controllability 433.4
controllable 433.14
controlled 106.13, 359.15, 428.13, 670.11
controlled association 92.33
controlled experiment 942.1
controlled force 462.22
controlled substance 86.5, 87.3
controlled vocabulary 530.1
controller 574.2, 628.7, 729.12, 1041.14, 1042.18
controllership 573.1, 628.6
controlling (n) 1022.2 (a) 417.15, 428.11, 573.12, 612.17, 997.24
control means 1041.3
control mechanism 1041.14
control of electromagnetic radiation for civil defense 460.2
control one's appetites 668.6
control oneself 106.7, 668.6
control panel 1034.7, 1041.16
control program monitor 1042.12
control room 1034.7
control station 1036.6
control system 1041.5
control the carnal man 668.6
control the fleshy lusts 668.6
control the old Adam 668.6
control the price of 630.11
control tower 184.22, 272.6
contronym 530.5
controversial 110.26, 935.19, 971.17
controversialist 935.12
controversiality 971.1
controversial point 938.10
controversion 335.2, 958.2
controversy 456.5, 457.1, 789.1, 935.4, 938.10
controvert 335.4, 451.6, 541.11, 779.4, 958.5
controvertibility 971.2
controvertible 958.9, 971.17
contumacious 156.8, 327.10, 361.12
contumaciousness 327.2, 361.4
contumacy 327.2, 361.4
contumelious 141.13, 142.9, 156.8, 157.8, 512.13, 513.8
contumeliousness 141.5
contumely 142.1, 156.2, 157.1, 510.7, 513.2
conturbation 917.1
contuse 393.13
contusion 85.38
contusive 671.16
conundrum 522.9, 938.10, 971.3, 1013.7
conurbation 230.1
convalesce 396.19
convalescence 396.8
convalescent 396.23
convalescent home 91.21
convected heat 1019.1
convector heat 1019.1
convene 420.11, 770.17
convener 574.5
convenership 573.4
convenience (n) 12.10, 121.2, 223.1, 387.4, 402.1, 449.9, 843.1, 995.1, 1014.2, 1040.3 (a) 387.20, 405.19
convenience-food 830.4
convenience foods 10.5
conveniences 121.3, 385.4
convenience store 736.1
convenient 121.11, 223.15, 387.20, 405.19, 843.9, 995.5, 1014.15
convent 703.6
convenitical 703.16
conventicle 703.1, 770.2
convention 373.1, 419.2, 423.4, 437.1, 437.2, 541.5, 578.1, 579.1, 580.3, 609.8, 770.2
conventional 373.13, 419.4, 437.10, 499.6, 579.5, 580.8, 687.7, 842.12, 867.6, 869.9, 1005.8
conventional grip 750.2
conventionalism 579.1
conventionalist 579.3, 867.2
conventionality 579.1, 867.1, 1005.2
conventionalization 580.1
conventionalize 580.5
conventionalized 580.7
conventional medicine 90.13
conventional phrase 529.1
conventional programming language 1042.13
conventional representation 349.1
conventional symbol 517.2
conventional usage 579.1
conventional weapons 462.1
conventional wisdom 864.8, 920.5, 953.6, 974.1
conventioneer 617.11
conventioner 617.11
convention hall 197.4
conventionist 617.11
conventions, the 579.2
conventual (n) 699.16, 699.17 (a) 698.14
conventual prior 699.16
converge 169.2, 208.10, 223.7, 770.16, 800.11
convergence 169.1, 208.8, 223.1, 238.4, 770.1, 800.1
convergence of events 843.4
convergent 169.3
convergent evolution 861.3
convergent strabismus 28.5
converging (n) 169.1 (a) 169.3, 208.13
conversable 343.10
conversableness 343.3, 540.1
conversance 587.5
conversant 413.26
conversant with 373.16, 928.19
conversate 343.1
conversation 343.1, 524.1, 541.1, 582.4
conversational 343.9, 523.20, 540.9, 541.12
conversational English 523.5
conversational interchange 541.1
conversationalism 523.5
conversationalist 524.17, 541.7
conversational partner 541.7
conversationist 541.7
conversation piece 870.5
converse (n) 205.4, 215.3, 343.1, 541.1, 582.4 (v) 343.6, 524.19, 541.8 (a) 215.5, 777.8, 779.6
converse, the 779.2
converser 541.7
converse with 541.8
conversing 541.1

conversion 389.1, 392.5, 482.1, 685.4, 746.3, 852.1, 858.1, 858.6, 892.2, 990.3
conversion disorder 92.14
conversion factor 630.2
conversion value 630.2
convert (n) 363.5, 572.2, 692.4, 858.7 (v) 205.5, 389.4, 685.6, 737.24, 852.7, 858.11, 863.4, 892.9, 953.18
converted 392.13, 685.9, 692.10, 852.10, 858.19, 990.9
converted split 750.2
converter 858.9, 858.10
convertibility 728.9, 790.1, 854.1, 858.1, 863.3
convertible 728.31, 790.8, 858.18, 863.5
convert into cash 728.29, 734.8
convertor 1035.11
convert to use 387.14
convex (n) 283.3 (a) 279.10, 282.8, 283.13
convexed 283.13
convexedness 283.1
convexity 279.1, 282.1, 283.1, 517.7
convex mirror 29.6
convexness 283.1
convexoconcave 279.10
convey 176.12, 239.15, 343.7, 518.8, 524.22, 551.8, 629.3
conveyability 343.4
conveyable 176.18, 343.11, 629.5
conveyance 179.1, 343.2, 482.1, 629.1
conveyancing 629.1
convey an impression of 349.8
convict (n) 429.11, 660.9 (v) 598.20, 602.3
convicted 602.6
conviction 124.1, 602.1, 953.5, 970.5
convictional 953.25, 953.26
convict release 431.2
convince 375.23, 858.16, 953.18, 973.9
convinced 953.21, 970.21
convincedness 953.1
convince oneself 953.19
convince otherwise 379.3
convince to the contrary 379.3
convincing 953.26, 957.16
convincingness 953.8
convivial 582.23, 743.28
conviviality 109.1, 582.3, 743.3
convocation 420.5, 423.4, 580.4, 770.2
convoke 420.11, 770.17
convoking 420.5
convolute 281.4, 545.7
convoluted 281.6, 545.8, 799.4
convolutedness 281.1
convolution 279.1, 281.1, 545.1, 799.1, 914.1
convolutional 281.6
convolve 281.4
convoy (n) 769.5, 1008.14 (v) 182.46, 769.8
convulse 26.7, 96.18, 743.21, 811.4, 917.10
convulsed 26.9, 96.25, 810.13
convulsion 85.6, 85.9, 105.9, 116.4, 152.8, 395.3, 671.5, 811.1, 860.1, 917.6, 926.7
convulsive 671.23, 917.19
convulsive therapy 92.35
coo 52.10, 60.5, 524.25
co-occur 836.4
co-occurrence 769.1, 836.1
co-occurring 836.5
cook (n) 11.3, 577.8 (v) 11.5, 354.17, 393.11, 395.11, 965.5, 1019.22, 1020.17
cook accounts 628.10
cookbook 11.4, 554.8
cooked 11.7, 354.30, 393.29, 965.8
cooked-up 354.29, 965.8
cooker 11.4, 1020.10
cookery 11.1, 11.4, 1020.10
cookery book 554.8
cook for 7.17, 385.9
cookhouse 8.17, 11.4
cookie 10.43, 104.10
cookie-cutter 778.7, 781.5, 812.8, 867.6
cookie-cutter copy 778.3, 785.3
cooking (n) 11.1, 354.9, 1020.1 (a) 11.6
cooking area 11.4
cooking with gas 409.14
cookoff 457.3
cook one's goose 395.11, 412.9, 1012.16
cook out 8.21
cookout 8.6
cookroom 11.4
cookshack 8.17
cookshop 8.17
Cook's tour 20.3
cook the accounts 354.17
cook the books 354.17, 482.16, 628.10
cook up 11.5, 354.18, 365.8, 381.9, 892.12, 965.5
cookware 11.4
cool (n) 106.2, 123.1, 670.1, 781.1, 855.1 (v) 379.4, 428.7, 465.7, 670.7, 1024.10 (a) 35.16, 94.9, 102.6, 106.12, 122.10, 123.3, 141.12, 142.9, 173.12, 344.10, 494.8, 583.6, 589.9, 670.13, 855.12, 920.18, 999.13, 1023.12, 1023.16
cool acceptance 123.1
coolant 1024.7, 1024.8
cool as a cucumber 106.12, 123.3, 129.2
cool breeze 318.4
cool cat 659.1
cool color 35.3, 35.6
cool customer 415.6
cool down 106.7, 428.7
cooled 1024.13
cooler 10.49, 429.9, 757.2, 1024.3
coolerman 1024.6
cool head 129.1, 920.6
coolheaded 106.12, 129.2, 920.18
coolheadedness 106.2, 920.6
coolhouse 1024.6, 1069.11
cooling (n) 428.1, 635.2, 1024.1 (a) 1024.12
cooling breeze 318.4
cooling down 428.1, 635.2
cooling off 428.1, 465.2, 635.2, 731.10
cooling-off 670.15
cooling off of the economy 633.4
cooling-off period 465.2, 465.5, 857.3
cooling of the economy 633.4
cooling one's heels 846.3
cooling system 317.10
cooling tower 1024.6
coolish 1023.12
cool it 106.7, 107.5, 465.9, 670.5, 1014.12
cool jazz 708.9
cool judgment 920.7
cool million 618.2
coolness 94.1, 102.1, 106.2, 123.1, 141.4, 344.3, 494.1, 583.2, 589.1, 920.6, 1023.1, 1023.3
cool off 106.7, 428.7
cool off the economy 633.6, 731.21
cool of the evening, the 315.2
cool one's heels 130.8, 329.2, 846.14
cool one's jets 329.2
coolth 1023.1
cool the economy 633.6, 731.21
coom 1020.16, 1021.2
coon 311.22
coon's age 827.4
co-op 228.14, 736.1
coop (n) 212.3, 228.22, 429.7, 429.9, 476.1 (v) 212.5, 429.12
cooped 212.10
cooped up 212.10
cooperant 450.5, 899.4
cooperate 324.3, 450.3, 476.6, 777.6, 788.6, 863.4, 899.2
cooperating 450.5, 777.9, 788.9, 800.12
cooperation 449.10, 450.1, 476.2, 582.6, 777.3, 788.1, 863.1, 899.1
cooperative (n) 228.14, 476.1, 617.1, 736.1 (a) 324.5, 449.22, 450.5, 476.9, 587.16, 777.9, 777.11, 788.9, 800.12, 899.4, 901.23
cooperative credit union 622.1
cooperativeness 324.1, 450.1
cooperative society 476.2, 617.1
cooperator 616.4
coop in 212.5, 429.12
co-opt 371.13
co-optation 371.1
co-option 371.1
coop up 212.5, 429.12
coordinate (n) 784.3 (v) 264.3, 788.7, 790.6, 808.10 (a) 264.4, 790.8, 899.4
coordinate clause 529.1
coordinated 413.22
coordinated operations 458.4
coordinated panel 1041.16
coordinates 159.1, 211.1, 300.5
coordinating conjunction 530.3
coordination 264.2, 413.1, 788.4, 790.2, 808.2, 1041.7
coordinator 808.5
cootie 311.36
cop (n) 282.5, 1008.16 (v) 472.9, 482.16
copacetic 999.13
cop a feel 223.10
cop a plea 351.7, 369.7
coparcenary 479.2
coparcener 479.5
co-parent (n) 559.5, 560.8 (v) 449.16
co-parenting 449.3
copartner 476.4, 588.3, 616.2
copartnership 450.2, 476.1
copartnery 450.2, 476.1
cope (n) 702.2, 1073.2 (v) 295.19, 385.12, 457.18, 995.4
coped 295.31
Copernican universe 1073.1
copestone 407.3
cope with 321.6, 328.9, 387.12, 457.17
cophosis 49.1
copiable 336.10
copied 336.8, 778.7, 784.10
copier 336.4, 547.13
copilot (n) 185.1 (v) 184.37
copious 247.8, 257.17, 538.11, 884.8, 890.9, 991.7
copiousness 247.3, 257.6, 538.2, 890.1, 991.2
cop it 307.19
copkiller 462.19
copolymeric 1060.9
copolymerize 1060.8
copolymerous 1060.9
cop out 362.7, 368.9, 369.7, 467.5, 468.2, 584.7, 858.13, 903.7
cop-out 368.2, 467.1, 468.1, 600.4
copper (n) 7.11, 728.7, 728.20, 1008.16 (a) 40.4, 1058.17
copper-colored 40.4
copperish 40.4
copperplate (n) 295.13, 713.6 (v) 295.26
copperplated 295.33
copper-red 41.6
copperware 735.4
coppery 40.4, 1058.17
coppice 310.14, 310.15
copping out 163.2
coprocessor 1042.2
coprolite 12.4
coprolith 12.4
coprological 513.8
coprologize 513.6
coprology 513.3
coprophilia 75.11
coprophiliac 75.16
cops, the 1008.16
copse 310.14, 310.15, 770.7
copsewood 310.15, 310.17
copsy 310.40
copter 181.5
copula 75.7, 530.3, 530.4
copulate (v) 75.21, 562.14, 770.16, 800.5 (a) 800.13

copulation 75.7, 800.1
copulative (n) 530.3 (a) 530.17, 800.16
copulative conjunction 530.3
copy (n) 78.1, 336.3, 349.5, 547.10, 548.4, 552.3, 554.5, 708.28, 712.10, 778.3, 785.1, 849.2, 862.2 (v) 78.7, 336.5, 349.12, 547.19, 621.4, 712.19, 778.6, 784.7, 785.8, 849.7, 873.5, 874.3
copy after 336.7
copybook hand 547.5
copyboy 353.4, 577.5
copycat (n) 336.4 (v) 336.6
copycat crime 336.1, 655.2
copy chief 555.4
copy-edit 548.17
copy editor 548.13, 554.2, 555.4, 938.17
copyeditor 554.2
copyhold 471.10
copyholder 548.13
copying 336.1, 621.2, 784.1, 874.1
copyist 336.4, 547.13, 716.1
copy machine 714.5
copyman 555.4
copy out 547.19
copyreader 548.13, 555.4
copyright (n) 210.3, 471.4, 642.2, 1008.3 (v) 210.5, 397.8, 1008.18
copyrighted 210.7, 471.8, 1008.21
copyright infringer 483.9
copyright page 554.12
copywriter 352.9, 547.15, 718.4
copywriting 552.1
coquet (n) 998.10 (v) 562.20, 998.14
coquetry 562.9, 998.8
coquette 104.11, 377.4, 562.11
coquettish 364.6, 377.8, 562.23
coquettish glances 562.9
coquettishness 364.3, 562.9
coquet with 930.10
coquillage 10.25
Cora 682.5
coral 41.8
coral-colored 41.8
coral head 235.2
coral heads 1006.5
coral island 235.2
coralline 41.8
coral-red 41.8
coral reef 235.2, 276.2, 283.9
corbel 901.14
cord 271.2, 1032.21, 1054.3
cordage 257.2, 271.3, 1054.3
cordate 279.15
cordial (n) 9.1, 10.49, 86.8, 88.15 (a) 9.3, 93.18, 97.6, 143.14, 187.16, 581.3, 585.11, 587.16
cordial friendship 587.8
cordiality 93.5, 97.1, 143.2, 187.9, 581.1, 585.1, 587.6
cordially 820.5
cordially yours 820.5
cordial understanding 788.2
cordial welcome 187.1, 585.2
cordiform 279.15
cordillera 237.6
cordilleran belt 237.6
cording 271.3
cordite 462.14
cordless 1032.30
cordless phone 347.4
cordon (n) 429.2, 646.5, 1008.9, 1012.4 (v) 212.5, 429.13, 773.6
cordon bleu 413.11, 646.5
cordon bleu cook 11.3
cordoned 212.10, 429.20
cordoned off 212.10, 429.20
cordoned-off 773.8
cordoning 212.1
cordoning off 429.2
cordon off 212.5, 429.13, 773.6
cords 5.18
corduroy (n) 288.2 (a) 288.6, 290.4
corduroyed 290.4
corduroys 5.18
cordwood 1054.3
core (n) 196.5, 199.2, 207.2, 208.2, 230.6, 275.3, 518.1, 557.2, 767.2, 819.1, 997.6, 1042.7 (a) 208.12, 230.11, 819.4
core city 230.6
core-city 230.11
core curriculum 568.8
corelate 777.5
corelated 777.8
corelation 777.1
corelational 777.8
corelative 777.8
core of one's being 93.3, 208.2
corequisite 567.5
corespondent 599.6
core storage 1042.7
coriaceous 1049.4
Corinthian (n) 198.6, 717.2 (a) 501.21
corium 2.4
cork (n) 180.11, 293.4, 295.3, 298.2 (v) 38.7, 293.7, 295.21, 428.8
corker 999.7
corkiness 1066.1
corking 999.13
corking up 474.1
cork jacket 397.6
corkscrew (n) 192.9, 281.2, 292.10 (v) 281.4 (a) 281.8
corkscrewy 281.8
cork up 428.8, 429.12, 474.5
corky 109.12, 260.13, 1066.9
corm 310.22, 310.33
cormorant 672.3
corn (n) 10.4, 85.39, 283.4, 310.5, 489.9, 974.3 (v) 397.9
cornball 842.17
corn belt 233.1
corn bread 10.29
corncob 89.6, 310.29
corncob pipe 89.6
corncrib 386.7
corn dab 10.29
corn dodger 10.29
corn dolly 349.6
cornea 2.9
corned 88.33
corned beef 10.14
cornemuse 711.9
corner (n) 164.1, 197.3, 258.3, 278.2, 284.7, 346.4, 469.3, 737.20, 752.3, 754.1, 756.3, 1013.6 (v) 469.6, 733.7, 737.26, 914.6, 1013.16
corner area 752.1
cornerback 746.2
cornered 278.6, 1006.13, 1013.25
corner flag 752.1
corner hit 749.6
corner in 737.20
cornering 469.3, 733.1
corner kick 752.3
corner man 747.2
corner of the eye 2.9, 27.9
corner of the memory 989.1
corner on, a 469.3
corner on the market 737.20
cornerstone 901.7, 997.6
corner store 736.1
corner the market 469.6, 737.26
corner throw 747.3
cornet 282.5
cornettist 710.4
corn-fed 257.18
cornfield 1069.9
cornflower 45.3
corn glucose syrup 66.3
corn god 1069.4
cornhusk 295.16
cornhusking 582.14
cornice 198.5
cornicle 285.4
corniculate 285.9, 285.14
cornification 285.1, 1046.5
cornified 285.9, 1046.13
corniform 279.11
cornify 1046.7
corniness 117.3
corning 397.2
Cornish wrestling 457.10
corn pit 737.7
corn pone 10.29
cornrow 3.7
cornrows 1016.14
corn shuck 295.16
corn shucking 582.14
corn snow 1023.8
corn spirit 678.11
cornstarch 1062.5
cornstarchy airs 141.1
corn sweet 66.3
corn sweetener 66.3
corn syrup 66.2, 66.3
corn tash 10.29
cornucopia 386.1, 386.4, 991.3
cornuted 285.9
corny 117.9, 842.17
corny joke 489.9
corolla 310.28
corollary 254.1, 769.3, 887.1, 946.4
corolla tube 310.28
corona 89.4, 171.2, 280.2, 310.28, 1025.14, 1026.6, 1073.13
coronach 115.6, 115.6
corona discharge 1025.13
coronagraph 1073.17
coronal 280.11
corona lucis 1026.6
coronary 85.19
coronary disease 85.19
coronary thrombosis 85.19
coronation 417.12, 615.3
coroner 90.4, 307.17
coronet 280.2, 498.6, 647.2, 647.3
corpora 770.11
corporal (n) 575.18, 575.19, 703.10 (a) 604.22, 1052.10
corporal entity 2.1
corporality 1052.1
corporalize 1052.9
corporal punishment 602.1, 604.4
corporal's guard 885.2, 992.2
corporate 617.16, 800.12, 805.6
corporate culture 724.4
corporate headquarters 739.7
corporate practice 597.4
corporate stock 738.2
corporation 2.19, 739.1
corporational 805.7
corporative 805.7
corporeal 1052.10
corporeal entity 2.1
corporeal hereditament 471.1, 479.2
corporeality 1052.1
corporealization 1052.8
corporealness 1052.1
corporeity 1052.1
corporeous 1052.10
corporify 1052.9
corposant 1019.13, 1025.13
corps 461.21, 461.22, 617.1, 617.7, 770.3
corps de ballet 705.3, 705.3, 707.11
corpse 270.8, 307.15
corpse candle 1026.2
corpselike 201.8, 270.20, 307.28
corpselikeness 307.11
corpse pose 201.2
corpse reviver 88.14
corps of advisers 423.1
corpulence 257.8, 269.2
corpulent 257.18, 269.8
corpus 554.7, 728.15, 770.11, 928.1, 928.9, 1052.3
corpus, the 792.3
corpuscle 305.4
corpuscular 258.14, 305.19
corpus delicti 307.15
corpus juris 673.5
Corpus Juris Civilis 673.8
corral (n) 196.6, 212.3 (v) 212.5, 472.9, 770.18, 1070.8
corralled 212.10
corralling 770.1
correct (v) 338.4, 392.12, 396.13, 510.17, 604.9, 867.3, 977.2 (a) 339.12, 504.15, 530.17, 533.7, 579.5, 637.3, 687.7, 973.16
correctable 396.25
correct copy 548.17
correct deportment 321.2
correct distance and maintain the bearings 182.51
correct ear 48.3
correct English 523.4
correct grammar 530.1

correct in one's behavior 504.15
correct in one's manners 504.15
correction 300.1, 392.4, 396.6, 510.5, 604.1
correctional 604.22
correctional facility 429.8
correctional institution 567.9
correctional officer 429.10
correction facility 429.8
correction fluid 37.4
corrections officer 429.10
correctitude 504.3, 637.2
corrective (n) 86.1 (a) 86.39, 392.16, 604.22
corrective action 1041.7
correctness 339.3, 504.3, 533.1, 579.1, 637.2, 973.5
correlate (n) 777.4, 784.3 (v) 775.6, 777.5
correlated 775.9, 777.8
correlation 775.2, 777.1, 943.1
correlational 777.8
correlative (n) 777.4, 784.3 (a) 769.9, 775.8, 777.8, 784.13, 943.8
correlative conjunction 530.3
correlativism 777.1
correlativity 777.1
correspond 203.5, 343.8, 455.2, 553.10, 777.7, 778.4, 784.7, 788.6, 790.5, 867.3, 899.2
correspondence 264.1, 343.1, 455.1, 549.1, 553.1, 777.1, 778.1, 781.1, 784.1, 788.1, 790.1, 867.1, 899.1
correspondence course 567.5, 568.8
correspondence principle 1038.2
correspondent (n) 551.5, 553.8, 555.4, 777.4, 784.3 (a) 777.10, 778.8, 781.5, 784.11, 788.9, 790.8
corresponding 455.3, 775.9, 777.10, 778.8, 784.11, 788.9, 790.8, 867.6, 991.6
correspond to 775.5, 777.7
correspond with 553.10
corridor 184.33, 189.5, 197.18, 231.1, 383.3
corridor of time 827.3
corridors of power 18.1
corridors of power, the 575.14, 612.3
corridors of time 821.3
corrie 237.7, 237.7, 284.8
Corrigan 678.8
corrigenda 392.4
corrigendum 975.3
corrigibility 396.9, 433.4
corrigible 392.17, 396.25, 433.14
corrival 452.2
corroborant 86.44
corroborate 334.6, 957.11
corroborated 957.20, 973.13
corroborating 957.18
corroboration 957.4, 970.8
corroborative 901.23, 957.18
corroboratory 334.8, 957.18
corroboratory evidence 957.4
corrode 252.6, 393.21, 713.10, 806.3, 1044.7
corroded 393.43
corroding 144.23, 393.44, 1000.12
corrosion 252.3, 393.6, 806.1, 1044.2
corrosionproof 15.20
corrosive (n) 1020.15 (a) 110.17, 144.23, 393.44, 544.11, 806.5, 1000.12
corrosiveness 110.1, 144.8
corrugate (v) 288.5, 290.3, 291.6 (a) 290.4, 291.8
corrugated 288.6, 288.7, 290.4, 291.8
corrugation 288.2, 290.1, 291.3
corrupt (v) 80.17, 378.3, 393.12, 393.22, 569.3, 654.10, 797.12, 858.15, 1000.6 (a) 378.4, 393.40, 645.16, 654.14, 975.16
corrupt administration 389.1
corrupted 80.20, 645.16, 654.14
corruptedness 645.1, 654.5
corruptibility 645.9, 828.1
corruptible 378.4, 645.23, 828.7
corrupting 393.44, 1000.12
corruption 80.7, 265.2, 378.1, 393.2, 393.6, 489.8, 525.5, 526.6, 531.2, 569.1, 645.1, 654.5, 797.3, 806.1, 858.5, 1000.3
corruption of speech 531.1
corruptive 393.44, 1000.12
corruptness 645.1, 654.5
corsage 310.25
corsair 483.7
corselet 5.23
corset 5.23, 901.2
cortege 309.5, 769.6
cortège 812.3
cortex 206.2, 295.3, 295.15, 460.3
cortical 2.27, 206.7, 295.32
cortical tissue 295.3
coruscant 1025.35
coruscate 920.11, 1025.24
coruscating 1025.35
coruscation 1025.7
corybantic 669.9, 926.30
corymb 310.27
coryphaeus 574.6
coryphée 705.3, 707.1
Cosa Nostra 660.10, 732.1
cosh 902.20
cosign 332.12, 438.9
cosignage 438.3
cosignatory 332.7
cosigned 436.8
cosigned promissory note 438.3
cosigner 332.7
cosmetic 206.7, 276.5, 401.9, 992.9, 1016.22
cosmetic dermatitis 85.34
cosmetician 1016.12
cosmeticize 1016.15
cosmeticized 1016.22
cosmetic measure, a 992.1
cosmetics 33.2, 206.1, 376.1, 735.6, 787.1, 1016.11
cosmetic surgery 90.2, 1016.10
cosmetize 1016.15
cosmetized 1016.22
cosmetologist 1016.12
cosmetology 1016.10
cosmic 247.7, 864.14, 1073.24
cosmical 864.14, 1073.24
cosmicality 864.1
cosmic consciousness 689.9
cosmic constant 158.6
cosmic dust 1051.5, 1073.15
cosmic evolution 1073.18
cosmic noise 1073.6
cosmic particle 1037.4
cosmic particles 1075.10
cosmic philosopher 1073.21
cosmic philosophy 1073.18
cosmic ray bombardment 1037.3, 1075.10
cosmic ray counter 1075.7
cosmic space 1073.3
cosmic stepping-stone 1075.5
cosmic string 1073.6
cosmic time 821.1
cosmic vibration 689.6
cosmism 1073.18
cosmist 1073.21
cosmochemist 1073.22
cosmochemistry 1073.19
cosmogener 1073.21
cosmogenist 1073.21
cosmogonal 1073.24
cosmogonic 1073.24
cosmogonical 1073.24
cosmogony 1073.18
cosmographer 1073.21
cosmographic 1073.24
cosmographical 1073.24
cosmographist 1073.21
cosmography 1073.18
cosmologic 1073.24
cosmological 1073.24
cosmological model 1073.1
cosmologist 952.8, 1073.21
cosmology 1073.18
cosmonaut 1075.8
cosmonautical 1075.13
cosmonautics 1075.1
cosmopolitan (n) 227.4, 413.17 (a) 177.40, 312.16, 413.28, 578.13, 864.14, 979.8
cosmopolitanism 864.1, 979.1
cosmopolite (n) 178.1, 227.4, 310.3, 311.3, 413.17 (a) 413.28
cosmorama 33.7
cosmos 794.1, 1073.1
cosmotheism 675.5, 952.5
cosmotheist 675.16
cosmotheistic 675.25
cossack 461.12
cosset (n) 104.15 (v) 427.6, 449.16, 562.16
cosseting 427.3
cost (n) 473.1, 626.3, 630.1 (v) 626.5, 630.13
cost- 283.3
cost accountant 628.7
cost accounting 628.6
cost-accounting system 628.6
cost an arm and a leg 632.6
cost a packet 632.6
cost a pretty penny 632.6
costar (n) 707.6 (v) 704.29
costate 290.4
cost card 628.4
cost-conscious 484.9
cost-consciousness 484.2
cost-effective 635.6
cost-effectiveness 635.2
cost-efficient 635.6
coster 730.5
costermonger 730.5
costi- 283.3
cost inflation 632.3
costing 626.1, 628.6
costing out 628.1
costing-out 626.1
costive 293.11
costiveness 293.3
cost keeper 628.7
costless 634.5
costlessness 634.1
costliness 632.1
cost little 633.5
costly 632.11
cost money 632.6
cost much 632.6
cost nothing 633.5
costo- 283.3
cost of living 626.3, 731.8
cost-of-living allowance 626.3
cost-of-living index 626.3, 630.4, 731.8, 731.9
cost out 626.5
cost-push 632.3
cost-push inflation 632.3
costs 626.3
cost sheet 628.4
cost system 628.6
costume (n) 5.1, 5.6, 5.9, 704.17 (v) 5.41
costumed 5.45
costume design 717.5
costume designer 704.23, 716.9
costume jewelry 498.5
costumer 5.33, 704.23
costumery 5.1, 5.9
costumier 5.33
cost you 632.6
cot 228.8
cot death 85.2
cote 228.8
côte 234.2
côtelette 10.19
côtelette de mouton 10.19
côtelette de porc frais 10.19
côtelette de veau 10.15, 10.19
cotenancy 476.1
cotenant 476.4
coterie 582.5, 617.6, 770.3
coterminous 223.16, 778.8, 836.5
coterminousness 223.3
cothurned 704.34
cothurnus 704.5
cotillion 705.2
cotillon 705.2
Cotsworth calendar 832.8
cottage 228.8, 554.15
cottage industry 892.3
cottager 227.7, 227.10
cotter 227.7
cottier 227.7
cotton 4.1, 86.33
cotton belt 233.1
Cotton Bowl 746.1

cotton broker 730.9
cotton on 989.11
cotton-picking 661.12
cotton plantation 1069.8
cottontail 311.23
cotton to 104.21, 455.2, 587.9
cottony 1047.15
cottony cloud 319.1
cotyledon 310.19
couch (n) 228.26, 229.1, 901.19 (v) 20.6, 274.5, 346.9, 524.22, 532.4, 913.4, 913.11
couch, the 92.6
couchant 201.8, 274.7
couche 296.1
couché 201.8
couched 532.5
couch in terms 532.4
couch one's lance 457.14
couch potato 331.8, 402.1, 761.6, 918.1
cougar 311.21
cough 2.21
cough drops 86.16
coughing 85.9
cough medicine 86.16
cough syrup 86.16
cough up 475.3, 624.16, 909.25, 909.27
could be 966.4, 968.4
couldn't care less about 157.3
coulee 199.4, 237.7
couleur de rose 124.11
coulisse 704.16, 704.20
couloir 237.7
council (n) 422.1, 423.1, 541.5, 574.11, 595.1, 613.3, 617.1, 770.2 (a) 423.5
council fire 423.1, 541.5
council house 228.1
councillor 575.16
councilman 575.16, 610.3
councilmanic 423.5
council of ministers 423.1
Council of Nicaea 423.4
council of state 423.1, 613.3
Council of Trent 423.4
council of war 423.1, 541.5
councilwoman 575.16
counsel (n) 422.1, 422.3, 449.2, 597.1, 597.4, 931.2 (v) 92.36, 422.5, 541.10, 573.9
counselee 422.4
counseling 92.6, 422.1
counseling service 92.10
counsel of perfection 125.4
counselor 92.10, 413.11, 422.3, 597.1
counselor-at-law 597.1
count (n) 244.2, 599.1, 608.4, 609.21, 745.3, 766.3, 1017.6, 1017.9, 1017.11 (v) 244.4, 708.44, 894.10, 946.8, 946.15, 997.12, 1017.17
countable 1017.25
countable noun 530.5
count as 349.10
count calories 7.19, 8.20, 270.13, 515.4
count card 758.2
count down 816.3
countdown 816.2, 1074.9
counted on 130.14
countenance (n) 33.4, 106.2, 216.4, 443.3, 449.4, 509.1 (v) 134.7, 375.21, 443.10, 449.14, 509.9
counter (n) 205.4, 217.7, 506.1, 548.6, 728.12, 736.6, 739.1, 759.15, 759.18, 759.21, 901.15, 1037.7 (v) 335.4, 451.3, 451.4, 460.10, 506.4, 600.10, 779.4, 789.5, 900.6, 958.5, 1012.15 (a) 163.12, 335.5, 451.8, 779.6, 787.4, 1011.13
counter,the 779.2
counteraccusation 939.2
counteract 215.4, 338.5, 451.3, 777.7, 779.4, 900.6, 1012.15
counteractant (n) 900.3 (a) 86.41, 900.8
counteracting 338.6, 900.8
counteraction 86.26, 163.4, 338.1, 451.1, 453.1, 900.1
counteractive (n) 900.3 (a) 338.6, 900.8, 1011.13
counteragent 900.3
counterattack (n) 459.1, 900.5 (v) 459.17, 900.6
counterbalance (n) 264.2, 297.4, 338.2, 779.2, 900.4 (v) 297.10, 338.5, 779.4, 790.6, 855.7, 900.7
counterbalanced 900.9
counterbalancing (n) 338.1, 900.2 (a) 338.6, 779.6, 900.9
counterblast 506.1, 900.4, 900.5, 939.2
counterblow 506.1, 900.5
countercathexis 92.34
counterchange (n) 863.1 (v) 863.4
countercharge (n) 599.3, 939.2 (v) 599.11, 939.5
countercheck (n) 779.2, 900.4, 1012.7 (v) 779.4, 900.6, 1012.10
counterclaim (n) 338.3, 598.1, 939.2 (v) 939.5
counterclockwise 220.4
countercoup 900.5
counterculture (n) 333.1, 868.2, 900.5 (a) 333.6, 868.6
countercurrent 238.12, 451.1, 900.4
counterdemand 338.3
counterdemonstration 333.2
counterdemonstrator 1008.13
counter drug 86.4
counterespionage 938.9
counterfeit (n) 354.13, 728.10, 785.1, 862.2 (v) 336.5, 354.18, 354.21, 500.12, 728.28, 784.7 (a) 336.8, 354.26, 784.10, 862.8
counterfeited 354.26, 500.16
counterfeiter 336.4, 357.1, 728.25
counterfeiting 336.1, 350.1, 728.24
counterfeit money 728.10
counterfire 900.5
counterflow 238.12
counterflux 238.12
counterfoil 517.13
counterforce 900.4
counterglow 1025.15
counterindoctrinate 858.15
counterindoctrination 858.5
counterinfluence 900.4
countering 335.2, 453.1
counterinsurgency 900.5
counterintelligence 345.4, 576.12, 938.9
counterintelligence agent 576.9
counterinvestment 92.34
counterirritant 86.26, 86.32, 900.3
counterman 577.7
countermand (n) 444.2, 445.1 (v) 445.2, 1012.15
countermarch 163.7
countermarching 163.4
countermark 517.11, 517.13, 527.10
countermeasure 86.26, 900.5
countermine (n) 460.5 (v) 381.9
countermotion 163.4
countermove 995.2
countermovement 163.4
counteroffensive 459.1
counteroffer 439.1
counterorder (n) 445.1 (v) 445.2
counterpane 295.10
counterpart 777.4, 784.3, 785.3, 790.4
counterpin 295.10
counterplot (n) 381.5 (v) 381.9
counterplotter 381.7
counterpoint 708.20, 720.7, 779.2
counterpoise (n) 338.2, 779.2, 900.4 (v) 338.5, 779.4, 790.6
counterpoised 779.6
counterpoison 86.26
counterpole 779.2
counterpoles 215.2
counterpose 779.4, 900.6, 943.4
counterposition 779.1, 900.1
counterpressure 900.4
counterproductive 19.15, 900.8, 923.10, 996.5, 1000.12, 1012.18
counterproductiveness 19.3, 996.1
counterproductivity 19.3
counterproposal 439.1
counterpunch 506.1
counterreply 939.2
counterrevolution 860.1, 900.5
countersecure 438.9
counter service 8.11
countersign (n) 517.11, 517.12, 527.10 (v) 332.12, 436.4, 438.9
countersignature 332.4, 527.10
countersigned 332.14
countersink 275.9, 292.15
counterspy 576.9
counterstamp 527.10
counterstatement 600.2, 939.2
counterstep 900.5
counterstroke 506.1, 900.5
countersuit 598.1
countersun 1025.14
countertenor (n) 58.6, 709.5 (a) 58.13
counterterm 779.2
counterterrorism 900.5
counter to one's preferences 99.7
countervail 338.5, 451.3, 779.4, 790.6, 900.6
countervailing (n) 900.2 (a) 338.6, 779.6, 900.8, 900.9
countervailing force 900.4
counterweigh 338.5
counterweight 338.2, 704.20, 900.4
counterword 526.11, 539.2
counterwork 451.3, 779.4, 900.6, 1012.15
counterworking (n) 451.1, 900.1 (a) 900.8
countess 608.6
count for 349.10
count heads 1017.17
count in 772.3
counting (n) 1017.9 (a) 772.6
counting hands 371.6
counting heads 371.6
counting noses 371.6
counting on the fingers 1017.9
countless 247.8, 823.3, 884.10
countless as the sands 884.10
countless as the stars 884.10
countlessness 247.3, 823.1, 884.1
count noun 530.5
count of 1017.13
count on 124.6, 380.6, 953.16
count one's bridges before they are crossed 124.8
count one's chickens before they are hatched 124.8, 414.14, 493.5, 975.11
count out 773.4
countrification 233.4
countrified 233.7
countrify 233.5
country (n) 231.1, 232.1, 596.5 (a) 233.6
country, the 233.1, 234.1
country-and-western music 708.11
country-and-western singer 710.14
country-born 233.7
country-bred 233.7
country bumpkin 606.6
country club 617.3
country-club set 618.6
country cousin 559.3
country dance 705.2
country doctor 90.4
country estate 228.5
country-fashion 233.7
country-fried 11.7
country gentleman 227.10, 470.2
country gentlewoman 227.10, 470.2
country house 228.5
countryman 227.5, 232.7, 606.6, 1069.5
country music 708.11
country of origin 232.2
country rock 708.10, 1058.7
country seat 228.5
countryside 233.1
country singer 710.13

country store 736.1
country-style 233.7
country town 230.2
countrywide 864.14
countrywoman 227.5, 232.7, 606.6
count sheep 23.3
count the beats 708.44
count ties 177.23
count up 1017.19
count upon 124.6
county 231.5, 232.1
county building 230.5
county clerk 550.1
county commissioners 575.16
county convention 609.8
county council 423.1
county court 595.2
county courthouse 230.5
county fair 743.4
county hall 595.6
county jail 429.8
county library 558.1
county line 211.3
county police 1008.17
county seat 230.4
county site 230.4
county supervisor 575.16
county town 230.4
coup 327.4, 328.3, 403.2, 413.8, 415.3, 417.12, 418.1, 480.2, 830.3, 995.2
coup de foudre 104.3
coup de grâce (n) 308.10, 395.2, 820.4 (v) 308.18
coup de main 459.1
coup de maître 413.10
coup de plume 547.1
coup d'etat 417.12, 418.1
coup d'état 327.4, 480.2, 860.1
coup de théâtre 704.2
coup d'œil 27.4
couple (n) 784.5, 873.2 (v) 75.21, 563.14, 563.15, 770.16, 775.6, 800.5, 805.3, 805.4, 873.5
coupled 563.21, 769.9, 775.9, 800.13, 805.6, 873.8
coupledness 800.1
coupledom 563.9
couplet 720.10, 873.2
couple up 873.5
couple with 769.7
coupling 75.7, 800.1, 800.4, 805.1, 873.1, 1040.5
coupon 728.12, 738.4
coupon-clipper 611.15, 618.7, 737.14
coupon-clippers 331.11
coupon rate 738.5
coupure 460.5
courage 359.3, 492.1, 970.5
courage of one's convictions, the 359.4
courageous 359.14, 492.16
courageousness 492.1
courier 174.5, 353.1, 553.7, 574.7
courier service 353.1
course (n) 8.10, 10.7, 161.1, 162.1, 172.2, 177.1, 177.5, 182.6, 184.34, 238.4, 239.1, 296.1, 381.4, 383.1, 384.1, 463.1, 517.8, 567.5, 568.8, 751.1, 753.1, 757.1, 812.2, 850.3, 889.2, 896.2 (v) 177.20, 238.16, 382.9
course ahead 839.1
coursebook 554.1
course examination 938.2
course of action 995.2
course of events 831.4
course of events, the 896.2
course of law 598.1
course of study 568.8
course of time 821.4
courser 174.6, 311.10, 311.17, 382.5, 461.30
courses 12.9
course turf 743.11
courseware 1042.11
coursework 568.1
coursing (n) 382.2 (a) 238.24
court (n) 212.3, 228.7, 423.1, 562.7, 594.2, 595.2, 595.6, 613.1, 743.11, 747.1, 748.1, 769.6, 894.6 (v) 104.18, 138.9, 440.14, 562.21, 587.12 (a) 595.7
court calendar 549.11
court card 758.2
court case 598.1
court danger 493.6
court destruction 1006.7
court disaster 492.10
court dress 5.11
courteous 24.12, 155.8, 504.13, 582.22, 587.16
courteousness 143.3, 504.1
courtesan 665.15
courtesies 504.7
courtesy 24.3, 143.7, 155.1, 321.2, 504.1, 504.6, 582.1
courtesy title 648.1
courthouse 230.5, 595.6, 613.4
courthouse wedding 563.3
courtier 138.3, 166.2, 511.4
courtierly 511.8
courting 104.5, 440.5, 562.7
courting disaster 493.3
court jester 489.12
courtliness 136.2, 504.2, 504.6, 580.3
courtly 136.12, 504.14, 511.8
courtly behavior 504.2
courtly politeness 504.2
court-martial 595.4, 598.5
court of arbitration 595.2
Court of Arches 595.3
court of justice 595.2
court of law 595.2
Court of Peculiars 595.3
court of record 595.2
court order 420.6
court plaster 86.33, 803.4
courtroom 595.6
courts, the 594.2
courtship 104.5, 562.7
court shoes 5.27
courtside 747.3
court sport 744.1
court system 594.2
court tennis 748.1
courtyard 212.3
couscous 10.36
cousin 559.3
cousin-german 559.3
cousinhood 559.1
cousin once removed 559.3
cousinship 559.1
cousin twice removed 559.3
couturier 5.36, 716.9
couturière 5.36, 716.9
couvert 8.11
covalence 1060.4
covalent 1060.10
covariation 777.1
cove 76.5, 197.3, 242.1, 279.4, 284.5, 284.7
coven 690.3, 690.8
covenant (n) 436.2, 437.1 (v) 332.10, 437.5
covenantal 437.10
covenanted 437.11
covenanter 332.6
covenant of salt 437.1
covenantor 332.6
coventual 703.16
cover (n) 8.11, 10.7, 184.11, 199.3, 295.2, 295.5, 295.10, 346.1, 346.2, 346.4, 356.11, 376.1, 528.1, 554.14, 1008.1, 1009.3, 1028.1 (v) 35.14, 75.21, 78.12, 158.9, 177.20, 293.6, 293.7, 295.19, 338.4, 341.10, 346.6, 376.4, 759.25, 772.3, 800.5, 825.5, 910.5, 1008.18, 1028.5
coverage 257.1, 295.1, 295.2, 552.1, 555.3, 772.1
cover a lot of ground 772.3, 794.8
cover charge 8.11, 630.6
coverchief 5.25
covered 295.31, 346.11, 438.11, 772.5, 1008.21, 1031.3
covered bridge 383.9
covered stadium 463.1
covered tone 52.2
covered wagon 179.2
covered way 383.3
cover for 862.5
cover girl 1016.7
cover ground 162.2, 174.8, 177.18
covering (n) 35.12, 78.5, 206.2, 295.1, 295.2, 296.2, 346.1 (a) 295.35, 346.15, 772.6, 1008.23, 1028.6
covering materials 1054.2
covering one's rear-end 460.1
covering shorts 737.19
covering the evidence 951.2
covering up 346.1
coverlet 295.10
coverlid 295.10
cover man 745.2
cover memory 989.1
cover name 528.1
cover oneself with 376.4
cover one's path 415.9
cover one's rear-end 460.8
cover one's short 737.24
covers 295.10
cover story 376.1
covert (n) 3.18, 228.26, 295.2, 310.15, 310.17, 346.4, 1009.3 (a) 295.31, 345.12, 346.11, 519.5
covert activity 345.4
cover the same ground 849.9
cover the spectrum 783.2
cover the territory 341.10
cover the waterfront 341.10
covertness 345.4, 346.1
covert operation 345.4
covert operative 576.9
coverture 295.2, 346.4, 563.1, 1009.3
covert way 346.5
cover up 295.19, 345.8, 346.6, 354.21, 376.4
cover-up 345.3, 350.1, 376.1
coverup 5.29
cover up for 862.6
cover up one's tracks 346.6
cover version 336.3
cover with excuses 600.11
cover your ass 460.8
covet 100.18, 154.2, 651.4
coveted 100.29
coveter 100.12
coveting (n) 100.6 (a) 100.24, 100.27
covetous 100.27, 154.3, 651.5
covetousness 100.8, 154.1, 651.1, 654.3
covey 770.3, 770.6, 884.3
covin 356.4, 381.5
covinous 356.22
cow (n) 77.9, 311.6 (v) 127.20, 379.3, 612.15
cowabunga 116.2
co-walker 988.3
coward (n) 16.6, 491.5 (a) 491.10
cowardice 16.2, 127.1, 362.4, 433.1, 491.1
cowardliness 491.1
cowardly 16.12, 127.23, 362.12, 491.10
cowardship 491.1
cowbarn 228.20
cowboy 178.8, 671.10, 758.2, 1070.3
cowboy boots 5.27
cowboy hat 5.25
cowbyre 228.20
cowcatcher 1008.3
cow chips 12.4
cow country 233.2
cow-country 233.9
cowcutting horse 311.10
cowed 127.26, 491.10
cower 16.8, 138.7, 491.9, 913.8
cowering 138.14, 491.13
cow flops 12.4
cowgirl 178.8, 1070.3
cowhand 1070.3
cowherd 574.7, 1008.6, 1070.3
cowhide (n) 605.1 (v) 604.12
cowhiding 604.4
cowhouse 228.20
cowing 127.6
cowish 311.45, 922.15
cowishness 922.3
cow keeper 1070.2
cowl (n) 295.2 (v) 295.19
cowled 295.31
cowlick 3.6

cowlike 311.45
cowling 295.2
cowman 1070.2, 1070.3
co-work 899.2
coworker 616.5, 726.1
coworking (n) 899.1 (a) 899.4
coworking space 739.7
co-worship 696.1
cow pats 12.4
cowpoke 178.8, 1070.3
cow pony 311.10, 311.13
cowpuncher 178.8, 1070.3
cowrie 728.3
cowshed 228.20
cow town 211.5, 233.2
cowtown 230.3
cox 183.8
coxcomb 500.9, 704.6
coxcombical 500.17
coxcombry 500.4, 578.3
coxswain (n) 183.8, 574.7 (v) 182.14
coy 139.12, 562.23
coyness 139.4, 562.9
coyote 311.19
coze (n) 541.3 (v) 541.9
cozen 356.18
cozenage 356.8
cozener 357.3
coziness 95.1, 121.2
cozy 95.15, 121.11, 228.33, 541.12, 582.24, 1007.7
cozy chat 541.3
cozy fire 1019.13
cozy up to 562.21, 587.11
crab (n) 108.4, 110.11, 115.9, 311.29, 311.36, 906.7, 912.3 (v) 108.6, 115.16, 184.40, 1012.16 (a) 67.5
crabapple 67.2
crabbed 67.5, 110.19, 303.18, 522.14, 534.3, 799.4
crabbed hand 547.6
crabbedness 110.2, 522.2, 799.1
crabbiness 110.3
crabbing (n) 184.13 (a) 108.8, 115.20
crabby 108.8, 110.20, 115.20
crab louse 311.36
Crab Nebula 1073.7
crab one's deal 1012.11
crabs 85.18
crabwalk 164.2
crack (n) 47.5, 56.1, 56.2, 56.3, 85.38, 87.7, 224.2, 290.1, 292.1, 403.3, 489.7, 524.3, 802.4, 830.3, 902.4, 942.2, 1003.2, 1004.1 (v) 56.6, 56.7, 56.8, 128.8, 224.4, 290.3, 292.11, 292.12, 341.10, 393.13, 393.23, 802.12, 902.14, 940.2, 1004.4, 1020.24 (a) 413.22, 999.14
crackability 1050.1
crackable 1050.4
crackableness 1050.1
crack a book 570.12
crack a joke 489.13
crack a safe 482.15
crack a smile 116.7
crackbrain 926.16
crackbrained 922.22, 926.26
crack cocaine 87.7
crackdown 428.1
crack down on 428.7, 428.8, 459.15
cracked 58.15, 61.4, 224.7, 292.18, 393.27, 525.12, 802.23, 922.22, 926.27, 1004.8
cracked on 101.11
cracked voice 58.2, 525.1
cracker 10.30, 53.6, 227.10, 1066.2
crackerjack (n) 413.14, 659.2, 999.7 (a) 413.22, 999.13
crackers 926.27
crackers and cheese 10.9
crack habit 87.1
crackhead 87.21
crack house 87.20
cracking (n) 56.2, 341.4, 940.1, 1020.5 (a) 56.10, 56.11, 393.45
crackle (n) 47.5, 56.2, 85.38, 742.3 (v) 56.7
cracklin' bread 10.29
crackling (n) 56.2 (a) 56.10
crackling fire 1019.13
crackly 56.10
crack of dawn 314.2
crack of dawn, the 1025.10
crack of doom 307.1, 820.1, 839.3
crack of the whip 375.8
crack on 174.10, 182.20
crack one's brains 931.9, 989.20
crack one up 116.9, 743.21
crack on sail 174.11, 182.20
crack open 292.14
crackpot 870.4, 926.16, 927.4
crackpotism 927.1
crackpottedness 923.1
crack shot 413.11, 904.8
cracksman 483.3
crack the whip 417.13, 573.10, 612.14
crack up 21.5, 116.8, 128.8, 184.44, 806.3, 902.13, 926.21
crack-up 21.2, 92.14, 184.20, 393.1, 395.4, 802.3, 1011.2
crackup 85.8, 128.4
crack wide open 351.4, 941.4
crack wise 489.13
cradle (n) 79.13, 228.2, 232.2, 818.4, 886.8, 916.9 (v) 22.19, 449.16, 670.7, 901.21
cradle, the 301.5
cradle book 554.6
cradle-to-grave security 611.7
cradling 670.15
craft 180.1, 356.3, 413.1, 413.7, 415.1, 415.3, 712.2, 724.6, 920.3
crafted 892.18
craftiness 415.1, 645.3, 920.3
crafting 892.2
crafts 712.16
craftsman 413.11, 716.1, 726.6, 892.7
craftsmanship 407.3, 413.1, 892.2
craftspeople 726.6
craftsperson 726.6
craftswoman 726.6
craft union 727.2
craftwork 712.2
crafty 354.31, 356.22, 415.12, 494.8, 645.18, 920.15
crafty rascal 415.6
crag 200.3, 237.6, 285.4, 1059.1
cragged 288.7
cragginess 288.1
craggy 288.7, 1059.12
cragsman 193.6
craig 1059.1
cram (n) 570.3, 794.3 (v) 8.25, 568.11, 570.14, 672.4, 770.18, 794.7, 902.12, 989.18, 993.15, 994.4, 1045.9
crambo 720.3, 720.9
crambo clink 720.3
crambo jingle 720.3
cram down one's throat 424.8, 478.20, 953.18
cram-full 794.11
cram in 191.7, 770.18
crammed 770.22, 794.11, 993.20, 994.6, 1045.12
crammed full 1045.12
crammer 571.5
cramming (n) 568.4, 570.3 (a) 672.6
cramp (n) 26.2, 85.6, 96.5, 428.3, 917.6, 1012.1 (v) 16.10, 212.6, 260.7, 260.8, 428.9, 800.7, 1012.11, 1012.16 (a) 270.14, 522.14
cramped 210.7, 212.10, 258.10, 260.12, 270.14, 428.15, 534.3, 980.10
cramped hand 547.6
cramped ideas 980.1
crampedness 270.1, 522.2
cramping (n) 428.3 (a) 26.10, 428.12
cramp one's style 428.9, 992.8, 1012.11, 1012.16
cramps 26.2, 85.29
cramp up 260.8
cram the mind 570.6
cram the mind with 989.17
cram up 570.14
cram with facts 568.11
crane (n) 912.3, 1020.12 (v) 27.15, 267.5, 325.4
crane one's neck 267.5
crane the neck 27.15
cranial 198.15
craniologist 198.9
craniology 198.9, 312.10
craniometry 312.10
craniosacral nervous system 2.14
cranium 198.8
crank (n) 87.4, 108.4, 110.11, 115.9, 278.2, 364.1, 605.3, 870.4, 906.4, 924.7, 926.18, 927.2, 927.4, 1040.5 (v) 204.12, 278.5, 906.9, 915.9 (a) 927.5
crank call 347.13
cranked up 251.7
crank in 906.9
crankiness 110.2, 204.8, 364.2, 900.1, 923.1, 927.1
crankish 927.5
crankism 927.1
crankle (n) 291.3 (v) 204.12
crankled 204.20
cranklety 291.8
crank out 547.21, 718.6, 892.8
cranks 489.7
crank up 251.4, 904.13
cranky 108.8, 110.19, 115.20, 364.5, 789.6, 900.8, 927.5
crannog 241.3
cranny 197.3, 224.2, 290.1, 346.4
crap (n) 12.2, 12.4, 87.9, 354.14, 520.3 (v) 12.13
crape 115.7
crapehanger 112.14
crap game 759.8
crapola 520.3
crap out 410.10
crapper 12.10, 12.11
crappy 12.20, 71.5, 80.23, 1000.8
craps 759.8, 873.3
craps bet 759.3
crapshoot 457.3, 972.1, 972.6, 972.9
crap shooter 759.21
crap shooting 759.8
craps table 759.16
crapulence 88.2, 669.1, 672.1
crapulency 669.1, 672.1
crapulent 88.31, 669.7, 672.6
crapulous 88.31, 669.7, 672.6
crapulousness 88.2, 669.1
crash (n) 53.3, 56.1, 87.1, 184.20, 194.1, 252.2, 393.1, 395.4, 410.3, 412.1, 625.3, 737.5, 902.3, 1011.2, 1042.18 (v) 22.14, 22.18, 53.7, 56.6, 87.22, 184.44, 189.8, 194.5, 214.5, 225.7, 238.22, 393.24, 410.12, 625.7, 633.6, 902.13
crash course 568.8
crash diet 7.13, 515.2
crash-diet 270.13
crash dive 182.8, 367.1
crash-dive 182.47
crasher 214.3
crash helmet 1008.3
crash in 214.5
crashing 53.11, 56.11, 902.24
crashing bore 96.2, 118.4
crash into 902.13
crash-land 184.43
crash-landing 184.18, 184.20
crash of thunder 56.5
crash pad 228.1
crash the gates 214.5
crashworthiness 1007.1
crashworthy 1007.7
crasis 537.4, 767.4
crass 247.12, 269.8, 497.11, 505.6, 922.15
crassamentum 1045.7
crass behavior 505.1
crassness 497.2, 505.1, 922.3
crate (n) 179.10, 195.1, 386.6 (v) 212.9, 295.20
crated 212.12
crater 237.7, 275.2, 284.2, 913.1, 1004.1
cratered 284.17
craterlike 284.16
crater-shaped 284.16
crating 212.2

C ration 10.6
craunch (n) 58.3 (v) 58.10
cravat 86.33
crave 100.18, 440.9, 440.11
crave after 100.18
craven (n) 491.6 (a) 491.12
cravenness 491.3
craving (n) 100.6 (a) 100.24
craw 2.18, 270.3
crawdaddy 311.29
crawfish (n) 311.29 (v) 163.6
crawfish out 163.6, 363.8
crawl (n) 175.2, 177.17, 182.11, 760.8 (v) 74.7, 138.7, 175.6, 177.26, 201.5, 274.5, 827.7, 913.9
crawl after 100.18
crawl in 22.18
crawling (n) 177.17, 913.3, 1034.21 (a) 138.14, 175.10, 177.39, 201.8, 221.15, 311.47, 770.22, 884.9
crawl into one's shell 346.8
crawl out of 369.9, 600.11
crawl out of the woodwork 33.8
crawl space 386.6
crawl with 221.7, 884.5, 910.6, 991.5
crawly 74.11, 917.21
cray-cray 926.27
crayfish 311.29
crayon (n) 712.12, 712.18 (v) 35.14, 712.19
crayon drawing 712.12
crayon engraving 713.5
crayoning 35.12
crayonist 716.3
crayons 35.8
craze (n) 47.5, 85.38, 100.8, 101.1, 105.8, 224.2, 364.1, 578.5, 926.12, 1004.1 (v) 47.7, 224.4, 393.13, 802.12, 926.24, 1004.4
crazed 224.7, 393.27, 926.26, 1004.8
craziness 923.1, 926.1, 926.2
crazy (n) 926.16 (a) 47.9, 265.10, 922.22, 923.8, 923.11, 926.27
crazy about 101.11, 104.30
crazy as a loon 926.27
crazy fancy 926.12
crazy for 100.22
crazy idea 364.1, 932.7
crazy like a fox 415.12, 920.15
crazy mixed-up 985.12
crazy-paving 47.4
crazy quilt 47.6, 972.1
crazy-quilt 782.1, 810.3
crazy to 100.22
crazywork 47.4
creak (n) 58.4, 58.5 (v) 58.7, 58.8
creakiness 58.1
creaking (n) 58.5 (a) 58.14
creaky 58.14
cream (n) 10.48, 37.2, 86.11, 249.5, 607.2, 997.7, 999.8, 1056.3, 1062.5 (v) 320.5, 412.9, 1062.10 (a) 37.8, 43.4
cream, the 371.12
cream-colored 43.4
cream cracker 10.30
creamed 412.15
creamer 802.7
creamery 739.3
cream horn 10.41
creaminess 37.1, 1056.5, 1062.1, 1063.1
creaming 412.3
cream it 745.5
cream off 999.11
cream of society 578.6
cream of the crop 578.6, 999.8
cream of the jest 489.6
cream puff 10.41, 77.10
cream separator 802.7
cream soup 10.10
cream tea 8.6, 582.13
creamy 35.22, 37.8, 43.4, 1056.9, 1062.11
crease (n) 291.1, 291.3, 749.1 (v) 291.5, 291.6, 713.9
creased 291.7, 291.8, 713.11
creasing 291.1, 291.4
create 262.7, 337.4, 818.10, 886.10, 892.8, 986.14
create a disturbance 810.10
create a riot 810.10
create a role 704.30
create a tempest in a teapot 355.3
created 763.6, 892.18
created being 305.2, 763.3
created nature 1073.1
created universe 1073.1
creating 677.17
creating again 78.1
creating anew 78.1
creating once more 78.1
creation 262.5, 266.1, 677.13, 712.9, 818.1, 892.1, 893.1, 1073.1
creational 892.14
creationism 818.4, 1073.18
creation of the brain 986.5
creation science 818.4, 1073.18
creative 265.11, 337.5, 354.31, 638.3, 645.16, 674.6, 677.17, 712.20, 818.15, 890.9, 892.16, 986.18
creative ability 986.2
creative accounting 625.1
creative artist 986.12
creative effort 892.1
creative imagination 720.11, 986.2
creativeness 337.1, 986.3
creative power 986.2
creative thought 920.8, 931.1, 986.2
creative writer 547.15, 718.4, 986.12
creative writing 547.2, 718.2
creativity 337.1, 920.8, 986.3
Creator 677.2
creator 716.1, 726.1, 886.4, 892.7
creatural 312.13, 763.6
creature 138.3, 250.2, 305.2, 311.2, 312.5, 332.6, 384.4, 432.6, 575.5, 576.1, 577.1, 616.8, 763.3, 893.1
creature comfort 10.1
creature comforts 95.1, 121.3
creaturely 312.13
creature of habit 373.3
creature of impulse 365.6
creature of the imagination 986.5
crèche 567.2
credence 703.12, 953.1
credenda 676.2, 953.3
credential 509.4, 549.6
credentials 405.4, 443.6, 517.11
credibility 644.3, 662.3, 953.8, 968.3
credibility gap 354.8, 456.2, 600.4, 645.3, 955.2, 955.3
credible 935.20, 953.24, 968.7
credit (n) 150.2, 255.8, 438.1, 622.1, 627.1, 628.5, 639.2, 646.1, 662.3, 888.1, 894.1, 953.1, 953.8 (v) 150.4, 622.5, 628.8, 953.10
creditable 509.20, 644.13, 662.15, 953.24
credit account 622.2
credit agency 622.1
credit bureau 622.1
credit card 622.3, 733.4
credit crunch 619.1, 623.2
credited 622.8, 888.6, 953.23
credit history 622.3, 733.4
crediting (n) 150.2, 639.2 (a) 150.5
credit instrument 622.3
credit insurance 622.1
credit life insurance 622.1
credit limit 622.3, 733.4
credit line 622.1, 888.2
credit man 622.4
credit memorandum 622.3
credit note 728.11
creditor 620.3, 622.4
credit rating 622.1, 729.6
creditress 622.4
credit risk 622.1
credits 627.1, 871.6
credit slip 622.3
credit squeeze 622.1
credit standing 622.1, 729.7
credit to one's account 622.5
credit union 617.1, 620.4, 622.1
credit with 622.5, 888.4
creditworthiness 729.7
creditworthy 729.18
credo 675.1, 676.2, 953.3
credulity 953.1, 954.1, 982.1
credulous 923.8, 953.22, 954.8
credulousness 954.1
credulous person 358.1
creed 334.1, 381.4, 675.1, 676.2, 953.3
creedal 953.27
creedal statement 953.3
creedbound 687.8, 980.10
creedless 955.8
creek 238.1, 242.1
creek bed 239.2
creeky 238.23
creep (n) 175.2, 177.17, 660.5 (v) 74.7, 138.7, 175.6, 177.26, 346.9, 827.7
creeper 310.4, 310.33
creepers 5.30
creep in 189.7, 214.5, 617.14
creepiness 127.2
creeping (n) 175.1, 177.17, 259.1, 1034.21 (a) 175.10, 177.39, 221.15, 311.47
creeping crud, the 85.1
creeping feeling 128.1
creeping flesh 99.2
creeping of the flesh 74.4, 133.2
creeping socialism 611.6
creeping thing 311.2
creep into a corner 583.4
creep out of 369.9
creeps 74.4, 127.5, 128.2, 1023.2
creep up on 131.6
creep with 221.7, 884.5, 910.6, 991.5
creepy 74.11, 127.31, 1000.8
creepy-crawly (n) 311.32 (a) 74.11, 917.21
creepy feeling 128.1
cremate 309.20, 1020.25
cremated 1020.30
cremation 309.2, 1020.5
cremator 1020.13
crematorium 309.9, 1020.13
crematory 309.9, 1019.13, 1020.13
crème de la crème 249.5, 371.12, 413.10, 578.6, 999.8
Cremona 711.5
crena 289.1
crenate 289.5
crenated 289.5
crenation 289.2
crenature 289.2
crenel 289.3
crenelate 289.4
crenelation 289.2
crenellate 460.9
crenellated 289.5, 460.12
crenulate (v) 289.4 (a) 289.5
crenulation 289.2
creole 523.11
creole language 523.11
creolized language 523.11
crêpe 10.45
crepehanger 112.14
crepehanging 112.24, 125.16
crepe rubber 1048.3
crêpe suzette 10.45
crepitant 56.10
crepitate 56.7
crepitation 56.2
crepuscle 315.2
crepuscular 315.8
crepuscular light 315.3, 1027.2
crepuscule 314.3, 315.3
crescendo (n) 53.3, 251.1, 259.1, 708.25 (v) 53.7, 251.6, 259.4, 259.5 (a) 53.11, 708.53
crescendoed 259.10
crescendoing 251.8
crescent (n) 230.9, 279.5, 280.8, 647.2, 1073.11 (a) 14.3, 251.8, 259.12, 279.11
crescentic 279.11
crescentiform 279.11
crescentlike 279.11
crescent moon 279.5, 1073.11
crescent-shaped 279.11
cresset 1026.3

crest (n) 3.6, 3.16, 198.2, 198.4, 237.6, 289.2, 647.2, 916.4 (v) 198.10
crested 3.29, 198.13
crestfallen 112.25, 132.5, 137.14
cretaceous 37.7
cretic 720.8
cretin 924.8
cretinism 922.9
cretinistic 922.22
cretinous 922.22
crevasse (n) 237.7, 275.2, 813.2 (v) 292.11
crevasses 1006.5
crevice 224.2
crew 185.4, 577.11, 617.6, 617.7, 706.4, 726.2, 745.2, 770.3
crew chief 185.4, 185.5
crewcut 1016.14
crewman 183.1, 185.4
crewmate 185.4
crewmember 185.4
crew trainer 181.10
crib (n) 197.2, 228.4, 228.9, 341.3, 386.6, 386.7, 665.9, 759.19 (v) 212.6, 336.5, 356.18, 429.12, 482.16, 482.19, 621.4
crib, the 301.5
cribber 483.9
cribbing 482.8, 621.2
cribble (n) 79.13 (v) 713.9
crib death 85.2
cribose 292.20
cribriform 292.20
cribriformity 292.8
cribrosity 292.8
crib sheet 482.8
crick (n) 26.2, 58.5, 238.1 (v) 58.7
cricket 53.6, 311.35, 637.2, 649.2
cricket ground 743.11
cricking 58.5
cri du coeur 115.3
cri du cœur 440.2
cried up 509.19
crier 353.3
crime 655.1, 655.2, 674.3, 674.4, 1000.3
crime against humanity 144.11, 655.2
crime fighting 604.1
crime-infested 655.5
crime of passion 153.1, 308.2
crime-ridden 655.5
crime scene 159.2
crime watch 825.3, 1008.2
crime wave 265.2
criminal (n) 593.1, 645.10, 660.9 (a) 638.3, 645.16, 654.16, 655.5, 656.3, 674.6, 1000.7
criminal act 655.2
criminal assault 665.6
criminal behavior 671.3
criminal cohabitation 665.7
criminal congress 665.7
criminal contempt 505.2
criminal conversation 665.7
criminal court 595.2
criminal identification 517.11
criminal insanity 926.1
criminal investigation 938.4
criminal involvement 656.1
criminalism 674.3
criminality 638.1, 645.1, 654.1, 655.1, 656.1, 674.3
criminalize 444.3, 586.6
criminal jurisdiction 594.1
criminal justice system 594.2
criminal-justice system 594.2
criminal law 673.5
criminal negligence 340.1
criminal practice 597.4
criminal syndicalism 418.2, 611.4
criminal syndicalist 860.3
criminal tendency 655.1
criminal trial 598.5
criminate 599.10
crimination 599.2
criminatory 599.14
criminological 673.12
criminology 673.7
criminosis 655.1
criminous 655.5
crimp (n) 3.5, 290.2, 291.1, 291.3, 357.3, 483.10 (v) 281.5, 289.4, 290.3, 291.5, 291.6, 482.20, 1012.16 (a) 1051.13
crimped 290.4, 291.7, 291.8
crimper 281.3, 483.10
crimping 482.9
crimping iron 281.3
crimple 291.6
crimpy 291.8
crimson (n) 41.1 (v) 41.4, 41.5, 105.19, 139.8 (a) 41.6
crimsoning 41.3, 139.5
crine 3.4
cringe (n) 903.3 (v) 16.8, 127.13, 138.7, 168.3, 491.9, 903.7, 913.8
cringe-inducing 971.27
cringe-making 971.27
cringer 138.3
cringe to 433.10
cringeworthy 971.27
cringing (n) 138.2 (a) 138.14, 491.13
cringle 180.14
crinite 3.24
crinkle (n) 281.1, 290.1, 291.3 (v) 52.12, 281.4, 288.5, 290.3, 291.6
crinkled 288.7, 291.8
crinkling 281.1
crinkly 290.4, 291.8
crinose 3.24
crinosity 3.1
cripple (n) 85.45 (v) 16.10, 19.9, 393.14, 1012.11
crippled 19.16, 393.30
crippled, the 85.45
crippling 393.1
crippling attack 459.1
crisis 729.8, 731.10, 843.4, 997.4, 997.6, 1006.1
crisis archeology 842.4
crisis management 843.5
crisp (n) 10.41 (v) 281.5, 291.5 (a) 9.3, 281.9, 521.11, 537.6, 1023.12, 1023.14, 1050.4, 1051.13
crisped 281.9
crispiness 1050.1
crispness 537.1, 1023.1, 1050.1, 1051.3
crispy 9.3, 281.9, 1050.4
crisscross (n) 170.1, 527.10, 740.1 (v) 170.6, 740.6 (a) 170.8
crisscrossed 170.8
criterion 300.2, 786.1, 869.4, 942.2
critic 341.7, 496.6, 510.9, 547.15, 556.4, 596.1, 704.27, 718.4, 723.4, 866.3, 946.7
critical 339.12, 341.15, 495.9, 510.23, 556.6, 723.6, 843.10, 944.7, 946.16, 997.22, 1006.9, 1006.12, 1013.17
critical altitude 184.35
critical analysis 723.1
critical approach 723.3
critical bibliography 946.2
critical care 197.25
critical commentary 723.1
critical discernment 944.2
critical edition 341.2
critical evaluation 723.1
critical idealism 1053.3
critical interpretation 723.1
criticality 339.3, 843.1
critical journal 946.2
critical juncture 843.4
critically ill 85.56
critical mass 1038.10
critical moment 843.5
criticalness 339.3, 495.1, 843.1, 944.1, 1006.2
critical niceness 944.1
critical notice 723.2, 946.2
critical of 108.7
critical point 843.4, 997.6
critical realism 1052.6
critical review 556.2, 946.2
critical revision 341.4
critical success 704.4
critical theory 723.3
critical thinking 920.1
critical treatise 723.2
critical treatment 723.2
criticaster 929.6, 946.7
criticism 341.8, 510.4, 556.2, 723.1, 946.2
criticism of the arts 723.1
criticize 510.14, 556.5, 723.5, 946.14
criticizer 510.9, 946.7
critickin 946.7
criticule 946.7
critique (n) 556.2, 723.1, 946.2 (v) 723.5, 946.14
critter 311.2, 311.6, 311.10
croak (n) 58.3, 525.1 (v) 58.9, 60.5, 115.15, 133.10, 307.19, 308.14, 525.7
croaked 307.29
croaker 90.4, 108.3, 311.26
croaking 58.15, 108.7, 525.12
croaky 58.15
crock, a 354.11, 520.3
crock (n) 311.12, 355.1, 742.2 (v) 88.23
crocked 88.33
crockery 195.1, 742.2
crocko 88.33
crocodile 311.24, 812.3
crocodile tears 354.6
Crocodilia 311.24
crocodilian (n) 311.24 (a) 311.47
Croesus 618.8
croft 231.4, 1069.8
crofter 227.7, 1069.5
croissant 10.31, 10.41
cromlech 309.16, 549.12
cromulent 100.30
crone 304.3
cronk 60.5
Cronus 821.2
cronut 10.44
crony 588.3, 616.1
cronyism 609.35
crook (n) 164.1, 204.3, 273.2, 278.2, 279.2, 357.4, 417.9, 483.1, 593.1, 647.4, 660.9, 702.3, 901.2, 1020.12 (v) 164.5, 204.9, 265.5, 278.5, 279.6
crookback 265.3
crookbacked 265.13
crookbilled 279.8
crooked 204.14, 204.20, 265.10, 265.11, 278.6, 279.8, 354.31, 645.16, 654.15
crookedbacked 265.13
crooked dice 759.8
crookedness 204.8, 265.1, 278.1, 279.1, 645.1
crooked politician 610.5
crooknosed 279.8
crook the elbow 88.25
croon (n) 708.13 (v) 708.38
crooner 710.13
crooning 708.13
crop (n) 2.18, 3.4, 283.6, 310.2, 472.5, 605.1, 770.7, 887.1, 893.2, 1016.14, 1069.15 (v) 8.28, 255.10, 268.6, 1069.16, 1069.19
crop circle 310.8
cropduster 185.1
crop-dusting 184.9
crop-eared 48.15
crop farm 1069.8
crop-farmer 1069.5
crop farming 1069.1
crop herbs 1069.19
cropland 1069.8
crop of hair 3.4
crop out 31.5, 33.8
cropped 268.9
cropper 194.3, 410.3, 1069.5
cropping 8.1
crop top 5.24
crop up 818.13, 831.6
croquembouche 10.41
croquet lawn 743.11
crosier 273.2, 417.9, 647.4, 702.3
cross (n) 96.8, 170.4, 273.2, 527.10, 549.12, 605.5, 647.1, 647.2, 696.10, 702.3, 797.8, 1011.1, 1012.6 (v) 132.2, 169.2, 170.6, 177.20, 182.13, 335.4, 451.3, 451.6, 696.14, 797.13, 900.6, 910.8, 938.22, 1012.15 (a) 110.19, 152.28, 170.8, 170.9, 170.10, 451.8, 789.6, 797.15

cross a bridge before one comes to it 401.7
crossarm 170.5
crossbar (n) 170.5, 746.1, 752.1 (v) 170.6
crossbarred 170.11
crossbar switching 347.7
cross bitt 170.5
cross block 746.3
cross-bombard 1038.17
crossbones 170.4, 307.2, 399.3
crossbow 462.7
crossbred 78.17, 797.15
crossbreed (n) 797.8 (v) 78.8, 797.13
crossbreeding 78.2, 797.4
cross-check (n) 938.3, 943.2, 970.8 (v) 943.5, 970.12
cross-checked 957.20
cross-country 161.14
cross-country course 753.1
cross-country cycling 744.1
cross-country flying 184.1
cross-country race 753.3
cross-country racing 755.2
cross-country skier 753.2
cross-country skiing 753.1
crosscourt (n) 170.1 (a) 170.9
crosscurrent 238.4, 318.1, 451.1, 900.4
crosscut (v) 170.6 (a) 170.8
cross-disciplinary 568.19, 864.13
cross-disciplinary knowledge 928.6
cross-dissolve 706.6
cross-dresser 75.16
cross-dressing 75.11
crossed 132.5, 170.8, 170.10, 797.15
crossed fingers 354.5
crossed in love 99.10
cross-examination 598.5, 598.8, 935.4, 938.13
cross-examine 938.22
cross-examiner 541.7, 938.16
cross-eye 28.5
cross-eyed 28.12
cross-eyedness 28.5
cross-eyes 28.6
cross-fertilization 78.3
cross-fertilize 78.10, 890.8
crossfire 459.9, 863.1
crossflow 238.4
cross-grained 110.19, 288.6, 294.6, 361.11
crossgrained 335.5
cross-grainedness 110.2, 294.2, 335.1
crossgrainedness 361.3
crosshatch 712.19, 713.9
cross-hatching 170.3, 517.6, 713.2, 1027.6
crossing (n) 169.1, 170.1, 170.2, 177.1, 182.6, 182.10, 335.2, 451.1, 797.4 (a) 169.3, 170.8
crossing one's fingers 959.1
crossing-out 170.3
crossing-over 858.3
crossing over and under 170.3
crossing point 169.1
crossing sweeper 79.16
crossing the Styx 307.8
cross-interrogate 938.22
cross-interrogation 938.13
cross-interrogator 938.16
cross-interrogatory 938.10
crosslike 170.10
cross moline 647.2
cross-multiply 1017.18
crossness 110.2
cross off 255.12
cross one's fingers 124.7, 130.8, 955.6
cross one's fingers behind one's back 959.4
cross one's heart 334.6, 436.4
cross one's heart and hope to die 334.6, 436.4
cross one's mind 931.18
cross one's palm with 624.16
cross one's path 831.6
cross one up 131.7
crossopterygian 311.30
cross out 255.12, 395.16
crossover 170.2, 704.8, 750.2
crossover network 50.8
crosspatch 110.11, 789.4
crosspiece 170.5
cross-pollinate 78.8, 78.10, 890.8
cross-pollination 78.3
cross-pollinize 78.10
cross-purposes 451.2, 456.2, 779.1
cross-question (n) 938.10 (v) 938.22
cross-questioner 938.16
cross-questioning 938.13
cross-refer 957.14
cross-reference (n) 957.5 (v) 957.14
crossroad 170.2
crossroads 169.1, 230.2, 843.4
crossruff 758.3
cross-section 170.1, 349.7, 793.1
cross-sex friendship 587.8
cross-shaped 170.10
cross-staff 273.2, 417.9, 702.3
cross stitch 741.1
cross-stitching 741.1
cross swords 454.3, 456.11, 457.13, 789.5, 935.16
cross swords with 457.17
cross-talk 541.1
cross the border 189.11
cross the path of 223.11
cross the Rubicon 359.8, 843.7
cross the Stygian ferry 307.20
cross the threshold 189.7
cross to bear 96.8
cross to be borne 96.8
cross-training 84.2
cross-ventilate 317.11
cross-ventilation 317.9
crosswalk 170.2
crossway (n) 170.2 (a) 170.9
crossways 170.9, 204.19, 740.8
crosswind 184.32, 318.1, 900.4
crosswind force 184.27
crosswise 170.9, 204.19, 740.8, 1012.17, 1013.19
crosswise motion 172.2
crosswiseness 204.1
crossword 522.9
crossword puzzle 522.8
crostato 10.9
crotch 2.13, 171.4
crotched 171.10, 278.6
crotchet 278.2, 364.1, 709.14, 927.2
crotchetiness 364.2, 900.1, 927.1
crotchety 364.5, 900.8, 927.5
crouch (n) 913.3 (v) 138.7, 274.5, 433.10, 491.9, 913.8
crouch before 433.10
crouch down 913.8
crouched 274.7
crouching 138.14, 433.16
croup 217.4
croupier 574.4
crow (n) 38.4, 116.4, 525.1, 906.4 (v) 60.5, 116.8, 454.5, 502.9, 524.25
crowbait 307.15, 311.12
crowbar (n) 192.9, 906.4, 1040.7 (v) 906.8
crow call 517.16
crowd (n) 48.6, 582.5, 617.6, 770.3, 770.4, 918.2 (v) 162.4, 401.4, 401.5, 770.16, 794.7, 884.5, 902.12, 993.15, 1012.12, 1045.9
crowd, the 606.2
crowded 270.14, 401.11, 770.22, 884.9, 993.20, 1045.12
crowdedness 270.1, 1045.1
crowdfunding 729.2
crowd in 189.7, 191.7, 214.5
crowding 884.9
crowd of sail 180.14
crowd on sail 182.20
crowd out 862.5
crowd-pleaser 377.3, 907.2
crowd-pleasing argument 936.3
crowd sail 174.11
crowdsourcing 726.1
crowing (n) 502.4 (a) 502.13
crow like a rooster 502.9
crown (n) 2.8, 198.2, 198.4, 198.5, 198.7, 249.3, 280.2, 310.11, 407.3, 411.1, 498.6, 554.4, 646.3, 647.2, 647.3, 728.4, 728.8, 748.1, 794.5, 1026.6 (v) 198.10, 295.21, 407.6, 615.12, 646.8, 662.13, 1002.5
Crown, the 417.8, 612.3
Crown court 595.2
crowned 198.13
crowned head 575.8
crowned with laurel 646.9
crowned with success 409.14
crown green 750.3
crowning (n) 615.3 (a) 198.11, 198.12, 249.14, 407.9, 820.11
crowning achievement 893.1, 1002.4
crowning glory 3.4
crowning of the edifice 407.3
crowning principle 932.4
crowning touch 820.4
crown jewel 498.6
crownless 198.14
crownlike 280.11
crown of thorns 96.8
crown post 273.4
crown prince 608.7
crown princess 608.8
crown roast 10.16
crown with laurel 646.8
crown with success 409.11
crow over 502.9
crow's-feet 291.3
crow's nest 27.8
crow to pick 589.5
crow to pluck 456.7
CRT spot 1036.11
crucial 843.10, 886.14, 997.22, 997.23
cruciality 843.1, 997.4
crucial moment 843.5
crucialness 997.4
crucial period 843.4
crucial point 997.6
crucial test 942.2
cruciate (v) 170.6 (a) 170.10
cruciation 96.7, 170.1
crucible 797.9, 858.10, 942.2, 1060.6
crucifer 701.2
cruciferous 170.10
crucified 26.9, 96.25
crucifix 170.4, 696.10
crucifixion 26.6, 96.7, 308.1, 604.6
cruciform (n) 170.4 (a) 170.10
crucify 26.7, 96.18, 604.16, 661.9, 1000.6
crud 1004.1
crud, the 85.1
cruddy 1000.8
crude (n) 406.5, 1056.4 (a) 35.20, 98.18, 406.10, 406.12, 497.11, 501.20, 505.6, 534.2, 661.12
crude but effective 387.20
crude estimate 951.4
crudeness 98.2, 406.4, 497.2, 501.3, 505.1, 534.1, 661.3, 666.3, 922.3
crude oil 1056.4
crude stuff 406.5
crudites 10.9
crudités 10.37
crudity 406.4, 497.2, 661.3
cruel 26.10, 144.26, 146.3, 308.24, 671.21
cruel and unusual punishment 389.2, 604.1
cruel disappointment 132.1
cruelhearted 144.26
cruelness 144.11
cruelty 144.11, 144.12, 146.1
cruelty-free 999.21
cruet 703.11
cruise (n) 177.5, 182.6 (v) 177.21, 182.13, 184.36, 409.10
cruise control 1041.3
cruise-goer 178.1
cruise missile 462.18
cruiser 178.1, 179.11, 180.4, 180.6, 180.7
cruiser weight 297.3
cruise ship 180.1, 180.5
cruise to nowhere 177.5
cruising 182.1, 184.1

cruising missile 1074.4
cruising sailor 183.1
cruising speed 184.31
cruller 10.44
crumb (n) 248.3, 258.7, 793.3, 1051.5 (v) 771.6, 1051.9
crumbcruncher 302.9
crumbcrusher 302.9
crumbgrinder 302.9
crumble (n) 1051.5 (v) 16.9, 252.6, 393.22, 395.22, 806.3, 842.9, 1051.9, 1051.10
crumble into dust 393.22, 806.3
crumble to dust 395.22, 1051.10
crumbliness 1050.1, 1051.3
crumbling (n) 806.1, 1051.4 (a) 16.15, 393.45, 842.14
crumbly 16.14, 1050.4, 1051.13
crumb of comfort 121.4
crumbsnatcher 302.9
crumminess 661.3, 998.2
crummy 250.6, 661.12, 998.21, 1000.8
crump (n) 52.3, 56.1, 58.3, 902.3 (v) 52.15, 56.6, 58.10, 902.13
crumpet 1016.8
crumple (n) 291.3 (v) 265.5, 288.5, 291.6
crumpled 265.10, 288.7, 291.8
crunch (n) 58.3, 619.1, 671.8, 843.4, 843.5, 902.3, 997.4, 1013.5 (v) 8.27, 58.10, 802.13, 902.13, 1051.9
crunchability 1050.1
crunchable 1050.4
crunched 265.10
crunches 84.2
crunchie 461.10
crunch numbers 1042.21
crupper 217.4
crusade 458.3, 886.9
crusade for 509.13
crusading 458.21, 692.11
crush (n) 100.2, 104.3, 260.2, 770.4, 794.3, 1063.2 (v) 112.18, 112.19, 128.10, 137.5, 260.8, 412.10, 428.8, 432.9, 802.13, 958.5, 1051.9, 1063.5
crushability 1050.1
crushable 1050.4
crushableness 1050.1
crushed 96.26, 112.29, 128.14, 132.5, 137.14, 412.17, 428.14, 432.15, 1051.11
crushed ice 1023.5
crusher 820.4, 958.3, 1051.7
crushing (n) 96.6, 412.3, 428.2, 432.4, 1051.4 (a) 98.21, 98.24, 137.15, 725.18, 1013.18
crushing burden 1001.1
crushing poverty 619.2
crushing rejoinder 958.2
crush one 98.16
crush one's hope 132.2
crush one's hopes 125.11
crush under an iron heel 612.15
crust (n) 10.28, 142.3, 206.2, 234.1, 295.14, 607.2 (v) 295.27
crustacean (n) 311.29, 311.31 (a) 311.50
crustaceous 311.50
crustal plate 235.1
crustal segment 235.1
crusted 1046.13
crustiness 110.2, 110.3, 505.3
crust of bread 10.28
crusty 110.20, 142.10, 505.7, 1046.13
crutch (n) 171.4, 273.2, 901.2 (v) 449.12, 901.21
crutch-stick 273.2
crux 170.4, 522.8, 997.6, 1013.7, 1013.8
cry (n) 59.1, 60.1, 115.2, 115.3, 116.2, 352.4, 440.2, 526.9, 552.6 (v) 13.5, 59.6, 60.2, 115.12, 115.13, 116.6, 352.13
cry aloud 59.9
cry at the top of one's voice 59.9
crybaby 16.6, 115.9
cry back 859.5
cry back to 859.6
cry before one is hurt 115.12, 400.3
cry bloody murder 59.6
cry blue murder 59.6
cry down 510.13, 512.8
cry for 100.16, 421.5, 440.11, 963.9
cry for joy 116.6
cry for quarter 145.6
cry for the moon 967.5
cry havoc 399.5, 400.3
crying (n) 115.2 (a) 59.10, 60.6, 115.21, 421.9, 997.22
crying evil 1000.3
crying shame 661.5
crymoanesthesia 1024.2
crymotherapy 1024.2
cryo-aerotherapy 1024.2
cryocautery 1024.2
cry of wolf 400.2
cryogen 1024.7
cryogenic 1023.20
cryogenics 1023.1, 1024.1
cryological 1023.20
cryology 1023.1
cry oneself blind 115.12
cry one's eyes out 115.12
cryonics 1023.1
cryopathy 1023.2, 1024.2
cryosphere 1023.5
cryospheric 1023.14
cry out 59.8, 115.13, 352.13
cry out against 333.5, 379.3, 510.13, 599.10
cry out for 421.5, 440.11, 963.9
cry out upon 510.13
cry over spilled milk 113.6
cry over spilt milk 355.3
cry pax 433.8
crypt 197.2, 266.3, 284.2, 309.16, 703.9
cryptanalysis 341.8, 523.11
cryptanalyst 341.7
cryptic 345.11, 346.13, 519.5, 519.7, 522.17
cryptical 522.17
cryptic meaning 519.2
cryptic mimicry 336.2
crypticness 345.1
crypto 357.11
cryptoanalysis 345.6
cryptoanalytics 345.6
cryptogram 345.6, 522.7
cryptograph 345.6
cryptographer 341.7, 345.6
cryptographic 345.16
cryptographical 345.16
cryptography 341.8, 345.6, 523.11, 547.1
cryptologist 341.7
cryptology 341.8
cryptonym 527.3
cryptonymic 528.3
cryptonymous 528.3
cry quits 370.7, 433.8
cry shame upon 510.13, 599.10
cry sour grapes 600.9
crystal (n) 8.12, 87.4, 1023.8 (a) 36.7, 37.7, 1029.4, 1059.12
crystal ball 839.1, 962.2, 962.3
crystal clarity 521.2
crystal clear 31.7, 348.8, 521.11, 1029.4
crystal-clearness 31.2, 348.3, 1029.1
crystal gazer 962.4
crystal gazing 962.2
crystaline clarity 521.2
crystal lattice 1059.7
crystalline 521.11, 1029.4, 1059.12
crystalline compound 1058.1
crystalline element 1058.1
crystallinity 521.2, 1029.1
crystallization 1046.5, 1059.8
crystallize 807.5, 1029.3, 1046.8, 1059.10
crystallized 1046.13
crystallographic 1058.18
crystallography 1058.10, 1059.9
crystal pickup 50.11
crystal system 1059.7
crystal vision 689.8
cry to 440.11
cry uncle 16.9, 127.13
cry up 352.15, 509.11, 509.12
cry upon 440.11, 599.10
cry wolf 400.3
cub (n) 302.5, 302.10 (v) 1.3 (a) 374.4, 406.11
Cuban 89.2
cubbish 406.11
cubbishness 406.4
cubby 197.3, 258.3, 346.4
cubbyhole 197.3, 258.3, 346.4
cube (n) 883.4 (v) 877.2, 879.3, 1017.18
cubed 278.9
cube farm 197.6
cubehead 87.21
cube root 883.4
cubes 87.10, 759.8
cube-shaped 278.9
cubic 158.10, 278.9
cubical 278.9
cubic footage 257.2
cubicle 197.3, 197.6, 197.7, 739.7
cubic measure 300.4
cubiculum 197.7
cubic yardage 257.2
cubiform 278.9
cuboid 278.9
cub reporter 552.9, 555.4
cucaracha 311.36
cucking stool 605.3
cuckold 665.22
cuckoldry 104.5, 665.7
cuckoo (n) 336.4, 710.23 (v) 60.5 (a) 926.27
cud 8.2, 89.7
cud-chewing 8.32, 311.45
cuddle 121.10, 562.17
cuddlesome 104.24
cuddlesomeness 104.6
cuddle up 121.10
cuddliness 104.6
cuddling 562.1
cuddly 104.24
cuddy 197.9, 311.15
cudgel 604.12, 902.20
cudgeling 604.4
cudgel one's brains 931.9, 989.20
cue 3.7, 217.6, 517.9, 551.3, 551.4, 704.10, 704.21, 978.4, 989.5
cue ball 760.1
cuesta 237.5
cue stick 760.1
cue word 517.9
cuff (n) 604.3, 902.8 (v) 604.11, 902.19
cuff link 498.6
cuffs 428.4
cuirassier 461.12
cuisine 10.1, 11.1, 11.4
cuisinier 11.3
cuisinière 11.3
cul-de-sac 293.3, 1013.6
culex 311.37
culinarian 11.3
culinary 11.6
culinary art 11.1
culinary artist 11.3
culinary concoction 10.7
culinary masterpiece 10.7
culinary preparation 10.7
culinary science 11.1
cull 255.10, 371.14, 472.11
cullibility 954.2
cullible 954.9
culling 773.2, 808.3
culling out 773.2
cull out 773.6
culm 310.21, 391.4, 1021.2
culminate 198.10, 407.6, 1002.5
culminating 198.12, 407.9, 820.11
culmination 198.2, 407.2, 794.4, 820.1, 1002.3
culminative 794.13, 820.11
culpa 340.1
culpability 656.1
culpable 510.25, 656.3
culpable negligence 340.1
culpably negligent 340.10
culprit 593.1, 599.6, 660.8
cult 617.6, 675.2, 696.1, 697.1, 701.1, 953.3
cult figure 662.9, 678.3, 786.4
cult following 104.1
cult hero 662.9
cultish 692.8, 697.7

cultism 675.2, 692.1, 696.1, 697.1, 701.1
cultist (n) 675.15, 697.4 (a) 692.8
cultistic 692.8
cultivate 24.7, 392.10, 449.16, 568.13, 587.12, 892.9, 1069.17
cultivated 392.13, 496.8, 504.16, 928.21
cultivated land 1069.9
cultivated plant 310.3
cultivated taste 496.1
cultivate the friendship of 587.12
cultivate the soil 405.12
cultivating 1069.13
cultivation 392.3, 496.1, 504.4, 568.3, 892.2, 1069.1, 1069.12, 1069.13
cultivation of the mind 392.3
cultivator 892.7, 1069.5
cult movie 706.2
cult of personality 662.6
cultrate 285.8
cult status 509.5, 675.2
cultural 568.18, 606.8
cultural anthropology 312.10
cultural appropriation 773.3
cultural awareness 24.2
cultural center 208.7
cultural change 373.2
cultural commentator 718.4
cultural community 227.1
cultural diffusion 797.1
cultural diversity 797.1
cultural drift 373.2
cultural geography 312.10
cultural lag 373.2
cultural layer 296.1
cultural literacy 570.1
culturally disadvantaged student 572.4
cultural memory 92.29
cultural studies 312.10
culture (n) 312.1, 373.2, 392.3, 496.1, 504.4, 928.5, 1069.1, 1069.13 (v) 1069.17, 1070.6
culture area 373.2
culture center 373.2
culture complex 373.2
culture conflict 373.2
cultured 392.13, 496.8, 504.16, 928.21
cultured pearl 498.6
culture gap 456.1, 780.1, 787.1
culture pattern 321.1, 373.2
culture shock 226.3
culture trait 373.2
culture vulture 496.6
cultus 696.1, 701.1
culvert 239.2
Cumaean sibyl 962.6
cumber (n) 297.7 (v) 297.13, 1012.11
cumbered 297.18
Cumberland wrestling 457.10
cumbersome 257.19, 297.17, 414.20, 1012.18, 1013.19
cumbersomeness 257.9, 297.2, 414.3, 1013.9
cumbrance 297.7, 1012.6
cumbrous 257.19, 297.17, 534.3, 1012.18
cumbrousness 257.9, 297.2, 534.1
cummerbund 5.11, 5.19
cumulate (v) 386.11, 770.18 (a) 770.21
cumulation 386.1, 472.2, 770.9
cumulative 253.8, 770.23, 957.16
cumulative distribution function 968.2
cumulative dividend 738.7
cumulative system 609.18
cumulative voting 371.6, 609.18
cumuliform 319.8
cumulonimbiform 319.8
cumulonimbus 319.2
cumulostratus 319.2
cumulous 319.8
cumulus 319.2
cunctation 846.5
cuneal 546.8
cuneate 278.8
cuneated 278.8
cuneiform (n) 546.2 (a) 278.8, 546.8
cunnilingus 75.7
cunning (n) 354.4, 356.3, 413.1, 415.1, 920.3 (a) 354.31, 356.22, 413.22, 413.30, 415.12, 920.15
cunning as a fox 415.12
cunning as a serpent 415.12
cunningness 415.1, 920.3, 1016.4
cunning of the serpent, the 415.1
cup (n) 195.1, 196.4, 284.2, 411.1, 549.12, 646.3, 749.1, 751.1, 752.1, 753.1, 755.1, 964.2 (v) 91.27, 176.17, 284.12, 284.13
cup, the 88.13
cupbearer 577.5
cupboard 195.1, 386.6
cupboard lover 357.8
cupcake 10.42
cupel 1020.24
cupellation 1020.5
cupful 196.4
cupholder cuisine 8.6
cupholder meal 8.6
Cupid 104.7
cupid 104.8
cupidinous 100.27
cupidity 100.8
cupidon 104.8
Cupid's bow 279.3
Cupid's-bow 279.10
Cupid's itch 85.18
cup of bitterness 96.8
cup of tea 866.1
cupola 272.6, 279.4, 295.6
cupped 284.16
cupping 91.20, 192.3
cupreous 40.4, 1058.17
cuprous 1058.17
cups 8.12
cup-shaped 284.16
cup that cheers, the 88.13
cur 311.18, 660.6, 797.8
curability 396.9
curable 392.17, 396.25
curacy 698.2, 698.9
curate (n) 699.2 (v) 938.25
curate's egg 1003.2
curative 86.39, 396.22
curative measures 91.14
curator 574.4, 729.12, 1008.6
curatorial 397.12, 1008.23
curatorship 386.9, 397.1
curb (n) 211.6, 383.6, 428.1, 737.7, 1012.7 (v) 175.9, 428.7, 1012.10
curb bit 1012.7
curb broker 737.10
curbed 428.13
curb exchange 737.7
curbing 211.6, 383.6
curb market 737.7
curb oneself 668.6
curb service 8.11
curbstone 211.6, 383.6
curd (n) 1045.7, 1062.5 (v) 1045.10
curded 1045.14
curdle 67.4, 1045.10, 1062.10
curdled 1045.14, 1062.12
curdle the blood 127.15
curdling 803.1, 1045.4, 1062.2
cure (n) 86.1, 91.14, 396.7, 615.1, 698.9, 1008.2 (v) 86.38, 91.24, 374.2, 396.15, 397.9, 405.6, 1046.8, 1066.6
curé 699.5
cure-all 86.3
cured 405.16
cureless 125.15
curelessness 125.3
cure of souls 698.9
cure oneself of 374.3
curfew 315.5, 444.1
Curia 595.3
curia 595.1
curiage 1037.1
curial 595.7
curie 1037.6
curiescopy 1037.8
curing (n) 11.2, 396.7, 397.2, 1046.5 (a) 86.39
curio 870.5, 998.5
curiosity 100.1, 122.2, 570.5, 870.5, 981.1, 983.1, 983.2
curious 339.10, 870.11, 938.36, 938.37, 981.5, 983.15, 983.16
curious as a cat 981.5
curious mind 981.1
curiousness 870.3, 981.1
curl (n) 3.5, 279.2, 281.2 (v) 279.6, 281.5
curled 281.9
curler 281.3, 916.4
curlicue 281.2
curling iron 281.3
curl one's hair 127.15
curl one's lip 508.9
curl one's lip at 157.3
curlpaper 281.3
curl up 20.6, 121.10
curl upwards 193.8
curly 281.9
curmudgeon 110.11, 304.2, 452.3, 484.4
currency 352.4, 578.2, 728.1, 864.2, 869.2
current (n) 161.1, 172.2, 238.4, 318.1, 896.2, 1032.2 (a) 352.17, 373.13, 552.15, 578.11, 761.13, 831.9, 838.2, 864.12, 869.9, 928.27
current account 622.2
current affairs 551.1, 552.1, 831.3
current assets 471.7
current-control circuit 1041.6
current events 551.1, 831.3
current flow 1032.2
current gain 1032.17
current of air 318.1
current of events 831.4
current of fashion 578.1
current of thought 931.4
current saying 974.1
current yield 738.5
curricular 568.19
curriculum 568.8
curriculum vitae 557.2, 719.1
curried 11.7, 68.7
curry (n) 10.11 (v) 11.5, 79.21, 1044.8, 1070.7
currycomb 1070.7
curry favor 138.9
curse, a 998.5
curse (n) 96.8, 513.1, 513.4, 602.1, 691.1, 1000.4, 1001.1, 1011.1 (v) 513.5, 513.6, 694.5, 1000.6
curse, the 12.9
cursed 513.9, 1000.10
curse God and die 125.10
curse of Eve, the 12.9
curse of Mexico 758.2
curse of Scotland 758.2
curse one's folly 113.6
curse up hill and down dale 513.5
curse with bell, book, and candle 513.5
cursing (n) 513.3 (a) 513.8
cursive 547.22
cursor 1042.18
cursoriness 276.1, 325.1, 340.2
cursory 248.6, 276.5, 325.5, 340.11, 401.9
cursory inspection 938.5
curt 268.8, 344.9, 505.7, 537.6
curtail 252.7, 255.9, 260.7, 268.6, 428.7, 480.21
curtailed 252.10, 268.9
curtail expenses 635.5
curtailment 252.4, 255.2, 260.1, 268.3, 428.1, 480.6, 635.2
curtain (n) 295.2, 345.3, 346.2, 704.7, 704.16, 704.20, 820.1, 1012.4, 1028.1 (v) 295.19, 346.6, 1028.5
curtain aurora 1025.16
curtain call 704.7
curtain-climber 302.9
curtained 295.31, 1028.7
curtained-off 802.20
curtaining (n) 295.1 (a) 1028.6
curtain lifter 704.7
curtain off 212.5, 213.8, 802.8

curtain raiser 704.7, 708.26, 816.2, 818.5
curtains 307.1, 820.1
curtain speech 543.2
curtal 268.8
curtate 268.8
curtilage 212.3
curtness 268.1, 344.2, 505.3, 537.1
curtsy (n) 155.2, 585.4, 913.3 (v) 155.6, 433.10, 585.10, 913.9
curule chair 417.10
curvaceous 279.7, 1016.18
curvaceousness 279.1, 1016.3
curvate 279.7
curvated 279.7
curvation 279.1
curvature 279.1
curve (n) 164.1, 278.2, 279.2, 356.6, 756.3 (v) 164.3, 164.5, 278.5, 279.6 (a) 279.7
curve ball 750.2
curveball 356.6
curved 279.7
curve inward 284.12
curves 1016.3
curvesome 279.7
curvet (n) 366.1, 366.2 (v) 177.34, 366.5, 366.6, 743.23
curviform 279.7
curvilineal 279.7
curvilinear 279.7
curving (n) 279.1 (a) 279.7
curvy 204.20, 279.7, 1016.18
cushiness 121.2
cushion (n) 51.4, 213.5, 670.3, 901.20, 1008.3, 1047.4 (v) 51.9, 120.5, 670.8, 901.21, 1008.18, 1047.6
cushioncraft 179.22, 181.7
cushioned 121.11
cushioniness 121.2
cushioning (n) 1047.5 (a) 670.14
cushiony 121.11
cushty 999.18
cushy 121.11, 1014.13
cusp 2.8, 285.3, 843.4, 997.6
cuspate 285.9
cuspated 285.9
cusped 285.9
cuspid 2.8
cuspidal 285.9
cuspidate 285.9, 285.14
cuspidated 285.9
cuss (n) 513.4 (v) 513.6
cussed 110.20, 144.20
cussedness 110.3, 144.5, 361.3
cussing 513.3
cussing-out 510.6
cuss like a sailor 513.6
cuss out 510.18, 513.7
cuss word 513.4
custard 10.40, 10.46
custard pie 10.41
custodial 339.13, 397.12, 1008.23
custodian 79.14, 90.11, 429.10, 574.4, 1008.6
custodianship 339.4, 387.2, 397.1, 429.5, 635.1, 1008.2
custody 339.4, 386.5, 397.1, 429.5, 573.4, 1008.2
custom (n) 321.1, 373.1, 373.3, 373.5, 578.1, 579.1, 731.6, 733.3, 842.2 (a) 892.18
customariness 373.6
customary 373.13, 579.5, 687.7, 842.12, 869.9
custom-build 892.8
custom-built 892.18
custom credit card 622.3
customer 387.9, 731.6, 733.4
customer agent 733.5
customer base 733.3
customer care 731.6
customer-gouging 356.8
customers 733.3
customer's broker 737.10
customer service 731.6
customhouse 630.10
customize 405.8
customized 405.17
custom-made 5.48, 892.18
custom-make 5.41, 892.8
customs 630.10
customs agent 630.10, 770.15
customs union 617.1
custos 709.12
cut (n) 85.38, 96.5, 156.2, 157.2, 222.4, 224.2, 245.1, 251.3, 252.4, 255.2, 262.1, 268.5, 289.1, 290.1, 290.2, 296.2, 403.3, 457.1, 459.3, 477.5, 508.2, 517.5, 624.7, 630.6, 631.1, 633.4, 713.5, 758.1, 793.1, 793.3, 802.4, 865.4, 902.4, 902.8, 908.2, 1016.14 (v) 16.11, 26.7, 68.5, 96.17, 152.21, 157.5, 204.11, 222.9, 222.10, 224.4, 252.7, 255.10, 255.12, 262.7, 268.6, 285.6, 289.4, 290.3, 292.11, 299.3, 340.7, 393.13, 442.5, 477.6, 549.15, 557.5, 604.12, 631.2, 633.6, 713.9, 715.5, 758.5, 793.6, 797.12, 802.11, 857.12, 902.15, 908.3, 909.17, 1023.10, 1064.5, 1069.17, 1069.19 (a) 16.19, 96.23, 224.7, 262.9, 290.4, 299.4, 393.27, 537.6, 633.9, 713.11, 802.23
cut above, a 249.12
cut a corner 268.7, 340.8
cut across (v) 170.6, 204.11, 268.7 (a) 170.8
cut a dash 501.13, 662.10
cut a deal 437.5
cut a dido 366.6, 743.23
cut adrift 802.8
cut a far 909.29
cut a figure 501.13, 662.10
cut a figure in society 578.9
cut along 174.9
cut a melon 738.13
cut-and-dried 117.9, 405.19, 964.9, 965.7
cut-and-dry 965.7
cut and paste 1042.21
cut-and-paste 1042.18
cut and run 188.12, 222.10, 368.10, 368.11
cut and thrust 457.13, 459.16, 935.16
cut and try (n) 942.1 (v) 942.8
cut-and-try 942.11
cutaneous (n) 91.17 (a) 2.27, 295.32
cutaneous sense 73.1
cut apart 224.4
cut ass 368.11
cut a swath 409.10, 501.13
cut at 508.9
cut away 255.10, 802.11
cut back 252.7, 268.6, 635.5
cutback (n) 252.4, 268.3, 635.2 (a) 252.10
cut both ways 777.7
cut capers 366.6, 743.23
cut card 759.11
cut classes 222.9
cut corners 268.7, 340.8, 635.5
cut crosswise 204.11
cut dead 156.5, 157.5
cut diagonally 204.11
cut direct 157.2
cut down 252.7, 268.6, 308.13, 308.18, 395.19, 459.25, 635.5, 913.5
cut down expenses 635.5
cut down to size (v) 249.7, 252.7, 512.8 (a) 137.13
cute 356.22, 413.22, 415.12, 645.18, 1016.17
cute chick 1016.8
cuteness 415.1, 1016.4
cutesy 415.12, 1016.21
cutesy-poo 415.12, 1016.21
cute trick 415.3
cut flowers 310.24
cut free 431.6
cut glass 715.3
cut ice 894.10, 997.12
cuticle 2.4, 295.3
cuticular 2.27, 206.7, 295.32
cutie 302.7, 1016.8
cutie pie 1016.8
cutification 415.1, 1016.10
cutify 1016.15
cut in 214.5, 214.6, 772.3
cut in two 802.11, 875.4
cutis 2.4
cut it 18.11, 328.6
cut it fine 973.11
cut it out 857.6
cutlass 462.5
cutlery 8.12, 1040.2
cutlet 10.13, 10.15, 10.19
cutline 937.2
cut loose 120.6, 182.48, 369.6, 430.19, 431.6, 431.7, 671.15, 743.24, 802.8, 802.11, 810.10
cut lots 759.23
cut no ice 391.8, 776.4, 998.11
cut off (v) 255.10, 308.13, 395.12, 480.21, 480.23, 773.4, 802.8, 802.11, 857.10 (a) 473.8
cutoff 211.3, 268.5, 395.2, 857.2
cut-off man 745.2
cut off one's nose to spite one's face 361.7
cut off one's spurs 447.3
cutoff point 211.3
cut off short 268.6, 857.12
cut off with a shilling 480.23
cut off without a cent (v) 480.23 (a) 473.8
cut off without a penny 619.6
cut of meat 10.13
cut of one's jib 33.4, 262.3
cut one down to size 137.6, 395.11, 1012.16
cut one in 477.6
cut one off at the knees 395.11
cut one's coat according to one's cloth 413.20, 635.4
cut one's eyeteeth 303.9
cut one short 51.8
cut one's losses 107.5, 163.7, 494.6
cut one's own throat 414.14
cut one's teeth 818.8
cut one's wisdom teeth 303.9
cut open 292.11
cut out (v) 188.7, 192.10, 222.10, 255.10, 372.2, 381.8, 390.4, 395.14, 773.4, 773.5, 802.8, 862.5 (a) 965.7
cut out for 413.29
cut out for one 866.5
cut out of one's will 480.23
cut plug 89.7
cut price 633.2
cut-price 633.9
cut prices 633.6
cutpurse 483.2
cut rate 633.2
cut-rate 633.9
cut short (v) 268.6, 395.12, 857.11 (a) 268.9, 795.5
cut some ice 997.12
cutter 2.8, 5.34, 268.4, 802.7, 1040.2
cut the cards 759.23
cut the cheese 909.29
cut the deck 759.23
cut the first turf 818.10
cut the ground from under 19.10, 958.4
cut the ground from under one 1012.15
cut the ground from under one's feet 958.4
cut the hair 3.22
cut the knot 802.8
cut the matter short 537.5
cut the mustard 18.11, 328.6, 409.12, 788.8, 942.10, 991.4
cut the pie 477.6
cut the ribbon 818.12
cut the throat 308.18
cutthroat (n) 308.11, 593.3 (a) 308.24, 457.23, 632.12
cutthroat competition 457.2
cut through 268.7
cutting (n) 255.2, 310.3, 310.33, 477.1, 526.3, 530.2, 537.4, 706.6, 758.1, 793.3, 797.3, 802.2, 1069.15 (a) 17.14, 68.6, 105.31, 144.23, 156.8, 285.8, 544.11, 671.16, 1023.14, 1064.8
cutting blowpipe 1020.14
cutting edge 165.1, 211.4, 216.2, 285.2, 818.1
cutting in two 875.1
cuttingness 68.1, 544.3
cutting of supply lines 459.5
cutting one's losses 494.1
cutting out 192.1

cutting-out 773.1
cutting remark 508.2
cuttings 557.4
cutting the pie 477.1
cutting through 292.1
cutting torch 715.4, 1020.14
cutting words 510.7
cut to 788.7
cut to pieces 308.18, 412.9, 802.13, 958.4
cut to ribbons 308.18
cut to the heart 96.17
cut to the quick (v) 96.17, 152.21 (a) 96.23, 393.27
cut transversely 204.11
cut two ways 777.7
cut under 734.8
cut up (v) 96.17, 112.19, 322.4, 477.6, 510.15, 743.23, 793.6, 802.18, 810.11 (a) 96.26, 112.29
cutup 322.3, 489.12, 743.18
cut-up and torn-up 112.26
cut up root and branch 395.14
cut up rough 322.4, 810.11
cut work out for 573.10
cwm 237.7, 284.8, 284.9
cyan 45.1
cyanean 45.3
cyaneous 45.3
cyanic 45.3
cyanide 1001.3
cyanosis 45.1, 85.9
cyanotic 45.3
cyanotype 714.5
cyberbullying 127.6
cyberharassment 127.6
Cyber Monday 733.1
cybernated 1041.22
cybernated factory 739.3
cybernation 1041.1, 1041.3
cybernetic 1041.24
cybernetic control 1041.3
cyberneticist 1041.19
cybernetics 1041.2
cybernetic technologist 1041.19
cybernion 1041.13
cybersex 75.11
cyberspace 1042.19
cyberstalking 127.6
cyberterrorism 127.7
cyborg 1041.12
cybrarian 550.1, 558.3
cybrarianship 558.2
cyc 704.20
cyclamates 66.2
cycle (n) 179.8, 280.2, 812.2, 815.1, 824.4, 850.3, 914.2, 1038.7 (v) 177.33, 850.5, 914.5
cycler 178.11
cycles 1034.12
cycles per second 1034.12
cyclic 280.11, 850.7, 1038.18
cyclical 280.11, 812.8, 849.13, 850.7
cyclicality 849.1, 850.2
cyclical motion 850.2
cyclicalness 850.2
cyclical unemployment 331.3
cycling 177.6
cycling shorts 5.18
cyclist 178.11
cyclo-cross 744.1
cycloid (n) 92.12, 280.7 (a) 280.11
cycloidal 280.11
cycloid personality 92.11
cyclolith 549.12
cyclometer 174.7
cyclone 105.9, 317.4, 318.13, 671.4
cyclone cellar 197.17, 1009.3
cyclonic 317.13, 318.22, 915.15
cyclopean 15.17, 28.12, 257.20
cyclopean concrete 1054.2
cyclopedia 554.9, 928.9
Cyclops 15.6
cyclorama 33.7, 704.20, 712.10
cyclostome 311.30
cyclothyme 92.12
cyclothymia 92.11, 926.5
cyclothymic 92.12
cyclothymic personality 92.11
cygnet 302.10, 311.27
cylinder 282.4
cylinder press 548.9
cylindric 282.11
cylindrical 239.16, 282.11
cylindrical coordinates 300.5
cylindricality 282.1
cylindroid (n) 282.4 (a) 282.11
cylindroidal 282.11
cymatium 198.5
cymbaler 710.11
cymbalist 710.11
cymbiform 284.16
cyme 310.27
cymose inflorescnce 310.27
cynegetic 382.11
cynegetics 382.2
cynic 125.7, 510.9, 512.6, 590.2, 955.4
cynical 125.16, 508.13, 510.23, 590.3
cynicism 125.6, 508.5, 590.1
cynosural 208.13
cynosure 208.4, 574.8, 662.9, 786.4, 907.2, 1016.6
Cynthia 1073.12
Cynthian 1073.25
cypress 115.7
cypress lawn 115.7
Cyprian 665.16
Cyrenaic (n) 663.3 (a) 95.18, 663.5
Cyrenaic hedonism 663.1
Cyrenaicism 95.4, 663.1
cyst 85.39, 283.4
cystocarp 305.13
cytocentrum 305.5
cytokinesis 305.16
cytoplasm 305.4
cytotaxonomy 527.1
czar 575.9, 575.13
czardom 417.8
czarina 575.10
czarism 612.8
D 87.10, 882.9
dab (n) 10.24, 248.2, 413.14, 902.7, 1004.3 (v) 35.14, 287.5, 295.24, 902.18
dabble 80.18, 331.13, 930.10, 998.14, 1065.12
dabbler 929.6, 930.7, 998.10
dabbling (n) 998.8 (a) 930.14
dab hand 413.13
dabster 929.6
dacoit 483.4
dactyl 720.8
dactylic 720.17
dactylic hexameter 720.7
dactylion 73.5
dactylogram 517.7
dactylograph 517.7
dactylology 49.3, 517.14
dactylonomy 1017.9
dad 560.10, 842.8
dad bod 283.3
dadburned 513.10
daddums 560.10
daddy 560.10
daddy longlegs 311.32
daddyo 560.10
daddy's boy 561.3
daddy's girl 561.3
Daddy Warbucks 618.7
dado (n) 199.2, 290.1, 901.8 (v) 290.3
dadoed 290.4
daduchus 699.15
daedal 47.9, 413.22, 799.4
Daedalian 413.22
Daedalus 185.9
daemon 678.5, 678.12, 920.8
daemonium meridianum 314.4
daeva 680.6
daffiness 923.1, 926.2
daffy 923.9, 926.27
daft 923.8, 926.26
daftness 923.1, 926.1
dagger (n) 170.4, 462.5, 1040.2 (v) 459.25
daggle 202.6
dagoba 703.4
daguerreotype (n) 714.4 (v) 714.14
daguerreotypist 716.5
dagwood 10.32
daily (n) 79.14, 555.1, 555.2 (a) 849.13, 850.8
daily bread 10.1, 449.3
daily communicant 692.4, 696.9
daily communion 692.1
daily double 759.4
daily dozen 84.2
daily grind 849.4
daily grind, the 118.1, 373.5, 812.2
daily life 373.5, 812.2
daily newspaper 555.2
daily racing form 757.4
daily round, the 118.1, 781.2
daily routine, the 781.2
daily woman 79.14
daimio 608.4
daimonion 920.8
daintiness 16.2, 79.1, 248.1, 294.3, 298.1, 495.3, 496.1, 1016.4
dainty (n) 10.8 (a) 8.33, 16.14, 63.8, 79.25, 248.7, 294.8, 298.12, 495.11, 496.8, 1016.19
dairy 386.8, 739.3
dairy bar 386.8
dairy cattle 311.6
dairy cow 311.6
dairy cows 311.6
dairy drink 10.49
dairy farm 1070.5
dairy farmer 1070.2
dairy farming 1070.1
dairyman 1070.2
dairy product 10.48
dais 417.10, 901.13
daisy 999.7
daisy chain 310.25
daisy-clipping 184.8
daisycutter 757.2
daisy-wheel printer 1042.9
Dalai Lama 575.9, 699.14
dale 237.7, 284.9
Dalkon shield 86.23
dalliance 104.5, 175.3, 562.1, 562.9, 846.3, 998.8
dallier 331.8, 846.6, 998.10
dally 175.8, 331.14, 562.14, 846.12, 998.14
dally away 486.5
dallying (n) 104.5, 175.3, 331.4, 846.3, 998.8 (a) 175.11, 846.17
Dalmatian 47.6
Daltonism 30.3
dam (n) 241.1, 560.11, 757.2, 1012.5 (v) 293.7, 857.11
damage (n) 393.1, 473.1, 630.1, 996.2, 1000.3 (v) 393.9, 1000.6
damageability 1050.1
damage control 338.1, 396.6
damaged 393.27, 432.16, 1003.4
damaged goods 432.1
damage one's good name 512.9
damages 603.3, 624.3, 626.3
damaging 393.27, 393.44, 1000.12
damascene 47.4
damask 41.6, 41.8
Dame 77.8
dame 302.7, 304.3, 571.2, 575.2, 608.6
dame 77.5, 77.6
Dame Fortune 964.3, 972.2
Dame Nature 677.8
damn, a 998.5
damn (v) 395.10, 510.13, 513.5, 513.7, 602.3, 682.6 (a) 513.9
damnability 1000.1
damnable 513.9, 654.16, 1000.10
damnation 395.1, 510.3, 513.1, 602.1
damnation alley 759.12
damnatory 510.22, 513.8, 602.5
damndest 403.16
damned 513.9, 680.17, 695.18, 1000.10
damned, the 680.1
damned-if-you-do-and-damned-if-you-don't 1013.7
damned little difference 784.15
damned spirits 680.1
damn fool 924.1
damn-fool 923.9
damning 957.16
damning evidence 957.3
damning with faint praise 156.2
damn with faint praise 156.4, 510.13
damoiselle 302.6

Damon and Pythias 588.6
damp (n) 51.4, 112.14, 379.2, 1065.1, 1067.1 (v) 16.10, 51.9, 112.18, 252.7, 379.4, 670.6, 670.8, 781.4, 1012.10, 1022.7, 1065.12 (a) 1065.15
damp down 428.8
damped 52.17
dampen 16.10, 51.9, 112.18, 252.7, 379.4, 670.6, 670.8, 1012.10, 1065.12
dampened 52.17
dampener 51.4
dampening (n) 252.1, 1065.6 (a) 670.14, 1065.18
dampen the spirits 112.18
damper 51.4, 112.14, 379.2, 1012.7, 1020.12
damper pedal 54.5
damping (n) 16.5, 252.1, 670.2, 1022.2, 1065.6 (a) 670.14
dampish 1065.15
dampness 12.7, 1065.1
dampproof 15.20, 1066.11
damp the spirits 112.18
damsel 77.6, 302.6
damsel in distress 302.6
dam up 293.7, 1012.10
dana 150.2
dance (n) 705.1, 705.2, 770.2, 917.4, 1025.8 (v) 109.6, 116.5, 705.5, 743.23, 917.12, 1025.25 (a) 705.6
dance around 368.8
dance attendance 138.8
dance attendance on 138.9, 769.8, 983.8
dance attendance upon 577.13
dance card 381.1
dance critic 547.15, 718.4
dance criticism 723.1
dance drama 705.1, 708.34
dance floor 705.4, 743.13
dance for joy 116.5
dance hall 197.4, 705.4, 743.13
dance music 708.8
dance notation 349.1
dance of death 307.2
dance-off (n) 705.2 (v) 705.5
dance on a hot griddle 1013.11
dance on the razor's edge 1006.7
dance palace 705.4
dancer 152.5, 705.3, 707.1
dancercise 84.2
dancercizing 84.2
dancery 705.4
dances 708.8
dance school 567.7
dance the war dance 454.3
dance through 1014.8
dance to a different tune 852.6
dance to another's tune 433.6
dance to another tune 363.6, 858.11
dance upon nothing 604.18
dancing (n) 705.1, 1025.8 (a) 95.16, 705.6, 917.18, 1025.36
dancing girl 707.1
dancing light 1025.8
dancing party 705.2
dancing pavilion 743.13
dander 152.6
dandiacal 578.14
dandified 500.17, 578.14
dandify 498.8
dandiprat 258.4
dandle 562.16
dandruff 80.7, 296.3
dandy (n) 500.9, 578.7, 999.7 (a) 500.17, 999.13
dandyish 578.14
dandyism 500.4, 578.3
danged 513.10
danger 971.6, 1006.1
danger money 624.4
dangerous 971.20, 1006.9
dangerous age, the 303.4
dangerous drug 87.3
dangerous ground 1006.1
dangerousness 1006.2
dangerous person 1006.1
danger sign 399.3
danger signal 400.1
dangersome 1006.9
danger to health 82.1
dangle (n) 202.2 (v) 138.11, 202.6, 348.5, 501.17, 916.10
dangle before one 377.6
dangle before the eyes 501.17
danglement 202.1
dangler 138.6, 166.2
dangling (n) 202.1 (a) 202.9, 804.5, 916.17
dangling modifier 531.1
dan grade 760.3
Daniel 684.1
Danish pastry 10.41
dank 1065.15
dankishness 1065.2
dankness 1065.2
danseur 705.3
danseuse 705.3
Dào 807.1
dap 382.10
dapper 578.13
dapperness 578.3
dapple (n) 47.3, 517.5 (v) 47.7, 517.19 (a) 47.12
dappled 47.12, 797.14
dappled-gray 39.4
dappledness 47.3
dapple-gray (n) 311.11 (a) 39.4
dappleness 47.3, 782.1
darb 999.7
Darby and Joan 104.17, 304.4, 873.2
dare (n) 454.2 (v) 142.7, 216.8, 404.3, 454.3, 492.9, 640.6, 1006.7
daredevil (n) 492.7, 493.4 (a) 493.9
daredevilry 493.3
daredeviltry 493.3
dare not 491.7
daresay 951.10, 953.11, 968.5
dare to 403.8
daring (n) 454.1, 492.4, 493.3, 501.4 (a) 454.7, 492.21, 493.9, 501.19
daringness 454.1
dark (n) 522.3, 930.3, 1027.1 (a) 30.9, 32.6, 38.8, 38.9, 110.24, 112.24, 133.16, 319.8, 345.11, 345.15, 522.15, 645.16, 654.16, 930.15, 1027.13, 1031.3
dark, the 345.1
dark age 930.3
Dark Ages 824.5
dark and gloomy 1027.14
dark as night 38.8, 1027.13
dark as pitch 38.8, 1027.13
dark as the inside of a black cat 1027.13
dark-blue 45.3
dark brown 40.3
dark chocolate 10.40
dark cloud 98.5, 1073.7
dark clouds 133.5
dark-colored 38.9, 1027.15
dark-complexioned 38.10
dark corner 346.4
dark depths 275.3
darken 30.7, 38.7, 105.19, 112.18, 319.7, 1004.6, 1027.9, 1027.12, 1031.2
darkened 30.10, 1004.10
darkened mind 926.1
darkening 38.5, 346.1, 1027.6
darken over 319.7, 1027.9
Darkest Africa 261.4
darkest hour 1027.1
dark glasses 29.3, 1028.2
dark-haired 38.13
dark horse 610.9, 930.6, 972.9
dark humor 489.1
darkish 38.9, 1027.15
darkishness 38.2, 1027.2
darkle 1027.12
dark lightning 1025.17
darkling 1027.13, 1027.16
dark matter 1073.7
dark meat 10.23
dark nebula 1073.7
darkness 30.1, 32.2, 38.1, 38.2, 112.7, 315.4, 522.3, 930.3, 1027.1, 1031.1
dark of night 315.4
dark secret 345.7
dark shade 1027.3
dark-skinned 38.10
darksome 38.9, 1027.13, 1027.15
darksomeness 38.2, 1027.2
dark time 1073.17
dark web 1042.19
darling (n) 104.9, 104.15, 302.3, 562.6 (a) 104.23
darn, a 998.5
darn 396.14, 513.5
darned 513.10
darning 741.1
dart (n) 174.6, 462.6, 1001.5 (v) 174.8, 904.10
dart ahead 174.12
darting pain 26.2
darts 744.1
dart to and fro 330.12
Darvon 86.12
Darwinianism 861.4
Darwinism 861.4
Darwinistic 861.8
dash (n) 17.2, 132.1, 174.3, 248.4, 401.1, 501.3, 501.4, 517.6, 544.4, 797.7, 902.4 (v) 112.18, 128.10, 132.2, 174.8, 238.22, 401.5, 412.11, 517.19, 904.10, 1012.15, 1065.12
dash ahead 174.12
dash at 459.18
dashboard 1008.3
dashboard dining 10.2
dashboard meal 8.6
dash down 913.5
dashed 112.22, 128.14, 132.5, 513.10
dashed hope 132.1
dashed hopes 125.5
dash for 161.9
dashing 174.15, 501.19, 578.13
dash into 902.13
dash off 188.10, 340.9, 365.8, 401.5, 547.21, 712.19, 718.6
dash of the pen 547.1
dash on 401.5
dash one's hope 132.2
dash ones' hopes 125.11
dash the cup from one's lips 125.11
dash to one's hopes 132.1
dastard (n) 491.6 (a) 491.12
dastardliness 491.3
dastardly 491.12
data 551.1, 770.11, 928.1, 935.7, 957.1, 1042.15
data, the 761.4
data bank 1042.1, 1042.15
data base 871.1
database 549.10, 871.1, 928.1, 1042.11, 1042.15
database management 1042.15
database management system 1042.11
data capture 1042.8, 1042.15
data entry 549.1
data file 1042.15
dataflow computer 1042.2
data-gathering 770.1, 938.4
data-handling system 1041.5
data highway 1042.16
data-input system 1041.5
data integrity 1042.15
data-interpreting system 1041.5
data management 549.1
data mining 549.1
data point 552.3
data processing 551.7, 1042.1
data record 1042.15
data-reduction system 1041.5
data retrieval 551.7
data scientist 726.7, 1042.17
data security 1042.18
data set 1042.15
data storage 551.7
data storage and retrieval 1042.1
data system 1041.5
data tablet 1042.4
data trail 1042.15
data transmission 347.2, 1036.8
data warehousing 734.2, 1042.15
data wrangler 1042.17
date (n) 104.11, 582.8, 704.11, 770.2, 824.4, 832.4 (v) 562.21, 770.16, 832.13, 842.9
date at 832.13
date back 832.13

datebook 549.11, 832.9
dated 832.15, 833.3, 837.7, 842.16
datedness 833.1
date from 832.13
dateless 822.3, 829.7, 842.10
datelessness 822.1
date line 832.4
dateline 832.13
datemark (n) 832.4 (v) 832.13
date movie 706.2
date of birth 850.4
date rape 75.11, 480.3, 665.6
date slip 832.9
date-stamp 832.13
date sugar 66.3
dating 104.5, 562.7, 832.1
dating agency 563.12
dating method 842.4
dating service 563.12
dative 530.9
datum 766.3, 928.1, 957.1
daub (n) 350.2, 712.10, 1004.3 (v) 35.14, 80.16, 295.24, 350.4, 712.19, 1004.6, 1056.8
dauber 716.1
daubster 716.1
daughter 77.7, 559.3, 561.3
daughter element 1038.10
daughterhood 561.6
daughter-in-law 564.2
daughterlike 561.7
daughterly 561.7
daughter of Eve 77.5, 312.5
daughter of joy 665.16
daughtership 561.6
daunt 127.18, 379.3, 612.15
daunted 127.25, 491.10
daunting 127.28
dauntless 359.14, 492.19
dauntlessness 492.2
davenport 229.1
David 492.7
David and Jonathan 588.6
Davy 240.3, 678.10
Davy Jones 240.3, 678.10
Davy Jones's locker 240.5, 275.4
dawdle (n) 175.5, 331.8 (v) 166.4, 175.8, 331.14, 827.9, 846.12
dawdler 175.5, 331.8, 846.6
dawdling (n) 175.3, 331.4, 846.3 (a) 175.11
dawn (n) 314.2, 818.1, 1025.10 (v) 1025.27 (a) 314.5
dawn chorus 60.1
dawning (n) 314.2, 928.2 (a) 314.5
dawnlight 314.3
dawn of day, the 314.2
dawn on 521.5
dawn raid 131.2
dawn's early light, the 314.3
dawn upon one 931.18
day 824.1, 824.2, 824.4, 832.4, 1025.10
dayblind 28.11
day blindness 30.2
daybook 549.11, 555.1, 628.4, 832.9, 871.6
day boy 572.3
daybreak 314.2, 818.1
day camp 225.1
daycare 1008.2
daycare center 567.2
day-crosser 368.5
daydream (n) 100.4, 976.1, 985.2, 986.9 (v) 984.3, 985.9, 986.17
daydreamer 985.2, 986.13
daydreaming (n) 92.19, 100.4, 984.1, 985.2, 986.8 (a) 984.8, 985.11, 986.25
day-dreamy 986.25
daydreamy 985.11
<number>-day forecast 317.7
day girl 572.3
Day-Glo (n) 35.4 (a) 35.20
day glow 1025.2, 1025.10
day help 577.2
day job 724.5
day laborer 726.2
day letter 347.14
daylight 224.1, 314.2, 352.4, 1025.10
daylight saving time 824.2, 832.3
daylight vision 27.1
daylong 827.12
day nursery 567.2
day of abstinence 515.3
Day of Atonement 658.3
day of doom 839.3
day off 20.3, 20.4, 222.4, 857.3
day of festivities 20.4
Day of Judgment 839.3
day of reckoning 839.3
day of rest 20.5, 402.1
day one 818.1
daypack 195.2
day-peep 314.2
day player 707.4
day-pupil 572.3
day sailing 760.2
days beyond recall 837.2
days gone by 837.1
day shift 825.3
dayshine 1025.10
day's march 261.2
days of old 837.2
days of wine and roses 1010.4
days of yore 837.2
dayspring 314.2
daystar 1073.4, 1073.13
daytide 1025.10
daytime 1025.10
daytime serial 1035.2
day-to-day, the 869.3
day trade 738.1
day-trade 729.17
day trader 737.10
day trading 738.1
day trip 20.3, 177.5
day-trip 177.24
day-tripper 178.1
day vision 27.1
daywear 5.1
dayworker 726.2
daze (n) 92.19, 985.3 (v) 30.7, 122.6, 971.13, 985.7, 1025.23
dazed 25.7, 30.10, 923.8, 971.25, 985.14
dazzle (n) 501.3 (v) 30.7, 122.6, 501.13, 985.7, 1025.23
dazzled 30.10, 985.14
dazzler 1016.8
dazzling 30.11, 1016.20, 1025.32
dazzling light 1025.4
dazzlingness 501.3
d-block 1060.2
D-day 459.13, 843.5
dea 678.2
deaccession (n) 629.1 (v) 629.3
deaccessioning 629.1
deacon 699.4, 699.10
deaconry 698.2
deaconship 698.2
deactivate 465.11, 771.8
deactivation 465.6, 771.3
dead (n) 51.1, 307.16 (a) 21.8, 22.22, 25.6, 25.8, 36.7, 52.17, 65.2, 117.6, 173.14, 293.9, 307.29, 331.20, 762.11, 820.9, 837.7, 842.15, 1027.17, 1055.5
dead, the 307.15
dead against 779.6
dead-alive 21.10
dead-and-alive 21.10
dead and buried 837.7
dead and done for 307.29, 762.11
dead and gone 307.29
dead as a dodo 307.30, 837.7
dead as a doornail 307.30
dead as a herring 307.30
dead asleep 22.22
dead as mutton 307.30
deadass 118.5
dead ball 746.3, 747.3
dead band 1041.10
dead beat 21.8
deadbeat 138.5
dead between the ears 922.17
dead body 307.15
dead broke 619.10
dead calm 173.5, 287.1
dead center 208.2, 329.1
dead cert 970.2
dead certainty 970.1, 970.2
dead cinch 970.2
dead-color 35.8
dead-drunk 88.32
dead duck 125.8
deaden 16.10, 25.4, 51.9, 94.8, 120.5, 670.6, 670.8, 1027.10
dead-end 293.9
deadend 293.3, 1013.6
dead-end kid 178.3
dead-end street 293.3
deadend street 1013.6
deadened 25.6, 52.17, 1027.17
deadening (n) 16.5, 120.1, 670.2 (a) 25.9, 86.47, 120.9, 670.14
deaden the pain 120.5
deadeye 904.8
deadfall 356.12, 759.19
deadfanny 118.5
dead flat 201.3
dead force 18.5
dead from the neck up 922.17
dead game 492.18
dead giveaway 351.2
dead hand 471.5
dead hand of the past 837.1
deadhead 634.3, 704.27
dead heat 757.3, 790.3, 836.3
deadhouse 309.9
dead in the Lord 307.29
dead in the water 19.18, 395.29
dead language 523.2
dead leaf 1050.2
dead letter 520.1
dead-letter office 553.7
dead level 201.3
dead lift 1013.2
deadline 211.3, 381.1, 820.3, 843.5
deadliness 82.3, 173.4, 307.11, 308.9, 1000.5
deadlock (n) 173.3, 293.3, 790.3, 857.2, 1013.6 (v) 857.11, 1012.13
deadlocked 790.7, 1013.24
deadlocked jury 596.5
dead loss 473.1
dead low water 274.2
deadly 82.7, 247.11, 307.28, 308.23, 395.26, 1000.12
deadly disease 85.2
deadly pale 36.7, 127.26
deadly pallor 36.2
deadly sin 655.2
deadly sin of envy 154.1
deadly weapons 462.1
dead man 307.15
dead march 115.6, 175.2, 309.5, 708.12
dead matter 548.4, 1055.1
dead meat 395.29, 820.10
deadness 25.1, 52.2, 65.1, 117.1, 1027.5
dead of night 51.1, 315.6, 1027.1
dead on arrival 307.29
dead-on-arrival 308.8
dead on one's feet 21.8
deadpan (n) 94.1, 522.5 (a) 522.20
dead past 837.1
dead person 307.15
dead pledge 438.4
dead reckoning 159.3, 182.2
dead right 973.16
dead ringer 349.5, 778.3
dead ringers 873.4
dead run 174.3
dead season 313.1
dead set 173.3
dead set against 325.5, 451.8, 510.21
dead set at 459.1
dead set on 359.16
dead shot 413.11, 904.8
dead silence 51.1
dead stand 173.3
dead-stick landing 184.18
dead-stick loop 184.16
dead-still 173.13
dead stop 173.3, 857.2
dead storage 386.5
dead straight 277.6
dead sure 970.14
dead-sure thing 970.2
dead time 1041.11
dead-tired 21.10

dead to 94.10, 930.12
dead to shame 142.11
dead to the world 22.22, 331.20, 984.7, 985.11
dead water 241.1
deadweight (n) 297.1, 297.2, 297.7, 1012.6 (a) 297.16
dead woman 307.15
dead wood 1054.3
deadwood 310.20, 391.4
dead zone 1041.10
deaf 25.6, 49.6, 361.13, 980.10, 984.7
deaf, the 49.2
deaf and dumb 49.6
deaf-and-dumb alphabet 49.3, 517.14
deaf-and-dumb person 49.2
deaf as a door 49.6
deaf as a doorknob 49.6
deaf as a doornail 49.6
deaf as an adder 49.6
deaf as a post 49.6
deaf as a stone 49.6
deaf-eared 49.6
deaf ears 49.1
deafen 49.5, 51.9, 53.7
deafened 49.6
deafening 15.22, 53.11
deaf-minded 980.10
deaf-mute (n) 49.2, 51.3 (a) 49.6
deaf-muteness 49.1, 51.2
deaf-mutism 49.1
deafness 49.1, 85.15, 361.5, 930.2
deaf to 94.10, 442.6, 930.12
deaf to pity 146.3
deaf to reason 980.10
deal (n) 244.2, 247.4, 296.2, 328.3, 404.1, 437.1, 468.1, 477.5, 731.4, 731.5, 758.1, 759.11, 1054.3 (v) 87.22, 477.8, 478.12, 731.15, 731.18, 758.5, 808.9, 902.14
deal a blow 902.14
deal a blow at 459.16
deal a check to 412.11
deal a crushing defeat 412.8
deal a deathblow 308.18
deal a deathblow to 395.12, 412.6
deal a knockout blow to 395.11
deal a smashing defeat 412.8
deal breaker 335.1
deal by 321.6
deal destruction 395.10
dealer 730.2, 732.4, 737.10
dealership 730.2
dealfish 49.6
deal hard measure to 425.5
deal harshly with 425.5
deal in 731.16, 772.3
deal in abstractions 864.9
deal in commercial paper 728.27
deal in futures 737.23
dealing 328.3, 343.1, 477.2, 731.1, 731.2, 758.1
deal in generalities 864.9
dealing in commercial paper 728.16
dealing of death 308.1
dealings 328.3, 343.1, 731.1, 775.1, 831.4
dealings of providence 677.13
deal in the marvelous 355.3
deal-making 731.2
deal off the bottom of the deck 356.18
deal one in 477.6
deal out 477.8, 478.12, 771.4, 808.9
deals 894.3
deal with 321.6, 328.9, 343.6, 387.12, 407.4, 541.11, 556.5, 604.9, 731.17, 775.5, 889.5
dean (n) 249.4, 304.5, 571.8, 574.3, 575.3, 699.9, 759.21 (a) 842.19
deanery 228.5, 417.7, 698.2, 703.7
dean of men 571.8
dean of the faculty 571.8
dean of women 571.8
deanship 249.1, 303.3, 417.7, 698.2
dean's list 871.6
dear (n) 104.9, 562.6 (a) 104.23, 632.10, 632.11
dear as the apple of one's eye 104.23
dear at any price 391.11
dear-bought 632.11
dearest wish 100.11
dearie 104.10
dearly beloved (n) 104.9 (a) 104.23
dearly love 104.20
dearly love to 100.15
dearness 632.1, 632.2
dear one 104.9
dearth 891.1, 992.3
dearth of ideas 987.1
Dearth Valley 1019.11
dear to one's heart 104.23
deary 562.6
Death 307.2
death 395.2, 820.1, 828.1, 1001.1
death 85.2, 307.1
death agony 307.8
deathbed (n) 307.8 (a) 846.18
deathbed repentance 113.4
death bell 309.6
deathblow 307.4, 308.10, 395.2, 412.1, 820.4
death-bringing 308.23
death by one's own hand 308.5
death camp 308.12
death cell 429.8
death certificate 549.6
death chair 605.5
death chamber 605.5
deathday 307.7
death-dealing (n) 308.1 (a) 308.23, 308.24
death-defying 493.9
death fire 1019.13
deathful 308.23
death grip 474.2
death groan 307.8
death house 429.8
death instinct 92.28
death knell 115.6, 307.1, 395.2
deathless 829.9, 855.18
deathlessness 829.3, 855.5
deathlike 307.28, 307.32
deathlike calm 173.5
deathlikeness 307.11
deathlike silence 51.1
deathliness 173.4, 307.11
deathly 307.28, 308.23
deathly hue 36.2
deathly pale 36.7, 307.28
deathly pallor 36.2
death mask 349.6, 785.1
death notice 307.13
death of the heart 96.1
death of the soul 96.1
death on 99.8, 103.7, 451.8, 510.21
death penalty 308.7, 602.1, 604.6
death rate 307.12
death rattle 307.8
death roll 307.13
death row 429.8
death's bright angel 307.2, 679.4
death sentence 602.1, 604.6
death's-head 307.2, 399.3
death song 115.6, 307.9
death squad 308.11
Death Star, the 1073.8
death-stricken 307.29
death stroke 307.4, 308.10, 820.4
death-struck 307.29
death struggle 307.8, 457.6
death throes 307.8
deathtime 307.7
death toll 307.12, 307.13
deathtrap 356.12
Death Valley 891.2
death warrant 395.2, 602.1, 604.6
deathwatch 307.8, 309.4
death wish 112.3
deb 578.7, 818.2
debacle 194.1, 395.4, 412.1, 860.1
débâcle 860.1
deball 255.11
deballed 19.19
deballing 255.4
debar 444.3, 773.4, 1012.12, 1012.14
debark 186.8
debarkation 186.2
debarment 773.1, 1012.2
debarred 773.7
debarring 773.1
debase 137.5, 265.6, 274.6, 389.4, 393.12, 447.3, 512.8, 661.8, 797.12, 913.4
debased 274.7, 654.14, 661.12, 913.12
debasement 137.2, 265.2, 274.1, 389.1, 393.3, 447.1, 654.5, 661.3, 797.3, 913.1
debase oneself 113.6, 661.7
debasing 661.11
debatable 971.17
debate (n) 457.1, 541.6, 543.2, 613.6, 935.4 (v) 362.7, 541.11, 543.10, 931.12
debater 543.4, 935.12
debating 541.6, 543.1
debating point 938.10
debauch (n) 88.5, 669.2 (v) 88.28, 393.12, 665.19, 665.20, 669.6, 743.24
debauched 654.14, 665.25, 669.8
debauchee 665.10, 669.3
debaucher 665.12
debaucherous 654.14
debauchery 665.3, 669.2
debauchment 665.3, 665.6, 669.2
debenture 728.11
debilitate 16.10, 19.9, 21.4, 85.50, 252.8
debilitated 16.12, 16.18, 19.15, 19.19, 21.7, 85.54, 303.18, 331.20
debilitating 16.20
debilitation 16.1, 16.5, 19.4, 21.1, 85.3
debility 16.1, 21.1, 85.3, 303.5
debit (n) 473.1, 626.1, 628.5 (v) 255.9, 628.8
debit card 622.3
debiting 626.1
deboarding 186.2
debonair 109.12
debonairness 109.3
debouch (n) 190.9 (v) 33.9, 190.11, 369.10, 909.25
debouchment 671.6
debrief 184.48, 771.8
debriefing 184.3
debris 256.1, 391.5, 1051.6
de Broglie wave 916.4
debt 621.1, 623.1
debt counseling 621.1
debtee 622.4
debt explosion 623.1
debt of honor 436.1
debt of nature 307.1
debtor 621.1, 623.4
debtor's prison 429.8
debt service 624.1
debt slave 432.7
debt slavery 432.1
debug 940.2
debugger 1042.13
debunk 977.2
debunker 512.6
debunking 977.1
debus 186.8
debut (n) 582.15, 704.12, 818.5 (v) 704.29, 818.9, 818.13
debutant 572.9, 818.2
debutante 578.7, 607.4
decade 824.2, 882.6
decadence 393.3, 654.5
decadency 393.3, 654.5
decadent 393.45, 654.14
decagon 882.6
decagonal 278.10, 882.22
decagram 882.6
decahedral 882.22
decahedron 882.6
decal 713.4, 803.4
decalcomania 713.4, 803.4
decalescence 1020.1
decaliter 882.6
Decalogue 882.6

decalogue 636.1
decameter 882.6
decamp 188.6, 188.14, 368.10, 370.6
decamping 222.4
decampment 188.1, 368.4, 370.2
decanal authority 417.7
decanal side 219.1
decant 79.22, 176.17, 192.12, 909.25
decapitate 604.16
decapitation 604.6
decapitator 604.7
decapod 882.6
decare 882.6
decarnate 988.8, 1053.7
decarnated 988.8, 1053.7
decastere 882.6
decastylos 882.6
decasyllabic 882.22
decasyllable 882.6
decathlon 744.1, 755.2, 882.6
decay (n) 71.2, 80.7, 393.6, 393.7, 806.1, 806.2 (v) 393.22, 806.3
decayed 393.40
decay of memory 990.1
decease (n) 307.1, 820.1 (v) 307.18
deceased 307.29, 837.7
deceased, the 307.15
decedent 307.15
deceit 356.3, 415.3
deceitful 354.31, 356.22, 415.12, 645.18
deceitfulness 354.4, 356.3, 645.3
deceivability 954.2
deceivable 954.9
deceive 354.19, 356.14, 415.9, 415.11, 643.7, 645.11, 665.20
deceived 930.13
deceive oneself 975.10
deceiver 336.4, 357.1, 593.1, 645.10, 660.9, 665.12, 759.22
deceiving (n) 356.1 (a) 356.21
decelerate 175.9, 428.7
deceleration 175.4, 252.2, 428.1
deceleration parachute 181.13
decemvir 882.6
decemvirate 882.6
decenary 1017.23
decencies 580.3, 637.2
decency 143.1, 427.2, 496.2, 504.3, 579.1, 637.2, 644.1, 664.2, 995.1
decennary 824.2, 882.6
decennial (n) 850.4 (a) 850.8, 882.22
decennium 824.2, 882.6
decent 143.13, 427.8, 496.9, 579.5, 637.3, 644.13, 664.5, 991.6, 995.5, 999.20
decentralization 171.1, 771.2
decentralize 771.7
decent sort of fellow, a 659.1
deception 346.1, 354.3, 356.1, 356.7, 759.13, 976.1
deceptive 356.21, 500.16, 936.10, 975.16, 976.9
deceptive cadence 709.23
deceptiveness 356.1
decertification 442.1
decertify 442.3
decibel 50.7
decide 323.2, 359.7, 375.22, 886.12, 894.8, 946.11, 970.11
decide against 444.5
decide between 371.14
decided 247.12, 334.8, 359.11, 820.9, 960.2, 970.20, 970.21, 997.21
decidedness 359.1
decided resemblance 784.4
decided upon 359.16
decide on 371.16
decide once and for all 420.9
decide upon 371.16
deciding vote 371.6
deciduous 194.11, 310.39, 310.44, 828.7
deciduous forest 310.12, 1069.8
deciduous plant 310.3
deciduous tooth 2.8
deciduous tree 310.10
decigram 882.6
deciliter 882.6
decillion 882.13
decima 882.14
decimal (n) 1017.3 (a) 882.22, 1017.23
decimal fraction 1017.7
decimalization 882.14
decimalize 882.15, 1017.18
decimal system 1017.4
decimate 308.17, 395.10
decimation 308.4, 395.1, 882.14
decimeter 882.6
decipher 341.10, 521.6, 940.2
decipherability 521.1, 521.3
decipherable 521.10, 521.12, 940.3
decipherer 341.7
deciphering 940.1
decipherment 341.3, 341.4, 940.1
decision 323.1, 359.1, 371.1, 598.9, 754.3, 946.5
decision-maker 381.6
decision-making 573.3
decisive 359.11, 420.12, 843.10, 845.9, 886.13, 953.26, 957.16, 960.2, 970.13
decisive defeat 412.3
decisive moment 843.5
decisiveness 15.1, 359.1, 845.3, 960.1
deck (n) 87.20, 197.21, 197.22, 199.3, 296.1, 758.2, 770.8, 901.13 (v) 5.39, 201.6, 412.7, 498.8, 902.17, 913.5
decked 5.45, 180.17, 274.7
decked out 498.11
decked-out 5.45
deck gun 1022.3
deckhand 183.6
deckhouse 197.9
deckie 183.6
deckle edge 289.2
deck officer 183.7
deck out 5.42, 498.8
deck shoes 5.27
deck up 5.42
declaim 352.13, 524.19, 543.10, 704.31
declaim against 510.13
declaimer 543.4
declamation 543.1, 543.2
declamatory 543.12, 545.8
declarable 630.15
declaration 332.3, 334.1, 352.2, 420.4, 524.3, 598.7, 953.7, 957.2
declaration of faith 953.7
declaration of policy 609.7
Declaration of Right 430.2
Declaration of the Rights of Man 430.2
declaration of war 458.6
declarative 334.8, 352.18
declaratory 334.8, 352.18
declare 334.5, 352.12, 420.8, 524.23, 953.12
declare a dividend 738.13
declare a moratorium 625.9
declare a recess 826.3
declared 334.9, 352.17
declare lawful 673.9
declare null and void 445.2
declare oneself 33.8
declare oneself against 451.3
declare oneself a party 466.6
declarer 758.3
declare roundly 352.12
declare war 457.13, 458.14
declaring oneself in 466.1
déclassé (n) 586.4 (a) 607.10
declassified 430.28
declension 194.1, 252.2, 393.3, 442.1, 526.3
declination 164.1, 194.1, 204.1, 300.5, 372.1, 393.3, 442.1
declinatory 372.4, 442.6
declinature 442.1
decline (n) 194.2, 204.5, 252.2, 393.3, 633.4, 738.9, 820.3, 911.1, 922.10 (v) 16.9, 85.48, 168.2, 194.6, 204.10, 252.6, 303.10, 372.2, 393.17, 442.3, 530.16, 633.6, 911.2, 1011.11
decline and fall 252.2
declined 204.16, 372.3
declined with thanks 372.3
decline of day 315.2
decline of life 303.5
decline politely 442.3
decline to accept 442.3
decline with thanks 442.3
declining (n) 372.1, 442.1 (a) 16.21, 168.5, 194.11, 204.16, 252.11, 303.17, 393.45
declining market 737.5
declining years 303.1, 303.5
declivate 204.16
declivitous 194.11, 204.16
declivity 204.5, 237.2
declivous 204.16
declutter 798.5
decluttering 798.2
decoagulate 1064.5
decoagulated 1064.6
decoagulation 1064.1
decoct 192.16, 405.7, 797.11, 1064.5
decoction 192.7, 192.8, 405.3, 797.2, 1020.2, 1061.2, 1064.3
decodable 940.3
decode 521.6, 940.2
decoder 341.7
decoding 341.3, 341.4, 551.7, 940.1
decollate 604.16
decollation 604.6
décolletage 6.3
decollete 5.47
décolleté (n) 6.3 (a) 6.13, 274.7
decolor 36.5
decolorant 36.4
decoloration 36.3
decolored 36.7, 36.8
decolorization 36.3
decolorize 36.5, 37.5
decolorized 36.8
decolorizer 36.4
decolorizing 36.3
decommission 390.4, 465.11
decommissioned 390.10
decommissioning 465.6
decompensation 92.17, 92.23
decomposable 393.47, 806.5
decompose 393.22, 806.3
decomposed 393.40
decomposing 806.5
decomposition 393.6, 393.7, 806.1, 1051.4
decompress 20.7, 106.7, 120.6, 299.3
decompressed 120.10, 299.4
decompression 20.1, 106.2, 120.1, 299.2
deconcentrate 771.7
deconcentration 771.2
decondition 82.4
decongest 86.38
decongestant 86.32
deconsecrate 447.4, 695.14
deconsecrated 695.15
deconsecration 447.2, 695.1
deconstruction 798.2
decontaminate 79.24, 601.4
decontaminated 79.27
decontamination 79.3, 600.5, 1037.1
decontrol 430.16
decontrolled 430.27
decor 229.1, 498.1, 704.20
decorate 253.4, 498.8, 545.7, 646.8, 1016.15
decorated 498.11, 545.11
decorated hero 492.7
decoration 254.4, 498.1, 646.5, 647.1, 712.1, 1016.10
decoration of honor 646.5
decorative 498.10, 712.20, 1016.22
decorative arts 712.1, 712.16
decorative composition 498.7
decorative style 498.7
decorator 716.11
decorator color 35.1
decorous 111.3, 496.9, 579.5, 580.8, 637.3, 664.5
decorousness 111.1, 496.2, 579.1, 637.2, 664.2
decorticate 6.8
decortication 6.1
decorum 496.2, 579.1, 580.3, 637.2, 664.2
decoupled 813.4

decoupling 813.1
decoy (n) 356.12, 357.5, 377.3, 733.6 (v) 356.20, 377.5
decoy duck 377.3
decrassify 79.22
decrease (n) 194.1, 252.1, 255.2, 260.1, 393.3, 473.2, 913.1 (v) 244.4, 245.4, 252.6, 252.7, 255.9, 260.7, 473.5
decreased 252.10
decrease in temperature 1023.1
decreasing 252.11
decree (n) 352.2, 420.4, 673.3, 946.5, 964.1 (v) 323.2, 420.8, 613.10, 673.9, 946.13, 964.7
decree absolute 566.1
decree-law 420.4
decreement 420.4
decree nisi 566.1
decree of nullity 566.1
decrement 252.1, 252.3, 255.2, 255.7, 473.2
decrepit 16.15, 85.54, 303.18, 393.33, 922.23
decrepitate 56.7
decrepitation 56.2
decrepitude 16.3, 85.3, 303.5
decreptitude 922.10
decrescence 252.1
decrescendo (n) 52.1, 252.2, 708.25 (a) 52.16, 252.11, 708.53
decrescent (n) 1073.11 (a) 252.11
decrescent moon 1073.11
decretal (n) 420.4 (a) 420.13
decretive 420.13
decretory 420.12, 420.13
decretum 420.4
decrial 510.3, 512.1
decrier 512.6
decriminalization 443.3, 673.2
decriminalize 443.11, 673.9
decriminalized 443.15, 673.11
decry 510.13, 512.8
decrying 510.3, 512.1
decrypt 940.2
decryption 940.1
dective 1008.15
Decuma 964.3
decumbence 201.2
decumbency 201.2
decumbent 201.8
decuple 882.22
decurion 882.6
decurrence 194.2
decurrent 194.11, 238.24
decurtate 268.8
decurvation 279.1
decurvature 279.1
decurve 279.6
decussate (v) 170.6 (a) 170.8
decussated 170.8
decussation 170.1
dedaub 35.14
dedicate 477.11, 685.5
dedicated 101.9, 359.11, 587.21, 652.5, 685.8, 692.8, 696.16
dedicate oneself to 509.13
dedicate to 387.13
dedication 101.2, 359.1, 477.4, 554.12, 587.7, 641.1, 652.1, 685.3
dedication to duty 641.2
deditician 430.11
deduce 192.14, 935.15, 946.10, 951.10
deducible 935.23
deduct 252.7, 255.9, 631.2
deductible (n) 1008.4 (a) 630.16
deduction 252.1, 255.1, 255.7, 630.9, 631.1, 775.1, 935.3, 946.4
deductive 255.13, 935.22
deductive power 920.1
deductive reasoning 935.3
deed (n) 328.3, 437.1, 492.6, 549.5 (v) 629.3
deeda 87.10
deedholder 470.2
deeding 629.1
deed of release 475.2
deed of trust 438.4
deed over 629.3
deeds of derring-do 492.4
deejay 1034.23
deely-bobber 1052.5
deem 946.8, 946.9, 951.10, 953.11
deemed 951.14
deeming 946.1
de-emphasize 252.9, 670.6, 998.12
de-emphasized 252.10
deemster 596.2
deem trustworthy 953.17
de-energize 19.9
deep (n) 275.2 (a) 35.17, 54.11, 93.24, 158.11, 207.6, 247.6, 269.6, 275.11, 415.12, 522.16, 920.17, 928.21
deep, the 240.1, 275.4
deep as a well 275.12
deep as China 257.20
deep as hell 275.12
deep asleep 22.22
deep as the ocean 257.20, 275.12
deep as the sea 275.12
deep black 38.8
deep-blue 45.3
deep blue sea, the 240.1
deep-buried 275.13
deep-colored 35.17, 35.19
deep-cut 275.11
deep dark secret 345.5
deep-discount 633.9
deep-dish pie 10.41
deep-down 275.11
deep-downness 275.1
deep-dye 35.14, 855.9
deep-dyed 35.18, 373.18, 794.10, 855.13
deep-dyed falsehood 354.12
deep-echoing 54.11
deepen 119.2, 158.9, 251.5, 269.4, 275.9
deepened 119.4, 251.7
deep-engraven 275.11, 855.13
deepening 119.1, 251.2, 275.8
deepest 199.7, 275.16
deepest mind 919.3
deepest recesses 207.2
deep-fat fried 11.7
deep-fat fry 11.5
deep-felt 93.24
deep-fixed 275.11, 373.18, 855.13
deep freeze 1023.3, 1024.5
deep-freeze 1024.11
deep-freeze, the 1023.4
deep-freezer 1024.5
deep freezing 1024.1
deep-freezing (n) 397.2 (a) 1024.12
deep-fried 11.7
deep-frozen 1024.14
deep-fry 11.5
deep-frying 11.2
deep future 839.1
deep-going 275.11
deepgoing 93.24
deep-grounded 855.13
deep in debt 623.8
deepish 275.11
deep knowledge 928.6
deep-laid 275.11, 415.12, 799.4, 855.13
deep-laid plot 381.5
deep-laid scheme 381.5
deep-lying 275.11
deeply involved 898.5
deeply involved in debt 623.8
deepmost 275.16
deep mourning 115.7
deepmouthed 54.11
deepness 54.1, 275.1, 522.2
deep night 1027.1
deep-pitched 54.11
deep pocket 618.7
deep pockets 618.1, 618.3
deep-reaching 275.11
deep-rooted 275.11, 373.18, 855.13
deep-rooted belief 953.5
deep-rootedness 275.1, 855.2
deeps 158.1, 275.3
deeps, the 275.4
deep-sea 182.58, 240.8, 275.15
deep sea, the 240.1, 275.4
deep-sea diver 240.7, 367.4
deep-sea diving 367.3
deep-sea man 183.1
deep-seated 275.11, 373.18, 767.7, 855.13
deep-seatedness 275.1, 855.2
deep-sea trench 275.4
deep secret 345.5
deep sense 93.1
deep-set 275.11, 373.18, 855.13
deep-settled 275.11, 373.18, 855.13
deep-sinking 275.11
deep six 309.5, 309.16, 390.3
deep-six 308.14, 370.5, 390.7
deep-sixed 307.29
deep sleep 22.5
deepsome 275.11
deep-sounding 54.11
Deep South 231.7
deep space 158.1, 261.1, 275.3, 1073.3
deep-space ship 1075.2
deep strike 459.1
deep structure 518.1, 530.2
deep study 983.3
deep-sunk 275.11
deep-sunken 275.11
deep-think 931.1
deep thinking 931.3
deepthinking 931.21
deep thought 931.3, 983.3
deep-thrilling 105.30
deep throat 551.5
deep-toned 54.11
deep-troubled 96.26
deep water 240.1
deep-water 275.15
deepwater sailor 183.1
deep web 1042.19
deep-worn 393.31
deer 311.5
deerlet 311.5
deerlike 311.45
deer tick 311.37
de-escalate 252.7, 670.6, 913.4
de-escalation 252.1, 670.2, 913.1
deescalation 464.7
deface 265.7, 1004.4, 1015.5
defaced 265.12, 1004.8, 1015.6
defacement 265.3, 1004.1, 1015.1
de facto 761.13, 761.15
de facto possession 469.1
defalcate 389.4
defalcation 389.1, 795.2, 911.1
defamation 512.2
defamation of character 512.2
defamatory 512.13
defame 512.9, 661.9
defamer 512.6
defang 16.10, 19.9
default (n) 222.4, 327.1, 340.1, 435.1, 623.2, 625.1, 795.2, 911.1 (v) 222.7, 340.6, 473.4, 625.6, 751.4
defaulter 625.5
defaulting 625.10
defeasance 445.1
defeasible 958.10
defeat (n) 132.1, 410.1, 412.1, 412.3, 1012.3 (v) 132.2, 249.7, 395.11, 411.5, 412.6, 958.5, 1012.15
defeated 132.5, 412.14, 820.9
defeated candidate 610.9
defeatee 412.5
defeater 411.2
defeat expectation 132.2
defeat hope 132.2
defeating 411.7, 1012.20
defeatism 125.6, 335.1, 491.2
defeatist (n) 125.7 (a) 125.16
defeat of time 827.1
defeat time 827.6
defeat utterly 412.8
defecate 12.13, 909.22
defecation 12.2, 12.4, 909.6
defect (n) 85.1, 795.2, 1003.2, 1004.1 (v) 188.17, 190.16, 222.8, 335.4, 363.7, 370.6, 435.3, 858.13
defectibility 1003.1
defection 188.1, 190.7, 222.4, 335.2, 363.2, 370.2, 625.1, 852.1, 858.3
defective (n) 85.45, 924.8 (a) 795.4, 975.16, 992.9, 1003.4, 1004.8

defective birth 870.6
defective fetus 870.6
defectiveness 795.1, 911.1, 975.1, 992.4, 1003.1
defective verb 530.4
defective vision 85.14
defective year 824.2
defectless 1002.6
defectlessness 1002.1
defect of sight 28.1
defect of vision 28.1
defector 190.10, 363.5, 858.8
defeminization 19.5
defence 460.1
defend 458.17, 460.8, 600.10, 1008.18
defendable 460.15
defendant 452.3, 598.11, 599.6, 935.12, 938.19, 939.3
defend a right 642.6
defended 1008.21
defender 460.7, 600.8, 616.9, 749.2, 752.2, 1008.5
defending 460.11
defend oneself 460.8, 900.6
defend tooth and nail 460.8
defend to the death 460.8
defend to the last breath 460.8
defenestrate 308.18, 604.16, 909.13
defenestration 308.1, 604.6, 909.1
defense 460.1, 598.6, 600.2, 747.3, 749.2, 749.5, 754.3, 900.5, 935.4, 939.2, 1008.1, 1012.5
defense attorney 597.1
defense capability 460.2
defense cuts 465.6
defense forces 461.20
defense hit 749.6
defense in depth 460.1
defense lawyer 597.1
defenseless 19.18, 584.12, 1006.14
defenselessness 19.4, 406.3, 584.4, 1006.3
defense mechanism 92.23, 368.1, 460.1, 990.3
defense of a thesis 935.4
defense plant 739.3
defense reaction 92.23, 368.1
defenses 460.1
defense work 460.4
defensibility 600.7, 649.1
defensible 460.15, 600.14, 649.7
defensive 460.11, 600.13, 1008.23
defensive, the 460.1
defensive back 746.2
defensive board 747.1
defensive platoon 746.2
defensive team 746.2
defensive zone 749.1
defer 163.6, 168.3, 329.5, 332.11, 846.9
deference 155.1, 326.1, 433.1, 434.1, 504.1, 641.1
deferential 155.8, 326.3, 433.16, 504.13, 641.13
deferential regard 155.1
deferment 846.4
defer payment 622.7
deferral 846.4
deferred assets 471.7
deferred payment 624.1
deferred payments 623.2
defer to 155.4, 326.2, 433.9, 434.2
defer to one's duty 641.9
defial 454.1
defiance 114.2, 327.2, 335.1, 361.4, 453.1, 454.1, 458.6
defiance of authority 327.2, 418.1
defiance of time 827.1
defiant 114.5, 327.8, 327.10, 361.12, 418.5, 454.7
deficiency 250.3, 795.1, 795.2, 992.4, 1003.1, 1003.2
deficiency disease 85.11
deficient 250.7, 340.12, 795.4, 911.5, 992.9, 1003.4
deficit 255.8, 623.1, 623.2, 795.2, 911.1, 992.4
deficit financing 623.2, 729.2
deficit spending 626.1
defile (n) 237.7, 270.3, 383.3 (v) 80.17, 177.30, 389.4, 393.12, 512.10, 654.10, 661.9, 665.20, 1000.6
defiled 80.21, 665.23
defilement 80.4, 389.1, 393.2, 512.2, 665.6, 1000.3
defiler 665.12
definability 341.6
definable 341.17, 518.10
define 210.4, 341.10, 349.9, 517.19, 521.6, 527.11, 855.9, 865.10
defined 31.7, 210.6, 521.11, 865.12, 959.8
definer 341.7
defining 210.9, 341.15, 809.7
defining moment 722.4, 843.5, 997.4
defining vocabulary 530.1
definite 31.7, 50.16, 210.6, 359.11, 521.11, 865.12, 960.2, 970.13
definite article 530.6
definiteness 31.2, 334.2, 359.1, 865.2, 960.1, 970.1
definite odor 69.1
definition 31.2, 210.1, 341.1, 341.5, 518.3, 521.2, 527.2, 865.8, 959.2, 1035.5
definitional 341.14
definitive 210.9, 247.12, 417.15, 820.11, 820.12, 960.2
definitiveness 820.2
definitive work 554.1
deflagrate 1020.24
deflagration 1019.14, 1020.5
deflate 19.10, 137.4, 252.7, 260.10, 633.6, 913.4, 958.4
deflated 252.10, 260.14, 913.12, 958.7
deflater 512.6
deflation 137.2, 252.1, 260.4, 410.3, 633.4, 731.10, 913.1
deflationary 260.11, 633.7, 731.23
deflationary spiral 633.4
deflect 164.5, 204.9, 279.6, 379.4, 1012.14
deflected 164.8
deflection 164.2, 204.1, 204.3, 278.2, 279.3, 379.2, 1036.12
deflectional 204.13
deflection-modulated display 1036.11
deflective 164.8
deflector 1035.11
deflexure 164.2, 204.1
deflorate 480.15
defloration 480.3, 665.6
deflower 393.12, 480.15, 665.20
deflowering 665.6
deflowerment 480.3
defluent 238.24
defluxion 190.4, 194.1, 238.4
defocus (n) 32.2 (v) 32.4
defoliant 1001.3
defoliate 802.14
defoliation 802.6
deforest 1069.18
deforestation 1069.3
deform 263.3, 265.7, 350.3, 852.7, 1004.4
deformation 265.3, 350.1, 393.3, 1004.1
deformed 265.12, 870.13, 1004.8, 1015.8
deformity 85.1, 85.45, 265.3, 870.3, 1004.1, 1015.2
defraud 356.18, 389.4, 482.13
defrauder 357.3
defrauding 356.1
defray 624.18
defrayal 624.1
defrayer 624.9
defray expenses 624.18
defrayment 624.1
defrock 447.4, 661.8, 909.19
defrocking 447.2, 909.4
defrost 1020.21
deft 413.22
deftness 413.1
defunct 307.29, 762.11, 820.9, 837.7
defunct, the 307.15
defuse 120.5, 464.8, 465.7, 670.6
defusing 120.1, 670.2
defy (n) 454.2 (v) 216.8, 327.6, 435.4, 453.2, 454.3, 458.14, 492.9, 1012.15
defy authority 418.4
defy belief 955.7
defy comprehension 522.10
defy danger 493.6, 1006.7
defying (n) 454.1 (a) 454.7
defying belief 955.10
defying gravity 193.1
defy time 827.6
dégagé 106.15, 340.11, 581.3
degauss 1032.27
degeneracy 393.3, 654.5
degenerate (n) 660.4 (v) 119.3, 393.12, 393.16, 654.9, 810.8, 852.6, 858.13, 861.5, 1011.11 (a) 393.45, 654.14, 852.10, 858.20
degenerateness 393.3, 654.5
degeneration 393.3, 654.5, 852.1, 858.3, 861.1, 1041.6
degenerative 393.27, 861.8
degenerative change 852.1
deglutition 8.1
degradability 393.6
degradable 393.47, 806.5
degradation 393.3, 393.6, 447.1, 645.2, 654.5, 661.3, 661.4, 806.1, 909.4, 913.1
degrade 137.5, 393.12, 447.3, 512.8, 661.8, 909.19
degraded 645.17, 654.14, 661.12
degrade oneself 661.7
degrading (n) 447.1 (a) 156.8, 661.11
degree 245.1, 300.2, 300.3, 607.1, 648.6, 708.29, 709.20, 807.2
degree-granting institution 567.5
degrees 161.3, 572.8
degust 62.7
dehisce 292.16, 310.34
dehiscence 292.2
dehiscent 292.18
dehiscent fruit 10.38
dehortation 379.1
dehumanize 144.15
dehumanized 144.26
dehumidification 1066.3
dehumidifier 1066.4
dehumidify 1066.6
dehydrant 1066.4
dehydrate 397.9, 1066.6
dehydrated 1066.9
dehydrated foods 10.5
dehydrating 1066.10
dehydration 397.2, 1066.1, 1066.3
dehydrator 1066.4
dehydrofreezing 1024.1
de-ice 1020.21
deification 155.1, 509.5, 662.8, 697.2, 912.1
deified 662.18, 912.9
deify 155.4, 509.12, 662.13, 697.5, 912.6
deifying 155.9
deign 137.8, 141.8, 441.2
deigning 137.3
deism 675.5, 692.1
deist 675.16
deistic 675.25
deity 677.1, 678.2
déjà vu 689.6, 989.3
deject 112.18
dejecta 12.3
dejected 110.24, 112.22
dejectedness 112.3
dejection 12.2, 12.3, 110.8, 112.3
dejecture 12.3
déjeuner à la fourchette 8.6
dejunk 798.5
de jure 673.11
de jure possession 469.1
deke 749.7
deking 749.3
dekko 27.3
delaminate 296.5
delamination 296.4
delation 599.1
delative 530.9

delator 551.6, 599.5
delatorian 599.14
delay (n) 175.4, 846.2, 1012.1 (v) 175.8, 175.9, 329.2, 390.6, 846.8, 846.9, 846.12, 1012.10
delayed 175.12, 846.16
delayed action 175.3
delayed-action 846.16
delayed reaction 846.2
delaying 175.11, 846.17
delaying action (n) 846.2 (v) 460.10
delaying tactic 175.3, 846.2
delay of game 846.2
dele 395.16
delectability 63.1, 97.3
delectable 63.8, 97.10
delectableness 97.3
delectate 95.10
delectation 95.2
delectus 554.7
delegate (n) 371.7, 576.2 (v) 478.16, 615.10, 862.7
delegated 615.19
delegated authority 417.1, 615.1
delegation 417.12, 478.2, 576.13, 615.1, 862.1
delete 255.12, 395.16, 802.8, 820.6
deleted 222.11, 820.9
deleterious 996.6, 1000.12
deleteriousness 1000.5
deletion 255.5, 395.7
deli 8.17
deliberate (v) 362.7, 541.10, 541.11, 931.12 (a) 175.10, 380.8, 402.6, 494.8
deliberate aggravation 119.1
deliberate blindess 340.2
deliberated 380.8, 935.21
deliberate falsehood 354.9
deliberate interference 1034.21
deliberately provoked 119.4
deliberate negligence 327.1
deliberateness 175.1, 380.3, 402.2, 494.1
deliberate over 931.13
deliberate stages 494.1
deliberate upon 541.11, 931.13
deliberating 931.21
deliberation 175.1, 380.3, 402.2, 494.1, 541.6, 613.6, 931.2
deliberative 423.5, 613.11, 931.21
deliberative assembly 423.1
deliberative body 423.1
delicacy 10.8, 16.2, 24.3, 85.3, 93.4, 93.6, 143.3, 248.1, 270.4, 294.3, 298.1, 339.3, 495.3, 496.1, 664.2, 780.2, 944.1, 973.5, 1006.2, 1016.4, 1047.1, 1050.1
delicate 16.14, 24.12, 35.22, 63.8, 93.20, 143.16, 248.7, 270.16, 294.8, 298.12, 339.12, 495.11, 496.8, 664.5, 944.7, 973.17, 1006.12, 1013.17, 1016.19, 1047.8, 1050.4
delicate features 1016.3
delicate health 85.3
delicate issue 456.7
delicateness 495.3, 1016.4
delicatessen 8.17
delicate subject 152.11
delicious 8.33, 63.8, 97.7, 97.10, 999.13
deliciousness 62.1, 63.1, 97.3
delict 674.4
delictum 674.4
delight (n) 95.2, 896.1 (v) 95.10, 95.12, 116.5, 502.9, 743.21
delighted 95.15, 743.26
delightful 63.8, 97.7, 743.27
delightfulness 97.2
delight in 63.5, 95.13
delighting 116.10
delights 1016.3
delight the palate 63.4
Delilah 665.15
delimit 210.4, 517.19, 959.3
delimitate 210.4
delimitation 210.1, 211.3
delimited 210.6, 959.10
delimited field 212.3
delineate 211.9, 349.8, 349.9, 381.11, 712.19
delineated 211.14
delineating in the imagination 986.6
delineation 211.2, 349.1, 349.2, 381.3, 517.6, 712.4, 712.12, 722.1
delineative 349.14
delineator 716.2, 716.3
delineatory 211.14, 349.13
delinkage 776.1, 802.1, 813.1
delinked 813.4
delinquence 625.1
delinquency 322.1, 327.1, 435.1, 625.1, 638.1, 654.1, 655.2, 674.3, 911.1
delinquent (n) 593.1, 625.5, 660.8 (a) 625.10, 638.3
deliquesce 252.6, 1064.5
deliquescence 252.3, 1064.1
deliquescent 252.11, 1064.6
deliquiation 1064.1
deliquium 1064.1
delirious 85.58, 93.18, 101.12, 105.25, 926.31
deliriousness 926.8
delirium 85.7, 92.18, 105.8, 926.8, 986.5
delirium alcoholicum 926.9
delirium ebriositatis 926.9
delirium mussitans 926.8
delirium tremens 88.3, 917.2, 926.9, 976.7
delitescence 34.1, 519.1
delitescent 519.5
deliver 120.6, 176.10, 328.6, 398.3, 407.4, 409.7, 431.4, 478.13, 524.22, 629.3, 745.5, 892.11
deliverable 176.18, 398.4
deliver a lecture 543.11
deliver a message 343.7
deliver an address 543.9
deliverance 120.2, 148.2, 369.1, 398.1, 431.1, 478.1, 629.1, 946.5
deliver an ultimatum 421.5
delivered 148.7, 431.10
deliverer 397.5, 592.2
deliver judgment 946.13
deliver one's charge to the jury 598.18
deliver oneself 369.6
deliver oneself from 431.8
deliver over 478.13
deliver the wrong message 265.6
deliver the wrong signal 265.6, 350.3
deliver up one's arms 433.8
delivery 1.1, 369.1, 398.1, 431.1, 478.1, 524.5, 629.1, 745.3, 750.2
delivery person 353.5
delivery price 738.9
delivery room 197.25
dell 237.7, 284.9
delocalize 176.11
delouse 79.24
delousing 79.3
Delphian oracle 962.7
Delphic oracle 962.7
Delphic sibyl 962.6
Delphic tripod 962.7
Delta 231.7
delta 171.4
delta 236.1, 283.9
deltaic 283.20
deltal 283.20
deltalike 171.8
delta plain 236.1
deltaplanform jet 181.3
delta-shaped 171.8
deltoid 171.8, 259.11, 278.8, 876.3, 878.4
deltoidal 171.8
delubrum 703.4
deludable 954.9
delude 356.14
deluded 92.39, 926.26, 926.28, 926.31
deluded belief 976.1
delude oneself 975.10
deluder 357.1
deluding 976.9
deluge (n) 238.5, 238.6, 316.2, 770.4, 993.2, 1065.6 (v) 238.17, 367.7, 993.14, 1065.14
Deluge, the 238.6
deluged 238.25, 1065.17
deluge set 1022.3
delusion 92.18, 354.3, 356.1, 975.1, 976.1
delusional 356.21, 976.9
delusionary 976.9
delusions of grandeur 501.2
delusive 356.21, 975.16, 976.9
delusiveness 356.1, 976.2
delusory 356.21, 976.9
deluxe 501.21, 533.9
delve 284.15, 938.31, 1069.17
delve for 938.30
delve into 938.23
delver 938.18
delving 938.38
demagnetize 1032.27
demagogic 543.12
demagogical 543.12
demagogism 543.1
demagogue (n) 375.11, 543.4 (v) 543.10
demagoguery 543.1
demagogy 543.1, 612.4
demand (n) 192.6, 421.1, 440.1, 630.6, 642.1, 643.1, 733.3, 734.1, 938.10, 963.2 (v) 192.15, 420.9, 420.11, 421.5, 424.5, 440.9, 630.12, 643.4, 938.20, 963.9
demand assurances 1007.3
demand attention 983.11
demand bill 728.11
demand curve 630.4
demand draft 728.11
demanded 643.8
demand for 963.2
demanding 21.13, 339.12, 421.9, 425.6, 440.18, 1013.17
demandingness 421.4, 425.1
demand payment 628.11
demand-pull inflation 632.3
demarcate 210.4, 477.9, 517.19, 780.6, 865.10, 944.4
demarcated 210.6
demarcation 210.1, 773.1, 780.4, 944.3
demarche 995.2
démarche 328.3, 404.1, 889.2
demark 944.4
demasculinization 19.5
demasculinize 19.12, 77.12
demasculinized 19.19
dematerialization 34.1, 689.19, 1053.5
dematerialize 34.2, 689.20, 764.4, 1053.6
deme 559.4
demean 137.5
demeaning 250.6, 661.11
demean oneself 137.7, 137.8, 141.8, 321.4, 661.7
demeanor 33.4, 321.1
demeanored 321.7
dement (n) 926.15 (v) 926.24
demented 671.18, 926.26
dementedness 926.1
dementia 926.1
dementia a potu 926.9
dementia praecox 926.4
demerger 802.1
Demerol 86.12
demesne 231.2, 471.6, 1069.8
demesne farm 1069.8
Demeter 890.5, 1069.4
demigod 492.7, 659.5, 678.3
demigoddess 492.7, 659.5, 678.3
demilegato 708.30
demilitarization 465.6
demilitarize 465.11
demilitarized zone 463.2, 465.5
demilune 1073.11
demimondaine 665.15
demimonde 665.15
demi-permanent 35.18
demirep 665.15
demise (n) 307.1, 629.1, 820.1 (v) 629.3
demi-sec champagne 88.17
demised 307.29
demisemiquaver 709.14
demission 448.1
demit 448.2
demitint 35.7, 713.2

demiurgic 892.16
demivolt 366.1
demo 333.2, 770.2
demob 771.8
demobilization 431.2, 465.6, 771.3
demobilize 431.5, 465.11, 771.8
demobilized 431.10, 465.12
democracy 476.2, 612.4
Democrat 609.27
democratic 612.16
democratic centralism 611.5
Democratic Party 609.24
democratism 612.7
democratize 611.16
demographic 312.13, 606.8
demographical 606.8
demographics 227.1, 312.10, 606.1
demography 227.1, 312.10, 606.1
demoiselle 302.6
demolish 395.17, 802.13, 802.15, 958.5
demolisher 395.8
demolishing 395.26
demolishment 395.5
demolition 395.5, 958.2
demolitionary 395.26
demon 101.5, 593.6, 671.9, 678.5, 678.12, 680.6, 920.8
demonetization 728.23
demonetize 728.26
demoniac (n) 926.15 (a) 144.26, 654.13, 680.17, 1000.10
demoniacal 105.25, 144.26, 654.13, 680.17, 926.29
demonianism 680.14
demoniast 680.15
demonic 105.25, 654.13, 680.17, 926.29, 1000.10
demonical 680.17, 926.29, 1000.10
demonic energy 17.1
demonish 680.17
demonishness 680.13
demonism 680.14, 690.2, 697.1
demonist 680.15
demonize 680.16, 691.9
demonized 926.29
demonkind 680.1
demonlike 680.17
demonography 680.14
demonolater 680.15, 697.4
demonolatrous 697.7
demonolatry 680.14, 697.1
demonologer 680.15
demonologist 680.15
demonology 680.14, 690.2
demonomancy 680.14
demonomist 680.15
demonomy 680.14
Demon Rum, the 88.13
demonry 680.14
demons 680.1
demonstrability 957.7, 970.3
demonstrable 348.13, 761.15, 957.19, 970.15
demonstrable existence 761.2
demonstrable fact 761.3
demonstratable 957.19, 970.15
demonstrate 333.5, 341.10, 348.5, 349.11, 501.17, 521.6, 568.10, 957.8, 957.10, 957.13, 1017.21
demonstrate against 333.5
demonstrated 348.13, 957.20, 973.13
demonstrate one's ability 413.20
demonstrate respect for 155.5
demonstrating 348.9, 957.17
demonstration 333.2, 341.4, 348.2, 349.1, 501.4, 770.2, 786.2, 935.1, 957.3, 957.5
demonstrational 957.17
demonstrative 93.17, 104.26, 341.15, 343.10, 348.9, 517.23, 587.19, 957.17
demonstrativeness 93.9, 104.2, 348.4
demonstrator 341.7, 1008.13
demon worship 680.14, 697.1
demon worshiper 680.15, 697.4
demoralization 127.6, 654.5
demoralize 127.20, 128.10, 654.10
demoralized 128.14
demos 606.1
Demosthenes 543.6
Demosthenian 544.8
Demosthenic 544.8
demote 447.3, 909.19, 913.6
demoted 274.7
demotic 523.20
demotic character 546.2
demotic language 523.6
demotion 393.3, 447.1, 661.4, 909.4, 913.1
demotivate 379.4
demotivation 112.3, 379.2
dempster 596.2
demulcent (n) 86.11, 1056.3 (a) 86.40, 120.9, 670.16, 1047.16
demulsion 670.2
demur (n) 325.2, 333.2, 453.1 (v) 325.4, 333.5, 362.7
demure 111.3, 139.12, 500.19
demureness 111.1, 139.4, 500.6
demurity 139.4
demurral 325.2
demurrer 333.2, 333.3, 598.6, 600.2
demurring 325.7, 362.11
demystify 341.10, 521.6
demythologization 341.4
demythologize 341.10
demythologizer 341.7
demythologizing 341.15
den 197.6, 197.8, 228.26, 228.28, 346.4, 654.7, 739.7, 739.8, 1009.5
denary 882.22
denationalization 731.7
denationalize 611.16
denaturalization 797.3
denaturalize 797.12
denature 393.12, 797.12, 852.7
denaturing 393.2
dendriform 171.10, 310.39
dendrite 2.14
dendritic 171.10, 310.39
dendrochronology 832.1
dendroid 310.39
dendroidal 310.39
dendrolater 697.4
dendrologic 310.40
dendrological 310.40
dendrologist 1069.7
dendrology 310.13
deniability 930.2, 971.2
deniable 971.17
denial 92.24, 335.2, 363.3, 372.1, 442.1, 444.1, 451.1, 473.1, 600.2, 668.1, 955.1, 958.2
denial of due credit 151.1
denial of proper credit 151.1
denied 372.3, 958.7
denied due credit 151.5
denied proper credit 151.5
denied to 967.9
denier 271.1
denigrate 38.7, 510.12, 512.10
denigration 38.5, 510.2, 512.2
denization 226.3
denizen (n) 227.2 (v) 225.9
denizen of the deep 311.29
denizens of hell 680.1
denizens of the air 678.7
denizens of the forest 311.1
denizens of the jungle 311.1
denizens of the wild 311.1
den of iniquity 654.7, 665.9
den of thieves 228.28, 483.1
den of vice 665.9
denominate (v) 517.17, 517.18, 527.11, 865.11 (a) 527.14
denominated 527.14
denomination 517.3, 527.2, 527.3, 617.5, 675.3, 809.3, 865.6
denominational 617.19, 675.26
denominationalism 617.13, 675.4
denominationalist 675.18
denominative 517.23, 527.16, 809.7
denominator 1017.7, 1017.12
denotation 517.3, 518.1, 526.14
denotational 518.10
denotative 517.23, 518.10
denote 517.17, 517.18, 518.8, 957.8
denouement 722.4, 820.1, 940.1
denounce 510.13, 514.2, 599.7, 602.3
denounced 599.15
denouncement 510.3, 599.1, 602.1
dense 269.8, 310.43, 763.7, 770.22, 922.15, 1045.12, 1046.10
dense body 689.18
dense fog 319.3
densen 1045.9
denseness 922.3, 1045.1
densification 1045.3
densify 1045.9
densimeter 1045.8
densitometer 1045.8
density 763.1, 922.3, 1045.1, 1046.1
density altitude 184.35
density control 1041.8
dent (n) 284.6, 517.7 (v) 284.14
dental 90.15
dental care 90.3
dental floss 86.22
dental hygienist 81.3
dental medicine 90.3
dental pulp 1063.2
dental record 517.11
dental surgeon 90.6
dentate 289.5, 474.9
dentated 289.5
dented 284.17
dentelle 554.15
denticle 285.4
denticulate 285.14
denticulation 285.1, 289.2
dentiform 285.14
dentifrice 79.17, 86.22
dentil 289.2
dentil band 289.2
dentine 2.8
dentist 90.6
dentistry 90.3
dentition 2.8, 285.1
dentoid 285.14
denudant 6.18
denudate 6.5
denudated 6.12
denudation 6.1, 473.1
denudatory 6.18
denude 6.5, 480.24, 802.14
denuded 6.12, 473.8
denuded of 992.13
denudement 6.1
denunciate 510.13, 599.7, 602.3
denunciation 510.3, 513.1, 514.1, 599.1, 602.1
denunciatory 510.22, 513.8, 514.3, 599.13, 602.5
Denver boot 1012.7
deny 335.4, 363.8, 372.2, 442.4, 444.3, 451.6, 955.5, 958.5
denying 335.5
denying oneself 668.2
deny oneself 667.3, 668.6, 668.7
deny oneself not at all 669.4
deny oneself nothing 669.4
deny oneself to 442.5, 586.5
deobstruct 292.12
deodorant (n) 72.3, 1016.11 (a) 72.6
deodorization 72.2, 79.3
deodorize 72.4, 79.24, 354.16
deodorizer 72.3
deodorizing (n) 72.2 (a) 72.6
deontology 636.2
deoxyribonucleic acid 305.9
depart 34.2, 188.6, 190.12, 222.8, 307.18, 368.10, 538.9, 802.8
departed 188.19, 222.11, 307.29, 837.7
departed, the 307.15
departed spirit 988.1
departed this life 307.29
département 231.5
departer 190.10
depart from 164.3, 370.5, 780.5
depart from the prepared text 365.8
departing 164.7, 188.18, 780.7

department 231.1, 231.2, 568.8, 594.4, 724.4
departmental citation 646.6
departmentalize 802.18
departmentalized 802.20
department chair 571.8
department head 571.8, 574.2
Department of Energy 1038.15
department of investigation 938.4
department of knowledge 928.10
department of philosophy 952.1
department store 736.1
depart this life 307.18
departure 34.1, 164.1, 188.1, 188.4, 190.2, 222.4, 307.1, 538.4, 780.1
depend 202.6, 959.6, 971.11
dependability 644.6, 970.4
dependable 644.19, 970.17, 1007.5
dependableness 644.6, 970.4
dependence 124.1, 202.1, 432.3, 616.9, 775.2, 953.1
dependence on 953.1
dependency 202.1, 432.3, 469.1
dependency-prone 87.25
dependency state 432.6
dependent (n) 138.6, 166.2, 432.6, 577.1 (a) 202.9, 432.13, 953.22, 959.9, 971.18
dependent on 897.6, 959.9
dependent state 432.6
depending 202.9, 953.22, 959.9, 971.18
depending on 959.9
depending on circumstances 959.9
depend on 432.12, 887.5, 953.16, 953.17, 959.6
depend upon 953.16
depersonalization 92.20
depict 349.8, 349.9, 704.30, 712.19
depicter 716.2
depicting in the imagination 986.6
depiction 349.1, 349.2
depictive 349.13, 349.14
depictment 349.1
depilate 6.8
depilation 6.4, 1016.14
depilatory 6.4
depilous 6.17
deplane 186.8
deplaning 186.2
deplete 388.3, 473.5, 486.4, 909.22
depleted 388.5, 473.7
depletion 252.3, 255.2, 388.1, 473.2, 909.6
depletion allowance 478.8
deplorability 98.5
deplorable 98.20, 113.10, 661.11, 1000.9
deplorableness 98.5
deplore 113.6, 115.10
deploy 159.11, 171.5, 259.6, 405.6, 957.12
deployed 159.18, 458.22
deployment 159.6, 171.1, 259.1, 387.1, 458.2, 771.1, 807.1, 808.1
deploy one's forces 405.6
deploy one's resources 405.6
deplume 447.3, 480.24, 661.8, 909.19
depluming 447.1, 661.4, 909.4
depone 334.6, 957.9
deponent 957.6
deponent verb 530.4
depopulate 308.17, 909.16
depopulation 909.3
deport 176.10, 190.16, 773.5, 909.17
deportation 190.7, 773.2, 909.4
deported 773.7
deported population 160.4
deportee 160.4
deportment 33.4, 321.1
deport oneself 321.4
deposal 160.2, 447.2, 448.1, 909.5
depose 160.6, 334.6, 418.4, 447.4, 909.19, 913.6, 953.12, 957.9
deposed 334.9
deposit (n) 159.6, 256.2, 438.3, 624.1, 729.14, 1045.5, 1058.7 (v) 78.9, 159.14, 346.7, 386.10, 438.10, 1045.11
depositary 470.5, 729.12
deposited 438.12
deposition 159.6, 256.2, 334.3, 447.2, 549.6, 598.7, 953.4, 957.2, 1059.8
deposit margin 737.23
depository 195.1, 386.6, 470.5, 729.12, 729.13
deposits 256.2
deposit slip 622.3
depot 386.6
depot park 462.2
depravation 393.3, 654.5
deprave 393.12, 1000.6
depraved 654.14, 661.12
depravedness 393.3, 654.5
depravity 654.5, 661.3
deprecate 335.4, 510.12, 950.2, 998.12
deprecate oneself 137.7, 139.7
deprecation 510.2, 512.1, 950.1
deprecative 139.10, 510.22
deprecatory 139.10, 510.22, 512.13
depreciate 252.7, 255.9, 473.5, 510.12, 512.8, 631.2, 633.6, 950.2, 998.12
depreciation 252.1, 255.2, 393.3, 473.2, 510.2, 512.1, 631.1, 633.4, 950.1
depreciative 510.22, 512.13
depreciator 512.6
depredate 395.10, 482.17
depredation 395.1, 482.6
depredator 483.6
depredatory 395.26
depress 112.18, 252.7, 274.6, 275.9, 284.14, 913.4
depressant (n) 86.12, 87.3 (a) 86.45, 112.30
depressed 92.39, 96.20, 112.22, 115.18, 274.7, 284.17, 913.12, 926.28, 1011.14
depressed area 619.3
depressed class 606.4
depressed population 619.3
depressing 98.20, 112.30
depression 92.14, 92.16, 96.6, 98.5, 112.3, 252.1, 274.1, 274.3, 275.8, 284.1, 284.2, 289.1, 331.3, 731.10, 913.1, 926.5, 1011.6
Depression Era 824.5
depression of spirit 112.3
depressive (n) 112.13, 926.15 (a) 98.20, 112.30, 926.28
depressive psychosis 926.5
deprival 480.6
deprivation 222.1, 442.1, 447.2, 473.1, 480.6, 619.2, 762.1, 802.6, 909.4, 992.4
deprivation of freedom 432.1
deprivative 480.25
deprive 480.21, 909.19
deprived 210.7, 307.34, 619.8
deprived of 473.8, 992.13
deprived of reason 926.26
deprive of 480.21
deprive of freedom 432.8
deprive of life 308.13
deprive of office 447.4
deprive of sight 30.7
deprive of sleep 21.4
deprive one of 442.4
depriving of sight 30.1
depth 158.1, 207.1, 257.1, 269.2, 275.1, 275.2, 709.4, 920.5
depth bomb 462.20
depth charge 462.20
depth indicator 275.6
depth interview 92.6
depthless 248.6, 276.5
depthlessness 276.1
depth of field 27.1
depth of misery 96.6
depth of thought 985.2
depth of water 275.6
depth perception 27.1
depth psychology 92.6
depths 199.1, 274.4, 275.3
depths, the 275.4
depths of one's being 767.5
depths of outer space 158.1
depths of space 261.1
depths of winter 1023.3
depth sounding 275.6
depurant 79.17
depurate 79.18, 79.22
depuration 79.4
depurative 79.28
deputation 417.12, 576.13, 615.1, 862.1
deputative 576.16
depute 576.15, 615.10, 862.7
deputize 18.10, 576.14, 576.15, 615.10, 862.5, 862.7
deputized 615.19
deputy (n) 466.3, 574.1, 576.1, 597.1, 615.9, 616.6, 862.2, 1008.15 (a) 576.16, 862.8
deputy sheriff 1008.15
deputyship 862.1
deracinate 160.6, 192.10, 395.14
deracinated 160.10
deracination 160.1, 192.1, 395.6
derail 410.15, 985.6, 1012.15
derailing 412.1, 1012.3
derailment 410.3, 412.1, 1012.3
derange 85.50, 811.2, 926.24
deranged 810.13, 926.26
derangement 810.1, 810.6, 811.1, 870.1, 926.1
Derby 757.1
derby 457.3, 457.12
deregulate 430.16, 611.16
deregulated 430.27
deregulation 430.9, 1014.6
dereism 92.23, 976.1, 986.7
dereistic 976.9, 986.24
dereistic thinking 92.23, 986.7
derelict (n) 331.9, 370.4, 586.4, 660.2, 828.4 (a) 340.10, 370.8, 390.10, 393.33, 586.10, 645.20
dereliction 327.1, 340.1, 370.2, 435.1, 645.5, 655.2, 1000.1
dereliction of duty 645.5
derequisition 475.1
deride 142.7, 157.3, 454.4, 508.8
de rigueur 579.5, 641.15
derision 142.2, 454.1, 508.1, 508.7
derisive 142.10, 156.7, 454.7, 508.12, 510.22, 512.13
derisory 508.12, 512.13
derivable 935.23
derivable from 888.6
derivation 192.5, 479.1, 518.6, 526.2, 526.3, 526.16, 560.4, 621.2, 886.5, 887.1, 946.4
derivational 526.20, 526.22, 887.6, 888.6
derivation from 888.1
derivative (n) 526.2, 887.1 (a) 336.9, 887.6, 888.6, 891.5
derivative action 1041.3
derivative title 469.1
derive 192.14, 472.8, 479.6, 946.10, 951.10
derived adjective 530.3
derived authority 417.1
derived four-channel system 50.11
derive from 479.6, 621.4, 887.5, 888.5
derive pleasure from 95.13
deriving 621.2
derm 2.4
derma 2.4
dermal 2.27, 295.32
dermatitis 85.35
dermatogen 295.3
dermic 2.27, 295.32
dermis 2.4, 295.3
dernier cri 841.2
dernier ressort 1009.2
derogate 255.9, 661.7
derogate from 512.8
derogation 255.2, 393.3, 512.1
derogative 512.13
derogator 512.6
derogatory 512.13, 661.10
derrick 272.6, 912.3
derrière 217.4
derring-do 492.4

derringer 462.10
dervish 667.2, 675.23, 699.12
desacralization 695.1
desacralize 695.14
desacralized 695.15
descant (n) 556.1, 708.4, 708.22, 708.26 (v) 538.7, 556.5, 708.38
descanter 556.3
descend 137.8, 141.8, 172.5, 184.43, 194.5, 204.10, 297.15, 629.4, 661.7
descendancy 560.4
descendant (n) 561.3, 817.4, 835.2 (a) 194.11
descendants 559.5, 561.1
descender 548.6
descend from 887.5
descending (n) 172.2, 194.1 (a) 172.8, 194.11, 204.16
descending order 807.2
descend on 459.14
descend to particulars 766.6, 865.9
descend upon 194.10, 459.14
descension 194.1
descent 137.2, 172.2, 194.1, 204.5, 275.8, 393.3, 560.4, 560.5, 561.1, 812.2, 815.1, 858.1, 913.1, 1011.3, 1074.9
descent on 459.1
descent upon 459.1
descramble 521.6
describability 341.6
describable 341.17
describe 341.10, 349.9, 865.10
describe a circle 914.5
description 341.1, 349.2, 722.1, 809.3, 865.8
descriptive 341.14, 349.14, 523.19
descriptive grammar 530.1
descry 27.12, 521.9, 941.5
desecrate 80.17, 389.4, 393.12, 661.9, 694.4
desecration 389.1, 638.2, 694.2
deselect (n) 370.4 (v) 372.2
desensitization 25.3
desensitize 25.4, 94.7
desensitized 25.8, 94.13
desert (n) 158.4, 236.1, 506.2, 891.2, 999.1, 1066.2 (v) 188.9, 222.8, 363.7, 368.10, 370.5, 566.5, 645.12, 858.13 (a) 891.4, 1066.7
desert a sinking ship 188.9, 363.7, 858.13
deserted 222.15, 340.14, 370.8, 390.10, 584.12
desertedness 222.2
deserter 363.5, 370.2, 491.6, 694.3, 858.8
desert fathers 584.5
desertification 891.2
desertion 188.1, 222.4, 363.2, 368.4, 370.2, 566.1, 584.4, 694.1, 858.3
desertion of principle 468.1
desertion under fire 491.3
desert island 891.2
desertization 891.2
desert of time 827.3
desert one's principles 468.2
desert rat 227.10, 1058.9
deserts 506.2
desert saints 584.5
desert sands 891.2
desert under fire 491.8
deserve 639.5
deserved 639.9, 649.7
deservedness 639.1
deserve punishment 604.21
deserving 509.20, 639.10
deservingness 639.1
deservings 639.3
desex 19.12, 255.11
desexualize 19.12
déshabillé 5.20
desi 745.2
desiccant 1066.10
desiccate 393.18, 397.9, 1066.6
desiccated 393.35, 1066.9
desiccation 397.2, 1066.3
desiccative (n) 1066.4 (a) 1066.10
desiccator 1066.4
desiderate 100.14
desideration 100.1, 100.11, 380.1, 963.2
desiderative (n) 530.13 (a) 100.21
desideratum 100.11, 380.1, 963.2
desiderium 100.5
design (n) 356.6, 380.1, 381.1, 381.3, 415.3, 498.7, 518.2, 554.12, 578.1, 709.11, 712.1, 712.8, 712.9, 712.12, 717.4, 722.4, 892.2 (v) 5.41, 380.4, 381.8, 712.19, 892.8, 892.12 (a) 717.7
design a prototype 381.10
designate 371.19, 436.5, 517.18, 527.11, 576.15, 615.11, 809.6, 865.11
designate an agent 862.7
designate a proxy 862.7
designated 371.26, 517.24, 527.14
designated driver 178.10, 494.1
designated hitter 745.2
designated runner 745.2
designating 527.2, 865.6
designation 371.8, 436.2, 517.3, 527.2, 527.3, 615.2, 809.3, 865.6
designative 517.23
design body 689.17
designed 380.8, 381.12
designee 371.1
designer (n) 381.6, 704.23, 716.9, 717.6, 892.7 (a) 717.7
designer drug 86.5, 87.3
designer food 10.1
designer gene 305.9
designer jeans 5.18
designer label 578.1
designer stubble 3.8, 288.3
designer water 1065.3
design flaw 1003.2
designing (n) 712.1 (a) 381.13, 415.12
designless 520.6, 972.16
designlessness 972.3
design specialty 712.16
desinence 857.1
desipience 923.1
desirability 100.13, 104.6, 371.11, 995.1
desirable 75.25, 97.6, 100.30, 371.24, 585.12, 995.5
desire (n) 75.5, 100.1, 100.11, 104.1, 124.1, 323.1, 380.1, 440.1 (v) 75.20, 100.14, 101.6, 124.6, 323.2, 380.4, 440.9
desire body 689.17
desire concentration 92.34
desired 100.29, 585.12, 839.8, 869.8
desire for knowledge 981.1
desire for oneself 154.2
desireful 100.21
desire guidance 422.7
desireless 102.8
desirelessness 102.3
desirer 100.12
desires of the flesh 75.5
desiring 100.21
desirous 100.21, 101.8, 104.25
desirous of 100.22, 154.3
desist 390.4, 857.6
desistance 390.2, 857.1
desist from 370.7, 390.4
desisting 390.2
desk 229.1, 703.13, 739.1, 901.15
desk, the 698.1
desk calendar 549.11
desk job 724.5
desk jockey 726.2
desk lamp 229.1
desks 710.12
desk telephone 347.4
desktop 739.1, 1042.18
desktop computer 1042.2
desktop publishing program 1042.11
desolate (v) 98.12, 112.19, 395.10, 909.16 (a) 96.26, 98.20, 112.28, 584.12, 891.4
desolated 112.29, 395.28
desolateness 98.4, 112.12, 222.2
desolating 98.23, 395.26
desolation 96.6, 98.4, 112.12, 395.1, 584.4, 891.2, 909.3
désolé 112.28
despair (n) 96.6, 112.3, 125.2 (v) 112.16, 125.10
despaired of 307.32
despairing 112.22, 125.12
despair of 125.10
desperado 308.11, 593.3, 660.9
desperate 125.12, 493.8, 926.30, 1013.26
desperate criminal 660.9
desperateness 125.2, 493.2
desperate situation 1006.1
desperation 125.2
despicability 98.2
despicable 98.18, 661.12, 998.21, 1000.9
despicableness 98.2, 661.3, 998.2, 1000.2
despisal 372.1
despise 103.5, 157.3, 372.2, 454.4, 510.12
despised 99.9, 372.3
despising (n) 103.1, 372.1 (a) 103.7, 372.4
despite 103.1, 144.6, 156.2, 157.1, 454.1
despiteful 103.8, 144.21, 589.10
despitefulness 103.1, 589.3
despoil 393.12, 395.10, 480.24, 482.17, 665.20, 1000.6
despoiled 393.42
despoiled of 473.8
despoiler 483.6, 665.12
despoiling 482.6
despoilment 395.1, 473.1, 482.6, 665.6
Despoina 682.5
despoliation 395.1, 473.1, 482.6, 1000.3
despond (n) 96.6 (v) 112.16, 125.10
despondence 112.3
despondency (n) 96.6, 112.3, 125.2 (v) 112.16
despondent 112.22, 125.12
desponding 112.22
despot 575.13
despotic 417.16, 612.16
despotism 612.4, 612.8, 612.9
despotize 612.15
desquamate 6.11, 296.5
desquamation 2.5, 6.1, 296.4
desquamative 6.18
dessert 8.10, 10.7, 10.8, 66.2
dessert dish 8.12
desserter 368.5
dessert menu 871.5
desserts 604.1, 639.3
dessert spoon 8.12
destabilization 810.1
destabilize 791.3, 810.9
destigmatization 600.1, 601.1
destigmatize 600.9, 601.4
destigmatizing 600.1, 601.1
destinal 839.8, 972.15
destinate 964.7
destination 186.5, 380.2, 553.9, 820.1, 964.2
destination wedding 563.3
destine 380.4, 477.9, 964.7
destined 839.8, 963.15, 964.9
destiny 477.5, 820.1, 839.2, 964.2, 972.1
destiny's darling 1010.6
destitute 473.8, 619.9, 625.11
destitute of 992.13
destitute of life 307.29
destitution 619.2, 992.4
desto 708.55
de-stress 120.5
destress 120.6
destrier 311.10
destroy 255.10, 308.13, 393.10, 395.10, 412.6, 671.11, 1000.6, 1012.15
destroyed 393.28, 395.28
destroyer 180.6, 180.7, 395.8, 593.5
Destroyer, the 677.3
destroyer escort 180.6
destroyer fleet 461.27
destroying 395.26
destructibility 16.2
destructible 16.14

destruction 255.3, 308.1, 393.1, 395.1, 412.1, 473.1, 671.1, 806.1, 1000.3, 1001.1
destruction of life 308.1
destructive 82.7, 308.23, 395.26, 671.16, 806.5, 1011.15
destructive criticism 115.4
destructive distillation 79.4, 1020.5
destructive metabolism 2.20
destructiveness 82.3, 671.1
desubstantialize 1053.6
desuete 390.10
desuetude 370.1, 390.1
desultoriness 538.3, 851.1, 854.2, 971.6
desultory 164.7, 538.13, 810.12, 851.3, 854.7, 917.18, 945.6, 971.20
detach 615.10, 615.17, 771.8, 802.10
detachable 802.20
detached 94.13, 344.10, 430.21, 583.6, 584.8, 649.9, 776.6, 802.20, 802.21, 804.4, 872.8, 979.12, 982.3
detached retina 28.5
detach for service 615.17
detachment 94.4, 102.2, 344.3, 461.22, 583.2, 584.1, 649.3, 770.3, 771.3, 773.2, 793.1, 802.1, 872.2, 979.5, 982.1
detail (n) 339.3, 461.22, 498.7, 766.3, 770.3, 793.1, 796.2 (v) 477.9, 538.7, 615.10, 766.6, 801.7, 861.6, 865.9, 1017.19
detailed 339.12, 349.14, 766.9, 865.12
detailing 538.6, 766.5, 801.2
detail man 730.4
details 349.2, 998.4
details, the 761.4
detain 175.9, 429.12, 846.8, 1012.10
detained 175.12, 429.19, 846.16
detainee 429.11
detainment 429.3, 1012.1
detangle 431.7
detect 941.5, 941.8
detectability 31.1
detectable 31.6, 941.10
detectable odor 69.1
detection 938.4, 941.1, 1036.9
detective 576.10, 938.16, 981.2, 1008.15
detective work 938.4
detector 1035.11
détente 465.1, 609.5
detention 175.4, 429.3, 474.1, 846.2, 1012.1
detention camp 228.29, 429.8
detention cell 429.8
detention center 212.3, 429.8
detention home 429.8
deter 127.18, 379.4, 1012.14
deterge 79.18
detergent (n) 79.17 (a) 79.28
deteriorate 119.2, 119.3, 393.9, 393.16, 842.9, 852.6, 1011.11
deteriorated 119.4, 393.27
deteriorating 393.45
deterioration 119.1, 393.3, 852.1
determent 379.1, 379.2, 1012.2, 1012.4
determinability 300.7, 957.7
determinable 300.14, 940.3, 941.10
determinacy 970.1
determinant (n) 211.3, 560.6, 886.1 (a) 211.11
determinate 210.6, 865.12, 960.2, 970.13, 970.20
determinateness 359.1, 970.1
determination 210.1, 300.1, 323.1, 359.1, 361.1, 380.1, 403.1, 940.1, 941.1, 942.2, 946.5, 957.3, 970.8
determinative (n) 530.6, 546.2, 886.1 (a) 210.9, 211.11, 820.12, 886.13, 953.26, 957.16
determine 161.5, 210.4, 323.2, 359.7, 375.22, 380.4, 570.6, 820.6, 865.11, 886.12, 894.8, 941.2, 946.11, 957.10, 970.11, 1017.18
determined 210.6, 359.11, 403.16, 839.8, 957.20, 964.8, 970.20, 970.21, 973.13
determinedness 359.1
determined upon 359.16
determine once for all 359.7
determiner 530.6, 560.6
determine upon 371.16
determining (n) 941.1 (a) 210.9, 211.11, 766.8
determinism 839.1, 964.4
determinist 964.5
deterministic 963.15, 964.10
deterrence 379.1, 609.5, 1012.2
deterrent (n) 379.2, 1012.4 (a) 127.28, 379.5, 399.7, 1012.19
deterrent capacity 460.1
deterrent example 399.1
deterring 127.28, 1012.19
detersion 79.2
detersive 79.28
detest 99.3, 103.5
detestable 98.18, 103.8, 1000.9
detestableness 1000.2
detestation 103.1, 103.3
detested 99.9
detester 103.4
dethrone 447.4
dethronement 447.2
detonate 56.8, 671.14, 904.12, 1021.8
detonating 671.24
detonating powder 462.15
detonation 56.3, 671.7, 904.4
detonator 462.15, 1021.4
detour (n) 164.1, 279.3, 383.1, 383.4, 914.3 (v) 164.3, 279.6, 914.4
detox 87.1
detoxicate 87.22
detoxification 87.1
detoxify 87.22, 516.2
detract 255.9, 985.6
detract attention 985.6
detract from 252.9, 512.8
detraction 252.5, 255.1, 255.2, 512.1
detractor 333.3, 510.9, 512.6
detractory 512.13
detrain 186.8
detriment 393.1, 473.1, 996.2, 1000.3
detrimental 996.6, 1000.12, 1011.13
detrimentalness 1000.5
detrital 1051.11
detrited 1051.11
detrition 1044.2, 1051.4
detritus 256.1, 1051.6
de trop 993.16, 993.17
detrude 909.13, 913.4
detrusion 909.1, 913.1
detune 810.8
deuce 748.2, 758.2, 790.3, 873.3
deuce-ace 876.1
deuced 513.10
deuce shot 714.8
deus 678.2
deus ex machina 722.4
Deus Fidius 649.4
deuteragonist 704.10
deuteranopia 30.3
deuterate 1060.8
deuterium 1038.5
deuterium nucleus 1038.6
deuterogamist 563.11
deuteron 1038.6
Deutsche Industrie Normen 714.9
deva 678.2
devachan 681.8
devaloka 681.8
devaluate 633.6, 728.26
devaluation 633.4, 728.23
devalue 393.12, 633.6, 728.26
devaluing 252.5
devastate 395.10, 909.16
devastated 395.28
devastating 395.26, 1016.21
devastating attack 459.1
devastation 395.1, 909.3
develop 14.2, 251.6, 259.4, 259.5, 259.7, 303.9, 348.5, 351.4, 392.7, 392.10, 538.7, 568.13, 714.15, 861.5, 861.6, 887.4, 892.12, 1002.5
developable 259.9
develop a method 384.6
develop at thesis 556.5
developed 14.3, 259.12, 303.13, 392.13, 794.9, 1002.9
developed nation 232.1
developed thought 931.5
developed world 731.8
developer 381.6, 714.13, 892.7
developing 861.8
developing world 430.12, 619.3
develop into 858.17
develop late 846.10
development 14.1, 78.6, 251.1, 259.3, 303.6, 392.2, 538.6, 568.3, 708.24, 722.4, 858.1, 861.1, 887.1
developmental 538.15
developmental change 861.1
developmental genetics 305.9
developmental test 92.9
developmental tool 1042.11
devi 678.2
deviability 854.2
deviable 854.7
deviance 164.1, 204.1, 638.1, 782.1, 914.1
deviancy 164.1, 638.1, 914.1, 927.1, 975.1
deviant (n) 75.16, 868.3 (a) 164.7, 204.13, 638.3, 852.10, 868.5, 927.5, 975.16
deviate (n) 75.16 (v) 164.3, 164.5, 204.9, 538.9, 654.9, 688.8, 787.2, 852.6, 914.4, 975.9
deviate from 780.5
deviate from the path of virtue 654.9
deviate from the truth 354.19
deviating 164.7, 538.13, 780.7, 782.3, 914.7
deviation 161.4, 164.1, 171.1, 204.1, 265.1, 538.4, 780.1, 782.1, 852.1, 868.1, 870.1, 914.1, 914.3, 927.1, 975.2
deviational 975.16
deviationism 868.1
deviationist (n) 868.3 (a) 868.5
deviative 164.7, 204.13, 265.10, 538.13, 780.7, 782.3, 851.3, 870.9, 914.7, 927.5, 975.16
deviatory 164.7, 782.3
device 91.19, 356.6, 376.1, 381.1, 384.3, 384.4, 415.3, 462.20, 517.1, 527.10, 536.1, 546.1, 647.2, 722.4, 974.4, 995.2, 1040.1
devices 384.2, 415.4
devil (n) 144.14, 318.12, 322.3, 493.4, 548.12, 589.6, 593.3, 593.6, 660.2, 660.3, 671.9, 680.2, 680.6 (v) 11.5, 96.13
devil and all, the 864.4
devil and the deep blue sea, the 371.3
devil dog 183.4
devil dogs 461.28
devildom 680.13
deviled 11.7, 96.24
deviled eggs 10.26
devil-god 678.2, 697.3
devil incarnate 144.14, 593.6
deviling 680.7
devilish 144.26, 322.6, 654.13, 680.17, 682.8, 1000.10
devilishness 322.2, 654.4, 680.13
devilize 680.16
devilkin 680.7
devil-like 680.17
devil lore 680.14
devil-made-me-do-it defense, the 600.2
devil-may-care 102.7, 106.15, 493.8
devil-may-careness 493.2
devilment 96.2, 144.5, 322.2
devil-ridden 926.29
devilry 144.5, 322.2, 654.4, 680.14
devil's advocate 935.12
devil's bedposts 758.2
devil's bones 759.8
devils' chorus 61.2

devilship 680.13
Devil's Island 429.8
devil's own luck 1011.5
Devil's pitchfork, the 680.13
devil's tattoo 55.1
devil's teeth 759.8
devil to pay, the 603.1, 1013.4
deviltry 144.5, 322.2, 654.4, 1000.1
devil worship 680.14, 697.1
devil-worship 680.14
devil worshiper 697.4
devil-worshiper 680.15
devious 164.7, 204.13, 645.16, 799.4, 914.7, 920.15
deviousness 164.1, 204.1, 538.5, 645.1, 914.1, 920.3
devirginate 480.15
devirgination 480.3
devisable 478.23, 629.5
devise (n) 478.10 (v) 381.8, 478.18, 892.8, 892.12
devised 381.12
devisee 479.4
deviser 381.6, 892.7
devising 892.1, 892.2
devitalization 16.5
devitalize 16.10, 19.12, 85.50
devitalized 16.18, 19.19
devitalizing 16.20
devitrify 1031.2
devoid 222.14, 762.8
devoid of 992.13
devoid of truth 354.25
devoir 641.1
devolute 615.10
devolution 205.1, 393.3, 394.1, 417.12, 615.1, 629.2, 861.1
devolutional 205.7
devolutionary 615.19, 861.8
devolve 394.4, 615.10, 629.4
devolvement 417.12, 615.1
devolve upon 615.10, 629.3, 641.7
Devonshire cream 1045.7
devote 387.13, 477.11, 685.5, 724.10
devoted 101.9, 104.26, 326.3, 359.11, 434.4, 587.21, 644.20, 652.5, 685.8, 692.8, 964.9, 983.17
devoted friend 588.2
devoted friendship 587.8
devotedness 101.2, 587.7, 644.7, 692.1
devoted to 104.29, 983.17
devoted to studies 570.17
devotee 100.12, 101.4, 104.11, 616.8, 692.4, 926.18
devotee of Bacchus 88.11
devote oneself 724.10
devote oneself to 328.8, 359.8, 404.3, 509.13, 724.11, 983.5
devote the mind to 931.10, 983.5
devote to 387.13
devoting 477.4
devotion 101.2, 104.1, 359.1, 477.4, 587.7, 641.1, 644.7, 652.1, 685.3, 692.1, 696.1
devotional 692.8, 696.16
devotionalist 692.4
devotions 696.4, 696.8
devotion to duty 641.2
devour 8.22, 95.13, 187.11, 395.10, 672.4, 954.6
devoured by 93.23
devoured by desire 100.24
devourer 8.16
devouring (n) 8.1 (a) 100.27
devouring element 1019.13
devout 101.9, 434.4, 692.8, 696.16, 953.21
devoutness 101.2, 692.1
De Vries theory 560.6
dew (n) 1065.4 (v) 1065.12
dewal 703.2
dewdrop 282.3
dewdrops 1065.4
dewiness 301.3, 841.1, 1065.1
dewing 1065.6
deworm 1070.7
dew point 1019.3, 1065.2
dewpoint 317.4
dew pond 241.1
dewy 301.9, 301.10, 841.7, 1065.15
dewy-eyed 986.24
Dexedrine 86.9
dexies 87.4
dexter 219.4
dexterity 219.2, 413.1, 920.2
dexterous 219.5, 413.22, 920.14
dexterousness 413.1
dextral 218.7, 219.4
dextrality 219.2
dextran 2.25
dextroamphetamine sulfate 86.9
dextrocardial 219.4
dextrocerebral 219.4
dextrocular 219.4
dextrocularity 219.2
dextroduction 219.2
dextrogyrate 219.4
dextrogyration 219.2
dextrogyratory 219.4
dextromanual 219.5
dextropedal 219.4
dextrorotary 219.4
dextrorotation 219.2
dextrorse 219.4
dextrose 66.3
dextrosinistral 219.6
dextrousness 413.1
dextroversion 219.2
dey 575.12
Dhammapada 683.9
dharana 691.3
dharma 767.4
dhoti 5.19
dhyana 691.3
diabetes 85.21
diabetic 85.61
diabetic diet 7.13
diable 680.2
diablerie 680.14, 690.2
diablo 680.2
diabolic 144.26, 654.13, 680.17, 1000.10
diabolical 144.26, 654.13, 680.17, 1000.10
diabolism 680.14, 690.2
diabolist 680.15, 690.5
diabolize 680.16, 691.9
diabology 680.14
diabolology 680.14
diabolus 680.2
diacaustic 279.2
diachronic 837.8
diaconicon 703.9
diaconicum 703.9
diaconus 699.4
diacritic (n) 546.1 (a) 780.9
diacritical 780.9
diacritical mark 546.1
diacritical mark or sign 530.15
diadem 280.2, 498.6, 647.3
diaeresis 720.7, 802.5
diagnosable 341.17
diagnose 90.14, 91.24, 341.9
diagnosis 91.12, 341.1, 946.5
diagnostic (n) 1042.18 (a) 90.15, 341.14, 517.23, 780.9
diagnostic procedure 91.12
diagnostic radiology 91.7
diagnostics 91.11, 341.8
diagonal (n) 170.5, 204.7, 277.2, 517.6 (a) 204.19
diagonality 204.1
diagonalize 204.11
diagram (n) 349.1, 381.3, 712.12, 801.4 (v) 349.8, 381.10, 530.16, 712.19, 801.7
diagrammatic 381.14, 517.23
dial 216.4
dialect (n) 523.1, 523.7, 532.1 (a) 523.22
dialectal 523.22
dialect atlas 523.7
dialectic (n) 541.6, 935.2, 935.5 (a) 935.19, 935.22
dialectical 935.19, 935.22
dialectical materialism 611.5, 1052.6
dialectical materialist 1052.7
dialectician 523.15, 921.1, 935.11, 952.8
dialecticism 935.2, 935.4
dialectics 935.2, 935.4
dialectological 523.22
dialectologist 523.15
dialog box 1042.10
dialogist 541.7
dialogue 541.2, 706.3, 722.4, 935.5
dial telephone 347.4
dial tone 347.13
dialysis 806.2
dialytic 806.6
dialyze 806.4
diamagnetic 908.4, 1032.31
diamagnetism 908.1, 1032.7
Diamantina Fracture 275.5
diameter 158.1, 257.1, 269.3, 277.2, 819.1, 875.3
diametral 819.4
diametric 779.7
diametrical 779.7
diametrically opposed 779.7
diametrically opposite 779.7
diamond (n) 659.1, 743.11, 745.1, 999.5, 1046.6 (v) 498.9 (a) 278.11
diamond broker 730.9
diamond in the rough 263.2, 406.5, 659.1
Diamond Jim Brady 486.2
diamond jubilee 850.4
diamondlike 1046.10
diamonds 758.2
Diamond Sutra, The 683.9
Diana 1073.12
Diana complex 92.22
diapason 158.2, 708.3, 709.6, 709.20, 711.22
diapason pitch 709.4
diaper rash 85.36
diaphane (n) 1029.2 (a) 1029.4
diaphaneity 1029.1
diaphanous 248.7, 270.16, 1025.31, 1029.4
diaphanousness 270.4, 1029.1
diaphone 517.15
diaphonic 61.4
diaphony 61.1
diaphoresis 12.7
diaphoretic (n) 86.30 (a) 12.22
diaphragm 2.18, 2.22, 50.8, 86.23, 213.5, 819.1
diapositive 714.3
diarist 547.15, 718.4, 719.3, 832.10
diaristic 832.15
diarize 549.15, 871.8
diarrhea 12.2, 85.9, 85.29
diarrhea of the mouth 538.2, 540.2
diary 549.11, 555.1, 719.1, 832.9, 871.6
diaskeuasis 341.4
diaskeuast 341.7, 555.4
diaspora 771.1, 771.3
diastase 7.10
diastatic 298.17
diaster 305.16
diastole 259.2, 850.3, 916.3
diastrophism 671.5
diatessaron 709.20
diathermal 1019.31
diathermic 1019.31
diathermy 91.5
diathesis 560.6, 978.3
diatom 258.7
diatomaceous 310.37
diatomic 1038.18
diatonic interval 709.20
diatonic scale 709.6
diatonic semitone 709.20
diatribe 510.7, 543.2
diavolo 680.2
dib 382.10
dibasic 1038.18
dibber 382.6
dibble 382.10, 1069.18
dibbler 382.6
dibrach 720.8
dice (n) 759.8 (v) 879.3
dice bet 759.3
diced 278.9
dice gospeller 759.21
dice point 759.9
dice roll 759.9
dicey 759.27, 971.16, 971.19, 972.15, 1006.10
diceyness 971.6, 1006.2
dichaeologia 600.5

dichotomize 802.11, 873.5, 875.4
dichotomized 873.6
dichotomous 802.20, 873.6, 875.6
dichotomy 802.2, 873.1, 875.1
dichroism 47.1
dichromatic 35.16, 47.9
dichromatism 30.3, 47.1
dichromic 47.9
dick 576.11, 1008.16
dick around 923.6
dicker (n) 437.1, 731.5 (v) 731.18
dickering 731.3
dickey 5.15, 5.31, 311.15
dicking around 923.1
dickish 922.17, 923.10
dicky-bird 311.27
dicot 310.3
dicotyl 310.3
dicotyledon 310.3
dictate (n) 419.1, 420.1, 673.3, 974.2 (v) 420.8, 420.9, 424.5, 612.14, 963.8
dictated 419.4, 420.12, 424.11
dictate peace 465.9
dictates of Mrs. Grundy 579.2
dictates of society 579.2
dictating 420.13
dictation 420.1, 568.2, 673.3
dictator 575.13
dictatorial 141.11, 417.16, 612.16
dictatorialness 417.3
dictatorship 417.7, 573.4, 612.4, 612.8
dictatorship of the proletariat 611.5
dictature 417.7
diction 529.2, 532.1
dictionary 554.9, 871.4
dictionary catalog 554.9
dictionary editor 554.2
dictionary meaning 518.1
dictum 334.1, 419.2, 420.4, 524.3, 946.5, 974.1, 974.2
didact 422.3
didactic 419.4, 422.8, 568.18, 720.16, 970.22
didacticism 568.1
didactics 568.1
didactive 419.4
didder (n) 105.5, 917.3 (v) 917.11, 1023.9
didders 1023.2
diddle (n) 356.9 (v) 75.21, 331.13, 331.14, 356.14, 356.19
diddle around 998.15
diddle away 486.5
diddle-daddle 331.14
diddler 331.8, 357.4
diddling 75.7, 356.9
diddling around 998.9
diddly 762.3
diddly squat 762.3
dido 366.2, 743.5
die (n) 713.8, 785.6, 786.6, 901.8 (v) 34.2, 307.18, 393.17, 395.23, 410.16, 762.6, 820.7, 837.6, 1022.8
die aborning 391.8, 410.15
die a natural death 307.23
die at one's post 360.6
die a violent death 307.23, 308.21
die away 34.2, 168.2, 252.6, 762.6, 820.7, 1022.8
die by one's own hand 308.22
diectic 935.19
died aborning 410.18
die down 173.8, 252.6, 1022.8
die fighting 307.22, 359.8
die for 100.14
die for one's country 307.24
die game 360.6
die hard 359.8, 360.6, 361.7, 453.4
die-hard 611.17
diehard (n) 361.6, 452.3, 611.9, 853.4 (a) 853.8
die-hardism 611.1
die in harness 307.22, 360.6
die in one's boots 360.6
die in the attempt 360.6
die in the last ditch 307.22, 360.6
die in the Lord 307.20
die laughing 116.8
dielectric (n) 1032.14 (a) 1032.36
dielectric heat 1019.1
dielectric heating 1020.1
die like a man 307.22
die of embarrassment 139.8
die off 34.2, 173.8, 252.8
die on the vine 16.9, 393.18
die out 34.2, 307.25, 762.6, 1022.8
diesel (n) 1043.3 (a) 904.17
diesel-dyke 75.15
diesel-electric 904.17
diesel-propelled 904.16
dies non 20.5
diet (n) 7.13, 423.1, 613.1, 770.2 (v) 7.19, 8.20, 270.13, 668.6
dietary (n) 7.13 (a) 7.23
dietary deficiency 992.6
dietary fiber 7.3
die temper 1046.4
dietetic 7.23, 8.31
dietetics 7.13, 7.16
diethyltoluamide 1001.3
dietic 7.23
dietician 90.11
dieting 7.13, 8.1, 270.9
dietitian 7.15, 90.11
diet of cake, a 994.3
dietotherapeutics 7.16
dietotherapy 7.16
diet pills 87.4
die trying 360.6, 403.12, 403.13
die with delight 95.12
die with one's boots on 307.22, 359.8, 360.6
die with pleasure 95.12
diff 1042.18
differ 333.4, 456.8, 780.5, 782.2, 787.2, 789.5
difference (n) 255.6, 255.8, 333.1, 456.2, 647.2, 780.1, 782.1, 787.1, 789.1, 791.1, 852.1, 870.1, 1017.6 (v) 780.6
difference of form 526.3
difference of opinion 456.2, 780.1
differencing (n) 647.2, 780.4 (a) 780.9
different 780.7, 782.3, 787.4, 841.11, 865.12, 870.9, 927.5
different as night and day 865.12
different as night from day 787.5
different ball game 780.3
different breed of cat 780.3
differentia 517.1, 780.2, 865.4
differentiable 944.9
differential (n) 780.2, 865.4, 1040.5, 1040.9 (a) 780.9, 809.7, 944.7, 1017.23
differential anesthetic 86.15
differential gap 1041.10
differential gear 1040.9
differential gearing 1040.9
differential purchase 906.2
differentiate 517.17, 780.6, 782.2, 865.10, 944.4
differentiated 780.7
differentiatedness 780.1
differentiating 780.9
differentiation 517.3, 780.4, 782.1, 865.1, 865.8, 944.3, 1017.2
differentiative 780.9
differentness 865.1, 927.1
different story, a 780.3
different thing, a 780.3
differing 325.5, 333.6, 456.15, 780.7, 789.6
differ in opinion 456.8
difficile 1013.17
difficult 361.11, 495.10, 522.14, 1011.13, 1013.17
difficulties 619.1, 1011.1
difficultness 361.3, 1013.1
difficult question 938.10
difficulty 96.2, 456.2, 522.2, 1011.1, 1012.4, 1012.6, 1013.1
diffidence 127.3, 139.2, 325.2, 362.3, 955.2
diffident 127.23, 139.10, 325.7, 362.11
diffluent 238.24
diffract 164.5, 771.4
diffracted 164.8
diffracted wave 916.4
diffraction 164.2, 771.1, 916.4
diffractional 771.11
diffractive 164.8, 771.11
diffuse (v) 164.5, 171.6, 176.10, 221.7, 299.3, 352.10, 771.4, 802.13, 804.3 (a) 164.8, 299.4, 538.11, 771.9, 864.13, 991.7
diffused 164.8, 299.4, 352.17, 473.7
diffuse light 1025.23
diffuse nebula 1073.7
diffuseness 299.1, 538.1
diffusing screen 1028.4
diffusion 164.2, 171.2, 221.3, 299.2, 352.1, 473.2, 538.1, 771.1, 802.3, 804.1
diffusive 221.14, 538.11, 771.11
diffusiveness 538.1
dig (n) 156.3, 284.4, 902.2, 902.4 (v) 93.11, 275.9, 284.15, 292.14, 521.8, 570.12, 725.14, 749.7, 902.12, 928.12, 938.31, 1043.4, 1069.17, 1069.19
digamist 563.11
digamous 563.19
dig around for 981.3
dig at 156.6, 508.9
digenesis 78.6
digenetic 78.16
digest (n) 557.1, 673.5, 808.4 (v) 7.18, 134.8, 187.13, 388.3, 521.7, 570.7, 673.10, 809.6, 931.12, 931.13
digestant 7.9
digested 268.9
digester 7.9, 1063.4
digestibility 7.2
digestible 7.21, 8.33
digestif 9.1
digestion 2.17, 7.8, 187.6, 388.1, 570.2, 1063.3
digestive (n) 7.9 (a) 2.31, 7.22, 187.17
digestive juice 13.2
digestive secretion 13.2
digestive secretions 2.17, 7.8
digestive system 2.17, 2.18, 7.8
digest of law 673.5
dig for 938.30
digger 192.9, 284.10, 938.18
digging (n) 275.8, 284.11 (a) 938.38
digging out 192.2
diggings 228.4, 284.4, 1058.6
digging up 941.1
dight 5.39, 5.43
digicam 714.11
dig in 359.9, 460.9
dig in one's heels 333.5, 855.11
dig into 938.23
digit 73.5, 199.5, 1017.3
digital (n) 1042.18 (a) 474.9, 1017.23
digital art 713.1
digital artist 714.2, 716.5
digital audio broadcasting 347.3
digital audio tape 50.12
digital camera 714.11
digital compression 347.18
digital computer 1042.2
digital computers 1042.1
digital data reducing system 1041.5
digital detox 344.1, 1033.1
digital disc 50.12
digital feedback control 1041.3
digitalin 86.9
digitalis 86.9
digital native 866.3, 1042.18
digital phone 347.4
digital photography 714.1
digital radio 343.5, 1034.1
digital recording 50.12
digital stereo 50.12
digital television 1035.1, 1035.11
digital transcription 50.12
digital TV 1035.1
digital video disc 50.12

digital video recorder 1035.11
digitate 474.9
digitated 474.9
digitization 1042.1
digitize 258.9, 1042.21
digitized 258.12
digits 474.4
diglot 523.16
dignification 662.8, 696.2
dignified 111.3, 136.12, 544.14
dignifiedness 136.2
dignify 580.5, 662.12
dignitary 997.8
dignities 504.7
dignity 111.1, 136.2, 533.1, 544.6, 580.1, 662.4, 698.5, 997.2, 997.8
dig one in the ribs 517.22
dig one's heels in 359.9, 361.7
dig one's own grave 414.14
dig out 188.10, 192.10, 284.15, 938.34
digraph 524.12, 546.1
digraphic 524.30
digress 164.3, 204.9, 538.9, 813.3, 914.4
digression 164.1, 204.1, 538.4, 813.1, 914.1, 914.3
digressive 164.7, 204.13, 538.13, 914.7
digressiveness 538.3
digs 228.4
dig up 192.10, 192.11, 472.9, 552.11, 770.18, 941.4, 981.3
dig up dirt 552.11
dig up the past 989.10
dihedral 218.7
dijn 988.1
Dijon mustard 10.12
dik-dik 311.5
Dike 649.4
dike (n) 224.2, 241.1, 290.2 (v) 284.15
dike 1012.5, 1058.7
diktat 420.4
dilapidate 393.9
dilapidated 16.16, 393.33, 806.5, 810.15, 842.14
dilapidation 393.1, 393.6, 806.1
dilatant 259.9
dilatation 259.2, 283.4, 355.1, 538.6
dilatative 538.15
dilate 259.4, 259.5, 283.11, 538.7
dilated 259.13
dilating 259.2, 538.6
dilation 251.1, 259.2, 283.4, 355.1, 538.6
dilative 538.15
dilatoriness 175.3, 331.5, 846.5
dilatory 175.11, 325.6, 331.19, 846.17
dildock 759.22
dilemma 371.3, 935.6, 971.3, 1013.7
dilemmatic 1013.23
dilettante (n) 101.4, 496.6, 866.3, 929.6, 930.7, 998.10 (a) 930.14
dilettantish 930.14
dilettantism 496.4, 930.5
dilettantship 930.5
diligence 330.6, 339.2, 360.1, 570.4, 983.1
diligent 330.22, 339.11, 360.8, 570.17, 983.15
dill pickle 10.9, 67.2
dilly 999.7
dillydallier 331.8, 846.6
dilly-dally 846.8
dillydally 175.8, 331.14, 846.12
dillydallying (n) 175.3, 331.4, 846.3 (a) 175.11, 846.17
dilogical 539.4
diluent (n) 1064.4 (a) 1064.8
dilute (v) 16.11, 252.8, 270.12, 299.3, 771.5, 797.12, 1065.12 (a) 65.2, 299.4
diluted 16.19, 65.2, 252.10, 270.16, 299.4, 771.9
dilutedness 270.4
dilution 16.5, 65.1, 270.4, 299.2, 771.1, 797.3
diluvium 256.2
dim (n) 1027.2 (v) 25.5, 30.7, 32.4, 36.5, 1027.9, 1027.12 (a) 28.13, 32.6, 36.7, 52.16, 522.15, 922.16, 1027.15
dim-bulb 924.4
dime (n) 728.7, 998.5 (v) 551.13
dime a dozen, a 633.8, 991.7
dime-a-dozen 998.21
dime bag 87.20
dimension 158.1, 257.1
dimensional 158.10
dimension control 1041.8
dimensions 257.1
dimeric 1060.9
dimerous 1060.9
dime store 736.1
dime-store 633.8
dimeter 720.7
dim-eyed 28.13
dim eyes 28.2
dimidiating 647.2
diminish 120.5, 137.5, 168.2, 252.6, 252.7, 255.9, 270.11, 393.18, 600.12, 670.6, 959.3
diminished 137.13, 252.10
diminished capacity 926.1
diminished interval 709.20
diminished responsibility 600.5
diminishing 168.5, 252.11, 670.14
diminishing returns 473.3
diminishment 120.1, 252.1
diminish oneself 137.7
diminuendo (n) 252.2, 260.1, 708.25 (a) 252.11, 708.53
diminuitive 530.2
diminution 120.1, 252.1, 255.2, 557.1, 670.2, 913.1
diminutive (n) 258.4, 527.7 (a) 258.12, 527.15
diminutiveness 248.1, 258.1
dim light 1027.2
dimmed 36.7, 1027.15
dimmed lights 1027.2
dimmer 704.18
dimming 36.3, 1027.2, 1027.6
dimmish 1027.15
dimness 32.2, 36.2, 52.1, 922.3, 1027.2, 1031.1
dim out 1027.9
dimout 1027.7
dim pat 837.3
dimple (n) 284.6 (v) 284.14
dimpled 284.17
dimpsy 1027.15
dim recollection 990.1
dim-sighted 28.13, 30.9, 922.14
dim-sightedness 28.2, 922.2
dimsightedness 30.1
dim sum 10.33
dim view 510.1
dimwit 924.2
dim-witted 922.16
dim-wittedness 922.3
din (n) 53.3, 810.5 (v) 53.7, 849.10
dinamode 17.7
dinch 1022.7
dine 8.18, 8.21
dine not wisely but too well 669.5
dine out 8.21
diner 8.6, 8.16, 8.17, 179.15, 197.11
dinero 728.2
diner-out 8.16
dinette 8.17, 197.11
dine with Duke Humphrey 515.4
ding (n) 54.3, 156.3 (v) 54.8, 849.10
ding-a-ling 54.3, 924.3
dingbat 924.3
Dingbelle 680.7
dingdong (n) 54.3, 781.2, 849.4, 924.3 (v) 54.8 (a) 849.15
dingdong theory 523.13
dinge 38.7
dinger 745.3
dinginess 38.3, 80.1
dinging (n) 54.3 (a) 54.13
dingle 54.3, 237.7, 284.9
dingleberry 12.4
dingo 311.19
dingus 1052.5
dingy 36.7, 38.11, 39.4, 80.22
dining (n) 8.1 (a) 8.31
dining car 8.17, 179.15, 197.11
dining compartment 179.15
dining hall 8.17, 197.11
dining room 8.17, 197.11
dining table 229.1
dining utensils 8.12
din in the ear 53.7, 849.10
din into 849.10
dinkiness 258.1
dinkum 973.15
dinkum oil 973.4
dinky 250.6, 258.10, 258.11, 807.8, 998.18
dinner (n) 8.6 (v) 8.21
dinner clothes 5.11
dinner club 88.20
dinner dance 705.2
dinner-dance 705.2
dinner dress 5.11
dinner gown 5.11
dinner jacket 5.11
dinner party 8.6, 8.9
dinner roll 10.31
dinner service 735.4
dinner theater 704.1, 704.14
dinner theatre 743.13
dinnertime 315.2
dinnerware 735.4
dinosaur 257.14, 311.24
dinosaurian 257.20
dinotherian 257.20
dint (n) 18.1, 284.6, 517.7, 902.4 (v) 284.14
diocesan conference 423.4
diocesan court 423.4
diocese 231.5, 698.8
Diogenes 584.5
Diomedes and Sthenelus 588.6
Dionaea 356.12
Dionysiac 926.30
Dionysus 88.2, 704.26, 890.5, 1069.4
dioptrics 1025.22
diorama 33.7, 712.11
dip (n) 10.9, 10.12, 79.5, 79.9, 204.5, 237.7, 284.2, 367.2, 483.2, 1026.2 (v) 35.14, 79.19, 176.17, 184.40, 204.10, 367.7, 517.22, 701.16, 1065.14
dip a flag 517.22
dip down 194.5
dipeptide 7.6
diphthong 524.12
diphthongal 524.30
diphyletic 560.18
dip into 570.13, 938.26
diplegia 85.27
diploid 305.21
diploid number 305.8
diploma 443.5, 549.6
diplomacy 413.1, 415.2, 466.1, 609.5
diplomat 413.11, 415.8, 576.6
diplomatic (n) 576.6, 609.5 (a) 413.22, 415.12, 466.8, 576.17, 609.43
diplomatic agent 576.6
diplomatic code 580.3
diplomatic corps 576.7
diplomatic courier 353.1
diplomatic doctrine 609.5
diplomatic immunity 430.2, 430.8, 601.2
diplomatic language 523.11
diplomatic mission 576.7
diplomatic pouch 195.2
diplomatics 415.2, 609.5
diplomatic service 576.7
diplomatic staff 576.7
diplomatic text 341.2
diplomatist 413.11, 415.8, 576.6
diplopia 28.1
diplopod 311.32
dipnoan 311.30
dipody 720.7
dip one's hands into 480.19
dipped 1065.17
dipping (n) 79.5, 367.2 (a) 204.16
dipping sauce 10.12
dipping the colors 155.2
dipping the ensign 155.2
dippy 923.9, 926.27
dip snuff 89.14
dipso 88.12
dipsomania 87.1, 88.3, 926.3

dipsomaniac 88.11
dipsy-doodle (n) 356.9, 357.4, 376.1 (v) 356.19
dip the beak 88.25
dip the colors 155.5
dip the ensign 155.5, 182.52
dip the pen in gall 512.12
diptych 549.11, 712.10
Dirac theory 1038.2
diradical 1060.2
Dirae, the 680.10
dire 98.19, 127.30, 133.16, 1000.9, 1011.14, 1011.15
direct (n) 709.12 (v) 161.5, 182.14, 208.10, 239.15, 420.8, 422.5, 553.13, 568.10, 568.11, 573.8, 612.11, 612.12, 708.45, 889.5, 894.8 (a) 161.12, 277.6, 416.5, 430.23, 499.7, 521.11, 533.6, 535.3, 560.18, 644.17, 812.8, 973.17
directable 161.13
direct access 1042.8, 1042.18
direct action 328.1
direct address 1042.18
direct apprehension 934.1
direct attention to 957.14, 983.10
direct broadcast 1035.2
direct cinema 706.1
direct communication 683.10
direct costs 626.3
direct-current circuit 1041.6
direct democracy 612.4
direct deposit 728.14, 729.14
direct distance dial 347.13
direct distance dialing 347.13
direct distance nondialing 347.13
directed 161.13
directedness 380.3
directed verdict 598.9, 965.1
direct examination 598.8, 938.13
direct free kick 752.3
direct hit 459.7
directing 573.12, 612.18
direct initiative 613.8
direction 159.1, 161.1, 375.2, 383.1, 419.1, 420.3, 422.1, 517.4, 553.9, 568.1, 573.1, 612.1, 704.13, 889.1, 896.2
directional 159.19, 161.12, 161.13
directionality 161.1
direction finder 574.9, 1036.4
direction-finder station 1034.6, 1036.6
directionize 161.5
direction line 161.1
direction post 517.4
directions 568.6
direction transmission 1034.16
directive (n) 420.3 (a) 161.13, 375.25, 420.13, 422.8, 573.12
direct line 277.2, 347.17, 560.4
direct mail 553.4
direct-mail 553.14
direct-mail advertising 553.4
direct-mail selling 553.4, 734.2
direct marketing 347.13, 734.2
directness 277.1, 416.1, 499.2, 521.2, 533.1, 535.1, 644.4
direct nomination 609.11
direct object 530.2
direct one's attention to 983.5
direct one's course 177.18
direct one's course to 177.25
direct oneself 161.7, 380.7
direct opposite, the 779.2
director 558.3, 574.1, 574.3, 575.6, 704.23, 706.4, 710.17, 730.1
directorate 573.4, 574.11, 575.14
direct order 420.1
director general 574.1
directorial 573.12
director of photography 706.5
directorship 249.3, 417.7, 417.10, 573.4
directory (n) 423.1, 549.9, 549.11, 551.1, 554.9, 574.10, 574.11, 1042.18 (a) 573.12
direct outward 206.5
direct perception 934.1
direct primary 609.15
direct proportion 777.1
direct ratio 777.1
direct relationship 777.1
directrix 277.2
direct selling 734.2
direct signal 1034.10
direct taxation 630.9
direct the eyes 27.13
direct the mind upon 931.11
direct tide 238.13
direct to 161.6, 983.10
direct to the attention 983.10
direct vote 371.6
direful 127.30
dire necessity 619.2, 963.4
direness 98.3, 127.2, 133.6, 1000.2
direption 482.6
dire straits 619.1
dirge (n) 115.6, 309.4, 309.5, 309.6 (v) 115.10
dirgelike 115.22, 309.22
dirigible (n) 181.11 (a) 161.13
dirigible balloon 181.11
dirk 459.25
dirt (n) 80.6, 234.1, 551.2, 552.8, 666.4 (v) 80.15
dirtbag 660.5
dirt bike 179.8
dirt-biking 744.1
dirt cheap 633.8
dirt-encrusted 80.22
dirt farm 1069.8
dirt farmer 1069.5
dirt-free 79.25
dirtied 80.21
dirtiness 38.3, 80.1, 665.5, 666.4, 1062.4
dirt poor 619.10
dirt road 288.2
dirt track 756.1
dirty (v) 38.7, 80.15, 1004.6 (a) 38.11, 80.22, 318.22, 319.8, 513.8, 650.10, 654.15, 661.12, 665.29, 666.9, 1062.14
dirty blond 35.9
dirty bomb 462.20
dirty crack 489.7
dirty deal 356.6
dirty dig 156.3
dirty game 645.6
dirty hands 656.1
dirtying 80.4
dirty joke 489.6
dirty language 513.3
dirty liar 357.9
dirty lie 354.12
dirty look 27.5, 152.2, 510.8
dirty-minded 654.15
dirty mouth 513.3
dirty movie 666.4
dirty name 513.4
dirty old man 665.11
dirty one's hands 80.16, 137.8, 141.8, 661.7
dirty politician 610.5
dirty politics 609.14
dirty pool 356.5, 609.14, 645.6, 650.2
dirty sea 238.14
dirty shame 661.5
dirty sky 319.4
dirty story 489.6
dirty talk 513.3, 666.4
dirty trick 356.6, 645.6
dirty tricks 609.14
dirty up 80.15
dirty water 238.14
dirty weather 316.4, 671.4
dirty wind 318.11
dirty word 513.4, 526.6
dirty work 645.6, 725.4
Dis 682.5
dis 156.6
disability 19.2, 85.1, 603.2, 996.2
disability insurance 624.6
disable 19.9, 85.50, 393.14
disabled 16.18, 19.16, 393.30, 820.9
disabled person 85.45
disablement 19.2, 393.1
disabuse 977.2
disabused 977.5
disabusing 977.4
disaccharide 7.5
disaccommodate 996.4
disaccommodation 996.3
disaccord (n) 333.1, 451.2, 456.1, 589.2, 780.1, 789.1, 868.1 (v) 456.8, 789.5
disaccordance 780.1, 789.1, 868.1
disaccordant 451.8, 456.15, 780.7, 789.6
disaccord with 780.5
disaccredit 442.3
disaccreditation 442.1
disaccustom 374.2
disaccustomed 374.4
disaccustomedness 374.1
disaccustom oneself 374.3
disadvantage (n) 603.2, 996.2, 1012.6, 1013.3 (v) 996.4, 1000.6
disadvantaged 250.6, 619.8
disadvantaged, the 606.4, 619.3
disadvantagedness 619.2
disadvantageous 996.6, 1000.12
disadvantageousness 996.1
disaffect 379.4, 456.14
disaffected 99.8, 589.11, 645.20
disaffection 99.1, 379.2, 456.4, 589.2, 645.5
disaffiliated 776.6
disaffinity 93.7, 99.1, 456.1, 589.1, 908.1
disaffirm 335.4
disaffirmance 335.2
disaffirmation 335.2
disaffirming 335.5
disagree 333.4, 442.3, 456.8, 789.5, 935.16
disagreeability 98.1, 110.2
disagreeable 64.5, 98.17, 110.19, 144.16, 789.6
disagreeableness 98.1, 110.2, 144.1
disagreeing 325.5, 333.6, 456.15, 780.7, 789.6
disagreement 325.1, 333.1, 442.1, 456.2, 510.1, 775.1, 779.1, 780.1, 789.1, 868.1, 935.4
disagree with 82.4, 333.4, 780.5
disallow 335.4, 442.3, 444.3, 510.10, 625.6
disallowance 335.2, 442.1, 444.1
disallowed 444.7
disallowing 335.5
disambiguate 341.12, 521.6, 798.5
disannul 445.2
disappear 32.3, 34.2, 188.9, 222.8, 346.8, 395.23, 762.6, 828.6, 837.6
disappearance 32.1, 34.1, 222.4, 346.1, 368.4
disappeared 222.11
disappearing (n) 34.1 (a) 34.3, 368.16
disappearing act 34.1, 368.4
disappear into thin air 34.2
disappoint 96.16, 98.15, 108.5, 125.11, 132.2, 977.2
disappointed 108.7, 132.5, 408.3, 510.21, 977.5
disappointing 98.20, 108.9, 132.6
disappointment 93.7, 96.6, 98.6, 108.1, 125.5, 132.1, 408.1, 410.3, 510.1, 977.1, 992.1
disappoint one's expectations 132.3
disapprobation 99.1, 152.1, 333.1, 510.1, 661.1
disapprobatory 510.21
disapproval 99.1, 152.1, 333.1, 372.1, 510.1, 512.1
disapprove 372.2, 510.10, 661.9
disapproved 372.3
disapprove of 99.3, 99.5, 510.10, 512.8
disapprover 510.9
disapproving 99.8, 510.21
disarm 19.9, 465.11
disarmament 465.6
disarmament treaty 464.7
disarmed 19.16
disarming 504.17

disarrange 160.5, 810.9, 811.2, 813.3, 917.10
disarranged 160.9, 810.13, 811.5
disarrangement 160.1, 810.1, 811.1
disarray (n) 810.1 (v) 6.7, 811.2
disarticulate 160.5, 802.8, 802.16
disarticulated 802.21, 810.12
disarticulation 160.1, 802.1, 810.1
disassemble 395.17, 802.15
disassembly 395.5, 802.6
disassimilation 2.20, 7.12
disassociate 802.8
disassociation 776.1, 802.1
disaster 308.8, 395.4, 671.5, 1011.2
disaster area 1011.2
disastrous 395.26, 671.23, 1011.15
disastrous defeat 412.4
disavow 335.4, 363.8
disavowal 335.2, 363.3, 372.1
disavowing 335.5
disbalance 791.3
disband 465.11, 771.8, 802.19
disbanding 465.6
disbandment 465.6, 771.3
disbar 447.4, 909.19
disbarment 447.2, 909.4
disbarring 447.2
disbelief 695.5, 955.1, 971.2
disbelieve 695.14, 955.5, 956.3
disbelieved 955.12
disbeliever 695.11, 955.4
disbelieving 695.19, 955.8
disbodied 1053.7
disburden 120.7, 298.6, 909.23, 1014.9
disburdened 298.11
disburdening (n) 120.3, 298.3, 480.6, 1014.6 (a) 298.16
disburdenment 480.6
disburden of 480.21
disburden one's heart 351.7
disbursal 477.2, 624.1, 626.1
disbursals 626.3
disburse 477.8, 626.5
disbursement 477.2, 626.1
disbursements 626.2
disburser 626.4
disbursing 624.21
disc 50.12, 549.10
discalceate 6.15
discalced 6.15, 667.4
discard (n) 370.4, 372.1, 390.3, 773.2 (v) 370.5, 372.2, 390.7, 909.13
discarded 370.8, 372.3, 390.11, 958.7
discarding 390.3
discarnate 988.8, 1053.7
discase 6.7
discased 6.12
discasing 6.2
discept 935.16
disceptation 935.4
disceptator 935.12
discern 27.12, 521.9, 928.12, 941.5
discerned 928.26
discernible 31.6, 348.8, 928.25, 941.10
discernibleness 31.1
discerning 920.16, 944.8
discernment 27.1, 496.1, 920.4, 920.7, 944.2
discharge (n) 2.24, 12.1, 12.3, 12.6, 56.3, 85.9, 120.2, 190.1, 190.4, 328.2, 407.1, 430.8, 431.2, 434.1, 437.4, 601.1, 624.1, 627.2, 671.7, 904.4, 908.2, 909.1, 909.5, 909.7, 1032.6 (v) 12.12, 13.5, 56.8, 190.15, 328.9, 407.4, 430.14, 431.5, 434.3, 437.9, 601.4, 624.13, 671.13, 671.14, 771.8, 904.12, 908.3, 909.13, 909.19, 909.23, 909.25
discharged 407.10, 624.22
dischargee 909.12
discharge one's duty 641.10
discharge one's function 434.3
discharge the office of 724.13
discharging cargo 909.6
discharging freight 909.6
disciple 101.4, 166.2, 572.2, 616.8, 684.2, 692.4, 858.7
disciplehood 572.2
disciples 617.5
discipleship 101.2, 166.2, 572.2, 692.1
disciples of Christ 687.3
disciplinarian 575.13
disciplinary 568.18, 604.22, 928.28
disciplinary action 604.1
disciplinary measure 604.1
discipline (n) 210.2, 359.5, 425.1, 568.3, 568.8, 604.1, 612.1, 668.1, 724.4, 807.3, 928.10, 937.1 (v) 210.5, 425.4, 568.13, 604.9, 612.11, 867.3
disciplined 134.9, 210.7, 425.6
discipline oneself 668.6
discipliner 604.7
disc jockey 1034.23
disclaim 335.4, 363.8, 372.2, 442.3
disclaimer 335.2, 363.3, 442.1, 475.2
disclaiming 335.5
disclamation 335.2, 363.3, 372.1, 442.1
disclosable 941.10
disclose 292.12, 348.5, 351.4, 517.17, 524.22, 551.8, 941.4, 957.9
disclosed 31.6, 292.17, 348.10, 351.9
disclosing (n) 351.1 (a) 351.10
disclosive 348.9, 351.10
disclosure 33.1, 292.1, 334.1, 343.2, 348.1, 351.1, 352.1, 517.3, 941.1, 957.2
disco 705.4, 743.13
discobolus 904.7
discography 708.1, 871.3
discoid 280.11
discolor (n) 1004.2 (v) 36.5, 36.6, 517.19, 1004.6
discoloration 36.3, 517.5, 1004.2
discolored 36.7, 1004.10
discolorment 1004.2
discombobulate 105.14, 985.7
discombobulated 810.16, 985.12
discombobulation 985.3
discomfirmatory 958.6
discomfit 96.15, 127.19, 412.8, 985.7, 1012.15
discomfited 96.22, 412.14, 810.13
discomfiture 96.4, 132.1, 412.2, 810.1, 985.3, 1012.3
discomfort (n) 26.1, 96.1, 98.1, 98.5 (v) 96.16, 98.14
discomforted 96.22
discomforting 98.20
discommend 510.12
discommendable 510.24
discommendation 510.2
discommode 996.4, 1013.13
discommodious 844.6, 996.7
discommodity 996.3
discompose 96.12, 96.13, 96.15, 105.14, 810.9, 811.4, 917.10, 971.12, 985.7
discomposed 96.22, 105.23, 810.13, 810.16, 917.16, 971.24, 985.12
discomposing 971.27
discomposure 96.1, 96.4, 810.1, 811.1, 917.1, 971.3, 985.3
disconcert (n) 971.3 (v) 96.15, 98.13, 105.14, 127.19, 971.12, 985.7, 1012.15
disconcerted 96.22, 810.13, 971.24, 985.12
disconcertedness 98.6, 810.1, 811.1, 971.3
disconcerting 98.21, 127.28, 971.27, 1012.20
disconcertingness 127.2
disconcertion 96.4, 971.3, 985.3, 1012.3
disconcertment 96.4, 971.3
disconfirm 958.4
disconfirmation 958.1
disconfirmed 958.7
disconformity 435.1, 780.1, 868.1
discongruity 780.1
disconnect (n) 776.1 (v) 802.8, 813.3, 851.2
disconnected 776.6, 802.21, 804.4, 813.4, 851.3, 926.28
disconnectedness 802.1, 813.1, 851.1
disconnection 92.20, 776.1, 802.1, 813.1
disconsolate 96.26, 112.28, 115.19, 125.12
disconsolateness 112.12, 125.2
disconsolation 112.12
disconsonant 61.4
discontent (n) 96.1, 108.1, 110.1, 112.2, 152.1, 510.1 (v) 96.12, 108.5
discontented 108.7, 110.17, 112.21, 510.21
discontentedness 108.1, 510.1
discontentment 108.1, 510.1
discontinuance 390.2, 813.1, 857.1
discontinuance wage 624.4
discontinuation 813.1, 820.1, 857.1
discontinue 293.8, 374.3, 390.4, 668.8, 813.3, 857.6
discontinued 390.10, 813.4
discontinuity 160.1, 224.1, 795.2, 802.1, 804.1, 813.1, 851.1, 852.2
discontinuous 224.5, 802.20, 804.4, 810.12, 813.4, 851.3
discontinuousness 813.1
discord 53.3, 58.2, 61.1, 456.1, 789.1
discordance 61.1, 456.1, 780.1, 789.1
discordancy 61.1, 456.1, 789.1
discordant 35.21, 61.4, 456.15, 589.9, 779.6, 780.7, 789.6
discordant couple 566.1
Discordia 456.1
discord with 333.4
discotheque 705.4
discothèque 743.13
discount (n) 631.1 (v) 372.2, 630.11, 631.2, 728.27, 959.5
discount broker 730.9
discounted 372.3
discountenance (n) 96.4 (v) 451.7, 510.11, 1012.15
discounter 729.11
discount house 736.1
discounting 372.1, 728.16
discount notes 728.27
discount oneself 137.7
discount rate 623.3
discount store 736.1
discount ticket 634.2
discourage 112.18, 127.18, 379.4, 1012.14
discouraged 112.22
discouraged workers 331.11
discouragement 112.3, 379.2, 1012.2
discouraging 112.30, 127.28, 379.5, 1012.19
discourse (n) 524.1, 541.1, 543.3, 556.1, 568.7, 935.1 (v) 543.9, 556.5, 568.16
discourse about 541.11
discourse of reason 935.1
discourser 541.7, 543.5, 556.3
discourse with 541.8
discoursive 556.6
discourteous 151.4, 156.7, 497.10, 505.4
discourteousness 505.1
discourtesy 25.1, 156.1, 321.2, 322.1, 505.1
discover 27.12, 351.4, 570.6, 852.9, 892.12, 941.2
discoverable 928.25, 941.10
discovered 892.19
discoverer 892.7
discovering 351.1
discover itself 941.9
discover oneself 33.8, 941.2
discover serendipitously 941.3
discover to one's cost 941.2

discovery 351.1, 472.6, 598.12, 852.4, 941.1
discredit (n) 661.1, 955.1 (v) 512.8, 661.8, 955.5, 958.4
discreditable 661.10
discreditableness 661.2
discredited 661.13, 955.12, 958.7
discrediting 512.1, 958.2
discreet 344.10, 345.15, 494.8, 920.19
discreetness 344.3, 345.1, 920.7
discrepancy 255.8, 779.1, 780.1, 789.1
discrepant 779.6, 780.7, 789.6
discrete 771.9, 776.6, 780.7, 802.20, 804.4, 813.4
discrete four-channel system 50.11
discrete matter 937.1
discreteness 768.1, 776.1, 780.1, 780.4, 802.1, 804.1, 813.1
discretion 323.1, 344.3, 345.1, 371.2, 371.10, 430.6, 494.1, 920.7, 961.1
discretional 324.7, 371.22
discretionary 324.7
discretive 813.4
discriminable 780.7, 944.9
discriminate (v) 650.8, 780.6, 944.4, 944.5 (a) 944.7
discriminate against 980.8
discriminated 780.7
discriminateness 944.1
discriminating 371.23, 495.9, 496.8, 780.9, 920.19, 944.7
discriminatingness 495.1, 944.1
discriminating taste 944.1
discrimination 371.10, 495.1, 496.1, 533.1, 650.3, 780.4, 920.7, 944.1, 946.1, 980.4
discriminative 495.9, 780.9, 920.19, 944.7
discriminativeness 495.1, 944.1
discriminatory 650.9, 780.9, 944.7, 980.12
discrown 447.4
discrownment 447.2
disculpation 601.1
discursion 164.1, 538.4
discursive 164.7, 177.37, 538.13, 556.6, 914.7, 920.12, 935.22
discursiveness 538.3
discursive reason 919.1, 935.1
discursive reasoning 935.3
discus 280.2, 904.5
discuss 541.10, 541.11, 556.5
discussant 556.3
discusser 556.3
discussion 541.5, 541.6, 556.1
discussion group 423.3
discuss with 541.10
discus thrower 904.7
disdain (n) 141.5, 142.1, 157.1, 372.1, 454.1 (v) 157.3, 372.2, 454.4, 495.8, 510.12
disdained 372.3
disdainful 141.13, 142.9, 157.8, 372.4, 454.7
disdainfulness 141.5, 157.1
disease (n) 85.1, 96.5, 1000.5, 1001.1 (v) 85.51
disease-causing 85.53
disease-causing agent 85.42
diseased 85.55, 85.60
diseased mind 926.1
disease-fighting (n) 91.1 (a) 86.39
disease of the digestive tract 85.29
disease of the eye 85.14
disease of the workplace 85.32
disease of vision 85.14
disease prevention 83.5
disease-producing 85.53
disease-producing microorganism 85.42
disedge 286.2
disembark 182.15, 186.8
disembarkation 182.5, 186.2
disembarkment 186.2
disembarrass 120.7, 431.7, 1014.9
disembarrassed 430.26
disembarrassment 120.3, 431.3, 1014.6
disembodied 988.8, 1053.7
disembodied spirit 988.1
disembodiment 689.19, 1053.5
disembody 689.20, 764.4, 1053.6
disembogue 190.11, 909.25
disemboguement 909.7
disembowel 192.13
disembowelment 192.4, 308.5
disembroil 431.7, 798.5, 1014.9
disembroilment 431.3
disemplane 186.8
disemploy 909.19
disemployment 909.5
disempower 418.4
disenable 19.9, 967.6
disenchant 977.2
disenchanted 99.8, 132.5, 510.21, 977.5
disenchanting 379.5, 977.4
disenchantment 510.1, 859.1, 977.1
disencumber 120.7, 298.6, 1014.9
disencumbered 298.11
disencumbering 298.16
disencumberment 298.3
disencumbrance 120.3, 1014.6
disendow 480.23
disendowment 480.7
disenfranchise 432.8
disenfranchised 19.18, 432.14
disenfranchisement 432.1
disengage 163.6, 431.7, 802.8, 802.10, 1014.9
disengaged 331.18, 369.11, 430.21, 802.21
disengagement 163.2, 431.3, 802.1, 1014.6
disentangle 192.10, 277.5, 431.7, 798.5, 940.2, 1014.9
disentanglement 192.1, 431.3, 798.2, 940.1, 1014.6
disenthrall 431.4
disenthrallment 431.1
disenthrone 447.4
disenthronement 447.2
disentitle 480.21
disentitlement 480.6, 640.1
disentomb 192.11
disentombment 192.2
disentwine 431.7
disentwining 431.3
disequalization 780.4
disequalize 780.6
disequilibrate 791.3
disequilibrium 791.1
disertitude 544.1
disesteem (n) 156.1, 510.1, 661.1 (v) 156.4
diseur 543.7, 707.2
diseuse 543.7, 707.2
disfavor (n) 99.1, 456.4, 510.1, 661.1 (v) 99.3, 510.10
disfellowship (n) 909.4 (v) 586.6, 909.17
disfiguration 1004.1
disfigure 265.7, 1004.4, 1015.5
disfigured 265.12, 1004.8, 1015.6
disfigurement 265.3, 1004.1, 1015.1
disfranchise 432.8
disfranchised 432.14
disfranchisement 432.1
disgorge 475.3, 671.13, 909.25, 909.26
disgorgement 909.7, 909.8
disgrace (n) 137.2, 512.1, 638.2, 654.3, 661.5 (v) 137.4, 512.8, 661.8
disgraced 661.13
disgraceful 638.3, 654.16, 661.11
disgracefulness 661.2
disgrace oneself 661.7
disgrace to one's name, a 661.5
disgrade 447.3
disgrading 447.1
disgruntle 108.5
disgruntled 108.7, 510.21
disgruntlement 108.1, 510.1
disguise (n) 5.9, 346.2, 354.3, 356.11, 787.1 (v) 346.6, 350.3, 354.16, 787.3
disguised 5.45, 32.5, 346.13
disguised message 551.4
disguise oneself 346.8
disgust (n) 99.2 (v) 64.4, 98.11, 99.6
disgusted 96.20, 103.7, 994.6
disgusting 80.23, 98.18, 98.19, 661.12, 1000.9
disgustingly rich 618.15
disgustingness 64.3, 80.2, 98.2, 1000.2
dish (n) 8.10, 8.12, 10.7, 745.1, 747.3, 1016.8, 1035.11 (v) 176.17, 284.12, 284.13, 395.11, 747.4, 1012.15
dishabille 5.20
disharmonic 61.4
disharmonious 61.4, 456.15, 789.6
disharmony 61.1, 456.1, 789.1, 810.1
dishearten 108.5, 112.18, 127.18, 1012.14
disheartened 112.22
disheartening 108.9, 112.30, 127.28, 132.6, 661.11
disheartenment 112.3
dished 132.5, 284.16
disherison (n) 480.7 (v) 480.23
disher-upper 747.2
dishes 8.12
dishevel 810.9, 811.2
disheveled 810.14
dishevelment 810.1
dish fit for a king 10.7
dishing 284.16
dishlike 284.16
dish of the day 10.7
dishonest 354.31, 354.32, 354.34, 645.16
dishonest race 757.3
dishonesty 354.4, 354.8, 356.8, 645.1
dishonor (n) 156.1, 625.1, 645.1, 661.1 (v) 156.5, 625.6, 661.8, 694.4
dishonorable 645.16, 661.10
dishonorable discharge 909.5
dishonorableness 661.2
dishonored 661.13
dishonored bill 625.1
dishonoring 625.1
dish out 176.17, 477.8, 478.12, 643.6
dishpan 79.12
dish-shaped 284.16
dish the dirt 552.12
dish up 176.17, 385.7, 439.5
dishware 8.12
dishwasher 79.12, 79.15
dishwashing liquid 79.17
dishwashing powder 79.17
dishwater (n) 16.7, 80.9, 391.4 (a) 65.2
dishwiper 79.15
dishy 97.8, 100.30, 377.8, 1016.21
disillude 977.2
disillusion (n) 510.1, 977.1 (v) 108.5, 132.2, 977.2
disillusionary 977.4
disillusioned 132.5, 510.21, 977.5
disillusioning 977.4
disillusionize 977.2
disillusionment 132.1, 510.1, 977.1
disillusive 977.4
disimprove 393.9, 393.16
disimprovement 393.1
disincarnate 689.20, 1053.6
disincarnation 689.19, 1053.5
disincentive 379.2
disinclination 99.1, 139.3, 325.1
disinclination to believe 956.1
disinclination to communicate 344.1
disincline 139.7, 379.4
disinclined 99.8, 139.12, 325.5
disinclined to believe 956.4
disinclined to communicate 344.8
disinclining 379.5
disinfect 79.18, 79.24
disinfectant (n) 79.17, 86.21, 1001.3 (a) 79.28, 86.43
disinfected 79.27
disinfection 79.3

disinfest 79.24
disinfestation 79.3
disinform 350.3, 569.4
disinformation 350.1, 354.9, 354.10, 569.2
disinformational 569.6
disinformative 354.25
disinforming 354.9
disingenuous 354.32, 645.18, 936.10
disingenuousness 354.5, 645.3, 936.1
disinherit 480.23
disinheritance 480.7
disintegrable 806.5
disintegrate 16.9, 308.18, 393.22, 393.23, 395.17, 395.22, 771.8, 802.9, 806.3, 810.8, 1050.3, 1051.9, 1051.10
disintegrated 806.5, 1051.11
disintegrating 16.15, 393.45, 806.5
disintegration 16.2, 393.6, 395.1, 771.3, 802.3, 806.1, 810.1, 1051.4
disintegration series 1038.8
disintegrative 806.5
disinter 192.11, 941.4
disinterest (n) 94.4, 102.2, 467.2, 649.3, 652.1, 982.1 (v) 379.4
disinterested 94.13, 102.7, 649.9, 652.5, 979.12, 982.3
disinterestedness 649.3, 652.1, 979.5, 982.1
disinterment 192.2
disintoxicate 87.22
disintricate 798.5
disinvestment 729.4
disinvolve 431.7, 798.5, 1014.9
disinvolvement 431.3, 798.2, 1014.6
disjoin 780.6, 802.8, 804.3, 806.3, 813.3
disjoined 780.7, 802.21
disjoin oneself 333.4
disjoint (v) 160.5, 802.8, 802.16 (a) 802.21
disjointed 160.9, 802.21
disjointing 160.1, 802.1
disjointure 802.1
disjunct 776.6, 802.21, 810.12
disjunction 773.2, 775.1, 776.1, 780.4, 802.1, 804.1, 806.1, 810.1, 813.1
disjunctive (n) 530.3 (a) 371.22, 802.25, 806.5, 813.4
disjunctive conjunction 530.3
disjuncture 776.1
disk 280.2, 296.2, 549.10, 915.4, 1042.6
disk cartridge 549.10
disk clutch 1040.10
disk drive 1042.5
diskette 549.10, 1042.6
disk flower 310.27
disk galaxy 1073.6
disk jockey 1034.23
disklike 280.11
disk operating system 1042.12
disk pack 1042.6, 1042.7
dislikable 64.5, 98.17, 99.7
dislike (n) 96.1, 99.1, 103.1, 103.3, 589.3 (v) 99.3, 103.6
disliked 99.9
dislocate 160.5, 802.16, 811.2
dislocated 160.9, 802.21, 810.13
dislocating 160.8
dislocation 160.1, 802.1, 804.1, 811.1
dislocatory 160.8
dislodge 160.6, 176.11, 431.7, 909.15
dislodged 160.9
dislodgment 160.2, 431.3, 909.2
disloyal 363.11, 645.20
disloyalty 363.2, 645.5
dismal 39.4, 98.20, 112.24, 117.6, 125.12, 125.16, 309.22
dismalness 98.5, 112.7, 117.1, 125.6
dismals 112.6
dismal science, the 731.11
dismantle 395.17, 802.15
dismantlement 395.5, 802.6
dismask 351.4
dismay (n) 127.1 (v) 98.14, 127.19, 971.12
dismayed 127.25, 491.10, 971.24
dismaying 98.20, 127.28, 971.27
dismayingness 127.2
dismember 604.15, 802.14, 804.3
dismembered 802.23, 804.4
dismemberment 604.2, 802.6, 804.1
dismiss 102.4, 157.6, 372.2, 431.5, 447.4, 601.4, 771.8, 908.3, 909.18, 909.19, 958.5, 984.4
dismissal 157.2, 372.1, 431.2, 447.2, 601.1, 771.3, 908.2, 909.5
dismiss all doubt 970.11
dismissal wage 624.4
dismissed 372.3, 958.7
dismissed out of hand 372.3
dismiss from one's thoughts 148.5, 984.4, 990.6
dismiss from the mind 933.3
dismissive 141.13, 372.4
dismiss out of hand 372.2
dismiss with a laugh 984.4
dismount 160.6, 194.7, 802.15
dismounting 802.6
disobedience 325.1, 327.1, 418.1, 418.2, 442.1, 454.1
disobedient 325.5, 327.8, 418.5, 442.6
disobey 327.6
disobey the law 674.5
disoblige 156.5, 996.4
disobliging 144.18
disorder (n) 85.1, 263.1, 322.1, 418.2, 782.1, 804.1, 810.1, 811.1, 852.1, 917.1, 971.4, 985.3 (v) 85.50, 263.3, 810.9, 811.2
disordered 92.39, 804.4, 810.12, 810.13, 811.5, 971.19, 985.12
disordered mind 926.1
disordered reason 926.1
disorderliness 322.1, 418.2, 671.3, 810.1
disorderly 263.4, 322.5, 418.6, 671.19, 782.3, 810.13, 851.3
disorderly conduct 322.1
disorderly house 665.9
disorganization 393.6, 395.1, 406.1, 418.2, 771.3, 806.1, 810.1, 811.1, 985.3
disorganize 771.8, 806.3, 810.9, 811.2, 985.7
disorganized 418.6, 810.13, 985.12
disorient 811.2, 985.7
disorientate 985.7
disorientated 985.12
disorientation 92.18, 161.4, 926.1, 985.3
disoriented 926.26, 971.24, 985.12
disown 335.4, 363.8, 372.2, 480.23
disowned 372.3, 586.10
disowning (n) 363.3 (a) 335.5
disownment 335.2, 363.3, 372.1, 480.7
disparage 156.4, 157.3, 255.9, 510.12, 512.8, 661.9, 950.2
disparagement 156.1, 157.1, 255.2, 510.2, 512.1, 513.2, 661.6, 950.1
disparager 512.6
disparaging 156.7, 510.22, 512.13
disparaging remark 512.4
disparate 780.7, 787.4, 791.4
disparity 333.1, 456.2, 780.1, 787.1, 789.1, 791.1
dispart 224.3, 292.11
disparted 224.6
dispassion 94.1, 94.4, 102.2, 106.1, 649.3, 670.1
dispassionate 94.9, 102.7, 106.10, 649.9, 670.13, 979.12
dispassionateness 94.1, 106.1, 649.3, 979.5
dispatch (n) 174.1, 308.1, 328.2, 330.3, 407.1, 551.1, 552.4, 553.2, 845.3 (v) 8.22, 172.6, 176.15, 308.13, 328.9, 401.4, 407.4, 553.12
dispatch-bearer 353.1
dispatched 407.10
dispatcher 178.13
dispatchful 330.18
dispatch-rider 353.1
Dis pater 682.5
dispel 34.2, 771.5, 802.19, 909.21
dispel one's illusions 977.2
dispensability 998.1
dispensable 477.12, 600.14, 993.17, 998.17
dispensary 86.36, 197.25
dispensation 443.1, 443.2, 475.1, 477.2, 573.3, 601.2, 612.1, 642.2, 677.13, 771.1
dispensations of providence 677.13
dispensatory 86.36, 86.37
dispense 430.14, 443.9, 477.8, 478.12, 734.9, 771.4
dispensed 430.30
dispensed with 475.5
dispense from 430.14, 601.4
dispenser 86.35
dispense with 390.5, 430.14, 475.3
dispensing 477.2
dispeople 909.16
dispeoplement 909.3
dispersal 771.1, 771.3, 802.3, 804.1
disperse 34.2, 164.5, 171.6, 259.6, 299.3, 477.8, 771.4, 771.8, 802.13, 802.19, 804.3
dispersed 164.8, 299.4, 771.9, 802.21, 810.12
dispersedness 299.1
dispersion 34.1, 164.2, 171.2, 259.1, 299.2, 477.2, 771.1, 771.3, 804.1
dispersive 771.11
dispirit 112.18
dispirited 112.22, 118.11
dispiritedness 112.3, 118.3
dispiriting 112.30
displace 160.5, 176.11, 447.4, 835.3, 862.5, 909.19
displaced 160.9
displaced meaning 518.1
displaced person 160.4, 178.5, 368.5, 586.4, 774.3
displaced population 160.4
displacement 92.23, 160.1, 275.7, 447.2, 852.3, 862.1
displacing 909.5
display (n) 33.2, 33.7, 206.4, 216.1, 348.2, 352.1, 501.4, 554.7, 1036.11, 1042.9, 1042.18 (v) 206.5, 348.5, 352.11, 501.17, 517.17, 957.8
displayable 348.13
display ad 352.6
display case 1029.2
displayed 348.13
displaying (n) 206.4 (a) 348.9
display room 197.24
display station 1036.6
displease 98.10, 108.5
displeased 99.8, 108.7, 510.21
displeasing 64.5, 98.17, 99.7, 108.9
displeasingness 98.1
displeasure 96.1, 98.1, 99.1, 112.2, 152.1, 510.1
displosion 56.3
displume 447.3, 480.24, 661.8, 909.19
displuming 447.1, 661.4, 909.4
disport 743.23
disposable 388.6
disposable camera 714.11
disposable goods 388.2
disposable income 627.1
disposable item 388.2
disposable lenses 29.3
disposable resources 384.2
disposal 159.6, 387.7, 390.3, 475.1, 477.2, 573.3, 629.1, 773.2, 807.1, 808.1
disposal of the dead 309.1
dispose 159.11, 161.7, 375.22, 477.8, 808.9, 894.7, 894.8
disposed 324.5, 808.14, 978.8
disposed of 407.10, 475.5

disposed to doubt 956.4
dispose of 8.22, 308.13, 328.9, 390.7, 395.12, 407.4, 475.3, 478.21, 773.5, 820.6, 958.5
disposition 159.6, 323.1, 381.1, 417.5, 458.2, 475.1, 477.2, 573.3, 612.1, 629.1, 767.4, 773.2, 807.1, 808.1, 896.1, 978.3
dispositional 978.7
dispositioned 978.8
disposition to believe 954.1
dispossess 480.23, 909.15
dispossessed, the 606.4, 1011.7
dispossessed of 473.8
dispossession 473.1, 480.7, 909.2
dispraise (n) 510.2 (v) 510.12
dispread (v) 771.4 (a) 771.9
disprize 157.3
disproof 335.2, 958.1
disproportion (n) 265.1, 789.2, 791.1, 810.1 (v) 265.7, 791.2
disproportionate 355.4, 789.6, 789.8, 791.4, 810.12
disproportionateness 789.2
disproportionate reaction 92.16
disprovable 958.10
disproval 958.1
disprove 335.4, 958.4
disproved 958.7
disproving 958.1
disputability 971.2
disputable 971.17
disputant (n) 452.3, 461.1, 935.12 (a) 457.22
disputation 457.1, 935.4
disputatious 110.26, 453.5, 456.17, 789.6, 935.19
disputatiousness 110.7, 457.1, 935.13
dispute (n) 453.1, 456.5, 457.1, 935.4, 938.12 (v) 333.5, 335.4, 453.3, 456.11, 457.21, 935.16, 955.6
disputed 955.12, 958.7
disputed election 609.15
disputing 453.5, 935.19
disqualification 19.2, 406.1
disqualified 19.16, 406.9
disqualify 19.11, 967.6
disquiet (n) 96.1, 105.5, 126.1, 127.5, 128.1, 135.1, 917.1 (v) 96.12, 96.16, 105.14, 126.4, 127.15, 917.10
disquieted 96.22, 105.23, 126.7, 127.25, 917.16
disquieting 105.30, 126.10, 127.28
disquietingness 127.2
disquietude 105.5, 126.1, 127.5, 128.1, 135.1, 917.1
disquisition 556.1, 568.7
disquisitional 556.6
disquisitor 556.3
disrecollect 990.5
disrecollected 990.8
disrecommendation 510.5
disregard (n) 102.2, 148.1, 157.2, 340.1, 372.1, 435.1, 454.1, 984.1 (v) 134.8, 148.4, 157.6, 327.6, 340.6, 372.2, 435.3, 454.4, 959.5, 979.7, 982.2, 984.2, 998.12
disregardant 340.11, 984.6
disregarded 148.7, 340.14
disregarder 340.5
disregardful 102.7, 144.18, 340.11, 435.5, 454.7, 984.6
disregardfulness 102.2, 144.3, 340.2, 984.1
disregard the distinction between meum and tuum 482.13
disregard the law 674.5
disrelated 776.6
disrelish (n) 99.1, 325.1 (v) 99.3, 103.6
disremember 990.5
disremembered 990.8
disrepair 391.1, 393.1
disreputability 661.2
disreputable (n) 660.1 (a) 661.10
disreputable gambling house 759.19
disreputableness 661.2
disreputable person 660.1
disrepute 661.1
disrespect (n) 142.2, 156.1, 327.1, 505.2, 510.1 (v) 156.4
disrespected 156.9
disrespectful 142.10, 156.7, 505.4
disrespectfulness 142.2, 156.1, 505.2
disrobe 6.7
disrobed 6.13
disrobement 6.2
disrobing 6.2, 802.6
disrupt 160.5, 802.13, 811.3, 1012.15
disruption 160.1, 322.1, 395.1, 418.2, 456.4, 802.3, 810.1, 810.4
disruptive 322.5, 806.5
disruptiveness 322.1
disruptive technology 395.1
diss 137.5, 156.6
dissatisfaction 96.1, 108.1, 132.1, 152.1, 333.1, 510.1
dissatisfactoriness 108.2
dissatisfactory 108.9
dissatisfied 108.7, 132.5, 510.21
dissatisfied customer 108.3, 333.3
dissatisfiedness 108.1
dissatisfy 108.5, 132.2
dissect 801.6, 802.17
dissection 801.1, 802.5
disseise 480.23
disseisin 480.7
dissemblance 354.3, 787.1
dissemble 346.6, 354.21
dissembler 336.4, 357.1, 357.8, 693.3
dissembling (n) 354.3 (a) 354.33
disseminate 176.10, 343.7, 352.10, 771.4, 1069.18
disseminated 352.17, 771.9
dissemination 348.1, 352.1, 771.1, 1069.14
disseminative 771.11
dissension 333.1, 451.2, 456.3, 789.1
dissent (n) 115.4, 325.1, 333.1, 442.1, 453.1, 456.3, 456.5, 510.1, 675.10, 780.1, 789.1, 868.1, 900.1 (v) 333.4, 442.3, 453.3, 782.2, 789.5, 868.4, 900.6, 935.16
dissenter 333.3, 675.20, 789.4, 868.3
dissent from 333.4, 510.10, 900.6
dissentience 333.1, 453.1
dissentient (n) 333.3, 452.3 (a) 333.6, 451.8, 453.5, 456.15, 675.28, 900.8
dissenting 333.6, 442.6, 453.5, 510.21, 868.5, 935.19
dissepiment 213.5
dissert 556.5
dissertate 556.5
dissertate on 541.11
dissertation 556.1
dissertational 556.6
dissertator 556.3
disserve 1000.6
disservice 144.13, 650.4
disserviceable 996.6, 1000.12
dissever 802.11
disseverance 802.2
disseverment 802.2
dissidence 333.1, 456.3, 789.1
dissident (n) 333.3, 452.3 (a) 333.6, 456.15, 789.6, 868.5, 900.8
dissilience 671.6, 802.3
dissiliency 671.6, 802.3
dissilient 671.24, 802.24
dissimilar 780.7, 787.4, 943.9
dissimilarity 780.1, 787.1
dissimilate 787.3
dissimilated 524.30
dissimilation 524.12, 787.1
dissimilative 2.31
dissimilitude 787.1
dissimulate 354.21
dissimulation 354.3
dissimulator 336.4, 357.1, 357.8, 693.3
dissipate 34.2, 387.13, 473.5, 473.6, 486.3, 665.19, 669.6, 771.5
dissipated 252.10, 388.5, 473.7, 486.9, 665.25, 669.8, 771.9
dissipate one's illusions 977.2
dissipater 669.3
dissipating 387.1
dissipation 34.1, 252.3, 387.1, 473.2, 486.1, 665.3, 669.2, 771.1
dissipationless 1014.14
dissipative 486.8, 771.11
dissociability 583.1
dissociable 583.5
dissociableness 583.1
dissociate 802.8, 806.4
dissociated 92.39, 776.6, 926.28
dissociate oneself from 510.10
dissociation 92.20, 92.23, 776.1, 806.2, 1038.8
dissociation of personality 92.20, 926.4
dissociative 806.6
dissociative disorder 92.14, 92.18, 92.20
dissogeny 78.2
dissolubility 1064.2
dissoluble 802.26, 1064.9
dissolubleness 1064.2
dissolute 654.14, 665.25, 669.8
dissoluteness 654.5, 665.3
dissolution 34.1, 252.3, 307.1, 307.12, 393.6, 395.1, 771.3, 802.3, 804.1, 806.1, 1064.1
dissolutional 1064.7
dissolution of marriage 566.1
dissolutive 1064.7
dissolvability 1064.2
dissolvable 802.26, 1064.9
dissolvableness 1064.2
dissolve (n) 706.6 (v) 34.2, 395.10, 762.6, 771.5, 771.8, 806.3, 828.6, 1064.5
dissolve in tears 115.12
dissolve into chaos 810.8
dissolvent (n) 1064.4 (a) 1064.8
dissolve one's marriage 566.5
dissolver 1064.4
dissolving (n) 34.1, 1064.1 (a) 34.3, 1064.7
dissolving agent 1064.4
dissonance 61.1, 780.1, 789.1
dissonancy 61.1
dissonant 61.4, 780.7, 789.6
dissonant chord 61.1
dissuade 379.3, 422.6
dissuading 379.5
dissuasion 379.1
dissuasive 379.5
distaff (n) 77.5, 740.5, 915.5 (a) 77.13
distaff side 559.2, 560.4
distaff side, the 77.3
distal 261.8
distance (n) 158.8, 159.2, 209.2, 261.1, 267.1, 300.3, 344.3, 583.2, 751.3 (v) 249.10
distance, the 261.3
distance across 269.1
distance between 224.1
distance crossways 269.1
distance crosswise 269.1
distanced 802.21
distance education 567.5, 568.1
distance learning 567.5
distance-learning course 568.8
distance of time 827.3, 837.3
distance oneself 261.7
distance runner 755.1
distance running 84.2
distance through 269.2
distancing (n) 261.1 (a) 802.25
distant 52.16, 141.12, 261.8, 344.10, 583.6, 589.11, 776.8, 982.3
distant early warning Line 460.2
distant future 839.1
distantness 141.4
distant past 837.3
distant perspective 158.4
distant prospect 158.4
distant relation 559.2
distant sound 52.1
distaste 99.1, 325.1, 510.1

distasteful 64.5, 98.17, 98.22, 99.7
distastefulness 64.1, 98.1
distemper (n) 35.8, 85.41 (v) 35.14, 96.13
distend 259.4, 259.5, 283.11, 1048.4
distended 257.18, 259.13, 283.15, 993.20
distended belly 2.18
distension 259.2, 283.4, 993.7, 1048.2
distensive 259.9
distich 720.10, 873.2, 974.1
distill 79.22, 88.30, 190.14, 192.16, 238.18, 798.4, 1020.20, 1067.8
distillate 192.8, 196.5, 887.1
distillation 79.4, 190.5, 192.7, 192.8, 196.5, 238.7, 798.2, 893.3, 1020.5, 1045.4, 1067.5
distilled 798.7
distilled essence 196.5
distilled water 1065.3
distiller 88.19, 88.21
distillery 88.21, 739.3
distilling 1020.5
distill out 192.16
distinct 31.7, 50.16, 348.8, 521.11, 780.7, 802.20, 865.12
distinction 136.2, 247.2, 533.1, 608.2, 646.1, 662.5, 780.1, 780.2, 780.4, 865.8, 943.1, 944.3, 997.2, 999.2
distinction without a difference, a 778.3, 790.3, 945.2
distinction without a difference 780.2, 963.6
distinctive 50.16, 349.15, 780.9, 809.7, 865.13, 944.7
distinctive feature 865.4
distinctiveness 865.1, 943.1, 944.3
distinctness 31.2, 348.3, 521.2, 780.1
distingué 662.16
distinguish 27.12, 662.12, 780.6, 865.10, 937.3, 941.5, 944.4, 989.11
distinguishable 928.25, 944.9
distinguish between 944.6
distinguished 247.9, 249.12, 646.9, 662.16, 780.7, 865.12, 865.13, 997.19
distinguished ancestry 607.3
Distinguished Conduct Medal 646.6
Distinguished Flying Cross 646.6
distinguished heritage 607.3
Distinguished Service Cross 646.6
Distinguished Service Medal 646.6
Distinguished Service Order 646.6
Distinguished Unit Citation 646.6
distinguishing (n) 780.4 (a) 349.15, 780.9, 944.7
distinguish in thought 944.4
distinguishment 941.1, 944.3, 989.4
distort 164.5, 263.3, 265.5, 342.2, 350.3, 354.16, 393.12, 936.8, 980.9, 1004.4
distorted 164.8, 265.10, 342.3, 354.26, 975.16, 1004.8
distorted conception 976.1
distorted image 350.2
distorting mirror 29.6
distortion 50.13, 164.2, 265.1, 342.1, 350.1, 350.2, 354.9, 936.1, 975.1, 1004.1
distortive 265.9
distract 379.4, 811.4, 926.24, 985.6
distract attention from 346.6
distracted 105.25, 971.24, 984.6, 985.10
distractedness 985.1
distracting 105.30, 971.27
distraction 926.1, 984.1, 985.1
distract the attention 985.6
distrain 480.20, 603.5
distraint 480.5, 603.3
distraught 926.26, 971.24, 985.10
distress (n) 26.1, 96.4, 96.5, 96.8, 98.5, 126.1, 480.5, 603.3 (v) 26.7, 96.16, 98.14, 126.4, 1000.6, 1013.13
distressed 26.9, 96.22, 1013.20
distressed, the 619.3
distressful 98.20, 126.10
distressfulness 98.5
distressing 26.10, 98.20, 126.10, 1000.12
distress sale 734.3
distributable 477.12
distributary 238.3
distribute 352.10, 477.8, 478.12, 478.13, 771.4, 793.6, 808.9, 809.6
distributed 352.17, 771.9
distributed costs 626.3
distribution 477.2, 771.1, 808.1
distributional 477.13
distribution system 1032.19
distributive 477.13, 771.11
distributive operation 1017.2
distributor 213.4, 385.6, 730.2
distributorship 730.2
district (n) 159.1, 231.1, 231.5 (v) 802.18
district attorney 597.1
district court 595.2
districting 802.1
district leader 610.12
distrust (n) 153.2, 494.2, 955.2 (v) 153.3, 955.6
distrusted 955.12
distrustful 153.5, 494.9, 955.9
distrustfulness 153.2, 494.2, 955.2
distrust oneself 139.7
disturb 96.13, 96.16, 98.13, 98.14, 105.14, 126.4, 810.9, 811.4, 917.10, 971.12, 985.7, 1013.13
disturbance 96.4, 105.4, 126.1, 671.2, 810.1, 810.4, 811.1, 917.1, 971.3, 985.3
disturbed 92.39, 96.21, 96.22, 105.23, 126.7, 810.13, 917.16, 926.28, 971.24, 985.12
disturbed mind 926.1
disturbing 98.21, 98.22, 105.30, 126.10, 971.27
disunify 782.2
disunion 456.4, 789.1, 802.1
disunite 456.14, 589.7, 802.8
disunited 589.11, 802.21
disunity 456.4, 789.1
disusage 390.1
disuse (n) 370.1, 390.1, 842.3 (v) 390.4
disused 370.8, 390.10, 842.16
disvaluation 510.2
disvalue 510.12
ditch (n) 224.2, 237.7, 239.1, 290.2, 460.5, 750.3, 1012.5 (v) 184.43, 224.4, 290.3, 368.7, 390.7, 475.3
ditched 290.4
ditchwater 80.9
dit-da artist 347.16
ditheism 675.5
ditheist 675.16
ditheistic 675.25
dither (n) 105.6, 917.3 (v) 362.8, 540.5, 922.12, 971.10, 1023.9
dithering 922.22
dithers 105.5, 128.2, 1023.2
dithery 1023.16
dithyrambic 720.16
ditto (n) 778.3, 790.4, 849.1, 849.5 (v) 332.9, 336.5, 778.6, 785.8, 790.5, 849.7, 874.3
ditto copy 785.5
ditty 708.14
ditz 924.7
ditziness 922.7, 984.1, 985.5
ditzy 854.7, 922.20, 923.9, 984.6, 985.16
diuretic (n) 79.17, 86.17 (a) 79.28, 86.48
diurnal 850.8
diuturnal 827.10
diva 707.6, 710.13
divagate 164.3, 164.4, 177.23, 204.9, 984.3, 985.9
divagation 164.1, 177.3, 204.1
divagational 204.13
divagatory 177.37
divan 423.1, 613.3
divaricate (v) 164.3, 171.5, 171.7, 292.11, 782.2 (a) 171.8, 782.3
divaricate from 780.5
divaricating 171.8
divarication 164.1, 171.1, 171.3, 782.1
dive (n) 88.20, 182.8, 184.13, 194.3, 228.28, 252.2, 367.1, 633.4, 665.9, 759.19 (v) 182.47, 182.56, 184.41, 252.6, 275.9, 367.6, 633.6
dive bar 88.20
dive-bomb 459.23
dive bomber 181.9
dive in 818.7
dive into 401.7, 725.15
diver 182.12, 367.4
diverge 164.3, 164.5, 171.5, 204.9, 456.10, 771.4, 780.5, 782.2, 787.2, 802.19, 852.6
diverge from 780.5
divergence 164.1, 171.1, 204.1, 261.1, 456.4, 771.1, 780.1, 782.1, 787.1, 789.1, 852.1, 870.1, 927.1
divergency 171.1, 780.1
divergent 171.8, 204.13, 780.7, 782.3, 787.4, 789.6, 802.20, 852.10, 870.9, 927.5
diverging 171.8, 780.7
divers 780.7, 783.4, 797.14, 884.7
diverse 780.7, 783.4, 787.4
diverse-colored 47.9
diverse control 1041.8
diversification 780.4, 782.1, 783.1, 852.1
diversified 780.7, 782.3, 783.4
diversiform 782.3, 783.3
diversify 780.6, 782.2, 783.2, 852.6, 852.7
diversion 164.1, 356.11, 389.1, 459.1, 743.1, 852.1, 985.1
diversionary attack 459.1
diversity 333.1, 780.1, 782.1, 783.1, 787.1, 789.1, 852.1
divert 164.5, 379.4, 389.4, 743.21, 985.6
divert attention 985.6
diverted 743.26
diverting 743.27
divertisement 743.1
divertissement 704.7, 743.1
divert the thoughts 985.6
divest 6.5, 480.21, 480.24
divested 6.12, 473.8
divestiture 6.1, 802.6
divestment 6.1, 473.1, 480.6, 729.4, 802.6
divest of freedom 432.8
divest of office 447.4
divesture 6.1
dividable 1017.25
dividableness 802.1
divide (n) 237.6, 272.5 (v) 171.5, 211.8, 213.8, 244.4, 292.11, 300.10, 456.10, 456.14, 477.6, 589.7, 773.6, 780.6, 793.6, 801.6, 802.8, 802.18, 808.11, 809.6, 875.4, 944.4, 1017.18
divide by four 881.3
divide by two 875.4
divided 456.15, 589.11, 773.8, 802.21, 875.6
divided attention 985.1
dividedness 456.2, 456.4
divided spectacles 29.3
divide fifty-fifty 477.6
divide in half 875.4
divide in thirds 878.3
divide in three 878.3
divide into four 881.3
divide into shares 477.6
divide in two 875.4
dividend 477.5, 624.7, 627.1, 738.7, 993.5, 1017.12
dividends 472.3, 627.1
divide on 333.4
divide pro rata 477.7

divider 875.3
divide up 477.6, 802.18
divide with 476.6, 477.6
dividing (n) 477.1 (a) 802.25
dividing fifty-fifty 875.1
dividing in two 875.1
dividing line 213.5, 802.4
dividing wall 213.5
divinability 962.8
divinable 962.13
divination 689.10, 690.1, 839.1, 961.1, 962.2
divinator 962.4
divinatory 961.7, 962.11
divine (n) 676.3, 699.2 (v) 133.11, 934.4, 940.2, 951.10, 962.9 (a) 97.9, 676.4, 677.16, 678.16, 685.7, 999.15, 1016.20
divine afflatus 375.9, 920.8, 986.2
divine breath 306.2, 919.4
divine creation 818.4
divine discontent 108.1
divine essence 677.1
divine faculty, the 935.1
divine healer 90.9
divine healing 91.2
divine inspiration 683.10
Divine Liturgy, the 701.8
divine messenger 679.1
Divine Mind 677.6
divineness 677.1, 685.1
divine providence 677.13
diviner 689.16, 690.5, 962.4
divineress 962.4
divine revelation 683.10
divine right 417.1, 642.1
divine service 696.8
divine spark 306.2, 919.5
diving 182.11, 184.13, 367.3, 760.8
diving bell 367.5
diving bird 311.27
diving boat 367.5
diving chamber 367.5
diving goggles 367.5
diving helmet 367.5
diving hood 367.5
diving mask 367.5
diving suit 367.5
divining 962.2
divining rod 962.3
divining stick 962.3
divinity 676.1, 677.1, 678.2, 685.1
divinity student 676.3
divisibility 802.1, 1017.12
divisible 477.12, 802.26
division 171.1, 213.5, 231.1, 456.2, 456.4, 461.22, 461.27, 477.1, 607.1, 613.6, 617.4, 617.10, 675.3, 708.24, 709.18, 754.2, 770.3, 773.3, 780.4, 793.1, 801.1, 802.1, 809.1, 809.2, 875.1, 944.3, 1017.2, 1017.12
divisional 809.7
divisionary 809.7
division championship 745.1, 746.1
division in the camp 456.4
division line 211.3
division of labor 892.3
division of philosophy 952.1
divisions 196.1
divisive 456.17
divisiveness 456.3
divisor 1017.12
divorce (n) 566.1, 802.1 (v) 566.5, 802.8
divorcé 566.2
divorced 566.7, 802.21
divorce decree 566.1
divorced man 566.2
divorced person 566.2
divorced woman 566.2
divorcement 566.1, 802.1
divorcer 566.2
divot 310.6
divulgate 351.5
divulgation 351.2
divulge 348.5, 351.5, 352.11
divulgement 351.2
divulgence 351.2, 352.1
divulging 351.2
divvied 477.12
divvy (n) 477.1 (v) 477.6, 477.10, 802.18
divvying 477.2
divvying up 477.1
divvy out 477.6
divvy up 477.6, 802.18
divvy up with 476.6
Dixie 231.7
Dixieland 231.7, 708.9
dizen 5.42, 498.8
dizened 498.11
dizenment 498.2
dizziness 16.1, 85.9, 85.15, 922.7, 984.1, 985.4, 985.5
dizzy (v) 985.8 (a) 16.12, 88.31, 854.7, 922.18, 922.20, 923.8, 923.9, 926.31, 985.15, 985.16
dizzying height 237.6
dizzying heights 272.2
dizzy round 915.2
dizzy rounds, the 743.7
D-list (n) 250.2 (a) 250.6
DNA 560.6
DNA double helix 305.9
DNA fingerprinting 305.9
DNA print 517.11
DNA profiling 801.1
DNA test 305.1
DNA testing 305.9
do (n) 3.15, 582.12, 743.4, 770.2 (v) 11.5, 107.6, 177.19, 177.20, 221.8, 246.2, 321.4, 328.6, 328.8, 336.5, 349.12, 356.19, 387.17, 407.4, 434.3, 708.39, 724.11, 788.8, 886.10, 892.11, 940.2, 991.4
DOA (n) 87.18 (a) 307.29
do a bad turn 144.15
doability 966.2
do a bit 500.12
doable 889.10, 940.3, 966.7, 995.5
do a comparative study 943.4
do a cosmetic job 206.6
do a cosmetic job on 787.3
do active duty 458.17
do a deal 437.5, 468.2, 731.18
do a disservice 650.7
do a fade-out 34.2
do a favor 143.12, 449.19
do a flip-flop 363.6, 859.5
do again 849.7
do a good deed 143.12
do a good turn 143.12
do a grave injustice 650.7
do a great wrong 650.7
do a gross injustice 650.7
do a hand's turn 725.12
do a hitch 825.5
do a job 482.16
do a job on 457.13, 512.9
do a kind deed 143.12
do a kindness 143.12
do a land-office business 1010.9
do a lick of work 725.12
do-all 577.9
do all in one's power 403.13
do all one can 403.13
do all right by oneself 409.10, 618.10, 1010.9
do all the talking 542.3
do a mischief 1000.6
do amiss 655.4, 975.12
do a mitzvah 143.12
do an about-face 163.10, 363.6, 852.7, 858.11, 859.5
do an about-turn 163.10
do an ill office to 1000.6
do an impression 336.6
do an impression of 349.12
do a number on 356.19, 512.9
do anyhow 340.9
do a 180 852.7
do a procedure 90.14
do a repeat 849.7
do a right-about-face 163.10
do a service 449.19
do a slow burn 152.18
do as much as in one lies 403.13
do a snow job on 375.23
do a solid 143.12
do as one pleases 323.3, 418.4, 430.20
do as one says 326.2
do as one would be done by 652.4
do as others do 578.10, 867.4
do a stint 825.5
do a striptease 6.7
do as well as one can 995.4
do as you would be done by 143.11
do at one's convenience 402.4
do at one's leisure 402.4
do at one's own peril 641.9
do at one's own risk 641.9
do at one's pleasure 402.4
do a tour 825.5
do a tour of duty 825.5
do at the last moment 401.8
do a U-turn 363.6
do a vanishing act 34.2
do away with 308.13, 395.12, 445.2, 909.21
do away with oneself 308.22
do a world of good 449.11, 999.10
do battle 457.16
dobbin 311.10
do business 450.3, 731.15
do business as usual 869.7
do business with 731.17
do by 321.6
do by halves 340.9
doc 90.4
do carelessly 340.9
docent 571.1
dochmiac 720.8
docile 324.5, 433.13, 570.18
docility 324.1, 433.3, 570.5
docimasy 801.1, 942.2
dock (n) 184.24, 217.6, 386.6, 595.6, 704.16, 1009.6 (v) 182.15, 186.8, 255.9, 255.10, 268.6
dockage 630.6, 1009.6
docked 268.9, 537.6, 795.5
docker 183.9
docket (n) 517.13, 549.4, 549.5, 549.11, 871.5, 871.6, 965.3 (v) 549.15, 628.8, 965.6
docketing 549.14
dock gate 239.11
dockhand 183.9
docking 186.2, 268.3, 1075.2, 1075.9
docking maneuver 1075.2
docking pilot 183.8
docking station 1042.4
dockside 1009.6
dock-walloper 183.9
dockworker 183.9
dockyard 739.1, 739.3, 1009.6
do credit to 509.15
doctor (n) 90.4, 396.10, 648.6, 704.22, 726.4, 921.1 (v) 90.14, 91.24, 91.29, 354.17, 396.14, 449.11, 797.12
doctor accounts 628.10
doctoral 568.19
doctoral candidate 556.3, 572.8
doctoral degree 648.6
doctorate 648.6
doctored 265.11, 354.30
doctoring 797.3
Doctor of Dental Medicine 90.6
Doctor of Dental Science 90.6
Doctor of Dental Surgery 90.6
Doctor of Divinity 699.2
Doctor of Medicine 90.4
doctor-patient confidentiality 345.5
doctor's degree 648.6
doctor's oral 938.2
doctor up 797.12
doctrinaire (n) 951.7, 970.7, 980.5 (a) 970.22, 980.12
doctrinairism 951.1
doctrinal 676.4, 953.27
doctrinalism 676.1
doctrinality 951.1
doctrinal statement 953.3
doctrinarian (n) 951.7 (a) 970.22
doctrinarity 951.1
doctrinary 676.4
doctrine 675.1, 676.2, 952.2, 953.2
doctrine of inference 935.2
doctrine of terms 935.2
doctrine of the judgment 935.2
doctrinism 676.1

docudrama 706.1, 1035.2
document (n) 547.10, 549.5 (v) 549.15, 719.4, 766.6, 957.11, 957.13
documental 549.18
documentalist 550.1
documentary (n) 1035.2 (a) 549.18, 719.6, 957.16, 973.13
documentary film 706.1
documentary observer 722.6
documentation 549.1, 719.1, 957.1, 957.4
documentational 549.18
documented 549.17, 719.6, 957.16
docutainment 706.1
dodder 16.8, 303.10
doddered 303.18
doddering 16.16, 303.18, 922.23
doddery 303.18, 922.23
dodecagonal 278.10
dodecahedral 278.10
dodecaphonism 61.1
dodecaphony 61.1
dodecuple scale 709.6
dodge (n) 356.6, 356.8, 368.1, 415.3, 903.3, 936.4, 995.2 (v) 157.7, 164.6, 340.8, 344.7, 368.8, 368.9, 415.9, 903.7, 914.4, 936.9
dodger 10.29, 340.5, 357.1, 415.6, 1008.3
dodgery 356.4
dodginess 971.6, 1006.2
dodging (n) 344.4, 368.2, 936.5 (a) 164.9
dodgy 164.9, 645.18, 854.7, 971.19, 1006.10
dodo 842.8
dodo head 924.4
Dodona 962.7
do double duty 725.13
do down 137.4
do down to the ground 407.7
do duty 458.17, 701.15, 724.13
doe 77.9, 311.5, 311.8, 311.23
do easily 1014.8
doeling 311.8
do'er 991.4
doer 330.8, 726.1
do everything one can 403.13
do evil 1000.6
do ex gratia 324.4
do famously 409.7
doff 6.6, 802.10
doffing 802.6
doff one's cap to 155.5, 509.14
do for 308.13, 395.11, 449.18, 577.13, 604.10
do for oneself 430.20
dofunny 1052.5
dog (n) 2.7, 76.8, 199.5, 311.12, 311.16, 347.4, 660.6, 1015.4 (v) 96.13, 126.5, 166.3, 382.8, 382.9, 1012.12
dog and pony show 33.7
dog-ass 1000.8
Dogberry 1008.16
dogcart 179.3
dog-cheap 633.8
dog clutch 1040.10
dog-day cicada 311.35
dog days 313.3, 1019.7
doge 575.7
dog-ear (n) 291.1 (v) 291.5
dog-eared 48.15, 291.7, 393.31
dog eat dog 418.2
dog-eat-dog 146.3
dogface 461.10
dogfight 457.4
dog flea 311.36
dog food 10.4
dogged 96.24, 126.8, 360.8, 361.8
doggedness 360.1, 361.1
dogged perseverance 360.1
doggerel (n) 720.3 (a) 508.14, 534.2
doggie paddle 182.11
dogging 96.2, 166.1, 382.1
doggish 311.41
doggo 346.14
doggone 513.10
doggoned 513.10
doggy 311.41
doggy bag 478.4, 993.5
doghouse 228.21, 258.3, 510.1
dog-hungry 100.25
dogie 178.3, 302.10, 311.6, 370.4
dog in the manger 651.3, 1012.9
dog-in-the-manger 108.7
dog it 368.9, 368.11
dogleg (n) 164.1, 204.8, 278.2, 751.1 (v) 164.5, 204.9 (a) 204.20
doglegged 164.7, 204.20, 278.6
doglike 311.41, 326.3
doglike devotion 326.1
doglike obedience 326.1
dogma 675.1, 676.2, 952.2, 953.2, 953.3
dogmatic 361.8, 361.13, 687.8, 953.21, 953.27, 970.22, 980.12
dogmatical 970.22
dogmaticalness 970.6
dogmatism 361.1, 361.5, 687.5, 970.6
dogmatist 361.6, 687.6, 970.7, 980.5
dogmatize 970.10
dogmatizer 970.7
dogmatizing 970.22
do good 143.12, 449.11, 999.10
do-gooder 143.8
do-goodism 143.4
do good works 143.12
dog paddle 182.11
dog-paddle 182.56
dog-paddling 760.8
dog pound 228.21
dog race 457.12
dog racing 457.11
dog's breakfast 797.6
dogsled 179.20
dog's life 1011.1
Dog Star 1073.4
dog tag 517.11
dog the footsteps of 835.3, 938.35
dog-tired 21.10
dogtooth 2.8, 289.2
dogtrot (n) 174.3, 175.2 (v) 175.6
dog wagon 8.17
dogwatch 825.3
dog-weary 21.10
dog whistle 517.16
dog year 824.2
do hands down 1014.8
dohickey 1052.5
do homage 433.10
do homage to 155.5
do honor 646.8
do honor to 155.5
do ill 1000.6
do in 21.4, 21.6, 308.14, 395.11, 395.12, 412.9, 857.11
do in a half-assed way 340.9
do in any old way 340.9
do in a pinch 991.4
do in a slip-shod fashion 340.9
do independently 324.4
doing (n) 321.1, 328.1, 328.3, 831.3, 892.5 (a) 831.9
doing business 731.2
doing nicely 83.10
doings 321.1, 328.3, 330.1, 775.1, 831.4
doing time 428.15, 429.21
do in one's own sweet way 430.20
do in spades 999.11
do it 75.21, 991.4
do it according to Hoyle 867.4
do it by the book 867.4
do it fair and square 649.5
do it on the run 330.10
do it or know why not 403.14
do it to death 993.10
do-it-yourself 892.18
dojigger 1052.5
dojiggy 1052.5
dojo 760.3
do justice to 8.24, 63.5, 95.13, 434.2, 600.9, 641.10, 649.5
dokhma 309.16
dolce 708.53
dolce far niente 331.4, 402.2
doldrums 112.6, 173.5, 231.3, 318.9
dole (n) 248.2, 477.2, 477.5, 478.6, 478.8, 793.1, 992.5 (v) 477.8, 478.12
dole, the 143.5
doleful 112.26, 145.8
dolefulness 112.11
dolefuls 112.6
dole out 477.8, 478.12, 771.4
do-less 331.19
do-lessness 331.5
dolichocephalic people 312.2
do like 336.5
doling 477.2
doling out 477.2, 624.1
dolittle 331.8
doll 77.6, 104.14, 258.6, 302.7, 349.6, 562.6, 659.2, 743.16, 1016.8
dollar 728.7, 728.8
dollar bill 728.5, 728.7
dollar crisis 729.8
dollar diplomacy 609.5
dollar gap 623.2, 729.8
dollar imperialism 609.5
dollars 728.1
dollars to doughnuts 972.8
doll-baby 104.14
dolled up 5.46
dollhouse 258.3, 743.16
dollish 301.12
doll-like 301.12
dollop 257.10, 793.3
dolls 87.4, 87.5
doll up 5.42, 498.8, 1016.15
dolly 349.6
dolmen 309.16, 549.12
dolor 26.1, 96.5
dolorific 98.20
dolorifuge 670.3
dolorogenic 98.20
dolorous 98.20, 112.26
dolorousness 112.11
dolorous tirade 115.3
dolphin 311.29
dolt 414.8, 924.2
dolthead 924.4
doltish 922.15
doltishness 922.3
Dom 648.5
domain 231.2, 232.1, 471.6, 724.4, 809.3, 809.4, 928.10
domain name 1042.18
domain of the impossible, the 967.1
domain of the possible, the 966.1
domajig 1052.5
domajigger 1052.5
domal 228.32
dome (n) 197.4, 198.7, 237.1, 237.6, 272.6, 279.4, 295.6, 746.1 (v) 279.6, 295.21
domed 295.31
domed stadium 463.1, 746.1
Domesday Book 549.11
domestic (n) 577.2 (a) 228.32, 584.10
domesticability 433.4
domesticable 433.14
domestic animals 311.1
domesticate 159.17, 373.9, 432.11
domesticated 228.34, 432.15, 433.15
domestication 373.7, 432.4
domestic cat 311.20
domestic drudge 577.9
domestic economy 573.6
domestic fowl 311.28
domestic help 577.2
domesticity 228.3
domesticize 373.9
domestic mail 553.4
domestic management 573.6
domestic science 11.1
domestic servant 577.2
domestic violence 671.1
domestic wine 88.17
domestic worker 726.2
domical 279.13
domicile (n) 228.1 (v) 225.7, 225.10
domiciled 225.14
domiciliary 228.32
domiciliary visit 938.15
domiciliate 225.7, 225.10
domiciliated 225.14
domiciliation 225.3
domina 77.5

dominance 417.6, 894.1
dominancy 417.6
dominant (n) 709.14, 709.15 (a) 249.14, 411.7, 417.15, 612.17, 864.12, 894.14, 997.24
dominant character 560.6
dominant chord 709.17
dominant note 709.14
dominate 31.4, 272.11, 432.8, 612.14, 864.10, 894.11
dominate the field 411.6
dominating 272.14
domination 31.3, 417.6, 432.1, 612.2, 612.9, 894.1
dominations 679.3
domineer 612.15
domineering (n) 141.1, 417.3, 612.9 (a) 141.9, 417.16
domineeringness 141.1, 417.3
domineer over 612.15
dominion 231.2, 232.1, 249.3, 417.5, 417.6, 469.2, 612.1, 612.2, 814.1
dominion rule 612.4
dominions 679.3
dominium 469.2
domino 356.11
domino effect 886.3, 887.3, 972.5
domino mask 356.11
domitable 433.14
domus 228.1
don (n) 76.7, 571.1 (v) 5.43
doña 77.8, 608.6
donability 966.3
donable 477.12, 966.8
Donar 56.5
donate 385.7, 478.12
donate to 478.14
donation 143.7, 478.1, 478.6
donation store 635.1
Donatist (n) 688.5 (a) 688.9
donative (n) 478.5, 478.6 (a) 478.25
donator 478.11
done 11.8, 21.8, 393.36, 407.11, 820.9, 892.17
done and done 407.11
done deal 328.3, 407.1
donee 479.3, 479.4
done for 307.29, 307.32, 393.29, 395.29, 412.14, 762.11, 820.10
done in 21.8, 393.29, 395.29, 412.15
doneness 11.8
done to a T 1002.9
done to a turn 11.8
done to perfection 11.8
done up 21.8, 393.36
done with 390.10, 407.11, 820.9
dong 54.8
donga 237.7
donging 54.3
donjon 460.6
Don Juan 104.12, 357.1, 377.4, 562.12, 665.10
donkey 311.15, 361.6, 924.2
donkey's years 827.4
donkey work 725.4
donna 77.8
donné datum 761.3
donnée 959.2
donnish 568.19, 570.17, 571.11, 928.22
donnishness 928.5
donnybrook 53.4, 456.5, 810.4
donnybrook fair 456.5, 810.4
do no evil 653.4
do no harm 999.10
donor 385.6, 478.11
donor egg 305.12
Do Not Call list 347.4
do nothing 329.2, 331.12, 853.6
do-nothing (n) 331.8 (a) 329.6, 331.19
do nothing in excess 670.5
do-nothingism 329.1
do-nothingness 329.1, 331.5
do-nothing policy 329.1
do not take 19.7
Don Quixote 608.5, 986.13
donsie 1011.14
don't 444.1
don't ask don't tell 458.20
don the mantle of 835.3, 862.5
don't know 362.5
don't let the chance slip by 843.8
do number one 12.14
donut 10.44
do obeisance 433.10
doobie 87.11
doodad 498.4, 1052.5
doodle (n) 712.12, 924.1 (v) 331.13, 331.14, 547.20, 708.42, 712.19
doodle-brained 923.9
doodlebug 962.3, 1074.4
doodler 331.8, 716.2
doodlesack 711.9
doo-doo 12.4
doodoohead 924.4
do offhand 340.9, 365.8
do of one's own accord 324.4
do of one's own free will 324.4
do of one's own volition 324.4
doohickey 1052.5
doojee 87.9
doom (n) 307.1, 395.2, 602.1, 820.1, 839.2, 839.3, 946.5, 963.7, 964.2 (v) 602.3, 682.6, 946.13, 964.7, 1000.6
doomed 125.13, 307.32, 395.28, 839.8, 964.9
doomed hope 124.1, 125.4
doomed hopes 124.1
doomful 133.16, 395.26, 1011.14
doomfulness 133.6
doom oneself 308.22
doomsayer 127.8
doomsday 839.3
doomsdayer 112.14
doomsman 596.2
doomster 596.2
doom to perdition 682.6
doomwatcher 1072.3
do one an injustice 650.7
do one a wrong 650.7
do one better 999.11
do one proud 136.6
do one's best 403.13, 725.9
do one's bidding 326.2
do one's bit 307.24, 324.3, 641.10
do one's damndest 403.14
do one's damnedest 330.13, 403.13
do one's darndest 403.14
do one's duty 8.24, 434.3, 641.10
do oneself in 308.22
do oneself proud 8.24, 407.7, 409.10
do one's heart good 95.6, 95.8, 136.6
do one's homework 405.13
do one's level best 403.13
do one's number 724.12
do one's office 434.3
do one's own thing 430.20, 435.3, 872.6
do one's part 324.3, 328.6, 476.6, 641.10
do one's share 476.6
do one's thing 328.4, 866.4, 889.8
do one's utmost 403.13
do one's worst to 389.5
do on one's own 430.20
do on one's own hook 430.20
do on one's own initiative 430.20
do on one's say-so 430.20
do on the fly 172.5, 401.5
do on the run 172.5, 401.5
door 189.5, 189.6, 190.9, 292.6
door chimes 54.4
doorframe 266.4
doorjamb 189.6, 273.4
doorkeeper 699.4, 704.23, 1008.12
doorman 1008.12
doormat 3.14, 16.6, 138.4, 358.2
door-opening 816.4, 818.16
doorpost 189.6, 273.4
doorsill 901.9
doorstep 193.5
doorstone 901.9
doorstop 1012.7
door-to-door 794.10
door-to-door salesman 730.4
doorway 189.6, 292.6
do out of 356.18, 480.21
do over 78.7, 849.7, 858.11
do-over 849.1, 858.1, 874.2
do over again 849.8
doo-wop 708.8
doozy 999.7
dope (n) 25.3, 86.5, 87.3, 714.10, 732.3, 924.2, 1021.1 (v) 22.20, 25.4, 91.25, 120.5, 940.2, 962.9 (a) 999.13
dope, the 551.1, 761.4
doped 22.21, 25.8
dope den 87.20
doped up 22.21
do penance 113.7, 338.4, 658.6
dope out 940.2, 962.9, 1017.18
dope pusher 732.4
doper 87.21
dope smuggling 732.2
dopester 962.5
dope up 120.5
dopey 173.14, 331.20, 922.16, 923.9, 985.14
dopiness 331.6, 922.3
doping 120.1
doping up 120.1
Doppelganger 873.4
Doppelgänger 778.3, 988.3
Doppler effect 160.1
Doppler signal 1036.11
do-re-mi (n) 709.7, 728.2 (v) 708.38
do, re, mi, fa, sol, la, ti, do 709.7
Dorian mode 709.10
Dorian tetrachord 709.8
Doric (n) 198.6, 717.2 (a) 534.2
do right 321.5, 649.5
do right by 143.9
dork 660.5
dorky 923.9
dorm 228.15
dormancy 173.4, 329.1, 331.1, 519.1
dormant 22.22, 173.14, 329.6, 331.20, 519.5
dormant partner 616.2
dormition 22.1
dormitory 228.15
dormitory room 197.7
dorm room 197.7
dorsal 217.10
dorsal region 217.3
dorsum 217.3, 524.18
dosage 86.6, 643.2
dose (n) 85.18, 86.6, 87.20, 244.2, 793.5, 1037.8 (v) 91.25, 643.6
dose equivalent 1037.6
dose of one's own medicine, a 506.2
do service 138.8, 504.11, 577.13, 696.11
do service for 449.18
dose with 643.6
dosing 643.2
do some heavy thinking 931.9
do something 328.5
do something about 328.5
do something about it 216.8
do something mutually beneficial 468.2
doss (n) 22.2, 225.3, 901.19 (v) 22.14
doss down 22.18, 225.7
dosshouse 228.15
dossier 549.1, 549.5, 719.2
do standing on one's head 1014.8
do suit and service 326.2
dot (n) 47.3, 159.1, 248.2, 258.7, 517.5, 709.12 (v) 47.7, 224.3, 517.19, 771.4, 771.6
dotage 303.5, 922.10, 954.1
dotal 478.26
dotard 304.2, 924.9
dotardism 922.10
dot-com 1042.18
dote 922.12, 926.20
dote on 104.18
dote upon 104.18
do the best one can 403.13, 995.4
do the best one knows how 403.13
do the bidding of 138.8

do the chores 725.12
do the crazy act 923.6
do the deadman's float 182.56
do the dirty work of 138.8
do the disappearing act 368.10
do the fair thing 649.5
do the goose step 177.30
do the handsome thing 649.5
do the heart good 109.7
do the honors 504.11, 585.8, 587.14
do the honors for 155.5
do the honors of the house 585.9
do the job 407.4, 788.8
do the lock step 177.30
do the math 380.6, 570.6, 940.2, 1017.18
do the needful 641.10
do the prep work 405.6
do the proper thing 321.5
do the right thing 321.5, 641.10, 653.4
do the right thing by 434.2, 649.5
do the same old thing 118.6
do the spadework 405.12
do the trick 328.6, 387.17, 407.4, 409.11, 788.8, 991.4, 995.3
do the unexpected 131.7
do the usual thing 869.7
do the will of 326.2
do things by the book 580.6
do time 429.18, 825.5
doting 303.17, 922.23, 923.8, 954.8
dot-matrix printer 1042.9
do to 328.6, 643.5
do to a frazzle 407.7
do to a T 407.7
do to a turn 11.5, 407.7
do to death 308.13
dot one's i's and cross one's t's 973.11
do too many things at once 993.10
do to perfection 11.5, 407.7, 1002.5
dots 87.10
dot-sequential television 1035.5
dotted 47.13, 224.6, 771.10
dotted line 517.6
dottedness 47.3
dottiness 926.2, 927.1
dotty 47.13, 926.27, 927.5
do twice over 993.10
Douay Bible 683.2
double (n) 164.1, 291.1, 349.5, 704.10, 745.3, 750.2, 778.3, 785.3, 862.2, 873.2, 988.3 (v) 163.8, 251.5, 291.5, 745.5, 785.8, 819.3, 849.7, 873.5, 874.3 (a) 354.31, 645.21, 873.6, 874.4
double acrostic 489.8
double agent 357.10, 576.9
double a point 182.30
double as 862.5
double axel 760.7
double back 163.8
double-barreled 997.17
double bind 1013.7
double-blind experiment 942.1
double bogey (n) 751.3 (v) 751.4
double-charge 632.7
double-check (n) 970.8 (v) 957.11, 970.12, 1017.21
double-checked 957.20
double chin 257.8
double contingency 971.8
double contraoctave 709.9
double corposant 1025.13
double cross 356.9, 645.8
double-cross 356.14, 645.14
double-crosser 357.10, 551.6
double-crossing 645.22
double-crust pie 10.41
doubled 291.7, 849.12, 873.6, 874.4
double dare 454.2
double-dare 454.3
double date 582.8
double-dealer 357.1, 357.10, 660.9
double-dealing (n) 354.4, 645.6 (a) 354.31, 356.22, 645.21
double-dig 1069.17
double-dip 874.3
double-dot display 1036.11
double Dutch 520.3, 522.7
double-dye 35.14
double-dyed 35.18
double eagle (n) 728.4, 751.3 (v) 751.4
double-edged 17.14, 285.8
double entendre 489.6, 539.1, 539.2
double entry 628.5
double-entry accounting 628.6
double-entry bookkeeping 628.6
double exposure 714.5
double-faced 354.31, 873.6
double-facedness 354.4
double fault 748.2
double-fault 748.3
double for 576.14, 862.5
doubleganger 988.3
double harness 873.2
double-harness 873.5
doublehearted 354.31
doubleheartedness 354.4
double helix 281.2
double image 1035.5
double in brass 413.21
double jeopardy 1006.1
double-jointed 1047.9
double killing 745.3
double life 354.4
double march 177.13
double meaning 522.7, 539.1
double-minded 354.31, 362.9
double-mindedness 362.1
double mordent 709.18
doubleness 354.4, 645.6, 873.1
doubleness of heart 354.4
double or nothing 759.3
double over 291.5
double personality 92.20
double pinochle 750.2
double play 745.3
double-prop 181.2
double-quick (n) 177.13, 401.3 (a) 174.15, 401.11
double-quick time 401.3
double rainbow 95.2, 316.8, 1025.14
double reed 711.6, 711.8
double-reed instrument 711.8
double-reef 182.50
double reference 539.1
double rhyme 720.9
doubles 748.1
double sap 460.5
double sawbuck 728.7
double sideband 1034.14
double-sided 873.6
double sight 28.1
double space 224.1
doublespeak (n) 523.9, 609.37, 936.3 (v) 936.9
doubles sideline 748.1
double standard 354.4
double-story 296.6
double-strength 15.15
doublet 526.2, 873.2
double take 817.1, 846.2
double-talk 520.2, 538.2
doubletalk (n) 524.12, 936.3 (v) 936.9
double-talker 357.9
double-team 746.5, 747.4, 873.5
double-think 873.1
double time 177.13, 401.3, 478.5
double-time (v) 401.5 (a) 401.11
doubleton 873.3
double-tongue 708.42
double-tongued 354.31
doubletree 170.5
double under 291.5
double up 805.4, 874.3
double vision 28.1
double whammy 513.1, 1000.4
double whammy on, a 1011.12
double wheel 163.9
double whole note 709.14
double wood 750.2
double zero 759.12
doubling 196.3, 291.1, 849.1, 873.1, 874.1
doubling over 291.1
doubloon 728.4
doublure 196.3
doubt (n) 127.4, 153.2, 695.6, 955.2, 971.2 (v) 153.3, 494.5, 695.14, 955.6, 971.9
doubtable 955.10, 969.3, 971.17
doubted 955.12
doubter 695.12, 955.4
doubtful 645.16, 695.20, 955.9, 955.10, 969.3, 971.17, 1006.11
doubtfulness 955.2, 955.3, 969.1, 971.2, 1006.2
doubting 955.9, 971.16
doubting Thomas 695.12, 955.4
doubtless 953.21, 970.16
doubtlessness 970.3
doubt not 953.14, 970.9
doubt oneself 139.7, 955.6
doubt one's word 955.6
doubt the truth of 955.6
douche (n) 79.5, 79.8, 86.17, 1065.8 (v) 79.19, 1065.12, 1065.13
douching 79.5
dough 461.7, 728.2, 1047.4, 1062.5
doughboy 461.7
doughfoot 461.7, 461.10
doughiness 1047.2, 1062.2, 1063.1
doughnut 10.42, 10.44
doughnut hole 10.42, 10.44
doughnut shop 8.17
doughtiness 492.1
doughty 15.15, 492.16
doughy 1047.9, 1047.12, 1062.12, 1063.6
do unto others as you would have others do unto you 143.11, 652.4
do up 21.6, 396.14, 397.11, 770.20, 800.9
do up brown 407.7, 794.8, 999.11
dour 110.24, 144.24, 361.9, 425.6, 425.7
dourness 110.8, 361.2, 361.3
douse 367.7, 1022.7
do usiness 724.12
dousing 367.2, 1022.2
dove 311.27, 416.3, 464.6, 465.2, 657.4
Dove, the 677.12
dove-colored 39.4
dovecote 228.23
dove-gray 39.4
dovelike 311.48, 433.15, 464.10, 657.6
dovelikeness 433.5, 464.4, 657.2
dove of peace 464.6, 670.3
Dover sole 10.24
do very well 409.7
dovetail (n) 777.2, 800.4 (v) 191.5, 777.5, 777.6, 788.6, 800.8
dovetailed 777.9
dovetailing 788.10
do violence to 389.5, 435.4
dovishness 464.4
do voluntarily 324.4
dowager 77.5, 304.3, 566.4, 575.2, 607.4
dowager queen 566.4
dowdiness 810.6
dowdy (n) 10.41 (a) 393.32
dowel 283.3
do well 1010.7
dower (n) 413.4, 478.9 (v) 478.17 (a) 478.26
dowered 478.26
dowhacky 1052.5
do what is expected 641.10
do what is right 321.5
do what lies in one's power 403.13
do what one can 403.10
do what one chooses 430.20
do what one has to do 641.10
do what one is told 326.2
do what one likes 430.20
do what one set out to do 409.8
do what one wishes 430.20
do with 387.10, 387.12, 995.4
do with a vengeance 794.8, 999.11
do with both eyes shut 1014.8

do with one's hands tied behind one's back 1014.8
do without 390.5, 475.3, 668.7
Dow Jones 438.1
Dow-Jones Industrial Average 737.1
down (n) 3.8, 3.19, 194.1, 236.1, 237.4, 294.3, 298.2, 746.3, 1011.3, 1047.4 (v) 8.22, 88.24, 134.8, 194.5, 270.12, 913.5 (a) 85.56, 85.59, 112.22, 115.18, 173.13, 194.11, 274.8, 412.14, 549.17
down-and-dirty 146.3
down-and-out (n) 619.4 (a) 395.28, 619.9, 820.10
down-and-out, the 619.3
down-and-outer 619.4
down-at-heel 393.32
down at heels 619.8
down-at-heels 393.32
down at the heel 619.8, 810.15
down-at-the-heel 393.32
down-at-the-heels 393.32
downbear 913.4
downbeat (n) 709.26, 850.3 (a) 112.30, 125.16
downbend 194.1
down card 759.10
downcast (n) 913.2 (a) 112.22, 194.12, 913.12
downcastness 112.3
downcome 194.1
down comforter 295.10
downcoming 194.11
downcurve 194.1
down-curving 279.8
downdraft 317.4, 318.1
Down East 231.7
Down-Easter Yankee 227.11
downer (n) 96.2, 112.3, 125.2, 194.2, 1011.1 (a) 112.30
downers 87.5
downfall 194.1, 316.2, 395.3, 410.3, 412.1, 913.2
downfalling 194.11
down feather 3.16
downflow 194.1, 238.4, 316.2
down for the count 619.10
downgoing 194.11
downgrade (n) 194.1, 194.2, 204.5 (v) 252.7, 447.3 (a) 204.16
downgrading 447.1
down-hanging 194.12
downhearted 112.22
downheartedness 112.3
downhill (n) 204.5 (a) 194.11, 204.16
downhill all the way 1014.13
downhill course 753.1
downhill race 753.3
downhill racer 753.2
downhill skiing 753.1
down-home 121.11, 233.8, 581.3, 798.6
downiness 3.1, 287.1, 294.3, 298.1, 1047.1
down in flames 820.10
downing 8.1
downing of arms 465.2
Downing Street 610.1
down in the dumps 112.22
down in the mouth 112.22, 125.12
down in the world 1011.14
downland 237.1, 310.8
download (n) 1042.18 (v) 1042.21
down low 345.1
down low, the 345.1
down on 99.8, 510.21
down one's alley 866.5
down one's arms 465.11
down on one's luck 1011.14
down on one's uppers 619.8
down pat 928.26
down payment 624.1
downplay 252.9, 670.6, 998.12
downplayed 252.10
downplaying 252.1
downpour 194.1, 238.4, 316.2, 913.2
downpouring 913.2
down-reaching 194.11
downright 200.11, 247.12, 644.17, 794.10, 960.2
downright lie 354.12
downrush 194.1, 318.1
downs 87.5, 236.1, 237.1, 272.3, 310.8
downscale 250.6, 619.7
downshifting 909.5
downside 96.2, 199.1
downside, the 1011.1, 1013.3
downsinking 194.11
downsize 252.7
downsizing 252.1
downspout 239.8
Down's syndrome 922.9
downstage 704.16
downswing 750.2, 751.3
downtempo 708.54
down the drain 473.7, 486.9, 762.11
down the rathole 486.9
down the spout 486.9
down the tube 395.29, 473.7, 762.11
down the tubes 395.29, 820.10
downthrow 913.2
downthrown 913.12
downthrust 913.1
downthrusting 913.1
down tick 194.1
down-tick 194.5
downtick 252.2, 393.3, 731.10
downtime 20.2, 402.1, 826.1, 846.2, 1042.18
down to bedrock 619.7
down-to-earth 987.6
down-to-earthness 987.2
down to one's last cent 619.10
downtown (n) 230.6 (a) 230.11
downtrend 194.1, 252.2, 393.3
down-trending 172.8
down trip 112.3
downtrod 432.16
downtrodden 432.16
downturn 194.1, 252.2, 393.3, 731.10
downturned 194.12
down under 231.6
down vest 5.14
downward 172.8, 194.11
downward curve 252.2
downwardly mobile 607.10
downward mobility 393.3, 607.1, 852.1
downward motion 172.2
downward slope, the 303.5
downward trend 194.1, 252.2, 393.3
downwash 184.30
downwind (v) 184.43 (a) 161.14
downwind leg 184.18
downy 3.27, 287.10, 294.8, 298.10, 1047.14
downy sleep 22.4
do wonders 409.7
do wrong 650.7, 654.8, 655.4, 1000.6
do wrong by 389.5, 650.7, 1000.6
do wrong to 389.5
dowry (n) 413.4, 478.4, 478.9 (a) 478.26
dowse for water 962.9
dowser 690.5, 962.3
dowse sail 182.50
dowsing 962.3
dowsing rod 962.3
doxologize 696.12
doxology 696.3, 708.17
doxy 665.17
doyen 304.5, 575.3
doyenne 304.5, 575.3
doze (n) 22.2 (v) 22.13
dozen 882.7
dozens, the 456.6, 490.1
doze off 22.16
dozer 179.18
doziness 22.1
dozing 985.11
dozy 22.21
drab (n) 665.14, 810.7 (a) 40.3, 781.6, 1027.17
drabble 80.19, 202.6
drabbled 80.21
drabble in the mud 80.19
drabbletailed 810.15
drabness 39.1, 1027.5
Draconian 144.26
Dracula 127.9
draff 256.2, 391.4
draft (n) 8.4, 86.6, 88.7, 275.7, 318.1, 381.3, 421.1, 458.8, 461.18, 547.10, 557.1, 615.7, 708.28, 712.12, 728.11, 905.1 (v) 192.12, 381.11, 547.19, 615.17, 712.19, 756.4
draft beer 88.16
draft call 615.7
draft dodger 368.5
drafted man 461.18
draftee 461.18
draft horse 311.13
draftiness 318.14
drafting 192.3, 615.7, 712.4
draft lottery 759.14
draft off 192.12
draftsman 716.3
draftsmanship 712.4, 712.8
draftswoman 716.3
drafty 318.21
drag (n) 87.1, 89.10, 96.2, 112.14, 118.1, 118.5, 125.7, 175.4, 177.12, 184.27, 297.7, 894.2, 900.4, 905.2, 907.1, 996.2, 1012.7, 1044.1 (v) 87.22, 89.14, 166.4, 175.6, 175.8, 177.28, 202.6, 287.5, 827.7, 846.8, 905.4, 907.4
drag a lengthening chain 827.7
drag along 175.6, 781.3, 827.7
drag and drop 1042.18
drag at one's chariot wheel 432.9
drag before the public 352.11
drag bunt 745.3
drag component 184.27
drag direction 184.27
drag down 472.9, 479.6, 624.20
dragée 86.7
drag force 184.27
dragged in 776.8
dragged into 898.5
dragged out 267.8
dragged-out 393.36, 827.11
dragger 382.6
dragginess 117.1
dragging (n) 846.2, 905.1 (a) 175.11, 907.5
dragging down 472.1
dragging of the feet 325.1
dragging one's feet 362.3, 846.2
dragging out 267.4
dragging-out 827.2
dragging pace 175.2
draggle 80.19, 202.6, 217.8, 905.4
draggled 80.21, 810.15
draggletailed 810.15
draggy 117.6
drag in 213.6, 776.5
drag in by the heels 213.6
drag in the mud 393.12
drag into 898.2
drag into court 598.13
drag into the limelight 352.15
drag its slow length along 827.7
dragnet 356.13, 382.1, 480.2, 938.15
dragnet clause 613.9
dragoman 341.7, 574.7
drag on 118.6, 781.3, 821.5, 827.7, 856.3
dragon 110.11, 671.9
drag one down 112.15
drag one's banner in the dust 661.7
drag one's feet 175.6, 362.7, 827.9, 846.8, 846.11
dragonfly 311.32
dragoon (n) 461.12 (v) 127.20, 424.4, 424.7
drag out 175.6, 192.14, 267.6, 538.8, 827.9, 846.9
drag queen 75.15
drag racing 756.1
drag ratio 184.27
drag sail 1012.7
drag sheet 1012.7
drag through the gutter 512.10
drag through the mud 512.10
drag up 912.8

drain (n) 80.12, 190.4, 239.5, 388.1, 421.1, 473.2 (v) 19.9, 36.5, 190.13, 192.12, 255.9, 387.16, 388.3, 473.5, 480.21, 480.24, 486.4, 909.22, 1066.6
drainage 190.4, 192.3, 909.6, 1066.3
drainage pattern 238.1
drain cock 239.10
drained 16.18, 21.10, 36.8, 85.54, 388.5, 891.4
drained of color 36.7, 36.8
draining (n) 21.2, 192.3, 909.6 (a) 16.20, 21.13, 393.45, 421.9
drain of color 36.5
drain off 480.13
drain of resources 388.3
drain out 190.13
drain the cup 8.29, 88.24
drain the cup of misery to the dregs 96.19
drake 76.8, 311.28
drakestone 1059.4
dram (n) 8.4, 88.7, 248.2, 793.5 (v) 88.24
drama 349.1, 704.1, 706.2
drama critic 547.15, 718.4
drama queen 93.1
dramatic 93.19, 501.24, 704.33, 708.50, 720.16
dramatical 704.33
dramatic art 704.2
dramatic criticism 723.1
dramatic form 704.2
dramatic irony 704.2
dramaticism 704.2
dramatico-musical 708.51
dramatic overture 708.26
dramatic poem 720.4
dramatics 93.9, 348.4, 501.4, 704.2
dramatic series 1035.2
dramatic soprano 709.5
dramatic stroke 704.2
dramatic structure 704.2
dramatism 704.2
dramatis personae 707.11, 871.6
dramatist 547.15, 704.22, 718.4
dramatization 349.4, 704.2
dramatize 348.5, 500.12, 704.28, 997.16
dramatizer 704.22, 707.2
dramaturge 704.22
dramaturgic 704.33
dramaturgical 704.33
dramaturgy 704.2
drama-writing 547.2, 718.2
dramshop 88.20
drape (n) 202.4, 295.2, 1028.1 (v) 5.39, 202.6
draped 201.8
drape oneself 20.6, 201.5, 913.11
draper 5.33
drapery 4.1, 5.1, 295.2, 1028.1
drastic 671.16
draw (n) 221.4, 237.7, 377.3, 759.10, 790.3, 836.3, 905.2, 907.1 (v) 89.14, 192.10, 192.12, 260.7, 267.6, 349.8, 349.9, 377.5, 472.8, 479.6, 604.17, 712.19, 751.4, 790.5, 894.9, 905.4, 907.4
draw a bead on 208.10, 380.4, 459.22
draw a blank 410.10, 990.5
draw a comparison 943.4
draw a conclusion 946.10
draw a deep breath 120.8
draw a distinction 944.6
draw a gun on 459.21
draw a line 780.6
draw a mental picture 951.10
draw and kick game 747.3
draw and quarter 604.15, 802.14
draw an inference 946.10
draw a parallel 775.6, 943.4
draw apart 802.8
draw a picture 712.19
draw a red herring across the trail 356.16
draw aside 164.6
draw a straight furrow 644.10
draw a subtle distinction 944.4
draw back 127.13, 163.6, 168.3, 903.7
drawback 631.1, 996.2, 1003.2, 1012.4
draw blood 393.13, 902.14
draw boundaries 210.4
draw breath 306.8
drawbridge 383.9
drawcard 377.3
draw cock 239.10
draw distinctions 944.4
draw down 886.11
drawdown 252.4, 255.2
drawer 195.1, 377.3, 386.6, 716.2, 716.3
draw first blood 457.14
draw forth 192.14
draw from 192.12, 479.6
draw in 168.3, 187.12, 260.7, 270.11, 377.5, 712.19, 898.2, 906.9
drawing (n) 192.1, 192.3, 349.1, 381.3, 712.4, 712.12, 712.16, 713.1, 759.14, 905.1 (a) 905.6, 907.5
drawing card 377.3, 907.2
drawing forth 192.5
drawing lots 759.1
drawing of water 725.4
drawing out 192.1, 192.5
drawing-out 827.2
drawing paper 712.18
drawing pencil 712.18
drawing room 179.15, 197.5, 197.10, 578.6
drawing the line 780.4
draw in one's claws 168.3
draw in one's horns 137.7, 168.3, 494.5
drawl (n) 175.1, 524.8 (v) 524.25, 525.7
drawling 525.12
draw lots 759.23
drawly 525.12
draw man 1058.9
drawn 21.9, 267.8, 270.20, 790.7
draw near 167.3, 223.7, 839.6, 840.2
draw nigh 167.3, 223.7, 840.2
drawn-out 259.11, 267.8, 827.11
drawn to 167.4
draw off 163.6, 192.12, 480.13
draw off the attention 985.6
draw on 104.22, 377.5, 387.14, 831.6, 839.6, 840.2, 886.11, 894.9
draw one out 938.21
draw on futurity 845.5
draw on the future 845.5
draw out 192.10, 192.14, 267.6, 538.8, 827.9
draw over 375.23
draw poker 758.4, 759.10
draw rein 175.9, 857.11
draw straws 759.23
drawstring bag 195.2
draw taut 906.9
draw tears 112.19
draw the attention 983.11
draw the breath of life 306.8
draw the color line 980.8
draw the curtains 1028.5
draw the fangs 286.2
draw the line 210.5, 944.4, 980.8
draw the line at 325.3
draw the longbow 354.19, 355.3, 502.6
draw the purse strings 625.6
draw the sword against 457.14, 459.14
draw the teeth 16.10, 286.2
draw the veil 351.4
draw to a close 820.7, 857.6
draw to a head 12.15, 407.8
draw to a peak 238.22
draw together 260.7, 770.18
draw towards 907.4
draw up 547.19, 807.5, 857.7, 912.8
draw up a plan 381.10
draw up a will 478.18
draw upon 387.14
draw wages 624.20
dray 179.2
drayage 630.7, 905.1
dray horse 311.13
drayman 178.9
dread (n) 96.1, 105.5, 126.1, 127.1, 130.3 (v) 127.10, 130.5 (a) 127.30
dreaded 127.30
dreadful 98.19, 127.30, 155.12, 247.11, 1000.9, 1015.11
dreadfulness 98.3, 127.2, 1000.2, 1015.2
dreading 130.12
dreadless 492.19
dreadlock 3.7
dreadlocks 1016.14
dream (n) 100.9, 124.4, 976.1, 976.7, 985.2, 986.9, 999.7, 1016.8 (v) 951.10, 985.9, 986.17
dream analysis 92.6
dreamboat 104.10, 1016.8
dream-born 986.20
dream-built 986.20
dreamcatcher 914.2
dream come true, a 1002.3
dream come true 986.7
dream-created 986.20
dreamer 22.12, 124.5, 952.8, 986.13
dreamer of dreams 986.13
dreamery 986.7, 986.8
dream factory 706.4
dream factory, the 1035.1
dreamful 986.25
dreamfulness 986.8
dream girl 104.14
dreaminess 986.8
dreaming (n) 985.2, 986.8 (a) 985.11, 986.25
dreaming sleep 22.1, 22.5
dreamland 22.2, 976.1, 986.11
dreamless sleep 22.5, 107.1
dreamlike 764.6, 976.9, 986.25
dreamlikeness 986.8
dreamlike thinking 92.23
dream of 100.20, 986.17
dream of other things 985.9
dream on 986.17
dream palace 706.7
dreamscape 976.1
dream sleep 22.1
dream state 92.19
dream-stricken 986.25
dream symbolism 92.6
dream team 744.1
dream up 892.12, 986.14
dream vision 976.1
dream world 986.11
dreamworld 976.1
dreamy 22.21, 670.15, 976.9, 985.11, 986.25
dreamy abstraction 985.2
dreamy-eyed 986.25
dreamy-minded 986.25
dreamy-souled 986.25
drear 112.24
dreariness 98.5, 112.7, 117.1
drearisome 112.24, 117.6, 118.9
drearisomeness 112.7, 117.1, 118.2
dreary 39.4, 98.20, 112.24, 117.6, 118.9, 133.16
dredge (n) 180.1, 284.10 (v) 192.10, 284.15, 771.6, 797.11, 912.8, 1043.4
dredge out 192.10
dredger 284.10
dredge up 192.10, 770.18, 912.8
dredging 192.1
dregs 256.2, 391.4, 606.3, 893.3
dregs of society 606.3, 660.11
drench (n) 8.4, 88.7, 1065.7 (v) 993.15, 1065.13, 1070.7
drenched 88.31, 993.20, 1065.17
drenched with sweat 12.22
drencher 316.2
drenching (n) 1065.7 (a) 1065.18
drenching rain 316.2
dress (n) 5.1, 5.6, 5.16, 33.4, 647.1 (v) 5.39, 79.20, 198.10, 287.5, 385.8, 405.6, 498.8, 890.8, 1044.8, 1056.8, 1069.17 (a) 5.45
dressage 1070.1
dress circle 704.15
dress clothes 5.11
dress code 5.1
dress designer 716.9

dress down 5.42, 510.18, 604.14
dress-down clothes 5.20
dress-down day 5.20
dressed 5.45, 405.16
dressed-down 5.47
dressed to advantage 5.46, 578.13
dressed to kill 5.46, 578.13
dressed to the nines 5.46, 578.13
dressed to the teeth 578.13
dressed up 5.46, 354.26
dresser 704.23
dress in 5.43, 5.44
dressing 5.1, 10.12, 10.27, 86.33, 198.3, 510.6, 890.4, 1044.2, 1069.13
dressing-down 510.6, 604.5
dressing room 197.15, 704.16
dressing ship 487.1
dressing up 5.10
dressmaker 5.36
dressmaker's model 786.5
dressmaking 5.32
dress parade 812.3
dress rehearsal 704.13
dress ship 182.52, 487.2
dress suit 5.11
dress the hair 3.22
dress the wounds 91.24
dress to kill 5.42, 578.9
dress uniform 5.11
dress up 5.42, 354.16, 498.8
dress-up clothes 5.10
dress whites 5.11
dressy 5.46, 501.19, 578.12
dressy clothes 5.10
Dreyer's New General Catalog 1073.8
dribble (n) 13.3, 190.5, 238.7, 248.2, 747.3 (v) 13.6, 190.14, 238.18, 747.4, 752.4
dribble away 393.19, 473.5, 486.5
dribbling 1065.17
driblet 248.2
dried 1066.9
dried beef 10.14
dried flower 310.25
dried raisin sweetener 66.3
dried-up 260.13, 393.35, 891.4, 1066.9
drier 35.8, 712.18, 1066.4
drift (n) 161.1, 164.1, 172.2, 184.28, 238.4, 518.1, 557.2, 756.3, 770.5, 770.10, 896.2, 1034.21 (v) 164.4, 177.23, 182.29, 182.54, 184.36, 329.2, 331.15, 770.19
driftage 164.1, 172.2, 238.4
drift along 162.3
drift anchor 1012.7
drift angle 184.28
drift away 168.2
drifter 160.4, 178.2, 331.9, 382.6, 660.2, 828.4
drifting (n) 164.1, 177.3 (a) 172.8, 177.37
drifting snow 1023.8
driftless 972.16
drift netter 382.6
drift off 22.16
drift off course 182.29
drift off to sleep 22.16
drift sail 1012.7
driftway 182.9
drift with the current 182.29, 331.15, 1014.12
driftwood 1054.3
drill (n) 84.2, 285.3, 328.1, 373.4, 568.3, 570.3, 725.6, 1040.2, 1040.6, 1040.7 (v) 275.9, 284.15, 292.15, 568.13, 570.12, 1043.4, 1069.18
drill, the 384.1
drilldown 245.2, 801.4
driller 284.10, 571.6, 1058.9
drill hole 292.3
drilling 192.1, 275.8, 568.3
drill into 568.12
drillmaster 571.6
dri mol 66.3
dri-mol 66.3
drimol 66.3
drink (n) 8.4, 10.49, 88.7, 88.9, 88.13, 240.1, 1061.2 (v) 8.29, 87.22, 88.24, 187.11, 187.13
drinkable (n) 10.49 (a) 8.34
drink a stirrup cup 188.16
drink a toast to 88.29
drink bottoms-up 88.24
drink deep 88.24
drinker 88.11
drink hard 88.24
drink in 8.29, 187.13, 570.7, 983.5
drinking (n) 8.3, 88.4, 187.4 (a) 88.35
drinking age 303.2
drinking bout 88.5, 743.6
drinking habit 87.1
drinking saloon 88.20
drinking vessel 195.1
drinking water 1065.3
drink in with rapt attention 983.5
drink like a fish 88.24
drink off 8.29, 88.24
drink offering 696.7
drink one's fill 88.24
drink seriously 88.24
drink to 8.29, 88.29
drink to the health of 88.29
drink up 8.29, 88.24, 187.13, 1066.5
drip (n) 118.5, 190.5, 238.7 (v) 190.14, 238.18, 1065.11
drip-dried 1066.9
drip-dry 1066.6
dripping (n) 190.5, 238.7 (a) 1065.17
drippings 190.5
dripping wet 1065.17
dripple 238.18
dripproof 1066.11
drippy 316.11
drisk 319.3
dri sweet 66.3
dri-sweet 66.3
drisweet 66.3
drive (n) 17.2, 18.1, 100.1, 174.4, 177.7, 330.7, 365.1, 375.6, 401.1, 458.3, 459.1, 544.3, 770.5, 886.9, 902.1, 904.1, 1040.3, 1042.5 (v) 172.6, 177.33, 182.29, 184.37, 284.15, 330.13, 382.9, 424.4, 459.17, 573.9, 725.16, 748.3, 751.4, 756.4, 757.5, 902.11, 902.12, 904.9, 926.25, 1070.8
drive a bargain 731.18
drive a hard bargain 731.18
drive ahead 162.4
drive an entering wedge 843.7
drive a roaring trade 1010.9
drive at 380.4
drive away 771.5, 908.3
drive back 460.10, 908.3
drive-by shooting 308.1
drive crazy 926.24
drive dull care away 109.9, 743.22
drive from one's thoughts 984.4
drive hard 459.19
drive home to 953.18
drive in 191.7
drive-in 8.17, 706.7
drive-in restaurant 8.17
drive insane 926.24
drive-in theater 706.7
drive into a corner 1013.16
drive into one's head 989.17
drive into the ground 538.8, 993.10
drive into the open 909.14
drivel (n) 13.3, 520.2 (v) 13.6, 520.5, 522.10, 922.12, 926.20
drivel away 486.5
driveling 922.22
driveling idiot 924.8
drive mad 926.24
driven from pillar to post 1013.26
driven snow 37.2, 1023.8
drive off 908.3
drive on 162.4, 330.13, 375.16, 401.4, 902.11
drive one crazy 128.9
drive one mad 152.25
drive oneself 330.13, 725.10
drive one up the wall 1013.13
drive out 909.14
driver 178.9, 178.10, 575.13, 577.4, 756.2, 889.4, 904.6
drive recklessly 1006.7
driver's license 443.6
driver's license number 517.11
driver's seat 417.10
drive stakes 225.11
drive-through 8.6, 8.11, 8.17
drive-thru 8.17
drive-thru meal 8.6
drive time 1034.6
drive to despair 125.11
drive to desperation 125.11
drive together 770.18
drive to leeward 182.29
drive to ruin 395.25
drive to the bad 395.25
drive to the dogs 395.25
drive to the wall 625.8, 1013.16
drive train 1040.4
drive up the wall 96.13, 926.24
driving (n) 177.6, 756.3 (a) 172.7, 316.11, 330.23, 375.25, 424.10, 459.29, 544.11, 902.23, 904.14, 926.34
driving age 303.2
driving force 375.1, 902.1, 904.1
driving horse 311.13
driving power 902.1
driving rain 316.2
driving range 751.1
driving under the influence 88.5
drizzle (n) 316.1 (v) 316.10
drizzling 316.11
drizzling mist 319.3
drizzly 316.11
Dr. Jekyll and Mr. Hyde 873.1
Dr Johnson 541.7
drogue 317.8, 1008.3, 1012.7
drogue chute 181.13
droit 642.1
droit du seigneur 387.7
droll 488.4, 489.15
drollery 488.1, 489.3
drollness 488.1, 489.3
-drome 743.15
drome 184.22
dromedary 311.5
drone (n) 76.8, 175.5, 311.34, 331.11, 525.4, 708.22, 711.9, 781.2, 812.2, 849.4 (v) 52.13, 525.9, 781.3
drone bass 708.22
drone on 525.9
droning (n) 52.7, 525.4 (a) 50.15, 52.20, 61.4
dronish 331.19
drony 331.19
drool (n) 13.3, 520.2 (v) 13.6, 520.5, 922.12, 926.20
drooling 922.22
drooly 97.8
droop (n) 177.12, 194.2, 202.2 (v) 16.9, 21.5, 85.48, 112.16, 194.6, 202.6, 393.18
droop-eared 48.15
drooping 16.12, 16.21, 21.7, 112.22, 194.11, 202.10, 393.45, 804.5
drooping spirits 112.3
droopy 16.12, 21.7, 112.22, 202.10, 331.20
drop (n) 88.7, 190.5, 194.1, 204.5, 238.7, 248.2, 249.2, 252.2, 258.7, 282.3, 346.4, 367.1, 393.3, 553.9, 605.5, 704.20, 753.1, 857.3 (v) 1.3, 6.6, 16.9, 21.5, 25.5, 78.9, 157.5, 190.14, 194.5, 204.10, 238.18, 252.6, 297.15, 308.18, 367.6, 370.7, 374.3, 390.4, 473.4, 475.3, 633.6, 904.12, 908.3, 913.5, 913.7
drop a bomb 410.10, 459.23
drop a bombshell 131.7
drop a brick 131.7, 414.12, 975.15
drop a dime 551.13
drop a flag 746.5
drop a hint 399.5
drop a letter 176.15
drop a line 343.8, 553.10
drop all idea of 370.7
drop anchor 159.17, 186.8

drop a pop-up 414.12
drop around 177.25, 582.19
drop asleep 22.16
drop a tear 115.12
drop by 177.25, 189.7, 582.19
drop by the wayside 16.9, 21.5, 410.12, 911.3
drop cloth 295.9
drop cookie 10.43
drop curtain 704.20
drop dead 307.21
drop-dead gorgeous 1016.21
drop-dead list 871.1
drop down 194.5
dropdown menu 1042.18
drop-forge 262.7
drop from one's thoughts 990.7
drop from sight 346.8
drop from the clouds 131.6
drop head 937.2
drop in 177.25, 189.7, 582.19
drop in a bucket 248.2
drop in on 131.7
drop in one's tracks 21.5, 85.47, 308.18
drop in temperature 1023.1
drop in the bucket, a 248.5, 992.1
drop in the bucket 992.5, 998.5
drop in the ocean, a 248.5, 992.1
drop in the ocean 248.2, 992.5, 998.5
drop into a good thing 1010.11
drop into place 807.5
drop it 106.7, 857.6
drop kick 902.9
droplet 258.7, 282.3
drop like a hot potato 370.7
dropline 937.2
drop off 22.16, 194.5, 252.6, 307.19
drop on 194.10
drop one's eyes 27.19
drop one's gaze 27.19
drop one's guard 406.6, 493.5
drop one's jaw 122.5
drop out 333.4, 370.5, 868.4
dropout 868.3
drop out of society 584.7
drop pass 749.3
dropped 1.4, 252.10
dropped eggs 10.26
dropped from the clouds 131.10
dropping (n) 194.1 (a) 194.11, 204.16
dropping anchor 186.2
dropping out 333.1, 370.3
droppings 12.4
drops 86.4, 86.6
drop scene 704.20
drop serene 30.1
drop-ship 176.15
dropshop 924.3
dropsical 85.61, 259.13
dropsy 85.9, 259.2
drop the ball 410.10, 414.12, 975.15
drop the curtain 820.6
drop the hook 182.15
drop the mooring 182.18
drop the other shoe 817.5
drop the subject 984.4
dross 256.2, 1020.16
drought 100.7, 992.4, 1066.1
drought-stricken 1066.7
droughty 100.26, 1066.7
drove (n) 770.5 (v) 1070.8
drover 574.7, 1070.3
drown 307.23, 308.19, 367.7, 428.8, 1011.10, 1065.14
drown care 743.22
drowned 238.25, 275.14, 307.31, 1065.17
drowned coast 234.2
drowning 307.5, 308.6, 604.6, 1065.6
drowning rain 316.2
drown one's sorrows 88.24
drown one's troubles 88.24
drown out 53.8
drowse (n) 22.2 (v) 22.13
drowse off 22.16
drowsiness 22.1, 331.6
drowsing 985.11
drowsy 22.21, 670.15
Dr Pangloss 124.5, 929.5
drub (n) 902.4, 902.10 (v) 412.9, 604.12, 902.16, 902.22
drubbing 412.1, 604.4, 902.4
drudge (n) 577.1, 577.2, 726.3 (v) 330.10, 360.3, 577.13, 725.14
drudgery 725.4
drudging 725.17
drug (n) 25.3, 86.4, 86.5, 87.3, 670.3, 735.2 (v) 22.20, 25.4, 91.25, 94.8, 670.6
drug abuse 87.1
drug abuser 87.21
drug addict 87.21
drug addiction 87.1, 926.3
drug czar 87.1
drug dealer 87.21
drug dependence 87.1
drug experience 87.1
drugged 22.21, 25.8, 94.9, 331.20
drugged sleep 22.5
drugged with sleep 22.21
drugging 670.2
druggist 86.35
druggy 87.21
drug habit 87.1
drug habituation 87.1
drug house 87.20
drug intoxication 87.1
drug lord 732.4
drug mule 732.4
drug of choice 87.3
drug on the market 735.2, 993.2
drug pusher 732.4
drug pushing 87.2
drug rush 85.36
drug-runner 732.4
drugs 732.3
drug seller 87.21
drug smuggler 732.5
drugstore 86.36
drugstore complexion 1016.11
drugstore cowboy 918.1
drug test 87.1
drug testing 938.6
drug traffic 732.1
drug trafficking 87.2
drug trip 986.5
drug use 87.1
drug user 87.21
Druid 697.4, 699.15, 962.4
Druidess 699.15
Druidism 697.1
druid stone 1059.1
drum (n) 55.1, 282.4, 711.16 (v) 55.4, 60.5, 316.10, 708.44, 849.10, 916.12
drumbeat 55.1
drumbeating 352.5
drum circle 710.12
drum corps 710.12
drumfire 55.1, 459.9
drumhead 2.10
drumhead court-martial 595.4
drumhead justice 649.1
drum into 849.10
drum into one's head 568.12
drum into one's skull 568.12
drum kit 711.16
drumlin 237.4
drum major 710.17
drum-major's baton 273.2
drummer 710.10, 730.4
drumming (n) 55.1, 902.4, 916.3 (a) 55.7, 316.11
drumming out 909.5
drum music 55.1
drum out 447.4, 773.4, 909.14, 909.19
drum printer 1042.9
drum roll 902.4
drum-shaped 282.11
drumstick 10.23, 177.14, 711.16
drum up 472.9, 770.18
drum up attention 983.10
drunk (n) 88.6, 88.11, 88.12 (a) 88.31, 93.18, 985.15
drunk and disorderly 88.31
drunkard 88.11, 660.2
drunk as a fiddler 88.31
drunk as a lord 88.31
drunk as an owl 88.31
drunk as a piper 88.31
drunk as a skunk 88.31
drunk driving 87.1
drunken 88.31, 88.35, 985.15
drunken brawl 53.3
drunken carousal 88.5
drunkenness 8.3, 88.1, 669.1, 985.4
drunken revelry 88.5
drunk tank 429.8
drupe 10.38
druthers 371.5, 430.6
Druze 675.23
Druzism 675.13
dry (n) 611.9, 668.5 (v) 397.9, 480.24, 1066.6 (a) 58.15, 67.5, 100.26, 117.6, 118.9, 219.4, 508.13, 516.3, 535.3, 611.17, 668.11, 891.4, 987.5, 1066.7
dryad 678.9
dry ammunition 462.17
dry as a bone 1066.7
Dryasdust 929.5
dry as dust 117.6, 1066.7
dry-as-dust 118.9
dryasdust (n) 118.4, 842.5 (a) 570.17
dry bed 239.2
dry behind the ears 413.28
dry bones 307.15
dry cereal 10.34
dry-clean 79.18
dry cleaner 79.15
dry cleaning 79.2
dry-cure 397.9
dry-curing 397.2
dry dock 1009.6
dryer 1066.4
dryer sheet 70.6
dry-eyed 28.13, 94.11
dryfarm 1069.16
dry fruit 10.38
dry gangrene 85.40
dry goods 5.4, 735.3
dry goods dealer 5.33
dry heaves, the 909.8
dry humor 489.1
Dry Ice 1023.5, 1024.7
dry ice 316.5
drying (n) 260.3, 397.2, 1066.3 (a) 1066.10
drying oil 1056.1
drying out 87.1
drying up 260.3, 1066.3
drying-up 992.4
dry land 234.1
dryness 58.2, 67.1, 100.7, 117.1, 891.1, 987.1, 1066.1
dry nurse 1008.8
dry-nurse 8.19, 449.16
dry off 1066.6
dry offset 548.1
dry out 87.22, 516.2, 668.8
dry plate 714.10
drypowder extinguisher 1022.3
dry rot 393.7, 1001.2
dry rub 63.3
dry run 184.11, 405.1, 458.4, 942.3
dry-salt 397.9
dry season 313.1
dry-shod 1066.11
dry storage 386.5
dry stream 238.1
dry up 260.9, 388.4, 393.18, 990.5, 1066.6
drywall 1054.3
dry wine 88.17
dry wit 489.1
dry-witted 489.15
dry womb 891.1
DSL 1042.19
D string 711.5
DT's , the 917.2
duad 873.2
duadic 873.6
dual (n) 530.8 (a) 873.6
dual citizen 227.4
dual citizenship 226.2
dual-control trainer 181.10
dualism 675.5, 873.1, 952.6
dualist 675.16
dualistic 873.6
duality 873.1
dualize 873.5
dualized 873.6, 874.4
dual personality 92.20

dual pricing 630.3
dual-purpose 873.6
dual purpose fund 737.16
dual slalom 753.3
dual slalom course 753.1
duarchy 612.4
dub (n) 414.9, 751.2 (v) 287.5, 527.11
dubbed 527.14
dubbing 527.2
dubiety 362.1, 955.2, 971.2
dub in 862.4
dubious 356.21, 362.9, 645.16, 695.20, 955.9, 955.10, 969.3, 971.17, 1006.11
dubiousness 362.1, 955.2, 969.1, 971.2, 1006.2
dubitable 955.10, 969.3, 971.17
dubitancy 971.2
dubitante 695.12
dubitation 971.2
ducal 608.10
ducat 728.4
duce 574.6, 575.13
duchess 608.6
duchy 231.5, 232.1
duck (n) 76.5, 311.28, 367.2, 368.1, 412.5, 562.6, 758.2, 903.3, 913.3 (v) 164.6, 168.3, 344.7, 367.7, 368.8, 368.9, 754.4, 903.7, 913.8, 913.9, 1065.14
duck and run 368.11
duckboards 295.9
duck bumps 1023.2
duck call 517.16
duck duty 368.9
duck farm 1070.5
duck fit 152.8
ducking 367.2, 368.2, 754.3, 913.1, 1065.7
ducking stool 605.3
duckling 302.10, 311.28, 562.6
duck out 222.8, 368.11, 368.12
duckpin 750.1
duckpin bowling 750.1
duckpins 750.1
duck responsibility 468.2
ducks 5.18, 104.14, 562.6
duck soup 1014.4
duck-squeezer 1072.3
ducktail 1016.14
duck the issue 467.5
ducky (n) 104.14 (a) 999.13
duct 2.23, 239.1
ductibility 1047.2
ductile 433.13, 1014.15, 1047.9
ductility 433.3, 1014.2, 1047.2
duct tape 86.33
dud (n) 19.6, 400.2, 410.2, 410.5, 410.8, 610.9, 764.2 (v) 5.39 (a) 391.9
dude 76.5, 500.9
duded-up 578.13
dude ranch 1070.5
dudette 77.6
dudgeon 152.7
duds 5.1
due (n) 623.1, 639.2, 642.1 (a) 130.13, 623.10, 637.3, 639.7, 639.10, 649.7, 888.6, 991.6
due bill 728.11
due course 845.1
duel (n) 457.7, 754.3 (v) 457.13
dueler 461.1
dueling 457.8
duelist 461.1
duel to the death 457.6
dueness 639.1, 649.1
duenna 571.2, 577.8, 769.5, 1008.7
due process 598.1, 673.1
due punishment 639.3
due reward 639.3
dues 623.1, 630.6, 639.3
due season 843.3
due sense of 920.6
dues-paying 617.19
dues-paying member 617.11
duet 450.1, 708.18, 873.2
duettino 708.18
duettist 710.1
duff 975.15
duffel 385.4, 471.3
duffer 414.7, 414.9, 751.2, 930.7
duffle bag 195.2
dufus 922.17
dufus-assed 922.17
dugout 284.5, 346.4, 460.5, 745.1, 1009.3
dugs 283.6
duke 608.4, 759.10, 902.5
dukedom 232.1, 608.9
duke it out 457.17
duke-out 457.4
dukkha 604.1
dulce de leche 10.40
dulcet 97.6, 708.48
dulcetness 708.2
dulcification 465.1, 670.2
dulcify 66.4, 465.7, 670.7
Dulcinea 104.13
dulcitude 66.1
dulcorate 66.4
dulia 696.1
dull (v) 16.10, 25.4, 36.5, 51.9, 94.7, 120.5, 286.2, 670.6, 1027.10 (a) 16.12, 25.6, 36.7, 39.4, 52.17, 94.9, 94.13, 106.10, 117.6, 118.9, 173.14, 286.3, 331.20, 535.3, 721.5, 922.16, 987.5, 1005.7, 1027.17
dullard (n) 924.2 (a) 922.15
dullardism 922.3
dull as dish water 117.6
dull-brained 922.16
dull-eared 49.6
dulled 52.17, 286.3
dull-edged 286.3
dullhead 924.4
dull-headed 922.16
dull-headedness 922.3
dull hearing 49.1
dulling (n) 16.5, 120.1, 670.2 (a) 25.9, 120.9, 670.14
dullish 286.3
dullness 16.1, 25.1, 36.1, 36.2, 39.1, 52.2, 65.1, 94.1, 94.4, 96.1, 106.1, 117.1, 118.2, 286.1, 331.6, 721.2, 922.3, 987.1, 1005.1, 1027.5
dull of hearing 49.6
dull of mind 922.16
dull-pated 922.16
dull-pointed 286.3
dull roar 51.1
dull-sighted 28.13
dull-sightedness 28.2
dull the pain 120.5
dull thud 52.3, 410.2
dull tool 16.6, 118.5, 410.8, 414.7
dull-witted 922.16
dull-wittedness 922.3
duly constituted 417.15
duly noted 549.17
dumb 51.12, 311.39, 344.9, 525.13, 922.15, 923.8, 930.11, 1010.13, 1055.5
dumb animal 311.2
dumbbell 84.1, 725.7, 924.4
dumb blond 922.4, 924.4
dumb bunny 924.4
dumb cluck 924.4
dumb creature 311.2
dumb down 497.9, 922.12
dumbfound 51.8, 122.6
dumbfounded 51.12, 122.9
dumbfoundment 122.1
dumb friend 311.2
dumbhead 924.4
dumbheaded 922.17
dumbing down 497.8
dumb luck 972.1
dumbness 51.2, 344.2, 922.3
dumbo 924.3, 924.4
dumb rabies 926.6
dumb show 349.4, 517.14
dumbstricken 51.12
dumbstruck 51.12, 122.9
dumb thing to do 923.4
dumb trick 923.4, 975.6
dumbwaiter 912.4
dumb with grief 112.26
dum-dum 924.4
dumdum bullet 462.19
dummy (n) 51.3, 336.3, 349.6, 354.13, 384.4, 548.2, 575.5, 576.1, 616.8, 758.3, 764.2, 786.5, 862.2, 924.4, 998.7 (a) 336.8, 354.26, 862.8
dummy run 942.3
dummy share 738.3
dummy up 51.6
dump (n) 80.11, 80.12, 137.2, 156.3, 228.11, 228.28, 370.4, 386.1, 386.6, 391.6, 462.2 (v) 137.5, 159.12, 159.15, 390.7, 475.3, 734.8, 737.24, 909.23
dump altitude 184.41, 184.43, 194.5
dumpcart 179.3
dumpiness 257.8, 268.2
dumping 159.6, 390.3, 391.4, 391.6, 475.1
dumpish 110.24, 112.25
dumpishness 110.8, 112.8
dumpling 10.33, 257.12
dump on 137.5, 156.6, 157.3
dumps 110.10, 112.6
dump site 80.12, 370.4
dumpsite 391.6
Dumpster 391.7
dumpy 257.18, 258.13, 268.10
dun (n) 311.11, 421.1, 622.4, 628.3 (v) 421.5, 440.12, 628.11 (a) 40.3
Dun & Bradstreet rating 622.1, 729.6
dun-brown 40.3
dunce 924.2, 930.7
duncery 922.3
duncical 922.15
duncish 922.15
dunderhead 924.4
dunderheaded 922.17
dunderheadedness 922.4
dunderpate 924.4
dun-drab 40.3
dune 237.4, 770.10
dung (n) 12.4, 890.4 (v) 12.13
dungarees 5.18
Dungeness crab 311.29
dungeon 429.8
dunghill (n) 80.10 (a) 491.12
dunghill fowl 311.28
dunghilly 491.12
dungy 12.20
dunk 79.19, 367.7, 747.4, 751.4, 1065.14
dunked 1065.17
dunking 367.2, 1065.7
dunnage 471.3
dunner 622.4, 770.15
dunning (n) 440.3 (a) 440.18
dun-olive 40.3
dun-white 37.8
duo 708.18, 873.2
duodecillion 882.13
duodecimal 882.24
duodecimal system 1017.4
duodecimo (n) 258.6, 882.7 (a) 258.12
duodenal 882.24
duodenary 882.24
duologue 541.2
dupability 954.2
dupable 954.9
dupable person 358.1
dupe (n) 138.3, 358.1, 384.4, 416.3, 508.7, 576.3, 759.22, 954.4 (v) 356.14, 785.8, 874.3, 923.7
dupe and ditto 785.3
duper 357.1
dupery 356.1
duple 873.6
duple meter 720.6
duplet 1033.3
duple time 709.24
duplex (n) 228.5, 228.14 (a) 873.6
duplex apartment 228.13
duplex house 228.14
duplexity 873.1
duplicable 336.10
duplicate (n) 349.5, 548.3, 778.3, 785.3, 874.1 (v) 78.7, 778.6, 785.8, 849.7, 873.5, 874.3, 883.6 (a) 778.7, 784.11, 874.4
duplicate bridge 758.3
duplicated 849.12, 873.6, 874.4
duplicate plate 548.8
duplication 78.1, 336.3, 785.2, 785.3, 849.1, 873.1, 874.1, 883.4, 993.4

duplication of effort 993.4
duplicative 849.14, 993.17
duplicature 291.1
duplicitous 354.31, 873.6
duplicity 354.4, 356.3, 645.6, 873.1
DuPont 618.8
duppy 988.1
durability 763.1, 827.1, 853.1, 1049.1
durable 15.15, 763.7, 827.10, 853.7, 1049.4
durable goods 735.4
durableness 827.1, 853.1
durables 735.4
duramen 1054.3
durance 429.3
durance vile 429.3
duration 158.8, 821.1, 824.3, 827.1, 829.1, 853.1
durational 821.7
durative (n) 530.12 (a) 821.7
dure 1046.10
duress 18.1, 424.3, 429.3, 963.1
durity 1046.1
dusk (n) 315.3, 1025.10, 1027.2 (v) 1027.12 (a) 38.9, 315.8, 1027.15
dusk-dark 315.3
duskiness 38.2, 315.3, 1027.2
dusking-tide 315.3
dusking time 315.3
duskish 315.8
duskishness 315.3
duskness 38.2, 1027.2
dusky 38.9, 38.11, 315.8, 1027.15
dust (n) 80.6, 87.7, 87.18, 234.1, 298.2, 307.15, 391.4, 391.5, 1051.5, 1066.2 (v) 79.18, 80.15, 771.6
dust ball 1051.5
dustbin 391.6, 391.7
dust bowl 233.1, 891.2
dust bunny 1051.5
dust cloud 1038.16, 1051.5, 1073.7
dust cover 295.18, 554.14
dust-covered 1051.11
dust-dark 315.3
dust devil 318.13, 1051.5
dusted 771.10
dust-gray 39.4
dustheap 391.6
dustiness 117.1, 1051.1
dusting 604.4
dust in the eyes 415.3
dust jacket 295.18, 554.14
dust kitten 1051.5
dustman 22.11
dust of ages 842.1
dust off 79.18, 902.17
dust one's jacket 604.14
dustproof 293.12
dust ruffle 295.10
dust storm 318.12
dust the batter off 745.5
dust thrown in the eye 376.1
dusttight 293.12
dustup 53.4, 456.5, 457.1, 810.4
dusty 39.4, 80.22, 117.6, 118.9, 177.41, 842.14, 1051.11, 1066.7
dusty-dark 315.3
Dutch 750.2
Dutch auction 734.4
Dutch courage 87.1, 88.1, 492.1
Dutch lottery 759.14
Dutch-treat 624.18
Dutch uncle 422.3
duteous 326.3, 434.4, 641.13
duteousness 326.1, 641.2
dutiable 630.15
duties 155.3
duties and responsibilities 641.1
dutiful 155.8, 326.3, 434.4, 641.13, 692.8
dutifulness 326.1, 434.1, 641.2, 692.1
duty 155.1, 387.5, 421.1, 630.9, 641.1, 643.3, 696.8, 701.3, 724.2, 724.3
duty-bound 641.16
duty calls one to 641.5
duty-free 630.16
duty-free shop 386.6
duty visit 582.7
duumvirate 450.1, 612.4
duvet 295.10
DVD 549.10
DVD burner 549.10
dwarf (n) 248.2, 258.5, 678.8 (v) 252.9 (a) 258.13
dwarfed 258.13, 265.12, 992.10
dwarfish 258.13, 992.10
dwarfishness 258.1
dwarfling 258.5
dweeb 660.5, 924.3
dwell 225.7, 827.6
dweller 227.2
dwellers 227.1
dwell in 221.6, 761.11
dwell in an ivory tower 1009.8
dwelling (n) 225.1, 228.1, 228.5 (a) 225.13
dwelling house 228.5
dwelling place 228.1
dwelling upon 849.2
dwell on 118.8, 507.5, 827.9, 849.9, 989.12, 997.14
dwell upon 118.8, 507.5, 989.12
dwindle 16.9, 34.2, 85.48, 168.2, 173.8, 252.6
dwindling (n) 252.2, 260.1 (a) 168.5, 173.12, 252.11, 393.45
DX code 714.9
dyad 873.2
dyadic 873.6
dyarchy 612.4
dybbuk 680.6, 988.1
dye (n) 35.8 (v) 35.14, 797.11
dyed 35.17
dyed-in-the-wool 35.18, 373.18, 794.10, 855.13
dyeing 35.11
dye in the wool 35.14, 855.9
dye one's hands in blood 308.15
dyestuff 35.8
dying (n) 252.1, 307.1, 307.14, 393.3, 1022.2 (a) 85.54, 135.6, 168.5, 307.32, 828.7
dying away (n) 252.1 (a) 52.16
dying breath 307.8
dying day 307.7
dying down 173.3
dying for 100.22
dying hour 307.7
dying off 252.1
dying quail 745.3
dying star 1073.8
dying to 100.21, 100.22, 101.8
dying words 817.1, 820.1
dyke 75.15, 76.9
dykey 75.30
Dylan 183.1, 240.3
dynamic 17.13, 18.12, 330.23, 1039.9
dynamical 1039.9
dynamic economics 731.11
dynamic energy 17.1
dynamic lift 184.26
dynamics 18.7, 172.1, 1039.3
dynamic speaker 50.8
dynamic symmetry 264.1
dynamic wind rose 318.15
dynamism 17.1, 330.7
dynamitard 395.8
dynamite (n) 462.14 (a) 999.13
dynamiter 395.8
dynamize 17.10
dynamoelectric 1032.30
dynast 575.8
dynastic 417.17
dynasty 612.1, 835.2
dyne 17.7
dyotheism 675.5
dysarthria 525.1
dysentery 12.2, 85.9, 85.29
dysfunction 638.1
dysfunctional 638.3, 996.5
dyslalia 525.1
dyslogia 525.1
dysmerogenesis 78.6
dysmerogenetic 78.16
dyspepsia 85.9, 85.29
dyspeptic (n) 85.43 (a) 85.61, 110.23
dysphasia 525.1
dysphemia 525.3
dysphemism 513.3, 513.4, 534.1, 1015.1
dysphemistic 513.8, 534.2, 1015.6
dysphemize 513.6, 1015.5
dysphemized 1015.6
dysphonia 525.1
dysphonic 525.12
dysphrasia 525.1
dyspnea 21.3, 85.9
dyspneic 21.12
dysteleological 972.16
dysteleology 972.3
dysthymia 926.5
dystopia 986.11
each 864.15
each and all 864.15
each and every (n) 792.3 (a) 864.15
each and every one 864.4
each one 864.15
each other 777.4
eager 100.21, 101.8, 130.11, 135.6, 324.5, 330.17, 404.8, 405.16, 441.4
eager assent 332.1
eager attention 48.1
eager beaver 101.5, 330.8
eager expectation 130.2
eagerness 17.2, 100.1, 101.1, 135.1, 324.1, 401.2, 441.1, 896.1, 1019.2
eagerness to serve 326.1
eagle (n) 27.11, 174.6, 193.7, 311.27, 647.1, 647.2, 647.5, 728.4, 751.3 (v) 751.4
eagle eye 27.10, 339.4
eagle-eyed 27.21, 339.13
eagle freak 1072.3
eaglet 311.27
eagle-winged 174.15
eagre 238.14
ear (n) 2.10, 48.1, 48.2, 48.7, 283.3, 310.29, 944.1, 983.1 (a) 2.28
earache 26.5, 85.15
ear buds 50.8
ear-deafening 53.11
ear disease 85.15
eardrops 86.11
eardrum 2.6, 2.10
eared 48.15
ear for, an 48.3, 413.5
ear for music 48.3, 708.31
earful 524.3
ear guard 1008.3
earing 180.14
earl 608.4
earldom 232.1, 608.9
earless 49.6
earlier 274.8, 834.4, 845.10
earlier state 834.1
earliest 216.10
earliest inhabitant 227.3
earlike 48.15
earliness 833.1, 834.1, 845.1
earl marshal 575.20
earlobe 2.10, 202.4
earlock 3.5
early 818.15, 833.3, 834.4, 837.10, 837.12, 845.7
early bird 314.1, 845.4
early comer 845.4
early days 301.1, 818.3
early death 307.4
early edition 554.6, 555.2
early grave 307.4
early hour 845.1
early-onset 818.15
early retirement 390.1, 448.1
early riser 845.4
early-season 313.9
early stage 845.1
early start 845.1
early symptom 399.3
early times 837.2
early warning 551.3
early warning system 399.3
early wood 1054.3
early years 301.1
earmark (n) 517.1, 517.5, 865.4 (v) 436.5, 477.9, 517.20, 865.10
earmarking 436.2, 477.3
ear-minded 48.15
ear-mindedness 48.3
earn 472.8, 624.20, 627.3, 639.5
earn a bad name 661.7
earn a livelihood 385.11
earn a living 385.11

earned 639.9
earned income 627.1
earned run 745.3
earned-run average 745.4
earnest (n) 438.2, 624.1 (a) 101.9, 111.3, 359.11, 983.15, 997.20
earnest money 438.2, 624.1
earnestness 101.2, 111.1, 359.1, 983.1
earnings 472.1, 472.3, 624.4, 627.1
earn one's keep 385.11, 725.12
ear, nose, and throat 48.9
earn out 472.12
earn reproach 661.7
ear of corn 310.29
earphone 50.8
earpiece 347.4
ear piercing 292.3
ear-piercing 53.11, 58.14
ear-reach 48.4
earreach 223.2
ear-rending 53.11
earring 280.3, 498.6
ear-shaped 48.15
earshot 48.4, 223.2
ear-splitting 53.11, 58.14
ear-tag 1070.7
Earth 1073.9, 1073.10
earth (n) 199.3, 201.3, 228.26, 234.1, 307.15, 1009.3, 1052.2 (a) 234.4
earth artist 716.6
earth-based religion 675.14
earthborn 312.13, 606.8
earthbound 234.4, 987.5
earth closet 12.10
earthen 234.5, 742.7
earthenware 735.4
earth flax 1022.5
earthiness 497.2, 663.2, 666.3, 695.2, 987.2
Earth insertion 1075.2
earthliness 695.2, 1052.6
earthling 312.5, 695.10
earthlings 312.1
earthly 234.4, 695.16, 1052.10
earthly minded 695.16
earthly-mindedness 695.2
earth metal 1058.3
earthmover 1040.3
earthmoving machinery 1040.3
earthnut 310.22
earth orbit 1075.2
earthquake 671.5
earth satellite 1075.6
earth science 234.1, 1071.1
earth sciences 1071.1
earth scientist 1071.2
earth's crust 234.1
earthshaker 131.2
earthshaking 53.11, 997.17
earth-shattering 894.13, 997.20, 997.23
earthshine 1025.12
earth spirit 678.6
earthwork 460.4, 549.12, 1012.5
earthworm 311.38
earthy 234.5, 312.13, 497.11, 606.8, 663.6, 666.8, 695.16, 987.6
ear-to-ear grin 116.3
ear trumpet 48.8
earwax 2.24
earwitness 48.5, 957.6
earworm 422.2
ease (n) 20.1, 95.1, 107.1, 120.1, 121.1, 402.1, 449.1, 533.1, 544.2, 581.1, 1010.1, 1014.1 (v) 20.7, 120.5, 120.6, 121.6, 252.8, 298.6, 430.13, 449.11, 600.12, 670.7, 670.9, 804.3, 959.5, 1014.7, 1047.6
eased 175.12, 298.11
easeful 121.11
ease in 191.3
easel 712.18
easel picture 712.13
ease matters 120.5
easement 120.1, 121.4, 298.3, 471.4
ease of 480.21
ease of belief 954.1
ease off 20.7, 164.6, 175.9, 670.9, 804.3
ease-off 175.4
ease oneself 12.12
ease one's load 120.7
ease out 773.4
ease the helm 182.31
ease the rudder 182.31
ease the way 1014.7
ease up 20.7, 175.9, 670.9
ease-up 175.4
ease up on 145.4, 427.5
ease up to 167.3
easier said than done 1013.17
easily attained 223.15
easily first 249.15
easily reached 223.15
easily taken in 954.8
easily understood 521.10
easiness 121.2, 340.2, 426.2, 427.1, 581.1, 954.2, 979.4, 1014.1, 1047.1
easing (n) 120.1, 252.1, 298.3, 670.2, 1014.5, 1047.5 (a) 120.9, 298.16, 670.14, 1047.16
easing off 252.1
easing of relations 465.1
easing of tension 120.1
easing of the load 120.3
easing of the way 449.5
East 231.6, 231.7
east (n) 161.3 (a) 161.14
East and West 758.3
eastbound 161.14
East Coast 231.7
East End 230.6
easter (n) 318.8 (v) 161.8
Easter bunny 478.11
Easter egg 472.6
easterly (n) 318.8 (a) 161.14
eastermost 161.14
eastern 161.14
Eastern Christianity 675.7
Easterner 227.11
Eastern grip 748.2
Eastern Hemisphere 231.6
easternmost 161.14
Eastern Orthodox Church 675.9
Eastern Orthodoxy 675.9
Eastern-Rite Christian 675.19
Eastern Rites 675.8
Eastern Seaboard 231.7
Eastern Standard Time 832.3
Eastern time 832.3
Easter sepulcher 703.9
Eastertide 313.2
easting 161.3
eastland 231.6, 231.7
eastlander 227.11
East Side 230.6
eastward 161.3
east wind 318.8
easy 95.15, 106.15, 107.7, 121.11, 121.12, 143.14, 175.10, 298.12, 331.19, 402.6, 426.5, 427.7, 533.6, 544.9, 581.3, 633.7, 665.26, 804.5, 954.9, 1010.12, 1014.13, 1047.8
easy as falling off a log 1014.13
easy as pie 1014.13
easy chair 229.1
easy circumstances 618.1, 1010.1
easy come 486.8
easy come easy go 443.14
easy death 307.6
easy end 307.6
easy-flowing 1014.14
easy go 486.8
easy going 1014.1
easygoing 102.7, 106.15, 107.7, 340.11, 426.5, 427.7, 430.21, 581.3, 846.17
easygoingness 102.2, 106.5, 426.2, 427.1, 581.1
easy lay 665.14
easy listening (n) 52.1 (a) 52.16
easy mark 19.6, 358.2, 954.4
easy mind 106.2
easy money 472.6
easy-natured 143.14
easy of belief 954.8
easy on the eyes 1016.21
easy-paced 175.10
easy pickings 358.2
easy purse strings 485.1
easy question 938.10
easy race 757.3
easy rider 178.3
easy-running 1014.14
easy slope 204.4, 237.2
easy street 95.5, 1010.1
easy target 1014.3
easy temper 106.1
easy terms 633.2
easy thing 1014.3
easy to be seen 348.8
easy to come by 966.8
easy to find 167.5
easy to get along with 143.14
easy to speak to 343.10
easy touch 358.2
easy to understand 521.10
easy victory 411.1
easy virtue 665.4
easy winner 411.2
easy woman 665.14
easy word 526.1
eat 8.20, 134.8, 187.11, 388.3, 393.21, 713.10
eatable 8.33
eatables 10.1
eatage 10.4
eat away 255.9, 393.21
eat away at 393.13
eat crow 137.7, 363.8, 433.11
eat dirt 137.7, 433.11
eat, drink, and be merry 88.28, 406.7, 669.6, 743.25
eaten 393.43
eaten up 388.5
eaten up with curiosity 981.5
eater 8.16
eater-out 8.16
eatery 8.17
eat everything in sight 8.25
eat heartily 8.24
eat high on the hog 409.10
eat humble pie 137.7, 363.8, 433.11
eating (n) 8.1, 187.4 (a) 8.31
eating disorder 7.13, 92.14, 672.1
eating house 8.17
eating place 8.17, 739.1
eating tobacco 89.7
eating up 388.1
eat into 393.21
eat less 515.4
eat like a bird 8.26, 515.4
eat like a horse 672.4
eat nothing 515.4
eat off the same trencher 582.17
eat one out of house and home 672.4
eat one's fill 8.25
eat one's hat 363.8
eat one's head off 672.4
eat one's heart out 112.17, 154.2
eat one's words 137.7, 363.8
eat out 8.21, 713.10
eat out of house and home 480.24, 619.6
eat out of one's hands 432.12
eats 10.2
eat sparingly 515.4, 668.6
eat the bread of idleness 331.15
eat the dust of 166.3
eat the wind out of 182.26
eat to live 668.6
eat up 8.22, 8.24, 95.13, 388.3, 954.6
eat up the road 174.9
eat up the track 174.9
eau 1065.3
eau de Cologne 70.3
eau de parfum 70.2
eau de rose 70.3
eaves 295.6
eavesdrop 48.10, 981.3
eavesdropper 48.5, 981.2
eavesdropping 48.2, 981.1
eaves trough 239.3
ebb (n) 34.1, 168.1, 173.3, 238.12, 238.13, 252.2, 393.3 (v) 16.9, 168.2, 172.5, 173.8, 238.16, 252.6, 393.17
ebb and flow (n) 238.13, 916.5 (v) 238.22, 850.5, 854.5, 916.13
ebb away 252.6
ebbing (n) 172.2, 173.3 (a) 168.5, 173.12, 393.45

ebb of life 307.1
ebb tide 238.13, 274.2
Eblis 680.4
Ebola virus 85.42
ebon (n) 38.4 (a) 38.8, 1027.13
ebonize 38.7
ebony (n) 38.1, 38.4 (a) 38.8, 1027.13
e-book 554.3
ebriosity 88.3
ebullience 105.4, 320.3, 330.2, 1020.2
ebulliency 320.3, 1020.2
ebullient 105.20, 109.11, 320.6, 330.17, 1019.25
ebulliometry 1019.21
ebullition 105.4, 320.3, 671.2, 917.1, 1020.2
e-business 1042.19
e-card 553.3
eccentric (n) 868.3, 870.4, 927.3 (a) 160.12, 488.4, 851.3, 854.7, 868.6, 870.9, 870.11, 927.5
eccentric inclination 1073.16
eccentricity 488.1, 851.1, 854.2, 865.4, 868.2, 870.1, 923.1, 927.1, 978.3
ecchymose 12.17
ecchymosed 12.23
ecchymosis 12.8, 85.38
ecclesiarch 575.1, 699.8, 699.9
ecclesiast 699.8
ecclesiastic (n) 699.2 (a) 698.13
ecclesiastical 698.13, 703.15
ecclesiastical calendar 701.12, 832.8
ecclesiastical council 423.4
ecclesiasticalism 698.2
ecclesiastical mode 709.10
ecclesiastical office 698.5
ecclesiological 676.4
ecclesiology 698.2
eccrine 13.8
eccrinology 13.4
eccrisis 12.1
ecderon 2.4
ecderonic 2.27
ecdysiast 6.3, 705.3, 707.1
ecdysis 6.1
echelon 184.12, 245.2, 458.2
echinate 285.10
echinoderm 311.31
echo (n) 54.2, 55.1, 93.5, 336.1, 336.4, 708.23, 711.17, 785.7, 849.1, 849.5, 874.2, 903.1, 939.1, 1036.11 (v) 48.12, 50.14, 54.7, 93.11, 332.9, 336.5, 849.7, 849.11, 873.5, 939.4, 1036.16
echo back 54.7
echo chamber 54.5
echoed 849.12
echoer 336.4
echoic 54.12, 336.9, 349.13, 526.20, 849.14, 939.6
echoic word 526.17
echoing (n) 874.1 (a) 54.10, 54.12, 849.14, 939.6
echoist 336.4
echolalia 849.4, 963.5
echoless 51.10
echolocation 275.6
echopraxia 963.5
echo pulse 1036.10
echo signal 1036.11
echo sounding 275.6
echovirus 85.42
e-cigarette 89.5
éclair 10.41
éclaircissement 341.4
eclampsia 85.6, 917.6
eclamptic 917.19
éclat 17.4, 352.4, 501.4, 509.2, 662.1
eclectic 371.23, 797.14, 805.5
eclectical 371.23
eclecticism 371.10, 675.4, 797.1
eclipse (n) 34.1, 295.1, 346.1, 1027.8, 1073.11, 1073.13 (v) 30.7, 249.8, 295.19, 346.6, 1027.9
eclipsed 295.31, 346.11, 1027.13
eclipse of the moon 1073.11
eclipse of the sun 1073.13
eclipsing (n) 295.1, 1027.6 (a) 249.12
eclipsing binary X-ray pulsar 1073.8
ecliptic 280.3, 1073.16
eclogic 720.16
eco 731.11
ecobabble 523.9, 523.10
ecocatastrophe 1072.2
ecocentric 1072.3
ecocide 308.1, 1072.2
ecofreak 1072.3
eco-friendly 397.12
école 567.1
ecological 209.9
ecological footprint 517.7
ecology 397.1, 1072.1
ecology, the 1072.1
e-commerce 733.1, 734.2, 736.2
econ 731.11
economese 523.10
econometrics 731.9, 731.11
economic 633.7, 635.6, 729.20, 731.23
economical 633.7, 635.6
economicalness 635.1
economical of words 344.9
Economic and Social Council 614.2
economic authority 731.12
economic class 607.1, 617.2
economic community 617.1
economic cycle 731.10
economic depression 731.10
economic determinism 731.11
economic expansion 731.10
economic expert 731.12
economic growth 731.10
economic indicator 731.9
economic planning 635.1
economic policy 731.7
economics 729.1, 731.11
economic science 731.11
economic sector 731.7
economic self-sufficiency 609.4, 731.7
economic stagnation 1011.6
economic status 607.1
economic support 449.3
economic system 731.7
economic theory 731.7
economism 731.11
economist 729.9, 731.12
economization 635.2
economize 635.4
economizer 635.3
economizing (n) 635.2 (a) 635.6
economy (n) 484.1, 635.1, 731.7 (a) 633.7
economy class 607.7
economy of assumption 484.1
economy of language 537.2
economy of means 484.1, 635.1
economy of scale 633.2
economy of words 344.2, 537.2
economy prices 633.2
economy size 257.4
economy-size 257.16
ECOSOC commission 614.2
ecosphere 305.1, 306.7; 317.2
ecosphere, the 1072.1
ecosystem 228.18, 1072.1
ecotourist 178.1
ecotoxic 64.7
ecphonesis 59.2
ecru 39.4
ecstasiate 95.10
ecstasiating 95.17
ecstasies 95.2
ecstasis 691.3
ecstasy 87.4, 93.2, 95.2, 104.2, 105.8, 683.10, 691.3, 986.2
ecstatic (n) 689.13 (a) 95.17, 105.25, 116.10, 985.11
ectoblast 2.4
ectoderm 2.4, 305.4
ectodermal 2.27, 295.32
ectodermic 2.27, 295.32
ectomorph 92.12, 270.8
ectomorphic 270.16
ectomorphism 92.11
ectomorphy 92.11
ectoplasm 305.4, 689.7
ectoplasmic 988.7
ectoplasy 689.7
ectype 785.1
ecumenic 450.5, 864.14
ecumenical 450.5, 864.14, 979.8
ecumenical council 423.4
ecumenicalism 450.1, 864.1, 979.1
ecumenicism 450.1, 450.2, 979.1
ecumenicist 979.6
ecumenicity 864.1, 979.1
ecumenicize 864.9
ecumenism 450.1, 670.1, 805.1, 979.1
ecumenist 979.6
ecumenistic 979.8
ecumenization 864.1
eczema 85.34, 85.35
edacious 672.6
edacity 672.1
Eddas, the 683.7
Eddic 683.14
eddies 184.29
eddy (n) 105.4, 238.12, 318.11, 915.2 (v) 238.21, 915.11
Eddy kite 181.14
edema 85.9, 251.1, 259.2, 283.4, 993.7
edematous 85.60, 85.61, 259.13, 1047.11
Eden 986.11
Edenic 986.23
edental 286.4
edentate 286.4
edentulous 286.4
edge (n) 17.5, 68.1, 198.2, 211.4, 249.2, 277.2, 285.1, 285.2 (v) 211.10, 218.4, 218.5, 285.7
edged 17.14, 211.12, 285.8
edge in 189.7, 213.6, 214.5
edgeless 286.3
edge off 164.6
edge out 249.9, 411.3, 412.6
edges 211.1
edgestone 211.6, 383.6
edge tool 285.2, 1040.2
edge up to 167.3
edginess 105.10
edging 211.7
edgy 105.28, 128.11, 135.6
edible 8.33
edible bird 10.22
edible lactose 66.3
edibles 10.1, 735.7
edict 352.2, 420.4, 673.3, 946.5
edictum 420.4
edification 392.1, 568.1, 928.4, 999.4
edifice 228.5, 266.2
edificial 266.6, 892.15
edify 392.9, 568.10
edifying 568.18
Edison effect 1033.4
edit 255.12, 341.11, 392.12, 547.19
edited text 341.2
edited version 547.10
editing 255.5, 341.4, 392.4, 706.6
edition 341.2, 554.5, 708.28
editor 341.7, 554.2, 555.4, 556.4, 706.4, 938.17, 946.7, 1042.11
editorial (n) 552.3, 556.2 (a) 341.15, 555.5, 556.6
editorialist 556.4
editorialize 547.21, 552.11, 718.6
editorial style 532.2
editorial writer 555.4, 556.4
editorial writing 547.2, 718.2
editor-in-chief 554.2
edit out 255.12
educability 570.5
educable 570.18
educate 392.9, 551.8, 568.10
educated 392.13, 570.16, 928.18, 928.21
educated class 572.8, 607.5
educated ear 944.1
educated guess 951.4
educated language 523.4
educated man 572.8
educated speech 523.4
educated woman 572.8
educatee 572.1
educating 568.18
education 392.3, 568.1, 570.1, 928.4
educational 551.18, 568.18
educational administrator 571.8

educational counseling 422.1
educational film 706.1
educational institution 567.1
educationalist 571.1
educationist 571.1
educative 551.18, 568.18
educator 571.1
educatory 568.18
educatress 571.2
educe 192.14
educible 192.17
eduction 192.5
eductive 192.17
edulcorate 66.4, 79.22
edulcoration 66.2, 79.4
edutainment 1035.2
eel 10.24
eellike 281.7, 311.49
eelshaped 281.7
eentsy-weentsy 258.11
eerie 122.11, 127.31, 307.28, 870.15, 988.9
eeriness 127.2, 307.11, 870.7, 988.4
Eeyore 112.13, 125.7
efface 395.16
effaceable 990.10
effaced 990.8
efface from the memory 990.6
effacement 395.7
efface oneself 139.7
effect (n) 18.1, 33.3, 380.1, 518.1, 775.4, 820.1, 831.1, 835.2, 887.1, 893.1, 894.1 (v) 328.6, 384.5, 407.4, 437.9, 886.10, 886.11, 892.10
effect a sale 734.8
effected 407.10
effectible 966.7
effective 18.12, 18.14, 384.8, 387.21, 544.11, 889.9, 894.13, 995.6
effectiveness 18.1, 249.3, 387.3, 544.3
effective rejoinder 958.2
effective style 544.1
effectivity 18.1
effect one's escape 369.6
effector 886.4, 892.7
effector organ 2.14
effects 385.4, 471.1, 735.1
effectual 18.14, 387.21, 886.13, 886.14, 889.9, 894.13, 973.13, 995.6
effectuality 18.1
effectuate 328.6, 407.4, 437.9, 886.10, 892.10, 892.11
effectuated 407.10, 892.17
effectuation 328.2, 407.1, 437.4, 892.4, 892.5
effeminacy 77.2
effeminate (n) 77.10 (v) 77.12 (a) 16.14, 75.30, 77.14
effeminate male 77.10
effeminateness 77.2
effemination 77.11
effeminatize 77.12
effeminization 19.5, 77.11
effeminize 19.12, 77.12
effeminized 19.19
effendi 648.3
effervesce 57.2, 101.7, 320.4
effervescence 57.1, 105.4, 320.3, 330.2
effervescency 320.3
effervescent 57.3, 105.20, 320.6, 330.17
effervescing 57.1
effete 16.12, 16.18, 19.15, 117.6, 388.5, 393.36, 393.45
effeteness 19.4, 117.1, 391.2, 393.3
efficacious 18.14, 384.8, 387.21, 889.9, 894.13
efficacy 18.2, 387.3
efficiency 18.2, 387.3, 413.1
efficiency engineering 573.7
efficiency expert 573.7
efficient 18.14, 387.21, 413.24, 635.6, 889.9, 995.6
efficient cause 886.3
effigy 349.5, 697.3
effloresce 295.27, 310.35, 1051.10
efflorescence 85.36, 310.26, 1051.1, 1051.5
efflorescent 310.38, 1051.11
effluence 190.4
effluent (n) 12.3, 238.3, 391.4 (a) 190.19
effluvial 1067.9
effluvious 69.9
effluvium 69.1, 71.1, 689.7, 1001.4, 1067.1
efflux 190.4
effluxion 190.4
efflux tube 239.6
effort 328.3, 403.1, 403.2, 404.1, 725.1, 995.2
effortful 725.18
effortfulness 725.5
effortless 1014.13
effortlessness 1014.1
effrontery 142.1
effulgence 1025.4
effulgent 1025.32
effuse (v) 12.12, 190.11, 190.15 (a) 991.7
effused 190.19
effusion 12.1, 190.4, 190.6, 538.2, 540.1
effusive 190.19, 343.10, 538.11, 540.9, 587.19
effusiveness 538.2, 540.1
effusive rock 1059.1
egalitarianism 612.4
egest 12.12, 909.26
egesta 12.3, 909.8
egestion 12.1, 909.8
egestive 12.19
egg (n) 305.12, 305.15, 753.3, 886.7 (v) 459.27
eggbeater 181.5, 797.9, 917.9
egg cell 305.12
eggement 375.4
egghead 141.7, 572.10, 928.11, 929.1
egg in one's beer 121.3, 993.2
egglike 305.23
egg on 375.16, 886.11
egg on one's face 96.4, 98.6, 137.2
eggplant 10.35
eggs 10.26
egg salad 10.26
eggs Benedict 10.26
egg-shaped 280.12
eggshell (n) 16.7, 305.15, 1050.2 (a) 35.22, 37.8
egg tempera 712.13
egg white 305.15, 1062.5
eggy 305.23
ego 92.28, 140.3, 865.5, 919.4
egocentric (n) 140.5 (a) 94.9, 140.10
egocentricity 140.3
egocentrism 140.3
egocentristic 140.10
ego defense 92.23
ego defenses 460.1
egohood 865.1
ego-id conflict 92.28
ego ideal 92.28, 786.4
ego-involve 375.12
egoism 140.3
egoist 118.4, 136.3, 140.5
egoistic 140.10
egoistical 140.10
egoisticalness 140.3
egoistic ethics 636.2
ego-libido 92.28
egomania 140.4
egomaniac 140.10
ego massage 95.1, 511.1
egotism 104.1, 140.3, 651.1
egotist 140.5, 651.3
egotistic 136.9, 140.10
egotistical 136.10, 140.10, 651.5
egotisticalness 140.3
ego trip 140.1, 651.1
ego-trip 140.6, 651.4
egregious 247.10, 247.12, 794.10, 993.16, 1000.9
egregiousness 993.1, 1000.2
egress (n) 188.1, 190.2, 190.9, 239.1, 909.6 (v) 190.12
egression 190.2
Egyptian darkness 1027.1
Egyptian deities 678.4
Egyptology 842.4
eider 3.19
eiderdown 3.19, 295.10, 1047.4
eidetic 989.22
eidetic image 349.5, 986.6
eidetic imagery 989.2
eidetic memory 989.2
eidolon 33.3, 976.4, 986.5, 988.1
eight 617.7, 758.2, 882.4
eight bells 314.4
eight-card stud 758.4
18-hole course 751.1
18 holes 751.3
18mo 554.4
eighteenmo 554.4
Eighteenth Amendment 668.3
eighteen-wheeler 179.12
18-yard box 752.1
eighter 882.4
eightfold 882.20
Eightfold Path 882.4
eightfold way 1018.1
eighth (n) 709.9 (a) 882.20
eighth note 709.14
eighth rest 709.21
800 number 347.4
800-pound gorilla 997.9
eight-spot 758.2
8vo 554.4, 882.4
eighty 882.7
eighty-eight 711.17
eighty-six 390.7
Einsteinian universe 1073.1
Einstein theory 158.6
eisegesis 342.1
eisegetical 342.3
Eisenhower Doctrine 609.5
eisteddfod 770.2
either (n) 864.5 (a) 872.7
either-or 539.4, 873.6
ejaculate 59.7, 75.24, 904.11, 909.25
ejaculation 12.1, 59.2, 904.2, 909.7
ejaculative 909.30
ejaculatory 59.11, 75.27, 904.15
eject 13.5, 671.13, 773.5, 802.8, 904.12, 908.3, 909.13
ejecta 12.3, 904.5
ejectamenta 12.3, 904.5
ejected 773.7
ejectee 909.12
ejection 12.1, 12.3, 190.3, 773.2, 904.4, 908.1, 909.1
ejection capsule 397.6
ejection seat 369.3, 397.6
ejective 904.15, 909.30
ejectment 909.1
ejector 909.11
ejector seat 369.3, 397.6
eke 794.6
eke out 385.12, 794.6
eke out a living 619.5
eke out an existence 856.5
eke out one's income 635.4
el 179.14
elaborate (v) 392.10, 538.7, 545.7, 861.6, 892.8 (a) 339.11, 498.12, 501.21, 533.9, 799.4
elaborated 533.9
elaborateness 498.2, 501.5
elaboration 355.1, 392.2, 498.1, 538.6, 849.2, 861.1, 892.2
élan 17.4, 101.1, 109.4
eland 311.5
élan vital 17.4, 306.2, 767.5, 886.7, 919.5
elapse 821.5, 837.6
elapsed 837.7
elasmobranch 311.30
elastic (n) 1048.3 (a) 259.9, 396.23, 1047.9, 1048.7
elastic band 1048.3
elastic bandage 86.33
elasticity 15.2, 1047.2, 1048.1
elasticize 1048.6
elastomer 1048.3
elate (v) 109.8, 136.6 (a) 95.17, 116.10, 502.13
elated 95.17, 109.11, 116.10, 136.10, 502.13
elation 95.2, 116.1, 502.4
elative 530.9
elbow (n) 2.7, 278.2, 800.4, 906.5 (v) 278.5, 902.12
elbow, the 909.5
elbow bender 88.12
elbow crooker 88.12
elbow grease 725.1

elbow in 214.5
elbow in the ribs 517.15
elbowroom 158.3, 430.4
eld 303.5, 304.2, 837.2, 842.1, 842.8
elder (n) 304.2, 304.5, 575.1, 575.16, 699.2, 699.10, 842.8, 921.1, 997.8 (a) 834.4, 842.19
eldercare 91.21
elder hostel 228.15
elderliness 303.5, 842.1
elderly 303.16, 842.10
elders 560.7
eldership 303.3, 842.1
elder statesman 413.11, 610.2, 921.1
eldest (n) 304.5 (a) 842.19
El Dorado 986.11
Eldorado 618.4
eldritch 988.9
elds 304.4
e-learning 567.5
elect (n) 371.12, 607.2, 608.1, 999.8 (v) 371.13, 371.20, 609.41, 615.11 (a) 371.26, 495.13, 999.16
elect, the 692.5
elected 371.26
elected by acclamation 371.26
elected official 610.11
election 371.1, 371.9, 417.12, 609.15, 698.10, 964.4
election district 609.16
electioneer (n) 610.10 (v) 609.40
electioneering 609.12
election fraud 609.18
election returns 549.7, 609.21
elective 324.7, 371.22, 371.23
elective course 568.8
elector 371.7, 609.23
electoral 371.23
electoral college 371.7, 609.22
electoral district 231.5
electoral mandate 417.1
electorate 227.1, 231.5, 371.7, 609.22
electors 609.22
Electra complex 92.22
electric (n) 179.17 (a) 105.30, 375.27, 904.17, 1032.30
electrical 1032.30
electrical appliance 1032.21
electrical charge 1032.5
electrical circuit 1032.4
electrical communication 347.1
electrical device 1032.21
electrical energy 17.1
electrical engineer 1032.23, 1043.2
electrical engineering 1043.1
electrical field 1032.3
electrical oscillation 916.1
electrical science 1032.1
electrical shock 916.3
electrical transcription 50.12, 1034.18
electrical unit 1032.1
electric attraction 1032.11
electric blanket 295.10
electric-blue 45.3
electric car 179.17
electric chair 605.5
electric charge 1032.5
electric conduction 1032.14
electric cord 1032.21
electric current 1032.2, 1033.6
electric detonator 462.15
electric discharge 1032.6
electric exploder 462.15
electric eye 1033.11
electric fan 318.18
electric field 1032.3
electric flow 1032.2
electric heat 1019.1
electric-heat 1020.17
electric-heated 1020.29
electric horsepower 1032.18
electrician 704.24, 1032.22
electricity 105.3, 174.6, 347.2, 1025.20, 1032.1
electric Kool-Aid 87.10
electric light 1025.19
electric light bulb 1026.1
electric meter 1032.21
electric potential 1032.12
electric power 18.4, 1032.18
electric-powered 1032.30
electric refrigeration 1024.1
electric refrigerator 1024.4
electric repulsion 1032.11
electric resistance 1032.13
electric shock 916.3
electric storm 316.3
electric stream 1032.2
electric train 179.14
electric unit 1032.1
electric wave 1034.11
electric wire 1032.21
electrification 105.11, 1032.24
electrified 131.13, 1032.30, 1032.34
electrify 17.10, 105.14, 131.8, 1032.26
electrifying (n) 1032.24 (a) 122.12, 131.11, 830.5, 1032.30
electroaffinity 1032.11
electroballistic 1032.33
electrobiological 1032.33
electrobiologist 1032.23
electrocardiogram 91.9
electrocardiography 91.12
electrocautery 91.5, 1020.15
electrochemical 1032.30, 1032.33, 1060.9
electrochemist 1032.23
electrocoagulation 91.5
electrocoating 295.13, 1032.25
electroconvulsive therapy 92.35
electrocorticogram 91.9
electrocute 604.16
electrocution 604.6
electrocutioner 604.7
electrodynamic 1032.30, 1039.9
electroencephalogram 91.9
electroencephalograph 91.9
electroencephalography 91.12
electroetching 1032.25
electrogalvanization 1032.25
electrogalvanize 1032.28
electrogild 1032.28
electrogilding 1032.25
electrograving 1032.25
electrokinetic 1032.30
electrolier 1026.6
electrolysis 806.2, 1016.14, 1032.25
electrolyte 1032.25
electrolytic 806.6, 1032.32
electrolyze 806.4, 1032.28, 1060.8
electromagnet 907.3
electromagnetic 1032.31
electromagnetic field 1032.3, 1032.9
electromagnetic induction 1032.15
electromagnetic induction of currents 1032.15
electromagnetic lifting magnet 907.3
electromagnetic radiation 916.4, 1025.5, 1032.10
electromagnetic spectrum 1032.10
electromagnetic theory 1018.1
electromagnetic wave 916.4, 1034.11
electromagnetism 1032.7
electromagnetize 1032.27
electromechanical 1032.30
electrometallurgical 1032.33
electrometallurgist 1032.23, 1058.12
electrometallurgy 1058.11
electrometric 1032.30
electromotive 1032.30
electromotive force 1032.12
electromotivity 1032.12
electromyogram 91.9
electromyography 91.12
electron 258.8, 1033.3
electron affinity 1033.3
electronarcosis 25.1
electron beam 1033.5
electron capture 1033.3
electron cloud 1033.3, 1033.6
electron current 1033.6
electron diffraction 1033.5
electron dynamics 1033.1
electronegative 1032.35
electron emission 1033.5, 1037.3
electron flow 1033.6
electron gas 1033.6
electronic 1033.15, 1039.7, 1040.14
Electronic Age 824.6
electronic ankle bracelet 428.4
electronic banking 1041.5
electronic book 554.3
electronic brain 1041.17, 1042.2
electronic carillon 711.18
electronic cigarette 89.5
electronic circuit 1033.8, 1034.9
electronic commerce 736.2
electronic communication 347.1
electronic communications 343.5
electronic computer 1041.17
electronic conductance 1033.9
electronic control 1041.3
electronic cop 1036.5
electronic cottage 1041.5
electronic current 1033.6
electronic data processing 551.7, 1042.1
electronic data processor 1042.2
electronic device 1033.13
electronic effect 1033.4
electronic engineering 1033.1
electronic hearing aid 48.8
electronic instrument 711.1
electronic journalism 552.1, 1034.18, 1035.2
electronic mail 347.13, 347.18, 353.6, 553.1, 553.4, 1042.19
electronic mail service 553.7
electronic measuring device 1033.13
electronic-mechanical control 1041.3
electronic media 551.5
electronic meter 1033.13
electronic money 728.1, 728.11
electronic navigation 184.6
electronic organizer 1041.17
electronic politics 609.1
electronic printer 1042.9
electronic refrigeration 1024.1
electronic refrigerator 1024.4
electronic resistance 1033.9
electronic revolution 860.1
electronic rights 642.2
electronics 347.3, 1033.1
electronics engineer 1033.14, 1043.2
electronic signature 332.4
electronics physicist 1033.14
electronic spreadsheet 871.1, 1042.11
electronic surveillance 48.2, 938.9
electronic switching 347.7
electronic tester 1033.13
electronic testing device 1033.13
electronic virus 1042.11
electronic warfare 457.1, 458.1
electron layers 1033.3
electron micrograph 714.3
electron microscopy 1033.1
electronography 548.1
electron optics 29.7, 1033.1
electron pair 1033.3
electron physics 1033.1
electron-positron pair 1033.3
electron ray 1033.5
electron-ray tube 1033.11
electron shells 1033.3
electron shower 1037.3
electron spin 1033.3
electron state 1033.3
electron stream 1033.6
electron theory of atoms 1033.2
electron theory of electricity 1033.2
electron theory of solids 1033.2
electron transfer 1033.3
electron tube 1033.10, 1035.11
electron volt 1033.7
electroosmosis 187.6
electrophysicist 1032.23
electrophysics 1033.1
electrophysiological 1032.33
electrophysiologist 1032.23

electroplate (n) 295.13 (v) 295.26, 1032.28
electroplated 295.33
electroplating 295.13, 1032.25
electropneumatic 1032.30
electropositive 1032.35
electropower 18.4
electropult 184.8
electroscopic 1032.30
electrosection 91.5
electroshock 1032.6
electrostatic 1032.30, 1039.8
electrostatic field 1032.3
electrostatic induction 1032.15
electrostatic printer 1042.9
electrostatic printing 548.1
electrostatic spraying system 1041.5
electrostatic tube of force 1032.3
electrosurgery 91.5
electrotechnical 1032.33
electrotechnician 1032.22
electrotechnologist 1032.23
electrotherapeutics 91.5
electrotherapy 91.5
electrothermal 1032.30
electrotype (n) 548.8 (v) 548.15
electrotyper 548.12
electrovalence 1060.4
electrovalent 1060.10
electuary 86.4
eleemosynary 143.15, 478.22, 634.5
elegance 339.3, 484.1, 496.1, 498.2, 500.5, 501.5, 504.4, 533.1, 544.2, 578.3, 580.3, 664.2, 1016.1
elegancies 504.7, 580.3
elegancy 533.1
elegant 496.8, 498.12, 500.18, 501.21, 533.6, 544.9, 578.13, 664.5, 999.12, 1016.17
elegant penmanship 547.5
elegant variation 545.4
elegiac (n) 720.7 (a) 115.22, 309.22, 720.16
elegiacal 115.22, 720.16
elegiac couplet 720.7
elegiac distich 720.7
elegiac pentameter 720.7
elegist 309.7, 720.12
elegize 115.10, 720.14
elegy 115.6
element 209.4, 766.3, 796.2, 886.1, 1020.10, 1052.2, 1060.2
elemental (n) 678.6 (a) 199.8, 317.13, 767.9, 818.15, 886.14, 1060.9
elemental spirit 678.6
elementarity 798.1
elementary 199.8, 767.9, 796.5, 798.6, 818.15, 886.14, 1060.9
elementary education 568.5
elementary mathematics 1017.1
elementary or subatomic particle 1038.6
elementary particle 1052.2
elementary school 567.3
elementary unit 1052.2
elements 196.1, 568.5, 701.7, 763.2, 818.6
elements, the 317.3
elenchus 935.5, 958.3
elephant 87.18, 257.14, 311.4
elephant driver 178.9
elephantiasis 993.1
elephantine 117.6, 257.19, 257.20, 311.46, 534.3, 993.16
elephant in the room 974.2
elephantlike 311.46
elephant skin 295.15
elevate 109.8, 200.9, 272.13, 392.9, 446.2, 662.13, 912.5, 912.6
elevated (n) 179.14 (a) 88.33, 136.11, 247.9, 251.7, 272.14, 544.14, 545.8, 652.6, 662.18, 912.9, 997.19
elevated land 237.1
elevate one's mood 109.7
elevating 912.10
elevation 193.1, 200.4, 251.1, 272.1, 272.2, 381.3, 446.1, 544.6, 652.2, 662.5, 662.8, 912.1
elevator 386.6, 386.7, 912.4
elevator talk 524.2
elevatory 912.10
eleven 617.7, 746.2, 882.7
elevenses 8.6
eleventeen 884.2
eleventeenth 882.25
eleventh 882.23
eleventh hour 315.5, 843.5, 846.1
eleventh-hour 843.10, 846.18
eleventh-hour rescue 381.5
elf 258.5, 302.4, 322.3, 678.8, 680.7
elf child 680.11
elfdom 870.7
elfenfolk 678.7
elfin 258.13, 678.17
elfish 322.6, 678.17, 680.18
elfishness 322.2
elflike 678.17
elflock 3.4
elicit 192.14, 375.13, 886.11
elicitation 192.5
elicitory 192.17
elide 268.6, 773.5
elided 268.9
eligibility 371.11, 772.1
eligible 371.24, 563.20
eliminant 12.19, 909.30
eliminate 12.12, 255.10, 308.16, 390.7, 395.14, 762.7, 773.5, 909.21, 909.22
elimination 12.1, 34.1, 255.3, 308.2, 390.3, 395.6, 773.2, 909.6
elimination diet 7.13
eliminative 12.19
elision 268.3, 537.4
elite (n) 249.5, 371.12, 578.6, 607.2, 608.1, 617.6, 999.8 (a) 495.13, 578.16, 999.16
elite group 617.6
elite troops 461.15, 461.23
elitism 141.3, 612.4
elitist (n) 141.7 (a) 141.11, 928.23
elixir 86.3, 86.4, 192.8, 196.5, 767.2
elixirate 192.16
elixir of life 86.3
elixir vitae 86.3
Elizabethan theater 704.14
elk 311.5
ell 254.3, 278.2
ellipse 279.2, 280.6
ellipsis 268.3, 537.4
ellipsoid (n) 282.2 (a) 279.13, 280.12, 282.9
ellipsoidal 282.9
elliptic 268.9, 279.13, 280.12, 537.6
elliptical 267.9, 268.9, 279.13
elliptical galaxy 1073.6
elliptical trainer 84.1
elocute 543.10
elocution 524.1, 543.1
elocutionary 543.12
elocutioner 543.7
elocutionist 543.7, 543.8
éloge 509.5
Elohim 677.2
Elohist 683.11
elongate 267.6
elongated 267.8, 267.9
elongation 267.4
elope 368.10
elopement 188.1, 368.4, 563.3
eloper 368.5
elopment 369.1
eloquence 524.4, 543.1, 544.1
eloquent 524.31, 543.12, 544.8
eloquent tongue 544.1
else 780.8
elsewhere 985.11
el supremo 575.4
elucidate 341.10, 521.6
elucidation 341.4
elucidative 341.15
elucidatory 341.15
elucubrate 570.12, 725.13
elude 368.7, 369.9, 415.11, 1012.15
elude one 522.10
eludible 368.14
elusion 368.1, 415.5
elusive 368.15
elusiveness 368.1
elusory 368.15
elute 79.22
elution 79.4, 79.5
elutriate 79.22
elutriation 79.4, 79.5
elvish 322.6, 680.18
Elysian 97.9, 681.12
Elysian fields 95.5, 681.9, 839.2
Elysium 95.5, 681.9
elytron 295.15
Elzevir 258.6
Elzevir edition 258.6
em 548.6, 548.7
emacerate 260.9, 270.12
emacerated 260.13, 270.20
emaceration 260.3, 270.6
emaciate (v) 260.9, 270.12, 393.19 (a) 270.20
emaciated 260.13, 270.20, 393.35
emaciation 85.9, 260.3, 270.6, 393.4
email (n) 347.13, 347.18, 553.1, 553.4, 1042.19 (v) 176.15
email address 553.9, 1042.18
email box 553.6
emanate 171.6, 190.11, 835.3
emanate a smell 69.6
emanate from 887.5
emanating 190.18
emanation 69.1, 171.2, 190.1, 689.7, 1025.1
emanational 13.7
emanative 13.7, 69.9, 190.18
emanatory 13.7
emancipate 431.4
emancipated 430.21, 431.10
emancipated slave 430.11
emancipating 592.4
emancipation 431.1
Emancipation Proclamation 431.1
emancipative 592.4
emancipator 398.2, 592.2
emanent 190.18
Emanuel Swedenborg 684.3
emarginate 285.14
emasculate (v) 19.12, 77.12, 255.11, 393.14 (a) 19.19
emasculated 19.19, 75.29, 393.30
emasculation 19.5, 255.4
embalm 70.8, 309.21, 397.10, 829.5
embalmed 397.13, 829.9
embalmed corpse 307.15
embalmer 309.8
embalming 309.3, 397.3
embalming fluid 88.14, 397.4
embalm in the memory 989.12
embalmment 309.3
embankment 234.2, 383.7, 770.10, 901.4, 1009.6, 1012.5
embarassing defeat 412.4
embargo (n) 293.1, 444.1, 625.2, 773.1 (v) 293.7, 444.3, 773.4
embargoed 773.7
embark 176.15, 182.19, 188.15
embarkation 182.5, 188.3, 818.5
embark in 404.3
embarkment 188.3, 818.5
embark on 818.9
embark upon 404.3
embarras de choix 371.3
embarras de richesses 618.1
embarrass 96.15, 98.13, 137.4, 898.2, 971.12, 985.7, 996.4, 1012.11, 1013.15
embarrassed 96.22, 137.14, 139.13, 623.8, 971.24, 985.12, 1013.20
embarrassed circumstances 619.1
embarrassing 98.21, 137.15, 971.27
embarrassing position 1013.4
embarrassing situation 1013.4
embarrassment 96.4, 98.6, 137.2, 139.4, 898.1, 971.3, 985.3, 1012.6, 1013.4
embarrassment of riches 993.2
embarrass oneself 975.14

embassage 552.4
embassy 228.5, 552.4, 576.7, 615.1, 739.7
embattle 460.9
embattled 458.22, 460.12
embay 209.6
embayed 242.2
embed 191.5, 207.5, 855.9
embedded 855.13
embedded journalist 458.8
embed itself in the mind 931.19
embedment 191.1, 855.2
embellish 354.16, 355.3, 392.10, 498.8, 545.7
embellished 354.26, 355.4, 392.13, 498.11, 545.11
embellishing 498.10
embellishment 355.1, 392.2, 498.1, 545.4, 709.18, 993.4
ember 256.2, 1019.16
embezzle 389.4, 482.13
embezzlement 389.1, 482.1
embezzler 483.1
embitter 110.16, 112.19, 119.2, 152.24, 393.9, 589.7
embittered 110.23, 119.4, 152.26, 393.27
embittering 119.1
embitterment 96.3, 119.1
emblazon 35.14, 498.8, 501.17, 509.12
emblazonment 498.1
emblazonry 35.11, 498.1
emblem 517.2, 647.1, 786.2
emblematic 517.23
emblematical 517.23
emblematize 517.18
embodied 1052.11
embodied in 796.4
embodiment 196.1, 348.1, 349.4, 349.7, 763.4, 767.2, 772.1, 792.1, 796.1, 1052.1, 1052.8
embody 348.5, 349.11, 763.5, 772.3, 796.3, 1052.9
embodying 349.13, 796.4
embody in words 532.4
embolden 375.21, 449.14, 492.15
emboldening 492.8
embolism 293.3
embolus 293.3, 1045.7
embonpoint 2.18, 257.8
embosom 209.6, 346.7, 474.7, 562.18
embosomed 159.18
emboss 283.12
embossed 283.18, 715.7, 855.13
embosser 30.6
embossing 715.1
embossment 283.2, 517.7, 715.3
embouchure 292.4, 711.6
embow 279.6
embowed 279.10
embox 295.20
embrace (n) 474.2, 562.3, 585.2, 585.4, 800.4 (v) 209.6, 295.20, 371.15, 474.6, 474.7, 480.14, 562.18, 585.9, 772.3, 800.5, 800.11, 803.6
embrace a belief 953.13
embraced 371.26, 772.5
embracement 209.5, 371.4, 562.3, 772.1
embrace reality 977.3
embracing 209.8, 772.6
embrangle 799.3
embrangled 799.4
embrasure 289.3
embrasured 289.5
embrocate 91.25, 1056.8
embrocation 86.11, 1056.3
embroider 354.16, 498.8, 545.7
embroidered 354.26, 355.4, 545.11
embroiderer 741.2
embroideress 741.2
embroidery 355.1, 498.1, 545.4, 741.1
embroidery hoop 741.3
embroil 811.4
embroilment 105.4, 456.5, 457.4, 671.2, 810.4, 917.1
embrown 40.2
embryo 305.14, 886.7
embryology 1068.3
embryonic 258.14, 305.22, 406.12, 795.4, 818.15, 886.14
embus 188.15
emcee (n) 574.4, 704.23, 743.20, 1034.23 (v) 573.9
emend 392.9, 392.12, 396.13
emendable 392.17, 396.25
emendate 392.12
emendation 341.4, 392.4, 396.6
emendator 341.7
emendatory 392.16
emended 392.13
emender 341.7
emerald (n) 44.1 (a) 44.4
Emerald City 986.11
emerald-green 44.4
emerge 31.4, 33.8, 190.11, 369.10
emerge from 887.5
emergence 33.1, 190.1, 369.1
emergency 197.25, 843.4, 997.4, 1006.1, 1013.4
Emergency Broadcast System 460.2
emergency exit 369.3
emergency funds 386.3
emergency kit 405.3
emergency medical technician 90.11, 398.2
emergency money 728.1
emergency preparedness 405.4
emergency rations 10.6
emergency room 197.25
emergent 190.18, 839.8, 843.10
emerging (n) 190.1 (a) 190.18
emerita 448.3
emeritus (n) 571.3 (a) 448.3, 837.10
emeritus status 448.1
emersion 190.2
emery 287.8
emesis 909.8
emetic (n) 64.3, 79.17, 86.17, 86.18 (a) 79.28, 86.49
emiction 12.5
emigrant 178.5, 190.10, 774.4
emigrate 177.22, 188.17, 190.16
emigration 177.4, 190.7
émigré 178.5, 190.10, 368.5, 774.3
Eminence 648.2
eminence 237.4, 247.2, 272.1, 272.2, 283.2, 417.4
eminence 662.4, 662.5, 662.9, 894.1, 997.2
éminence grise 415.8, 610.6, 894.6
eminent 247.9, 249.12, 272.14, 283.14, 417.15, 662.18, 997.19
eminent domain 417.1, 417.6, 480.5
emir 575.9, 608.7, 648.3
emirate 417.7
emissary 353.1, 576.2, 576.6
emissile 283.14
emission 12.1, 190.1, 909.7
emission control 1072.1
emission nebula 1073.7
emissive 909.30
emit 12.12, 13.5, 190.15, 352.14, 524.22, 909.24, 1067.8
emit a smell 69.6
emit a sound 50.14
emitter junction capacitance 1032.16
emitter signal voltage 1033.7
emitting 190.1
emm 87.14
Emmanuel 677.10
emmet 311.33
Emmy 646.2
emoji 1042.18
emollient (n) 86.11, 1056.3 (a) 86.40, 120.9, 1047.16, 1056.10
emolument 624.5
emote 93.13, 500.12, 704.29
emotiometabolic 93.17
emotiomotor 93.17
emotiomuscular 93.17
emotion 93.1, 105.1, 978.1
emotionable 93.20
emotional 93.17, 105.28, 978.7
emotional appeal 93.9
emotional blackmail 421.1
emotional charge 93.1
emotional coloring 93.1
emotional crisis 105.6
emotional deadness 94.1
emotional disorder 92.14
emotional dissociation 92.20
emotional health 83.1
emotional instability 92.14, 93.9, 105.10
emotional insulation 92.23
emotional intelligence 93.1
emotionalism 93.9, 105.10
emotionalistic 93.19
emotionality 93.9
emotionalization 93.9
emotionalize 93.13, 704.29
emotionalizing 93.9
emotional life 93.1
emotionally dead 94.9
emotionally disturbed student 572.4
emotionally numb 94.9
emotionally paralyzed 94.9
emotionally unstable 105.28
emotional nuance 93.1
emotional numbness 94.1
emotional paralysis 94.1
emotional quotient 93.1
emotional release 92.25, 120.2
emotional response 989.1
emotional shade 93.1
emotional shock 92.17
emotional stability 855.1
emotional support 901.1
emotional symptom 92.18
emotional trauma 85.25, 92.17
emotionless 94.9
emotionlessness 94.1
emotiovascular 93.17
emotive 93.17, 93.19, 93.22
emotive meaning 518.1
emotiveness 93.9
emotivity 93.9, 978.1
empath 689.13
empathetic 24.12, 93.20, 147.3, 455.3, 788.9
empathic 24.12, 147.3, 455.3
empathize 455.2
empathize with 93.11, 147.2
empathy 24.3, 93.5, 145.1, 455.1
empeople 225.9
empeopled 225.12
empeoplement 225.2
emperor 575.8
emperorship 417.8
empery 232.1, 417.5, 417.8, 612.1
emphasis 334.1, 524.10, 709.25, 720.7, 997.1
emphasize 997.14
emphasized 997.21
emphatic 334.8, 334.9, 544.13, 997.21
emphatic denial 335.2
empierce 292.15
empiercement 292.3
empire 232.1, 417.5, 417.8, 612.1
empirical 761.15, 942.11, 957.16, 1052.10
empirical existence 761.2
empirical fact 761.3
empirical politics 609.1
empiricism 636.2, 942.1, 1052.6
empiricist 942.6
emplace 159.11
emplaced 159.18
emplacement 159.1, 159.6, 901.13
emplane 188.15
emplanement 188.3
employ (n) 387.1, 577.12, 724.1 (v) 328.8, 387.10, 387.13, 615.14, 724.10, 725.8
employable 384.8, 387.18, 387.23
employed 330.21, 387.24, 615.20
employee 432.5, 577.3, 616.6, 726.2
employee demands 727.1
employee rights 727.1
employees 577.11
employer 249.4, 387.9, 574.3, 575.1
employer rights 727.1
employing 387.8

employment 328.1, 387.1, 387.8, 577.12, 615.4, 724.1, 724.5, 725.4
employment contract 437.1
employ oneself in 328.8, 724.11
employ time 821.6
empoison 85.52
emporium 736.1, 736.2
empower 18.10, 443.11, 576.15, 615.10
empowered 417.15, 443.17
empowerment 18.8, 417.12, 443.3, 615.1
empress 575.10
empressement 101.1
emprise 404.2
emptied 393.36
emptiness 96.1, 100.7, 117.1, 158.1, 222.2, 222.3, 284.1, 354.5, 391.2, 520.1, 762.1, 922.6, 998.3
emptiness of mind 933.1
emptor 733.5
empty (v) 190.13, 192.12, 909.22 (a) 19.15, 100.25, 117.6, 222.14, 284.16, 354.32, 391.13, 520.6, 522.20, 762.8, 922.19, 930.11, 933.4, 936.10, 936.13, 998.19
empty-calorie 8.31
empty ceremony 580.4
empty claim 640.1
empty formality 580.4
empty gesture 354.6
empty-handed 992.12
empty hands 465.2
empty-headed 922.13, 922.19, 930.11, 933.4, 985.16, 990.9
empty-headedness 922.6, 930.1, 933.1, 985.5
emptying 192.3, 909.6
empty into 238.16
empty-minded 922.19
empty-mindedness 922.6
empty name 527.3
empty-nester 560.8
empty-noddled 922.19
empty of 992.13
empty out 909.22
empty-pated 922.19
empty pocket 619.2
empty purse 619.2
empty-skulled 922.19
empty sound 520.1
empty space 158.1, 184.32, 222.3, 1073.3
empty stomach 100.7
empty suit 16.6, 500.7, 998.7
empty talk 354.11
empty threat 514.1
empty title 527.3
empty view 158.4
empty word 530.3
empty words 936.3
empurple 46.2
empurpled 46.3
empyreal 97.9, 681.12, 1073.25
empyrean (n) 1073.2 (a) 97.9, 677.16, 681.12, 1073.25
empyrean, the 681.4
em quad 548.7
em space 224.1
emulate 336.7, 457.18, 786.7, 999.11
emulation 336.1, 457.2
emulative 336.9
emulator 452.2, 1042.18
emulous 457.23
emulousness 154.1
emulsification 803.1, 1062.7
emulsifier 797.9, 1062.7
emulsify 797.10, 1062.10
emulsion 714.10, 714.13, 1062.7, 1064.3
emulsionize 1062.10
emulsive 1062.11
emulsoid 1062.7
emunctory 2.23, 190.9
en 548.6, 548.7
enable 18.10, 384.6, 405.8, 443.11, 772.3, 966.5
enablement 18.8, 405.2, 772.1
enabling 443.3
enact 328.9, 348.5, 349.12, 407.4, 613.10, 673.9, 704.30
enacting 349.4
enacting clause 613.9
enaction 613.5
enact laws 613.10
enactment 328.2, 348.2, 349.4, 613.5, 673.2, 673.3, 704.8
enamel (n) 2.8, 35.8, 287.2, 295.12 (v) 35.14, 295.24 (a) 742.7
enameled 35.17
enameler 716.7
enameling 35.12
enamelist 716.7
enamel kiln 742.5
enamelware 735.4, 742.2
enamelwork 712.16
enamor 104.22
enamored 104.27
enamored of 104.29
enantiomorphic 264.4
enantiosis 539.1, 779.3, 873.1
enate (n) 559.2, 560.4 (a) 559.6, 560.18, 775.10, 784.13
enatic 560.18
enation 559.1, 775.3
encage 429.12
encamp 225.11
encampment 225.4, 228.29, 463.3
encapsulate 268.6, 295.20, 557.5, 849.8
encapsulated 268.9, 295.31
encapsulation 268.3, 557.1
encapsuled 212.12, 295.31, 537.6
encase 212.6, 212.9, 295.20
encased 212.12, 295.31
encasement 212.2, 295.17
enceinte 78.18
encephalic 198.15
encephalitic 85.61
encephalitis lethargica 22.6
encephalogram 91.9
encephalograph 91.9
encephalon 2.15, 919.6
enchain 19.10, 428.10
enchant 95.10, 377.7, 691.8, 983.13
enchanted 95.17, 104.27, 122.9, 691.12, 870.16, 983.18, 986.25
enchanter 357.1, 377.4, 690.9
enchanting 97.7, 377.8, 691.11, 894.13, 983.20
enchantingness 122.3
enchantment 95.2, 97.2, 104.2, 377.1, 690.1, 691.2, 870.8, 894.1, 1000.4
enchantress 377.4, 690.9, 1016.7
enchase 713.9
enchased 713.11
enchasing 713.2
enchiridion 554.8
enchymatous 259.13
encincture (n) 209.5, 210.1 (v) 209.7
encinctured 209.11
encipher 345.10, 522.12
enciphered 345.16
encircle 209.7, 212.5, 280.10, 459.19, 772.3, 914.5
encircled 209.11, 210.6
encirclement 209.5, 459.5
encircling 209.8, 772.6
enclasp 209.6
enclave 212.3, 231.4
enclitic 254.2, 526.3, 526.4
enclose 158.9, 207.5, 209.6, 210.4, 211.8, 212.5, 429.12, 772.3
enclosed 209.10, 212.10, 429.19
enclosed, the 196.6
enclosed space 197.2
enclosing 209.8, 212.11, 772.6
enclosure 196.6, 209.5, 212.1, 212.3, 231.4, 429.7, 460.4
enclothe 5.39
encloud 319.7, 1027.9
encode 345.10, 522.12
encoded 345.16
encoder 1035.8
encoding 551.7
encoffin 309.19
encoffinment 309.1
encomiast 509.8
encomiastic 509.16
encomium 509.5
encompass 158.9, 209.6, 212.5, 280.10, 295.20, 459.19, 772.3, 792.8, 800.5, 805.3, 914.5
encompassed 209.10, 772.5
encompassing (n) 209.5 (a) 209.8, 772.6
encompassment 209.5, 459.5, 772.1, 805.1
encompass with shadow 1027.9
encore (n) 509.2, 704.7, 849.6, 874.2 (v) 509.10
encounter (n) 223.4, 457.3, 902.3 (v) 167.3, 216.8, 223.11, 451.5, 457.15, 831.8, 902.13, 941.3
encounter danger 1006.6
encourage 109.7, 121.6, 375.15, 375.21, 422.6, 449.14, 449.17, 492.15
encouragement 121.4, 375.5, 375.7, 449.4, 492.8
encourager 121.5, 375.10, 616.9
encouraging 109.16, 121.13, 124.12, 375.27
Encratic 668.10
Encratism 668.2
Encratite 668.4
encrimson 41.4
encroach 214.5, 640.8, 910.9
encroacher 214.3, 774.2
encroachment 214.1, 393.1, 640.3, 655.1, 674.3, 910.3
encroach upon 640.7
encrust 295.27
encrustation 295.14
encryption 1042.19
enculturate 373.9
enculturation 226.3, 373.2, 392.3
encumber 253.4, 297.13, 1012.11
encumbered 297.18, 623.8
encumbering 1012.18
encumbrance 96.8, 297.7, 432.6, 1012.6
encyclical 352.2
encyclical letter 352.2
encyclopedia 554.9, 928.9
encyclopedic 772.7, 864.14, 928.21
encyclopedic knowledge 928.6
encyclopedist 547.15, 718.4
encyst 212.9
end (n) 211.3, 256.1, 307.1, 375.1, 380.2, 395.2, 407.2, 472.3, 477.5, 518.2, 746.2, 793.3, 794.5, 820.1, 857.2, 886.3, 940.1, 964.2 (v) 308.13, 395.12, 395.23, 407.6, 820.6, 857.6, 887.4, 911.3
end, the 820.1
end-all 820.4
endamage 393.9
endanger 1006.6
endangered 523.23, 1006.13
endangered species 1068.1
endangerment 1006.1
endear 104.22
endearing 97.7, 104.24
endearment 377.3, 562.5
endeavor (n) 328.3, 403.1, 403.2, 725.1 (v) 403.5, 404.3, 725.9
endeavor to 403.8
ended 407.11, 820.9
endemic 85.62, 226.5
ender 820.4
endermatic 2.27, 295.32
endermic 2.27, 295.32
enderon 2.4
en déshabillé 5.47, 6.13
endgame 857.2
end happily 940.2
end in a point 285.6
ending (n) 307.1, 407.2, 820.1, 857.1, 857.2 (a) 820.11
end in itself 380.2
end in view 375.1, 380.2, 886.3
endleaf 554.12
endless 538.12, 812.8, 823.3, 829.7, 856.7, 884.10
endless chain 812.2
endlessness 812.1, 823.1, 829.1
endless round 812.2
endless supply 991.3
endless task 408.1
endless time 829.2

end line 746.1
endmost 820.12
endocardium 2.16
endocentric compound 526.4
endocentric construction 529.1
endocrine (n) 13.2 (a) 13.8
endocrine disease 85.21
endocrinism 85.21
endocrinology 13.4
endocrinopathy 85.21
endoderm 2.4, 305.4
endodontist 90.6
end of burning 1074.9
end of hostilities 465.5
end of life 307.1
end of one's rope 1013.6
end of one's tether 21.1, 1013.6
end of the earth 261.4
end of the line 186.5, 307.1, 820.1, 857.2
end of the line, the 383.7
end of the rainbow 986.10
end of the rainbow, the 261.4
end of the road 307.1, 820.1
end of the world 395.2
endogamic 78.17
endogamous 78.17
endogamous group 617.2
endogamy 78.2
endogenous depression 92.14
endogenous metabolism 2.20
endolymph 2.10
endome 295.21
endomitosis 305.16
endomorph 92.12
endomorphic 257.18
endomorphism 92.11
endomorphy 92.11, 257.8
end one's days 307.18
end one's life 307.18
endoplasm 305.4
endopsychic 919.7
endorse 332.12, 371.15, 438.9, 441.2, 449.14, 509.9, 609.41
endorsed 332.14
endorsee 479.3
endorsement 332.4, 441.1, 509.1, 527.10
endorser 332.7, 616.9
endorsing 441.4
endoskeleton 2.2
endosmosis 187.6
endosmotic 187.17
endothelium 2.4
endow 18.10, 385.7, 449.15, 478.17, 618.9, 892.10
endowed 385.13, 413.29, 478.26
endowed chair 571.10
endowed with 469.9
endowed with beauty 1016.17
endowed with life 306.12
endowment 18.8, 385.1, 413.4, 449.3, 478.1, 478.9, 560.6
endow with 478.17
endow with life 306.10
endpaper 554.12
endpleasure 95.1
end point 820.1
end-point control 1041.8
end product 893.1, 1038.10
end result 887.1, 940.1
end rhyme 720.9
endsheet 554.12
end stage 820.1
end-stage 820.12
end state 887.1, 940.1
end stop 530.15
end-stop 857.6
end the life of 308.13
end-to-end 223.16
endue 5.39, 18.10
endued 5.45
end up 186.6, 820.6, 820.7, 887.4, 946.10
end up in smoke 410.13, 911.3
endurable 107.13
endurance 15.1, 134.1, 360.1, 827.1, 853.1, 856.1
endurance race 457.12
endurant 134.9
endure 134.5, 148.4, 267.5, 306.11, 360.2, 443.10, 453.2, 626.7, 761.9, 821.5, 827.6, 831.8, 853.5, 856.3, 1049.3
endure forever 829.6
enduring 134.9, 267.7, 360.8, 763.7, 827.10, 853.7, 989.22
end use 387.5
end user 387.9
endways 223.16
endwise 223.16
endzone 746.1, 749.1
enema 79.5, 79.17, 86.17, 86.19, 1065.8
enemies list 871.1
enemy (n) 452.1, 589.6 (a) 451.8, 458.20
enemy aircraft 181.9
enemy atrocities 458.11
enemy line 463.2
enemy prisoner of war 429.11
energetic 17.13, 18.12, 330.17, 330.22
energeticalness 330.6
energetics 1039.3
energid 17.7, 305.4
energize 17.10, 306.10, 375.12, 1032.26
energized 9.4
energizer 17.6, 375.10
energizing (n) 17.8 (a) 9.3, 17.15, 306.13, 375.27
energumen 101.4, 926.15, 926.18
energy (n) 15.1, 17.1, 17.4, 18.1, 330.2, 330.6, 725.1 (a) 1021.9
energy bar 10.43
energy charge 92.34
energy drink 10.49
energy efficient 17.15
energy level 1033.3, 1038.15
energy metabolism 2.20, 7.12
energy source 17.1, 1021.1
energy vampire 17.1, 1032.6
enervate 16.10, 19.12, 21.4, 85.50, 764.4
enervated 16.18, 19.15, 19.19, 21.7, 85.54, 331.20
enervating 16.20
enervation 16.5, 19.4, 21.1, 85.3, 331.6
enface 547.19
enfant terrible 302.4, 322.3, 427.4, 868.3
enfeeble 16.10, 19.9, 85.50, 252.8
enfeebled 16.18, 21.7
enfeeblement 16.1, 16.5, 21.1
enfeebling 16.20
enfeoff 478.16, 629.3
enfeoffed 469.9
enfeoffment 478.2, 629.1
enfilade (n) 459.9 (v) 459.22
enflame 375.18
enfold 207.5, 209.6, 291.5, 295.20, 562.18
enfolded 209.10
enfolding 209.8
enfoldment 209.5, 291.4, 562.3
enforce 387.11, 424.4, 437.9, 673.9
enforceable 673.11
enforced respite 20.2
enforcement 424.1, 437.4
enforce one's claim 480.13
enforcer 461.1, 749.2
enforce the law 1008.18
enforce upon 643.6
enforcing 643.2
enframe 211.10
enframement 211.4
enfranchise 18.10, 431.4, 443.11, 772.3
enfranchised 371.24, 443.17
enfranchisement 18.8, 371.6, 431.1, 443.3, 772.1
engage 375.22, 377.6, 403.6, 436.5, 437.5, 457.16, 615.14, 724.10, 777.6, 898.2, 983.13
engagé 330.21
engage attention 983.11
engaged 330.21, 436.8, 437.11, 458.22, 476.8, 563.18, 983.17
engaged in thought 931.22
engage in 328.8, 404.3, 724.11
engage in a blood sport 382.9
engage in a conversation 541.8
engage in battle 457.16, 458.13
engage in combat 457.16
engage in hostilities 458.13
engage in personalities 512.10
engage in small talk 541.9
engagement 104.5, 375.3, 404.1, 436.2, 436.3, 457.3, 476.1, 562.8, 582.8, 615.4, 704.11, 724.5, 777.3, 898.1, 983.3
engagement book 549.11, 582.8
engagement ring 498.6
engage oneself 404.3, 476.5
engage the attention 983.13
engage the mind 983.13
engage the thoughts 931.20, 983.13
engage with 457.17
engaging 97.7, 377.8, 983.20
en garde (n) 760.4 (a) 399.8
engender 78.8, 818.14, 886.10, 890.7, 892.12
engenderer 886.4, 892.7
engendering 78.2, 892.1
engenderment 78.2, 892.1
engild 35.14, 43.3
engine 858.10, 1040.3, 1075.9
engine driver 178.12
engineer (n) 178.12, 381.6, 461.14, 726.7, 892.7, 1043.2 (v) 381.9, 409.12, 415.10, 573.8, 886.10, 892.11, 1043.4
engineered 354.30
engineering 381.5, 892.2, 928.4, 1039.6, 1043.1
engineers 1039.6
engineman 178.12
engine part 1040.3
engine-room officer 183.7
enginery 1040.3
engines of war 462.11
engird 209.7
Englishable 341.17
English as it is spoken 523.5
English breakfast 8.6
English Channel 239.1
English garden 1069.10
Englishing 341.3
Englishism 523.8
English literature 547.12, 718.1
English muffin 10.31
English rose 647.6
English-speaking 524.31
English system of measurement 300.1
engorge 8.25, 187.11, 395.10, 672.4, 994.4
engorged 994.6
engorgement 187.4, 993.3, 994.1
engraft 191.6, 800.7, 855.9
engrafted 855.13
engrafting 191.1
engrail 47.7
engrailed 47.9
engram 92.29, 989.1
engrave 93.16, 284.14, 290.3, 498.9, 517.19, 548.14, 549.15, 713.9, 715.5, 855.9, 989.17
engraved 284.17, 290.4, 713.11, 715.7, 855.13
engraved invitation 440.4
engravement 713.2
engraven 715.7
engrave on 93.16
engraver 550.1, 716.6, 716.8
engraver's proof 548.5
engraving 284.11, 290.1, 517.5, 712.1, 712.10, 712.16, 713.2, 715.1
engraving tool 713.8
engross 187.13, 259.8, 469.6, 547.19, 733.7, 737.26, 931.20, 983.13
engrossed 547.22, 931.22, 983.17, 985.11
engrossed in 983.17
engrossed in thought 931.22
engrossing 983.20
engrossment 187.6, 360.1, 469.3, 547.1, 547.10, 570.3, 931.3, 983.3, 985.2
engross the mind 983.13
engross the thoughts 931.20, 983.13
engulf 187.11, 238.17, 367.7, 395.21, 993.14
engulfed 238.25, 275.14, 1065.17
engulfment 187.4, 238.6, 367.2
enhance 119.2, 251.5, 392.9, 912.7
enhanced 119.4, 251.7, 392.13

enhancement 119.1, 251.2, 355.1, 392.1
enharmonic (n) 709.14 (a) 709.27
enharmonic diesis 709.20
enharmonic interval 709.20
enharmonic note 709.14
enharmonic scale 709.6
enharmonic tetrachord 709.8
enharmonic tie 709.12
enigma 345.5, 522.7, 522.8, 930.6, 938.10, 971.3, 971.8, 1013.7
enigmatic 122.10, 345.11, 522.17, 539.4, 930.16, 971.27, 974.6
enigmatical 522.17
enigmaticalness 522.6
enigmatic question 522.8
enisle 235.5
enjoin 420.8, 422.6, 428.7, 444.3, 643.4
enjoinder 422.1, 428.1, 444.1
enjoining 428.1
enjoy 63.5, 95.13, 469.4
enjoyable 97.6
enjoyableness 97.1
enjoy a certain position 765.5
enjoyer 387.9, 470.1
enjoy good health 83.6
enjoy good relations with 587.9
enjoying health 83.8
enjoyment 95.1, 743.1
enjoyment of property 387.7
enjoy oneself 95.14
enjoy one's own company 583.4
enjoy prosperity 1010.7
enjoy single blessedness 565.5
enjoy the use of 387.10
enkindle 105.12, 375.18, 1020.22
enkindled 1019.27
enkindling 1020.27
enlace 740.6
enlaced 740.7
enlacement 740.1
enlarge 119.2, 251.4, 257.15, 259.4, 259.5, 538.7, 714.15, 861.6
enlarged 119.4, 251.7, 259.10
enlargement 119.1, 251.1, 259.1, 355.1, 538.6, 714.5, 785.5, 861.1
enlarge on 861.6
enlarge the mind 568.10
enlarge upon 538.7
enlarging 538.15
enleagued 805.6
enlighten 341.10, 392.9, 521.6, 551.8, 568.10, 977.2, 1025.28
enlightened 920.19, 928.18, 977.5, 1025.39
enlightener 551.5
enlightening 341.15, 551.18, 568.18, 977.4, 979.13
enlightenment 341.4, 392.3, 551.1, 568.1, 928.4, 941.1, 977.1
enlist 191.4, 375.22, 476.5, 615.17, 617.14, 825.5
enlisted man 461.8
enlistee 461.18, 617.11
enlistees 461.26
enlisting 458.8
enlist into service 387.14
enlistment 187.2, 375.3, 549.14, 615.7, 825.4
enlist under the banner of 450.4
enliven 9.2, 17.10, 105.13, 109.7, 306.10, 375.20, 743.21
enlivened 9.4, 306.12
enlivening 17.15, 109.16, 375.26
enlivenment 9.1, 17.8, 375.9
enmesh 356.20, 480.17, 898.2, 1012.11, 1013.15
enmeshed in 898.5
enmeshment 356.1, 898.1
enmist 319.7
enmity 99.2, 103.2, 451.2, 456.1, 457.1, 589.1
ennead 882.5
enneadic 882.21
enneagon 882.5
Enneagram 689.4
enneahedral 882.21
enneahedron 882.5
enneastyle 882.21
enneastylos 882.5
ennoble 446.2, 662.13
ennobled 136.12, 608.10, 662.18
ennoblement 446.1, 662.8
ennui 96.1, 118.3, 331.6
enormity 156.2, 247.1, 257.7, 655.2, 661.3
enormous 247.7, 257.20, 993.16, 1000.9
enormousness 247.1, 257.7, 993.1
enough (n) 991.1 (a) 107.11, 991.6
enough and then some 991.2
enough and to spare 991.2, 993.2
enough in all conscience 993.2, 994.1
enough said 399.1
enough to drive one mad 98.25
enough to get by on 991.1
enough to go around 991.1
enough to live on 991.1
enough to make a preacher swear 98.25
enough to provoke a saint 98.25
enough to try the patience of Job 98.25
enough to wake the dead 53.11
enough to wake the seven sleepers 53.11
enplane 188.15
enplanement 188.3
en quad 548.7
enqueue 812.6
enrage 105.12, 152.25, 1020.18
enraged 152.32, 671.18
enragement 152.5
en rapport 455.3
enrapture 95.10, 104.22, 377.7
enraptured 95.17, 104.27, 105.25, 122.9
enravish 95.10, 377.7
enravished 95.17, 122.9
enravishing 97.7, 377.8
enravishment 97.2
en règle 807.6
enrich 7.20, 392.9, 498.8, 545.7, 618.9, 890.8
enriched 392.13
enricher 890.4
enriching 890.11
enrichment 7.14, 392.1, 890.3
enrobe 5.39
enroll 191.4, 549.15, 570.11, 615.17, 617.14, 871.8
enrolled 549.17
enrollee 461.18, 617.11
enrollment 187.2, 549.14, 615.7, 871.7
ens 761.2
ensanguine 1004.7
ensanguined 1004.11
ensate 285.13
ensconce 159.16, 159.17, 346.6
ensconced 159.18
ensconce oneself 159.17
enscroll 549.15
ensemble 5.6, 229.1, 707.11, 710.12, 710.16, 797.5
ensemble, the 792.3
ensemble music 708.18
ensemble singing 708.18
ensepulcher 309.19
enshrine 212.5, 309.19, 662.13, 685.5, 912.6
enshrined 662.18, 912.9
enshrine in the memory 989.12
enshrinement 662.8, 685.3, 912.1
enshroud 5.39, 295.20, 346.6
ensiform 285.13
ensign 575.19, 647.1, 647.7
ensilage 10.4
enskied 685.8
ensky 662.13, 685.5, 912.6
enskyed 662.18
enskying 662.8, 685.3
enskyment 662.8
enslave 432.8, 480.19, 612.15
enslaved 432.14
enslavement 432.1, 480.4
ensnare 356.20, 377.5, 382.9, 480.17, 941.7
ensnarement 356.1
ensnarl 356.20, 1012.11
en space 224.1
ensphere 209.7, 260.8
enstamp 548.14
ensue 815.2, 835.3, 887.4
ensue from 887.5
ensuing (n) 835.1 (a) 815.4, 835.4, 887.6
ensure 438.9, 970.11, 1008.18
ensured 438.11
ensuring 970.8
entail (n) 479.2 (v) 478.18, 517.17, 519.4, 629.3, 772.4, 886.12
entailed 420.12, 887.6, 963.12
entailment 629.1, 772.2, 963.1
entangle 356.20, 480.17, 797.10, 799.3, 898.2, 985.7, 1012.11, 1013.15
entangled 799.4
entangled in 898.5
entanglement 104.5, 356.1, 799.1, 800.1, 898.1
entelechy 763.3, 767.2
entente 437.2, 587.3, 788.2
entente cordiale 437.2, 587.3
enter 33.8, 189.7, 191.3, 549.15, 617.14, 628.8, 818.9, 871.8
enter a caveat 379.3
enter a plea 598.19
enter a pleading 598.19
enter a protest 333.5
entered 549.17, 871.9
entering (n) 549.14 (a) 186.9, 189.12
enter into 476.5, 796.3, 800.5, 818.9
enter into a gentlemen's agreement 436.5
enter into competition with 457.18
enter into one's view 332.9
enter into one's views 455.2
enter into possession of 472.8
enter into the feelings of 332.9, 455.2
enter into the ideas of 332.9, 455.2
enter into the spirit of 93.11
enter key 1042.18
enter on 404.3, 725.15, 818.9
enteron 207.4
enter one's mind 931.18
enter orbit 1075.12
enterovirus 85.42
enterprise 17.2, 328.3, 330.7, 381.1, 403.1, 404.1, 492.4, 492.6, 617.9, 724.1
enterpriser 381.6, 730.1
enterprise zone 230.6, 739.3
enterprising 17.13, 330.23, 404.8, 492.21
enterprisingness 330.7
entertain 474.7, 582.20, 585.8, 743.21, 931.14
entertain a belief 953.13
entertain a feeling 93.10
entertain an opinion 953.13
entertain a theory 951.9
entertain doubts 955.6
entertained 743.26
entertainer 707.1
entertain guests 585.8
entertain ideas 931.8
entertaining 743.27
entertainment 8.5, 95.1, 582.11, 704.12, 743.1, 743.13
entertainment industry 743.13
entertainment industry, the 704.1
entertain respect for 155.4
entertain the hope 124.6
entertain the idea of 931.16
entertain the inner man 8.20
entertain thoughts of 931.16
enter the arena 609.39
enter the arena with 457.16
enter the church 692.7
enter the lists 609.39
enter the ring with 457.16
enter upon 404.3, 818.9
enter with a will 324.3
enthrall 95.10, 377.7, 432.8, 983.13
enthralled 122.9, 432.14, 983.18

enthralling 97.7, 377.8, 983.20
enthrallment 377.1, 432.1
enthrone 615.12, 662.13
enthroned 662.18
enthronement 615.3, 662.8
enthrone one's own will 418.4
enthuse 17.10, 101.7
enthused 101.10
enthusiasm 17.4, 101.1, 324.1, 544.5, 926.12, 983.2
enthusiast 101.4, 330.8, 770.15, 926.18, 986.13
enthusiastic 17.13, 93.18, 101.10, 324.5, 544.13, 983.16
enthusiastic about 101.10
enthymematic 935.22
enthymematical 935.22
enthymeme 935.6
entice 377.5
enticement 377.1
enticer 377.4
enticing 375.27, 377.8
enticingness 122.3
entify 763.5
entincture 797.11
entire (n) 76.8, 311.10 (a) 792.9, 794.9, 960.2, 1002.7
entire horse 76.8, 311.10
entireness 794.1, 1002.2
entire satisfaction 107.1
entirety 792.1, 794.1
entirety, the 792.3
entitle 443.11, 527.11
entitled 443.17, 639.9
entitledness 639.1
entitled to 639.10
entitlement 436.1, 443.3, 639.1
entitlement generation 651.1
entity 306.4, 761.1, 761.2, 763.3, 792.2, 872.4, 1052.4
entoderm 2.4
entoil 356.20, 1012.11
entomb 212.6, 309.19
entombment 309.1
entourage 166.2, 209.1, 769.6
entr'acte 704.7, 826.1
entrails 2.16, 2.18, 207.4
entrain 177.33, 188.15
entrainment 188.3
entrammel 428.10, 1012.11
entrance (n) 187.3, 189.1, 189.5, 191.1, 197.19, 214.1, 239.1, 292.6 (v) 22.20, 95.10, 377.7, 691.7
entranced 95.17, 122.9, 986.25
entrance fee 630.6
entrance hall 197.19
entrancement 97.2, 691.2
entrancer 357.1
entranceway 189.5, 197.19
entrancing 97.7, 377.8, 691.11
entrant 189.4, 452.2, 572.9, 818.2
entrap 356.20, 429.15, 480.17, 1012.11
entrapment 356.1, 377.1
entreat 440.11
entreating 440.17
entreaty 375.5, 440.2, 696.4
entree 8.10, 10.7, 187.3, 189.1
entrée 8.10, 187.3, 189.1
entremets 8.10
entrench 214.5, 460.9, 855.9
entrenched 460.12, 853.7, 855.13
entrenchment 214.1, 290.2, 460.5, 855.2
entrepôt 386.6
entrepreneur 381.6, 730.1
entrepreneurial 730.12
entresol 197.23
entropic 810.12, 971.19
entropy 173.4, 263.1, 551.7, 804.1, 810.1, 852.1, 971.1
entrust 478.16, 615.10, 622.6
entrusting 615.1
entrustment 478.2, 615.1
entrust with information 551.11
entry 187.3, 189.1, 189.5, 197.19, 292.6, 549.4, 549.14, 628.5
entry fee 630.6
entry level 818.1
entry-level 798.6, 818.16
entry-level employee 818.2
entry visa 443.7
entryway 189.5, 197.19
entwine 740.6, 1012.11
entwined 740.7
entwinement 740.1
entwining (n) 740.1 (a) 740.8
enucleate 192.10, 255.10
enucleation 192.1
enumerable 1017.25
enumerate 244.4, 801.7, 871.8, 1017.17
enumerated 871.9
enumeration 801.2, 871.1, 1017.9
enumerative 801.9, 1017.24
enunciate 334.5, 352.12, 524.22
enunciated 334.9, 524.29
enunciation 334.1, 352.2, 524.5
enunciative 334.8, 352.18
enunciator 353.3
enunciatory 334.8
envelop 5.39, 209.6, 295.20, 346.6
envelope (n) 206.2, 295.18, 662.6 (v) 459.19
enveloped 209.10, 295.31
enveloping 209.8, 295.35
envelopment 209.5, 212.1, 291.4, 295.1, 295.18, 459.5
envenom 85.52, 110.16, 589.7, 1000.6
envenomed 82.7, 144.22
envenoming 393.2
enviable 100.30
envious 108.7, 153.5, 154.3
enviousness 154.1
environ 158.9, 209.6
environal 209.9
environed 209.10
environing 209.8, 766.8
environing circumstances 209.1, 766.2
environing phenomena 831.4
environment 159.1, 209.1, 209.5, 228.18, 766.2
environment, the 209.4, 1072.1
environmental 209.9, 766.8
environmental activism 397.1
environmental activist 1072.3
environmental artist 716.6
environmental assessment 1072.1
environmental auditing 1072.1
environmental conservation 397.1
environmental control 1072.1
environmental destruction 1072.2
environmental disease 85.32
environmental engineer 1043.2
environmental engineering 1043.1
environmental hazard 85.32
environmental impact analysis 1072.1
environmentalism 397.1
environmentalist 1072.3
environmentally conscious 1072.1
environmentally friendly 1072.1
environmental management 1072.1
environmental monitoring 1072.1
environmental policy 1072.1
environmental pollutant 1001.3, 1072.2
environmental pollution 82.1, 1000.3, 1072.2
environmental protection 1072.1
environmental science 1072.1
environment-friendly 397.12
environmentology 1072.1
environs 159.1, 209.1, 223.1, 231.1
envisage 130.5, 380.5, 772.3, 839.6, 931.17, 961.5, 986.15
envisaged 380.8, 772.5, 839.8
envisagement 381.1, 772.1, 839.1, 961.1
envisaging (n) 986.6 (a) 772.6
envision 130.5, 380.5, 839.6, 931.17, 961.5, 986.15
envisioned 380.8, 839.8
envisioning 986.6
envisionment 839.1, 961.1
envoi 254.2, 720.10, 817.1, 820.1
envoy 576.2, 576.6
envoy extraordinary 576.6
envy (n) 108.1, 153.1, 154.1, 654.3, 655.3 (v) 154.2
envying 154.3
enweb 356.20
enwrap 5.39, 209.6, 212.9, 295.20
enwrapment 212.2, 295.1
enwrapped 212.12, 295.31
enwrapping (n) 295.1 (a) 209.8
Enyo 458.12
enzyme 7.9, 7.10
enzymic 298.17
enzymologist 7.15
enzymology 7.16
eolian deposit 234.1, 1059.6
eolith 842.6
eolithic 842.20
eon 824.4
eonian 829.7
eons 823.1
Eos 314.1
epact 255.8, 832.5
epagoge 935.3
epagogic 935.22
Epaminondas and Pelopidas 588.6
eparch 575.12
epaulet 647.5
épée fencing 760.4
epeirogeny 237.6
epenthetic vowel 524.12
ephemera 557.4, 828.5
ephemeral (n) 310.3, 828.5 (a) 307.33, 310.44, 764.5, 828.7
ephemerality 764.1, 828.1
ephemeralness 764.1, 828.1
ephemerid 828.5
ephemerides 828.5
ephemeris 555.1, 828.5, 832.8
ephemeron 828.5
ephor 596.2
epiblast 2.4
epic (n) 413.10, 719.2 (a) 257.20, 720.16, 722.9
epical 257.20, 722.9
epicalyx 310.28
epicanthic fold 2.9
epicanthus 2.9
epicarp 295.3
epicarpal 2.27, 295.32
epicedial 115.22
epicedium 115.6
epicence 75.17
epicene 75.31
epicenism 75.12, 77.2
epicenity 75.12, 77.2
epicenter 208.5, 671.5
epicentral 208.11
epic fail 975.3
epic film 706.2
epic poet 720.12
epicranium 198.8
epic theater 704.1
epicure 8.16, 496.6, 663.3
epicurean (n) 496.6, 663.3 (a) 11.6, 63.8, 95.18, 663.5
Epicureanism 952.3
epicureanism 8.15, 95.4, 496.4, 663.1, 672.2
epicurism 8.15, 496.4, 663.1, 672.2
epicycle 280.7
epicyclic 280.11
epicyclic train 1040.4
epicycloid 280.7
epidemial 85.62
epidemic (n) 85.5 (a) 85.62, 864.12, 991.7
epidemicity 85.4
epidemiologist 81.3
epidemiology 81.2, 85.4
epidermal 2.27, 276.5, 295.32
epidermic 2.27, 206.7, 295.32
epidermis 2.4, 206.2, 276.1, 295.3
epigenesis 78.6
epigenetic 78.16
epiglottis 2.22, 524.18
epigram 489.7, 537.3, 974.1
epigrammatic 537.6, 974.6
epigrammatical 537.6, 974.6

epigrammatist 489.12
epigrammatize 974.5
epigraph 546.5, 937.2, 974.4
epigrapher 719.3
epigraphic 312.13, 549.18
epigraphy 341.8, 719.1, 842.4
epilepsy 85.6, 917.6
epileptic (n) 85.43 (a) 85.61
epilogue 254.2, 704.7, 793.2, 817.1, 820.1
Epimenides 921.4
epinephrine 86.9
epiphanic 348.9, 683.13
epiphany 31.1, 33.1, 348.1, 683.10, 934.1
epiphenomenalism 1052.6
epiphytotic 85.62
episcopacy 417.7, 698.2
episcopal 698.13
Episcopalian 675.20
episcopalian 698.13
episcopalianism 698.3
episcopal vestments 702.1
episcopate 698.2
episode 213.2, 538.4, 722.4, 813.1, 831.2, 926.7
episodic 213.9, 538.13, 813.4
epispastic 86.31
episperm 295.15
episteme 413.9
epistemological idealism 1053.3
epistemological logic 935.2
epistemological realism 1052.6
epistemological realist 1052.7
epistle 553.2
Epistles 683.4
Epistle side 219.1
epistolary 553.14
epistolary communication 553.1
epistolary intercourse 553.1
epitaph 309.18
epitaphic 309.22
epitaphist 309.7
epitasis 917.6
epithalamic 563.18
epithalamium 563.3
epithalamy 563.3
epithelium 2.4
epithem 86.33
epithet (n) 513.4, 527.3, 527.7, 974.4 (v) 513.7
epithetic 513.8, 527.15
epithetical 513.8, 527.15
epithetize 513.7
epitome 268.3, 349.7, 557.1, 659.4, 767.2, 786.4, 1002.4
epitomist 268.4
epitomization 268.3
epitomize 268.6, 786.7
epitomized 268.9
epitomizer 268.4
epitrite 720.8
epizootic 85.62
epoch 824.5
epochal 850.7
epoch-making 997.23
epode 720.10
eponym 526.2, 527.3
eponymic 527.16
eponymous 527.16
eponymy 526.16
epopt 699.15
epos 719.2, 720.5
epoxy resin 803.4
Epsom salts 86.17
equability 106.3, 781.1
equable 670.13, 781.5
equal (n) 790.4, 862.2 (v) 203.4, 790.5, 790.6, 999.11 (a) 203.6, 264.4, 477.13, 778.8, 781.5, 790.7, 863.5
equality 264.1, 649.1, 778.1, 790.1
equalization 264.2
equalize 201.6, 264.3, 287.5, 781.4, 788.7, 790.6
equalized 790.7
equalizer 462.10, 820.4
equalizing (n) 790.2 (a) 863.5, 900.9
equalizing pulse 1035.4
equal on both sides 264.4
equal opportunity 790.2, 843.2
equal opportunity employer 249.4, 574.3
equal out 790.6
equal rights 790.1
Equal Rights Amendment 431.1
equal share 477.5
equal temperament 709.4
equal time 1035.2
equal to 18.14, 107.11, 405.18, 413.24, 991.6
Equanil 86.12
equanimity 106.3, 781.1
equanimous 106.13, 790.9
equate 203.5, 775.6, 790.6
equating 790.2
equation 790.1, 790.2, 1017.2
equator 231.3, 280.3, 819.1, 875.3, 1019.11, 1073.16
equator coordinates 300.5
equatorial 819.4, 1019.24
equatorial low 318.9
equerry 577.4, 1070.2
equestrian (n) 178.8 (a) 311.45
equestrian director 704.23, 707.3
equestrienne 178.8
equiangular 790.10
equibalanced 790.9
equid 311.5
equidimensional 790.10
equidistance (n) 203.1, 208.1, 819.2 (v) 203.5
equidistant 203.6, 208.11, 819.4
equilateral 264.4, 790.10
equilibration 790.2
equilibrious 106.13
equilibrist 707.3
equilibrium 106.3, 264.1, 329.1, 533.2, 670.1, 777.1, 781.1, 790.1, 812.1, 855.1, 900.2
equilibrize 781.4
equine (n) 311.5, 311.10 (a) 311.45
equinoctial (n) 318.11, 1073.16 (a) 313.9, 1073.25
equinoctial circle 1073.16
equinoctial colure 1073.16
equinoctial line 1073.16
equinox 313.7, 1073.16
equip 5.41, 385.8, 405.8, 892.10
equipage 179.5, 385.4
equiparant 790.8
equipment 385.1, 385.4, 405.1, 405.2, 413.4, 749.4, 750.1, 752.1
equipoise 338.2, 790.1
equipollence 777.1, 790.1
equipollent (n) 790.4 (a) 777.10, 790.8
equiponderance 790.1
equiponderant 790.9
equiponderate 338.5
equiponderous 790.9
equipped 385.13, 405.16
equiproportional 790.10
equisided 790.10
equisized 790.10
equispaced 203.6, 790.10
equitability 979.5
equitable 649.7, 649.9, 979.12
equitable interest 471.4
equitable jurisdiction 594.1
equitableness 649.1
equitant 295.36
equitation 177.6
equity 471.4, 649.1, 738.2, 790.1
equity capital 728.15, 737.19
equity loan 438.4
equity security 738.2
equivalence 777.1, 778.1, 784.1, 788.1, 790.1, 943.3
equivalency 790.1
equivalent (n) 338.2, 778.3, 784.3, 790.4, 862.2 (a) 777.10, 778.8, 784.11, 788.9, 790.8, 862.8, 863.5
equivocacy 539.1
equivocal (n) 539.2 (a) 344.11, 354.34, 522.13, 539.4, 779.8, 797.14, 936.14, 971.16
equivocality 489.8, 539.1, 539.2, 789.2, 873.1, 971.5
equivocalness 539.1, 789.2, 936.1, 971.5
equivocate 344.7, 354.19, 362.8, 368.8, 539.3, 914.4, 936.9
equivocation 344.4, 354.9, 362.2, 368.1, 522.1, 539.2, 779.3, 873.1, 936.1, 936.5
equivocator 357.9, 362.5, 936.7
equivocatory 539.4, 914.7, 936.14
equivoke 520.2
equivoque 489.8, 539.2
era 824.5
eradicable 255.13, 990.10
eradicant 1001.3
eradicate 192.10, 255.10, 395.14, 762.7, 773.5
eradication 192.1, 255.3, 395.6, 773.2
eradicative 192.17, 395.27
eradicator 308.11, 395.9
Era of Good Feeling 824.5
era of prosperity 1010.4
erasable 990.10
erase 255.12, 308.14, 395.16, 820.6, 1044.7
erase all doubt 970.11
erased 990.8
erase from the memory 990.6
eraser 395.9
erasing 1044.2
erasure 34.1, 255.3, 255.5, 395.7, 1044.2
Erato 710.22, 720.11, 986.2
Erebus 682.5, 1027.1
erect (v) 200.9, 266.5, 892.8, 912.5, 1043.4 (a) 136.8, 200.11, 644.13, 912.9
erect bearing 136.2
erectile 912.10
erecting 200.4
erection 75.5, 200.4, 228.5, 266.2, 892.2, 912.1
erective 912.10
erectness 200.1, 644.1
erectness of posture 200.1
erector 912.3
eremite 565.2, 584.5, 667.2
eremitic 584.10, 667.4, 982.3
eremitical 584.10, 667.4
eremitism 584.2, 667.1
Erewhon 986.11
erg 17.7
ergonomically 717.7
ergonomics 717.5
ergonomy 717.5
ergophobia 331.5
ergophobic 331.19
ergotism 85.31
Erinyes, the 152.10, 507.3, 680.10
Eris 456.1
eristic (n) 935.4, 935.12 (a) 456.17, 935.19
eristical 456.17, 935.19
erlking 680.7
ermine 647.2, 647.3
ermines 647.2
erminites 647.2
erminois 647.2
erode 34.2, 168.2, 252.6, 255.9, 388.3, 393.20, 393.21, 473.5, 806.3, 1044.7
erode away 388.3, 393.19, 1044.7
eroded 252.10, 388.5, 393.34, 393.43, 473.7
eroding 168.5, 393.44
erogenic 75.25
erogenous 75.25
eromania 75.5
Eros 104.1, 104.7
erose 289.5, 782.3
erosion 252.3, 255.1, 388.1, 393.5, 473.2, 806.1, 1044.2
erosive 255.13, 393.44, 806.5, 1044.10
erotic 75.25, 104.25, 665.29, 720.16
erotica 547.12, 663.2, 718.1
erotic art 666.4
eroticism 75.5, 665.5
eroticizing 75.26
erotic literature 547.12, 666.4, 718.1
eroticomania 665.5
eroticomaniac 665.11
eroticomaniacal 665.29
erotism 75.5
erotogenic 75.25
erotographomania 666.4
erotology 666.4

erotomania 75.5, 665.5
erotomaniac 75.16, 665.11
erotomaniacal 665.29
err 164.4, 410.14, 654.9, 655.4, 688.8, 948.2, 975.9
errability 971.7
errable 971.22
errancy 971.7, 975.1
errand 615.1, 724.2
errand boy 353.4, 432.5, 577.5
errand girl 577.5
errant 164.7, 177.37, 971.22, 975.16
errantry 164.1, 177.3, 652.2
errata 554.12
erratic (n) 927.3 (a) 164.7, 364.6, 782.3, 810.12, 851.3, 854.7, 870.9, 927.5, 971.16
erraticism 364.3, 854.2, 870.1, 927.1, 971.1
erraticness 851.1, 927.1, 971.1
erratum 975.3
errhine 2.32
erring 654.12, 975.16, 975.18
erring sister 665.16
erroneous 354.25, 531.4, 688.9, 975.16, 976.9, 1003.4
erroneousness 354.1, 975.1, 1003.1
error 342.1, 410.4, 414.5, 654.3, 655.2, 688.2, 745.3, 748.2, 948.1, 975.1, 975.3
error in judgment 948.1
error-prone 971.22
ersatz (n) 862.2 (a) 336.8, 354.26, 784.10, 862.8
erstwhile 814.5, 837.10
erubescence 41.3
erubescent 41.11
eruct 671.13, 909.25, 909.28
eructate 909.28
eructation 671.6, 909.7, 909.9
eructative 909.30
erudite 570.16, 928.21
eruditeness 928.5
erudition 570.1, 570.4, 920.5, 928.5
erupt 33.9, 85.47, 190.11, 369.10, 671.13, 818.13, 909.25
eruption 85.36, 105.9, 152.9, 671.6, 909.7
eruptive 105.28, 671.24
eruptiveness 105.10
erythema 41.1
erythematous 41.9
Erythraean sibyl 962.6
erythrism 41.1
erythristic 41.10
erythrocyte 2.25
erythroderma 41.1
erythromycin 86.29
escadrille 461.27, 461.29
escalade (n) 193.1, 459.4 (v) 193.11, 459.20
escalate 912.5
escalation 251.2, 912.1
escalator 193.3, 912.4
escalator clause 613.9, 624.4, 959.2
escalator plan 624.4
escalatory 912.10
escalier 193.3
escallop 10.15
escapable 368.14
escapade 404.2, 743.6
escape (n) 92.23, 188.1, 190.9, 222.4, 368.1, 369.1 (v) 190.12, 222.8, 368.7, 369.6, 431.8
escape artist 369.5
escape attention 984.5
escape by the skin of one's teeth 369.8
escape clause 369.4, 959.2
escaped 369.11
escapee 368.5, 369.5
escape earth 1075.12
escape hatch 346.5, 369.3, 369.4, 600.4, 959.2
escape into fantasy 92.23
escape key 1042.18
escape mechanism 92.23, 460.1
escape notice 32.3, 519.3, 984.5
escape one 522.10, 522.11, 984.5, 990.7
escape one's lips 524.27
escape prison 369.6
escaper 369.5
escape route 346.5
escape the memory 990.7
escape velocity 174.2, 1075.1, 1075.9
escapeway 346.5, 369.3, 959.2
escape with a whole skin 369.7
escape without penalty 369.7
escapism 92.23, 369.1
escapist 369.5, 986.13
escapologist 369.5
escapology 369.1
escargot 10.25
escarpment 200.3, 237.2
eschar 85.37, 295.14
eschara 703.12
escharotic (n) 1020.15 (a) 17.14, 68.6
eschatological 839.8
eschatology 820.1, 839.3
eschaton 395.2
escheat 603.3
escheatment 603.3
eschew 668.7
eschewal 668.2
eschew self-advertisement 139.7
escort (n) 104.11, 104.12, 769.5, 1008.7, 1008.14 (v) 769.8
escritoire 901.15
escrow 386.5, 438.2
escuela 567.1
esculent 8.33
escutcheon 647.2
esemplastic 986.18
esemplastic imagination 986.2
esemplastic power 920.1, 986.2
esexual 75.29
e-signature 332.4, 1042.11
esker 237.5
esne 432.7
esophagus 2.18
esoteric (n) 689.11 (a) 345.11, 345.14, 519.5, 519.7, 522.16, 689.23, 767.7, 865.12, 870.15, 952.10
esoterica 345.5, 689.1
esoterical 689.23
esotericism 522.2, 689.1
esoteric meaning 519.2
esoteric reality 767.5
esoterics 689.1
esoterism 689.1
esotery 522.2, 689.1
esotropia 28.5
espadrilles 5.27
especial 865.12
Esperanto 523.11
espial 27.2, 938.9, 941.1
espionage 27.2, 938.9
espionage agent 576.9
esplanade 383.2
espousal 371.4, 436.3
espousals 563.3
espouse 371.15, 509.13, 563.15, 600.10
espouse a belief 953.13
espouse a theory 951.9
espoused (n) 563.6 (a) 371.26, 563.21
espousement 563.3
espouser 563.6
esprit 93.3, 109.4, 450.1, 455.1, 489.1, 920.2
esprit de corps 450.1, 455.1, 587.2, 587.3, 617.13
esprit d'escalier 931.5
espy 27.12, 941.5
Esquire 648.3
esquire (n) 76.7, 104.12, 608.4 (v) 562.21
esquire (n) 769.5 (v) 769.8
ess 279.11
essay (n) 403.2, 547.10, 556.1, 942.2 (v) 403.6, 942.8
essayer 942.6
essayist 547.15, 556.3, 718.4
essayistic 556.6
essay-writing 547.2, 718.2
esse 761.1, 767.2
essence 69.1, 70.2, 192.8, 196.5, 518.1, 557.2, 761.1, 767.2, 792.6, 893.3, 932.1, 937.1, 997.6, 999.8
essenced 70.9
essence of life 306.2, 919.5
Essence of the Universe, the 677.3
Essene 675.21
essential (n) 767.2, 963.2, 997.6 (a) 192.18, 199.8, 767.9, 798.6, 963.13, 997.23
essential amino acid 7.6
essential element 7.11
essential facts 761.4
essentiality 767.1, 963.3
essentialization 79.4
essentialize 79.22, 192.16
essential matter 997.6
essential nature 767.2, 767.5
essentialness 963.3
essential oil 70.2, 1056.1
essential principle 767.2
essentials 761.4, 818.6, 963.2
essive 530.9
establish 159.16, 352.15, 373.9, 673.9, 818.11, 855.9, 886.10, 892.10, 957.10, 970.11
establishable 957.19
establish connection 343.8
established 159.18, 373.13, 373.18, 761.15, 842.12, 855.13, 957.20, 970.20, 973.13
Established Church 675.11
established fact 761.3
established way 373.1
establisher 892.7
establishing 818.1
Establishment 997.8
establishment 159.6, 159.7, 249.5, 266.2, 617.8, 736.1, 739.1, 809.4, 818.1, 853.1, 855.2, 892.4, 957.3, 970.8
Establishment, the 575.14, 612.3, 894.6
establish residence 159.17
estate 228.7, 245.2, 471.4, 607.1, 765.1, 809.2
estate agent 730.9
estate and effects 471.1
estate of freehold 471.5
esteem (n) 155.1, 509.1, 662.3, 696.1, 894.1, 997.2 (v) 104.20, 155.4, 509.9, 946.8, 953.11, 997.13
esteemed 104.23, 155.11, 662.15, 997.19
ester 1056.1
esterify 1060.8
esthesia 24.2
esthesis 24.2
esthetic 1016.17
esthetic criticism 723.1
estimable 155.12, 300.14, 509.20, 644.13, 662.15, 894.13, 997.19, 999.12, 1017.25
estimableness 509.7, 644.1
estimate (n) 300.1, 946.3, 953.6, 971.8 (v) 300.10, 946.9, 953.11, 1017.18
estimating 1017.24
estimation 155.1, 300.1, 630.3, 662.3, 946.3, 953.6, 1017.10
estimative 300.12, 1017.24
estimator 300.9, 1017.15
estivate 173.9, 313.8
estivating 173.14
estivation 173.4, 313.3
estoile 882.2
estop 1012.14
estoppel 1012.2
estrade 901.13
estral 75.28
estral cycle 75.5
estrange 456.14, 589.7, 802.8
estranged 566.7, 589.11, 802.21
estrangement 456.4, 566.1, 589.2, 802.1
estreat 603.5
E string 711.5
estrous 75.28, 850.8
estrous cycle 75.5
estrual 75.28
estrum 75.5
estrus 75.5
estuarine 182.58, 234.6, 242.2
estuarine area 240.4
estuary 190.9, 242.1
esurience 100.8
esurient 100.27, 672.6
étang 241.1
etc (n) 559.4 (a) 547.26

etch 713.10
etcher 716.8
etchhing 713.2
etching 712.1, 713.5
etching ball 713.8
etching ground 713.8
etching varnish 713.8
eternal 420.12, 677.17, 823.3, 829.7
eternal damnation 395.1, 682.1
eternal feminine, the 77.1
eternal home 839.2
eternalization 829.4
eternalize 829.5
eternal life 681.2, 829.3
eternally the same 677.17
eternalness 829.1
eternal object 932.2
eternal re-creation 829.4
eternal recurrence 829.4
eternal rest 307.1
eternal return 280.2, 829.4
eternal return, the 850.2
eternal sleep 307.1
eternal triangle 104.5
eternal universal 932.2
eternal verities 973.1
eternal youth 829.3
eterne 829.7
eternity, an 829.2
eternity 822.1, 823.1, 827.4, 829.1
eternize 829.5
Etesian winds 318.8
ether 25.3, 86.15, 272.2, 298.2, 317.1, 764.3, 1024.7, 1073.2
ethereal 270.16, 272.14, 298.10, 299.4, 317.12, 681.12, 764.6, 986.22, 988.7, 1053.7, 1067.9
ethereality 270.4, 298.1, 299.1, 764.1, 1053.1, 1067.3
etherealization 299.2, 689.19, 1067.5
etherealize 299.3, 689.20, 764.4
etherialism 1067.3
etheric 988.7
etheric body 689.17
etheric double 988.3
etheric self 988.3
etherification 1067.5
etherify 1067.8
etherize 25.4, 1067.8
ether space 1073.3
ethic 636.1
ethical 636.6, 641.13, 644.13
ethical code 636.1
ethical drug 86.4
ethical formalism 636.2
ethical hedonism 663.1
ethical investment 729.4
ethicality 636.3
ethicalness 636.3
ethical philosophy 636.2
ethical self 92.28, 636.5, 865.5
ethical system 636.1
ethics 636.1, 641.1, 952.2
ethnic (n) 312.5 (a) 559.7
ethnic cleansing 308.4
ethnic community 227.1
ethnic diversity 797.1
ethnic group 312.1, 617.4
ethnicism 312.1
ethnicity 312.1, 559.4, 773.3
ethnic joke 489.6
ethnic literature 718.1
ethnic majority 312.2
ethnic minority 312.2
ethnic music 708.11
ethnic vote 609.31
ethnoarchaeology 312.10
ethnobiology 1068.3
ethnocentric 617.18, 773.9
ethnocentricity 617.13
ethnocentrism 773.3
ethnographer 312.10
ethnographic 312.13
ethnography 312.10
ethnological 312.13
ethnologist 312.10
ethnology 312.10
ethnomusicologist 710.20
ethnomusicology 708.11
ethological 321.7, 636.6
ethology 321.3
ethonomics 636.2
ethos 373.2, 636.1, 767.4, 932.8, 953.6, 978.5
ethyl chloride 86.15, 1024.7
ethylene glycol 1024.8
etiolate 19.12, 36.5, 37.5
etiolated 16.12, 16.18, 19.15, 36.7, 36.8, 117.6, 393.34, 393.36
etiolation 16.1, 19.4, 36.3, 37.3, 117.1, 393.3
etiological 886.13
etiology 886.1, 888.1
etiquette 321.2, 373.1, 496.1, 504.3, 579.1, 580.3
étoffe 4.1
Etruscan 554.15
ettings 472.3
étude 556.1
étuvée 10.11
etymologer 523.15
etymologic 526.20
etymological 526.20
etymologist 523.15, 526.15
etymology 518.6, 526.16, 719.2
etymon 526.2, 526.16
eucalyptus 70.4
eucaryotic cell 305.4
Eucharist 701.7
eucharist 150.2
Eucharist, the 701.4
eucharistic 701.18
eucharistical 701.18
Eucharistic rites 701.8
euchre 356.18
euchromosome 305.8
eudaemonic 95.18
eudaemonics 636.2
eudaemonism 95.4
eudaimonia 95.2
eudemonism 95.4
eudiometer 1067.7
eugenics 392.1, 560.6
euhemerism 341.4
euhemerist 341.7
euhemeristic 341.15
euhemerize 341.10
eulogist 309.7, 509.8
eulogistic 309.22, 509.16
eulogium 509.5
eulogize 509.12
eulogizer 309.7, 509.8
eulogy 115.6, 309.4, 509.5, 543.2, 646.4
Eumenides, the 152.10, 507.3, 680.10
eumerogenesis 78.6
eumerogenetic 78.16
eumitosis 305.16
eunuch 19.6, 75.9
eunuchize 255.11
eunuchized 19.19, 75.29
euonym 527.3
eupathy 107.1
eupepsia 83.2
eupeptic 7.22, 83.8, 95.15, 107.7, 109.11
eupeptic mein 109.1
euphemism 500.5, 526.9, 533.3, 862.2
euphemistic 500.18
euphemize 344.7
euphonic 533.8, 708.48
euphonical 533.8
euphonious 533.8, 708.48
euphony 533.2, 708.3
euphoria 95.1, 107.1
euphoric 95.15, 107.7, 109.11, 116.10
euphoric mein 109.1
euphuism 500.5, 533.3, 536.1
euphuist 533.5, 545.5
euphuistic 500.18, 533.9, 545.8
euphuistical 533.9
Eurasia 231.6, 235.1
Eurasia Basin 275.5
Eurasian 797.8
Eurasian landmass 235.1
Eurasian plate 235.1
euripus 242.1
Euroclydon 318.8
Eurojargon 523.10
Europe 231.6, 235.1
European Boxing Union 754.1
European plan 8.11
European roulette 759.12
European wheel 759.12, 759.16
Eurotrash 250.2
Eurus 318.2
Euryale 690.9
eurythmic 264.4
eurythmics 264.1, 568.9
eurythmy 264.1
eustachian tube 2.10, 2.23
Euterpe 710.22, 720.11, 986.2
euthanasia 307.6, 308.1
euthanasiast 308.11
euthanatize 308.13
euthenics 392.1
eutrophication 1072.2
evacuate 12.13, 188.9, 370.5, 909.22, 909.24
evacuation 12.2, 188.1, 190.2, 370.1, 909.6
évacué 178.5
evacuee 160.4, 178.5, 368.5
evadable 368.14
evade 164.6, 344.7, 368.7, 369.6, 415.11, 467.5, 645.11, 903.7, 936.9
evader 344.5, 357.9, 369.5
evade responsibility 468.2
evade the issue 467.5, 936.9
evaluate 300.10, 630.11, 723.5, 801.8, 946.9
evaluated 630.14
evaluating 946.3
evaluation 300.1, 630.3, 801.3, 946.3
evaluative 723.6, 946.16
evaluative criticism 946.3
evaluator 300.9
evanesce 34.2, 828.6
evanescence 34.1, 168.1, 258.2, 764.1, 828.1
evanescent 34.3, 168.5, 258.14, 764.6, 828.7
evangel 353.2, 552.2, 699.6
evangelic 683.11
Evangelical (n) 675.20 (a) 675.28
evangelical 683.11, 687.7, 687.8
Evangelicalism 675.10
evangelicalism 687.5, 692.3
evangelicalist 699.6
evangelism 543.3, 692.3
evangelist 353.2, 543.5, 684.2, 696.9, 699.6, 858.9
evangelistic 683.11, 698.13
evangelization 858.6
evangelize 858.16, 953.18
Evangels 683.4
evaporability 1067.4
evaporable 1067.10
evaporate 34.2, 397.9, 762.6, 771.5, 828.6, 1066.6, 1067.8
evaporated 1066.9
evaporating 34.3
evaporation 34.1, 397.2, 473.2, 771.1, 1065.3, 1066.3, 1067.5
evaporative 1066.10, 1067.10
evaporator 1066.4, 1067.6
evasion 344.4, 345.1, 368.1, 369.1, 415.5, 467.1, 520.2, 903.3, 936.5
evasion of responsibility 468.1
evasive 164.9, 344.11, 345.15, 368.15, 645.16, 914.7, 936.14
evasive action 368.1
evasiveness 345.1, 368.1, 645.1
evasive reasoning 936.1
evasive reply 939.1
Eve 77.5
eve 315.2
even (n) 315.2 (v) 201.6, 264.3, 287.5, 781.4, 790.6 (a) 201.7, 203.6, 264.4, 277.6, 287.10, 467.7, 649.7, 670.13, 781.5, 790.7, 850.7, 863.5, 973.17, 1017.23
even break 759.6, 790.2, 843.2, 972.7
even chance 759.6, 966.1, 972.7
evenhanded 649.7, 649.9, 979.12
evenhandedness 649.1, 979.5
evening (n) 264.2, 315.2, 790.2 (a) 315.8
evening bag 195.2
evening damp 1065.4
evening devotions 696.8
evening dress 5.11
evening gown 5.11
evening meal 8.6
evening mist 316.1

evening of one's days 303.5
evening of the score 507.1
evening prayers 696.8
evening's close 315.2
evening services 696.8
evening star 1073.4
evening twilight 315.3
evening up 790.2
evening wear 5.11
even lot 738.3
even money 790.3
evenness 106.1, 201.1, 264.1, 287.1, 670.1, 781.1, 790.1, 850.1
even odds 759.6, 972.7
even off 790.6
even out 670.7, 781.4
evensong (n) 696.8 (a) 315.8
evensong hour 315.2
evensong time 315.2
even stephen 477.13
even-steven 264.4, 790.7
even-steven trade 863.2
event 743.9, 766.1, 831.1, 831.2, 887.1
even temper 106.1
even-tempered 106.10, 670.13
even tenor 781.2, 807.1
even-tenored 173.12
eventful 831.10
even the score 506.7, 507.4, 624.12
event horizon 843.5, 1073.8
eventide 315.2
even-toed ungulate 311.5
even trade 863.2
eventual 820.12, 831.11, 839.8
eventuality 766.1, 831.1, 839.1, 839.4, 887.1, 897.1, 966.1
eventuate 831.5, 887.4
eventuating 831.9
eventuation 831.1, 887.1
even up 264.3, 790.6
ever 820.5
ever-abiding 829.7
ever-bearing 829.8
ever-being 829.7
ever-blooming 829.8
ever-changing 854.6
ever-durable 829.7
ever-during 829.7
ever-duringness 829.1
ever-fresh 829.9
everglade 243.1
evergreen (n) 310.3, 310.10 (a) 310.39, 310.44, 827.10, 829.8, 841.7
evergreen forest 1069.8
everlasting 118.9, 677.17, 829.7, 829.9
everlasting fire 682.2
everlasting moment 822.1
everlastingness 829.1
everlasting torment 682.2
everliving 829.7
everness 829.1
ever-new 829.8, 841.7
ever-recurring 849.13
eversion 205.1
ever so many 884.6
evert 205.5
everted 205.7
every 864.15
every bit a 413.22
everybody 312.4, 606.1, 864.4
everybody and his brother 770.4
everybody and his uncle 770.4
everybody's fool 508.7
everyday 373.13, 499.6, 523.20, 798.6, 847.4, 850.6, 869.9
every inch a king 417.17, 608.10
every living soul 864.4
Everyman 606.1, 606.5, 864.3
everyman 864.3
every man for himself 418.6
every man Jack 864.4
every mother's son 864.4
every one 864.15
everyone 312.4, 606.1, 864.4
everyone and his brother 864.4
every other 850.7
ever-young 829.8
ever yours 820.5
everything 792.3, 864.4
everything bagel 10.31
everything but the kitchen sink 783.1, 792.3, 797.6
everything from soup to nuts 792.3
everything that is 1073.1
everywhere 221.13
Everywoman 606.1
everywoman 864.3
evict 160.6, 480.23, 909.15
evicted 160.10
evictee 586.4, 909.12
eviction 160.1, 480.7, 773.2, 909.2
evictor 909.11
evidence (n) 31.2, 348.1, 348.3, 517.9, 551.1, 598.8, 935.5, 957.1 (v) 348.5, 957.8
evident 31.6, 31.7, 348.8, 957.20
evidential 348.9, 517.23, 957.16
evidentiary 957.16
evidentness 31.2, 348.3
evil (n) 654.1, 654.3, 655.2, 1000.1, 1000.3, 1001.1, 1013.3 (a) 133.16, 638.3, 654.16, 1000.7
evil, the 660.11
evil child 660.8
evil courses 655.1
evil day 1011.6
evil dispensation 1011.5
evil-disposed 144.19
evil disposition 144.4
evildoer 144.14, 593.1, 660.8
evildoing (n) 655.1 (a) 655.5
evil eye 27.5, 144.4, 513.1, 691.1, 1000.4
evil-eyed 1000.11
evil-faced 1000.11
evil-fashioned 1000.11
evil-favored 1000.11, 1015.7
evil fortune 1011.5
evil genius 680.6, 1000.4
evil-gotten 1000.11
evilhearted 654.15
evil hour 844.2
evil-hued 1000.11
evil humor 110.1
evil-humored 110.18
evil intent 144.5
evil-looking 1000.11, 1015.7
evil man 660.8
evil-minded 654.15, 1000.11
evil nature 654.1
evilness 654.4, 1000.1
evil person 660.8
evil portent 399.2
evil-qualitied 1000.11
evil reputation 661.1
evil repute 661.1
evil-shaped 1000.11
evil-smelling 71.5
evil speaking 513.3
evil spirit 680.6
evil spirits 678.5, 680.1
evil star 1000.4, 1011.5
evil-starred 133.16, 1011.14
evil temper 110.1
evil-tempered 110.18
evil woman 660.8
evince 348.5, 957.8
evincement 348.1
evincible 957.19
evincive 348.9, 957.17
eviscerate 16.10, 192.13
eviscerated 16.18
evisceration 16.5, 192.4
evocation 192.5, 349.2, 420.5, 690.4, 691.4
evocative 192.17, 349.14, 989.21
evoke 192.14, 349.9, 375.13, 420.11, 690.11, 784.7, 886.11, 989.9
evoke a response 903.8
evoke from the dead 690.11
evolute 281.2
evolution 392.2, 861.1, 1017.2
evolutional 861.8
evolutionary 861.8
evolutionary change 861.1
evolutionism 636.2, 861.4
evolutionist 861.8
evolutionistic 861.8
evolve 192.10, 392.10, 538.7, 861.5, 892.8, 892.12
evolve into 858.17
evolvement 192.1, 861.1
evolving (n) 861.1 (a) 861.8
evulgate 351.5
evulgation 351.2, 352.1
evulse 192.10
evulsion 192.1
ewe 77.9, 311.7
ewe lamb 77.9, 311.7
ewer 79.12
ex 170.4
exacerbate 26.7, 96.14, 110.16, 119.2, 251.5, 393.9, 589.7
exacerbated 119.4, 393.27
exacerbation 96.3, 105.11, 119.1, 251.2
exact (v) 192.15, 421.5, 424.5, 480.22, 630.12, 643.4, 963.9 (a) 339.12, 533.6, 580.10, 766.9, 944.7, 973.17
exacta 759.4
exact counterpart 778.3
exact description 349.2
exacted 643.8
exacting 192.17, 339.12, 421.9, 425.6, 495.9, 632.12, 1013.17
exactingness 339.3, 425.1
exaction 192.6, 421.1, 630.6, 643.1
exactitude 339.3, 533.1, 973.5
exactive 192.17
exact likeness 349.5
exactly alike 778.7
exact mates 873.4
exact measure 991.1
exactment 630.6
exactness 339.3, 973.5
exact point 159.1
exact revenge 507.4
exact science 928.10
exact spot 159.1
exact time, the 832.2
exact truth, the 973.3
exaggerate 119.2, 251.5, 265.6, 350.3, 354.19, 355.3, 910.4, 949.2, 993.10, 993.11
exaggerated 355.4, 949.3, 993.16
exaggerated lengths 355.1
exaggerated respect 155.1
exaggerate one's own merits 502.6
exaggerating (n) 355.1 (a) 355.5
exaggeration 119.1, 251.2, 350.1, 354.9, 354.11, 355.1, 532.2, 910.1, 949.1, 993.1
exaggerative 355.5
exaggerator 502.5
exalt 109.8, 155.4, 251.4, 446.2, 509.12, 662.13, 685.5, 696.12, 912.6
exaltation 95.2, 272.1, 446.1, 509.5, 652.2, 662.5, 662.8, 685.3, 696.2, 912.1
exalted 95.17, 109.11, 247.9, 272.14, 608.10, 652.6, 662.18, 685.8, 912.9
exaltedness 662.5
exalt to the skies 662.13
exam 938.2
examen 938.2
examinant 938.17, 938.19
examinate 938.19
examination 27.6, 91.12, 541.2, 541.6, 556.1, 598.5, 935.4, 938.2, 938.3, 938.12
examinational 938.37
examination by ear 48.1
examination of conscience 113.3
examination room 197.25
examinatorial 938.37
examine 27.14, 90.14, 541.11, 570.12, 938.21, 938.24
examine by ear 48.10
examine cursorily 938.26
examinee 938.19
examine one's conscience 113.6
examine point by point 938.25
examiner 541.7, 801.5, 938.16, 938.17
examine side by side 943.4
examine the books 628.9
examine thoroughly 938.25
examining 938.37
examining room 197.25
examining side by side 943.1
example (n) 62.4, 349.7, 399.1, 786.2, 957.5 (v) 957.13

exanimate 307.29, 331.20, 1055.5
exarch 575.12
exasperate 96.13, 98.15, 119.2, 152.24
exasperated 96.21, 119.4, 135.6, 152.27
exasperating 98.22, 119.5
exasperation 96.2, 98.7, 105.11, 119.1, 152.1, 375.4
exasperative 119.5
Excalibur 462.5
ex cathedra 970.18
excavate 192.10, 192.11, 275.9, 284.15, 292.14, 941.4, 1043.4
excavation 192.1, 224.2, 275.8, 284.4, 284.11, 941.1
excavator 192.9, 284.10
excecate (v) 30.7 (a) 30.10
excecation 30.1
exceed 247.5, 249.6, 910.4, 993.9
exceeding 249.12
excel 249.6, 999.11
excel at 413.18
excel in 413.18
excellence 249.1, 496.1, 662.5, 997.1, 999.1
Excellency 648.2
excellent 249.12, 413.22, 496.7, 662.18, 999.12
excellent accommodations 121.3
excellent companion 582.16
excellent manners 504.3
excelling 249.12
except 255.10, 372.2, 430.14
excepted 372.3, 430.30, 773.7
exception 122.2, 333.2, 372.1, 421.2, 430.8, 510.4, 600.2, 773.1, 870.5, 959.1
exceptionable 108.10, 510.24
exceptional 122.10, 247.10, 572.12, 773.9, 865.12, 870.14, 927.5, 997.19
exceptionality 870.2
exceptionalness 870.2
exception to the rule 780.3
excerpt (n) 557.3 (v) 371.14
excerpta 557.4
excerption 557.3
excerpts 557.4
excess (n) 256.4, 355.1, 632.4, 640.1, 669.1, 910.1, 993.1 (a) 993.17
excess baggage 391.1
excessive 355.4, 632.12, 640.10, 669.7, 671.16, 993.16
excessive emotion 105.10
excessive force 144.11
excessive in one's praise 509.18
excessive interest 623.3
excessive irritability 128.1
excessiveness 632.4, 669.1, 926.11, 993.1
excessive praise 509.5, 511.3
excess of feeling 93.9
exchange (n) 343.1, 347.12, 490.1, 506.1, 541.1, 629.1, 731.2, 737.7, 854.3, 862.1, 862.2, 863.1 (v) 629.3, 731.15, 852.7, 854.5, 862.4, 863.4
Exchange, the 737.7
exchangeability 863.3
exchangeable 863.5
exchange blows 457.13
exchange colors 182.52, 517.22
exchanged 863.5
exchange fisticuffs 457.13
exchange floor 737.7
exchange greetings 585.10
exchange ideas 541.11
exchange letters 553.10
exchange observations 541.10, 943.6
exchange of blows 457.4
exchange of letters 553.1
exchange of views 541.5, 541.6
exchange of vows 436.3
exchange opinions 541.11
exchange rate 728.9
exchange reaction 1038.8
exchange shots 457.17
exchange views 541.10, 541.11, 943.6
exchange visit 582.7
exchange visits 582.19
exchange words 541.8
exchequer 386.6, 728.14, 729.13
exchequer bill 728.11
excise 192.10, 255.10, 802.11
exciseman 630.10, 770.15
excision 192.1, 255.3
excitability 93.9, 105.10, 110.2
excitable 105.28, 110.19, 128.11
excitableness 105.10
excitation 105.11, 375.4
excite 24.7, 105.12, 375.17, 917.10, 983.12, 1020.18
excite attention 983.10
excited 75.27, 93.18, 93.23, 105.20, 135.6, 917.16, 983.16
excited imagination 986.4
excitedness 105.1
excited state 1033.3
excite easily 105.16
excite interest 983.12
excitement 93.2, 105.1, 105.11, 135.1, 375.4, 917.1, 1019.2
excite notice 983.11
excite one's interest 983.12
exciter 375.11
exciting 100.30, 105.30, 375.27, 377.8, 544.13, 983.19
exclaim 59.7, 524.24, 524.25
exclaim against 333.5, 510.13
exclaim at 333.5, 453.3
exclamation 59.2, 524.3
exclamatory 59.11
exclamatory adjective 530.3
exclamatory noun 530.3
excludability 773.1
exclude 255.10, 293.6, 372.2, 444.3, 510.10, 773.4, 909.13, 909.17, 1012.14
excluded 293.9, 372.3, 773.7, 967.7
exclude from 444.3
excluding 773.9
exclusion 255.3, 293.1, 372.1, 444.1, 510.1, 773.1, 909.4, 959.1
exclusionary 293.9
exclusive (n) 552.3 (a) 157.8, 210.9, 293.9, 371.23, 444.6, 469.11, 495.13, 583.6, 617.18, 773.9, 872.7
exclusive jurisdiction 594.1
exclusiveness 157.1, 495.5, 583.3, 617.13, 773.3
exclusive possession 469.3
exclusive right 642.1
exclusivity 157.1, 495.5, 583.3, 617.13, 773.1
exclusory 773.9
excogitate 931.11
excogitating 931.21
excogitation 931.1
excogitative 931.21
excommunicate 372.2, 447.4, 513.5, 602.3, 909.17
excommunicated 372.3
excommunication 372.1, 447.2, 513.1, 602.1, 909.4
excommunicative 513.8
excommunicatory 513.8
ex-con 660.9
ex-convict 429.11
excoriate 6.8, 510.20
excoriated 96.25
excoriation 6.1, 96.7, 510.3
excrement 12.3, 80.7
excremental 12.20, 71.5, 80.23
excrementary 12.20
excrementitious 80.23
excrescence 14.1, 85.39, 259.3, 283.2, 517.7
excrescency 283.2
excrescent 283.14
excrescential 283.14
excreta 12.3
excrete 12.12, 13.5, 190.15
excretion 12.1, 13.1, 190.6, 909.6
excretionary 12.19
excretive 12.19
excretory 12.19, 13.7, 190.20
excruciate 26.7, 96.18, 98.12
excruciating 24.13, 26.10, 98.23
excruciatingness 98.4
excruciating pain 26.6
excruciation 26.6, 96.7, 98.4
exculpate 148.3, 600.9, 601.4
exculpated 148.7
exculpation 148.2, 600.1, 601.1
excurse 164.4, 538.9
excursion 164.1, 177.5, 204.1, 538.4, 914.1, 914.3
excursionist 178.1, 918.3
excursive 164.7, 204.13, 538.13, 914.7
excursus 164.1, 538.4, 556.1, 914.1
excurvate 283.13
excurvated 283.13
excurvation 279.1, 283.1
excurvature 279.1, 283.1
excurved 283.13
excusability 600.7
excusable 600.14
excusatory 600.13
excuse (n) 148.2, 376.1, 600.4, 601.1, 658.2, 886.2 (v) 148.3, 430.14, 600.11, 601.4
excused 148.7, 430.30, 773.7
excused absence 222.4
excuse-me hit 745.3
excuser 600.8
excusing 600.13
exec 575.17
execrable 98.18, 513.9, 654.16, 661.12, 1000.10
execrableness 661.3
execrate 103.5, 510.19, 513.5, 513.6
execrating 510.22
execration 103.1, 103.3, 510.7, 513.1
execrative 103.7, 510.22
execratory 510.22, 513.8
execu-crime 655.2
executant 710.1, 726.1
execute 308.13, 328.7, 328.9, 407.4, 434.3, 437.9, 604.16, 708.39, 892.11
execute a coup d'état 417.14
execute a maneuver 182.46
execute a will 478.18
execute by firing squad 604.16
executed 407.10, 892.17
execution 307.5, 308.1, 308.7, 328.2, 407.1, 434.1, 437.4, 480.5, 604.6, 708.30, 889.1, 892.5
executional 892.14
executioner 308.11, 604.7
executionist 604.7
execution of judgment 946.5
executive (n) 574.3, 575.6, 610.2, 726.4, 889.4 (a) 501.21, 573.14, 612.16, 612.18, 632.11
executive, the 574.11
executive arm 574.11
executive branch 574.11, 613.2
executive committee 574.11
executive council 574.11
executive decision 359.1
Executive Department 613.2
executive development specialist 615.5
executive director 574.3
executive editor 554.2
executive function 573.3
executive hierarchy 574.11
executive office 739.7
executive officer 574.3, 575.17, 576.1, 616.6
executive order 419.2
executive park 739.7
executive privilege 430.2
executive recruiter 615.5
executive recruiting 615.4
executive recruitment consultant 615.5
executive role 573.3
executive search 615.4
executive search agency 615.5
executive search firm 615.5
executive secretary 574.3
executive session 345.2
executive suite 739.7
executive veto 613.7
executor 574.4, 726.1, 892.7
executorship 615.1
executrix 726.1, 892.7
exegesis 341.4, 341.5
exegesist 341.7
exegete 341.7, 723.4
exegetic 341.14, 341.15

exegetical 341.14, 341.15, 556.6, 723.6
exegetics 341.8, 723.1
exegetist 341.7
exemplar 349.7, 659.4, 786.2, 869.4, 932.2, 1002.4
exemplariness 509.7
exemplary 349.15, 399.7, 509.20, 786.8, 1002.9
exemplary citizen 659.3
exemplification 341.4, 349.1, 349.7, 786.2, 957.5
exemplificative 341.15
exemplify 341.10, 349.11, 786.7, 957.13
exempt (v) 430.14, 601.4 (a) 430.30
exempted 430.30
exempt from 601.4
exemptible 600.14
exemption 148.2, 430.8, 443.2, 601.2, 773.3, 959.1
exemption from hostilities 464.1
exequatur 615.1
exequial 309.22
exequies 309.4
exercise (n) 81.2, 84.2, 328.1, 387.1, 568.3, 568.7, 570.3, 580.4, 615.4, 724.2, 725.6, 889.1 (v) 84.4, 96.13, 328.8, 387.10, 568.13, 725.8, 983.13
exercise a right 642.6
exercise bike 84.1
exercise book 554.10
exercise care 339.7
exercised 387.24
exercise discrimination 944.5
exercise influence 894.9
exercise judgment 946.8
exercise machine 84.1
exercise of memory 989.3
exercise one's discretion 371.13
exercise one's franchise 371.18
exercise one's option 371.13
exercise one's suffrage 371.18
exerciser 725.7
exercises 580.4, 696.8
exercise self-control 668.6
exercise self-restraint 668.6
exercise skill 413.20
exercise sovereignty 417.13
exercise systems 84.2
exercise tact 944.5
exercise the elbow 88.25
exercise the functions of 724.13
exercise the mind 931.8
exercise the right of angary 480.20
exercise the right of eminent domain 480.20
exercise track 84.1
exercise walk 177.27
exercise walker 178.6
exercising 725.6
exert 387.10, 725.8
exerted 387.24
exert influence 894.9
exertion 387.1, 403.1, 725.1
exert oneself 403.5, 403.12, 725.9
exert pressure 440.12
exert strength 15.12
exfiltrate 163.6, 190.15
exfiltration 163.2, 190.2, 190.6
exfoliate 6.11, 296.5, 802.12
exfoliation 6.1, 296.4, 802.3
exfoliatory 6.18
ex gratia 323.4, 324.7
exhalation 2.21, 52.4, 69.1, 190.4, 1067.1, 1067.5
exhale 69.6, 909.24, 1067.8
exhaust (n) 184.30, 190.4, 190.9, 1001.4, 1074.8 (v) 16.10, 19.12, 21.4, 98.16, 190.13, 192.12, 387.13, 388.3, 480.24, 486.4, 909.22, 909.24, 909.25, 993.10
exhausted 16.18, 21.10, 85.54, 388.5, 393.36, 891.4
exhaustedness 21.2
exhaust every move 360.5
exhaust fan 318.18
exhaust fumes 1001.4
exhaust gas 1001.4
exhaustible 388.6
exhausting (n) 387.1, 388.1, 909.6 (a) 16.20, 21.13, 98.24, 725.18
exhaustion 16.1, 16.5, 21.2, 85.3, 85.8, 252.3, 388.1, 473.2, 909.6
exhaustion delirium 926.8
exhaustion psychosis 926.8
exhaustive 247.6, 269.6, 407.12, 792.9, 794.10
exhaustiveness 772.1, 792.5, 794.1
exhaustive study 938.4
exhaustless 823.3, 991.7
exhaustlessness 823.1
exhaust price 738.10
exhibit (n) 33.7, 348.2, 704.12, 957.1 (v) 206.5, 348.5, 501.17, 957.8
exhibitable 348.13
exhibited 348.13
exhibition game 942.3
exhibition 33.7, 348.2, 501.4, 554.7, 704.12
exhibitional 348.9
exhibitioner 572.7
exhibition hall 197.4
exhibitionism 6.1, 75.11, 501.4, 666.2
exhibitionist 6.3, 75.16, 501.11
exhibitionistic 501.19, 666.6
exhibition room 197.24
exhibitive 348.9, 517.23
exhibit one's wares 501.16
exhibitor 704.23
exhibit the form of 33.10
exhilarate 9.2, 17.10, 105.13, 109.7, 375.20, 743.21
exhilarated 9.4, 95.15, 105.20, 109.11
exhilarating 9.3, 17.15, 105.30, 109.16, 375.26
exhilaration 9.1, 17.8, 95.2, 105.1, 105.11, 109.2, 375.9
exhilarative 17.15
exhort 375.14, 422.6, 492.15
exhortation 375.3, 375.5, 422.1, 458.7, 543.2
exhortative 375.29, 422.8
exhortatory 375.29, 422.8, 568.18
exhumation 192.2, 941.1
exhume 192.11, 941.4
exigence 421.4, 963.4, 997.4
exigency 375.6, 421.4, 843.4, 963.4, 997.4
exigent 339.12, 421.9, 425.6, 843.10, 963.12, 997.22
exiguity 248.1, 258.1, 270.4, 885.1, 992.2
exiguous 258.10, 885.5, 992.10
exiguousness 248.1, 992.2
exile (n) 160.4, 178.5, 190.7, 586.4, 604.2, 773.2, 774.3, 909.4 (v) 190.16, 586.6, 773.5, 909.17
exiled 160.10, 773.7
exilement 909.4
exility 270.4
exing 170.4
exist 221.6, 306.8, 761.8, 827.6
existence, an 763.3
existence 221.1, 306.1, 761.1, 1052.1
existent 306.12, 761.13, 838.2
existentialism 761.7
existential vacuum 96.1
existential woe 96.1
exist in 761.11
existing 761.13, 838.2
existing conditions 766.2
existing situation 766.2
exit (n) 188.1, 190.2, 190.9, 239.1, 307.1, 368.4, 383.3 (v) 34.2, 188.6, 190.12, 222.8, 369.10
exit poll 371.6, 938.14
exit strategy 192.1
exit visa 443.7
ex libris 517.13
exobiology 1073.19
exocentric compound 526.4
Exocet missile 462.18
exocrine 13.8
exode 704.7
exodontic 90.15
exodontist 90.6
exodus 188.1, 190.2, 704.7
ex officio 417.15
exogamic 78.17
exogamous 78.17
exogenous metabolism 2.20
exomorphic 206.7
exon 305.9
exonerate 148.3, 601.4
exonerated 148.7
exoneration 148.2, 601.1
exonerative 148.6
exonizing 305.9
exophthalmic 283.16
exorbitance 355.1, 632.4, 993.1
exorbitancy 632.4, 993.1
exorbitant 355.4, 421.9, 632.12, 671.16, 993.16
exorbitant demand 421.1
exorbitant interest 623.3
exorbitant price 632.3
exorbitation 164.1
exorcisation 690.4
exorcise 690.12
exorciser 690.7
exorcism 690.4, 691.1
exorcist 690.7, 699.4
exorcista 699.4
exordial 814.4
exordium 816.2
exoskeletal 206.7
exoskeleton 206.2, 295.15
exosmosis 187.6
exosmotic 187.17
exosphere 198.2
exostosis 85.39
exoteric 521.10
exotic (n) 310.3 (a) 35.19, 122.11, 261.8, 377.8, 774.5, 776.6
exotic dancer 707.1
exotropia 28.5
expand 158.9, 251.4, 259.4, 259.5, 259.6, 267.6, 269.4, 299.3, 538.7, 771.4, 861.6, 864.9
expanded 251.7, 259.10
expanding 251.8, 538.15
expanding bullet 462.19
expanding economy 731.10, 1010.5
expanding universe 1073.1
expanding universe theory 1073.18
expand on 538.7, 861.6
expand one's consciousness 976.8
expand upon 538.7
expanse 158.1, 158.2, 158.5, 247.1, 257.1, 269.1
expanse tract 158.1
expansible 259.9
expansile 259.9
expansion 158.1, 251.1, 257.1, 259.1, 355.1, 538.6, 731.10, 771.1, 861.1
expansional 259.9
expansionism 458.11, 609.5
expansion slot 1042.3
expansive 158.11, 257.17, 259.9, 269.6, 343.10, 540.9
expansiveness 257.6
ex parte 957.16
expatiate 538.7
expatiating 538.15
expatiation 538.6
expatriate (n) 178.5, 190.10, 586.4 (v) 177.22, 188.17, 190.16, 773.5, 909.17
expatriated 160.10
expatriation 177.4, 190.7, 363.3, 773.2, 909.4
expect 124.6, 130.5, 380.6, 839.6, 951.10, 953.11
expectance 130.1
expectancy 130.1, 843.1
expectant 124.10, 130.11, 961.7
expectant waiting 130.3
expectation 123.1, 124.1, 130.1, 639.1, 839.1, 961.3, 968.1
expectation of life 827.5
expectations 130.4, 639.1
expected 123.3, 130.13
expected of 130.14
expecting 78.18, 123.3, 130.11
expect it of 130.10
expectorant 86.32

expectorate 13.6
expectoration 13.3
expect to 130.9
expedience 828.1, 843.1, 995.1, 999.1
expediency 637.2, 843.1, 995.1
expedient (n) 381.5, 384.3, 415.3, 995.2, 1009.2 (a) 387.18, 637.3, 828.7, 843.9, 959.8, 995.5, 999.12
expedients 415.4
expedite 162.5, 176.10, 176.15, 401.4, 449.17, 1014.7
expedite one's affair 995.3
expediter 381.6, 384.4, 576.3
expediting 449.5, 1014.5
expedition 174.1, 177.5, 330.3, 404.2, 449.5, 458.3, 845.3, 1014.5
expeditionary 177.36
expeditionary force 461.20
expeditious 174.15, 330.18, 401.9, 845.9
expeditiousness 330.3, 401.2, 845.3
expel 12.12, 176.10, 447.4, 773.5, 802.8, 909.13, 909.17, 909.19, 909.25
expelled 773.7
expellee 586.4, 909.12
expeller 909.11
expend 387.13, 388.3, 486.4, 624.14, 626.5
expendability 998.1
expendable 388.6, 862.10, 993.17, 998.16
expended 473.7, 624.22
expender 626.4
expending 387.1, 388.1
expenditor 626.4
expenditure 387.1, 388.1, 473.2, 626.1, 630.1
expenditures 628.1
expend one's anger on 152.16
expense 473.1, 626.1, 626.3, 630.1
expense account 622.2, 626.3
expenseless 634.5
expenselessness 634.1
expenses 626.3
expensive 632.11
expensiveness 632.1
experience (n) 24.1, 413.9, 831.2, 928.1 (v) 24.6, 93.10, 831.8
experienced 373.15, 413.28
experienced hand 413.11
experience imaginatively 986.14
experiences 719.1
experience vicariously 986.14
experiment (n) 403.2, 942.1 (v) 403.10, 942.8
experimental 403.16, 942.11
experimental animal 942.7
experimental design 942.1
experimental engineer 942.6
experimental film 706.1
experimentalism 942.1
experimentalist 942.6
experimentalize 942.8
experimental logic 935.2
experimental method 942.1
experimental proof 942.1
experimental sample 942.4
experimental science 928.10
experimental scientist 928.11
experimental subject 942.7
experimental theater 704.1
experimental verification 942.1
experimentation 942.1
experimentee 942.7
experimenter 942.6, 951.7
experimentist 942.6
experiment station 942.5
experiment upon 942.8
expert (n) 413.11, 422.3, 496.6, 866.3, 928.11 (a) 413.22, 866.5, 1002.9
expert at 413.27
expert consultant 413.11
expert in 928.19
expert in decor 716.11
expertise 413.1, 496.4, 865.4, 928.1, 928.6
expertism 496.4
expertness 413.1
expert rifleman 461.9
expert's slope 753.1
expert's trail 753.1
expert systems 1042.20
expert witness 551.5
expiable 600.14
expiate 338.4, 658.4
expiation 338.1, 658.1
expiatory 338.6, 658.7
expiatory offering 658.1
expiatory sacrifice 658.1
expiration 2.21, 307.1, 820.1, 1067.1
expiration date 820.3
expiratory 2.32
expire 307.18, 395.23, 762.6, 820.7, 821.5, 909.24
expired 762.11, 837.7
expiring 307.32
expiry 307.1, 820.1
explain 341.10, 521.6, 568.16, 600.9, 600.11, 940.2, 1014.7
explainability 600.7
explainable 341.17, 940.3
explainableness 341.6
explain away 341.10, 600.12, 936.8
explainer 341.7
explaining 341.15
explain oneself 341.10
explanation 341.4, 518.3, 600.1, 786.2, 886.2, 940.1, 951.1, 951.2
explanatory 341.15
explanatory remark 341.5
expletive (n) 59.2, 513.4, 526.6, 849.3, 993.4 (a) 993.17
explicability 341.6, 600.7
explicable 341.17, 888.6, 940.3
explicate 341.10, 521.6, 538.7, 723.5
explication 341.4, 538.6
explicative 341.15, 723.6
explicator 341.7, 723.4
explicatory 341.15
explicit 348.8, 518.10, 521.11, 644.17, 960.2
explicitness 521.2, 960.1
explodable 671.24
explode 33.9, 56.8, 105.16, 152.20, 251.6, 395.18, 410.13, 671.14, 958.4, 1021.8
exploded 955.12, 958.7
exploded view 801.4
exploder 462.15
exploding 56.11
exploit (n) 328.3, 492.6 (v) 387.15, 387.16, 632.7, 999.11
exploitable 387.23, 954.9
exploitation 387.8
exploitative 387.19
exploiter 381.7, 387.9
exploitive 387.19
exploit one's position 387.16
exploration 404.2, 938.8, 938.15, 942.1
explorational 938.37
explorative 938.37
exploratory 816.4, 938.37, 941.10
exploratory examination 938.6
exploratory ship 1075.2
exploratory survey 938.8
explore 938.23, 938.31
explorer 178.1, 816.1, 981.2
explosible 671.24
explosion 53.3, 56.3, 105.9, 152.9, 251.2, 671.7, 958.1
explosive (n) 462.14, 524.12 (a) 56.11, 105.28, 110.25, 671.24, 1006.9
explosive bullet 462.19
explosiveness 105.10
explosives 462.1
explosivity 105.10
expo 348.2
exponent 341.7, 349.7, 556.4, 576.1, 616.9, 786.2, 883.4
exponential 1017.23
exponential growth 251.1
exponentiation 883.4
export (n) 190.8 (v) 176.10, 176.15, 190.17, 731.17, 1042.21
exportable 176.18
export and import 731.2
exportation 190.8
exporter 730.2
exporting 190.8
exposable 941.10
expose 6.5, 292.12, 351.4, 661.9, 941.4, 958.4, 977.2, 1006.6
exposé 351.1, 958.1
exposed 6.12, 31.6, 292.17, 317.12, 318.23, 348.10, 897.5, 958.7, 1006.15, 1037.11
exposed nerve 24.4
exposed to 897.6
exposed to view 31.6
expose gradually 861.7
expose itself 941.9
expose oneself 33.8, 1006.7
expose oneself to 897.3
expose to infamy 661.9
expose to view 348.5
exposing (n) 6.1 (a) 351.10
exposit 341.10, 568.16
exposition 33.7, 341.4, 348.2, 351.1, 556.1, 568.7, 708.24, 736.2
expositional 348.9
expositive 341.15, 349.14, 556.6
expositor 341.7, 543.5, 556.3, 556.4
expositorial 556.6
expository 341.15, 348.9, 556.6
expository prose 721.1
expository scene 704.7
expository writing 547.2, 718.2
ex post facto 835.4, 837.12
ex post facto examination 307.17
expostulate 333.5, 379.3, 422.6
expostulation 333.2, 379.1, 422.1
expostulative 333.7, 422.8
expostulatory 333.7, 379.5, 422.8
exposure 6.1, 31.1, 31.2, 33.1, 159.3, 348.2, 351.1, 352.4, 662.1, 714.9, 897.2, 941.1, 958.1, 1006.3, 1037.8
exposure meter 714.9, 1025.21
expound 341.10, 556.5, 568.16
expounder 341.7, 543.5, 556.4
expounding 341.4
express (n) 179.14, 353.1 (v) 176.15, 192.16, 334.5, 348.5, 349.9, 517.17, 524.22, 532.4, 957.8 (a) 174.15, 348.8, 521.11, 865.12, 960.2, 973.17
expressable 176.18
expressage 630.7
express an opinion 946.8
express a wish for 440.9
express bus 179.13
express by words 532.4
expressed 532.5
expressed desire 440.1
express general agreement 332.11
expressing 192.1
express intention 380.3
express in words 532.4
expression 192.1, 192.7, 348.1, 517.3, 524.2, 524.3, 526.1, 529.1, 532.1, 544.1, 708.30, 974.1
expressionism 350.1
expressionist criticism 723.1
expressionless 344.10, 522.20
expressionlessness 344.3, 522.5
expression mark 709.12
expression of ideas 532.2
expressive 348.9, 349.14, 517.23, 518.10, 544.10
expressiveness 518.5, 544.1
express lane 401.1
express mail 553.4
express-mail 176.15
express messenger 174.5
expressness 380.3
express one's appreciation 150.4
express regret 658.5
express sympathy for 147.2
express the belief 953.12
express train 174.6, 179.14
expropriate 389.4, 480.20, 480.23
expropriation 480.5, 480.7, 909.2
expropriator 480.11

expropriatory 480.25
expugnable 1006.16
expulsion 12.1, 447.2, 773.2, 909.1, 909.7
expulsive 909.30
expunction 395.7
expunge 255.12, 395.16, 820.6
expunged 820.9
expunge from the record 148.3
expunger 395.9
expurgate 79.18, 255.12
expurgated 79.26
expurgation 79.2, 255.5
expurgatory 79.28
exquisite (n) 500.9 (a) 24.13, 26.10, 63.8, 97.7, 339.12, 495.11, 500.18, 578.13, 999.15, 1016.19
exquisite manners 504.3, 580.3
exquisiteness 24.3, 97.2, 339.3, 495.3, 500.5, 999.2, 1016.1
exquisite torment 26.6
exquisite torture 26.6
exsanguinated 36.7
exsanguination 36.2
exsanguine 36.7
exsanguineous 36.7
exsect 192.10
exsection 192.1
exsiccant 1066.10
exsiccate 1066.6
exsiccated 1066.9
exsiccation 1066.3
exsiccative (n) 1066.4 (a) 1066.10
exsiccator 1066.4
exsufflation 2.21, 690.4
extant 256.7, 306.12, 761.13, 838.2
extemporaneous 365.12, 406.8
extemporaneousness 365.5, 406.1
extemporariness 365.5
extemporary 365.12
extempore (n) 365.5, 708.27 (a) 365.12
extemporization 365.5
extemporize 365.8, 406.6
extemporized 406.8
extemporizer 365.6
extend 158.9, 251.4, 259.4, 259.5, 259.6, 261.5, 267.5, 267.6, 269.4, 277.5, 439.4, 478.12, 538.8, 757.5, 827.6, 827.9, 846.9, 856.4, 864.9, 1048.4
extend a line of credit 622.6
extend amnesty 601.4
extend an invitation 440.13
extend courtesy 504.11
extend credit 622.6
extended 158.11, 251.7, 259.10, 267.8, 518.10, 538.12, 827.11
extended care 91.21
extended family 559.5, 617.2
extended trot 174.3
extended-wear lenses 29.3
extend gratitude 150.4
extendibility 1047.2
extendible 1047.9
extending 158.11
extending everywhere 823.3
extend out 261.5, 267.5
extend over 295.30
extend sympathy 121.6
extend thanks 150.4
extend the right hand of friendship 585.9
extend the right of friendship 587.12
extend throughout 221.7
extend to 261.6
extend to the side 269.4
extensibility 1047.2, 1048.1
extensible 1047.9
extensile 259.9, 1047.9, 1048.7
extension 3.13, 158.1, 202.3, 251.1, 254.1, 254.3, 257.1, 259.1, 267.1, 267.4, 347.4, 518.1, 815.1, 827.2, 856.1, 1048.2
extensional 259.9, 518.10
extension ladder 193.4
extensionless 1053.7
extension of time 846.4
extensive 158.11, 247.7, 257.17, 259.9, 267.7, 269.6, 864.13
extensive knowledge 928.6
extensiveness 158.5, 257.6, 275.1, 864.2
extensive study 570.3
extent 158.1, 158.5, 244.1, 245.1, 257.1, 261.1, 267.1, 269.1, 300.3
extenuate 16.10, 252.8, 600.12, 670.6
extenuating 600.13, 959.7
extenuating circumstances 600.5, 959.1
extenuation 16.5, 252.1, 600.5
extenuative (n) 600.5 (a) 600.13
extenuatory 959.7
exterior (n) 33.2, 206.2, 712.11 (a) 206.7, 774.5
exteriority 206.1, 276.1, 774.1
exteriorization 206.4
exteriorize 206.5
exteriorized protoplasm 689.7
exterior paint 35.8
exterminate 308.13, 308.17, 395.14, 762.7, 909.21
extermination 308.1, 395.6
exterminative 395.27
exterminator 308.11, 395.8
exterminatory 395.27
external (n) 206.2 (a) 206.7, 768.3, 774.5
external appearance 33.2
external combustion 1043.3
external ear 2.10, 48.7
external frustration 92.17
external gear 1040.9
external hard drive 1042.5
externality 206.1, 768.1
externalization 206.4
externalize 206.5, 1052.9
externalness 206.1
external organ 2.7
externals 33.2
external secretion 13.1
exterrestrial 206.9, 1073.26
exterritorial 206.9
extinct 34.4, 307.29, 762.11, 820.9, 837.7, 842.15
extinction 34.1, 252.3, 255.3, 307.1, 307.12, 395.6, 1022.2
extinction level event 395.2
extinguish 249.8, 255.10, 395.15, 428.8, 820.6, 1022.7, 1027.11
extinguished 1022.11
extinguisher 395.9, 1022.3
extinguishing 1022.2
extinguishment 307.1, 395.6, 428.2, 1022.2, 1027.6
extirpate 255.10, 395.14, 762.7
extirpation 192.1, 255.3, 395.6
extirpative 255.13, 395.27
extirpatory 395.27
extol 509.12, 696.12
extoller 509.8
extolment 509.5, 696.2
extort 192.15, 421.5, 480.22, 482.13
extortion 192.6, 421.1, 480.8, 482.3, 632.5
extortionary 192.17
extortionate 192.17, 421.9, 480.26, 632.12
extortionate demand 421.1
extortionateness 632.4
extortionate price 632.3, 632.5
extortioner 480.12
extortionist 480.12
extortive 192.17
extra (n) 253.1, 254.4, 555.2, 704.10, 706.4, 707.7, 768.2, 993.5 (a) 253.10, 390.12, 768.4, 848.3, 993.18
extra added attraction 254.4
extra allowance 624.6
extra-base hit 745.3
extraclassroom 568.20
extract (n) 70.2, 192.8, 557.3, 893.3, 1061.2 (v) 79.22, 192.10, 255.9, 371.14, 398.3, 892.9, 946.10
extracted 892.18
extracted material 1058.1
extracted matter 1058.1
extract information 938.22
extracting 192.1
extraction 79.4, 190.2, 192.1, 192.8, 255.2, 557.3, 560.4, 892.2, 905.1
extraction of roots 1017.2
extractive 192.17
extractive metallurgy 1058.11
extractor 192.9
extract roots 1017.18
extracts 557.4
extracurricular 568.20
extracurricular relations 665.7
extracurricular sex 665.7
extra dash 254.4
extradictionary 712.21
extradite 176.10, 481.4, 909.17
extradition 481.1, 909.4
extra dividend 738.7
extrados 206.2
extra edition 555.2
extra extra large 257.23
extra extra large size 257.4
extragalactic 206.9, 1073.25
extra innings 745.3
extrajudicial 674.6
extrajudicial oath 334.4
extra-large 257.23
extra large size 257.4
extralateral 206.9
extraliminal 206.9
extramarginal 92.42
extramarital 665.27
extramarital relations 665.7
extramarital sex 665.7
extramundane 206.9, 681.12, 870.15, 1053.7, 1073.26
extramural 206.9, 567.13, 568.19
extraneous 768.3, 774.5, 776.6, 776.7, 787.6
extraneousness 768.1, 774.1
extranuclear 1038.19
extraordinarily like 784.15
extraordinariness 122.3, 870.2
extraordinary 122.10, 131.10, 247.10, 865.12, 870.14, 997.19
extraordinary worth 632.2
extraorganismal 768.3
extraorganismic 768.3
extrapolar 206.9
extrapolate 839.6
extrapolated 839.8
extrapolation 254.1, 839.1, 1017.2
extraprovincial 206.9
extra sec champagne 88.17
extrasensory 689.24
extrasensory perception 24.5, 343.1, 689.8, 934.1
extrasolar 206.9, 1073.26
extraterrene 1073.26
extraterrestrial (n) 870.4 (a) 206.9, 681.12, 774.5, 870.15, 1073.26
extraterrestrial visitor 1075.8
extraterritorial 206.9
extraterritoriality 206.1
extratribal 206.9
extravagance 355.1, 486.1, 501.3, 538.2, 632.4, 669.1, 926.11, 991.2, 993.1, 993.2, 993.4
extravagancy 993.1, 993.2
extravagant 355.4, 486.8, 501.20, 501.21, 502.12, 538.11, 632.12, 669.7, 671.16, 923.11, 926.32, 986.20, 991.7, 993.16
extravaganza 354.10, 501.3
extravagation 501.3
extravasate 12.12, 12.17, 190.15, 909.25
extravasated 190.19
extravasation 12.1, 12.3, 190.6, 909.7
extravehicular 1075.13
extreme (n) 355.1, 794.5, 820.2, 993.1 (a) 24.13, 211.11, 247.13, 261.12, 327.11, 355.4, 611.20, 669.7, 671.16, 820.12, 926.32, 993.16
extreme cold 1023.1
extreme heat 1019.5
extreme height 272.2
extreme innerness 275.1
extreme left 611.4
extreme left wing 611.4
extreme left-wing 611.20

extreme left-winger 611.12
extreme limit 198.2
extremely cold 1023.14
extremely high frequency 1034.12
extremely hot 1019.25
extremeness 926.11
extreme penalty 604.6
extreme right 611.4
extreme rightism 611.4
extreme right wing 611.4
extreme right-winger 611.9
extremes 993.1
extreme sport 744.1
extreme temperatures 1075.10
extreme tension 993.7
extreme unction 307.8, 309.4, 701.4, 701.5
extremism 327.3, 355.1, 392.5, 611.4, 926.11, 993.1
extremist (n) 327.5, 392.6, 611.12 (a) 611.20, 926.32
extremistic 327.11, 611.20
extremity 96.6, 198.2, 199.5, 211.3, 307.8, 671.1, 794.5, 820.2, 843.4, 993.1, 1013.6
extricable 398.4
extricate 192.10, 398.3, 431.7, 1014.9
extricated 431.10
extricate oneself 431.8
extrication 192.1, 369.1, 398.1, 431.3, 1014.6
extrinsic 206.7, 580.7, 768.3, 774.5, 776.7
extrinsicality 206.1, 580.1, 768.1, 774.1
extrospective 92.41
extroversion 92.11, 343.3
extroversive 92.41
extrovert (n) 92.12 (a) 92.41
extroverted 92.41, 343.10
extrovertedness 92.11
extrude 190.11, 283.10, 892.8, 909.13
extruded plastic 1054.6
extruding 283.14
extrusion 12.1, 190.1, 283.2, 909.1
extrusive 909.30
extrusive rock 1059.1
exuberance 95.2, 109.4, 430.3, 538.2, 890.1, 991.2
exuberant 93.18, 109.14, 310.43, 430.24, 538.11, 890.9, 991.7, 1010.13
exuberate 991.5
exudate (n) 12.3, 12.7 (v) 12.12, 190.15
exudation 12.1, 12.3, 12.7, 13.1, 190.6, 1065.1
exudative 12.19, 13.7, 190.20
exude 12.12, 12.16, 13.5, 190.15, 1065.11
exude cheerfulness 109.6
exuding (n) 190.6 (a) 190.20
exult 116.5, 502.9
exultant 95.17, 116.10, 502.13
exultation 116.1, 502.4
exult in 136.5
exulting 116.10, 502.13
exurb 230.1
exurbanite 227.6
exurbia 230.1
exuviae 2.5
exuvial 6.18
exuviate 6.10
exuviation 6.1
ex voto offering 696.7
eye (n) 2.9, 27.1, 27.3, 27.9, 280.5, 573.2, 576.11, 944.1, 953.6, 978.2, 1008.1 (v) 27.13, 27.14, 27.15, 562.20, 918.5 (a) 2.28, 27.20
eye, the 27.3
eye askance 127.10
eyeball (n) 2.9, 27.9 (v) 27.13, 938.24 (a) 27.20
eyeballing 300.1
eyeball inspection 27.6
eyeball to eyeball 779.6
eyeball-to-eyeball 215.5, 216.10
eyeball-to-eyeball encounter 541.5
eyebath 86.11
eyebrow pencil 1016.11
eyebrows 3.12
eye candy 1016.1
eye-catching 377.8, 907.5
eye defect 85.14
eye disease 85.14
eyedrops 86.11
eye-filling 1016.21
eye for, an 413.5
eye for an eye, an 506.3, 863.1
eye for an eye 658.1
eyeful 1016.6
eyeglass 29.3
eyeglasses 27.9, 29.3
eye hungrily 100.19
eyelashes 3.12
eyeless 30.9
eyelessness 30.1
eyelet 280.5
eyelid 2.9, 27.9
eyeliner 1016.11
eye makeup 1016.11
eye memory 989.1
eye-minded 27.21
eye-mindedness 27.1
eye of the hurricane 173.5
eye of the mind 989.1
eye of the storm 208.2, 671.4
eye-opener 88.9, 131.2
eye-opening 122.12, 131.11, 351.10
eye patch 30.5
eyepiece 29.2
eye-popper 122.2
eye-popping 105.30, 105.32, 131.11
eyer 918.1
eyereach 31.3
eye rhyme 720.9
eye-rolling 108.8
eyesalve 86.11
eyes bigger than one's stomach 100.7
eye-servant 368.3
eye-server 368.3
eyeshade 1028.2
eye shadow 1016.11
eyeshield 1028.2
eyeshot 27.7, 31.3
eyesight 27.1, 31.3
eyes-only 345.11, 345.14
eyes-only information 345.5
eyesore 1004.3, 1015.4
eyestrain 21.1, 28.2
eyetooth 2.8
eye up 562.21
eyewash 86.11, 354.14, 511.1, 1056.3
eyewear 27.9
eyewitness (n) 918.1, 957.6 (a) 957.16
eyrie 228.23
Ezekiel 399.4, 684.1
fab 999.13
Fabian (n) 392.6, 611.14 (a) 392.16, 611.22
Fabianism 392.5, 611.6
Fabian policy 846.5
Fabian socialism 611.6
Fabian socialist 611.14
fable (n) 354.10, 722.4 (v) 722.7
fabled 662.16
fableist 722.5
fabler 722.5
fabric 4.1, 196.5, 228.5, 266.1, 266.2, 266.4, 740.1, 763.2
fabricable 1047.9
fabricate 354.18, 796.3, 892.8, 892.12, 986.14
fabricated 354.29, 892.18, 892.19, 986.21
fabrication 266.1, 354.10, 796.1, 892.1, 892.2, 986.3, 986.5
fabricational 892.14
fabricative 892.16
fabricator 357.9, 726.1
fabulist 357.9, 722.5
fabulize 722.7
fabulous 122.10, 247.10, 354.29, 678.15, 722.8, 870.14, 986.21, 993.16
fabulousness 870.2, 993.1
facade 33.2, 206.2, 354.3, 376.1, 500.1
façade 216.1, 354.3
face (n) 33.4, 136.1, 142.3, 200.3, 206.2, 216.1, 216.4, 237.2, 354.3, 458.11, 548.6, 630.2, 662.2, 662.4 (v) 35.14, 130.5, 196.7, 215.4, 216.8, 216.9, 295.23, 295.25, 451.5, 454.3, 492.10, 840.2
face about 163.10
face card 758.2
face cream 1056.3
faced 296.6
face down 453.3, 492.11
face-first 162.6, 165.3
faceless 781.5, 945.6
facelessness 945.2
facelift (n) 90.2, 396.4 (v) 396.17
facelifting 396.4
face mask 1008.3
face-mask tackle 746.3
face of brass 142.2
face off 749.7
face-off circle 749.1
face-off spot 749.1
face out 359.10, 453.3, 454.3, 492.11
face painting 712.3
faceplant 204.4
faceprint 714.3
face-saver 468.1
facet 33.3, 206.2, 216.1, 766.3, 793.4
face that launch'd a thousand ships, the 1016.7
face that would stop a clock 1015.3
face the facts 433.6
face the music 433.6, 492.10, 604.20
facetiae 489.7
face time 587.5, 769.2
facetious 489.15
facetiousness 489.2, 489.7
face to face 779.6
face-to-face 215.5, 223.16
face to the right-about 163.10
face up 492.10
face upon 216.9
face up to 453.3, 492.10, 1006.7
face value 630.2, 738.9
face with 216.8
facial 1016.10, 1044.3
facial appearance 33.4
facial expression 33.4
facial hair 3.8
facial massage 1044.3
facies 216.4
facile 433.13, 544.8, 544.9, 570.18, 1014.13, 1047.9
facileness 1014.1
facilitate 162.5, 384.6, 384.7, 449.17, 1014.7
facilitating (n) 1014.5 (a) 384.8
facilitation 449.5, 1014.5
facilitator 381.6, 384.4, 449.7, 576.3, 892.7
facilities 385.3, 385.4
facility 18.2, 385.4, 413.1, 433.3, 449.9, 544.2, 570.5, 739.1, 1014.1, 1040.3, 1047.2
facility in writing 547.2, 718.2
facility of speech 524.4
facing (n) 196.3, 295.12 (a) 206.7, 215.5, 216.11, 218.6
facing death 307.32
facing machine 1040.6
facsimile (n) 336.3, 347.15, 349.5, 548.3, 778.3, 785.1, 785.3, 785.5 (v) 785.8 (a) 347.21
facsimile broadcasting 1035.3
facsimile transmission 347.4, 714.3
fact 761.3, 766.3, 831.2, 957.1, 973.1
fact-based 719.6, 722.8
fact bite 761.3
fact checker 554.2
fact-checker 938.17
fact distribution 1041.7
fact-find 938.23
fact finder 938.18
fact-finding 938.37, 938.38
facticity 761.2
faction 456.3, 617.4, 617.13, 675.3, 770.3, 789.1
factional 456.17, 617.19
factionalism 617.13
factionist 675.18

faction-ridden 456.15
factious 327.11, 456.17, 935.19
factiousness 327.3, 456.3
factitious 354.26
factitiousness 354.2
factless 975.16
factlet 761.3
fact of experience 761.3
fact of life 551.1
fact of the matter 761.3
factoid 552.3, 761.3
factor (n) 560.6, 574.4, 576.3, 766.3, 796.2, 883.4, 886.1 (v) 801.8, 1017.18
factorial 883.4
factor in 803.8, 953.17
factoring 801.3
factor into 953.17
factorization 883.4
factorize 798.4, 801.7, 1017.18
factor out 802.8, 1017.18
factorship 615.1
factory 739.3
factory belt 739.3
factory district 739.3
factory farm 1070.5
factory-farm 1069.18
factory farming 1069.1, 1070.1
factory floor 726.2
factory-fresh 390.12, 841.9
factory-new 841.9
factory outlet 736.1, 736.2
factory outlet center 736.2
factory store 386.6
factory town 739.2
factory worker 607.9, 726.2
factotum 577.9, 726.2
facts 551.1, 928.1, 957.1
facts, the 761.4
fact sheet 551.1, 761.4, 957.4
facts of the case, the 761.4
facts of the matter, the 761.4
factual 761.15, 957.16, 970.15, 973.13, 973.16
factual base 928.1
factual information 551.1
factualism 973.5
factuality 761.2, 970.3
factualness 973.5
facula 1025.6
facultative referendum 613.8
faculties 919.2
faculty 18.2, 413.4, 417.1, 571.9, 642.1
faculty members 571.9
faculty of speech, the 524.1
facund 544.8
facundity 544.1
facy 142.10
fad 364.1, 409.3, 578.5
fad diet 7.13
faddiness 578.5
faddish 364.6, 578.15, 841.13
faddishness 364.3, 578.5
faddism 364.3, 578.5
faddist 101.4, 578.5
faddy 578.15
fade (n) 34.1, 706.6 (v) 16.9, 34.2, 36.5, 36.6, 37.5, 85.48, 168.2, 303.10, 393.17, 393.18, 751.4, 757.5, 759.25, 762.6, 828.6, 837.6, 842.9, 903.7 (a) 117.9
fade away 34.2, 168.2, 393.18, 395.23, 762.6, 837.6
fadeaway 34.1
fade away from the memory 990.7
faded 36.7, 393.34, 837.7
fadedness 36.2
fade in 33.8
fade-in 706.6, 1034.16
fade into the distance 168.2
fadeless 35.18, 829.9
fade like a shadow 828.6
fade out 34.2, 36.6, 762.6
fade-out 252.1, 706.6, 1034.16, 1034.21
fadeout 34.1, 1027.7
fade to black 706.6
fading (n) 34.1, 36.3, 393.3, 1034.21 (a) 16.21, 34.3, 168.5, 303.17, 307.32, 393.45, 828.7
fading fast 393.45
fad word 526.9
faerie 678.7, 870.7, 986.11
faery 678.17
fag (n) 75.15, 77.10, 89.5, 725.4, 726.3 (v) 21.6, 725.14, 725.16
fag end 256.1, 820.2
fag-end 793.3
fagged 21.8
fagged out 21.8
faggot 75.15
faggoty 75.30
fagot 770.8, 1021.3
Fahrenheit 1019.30
Fahrenheit scale 1019.19
fail 16.9, 85.48, 132.2, 250.4, 303.10, 340.6, 393.17, 408.2, 410.9, 410.17, 625.7, 645.12, 704.28, 911.2, 992.8, 1003.3
failed 391.9, 410.18, 625.11
failed expectation 132.1
fail ignominiously 410.13
fail in 992.8
failing (n) 393.3, 654.2, 1003.2 (a) 16.21, 85.54, 393.45, 410.18, 795.4, 992.9
fail in one's duty 340.6
fail miserably 410.13
fail of one's ambitions 132.4
fail of one's hopes 132.4
fail of success 410.9
fail-safe 1007.5
fail to appear 222.7
fail to indict 600.9
fail to pull out 184.44
fail to remember 990.5
fail to satisfy 108.5
failure 19.3, 132.1, 250.3, 340.1, 393.3, 408.1, 410.1, 410.7, 412.1, 435.1, 625.3, 625.4, 654.2, 655.2, 704.4, 911.1, 975.3, 990.2, 1003.2
failure is not an option 360.1
failure of nerve 393.3
failure to indict 600.1
failure to pay 625.1
fain 324.5
faineancy 331.5
fainéant (n) 331.8 (a) 331.19
fain of 100.22
faint (n) 25.2 (v) 16.9, 21.5, 25.5 (a) 16.12, 21.7, 32.6, 36.7, 52.16, 85.56, 362.12
faintheart 491.1, 491.4, 491.5
fainthearted 362.12, 491.10
faintheartedness 362.4, 491.1
faint hope 124.3
fainting (n) 85.9 (a) 21.7
faintish 16.12, 85.56
faintishness 16.1
faint likelihood 969.1
faintly like 784.15
faintness 16.1, 21.1, 32.2, 36.2, 52.1, 362.4
fain to 100.22
faint praise 512.1
faint resemblance 784.4
faint-sounding 52.16
faint suggestion 551.4
faint-voiced 52.16
fair (n) 736.2, 743.4 (a) 36.9, 37.8, 79.25, 97.6, 97.11, 133.17, 504.13, 521.12, 639.8, 644.13, 649.7, 968.6, 979.12, 999.12, 999.20, 1005.7, 1010.13, 1016.18, 1019.24, 1066.8
fair and square 644.14, 649.7
fair catch 746.3
fair copy 349.5, 547.10, 785.1
Fair Deal 609.6
faired 286.3
fair expectation 968.1
fair field 843.2
fair field and no favor, a 649.3
fair game 508.7, 843.2
fairground 743.14
fair-haired 37.9
fair-haired boy 104.15
fair hand 547.5
fairing 478.4
fairish 999.20, 1005.7
fairishness 999.3, 1005.1
fair-minded 649.8
fair-mindedness 649.2
fair name 662.2
fairness 36.2, 37.1, 644.1, 649.2, 979.5, 999.1, 1016.2
fair play 649.2
fair prospect 124.1
fair sex, the 77.3
fair shake 649.2, 790.2, 843.2, 972.7
fair-spoken 504.15, 504.17, 511.8
fair thing, the 649.2
fair to middling 1005.7
fair trade 630.5, 731.1
fair-trade 630.11
fair-trade agreement 630.5
fair-trading 630.5
fair value 630.2
fairway 182.10, 184.23, 310.7, 743.11, 751.1
fair weather 97.4, 317.3, 1010.4, 1019.7
fair-weather friend 357.8
fair-weather sailor 183.1
fair wind 318.10
fair words 504.5, 511.1
fairy (n) 75.15, 298.2, 678.8 (a) 678.17
fairyfolk 678.7
fairy godmother 478.11, 592.1, 659.5, 678.12
fairyish 678.17
fairyism 678.14
fairyland 678.7, 986.11
fairylike 678.17
fairy lore 678.14
fairy man 678.8
fairy queen 678.8
fairy ring 280.2
fairy tale 354.11
fairy woman 678.8
fait accompli 328.3, 407.1, 761.3, 973.2
faith 101.2, 124.1, 326.1, 434.1, 436.1, 617.5, 644.7, 653.3, 675.1, 692.1, 886.9, 953.1, 953.3, 970.5
faith, the 687.2
faith-based 685.7
faithful (n) 644.8 (a) 101.9, 104.26, 326.3, 349.14, 360.8, 434.4, 587.21, 644.20, 687.7, 692.8, 784.16, 853.7, 953.21, 970.17, 973.17
faithful, the 692.5, 953.9
faithful copy 785.1
faithful friend 588.2
faithful love 104.1
faithfully 820.5
faithfully yours 820.5
faithfulness 101.2, 326.1, 434.1, 644.7, 692.1, 853.1, 973.5, 973.7
faithful rendering 973.7
faithful servant 138.3, 692.4
faithful translation 341.3
faith healer 90.9
faith healing 90.13, 91.2
faithless 354.31, 363.11, 645.20, 695.19, 955.8
faithlessness 354.4, 363.2, 645.5, 695.5
faith of our fathers 687.2
faithworthiness 644.6, 970.4
faithworthy 644.19, 970.17
fake (n) 354.13, 356.7, 357.6, 500.7, 747.3, 785.1, 862.2 (v) 336.5, 354.17, 354.18, 354.21, 365.8, 500.12, 747.4 (a) 336.8, 354.26, 500.16, 784.10, 862.8
faked 354.26, 500.16
fake fur 4.2
fakement 354.13, 356.7, 415.3
fake one out 356.15
fake out 249.8, 354.19
fakeout 354.3
faker 336.4, 357.1, 357.6
fakery 336.1, 354.3, 356.4
fake someone out 356.16
fake tan 1016.10
fake up 340.9
faking 354.3
fakir 667.2, 699.12
falafel 10.9
Falak al Aflak 681.7
falcade 366.2
falcate 279.11
falciform 279.11
falcon (n) 311.27, 647.2 (v) 382.9
falconer 382.5
falconry 382.2

fall (n) 3.13, 194.1, 194.3, 202.2, 204.5, 238.11, 252.2, 313.4, 316.1, 367.1, 393.3, 394.2, 395.3, 410.3, 412.1, 474.3, 655.3, 913.2 (v) 194.5, 194.8, 202.6, 204.10, 252.6, 307.18, 316.10, 367.6, 393.17, 394.4, 395.22, 410.12, 412.12, 633.6, 654.9, 831.5, 1011.10 (a) 313.9
fall aboard 182.41
fall about 116.8
fallacious 354.25, 356.21, 688.9, 936.10, 936.11, 975.16, 976.9
fallaciousness 354.1, 356.1, 936.1, 975.1, 976.2
fall across 223.11
fallacy 354.1, 356.1, 688.2, 936.1, 936.3, 975.1
fall afoul of 902.13
fall again into 394.4
fall all over 138.9
fall all over oneself 101.6, 324.3, 401.5, 403.11
fall all over one with gratitude 150.4
fall among 223.11
fall apart 128.7, 393.23, 802.9
fall apart at the seams 128.7, 802.9
fall asleep 22.16, 307.18
fall asleep at the switch 984.3
fall astern 163.5, 217.8
fall at one's feet 138.7, 433.10
fall at the feet of 155.6
fall a victim to 85.47
fall away 204.10, 252.6, 363.7, 393.17, 911.2
fall back 163.6, 217.8, 393.16, 394.4, 903.7
fallback 163.2, 903.3
fall back on 387.14
fall back to prepared positions 460.10
fall back upon 387.14
fall behind 163.5, 166.4, 217.8
fall behindhand 166.4
fall between two stools 362.7, 410.12
fall by the wayside 16.9, 21.5, 391.8, 410.12, 911.3
fall dead 307.21, 410.12
fall down 182.29, 194.5, 194.8, 410.12, 911.3, 1003.3
fall down before 155.6
fall down dead 307.21
fall down on one's knees 658.5
fall down on the job 410.12
fall due 623.7
fallen 11.9, 252.10, 307.29, 395.28, 412.14, 654.12, 663.6, 665.28, 694.6, 695.18, 913.12
fallen angel 660.4
fallen chest 2.19
fallen countenance 132.1
fallen from grace 694.6
fallen humanity 312.6
fallen nature 663.2
fallenness 654.1
fallen state 654.1, 663.2
fallen woman 665.16
fall flat 117.4, 194.8, 410.12, 911.3
fall flat as a pancake 117.4
fall flat on one's face 410.12, 975.15
fall for 104.21, 953.10, 954.6
fall foul of 223.11, 902.13
fall from favor 661.7
fall from grace (n) 394.2, 655.3, 694.1 (v) 394.4, 654.9, 661.7
fall from one's high estate 661.7, 1011.11
fall from the lips 524.27
fall guy 358.2, 412.5, 862.3
fall head and ears in love 104.21
fall headlong 194.8
fall head over heels in love 104.21
fallibility 971.7, 975.1, 1003.1
fallible 971.22, 1003.4
fallible observer 722.6
fall in 260.10, 326.2, 393.24, 410.12, 807.5, 812.6
fall in a faint 25.5
falling (n) 194.1 (a) 194.11, 202.9, 204.16, 393.45, 913.12
falling action 722.4
falling-away 204.5
falling back 394.1
falling barometer 399.3
falling down and worshiping 696.1
falling glass 399.3
falling in love 104.3
falling leaf 184.15
falling loosely 202.9
falling-off 204.5, 393.3, 670.2
falling-out 456.4
falling short (n) 911.1, 992.1 (a) 132.6
falling shy 992.1
falling sickness 85.6, 917.6
falling star 1073.15
falling terminal 524.9
fall in line 326.2, 332.9, 579.4, 812.6, 867.4
fall in love 104.21
fall in price 633.6
fall in the way of 221.6
fall into 404.3, 479.7, 897.4
fall into a brown study 931.12
fall into a habit 373.11
fall into confusion 810.8
fall into decay 393.22
fall into despair 125.10
fall into disrepute 661.7
fall into disuse 390.9
fall into error 688.8, 975.9
fall in together 788.6
fall into line 332.9, 579.4, 807.5, 867.4
fall into one's hands 479.8
fall into order 807.5
fall into place 807.5
fall into rank 807.5, 812.6
fall into raptures 95.12
fall in with 169.2, 332.9, 441.3, 450.4, 455.2, 582.17, 867.3, 867.4, 897.4, 941.3
fall just right 843.6
fall line 237.2, 753.1
fall of Adam 655.3
fall of day 315.2
fall off 194.5, 204.10, 252.6, 363.7, 393.17, 802.9
fall of man 655.3
fall of the cards 759.2
fall of the curtain 820.1
fall of the leaf 313.4
fall of the year 313.4
fall on 194.10, 459.14, 941.3, 972.11
fall on deaf ears 49.4, 984.5
fall on evil days 1011.11
fall on one's face 194.8
fall on one's knees 138.7, 145.6, 150.4, 155.6
fall on one's knees before 433.10
fall on one's knees to 440.11
fall on the ear 48.12
fallopian tube 2.23
fallopian tubes 2.13
fall out 456.10, 887.4
fallout 1037.1, 1038.16, 1051.5
fallout shelter 1009.3, 1038.16
fall over 138.9, 194.8
fall over backward 403.11
fall over backwards 101.6
fallow (n) 1069.8 (v) 1069.17 (a) 36.7, 43.4, 331.18, 406.14, 891.4, 933.4
fallow deer 311.5
fallowing 1069.13
fallow mind 933.1
fallowness 43.1, 891.2
fall prostrate 194.8
falls 238.10, 238.11
fall senseless 25.5
fall short 132.3, 250.4, 410.12, 795.3, 911.2, 992.8, 1003.3
fall shy 992.8
fall silent 51.7
fall through 410.12, 911.3
fall to 8.20, 404.3, 641.5, 725.15, 818.7
fall to a low ebb 252.6
fall to loggerheads 457.17
fall to one 479.8, 641.7
fall to one's lot 479.8, 972.11
fall to one's share 479.8
fall to pieces 128.7, 393.22, 393.23, 395.22, 802.9, 806.3, 1050.3, 1051.10
fall to the ground 395.22, 410.12, 911.3
fall to work 725.15
fall under one's notice 983.11
fall upon 131.6, 186.7, 223.11, 459.14
fall wind 318.1
fall with 450.4
false 354.25, 354.31, 356.21, 356.22, 645.20, 674.7, 693.5, 975.16, 976.9
false air 354.3
false alarm 400.2, 410.8
false appearance 976.2
false belief 976.1
false cadence 709.23
false charge 599.4
false claim 640.1
false color 354.3
false coloring 265.2, 350.1, 354.9
false colors 356.11
false-dealing 354.31
false dew 1065.4
false dice 759.8
false doctrine 688.2
false echoes 1036.12
false economy 635.1
false eyelashes 3.13
false face 356.11, 645.6
false friend 357.8
false front 216.1, 354.3, 356.11, 500.1, 501.4
false fruit 10.38
false god 678.2
false hair 3.13
falsehearted 354.31, 356.22, 645.18, 645.21
falseheartedness 354.4, 356.3, 645.6
falsehood 265.2, 354.1, 354.8, 354.11
false hope 124.4
false horizon 201.4
false image 33.5, 350.2
false light 976.2
falsely color 354.16
falsely colored 265.11, 354.26
false memory 990.2
false modesty 500.6
false money 728.10
false move 975.4
false music 708.20
false name 527.8
false negative 354.1
falseness 354.1, 354.4, 356.1, 356.3, 645.3, 645.5, 693.1, 975.1, 976.2
false note 61.1, 975.4
false oath 354.9
false piety 354.6, 693.1
false plea 354.9
false positive 354.1, 400.2
false pretense 354.3
false pretenses 350.1
false pretension 354.3
false-principled 354.31
false reasoning 936.1
false show 354.3, 500.1, 976.2
false statement 354.11
false step 975.4
false swearing 354.9
false title 640.1
falsetto (n) 58.6, 525.1, 709.5 (a) 58.13, 708.50
false witness 357.9, 599.4
falsies 5.24
falsification 265.2, 350.1, 354.9
falsified 265.11, 354.26
falsifier 357.9
falsify 265.6, 350.3, 354.16, 354.19, 645.11
falsify accounts 628.10
falsifying 354.9
falsity 354.1, 354.3, 354.11, 645.5, 975.1
falter (n) 325.2, 362.3, 709.19, 917.3, 917.8 (v) 125.10, 175.8, 325.4, 362.7, 491.8, 525.8, 917.11, 917.15, 971.10
faltering (n) 325.2, 362.3, 525.3 (a) 175.10, 325.7, 362.11, 525.13

fam 559.5
fame 247.2, 352.4, 662.1, 997.2
famed 662.16
familial 560.18
familiar (n) 588.1, 678.12 (a) 117.9, 142.9, 373.13, 523.20, 581.3, 582.24, 587.19, 869.9, 928.27
familiar as household words 928.27
familiar friend 588.1
familiar friendship 587.8
familiarity 581.1, 582.1, 587.5, 640.2, 928.1, 928.3
familiarization 373.7, 405.1, 551.1
familiarize 373.9, 551.8
familiarized 373.15, 405.16
familiarness 117.3
familiar ring, a 117.3
familiar spirit 678.12
familiar story 974.3
familiar tune 974.3
familiar with 373.16, 928.19
family (n) 527.1, 559.2, 559.4, 559.5, 560.4, 561.1, 617.2, 809.5, 835.2, 1060.2, 1068.1 (a) 559.7, 560.18
family connection 559.1, 564.1
family counselor 466.5
family doctor 90.4
family favor 784.2
family feeling 788.3
family-friendly 559.6
family homestead 228.2
family jewels 2.13
family leave 78.1
family likeness 784.2
family man 76.10
family member 559.2
family name 527.5
family of man, the 312.1
family planning 891.1
family plot 309.15
family practice 90.1, 90.13
family relationship 775.3
family resemblance 784.2
family reunion 582.10
family room 197.12
family secret 345.5
family service 1008.2
family size 257.4
family-size 257.16
family-sized 257.23, 559.6
family-style 559.6
family therapy 92.6
family tie 559.1
family tree 560.5, 815.1
family values 449.3
family way, the 78.5
famine 891.1, 992.4
famine price 632.3
famish 307.23, 484.5
famished 100.25, 992.12
famishing 100.25
famous 247.9, 662.16, 999.12
famous last words 817.1
famousness 352.4, 662.1
famous person 997.8
fan (n) 101.5, 166.2, 171.4, 221.5, 317.10, 318.18, 509.8, 616.9, 866.3, 904.6, 926.18, 1024.3 (v) 105.12, 259.6, 317.11, 375.17, 410.10, 745.5, 758.5
fanatic (n) 101.4, 361.6, 692.4, 870.4, 926.15, 926.18, 980.5 (a) 361.8, 671.22, 926.32
fanatical 101.12, 361.8, 692.11, 926.32, 980.10
fanaticalness 926.11
fanaticism 101.3, 361.1, 671.2, 692.3, 886.9, 926.11, 980.1
fan base 918.2
fanciable 986.26
fancied 354.29, 762.9, 986.19
fancied up 5.46
fancier 100.12, 101.4, 770.15, 986.12
fanciful 364.5, 762.9, 764.6, 870.12, 932.9, 986.20
fancifulness 364.2
fanciness 498.2
fan club 101.5, 509.8
fancy (n) 100.1, 100.3, 104.1, 323.1, 364.1, 365.1, 371.5, 932.1, 976.3, 986.1, 986.5 (v) 100.14, 104.18, 951.10, 953.11, 986.14 (a) 8.33, 413.22, 498.12, 501.18, 501.21, 545.11, 632.11, 632.12, 993.16
fancy-born 986.20
fancy-bred 986.20
fancy-built 986.20
fancy diving 367.3
fancy dog 311.16
fancy dress 5.10
fancy-dress ball 705.2
fancy-framed 986.20
fancy-free 565.7
fancy man 665.18
fancy price 632.3
fancy talk 502.2
fancy up 5.42
fancywork 741.1
fancy-woven 986.20
fancy-wrought 986.20
fandangle 520.2
fane 703.2
fanfare 53.5, 116.2, 487.1, 517.16, 554.15
fanfaron (n) 502.5, 503.2 (a) 502.10
fanfaronade 487.1, 501.4, 502.1, 503.1
fanfaronading 502.10
fanfic 718.1
fang 2.8, 285.4, 1001.5
fanged 285.14, 474.9
fangotherapy 91.4
fangs 474.4
fan-jet engine 181.1
fanlike 171.8, 259.11
fan mail 553.4
fan marker 184.19
fanned 259.11
fanning (n) 171.1, 317.9 (a) 259.11
fanning out 171.1, 259.1
fanny 217.5
fanny pack 195.2, 729.15
fanon 703.10
fan out 171.5, 259.6, 771.4
fans 918.2
fan-shape 259.11
fan-shaped 171.8, 259.11, 876.3
fantabulous 999.13
fantail 217.6, 217.7
fantasied 354.29, 364.5
fantasist 986.12
fantasize 354.18, 986.14
fantasize about 354.18
fantasizing 92.23
fantasque 986.20
fantast 986.12
fantastic 122.10, 247.10, 354.29, 364.5, 762.9, 870.12, 923.11, 976.9, 986.20
fantastical 364.5, 870.12, 923.11, 986.20
fantasticality 364.2, 870.3
fantasticalness 923.3
fantasticism 986.1
fantastic notion 364.1
fantasy (n) 92.23, 100.1, 364.1, 870.8, 976.4, 985.2, 986.1, 986.5 (v) 985.9, 986.17
fantasy baseball 745.1
fantasy football 746.1
fantasying 985.2, 986.8
fantasy sport 744.1
fan the embers 989.12
fan the fire 105.12
fan the flame 105.12, 375.17, 456.14, 1020.22
fantoccino 349.6
fantoccio 349.6
fantoche 349.6
fanzine 101.5
far 261.8
farad 1032.16
far ahead 845.8
far and away the best 249.13
faraway 261.8, 985.11
farce 10.27, 489.1, 508.6, 704.6, 998.5
farcer 704.22, 707.9
farcical 488.6, 489.15, 508.14, 704.35
farcicality 488.2
farcicalness 488.2
farcist 704.22, 707.9
far cry, a 780.1
far cry 261.2
fardel 96.8, 770.8
fare (n) 10.1, 10.3, 178.1, 630.6 (v) 8.20, 177.18, 177.21, 765.5, 887.4
Far East 231.6
fare forth 177.18
far-embracing 864.13
fare well 409.7, 1010.7
farewell (n) 188.4 (a) 188.18
farewell address 543.2
farewell performance 704.12, 708.33
farewells 585.3
far-extending 864.13
far-famed 662.16
far-fetched 355.4, 776.8, 969.3
far-fetched story 354.11
far-flung 261.8, 267.7, 864.13
far-flying 864.13
far from it 787.5
far future 839.1
far-going 864.13
fargoing 267.7
far gone 85.56, 87.23
far-gone 88.31, 393.36, 898.5
far-heard 662.16
far horizon 158.4
far horizon, the 261.3
farina 1051.5
farinaceous 310.36, 1051.11
farinaceous plant 310.5
farm (n) 228.5, 739.1, 745.1, 1069.8, 1070.5 (v) 233.5, 615.16, 1069.16, 1070.6 (a) 233.6, 1069.20
farm belt 231.7, 233.1
farmboy 1069.5
farm club 745.1
farm country 233.1
farm economics 1069.1
farm economy 1069.1
farmed-out work 892.3
farmer 606.6, 630.10, 1069.5
farmerish 233.7
farmers' market 736.2
farmery 1069.8
farmgirl 1069.5
farmhand 1069.5
farmhold 1069.8
farmhouse 228.5
farming (n) 1069.1 (a) 1069.20
farm interests 609.31
farm laborer 1069.5
farmland 233.1, 1069.8
farmlet 1069.8
farm machinery 1040.3
farm out 615.16
farmplace 1069.8
farm pond 241.1
farmscape 712.11
farmstead 228.6, 1069.8
farm system 745.1
farm team 745.1
farm-to-fork 7.21
farm-to-table 7.21
farm worker 1069.5
farmyard 1069.8
farness 261.1
far-off 261.8
far-offness 261.1
far out 247.13, 841.13, 868.6
far past 837.3
far piece 261.2
farrago 354.11, 810.3
far-ranging 864.13
far-reaching 158.11, 267.7, 864.13
farrier 726.8, 1070.2
farrow (n) 302.10, 561.2 (v) 1.3
farrowing 1.1
farseeing 27.21, 920.16, 961.7
farseeingness 920.4, 961.1
farsight 27.1
farsighted 27.21, 28.11, 920.16, 961.7
farsightedness 27.1, 28.4, 920.4, 961.1
far-spread 864.13
far-spreading 864.13
far-stretched 864.13
fart, a 762.3
fart (n) 71.3, 660.5, 909.10 (v) 909.29
fart around 998.15

farther 253.10, 261.10
farthermost 261.12
farthest 261.12, 820.12
farthest bound 820.2
farthest off 261.12
farthest out 841.14
farthest outpost 216.2
farthing 248.2, 728.8, 881.2, 998.5
farthing dip 1026.2
farting 1067.3
farting around 998.9
fartlek 84.2
fasces 417.9, 647.1, 770.8
fascia 2.3, 201.3, 216.1, 271.4, 280.3
fascicle 554.13, 793.2
fascicled 770.21
fasciculated 770.21
fascinate 95.10, 104.22, 105.15, 377.7, 691.8, 983.12, 983.13
fascinated 104.27, 122.9, 691.12, 983.16, 983.18
fascinated attention 983.4
fascinating 97.7, 122.10, 377.8, 691.11, 983.20
fascination 97.2, 100.3, 101.1, 122.1, 122.3, 377.1, 691.2, 926.12, 926.13
fascinator 377.4
fascine 770.8
fascism 612.4, 612.7, 612.9, 980.4
fascist 612.16
fascistic 612.16
fashion (n) 5.1, 33.3, 262.1, 266.1, 373.1, 384.1, 532.2, 578.1, 765.4 (v) 262.7, 892.8
fashionability 578.2
fashionable (n) 578.7 (a) 578.11, 841.13
fashionableness 578.2
fashionable society 578.6
fashion design 5.32, 712.16, 717.5
fashion designer 5.36
fashioned 262.9, 892.18
fashioning 262.5, 266.1, 796.1, 892.2
fashionista 5.1, 578.7
fashion plate 500.9, 578.7
fashion roadkill 5.1
fast (n) 515.2, 668.2, 701.12 (v) 515.4, 668.7 (a) 35.18, 174.15, 293.12, 373.18, 587.21, 665.25, 800.14, 855.12, 855.16, 970.17
fast and loose 854.7
fast asleep 22.22
fast break 747.3
fast day 515.3, 701.12
fast deal 356.6
fast driver 756.2
fast-dye 35.14
fast-dyed 35.18
fasten 293.6, 428.10, 800.7, 855.8
fasten a quarrel on 456.13
fasten down 855.8
fastened 293.9, 800.14, 855.14, 855.16
fastener 800.3
fastening 800.3
fasten itself on the mind 931.20
fasten on 599.8
fasten oneself upon 138.11
fasten one's eyes upon 27.15
fasten up 202.8
fasten upon 480.16, 643.4, 888.4
faster than sound 50.17, 174.16
fast food 8.6, 10.1, 10.2
fast-food 387.20, 405.19, 830.4
fast-food restaurant 8.17
fast-forward 174.3, 401.3
fast friend 588.2
fast friendship 587.8
fast-growing 14.3, 251.8, 259.12
fasthold 460.6
fastidious 79.25, 495.9, 496.8, 644.15, 944.7
fastidiousness 79.1, 495.1, 496.1, 644.2, 944.1
fasting (n) 270.9, 515.1, 658.3, 667.1 (a) 100.25, 515.5, 668.10
fast lane 174.3, 669.2
fast-lane 100.28
fastnacht 10.44
fastness 174.1, 460.6, 587.7, 665.3, 855.1
fast pace 669.2
fast pile 1038.13
fast rate 174.1
fast-rising 251.8
fast surface 748.1
fast telegram 347.14
fast time 832.3
fast track 174.3, 249.5, 578.6
fast-track 100.28
fastwalk 383.2
fat (n) 7.7, 993.4, 999.8, 1056.1 (v) 259.8 (a) 257.18, 259.13, 268.10, 269.8, 297.16, 472.16, 618.14, 922.15, 991.7, 1010.13, 1056.9
fatal 308.23, 395.26, 839.8, 972.15, 997.20, 1011.14, 1011.15
fatal accident 307.5, 308.8
fatal attraction 665.15
fatal blow 308.10
fatal disease 85.2
fatal flaw 16.2, 16.4, 1006.4
fatal hour 307.7
fatalism 106.2, 134.2, 964.4
fatalist 964.5
fatalistic 964.10
fatality 133.6, 133.7, 308.8, 308.9, 964.2
fatality list 307.13
fata morgana 976.6, 1025.13
fat as a hog 257.18
fat as a pig 257.18
fat as a quail 257.18
fat as bacon 257.18
fat-assed 257.18
fat cat 618.7
fat chance 969.1
fat city 1010.1
fate (n) 395.2, 477.5, 820.1, 839.2, 963.7, 964.2, 972.1 (v) 477.9, 964.7
fated 839.8, 963.15, 964.9
fated moment 824.1
fatedness 963.7
fateful 133.16, 395.26, 963.15, 964.9, 997.20, 997.22
fateful moment 824.1
fatefulness 133.6, 963.7
Fates 964.3
Fates, the 839.2
fate worse than death 665.6
fat-faced type 548.6
fat-free 7.21
fat-free diet 7.13
fathead 924.4
fatheaded 922.17
fatheadedness 922.4
Father 648.5
father (n) 699.5, 886.4, 892.7, 997.8 (v) 818.14, 886.10, 888.5
father (n) 76.10, 304.5, 559.3, 560.9 (v) 78.8
Father Christmas 678.13
father complex 92.22
father confessor 699.5
father figure 92.31
father fixation 92.21
Fatherhood 677.1
fatherhood 559.1, 560.2
father image 92.29, 92.31
father in Christ 699.5
fathering 78.2
father-in-law 564.2
fatherland 228.2, 232.2
fatherless 19.18, 307.34, 584.12
fatherlessness 584.4
fatherlike 560.17
fatherliness 560.2
father love 104.4
fatherly 560.17
fatherly eye 1008.2
Father of Lies 357.9
fathers 560.7
Fathers, the 684.2
fathership 560.2
fathers of the church 684.2
father's side 560.4
father surrogate 92.31
father symbol 92.30
Father Time 304.2, 821.2
father upon 888.4
fathom 275.10, 300.10, 521.7, 928.12, 938.23, 940.2
fathomable 300.14, 521.10
fathomableness 521.1
fathomage 275.6
fathoming 275.6
fathomless 275.12
fathomlessness 275.1
fatidic 839.8, 962.11, 972.15
fatidical 962.11
fatigue (n) 16.1, 16.5, 21.1, 85.9, 331.6, 725.4 (v) 21.4, 21.5, 118.6
fatigued 16.18, 21.7, 393.36
fatigue disease 21.1
fatigues 5.1
fatiguesome 21.13
fatigue syndrome 21.1
fatiguing 16.20, 21.13, 118.10
fatling 311.6
fatness 257.8, 268.2, 269.2, 297.1, 1056.5
fat of the land 991.2, 1010.1
fat part 704.10
fat person 257.12
fat purse 618.1
fat shaming 127.6
fatso 257.12
fatten 8.19, 251.4, 257.15, 259.8, 269.5, 392.9, 890.8, 1010.8, 1070.6
fattening (n) 251.1 (a) 8.33, 890.11
fatten on 8.28, 138.12
fatten up 7.17, 8.19
fatten upon 8.28
fattiness 1056.5
fattish 257.18
fattishness 257.8
fatty (n) 257.12 (a) 1056.9
fatty acid 7.7
fatty oil 1056.1
fatuitous 19.15, 391.13, 764.6, 923.8
fatuity 19.3, 391.2, 923.1, 933.1
fatuous 19.15, 391.13, 764.6, 923.8, 933.4, 998.19
fatuousness 923.1
fat-witted 922.16
faubourg 230.1
fauces 2.18
faucet 239.10, 293.4
fault (n) 224.2, 654.2, 655.2, 748.2, 975.1, 975.3, 1003.2, 1004.1 (v) 115.15, 510.12, 748.3
fault-block mountain 237.6
fault-find 510.15
faultfind 510.12
faultfinder 108.3, 115.8, 510.9, 946.7
faultfinding (n) 115.4, 510.4, 512.1 (a) 108.7, 115.19, 510.23
faultful 975.16
faultiness 975.1, 1003.1
faulting 237.6
faultless 657.6, 973.16, 1002.6
faultlessness 657.1, 973.5, 1002.1
fault line 748.2
fault scarp 237.2
faulty 531.4, 656.3, 936.11, 975.16, 1003.4, 1004.8
faulty comparison 531.1
faulty coordination 531.1
faulty eyesight 28.1
faulty grammar 531.1
faulty punctuation 531.1
faulty reasoning 975.1
faulty reference 531.1
faulty subordination 531.1
faulty syntax 531.1, 975.7
faun 678.11
fauna 311.1, 1068.1
faunal 1068.4
Faunus 678.11
Faust 690.5
Faustianism 108.1
fauteuil 704.15
faux 336.8
faux pas 975.5
favela 230.6
faveolate 284.17
favicon 1042.19
favonian 318.21
Favonius 318.2

favor (n) 33.4, 100.3, 143.7, 145.1, 155.1, 216.4, 249.1, 371.5, 449.4, 478.7, 509.1, 553.2, 587.3, 642.2, 662.3, 894.1, 894.2, 989.6, 999.4 (v) 100.14, 143.9, 155.4, 371.17, 392.9, 427.6, 449.11, 449.14, 449.17, 449.19, 509.9, 650.8, 784.7, 999.10
favorable 124.12, 133.17, 324.5, 441.4, 449.22, 509.17, 587.15, 843.9, 995.5, 999.12
favorable attention 48.2
favorable disposition 324.1
favorableness 133.8, 324.1, 449.10, 843.1, 999.1
favorable opportunity 843.3
favorable prospect 968.1, 972.8
favorable regard 587.3
favorable termination 409.1
favorable vote 509.1
favorable wind 184.32, 318.10
favorably disposed 324.5
favorably impressed with 95.15
favorably inclined 324.5
favorably situated 894.14
favored 371.25, 430.30, 509.19, 1010.14
favorer 588.1, 616.9
favoring (n) 427.3 (a) 133.17, 371.25, 384.8, 509.17, 784.10
favorite (n) 104.15, 662.9, 757.2 (a) 104.23, 509.19, 587.19
favorite of the gods 1010.6
favorite son 610.9
favoritism 371.5, 650.3, 980.3
favors of office 609.36
favor with 478.15, 478.17
fawn (n) 302.10, 311.5 (v) 1.3, 138.7 (a) 40.3
fawn-colored 40.3
fawner 138.3
fawnery 138.2
fawning (n) 138.2, 511.1 (a) 138.14, 511.8
fawningness 138.2
fawn upon 138.9, 511.5
fax (n) 347.4, 347.15, 785.5 (v) 785.8 (a) 347.21
fax number 347.12
fax transmission 714.3
fay (n) 678.8 (a) 678.17
faze 127.18
fazing 127.28
FBI agent 576.10
f-block 1060.2
F clef 709.13
fealty 326.1, 641.1, 644.7
fear (n) 96.2, 103.3, 126.1, 127.1, 128.1, 362.4, 491.1 (v) 127.10, 362.7
fear and trembling 127.5
feared 127.22
fear for 133.10
fearful 126.7, 127.23, 127.28, 128.11, 247.11, 491.10
fearfulness 127.2, 127.3
fear God 692.6
fearing 127.23
fear-inspiring 127.28, 514.3
fearless 492.19
fearlessness 492.2
fear of God 692.2
fear of missing out 844.5
fearsome 127.23, 127.28
fearsomeness 127.2
fear-stricken 127.22
fear-struck 127.22
feasance 436.2
feasibility 889.3, 966.2, 995.1, 1014.2
feasible 889.10, 966.7, 995.5, 995.6, 1014.15
feasible, the 966.1
feast (n) 8.9, 10.1, 20.4, 95.3, 701.12, 743.4 (v) 8.24, 95.8, 743.25
feast and famine 972.5
feast day 20.4
feasting 8.1
feast of the soul 95.3
feast on 8.20, 8.28, 95.13
feast one's eyes on 27.15
feast upon 8.28
feat 328.3, 413.8, 413.10, 492.6
feather (n) 3.16, 3.18, 298.2, 809.3, 998.5 (v) 3.21, 182.53, 184.40, 196.7, 498.9
feather an oar 182.53
feather bed 295.10, 1047.4
featherbedding 993.4
featherbrain 924.7
featherbrained 922.20, 985.16
feathered 3.28, 498.11
feathered friends 311.27
featheredge 211.4, 285.2
featheredged 285.8
feathered songster 710.23
featherhead 924.4, 924.7
featherheaded 922.17, 985.16
featheriness 1047.1
feathering 3.18
feather in one's cap, a 411.1
feather in one's cap 646.3
feather in the wind 854.4
featherlike 3.27
feather one's nest 387.16, 389.4, 618.10
feather out 3.21
feathers 3.18, 5.1, 295.3, 1047.4
feathers fly 457.13
featherweight (n) 258.4, 297.3 (a) 298.13, 895.3
feathery 3.27, 298.10, 1047.14
featliness 413.2
featly 413.23
feature (n) 33.3, 33.4, 556.1, 706.1, 735.2, 793.4, 796.2, 865.4, 866.2, 997.7 (v) 348.5, 704.28, 865.11, 866.4, 983.10, 997.14, 997.15 (a) 866.5
feature attraction 707.6
featured 348.12, 866.5
featured actor 707.2
featured player 706.4
feature editor 555.4
feature fatigue 1033.4
feature film 706.1
feature-length film 706.1
featureless 222.14, 263.4, 812.8, 864.11
featurelessness 812.1
features 33.4, 211.2, 216.4, 262.3
feature story 552.3
feature writing 547.2, 718.2
featuring 348.4, 865.6
febricity 85.7
febrifugal 86.41
febrifuge 86.14
febrile 85.58, 93.18, 101.12, 105.22
febrility 85.7, 917.1
fecal 12.20, 71.5, 80.23
feces 12.4, 256.2
feckless 19.15, 391.9, 406.15
fecklessness 391.2, 406.2
feculence 12.4, 80.2
feculent 12.20, 71.5, 80.23
fecund 538.11, 890.9, 986.18
fecundate 78.10, 890.8
fecundation 78.3, 890.1, 890.3
fecundative 78.15
fecundatory 890.11
fecundify 78.10, 890.8
fecundity 538.2, 890.1, 986.3
fed 576.10, 1008.15
Federal 576.10
federal (n) 1008.15 (a) 612.16, 805.7
federal assembly 613.1
Federal Aviation Agency 184.7
Federal Bureau of Investigation 576.10, 1008.17
Federal Communications Commission 1034.16
federal court 595.2
federalese 523.10, 609.37, 612.10
Federal Government 613.2
federal government 612.4
federalism 612.4, 612.7
federalist 612.16
federalistic 612.16
Federalist Party 609.24
federalization 805.1
federalize 805.4
federal prison 429.8
Federal Reserve Bank 729.14
Federal Reserve note 728.5
Federal Reserve System 729.14
federate (v) 450.3, 805.4 (a) 805.6
federated 805.6
federation 232.1, 450.2, 612.4, 617.1, 805.1
Fédération Internationale de Hockey 749.4
Fédération Internationale de Ski 753.1
Federation of International Football Associations 752.1
federative 805.7
feds 1008.16
fed to the gills 994.6
fed to the teeth 994.6
fed up 118.11, 994.6
fed-upness 994.2
fee (n) 478.5, 624.5, 630.6 (v) 624.10
feeble 16.12, 19.13, 32.6, 52.16, 85.54, 303.18, 362.12, 922.21, 936.12
feeble-eyed 28.13
feebleminded 362.12, 922.21
feeblemindedness 362.4, 922.8
feebleness 16.1, 19.1, 32.2, 52.1, 85.3, 303.5, 362.4, 922.8
feed (n) 8.5, 10.4, 704.10, 747.3, 749.3 (v) 7.17, 8.18, 8.20, 95.8, 306.11, 375.21, 385.9, 449.16, 890.8, 1020.22, 1021.8, 1070.6, 1070.7
feedback 50.13, 903.1, 1041.6
feedback circuit 1041.6
feedback control 1041.3
feedback loop 1041.6
feedback system engineer 1041.19
feedback system engineering 1041.2
feeder 8.16, 238.3, 704.10, 707.2
feeder airline 184.10
feeder plant 739.3
feeding (n) 7.1, 8.1 (a) 8.31
feeding frenzy 8.9, 457.2
feed on 8.28, 138.12
feed one a line 356.16
feed one's face 8.20
feed the fire 105.12, 375.17, 1020.22
feed the fish 909.26
feed upon 8.28
fee-faw-fum 127.9, 680.9
feel (n) 73.1, 73.3, 209.3, 294.1, 413.6, 944.1 (v) 24.6, 33.10, 73.6, 93.10, 223.10, 562.16, 831.8, 934.4, 951.10
feel about it 978.6
feel around 938.32
feel ashamed of oneself 137.9
feel at home 121.8, 430.18, 581.2
feel at liberty 430.18
feel aversion for 103.6
feel awful 85.46
feel better about 120.8
feel cheap 137.9
feel comfortable with 413.18
feel confident 124.6
feel contempt for 157.3
feel creepy 74.7
feel crummy 85.56
feel deeply 93.10
feel disgust 99.4
feel dragged out 21.5
feel easy 121.8
feel entitled 141.8
feeler 3.10, 73.4, 439.1, 938.10, 942.4
feel fine 83.6
feel fit 83.6
feel for 93.11, 145.3, 938.32
feel free 430.18
feel free as a bird 430.18
feel funny 74.7
feel good 83.6, 95.6, 95.12
feel happy 95.12
feel hungry 100.19
feel hurt 152.12
feel ill 85.46
feeling (n) 24.1, 73.1, 73.2, 93.1, 145.1, 209.3, 934.3, 944.1, 951.5, 952.2, 953.6, 962.1, 978.1, 978.4 (a) 24.9, 93.17, 934.5, 938.37
feeling awful 85.56
feeling evil 110.17

feeling faint 21.7, 85.56
feeling for 413.5, 896.1
feeling for language 532.2
feeling for words 532.2
feeling in one's bones 93.1, 133.1, 934.3, 951.5
feeling low 112.22
feeling no pain 88.33
feeling of identity 455.1
feeling of kinship 143.1
feeling of relief 120.4
feeling one's oats 83.8
feeling out 942.2
feeling-out 439.1
feelings 24.3, 93.1, 978.4
feeling something terrible 85.56
feeling the pinch 619.7
feeling tone 978.1
feeling up 73.2
feel in one's bones 93.10, 133.9, 934.4, 961.6
feel in one's breast 93.11
feel in one's gut 93.10
feel in one's viscera 93.10
feel intuitively 934.4
feel like a million 83.6
feel like a million dollars 83.6
feel like a new person 83.7, 396.20, 852.6, 858.12
feel like hell 85.46
feel like the walking dead 85.46
feel no obligation 151.3
feel no remorse 114.3
feel nothing 114.3
feel of 73.6
feel oneself again 120.8
feel one's oats 17.11, 83.6
feel one's way 30.8, 162.4, 339.7, 403.10, 494.5, 938.32
feel out 942.9
feel out of place 872.6
feel pain 26.8
feel relief 120.8
feel resentment 152.12
feel right 95.6
feel small 137.9
feel something terrible 85.46
feel sore 152.12
feel sorrow for 145.3
feel sorry for 145.3
feel superior to 157.3
feel sure 953.14, 970.9
feel the ground sliding from under one 1006.8
feel the pangs 26.8
feel the pulse 942.9
feel the want of 963.9, 992.7
feel the wind of change 133.9
feel under an obligation 150.3
feel under the weather 85.46
feel unsure 971.9
feel up 73.8, 223.10, 562.16
feel with 147.2
feel with the fingertips 73.6
fee position 469.1
fee simple 469.1
fee simple absolute 469.1
fee simple conditional 469.1
fee simple defeasible 469.1
fee simple determinable 469.1
feet 548.6
fee tail 469.1
feet of clay 16.4
feign 354.21, 500.12
feigned 354.26, 500.16
feigned belief 500.1
feigning 354.3
feint (n) 354.3, 356.6, 376.1, 415.3, 459.3, 746.3, 754.3, 760.4 (v) 459.16, 754.4
feist 110.11
feistiness 110.3, 110.4, 327.2, 359.3, 361.3, 456.3, 935.13
feisty 17.13, 110.20, 110.25, 327.10, 359.14, 361.11, 456.17, 935.19
feldspar 742.3
felicific 97.6
felicitate 149.2
felicitation 149.1
felicitous 97.6, 496.9, 509.16, 533.7, 544.8, 788.10, 843.9, 995.5
felicitousness 97.1, 533.1, 544.1, 843.1
felicity 95.2, 109.1, 413.5, 496.2, 533.1, 544.1, 788.5, 1010.1, 1010.2
felid 311.42
feline (n) 311.3, 311.20 (a) 311.42, 345.12, 415.12
fell (n) 4.2, 236.1, 237.3, 295.3 (v) 201.6, 308.18, 395.19, 412.10, 904.12, 913.5 (a) 127.30, 144.26, 308.23
fellah 606.6
fellate 75.22
fellatio 75.7
fellation 75.7
felled 412.17
feller 76.5
fellow (n) 76.5, 90.4, 104.12, 302.5, 312.5, 349.5, 571.1, 571.4, 588.1, 588.3, 616.1, 617.11, 769.4, 784.3, 790.4 (a) 450.5, 769.9
fellow citizen 227.5
fellow commoner 572.7
fellow companion 588.3
fellow conspirator 616.3
fellow countryman 227.5
fellow countrywoman 227.5
fellow creature 312.5, 588.1
fellow feeling 93.5, 104.1, 143.1, 145.1, 450.1, 455.1, 587.3
fellow heir 479.5
fellowman 588.1
fellow member 616.1
fellowship (n) 450.1, 450.2, 455.1, 478.8, 571.10, 582.2, 582.4, 582.6, 587.2, 617.3, 646.7, 675.3, 769.2 (v) 582.17
fellow student 572.3, 588.3
fellow townsman 227.5
fellow traveler 178.1, 332.6, 611.13, 769.5
fellow worker 616.5
felly 280.4
felo-de-se 308.5
felon 85.37, 593.1, 660.9
felonious 645.16, 655.5, 674.6
feloniousness 645.1, 655.1
felony 655.2, 674.4
felsic rock 1059.1
felt (n) 4.1 (v) 740.6
fem 77.14
female (n) 75.1, 77.4 (a) 77.13
female being 77.4
female chauvinism 590.1
female chauvinist 590.2, 980.5
female-chauvinistic 590.3
female circumcision 701.9
female gamete 305.12
female homosexual 75.15
female impersonator 707.1
female line 560.4
femaleness 75.1, 77.1, 303.2
female organs 2.13
female rhyme 720.9
female sex, the 77.3
female suffrage 609.17
feme 563.8
feme covert 77.5, 563.8
feme sole 77.5, 565.4
feminacy 77.1
feminality 77.1
femineity 77.1
feminine (n) 530.10 (a) 77.13
feminine caesura 720.7
feminineness 77.1
feminine rhyme 720.9
feminine wile 77.1, 665.6
femininity 75.1, 77.1, 77.3, 303.2
feminism 77.1, 77.2, 642.4, 980.4
feminist 77.5, 642.5, 980.5
feminization 77.11
feminize 77.12
femme 77.5
femme fatale 377.4, 665.15
fen 243.1
fence (n) 212.4, 460.4, 467.1, 479.3, 732.6, 750.2, 1012.5 (v) 212.7, 368.8, 457.13, 460.9, 479.6, 732.7, 936.9, 1008.18
fenced 212.10
fenced-in 212.10
fence in 212.5, 212.7, 429.12
fence off 213.8, 773.6
fenceposts 750.2
fencer 461.1
fencer's mask 1008.3
fences 745.1
fence-sitter 362.5, 467.4
fence-sitting (n) 362.1, 467.1 (a) 246.3, 362.9, 363.12
fence-straddler 362.5, 467.4
fence-straddling (n) 362.1, 467.1 (a) 362.9, 363.12
fence up 212.7, 429.12
fencing 212.4, 344.4, 457.8, 760.4, 936.5
fencing-in 212.1
fend 460.10, 1008.18, 1012.14
fender 213.5, 1008.3, 1020.11
fend for oneself 430.20
fend off 460.10, 908.3, 1012.14
fenestra 292.1
fenestrated 292.19
feng shui 498.1
Fenian 860.6
fenland 243.1
fenny 243.3, 1065.15
Fensalir 681.10
feodal 471.9
feodum 469.1
feoffee 470.2, 479.4
feoffor 478.11
feral 105.25, 144.26, 308.23, 309.22, 311.39, 671.21
feria 743.4
ferial 20.10
ferine 671.21
fermata 709.12, 857.3
ferment (n) 10.28, 105.4, 152.7, 298.4, 320.3, 330.4, 671.2, 852.5, 917.1 (v) 67.4, 298.7, 320.4, 375.17, 671.12, 917.10, 1060.8
fermentation 67.3, 105.4, 298.4, 320.3, 917.1
fermentative 298.17
fermenting 298.17
Fermi-Dirac statistics 968.2
fern 310.4
fern seed 691.6
ferocious 105.25, 144.26, 458.20, 671.21
ferociousness 144.11, 671.1
ferocity 144.11, 458.10, 671.1
ferret 27.11, 311.22
ferret-eyed 27.21
ferret out 938.34, 941.4
ferric 1058.17
ferrier 183.5
Ferris wheel 743.15
ferroconcrete 1054.2
ferromagnetic 1032.31
ferromagnetism 1032.7
ferrotype 714.4
ferrous 1058.17
ferruginous 40.4, 41.6, 1058.17
ferry (n) 383.3 (v) 176.13, 184.36
ferryman 183.5
ferry rocket 1075.2
fertile 890.9, 986.18, 991.7
fertile imagination 986.3
fertile material 1038.10
fertile mind 986.3
fertility 538.2, 890.1, 986.3, 991.2
fertility cult 890.5
fertility drug 86.32
fertility god 678.11, 1069.4
fertility pill 86.32
fertility rate 78.1
fertility rite 701.9
fertility symbol 92.30
fertilization 78.3, 890.3
fertilize 78.10, 890.8, 1069.17
fertilizer 890.4
fertilizing 78.15, 890.11
ferule 604.1, 605.2
fervency 93.2, 101.2, 544.5, 1019.2
fervent 93.18, 101.9, 105.22, 330.22, 544.13
fervent hope 124.1
fervid 93.18, 100.24, 101.9, 105.22
fervidity 1019.2
fervidness 93.2, 101.2, 1019.2
fervor 93.2, 101.2, 104.1, 324.1, 330.6, 544.5, 1019.2
fervorless 102.6
fervorlessness 102.1
Fescennine 666.9

fescenninity 666.4
fess 647.2
fessing up 351.3
fess point 647.2
fess up 351.7
fest 708.32
festal 20.10, 487.3, 743.28
festal board 8.9
fester (n) 85.37 (v) 12.15, 26.7, 393.22
festering (n) 12.6, 26.4, 85.37, 393.2 (a) 12.21, 26.11, 393.40, 989.25
fester in the mind 989.13
festinate (v) 401.5 (a) 401.9
festination 401.3
festival 708.32, 743.4
festival day 20.4
festive 487.3, 582.23, 743.28
festive occasion 95.3, 743.4
festivity 95.3, 116.1, 487.1, 582.3, 582.11, 743.3, 743.4, 770.2
festoon (n) 279.2, 310.25 (v) 545.7
festooned 498.11, 545.11
festoons 498.3
Festschrift 554.7, 770.11
fetal 305.22, 406.12, 818.15
fetch (n) 158.2, 356.6, 415.3, 988.1, 988.3 (v) 176.16, 177.18, 182.35, 186.6, 377.6, 630.13, 902.14, 946.10
fetch about 163.9, 182.30
fetch and carry 138.8, 176.16
fetch away 182.29
fetch breath 306.8
fetch down 913.5
fetcher 1016.8
fetching 97.7, 377.8
fetching-up 568.3
fetch up 182.33, 568.13, 857.7
fetch up all standing 182.33, 857.7
fetch up at 186.6
fete 95.3, 582.11, 743.4, 770.2
fête champêtre 8.6, 743.4
fete day 20.4
fetichism 697.1
fetid 64.7, 71.5, 80.23, 98.18, 1000.9, 1067.9
fetid air 1067.1
fetidity 71.1, 71.2
fetidness 64.3, 71.1, 71.2, 80.2
fetish (n) 691.5, 697.3 (v) 697.5
fetishism 75.11, 675.6, 690.1, 697.1
fetishist 75.16, 697.4
fetishistic 690.14, 697.7
fetishization 697.2
fetishize 697.5
fetlock 3.6, 199.5
fetor 64.3, 71.1
fetter (n) 428.4, 1012.7 (v) 428.10, 800.10, 1012.11
fettered 428.16
fettle (n) 84.1, 765.3 (v) 79.20
fettuccine 10.33
fetus 305.14
feud (n) 456.5, 469.1, 507.1, 589.4 (v) 456.11, 457.13
feudal 417.16, 432.13, 471.9
feudalism 432.1, 612.7
feudality 432.1, 612.7
feudal system 612.4
feudatory (n) 470.2, 577.1 (a) 432.13, 471.9
feuder 461.1
feuille 296.2
fever (n) 85.7, 85.9, 105.7, 758.2, 882.1, 917.1, 926.7, 1019.1 (v) 85.47
fever blister 85.37, 320.1
fevered 85.58, 93.18
fever heat 85.7, 105.7, 1019.1
feverish 85.58, 93.18, 101.12, 105.22, 401.9, 917.16, 1019.25
feverishness 85.7, 401.2, 917.1, 1019.1
fever of excitement 105.7
feverous 85.58
fever pill 86.14
fever pitch 105.7
fever-reducer 86.14
fever ward 197.25
few, a 883.1, 884.2, 885.2
few 248.6, 250.8, 885.4
few, the 885.3
few and far between 771.9, 848.2, 885.5, 992.11
fewer 885.6
fewness 248.1, 250.3, 885.1
fey 870.15, 927.5
feyness 689.8
fiancé 104.16
fiancée 104.16
fiasco 132.1, 410.6
fiat 420.4, 443.3
fiat money 728.5
fib (n) 354.11 (v) 354.19
fibber 357.9
fibbery 354.8
fibbing 354.8
fiber 4.1, 7.3, 271.1, 305.1, 767.4
fiber art 712.2
fiber cable 347.17
fibered 271.7
Fiberglas racket 748.1
fiberglass 295.23
fiber-optic cable 347.17
fiber optics 29.7, 1025.22
Fibonacci numbers 1017.8
fibril 271.1
fibrilla 271.1
fibrillation 85.9, 851.1, 916.3
fibrilliform 271.7
fibroid 271.7
fibrous 271.7, 294.7, 1049.4
fibster 357.9
fice 110.11
fiche 785.4
fickle 362.9, 364.6, 645.20, 828.7, 854.7, 971.16
fickle finger of fate, the 972.2
fickleness 362.1, 364.3, 645.5, 854.2, 971.1
fictile 1047.9
fictility 1047.2
fiction 354.10, 354.11, 547.10, 722.1, 986.3, 986.5
fictional 354.29, 719.7, 722.8, 986.21
fictionalization 354.9, 986.3
fictionalize 354.18, 722.7, 986.14
fictionalized 354.29, 722.8, 986.21
fictioneer 547.15, 718.4
fictionist 722.5
fiction of the mind 986.5
fiction writer 547.15, 718.4
fictitious 354.26, 354.29, 986.21
fictitious name 527.8
fictive 354.26, 986.21
fid 89.7
fiddle (n) 356.9 (v) 396.14, 708.41, 998.15
fiddle around 396.14, 998.15
fiddlebow 711.5
fiddledeedee 520.2
fiddle-faddle (n) 520.2 (v) 998.15
fiddler 710.5
Fiddler's Green 986.11
fiddlestick 711.5
fiddlesticks 520.2
fiddlestring 711.20
fiddle with 998.14
fiddling 354.9, 998.8
fiddling around 998.9
fideicommissary heir 479.5
fideism 953.1
fideist 953.9
fideistic 953.21
fidelity 101.2, 360.1, 434.1, 644.7, 973.5
Fides 649.4
Fides populi Romani 649.4
Fides publica Romani 649.4
fidget 105.18, 128.6, 917.13
fidgetiness 105.5, 128.1, 330.4, 917.5
fidgeting (n) 917.5 (a) 128.12
fidgets 105.5, 128.1, 917.1, 917.5
fidgety 105.27, 128.12, 330.20, 917.16, 917.19
fiducial 855.12, 953.25
fiduciary (n) 470.5 (a) 438.13, 728.30, 953.24, 953.25
fiduciary heir 479.5
fidus Achates 616.7
fiefdom 469.1
field 158.1, 158.4, 184.22, 209.2, 212.3, 231.2, 231.4, 310.8, 430.4, 463.1, 463.2, 568.8, 647.2, 724.4, 743.11, 745.1, 746.1, 749.4, 752.1, 757.3, 865.7, 866.1, 928.10, 937.1, 1042.18, 1069.9
field, the 452.2
field archery 744.1
field army 461.22
field artillery 462.11
field-based 724.16
field day 20.4, 743.4, 743.10
field dog 311.17
field emission 1033.5
fielder 745.2
field event 755.2
field general 746.2
field glass 29.4
field glasses 29.4
field goal 746.3, 747.3
field guide 554.8
field hockey 749.4
Field Hockey Association of America 749.4
field hockey game 749.6
field hockey match 749.6
field hockey team 749.5
field holler 708.11
field house 755.1
field ice 1023.5
fielding average 745.4
field magnet 907.3
field marshal 575.17
field of battle 463.2
field of blood 308.12, 463.2
field of bloodshed 308.12, 463.2
field of electrical force 1032.3
field officer 575.17
field of inquiry 928.10
field of slaughter 463.2
field of study 928.10
field of view 27.1, 31.3
field of vision 27.1, 27.7, 31.3
field rations 10.6
field-sequential television 1035.5
fields of Aalu 681.9
field spirit 678.11
field station 942.5
field-tested 942.12
field train 461.22
fieldwork 413.9
fiend 87.21, 101.5, 593.6, 671.9, 680.6
fiend from hell 593.6, 680.6
fiendish 144.26, 654.13, 680.17, 1000.10
fiendishness 144.11, 654.4, 680.13
fiendlike 144.26, 654.13, 680.17
fierce 17.14, 105.25, 105.29, 144.26, 152.32, 458.20, 671.16, 671.21
fierceness 17.5, 144.11, 458.10, 671.1
fierce temper 110.4
fieriness 68.2, 544.5, 1019.12
fiery 26.11, 41.6, 85.58, 93.18, 101.9, 105.22, 105.29, 110.25, 544.13, 671.22, 1019.26, 1020.26, 1025.39
fiery cross 458.11
fiery crostarie 458.11
fiery furnace 1019.11
fiery ordeal 96.9
fiery temper 110.4
fiesta 95.3, 743.4
Fiesta Bowl 746.1
fife 708.42
fife and drum corps 710.12
fifer 710.4
Fifinella 680.7
fifteen 882.7
fifteen minutes of fame 247.2, 662.6
15-year mortgage 438.4
fifth (n) 709.20, 882.1, 882.14 (a) 882.17
Fifth Amendment 51.1
fifth column 357.11
fifth-column 645.22
fifth-column activity 645.7
fifth columnist 357.11, 363.5, 551.6

fifth force 1038.6
fifth-generation computer 1042.2
fifth starter 745.2
fifth wheel 768.2, 993.2, 993.4
fiftiesh 303.14
fifty 882.7
fifty cents 728.7
fifty-dollar bill 728.7
fifty-fifty (n) 875.2, 972.7 (a) 264.4, 467.7, 477.13, 790.7, 797.14
55+ community 209.1
fifty percent 875.2
fig 5.10, 998.5
fight (n) 456.5, 457.3, 457.4, 458.10, 725.3, 754.3 (v) 35.15, 451.4, 456.11, 457.13, 458.13, 725.11, 754.4
fight a duel 457.13
fight against 451.4
fight a holding action 460.10
fight back 106.8, 451.4, 453.3, 900.6
fight down 106.8
fighter 181.9, 461.1, 754.2
fighter pilot 185.3
fight fire 1022.7
fight fire with fire 506.4
fight for 457.20
fight game, the 754.1
fight hammer and tongs 457.17
fight hand-to-hand 457.15
fighting (n) 457.1, 457.9, 458.1, 754.1 (a) 457.22, 458.20
fighting at close quarters 457.1
fighting chance 972.9
fighting cock 461.1, 492.7
fighting force 18.9
fighting machine 461.20
fighting mad 152.30
fighting man 461.6
fighting spirit 492.1
fighting weight 297.3
fighting words 454.2
fight it out 457.17
fight like devils 457.17
fight off 460.10, 908.3
fight one's battles over again 849.8
fight one's way 162.4, 457.13, 725.11
fight over 457.21
fight plan 754.3
fights, the 457.9, 754.1
fight shy 127.12, 168.3
fight shy of 325.4, 368.6
fight the good fight 457.13, 653.4, 692.6
fight the good fight for 509.13
fight tooth and nail 457.17
fight to the death (n) 457.6 (v) 457.17
fight to the finish 457.17
fight to the last ditch (n) 457.6 (v) 453.4
fight with 457.17
fight with no quarter given 457.6
fig leaf 346.2
figment 354.10, 986.5
figmental 354.29, 986.21
figment of the imagination 976.4, 986.5
fig out 5.42, 498.8
fig up 5.42
figural 517.23, 519.10, 1017.23
figurant 705.3, 707.7
figurante 705.3, 707.7
figurate 1017.23
figuration 211.2, 262.1, 262.5, 349.1, 349.7
figurative 349.13, 517.23, 518.10, 519.10, 536.3, 545.11, 1017.23
figurative language 536.1
figurativeness 536.1
figure (n) 33.3, 33.5, 92.32, 211.2, 262.1, 262.4, 349.6, 381.3, 498.7, 501.4, 536.1, 545.4, 630.1, 662.1, 662.9, 708.24, 758.2, 865.4, 935.6, 976.4, 997.8, 1017.3, 1052.3 (v) 262.7, 349.11, 381.8, 498.9, 517.18, 536.2, 662.10, 935.17, 946.9, 1017.18
figured 381.12, 498.11, 536.3, 545.11
figured bass 708.22
figured style 536.1
figure eight 92.30
figure-ground 92.32
figurehead 216.3, 349.6, 575.5, 576.1, 616.8, 647.1, 998.7
figure in 476.5, 1017.18
figure of comparison 943.1
figure of fun 508.7, 924.1
figure of speech 536.1, 545.4
figure on 380.6, 1017.18
figure out 380.6, 570.6, 940.2, 1017.18
figurer 716.6, 1017.15
figures 1017.1, 1017.14
figure skates 179.21
figure skating 760.7
figure to oneself 986.14
figure up 1017.19
figurine 349.6
figuring 381.1, 1017.10
figurist 716.6
filament 3.17, 271.1
filamentary 3.23, 271.7
filamentous 3.23, 271.7
filamentule 3.17
filature 271.1
filch 482.13
filcher 483.1
filching 482.1
file (n) 461.22, 549.5, 549.10, 647.2, 719.2, 812.2, 871.3, 1042.15, 1042.18 (v) 177.30, 285.7, 287.8, 386.10, 549.15, 809.6, 812.7, 871.8, 1044.7
file a claim 598.15
file and forget 345.7, 346.7
file away 255.9, 386.10
filed 386.15, 549.17, 809.8, 871.9
file folder 195.1, 1042.18
file for 440.9
file for divorce 566.5
file format 1042.18
file leader 574.6
file off 177.30, 812.7
files 549.3
file server 1042.19
file sharing 1042.18
filet 10.14, 10.18
file 13 391.7
file to a point 285.7
file transfer protocol 1042.18
fili 710.14, 720.12
filial 104.26, 561.7
filial love 104.4
filiated 775.9
filiate to 888.5
filiation 559.1, 560.4, 561.4, 775.1, 812.2
filibuster (n) 543.2, 613.6, 1012.8 (v) 540.7, 613.10, 846.11
filibusterer 1012.8
filibustering 613.6
filiform 3.23, 271.7
filigree (n) 170.3, 254.4 (v) 498.9
filigreed 170.11
filing 613.6, 809.1, 871.7, 1044.2
filing card 549.10
filing clerk 550.1
filings 256.1, 391.4, 1051.5
filing system 871.3
fill (n) 266.3, 794.3, 994.1 (v) 159.15, 196.7, 198.10, 221.7, 293.7, 385.7, 434.2, 469.4, 772.3, 794.7, 849.8, 993.8, 994.4
fill an office 609.42, 724.14
filled 794.11
filled out 538.12
filled to overflowing 993.20
filled with 221.15
filler 196.3, 311.13, 530.2, 538.6, 849.3
fillet 10.14, 271.4, 280.3
fill horse 311.13
fill in 276.3, 538.7, 551.9, 772.3, 794.6
fill-in 862.2
fill in for 825.5, 862.5
filling (n) 191.2, 196.3, 254.4, 740.3, 849.3, 993.4 (a) 794.13, 994.7
filling in the empty places 538.6
fillip (n) 254.4, 375.7, 902.7 (v) 105.13, 902.18
fill one's pockets 618.10
fill out 251.4, 259.5, 259.8, 282.6, 437.9, 538.8, 549.15, 772.3, 794.6
fill the air 53.7
fill the bill 384.7, 387.17, 405.15, 788.8, 991.4, 995.3
fill the measure of 794.7
fill the mind 931.20
fill the shoes of 835.3, 862.5
fill time 821.6
fill to overflowing 794.7
fill to the brim 794.7
fill up 196.7, 276.3, 293.7, 385.7, 385.9, 794.7, 994.4, 1021.8
fill with doubt 955.7
filly 77.9, 302.7, 302.10, 311.10, 757.2
film (n) 295.12, 296.2, 319.3, 549.10, 706.1, 714.10 (v) 32.4, 295.19, 349.8, 706.8, 714.14 (a) 706.9
film actor 706.4
film actress 706.4
film buff 866.3
film clip 557.3
film company 706.4
film crew 706.4
filmdom 706.1
filmed 295.31
film editing 706.6
film editor 706.4
filmed-over 295.31
film-eyed 28.13
film gauge 714.9
filmic 706.9
filminess 32.2, 294.3, 1029.1
filmistic 706.9
filmmake 706.8
filmmaker 706.4
filmmaking 706.1
film noir 706.2
filmography 871.3
film over 295.19
film pickup 1035.2
film rating 714.9
films 706.1
films, the 706.1
film set 706.4
film speed 714.9
film star 707.4
film studio 706.4
film theater 706.7
filmy 32.6, 294.8, 1029.4
filmy-eyed 28.13
filo 10.41
Filofax 549.11
filoplume 3.16
filter (n) 79.13, 292.8, 1028.4 (v) 79.22, 190.15, 192.16, 238.18
filterable virus 85.42
filtered 79.26
filter in 187.13, 189.10
filtering 79.4, 190.6
filter out 192.16, 773.4
filter tip 89.5
filth 80.7, 513.3, 666.4, 1000.2
filthied 80.23
filthiness 80.2, 666.4
filthy 80.23, 666.9, 1000.9
filthy language 513.3
filthy lucre 472.3, 728.1
filthy rich 618.15
filthy weed 89.1
filtrate 79.22, 190.15
filtration 79.4, 190.6
fimbria 211.7
fimbriate 211.12
fimbriated 211.12
fimbriation 211.7
fin 182.11, 728.7, 882.1
finagle 356.18, 381.9, 415.10
finagler 381.7, 610.6
finagling (n) 381.5 (a) 356.22
final (n) 938.2 (a) 188.18, 407.9, 420.12, 820.12, 831.11, 887.6, 957.16, 960.2
final blow 395.2
final cause 375.1, 380.2, 886.3
final draft 547.10
final dress 704.13
finale 704.7, 820.1
final examination 938.2
final extremity 307.8
Final Four 747.1

final gun 746.3
final hour 307.7
final instructions 568.6
finalist 452.2
finality 839.4
finalization 407.2, 820.1
finalize 407.6, 820.8
finalizing (n) 820.1 (a) 407.9
final lot 964.2
final notice 399.1
final offer 439.3
final resting place 309.15
final say, the 894.1
final solution 820.1
final solution, the 308.4
final stroke 308.10, 407.3, 820.4
final summons 307.1
final touch 407.3
final twitch 820.1
final warning 399.1
final whistle 857.2
final will 323.1
final wishes 323.1
final word 439.3
final words 307.9, 820.1
finance (n) 729.1 (v) 449.12, 449.15, 478.19, 624.18, 729.16
finance capitalism 611.8
finance capitalist 729.9
finance company 620.4
financer 478.11, 729.10
finances 728.14, 729.1
financial 728.30, 729.20, 731.23
financial advisor 628.7
financial aid 478.8
financial assistance 478.8
financial backing 729.2
financial commitment 623.1, 897.1
financial condition 729.6
financial corporation 620.4
financial crisis 729.8
financial distress 619.1
financial district 230.6, 737.8
financial embarrassment 619.1
financial expert 729.9
financial industry 729.1
financial institution 739.1
financial interests 609.31
financially burdened 897.5
financially distressed 619.7
financially embarrassed 619.7
financial obligation 897.1
financial officer 729.12
financial package 624.4
financial penalty 603.3
financial remuneration 624.4
financial resources 386.2
financial support 729.2
financial world 729.1
financier (n) 620.3, 729.9, 730.1 (v) 729.17
financing 621.1, 729.2
find (n) 472.6, 941.1, 999.5 (v) 186.6, 385.7, 570.6, 941.2, 946.10, 946.11, 946.13
findable 941.10, 966.8
find a clue to 940.2
find against 946.13
find a husband for 563.14
find a line of position 159.11
find a loophole 369.9
find a mate for 563.14
find an indictment against 598.15
find an opening 292.13
find an out 600.9
find a phrase for 532.4
find a way 384.6
find a wife for 563.14
find balance 670.5
find common ground 777.5
find credence 953.20
finder 29.5
find fault 115.15, 510.15
find fault with 510.12
find favor with 509.15
find for 946.13
find guilty 602.3
find hard to believe 955.5
finding 385.1, 472.6, 940.1, 941.1, 946.5
finding list 574.10, 871.3
finding out 941.1
finding-out 940.1
find it hard going 619.5
find it in one's heart 324.3, 332.8
find means 384.6
find one's account in 387.15
find one's advantage in 387.15
find oneself 941.2
find oneself at 221.8
find one's heart 324.3
find one's tongue 524.21
find one's way into 189.7
find out 551.14, 570.6, 940.2, 941.2, 970.11
find out about 570.6
find out the hard way 941.2
find refuge 1009.8
find sanctuary 1009.8
find the answer 940.2
find the key of 940.2
find the key to 341.10
find the solution 940.2
find the spot 159.11
find time 821.6
find time for 449.13
find vent 190.13, 352.16, 369.10
find words for 532.4
find words to express 524.22, 532.4
fine (n) 603.3 (v) 603.5, 764.4 (a) 8.33, 83.8, 97.6, 258.11, 270.16, 285.8, 294.8, 299.4, 339.12, 495.11, 496.8, 498.12, 501.21, 764.6, 944.7, 973.17, 999.12, 1016.19, 1051.11, 1066.8
fine and dandy 999.13
fine art 712.1
fine artist 716.1
fine art of living 496.4
fine arts 712.1
fine chemicals 1060.2
fine-combed 339.11
fine dining 8.1
fine distinction 780.2, 944.3
fine down 392.11
fine-drawn 270.16, 294.8
fine edge 285.2
fine-edged 285.8
fine feather 5.10, 83.2
fine fettle 83.2, 807.3
fine flavor 63.1
fine gentleman 500.9
fine-grained 294.8
fine-grainedness 294.3
fine hair 3.19
fine hand 547.5
fine how-de-do 810.2
fine how-do-you-do 1013.5
fine Italian hand 415.1
fine kettle of fish 1013.5
fine lady 500.10
fine linen 1010.1
fineness 24.3, 270.4, 294.3, 299.1, 495.3, 498.2, 764.1, 973.5, 999.1
fineness of feeling 93.4
fineness of grain 294.1
fine person 659.1
fine point 780.2
fine print 865.6, 959.2
fine print at the bottom 959.2
finer 249.12
fine rain 316.1
finery 5.1, 5.10, 498.3
fine shape 83.2
fine-spoken 504.17, 511.8
finespun 270.16, 294.8
finesse (n) 381.5, 413.1, 415.1, 496.1, 758.3, 944.1 (v) 381.9, 415.9
fine state of affairs 1013.4
fine talk 502.2
fine-toned 708.48
fine-tooth comb 339.3
fine-toothed 339.11
fine-tune 392.11, 437.8, 808.13, 852.7, 1002.5
fine-tuned 339.11
fine-tuning 339.3, 392.4, 808.2
fine whack 83.2
fine writer 545.5
fine writing 545.4, 547.5
finger (n) 2.7, 73.5, 88.7, 517.4 (v) 73.6, 308.20, 517.18, 551.13, 599.7, 888.4
finger, the 508.3
finger alphabet 49.3
fingerboard 711.5, 711.17
finger bowl 79.12
fingerbowls 8.12
finger buffet 8.9
finger-drying 3.15
fingered 474.9
finger guard 1008.3
finger in every pie, a 330.9
fingering 73.2, 517.3, 708.30
finger-licking 8.33
finger-lickin' good 63.8
fingerling 258.4, 311.29
finger mark 517.7
fingernails 474.4
finger of death 307.1
finger painter 716.4
finger painting 712.13
finger pillory 605.3
finger-pointing 599.1
finger post 517.4
fingerpost 574.7
fingerprint 517.7, 517.11
finger ring 280.3
finger-roll 747.4
fingers 474.4
fingers all thumbs 414.20
finger's breadth 223.2, 270.1
fingersmith 483.2
fingerspelling 49.3
fingerstone 1059.4
finger's width 223.2, 270.1
fingertip caress 73.1
finical 339.12, 495.10, 766.9, 983.15
finicality 339.3, 495.2
finicalness 339.3, 495.2, 983.4
finickiness 339.3, 495.2, 983.4
finicking 339.12, 495.10, 766.9, 983.15
finickingness 339.3, 495.2
finicky 339.12, 495.10, 766.9, 983.15
finikin 495.10
finis 820.1
finish (n) 211.3, 264.1, 287.2, 294.1, 407.2, 413.8, 496.1, 504.4, 533.1, 757.3, 820.1, 1002.2 (v) 287.7, 308.13, 388.3, 392.11, 395.12, 407.6, 820.6, 820.8, 958.5
finished 264.4, 287.11, 307.29, 388.5, 393.29, 395.29, 407.11, 413.26, 533.6, 762.11, 820.9, 837.7, 1002.9
finished book 554.3
finished up 407.11
finished version 547.10
finisher 5.34, 407.3, 820.4, 958.3
finish in front 411.3
finishing (n) 388.1, 392.4, 407.2, 820.1, 892.2 (a) 407.9, 820.11
finishing stroke 407.3, 820.4
finishing touch 407.3, 820.4
finish line 755.1, 820.1
finish off 308.13, 388.3, 395.12, 407.6, 820.8
finish off a play 749.3
finish up 407.6, 820.6, 820.8
finish with 820.6
finite 210.7, 312.13, 1017.23
finite verb 530.4
finitude 828.1
fink (n) 551.6, 727.8 (v) 551.13, 727.11
finnan haddie 10.24
Finnbeara 678.8
finniff 882.1
Finnish bath 79.8
Finno-Ugric 523.12
fiord 242.1
fire (n) 17.2, 26.3, 85.7, 93.2, 101.2, 105.7, 375.9, 459.8, 544.5, 1019.13, 1025.20, 1026.1, 1052.2 (v) 11.5, 17.10, 105.12, 375.17, 375.18, 375.20, 671.14, 742.6, 745.5, 904.10, 904.12, 909.19, 1020.17, 1020.22, 1066.6, 1074.13
fire alarm 400.1
fire and brimstone 682.2
fire-and-brimstone 682.8
fire and fury 105.8
fire ant 311.33
fire apparatus 1022.3
firearm 462.10
fire a salute 155.5, 487.2
fire a shot at 459.22

fire at 459.22, 459.28
fire a volley 459.22
fireball 1019.13, 1025.17, 1073.15
fireballing 745.3
fire beetle 1026.5
fire bell 400.1
fireboard 1020.11
firebolt 1025.17
firebomb 462.20
firebox 1020.10
firebrand 375.11, 671.9, 1019.16, 1021.4
fire break 1022.5
firebrick 742.2, 1054.2
fire brigade 1022.4
fire buff 1020.8
firebug 1020.8
fire-chaser 1022.4
fireclay 742.3
firecracker 53.6
fire-cured 89.2
fire curtain 704.16
fired 11.7, 105.20, 375.31, 742.7
firedamp 1001.4, 1067.1
fire department 1022.4
firedog 47.6, 1020.12
fired-up 983.16
fire-eater 110.11, 461.1, 493.4, 671.10, 1022.4
fire-eating (n) 493.3 (a) 493.9
fire engine 41.1, 1022.3
fire escape 190.9, 193.3, 369.3
fire extinguisher 1022.3
fire fight 457.4
firefighter 1022.4
fire fighting 1022.2
fire flag 400.1
firefly 1025.7, 1026.5
fireguard 1008.10, 1020.11
fire hook 1020.12
fire hose 239.6, 1022.3
firehouse 230.5
fire hydrant 239.12, 1022.3
fire iron 1020.12
fire ladder 193.4
firelike 1019.26
fire line 1022.5
firelit 1025.39
fire main 239.7
fireman 178.13, 183.6, 745.2, 1022.4
fire-new 841.10
fire off 818.7, 904.12
fire of genius 720.11, 920.8
fire one's imagination 375.20
fire patrolman 1008.10
firepit 1020.11
fireplace 228.2, 1020.11
fireplace tool 1020.12
fireplug 239.12, 1022.3
firepower 18.9, 459.8
fire prevention 1022.5
fireproof (v) 15.14, 1022.6 (a) 15.20, 1022.10, 1049.5
fireproofed 1022.10
fireproofing 1022.5
fireproof material 1022.5
firer 375.10
fire raid 459.4
fire-raising 1020.7
fire-red 41.6
fire resistance 1022.1, 1022.5
fire-resistant 1022.10
fire-resistant material 1022.5
fire-resisting 15.20, 1022.10
fire-resisting material 1022.5
fire-resistive 1022.10
fire-resistive material 1022.5
fire retardant 1022.5
fire-retardant 1022.10
fire-retardant material 1022.5
fire-retarded 1022.10
fire sale 734.3
fire screen 1020.11
fireside 228.2, 1020.11
fireside chat 552.2
fire spirit 678.6
fire station 230.5
firestorm 395.1, 671.4, 1019.9
fire the parting shot 939.5
fire tongs 1020.12
fire tower 272.6
firetrap 356.12
fire trench 460.5
fire truck 179.12
fire up 105.16, 152.19, 1020.17
fire upon 459.22
fire wall 1022.5
firewall 1042.11
firewalled 1007.4
fire warden 397.5, 1008.10, 1022.4
firewater 88.13
firewood 1021.3, 1054.3
fireworks 459.8, 1019.17
fireworm 1026.5
fire worship 697.1, 1020.7
fire worshiper 697.4, 1020.8
firing 375.4, 375.9, 447.2, 459.8, 904.2, 909.5, 1020.4, 1021.1
firing area 1074.7
firing line 463.2
firing squad 604.6
firing table 1074.10
firing test 1074.1
firing tube 1074.10
firm (n) 617.9, 739.1 (v) 855.7, 1046.7 (a) 15.18, 293.12, 359.12, 361.9, 425.7, 587.21, 644.20, 687.7, 763.7, 770.22, 800.14, 853.7, 855.12, 855.15, 970.17, 1007.5, 1045.12, 1046.11
firmament 1073.2
firm as Gibraltar 15.18, 855.12
firm belief 953.5
firm bid 439.3
firm foundation 901.6
firm friendship 587.8
firm ground 901.6
firm hand 425.3
firm hold 474.2
firming 15.5, 1046.5
firmly established 855.13
firm-minded 359.15
firmness 15.3, 359.2, 361.2, 425.2, 587.7, 644.7, 763.1, 781.1, 853.1, 855.1, 855.3, 970.4, 1045.1, 1046.2
firmness of mind 359.2
firmness of spirit 359.2
firm price 439.3
firm resolve 359.1
firm up 855.7, 855.8
firmware 1042.7
firn 1023.5
first (n) 745.1, 818.3 (a) 165.3, 216.10, 249.14, 814.4, 818.15, 818.17, 834.4, 841.11
first aid 91.14
first-aid 86.39
First Amendment 348.1, 430.1
first among equals 249.4
first and last 872.9
first appearance 818.5
first approach 556.1
first arrival 845.4
first attempt 403.2
first bagger 745.2
first base 745.1
first-base coach 745.2
first baseman 745.2
first-base umpire 745.3
first blush 314.2, 818.3
first-born (n) 304.5 (a) 842.19
first brightening 314.2
first cameraman 706.5
first car 818.1
first cause 886.3
first chair 413.13, 710.19, 814.1
first choice 371.1
first-chop 999.18
first class 607.2
first-class 249.13, 999.17
first-class mail 553.4
first comer 227.3, 845.4
first course 8.10
first cousin 559.3
first crack 845.1
first crack out of the box 818.1
first date 818.1
First day 20.5
first-degree burn 85.38, 1019.13, 1020.6
first-degree murder 308.2
first down 746.3
first draft 547.10, 942.2
first edition 337.3, 554.6
first episode 816.2
first ever (n) 818.3 (a) 818.15, 841.11
First Families of Virginia 607.2, 608.1
first fiddle 997.9
first finger 73.5
first floor 197.23
first fruits 627.1, 887.1
first glance 818.3
firsthand 337.5, 841.7, 957.16
first home 818.1
first impression 713.5, 818.3
first in line 216.2
first inning 818.3
first in the field 337.5
first job 818.1
first kiss 818.1
first lady 575.2
first language 523.3
first lap 818.3
first leg 818.3
first lieutenant 575.17
first light 314.2, 314.3, 845.1
first line 216.2
first line of battle 216.2
first line of defense 461.23, 461.27
firstling (n) 304.5 (a) 842.19
first look 938.5
first man 575.18
first mate 183.7
first mortgage 438.4
first move 818.3
first name 527.4
first-nighter 704.27
first of all 818.15
first on the scene 845.4
first option 733.2
first order 997.1
first person 530.7
first-person past narrator 722.6
first-person present narrator 722.6
first philosophy, the 689.3
first place 249.3
first principles 818.6, 935.7
first prize 249.3, 411.1, 646.2
first quarter 1073.11
first-rate 249.13, 413.22, 999.17
first-rateness 999.1
first-rater 413.14, 999.6
first reader 818.6
first reading 613.6
first refusal 733.2
first round 818.3
first sergeant 575.18, 575.19
first sight 818.3
first stage 818.3, 845.1
first step 818.3
first steps 568.5, 818.6
first stone 901.7
first story 197.23
first strike 459.1
first-strike capacity 459.1
first string 617.7
first team 617.7, 746.2
first theology, the 689.3
first tragedian 707.6
first violinist 710.19
First World 731.8
firth 242.1
fisc 729.13
fiscal 728.30, 729.20, 731.23
fiscal policy 731.7
fiscal year 824.2, 825.4
fish (n) 10.24, 182.12, 311.3, 311.29, 311.30, 358.2, 728.7, 759.18 (v) 382.10
fish and chips 10.24
fish ball 10.24
fish bowl 210.2
fish cake 10.24
fish culture 1070.1
fish day 515.3, 668.2
fish-eating bird 311.27
fish eggs 10.24, 305.15
fisher 382.6
fisherman 183.1, 382.6
fishery 382.3
fisheye, the 27.5
fish for 440.14, 938.30
fish for compliments 140.6
fish fork 8.12
fish fry 8.6
fishhook 356.13, 758.2
fishiness 645.1

fishing (n) 382.3 (a) 382.11, 938.38
fishing expedition 938.4
fishing fleet 180.10
fishing license 443.6
fishing question 938.10
fish-kiss 562.4
fish knife 8.12
fishlike 311.49
fish market 736.2
fish meal 890.4
fish or cut bait 328.5
fish out 938.34
fish out of water, a 789.4
fish out of water 868.3
fish pie 10.24
fishpond 228.24, 241.1
fish position 753.3
fish stick 10.24
fish story 354.11, 502.2
fishtail (n) 182.11 (v) 184.40, 756.4
fishtail down 184.43
fishtailing 184.13
fishtail landing 184.18
fish to fry 724.2
fish up 912.8, 941.4
fishworm 311.38
fishy 311.49, 356.21, 522.20, 645.16
fishy transaction 356.8
fissile 224.7, 802.26, 1038.20, 1050.4
fissility 1050.1
fission (n) 802.2, 806.2, 1038.8 (v) 802.13, 806.3, 806.4, 875.4, 1038.17
fissionable 802.26, 1038.20
fissionable material 1038.10
fission particles 1038.16
fission products 1037.5
fission reaction 1038.8
fissural 224.7
fissure (n) 224.2, 290.1, 802.4, 813.2 (v) 292.11, 393.23, 802.11, 802.12
fissured 224.7
fist 462.4, 517.4, 547.3
fist bump (n) 116.2 (v) 517.22
fistfight 457.4
fistful, a 991.2
fistful 884.3
fistic sport, the 754.1
fisticuffs 457.9, 754.1
fist pump (n) 116.2 (v) 517.22
fistula 2.23, 85.37, 292.1
fit (n) 85.6, 105.9, 152.8, 330.4, 405.2, 671.5, 825.1, 917.6, 926.7 (v) 5.41, 159.9, 323.2, 385.8, 405.8, 568.13, 775.5, 777.6, 788.7, 788.8, 790.6, 852.7, 867.3, 995.3 (a) 83.8, 83.12, 371.24, 405.17, 413.24, 533.7, 637.3, 639.8, 649.7, 788.10, 843.9, 991.6, 995.5
fitaerobics 84.2
fit and fine 83.8
fit as a fiddle 83.9
fit for 413.24
fit for a gourmet 63.8
fit for a king 63.8, 999.12
fit for occupation 225.15
fit for release 398.4
fit for sea 180.18
fit for society 582.22
fit for the dust hole 393.36
fit for the junkyard 391.11
fit for the wastepaper basket 393.36
fitful 810.12, 813.4, 851.3, 854.7, 917.19
fitfulness 813.1, 851.1
fitful sleep 22.2
fit in 159.9, 191.8, 867.4
fit-in split 750.2
fit like a glove 777.6, 788.8, 995.3
fit like a second skin 995.3
fitness 18.2, 81.2, 83.1, 84.1, 371.11, 405.4, 496.2, 637.2, 788.5, 843.1, 995.1
fitness center 84.1
fitness for society 582.1
fitness-walk 84.4
fitness walking 84.2
fit of abstraction 985.2
fit of anger 152.8
fit of crying 115.2
fit of laughter 116.4
fit of temper 152.8
fit out 5.41, 385.8, 405.8
fits and starts 851.1, 917.2
fits one like a glove 866.5
fitted 371.24, 385.13, 405.17, 413.24, 788.10
fitted for 413.24
fittedness 371.11, 405.4, 788.5
fitted out 385.13
fitted sheet 295.10
fitter 5.35
fit the pattern 786.7
fitting (n) 405.2, 852.1 (a) 387.18, 496.9, 533.7, 637.3, 788.10, 843.9, 995.5
fittingness 496.2, 533.1, 637.2, 843.1, 995.1
fitting out 385.1, 405.2
fitting room 197.15
fittings 385.4
fit to a T 788.8, 995.3
fit to be tied 152.30
fit to bust 794.11
fit to eat 63.8
fit together 788.6
fit to kill 5.46
fit to live in 225.15
fit up 385.8
five 617.7, 747.2, 758.2, 882.1
five-alarm 15.22, 1019.25
five-and-dime 736.1
five-and-ten (n) 736.1 (a) 633.8
five and twenty 882.7
Five Books of Moses 683.3
five bucks 882.1
five-card draw 759.10
five-card stud 758.4, 759.10
five cents 728.7
five centuries 882.9
five C's 882.9
five-dollar bill 728.7
five-dollar gold piece 728.4
five dollars 882.1
five-dollar word 526.10, 545.3
five-em space 548.7
fivefold (v) 882.16 (a) 882.17
five hundred 882.9
five-hundred-dollar bill 728.7
five hundred dollars 728.7
five-minute gun 400.1
five o'clock shadow 3.8, 288.3
five-o'clock tea 582.13
five of a kind 758.4
five on the floor 1040.9
five-part time 709.24
five-percenter 609.30, 894.6
fivepin 750.1
fivepin bowling 750.1
five-pointed star 882.1
fiver 728.7, 728.8, 882.1
five second rule 600.5
five-second rule 747.3
five senses 24.5
fivesome 882.1
five-speed 1040.9
five-spot 728.7, 758.2, 882.1
five-star general 575.17
five-step approach 750.2
5-2 offense 752.3
527 group 609.29
fivish 884.7
fix (n) 87.20, 159.3, 182.2, 371.3, 765.1, 971.3, 995.2 (v) 159.11, 159.16, 161.5, 210.4, 244.4, 255.11, 262.7, 292.15, 308.14, 359.7, 373.9, 378.3, 392.11, 395.11, 396.14, 405.6, 412.9, 420.9, 437.8, 506.7, 604.10, 788.7, 800.7, 808.9, 808.10, 855.9, 865.11, 946.11, 957.10, 965.5, 970.11
fixable 378.4, 396.25
fixate 92.36, 926.25
fixated 926.33
fixating 983.16
fixation 92.15, 92.21, 159.6, 159.7, 173.2, 855.2, 926.13, 1012.1
fixative 70.2, 712.18, 803.4
fixed 159.18, 173.13, 210.6, 359.12, 373.18, 412.15, 800.14, 807.7, 808.14, 842.12, 853.7, 855.14, 855.16, 865.12, 957.20, 959.8, 960.2, 965.8, 970.20, 983.18
fixed asset 729.13
fixed assets 471.7
fixed belief 970.5
fixed capital 728.15
fixed disk 1042.6
fixed-do system 709.7
fixed expression 529.1
fixed feast 20.4
fixed idea 926.13
fixed income 624.4
fixed in the mind 989.25
fixed mind 361.1
fixedness 359.2, 373.6, 853.1, 855.2
fixed oil 1056.1
fixed opinion 953.5
fixed-point notation 1017.4
fixed price 738.9
fixed purpose 380.1
fixed race 757.3
fixed-rate mortgage 438.4
fixed regard 983.4
fixed resolve 359.1
fixed stars 1073.4
fixed station 1036.6
fixed upon 359.16
fixed-wing aircraft 181.1
fixer 396.10, 597.3, 609.30, 714.13
fixing 159.6, 255.4, 292.3, 396.6, 865.6
fixing bath 79.9, 714.13
fixing to 405.16
fix in the memory 989.17
fix in the mind 570.8, 989.17
fix-it shop 739.5
fixity 173.2, 361.2, 855.2
fixity of purpose 359.2, 359.4
fix on 161.5, 888.4, 983.8
fix one's attention 983.11
fix one's eyes upon 27.15
fix one's gaze 27.15
fix one's position 159.11
fix one's thoughts 931.10
fix one's wagon 506.7, 604.10
fix responsibility for 599.8
fix the blame for 599.8
fix the burden of 888.4
fix the date 832.13
fix the mind on 931.10
fix the paternity of 888.5
fix the price of 630.11
fix the responsibility for 888.4
fix the thoughts on 983.5
fix the thoughts upon 931.10
fix the time 832.11
fix to 405.10
fix together 800.5
fixture 254.1, 855.2, 1040.3
fixtures 385.4, 735.4
fix up 385.8, 396.14, 396.15, 396.17, 405.6, 405.7, 465.8, 498.8, 808.12
fix-up 396.6, 582.8
fix upon 371.16
fizz (n) 57.1, 320.3 (v) 57.2, 320.4
fizzle (n) 57.1, 132.1, 320.3, 410.2 (v) 57.2, 132.3, 320.4, 410.13, 1022.8
fizzle out 16.9, 132.3, 410.13, 820.7, 891.3, 911.3, 1022.8
fizzling (n) 57.1 (a) 57.3
fizz out 410.13
fizzy 320.6, 1067.9
fjord 242.1
flabbergast 122.6
flabbergasted 122.9, 131.13
flabbiness 16.1, 19.1, 1047.3, 1063.1
flabby 16.12, 19.13, 1047.10, 1063.6
flabelliform 259.11
flabellum 318.18
flaccid 16.12, 1047.10
flaccidity 16.1, 1047.3
flaccidness 1047.3
flack 33.2, 352.5, 352.9
flackery 352.4
flag (n) 310.19, 383.6, 646.3, 647.7, 751.1, 1054.2 (v) 16.9, 21.4, 21.5, 85.48, 175.8, 295.22, 393.18, 498.9, 517.22

flag down 517.22, 745.5, 857.11
flagella 305.5
flagellant (n) 667.2 (a) 667.4
flagellate 604.12
flagellate oneself 113.6, 658.6, 667.3
flagellation 604.4, 658.3, 667.1
flagelliform 271.7
flagellum 271.1, 310.20, 605.1
flageolet tone 709.16
flagged 517.24
flagging (n) 175.4, 383.6 (a) 16.21, 21.7, 175.10, 393.45
flagitious 654.16
flagitiousness 654.4
flagman 399.4
flag of truce 465.2
flag on the play 746.3
flagrance 348.4
flagrancy 348.4, 501.3, 666.2
flagrant 247.12, 348.12, 501.20, 654.16, 661.12, 666.6, 1000.9, 1019.27
flagrant falsehood 354.12
flagship 818.17
flagstaff 273.1
flagstick 751.1, 753.1
flagstone 383.6, 1054.2
flag waver 591.3
flag-waving 591.2
flagwaving 591.4
flail 604.12, 902.16, 1051.9
flail at 459.16
flail away at 459.16
flailing 604.4, 1051.4
flair 18.2, 413.4, 413.5, 501.4, 712.6, 920.2, 944.2
flak 456.3, 462.11, 510.4
flake (n) 87.7, 296.3, 870.4, 926.16, 927.4, 1023.8 (v) 6.11, 47.7, 296.5, 1050.3, 1051.9
flaked-out 22.22
flake off 6.11, 188.7
flake out 22.14
flake pastry 10.41
flakiness 296.4, 364.3, 1050.1, 1051.3
flaking 1051.4
flaky (n) 87.21 (a) 296.7, 364.5, 923.9, 926.27, 927.6, 1050.4, 1051.11
flam (n) 354.11, 354.14, 356.7 (v) 356.19
flambeau 1021.4, 1026.3
flamboyance 498.2, 501.3, 1025.4
flamboyancy 498.2, 545.1, 1025.4
flamboyant 498.12, 545.8, 1025.32
flame (n) 104.1, 104.12, 1019.13, 1025.6, 1026.1 (v) 41.5, 1019.22, 1020.23, 1020.24, 1025.23
flame-colored 41.6
flame mail 347.13
flamen 699.15
flame out 184.45, 1022.8
flameout 1022.2
flameproof (v) 1022.6 (a) 15.20, 1022.10
flame-red 41.6
flame up 105.16, 152.19, 1019.22
flaming (n) 1020.5 (a) 41.6, 93.18, 101.9, 105.22, 545.8, 671.22, 1019.27, 1025.32, 1025.34
flaming torch 1026.3
flammability 1020.9
flammable (n) 1021.1 (a) 1020.28
flammable material 1021.1
flan 10.46
flanch 647.2
flâner 177.28
flânerie 177.8, 331.4
flâneur 331.8
flâneuse 331.8
flange 211.4, 283.3
flank (n) 218.1 (v) 218.4, 459.17, 460.8, 914.5
flank attack 459.1
flanked 218.7
flanker 746.2
flanker back 746.2
flanking 218.6
flank speed 174.3
flannel cake 10.45
flannels 5.18, 5.22
flap (n) 53.4, 56.1, 105.6, 283.3, 295.4, 296.2, 330.4, 671.2, 902.8, 917.1, 917.4 (v) 56.6, 202.6, 902.16, 902.19, 916.11, 917.12
flapcake 10.45
flapdoodle 520.3
flap-eared 48.15
flapjack 10.45
flap one's jaw 524.20
flappable 105.28, 110.19
flapper 182.11, 989.5
Flapper Era 824.5
flapping 56.11, 804.5
flap the memory 989.19
flare (n) 259.1, 400.1, 517.15, 671.7, 1019.14, 1025.6, 1026.3, 1035.5 (v) 259.6, 1019.22, 1025.23
flared 259.11
flared-out 259.11
flare out 259.6
flare path 184.19
flare up 33.9, 105.16, 152.19, 1019.22
flare-up 105.9, 152.9, 671.7, 1019.14
flaring 35.20, 259.11, 501.20, 1019.27, 1025.34
flash (n) 27.4, 105.3, 174.6, 365.1, 413.14, 552.5, 671.7, 830.3, 934.3, 1019.14, 1025.6 (v) 6.7, 33.8, 33.9, 347.20, 501.17, 517.22, 1025.23
flash across the mind 931.18
flash back 939.4
flashback 989.3
flash burn 85.38, 1038.16
flash card 570.3
flash drive 1042.5
flash fire 1019.14
flash flood 238.5
flash-frying 11.2
flashiness 498.2, 501.3, 545.1
flashing (n) 6.1, 6.2, 928.2 (a) 501.19, 828.8, 1025.34, 1025.36
flashing light 400.1
flashing point 671.7, 1019.13
flash in the pan (n) 19.6, 400.2, 409.3, 410.5, 410.7, 764.2, 828.5 (v) 410.13, 891.3
flash mob 617.4, 770.2
flash of insight 934.1
flash of light 1025.6
flash of lightning 1025.17
flash of wit 489.7
flash on 931.16, 989.9
flash on the mind 989.15
flash-pasteurize 79.24
flashpoint 671.7, 1019.3, 1019.5, 1019.13
flash price 738.9
flash up 105.16
flash upon one 131.6
flashy 35.20, 498.12, 501.19, 545.8, 545.11, 1025.34
flat (n) 197.23, 201.3, 228.13, 228.13, 236.1, 276.2, 287.3, 704.20, 709.14, 746.3, 759.22 (a) 35.22, 36.7, 52.17, 61.4, 65.2, 117.6, 118.9, 158.10, 173.14, 201.7, 201.8, 236.2, 260.14, 270.17, 274.7, 277.6, 286.3, 287.10, 524.30, 619.10, 721.5, 781.5, 960.2, 1027.17
flat as a billiard table 201.7
flat as a board 201.7
flat as a bowling green 201.7
flat as a pancake 201.7
flat as a table 201.7
flat as a tennis court 201.7
flat-ass 619.10
flatbed cylinder press 548.9
flat broke 619.10
flat calm 173.5
flatcar 179.15
flat-chested 270.17
flat coat 35.8
flat contradiction 335.2
flat country 236.1
flat denial 335.2
flat failure 410.2
flatfish 10.24, 311.30
flatfoot 265.3, 576.11, 1008.16
flatfooted 265.12
flathat 184.42
flathatting 184.17
flat joint 759.19
flatland 201.3, 236.1
flatlet 228.13
flatline 307.19
flatliner 307.15
flat market 737.3
flatmate 227.8, 588.3
flatness 52.1, 52.2, 61.1, 65.1, 96.1, 117.1, 201.1, 277.1, 286.1, 287.1, 721.2, 1027.5
flat on one's back 85.59, 201.8
flat on one's belly 201.8
flat on one's face 201.8
flat-out 960.2
flat-out speed 174.3
flat racing 757.1
flat refusal 442.2
flats 5.27, 201.3, 228.14, 236.1, 274.3, 276.2
flat-screen 1042.22
flat-screen display 1042.9
flat silver 8.12
flat-slab construction 266.2
flat spin 184.15
flat store 759.19
flatten 201.6, 260.10, 274.6, 277.5, 286.2, 287.5, 294.4, 395.19, 412.10, 781.4
flattened 201.7, 412.17
flattened-strand rope 271.2
flattener 287.4
flattening 395.5
flatten oneself 913.11
flatten out 184.43
flatter 138.7, 149.2, 440.12, 509.12, 511.5
flatterer 138.3, 509.8, 511.4
flattering 138.14, 149.3, 440.18, 509.16, 511.8
flattering remark 509.6
flattering tongue 511.2
flatter oneself 502.8
flattery 138.2, 149.1, 375.7, 509.5, 509.6, 511.1
flattie 1008.16
flat tire 118.5, 1012.6
flattop 180.6, 180.8, 1016.14
flatulence 259.2, 545.1, 909.10, 1067.3
flatulency 259.2, 545.1, 909.10
flatulent 259.13, 501.22, 545.9, 909.30
flat universe 1073.1
flatuosity 909.10, 1067.3
flatuous 909.30
flatuous melancholia 926.5
flatus 71.3, 259.2, 318.3, 909.10, 1067.3
flatware 8.12, 735.4
flat wash 35.8
flaunt (n) 501.4, 916.2 (v) 348.5, 501.17, 916.11
flaunter 501.11
flaunting (n) 501.4, 916.2 (a) 35.20, 501.19, 501.20, 545.8
flautist 710.4
flavescent 43.4
flavor (n) 62.1, 63.3, 865.4 (v) 63.7, 797.11
flavor control 1041.8
flavored 62.9
flavored brandy 88.15
flavor enhancer 63.3
flavorer 63.3
flavorful 62.9, 63.9
flavorfulness 63.1
flavoriness 63.1
flavoring 63.3
flavorless 65.2
flavorlessness 65.1
flavor of the month 578.1, 865.2
flavor of the week 578.1
flavorous 62.9, 63.9
flavorousness 63.1
flavorsome 63.9, 97.10
flavorsomeness 63.1, 97.3
flavory 62.9, 63.9
flaw (n) 224.2, 318.5, 654.2, 975.1, 1003.2, 1004.1 (v) 1004.4
flawed 654.12, 674.6, 936.11, 975.16, 1004.8

flawed argument 936.3
flawed judgment 948.1
flawed logic 975.1
flawedness 975.1
flawless 973.16, 1002.6
flawlessness 973.5, 1002.1
flawy 318.21
flax 604.14
flax-colored 43.4
flaxen 43.4
flaxen-colored 43.4
flaxen-haired 37.9
flaxseed 310.31
flay 6.8, 480.24, 510.20, 604.12, 802.14
flaying 96.7, 510.3
flea 311.36, 366.4
fleabag 228.15
fleabite 998.5
flea-bitten 47.13
flea fair 736.2
flea in one's ear, a 372.1, 442.2, 510.5
flea in one's ear 399.1
flea in one's nose 364.1
flea in the ear 422.2
fleam 204.4
flea market 734.3, 736.2
fleapit 706.7
flea powder 87.9
flèche 272.6, 285.4
fleck (n) 3.6, 47.3, 248.2, 258.7, 517.5, 1004.3 (v) 47.7, 517.19
flecked 47.13
fleckered 47.13
flection 164.2, 278.1, 279.3, 291.1
flectional 164.8, 291.7
flector tuning 1036.8
fled 369.11
fledge 3.21, 303.9
fledging 818.2
fledgling (n) 302.1, 302.5, 302.10, 311.27, 572.9, 841.4 (a) 301.10, 406.11, 841.7
flee 34.2, 188.12, 368.10, 369.6, 762.6
fleece (n) 3.2, 3.4, 3.19, 4.2, 37.2, 295.3, 1047.4 (v) 6.5, 356.18, 480.24, 482.17, 632.7
fleeced 619.8
fleecer 357.4
fleece-white 37.7
fleeciness 3.1
fleecy 3.24, 1047.14
fleecy cloud 319.1
fleecy-white 37.7
fleeing 222.4
fleer (n) 368.5, 508.2, 508.4 (v) 508.9
fleer at 156.5, 489.13
fleering (n) 508.1 (a) 508.12
fleet (n) 180.10, 461.27, 770.3 (v) 174.8, 828.6 (a) 174.15, 413.23, 828.8
fleet admiral 575.19
fleet-footed 174.15
fleeting 34.3, 168.5, 764.5, 828.7
fleeting impulse 365.1
fleetingness 168.1, 764.1, 828.1
fleetness 828.2
Fleet Street 555.3
flesh 10.13, 75.2, 295.3, 305.1, 312.1, 312.8, 559.2, 663.2, 1052.3
flesh, the 663.2
flesh and blood 2.1, 312.5, 559.2
flesh-colored 41.8
flesh-eater 8.16
flesh-eating 8.31
fleshiness 75.2, 257.8, 1063.1
fleshing-out 538.6
fleshless 270.17
fleshlessness 270.5
fleshliness 663.2, 665.5
fleshly 75.25, 312.13, 654.12, 663.6, 665.29, 686.3, 1052.10
fleshly, the 686.2
fleshly delight 95.1
fleshly lust 75.5
flesh out 538.7, 861.6, 1002.5
flesh peddler 615.5
flesh-pink 41.8
fleshpot 654.7
fleshpots 228.28, 1010.1
fleshpots of Egypt 1010.1
flesh wound 85.38
fleshy 257.18, 1063.6
fleur-de-lis 647.1, 647.2
flex (n) 279.3 (v) 279.6, 1048.4
flexed 164.8, 278.6, 279.7
flexibility 413.3, 426.2, 433.3, 854.1, 867.1, 1014.2, 1047.2, 1048.1
flexible 291.7, 413.25, 426.5, 433.13, 854.6, 867.5, 1014.15, 1047.9, 1048.7
flexible supports 630.5
flexile 1047.9, 1048.7
flexility 1047.2
flexitarian 668.4
flexitarianism 668.2
flexitime 624.6, 825.3
flex one's muscles 405.13
flextime 624.6, 825.3
flexular 281.6
flexuose 281.6
flexuosity 204.8, 281.1
flexuous 204.20, 279.7, 281.6, 1047.9
flexuousness 281.1, 1047.2
flexural 278.6, 279.7, 291.7
flexure 164.2, 278.1, 279.3, 291.1
flibbertigibbet 924.7, 985.5
flick (n) 52.3, 73.1, 517.5, 706.1, 902.7, 905.3, 1004.3 (v) 73.6, 902.18, 905.5, 917.12
flicker (n) 706.1, 917.4, 1019.13, 1025.8 (v) 917.12, 1019.22, 1025.25
flickering (n) 1025.8 (a) 828.8, 851.3, 854.7, 917.18, 1019.27, 1025.36
flickering flame 1019.13
flickering light 1025.8
flicker of an eye 27.4
flickers, the 706.1
flickery 917.18, 1025.36
flick of the eye 27.4
flick of the eyelash 517.15
flick one on the raw 93.14
flicks, the 706.1
flick through 938.26
flicky 917.18, 1025.36
flier 174.5, 179.14, 185.1, 352.8, 707.3, 737.19, 759.2
flies 704.16
flight 92.23, 172.2, 174.1, 177.4, 184.1, 184.9, 188.1, 368.4, 369.1, 461.29, 462.6, 709.18, 770.6, 884.3, 1074.9
flight attendant 185.4, 577.5
flight crew 185.4
flight deck 184.23
flighted 3.28
flight engineer 185.1
flight feathers 3.18
flight formation 184.12
flightiness 364.3, 854.2, 922.7, 984.1, 985.5
flight instrument 181.1
flightless bird 311.27
flight of fancy 354.11, 986.1, 986.7
flight of stairs 193.3
flight of time 821.4
flight of wit 489.7
flight operation 184.11
flight path 184.33, 383.1
flight pay 624.4
flight plan 184.3
flight position 753.3
flight recorder 549.10
flight simulator 181.10
flight strip 184.23
flight test 942.3
flight tester 185.6
flight training 184.3
flighty 364.6, 854.7, 922.20, 926.26, 984.6, 985.17
flimflam (n) 354.11, 354.14, 356.1, 364.1 (v) 356.19
flimflam flam 356.9
flimflam man 357.4
flimflammer 357.4
flimflammery 356.1
flimsiness 16.2, 270.4, 299.1, 764.1, 998.3, 1050.1
flimsy (n) 547.10 (a) 16.14, 270.16, 299.4, 764.7, 936.12, 998.19, 1029.4, 1047.10, 1050.4
flinch (n) 903.3 (v) 127.13, 131.5, 168.3, 325.4, 362.7, 903.7
fling (n) 403.3, 743.6, 904.3 (v) 159.13, 174.8, 904.10
fling at 459.28
fling down the gauntlet 458.14
flinger 904.7
flinging 904.2
flinging woo 562.2
fling off 188.11, 524.22, 909.21
fling-on clothes 5.20
fling oneself at 562.21
fling oneself at one 439.7
fling out 188.11
fling woo 562.15
flint 1021.4, 1046.6
flint and steel 1021.4
flinthearted 94.12, 144.25
flintheartedness 94.3
flintiness 94.3, 146.1, 359.2, 361.2, 1046.1
flintlike 1046.10, 1059.11
flintlock 462.10
flinty 94.12, 146.3, 359.12, 361.9, 1046.10, 1059.11
flip (n) 363.1, 749.3, 902.7, 904.3, 905.3 (v) 105.17, 128.8, 779.5, 902.18, 904.10, 905.5, 917.12 (a) 142.10, 540.9
flip a coin 759.23
flip-flop (n) 363.1, 852.1, 858.1, 859.1 (v) 205.5, 205.6, 364.4, 852.7, 859.5
flip-flop circuit 1041.6
flip-flopped 205.7
flip-flopper 362.5
flip-flops 5.27
flip of a coin 759.2, 972.1
flip one's lid 105.17, 128.8, 152.20, 926.22
flip one's wig 105.17, 128.8, 152.20, 926.22
flip out 105.17, 152.18, 926.22
flippancy 142.2, 489.4, 508.1, 984.1
flippant 142.10, 156.7, 340.11, 493.9, 508.12
flipped 205.7, 926.27
flipper 182.11, 704.20
flipper turns 184.16
flip phone 347.4
flipping a coin 759.1
flippy 870.11
flip side 215.3
flip side, the 205.4, 779.2
flip through the pages 938.26
flirt (n) 104.11, 377.4, 562.11, 902.7, 905.3, 998.10 (v) 377.5, 562.20, 902.18, 905.5, 998.14
flirtation 104.5, 377.1, 562.9, 998.8
flirtatious 364.6, 377.8, 562.23
flirtatiousness 562.9
flirtiness 562.9, 998.8
flirting with death 493.3
flirt with 377.5
flirt with death 493.6
flirt with the idea 931.12
flirty 562.23
flit (n) 75.15, 174.1, 917.4 (v) 174.8, 177.18, 177.22, 177.23, 177.35, 821.5, 828.6, 917.12
flite 456.11
fliting 456.5
flitter (n) 917.4 (v) 917.12
flitting (n) 177.3 (a) 177.37, 828.7, 854.7
float (n) 180.11 (v) 176.13, 182.54, 182.56, 193.10, 287.9, 298.8, 298.9, 738.12, 818.11, 904.13, 916.11, 1065.14
floatability 298.1
floatable 298.14
float a bond issue 738.12
float a loan 620.5, 621.3
float around 177.23
floater 178.2, 609.23
float high 298.8
float in a sea of doubt 971.9
floating (n) 182.11, 609.18, 818.5 (a) 177.37, 182.60, 298.14, 802.22
floating bridge 383.9
floating capital 728.15
floating crap game 759.8

floating cushion 397.6
floating debt 623.1
floating game 759.8
floating hotel 180.5
floating island 235.2
floating palace 180.5
floating-point notation 1017.4
float in space 1075.12
float in the air 52.9, 193.10
float on one's back 182.56
floatplane 181.8
floats 704.18
float seaplane 181.8
float up 193.9
floaty 298.14
floccose 3.24, 296.7
floccule 296.3
flocculent 3.24, 296.7, 1047.14
flocculus 296.3
flock (n) 3.6, 296.3, 696.9, 700.1, 770.4, 770.5, 770.6, 884.3 (v) 770.16
flocks 884.3
flock to 450.4
flock together 582.17, 769.7, 770.16
flocky 3.24
floe 1023.5
flog 375.14, 604.12
flog a dead horse 391.8, 993.12
flogging 375.3, 604.4
flog oneself 725.10
flo malt 66.3
flo-malt 66.3
flomalt 66.3
flood (n) 238.5, 238.6, 238.13, 247.3, 251.1, 272.8, 316.2, 316.4, 704.18, 770.4, 991.2, 993.2 (v) 238.16, 238.17, 991.5, 993.8, 993.14, 1065.14
Flood, the 238.6
flooded 238.25, 275.14, 1065.17
flooded with light 1025.39
floodgate 190.9, 239.11
flood-hatch 239.11
flooding 1065.6
floodlight (n) 704.18, 1025.19 (v) 1025.28
floodlit 1025.39
floodmark 300.6
flood negative 182.47
flood of light 1025.4
flood of tears 115.2
flood plain 236.1
floodproof 1066.11
flood the market 993.14
flood the market with 734.8
flood the tanks 182.47
flood tide 238.13, 272.8
flood with light 1025.28
floor (n) 197.23, 199.3, 199.4, 201.3, 211.3, 296.1, 463.1, 630.4, 901.6, 901.13 (v) 295.22, 412.7, 913.5, 958.5, 971.14
floorboards 295.9
floor broker 737.10
floor cover 295.9
floor covering 199.3, 295.9
floored 295.31, 412.14, 971.26
floor enamel 35.8
floorer 522.8, 958.3
floor exercise 760.5
floor hockey 749.1
flooring 199.3, 295.9, 901.6, 1054.2
floor it 174.9, 330.14
floor lamp 229.1
floor leader 610.3
floorman 574.2, 737.10
floor manager 574.2
floor price 630.4
floor trader 737.10
floorwalker 574.2, 730.3
floozy 665.14
flop (n) 56.1, 194.3, 410.2, 410.8, 414.5, 704.4, 917.4 (v) 22.18, 194.6, 202.6, 410.10, 704.28, 747.4, 852.6, 917.12
flop down 194.6
flop-eared 48.15
flophouse 228.15
flopperoo 410.2
floppiness 804.2, 1047.3
flopping 747.3
floppy (n) 549.10, 1042.6 (a) 16.12, 202.10, 1047.10
floppy disk 1042.6
floppy disk drive 1042.5
floppy disL 549.10
flop sweat 127.3, 139.4
Flora 1069.4
flora 310.1, 1068.1
flora and fauna 305.1
floral 310.38
floral decoration 498.1, 712.16
floral decorator 716.11
floral envelope 310.28
floral leaf 310.19
floreate (v) 310.35 (a) 310.38
florescence 301.1, 310.26
florescent 14.3, 259.12, 301.9, 310.38
floret 310.24
floriate 310.38
floriated 310.38
floricultural 310.38
floriculture 310.24, 1069.2
floriculturist 1069.6
florid (n) 709.18 (a) 41.9, 310.38, 498.12, 545.11, 986.20
Florida water 70.3
floridity 41.1, 498.2, 536.1, 545.4
floridness 41.1, 498.2, 545.4
florid phrase 709.18
florid style 536.1
florilegium 554.7, 557.4, 770.11
florin 728.8
florist 1069.6
floscule 310.24
floss 3.19, 1047.4
flossiness 1047.1
flossy 3.27, 271.7, 501.18, 1047.14
flotation 738.6, 818.5
flotation device 397.6
flotilla 180.10, 461.27
flotsam 370.4
flotsam and jetsam 370.4
flounce (n) 177.12, 211.7, 291.1, 905.3, 917.8 (v) 177.28, 291.5, 366.6, 498.9, 743.23, 905.5, 917.15
flounced 291.7
flounce off 188.11
flounce out 188.11
flouncy 498.12, 501.19
flounder (n) 10.24, 917.8 (v) 182.55, 194.8, 414.11, 854.5, 915.13, 917.15, 971.9, 1013.11
flour (n) 10.34, 37.2, 1051.5 (v) 771.6, 1051.9
flouriness 1051.1
flourish (n) 254.4, 498.1, 501.4, 517.16, 536.1, 545.4, 708.27, 709.18, 916.2 (v) 14.2, 17.11, 83.6, 259.7, 303.9, 310.34, 310.35, 348.5, 407.8, 501.17, 502.6, 545.7, 662.10, 916.11, 1010.8
flourishing (n) 303.6, 916.2 (a) 14.3, 251.8, 259.12, 310.43, 890.9, 1010.13
flourishing condition 1010.1
flourish of rhetoric 545.4
flourish of trumpets 53.5, 487.1
flour mill 739.3
floury 1051.11
flout (n) 156.2, 508.2 (v) 156.5, 327.6, 435.4, 454.4, 508.9
flouting 156.2
flouting the law 674.3
flout the law 674.5
Flow 12.9
flow (n) 172.2, 177.16, 184.29, 238.4, 238.13, 533.1, 544.2, 896.2, 991.2, 1061.1 (v) 12.18, 172.5, 177.18, 177.35, 190.13, 202.6, 238.16, 821.5, 991.5, 1014.10
flow 12.1, 12.9
flowage 1061.1
flow back 238.16
flow chart 381.3, 801.4
flow control 1041.8
flow-control system 1041.5
flow diagram 381.3
flower (n) 310.24, 310.33, 536.1, 767.2, 999.8 (v) 303.9, 310.35, 498.9, 861.5, 1010.8
flowerage 310.1, 310.26
flower arrangement 310.25, 498.1
flower bed 1069.10
flower bud 310.23
flower child 868.3
flowered 310.38, 498.11
floweret 310.24
flower gardening 1069.2
flower girl 563.4
flower-growing 1069.2
flower head 310.27
floweriness 498.2, 545.4
flowering (n) 310.26, 861.1 (a) 14.3, 259.12, 301.9, 310.38, 1010.13
flowering plant 310.3
flowering time 301.1
flowerlike 310.38, 1016.19
flower nymph 678.9
flower of age 303.2
flower of life 301.1
flower power 143.4
flowers 554.7, 557.4
flowers of rhetoric 545.4
flowers of speech 545.4
flower vegetable 10.35
flowery 70.9, 310.38, 498.12, 536.3, 545.11
flowery style 536.1
flow from 887.5
flow in 189.9, 238.16
flowing (n) 177.16, 238.4 (a) 172.8, 202.9, 238.24, 533.6, 533.8, 544.9, 547.22, 1061.4
flowing bowl, the 88.13
flowing locks 3.5
flowing periods 533.1
flowing stream 238.1
flowing tongue 540.1
flowing toward 167.1
flowing tresses 3.5
flowing well 241.1
flow into 238.16
flowmeter 1061.3
flown 369.11
flow of air 318.1
flow of blood 308.1
flowoff 190.4
flow of ideas 931.4
flow of thought 931.4
flow of time 821.4
flow of words 538.2, 540.1
flow on 162.3, 295.24, 821.5, 1065.14
flow out 190.13, 238.16
flow over 238.17
flow together 770.16
flow with milk and honey 991.5
flu 85.16
flub (n) 414.5, 975.6 (v) 414.12
flub the dub 414.12
fluctuant 916.15
fluctuate 362.8, 364.4, 851.2, 854.5, 916.10
fluctuating 362.10, 851.3, 854.7, 916.15
fluctuation 362.2, 851.1, 854.3, 916.1
fluctuational 916.15
fluctuations 738.9
flue 3.19, 239.14, 298.2, 1020.11, 1047.4
flue cleaner 79.16
flue-cured 89.2
fluegelhornist 710.4
fluency 238.4, 533.1, 538.2, 540.1, 544.2, 1061.1
fluent 172.8, 238.24, 533.6, 533.8, 540.9, 544.9, 1061.4
fluent tongue 540.1
flue pipe 239.14
fluff (n) 3.19, 294.3, 298.2, 414.5, 975.7, 1047.4 (v) 704.31, 975.15, 1047.6
fluffhead 924.4
fluffheaded 923.9
fluffiness 3.1, 294.3, 298.1, 922.7, 1047.1
fluff one's lines 990.5
fluff up 1047.6
fluffy 3.27, 294.8, 298.10, 922.20, 1047.14
fluid (n) 1061.2, 1067.1, 1067.2 (a) 533.8, 854.6, 1061.4
fluidal 1061.4
fluid dynamics 1039.4
fluid extract 1061.2

fluidic 1061.4
fluidics 1039.4
fluidification 1064.1
fluidify 1064.5
fluidity 854.1, 1061.1, 1067.3
fluidization 1064.1, 1067.5
fluidize 1064.5, 1067.8
fluid mechanics 1061.1, 1061.2
fluidmeter 1061.3
fluid motion 238.4
fluid movement 238.4
fluidness 1061.1
fluid operations 458.4
fluke (n) 10.24, 972.6, 1010.3 (v) 411.3
flukiness 972.1
fluky 972.15
flumadiddle 1052.5
flume (n) 190.9, 237.7, 239.2, 239.3 (v) 176.14
flummery 520.2
flummox (n) 985.3 (v) 410.10, 971.12, 985.7, 1012.15
flump (n) 52.3 (v) 52.15, 194.6
flump down 194.6
flunk (n) 410.5 (v) 410.9, 410.17
flunk out 410.9, 410.17
flunky 138.3, 166.2, 250.2, 432.5, 577.1, 577.6, 616.8, 726.2
flunkyism 138.2
fluoresce 1025.26
fluorescence 1025.13
fluorescent 35.20
fluorescent lamp 1026.1
fluorescent light 1025.19, 1026.1
fluorescent paint 1037.5
fluorescent tube 1026.1
fluoridate 1060.8
fluoride 86.22
fluorinate 1060.8
fluoroscopy 91.7, 1037.8
flurried 917.16
flurry (n) 105.4, 174.1, 316.1, 318.5, 330.4, 401.1, 503.1, 738.9, 917.1, 985.3, 1023.8 (v) 105.14, 917.10, 985.7
flush (n) 35.2, 41.3, 79.5, 83.1, 85.7, 105.2, 139.5, 238.6, 238.9, 753.1, 758.4, 1019.1, 1019.12, 1025.2 (v) 41.5, 79.19, 105.19, 109.8, 136.6, 139.8, 152.14, 201.6, 238.16, 382.9, 1019.22, 1065.13 (a) 41.9, 83.12, 83.13, 201.7, 618.14, 618.15, 790.7, 794.11, 991.7
flushed 41.9, 83.13, 85.58, 93.18, 95.17, 105.22, 109.11, 116.10, 136.10, 139.13, 502.13, 1019.25
flushed with anger 152.29
flushed with joy 95.16
flushed with pride 136.10
flushed with success 411.7
flushed with victory 411.7
flushing (n) 41.3, 79.5, 139.5 (a) 41.11, 1025.30
flushing out 79.5
flush it 410.17
flushness 201.1
flush of the morning 314.2
flush out 79.19, 909.22
flush syndrome 41.3
flush with money 618.14
fluster (n) 105.6, 330.4, 503.1, 917.1, 985.3 (v) 105.14, 985.7
flusteration 105.6
flustered 88.31, 105.23, 917.16, 985.12
flustration 105.6
flute (n) 8.12, 290.1 (v) 290.3, 291.5, 524.25, 708.42
fluted 290.4, 291.7
fluting 290.1
flutist 710.4
flutter (n) 50.13, 55.1, 105.5, 105.6, 330.4, 401.1, 709.19, 737.19, 738.9, 916.3, 917.4, 985.3, 1025.8 (v) 55.4, 105.14, 105.18, 916.10, 916.11, 917.10, 917.12, 985.7, 1025.25
flutteration 917.1
fluttered 985.12
flutteriness 330.4
fluttering (n) 50.13, 1025.8 (a) 55.7, 184.50, 917.18, 1025.36
fluttering the eyelids 28.7
flutter kick 760.8
flutter the dovecot 917.10
fluttery 105.27, 128.12, 917.18, 985.16, 1025.36
fluvial 238.23
fluviatic 238.23
fluviatile 238.23
fluviation 238.1
fluviograph 238.15
fluviology 1039.4
fluviomarine 234.6, 238.23, 242.2
fluviometer 238.15
fluvioterrestrial 234.4
flux (n) 12.1, 12.2, 12.9, 85.9, 85.29, 172.2, 238.4, 238.13, 742.3, 1025.21, 1061.1, 1064.4 (v) 91.24, 805.3, 1020.21, 1064.5
flux and reflux 238.13, 916.5
flux collector 1073.17
fluxible 1061.4
fluxile 1061.4
fluxility 1061.1
fluxion 1061.1
fluxional 238.24, 1061.4
fluxionary 1061.4
fluxive 238.24
flux of time 821.4
flux of words 538.2, 540.1
fly (n) 295.4, 311.32, 356.13, 745.3 (v) 34.2, 174.8, 176.12, 177.35, 184.36, 184.37, 188.12, 193.10, 368.10, 745.5, 762.6, 821.5, 828.6, 916.11
fly a kite 942.9
fly aloft 193.10
fly apart 802.9
fly at 459.18
fly back 903.6
fly ball 745.3
fly blind 184.37
flyblown 80.23, 393.42
flyboy 185.1, 185.3
flyby 1075.9
fly-by-night 645.19, 828.7
fly by the seat of one's pants 184.37, 415.9
fly down 184.43
flyer 757.2
fly-fish 382.10
fly-fishing 382.3
fly floor 704.16
fly gallery 704.16
fly in formation 184.37
flying (n) 184.1 (a) 34.3, 87.24, 172.8, 174.15, 184.50, 401.9, 828.7
flying and landing guides marker 184.19
flying bathtub 181.7
flying bedstead 181.7
flying boat 181.8, 181.9
flying bomb 1074.4
flying bridge 383.2, 383.9
flying buttress 901.4
flying cadet 185.3
flying circus 184.1, 184.10
flying classroom 181.10
flying colors 409.3, 411.1
flying column 461.22
flying crow's nest 181.7
Flying Dutchman 178.2, 183.1, 988.2
flying fish 311.30
flying horses 743.15
flying jump 366.1
flying lessons 184.3
flying machine 181.1
flying mare 474.3
flying motorcycle 181.7
flying platform 181.7
flying ring 181.7
flying rumor 552.6
flying sap 460.5
flying saucer 1075.3
flying speed 184.31
flying squad 727.7
flying squadron 727.7
flying start 174.4, 249.2, 756.3, 818.1
flying visit 582.7
flying walkway 383.2, 383.9
fly in the face of 327.6, 335.4, 451.3, 453.3, 454.4, 779.4, 900.6
fly in the face of facts 948.2
fly in the face of reason 967.4
fly in the face of the law 674.5
fly in the ointment 1000.3, 1003.2, 1012.4
fly in the teeth 454.4
fly in the teeth of 216.8, 451.3, 453.3
fly into a passion 105.16, 152.20
fly into a rage 152.20
fly into a temper 152.20
fly into the face of danger 492.10
flyleaf 554.12
fly left seat 184.37
fly low 174.9
flyman 704.24
fly off 164.6
fly off at a tangent 152.20
fly off on a tangent 171.5
fly off the handle 105.17, 152.20
fly on instruments 184.37
fly on the wall 27.7, 48.5
fly open 292.11
fly out 152.20, 745.5
fly over 812.7
flyover 170.2, 383.3, 383.9, 812.3
fly past 812.7
flypast 812.3
fly right 653.4
fly right seat 184.37
flyspeck (n) 248.2, 258.7, 1004.3 (v) 1004.5
fly storm warnings 400.3
fly the coop 369.6
flyting 490.1, 935.4
fly to 1009.7
flytrap 356.12
fly up 193.9
flyweight 297.3
flywheel effect 812.2
FM band 1034.13
FM broadcasting 1034.16
FM signal 1034.10
FM station 1034.6
foal (n) 302.10, 311.10, 757.2 (v) 1.3
foaled 1.4
foam (n) 13.3, 37.2, 298.2, 320.2, 1022.3, 1047.4, 1065.5 (v) 320.4, 320.5, 671.12
foam at the mouth 152.15, 926.20
foam extinguisher 1022.3
foam-flecked 320.7
foaminess 298.1
foaming 320.3
foaming at the mouth 105.25, 152.32, 926.30
Foamite 1022.3
foam over 320.4
foam-rubber mattress 901.20
foam-white 37.7
foamy 298.10, 320.7, 1047.11
fob (n) 195.2, 498.6 (v) 356.18
fob off 862.4
fob off as 350.3
fob off on 643.7
fob on 643.7
focal 169.3, 208.13, 249.14, 819.4, 997.23
focalization 169.1, 208.8
focalize 208.10
focal point 169.1, 208.4, 907.2
focus (n) 169.1, 208.4, 208.8, 767.2, 907.2 (v) 208.10, 819.3
focused 169.3, 920.13, 931.21
focus group 793.1
focusing (n) 208.8 (a) 169.3
focusing on 865.6
focus of attention 208.4, 937.1
focus of interest 937.1
focus on 865.11, 889.6, 931.10, 937.3, 983.8, 983.10
focus one's thoughts 931.10
focus the attention 983.11
focus the mind on 983.5
fodder (n) 10.4 (v) 8.18, 1070.7
foe 452.1, 589.6
foehn 318.6
foeman 452.1, 589.6
f off 188.7, 222.10

fog (n) 184.32, 310.5, 319.3, 522.3, 985.3, 1065.4 (v) 32.4, 295.19, 319.7, 971.15, 985.7
fog alarm 400.1, 517.15
fog bank 319.3
fog bell 400.1, 517.15
fogbound 319.10, 522.15, 971.19
fogbow 316.8, 1025.14
fog computing 1042.1, 1042.12
fogdog 316.8
fog drip 316.1, 319.3, 1065.4
fogged 295.31, 985.13
fogged in 295.31
fogged-in 319.10
fogginess 32.2, 319.4, 522.3, 971.4, 1065.1
fogging 295.1
foggy 32.6, 319.10, 522.15, 922.18, 971.19, 985.13
foghorn 399.3, 400.1, 517.15
fog in 319.7
fog signal 400.1, 517.15
fog up 263.3
fog whistle 517.15
fogy 842.8, 853.4, 924.9
fogyish 842.17, 853.8
fogyishness 842.3
fogyism 853.3
föhn 318.6
foible 654.2, 1003.2
foie de veau 10.15
foil (n) 296.2, 412.2, 462.5, 498.7, 707.2, 1012.3 (v) 132.2, 415.11, 1012.15
foiled 132.5
foil fencing 760.4
foiling 132.1, 415.5, 1012.3
foilsman 461.1
foison 991.2
foist 776.5
foist in 213.6, 214.5
foist off 862.4
foist off as 350.3
foist on 643.7
foist oneself upon 214.5
fold (n) 212.3, 284.2, 291.1, 296.2, 700.1 (v) 260.10, 291.5, 293.8, 410.10, 562.18, 625.7, 819.3
foldable 260.11, 291.7
fold belt 237.6
fold-belt mountain 237.6
fold-dance 705.5
folded 291.7
folder 195.1, 352.8, 554.11, 554.17
folderol 498.3, 520.2, 708.24, 998.5
fold in 291.5
folding (n) 237.6, 291.4, 554.14 (a) 291.7
folding green 728.6
folding ladder 193.4
folding money 728.6
fold mountain 237.6
fold one's arms 329.2, 331.12
fold on itself (n) 291.1 (v) 291.5
fold over 291.5
fold to the heart 562.18
fold up 260.10, 291.5, 293.8, 410.10, 625.7, 820.6
foliaceous 296.6
foliage 310.18
foliage bud 310.23
foliaged 44.4, 310.41
foliate (v) 1017.17 (a) 310.41
foliated 296.6, 310.41
foliation 296.4, 310.18, 1017.9, 1059.8
folio 554.4, 554.12, 554.17, 793.2
foliole 310.19
foliose 310.41
folk (n) 227.1, 312.1, 559.4, 559.5, 606.1 (a) 606.8, 720.16, 842.12
folk art 712.1
folk ballad 708.11
folk dialect 523.7
folk etymology 526.16, 975.7
folk guitarist 710.5
folk hero 662.9
folk history 719.2, 842.2
folkie 710.13
folk literature 547.12, 718.1
folklore 678.14, 842.2, 954.3
folkloric 678.15, 842.12
folk motif 842.2
folk music 708.11
folk-music festival 708.32
folk rock 708.10
folk-rock singer 710.14
folks 559.2, 559.5, 606.1
folk school 567.3
folksiness 581.1
folk-sing 708.32
folk singer 710.13, 710.14
folk singing 708.13
folk song 708.11
folk speech 523.7
folksy 581.3
folktale 719.2, 842.2
Folkvang 681.10
folkway 321.1, 373.1
folkways 373.2
follicle 310.30
follow (n) 382.1 (v) 27.13, 138.11, 166.3, 203.5, 217.8, 250.4, 328.8, 336.7, 382.8, 422.7, 434.2, 521.7, 562.21, 744.2, 784.7, 786.7, 803.7, 815.2, 817.5, 835.3, 866.4, 867.3, 887.4, 938.30, 938.35, 957.10
follow a clue 938.35
follow a course 161.10, 182.28
follow advice 422.7
follow after 835.3
follow a hands-off policy 853.6
follow as a matter of course 957.10
follow as an occupation 328.8, 724.11
follow at heel 138.11
follow a trade 724.12
follow close upon 223.12
follower 101.4, 104.11, 138.6, 166.2, 250.2, 382.4, 572.2, 577.1, 616.8, 692.4, 696.9
followers 606.2, 617.5, 769.6
followership 101.2, 572.2, 692.1, 769.6
followers of Christ 687.3
follow-focus shot 714.8
follow from 887.5, 957.10
follow hard upon 835.3
follow implicitly 422.7
following (n) 166.1, 166.2, 336.1, 382.1, 769.6, 815.1, 835.1, 938.9, 1042.19 (a) 166.5, 382.11, 784.10, 815.4, 835.4, 887.6, 935.23
following spot 704.18
following the letter 973.15
following wind 318.1, 318.10
follow in the footsteps 166.3
follow in the footsteps of 336.7
follow in the steps of 166.3, 336.7
follow in the trail of 166.3
follow in the wake of 166.3, 336.7
follow like sheep 336.7
follow on 835.3, 887.5
follow one's conscience 375.24
follow one's nose 69.8, 161.10
follow on the heels of 166.3, 815.2
follow protocol 504.10, 580.6
follow righteousness 692.6
follow spot 704.18
follow suit 336.7
follow the beam 184.37
follow the beaten path 373.12, 867.4
follow the beaten track 373.12
follow the book 326.2
follow the crowd 138.11, 578.10, 867.4
follow the example of 336.7
follow the fashion 578.10, 867.4
follow the golden rule 143.11
follow the hounds 382.9
follow the lead of 326.2
follow the party line 609.41
follow the ponies 759.25
follow the rules 579.4, 867.4
follow the scent of 938.35
follow the seasons 177.23
follow the straight and narrow 653.4
follow the trail of 938.35
follow the trail to 888.5
follow the via media 467.6
follow through 360.5, 817.5
follow-through 750.2, 751.3, 817.1
follow to a conclusion 794.8
follow up 360.5, 382.8, 794.8, 812.4, 817.5, 835.3, 938.35
follow-up 91.10, 382.1, 552.3
followup 817.1, 835.2
follow up an inquiry 938.20
follow upon 835.3
follow up the attack 459.17
folly 923.1, 923.4
foment (n) 917.1 (v) 105.12, 120.5, 375.17, 1020.17
fomentation 105.11, 375.4, 671.2
fomenter 375.11
fomenting 375.28
fond 104.26, 124.10, 923.8, 954.8
fond embrace 562.3
fond hope 124.1, 125.4
fond illusion 356.1, 976.1
fondle 73.8, 449.16, 474.7, 562.16
fondling 73.1, 73.2, 104.15, 562.1
fondness 93.6, 100.2, 104.1, 954.1
fondness for society 582.1
fondness for the bottle 88.2
fond of 100.22, 104.29
fond of society 582.22
fond remembrance 837.4
fondue fork 8.12
font 238.9, 386.4, 548.6, 701.6, 703.11, 886.6
fontanel 292.1
food 7.3, 10.1
food additive 7.4, 397.4
food allotment 10.6
food and drink 10.1, 10.5
food chain 7.1
food coloring 35.8
food court 739.1
food cycle 7.1
food fish 10.24, 311.30
food for powder 461.6
food for thought 931.7
food for worms (n) 307.15 (a) 307.29
food freezing 1024.1
food group 7.1
foodie 8.16
food intake 7.1
food items 735.7
food mill 1063.4
food plant 310.3
food poisoning 85.29, 85.31
food preparation 11.1
food preparer 11.3
food preservation 397.2
food processing 11.1
food processor 797.9, 1063.4
food pyramid 7.1
food stamps 478.8
foodstuff 10.1
food supply 10.5
food value 7.1
foofaraw 105.6, 330.4, 498.3, 671.2, 810.4
foo fighter 1075.3
foofooraw 53.4, 456.6
fool (n) 358.1, 508.7, 707.10, 924.1, 930.7 (v) 356.15, 923.6, 998.14 (a) 923.8
foolable 923.12, 954.9
fool around 490.6, 743.23, 923.6, 998.15
fool around with 214.7, 942.8
fool away 486.5
fooler 357.1
foolery 489.5, 508.2, 923.1
foolhardiness 492.4, 493.3
foolhardy 492.21, 493.9
fool-hasty 401.11
foolheaded 923.8
foolheadedness 923.1
fooling (n) 356.1, 489.5, 490.1, 490.2, 508.1, 998.8 (a) 490.7, 508.12
fooling around 490.1, 490.3, 923.1, 998.9

foolish 322.6, 520.7, 922.13, 923.8, 923.11, 998.19
foolish hope 125.4
foolishness 322.2, 922.1, 923.1, 933.1, 985.5, 998.3
foolish thing 923.4
fool mistake 975.6
fool notion 364.1, 932.7
foolproof 15.20, 1014.15
foolscap 547.4
fool's errand 125.8, 391.3
fool's paradise 124.4, 976.1
fool's trick 923.4
fool with 214.7, 998.14
foot (n) 2.7, 180.14, 199.2, 199.5, 720.7 (v) 174.8, 177.27, 177.28, 182.21, 182.54, 705.5
footage 267.1, 706.5
foot-and-mouth disease 85.41
footbacker 178.6
football 746.1, 746.2, 752.1
football equipment or gear 746.1
footballer 752.2
football field 743.11
football game 746.3
footballing 746.1
football player 746.2
footballs 87.4
football season 313.1
football team 746.2
footband 554.14
footbath 79.8
footboy 577.5
footbridge 383.9
foot-dragger 175.5
foot-dragging (n) 175.1, 325.1, 846.2, 1012.1 (a) 175.10, 325.6, 846.17, 1012.19
footed 199.9
footed arrow 462.6
footer 750.3
footfall 177.11
foot fault 748.2
foot-fault 748.3
foot fetish 75.11
footgear 5.27
foot guard 1008.3
Foot Guards 461.15
foothills 233.1, 237.1, 274.3
foothold 474.2, 901.5, 906.2
footing 159.2, 177.8, 199.2, 245.2, 266.3, 474.2, 607.1, 624.5, 757.1, 765.1, 894.4, 901.5, 901.6, 906.2, 978.2, 1017.10
footing it 177.8
foot in the door, a 187.3, 189.5
foot it 177.27
footle 331.13
footlights 704.18, 1025.4
footlights, the 704.1
footling 248.6, 998.17
foot locker 195.1
footlong 10.21
footloose 177.37, 430.21
footloose and fancy-free 177.37, 430.21
footman 577.6
footmark 517.7
footnote 254.2, 341.5, 549.4
footpace 175.2
footpad 483.5
foot passenger 178.6
footpath 383.2
foot patrol 179.11
foot pavement 383.2
footplate 901.5
footplate man 178.13
foot-pound 17.7
footprint 517.7, 1042.18
footrace 457.12
footrail 901.5
footrest 193.5, 901.5
foots 704.18
footslog 177.28, 177.30
footslogger 178.6, 461.10
footslogging 177.8
foot soldier 178.6, 461.9
footsore 21.7
footstalk 310.21, 901.8
footstep 177.11, 193.5, 517.7
footstone 549.12, 901.7
foot the bill 624.18
foot traveler 178.6
foot up 1017.19
footway 383.2
footwear 5.27
foot-weary 21.7
footwork 754.3
foozle (n) 410.6, 414.5, 975.6 (v) 410.14, 975.15
foozler 414.9
fop 500.9, 578.7
foppery 500.4, 578.3
foppish 500.17, 578.14
foppishness 500.4, 578.3
forage (n) 10.4, 938.15 (v) 8.18, 385.9, 482.17, 938.31
forage grass 310.5
forager 483.6
foraging 482.6
for all the world like 784.15
for all to see 31.7
foramen 292.1
foray (n) 459.4, 482.6 (v) 459.20, 482.17
forayer 483.6
forbade 444.7
forbear 134.4, 145.4, 329.3, 390.5, 668.7
forbearance 134.1, 145.1, 148.1, 368.1, 668.1, 979.4
forbearant 145.7, 427.7, 979.11
forbearing (n) 134.1, 427.1 (a) 134.9, 148.6, 979.11
forbearingness 134.1
forbid (v) 444.3, 1012.14 (a) 444.7
forbiddance 444.1, 1012.2
forbidden 444.7, 967.7
forbidden fruit 100.11, 377.3, 444.1, 928.8
forbidden ground 444.1
forbidden love 104.5
forbidden territory 444.1
forbidding (n) 444.1 (a) 98.18, 344.10, 444.6, 1012.19, 1015.11
forbidding countenance 1015.3
forbiddingness 1015.2
force (n) 15.1, 17.1, 18.1, 238.11, 244.1, 330.7, 424.2, 518.1, 544.3, 577.11, 671.1, 887.2, 894.1, 902.1, 973.6 (v) 375.12, 424.4, 643.6, 665.20, 902.12, 963.8, 1069.17
force, the 689.8, 1008.17
force back 908.3
force bed 1069.11
forced 325.5, 534.3, 725.18, 776.8, 963.14
forced draft 174.3
forced labor 725.4
forced-labor camp 429.8
forced landing 194.3
forced march 177.10, 401.3
forced marriage 563.3
force down one's throat 643.6
forced resignation 447.2, 448.1
forced retirement 448.1
forced separation 909.5
force-feed 7.17, 8.19
force field 429.5
force from 480.22
forceful 15.15, 17.13, 18.12, 330.23, 544.11, 997.21
forcefulness 18.1, 330.7, 544.3
force in 191.7
force into a mold 867.3
forceless 19.13, 895.3
forcelessness 19.1, 895.1
force majeure 18.1, 963.7
forcemeat 10.13, 10.27
force of arms 458.1
force of friction 1044.5
force of gravity 18.6
force of habit 373.3
force of inertia 18.5
force of life 18.5, 306.2
force of nature 305.1
force of viscosity 1044.5
force one's hand 424.4
force one's thoughts from 984.4
force one's way 162.4
force open 292.14
force out 192.15, 447.3, 909.14
force-out 745.3
force out of place 160.5
forceps 192.9
forces 18.9, 461.23
forces of law and order 1008.17
forces of nature 317.3
force to the wall 395.25
force upon 439.9, 478.20, 643.6
forcible 15.15, 17.13, 18.12, 424.12, 544.11, 997.21
forcible removal 160.1
forcible seizure 480.2, 671.3
forcible shift 160.1
forcing 424.1, 643.2
forcing bed 886.8, 1069.11
forcing house 1069.11
forcing on 643.2
forcing pit 1069.11
Ford 618.8
ford 276.2, 383.3
ford 910.8
fore (n) 216.1, 751.1 (v) 751.4 (a) 216.10, 834.4, 837.10
fore-and-aft rigged 180.17
fore-and-aft sail 180.14
forearm (n) 2.7, 906.5 (v) 405.11, 494.6
forearmed 130.11
forearming 494.3
forebear 816.1
forebearance 390.2, 427.1
forebearing 427.7
forebears 560.7
forebode 133.10, 399.6, 514.2, 962.9
foreboding (n) 93.1, 126.1, 127.4, 133.2, 399.2, 514.1, 934.3, 961.3, 962.1 (a) 126.7, 133.16, 399.8, 514.3, 962.12
forebodingness 126.1
forecast (n) 317.7, 961.1, 962.1 (v) 381.8, 962.9 (a) 962.14
forecaster 962.4
forecasting (n) 317.5, 962.1 (a) 962.11
forecastle 216.3
forecasts 1041.7
forechecking 749.3
foreclose 480.23, 1012.14
foreclosure 480.7, 1012.2
foreconscious (n) 92.28 (a) 92.42
forecourt 747.1, 748.1
foredate 833.2
foredated 833.3
foredawn 314.3
foredeck 216.3
foredestiny 964.1
foredoom (n) 964.2 (v) 964.7
foredoomed 125.13, 964.9
foredoomed hope 125.4
fore edge 554.12
forefathers 560.7
forefeeling 133.1, 934.3
forefinger 73.5
forefoot 199.5
forefront 165.1, 211.4, 216.1, 216.2
foreglance 961.1
foregleam 961.1
foreglimpse (n) 961.1 (v) 845.6, 961.5
foreglimpsed 962.14
foregoer 816.1
foregoing (n) 165.1 (a) 165.3, 814.5, 834.4, 837.11
foregone 964.8
foregone conclusion 409.2, 964.1
foreground 216.1, 223.1
foreground detail 498.7
foregut 2.18
forehand (n) 216.1 (a) 216.10, 845.7
forehanded 494.10, 635.6, 845.7, 961.7
forehandedness 494.3, 635.1, 961.1
forehead 216.5
foreign 206.9, 768.3, 774.5, 776.6
foreign accent 524.8
foreign affairs 609.5
foreign body 774.2
foreign-born 774.5
foreign correspondent 555.4
foreign currency 728.9
foreign denominations 728.9
foreign element 774.2
foreigner 773.3, 774.3, 870.4
foreign exchange 728.9
foreign-exchange trading 737.19

foreign film 706.2
foreign influx 189.3
foreign intruder 774.2
foreign intrusion 774.2
foreignism 526.7
foreign language 523.1
foreign language film 706.2
foreign-language study 523.13
foreign-looking 774.5
foreign money 728.9
foreignness 206.1, 768.1, 774.1
foreign office 576.7
foreign-owned plant 739.3
foreign policy 609.5
foreign service 576.7
foreign service officer 576.6
foreign threat 458.11
forejudge 947.2, 980.7
forejudged 947.3
forejudgment 947.1, 980.3
forejumper 753.2
foreknow 961.6
foreknowable 962.13
foreknowableness 962.8
foreknower 962.4
foreknowing (n) 961.3 (a) 961.7
foreknowledge 928.3, 961.3, 964.1
foreknown 962.14
foreland 216.1, 283.9
foreleg 177.14
forelock 3.6
foreman 574.2, 596.6
foreman of the jury 596.6
foremanship 573.4
foremast 216.3
foremeant 380.9
forementioned 814.5
foremost 165.3, 216.10, 249.14, 814.4, 818.17, 997.24
forename 527.4
forenamed 814.5
forenoon (n) 314.1 (a) 314.5
forensic (n) 543.2 (a) 90.15, 543.12, 594.6, 673.12
forensic address 543.2
forensic chemistry 673.7
forensic medicine 673.7
forensic psychiatry 673.7
forensics 457.1, 543.1
forensic science 673.7
forensic tool 517.11
foreordain 964.6
foreordained 964.8
foreordainment 964.1
foreordination 964.1
forepart 216.1
forepaw 199.5
forepeak 216.3
foreperson 596.6
foreplay 75.7
forepleasure 95.1
forequarter 216.1
foreroom 197.5
forerun 133.13, 816.3, 834.3, 845.6
forerunner 133.4, 353.2, 405.5, 574.6, 753.2, 816.1, 834.2
forerunning 133.15, 399.8
foresee 130.5, 130.6, 380.6, 839.6, 845.6, 961.5, 962.9
foreseeability 961.3, 962.8
foreseeable 961.8, 962.13, 968.6
foreseeing (n) 961.1 (a) 494.10, 920.16, 961.7, 962.11
foreseen 130.13, 839.8, 961.8, 962.14
foreseer 962.4
foreshadow (n) 133.3 (v) 133.9, 349.11, 814.2, 962.10
foreshadowed 133.14
foreshadower 133.4
foreshadowing (n) 133.3 (a) 133.15
foreshore 234.2
foreshorten 268.6
foreshortened 268.9
foreshortening 268.3
foreshow 133.9, 962.10
foreshowing (n) 133.3, 962.1 (a) 133.15
foreshown 133.14, 962.14
foreside 216.1
foresight 381.1, 494.3, 689.8, 839.1, 845.1, 920.4, 961.1, 962.1
foresighted 494.10, 845.7, 920.16, 961.7
foresightedness 494.3, 920.4, 961.1
forest (n) 310.12, 310.13, 1069.8 (v) 1069.18 (a) 310.40
forestage 704.16
forestal 310.40
forestall 130.6, 356.14, 469.6, 845.6, 1012.14
forestalling (n) 368.1, 1012.2 (a) 130.11, 1012.19
forestallment 368.1, 469.3
forestation 1069.3
forest conservation 397.1
forest cover 310.13
forested 310.40
forester 1008.6, 1069.7
forest fire 1019.13
forest firefighter 1022.4
forest god 678.11, 1069.4
forest-green 44.4
forest land 310.13
forest management 397.1, 1069.3
forest manager 1069.7
forest preserve 310.13, 397.7, 1009.1
forest product 1054.3
forest ranger 397.5, 1008.6, 1069.7
forest reserve 397.7
forestry 310.13, 1069.3
forests 233.2
forest spirit 678.11
foretaste (n) 10.9, 961.4 (v) 845.6, 961.5
foretell 839.6, 962.9
foretellable 962.13
foretellableness 962.8
foreteller 962.4
foretelling (n) 962.1 (a) 962.11
forethink 380.7
forethought 339.1, 380.3, 381.1, 494.3, 961.2
forethoughted 494.10, 920.16, 961.7
forethoughtful 494.10, 920.16, 961.7
forethoughtfulness 494.3
foretime 837.1, 837.2
foretoken (n) 133.3 (v) 133.11, 962.10
foretokened 133.14
foretokening (n) 133.3 (a) 133.15
foretold 962.14
foretooth 2.8
forever 823.1, 829.2
foreverness 829.1
forewarn 133.10, 399.6
forewarned 130.11
forewarning (n) 399.2 (a) 133.15, 399.8, 962.11
forewisdom 961.3
foreword 216.1, 554.12, 793.2, 816.2
forfeit (n) 438.3, 473.1, 603.3 (v) 473.4, 475.3 (a) 473.7
forfeited 473.7, 475.5
forfeit one's good opinion 661.7
forfeiture 473.1, 603.3
forfend 444.3
for free 634.5
forgather 770.16
forgathering 770.1, 770.2
forge (n) 739.4, 1020.11 (v) 262.7, 336.5, 354.18, 728.28
forge ahead 162.4, 216.7, 330.13
forged 262.9, 336.8, 354.29, 892.18
forgeman 726.8
forger 336.4, 357.1, 726.8, 728.25
forgery 336.1, 350.1, 354.10, 354.13, 728.10, 728.24, 785.1
forget 148.5, 984.4, 990.5
forget about it 984.4
forgetful 144.18, 340.11, 990.9
forgetfulness 144.3, 340.2, 933.1, 990.1
forget it 106.7, 984.4
forget nothing 494.6
forget oneself 152.17
forget one's lines 990.5
forget one's own name 990.4
forget one's place 142.7
forgettable 990.10
forget the odds 1006.7
forgetting (n) 990.1 (a) 990.9
forgetting nothing 494.8
forget to remember 990.5
forging 266.1
forgivable 600.14
forgivableness 600.7
forgive 145.4, 148.3, 601.4, 625.9, 990.6
forgive and forget 148.5, 465.10
forgiven 148.7
forgiveness 145.1, 148.1, 464.7, 601.1, 990.1
forgiveness of sin 148.2
forgiving 148.6, 427.7
forgivingness 148.1
forgo 329.3, 370.7, 390.5, 475.3, 668.7
forgoing 475.1, 668.1
forgone 475.5
forgotten 148.7, 151.5, 837.7, 990.8
forgotten man, the 619.3
for-instance 786.3
fork (n) 171.4, 238.3, 278.2, 310.20, 1040.8 (v) 171.7, 176.17, 278.5, 626.5, 875.4, 904.10, 1069.17
fork bender 689.11
forked 171.10, 278.6, 875.6
forked lightning 1025.17
forking (n) 171.3, 875.1 (a) 171.10, 875.6
fork it in 672.4
forklift 912.3
fork lightning 1025.17
forklike 171.10
fork out 478.12, 624.14, 626.5
fork over 478.12, 478.13, 624.14, 624.16
forks 8.12
fork up 478.12
for lagniappe 993.18
for life 827.13
forlorn 112.28, 125.12, 584.12
forlorn hope 125.4, 132.1
forlornness 112.12, 125.2, 584.4
forlorn of 992.13
for love 634.5
form (n) 2.2, 33.3, 33.5, 92.32, 228.26, 262.1, 262.4, 262.6, 266.1, 373.4, 384.1, 419.2, 419.3, 498.7, 549.5, 572.11, 579.1, 580.1, 673.3, 701.3, 708.5, 709.11, 757.4, 765.3, 765.4, 786.6, 808.1, 809.3, 869.4, 976.4, 988.1, 1052.3, 1053.3 (v) 262.7, 262.8, 266.5, 568.13, 796.3, 807.5, 892.8, 892.10
formability 570.5, 1047.2
formable 570.18, 1047.9
form a conviction 953.13
form a hypothesis 951.9
formal (n) 580.4, 705.2 (a) 111.3, 262.9, 266.6, 501.22, 504.14, 527.15, 530.17, 534.3, 579.5, 580.7, 701.18, 765.6, 807.6
formal agreement 437.1
formal argument 935.5
formal cause 886.3, 932.2
formal contrast 526.3
formaldehyde 88.14, 397.4
formal dress 5.11
formal education 568.1
formal fallacy 936.3
formalin 397.4
form a line 812.6
formalism 500.5, 580.2, 693.2, 701.1
formalist (n) 693.3, 701.2, 867.2, 929.5 (a) 580.7
formalist criticism 723.1
formalistic 500.18, 580.7, 867.6
formalities 504.7, 580.3
formality 111.1, 500.5, 501.6, 579.1, 580.1, 580.4, 673.3, 701.3, 869.4
formalization 580.1, 869.5
formalize 262.7, 437.7, 580.5, 869.6
formal language 523.4, 1042.13

formal logic 935.2
formal meal 8.8
formalness 580.1
formal observance 487.1
formals 5.11
formal speech 543.2
formal visit 582.7
formal written language 523.4
form a mental picture of 986.15
form a mutual admiration society with oneself 502.8
form an estimate 946.9
form an opinion 946.8
form a part of 796.3
form a series 812.4
format (n) 262.1, 266.1 (v) 262.7, 783.2
formation 184.12, 262.1, 262.5, 266.1, 526.4, 746.3, 796.1, 807.1, 808.1, 892.2, 892.4
formational 262.9, 808.15, 892.14
formation flying 184.12
formative (n) 526.3, 530.2 (a) 262.9, 796.5, 818.15, 886.13, 892.16, 1047.9
formativeness 1047.2
form a unity 792.7
form a whole 792.7
form class 530.3
formed 262.9, 266.6, 892.18
formed of 796.4
fomentation 86.33
former 814.5, 834.4, 837.10, 842.19
former times 837.1
form-fitting 293.12
form four 879.3, 880.2
form fours 879.3
form-function unit 530.2
form-giving cause 932.2
formication 74.4, 917.5
formicative 74.11
formidability 1013.1
formidable 127.30, 247.10, 997.20, 1013.17
formidable defenses 94.3
formidableness 247.1
form ideas 931.8
forming 262.5, 808.1, 892.2
forming a part of 772.5
formless 263.4, 538.11, 810.12, 870.9
formlessness 263.1, 538.1
form of government 612.1
form of life 305.2
form of service 701.3
form of speech 532.2
form of worship 701.3
formol 397.4
forms 1042.10
form squares 879.3
form the foundation of 901.21
formula 381.4, 419.2, 419.3, 673.3, 701.3, 869.4, 974.2
Formula car racing 756.1
formulaic 701.18, 974.6
formular 701.18
formularist 701.2
formularize 532.4
formulary (n) 419.3, 673.3, 701.3, 869.4 (a) 419.4, 580.7, 701.18
formulate 392.10, 524.22, 532.4, 547.21, 673.9, 718.6, 892.8, 892.12
formulated 532.5
formulated belief 953.3
formulation 262.5, 532.1, 808.1, 892.2
formulist 701.2
formulistic 974.6
form up 808.9
form word 530.3
fornicate 75.21, 665.19
fornication 75.7, 665.7
fornicator 665.13
fornicatress 665.13
fornicatrix 665.13
for no other ears 345.14
for nothing 634.5
for one's health 81.5
for real 761.15
forsake 370.5, 645.12
forsaken 99.10, 222.15, 370.8, 584.12, 586.10
forsake the world 584.7
forsaking 370.1
forsaking of the world 584.1
forswear 335.4, 363.8, 370.7, 372.2, 475.3, 668.8
forswearing 335.2, 363.3, 370.3, 475.1, 645.3
forswear oneself 354.20, 645.12
forswear speaking 51.5
forswear speech 51.5
forswear violence 464.8
forsworn 354.34, 363.11, 372.3, 475.5, 645.18
fort 460.6, 1009.3
forte (n) 53.3, 413.4, 708.25, 865.4, 866.1 (a) 53.11, 708.53
forté 231.2
forthcome 840.2
forthcoming (n) 33.1, 167.1, 840.1 (a) 167.4, 190.18, 405.22, 839.8, 840.3
forthcomingness 840.1
for the best 999.16
for the birds 98.25
for the gods 63.8
for the people 612.4
forthright 644.17
forthrightness 644.4
fortification 7.14, 15.5, 460.4, 957.4
fortified 251.7, 460.12, 1046.13
fortified tunnel 460.5
fortified wine 88.17
fortify 7.20, 9.2, 15.13, 253.5, 460.9, 797.12, 957.11
fortifying (n) 15.5, 797.3 (a) 9.3
fortiori reasoning, a 935.3
fortissimo (n) 53.3, 708.25 (a) 53.11, 708.53
fortitude 15.1, 134.1, 359.4, 492.5, 653.3
Fort Knox 729.13
fortnight 824.2, 882.7
fortnightly (n) 555.1 (a) 850.8
fortress 460.6
fortuitous 766.7, 768.4, 972.15
fortuitousness 972.1
fortuity 972.1, 972.6
Fortuna 964.3, 972.2
fortunate 133.17, 409.14, 843.9, 972.15, 1010.14
Fortunate Islands 681.9
Fortunate Isles 681.9
fortunateness 133.8, 1010.2
fortunate outcome 409.1
Fortunatus's cap 691.6
Fortune 972.2
fortune 1010.2
fortune 618.1, 759.2, 964.2, 972.1
fortune cookie 10.43
Fortune 500 731.1
fortune hunter 651.3
fortuneless 619.9, 1011.14
fortunes 719.1
fortune's child 1010.6
fortune's favor 1010.2
fortune's favorite 1010.6
fortune's fool 1011.7
Fortune's wheel 759.16, 964.2
fortune-tell 962.9
fortuneteller 962.4
fortunetelling (n) 962.2 (a) 962.11
for two 873.7
forty 231.4, 882.7
forty-five 462.10
forty-four 462.10
fortyish 303.14
forty-niner 178.1, 1058.9
forty-ninth parallel 231.7
forty winks 22.3
forum 230.8, 423.3, 463.1, 541.6, 595.1, 770.2
for want of 992.13
forward (n) 749.2, 752.2 (v) 162.5, 176.15, 384.7, 392.9, 401.4, 449.17, 478.13, 553.12, 886.12, 902.11, 904.9, 995.3 (a) 101.8, 142.9, 162.6, 214.9, 216.10, 324.5, 359.15, 493.9, 666.6, 845.8
forwardal 162.1
forwarding (n) 162.1, 401.3, 449.5 (a) 384.8
forward jump 162.1
forward leap 162.1
forward line 216.2, 749.2
forward look 839.1
forward-looking 162.6, 841.13
forward motion 162.1, 172.2
forwardness 101.1, 214.2, 324.1, 359.6, 361.3, 493.3, 666.2, 845.2
forward observer 1008.10
forward pass 746.3, 904.3
forward spring 162.1
forward wall 746.2
fosse 290.2, 460.5
fossil (n) 256.1, 842.6, 842.8 (a) 842.13
fossil fish 311.30
fossil footprint 517.7
fossil fuel 1021.1
fossil-fuel 1021.9
fossil hunter 842.5
fossil hunting 842.4
fossilization 1046.5
fossilize 842.9, 1046.7
fossilized 303.18, 842.13, 1046.13
fossil man 842.7
fossil oil 1056.4
fossil print 517.7
fossil record 842.6
foster (v) 8.19, 162.5, 339.9, 375.12, 375.21, 392.9, 449.16, 474.7, 568.13, 1008.19 (a) 559.6
foster a belief 953.13
fosterage 449.3, 449.4, 1008.2
foster an idea 931.16
foster brother 559.3
foster care 449.3
foster child 432.6, 561.3
foster father 560.9
foster home 1009.4
fostering (n) 385.3, 449.3, 568.3, 1008.2 (a) 449.20, 1008.23
foster in the mind 931.20
fosterling 302.9
foster mother 560.11
foster sister 559.3
foster the hope 124.6
fou 926.15
foul (n) 650.2, 745.3, 746.3, 747.3, 749.3, 749.6, 752.3, 754.3 (v) 80.17, 293.7, 389.4, 480.17, 747.4, 855.10, 902.13 (a) 64.7, 69.10, 71.5, 80.23, 82.5, 98.18, 173.14, 293.11, 318.22, 393.40, 513.8, 650.10, 654.16, 661.12, 666.8, 666.9, 680.17, 1000.9, 1015.11
foul ball 745.3
foul breath 71.1
fouled 80.21, 293.11
fouled up 393.29, 799.4, 810.16
fouled-up 414.22
fouling 389.1, 393.2
fouling out 747.3
foul invective 513.4
foul lane 747.1
foul language 513.3
foul line 745.1, 747.1, 750.1
foul matter 80.7
foul mouth 513.3
foulmouthed 144.23, 513.8, 666.9
foulness 64.3, 71.2, 80.2, 98.2, 393.7, 654.4, 661.3, 666.4, 1000.2
foul odor 71.1
foul one's own nest 80.17, 389.4, 661.7
foul out 747.4
foul-out 745.3
foul play 308.2, 356.4, 645.6, 650.2, 1000.3
foul pole 745.1
foul shot 747.3
foul-smelling 71.5
foul-spoken 666.9
foul-tasting 64.5
foul the anchor 182.15
foul-tongued 666.9
foul trouble 747.3
foul up 393.11, 414.12, 799.3, 811.3, 975.15, 1012.16
foul-up 414.5, 414.9, 810.2, 975.6

foul weather 671.4
foul weather gear 5.13
foul wind 900.4
foumart 311.22
found 159.16, 262.7, 715.5, 818.11, 855.9, 886.10, 892.10, 1020.24
foundation 159.7, 199.2, 405.1, 478.9, 600.6, 617.8, 750.2, 818.1, 855.6, 892.4, 901.6, 935.7, 1016.11
foundational 199.8, 818.15
foundation cream 1016.11
foundation garment 5.23, 901.2
foundation stone 901.7
founded 262.9
founded on 901.24, 957.16
founder (n) 892.7 (v) 85.49, 182.44, 194.6, 275.9, 367.8, 393.24, 410.11, 1011.10
foundered 1013.27
foundering 194.11, 297.18
founder member 892.7
founding 715.1
founding father 892.7
founding member 892.7
founding partner 892.7
foundling 370.4
found money 472.6
found nowhere 762.5
found object 715.2
found on 199.6
foundry 739.4
foundry proof 548.5
found wanting 992.9, 1003.4
fount 238.9, 386.4, 886.6
fountain (n) 193.1, 238.9, 386.4, 886.6 (v) 193.9
fountainhead 238.2, 818.4, 886.6
Fountain of Youth 986.11
fountain of youth 829.3
fountain syringe 1065.8
4 879.1
four (n) 758.2, 879.1 (a) 879.4
four and twenty 882.7
four-bagger 745.3
four-ball match 751.3
four bits 728.7
four-channel stereo system 50.11
four corners of the earth 261.4, 1073.10
4º 881.2
4-D 714.1
four-dimensional geometry 158.6
4-D movie 706.1
four-dimensional space 158.6
four elements, the 1052.2
four-em space 548.7
four-eyed 29.11
four-flush 354.21
fourflusher 357.6
four-flushing 354.3
fourfold (v) 880.2 (a) 880.3
fourfoldness 879.2, 880.1
four-foot octave 709.9
Four Freedoms, the 430.1
Four Hundred, the 578.6, 607.2, 608.1
Fourierist 611.14
Fourieristic 611.22
four-in-hand 179.5
four-leaf clover 691.5, 879.1
four-legged 879.4
four-legged friend 311.2
four-letter 523.21
four-letter word 513.4, 526.6
four-line octave 709.9
fourness 879.2
four of a kind 758.4
four of clubs 758.2
401K 729.3
four-part (n) 708.18 (a) 708.50, 880.3
four-part diaphony 879.1
four-part time 709.24
fourpence 728.8
fourpenny 728.8
four-percenter 609.30
four-ply 880.3
4.0 GPA 646.1
four-rayed 879.4
fourscore 882.7
four-score and ten 882.7
four-sided 218.7
foursome 751.2, 879.1
four-spot 758.2
foursquare 278.9, 644.14, 879.4
four-star general 575.17
four-step approach 750.2
four-tailed bandage 86.33
fourteen 882.7
fourteenth 882.25
fourth (n) 709.17, 709.20, 881.2 (a) 881.5
fourth-class 1005.9
fourth dimension 158.6
fourth-dimensional 158.10
fourth down 746.3
fourth estate 552.9
fourth estate, the 552.1, 555.3
fourth-generation computer 1042.2
fourth generation language 1042.13
Fourth-of-July orator 502.5
fourth part 881.2
fourth person 530.7
fourth power 883.4
fourth-rate 1005.9
fourth-rateness 1005.3
fourth-rater 1005.5
4to 554.4, 881.2
four-up 179.5
four walls 197.1
four-wheel drive 179.9
four-wheeler 179.4
fowl (n) 10.22, 311.27, 311.28 (v) 382.9
fowls of the air 311.27
fox 311.19, 415.6
foxed 47.13, 1004.10
fox fire 1019.13, 1025.13
foxhole 284.5, 346.4, 460.5, 1009.3
foxhole buddy 461.6
foxhunt 382.2
foxhunting 382.2
foxiness 415.1, 920.3
foxing 1004.2
foxlike 311.41
foxtrot 705.5
foxtrotter 705.3
foxy 40.4, 311.41, 415.12, 920.15, 1004.10
foyer 197.19
frabjous 743.27
fracas 53.3, 456.5, 457.5, 810.4
fracking 1059.9
fraction 609.24, 793.1, 1017.7, 1017.12
fractional 793.7, 1017.23
fractional currency 728.1
fractional lot 738.3
fractional note 728.5
fractionate 1067.8
fractionation 1067.5
fractious 110.19, 325.5, 327.10, 361.12, 451.8, 453.5
fractiousness 110.2, 325.1, 327.2, 361.4, 451.2, 453.1
fracturable 16.14, 1050.4
fracturableness 1050.1
fracture (n) 85.38, 224.2, 802.4 (v) 224.4, 393.13, 393.23, 802.12, 1050.3
fracture one 743.21
fractureproof 1049.5
frag 308.18
fragile 16.14, 764.7, 828.7, 1050.4
fragile health 85.3
fragility 16.2, 85.3, 764.1, 1050.1
fragment (n) 248.2, 793.3 (v) 395.17, 782.2, 802.13, 1050.3, 1051.9
fragmentable 16.14
fragmentary 16.15, 793.7, 802.24, 813.4
fragmentate 1050.3
fragmentation 771.1, 802.3, 806.1, 1051.4
fragmented 16.15, 456.15, 802.24, 1051.11
fragmenting 393.45
fragmentize 802.9, 802.13, 1050.3
fragmentized 802.24
fragmentizing 802.3
fragments 557.4
fragrance 69.1, 70.1
fragrance control 1041.8
fragrance-free 72.5
fragrant 69.9, 70.9
fragrant as new-mown hay 70.9
fragrant weed 89.1
fraid-cat 491.5
fraidy-cat 491.5
frail (n) 302.7 (a) 16.14, 85.54, 270.16, 312.13, 362.12, 654.12, 764.7, 828.7, 1050.4
frail health 85.3
frail humanity 312.6
frailness 270.5, 764.1
frail sister 665.14
frailty 16.2, 85.3, 270.4, 312.8, 362.4, 654.2, 1003.2, 1050.1
frame (n) 2.1, 2.2, 195.1, 199.2, 211.2, 211.4, 262.1, 262.4, 266.1, 266.4, 599.4, 714.10, 745.3, 750.2, 766.2, 767.4, 901.10, 965.2, 978.4, 1052.3 (v) 211.10, 262.7, 381.8, 381.9, 532.4, 599.12, 892.8, 892.12, 965.5
framed 262.9, 965.8
framed-up 965.8
frame of mind 978.4
frame of reference 959.2, 978.2
framer 381.6
frame up 381.9, 599.12
frame-up (n) 354.13, 381.5, 599.4, 965.2 (v) 965.5
framework 2.2, 211.2, 266.4, 978.2
framing 266.4, 892.2
franchise (n) 371.6, 430.8, 443.5, 609.17, 642.2, 730.2 (v) 443.11
franchised 443.17
Franciscan (n) 667.2 (a) 667.4
Franciscanism 667.1
franctireur 461.16
frangibility 16.2, 1050.1
frangible 16.14, 1050.4
frangibleness 16.2
frangipani 70.4
Franglais 523.10
frank (n) 553.5 (a) 343.10, 416.5, 430.23, 535.3, 540.9, 644.17, 666.8
frankalmoign 469.1, 471.5
Frankenfood 10.1
Frankenstein 127.9
Frankenstein's monster 593.6
frankfurter 10.21
frankhearted 644.17
frankincense 70.4
franklin 430.11
Franklin D Roosevelt 543.6
frankness 343.3, 535.1, 540.1, 644.4, 666.3
frantic 101.12, 105.25, 330.24, 671.18, 926.30, 985.10
franticness 330.9
frappé 10.47
frat brother 617.11
frater 559.3
fraternal 143.13, 587.15
fraternal feeling 143.1
fraternalism 450.2, 587.2
fraternal order 617.3
fraternal society 617.3
fraternal twins 873.4
fraternity 450.2, 559.1, 582.6, 587.2, 617.3
fraternity brother 617.11
fraternity house 228.15
fraternity man 617.11
fraternization 450.2, 582.6, 587.2, 645.7
fraternize 582.17, 645.15
fraternizer 357.11
fraternize with 587.9
fratricidal 395.26
fraud 354.3, 354.13, 356.8, 357.6, 389.1, 482.1, 500.7, 645.3, 674.3
fraudulence 356.8, 645.1
fraudulency 356.8, 645.1
fraudulent 356.22, 482.21, 638.3, 645.16, 674.6
fraudulent voter 609.23
fraught 297.18, 794.12
fraught with danger 1006.9
fraught with doom 133.16

fraught with meaning 518.10
fray (n) 85.38, 457.4 (v) 393.13, 393.20, 1044.7
frayed 393.32
frayed nerves 128.4
frazil 1023.5
frazzle (n) 85.38 (v) 21.6, 126.4, 393.13, 393.20, 1044.7
frazzled 21.8, 393.32, 393.36
frazzled nerves 128.4
freak (n) 87.21, 100.12, 101.5, 364.1, 789.4, 866.3, 868.3, 870.4, 870.6, 926.18, 927.4, 972.6 (a) 870.13
freak accident 972.6
freaked out 105.25
freaked-out 95.17, 101.11, 870.11, 926.27
freakery 854.2
freakiness 927.1
freakish 364.5, 854.7, 870.13, 927.5
freakish inspiration 364.1
freakishness 265.3, 364.2, 854.2, 870.3, 927.1
freak occurrence 972.6
freak of nature 870.6
freak out 95.11, 105.17, 128.8, 926.22, 976.8, 986.17
freak out on 105.18
freak show 907.2
freak someone out 128.10
freaky 870.11, 870.13
frecked 47.13
freckle (n) 47.3, 517.5, 1004.1 (v) 47.7, 517.19, 771.6, 1004.5
freckled 47.13, 771.10, 1004.9
freckle-faced 1004.9
freckliness 47.3
freckly 47.13, 1004.9
free (v) 120.6, 192.10, 292.12, 398.3, 430.13, 430.14, 431.4, 431.7, 601.4, 802.10, 804.3, 1014.9 (a) 222.15, 292.17, 324.7, 331.18, 343.10, 369.11, 402.5, 430.21, 430.31, 431.10, 485.4, 634.5, 644.17, 665.25, 802.22
free-acting 430.23
free admission 634.2
free agent 430.12
free and clear 469.8, 624.23
free-and-clear possession 469.1
free-and-clear title 469.1
free and dry 1007.6
free and easy 106.15, 109.12, 340.11, 430.21, 581.3, 582.23, 868.6
free as a bird 340.11, 369.11, 430.21
free as air 430.21, 634.5
free association 92.33
free as the wind 430.21
freebase 87.22
freebasing 87.2
freebee 634.5
freebie (n) 254.4, 478.4, 634.1 (a) 634.5
freeboot 482.17, 482.18
freebooter rapparee 483.6
freebooting 482.6, 482.7
freeborn 430.21
freeby 634.5
free choice 323.1, 371.1, 430.6
Free Church 675.11
free citizen 430.11
free city 232.1
free climbing 760.6
free companion 461.17
free competition 430.9
free country 232.1
free course 430.4
freed 430.21, 431.10
free decision 430.6
free diver 367.4
freedman 430.11
freedom 369.1, 402.1, 430.1, 443.4, 485.1, 581.1, 601.2, 642.2, 644.4, 1014.1
freedom abused 640.2
freedom fighter 327.5, 461.16
freedom from fear 430.1
freedom from illusion 987.2
freedom from want 430.1
freedom from war 464.1
freedom of movement 430.1
freedom of speech 430.1
freedom of speech and expression 430.1
freedom of the house 585.1
freedom of worship 430.1
freedwoman 430.11
free economy 611.8
free electron theory of metals 1033.2
free enterprise 430.9, 609.4, 611.8
free-enterprise 611.23
free-enterprise economy 611.8, 731.7
free-enterprise system 611.8
free exercise 84.2
free fall 174.4, 633.4
free-fall (n) 194.1, 367.1, 393.3 (v) 367.6
free-floating 430.22, 802.20, 802.22
free-for-all 53.4, 457.5, 810.4
free form 526.1
freeform 430.22
free for nothing 634.5
free for the asking 634.5
free from 120.6
free gift 478.4
free giver 485.2
free-going 430.23
free gratis 634.5
free gratis for nothing 634.5
free hand 323.1, 430.4, 443.4, 485.1
freehand 430.23, 712.21
freehand drawing 712.4
freehanded 430.23, 485.4
freehandedness 485.1
freehearted 143.15, 485.4
freeheartedness 485.1
free hit 749.6
freehold (n) 234.1, 469.1, 471.5 (a) 471.10
freeholder 227.7, 470.3, 610.3
freeing (n) 120.2, 369.1, 398.1, 431.1, 431.2, 431.3, 909.6, 1014.6 (a) 592.4
free kick 746.3, 752.3
free lance 461.17, 547.15
freelance (n) 430.12, 461.17, 718.4, 726.2 (v) 430.20, 547.21, 718.6, 747.4 (a) 430.22
freelancer 726.2
freelance reporter 555.4
freelance worker 577.3, 726.2
freelance writer 547.15, 718.4
freelancing 747.3
free liver 669.3
free living 669.2
free-living 669.8
freeload 634.4
freeloader 138.5, 331.11, 585.6, 634.3
free love 75.18, 104.1, 665.7
freeloving 665.27
free-lovism 104.1, 665.7
free man 566.2
freeman 430.11
freemarket 731.1
free-market economy 731.7
freemasonry 450.2, 587.2
free morpheme free form 526.3
free-moving 430.23
free nation 232.1
freeness 343.3, 485.1, 634.1, 644.4
free of 430.31
free of charge 634.5
free of cost 634.5
free of expense 634.5
free oneself 369.6
free oneself from 431.8
free pardon 601.1
free pass 634.2
free play 430.4
free port 1009.6
freer 592.2
free radical 1060.2
free-range 430.26
free-range parent 559.1
free-ranging 430.26
free ride 634.1, 745.3
free rider 634.3
free safety 746.2
free scope 430.4
free skating 760.7
free socage 469.1
free-speaking 343.10, 524.31, 644.17
free speech 430.1
free-spending 485.4
free spirit 430.12, 868.3
free-spirited 430.22
free-spoken 343.10, 430.23, 524.31, 644.17
freestanding 430.22, 802.20
freestyle 182.11
freestyle skier 753.2
freestyle skiing 753.1
free swimming 182.11
free television 1035.1
freethinker 430.12, 695.13, 868.3, 979.6
freethinking (n) 430.10, 695.7, 979.2 (a) 430.25, 695.21, 979.9
free thought 430.10, 695.7, 979.2
free throw 747.3
free-throw lane 747.1
free-throw line 747.1
free ticket 634.2, 745.3
free time 402.1
free-tongued 343.10, 644.17
free trade 430.9, 609.4, 731.1
free trade area 617.1
free-trade economy 731.7
free trader 430.12
free translation 341.3
free up 1014.9
free verse 720.6
freeware 1042.11
free weights 84.2
freewheeling 430.22
free will 323.1, 324.2, 371.1, 430.6
freewill 324.7
free with one's money 485.4
free woman 566.2
freewoman 430.11
free-working 430.23
freezable 1024.12
freeze (n) 173.3, 625.2, 1023.3 (v) 25.4, 94.8, 127.11, 127.17, 173.7, 329.2, 397.9, 525.7, 704.31, 829.5, 855.7, 855.10, 857.7, 857.11, 1023.9, 1023.10, 1024.11, 1046.8
freeze, the 589.1
freeze-dried 1066.9
freeze-dry 397.9, 1023.10, 1024.11, 1066.6
freeze-drying 397.2, 1066.3
freeze-frame 706.6
freeze out 773.4, 909.14
freeze over 1023.11
freezer 11.4, 1024.5
freezer, the 1023.4
freezer locker 1024.6
freezer ship 1024.4
freeze solid 1024.11
freeze the ball 747.4
freeze the blood 127.15
freeze the puck 749.7
freeze to 474.6, 803.6
freeze to death 1023.9
freeze up 173.7
freezing (n) 397.2, 1024.1 (a) 1023.14, 1023.16, 1024.12
freezing cold 1023.14
freezing machine 1024.5
freezing mixture 1024.7
freezing point 1019.3, 1023.1
freezing rain 1023.5
freezing weather 1023.3
freezing wind 318.7
freight (n) 179.14, 196.2, 297.7, 630.7, 643.3, 1012.6 (v) 159.15, 176.12, 176.15, 297.13, 794.7
freightage 630.7
freight car 179.15
freighted 297.18, 794.12
freighted with doom 133.16
freighted with significance 518.10
freighter 179.14, 180.1
freighting 643.1
freight train 179.14
French bread 10.28
French Canadian 523.7
French door 189.6
French doughnut 10.44
French fleur-de-lis 647.6

French fries 10.35
French harp 711.10
French-horn player 710.4
French hours 268.1
Frenchism 523.8
French kiss 562.4
French leave 222.4, 368.4, 369.1
French literature 547.12, 718.1
French pastry 10.41
French pitch 709.4
French toast 10.41
frenetic 101.12, 330.24, 926.30
frenzied 101.12, 105.25, 330.24, 671.18, 926.30
frenziedness 330.9
frenzy (n) 85.6, 101.3, 105.8, 152.10, 671.2, 917.1, 926.7, 985.3, 986.2 (v) 105.12, 152.25, 926.24
frenzy of desire 100.8
frenzy of lust 75.5
Freon 1024.7
frequence 221.4, 847.1
frequency 50.2, 847.1, 916.1, 916.4, 1034.12
frequency band 916.1, 916.4, 1034.13
frequency curve 968.2
frequency distribution 968.2
frequency modulation 1034.14
frequency polygon 968.2
frequency spectrum 916.1, 916.4, 1034.12
frequent (v) 221.10, 847.3 (a) 373.14, 847.4, 849.13
frequent as a customer 731.17
frequentative (n) 530.13 (a) 847.4
frequenter 221.5, 585.6
frequent flier 184.10
frequent flyer 184.10
frequenting 221.4
frequently asked question 938.10
Frere's type 30.6
fresco (n) 35.12, 712.10 (v) 35.14
frescoing 35.12
fresh (n) 238.1, 238.5 (a) 9.3, 79.25, 83.13, 142.10, 253.10, 318.21, 337.5, 390.12, 414.17, 838.2, 841.7, 841.8, 989.22, 1002.8, 1023.12
fresh air 72.2
fresh as a daisy 79.25, 83.13, 841.7
fresh as April 83.13
fresh as a rose 83.13
fresh as the morning dew 841.7
fresh breeze 318.4
freshen 9.2, 79.18, 317.11, 318.19, 392.11, 1023.10, 1024.10
freshened up 9.4
freshening 72.6
freshening up 9.1
freshen the air 72.4
freshen up 9.2
freshet 238.1, 238.5
fresh-faced 83.13, 301.9
fresh foods 10.5
freshie 572.6
freshman 572.6, 572.9, 818.2
freshman year 818.4
freshness 72.2, 79.1, 142.2, 301.3, 337.1, 841.1, 1023.1
fresh off the assembly line 390.12
fresh out of 911.5, 992.13
fresh start 818.1, 856.2, 858.2
fresh up 9.2
fresh water 1065.3
freshwater fish 311.30
freshwater lake 241.1
fresh-water nymph 678.10
fresh-water sailor 183.1
fret (n) 26.5, 96.3, 105.6, 152.7, 170.3, 647.2, 759.12 (v) 26.7, 96.14, 110.14, 112.17, 115.15, 126.5, 126.6, 135.4, 152.15, 152.24, 393.13, 393.20, 917.10, 1044.7
fret and fume 115.15, 126.6
fret at 510.16
fretful 110.22, 115.19, 135.6, 330.20
fretfulness 110.2, 110.6, 135.1
fretted 126.8, 740.7
fretting (n) 126.2, 135.1, 1044.2 (a) 26.13, 126.10, 135.6, 1044.10
fretwork 170.3
Freudian fixation 92.21
Freudianism 92.2
Freudian psychology 92.2
Freudian slip 975.4
Frey 890.5, 1069.4
Freya 104.7, 1016.9
friability 1050.1, 1051.3
friable 1050.4, 1051.13
friableness 1050.1
friar 699.16
friarhood 698.4
friar's lantern 1025.13
friary 703.6
fribble (n) 498.4, 500.9, 998.5, 998.10 (v) 331.13, 998.14 (a) 998.19
fribble away 486.5
fribbling 998.19
fricandeau 10.15
fricassee (n) 10.11 (v) 11.5
fricasseed 11.7
frication 57.1, 73.2, 1044.1
fricative (n) 524.12 (a) 524.30, 1044.9
fricatrice 75.14
fricking around 998.9
friction (n) 73.2, 451.2, 456.1, 589.3, 900.1, 900.4, 1044.1 (a) 1044.9
frictional 1044.9
frictional resistance 1044.1
frictional rustling 57.1
friction clutch 1040.10, 1044.5
friction drive 1044.5
friction gearing 1044.5
friction head 1044.5
frictionize 1044.6
frictionless 455.3, 524.30, 1014.14
frictionless continuant 524.12
frictionlessness 287.1, 455.1
friction match 1021.5
friction pile 1044.5
friction saw 1044.5
friction welding 1044.5
Friday 832.4, 964.2
Friday the thirteenth 964.2
fridge 11.4, 1024.4
fried 11.7, 87.24, 88.33
friedcake 10.44
fried eggs 10.26
fried fish 10.24
Friedmann universe 1073.1
friend 588.1
friend at court 597.1, 616.9, 894.6
friend in court 597.1, 616.9, 894.6
friend indeed 588.2
friend in need 588.2
friendless 19.18, 584.12, 872.8
friendlessness 584.4
friendlike 587.15
friendliness 121.2, 582.1, 585.1, 587.1
friendly 121.11, 228.33, 449.22, 582.22, 585.11, 587.15
friendly chat 541.3
friendly fire 459.1, 460.1
friendly game 759.7
friendly relations 587.3
friendly talk 541.3
friendly with 587.17
friend of 588.2
friend of one's bosom 588.1
friendship 587.1
friends with 587.17
friends with benefits 104.5
frig 75.21
frig around 998.15
Frigg 563.13
frigging around 998.9
fright (n) 127.1, 131.3, 1015.4 (v) 127.15
frighten 127.15, 131.8
frighten away 127.15
frightened 127.25, 128.11, 400.4
frightened out of one's mind 127.26
frightened out of one's wits 127.26, 400.4
frightened to death 127.25, 400.4
frightener 127.9
frightening (n) 127.6 (a) 127.28
frightening drug experience 87.1
frighteningness 127.2
frightening off 379.1
frighten off 127.21, 379.3
frighten out of one's senses 127.17
frighten out of one's wits 127.15, 127.17, 400.3
frighten to death 400.3
frightful 127.28, 247.11, 1015.11
frightful bore 118.4
frightfully rich 618.14
frightfulness 127.2, 1015.2
frigid 75.29, 94.9, 344.10, 583.6, 1023.14
Frigidaire 1024.4
frigidarium 1024.6
frigidity 75.2, 75.9, 94.1, 344.3, 583.2, 1023.1
Frigid Zone 231.3
Frigid Zones 1023.4
frigorific 1024.12
frijoles 10.35
frill (n) 211.7, 254.4, 291.1, 545.4, 993.4 (v) 291.5
frilled 498.12
frillery 498.3
frilliness 498.3
frilling 211.7, 498.3
frills 498.3, 993.4
frills and furbelows 498.3
frilly 498.12, 501.19
fringe (n) 3.6, 206.2, 211.4, 211.7, 751.1 (a) 206.7
fringe area 1035.5
fringe benefit 624.6
fringed 211.12
fringes 211.1
fringe theater 704.1
fringing 211.11
fringing forest 310.12
fringy 868.6
frippery 5.10, 498.3, 993.4, 998.5
frisk (n) 366.2, 743.5, 938.15 (v) 116.5, 177.34, 366.6, 743.23, 938.31
frisker 743.18
friskiness 109.4
frisky 109.14, 330.17
frit 127.25, 128.11, 400.4
frith 242.1, 310.15, 310.17
fritter 10.44
fritter away 486.3, 486.5
fritter away time 331.13
frittering away 486.1
fritzed 393.38
fritz out 393.26
frivol 923.6, 998.15
frivolity 109.5, 298.1, 489.4, 493.2, 923.1, 985.5, 998.3
frivolous 109.15, 298.10, 493.9, 598.21, 810.12, 922.20, 985.16, 998.19
frivolousness 364.3, 922.7, 923.1, 984.1, 985.5, 998.3
frizz (n) 3.5 (v) 11.5
frizzed 281.9
frizziness 3.1
frizzle (n) 3.5 (v) 11.5
frizzled 281.9
frizzly 281.9, 294.7
frizzy 281.9, 294.7
frock (n) 5.3, 5.6, 5.16, 702.2 (v) 5.40, 698.12
frog 311.26, 366.4
froggy 311.47
frog kick 760.8
frogman 182.12, 183.4, 367.4
frogskin 728.7
frogskins 728.6
frolic (n) 489.10, 743.5 (v) 109.6, 116.5, 743.23
frolicker 743.18
frolicsome 109.14, 743.29
frolicsomeness 109.4
fromage 10.48
from away 222.12
from better to worse 393.45
from hell 98.20
from hell to breakfast 771.9

from high to low 137.8
from home 222.12
from Missouri 955.9
from on high 681.12
from out in left field 131.10
from the heart 93.24
from the horse's mouth 970.18
from the sticks 233.8
frond 310.19, 310.20
frondage 310.18
frondescence 310.18
frondeur 108.3
front (n) 33.2, 165.1, 184.32, 206.1, 206.2, 216.1, 216.2, 317.4, 354.3, 376.1, 466.3, 500.1, 575.5, 609.33 (v) 215.4, 216.7, 216.8, 451.5, 453.3, 454.3, 492.10, 814.2 (a) 206.7, 216.10, 524.30, 818.17
front, the 463.2
frontage 159.3, 216.1
frontal (n) 216.1, 703.12 (a) 216.10, 818.17
frontal assault 459.1
frontal attack 459.1
frontal system 317.4
front and center 165.1
front burner 216.1, 997.1
front-burner issue 997.6
front elevation 216.1
front for 216.7, 576.14, 862.6
front four 746.2
frontier (n) 211.3, 211.5, 216.1, 233.2, 261.4, 930.6 (a) 211.11
frontier post 211.5
frontiersman 227.10, 816.1
frontiers of knowledge 930.6
fronting 216.11
frontispiece 216.1, 816.2
front line 211.4, 216.2, 463.2
front man 216.1, 466.3, 575.5
front marker 751.1
front matter 216.1, 254.2, 554.12, 793.2, 816.2
front nine 751.1
front office 216.1
front on 216.9
front page 216.1
front-page 552.13
front-porch campaign 609.13
front position 814.1
front rank 216.2
front room 197.5
frontrunner 216.2, 757.2, 816.1
front-running 216.10
front seat 216.1, 814.1
front view 216.1
front yard 216.1
frost (n) 410.2, 589.1, 1023.3, 1023.7 (v) 37.5, 39.3, 66.4, 198.10, 1023.10, 1023.11, 1030.3
frost-beaded 1023.17
Frost Belt 231.7
frostbite (n) 1023.2 (v) 1023.10
frostbitten 1024.14
frostbound 1023.17
frost-checkered 1023.17
frost-covered 1023.17
frosted (n) 10.49 (a) 37.7, 94.9, 1023.17, 1030.4
frosted glass 1028.4
frosted lens 1028.4
frosted-over 1023.17
frost-fettered 1023.17
frost-gray 39.4
frostiness 37.1, 94.1, 102.1, 344.3, 583.2, 589.1, 1023.1
frosting 10.40, 37.3, 198.3
frostlike 1023.17
frost line 1023.7
frostnipped 1024.14
frost over 1030.3
frost-rent 1023.17
frost-riven 1023.17
frost smoke 319.3, 1023.7
frosty 37.7, 39.5, 94.9, 344.10, 583.6, 589.9, 1023.17, 1030.4
frosty-faced 1023.17
frosty-whiskered 1023.17
froth (n) 13.3, 256.2, 298.2, 320.2, 998.4, 998.5, 1065.5 (v) 320.4, 320.5
froth at the mouth 926.20
frothiness 298.1, 320.3, 922.7
frothing 320.3
frothing at the mouth 105.25, 152.32, 926.30
froth up 320.4
frothy 298.10, 320.7, 501.19, 922.20, 998.19
frottage 73.2, 1044.1
froufrou 52.6, 498.3, 993.4
froward 327.8, 361.11
frowardness 327.1
frown (n) 110.9, 152.2, 265.4, 510.8 (v) 110.15, 152.14
frown at 510.10
frown down 510.10
frowned-upon behavior 322.1
frowning 110.24, 111.3
frown on 510.10
frowns of fortune 1011.5
frown upon 510.10
frowst 71.1, 71.2
frowstiness 71.2
frowsty 71.5, 393.42
frowsy 393.42
frowy 71.5, 393.41
frowziness 71.2, 810.6
frowzy 71.5, 393.42, 810.15
frozen 94.9, 127.26, 210.9, 386.15, 800.14, 829.9, 853.7, 855.15, 855.16, 1023.16, 1024.14
frozen assets 471.7, 623.1
frozen black hole 1073.8
frozen custard 10.47
frozen dessert 10.47
frozen-food locker 1024.6
frozen foods 10.5
frozen in 1023.19
frozen meal 8.5
frozenness 853.1
frozen out 1023.19
frozen pudding 10.47
frozen solid 1024.14, 1046.13
frozen to death 1023.16
frozen water 1023.5
frozen yogurt 10.47
fructiferous 890.9, 890.10
fructification 890.1, 890.2, 892.5, 892.6
fructificative 890.11
fructify 78.10, 890.7, 890.8, 892.13
fructose 66.3
fructose intolerance 85.22
fructose sweetener 66.3
fructuous 995.5
fructuousness 892.5
frugal 484.7, 633.7, 635.6, 668.9, 992.10
frugality 484.1, 635.1, 668.1
frugalness 635.1
frugal to excess 484.7
frugivore 8.16
fruit (n) 10.38, 75.15, 310.4, 310.31, 472.5, 561.1, 887.1, 893.1 (v) 892.13
fruitarian (n) 8.16, 668.4 (a) 8.31, 668.10
fruitarianism 668.2
fruitbearing 890.10
fruit belt 233.1
fruit bowl 8.12
fruitcake 10.42, 75.15, 926.16
fruitcakey 926.27
fruit cocktail 10.38
fruit compote 10.38
fruit cup 10.38
fruit dish 8.12
fruit-eating bird 311.27
fruitful 890.9
fruitfulness 387.4, 890.1, 995.1
fruitgrower 1069.6
fruit-growing 1069.2
fruitiness 70.1
fruiting (n) 892.6 (a) 1010.13
fruiting body 10.38
fruition 95.1, 407.1, 794.4, 892.6
fruit juice 10.49
fruit knife 8.12
fruitless 19.15, 391.12, 410.18
fruitlessness 391.2, 891.1
fruitlike 310.36
fruit of one's loins 893.1
fruit pie 10.41
fruits 10.38, 472.3, 627.1
fruit salad 10.37, 10.38
fruits and vegetables 310.4
fruits de mer 10.24
fruit soup 10.38
fruit tree 310.10
fruity 63.9, 70.9, 310.36, 926.27
frumious 101.12
frump 304.3, 810.7
frumpish 810.15
frumpishness 810.6
frumps 110.10
frumpy 810.15
frustaneous 391.9
frustrate 132.2, 412.11, 415.11, 900.7, 1012.15
frustrated 75.29, 132.5
frustrater 1012.8
frustrating 1012.20
frustration 92.17, 132.1, 412.2, 415.5, 900.2, 1012.3
fry (n) 10.7, 302.10, 311.29, 561.2 (v) 11.5, 40.2, 604.16, 1019.22, 1020.17
fry cook 11.3
fryer 302.10, 311.28
frying 11.2
fry up 11.5
f-stop 714.9
FUBAR 799.4
fubsiness 257.8
fubsy 257.18
fuchsia 41.8, 46.3
fucoid 310.37
fud 842.8
fuddle (n) 88.1, 985.3 (v) 88.23, 971.13, 985.7
fuddlebrained 922.18, 985.13
fuddled 88.33, 923.8, 971.25, 985.13
fuddledness 88.1
fuddlement 88.1, 985.3
fuddy-duddiness 842.3
fuddy-duddy (n) 495.7, 842.8, 924.9 (a) 842.17
fuddy-duddyism 853.3
fudge (n) 10.40, 520.2 (v) 340.8, 354.16, 354.18, 356.18, 628.10, 936.9
fudge and mudge (n) 368.1, 936.1 (v) 362.8, 368.8
fudge in 213.6
fudge together 892.8
fudge up 340.9
fudging 368.1, 936.1
fuel (n) 756.1, 1021.1, 1056.4, 1074.8 (v) 385.9, 1021.8 (a) 1021.9
fuel additive 1021.1
fuel dope 1021.1
fuel injection 1043.3
fuel oil 1056.4
fuel ship 1075.2
fuel starter 1021.1
fuel up 1021.8
fug 71.1, 1019.6
fugacious 828.7
fugaciousness 828.1
fugacity 828.1
fugato 708.19
-fuge 909.11
fugitate 368.10, 909.17
fugitation 368.4, 909.4
fugitive (n) 368.5, 369.5, 660.9 (a) 34.3, 168.5, 177.37, 368.16, 369.11, 764.5, 828.7
fugitiveness 168.1, 764.1
fugitivity 168.1
fugleman 249.4, 574.6, 816.1
fugue 92.19, 708.19, 990.2
fugue form 709.11
fugue state 92.19
fuhgeddaboudit 984.4
führer 574.6, 575.13
fulcrum 208.2, 901.2, 906.3, 915.5
fulcrumage 906.1
fulfill 328.7, 407.4, 434.2, 437.9, 794.6, 991.4
fulfill a short sale 737.24
fulfilled 107.7, 407.10
fulfilling 407.9, 794.13
fulfillment 92.27, 107.1, 407.1, 434.1, 437.4, 794.4
fulfill one's duty 641.10
fulfill one's military obligation 458.17
fulfill one's role 434.3
fulgent 1025.32
fulgentness 1025.4

fulgid 1025.32
fulgidity 1025.4
fulgor 1025.4
fulgurant 1025.34
fulgurant pain 26.2
fulgurate 1025.23
fulgurating 1025.34
fulguration 671.7, 1025.17
fuliginosity 38.3
fuliginous 38.11
fuliginousness 38.3
full (n) 794.2 (a) 35.17, 53.11, 54.10, 88.31, 107.9, 247.6, 257.18, 269.6, 269.8, 293.11, 430.27, 766.9, 770.22, 794.9, 794.11, 991.7, 994.6, 1002.7
full age 303.2
full amount 244.1
full-armed 460.14
full assembly 423.1
full authority 443.4
fullback 746.2
full beard 3.8
full-bellied 257.18
full blast 18.1, 53.5
full-blooded 15.15, 41.9, 607.10, 608.11
full bloom 303.2, 310.26
full blow 310.26
full-blown 257.22, 303.13
full board 385.3
full boat 244.1, 758.4
full-bodied 63.9, 269.8
full-bodied flavor 63.1
full-bosomed 257.18
full-buttocked 257.18
full career 162.1
full-charged 794.12
full circle 280.2, 914.2, 915.1
full color 35.7
full-colored 35.17
full consent 430.6
full count 745.3
full development 407.2
full dress 5.11
full-dress 794.9
full-dress suit 5.11
full-dress uniform 5.11
full-face 216.10
full-faced 548.20
full faith 438.1
full faith and credit 953.1
full feather 5.10
full fig 5.10
full-figured 257.18
full-finger grip 751.3
full-fingertip grip 750.2
full flavor 63.1
full-flavored 63.9
full-fledged 14.3, 257.22, 259.12, 303.13, 794.9
full force 18.1
full-formed 257.22
full-fraught 794.12
full frontal 6.3, 216.1
full-frontal 216.10
full-frontal nudity 6.3
full gallop 174.3
full-grown 14.3, 257.22, 259.12, 303.13, 407.13, 794.9
full growth 257.3, 303.2
full house 704.12, 758.4, 794.3
full-laden 794.12
full-length 267.7
full lot 738.3
full many 884.6
full meal 8.8
full measure 794.3, 991.2
full military rites 309.1
full monty, the 792.4
full moon 1073.11
fullmouthed 53.12
full name 527.3
full nelson 474.3
fullness 53.1, 54.1, 247.1, 269.1, 792.5, 794.2, 812.1, 991.2, 994.1, 1002.2
full of 994.6
full of beans 17.13, 83.9, 330.24, 975.18
full of beans and feeling one's oats 109.14
full of bull 975.18
full of business 330.21
full of crap 975.18
full of Dutch courage 88.34
full of enthusiasm 101.10
full of fight 458.20
full of go 330.17
full of grace 679.6
full of hate 589.10
full of hatred 589.10
full of holes 393.32
full of hope 124.10
full of hot air 975.18
full of incident 831.10
full of integrity 644.13
full of it 975.18
full of life 101.8, 330.17
full of life and vigor 83.8
full of meaning 518.10
full of mischief 322.6
full of of piss and vinegar 83.9
full of old nick 322.6
full of oneself 140.12
full of pep 17.13, 330.17
full of piss and vinegar 17.13, 109.14, 544.11
full of pizzazz 17.13
full of point 518.10
full of promise 124.12, 133.17
full of prunes 975.18
full of remorse 113.8
full of risk 1006.10
full of sound and fury 503.4
full of substance 518.10
full of the devil 322.6
full-on 17.13
full particulars 766.2
full power 443.4, 615.1
full pratique 443.7
full price 244.1
full report 351.2
full sail 180.14
full-scale 257.22, 794.9
full scope 430.4
full score 708.28
full shot 714.8
full size 257.3
full-size 257.22
full-sized 257.22
full-spectrum light 1025.19
full speed 174.3
full stop 173.3, 857.2
full-strength 15.15
full sun 1025.10
full swing 430.4
full-throated 53.12
full tide 238.13
full-tilt boogie 708.10
full-time 825.3
full-time worker 726.2
full to bursting 794.11
full-up 107.9
full vowel 524.11
full wine 88.17
fully developed 14.3, 259.12, 303.13, 407.13, 1002.9
fully fledged 14.3, 303.13
fully laden 794.11
fully realized 407.12
fulmar 311.27
fulminant 671.24
fulminate 56.8, 671.14
fulminate against 510.13, 510.19, 513.5
fulminating 56.12, 105.25, 671.24
fulminating mercury 462.15
fulmination 56.3, 510.3, 513.1, 671.7, 1025.17
fulminatory 513.8, 671.24
fulsome 64.7, 71.5, 98.18, 504.17, 509.18, 511.8, 545.8, 545.9, 661.12, 666.9, 1000.9
fulsomeness 98.2, 504.5, 545.1, 661.3, 1000.2
fulvous 40.3
Fu Manchu mustache 3.11
fumarole 239.14
fumble (n) 414.5, 746.3 (v) 414.11, 746.5, 811.3, 938.32
fumbled 414.21
fumble-fist 414.9
fumbler 414.8
fumbling (n) 414.4 (a) 414.20
fumblitis 414.3
fume (n) 69.1, 105.4, 152.7, 671.2, 917.1, 1020.16, 1067.1 (v) 152.15, 397.9, 671.12, 909.24, 1019.23, 1067.8
fumes 1067.1
fumes of fancy 986.1
fumigant 72.3, 86.21, 1001.3
fumigate 70.8, 72.4, 79.24, 1067.8
fumigated 72.5
fumigation 72.2, 79.3, 1067.5
fumigator 70.6, 72.3, 86.21
fuming (n) 397.2 (a) 152.32, 1019.27, 1067.9
fumy 1067.9
fun (n) 95.1, 97.1, 109.5, 489.6, 743.2 (v) 489.13 (a) 97.8, 743.27
funambulism 454.1, 492.4, 493.3
fun and games 743.2
function (n) 328.1, 380.1, 387.5, 530.2, 580.4, 582.10, 615.4, 641.1, 701.3, 724.1, 724.3 (v) 328.4, 724.13, 889.5, 889.7
functional 92.37, 328.10, 387.18, 530.17, 724.16, 889.9, 889.11, 889.12
functional calculus 935.2
functional design 387.6
functional food 10.1
functional furniture 387.6
functional housing 387.6
functional illiteracy 930.4
functionalism 387.6
functionalist 716.10
functionality 387.3
functionally illiterate 930.13
functionary 575.15, 576.3, 889.4
function as 889.8
function class 530.3
functioning (n) 328.1, 889.1 (a) 328.10, 889.11
function key 1042.18
functionless 391.14
functionlessness 391.1
function word 526.1, 530.3
fund (n) 386.2, 478.9, 728.14, 728.15, 738.2, 770.11 (v) 385.7, 449.12, 478.19, 624.18, 729.16
fundable 478.23
fundament 199.1, 901.6
fundamental (n) 50.2, 767.2, 901.6, 997.6 (a) 199.8, 767.9, 798.6, 818.15, 886.14, 963.12, 997.23
fundamental colors 35.7
fundamental idea 932.4
fundamentalism 425.2, 675.7, 687.5, 692.3
fundamentalist (n) 687.4, 692.4 (a) 425.7, 687.8
fundamentality 767.1, 798.1
fundamental particle 1038.6, 1052.2
fundamentals 963.2
fundamental tone 50.2
funded debt 623.1
funder 478.11, 729.10
funding 729.2
fund-raise 770.18
fundraiser 478.9, 729.10
fundraising 440.5
fund-raising dinner 609.12
funds 384.2, 471.7, 728.14
funebrial 112.24, 309.22
funebrious 309.22
funebrous 309.22
funeral (n) 309.5, 580.4, 812.3 (a) 309.22
funeral car 309.10
funeral ceremony 309.4
funeral coach 309.10
funeral customs 309.1
funeral director 309.8
funeral home 309.9
funeral hymn 309.6
funeral march 115.6, 175.2, 708.12
funeral oration 115.6, 309.4, 543.2
funeral parlor 309.9, 739.1
funeral pile 309.9
funeral procession 309.5
funeral pyre 1019.13
funeral ring 309.6
funeral rites 309.4
funeral sermon 309.4
funeral service 309.4
funeral song 115.6
funeral urn 309.12

funeral vessel 309.12
funerary 309.22
funerary customs 309.1
funerary urn 309.12
funerary vessel 309.12
funereal 38.9, 112.24, 125.16, 309.22, 701.18, 1027.14
funereality 38.2
funerealness 112.11
funest 1011.14
fun fair 743.14
fungi 311.3
fungicide 1001.3
fungiform 310.37
fungoid 310.37
fungosity 85.39
fungous 310.37
fungus 85.39, 85.42, 310.3, 310.4, 1001.2
funhouse 743.15
funicular (n) 179.14, 383.8 (a) 271.7
funicular railway 383.8
funiculate 271.7
funicule 310.21
funiculus 310.21
funiosity 488.2
funk (n) 69.1, 71.1, 112.3, 127.1, 491.5 (v) 127.11, 127.13, 127.15, 491.8
funker 491.5
funk hole 1009.3
funkiness 71.2
funking 491.10
funk out 491.8
funks 112.6
funky 69.10, 71.5, 112.23, 491.10
fun-loving 95.18
funmaker 322.3, 743.18
funmaking 743.2
funnel (n) 169.1, 239.6, 239.14, 282.5 (v) 169.2, 176.14, 239.15
funnel breast 284.2
funnel-breasted 284.16
funnel chest 284.2
funnel-chested 284.16
funnel cloud 105.9, 318.13
funnelform 282.12
funnelled 282.12
funnellike 282.12
funnel-shaped 282.12, 284.16
funnies 712.15
funnies, the 489.1
funniness 488.1, 489.2
funny 488.4, 489.15, 522.18, 539.4, 870.11, 927.5, 927.6, 955.10, 971.27
funny as a crutch 112.21
funny bone 489.11
funny business 345.4, 356.3, 489.5
funny farm 926.14
funny feeling 127.4, 128.1, 399.2, 934.3
funny ha-ha 488.5
funnyman 489.12, 707.9
funny money 728.10
funny paper 712.15
funny peculiar 522.18, 539.4, 971.27
funny side, the 488.1
funny story 489.6
funny thing 870.5
funplex 743.15
fun-sized 258.12
funsome 743.27
funster 743.18
fun time 95.5
fur (n) 3.2, 3.19, 4.2, 295.3, 647.2 (v) 196.7
furbelow 211.7
furbish 287.7, 392.11, 396.17, 498.8, 1044.8
furbished 287.11
furbishment 396.4
furbish up 392.11
furcal 278.6
furcate (v) 171.7, 278.5 (a) 171.10, 278.6
furcation 171.3, 278.2
furcula 171.4
furculum 171.4
fur farm 1070.5
fur farming 1070.1
furfur 80.7
furfuraceous 296.7, 1051.11
furfuration 296.4
Furies, the 152.10, 507.3, 680.10
furious 101.12, 105.25, 105.29, 152.32, 401.9, 493.8, 671.16, 671.18, 926.30
furiousness 401.2, 493.2, 671.1
furious rabies 926.6
furious rage 152.10
furl 182.50, 915.10
furlough (n) 20.3, 222.4, 331.3, 402.1 (v) 909.19
furloughing 909.5
furnace 739.4, 742.5, 1019.11, 1020.10, 1038.13
furnish 385.7, 385.8, 405.8, 478.15, 892.13
furnish accommodations 385.10
furnished 385.13
furnisher 385.6
furnish evidence 957.8
furnishing 385.1, 405.2
furnishings 5.2, 229.1, 385.4, 735.5
furnishings design 712.16
furnishment 385.1, 478.1
furnishments 229.1, 385.4
furnish support 449.12, 901.21
furniture 229.1, 385.4, 548.2, 735.5
furniture arrangement 498.1
furniture broker 730.9
furniture design 229.1, 712.16, 717.5
furniture designer 716.9
furniture piece 229.1
furniture style 229.1
furor 93.2, 100.8, 105.8, 152.10, 671.2, 926.1, 926.7, 926.12
furore 105.8
furor epilepticus 926.7
furred 3.24
furrier 5.33, 5.35
furriness 3.1
furring 4.2
furrow (n) 224.2, 284.6, 290.1, 291.3 (v) 224.4, 284.15, 290.3, 291.6, 713.9
furrowed 290.4, 291.8, 713.11
furrowing 1069.13
furry 3.24, 3.27, 295.32, 1047.14
furry creatures 311.1
furry friend 311.2
further (v) 162.5, 449.17 (a) 253.10, 261.10, 841.8
furtherance 162.1, 392.1, 446.1, 449.5, 861.1
furthering (n) 162.1 (v) 446.2
further look 938.7
furthermost 261.12
further oneself 162.2
furthersome 449.21
furthest 247.13, 261.12
furtive 345.12, 346.14, 356.22
furtiveness 345.4, 356.3
furuncle 85.37, 283.4
furunculus 85.37
Fury 680.10
fury 926.7
fury 93.2, 101.3, 105.8, 110.11, 110.12, 152.10, 593.7, 671.2, 671.9
fury of desire (n) 100.8 (a) 100.24
fury of lust 75.5
fuscous 40.3, 1027.15
fuse (n) 462.15, 1008.3, 1021.4 (v) 450.3, 770.16, 778.5, 797.10, 803.9, 805.3, 1020.21, 1020.24, 1064.5
fused 805.5, 1020.31
fusee 1021.5, 1026.3
fusibility 1020.3, 1064.2
fusible 1020.31, 1064.9
fusiform 270.15, 285.12
fusil 647.2
fusileer 461.9
fusillade (n) 56.3, 459.9, 604.6, 902.4, 904.4 (v) 459.22
fusilli 10.33
fusing (n) 1064.1 (a) 805.7, 1064.7
fusion (n) 450.2, 708.10, 778.2, 797.1, 805.1, 872.1, 1020.3, 1038.9, 1058.4, 1064.1 (a) 797.15
fusional 523.23
fusion cuisine 10.1
fusion politics 609.1
fusion reaction 1038.9
fusiony 797.15
fuss (n) 105.6, 330.4, 355.2, 456.5, 495.7, 498.3, 503.1, 671.2, 810.4, 917.1 (v) 105.14, 115.15, 126.6, 135.4, 330.12, 495.8
fuss and feathers 501.4
fuss at 510.16
fussbudget 112.14, 126.3, 495.7
fuss-budgety 495.10
fussed 985.12
fusser 495.7
fussiness 330.4, 339.3, 495.2
fussing 330.20
fuss over 495.8
fuss over one 143.10
fusspot 495.7
fussy 105.27, 330.20, 339.12, 495.10, 498.12, 766.9, 926.33
fussy eater 8.16
fust 173.9, 842.9
fustian (n) 520.2, 545.2 (a) 545.9
fustigate 510.20, 604.12
fustigation 510.3, 604.4
fustiness 71.2, 117.3
fusty 71.5, 117.9, 393.42, 842.14
futharc 546.3
futhark 546.3
futile 19.15, 125.13, 391.13, 410.18, 923.8, 996.5, 998.19
futility 19.3, 125.1, 125.4, 391.2, 410.1, 520.1, 996.1, 998.3
futon 901.19, 901.20
future (n) 104.16, 530.12, 839.1, 964.2 (a) 839.8, 840.3
future, the 821.1, 839.1
future grain 738.11
future perfect 530.12, 839.1
future prospects 130.4
futures 738.11
future state 839.2
future tense 839.1
future time 835.1
futurism 839.1
futuristic 839.8
futuristic film 706.2
futuristics 839.1
futurity 839.1, 839.4, 840.1
futz around 743.23
fuzz (n) 3.2, 3.19, 294.3, 298.2 (v) 295.19, 971.15
fuzz, the 1008.16
Fuzzbuster 1036.5
fuzziness 3.1, 32.2, 263.1, 294.3, 522.3, 971.4
fuzzing 295.1
fuzzword 523.5, 526.6
fuzzy 3.24, 3.27, 32.6, 263.4, 294.8, 522.15, 971.19
fuzzyheaded 971.19
fuzzy math 1017.1
fuzzy memory 990.1
F-word 513.4
fylfot 170.4, 691.5
G 297.5, 728.7, 882.10
gab (n) 292.4, 524.1, 540.3 (v) 524.20, 540.5
gabber 540.4
gabbiness 540.1
gabble (n) 520.2, 525.4, 540.3 (v) 60.5, 520.5, 525.9, 540.5
gabbler 540.4
gabbling 540.10
gabby 540.9
Gabriel 353.2, 679.4
Gabriel's horn 53.5
Gabriel's trumpet 53.5, 820.1
gaby 924.4
gad (n) 178.2, 375.8 (v) 177.23
gad about 177.21, 177.23
gadabout 178.2
gad around 177.21, 177.23
gadding (n) 177.3 (a) 177.37
gadfly 375.8, 375.10
gadget 384.4, 1040.1, 1052.4
gadgetry 384.3, 1040.1
Gaea 1069.4, 1073.10
gaff 759.16
gaffe 923.4, 975.5
gaffer 304.2, 574.2
gaff-rigged 180.17

gag (n) 51.4, 428.4, 489.6, 704.8 (v) 19.10, 51.8, 99.4, 428.8, 428.10, 909.26
gaga 923.8, 926.27, 985.16
gaga over 101.11
gage 87.11, 438.2
gagging 909.8
gaggle (n) 770.6 (v) 60.5
gag line 489.6
gagman 489.12, 704.22
gag on 955.5
gag order 444.1
gagster 489.12
gag writer 489.12, 704.22
Gaia 1073.10
gaiety 35.4, 95.2, 109.4, 498.3, 501.3, 582.3, 743.3
gain (n) 251.1, 472.3, 746.3, 999.4, 1032.17, 1041.11 (v) 186.6, 251.6, 375.23, 392.7, 411.3, 472.8, 479.6, 897.4
gain access 292.12
gain admission 189.7
gain admittance 189.7
gain a footing 894.12
gain a good knowledge of 570.9
gain a hearing 48.12, 894.12
gain a hold upon 612.12, 894.12
gain altitude 184.39, 193.10
gain a thorough knowledge of 570.9
gain authority 417.14
gain by 472.12
gain command of 570.9
gain entree 189.8
gainer 367.1
gainful 387.22, 472.16, 624.21
gainful employment 724.5
gainfulness 472.4
gain ground 162.2, 174.10, 392.7
gain influence 894.12
gaining 472.1
gaining altitude 193.1
gain knowledge 570.6
gain knowledge of 570.6
gainless 391.12
gain on 174.13
gain one's end 409.8
gain one's liberty 369.6
gain over 375.23
gain recognition 662.11
gains 251.3, 472.3, 627.1
gainsay 335.4, 451.6
gainsaying 335.2
gain strength 251.6, 392.8, 396.19
gain the ascendancy 411.6
gain the confidence of 953.20
gain the friendship of 587.10
gain the upper hand 411.6, 417.14
gain the whip hand 411.6
gain time 845.5
gain to windward of 182.26
gain understanding of 570.6
gain upon 167.3, 174.13
gain weight 259.8
gait 172.4, 177.12
gaited horse 311.14
gal 77.6, 302.7, 312.5
gala (n) 501.4, 743.4 (a) 487.3, 743.28
gala affair 743.4
galactic 158.10, 247.7, 864.14, 884.10, 1073.25
galactic circle, the 1073.6
galactic cluster 1073.5, 1073.6
galactic coordinates 1073.6
galactic distance 261.1
galactic latitude 1073.6
galactic longitude 1073.6, 1073.16
galactic nebula 1073.6, 1073.7
galactic noise 1073.6
galactic nucleus 1073.6
galactic pole 1073.6
galactosemia 85.22
gala day 20.4, 743.4
galaxy 662.9, 770.4, 1073.6
Galaxy, the 1073.6
gale 105.9, 318.11
galeated 279.20
gale-force 318.22
galeiform 279.20
Galen 90.12
gales of laughter 116.4
gale warning 400.1
gal Friday 616.7
galilee 197.19
galimatias 520.2
gall (n) 13.2, 64.2, 85.38, 96.3, 96.8, 110.1, 142.3, 144.7, 152.3, 283.3, 493.1, 505.1 (v) 26.7, 96.14, 393.13, 1044.7
gall and wormwood 64.2, 96.8
gallant (n) 104.12, 492.7, 500.9, 504.9, 665.10 (a) 492.16, 501.19, 504.14, 665.25
gallantness 492.1, 504.2
gallantry 492.1, 504.2, 562.7, 665.3
gallantry beyond the call of duty 492.1
gallantry under fire 492.1
gallbladder 2.16
gallbladder disease 85.23
galled 26.11, 96.21
gallery 27.8, 48.6, 197.4, 197.18, 197.21, 197.22, 197.24, 296.1, 383.3, 386.9, 460.5, 704.15, 712.17, 901.13
gallery forest 310.12
galley 11.4, 180.3, 197.14, 548.5
galley chase 548.2
galley proof 548.5
galleys 604.2
galley slave 183.5, 432.7, 726.3
galliard 366.1
Gallicism 523.8
gallimaufry 797.6
gallinaceous 311.48
galling (n) 1044.2 (a) 26.13, 98.22, 1044.10
gallipot 86.35
gallium arsenide chip 1042.3
gallivant 177.23, 562.20
gallivanting (n) 177.3 (a) 177.37
gallonage 257.2
galloon 211.7
gallop (n) 174.3, 177.12 (v) 174.8, 177.34
galloper 311.14
galloping 174.15
galloping dominoes 759.8
Galloway 311.10
gallows 605.5
gallows, the 604.6
gallows bird 660.9
gallows humor 489.1
gallows-tree 605.5
Gall's serrated type 30.6
galluses 202.5
galoot 924.3
galore 991.7
Galtonian theory 560.6
galvanic 105.30, 375.27, 1032.30
galvanic shock 1032.6
galvanization 105.11, 1032.25
galvanize 17.10, 105.13, 295.26, 375.12, 1032.26, 1032.28
galvanized 295.33
galvanizer 375.10
galvanizing 375.27
galvanometric 1032.30
galvanoscopic 1032.30
gam (n) 2.7, 770.5 (v) 541.9
gamb 177.14
gambade 366.2
gambado (n) 366.2 (v) 366.6
gambit 356.6, 403.2, 415.3, 818.3
gamble (n) 759.2, 971.8, 972.1 (v) 759.23, 759.25, 897.3, 962.9, 972.12, 1006.6, 1006.7
gamble away 486.3
gamble on 759.24, 953.16, 970.9
gambler 759.21, 951.8
Gamblers Anonymous 449.2
gambler's chance 759.2
gamble with 1006.6
gambling 732.1, 743.9, 758.1, 759.1
gambling chance 759.2, 972.9
gambling den 759.19
gambling game 743.9, 759.7
gambling games 758.1
gambling hall 759.19
gambling house 228.27, 759.19
gambling odds 759.6
gambling table 759.16
gambling wheel 759.16
gambol (n) 366.2, 743.5 (v) 109.6, 116.5, 366.6, 743.23
gamboler 743.18
gambrel 177.14
game (n) 10.13, 100.11, 104.9, 311.1, 380.2, 381.1, 381.5, 382.7, 415.3, 457.3, 508.7, 724.6, 743.2, 743.9, 743.16, 744.1, 745.3, 746.3, 747.3, 748.2, 758.1, 758.3, 759.7 (v) 759.23 (a) 324.5, 359.14, 393.30, 492.17
game at which two can play 506.3
game bird 311.27
game changer 518.1, 518.5
game-changer 744.1
game-changing 997.17
gamecock 461.1, 492.7
game face 467.4
game fish 311.29, 311.30
game fowl 311.28
gamekeeper 382.5, 1008.6
game loser 412.5
gameness 324.1, 359.3, 492.5
game of chance 759.7
game over 410.2
game plan 381.1, 381.2, 746.3
game point 748.2
game preserve 397.7, 1009.1
game reserve 397.7
game room 197.12
games 457.3, 755.1, 755.2, 894.3
game sanctuary 1009.1
game, set, match 748.2
game show 1035.2
gamesman 610.6
gamesmanship 415.1, 457.2
gamesome 109.14, 743.29
gamesomeness 109.4
gamester 759.21
gametangium 305.10
gamete 305.10
game theory 968.2
gametic 78.16, 305.20
game time 744.1
gametophore 305.10
gametophyte 305.10, 310.3
game to the end 359.14, 360.8
game to the last 359.14, 360.8
game two can play, a 506.3
game warden 397.5, 1008.6
game-winning 411.7
gamic 75.25, 305.20
gamin 178.3, 302.4
gamine 178.3
gaminess 68.3, 71.2, 492.5
gaming 743.2, 759.1
gaming house 759.19
gaming license 443.6
gammacism 525.5
gamma decay 1038.8
gammadion 170.4, 691.5
gamma globulin 86.27
gamma radiator 1037.5
gamma ray 1025.5
gamma ray counter 1075.7
gamma rays 1032.10
gammer 560.16
gammerstang 270.8
gammon (n) 354.14, 520.2 (v) 354.21, 356.14
gammy 560.16
gamone 305.10
gamp 295.7
gams 177.15
gamut 158.2, 709.6, 812.2
gamy 68.8, 71.5, 393.41
gander, a 27.3
gander 76.8, 311.28
Gandhi 921.2
ganef 483.1
gang (n) 577.11, 617.1, 770.3, 770.5 (v) 805.4
gang around 770.16
gangbang 75.7, 480.3
gangdom 660.10
ganger 574.2
gangland 660.10
gangland-style execution 308.2
gangleader 660.10
gangle-shanked 270.18
gangleshanks 270.8
gangliness 270.5
gangling 270.17, 272.16

ganglion 2.14, 208.5
ganglord 660.10
gangly 270.17, 272.16
gang member 593.3, 660.9
gangplank 189.5
gangrene (n) 80.7, 85.40 (v) 393.22
gangrened 85.60, 393.40
gangrenous 85.60, 393.40
gangsta rap 708.7
gangster 483.4, 593.1, 593.3, 660.9, 660.10
gangsterism 660.10
gangue 1058.7
gang up 770.16, 805.4
gang up on 459.14
gang up with 582.18
gang violence 655.1, 655.2
gangway 189.5
gangway ladder 193.4
ganja 87.11
gantlet, the 604.2
gantry crane 912.3
Ganymede 577.5
gaol (n) 429.8 (v) 429.14
gaolbird 429.11, 660.9
gaoler 429.10
gap (n) 158.8, 224.1, 224.2, 237.5, 284.9, 292.1, 780.1, 787.1, 795.2, 802.4, 813.2 (v) 224.4, 292.16
gape (n) 27.5, 224.2, 292.1, 292.2 (v) 27.15, 122.5, 292.16, 918.5, 981.3
gaper 918.1
gapes 85.41
gapes, the 292.2
gaping (n) 292.2 (a) 122.9, 130.11, 224.7, 259.11, 275.12, 292.18
gaping chasm 1006.1
gaping depths 275.3
gapless 812.8
gaplessness 812.1
gapped 804.4
gappy 224.7
gap year 567.5
garage 197.27, 386.6, 739.5
garage band 710.12
garage sale 734.3
garb (n) 5.1, 33.4 (v) 5.39
garbage 80.9, 87.9, 391.4, 520.3, 522.7
garbage bag 391.7
garbage can 391.7
garbage collector 79.16
garbage disposal 391.7
garbage dump 80.12, 370.4, 391.6
garbage grinder 391.7
garbage incinerator 1020.13
garbage pail 391.7
garbage truck 179.12
garbagey 998.21
garbed 5.45
garble (n) 522.7 (v) 265.6, 342.2, 350.3, 354.16, 522.12, 811.3
garble accounts 628.10
garbled 265.11, 342.3, 354.26, 520.6, 522.14, 795.5, 975.19
garbless 6.13
garbling 342.1, 350.1
garbology 391.6
garçon 302.5, 577.4
garden (n) 554.7, 1069.10 (v) 1069.16 (a) 310.38, 499.6, 798.6, 864.16, 1005.8
garden apartment 228.13
gardenburger 10.32
gardener 577.4, 1069.6
garden flower 310.24
garden gnome 678.8
garden hose 239.6
gardening 310.24, 1069.2
Garden of Eden 986.11
garden of remembrance 309.15
garden of rest 309.15
garden of the Gods 681.9
garden of the Hesperides 681.9
garden path 383.1, 383.2
garden plant 310.3
garden spot 1069.10
garden suburb 230.1
garden tool 1040.1, 1040.8
garden variety 869.3
garden-variety 499.6, 1005.8
Gargantuan 247.7
gargantuan 257.20
gargle (n) 79.17, 86.22, 88.7 (v) 79.19, 88.24
gargling 88.4
gargoyle 239.8, 1015.4
gargoylish 1015.8
garish 35.20, 497.10, 501.20, 545.8, 1025.32
garishness 35.5, 545.1
garland (n) 280.2, 310.25, 554.7, 646.3, 647.2, 720.5 (v) 498.9
garment (n) 5.3 (v) 5.39
Garment District 5.32
garmented 5.45
garment industry, the 5.32
garmentless 6.13
garmentmaker 5.34, 741.2
garment-making 5.32, 741.1
garments 5.1
garmenture 5.1
garmentworker 5.34
garner (n) 386.7 (v) 386.11
garnered 386.14
garner up 386.11
garnish (n) 498.1 (v) 480.20, 498.8
garnished 498.11
garnishee 480.20
garnishment 480.5, 498.1
garniture 498.1
garret 197.16
garrison (n) 10.6, 460.6, 461.22, 1008.9 (v) 460.9
garrisoned 460.14
Garrison finish 757.3
garrison house 460.6
garrison state 458.9, 612.4
garron 311.12
garrote (n) 308.6, 604.6 (v) 308.19, 604.16
garroter 308.11, 604.7
garroting 308.6
garrulity 540.1
garrulous 538.15, 540.9
garrulousness 540.1
Garter 575.20
garter 646.5
garter belt 5.23
Garter King of Arms 575.20
gas (n) 86.15, 409.4, 502.2, 520.3, 540.3, 909.9, 909.10, 1021.1, 1025.20, 1056.4, 1067.2, 1067.3 (v) 385.9, 520.5, 540.5 (a) 904.17
gas attack 459.1
gasbag 181.11, 502.5, 540.4
gas black 38.6
gas chamber 308.12, 605.5
gas chamber, the 604.6
Gascon (n) 502.5 (a) 502.10
gasconade (n) 502.1 (v) 454.5, 502.6, 503.3
gasconader 502.5
gasconading 502.10
gas conduction 1032.14
gasconism 502.1
gaseity 1067.3
gaseous 299.4, 764.6, 1067.9
gaseousblanket 317.2
gaseous envelope 317.2
gaseous environment 317.2
gaseous medium 317.2
gaseous nebula 1073.7
gaseousness 1067.3
gaseous state 1067.3
gas gangrene 85.40
gas-guzzling 1021.9
gash (n) 85.38, 224.2, 289.1, 290.1, 391.4, 517.5 (v) 224.4, 289.4, 290.3, 393.13, 517.19, 802.11
gas heat 1019.1
gas-heat 1020.17
gas-heated 1020.29
gashed 289.5, 290.4
gasification 1067.5
gasified 1067.9
gasiform 1067.9
gasify 1067.8
gas jet 1020.10
gasket 293.5
gaslight 1025.19
gaslike 1067.9
gaslit 1025.39
gas main 239.7
gas meter 1067.7
gasolier 1026.6
gasoline (n) 1025.20, 1043.3, 1056.4 (a) 904.17
gasoline-propelled 904.16
gasometer 1067.7
gasp (n) 2.21 (v) 21.5, 524.25, 1019.22
Gaspar 921.5
gasping 21.3
gasping for breath 21.12
gas-powered 1021.9
gasproof 293.12
gas-propelled 904.16
gas refrigeration 1024.1
gas refrigerator 1024.4
gasser 409.4, 704.4
gassiness 259.2, 540.1, 1067.3
gassing 604.6
gas station 739.1
gassy 259.13, 501.22, 502.12, 540.9, 545.9, 1067.9
gastight 293.12
gastric 2.31
gastric antacid 86.25
gastric digestion 2.17, 7.8
gastric glands 2.17, 7.8
gastric juice 2.17, 7.8, 13.2
gastritis 85.29
gastroenteritis 85.29
gastrointestinal disease 85.29
gastrointestinal tract 2.17, 7.8
gastrology 8.15
gastronome 8.16
gastronomic 11.6
gastronomical 8.31
gastronomics 8.15
gastronomy 8.1, 8.15, 11.1, 496.4, 672.2
gastropod 311.3
gastropub 8.17
gas up 385.9
gat 292.1, 462.10
gate 189.5, 189.6, 239.4, 239.10, 239.11, 627.1, 757.1, 918.2, 1012.5, 1058.5
gate, the 909.5
gâteau 10.42
gatecrash 189.8
gate-crasher 214.3, 585.6, 774.4
gated community 209.1
gatehouse 228.9
gatekeeper 1008.12
gatekeeping 189.1
gatepost 189.6, 273.4
gate receipts 627.1
gateway 189.6, 1042.19
gateway drug 87.3
gather (n) 291.1 (v) 14.2, 259.7, 291.5, 318.19, 472.11, 770.16, 770.18, 800.5, 840.2, 946.10, 951.10, 1069.19
gather around 770.16, 807.5
gather courage 492.12
gathered 291.7, 386.14, 770.21, 800.13, 892.18
gatherer 770.15
gather flesh 259.8
gather head 162.2
gather in 472.11, 770.18, 1069.19
gathering (n) 85.37, 472.2, 554.14, 582.10, 681.11, 770.1, 770.2, 770.9, 793.2, 800.1, 1069.15 (a) 840.3
gathering clouds 133.5, 399.3, 1006.1
gathering dust 340.14
gathering evidence 938.4
gathering of the clouds 1027.6
gathering place 228.27
gather into barns 386.11
gather knowledge 570.6
gather materials 1054.7
gather one's thoughts 931.10
gather the news 552.11
gather together 770.18
gather to oneself 472.11
gather up 912.8
gather way 162.2, 182.21
Gatling gun 462.10
gator 311.24
Gator Bowl 746.1
Gatsbyesque 501.18
gauche 414.20, 497.10, 930.11, 996.7

gaucheness 996.3
gaucherie 233.3, 414.5, 996.3
gaucho 178.8, 1070.3
gaud 498.4, 998.5
gaudery 498.3, 501.3
gaudiness 33.2, 35.5, 497.2, 498.2, 501.3, 545.1, 998.2
gaudy 35.20, 497.11, 501.20, 545.8, 998.21
gauge (n) 257.1, 300.2, 517.4 (v) 257.15, 300.10, 801.8, 946.9
gaugeable 300.14
gauged 300.13
gauger 300.9
gauging 300.1, 801.3, 946.3
gauleiter 575.12
gaum 1062.5
gauminess 1062.2
gaumy 1062.12
gaunt 270.17, 270.20, 891.4
gauntlet 454.2
gauntness 270.5
gauping 122.9
gauss 1032.9
Gautama Buddha 684.4
gauze 86.33, 319.3
gauziness 270.4, 1029.1
gauzy 270.16, 294.8, 764.6, 1029.4
gavel 417.9
gavelkind 469.1, 479.2
Gawain 608.5
gawk (n) 414.8, 924.5 (v) 27.15, 122.5, 981.3
gawkiness 270.5, 414.3
gawkish 414.20
gawkishness 414.3
gawky (n) 924.5 (a) 270.17, 414.20
gawp 27.15
gay 35.19, 75.30, 88.31, 95.16, 109.14, 501.19, 582.23, 665.25, 743.28
gay bar 88.20
gay-colored 35.19
gay deceiver 336.4, 357.1, 665.10
gay dog 665.10
gay-friendly 75.30
gay lib 431.1
gay liberation 431.1
gay marriage 563.1
gayness 109.4
Gay Nineties 824.5
gay person 75.14
gay pride 75.14
gay rights 75.14, 642.3
gaze (n) 27.5 (v) 27.15, 122.5
gaze at 27.13
gazebo 27.8, 228.12
gazehound 311.16
gazelle 174.6, 311.5, 366.4
gaze open-mouthed 27.15
gazer 918.1
gazer-on 918.1
gazette 549.8, 555.1, 555.2
gazetteer 554.9, 555.4, 574.10, 871.4
gaze upon 27.13
gazillion 884.4
gazing 122.9
gazingstock 508.7
G clef 709.13
Ge 1073.10
geanticlinal 279.7
geanticline 279.3
gear (n) 5.1, 5.2, 180.12, 271.3, 385.4, 471.3, 749.4, 752.1, 1040.4, 1040.5, 1040.9 (v) 385.8 (a) 999.13
gearbox 1040.9
geared 87.24, 788.10
geared up 87.24
gearhead 178.12, 381.6
gearing 1040.9
gearshift 1040.9
gear to 788.7, 867.3
gear tooth 1040.9
gear train 1040.9
gear up 405.13
gearwheel 1040.5, 1040.9
gee 164.6
gee-gee 757.2
geek 413.14, 414.8
geek chic 5.1
geekdom 1042.1
geekhood 1042.1
GEE navigation 1036.3
geest 1059.1
geezed 87.24
geezer 304.2
gegenschein 1025.15
Gehenna 682.1, 839.2
Geiger counter 1032.21
geisha 705.3, 707.1
geisha girl 705.3, 707.1
geist 919.4
gel (n) 704.18, 1062.5, 1064.3 (v) 269.5, 1045.10, 1062.10
gelände jump 366.1
geländesprung 366.1
gelatin 10.40, 704.18, 1062.5
gelatinate 1045.10
gelatination 1045.4
gelatine 1062.5
gelatin filter 1028.4
gelatinity 803.3, 1062.2
gelatinization 1045.4
gelatinize 1045.10
gelatinized 1045.14
gelatinous 1062.12
gelatinousness 803.3, 1062.2
gelation 1062.2
gelato 10.47
geld 77.12, 255.11
gelded 19.19, 891.4
gelding 19.6, 75.9, 255.4, 311.10, 757.2
gelid 1023.14, 1024.14
gelidity 1023.1
gelignite 462.14
gelled 1045.14
gelling 1045.4
gel mineral 1058.1
gelt 728.2
gem (n) 498.6, 659.1, 999.5, 1059.7 (v) 498.9
Gemara 683.5
Gemaric 683.12
gem carver 716.6
gem-cutting 715.1
gem engraver 716.8
geminate (v) 874.3 (a) 874.4
geminated 874.4
gemination 874.1
Gemini 873.4
gemma 310.23
gemmate 310.34
gemmation 14.1, 259.3
gemmula 310.23
gemmule 310.23
gem of the first water 999.8, 1059.7
gemstone 1059.7
gen 551.1
gen, the 551.1, 761.4
gendarme 1008.16
gender 75.1, 530.10
gender-based 75.31
gender bender 75.2
gender-bending 75.31
gender equality 778.1, 790.1
gender fluid 75.2
gender-fluid (n) 75.14 (a) 75.31
gender fluidity 75.2
gender gap 456.1
genderism 75.10
genderize 75.19
gender-neutral 75.31
gender-related 75.31
gender-sensitive 75.31
gender-specific 75.31
gene 305.9, 560.6
genealogical 560.18
genealogical tree 560.5
genealogist 550.2
genealogy 549.9, 560.5
gene complex 305.9
gene disease 85.12
gene flow 305.9
gene mapping 305.9
gene pool 305.9
general (n) 575.17 (a) 312.16, 476.9, 497.14, 612.17, 864.11, 869.8, 945.5, 951.13, 971.19
general acclamation 332.5
general agreement 332.1, 332.5
general anesthetic 25.3, 86.15
General Assembly 614.2
general assembly 613.1
general audience 706.1
general aviation 184.1
general belief 953.6
General Catalogue of Printed Books 558.4
general consent 332.5
general court-martial 595.4
general delivery 553.4
general demurrer 598.6, 600.2
general drift, the 896.2
general election 371.9, 609.15
general expenses 626.3
general headquarters 208.6
general hospital 91.21
general idea 864.8, 932.3
general information 551.1
generalism 928.6
generalissimo 575.17
generality 246.1, 772.1, 792.6, 864.1, 869.2, 932.3, 945.1, 945.2, 971.4
generalization 373.1, 864.1, 864.8, 935.3
generalize 864.9, 935.15, 951.9
generalized 864.11, 951.13
generalized proposition 864.8
general knowledge 928.6
general lien 438.5
generally accepted 373.13
generally admitted 928.27
generally capable 413.25
general medicine 90.13
general officer 575.17
general of the air force 575.17
general of the army 575.17
general order 420.3
general outlook 317.7
general partner 616.2
general post office 553.7
general practice 90.1, 90.13
general practitioner 90.4
general principle 419.2
general prior 699.16
general public 227.1
general public, the 606.1
general purpose computer 1042.2
general relativity theory 1018.1
general servant 577.9
generalship 458.5, 573.4
general store 736.1
general strike 327.4, 727.5
General Stud Book 757.1
general tendency, the 896.2
general theory of relativity 158.6
general truth 419.2, 974.2
general uprising 327.4
general voice 332.5
generate 78.8, 886.10, 890.7, 892.12, 1032.26
generation 78.2, 78.6, 824.4, 827.5, 892.1
Generation D 1042.1
generation gap 456.1
generation of Adam, the 312.6
generation of man 312.1
Generation X 302.2
Generation Y 302.2
generative 2.29, 78.16, 886.14, 892.16
generative grammar 530.1
generator 886.4
generic 864.11
generic name 86.4
generosity 143.4, 485.1, 585.1, 652.2, 991.2
generous 143.15, 148.6, 247.8, 257.17, 427.8, 478.22, 485.4, 585.11, 652.6, 890.9, 979.11, 991.7
generousness 257.6, 427.2, 485.1, 652.2, 890.1, 979.4, 991.2
generous to a fault 478.22, 652.6
genesiology 560.6
genesis 1.1, 78.6, 818.4, 861.3, 886.5, 892.1
gene splicing 305.9
gene-string 305.8
gene therapy 305.9
genethliac 1073.23
genethliac astrology 1073.20
genethliacism 1073.20
genethliacs 1073.20
genethlialogy 1073.20

genetic 78.16, 305.18, 559.6, 559.7, 560.19, 767.8, 861.8, 886.14
genetically modified 852.10
genetically related 775.10
genetic code 560.6
genetic counseling 305.9
genetic disease 85.12
genetic drift 305.9
genetic engineering 305.9, 560.6
genetic fingerprint 517.11
genetic fingerprinting 305.9, 560.6
genetic individual 305.2
genetic makeup 767.4
genetic material 305.9
genetic profile 305.9
genetic relationship 559.1
genetic resemblance 784.2
genetics 560.6
genetic screening 305.9
genetoid 305.10
gene transfer 305.9
gene-transmitted disease 85.12
gene transplantation 305.9
genetrix 560.11
genial 78.16, 97.6, 109.11, 143.14, 582.22, 585.11, 587.16, 1019.24
geniality 97.1, 109.1, 143.2, 582.1, 582.3, 585.1, 587.6
genic 305.18, 560.19
geniculate 278.6
geniculated 278.6
genie 680.6, 988.1
genital 2.29, 78.16
genitalia 2.13, 75.1
genitals 2.13, 75.1
genitive (n) 530.9 (a) 78.16
genitor 560.9
genius 18.2, 249.4, 375.9, 413.4, 413.5, 413.11, 413.12, 413.13, 678.5, 678.12, 680.6, 767.4, 920.2, 920.8, 929.3, 986.2, 999.6
genius domus 678.12
genius familiae 678.12
genius for 413.5
genius loci 678.12
genius tutelae 678.12
genocidal 308.24
genocide 308.1, 308.4, 655.2
genogram 560.5
genome 305.8
genotype 305.9, 786.1, 809.5
genre 262.1, 712.7, 809.3
genre painter 716.4
gens 559.4, 617.2
gent 76.4, 76.5
genteel 496.9, 504.16, 578.13, 607.10, 608.10
genteel comedian 707.9
genteelness 496.2, 504.4, 608.2
genteel poverty 619.1
gentile (n) 688.6, 695.11 (a) 559.7, 688.10
gentilic 559.7
gentilism 688.3
gentilities 504.7
gentility 496.2, 504.4, 607.2, 607.3, 608.2
gentle (v) 373.9, 432.11, 670.7, 1047.6, 1070.7 (a) 52.16, 143.14, 145.7, 175.10, 298.12, 427.7, 433.15, 504.16, 607.10, 608.10, 670.10, 1047.8
gentle as a lamb 433.15, 670.10
gentle breeze 318.4
gentle contact 223.5
gentled 432.15
gentlefolk 607.2, 608.1, 608.3
gentlefolks 608.3
gentle hint 551.4
gentleman 76.4, 76.7, 577.4, 607.4, 608.4, 644.8, 659.1
gentleman and a scholar, a 659.1, 929.3
gentleman-at-arms 1008.14
gentleman-farmer 1069.5
gentlemanlike 76.12, 504.16, 607.10, 608.10
gentlemanlikeness 76.1, 504.4
gentlemanliness 76.1, 504.4
gentlemanly 76.12, 504.16, 607.10, 608.10
gentleman of leisure 331.8
gentleman's agreement 437.1
gentleman's gentleman 577.4
gentle melancholy 112.5
gentlemen's agreement 436.2, 437.1
gentleness 52.1, 93.6, 143.2, 145.1, 145.2, 298.1, 427.1, 433.5, 504.4, 670.1, 1047.1
gentlepeople 608.3
gentleperson 496.6
gentle sex, the 77.3
gentle sleep 22.4
gentle slope 204.4, 237.2
gentle touch 298.1
gentle wind 318.4
gentlewoman 77.5, 577.8, 608.6
gentlewomanlike 77.13
gentlewomanliness 77.1
gentlewomanly 77.13
gentling (n) 432.4 (a) 670.15
gentrification 392.1, 644.1
gentrified 392.13
gentrify 392.9
gentry 606.1, 607.2, 608.3
gents', the 12.10
genuflect 155.6, 433.10, 696.11, 913.9
genuflection 155.2, 696.4, 913.3
genuine 416.6, 644.14, 644.17, 761.15, 973.15
genuine article 337.3
genuine article, the 761.2, 973.4
genuineness 416.2, 644.4, 973.7
genus 527.1, 809.3, 809.5, 1068.1
genus Homo 312.1
geocache 295.1
geocaching 295.1, 1071.1
geocentric 208.11
geocentric longitude 1073.16
geodesic 300.12
geodesical 300.12
geodesic dome 279.4
geodesist 300.9, 1017.16
geodesy 159.8
geodetic 159.19, 300.12
geodetical 300.12
geodetic engineer 300.9
geodetic longitude 1073.16
geodetic satellite 159.8, 1075.6
geodynamic 1039.9
geoengineering 1058.10
geographer 1071.2
geographic 159.19
geographical 231.8
geographical information system 1071.1
geographically limited 231.9
Geographic Information System 159.8
geographic longitude 1073.16
geography 159.8, 1071.1
geoid 282.2
geolocation 1042.18, 1071.1
geological fold 291.1
geological map 159.5
geological past 837.3
geological record 1071.1
geological science 1071.1
geological sediment 1059.6
geological time period 824.2
geologist 1058.12, 1071.2
geology 1058.10, 1059.9, 1071.1
geomagnetic pole 1032.8
geomagnetic storm 1032.9
geomancer 962.4
geometer 1017.16
geometric 1017.22
geometrical 1017.22
geometrical horizon 201.4
geometrical optics 1025.22
geometrical progression 1017.8
geometrician 1017.16
geometric proportion 1017.7
geometric ratio 1017.7
geometry 278.3, 568.3
geophilous 234.4
geophysical satellite 1075.6
geopolitical 609.43
geopolitics 609.2
geoponic 1069.20
geoponical 1069.20
geoponics 1069.1
geo probe 1075.6
georama 33.7
george 439.8
George Fox 684.3
geoscience 1059.9, 1071.1
geoscientist 1071.2
geospatial 159.19
geosphere 1073.10
geostatic 1039.8
geostationary orbit 1075.2
geostationary satellite 1075.6
geostrophic wind 318.1
geosynchronous satellite 1075.6
geosynclinal 279.7
geosyncline 279.3
geotag 1042.18
geotagging 1042.18
geotechnical engineering 1043.1
geothermal energy 1021.1, 1021.7
geothermal gradient 1021.1
geothermal heat 1021.1
geothermal power 18.4
geotropism 297.5
geriatric (n) 304.2 (a) 303.16, 303.18
geriatric medicine 303.8
geriatrics 303.8
germ 85.42, 258.7, 295.16, 305.14, 886.7
german (n) 559.2 (a) 559.6
germane 559.6, 775.11
germaneness 775.4
German goiter 2.19
Germanic 523.12
Germanism 523.8
German tinder 1021.6
germ-carrying 85.62
germ cell 75.7, 305.4, 305.10, 560.6
germen 305.14
germicidal 86.43
germicide 86.21, 1001.3
germinal 78.15, 258.14, 305.22, 886.14, 890.11, 986.18
germinal imagination 986.3
germinant 305.22
germinate 14.2, 259.7, 310.34, 890.8
germinate from 887.5
germination 14.1, 78.3, 259.3, 310.32
germinational 305.22
germinative 305.22
germiparous 305.22
germ-laden 82.7
germ layer 305.4
germline insertion 305.9
germling 310.10, 310.31
germ plasm 305.4, 305.10, 560.6
germ warfare 458.1
Geronimo 458.7
gerontic 303.16
gerontocracy 612.4
gerontology 303.8
gerrymander (n) 609.16 (v) 415.10, 609.38
gerrymandered district 609.16
gerrymandering 356.8
gerund 530.5
gerundive 530.3
gest 492.6
gestalt 33.3, 92.32, 209.1, 211.2
Gestalt psychology 92.2
gestate 78.12, 886.10
gestating 78.18
gestation 78.5
gestational diabetes 85.21
gestatory 818.15
gesticulate 517.21
gesticulation 321.1, 517.14
gesticulative 517.25
gesticulatory 517.25
gestural 517.25
gesture (n) 328.3, 517.14, 551.4 (v) 517.21
gesture language 517.14
gestures 321.1
get (n) 472.3, 559.5, 561.2, 627.1 (v) 48.11, 78.8, 85.47, 96.13, 174.9, 176.16, 188.7, 308.14, 472.8, 479.6, 480.13, 521.8, 570.6, 761.12, 886.11, 897.4, 940.2, 941.2, 971.14
get a bang out of 95.13
get a base hit 745.5
get a bearing 159.11
get a black eye 661.7

getable 966.8
getableness 966.3
get aboard 745.5
get about 177.21, 396.20
get a break 1010.11
get abroad 352.16
get a bun on 88.26
get a charge out of 95.13
get a corner on 469.6, 737.26
get acquainted 587.10
get across 48.12, 343.7, 518.8, 521.6, 568.10, 989.17
get a fix on 159.11, 521.8, 970.11
get afloat 352.16
get a foothold 474.5, 906.8
get a footing 159.17
get a free pass 745.5
get a free ride 745.5
get after 96.13, 166.3, 389.7, 983.8
get a glimpse of 27.12
get a good pennyworth 633.5
get a grip 106.7
get a grip on oneself 106.7
get a handle on 208.10
get a hard-on 75.20
get ahead 162.2, 165.2, 249.10, 251.6, 392.7, 409.10, 1010.7
get ahead of 216.7, 845.6, 910.8
get a head start 165.2, 845.6
get a hold on 926.25
get a hustle on 401.6
get a kick out of 95.13
get a laugh 116.9
get a leg up on 411.6
get a life 328.5
get a lift out of 95.13
get a little on the side 665.19
get all balled up 1013.12
get all bollixed up 1013.12
get all in a lather 12.16
get all snarled up 1013.12
get all tangled up 1013.12
get a load of 27.12, 983.6
get a load off one's feet 20.6
get a load off one's mind 351.7, 524.21
get a loan 621.3
get a lock on 970.11
get along 162.2, 188.6, 303.10, 392.7, 409.12, 455.2, 856.5
get along in years 303.10
get along on 995.4
get along on a shoestring 635.4
get along with 455.2
get along without 475.3
get a move on 174.9, 401.6
get a navigational fix 159.11
get an earful 48.11
get an erection 75.20
get an eye for an eye and a tooth for a tooth 506.6
get an eyeful of 27.12
get an impression 93.10
get an income 624.20
get a noseful of 69.8
get a piece of the action 759.25
get a purchase 906.8
get a reaction 903.8
get a reading 942.9
get a reputation 662.11
get a response 903.8
get a rise out of 903.8
get a rough idea 223.8
get around 177.21, 352.16, 356.14, 368.7, 413.19, 415.11, 431.8, 511.6
get around to 405.6
get a rush 87.22
get a rush out of 95.13
get a sense 942.9
get a shellacking 604.19
get a sounding 942.9
get a stranglehold on 19.10, 411.6, 428.10
get at 186.7, 378.3, 389.7, 894.9, 970.11
get-at-able 966.8
getatable 167.5
get-at-ableness 894.5, 966.3
getatableness 167.2
get a tan 1020.19
get away 188.6, 188.8, 369.6
getaway 20.3, 174.4, 188.1, 188.2, 369.1
get away from 368.7
get away from it all 20.9, 743.22
get away with 369.7
get away with it 409.11
get away with murder 369.7
get a whiff of 69.8, 941.6
get a wiggle on 401.6, 845.5
get a wrong impression 948.2
get back 481.6
get back at 506.4, 863.4
get back in shape 396.20
get back on one's feet 83.7
get back to 343.8
get back to earth 977.3
get backwards 342.2
get before 165.2
get behind 163.5, 166.4, 217.8, 449.13
get better 396.19
get between one's finger and thumb 480.14
get bigger 14.2
get bogged down 911.3
get busy 725.15
get butterflies in one's stomach 126.6
get by 369.7, 385.12, 409.11, 409.12, 765.5, 839.7, 942.10, 984.2, 984.5, 991.4
get by heart 989.16
get by hook or by crook 384.6
get by on 995.4
get by on little 635.4
get by osmosis 570.7
get by rote 570.8
get by with 369.7
get chummy with 587.11
get clear of 369.6, 431.8
get close to 587.11
get cold feet 491.8
get control of 894.12
get cozy with 587.11, 894.9, 894.12
get cracking 401.6, 725.15, 818.11
get cutting 330.14
get done 407.6
get down 8.22, 87.22, 194.7, 913.8
get down cold 570.9
get down from one's high horse 137.7
get down on one's haunches 913.8
get down on one's knees 155.6
get down on one's marrow-bones 440.11
get down on one's marrowbones 658.5
get down pat 570.9
get down to 818.7
get down to brass tacks 865.9
get down to business 330.11, 725.15
get down to cases 865.9
get down to nuts and bolts 938.25
get down to the nitty-gritty 865.9
get down to work 725.15
get drunk 88.26
get even with 506.7, 507.4, 624.12, 863.4
get excited 105.16, 135.4
get excited about 101.6
get exposure 352.16
get for one's pains 639.6
get free 369.6
get free of 431.8
get fresh 142.7
get from 192.14
get frostbite 1023.9
get funny 923.6
get-go 818.1
get going 188.7, 401.6, 404.3, 725.15, 818.8, 843.8
get good wood on it 745.5
get hands on 480.14
get healthy 83.7
get hep to 551.14
get hers 639.6
get high 88.26
get high on 95.13, 105.18
get his 639.6
get hitched 563.15
get hold of 343.8, 472.9, 480.14, 521.7, 570.6
get hold of an idea 953.13
get hold of oneself 106.7
get hold of the wrong end of the stick 948.2
get home free 855.11
get hot under the collar 105.17, 152.18
get huffy 152.13
get hung up 911.3
get hurt 604.19
get in 186.6, 189.7, 193.12, 214.5, 472.11, 770.18
get in a bind 1013.12
get-in-able 966.8
get in a box 1013.12
get in a hole 1013.12
get in a jam 1013.12
get in a mess 1013.12
get in a pincers 459.19
get in a rut 373.12
get in a word edgewise 524.21
get in back of 449.13
get in behind 449.13
get in connection with 343.8
get in contact with 343.8
get in formation 812.6
get in front of 165.2
get in good with 587.13
get in hot water 1013.12
get in line 812.6, 867.4
get in on 214.5, 476.5
get in one's hair 96.13, 98.14
get in one's own way 414.11
get in on the ground floor 818.8
get in order 808.8
get in position 807.5
get in the act 476.5
get in the family way 78.11
get in the good graces of 587.13
get in the harvest 1069.19
get in there 818.8
get in the soup 1013.12
get in the swim 578.10
get in the way 1012.12
get into 5.43, 189.8, 617.14
get into a dither 105.17, 135.4
get into a scrape 1013.12
get into a stew 105.17, 135.4
get into a swivet 105.17
get into a tizzy 105.17
get into character 704.32
get into condition 405.13
get into debt 623.6
get into favor 587.13
get into harness 405.13
get into mischief 322.4
get into one's clutches 480.14
get into one's grasp 480.14
get into one's head 521.8, 570.6, 989.17
get into one's hold 480.13
get into one's possession 480.13
get into one's thick head 521.8
get into one's thick skull 989.17
get into shape 405.13
get into the good graces of 138.10
get into the way of 373.11
get into the zone 409.10
get into trouble 1000.6, 1013.12
get in touch 343.8
get involved 476.5
get in with 138.10, 587.13, 894.12
get it 521.8, 604.19, 941.2
get it coming and going 604.19
get it in the neck 604.19
get it into one's head 953.11, 953.13
get it off one's chest 120.7, 351.7, 933.3
get it off one's mind 933.3
get it out of one's head 106.7
get it out of one's mind 106.7
get it out of one's system 351.7
get it over 407.6, 820.6
get it over with 407.6, 857.11
get it straight 973.10
get it together 106.8, 208.10, 392.9, 808.8, 858.12
get it wrong 975.10
get justice 639.6
get killed 308.21
get laid 75.21

get laryngitis 51.7
et left 410.10
get letter-perfect 989.16
get leverage 906.8
get loose 802.9
get lost 188.7, 430.17
get mad 152.18
get miffed 152.13
get mired 911.3
get mired down 911.3
get moving 401.6
get next to 138.10, 587.11, 587.13
get no better fast 393.16
get no place fast 175.6
get nowhere 19.7, 410.13
get nowhere fast 175.6
get off 75.24, 87.22, 188.8, 194.7, 352.14, 369.7, 431.9, 818.8
get off a joke 489.13
get off-base 327.6, 975.9
get off cheap 369.7
get off easy 369.7
get off lightly 369.7
get off on a technicality 369.7
get off one's back 430.17
get off one's case 430.17
get off one's duff 330.14
get off one's tail 430.17
get off on the wrong foot 1013.11
get off scot-free 430.18, 431.9
get off the dime 188.8, 328.5, 330.14, 843.8
get off the ground 184.38, 818.8, 904.13
get off the hook 600.9
get off the mark 904.13
get off the subject 538.9
get off the track 984.3
get off to a bad start 1013.11
get off to a good start 818.8
get on 5.43, 87.22, 96.13, 188.6, 193.12, 303.10, 409.10, 409.12, 765.5, 856.5, 1010.7
get on credit 621.3
get one down 96.13, 112.18, 1013.13
get one over a barrel 424.8
get one's act together 858.12
get one's back up 152.13, 152.17, 152.23, 152.24
get one's bearings 161.11
get one's blood up 152.17
get one's comeuppance 639.6
get one's credentials 409.7
get one's dander up 152.18, 152.23
get one's desserts 604.19, 639.6
get one's ducks in a row 392.9, 808.8, 858.12
get one's dues 639.6
get oneself a deal 731.19
get oneself in a sulk 110.14
get oneself in a tizzy 152.18
get one's eye 377.6
get one's feet on the ground 977.3
get one's feet wet 818.8, 818.10
get one's fingers burned 604.19
get one's fingers on 472.9, 480.14
get one's foot in the door 189.7
get one's goat 96.13, 152.23
get one's gorge up 152.17
get one's hackles up 152.18, 152.23
get one's hands dirty 80.16, 661.7
get one's hands on 472.9, 480.14
get one's hooks into 472.9
get one's hopes up 124.7
get one's house in order 405.13, 808.10
get one's Irish up 152.18, 152.23
get one's jollies 743.22
get one's just desserts 604.19
get one's kicks 743.22
get one's knuckles rapped 604.19
get one's mitts on 472.9
get one's money's worth 633.5
get one's monkey up 152.18
get one's second wind 396.20
get one's sword 405.13
get one's teeth into 403.5
get one's teeth into it 725.15
get one's way 323.3
get one's wish 323.3
get one under one's thumb 424.8
get one wrong 342.2
get on good terms with 587.13
get on in the world 618.10, 1010.9
get on in years 303.10
get on line 812.6
get on one's high horse 141.8
get on one's nerves 58.11, 96.14, 128.9
get on swimmingly 1010.7
get on the bandwagon 138.11, 332.9, 578.10, 609.41, 867.4
get on the cuff 621.3
get on the good side of 138.10, 587.13
get on the in with 587.13
get on the job 725.15
get on the right side of 138.10, 587.13
get on the scoreboard 746.5
get on the ticket 610.13
get on the wagon 374.3, 668.8
get on the water wagon 668.8
get on tick 621.3
get on well 1010.7
get on well with 587.9
get on with 455.2
get organized 106.7
get out 188.7, 190.12, 192.10, 351.8, 352.14, 369.6, 431.7, 548.14
get out a sheet-anchor 494.6
get out from under 120.8, 1014.9
get out in the open 351.4, 352.11
get out of 192.14, 368.7, 368.9, 369.6, 431.8, 431.9
get out of a jam 431.8
get out of bed 23.6
get out of commission 393.26
get out of gear 393.25
get out of joint 393.25
get out of kilter 393.26
get out of line 868.4, 975.9
get out of one's depth 367.8
get out of one's face 430.17
get out of one's hair 430.17
get out of order 393.25
get out of the way of 164.6, 368.6
get out of whack 393.26
get out on the wrong side of the bed 110.13
get over 172.5, 343.7, 392.8, 396.20, 521.5, 521.6
get over it 83.7
get over the ground 162.2, 174.8
get over with 820.6
get palsy-walsy with 587.11
get palsy with 587.11
get past 984.2
get physical 75.20
get pickled 88.26
get plastered 88.26
get precise 865.9
get quit of 390.7, 431.8, 773.5
get quits with 624.12
get ready 405.6, 405.13
get ready to 405.10
get real 920.10
get red 105.19
get red in the face 139.8
get religion 692.7
get rich 618.10
get rid of 308.16, 390.7, 395.12, 431.8, 475.3, 734.8, 773.5, 909.21
get right 940.2
get rolling 188.7, 725.15
get round 415.11
get satisfaction 506.5
get scent of 551.15
get sea room 182.37
get set 405.13
get set for 405.10
get shut of 390.7, 773.5
get sidetracked 538.9
get smart 142.7
get some air 177.24
get some sack time 22.14
get some shut-eye 22.14
get something out of one's system 120.8
get something under one's control 18.11
get something under one's thumb 18.11
get somewhere 162.4
get sore 152.18
get squared away 818.8
get square with 624.12
get stage fright 525.7
get stars in one's eyes 101.7
get started 818.13
get taller 14.2
get taped 570.9
getter 479.3
get the advantage 411.6
get the ascendancy 249.6
get the ball rolling 818.7
get the benefit of 639.6
get the benefit of the doubt 953.15
get the best of 411.5, 412.6, 415.11
get the better 411.5, 412.6, 415.11
get the blues 112.15
get the breaks 1010.11
get the cold shoulder 340.8
get the color back in one's cheeks 83.7
get the drift 521.8
get the drop on 411.6, 459.21
get the ear of 894.9
get the edge 249.6
get the edge on 411.6
get the facts 551.14
get the floor 613.10
get the go-by 340.8
get the golden handshake 448.2
get the golden parachute 448.2
get the green light 188.8
get the hang of 373.11, 521.8, 570.9
get the hell out 188.7, 368.11
get the idea 521.8
get the impression 934.4
get the inside track 894.12
get the jump on 411.6
get the knack of 373.11, 570.9
get the last laugh 411.3
get the lay of the land 27.13, 161.11
get the lead out 174.9, 330.14, 401.6
get the lie of the land 161.11
get the mastery of 894.12
get the meaning of 521.7
get the message 521.8
get the munchies 8.20
get the picture 328.5, 521.8
get the power into one's hands 417.14
get there 186.6, 409.10
get there first 845.5
get the shortend of the stick 1011.9
get the show on the road 818.7
get the upper hand 417.14
get the wind up 127.11
get the word 521.8
get the worst of it 412.12
get things into proportion 925.2
get through 189.8, 328.7, 407.5, 407.6, 839.7
get through one's head 521.8
get through one's thick head 521.8
get through one's thick skull 570.6
get through to 48.12, 343.8
get through with 407.6, 820.6
getting 472.1, 479.1, 570.2
getting ahead 472.3
getting a load off one's mind 351.3
getting along 303.17
getting along in years 303.17
getting around 368.1, 415.5
getting away 473.1

getting even 507.1
getting hitched 563.1
getting hold of 472.1, 570.2
getting in condition 405.1
getting in shape 405.1
getting off 186.2
getting on 303.17
getting on in years 303.17
getting ready 405.1
getting rid of 475.1
getting round 415.5
getting spliced 563.1
getting the hang of 570.2
getting the hell out 368.4
getting underway 375.2
getting up in years 303.17
getting with child 78.3
get tired 21.5
get to 48.12, 126.5, 186.6, 261.6, 343.8, 378.3, 818.7
get to be 761.12, 818.13
get to do 375.22
get together 332.10, 450.3, 472.11, 770.18
get-together 582.10, 770.2
get together with 450.4
get to know one another 587.10
get too big for one's breeches 140.6
get to one 93.15
get to one's feet 200.8
get top billing 704.29, 997.12
get to the bottom line 537.5
get to the bottom of 341.10, 940.2
get to the core 798.5
get to the essence 798.5
get to the heart of 341.10, 570.9, 940.2
get to the heart of the matter 208.10
get to the nitty-gritty 537.5
get to the point 931.10
get tough 15.12, 359.9
Getty 618.8
get under control 428.7, 612.14
get under one's skin 93.14, 96.13
get underway 182.19, 188.6, 404.3, 818.8
get up 5.42, 23.4, 23.6, 200.8, 405.7, 570.14, 892.8
getup 5.2, 5.9, 266.1, 330.7, 796.1
get-up-and-get 330.7
get-up-and-go 17.3, 330.7
get up early 330.16
get up in 570.9
get up late 846.7
get up on 989.18
get up one's nerve 492.12
get up on the wrong side of the bed 456.11
get up steam 405.9
get up the courage 492.12
get up the nerve 492.12
get-up time 314.1
get up to speed 521.8
get used to 373.11
get warm 223.8
get well 83.7, 396.20
get well out of 369.6, 431.8
get what is coming to one 639.6
get what one is asking for 604.20
get wind of 48.11, 69.8, 551.14, 551.15, 941.6
get wise to 551.14
get with child 78.10
get with it 328.5, 725.15
get with young 78.10
get word 48.11, 551.14
get word-perfect 989.16
get worse 119.3, 393.16
get wrong 342.2, 948.2
gewgaw 498.4, 743.16, 998.5
geyser 238.9, 1019.10
ghastliness 36.2, 127.2, 307.11, 1015.2
ghastly 36.7, 37.7, 127.30, 307.28, 1015.11
ghee 1061.2
ghetto (n) 230.6 (a) 230.11
ghetto, the 80.11
ghetto blaster 50.11
ghetto-dwellers 606.4, 619.3
ghettoize 773.6
ghettoized 619.8, 773.8
ghost (n) 127.9, 547.15, 718.4, 862.2, 988.1, 1035.5 (v) 182.54, 547.21, 576.14, 718.6, 813.3, 862.5
ghostbuster 1053.4
ghostbusting 1053.1
ghost dance 690.3, 701.9
ghost-haunted 988.10
ghost-hunter 1053.4
ghost-hunting 1053.1
ghosting 813.1
ghostish 988.7
ghostlike 307.28, 988.7
ghostlikeness 307.11
ghostliness 307.11, 988.4, 1053.1
ghostly 307.28, 988.7, 1053.7
ghost of a chance, a 969.1, 972.9
ghost of a chance 966.1
ghost-raiser 1053.4
ghost-raising 1053.1
ghost-ridden 988.10
ghost story 354.11
ghost town 230.1
ghost word 526.8, 526.11
ghostwrite 547.21, 576.14, 718.6, 862.5
ghost writer 576.1
ghostwriter 547.15, 718.4, 862.2
ghosty 988.7
ghoul 127.9, 483.1, 593.6, 680.6
ghoulish 127.30, 680.17, 981.5, 1000.10
ghoulishness 127.2, 981.1
GI 461.7
giant (n) 15.6, 257.13, 272.7 (a) 257.20, 272.16
giant black hole 1073.8
giant clam 311.29
giantess 257.13
giantism 257.5, 257.7, 993.1
giant-killer 308.11
giantlike 257.20
giantlikeness 257.7
giant of learning 929.3
giant size 257.4
giant-size 257.23
giant slalom 753.3
giant slalom course 753.1
giant slalom racer 753.2
giant step 261.2
giant stride 261.2
gib 311.20
gibber (n) 520.2, 525.4, 540.3 (v) 520.5, 522.10, 525.9, 540.5
gibbering (n) 525.4 (a) 540.10
gibberish 520.2, 522.7, 523.9
gibbet (n) 605.5 (v) 604.17, 661.9
gibble-gabble (n) 520.2, 540.3 (v) 520.5, 540.5
gibble-gabbler 540.4
gibbose 279.10, 283.13
gibbosity 283.1, 283.2
gibbous 265.13, 279.10, 283.13
gibbous moon 1073.11
gibbousness 283.1, 283.2
gib-cat 311.20
gibe (n) 156.2, 489.7, 508.2 (v) 508.9
gibe at 156.5, 489.13
gibing retort 508.2
giblets 2.16, 10.20, 10.23, 207.4
Gibraltar 15.8
GI bride 563.5, 563.8
giddiness 923.1, 984.1, 985.4, 985.5
giddy 88.31, 854.7, 917.16, 926.31, 984.6, 985.15, 985.16
giddy as a goose 985.16
giddybrain 924.7
giddy-brained 985.16
giddyhead 924.7
giddy-headed 985.16
giddypate 924.7
giddy-pated 985.16
giddy-witted 985.16
gift (n) 413.4, 478.4, 634.1, 920.2 (v) 478.12, 478.14
gift card 478.4
gift certificate 478.4
gifted 413.29, 572.12, 920.14
gifted child 413.12
giftedness 920.2
gifted person 413.12
gifted student 572.4
gifter 478.11
gift for 413.5
gift from on high 472.7
gift horse 478.4
gifting 478.1
giftlike 634.5
gift of expression 544.1
gift of gab 532.2, 540.1, 540.2, 544.1
gift of the gab 532.2, 544.1
gift of tongues 522.7, 692.3
gifts 920.2
gift tax 630.9
giftware 735.6
gift with 478.12, 478.14
gift wrap 295.18
gift wrapping 295.18
gig (n) 704.11, 724.5 (v) 382.10
giga 257.20
gigabit 1042.14
gigabucks 618.3
gigabyte 882.10, 1042.18
gigaflop 410.2
gigamaree 1052.5
gigantean 257.20
gigantesque 15.17, 247.7, 257.20
gigantic 15.17, 247.7, 257.20, 272.16, 993.16
giganticness 257.7
gigantism 247.1, 257.5, 257.7, 993.1
gig economy 731.7
giggle (n) 116.4 (v) 116.8
gigolo 104.12, 138.5, 562.12, 665.18
gigot 10.16, 177.14
gigster 311.13
GI Joe 461.7
gilbert 1032.7
gild 35.14, 43.3, 97.5, 295.24, 354.16, 545.7
gilded 43.4, 354.27, 498.12
Gilded Age 824.5, 824.5
gildedness 43.1
gilding 35.12, 498.3, 600.5
gilding the lily 355.1, 768.2
gild the lily 97.5, 355.3, 392.10, 545.7, 993.12
gill 104.13, 238.1, 284.9
gill net 356.13
gilt (n) 77.9, 311.9, 354.3, 498.3, 728.2 (a) 43.4, 1058.17
gilt-edge 999.15
gilt-edged 999.15
gimbal 915.5
gimcrack (n) 498.4, 743.16, 998.5, 1040.1 (a) 16.14
gimcrackery 993.4, 998.4
gimcracky 16.14, 998.21
gimlet eye 27.10
gimme 478.4, 634.1
gimmick 356.6, 377.3, 415.3, 722.4, 759.16, 995.2, 1040.1, 1052.5
gimmicked-up 498.12
gimmickery 356.1
gimmickry 356.1, 415.4, 498.3, 501.3
gimmick up 498.8
gimmicky 356.22, 415.12, 501.19
gimpy 16.14
gin (n) 356.12 (v) 356.20, 773.6
ginchy 75.25, 377.8
gin drinker's liver 88.3
ginger 17.3, 68.2
gingerbread (n) 10.42, 498.3, 993.4 (a) 498.12
gingerbread man 349.6
gingerbread woman 349.6
gingerbready 498.12
ginger-haired 41.10
gingerliness 494.1
gingerly 494.8
gingery 544.12
ginhound 88.12
gin mill 88.20
ginormous 247.7
ginseng 86.8
gin up 892.8
giraffe 311.5
gird 15.13, 209.7, 800.9
girding 209.5, 800.3

girdle (n) 5.23, 271.4, 280.3, 901.2 (v) 209.7, 280.10, 800.9, 914.5
girdled 209.11
girdle the globe 914.5
girdling 209.5
gird one's loins 458.19
gird up one's loins 15.10, 15.13, 405.13, 458.19, 725.15
girja 703.2
girl 77.5, 87.7, 104.14, 302.6, 304.3, 577.8
girlchild 302.6
girl flick 706.2
girl Friday 577.3
girlfriend 104.13, 588.1, 588.3
girlhood 301.2, 302.2
girlie 302.6
girlish 77.13, 270.16, 301.11, 406.11
girlishness 77.1, 301.4
girl-like 301.11
girl-likeness 301.4
girl next door 864.3
girl next door, the 606.1
Girl Scout 999.6
girls' room 12.10
girl thing, a 77.1
girl-watcher 918.1
girly man 77.2
girt (n) 280.3, 901.18 (v) 800.9 (a) 209.11
girth (n) 257.1, 280.3, 819.1, 901.18 (v) 800.9
GI's 12.2
gismo 1052.5
gist 196.5, 518.1, 557.2, 767.2, 792.6, 937.1, 997.6
git 174.9, 188.7
git-go 818.1
give (n) 1047.1, 1047.2, 1048.1 (v) 343.7, 385.7, 478.12, 524.22, 629.3, 634.4, 643.6, 888.3, 1047.7, 1048.5
give a bad name 512.10, 661.9
give a bad rap 650.6
give a bad time to 96.13
give a bang 95.11
give a bawling out 510.18
give a beating 604.12
give a big hand 150.4, 509.10
give a black eye 393.13, 512.10, 661.9
give a black mark 661.9
give a blank check 443.12
giveable 478.23
give a boost 449.11, 912.7
give a boost to 251.5, 509.11
give a bouquet 509.14
give a break 9.2, 145.4
give a breather 9.2
give a breath of fresh air 9.2
give a briefing 184.48, 568.15
give a broad hint 422.5
give absolution 148.3, 601.4
give a bum steer 356.16
give a buz 347.19
give a buzz 347.19
give a call 347.19
give a chance to 966.5
give a charge 95.11
give a cheer 116.6
give acknowledgement 939.4
give a color to 354.16
give a come-hither look 377.5
give a coup d'œil 27.17
give a cursory look 938.26
give a dekko 938.26
give a direct order 420.8
give a dirty look 152.14
give admittance to 187.10
give a dog a bad name 512.10, 661.9
give a dressing-down 604.14
give advance notice 399.5, 399.6
give a face lift 498.8
give a fair shake 649.5
give a false alarm 400.3
give a false coloring 265.6, 342.2, 350.3, 354.16
give a false idea 342.2
give a false impression 342.2
give a figure to 1017.17
give a fillip to 105.13
give a fling at 403.7
give a for-instance 957.13
give a free course to 426.3
give a free hand 430.15, 443.12
give a fresh lease on life 396.15
give a going-over 510.18, 604.10
give a good account of oneself 409.10
give a guess 951.11
give a hand 449.11, 509.10
give a head's up 399.6
give a hearing to 48.10, 598.18, 946.12
give a helping hand 449.11
give a high five 517.22, 585.10
give a hint 422.5, 989.19
give air to 352.11
give a jingle 347.19
give a job to 615.14
give a jolt 131.13
give a knockdown 587.14
give a leg up 449.11, 912.7
give a lesson 568.16
give a lesson to 568.10
give a lick and a promise 206.6, 276.4, 340.7, 340.8
give a lift 109.7, 449.11, 912.7
give a line of credit 622.6
give a loose translation 341.13
give a low five 585.10
give a miss to 368.6
give an account of 551.8, 552.11, 719.5, 722.7
give an alarm 400.3, 517.22
give an appreciation 946.9
give an assignment 568.17
give an assist 449.11
give and go 747.4
give-and-go (n) 749.3 (v) 749.7
give and take (n) 450.1 (v) 338.4, 457.13, 468.2, 506.4, 649.5, 863.4, 935.16
give-and-take (n) 338.2, 468.1, 490.1, 506.1, 541.1, 649.1, 731.2, 863.1 (a) 863.5
give an ear 48.10
give an encore 849.8
give an entree 187.10
give a new lease on life 306.10, 396.15, 841.5
give an examination 938.24
give an exclamation 59.7
give an idea of 568.10
give an impetus 902.11
give an impression of 349.12
give an impulse to 449.17
give an inch and take an ell 640.7
give an inkling of 551.10
give an introduction 587.14
give an obolus to Charon 307.20
give a nod 206.6
give a nod of assent 332.12
give an open invitation 443.12
give an open mandate 443.12
give an opinion 946.8
give an order 420.8
give answer 939.4
give a once-over-lightly 206.6, 938.26
give a party 582.20, 585.8
give a performance 704.28
give a piece of advice 422.5
give a piece of one's mind 510.18
give a piece of the action 772.3
give a pink slip 447.4
give a pointer to 551.11
give a posy 509.14
give a promise 436.4
give a push 904.13
give a push in the right direction 161.5
give a quick look 938.26
give a quid pro quo 506.6
give a rap on the knuckles 604.11
give a raw deal 650.6
give a report 552.11
give a reprieve 601.5
give a ring 347.19
give a rotten deal 650.6
give a rough idea 223.8
give a royal welcome 187.10
give a run for one's money 457.18
give a rush 95.11
give as a gift 478.12
give as an excuse 600.11
give a second chance 145.4
give as good as one gets 506.6, 863.4
give as good as was sent 506.6
give a shot in the arm 9.2
give a shout of laughter 116.8
give a shove 904.13
give a shriek of laughter 116.8
give a sidelong look 27.18
give a signal 517.22
give as lagniappe 478.12
give as much as one takes 863.4
give a spin 265.6
give a square deal 649.5
give assent 332.8
give a start 904.13
give a suggestion 989.19
give a surprise party 131.7
give a talk 543.9
give a thrashing 604.12
give a thrill 105.15
give a tone to society 578.9
give a transfusion 91.27
give a trial to 942.8
give a try 403.7, 942.8
give a tryout 942.8
give attention 48.10
give a turn to 852.7
give a twist to 852.7
give audience to 48.10
give a warm reception to 585.9
give away 351.6, 390.7, 393.23, 475.3, 478.21, 563.14
giveaway (n) 351.2 (a) 633.9
giveaway show 1035.2
give a whammy 691.10
give a whipping 604.12
give a wide berth 368.6, 903.7
give a wide berth to 261.7
give a write-up 352.15
give a wrong idea 350.3
give back 396.11, 481.4
give battle 457.16
give being to 892.12
give benediction 696.14
give birth 1.3, 78.13, 306.10
give birth to 306.10, 818.14, 886.10
give bridle to 430.15
give by way of information 551.8
give care to 91.24
give carte blanche 443.12
give chase 382.8
give cheerfully 485.3
give comfort 121.6
give concern 126.4
give confidential information 551.11
give consent 441.2
give credence to 953.10
give credit 150.3, 150.4, 620.5, 622.6
give credit to 953.10
give credit where credit is due 646.8, 662.12
give danger a wide berth 1007.3
give directions 568.15
give directions to 161.6
give dispensation from 430.14
give due credit 150.3
give ear 48.10
give ear to 983.7
give emphasis to 997.14
give encouragement 375.21
give entrance 187.10
give evidence 517.17, 957.9
give expression 524.22
give expression to 532.4
give fair warning 399.5
give faith to 953.10
give forgiveness 148.3
give forth 352.14
give forth a sound 50.14
give free course to 669.4
give freely 478.12, 485.3
give free play to the emotions 93.13
give free rein 443.12
give free rein to 426.3, 430.15, 669.4
give free rein to the imagination 986.14
give full authority 443.12

give full particulars 766.6
give full play 430.15
give full power 443.12
give generously 478.12
give good reasons for 600.9
give good returns 387.17
give greater draft fore and aft 182.49
give ground 163.6, 433.7, 903.7
give ground for expecting 133.12
give hail Columbia 510.18
give head 75.23
give heed 983.8
give heed to 983.5
give hell 510.18
give help 449.11
give her beans 182.20
give homework 568.17
give hope 124.9
give in 250.5, 433.7, 478.13
give in addition 478.12
give in charge 478.16, 615.10
give indication of 957.8
give in exchange 506.4, 731.15
give in kind 506.6
give in marriage 563.14
give in return 506.4
give insight 341.10
give instruction 568.10
give instructions 568.15
give into the bargain 478.12
give in trust 478.16
give it a go 942.8
give it all one's got 403.14
give it a second thought 494.5
give it no more thought 984.4
give it once over lightly 276.4
give it one's all 403.13
give it one's best shot 403.14
give it the gas 174.9
give it the gun 174.9, 401.6
give it to 510.18, 604.10
give leave 443.9
give lessons in 568.10
give life to 306.10
give light 1025.23
give lip service 354.23
give little weight to 998.12
give measure for measure 506.6
give mind to 983.5
give momentum 902.11
give moral support to 449.14
give more matter and less art 537.5
give more than one's share 485.3
give mouth honor 354.23, 693.4
given, a 973.2
given (n) 761.3, 959.2 (a) 373.18, 478.24, 634.5, 761.15, 951.14, 959.8, 978.8
given a blessing 509.19
given a turn 131.13
given birth 1.4
give new life to 105.13, 449.11, 449.12
given fact 761.3
given name 527.4
give no cheer 96.12
give no comfort 96.12
give no credence to 955.5
give no heed 984.2
give no joy 96.12
give no pleasure 96.12
give no quarter 146.2
give notic 399.5
give notice 133.13, 352.12, 551.8
give notification 551.8
give no trouble 1014.10
given to drink 88.35
given up 307.32
given up for dead 307.32
give occasion to 886.10
give odds 759.25
give off 12.12, 13.5, 190.15, 909.24, 1067.8
give offense 98.11, 152.21
give offense to 156.5
give official sanction 443.11
give off waves of heat 1019.22
give of oneself 485.3
give of one's substance 485.3
give one a bad time 1013.13
give one a bellyful 118.6
give one a big send-off 188.16
give one a black eye 38.7, 512.9
give one a blank check 430.15
give one a charge 105.15
give one a dirty look 27.16
give one a dose of one's own medicine 506.6
give one a fright 127.15
give one a hard time 98.14, 115.16, 510.18, 1012.16, 1013.13
give one a kick 95.11, 105.15
give one a knuckle sandwich 457.13
give one a lesson 604.9
give one a lift 105.15
give one a lump in the throat 93.14
give one another chance 148.4
give one a pain 96.13, 98.14
give one a pain in the ass 98.14, 118.6
give one a pain in the butt 98.14
give one a pain in the neck 98.14
give one a rain check 846.9
give one a red face 137.4
give one a reputation 662.14
give one a revelation 131.7
give one a scare 127.15
give one a send-off 188.16
give one a snow job 356.15
give one a tip 551.11
give one a tongue-lashing 510.17
give one a tough row to hoe 96.16
give one a turn 105.14, 127.15, 131.8
give one a whammy 27.16
give one carte blanche 430.15
give one goose-flesh 127.15
give one gray hair 96.16, 98.15, 1013.13
give one his comeuppance 506.5, 604.10
give one his desserts 506.5, 604.9
give one his gruel 604.10
give one his head 426.3, 430.15
give one his just desserts 506.5, 604.9
give one leeway 430.15
give one line 430.15
give one pause 931.18
give one room 430.15
give one rope 430.15
give one's best 504.12
give one's best regards 504.12
give one's blessing 143.11, 696.14
give one's blessing to 441.2
give one's compliments 504.12
give one's countenance to 449.14
give oneself 449.18
give oneself airs 140.6, 141.8, 157.7, 501.14
give oneself for 509.13
give oneself over to 112.16
give oneself over to pleasure 743.22
give oneself up 125.10, 433.6
give oneself up to 112.16, 359.8, 404.3, 669.4, 983.5
give oneself up to reverie 985.9
give one's eyeteeth for 100.17
give one's fair share 478.14
give one's hand to 563.15
give one short shrift 442.5
give one's imprimatur 332.12
give one's kingdom in hell for 100.17
give one's life for one's country 307.24
give one's love 504.12
give one's mind to 983.5
give one some skin 585.10
give one space 430.15
give one's parole 436.4
give one's regards 504.12, 585.10
give one's right arm for 100.14
give one's share 478.14
give one's support to 449.14
give one's thanks 150.4
give one's undivided attention 983.8
give one's voice for 332.8
give one's walking papers 909.20
give one's word 436.4, 957.9
give one's word of honor 436.4
give one the ax 909.20
give one the beady eye 157.3
give one the boot 909.20
give one the creeps 74.7, 127.15
give one the evil eye 27.16
give one the finger 454.3
give one the fish eye 27.16
give one the fish-eye 157.3
give one the freedom of the house 585.9
give one the glad eye 27.14
give one the hairy eyeball 157.3
give one the lie 955.6
give one the lip 142.8
give one the red carpet treatment 646.8
give one the runaround 368.7
give one the sack 909.20
give one the slip 369.9
give one the stink eye 157.3
give one the willies 74.7, 127.15
give one tit for tat 506.6
give one trouble 1013.13
give one what for 510.18
give one what is coming to him 506.5
give origin to 886.10
give out 13.5, 16.9, 21.5, 351.5, 352.11, 388.4, 393.26, 477.8, 478.12, 478.13, 909.24
give out a hint 551.10
give out a smell 69.6
give out with 524.22
give over 125.10, 370.7, 390.4, 433.8, 478.13, 857.6
give over to 387.13
give pain 26.7
give pause 133.10, 983.12
give permission 332.12, 443.9
give place 163.6
give place to 368.6, 862.4
give pleasure 95.6
give power 443.11
give prospect of 133.12
give publicity 352.15
give quarter 145.4
giver 478.11
give rain to 430.15
give reason for 341.10
give recognition 150.4
give refuge to 187.10
give release 120.6
give relief 120.5
give respite 120.6
give rise to 886.10, 892.12
give room for 443.9
give rope enough to 426.3
give salvation 685.6
give sanctuary to 187.10
give satisfaction 396.13, 457.13, 481.5, 658.4
give shelter to 187.10
give sign 348.5
give someone lip 454.4
give sorrow words 115.10
give special attention to 983.8
give support 449.12, 901.21
give surcease 120.6
give thanks 150.4, 696.12, 696.13
give the air 909.18
give the asking price 733.9
give the ax 909.20
give the battle cry 458.18
give the benefit of the doubt 600.12, 953.15
give the bird 508.10
give the Bronx cheer 508.10
give the bum's rush 773.5, 909.13
give the business 308.14, 356.19
give the chuck to 909.13
give the coat off one's back 485.3
give the cold shoulder 156.5, 157.5, 340.8, 909.17
give the cold shoulder to 368.6
give the come-on 377.5
give the coup de grâce to 395.12

give the cue 551.10, 989.19
give the devil 510.18
give the devil his due 600.12, 649.5
give the evil eye 513.5, 691.10, 1000.6
give the eye 27.14
give the facts 551.8
give the feeling of 33.10
give the finishing strokes 407.6
give the finishing touches 407.6
give the freedom of 430.15
give the game away 351.6
give the gate 447.4, 909.18, 909.20
give the glad hand 585.9
give the go-ahead 332.12, 443.9
give the go-by 156.6, 157.5, 157.6, 340.8
give the golden handshake 447.4
give the golden parachute 447.4
give the good word 552.11
give the go sign 443.9
give the green light 332.12, 443.9
give the high sign 399.5, 517.22
give the hook 909.13
give the kiss of death to 308.20
give the kiss-off 157.5
give the lie to 335.4, 958.4
give the malocchio 691.10
give the meaning 341.10
give the mind to 570.12, 931.10
give the nod 332.12, 371.14, 443.9, 517.22
give the nod to 862.7
give the OK 332.12
give the old heave-ho 909.13
give the once-over 27.14, 938.24, 938.26
give the pink slip 909.19
give the pleasure of one's company 221.8
give the quietus 308.18, 820.6
give the quietus to 395.12
give the raspberry 508.10
give the red-carpet treatment 155.5, 585.9
give the reins to 426.3, 430.15
give the runaround 368.7, 415.11
give the run of 430.15
give the shirt off one's back 478.12, 485.3
give the shock of one's life 131.8
give the short end of the stick 389.6
give the shoulder 157.5
give the show away 351.6
give the silent treatment 909.17
give the slip 368.7, 415.11
give the stick 604.12
give the third degree 938.22
give the word 420.8, 443.9
give the word of command 420.8
give the works 308.14
give thought to 931.11, 983.5
give three cheers 116.6
give thumbs up 332.12
give tick 622.6
give tidings of 552.11
give tit for tat 624.11, 863.4
give title to 629.3
give to 387.13, 478.14
give token 348.5, 517.17
give tongue 59.9, 60.2, 524.22
give top billing to 704.28, 997.15
give to the world 352.11
give to understand 953.18
give umbrage 152.21
give until it hurts 485.3
give up 125.10, 370.7, 374.3, 390.4, 433.7, 433.8, 448.2, 475.3, 522.11, 668.8, 930.10
give up alcohol 516.2
give up all expectation 125.10
give up all hope 125.10
give up as a bad job 370.7
give up hope 125.10
give up on 370.7
give up one's post 448.2
give up the ball 746.5
give up the crown 448.2
give up the ghost 307.18
give utterance 524.22
give vent to 351.5, 352.11, 524.21, 909.24
give voice 59.9, 60.2, 524.22
give voice to 352.13, 524.21, 576.14
give warning 399.5
give way 16.9, 112.16, 125.10, 182.53, 194.6, 393.23, 433.7, 468.2, 633.6, 802.9, 1047.7
give way to 427.6, 430.19, 433.9
give way to tears 115.12
give what-for 604.10
give with an open hand 485.3
give with both hands 485.3
give word 343.7, 551.8
give word for word 989.16
give words to 349.9, 532.4
giving (n) 143.4, 343.2, 478.1, 629.1, 643.2, 759.1 (a) 478.22, 485.4, 1047.9
giving back 481.1
giving birth (n) 1.1 (a) 1.4
giving forth 190.1
giving in 433.2
givingness 485.1
giving out 190.1, 477.2
giving over 433.2, 473.1
giving up 433.2, 473.1, 475.1
giving up the fort 433.2
giving voice 524.5
giving way 468.1
gizmo 1040.1, 1052.5
gizzard 10.20
glabrate 287.10
glabrescent 287.10
glabriety 287.1
glabrous 6.17, 287.10
glabrousness 287.1
glace 10.47
glacé 287.11, 1025.33
glaciable 1024.12
glacial 1023.14, 1024.14
glacial boulder 1059.5
glacial deposit 1059.6
glacial epoch 824.5
glacial lake 241.1
glacial movement 896.2
glaciarium 743.11
glaciate 1023.10, 1024.11
glaciation 1023.5, 1024.1, 1046.5
glacier 1023.5
glacieret 1023.5
glacification 1024.1
glacis 204.4, 237.2
glad 95.15, 95.16, 109.11, 109.16
gladden 95.9, 109.7
gladdening 109.16
glade 158.4, 243.1
glad eye (n) 27.3, 27.5 (v) 585.9
glad hand 585.9
glad hand, the 585.2
gladiate 285.13
gladiator 461.1
gladiatorial 458.20
gladness 95.2, 109.1
glad rags 5.10
gladsome 95.15, 109.11, 743.28
gladsomeness 109.1
Glad Tidings 683.4
glad tidings 552.2
glair 305.15, 1062.5
glairy 1062.12
glam 377.8
glamorize 662.13, 1016.15
glamorous 377.8, 662.19, 691.11, 1016.20
glamorousness 122.3
glamour (n) 97.2, 377.1, 662.6, 690.1, 691.1, 1016.5 (v) 691.8
glamour girl 1016.7
glamping 463.3
glance (n) 27.4, 73.1, 223.5, 517.15, 938.5, 1025.6 (v) 27.17, 73.7, 164.6, 223.10, 287.7, 517.22, 1025.23
glance at 27.17, 551.10, 938.26
glance neither to the right nor to the left 982.2
glance off 164.6
glance of the eye 27.4
glance over 570.13
glance through 570.13
glance upon 27.17
glancing (n) 73.1 (a) 218.6, 223.17
glancing light 1025.8
gland 2.23, 13.2, 293.5
gland disease 85.21
glanders 85.41
glandular 13.8, 93.17
glandular disease 85.21
glandulous 13.8
glans clitoridis 2.13
glans penis 2.13
glare (n) 27.5, 152.2, 352.4, 501.3, 510.8, 1025.4 (v) 27.16, 30.7, 31.4, 152.14, 348.7, 501.13, 1025.23
glare-eyed 28.12
glaring 31.7, 35.20, 247.12, 348.12, 501.20, 1025.32
glaring light 1025.4
glaring look 27.5
glary 1025.32
glasnost 612.7
glass (n) 16.7, 29.2, 29.4, 29.6, 195.1, 287.3, 317.8, 498.5, 742.2, 747.1, 1019.20, 1029.2, 1050.2, 1054.2 (v) 295.23 (a) 1029.5
glassblower 716.7
glass ceiling 980.4, 1012.1, 1012.5
glass cutter 716.7
glass decorator 716.7
glass design 712.16
glasses 8.12, 29.3
glass house 1050.2
glasshouse 228.12, 1069.11
glassiness 1029.1
glass jaw 1050.2
glasslike 1029.5
glasslikeness 1029.1
glassmaking 712.2
glass printing 713.4
glass wall 1012.1
glassware 8.12, 735.4, 1029.2
glasswork 1029.2
glassy 287.11, 522.20, 1025.33, 1029.5
Glathsheim 681.10
glaucescence 37.1, 39.1, 44.1
glaucescent 37.8, 39.4, 44.4
glaucoma 30.1, 85.14
glaucomatous 30.9
glaucous 37.8, 39.4, 44.4
glaucous-green 44.4
glaucousness 37.1, 39.1, 44.1
glaze (n) 10.40, 35.8, 287.2, 742.3, 1023.5 (v) 35.14, 66.4, 287.7, 295.23, 742.6, 1023.11
glaze and icing sugar 66.3
glazed 287.11, 522.20, 742.7
glazed doughnut 10.44
glazed frost 1023.5
glazed-over 522.20
glaze frost 1023.7
glaze icing sugar 66.3
glaze over 1023.11
glazer 716.7
glazing 35.12
glazomania 549.1
gleam (n) 248.4, 1025.2, 1025.5, 1025.6 (v) 33.9, 662.10, 1025.23
gleaming 287.11, 1025.30
gleaming smile 116.3
gleam in one's father's eye, a 886.7
gleam of hope 124.3
gleam of light 1025.6
gleamy 1025.30
glean 371.14, 472.11, 946.10, 1069.19
gleaning 472.2, 1069.15
gleanings 472.3, 557.4
glean knowledge 570.6
glebe 234.1, 698.9, 703.7
glee 95.2, 109.5, 708.14
glee club 708.18, 710.16
gleeful 109.15
gleefulness 109.5
gleeman 710.14
gleesome 109.15
gleet 2.24, 12.6
glen 237.7, 284.9
glen nymph 678.9

glib 504.17, 540.9, 544.8, 1014.13
glibness 504.5, 540.1, 544.1
glib tongue 415.6
glide (n) 177.16, 184.13, 194.4, 524.12 (v) 177.35, 182.54, 184.36, 194.9, 287.9, 821.5, 1014.10 (a) 524.30
glide-bomb 459.23
glide landing 184.18
glider 181.12
glider train 181.12
gliding (n) 177.16, 184.1 (a) 184.50
gliding joint 800.4
gliding machine 181.12
glim 1026.1
glimmer (n) 551.4, 1025.7 (v) 1025.24
glimmering (n) 551.4, 930.5, 1025.7 (a) 1025.35
glimmering goal 100.11
glimmer of hope 124.3
glimmerous 1025.35
glimmery 1025.35
glimpse (n) 27.4, 930.5 (v) 27.12, 27.17
glint (n) 1025.2, 1025.6 (v) 27.17, 1025.23
glinting 1025.30
glisk 1025.24
glissade (n) 194.4 (v) 177.35, 194.9
glissando 194.4, 708.30
glisten (n) 1025.7 (v) 1025.24
glistening 1025.35
glister (n) 1025.2, 1025.7 (v) 1025.24
glistering 1025.35
glitch 393.1, 410.5, 1003.2, 1012.6
glitchy 410.18
Glitnir 681.10
glitter (n) 501.3, 1025.7 (v) 501.13, 662.10, 1025.24
glitterati 578.6, 618.6
glittering (n) 1025.7 (a) 501.19, 1025.35
glittering generality 864.8
glittery 1025.35
glitz 33.2, 35.5, 498.3, 501.3, 545.1
glitzed-up 498.12
glitz up 498.8
glitzy 35.20, 498.12, 501.18, 501.19, 545.8
gloam (n) 315.3 (v) 1027.12
gloaming 315.3, 1027.2
gloat 502.9
gloating (n) 144.6, 502.4 (a) 502.13
gloat over 502.9
glob 257.10, 282.2
global 282.9, 772.7, 792.9, 794.9, 864.14, 960.2
global ecology 1072.1
global ecosystem 1072.1
Global English 523.4
globalism 864.1
globality 864.1
globalization 864.1
globalize 864.9
globalized 864.14
Global Positioning System 159.8, 573.1, 1071.1
global village 864.4
global warming 317.4, 1019.7
globate 282.9
globe (n) 282.2, 1028.3, 1073.10 (v) 282.7
globed 282.9
globe-girdler 178.1
globe-girdling 177.36
globelet 282.2
globelike 282.9
globe-shaped 282.9
Globe Theatre 704.14
globe-trot 177.21, 918.6
globe-trotter 178.1
globe-trotting (n) 177.1 (a) 177.36
globetrotting 918.4
globoid (n) 282.2 (a) 282.9
globose 282.9
globoseness 282.1
globosity 282.1
globular 282.9
globular cluster 1073.5, 1073.8
globularity 282.1
globular lightning 1025.17
globularness 282.1
globule 282.2, 320.1
globulin 2.25, 7.6
glocal 864.12
glocalization 611.8
glocalize 864.10
glochidiate 288.9
glomerate 770.21
glomeration 770.9
glomerulus 282.2
glom on to 472.9, 480.14
gloom (n) 112.7, 1027.3, 1027.4 (v) 110.15, 1027.9, 1027.12
gloom and doom 96.6, 112.3, 125.2
gloomful 1027.14
gloominess 112.7, 125.6, 1027.4
glooming (n) 315.3 (a) 1027.14
gloomster and doomster 112.14
gloomy 112.24, 125.16, 133.16, 319.8, 1027.14
gloomy Gus 112.13, 125.7
gloomy outlook 125.6
glop 80.8, 1062.5, 1062.8
gloppy 80.23, 810.15, 1062.12
Gloria 696.3
Gloria in Excelsis 696.3
Gloria Patri 696.3
glorification 509.5, 662.8, 685.3, 696.2
glorified 662.18, 679.6, 681.12, 685.8
glorify 509.12, 662.13, 685.5, 696.12
glorify the Lord 696.12
glorious 88.31, 247.9, 501.21, 662.19, 677.17, 999.15, 1016.20
gloriousness 1016.5
glory (n) 171.2, 247.2, 280.2, 501.5, 509.5, 646.1, 662.1, 662.6, 696.2, 997.2, 1025.4, 1025.14 (v) 116.5, 502.9
glory days 837.2
glory hole 197.17, 386.6
glory in 136.5
gloss (n) 276.1, 287.2, 341.3, 341.5, 342.1, 354.3, 376.1, 554.9, 556.2, 600.5, 1025.2 (v) 35.14, 287.7, 295.24, 341.11, 342.2, 354.16 (a) 35.22
glossal 62.10
glossarial 341.15, 871.9
glossarist 523.15, 556.4
glossary 341.3, 554.9, 554.12, 871.4
glossematic 518.12, 530.17
glossematics 530.1
glosseme 518.6
glossiness 287.1
glossing 35.12
gloss of novelty 841.1
glossographer 523.15, 526.15, 556.4
glossographic 526.20
glossographical 526.20
glossography 526.14
glossolalia 520.2, 522.7, 523.10, 689.6, 692.3
glossological 523.19
glossology 523.13, 527.1
gloss over 340.6, 346.6, 354.16, 376.4, 600.12
glossy (n) 714.5 (a) 287.11, 1025.33
glottalic airstream 524.12
glottalization 524.12
glottalized 524.30
glottal stop 524.12
glottis 524.18
glottochronological 523.19
glottological 523.19
glottology 523.13
glove (n) 5.31, 454.2 (v) 745.5
glove compartment 195.1
glove man 745.2
glove puppet 349.6
glover 5.33
glow (n) 17.4, 35.2, 41.3, 83.1, 314.3, 544.5, 1016.1, 1019.12, 1025.2 (v) 41.5, 83.6, 105.18, 105.19, 109.6, 662.10, 1016.16, 1019.22, 1020.17, 1025.23
glow discharge 1033.5
glower (n) 27.5, 110.9, 152.2 (v) 27.16, 110.15, 152.14
glowering 110.24
glowering look 27.5
glowing 35.16, 41.6, 41.9, 93.18, 95.16, 101.10, 105.22, 109.11, 544.13, 1016.20, 1019.27, 1025.30, 1025.39
glowing health 83.2
glowing smile 116.3
glowworm 1025.7, 1026.5
glue (n) 803.4, 1062.5 (v) 800.5, 803.9
glued 800.14
gluelike 1062.12
gluelikeness 1062.2
glue on 253.4
glue-sniffing 87.1
glue the mind to 931.10
gluey 803.12, 1045.12, 1062.12
gluiness 803.3, 1045.1, 1062.2
gluing 800.3
gluing-off 554.14
glum 110.24, 112.25
glume 310.19
glumness 110.8, 112.8
glut (n) 256.1, 892.5, 993.3, 994.1 (v) 8.25, 118.6, 672.4, 993.15, 994.4
gluteal 217.10
gluteal region 217.4
gluten 7.6, 803.4, 1062.5
gluten-free diet 7.13
glutenous 803.12, 1062.12
glutinose 1062.12
glutinosity 803.3, 1062.2
glutinous 803.12, 1062.12
glutinousness 1062.2
glut oneself 672.5
glut on the market 633.1
glutted 993.20, 994.6
glutting 672.6
glutton 8.16, 100.12, 311.22, 672.3
gluttonize 8.25, 672.4, 993.15
gluttonizing 672.6
gluttonous 8.31, 100.27, 669.7, 672.6, 993.16
gluttonousness 672.1
gluttony 8.1, 100.8, 654.3, 655.3, 669.1, 672.1, 993.1
glyceride 7.7
glycerin 1056.2
glycerinate 1056.8
glycerine 1056.2
glycerinize 1056.8
glycerol 1056.1
glycerolate 1056.8
glycerol-cholesterol 7.7
glyceryl ester 1056.1
glycogen 7.5
glyph 715.2, 715.3
glyphic 713.11, 715.7
glypt- 713.11
glyptic 713.12, 715.7
glyptical 713.12
glyptic artist 716.6
glypto- 713.11
glyptograph 715.3
glyptographer 716.8
glyptographic 713.12
glyptographic artist 716.6
G-man 576.10, 1008.15
gnarl (n) 265.1, 283.3, 310.11 (v) 60.4, 152.14, 265.5, 288.4, 294.4
gnarled 283.17, 288.8
gnarly 283.17, 288.8, 999.13, 1000.8
gnash (n) 8.2 (v) 8.27
gnasher 2.8
gnashing of teeth 152.3
gnash one's teeth 115.11, 152.14
gnat 258.7, 311.32
gnaw 8.27, 26.7, 393.21, 1044.7
gnaw at the root of 393.21
gnaw away 1044.7
gnawer 311.3
gnawing (n) 26.2, 26.5 (a) 26.10, 1044.10
gnawing of the bowels 26.5
gnawing pain 26.2
gneiss 1059.1
gnocchi 10.33

gnome 258.5, 678.6, 678.8, 974.1
gnomelike 678.17
gnomes of Zurich, the 729.1
gnomic 537.6, 974.6
gnomish 678.17
G-note 728.7
gnotobiotics 1070.1
gnu 311.5
go (n) 328.3, 330.7, 403.3, 457.3, 743.9, 825.1, 825.2 (v) 34.2, 158.9, 159.9, 161.7, 162.2, 168.2, 172.5, 177.18, 177.19, 188.6, 261.5, 307.18, 328.5, 395.23, 409.7, 761.12, 762.6, 889.7, 896.3 (a) 889.9
go aboard 182.35, 188.15, 193.12
go about 163.9, 177.23, 182.30, 384.5, 404.3, 914.5
go-about 178.2
go about one's business 724.10
go abroad 177.21
go across 521.5, 910.8
goad (n) 375.8 (v) 375.15, 902.11, 902.12, 1070.8
goading 375.5
goad on 375.16
go adrift 164.4
go after 166.3, 176.16, 382.8, 815.2, 835.3
go against 451.3, 457.16, 510.10, 779.4, 900.6
go against the current 162.4
go against the grain 96.14, 128.9, 288.5, 900.6
go aground 182.42
go ahead 162.2, 330.13, 392.7, 818.7
go-ahead (n) 162.1, 330.7, 441.1, 443.1, 509.1 (a) 162.6, 330.23
go-ahead, the 332.4
go ahead of 814.2
go ahead with 328.5
goal 186.5, 375.1, 380.2, 409.5, 749.1, 749.4, 749.6, 752.1, 752.3, 820.1
go a la canona 87.22
goal area 752.1
goalie 749.2, 752.2, 1008.9
goal judge 749.3
goalkeeper 749.2, 749.5, 752.2, 1008.9
goal kick 752.3
go all colors 105.19
goal line 746.1, 749.1, 749.4, 752.1
go all lengths 403.15, 407.7
go all out 174.9, 330.13, 360.7, 403.14, 407.7, 430.19, 725.9, 794.8
go all the way 75.21, 360.5
goalminder 749.2
goal mouth 749.4
go aloft fly aloft 184.38
go along 162.2, 177.18, 324.3, 332.9, 441.2, 765.5, 856.3
go along for the ride 769.7
go alongside 182.35, 203.4
go along with 332.9, 332.11, 422.7, 433.6, 441.2, 443.10, 450.4, 769.7, 788.6, 836.4, 899.3
go along with the crowd 332.9
goal-oriented 375.25
goalpost 746.1, 749.4, 752.1
goal posts 750.2
goaltender 749.2, 752.2, 1008.9
go amiss 410.15, 911.4, 975.9
go and do 328.6
go and get 176.16
go ape 105.17, 926.22
go ape over 101.7
go around 172.5, 209.6, 850.5, 914.4, 914.5, 914.6, 915.9, 991.4
go around and around 538.10
go around in circles 391.8, 914.5, 971.9, 1013.11
go around Robin Hood's barn 914.4
go around with 582.17, 587.9
go as 349.10, 527.13
go ashore 186.8
go as one pleases 418.4, 430.20
go ass over elbows 205.6
go astern 182.34
go as the crow flies 161.10, 268.7
go astray 164.4, 410.15, 538.9, 654.9, 688.8, 911.4, 975.9
go astray from 473.4
go-as-you-please 430.21
go at 177.19, 404.3, 459.14, 459.15
goat 311.5, 311.8, 311.12, 366.4, 508.7, 665.11, 862.3
go at a snail's pace 175.6
goatee 3.8
goateed 3.25
go at flank speed 182.21
go at full blast 174.9
go at full steam 174.9
go at full tilt 174.9
goat god, the 678.11
go at hammer and tongs 101.6
goatherd 574.7, 1070.3
goatish 75.27, 311.45, 665.29
goatishness 75.5, 104.2, 665.5
go at it ass-backwards 414.12
go at it hammer and tongs 457.17
go at it tooth and nail 457.17
go at large 430.18
go at liberty 369.7, 431.9
goatlike 311.45
go at the double 401.5
go at tooth and nail 101.6
go at warp speed 174.8
go away 34.2, 168.2, 171.5, 188.6
go AWOL 222.9, 368.10
go awry 975.9
gob 8.2, 183.1, 183.4, 244.2, 257.10, 282.2, 292.4, 770.9, 793.3
go back 163.6, 163.8, 217.8, 849.11, 859.5, 989.9
go back on 370.5, 445.2, 645.12
go back on one's word 370.5, 645.12
go back over 938.27, 989.9
go back to 221.9, 856.6, 859.6
go back to go 859.5
go back to square one 859.5
go back to the drawing board 163.7, 859.5
go backwards 163.5, 217.8
go bad 67.4, 393.22
go-bag 405.3
go bail for 431.5, 436.5
go bananas 105.17, 926.22
go bankrupt 410.9, 625.7
go bathing 182.56
go bats 926.22
gobbet 8.2, 248.2, 257.10, 282.2, 793.3
gobble 8.23, 60.5, 187.11, 388.3, 395.10, 672.4
gobble down 8.23, 672.4
gobbledygook 520.2, 522.7, 523.9, 545.2, 609.37
gobbler 76.8, 311.28, 672.3
gobble up 388.3, 395.10, 469.6, 954.6
gobbling (n) 8.1 (a) 100.27, 672.6
go beddy-bye 22.17
go before 165.2, 814.2, 816.3, 834.3, 845.6
go behind 163.5, 166.3
go belly up 307.19, 625.7, 1011.11
go below 182.47
go berserk 671.15, 810.10, 926.20
go beside 203.4
go between 213.6, 384.7, 466.6
go-between 213.4, 341.7, 353.1, 384.4, 466.3, 563.12, 576.4
go beyond 910.4, 993.9
go beyond belief 969.2
go beyond reason 969.2
go beyond the bounds of reason 969.2
go blank 704.31
goblet 8.12
goblin 127.9, 678.8, 680.8
go blind 30.8
go blooey 393.26
go bonkers 926.22
go bonzo 926.22
go broke 473.4, 625.7
gobs 247.4, 257.10, 618.3
gobsmacked 122.9
go bughouse 926.22
go bust 625.7
go by 527.13, 821.5, 867.3, 910.8
go-by 156.3
go-by, the 157.2
go by air 184.36
go by airline 184.36
go by fits and starts 851.2
go by plane 184.36
go by rail 177.33
go by ship 182.13
go by the board 182.45, 395.22
go by the book 973.11
go by the name of 527.13
go by the rule book 146.2
go camping 225.11
go-cart 179.6
go-carting 744.1
go clean counter to 900.6
Goclenian sorites 935.6
go cold turkey 87.22
go contra 335.4, 510.10
go contrary to 779.4
go counter to 327.6, 335.4, 900.6
go crabwise 172.5, 218.5
go crackers 926.22
go crazy 926.22
go cuckoo 926.22
God 677.2
god 659.5, 677.1
god 678.2
go dancing 705.5
god-awful 1000.8
godawful mess 810.3
godchild 438.7
goddamn 513.9
goddamned 513.9
goddaughter 77.7, 438.7
goddess 659.5, 677.1, 678.2
goddesslike 1016.18
go dead 410.16
go dead slow 175.6
go deaf 49.4
go deep 93.14
go deep into 938.25
godet 191.2
go-devil 179.16
godfather 76.10, 438.6
God-fearing 155.9, 692.9, 692.10, 953.21
God-fearing man 692.4
godforsaken 222.15, 261.9, 584.12
godforsaken place 261.4
God-given 478.24
Godhead 677.9
godhead 677.1
godhood 677.1
God Incarnate 677.11
go directly 161.10
go dirt cheap 633.5
godkin 678.3
God knows where 261.4
godless 695.17, 695.18
godlessness 694.1, 695.3
godlet 678.3
godlike 247.9, 662.18, 677.16, 678.16, 692.9
godlikeness 677.1, 692.2
godliness 653.1, 677.1, 685.1, 692.2
godling 678.3
godly 653.5, 677.16, 692.9
godly-minded 692.9
godly-mindedness 692.2
godmother 77.7, 438.6
go down 182.44, 194.5, 194.6, 367.8, 393.17, 410.11, 412.12, 754.4, 831.5, 953.20
go down for the count 754.4
go downhill 16.9, 194.5, 204.10, 393.17, 410.11, 1011.11
go down like a stone 367.8
go down on 75.23
go down on one's knees 137.7
go down on one's knees to 440.11
go downon strikes 745.5
go down swinging 745.5
go down the drain 163.5, 473.6
go down the tubes 163.5, 395.22, 473.6

go down with flying colors 360.6, 453.4
godparent 438.6
gods, the 678.1
God's acre 309.15
God's board 703.12
God's country 232.2
God's creation 312.7
godsend 472.7, 999.5
God's gift 140.1
godship 677.1
God's image 312.7
gods of the netherworld 680.5
godson 76.10, 438.7
Godspeed 188.4
God's penny 438.2, 624.1
God's throne 681.4
God's truth 973.4
God's will 963.7, 964.2
God the Holy Ghost 677.12
go Dutch 624.18, 790.5, 875.4
go easily 1014.10
go east 161.8
go easy 1014.12
go easy on 145.4, 427.5
goer 174.5, 178.1, 190.10
go even stephen 476.6
go even stephen with 477.6
go eyeball-to-eyeball with 451.5, 454.3, 492.10
go far 409.10
go far afield 969.2
go fast 162.2, 174.8
gofer 432.5, 577.3, 577.5
go fetch 176.16
goffer (n) 290.2 (v) 290.3
goffered 290.4
go fifty-fifty 468.2, 476.6
go fifty-fifty with 477.6
go fishing 382.10
go flat out 174.9, 403.13, 430.19
go for 101.6, 104.19, 161.9, 176.16, 349.10, 380.4, 449.14, 459.15, 954.6
go for a burton 307.19, 410.10
go for a drive 177.33
go for an airing 177.24
go for an outing 177.24
go for a ride 177.24, 177.33
go for a song 633.5
go for a spin 177.33
go for a Sunday drive 177.33
go for a walk 177.24, 177.29
go for broke (n) 458.7 (v) 359.8, 360.7, 403.13, 403.14, 407.7, 493.6, 972.12
go for it 403.7, 403.14
go for nickels and dimes 633.5
go for peanuts 633.5
go forth 188.8, 352.16
go for the brass ring 403.7, 457.13
go for the deck 184.41
go for the jugular 144.15, 671.11
go forward 162.2, 392.7
go free 369.7, 431.9
go from bad to worse 119.3
go from home 188.17
go from push to shove 119.3
go full speed ahead 182.21
go full speed astern 182.21, 182.34
go full steam ahead 330.13
go full tilt at 459.18
go gaga 101.7
go gangbusters 330.14
go get 176.16
go-getter 330.8, 726.1
go-getting (n) 330.7 (a) 17.13, 162.6, 330.23
goggle (n) 27.5 (v) 27.15, 28.9, 283.11 (a) 283.16
goggled 29.11, 283.16
goggle-eyed 28.12
goggle eyes 2.9, 27.9, 28.6
goggler 918.1
goggles 29.3, 1008.3, 1028.2
go-go 17.13, 430.24, 928.17
go-go dancer 705.3, 707.1
go great guns 409.7, 1010.7
go gunning for 938.30
go halfers 875.4
go halvers 476.6
go halves 476.6, 790.5
go halvsies 476.6, 624.18
go halvsies with 477.6
go hand in glove with 778.4
go hand in hand 836.4
go hand in hand with 450.4, 455.2, 769.7, 899.3
go hard with 96.19, 1011.8
go hat in hand to 440.11
go haywire 128.8, 393.26, 923.6
go head over heels 205.6
go hell-bent for leather 174.9
go hog wild 101.6, 105.17, 926.22
go home 163.8, 307.20
go home feet first 307.19, 307.20
go hungry 515.4
go hunting 382.9
go ill with 1011.8
go in 189.7, 270.11
go in advance 405.12, 814.2
go in business for oneself 159.17
go in circles 914.4
go in debt 623.6
go in for 328.8, 371.15, 404.3, 570.15, 866.4
going (n) 34.1, 162.1, 172.1, 177.1, 188.1, 307.1 (a) 172.8, 177.36, 307.32, 889.11
going about 552.15
going afoot 177.8
going against the current 900.1
going against the tide 900.1
going all the way 75.7
going along with 433.1
going around 552.15
going around in circles 971.24, 985.15
going ashore 186.2
going away 307.1
going back on 445.1
going backwards 172.2
going belly up 473.3
going between (n) 384.3 (a) 466.8
going both ways 75.10
going down of the sun 315.2
going for broke 493.3
going forward 162.1
going near 167.1
going off 307.1
going on (n) 172.2 (a) 405.22, 831.9, 889.11
going on all fours 177.17
going on foot 177.8
going out 190.2, 1022.2
going-out-of-business sale 734.3
going out with 104.5
going over 363.2, 849.2
going-over 510.6
going over to the opposition 363.2
going rate 630.2
goings-on 321.1, 330.1, 831.4
going steady 104.5
going strong 15.21, 1010.13
going the rounds 552.15
going through 849.2
going to bed with 75.7
going together 104.5
going to happen 840.3
going too far 355.1
going to pieces 393.45
going to the polls 609.18
going to the wall 473.3
going toward 167.1
go in harm's way 492.10, 493.6, 1006.7
go in hock 623.6
go in hock for 622.7
go in one ear and out the other 990.7
go in opposition to 451.3, 900.6
go in partners 805.4
go in partnership 805.4
go in pursuit of 382.8, 938.30
go in search of 938.30
go in the lead 165.2
go in the rear of 166.3
go in the tank 965.5
go into 189.7, 404.3, 476.5, 541.11, 556.5, 617.14, 796.3, 818.9, 861.6, 938.23
go into action 328.5, 404.3, 818.7
go into a funk 127.11
go into a huddle 541.10, 770.16
go into a tailspin 152.20, 184.40, 393.17
go into a tantrum 152.15
go into convulsions 116.8
go into decay 393.22
go into detail 766.6, 861.6, 865.9
go into effect 889.7
go in together 899.2
go into heart and soul 324.3
go into hiding 346.8
go into hysterics 105.16, 128.7
go into litigation 598.13
go into mourning 115.17
go into one's pocket 479.8
go into orbit 914.5, 1075.12
go into outer space 1075.12
go into partnership with 450.3
go into politics 609.39, 610.13
go into raptures 95.12
go into receivership 625.7
go into retirement 584.7
go into reverse 163.7
go into seclusion 584.7
go into shock 85.47
go into the money market 621.3
go into training 570.11
go in with 450.4
go it alone 430.20
goiter 85.21
go kaput 393.26
go-karting 756.1
go kerflooey 393.26
go lame 85.49
Golconda 618.4
gold (n) 43.1, 618.1, 728.1, 728.20 (a) 43.4, 1058.17
goldanged 513.10
goldarned 513.10
goldbrick (n) 175.5, 331.8, 340.5, 356.10, 368.3 (v) 340.7, 368.9
goldbricker 331.8, 368.3
goldbricking 331.4, 368.2
gold bullion 1058.3
gold card 622.3
gold certificate 728.5
gold-colored 43.4
Gold Cup Race 757.1
gold depository 729.13
gold digger 562.11, 1058.9
gold dust 87.7, 1058.3
golden 43.4, 133.17, 632.10, 708.48, 999.15, 1058.17
Golden Age 824.5
golden age 1010.4
golden-ager 304.2
golden calf 697.3
golden days 1010.4
golden dream 124.4
golden era 1010.4
Golden Gate 750.2
Golden Gloves 754.1
golden goose 618.4
golden-haired 37.9, 43.5
golden handcuffs 478.8, 624.4
golden handshake 448.1
golden handshake, the 447.2
golden jubilee 850.4
golden mean 246.1, 467.3, 668.1, 670.1
goldenness 43.1
golden oldie 842.6
golden opportunity 843.3
golden parachute 448.1, 624.4
golden parachute, the 447.2
golden rule 419.2, 636.2, 974.2
golden saying 974.1
golden season of life 301.1
golden silence 51.1
golden slumbers 22.4
golden syrup 66.2, 66.3
golden time 1010.4
golden-toned 708.48
golden-tongued 708.48
golden touch, the 618.5
Golden Twenties 824.5
golden vision 100.11
golden-voiced 708.48
golden wedding anniversary 850.4
golden years, the 303.5
golden-yellow 43.4
gold fever 1058.8

gold-filled 1058.17
Goldilocks 35.9
Goldilocks economy 731.7
gold medal 646.2
gold mine 386.4, 618.4, 1058.6
gold miner 1058.9
gold mining 1058.8
gold nugget 728.20
gold panner 1058.9
gold piece 728.4
gold plate 295.13
gold-plate 295.26
gold-plated 295.33, 632.11, 1058.17
gold rush 1058.8
gold standard 419.2, 659.4, 728.21
gold star 646.5, 646.6
golem 924.8
golf (n) 751.1 (v) 745.5
golf bag 751.1
golf ball 751.1
golf balls 759.8
golf bet 759.3
golf cart 751.1
golf clubs 751.1
golf course 310.7, 743.11, 751.1
golf equipment 751.1
golfer 751.2
golf glove 751.1
golfing 751.1
golfing grip 751.3
golf links 743.11
golf shot 751.3
Golgi apparatus 305.5
Golgotha 309.15
Goliard 178.2
Goliath 15.6
go light 517.15, 1026.4
go like 336.5
go like a bat out of hell 174.9
go like a flash 174.8
go like a sewing machine 1014.10
go like a shot 174.8
go like a streak of lightning 174.8
go like blazes 174.9
go like blue blazes 174.9
go like clockwork 1014.10
go like greased lightning 174.8
go like lightning 174.8
go like the wind 174.8
go long 737.23
go mad 926.21
go marketing 733.8
gomme 66.3
Gomorrah 654.7
gonadal 13.8
gonads 2.13
go native 226.4
gondola 179.15, 180.1, 383.8
gondolier 183.5
gondoliere 183.5
Gondwana 235.1
gone 16.12, 21.8, 21.10, 34.4, 125.15, 188.19, 222.11, 307.29, 388.5, 473.7, 762.11, 837.7
go near 167.3
gone astray 160.11
gone away 34.4, 188.19
gone bad 393.40
gone before 307.29
gone begging 99.9
gone but not forgotten 307.29
gone-by 837.7, 842.15
gone feeling 16.1
gone for a burton 307.29
gone glimmering 762.11, 837.7
gone goose 125.8
gone gosling 125.8
gone missing 160.11
goneness 21.1
gone off 188.19
gone on 101.11, 104.30
gone out 842.15
gone out of one's head 990.8
goner 125.8
gone the way of all flesh 307.29
gone to a better land 307.29
gone to a better place 307.29
gone to a better world 307.29
gone to dust 1051.11
gone to glory 307.29
gone to hell 125.15
gone to hell in a handbasket 125.15, 395.29
gone to kingdom come 307.29
gone to pot 395.29
gone to rack and ruin 395.28
gone to seed 310.43, 414.18, 486.9, 842.14
gone to the dogs 395.29, 654.14
gone to waste 486.9
gone to wrack and ruin 393.33
gone west 307.29
gonfalon 458.11, 647.7
gonfanon 647.7
gong (n) 54.4, 517.10 (v) 54.8
gonged 87.24
Gongoresque 533.9, 545.8
Gongorism 533.3, 536.1
Gongorist 533.5, 545.5
Gongoristic 533.9
gonidangium 305.13
go night-night 22.17
goniometer 278.4
goniometry 278.3
gonorrhea 85.18
go north 161.8
go nowhere 410.9
go nuts 101.7, 926.22
go nutso 926.22
gonzo (n) 868.3, 870.3, 870.4, 924.3 (a) 868.6, 870.11
goo 93.8, 1062.5
good (n) 387.3, 999.4 (a) 63.8, 81.5, 97.6, 133.17, 143.13, 413.22, 509.20, 637.3, 644.13, 649.7, 653.5, 677.17, 692.9, 729.18, 973.14, 973.15, 991.6, 995.5, 999.12
good, the 692.5
good and mad 152.30
good and ready 405.16
good and tired 21.7, 118.11
good angel 113.4, 678.12
good appearance 1016.3
good as gold 143.13, 632.10
good at 413.22, 413.27
good auspices 133.8
good behavior 321.2, 326.1, 504.3, 637.2
good bone structure 1016.3
Good Book, the 683.2
good break 1010.3
good breeding 504.4
good buy 633.3
goodbye 188.4
good call 403.1
good cards 759.10
good case 935.10
good cause 143.6
good chance 759.6, 843.3, 966.1, 968.1, 972.8
good character 509.4, 644.1
good cheer 109.1, 109.2, 124.1, 582.3
good citizen 659.3
good citizenship 321.2, 591.1
good color 662.2
good company 582.16
good condition 83.2, 765.3, 807.3
good conduct 637.2
good conscience 636.3
good constitution 83.2
good cry 115.2
good deal 247.4
good decision 403.1
good deed 143.7
good deportment 504.3
good digestion 83.2
good disposition 143.2
good ear 944.1
good eater 672.3
good effect 1016.3
good egg 653.2, 659.2, 999.6
good English 523.4, 530.1
good enough 107.12, 991.6, 999.20
good example 659.4
good eye 944.1
good faith 644.7
good-faith 644.14
good features 1016.3
good feeling 93.5, 95.1, 894.1
goodfella 483.4
good fellow 588.5, 659.1
good-fellowship 582.2
good figure 1016.3
good fist 547.5
good flavor 63.1
good folk, the 678.7
good footing 587.3
good for 7.21, 81.5, 387.18, 449.21, 630.14, 729.18
good for a laugh 488.4
good form 579.1, 580.3
good-for-naught (n) 331.9, 660.2 (a) 391.11
good-for-nothing (n) 331.9, 660.2 (a) 331.19, 391.11
good fortune 972.1, 1010.2
Good Friday 515.3
good friend 588.2
good genius 678.12
good graces 587.3
good grammar 530.1
good guy 659.2
good hair 1016.14
good hand 413.13, 547.5, 759.10
good hand at 413.27
good head for 413.5
good health 83.2
good hearing 48.3
goodhearted 143.13
goodheartedness 143.1
good hope 124.1
good humor 109.2, 143.2
good-humored 143.14
good-humoredness 143.2
good idea 932.6
goodiness 693.1
good influence 392.1, 894.6
good in parts 1003.4
goodish 413.22, 999.20
goodishness 999.3
good Joe 659.2
good judge 496.6
good judgment 920.7, 946.1
good karma 455.1
good life, the 1010.1
goodliness 97.1, 637.2, 999.1, 1016.2
good-looker 1016.8
good-looking 1016.18
good looks 1016.3
good loser 412.5
good lot 659.1
good luck 972.1, 1010.2
good-luck charm 691.5
good-luck piece 691.5
goodly 97.6, 257.16, 999.12, 1016.18
good man 644.8
good management 635.1
good-mannered 504.15
good manners 321.2, 504.3, 580.3
good memory 989.2
good mixer 582.16
good move 403.1
good name 662.2, 731.6
good nature 143.2
good-natured 97.7, 143.14
good-natured banter 490.1
good-naturedness 143.2
good neighbor 478.11, 659.3
good-neighbor policy 609.5
goodness 63.1, 81.1, 97.1, 143.1, 637.2, 644.1, 653.1, 692.2, 999.1
goodness of heart 143.1
Good News 683.4
good news 552.2
good night's sleep 22.4
good odor 662.2
good offices 143.7, 449.1, 466.1
good old days 837.2
good old summertime 313.3
good old times 837.2
good omen 133.8
good one 489.6
good opportunity 843.3, 972.8
good pennyworth 633.3
good person 592.1, 659.1
good point 865.4
good points 1016.3
good possibility 966.1, 972.8
good price 632.3
good prognosis 124.1
good proportions 1016.3
good prospect 124.1
good prospects 124.1
good reason 600.6, 935.10
good reasoning 935.10
good reference 662.2

good relation 775.1
good rep 662.1
good report 662.2
good reputation 662.2
good repute 662.2
good review 509.3
good riddance 398.1
good right arm 901.2
goods 4.1, 471.1, 735.1
goods, the 18.2, 413.4, 551.1, 973.4
good Samaritan 143.8, 478.11, 592.1
good sense 920.6, 925.1
goods for sale 735.1
good shape 83.2, 807.3, 1016.3
good shot 904.8
good side of, the 587.3
good-sized 257.16
good society 578.6
good soldier 492.7
good sooth 973.1
good sort 659.1
good spirits 109.2
good sport 412.5
good sportsmanship 649.2
good state of health 83.2
good stewardship 635.1
good story 489.6
goods train 179.14
good sum 618.2
good supply 991.1
good taste 63.1, 496.1, 533.1
good-tasting 63.8
good temper 106.1, 143.2
good-tempered 143.14
good-temperedness 143.2
good terms 587.3
good thing 999.5
good things of life 121.3
Good Tidings 683.4
good time 95.5, 109.5, 743.2, 843.3
good times 1010.4
good to eat 8.33, 63.8
good track record 662.2
good trim 83.2, 807.3
good turn 143.7
good understanding 587.3, 920.5
good use 387.1
good vibes 455.1
good vibrations 455.1, 788.3
good ways 261.2
good weather 317.3
goodwill 143.4, 324.1, 449.4, 449.10, 587.3, 731.6
Goodwill clothes 5.5
good will toward man 143.4
good wishes 149.1, 504.8
good woman 644.8
good word 509.3, 552.2
good work 143.7
good works 143.6
goody (n) 10.8 (a) 693.5
goody bag 478.4
goody good-good 500.18
goody-goodiness 693.1
goody-goodness 500.5
goody-goody (n) 77.10, 500.11 (a) 354.33, 500.18, 653.5, 693.5
goody-goodyism 500.5
goody two-shoes (n) 77.10, 500.11 (a) 354.33
gooey 93.21, 803.12, 1062.12
gooeyness 1062.2
goof (n) 414.9, 924.3, 975.6 (v) 410.14, 414.12, 975.15
goof around 175.8
goofball 414.9
goofballs 87.5
goofed-up 414.22
goofer 414.9
go off 53.10, 56.8, 67.4, 164.6, 171.5, 188.6, 393.17, 409.7, 671.14, 831.5
go off at a tangent 164.6, 171.5
go off at half cock 401.7, 406.6
go off base 654.9
go off half-cocked 135.4, 401.7, 406.6, 844.4, 845.6, 903.5, 947.2
go off in all directions at once 971.9
go off on a tangent 164.4, 278.5, 538.9
go off one's head 926.21
go off one's nut 926.22
go off one's rocker 926.22
go off soundings 182.19
go off the air 34.2, 1034.25
go off the deep end 105.17, 926.22, 993.10
go off the rails 410.15
go off the track 926.22
go off to sleep 22.16
go off with 769.7
goofiness 922.4, 923.1, 926.2
goofing 368.2
goofing off (n) 175.3, 331.4, 368.2 (a) 984.8
goof off 175.8, 331.12, 340.7, 368.9
goof-off 175.5, 331.8, 340.5, 368.3
goof-off time 402.1
goofproof (v) 15.14 (a) 1014.15
goof up 414.12
goofus (n) 414.9, 927.4 (a) 927.6
goofy 923.9, 926.27, 927.6
google 1042.21
googly 356.6
googly eyes 27.9
googol 882.13, 884.4, 1017.5
googolplex 882.13, 884.4, 1017.5
goo-goo (n) 143.8 (a) 693.5
goo-goo eyes 562.9
gook 1062.5, 1062.8
gooky 1062.12
go on 152.15, 162.2, 188.6, 321.4, 360.2, 409.12, 540.5, 765.5, 810.11, 827.6, 827.7, 831.5, 856.3, 856.5
goon 461.1, 593.4, 616.8, 671.10, 727.7, 727.8
go on a bender 88.28, 743.24
go on a binge 88.28, 743.24
go on about 101.7, 538.8, 856.5
go on a cruise 177.21
go on a crusade 458.16
go on a crusade against 458.14
go on a diet 7.19, 8.20
go on a fishing expedition 938.30
go on a honeymoon 563.16
go on a journey 177.21
go on a junket 177.21
go on all fours 177.26
go on all fours with 788.6
go on and on 823.2, 827.7, 829.6
go on an ego trip 140.6, 651.4
go on an expedition 177.21
go on a pilgrimage 177.21
go on a rampage 671.15, 810.10
go on a sightseeing trip 177.21
go on a spending spree 626.5
go on a spree 88.28, 743.24
go on a tour 918.6
go on a trip 976.8, 986.17
go on a voyage 182.13
go on a wartime footing 458.19
go on a wild-goose chase 391.8
go on a wrong tack 410.15
go on bended knee to 440.11
go on board 188.15, 193.12
go once over lightly 340.8
go one better 249.6, 415.11, 999.11
go one-on-one with 451.5, 454.3, 492.10, 999.11
go one's own way 430.20
go one's way 188.6
go on forever 118.6, 823.2, 829.6
go on furlough 20.9, 222.8
go on hands and knees 177.26
go on holiday 222.8
go on horseback 177.34
go on leave 20.9, 222.8
go on one's beat 1008.20
go on over 101.7
go on parade 177.30, 812.7
go on safari 177.21
go on shipboard 182.13, 188.15
goon squad 727.7
go on strike 727.10, 857.8
go on the air 1034.25
go on the blink 393.26
go on the bum 177.23
go on the defensive 460.10
go on the fritz 393.26
go on the heel and toe 177.27
go on the merry-go-round 743.24
go on the road 177.21
go on the rocks 410.9, 625.7, 1011.10
go on the shoals 1011.10
go on the stump 543.9
go on the town 743.24
go on the wagon 516.2, 668.8
go on the warpath 458.15
go on tick 622.7
go on tiptoe 177.26
go on vacation 222.8
go onwards and upwards 193.8
go on welfare 619.5
go on with 856.5
go on with the show 856.5
goop 1062.5
goopy 1062.12
goose (n) 311.28, 759.16, 924.6 (v) 375.15
gooseboy 1070.3
goose bumps 74.4, 127.5, 288.2
goosebumps 1023.2
goose call 517.16
goosedrownder 316.2
goose egg 762.3
gooseflesh 74.4, 127.5, 288.2, 1023.2
goosegirl 1070.3
goose grass 285.5
gooseherd 1070.3
gooseneck 759.16
goose pimples 74.4, 288.2, 1023.2
goose step 177.13, 867.1
goose-step (v) 177.30, 867.4 (a) 365.11, 373.14
goose up 17.10
goosey 24.12
goosiness 127.3
goosing 375.5
goosy 127.23, 311.48
go out 158.9, 190.12, 261.5, 307.18, 390.9, 727.10, 820.7, 1022.8, 1027.12
go out for 328.8, 404.3, 744.2
go out like a lamb 670.5
go out like a light 25.5
go out of bounds 868.4
go out of business 293.8, 625.7
go out of one's depth 493.5, 1006.7
go out of one's gourd 926.22
go out of one's skull 128.8, 926.22
go out of one's tree 926.22
go out of one's way 339.7, 403.11, 425.4, 649.5, 914.4
go out of one's way to avoid 157.7
go out of print 34.2
go out of style 842.9
go out of the way 164.3, 403.11, 652.3
go out of use 842.9
go out on a limb 493.5, 951.11, 1006.7
go out on strike 857.8
go out the window 395.22
go out with the ebb 307.18
go out with the tide 168.2
go over 177.20, 363.6, 363.7, 409.7, 570.12, 704.32, 849.8, 938.22, 938.24
go over again and again 849.9
go over and over 849.9
go over big 95.7, 409.7
go overboard 182.45, 993.10
go over like a lead balloon 117.4, 410.10
go over one's head 522.10, 522.11, 984.5
go overseas 177.21
go over step by step 938.25
go over the board 182.45
go over the ground 177.20
go over the hump 87.22
go over the same ground 849.8
go over the side 182.45
go over the top 193.11, 459.18
go over the wall 431.8
go over to the enemy 645.15
go over to the great majority 307.20
go over to the majority 307.20

go over with a bang 95.7, 409.7
go over with a fine-tooth comb 938.25
goozle 2.19
go partners 450.3
gopher 1042.18
go phut 410.13
go pit-a-pat 55.4, 105.18, 916.12, 917.12
go pitter-patter 55.4
go places 409.10
go places and do things 743.24
go public 120.7, 738.12
go public with 352.11, 352.15
gorbellied 257.18
gorbelly 257.12
Gordian knot 799.2, 1013.7
gore (n) 2.25, 191.2, 308.1 (v) 292.15, 459.26
gorge (n) 2.18, 237.7, 293.3 (v) 8.25, 672.4, 993.15, 994.4
gorged 993.20, 994.6
gorge oneself 8.25
gorgeous 35.19, 501.20, 1016.20
gorgeousness 35.4, 501.3, 501.5, 1016.5
gorger 672.3
gorging (n) 8.1 (a) 672.6
Gorgon 690.9
go right through 1023.10
gorilla 15.7, 308.11, 461.1, 593.4, 671.10
gorilla pills 87.5
goring 292.3
gorked 87.24
gormand 672.3
gormandize 672.4
gormandizer 672.3
go round 172.5, 209.6, 850.5, 914.5, 915.9
go-round 850.2, 914.2
go round about 538.10, 914.4
go roundabout 914.4
go round again 849.11
go round and round 914.5
go round Robin Hood's barn 538.10
go round the bend 926.22
gory 2.33, 41.7, 308.24, 1004.11
go scot free 369.7, 431.9
go scot-free 430.18
go separate ways 771.8, 802.19
go shares 476.6, 790.5
gosh-awful 1000.8
goshdarn 513.10
Goshen 986.11
go shopping 733.8
go short 737.24
go sideways 172.5, 218.5
go sign 443.1
gosling 302.10, 311.28
go slow 162.4, 175.6, 402.4
go-slow 175.10, 846.17
go slowly 175.6
go-slow policy 609.4
go slumming 918.6
go so far as to 640.6
go soft 16.9
go soft at the edges 32.4
go solo 872.6
go sour 67.4
go south 161.8, 410.11
Gospel 683.11
gospel (n) 552.2 (a) 683.11
gospel (n) 953.3, 973.3 (a) 973.13
Gospel, the 683.4
gospel, the 973.4
Gospels 683.4
Gospel side 220.1
gospel song 696.3
gospel truth 687.1, 973.3
gospel truth, the 973.4
gossamer (n) 271.1, 298.2 (a) 248.7, 270.16, 271.7, 294.8, 764.6, 986.22, 1029.4
gossameriness 270.4, 294.3, 298.1, 1029.1
gossamery 16.14, 271.7, 294.8, 298.10, 764.6, 1029.4
gossip (n) 354.11, 540.3, 541.4, 551.4, 552.7, 552.9, 588.3, 981.2 (v) 354.16, 540.5, 541.9, 552.12
gossip column 552.8
gossip columnist 552.9
gossiper 552.9
gossiping (n) 552.7 (a) 552.14
gossipmonger 551.5, 552.9
gossipmongering 552.7
gossipry 552.7
gossipy 343.10, 540.9, 552.14, 981.5
go steady 562.14
go step by step 494.5
go straight 161.10, 277.4, 392.9
go straight on 161.10
go straight to the point 161.10
go swimming 182.56
gotcha question 552.3, 938.10
Goth 497.7
Gothamite 921.6
go the distance 15.11, 360.5, 827.6
go the dizzy rounds 743.24
go the extra mile 324.3, 339.7, 425.4, 649.5
go the limit 360.7, 403.14, 407.7, 669.5, 794.8
go the long way around 914.4
go the other way 682.7
go the round 914.5
go the rounds 177.23, 352.16
go the same round 849.8
go the the mat with 451.4
go the way of all flesh 307.18
go the whole hog 359.10, 360.7, 794.8
go the whole length 403.15, 407.7
go the whole nine yards 359.10, 360.7
go the whole way 407.7, 794.8
Gothic 497.12, 842.13, 930.13, 986.20
Gothicism 497.3, 930.3
Gothis 198.6
go through 189.8, 328.7, 486.3, 626.5, 704.32, 831.8, 938.31, 1023.10
go through a change 852.6
go through channels 867.4
go through fire and water 360.5, 403.15, 492.10, 1006.7
go through hell 96.19
go through hell and high water 360.7
go through one 93.14
go through one's paces 501.16
go through one's part 704.32
go through phases 854.5
go through the length and breadth of the land 352.16
go through the motions 354.21
go through the roof 152.17
go through the school of hard knocks 570.10
go through with 328.5, 827.6
go through with it 360.5
go tit-for-tat 777.7
go to 177.25, 221.8, 261.6
go to a better land 307.20
go to a better life 307.20
go to a better place 307.20
go to a better world 307.20
go to Abraham's bosom 307.20
go to a funeral 115.10
go to all lengths 407.7, 794.8
go to and fro 916.13
go to an extreme 993.10
go to any length 360.5
go to any lengths 360.5
go to a watery grave 307.23
go to bat for 449.13, 600.10, 901.21, 1008.18
go to bed 20.6, 22.17
go to bed betimes 22.13
go to bed with 75.21
go to bed with the chickens 20.8
go to Davy Jones's locker 182.44, 307.23
go to do 404.3
go toe-to-toe 457.13
go to extremes 355.3, 993.10
go to foreign places 177.21
go to foreign shores 177.21
go to get 176.16
go together 769.7, 788.6
go to glory 307.20, 395.24
go to great lengths 101.6, 339.7, 403.15
go to great pains 339.7
go to ground 346.8
go-to guy 577.3
go to hell 395.24, 682.7
go to hell in a handbasket 395.24
go to it 725.15
go-to-itiveness 330.7
go to kingdom come 307.20
go to law 598.13
go to loggerheads 457.17
go to make up 796.3
go too far 493.5, 910.9, 993.10
go to one's head 88.22, 140.7, 926.23, 985.8
go to one's heart 93.14
go to one's last home 307.20
go to one's long account 307.20
go to one's rest 307.20
go to one's reward 307.20
go to perdition 395.24
go to pieces 16.9, 128.7, 393.22, 395.22, 802.9
go to pot 395.24, 473.6, 625.7, 1011.11
go to press 548.18
go to rack and ruin 395.24, 806.3
go to rest 20.6
go to ruin 395.24, 625.7
go to school 570.11
go to sea 182.13, 182.19
go to sea in a sieve 493.5, 1006.7
go to seed 395.24, 473.6, 1011.11
go to shivers 395.24
go to show 957.8
go to sleep 22.16
go to smash 395.24, 410.12
go to smithereens 395.24
go to Tap City 473.4
go to the bad 393.16, 395.24, 654.9
go to the bathroom 12.12
go to the bitter end 360.5
go to the bottom 182.44, 367.8
go to the deuce 395.24
go to the devil 395.24, 682.7
go to the dogs 395.24, 473.6, 625.7, 654.9, 1011.11
go to the electorate 609.40
go to the expense of 626.5
go to the happy hunting grounds 307.20
go to the mat with 457.13
go to the other place 682.7
go to the polls 371.18
go to the toilet 12.12
go to the trouble 403.11
go to the voters 609.40
go to the wall 307.19, 395.24, 410.9, 625.7
go to town 330.14, 409.7
go to war 457.13, 458.15
go toward 167.3, 169.2
go to waste 473.6
go to windward 182.25
go treat 624.19
gotten on the wrong side of the blanket 674.7
gouache 35.8, 35.12, 712.13
gouge (n) 284.6, 289.1, 290.1 (v) 30.7, 284.15, 289.4, 290.3, 292.15, 356.19, 632.7
gouged 290.4
gouge out 192.10, 284.15, 292.15
gouging (n) 632.5 (a) 632.12
goulash 10.11
go under 395.24, 410.11, 412.12, 625.7
go under a false name 527.13
go under an alias 346.8
go under an assumed name 527.13
go under false pretenses 354.22
go underground 346.8
go under the knife 91.29
go under the name of 527.13
go unrestrained 430.19
go up 193.8, 251.6, 395.24, 625.7, 671.14
go up against 457.15, 457.16
go up blind alleys 538.9

go uphill 204.10
go up in flames 1020.23
go up in one's lines 990.5
go up in smoke 34.2, 410.13, 473.6, 828.6, 911.3, 1020.25
go up like a rocket and come down like a stick 410.13
go upon 404.3
go up the nose 68.5
go up the spout 395.22
go up the wall 126.6, 128.8
go up to with hat in hand 894.9
gourmand 8.16, 496.6, 663.3, 672.3
gourmandise 8.1, 672.2
gourmandism 672.2
gourmandizer 672.3
gourment dining 8.1
gourmet (n) 8.16, 496.6, 663.3 (a) 8.33, 63.8
gourmet eating 8.1
gourmet food 10.8
gourmet quality 63.1
gout 85.22
goût 62.1, 63.2
gouty 85.61
govern 417.13, 428.7, 573.8, 612.11, 894.8
governability 433.4
governable 433.14
governance 417.5, 573.1, 612.1, 1008.2
governess 571.2, 575.2, 1008.7
governing 417.15, 573.12, 612.17
governing board 567.12, 574.11
governing body 574.11
governing organization 755.1
government 231.5, 417.5, 573.1, 609.2, 612.1, 1008.2
government, the 612.3
government agency 613.2
governmental 609.43, 612.16
governmentalism 609.4, 612.7
governmental leadership 609.3
government archives 549.2
government by committee 450.1
government circles 612.3
government control 609.4
government employee 575.15
government holiday 850.4
government issue 385.4
government-issue 609.44
government man 1008.15
government mark 517.13
government note 728.5
government office 739.1
government of the people 612.4
government papers 549.2
government stamp 517.13
government surplus 256.4
governor 429.10, 560.9, 574.1, 575.6, 575.12, 610.2, 1008.3, 1008.6, 1041.14
governor, the 560.10
governor-general 575.12
governorship 417.7, 417.10, 573.4
governor's mansion 228.5
go wading 182.56
go way back 587.9
go well 1010.7
go west 161.8, 307.19
go whole hog 407.7, 669.5
go wild 330.14
go with 223.12, 328.5, 332.9, 371.13, 404.3, 769.7, 788.6, 899.3
go without 668.7
go without saying 348.7, 970.9
go with the crowd 867.4
go with the current 332.9, 578.10
go with the flow 107.5, 331.15, 578.10
go with the party 609.41
go with the stream 138.11, 162.3, 578.10
go with the tide 578.10, 867.4, 1014.12
gowk 414.9, 924.4
gown (n) 5.3, 5.16, 702.2 (v) 5.40
gowned 5.45
gownsman 726.4
go woolgathering 985.9
go wrong 132.3, 393.25, 395.24, 410.15, 654.9, 688.8, 975.9
goy 688.6
goyim 688.6
goyish 688.10
grab (n) 480.2 (v) 101.6, 472.9, 480.14, 480.18, 640.8, 745.5, 931.19, 983.13
grab all of 469.6
grab at 101.6
grab bag 759.14, 797.6
grabbiness 651.1
grabbing 480.2
grabble 938.32, 1069.19
grabby 100.27, 472.15, 480.26, 651.5
graben 237.7
grab hold of 480.14
grab one 931.18
grab some R and R 20.8
Grace 648.2
grace (n) 677.15, 685.3, 696.4, 709.18, 999.1, 1016.1 (v) 662.12, 1016.15
grace (n) 97.2, 143.2, 143.4, 143.7, 145.1, 148.2, 150.2, 413.1, 478.7, 496.1, 533.1, 544.2, 601.1, 601.3, 636.5 (v) 498.8
graceful 413.22, 413.23, 496.8, 504.13, 533.6, 544.9, 1016.17
graceful gesture 504.6
gracefulness 496.1, 504.1, 533.1, 544.2, 1016.3
graceless 414.20, 534.2, 654.18, 695.18, 1015.9
gracelessness 414.3, 534.1, 695.4, 1015.1
grace note 708.27, 709.18
grace of expression, the 532.2
grace period 625.2
graces 500.1, 501.2, 504.7
Graces, the 1016.9
grace under pressure 106.2
grace with 478.17
gracile 270.16, 496.8, 533.6, 1016.17
gracility 270.4, 496.1, 533.1, 535.1, 1016.3
graciosity 427.2, 496.1
gracious 97.6, 143.13, 427.8, 485.4, 496.8, 504.13, 581.3, 585.11, 587.16
gracious life 1010.1
gracious living 496.1, 1010.1
graciousness 97.1, 143.1, 427.2, 485.1, 496.1, 504.1, 581.1, 585.1
grad 572.8
gradate 808.11
gradation 245.3, 524.13, 607.1, 807.2, 808.3, 812.2
gradational 245.5
grade (n) 204.4, 245.1, 572.11, 607.1, 760.3, 809.2 (v) 201.6, 204.10, 245.4, 257.15, 287.5, 300.10, 808.11, 809.6, 944.4, 1043.4
grade A (n) 999.8 (a) 999.14
Grade B movie 706.1
grade crossing 170.2
graded 808.14, 809.8
graded school 567.3
grade insignia 647.5
grade point average 568.7
grades 568.7
grades, the 567.3
grade school 567.3
grade schooler 572.3
gradient (n) 200.5, 204.4 (a) 193.14
gradient wind 318.1
gradin 703.12, 901.14
grading 245.3, 568.7, 809.1
grad student 572.8
gradual 175.10, 245.5
gradual change 852.1, 861.1
gradualism 175.1, 245.3, 392.5, 861.3
gradualist 392.6
gradualistic 392.16
gradual revelation 861.2
graduate (n) 413.11, 572.8 (v) 245.4, 257.15, 300.10, 392.7, 409.7, 446.2, 944.4 (a) 568.19, 572.12
graduate assistant 571.4
graduated 245.5
graduated cylinder 278.4, 1060.6
graduate degree 570.3
graduated scale 300.2
graduated taxation 630.9
graduate-professional 568.19
graduate school 567.5
graduate student 572.8
graduation 245.3, 446.1, 580.4
graduation exercises 580.4
gradus 554.8, 554.10, 871.4
graffito 546.5, 712.12
graft (n) 191.1, 191.2, 356.8, 378.1, 482.1, 482.11, 609.34, 609.35 (v) 191.6, 800.7, 1069.17
grafter 483.1, 610.5
grafting 191.1
Graf Zeppelin 181.11
graham cracker 10.30
grain (n) 10.4, 248.2, 258.7, 294.1, 310.5, 310.31, 767.4, 809.3, 978.3, 1051.6 (v) 35.14, 294.4, 1051.9, 1051.10
grain bin 386.7
grain broker 730.9
grain-eater 8.16
grain-eating 8.31
grained 294.6
grain elevator 386.7
grain-fed 257.18
graininess 294.2, 1051.2
grain of salt 959.1
grain of sand 258.7, 1059.2
grainy 288.6, 294.6, 1051.12
grallatorial 182.58
gramarye 690.1
gramfer 560.14
gramicidin 86.29
graminaceous 310.42
graminaceous plant 310.5
gramineous 310.42
gramineous plant 310.5
graminivore 8.16
graminivorous 8.31
grammalogue 546.2
grammar 523.14, 530.1, 532.1, 554.1, 554.10, 568.3, 818.6
grammarian 523.15, 526.15
grammarless 930.13
grammar school 567.3, 567.4
grammatic 523.19
grammatical 523.19, 530.17
grammatical analysis 530.1
grammatical error 975.7
grammatical gender 530.10
grammaticality 530.1
grammatical meaning 518.1
grammaticalness 530.1
grammatical theory 530.1
grammaticaster 523.15, 929.6
grammaticize 530.16
grammatist 523.15
grammy 560.16
gram-negative bacteria 85.42
gramophone 50.11
gramp 560.14
grampa 560.14
gramper 560.14
gram-positive bacteria 85.42
gramps 304.2, 560.14
granary 386.7
grand (n) 728.7, 882.10 (a) 136.12, 247.6, 257.16, 501.21, 544.14, 662.18, 997.17, 999.12
grandam 304.3, 560.15
grandaunt 559.3
grand ballroom 197.4
grandchild 561.3
grandchildren 561.1
grand climacteric 303.7
grand cordon 646.5
granddad 560.14
granddada 560.14
granddaddy 560.14
grand dame 607.4
granddaughter 77.7, 561.3
grand design 792.3
grand drape 704.16
grand duchess 575.10, 608.6
grand duchy 232.1
grand duke 575.8, 608.4
grande dame 500.10
grandee 607.4, 608.4
grandeur 136.2, 247.1, 257.6, 501.5, 544.6, 662.5

grandfather (n) 76.10, 304.2, 560.13 (v) 430.14
grandfather clause 430.8
grandfathered 430.30
grandfathered rights 430.2
grandfatherhood 560.1
grandfathering 430.8
grandfatherly 560.17
grand finale 820.1
grandiloquence 355.1, 501.7, 526.10, 532.2, 545.1
grandiloquent 355.4, 501.22, 545.8
grandiose 501.21, 545.8
grandioseness 545.1
grandiosity 257.6, 501.5, 545.1
grandisonant 545.8
grand jeté 366.1
grand juror 596.6
grand jury 596.5
grand juryman 596.6
Grand Lama 699.14
grand larceny 482.2
grandma 560.16
grandmamma 560.16
grandmammy 560.16
grand master 413.13, 417.7
grandmaternal 560.17
grandmother 77.7, 304.3, 560.15
grandmotherhood 560.1
grandmotherly 560.17
Grand National 757.1
grandnephew 559.3
grandness 247.1, 257.6, 501.5
grandniece 559.3
grand opera 708.34
grandpa 76.10, 560.14
grandpap 560.14
grandpapa 560.14
grandpappy 560.14
grandparent 560.8
grandparentage 560.1
grandparental 560.17
grandparenthood 560.7
grandparents 560.7
grandpaternal 560.17
grandpop 560.14
grand prior 699.16
grandsire 304.2, 560.13
grand slam 409.5, 411.1, 758.3
grand-slam home run 745.3
grand-slammer 745.3
grandson 76.10, 561.3
grandstand (n) 27.8, 48.6, 745.1 (v) 413.20, 501.16
grandstander 501.11
grandstanding 501.1
grandstand player 501.11
grand style, the 532.2, 712.7
grand theft 482.2
grand total 792.2
grand tour 177.5, 918.4, 1075.1
granduncle 559.3
grand unified theory 1018.1
grand vizier 575.7
granfer 560.14
grange 228.6, 1069.8
granger 1069.5
granite 1046.6, 1059.1
granitelike 1046.10, 1059.11
graniteware 735.4
granitic 1046.10, 1059.11
granivore 8.16
granivorous 8.31
granma 560.16
grannam 560.16
granny 304.3, 495.7, 560.16, 842.8
granny chic 5.1
granny flat 228.13
granny glasses 29.3
grant (n) 417.12, 443.5, 478.1, 478.8, 642.2, 646.7, 959.1 (v) 332.11, 351.7, 441.2, 443.9, 478.12, 951.10, 959.5
grant absolution 148.3, 601.4
grant a decree of nullity 566.5
grant a divorce 566.5
grant a final decree 566.5
grant amnesty 601.4
grant amnesty to 148.3
grant an annulment 566.5
grant a reprieve 601.5
grant bail to 431.5
grant citizenship 226.4
granted 332.14, 478.24, 951.14
granted for the sake of argument 951.14
grantee 479.4
grant exemption 148.3
grant forgiveness 148.3
Granth 683.7
granther 560.14
grant immunity 148.3, 430.14, 601.4
grant-in-aid 478.8
granting 478.1
grantor 478.11
grant remission 148.3, 601.4
granular 258.14, 294.6, 1051.12
granularity 294.2, 1051.2
granular snow 1023.5, 1023.8
granular sweetener 66.3
granular texture 294.1
granulate (v) 288.4, 294.4, 396.21, 1046.8, 1051.9, 1051.10 (a) 1051.12
granulated 288.6, 294.6, 1046.13, 1051.12
granulated sugar 66.2, 66.3
granulation 288.1, 294.2, 1035.5, 1046.5, 1051.2, 1051.4
granulator 1051.7
granule 248.2, 1051.6, 1059.6
granulet 1051.6
granulization 1051.4
granulize 1051.9
grape 310.4
grape, the 88.17
grape ranch 1069.10
grapery 1069.10
grapes of wrath 152.5
grapevine 310.4, 551.6, 552.6, 552.10
grapevine, the 551.5
grapevine telegraph 552.10
graph (n) 47.4, 381.3, 546.1, 712.12, 801.4 (v) 381.10, 801.7
graphanalysis 547.3
grapheme 523.14, 546.1
graphemic 523.19, 546.8
graphemics 546.3
graphic 349.13, 349.14, 544.10, 547.22, 712.21
graphic abbreviation 557.1
graphic account 349.2
graphical 547.22
graphic artist 713.1, 716.3, 716.8
graphic arts 548.1, 712.1, 712.16, 713.1
graphic design 713.1
graphic designer 713.1
graphic narration 722.1
graphicness 544.1
graphic panel 1041.16
graphics 713.1, 1042.18
graphic scale 159.5
graphics design 717.5
graphics printer 1042.9
graphics tablet 1042.2
graphics terminal 1042.9
graphing 381.1
graphite 1056.2
graphite racket 748.1
graphite rubbing 1044.2
graphitic 1058.15
graphoanalytic 547.22
graphoanalytical 547.22
graphologic 547.22
graphological 547.22
graphologist 547.14
graphology 547.3
graphomania 547.2, 718.2
graphomaniac 547.25
graphomaniacal 547.25
graphometer 278.4
graphometric 547.22
graphometrical 547.22
graphometrist 547.14
graphometry 547.3
graphorrhea 547.2, 718.2
graphoscope 1042.2
graphospasm 547.2
graphotype 713.5
graph paper 47.6
graphy 546.1
grapple (n) 474.2 (v) 457.13, 474.6, 480.14, 800.7
grappler 461.3
grapple with 451.4, 457.13, 457.17, 492.10
grappling 457.10
grasp (n) 158.2, 474.2, 612.2, 901.11, 928.3 (v) 474.6, 480.14, 521.7, 803.6, 928.12
graspability 521.1
graspable 521.10, 928.25
grasp by the lapels 440.12
grasped 928.26
grasping (n) 100.1, 100.8 (a) 100.27, 421.9, 472.15, 474.8, 480.26, 651.5
graspingness 100.8, 651.1
grasp the meaning 521.7
graspy 100.27, 480.26, 651.5
grass (n) 44.1, 87.11, 310.5, 310.8, 748.1 (v) 957.9
grass court 310.7, 748.1
grass-cutting 184.8
grass-eater 8.16
grass-eating 8.31
grass green 751.1
grass-green 44.4
grasshopper (n) 311.35, 366.4 (a) 406.15
grassland 233.1, 234.1, 236.1, 310.8, 1069.8
grasslike 310.42
Grassmann's law 524.13
grassplot 310.7
grassroots (n) 199.1, 233.1, 607.7, 886.5 (a) 199.8, 606.8, 798.6, 997.23
grassroots campaign 609.13
grassroots movement 609.33
grass skiing 753.1
grass surface 748.1
grasstrack 756.1
grass veld 236.1, 310.8
grass widow 566.2
grass widower 566.2
grasswidowhood 566.1
grassy 44.4, 310.36, 310.42
grate (n) 170.3, 292.8, 808.5, 1020.11, 1020.12 (v) 26.7, 58.10, 61.3, 96.14, 170.7, 1044.7, 1051.9
grated 170.11, 1051.11
grateful 97.6, 150.5, 585.12
grateful dead 988.1
gratefulness 150.1
grate on 58.11, 96.14, 128.9
grater 1051.7
grate upon the ear 58.11
gratification 95.1, 107.1, 427.3
gratified 95.15, 107.7
gratify 8.18, 95.8, 97.5, 107.4, 136.6, 427.6
gratifying 97.6, 585.12
gratify oneself 651.4
grating (n) 170.3, 808.5, 1020.12, 1051.4 (a) 26.13, 58.16, 61.4, 61.5, 128.15, 789.6
gratis 634.5
gratitude 150.1
gratuitous 142.10, 324.7, 478.24, 634.5, 810.12, 993.17
gratuitousness 324.2, 634.1
gratuity 150.2, 378.2, 478.5, 634.1, 993.5
gratulant 149.3
gratulate 149.2
gratulation 149.1
gratulatory 149.3
graupel 1023.6
gravamen 518.1, 767.2, 792.6, 997.6
gravamen of a charge 599.1
grave (n) 307.1, 309.16, 549.12 (v) 549.15, 713.9, 715.5, 989.17 (a) 26.10, 38.9, 54.11, 106.14, 111.3, 112.24, 136.12, 247.6, 297.16, 544.14, 580.8, 661.12, 997.20
grave, the 682.1, 839.2
grave affair 997.3
grave as an undertaker 111.3
graveclothes 309.14
graved 713.11
gravedigger 284.10, 309.8
grave injustice 650.4
gravel (n) 383.6, 1051.6, 1054.2, 1059.3, 1059.6 (v) 96.14
gravel-blind 28.13
gravel-blindness 28.2
gravelish 294.6
gravelliness 1051.2

gravelly 54.11, 288.7, 294.6, 1051.12, 1059.12
gravelstone 1059.4
graven 713.11, 715.7, 855.13
graveness 38.2, 997.3
graven image 697.3
graveolence 71.1
graveolent 71.5
grave pit 309.16
graver 713.8, 716.6, 716.8
grave robber 483.1
grave-robbing 482.10
graverobbing 192.2
graveside 309.22
graveside oration 115.6
graveside service 309.4
grave sin 655.2
gravesite 309.16
gravestone 309.17, 549.12
graveyard 309.15
graveyard shift 825.3
graveyard vote 371.6
gravid 78.18
gravidity 78.5
gravidness 78.5
gravimetric analysis 801.1
graving 517.5, 713.2
gravisphere 297.5
gravitas 111.1, 136.2, 544.6, 580.1, 997.3
gravitate 194.5, 297.15
gravitate toward 896.3
gravitation 194.1, 297.5, 907.1
gravitational 297.20
gravitational astronomy 1073.19
gravitational collapse 1073.8
gravitational field 297.5
gravitational pull 297.5
graviton 297.5
gravity (n) 106.4, 111.1, 112.7, 136.2, 297.1, 297.5, 544.6, 580.1, 907.1, 997.1, 997.3 (a) 904.17
gravity dam 1012.5
gravity-defying 193.14
gravity wave 238.14
gravity wind 318.1
gravlax 10.24
gravure 548.1
gravy 472.6, 478.5, 624.6, 728.2, 1061.2, 1062.5
gravy train 618.4
gray (n) 35.9, 39.1, 311.11, 1037.6 (v) 39.3 (a) 36.7, 39.4, 112.24, 303.16, 781.6
gray area 467.3, 539.1, 819.2, 971.8
grayback 311.36
graybeard 39.2, 304.2
gray-bearded 39.5, 303.16
gray-black 39.4
gray-brown 39.4
gray-colored 39.4
gray-crowned 303.16
gray-drab 39.4
grayed 39.4
gray eminence 415.8, 610.6, 894.6
gray goods 1042.2
gray hair 3.3
gray-hair 39.2
gray-haired 39.5, 303.16
gray-haired person 39.2
gray hairs 303.5
gray-headed 39.5, 303.16
gray-headed person 39.2
gray-hued 39.4
graying temples 3.3
grayish 39.4
grayish-brown 40.3
grayishness 39.1
gray literature 547.10
gray market 732.1
gray marketeer 732.4
gray matter 919.1, 919.6
grayness 36.2, 39.1, 303.5, 315.2
gray noise 52.4
gray of the evening 315.2
gray out 25.5, 184.46
grayout 25.2, 184.21
gray-speckled 39.4
gray-spotted 39.4
gray-toned 39.4
grayware 1042.11
gray water 391.4
gray-white 37.8
gray with age 303.16
gray with fear 127.26
graze (n) 73.1, 223.5 (v) 8.18, 8.28, 73.7, 223.10, 570.13, 733.8, 902.18, 1035.15, 1044.7
graze by 223.10
grazer 311.3
graze the surface 276.4
grazier 1070.2
grazing (n) 8.1, 73.1, 310.8, 1044.2, 1070.1 (a) 73.12, 223.17
grazing country 233.1
grazing land 310.8
grazing region 233.1
grease (n) 478.5, 511.1, 728.2, 1056.1 (v) 287.5, 378.3, 1014.7, 1056.8
grease-burner 11.3
greased 287.12
greased lightning 174.6
greased palm 375.7
grease gun 1056.7
grease job 1056.6
grease monkey 185.6, 1040.12
grease one's palm 375.23
greasepaint 704.17, 1016.11
grease pit 1056.7
grease rack 1056.7
grease the palm 378.3, 624.16
grease the ways 1014.7
grease the wheels 1014.7, 1056.8
greasiness 287.1, 1056.5
greasing 1014.5, 1056.6
greasing of the wheels 449.5
greasy 287.12, 1056.9
greasy grind 572.10, 726.3, 929.4
greasy spoon 8.17
great (n) 247.1, 413.14, 711.17 (a) 78.18, 247.6, 249.14, 257.16, 417.15, 652.6, 662.18, 997.17, 999.12
great, the 997.8
great abundance 991.2
great ado 1013.3
great age 842.1
Great American novel 718.1
great attractor 1073.6
great-aunt 559.3
great beauty 1016.7
great beyond, the 839.2
great big 257.20
Great Britain 232.4
great calorie 1019.19
great cause 886.9
great circle 280.3, 1073.16
great-circle course 277.2
greatcoat 5.13
great cost 632.1
great deal 247.4
great distance 261.2
Great Divide 272.5
Great Divide, the 261.4, 307.1
great doings 743.4, 997.5
great effort 725.1
greaten 259.5
greatening 251.1
greater 249.12, 272.19
greater city 230.1
greater gods, the 678.1
greater number, a 883.1
greater number, the 883.2
greater part 883.2
greatest 247.13, 249.13, 999.16
greatest, the 249.4
greatest common divisor 883.4
greatest common factor 883.4
greatest good of the greatest number 143.4
greatest hits 708.33
greatest number, the (n) 883.2 (a) 883.9
great expectations 124.1
great friend 588.2
great fun 743.2
great go 938.2
great-grandaunt 559.3
great-grandchildren 561.1
great-grandfather 560.13
great-grandmother 560.15
great-granduncle 559.3
great heart 485.1, 652.2
greathearted 143.15, 485.4, 492.16, 652.6
greatheartedness 143.4, 485.1, 492.1, 652.2
great hereafter, the 839.2
great honor 646.1
great house 228.7
great hundred 882.8
great idea 932.6
great lady 575.2
great leveler 307.2
greatly daring 454.7
great majority, the 307.16
great man 997.8
Great Mother 677.8
greatness 78.5, 247.1, 249.1, 257.1, 257.6, 417.4, 652.2, 662.5, 997.2
greatness of heart 652.2
greatness of soul 652.2
greatness of spirit 652.2
great octave 709.9
great of heart 652.6
great of soul 652.6
great one for 101.5
great out-of-doors, the 206.3
great person 662.9
Great Plains 231.7
great plenty 991.2
great point 997.6
great price 632.2
great reach 247.1
great reader 572.1
great respect 155.1
great room 197.5
greats 938.2
great satisfaction 95.1
great scale 709.6
great scope 247.1
great sea 240.1
great seal 647.3
Great Society 609.6
great soul 659.6, 921.1
great-souled 652.6
great-sounding 545.8
Great Spirit, the 677.2
great-spirited 652.6
great success 409.3
great talker 540.4
great-uncle 559.3
great unknown, the 839.2
great unnumbered, the 606.2
great unwashed 497.6
great unwashed, the 606.2
great value 632.2
great wall of galaxies 1073.6
great white throne, the 681.4
Great White Way, the 704.1
great wind 318.11
great with child great with young 78.18
great woman 997.8
great work 554.1
great wrong 650.4
great year 824.4
grec 759.22
Greco-Roman wrestling 457.10
greed 100.8, 651.1, 655.3, 672.1
greediness 100.8, 672.1
greedy 100.27, 472.15, 651.5, 672.6
greedy as a hog 100.27
greedy eater 672.3
greedygut 672.3
greedyguts 672.3
greedy pig 100.12
Greek 198.6, 522.7, 617.11
greek 759.22
Greek and Roman deities 678.4
Greek archaeology 842.4
Greek calends 822.2
Greek chorus 704.10
Greek Corinthian 198.6
Greek Ionic 198.6
Greek kalends 822.2
Greek mode 709.10
Greek Orthodox Church 675.9
Greek theater 704.14
Greek to one 522.13
green (n) 35.13, 44.1, 310.7, 728.2, 750.3, 751.1 (v) 44.3 (a) 44.4, 67.5, 83.13, 153.5, 209.9, 301.10, 310.36, 406.11, 414.17, 841.7, 841.10, 930.11, 954.9, 989.22
green apple 67.2
green around the gills 36.7, 85.57

green as grass 44.4, 414.17
greenback 478.19
greenbacks 728.6
greenbelt 230.6
Green Berets 461.15
green blindness 30.3
green-blue 44.4
green book 549.8
green bowling 750.3
green building 266.2
green card 443.7
green cloth 759.16
green energy 17.1, 1021.1
greener 358.2
greener pastures 124.1
greenery 310.1, 310.18
green-eyed 153.5, 154.3
green-eyed monster 153.1
green flash 1025.6, 1025.10
green goods 728.10, 735.7
greengrocer's apostrophe 546.4
greenhorn (n) 358.1, 414.7, 572.9, 774.4, 818.2, 930.7 (a) 374.4
greenhornism 930.1
greenhouse 228.12, 1069.11
greenhouse effect 1019.7
greenhouse gas 1001.4
greenhouse plant 310.3
greenie 87.4
green in the eye 153.1, 930.1
greenish 44.4
greenish-blue 44.4
greenishness 44.1
greenish-yellow 43.4, 44.4
Greenland 235.1, 261.4, 1023.4
green light 441.1, 443.1, 509.1, 517.15, 1026.4
green light, the 188.2, 332.4
greenmail 737.19
Green Man 678.11
green man 1069.4
greenness 44.1, 67.1, 301.3, 406.4, 414.2, 841.1, 930.1, 954.2
Green Panther 1072.3
Green Party 609.24
green plant 310.3
green plants 310.1
green revolution 860.1, 1069.1
greenroom 197.20, 704.16
greens 10.35, 10.37, 310.1
greensick 44.4
greensickness 44.1
greenstick fracture 85.38
green stuff 728.2, 728.6
greensward 310.6
green thumb 1069.6, 1069.12
Greenwich mean time 832.3
Greenwich time 832.3
green with envy 154.3
green with jealousy 153.5
greeny 358.2, 818.2, 930.7
greenyard 310.7
greet 524.26, 585.10
greeter 585.5
greeting 524.3, 585.4
greeting card 553.3
greetings 186.4, 504.8, 585.3
greet the day 23.6
greet with a kiss 585.10
greet with skepticism 955.6
grefa 87.11
gregal 318.8
gregale 318.8
gregarious 540.9, 582.22
gregariousness 540.1, 582.1
gregau 318.8
grege 40.3
Gregorian calendar 832.8
Gregorian chant 708.20
Gregorian mode 709.10
greige (n) 39.1 (a) 39.4
gremlin 678.8, 680.7, 1012.6
grenade 462.20
grenade launcher 462.21
grenadier 272.7, 461.9
Grenadier Guards 461.15
grep 1042.18
greyhound 174.6
grid (n) 170.3, 704.16, 1020.12, 1035.5 (v) 170.7
gridded 170.11
griddle (n) 1020.12 (v) 11.5
griddlecake 10.45
grid emission 1033.5
gridiron 170.3, 704.16, 743.11, 746.1, 1020.12
grid line 159.5
gridlock 173.3, 293.3, 1012.1
grid start 756.3
grief 96.5, 96.6, 98.5, 112.10, 113.1, 1011.2
grieful 112.26
griefless 114.4
grief-stricken 112.26
grievance 96.8, 115.4, 152.4, 333.2, 650.4, 1000.3, 1001.1
grievance committee 333.2
grieve 96.17, 98.14, 112.17, 112.19, 115.10, 145.5, 152.21
grieved 96.23, 112.26
grieve for 147.2
griever 115.8, 309.7
grieve with 147.2
grieving (n) 115.1 (a) 115.18
grieving heart 112.9
grievous 98.20, 112.26, 145.8, 1000.9, 1011.15
grievousness 98.5, 112.11
griffe 797.8
griffin 647.2
griffonage 547.6
grift 356.8, 415.3, 759.13
grifter 759.22
grig 382.10
grill (n) 8.17, 10.7, 10.13, 1020.12 (v) 11.5, 604.15, 938.22
grill, the 938.13
grille 170.3
grilled 11.7
griller 1020.12
grilling (n) 11.2, 938.13 (a) 1019.25
grillroom 8.17
grillwork 170.3
grilse 311.29
grim 96.20, 98.19, 110.24, 111.3, 112.21, 112.24, 125.12, 127.30, 144.24, 361.9, 425.6, 1000.8, 1015.7
grimace (n) 110.9, 265.4, 917.3 (v) 26.8, 99.5, 110.15, 265.8, 704.31
grimace at 510.10
grimacer 707.5
grimalkin 311.20, 593.7
grime (n) 80.6 (v) 80.15
grim-faced 111.3, 1015.7
griminess 38.3, 80.1
Grimm's law 524.13
grimness 96.1, 98.3, 110.8, 111.1, 112.2, 112.7, 127.2, 144.9, 361.2, 425.1
grim reality 761.2
Grim Reaper 307.2
grim-visaged 111.3, 1015.7
grimy 38.11, 80.22
grin (n) 116.3 (v) 116.7
grin and abide 134.7
grin and bear it 109.10, 134.7, 433.6, 492.14
grin at 508.8
grinch 112.14, 1012.9
grind (n) 58.3, 570.3, 572.10, 725.4, 726.3, 929.4 (v) 8.27, 26.7, 58.10, 285.7, 287.8, 547.21, 570.12, 612.15, 725.14, 802.13, 1044.7, 1051.9
grind, the 373.5
grind away 827.6
grind down 612.15
grinder 2.8, 10.32, 1040.6, 1051.7
grind house 706.7
grind in 375.14, 568.12
grinding (n) 570.3, 1044.2, 1051.4 (a) 26.13, 58.16, 98.24, 417.16, 725.17, 1044.10
grinding halt 857.2
grinding pain 26.2
grind on 827.6, 856.3
grind one's teeth 152.14
grind organ 711.14
grind out 718.6, 892.8
grindstone 1051.7
grind to a halt 857.7
grind to dust 1051.9
grind to powder 1051.9
grind up 1051.9
grin like a Cheshire cat 116.7
grin like a chessy-cat 116.7
grinning (n) 116.3, 508.1 (a) 508.12
grinning skull 307.2
grip (n) 17.5, 413.1, 417.5, 474.2, 612.2, 748.2, 750.2, 901.11, 917.6, 928.3 (v) 474.6, 480.14, 926.25, 983.13
grip car 179.17
gripe (n) 26.5, 115.5, 612.2, 619.2 (v) 26.7, 96.13, 108.6, 115.16
griped 96.21
griper 108.3, 108.4, 115.9
gripes 26.5
griping (n) 115.5 (a) 26.10, 26.12, 108.7, 108.8, 115.20
gripman 178.12
grip of iron 474.2
grip of steel 474.2
gripped 926.33, 983.18
gripping 474.8, 926.34, 983.20
grisaille 39.1
grisard 39.2
Griselda 134.3
Griselda-like 134.9
griseous 36.7, 37.7, 39.4
griseousness 36.2
grisette 665.14
grisliness 127.2, 307.11, 1015.2
grisly 127.30, 307.28, 1015.11
grist 386.2, 1051.5, 1054.1
grist for the mill 386.2
gristle 1049.2
gristly 1049.4
grit (n) 294.2, 359.3, 492.5, 1051.6 (v) 96.14
gritless 491.11
gritlessness 491.2
grit one's teeth 359.8
grits 10.2, 1051.5
gritted teeth 359.3
grittiness 294.2, 492.5, 1051.2
gritty 294.6, 359.14, 492.18, 1046.10, 1051.12, 1059.12
grizzle (n) 3.3, 311.11 (v) 37.5, 39.3, 110.14, 115.14 (a) 39.4
grizzled 37.7, 39.4, 39.5
grizzled veteran 413.16
grizzliness 37.1
grizzling 37.3
grizzly 37.7, 39.4
grizzly bear 110.11
groan (n) 58.3, 115.3, 115.4 (v) 58.9, 115.13, 115.15, 318.20
groaning 115.4
groaning board 8.9
groat 248.2, 728.8
groats 1051.5
grocer 385.6, 736.1
groceries 10.2, 10.5, 735.7
grocery 10.5, 735.7
grocery list 871.1
grocery store 736.1
grody 98.18
grog (n) 88.13 (v) 88.24
grog blossom 88.3
groggery 88.20
groggy 16.16, 173.14, 985.14
grogshop 88.20
groin 2.13, 171.4, 901.4, 1009.6, 1012.5
grok 343.6, 521.8, 934.4
grokking 343.1
Grolier 554.15
grommet 280.5
gronk 80.7
groom (n) 563.5, 1070.2 (v) 79.20, 568.13, 808.12, 1070.7
groomed 405.16
groomer 571.6
grooming 568.3
groomsman 563.4, 616.6
groove (n) 224.2, 290.1, 373.5, 383.2, 548.6, 756.3 (v) 224.4, 284.15, 290.3, 713.9
grooved 290.4, 713.11
groove on 95.13
groovy 578.15, 928.17, 999.13
grope 223.10, 938.32, 971.9
grope for 938.32
grope in the dark 30.8, 930.9, 938.32
groping 930.11, 938.37
gross (n) 472.3, 627.1, 751.3, 882.8 (v) 472.12, 627.4 (a) 64.7, 80.23, 98.18, 247.12, 257.18,

269.8, 294.6, 310.43, 497.11, 505.6, 534.2, 661.12, 663.6, 666.8, 792.9, 922.15, 1000.8, 1000.9
gross amount 792.2
gross behavior 505.1
gross body 689.18
gross credulity 954.1
gross domestic product 472.5
gross error 975.3
gross exaggeration 350.2
gross falsehood 354.12
gross-headed 922.16
gross ignorance 930.1
gross income 624.4, 627.1
gross injustice 650.4
gross interest 623.3
gross lift 184.26
grossly overpriced 632.12
gross national product 731.7, 731.9, 892.1, 893.1
grossness 80.2, 98.2, 257.8, 269.2, 294.2, 497.2, 505.1, 534.1, 661.3, 663.2, 666.3, 922.3, 1000.2
gross one out 64.4
gross out 98.11, 99.6
gross profit 472.3
gross profit margin 627.1
gross receipts 627.1
gross weight 297.1
gross-witted 922.16
grot 284.5
grotesque (n) 712.9 (a) 265.12, 870.13, 923.11, 986.20, 1015.8
grotesqueness 870.3
grotesquerie 870.3
grotto 284.5
grotty 80.23, 1015.6
grouch (n) 108.4, 110.11, 115.9, 1012.9 (v) 108.6, 110.14, 115.16
grouchiness 110.3
grouchy 108.8, 110.20, 115.20
ground (n) 35.8, 159.2, 199.3, 199.4, 201.3, 209.2, 212.3, 231.1, 234.1, 275.4, 375.1, 463.1, 600.6, 712.18, 886.1, 901.6, 935.7, 957.1 (v) 159.16, 182.42, 210.5, 428.9, 429.12, 568.10, 745.5, 855.9, 913.5, 1032.29 (a) 199.7, 1051.11
ground bait 356.13, 377.3
ground ball 745.3
ground-based observatory 1073.17
ground bass 708.22
ground beef 10.14
groundbreaker 816.1
groundbreaking 404.8
ground cloth 295.9
ground clutter 1036.12
ground combat 457.4
ground-controlled approach 184.19
ground control of aircraft 1036.9
ground cover 310.17, 310.33
ground covering 199.3
ground crew 185.5
ground down 432.16
grounded 428.13, 429.19, 766.8, 855.13, 855.16, 1013.27
grounded on 901.24, 957.16
ground-effect machine 179.22, 181.7
ground elevation 184.35
ground engineer 185.6
grounder 745.3
ground floor 197.23, 845.1
ground fog 319.3
ground forces 461.23
ground frost 1023.7
ground glass 1028.4
ground hard and fast 182.42
groundhog 133.5, 284.10, 311.22
ground ice 1023.5
grounding 405.1, 568.5, 604.5
groundless 764.8, 936.13, 958.8
groundless rumor 552.7
ground-level 199.7
groundling 48.6, 312.5, 497.6, 704.27
ground log 174.7
ground loop 184.8, 184.16
groundman 1032.22
ground on 199.6
ground one's arms 465.11
ground out 745.5
ground plan 381.1, 381.3
groundpounder 461.10
ground rent 630.8
ground rule 419.2
grounds 223.1, 256.2, 310.7, 471.6, 600.2, 600.6, 886.1, 901.6, 935.5, 957.1, 959.2
ground school 184.1
groundsel 901.9
grounds for belief 957.1
grounds for war 456.7
groundsheet 295.9
groundskeeping 1069.2
ground speed 174.1, 184.31
ground state 1033.3
ground swell 238.14, 609.33
ground test 1074.1
ground tester 185.6
ground troops 461.23
groundwater 1065.3
groundwater pollution 1072.2
ground wave 1034.11
groundwork 405.1, 818.6, 901.6
ground zero 1038.16
group (n) 244.2, 617.1, 617.6, 675.3, 710.12, 712.7, 770.3, 770.7, 784.5, 809.2, 1060.2 (v) 257.15, 770.16, 770.18, 801.8, 808.11, 809.6
group analysis 92.6
group dynamic 375.1
grouped 808.14, 809.8
group effort 449.2
group grope 75.7
group hug 562.3
groupie 101.5, 697.4
grouping 617.1, 617.6, 712.8, 770.3, 770.7, 770.9, 801.3, 808.3, 809.1, 809.2
group memory 989.1
groupment 770.3, 770.7
group of advisers 423.1
group practice 90.13
group pressure 609.29
group psychology 92.6
group sex 75.7
group shot 714.8
group therapy 926.19
groupware 1042.11
groupy 166.2
grouse (n) 115.5 (v) 108.6, 115.16
grouser 108.3, 115.9
grousing (n) 115.5 (a) 108.8, 115.20
grout 295.25
grove 284.9, 310.14, 770.7
grovel 138.7, 177.26, 201.5, 274.5, 433.10, 665.19, 913.9, 915.13
groveler 138.3
groveling (n) 138.2, 913.3 (a) 138.14, 201.8
groves of Academe, the 567.5
grow 14.2, 251.6, 259.7, 272.12, 303.9, 310.34, 761.12, 861.5, 892.9, 1069.16, 1070.6
grow apart 589.7, 802.8
grow better 392.7
grow bright 1025.27
grow cold 1023.9
grow dark 1027.12
grow dim 1027.12
grower 892.7, 1069.5, 1069.6
grow fat 1010.8
grow from 887.5
grow hair 3.20
growing (n) 892.2, 1069.12 (a) 14.3, 251.8, 259.12, 301.10
growing like a mushroom 251.8
growing like a weed 14.1
growing old 303.17
growing pains 301.7
growing season 313.3
growing up 14.1, 259.3
grow into 858.17
growl (n) 54.2, 56.4, 58.3 (v) 56.9, 58.9, 60.4, 115.15, 152.14, 318.20, 524.25
growler 108.3, 1023.5
grow light 1025.27
grow like a weed 14.2, 259.7
growling (n) 54.2 (a) 54.12, 60.6, 108.7, 110.19
grow lush 310.34
grown 14.3, 259.12, 303.12, 892.17, 892.18
grown man 304.1
grown old 842.13
grown old in years 303.16
grown-up 14.3, 259.12, 303.12
grownup 304.1
grown-upness 303.2
grown woman 304.1
grow old 303.10, 304.6, 842.9
grow on 104.22
grow on one 104.22, 373.10
grow out of 14.2, 259.7, 887.5
grow over 910.5
grow pale 36.6, 127.11
grow red 41.5
grow rich 618.10, 1010.9
growth 14.1, 85.9, 85.39, 251.1, 259.3, 303.6, 310.2, 310.32, 731.10, 858.1, 861.1
growth factor 7.3
growth force 306.2
growth fund 737.16
grow thick 269.5
growth regulator 7.3
growth ring 310.11
grow to 803.6
grow together 800.11, 803.6
grow uncontrollably 14.2, 259.7
grow up 14.2, 193.8, 259.7, 272.12, 303.9, 407.8
grow weak 16.9
grow weaker 16.9
grow weary 21.5
grow whiskers 303.10, 842.9
grow worse 119.3, 393.16
grrr 54.2
grub (n) 10.2, 302.12, 726.3 (v) 284.15, 725.14
grubbery 10.2
grubbies 5.20
grubbiness 80.1, 810.6
grubbing (n) 472.2 (a) 725.17
grubby 80.22, 810.15, 910.11
grub out 192.10
grubstake (n) 729.2 (v) 729.16
grubstaker 729.10
Grub Street writer 547.16, 718.5
grub up 192.10, 472.9, 938.34
grudge (n) 99.2, 103.1, 152.4, 589.5 (v) 154.2, 325.3, 442.4, 484.5
grudgeful 507.7
grudgefulness 507.2
grudge match 451.1
grudging (n) 154.1 (a) 154.3, 325.6, 484.8, 589.10
grudging consent 325.1
grudgingness 154.1, 325.1
grudging thanks 151.1
gruel (n) 16.7, 270.7, 1062.5 (v) 16.10
grueling 16.20, 21.13, 604.22, 725.18, 1013.18
gruelly 65.2
gruesome 127.30, 307.28, 1015.11
gruesomeness 127.2, 307.11, 1015.2
gruff 58.15, 110.19, 505.7
gruffness 58.2, 110.2, 505.3
grum 110.24, 112.25
grumble (n) 54.2, 56.4, 58.3 (v) 56.9, 58.9, 60.4, 115.15
grumbler 108.3, 115.9
grumbling (n) 54.2, 115.4 (a) 108.7, 110.19
grumbly 110.19
grume 2.25, 1045.7
grumly 1031.3
grumness 110.8, 112.8
grumous 1045.14, 1062.12
grump (n) 108.4, 110.11 (v) 108.6, 110.14, 115.16
grumpiness 110.3
grumpish 110.20
grumpishness 110.3
grumps 110.10
grumpy 110.20
Grundy 579.3
Grundyism 579.1
grunge 708.10
grunginess 80.1, 98.2

grungy 80.22, 80.23, 98.18
grunt (n) 60.1, 432.5, 461.7, 461.10, 607.9 (v) 60.3, 115.15, 524.25
grunt-and-groaner 461.3
grunt and sweat 725.11
gruntle 60.3
grunt work 725.4
grunt worker 607.9
gr wt 297.1
G-spot 75.5
G string 711.5
G-string 5.19, 901.2
G suit 297.5, 1075.11
guacamole 10.9, 10.12
guano 12.4, 890.4
guarantee (n) 334.4, 436.1, 438.1, 438.6 (v) 334.6, 436.4, 438.9, 1008.18
guaranteed 436.8, 438.11, 970.20, 1007.5
guaranteed annual income 478.8, 611.7, 624.4
guaranteed annual wage 624.4
guaranteed income 611.7, 624.4
guaranteed income plan 624.4
guarantor 332.7, 438.6
guarantorship 438.8
guaranty (n) 438.1, 438.6 (v) 438.9
guard (n) 178.13, 339.4, 429.10, 460.1, 460.7, 746.2, 769.5, 1008.1, 1008.3, 1008.9 (v) 397.8, 428.7, 460.8, 747.4, 769.8, 1008.18
guard against 460.8, 494.6
guard dog 311.16, 460.7, 1008.11
guard duty 339.4
guarded 339.13, 344.10, 428.13, 494.8, 494.9, 956.4, 1008.21
guardedness 339.4, 344.3, 494.1, 956.1
guarded secret 345.5
guarder 1008.9
guardhouse 429.8
guardhouse lawyer 597.1, 935.12
guardian (n) 429.10, 574.4, 678.12, 1008.6 (a) 1008.23
guardian ad litem 1008.6
guardian angel 113.4, 460.7, 636.5, 678.12, 679.1, 1008.6
Guardian of Mankind, the 677.5
guardianship 339.4, 386.5, 387.2, 397.1, 573.4, 1008.2
guardian spirit 678.12
guarding (n) 429.5 (a) 460.11, 1008.23
guardless 1006.14
guard one's honor 136.7
guardrail 1008.3
guards 461.15, 1008.14
guardsman 1008.9, 1008.14
guardsmen 461.15
Guarnerius 711.5
Guatemala Trench 275.5
gubbish 522.7
gubernatorial 612.16
guck 1062.8
guddler 382.6
gudgeon 358.1, 915.5
guerdon (n) 624.3 (v) 624.10
guerrilla 461.16, 671.9
guerrilla art 712.1
guerrilla marketing 731.13
guerrilla theater 704.1
guerrilla warfare 458.1
guess (n) 951.4, 971.8 (v) 940.2, 946.9, 951.11, 953.11, 962.9
guessed 951.14
guesser 951.8
guessing 971.24
guess right 940.2
guesstimate (n) 951.4, 971.8 (v) 951.11, 962.9
guesswork 930.6, 942.1, 951.3, 951.4, 962.1
guessworker 951.8
guest (n) 227.8, 585.6, 828.4 (v) 585.8
guestbook 549.11
guesthouse 228.15
guestimation 962.1
guest list 585.6
guest of honor 585.6
guest pass 634.2
guest register 549.11
guest room 197.7
guest ticket 634.2
Guevarist 860.6
guff 520.3, 540.3
guffah 59.1
guffaw (n) 116.4 (v) 116.8
guggle 52.11, 60.5, 320.4
guggling 52.19
guidable 161.13
guidance 159.3, 422.1, 449.2, 449.4, 568.1, 573.1, 1008.2
guidance center 208.5
guidance counseling 422.1
guidance counselor 466.5
guidance system 1075.2
guide (n) 239.3, 341.7, 422.3, 517.4, 571.1, 574.7, 678.12, 769.5, 816.1, 988.1 (v) 161.5, 165.2, 182.14, 422.5, 568.10, 573.9, 769.8, 816.3, 894.8
guideboard 517.4
guidebook 551.1, 554.8, 574.10
guided 161.13
guided control 1074.9
guided imagery 90.13
guided meditation 92.6
guided missile 1041.18, 1074.3
guided missile cruiser 180.6
guide dog 30.6, 311.16
guided tour 918.4
guided wave 916.4
guideless 19.18, 416.5
guideline 381.1, 419.2, 869.4
guidelines 381.1
guide oneself 321.4
guidepost 517.4, 574.7
guider 574.7
guiding 573.12
guiding light 375.1, 375.9, 574.8
guiding principle 419.2, 932.4
guiding principles 381.4
guiding star 375.1, 574.8
guidon 647.7
Guidonian syllables 709.7
guild 617.1, 617.3, 727.2
guildsman 617.11
guild socialism 611.6
guile 356.3, 415.1
guileful 356.22, 415.12, 920.15
guilefulness 920.3
guileless 644.18, 923.12, 953.22
guilelessness 416.1, 644.5
guillotine (n) 605.5, 613.6, 857.5 (v) 604.16
guillotine, the 604.6
guilt 656.1
guilt by association 888.1
guilt complex 656.1
guilt feelings 656.1
guiltiness 656.1
guiltless 653.6, 657.6
guiltlessness 653.2, 657.1
guilt someone 656.2
guilty 602.6, 656.3
guilty as hell 656.3
guilty conscience 656.1
guilty involvement 656.1
guilty verdict 602.1
guinea 728.4, 728.8
guinea cock 311.28
guinea fowl 311.28
guinea hen 77.9, 311.28
guinea pig 311.22, 942.7
guisard 357.7, 707.1
guise 5.1, 33.3, 33.4, 295.2, 321.1, 376.1, 384.1, 765.4
guitarist 710.5
guitar-picker 710.5
gulag 429.8
gulch 237.7, 239.2
gules 647.2
gulf 224.2, 238.12, 240.2, 242.1, 275.2, 284.4, 292.1
Gulf Coast 231.7
gulfed 242.2
gulflike 242.2
gulfweed 310.4
gulfy 238.24, 242.2, 915.15
gull (n) 358.1 (v) 356.14, 356.18, 923.7
Gullah 523.7
gulled 923.8
gullet 2.18
gullibility 923.2, 954.2, 982.1
gullible 923.12, 953.22, 954.9
gullible person 358.1
Gulliver 178.2
gully (n) 237.7, 239.2 (v) 290.3
gullyhole 239.2
gullywasher 316.2
gulosity 672.1
gulp (n) 2.21, 8.4, 187.4 (v) 8.23, 8.29, 187.11, 672.4
gulp down 8.23, 187.11, 672.4, 954.6
gulping (n) 8.1, 8.3, 187.4 (a) 672.6
gum (n) 803.4, 1048.3, 1057.1, 1062.6 (v) 8.27, 803.9, 1012.16
gumbo (n) 10.10, 797.6, 1062.5, 1062.8 (a) 234.5, 1062.12
gumboil 85.37
gumbolike 1062.12
gum elastic 1048.3
gumlike 1057.3, 1062.12
gumlikeness 1062.2
gummed up 393.29
gummed-up 414.22
gumminess 803.3, 1062.2
gummous 803.12, 1057.3, 1062.12
gummy 803.12, 1057.3, 1062.12
gumption 330.7
gum resin 1057.1
gums 2.12
gumshoe (n) 576.11, 1008.16 (v) 177.26, 346.9
gumshoeing 177.17
gumshoe man 576.11
gum up 19.9, 393.11, 414.12, 803.9, 1012.11, 1012.16
gum up the works 414.12, 1012.11, 1012.16
gun (n) 308.11, 461.17, 462.10, 593.4, 746.3, 857.2, 904.4, 904.8 (v) 382.9, 904.12
gun battle 457.4
gunboat 180.6
gunboat diplomacy 461.27, 609.5
gunboats 5.27
gun control 437.2
guncotton 462.14
gundog 311.17, 382.5
gun down 308.14, 308.18
gunfight 459.8
gunfire 459.8, 904.4
gun for 904.12, 938.30
gung ho (n) 458.7 (a) 17.13, 101.8, 101.10
gunk 80.8, 803.4, 1062.5, 1062.8
gunkholing 182.1
gunkiness 1062.2
gunky 80.23, 803.12, 1062.12
gun loader 183.6
gun make 462.10
gunman 308.11, 461.17, 593.3, 904.8
gunmetal 39.1
gunner 183.6, 185.4, 461.11, 747.2, 904.8
gunnery 462.3, 904.2
gunnery mission 184.11
gunnery sergeant 575.19
gunning 382.2, 904.2
gun park 462.2
gun part 462.10
gunplay 459.8
gunpowder 462.14
gun room 462.2
gunrunner 732.5
gunrunning 732.2
guns 461.11, 462.11
gunsel 308.11, 593.4, 671.10
gunshot 56.3, 223.2, 904.4
gun-shy 127.23, 128.12
gunslinger 737.11
gun to one's head, a 424.3
gun-toting 460.14
gurge (n) 238.12, 915.2 (v) 238.21, 915.11
gurgle 52.11, 238.18, 320.4
gurgling 52.19
gurney 901.19
guru 571.1, 575.1, 659.6, 699.13, 699.14, 921.1
gush (n) 190.4, 193.1, 238.4, 238.9, 251.1, 511.2, 538.2, 540.1, 671.6, 991.2 (v) 93.13,

101.7, 190.13, 193.9, 238.16, 238.20, 540.5, 991.5
gushiness 540.1
gushing (n) 538.2 (a) 93.21, 238.24, 511.8, 538.11
gushing rain 316.2
gush out 190.13
gush over 101.7
gushy 538.11, 540.9
gusset 191.2
gussied up 5.46
gussy up 5.42, 498.8, 1016.15
gust 62.1, 100.2, 105.9, 318.5, 865.4
gustable 8.33, 62.8, 63.8
gustation 62.6
gustative 62.8
gustatory 62.8
gustatory cell 62.5
gustatory delightfulness 63.1
gustiness 318.14
gusto 17.2, 17.4, 63.2, 93.2, 95.1, 100.2, 101.1, 109.4
gusty 318.21
gut (n) 2.19, 93.3, 242.1 (v) 192.13, 395.10, 482.17 (a) 93.17, 207.6, 365.11, 767.9, 997.23
gut-ache 26.5
gut course 568.8
gut feeling 365.1, 934.3
gut it out 216.8
gutless 16.12, 16.17, 491.11
gutlessness 16.2, 491.2, 491.4
gutless wonder 16.6
gut reaction 93.1, 365.1, 934.2
gut response 365.1
guts 2.16, 2.19, 15.1, 68.2, 93.3, 196.1, 207.4, 359.3, 492.3, 767.5
guts, the 767.3
gut sensation 93.1
gut sense 93.1
gutsiness 15.1, 492.1
gutsy 15.15, 359.14, 492.18
gutta-percha 1048.3
gutta serena 30.1
guttation 1065.4
gutted 395.28, 1020.30
gutter (n) 239.3, 239.5, 290.2, 383.6, 654.7, 750.1 (v) 917.12, 1025.25 (a) 661.11, 666.8
gutter ball 750.2
guttering (n) 1025.8 (a) 851.3, 854.7, 917.18, 1019.27
guttermouth 497.6
guttersnipe 178.3, 497.6
guttiness 492.1
gutting 192.4
guttle 8.25, 672.4
guttler 672.3
guttling 672.6
guttural (n) 524.12 (a) 58.15, 524.30, 525.12
guttural accent 524.8
gutturalism 58.2
gutturality 58.2
gutturalness 58.2
gutty 15.15, 359.14, 492.18
gut with fire 395.10
gut-wrenching 105.30
guy 76.5, 901.2
guyed 901.24
guyline 901.2
guyliner 1016.11
guyot 237.6, 240.5
guy thing, a 76.1
guywire 901.2
guzzle (n) 2.19, 8.4, 88.6, 88.7 (v) 8.29, 88.24, 672.4
guzzler 88.11
guzzling (n) 8.3, 88.4 (a) 672.6
gym 84.1, 463.1, 567.11, 743.11
gymkhana 457.3, 743.10
Gymnasium 567.4
gymnasium 567.11, 743.11
gymnasium 84.1, 197.12, 463.1
gymnastic 743.30
gymnastic exercise 84.2
gymnastics 84.2, 568.9, 744.1, 760.5
gymnosophical 6.14
gymnosophist 6.3, 668.4
gymnosophy 6.3, 668.2
gymnosperm 310.3
gym shorts 5.18
gynaeceum 563.10
gynandrian 75.31
gynandrism 75.12
gynandroid 75.17
gynandrous 75.31
gynandry 75.12
gynarchy 612.5
gynecic 77.13
gynecocracy 612.5
gynecoid 77.13
gynecological 90.15
gynecomania 75.5, 665.5
gynecomaniac 665.11
gynecomaniacal 665.29
gynic 77.13
gynocracy 612.5
gynoecium 310.28
gynophore 310.21
gyp (n) 77.9, 311.16, 356.9, 357.4 (v) 356.19
gyp artist 357.4
gyp joint 228.28, 356.8
gypper 357.4
gypsy 178.4
gypsy cab 179.13
gypsydom 177.3
gypsyish 177.37
gypsylike 177.37
gypsy rehearsal 704.13
gypsy run 704.13
gypsy run-through 704.13
gyral 915.15
gyrate 172.5, 915.9
gyrating 915.14
gyration 915.1
gyrational 172.8, 915.15
gyratory 172.8, 915.15
gyre (n) 281.2, 914.1, 915.2 (v) 914.5, 915.9
gyrene 183.4
gyrenes 461.28
gyre upward 193.10
gyring 914.1, 915.1
gyring up 193.1
gyro 10.32, 181.5
gyrocompass 574.9
gyron 647.2
Gyropilot 574.7
gyroplane 181.5
gyroscopic 915.15
gyroscopic compass 574.9
Gyrosin compass 574.9
gyrostatic 915.15
gyrostatic compass 574.9
gyrostatics 915.8
gyve 428.10
gyves 428.4
H 87.9, 753.1
Habakkuk 684.1
habeas corpus 430.2
haberdasher 5.33
habiliment 5.1
habilimentation 5.32
habilimented 5.45
habilitate 5.39
habit (n) 5.1, 5.6, 87.1, 373.3, 500.2, 702.1, 767.4 (v) 5.41
habitability 225.6
habitable 225.15
habitancy 225.1, 227.1
habitant 227.2, 227.9
habitat 159.1, 209.1, 225.1, 228.18
habitation 225.1, 228.1
habited 5.45
habit of life 321.1
habit of mind 931.1
habit of thought 931.1
habit pattern 373.3
habitual 373.14, 807.6, 847.4, 869.9
habitual criminal 859.3
habitual criminality 655.1, 674.3
habitual drunkenness 88.3
habitual liar 357.9
habitual lying 354.8
habitualness 373.6, 847.1, 864.2
habitual offender 859.3
habitual smoking 89.10
habituate 373.9
habituated 373.17
habituation 373.7
habitude 373.3
habitué (n) 221.5, 582.16, 585.6 (a) 373.17
hachis 10.13
hachure 159.5, 170.3, 517.6
hacienda 228.6, 1069.8
hack (n) 2.21, 178.9, 178.10, 179.13, 289.1, 311.12, 311.13, 403.3, 414.8, 517.5, 547.16, 610.4, 718.5, 726.3 (v) 177.34, 328.6, 407.4, 802.11
hackathon 1042.13
hackdriver 178.10
hacked 152.30, 795.5
hacker 414.7, 751.2, 1042.17
hacking 802.2, 1042.1, 1042.13, 1042.18
hacking out a deal 731.3
hack it 18.11, 328.6, 409.8, 409.12, 942.10, 991.4
hackle (n) 3.16, 3.18 (v) 79.21
hackman 178.9, 178.10
hackney (n) 311.13 (a) 117.9
hackneyed 21.11, 117.9, 373.14, 864.16, 928.27
hackneyed expression 526.9, 864.8
hackneyedness 117.3
hackneyed saying 974.3
hack off 802.11
hack out a deal 731.18
hack through 802.11
hacktivist 330.8
hack writer 547.16, 718.5
hacky 178.9, 178.10
hadal zone 275.4
had as soon 371.17
had best 641.3
had better 641.3
Hades 682.1, 682.3, 682.5, 839.2
had it 762.11
Hadith 683.6
had rather 371.17
had sooner 371.17
Haeckelism 861.4
haft 901.11
hag 304.3, 593.7, 690.8, 1015.4
haggadah 701.10
Haggai 684.1
haggard 21.9, 36.7, 105.25, 112.22, 270.20, 307.28, 926.32
haggardness 36.2, 270.5, 307.11
haggle (n) 731.3 (v) 731.18
haggling 731.3
Hagiographa 683.3
hagiographic 719.6
hagiographical 719.6
hagiography 719.1
hagiology 719.1
hag-ridden 691.13
hagride 691.9
ha-ha (n) 116.4, 224.2, 290.2 (v) 116.8
hail (n) 59.1, 585.4, 884.3, 1023.6 (v) 59.6, 332.8, 509.10, 517.22, 524.26, 585.10, 1023.11
hail and speak 182.52
hail-fellow-well-met 582.23
Hail Mary 696.4
hail one's wind 182.24
hailstone 1023.6
hailstorm 1023.6
hair 3.2, 223.2, 248.2, 270.1, 271.1, 295.3, 704.23, 998.5
hairbreadth 223.2, 270.1
hairbreadth escape 369.2
hair coloring 1016.14
haircut 3.15, 1016.14
hairdo 3.15, 1016.14
hairdresser 1016.12
hairdressing 1016.10, 1016.14
hairdressing salon 1016.13
hairdryer 1066.4
hair extensions 3.13, 3.14
hair hygrometer 1065.10
hairiness 3.1, 1013.1
hairless 6.17
hairlessness 6.4
hairlet 3.2
hairlike 3.23, 271.7
hairline 517.6, 780.2
hairline crack 224.2, 292.1
hair loss 6.4
hair of the dog 88.8, 88.9
hair of the dog that bit one 88.8
hairpiece 3.14
hairpin (n) 164.1, 204.8, 753.1, 756.3 (v) 164.5 (a) 204.20
hairpin curve 756.3

hairpin turn 279.3
hair-raiser 127.9
hair-raising 127.28, 127.29
hair remover 6.4
hair replacement 1016.14
hair salon 1016.13
hairsbreadth 223.2, 270.1
hair shirt 113.3, 658.3
hair space 224.1, 548.7
hairsplitter 936.7
hairsplitting (n) 495.4, 510.4, 936.5, 944.3 (a) 495.12, 510.23, 936.14
hairstyle 3.15, 1016.14
hair styling 1016.14
hairstylist 1016.12
hair-trigger (n) 365.2 (a) 174.15, 365.9
hair weave 3.14
hairy 3.24, 271.7, 288.9, 294.7, 295.32, 988.9, 1000.8, 1006.10, 1013.17
hairy-chested 76.13
hairy eyeball 27.5
hajj 177.5, 696.8
hajji 178.1, 699.12
hakim 575.9
halberdier 461.6
halcyon 97.11, 173.12, 464.9, 1010.13
halcyon bird 133.5
halcyon days 107.1, 317.3, 1010.4
hale (v) 905.4 (a) 15.15, 83.12
hale and hearty 83.12
haleness 83.3
hale old age 303.5
half (n) 477.5, 746.3, 747.3, 749.6, 819.2, 875.2 (a) 477.13, 875.5
half a C 728.7
half a chance 972.7
half-acre 230.6
half a dozen 882.2
half a gale 318.11
half a hundred 882.7
half a jiffy 830.3
half a mind 323.1
half a mo 828.3, 830.3
half-and-half (n) 875.2 (a) 467.7, 477.13, 790.7, 797.14
half-and-half measures 467.3
half an eye 27.4
half an idea 951.5
half-animal 311.39
half a notion 323.1
half a second 830.3
half a shake 830.3
half asleep 22.21
half-ass 930.14
half-assed 250.6, 340.12, 414.15, 414.22, 930.14
half-awake 985.11
halfback 746.2
half-baked 406.10, 406.11, 845.8, 922.22, 930.14, 1003.4
half-Beaufort scale 318.15
half-belief 955.2
half believe 955.6
half-blind 28.13
half blood 797.8
half-blooded 797.15
half-bred (n) 797.8 (a) 797.15
half-breed (n) 797.8 (a) 797.15
half brother 559.3
half cadence 709.23
half-caste (n) 797.8 (a) 797.15
half circle 280.8
half-clothed 6.13
half-cocked 406.11, 845.8, 930.14
half-conscious 25.8
half court line 748.1
half crown 728.4, 728.8
half day 824.2
half-dead 118.11, 307.32
half-deaf 49.6
half-dollar 728.7, 728.8
half-done 340.14
half-dressed 5.47
half eagle 728.4
half-face view 218.1
half-famished 100.25
half-frozen 1023.16, 1062.11
half G 728.7
half-god 678.3
half grand 728.7
half-grown 406.11
half-hardy 310.44
half-heard 52.16
halfhearted 16.17, 102.6
halfheartedness 102.1, 354.5
halfhearted thanks 151.1
half-holiday 20.4
half-human 311.39
half-know 930.10
half-learned 930.14
half-learning 930.5
half-life 1037.1, 1037.6
half-light 35.7, 314.3, 1027.2
half-lit 1027.15
half-mast 517.22
half measures 467.3
half-melted 1062.11
half-moon 279.5, 1073.11
half nelson 474.3
half note 709.14
half-open 292.18
halfpenny 728.8, 998.5
half pint 258.4
half-pint 258.10
half points 161.3
half-price 633.9
half rations 992.5, 992.6
half relief 715.3
half-remembered 990.8
half rest 709.21
half rhyme 720.9
half scholar 929.6
half-seas over 88.33
half-seen 32.6
half sister 559.3
half space 224.1
half-starved 100.25, 992.12
half step 177.13, 709.20
halftime 746.3, 825.3, 826.1
halftime intermission 826.1
half tint 35.7, 713.2
half-title page 554.12
halftone 35.7, 709.20
halftone engraving 548.1
half-true 265.11, 354.26
half-truth 354.11
half-visibility 32.2
half-visible 32.6
halfway 208.11, 819.4, 875.5
halfway house 429.8, 819.2, 1009.4
halfway line 752.1
halfway mark 875.3
halfway measures 467.3
halfway point 819.2
halfway station 1075.5
half-wit 924.2, 924.8
half-witted 922.22
half-wittedness 922.9
half-yearly 850.8
halieutic 382.11
halieutical 382.11
halieutics 382.3
halitosis 71.1
hall 189.5, 197.4, 197.18, 228.5, 463.1, 567.10, 704.14
hallelujah 116.2, 696.3
hallmark (n) 517.1, 517.13, 865.4 (v) 517.20
hall of fame 662.6
hall of famer 413.15
halloo (n) 59.1 (v) 59.6, 524.26
hallow 487.2, 685.5
hallowday 701.12
hallowed 677.17, 685.8, 842.12
hallowedness 685.1
Halloween 690.3
hallowing 685.3
halls of ivy, the 567.5
halls of learning, the 567.5
hallucinate 976.8
hallucinated 926.26
hallucinating 926.31
hallucination 92.18, 356.1, 689.6, 976.7, 986.5
hallucinational 976.10
hallucinative 976.10
hallucinatory 356.21, 976.10
hallucinogen 86.13, 87.3
hallucinogenic 86.46, 976.10
hallucinogenic drug 87.3
hallucinosis 976.7
hallway 189.5, 197.18
halo 171.2, 280.2, 662.6, 1025.14
halo effect 894.1
halogenate 1060.8, 1067.8
halogen gas 1067.2
halt (n) 20.2, 173.3, 846.2, 857.2, 1012.2, 1013.6 (v) 16.8, 173.8, 175.8, 177.28, 525.8, 857.6, 857.7, 857.11, 1012.13 (a) 393.30
halter (n) 428.4, 605.5 (v) 800.10
halting (n) 857.1, 1012.2 (a) 175.10, 393.30, 525.13, 534.3, 851.3
halting meters 720.3
halve 476.6, 802.11, 873.5, 875.4
halved 875.6
halved hole 751.3
halvers 477.13
halving 873.1, 875.1
halvsies 875.2
ham (n) 2.7, 177.14, 230.2, 704.8, 707.5, 1034.24 (v) 355.3, 500.12, 704.31 (a) 704.33
ham actor 707.5
hamadryad 678.9
ham-and-egger 606.5
hamartia 975.1
hamate 279.8
hamburger 10.14, 10.32
hamburger joint 8.17
hamburger stand 8.17
ham-fisted 414.20, 534.2
ham-fistedness 414.3, 534.1
ham-handed 414.20, 534.2
ham-handedness 414.3, 534.1, 1013.9
hamiform 279.8
Hamito-Semitic 523.12
ham it up 93.13, 355.3, 500.12, 501.16, 704.31
Hamlet 542.2
hamlet 230.2, 231.5
hammada 237.3
hammed up 500.15
hammer (n) 2.10, 1040.7, 1051.7 (v) 671.11, 725.14, 849.10, 902.16, 931.9
hammer and sickle 647.1
hammer at 725.13
hammer away 360.3, 725.14
hammer away at 849.9, 931.9
hammered 715.7
hammered-out 262.9
hammerhead 361.6
hammer home 997.14
hammering 709.14, 902.3
hammering out a deal 731.3
hammer into one's head 989.17
hammerlock 474.3
hammer out 262.7, 340.9, 541.11, 892.8
hammer out a bargain 332.10
hammer out a deal 731.18
hamminess 93.9
hamming 704.8
hamming up 704.8
hammock 237.4
hammy 93.19, 704.33
hammy acting 704.8
ham operator 1034.24
hamper (n) 428.4, 1012.6 (v) 212.9, 297.13, 428.10, 1012.11
hampered 297.18, 428.16
hampering (n) 1012.1 (a) 1012.18
ham radio 1034.16
ham shack 1034.6
ham station 1034.6
hamster wheel 373.5, 849.4
hamster-wheel 118.10, 849.14
hamstring 19.9, 19.10, 393.14, 395.11, 1012.11
hamstringing 393.1
hamstrung 19.16, 393.30
hamulate 279.8
hand (n) 2.7, 183.6, 218.1, 312.5, 328.3, 413.1, 417.5, 449.2, 509.2, 517.4, 527.10, 547.3, 612.2, 726.1, 726.2, 758.2, 758.3, 793.4 (v) 478.13, 629.3
hand and glove 587.19
hand around 477.8
hand a sail 182.50
hand at, a 413.27
hand back 481.4
handbag 195.2, 729.15
handbags at dawn 456.6
handbag situation 456.6

handball 1048.3
handbarrow 179.3
handbill 352.8
handbook 554.8, 574.10, 759.19
handbreadth 269.3
handcar 179.16
handcart 179.3
hand-check 747.4
handclap 509.2
handclapping 509.2
handclasp 585.4
hand composition 548.2
handcrafted 892.18
hand cream 1016.11
handcuff 19.10, 428.10, 800.9, 1012.11
handcuffed 428.16
handcuffs 428.4
hand down 478.18, 629.3
hand down a sentence 946.13
hand down a verdict 946.13
handed 218.7
handed down 373.13, 842.12
handedness 218.1
handfasting 436.3
hand for, a 413.5
hand forward 176.10
handful 248.2, 885.2, 1013.2
handful of thumbs 414.3
hand gallop 174.3
hand grenade 462.20
hand guard 1008.3
handgun 462.10
handheld computer 1042.2
handhold 474.2
handicap (n) 85.1, 297.7, 603.2, 751.3, 791.1, 996.2, 1012.6 (v) 297.13, 603.4, 1012.11
handicapped 393.30
handicapped, the 85.45
handicapped golfer 751.2
handicapped person 85.45
handicapped student 572.4
handicapper 759.6
handicapping 757.1
handicraft 712.2, 724.6, 892.2
handicrafted 892.18
handicraftsman 726.6
hand in 478.13
handiness 223.1, 413.1, 1014.2
hand in glove 450.5, 587.19
hand-in-glove 769.9, 800.13
handing over 370.3
hand-in-hand 223.14, 587.19, 769.9, 800.13
hand in one's resignation 448.2
hand it to 250.5, 509.14
hand it to one 509.12, 646.8
handiwork 328.3, 725.4, 892.2, 893.1
hand job 75.8
handkerchief 5.25, 5.31
hand laundry 79.11
handle (n) 283.3, 376.1, 527.3, 648.1, 901.11 (v) 73.6, 182.14, 321.6, 328.9, 387.10, 387.12, 541.11, 556.5, 573.8, 731.16, 889.5, 1070.7
handleability 1014.2
handleable 433.14, 1014.15
handlebar mustache 3.11
handlebars 3.11
handle it just right 409.8
handle oneself 321.4
handle oneself well 413.20
handler 551.5, 571.6, 754.2, 889.4
handle to one's name 648.1
handle with gloves 339.7
handle with kid gloves 339.7, 427.5
handle with velvet gloves 427.5
handling 73.2, 328.2, 387.2, 387.8, 556.1, 573.1, 889.1
handlist 574.10, 871.3
hand loom 740.5
hand lotion 1016.11, 1056.3
handmade 892.18
handmaid 384.4, 577.8
handmaiden 384.4, 577.8
hand-me-down 842.18
hand-me-downs 5.5
hand-minded 73.10
hand-mindedness 73.1
hand miner 1058.9
hand mirror 29.6
hand of death 307.1
hand off 747.4
handoff 746.3, 747.3
hand of friendship 465.2
hand of glory 691.1
hand on 176.10, 343.7, 478.18, 629.3
hand one's name down to posterity 662.13
hand one's walking papers 447.4
hand organ 711.14
hand out 477.8, 478.12, 478.13
handout 352.3, 352.8, 449.4, 478.6, 478.8, 551.1
hand over 176.10, 370.7, 433.8, 475.3, 478.13, 624.15, 629.3
handover 475.1
hand over one's sword 433.8
hand-painted 742.7
handpick 371.14
handpicked 371.25, 371.26, 999.16
handprinting 547.4
handprop 704.17
hand puppet 349.6
handrail 1008.3
hand ride 757.3
hands 18.9, 417.5, 474.4, 612.2, 1008.2
hands across the sea 587.3
hand sanitizer 79.17
handsel (n) 438.2, 478.4 (v) 438.10
handset 347.4
handshake (n) 436.2, 437.3, 585.4 (v) 138.9
handshaker 138.4
hand signal 517.14
hand soap 79.17
hands-off 427.8, 430.25, 443.14, 853.8
hands-off policy 368.1
handsome 485.4, 652.6, 1016.17
handsome fortune 618.1
handsomeness 1016.1
handsome thing, the 649.2
hands-on 476.8
hands-on experience 413.9
handspike 906.4
handspring 205.2, 366.1
handstaff 273.2
handstand 205.2
hand's turn 725.4
hand-to-hand 457.4
hand-to-hand combat 457.4
hand-to-hand fight 457.4
hand-to-hand snap 746.3
hand-to-mouth 406.15, 991.6
hand-to-mouth existence 619.2
hand tool 1040.1, 1040.7
hand-turned 742.7
hand-turned wheel 742.4
hand up an indictment 599.7
hand vote 371.6
hand-waving 321.1
handwork 725.4, 892.2
handwoven 740.7
hand-wringing (n) 917.1 (a) 105.26
handwriting 546.5, 547.3
handwriting expert 547.14
handwriting on the wall 399.3
handwriting on the wall, the 964.2
handwriting recognition 547.14, 1042.1
handwriting style 547.4
handwritten 547.22
handy 223.15, 258.12, 384.8, 387.20, 413.22, 1014.15
handy at 413.27
handyman 396.10, 413.11, 577.4, 577.9
handyperson 577.9
handywoman 413.11
hang (n) 202.2, 204.5, 413.6 (v) 193.10, 202.6, 202.8, 221.10, 225.7, 604.17, 846.11, 959.6, 971.11
hang about 138.11, 221.10, 223.12, 331.14, 846.12
hang a left 164.3
hang a 180 859.5
hangar 184.24, 197.27, 739.5
hang a right 164.3
hang around 138.11, 221.10, 223.12, 331.12, 331.14
hang around with 582.18, 769.7
hang back 166.4, 325.4, 362.7, 846.11, 903.7
hang behind 166.4
hang by a hair 971.11, 1006.7
hang by a thread 971.11, 1006.7, 1006.8
hang by the eyelids 971.11
hang by the neck 604.17
hang crape 112.15
hangdog 137.14, 138.14
hangdog look 110.9, 137.2
hang down 202.6
hanger 202.4, 202.5, 310.13, 937.2
hanger-on 138.6, 166.2, 432.6, 577.1, 610.8, 616.8
hang fire 173.9, 329.2, 410.13, 846.9, 846.11, 857.7, 857.9, 891.3
hang glider 181.12
hang heavy on one's hands 993.8
hang in 15.11, 134.6, 306.11, 359.9, 360.7, 492.14, 827.6, 856.5
hang in doubt 971.10
hang in effigy 661.9
hanging (n) 202.1, 202.4, 204.5, 295.2, 582.2, 604.6, 704.20 (a) 194.12, 202.9, 804.5
hanging buttress 901.4
hanging by a thread 307.32, 1006.12
hanging fixture 1026.6
hanging gardens 204.4
hanging in 856.1hanging in there 360.8
hanging on (n) 856.1 (a) 959.9
hanging out (n) 582.2 (a) 31.6, 348.12
hanging over one's head 840.3
hanging valley 237.7
hang in space 1075.12
hang in suspense 971.11
hang in the balance 971.11
hang in there 134.5, 134.6, 359.9, 360.7, 492.14, 827.6
hang like a millstone 297.12
hang like a millstone round one's neck 1012.11
hang loose 106.9
hangman 308.11, 604.7
hangman's rope 605.5
hang off 325.4
hang on 306.11, 360.4, 474.6, 599.8, 803.6, 887.5, 888.4, 959.6
hang one's head 112.15, 137.9
hang one's lip 110.15
hang on every word 48.10
hang on for dear life 360.7, 474.6
hang on like a bulldog 360.4
hang on like a leech 360.4
hang on one's words 983.5
hang on the lips 983.5
hang on the lips of 48.10
hang on the skirts of 138.11, 166.3
hang on the sleeve of 138.11
hang on to 474.6
hang open 292.16
hang out 31.5, 202.7, 221.10, 225.7, 348.7, 941.9
hangout 228.27
hang out at 847.3
hang out one's shingle 724.12
hang out to dry 1066.6
hang out with 582.18, 769.7
hang over 202.7, 295.30, 840.2
hangover 88.1, 835.1
hang over one's head 840.2, 971.10
hangry 100.25, 100.27, 992.12
hang the expense 486.3
hang the jury 598.19
hang together 450.3, 788.6, 800.11, 803.6
hang tough 15.11, 87.22, 134.6, 216.8, 359.9, 360.7, 453.3, 492.14, 827.6, 855.11, 856.5, 1049.3

hang up 202.8, 347.19, 410.13, 846.9, 857.6
hang-up 846.2, 926.13, 1012.4
hangup 1003.2
hang upon 971.11
hang up one's hat 159.17
hang up one's shingle 159.17
hang up one's spurs 448.2
hang upon the skirts of 223.12
hang with 582.18, 769.7
hank 271.2
hanker after 100.18
hankerer 100.12
hanker for 100.18
hankering (n) 100.5 (a) 100.23
hanky-panky 75.7, 104.5, 356.5
Hansard 549.8
Hanswurst 707.10
hant (n) 988.1 (v) 988.6
hap (n) 831.2, 972.1, 972.6 (v) 831.5, 972.11
ha'penny 728.8
haphazard (n) 972.4 (a) 340.12, 406.8, 810.12, 851.3, 972.16
haphazardness 340.3, 810.1
hapless 1011.14
haploid 305.21
haploid number 305.8
haplomitosis 305.16
happen 831.5, 972.11
happen along 972.11
happen as expected 973.12
happen by chance 972.11
happening (n) 328.1, 831.2, 972.6 (a) 578.11, 831.9
happenings 552.1
happening upon 941.1
happen on 941.3, 972.11
happen over and over 849.11
happenstance 768.2, 831.2, 972.1, 972.6
happen to be 761.8
happen together 899.2
happen upon 941.3
happify 95.9
happiness 95.2, 107.1, 109.1, 496.2, 1010.1
happy 88.31, 95.16, 107.7, 109.11, 133.17, 496.9, 533.7, 788.10, 843.9, 995.5
happy accident 941.1
happy as a clam 95.16, 109.11
happy as a clam at high water 95.16
happy as a king 95.16
happy as a lark 95.16, 109.11
happy as a pig in poo 95.16
happy as the day is long 95.16
happy camper 95.2
happy chance 972.1
happy coincidence 843.3
happy couple 563.9
happy ending 820.1, 940.1
happy expectation 124.1
happy face 95.2
happy family 455.1
happy few 249.5
happy fortune 1010.2
happy-go-luckiness 406.2
happy-go-lucky 406.15
happy hour 20.2, 95.5
Happy Isles 681.9, 839.2
happy medium 246.1, 467.3, 468.1, 670.1, 819.2
happy outcome 940.1
happy thought 489.7
Happy Valley 986.11
hara-kiri 308.5, 701.9
harangue (n) 543.2, 568.7 (v) 543.10, 568.16
haranguer 543.4
harass 21.4, 96.13, 98.15, 126.5, 127.20, 389.7, 459.19, 1000.6, 1013.13
harassed 96.24, 126.8, 1013.20
harasser 96.10
harassing 98.22, 126.10
harassment 96.2, 98.7, 126.2, 389.3
harbinger (n) 133.4, 353.2, 816.1 (v) 133.13
harbor (n) 186.5, 242.1, 1009.1, 1009.6 (v) 225.10, 474.7, 1008.18
harbor a design 380.4
harbor a feeling 93.10
harborage 1009.1, 1009.6
harbor a grudge 589.8
harbor an idea 931.16
harbor doubts 955.6
harbor of refuge 1009.1
harbor pilot 183.8
harbor resentment 152.12
harbor revenge 507.5
harborside 1009.6
harbor the hope 124.6
hard 15.15, 26.10, 64.6, 88.37, 94.12, 114.5, 144.24, 144.25, 146.3, 330.22, 361.9, 361.10, 425.7, 522.14, 524.30, 654.17, 665.29, 761.15, 763.7, 973.13, 973.14, 1011.13, 1013.17, 1045.12, 1046.10, 1049.4
hard act to follow 999.6
hard-and-fast 419.4, 420.12
hard-and-fast rule 869.4
hard as a rock 1046.10
hard as nails 15.15, 146.3, 1046.10, 1049.4
hard-ass 1013.17
hard at it 330.21, 725.17
hard at work 330.21
hardball 745.1, 997.3, 1006.1
hardball and the nitty-gritty 761.2
hard bargain 731.5
hard binding 554.14
hard-bitten 361.10
hard-bittenness 361.2
hard blow 96.5, 1011.2
hard-bodied 15.15
hardbody 15.6
hard-boil 1046.8
hard-boiled 15.18, 361.10, 1046.10
hard-boiled eggs 10.26
hard book 554.3
hardbound 554.3
hardbound book 554.3
hard case 619.4, 1011.1, 1011.7
hard cash 624.1, 728.1
hard-charging 15.15
hard contest 457.3
hard copy 547.10
hard core 708.10
hardcore 361.9, 671.22
hardcore pornography 666.4
hard court 748.1
hardcover 554.3
hardcover book 554.3
hard currency 728.1
hard disk 549.10, 1042.6
hard disk drive 1042.5
hard drinker 88.11
hard drinking 87.1, 88.4
hard-drinking 88.35
hard drive 1042.5
hard drug 87.3
hard-earned 725.18, 1013.17
har-de-har 116.8
hard eighteen 759.11
harden 15.13, 94.6, 373.9, 1046.7, 1049.3, 1059.10
hardened 25.6, 94.12, 114.5, 144.25, 373.15, 654.17, 1046.13, 1049.6
hardenedness 94.3
hardener 1046.4
hardening (n) 15.5, 373.7, 853.1, 1045.3, 1046.4, 1046.5 (a) 1046.14
hardening agent 1046.4
hardening of the arteries 1046.5
harden one's heart 94.6, 114.3, 146.2, 442.3
hard fact 761.3
hard-favored 1015.7
hard-featured 1015.7
hard feelings 93.7, 152.3, 589.4
hardfisted 484.9
hardfistedness 484.3
hard-fought 725.18, 1013.17
hard freeze 1023.3
hard frost 1023.3, 1023.7
hard goods 735.4
hard hat 591.3, 611.9, 1008.3
hardhead 361.6, 987.3
hardheaded 361.8, 956.5, 987.6
hardheadedness 361.1, 956.1, 987.2
hard heart 94.3
hardhearted 25.6, 94.12, 144.25, 654.17, 1046.10
hardheartedness 93.7, 94.3, 144.10, 654.6
hard hexachord 709.8
hard-hit ball 745.3
hard-hitting campaign 609.13
hardihood 142.1, 492.5
hardiness 15.1, 83.3, 492.5, 1049.1
hard information 551.1
hard job 725.5, 1013.2
hard knocks 1011.1
hard labor 604.2, 725.5
hard landing 1075.2, 1075.9
hard lenses 29.3
hard life 1011.1
hard line 361.2, 425.1, 458.10, 687.5
hard-line 361.9, 425.6, 458.21, 671.22
hardline 687.8
hard-liner 361.6, 461.5
hard lines 1011.5
hard liquor 10.49, 88.13
hard look 27.14
hard lot 1011.1
hard luck 1011.5
hard-luck guy 1011.7
hard luck story 115.4
hardly a chance 972.9
hardly any 885.4
hardly anything 248.5, 998.6
hardly expect 131.4
hardly give one time to breathe 96.13
hardly have time to breathe 401.8
hardly like 787.4
hardly possible 969.3
hardly the thing 638.3
hardly touch 276.4
hardly wait 135.4
hard man with a buck 484.4
hard market 737.1
hard master 575.13
hard money 728.4
hard-mouthed 361.10
hardness 15.3, 94.3, 114.2, 144.9, 144.10, 146.1, 294.2, 425.2, 522.2, 654.6, 1013.1, 1045.1, 1046.1, 1049.1
hardness of hearing 49.1
hardness of heart 94.3, 114.2, 144.10, 654.6, 1046.1
hardness scale 1046.4
hardness test 1046.4
hard news 552.1
hardnose 361.6, 671.10
hard-nosed 361.10, 453.5
hard-nosedness 361.2
hard nut to crack 522.8, 799.2, 1013.2, 1013.7
hard of belief 955.10, 956.4
hard-of-hearing 49.6
hard-of-hearing, the 49.2
hard-of-hearing aid 48.8
hard of heart 144.25
hard-on 75.5
hard on the eyes 1015.6
hard palate 524.18
hardpan 199.1, 901.6
hard pinch 619.1
hard plight 1011.1
hard porn 547.12, 718.1
hard-pressed 401.11, 1013.26
hard pull 1013.2
hard put to it 1013.20
hard resin 1057.1
hard road to travel 1013.2
hard rock 708.10
hard roll 10.31
hard row of stumps 1013.2
hard row to hoe (n) 1011.1, 1013.2 (v) 1011.9
hard-run 401.11
hard sell 375.3, 440.3, 734.2
hard-selling 375.29
hard-set 361.10
hard seventeen 759.11
hard shadow 1035.5
hard-shell (n) 94.3, 842.8 (a) 361.9, 425.7, 453.5
hardship 619.1, 1011.1
hard skill 928.4
hard stuff 87.9, 88.13

hardtack 10.30
hard times 1011.6
hard to believe 955.10
hard to find 992.10
hard to please 495.10
hard to understand 522.14
hard truth, the 973.3
hard up 619.7, 1013.26
hard usage 387.1
hard use 387.1
hard-visaged 1015.7
hardware 735.4, 1041.17, 1042.2
hardware description language 1042.13
hard water 1065.3
hard way, the 725.5, 1013.1
hard wear 387.1, 393.5
hard winter 1023.3
hardwiring 1033.8, 1042.3
hard-won 725.18
hardwood (n) 747.1, 1054.3 (a) 310.39
hardwood tree 310.10
hard word 526.1, 526.10
hard words 510.7, 545.3
hard work 360.1, 725.5
hardworking 330.22, 725.17
hardy 15.15, 83.12, 142.9, 310.44, 492.16, 827.10, 1049.4
hardy-har 488.5
hardy-har-har 488.5
hare 174.6, 311.23
harebrain (n) 924.7 (a) 985.16
harebrained 364.5, 493.9, 985.16
harebrained idea 364.1
harebrainedness 493.3
harefoot 199.5
harelip 265.3
harem 563.10
harem girl 665.15
Hare system 371.6, 609.18
Hargrave kite 181.14
har-har-har 488.5
haricots 10.35
hark 48.10, 983.7
hark back 859.5, 989.9
hark back to 859.6
harking back 989.3
Harleian 554.15
Harlem tennis 759.8
Harlequin 707.10
harlequin (n) 47.4, 47.6, 707.10 (v) 47.7 (a) 47.9
harlequinade 489.5
harlequin glasses 29.3
harlot (n) 665.14, 665.16 (a) 665.28
harlotry 665.8
harm (n) 393.1, 996.2, 1000.3, 1001.1 (v) 393.9, 996.4, 1000.6
harmattan 318.6, 318.12
harmed 393.27
harmful 82.5, 144.20, 996.6, 1000.12, 1011.13
harmfulness 82.1, 144.5, 1000.5
harmless 999.21, 1002.8, 1007.5
harmlessness 999.9, 1007.1
harmless teasing 490.1
harmonic (n) 50.2, 709.16 (a) 708.49, 916.15
harmonica 711.10
harmonic close 708.24
harmonic intrval 709.20
harmonic minor 709.6
harmonic motion 916.1
harmonicon 711.10
harmonic progression 709.2, 1017.8
harmonic proportion 1017.7
harmonics 50.5, 708.3, 709.1
harmonic tone 709.16
harmonious 35.16, 97.6, 264.4, 450.5, 455.3, 533.8, 587.15, 708.49, 788.9, 807.6, 867.6, 899.4
harmoniousness 97.1
harmonious sound 708.1
harmonist 710.20
harmonization 264.2, 708.5, 709.2, 788.4, 808.2
harmonize 264.3, 450.3, 455.2, 465.8, 708.35, 708.46, 781.4, 788.6, 788.7, 808.10, 867.3, 899.2
harmonized 450.5, 808.14
harmonizer 466.3, 710.20
harmonize with 455.2
harmonizing 708.49
harmonograph 916.8
harmony 264.1, 332.5, 450.1, 455.1, 464.1, 533.2, 587.3, 681.5, 708.3, 709.1, 788.1, 807.1, 867.1
harmony of the spheres 708.3, 1073.4
harness (n) 5.2, 181.13, 385.4, 385.5, 460.3 (v) 800.10, 1070.7
harness racer 178.9
harness racing 757.1
harness up 800.10
harp (n) 711.3, 711.10 (v) 856.5
harper 710.5
harping (n) 849.4, 983.4 (a) 118.9, 849.15
harpist 710.5
harp on 118.8, 849.9, 997.14
harp on the same string 118.8
harpoon (n) 462.8 (v) 480.17
harpoon log 174.7
harpsichord 711.12
harpsichordist 710.7
harp upon 118.8
harp upon one thing 118.8
harpy 110.12, 480.12, 593.6
harridan 665.14, 1015.4
harried 96.24, 126.8
harrier 96.10, 174.5
harrow (n) 285.4 (v) 26.7, 96.18, 287.5, 1069.17
harrowed 26.9, 96.25
harrowing (n) 1069.13 (a) 26.10, 98.23
harrow the ear 58.11
harry 96.13, 126.5, 389.7, 459.14, 459.19
harrying 96.2, 389.3
harry out 909.14
harry to destruction 395.25
harsh 17.14, 26.10, 35.21, 58.15, 61.4, 61.5, 64.6, 68.6, 98.20, 98.24, 144.24, 146.3, 288.7, 425.6, 505.7, 525.12, 534.2
harsh-colored 35.21
harsh criticism 510.4
harshen 26.7, 144.15, 288.4
harshness 17.5, 58.2, 61.2, 68.1, 98.4, 98.5, 98.8, 144.9, 146.1, 288.1, 425.1, 505.3, 525.1, 534.1, 671.1
harsh-sounding 58.15
harsh-tongued 144.23
hart 76.8, 311.5
hartebeest 311.5
harum-scarum 493.8, 671.20
harumscarum 493.4
haruspex 962.4
haruspical 962.11
haruspication 962.2
haruspicy 962.2
harvest (n) 313.4, 472.5, 887.1, 893.2, 1069.15 (v) 472.8, 472.11, 892.9, 1069.19
harvested 892.18
harvester 1069.5
harvest festival 743.4
harvest home 313.4, 743.4
harvesting 892.2, 1069.15
harvestman 311.32, 1069.5
harvest mite 311.36
harvest moon 1073.11
harvest time 313.4
has-been (n) 842.8 (a) 837.7, 842.16
hash (n) 10.13, 87.8, 410.6, 414.5, 797.6, 810.3 (v) 797.10
hashed 795.5
hashed up 393.29
hashed-up 414.22
hashery 8.17
hash house 8.17
hash mark 647.2, 647.5, 746.1
hash out 541.11
hash over 541.11
hashtag 1042.18
hash up 393.11, 414.12
Hasid 675.21
Hasidic 675.30
Hasidism 675.12
haslet 10.20
hasp 800.8
hassle (n) 119.1, 456.6, 725.3, 810.4, 935.4 (v) 98.15, 119.2, 456.12, 510.16, 725.11, 935.16, 1000.6
hassling 457.1
hassock 310.2, 770.7
hastate 285.12
haste (n) 135.1, 174.1, 365.2, 401.1, 493.2, 845.2 (v) 174.8, 401.4
hasteless 402.6
hastelessness 402.2
hasten 135.4, 162.5, 174.8, 174.10, 401.4, 401.5, 449.17, 1014.7
hastening 401.3, 1014.5
hasten off 188.10
hasten on 375.16, 401.4
hasten someone's end 308.13
hastiness 340.2, 365.2, 401.2, 406.2, 493.2, 845.2
hasty 110.25, 135.6, 174.15, 365.9, 401.9, 406.8, 493.8, 830.5, 845.8
hasty conviction 954.1
hasty retreat 368.4
hat (n) 5.25 (v) 5.40, 295.21
hatch (n) 189.6, 561.2 (v) 1.2, 78.12, 354.18, 381.9, 517.19, 712.19, 713.9, 892.12, 986.14, 1070.6
hatch a plot 381.9
hat check 728.12
hat-check girl 577.5
hatched 1.4, 354.29
hatchel 79.21
hatchery 886.8
hatchet face 270.5
hatchet-faced 270.19, 1015.7
hatchet job 395.5, 512.4
hatchet man 308.11, 461.1, 512.6, 593.4, 604.7, 610.8
hatching 1.1, 170.3, 517.6, 713.2, 892.1, 1027.6
hatchment 647.2
hatch up 381.9, 892.12
hatchure 170.3
hatchway 189.6
hate (n) 99.2, 103.1, 103.3, 589.3 (v) 93.12, 99.3, 103.5, 589.8
hate crime 103.1
hateful 98.18, 103.8, 144.20, 589.10, 1000.9
hatefulness 98.2, 103.2, 144.5, 1000.2
hate oneself for one's actions 113.6
hater 103.4
hate someone's guts 103.5
hat hair 1016.14
hat head 1016.14
hathi 311.4
hating 103.7
hatmaker 5.37
hatmaking 5.32
hatred 99.2, 103.1, 589.3
hatted 5.45
hatter 5.37
hatting 5.32
hat trick 749.3, 876.1
haugh 310.8
haughland 310.8
haughtiness 136.1, 141.1
haughty 136.9, 141.9, 157.8, 272.14
haughty airs 141.1
haul (n) 261.1, 472.3, 480.10, 482.11, 725.2, 905.2 (v) 176.13, 182.24, 182.48, 725.10, 905.4
haulage 630.7, 905.1
haul around 852.6
haul ass 188.7, 222.10
haul down 182.48, 913.4
haul down the flag 433.8
haul in 745.5
hauling (n) 905.1 (a) 905.6
hauling down 913.1
haul into court 598.13
haulm 310.21
haul off 182.24, 182.36
haul over the coals 510.18
haul round 182.30
haul the wind 182.24
haul to 182.24
haul up 182.24, 182.33, 912.8
haunch 218.1
haunches 217.4

haunt (n) 228.27, 988.1 (v) 98.16, 126.5, 166.3, 221.10, 988.6
haunted 126.8, 988.10, 989.23
haunted with fear 127.22
haunter 221.5, 585.6
haunting 849.13, 989.25
haunt one's thoughts 989.13
haunt the memory 98.16
haute couture 5.32, 578.1
haute cuisine 11.1
hauteur 141.1, 157.1, 272.1
haut monde 578.6, 607.2, 608.1
Havana 89.2, 89.4
Havana seed 89.2
have, a 470.1
have 1.3, 334.5, 356.19, 424.4, 443.10, 469.4, 474.7, 479.6, 521.7, 831.8, 928.12, 989.11
have a baby 1.3
have a bad time 1011.9
have a bad time of it 96.19
have a ball 95.14, 582.21, 743.22
have a bath 79.19
have a beef with 456.9
have a bellyful 994.5
have a bellyful of 99.4
have a bent for 413.18
have a bias 371.17
have a big bazoo 351.6, 540.8
have a big hand for 509.10
have a big mouth 351.6, 540.5, 540.8
have a blast 95.14
have a blind side 30.8
have a blind spot 30.8, 980.6
have a BM 12.13
have a bone in one's throat 525.7
have a bone to pick 451.7
have a bone to pick with 456.9, 589.8
have about enough of 994.5
have a bowel movement 12.13
have a bright idea 886.10
have a brush with 457.17
have a bump for 413.18
have a bun in the oven 78.12
have a care 339.7, 494.7
have a case 957.10, 957.15
have a catch 959.4
have a cat fit 152.15
have accounts to settle 507.5
have a certain sameness 118.6
have a certain state 765.5
have a chance 966.4, 972.13
have a chance at 972.13
have a charmed life 1010.11
have a chill 1023.9
have a chip on one's shoulder 456.13
have a claim 642.6
have a clean bill of health 83.6
have a clear conscience 657.5
have a close call 369.8
have a close shave 369.8
have a comedown 1011.11
have a conniption 152.15
have a conniption fit 152.15
have a cotton habit 87.22
have a cozy chat 541.9
have a crack at 942.8
have a crack at have a try at 403.7
have a crow to pick 589.8
have a crow to pick with 507.5
have a crow to pluck 451.7
have a crow to pluck wit 456.9
have a cruel streak 144.15
have a crush on 104.19
have a deadline 401.8
have a dekko 27.13
have a demon 926.20
have a devil in one 110.13
have a disaffinity for 99.3
have a dram 88.24
have a drink 88.24
have a drop too much 88.27
have a dry run 942.8
have a duck fit 152.15
have a dummy run 942.8
have a faculty for 413.18
have a falling-out 456.10
have a fancy for 100.14, 104.18
have a feeling 934.4
have a fine time of it 1010.10
have a finger in 214.7, 476.5
have a finger in the pie 214.7, 476.5
have a fit 105.16, 926.20
have a fix on 941.6
have a flair for 413.18
have a fling at 403.7, 508.9, 972.13
have a fondness for 104.18
have a free hand 430.18
have a free mind 430.20
have a friendly chat 541.9
have a funny feeling 934.4
have a gift for 413.18
have a go 328.5, 403.7, 825.5, 942.8
have a go at 328.8, 403.7, 818.9
have a gold mine 618.10
have a good appetite 8.24, 100.19
have a good chance 966.4, 968.4
have a good command of 413.18, 928.12
have a good head for 413.18
have a good head on one's shoulder 925.2
have a good knowledge of 928.13
have a good memory 989.9
have a good mind to 324.3
have a good notion 380.5
have a good thing going 409.10, 1010.7
have a good time 95.14, 743.22
have a good time of it 1010.10
have a green thumb 1069.16
have a grudge 152.12
have a guzzle soak 88.24
have a hand for 509.10
have a handful of thumbs 414.11
have a hand in 476.5, 886.12
have a happy result 887.4
have a hard time of it 1011.9, 1013.11
have a head 320.4
have a head on one's shoulders 920.10
have a healthy lead 249.10
have a heart of gold 143.11
have a heart of stone 94.5
have a heart-to-heart 541.9
have a hemorrhage 152.20
have a high incidence 847.3
have a high opinion of 155.4
have a high profile 31.5
have a hold over 894.11
have a hunch 93.10, 133.9, 934.4, 953.11, 961.6
have a jag on 88.27
have a job 724.12
have a joker in the deck 959.4
have a key to the executive washroom 997.12
have a kicker 959.4
have a lech 75.20
have a lech for 100.18
have a leg to stand on 935.17
have a lie-down 20.6
have a little learning 930.10
have a little talk 541.9
have all one can stand 994.5
have all one can take 994.5
have all one's marbles 920.10, 925.2
have all one's wits about one 339.8, 920.10
have all the earmarks of 33.10, 784.7
have all the features of 33.10, 784.7
have all the luck 1010.11
have all the money in the world 618.12
have all the signs of 784.7
have all to oneself 469.6
have a long face 110.15
have a long nose 981.4
have a look 27.13
have a look at 570.13, 931.14, 983.5
have a look-see 27.13
have a lot going for 133.12
have a lot going for one 413.18
have a lot on one's mind 931.8, 983.5
have a lot on one's plate 330.10, 983.5
have a lot to do with 894.10
have a lot to learn 930.9
have a lot to say about 894.10
have a low IQ 922.12
have a low opinion of 510.10
have a meeting of the minds 788.6
have a mind 380.5
have a mind like a sieve 990.4
have a mind of one's own 359.8
have a mind to 100.14, 323.2
have a mint 618.12
have a misery 26.8
have a mishap 1011.10
have a mortgage-burning party 624.13
have a mote in the eye 28.8
have an account with 731.17
have an ague 917.11
have an alias 527.13
have an alibi 600.11
have an anchor to windward 494.6
have an attitude 108.6, 115.16
have an attraction 907.4
have an audience of one 542.3
have an aversion to 99.3
have and hold 469.4, 474.7
have an ear for 48.11, 413.18
have an early night 22.13
have a near miss 223.10
have an edge 285.6
have an entree 189.7
have a nerve 142.7
have a nervous breakdown 128.7
have an escape hatch 368.8, 415.9
have a nest egg 635.4
have an eye for 104.19, 413.18
have an eye on 938.35, 1008.19
have an eye out 27.13
have an eye out for 130.8
have an eye to 100.14, 380.5, 983.9
have an eye to the future 961.5
have an idea 953.11
have an idea of 931.16
have an impediment in one's speech 525.7
have an impression 953.11
have an in 189.7, 894.10
have an income of 479.6
have an inkling 953.11
have an inspiration 986.15
have an intimation 133.9
have an in with 587.9
have a nip 88.24
have an itching palm 100.18
have an itchy palm 100.18
have an opportunity 972.13
have another crack 856.6
have another go 856.6
have another shot 856.6
have another thing coming 977.3
have another think coming 975.10
have another try 856.6
have a notion 380.5
have an out 368.8, 415.9, 600.11
have an overdose 994.5
have ants in one's pants 105.18, 917.11, 917.14
have an understanding 436.5
have an upright carriage 200.7
have a part 898.3
have a part in 476.5
have a party 582.20
have a penchant 371.17, 896.3
have a penchant for 100.14
have a percentage 476.6
have a picture of 986.15
have a piece of 476.6
have a powwow with 422.7
have a premonition 133.10, 961.6
have a presentiment 133.10, 961.6
have a red face 139.8, 656.2
have a rehearsal 942.8
have a relapse 394.4
have a relish of 63.6

have a reversal 473.4
have a right 642.6
have a rightful claim to 639.4
have a rightful claim upon 639.4
have a right to 639.4
have a role 898.3
have a rough time 1013.11
have a run 578.9
have a run of luck 1010.11
have as a fulcrum 959.6
have as a guest 225.10
have as a lodger 225.10
have a say 371.18
have a screw loose 926.20, 926.22
have a second look 849.7
have a sensation 93.10
have a sense 953.11
have a setback 473.4
have a short attention span 984.3
have a short fuse 105.17, 110.13
have a short memory 990.4
have a short memory span 990.4
have a shot at 403.7, 972.13
have a show of hands 371.21
have a slanging match 490.5
have a slight chance 972.13
have a small chance 972.13
have as many phases as the moon 364.4, 854.5
have a soft place in one's heart 93.12
have a soft spot for 63.5
have a soft spot in one's heart 93.12
have a soft spot in one's heart for 100.14, 104.18
have as one's master 570.11
have a stake in 476.6
have a storm in a teapot 998.13
have a story 600.11
have a string attached 959.4
have a stroke of luck 1010.11
have a strong effect 93.15
have a swelled head 140.6
have at 404.3, 457.14, 459.14
have a tabe at 403.7
have a talent for 413.18
have a talk with 541.8
have a tantrum 105.16
have a tapeworm 100.19
have a taste for 100.14, 866.4
have a temper 110.13
have a temper tantrum 105.16
have a tempest in a teacup 998.13
have a tendency 896.3
have a tender heart 93.12
have a test run 942.8
have a theory 951.9
have a thick skin 94.5
have a thing about 24.6, 926.25
have a thorough knowledge of 928.13
have a tiger by the tail 1013.12
have at it 725.15
have a title to 639.4
have at one's command 469.4
have at one's elbow 422.7
have at one's fingertips 928.13, 989.16
have a tongue in one's head 544.7
have a tough row to hoe 1011.9
have a try 403.7
have authority 417.13
have a very red face 137.9
have a voice 371.18
have a voice in 476.5
have a way out 415.9
have a way with 413.18
have a way with one 894.10
have a weakness for 104.18, 866.4
have a weakness in one's heart for 100.14
have a whack at 403.7
have a whirl 403.7
have a white night 23.3
have a willing heart 324.3
have a will of one's own 359.8, 430.20
have a wolf in one's stomach 100.19
have a word with 541.8
have a word with one 399.5, 422.5
have a yellow streak 491.7
have a yen for 100.16
have bad luck 1011.9
have bang to rights 957.15
have bats in one's belfry 926.22
have bats in the belfry 926.20
have been around 413.19
have been around the block 413.19
have been through the mill 413.19
have being 761.8
have better things to do 844.3
have birth 1.2
have blinders on 30.8
have blood in one's eyes 359.8
have blood on one's hands 308.15
have breakfast 8.21
have by heart 989.16
have by rote 989.16
have champagne tastes on a beer budget 486.7
have charisma 894.10
have chilblains 1023.9
have childlike faith in 953.15
have children 1.3
have clean hands 657.5
have clout 417.13
have clout with 894.11
have cold feet 491.7
have coming 639.4
have coming in 479.6
have coming out of one's ears 884.5
have confidence 953.14
have confidence in 953.15, 953.17
have confidential information 345.7
have connection with 775.5
have consideration for 143.10
have constantly in one's thoughts 931.20
have control of 612.12
have conversations 541.10
have currency 352.16, 864.10
have cut one's eyeteeth 413.19
have cut one's wisdom teeth 413.19
have dead to rights 941.8, 957.15
have dealings with 343.6, 731.17
have deep feelings 93.12
have deep pockets 618.11
have designs on 100.14, 104.19, 380.4
have devil 926.20
have dibs on 421.6
have difficulty 1013.11
have dinner 8.21
have done with 370.7, 390.4, 475.3, 857.6
have doubts 955.6
have down cold 928.13
have down pat 928.13
have drag 894.10
have drugs 87.22
have duck bumps 1023.9
have eating out of one's hand 432.10
have effect 889.7
have egg on one's face 414.14, 975.14
have energy 17.11
have enough 412.12, 994.5
have every appearance of 33.10, 784.7
have every indication of 33.10, 784.7
have every intention 380.4, 380.5
have every sign of 33.10
have everything going one's way 1010.7
have everything to learn 930.8
have evidence 957.15
have exclusive possession of 469.6
have exclusive rights to 469.6
have eyes for 104.19
have eyes in the back of one's head 27.14
have faith 692.6
have faith in 953.15
have favorable odds 968.4
have foreplay 75.23
have for one's own 469.5
have for one's very own 469.5
have free play 889.7
have free scope 430.18
have friends in high places 894.10
have full play 894.10
have fun 582.21, 743.22
have game 413.19
have going for it 421.6
have going for one 421.6, 469.4
have good chemistry 587.11
have good prospects 124.9
have goose bumps 74.7
have goosebumps 1023.9
have gooseflesh 74.7
have goose pimples 1023.9
have got to 963.10
have green in the eye 153.3
have had it 135.5, 994.5
have had its day 837.6
have had one's day 303.11
have half a mind 380.5
have half a mind to 323.2
have half a notion 380.5
have half a notion to 323.2
have high visibility 31.5
have hold of 521.8, 928.12
have hoped for better 132.4
have hot pants for 75.20
have impact 518.8
have in contemplation 130.5
have independent means 618.11
have influence 894.10
have influence over 894.11
have information about 928.12
have in hand 404.4, 469.4, 612.12
have in mind 130.5, 148.4, 380.5, 518.9, 931.16, 931.20, 989.12
have in one's eye 983.9
have in one's grasp 469.4
have in one's hands 417.13
have in one's head 928.13
have in one's pocket 894.11
have in one's possession 469.4
have in one's power 612.12
have in prospect 130.5
have in reserve 386.13
have inside information 551.15
have in sight 27.12
have in store 386.13
have in store for 964.7
have intercourse 75.21
have in tow 769.8
have in view 380.5
have it 307.19, 820.7, 940.2
have it all one's own way 612.12, 1014.11
have it all one's way 323.3, 411.4
have it all over 249.6, 249.7
have it bad 104.19
have it both ways at once 354.24
have it break good for one 1010.11
have it coming 604.21
have it down pat 521.8
have it easy 1014.11
have it in for 99.3, 103.6, 144.15, 589.8
have it in the bag 1014.11
have it in the genes 767.6
have it made 409.10, 1010.7
have it out 457.17, 935.16
have it out of 604.10
have it reported 551.14
have it soft 1014.11
have its place 159.9
have its seat in 159.10
have its slot 159.9
have its time 820.7
have it taped 521.8, 928.13
have it up to here 994.5
have it wrapped up 409.10
have knowledge of 928.12
have legs 409.7, 704.28
have leverage 894.10

have life 306.8
have little in common 787.2
have little recall 990.4
have little to say 51.5, 344.6
have little weight 298.6
have long ears 48.10
have lots of laughs 743.22
have low self-esteem 139.7
have lunch 8.21
have magnetism 894.10
have many irons in the fire 330.10, 783.2
have means 618.11
have mercy upon 145.4
have method in one's madness 920.10
have mixed feelings 362.6, 539.3, 971.9
have money 618.11
have money to burn 618.12
have more than one can hold 88.27
have much ado with 1013.11
have much to answer for 656.2, 674.5
haven (n) 186.5, 1009.1, 1009.6 (v) 1008.18
have need to 963.10
have nine lives 306.11, 1007.2
have no affectations 416.4
have no alibi 656.2
have no alternative 963.11
have no association with 368.6
have no attention span 984.3
have no bearing 776.4
have no bounds 823.2, 829.6
have no business with 776.4
have no chance 972.14
have no choice 963.11
have no claim upon 640.5
have no clout 998.11
have no conception 930.10
have no desire for 102.4
have no diffidence 953.14
have no doubt 953.14, 970.9
have no ears 49.4
have no end 823.2, 829.6
have no expectation 131.4
have no false modesty 140.6
have no fight left 433.7
have no hand in 329.4, 668.7
have no idea 930.10
have no kick coming 107.5
have no liking for 99.3
have no limit 823.2
have no limits 829.6
have no lower to go 393.17
have no measures with 456.8
have no misgivings 953.14
have no more 473.4
have no objection 441.2
have no opportunity 972.14
have no option but 963.11
have no patience with 135.5
have no plan 406.6
have no problem with 332.8, 521.7, 788.6
have no pull 998.11
have no qualms 953.14
have no recollection of 990.5
have no regrets 114.3
have no relish for 102.4
have no remedy 125.9
have no remembrance of 990.5
have no remorse 114.3
have no reservations 953.14
have no respect for 510.10
have no right to 640.5
have no second thoughts 953.14
have no secrets 348.6, 521.4
have no self-doubt 140.6
have no shame 114.3
have no staying power 16.9
have no stomach for 491.8
have not a hope 125.9
have not a prayer 125.9
have no taste for 99.3, 102.4
have nothing but time 402.3
have nothing in common 787.2
have nothing on 250.4, 331.16
have nothing to complain about 107.5
have nothing to do 331.16
have nothing to do with 329.4, 368.6, 442.3, 583.4, 586.5, 668.7, 776.4
have nothing to go on 930.9
have nothing to hide 657.5
have no thought of 131.4
have no time for 99.3, 156.4, 984.2
have no time to lose 401.8
have no time to spare 401.8
have no title to 640.5
have no truck with 157.7, 368.6, 586.5
have-nots, the 606.4, 619.3
have no turns 277.4
have no use for 99.3
have occasion for 963.9
have on 5.44
have one dead to rights 429.15
have one foot in the grave 16.8, 303.11
have one for the road 188.16
have one on the ropes 1013.16
have one's back to the wall 1006.8, 1013.11
have one's cake and eat it 651.4
have one's cake and eat it too 354.24
have one's credit good for 622.7
have one's doubts 955.6, 971.9
have one's druthers 323.3, 371.13, 430.18
have one's ear 48.12
have one's eye on 27.12, 100.14
have one's eyes opened 977.3
have one's fill 994.5
have one's flesh crawl at the thought of 99.5
have one's fling 430.19, 669.6, 743.24
have one's friend 12.18
have one's hand in the till 482.13
have one's hands full 330.10, 1013.11
have one's hands in 404.4, 724.11
have one's hands tied 19.7
have one's head in the clouds 986.17
have one's head screwed on right 920.10
have one's heart bleed for 145.3
have one's heart go out to 145.3
have one's heart in one's mouth 126.6, 127.10
have one's heart in the right place 143.11
have one's heart miss a beat 126.6
have one's heart's desire 107.5
have one's heart set on 100.17
have one's heart skip a beat 126.6, 127.10
have one's heart stand still 126.6, 127.10
have one's hide 604.10
have one's innings 825.5
have one's marriage annulled 566.5
have one's measure 941.8
have one's mind made up 947.2
have one's moments 1010.11
have one's name in lights 704.29
have one's name on the danger list 1006.8
have one's nerve 142.7
have one's nose in a book 570.12
have one's nose out of joint 152.12
have one's number 941.8
have one's options reduced 963.11
have one's own way 417.13, 430.20
have one's period 12.18
have one's place in the sun 1010.10
have one's pride 136.4
have one's revenge 507.4
have one's say 334.5, 524.21
have one's time 307.19
have one's way 323.3
have one's way with 412.10
have one's will 323.3
have one's will of 480.15
have one's wits about one 925.2
have one's words stick in one's throat 51.5
have one's work cut out 1013.11
have one to know 551.8
have on one's hands 404.4, 656.2
have on one's mind 931.20
have on one's shoulders 404.4
have on the brain 849.9, 931.20
have on the edge of one's consciousness 989.20
have on the tip of one's tongue 989.20
have on the tip of the tongue 990.5
have origin 818.13
have other fish to fry 330.10, 844.3
have other things to do 330.10
have over a barrel 417.13
have partiality 371.17
have perfect pitch 48.11
have permission 443.13
have personality 894.10
have pity 145.4
have place 159.9
have play 889.7
have plenty of time 402.3
have plenty on the ball 413.18
have power 417.13, 612.12
have power over 894.11
have preference 371.17
have prestige 155.7
have priority 814.2
have prior knowledge 961.6
have promise 133.12
have proof 957.15
have pull 894.10
have pull with 894.11
have qualms 127.10, 325.4
have quite enough 994.5
haver (n) 470.1 (v) 540.5
have rather 371.17
have reason to hope 124.6
have recourse to 387.14
have regard for 143.10, 983.9
have regard to 937.3
have repercussions 903.6
have reservations 955.6
have rocks in one's head 926.22
have rotten luck 1011.9
have run its course 837.6
have run out 837.6
haves, the 618.6
haves and have-nots 607.1
have savvy 413.19, 920.10
have scruples 325.4
have second thoughts 113.7, 163.7, 363.6, 494.5, 931.15
have secret information 345.7
have seen better days 303.11, 393.16, 619.5, 1011.11
have seen one's best days 303.11
have seen one's day 303.11
have sewed up 970.9
have sex 75.21
have sexual relations 75.21
have simple faith in 953.15
have smarts 920.10
have someone's number 521.9
have something at hand 223.8
have something at one's fingertips 223.8
have something hanging over one's head 1006.8
have something laid by 386.13
have something laid by for a rainy day 386.13
have something on 957.15
have something on one's mind 931.8
have something on the ball 413.18
have something to draw on 386.13
have something to spare 413.18
have something up one's sleeve 386.13, 415.9
have sown one's wild oats 303.9
have stars in one's eyes 95.12, 986.17
have sticky fingers 100.18
have subject 432.10

have suction 894.10
have suffrage 476.5
have suspicions 955.6
have tenure 825.5
have tenure of 469.4
have tenure of appointment 825.5
have that or nothing 963.11
have the abdabs 74.7
have the appearance of 33.10
have the ascendancy 249.6, 612.14
have the audacity 142.7
have the authority 249.11
have the bar sinister 1.2
have the blues 110.14, 112.15
have the cards stacked against one 1013.11
have the chances against one 1006.8
have the cheek 142.7
have the cold creeps 74.7
have the cold shivers 1023.9
have the conn 182.14
have the courage of one's convictions 492.9
have the credentials 405.15
have the creeps 74.7
have the curse 12.18
have the deed for 469.5
have the ear of 587.9, 953.20
have the edge 249.6
have the facts 551.15
have the fidgets 105.18, 128.6, 917.13
have the final say 939.5
have the flavor of 63.6
have the floor 613.10
have the force of 518.8
have the friendship of 587.9
have the function of 889.8
have the gall 142.7
have the game in one's hands 1014.11
have the game in one's own hands 411.4, 612.12
have the gift of gab 544.7
have the gift of the gab 544.7
have the golden touch 618.10
have the goods on 941.7, 957.15
have the guts 492.9
have the hang of it 413.18
have the heebie-jeeies 74.7
have the idea 886.10, 953.11
have the impression 934.4
have the inside track 894.10
have the jitters 128.6, 917.11
have the job of 889.8
have the killer instinct 144.15
have the knack 413.18
have the last laugh 411.3
have the last word 249.11, 323.3, 886.12, 894.8, 939.5, 958.4
have the latchstring out 585.7
have the law in 598.13
have the look of 33.10
have the makings of 968.4
have the mandate 417.13
have the mastery of 612.14
have the mission of 889.8
have them rolling in the aisles 743.21
have the munchies 8.20
have the nerve 492.9
have the odds against one 1006.8
have the opinion 953.13
have the power 417.13
have the prerequisites 405.15
have the qualifications 405.15
have the right 417.13
have the right touch 413.18
have the ring of truth 973.9
have the role of 889.8
have the run of 430.18
have the runs 12.13
have the say 249.11, 417.13, 894.8
have the say-so 18.11, 417.13, 894.8
have the sense 953.11
have the sense of 518.8
have the shakes 105.18, 917.11
have the sway 612.13
have the time of one's life 95.14
have the top place 198.10
have the top spot 198.10
have the touch 413.18
have the trots 12.13
have the upper hand 612.14
have the use of 387.10
have the wherewithal 384.6, 618.11
have the whip hand 249.11, 417.13
have the wind of 182.26
have the world at one's feet 409.10
have the wrong way round 342.2
have thoughts about 931.16
have tied to one's apron strings 432.8
have time 402.3
have time enough 402.3
have time to spare 402.3
have title to 469.5
have to 424.9, 963.10
have to do with 476.5, 775.5, 889.6
have to fall back upon 386.13
have to hand it to 509.14
have too many irons in the fire 404.6, 993.10
have too much 994.5
have too much of a good thing 994.5
have too much on one's plate 404.6, 993.10
have to one's discredit 656.2
have to one's name 469.5
have to run for it 1006.8
have total recall 989.9
have trouble 1011.9, 1013.11
have truck with 343.6, 731.17
have tunnel vision 980.6
have two minds 362.6
have two strikes against one 1013.11
have under consideration 931.16
have under control 612.12
have under one's thumb 417.13, 432.8
have up one's sleeve 390.5
have up the gazoo 884.5
have veto power over 894.8
have way upon 182.19
have weight 297.10
have well in hand 612.12
have what it takes 15.9
have what one says go 417.13
have whiskers 303.10, 842.9
have words 456.11, 935.16
have words with 510.17
have young 1.3
having 469.9
having a baby 1.1
having and holding 469.9
having a part 476.1
having a share 476.1
having a voice 476.1
having had one too many 88.31
having high self-esteem 140.8
having high self-valuation 140.8
having intercourse 75.7
having life (n) 306.1 (a) 306.12
having no religious preference 695.15
havings 471.1
having sex 75.7
having sight 27.20
having title to 469.1
having vision 27.20
havoc (n) 395.1, 1000.3 (v) 395.10
haw 164.6, 525.8
hawk (n) 27.11, 311.27, 461.5, 591.3 (v) 13.6, 382.9, 734.9
hawk, the 318.7
hawk call 517.16
hawker 730.5
hawkeye 27.10**hawk-eyed** 27.21, 339.13
hawking (n) 375.3, 382.2, 734.2 (a) 525.12
Hawking radiation 1073.8
hawking voice 525.1
hawkish 458.21, 459.30, 591.4
hawkishness 458.10
hawklike 311.48
hawkshaw 576.11
hawser 905.1
hay (n) 10.4, 87.11 (v) 1069.19
hay, the 901.19
hayburner 757.2
haycock 770.10
hay fever 85.34
hayfield 1069.9
hayloft 197.16, 386.7
haymaker 754.3, 1069.5
haymish 581.3
haymow 386.7, 770.10
hayrick 386.7, 770.10
hayseed (n) 227.10, 310.31, 606.6, 924.5 (a) 233.8
haystack 770.10
haywagon 179.2
haywire 393.38, 810.13, 926.27, 927.6
hazard (n) 751.1, 759.2, 759.3, 971.6, 972.6, 1006.1, 1012.4 (v) 640.6, 759.24, 759.25, 972.11, 1006.6, 1006.7
hazard a conjecture 951.11
hazarder 759.21
hazarding 759.1
hazard of the die 759.2, 759.9
hazardous 759.27, 971.20, 1006.10
hazardous materials 391.4, 1006.1
hazardousness 1006.2
hazardous waste 391.4
hazard pay 150.2, 254.4
haze (n) 87.10, 319.3, 985.3, 1065.4 (v) 319.7, 490.5
hazel 40.3
haziness 32.2, 263.1, 319.4, 971.4
hazing 490.2
HAZMAT 391.4
hazy 32.6, 263.4, 319.10, 522.15, 971.19, 985.13
hazy idea 951.5
hazy recollection 990.1
H-blast 1038.16
H-bomb 462.20
he 76.4, 865.5
he- 76.12
head (n) 2.7, 3.4, 12.10, 87.21, 101.5, 180.14, 198.4, 198.5, 198.7, 216.1, 216.1, 238.2, 249.4, 283.9, 310.27, 312.5, 320.2, 554.12, 557.1, 574.2, 712.14, 752.3, 809.2, 886.5, 902.2, 919.1, 919.6, 920.9, 937.1, 937.2, 1065.3 (v) 161.7, 165.2, 198.10, 216.7, 297.15, 573.8, 612.11, 752.4, 814.2, 896.3, 937.3 (a) 198.11, 216.10, 573.12, 612.17, 818.17
headache 26.5, 85.9, 85.25, 96.2, 118.5, 1013.3, 1013.7
headache powder 86.12
headachy 26.12
head and shoulders above 249.13, 999.14
head away from 182.36
headband 554.14
headbanger 924.4
headbanging 424.3
headcase 926.15, 926.16
head cheese 997.11
head chef 11.3
headchute 239.5
headcloth 5.25
headclothes 5.25
head count 227.1, 871.6, 1017.11
headdress 3.15, 5.25
headed 198.13
headed group 529.1
header 194.3, 367.1, 752.3
head for 161.9
head for blue water 182.19
head for the bottom 633.6
head gate 239.11
headgear 5.25
head honcho 575.4
headhunt 615.14
headhunter 308.11, 615.5
head in 857.7
headiness 69.2

heading (n) 161.1, 165.1, 184.34, 198.4, 216.1, 527.3, 573.2, 809.2, 937.1, 937.2 (a) 165.3, 198.12
heading up 573.2
head in the clouds 933.1, 984.1
head into 182.41, 216.8, 492.10, 818.7
headlamp 1025.19
headland 237.2, 283.9
headless 198.14, 922.13
head librarian 558.3
headlights 283.7
headline (n) 937.2 (v) 704.28, 937.3, 997.15
headline attraction 707.6
headliner 377.3, 707.6
headlock 474.3
headlong 174.15, 204.18, 365.9, 401.10, 493.8, 830.5
headlong plunge 174.3, 174.4
headlong rush 174.3
head louse 311.36
headman (n) 574.2, 575.3, 575.16 (v) 749.7
headmanning 749.3
headmaster 571.8
headmistress 571.8
headmost 165,3, 198.11, 216.10, 249.14, 814.4
head off 164.6
head office 739.7
head of hair 3.4
head of household 227.7
head of service 558.3
head of state 575.7
head of the class 999.8
head of the slate 610.9
head of the ticket 610.9
head-on 216.10
head-on attack 459.1
head-over-heels 205.7
head over heels in 898.5, 983.17
head over heels in love 104.28
headphone 347.5
headphones 50.8
headpiece 5.25, 198.4, 198.7, 919.1
headquarters 208.6, 739.7
headrace 239.2
head register 58.6
head resistance 184.27
headroom 158.3, 224.1
heads 215.3, 759.2
headset 50.8, 347.5
headship 249.3, 417.7, 573.4
headshrinker 92.10
headsman 604.7
head-splitting 53.11
headspring 886.6
headstand 205.2
head start 249.2, 845.1
headstock 915.7
headstone 549.12, 901.7
head straight for 161.10
headstream 238.2, 886.6
headstrong 361.8, 418.5
headstrongness 361.1
head the line 165.2
head the table 814.2
head to leeward 182.23
head tone 58.6
head-to-toe 772.5
head toward 182.35
head to wind 182.17
head to windward 182.24
head trip 931.6
head-turning 31.6
head up 216.7, 573.8, 814.2, 818.10, 937.3
head voice 58.6, 709.5
headwaiter 577.7
headwater 238.2, 886.6
headwaters 238.2
headway 158.3, 162.1, 182.9, 392.1
headwear 5.25
head wind 184.32, 451.1
headwind 318.1, 318.10, 900.4
headwork 570.3, 931.1
heady 69.10, 70.9, 88.36, 105.30, 320.7, 418.5
heal 91.24, 396.15, 396.21
healer 90.9
healing (n) 91.1, 91.2, 396.7 (a) 86.39
healing agent 86.1
healing arts 91.1
healing quality 86.1
healing virtue 86.1
heal itself 396.21
heal over 396.21
health (n) 8.4, 83.1, 88.10, 869.1 (a) 90.15
health and fitness 83.1
health awareness program 83.5
health care 83.5, 90.1
health-care delivery 90.1
health-care delivery plan 83.5
health-care delivery service 83.5
health-care industry 90.1
health-care policy 83.5
health-care professional 90.8, 726.4
health-care provider 90.8
health center 91.21
health club 83.5, 84.1
health commissioner 83.5
health-conscious 83.14
health department 83.5
heal the breach 465.8
health-enhancing 81.5
health examination 938.6
health food 7.3, 10.1
healthful 7.21, 81.5, 83.8
healthfulness 7.2, 81.1, 83.2
health-giving 81.5
health hazard 82.1
healthiness 81.1, 83.2, 999.1
health insurance 83.5, 90.1, 611.7, 624.6
healthless 85.54
healthlessness 85.3
health maintenance 83.5
health maintenance organization 83.5, 90.4, 90.13
health management 83.5
health physicist 81.3
health physics 81.2
health plan 83.5
health policy 83.5
health-preserving 81.5
health-protecting 83.14
health protection 83.5
health resort 91.23, 228.27
health service 83.5
health spa 83.5, 84.1, 228.27
healthwalking 84.2
healthy 81.5, 83.8, 257.16, 999.12
healthy body 83.2
healthy constitution 83.2
healthy economy 731.7
healthy glow 35.2
healthy hue 35.2
healthy meal 8.8
healthy mind 925.1
healthy-minded 925.4
healthy mind in a healthy body, a 925.1
heal up 396.13, 396.15
heap (n) 179.10, 244.2, 247.4, 257.10, 386.1, 770.4, 770.10 (v) 159.15, 478.12, 770.19
heap dirt upon 512.10
heaped 386.14, 770.21
heaped on 643.8
heaped-up 884.6
heaping on 643.1
heaping up 472.2
heaps 618.3
heaps of gold 618.2
heap up 159.15, 386.11, 472.11, 770.19
heap upon 478.15, 485.3
hear 24.6, 48.10, 48.11, 551.15, 598.18, 946.12, 983.7
hear a big hand for 509.10
hearable 50.16
hear a different drummer 327.6, 333.4, 789.5, 868.4
hear confession 148.3, 701.17
heard 50.16
hearer 48.5, 479.3
hear from 48.11
hearing (n) 24.5, 48.1, 48.2, 48.4, 598.5, 938.2, 938.4, 942.3 (a) 48.13, 48.14
hearing aid 48.8, 49.3
hearing dog 30.6
hearing ear dog 311.16
hearing-impaired 49.6
hearing impairment 49.1
hearing loss 49.1
hearing organ 2.10, 48.7
hear it for 509.10
hearken 48.10
hearkener 48.5
hearken to 326.2, 983.7
hear loud and clear 521.8
hear nothing 984.2
hear of 48.11, 443.10
hear out 48.10
hear say 551.15
hearsay (n) 552.6 (a) 957.16
hearsay evidence 958.1
hearse (n) 309.10 (v) 309.19
hear shots fired in anger 458.17
heart 2.16, 10.20, 93.2, 93.3, 104.1, 196.5, 207.2, 208.2, 306.2, 492.5, 767.2, 767.5, 819.1, 919.4, 978.4, 997.6
heartache 96.6, 112.9
heart and soul 767.2, 767.5
heart attack 85.19
heartbeat 306.2, 916.3
heartblood 306.2
heartbreak 98.4, 112.9
heartbreaker 562.12
heartbreaking 98.23, 145.8
heartbroken 112.29
heartbrokenness 112.9
heartburn 26.5, 85.29, 153.1
heartburning 152.3, 153.1
heart condition 85.19
heart disease 85.19
hear tell of 48.11, 551.15
hearten 17.10, 109.7, 121.6, 375.21, 449.14, 492.15
heartening (n) 492.8 (a) 109.16, 121.13, 124.12
heart-expanding 105.30
heart failure 85.19
heartfelt 93.24
heartfelt apology 113.4
heartfelt grief 112.10
heartgrief 112.10
hearth 228.2, 559.5, 1020.11
hearth and home 228.2
hearthside 559.5, 1020.11
hearthstone 79.17, 228.2, 1020.11
heartiness 15.1, 17.2, 83.3, 93.2, 101.2, 109.4, 582.3, 585.1, 587.6
heartland 207.3, 231.1
heartlands 231.7
heartless 94.9, 94.13, 112.22, 144.25, 146.3, 491.11, 654.17
heartlessness 94.1, 94.4, 112.3, 144.10, 146.1, 491.2, 654.6
heartlike 279.15
heart of gold 143.1, 485.1, 999.9
heart of hearts 93.3, 207.2, 767.5
heart of oak 15.8, 492.5, 1046.6
heart of stone 94.3, 114.2, 144.10, 146.1, 654.6
heart of the matter 537.1, 819.1
heartquake 105.5, 127.5
heartrending 98.23, 145.8
heart-robbing 97.7
hearts 87.4, 758.2
hearts-and-flowers 93.8
heart's blood 306.2
heart's core 93.3, 767.5
heart's desire 100.1, 100.11
heart's ease 121.4
heart-shaped 279.15
heartsick 96.26, 112.28
heartsickening 98.23
heartsickness 98.4, 112.9
heart-sink (n) 96.8 (v) 98.14
heartsmitten 104.27
heartsore 112.28
heartsoreness 112.9
heart-stirring 105.30
heart-stopper 105.1
heart-stopping 105.30
heart strain 21.1
heart-stricken 96.26, 112.29
heartstrings 93.3
heart-struck 96.26, 112.29
heartstruck 104.27
heart surgery 85.19
The Heart Sutra 683.9
heart-swelling 105.30

heart-thrilling 105.30
heartthrob 104.10, 916.3
heart-to-heart (n) 541.3 (a) 644.17
heart-to-heart talk 541.3
heart trouble 85.19
heartwarming 97.6, 97.7, 109.16
heartwood 1054.3
heartwounding 98.23
heartwrenching 112.27
hearty (n) 183.1, 588.5 (a) 15.15, 17.13, 83.12, 93.18, 101.9, 109.14, 582.23, 585.11, 587.16
hearty assent 332.1
hearty eater 672.3
hearty enjoyment 95.1
hearty laugh 116.4
hearty meal 8.8
hearty welcome 585.2
hear what one is saying 521.8
heat (n) 68.2, 75.5, 85.7, 93.2, 101.2, 105.7, 152.5, 457.12, 544.5, 755.2, 1008.16, 1019.1 (v) 11.5, 105.12, 375.17, 1020.17 (a) 1021.9
heat barrier 1075.2
heated 11.7, 93.18, 101.9, 105.22, 671.22, 1019.25, 1020.29
heated imagination 986.4
heatedness 101.2, 1019.1
heated up 119.4, 1020.29
heater 462.10, 1019.11, 1020.10
heat exchange 1020.1
heat exhaustion 85.28
heath 236.1, 310.8, 891.2
heat haze 1019.7
heathen (n) 688.7, 695.11 (a) 688.11, 695.19, 697.7, 930.13
heathendom 688.4
heathen god 678.2
heathenish 688.11
heathenism 688.4, 697.1, 930.3
heathenry 688.4
heathered 35.22
Heath Robinson device 799.2
heat index 317.4
heating (n) 1019.1, 1020.1 (a) 1020.26
heating duct 1020.10
heating element 1020.10
heating method 1020.1
heating pipe 1020.10
heating system 1020.1
heating tool 1020.14
heating-up 251.2
heat lamp 1020.10
heat lightning 1025.17
heat prostration 85.28
heat pump 317.10
heat rash 85.36
heat shield 1075.2
heat source 1021.1
heatstroke 85.28
heat-temper 1046.7
heat-tempered 1046.15
heat the economy 632.9, 731.21
heat therapy 91.4
heat transfer 1019.1
heat-treated 1046.15
heat treating 1046.4
heat up 11.5, 119.2, 251.5, 375.17, 589.7, 1020.17
heat up the economy 632.9, 731.21
heat wave 317.3, 1019.7
heave (n) 238.14, 725.2, 904.3, 905.2, 912.2 (v) 99.4, 105.18, 182.48, 182.55, 238.22, 725.10, 904.10, 905.4, 909.26, 912.5
heave aloft 200.9
heave alongside 182.35
heave a peak 182.48
heave a sigh of relief 120.8
heave at 459.28
heave down 182.43
heave-ho 372.1, 909.5
heave in sight 33.8
heave in together 182.46
Heaven 307.3, 681.1, 839.2, 964.3, 986.11
heaven 95.2, 97.1, 198.2, 272.2, 1010.4, 1073.2
heaven-aspiring 272.15
heaven-high 272.15
heavenish 681.12
heaven-kissing 272.15
heavenliness 677.1, 685.1, 692.2, 1016.5
heavenly 97.9, 677.16, 679.6, 681.12, 685.7, 692.9, 986.23, 999.15, 1016.20, 1073.25
heavenly being 679.1
heavenly body 1073.4
Heavenly City 681.3
Heavenly City of God 681.3
heavenly hierarchy 679.2
heavenly host 679.2
heavenly-minded 692.9
heavenly-mindedness 692.2
Heaven of heavens 681.4
Heaven on earth 986.11
heaven-reaching 272.15
heavens 198.2, 272.2
heavens, the 1073.2
Heaven's designation 681.1
heaven-sent 843.9, 995.5
heavenwide 864.14
heave offering 696.7
heave out 909.13
heave out a sail 182.20
heave overboard 390.7
heaver 904.7
heave round 182.30, 182.48
heaves 85.41
heaves, the 909.8
heave short 182.48
heave the gorge 909.26
heave the lead 275.10
heave the log 182.48
heave to 182.24, 182.33
heavier-than-air craft 181.1
heavily committed 897.5
heavily muscled 15.16
heaviness 22.1, 78.5, 98.8, 112.1, 117.1, 297.1, 331.6, 534.1, 1062.2
heaviness of heart 112.1
heaving (n) 105.5, 904.2, 905.1, 909.8 (a) 2.32
heaving aloft 200.4
heaving up 200.4
heavy (n) 257.12, 704.10, 707.2 (a) 22.21, 54.11, 78.18, 98.24, 112.20, 117.6, 173.14, 247.6, 269.8, 297.16, 310.43, 319.8, 331.20, 524.30, 534.3, 704.34, 725.18, 763.7, 922.16, 997.20, 999.13, 1013.18, 1045.12, 1062.12
heavy-armed 460.14
heavy artillery 462.11
heavy as lead 297.16
heavy blow 318.11
heavy chemicals 1060.2
heavy cruiser 180.6
heavy demand 421.1
heavy dragoon 461.12
heavy drinker 88.11
heavy drinking 88.3
heavy duty 387.1
heavy-duty 1049.4
heavy-eyed 22.21
heavy eyelids 22.1
heavy field artillery 462.11
heavy-footed 534.2
heavy-footedness 534.1
heavy hand 425.3, 612.9
heavy-handed 25.6, 414.20, 534.2
heavy-handedness 414.3, 534.1
heavy harmony 708.3
heavy heart 96.6, 112.1
heavyhearted 112.20
heavyheartedness 112.1
heavy hitter 894.6
heavy hydrogen 1038.5
heavy industry 892.3
heavy jack 618.3
heavy-laden 126.9, 794.12
heavy lead 707.6
heavy lettuce 618.3
heavy lift 1013.2
heavy lifting 360.1, 725.5
heavy loser 625.4
heavy machinery 1040.3
heavy meal 8.8
heavy metal 708.10, 1060.2
heavy momma 575.4, 997.9
heavy money 618.3
heavy particle 1037.4
heavy particle counter 1075.7
heavy petting 562.2
heavy rain 316.2
heavy right foot 174.3
heavy scene 997.3
heavy sea 238.14
heavyset 257.18, 269.8
heavy sin 655.2
heavy sky 319.4
heavy sledding 1013.2
heavy sleep 22.5
heavy-smelling 71.5
heavy smoker 87.21
heavy swell 238.14
heavy thinking 931.1
heavy water 1065.3
heavy weather 1011.6
heavyweight (n) 257.12, 297.3, 894.6, 997.8 (a) 297.16, 997.17
heavy wine 88.17
heavy with child 78.18
heavy with meaning 133.15
heavy with sleep 22.21
heavy with young 78.18
hebdomadal 850.8
hebdomadary 850.8
hebdomal 882.19
Hebe 577.5
hebephrenia 926.4
hebephreniac 926.17
hebephrenic schizophrenia 926.4
hebetate 94.7
hebetude 94.4, 331.6, 922.3
hebetudinous 94.13, 331.20, 922.16
Hebraism 675.12
Hebrew (n) 675.21 (a) 675.30
Hebrew calendar 832.8
Hebrewism 675.12
Hebrides, the 1023.4
Hecate 1073.12
hecatomb 308.3, 395.1, 696.7, 882.8
heckle 59.6, 79.21, 96.13
heckled 96.24
heckler 96.10
heckling 59.1
hectic (n) 41.3, 1019.12 (a) 41.9, 85.58, 101.12, 105.22, 330.24
hectic flush 41.3, 85.7, 1019.12
hecticness 917.1
hectograph 548.14, 785.8
hectograph copy 785.5
hectography 785.2
Hector 492.7
hector (n) 502.5, 503.2 (v) 96.13, 127.20, 503.3
hectored 96.24
hectorer 503.2
hectoring (n) 127.6, 503.1 (a) 503.4, 514.3
hedge (n) 211.3, 494.1, 959.1 (v) 210.5, 212.7, 368.8, 494.6, 936.9, 959.3
hedge about 210.5, 959.3
hedged 210.7, 212.10, 959.10, 987.5
hedged about 210.6, 959.10
hedged about by 959.9
hedged by 959.9
hedged in 428.15
hedged-in 212.10
hedge fund 729.4
hedgehog 311.22, 462.21, 1074.10
hedgehop 184.42
hedgehopping 184.17
hedge in 210.4, 212.5, 212.7
hedge one's bets 494.6
hedge out 212.7
hedger 936.7
hedge trimmer 1040.8
hedging (n) 210.2, 494.1, 936.5, 959.1 (a) 325.7, 936.14
hedging-in 212.1
hedging one's bets 494.1
hedonic 95.18, 663.5
hedonic calculus 663.1
hedonics 95.4, 663.1
hedonic treadmill 95.4, 373.5
hedonism 95.4, 636.2, 651.1, 663.1, 669.2
hedonist 663.3
hedonistic 95.18, 651.5, 663.5

heebie-jeebies 127.5, 128.2, 917.1
heebie-jeebies, the 926.10
heed (n) 339.1, 434.1, 494.1, 983.1 (v) 48.10, 326.2, 339.6, 434.2, 983.6
heedful 143.16, 339.10, 494.8, 983.15
heedfulness 143.3, 339.1, 494.1, 983.1
heeding 48.1, 434.1
heedless 25.8, 102.7, 144.18, 340.11, 365.10, 406.15, 982.3, 984.6, 990.9
heedlessness 25.2, 102.2, 144.3, 340.2, 365.3, 406.2, 493.2, 982.1, 984.1, 990.1
heed one's better self 113.6
hee-haw (n) 116.4 (v) 116.8
hee-hee (n) 116.4 (v) 116.8
heel (n) 199.5, 217.1, 217.7, 660.5 (v) 163.9, 164.3, 166.3, 182.43, 385.8, 754.4
heel-and-toe racing 755.2
heelball rubbing 1044.2
heeled 87.25, 385.13, 460.14
heeler 138.6, 609.27, 610.8
heeling (n) 166.1 (a) 791.5
heel of Achilles 16.4, 1006.4
heelpiece 217.1
heffalump 311.4
heft (n) 297.1 (v) 297.10, 912.5
heftiness 15.2, 257.8, 297.1
hefting 297.9
hefty 15.15, 257.18, 297.16, 725.18, 1013.18
Hegelian (n) 1053.4 (a) 952.12, 1053.8
Hegelian idea 932.2
Hegelianism 1053.3
hegemonic 249.14, 417.15, 612.17
hegemonical 249.14
hegemonistic 417.15, 612.17
hegemony 249.1, 249.3, 417.6, 417.7
hegira 188.1, 368.4
he-goat 76.8, 311.8
heh heh 116.4
Heideggerian 952.12
heifer 77.9, 302.7, 311.6
height 158.1, 237.6, 245.1, 249.3, 257.1, 272.1, 272.2, 709.4, 912.1, 1002.3
heighten 119.2, 251.5, 272.13, 912.5
heightened 119.4, 251.7
heightening 119.1, 251.2, 355.1
heighth 272.1
height of fashion 578.1
height of one's ambition, the 100.11
heights 237.1, 272.2
heinous 98.18, 654.16, 661.12, 1000.9
heinousness 98.2, 144.11, 654.4, 661.3, 1000.2
heir 256.3, 479.5, 561.3, 817.4, 835.2
heir apparent 479.5, 608.7
heir at law 479.5
heir by destination 479.5
heiress 479.5, 561.3
heir expectant 479.5
heir general 479.5
heir in tail 479.5
heirloom 479.2
heirloom plant 310.3, 1069.2
heirloom seed 310.31, 1069.2
heir of entail 479.5
heir of the body 479.5
heir presumptive 479.5, 608.7
heirs 561.1
heirship 479.2
Heisenberg principle 971.1
Heisenberg's principle 972.1
heist (n) 482.4 (v) 482.16, 912.5
Hel 682.3, 682.5
held 386.15, 429.19, 469.8, 855.16, 901.24, 926.33, 953.23, 983.18
held back 386.15, 390.12
held dear 104.23
heldentenor 709.5
held in awe 662.18
held in consideration 155.11
held in esteem 662.15
held in favor 155.11
held in pledge 438.13
held in regard 155.11
held in reserve 386.15, 390.12
held in respect 155.11
held in trust 438.13
held out 390.12
held up 846.16
Helen of Troy 1016.9
heliacal 1073.25
helical 281.8, 914.7, 915.15
helical gear 1040.9
helicline 204.4
helicoid (n) 915.2 (a) 281.8
helicoidal 281.8
Helicon 720.11
helicopter 181.5, 181.9
helicopter gunship 181.9
helicopter parent 559.1
helicopter skiing 753.1
helidrome 184.22
heliocentric longitude 1073.16
heliochrome 714.3
heliochromy 714.1
Heliogabalus 663.3
heliograph 517.15, 714.3
heliographic 1025.41
heliography 1025.22
heliolater 697.4
heliolatrous 697.7
heliological 1025.41
heliology 1025.22
heliometry 1025.22
Helios 1073.14
heliostat 1073.17
heliotherapy 91.4
heliotrope 70.2
heliotype 714.4
helipad 184.23
heliport 184.22, 901.13
heli-skiing 753.1
helium nucleus 1038.6
helix 2.10, 281.2, 915.2
Hell 307.3, 839.2,1023.4
hell 38.4, 96.7, 275.3, 429.7, 682.1, 759.19, 810.5, 1019.11
hell around 743.24, 810.11
hell-bent on 359.16
hellborn 654.13, 682.8
hell broke loose 53.4
hellcat 493.4, 593.3, 593.7, 671.9
hell-driver 174.5
Hellenic 523.12
Hellespontine sibyl 962.6
hellfire 682.2
hellfire preacher 543.5
hellhag 593.7
hellhole 80.3, 654.7
hellhound 593.6, 671.9, 680.6
hellion 593.4, 671.9, 680.6
hellish 127.28, 144.26, 654.13, 671.18, 680.17, 682.8, 1000.10
hellish host 680.1
hellishness 654.4
hellkite 593.6, 680.6
hell let loose 53.3
hello 59.1, 585.4
hell on earth 26.6
hell-raiser 593.3, 671.9
hell's kitchen 230.6
hellspawn 561.5, 680.1
hell to pay 1013.5
hell upon earth 96.7
helm (n) 417.10, 573.5, 612.2 (v) 182.14
helm, the 573.1
helmet 5.25, 647.2, 1008.3
helmetlike 279.20
helmet of hair 3.4
helmet-shaped 279.20
helminth 311.38
helmsman 183.8, 574.7
helmsmanship 161.1, 182.4
helot 138.3, 432.7
helotism 138.1, 432.1
helotry 138.1, 432.1
help (n) 86.1, 449.1, 478.8, 577.2, 577.11, 592.1, 616.6 (v) 86.38, 143.12, 449.11, 478.19, 577.13, 999.10, 1012.14
help, the 577.11
help a lame dog over a stile 449.11
help along 1014.7
help bear one's grief 147.2
help decide 476.5
helpdesk 1042.18
helper 432.5, 449.7, 592.1, 616.6
helpful 143.16, 384.8, 387.18, 449.21, 999.12
helpfulness 143.3, 387.3, 449.10, 999.1
helping (n) 8.10, 477.5, 793.5 (a) 449.20, 577.14
helping along 449.5
helping hand 449.2, 592.1
helping verb 530.4
help in time of need 449.2
helpless 19.18, 88.32, 584.12, 1006.14
helplessness 19.4, 584.4, 1006.3
helpmate 563.6, 563.8, 616.6
helpmeet 563.6, 563.8, 616.6
help oneself to 480.19
help on its way 1014.7
help out 1014.7
help to 478.12
help up 912.7
helter-skelter (n) 401.1, 810.3, 810.4 (a) 802.21, 810.16
helve 901.11
hem (n) 211.4, 211.7 (v) 211.10, 212.7, 268.6, 428.9, 525.8
he-man 15.6, 76.6, 492.7
hem and haw 344.7, 362.7, 368.8, 525.8
hemangioma 517.5, 1004.1
he-mannish 76.13
hematal 2.33
hematic 2.33
hematic disease 85.20
hematopathology 85.20
hematoscope 2.25
hematoscopy 2.25
hemeralopia 30.2
hemeralopic 30.9
hemic disease 85.20
hemicrania 26.5
hemicycle 280.8
hemidemisemiquaver 709.14
hem in 211.10, 212.5, 212.7, 428.9, 429.12, 459.19
hemiplegia 85.27
hemisphere 231.2, 793.4, 875.2
hemispheric 282.9
hemispherical 282.9
hemlock 604.6, 1001.3
hemmed 212.10
hemmed in 428.15
hemmed-in 209.10, 212.10
hemming 741.1
hemming-in 212.1
hemocyte 2.25
hemoglobin 2.25, 7.6
hemometer 2.25
hemophilia 85.20
hemorrhage (n) 12.8, 85.9, 1061.1 (v) 12.17
hemorrhaging 12.23
hemorrhea 12.8
hemorrhoids 85.37
hemothymia 926.1, 926.7
hemp 87.11, 605.5
hen 77.6, 77.9, 304.3, 311.28, 758.2
henchman 138.6, 166.2, 460.7, 577.1, 610.8, 616.8
hencoop 228.22
hencote 228.22
henhearted 491.10
henheartedness 491.1
henhouse 228.22
henna (n) 41.1 (v) 41.4 (a) 40.4
hennery 228.22
hen night 487.1
henotheism 675.5
henotheist 675.16
henpeck 510.16, 612.15
henpecked 326.5, 432.16
henry 87.9, 1032.15
Henry Morgan 483.7
hen scratches 350.2, 547.7
hen-talk 523.10
hen track 522.4
hen tracks 350.2, 547.7
hen turkey 311.28
hep 928.17
hepatic disease 85.23
Hephaestus 726.8
hepped up over 101.11

heptachord 882.3
heptad 882.3
heptadic 882.19
heptagon 882.3
heptagonal 278.10, 882.19
heptahedral 882.19
heptahedron 882.3
heptamerous 882.19
heptameter 720.7, 882.3
heptangular 882.19
heptapody 720.7
heptarchy 882.3
heptastich 720.10, 882.3
Heptateuch 882.3
heptathlon 755.2
heptatomic 1038.18
hep to 928.16
her 77.4, 87.7, 865.5
Hera 563.13
Heraclitean 952.12
herald (n) 133.4, 165.1, 353.2, 575.20, 576.2, 576.5, 816.1 (v) 133.13, 352.13, 816.3, 834.3
herald abroad 352.13
herald angel 353.2
heraldic 352.18
heraldic device 647.2
heraldic officials 647.2
heraldry 501.6, 647.1
herb 87.11, 310.3, 310.4, 310.33
herbaceous 310.36
herbaceous plant 310.3
herbage 310.1, 310.8
herbal 310.36
herbarium 1069.10
herbicide 1001.3
herbivore 8.16, 311.3
herbivorism 8.1
herbivority 8.1
herbivorous 8.31
herbivorousness 8.1
herbose 310.36
herbous 310.36
herbs 86.4
herb tea 86.8
herby 310.36
herculean 15.17, 257.20, 725.18, 1013.17
herculean task 1013.2
Hercules 15.6, 901.3
Hercules and Iolaus 588.6
herd (n) 574.7, 770.5, 1008.6 (v) 573.9, 1070.8
herd, the 606.2
herdboy 1070.3
herded 770.21
herder 1070.3
herding 1070.1
herdsman 574.7, 1070.3
herd together 582.17, 770.16
herd up 1070.8
hereafter (n) 839.1 (a) 839.8
hereafter, the 681.2, 839.2
here-and-now 1052.10
here and now, the 761.2, 838.1, 987.2
hereditability 560.6
hereditable 560.20
hereditament 471.1, 479.2
hereditary 305.18, 560.19, 767.8
hereditary character 305.9
hereditary disease 85.12
hereditary nobility 608.1
heredity 305.9, 560.6
here lies 309.18
hereness 221.1
hereralopic 28.11
heresiarch 688.5
heresy 688.2, 789.2, 868.2, 955.1, 975.1
heretic 688.5, 695.11, 868.3
heretical 688.9, 789.9, 868.6, 955.8, 975.16
here today and gone tomorrow 828.7
here today gone tomorrow 34.3
Her Excellency 648.2
Her Highness 648.2
her honor 596.1
heritability 560.6
heritable (n) 479.2 (a) 560.20, 629.5
heritage 479.2, 560.6
heritage tourism 177.1
heritance 479.2
heritor 479.5
herky-jerky 671.23, 813.4, 851.3, 917.19
herky-jerky motion 745.2
Her Ladyship 648.2
Her Majesty 648.2
Her Majesty's Government 612.3
Her Majesty's Ship 180.6
hermaphrodite (n) 75.17 (a) 75.31
hermaphroditic 75.31
hermaphroditism 75.12
hermeneut 341.7
hermeneutic 341.14
hermeneutical 341.14
hermeneutics 341.8, 723.1
Hermes 353.1
hermetic 15.20, 293.12, 345.11
hermetical 293.12
hermetically sealed 15.20, 293.12
hermeticism 345.5
hermetics 345.5, 689.1
hermetism 345.5
hermit 584.5, 667.2, 699.16, 870.4
hermitage 703.6, 1009.5
hermitess 584.5
hermitic 584.10
hermitical 584.10
hermitish 584.10
hermitism 584.2
hermitlike 584.10
hermitry 584.2
hero 10.32, 411.2, 492.7, 659.5, 662.9, 678.3, 704.10, 707.6, 786.4
Herod 503.2
heroic 247.9, 257.20, 492.16, 652.6, 708.50, 720.16, 842.12
heroic act 492.6
heroical 257.20
heroicalness 492.1
heroic couplet 720.7
heroic deed 492.6
heroic legend 662.7
heroic myth 662.7
heroics 492.6, 493.1, 502.1
heroic tenor 709.5
heroin addict 87.21
heroin addiction 87.1
heroine 492.7, 659.5, 662.9, 678.3, 704.10, 707.6
heroin habit 87.1
heroin user 87.21
heroism 247.2, 492.1, 652.2
herolike 492.16
heronry 228.23
hero's welcome 186.4
hero worship 104.1, 155.1, 509.5, 697.1
hero-worship 155.4, 509.12, 697.5
hero-worshiper 697.4
hero-worshiping 155.9, 509.18, 697.7
herpes 85.18, 85.35
herpes zoster 85.25
herring pond, the 240.1
herself 77.4, 575.4, 865.5
Hershey bar 647.2, 647.5
herstory 549.1, 719.1
hertz 1034.12
Hertzian wave 1034.11
Hertzsprung-Russell diagram 1073.8
her worship 596.1
hesistant 494.8
hesitance 325.2, 362.3
hesitancy 325.2, 362.3, 494.1, 971.1
hesitant 325.7, 362.11, 971.16
hesitant approach 439.1
hesitate 325.4, 362.7, 525.8, 846.11, 971.10
hesitating (n) 362.3 (a) 325.7, 362.11, 525.13, 971.16
hesitation 175.1, 325.2, 362.3, 494.1, 525.3, 846.5, 955.2, 971.1
Hesper 1073.4
hesperidium 10.38
Hesperus 1073.4
hest 420.1
Hestia 228.30
hestia 703.12
het 1020.29
hetaera 665.15
heteratomic 1038.18
heteroatomic 1038.18
heterochromatin 305.7
heterochromosome 305.8
heteroclite 851.3, 870.9
heterocycle 1038.7
heterocyclic 1038.18
heterodox 333.6, 688.9, 789.9, 868.6, 975.16
heterodoxy 688.1, 789.2, 868.2, 975.1
heterodyne 1034.28
heterogamy 78.3
heterogeneity 780.1, 783.1, 789.2, 791.1
heterogeneous 780.7, 783.4, 797.14
heterogenesis 78.6
heterogenetic 78.16
heteromerous 1060.9
heteromorphic 783.3, 870.9
heteromorphism 783.1, 870.1
heteromorphous 783.3
heteronomous 612.16
heteronomy 612.4
heteronuclear 1038.19
heterophyte 310.4
heterosexism 75.10
heterosexual 75.13
heterosexuality 75.2, 75.10
heterothermic 1023.20
heterotopia 160.1, 852.3
heterotopic 160.8
heterotrophic organism 305.2
heterotropia 28.5
hetman 575.17
het up 105.22, 152.30, 1020.29
heuristic 935.22, 938.37, 942.11
hew 262.7, 802.11
hew down 913.5
hewing of wood 725.4
hewn 262.9, 802.23
hew out 262.7
hex (n) 513.1, 690.8, 691.1, 1000.4 (v) 513.5, 691.9, 1000.6, 1011.12
hexachord 709.8, 882.2
hexad (n) 882.2 (a) 882.18
hexadecimal system 1017.4
hexadic 882.18
hexagon 882.2
hexagonal 278.10, 882.18
hexagram 882.2
hexahedral 278.10, 882.18
hexahedron 882.2
hexameter 720.7, 882.2
hexangular 882.18
hexapartite 882.18
hexapod 311.32, 882.2
hexapody 720.7, 882.2
hexarchy 882.2
hexastich 720.10, 882.2
hexastyle (n) 882.2 (a) 882.18
Hexateuch 683.3, 882.2
hexatomic 1038.18
hexatonic 882.18
hexavalent 882.18
hex sign 914.2
heyday 1010.4
heyday of the blood 301.1
heyday of youth 301.1
hey presto 852.13
HF pulse 1036.10
HHH 1019.25
H-hour 459.13, 843.5
hi 59.1
hiatal 224.7
hiatus 158.8, 224.1, 292.1, 795.2, 813.2
hiatus of learning 930.1
hibernal 313.9, 1023.14
hibernate 22.15, 173.9, 313.8, 329.2, 331.16, 519.3
hibernating 173.14, 519.5
hibernation 22.2, 173.4, 313.6, 331.1
Hibernicism 523.8
hiccup (n) 2.21, 909.9, 968.2, 1012.6 (v) 909.28
hic jacet 309.18
hick (n) 227.10, 414.9, 416.3, 606.6, 924.5 (a) 233.8
hickdom 233.1
hickey 85.37, 1004.1, 1052.5

hickified 233.8
hickishness 233.3
hicklike 233.8
hick town 230.3
hicky 233.8
hid 346.11
hidalgo 608.4
hidden 32.5, 345.11, 346.11, 519.5, 519.7, 522.16
hidden agenda 375.1, 947.1
hidden danger 356.12
hidden depths 32.1
hidden hand 894.6
hidden meaning 519.2
hiddenness 345.1, 346.1
hidden out 346.14
hidden treasure 472.6
hide (n) 3.2, 4.2, 295.3, 296.2 (v) 34.2, 346.6, 346.8, 386.11, 412.9, 604.14
hide away 346.7, 346.8
hideaway 346.4, 584.6, 1009.5
hidebound (n) 500.6 (a) 425.7, 500.19, 687.8, 867.6, 980.10
hideboundness 687.5, 980.1
hide one's face 137.9, 139.7
hide one's face in shame 113.6
hide one's hand 415.9
hide one's head in the sand 148.4, 362.7, 368.13, 984.2
hide one's light under a bushel 139.7, 346.6
hide one's trail 346.6
hideous 98.19, 127.30, 1015.11
hideousness 98.3, 127.2, 1015.2
hide out 346.8
hideout 346.4, 1009.5
hide under 376.4
hidey-hole 197.3, 346.4, 584.6, 1009.5
hiding (n) 295.1, 345.1, 346.1, 346.4, 412.1, 604.5 (a) 346.15
hiding one's light under a bushel 139.2
hiding place 346.4, 1009.5
hie 174.8, 177.18
hiemal 313.9, 1023.14
hie on 375.16, 401.4
hie oneself to 177.25
hierarch 699.8
hierarchal 698.16
hierarchic 245.5, 809.8
hierarchical 245.5, 698.16, 809.8
hierarchy 245.2, 417.7, 575.14, 607.1, 612.4, 698.7, 801.4, 807.2, 808.4, 809.1, 809.4
hieratic 580.8, 698.16
hieratical 580.8
hieratic symbol 546.2
hierocracy 612.4, 698.7, 699.1
hierocratic 698.16
hierodule 699.15
hieroglyph 349.1, 546.2
hieroglyphic (n) 349.1, 546.2 (a) 345.16, 546.8
hieroglyphical 546.8
hieroglyphics 546.2
hieromonach 699.16
Hieronymian 584.5
Hieronymite 584.5
hierophant 699.15
hieros 699.15
hie to 177.25
hi-fi (n) 50.11 (a) 50.16
hi-fi fan 50.11
hi-fi freak 50.11
hi-fructose corn syrup 66.3
higgle 731.18
higgledy-piggledy (n) 810.3 (a) 810.16
higgler 730.5
higgling 731.3
high, a 88.1, 105.1
high (n) 22.6, 87.1, 317.4, 567.4, 738.9, 1040.9 (a) 58.13, 64.7, 68.8, 71.5, 87.24, 88.33, 95.17, 105.20, 109.11, 136.11, 158.11, 247.9, 272.14, 393.41, 524.30, 608.10, 632.11, 652.6, 662.18, 912.9, 993.16
high aim 100.9
high-altitude flying 184.1
high-altitude research rocket 1074.6
high-altitude wind 318.1
high and dry 855.16, 1007.6, 1013.27, 1066.7
high and mightiness 662.5
high-and-mightiness 141.3
high-and-mighty 141.11, 662.18
high as a kite 88.33, 109.15
high as a steeple 272.14
highball (n) 88.9, 759.10 (v) 174.9
high beams 1025.4
high birth 607.3, 608.2
high blood pressure 85.9, 85.19
highborn 607.10, 608.11
highbred 504.16, 607.10, 608.11
highbrow (n) 141.7, 929.1 (a) 928.23
highbrowed 928.23
highbrowish 928.23
high caliber 249.1
high-caliber 999.14
high-calorie diet 7.13
high camp 497.1
high-camp 497.14
high-card trick 758.3
high-caste 608.11
high chief 575.8
High Church 675.11
High-Church 701.18
High-Churchism 675.11
High-Churchist 701.2
High-Churchman 701.2
high-class 999.14
high color 41.1
high-colored 35.19
high cost 632.1
high country 237.1
high court 595.2
high culture 928.5
high day 20.4
high-definition 349.14
high-definition television 1035.1, 1035.5
high-definition TV 1035.1
high-density lipoprotein 7.7
high descent 608.2
high diver 367.4
high diving 367.3
high dudgeon 152.7
high-energy particle 1037.4
higher 249.12, 272.19
higher echelons 575.14
higher education 567.5
higher ground 272.2, 272.4
higher-income 618.14, 1010.12
higher-income group 607.2
higher learning 567.5
higher mathematics 1017.1
higher tax bracket 607.2
higher-up 249.4, 610.7
higher-ups 249.5, 575.14
highest (n) 249.3 (a) 198.11, 249.13, 272.19, 677.17, 997.24
high estate 607.3
highest category 932.2
highest common factor 883.4
highest degree (n) 794.5 (a) 999.17
highest level 198.11
highest pitch 198.2, 1002.3
highest point 198.2
highest-quality 249.13
highest-ranking 249.14
highest type 786.4, 1002.4
highest unitary principle of thought 932.2
high explosive 462.14
high-explosive charge 1074.8
high-explosive shell 462.19
highfalutin (n) 502.2, 545.2 (a) 136.11, 141.9, 501.18, 502.12, 545.8
high-faluting 141.9
highfaluting (n) 502.2 (a) 136.11, 501.18, 502.12
highfaluting ways 501.2
highfalutin ways 501.2
high fashion 578.1
high feather 83.2
high-fidelity 50.16
high-fidelity system 50.11
high finance 729.1
high-five (n) 116.2, 487.1 (v) 116.6, 487.2
high flavor 68.3
high-flowing 545.8
high-flown 136.11, 141.9, 355.4, 501.18, 502.12, 545.8, 923.11
high-flown diction 545.1
high-flying 100.28, 501.18, 545.8
high fog 319.1
high frequency 1034.12
high-frequency 1034.28
high-frequency amplification 1034.15
high-frequency direction finder 1036.4
high-frequency pulse 1036.10
high-frequency telephony 347.4
high-frequency treatment 91.5
high-frequency wave 1034.11
high fructose corn syrup 66.3
high-geared 174.16
high glee 109.5
high goal 100.9
high-grade 999.14
high ground 249.2
high growth rate 731.10
high hand 612.9
high-handed 417.16
high-handedness 417.3
high-hat (v) 157.5 (a) 141.14
high-hatted 141.14
high-hattedness 141.6
high-hattiness 141.6
high-hatty 141.14
high-headed 136.11, 141.9
high heels 5.27
High Holiday 20.4
High Holy Day 20.4
high hopes 124.1
high horse 141.1
high ideals 644.1
high income 618.1
high-income 1010.12
high-intensity runway approach lights 184.19
high IQ 920.2
high jinks 743.4
high jump 366.1
high jumper 366.4
high king 575.8
highland (n) 237.1, 272.3 (a) 233.6, 272.17
Highland fling 366.1
high landing 184.18
highlands 233.1, 237.1, 272.3
high-level language 1042.13
high-level talk 541.5
high life 578.6, 607.2, 608.1
highlight (n) 997.7, 1025.1 (v) 348.5, 517.17, 547.19, 865.11, 983.10, 997.14, 1025.28
highlighted 348.12, 997.21
highlighter 712.18
highlighting 348.4, 517.3, 865.6
highlights 1025.19
high liver 669.3
high living 669.2
high-living 669.8
high lope 174.3
high-low 759.10
highly colored imagination 986.4
highly considered 155.11
highly emotional 105.28
highly esteemed 662.15
highly flavored 68.8
highly regarded 662.15
highly reputed 662.15
highly respectable 644.13, 662.15
highly satisfied 107.9
highly seasoned 68.8
highly strung 105.28, 110.21, 128.11
highly touted 509.19
high-maintenance 339.12, 360.8
high man on the totem pole 997.9, 997.11
High Mass 701.8
high-mettled 105.28
high-minded 136.11, 644.13, 652.6
high-mindedness 644.1, 652.2
high-muck-a-muck 997.9
high-muckety-muck 997.9
Highness 648.2
highness 58.1, 68.3, 272.1, 632.1
high noon 198.2, 314.4
high-noon 314.6
high-nosed 136.11, 141.9
high note 1010.3

high-occupancy vehicle 179.13
high office 417.10
high old time 743.2
high on the hog 1010.12
high opinion 155.1
high order 997.1
high-paid 472.16
high-paying 472.16
high-performance 18.12
high pitch 709.4
high-pitched 58.13, 272.14
high place 662.4
high places 417.2
high plateau 237.3
highpockets 272.7
high point 997.6, 1010.4
high post 747.3
high-potency 18.12
high-powered 18.12, 997.17
high pressure 375.3, 424.3, 440.3, 997.4
high-pressure (v) 375.14, 424.8 (a) 18.12, 317.13, 997.22
high-pressure area 184.32, 317.4
high-pressure methods 424.3
high-pressure salesmanship 734.2
high price 632.3
high-priced 632.11
high price tag 632.3
high priest 575.3, 575.4, 699.9, 699.10, 699.11
high priestess 15.6
high-principled 644.13
high principles 644.1
high-priority 997.22
high profile 31.2
high-profile 31.7
high-protein diet 7.13
high purpose 100.9
high-quality 999.14
high rank 607.3, 997.1
high-reaching 100.28, 272.14
high regard 155.1
high relief 283.2, 348.4, 715.3
high-rent 632.11
high repute 662.2
high resolution 31.2
high-rise (n) 228.14 (a) 272.14
high-rise apartment building 228.14
high road 1014.4
highroad 1014.1
high roller 759.21
high school 567.4
high schooler 572.3
high school football 746.1
high sea 240.1
high seas 240.1
high season 177.5
high-seasoned 68.7
high self-esteem 140.1
high self-valuation 140.1
high-set 272.14
high sign 399.3, 517.15
high society 578.6, 607.2, 608.1
high-society 578.16, 607.10
high-sounding 58.13, 545.8
high-sounding words 545.3
high-specific activity 1037.1
high-speed 174.16
high-speed embosser 30.6
high-speed Internet 1042.19
high-spirited 105.28, 322.6
high spirits 95.2, 109.2, 109.4, 322.2
high spot 997.7
high-stakes 632.11
high-stakes gambler 759.21
high standard of living 1010.1
high standing 247.2
high status 607.3
high-stepper 311.14
high street 230.6
high-strung 105.28, 110.21, 128.11
high-sulfur 1021.9
high summer 313.3, 1019.7
high-swelling 502.12
hightail 174.9, 188.12
hightail it 188.7
high tar 89.5
high-tasted 68.8
high tax bracket 618.1
high tea 8.6, 582.13
high-tech (n) 928.10 (a) 928.28
high technology 928.10
high tension 1032.12
high-tension 18.12, 1032.34
high terrain 237.1
high-test 999.14
high tide 238.13, 272.8
high time 743.2, 843.3, 846.1
high-toned 58.13, 136.11, 501.18
high treason 645.7
high-up 272.14
high value 632.2
high-velocity 174.16
high visibility 31.2
high-visibility 31.6
high volume 53.1
high water 238.13, 272.8
high-water mark 211.3, 300.6
highway 383.5
highway interchange 170.2
highwayman 483.5
highway patrol 1008.17
highway robber 483.5
highway robbery 482.3, 632.5
highway sign 352.7
highway trailer 179.19
high wind 318.11
high wire 971.8
high-wire artist 707.3
high words 152.9
high-wrought 498.12
high-yield 472.16
high-yielding 472.16
hijack 424.7, 482.20
hijacker 483.5, 483.7
hijacking 482.3
hike (n) 177.10, 251.1, 912.2 (v) 177.30, 251.4, 259.4, 912.5
hiked 251.7, 259.10
hiker 178.6
hike up 251.4, 259.4
hiking 177.8, 259.1, 912.1
hiking trail 383.2
hilarious 109.15, 488.4, 743.28
hilariousness 109.5, 488.1
hilarity 109.5, 116.4, 488.1
hill (n) 237.4, 272.4, 283.3, 745.1, 770.10 (v) 770.19
hillbilly (n) 227.10, 606.6 (a) 233.8
hillbilly music 708.11
hill country 237.1
hill-dwelling 272.17
Hiller-CNR machine 181.7
hill heaped upon hill 237.6
hillock 237.4
hillocky 283.15
hill of beans, a 762.3
hill of beans 998.5
hill rating 753.1
hills 237.1
hillside 204.4, 237.2
hilly 237.8, 272.18
hilly country 237.1
him 76.4, 87.9, 865.5
Himinbjorg 681.10
himself 76.4, 575.4, 865.5, 997.11
hind (n) 77.9, 311.5, 606.6 (a) 217.9
hind end 217.1, 217.5
hinder (v) 428.7, 460.10, 846.8, 1012.10 (a) 217.9
hinderer 1012.8
hindering (n) 1012.1 (a) 1012.17
hindermost 217.9
hinder part 217.1
hindgut 2.18
hindhand 217.9
hindhead 217.1
hind leg 177.14
hind legs 177.15
hindmost 217.9
hind part 217.1
hindquarter 217.3
hindrance 428.1, 846.2, 1012.1
hindsight 989.3
hind tit 432.2
Hindu 675.24
Hindu calendar 832.8
Hindu deities 678.4
Hinduism 675.14
Hindu mode 709.10
Hindu triad 677.9
Hindu trinity 677.9
hinge (n) 800.4, 843.4, 915.5 (v) 800.8, 959.6
hinged joint 800.4
hinge on 887.5, 959.6
hinging on 959.9
hinging post 273.4
hingle 915.5
hinky 645.16
hinny 311.15, 797.8
hint (n) 62.3, 248.4, 256.1, 399.1, 422.2, 517.3, 517.9, 519.2, 551.4, 797.7, 951.5, 989.5 (v) 133.11, 133.12, 517.17, 519.4, 551.10
hint at 422.5, 551.10
hinted 519.7
hinterland (n) 206.3, 207.3, 209.2, 231.1, 233.2, 261.4 (a) 207.7, 233.9
hinterlander 227.10
hip (n) 218.1, 800.4 (a) 578.11, 928.17
hip bath 79.8
hip hop 708.7
hiphuggers 5.18
hipness 578.3, 928.3
hipped on 101.11
hippety-hop (n) 177.11, 366.1 (v) 177.28, 366.5
hippic 311.45
hippie (n) 868.3 (a) 868.6
hippiedom 868.2
hippiness 257.8
hippo 257.12, 257.14, 311.4
hip-pocket 474.5
Hippocrates 90.12
Hippocratic 90.15
Hippocratic countenance 307.11
Hippocratic face 307.11
Hippocratic oath 334.4
Hippocrene 720.11
hippodrome 463.1
hippopotamic 257.19
hippopotamus 257.14, 311.4
hippy 257.18
hipster 868.3
hiragana 546.2
hircine 311.45
hire (n) 615.6, 624.4, 630.6 (v) 615.14, 615.15, 615.16
hired 615.20, 624.22
hired applauder 704.27
hired car 179.13
hired girl 577.8
hired gun 461.17, 671.9
hired hand 577.3
hired help 577.11
hired killer 308.11, 461.17, 671.9
hired man 577.3
hireling (n) 461.17, 577.3 (a) 615.20, 645.23
hire out 615.16
hire purchase 621.1, 624.1, 733.1
hire purchase plan 622.1, 624.1
hirer 470.4
hi-res 31.2
hiring 615.4, 615.6
hirsute 3.24, 3.27, 288.9, 294.7
hirsuteness 3.1
his 76.4, 87.9
his and hers 784.5
His Excellency 648.2
His Grace 648.5
His Highness 648.2
His Holiness 648.5
his honor 596.1
His Lordship 648.2
his lordship 596.1
His Majesty 648.2
His Majesty's Government 612.3
His Majesty's Ship 180.6
his nibs 997.11
hispid 3.24, 285.9, 288.9
hispidity 3.1, 288.1
hispidulous 3.24
His Reverence 648.5
hiss (n) 57.1, 59.1, 508.3, 510.8, 525.1 (v) 57.2, 60.4, 108.6, 320.4, 508.10, 524.25
hissing (n) 50.13, 57.1, 508.1, 508.3 (a) 57.3, 508.12

histogenesis 78.6
histogenetic 78.16
histology 266.1
historian 550.2, 718.4, 719.3, 832.10
historic 719.6, 842.13, 997.19
historical (n) 549.2 (a) 719.6, 722.8, 761.15, 970.15, 973.13
historical approach 719.1
historical discipline, the 719.1
historical error 833.1
historical film 706.2
historical linguistics 526.16
historically accurate 719.6
historical materialism 1052.6
historical materialist 1052.7
historical method 719.1
historical painter 716.4
historical present 530.12, 838.1
historical present tense 837.5
historical program 609.6
historical records 549.2
historical research 719.1
historical truth 973.1
historic comedy 704.6
historicity 761.2, 973.1
historicize 719.4
historicized 719.6, 722.8
historied 719.6
historify 719.4
historiographer 718.4, 719.3, 832.10
historiographical 719.6
historiography 719.1
history (n) 549.1, 719.1, 837.1, 989.6 (a) 395.29
history of ideas 932.2
history of illness 85.3
history of printing 548.1
histrio 707.2
histrion 707.2
histrionic 93.19, 348.9, 500.15, 501.24, 704.33
histrionic art 704.2
histrionics 93.9, 501.4, 704.2, 704.8
histrionism 704.2
histrionize 500.12
his worship 596.1
hit (n) 87.20, 105.3, 308.2, 409.4, 409.5, 413.8, 510.4, 704.4, 708.7, 745.3, 759.11, 902.4, 999.5 (v) 93.15, 177.19, 186.6, 223.10, 308.14, 440.15, 459.14, 510.14, 745.5, 751.4, 788.6, 902.13, 902.14, 904.12, 931.19, 941.2
hit a clam 61.3
hit a clinker 61.3
hit a clip 902.14
hit a fly 745.5
hit against 902.13
hit a happy medium 246.2
hit a home run 745.5
hit and miss 942.1
hit-and-miss 340.12
hit-and-run (v) 910.7 (a) 491.12
hit-and-run attack 459.1
hit-and-run driver 178.10
hit-and-run play 745.3
hit a nerve 24.8, 903.8
hit a nerve ending 24.8
hit a sacrifice fly 745.5
hit a slump 393.17
hit a snag 1013.11
hit a sour note 61.3
hit a streak of luck 1010.11
hit at 459.16
hit back at 506.4
hit below the belt, a 650.2
hit below the belt 650.6, 754.4
hit bottom 112.16, 199.6, 393.17, 852.6
hitch (n) 26.2, 177.12, 825.4, 905.3, 1012.4, 1013.8 (v) 177.28, 177.31, 563.14, 800.8, 905.5, 1070.7
hitch and hike 916.13
hitch a ride 177.31
hitched 563.21
hitchhike 177.31
hitchhiker 178.6
hitchhiking 177.8
hitching 177.8
hitching post 273.4
hitch on 253.4
hitch one's wagon to a star 100.20
hitch up 800.10
hit for 161.9
hit home 24.8, 903.8
hit-in 749.6
hit it 409.9, 940.2
hit it big 1010.11
hit it off 587.9
hit it off with 455.2
hit it on the nose 940.2, 973.10
hit it out 745.5
hit it right on the button 745.5
hit it right on the screws 745.5
hit like lightning 459.14
hit list 871.1
hit man 308.11, 604.7, 671.9
hit off 336.6, 349.8
hit-off 336.1
hit off on 336.6
hit on 439.8
hit one close to home 518.8
hit one for 621.3
hit one in the eye 31.4, 348.7
hit one like a ton of bricks 112.18
hit one's stride 409.10
hit one where he lives 24.8
hit one where one lives 96.17, 152.21, 518.8
hit-or-miss 340.12, 810.12, 942.11, 971.19
hit-or-missness 971.1
hit out at 459.16
hit out for 161.9
hit parade 578.2
hit pay dirt 1058.14
hit rock bottom 112.16, 393.17, 1011.11
hits 1042.19
hit show 704.4
hitter 745.2
hit the ball 330.14, 725.13
hit the books 570.12
hit the booze 88.25
hit the bottle 88.25
hit the brake pedal 857.11
hit the brakes 1012.13
hit the bricks 727.10
hit the bull's-eye 973.10
hit the campaign trail 609.40
hit the canvas 754.4
hit the ceiling 105.17, 152.20
hit the deck 23.6
hit the dirt 913.11
hit the eye 31.4
hit the ground 913.11
hit the hay 22.18
hit the high spots 276.4, 340.8, 557.5, 570.13, 938.26
hit the jackpot 409.9, 618.10
hit the mark 93.15, 409.9
hit the nail on the head 940.2, 973.10
hit the panic button 127.11
hit the road 177.23, 188.7
hit the roof 152.17
hit the sack 22.18
hit the sauce 88.25
hit the shops 733.8
hit the silk 184.47
hit the skids 16.9, 393.17, 1011.9
hit the spot 95.7
hit the streets 352.16
hit the trail 177.21, 177.23, 188.7
hitting 621.1
hitting the booze 88.4
hitting the bottle 87.1, 88.4
hitting the sauce 88.4
hitting up 87.2, 621.1
hit town 186.6
hit tune 708.7
hit up 440.15, 621.3
hit upon 186.7, 194.10, 941.3
hit upon a solution 940.2
hit with the good wood 745.5
hive (n) 228.25, 739.2, 770.6, 884.3 (v) 159.17, 770.16
hive mind 92.28, 842.2
hive of activity 330.5
hive off 771.4, 886.12, 890.7
hive of industry 739.2
hives 85.34, 85.35, 85.36
hiving-off 892.4
HIV-positive 85.61
Hlithskjalf 681.10
hoagy 10.32
hoar (n) 1023.7 (a) 37.7, 39.4, 39.5, 303.16
hoard (n) 386.1, 472.3, 770.11 (v) 386.11, 390.5, 733.7
hoarded 386.14
hoarder 770.15
hoarding 484.3
hoard up 386.11
hoarfrost 1023.7
hoar-frosted 1023.17
hoariness 37.1, 39.2, 303.5
hoarse 58.15, 61.5, 525.12
hoarseness 58.2, 525.1
hoarstone 549.12
hoary 37.7, 39.4, 39.5, 303.16, 842.10, 842.12, 1023.17
hoary age 303.5, 842.1
hoary eld 842.1
hoary-haired 39.5
hoary-headed joke 489.9
hoax (n) 354.13, 356.7 (v) 356.14
hoaxability 954.2
hoaxable 954.9
hoaxer 357.1
hoaxproof 956.5
hob 678.8, 680.8, 901.14, 1020.11
hobbit 258.5
hobble (n) 175.2, 177.12, 428.4, 1013.5 (v) 19.10, 175.6, 177.28, 393.14, 428.10, 1012.11
hobbled 175.10
hobbledehoy 302.5
hobbling (n) 393.1 (a) 175.10, 393.30
hobby (n) 724.7 (a) 724.17
hobbyhorse (n) 724.7 (v) 182.55
hobbyist 101.4
hobgoblin 127.9, 680.7, 680.8
hobnailed 233.7
hobnobbing 582.2
hobnob with 582.17, 587.9
hobo (n) 178.3, 195.2, 331.9, 440.8, 619.4, 660.2, 828.4, 870.4 (v) 177.23
hobo camp 228.29
hoboism 177.3, 331.5
hobo jungle 228.29
Hobson's choice 371.3, 428.3, 963.6, 970.1
hock (n) 177.14, 438.2 (v) 438.10
hocked 438.12
hockey 749.1
hockey equipment or gear 749.1
hockey field 749.4
hockey game 749.3
hockey match 749.3
hockey mom 77.7
hockey rink 749.1
hockey skates 179.21
hockey team 749.2
hocking 620.1
hock shop 620.4
hocus (n) 87.14 (v) 356.19
hocus-pocus (n) 356.5, 356.6, 520.2, 689.1, 691.4 (v) 356.14, 356.19
ho-dad 142.6
hodgepodge 770.13, 797.6, 810.3
Hodgkin's disease 85.20
hoe (n) 1040.8 (v) 1069.17
hoecake 10.29
hoedown 705.2
hoeing 1069.13
hog (n) 76.8, 80.13, 87.18, 311.5, 311.9, 651.3, 672.3 (v) 469.6, 480.19, 651.4
hogan 228.10
hogback 237.5
hog call 517.16
hog cholera 85.41
hogdeer 311.5
hog for, a 100.27
hogger 178.12
hogging 469.11
hoggish 80.24, 100.27, 311.45, 469.11, 672.6
hoggishness 80.2, 100.8, 672.1
hoggy 472.15
hoghead 178.12
hog heaven 1010.1
hogherd 1070.3
hog it down 672.4

hogpen 80.11
hog's-back 237.5
hog-tie 428.10
hogtie 19.10
hogtied 19.16
hog wallow 243.1, 1062.9
hogwash 354.14, 391.4, 520.3
hog-wild 105.25
ho-ho (n) 116.4 (v) 116.8
ho-hum 117.6, 781.6
hoick 184.39
hoi polloi 250.2, 497.6
hoi polloi, the 606.2
hoist (n) 912.2, 912.3 (v) 912.5
hoist a banner 517.22
hoist sail 182.20
hoist the blue Peter 182.19, 182.52, 188.15
hoist the white flag 465.9
hoity-toitiness 141.1
hoity-toity (n) 141.1 (a) 141.9, 607.10
hoke (n) 354.14, 704.8 (v) 336.5
hoke comic 707.9
hoked-up 336.8
hoke up 336.5, 354.18
hokey 117.9, 336.8
hokey-pokey 356.5
hokum 354.14, 520.3, 704.8
hokum act 704.7
hokum comic 707.9
hold (n) 197.17, 386.6, 429.5, 460.6, 469.1, 474.2, 480.2, 612.2, 709.12, 894.1, 901.5, 901.11, 906.2 (v) 87.22, 158.9, 329.3, 334.5, 386.11, 428.7, 429.12, 469.4, 474.6, 474.7, 761.8, 772.3, 803.6, 827.6, 853.5, 855.7, 856.4, 857.6, 901.21, 926.25, 946.8, 946.10, 946.11, 953.11, 973.8, 983.13, 991.4
hold a boat race 965.5
hold a brief for 449.14, 576.14
hold a candle to 943.7
hold a card 617.15
hold accountable 641.12
hold aces 1010.11
hold a close wind 182.25
hold a conference 541.10
hold a farthing candle to the sun 391.8
hold a funeral 309.19
hold against 599.8
hold a grudge 152.12
hold a gun to one's head 424.4
hold a heading 161.7
hold a high opinion of 155.4
hold all the aces 18.11, 249.11, 612.12
hold aloof 157.7, 368.6
hold aloof from 668.7
hold a loose rein 426.3
hold a low opinion of 156.4
hold a meeting 770.17
hold a middle course 467.6
hold an idea 931.16
hold answerable 641.12
hold a pistol to one's head 514.2
hold a post 609.42
hold a press conference 352.12
hold as 953.11
hold a séance 689.21
hold a session 770.17
hold a sitting 689.21
hold a summit 541.10
hold at arm's length 157.7
hold at bay 428.7, 460.10
hold a tight hand upon 425.4
hold a wake 115.10
hold away from 261.7
hold back 106.8, 175.9, 386.12, 390.5, 428.7, 442.4, 484.6, 668.6, 668.7, 846.8, 1012.10
holdback 1012.1, 1012.7
hold beneath contempt 157.3
hold beneath one 157.3
hold by 434.2
hold captive 429.14, 432.8
hold cheap 157.3
hold communication 343.6
hold control 1041.8
hold court 946.12
hold dear 104.20, 155.4
hold down 428.8, 432.8
hold down a job 724.12
holder 195.1, 470.1, 479.3
holder of the legal estate 470.5
hold everything 846.12
hold fast 359.9, 360.4, 428.7, 474.6, 803.8, 855.11
hold for 161.9
hold for ransom 482.20
hold forth 439.4, 540.5, 543.10, 568.16
hold forth without interruption 542.3
hold good 935.17, 957.10, 973.8
hold in 428.7, 474.5
hold in abomination 103.5
hold in bondage 432.8
hold in captivity 429.14, 432.8
hold in check 175.9, 428.7, 670.6
hold in consideration 155.4
hold in contempt 142.7, 156.4, 157.3, 510.12, 512.8
hold in custody 429.12
hold in derision 454.4, 508.8
hold in esteem 155.4
hold in fee simple 469.5
holding (n) 87.2, 231.4, 469.1, 471.4, 474.1, 738.3, 946.5 (a) 87.25, 469.9, 474.8, 901.23, 926.34, 983.20
holding back 362.3, 442.1
holding capacity 257.2
holding cell 429.8
holding company 737.16
holding in 474.1
holding in remembrance 989.23
holding in suspension 846.4
holding one's breath 130.11
holding out 856.1
holding pattern 184.18
holdings 386.2, 471.1, 738.2, 738.3, 770.11
holding the reins 573.13
holding together 803.10
holding up 846.4
holding up together 943.1
hold in hand 612.12
hold in leading strings 432.8
hold in leash 428.7, 432.8
hold in low esteem 156.4
hold in mind 983.9, 989.12
hold in one's affections 104.20
hold in one's heart 104.20
hold in one's thoughts 989.12
hold in restraint 429.12
hold in reverence 155.4
hold in solution 1064.5
hold in subjection 432.8
hold in swaddling clothes 432.8
hold in thrall 104.22, 432.8
hold in view 27.13
hold it against 589.8
hold jubilee 487.2
hold membership 617.15
hold no brief 467.5, 649.6
hold no brief for 102.4, 510.10
hold off 325.4, 390.5, 460.10, 846.9, 846.11, 908.3
hold office 609.42, 724.14, 825.5
hold on 161.5, 360.4, 474.6, 737.23, 803.6, 827.6, 846.12, 856.3
hold on a course 182.28
hold one's breath 51.5, 122.5, 130.8, 173.7, 846.12
hold one's course 161.10, 856.3
hold oneself aloof 344.6, 583.4
hold oneself erect 136.4
hold oneself in readiness 405.10, 405.14
hold oneself stiff 200.7
hold oneself straight 200.7
hold one's eye 27.15
hold one's feet to the fire 424.8, 894.7
hold one's gaze 27.15
hold one's ground 216.8, 359.9, 361.7, 453.3, 453.4, 474.5, 855.11
hold one's hand 329.3, 370.7, 449.14
hold one's head above water 385.12
hold one's head high 136.4
hold one's nose in the air 141.8
hold one's own 359.9, 453.4, 474.5, 855.11
hold one's peace 51.5
hold one's sides 116.8
hold one's temper 106.7
hold one's tongue 51.5, 344.6, 345.7, 494.7
hold one's way 856.3
hold on like a bulldog 474.6, 803.8
hold on to 474.6, 474.7
hold opposite views 456.8
hold out 15.10, 359.9, 360.4, 361.7, 439.4, 453.2, 453.4, 727.10, 827.6, 855.11
holdout 727.6
hold out against 442.3
hold out a helping hand 449.11
hold out an expectation 436.4
hold out for 457.20, 731.18
hold out hope 124.9, 133.12
hold out on 345.7, 484.6
hold out promise 124.9
hold out the hand 585.9
hold out the olive branch 465.9
hold out the right of fellowship 587.12
hold over 846.9
holdover 256.1, 610.11
hold over one's head 514.2
hold prisoner 429.14
hold responsible 641.12
hold spellbound 983.13
hold steady 856.3
hold steady for 161.10
hold still for 134.6
hold sway 612.13
hold talks 541.10
hold the attention 983.11
hold the belief 953.13
hold the course 182.28
hold the field 249.10
hold the fort 460.10
hold the helm 612.12
hold the interest 983.13
hold the line 460.10
hold the market 737.25
hold the memory of 989.12
hold the mirror up to nature 349.11
hold the phone 347.19
hold the prerogative 417.13
hold the promptbook 989.19
hold the proxy of 576.14
hold the purse strings 573.8, 729.16
hold the reins 573.9, 612.12
hold the scales 297.10, 946.12
hold the thought 931.16
hold the wire 347.19
hold tight 474.6
hold together 450.3, 788.6, 800.11, 803.6, 973.8
hold true 973.8
hold under house arrest 429.14
hold up 15.10, 175.9, 298.8, 360.4, 428.7, 449.12, 453.2, 482.14, 501.17, 632.7, 846.8, 846.9, 855.11, 901.21, 912.5, 942.10, 973.8, 1012.10
holdup 175.4, 482.3, 632.5, 846.2, 1012.1, 1041.11
hold up as a model 786.7
hold up as an example 997.13
hold-up bill 613.9
hold up in the wash 942.10, 973.8
holdup man 483.5
hold up one's end 328.6
hold up one's end of the bargain 328.6
hold up one's hand 371.18
hold up one's head 136.4, 492.14
hold up the hand 517.22
hold up the mirror to 351.4
hold up together 770.18, 943.4
hold up to notice 983.10
hold up to public ridicule 661.8
hold up to public shame 661.8
hold up to reprobation 510.13
hold up to shame 661.8
hold up to view 351.4
hold water 935.17, 957.10, 973.8
hold with 332.8, 441.2, 509.9
hold with the hare and run with the hounds 138.11

hold your horses 846.12
hold your water 846.12
hole (n) 80.11, 184.32, 197.2, 197.17, 224.2, 228.11, 228.26, 228.28, 258.3, 275.2, 284.2, 284.5, 292.1, 292.3, 346.4, 409.5, 654.7, 751.1, 795.2, 1003.2, 1013.6 (v) 191.3, 292.15
hole, the 429.8
hole-and-corner 345.12
holed 260.14, 292.19
holed up 346.14
hole in one 409.5
hole-in-one 751.3
hole-in-the-wall 197.3, 228.9, 258.3
hole out 751.4
holeproof 15.20, 293.13
hole punch 713.8, 786.6
hole to creep out of 369.4
hole up 346.8
holey 292.19, 393.32
holeyness 288.1
holiday (n) 20.3, 20.4, 222.4, 402.1, 487.1, 701.12, 826.1, 857.3, 1010.4 (v) 20.9 (a) 20.10
holiday company 177.5
holiday-making 743.3
holidays 624.6
holier-than-thou 354.33, 692.11, 693.5
Holiness 648.5
holiness 685.1, 692.2
holism 792.5
holistic 792.9, 864.14
holistic approach 792.5
hollandaise 10.12
holler (n) 59.1, 115.5, 237.7 (v) 59.6, 115.16, 333.5
hollering 59.10
holler out 59.8
hollo (n) 59.1 (v) 59.6
hollo after 382.8
hollow (n) 197.2, 237.7, 275.2, 284.2, 292.1 (v) 284.12, 284.13 (a) 54.11, 117.6, 222.14, 284.16, 354.32, 391.13, 922.19, 936.10
hollowed 284.16
hollow-eyed 21.9, 270.20
hollow hunger 100.7
hollow man 16.6, 500.7, 764.2, 998.7
hollow mockery 354.5
hollowness 54.1, 117.1, 222.2, 284.1, 354.5, 391.2, 913.1, 922.6
hollow out 284.13
hollow pretense 354.3
hollow shell 284.2
hollow threat 514.1
hollow truce 465.5
hollow ware 8.12, 735.4
holly 44.4
holly-green 44.4
Hollywood 706.1
Hollywood ending 820.1, 969.1
holm 235.2, 243.1
holocaust 96.7, 308.1, 308.3, 395.1, 696.7
Holocaust, the 308.4
holocephalan 311.30
holocrine 13.8
hologram 714.5
holograph (n) 337.3, 547.3, 547.10, 549.5 (a) 547.22
holographic 547.22
holographical 547.22
holt 310.14
holy 677.17, 685.7, 692.9
holy, the 685.2
Holy Bible 683.2
Holy Church 687.3
Holy City 681.3
Holy Communion 701.7
holy day 20.4, 701.12, 850.4
holy father 699.5
Holy Ghost, the 121.5, 677.12
holy ground 1009.5
Holy Joe 699.2
Holy Land 986.11
holy man 659.6
holy matrimony 563.1
holy mess 810.3, 1013.5
holy-minded 692.9
holy-mindedness 692.2
holy mother 699.17
holy of holies 197.8, 703.4, 703.5, 1009.5
holy of holies, the 685.2
holy orders 565.1, 698.1, 698.10, 699.4, 701.4
Holy Orthodox Catholic Apostolic Church 675.9
holy place 208.7, 703.4
holy rite 701.3
Holy Roman Emperor 575.9
Holy Sacrament, the 701.7
Holy Scripture 683.2
Holy Spirit, the 121.5, 677.12
holystone 79.17
holy table 703.12
holy terror 127.9, 302.4, 427.4, 593.2, 593.4, 671.10
holytide 701.12
holy war 458.3
holy water 696.10
holy-water basin 703.10
holy-water font 703.11
holy-water stoup 703.10
holy wedlock 563.1
Holy Willie 693.3
Holy Writ 683.2
homage 155.1, 155.2, 326.1, 433.1, 509.5, 641.1, 644.7, 696.1
homager 432.7, 577.1
homaloid 201.3
homaloidal 201.7
hombre 76.4, 87.9
home (n) 228.2, 228.18, 232.2, 1009.4 (a) 228.32, 1007.6
home appliance 1040.3
home away from home 228.8
home-based 724.16
homebody 584.5
homebound 85.54, 584.10
home boy 227.5, 588.4
homeboy 588.3, 588.4
homebred 226.5
home brew 88.16, 88.18
home care 90.1
homecoming 186.3
home computer 1042.2
home-cooked meal 8.8
home cooking 8.8
homecroft 1069.8
home defense army 461.25
home economics 11.1, 573.6
home equity loan 438.4
homefarm 1069.8
homefelt 93.24
homefolk 559.5
homefolks 559.5
home free 1007.6, 1007.7
home front 724.4
home front, the 232.2
home furnishings 229.1, 735.4, 735.5
home girl 227.5
homegirl 588.4
home ground 232.2
home-grown 226.5
home guard 461.24
home in 798.4
home in on 159.11, 208.10
home-keeping 173.15
homeland 228.2, 232.2
homeless 160.10, 584.12, 619.9, 854.7, 872.8
homeless, the 606.4, 619.3, 1011.7
homelessness 584.4, 619.2
homeless person 160.4, 331.10, 619.4, 828.4
homeless shelter 228.29
homeless waif 178.3
homelike 121.11, 225.15, 228.33
homelikeness 121.2
homeliness 121.2, 137.1, 497.5, 499.1, 581.1, 1015.1
homely 121.11, 137.10, 228.33, 497.14, 499.6, 535.3, 581.3, 606.8, 798.6, 1015.6
homely as a mud fence 1015.6
homely enough to sour milk 1015.6
homely enough to stop a clock 1015.6
homemade 892.18
homemaker 575.2
homemaking 228.3, 573.6
home management 11.1
home office 197.6, 208.6, 739.7, 739.8
home on 1036.17
homeopathic 90.15
homeopathy 90.13
homeostasis 855.1
homeowner 227.7
home page 1042.18, 1042.19
home permanent 3.15
home place 228.2
home plate 186.5, 745.1
home-plate umpire 745.3
home port 1009.6
homer (n) 353.6, 409.5, 745.3 (v) 745.5
home reserve 461.24
home reserves 461.25
Homeric 257.20, 720.16
Homeric laughter 116.4
home roof 228.2
homeroom 208.6
home rule 430.5, 612.4
home run 409.5, 745.3
home schooling 567.3, 568.1, 568.5
home shopping 733.1, 736.2
homesick 100.23, 112.23
homesickness 100.5, 112.5
homesite 228.5
homespun (n) 535.1 (a) 288.6, 416.6, 497.14, 499.6, 535.3, 798.6, 892.18
home station 1036.6
homestead 228.2, 1069.8
homesteader 227.9, 470.4
homestretch 820.3
homestyle 892.18
home sweet home 228.2
home thrust 459.3, 510.4
hometown 228.2
hometowner 227.5
home truth 974.2
home truth, the 973.3
home turf 228.1, 894.4
home tutor 571.1
homeward 186.9
homeward-bound 186.9
homework 568.7, 724.2
home worker 726.2
homey 121.11, 228.33, 581.3
homeyness 121.2, 228.2, 581.1, 798.1
homicidal 308.24
homicidal mania 926.1, 926.7
homicidal maniac 308.11, 926.15
homicide 308.2, 308.11
homiletic 568.18
homiletical 568.18
homiletics 543.1
homilist 543.5, 571.7, 699.3
homily 543.3, 556.1, 568.7
hominal 312.13
hominess 228.2
homing pigeon 353.6
hominid (n) 842.7 (a) 312.14
Hominidae 312.1
hominids 312.1
homish 228.33
hommage 509.5
homme 76.4
homo 75.15, 312.1
homocentric 208.14, 312.13
homocycle 1038.7
homocyclic 1038.18
homoerotic 75.30
homoeroticism 75.10
homo faber 312.7
homogeneity 778.1, 781.1, 798.1
homogeneous 778.7, 781.5, 784.10, 798.6, 812.8
homogenesis 78.6
homogenetic 78.16
homogenize 781.4, 797.10
homogenized 812.8
homogenizer 797.9
homogeny 778.1
homograph 526.1, 778.3
homologize 788.7
homologous 775.8, 777.10
homologous chromosomes 305.8
homology 775.1
homonuclear 1038.19
homonym 526.1, 778.3

homophile 75.14
homophilia 75.10
homophone 526.1, 778.3
homophonic 708.49
homophony 708.3, 708.21
homopolymerize 1060.8
Homo sapiens 312.1
homosexism 75.10
homosexual (n) 75.14 (a) 75.30
homosexualism 75.10
homosexualist 75.14
homosexuality 75.2, 75.10
homosexual marriage 563.1
homunculus 258.5
hon 104.10, 562.6
honcho 249.4, 574.6, 575.4, 997.11
hone 285.7
honed edge 285.2
hone for 100.16
honest 499.7, 644.13, 644.16, 653.5, 973.15
honest and aboveboard 644.14
honest as the day is long 644.14
honest gambling house 759.19
honest man 644.8, 659.1
honest sweat 12.7
honest-to-God 761.15, 973.15
honest-to-God truth, the 973.4
honest-to-goodness 973.15
honest truth, the 973.3
honest woman 644.8
honesty 644.1, 644.3, 973.7
honey (n) 10.40, 66.2, 66.3, 104.10, 562.6, 803.4, 999.7, 1016.8, 1062.5 (v) 66.4, 511.6
honeybee 311.34
honey blond 35.9
honey-blond 37.9
honey bun 104.10
honeybun 562.6
honeybunch 104.10, 562.6
honey-bunny 104.10, 562.6
honey child 562.6
honey-colored 43.4
honeycomb (n) 66.2, 284.6, 292.8 (v) 221.7, 284.14, 292.15, 393.15, 395.20
honeycombed 221.15, 284.17, 292.19
honeydew 66.2
honeyed 66.5, 97.6, 511.8, 708.48
honeyed phrases 511.1
honeyed words 377.3, 504.5, 511.1, 562.5
honeymoon (n) 20.3, 563.3, 1010.4 (v) 563.16
honeymooner 563.5
honeymooners 104.17, 563.9
honey-mouthed 504.17, 511.8
honey mustard 10.12
honeypie 104.10
honeypot 66.2
honeysweet 66.5
honey-tongued 504.17, 511.8
honey trap 938.10
honi bake 66.3
honi-bake 66.3
honibake 66.3
honi flake 66.3
honi-flake 66.3
honing (n) 100.5 (a) 100.23
honk (n) 53.5 (v) 53.10, 60.5
honk the horn 53.10
honky-tonk 88.20
Honor 648.2
honor (n) 155.1, 471.6, 509.5, 644.1, 646.1, 648.1 (v) 155.4, 437.9, 487.2, 624.13, 646.8
honor (n) 662.3, 662.4, 664.1, 696.1, 888.1, 997.2 (v) 662.12, 696.11
honor a bill 624.18
honorable 155.12, 644.13, 646.10, 662.15
Honorable, the 648.8
honorable descent 608.2
honorable mention 509.3, 646.4
honorableness 644.1
honorarium 478.5, 478.8, 624.3, 624.5
honorary 646.10, 648.7
honorary member 617.11
honor before 371.17
honored 155.11, 646.9, 662.15, 662.16
honored guest 662.9
honoree 662.9
honorific (n) 527.3, 648.1 (a) 155.8, 527.15, 646.10, 648.7
honorificabilitudinitatibus 545.3
honoring (n) 434.1 (a) 696.16
honoring the occasion 487.1
honor one's obligations 434.3
honor point 647.2
honor roll 871.6
honors 758.3, 938.2
honors cards 758.3
honors of the house 585.1
honor system 952.2
honor the occasion 111.2
honor trick 758.3
hoo 60.5
hooch 88.14, 88.18
hooch hound 88.12
hood (n) 295.2, 322.3, 461.1, 593.4, 660.5, 671.10, 702.2 (v) 5.40, 295.19, 295.21
hoodang 582.12
hooded 5.45, 295.31
hoodlum 322.3, 461.1, 483.4, 593.4, 671.10
hoodlumism 322.1
hoodoo (n) 675.6, 690.1, 691.5, 1000.4 (v) 691.9, 1011.12 (a) 690.14
hoodwink 30.7, 356.17
hoodwinkable 954.9
hoodwinked 30.10, 930.13
hoodwinking 30.1, 356.1
hoody 671.20
hooey 354.14, 520.3
hoof (n) 199.5 (v) 705.5
hoof-and-mouth disease 85.41
hoofbeat 177.11
hoofed 199.9, 311.45
hoofer 178.6, 705.3, 707.1
hoofing 177.8, 705.1
hoofing it 177.8
hoof it 177.27, 705.5
hoofmark 517.7
hoofprint 517.7
hoo-ha 53.4, 330.4, 456.6, 810.2, 917.1
hook (n) 180.16, 278.2, 279.2, 283.9, 356.13, 377.3 (v) 278.5, 279.6, 356.20, 472.9, 480.17, 482.16, 751.4, 800.8
hookah 89.6
hook and hook in 375.23
hook-and-ladder 1022.3
hook-and-ladder truck 179.12
hook a ride 177.31
hook ball 750.2
hooked 87.25, 278.6, 279.8, 563.21, 740.7
hooked into 898.5
hookedness 278.1, 279.1
hooker 180.1, 665.16
hookey 368.4
hook in 356.20
hooking 800.3
hook ladder 193.4
hooklike 279.8
hook-nosed 279.8
hooks 474.4
hook-shaped 279.8
hook up 450.3, 800.10
hookup 104.5, 450.2, 800.1, 805.1, 1034.8
hook up with 805.4
hooky 222.4, 368.4, 369.1
hooligan 322.3, 461.1, 497.6, 593.4, 660.5
hooliganish 497.13
hooliganism 322.1, 497.4
hoop 280.3, 743.16, 747.1
hooper 747.2
hoopla 116.1, 352.4, 355.1, 743.3
hoopla campaign 609.13
hoops 747.1
hoop sport 747.1
hoopster 747.2
hooray (n) 59.1, 116.2 (v) 116.6
hoosegow 429.9
hoot, a 762.3, 998.5
hoot (n) 59.1, 489.6, 508.3 (v) 59.6, 60.5, 508.10
hoot down 508.8
hootenanny 708.32, 1052.5
hooter 283.7, 400.1
hooting (n) 508.1 (a) 508.12
hootmalalie 1052.5
hooved 311.45
hop (n) 87.16, 177.11, 184.9, 366.1, 705.2 (v) 174.9, 177.28, 184.36, 366.5, 705.5
hop along 174.9
hopdog 87.21
hope (n) 100.1, 100.9, 100.11, 124.1, 130.2, 653.3, 953.1, 966.1, 1009.2 (v) 124.6, 130.5, 839.6
hope against hope 124.6
hope and pray 124.6
hope deferred 125.5, 132.1
hoped-for 100.29, 130.13, 839.8
hope for 100.16, 124.6, 839.6
hope for the best 124.7
hopeful (n) 100.12, 124.5, 302.1, 610.9 (a) 109.11, 124.10, 130.11, 968.6
hopefulness 109.1, 124.1
hopeful prognosis 124.1
hope in 124.6, 953.15
hopeless 94.13, 125.12, 307.32, 414.15, 967.7
hopeless case 125.8, 410.8
hopeless condition 85.2
hopelessness 94.4, 112.3, 125.1, 967.1, 972.10
hopeless situation 125.8
hopemonger 124.5
hoper 124.5
hopes 124.1, 130.4
hope to die 334.6
hope to God 124.6
hophead 87.21
hop in 189.7, 193.12
hoping (n) 124.1 (a) 100.21, 124.10
hoping against hope 124.1
hop it 174.9
hoplite 461.6
hop off 184.38
hopoff 184.8
hop-o'-my-thumb 258.5
hop out 190.11
hopped up 105.20
hopped-up 87.24, 135.6, 251.7
hopper 311.35, 366.4
hopper car 179.15
hoppergrass 311.35
hopping (n) 366.3 (a) 105.27, 366.7
hopping mad 152.30
hopple (n) 428.4 (v) 428.10
hoppytoad 311.26
hop, skip, and jump 366.1
hoptoad 311.26
hop to it 401.6, 725.15, 845.5
hop up 251.5
horde (n) 770.4 (v) 770.16
horde, the 606.2
horehound 86.16
horizon 27.1, 31.3, 201.4, 261.3
horizontal (n) 201.3 (a) 201.7, 277.6
horizontal axis 201.3
horizontal bar 725.7, 760.5
horizontal fault 201.3
horizontality 201.1
horizontal line 201.3
horizontally mobile 607.10
horizontal mobility 607.1, 852.1
horizontalness 201.1, 277.1
horizontal parallax 201.3
horizontal plane 201.3
horizontal projection 201.3
horizontal surface 201.3
horizontal synchronizing pulse 1035.4
horizontal union 727.2
horme 100.1
hormic 100.21
hormonal 2.29, 13.8
hormone 13.2, 86.32
hormone replacement therapy 86.32
hormonic 13.8
hormonology 13.4
horn (n) 50.8, 53.6, 237.6, 285.4, 347.4, 400.1, 711.6, 901.18 (v) 459.26
hornbook 554.10, 568.5, 818.6

horndog 75.16
horned 279.11, 285.9
horned moon 1073.11
horner 710.4
hornet 311.34
hornet's nest 228.25, 1006.1, 1013.3
Horneyan psychology 92.2
hornification 1046.5
hornified 1046.13
hornify 1046.7
horn in 214.5
horniness 75.5, 104.2, 665.5
hornist 710.4
hornless cow 311.6
hornlike 279.11
horn-mad 153.5
horn-madness 153.1
horn of Amalthea 991.3
horn of plenty 991.3
horn player 710.4
horn-rimmed glasses 29.3
horns 680.13
horn-shaped 279.11
horns of a dilemma 971.3, 1013.7
hornswoggle 356.14
hornswoggler 358.2
horny 75.27, 285.9, 665.29, 1046.10
horologe 832.6
horologer 832.10
horologic 832.15
horological 832.15
horologist 832.10
horologium 832.6
horology 821.1, 832.1
horometric 832.15
horometrical 832.15
horometry 832.1
horoscope 1073.20
horoscoper 1073.23
horoscopist 1073.23
horoscopy 962.2, 1073.20
horotelic 861.8
horotely 861.3
horrendous 98.19, 127.30
horrible 98.19, 127.30, 247.11, 1000.9, 1015.11
horribleness 98.3, 127.2, 1000.2, 1015.2
horrid 98.19, 127.30, 1000.9, 1015.11
horridness 98.3, 1015.2
horrific 98.19, 127.30
horrification 127.1, 127.7
horrified 127.26
horrify 98.11, 127.17
horrifying 98.19, 127.30
horripilant 288.6
horripilate 127.15, 288.4, 1023.9
horripilation 127.5, 288.2, 1023.2
horror 96.7, 99.2, 127.1, 127.2, 127.9, 638.2, 1015.4
horrors, the 926.10
horror-stricken 127.26
horror-struck 127.26
hors de combat 19.17, 412.14
hors d'oeuvre 8.2, 10.7, 10.9, 62.4
horse (n) 15.8, 87.9, 311.5, 311.10, 725.7, 757.2, 901.16 (v) 912.7
horse about 810.11
horse around 322.4, 743.23, 810.11, 923.6, 998.15
horseback 237.5
horsebacker 178.8
horseback rider 178.8
horseback riding 177.6
horse blanket 295.11
horse box 179.17
horsecar 179.17
horsecart 179.3
horsecloth 295.11
horse doctor 90.7
horse-faced 270.19, 1015.7
horse farm 1070.5
horsefeathers 520.3
horseflesh 311.10
Horse Guards 461.15
horsehair 3.2, 711.20
horseherd 1070.3
horse latitudes 173.5, 231.3, 318.9
horselaugh (n) 116.4 (v) 116.8
horseless 1041.23
horselike 311.45
horseman 178.8
horsemanship 177.6, 413.1, 1070.1
horse marine 183.4
horse of a different color 780.3
horse parlor 759.19
horseplay 322.1, 489.5
horsepower 18.4
horsepower-hour 17.7
horsepower-year 17.7
horse race 457.3, 457.12, 609.15, 757.3
horse-race 457.19
horse racer 174.5
horse racing 457.11, 757.1
horseracing bet 759.3
horseracing bets 757.4
horseradish 10.12
horse-ride 177.34
horserider 178.8
horse riding 177.6
horse room 759.19
horse sense 24.5, 920.6
horseshoe 279.5
horseshoe magnet 907.3
horseshoer 1070.2
horse soldier 178.8
horse trade 731.5
horse-trade 731.15
horse trader 357.3, 415.6
horsetrading 731.2, 731.3
horse training 1070.1
horsewhip (n) 605.1 (v) 604.12
horse-whipping 604.4
horse whisperer 90.7
horsewoman 178.8
horse wrangler 1070.3
horsing around 923.1, 998.9
horst 237.5
horsy 311.45
hortation 375.3, 422.1
hortative 375.29, 422.8
hortatory 375.29, 422.8, 568.18
hortatory address 543.2
horticultural 310.38, 1069.21
horticulture 310.24, 1069.2
horticulturist 1069.6
hortorium 310.24
hortulan 310.38
hosanna 116.2, 696.3
hose (n) 5.28, 239.6 (v) 356.19, 1065.12
Hosea 684.1
hose down 79.19, 1065.12
hose out 79.19
hosepipe 239.6
hoser 357.4
hosier 5.33
hosiery 5.28, 5.32
hosing 356.9, 1065.6
hosing down 1065.6
hospice 91.21, 228.15, 1009.4
hospice care 197.25
hospice caregiver 90.10
hospitable 121.13, 143.15, 187.16, 485.4, 582.22, 585.11, 587.16
hospitableness 585.1
hospital 91.21
hospital administrator 90.11
hospital cleanliness 79.1
hospital gangrene 85.40
hospitality 121.2, 143.4, 187.1, 187.9, 225.3, 485.1, 582.1, 585.1, 587.6
hospitality hour 582.10
hospitalization 91.14
hospitalize 85.50
hospitalized 85.59
hospital room 197.25
hospital ship 180.6
hospital steward 183.6
hospitium 1009.4
hospodar 575.12
hoss 311.10
Host 701.7
host (n) 461.23, 585.5 (v) 585.8
host 743.20, 770.4, 770.5, 884.3, 1034.23, 1035.13
hostage 429.11, 438.2
hostages to fortune 561.1
hostel 228.15
hostelry 228.15
hostess 185.4, 577.5, 577.7, 585.5
hostile 38.9, 98.17, 99.8, 451.8, 458.20, 589.10, 779.6, 789.6, 900.8, 1011.13
hostile criticism 510.4
hostile expedition 458.3
hostile look 27.5
hostile reaction 453.1
hostile takeover 737.19
hostile witness 599.5
hostilities 458.1
hostility 38.2, 93.7, 98.1, 99.2, 215.1, 451.2, 457.1, 458.10, 589.3, 779.1
hostler 1070.2
host of heaven 679.2
host of hell 680.1
hot (v) 1020.17 (a) 41.6, 68.7, 75.27, 75.28, 85.58, 93.18, 101.9, 105.22, 110.25, 152.30, 223.14, 368.16, 482.23, 662.16, 665.29, 671.22, 709.29, 759.27, 841.10, 941.10, 999.13, 1019.25, 1020.29, 1032.34, 1037.11
hot about 101.11
hot air 502.2, 520.3, 540.3, 545.2, 1019.9
hot-air artist 502.5, 540.4
hot-air balloon 181.11
hot-air balloonist 185.7
hot-air heat 1019.1
hot-air-heat 1020.17
hot-air-heated 1020.29
hot and bothered 75.27, 152.30
hot and humid 1019.25
hot as a three-dollar pistol 1019.25
hot as blazes 1019.25
hot as fire 1019.25
hot as hell 1019.25
hot as pepper 68.7
hot as the hinges of hell 1019.25
hot bath 91.4
hotbed 208.5, 886.8, 890.6, 1069.11
hot blood 75.5, 110.4
hot-blooded 75.27, 101.9, 1019.29
hotbox 915.6
hot button 375.2
hot-button issue 997.5
hot cake 10.45
hot cereal 10.34
hot chocolate 10.49
hotchpot 797.6
hotchpotch 797.6
hot corner 745.1
hot-corner man 745.2
hot day 1019.8
hotdog (n) 10.21, 501.11 (v) 413.20, 501.16, 753.4
hotdogging 753.1
hotdog skiing 753.1
hotdog stand 8.17
hot economy 632.3
hotel 228.15, 739.1
hôtel 228.7
hotel broker 730.9
hotel detective 576.10
hot enough to fry an egg on 1019.25
hot enough to roast an ox 1019.25
hot flash 85.9
hot flush 85.9
hotfoot 174.9, 401.6
hotfooting 401.3
hot for 101.11
hot goods 482.11, 732.3
hot hand 972.6, 1010.3
hothead 110.11, 671.9
hotheaded 105.29, 110.25, 493.8, 671.22
hotheadedness 110.4, 493.2
hothouse 1069.11
hothouse plant 16.6, 310.3
hot humid hazy 1019.7
hot iron 1020.15
hot items 732.3
hot jazz 708.9
hot key 1042.18
hot lead 517.9

hot lick 708.27
hot line 347.13, 347.17
hot link 1042.19
hotlist 1042.18
hot lunch 8.6
hot mess 406.5, 1013.7
hot-metal typesetting 548.2
hotness 68.2, 1019.1
hot number 75.4
hot nuts 75.5
hot off the griddle 841.10
hot off the press 352.17, 552.15, 841.10
hot on 101.11
hot pants 5.18, 75.5, 104.2
hot poo 999.7
hot pot 10.11
hot potato 96.2
hot-press 287.6
hot property 480.10, 482.11
hot pursuit 382.1
hot rock 413.14
hot rocks 75.5
hot rod 179.9
hot-rod racing 756.1
hots, the 75.5
hotsaucing 568.3
hot seat 605.5, 1013.5
hot seat, the 604.6
hot-selling 100.30
hotshot 501.11
hot shower 79.8
hot spell 1019.7
hot spot 24.4, 743.13, 1006.1, 1013.5
hot spring 91.23, 1019.10
hotspur 110.11, 493.4, 671.9
hot-stove league 744.1
hot stuff 413.14, 662.9
hotted up 119.4, 1020.29
hot temper 110.4
hot-tempered 110.25
hottest 841.10
hottie 75.4, 1016.8
hot tip 551.2
hot to trot 75.27, 665.29
hot tub 79.8, 84.1
hot under the collar 105.22, 152.30
hot up 119.2, 251.5, 1020.17
hot war 458.1
hot water 1013.5, 1019.10
hot-water-heat 1020.17
hot-water-heated 1020.29
hot-water pipe 1020.10
hot wave 1019.7
hot weather 317.3, 1019.7
hot wind 318.6, 1019.5
Houdini 369.5
hound (n) 101.5, 311.16, 311.17, 660.6 (v) 96.13, 126.5, 166.3, 382.8, 382.9, 389.7
hounded 96.24, 126.8
hounding 96.2, 166.1, 382.1, 389.3
hound on 375.16
houndstooth 47.4
hound to destruction 395.25
hour 824.1, 824.2, 832.2
hourglass 260.1, 832.6
hourglass figure 260.1
hourglass of time 821.3
hour hand 517.4
houri 665.15, 1016.9
hourly 850.8
hourly worker 577.3, 607.7, 726.2
House 613.2
house (n) 48.6, 197.9, 228.5, 266.2, 423.1, 559.4, 559.5, 560.4, 617.9, 703.6, 704.14, 704.27, 736.1, 739.1, 759.19, 918.2, 1073.20 (v) 225.10, 385.10
house and grounds 228.5
house and lot 228.5
house ant 311.33
house arrest 429.3, 429.6, 604.2
houseboat 228.5
housebound 85.54, 331.18
houseboy 577.4
housebreak 373.9, 432.11, 482.15, 568.13
housebreaker 483.3
housebreaking 373.7, 482.5, 568.3
housebroke 432.15
housebroken 228.34, 373.15, 432.15, 433.15, 504.15
housebrokenness 433.4
housebug 311.37
house built on sand 16.7
house cat 311.20
houseclean 79.18
housecleaner 79.14
housecleaning 79.2
housed 225.14, 295.31
house decorator 716.11
house detective 227.2, 576.10
house dick 576.10
house divided against itself 456.4
house flag 647.7
house furnishings 229.1
household (n) 228.2, 559.5 (a) 228.32, 499.6, 869.9, 928.27
household effects 229.1, 471.1
householder 227.7, 470.2
household franchise 609.17
household gods 678.12
household goods 229.1
householding 228.3
household possessions 471.1
householdry 228.3
household servant 577.2
household troops 461.15
household words 535.1
househusband 76.10
house in 212.5
housekeep 228.31
housekeeper 574.4, 577.8, 577.10
housekeeping 228.3, 573.6
houseless 160.10
house lights 1025.4
houselights 704.18
housemaid 79.14, 577.8
houseman 577.4
housemistress 575.2
housemother 575.2
house numbers 759.12
house of assembly 613.1
house of assignation 665.9
house of cards 16.7, 1006.1, 1050.2
house of correction 429.8
house of death 309.16
house of detention 429.8
house of God 703.1
house of ill repute 665.9
house of joy 665.9
house of life 1073.20
house of prayer 703.1
house of prostitution 665.9
House of Representatives 613.2
House of Representatives committee 613.2
house of worship 703.1
house organ 555.1
house-owner 227.7
house physician 90.4
house plan 381.3
houseplant 310.3
house-poor 619.7
house-proud 136.8
houseroom 228.1
house-search 938.15
house-sitting 1008.1
house steward 577.10
house-to-house 794.10
house-to-house combat 457.4
housetop 295.6
house trailer 179.19, 228.17
house-train 568.13
housewares 229.1, 735.4
housewarming 770.2
housewife 77.7, 575.2
housewifery 228.3, 573.6
housing (n) 184.24, 225.3, 228.1, 228.4, 295.2, 295.11, 1034.3 (a) 892.15
housing bill 225.3
housing development 225.3
housing problem 225.3
housing project 225.3
hovel 80.11, 228.11
hover 184.36, 193.10, 202.8, 298.9, 362.7, 840.2
hovercar 179.22, 181.7
Hovercraft 179.22, 181.7
hovering 184.50
hover over 223.12
hoverport 1009.6
how, the 384.1
howdah 901.17
how-do-you-do 585.4, 1013.5
Howe's American type 30.6
however, a 1012.4
howevers 421.3
how it goes 765.2
how it is 765.2, 973.4
howitzer 462.11
howl (n) 53.3, 58.4, 59.1, 60.1, 115.3, 115.5, 333.2 (v) 58.8, 59.6, 60.2, 115.13, 115.16, 318.20, 333.5
howler 489.6, 975.6
howling (n) 50.13, 60.1, 115.1 (a) 58.14, 60.6, 105.25, 115.19, 247.11
howling success 409.4
howling wilderness 891.2
howl like all the devils of hell 53.9
howsomevers 421.3
how the land lies 765.2
how they fall 972.1
how things are 765.2, 973.4
how things stack up 765.2
how things stand 765.2, 766.2
how-to, the 384.1
how-to book 554.8
hoyden (n) 76.9, 302.8 (a) 76.14
H2O 1065.3
huaca 678.1
hub 169.1, 208.2, 208.5, 915.5, 1020.11, 1040.5
hubble-bubble 89.6
Hubble classification 1073.6
hubbub 53.3, 59.4, 330.4, 671.2, 810.4, 917.1, 935.4
hubby 563.7
hub of industry 739.2
hubris 136.1, 141.2, 142.1, 493.1, 640.2, 970.5
hubristic 141.11, 142.9, 493.7, 640.11, 970.21, 993.16
huckster (n) 352.9, 730.5 (v) 731.18, 734.9
huckstering 355.1, 375.3, 734.2
hucksterism 352.5, 734.2
huddle (n) 541.5 (v) 223.12, 422.7, 770.16
huddled masses 497.6
Hudibrastic 720.16
Hudibrastic verse 720.3
hue (n) 35.1, 35.6, 767.4 (v) 35.14
hue and cry 53.3, 59.4, 352.4, 382.1, 400.1
hue cycle 35.7
hued 35.17
hueless 36.7
huelessness 36.1
huff (n) 152.7 (v) 127.20, 152.24, 259.4, 318.19
huff and puff 725.11
huff-duff 1036.4
huffed 152.27
huffiness 110.2, 110.3
huffing 2.32
huffish 110.20
huffishness 110.2, 110.3
huffy 110.20, 152.27
hug (n) 474.2, 562.3, 585.2, 585.4 (v) 223.12, 474.6, 474.7, 480.14, 562.18, 585.9, 803.6
huge 15.17, 247.7, 257.20
hugeness 247.1, 257.7
hugger-mugger (n) 345.1, 345.4 (v) 345.8 (a) 345.12, 810.16
hugger-muggery 345.1
hugging 562.1
huggy 257.18
Hughes 618.8
hug oneself 116.5, 136.5, 502.8
hug the coast 182.39
hug the deck 201.5
hug the earth 274.5
hug the figure 803.8
hug the ground 201.5
hug the land 182.39, 223.12
hug the shore 182.39, 223.12
hula girl 705.3
hula hoop 743.16
hulk 15.7, 180.1, 257.11, 257.13, 393.8, 1052.3

hulkiness 257.9, 414.3, 1013.9
hulking 257.19, 414.20, 1013.19
hulkingness 257.9
hulky 257.19, 414.20, 1013.19
hull (n) 180.1, 295.16, 310.30 (v) 6.9
hullabaloo 53.4, 59.4, 105.3, 330.4, 810.4
hum (n) 50.13, 52.4, 52.7, 708.13, 812.2 (v) 52.13, 525.8, 708.38, 781.3
human (n) 312.5 (a) 143.13, 145.7, 312.13
human behavior 321.3
human being 306.4, 312.5
human beings 312.1
hum and haw 344.7, 362.7, 525.8
human dynamo 17.6, 330.8
humane 143.13, 145.7, 427.7
human ecology 312.10
humane letters 547.12, 718.1
humaneness 143.1, 427.1
human engineering 717.5
human equation 312.8
human error 975.1, 975.3
human factor 865.1
human factors engineering 717.5
human fallibility 312.8
human family 312.1
human frailty 16.2, 312.8
human geography 312.10
human growth hormone 14.1
human immunodeficiency virus 85.42
human interest 93.9
human-interest 93.22
humanism 312.11, 695.7, 928.5
humanist 695.13, 929.3, 1052.7
humanistic 312.13, 695.16
humanistic scholarship 928.5
humanitarian (n) 143.8, 478.11 (a) 143.15
humanitarianism 143.4
humanity 143.1, 145.1, 312.1, 312.6, 312.8, 427.1
humanization 312.9
humanize 312.12
humanizing 312.9
humankind 312.1
humanly possible 966.6
human mountain 257.12
human nature 312.6, 312.8
humanness 312.8
humanoid (n) 842.7 (a) 312.14, 842.11
human paleontology 842.4
human race 312.1
human resources 18.9
human rights 430.2, 642.3
human sacrifice 696.7
human shield 460.3
human species 312.1
human weakness 312.8
human wreck 660.2
humble (v) 137.4, 412.10, 432.9, 447.3 (a) 113.9, 134.10, 137.10, 139.9, 250.6, 433.15, 606.8, 652.5, 692.10
humble apology 113.4
humbled 113.9, 137.13, 137.14, 412.17, 432.15
humblehearted 137.11
humble-looking 137.10
humble-minded 137.11
humbleness 134.2, 137.1, 250.1, 1005.3
humble oneself 113.7, 137.7
humble oneself before 696.11
humble servant 577.2
humble-spirited 137.11
humblest 137.10
humble-visaged 137.10
humbling (n) 432.4, 447.1 (a) 137.15
humbug (n) 354.3, 354.7, 354.14, 356.7, 357.6, 520.2 (v) 356.14
humbugable 954.9
humbuggery 354.3, 354.7, 354.14
humdinger 999.7
humdrum (n) 118.1, 849.4 (a) 118.9, 721.5, 781.6, 849.15
humdrumminess 118.2
humdrumness 118.2
humdrum toil 725.4
Humean 695.20, 952.12
humect 1065.12
humectant 1065.18
humectate 1065.12
humectation 1065.1
humid 1019.28, 1065.15
humidification 1065.2, 1065.6
humidifier 1065.3
humidify 1065.12
humidity 317.4, 1019.6, 1065.2
humidity control 1041.8
humidity wind rose 318.15
humidness 1019.6, 1065.2
humidor 89.4, 1065.10
humid weather 1019.7
humiliate 98.13, 137.4, 156.5, 432.9, 447.3, 661.8
humiliated 137.14, 432.15
humiliating 98.21, 137.15, 156.8, 661.11
humiliation 96.4, 98.6, 137.2, 156.2, 157.2, 432.4, 447.1, 661.5
humiliative 137.15, 661.11
humility 134.2, 137.1, 139.1, 250.1, 433.5, 652.1
Humism 695.6
Humist 695.12
hummer 174.5
humming (n) 52.7, 708.13 (a) 52.20, 60.6
hummock 237.4
hummocky 283.15
hummum 79.8
hummus 10.9
humongous 247.7, 247.10, 257.20
humongousness 247.1, 257.7
humor (n) 2.24, 2.25, 92.11, 364.1, 489.1, 767.4, 978.3, 978.4 (v) 427.6
humoral 2.33, 13.8
humoring 427.3
humorist 489.12, 547.15, 718.4
humorless 112.21
humorlessness 111.1, 112.2
humorous 488.4, 489.15, 743.27
humorousness 488.1, 489.2
humors 767.4
humorsome 364.5, 489.15
humorsomeness 364.2, 489.3
hump (n) 237.6, 283.3 (v) 174.9, 279.6, 330.14, 401.6, 725.9
humpback 265.3
humpbacked 265.13, 279.10
hump day 832.4
humped 265.13, 279.10, 283.13
hump it 174.9, 401.6, 725.9
hump oneself 401.6, 725.9
hump speed 184.31
humpy 279.10
humus 890.4
hun 395.8
hunch (n) 93.1, 133.1, 283.3, 399.2, 934.3, 951.4, 951.5, 962.1 (v) 279.6, 913.8
hunchback 265.3
hunchbacked 265.13
hunch down 913.8
hunched 279.10
hunch over 913.8
hunchy 279.10
hundred 231.5, 882.8
hundred-dollar bill 728.7
hundredfold 882.29
hundred-percent American 591.3
hundred-percenter 591.3
hundredth 882.29
hundred-to-one shot 972.9
hundredweight 882.8
hung 202.9
Hungarian goulash 10.11
hunger (n) 8.1, 100.6, 100.7, 896.1 (v) 8.20, 100.19
hunger after 100.18
hunger for 100.19
hunger for knowledge 570.12
hunger for learning 570.5
hungering 100.24, 100.25
hunger pain 26.2
hunger pang 26.2
hunger strike 515.1
hung jury 596.5
hungover 88.27
hungriness 100.7
hungry 100.24, 100.25, 992.12
hungry as a bear 100.25
hungry for knowledge 570.18
hungry ghost 100.6
hungry mouth 8.16
hung up 96.22, 846.16, 926.33
hunk 15.6, 75.4, 76.6, 244.2, 257.10, 770.9, 793.3, 1016.8
hunker 913.8
hunker down 913.8
hunky 15.15, 76.13, 1016.18
hunky-dory 999.13
Hunt 618.8
hunt (n) 382.2 (v) 382.8, 382.9, 389.7
hunt (n) 938.15 (v) 938.30, 938.31
hunt down 382.9, 938.35, 941.2
hunted, the 382.7
hunter 311.13, 311.17, 382.4, 382.5, 904.8, 938.18
hunter-killer submarine 180.9
hunter's moon 1073.11
hunt for 938.30
hunting (n) 382.1, 382.2, 938.15 (a) 382.11
hunting cry 59.3
hunting dog 311.17
hunting expedition 177.5
hunting license 443.6
hunting season 313.1
Huntington's chorea 85.25
hunting trip 177.5
hunt out 909.14, 938.34
huntress 382.5
huntsman 382.5
hunt through 938.31
hunt up 938.30
hurdle (n) 366.1, 1012.4, 1013.8 (v) 366.5
hurdler 366.4
hurdle race 366.3, 757.1
hurdle racer 366.4
hurdles 755.2
hurdles, the 366.3
hurdling 366.3, 755.2
hurdy-gurdist 710.9
hurdy-gurdy 711.14
hurdy-gurdyist 710.9
hurdy-gurdy man 710.9
hurl (n) 904.3 (v) 99.4, 159.13, 904.10
hurl a brickbat 156.6
hurl against 459.28
hurl at 459.28
hurl at the head of 459.28
hurl defiance 454.3
hurler 745.2, 904.7
hurley 749.4
hurl forth 671.13
hurling 749.4, 904.2
hurly-burly 105.4, 917.1
hurrah (n) 59.1, 116.2 (v) 116.6
hurrah campaign 609.13
hurrah's nest 797.6, 799.2, 810.3
hurray (n) 116.2 (v) 116.6
hurricane 105.9, 318.11, 400.1, 671.4
hurricane-force 318.22
hurricane-hunter aircraft 317.8
hurricane warning 317.7, 400.1
hurricane watch 317.7, 400.1
hurried 401.9, 401.11, 493.8
hurriedness 401.2, 493.2
hurry (n) 105.4, 174.1, 401.1 (v) 172.5, 174.8, 401.4, 401.5
hurry about 330.12
hurry along 401.4
hurry away 188.10
hurrying 401.3
hurry on 375.16, 401.4, 401.5
hurry-scurry (n) 105.4, 401.1 (v) 401.5
hurry through 401.5
hurry up 174.10, 401.4, 401.5
hurst 310.14
hurt (n) 26.1, 85.38, 96.5, 393.1, 996.2, 1000.3 (v) 26.7, 26.8, 96.17, 96.19, 152.21, 393.9, 393.13, 902.13, 1000.6 (a) 26.9, 96.23, 393.27
hurtful 26.10, 1000.12

hurtfulness 1000.5
hurting (n) 26.1, 393.1 (a) 26.9, 26.10, 619.10
hurtle 174.8, 902.12, 902.13
hurtless 999.21
hurtlessness 999.9
hurt one's feelings 96.17, 152.21
hurt the ears 61.3
husband (n) 76.10, 563.7, 575.1 (v) 386.12, 635.4
husband and wife 563.9
husbandhood 563.1
husbandless 565.7
husbandly 104.26, 563.18
husbandman 1069.5
husband one's resources 386.12, 405.11, 635.4
husbandry 573.1, 635.1, 1069.1
husband swapping 75.7
husband-to-be 104.16
hush (n) 51.1, 57.1 (v) 51.7, 51.8, 57.2, 252.9, 345.8, 670.7
hushcloth 51.4
hushed 51.10, 52.16, 173.12, 670.11
hushed attention 48.1
hushed expectancy 130.3
hushed-up 345.11
hush-hush (v) 51.8, 345.8 (a) 345.11
hush-hush matter 345.5
hushing (n) 57.1, 670.2 (a) 57.3, 670.15
hush money 378.2, 624.5
hush of hight 51.1
hush of night 315.6
hush one up 51.8
hush puppy 10.29
hush up 51.5, 345.8
hush-up 345.3
husk (n) 295.16, 310.30 (v) 6.9
huskiness 15.2, 58.2
husking 582.14
husking bee 582.14
husks 256.1, 391.4
husky 15.15, 58.15
hussar 461.12
Husserlian 952.12
hussy 142.5, 665.14
hustings 901.13
hustings, the 543.1
hustle (n) 330.7, 401.1, 482.4, 902.2 (v) 330.13, 356.19, 401.4, 401.5, 725.13, 902.12, 917.11
hustle out 909.18
hustler 174.5, 330.8, 357.4, 665.16, 759.22
hustle up 401.4
hustling 174.15, 330.23, 665.28
hut 228.9
hutch (n) 228.9, 386.6 (v) 386.10
hutment 228.9
hutzpa 142.2
Huygens' principle 916.4
huzzah (n) 59.1, 116.2 (v) 116.6, 509.10
Hyades 678.9, 1073.8
hyalescence 1029.1
hyalescent 1029.5
hyaline (n) 1073.2 (a) 1029.5
hyalinocrystalline 1029.5
hybrid (n) 526.11, 797.8 (a) 797.15
hybrid bike 179.8
hybrid chip 1042.3
hybrid computer 1042.2
hybridism 526.11, 797.4
hybridization 797.4
hybridize 797.13
hybrid word 526.11
Hydra 890.6
hydracid 1060.3
Hydraheaded 78.14
hydrant 239.12, 1022.3, 1065.8
hydrate 1060.8
hydrated 1065.16
hydraulic 1039.7, 1039.11, 1065.16
hydraulic engineer 1043.2
hydraulic engineering 1043.1
hydraulic-fill dam 1012.5
hydraulic lift 912.3
hydraulic mining 1058.8
hydraulic power 18.4
hydraulics 1039.4, 1061.2, 1065.9
hydraulic tailgate 912.3
hydrazine 1074.8
hydridizing 1069.14
hydrodynamic 1039.11, 1065.16
hydrodynamics 238.4, 1039.4
hydroelectric 1021.9, 1032.30
hydroelectric energy 17.1
hydroelectricity 1032.18
hydroelectric plant 1032.19
hydroelectric power 17.1, 18.4, 1021.7, 1032.18
hydrogen 7.11
hydrogenate 1060.8, 1067.8
hydrogenated fat 1056.1
hydrogen blast 1038.16
hydrogen bomb 462.20, 1038.16
hydrogen-bomb 459.23
hydrogen cloud 1073.7
hydrogen peroxide 86.21
hydrogen sulfide 71.3
hydrograph 1065.10
hydrographer 240.7
hydrographic 240.8
hydrographical 240.8
hydrography 240.6, 1039.4, 1065.9
hydrokinetics 1039.4
hydrol 1065.3
hydrolase 7.10
hydrologic 1039.11
hydrological cycle 1065.3
hydrology 1039.4, 1061.1, 1065.9
hydrolysis 806.2
hydrolyst 806.2
hydrolyte 806.2
hydrolytic 806.6, 1032.32
hydrolyze 806.4
hydromancy 962.3
hydromechanic 1039.11
hydromechanical 1039.7, 1039.11
hydromechanics 1039.4
hydrometallurgy 1058.11
hydrometeor 1065.3
hydrometeorological 316.12
hydrometeorology 316.9, 317.5
hydrometer 1045.8, 1061.3
hydrometric 1039.11
hydrometrical 1039.11
hydrometry 1039.4
hydropathic 90.15
hydropathy 91.3
hydrophobia 85.41, 926.6
hydrophyte 310.3
hydropic 85.61
hydroplane (n) 181.8 (v) 184.36
hydropot 668.4
hydrops 85.9
hydrosphere 240.1, 1065.3
hydrostat 1065.10
hydrostatic 1039.11
hydrostatic head 1065.3
hydrostatics 1039.4
hydrotherapeutics 91.3, 1065.9
hydrotherapy 91.3, 1065.9
hydrothermal water 1065.3
hydrous 1065.16
hydroxy aldehyde 7.5
hydroxy ketone 7.5
hydroxylate 1060.8
hyena 311.19, 593.5, 660.6
hyetal wind 318.15
hyetograph 316.7
hyetographic 316.12
hyetography 316.9, 317.5
hyetological 316.12
hyetology 316.9
hyetometer 316.7
hyetometric 316.12
hyetometrograph 316.7
hyetometrographic 316.12
Hygeia 83.1
hygeian 81.5
hygeist 81.3
hygenics 79.3
hygge 121.11
hygiene 79.3, 81.2
hygienic 79.27, 81.5
hygienical 81.5
hygienics 81.2
hygienist 81.3
hygienize 79.24
hygric 1065.19
hygrodeik 1065.10
hygrograph 1065.10
hygrology 1065.9
hygrometer 317.8, 1065.10
hygrometric 1065.19
hygrometry 1065.9
hygrophilous 1065.19
hygroscope 1065.10
hygroscopic 1065.19
hygrostat 1065.10
hygrothermal 1065.19
hygrothermograph 1065.10
hyle 1052.2
hylic 1052.10
hylomorphism 1052.6
hylomorphous 1052.12
hylotheism 675.5, 1052.6
hylotheist 675.16
hylotheistic 1052.12
hylozoic 1052.12
hylozoism 952.5, 1052.6, 1053.3
hylozoistic 1052.12
Hymen 563.13
hymen 2.6, 563.3
hymeneal (n) 563.3 (a) 563.18
hymeneal rites 563.3
hymn (n) 150.2, 696.3, 708.14, 708.17 (v) 696.12, 708.38
hymnal (n) 696.3, 708.28 (a) 708.50
hymnbook 708.28
hymner 710.13
hymnist 710.20
hymnody 696.3, 708.17
hymn of praise 696.3
hymnographer 710.20
hymnography 696.3
hymnologist 710.20
hymnology 696.3, 708.17
hymn-tune 708.17
hypabyssal rock 1059.1
hypallage 205.3
hype (n) 87.20, 352.4, 355.1, 509.3, 949.1 (v) 355.3, 375.14, 509.11, 509.12, 949.2
hyped 105.26, 355.4, 502.12
hyped up 105.26
hyper 105.26, 330.24
hyperacid 67.6
hyperacidity 67.1
hyperactive 330.24
hyperactivity 330.9
hyperbatic 205.7
hyperbaton 205.3
hyperbola 279.2
hyperbole 350.1, 355.1, 993.1
hyperbolic 279.13, 993.16
hyperbolical 355.4, 355.5, 993.16
hyperbolic orbit 1073.16
hyperbolism 355.1
hyperbolize 355.3
hyperboreal blast 318.7
hyperborean 161.14, 261.9, 1023.14
hyperborean blast 318.7
hypercathexis 92.34, 926.13
hypercorrection 975.7
hypercritical 495.12, 510.23
hypercriticalness 510.4
hypercriticism 495.4, 510.4
hyperdulia 696.1
hyperelegance 533.3
hyperelegant 533.9
hyperemia 993.3
hyperemic 993.20
hyperesthesia 24.3
hyperesthetic 24.12
hyperform 975.7
hyperglycemia 85.21
Hyperion 1016.9, 1073.14
hyperkinesia 330.9
hyperkinesis 330.9
hyperkinetic 330.24
hyperlink 1042.19
hypermedia 1042.20
hypernormal 870.15
hypernym 809.2
hyperopia 28.4
hyperorthodox 687.8
hyperorthodoxy 687.5
hyperpathia 24.3
hyperpathic 24.12
hyperphagia 672.1
hyperphagic 672.6
hyperphysical 870.15
hyperphysics 689.3

hyperplasia 257.5
hyperpyretic 85.58
hyperpyrexia 85.7
hypersensitive 24.12, 110.21, 495.12
hypersensitiveness 110.5
hypersensitivity 24.3, 110.5, 495.4
hypersexual 75.25
hypersonic 50.17, 174.16, 184.49
hypersonic speed 174.2
hyperspace 269.2
hypertension 85.9, 85.19
hypertensive 85.61
hypertext 1042.20
hyperthermia 85.7
hyperthermic 85.58
hyperthymia 93.9, 105.10
hyperthymic 93.19, 105.28
hyperthyroidism 85.21
hypertrichosis 3.1
hypertrophied 14.3, 259.12, 993.16
hypertrophy (n) 257.5, 993.1 (v) 14.2, 259.7
hypesthesia 25.1
hyphenate (n) 227.4 (v) 530.16
hyphenated American 227.4
hyping 509.17
hypnic 315.9, 377.8, 690.14
hypnoid 22.24
hypnoidal 22.24
hypnology 22.8
Hypnos 22.11
hypnosis 22.7, 691.3
hypnotherapeutic 92.38
hypnotherapist 92.10
hypnotherapy 22.7, 92.6
hypnotic (n) 22.10 (a) 22.23, 22.24, 86.45, 120.9, 377.8, 690.14, 983.20
hypnotic sleep 22.7
hypnotic somnolence 22.7
hypnotic suggestion 22.8
hypnotic trance 92.19
hypnotism 22.8
hypnotist 22.9
hypnotization 22.8
hypnotize 22.20, 377.7, 691.7, 894.11, 983.13
hypnotized 25.6, 122.9, 691.12, 983.18
hypnotizer 22.9, 357.1
hypo 714.13
hypoaeolian mode 709.10
hypochondria 85.3, 112.4
hypochondriac (n) 85.43, 926.15 (a) 92.39, 112.22
hypochondriacal 112.22, 926.28
hypochondriasis 85.3, 112.4
hypochromia 36.2
hypochromic 36.7
hypochromic anemia 36.2
hypocoristic (n) 527.7 (a) 527.15
hypocrisy 354.6, 356.3, 500.1, 645.3, 693.1, 873.1
hypocrite 336.4, 357.8, 693.3
hypocritic 354.33
hypocritical 354.33, 376.5, 500.16, 511.8, 693.5, 873.6
hypocriticalness 354.6
hypocycloid 280.7
hypoderma 2.4
hypodermal 2.27
hypodermic (n) 91.16 (a) 2.27
hypodermic injection 91.16
hypodermic needle 285.3
hypodermic syringe 285.3
hypodermis 2.4
hypodorian mode 709.10
hypogeal 275.13
hypoglycemia 85.21
hypoionian mode 709.10
hypolocrian mode 709.10
hypolydian mode 709.10
hypomixolydian mode 709.10
hyponym 527.3, 809.2
hypophrygian mode 709.10
hypoplasia 795.1
hypoplastic 795.4
hypospray 91.16
hypostasis 530.5, 763.4, 767.2, 1052.2
Hypostatic Union, the 677.11
hypostatize 763.5
hypotaxis 530.2
hypotension 85.9
hypothec 438.4
hypothecate 438.10, 951.9
hypothecation 438.4, 951.1
hypothermia 85.7, 1019.1, 1024.2
hypothermic 1023.20
hypothermy 1024.2
hypothesis 935.7, 951.1, 951.2, 952.2
hypothesis ad hoc 935.7
hypothesis and verification 935.3
hypothesist 951.7
hypothesize 935.15, 951.9
hypothesizer 951.7
hypothesizing 951.1
hypothetic 951.13
hypothetical 935.22, 951.13, 952.10
hypotheticalness 951.6
hypothetico-deductive method 935.3
hypothymia 25.1
hypothyroidism 85.21
hypsographic 272.20, 300.12
hypsographical 300.12
hypsography 272.9
hypsometer 272.9
hypsometric 300.12
hypsometrical 272.20, 300.12
hypsometry 272.9
hysteresis 1032.7, 1041.11
hysteresis curve 1032.7
hysteria 105.8
hysteric 92.39, 93.19, 101.12
hysterical 92.39, 93.19, 101.12, 105.25, 488.5, 926.30
hysterical aphonia 525.6
hysterical mutism 51.2
hysteromania 665.5
hysteromaniac 665.14
hysteromaniacal 665.29
hysteron proteron 205.3, 810.3, 936.3
I 865.5, 872.3
I, the 919.4
iamb 720.8
iambic (n) 720.8 (a) 720.17
iambic pentameter 720.7
iambus 720.8
iatric 86.39, 90.15
iatrochemical 1060.9
ibuprofen 86.12
IC analysis 526.3, 530.2
Icarus 185.9
ice (n) 10.47, 87.4, 287.3, 498.5, 1023.5, 1024.7, 1050.2 (v) 66.4, 198.10, 308.14, 749.7, 1023.11, 1024.10, 1024.11 (a) 1024.14
Ice Age 824.5
ice age 837.3, 1023.3
ice bag 1024.3
ice banner 1023.5
ice barrier 1023.5
ice belt 1023.5
iceberg 1023.5
iceblink 1025.9
ice-blue 45.3
icebound 428.15, 1023.19
icebox 429.9, 1024.4
icebox cookie 10.43
icebreaker 180.6
ice bucket 1024.3
icecap 1023.5
ice cave 1023.5
ice chest 1024.4
ice climbing 760.6
ice cloud 319.2
ice-cold 1023.14, 1024.14
ice-cool 1024.10
ice-cooled 1024.13
ice cream 10.47
ice-cream cone 10.47, 282.5
ice-cream float 10.47
ice-cream freezer 1024.5
ice-cream headache 1023.2
ice-cream parlor 8.17
ice cream sandwich 10.47
ice-cream soda 10.47
ice-cream sundae 10.47
ice crystal 1023.5
ice cube 1024.3
ice-cube machine 1024.5
ice cubes 1023.5, 1024.7
iced 965.8, 970.20, 1024.13
ice dancing 760.7
ice dike 1023.5
ice-encrusted 1023.14
icefall 1023.5
ice field 1023.5
ice fishing 382.3
ice floe 1023.5
ice foot 1023.5
ice front 1023.5
ice hockey 749.1
ice house 1024.4
icehouse 1024.5
ice island 1023.5
Iceland 1023.4
Iceland pony 311.10
icelike 1023.14, 1024.14
ice machine 1024.5
ice maiden 94.1, 110.12
ice milk 10.47
ice needle 1023.5
ice over 1023.11
ice pack 1023.5, 1024.3
ice pail 1024.3
ice pinnacle 1023.5
ice plant 1024.5
icequake 1023.5
ice raft 1023.5
ice rink 743.11, 749.1
ice sculpture 715.1
ice sheet 1023.5
iceshockle 1023.5
ice-skate 177.35
ice skates 179.21
ice skating 760.7
ice sky 1025.9
ice storm 1023.5
ice the puck 749.7
ice up 1023.11
ice water 10.49
I Ching 962.2
ichnite 517.7
ichnography 381.3, 712.5
ichnolite 517.7
ichor 2.24, 2.25, 12.6
ichorous 2.33
icicle 1023.5, 1050.2
iciness 94.1, 102.1, 344.3, 583.2, 589.1, 1023.1
icing 10.40, 198.3, 749.3
icing on the cake, the 407.3
icing the cake 407.3
icing the puck 749.3
ickiness 80.2
icky 64.7, 80.23, 1000.8
icon 33.3, 349.5, 517.2, 518.6, 712.10, 785.1, 862.2, 1042.18, 1042.19
iconic 518.12
iconoclasm 395.1, 695.9, 868.2
iconoclast 395.8, 675.15, 695.10
iconoclastic 695.22
iconoclasticism 695.9
iconoduly 697.1
iconography 349.1, 517.2
iconolagny 666.4
iconolater 697.4
iconolatrous 697.7
iconolatry 697.1
iconology 517.2
iconoscope 1035.10
icosahedral 278.10
icteric 43.6
icterical 43.6
icterus 43.2, 85.9, 85.23
ictus 85.6, 524.10, 709.25, 720.7, 917.6
icy 94.9, 313.9, 344.10, 583.6, 589.9, 1023.14, 1024.14
icy blasts 318.7
icy calm 106.2
icy clutch of dread 127.5
icy-cold 1024.14
icy fingers 127.5
icy nerves 129.1
icy wind 318.7
id 92.28, 934.2
ID card 517.11
idea 248.4, 380.1, 381.1, 422.1, 518.1, 931.1, 932.1, 951.5, 952.2, 953.6
idea, the 886.2
idea afloat 552.6
ideaed 932.10
ideal (n) 100.11, 375.1, 659.4, 786.4, 869.4, 932.2, 986.7,

1002.4 (a) 786.8, 869.8, 932.9, 951.13, 986.23, 1002.6
idealism 100.9, 652.2, 932.2, 952.4, 986.7, 1053.3
idealist (n) 124.5, 952.8, 986.13, 1053.4 (a) 1053.8
idealistic 124.11, 652.6, 986.24, 1053.8
ideality 986.7
idealization 92.23, 689.19, 976.2, 986.7
idealize 689.20, 697.5, 949.2, 986.16
idealized 986.23
idealogue 952.8
ideals 100.9
ideal type 662.9, 786.4, 869.4
ideate (n) 932.2 (v) 931.8, 931.16, 986.14
ideation 920.1, 928.3, 931.1
ideational 920.12, 931.21, 932.9, 952.10, 978.7, 986.18
ideational agnosia 990.2
ideational frame of reference 978.2
ideative 931.21, 986.18
ideatum 932.1, 932.2
idée fixe 926.13
idée-force 932.2
idem 778.3
ident 1035.6
identic 778.7
identical 778.7, 784.10, 790.8, 873.6
identicalness 778.1
identical rhyme 720.9
identical same 778.3
identical twins 873.4
identifiable 31.7
identification 24.3, 92.23, 92.33, 93.5, 517.3, 517.11, 527.2, 778.2, 989.4, 1035.6
identificational 517.23
identification badge 517.11
identification card 517.11
identification mark 517.11
identification tag 517.11
identified as 527.14
identify 517.17, 527.11, 775.6, 778.5, 941.5, 989.11, 1036.17
identifying 517.23
identify oneself with 332.9
identify with 93.11, 455.2
identity 455.1, 778.1, 784.1, 790.1, 865.1, 872.1
identity card 517.11
identity crisis 92.15
identity theft 480.1, 482.3
identity theory of mind 1052.6
ideocracy 612.4
ideogram 349.1, 517.2, 546.2
ideogrammatic 546.8
ideogrammatic character 546.1
ideogrammic 546.8
ideogrammic character 546.1
ideograph 546.2
ideographic 349.13, 517.23, 546.8, 547.26
ideographic character 546.1
ideological 932.9, 952.10, 978.7
ideologist 953.9
ideologue 953.9
ideology 932.8, 952.2, 953.3, 978.5
ideophone 546.1
ides 832.4
Ides of March 964.2
idiochromosome 305.8
idiocrasy 865.4, 927.1
idiocratic 865.13, 927.5
idiocratical 927.5
idiocy 922.9, 923.1
idioglossia 525.1
idiolalia 525.1
idiolect 523.1, 523.7
idiom 523.1, 523.7, 529.1, 532.1
idiomatic 518.10, 523.22
idioplasm 305.10
idiosyncrasy 337.1, 500.2, 517.1, 865.4, 927.1, 927.2, 978.3
idiosyncratic 312.15, 364.6, 517.23, 780.9, 865.13, 927.5
idiosyncratical 927.5
idiot 924.8, 926.15
idiot box 1035.11
idiotic 922.22, 923.8
idiotic grin 116.3
idiotism 529.1, 922.9
idle (v) 173.9, 175.6, 175.9, 329.2, 331.12, 998.14 (a) 173.13, 175.10, 329.6, 331.18, 391.13, 402.5, 936.13, 998.19
idle away 486.5
idle away time 331.13
idle chat 541.4
idle chatter 540.3
idle chatterer 540.4
idle fancy 986.5
idle hands 331.2
idle hours 331.2, 402.1
idleness 175.1, 329.1, 331.2, 998.3
idler 178.3, 331.8, 340.5
idle rich 331.11
idle talk 540.3, 541.4, 552.7
idle threat 514.1
idle wish 323.1
idling 331.4, 998.8
idol (n) 104.15, 349.5, 659.5, 662.9, 678.2, 697.3, 786.4 (v) 697.5
idolater 101.4, 688.7, 696.9, 697.4
idolatress 697.4
idolatric 697.7
idolatrical 697.7
idolatrize 697.5
idolatrizer 697.4
idolatrous 155.9, 509.18, 688.11, 697.7
idolatrousness 697.1
idolatry 104.1, 155.1, 509.5, 511.3, 688.4, 696.1, 697.1
idolify 697.5
idolism 104.1, 697.1
idolist 697.4
idolistic 697.7
idolization 104.1, 155.1, 697.2
idolize 104.20, 155.4, 509.12, 511.7, 696.11, 697.5
idolized 662.18
idolizer 101.4, 697.4
idolizing (n) 509.5 (a) 155.9, 697.7
idoloclast 395.8, 695.10
idolodulia 697.1
idolomancy 697.1
idolum 976.4, 988.1
idol worship 697.1
idol worshiper 697.4
idol worshiping 697.7
I don't know what 528.2
idyllic 97.9, 464.9, 720.16
idyllist 720.12
IF amplification 1034.15
IF audio signal 1035.4
iffy 971.17, 972.15
IF pulse 1036.10
ifs 421.3
IF video signal 1035.4
igloo 228.10, 279.4, 1023.4, 1023.8
igneous 1019.26
igneous rock 1059.1
ignescence 1019.15
ignescent 1019.27
ignis fatuus 976.1, 1019.13, 1025.13
ignite 152.19, 1020.22
ignited 1019.27
igniter 1021.4
ignition 1019.13, 1020.4, 1074.9
ignition point 1019.13
ignition system 1021.4
ignition temperature 1019.13
ignobile vulgus 606.2
ignobility 98.2, 497.5, 661.4
ignoble 98.18, 497.15, 661.10
ignobleness 98.2
ignominious 638.3, 661.10
ignominious defeat 412.4
ignominiousness 661.4
ignominy 638.2, 661.4
ignoramus 572.9, 924.1, 930.7
ignorance 340.2, 374.1, 414.2, 922.1, 930.1, 933.1
ignorant 340.10, 374.4, 414.17, 922.13, 930.11, 933.4
ignorantism 930.1
ignorantness 930.1
ignoratio elenchi 935.5
ignore 134.8, 148.4, 157.6, 327.6, 340.6, 372.2, 600.12, 773.4, 979.7, 984.2
ignored 151.5, 340.14, 372.3, 773.7
ignore grammar 531.3
ignore opportunity's knock 844.5
ignorer 340.5
ignoring 372.1
II 873.2
III 876.1
ileum 2.18
ilk 767.4, 809.3
ill (n) 1000.3 (a) 85.56, 133.16, 144.16, 1000.7
ill-adapted 789.7
ill-advised 365.11, 414.21, 923.10, 996.5
ill-affected 110.18, 144.19, 1000.11
ill-assorted 789.7
ill at ease 96.22
illation 946.4
illative 530.9
illaudable 510.24
ill-balanced 791.5
ill-balanced sentences 534.1
ill-behaved 505.5
ill blood 589.4
ill-boding 133.16
ill-bred 497.12, 505.6
ill-bred fellow 497.6
ill breeding 497.3, 505.1
ill-chosen 789.7
ill-conceived 1000.11
ill-conditioned 144.19, 505.5
ill-conducted 414.21
ill-considered 365.11, 414.21, 493.7, 844.6, 845.8, 923.10, 996.5
ill-contrived 414.21, 923.10
ill day 1011.6
ill-defined 32.6, 971.19
ill-definedness 971.4
ill-devised 365.11, 414.21, 923.10
ill-digested 406.11
ill-disciplined 327.8
ill-disposed 110.18, 144.19, 589.10
ill-disposedness 144.4
ill disposition 144.4
ill-done 414.21
ill done-by 132.5
ill-educated 930.13
illegal 444.7, 638.3, 650.9, 674.6
illegal commerce 732.1
illegal drug 86.5, 87.3
illegal gambling house 759.19
illegal immigrant 368.5
illegality 638.1, 650.1, 674.1, 674.4
illegal operations 732.1
illegal traffic 732.1
illegibility 522.4
illegible 522.19
illegible handwriting 547.6
illegitimacy 561.5, 674.2
illegitimate (n) 561.5 (a) 354.26, 674.6, 674.7
illegitimate business 732.1
illegitimate child 561.5
illegitimateness 674.2
illegitimation 674.2
ill-equipped 406.9, 992.12
ill-executed 414.21
ill fame 661.1
ill-fashioned 1000.11
ill-fated 133.16
ill-fated life 1011.4
ill-fatedness 133.7
ill-favor 661.1
ill-favored 1000.11, 1015.7
ill-favoredness 1015.1
ill-featured 1015.7
ill feeling 589.4
ill-fitted 406.9, 789.7
ill-flavored 64.5
ill fortune 1011.5
ill-found 992.12
ill-founded 936.13
ill-furnished 406.9, 992.12
ill-gauged 923.10
ill-got 645.16
ill-gotten 645.16, 1000.11
ill-gotten gains 482.11

ill hap 1011.2
ill health 82.1, 85.3
ill humor 108.1, 110.1, 935.13
ill-humored 110.18, 935.19
illiberal (n) 980.5 (a) 484.9, 651.6, 980.10
illiberality 484.3, 651.2, 980.1
illicit 444.7, 665.27, 674.6
illicit business 356.8, 674.1, 732.1
illicit love 104.5
illicitness 674.1
ill-imagined 923.10
illimitability 823.1
illimitable 430.27, 823.3
illimited 823.3
ill-informed 930.11
ill-intentioned 144.19
illiquid 625.11
illiteracy 930.4
illiterate (n) 930.7 (a) 930.13
illiterateness 930.4
illiterate speech 523.6
illiterati 930.7
ill-judged 923.10
ill-lighted 1027.14
ill-lit 1027.14
ill-looking 1000.11, 1015.7
ill luck 1011.5
ill-made 265.12, 1015.8
ill-managed 414.21
ill-mannered 505.5
ill manners 505.1
ill-marked 32.6
ill-matched 789.7, 791.4
ill-mated 789.7
ill nature 110.1, 144.4
ill-natured 110.18, 144.19
illness 85.1, 96.5
ill off 619.7, 992.12, 1011.14
illogic 936.2
illogical 936.11, 975.16
illogicality 936.2
illogicalness 936.2
ill-omened 133.16
ill-omenedness 133.7
ill person 85.43
ill-proportioned 265.12, 1015.8
ill-provided 406.9, 992.12
ill-qualified 414.19
ill repute 661.1
ill-requited 151.5
ill-rewarded 151.5
ill-seasoned 844.6
ill-served 132.5
ill service 144.13
ill-shaped 265.12, 1000.11, 1015.8
ill-smelling 71.5
ill-sorted 789.7, 791.4
ill-sounding 534.2
ill-starred 133.16, 844.6, 1011.14
ills the flesh is heir to 1000.3
ill success 410.1, 1011.4
ill-suited 789.7, 996.5
ill temper 110.1
ill-tempered 110.18
ill-time 844.3
ill-timed 789.7, 844.6, 996.5
ill-treat 389.5
ill-treatment 389.2
ill turn 144.13
illume 1025.28
illuminance 1025.1
illuminant (n) 1025.20, 1026.1 (a) 1025.30
illuminate (n) 921.1 (v) 35.14, 341.10, 348.5, 498.9, 521.6, 1025.28
illuminated 88.33, 1025.39
illuminati 413.11, 929.2
illuminating 341.15, 551.18, 568.18, 1025.40
illuminating gas 1025.20
illumination 35.11, 341.4, 498.1, 568.1, 712.10, 928.2, 928.4, 1025.1, 1025.19
illuminative 341.15
illuminator 716.2, 1026.1
illumine 568.10, 1025.28
illumining 1025.40
ill-usage 389.2
ill use 387.1
ill-use (n) 389.2 (v) 387.16, 389.5
illusion 356.1, 691.2, 764.3, 975.1, 976.1, 986.5
illusional 976.9
illusionary 691.11, 976.9
illusionism 976.2
illusionist 357.2, 690.6, 976.2
illusive 356.21, 691.11, 936.10, 976.9
illusiveness 976.2
illusoriness 976.2
illusory 356.21, 691.11, 762.9, 764.6, 975.16, 976.9, 986.19
illustrate 341.10, 349.11, 957.8, 957.13
illustrating 349.13
illustration 341.4, 349.1, 712.10, 712.16, 786.2, 957.5
illustrational 349.13
illustrative 341.15, 349.13
illustrator 716.2
illustrious 247.9, 662.19
illustriousness 247.2, 662.6
ill-ventilated 173.16
ill will 93.7, 144.4, 589.4
ill wind 1000.4, 1011.5
ill wishes 513.1
image (n) 33.2, 33.3, 33.5, 92.29, 349.2, 349.5, 500.1, 517.1, 536.1, 712.10, 714.3, 785.1, 932.1, 976.4, 986.6, 1035.5 (v) 349.11, 931.17, 986.15
image breaking 695.9
image-building 986.6
image capture 714.1
imageless 933.5
imageless thought 931.1
image-maker 352.9
imagemaker 352.9
image of, the 778.3, 784.3
imager 716.2
imagery 349.1, 349.2, 536.1, 986.5, 986.6
imagery study 986.6
image worship 697.1
image-worshiper 697.4
imaginability 966.1
imaginable 951.15, 966.6, 986.26
imaginary 762.9, 764.6, 776.8, 976.9, 986.19, 1017.23
imagination 976.3, 986.1, 986.5
imaginational 986.19
imaginative 337.5, 544.10, 712.20, 932.9, 986.18
imaginative exercise 986.7
imaginative narrative 722.1
imaginativeness 986.1
imagine 931.17, 951.10, 953.11, 986.14
imagined 762.9, 986.19
imagineer (n) 986.12 (v) 986.14
imagineering 986.3
imaginer 986.12
imaging 92.25, 349.1, 986.6
imagining 986.1, 986.5
imagism 986.6
imagist 720.12
imagistic poetry 986.6
imago 33.3, 92.29, 932.1
imam 575.9, 699.12
imbalance 265.1, 791.1
imbecile (n) 924.8 (a) 16.12, 922.22, 923.8
imbecilic 922.22, 923.8
imbecility 19.2, 922.9, 923.1
imbibe 8.29, 88.24, 187.11, 187.13, 570.7
imbiber 88.11
imbibing 8.3, 88.4, 187.4, 570.2
imbibition 8.3, 187.4
imbibitory 187.16, 187.17
imbricate (v) 295.30 (a) 295.36
imbricated 295.36
imbrication 295.4
imbroglio 456.5, 1013.4
imbrue 797.11, 1065.13
imbruement 1065.7
imbue 35.14, 221.7, 375.20, 568.12, 797.11, 1065.13
imbued 35.17, 221.15
imbued with 93.23
imbued with life 306.12
imbuement 221.3, 568.2, 797.2, 1065.7
imbue with life 306.10
imitable 336.10
imitate 336.5, 517.21, 621.4, 784.7, 849.7
imitated 784.10
imitation (n) 78.1, 336.1, 336.3, 349.4, 354.13, 508.6, 621.2, 784.1, 785.1, 849.1, 862.2, 874.1 (a) 336.8, 354.26, 784.10, 862.8
imitation fur 4.2
imitation leather 4.2
imitative 336.9, 349.13, 849.14
imitator 336.4
immaculacy 79.1, 644.1, 653.2, 657.1, 664.1
immaculate 79.25, 644.13, 653.6, 657.7, 664.4, 1002.6
Immaculate Conception, the 679.5
immaculateness 79.1, 653.2, 657.1, 664.1, 1002.1
immanence 221.1, 767.1
immanent 221.12, 767.7
immanent cause 886.3
immaterial 762.9, 764.5, 776.7, 988.8, 998.17, 1053.7
immaterialism 1053.3
immaterialist (n) 1053.4 (a) 1053.8
immaterialistic 1053.8
immateriality 32.1, 299.1, 764.1, 776.1, 976.2, 988.1, 998.1, 1053.1, 1053.2
immaterialization 689.19
immaterialize 689.20, 1053.6
immaterialness 1053.1
immature 301.10, 406.11, 414.17, 795.4, 841.7, 922.24, 930.14, 1003.4
immatureness 406.4
immaturity 301.3, 406.4, 414.2, 795.1, 841.1, 922.11, 923.2, 1003.1
immeasurability 823.1
immeasurable 247.7, 823.3, 884.10
immediacy 221.1, 223.1, 830.1, 845.3, 963.4
immediate 221.12, 223.16, 223.19, 401.9, 812.8, 830.4, 838.2, 840.3, 845.9
immediate apprehension 934.1
immediate cause 886.3
immediate cognition 934.1
immediate constituent analysis 526.3, 530.2
immediate dislike 93.7
immediate family 559.2
immediate foreground 223.1
immediate future 839.1, 840.1
immediate intuition 683.10
immediate neighbor 223.6
immediateness 830.1, 845.3
immediate perception 934.1
immediate prospect 839.1
immediate purpose 387.5
immediate resources 728.18
immedicable 125.15
immedicableness 125.3
Immelmann turn 184.16
immelodious 61.4
immemorial 373.13, 829.7, 837.10, 842.10, 842.12
immemorial usage 842.2
immemorial wisdom 842.2
immense 247.7, 257.20, 823.3, 999.15
immenseness 257.7
immensity 247.1, 257.7, 823.1
immerge 367.7
immergence 367.2
immerse 367.7, 701.16, 983.13
immersed 275.14, 1065.17
immersed in 898.5, 983.17
immersed in thought 931.22
immersible 367.9
immersion 367.2, 701.6, 983.3, 1065.6
immersive 367.9
immethodical 810.12, 851.3
immigrant (n) 178.5, 189.4, 227.4, 227.9, 774.4 (a) 186.9
immigrate 177.22, 189.11
immigration 177.4, 189.3
imminence 130.1, 167.1, 514.1, 839.1, 840.1

imminency 840.1
imminent 130.13, 167.4, 514.3, 839.8, 840.3
imminent threat 514.1
immingle 797.10
immiscibility 804.1
immiscible 789.6
immission 187.2
immit 187.10
immix 797.10
immixture 797.1, 797.5
immobile 173.13, 329.6, 853.7, 855.15
immobility 173.2, 329.1, 331.1, 853.1, 855.3
immobilization 855.3
immobilize 855.7
immoderacy 430.3, 669.1, 993.1
immoderate 430.24, 632.12, 669.7, 671.16, 993.16
immoderateness 632.4, 669.1, 993.1
immoderation 632.4, 669.1, 993.1
immodest 140.11, 666.6
immodesty 140.4, 666.2
immolate 308.13
immolate before 696.15
immolation 308.1, 696.7
immoral 638.3, 645.16, 654.11
immorality 654.1
immortal (n) 662.9, 677.1, 678.2 (a) 249.15, 662.18, 677.17, 829.9, 855.18
immortality 306.1, 662.7, 681.2, 822.1, 829.3, 855.5
immortalization 662.8, 829.4
immortalize 662.13, 719.4, 829.5
immortalized 662.18
immortal life 681.2
immortal name 662.7
immortals 759.10
immortals, the 678.1
immotile 855.15
immotility 855.3
immotive 173.13
immovability 94.1, 361.2, 853.1, 855.3, 1046.3
immovable 94.9, 359.12, 361.9, 855.15, 1046.12
immovable feast 850.4
immovableness 853.1, 855.3
immoveables 471.6
immundity 80.1
immune 83.14, 430.30, 453.5, 1007.4
immune globulin 86.27
immune response 83.2
immune system 83.2, 83.4
immunity 83.4, 91.15, 148.2, 430.8, 601.2, 642.2, 1007.1
immunity theory 91.15
immunization 83.4, 91.15
immunization therapy 91.15
immunize 91.28
immunized 1007.4
immunizing 1008.23
immunochemistry 91.15
immunodeficiency 91.15
immunoglobulin 7.6
immunology 91.15
immunosuppressive drug 86.27
immunotherapy 91.15
immuration 429.3
immure 212.6, 429.12, 429.14
immured 212.10, 429.21
immurement 212.1, 429.3
immutability 361.2, 829.1, 853.1, 855.4, 1046.3
immutable 360.8, 361.9, 677.17, 781.5, 827.10, 853.7, 855.17, 1046.12
imp (n) 302.4, 322.3, 678.8, 680.7, 793.4 (v) 191.6
impact (n) 18.1, 518.1, 671.8, 887.2, 902.3, 1074.9 (v) 191.7, 886.10, 889.6, 902.13
impact area 1074.7
impacted 855.16
impactful 18.12
impaction 191.1
impactment 191.1
impact on 886.10, 889.6
impact printer 1042.9
impactproof 1049.4
impact-resistant 1049.4
impact statement 801.3
impair (v) 16.10, 255.9, 393.9, 1000.6 (a) 872.9, 1017.23
impaired 393.27, 1003.4
impaired hearing 49.1
impaired vision 28.1
impairment (n) 255.2, 393.1, 806.1, 996.2, 1003.1 (v) 49.4
impairment of motor function 85.27
impairment of speech 525.1
impale 96.18, 292.15, 459.25, 604.15, 661.9
impaled 96.25
impalement 292.3, 459.10, 604.2, 604.6, 647.2
impaling 647.2
impalpability 258.2, 764.1, 1053.1
impalpable 258.14, 764.5, 1051.11, 1053.7
impanation 701.7
impanel 549.15, 598.16, 871.8
impanel a jury 598.16
impanelment 549.14, 598.4
imparadise 95.10
imparadised 95.17
impart 176.10, 343.7, 351.4, 478.12, 524.22
impartability 343.4
impartable 176.18, 343.11, 478.23
impartation 343.2, 478.1
imparter 478.11
impartial 467.7, 649.9, 979.12
impartial arbitrator 466.4
impartiality 467.1, 649.3, 670.1, 945.1, 979.5
impartibility 1045.2
impartible 800.15, 1045.13
imparting 343.2
imparting a spin 354.9
impartment 343.2, 478.1
impart spin 354.16, 894.7
impassability 293.2
impassable 293.13
impasse 293.3, 790.3, 1013.6
impassibility 25.1, 94.1
impassible 25.6, 94.9
impassion 105.12, 375.17
impassioned 93.18, 101.9, 104.25, 105.20, 544.13
impassionedness 93.2, 101.2, 544.5
impassioning 375.4
impassive 25.6, 94.9, 106.10, 134.9, 173.12, 344.10, 522.20, 855.12, 982.3
impassiveness 94.1, 106.1, 344.3, 982.1
impassivity 94.1, 106.1, 344.3, 522.5, 982.1
impatience 101.1, 135.1, 365.2
impatient 101.8, 135.6, 365.9
impatientness 135.1
impatient of control 327.10
impatient of discipline 327.10
impeach 510.13, 598.15, 599.7
impeachability 656.1
impeachable 510.25, 656.3
impeachableness 656.1
impeached 599.15
impeacher 599.5
impeachment 447.2, 510.3, 598.3, 599.1
impeccability 657.1, 657.3, 973.5, 1002.1
impeccable 657.7, 973.16, 1002.6
impeccableness 657.3
impecuniosity 619.1
impecunious 619.7
impecuniousness 619.1
impedance 1032.13
impedance matching 1041.7
impede 175.9, 846.8, 1012.10, 1012.11
impeded 175.12
impeder 1012.8
impediment 293.3, 1012.1, 1012.6
impedimenta 385.4, 471.3, 1012.6
impedimental 1012.18
impeding 1012.18
impeditive 1012.18
impel 172.6, 375.12, 424.4, 902.11, 904.9, 926.25, 963.8
impelled 375.30
impellent (n) 902.1 (a) 902.23
impeller 375.10, 904.6
impelling 172.7, 375.25, 902.23, 926.34
impelling force 902.1
impend 130.10, 202.7, 840.2
impendence 202.3, 840.1
impendency 202.3, 840.1
impendent 202.11, 840.3
impending 202.11, 840.3
impend over 202.7
impenetrability 15.4, 293.2, 522.1, 967.3, 1045.1, 1046.1
impenetrable 15.19, 293.13, 310.43, 522.13, 967.9, 1031.3, 1045.12
impenetrable wall 1012.5
impenitence 114.2
impenitent 114.5
impenitentness 114.2
imperative (n) 419.2, 420.1, 530.11, 641.1, 963.4 (a) 417.15, 417.16, 420.12, 420.13, 424.10, 424.11, 544.11, 641.15, 963.12, 963.13, 997.22
imperativeness 417.3, 963.4, 997.4
imperatorial 417.17
imperceptibility 32.1, 258.2
imperceptible 32.5, 258.14
imperception 25.1
imperceptive 25.6, 922.14
imperceptiveness 25.1, 922.2
imperceptivity 25.1
impercipience 25.1, 340.2, 922.2
impercipiency 922.2
impercipient 25.6, 922.14, 930.12
imperfect (n) 530.12 (a) 250.7, 393.27, 795.4, 992.9, 1003.4
imperfect cadence 709.23
imperfection 250.3, 654.2, 795.1, 911.1, 992.4, 1003.1, 1003.2
imperfective 530.13
imperfect knowledge 930.5
imperfectness 1003.1
imperfect usufruct 387.7
imperfect vision 28.1
imperforate 293.10
imperforation 293.2
imperial (n) 3.8, 554.4 (a) 417.16, 417.17
Imperial Highness 648.2
imperialism 417.8, 609.5, 612.7
imperialist 611.9
imperialist threat 458.11
Imperial Majesty 648.2
imperil 1006.6
imperiled 1006.13
imperilment 1006.1
imperious 141.11, 417.16, 417.17, 420.13, 424.10, 641.15, 997.22
imperiousness 141.3, 417.3
imperishability 829.3, 855.5
imperishable 829.9, 855.18
imperium 249.3, 417.5
impermanence 828.1, 854.1
impermanency 828.1
impermanent 828.7, 854.6
impermeability 293.2, 1045.1
impermeable 293.13, 1045.12
impermissibility 674.1
impermissible 674.6
impersonal 344.10, 580.7, 649.9, 768.3, 945.6, 979.12, 982.3
impersonality 344.3, 580.1, 768.1, 945.2, 973.1, 979.5
impersonal verb 530.4
impersonate 336.6, 349.11, 349.12, 354.22, 704.30
impersonation 336.1, 349.4, 704.8
impersonator 336.4, 357.6, 357.7, 707.1
impersuadability 895.2
impersuadable 895.4
impersuasibility 895.2
impersuasible 895.4
impertinence 142.2, 214.2, 454.1, 776.1

impertinent 142.10, 214.9, 454.7, 505.4, 776.7
imperturbability 106.1, 173.1, 855.1
imperturbable 94.9, 106.10, 855.12, 982.3
imperturbableness 106.1
imperturbation 106.2
impervious 15.20, 94.12, 293.13, 895.4, 967.9
imperviousness 94.3, 293.2, 895.2, 967.3
imperviousness to light 1031.1
impervious to light 1031.3
impervious to persuasion 956.4
impetrate 440.11
impetration 440.1, 440.2, 696.4
impetuosity 17.4, 401.2, 493.2, 671.1
impetuous 17.13, 105.29, 135.6, 365.9, 401.10, 493.8, 828.7, 830.5, 854.7
impetuousity 365.2
impetuousness 135.1, 365.2, 401.2, 493.2
impetus 17.4, 174.4, 375.1, 902.1
impiety 694.1, 694.2, 695.3
impignorate 438.10
impinge 214.5, 223.10, 902.13
impingement 214.1, 223.5, 902.3
impingence 223.5
impingent 223.17
impinge on one's consciousness 931.18
impinge on the eye 31.4
impinging 223.17
impious 694.6, 695.17
impiousness 694.1
impish 322.6, 680.18
impishness 322.2
implacability 361.2, 507.2
implacable 361.9, 507.7
implacableness 507.2
implant 191.6, 191.8, 568.12, 855.9, 1069.18
implantation 191.1, 568.2, 855.2
implanted 373.18, 767.7, 855.13
implant in 213.6
implausibility 955.3, 969.1
implausible 955.10, 969.3
implead 598.13, 598.19
implement (n) 384.4, 576.3, 1040.1 (v) 328.7, 407.5, 437.9
implementable 328.10
implemental 384.8
implementation 328.2, 407.1, 889.1
implemented 407.10
implementer 576.3
impletion 794.2
impliability 361.2, 425.2
impliable 361.9, 425.7
implicate 519.4, 599.10, 772.4, 799.3, 898.2
implicated 476.8, 519.7, 599.15, 656.3, 775.9, 799.4, 898.4
implicated in 898.5
implicate oneself 351.7
implication 518.1, 519.2, 551.4, 599.1, 599.2, 656.1, 772.2, 898.1
implicational 519.6
implicative 517.23, 519.6
implicatory 519.6
implicit 51.11, 519.8, 767.7, 957.16, 960.2
implicit belief 953.5
implicit consent 441.1
implied 518.11, 519.7, 519.8
implied consent 443.1
implied meaning 518.1, 519.2
implied threat 514.1
implode 260.10
imploration 440.2, 696.4
implore 422.6, 440.11, 696.13
implore counsel 422.7
implore mercy 433.8
imploring (n) 440.2 (a) 440.17, 696.16
implosion 260.4
imply 133.12, 518.8, 519.4, 551.10, 599.7, 772.4, 957.8
impolicy 414.6
impolite 497.12, 505.4
impoliteness 497.3, 505.1
impolitic 414.21, 923.10, 996.5
impolitical 996.5
impoliticalness 996.1
impoliticness 996.1
imponderabilia 298.5
imponderability 258.2, 298.5, 764.1, 1053.1
imponderable 258.14, 298.18, 764.5, 1053.7
imponderableness 298.5
imponderables 298.5
imponderous 298.10
imporosity 1045.1
imporous 1045.12
import (n) 187.7, 189.1, 518.1, 518.5, 519.2, 887.2, 997.1 (v) 176.10, 187.14, 191.3, 518.8, 519.4, 731.17, 997.12, 1042.21
importable 176.18
importance 417.4, 518.5, 662.5, 894.1, 997.1
important 417.15, 662.17, 894.13, 997.17
important message 352.6
important money 618.3
important person 575.3, 662.9, 997.8
important thing 997.6
importation 187.7, 189.1
imported wine 88.17
importer 730.2
importing 187.7, 189.1
importless 520.6
importunacy 359.6, 421.4
importunate 98.22, 359.15, 421.9, 440.18, 963.12
importunateness 359.6, 421.4, 440.3
importune (v) 375.14, 439.7, 440.12 (a) 98.22
importunity 421.4, 440.3
impose 214.5, 420.9, 421.5, 424.5, 548.16, 630.12, 643.4, 701.15
impose a penalty on 603.4
impose by force 643.6
imposed 420.12, 643.8
imposed peace 464.2
impose on 214.5, 640.7, 643.4, 643.7, 776.5
impose one's will 323.3
impose on one for 421.5
impose sanctions on 603.4
impose upon 214.5, 387.16, 643.7, 996.4
imposing 136.12, 257.18, 501.21, 997.20
imposing an onus 643.1
imposingness 501.5
imposition 96.8, 214.1, 356.8, 421.1, 548.2, 630.9, 640.2, 643.1, 650.4, 1012.6
impossibilism 967.1
impossibility 125.1, 870.2, 955.3, 967.1, 972.10
impossible (n) 967.1 (a) 108.10, 125.14, 870.12, 967.7, 972.18, 1017.23
impossible, the 967.1
impossible dream 976.1
impossibleness 967.1
impost 421.1, 630.9
imposter 336.4
impostor 336.4, 354.13, 357.6
imposture 336.1, 354.3, 354.7, 356.8
impotable 64.8
impotence 16.1, 19.1, 75.2, 75.9, 391.2, 426.1, 891.1, 895.1
impotency 16.1, 19.1, 895.1
impotent (n) 19.6 (a) 16.12, 19.13, 75.29, 391.9, 426.4, 891.4, 895.3
impound 212.5, 429.12, 480.20
impounded 429.19
impoundment 429.1, 480.5
impoverish 388.3, 480.24, 619.6, 625.8
impoverished 388.5, 619.8, 992.10, 992.12
impoverishment 388.1, 473.2, 619.2, 992.4
impracticability 967.2
impracticable 967.8, 996.5
impractical 951.13, 967.8, 986.24, 996.5, 1013.19
impracticality 967.2, 986.7, 1013.9
imprecate 440.11, 513.5
imprecation 440.2, 513.1
imprecatory 513.8
imprecise 426.4, 531.4, 971.16, 971.19, 975.17, 1003.4
imprecision 340.4, 426.1, 971.4, 975.2
impregnability 15.4, 855.5
impregnable 15.19, 855.18
impregnate 78.10, 568.12, 797.11, 890.8, 1065.13
impregnated 78.17
impregnation 78.3, 568.2, 797.2, 890.3, 1065.7
impresario 574.1, 704.23
impress (n) 284.6, 517.7, 548.3, 713.5, 785.5, 865.4, 887.2 (v) 93.15, 155.7, 284.14, 377.6, 387.14, 480.20, 482.20, 517.19, 548.14, 568.12, 615.17, 662.10, 855.9, 931.19, 989.17
impressed 93.23, 713.11, 855.13
impressed by 93.23
impressed with 93.23, 953.21
impressed with oneself 140.12, 501.22
impress forcibly 93.15
impressibility 24.2
impressible 24.11, 1047.9
impression 33.3, 93.1, 262.1, 284.1, 284.6, 336.1, 349.2, 517.7, 548.3, 554.5, 568.2, 713.5, 785.5, 865.4, 887.2, 932.1, 934.3, 951.5, 953.6
impressionability 24.2, 93.4, 570.5, 894.5, 1047.2
impressionable 24.11, 93.20, 570.18, 894.15, 923.12, 1047.9
impressionistic 951.13
impressive 105.30, 501.21, 544.11, 953.26, 999.14
impressiveness 377.2, 501.5, 544.3
impressment 424.3, 458.8, 480.5, 482.9, 615.7
impress one 983.11
impress on the mind 989.17
impress upon 93.16
impress upon the memory 568.12
impress upon the mind 568.12
imprimatur 332.4, 443.6, 554.12
imprint (n) 284.6, 517.7, 517.13, 548.3, 554.12, 713.5, 887.2 (v) 284.14, 517.19, 548.14, 855.9, 989.17
imprinted 713.11, 855.13
imprison 212.5, 429.14
imprisoned 212.10, 429.21
imprisonment 212.1, 429.3, 604.2
improbability 131.1, 870.5, 955.3, 962.1, 969.1, 972.9
improbable 131.10, 776.8, 962.13, 969.3, 972.18
improbity 354.4, 645.1
impromptu (n) 365.5, 708.27 (a) 365.12, 406.8
improper 322.5, 497.10, 531.4, 534.2, 638.3, 640.10, 654.16, 666.5, 789.7, 844.6, 996.5, 1000.7
improper fraction 1017.7
improperness 638.1, 650.1, 1000.1
improper suggestion 439.2
impropriety 322.1, 497.1, 526.6, 534.1, 638.1, 640.1, 650.1, 655.2, 666.1, 789.3, 844.1
improv 365.8
improvable 392.17, 396.25
improve 387.15, 392.7, 392.9, 396.19, 568.13, 852.6, 852.7, 1002.5
improved 392.13, 852.10
improvement 162.1, 392.1, 396.1, 568.3, 852.1, 858.2
improve on 249.6
improve one's mind 568.10
improve the mind 570.6
improve the occasion 387.15, 843.8
improve the shining hour 330.16

improve upon 392.9
improvidence 406.2, 493.1
improvident 406.15, 493.7
improving 392.15
improving the mind 570.1
improvisate 365.8
improvisation 365.5, 406.1, 704.8, 708.27, 892.1, 995.2
improvisational 995.7
improvisator 365.6, 543.7, 710.13
improvisatorial 365.12
improvisatory 365.12
improvise 365.8, 406.6, 704.29, 892.8, 892.12
improvised 365.12, 406.8, 704.33, 995.7
improviser 365.6
improvising 365.5
improvision 365.5
improviso 365.12
improvisor 365.6
improvvisatore 365.6
imprudence 493.1, 923.2, 923.4, 945.1
imprudent 493.7, 923.10, 945.5
impubic 406.11
impudence 142.2, 156.1, 454.1, 493.1
impudent 142.10, 156.7, 454.7, 493.7
impudicity 666.2
impugn 335.4, 510.13, 599.10
impugnation 451.1
impugned 599.15, 958.7
impugner 599.5
impugnment 335.2, 451.1, 599.2
impuissance 19.1
impulse 18.4, 365.1, 375.6, 845.2, 902.1, 934.2, 963.5
impulse buy 365.1
impulse-buy 365.7, 733.8
impulse buying 733.1
impulse-control disorder 92.14
impulse of life 306.2
impulse recorder 1075.7
impulsion 375.6, 902.1, 904.1
impulsive 364.6, 365.9, 375.25, 401.10, 782.3, 828.7, 830.5, 845.8, 854.7, 902.23, 934.6, 963.14
impulsiveness 365.2, 401.2, 845.2, 854.2
impulsivity 365.2, 401.2, 845.2, 854.2
impunity 601.2
impure 80.20, 534.2, 654.12, 665.23, 666.9, 1003.4
impurity 80.1, 534.1, 654.1, 665.1, 774.2, 1003.1
imputable 510.25, 888.6
imputation 510.4, 512.4, 599.1, 661.6, 888.1
imputative 599.13
impute 599.7, 888.3
imputed 888.6
impute shame to 661.8
impute to 888.4
in, an 587.3
in (n) 187.3, 189.5 (a) 189.12, 476.8, 578.11, 587.18, 841.13, 1007.6
in a backwater 584.8
in a bad humor 110.17
in a bad way 85.56, 393.36, 1006.13
in abeyance 173.14, 390.12, 846.16
inability 19.2, 414.1
inability to believe 955.1
in a bind 846.16, 1013.22
in a blaze 1019.27, 1025.39
in a blue funk 127.25
in a bother 105.21
in a botheration 985.12
in a box 1013.22
in Abraham's bosom 307.29
in a brown study 931.21
inaccessibility 344.3, 583.2, 967.3
inaccessible 261.9, 344.10, 583.6, 967.9
in accord 455.3, 708.49, 788.9, 867.6
in accordance 788.9
inaccordance 780.1, 789.1, 868.1
inaccordant 780.7, 789.6
inaccuracy 340.4, 350.1, 948.1, 971.4, 975.2, 1000.1, 1003.1
inaccurate 340.13, 971.19, 975.17, 1000.7, 1003.4
inaccurateness 975.2
in a class by itself 249.15, 780.8, 999.17
in a cloud 346.11
in a corner 1013.25
inacquiescent 442.6
in action 328.10, 889.11
inaction 173.2, 329.1, 331.1
inactivate 19.9
inactive 173.14, 329.6, 331.17, 402.6
inactive market 737.3
inactiveness 331.1
inactivity 20.1, 173.2, 329.1, 331.1, 402.2
in a dark corner 346.14
in a daze 985.14
in a dead calm 173.17
in a delicate condition 78.18
inadept 414.15
inadeptness 414.1
inadequacy 19.2, 108.2, 250.3, 414.1, 791.1, 795.1, 911.1, 992.1, 1003.1, 1003.2
inadequate 19.15, 108.9, 250.7, 414.19, 791.4, 795.4, 911.5, 992.9, 1003.4
inadequateness 992.1, 1003.1
in a dilemma 971.25, 1013.23
in a direct line 560.18
in a dither 105.21
in adjustment 807.7
inadmissibility 108.2, 773.1, 789.3
inadmissible 108.10, 773.9, 776.7, 789.7
inadmissible evidence 958.1
in advance of one's age 920.17
in adverse circumstances 1011.14
inadvertence 340.1, 975.4, 984.1
inadvertency 340.1, 975.4, 984.1
inadvertent 340.10, 365.10, 365.11, 984.6
inadvisability 923.2, 996.1
inadvisable 923.10, 996.5
in a fair way 968.6
in a ferment 105.21
in a fever 85.58
inaffable 505.4
in a fix 971.24, 1013.22
in a flurry 105.21
in a fluster 105.21
in a flutter 105.21
in a fog 346.11, 985.13
in a foofaraw 105.21
in a frenzy of desire 100.24
in a fright 127.25
in a fume 152.32
in a funk 127.25
in a fury 152.32
in a glow 1019.27
in a good mood 324.5
in a good state of preservation 397.13
in agreement 332.15, 450.5, 788.9
in a haze 346.11
in a hole 1013.22
in a huff 152.31
in a jam 971.24, 1011.14, 1013.22
in a jumble 985.12
in a lather 105.21, 135.6, 152.30
inalienable 767.7, 800.15
inalienable right 642.1
in a line 277.6
inalterability 853.1, 855.4
inalterable 360.8, 853.7
inalterableness 853.1
in a maze 971.24
in ambuscade 346.14
in ambush 346.14
in a mess 810.16, 1013.22
in a mist 346.11
inamorata 104.13
inamorato 104.12
in a muddle 985.13
inane 19.15, 65.2, 117.6, 222.14, 391.13, 520.6, 762.8, 764.6, 922.19, 923.8, 930.11, 933.4, 998.19
inanimate (n) 530.10 (a) 307.29, 331.17, 331.20, 1055.5
inanimated 1055.5
inanimate matter 1055.1
inanimateness 1055.2
inanimate object 1052.4
inanimation 331.6, 1055.2
inanition 16.5, 21.2, 222.2
inanity 19.3, 65.1, 117.1, 222.3, 391.2, 520.1, 762.1, 922.6, 923.1, 930.1, 933.1, 998.3
in anticipation 130.11, 405.21
in an uproar 105.21
in A-1 condition 83.8
in a panic 127.27
in a passion 152.32
in a pet 152.31
in a pickle 971.24, 1011.14, 1013.22
in a position to 897.6
in a pother 105.21, 985.12
inappealable 960.2, 970.15
inappetence 94.4, 102.3
inappetent 102.8
in apple-pie order 807.7
inapplicability 391.1, 776.1, 789.3
inapplicable 391.14, 776.7, 789.7
inapposite 776.7, 789.7
inappositeness 776.1, 789.3
inappreciability 258.2
inappreciable 258.14, 998.17
inapprehensibility 522.1
inapprehensible 522.13
inappropriate 497.10, 638.3, 640.10, 666.5, 776.7, 789.7, 844.6, 996.5
inappropriateness 497.1, 638.1, 640.1, 666.1, 789.3, 844.1, 996.1
in a predicament 1006.13, 1013.21
in a pretty pass 1013.21
in a pretty pickle 1011.14, 1013.22
inapt 414.15, 789.7, 996.5
inaptitude 414.1, 789.3, 996.1
inaptness 414.1, 789.3
in a pucker 105.21, 126.7, 985.12
in a quandary 1013.23
in a quiver 105.21, 128.12
in a rage 152.32
inarch 191.6
in a reverie 985.11
in armor 460.13
in arms 301.12, 405.16, 460.14
in arrears 623.10, 625.10, 795.4
inarticulacy 525.2
inarticulate 51.12, 139.12, 522.13, 525.12
inarticulateness 51.2, 522.1, 525.2
inarticulation 525.2
in articulo mortis 307.32
inartificial 406.13, 416.6, 499.7, 973.15
inartificiality 406.3, 416.2, 499.2, 973.7
inartistic 1015.10
in a rut 373.17
in ascendancy 249.12, 411.7, 612.17, 894.14
in a scrape 971.24, 1013.22
in a shocking humor 110.17
in a snit 152.27, 152.31
in a sorry plight 1013.21
in a sound sleep 22.22
in a spin 917.16
in a spot 1013.22
in a stable state 855.12
in a state of flux 854.7
in a state of nature 6.14, 406.13
in a state of suspense 971.18
in a stew 105.21, 126.7, 135.6, 152.31, 971.24, 985.12
in a stupor 22.21, 94.13
in a sweat 12.22, 105.21, 135.6
in a swivet 105.21
in a temper 152.31
in a tight spot 1011.14, 1013.22
in a tizzy 105.21, 985.12
in a trance 691.12, 986.25, 990.9

in a transport 105.25
in a transport of delight 95.17
in attendance 221.12
inattention 102.2, 340.1, 435.1, 923.2, 982.1, 984.1, 985.1
inattentive 102.7, 340.10, 414.15, 435.5, 982.3, 984.6
inattentiveness 414.1, 984.1
in a turmoil 105.21
in a twitter 105.21
inaudibility 51.1, 52.1
inaudible 51.10
inaugural (n) 543.2, 580.4 (a) 814.4, 816.4, 818.15
inaugural address 543.2, 818.5
inaugurate 191.4, 615.12, 818.11, 841.5, 886.10, 892.10
inauguration 159.7, 187.2, 580.4, 615.3, 818.5, 892.4
inaugurator 892.7
inauguratory 818.15
inauspicious 133.16, 844.6, 1000.7, 1011.14
inauspiciousness 133.7, 844.1, 1000.1, 1011.4
inauthentic 936.11, 975.19
in a watery grave 307.31
in a wax 152.31
in awe 122.9, 155.9
in awe of 122.9
in a world of one's own 984.7
in a zone 87.24
in bad 661.13
in bad humor 112.21
in bad odor 661.13
in bad odor with 589.13
in bad repute 661.13
in bad spirits 112.21
in bad taste 497.10, 534.2
in bad with 589.12, 589.13
in battle array 405.16, 458.22
in being 761.13
inbeing 767.1
in bits 393.27
in black and white 547.22, 549.17
in bloom 310.38
in blossom 310.38
in board 347.8
in bold relief 31.7, 283.18, 348.12
in bondage 432.14
in bonds 428.16, 432.14
inborn 767.8
inborn aptitude 413.5
inborn capacity 560.6
inborn predisposition 560.6
inborn proclivity 934.2
inborn susceptibility 560.6
inborn tendency 560.6
inbound 186.9, 189.12
in bounds 746.3
inbounds marker 746.1
inbred 78.17, 767.8
inbreed 78.8
inbreeding 78.2
in buckram 580.9
in cahoots 450.5, 805.6
incalculability 823.1, 971.1
incalculable 823.3, 884.10, 930.16, 971.16
incalculable, the 930.6
incalescence 1019.1
in-camera 293.9
incandesce 1019.22, 1025.23
incandescence 1019.5, 1019.12, 1025.2
incandescent 1019.27, 1025.30
incandescent body 1026.1
incandescent light 1025.19
incandescent point 1026.1
incantation 690.4, 691.4
incantational 690.14
incantatory 690.14
incapability 19.2, 406.1, 414.1
incapable (n) 85.45, 414.7 (a) 19.14, 406.9, 414.19
incapable of life 307.32
incapacious 270.14
incapaciousness 270.1
incapacitate 19.9, 85.50, 393.14
incapacitated 16.18, 19.16, 393.30
incapacitation 19.2, 393.1
incapacity 16.3, 19.2, 414.1, 891.1, 922.1
in captivity 429.21, 432.14
incarcerate 212.5, 429.14
incarcerated 212.10, 429.21
incarceration 212.1, 429.3, 604.2
incarmined 41.6
incarnadine (v) 41.4 (a) 41.8
incarnate (v) 348.5, 349.11, 763.5, 796.3, 1052.9 (a) 33.11, 306.12, 677.16, 1052.11
incarnated 677.16
incarnating 348.9, 349.13, 796.4
incarnation 33.1, 348.1, 349.4, 763.4, 767.2, 796.1, 1052.8
Incarnation, the 677.11
incarnational 348.9
In Case of Emergency 405.4
in cash 618.14
incautious 493.7, 984.8
incautiousness 493.1
incendiarism 1020.7
incendiarize 1020.25
incendiarized 1020.30
incendiary (n) 375.11, 462.20, 671.9, 1020.8 (a) 375.28, 1020.27
incendiary bomb 462.20
incendive 1020.27
incense (n) 70.1, 70.4, 504.5, 511.1, 696.7, 696.10 (v) 70.8, 105.12, 152.24, 375.17
incense-breathing 70.9
incense burner 70.6
incensed 152.28
incensory 70.6
incentive (n) 375.7, 902.1 (a) 375.28
incentive pay 478.5
inception 818.4, 818.5, 886.5, 892.4
inception of pregnancy 78.4
inceptive 818.15
incertitude 971.1
incessancy 812.1, 829.1, 847.2
incessant 812.8, 829.7, 847.5, 849.13, 856.7
incest 75.11, 665.7
incestuous 665.27
incestuousness 75.11
inch, an 223.2
inch (n) 223.2 (v) 175.6, 177.26
in chains 428.16, 432.14
inch along 175.6, 177.26
in character 130.14, 865.13
in charge 429.22, 573.13, 612.17
in check 428.13
inch forward 162.4
in chief 612.17
in childbed 85.59
inchoate 263.4, 406.11, 810.12, 818.15, 971.19
inchoateness 971.4
inchoation 818.4
inchoative (n) 530.13 (a) 818.15
inch one's way up 193.11
in chorus 708.49
inch up 193.11
inchworm 311.38
incidence 831.1, 847.1
incident 722.4, 766.1, 831.2
incidental (n) 709.18, 766.3, 768.2 (a) 766.7, 768.4, 776.7, 831.9, 843.11, 848.3, 972.15
incidental information 551.1
incidental note 709.18
incidental power 894.1
incidental product 893.3
incidental remark 213.2
incidental to 959.9
incident light 1025.9
incident to 897.6, 959.9
incinerate 308.18, 309.20, 395.10, 395.19, 1020.25
incinerated 1020.30
incineration 309.2, 390.3, 1020.5
incinerator 1020.13
incinerator ash 391.4
incipience 818.4
incipiency 818.4
incipient 818.15
in circulation 352.17, 552.15
incise 224.4, 289.4, 290.3, 292.11, 393.13, 549.15, 713.9, 802.11
incised 289.5, 290.4, 713.11, 715.7
incising 713.2
incision 85.38, 224.2, 289.1, 290.1, 713.2
incisive 17.13, 17.14, 144.23, 544.11, 920.16
incisiveness 144.8, 544.3, 920.4
incisor 2.8
incisural 289.5
incitation 375.4
incite 105.12, 375.17, 422.6, 492.15, 886.11, 902.11, 1020.18
incitement 105.11, 152.11, 375.4, 375.7, 902.1
inciter 375.11
inciting 375.28
incitive 375.28
incivility 497.3, 505.1
inclemency 144.9, 146.1, 671.1, 1023.1
inclement 144.24, 146.3, 318.22, 1023.14
inclination 100.3, 155.2, 161.1, 194.1, 204.2, 204.4, 323.1, 371.5, 413.5, 650.3, 896.1, 978.3, 980.3
inclinational 204.15, 896.4, 978.7
inclination of the balance 791.1
inclination of the head 155.2
inclination to believe 954.1
inclinatory 204.15, 896.4
incline (n) 193.3, 204.4, 237.2 (v) 161.7, 204.10, 297.15, 324.3, 375.22, 894.7, 896.3
inclined 204.15, 324.5, 375.30, 978.8
inclined plane 204.4, 1040.5
inclined to believe 954.8
inclined to forget 990.9
inclined toward 100.22
incline the head 155.6
incline toward 371.17, 978.6
inclining 204.15, 896.4
in clover 95.15, 618.14, 1010.12
include 187.10, 207.5, 212.5, 772.3, 800.5, 805.3, 937.3
included 772.5, 898.4
include oneself out 190.12, 222.7
include out 372.2
including 772.6, 796.4
including out 959.1
inclusion 191.2, 209.5, 212.1, 450.2, 772.1, 805.1, 898.1
inclusion-exclusion 210.1
inclusive 772.6, 781.5, 792.9, 800.12, 945.6, 979.12
inclusiveness 772.1, 792.5, 794.1, 864.1
inclusive of 796.4
inclusivism 772.1
incog 346.13
incogitant 933.4
incognita 357.7
incognito (n) 345.2, 356.11, 357.7, 528.1 (a) 345.13, 346.13, 528.3
incognizability 522.1
incognizable 522.13, 930.16
incognizance 930.2
incognizant 930.12
incoherence 160.1, 522.1, 789.2, 802.1, 804.1, 806.1, 810.1, 813.1, 926.8, 971.4
incoherent 522.13, 789.8, 802.20, 804.4, 810.12, 813.4, 926.31, 971.19
in color 35.17
in combat 458.22
incombustibility 1022.1
incombustible 1022.9
income 189.1, 472.3, 624.4, 627.1
income after deductions 624.4
income fund 737.16
incomer 189.4, 227.9
income tax 630.9
incoming (n) 189.1 (a) 186.9, 189.12
incoming population 189.3
incommensurability 787.1, 789.2
incommensurable 776.6, 787.6, 789.8, 943.9
incommensurableness 787.1

incommensurate 108.9, 787.6, 789.8
in commission 387.25, 807.7
incommode 996.4
incommodious 270.14, 996.7
incommodiousness 270.1
incommodity 996.3
in common 476.9
incommunicability 122.4
incommunicable 122.13
incommunicableness 122.4
incommunicado 346.11
incommutability 855.4
incommutable 855.17
incomparability 249.1, 787.1
incomparable 249.15, 776.6, 787.6, 943.9
incomparableness 787.1
incompatibility 456.1, 583.1, 589.1, 780.1, 789.2
incompatible 583.5, 589.9, 780.7, 789.6, 789.8
incompatibleness 456.1, 589.1
incompetence 19.2, 250.3, 406.1, 414.1, 992.1
incompetency 19.2, 250.3, 406.1, 414.1, 992.1
incompetent (n) 19.6, 414.7 (a) 19.14, 250.7, 406.9, 414.19, 992.9
in competition 457.23
incomplete 793.7, 795.4, 992.9, 1003.4
incomplete antibody 86.27
incompleteness 795.1, 813.1, 992.4, 1003.1
incomplete pass 746.3
incompletion 795.1
incomplex 798.8
in complicity 599.15
incomprehensibility 522.1, 823.1
incomprehensible 122.10, 522.13, 823.3, 870.12
incomprehension 922.2, 930.2
incompressibility 1045.1, 1046.2
incompressible 1045.12, 1046.11
inconceivability 522.1, 870.2, 955.3, 967.1
inconceivable 122.10, 870.12, 955.10, 967.7
in concert 450.5, 455.3, 708.49
inconcinnate 534.2
inconcinnity 534.1
inconcinnous 534.2
inconclusive 936.11, 936.12, 958.8
inconclusiveness 936.2
in concord 708.49
in condition 83.8, 83.12, 765.7, 807.7
in confinement 429.19
in conflict 362.9
in conformity 326.3
in conformity with the evidence 973.13
in conformity with the facts 973.13
incongruence 456.1
incongruency 456.1
incongruent 780.7
incongruity 488.1, 780.1, 789.2, 868.1, 936.2, 996.1
incongruous 35.21, 488.4, 780.7, 789.8, 936.11, 996.5
inconnection 776.1
inconsequence 776.1, 998.1
inconsequent 776.7, 789.8, 936.11
inconsequential 248.6, 936.11, 998.17
inconsequentiality 248.1, 998.1
inconsequentialness 248.1
inconsiderable 248.6, 998.17
inconsiderableness 248.1, 998.1
inconsiderate 144.18, 340.11, 365.10, 505.6, 923.10
inconsiderateness 25.1, 144.3, 340.2, 365.3, 505.1, 643.1
inconsideration 144.3, 340.2, 365.3, 505.1, 923.2, 984.1
inconsistency 779.1, 780.1, 782.1, 789.2, 804.1, 854.2, 868.1, 936.2
inconsistent 362.10, 776.6, 779.6, 780.7, 782.3, 789.8, 804.4, 854.7, 936.11
inconsolability 112.12
inconsolable 112.26, 112.28
inconsolableness 112.12
inconsonance 780.1, 789.2
inconsonant 776.6, 780.7, 789.8
inconspicuous 32.6
inconspicuousness 32.2
inconstancy 362.1, 364.3, 645.5, 782.1, 851.1, 854.2
inconstant 364.6, 435.5, 645.20, 782.3, 828.7, 851.3, 854.7
in contact 223.17
incontestability 970.3
incontestable 15.19, 970.15
incontinence 100.8, 430.3, 486.1, 665.2, 669.1, 993.1
incontinent 430.24, 486.8, 665.24, 669.7, 993.16
in control 670.11
incontrovertibility 970.3
incontrovertible 957.16, 970.15
incontrovertible evidence 957.3
incontrovertible proof 957.3
inconvenience (n) 643.1, 844.1, 996.1, 996.3, 1012.6, 1013.3, 1013.9 (v) 640.7, 811.4, 996.4, 1013.13
inconvenienced 1013.20
inconveniency 996.1, 996.3
inconvenient 844.6, 996.7, 1013.19
inconvenientness 996.3
inconvertibility 853.1, 855.4
inconvertible 625.13, 855.17
inconvertibleness 853.1
inconvincibility 956.1
inconvincible 956.4
incorporate (v) 772.3, 796.3, 805.3, 1052.9 (a) 1053.7
incorporated 617.16, 800.13, 805.5, 1052.11
incorporating 772.6, 805.7
incorporation 450.2, 772.1, 796.1, 805.1, 1052.8
incorporative 523.23, 805.7
incorporeal (n) 988.1, 1053.2 (a) 764.5, 988.7, 1053.7
incorporeal being 988.1
incorporeal entity 988.1
incorporeal hereditament 471.1, 479.2
incorporeality 299.1, 764.1, 1053.1
incorporealness 1053.1
incorporeity 988.1, 1053.1, 1053.2
incorporeous 1053.7
incorrect 531.4, 534.2, 638.3, 975.17
incorrectness 534.1, 638.1, 975.2
incorrect usage 531.1
incorrigibility 125.3, 361.4
incorrigible 125.15, 361.12, 373.18, 654.18
incorrupt 653.7, 657.6
incorrupted 653.7
incorruptibility 644.6, 829.3, 855.5
incorruptible 644.19, 829.9, 855.18
incorruption 829.3
incorruptness 653.2, 657.2
in costume 5.45
in course of preparation 405.22
incrassate (v) 269.5, 1045.10, 1062.10 (a) 259.13, 803.12, 1045.14
incrassated 1062.12
incrassation 803.1, 1062.2
increase (n) 119.1, 193.1, 251.1, 251.3, 253.1, 254.1, 259.1, 392.1, 883.4, 912.1 (v) 14.2, 119.2, 244.4, 245.4, 251.4, 251.6, 253.5, 259.4, 259.5, 259.7, 883.6
increased 119.4, 251.7, 259.10, 883.8
increase of temperature 1020.1
increase pressure 119.2
increase tension 119.2
increase the chances 968.4
increase the temperature 1020.17
increasing 251.8
increate 761.14
incredibility 870.2, 955.3, 969.1
incredible 122.10, 247.10, 870.12, 923.11, 955.10, 969.3
increditability 870.2
incredulity 695.6, 955.1, 956.1
incredulous 695.20, 955.8, 956.4
incredulousness 956.1
increment 251.1, 254.1
incremental 251.8
incremental change 861.1
increscent 1073.11
increscent moon 1073.11
incriminate 599.10
incriminated 599.15
incriminate oneself 351.7
incriminating 599.14
incriminating evidence 958.1
incrimination 599.2
incriminator 599.5
incriminatory 599.14
in critical condition 307.32
in-crowd 578.6, 582.5, 617.6
incrust 295.27
incrustation 295.1, 295.14
incrusted 1046.13
incubate 78.12
incubation 78.5
incubator 886.8
incubator baby 302.9
incubus 127.9, 297.7, 680.6, 986.9
inculcate 568.12, 989.17
inculcated 373.18
inculcation 568.2
inculpability 657.3
inculpable 657.8
inculpate 599.10
inculpated 599.15, 656.3
inculpation 599.2, 656.1
inculpative 599.14
inculpatory 599.14
incumbency 297.7, 641.2, 698.9, 724.5
incumbent (n) 227.2, 470.4, 610.11, 699.7 (a) 202.11, 295.36, 297.17, 641.17
incumbent on 641.14
incunabula 301.5, 818.4
incunabular 818.15
incunabulum 554.6
incur 897.4
incurability 125.3
incurable (n) 85.43 (a) 125.15, 308.23
incur a debt 623.6
incur a responsibility 641.8
incur costs 626.5
incur danger 1006.6
incur discredit 661.7
incur disgrace 661.7
incur dishonor 661.7
incur expenses 626.5
incuriosity 102.2, 982.1, 984.1
incurious 102.7, 982.3, 984.6
incuriousness 982.1
incur loss 473.4
incursion 189.2, 214.1, 459.4, 910.3
incursionary 459.29
incursive 459.29
incurvate (v) 279.6 (a) 279.7, 284.16
incurvated 279.7
incurvation 279.1, 284.1
incurvature 279.1, 284.1
incurve 279.6, 284.12
incurved 279.7, 284.16
incurving 279.7, 284.16
incus 2.10
in custody 429.22
indagate 938.23
indagation 938.4
indagative 938.37
indagator 938.17
in danger 85.56, 1006.13
in danger of 897.6
in darkness 30.9, 930.15
in Davy Jones's locker 307.31
in deadly peril 1006.13
in debt 623.8, 897.5
indebted 623.8, 729.19, 897.5
indebtedness 623.1, 897.1
indebted to 150.5, 641.16

indebtment 623.1
indecency 75.5, 497.1, 665.1, 666.1
indecent 497.10, 665.23, 666.5
indecent assault 480.3
indecent exposure 6.1
indecent proposal 439.2
indeciduous 829.8
indecipherability 522.4
indecipherable 522.19
indecision 329.1, 362.1, 971.1
indecisive 16.17, 263.4, 362.9, 854.7, 958.8, 971.16, 971.19
indecisiveness 16.2, 263.1, 362.1, 971.1, 971.4
indecorous 497.10, 534.2, 638.3, 666.5
indecorousness 497.1, 534.1, 638.1, 666.1
indecorum 497.1, 638.1, 666.1
in deep 898.5
in deep doo-doo 1013.22
in deep trouble 1013.21
in deep water 1013.21
indefatigability 330.6, 360.1
indefatigable 330.22, 360.8, 856.7
in default 795.4
in default of 992.13
indefeasibility 855.4, 963.7
indefeasible 855.17, 963.15
indefectibility 1002.1
indefectible 1002.6
indefective 1002.6
indefensibility 108.2, 650.5
indefensible 108.10, 650.12
indefinability 522.6
indefinable 122.13, 522.18, 971.19
indefinableness 122.4, 971.4
indefinite 32.6, 263.4, 864.11, 945.6, 971.19
indefinite article 530.6
indefiniteness 32.2, 263.1, 945.2, 971.4
indefinite pronoun 530.5
indefinite quantity 244.2
indehiscent fruit 10.38
indeliberate 365.11
indeliberation 365.4
indelibility 855.5
indelible 35.18, 93.24, 855.18, 989.25
indelibly impressed 855.13
indelibly impressed on the mind 989.25
indelibly in the mind 989.17
indelicacy 497.1, 666.1
indelicate 497.10, 666.5
indelicate language 513.3
in demand 100.29, 734.14
indemnification 338.1, 481.2, 624.3, 658.1
indemnificatory 338.6, 481.7
indemnify 338.4, 438.9, 481.5, 506.5, 624.10
indemnity 148.2, 338.1, 438.1, 438.3, 601.2, 624.3, 658.1
indemonstrability 971.1
indemonstrable 971.16
indent (n) 284.6, 420.5, 421.1, 440.1, 480.4, 517.7 (v) 284.14, 289.4, 420.11, 421.5, 440.9, 480.19, 913.4
indentation 284.6, 284.11, 289.1, 294.1, 517.7
indented 284.17, 289.5
indenter 1046.4
indention 284.6, 517.7
indenture (n) 284.6, 615.8 (v) 615.18
indentured 615.21
indentured servant 432.7
indentureship 432.1
independence 136.1, 232.6, 324.2, 359.5, 430.5, 449.6, 458.11, 467.1, 609.26, 618.1, 776.1
independent (n) 430.12, 467.4, 609.28, 611.10, 868.3 (a) 136.8, 324.7, 359.15, 430.22, 449.23, 467.7, 565.7, 609.45, 611.18, 618.14, 776.6, 802.20
independent clause 529.1
independent contractor 726.2
independent film 706.1
independently rich 618.14
independently wealthy 618.14
independent means 430.5
independent of one's will 963.14
independent witness 970.8
in-depth 269.6
indescribability 122.4
indescribable 122.13, 870.14
in despair 125.12
in desperate case 1006.13
in desperate straits 1013.26
indestructibility 829.1, 855.5
indestructible 829.7, 855.18, 1049.5
in detention 429.19, 429.22, 572.13
indeterminable 971.19
indeterminableness 971.4
indeterminacy 775.2, 971.1, 972.1
indeterminacy principle 971.1
indeterminancy principle 968.2
indeterminate 263.4, 522.15, 768.4, 775.7, 864.11, 971.19, 972.15
indeterminateness 263.1, 522.3, 971.4, 972.1
indetermination 971.1
indeterminism 971.1
indevotion 695.1
indevotional 695.15
indevout 695.15
indevoutness 695.1
index (n) 73.5, 159.5, 196.1, 444.1, 517.1, 517.4, 549.11, 551.4, 554.9, 554.12, 558.4, 574.10, 801.4, 808.4, 865.4, 871.7, 883.4 (v) 549.15, 809.6, 871.8
index card 549.10
indexed 549.17, 809.8, 871.9
indexes 1017.14
index finger 73.5, 517.4
index fossil 842.6
indexical 809.8
indexing 549.14, 809.1, 871.7
indexterity 414.1
India 235.1
Indian 312.3
Indiana ballot 609.19
Indianapolis Motor Speedway 756.1
Indian buffalo 311.6
Indian club 725.7
Indian file 812.2
Indian hay 87.11
Indian heat 1019.5
Indian mode 709.10
Indian plate 235.1
Indian pony 311.10
Indian reservation 397.7
Indian ridge 237.5
Indian summer 313.5, 1019.7
in diapers 301.12
India rubber 395.9
indicant 133.3, 517.1
indicate 133.11, 161.5, 348.5, 517.17, 518.8, 551.10, 865.11, 957.8
indicated 133.14, 519.7, 963.13
indicating 517.23
indication 85.9, 133.3, 348.1, 517.3, 551.4, 957.1
indicative (n) 530.11 (a) 133.15, 348.9, 517.23, 518.10, 519.6, 957.16
indicativeness 517.3
indicator 517.1
indicator card 759.11
indicatory 348.9, 517.23
indices 1017.14
indict 510.13, 598.15, 599.7, 888.4
indictability 656.1
indictable 510.25, 656.3
indictableness 656.1
indicted 599.15
indictment 510.3, 598.3, 599.1, 888.1
indictor 599.5
indie 430.12, 706.1
indifference 25.2, 94.4, 102.1, 106.5, 173.4, 325.1, 331.6, 340.2, 426.1, 435.1, 467.2, 695.1, 945.1, 979.5, 982.1, 984.1, 998.1, 1005.1
indifferent 65.2, 94.13, 102.6, 106.15, 325.6, 340.11, 426.4, 467.7, 695.15, 930.12, 945.5, 979.12, 982.3, 984.6, 1005.7
indifferentism 102.1, 695.1, 982.1
indifferentist 695.15
indifferentistic 695.15
indifferentness 102.1, 467.2, 982.1
in difficulties 623.8
indigence 619.2
indigene 227.3
indigenity 226.1
indigenization 226.3
indigenize 226.4
indigenized 226.6
indigenous 226.5, 767.8
indigenousness 226.1, 767.1
indigent (n) 619.4 (a) 619.8
indigestibility 82.2
indigestible 82.6
indigestion 85.9, 85.29
indignant 152.28, 510.21
indignant displeasure 152.4
indignation 152.4, 510.1
indignation meeting 333.2
indignity 156.2, 512.1
indigo (n) 35.13, 45.1 (a) 45.3
indirect 164.7, 204.13, 356.22, 538.14, 645.16, 831.11, 914.7
indirect authority 417.1
indirect costs 626.3
indirect free kick 752.3
indirect initiative 613.8
indirection 164.1, 204.1, 356.3, 538.5, 645.1, 914.1
indirectness 204.1, 354.5
indirect object 530.2
indirect power 894.1
indirect question 204.1
indirect taxation 630.9
in dire straits 623.8
in disagreement 780.7
indiscernibility 32.1, 945.2
indiscernible 32.5, 258.14, 945.6
indiscerptibility 1045.2
indiscerptible 1045.13
indiscipline 327.1, 418.1, 430.3, 669.1
indisciplined 327.8
in discredit 661.13
indiscreet 493.7, 666.5, 923.10, 945.5
indiscreetness 666.1, 923.2, 945.1
indiscretion 351.2, 493.1, 655.2, 666.1, 923.2, 923.4, 945.1, 975.5
indiscriminate 797.14, 810.12, 864.13, 945.5, 972.16
indiscriminateness 810.1, 945.1
indiscrimination 102.2, 945.1, 963.6
indiscriminative 945.5
in disfavor 661.13
in disgrace 661.13
in disguise 346.13
in dishabille 5.47, 6.13
in disorder 810.13
indispensability 963.3
indispensable (n) 963.2 (a) 963.13, 997.23
indispensable content 196.5
indispensableness 963.3
indispose 85.50, 379.4
indisposed 85.56, 325.5, 344.8
indisposedness 325.1
indisposed to believe 956.4
indisposed to talk 344.9
indisposition 85.1, 325.1
indisposition to speak 344.1
indisputability 970.3
indisputable 348.8, 761.15, 957.16, 960.2, 970.15
indisputable evidence 957.3
indisputable fact 761.3
indisputable truth 973.3
in dispute 971.17
in disrepair 391.14, 393.37
in disrepute 661.13
indissolubility 1045.2
indissoluble 800.15, 1045.13
indissolvable 1045.13

indistinct 32.6, 52.16, 522.15, 525.12, 945.6, 971.19
indistinction 945.2
indistinctive 945.6
indistinctness 32.2, 52.1, 522.3, 945.2, 971.4
indistinct speech 525.1
indistinguishability 32.2, 778.1
indistinguishable 32.6, 778.7, 945.6
indistinguishableness 945.2
in distress 26.9
indisturbance 106.2
indite 547.21, 718.6, 892.8
inditement 547.2, 718.2
inditer 547.15, 718.4
inditing 547.2, 718.2
individual (n) 305.2, 312.5, 763.3, 872.4 (a) 312.15, 517.23, 865.12, 872.7
individual, the 865.3
individual essence 919.5
individual freedom 430.5
individual identity 865.1
individualism 140.3, 430.5, 611.8, 651.1, 865.1, 865.4, 978.3
individualist (n) 140.5, 430.12, 651.3, 789.4 (a) 865.12
individualistic 430.22, 611.23, 651.5, 789.9, 865.12
individuality 312.5, 865.1, 872.1, 872.4
individualization 780.4, 865.7
individualize 780.6, 865.9
individualized 517.24
individualizing 780.9
individualness 865.1
individual responsibility 430.7
Individual Retirement Account 729.3
individual space 158.7
individual speech 523.1
individual speech habits 523.1
individuate 780.6, 872.6
individuating 780.9
individuation 780.4
indivisibility 872.1, 1045.2
indivisible 798.6, 800.15, 855.18, 872.7, 1045.13
indocile 325.5, 327.9, 361.12
indocility 325.1, 327.1, 361.4
indoctrinate 568.12, 569.4, 858.15
indoctrinated 226.6
indoctrination 568.2, 569.2, 858.5, 858.6
indoctrinational 569.6
Indo-European 523.12
Indo-Iranian 523.12
indolence 173.4, 175.1, 329.1, 331.5
indolent (n) 331.7 (a) 175.10, 331.19
indomitability 15.4, 361.4
indomitable 15.19, 360.8, 361.12
indoor 207.6
indoor game 743.9
indoor gardening 1069.2
indoor sport 744.1
indoor tennis 748.1
in doubt 955.9, 971.17
Indra 56.5
indraft 189.2, 318.1
indrawing 189.2
indubious 970.16
indubitability 970.3
indubitable 348.8, 970.15
indubitableness 970.3
induce 192.14, 375.22, 422.6, 886.11, 894.7, 946.10
induced drag 184.27
inducement 375.3, 375.7, 377.1, 478.5
inducer 375.10
inducive 375.25
induct 191.4, 615.12, 615.17, 818.11
inductance 1032.15
inductee 461.18, 572.9
inductile 1046.12
inductility 1046.3
induction 187.2, 615.3, 615.7, 698.10, 818.5, 818.6, 935.3, 946.4, 1032.15
induction cooking 11.2
induction heat 1019.1
induction heating 1020.1
inductive 935.22
inductive method 935.3
inductive reactance 1032.13
inductive reasoning 935.3
inductivity 1032.15
indulge 107.4, 427.6, 443.10, 669.4
indulged 148.7, 427.9
indulge in 95.13, 669.4
indulge in easy vices 669.4
indulge in overkill 355.3
indulge in wish fulfillment 986.17
indulgence 134.1, 143.3, 148.1, 427.3, 443.2, 642.2, 669.1, 979.4
indulgent 134.9, 143.16, 427.8, 430.25, 443.14, 669.7, 979.11, 983.17
indulge one's appetite 672.4
indulge one's appetites 669.4
indulge oneself 418.4, 651.4, 669.4
indulge with 478.15
in dumb show 517.25
in durance vile 429.21
indurate (v) 94.6, 1046.7 (a) 1046.13, 1046.15
indurated 94.12, 144.25, 654.17, 1046.13, 1046.15
induration 94.3, 114.2, 144.10, 146.1, 1046.1, 1046.5
indurative 1046.14
industrial 724.16, 731.22, 742.7, 892.14
industrial action 727.5
industrial age 824.5
industrial archeology 842.4
industrial area 739.3
industrial art 712.1, 712.2
industrial ceramics 742.2
industrial city 230.1
industrial crop 1069.15
industrial design 712.2, 717.5
industrial engineer 1043.2
industrial engineering 573.7, 1043.1
industrial estate 739.3
industrial instrumentation 1040.11
industrialism 731.13
industrialist 730.1, 892.7
industrialization 731.14, 892.3
industrialize 731.20, 892.11
industrialized nation 232.1
industrial nation 232.1
industrial park 739.3
industrial production 892.3
industrial psychologist 92.10
industrial relations 727.1
industrial school 429.8, 567.9
industrial-strength 15.15
industrial town 739.2
industrial union 727.2
industrial waste 391.4, 893.3
industrial worker 607.9, 726.2
industrial zone 739.3
industrious 330.22, 339.11, 360.8, 725.17
industriousness 330.6, 339.2, 360.1
industry 330.6, 339.2, 360.1, 617.9, 724.2, 725.4, 731.1, 892.3
industry leader 730.1
industry standard 385.4
in Dutch 661.13, 1013.22
in duty bound 641.16
indwell 221.6, 767.6
indweller 227.2
indwelling (n) 767.1 (a) 221.12, 767.7
indwellingness 221.1
indwelling spirit 306.2, 767.5
Indy car racing 756.1
in earnest 101.9, 111.3
inearth 309.19
inebriant (n) 88.13 (a) 88.36
inebriate (n) 88.11 (v) 88.22 (a) 88.31
inebriated 88.31
inebriating 88.36
inebriation 88.1
inebriative 88.36
inebriety 88.1
inebrious 88.31
in eclipse 346.11
in ecstasies 95.17
in ecstasy 105.25
inedible 64.8
ineducability 922.3
ineducable 922.15
ineducation 930.4
ineffability 122.4, 685.1
ineffable 122.13, 685.7, 870.14
ineffable, the 685.2
ineffableness 122.4
ineffaceability 855.5
ineffaceable 855.18
in effect 387.25, 761.13
ineffective 19.14, 19.15, 391.9, 410.18, 414.19, 895.3
ineffectiveness 19.3, 391.2, 414.1, 895.1
ineffectual 19.15, 391.9, 410.18, 414.19, 891.4, 895.3
ineffectuality 19.3, 391.2, 414.1, 895.1, 998.1
ineffectualness 19.3, 891.1
inefficacious 19.15, 410.18, 895.3
inefficaciousness 19.3, 895.1
inefficacy 19.3, 391.2, 895.1
inefficiency 19.2, 414.1
inefficient 19.14, 414.15
inelastic 361.9, 1046.11, 1046.12, 1050.4
inelasticity 361.2, 1046.2, 1046.3, 1050.1
inelegance 414.3, 497.1, 534.1, 666.1, 1015.1
inelegancy 497.1, 534.1, 666.1
inelegant 414.20, 497.10, 534.2, 666.5, 1015.6
ineluctability 963.7, 970.1
ineluctable 963.15, 970.13
in embarrassed circumstances 623.8
in embryo 405.22, 406.12, 818.15, 886.14
inenarrability 122.4
inenarrable 122.13, 685.7
inenarrable, the 685.2
inenarrableness 685.1
inept 19.14, 414.15, 789.7, 922.13, 923.8, 996.5
ineptitude 19.2, 922.1, 923.1, 996.1
ineptness 414.1
inequal 288.6
inequality 288.1, 607.1, 650.1, 650.3, 780.1, 782.1, 789.1, 791.1
inequality of dealing 650.1
inequality of treatment 650.1
in equilibrium 855.12
in equipoise 106.13
inequitable 650.9
inequitableness 650.1
inequity 650.1, 791.1
ineradicability 855.5
ineradicable 855.18
inerasable 855.18
inerasableness 855.5
inerrability 970.1
inerrable 970.19, 973.17
inerrancy 970.1
inerrant 970.19, 973.17
in error 354.25, 975.18
inert 173.14, 329.6, 331.20, 467.7, 855.17, 1055.5
inert gas 1060.2, 1067.2
inertia 173.4, 175.1, 329.1, 331.1, 331.5, 855.3
inert matter 1055.1
inertness 173.4, 175.1, 329.1, 855.3, 1055.2
inerudite 930.13
inerudition 930.4
inescapable 761.15, 963.15
inescapable fact 761.3
inescapableness 963.7
in escrow 438.12, 438.13
inescutcheon 647.2
inessential, an 998.6
inessential (n) 768.2, 998.4 (a) 766.7, 768.4, 998.17
inessentiality 998.1

inessive 530.9
inestimable 632.10
inevasible 963.15
inevasibleness 963.7
in every one's mouth 552.15
in everyone's mouth 662.16, 928.27
in evidence 31.6
inevitability 424.1, 963.7, 964.2, 970.1
inevitable 424.11, 963.15, 964.9, 970.13
inevitable accident 963.7
inevitableness 963.7
inexact 340.13, 971.19, 975.17, 1003.4
inexactitude 340.4, 945.1, 975.2, 1003.1
inexactness 340.4, 971.4, 975.2, 1003.1
in excess 993.17
inexcitability 94.1, 102.2, 106.1, 117.1, 123.1, 129.1
inexcitable 94.9, 102.7, 106.10, 117.6, 123.3, 129.2
inexcitableness 106.1
inexcusability 650.5
inexcusable 650.12
inexecution 408.1
in exercise 889.11
inexertion 331.5
inexhaustibility 823.1
inexhaustible 823.3, 884.10, 991.7
in existence 761.13
inexistent 762.8
inexorability 361.2, 425.2, 963.7
inexorable 146.3, 361.9, 425.7, 963.15
inexorableness 146.1
inexpectance 131.1
inexpectancy 131.1
inexpectant 131.9
in expectation 130.11
inexpectation 125.1, 131.1, 830.2
inexpedience 414.6, 844.1, 923.2, 996.1, 1000.1
inexpediency 414.6, 996.1
inexpedient 844.6, 923.10, 996.5, 1000.7
inexpensive 633.7
inexpensiveness 633.1
inexperience 301.3, 374.1, 414.2, 930.1
inexperienced 301.10, 374.4, 414.17, 923.12, 930.11, 930.14
inexpert 414.15
inexpertness 414.1
inexpiable 650.12
inexpiableness 650.5
inexpiable sin 655.2
inexplicability 522.6
inexplicable 522.18, 972.16
inexplicit 539.4, 971.16
inexplicitness 539.1
inexpressibility 122.4, 685.1
inexpressible 122.13, 685.7
inexpressible, the 685.2
inexpressive 522.20
inexpressiveness 522.5
inexpugnability 15.4, 855.5
inexpugnable 15.19, 855.18
inextensibility 1046.3
inextensible 1046.12
inextensile 1046.12
inextension 1053.1
inextensional 1046.12
inextinguishability 855.5
inextinguishable 855.18
in extremis 307.32, 1006.13, 1013.26
in extremities 1013.26
inextricability 522.6, 855.3
inextricable 522.18, 799.5, 855.16
infallibilism 970.1, 970.6
infallibilist 970.7
infallibility 970.1, 1002.1
infallible 970.19, 973.17, 1002.6
infamous 638.3, 645.17, 654.16, 661.10, 1000.9
infamousness 654.4, 661.4, 1000.2
infamy 352.4, 638.2, 654.3, 661.4
infancy 19.2, 301.3, 301.5, 303.1, 818.4
infant (n) 302.1, 302.9, 416.3, 657.4, 818.2 (a) 301.12, 795.4, 818.15
infanta 608.8
infant care 1008.2
infanticide 696.7
infanticipating 78.18
infantile 301.12, 818.15, 922.24
infantile fixation 92.21
infantile paralysis 85.27
infantile sexuality 75.5
infantilism 922.9, 922.11
infantine 301.12, 922.24
infantry combat 457.4
infantry division 461.22
infantryman 178.6, 461.9
infant school 567.2
infants' wear 5.30, 735.3
infantwear 5.30
infarct 293.3
infarcted 293.11
infarction 293.3
in fashion 578.11
in fat city 1010.12
infatuate (n) 101.4, 104.11, 926.18 (v) 104.22, 377.7, 923.7, 926.25 (a) 104.27
infatuated 101.12, 104.27, 923.8, 926.33, 954.8
infatuatedness 104.3
infatuated with 101.10
infatuation 100.2, 101.3, 104.3, 923.5, 926.12, 954.1
in favor 324.5, 587.18, 662.15, 662.16
in favor of 509.17
in fear 127.23
infect 80.17, 85.51, 375.20, 393.12, 797.12, 1000.6, 1037.10
infected 80.20, 85.60, 1037.11
infectee 80.13
infection 80.4, 85.4, 85.13, 375.9, 393.2, 1000.3
infectious 82.7, 85.62
infectious disease 85.13
infectiousness 82.3, 85.4
infective 82.7, 85.62
infectivity 82.3
infecund 891.4, 987.5
infecundity 891.1, 987.1
in fee 469.8
in fee simple 469.8
infelicitous 531.4, 534.2, 789.7, 844.6, 996.5
infelicity 96.6, 112.2, 531.2, 534.1, 789.3, 844.1, 996.1
infeodation 478.2
infer 519.4, 935.15, 946.10, 951.10
inferable 935.23
inference 519.2, 935.3, 946.4, 951.3
inferential 519.6, 935.22
inferior (n) 250.2, 432.5, 577.1 (a) 19.14, 250.6, 274.8, 432.13, 911.5, 998.16, 998.17, 1000.7, 1005.9
inferior court 595.2
inferiority 19.2, 250.1, 432.2, 870.1, 911.1, 998.1, 1000.1, 1005.3
inferiority complex 92.22, 139.2
inferiorness 1005.3
inferior planet 1073.9
infernal 144.26, 654.13, 682.8, 1000.10
infernal pit 275.3
infernal regions 682.1
inferno 682.1, 1019.11
inferred 519.7, 951.14
infertile 891.4, 987.5
infertility 891.1, 987.1
infest 910.6
infestation 910.2
infested 910.11
infestive 112.21
infestivity 112.2
infestment 910.2
infeudate 478.16
infeudation 478.2
infidel (n) 688.6, 695.11 (a) 688.10, 695.19
infidelic 688.10, 695.19
infidelism 688.3, 695.5
infidelity 104.5, 645.5, 688.3, 695.5, 955.1
infield 743.11, 745.1, 755.1, 757.1
infielder 745.2
infield grass 745.1
infield turf 745.1
infighting 456.3, 457.1, 457.9
infiltrate 187.13, 189.10, 214.5, 459.17, 797.11, 1065.13
infiltration 187.6, 189.1, 214.1, 459.1, 797.2, 1065.7
infiltrator 214.3
in fine feather 5.46, 83.9
in fine fettle 83.8, 807.7
in fine shape 83.8
in fine whack 83.9
infinite 158.11, 221.13, 247.7, 257.20, 267.7, 677.17, 823.3, 829.7, 884.10, 1017.23
infinite duration 829.1
infinitely continuous 823.3
infinitely extended 823.3
infiniteness 823.1
infinite number 1017.5
infinitesimal 258.14
infinitesimalness 258.2
infinite space 158.1
infinite spirit 677.7
infinite variety 783.1
infinitive 530.4
infinitude 823.1, 884.1, 1017.5
infinity 158.1, 221.2, 247.1, 261.1, 267.1, 823.1, 829.1, 884.1, 1017.5
infinity pool 743.12
infirm 16.15, 16.18, 85.54, 303.18, 362.12, 654.12, 764.7, 854.7, 922.21, 971.20
infirm, the 85.43
infirmary 91.21
infirmity 16.3, 85.1, 85.3, 303.5, 362.4, 654.2, 922.8, 971.6, 1003.2
infirmity of age 303.5
infirmity of purpose 362.1
infirmity of will 16.2
infirm of purpose 16.17, 362.9
infirm of will 16.17
infirm old age 303.5
infix (n) 213.2, 254.2, 526.3 (v) 191.8, 253.4, 568.12, 855.9, 989.17
infixal 526.22
infixation 526.3, 568.2
infixed 373.18, 767.7, 855.13
infixing 191.1
infixion 568.2, 855.2
inflame 17.10, 26.7, 41.4, 105.12, 119.2, 152.24, 375.17, 1020.18, 1020.22
inflamed 26.11, 41.6, 85.58, 85.60, 105.20, 671.22, 1019.27
inflamer 375.11
in flames 1019.27
inflame with love 104.22
inflaming 1020.27
inflammability 105.10, 1020.9
inflammable (n) 1021.1 (a) 105.28, 1020.28
inflammable material 1021.1
inflammation 26.4, 85.9, 85.10, 105.11, 375.4
inflammative 1020.27
inflammatory 105.30, 375.28, 1020.27
inflammatory disease 85.10
inflatable 259.9
inflatable slide 369.3
inflate 140.7, 251.4, 259.4, 355.3, 545.6, 632.9, 993.13
inflated 251.7, 259.13, 355.4, 501.22, 502.12, 545.9
inflatedness 545.1
inflation 251.1, 259.2, 355.1, 501.7, 532.2, 545.1, 626.3, 630.4, 632.3, 731.10, 993.7
inflationary 259.9, 632.12, 731.23
inflationary gap 632.3
inflationary prices 632.3
inflationary spiral 630.4, 632.3
inflationary trend 632.3
inflationary universe 1073.1
inflect 279.6, 524.28, 530.16
inflected 523.23

inflection 278.2, 279.3, 524.6, 526.3, 530.2
inflectional 523.23, 526.22
inflection of voice 524.6
inflective 164.8, 526.22
inflexibility 359.2, 361.2, 425.2, 855.3, 963.7, 1046.3
inflexible 359.12, 361.9, 425.7, 855.15, 895.4, 963.15, 1046.12
inflexible will 361.1
inflict 328.6, 643.5
inflict a penalty on 603.4
inflict capital punishment 604.16
inflicted 643.8
infliction 96.8, 604.1, 643.1, 1001.1
inflictive 604.22
inflict on 643.4
inflict pain 26.7
inflict upon 604.9
in flight 368.16
in-flight training 184.1
in flood 238.25
inflooding (n) 189.2 (a) 189.12
inflorescence 310.26
inflorescent 310.38
inflow (n) 189.2, 238.4, 318.1 (v) 189.9
in flower 310.38
inflowing 189.12
influence (n) 18.1, 249.3, 375.2, 415.4, 417.4, 894.1, 894.6 (v) 375.22, 886.10, 886.11, 886.12, 889.6, 894.7, 980.9
influenceability 894.5
influenceable 894.15
influenced 650.11, 980.12
influence peddler 415.8, 609.30, 610.5, 894.6
influence peddling 609.29, 894.3
influencer 894.6
influent 189.12
an influential 894.6
influential 417.15, 894.13
influentiality 894.1
influentialness 417.4
influenza 85.16
influx 189.2, 214.1
info 551.1
infobit 1042.14
in focus 31.7
infold 291.5
infolding 291.4
infoldment 291.4
infomercial 352.6
infopreneur 551.5
in force 18.12, 387.25, 761.13, 889.11
inform (v) 221.7, 351.6, 375.20, 551.8, 552.11, 568.10 (a) 263.4
inform against 551.12, 599.7
informal 523.20, 581.3
informal agreement 437.1
informality 581.1
informal language 523.5
informal meal 8.7
informalness 581.1
informal vote 371.6
informant 551.5, 552.9, 938.19, 957.6
informatics 1042.1
information 343.1, 551.1, 552.1, 568.1, 598.3, 599.1, 928.1, 957.1, 1042.15
information, the 761.4
information against 599.1
informational 551.18, 568.18
information center 551.5, 558.1
information explosion 251.2, 347.1, 551.7
information fatigue 928.6
information machine 1041.17
information media 551.5
information medium 551.5
information network 551.5
information officer 551.5
information overload 551.1
information processing 551.1, 551.7, 1042.1
information processor 1042.2
information retrieval 551.7
information revolution 860.1
information science 558.2, 1042.1
information storage 989.1
information superhighway 551.7, 1042.19
information technology 551.7
information theory 343.5, 347.1, 551.7, 1041.2
informative 551.18, 552.13, 568.18
informatory 551.18
informed 405.16, 551.17, 928.15, 928.18
informed in 928.19
informed of 928.16
informer 357.10, 540.4, 551.5, 551.6, 552.10, 599.5, 957.6
informing (n) 343.2 (a) 551.18
inform on 351.6, 551.12, 599.7, 645.14
infotainment 1035.2
infract 674.5
infraction 327.1, 435.2, 638.1, 655.1, 674.3, 746.3, 747.3, 749.3, 749.6, 910.3
infra dig 250.6, 497.12, 661.11
infra indignitatem 661.11
infrangibility 1045.2, 1049.1
infrangible 15.18, 1045.13, 1049.5
infrarace 312.1
infrared 41.6
infrared astronomy 1073.19
infrared light 1025.1
infrared observatory 1073.17
infrared radiation 1032.10
infrared ray 1025.5
infrared spectroscopy 29.7
infrasonic frequency 50.6
infrastructural 266.6
infrastructure 199.2, 250.2, 266.3, 574.11, 901.1, 901.6, 901.10
infrequence 848.1
infrequency 848.1, 885.1
infrequent 848.2, 885.5, 992.11
infrigidation 1024.1
infringe 214.5, 435.4, 621.4, 640.8, 674.5, 910.9
infringe a copyright 482.19
infringement 214.1, 327.1, 393.1, 435.2, 482.8, 621.2, 640.3, 655.1, 674.3, 910.3
infringement of copyright 480.4, 482.8
in front 216.10
in full bloom 14.3, 303.13
in full cry 382.11
in full dress 5.46
in full feather 5.46
in full force 15.21
in full swing 15.21, 330.19, 1010.13
in full view 31.6
infundibular 282.12, 284.16
infundibuliform 282.12, 284.16
in funds 618.14
infuriate (v) 105.12, 152.25, 589.7 (a) 152.32, 671.18
infuriated 152.32
infuriation 105.11, 152.5
infuscate 40.2
infuscation 40.1
infuse 191.3, 192.16, 375.20, 568.12, 797.11, 1064.5, 1065.13
infuse life into 105.13
infusibility 1045.2
infusible 1045.13
infusion 10.49, 191.1, 192.7, 192.8, 375.9, 568.2, 701.6, 797.2, 797.7, 1061.2, 1064.1, 1064.3, 1065.7
infusive 375.26
ingate 239.4
ingathering 770.1
in gear 777.9
ingeminate 874.3
ingemination 874.1
ingenious 413.22, 415.12, 986.18
ingeniousness 413.1, 415.1
ingénu 416.5
ingenue 416.3, 704.10, 706.3, 707.2
ingenuity 413.1, 986.3
ingenuous 301.10, 416.5, 644.17, 930.11, 954.9
ingenuousness 416.1, 644.4, 930.1, 954.2
ingest 8.22, 187.11, 388.3, 570.7
ingesta 10.1
ingestion 2.17, 7.8, 8.1, 187.4, 388.1, 570.2
ingestive 187.16
ingle 228.2, 1019.13, 1020.11
inglenook 228.2, 284.7, 1020.11
ingleside 228.2, 1020.11
inglorious 137.10, 661.10, 661.14
inglorious defeat 412.4
ingloriousness 137.1, 661.4
in glory 679.6, 681.12
ingoing (n) 189.1 (a) 92.40, 189.12
ingoingness 92.11
in good case 83.8, 1010.12, 1010.13
in good condition 807.7
in good form 807.7
in good health 83.8
in good heart 124.10
in good odor 509.19, 662.15
in good set terms 529.5
in good shape 83.8, 807.7
in good spirits 109.11
in good taste 496.7
in good time 845.7
in good trim 807.7
in good with 587.18
ingot 728.20, 1058.5
ingraft 191.6
ingrain (v) 35.14, 855.9 (a) 35.18
ingrained 35.18, 373.18, 767.7, 855.13
ingrate 151.2
ingratiate oneself 138.10, 894.7
ingratiate oneself with 894.12
ingratiating 138.14, 504.17
ingratiation 138.2, 511.1
ingratitude 151.1
ingredient 766.3, 793.1, 796.2
ingredients 196.1, 763.2
ingress 189.1, 189.5, 239.1
ingression 189.1
ingressive 189.12
in grief 112.26
in-group 770.3
ingroup 617.6, 894.6
in-group, the 575.14
ingrowing 189.12
ingrown 855.13
inguen 171.4
ingurgitate 187.11
ingurgitation 187.4
inhabit 159.17, 225.7, 225.9, 761.11
inhabitability 225.6
inhabitable 225.15
inhabitancy 225.1
inhabitant 227.2
inhabitants 227.1
inhabitants of Pandemonium 680.1
inhabitation 225.1
inhabited 225.12
inhabited sculpture 717.1
inhabiter 227.2
inhabiting 225.1, 225.2
inhalant 86.4, 86.6, 87.3
inhalation 2.21, 187.5
inhale 69.8, 89.14, 187.12
inhalement 187.5
inhale snuff 89.14
in half 875.1
in hand 390.12, 404.7, 405.22, 469.8, 670.11, 807.6, 831.9, 889.11
in harbor 1007.6
inharmonic 61.4
inharmonious 35.21, 61.4, 456.15, 780.7, 789.6
inharmoniousness 61.1, 456.1, 780.1
in harmony 455.3, 788.9
inharmony 61.1, 456.1, 780.1
in harness 328.10, 330.21, 460.13
in health 83.8
in heat 75.28
in heaven 95.17
inhere 221.6, 767.6
inhere in 761.11
inherence 221.1, 767.1
inherent 221.12, 767.7, 934.6

inherent authority 417.1
inherent vice 16.2
inherit 479.7, 767.6, 815.2
inheritability 560.6
inheritable 560.20, 629.5
inheritance 471.1, 478.10, 479.2, 560.6
inheritance factor 560.6
inheritance tax 630.9
inherited 560.19, 767.8
inheritor 256.3, 479.5, 817.4, 835.2
inheritors 561.1
inheritress 479.5
inheritrix 479.5
inhibit 106.8, 428.7, 429.12, 444.3, 474.5, 1012.10
inhibited 428.13
inhibiting 210.7, 428.11, 1012.17
inhibiting antibody 86.27
inhibition 92.24, 428.1, 444.1, 474.1, 1012.1
inhibitive 428.11, 444.6, 1012.17
inhibit one's desires 668.6
inhibitory 444.6
in hiding 346.14
in high dudgeon 152.31
in high esteem 155.11
in high estimation 155.11
in high favor 662.15
in high feather 5.46, 83.9, 502.13
in high relief 31.7, 283.18, 348.12, 715.7
in high spirits 109.11
in hock 438.12, 623.8, 625.10
in hog heaven 1010.12
in hold 429.22
in holy orders 698.17
in hopes 124.10
inhospitable 144.16, 586.7, 589.9
inhospitableness 144.1, 586.1
in hospital 85.59
inhospitality 144.1, 586.1, 589.1
in hot pursuit 382.11
in hot water 1013.22
inhuman 144.26, 671.21, 680.17
inhumane 144.26
inhumaness 144.11
inhumanity 144.11, 144.12, 671.1
inhumation 309.1
inhume 309.19
in hysterics 105.25
in ignorance of 930.12
inimical 451.8, 458.20, 589.9, 779.6, 900.8, 1011.13
inimicality 589.1
inimicalness 451.2, 779.1
inimitability 249.1
inimitable 249.15
in intensive care 85.56
iniquitous 144.20, 650.9, 654.16, 655.5, 1000.7
iniquitousness 144.5, 650.1, 654.4
iniquity 650.1, 654.3, 655.2, 1000.1
in irons 428.16
inirritability 106.1
inirritable 106.10
initial (n) 546.1, 818.3 (v) 332.12, 546.6 (a) 818.15
initialing 546.5
initialization 818.3
initialize 1042.21
initial rhyme 720.9
initials 517.11, 527.10
initial substance 1052.2
Initial Teaching Alphabet 546.3
initiate (n) 572.9, 617.11, 818.2 (v) 191.4, 404.3, 568.14, 818.10, 818.11 (a) 413.26
initiated 413.26
initiation 159.7, 187.2, 568.5, 580.4, 701.9, 818.3, 818.5
initiation fee 624.5
initiative (n) 17.2, 328.3, 330.7, 404.1, 613.8, 889.2 (a) 187.18, 818.15
initiator 892.7
initiatory 187.18, 568.18, 814.4, 818.15
in its infancy 818.15
in its original carton 841.9
inject 87.22, 90.14, 191.3, 375.20, 1065.13
inject in 213.6
injecting 87.2
injection 86.6, 87.20, 91.16, 189.1, 191.1, 213.2, 214.1, 1065.7, 1075.2, 1075.9
inject oneself into 214.7
in jeopardy 1006.13
injest 1065.13
injudicial 674.6
injudicious 493.7, 923.10
injudiciousness 493.1, 923.2, 948.1
injunction 419.1, 420.2, 420.6, 428.1, 444.1, 773.1
injure 26.7, 389.5, 393.9, 393.13, 1000.6
injured 96.23, 393.27
injured party 598.11
injured pride 137.2
injure one's reputation 512.9
injurious 82.5, 393.27, 393.44, 996.6, 1000.12
injuriousness 82.1, 1000.5
injury 85.38, 96.5, 156.2, 389.2, 393.1, 473.1, 650.4, 655.2, 996.2, 1000.3
injury of one's reputation 512.2
injury to one's reputation 512.2
injustice 350.1, 640.2, 650.1, 650.4, 655.2, 791.1
ink (n) 38.4, 712.18 (v) 38.7
ink-black 38.8
in keeping 867.6
inkhorn 534.3, 545.8, 928.22
in kilter 807.7
inkiness 38.1
inkjet printer 1042.9
inkling 551.4, 797.7, 951.5
inkslinger 547.13, 718.3
inkslinging 547.1
ink spiller 547.13, 718.3
ink spilling 547.1
inkstained wretch 555.4, 718.3
inky 38.8, 1004.10
inky-black 38.8
inland (n) 207.3 (a) 207.7
inland navigation 182.1
Inland Revenue 630.10
inlands 207.3
inland sea 241.1
in-laws 564.2
inlay (n) 47.4, 191.2, 196.3 (v) 191.5, 191.8, 196.7
inlayer 196.3
in layers 296.6
inlaying 196.3
in leading strings 326.5, 428.13, 432.16
in league 805.6
inlet 189.5, 242.1, 292.1, 383.3
in letters of fire 997.21
in limbo 130.12, 971.18, 971.25
in line 867.6
in-line 812.9
in-line blading 744.1
in-line skating 177.16, 744.1
in liquor 88.31
in lockstep 867.6
in loco 843.9
in longhand 547.22
in love 104.28
in love with 104.29
in low relief 715.7
in low spirits 112.22
in luck 1010.14
in luxury 1010.12
inlying picket 1008.9
inmate 227.2, 429.11
in mesh 777.9
in-migrant 178.5, 189.4
in-migrate 177.22, 189.11
in-migration 177.4, 189.3
in mint condition 83.8, 390.12, 841.9
inmost 207.6, 345.13
inmost heart 93.3, 767.5, 919.3
inmost mind 919.3, 931.4
inmost recesses of the memory 989.1
inmost soul 93.3, 767.5
inmost thoughts 931.4
in motion 172.7
in mourning 115.18
in must 75.28
inn 228.15
in name only 376.5, 527.15
in nappies 301.12
innards 2.16, 196.1, 196.3, 207.4, 1040.4
in narrow circumstances 619.7
innascibility 761.5
innascible 761.14
innate 560.19, 767.8, 934.6, 978.7
innate ability 413.5
innate aptitude 413.5
innate idea 932.2
innateness 767.1
innate proclivity 934.2
in native buff 6.14
in nature's garb 6.14
in need 619.8
in need of rest 21.7
in negligee 5.47
inner (n) 207.2 (a) 207.6, 767.7, 865.12
inner arbiter 636.5
inner being 919.4
inner child 865.5
inner circle 423.1, 617.6
inner circle, the 575.14
inner city 230.6
inner-city 230.11
inner city, the 80.11
inner-directed 92.40, 375.30, 430.22, 789.9
inner-directedness 92.11
inner-directed person 789.4
inner-direction 375.2, 430.5
inner ear 2.10
inner essence 767.2
inner form 262.1
inner landscape 207.2
inner life 207.2
inner light 636.5
inner man 207.2, 865.5, 919.3, 919.4
inner mechanism 2.16, 207.4
inner mind 919.4
innermost 207.6, 345.13
innermost being 93.3
innermost recesses 207.2
innermost recesses of the heart 767.5
innermost thoughts 931.4
inner nature 207.2, 767.5
innerness 207.1, 767.1
inner person 767.5
inner planet 1073.9
inner reality 767.5
inner recess 207.2
inner recesses of the heart 93.3
inner recesses of the mind 919.3
inner reliever 745.2
inner sanctum 584.6, 1009.5
inner self 207.2, 865.5
inner sense 689.8
inner space 158.7, 275.4
innerspring mattress 901.20
inner station 1075.5
inner voice 641.2
inner workings 196.1, 1040.4
inness 207.1
inning 745.3, 825.2
innings 825.2
innocence 416.1, 499.2, 653.2, 657.1, 664.1, 930.1, 999.9
innocency 657.1
innocent (n) 302.3, 358.1, 416.3, 657.4, 953.9 (a) 148.7, 301.10, 416.5, 499.7, 653.6, 657.6, 664.4, 930.11, 953.22, 999.21
innocent as a lamb 657.6
innocent bystander 918.1
innocentness 657.1
innocent tumor 85.39
innocuous 137.10, 416.5, 600.14, 657.6, 999.21
innocuousness 137.1, 999.9
innominability 122.4
innominable 122.13
innominate 528.3
innovate 337.4, 841.5, 852.9
innovation 337.1, 337.2, 816.2, 841.2, 852.4, 892.1
innovational 852.11
innovationist 852.5

innovative 852.11, 986.18
innovator 816.1, 852.5
innoxious 999.21
innuendo 508.5, 512.4, 519.2, 551.4, 599.1
in numbers 709.28
innumerability 823.1, 884.1
innumerable 823.3, 884.10
innutritiousness 82.2
inobservance 435.1, 984.1
inobservant 435.5, 984.6
inoccupation 331.2, 331.3
inoculability 85.4
inoculable 85.62
inoculate 91.28, 191.3, 375.20, 568.12
inoculation 86.28, 91.16, 191.1, 568.2
inodorous 72.5
inodorousness 72.1
inoffensive 72.5, 600.14, 999.21
inoffensiveness 72.1, 999.9
in on 476.8
in one's armor 94.9
in one's bad books 589.13
in one's best bib and tucker 5.46
in one's birthday suit 6.14
in one's black books 589.13, 661.13
in one's clutches 432.14
in one's control 432.14
in one's cups 88.31
in one's element 121.12
in one's employ 577.14
in one's eye 130.13, 840.3
in one's good books 587.18, 662.15
in one's good graces 587.18
in one's grasp 469.8
in one's grip 469.8
in one's hands 432.14, 966.6
in one's name 469.8
in one's own hand 547.22
in one's pay 577.14
in one's pocket 378.4, 432.14, 894.15
in one's possession 469.8
in one's power 432.14, 966.6
in one's prime 303.13
in one's right mind 516.3, 925.4
in one's second childhood 922.23
in one's shell 94.9
in one's shirtsleeves 5.47
in one's sober senses 516.3
in one's teens 301.14, 882.25
inoperability 391.1, 967.2
inoperable 85.56, 125.15, 308.23, 391.14, 967.8
in operation 387.25, 889.11
inoperative 19.15, 391.14, 393.37
inoperativeness 391.1
inopportune 844.6, 996.5
inopportune moment 844.2
inopportuneness 844.1, 996.1
inopportunity 844.1
in opposition 333.6, 1011.13
in order 765.7, 807.7, 812.9
in orders 698.17
inordinacy 355.1, 669.1
inordinance 993.1
inordinate 355.4, 632.12, 669.7, 926.32, 993.16
inordinate desire 100.8
inordinateness 632.4, 669.1, 993.1
inorganic 1055.4, 1058.15, 1060.9
inorganic chemical 1060.2
inorganic chemist 1060.7
inorganic chemistry 1055.3
inorganic fertilizer 890.4
inorganic matter 1055.1
inorganic mineral 1058.1
inorganic sediment 1059.6
inorganic substance 1058.1
inorganized 1055.4
inornate 499.9
inornateness 499.4
in outline 211.14
in over one's head 19.14
in ovo 406.12, 886.14
in pain 26.9
in pantomime 517.25
in paradise 95.17
in parity 778.8
in partnership 805.6
inpatient 85.43, 227.2
in pawn 438.12
in perfect order 807.7
in peril 1006.13
in personam jurisdiction 594.1
in petto 32.5, 345.14
in phase (n) 916.4 (a) 836.6
in pieces 393.27, 802.23
in place 159.18, 221.12, 385.13, 855.13
in plain brown paper 346.13
in plain sight 31.6
in plain wrapping 346.13
in play 889.11
in plenty 991.7
in point 775.11
in poise 900.9
in polar opposition 779.7
in poor health 85.54
in poor taste 497.10
in port 1007.6
in possession of 469.9
in possession of one's faculties 516.3, 925.4
in possession of one's senses 925.4
inpour (n) 189.2 (v) 189.9
inpouring 189.12
in power 18.12
in practice 387.25, 889.11
in preparation 405.22
in price 633.6
in print 352.17, 548.19
in prison 429.21
in process 404.7, 405.22, 889.11
in production 405.22
in profusion 884.9
in progress 404.7, 405.22
in prose 721.4
in prospect 130.13, 840.3
in purdah 346.11
in pursuit 382.11
input (n) 189.1, 1042.15, 1042.18 (v) 1042.21
input device 1042.3, 1042.4
input-output 1042.15
input voltage 1033.7
in quantity 991.7
in Queer Street 619.7
inquest 307.17, 596.5, 598.5, 938.1
in question 971.17, 971.18
in quest of 382.11, 938.38
inquietude 96.1, 105.5, 126.1, 127.5, 917.1
inquire 938.20, 981.3
inquire after 938.20
inquire for 938.30
inquire into 556.5, 931.14
inquirendo 938.1
inquire of 938.20
inquirer 572.1, 938.16, 951.7, 981.2
inquiring (n) 938.1, 938.12 (a) 938.36, 981.5
inquiring mind 938.1, 981.1
inquiry 556.1, 598.5, 938.1, 938.10, 938.14
inquiry agent 576.10
inquiry into 938.4
Inquisition 938.4
inquisition (n) 938.13 (v) 938.22
inquisition 595.1, 598.5, 938.1
Inquisition, the 595.1
inquisitional 938.36
inquisitionist 938.16
inquisitive 214.9, 981.5
inquisitiveness 214.2, 570.5, 981.1
inquisitive person 981.2
inquisitor 938.16, 981.2
inquisitorial 938.36, 981.5
inquisitress 981.2
in rags 393.32, 619.8, 810.15
in rapport 455.3, 788.9
in raptures 95.17
in readiness 405.16, 405.21
in ready state 405.16
in receivership 625.11
in red letters 997.21
in reduced circumstances 619.7
in relief 283.18, 348.12, 715.7
in remission 428.13
in rem jurisdiction 594.1
in repair 765.7, 807.7
in reserve 405.21, 840.3
in residence 225.13, 228.32
in retirement 402.5, 448.3
in retrospect 989.21
in rhythm 709.28
in rivalry 457.23
inroad (n) 214.1, 393.1, 459.4, 910.3 (v) 459.20
in round terms 529.5
in ruins 393.33, 395.28
inrun 189.2, 753.1
in run position 753.3
inrush (n) 189.2, 318.1 (v) 189.9
inrushing 189.12
in rut 75.28, 105.22
ins 610.11
ins, the 575.14
in sackcloth and ashes 115.18
in safe keeping 1007.6
in safety 1007.6
insalata verde 10.37
insalubrious 82.5
insalubriousness 82.1
insalubrity 82.1
ins and outs 766.2, 972.5
insane 101.12, 671.18, 923.8, 926.26
insane asylum 926.14
insaneness 926.1
insanitary 82.5
insanitation 80.3
insanity 92.14, 811.1, 922.9, 923.1, 926.1
insatiability 100.8, 672.1, 993.3
insatiable 100.27, 480.26, 672.6
insatiable desire 100.8
insatiableness 993.3
insatiate 100.27
in scale 245.5
inscribe 546.6, 547.19, 549.15, 713.9, 855.9, 989.17
inscribed 547.22, 549.17, 713.11
inscribe in the memory 989.17
inscribe oneself 617.14
inscriber 716.8
inscribing 549.14
in script 547.22
inscript 713.2
inscription 309.18, 546.5, 547.1, 549.4, 549.12, 549.14, 554.12, 713.2, 974.4
inscriptional 549.18
inscrutability 522.1, 1031.1
•**inscrutable** 522.13
insculpture 715.5
insculptured 713.11
in search of 938.38
in season 313.9
insect 311.3, 311.31, 311.32, 660.6
insect-eating 8.31
insect-eating bird 311.27
insecticide 1001.3
insectile 311.51
insectivore 311.3
insectivorous 8.31
insectlike 311.51
insect powder 1001.3
insecure 971.20, 971.23, 1006.11, 1006.14
insecurity 971.6, 1006.2
in seisin 469.8
inseminate 78.10, 890.8, 1069.18
inseminated 78.17
insemination 78.3, 890.3, 1069.14
insensate 25.6, 144.26, 671.18, 671.21, 922.13, 923.8, 923.10, 923.11, 1055.5
insensate cruelty 144.11
insensateness 671.1, 923.1, 1055.2
insensibility 25.1, 94.2, 922.2, 930.2, 945.1, 990.1, 1055.2
insensible 25.6, 32.5, 94.10, 922.14, 930.12, 984.7, 1055.5
insensibleness 25.1, 94.2
insensible to 930.12
insensible to the past 990.9
insensitive 25.6, 94.12, 144.18, 144.25, 505.6, 945.5
insensitiveness 25.1, 94.3

insensitivity 25.1, 94.3, 102.2, 144.10, 505.1, 945.1, 980.2
insentience 25.1, 1055.2
insentient 25.6, 1055.5
inseparability 587.5, 803.1, 1045.2
inseparable 587.19, 800.15, 803.10, 1045.13
inseparable friend 588.1
inseparableness 587.5
insert (n) 191.2, 213.2, 352.8 (v) 189.7, 191.3, 549.15
insert in 213.6
insertion 189.1, 191.1, 191.2, 213.2, 352.8, 549.14, 1075.2, 1075.9
insert oneself 214.5
in service 387.25
in-service training 568.3
in session 770.21
inset (n) 159.5, 191.2 (v) 191.5
in set phrases 529.5
in set terms 529.5
in seventh heaven 95.17
inseverable 800.15
in shape 83.8, 83.12, 765.7, 807.7
in shards 393.27, 802.24
in shelter 1007.6
in shorthand 547.22, 547.27
in short supply 795.4, 992.11
in shreds 393.32, 802.23
inside (n) 207.2, 767.5, 819.1 (a) 207.6, 345.14, 819.4
inside dope 551.2
inside information 345.5, 551.2
inside job 381.5
inside layer 196.3
inside left 749.5, 752.2
inside man 576.9
inside out 205.7
inside position 756.3
insider 551.2, 617.11
inside rail 757.1
inside right 749.5, 752.2
insider information 552.10
insider trading 356.8, 551.2, 737.6
insides 2.16, 196.1, 207.4, 767.5
inside skinny 345.5
inside skinny, the 551.1, 761.4
inside the box 373.13
inside track 249.2, 894.2
inside trader 737.11
inside wire 551.2
insidious 356.22, 415.12, 645.16, 920.15
insidiousness 356.3, 415.1, 920.3
in sight 31.6
insight 689.8, 767.5, 920.4, 928.2, 932.6, 934.1, 944.2, 961.3
insightful 928.15, 944.8
insight meditation 92.6
insignia 517.1, 647.1
insignia of arm 647.5
insignia of branch 647.5
insignia of rank 647.5
insignificance 248.1, 250.1, 520.1, 998.1
insignificancy, an 998.6
insignificancy 998.7
insignificant 248.6, 520.6, 998.17
insincere 354.32, 500.15, 511.8, 645.18, 693.5, 936.10
insincere argument 936.3
insincerity 354.5, 500.1, 511.2, 645.3, 693.1, 936.1
insinuate 189.10, 191.3, 214.5, 422.5, 519.4, 551.10, 599.7
insinuated 519.7
insinuate in 213.6
insinuate oneself 138.10, 189.7
insinuate oneself into 617.14
insinuating 511.8, 512.13, 519.6, 920.15
insinuation 138.2, 189.1, 191.1, 213.2, 214.1, 422.2, 512.4, 551.4, 599.1, 894.1, 920.3
insinuative 519.6
insinuatory 519.6
insipid 16.17, 65.2, 117.6, 222.14, 721.5, 1005.7
insipidity 16.3, 65.1, 102.1, 117.1
insipidness 65.1, 117.1, 721.2
insist 334.5, 375.14, 421.8, 439.9
insistence 360.1, 375.5, 421.4
insistency 360.1
insistent 360.8, 421.9, 440.18, 997.22
insistent demand 421.1
insist on 421.8
insist upon 375.14, 421.8, 849.9, 959.4, 963.8
in slavery 432.14
in smithereens 802.24
insobriety 88.1
insociability 583.1
insociable 583.5
in society 578.16
insolate 1020.19, 1066.6
insolation 85.28, 1020.1, 1021.1, 1066.3
insole 196.3
insolence 114.2, 141.2, 142.1, 156.1, 454.1, 493.1, 505.2
insolent 114.5, 141.10, 142.9, 156.7, 156.8, 454.7, 493.7, 505.4
insolidity 299.1, 971.6, 1047.1
in solitude 584.11
insolubility 1045.2
insoluble 522.18, 1045.13
in solution 1064.6
insolvability 522.6
insolvable 522.18
insolvency 619.1, 622.1, 625.3
insolvent (n) 623.4, 625.4 (a) 619.9, 623.8, 625.11, 729.19
insolvent debtor 625.4
insomnia 23.1, 85.9
insomniac (n) 23.1 (a) 23.7
insomnious 23.7
insomnolence 23.1
insomnolency 23.1
insouciance 94.4, 102.2, 340.2, 982.1
insouciant 94.13, 102.7, 340.11, 982.3
in spate 238.25, 993.20
inspect 27.14, 938.24
inspection 27.6, 339.4, 570.3, 938.3, 1041.7
inspectional 938.37
inspection of books 628.6
inspector 574.2, 938.17, 1008.15
inspectorial 938.37
inspect the books 628.9
inspiration 2.21, 187.5, 365.1, 375.1, 375.9, 492.8, 677.15, 683.10, 720.11, 886.4, 920.8, 932.6, 934.1, 986.2
inspirational 375.26
inspiratory 2.32
inspire 109.7, 124.9, 187.12, 375.13, 375.20, 492.15, 886.11
inspire belief 953.18
inspire confidence 953.18
inspired 375.31, 533.7, 683.11, 986.18
inspired leader 574.6
inspire hope 124.9
inspirer 375.10, 886.4
inspire respect 155.7
inspiring 109.16, 124.12, 375.26, 544.14
inspirit 109.7, 124.9, 306.10, 375.20, 492.15
inspirited 306.12
inspiriting (n) 492.8 (a) 109.16, 124.12, 375.26
inspiriting force 306.2
inspiritment 492.8
inspissate (v) 269.5, 1045.9, 1045.10, 1062.10 (a) 803.12, 1045.14
inspissated 1045.14, 1062.12
inspissation 803.1, 1045.3, 1045.4, 1062.2
instability 16.3, 362.1, 782.1, 828.1, 854.2, 971.6, 1006.2
install 159.11, 159.16, 191.4, 615.12, 818.11, 892.10
installation 159.6, 159.7, 187.2, 615.3, 698.10, 739.1, 739.3, 818.5, 892.4
installations 385.4
installed 159.18
installment 159.7, 187.2, 554.13, 615.3, 624.1, 793.1, 818.5
installment buying 621.1, 733.1
installment credit 622.1
installment mortgage 438.4
installment plan 621.1, 622.1, 622.2, 624.1
instance (n) 375.5, 439.2, 766.3, 786.2, 786.3, 957.5 (v) 766.6, 957.13
instant (n) 824.1, 828.3, 830.3 (a) 401.9, 405.19, 421.9, 830.4, 840.3, 845.9, 997.22
instantaneity 830.1
instantaneous 268.8, 830.4, 845.9
instantaneousness 174.1, 268.1, 830.1, 845.3
instant dislike 99.1
instant gratification 95.1, 663.1, 669.1, 830.1
instant message 552.4, 553.4
instant messaging 553.1
instant obsolescence 388.2
instant replay 1035.3
instate 191.4, 615.12
instatement 187.2, 615.3
instatutory 674.6
instauration 396.1
in step 836.6, 867.6
instep 199.5
instigate 375.17, 886.11
instigating 375.28
instigation 375.4
instigative 375.28
instigator 375.11, 886.4, 892.7
instill 568.12, 797.11, 989.17
instillation 568.2, 797.2
instilled 373.18
instillment 568.2, 797.2
instinct 93.1, 365.1, 413.4, 934.2, 944.1, 951.5, 963.5
instinct for 896.1
instinctive 311.39, 767.8, 934.6, 963.14
instinctiveness 963.5
instinctual 311.39, 767.8, 934.6
instinct with life 306.12
in stir 429.21
institute (n) 567.1, 617.8 (v) 818.11, 886.10, 892.10
institute an inquiry 938.20
institute legal proceedings against 598.13
institute of higher learning 567.5
institution 373.1, 617.8, 673.3, 698.10, 701.3, 739.1, 818.1, 892.4
institutional 567.13
institutionalization 429.4
institutionalize 429.17
institution of higher education 567.5
institutive 886.13
institutor 892.7
in stock 469.8
in storage 386.15
in store 405.21, 469.8, 840.3, 964.9
in straitened circumstances 210.7, 619.7
in strong relief 31.7, 348.12
instruct 420.8, 422.5, 551.8, 568.10
instructable 570.18
instructed 928.18
instruction 419.1, 420.3, 422.1, 551.1, 568.1, 568.7, 928.4
instructional 568.18
instructions 568.6
instructive 419.4, 420.13, 422.8, 551.18, 568.18
instructor 185.1, 405.5, 422.3, 571.1, 571.3
instructorship 571.10
instructress 571.2
instrument (n) 91.19, 138.3, 300.2, 384.4, 549.5, 576.3, 1040.1 (v) 708.46, 1040.13
instrumental (n) 530.9 (a) 384.8, 387.21, 449.20, 708.51
instrumental conditioning 92.26
instrumentalism 942.1, 1052.6
instrumentalist 710.3
instrumentality 384.3, 387.3

instrumental logic 935.2
instrumental musician 710.3
instrumental score 708.28
instrumentate 708.46
instrumentation 300.1, 709.2, 1040.11, 1074.1
instrument carrier 1074.6
instrument flight 184.1
instrument flight rules 184.1
instrument flying 184.1
instrument in proof 957.2
instrument landing 184.18
instrument landing system 184.19
instrument of music 711.1
instrument panel 1034.7
instrument rocket 1074.6
instruments 704.18
instruments of destruction 462.1
in style 578.11
in subjection 432.14
insubordinate (n) 327.5 (a) 327.9, 418.5
insubordination 327.1, 418.1, 418.2, 454.1
insubstantial 270.16, 298.10, 299.4, 764.5, 828.7, 936.12, 971.20, 998.17, 1029.4, 1053.7
insubstantial image 986.5
insubstantiality 270.4, 299.1, 764.1, 885.1, 971.6
insubstantialize 1053.6
insufferable 98.25
insufferableness 98.9
insufficiency 19.2, 108.2, 248.1, 250.3, 276.1, 791.1, 911.1, 992.1
insufficient 108.9, 250.7, 791.4, 911.5, 992.9
insufficient funds 625.3
insufficientness 992.1
insufflation 2.21
insular (n) 235.4 (a) 231.9, 235.7, 584.8, 773.9, 776.6, 802.20, 872.8, 980.10
insularism 980.1
insularity 235.2, 773.3, 980.1
insulate 15.14, 235.5, 773.6, 1032.29
insulated 235.7, 773.8
insulating 1032.36
insulation 773.3, 1008.3
insulation resistance 1032.13
insulator 1032.14
insult (n) 156.2, 157.1, 454.2, 508.2 (v) 156.5, 157.3, 508.8
insulting 142.9, 156.8, 157.8
in Sunday best 5.46
insuperability 15.4, 967.2
insuperable 15.19, 967.8
insupportable 98.25
insupportableness 98.9
insuppressibility 361.4
insuppressible 361.12
insurance 438.1, 494.3, 1008.4
insurance adjuster 1008.4
insurance agent 1008.4
insurance broker 730.9, 1008.4
insurance company 1008.4
insurance man 1008.4
insurance papers 549.5
insurance policy 1008.4
insure 438.9, 970.11, 1008.18
insured 438.11, 1007.4
insured mail 553.4
insuree 438.7
insurer 332.7, 438.6
insurge 327.7
insurgence 327.4, 453.1
insurgency 327.4
insurgent (n) 327.5 (a) 327.11, 418.5, 860.5
insurgentism 327.3
insurmountability 967.2
insurmountable 967.8
insurrect 327.7
insurrection 327.4, 453.1
insurrectionary (n) 327.5 (a) 327.11, 860.5
insurrectionism 327.3
insurrectionist 327.5
insurrecto 327.5
insusceptibility 94.1
insusceptible 94.9
insusceptible of change 855.17
in suspense 130.12, 173.14, 971.18, 971.25
in suspension 1064.6
in swaddling clothes 301.12
in sync 708.49, 788.9, 836.6, 899.4, 1035.16
in synchronization 1035.16
intact 293.10, 301.10, 397.13, 664.6, 792.10, 794.9, 798.7, 841.7, 853.7, 960.2, 1002.7, 1007.4
intactness 406.3, 664.3, 794.1, 798.1, 841.1, 872.1, 1002.2
intaglio 712.16, 713.8, 715.3, 786.6
intaglio printing 548.1
intaglio rilevato 715.3
intaglio rilievo 715.3
in tails 5.46
intake 189.1, 189.5, 627.1
intangibility 258.2, 764.1, 1053.1
intangible 258.14, 764.5, 1053.7
intangible assets 471.7
intangibles 471.7
in tatters 393.32
in tears 115.21
in Technicolor 35.17
integer 792.1, 872.4
integrable 797.16
integral 792.9, 796.5, 872.7, 872.10, 1002.7, 1017.23
integral humanism 312.11
integrality 794.1, 872.1
integral part 793.4
integrant (n) 793.4, 796.2 (a) 796.5, 872.10
integrate 264.3, 790.6, 792.7, 797.10, 805.3, 872.5
integrated 772.5, 792.9, 800.13, 805.5, 872.10
integrated circuit 1042.3
integrated online system 558.4
integrated personality 92.27
integrated system 1041.5
integration 264.2, 450.2, 788.4, 790.2, 792.1, 797.1, 805.1, 872.1, 1017.2
integration of personality 92.27
integrative power 920.1
integrity 416.1, 644.1, 653.1, 792.1, 794.1, 798.1, 865.1, 872.1, 1002.2
integument 2.4, 206.2, 295.3
integumental 295.32
integumentary 295.32
intel 551.1
intellect 919.1, 920.1, 920.9, 921.1, 929.1
intellection 919.1, 928.3, 931.1
intellectual (n) 920.9, 921.1, 928.11, 929.1 (a) 919.7, 920.12, 928.23, 932.9, 978.7
intellectual acquirement 570.1
intellectual acquisition 570.1
intellectual attainment 570.1
intellectual basis 932.4
intellectual breakthrough 932.5
intellectual childishness 798.3
intellectual climate 978.5
intellectual curiosity 100.1
intellectual elite 929.2
intellectual exercise 931.1
intellectual faculty 919.1
intellectual frame of reference 978.2
intellectual genius 413.12
intellectual gifts 919.2
intellectual grasp 920.1
intellectual immaturity 798.3
intellectual inertia 982.1
intellectualism 920.1, 928.5
intellectualist 929.1
intellectualistic 928.23
intellectuality 570.4, 920.1, 928.5
intellectualization 92.23, 931.1
intellectualize 931.8, 935.15
intellectually childish 798.10
intellectually immature 798.10
intellectual object 932.1
intellectual pleasure 95.1
intellectual power 920.1
intellectual prodigy 413.12
intellectual property 471.1
intellectuals 919.2
intellectual talents 919.2
intellectual weakness 922.1
intelligence 551.1, 552.1, 570.5, 576.12, 678.5, 919.1, 920.1, 920.9, 928.1, 928.3, 938.9, 957.1
intelligence agency 345.4, 938.9
intelligence agent 576.9
intelligence bureau 576.12
intelligence department 576.12
intelligence-gathering 938.9
intelligence officer 576.9
intelligence quotient 920.1
intelligence service 576.12
intelligence testing 92.8
intelligence work 938.9
intelligent 570.18, 919.7, 920.12, 928.15
intelligent, the 921.3
intelligent agent 1042.11, 1042.20
intelligent design 1068.3
intelligent retrieval 1042.20
intelligentsia 929.2
intelligibility 518.5, 521.1, 925.1, 1014.1
intelligible 518.10, 521.10
Intelsat 1035.9
intemperance 88.2, 430.3, 486.1, 665.2, 669.1, 672.1, 993.1
intemperate 430.24, 486.8, 665.24, 669.7, 671.16, 672.6, 993.16
intemperateness 100.8, 669.1, 993.1
in tempo 836.6
intend 130.9, 380.4, 381.8, 518.9, 964.7
intendance 573.2
intendancy 573.2, 573.4
intendant 574.1, 575.6
intended (n) 104.16 (a) 380.8, 436.8, 518.11
intendment 380.1
intense 15.22, 17.13, 24.13, 35.19, 93.18, 101.9, 247.6, 671.16, 983.15
intense cold 1023.1
intense darkness 1027.1
intense heat 1019.5
intense thought 931.3
intensification 119.1, 251.2
intensified 119.4, 251.7
intensify 26.7, 119.2, 251.5, 251.6
intensifying 251.8
intension 518.1
intensional 518.10
intensity 17.1, 35.4, 53.1, 53.2, 101.2, 247.1, 671.1, 1025.21
intensity-modulated display 1036.11
intensive (n) 530.2 (a) 725.18, 794.10
intensive care 197.25
intensive care unit 197.25
intensive farming 1069.1
intent (n) 380.1, 518.2 (a) 101.9, 983.15, 983.17
intention 323.1, 375.1, 380.1, 381.1, 436.3, 518.2
intentional 323.4, 380.8
intentional fallacy 356.1
intentionality 380.3
intentional pass 745.3
intentive 983.15
intentiveness 983.1
intentness 101.2, 983.1, 983.3
intent on 101.9, 983.17
intent upon 359.16
inter 309.19
interact 582.17, 777.6
interacting 343.9, 777.9
interaction 343.1, 777.3
interactional 343.9
interactive (n) 1042.18 (a) 343.9, 777.9
interactive fiction 722.1
interactive system 1042.16
interaffiliate 800.6
interaffiliated 777.8
interaffiliation 777.2, 800.2
interagency 466.1
interagent 384.4, 466.3, 576.4
interalliance 777.2
interallied 777.8

interally 777.5
interassociate 777.5, 800.6
interassociated 777.8
interassociation 777.2, 800.2
interblend 797.10, 805.3
interbred 797.15
interbreed 797.13
interbreeding 797.4
intercalary 213.9, 832.15
intercalary year 824.2
intercalate 191.3, 213.6, 832.14, 1060.8
intercalated 832.15
intercalation 191.1, 213.2
intercede 466.6
interceder 466.3
intercept 48.10, 1012.10
interception 746.3, 1036.9
intercession 466.1, 677.14
intercessional 466.8, 677.16
intercession prayer 696.4
intercessive 677.16
intercessor 466.3, 597.1
Intercessor, the 677.12
intercessory 466.8
intercessory prayer 696.4
interchange (n) 170.2, 343.1, 383.3, 506.1, 731.2, 777.3, 863.1 (v) 343.6, 455.2, 731.15, 777.6, 863.4
interchangeability 863.3
interchangeable 176.18, 863.5, 945.6
interchanged 777.8, 863.5
interchange of speech 541.1
interchange of views 541.5
intercollegiate 567.13
intercom 50.11, 347.6
intercommunicate 343.6, 800.11
intercommunicating 800.16
intercommunication 343.1, 582.4, 777.3, 800.1
intercommunicational 343.9
intercommunication system 50.11, 347.6
intercommunicative 343.9
intercommunion 343.1, 476.2, 582.4
intercommunional 343.9
interconnect 740.6, 775.6, 777.5, 800.6
interconnected 777.8
interconnection 777.2, 800.2
intercosmic 1073.25
intercosmic space 1073.3
intercouple 777.5
intercoupled 777.8
intercoupling 777.2
intercourse 75.7, 343.1, 541.1, 582.4, 731.1, 775.1, 777.3, 800.1
intercross 170.6
intercrossing 170.1, 170.2
intercurrence 213.1
intercurrent 213.10
interdenominational 675.27
interdepend 777.5
interdependence 777.2
interdependency 777.2
interdependent 777.8
interdict (n) 420.6, 428.1, 444.1 (v) 444.3
interdiction 420.6, 444.1
interdictive 444.6
interdictory 444.6
interdictum 444.1
interdigitate 777.5, 800.6
interdigitation 777.2, 800.2
interdisciplinary 568.19, 864.13
interdisciplinary knowledge 928.6
interest (n) 375.7, 377.1, 387.4, 404.1, 449.4, 471.4, 472.3, 477.5, 617.4, 620.1, 623.3, 627.1, 642.1, 650.3, 651.1, 724.1, 738.7, 775.4, 831.3, 886.9, 894.2, 935.14, 981.1, 983.2, 997.1, 999.4 (v) 377.6, 775.5, 898.2, 983.12
interested 617.19, 650.11, 898.4, 980.12, 981.5, 983.16
interestedness 981.1
interest group 609.31, 617.4
interest-group politics 609.1
interest in 375.22
interesting 377.8, 983.19
interest lottery 759.14
interest oneself 898.3
interest payment 624.1
interest politics 609.1
interest rate 620.1, 623.3
interests 997.8
interests, the 575.14
interface (n) 211.3, 467.3, 800.2, 800.4, 1042.18 (v) 296.5, 777.5, 800.6, 800.11
interfacing 223.17
interfaith marriage 563.1
interfere 214.5, 1012.10
interference 50.13, 57.1, 214.1, 900.1, 916.4, 1012.1, 1034.21
interfere with 900.6
interfering 214.8
interferon 86.27
interfold 291.5
interfoliate 213.6
interfoliation 213.1
interfuse 213.7, 805.3
interfusion 213.3, 797.1
intergalactic 158.10, 1073.25
intergalactic distance 261.1
intergalactic matter 1075.10
intergalactic space 158.1, 1073.3
interim (n) 224.1, 813.2, 826.1, 846.2, 857.3 (a) 826.4
interim certificate 738.4
interim dividend 738.7
interior (n) 207.2, 207.3, 712.11, 819.1 (a) 207.6, 207.7, 345.13, 819.4
interior decorating 498.1
interior decoration 498.1
interior decorator 716.11
interior design 498.1, 712.16, 717.5
interior designer 716.11
interiority 207.1, 275.1
interior man 207.2
interior monologue 542.1, 722.6
interior paint 35.8
interjacence 213.1
interjacent 213.10
interjaculate 213.6
interject 191.3, 213.6, 524.24
interjection 191.1, 213.2, 214.1, 524.3, 530.3
interjectional 213.9
interjoin 777.5, 800.6
interjoinder 800.2
interknit (v) 740.6 (a) 740.7
interknitting 740.1
interlace 740.6, 777.6, 797.10
interlaced 170.12, 740.7
interlaced scanning 1035.3
interlacement 170.3, 740.1
interlacer 740.4
interlacery 740.1
interlacing (n) 740.1, 777.3 (a) 740.8
interlanguage 523.11
interlard 213.7, 797.10
interlarding 797.1
interlardment 213.3, 797.1
interleaf 213.6
interleave 797.10
interleaving 213.1
interlibrary loan 558.1
interline 196.7
interlinear 341.3
interlinear translation 341.3
interlineate 196.7
interlineation 196.3, 213.2, 254.2
interlining 196.3
interlink 777.5, 800.6
interlinkage 777.2
interlinked 775.9, 777.8
interlinking 777.2, 800.2
interlocation 213.1
interlock (n) 1008.3 (v) 777.5, 788.6, 800.6
interlocked 775.9, 777.8
interlocking 777.2, 800.2
interlocking directorate 574.11
interlocking grip 751.3
interlocution 213.2, 541.1, 541.2
interlocutor 541.7, 938.16
interlocutory 466.8, 541.12
interlocutory decree 566.1
interlocutress 541.7
interlocutrice 541.7
interlocutrix 541.7
interlope 214.5
interloper 214.3, 774.2
interloping 214.1
interlude (n) 20.2, 704.7, 708.24, 826.1, 857.3 (v) 826.3
intermarriage 563.1, 797.4
intermarry 563.15
intermeddle 214.7, 1012.10
intermeddler 214.4
intermeddling 214.2
intermediacy 213.1
intermedial 466.8
intermediary (n) 213.4, 384.4, 466.3, 576.4 (a) 213.10, 246.3, 384.8, 466.8, 819.4
intermediate (n) 384.4, 466.3, 576.4, 1040.9 (v) 466.6 (a) 213.10, 246.3, 466.8, 819.4
intermediate agent 466.3
intermediate frequency 1034.12
intermediate-frequency 1034.15
intermediate-frequency pulse 1036.10
intermediate-frequency signal 1036.11
intermediate pile 1038.13
intermediate school 567.4
intermediate schooler 572.3
intermediate slope 753.1
intermediate space 224.1
intermediate trainer 181.10
intermediation 384.3, 466.1
intermediator 466.3
intermediatory 466.8
intermedium 213.4, 384.4, 466.3, 576.4
interment 309.1, 346.1
intermesh 777.6
intermeshing 777.3
intermezzo 704.7, 708.24, 826.1, 857.3
intermigrate 177.22
intermigration 177.4
interminability 823.1, 829.1
interminable 267.7, 812.8, 823.3, 827.11, 829.7
interminate 823.3
intermingle 797.10
interminglement 797.1
intermingling 797.1
intermission 20.2, 120.2, 158.8, 224.1, 704.7, 746.3, 813.2, 826.1, 857.3
intermit 120.6, 813.3, 850.5, 851.2, 857.10
intermittence 813.1, 850.2, 851.1, 857.3
intermittency 850.2
intermittent 813.4, 850.7, 851.3
intermittent rain 316.1
intermittent showers 316.1
intermitting 851.3
intermix 797.10
intermixture 797.1, 797.5
intermutation 863.1
intern (n) 90.4, 207.2, 571.4 (v) 90.14, 429.14
internal (n) 207.2 (a) 90.15, 207.6, 767.7, 819.4, 919.7
internal clock 306.2
internal combustion 1043.3
internal fertilization 78.3
internal friction 1044.1
internal frustration 92.17
internal gear 1040.9
internality 207.1, 767.1
internalization 207.1
internalize 187.13, 207.5
internal medicine 90.13
internalness 207.1
internal organs 2.16
internal reality 767.1, 767.5
internal revenue agent 630.10
Internal Revenue Service 630.10
internal rhyme 720.9
internals 2.16, 207.4
internal secretion 13.1
internal struggle 457.4
international 312.16, 864.14
international agreement 437.2
international airspace 184.32
international alphabet flag 517.15

International Amateur Boxing Association 754.1
International Athletic Federation 755.1
international banker 729.9
international banking 729.1
International Boxing Federation 754.1
International Court of Justice 614.2
International Criminal Police Commission 1008.17
International Date Line 832.4
International Federation of Women's Hockey Associations 749.4
international fixed calendar 832.8
International Freestyle Skiers Association 753.1
international government 612.1
International Hockey Board 749.4
International Ice Hockey Federation 749.1
internationalism 232.6, 609.5, 864.1, 952.7
internationality 232.6
internationalization 864.1
internationalize 864.9
international language 523.11
international law 673.5
International Monetary Fund 729.14
international numeral pennant 517.15
international organization 614.3
International Phonetic Alphabet 546.3
international pitch 709.4
international relations 609.2
International scale 318.15
International Standard Book Number 517.13
International Tennis Federation 748.1
international water 240.1
internecine 308.23, 395.26
internecine combat 457.4
internecine struggle 457.4
internecive 395.26
interned 429.21
internee 429.11
Internet 347.18, 1042.16
Internet cafe 552.1, 1042.19
Internet forum 552.1
Internet of things 1042.19
Internet radio 1034.6
Internet service provider 1042.19
Internet startup 739.1
Internet television 1035.1
internetworked 777.8
internment 429.3
internment camp 429.8
internuncial neuron 2.14
internuncio 466.3, 576.4, 576.6
interpellant 938.37
interpellate 938.20
interpellation 938.1, 938.12
interpellator 938.16
interpenetrate 189.8, 213.7
interpenetrating 775.9
interpenetration 189.1, 213.3, 797.2
interpersonal communication 343.1
interphase 305.16
Interphone 347.6
interplanetary 1073.25
interplanetary explorer 1075.6
interplanetary monitoring satellite 1075.6
interplanetary rocket 1075.2
interplanetary space 158.1, 1073.3
interplanetary travel 1075.1
interplay (n) 343.1, 777.3, 863.1 (v) 777.6
interplaying 777.9
interpleader 576.4
Interpol 1008.17
interpolate 213.6
interpolation 191.1, 213.2, 254.2, 708.27, 1017.2
interpolative 213.9
interposal 213.1, 214.1
interpose 213.6, 214.5, 466.6
interposing 213.1
interposition 213.1, 214.1, 466.1
interpret 341.9, 708.39, 723.5, 940.2
interpretability 341.6, 518.5, 521.1
interpretable 341.17, 518.10, 521.10
interpretableness 341.6
interpretation 341.1, 518.3, 704.8, 940.1
interpretational 341.14
interpretation of dreams 92.6
interpretative 341.14, 556.6
interpreted 704.33
interpreter 341.7, 710.1, 723.4, 1042.13
interpretive 341.14, 556.6, 723.6
interpret the part 704.32
interracial marriage 563.1
interregnum 418.1, 612.4, 826.1
interrelate 775.6, 777.5
interrelated 775.9, 777.8
interrelation 775.2, 777.2
interrelationship 777.2
interresponsive 343.9
interrogate 343.8, 938.21, 981.3
interrogation 541.2, 938.10, 938.12
interrogational 938.36
interrogative (n) 938.10 (a) 343.9, 938.36
interrogator 541.7, 938.16
interrogatory (n) 938.10 (a) 343.9, 938.36
interrogatrix 938.16
interrupt 214.6, 813.3, 844.4, 857.10, 1012.10
interrupted 813.4
interrupted cadence 709.23
interrupter 347.2
interrupting 1012.17
interruption 158.8, 214.1, 224.1, 813.2, 826.1, 844.1, 857.3, 1012.1
interruptive 214.8, 1012.17
interscholastic 567.13
intersect 169.2, 170.6, 788.6
intersected 170.8
intersecting (n) 170.1 (a) 169.3, 170.8
intersection 170.1, 170.2, 383.3, 788.1
intersectional 170.8
intersection of minds 788.3
interseptum 213.5
intersession course 568.8
intersex 75.17
intersexualism 75.12
intersexuality 75.12
intersidereal 1073.25
intersow 213.7
interspace (n) 224.1 (v) 224.3
interspaced 224.6
interspacial 224.6
interspatial 224.5
intersperse 213.7, 797.10
interspersion 213.3
intersprinkle 213.7
interstellar 158.10, 1073.25
interstellar cloud 1073.7
interstellar distance 261.1
interstellar medium 1073.3
interstellar space 158.1, 1073.3
interstice 224.1
interstitial 224.5, 224.6
intertexture 170.3, 294.1, 740.1
interthread 740.6
interthreaded 740.7
interthreading 740.1
intertidal zone 238.13, 240.4
intertie 740.6, 777.5, 800.6
intertied 740.7, 777.8
intertieing 740.1
intertissue 740.6
intertissued 740.7
intertropical convergence zone 318.9
intertwine 740.6, 777.6, 797.10
intertwined 170.12, 740.7
intertwinement 170.3, 740.1
intertwining (n) 740.1, 777.3 (a) 740.8
intertwist 740.6
intertwisted 740.7
intertwisting 740.1
interurban 230.11
interval (n) 158.8, 224.1, 245.1, 292.1, 709.12, 709.17, 709.20, 795.2, 813.2, 824.1, 826.1, 826.1, 857.3 (v) 826.3
intervale 284.9
intervaled 224.6
intervallary 224.5
intervallic 224.5
interval training 84.2
intervene 213.6, 214.5, 466.6, 826.3, 1012.10
intervener 466.3
intervenience 213.1
intervenient 213.10, 214.8
intervening 213.10, 466.8
intervening sequence 305.9
intervening space 158.8, 224.1
intervenor 466.3
intervention 213.1, 214.1, 449.2, 466.1
interventional 466.8
interventionism 214.1, 466.1
interventionist 466.3
interview (n) 48.2, 541.2, 541.5, 552.3, 582.8, 938.11 (v) 938.21
interviewee 551.5, 938.19
interviewer 541.7, 555.4, 938.16
interview show 1034.18
interweave 740.6, 777.6, 797.10
interweavement 740.1
interweaving (n) 740.1, 777.3 (a) 740.8
interwed 563.15
interwork 777.6
interworking (n) 777.3 (a) 777.9
interwoven 170.12, 740.7
intestate 478.25
intestinal digestion 2.17, 7.8
intestinal fortitude 15.1, 492.3
intestinal juice 2.17, 7.8, 13.2
intestine (n) 2.18 (a) 207.6
intestines 2.18
intestine struggle 457.4
in the absence of 992.13
in the air 552.15
in the altogether 6.14
in the arms of Morpheus 22.22
in the ascendant 193.14, 249.12, 411.7, 612.17, 894.14
in the bag 965.8, 970.20
in the balance 971.18
in the best taste 496.7
in the big house 428.15, 429.21
in the blood 767.8
in the bloom of youth 301.9
in the bosom of the lodge 345.14
in the bud 305.22, 818.15
in the buff 6.14
in the cards 130.13, 840.3, 964.9, 968.6
in the chips 618.15
in the clear 430.21, 521.12, 657.6, 1007.6
in the clouds 985.11, 986.24
in the cold 340.14
in the cooler 429.21
in the cradle 301.12
in the crib 301.12
in the dark 930.15
in the depths 112.22
in the doghouse 661.13
in the doldrums 112.22
in the doleful dumps 112.22
in the driver's seat 573.13, 894.14
in the dumps 112.22
in the dust 137.13, 696.16
in the face of death 307.32
in the family way 78.18
in the field 458.22
in the fire 404.7
in the flesh 306.12
in the flower of youth 301.9
in the foreground 348.12
in the fresh air 72.5
in the gaseous state 1067.9
in the grand style 712.20
in the grave 307.29
in the gravy 618.15
in the gut 24.4
in the gutter 619.9, 654.14

in the habit of 373.17
in the hands of receivers 625.11
in the hole 623.8
in the hopper 404.7, 405.22
in the hot seat 1006.13
in the humor 324.5, 978.8
in the jaws of death 307.32
in the know 928.16, 928.17
in the land of Nod 22.22
in the land of the living 306.12
in the lap of Morpheus 22.22
in the life 665.28
in the limelight 662.17
in the making 405.22
in the market 733.10
in the market for 938.38
in the melting mood 115.21
in the mode 578.12
in the money 618.15, 757.6
in the mood 324.5, 978.8
in the neighborhood 223.16
in the news 552.15
in the nick of time 995.5
in the nursery 301.12
in the offing 840.3
in the oven 405.22
in the picture 928.18
in the pink 83.9, 807.7
in the pink of condition 83.8, 807.7
in the pipe 889.11
in the pipeline 381.12, 404.7, 405.22, 889.11
in the plenitude of power 15.21
in the raw 6.14, 406.13
in the red 619.9, 623.8, 625.10
in the right 637.3
in the right church but the wrong pew 160.11, 975.18
in the rough 406.12
in the saddle 405.16
in the same boat 790.7
in the same category 775.9
in the secret 928.16
in the sewer 654.14
in the shade 250.6
in the shadow of a rock 1007.6
in the soup 1013.22
in the state of nature 416.6
in the swim 578.11
in the train of 577.14
in the very grain 767.7
in the vicinity 223.16
in the way 1012.17
in the wind 831.9, 840.3
in the wings 346.11, 346.14
in the womb of time 840.3
in the works 381.12, 404.7, 405.22, 889.11
in the wrong 656.3
in the wrong box 160.11, 975.18
in the wrong pew 160.11
in the wrong place 160.11
in thing, the 578.4, 841.2
in thrall 432.14
intifada 327.4
intimacy 75.7, 104.1, 223.1, 582.1, 587.5, 775.1, 928.1
intimate (n) 588.1 (v) 422.5, 519.4, 551.10 (a) 207.6, 223.14, 228.33, 345.13, 582.24, 587.19, 800.13, 865.12
intimate acquaintance 587.5
intimate apparel 5.22
intimated 519.7
intimate discourse 541.3
intimate distance 223.2
intimate friend 588.1
intimate friendship 587.8
intimately related 559.6
intimate places 207.2
intimate with 928.19
intimation 248.4, 422.2, 517.9, 519.2, 551.4, 797.7, 934.3, 951.5
in time 836.6
intimidate 127.20, 379.3, 424.7, 503.3, 514.2, 612.15
intimidated 127.26, 491.10
intimidating 379.5, 514.3
intimidation 127.6, 379.1, 424.3, 503.1, 514.1
intinction 701.7
into 928.17
intolerability 98.9, 108.2
intolerable 26.10, 98.25, 99.7, 108.10, 247.12
intolerableness 98.9
intolerance 93.7, 135.2, 361.1, 589.3, 980.2
intolerant (n) 980.5 (a) 135.7, 361.8, 980.11
intoleration 135.2, 980.2
intonate 524.28, 708.38
intonated 524.30
intonation 50.2, 524.6, 708.13, 708.30, 709.2
intonation contour 524.6
intonation of foice 524.6
intonation pattern 524.6
intone 708.38
intorsion 281.1
intort 281.4, 740.6
into the past 837.12
in touch with reality 925.4
intoxicant 88.13
intoxicate 88.22, 105.15, 985.8
intoxicated 87.23, 88.31, 93.18, 105.25
intoxicating 88.36, 105.30
intoxicating liquor 88.13
intoxication 85.31, 88.1, 95.2, 105.8
intoxicative 88.36
intracardiac 91.17
intracoastal 207.8
intractability 327.1, 361.4, 1046.3
intractable 327.9, 361.12, 1046.12
intractableness 325.1
intractile 1046.12
intradermal 91.17
intrados 207.2
intragroupal 207.8
in training 414.17
intramarginal 207.8
intramedullary 91.17
intramontane 207.8
intramundane 207.8
intramural 207.8, 567.13, 568.19
intramuscular 91.17
intranet 1042.16, 1042.19
intransient 827.10
intransigence 361.2
intransigency 361.2
intransigent (n) 361.6, 452.3 (a) 361.9, 1046.12
intransigentism 361.2
intransitive (n) 530.4 (a) 530.17
intransitive verb 530.4
intransmutability 855.4
intransmutable 855.17
intransparency 1031.1
intransparent 1031.3
intrapreneur 381.6, 730.1
intrariverine channel 239.2
intraspinal 91.17
intraterritorial 207.8
intrathecal 91.17
intrauterine device 86.23
intravenous 91.17
intrepid 492.16
intrepidity 492.1
intrepidness 492.1
intricacy 281.2, 522.2, 799.1, 1013.1
intricate 522.14, 797.14, 799.4, 971.27, 1013.17
intricateness 799.1
intrigue (n) 104.5, 345.4, 381.5, 415.3, 645.3 (v) 377.7, 381.9, 415.10
intrigued 95.15
intriguer 357.10, 381.7, 415.7
intrigues 894.3
intriguing 97.7, 377.8, 381.13
in trim 180.19, 807.7
intrinsic 207.6, 221.12, 767.7, 865.13
intrinsicality 207.1, 767.1
intrinsic reality 767.5
intrinsic truth 974.2
intrinsic truth, the 973.3
introceptive 187.16
introduce 187.14, 191.3, 439.5, 568.14, 587.14, 814.3, 816.3, 818.11, 852.9
introduce in 213.6
introduce new blood 852.9
introducer 852.5, 892.7
introduction 187.7, 189.1, 191.1, 213.2, 554.12, 568.5, 587.4, 613.6, 704.7, 708.26, 793.2, 816.2, 818.5, 818.6, 852.4
introductive 187.18
introductory 187.18, 568.18, 818.15
introductory phrase 708.24
introductory study 556.1
Introit 696.3
introit 708.17
intromission 187.2, 191.1
intromissive 187.16
intromit 187.10, 191.3
intromittent 187.16
intron 305.9
intronizing 305.9
introspect 207.5, 931.12, 938.20
introspection 931.6
introspective 931.21, 931.22
in trouble 661.13, 1013.21
introversion 92.11, 205.1, 207.1, 344.3
introversive 92.40
introvert (n) 92.12 (v) 205.5, 207.5 (a) 92.40
introverted 92.40, 205.7, 344.10
introvertedness 92.11
intrude 189.7, 213.6, 214.5, 844.4, 910.9
intruder 189.4, 214.3, 774.2, 774.4
intrusion 189.1, 213.1, 214.1, 774.1, 844.1, 910.3
intrusive 189.12, 214.8, 330.24, 774.5, 844.6
intrusiveness 214.2
intrusive rock 1059.1
in trust 438.13
intuit 93.10, 934.4, 961.6
intuitable 961.8
intuition 93.1, 689.8, 920.4, 934.1, 934.3, 944.1, 951.5
intuitional 934.5
intuitionism 636.2, 934.1
intuitive 133.15, 934.5, 951.13, 961.7
intuitive impression 934.3
intuitive knowledge 934.1
intuitiveness 934.1
intuitive reason 934.1
intuitive understanding 934.1
intuitivism 934.1
intumescence 85.39, 259.2, 283.4
in tune 455.3, 708.49
intussuscept 205.5
intussusception 205.1
in two 802.20
inunction 1056.3, 1056.6
inunctum 1056.3
inundate 112.19, 238.17, 367.7, 395.21, 459.20, 910.7, 993.14, 1065.14
inundated 112.29, 238.25, 275.14, 910.10, 1065.17
inundation 238.6, 367.2, 538.2, 910.1, 991.2, 993.2, 1065.6
in unison 708.49
inurbane 233.7, 505.4
inurbanity 233.3, 505.1
inure 94.6, 373.9
inured 94.12, 373.15, 654.17
inuredness 94.3
inurement 373.7
inurn 309.19
inurning 309.1
inurnment 309.1
in use 387.25
inusitation 390.1
inutile 19.15
inutility 19.3, 391.1
invade 214.5, 459.20, 640.8, 910.6, 910.9
invader 214.3, 459.12
invading 459.29
invaginate 205.5
invaginated 205.7
invagination 205.1
invalid (n) 19.6, 85.43, 584.5 (v) 85.50 (a) 19.15, 85.54, 445.3, 936.11, 936.13, 1000.7
invalidate 19.11, 395.13, 445.2, 900.7, 958.4
invalidated 19.16, 958.7

invalidating 900.9
invalidation 445.1, 900.2, 958.1
invalid claim 640.1
invalided 85.59
invalidism 16.1, 16.3, 19.4, 85.3
invalidity 19.3, 85.3, 762.1, 936.2, 1000.1
invalid linking 776.2
invalid title 640.1
invaluable 632.10
invaluableness 632.2
invariability 118.1, 781.2, 853.1, 855.1
invariable 118.9, 781.5, 855.17
invariableness 853.1
invasion 214.1, 459.4, 640.3, 910.2
invasionary 459.29
invasive 189.12, 214.8, 459.29
invective (n) 508.5, 510.7, 513.2, 543.2 (a) 510.22
inveigh against 510.13
inveighing 510.22
inveigle 356.20, 377.5
inveiglement 377.1, 511.1
inveigler 377.4
invent 337.4, 354.18, 365.8, 818.10, 841.5, 852.9, 892.12, 931.16, 941.2, 986.14
invented 354.29, 892.19
invention 337.2, 354.10, 852.4, 892.1, 893.1, 941.1, 986.3, 986.5
inventive 415.12, 818.15, 892.16, 986.18
inventiveness 337.1, 415.1, 986.3
inventor 886.4, 892.7, 986.12
inventorial 871.9
inventoried 871.9
inventory (n) 196.1, 384.2, 386.1, 549.1, 628.4, 735.1, 770.1, 808.4, 871.1, 1017.11 (v) 628.9, 871.8, 1017.19, 1017.21
inventory-clearance sale 734.3
inventorying 549.14, 1017.9
inveracity 354.1, 645.3
inverse (n) 205.4, 215.3, 1017.12 (v) 205.5 (a) 215.5, 779.6
inverse, the 779.2
inversed 205.7
inverse peak voltage 1033.7
inverse proportion 777.1
inverse ratio 777.1
inverse relationship 777.1
inversion 163.3, 205.1, 1017.2
invert (n) 75.14 (v) 205.5, 779.5, 1060.8
invertebracy 362.4
invertebral 311.50
invertebrate (n) 16.6, 311.3, 311.31, 491.5 (a) 311.50, 362.12
inverted 205.7
inverted flight 184.9
inverted mordent 708.27, 709.18
inverted normal loop 184.16
inverted order 205.1
inverted outside loop 184.16
inverted spin 184.15
inverted sugar 66.3
inverted turn 709.18
invert sugar 66.3
invest 5.39, 18.10, 159.16, 191.4, 209.6, 295.20, 385.7, 459.19, 478.17, 615.10, 615.12, 626.5, 729.17
invested 5.45, 385.13, 478.26
invested authority 417.1
invested with authority 417.15
investigate 541.11, 938.23, 981.3
investigation 541.6, 938.4
investigational 938.37
investigation into first causes 952.1
investigation of the past, the 719.1
investigative 938.37
investigative agency 938.4
investigative bureau 938.4
investigative journalism 552.1
investigative journalist 555.4
investigative reporter 555.4
investigative reporting 547.2
investigator 576.10, 938.17, 942.6
investigatory 938.37
invest in 729.17
investing 615.1
investiture 5.1, 5.10, 159.7, 187.2, 187.7, 478.1, 615.1, 615.3, 698.10
investment 5.1, 18.8, 385.1, 459.5, 478.9, 615.1, 729.4
investment banker 729.11
investment banking 729.1, 729.5
investment company 737.16
investment credit 622.1
investment manager 628.7
investment portfolio 738.2
investment securities 738.1
investment trust 737.16
investor 729.9
investors on the sidelines 737.3
invest with power 18.10
inveteracy 373.6, 853.1, 855.2
inveterate 373.18, 827.10, 842.12, 855.13
inveterateness 373.6
invidia 154.1
invidious 144.20, 153.5, 154.3
invidiousness 144.5, 154.1
in view 31.6, 130.13, 221.12, 840.3
invigilation 339.4
invigorate 9.2, 15.13, 17.10, 105.13, 109.7, 306.10
invigorated 9.4
invigorating 9.3, 17.15, 81.5, 86.44, 109.16, 1023.12
invigoration 9.1, 15.5, 17.8
invigorative 17.15
invincibility 15.4, 18.3, 855.5, 970.4
invincible 15.19, 249.15, 360.8, 855.18, 970.17
inviolability 15.4, 644.6, 685.1, 872.1
inviolable 15.19, 644.19, 685.7
inviolableness 685.1
inviolate 644.13, 685.7, 853.7, 1002.8
invisibility 32.1, 258.2, 346.1, 522.4
invisible 32.5, 258.14, 346.12
invisible, the 32.1
invisible helper 678.12
invisible ink 345.6
invisible light 1025.1
invisible radiation 1025.5
invitation 375.7, 377.1, 439.1, 440.4
invitational 440.19
invitation to combat 454.2
invitatory 187.16, 440.19
invite (n) 440.4 (v) 375.21, 377.6, 440.13, 897.4, 983.12
invite attention 983.11
invited guest 585.6
invitee 585.6
invite ridicule 923.6
inviting 97.7, 187.16, 375.27, 377.8, 440.19, 983.19
invitingness 97.2, 187.9
in vitro 78.3
in vitro fertilization 78.3
invocation 420.5, 440.2, 690.4, 691.4, 696.4, 696.5
invocatory plea 440.2
invocatory prayer 440.2
in vogue 578.11
invoice (n) 628.3, 871.5 (v) 628.11
invoke 420.11, 440.11, 524.26, 690.11, 696.13, 957.12, 957.14
invoke benefits upon 696.14
involucre 310.19, 310.28
involucrum 310.19
involuntariness 365.4, 963.5
involuntary 325.5, 365.11, 424.11, 934.6, 963.14, 972.17
involuntary cooperation 898.1
involuntary impulse 365.1
involuntary muscle 2.3
involuntary presence 898.1
involuntary servitude 432.1
involute (n) 281.2 (a) 281.6
involuted 281.6, 799.4
involution 281.1, 393.3, 799.1, 898.1, 1017.2
involutional 281.6
involutional melancholia 926.5
involutional psychosis 926.5
involve 209.6, 517.17, 519.4, 545.7, 599.10, 772.4, 775.5, 799.3, 898.2, 957.8, 983.13, 1012.11, 1013.15
involved 330.21, 476.8, 519.7, 599.15, 623.8, 650.11, 656.3, 772.5, 775.9, 799.4, 898.4, 983.17
involved in 898.5
involved in debt 623.8
involve in 983.12
involvement 93.5, 104.5, 209.5, 466.1, 476.1, 599.2, 650.3, 656.1, 772.2, 799.1, 898.1, 983.3
involve oneself 466.6, 476.5
involve the interest 983.13
involve with 983.12
involving 775.11
invulnerability 15.4, 855.5, 895.2, 1007.1
invulnerable 15.19, 855.18, 895.4, 1007.5, 1008.21
in want 619.8
in want of 992.13
inward (n) 207.2 (a) 189.12, 207.6, 345.13, 767.7
inward-bound 189.12
inwardbound 186.9
inward monitor 636.5
inwardness 207.1, 767.1
inwards 2.16, 207.4
inweave 740.6
in white tie and tails 5.46
in with 587.18, 805.6
in-word 526.9
in working order 807.7, 889.9
in writing 547.22
inwrought 767.7, 855.13
iodine 7.11
I of the story, the 722.5
ion 258.8, 1032.25, 1038.4, 1060.2
ion engine 1074.2
Ionian Basin 275.5
Ionian mode 709.10
Ionic 198.6, 717.2
ionic (n) 720.8 (a) 1032.32
ionic conduction 1032.14
ionization 1032.25, 1038.8
ionization chamber 1037.7
ionization potential 1033.7
ionize 1032.28, 1060.8
ionizing event 1037.7
ionizing radiation 1037.1
ionogen 1032.25
ionogenic 1032.32
iota 248.2, 258.7
IOU 438.3, 728.11
IP address 1042.19
iPhone 347.4
iPod 50.11
ipse dixit 334.1, 420.4
ipseity 865.1
ipso facto 963.15
IQ meter 92.8
irascibility 105.10, 110.2, 361.3, 456.3
irascible 24.12, 105.28, 110.19, 361.11, 361.12, 456.17
irate 152.28
irateness 152.5
ire 152.5
ireful 152.28
irenic 464.10, 465.12
irenicism 464.4
irenics 465.1, 670.1
iridal 47.10
iridesce 47.8, 1025.26
iridescence 47.2, 854.4, 1025.18
iridescent 35.22, 47.10, 1025.37
iridial 47.10
iridian 47.10
iridiated 47.10
iridine 47.10
iridization 47.2
Iris 353.1
iris 2.9, 27.9, 47.6
irisated 47.10
irisation 47.2
irised 47.10
Irish 152.6
Irish bull 975.7

Irish confetti 462.18
Irish dividend 738.8
Irish Guards 461.15
Irishism 523.8
Irish pipes 711.9
Irish potato 10.35
Irish shamrock 647.6
Irish stew 10.11
Irish wake 309.4
iris recognition 549.10
irk (n) 118.1 (v) 96.13, 98.15, 118.6, 1013.13
irked 96.21, 118.11, 1013.20
irking 98.22
irksome 98.22, 118.10, 1013.18
irksomeness 98.7, 118.1, 118.2
iron (n) 7.11, 15.8, 39.1, 86.8, 179.8, 287.4, 747.1, 1046.6 (v) 277.5, 287.6, 1044.6 (a) 361.9, 425.7, 1058.17
Iron Age 824.5
Iron Age man 842.7
iron boot 612.9
ironbound 288.7, 425.7, 428.16
ironbound coast 234.2
ironbound security 345.3
ironclad 425.7, 460.13
ironclad agreement 437.1
ironclad hand 759.10
ironclad oath 334.4
ironclad proof 957.3
ironclad reasoning 935.10
iron crow 906.4
iron curtain 211.5, 345.3, 611.5, 1012.5
iron-curtain country 232.1
iron duke 759.10
iron entering the soul, the 96.9
iron-gray 39.4
iron grip 474.2
iron hand 417.5, 425.3, 428.4, 612.2, 612.9
ironhanded 425.7
iron-hard 15.15, 1046.10
ironhearted 492.16
iron heel 605.4, 612.9
ironic 489.15, 508.13, 519.6, 539.4, 779.8, 797.14
ironical 489.15, 508.13
ironic implication 519.2
ironic juxtaposition 215.1
ironic suggestion 519.2
ironist 489.12
ironize 539.3
ironlike 1046.10, 1058.17
iron maiden, the 96.7
Iron Maiden of Nuremberg 605.4
iron man 728.7
ironmongery 735.4
iron-nerved 129.2
iron nerves 129.1
iron out 465.8, 940.2
iron-pumping 744.1
iron rations 462.13
iron-red 41.6
iron rule 428.4
irons 428.4
irons in the fire 724.2
ironware 735.4
iron will 359.4, 855.1
iron-willed 855.12
irony 489.1, 508.5, 539.1, 779.3, 873.1
irradiance 1025.1
irradiancy 1025.1
irradiate (v) 91.26, 397.9, 1025.28, 1037.10 (a) 1025.39
irradiated 1025.39, 1037.11
irradiation 397.2, 1025.1
irradiative 1025.30
irrational 922.13, 923.10, 926.26, 926.32, 936.11, 1017.23
irrationality 922.1, 923.2, 926.1, 936.2
irreclaimability 125.3
irreclaimable 125.15, 473.7, 654.18
irreconcilability 361.2, 780.1, 789.2
irreconcilable (n) 452.3 (a) 361.9, 507.7, 589.11, 780.7, 789.8
irreconcilableness 507.2
irrecoverable 125.15, 837.7
irrecoverableness 125.3
irredeemability 125.3
irredeemable 125.15, 625.13, 654.18
irreducibility 872.1, 963.3
irreducible 767.7, 798.6, 799.5, 872.7, 963.13
irreducible content 196.5
irreducible fact 761.3
irreducibleness 963.3
irreductible 963.13
irreformability 125.3
irreformable 125.15, 654.18
irrefragability 970.3
irrefragable 970.15
irrefutability 970.3
irrefutable 957.16, 970.15
irrefutable logic 935.10
irregular (n) 461.16, 1005.6 (a) 265.10, 288.6, 581.3, 674.6, 782.3, 791.4, 810.12, 813.4, 851.3, 854.7, 870.9, 927.5, 1005.9
irregular galaxy 1073.6
irregularity 85.29, 265.1, 288.1, 294.2, 581.1, 782.1, 791.1, 810.1, 813.1, 851.1, 854.2, 870.1, 927.1
irregular verb 530.4
irrelation 776.1
irrelative 776.6, 776.7
irrelativeness 776.1
irrelevance, an 776.3
irrelevance 520.1, 776.1, 789.3, 844.1, 998.1
irrelevancy 776.1, 776.3, 789.3, 844.1, 998.1
irrelevant 776.7, 789.7, 844.6, 998.16
irreligion 694.1, 695.3
irreligionist 695.10
irreligious 694.6, 695.17, 955.8
irremediable 125.15, 395.28
irremediableness 125.3
irremissibility 650.5
irremissible 650.12
irremovability 855.3
irremovable 855.15
irreparability 125.3
irreparable 125.15
irrepentance 114.2
irreplaceability 963.3
irreplaceable 388.5, 963.13
irreprehensibility 657.3
irreprehensible 657.8
irreprehensibleness 657.3
irrepressibility 109.1, 361.4, 430.3
irrepressible 109.11, 361.12, 430.24
irrepressibleness 109.1, 430.3
irrepressible optimist 124.5
irreproachability 644.1, 657.3
irreproachable 644.13, 653.5, 657.8, 1002.6
irreproachableness 644.1, 657.3
irreprovable 657.8
irresilience 1046.3
irresiliency 1046.3
irresilient 1046.12
irresistibility 15.4, 424.1
irresistible 15.19, 18.12, 97.7, 247.6, 377.8, 424.10, 957.16, 963.15
irresistible force 424.2, 902.1
irresistible impulse 365.1, 926.13
irresolute 16.17, 362.9, 854.7, 971.16
irresoluteness 362.1
irresolution 16.2, 362.1, 971.1
irresolved 362.9
irresponsibility 418.1, 493.1, 645.4
irresponsible 418.5, 430.30, 493.7, 645.19, 854.7, 971.16
irretrievability 125.3, 855.4
irretrievable 125.15, 473.7, 855.17
irreverence 156.1, 694.1
irreverent 156.7, 694.6
irreversibility 125.3, 855.4
irreversible 125.15, 161.12, 373.18, 855.17
irrevocability 125.3, 855.4, 963.7
irrevocable 125.15, 420.12, 855.17, 963.15
irrevocable past, the 837.1
irrigate 16.11, 79.19, 1065.12, 1069.17
irrigation 79.5, 1065.6, 1069.13
irrigational 1065.18
irrigation ditch 239.2
irrigator 1065.8
irriguous 1065.18
irritability 24.3, 105.10, 110.2, 456.3
irritable 24.12, 105.28, 110.19, 128.11, 456.17
irritable man 452.3
irritable temper 110.4
irritant (n) 96.3 (a) 26.13
irritate 26.7, 96.14, 119.2, 128.9, 152.24, 393.9, 456.14, 589.7
irritated 26.11, 96.21, 119.4, 152.27, 393.27
irritating 26.13, 68.6, 98.22, 119.5
irritation 26.4, 96.3, 105.11, 119.1, 152.1, 375.4, 1011.1
irritative 26.13
irrupt 33.9, 189.7, 214.5, 818.13, 910.9
irruption 105.9, 214.1, 459.4
irruptive 189.12, 459.29
Isaac 684.1
Isaiah 684.1
isangoma 690.7
Iscariotic 645.22
ischemic heart disease 85.19
Ishmael 586.4
isinglass 1062.5
Isis 890.5
Islam 675.13
Islamic 675.31
Islamism 675.13
Islamistic 675.31
Islamite 675.23
Islamitic 675.31
island (n) 184.22, 235.2 (v) 235.5 (a) 235.7
island base 1075.5
island chain 235.2
island-dotted 235.7
island-dweller 235.4
islanded 235.7
islander 235.4
island group 235.2
island-hop 235.5
islandish 235.7
islandlike 235.7
islandman 235.4
islandologist 235.4
islandology 235.2
Islands of the Blessed 681.9
island universe 1073.6
islandy 235.7
isle 235.2
islesman 235.4
Isles of the Blessed 681.9
islet 235.2
isleted 235.7
ism 617.5, 675.2, 953.3
isness 761.1
isoantibody 2.25
isobar 317.4, 1038.5
isobaric 317.13, 1038.18
isobaric line 317.4
isochronal 836.5, 836.6, 850.7
isochronism 836.1
isochronize 836.4
isochronous 836.5, 836.6
isocracy 612.4
isocyclic 1038.18
isoenzyme 7.10
isogamy 78.3
isogenesis 78.6
isogenetic 78.16
isogeny 778.1
isogloss 523.7, 524.8
isoglucose 66.3
isogonic 790.10
isolate 235.5, 255.10, 429.13, 773.6, 801.6, 802.8, 1032.29
isolated 92.40, 173.12, 235.7, 345.13, 429.20, 584.8, 773.8, 776.6, 802.20, 802.21, 872.8
isolated case 872.4
isolate oneself 872.6
isolating 523.23

isolation 92.23, 345.2, 429.2, 584.1, 773.3, 801.2, 802.1, 872.2
isolationism 430.9, 584.1, 609.5, 952.7
isolationist 430.12, 584.5
isoline 159.5
isomaltulose 66.3
isomer 1038.5
isomerase 7.10
isomeric 1060.9
isomerize 1060.8
isomerous 1060.9
isometric (n) 317.4 (a) 317.13, 790.10
isometric exercise 84.2
isometric line 317.4
isometrics 84.2
isonuclear 1038.19
isopiestic 317.13
isopiestic line 317.4
isostasy 237.6
isoteric 1038.18
isotherm 317.4
isothermal 1019.30
isothermal line 317.4
isothermic 1019.30
isotone 1038.5
isotope 1038.5
isotopic 1038.18
isotronic 1041.24
Israelite (n) 675.21 (a) 675.30
Israelitic 675.30
Israelitish 675.30
Israelitism 675.12
issuance 33.1, 190.1, 352.1, 369.1, 477.2, 728.23, 738.6
issue (n) 190.1, 244.2, 352.1, 369.1, 554.5, 559.5, 561.1, 609.7, 738.6, 831.1, 886.9, 887.1, 893.1, 937.1, 938.10, 940.1, 997.6 (v) 33.8, 188.8, 190.11, 238.16, 244.4, 352.14, 352.16, 369.10, 477.8, 478.12, 548.14, 728.26, 738.12, 771.4, 818.13, 835.3, 887.4
issue, the 457.2
issue a caveat 422.6
issue a command 420.8
issue a manifesto 334.5, 352.12
issue an injunction 420.8
issue an injunction against 444.3
issue an invitation 440.13
issue an ultimatum 399.5, 421.5
issue a position paper 334.5
issue a prohibitory injunction 444.3
issue a statement 352.12
issue a summons 598.14
issue a white paper 352.12
issue a writ 420.8
issued 352.17
issue forth 1.2, 33.8, 188.8, 190.11, 369.10, 818.13
issue from 887.5
issueless 891.4
issue par 738.9
issue price 738.9
issue stock 738.12
issuing (n) 33.1, 190.1 (a) 190.18
issuing company 737.15
is the new 842.16
isthmian 270.14
isthmic 270.14
isthmus 260.1, 270.3
isthmus of the fauces 2.18
it 578.5, 865.5, 973.4
Italian bread 10.28
Italian hand 415.1
Italian ice 10.47
Italian paste 10.33
Italic 523.12
italic (n) 548.6 (a) 547.22
italicize 997.14
italicized 547.22, 997.21
itch (n) 74.3, 75.5, 85.35, 100.6 (v) 74.5, 917.13
itch for 75.20, 100.16
itch for knowledge 981.1
itchiness 74.3, 917.5
itching (n) 74.3, 85.9, 100.6 (a) 74.10, 75.27, 100.24, 665.29
itching for 100.22
itching palm 100.8
itching to 100.22
itch to 100.15, 135.4
itchy 24.12, 74.10, 665.29, 981.5
item 104.17, 549.4, 628.5, 735.2, 766.3, 793.1, 796.2, 872.4, 957.5
itemization 349.2, 766.5, 801.2, 865.7, 871.1, 871.7
itemize 766.6, 801.7, 865.9, 871.8, 957.13, 1017.19
itemized 871.9
itemized account 871.5
itemized bill 628.3
item of evidence 957.1
item on the agenda 937.1
items 196.1, 735.1, 871.1, 928.1
item veto 444.2, 613.7
iterate 849.8, 856.5
iterated 849.12
iteration 538.2, 849.2, 874.1
iterative (n) 530.13 (a) 538.11, 849.14
it girl 1016.8
ithyphallic 665.29, 666.9
itineracy 177.3
itinerancy 177.3
itinerant (n) 178.2 (a) 177.36
itinerary (n) 383.1, 574.10, 871.6 (a) 177.36
-itis 85.10
itself 865.5
itsy-bitsy 258.11
itsy-witsy 258.11
IV 879.1
ivied halls 567.5
ivories 2.8, 711.17, 759.8
ivory (n) 37.2, 287.3 (a) 37.8
ivory carver 716.6
ivory tickler 710.7
ivory tower 584.1, 584.6, 1009.5
ivory-towered 584.9
ivory-towerish 584.9
ivory-towerishness 584.1
ivory-towerism 584.1
ivory-towerist 584.5
ivory-towerite 584.5
ivory-white 37.8
ivy (n) 310.4 (a) 44.4
ivy-green 44.4
Ivy League 249.4
IX 882.5
Ixion's wheel 915.4
izzard 820.1
J 87.11
ja 770.4
jab (n) 459.3, 902.2, 902.4 (v) 87.22, 508.9, 754.4, 902.12, 902.14
jab at 508.9
jabber (n) 520.2, 525.4, 540.3 (v) 520.5, 525.9, 540.5
jabberer 540.4
jabbering 540.10
jabbing 754.3
jacal 228.10
j'accuse 599.9
jack (n) 183.1, 311.15, 647.7, 728.2, 750.3, 758.2, 901.8, 912.3, 1040.7 (v) 382.9
jack-a-dandy 500.9
jack afloat 183.1
jackal 138.3, 311.19, 616.8
jackanapes 500.9
jackass 311.15
jack-at-a-pinch 592.1
jackboot, the 424.3
jackdaw in peacock's feathers 357.6
jacker 382.5, 382.6
jacket (n) 5.13, 295.3, 295.16, 295.18, 554.14 (v) 5.40
jacketed 295.31
jacketing 295.18
jack field 1034.7
Jack Frost 1023.7
jacking off 75.8
jacking-up 510.6
jack-in-office 575.15, 610.11
jack-in-the-box 743.16
Jack-in-the-green 678.11
Jack Ketch 604.7
jackknife 367.1
jackleg 357.4
jackleg politician 610.5
jacklight 382.9
jacklighter 382.5
jack-of-all-trades 413.11, 726.2
jack off 75.22
jack of trumps 758.2
jack-o'-lantern 1025.13
jackpot 646.2, 758.4, 759.5
jack-pudding 707.10
jackrabbit 311.23, 366.4
jackroll 482.16
jacks 743.16
jackscrew 912.3
Jacksonian Age 824.5
jackstone 1059.4
jackstraw 764.2, 998.7
jack-tar 183.1
jack up 251.4, 510.18
jack with 214.7
jacky 183.1
Jacob 684.1
Jacobin 611.12
Jacobinic 860.6
Jacobinical 860.6
Jacobinism 611.4, 860.2
Jacob's ladder 193.4
jactation 502.1, 917.2
jactitate 917.11
jactitation 502.1, 917.2
jaculate 904.11
jaculation 904.2
jaculator 904.7
jaculatory 904.15
Jacuzzi 79.8, 84.1, 1044.3
jade (n) 311.12, 665.14 (v) 21.4, 21.5, 118.6, 994.4 (a) 44.4
jaded 21.7, 118.11, 331.20, 393.36, 994.6
jadedness 21.1, 118.3, 331.6, 994.2
jading 994.7
jag (n) 88.6, 285.4, 289.1 (v) 289.4
Jaganatha 697.3
jagged 278.6, 285.14, 288.7, 289.5, 782.3, 813.4
jagged edge 285.2
jaggedness 288.1
jaggy 288.7, 289.5
jaguar 47.6, 311.21
jaguar-man 680.12
jahannan 682.1
jail (n) 212.3, 429.8 (v) 212.5, 429.14
jailbird 429.11, 660.9
jailbreak 369.1
jail cell 429.8
jailed 212.10, 429.21
jailer 429.10, 604.8, 1008.9
jailhouse 429.8
jailing 212.1, 429.3, 604.2
Jainism 675.14
Jainist 675.24
jakes 12.4, 12.10
jalopy 179.10
jam (n) 10.40, 293.3, 765.1, 846.2, 884.3, 971.3, 1012.5, 1013.5, 1062.5 (v) 53.8, 293.7, 582.21, 708.43, 794.7, 800.8, 855.8, 855.10, 857.7, 884.5, 902.12, 993.15, 1012.12, 1036.15, 1045.9
Jamaica shorts 5.18
jamb 177.14, 273.4
jambe de mouton 10.16
jamboree 743.4
jam-full 794.11
jam in 189.7, 191.7, 1045.9
jammed 293.11, 800.14, 846.16, 855.16, 884.9, 993.20, 1045.12
jammed in 1045.12
jammedness 1045.1
jammer 1036.14
jammin' 249.13
jamming 1034.21, 1036.13
jamoke 660.5
jam-pack 794.7, 993.15
jam-packed 293.11, 770.22, 794.11, 884.9, 993.20, 1045.12
jam session 365.5, 708.32
jam through 613.10
jam-up (n) 794.3 (a) 999.13
jane 77.6, 87.11
Jane Doe 527.8, 606.5, 864.3
jangle (n) 53.3, 54.3, 58.3, 61.2, 456.1 (v) 54.8, 58.9, 61.3, 456.8, 789.5
jangled nerves 128.4
jangle the nerves 58.11, 128.9
jangling 58.16, 61.5, 789.6

jangly 58.16, 61.5
Jan Hus 684.3
janitor 79.14, 1008.6, 1008.12
janitress 79.14
jank 250.6
janky 250.6
Jansenist 554.15
Janus 873.1
Janus-faced 354.31
Janus-like 873.6
japan (n) 38.6 (v) 35.14, 38.7
Japanese bath 79.8
Japanese rising sun 647.6
japanning 35.12
Japan Trench 275.5
jape (n) 489.6, 508.2 (v) 489.13, 490.5, 508.9
japery 489.2, 508.1
japing (n) 490.2 (a) 508.12
jar (n) 58.3, 61.2, 131.3, 195.1, 456.1, 917.3 (v) 58.9, 61.3, 105.14, 131.8, 212.9, 456.8, 789.5, 917.11
jargon (n) 520.2, 522.7, 523.9, 523.11, 526.5 (v) 523.18
jargonal 523.21
jargoneer 523.17
jargonish 523.21
jargonist 523.17
jargonistic 523.20
jargonize 523.18
jargonizer 523.17
jargon word 526.5
jarhead 183.4
jar on 58.11, 128.9
jarred 131.13
jarring (n) 456.1, 789.1 (a) 58.16, 61.5, 105.30, 128.15, 131.11, 789.6, 917.20
jarring of sounds 61.2
jar upon the ear 58.11
jarvey 178.9
jar with 780.5
jasmine oil 70.2
Jason 183.1
jasper 76.5
Jataka 683.9
jaundice (n) 43.2, 85.9, 85.23, 153.1, 980.3 (v) 43.3, 980.9
jaundiced 43.6, 110.23, 153.5, 980.12
jaundiced eye 153.1, 980.3
jaundiced yellow 35.5
jaundice-eyed 153.5
jaundice of the soul 153.1
jaunt (n) 177.5, 177.10 (v) 177.21, 177.23
jauntiness 109.3, 501.3, 578.3
jaunting 177.1
jaunty 109.12, 501.19, 578.13
Java 275.5
java 10.49
javelin 462.8
javelin thrower 904.7
jaw (n) 2.12, 292.4 (v) 510.19, 524.20, 540.5
jawbone 375.14, 894.7
jawboning 375.3
jawbreaker 526.10, 545.3
jawbreaking 545.10, 1013.17
jaw-dropping 122.12
jawed 474.9
jaw-jaw 524.1, 540.3
jawless fish 311.30
jawline 2.12
jaws 292.4, 474.4
jawsmith 543.4
jaws of death 307.1
jawtwister 526.10, 545.3
jawtwisting 545.10
jay 87.7, 358.2, 540.4
jaywalk 177.27
jaywalker 178.6
jaywalking 177.8
jazz (n) 17.3, 708.9 (a) 708.51, 709.29
Jazz Age 824.5
jazz ballet 84.2
jazzed 709.29
jazzed up 709.29
jazzed-up 17.13, 251.7
Jazzercise 84.2
jazz festival 708.32
jazziness 501.3
jazzman 710.2
jazz musician 710.2
jazz stick 711.16
jazz up 17.10, 105.13, 251.5
jazzy 501.19, 708.51, 709.29
J-bar 753.1
j-bird 758.2
j-boy 758.2
jealous 153.5, 154.3
jealousness 153.1
jealousy 153.1, 154.1
Jean Lafitte 483.7
jeans 5.18
jebel 237.4
jeer (n) 59.1, 156.2, 508.2 (v) 508.9
jeer at 156.5
jeering (n) 156.2, 508.1 (a) 508.12
Jeff Bezos 618.8
Jehovah 677.2
Jehu 174.5, 178.9
jejune 65.2, 117.6, 270.20, 276.5, 891.4, 922.19, 992.10
jejuneness 65.1, 301.1, 992.2
jejunity 65.1, 117.1, 922.6, 992.2
jejunum 2.18
jell (n) 1062.5 (v) 1045.10, 1062.10
jelled 1045.14, 1062.12
jellied 1045.14, 1062.12
jellies 5.27
jellification 1045.4, 1062.2
jellify 1045.10, 1062.10
jelling 1045.4
Jell-O 10.40
jelly (n) 10.40, 1062.5 (v) 1045.10, 1062.10
jelly beans 87.4
jelly doughnut 10.44
jellyfish 16.6, 362.5, 491.5
jellying 1045.4
jellylike 1062.12
jellylikeness 803.3, 1062.2
jelly shoes 5.27
je ne sais quoi 528.2
jennet 311.15
jenny 77.9, 271.5, 311.15
jenny ass 311.15
jeopard 1006.6
jeopardize 1006.6
jeopardized 1006.13
jeopardous 1006.9
jeopardy (n) 1006.1 (v) 1006.6
jeremiad 115.3, 510.7, 543.2
Jeremiah 399.4, 684.1
Jeremianic 115.19
jerk (n) 414.9, 660.5, 905.3, 917.3, 924.3 (v) 105.18, 397.9, 904.10, 905.5, 917.13
jerk back 163.5
jerkiness 782.1, 851.1, 917.2
jerking (n) 397.2, 917.5 (a) 917.19
jerk off 998.15
jerk out 59.7
jerks, the 85.25
jerk up 912.5
jerkwater 998.18
jerkwater town 230.3
jerky (n) 10.13, 10.14 (a) 671.23, 782.3, 813.4, 851.3, 917.19
jerry (n) 12.11 (a) 16.14
jerry-built 16.14
Jersey hit 750.2
Jerusalem Bible 683.2
jest (n) 489.6, 508.2, 508.7, 998.5 (v) 489.13, 490.5
jest-book 489.6
jester 489.12, 707.10
jesting (n) 490.2 (a) 489.15
jestingstock 508.7
Jesuit 936.6, 936.7
Jesuitic 936.10
jesuitic 354.32
Jesuitical 415.12, 936.10
jesuitical 354.32
Jesuitism 415.1, 936.1, 936.4
jesuitism 354.5
Jesuitize 936.9
Jesuitry 415.1, 936.1
jesuitry 354.5
Jesus 677.10
Jesus Christ 677.10
jet (n) 38.4, 181.3, 193.1, 238.9, 671.6, 909.7, 1020.10, 1043.3 (v) 184.36, 190.13, 193.9, 238.20, 909.25 (a) 38.8, 184.49, 904.17
Jet Age 824.6
jet aircraft 181.3
jet-assisted takeoff 184.8
jetavator 1074.2
jet-black 38.8
jet blast 1074.8
jet bomber 181.9
jet bridge 189.5
jeté 366.1
jet engine 181.1
jet engineer 185.6
jet engineering 1039.6
jet exhaust 184.30
jet fighter 181.9
jet flight 184.1
jet injection 91.16
jet jockey 185.1
jet lag 21.1
jet liner 181.3
jet pilot 185.1
jet plane 174.6, 181.3
jetport 184.22
jet power 18.4, 184.25
jet-propelled 184.50, 904.16
jet propulsion 184.25, 1074.8
jetsam 370.4
jet set 178.1, 578.6, 608.1, 618.6
jet-set 578.16
jet-setter 178.1, 608.4
jetsetter 578.7
jet-skiing 744.1
jet stream 318.1
jetstream 184.32
jet tanker 181.9
jettison (n) 370.1, 390.3, 909.1 (v) 370.5, 390.7, 909.13
jettisoned 370.8
jettisoning 370.1
jetty (n) 901.4, 1009.6, 1012.5 (a) 38.8
jetway 189.5
jeu d'esprit 489.7
jeune fille 302.6
jeunesse 301.1
Jew 675.21
jewel (n) 104.15, 498.6, 659.1, 915.7, 999.5 (v) 498.9
jewel case 195.1
jeweled 498.11
jewelry 5.31, 498.5
jewelry box 195.1
jewelry design 712.16
jewelry maker 716.2
jewels 732.3
jewel smuggling 732.2
jewel thief 483.1
Jewish 675.30
Jewish calendar 832.8
Jewish holy days 701.13
Jewish Law, the 683.3
Jewish star 882.2
jewlery design 717.5
Jew's harp 711.10
Jezebel 593.7, 665.14, 665.15
jib 127.12, 164.6, 362.7, 903.7
jibber 525.4
jibbing 362.11
jib boom 216.3
jibe 182.30, 788.6, 852.6
jibe all standing 182.30
jiff 830.3
jiffy 830.3
jig (n) 356.13, 366.1, 905.3, 917.3 (v) 382.10, 905.5, 917.13
jigger (n) 88.7, 311.36, 382.6, 1052.5 (v) 905.5, 917.13
jiggery-pokery 354.14, 356.5
jigget 905.5, 917.13
jiggety 917.19
jiggins 924.8
jiggle (n) 905.3, 917.3 (v) 905.5, 917.11, 917.13
jiggler 917.9
jigsaw 802.11
jigsaw puzzle 522.8
jihad 458.3
jill 104.13, 302.7
jillion (n) 882.13, 884.4, 1017.5 (a) 884.6
jilt (n) 357.1 (v) 370.5, 390.7
jilted 99.10
jilter 357.1
jilting 370.1
Jim Crow 584.1, 773.3, 980.4
Jim Crow law 980.4

jim dandy (n) 999.7 (a) 999.13
jimjams 127.5, 128.2
jimjams, the 926.10
jimmy (n) 906.4 (v) 906.8
Jimmy Bungs 183.6
Jimmy Hicks 882.2
Jina 684.4
jingle (n) 54.3, 347.13, 720.7, 784.6, 849.4 (v) 54.8, 720.15
jingle-brained 922.17
jingle-jangle (n) 54.3, 849.4 (a) 849.15
jinglejangle 54.8
jingling (n) 54.3 (a) 54.13, 720.18, 784.17
jingo (n) 461.5, 591.3, 980.5 (a) 458.21
jingoish 458.21
jingoism 458.10, 591.2
jingoist (n) 461.5, 591.3 (a) 458.21, 591.4
jingoistic 458.21, 591.4
jink (n) 368.1 (v) 368.8
jinn 988.1
jinni 680.6
jinniyeh 680.6
jinrikisha 179.3
jinx (n) 513.1, 691.1, 1000.4 (v) 691.9, 1000.6, 1011.12
jitney 179.13
jitney driver 178.10
jitter 128.6
jitteriness 128.1, 917.1
jitters 128.2, 917.1
jittery 128.12, 917.16
jiva 306.2, 919.4
jivatma 306.2, 919.4
jive (n) 355.1, 520.3, 708.9 (v) 490.6, 708.43
jive turkey 924.4
jiving (n) 490.3 (a) 508.12
jo 104.13
Job 134.3
job (n) 328.3, 482.4, 724.1, 724.2, 724.3, 724.5, 831.3, 1042.18 (v) 615.15, 615.16, 731.16, 734.8
job action 727.5
jobber 213.4, 726.2, 730.2, 737.10
jobbernowl 924.4
jobbery 415.2, 609.34
jobbing 415.2, 731.2, 734.2, 737.18
job-control language 1042.13
jobholder 726.2
jobless 331.18
joblessness 331.3
Job-like 134.9
job lot 735.1
job printing 548.1
Job's comforter 125.7
job-share 450.3
job sharing 417.12, 862.1
job-sharing 450.1
job site 739.3
job vacancy 222.2
jock 76.6, 743.19, 757.2, 901.2
jockey (n) 174.5, 178.8, 757.2, 901.18 (v) 415.10, 457.18
Jockey Club 757.1
jockeying 457.2
jockey weight 297.3
jockstrap 76.6, 901.2
jocose 489.15
jocoseness 489.2
jocosity 489.2
jocular 109.15, 489.15
jocularity 109.5, 489.2
jocund 109.15
jocundity 109.5
jodhpurs 5.18
Joe 76.5
joe 10.49
Joe Blow 606.5, 864.3
Joe Citizen 606.1
Joe Doakes 606.5
Joel 684.1
Joe Miller 489.9
Joe Millerism 489.9
Joe Public 606.1
Joe Schmo 606.1
Joe Six-pack 864.3
Joe Sixpack 606.1, 606.5
Joe Tentpeg 461.7
jog (n) 175.2, 177.12, 283.3, 289.1, 902.2, 905.3, 917.3 (v) 84.4, 177.28, 902.12, 905.5, 917.11
jogger 989.5
jogging 84.2
joggle (n) 283.3, 289.1, 902.2, 905.3, 917.3 (v) 902.12, 905.5, 917.11
jogglety 917.20
joggling 917.20
joggly 917.20
jog on 162.3, 175.7, 856.3
jog the memory 989.19
jog trot 174.3, 175.2, 373.5
jog-trot 118.9, 849.15
jogtrot 175.6
Johannine Epistles 683.4
John 684.2
john 12.10, 12.11, 197.26, 758.2, 759.22
John Barleycorn 88.13
John Bull 232.5, 612.3
John Calvin 684.3
John Doe 527.8, 606.1, 606.5, 864.3
John Doe and Mary Roe 998.7
John Doe and Richard Roe 998.7
John Dogface 461.7
John Hancock 332.4, 527.10
John Knox 684.3
John Law 1008.16
Johnny 461.7
johnny 12.10, 12.11, 76.5
johnnycake 10.29
Johnny-come-lately 774.4, 818.2, 846.6
johnny house 12.10
Johnny-on-the-spot (n) 592.1, 845.4 (a) 845.9, 983.15
John Q Public 864.3
John Q. Public 606.1, 606.5
John's disease 85.41
John Smith 606.5
Johnsonese 545.1
Johnsonian 522.14, 545.8
John Wesley 684.3
John Wycliffe 684.3
joie de vivre 17.4, 95.1, 109.2
join (n) 800.4 (v) 223.9, 223.13, 238.16, 450.3, 450.4, 476.5, 563.14, 582.17, 615.17, 617.14, 770.18, 778.5, 796.3, 800.5, 800.11, 803.7, 805.3, 812.4, 899.2
join a tour 918.6
join battle 457.16
join battle with 451.4
joinder 800.1
joined 223.16, 769.9, 770.21, 775.9, 800.12, 800.13, 803.11, 805.5, 812.8
joined at the hip 769.9
joined the choir invisible 307.29
joined up 800.13
joined-up 769.9
joiner 582.16, 617.11
join forces 805.4
join fortunes with 805.4
join hands with 450.4
join in 450.3, 476.5, 541.8
join in fellowship 582.17
joining (n) 223.4, 253.1, 800.1, 800.4 (a) 800.16
joining of forces 450.1
joining of hands 450.1
joining the opposition 363.2
joining up 223.4
join in holy matrimony 563.14
join in the chorus 332.9
join issue 456.11, 457.16, 935.16
join issue upon 335.4
join one's ancestors 307.20
join oneself to 404.3, 449.13, 476.5
join oneself with 332.9, 509.13, 600.10
join one's fortunes with 450.4
joint (n) 10.13, 87.12, 224.2, 228.28, 429.9, 654.7, 665.9, 759.19, 800.4 (v) 800.8 (a) 450.5, 476.9, 769.9, 770.21, 777.11, 800.12, 805.5, 899.4
joint chairmanship 476.1
joint control 476.1
joint discussion 541.6
jointed 800.17
joint effort 450.1
join the angels 307.20
join the choir invisible 307.20
join the great majority 307.20
joint heir 479.5
join the majority 307.20
join the opposition 451.3
join the parade 578.10
jointless 812.8
jointlessness 812.1
join together 450.3, 563.14, 805.4
joint operation 450.1, 889.1
joint operations 458.4
joint ownership 476.1
joint resolution 613.5
joint return 630.9
joint-stock company 737.15
joint tenancy 476.1
joint the club 578.10
jointure 478.9, 800.1
join up 476.5, 617.14, 800.5
join up with 223.11, 450.4, 805.4, 899.3
join with 238.16, 253.4, 450.4, 805.4
joke (n) 489.6, 508.7, 998.5 (v) 489.13, 490.5
joker 76.5, 131.2, 322.3, 356.6, 357.1, 421.3, 489.12, 613.9, 758.2, 959.2, 1012.4, 1013.8
jokesmith 489.12, 704.22
jokester 322.3, 357.1, 489.12
joke with whiskers 489.9
joke writer 704.22
joking (n) 489.2, 490.2 (a) 489.15
joky 489.15
jollies 105.3, 461.28
jollification 743.3
jollify 743.24
jolliness 109.5
jollity 109.5, 582.3, 743.3
jolly (n) 183.4 (v) 490.6, 511.6, 743.24 (a) 88.31, 109.15, 582.23, 743.28
jolly fellow 588.5
jollying (n) 490.3 (a) 490.7
Jolly Roger 647.7
jolt (n) 88.7, 105.3, 131.3, 902.2, 917.3 (v) 105.14, 131.8, 177.28, 902.12, 917.11
jolted 131.13
jolterhead 924.4
jolterheaded 922.17
jolterheadedness 922.4
joltheaded 922.17
joltheadedness 922.4
joltiness 288.1, 917.2
jolting 105.30, 131.11, 917.20
jolty 288.6, 917.20
Jonah (n) 684.1, 1000.4 (v) 1011.12
jones 87.1, 87.9
jongleur 710.14, 720.12
Jophiel 679.4
Jordan 307.3
jordan 12.11
Jordan's bank 307.3
jornada 177.5
Joseph 684.1
Josephite 675.22
Joseph's coat 47.6
Joseph Smith 684.3
Joseph Surface 357.8, 693.3
josh 489.13, 490.6
josher 490.4
joshing (n) 489.2, 490.3, 508.1 (a) 489.15, 490.7, 508.12
Joshua 684.1
joss 697.3
joss stick 70.4
jostle (n) 902.2, 917.3 (v) 61.3, 456.8, 457.13, 482.14, 789.5, 902.12, 917.11
jostling (n) 482.3 (a) 61.5
jostling of sounds 61.2
jot 248.2, 258.7, 517.5
jot down 549.15
jot nor tittle 258.7
jotting 549.4
jottings 549.4
joule 17.7, 1019.19
jounce 917.11

jouncy 917.20
journal 549.11, 555.1, 628.4, 719.1, 832.9, 871.6, 915.6, 1040.5
journal bearing 915.7
journal box 915.6
journalese (n) 523.10 (a) 555.5
journalism 547.2, 552.1, 555.3, 718.2
journalist 552.9, 555.4
journalistic 555.5
journalize 628.8
journalizer 628.7
journey (n) 177.5 (v) 177.21
journeyer 178.1
journeying (n) 177.1 (a) 177.36
journeyings 177.2
journeyman (n) 413.11, 726.6, 892.7 (a) 413.24
journeyman work 893.1
journeys 177.2
journey's end 186.5, 820.1
journo 555.4
joust (n) 457.3 (v) 457.13
jouster 461.1
jovial 109.15, 582.23, 743.28
joviality 109.5, 582.3, 743.3
jowl 218.1
jowls 292.4
joy (n) 95.2, 109.5 (v) 95.12, 116.5, 502.9
joyance 95.2, 95.3
joyful 95.16, 109.15, 109.16, 743.28
joyfulness 95.2, 109.5
joy juice 87.6
joyless 96.20, 98.20, 112.21
joylessness 96.1, 98.5, 112.2
joyous 95.16, 109.15, 743.28
joyousness 109.5
joy pop 87.22
joy powder 87.7
joyride (n) 177.7 (v) 177.33
joyrider 178.10
joy stick 87.12
joystick 573.5, 1042.4
joy-to-stuff ratio 95.2
Jr 301.15
jube 703.10
jubilance 116.1
jubilant 95.17, 116.10, 502.13
jubilant display 116.1
jubilate 116.5, 487.2, 502.9
jubilation 95.3, 116.1, 502.4
jubilee 116.1, 487.1, 850.4
jubilize 487.2
Judaic 675.30
Judaical 675.30
Judaism 675.12
Judaist 675.21
Judas 357.10, 660.9
Judas goat 574.6
Judas Iscariot 357.10
Judas kiss 645.8
Judas-like 645.22
judder 847.3
juddering (n) 847.2, 917.2 (a) 847.5, 917.17
Judeo-Christian belief 675.7
Judeo-Christian religion 675.7
judge (n) 466.4, 496.6, 596.1, 754.3, 946.6 (v) 466.6, 594.5, 598.18, 598.20, 723.5, 801.8, 946.8, 953.11
judge advocate 597.1
Judge Advocate General 596.3
judge amiss 948.2
judge and jury 596.1
judge beforehand 947.2, 980.7
judge before the evidence is in 947.2
judged beforehand 947.3
judge not 979.7
judge on its own merits 649.6
judge on the merits 979.7
judge prematurely (v) 947.2 (a) 947.3
judger 946.6
judgeship 594.3
judging 946.1
judgmatic 920.19
judgmatical 920.19
judgment 594.2, 598.9, 602.1, 604.1, 677.14, 801.3, 920.7, 940.1, 944.2, 946.1, 952.2, 953.6
Judgment, the 839.3
judgmental 99.8, 495.9, 510.22, 946.16
judgmentalness 495.1
judgment call 946.1
Judgment Day 839.3
judgment day 946.4
judgment lien 438.5
judgment seat 595.5
judicative 594.6, 946.16
judicatorial 594.6
judicatory (n) 594.2, 595.1 (a) 594.6
judicature 594.2, 595.1, 595.2, 946.1
judicial 594.6, 595.7, 673.11, 920.19, 946.16
judicial activism 330.1
judicial astrology 1073.20
judicial circuit 231.2
judicial execution 308.7
judicial murder 308.7, 604.6
judicial oath 334.4
judicial process 594.2, 598.1
judicial punishment 604.1
judicial separation 566.1
judicial system 594.2
judiciary (n) 594.2, 595.1 (a) 594.6, 595.7, 946.16
judicious 494.8, 670.10, 920.19, 944.8, 946.16
judiciousness 494.1, 670.1, 920.7, 944.1
judo 760.3
jug (n) 429.9, 742.2 (v) 429.14
jug-bitten 88.33
jug ear 48.7
jug-earned 48.15
jugged 429.21
Juggernaut 697.3
juggins 924.8
juggle (n) 356.6 (v) 354.17, 356.14
juggled 354.30
juggler 357.2, 357.3, 707.3
juggler's trick 356.6
jugglery 356.5, 415.3
juggle the accounts 354.17
juggle the books 354.17
juggling 356.5
juggling act 356.5
jughead 311.12, 924.4
jugs 283.7
jugular vein 2.23
jugulate 308.18
jug wine 88.17
juice 10.49, 88.14, 756.1, 1032.2, 1061.2
juice bar 8.17
juice box 10.49
juiced up 1032.34
juicehead 88.12
juice joint 759.19
juiceless 1066.7
juicelessness 1066.1
juice up 1032.26
juiciness 63.1, 97.3, 301.3, 1061.1
juicing 10.49
juicy 63.8, 97.10, 301.10, 983.19, 1047.11, 1061.4
juicy morsel 552.8
juju 93.1, 675.6, 690.1, 691.5
jujuism 675.6, 690.1
juke (n) 368.1 (v) 368.8
jukebox 50.11
juke joint 743.13
Julian calendar 832.8
jumble (n) 522.7, 797.6, 810.3, 985.3 (v) 263.3, 522.12, 797.10, 810.9, 811.3, 945.3
jumbled 522.14, 797.14, 810.16, 985.12
jumble together 945.3
jumble up 797.10, 810.9
Jumbo 311.4
jumbo (n) 257.11, 257.14 (a) 257.16, 257.20
jumbo 993.16
jumbo jet 181.3
jumbo mortgage 438.4
jumbuck 311.7
jument 311.13
jump (n) 162.1, 177.11, 184.9, 193.1, 224.1, 249.2, 251.1, 366.1, 446.1, 747.3, 760.7 (v) 127.12, 131.5, 177.28, 184.47, 340.7, 366.5, 369.6, 446.2, 457.14, 459.15, 480.16, 756.4, 917.11
jump about 366.6
jump a claim 480.19
jump all over 510.18
jump a mile 127.12, 131.5
jump area 463.2
jump at 101.6, 371.14, 480.16
jump at the bidding of 138.8
jump bail 368.10
jump ball 747.3
jump down one's throat 152.16, 510.18
jump down someone's throat 152.20
jumped-up 140.11, 606.8
jumper 366.4, 367.4
jumpers 5.30
jump for joy 116.5
jump forward 162.2
jump head 937.2
jump-hop 366.1
jump in 189.7, 193.12, 214.6
jumpiness 127.3, 128.1, 917.1
jumping (n) 366.3, 753.1 (a) 366.7
jumping bean 366.4
jumping jack 366.4
jumping-off place 230.3, 261.4, 820.2
jumping-off point 188.5
jumping pain 26.2
jumping the shark 1035.2
jump jet 181.3
jumpmaster 185.8
jump off 184.38, 459.18, 818.7
jumpoff 366.1, 818.1
jump off the deep end 993.10
jump on 428.8, 510.18
jump on the bandwagon 336.7, 578.10
jump out 190.11
jump out of one's skin 127.11, 127.12, 131.5
jump out of the frying pan and into the fire 119.3
jump out of the frying pan into the fire 414.14
jump over 366.5
jump overboard 308.22
jumps 87.7, 128.2
jump ship 188.9, 222.9
jump shot 366.1
jump-start 818.11, 904.13
jump the gun 135.4, 845.6, 947.2
jump the track 393.16, 538.9
jump through a hoop 433.6
jump to a conclusion 947.2
jump turn 366.1
jump up 193.9, 200.8, 251.4, 949.2
jumpy 127.23, 128.12, 330.20, 917.16, 917.19
jumpy as a cat on a hot tin roof 128.12
jump zone 463.2
junction 223.3, 253.1, 383.3, 383.7, 770.1, 775.1, 796.1, 800.1, 803.2, 805.1, 899.1
junction buoy 517.10
juncture 223.4, 524.9, 766.1, 800.4, 824.1, 857.4
Jungian psychology 92.2
jungle 310.12, 799.2
jungle ballot 609.19
jungle cat 311.21
jungled 310.43
jungly 310.43
junior (n) 250.2, 302.1, 432.5, 572.6 (a) 250.6, 301.15, 835.4
junior chamber of commerce 617.9
Junior Circuit, the 745.1
junior high 567.4
junior high school 567.4
junior hockey 749.1
juniority 250.1, 301.3, 432.2
junior miss 302.8
junior officer 575.17
junior school 567.3

junior varsity 250.6
junk (n) 87.9, 354.13, 370.4, 391.5 (v) 370.5, 390.8, 909.13 (a) 370.8, 391.11
junk dealer 730.10
junked 87.24, 370.8, 390.11
junker 179.10
junket (n) 177.5 (v) 177.21
junketing 177.1
junk food 10.1
junkheap 179.10, 370.4, 391.6
junkie 87.21, 101.5
junking 390.3
junk jewelry 498.5
junk mail 553.4
junkman 730.10
junkpile 179.10, 370.4, 391.6
junk room 197.16
junk science 936.2
junky 354.26, 391.11
junkyard 391.6
junkyard dog 110.11, 460.7
Juno 563.13
Junoesque 1016.18
junta 423.1, 617.6, 770.3, 805.1
junto 617.6
Jupiter 1073.9
Jupiter Fidius 649.4
Jupiter Fulgur 1025.17
Jupiter Fulminator 1025.17
Jupiter Pluvius 316.6
Jupiter Tonans 56.5
jural 594.6
juridic 594.6, 946.16
juridical 594.6, 673.11, 946.16
jurisconsult 597.2
jurisdiction 231.2, 249.3, 417.5, 573.2, 594.1, 612.2, 615.1, 673.1, 1008.2
jurisdictional 594.6
jurisdictive 594.6
Juris Doctor 597.1
jurisprudence 673.7
jurisprudent (n) 597.2 (a) 673.12
jurisprudential 594.6, 673.12
jurist 597.2, 935.12
juristic 946.16
juristical 946.16
juror 596.6
jury 596.5
jury box 595.6
jury instructions 598.8
jury list 596.5, 871.6
juryman 596.6
jury of one's peers 596.5
jury panel 596.5
jury-rig (n) 365.5, 995.2 (v) 340.9, 365.8
jury-rigged 365.12, 995.7
jury-rigged expedient 995.2
jury selection 598.4
jury service 598.4
jury trial 598.5
jurywoman 596.6
jus 673.3
jus primae noctis 387.7
jussive (n) 530.11 (a) 420.13
just 533.7, 639.8, 644.13, 649.7, 653.5, 673.11, 677.17, 935.20, 973.14, 973.16, 979.12
just alike 778.7
just around the corner 387.20, 840.3
just a second 828.3
just as one thought 130.14
just as predicted 130.14
just be 761.10
just between the two 587.19
just dandy 999.13
just deserts 506.2
just desserts 604.1, 639.3
just do 246.2, 991.4
just enough 991.1
just expectation 639.1
Justice 649.4
justice 594.2, 596.1, 639.1, 644.1, 649.1
justice 653.3, 673.1, 790.1, 946.6, 979.5
justice of the peace 596.1
Justice of the Supreme Court 596.3
justiceship 594.3
justiciability 673.1
justiciable 598.21, 673.11, 674.6
justiciar 596.2
justiciary 596.2
justifiability 600.7, 649.1, 935.9
justifiable 443.15, 600.14, 649.7, 935.20
justifiable expectation 639.1
justifiable homicide 308.2
justifiableness 443.8, 649.1
justification 375.1, 548.2, 600.1, 649.1, 685.3, 952.2
justification by faith 685.3
justification by works 685.3
justification space 548.7
justificatory 600.13
justified 639.9, 649.7, 685.9
justifier 600.8
justify 548.16, 600.9, 601.4
justify hope 124.9
justifying 600.13
justifying space 548.7
justify one in supposing 551.10
Justinian Code 673.5
Justitia 649.4
just know 934.4, 961.6, 970.9
just like one 130.14
justness 644.1, 649.1, 935.9, 973.6, 979.5
just out 841.10
just plain nuts 926.27
just right 788.10, 1002.6
just right as rain 973.16
just say no 668.6
just see 986.15
just so 1002.6
just what the doctor ordered 788.10
just yesterday 837.1
jut 202.7, 295.30
jut out 283.10
jut over 202.7
jutting (n) 202.3 (a) 202.11, 283.14
jutty 901.4, 1009.6
juvenal (n) 302.1 (a) 301.9
juvenescence 301.1
juvenescent 301.9
juvenile (n) 302.1, 554.1, 707.2, 757.2 (a) 301.9, 406.11
juvenile book 554.1
juvenile court 595.2
juvenile delinquency 636.4, 638.1
juvenile delinquent 302.4
juvenile editor 554.2
juvenile lead 707.6
juvenility 301.1
juxtapose 223.13, 770.18
juxtaposed 223.16
juxtapose in opposition 779.4
juxtaposition 223.3, 253.1, 770.1
juxtapositional 223.16
K 745.3
kaama 311.5
kabala 689.1
kabballa 689.1
kablooey 56.4
kaboom 56.4
ka-ching 56.1, 729.13
Kaddish 696.4, 701.9
kaffir 688.6
kafuffle 810.2
kaid 575.9
kairos 824.1, 843.5
kairotic 843.10
kairotic moment 843.5
kairotic time 821.1
kaiser 575.9
kaiserdom 417.8
kaiserism 612.8
kaiser roll 10.31
kaisership 417.8
kakotopia 986.11
kale 728.2
kaleidoscope 47.6, 854.4
kaleidoscopic 35.16, 47.9, 263.4, 854.6
kaleidoscopical 47.9
kalian 89.6
Kama 104.7
kama 689.18
kamaloka 681.8
kamarupa 689.17
kamavachara 681.8
kame 237.4, 237.5
kamic body 689.17
kamikaze 181.9, 308.5
kamikaze attack 459.1
kana 546.2
kangaroo 366.4
kangaroo care 78.6
kangaroo cloture 857.5
kangaroo court 595.2
kanji 546.2
Kantian (n) 1053.4 (a) 952.12, 1053.8
Kantian idea 932.2
Kantianism 1053.3
kaolin 742.3
kapok 1047.4
kaput 125.15, 391.14, 393.29, 395.29, 412.14, 762.11, 820.10
Karaism 675.12
Karaite 675.21
Karaitism 675.12
karaoke 708.7, 708.15, 708.32
karate 760.3
karate chop 760.3
karma 839.2, 886.1, 887.1, 963.7, 964.2
karyokinesis 305.16
karyomitosis 305.16
karyosome 305.7
karyotin 305.7
katabatic wind 318.1
katakana 546.2
Katusha 1074.10
Katy-bar-the-door 53.4, 671.3
katzenjammer 88.1
kayak 180.1, 760.2
kayo (n) 25.2, 820.4 (v) 25.4, 820.6
kayo punch 820.4
kazoo 711.10
keck 99.4, 909.26
kedge 182.15, 182.48
kedge off 182.15
keel (n) 180.1, 199.2 (v) 182.44, 204.10
keelhaul 604.15
keelhauling 604.2
keel over 25.5, 182.44, 205.6
keelson 199.2
keel up 182.44
keen (n) 58.4, 115.3, 115.6 (v) 58.8, 115.10, 524.25 (a) 17.13, 17.14, 24.13, 58.14, 68.6, 93.18, 93.24, 101.8, 105.31, 144.23, 285.8, 324.5, 330.17, 339.14, 404.8, 405.16, 489.15, 671.16, 920.14, 981.5, 999.13, 1023.14
keen about 101.11, 983.16
keen desire 101.1
keen-edged 285.8
keener 309.7
keen eye 27.10
keen-eyed 339.13
keening (n) 115.1 (a) 58.14
keen interest 101.1
keenly sensitive 24.13
keenness 17.2, 17.5, 68.1, 101.1, 144.8, 285.1, 324.1, 339.5, 489.2, 920.2, 1023.1
keen-nosed 69.13
keen on 100.22, 101.11, 983.16
keen pleasure 95.1
keen satisfaction 95.1
keen-scented 69.13
keen sight 27.1
keen-sighted 27.21
keen-witted 489.15, 920.14
keen-wittedness 489.2, 920.2
keep (n) 10.3, 385.3, 429.5, 429.8, 449.3, 460.6 (v) 326.2, 385.7, 386.11, 386.12, 397.8, 428.7, 434.2, 449.12, 474.5, 474.7, 487.2, 701.14, 827.6, 855.7, 856.4, 989.12, 1008.18, 1070.6
keep a balance 863.4
keep abreast of the times 551.16
keep account of 551.16, 1017.20
keep accounts 628.8
keep a check on 551.16, 1017.20
keep a civil tongue in one's head 504.10
keep a firm hand on 425.4
keep a firm hold on 474.6
keep afloat 385.12, 901.21
keep after 389.7
keep a good leeway 261.7
keep a good margin 261.7

keep a good offing 261.7
keep a happy medium 467.6, 670.5
keep a high profile 31.5
keep alert 23.3, 339.8
keep a lid on 345.7
keep a light in the window 585.7
keep alive 306.11, 397.8, 829.5, 856.4
keep alive in one's thoughts 989.12
keep aloof 157.7, 368.6
keep a lookout for 130.6
keep a low profile 139.7, 346.8, 494.7
keep an account with 622.7
keep an ear to the ground 983.7
keep an eye on 27.13, 339.9, 551.16, 573.10, 938.35, 1008.19
keep an eye out 27.13, 339.8, 1007.3
keep an eye out for 130.8
keep an idea 931.16
keep an open house 585.7
keep an open mind 979.7, 982.2
keep a nose to the wind 339.8
keep apart 224.3, 773.6, 872.6
keep a safe distance 1007.2
keep a safe distance from 261.7
keep as a nest egg 386.12, 405.11
keep a sharp eye on 1008.19
keep a sharp lookout 339.8
keep aside 773.6
keep a stiff upper lip 106.9, 109.10, 492.14
keep a straight face 111.2
keep at 360.2, 389.7
keep at a distance 157.7, 344.6, 583.4
keep at a respectful distance 157.7, 261.7, 368.6, 494.7
keep at arm's length 157.7, 261.7, 460.10, 908.3
keep at bay 460.10
keep a tight hand on 428.7
keep a tight hand upon 425.4
keep a tight hold on 474.6
keep a tight rein 670.6
keep a tight rein on 425.4
keep a tight rein upon 612.15
keep at it 330.15, 360.2, 856.5
keep at one's beck and call 432.8
keep au courant 551.16
keep awake 23.3
keep a watch 825.5
keep away 222.7, 261.7
keep away from 261.7, 368.6
keep a weather eye on 27.13
keep a weather eye open 339.8, 494.7
keep a weather eye out 494.7, 983.8, 1007.3
keep bachelor quarters 565.5
keep back 175.9, 345.7, 386.12, 390.5, 428.7, 846.8, 1012.10
keep banker's hours 846.7
keep between us 345.7
keep body and soul together 306.11, 385.12
keep books 628.8
keep both feet on the ground 987.4
keep busy 330.15, 725.16
keep buttoned up 345.7
keep by one 386.12
keep calm 106.9
keep clear of 261.7, 368.6
keep close 345.7
keep close to 223.12
keep coming 849.11
keep company 562.14
keep company with 582.17, 587.9, 769.7
keep cool 106.9
keep count of 1017.20
keep current 841.6
keep dark 345.7
keep doggedly at 360.3
keep down 428.8, 432.8, 612.15
keep driving 330.15, 360.2
keeper 397.5, 429.10, 470.1, 907.3, 1008.5, 1008.6
keep everyone waiting 846.7
keep faith 644.9
keep faith with 434.2
keep fit 83.6
keep fresh 829.5
keep from 329.3, 345.7, 368.6, 428.7, 668.7, 1012.14
keep from harm 1008.18
keep from laughing 111.2
keep from spreading 428.9
keep going 330.15, 360.2, 856.3, 856.4
keep guard 1008.20
keep hands off 368.6, 430.16, 668.7
keep hanging in midair 362.8
keep her steady 182.28
keep hidden 346.7
keep hold of 474.6
keep hold of the land 223.12
keep hope alive 124.7
keep hoping 124.7
keep house 159.17, 228.31
keep in 428.7, 429.12, 474.5
keep in bounds 428.9
keep in check 428.7, 1012.10
keep in contact with 343.8
keep in countenance 375.21, 449.14, 509.9
keep in custody 429.12
keep in detention 429.12
keep in formation 182.46
keep informed 551.16
keeping (n) 264.1, 397.1, 429.5, 434.1, 474.1, 1008.2 (a) 397.12, 474.8
keeping a low profile 139.11
keeping apart 872.2
keeping flocks and herds 1070.1
keeping in 474.1
keeping in mind 989.23
keeping it real 337.1
keeping Lent 100.25, 515.5
keeping low visibility 139.11
keeping one's lip buttoned 51.2
keeping the faith (n) 434.1 (a) 692.8
keep in hand 390.5
keep in ignorance 345.7
keep in memory 989.12
keep in mind 931.16, 983.9, 989.12
keep in order 573.10
keep in petto 345.7
keep in practice 568.13
keep in reserve 386.12
keep in sight 27.13, 339.8, 983.9
keep in step 578.10, 836.4, 867.4
keep in store 386.12
keep in suspense 971.13
keep intact 397.8
keep in the background 139.7, 346.8, 583.4
keep in the center of one's attention 983.8
keep in the dark 345.7
keep in the middle of the road 467.5
keep in the right path 653.4
keep in touch 343.8
keep in view 27.13, 339.8, 983.9, 989.12
keep inviolate 397.8
keep in with 587.13
keep it a deep 345.7
keep it under one's hat 345.7
keep it up 134.5
keep late hours 846.7
keep moving 330.15
keep mum 51.5, 345.7
keep off 460.10, 908.3, 1012.14
keep off and on 362.8, 364.4
keep on 330.15, 360.2, 827.6, 856.3
keep on at 96.13
keep one company 769.7
keep one guessing 971.13
keep one in line 425.4
keep one on edge 126.4
keep one on pins and needles 126.4
keep one on shpilkes 126.4
keep one on tenterhooks 126.4, 971.12
keep one's chin up 109.10, 492.14
keep one's cool 106.6, 106.9, 123.2, 670.5, 855.11
keep one's counsel 51.5
keep one's course 161.10
keep one's distance 139.7, 157.7, 261.7, 344.6, 368.6, 583.4
keep one's ears open 48.10, 983.7
keep one's ear to the ground 48.10, 981.3
keep oneself to oneself 139.7, 344.6, 583.4, 872.6
keep oneself under control 668.6
keep one's esthetic distance 261.7
keep one's eye on 955.6, 981.3
keep one's eye on the ball 339.8, 983.8
keep one's eye peeled 494.7
keep one's eyes on the stars 100.20
keep one's eyes open 23.3, 27.13, 339.8, 494.7, 981.3, 983.8
keep one's eyes peeled 27.13, 339.8
keep one's eyes skinned 27.13
keep one's eyes upon 27.15
keep one's fingers crossed 124.7, 954.7
keep one's footing 359.9
keep one's freedom 565.5
keep one's hand in 568.13
keep one's head 106.9, 670.5
keep one's head above water 385.12, 409.13, 827.6, 1007.2
keep one's mouth shut 51.5
keep one's nose out 430.17, 982.2
keep one's nose to the grindstone 330.15, 360.3, 725.14
keep one's own counsel 344.6, 345.7
keep one's pants on 134.4
keep one's pecker up 109.10, 492.14
keep one's promise 434.2, 644.9
keep one's shirt on 106.9, 134.4
keep one's spirits up 109.10, 124.7
keep one's sword in its sheath 464.8
keep one's temper 106.7, 670.5
keep one's tongue between one's teeth 51.5
keep one's trap shut 51.6
keep one's wits about one 920.10
keep one's word 434.2, 644.9
keep one's yap shut 51.6
keep on good terms 587.9
keep on hand 386.12
keep on ice 397.9
keep on keeping on 330.15, 360.7, 856.3
keep on the go 330.15
keep on the safe side 494.6, 1007.3
keep on the straight and narrow path 653.4
keep on trucking 330.15, 360.7
keep out 773.4
keep out in the cold 773.4
keep out of 329.4
keep out of harm's way 494.7
keep out of mischief 321.5
keep out of sight 346.8
keep out of the way 222.7
keep out of the way of 261.7, 368.6
keep pace with 174.14, 790.5, 836.4, 899.3
keep pointed 161.10, 182.28, 182.46
keep posted 551.9, 551.16
keep quiet 51.5, 173.7
keep remote from 368.6
keep safe 397.8, 1007.2
keepsake 989.6
keep score 871.8
keep secret 344.6, 345.7, 346.7
keep silence 51.5

keep silent 51.5
keep smiling 124.7
keep snug 345.7
keep something for a rainy day 494.6
keep station 182.46
keep step with 790.5
keep still 51.5
keep tabs 1017.20
keep tabs on 494.7, 551.16, 1008.19
keep tally 1017.20
keep tempo 708.44
keep the ball rolling 330.15, 360.2
keep the change 485.3
keep the course 182.28
keep the door open 585.7
keep the ear to the ground 339.8
keep the even tenor of one's way 856.5
keep the faith 124.7, 434.2, 692.6
keep the golden mean 467.6
keep the heading 182.28
keep the home fires burning 585.7
keep the law 326.2
keep the lid on 428.8
keep the memory alive 989.12
keep them in stitches 743.21
keep the peace 464.8, 670.5, 670.7
keep the pot boiling 330.15, 360.2
keep the wolf from the door 385.12
keep the wound open 507.5
keep time 708.44, 821.6, 832.11, 836.4
keep to 346.8
keep together 450.3
keep to oneself 51.5, 344.6, 345.7, 474.5, 583.4
keep to the middle 246.2
keep to the middle way 670.5
keep to the spirit of 434.2
keep track of 551.16, 1017.20
keep troth 644.9
keep trying 360.2
keep under 106.8, 428.8, 432.8, 612.15
keep under control 428.7
keep undercover 346.6, 1008.18
keep under lock and key 429.14
keep under observation 27.13
keep under one's thumb 432.8, 612.14, 894.11
keep under wraps 345.7, 346.6
keep up 15.10, 360.2, 397.8, 578.10, 724.12, 856.4, 901.21
keep up a correspondence 553.10
keep up a fast pace 669.6
keep up a killing pace 669.6
keep up appearances 578.10
keep up on 551.16
keep up one's courage 492.14
keep uppermost in one's thought 983.8
keep up the good work 360.2
keep up the memory of 989.12
keep up-to-date 551.16
keep up to standard 867.4
keep up with 174.14
keep up with the Joneses 457.18, 578.10
keep vigil 339.8, 1008.20
keep warm 1019.22
keep watch 339.8, 1008.20
keep watch and ward 339.8, 1008.20
keep watch on 551.16
keep watch over 1008.19, 1008.20
keep within 207.5
keep within bounds 428.9, 668.6, 670.5, 670.6
keep within compass 635.4, 670.5
keep within limits 668.6
keep within one's budget 635.4
keep within the bosom of the lodge 345.7
keep within these walls 345.7
keep with it 856.3
keep your shirt on 846.12
kef 331.6
kegeling 750.1
kegling 750.1
keif 22.1
keister 217.5
Kekulé formula 1038.7
keloid 1004.1
keloidal 1004.8
kelp 310.4
kelpie 678.10
kemo sabe 588.3
ken (n) 27.1, 31.3, 928.1 (v) 27.12, 521.7, 928.12
kennel (n) 228.21, 239.5, 290.2, 311.16, 383.6, 770.5 (v) 212.5
keno 759.15
Kentucky Derby 757.1
Keogh plan 729.3
kept 386.15, 397.13
kept down 432.16
kept in 429.19
kept in remembrance 989.22
kept in reserve 386.15
kept mistress 665.17
kept-out 773.7
kept under 432.16
kept woman 665.17
kerb 211.6, 383.6
kerbstone 211.6, 383.6
kerchief 5.25
kerf 289.1
kerflooey 393.38, 395.29
kerfuffle 810.2
Kermandec Trench 275.5
kermis 743.4
kernel 10.39, 196.5, 208.2, 310.31, 767.2, 819.1, 997.6
kerosene 1025.20, 1056.4
kerosene-heated 1020.29
ketchup 10.12
ketone 7.5
ketosis 85.22
kettle-drummer 710.10
Ketubim 683.3
key (n) 35.1, 235.2, 292.10, 341.3, 347.2, 517.9, 548.6, 709.4, 709.15, 711.6, 747.1, 894.6, 1042.18 (v) 293.6, 549.15 (a) 208.11
keyboard (n) 711.17, 1042.4 (v) 548.15, 549.15, 1042.21
keyboarder 547.18, 548.12, 1042.17
keyboard instrument 711.12
keyboardist 710.7
keyboard player 710.7
keyboard wind instrument 711.13
keycard 292.10
keyed up 105.20
keyed-up 130.12
key figure 208.4
keyhole 747.1
key in (n) 548.6 (v) 1042.21
Keynesian economics 731.11
Keynesianism 731.11
keynote (n) 517.1, 543.3, 709.15, 865.4 (v) 865.10
keynote address 609.7
keynote presentation 543.3
keynoter 610.7
keynote speaker 543.4
keynote speech 609.7
keypad 1042.4
key person 574.1
key player 574.1
key point 997.6
key puncher 1042.17
keys 647.4, 711.17
key signature 709.12, 709.15
keystone 279.4, 745.1, 901.7, 997.6
keystone bagger 745.2
keystone sack 745.1
key to 788.7
key to the city 894.6
key trait 373.2
key up 105.12, 251.5
keyword 517.9, 526.1
khaki 40.3
khaki-colored 40.3
khakis 5.18
khamsin 318.6, 318.12
khan 575.9, 608.7, 648.3
khanum 608.6
khazer 672.3
khedive 575.12
kiack 703.2
kibble 1051.9
kibbutz 476.2, 1069.8
kibe 85.37, 1023.2
kibitz 214.7, 422.5
kibitzer 214.4, 422.3, 759.21, 918.1
kibitzing 214.2
kibosh 19.9, 820.6
kick (n) 17.3, 68.2, 105.3, 115.5, 333.2, 517.15, 551.4, 745.3, 746.3, 752.3, 759.10, 900.1, 902.9, 903.2 (v) 68.5, 87.22, 108.6, 115.16, 333.5, 374.3, 517.22, 668.8, 746.5, 752.4, 902.21, 903.6, 909.20
kick about 902.21
kick against 453.3
kick against the pricks 333.4
kick a habit 374.3
kick around 331.14, 389.6, 432.9, 541.11, 612.15, 902.21
kick-ass 18.12
kick back 20.7, 106.7, 329.2, 624.11, 631.2, 903.6
kickback 624.2, 631.1, 903.2
kickboxing 760.3
kick cold turkey 87.22
kick downstairs 773.5, 902.21, 909.13
kick down the ladder 359.8
kicked around 432.16
kicker 108.4, 115.9, 131.2, 421.3, 746.2, 959.2
kick in 307.19, 385.7, 478.14, 624.16, 818.7
kicking 115.5, 902.9
kicking downstairs 909.1
kicking out 909.1
kicking team 746.2
kicking upstairs 446.1, 447.2
kick in the face (n) 156.2 (v) 156.5
kick in the teeth 442.2
kick it up a notch 251.5
kick like a mule, a 903.2
kick like a mule 903.6
kick off 307.19, 439.5, 746.5, 752.4, 814.2, 818.7, 904.13
kickoff (n) 746.3, 752.3, 816.2, 818.1 (a) 816.4
kick off an attack 459.17
kickoff return 746.3
kick one in the teeth 442.5
kick oneself 113.6
kick out 902.21, 909.13
kick out against 451.3, 453.3
kick over the traces 327.7
kick pleat 291.2
kicks 95.1
kickshaw 10.8, 498.4, 743.16, 998.5
kick-start 174.8, 818.11, 904.13
kickstart 174.4
kick stick 87.12
kick the air 604.18
kick the beam 298.6, 992.8
kick the bucket 307.19
kick the habit 87.22, 412.7, 668.8
kick under the table 399.1
kick up a dust 503.3
kick up a fuss 115.16, 152.20, 810.11, 1013.14
kick up a hullabaloo 53.9
kick up a racket 53.9
kick up a row 115.16, 152.15, 152.20, 456.12, 810.11
kick up a shindy 810.11
kick up a storm 115.16, 152.20, 810.11, 1013.14
kick up dust 53.9
kick up one's heels 582.21, 743.24
kick upstairs 446.2, 447.4, 909.19
kick wheel 742.4
kicky 97.8
kid (n) 302.3, 302.10, 311.8 (v) 356.15, 489.13, 490.6
kid along 511.6
kid around 489.13, 998.15

kid brother 559.3
kidder 357.1, 490.4
kiddie 302.3
kiddie cam 549.10
kidding (n) 356.1, 489.6, 490.1, 490.3 (a) 490.7, 508.12
kidding around 490.1, 998.9
kiddish 301.11
kiddo 302.3
kiddy 302.3
kiddy pool 743.12
kid-glove politics 609.1
kid gloves 427.1
kid-glove treatment 427.1
kidnap 480.14, 482.20
kidnapper 480.12, 483.10
kidnapping 480.2, 482.9
kidney 2.16, 809.3, 978.3
kidney disease 85.24
kidneylike 279.16
kidneys 2.16, 10.20
kidney-shaped 279.16
kid oneself 954.6
kids 302.2, 559.5, 561.1
kid sister 559.3
kid stuff 1014.4
kidvid 1035.2
kif 87.11
Kilkenny cats 457.1
kill (n) 238.1, 308.1, 382.7 (v) 116.9, 255.10, 255.12, 308.13, 345.8, 395.12, 395.16, 428.8, 444.5, 613.10, 743.21, 820.6, 857.12
kill by inches 26.7, 96.18
kill-crazy 671.21
killer (n) 308.11, 593.3, 671.9, 999.7 (a) 999.13
killer-diller 999.7
killer instinct 330.7, 671.1
kill for 100.14
killing (n) 307.5, 308.1, 472.3, 671.3 (a) 21.13, 308.23, 725.18, 1016.21
killing field 463.2
killing fields 308.12
killing frost 1023.7
killing ground 463.2
killing pace 669.2
killjoy 112.14, 125.7, 1012.9
kill off 255.10, 308.13, 395.12
kill oneself 308.22
kill the clock 747.4
kill the fatted calf 487.2, 585.9
kill the goose that lays the golden egg 414.14, 486.4
kill the slain 993.12
kill time 331.13, 743.22, 821.6
kill two birds with one stone 472.12
kiln (n) 742.5, 1020.11 (v) 1066.6
kilo 882.10
kilobit 1042.14
kilobyte 882.10, 1042.14, 1042.18
kilocalorie 1019.19
kilocycle 882.10
kilocycles 1034.12
kilogram 882.10
kilogram-calorie 1019.19
kilogram-meter 17.7
kilohertz 882.10, 1034.12
kiloliter 882.10
kilometer 882.10
kilowatt-hour 17.7
kin 559.2, 559.5, 809.2, 809.3
kind (n) 559.4, 767.4, 809.3 (a) 143.13, 148.6, 427.8, 449.22, 587.15, 999.12
kind deed 143.7
kindergarten 567.2
kindergartner 572.3
kindest regards 504.8
kind heart 143.1
kindhearted 143.13
kindheartedness 143.1
kindle 17.10, 105.12, 152.19, 375.18, 886.11, 1020.18, 1020.22
kindled 1019.27
kindliness 143.1, 427.2
kindling (n) 1020.4, 1021.3, 1054.3 (a) 1020.27
kindlings 1021.3
kindling wood 1021.3
kindly 143.13, 427.8, 449.22
kindly act 143.7
kindly-disposed 143.13, 449.22
kindly disposition 143.1
kindness 143.1, 143.7, 145.1, 148.1, 427.2, 587.1, 999.1
kindness of heart 143.1, 999.9
kind offices 143.7
kindred (n) 559.1, 559.2 (a) 559.6, 560.18, 775.10
kindred soul 784.3
kindred spirit 582.6, 588.2, 784.3
kind regards 504.8
kind remembrances 504.8
kine 311.6
kinematic 1039.9
kinematical 1039.9
kinematics 172.1
kinescope 714.8, 1035.11
kinesiatrics 172.1
kinesic 517.25
kinesics 517.14
kinesiology 172.1
kinesipathy 172.1
kinesis 172.1
kinesitherapy 172.1
kinesthesia 24.5
kinesthetic 24.9
kinesthetic memory 989.1
kinetic 17.13, 1039.9
kinetical 1039.9
kinetic energy 17.1
kinetics 172.1, 1039.3
kinetic theory 1018.1
kinfolk 559.2
kinfolks 559.2
king 575.8, 608.7, 730.1, 743.17, 758.2, 997.10
king at arms 575.20
king crab 311.29
kingcraft 609.3
kingdom 232.1, 305.3, 527.1, 809.4, 809.5
kingdom Animalia 1068.1
kingdom come 986.11
Kingdom of God 681.3
king-emperor 575.8
kingfish 575.4
kinghood 417.8
King James Version 683.2
kinglet 575.8
kinglike 417.17, 608.10
kingliness 136.2
kingly 136.12, 417.17, 608.10
kingmaker 415.8, 610.6, 894.6
king of arms 575.20
king of hearts 758.2
King of Kings 677.2
King of Light, the 677.5
kingpin 575.4, 997.9
king post 273.4
king-post 901.8
King's English, the 523.4
kingship 249.3, 417.8, 608.9, 612.4
king size 257.4
king-size 247.7, 257.16, 257.20, 257.23
king's ransom 618.2
King's shilling, the 624.1
kink (n) 26.2, 281.2, 364.1, 927.2, 1003.2, 1004.1 (v) 281.5, 1004.4
kinked 281.9, 1004.8
kinky 281.9, 364.5, 868.6, 927.6
kinnery 559.2
kinoplasm 305.5
kinsfolk 559.2
kinship 455.1, 559.1, 775.3, 784.2
kinship group 617.2
kinsman 559.2
kinsmen 559.2
kinswoman 559.2
kiosk 228.9, 228.12, 736.3
kip (n) 901.19 (v) 22.14
kip down 22.18
kipper (n) 10.24, 311.29 (v) 397.9
kippered herring 10.24
kippered salmon 10.24
kippering 397.2
kirigami 712.2
kishkes 2.16, 207.4, 767.5
kismet 839.2, 964.2
kiss (n) 73.1, 223.5, 562.4, 585.4 (v) 73.7, 223.10, 562.19, 585.10
kissable 104.24
kiss and make up 465.10
kiss and tell 351.6
kiss-and-tell 351.10, 551.19
kiss-ass 138.14
kiss cheeks 585.10
kisser 216.4, 292.4
kiss goodbye 473.4, 475.3
kiss hands 585.10
kissing (n) 562.1 (a) 223.17
kissing and making up 465.3
kiss of death 308.2, 645.8, 820.4
kiss off 475.3, 908.3, 984.4
kiss-off 157.2, 372.1, 442.2, 908.2
kiss of life 2.21
kiss one off 442.5
kiss one's feet 138.7
kiss the book 334.6
kiss the hem of one's garment 138.7, 155.6
kiss the rod 433.11
kist 309.11
kit 195.1, 302.10, 311.20, 385.4, 471.3, 770.12
kit and caboodle, the 792.4
kitchen (n) 8.17, 11.4, 197.14, 739.8, 745.3 (a) 11.6
kitchen cabinet 423.1, 613.3
kitchener 11.3
kitchenette 11.4, 197.14
Kitchen Kaffir 523.11
kitchenmaid 577.8
kitchen midden 80.10, 391.6
kitchen police 461.22
kitchen sink 79.12, 797.8, 973.7
kitchen stuff 10.1
kitchenware 11.4, 735.4
kite (n) 181.1, 181.14, 728.10 (v) 193.10
kite a check 625.6, 728.28
kited check 625.3
kite-wind 318.8
kith and kin 559.2
kithless 584.12, 872.8
kithlessness 584.4
kit house 228.5
kitling 311.20
kitsch 497.1, 547.12, 712.9, 718.1
kitschy 497.14
kitten (n) 16.7, 302.3, 302.10, 311.20 (v) 1.3
kitten heels 5.27
kittenish 77.13, 109.14, 301.12, 311.42
kittenishness 109.4
kittenlike 301.12
kitty 311.20, 728.14, 750.3, 759.5
kitty-cat 311.20
kittycorner 204.19
kittycornered 204.19
Klaxon 53.6
klaxon 399.3, 400.1
kleig light 704.18
kleptomania 482.12
kleptomaniacal 482.21
klieg light 704.18, 1025.4
kloof 237.7
klutz 414.9, 924.3
klutziness 534.1, 922.4
klutzish 922.15
klutzy 534.2, 922.15
knack 413.6, 498.4
knave 322.3, 660.3, 758.2
knavery 356.4, 415.3, 645.2, 654.3
knavish 322.6, 645.17, 654.16
knavishness 645.2
knaydlach 10.33
knead 73.8, 262.7, 797.10, 1044.6, 1047.6
kneading 1044.3
knee (n) 2.7, 177.14, 278.2, 800.4 (v) 902.21
knee-cap 19.9
knee-deep 275.11, 276.5
knee guard 1008.3
knee-high 258.10, 274.7, 301.11
knee-high to a grasshopper 258.10, 274.7
knee jerk 365.1

knee-jerk (n) 903.1, 934.2 (a) 365.11, 373.14, 509.18, 903.9, 934.6, 953.22, 954.8, 963.14
knee-jerk agreement 954.1
knee-jerk assent 332.2
knee-jerk conservative 853.4
knee-jerk reaction 373.3, 963.5
knee-jerk response 903.1, 954.1
kneel 138.7, 155.6, 913.9
kneeling 155.2, 433.1, 913.3
kneeling stool 703.10
kneel to 433.10, 440.11
knee-shaped 278.6
knee-slapper 489.6, 489.9
kneesocks 752.1
knee-sprung 393.30
knees-up 582.12
knell (n) 54.3, 115.6, 307.1, 309.6 (v) 54.8, 115.10
knelling 54.3
knell-like 115.22
knez 608.7
knickers 5.18
knickknack 498.4, 743.16, 998.5
knickknackery 998.4, 998.5
knickknacks 735.6
knife (n) 462.5, 1040.2, 1040.7 (v) 459.25
knife, the 91.19
knife edge 971.6, 1013.4
knife-edge 285.2
knife-edged 285.8
knifelike 285.8
knife one 645.13
knife pleat 291.2
knife poised at one's throat 514.1
knifing 459.10
knight (n) 178.8, 460.7, 461.1, 504.9, 608.5, 743.17 (v) 446.2
knight-adventurer 608.5
knightage 608.1
knight bachelor 608.5
knight banneret 608.5
knight baronet 608.5
knight-errant 608.5
knight-errantry 652.2
knight-errantship 608.9
knighthood 458.5, 608.9
knighting 446.1
knight in shining armor 492.7
knightlike 492.16
knightliness 492.1, 504.2, 652.2
knightly 492.16, 504.14, 608.10, 652.6
knightly skill 458.5
knight of the plume 547.13, 718.3
knight of the quill 547.13, 718.3
knight of the road 178.3, 730.4
knight service 469.1
knit (v) 260.7, 291.6, 396.21, 740.6, 800.7, 800.11 (a) 740.7, 800.13
knit one's brow 931.9
knitted 260.12, 291.8, 740.7, 800.13
knitter 740.4, 741.2
knit the brow 110.15
knitting 260.1, 740.1
knitting machine 740.5
knit up 396.13, 396.15
knives 8.12
knob (n) 237.4, 282.2, 283.3 (v) 288.4, 294.4
knobbed 283.17, 294.7
knobbliness 288.1
knobbly 288.8
knobby 272.18, 283.17
knoblike 283.17
knobs 283.7
knock (n) 56.1, 510.4, 902.4 (v) 56.6, 510.14, 902.13, 902.14, 902.16
knock about 177.23, 389.5
knockabout 671.20
knock against 902.13
knock around 177.23, 541.11
knock-around clothes 5.20
knock back 8.29, 88.24
knock cold 902.17
knock dead 743.21, 1016.16
knock down 112.18, 128.10, 395.19, 472.9, 512.8, 631.2, 633.6, 734.11, 754.4, 902.14, 913.5, 958.4
knockdown 587.4
knock-down-and-drag-out (n) 456.6, 457.5 (a) 671.20
knock-down-and-drag-out fight 456.6
knockdown argument 935.10, 958.3
knocked flat 274.7
knocked out 21.8, 25.8
knocked-out 262.9
knocked silly 985.14
knocked-up 78.18
knocker 512.6
knockers 283.7
knock flat 128.10
knock for a loop 131.7, 902.17
knock head 604.14
knock heads 424.8
knock heads together 424.8, 425.4, 604.14
knock in 191.7
knocking (n) 512.1 (a) 56.11
knocking down 472.1
knocking knees 127.5
knocking off course 160.1
knocking up 78.3
knock in the head 308.18, 395.11, 820.6
knock into one's head 568.12
knock it off 51.6, 857.6
knock-knee 265.3
knock-kneed 265.12
knock off 20.8, 255.10, 307.19, 308.14, 340.9, 365.8, 407.4, 412.9, 482.16, 547.21, 718.6, 857.8
knockoff 336.3
knock off course 160.5
knock off one's feet 95.11
knock-on 886.3
knock one back 630.13
knock one dead 95.11
knock one down to size 137.6
knock-on effect 886.3
knock one for a loop 95.11
knock one off his perch 137.5
knock oneself out 403.14
knock one's eyes out 1016.16
knock one's head against 902.12
knock one's lights out 604.14
knock one's socks off 95.11, 122.6, 377.7
knock on the head 308.18, 395.11, 412.6
knock on wood 124.7, 954.7
knock out 19.10, 21.6, 25.4, 95.11, 262.7, 340.9, 395.11, 547.21, 718.6, 754.4, 820.6, 902.14
knockout 25.2, 411.1, 754.3, 820.4, 999.7, 1016.8
knockout blow 820.4
knockout drops 25.3, 87.6, 88.9
knock over 395.19, 482.16
knockover 482.4
knock senseless 25.4
knock stiff 25.4
knock the bottom out of 19.11, 633.6, 958.4, 1012.15
knock the chip off one's shoulder 454.3
knock the chocks out from under 958.4
knock the props from under one 1012.15
knock the props out from under 19.10, 958.4, 977.2
knock together 340.9
knock unconscious 25.4
knock under 433.6
knock up 78.10, 912.5
knoll 237.4
knot (n) 3.7, 265.1, 282.2, 283.3, 310.11, 522.8, 770.3, 770.7, 799.2, 800.3, 1013.7, 1045.6 (v) 265.5, 790.5, 799.3, 800.5, 1045.10
knotholes 759.12
knotmeter 174.7
knots 174.1, 184.31
knotted 283.17, 288.8, 291.8, 770.21, 775.9, 790.7, 799.4, 800.13, 1013.17
knottiness 522.2
knotting 800.1, 800.3
knotty 283.17, 288.8, 522.14, 1013.17
knotty point 522.8, 1013.7
knotty question 938.10
knout (n) 605.1 (v) 604.12
know 521.7, 551.15, 587.9, 831.8, 928.12, 970.9, 989.11
know, the 551.1
knowability 521.1
knowable 521.10, 928.25
know again 989.11
know a hawk from a handsaw 413.19, 944.6
know a little 930.10
know-all (n) 140.5 (a) 140.11
know all the answers 413.19, 928.13
know all the ins and outs 413.19, 928.13
know all the moves moves 413.19
know all the moves of the game 413.19
know all the tricks 413.19
know all the tricks of the trade 413.19
know a thing or two 413.19, 928.13
know a trick or two 415.10
know a trick worth two of that 415.11
know backwards 928.13
know backwards and forwards 413.19, 928.13
know beforehand 961.6
know by heart 928.13, 989.16
know by rote 928.13
know by sight 989.11
know damn well 928.13
know darn well 928.13
know down to the ground 928.13
know for certain 970.9
know from alpha to omega 413.19
know from A to Z 413.19
know from memory 989.16
know from nothing 930.8
know from the ground up 413.19
know full well 928.13
know-how 413.1, 928.1
know in advance 961.6
knowing (n) 928.1 (a) 380.8, 413.28, 415.12, 920.12, 920.15, 920.17, 928.15
knowing, the 921.3
knowingness 928.1
knowing one's place 155.10
knowing right from wrong 925.1
know in one's bones 133.9, 934.4
know inside out 521.8, 928.13
know instinctively 934.4
know it all 140.6
know-it-all (n) 140.5, 142.6, 413.11 (a) 140.11
knowledge 570.1, 920.1, 928.1
knowledgeable 570.16, 866.5, 920.17, 928.15
knowledge engineering 1042.20
knowledge gap 930.1
knowledge of the world 413.9
knowledge representation 1042.20
knowledge-seeking 938.38
knowledge without reason 934.1
knowledge without thought 934.1
know like a book 413.19, 928.13
know like the back of one's hand 413.19, 521.8, 928.13
known 928.26
known as 527.14
known by every schoolboy 928.27
known by measurement 300.13
known by the name of 527.14
know no bounds 823.2, 910.9, 993.8, 993.10
know no end 823.2
know no limit 823.2
know no limits 669.5
know not 930.10

know nothing 930.8
know-nothing (n) 930.7 (a) 930.11, 980.12
know-nothingism 611.4, 773.3, 930.1, 980.4
know nothing of 930.10
know not what 930.10
know no wrong 657.5
know one's onions 413.19, 928.13
know one's own mind 323.3, 359.8
know one's place 139.7
know one's stuff 413.19, 928.13
know one's way about 413.19
know one's way around 928.13
know something by heart 928.12
know something by rote 928.12
know something from memory 928.12
know the ropes 413.19, 928.13
know the score 413.19, 920.10, 928.13
know the ways of the world 413.19
know well 551.15, 570.9, 928.13
know what it's all about 413.19
know what's what 413.19, 920.10, 928.13, 944.6
know when one has had enough 668.6
know when the honeymoon is over. 987.4
know where the bodies are buried 345.7, 551.15
know which is which 944.6
know which side one's bread is buttered on 651.4
knub 294.1
knuckle (n) 800.4 (v) 725.9
knuckle down 433.6
knuckle down to 404.3, 725.15
knuckle dragger 671.10
knuckle-dusters 462.4
knuckle guard 1008.3
knucklehead 924.4
knuckleheaded 922.17
knuckleheadedness 922.4
knuckler 746.3
knuckles 462.4
knuckle to 433.10
knuckle under 433.6
knuckle under to 433.9
knucks 462.4
knur 283.3
knurl (n) 283.3 (v) 289.4
knurled 283.17, 288.8
knurly 283.17, 288.8
KO 395.11
kobold 678.8, 680.7
Kodak 714.11
kohen 699.11
kohl 1016.11
koine 523.11
kolkhoz 476.2
kona ame 66.3
kona-ame 66.3
K-1 bombsight 1036.2
konimeter 1051.8
koniology 1051.8
Kon Tiki 180.11
koodoo 311.5
kook 870.4, 926.16, 927.4
kookiness 926.2
kooky 870.11, 923.9, 926.27, 927.6
koozie 195.1
kop 237.4
kopje 237.4
Koran 673.8, 683.6
Koranic 683.14
Kore 682.5, 1069.4
kosher 8.33, 79.25, 637.3, 673.11, 867.6
kowtow (n) 155.2, 913.3 (v) 138.7, 155.6, 201.5, 433.10, 913.9
kowtower 138.3
kowtowing 913.3
kraal 231.4
K ration 10.6
K rations 515.2
Kraut 10.35
Kreis 231.5
Kremlin, the 228.5
kreplach 10.33
kriegspiel 458.4
Kriss Kringle 678.13
Kronos 821.2
kudos 509.3, 509.5, 646.4, 662.1
kurbash 605.1
Kuril Trench 275.5
kvetch (n) 108.4, 115.5, 115.9, 510.9 (v) 108.6, 115.16
kvetching 115.5
kvetchy 108.8, 115.20
Kwok's disease 85.34
K-Y 1056.2
kyle 242.1
kymograph 916.8
kyphosis 265.3
kyphotic 265.13
Kyrie Eleison 696.4
L 87.10, 254.3, 278.2, 704.16, 882.7
lab 739.6, 942.5
Laban dance notation system 349.1
labanotation 349.1
labarum 647.7
label (n) 517.13, 527.3, 647.2, 809.2, 809.3 (v) 517.20, 527.11, 864.9
labeled element 91.8
labeling 373.1, 864.1, 864.8
labellum 211.4
labia 2.13
labial (n) 524.12 (a) 211.13, 524.30
labialization 524.12
labialized 524.30
labia majora 2.13
labia minora 2.13
labiate 211.13
labiodental 524.12
labionasal 524.12
labium 211.4
labor (n) 1.1, 724.1, 724.2, 725.4 (v) 1.3, 330.10, 403.5, 724.12, 725.12, 849.9, 886.10, 917.15
labor against 451.4
laboratory 197.25, 739.6, 942.5
laboratory animal 942.7
laboratory technician 90.11
laboratory test 91.12
labor camp 429.8, 604.2
labor contract 437.1, 727.3
labor costs 626.3
labored 498.12, 534.3, 725.18, 849.15
labored breathing 21.3, 85.9
laborer 432.7, 577.3, 607.9, 726.2
labor force 726.2
labor for naught 391.3
labor in behalf of 449.18
labor in darkness 930.9
laboring (n) 538.6 (a) 725.17
laboring class 607.7
laboring man 607.9, 726.2
labor in one's vocation 724.12
labor interests 609.31
labor in vain (n) 391.3 (v) 391.8, 410.9, 473.5, 486.4
laborious 330.22, 725.18, 1013.17
laboriousness 330.6, 725.5, 1013.1
labor law 673.5
labor lost 391.3
labor market 726.2
labor negotiations 727.1
labor of Hercules 725.5
labor of love 143.7, 324.2, 478.2, 634.1
labor of Sisyphus 391.3
labor organizer 727.4
Labor Party 609.24
labor relations 727.1
labor resources 386.2
labor room 197.25
labor-saving 635.6, 1039.7, 1040.14
labor-saving device 449.9, 1040.3
labor the obvious 993.12
labor under 85.46, 831.8
labor under a disadvantage 1013.11
labor under a false impression 975.10
labor under difficulties 1013.11
labor union 617.1, 727.2
labor unionism 727.1
labor unionist 727.4
labor union official 727.4
Labour Party 609.24
lab rat 942.7
labrum 211.4
labyrinth 799.2
labyrinthian 799.4
labyrinthine 164.7, 265.10, 279.7, 281.6, 545.8, 799.4
lace (n) 4.1, 170.3, 271.4 (v) 604.12, 740.6, 797.12, 800.9
lace curtain 608.4
lace-curtain 578.16
laced 170.11, 740.7
lacelike 170.11
lacerability 1050.1
lacerable 1050.4
lacerate (v) 26.7, 96.18, 393.13, 802.14 (a) 289.5
lacerated 26.9, 96.25, 289.5, 393.27
lacerate the ear 58.11
lacerate the heart 112.19
laceration 85.38, 96.7, 802.2
lacery 170.3
lacework 170.3
laches 340.1, 435.1
Lachesis 964.3
lachryma 2.24, 115.2
lachrymal 2.33, 13.7, 115.21
lachrymose 13.7, 115.21
lachrymosity 115.2
laciness 270.4
lacing 170.3, 604.4, 740.1, 797.3
lack (n) 222.1, 619.2, 795.2, 992.4, 1003.1 (v) 619.5, 795.3, 911.2, 963.9, 992.7, 992.8
lackadaisical 102.7, 106.15, 331.20, 340.11, 846.17, 982.3
lackadaisicalness 102.2, 106.5, 331.6
lackbrained 922.13
lackbrainedness 922.1
lack emotion 982.2
lackey (n) 138.3, 577.1, 577.6, 616.8, 867.2 (v) 577.13
lack force 19.7
lacking 222.11, 473.8, 762.8, 795.4, 911.5, 992.9, 992.13, 1003.4
lacking give 1046.10
lackluster (n) 36.1, 1005.1, 1027.5 (a) 36.7, 1005.7, 1027.17
lack of affect 25.1, 94.1, 102.2
lack of agreement 531.1
lack of appetite 94.4, 102.3
lack of authority 418.1
lack of awareness 25.1, 922.2
lack of bite 286.1
lack of caring 94.4
lack of censorship 430.1
lack of ceremony 435.1
lack of charisma 895.1
lack of charm 895.1
lack of choice 963.6
lack of claim 640.1
lack of color 36.1
lack of concern 25.1
lack of concord 531.1
lack of consciousness 922.2
lack of contact 94.1
lack of convention 581.1
lack of conviction 955.1
lack of credentials 406.1
lack of definition 263.1
lack of depth 922.7
lack of eagerness 325.1
lack of enthusiasm 325.1
lack of feeling 25.1, 94.1, 102.2, 945.1
lack of feelings 987.2
lack of feeling tone 94.1
lack of finish 534.1
lack of food 515.2
lack of force 895.1
lack of foresight 340.2
lack of forethought 340.2
lack of heat 1023.1
lack of hindrance 1014.1
lack of incisiveness 286.1
lack of influence 895.1
lack of information 930.1
lack of integrity 354.4

lack of interest 982.1
lack of magnetism 895.1
lack of meaning 344.1
lack of memory 933.1
lack of message 344.1
lack of moral fiber 491.3
lack of motive 972.3
lack of parallelism 531.1
lack of personality 895.1
lack of pleasure 96.1
lack of polish 534.1
lack of power 895.1
lack of preparation 406.1
lack of principle 654.2
lack of refinement 945.1
lack of respect 156.1
lack of sanitation 80.3
lack of self-confidence 139.2
lack of sensitivity 923.2
lack of sentimentality 987.2
lack of sheen 1027.5
lack of smell 72.1
lack of sparkle 1027.5
lack of staying power 21.1
lack of substance 998.1
lack of title 640.1
lack of touch 94.1
lack of vision 30.1
lack of weight 298.1
lack of work 331.3
lack of zeal 325.1
lack preparation 406.6
lack regularity 851.2
lack the time 844.3
lackwit 924.2
lackwitted 922.13
lackwittedness 922.1
Laconian 344.5
laconic (n) 344.5 (a) 344.9, 537.6
laconicalness 344.2
laconicism 537.2
laconicness 537.2
laconics 537.2
laconism 344.2, 537.2
lacquer (n) 295.12 (v) 35.14, 295.24
lacquered 287.11
lacquering 35.12
lacquerwork 712.16
lacrimae rerum 112.11
lacrimal 2.33
lacrimate 13.5
lacrimation 13.1
lacrimatory (n) 115.2 (a) 2.33, 13.7, 115.21
lactate 8.19, 13.5
lactating 13.7
lactation 2.24, 13.1, 1061.1
lactational 13.7
lacteal 13.7, 1061.5
lacteous 13.7, 1061.5
lactescence 37.1, 1061.1
lactescent 37.7, 1061.5
lactic 1061.5
lactiferous 1061.5
lactometer 1045.8
lactose 66.3
lactose intolerance 85.22
lactovegetarian (n) 8.16 (a) 8.31
lactovegetarianism 7.13
lacuna 158.8, 224.1, 284.2, 292.1, 795.2, 813.2
lacunar 224.7
lacuscular 241.5
lacustral 241.5
lacustrian (n) 241.2 (a) 241.5
lacustrine 241.5
lacustrine dweller 241.2
lacustrine dwelling 241.3
lacy 170.11, 270.16
lad 76.5, 302.5
ladder 193.4
ladder pipe 1022.3
ladder truck 1022.3
laddie 302.5
lade 159.15, 297.13, 794.7
laden 297.18, 794.12
laden with doom 133.16
laden with significance 518.10
laden with sorrow 112.20
la-di-da (n) 500.1 (a) 500.15
ladies', the 12.10
ladies' man 104.12, 500.9, 562.12
ladies' night 487.1
Ladies' Professional Golfers' Association 751.1
ladies' room 12.10
ladies' wear 735.3
lading 159.6, 196.2, 297.7, 794.3
ladino 797.8
ladle (n) 195.1 (v) 176.17
ladle out 477.8
la dolce vita 95.5
Lady 648.2
Lady 77.8
lady 659.1, 758.2
lady 77.5, 77.8
lady 87.7, 104.13, 563.8, 607.4, 608.6, 644.8
Lady Bountiful 143.8, 478.11, 485.2
Lady chapel 703.3
lady fair 1016.7
Lady Fortune 964.3, 972.2
ladyfriend 104.13
lady-help 577.8
lady-in-waiting 577.8
lady-killer 104.12, 500.9, 562.12, 665.10
lady-killing 562.10
ladylike 77.13, 504.16, 607.10, 608.10
ladylikeness 77.1, 504.4
ladylove 104.13
Lady Luck 972.2
lady of the bedchamber 577.8
lady of the evening 665.16
lady of the house 470.2, 575.2
lady of the manor 470.2
Ladyship 648.2
ladyship 608.9
lady's maid 577.8
lady snow 87.7
lady superior 699.17
lag (n) 175.3, 175.4, 429.11, 846.2, 1041.11 (v) 166.4, 175.8, 331.14, 429.18, 833.2, 846.8, 911.2, 1020.24
lagan 370.4
lag back 166.4
lag behind 166.4, 217.8
laggard (n) 175.5, 331.8 (a) 325.6, 331.19, 846.17
laggardness 331.5
lagger 429.11
lagging (n) 175.3, 846.2 (a) 175.11, 846.17
lagniappe 254.4, 478.5, 624.6, 993.2, 993.5
lagoon 241.1
lagued 910.11
la guerre 458.1
laguna 241.1
laic (n) 700.2, 726.5 (a) 700.3
laical 700.3
laicism 695.1
laicization 695.1
laicize 695.14
laicized 695.15
laid aside 340.14
laid-back 106.15, 121.12, 129.2, 143.14, 173.12, 340.10, 402.6, 426.5
laid bare 6.12
laid low 85.56, 274.7, 393.36
laid on the shelf 19.17
laid-out 262.9
laid up 85.59, 386.14
laid up in lavender 397.13
lair 228.26, 228.28, 284.5, 346.4, 584.6, 1009.5
laird 608.4
Lais 665.15
laissez-aller (n) 329.1, 430.9 (a) 329.6
laissez-faire (n) 329.1, 340.1, 427.3, 430.9, 609.4, 611.8 (v) 329.4 (a) 329.6, 340.10, 853.8
laissez-faireism 329.1, 430.9, 609.4, 611.4, 611.8, 853.3
laity, the 700.1
lake 241.1
lake dweller 241.2
lake dwelling 228.5, 241.3
lake-dwelling 241.5
lakefront (n) 234.2 (a) 234.7
lake house 241.3
lakelet 241.1
lakelike 241.5
lake of fire and brimstone 682.2
lake pollution 1072.2
laker 241.2
lake sediment 1059.6
lakeshore (n) 234.2 (a) 234.7
lakeside 241.5
lakeside dweller 241.2
lakeside home 241.3
lakeside village 241.3
lakish 241.5
laky 241.5
lallation 525.1, 525.5
lam 188.7, 368.11
lama 565.2, 699.14, 699.16
Lamarckianism 861.4
Lamarckism 861.4
lamasery 703.6
lamb (n) 10.16, 302.3, 302.10, 311.7, 416.3, 465.2, 562.6, 657.4, 759.22, 1006.3 (v) 1.3
lambaste 412.9, 459.15, 510.18, 604.14, 902.16
lambasted 412.15
lambasting 412.1
lambdacism 525.5
lambency 73.1, 1025.2, 1025.8
lambent 73.12, 1025.36, 1025.39
Lambeth 703.8
Lambeth Palace 703.8
lambkin 302.3, 302.10, 311.7, 562.6
lamblike 137.11, 433.15, 464.10, 657.6
lamblikeness 433.5, 464.4, 657.2
lamb to the slaughter 862.3
lame (v) 19.9, 393.14, 1012.11 (a) 393.30, 410.18, 923.9
lamebrain 924.2
lamebrained 922.15
lame brains 926.2
lame duck 575.5, 610.11, 625.4, 737.11
lame excuse 376.1, 600.4
lamella 296.2
lamellar 296.6
lamellate 296.6
lamellated 296.6
lamellation 296.4
lamelliform 296.6
lament (n) 115.3 (v) 98.14, 115.10
lamentability 98.5
lamentable 98.20, 112.26, 1000.9
lamentableness 98.5
lamentation 98.5, 112.10, 115.1
lamenter 115.8, 309.7
lament for 145.3
lamenting (n) 115.1 (a) 115.18
lamentive 115.19
lame-o 19.14, 414.15
lame verses 720.3
lamia 593.6, 680.6, 690.8
lamina 296.2, 310.19, 1050.2
laminar flow 184.29
laminate (n) 296.2, 1054.6 (v) 296.5 (a) 296.6
laminated 296.6
laminated glass 296.2, 1008.3
laminated wood 296.2
lamination 296.4
laming 393.1
laminous 296.6
l'amour bleu 75.10
lamp 229.1, 1026.1
lampblack 38.6
lamping 1025.30
lamp light 1025.19
lamplit 1025.39
lampoon (n) 489.1, 508.6, 512.5 (v) 489.13, 508.11, 512.12
lampooner 489.12, 512.7
lampoonery 489.1, 512.5
lampoonist 512.7
lampshade 1028.3
lampwick 1026.7
lampyrid 1026.5
lanai 197.5, 197.21
lanate 3.24, 1047.14
lanated 3.24
lance (n) 461.12, 462.8 (v) 292.15, 459.25, 802.11, 904.10
lance corporal 575.18, 575.19
lance-jack 575.18
lancelike 285.12
Lancelot 608.5
lanceolar 285.12
lanceolate 285.12

lancer 461.12
lance sergeant 575.18
lanciform 285.12
lancinate 96.18
lancinated 96.25
lancinating pain 26.2
lancination 96.7
lancing 292.3
Land 231.5
land (n) 231.1 (v) 184.43, 186.8, 194.7
land (n) 232.1, 234.1, 471.6 (v) 472.9, 480.17
land a blow 902.14
land a rabbit punch 754.4
land attack 459.1
land breeze 318.4
land bridge 240.5
land broker 730.9
land crab 311.29
lande 236.1
landed 469.9, 471.8
landed estate 471.6
landed gentry 470.3, 608.3
landed interests 470.3
landed person 470.3
landed property 471.6
lander 1075.6
landfall 186.2
landfill 80.12, 370.4, 391.6
land flowing with milk and honey 890.6
landform 235.1
land grabber 357.3
land-grabber 483.1
landgrave 608.4
landholder 470.3
landholding (n) 469.2 (a) 469.9
landholdings 234.1
landing 184.18, 184.22, 186.2, 193.3, 296.1, 901.13, 1009.6
landing beach 463.2
landing crew 185.5
landing deck 184.23
landing field 184.22
landing pad 901.13
landing pattern 184.18
landing place 1009.6
landing run 184.18
landing signalman 183.6
landing speed 184.31
landing stage 193.3, 901.13, 1009.6
landing strip 184.23
landing three-point landing 184.18
land in the cooler 429.18
landlady 470.2
landless 619.9
landline 347.4
landlocked 207.7, 241.5, 428.15
landlocked water 241.1
landloper 178.3
landloping 177.37
landlord 470.2, 585.5
landlubber 183.2, 234.3
landman 234.3
landmark 517.10, 997.6
landmark decision 598.9
landmass 231.6, 234.1, 235.1
land measure 300.4
landmine 462.20
land of dreams 986.11
land of enchantment 986.11
land of faerie 986.11
land-office business 421.1, 1010.5
land of heart's desire 100.11, 986.11
Land of Liberty 232.3
land of milk and honey 95.5, 986.11
land of Nod 22.2
land of our fathers 232.2
land of plenty 986.11
land of Prester John 986.11
land of promise 986.11
land of the gods 681.8
Land of the Rose 232.4
Land of Youth 986.11
Land of Youth, the 839.2
land on 459.15, 604.10
land on like a ton of bricks 459.15
land on one's feet 1007.2
land operations 458.4
landowner 470.3, 575.3
landownership 469.2
landowning (n) 469.2 (a) 469.9
land pirate 357.3, 483.1
land-poor 619.7
lands 471.6
landscape 33.6, 712.11
landscape architect 716.10, 717.3, 1069.6
landscape architecture 717.1, 717.5, 1069.2
landscape design 712.16
landscape gardener 716.10, 717.3, 1069.6
landscape gardening 717.1, 1069.2
landscape painter 716.4
landscapist 716.4, 1069.6
land shark 357.3, 483.1
landside 184.22
landslide 194.4, 411.1, 609.21, 991.2, 993.2
landslide victory 411.1
landslip 194.4
landsman 227.5, 234.3, 588.4
land surveyor 300.9
land tenure 469.2
land up 820.7, 887.4
landwehr 461.25
lane 184.33, 383.3, 750.1, 755.1
langlauf 753.1
lang syne 837.2
language (n) 523.1, 524.1, 532.1, 1042.13 (a) 524.29
language element 523.14
language family 523.1, 523.12
language group 523.1
language origins 523.13
language pollution 525.5
language study 523.13
language type 523.1
language universal 523.11
langue 523.1
languid 16.12, 21.7, 22.21, 94.13, 173.14, 175.10, 331.20
languidness 94.4, 331.6
languish 16.9, 85.48, 112.16, 252.6, 393.18
languish for 100.16
languishing (n) 85.3, 100.5 (a) 16.21, 85.54, 100.23, 104.26, 112.22, 252.11, 393.45, 827.11
languishment 16.1, 16.5, 85.3, 100.5, 112.10, 252.1, 331.6
languor 16.1, 21.1, 22.1, 94.4, 118.3, 173.4, 175.1, 331.6
languorous 16.12, 173.14, 175.10, 331.20
languorousness 331.6
lank 270.17, 272.16
lankiness 270.5
lankness 270.5
lanky (n) 270.8 (a) 270.17, 272.16
lanolin 1056.3
lantern 272.6, 295.6, 1025.20, 1026.1
lantern fly 1026.5
lantern jaw 270.5
lantern-jawed 270.19
lanternlit 1025.39
lantern slide 714.5
lanthanide 1060.2
Laodicean 94.9, 102.6, 467.7, 695.15
Laodiceanism 102.1, 467.2, 695.1
Lao-tzu 684.4
lap (n) 8.4, 73.1, 216.1, 238.8, 295.4, 296.2, 457.12, 755.1, 756.3, 914.2 (v) 5.39, 8.30, 52.11, 73.9, 88.24, 165.2, 174.13, 209.6, 211.10, 238.17, 238.19, 291.5, 295.20, 295.30, 562.17, 914.5
lap at 238.17
lap dancer 6.3
lap dissolve 706.6
lapdog 104.15, 138.3, 311.16
lapel 291.1
lapel button 647.1
lapel pin 647.1
lapidarian 533.6, 713.12
lapidary (n) 716.6, 716.8 (a) 533.6, 713.12
lapidary quality 533.1
lapidate 308.18, 459.27, 604.16
lapidation 308.1, 459.11, 604.6
lapideous 1046.10, 1059.12
lapidific 1046.10
lapidifical 1046.10
lapidification 1046.5
lapidified 1046.13
lapidify 1046.7
lapin 311.23
lap of honor 755.1
lap of luxury 1010.1
lap over 238.17, 295.30
lapped 209.10
lappet 202.4, 291.1
lapping (n) 8.3, 238.8 (a) 52.19, 295.36
lap pool 743.12
lap robe 295.10
lapsarian 394.5, 859.7
lapse (n) 158.8, 163.1, 194.2, 252.2, 340.1, 393.3, 394.1, 655.2, 694.1, 820.3, 857.3, 858.1, 859.1, 975.4 (v) 163.5, 194.6, 205.5, 340.6, 393.17, 394.4, 654.9, 820.7, 821.5, 837.6, 858.13, 859.4, 975.9
lapse back 859.4
lapsed 205.7, 435.5, 654.12, 663.6, 694.6, 695.18, 837.7
lapsed nature 663.2
lapsedness 654.1
lapsed state 663.2
lapse into 858.17
lapse into disorder 810.8
lapse of memory 990.1
lapse of time 821.4, 824.1
lapsing (n) 394.2 (a) 394.5
lapsus 975.4
lapsus linguae 975.4
laptop 1042.2
laptop computer 1042.2
lap up 8.30, 88.24, 954.6
Laputa 986.11
larboard (n) 220.1 (a) 220.4
larcener 483.1
larcenist 483.1
larcenous 482.21
larcenousness 482.12
larceny 482.2
lard 392.9, 1056.8
lardaceous 1056.9
lardass 175.5, 257.12
lard-assed 257.18
larder 10.5, 197.14, 386.1, 386.6, 386.8
lardy 1056.9
lares and penates 228.30, 471.1, 678.12
large 247.7, 257.16, 485.4
large amount 244.2, 884.3
large as life 257.22
large calorie 1019.19
large charge 105.3
large hat size 140.4
large heart 485.1
largehearted 143.15, 485.4, 652.6
largeheartedness 143.4, 485.1, 652.2
large intestine 2.18
large-lettered 546.8
large meal 8.8
large-minded 979.8
large-mindedness 979.1
largeness 247.1, 257.1, 257.6, 257.8, 485.1
large number 1017.5
large order 8.8, 1013.2
large part 257.11
large person 257.12
larger than life 257.16, 257.20, 257.22, 993.16, 997.20
larger-than-life 247.7, 501.21
large-scale 257.16, 864.13
large size 257.4
large-size 257.16
large-sized 257.16
largess 143.7, 478.5, 485.1
largesse 485.1
large sum 618.2
larghetto (n) 708.25 (a) 708.54
larghissimo 708.25
largish 257.16
largishness 257.6
largo (n) 175.2, 708.25, 709.24 (a) 708.54

lariat 356.13
lark (n) 193.7, 710.23, 743.6 (v) 743.24
lark about 743.23
larking 743.3
larkish 743.29
larrup (n) 902.5 (v) 604.14, 902.17
larruping 604.5
larva 302.12, 305.14, 311.32, 988.1
larval 305.22
laryngismus 85.6
laryngitic 85.61
laryngitis 51.2
laryngospasm 85.6
larynx 524.18
lasagne 10.33
lascivious 75.27, 100.21, 104.25, 665.29
lasciviousness 75.5, 104.1, 665.5
laser beam 1025.5
laser disk 549.10
laser-induced fusion 1038.9
laser printer 1042.9
laser surgery 91.19
lash (n) 375.8, 605.1, 902.8 (v) 182.15, 375.15, 428.10, 510.20, 604.12, 800.9, 1070.8
lash and tie 182.15
lash back 903.6
lashed 800.13
lashes 3.12
lashing 604.4, 800.3
lashings 247.4
lash into a frenzy 375.17
lash into fury 152.25
lash out 902.8
lash out at 459.16
lash the waves 391.8
lash up 340.9, 365.8
lass 77.5, 104.13, 302.6
lassie 77.5, 104.13, 302.6
lassitude 16.1, 21.1, 331.6
lasso (n) 280.2, 356.13 (v) 480.17
last (n) 786.6, 820.1 (v) 267.5, 306.11, 360.2, 761.9, 821.5, 827.6, 853.5 (a) 188.18, 407.9, 820.12, 831.11, 837.11, 841.14
last agony 307.8
last breath 307.8, 820.1
last but not least 820.12
last call 582.10
last dab 820.4
last days 839.3
last debt 307.1
last-ditch 820.12, 995.7
last-ditcher 361.6, 452.3
last-ditch fight 457.6
last duty 309.4
last expedient 995.2
last extremity 307.8
last forever 823.2, 829.6
last frontier 211.5, 231.1
last gasp 307.8, 820.1
last-gasp 401.9
last home 309.16
last honors 309.4
last hope 124.3
last hour 307.7
last hurrah 820.1
lasting 360.8, 763.7, 821.7, 827.10, 827.11, 853.7, 855.17, 989.22, 1049.4
lasting fame 662.7
lasting friendship 587.8
lastingness 821.1, 827.1, 853.1, 855.4, 1049.1
lasting peace 464.1
last inning 820.3
Last Judgment 946.1
last lap 820.3
last legs 820.1
last lick 820.4
last long 827.6
last minute 846.1
last-minute 401.9, 846.18
last-minute lie 609.14
last muster 307.1
last name 527.5
last offer 439.3
last offices 309.4
last of the big spenders 486.2
last out 306.11, 360.4, 827.6, 827.8
last post 309.5, 517.16
last quarter 1073.11
last resort 381.5, 995.2, 1009.2
last resource 995.2, 1009.2
last rest 307.1
last rites 307.8, 309.4, 701.5
last round 820.3
last roundup 307.1
last-second 401.9
last service 309.4
last shift 995.2
last shot 403.3
last sleep 307.1
last stage 820.3
last stop 186.5, 820.1
last straw 152.11, 820.4, 886.3
last straw, the 135.3
last stroke 407.3
Last Summoner 307.2
Last Supper 701.7
last thing one expects, the 131.1
last things 820.1, 839.3
last throe 820.1
last touch 407.3
last trumpet 820.1
last will and testament 478.10
last word 249.3, 439.3, 518.1, 573.3, 939.2
last word, the 578.4, 841.2, 894.1, 1002.3
last words 307.9, 817.1, 820.1
Latakia 89.2
latch 293.6, 800.8
latchkey 292.10
latch on 138.11
latch on to 472.9, 480.14, 640.8
latch onto 138.11, 521.7
late 175.12, 307.29, 814.5, 833.3, 837.10, 841.12, 844.6, 846.16
late arrival 846.6
late bloomer 846.6
late-blooming 407.13
latecomer 846.6
late developer 846.6
late edition 555.2
lateen-rigged 180.17
late hour 846.1
late lamented 307.29
late lamented, the 307.15
late-life 303.16
late-model 841.9
latency 32.2, 173.4, 519.1
lateness 833.1, 835.1, 841.1, 844.1, 846.1
late night 315.6
late-night snack 315.6
late-night supper 315.6
latent 32.5, 173.14, 345.11, 346.11, 519.5
latent content 519.1
latent heat 1019.1
latent hostility 451.2
latent meaning 519.2
latent meaningfulness 519.1
latentness 519.1
latent violence 105.10
later 835.4, 839.8, 841.12, 846.18
lateral (n) 524.12, 904.3 (v) 218.5 (a) 218.6, 218.7, 524.30
lateral bud 310.23
lateral drift 184.28
laterality 218.1
lateralize 218.5
lateral pass 904.3
lateral root 310.22
lateral thinking 931.2, 986.2
lateral thought 931.2
Lateran Council 423.4
late riser 846.6
laterite 1059.1
lateritious 41.6
late-season 313.9
late shift 825.3
latest 838.2, 841.14
latest fad 841.2
latest fashion 5.1, 841.2
latest thing, the 578.4, 841.2
latest wrinkle 841.2, 932.5
latest wrinkle, the 578.4
late wood 1054.3
latex 1048.3, 1061.2
lath (n) 270.7, 271.4, 1054.3 (v) 295.23
lath and plaster 1054.2
lathe 858.10, 1040.6
lather (n) 12.7, 105.6, 135.1, 320.2, 1056.2 (v) 79.19, 320.5, 412.9, 604.14, 1056.8
lathered 412.15
lathered up 105.20
lathering 79.5, 412.1, 604.5
lathering up 105.11
lather up 105.12
lathery 320.7
lathhouse 228.12, 1069.11
lathing 1054.3
lath-legged 270.18
lathlegs 270.8
lathwork 1054.3
laticostate 269.7
latidentate 269.7
Latin America 231.6
Latinate 534.3
Latinate diction 545.3
Latin Christianity 675.7
Latinism 523.8
Latinist 929.3
Latinitaster 929.6
Latino 312.3
Latino literature 718.1
Latin school 567.4
latish 846.16
latitude 158.3, 159.5, 231.3, 269.1, 300.5, 426.2, 430.4, 979.1
latitude and longitude 159.1
latitudinarian (n) 430.12, 695.13, 979.6 (a) 430.25, 695.21, 979.9
latitudinarianism 430.10, 695.7, 979.2
lative 530.9
latke 10.45
latrate 60.2
latria 696.1
latrine 12.10, 12.11
latrine lawyer 597.1, 935.12
latrine rumor 552.6
latter 217.9, 837.11, 841.12
latter-day 841.13
Latter-day Saint 675.22
lattice (n) 170.3, 266.4, 292.8, 1038.7, 1038.13 (v) 170.7
latticed 170.11
latticelike 170.11
latticework 170.3, 266.4
laud (n) 150.2, 509.5, 696.2, 696.3 (v) 509.12, 696.12
laudability 509.7
laudable 509.20, 999.12
laudableness 509.7
laudanum 86.12
laudation 509.5, 696.2
laudator 509.8
laudatory 509.16
lauded 247.9
lauder 509.8
lauds 696.8
laugh (n) 116.4, 489.6 (v) 95.12, 109.6, 116.8
laughability 488.1
laughable 488.4, 923.11
laughableness 488.1
laugh all the way to the bank 472.12
laugh at 454.4, 508.8
laugh away 984.4
laugher 411.1
laughing (n) 116.4 (a) 95.16, 109.11
laughing academy 926.14
laughing gas 86.15
laughingstock 508.7
laugh in one's beard 116.8
laugh in one's face 454.4, 508.8
laugh in one's sleeve 116.8
laugh it up 116.8, 743.22
laugh off 984.4
laugh oneself silly 116.8
laugh on the wrong side of one's mouth 132.4
laugh-out-loud 508.13
laugh out of court 454.4, 508.8
laugh out of the other side of one's mouth 113.7
laugh outright 116.8
laughs 743.2
laughter 109.5, 116.4
laughter-loving 109.15
laugh to scorn 454.4, 508.8
laugh up one's sleeve 116.8

launch (n) 180.4, 818.1, 818.5, 1074.9 (v) 352.14, 404.3, 439.5, 818.11, 904.10, 904.13, 1074.13, 1075.12
launch a holy war on 458.14
launch an attack 459.17
launch a rumor 352.10
launch a vendetta 507.4
launched into eternity 307.29
launcher 462.21
launch forth 188.8, 818.8
launching 818.1, 818.5, 852.4
launching base 1075.5
launching mortar 1074.10
launching pad 818.1, 901.13, 1074.10
launching platform 1074.10
launching ramp 204.4
launching tower 1074.10
launching tube 1074.10
launching way 184.23
launch into 404.3, 725.15
launch into eternity 308.13
launch out against 459.14
launch pad 818.1, 1074.10
launch upon 404.3
launch vehicle 1075.9
launder 79.19
launderer 79.15
launderette 79.11
laundering 79.6
launder money 673.9
laundress 79.15
laundrette 79.11
Laundromat 79.11
laundry 79.6, 79.11
laundry list 871.1, 965.3
laundryman 79.15
laundry room 197.13, 739.8
laundrywoman 79.15
Laurasia 235.1
laureate (n) 249.4, 413.15, 720.12 (a) 646.9
laurel 498.6, 646.3
laurels 249.3, 411.1, 646.3
lava 1020.16, 1059.1
lavabo 79.5, 79.12
lavage 79.5, 86.19
lavalier 202.4
lavaliere 202.4
lavation 79.5
lavatory 12.10, 79.10, 79.12, 197.26
lave 79.19, 1065.13
lavement 86.19
lavender (n) 46.1 (a) 46.3
lavender-blue 46.3
lavender language 523.10
lavender oil 70.2
lavender water 70.3
laving 79.5, 1065.6
lavish (v) 478.12, 486.3, 486.7 (a) 485.4, 486.8, 545.11, 884.9, 991.7, 993.19
lavish care on 449.16
lavishness 486.1, 501.5, 991.2, 993.2
lavish oneself on 509.13
lavish upon 478.15, 485.3
lavish with 993.14
lavolta 366.1
lavosh 10.29
law (n) 417.1, 419.2, 420.4, 444.1, 673.3, 673.7, 752.3, 869.4, 974.2 (v) 598.13
Law, the 683.3
law, the 673.4, 1008.16
law-abiding 326.3, 644.13
law-abidingness 326.1
law and equity 673.6
law and order 464.2
lawbook 673.5
lawbreaker 593.1, 660.9
lawbreaking 327.1, 655.1, 674.3
law court 595.2
law enforcement 1008.1
law enforcement agency 1008.17
law enforcement agent 1008.15
law-enforcement professional 726.4
law enforcer 1008.15
law firm 597.4
lawful 443.15, 649.7, 673.11, 973.14, 973.15
lawful authority 417.1
lawfulness 443.8, 649.1, 673.1
lawful possession 469.1
lawgiver 610.3
lawless 327.8, 418.5, 674.6
lawlessness 327.1, 418.1, 640.2, 674.1
law library 558.1
lawlike 673.11
law-loving 644.13
lawmaker 610.3
lawmaking (n) 573.3, 613.5 (a) 613.11, 673.11
law member of a court-martial 597.2
lawn 310.7
lawn bowling 750.3
lawn bowls 750.3
lawn grass 310.5
lawn mower 1040.8
lawn-roller 287.4
lawn sprinkler 1065.8
lawn tennis 748.1
law of averages 972.1
law of conservation of mass 1038.2
law of definite proportions 1038.2
law of Dulong and Petit 1038.2
law of equivalent retaliation 506.3
law officer 597.1
Law of Moses 673.8, 683.3
law of multiple proportions 1038.2
law of nature 869.4
law of parity 1038.2
law of parsimony 484.1
law of retaliation 506.3
law of succession 479.2
law of the jungle 418.2
law of the jungle, the 424.2
law of the land 673.5
law-revering 644.13
lawsuit 598.1, 599.1
law unto oneself 359.4, 430.7
lawyer 597.1, 726.4, 935.12
lawyer-client confidentiality 345.5
lawyerlike 597.6
lawyerly 597.6, 598.21
lax 331.19, 340.10, 340.12, 426.4, 427.7, 430.24, 430.25, 443.14, 524.30, 654.12, 665.26, 804.5, 846.17, 971.19, 975.17, 1047.10
laxate 1047.6
laxation 1047.3, 1047.5
laxative (n) 79.17, 86.17 (a) 86.48
laxity 340.1, 426.1, 435.1, 654.2, 665.4, 804.2, 971.4, 975.2, 1047.3
laxness 340.1, 426.1, 427.1, 430.3, 804.2, 846.5, 1047.3
lax stewardship 406.2
lay (n) 159.3, 161.1, 708.4, 708.14, 759.3 (v) 75.21, 78.9, 120.5, 159.12, 159.14, 182.48, 201.5, 201.6, 287.5, 465.7, 643.4, 670.6, 690.12, 759.25 (a) 700.3
lay abbot 699.16
lay aboard 182.35
lay about 404.3
layabout 331.8
lay about one 457.14
lay a course 182.27
lay a course for 182.35
lay a false scent 346.6
lay a hand on 459.14, 1000.6
lay a heavy hand on 425.5
lay aloft 182.48
lay anchor 182.15
lay an egg 117.4, 410.10, 414.12, 459.23
lay a plot 381.9
lay aside 176.11, 390.6, 773.6, 846.9, 984.4
lay at 459.15
lay at one's door 599.9
lay at one's feet 439.4
lay a trap for 356.20
lay at the door of 888.4
lay a wager 759.25
lay away 386.10, 390.6
lay away from 182.36
layaway plan 624.1
layaway purchase 733.1
lay a wet blanket on 379.4
lay back 20.7, 106.7
layback spin 760.7
lay bare 6.5, 351.4, 941.4
lay before 216.8, 439.5
lay before the public 352.11
lay blame upon 510.13
lay brother 699.16, 700.2
lay by 182.17, 331.16, 386.10, 386.12, 390.6, 405.11, 846.9
lay by the heels 412.7, 429.15, 480.18, 913.5
lay charges 599.7
lay claim to 421.6
lay down 159.14, 182.43, 201.6, 296.5, 334.5, 370.7, 386.10, 420.9, 438.10, 624.15, 759.25, 951.12
lay down a bunt 745.5
lay down a plan 381.8
lay down one's arms 433.8, 465.11
lay down one's life for one's country 307.24
lay down one's tools 20.6, 857.8
lay down on the job 329.2
lay down the law 420.10, 573.8, 612.14, 970.10
lay eggs 1.3
lay emphasis on 997.14
layer (n) 296.1 (v) 296.5
layer cake 10.42
layered 296.6
layered fiberglass 296.2
layering 296.4
layer tint 159.5
layette 5.30
lay eyes on 27.12, 941.5
lay fee 469.1, 471.5
lay figure 349.6, 575.5, 712.18, 764.2, 786.5
lay flat 201.6
lay for 161.9, 182.35, 346.10
lay forward 182.48
lay ghosts 690.12
lay hands on 459.14, 480.14, 696.14, 701.15
lay hold of 472.9, 480.14
lay in 182.35, 386.10, 1054.7
lay in a store 386.10
lay in a supply 386.10
laying 759.1
laying bare 6.1, 351.1
laying odds 759.1
laying of charges 599.1
laying on 295.1, 643.1
laying on of hands 73.2, 696.5
laying open 292.1
laying over 295.1
laying waste 671.3
lay in provisions 405.11
lay in ruins 395.10
lay in store 386.10
lay in the earth 309.19
lay in the grave 309.19
lay in the lap of the gods 134.7
lay in the scales 297.10
lay into 457.14, 459.15, 510.20, 604.10
lay it down 745.5
lay it on 511.6, 545.6, 993.11
lay it on the line 216.8, 421.8, 535.2, 865.9
lay it on thick 295.24, 355.3, 500.12, 502.7, 509.11, 511.6, 545.6, 993.11
lay it on with a trowel 355.3, 511.6, 545.6, 993.11
lay level 201.6, 913.5
lay level with the ground 201.6
lay low 16.10, 201.6, 274.5, 308.18, 346.8, 913.5
layman 700.2, 726.5
lay me down to sleep 22.17
laymen 700.1
lay money on 953.16
lay odds 759.25
lay off 20.8, 210.4, 300.11, 331.16, 381.10, 390.4, 857.6, 857.8, 909.19
layoff 331.3, 909.5
lay officer 699.8
lay of the land 161.1, 766.2
lay of the land, the 765.2

lay on 295.19, 295.24, 457.14, 599.8, 604.12, 643.4, 643.6
lay on a color 712.19
lay on color 35.14
lay one's cards on the table 351.7
lay oneself open to 1006.7
lay oneself out 403.11, 725.9
lay one's finger on 517.18, 865.11
lay one's fingers on 941.2
lay one's hands on 941.2
lay one's mitts on 472.9
lay one's money down 624.15
lay on one 343.7, 624.16
lay on the line 1006.6
lay on the rack 26.7
lay on the table 390.6, 846.9
lay open 6.5, 292.11, 351.4, 1006.6
lay out 25.4, 201.6, 262.7, 300.11, 308.14, 309.21, 381.10, 438.10, 626.5, 913.5
layout 262.1, 381.1, 548.2, 759.12, 766.2, 807.1
lay out a course 182.27, 568.17
lay out boundaries 210.4
layout cloth 759.16
lay out money 729.17
lay over 225.8, 295.19, 846.9
layover 225.5
layperson 700.2, 930.7
laypersons 700.1
lay plans 381.8
lay siege to 459.19, 562.21
lay sister 700.2
lay stress upon 997.14
lay suit 758.3
lay the ax to the root of 395.14
lay the blame on 599.8
lay the dust 465.7
lay the finger on 599.7
lay the first stone 405.12, 818.10
lay the flattering unction to one's soul 120.5, 140.6, 511.5
lay the foundation 159.16, 405.12
lay the groundwork 405.12
lay the land 182.37
lay to 182.17, 331.16, 725.9, 888.4
lay together 75.21, 800.5
lay to heart 93.11
lay to one's charge 599.9, 888.4
lay to rest 309.19, 395.13, 820.6, 958.4
lay to the oars 725.9
lay under an interdict 444.3
lay under an interdiction 444.3
lay under contribution 387.14
lay under restraint 428.7
lay under the sod 309.19
lay up 85.50, 182.17, 296.5, 386.11
lay up a store 405.11
lay violent hands on 480.15
lay wait 346.9
lay wait for 346.10
lay waste 395.10, 671.11
lay with 75.21
laywoman 700.2
laywomen 700.1
lazaret 91.22, 386.6
lazaretto 91.22, 386.6
lazar house 91.22
laze 175.6, 331.12
laziness 175.1, 331.5, 340.2
lazing 331.4
lazy (v) 331.12 (a) 175.10, 331.19, 340.11, 402.6, 846.17
lazybones 331.7
lazyboots 331.7
lazy eight 184.13
lazy eye 28.6
lazylegs 331.7
lazy stream 238.1
lea 310.8
leach (n) 1064.3 (v) 79.22, 190.15, 238.18, 255.9, 1064.5, 1065.13
leachate 1064.3
leached 891.4
leaching 79.4, 190.6, 238.7, 1064.1, 1065.7
leaching away 473.2
leachy 292.20
lead (n) 39.1, 200.6, 249.1, 297.6, 311.13, 428.4, 517.4, 517.9, 573.1, 704.10, 706.3, 707.6, 709.12, 750.3, 758.3, 997.10 (v) 161.7, 165.2, 216.7, 249.11, 297.12, 297.15, 375.22, 417.14, 573.8, 612.11, 708.45, 769.8, 814.2, 816.3, 818.10, 886.11, 894.7, 896.3 (a) 1058.17
lead, the 165.1, 814.1
leadable 161.13
lead a charmed life 1007.2, 1010.11
lead a cloistered life 584.7
lead actor 707.2
lead actress 707.2
lead a dog's life 1011.9
lead an easy life 331.15
lead a retired life 584.7
lead astray 356.16, 665.20
lead block 746.3
lead by the nose 432.10, 612.14, 894.7, 894.11
lead down the garden path 265.6, 665.20
lead down the primrose path 665.20
leaden 36.7, 39.4, 117.6, 173.14, 297.16, 331.20, 534.3, 1058.17
leadenness 39.1, 117.1, 297.1, 534.1, 1027.1
leader 216.2, 249.4, 310.11, 311.13, 556.2, 574.6, 574.7, 575.3, 575.7, 610.2, 710.17, 735.2, 750.3, 816.1, 866.2, 938.10
leaderless 19.18
leader of men 574.6
leadership 249.3, 417.7, 573.4, 894.1
leadership group 617.6
leader writer 555.4, 556.4
leadfoot 756.2
lead-gray 39.4
lead in 816.3
lead-in 816.2
leading (n) 165.1, 573.1 (a) 165.3, 216.10, 249.14, 417.15, 573.12, 612.17, 814.4, 818.17, 997.24
leading actor 707.6
leading actress 707.6
leading article 556.2
leading candidate 610.9
leading card 866.2
leading edge 165.1, 818.1
leading idea 932.4
leading lady 704.10, 707.2, 707.6
leading light 997.10, 999.6
leading man 704.10, 707.2, 707.6
leading question 938.10
leading role 704.10
leading spirit 892.7
leading string 428.4
leading woman 704.10
lead into captivity 432.8
lead item 735.2, 866.2
lead off 814.2, 818.10
leadoff 818.1
leadoff hitter 745.2
leadoff man 816.1
leadoff woman 816.1
lead on 377.5, 573.8, 894.9
lead one a chase 368.7
lead one a dance 368.7
lead one down the garden path 645.14
lead one on a merry chase 368.7
lead one on a pretty dance 368.7
lead one to 375.22
lead one to believe 519.4, 551.8, 953.18
lead one to expect 124.9, 130.10, 133.12, 968.4
lead one to gather 551.10
lead one to understand 551.8
lead-pipe cinch 409.2, 970.2
lead role 704.10
lead-runner 816.1
lead singer 710.13
lead the dance 165.2
lead the field 216.7
lead the life of Riley 402.4, 1010.10
lead the mind astray 985.6
lead the pack 165.2, 216.7
lead the way 165.2, 786.7, 814.2, 816.3, 818.10
lead time 405.1, 845.1, 961.2
lead to 161.6, 261.6, 772.4, 886.12
lead to believe 375.23, 953.18
lead to the altar 563.15
lead up the garden path 265.6, 356.16
lead up to 405.12
leaf (n) 89.2, 296.2, 310.11, 310.19, 352.8, 554.12, 1054.5 (v) 310.34
leafage 310.18
leaf blade 310.19
leaf bud 310.23
leaf from someone else's book, a 621.2
leaf in 213.6
leafiness 310.18
leafing-in 213.1
leaflet 310.19, 352.8, 554.11
leaflike 296.6
leaf litter 310.17, 890.4
leaf metal 1058.3
leaf mold 310.17, 890.4
leaf out 310.34
leaf sight 29.5
leafstalk 310.21
leaf through 938.26
leaf vegetable 10.35, 310.4
leafy 44.4, 310.36, 310.41
leafy vegetable 10.35
league (n) 437.2, 450.2, 617.1, 745.1, 746.1, 750.1, 752.1, 805.1, 809.3 (v) 450.3, 770.16, 800.5, 805.4
league bowling 750.1
league championship 745.1
League Championship Series 745.1
leagued 770.21, 800.13, 805.6
League of Nations 612.6, 614.1
league pennant 745.1
leaguer 212.5
leaguered 212.10
league together 450.3
league with 617.14
leak (n) 12.5, 190.5, 292.1, 351.2, 369.1, 551.4, 552.10 (v) 190.14, 343.7, 351.4, 351.6, 473.6, 551.10
leakage 189.1, 190.5, 369.1, 473.2
leak away 473.6
leak in 189.10
leaking 190.5
leaking purse 486.1
leak out 190.14, 351.8, 369.10
leakproof 15.20, 1066.11
leaky 190.20, 292.19
lean (n) 204.2 (v) 204.10, 297.15, 324.3, 896.3 (a) 270.17, 535.3, 992.10
lean and hungry look 270.5
lean-cheeked 270.19
lean-faced 270.19
lean-fleshed 270.17
lean green 728.6
leaning (n) 100.3, 204.2, 371.5, 413.5, 650.3, 896.1, 968.1, 978.3, 980.3 (a) 204.15, 791.5, 896.4
leaning toward 100.22
leaning tower 204.2
lean-jawed 270.19
lean-limbed 270.18
lean-looking 270.17
lean-minded 922.13
leanness 270.5, 535.1, 992.2
lean on 424.8, 514.2, 894.9, 901.22, 953.16
lean on a broken reed 493.5
lean on it 330.14
lean over backward 324.3, 403.11
lean over backwards 649.5, 652.3, 979.7
lean-to 228.9

lean toward 100.14, 371.17, 978.6
lean upon 124.6
lean-witted 922.13
leap (n) 162.1, 193.1, 224.1, 245.1, 251.1, 366.1, 403.3, 816.2, 852.4 (v) 174.8, 366.5, 401.5
leap before one looks 401.7
leaper 366.4
leap forward 162.2
leapfrog (n) 366.1 (v) 366.5
leapfrogging 366.3
leap in 189.7
leaping (n) 366.3 (a) 95.16, 193.14, 366.7
leaping weir 1012.5
leap in the dark 759.2, 971.8
leap into the breach 843.7
leap like a startled gazelle 127.12
leap of faith 953.5
leap out 190.11
leap over 366.5
leap over the wall 369.6
leaps and bounds 162.1
leap to the eye 348.7
leap up 193.9
leap year 824.2, 850.4
learn 521.7, 551.14, 570.6, 928.14, 941.2
learn about 570.6
learn a lesson 570.10
learn all about 570.9
learn by doing 570.10
learn by experience 570.10
learn by heart 989.16
learn by rote 989.16
learned 570.16, 572.12, 920.17, 928.21
learned clerk 929.3
learned helplessness 19.4
learned man 929.3
learnedness 570.4, 928.5
learned person 929.3
learner 178.10, 572.1, 818.2
learner's permit 443.6
learn from 570.11
learning 570.1, 928.4, 941.1
learning by heart 989.3
learning center 558.1
learning curve 989.2
learning disabled student 572.4
learning impaired student 572.4
learning style 570.1
learn one's lines 704.32
learn the hard way 570.10
learn the ins and outs 570.9
learn the ropes 570.9
learn to live in one's own skin 107.5
learn verbatim 989.16
learn word for word 989.16
lease (n) 469.1, 615.6 (v) 225.7, 228.31, 615.15, 615.16
lease and release 629.1
lease-back 615.16
leased 615.20
leasehold (n) 469.1, 471.5 (a) 471.10
leaseholder 227.8, 470.4
leasehold mortgage 438.4
lease-lend 615.16, 620.5
lease out 615.16
leaser 227.8
leash (n) 428.4, 876.1 (v) 428.10, 800.9
leashed 428.16
least (n) 885.3 (a) 137.10, 250.8, 885.7
least common multiple 883.4
leather (n) 4.2, 1049.2 (v) 604.14
leather-bound book 554.3
leatherette 4.2
leather goods 735.3
leatheriness 1049.1
leathering 604.5
leatherlike 1049.4
leatherlikeness 1049.1
leatherneck 183.4
leathernecks 461.28
leather paper 4.2
leatherware 735.3
leathery 1049.4
leave (n) 20.3, 188.4, 222.4, 402.1, 441.1, 443.1, 750.2 (v) 188.6, 256.6, 307.27, 310.34, 340.7, 370.5, 443.9, 448.2, 478.18, 566.5, 802.8
leave a bad taste in one's mouth 99.6
leave alone 329.4, 430.16, 443.12, 853.6
leave a loose thread 340.7
leave a lot to be desired 108.5, 992.8
leave an aching void 112.19
leave a sinking ship 188.9, 363.7, 858.13
leave at the post 249.10
leave be 329.4, 430.17
leave behind 174.13, 249.10, 256.6, 307.27, 370.5
leave cold 190.12
leaved 44.4, 310.41
leave flat 188.9, 370.5
leave flatfooted 174.13
leave go 475.4
leave half-done 340.7
leave hanging in midair 362.8
leave high and dry 188.9, 370.5
leave holding the bag 356.14, 370.5
leave home 188.17
leave in the dark 345.7
leave in the dust 249.10
leave in the lurch 132.2, 249.10, 356.14, 370.5
leave it to one 443.12
leave looking 174.13
leave loose ends 340.7
leave much to be desired 108.5, 250.4
leaven (n) 10.28, 298.4, 852.5, 912.3 (v) 221.7, 298.7, 797.11, 959.3
leavened 959.10
leavening (n) 10.28, 298.4 (a) 298.17
leave no address 346.8
leave no avenue unexplored 360.5, 403.15
leave no chance 967.6
leave no escape 424.5
leave no loose ends 407.7
leave no margin for error 494.6
leave no option 424.5
leave no room for error 494.6
leave no stone unturned 360.5, 403.15, 494.6, 794.8, 938.33
leave nothing hanging 407.7
leave nothing to chance 494.6
leave nothing to say 958.4
leave nothing undone 794.8
leave no trace 34.2, 395.14, 762.6
leave no void 221.7
leave of absence 20.3, 222.4
leave off 370.7, 374.3, 390.4, 857.6
leave one cold 94.5, 117.4, 118.7
leave one in peace 430.16
leave one's card 582.19
leave oneself open to 897.3
leave oneself wide open 493.5, 1006.7
leave one's mark 662.10
leave one to gather 551.10
leave one to oneself 430.16
leave one to one's fate 370.5
leave one unmoved 94.5, 117.4
leave on the cutting-room floor 395.16
leave out 773.4
leave out in the cold 157.6, 340.8, 372.2, 773.4, 984.4
leave out nothing 494.6
leave out of account 959.5
leave out of one's calculation 340.6
leave over 256.6
leave quickly 188.10
leaver 190.10
leave room for 443.9
leave standing 174.13
leave-taking 188.4
leave the atmosphere 1075.12
leave the beaten path 868.4
leave the country 188.17
leave the door open to 443.10
leave the earth behind 193.10
leave the ground 184.38, 193.10
leave the nest 188.17, 303.9
leave the scene 34.2, 222.8
leave the stage 34.2
leave the straight and narrow 654.9
leave the way open to 443.10
leave things as they are 329.4, 853.6
leave to luck 759.24
leave to one's fate 188.9
leave unavenged 148.4
leave undone 340.7, 340.8, 408.2
leave unsatisfied 96.12
leave well enough alone 329.4, 430.16
leave word 343.7, 551.8
leaving (n) 188.1, 222.4, 370.1 (a) 188.18
leaving life 307.1
leaving much to chance 972.16
leaving no margin for error 494.8
leaving no room for error 494.8
leaving no stone unturned 494.8
leaving-out 773.1
leaving out nothing 494.8
leavings 256.1, 391.4, 893.3
leaving the earth behind 193.1
leaving the ground 193.1
leavy 310.41
lech 75.5, 100.6, 896.1
lecher 562.12, 660.4, 665.11
lecherous 665.29
lecherousness 665.5
lechery 562.10, 665.5
lecithin 7.7
lectern 703.13, 901.15
lection 341.2
lectionary 701.10
lector 571.7, 699.4
lecture (n) 510.5, 543.3, 568.7 (v) 510.17, 543.11, 568.16
lecture-demonstration 568.7
lecture hall 197.4, 567.11
lecturer 543.5, 571.3, 571.7
lecture room 567.11
lectureship 571.10
lecturing (n) 543.1 (a) 568.18
LED 1042.3
led astray 930.13
led by the nose 432.16
led captain 138.3
le dernier cri 578.4
ledge 201.3, 211.4, 296.1, 901.14
ledger 549.11, 628.4, 709.12, 871.5
ledger line 708.29
ledges 1006.5
lee (n) 218.2, 1008.1 (a) 218.6
lee anchor 218.2
leech (n) 138.5, 180.14, 311.37, 480.12, 803.4 (v) 91.27
leeching 91.20
leechlike 138.14
leechlike grip 360.1
lee helm 218.2
leek-green 44.4
leer (n) 27.3, 508.4, 517.15 (v) 27.14, 517.22
leer at 27.14
leeriness 494.2, 955.2, 956.1
leering (n) 508.1 (a) 508.12
leering look 27.3
leery 494.9, 955.9, 956.4
lees 256.2, 391.4, 893.3
lee sheet 218.2
lee shore 218.2, 1006.5
lee side 161.2, 218.2
lee tack 218.2
lee tide 218.2
leeward (n) 218.2 (a) 218.6
leeway 158.3, 182.9, 184.28, 224.1, 261.1, 430.4
lee wheel 218.2
left (n) 220.1, 609.24, 611.3, 611.11 (a) 188.19, 220.4, 256.7, 370.8
left a mile behind 250.7
left back 752.2
left bower 758.2
left brain 2.15
left-brain 723.6
left coast 231.7

left defenseman 749.2
left fence 750.2
left field 220.1
left fielder 745.2
left forward 747.2
left fullback 749.5
left guard 747.2
left half 752.2
left halfback 749.5
left hand 220.1
left-hand 218.7, 220.4, 414.20
left-handed 156.8, 204.13, 220.5, 414.20
left-handed compliment 156.2
left-handedness 220.2, 414.3
left-hander 220.3, 745.2
left hand opponent 758.3
left-hand pitcher 745.2
left-hand side 220.1
left hanging 795.4
leftism 611.3
leftist (n) 611.11 (a) 611.19
leftness 220.2
left-of-center 220.4, 265.10, 611.19
left-out 773.7
left out in the cold 773.7
leftover (n) 254.1, 993.5 (a) 256.7, 993.18
leftovers 256.1, 993.5
left side 220.1
left undone 340.14
left wing 220.1, 611.3, 611.11
left-wing 220.4, 611.19
left-wing conspiracy 609.24
left-winger 220.1, 609.27, 611.11
left-wing extremism 611.4
left-wing extremist 611.12
left-wingish 220.4
left wingman 749.2
lefty (n) 220.3, 745.2 (a) 220.5
leg (n) 2.7, 10.15, 10.23, 177.14, 182.6, 273.6, 793.4 (v) 177.27
legacy 478.10, 479.2, 627.1, 887.1
legal (n) 594.1 (a) 443.15, 549.17, 649.7, 673.11, 973.14
legal action 598.1
legal adviser 597.1
legal age 303.2
legal agreement 437.1
legal aid 597.1, 597.4
legal-aid practice 597.4
legal authority 417.1, 594.1
legal blindness 28.1, 30.1
legal branch 673.4
legal bucketing 737.18
legal case 598.1
legal chemistry 673.7
legal claim 469.1
legal code 673.5
legal contract 437.1
legal counsel 597.1
legal counselor 597.1
legal document 549.5
legal eagle 597.3
legalese 523.10
legal ethics 636.1
legal evidence 957.2
legal expert 597.1
legal fiction 354.11
legal firm 597.4
legal flaw 674.1
legal form 673.1
legal guardian 559.5
legal heir 479.5
legal holiday 20.4
legal incapacity 19.2
legal instrument 549.5
legal irregularity 674.1
legalis homo 303.2, 304.1
legalism 580.2, 673.1
legalist 597.1
legalistic 580.7, 673.12, 867.6
legality 443.8, 649.1, 673.1
legalization 443.3, 673.2
legalize 443.11, 673.9
legalized 443.15, 673.11
legalized killing 308.7
legal jointure 478.9
legally binding 673.11
legally blind 28.11, 30.9
legally responsible 897.5
legally separated 566.7
legal medicine 673.7
legal murder 604.6
legal order 420.6
legal pad 549.11
legal paper 549.5
legal possession 469.1
legal practice 597.4
legal practitioner 597.1
legal procedure 598.1
legal proceeding 598.1
legal process 598.1, 673.1
legal profession 597.4
legal remedy 598.1
legal representation 597.1
legal residence 225.1
legal responsibility 897.1
legal restraint 428.1
legal right 594.1
legal rights 430.2
legal science 673.7
legal separation 566.1
legal-sized 257.22
legal specialty 673.4
legal sway 594.1
legal system 594.2, 673.4
legal tender 728.1
legal-tender note 728.5
legal tribunal 595.2
legatary 479.4
legate 576.2, 576.6
legatee 479.4
legation 576.7, 576.13, 615.1, 739.7
legato (n) 708.25, 708.30, 709.14 (a) 708.53
legend 159.5, 341.5, 354.10, 662.7, 678.14, 719.1, 719.2, 842.2, 937.2
legendary 354.29, 662.16, 678.15, 719.6, 722.8, 842.12, 870.14, 986.21
léger 298.10
legerdemain 356.5
leggiero 708.53
leggings 5.18
leggy 272.16
legibility 521.3
legible 521.12
legion 461.22, 770.4, 884.3
legionary 461.6
legions 461.23
legislate 328.9, 613.10, 673.9
legislation 573.3, 613.5, 673.2, 673.3
legislative 613.11, 673.11
legislative assembly 613.1
legislative body 613.1
legislative caucus 609.9
legislative chamber 613.1
legislative immunity 430.8
legislative investigation 938.4
legislative lobby 609.32
legislator 575.16, 610.3
legislatorial 613.11
legislatrix 610.3
legislature 423.1, 613.1, 613.2, 613.5
legist 597.2
leg it 177.27
legit (n) 704.1 (a) 443.15, 673.11
legitimacy 417.1, 443.8, 600.7, 673.1, 973.7
legitimate (v) 443.11, 673.9 (a) 443.15, 600.14, 673.11, 704.33, 935.20, 973.14, 973.15
legitimated 443.15
legitimateness 673.1
legitimate stage 704.1
legitimate succession 417.12
legitimate theater 704.1
legitimation 443.3, 673.2, 772.1
legitimatization 673.2
legitimatize 673.9, 772.3
legitimization 772.1
legitimize 443.11, 673.9, 772.3
legitimized 443.15, 673.11
leg man 555.4
leg of lamb 10.16
leg of mutton 10.16
leg-pull 489.10, 508.2
leg-puller 357.1
legroom 158.3
legs 2.7
leg to stand on 376.1
legume 310.4, 310.30
legumen 310.30
légumes 10.35
legumin 1045.7
leguminiform 310.36
leguminose 310.36
leguminous 310.36
leg up, a 843.2, 912.2
leg up 249.2, 449.2
legwear 5.28
leg-weary 177.41
legwork 555.3, 938.4
lei 310.25
Leibnizian 124.11, 952.12
Leibnizian optimism 124.2
Leibnizian optimist 124.5
leiotrichous 287.10
leisure (n) 20.1, 329.1, 331.2, 402.1, 857.3 (a) 331.18, 402.5
leisure class 331.11
leisured 331.18, 402.5
leisureliness 175.1, 331.2, 402.2
leisurely 175.10, 402.6
leisurely gait 175.2
leisure time 857.3
leisurewear 5.20
leitmotiv 708.24
Le Mans start 756.3
lemma 310.19, 935.7
lemniscate 280.7
lemon (n) 67.2, 410.2 (a) 43.4
lemon-colored 43.4
lemon law 494.3, 1008.4
lemon sole 10.24
lemony 67.5
lemon-yellow 43.4
lemures 988.1
lend 620.5, 728.27
lend, the 620.2
lend a color to 600.12
lend a hand 328.5, 449.11
lend a helping hand 449.11
lend aid 449.11
lend an ear 48.10
lend an ear to 983.7
lend a willing ear 324.3
lend credit 662.14
lend distinction 662.14
lender 620.3
lending 620.1, 728.16
lending at interest 620.1
lending institution 620.4, 729.14
lending library 558.1
lending on security 620.2
lending rate 620.1, 623.3
lend-lease (n) 615.6, 620.2 (v) 615.16, 620.5
lend one's backing to 509.11
lend one's countenance to 449.14
lend oneself 449.18
lend oneself to 332.9, 449.14
lend one's name to 449.14, 509.11
lend one's offices 449.14
lend one's support to 449.14, 509.11
lend substance to 763.5
lend support 449.12, 901.21
lend wings to 449.17
length, a 267.2
length 158.1, 257.1, 261.1, 267.1, 300.3
length and breadth 792.3
length and breadth of the land, the 1073.10
lengthen 158.9, 251.4, 267.6, 827.9, 856.4
lengthened 267.8, 827.11
lengthening (n) 267.4, 827.2, 856.1 (a) 251.8
lengthen out 267.6, 827.9
lengthiness 267.1
length of time 827.3
length of years 303.5
lengthways 267.9
lengthwise 267.9
lengthy 267.7, 272.16, 538.12
lenience 134.1, 426.2, 427.1, 979.4
leniency 134.1, 143.3, 145.1, 426.2, 427.1, 443.2, 465.2, 670.2, 979.4, 1047.1
lenient 134.9, 143.16, 145.7, 426.5, 427.7, 443.14, 979.11
lenientness 427.1
lenify 670.6
Leninism 611.5

Leninist (n) 611.13, 860.3 (a) 611.21, 860.6
lenitive (n) 86.10, 670.3, 1056.3 (a) 86.40, 120.9, 670.16, 959.7, 1056.10
lenitude 331.6
lenity 143.2, 145.1, 145.2, 427.1, 670.1, 979.4, 1047.1
lens 2.9, 29.2
lens hood 1028.4
lensman 714.2, 716.5
lens opening 714.9
lens-shaped 279.12
Lent 515.3, 658.3
lent 620.6
Lenten 100.25, 515.5, 668.10, 992.10
Lenten diet 515.2
Lenten fare 515.2, 668.2, 992.6
lenticular 279.12
lenticular galaxy 1073.6
lenticularis 319.8
lentiform 279.12
lentiginous 296.7
lentigo 517.5, 1004.1
lentil 310.4
lentitude 175.1
lento 708.54
lentoid 279.12
lentor 175.1, 331.6, 1062.2
Leo 311.21
leonine 311.42
leopard 47.6, 311.21
leopard's spots 855.6
leotards 5.9
leper 586.4
lepidopteran 311.51
lepidopterous 311.51
lepidote 296.7
leporide 311.23
leppy 311.6
leprechaun 258.5, 678.8
leprous 85.61
lesbian (n) 75.14, 76.9 (a) 75.30
lesbianism 75.10
lesbian marriage 563.1
lesbie 75.15
lesbo 75.15
lese majesty 645.7
lesion 85.37, 85.38, 96.5
less (n) 885.3 (a) 250.6, 252.10, 885.6
less advanced 274.8
lessee 227.8, 470.4
lessen 120.5, 252.6, 252.7, 255.9, 600.12, 670.6
lessening (n) 120.1, 252.1, 260.1, 393.3, 670.2 (a) 252.11, 670.14
lesser 250.6, 252.10
lesser gods, the 678.1
lesser-known 528.3, 930.13
lesser nobility 608.3
lesser of two evils 371.3, 862.2
lesson 399.1, 510.5, 568.7
less semitone 709.20
less than nothing (n) 248.5 (a) 762.8
less than no time 828.3
less than perfect 1003.4
less than pleased 99.8, 108.7, 510.21
let (n) 615.6, 748.2, 1012.1 (v) 192.12, 443.9, 615.15, 615.16, 951.10 (a) 615.20
let a fart 909.29
let alone 329.4, 340.7, 368.6, 390.5, 430.16, 668.7, 853.6
let-alone principle 430.9
let ball 748.2
let be 329.4, 340.7, 430.16, 853.6, 951.10
let blood 91.27, 192.12, 308.15
let bygones be bygones 148.5, 465.10
let come in one ear and go out the other 984.2
let dangle 340.7
let daylight in 351.4
let down (v) 20.7, 132.2, 175.9, 356.14, 393.16, 645.14, 670.9, 913.4 (a) 108.7, 132.5
letdown 125.2, 132.1, 137.2, 175.4, 410.3, 670.2
let down easy 977.2
let down one's defenses 897.3
let down one's guard 897.3
let drive at 459.16
let drop 351.6, 524.24, 913.7
let fall 351.6, 524.24, 913.7
let fall into desuetude 370.5
let fall into disuse 370.5
let fester in the mind 989.12
let flow through one's fingers 486.3
let fly 904.10, 904.12
let fly at 459.16, 459.28
let get around 351.5
let go 148.4, 329.5, 340.6, 340.7, 390.4, 430.14, 430.19, 431.5, 475.4, 601.4, 743.24, 771.8, 804.3, 904.10, 909.19, 909.24
let go by 134.7, 668.7
let go by default 340.6
let go free 431.5
let go of 913.7
let go one's own way 430.15
let go the anchor 182.15
let grass grow under one's feet 166.4
lethal 82.7, 308.23, 1000.12
lethal blow 308.10
lethal chamber 605.5
lethal injection 604.6
lethality 308.9, 1000.5
lethargic 22.21, 94.13, 331.20
lethargicalness 94.4
lethargic hypnosis 22.7
lethargy 22.1, 22.6, 94.4, 102.2, 331.6, 922.3
let have 478.12
let have it 902.14
Lethe 682.4, 990.1
let heads roll 860.4
Lethean 682.8, 990.9
let her out 174.9
let her rip 174.9, 818.7
Lethe water 990.1
let in 187.10, 585.7
let in on 343.7, 351.5, 551.11, 977.2
let in on the know 551.11
let into 928.16
let into the secret 351.5
let it all hang out 120.7, 351.7, 430.19
let it be understood 521.6
let it go 148.5, 984.4
let it have its way 329.4
let it pass 148.5
let it ride 430.16, 853.6
let it roll 818.7
let know 551.8
let loose 430.19, 431.5, 431.6, 743.24, 904.10
let loose of 475.4
let money be no object 485.3
let nature take its course 430.16
let next to 551.11
let off (v) 430.14, 431.5, 601.4, 615.16, 671.14, 904.12 (a) 430.30
let off scot-free 601.4
let off steam 743.24
let off the hook 427.5, 431.5
let on 351.7, 354.21
let one down 132.3
let one go at will 430.15
let one have his head 430.15
let one have his own way 427.6
let one have it 459.15, 510.18, 604.10
let one have it with both barrels 459.15, 510.18
let one know 478.12
let one off easy 148.4
let one off this time 148.4
let one's angry passions rise 152.17
let one's attention wander 984.3, 985.9
let one's breath out 909.24
let oneself go 365.7, 393.16, 430.19, 743.22, 743.24
let oneself in for 1006.7, 1013.12
let one's hair down 120.7, 351.5, 430.19, 541.9, 581.2, 743.24
let one's imagination run riot 986.14
let one's imagination wild 986.14
let one's light shine 692.6
let one's mind run on other things 985.9
let one's mind wander 985.9
let one's thoughts wander 985.9
let one's voice be heard 348.6
let one's wits go bird's nesting 985.9
let on like 354.21
let out 192.12, 267.6, 351.4, 351.5, 431.5, 524.22, 615.16, 909.19, 909.24
let out on bail 431.5
let pass 134.7, 329.5, 984.2
let rankle in the breast 989.12
let ride 329.5, 340.6
let rip 904.10
let sleeping dogs lie 107.5, 430.16, 846.12
let slide 329.5, 340.6
let slip 329.5, 340.6, 351.6, 473.4, 984.4
let slip out 343.7, 351.4, 365.7, 551.10
let slip through one's fingers 473.4, 486.3, 844.5
let someone get away with murder 443.12
let something go 148.4
let something slide 846.11
let take its course 340.6
letter (n) 349.1, 523.14, 546.1, 546.2, 547.9, 547.10, 548.6, 552.4, 553.2 (v) 546.6 (a) 553.14
letter, the 973.5
letter bag 553.4
letter bomb 462.20
letter box 553.6
lettercard 553.3
letter carrier 353.5, 553.7
letter drop 553.6
lettered 546.8, 547.22, 547.24, 718.7, 928.21
letterer 547.13
letter file 871.3
letter from Uncle Sam 615.7
letterhead 517.13, 553.9
lettering 546.5, 547.1, 547.4
letter man 743.19
letter of credit 622.3, 728.11
letter of introduction 509.4, 517.11
letter of recommendation 509.4
letter of reference 509.4
letter of the law 673.1
letter-perfect 973.15, 973.16
letterpress 548.1, 548.3, 548.10
letterpress photoengraving 548.1
letters 546.3, 547.12, 549.1, 718.1, 928.5
letters of marque 482.7
letters of marque and reprisal 482.7
letters of the alphabet 546.3
letters patent 443.5
letterweight 297.6
letter writer 553.8
letter writing 553.1
let the air out of 260.10, 977.2
let the ayes have it 332.11
let the cat out of the bag 351.4, 351.6, 551.13
let the chance slip by 340.6
let the grass grow under one's feet 331.12, 340.6
let the matter stand 846.9
let the mind lie fallow 933.2
let the portcullis down 1009.7
let the wound heal 465.10
let things take their course 329.4, 853.6
letting down 331.2, 645.8
letting go 148.2, 475.1
letting one in on 343.2
letting out 351.2
let tomorrow take care of itself 406.7, 486.3
lettuce 728.2, 728.6
let up 20.7, 175.9, 252.6, 670.9, 804.3, 857.9
let-up 120.1

letup 20.2, 175.4, 252.1, 402.1, 670.2, 813.2, 826.1, 857.3
let up on 145.4
let well enough alone 107.5, 329.4, 368.6, 430.16, 668.7, 853.6, 984.2
leukemia 85.20
leukocyte 2.25
leukoderma 37.1
leukorrhea 2.24, 12.6
Levant 231.6
levant 368.10, 625.6
levanter 318.8, 625.5
levee 582.10, 770.2, 1012.5
level (n) 197.23, 201.3, 236.1, 245.1, 245.2, 287.3, 296.1, 607.1, 809.2 (v) 201.6, 287.5, 395.19, 781.4, 790.6, 913.5 (a) 201.7, 277.6, 287.10, 649.7, 781.5, 790.7
level as a plain 201.7
level at 459.22
level crossing 170.2
level green 750.3
level head 106.3, 920.6
levelheaded 106.13, 670.13, 920.18
levelheadedness 106.3, 920.6
leveling 395.5
leveling off 252.2
level landing 184.18
level line 201.3
levelness 201.1, 287.1, 790.1
level off 184.43, 781.4, 790.6
level-off 184.8
level of stress 524.10
level out 201.6, 781.4, 790.6
level plane 201.3
level playing field 649.1, 649.2, 790.1, 843.2, 972.7
levels 530.2
levels of meaning 539.1
level with 644.10
lever (n) 384.4, 906.4, 912.3, 1040.5, 1040.7 (v) 906.8
leverage 737.19, 894.1, 906.1, 1039.1
leveraged buyout 737.19, 805.1
leveret 311.23
leviable 630.15
Leviathan 311.29
leviathan 180.1, 257.14
levigate 287.8, 1051.9
levigated 1051.11
levigation 1044.2, 1051.4
levigator 1051.7
levin bolt 1025.17
levin brand 1025.17
levitate 193.8, 298.9, 912.5
levitation 193.1, 298.1, 689.6
levitational 298.15
levitative 298.15, 912.10
Levite 699.11
levity 109.3, 109.5, 298.1, 364.3, 489.4, 508.1, 984.1, 998.3
levoduction 220.2
levorotation 220.2
levorotatory 220.4
levoversion 220.2
levy (n) 421.1, 458.7, 461.18, 480.5, 615.7, 630.9 (v) 421.5, 458.18, 480.20, 615.17, 630.12, 643.4
levy a distress 603.5
levy blackmail 480.22
levying 615.7
levy war on 458.14
lewd 665.29, 666.9
lewdness 665.5, 666.4
Lewis-Langmuir theory 1038.2
lex 673.3
lexeme 518.6, 526.1
lexemic 518.12
lexical 518.12, 526.20
lexical form 518.6
lexical item 518.6
lexical meaning 518.1
lexicographer 341.7, 523.15, 526.15
lexicographic 523.19, 526.20
lexicographical 523.19, 526.20
lexicography 341.8, 526.14
lexicologic 526.20
lexicological 523.19, 526.20
lexicologist 523.15, 526.15
lexicology 518.7, 526.14
lexicon 523.1, 526.13, 527.1, 554.9, 871.4
lexicostatistical 523.19
lexigraphic 526.20, 546.8
lexigraphical 526.20
lexigraphic character 546.1
lexigraphy 526.14, 546.5
lexiphanic 545.8
lexiphanicism 526.10, 545.1, 545.3
lexis 526.13
lexological 518.12
lex talionis 506.3, 863.1
ley 310.8
lez 75.15
liabilities 626.3, 628.1
liability 623.1, 641.2, 896.1, 897.1, 897.2, 968.1, 996.2, 1006.3
liability to error 971.7
liable 602.6, 623.9, 641.17, 897.5, 968.6, 1006.15
liableness 897.2
liable to 897.6
liable to error 971.22
liaise 213.6, 384.7
liaise with 775.5
liaising 800.13
liaison 104.5, 213.4, 384.4, 466.3, 775.1, 800.1
liana 310.4
liar 357.9
liar of the first magnitude 357.9
libation 8.4, 10.49, 88.7, 696.7
libber 642.5
libeccio 318.8
libel (n) 354.12, 512.3, 598.7 (v) 512.11
libelant 357.9, 599.5
libelee 599.6
libeler 357.9, 512.6
libelous 512.13
liberal (n) 220.1, 430.12, 611.11, 979.6 (a) 220.4, 430.25, 443.14, 478.22, 485.4, 585.11, 611.19, 652.6, 864.13, 979.9, 991.7
liberal arts 568.3
liberal education 928.4
liberalism 430.9, 430.10, 611.3, 979.2
liberalist (n) 611.11, 979.6 (a) 611.19
liberalistic 611.19, 979.9
liberality 478.1, 478.5, 485.1, 585.1, 652.2, 979.2, 991.2
liberalization 430.10
liberalize 430.13
liberalizing 979.13
liberal-minded 979.9
liberalmindedness 979.2
liberalness 485.1, 652.2, 979.2, 991.2
Liberal Party 609.24
liberate 120.6, 192.10, 398.3, 430.13, 431.4, 802.10, 1014.9
liberated 430.21, 431.10
liberated woman 77.5
liberating 592.4, 979.13
liberation 369.1, 398.1, 430.10, 431.1, 482.1
liberator 592.2
libertarian (n) 430.12, 979.6 (a) 430.25, 979.9
libertarianism 430.10, 979.2
Libertarian Party 609.24
liberties 640.2
libertinage 665.3
libertine (n) 430.12, 562.12, 665.10 (a) 430.25
libertinism 430.10, 665.3
liberty 20.3, 430.1, 430.2, 430.8, 443.1, 443.5, 642.2, 843.2
liberty abused 640.2
libidinal 75.25, 100.21, 934.6
libidinal energy 92.28
libidinous 75.27, 100.21, 665.29
libidinousness 75.5, 665.5
libido 75.2, 92.28, 100.1, 104.1, 104.2, 934.2
libido arrest 92.21
libido fixation 92.21
Lib-Lab 611.11
librarian 550.1, 558.3, 574.4
librarianship 558.2
library 197.6, 386.6, 397.7, 554.5, 558.1, 739.1, 770.11, 1009.5
library and information services 558.2
library and information studies 558.2
library binding 554.14
library card 549.10
library catalog 558.4
library edition 554.5
library furniture 229.1
Library of Congress 549.3, 558.1
Library of Congress Catalog 558.4
library professional 558.3
library science 558.2
library services 558.2
library services director 558.3
librate 916.10
libration 916.1
librational 916.15
libration in latitude 916.1
libration in longitude 916.1
libration of the moon 916.1
libratory 916.15
librettist 704.22, 710.20, 720.12
libretto 704.21, 708.28
libretto writing 718.2
libretto-writing 547.2
Librium 86.12
Libyan sibyl 962.6
license (n) 417.12, 418.1, 430.1, 430.8, 443.1, 443.6, 581.1, 615.1, 640.2, 642.2, 665.3, 673.2, 810.2 (v) 443.11, 615.10, 673.9
licensed 430.30, 443.17
licensed pilot 185.1
licensed psychologist 92.10
licensed teacher 571.1
licensee 615.9
license fee 630.6
license plate 443.6
licensing 443.3
licensing agreement 437.1
licentiate 615.9
licentious 418.5, 430.24, 640.11, 665.25, 669.8
licentiousness 418.1, 430.3, 562.10, 640.2, 665.3, 669.2
lichen 310.4
lichhouse 309.9
licit 443.15, 673.11
licitness 443.8, 673.1
lick (n) 62.2, 73.1, 172.4, 248.4, 403.3, 708.27, 725.4, 902.5 (v) 8.30, 62.7, 73.9, 249.7, 412.9, 604.14, 971.14
lick and a promise, a 276.1, 340.3, 992.1
lick and a promise 795.1
licked 412.15, 971.26
lickerish 75.27, 100.21, 665.29
lickerishness 665.5
licking 8.1, 412.1, 604.5
lick in to shape 407.6
lick into shape 262.7, 568.13, 867.3, 1002.5
lick of work 725.4
lick one's chops 100.19
lick one's lips 100.19
lick one's shoes 138.7
lickspit 138.3
lickspittle (n) 138.3 (v) 138.7
lick the dust 137.7, 138.7, 412.12, 433.11
lick the feet of 138.7
lick the plate 8.24
lick the platter 8.24
lick to a frazzle 412.9
lictor 1008.15
lid 2.9, 5.25, 27.9, 293.4, 295.5
lidless 23.7, 339.13
lidless eye 339.4
lidless vigil 23.1
lido 234.2
lid poppers 87.4
lie (n) 159.3, 161.1, 354.11, 751.3 (v) 158.9, 159.10, 182.16, 201.5, 221.6, 354.19, 645.11
lie-abed 22.12, 175.5, 331.7
lie about 331.12
lie a course 182.27
lie across 170.6
lie ahead 839.6

lie ahull 182.17
lie along 182.43
lie along the shore 182.39
lie around 331.12
lie athwart 182.16
lie at the root of 886.10
lie back 329.2
lie back on one's record 331.15
lie beam on to the seas 182.32
lie behind 375.20
lie beneath 519.3
lie by 182.17, 223.9, 223.12, 331.16
lie close 346.8
lie close to the wind 182.25
lieder singer 710.13
lie detector 92.8
lied form 709.11
lie doggo 346.8
lie dormant 22.15, 329.2, 331.16, 519.3
lie down 20.6, 201.5, 274.5, 913.11
lie down and roll over for 326.2
lie down on the job 331.12, 368.9
lie fallow 331.16, 891.3
lie flat 201.5
lie flatly 354.19
liege (n) 432.7, 575.1, 577.1 (a) 432.13
liege lord 575.1
liege man 432.7, 577.1
liege subject 432.7
lie hard upon 297.13, 1011.8
lie heavy 297.10
lie heavy upon 297.13, 1011.8
lie hid 32.3, 346.8, 519.3
lie hidden 346.8
lie idle 331.16
lie in 1.3, 159.10, 182.35, 761.11
lie in Abraham's bosom 307.26
lie in ambush 346.10
lie in one's course 839.6
lie in one's power 18.11
lie in one's throat 354.19
lie in state 309.21
lie in the grave 307.26
lie in wait 346.9
lie in wait for 130.8, 346.10
lie just around the corner 839.6
lie like a trooper 354.19
lie limply 201.5
lie low 274.5, 329.2, 346.8, 494.7, 519.3
lien 438.4, 438.5, 469.1
lie near to the wind 182.17
lientery 12.2
lie off 182.17
lie off the land 182.17
lie on 297.11, 901.22, 959.6, 1011.8
lie on a level 201.5
lie on a level with 790.5
lie on one's back 201.5
lie on one's door 641.7
lie on one's face 201.5
lie on one's oars 368.9
lie on the shelf 331.16
lie on the surface 348.7
lie opposite 215.4
lie out of 600.11
lie over 295.30, 840.2
lie perdue 346.8
lie prone 201.5, 274.5
lie prostrate 201.5, 274.5
lie snug 346.8
lie still 173.7
lie supine 201.5, 274.5
lie through one's teeth 354.19
lie to 182.17, 331.16
lie together 75.21
lieu 159.1, 159.4
lie under 274.5, 897.3
lie under a necessity 963.10
lie under an obligation 150.3, 623.5
lie under the surface 519.3
lie up 182.17, 331.16
lie upon 641.7
lieutenancy 615.1
lieutenant 432.5, 575.17, 575.19, 576.1, 616.6, 1008.15
lieutenant colonel 575.17
lieutenant commander 575.19
lieutenant general 575.17
lieutenant governor 575.12
lieutenant junior grade 575.19
lie with 75.21, 959.6
Life 677.6
life 17.4, 17.6, 101.1, 109.4, 306.1, 312.5, 330.2, 430.2
life 719.1, 761.1, 763.3, 827.5, 831.4
life after death 681.2, 839.2
life-and-death 997.23
life-and-death struggle 457.6
life and letters 719.1
life belt 397.6
life beyond the grave 839.2
lifeblood 2.25, 306.2, 767.2
lifeboat 180.1, 369.3, 397.6, 398.2
life breath 306.2
life buoy 180.11, 369.3, 397.6
life care 90.1
life-care home 1009.4
life-changing 852.10
life cycle 306.2, 306.5
life drawing 712.4
life essence 306.2
life everlasting 829.3
life expectancy 303.1, 306.1, 306.5, 827.5
life-expired 19.17, 390.10
life force 17.4, 306.2, 767.5
life form 763.3
life-form 305.2
life-giving 78.15, 306.13
lifeguard 398.2, 1008.6
lifeguarding 760.8
Life Guards 461.15
Life Guardsman 1008.14
life hack 928.4
life history 719.1
life instinct 92.28
life insurance 624.6
life jacket 397.6
lifeless 117.6, 173.14, 307.29, 331.20, 1027.17, 1055.5
lifeless dead to the world 25.8
lifeless matter 1055.1
lifelessness 65.1, 117.1, 331.6, 1027.5, 1055.2
lifelike 349.14, 784.16, 973.15
lifelike image 986.6
lifelikeness 973.7
lifeline 369.3, 397.6, 1008.3
lifelong 827.13
lifemanship 457.2
life mask 349.6, 785.1
life member 617.11
life net 369.3, 397.6
life of ease 121.1, 1010.1
life of Riley 95.5, 1010.1
life of the party 17.6, 322.3, 489.12, 582.16
life on earth 306.4
life one's hand against 457.14
life-or-death 997.23
life-or-death struggle 457.6
life peer 608.4
life preserver 180.11, 397.6, 1008.3
life principle 306.2, 689.18, 919.5
life process 306.2
life-promoting 81.5
lifer 429.11
life raft 180.11, 369.3, 397.6
life records 549.2
life ring 397.6
lifesaver 397.5, 398.2, 1008.6
lifesaving 398.1, 760.8
lifesaving medal 646.6
life savings 728.14
lifesaving service 398.2
life science 1068.1, 1068.3
life scientist 1068.2
life's duration 827.5
life sentence 602.1
life-size 257.16
lifesize 257.3
life-sized 257.16, 257.22
life skill 928.4
life span 306.1, 821.4
lifespan 303.1, 827.5
life story 719.1
lifestyle 321.1, 371.5, 373.1, 765.4, 866.1
lifestyle drug 87.3
life-support 901.1
life-sustaining 901.23
life-sustainment 901.1
life's work 724.6
life table 968.2
life-threatening 85.53, 308.23, 1011.15
lifetime (n) 303.1, 306.1, 306.5, 827.5 (a) 827.13
lifetime member 617.11
life to come 681.2, 839.2
life vest 397.6
life-weariness 118.3
life-weary 118.11
lifework 724.6, 886.9
lift (n) 105.3, 177.7, 184.26, 238.14, 272.2, 317.2, 392.1, 449.2, 482.4, 753.1, 912.2, 912.3, 912.4, 1073.2 (v) 109.8, 176.12, 238.22, 336.5, 392.9, 482.16, 621.4, 624.13, 912.5
lift a finger 328.5, 403.6
lift a hand 403.6, 453.3
lift a hand against 451.3, 459.14, 900.6
lift component 184.26
lift direction 184.26
lifted 912.9
lifter 483.1, 912.3, 1020.12
lift force 184.26
lifting (n) 482.1, 621.2, 912.1 (a) 912.10
lifting body 181.1
lift off 802.10, 1075.12
liftoff 184.8, 188.2, 1074.9
lift one's voice 524.21
lift ratio 184.26
lifts 1073.2
lift temporarily 959.5
lift the hat 585.10
lift the veil 351.4
lift up 200.9, 818.11, 912.5, 937.3, 983.10
lift up one's heart 121.7
lift up the eyes 27.13
lift up the heart 696.11
lift up the voice 59.9
lift weights 84.4
ligament 2.3, 271.2
ligamental 271.7
ligate 800.5
ligating 800.3
ligation 271.2, 800.3
ligature 271.2, 548.6, 709.12, 800.3
liger 797.8
light (n) 33.3, 174.6, 314.2, 341.4, 551.1, 916.4, 978.2, 1021.4, 1025.1, 1025.21, 1026.1, 1029.2, 1032.10 (v) 184.43, 194.7, 1020.22, 1025.27, 1025.28, 1025.29 (a) 16.14, 35.22, 36.9, 37.8, 109.12, 270.16, 276.5, 298.10, 298.12, 317.12, 364.6, 413.23, 524.30, 665.26, 704.35, 922.20, 998.19, 1014.13, 1025.31
light air 318.4
light aircraft 181.11
light and shade 1025.19
light-armed 460.14
light as a feather 298.10
light as air 298.10
light as day 1025.30
light as gossamer 298.10
light at the end of the tunnel, the 100.11, 130.2, 940.1
light baritone 709.5
light-blue 45.3
lightboard 704.16, 704.18
light breeze 318.4
light bulb 1026.1
light-colored 36.9
light comedian 707.9
light dragoon 461.12
light eater 8.16
lighted 1025.39
lighted buoy 517.10
lightedness 1025.3
light emission 1025.2
light-emitting diode 1025.19
lighten 120.7, 298.6, 670.6, 1025.27, 1025.28
lightened 36.8, 298.11, 1025.39
lightening (n) 36.3, 120.3, 298.3, 670.2 (a) 298.16, 1025.40
lighten of 480.21

lighter (n) 1021.4 (v) 176.13
lighterage 630.7
lighterman 183.5
lighter-than-air aviation 184.1
lighter-than-air craft 181.11
lightface 548.20
light-faced 548.20
light fantastic, the 705.1
light filter 1028.4
light-fingered 482.21
light-fingered gentry 483.2
light fingers 482.12
light fixture 1026.6
light-footed 174.15, 413.23
light globe 1028.3
light hand 427.1
light harmony 708.3
lightheaded 16.12, 926.31, 985.15
lightheadedness 16.1, 985.4
light heart 109.3
lighthearted 109.12
lightheartedness 109.3
light heavyweight 297.3
light holder 1026.6
lighthouse 27.8, 272.6, 400.1, 517.10
lighthouse beacon 517.15
lighthouse keeper 399.4
light-hued 36.9
light industry 892.3
light infantryman 461.9
lighting (n) 1020.4, 1025.19 (a) 1020.27, 1025.40
lighting cameraman 706.5
lighting design 717.5
lighting up 1020.4
light-intensity control 1041.8
light into 457.14, 459.15, 604.10, 725.15
lightish 1025.31
lightish-blue 45.3
light-legged 174.15
lightless 1027.13
lightlessness 38.2, 1027.1
light lunch 8.6, 8.7
lightly touching 73.12
light meal 8.7
light meter 714.9, 1025.21
lightmindedness 984.1
light music 708.7
lightness 16.2, 35.6, 36.2, 37.1, 109.3, 270.4, 298.1, 364.3, 413.2, 665.4, 922.7, 998.3, 1025.3
lightning 174.6, 1025.17
lightning attack 459.1
lightning bug 1026.5
lightning conductor 1008.3
lightning express 179.14
lightninglike 830.4
lightning rod 1008.3
lightning speed 174.1, 174.2
lightning strike 1025.17
lightning-swift 830.4
lightning war 459.1
light of day 1025.10
light of heel 174.15
light of love 104.9
light of one's eye 104.9
light of one's life 104.9
Light of the World 677.10
light on 992.9
light opera 708.34
light out 188.10
light pen 1025.19, 1042.4
light-pervious 1029.4
light plot 704.18
light pollution 1072.2
lightproof 293.12, 1031.3
light punishment 604.3
light purse 619.1
light quantum 1025.21
light rain 316.1
light rein 427.1
light repast 8.7
lights 704.18, 953.6
light sculpture 712.16
light shield 1028.1
lightship 517.10
light show 33.7, 47.2, 1025.8
light sleep 22.2
lightsome 109.12, 1025.31
lightsomeness 109.3
light source 1025.1, 1025.20, 1026.1
lights out 22.18
lights-out 315.4
light texture 270.4
light the fuse 105.12, 375.18, 456.14
light the way 165.2
lighttight 293.12
light touch 73.1, 298.1
light tower 272.6
light up 105.12, 109.9, 1020.22, 1025.28
light upon 186.7, 194.10, 223.11, 941.3
light wave 1025.1
lightweight (n) 16.6, 250.2, 258.4, 297.3, 924.2, 998.7 (a) 16.14, 298.10, 298.13, 895.3
light wind 318.4
light wine 88.17
light within 636.5
light-year 1073.3
light-years 261.1
lignaloes 70.4
ligneous 310.40
ligniform 310.40
lignitic 1021.9
ligula 271.4
ligular 271.7
ligulate 271.7
ligule 271.4, 310.19
likability 100.13, 104.6
likable 63.8, 97.6, 100.30, 104.24
like (n) 104.1, 784.3, 790.4 (v) 63.5, 95.13, 100.14, 104.18, 371.14 (a) 775.8, 778.7, 784.10, 790.7
likeableness 104.6
like a bump on a log 329.6
like a chicken with its head cut off 971.24
like a drowned rat 1065.17
like a feather in the wind 854.7
like a fish out of water 160.11
like a furnace 1019.25
like a hog on ice 361.12
like a house afire 101.9
like an oven 1019.25
like a prune 303.18
like a sieve 292.20
like a sitting duck 19.18, 897.5
like best 371.17
like better 371.17
like cats and dogs 456.15
like Chinese mustard 68.7
like for like (n) 506.3 (a) 506.8
like grains of sand 804.4
like horseradish 68.7
like it is 765.2, 973.4
like it or lump it 963.11
likelihood 130.1, 897.1, 966.1, 968.1, 972.8
likelihoods 130.4
likeliness 897.1, 968.1
likely 788.10, 897.5, 966.6, 968.6, 978.8, 995.5, 1016.18
likely lad 659.2
likely story 600.4
likely to 897.6
like-minded 332.15, 455.3, 788.9
like-mindedness 332.5, 455.1
likemindedness 788.3
liken 943.4
likeness 33.3, 349.5, 712.10, 784.1, 784.3, 785.1, 790.1
like new 396.24, 841.9
likening 778.2, 784.1, 943.1
liken to 943.4
like of, the 784.3
like one possessed 926.30
like parchment 1066.7
like pulling teeth 1013.17
like putty 362.12, 923.12
like putty in one's hands 433.13
like sardines 293.11
like sardines in a can 884.9, 993.20
like shooting fish in a barrel 1014.13
like snow in August 848.2
likes of, the 784.3, 809.3
like Stentor 53.12
like Swiss cheese 292.19
like taking candy from a baby 1014.13
like the Rock of Gibraltar 853.7
like the sound of one's own voice 540.6
like to 100.15
like two peas in a pod 778.7
liking 100.2, 104.1, 323.1, 896.1, 1042.19
likker 88.14
lilac (n) 46.1 (a) 46.3
Lilienfeld technique 753.3
Lilith 680.4, 680.6
Lilliputian (n) 258.5 (a) 258.13
lilt (n) 708.4, 708.14, 709.22, 720.7 (v) 109.6, 116.5, 524.25, 708.38
lilting 708.48, 720.18
lily 37.2, 77.10
lily-liver 491.5
lily-livered 16.12, 491.10
lily-liveredness 491.1
lily-white 37.7
limation 1044.2
limb 2.7, 177.14, 211.4, 310.11, 310.20, 793.4, 906.4
limber (v) 1047.6 (a) 16.12, 1047.9
limberness 1047.2
limber up 405.13, 1047.6
limbic 211.11, 820.12
limbo 130.3, 390.2, 429.7, 682.1
limbs of Satan 660.11
limbus 211.4
lime (n) 37.2, 67.2, 356.13, 890.4 (v) 356.20, 1012.11
limejuicer 183.1
limekiln 742.5
limelight 352.4, 704.18
limen 24.2, 211.3
limestone 1059.1
limewater 1065.3
limey 183.1
Limeyland 232.4
liminal 211.11
limit (n) 198.2, 210.2, 211.3, 257.2, 794.5, 820.2 (v) 210.5, 211.8, 270.11, 428.9, 866.4, 959.3 (a) 211.11
limit, the 135.3
limitable 210.10
limital 210.10
limitary 210.9
limitation 210.2, 211.3, 270.1, 428.3, 471.4, 911.1, 959.1, 959.2
limitational 959.7
limitations 211.1
limitative 210.9, 428.12, 959.7
limit condition 211.3
limit control 1041.8
limited (n) 179.14 (a) 210.7, 231.9, 258.10, 270.14, 428.15, 670.11, 866.5, 959.10, 992.10
limited choice 371.3
limited edition 249.5, 865.2
limited liability corporation 739.1
limited monarchy 612.4
limited number 885.2
limited practice 90.13
limited veto 444.2, 613.7
limited war 458.1
limiter 1035.11
limiting (n) 210.1, 210.2, 780.4, 959.1 (a) 210.9, 211.11, 212.11, 428.12, 766.8, 820.12, 959.7
limiting condition 959.2
limiting factor 211.3
limitless 100.27, 430.27, 677.17, 823.3
limitlessness 823.1
limit of one's patience, the 135.3
limit of vision 31.3
limit oneself 668.6
limits 209.1, 211.1
limit-setting 210.1
limn 211.9, 349.8, 349.9, 712.19
limner 716.2
limnetic 241.5
limniad 678.10
limnimeter 241.4
limning (n) 349.1, 349.2 (a) 349.13
limnograph 241.4
limnologic 241.5
limnological 241.5

limnologist 241.4
limnology 241.4
limnophilous 241.5
limo 179.13
limoniad 678.9
limousine 179.13
limp (n) 175.2, 177.12 (v) 16.8, 175.6, 177.28 (a) 16.12, 202.10, 1047.10
limp as a dishrag 16.12
limp-cover book 554.3
limpet 803.4
limpid 521.11, 533.6, 1029.4
limpidity 31.2, 521.2, 533.1, 1029.1
limping 175.10, 393.30
limping meters 720.3
limpness 1047.3
limp-wristed 16.17, 75.30
linaloa 70.4
linchpin 997.6
lincture 86.4
linctus 86.4
Lindow man 842.7
line (n) 161.1, 180.10, 211.3, 216.2, 267.3, 271.2, 347.17, 381.4, 383.1, 383.7, 384.1, 463.2, 517.6, 517.8, 553.2, 559.4, 560.4, 560.5, 562.5, 609.4, 708.4, 708.22, 708.29, 709.12, 712.8, 713.2, 720.10, 722.4, 724.6, 735.1, 745.1, 746.1, 746.2, 746.3, 749.2, 809.3, 812.2, 812.3, 815.1, 835.2, 866.1, 896.2 (v) 196.7, 211.10, 295.25, 381.11, 517.19, 713.9, 808.9, 812.5
line, the 231.3, 461.23, 747.1
lineage 559.4, 560.4, 560.5, 561.1, 608.2, 812.2, 815.1, 835.2
lineal 277.6, 559.7, 560.18, 812.9, 835.4
lineality 277.1
lineament 865.4
lineaments 33.3, 33.4, 206.2, 211.2, 216.4, 262.3
linear 277.6, 812.9
linear calibration 1041.7
linear dimension 257.1
linearity 277.1
linear measure 257.1, 300.4
linear measures 267.1
linear operation 1041.6
linear system 1041.5
linear thinking 920.1
lineation 517.6
linebacker 746.2
linebred 78.17
linebreed 78.8
line breeding 1070.1
linebreeding 78.2
lined 713.11
line doggie 461.10
line dot-matrix printer 1042.9
line drawing 712.12
line drive 745.3
lined up 203.6
line editor 554.2
line engraver 716.8
line engraving 548.1
line in the sand 451.1
line item 626.3, 628.5
line-item veto 372.1, 444.2
line letter 30.6
lineman 178.13, 347.10, 752.2, 1032.22
linemen 746.2
linen 5.1, 5.15, 5.22, 295.10
linen closet 197.15
linens 735.3
line of action 384.1
line of advance 383.1
line of battle 463.2
line-of-battle ship 180.6
line of business 724.6, 866.1
line of circumvallation 211.3
line of country 724.4, 866.1
line of credit 622.1
line of defense 461.23
line of demarcation 211.3, 875.3
line of departure 188.5, 216.2
line of descent 560.4
line of direction 161.1
line of duty 641.1
line of endeavor 724.6
line of force 1032.9
line of goods 735.1
line of least resistance 464.4
line of march 161.1
line of position 159.3, 182.2
line of retreat 383.1
line of scrimmage 746.3
line of sight 27.1, 31.3
line of succession 479.2
line of supply 385.1
line of thinking 931.1
line of type 548.2
line of vision 27.1, 31.3
line of work 724.6
line one's pockets 472.12, 618.10
line out 708.38
line printer 1042.9
liner 180.1, 180.5, 196.3, 296.2, 745.3
line radio 347.3
liner notes 50.12
lines 33.4, 211.2, 228.29, 384.1, 704.10, 704.21, 706.3, 712.7
line-sequential television 1035.5
line shot 745.3
linesman 748.2, 749.2, 749.3, 752.3, 1032.22
line squall 318.11, 671.4
line storm 318.11
line umpire 748.2
line up 203.5, 808.9, 812.5, 812.6, 965.6
lineup 381.1, 746.3, 807.1, 871.6, 965.3
lineup batting order 745.2
line up for 130.8
line up one's ducks 405.11
line up with 450.4
linewoman 347.10
linga sharira 689.17, 689.18
linger 166.4, 175.8, 331.14, 827.7, 846.12, 856.3
linger behind 166.4
lingerer 175.5, 331.8
lingerie 5.22
lingering (n) 175.3, 331.4, 827.2, 846.3 (a) 54.12, 175.11, 827.11, 846.17
lingering death 748.2
linger on 827.7, 827.9
lingo 523.1, 523.9
lingua 62.5, 523.1
lingua franca 523.11
lingual 62.10, 523.19, 524.29
lingual delirium 926.8
linguiform 62.10
linguine 10.33
linguist 523.15, 523.16, 526.15
linguistic 343.9, 518.12, 523.19, 524.29
linguistic act 524.2
linguistic ambience 523.7
linguistic analysis 523.13
linguistic atlas 523.7
linguistic behavior 524.2
linguistic community 227.1, 523.7
linguistic finesse 532.2
linguistic form 518.6, 526.1
linguistician 523.15
linguistic intercourse 343.1
linguistic island 523.7
linguistics 518.7, 523.13
linguistic scholar 523.15
linguistic science 523.13
linguistic scientist 523.15, 526.15
linguistic structure 530.1
linguistic tact 532.2
linguistic terminology 523.13
linguistic theory 523.13
linguistic universal 523.11
lingulate 62.10
liniment 86.11, 1056.3
lining 196.3, 554.14, 713.2
lining-up 554.14
link (n) 213.4, 775.1, 800.4, 1026.3 (v) 177.28, 770.16, 775.6, 800.5, 805.3, 805.4, 812.4
linkage 775.1, 800.1, 805.1
linked 775.9, 800.13, 805.6, 812.8
linked up 805.6
linking (n) 775.1, 800.1, 800.3, 805.1 (a) 223.17, 530.17, 775.7, 800.16
linking verb 530.4
linking word 530.3
links 310.7, 743.11, 751.1
linksman 751.2
Link trainer 181.10
link up 770.16, 775.6, 800.5, 800.11, 803.7, 812.4
linkup 775.1, 800.1, 812.2
link up with 169.2, 775.5
link with 775.5
linn 238.11, 241.1
Linnaean 527.17
Linnaean method 527.1
linoleum-block print 713.5
Linotype 548.15
Linotyper 548.12
linseed 310.31
linsey-woolsey 288.6
lint 3.19, 86.33, 1051.5
lintel 189.6
lion 15.8, 311.21, 492.7, 647.2, 662.9, 997.9
lioness 77.9
lionhearted 492.16
lionheartedness 492.1
lionism 918.4
lionization 662.8
lionize 509.12, 662.13, 697.5, 918.6
lionizing (n) 509.5 (a) 509.18, 697.7
lionlike 311.42
lion's share 257.11, 477.5, 792.6, 883.2
lion tamer 707.3
lip (n) 142.4, 211.4, 283.3, 597.3, 711.6, 751.1 (v) 142.8, 524.22, 708.42
lip-clap 73.1
lip color 1016.11
lipid 7.7, 1056.1
lip off 939.5
lipoid 7.7
lipoprotein 7.7
liposuction 90.2
lipothymia 25.2
lipothymy 25.2
lipped 211.13
Lippes loop 86.23
lippitude 28.2
lip praise 693.2
lipread 49.4
lip reader 49.2
lipreader 341.7
lip reading 49.3
lipreading 341.3
lip rouge 1016.11
lips 2.12, 2.13, 292.4, 524.18
lip server 693.3
lip service 354.6, 693.2
lipstick (n) 1016.11 (v) 41.4
lip worshiper 693.3
liquated 1020.31
liquation 1020.3
liquefacient 1061.2, 1064.4
liquefaction 1020.3, 1061.1, 1064.1
liquefactive 1064.7
liquefiable 1061.4, 1064.9
liquefied 1020.31, 1061.4, 1064.6
liquefier 1061.2, 1064.4
liquefy 1020.21, 1047.6, 1064.5
liquefying (n) 1020.3, 1064.1 (a) 1061.4, 1064.7
liquesce 1064.5
liquescence 1020.3, 1064.1
liquescency 1064.1
liquescent 1064.6
liqueur 10.49, 88.15
liquid (n) 10.49, 524.12, 1061.2 (a) 524.30, 728.31, 1061.4, 1065.16
liquid air 1024.7
liquid assets 386.2, 471.7, 728.18
liquidate 255.10, 308.13, 308.16, 308.17, 395.14, 447.4, 624.13, 728.29, 737.24, 762.7, 773.5, 909.21
liquidated 395.28, 624.22, 773.7, 858.19

liquidating dividend 738.7
liquidation 308.2, 395.6, 447.2, 624.1, 737.19, 773.2
liquidator 624.9, 729.12
liquid conduction 1032.14
liquid-crystal display 1025.19
liquid diet 7.13
liquid extract 1061.2
liquid fuel 1074.8, 1075.9
liquid helium 1024.7
liquidity 1061.1
liquidization 1064.1
liquidize 1064.5
liquidizer 1065.3
liquidizing 1064.1
liquid-level control 1041.8
liquid lunch 87.1
liquidness 1061.1
liquid nitrogen 1024.7
liquid oxygen 1024.7, 1074.8
liquid state 1061.1
liquid sweetener 66.3
liquid waste 370.4, 391.4
liquidy 1061.4
liquor (n) 10.49, 86.12, 88.9, 88.13, 1061.2 (v) 88.25
liquor dealer 88.19
liquor-drinking 88.35
liquorish 88.35
liquor-loving 88.35
liquor store owner 88.19
liquor up 88.25
lisp (n) 57.1, 525.1 (v) 57.2, 525.7
lisping (n) 525.1 (a) 525.12
Lissajous curve 916.5
Lissajous figure 280.7, 916.5
lissome 1047.9
lissotrichous 287.10
list (n) 47.5, 196.1, 204.2, 211.4, 211.7, 212.3, 549.1, 871.1 (v) 48.10, 182.43, 194.8, 204.10, 211.10, 549.15, 615.17, 809.6, 871.8, 1069.17
listed 47.15, 871.9
listen 48.10, 326.2, 983.7
listen at 48.10
listener 48.5, 479.3, 1034.22
listener-in 48.5, 1034.22
listenership 1034.22
listen in 48.10, 347.19, 1034.27
listening (n) 48.1, 48.2 (a) 48.14
listening device 48.8
listening in 48.2
listen to 48.10
listen to reason 920.10, 979.7
listen with both ears 48.10, 983.7
listeriosis 85.31
listing (n) 549.14, 871.1, 871.7, 1069.13 (a) 204.15, 791.5
listless 16.12, 94.13, 102.7, 118.11, 331.20, 982.3
listlessness 16.1, 94.4, 102.2, 118.3, 331.6, 982.1
listmaker 547.15, 549.13
listmaking 549.1
list of agenda 965.3
list price 630.1
lists 463.1
list system 371.6, 609.18
lit 88.33, 1025.39
litany 696.4
Lit-Crit 723.3
literacy 570.4, 928.5
literal 341.16, 518.10, 521.11, 546.8, 547.22, 687.7, 973.15, 973.16, 987.5
literalism 687.5, 973.5, 973.7
literalist 687.8
literalistic 687.8
literality 973.5, 973.7
literal meaning 518.1
literal-minded 987.5
literalness 521.2, 973.5, 973.7
literal translation 341.3
literal truth 973.5
literary 547.24, 718.7, 928.22
literary analysis 723.3
literary art 547.2, 718.2
literary artifact 547.10
literary artisan 547.15
literary artist 547.15, 718.4
literary artistry 547.2, 718.2
literary canon 547.12, 718.1
literary composition 547.2, 718.2
literary craftsman 547.15, 718.4
literary critic 547.15, 718.4, 946.7
literary criticism 341.8, 723.3, 946.2
literary culture 928.5
literary device 536.1
literary evaluation 723.3
literary exegetics 723.3
literary flair 547.2, 718.2
literary hack 547.16, 718.5
literary hermeneutics 723.3
literary interpretation 723.3
literary journeyman 547.15, 718.4
literary language 523.4
literary lion 547.15
literary man 547.15, 929.3
literary piracy 482.8
literary pirate 483.9
literary power 547.2, 718.2
literary production 547.2, 547.10, 718.2
literary scholar 718.4
literary style 532.2
literary talent 547.2, 718.2
literary text 547.12, 718.1
literary theory 723.3
literary work 547.12, 718.1
literate (n) 929.1 (a) 570.16, 928.21
literati 929.2
literature 352.8, 547.10, 547.12, 718.1, 928.9
literature of the field 928.9
lithe 1047.9
litheness 1047.2
lithesome 1047.9
lithic 1059.11
lithification 1046.5, 1059.8
lithified sediment 1059.1
lithify 1046.7, 1059.10
lithograph (n) 713.5 (v) 713.9
lithographer 716.8
lithographic 713.12
lithographic stone 713.6
lithography 35.11, 548.1, 712.16, 713.3
lithogravure 548.1
lithoid 1046.10, 1059.12
lithoidal 1046.10, 1059.12
lithophotogravure 548.1
lithosphere 234.1, 295.14
lithotype 713.5
litigable 598.21, 673.11, 674.6
litigant (n) 452.3, 598.11 (a) 598.21
litigate 598.13, 673.9, 935.16
litigating 598.21
litigation 457.1, 598.1, 935.4
litigationist 598.11
litigator 598.11, 935.12
litigatory 598.21
litigious 110.26, 456.17, 598.21, 935.19
litigiousness 110.7, 456.3, 457.1, 935.13
litmus-paper test 942.2
litmus test 942.2
litotes 350.1
litter (n) 256.1, 302.10, 309.13, 391.5, 559.5, 561.2, 770.5, 810.3, 884.3, 901.19, 901.20 (v) 1.3, 811.2, 1070.7
litterateur 929.3
littérateur 547.15, 718.4
litter basket 391.7
litter bin 391.7
litterbug 810.7
littering 1.1
little, a 223.2
little (n) 248.2, 828.3 (a) 248.6, 250.7, 258.10, 268.8, 651.6, 661.12, 980.10, 998.17
little angel 302.9
little bird, a 552.10
little birdie, a 552.10
little birdy 399.1
little bit 248.2, 828.3
little bite 62.4
little-bitsy 258.11
little-bitty 258.11
little boys room 197.26
little boys' room 12.10
little brown jug 88.13
little bugger 302.3
little chance 972.9
little darling 302.9
little devil 322.3, 680.7
little Dick Fisher 879.1
little doll 302.9
little expectation 969.1
little extra 254.4
little fellow 302.3, 606.5
little fellow, the 998.7
little finger 73.5
little folk 606.4
little game 381.5, 415.3
little-girlish 77.13
little-girlishness 77.1
little girls room 197.26
little girls' room 12.10
little green man 678.11, 870.4, 1075.8
little green men 678.8
little guy 302.3
little guy, the 998.7
little guys 302.2
little innocent 302.3
Little Italy 230.6
Little Joe 879.1
little Joe from Kokomo 879.1
little kids 302.2
little known 661.14
Little League baseball 745.1
little learning, a 930.5
little man 606.5, 998.7
little men, the 678.7
little-minded 980.10
little-mindedness 980.1
little Miss Fixit 396.10, 466.3
little missy 302.6
little monkey 302.4, 322.3
little natural 882.3
littleness 248.1, 250.3, 258.1, 268.1, 651.2, 661.3, 980.1, 998.1
little old lady 304.3
little one 302.3
little ones 561.1
little opportunity 972.9
little people 561.1
little people, the 606.1, 678.7
little person 980.5
little Phoebe 882.1
little pitcher with big ears 48.5
little plate 62.4
little problem 1003.2
little rascal 322.3
little recall 990.1
little red schoolhouse 567.10
little retentivity 990.1
little shaver 302.3
little slam 758.3
little smack 62.4
little something, a 478.4
little squirt 302.3
littlest 250.8
little summer of St. Luke 313.5
little tad 302.3
little talk 541.3
little terror 302.4
little theater 704.14
little thing, a 998.6
little tin god 104.15, 662.9, 997.9
little toe 2.7
little too thick,a 955.10
little tot 302.3
little voice 52.4
little ways 223.2
little while 828.3
little white lie 354.11
little woman 563.8
littoral (n) 234.2, 240.4 (a) 182.58, 211.11, 234.7
littoral zone 234.2
lit to the gills 88.33
lit up 88.33, 1025.39
liturgic 580.8, 701.18
liturgical 701.18, 708.50
liturgical garment 5.1
liturgical garments 702.1
liturgical music 708.17
liturgics 701.1
liturgiology 701.1
liturgism 701.1
liturgist 701.2
liturgistic 701.18
liturgistical 701.18

liturgy 580.4, 696.8, 701.3
Liturgy, the 701.8
lituus 273.2, 279.2
livability 225.6
livable 225.15
live (v) 225.7, 306.8, 662.10, 761.8, 827.6 (a) 306.12, 330.17, 1019.27, 1032.34
live above one's means 669.5
live a cat-and-dog life 456.8
live action 1035.2
live a dog's life 1011.9
live again 306.9
live a life of ease 121.8, 331.15, 1010.10
live alone 565.5, 584.7
live ammunition 462.13
live and breathe 306.8
live and learn 570.10
live and let live 329.4, 430.16, 979.7, 982.2
live apart 566.5, 584.7
live as man and wife 563.17
live at 159.17
live audience 48.6
live ball 746.3, 747.3
live beyond one's means 486.7, 669.5
live by 437.9
live by one's wits 356.18, 415.9, 645.11
live by the sword and die by the sword 507.6
live coal 1019.16
lived-in 121.11
live down 658.4
live fast 669.6
live forever 829.6
live for the day 406.7, 486.3
live for the moment 663.4
live from hand to mouth 406.7, 619.5
live frugally 635.4, 668.6
live hard 669.6
live high 618.12, 669.4, 1010.10
live high on the hog 409.10, 618.12, 669.4, 1010.10
live in 225.7
live-in 207.6, 225.13
live in a dream world 986.16
live in a glass house 31.5, 493.5
live in an ivory tower 1009.8
live in clover 618.12, 1010.10
live-in help 577.2
live in hopes 124.6
live-in lover 588.1, 665.17
live-in maid 227.2, 577.8
live in one's memory 989.13
live in retirement 584.7
live in sin 225.7
live in the lap of luxury 618.12
live it up 95.14, 582.21, 669.4, 743.22
live large 95.14
livelihood 449.3
live like a pig 80.14
live like cat and dog 456.8
live like the grasshopper 406.7
liveliness 17.4, 68.2, 93.2, 101.1, 109.4, 306.1, 330.2, 544.4, 1048.1
livelong 827.13
live long and prosper 1010.7
lively 17.13, 68.7, 93.18, 101.8, 109.14, 174.15, 330.17, 544.12, 983.19, 1048.7
lively imagination 986.4
lively interest 981.1
lively market 737.2
lively pace 174.1
live matter 548.4
liven 17.10, 109.7
liven up 9.2, 17.10, 105.13
live off 138.12
live off of 138.12
live off the fat of the land 669.4, 1010.10
live on 8.28, 761.9, 827.6, 839.7
live on velvet 1010.10
live-out maid 577.8
live out of a suitcase 177.21
live outside the law 674.5
liver 2.16, 2.17, 7.8, 10.20
liver-brown 40.4
liver chestnut 311.11
liver-colored 40.4
liver death 85.2, 307.5
liver disease 85.23
liveried 5.45
liveried servant 577.6
liverish 85.61, 110.23
liverishness 110.1
liver rot 85.41
liver spot 2.4
liverwort 310.4
livery 5.2, 5.7, 647.1
livery servant 577.6
live show 1035.2
live simply 668.6
livestock 311.1
livestock farming 1070.1
live temperately 670.5
live the life of Riley 618.12, 1010.10
live through 396.20, 409.13, 827.6
live through it 360.4
live to a ripe old age 303.10
live to eat 672.4
live to fight another day 827.6
live together 225.7, 563.17
live upon 8.28
live upon nothing 484.5
live up to 434.2, 437.9
liveware 1042.17
live weight 297.1
live well 618.12, 669.4, 1010.10
live wire 330.8, 1032.5
live with 134.5, 979.7
live within one's income 635.4
live within one's means 670.5
live with it 360.4, 433.6
livid 36.7, 38.12, 39.4, 45.3, 46.3, 152.28, 307.28
livid-brown 40.4
lividity 39.1, 45.1, 46.1
lividness 36.2, 39.1, 45.1, 46.1
livid rage 152.10
livid with rage 152.28
living (n) 225.1, 306.1, 449.3, 698.9 (a) 17.13, 225.13, 305.17, 306.12, 761.13, 784.16, 1019.27
living, the 306.3
living and breathing, the 306.3
living apart 566.1
living as man and wife 563.1
living being 305.2, 306.4, 311.2
living death 96.7
living doll 659.2
living floor 296.1
living force 18.5, 306.2
living image 349.5
living in 225.13
living in sin 225.1
living issue 937.1
living language 523.2
living large 95.18
living matter 305.1
living nature 305.1
living passion 152.10
living person 306.4
living picture 349.5
living pledge 438.4
living quarters 225.3, 228.4
living rock 1059.1
living room 197.5
living soul 306.4, 312.5
living souls 227.1
living space 158.3, 158.4, 228.1
living thing 305.2, 306.4, 311.2, 763.3
living together 225.1
living wage 624.4
living will 478.10
lixiviate 79.22, 190.15, 238.18, 1064.5, 1065.13
lixiviation 79.4, 190.6, 238.7, 1064.1, 1065.7
lixiviator 79.13
lixivium 1064.3
lizard 311.24
lizardlike 311.47
llama 311.5
llano 236.1, 310.8
Lloyd's Register 549.9
load (n) 96.8, 196.2, 247.3, 297.7, 462.16, 477.5, 618.3, 643.3, 794.3, 1012.6 (v) 159.15, 196.7, 297.13, 354.17, 405.9, 794.7, 904.12, 1011.8, 1042.21
load control 1041.8
load down 297.13
loaded 88.33, 253.8, 297.18, 405.16, 618.15, 794.12, 843.10
loaded dice 759.8, 791.1
loaded for 405.18
loaded for bear 405.16, 938.38
loaded momen 843.5
loadedness 843.1
loaded with doom 133.16
loaded with meaning 518.10
loaded with shame 661.13
loader 183.9, 1042.13
load fund 737.16
loadie 88.12
loading 159.6, 297.7, 643.1
loading down 643.1
load line mark 300.6
load of crap 354.12
load off one's mind 120.3
loads 247.4, 618.3
loadsa 247.4
load the dice 356.18, 759.26
load the mind 570.6
load the mind with 989.17
load up 297.13
load waterline 300.6
load with care 96.16
load with ornament 545.7
load with reproaches 510.19
loaf (n) 257.10, 701.7 (v) 331.12
loafer 178.3, 331.8, 440.8
loafers 5.27
loafing 331.4
loaf of bread 10.28
loamy 234.5, 1047.12
loan (n) 620.2 (v) 620.5
loaned 620.6
loaner 620.3
loaning 620.1
loan office 620.4
loan officer 620.3, 729.11
loan shark 620.3, 622.4
loan-shark 620.5
loan-sharking 620.1, 732.1
loan translation 526.7
loan word 526.7
loath 99.8, 325.6
loathe 99.3, 103.5
loather 103.4
loathesome 103.8
loathing (n) 99.2, 103.1, 144.7 (a) 103.7, 144.19
loathly 1015.11
loathsome 98.18, 1000.9, 1015.11
loathsomeness 64.3, 98.2, 1000.2, 1015.2
loaves and fishes 472.7, 1010.1
lob (n) 904.3 (v) 748.3, 904.10, 912.5
lobar 202.12
lobate 202.12
lobated 202.12
lobation 202.4
lobbering 1062.2
lobbing 904.2
lobby (n) 197.19, 414.8, 609.32, 617.4, 894.3, 894.6 (v) 375.14, 609.38, 894.9
lobbyer 609.32
lobbying 375.3, 609.29, 894.3
lobbyism 609.29, 894.3
lobbyist 375.11, 609.32, 894.6
lobby through 613.10, 894.9
lobe 2.10, 202.4, 793.4
lobed 202.12
lobe-finned fish 311.30
loblolly 1062.5, 1062.9
lobo 311.19
lobscouser 183.1
lobster 311.29, 759.22
lobsterman 183.1, 382.6
lobster-red 41.6
lobster tour 825.3
lobster trick 825.3
lobular 202.12
lobule 2.10, 202.4, 793.4
lobus 202.4
local (n) 88.20, 179.14, 227.3, 227.6, 617.10, 727.2 (a) 231.9, 523.22
local anesthetic 25.3, 86.15
local area network 1042.16, 1042.19
local bus 179.13

local call 347.13
local case 530.9
local color 209.3, 722.4
local death 85.2
local dialect 523.7
locale 159.1, 209.2, 463.1, 704.19, 722.4
local express 179.14
local forecast 317.7
local government 612.1
Local Group, the 1073.6
local horizon 201.4
localism 523.7, 526.6, 609.4
locality 159.1, 228.18
localization 159.6, 611.8, 865.7
localize 159.11, 428.9
localized 231.9
localized war 458.1
local office 739.7
local oscillator signal 1036.11
local paper 555.2
local rag 555.2
local television 1035.1
local time 832.3
local union 727.2
local yokel 227.3
locatable 941.10
locate 159.11, 159.17, 161.5, 941.2
located 159.18
locating 159.6, 941.1
location 159.1, 159.6, 704.19, 706.4, 765.1, 941.1, 1069.8
locational 159.19
locative 530.9
locavore 159.1, 227.6
loch 241.1, 242.1
Loch Ness monster 311.29
lock (n) 3.5, 173.3, 239.11, 428.5, 474.3, 759.10, 970.2 (v) 293.6, 788.6, 800.8, 1012.12
lock away 212.5, 429.14
lock box 195.1
lockbox 346.4
lock down 212.5
lockdown 212.1, 429.1, 429.3
locked in 1035.16
locked up 429.21
locked-up page 548.8
locked-wire rope 271.2
locker 195.1, 386.6, 729.13, 1024.6
locker plant 1024.6
locker room 567.11
locket 498.6
lock gate 239.11
lock horns 456.12, 457.17, 900.6, 935.16
lock in 429.14, 474.5, 970.11
locking in 474.1
locking on 1036.8
locking signals 1036.8
locking-up 212.1, 429.1
lockjaw 85.6
lock on 1036.17
lock out 293.6, 727.10, 773.4
lockout 727.5, 773.1, 857.2
locks 3.4
lock step 177.12
lockstep (n) 177.13, 326.1, 867.1 (a) 365.11, 373.14
lock, stock, and barrel 386.1
lock the barn door after the horse is stolen 391.8, 414.14, 844.5
lock the door 1009.7
lock up 212.5, 293.6, 346.7, 429.14, 857.8
lockup 429.1, 429.8
loco (n) 85.41 (a) 926.27
loco disease 85.41
locofoco 1021.5
locoism 85.41
locomobile 1041.23
locomotion 172.3, 177.1
locomotive (n) 1043.3 (a) 177.36, 179.23, 1039.7, 1041.23
locomotor 1039.7
Locrian mode 709.10
locum 576.1
locum tenens 227.2, 576.1, 862.2
locus 159.1
locust 311.35
locution 523.1, 524.2, 526.1, 529.1, 532.1
lode 296.1, 386.4, 618.4, 1058.7
lode claim 1058.8
loden green 44.4
lodestar 208.4, 375.1, 574.8, 907.3, 1073.4
lodestone 100.11, 907.3
lodestuff 1058.7
lodge (n) 228.5, 228.8, 228.26, 617.3, 617.10 (v) 159.14, 225.7, 225.10, 385.10, 386.10, 855.9, 855.10
lodgeable 225.15
lodge a complaint 115.15, 599.7
lodge a plaint 599.7
lodged 225.14
lodged in one's mind 989.22
lodge in the mind 931.19
lodger 227.8, 470.4
lodging (n) 225.1, 225.3, 228.1, 228.4 (a) 225.13
lodging house 228.15
lodging place 228.1
lodgings 228.4, 385.3
lodgment 159.7, 225.3, 228.1, 228.4
loess 256.2, 1059.6
loft (n) 197.6, 197.16, 386.6, 739.1 (v) 751.4, 912.5
loftiness 136.2, 141.1, 247.2, 272.1, 501.1, 544.6, 545.1, 649.3, 652.2, 662.5
lofting 200.4
loft ladder 193.4
lofty 136.11, 141.9, 158.11, 247.9, 272.14, 501.18, 544.14, 545.8, 649.9, 652.6, 662.18, 912.9
lofty affectations 501.1
lofty airs 501.2
lofty ambition 100.10
lofty brow 216.5
lofty-minded 136.11
log (n) 174.7, 549.11, 628.4, 832.9, 1021.3, 1054.3 (v) 182.48, 549.15, 628.8
logan stone 916.9
logarithm 1017.1
logarithmic 1017.23
logbook 549.11, 628.4
log cabin 228.8
loge 704.15
logged 549.17
logger 1069.7
loggia 197.18
logging 549.14, 1069.3
logic 568.3, 931.1, 935.2, 935.9
logical 920.18, 931.21, 935.20, 973.14
logical analysis 541.6
logical category 932.2
logical circle 280.2
logical discussion 541.6
logical fallacy 936.3
logical form 932.2
logical impossibility 967.1
logicality 935.9
logicalize 935.15
logically impossible 967.7
logical necessity 920.5
logicalness 935.9
logical operation 1017.2
logical order 807.2
logical outcome 887.1
logical positivism 1052.6
logical sequence 815.1
logical thought 935.1
logicaster 935.11
logic bomb 1042.11
logic-chopper 936.6
logic-chopping (n) 936.5 (a) 936.14
logic circuit 1042.3
logic-defying 870.12, 969.3
logician 921.1, 935.11, 952.8
logicize 935.15
logic of the heart, the 93.1
logics 935.2
log in 1042.21
login 1042.18
loginess 331.6
logistic 458.4, 935.2
logistician 935.11
logistics 385.1
logjam 329.1, 846.2, 1012.5, 1013.6
log line 174.7
logo 210.3, 517.2, 517.13, 647.1
log-off 857.1
logoff 1042.18
logogram 349.1, 489.8, 517.2, 546.2
logogrammatic 546.8
logograph 349.1, 546.2
logographer 547.15, 718.4
logographic 546.8
logographic character 546.1
logogriph 489.8, 522.9
logogriphic 522.17
logomacher 935.12
logomachic 935.19
logomachical 935.19
logomachist 935.12
logomachize 935.16
logomachy 456.5, 457.1, 935.4
logomania 540.2
logometric 1017.23
logon 1042.18
logophile 523.15
logorrhea 520.2, 538.2, 540.2
Logos 677.7, 677.11
logos 526.1
logotype 210.3, 517.2, 517.13, 548.6
log out 1042.21
logroll 613.10, 863.4
logroller 609.30, 610.6
logrolling 609.29, 613.6, 863.2
logy 173.14, 331.20
log zs 22.14
loin 10.15, 217.3
loincloth 5.19
loinguard 5.19
loins 886.7
loiter 166.4, 175.8, 331.14, 846.12, 998.14
loiter about 331.12
loiter around 331.12
loiter away time 331.13
loiter behind 166.4
loiterer 175.5, 331.8
loitering (n) 175.3, 331.4, 998.8 (a) 175.11, 846.17
loiter out the time 331.13
Loki 680.5, 682.5
loll (n) 201.2 (v) 20.6, 201.5, 402.3
lollapalooza 999.7
loll around 331.12
loller 331.8
lolling (n) 331.4 (a) 201.8
lollop 401.4
lollop about 331.12
lolloping 257.21
lolly 1023.5
lollygag 175.8, 331.14, 562.15
lollygagger 175.5
lollygagging (n) 104.5, 175.3, 562.2 (a) 175.11
Lombard Street 729.1, 737.8
London fog 319.3
London special 319.3
lone 584.11, 872.7, 872.8, 872.9
loneliness 584.3, 872.2
lonely 584.11, 872.8
lonely heart 565.2
lonely-hearts 584.11, 872.8
lonely hearts club 563.12
loneness 584.3, 872.2
lone pair 1033.3
loner 430.12, 584.5, 651.3, 870.4
lonesome 584.11, 872.8
lonesomeness 584.3, 872.2
lone wolf 430.12, 651.3, 870.4
lone woman 565.4
long (n) 737.13, 827.4 (a) 267.7, 272.16, 538.12, 827.11
long account 737.13
long ago, the 837.2
longanimity 134.1, 148.1, 433.1
longanimous 134.9, 148.6, 433.12
long arm of the law 1008.17
long-awaited 130.13, 846.16
long ball 745.3
long-ball hitter 745.2, 894.6
long ballot 609.19
longbow 462.7
long-continued 827.11
long-continuing 827.11
long distance 347.9, 347.13
long-distance 261.8
long-distance call 347.13

long-distance communication 343.5
long-distance running 755.2
long division 1017.12
long dozen 882.7
long-drawn 827.11
long-drawn-out 267.8, 538.12, 827.11
long drink 88.9
long drink of water 257.13, 270.8, 272.7
long-eared 48.15
longed-for 100.29
long-established 373.18, 842.12, 855.13
longeval 827.10
longevity 83.3, 303.1, 303.5, 306.1, 306.5, 827.1
longevous 827.10
long-expected 130.13
long face 110.9, 111.1
long-faced 111.3, 112.20, 112.25
long for 100.16
long gone 307.29, 837.7
long-grain rice 10.36
long green 618.3
long green, the 728.6
longhair 842.8
longhair music 708.6
longhand 547.22
long haul 261.2, 725.5
longheaded 920.16
longheadedness 920.4
long home 309.16
long horse 725.7
longhouse 228.10
long hundred 882.8
longiloquence 538.2
longiloquent 538.12
longing (n) 100.5 (a) 100.23
longing eye 100.4
longing for the past 842.4
longinquity 261.1
long interest 737.13
long in the tooth 303.17, 413.28
longish 267.7
longitude 159.5, 231.3, 267.1, 300.5, 1073.16
longitude in arc 231.3
longitude in time 231.3
longitudinal 267.9
longitudinal wave 916.4
long johns 5.22
Long John Silver 483.7
long jump 366.1
long-lasting 267.7, 827.10, 1049.4
long-lastingness 827.1
long-legged 272.16
longlegs 272.7
long life 303.5, 306.1
long-limbed 272.16
long-lived 306.12, 827.10
long-livedness 827.1
long-lost 34.4, 222.11, 473.7
long market 737.1
long mordent 709.18
longness 267.1
long odds 759.6, 972.6, 972.9
long on looks 1016.21
long-pending 827.11
long pennant 647.7
long period 1060.2
long-playing record 50.12
long pull, a 905.2
long range 261.2
long-range 261.8, 267.7
long range aid to navigation 1036.3
long-range forecasting 317.5
long-range plan 381.1, 961.2
long-range planning 381.1
long reliever 745.2
long road 261.2
long rope 430.4
long run 261.2, 704.4, 839.1
longs 737.13
longshanks 272.7
longshoreman 183.9
long shot 261.2, 714.8, 759.3, 759.6, 969.1, 972.6, 972.9
long side 737.13
long sight 28.4
longsighted 28.11, 920.16, 961.7
longsightedness 28.4, 920.4, 961.1
longsome 267.7
long-spun 538.12
long standing 827.1, 853.1
long-standing 827.10, 842.12
long step 261.2
long-sufferance 134.1
long-suffering (n) 134.1, 148.1, 433.1, 979.4 (a) 106.10, 134.9, 134.10, 148.6, 433.12, 979.11
long suit 413.4, 866.1
long tail 731.10
long term 839.1
long-term 827.10
long-term forecast 317.7
long-term memory 989.1
long-term plan 381.1
long tether 430.4
long time 267.1, 827.4
long to 100.15
long-tongued 540.9
long trail 261.2
long vowel 524.11
long-wall mining 1058.8
long wave 1034.11
long way 261.2
long way around 164.1
long way around, the 914.3
long while 827.4
long-winded 118.9, 267.8, 538.12, 827.11
longwinded 540.9
long-windedness 118.2, 538.2, 540.1
long word 526.10, 545.3
long yardage 746.3
loo 12.10
looby 497.6, 606.6, 924.3
loobyish 497.13
look (n) 27.3, 33.3, 33.4, 248.4, 551.4 (v) 27.13, 27.15, 33.10, 938.30, 983.6
look about one 339.8, 494.7
look a fright 1015.5
look after 27.13, 339.9, 577.13, 1008.19
look after one's fences 609.38
look after one's own interests 651.4
look aghast 122.5
look a gift horse in the mouth 151.3
look agog 122.5
look ahead 961.5
look-alike 778.3, 784.3
look-alikes 784.5, 873.4
look alive 339.8, 983.8
look all over 938.33
look all over hell 938.33
look a mess 1015.5
look another way 27.19
look around 938.31
look around for 938.30
look aside 27.19
look as if butter would not melt in one's mouth 657.5
look as if butter wouldn't melt in one's mouth 106.6
look as if one has seen a ghost 127.11
look a sight 1015.5
look askance 27.18, 99.5
look askance at 510.10
look askant 27.18
look asquint 27.18, 28.9
look at 27.13, 918.5, 938.24
look at in the light of 978.6
look at it 978.6
look away 27.19
look back 989.9
look back upon things past 989.9
look bad 1015.5
look before one leaps 494.6, 1007.3
look better 392.7
look beyond 961.5
look big 454.5, 501.14
look black 27.16, 105.19, 110.15, 133.10
look black as thunder 110.15
look black upon 510.10
look bleak 125.9
look blue 112.15, 132.4
look closely at 938.25
look coldly upon 157.5
look daggers 27.16, 152.14
look dark 125.9
look down on 495.8
look down one's nose 27.18, 99.5, 141.8, 495.8
look down one's nose at 157.5, 372.2
look down over 272.11
look down upon 157.3, 272.11
looked-for 130.13, 839.8
looker 479.3, 918.1, 1016.8
looker-on 223.6, 918.1
look everywhere 938.33
look fit to kill 1016.16
look foolish 137.9
look for 124.6, 130.6, 440.14, 839.6, 938.30
look for a needle in a haystack 391.8, 967.5
look for high and low 938.30
look forth 33.8
look for time 821.6
look for trouble 454.3, 456.13
look forward to 130.6, 839.6, 961.5
look full in the face 27.15, 492.10
look good 1016.16
look green about the gills 85.46
look guilty 656.2
look high and low 938.30, 938.33
look in 189.7, 582.19
look-in 27.3, 582.7
looking 27.2
looking ahead 961.1
looking at from all angles 931.2
looking back 837.4, 989.3
looking fit to kill 1016.21
looking for 130.11, 938.38
looking for trouble 110.26
looking forward to 130.11
looking glass 29.6
looking on 216.11
looking out for number one 651.1
looking out on 216.11
looking out the window 984.8
looking up 124.12, 392.15
look in one's eyes 517.15
look in the eye 216.8, 454.3
look into 938.23
look into every hole and corner 938.33
look into the future 961.5
look kindly upon 324.3
look like 33.10, 133.11, 784.7
look like a million 1016.16
look like hell 1015.5
look like something the cat dragged in 1015.5
look like the cat that swallowed the canary 95.12, 656.2
look like the devil 1015.5
look lively 339.8, 983.8
look on 27.12, 27.13, 221.8, 918.5
look one in the eye 136.4, 492.10
look one in the face 136.4, 416.4
look one up 582.19
look only at one side of the shield 980.6
look on the bright side 124.8
look on the dark side 125.9
look on with the evil eye 691.9
look out 339.8, 494.7, 983.8
lookout 27.2, 27.8, 33.6, 339.4, 399.4, 724.1, 1008.10
look out for 130.6, 405.11, 1008.19
look out for number one 430.20, 651.4, 669.4
look out for numero uno 651.4
lookout man 399.4, 1008.10
look out upon 216.9
look over 27.14, 216.9, 938.24
look-over 938.3
look over one's shoulder 494.7
look right through 157.6
looks 33.4
look-see, a 27.3
look-see 938.3
look serious 111.2
look sharp 339.8, 494.7, 983.8
look silly 137.9
look something terrible 1015.5

look straight in the eye 27.15
look sullen 110.15
look sweet upon 562.20
look the other way 30.8, 329.4, 979.7, 984.2
look threatening 514.2
look through 938.31
look-through 938.3
look through rose-colored glasses 124.8
look to 130.6, 387.14, 405.11, 896.3, 983.5, 1008.19
look to be 33.10
look toward 216.9
look up 392.7, 938.30
look upon 27.12, 27.13, 931.17
look upon as 953.11
look upstairs and downstairs 938.33
lookup table 1042.13
look up to 155.4, 697.5
look with one's own eyes 339.8
look with scorn upon 157.3
looky-loo 178.1
loom (n) 740.5, 840.1 (v) 33.8, 193.8, 247.5, 514.2, 740.6, 839.6, 840.2
loomed 740.7
looming (n) 976.6 (a) 133.16, 840.3
looming in the distance 840.3
looming over 133.16
looming up 840.3
loom large 31.4, 247.5
loom of the land 234.2
loom up 514.2, 840.2
loon 926.16
looniness 926.2
loony (n) 926.16 (a) 923.9, 926.27
loony bin 926.14
loony left 611.4
loony tune 926.16
loony-tune 923.9, 926.27
loop (n) 184.16, 279.2, 280.2, 283.3, 745.1, 760.7, 914.2 (v) 184.40, 209.7, 279.6, 740.6
looper 745.3
loophole 27.8, 190.9, 369.4, 381.5
loop in 1032.26
looping the loop 184.16
looplet 280.2
loop the loop 184.40
loopy 923.9, 926.27, 927.6
loose (n) 430.1 (v) 431.6, 670.9, 802.10, 804.3, 1014.7 (a) 182.61, 202.10, 340.10, 369.11, 426.4, 430.21, 430.24, 531.4, 538.13, 581.3, 665.26, 802.22, 804.5, 810.15, 936.11, 971.19, 975.17, 1047.10
loose bowels 12.2
loose cannon 395.8, 1006.1
loose construction 534.1
loose constructionism 341.1
loose constructionist 341.7
loose end 971.8
loose ends 340.3, 408.1
loose-fitting 804.5
loose formation 184.12
loose for sea 182.18
loose-knit 802.22, 971.17
loose-leaf notebook 549.11
loose-limbed 1047.9
loose memory 990.1
loose-moraled 665.26
loose morals 665.4
loosen 431.6, 670.9, 802.10, 804.3, 1047.6
loosened 802.22
looseness 340.1, 426.1, 581.1, 665.4, 804.2, 810.6, 971.4, 975.2, 1047.3
looseness of the bowels 85.29
loosening (n) 426.1, 670.2 (a) 1047.16
loosen the purse strings 485.3, 626.5
loosen up 743.21, 743.22, 1047.7
loose one's grip on 475.3
loose purse strings 486.1
loose thread 975.4
loose tongue 540.1
loose translation 341.3
loose woman 665.14
loosey-goosey 340.10
loosing 431.2
loot (n) 482.11, 728.2 (v) 480.14, 482.17, 671.11
looter 483.6
looting (n) 480.9, 482.6, 671.3 (a) 482.22
lop (n) 238.14 (v) 202.6, 255.10 (a) 202.10
lope (n) 174.3 (v) 174.8, 177.34
lop-eared 48.15, 202.10
lop off 255.10
lopped 795.5
lopper 1045.10, 1062.10
loppered 1062.12
loppered milk 1045.7
loppering 1062.2
loppy 202.10
lopsided 265.10, 791.5
lopsidedness 265.1
loquacious 540.9
loquaciousness 540.1
loquacity 538.2, 540.1
loran 159.3, 182.2, 184.6, 1036.3
Lord 648.2, 677.2
lord 470.2, 575.1, 608.4
lord and master 575.1
Lord Buddha, the 677.4
Lord Chancellor 596.3
Lord Chief Justice 596.3
Lord Fauntleroy 77.10
lord-in-waiting 577.4
lord it over 612.15
Lord Justice 596.3
lordliness 136.2, 141.3, 417.3
lordling 608.4
lordly 136.12, 141.11, 417.16
lord mayor 575.16
lord of creation 312.7, 607.4, 997.8
Lord of Lords 677.2
lord of the bedchamber 577.4
lord of the manor 470.2, 575.1, 997.10
Lord of Wisdom, the 677.5
lordosis 265.3
lord paramount 575.1, 575.8
Lord's day 20.5, 701.12
Lordship 648.2
lordship 249.3, 417.7, 469.2, 608.9
lords of creation 249.5, 607.2, 894.6, 997.8
lords of creation, the 575.14
Lord's Prayer, the 696.4
Lord's Supper 701.7
Lord's table 703.12
lords temporal and spiritual 608.1
lore 678.14, 842.2, 928.9, 954.3
Lorelei 377.4
lorgnette 29.3
lorgnon 29.3
lorica 295.15
loricate (v) 295.27 (a) 295.31, 460.13
loricated 295.31, 460.13
lorication 295.15
lorn 584.12
lorry 179.12
lose 160.7, 410.9, 412.12, 473.4, 486.4, 990.5
lose altitude 184.41, 194.5
lose blood 12.17
lose caste 661.7
lose color 36.6
lose countenance 661.7
lose courage 127.11, 128.7, 491.8
lose credit 661.7
lose currency 842.9
lose distinctness 32.4
lose everything 473.4
lose face 250.5, 414.14, 661.7
lose flesh 270.13
lose ground 163.5, 175.9, 911.2
lose heart 112.16, 125.10
lose heat 1023.9
lose hope 125.10
lose interest 102.4
lose-lose 125.14
lose momentum 175.9
lose no time 401.5
lose novelty 842.9
lose one 522.10
lose one's bearings 164.4
lose one's cool 105.17
lose oneself in 983.5
lose one's good name 661.7
lose one's grip 85.48
lose one's head 923.6
lose one's hearing 49.4
lose one's heart 104.21
lose one's life 307.18
lose one's marbles 922.12, 926.22
lose one's mind 922.12, 926.21
lose one's nerve 491.8
lose one's senses 926.21
lose one's shirt 473.4, 625.7
lose one's sight 30.8
lose one's temper 152.17
lose one's touch 414.14
lose one's train of thought 990.5
lose one's vision 30.8
lose one's voice 51.7, 525.7
lose one's way 164.4
lose one's wits 926.21
lose out 410.10, 412.12, 473.4, 911.2
lose patience 135.5
lose possession 746.5
lose power 184.45
loser 125.7, 250.2, 410.2, 410.8, 412.5, 473.1, 625.4, 1011.7
lose resolution 32.4
lose self-control 128.7
lose sharpness 32.4
lose sight of 340.6, 435.3, 990.5
lose sleep 126.6
lose speed 175.9
lose strength 85.48
lose the chance 844.5
lose the day 412.12
lose the opportunity 844.5
lose the will to live 112.16
lose time 331.13
lose track of 160.7, 340.6
lose track of what one was saying 990.5
lose weight 270.13, 298.6
losing (n) 160.3, 473.1 (a) 757.6, 759.27
losing battle 125.1
losing game 410.1
losing hold of 473.1
losing one's touch 414.18
losings 473.3
losing streak 473.1
loss 34.1, 252.3, 393.1, 473.1, 746.3, 996.2
losses 473.3
loss leader 633.3, 735.2
loss of balance 85.15
loss of contact with reality 926.1
loss of face 661.4
loss of ground, a 996.2
loss of hearing 49.1
loss of honor 661.4
loss of hope 125.2
loss of innocence 977.1
loss of life 307.1
loss of memory 933.1, 990.2
loss of mind 926.1
loss of morale 393.3
loss of name 661.4
loss of one's illusions 977.1
loss of possession 746.3
loss of reason 926.1
loss of repute 661.4
loss of speech 525.6
loss of tone 393.3
loss of touch with reality 926.1
loss of vital signs 85.2
loss of voice 525.1
lost 34.4, 125.15, 412.13, 473.7, 486.9, 654.18, 695.18, 971.24, 985.11, 990.8
lost, the 680.1
lost-and-found 859.3
lost cause 125.8
lost forever 837.7
lost generation 302.2
lost in 983.17
lost in amazement 122.9
lost in thought 931.22, 985.11
lost in wonder 122.9
lost lamb 859.3
lost language 523.2

lost sheep 660.4
lost soul 660.4
lost souls 680.1
lost to 94.10, 473.7, 967.9
lost to all sense of honor 654.17
lost to shame 142.11, 654.17
lost to sight 34.4
lost to view 34.4
lost-wax process 715.1
lot (n) 231.4, 244.2, 247.4, 471.6, 477.5, 706.4, 738.3, 765.1, 770.7, 809.3, 893.4, 964.2, 972.1 (v) 477.9, 759.23
lot, the 792.3
lot alike, a 784.15
Lothario 104.12, 562.12, 665.10
lotion 70.3, 86.11, 1056.3
lots 247.4, 471.6, 884.2, 884.3, 991.2
lotsa 884.2
lots of laughs 743.2
Lot's wife 981.2
lottery 759.14
lottery money 759.14
lottery winner 409.6
lotto 759.14, 759.15
lot to do with, a 894.1
lot to say about, a 894.1
lotus-eater 331.8, 986.13
lotus-eating 173.4, 331.6
lotus land 124.4, 986.11
The Lotus Sutra 683.9
loud 15.22, 35.20, 53.11, 421.9, 497.11, 501.20
loud and clear 334.8, 521.11
loud color 35.5
loud-hailer 50.11, 53.6
loudish 53.11
loudishness 53.1
loudmouthed 53.12, 59.10
loudness 35.5, 50.1, 53.1, 497.2, 501.3
loud noise 53.3
loud pedal 54.5
loud-sounding 53.11
loudspeaker 50.8
loud-speaking 524.31
loud-spoken 524.31
loud-voiced 53.12, 59.10
lough 241.1
Lou Gehrig's disease 85.25
louis d'or 728.4
lounge (n) 88.20, 197.5, 197.20 (v) 20.6, 201.5, 331.12, 402.3
lounge around 331.12
lounge lizard 331.11
lounger 331.8
loungewear 5.20
lounging (n) 201.2, 331.4 (a) 201.8
lour 1027.12
louring 319.8
louse 311.36, 660.5
loused up 393.29, 799.4
loused-up 414.22
louse up 393.11, 414.12, 799.3, 975.15, 1012.16
louse-up 975.6
lousiness 910.2, 1000.2
lousy 910.11, 1000.8
lousy rich 618.15
lousy with 221.15, 884.9, 991.7
lout 414.8, 416.3, 497.6, 606.6, 924.5
loutish 233.7, 414.20, 497.13, 505.6
loutishness 414.3, 497.4, 505.1, 922.3
louver 239.13
louverwork 239.13
lovability 100.13, 104.6
lovable 100.30, 104.24
Love 104.7
Love 677.6
love (n) 104.9, 143.4, 455.1, 504.8, 562.6, 587.1, 653.3 (v) 104.18
love (n) 75.2, 100.2, 104.1 (v) 63.5, 93.12, 95.13, 100.14
love 748.2, 820.5, 1019.2
loveableness 104.6
love affair 104.5
love apple 10.35
love at first sight 104.3
lovebirds 104.17
love call 562.5
love charm 691.5
love child 561.5
loved 104.23
loved one 104.9
loved one, the 307.15
love game, the 104.5
love God 692.6
love handles 2.18
love-hate 215.5
love-hate relationship 104.1
love interest 93.9, 100.12, 104.11
love knot 104.8, 517.2
loveless 99.10, 102.8
lovelessness 102.3
love letter 562.13
love life 75.2
loveliness 97.2, 104.6, 1016.1
lovelock 3.5
lovelorn 99.10, 104.26
lovelornness 104.2
lovely 97.7, 104.24, 1016.17
lovely build 1016.3
lovely time 743.2
lovely to behold 1016.18
lovely weather for ducks 316.2
lovemaking 75.2, 75.7, 104.1, 562.1
love nest 582.9
love of country 591.2
love of God 692.1
love of humankind 143.4
love of man 143.4
love of mankind 143.4
love of one's country 104.1
love philter 75.6
lovepot 88.11
love potion 75.6
lover 100.12, 104.11, 562.6, 588.1, 616.9
loverboy 104.12, 665.10
loverlike 104.25
loverly 104.25
lover of beauty 496.5
lover of learning 929.3
lover of wisdom 921.1
lovers' quarrel 456.5
lovesick 104.26
lovesickness 104.2
lovesome 104.24, 104.26
lovesomeness 104.6
love song 708.14
love story 706.2
lovestruck 104.27
love-tap 902.7
love that dare not speak its name, the 75.10
love the sound of one's own voice 140.6, 540.5
love to 100.15
love to distraction 104.20
love to eat 672.4
love triangle 104.5
loving 104.26, 143.13, 339.10, 677.17
loving care 339.1
loving concern 104.1
loving couple 104.17
loving cup 646.3
loving-kindness 143.1, 587.1
lovingly 820.5
lovingness 104.2
loving touch 73.1
low (n) 317.4, 731.10, 738.9, 1040.9 (v) 60.2 (a) 52.16, 54.11, 112.22, 137.10, 248.6, 250.6, 268.8, 274.7, 307.32, 497.15, 510.21, 523.20, 524.30, 534.2, 606.8, 633.7, 654.16, 661.12, 666.8, 913.12
low-and-middle-income housing 228.1
lowball 759.10
low blood pressure 85.9
low-bodied 274.7
lowborn 606.8
lowbred 606.8
low-bred fellow 497.6
lowbrow (n) 930.7 (a) 930.13
lowbrowed 930.13
lowbrowish 930.13
low-budget picture 706.1
low-built 274.7
low-cal 7.21
low-calorie 7.21
low-calorie diet 7.13
low camp 497.1
low-camp 497.14
low-carbohydrate diet 7.13
low charge 633.2
low-cholesterol diet 7.13
Low Church 675.11
Low-Churchism 675.11
low class 1005.4
low-class 1005.9
low comedian 707.9
low-cost housing 228.1
low cunning 354.4, 415.1, 920.3
low-cut 5.47, 6.13, 274.7
low-definition 32.6
low den 759.19
low density 299.1
low-density lipoprotein 7.7
low-down 661.12
lowdown 957.1
lowdown, the 551.2, 973.4
low-down dirty shame 661.5
low ebb 274.2
lower (n) 110.9, 1027.4 (v) 110.15, 112.18, 133.10, 137.5, 152.14, 194.6, 252.7, 274.6, 275.9, 284.15, 447.3, 514.2, 633.6, 840.2, 913.4, 1027.12 (a) 250.6, 252.10, 274.8
lower animal 311.1, 311.31
lower case 548.6
lowercase 546.8, 548.20
lowercase letter 546.2
lower chamber 613.1
lower class 250.2, 607.7
lower-class 607.10
lower class, the 606.1
lower classes 607.7
lower deck 745.1
lowered 137.13, 252.10, 274.7, 913.12
lower forty-eight 231.7
lower frequencies 1034.12
Lower House 613.2
lower house 613.1
lowering (n) 194.2, 252.1, 275.8, 633.4, 913.1, 1027.4 (a) 110.24, 133.16, 202.11, 319.8, 514.3, 840.3, 1027.14
lowering oneself 137.3
lowering sky 319.4
lowering the body 309.4
lower limit 211.3
lower middle class 607.5
lowermost 199.7
lower oneself 137.8, 141.8, 661.7
lower one's guard 1006.7
lower one's sights 107.5
lower one's tone 137.7
lower one's voice 52.10
lower orders 250.2, 606.4, 607.7
lower ranks 250.2
lower sail 182.50
lower side 199.1
Lower Slobbovia 1023.4
lower status 432.2
lower strata 274.4
lower the body 309.19
lower the boom 420.10, 604.10
lower the boom on 459.15
lower the colors 433.8
lower the flag 433.8
lower the spirits 112.18
lower the voice 670.6
lower world 682.1
lowest 137.10, 199.7, 250.8, 274.8, 633.9
lowest common denominator 521.2, 864.3
lowest common multiple 883.4
low esteem 156.1
low estimate 156.1
low estimation 510.1
lowest layer 199.1
lowest level 199.1, 274.4
lowest of the low, the 274.4
lowest point 274.4
lowest stratum 199.1
low-fat 7.21
low-fat diet 7.13
low frequency 1034.12
low-frequency 1034.28
low-frequency wave 1034.11
low grade 1005.4
low-grade 250.6, 1005.9
low green tent 309.16

low growth rate 635.2
low-hanging fruit 1014.1
low house 309.16
low-hung 274.7
low-income group 607.7
lowing 60.6
low in self-esteem 139.10
low in the pecking order 250.6
low IQ 922.1
low key 139.3, 344.3
low-key 344.10, 496.7, 670.13
low-keyed 139.11, 344.10, 670.13
lowland (n) 236.1, 274.3 (a) 233.6
low landing 184.18
lowlands 233.1, 236.1, 274.3
low language 523.6
low-level 274.7
low-leveled 274.7
low-level language 1042.13
lowliest 137.10
lowlife 250.2, 660.2
lowlifer 660.2
lowlihood 137.1
lowliness 137.1, 250.1, 1005.3
low-load fund 737.16
lowly 99.9, 137.10, 250.6, 606.8
low-lying 233.6, 274.7
low-maintenance 121.11, 426.5
low man on the totem pole 250.2, 432.5, 818.2
Low Mass 701.8
low mental age 922.1
low-minded 497.15, 654.15
low-necked 5.47, 6.13, 274.7
lowness 52.1, 54.1, 112.3, 248.1, 250.3, 268.2, 274.1, 497.5, 661.3
lowness of spirit 112.3, 117.1
low on 992.9
low opinion 510.1
low order of importance 998.1
low order of probability 969.1
low pitch 709.4
low-pitched 54.11
low place on the totem pole 818.1
low point 1011.1
low post 747.3
low-pressure 317.13
low-pressure area 184.32, 317.4
low-pressure salesmanship 734.2
low price 633.2
low-priced 633.7
low price tag 633.2
low priority 998.1
low-priority 998.16
low profile 31.2, 32.2, 139.3, 344.3
low-profile 32.6
low quality 1005.4
low-quality 1005.9
low rating 510.5
low relief 283.2, 715.3
low-rent 98.17, 250.6, 501.20, 661.12, 998.18, 1000.8, 1005.9
low-res 31.2
low resolution 31.2
low ride 98.17, 661.12
low-ride 501.20, 1000.8, 1005.9
lowrider 179.9
low-rise 274.7
low road 654.1, 654.5
low roller 759.21
low rumbling 52.7
low-salt 7.21
low-salt diet 7.13
low season 177.5
low self-esteem 139.2
low-set 274.7
low-sized 274.7
low-sodium 7.21
low-sodium diet 7.13
low-sounding 52.16
low-spirited 112.22, 117.6
low spirits 112.3
low-statured 274.7
low sticker price 633.2
low tar 89.5
low tariff 633.2
low temperature 1023.1
low tension 1032.12
low-tension 1032.34
low-test 1005.9
low-thoughted 654.15
low tide 238.13, 274.2
low-toned 54.11
low turnout 885.2
low visibility 31.2, 139.3
low voice 52.4
low-voiced 52.16
low water 238.13, 274.2
low-water mark 211.3
lox 10.24, 1024.7, 1074.8
loxodrome 161.3
loyal 101.9, 326.3, 359.12, 360.8, 434.4, 587.21, 644.20
loyal friendship 587.8
loyalist 609.27
loyal opposition 609.24
loyal opposition, the 452.1
loyalty 101.2, 326.1, 359.2, 360.1, 641.1, 644.7
loyalty card 622.3
loyalty oath 334.4
lozenge 86.7, 647.2
LSD user 87.21
luau 386.4, 618.4, 991.2
lubber 183.2, 331.8, 414.8, 924.5
lubber line 161.3, 517.4
lubberliness 414.3, 497.4
lubberly 257.19, 414.20, 497.13
lube 1056.6
lube job 1056.6
lubric 287.12
lubricant (n) 287.4, 1056.2 (a) 1056.10
lubricate 287.5, 1014.7, 1056.8
lubricated 88.33, 287.12
lubricating (n) 1014.5, 1056.6 (a) 1056.10
lubricating agent 1056.2
lubricating oil 1056.2
lubrication 1056.6
lubricational 1056.10
lubricative 1056.10
lubricator 1056.2, 1056.7
lubricatory 1056.10
lubricious 665.29
lubriciousness 665.5
lubricity 287.1, 665.5, 1056.5, 1056.6
lubricous 287.12
lubrification 1056.6
lubrify 1056.8
lubritorium 1056.7
lubritory 1056.7
Lucas's type 30.6
lucence 1025.3, 1030.2
lucency 1025.3, 1030.2
lucent 1025.31, 1029.4, 1030.5
lucid 521.11, 533.6, 920.18, 925.4, 1025.31, 1029.4, 1030.5
lucid dreaming 22.5, 689.9
lucid interval 925.1
lucidity 31.2, 521.2, 533.1, 689.8, 925.1, 1025.3, 1029.1, 1030.2
lucid stillness 51.1
Lucifer 1073.4
lucifer 1021.5
luciferase 1025.13, 1026.5
luciferin 1025.13, 1026.5
Luck 972.2
luck 1010.2
luck 759.2, 971.1, 972.1
luckiness 133.8, 1010.2
luckless 1011.14
lucklessness 1011.4
luck of the draw 759.2
luck of the draw, the 972.1
luck out 1010.11
lucky 133.17, 759.27, 843.9, 972.15, 1010.14
lucky bean 691.5
lucky break 843.3, 1010.3
lucky charm 691.5
lucky devil 1010.6
lucky dog 1010.6
lucky piece 691.5
lucky shot 972.6
lucky streak 843.3
lucky strike 941.1, 1010.3
lucrative 387.22, 472.16, 624.21
lucrative interest 623.3
lucre 472.3, 618.1, 728.1
lucubrate 570.12, 725.13
lucubration 547.10, 556.1, 570.3, 931.2
luculent 1025.31
Lucullan 95.18
Lucullan banquet 8.9
Lucullan feast 95.3
Lucullus 8.16
luded out 87.24
ludicrous 488.4, 923.11
ludicrousness 488.1, 923.3
luetic 85.61
luff (n) 180.14 (v) 182.25
luff up 182.25
lug (n) 905.2 (v) 176.12, 905.4
luggage 195.1, 471.3
luggage train 179.14
lug in 213.6
lugs 89.2
lugubrious 112.26, 125.16
lugubriousness 112.11
Luke 684.2
luke 1019.24
lukewarm 94.9, 102.6, 695.15, 1019.24
lukewarmness 102.1, 1019.4
lukewarm piety 695.1
lukewarm support 512.1
lull (n) 20.2, 51.1, 173.5, 331.1, 813.2, 826.1, 857.3 (v) 120.5, 173.8, 670.7
lullaby 22.10, 708.14
lulling (n) 120.1, 670.2 (a) 670.15
lull in hostilities 465.5
lull to sleep 22.20
lulu 999.7
lumbago 85.9
lumbar 217.10
lumbar pack 195.2
lumbar region 217.3
lumber (n) 391.5, 759.21, 1012.6, 1054.3 (v) 175.7, 177.28, 414.11, 1012.11
lumberer 1069.7
lumbering (n) 177.8, 1069.3 (a) 175.10, 257.19, 414.20, 534.3
lumbering pace 175.2
lumberjack 15.8, 1069.7
lumberman 1069.7
lumber room 197.16, 386.6
lumberyard 386.6
lumbriciform 281.7
lumbricine 281.7
lumbricoid 281.7
lumen 1025.21
lumen meter 1025.21
lumeter 1025.21
Luminal 86.12
luminal 1025.41
luminance 1025.3, 1025.4
luminant (n) 1025.20, 1026.1 (a) 1025.30
luminaries 662.9
luminarist 716.4
luminary (n) 662.9, 997.10, 999.6, 1026.1, 1073.8 (a) 1025.41
luminate 1025.28
luminative 1025.30
luminesce 1025.26
luminescence 1025.13
luminescent 1025.38
luminiferous 1025.30
luminificent 1025.30
luminist 716.4
luminophor 1025.13, 1026.5
luminosity 1025.3
luminous 521.11, 677.17, 1025.30, 1025.39
luminous energy 1025.1
luminous flux 1025.21
luminous intensity 1025.21
luminousness 1025.3
luminous power 1025.21
lummox 414.9, 924.5
lump (n) 257.10, 283.3, 283.4, 414.9, 517.7, 770.9, 793.3, 1045.6 (v) 1045.10
lumped 770.21
lumpen (n) 606.4 (a) 233.7, 331.18, 661.12, 810.15
lumpenprole, the 606.4
lumpen proletariat 331.11
lumpen proletariat, the 606.4
lumper 183.9
lumpiness 263.1, 288.1, 294.2
lumping 257.19
lump in one's throat 93.9

lumpish 233.7, 257.19, 263.4, 297.17, 331.20, 414.20, 497.13, 922.15, 1045.14
lumpishness 257.9, 263.1, 297.2, 414.3, 497.4, 922.3
lump it 134.6
lump sum 728.13
lump together 800.5, 805.3, 945.3
lumpy 257.19, 263.4, 288.8, 294.7, 1045.14
Luna 1073.12
lunacy 923.1, 926.1
lunar 279.11, 1073.25
lunar base 1075.5
lunar caustic 1020.15
lunar city 1075.5
lunar colony 1075.8
lunar corona 1025.14
lunar eclipse 1027.8, 1073.11
lunar excursion module 1075.2
lunar halo 1025.14
lunar insertion 1075.2
lunar landscape 891.2
lunar mare 236.1
lunar module 1075.2
lunar month 824.2
lunar orbit 1075.2
lunar rill 284.9
lunar tide 238.13
lunar waste 891.2
lunary 1073.25
lunar year 824.2
lunate 279.11, 1073.25
lunatic (n) 924.1, 924.7, 926.15 (a) 926.26
lunatic asylum 926.14
lunatic fringe 611.12, 926.18
lunation 824.2
lunch (n) 8.6 (v) 8.21 (a) 927.6
lunch break 314.1, 402.1
lunch-bucket worker 726.2
lunch counter 8.17
luncheon 8.6
luncheonette 8.17
luncher 8.16
lunch hour 314.1
lunchiness 926.2
lunchmeat 10.13
lunchroom 8.17
lunchtime 314.1, 314.4
lunch wagon 8.17
lunchy 922.17, 923.9, 926.27
lung (n) 2.16 (a) 2.32
lung disease 85.16
lunge (n) 459.3, 760.4 (v) 177.28
lunge at 459.16
lungs 2.16, 2.22
luniform 279.11
lunker 257.11
lunkhead 924.4
lunkheaded 922.17
lunula 279.5
lunular 279.11, 1073.25
lunulate 1073.25
lunule 279.5
lupine 311.41, 480.26
lurch (n) 177.12, 204.3, 916.6, 917.8 (v) 177.28, 182.55, 194.8, 916.10, 917.15
lurcher 311.18
lurching 851.3, 916.17
lure (n) 356.13, 375.7, 377.3, 907.2 (v) 356.20, 375.22, 377.5, 907.4
lurid 35.20, 36.7, 41.6, 105.32, 307.28, 501.20, 545.8, 666.9
lurid imagination 986.4
luridness 35.5, 307.11, 501.3, 545.1
lurk 346.9, 519.3
lurking 346.14, 519.5, 840.3
lurking hole 346.3
lurking place 346.3
luscious 63.8, 97.10
lusciousness 63.1, 97.3
lush (n) 88.12 (v) 88.25 (a) 63.8, 310.43, 545.11, 890.9
lusher 88.12
lushness 545.4, 890.1
lushy 88.33
lust (n) 75.5, 100.6, 100.8, 323.1, 654.3, 655.3, 665.5 (v) 75.20, 100.14
lust after 75.20, 100.14, 100.18
luster (n) 287.2, 662.6, 824.2, 1016.5, 1025.2, 1026.6 (v) 287.7, 1025.23
lusterless 36.7, 1027.17
lusterlessness 1027.5
lust for 100.16
lust for knowledge 981.1
lust for learning 100.1
lustful 75.27, 100.21, 665.29
lustful leer 27.3
lustfulness 75.5, 665.5
lustihood 15.1
lustiness 15.1, 17.4, 83.3
lustless 16.12, 19.19
lustral 79.28, 658.7
lustrate 79.18
lustration 79.2, 658.3
lustrational 658.7
lustrative 658.7
lustrous 662.19, 1025.30, 1025.33
lustrum 824.2
lusts of the flesh 75.5
lusty 15.15, 17.13, 83.12, 257.18
luteal 13.8
lutenist 710.5
luteolous 43.4
luteous 43.4
lute player 710.5
lutescent 43.4
lute tablature 708.28
Lutheran 675.28
lutist 710.5
lutose 1051.11
lux 1025.21
luxate 160.5, 802.16
luxated 802.21
luxation 160.1, 802.1
luxuriance 498.2, 545.4, 890.1, 991.2
luxuriant 310.43, 498.12, 501.21, 545.11, 890.9, 991.7
luxuriate 310.34, 993.8
luxuriate in 95.13, 669.4
luxuriation 310.32
luxuries 121.3
luxurious 97.7, 121.11, 498.12, 501.21, 618.14, 632.11, 663.5
luxurious casino 759.19
luxuriousness 121.2, 498.2, 501.5, 618.1, 632.1, 663.1
luxury 95.1, 97.2, 501.5, 663.1, 993.4, 1010.1
luxury goods 735.1
luxury liner 180.5
luxury-loving 663.5
luxury price 632.3
lyase 7.10
lycanthrope 680.12
lycée 567.4
lyceum 197.4, 567.4
lych-gate 309.15
Lydian mode 709.10
lying (n) 201.2, 274.1, 354.8 (a) 201.8, 354.34
lying down 274.1
lying hid 346.14
lying-in 1.1
lying in ambush 840.3
lying in wait 346.14
lying low 519.5
lying pretension 376.1
lymph 2.24
lymphatic (n) 2.23 (a) 2.33, 13.7, 331.20
lymphoma 85.20
lynch 308.13, 604.17
lyncher 604.7
lynching 308.1, 604.6
lynch law 418.2
lynch mob 604.7
lynx 27.11, 311.21
lynx-eyed 27.21
Lyon 575.20
Lyon King of Arms 575.20
lyophilization 397.2
lyophilize 397.9
lypothymia 926.5
lyre 711.3
lyric 708.48, 708.50
lyrical 708.48, 720.16
lyric baritone 709.5
lyric bass 709.5
lyric cantata 708.18
lyric drama 708.34
lyricism 708.13
lyricist 710.20, 720.12
lyrico-dramatic 720.16
lyric poem 720.4
lyric poet 720.12
lyric poetry 720.1
lyric soprano 709.5
lyric stage 708.34
lyric tenor 709.5
lyric theater 708.34
lyric writing 718.2
lyric-writing 547.2
lyrist 710.5, 710.20, 720.12
lyse 395.10
Lysenkoism 861.4
lysin 86.27
lysis 395.1
lyssa 926.6
M 87.14, 882.10
ma 560.12
ma'am 77.8
Mab 678.8
macabre 127.30, 307.28, 988.9
macabreness 307.11
macadam 199.3, 383.6
macadamize 295.22
macaroni 10.33, 500.9
macaronic (n) 526.11 (a) 508.14
macaronicism 526.11
macaronics 720.3
macaronic verse 720.3
Macchiavelian 494.8
mace 417.9, 647.1
mace-bearer 1008.15
macerate 96.18, 260.9, 1047.6, 1063.5, 1065.13
macerated 1063.6, 1065.17
maceration 658.3, 667.1, 1063.3, 1065.7
macerator 1063.4
Mach 174.2
Mach cone 184.31
machete 462.5
Mach front 1038.16
Machiavel 357.1, 415.8
Machiavelli 357.1, 381.7
Machiavellian (n) 357.1, 415.8, 610.6 (a) 354.31, 381.13, 415.12
Machiavellian intrigues 894.3
Machiavellianism 354.4, 415.2
Machiavellianist 415.8
Machiavellic 415.12
Machiavellism 415.2
machicolate 289.4
machicolated 460.12
machicolation 289.3
machinate 381.9, 415.10
machination 356.4, 381.5, 415.4
machinations of the devil 655.1
machinator 357.10, 381.7, 415.7, 610.6
machine (n) 179.9, 385.4, 609.24, 617.1, 858.10, 1040.3, 1042.2 (v) 892.9, 1040.13
machine code 1042.13
machine composition 548.2
machine computation 1042.1
machined 892.18
machine gun (n) 462.10 (a) 847.5
machinegun 308.18
machine gunner 185.4, 461.11
machine language 1042.13
machinelike 1040.14
machine-made 892.18
machine part 1040.5
machine politician 610.1
machine politics 609.1
machiner 1040.12
machine-readable language 1042.13
machinery 384.3, 385.4, 1040.3, 1040.4
machine shop 739.3
machine-switching office 347.7
machine tool 1040.1, 1040.6
machine-usable 1042.22
machining 892.2
machinist 704.24, 1040.12
machismo 76.2, 492.1
Mach meter 174.7
Mach number 174.2
macho 76.13, 492.16
Mach one 174.2
Mach stem 1038.16
Mach two 174.2
Mach wave 184.31
mack 665.18

mackerel sky 47.6, 319.1
mackle 548.3
mackman 665.18
macro 257.20
macrobiotic 827.10
macrobiotic diet 7.13
macrochemical 1060.9
macroclimate 317.3
macroclimatic 317.13
macrocosm 1073.1
macrocosmos 1073.1
macroecology 1072.1
macroeconomics 731.7
macroevolution 861.3
macrogamete 305.10
macrography 547.1
macrolanguage 1042.13
macrolevel 246.1
macrology 538.2, 849.3
macrometeorology 317.5
macromolecule 1060.2
macronucleus 305.7
macronutrient 7.11
macrospore 305.13
mactation 696.7
macula 47.3, 517.5, 774.2, 1004.1, 1004.3
macular 47.13, 1004.9
maculate (v) 47.7, 1004.5 (a) 47.13, 654.12, 665.23, 1004.9
maculated 47.13, 1004.9
maculation 47.3, 1004.3
macule 47.3, 1004.3
mad (n) 152.5 (v) 926.24 (a) 105.25, 152.30, 493.8, 671.18, 923.8, 926.26, 926.30
mad about 101.11, 104.30
madam 77.8, 575.2, 665.18
madame 77.8, 648.4
mad apple 10.35
mad as a hatter 926.26
mad as a hornet 152.30
mad as a march hare 926.26
mad as a wet hen 152.30
mad as hell 152.30
madbrain (n) 493.4 (a) 493.9
madbrained 493.9
madcap (n) 489.12, 493.4 (a) 493.9
mad cow disease 85.41
Mad Decade 824.5
madden 105.12, 152.25, 589.7, 926.24
maddened 926.26
maddening 105.30
madder 41.4
madding 105.25, 926.30
mad dog 593.3, 671.9
made 262.9, 409.14, 892.17, 892.18
made easy 521.11
made flesh 677.16
made for 413.29
made-for-television movie 706.1, 1035.2
made-for-TV movie 1035.2
made homeless 160.10
madeleine 10.42
mademoiselle 77.8, 302.6
made of 796.4
made of iron 15.18
made of money 618.15
made out of 796.4
made out of whole cloth 892.19
made public 348.10, 352.17, 552.15
made sure 970.20
made to grovel 432.15
made to order 892.18
made-to-order 5.48
made-up 354.29, 892.19, 1016.22
made up of 796.4
mad for 100.22
madhouse 810.2, 926.14
Madison Avenue 352.5
madman 926.15
mad money 728.19
madness 105.8, 923.1, 926.1
mad on 100.22
Madonna, the 679.5
madperson 926.15
madrigal 708.18
madrigaletto 708.18
madrigalist 710.20
mad round 95.3, 582.7, 743.7
mad staggers 85.41
madstone 691.5
mad with lust 100.24
madwoman 926.15
Maecenas 478.11, 616.9, 729.10
maelstrom 238.12, 330.4, 915.2, 917.1
maenadic 926.30
maestro 413.13, 571.1, 710.1, 710.17
Mae West 397.6
maffick 53.9, 487.2, 810.11
mafficking (n) 743.3 (a) 53.13
maffle 52.10
Mafia 732.1
Mafia, the 660.10
mafic rock 1059.1
Mafioso 671.9, 732.4
mag 728.8, 756.1
magazine 386.6, 462.2, 555.1
magazine publishing 555.3
magazine section 555.2
magazine writer 547.15, 718.4
magazine writing 547.2, 718.2
magazinish 555.5
magaziny 555.5
Magdalen 113.5
mage 690.6
Magellanic clouds 1073.5
Magen David 882.2
magenta (n) 46.1 (a) 46.3
maggid 699.11
maggot 302.12, 311.32, 364.1, 927.2
maggot in the brain 364.1, 927.2
maggoty 64.7, 80.23, 364.5, 393.42, 927.5, 986.20
Magi 921.5
magian 690.14
magianism 690.1
magic (n) 662.6, 690.1, 976.2 (v) 420.11 (a) 662.19, 690.14
magic act 976.2
magical 662.19, 690.14, 870.16
magic away 482.20
magic belt 691.6
magic bullet 86.1, 86.29
magic carpet 691.6
magic circle 280.2, 690.3
magic formula 691.4
magician 357.2, 413.13, 690.6, 707.1, 852.5, 976.2
magic lantern 714.12
magic mushroom 87.19
magic realism 706.1
magic ring 691.6
magic show 704.1, 976.2
magic spectacles 691.6
magic spell 691.1
magic up 420.11
magic wand 691.6
magic word 691.4
magic words 691.4
magism 690.1
magisterial 136.12, 141.11, 249.14, 413.22, 417.16, 594.6, 970.18
magisterialness 141.3, 417.2, 417.3
magistracy 231.5, 417.7, 594.3
magistral 141.11, 413.22, 417.16
magistrality 417.3
magistrate 466.4, 574.3, 575.16, 596.1
magistrateship 417.7, 594.3
magistrature 417.7, 594.3
magistry 417.10
magma 797.5, 1059.1
magmatic rock 1059.1
magmatism 1059.8
Magna Carta 430.2, 673.8
magnanimity 100.10, 148.1, 247.2, 485.1, 652.2, 979.4
magnanimous 148.6, 247.9, 427.8, 485.4, 652.6, 979.11
magnanimousness 652.2
magnate 608.4, 618.7, 730.1, 997.8
magnesium 7.11
magnesium wheel 756.1
magnet (n) 100.11, 208.4, 907.3 (v) 907.4
magnetic 75.25, 894.13, 907.5, 983.20, 1032.31
magnetic attraction 1032.7
magnetic axis 1032.8
magnetic bearing 161.2
magnetic cartridge 50.11
magnetic circuit 1032.7
magnetic compass 574.9
magnetic conductivity 1032.7
magnetic core memory 1042.7
magnetic creeping 1032.7
magnetic curves 1032.7
magnetic declination 1032.7
magnetic dip 1032.7
magnetic directions 161.3
magnetic disk 549.10, 1042.6, 1042.7
magnetic drum 1042.6
magnetic elements 1032.7
magnetic field 1032.3, 1032.9
magnetic field of currents 1032.3
magnetic figures 1032.7
magnetic flux 1032.7
magnetic flux density 1032.9
magnetic force 1032.9
magnetic friction 1032.7
magnetic heading 161.2, 184.34
magnetic hysteresis 1032.7
magnetic inclination 1032.7
magnetic induction 1032.15
magnetic intensity 1032.9
magnetic lag 1032.7
magnetic memory 1032.7
magnetic moment 1032.7
magnetic needle 574.9, 907.3
magnetic north 161.3, 907.3
magnetic permeability 1032.7
magnetic pole 907.3, 1032.8
magnetic potential 1032.7
magnetic reluctance 1032.13
magnetic remanence 1032.7
magnetic repulsion 908.1
magnetic resistance 1032.13
magnetic resonance imaging 91.7, 91.9
magnetic retardation 1032.7
magnetic retentiveness 1032.7
magnetics 1032.7
magnetic storage 549.10
magnetic tape 549.10, 1042.6
magnetic tape unit 1042.6
magnetic track 549.10
magnetic tube of force 1032.9
magnetic variation 1032.7
magnetic viscosity 1032.7
magnetism 100.13, 377.1, 894.1, 907.1, 1032.7
magnetite 907.3
magnetization 1032.7
magnetize 22.20, 894.9, 907.4, 1032.27
magnetized 907.5
magnetometer 1075.7
magnetomotive force 1032.9
magnetomotivity 1032.9
magneto-optical disk 1042.6
magnetosphere 1073.10
magnetotelephonic 347.21
magnet school 567.1
Magnificat 696.3
magnification 119.1, 251.2, 259.1, 355.1, 509.5, 662.8, 696.2
magnificence 501.5, 999.2
magnificent 247.9, 501.21, 999.15
magnifico 607.4, 608.4
magnified 119.4, 251.7, 355.4, 662.18
magnifique 122.10
magnify 119.2, 251.5, 259.4, 355.3, 509.12, 662.13, 696.12
magniloquence 545.1
magniloquent 545.8
magnitude 244.1, 247.1, 257.1, 997.2, 1073.8
magnum opus 413.10, 554.1
magpie 540.4, 770.15
mag tape 1042.6
magus 690.6, 976.2
Mahamaya 976.2
maharani 575.10
mahatma 413.13, 659.6, 689.11, 921.1
Mahavira 684.4
Mahdi 574.6
mahogany (n) 287.3 (a) 40.4
mahogany-brown 40.4

mahout 178.9
mahzor 701.10
maid (n) 79.14, 302.6, 565.4, 577.8 (v) 577.13
maiden (n) 77.5, 302.6, 565.4, 605.5, 757.2 (a) 301.11, 565.7, 818.17, 841.7
maiden aunt 77.7
maidenhead 2.6, 301.2, 565.1, 664.3
maidenhood 77.1, 301.2, 565.1, 664.3, 841.1
maiden horse 757.2
maiden lady 565.4
maidenliness 77.1, 301.4
maidenly 77.13, 301.11, 565.7, 664.6, 841.7
maiden name 527.5
maiden speech 818.5
maiden state 565.1
maid-in-waiting 577.8
maid of all work 577.9
maid of honor 563.4
maidservant 577.8
maieutic 935.22
maigre 668.10
mail (n) 3.18, 295.15, 460.3, 553.4 (v) 176.15, 553.12
mailable 176.18, 553.14
mailbag 553.6
mail boat 353.6
mailboat 553.7
mailbox 553.6, 1042.19
mail car 353.6
mail carrier 353.5, 553.7
mailclad 460.13
mail clerk 553.7
mail coach 353.6
mail drop 553.6
mailed 460.13
mailed fist, the 424.3
mailer 353.6
mail-in 553.14
mailing 553.1
mailing list 553.4
mailing machine 553.6
maillot 5.29
maillot de bain 5.29
mailman 353.5, 553.7
mail-order 553.14
mail-order buying 733.1
mail-order goods 735.1
mail-order house 736.1
mail orderly 183.6
mail-order selling 553.4, 734.2
mail packet 353.6
mailplane 353.6
mail solicitation 553.4
mail train 353.6
mail truck 353.6
maim 19.9, 393.13, 393.14, 802.14
maimed 393.30
maiming 19.5, 393.1
main (n) 235.1, 239.7, 240.1 (a) 247.6, 249.14, 818.17, 997.24
main attraction 706.1, 997.7
main bearing 915.7
main body 792.6
main chance 972.8
main course 8.10, 10.7
main course, the 896.2
main current 896.2
main-current 896.4
main dish 10.7
main feature 866.2
main features 211.2
main force 18.1, 424.2
mainframe 1042.2
mainframe computer 1042.2
main idea 932.4
main interest 866.1
mainland (n) 235.1 (a) 235.6
mainlander 235.3
mainline (v) 87.22 (a) 896.4
mainlining 87.2
main man 588.4
main memory 1042.7
main office 208.6, 739.7
mainpernor 438.6
main plant 739.3
main point 557.2, 937.1, 997.6
mainprise 438.2
main rocket 1075.2
mains 1069.8
main sea 240.1
main sequence 1073.8
mainspring 375.1, 886.6
main squeeze 104.10
mainstay (n) 616.9, 901.2 (v) 901.21
main storage 1042.7
mainstream (n) 896.2 (a) 896.4
mainstream jazz 708.9
main street 230.6
main-street 230.11
main strength 18.1
maintain 334.5, 385.7, 397.8, 421.8, 449.12, 474.5, 600.10, 624.19, 827.6, 853.5, 856.4, 901.21, 953.11
maintain a household 228.31
maintain clearance 261.7
maintain connection 343.8
maintain continuity 812.4
maintain distance 261.7
maintained 901.24, 953.23
maintainer 616.9, 901.2
maintaining 901.23
maintain one's perspective 261.7
maintain position 182.46
maintain the heading 182.28
maintain the highest standards 425.4
maintain with one's last breath 334.5
maintenance 396.6, 397.1, 449.3, 474.1, 624.8, 827.1, 853.2, 856.1, 901.1
maintenance man 396.10
maintenance of membership 727.3
maintenance woman 396.10
main thing 997.6
Maioli 554.15
maître d' 577.7
maître d'hôtel 574.4, 577.7, 577.10
maize 43.4
majestic 136.12, 247.9, 417.17, 501.21, 544.14, 677.17
Majesty 648.2
majesty 136.2, 247.2, 417.8, 501.5, 544.6, 575.8
majolica painter 716.7
major (n) 304.1, 568.8, 575.17, 709.15 (a) 842.19, 997.17
major basilica 703.1
major chord 709.17
major deities, the 678.1
major-domo 577.10
majordomo 574.4
major form class 530.3
major general 575.17
major in 570.15, 866.4
major interval 709.17, 709.20
majority (n) 257.11, 303.2, 312.2, 792.6, 883.2 (a) 883.9
majority, the 307.16, 606.2
majority leader 610.3
majority rule 612.4
major key 709.15
major league 745.1
major-league 997.17
major mode 709.10
major operations 458.4
major orders 698.10, 699.4
major part 792.6
major party 609.24
major planet 1073.9
major player 894.6
major poet 720.12
major premise 935.7
Major Prophets 683.3
majors, the 745.1
major scale 709.6
major second 709.20
major suit 758.3
major surgery 91.19
major war 458.1
majuscular 546.8
majuscule (n) 548.6 (a) 546.8
make (n) 262.1, 266.1, 472.5, 627.1, 796.1, 809.3, 893.4, 978.3 (v) 87.22, 177.19, 182.35, 186.6, 238.16, 328.4, 328.6, 328.9, 405.7, 407.4, 424.4, 437.9, 472.8, 796.3, 858.11, 886.10, 892.8, 986.14
make a bargain 731.19
make a beeline 161.10, 268.7, 277.4
make a beginning 818.8
make a bequest 478.18
make a bet 759.25
make a bid 439.6, 733.9
make a bid for 403.9
make a big deal 949.2
make a big deal of 794.8, 993.10, 997.14
make a blind bargain 731.15
make a blunder 975.14
make a boast of 502.6
make a bold push 403.12
make a boner 975.15
make a boo-boo 975.15
make a break for 161.9
make a break for it 368.11
make a breakthrough 409.10, 852.9
make a brollyhop 184.47
make a bundle 472.12, 737.23
make a burst of speed 174.12
make a buy 733.7
make a call 347.19
make a cash payment 624.17
make a cat's-paw of 387.16
make a cautious move 403.10
make accounts square 624.13
make a change 852.7
make a chattel of 432.8
make a circuit 914.5
make acknowledgement 939.4
make acknowledgments of 150.4
make a clamor 59.8
make a clean breast 351.7
make a clean sweep 860.4, 909.22
make a close study of 938.25
make a colossal blunder 975.14
make a comeback 396.20
make a comfort stop 12.12
make a commotion 810.10
make a comparison 943.4
make a compromise 468.2
make a course correction 164.3
make acquaintance with 587.10
make acquainted 587.14
make a critical revision 547.19
make a cross-reference 957.14
make acute 119.2
make a dash 174.12
make a dash at 459.18
make a dash for 161.9
make a date 832.13
make a dead set against 451.3
make a dead set at 459.14
make a dead-stick landing 184.43
make a deal 437.5, 468.2, 731.18, 731.19
make a deal for 733.7
make a decision 371.16, 946.11
make a demand 421.5
make a dent 818.8
make a dent in 93.15, 894.12
make a determined resistance 453.3
make a detour 914.4
make a dicker 731.19
make a distinction 780.6, 944.6
make a doormat of oneself 138.7
make advances 343.8, 439.7, 587.12, 894.9
make a face 99.5, 265.8
make a face at 372.2
make a fair copy 547.19
make a false step 975.14
make a fast buck 472.12
make a faux pas 414.12, 975.14
make a federal case of 794.8, 949.2, 993.10, 997.14
make a federal case out of it 355.3
make a fine distinction 944.4
make a flight 184.36
make a fool of 356.15, 415.11, 923.7
make a fool of one 137.5
make a fool of oneself 414.14, 923.6
make a fortune 618.10
make a free throw 747.4
make a fresh start 856.6

make after 382.8
make a funny 489.13
make a fuss 330.12
make a fuss about 115.15, 997.13
make a fuss over 101.7
make a generalization 864.9
make a getaway 369.6
make a good end 307.22
make a good thing of 387.15, 472.12
make a go of it 409.7, 409.11
make a grab for 480.16
make a great show of 348.5, 501.17
make a hash of 414.12, 811.3
make a hat trick 749.7
make a hit 95.7, 409.7, 704.28
make a hit with 104.22
make a hog of oneself 672.5
make a hole in one 751.4
make a house call 90.14
make a household word of 352.15
make a journey 177.21
make a joyful noise unto the Lord 708.38
make a judgment call 946.8
make a killing 409.9, 411.3, 472.12, 737.23
make a landfall 182.38, 186.8
make a lapdog of 427.6
make a laughingstock of 508.8
make a leg 155.6, 913.9
make a light 1025.29
make a line 812.6
make a lip 110.15
make a living 385.11
make all clear for 1014.7
make allocations 477.9
make allowance 631.2
make allowance for 600.12, 959.5
make allowances for 148.4
make all square 396.13
make a long face 110.15, 111.2, 112.15
make a long story short 537.5
make a low bow 913.9
make a lucky strike 1010.11
make a man of 492.15, 999.10
make a mark 517.19
make a match 563.14
make a memorandum 549.15
make amends 338.4, 481.5, 506.5, 624.11, 658.4
make a mess of 80.17, 414.12, 811.3
make a mint 472.12
make a miscue 975.13
make a misstep 975.14
make a mistake 975.13
make a mockery of 435.4, 508.8
make a mockery of the law 674.5
make a monkey of 923.7
make a monkey of one 137.5
make a monkey of oneself 923.6
make a motion 439.5
make a moue 110.15
make a mountain out of a molehill 355.3, 997.14
make a mouth 265.8
make a move 757.5, 818.8
make a move on 439.8
make an adaptation 708.46
make an adjustment 468.2
make an ado 101.7
make an ado about 997.13
make an affidavit 953.12
make an all-out effort 403.5
make an allusion to 517.18, 551.10
make a name 662.11
make a name for oneself 662.11
make an announcement 352.12
make an appearance 33.8, 186.6, 221.8, 348.7
make an approximation 300.10
make an arrangement 468.2
make an arrest 429.15
make an assignment 568.17
make an attempt 403.6
make an auspicious beginning 818.8
make an edition 341.11
make an educated guess 962.9
make an effort 403.6
make an end of 395.12, 820.6
make an entrance 189.8, 704.29
make an entry 549.15, 628.8
make an error 745.5
make an estimation 946.9
make a new beginning 856.6
make a new man of 858.12
make an example of 604.9
make an exit 190.12
make an expedition 458.16
make an experiment 942.8
make angry 152.22
make an honest man of 563.15
make an honest woman of 563.15
make an idol of 697.5
make an impact upon 93.15
make an impression 48.12, 93.15, 931.19, 989.13
make an improvement 392.9
make an incursion 910.9
make an inroad 459.20
make an investment 729.17
make an irruption into 459.20
make an oath 334.6
make an obeisance 913.9
make an offer 733.9
make a noise 50.14, 53.9
make a noise in the world 409.10, 662.10, 1010.9
make an opening 292.13, 843.7
make a North River jibe 182.30
make a nosedive 367.6
make a note 549.15, 989.19
make an outcry 59.8, 115.13
make an overture 439.7
make a nuisance of oneself 96.13, 440.12
make an unforced error 748.3
make an uproar 53.9, 59.8
make a parachute jump 184.47
make a party to 898.2
make a pass 439.8, 914.5
make a passage 182.13
make a patsy of 356.19, 415.11
make a pawn of 387.16
make a peace offering 465.9
make a personal appearance 221.8
make a pest of oneself 440.12
make a pig of oneself 672.5
make a pile 472.12
make a pilgrimage 177.21
make a pinch 429.16
make a pitch for 352.15, 509.11
make a pit stop 12.12
make a play for 403.9, 439.8
make a plaything of 432.10
make a plea 598.19, 600.10
make a point 748.3
make a point of 359.7, 457.20, 959.4
make apology for 600.11
make application 440.9
make a practice of 373.11, 869.7
make a precipitate departure 368.10
make a prediction 962.9
make a present of 478.12
make a pretense 354.21
make a pretense of 376.3
make a pretext of 376.3
make a production of 997.16
make a prognosis 962.9
make a projection 381.8
make a promise 436.4
make a proof 548.14
make a prophecy 962.9
make a puppet of 432.10
make a purchase 733.7
make a quantum jump 852.9
make a quantum leap 852.9
make a quick buck 472.12
make a quick exit 368.10
make a racket 53.9
make a radical change 860.4
make a raid 459.20
make a rebuttal 939.5
make a recension 547.19
make a reconnaissance 938.28
make a regulation 673.9
make a report 352.12
make a request 440.9
make a requisition 440.9
make a resolute stand 453.4
make a resolution 359.7
make a reverence 913.9
make a round trip 280.10, 859.5, 914.5
make arrangements 381.8, 405.6
make arrangements for 405.11
make a run 182.13
make a run for 161.9
make a run for it 368.10
make a sacrifice 475.3, 652.3
make a sale 734.8
make a scene 93.13
make a selection 371.14
make as good as new 396.11
make a short sale 737.24
make a show 501.13
make a show of 348.5, 354.21, 500.12
make as if 354.21
make a sign 517.22
make a signal 182.52
make a slow start 846.10
make a sound 50.14
make a sounding 275.10
make a space 224.3
make a special case of 430.14
make a special effort 403.11
make a speech 543.9
make a spinnaker run 182.22
make a splash 501.13, 662.10
make a sport of 432.10
make a spurt 174.12
make assignments 477.9
make a stab at 403.7
make a stand 453.3
make a stand against 451.3, 453.3
make a statement 352.12, 524.23
make as though 354.21
make a stink 108.6, 115.16
make a stink about 333.5
make a stir about 997.13
make a strategic withdrawal 368.10
make a strong bid for 403.9
make a study of 570.12
make a success 409.10
make a sucker of 415.11
make a survey 938.29
make a sworn statement 953.12
make a syllabus 568.17
make at 182.35
make a tentative move 403.10
make a thrust 459.16
make a to-do 810.10
make a to-do over 101.7
make a touch 440.15
make a train 177.33
make a trial of 942.8
make a trip 177.21
make a try 403.7
make a U-turn 163.9, 852.7
make available 385.7, 478.12
make available to 478.15
make available to all 521.6
make a virtue of necessity 134.7, 387.15, 600.9
make a visit 582.19
make away with 308.13, 395.12
make a whole 792.7
make a widow 566.6
make a will 478.18
make a woman of 999.10
make a wrong step 975.14
make a wry face 26.8, 99.5, 110.15, 265.8
make a wry face at 510.10
make a wry mouth 265.8
make bad weather 182.40
make believe 354.21
make-believe (n) 986.5 (a) 354.26, 762.9, 986.21
make better 396.15
make bite the dust 412.7
make blind 30.7
make blood flow freely 457.17
make blooper 975.15
make bold 142.7, 640.6
make bold to 492.9
make bold to ask 440.9
make bold with 156.4
make bones about 325.4
make bones of 325.4

make book 759.25, 972.12
make book on 380.6, 953.16
make both ends meet 790.6
make Brownie points 662.11
make burst at the seams 794.7
make businesslike 731.20
make capital of 387.15
make capital out of 472.12
make certain 970.11
make chicken scratches 547.20
make chin music 524.20
make choice of 371.13
make clear 341.10, 348.5, 521.6, 1014.7
make cold 1023.10
make common cause 450.3
make common cause with 450.4, 805.4
make compensation 338.4, 658.4
make complex 251.5
make concessions 468.2
make conditional 959.4
make confession 701.17
make conform 867.3
make connection 343.8
make contact with 343.8
make contingent 959.4
make conversation 541.9
make court to 138.9
make crystal clear 521.6
make delivery 737.24
make dependent 432.8
make discrete 801.6
make dispositions for 405.11
make distinctions 944.4
make do 995.4
make do with 862.4, 892.12
make do without 668.7
make due provision for 385.7, 405.11
make dutiable 630.12
make economies 635.4
make ends meet 385.12, 635.4
make enemies 589.7
make every effort 403.15
make expiation 658.4
make eyes at 562.20
make fair promise 124.9, 133.12, 968.4
make fair weather 511.5
make false pretenses 354.22
make fast 428.10, 800.7, 855.8
make fast work of 401.5
make feel like a king 585.9
make feel like a queen 585.9
make fertile 890.8
make few demands 427.6
make for 161.9, 182.35, 401.5, 449.17
make for health 81.4
make four 879.3, 880.2
make free 142.7, 640.6
make free with 156.4, 480.19, 640.7
make frictionless 1014.7
make friends 587.10
make from scratch 841.5
make from the ground up 841.5
make fun 489.13
make fun of 489.13, 508.8
make game of 508.8
make go 889.5
make good 277.5, 338.4, 396.13, 409.10, 434.2, 481.5, 618.10, 624.11, 641.11, 644.9, 658.4, 794.6, 957.10, 1010.9
make good one's escape 369.6
make good one's promise 434.2
make good one's word 434.2
make good time 162.2, 174.8
make good use of 387.15
make goo-goo eyes at 377.5, 562.20
make hamburger of 802.13
make hamburger out of 412.9
make happy 95.9
make haste 174.8, 401.5
make haste slowly 494.5
make hay 387.15
make hay while the sun shines 330.16, 843.8
make head or tails of 341.10
make heads or tails of 521.7
make headway 162.2, 182.21, 392.7, 409.10, 1010.7
make heavy weather 182.40, 182.55
make heavy weather of it 725.11, 1011.9, 1013.11
make hen scratches 547.20
make hen tracks 547.20
make holiday 20.9
make human 312.12
make immortal verse 720.14
make imperative 641.12
make impossible 967.6
make incumbent 641.12
make innovations 852.9
make inquiry 938.20
make inquisition 938.22
make inroads 910.9
make it 18.11, 186.6, 409.10, 409.12, 839.7, 942.10
make it a condition 959.4
make it clear 521.6
make it felt 93.16
make it hot for one 604.10
make it one's business 328.8, 724.11
make it quits 658.4
make it tough for 1013.13
make it up 465.10, 481.5
make it up as one goes along 365.8, 406.7
make it with 75.21
make justice prevail 600.9
make knots 174.8, 182.21
make known 343.7, 351.5, 352.11
make land 182.38, 186.8
make late 846.8
make laugh 116.9
make laws 613.10
make leeway 182.29, 218.5
make legal 673.9
make legal and binding 437.7
make legendary 662.13
makeless 999.16
make lie down and roll over 432.10, 894.11
make life miserable 96.18
make life not worth living 96.18
make light 298.6
make lighter 298.6
make light of 950.2, 984.2, 998.12, 1014.12
make like 336.5, 354.21
make likely 133.12
make little of 157.6, 512.8, 950.2, 998.12, 1014.12
make look like a sieve 292.15
make look like Swiss cheese 292.15
make love 75.21, 562.14
make love not war 143.11, 464.8
make mad 152.22, 926.24
make magic 690.10, 976.8
make mandatory 420.9
make matters up 465.10, 658.4
make mention of 524.24
make merry 116.5, 487.2, 743.24
make merry with 489.14, 508.8
make mincemeat of 393.13, 395.17, 802.13
make mincemeat out of 412.9
make money 472.12, 618.10
make money by 472.12
make more acute 119.2
make more likely 968.4
make more than one 883.5
make mountains out of molehills 998.13
make moves 328.5
make much ado about 101.7, 997.13
make much ado about nothing 998.13
make much of 101.7, 355.3, 509.12, 997.13
make music 708.39
make necessity a virtue 387.15
make-nice 143.17
make no bones about 359.10
make no bones about it 421.8, 535.2, 644.12
make no difference 102.5, 391.8
make no doubt 970.11
make no mistake 970.11
make no never mind 776.4, 998.11
make no never-mind 102.5
make no provision 406.7
make no scruple of 359.10
make no sign 51.5, 345.7, 519.3
make nothing of 522.11, 950.2, 998.12
make obeisance 155.6
make obligatory 420.9
make of 341.10
make off 188.6, 368.10
make off with 482.13
make one 563.14, 778.5, 805.3, 872.5
make one a compliment 509.14
make one a protégé 1008.19
make one bristle 96.13
make one easy 106.6
make one fed-up 118.6
make one feel at home 585.9
make one feel like one of the family 585.9
make one feel small 137.4
make one feel this high 137.4
make one feel welcome 585.9
make one give in 432.9
make one hot under the collar 152.23
make one jealous 153.4
make one jump out of his skin 131.8
make one laugh 743.21
make one lose sleep 1013.13
make one puke 98.11
make one retch 98.11
make one's adieus 188.16
make one's appearance 33.8
make one say "uncle" 412.9, 432.9
make one's bed and lie on it 604.20
make one's blood boil 152.22, 152.25
make one's blood run cold 127.15
make one's bow 155.6, 704.29
make one's business 866.4
make one's case 957.10
make one's cause one's own 449.14
make one's choice 371.13
make one's compliments 504.11
make one's day 97.5
make one's debut 704.29, 818.9
make one see 349.9
make one see double 88.22
make oneself acquainted with 570.6
make oneself at home 121.8
make oneself comfortable 121.8
make oneself conspicuous 501.12
make oneself easy about 375.24, 953.19
make oneself easy on that score 953.19
make oneself felt 894.7
make oneself heard 48.12
make oneself known 662.11
make oneself master of 570.9
make oneself miserable 113.6, 658.6, 667.3
make oneself notorious 661.7
make oneself part of 476.5, 617.14
make oneself scarce 188.7, 222.8, 368.11
make oneself understood 521.6
make oneself useful 577.13
make one's escape 369.6
make one's exit 188.9, 190.12, 307.18
make one's field 570.15
make one's flesh creep 127.15, 127.17
make one's fortune 1010.9
make one's gorge rise 64.4
make one's hair stand on end 122.7, 127.15
make one's head reel 985.8
make one's head spin 985.8
make one's head swim 122.7, 522.10, 985.8
make one's heart bleed 112.19
make one shiver 1023.10
make one's home 159.17, 225.7
make one shudder 98.11
make one sick 98.11

make one sick in the stomach 98.11
make one sick to one's stomach 98.11
make one sing small 137.6
make one sit up 122.7
make one sit up and take notice 894.12
make one's life miserable 96.13
make one's mark 409.10, 501.13, 662.10, 1010.9
make one's mission 866.4
make one's mouth water 63.4, 377.6
make one's move 174.12, 843.7
make one's nerves tingle 127.15
make one's own 472.10, 480.19
make one's own way 430.20
make one's pile 618.10
make one's point 409.8, 953.18
make one's rounds 177.20, 914.5
make one's salutations 585.10
make one's skin crawl 58.11
make one stare 122.7
make one's teeth chatter 127.15, 1023.10
make one's tongue cleave to the roof of one's mouth 122.7
make one's voice heard 894.12
make one's way 162.4, 385.12, 392.9, 409.10
make one's way to 177.25
make one tiddly 88.22
make one tired 118.6
make one tremble 127.15
make one vomit 98.11
make out 27.12, 75.21, 385.12, 409.12, 437.9, 521.7, 521.9, 547.19, 549.15, 562.15, 765.5, 856.5, 928.12, 940.2, 941.5, 957.10, 989.11, 995.4
make out a report 552.11
make-out artist 562.12
make out like 500.12
make out like a bandit 409.10
make out of whole cloth 354.18
make over 78.7, 176.10, 629.3, 858.11
makeover 392.5, 852.3, 858.1
make overtures 343.8, 894.9
make payments on 624.10
make payments to 624.10
make payments towards 624.10
make pay through the nose 632.7
make peace 148.5, 465.9, 466.7, 894.12
make-peace 466.5
make place 292.13
make plain 341.10, 348.5
make pleasant 97.5
make plumb 788.7
make points 662.11
make port 186.8, 1009.8
make possible 443.9, 966.5
make precise 973.11
make preparations 405.6
make probable 968.4
make profit 472.12
make progress 162.2, 392.7, 1010.7
make progress against 162.2
make prolix 267.6
make propitiation 696.15
make proud 136.6
make provision 385.7, 405.11
make public 352.11
make putty of 432.10
make quits 506.7
Maker 677.2
maker 716.1, 720.12, 726.1, 726.6, 886.4, 892.7
make rapid strides 162.2, 174.8, 392.7
make ready 405.6
makeready 405.1, 548.9
make red 41.4
make redundant 909.19
make reference to 524.24, 957.14
make reparation 481.5, 624.11, 658.4
make reprisal 506.5
make requital 506.5
make reservations 421.7
make restitution 481.5, 506.5, 624.11, 658.4
make retribution 506.5
make right 277.5, 396.13, 658.4
make right prevail 600.9
make room 224.3, 292.13
make room for 959.5
make sacrifice to 696.15
make sad work of 414.11
make safe 1008.18
make sail 182.20
make sea room 182.37
make secure 855.8
make sense 521.4, 935.17
make sense of 341.10
make sense out of 521.7, 808.8
make sensitive 24.7
make shift 995.4
makeshift (n) 365.5, 384.4, 862.2, 995.2 (a) 365.12, 406.8, 862.8, 995.7, 1003.4
makeshifty 995.7
make short work of 395.11, 401.5, 407.4, 411.4, 1014.8
make sit up and beg 894.11
make small 258.9
make smell like roses 354.16
make so bold 640.6
make so bold as to 492.9
make something of 521.7
make something of it 454.3
makes one tick 767.6
make sore 152.23
make space 292.13
make special 865.10
make sternway 163.7, 182.21, 182.34
make strides 162.2, 174.8, 392.7
make suit to 562.21
make supplication 696.13
make sure 494.6, 855.8, 970.11, 1007.3
make sure against 405.11, 494.6
make sure of 375.24, 953.19, 970.11
make terms 437.6, 466.6
make the air blue 513.6
make the best of 387.15
make the best of a bad bargain 134.7
make the best of it 124.8, 134.7, 433.6
make the best of one's time 401.5
make the best of one's way 162.2, 174.8
make the butt of one's humor 489.13
make the cut 991.4
make the eyes water 68.5
make the flesh crawl 98.11
make the flesh creep 98.11
make the fur fly 456.11, 457.13
make the grade 18.11, 392.7, 409.12, 991.4
make the lion lie down with the lamb 465.9
make the mind a blank 933.2
make the most of 387.15, 999.11
make the most of it 134.7
make the most of one's time 330.16
make the round of 914.5
make the rules 573.8
make the scene 33.8, 177.25, 186.6, 409.10, 476.5
make the sign of the cross 701.15
make the sign of the cross upon 696.14
make the sparks fly 330.13
make the supreme sacrifice 307.24
make the welkin ring 53.7
make the world a safer place 465.9
make the worst of 125.9
make things difficult 967.6
make things hum 330.13
make time 174.8, 562.14
make time stand still 821.6
make too much of 355.3, 949.2
make to order 5.41, 892.8
make toward 182.35
make tracks 174.9, 188.12, 222.10, 368.11, 401.6
make trade-off 468.2
make tributary 432.8
make trouble 456.14, 810.10
make uncertain 971.15
make uniform 781.4, 788.7
make unintelligible 522.12
make unique 865.10
make unpleasant 98.10
make up 148.5, 354.18, 365.8, 405.7, 437.8, 465.8, 465.10, 548.16, 758.5, 770.18, 794.6, 796.3, 892.8, 892.12, 1016.15
makeup 196.1, 262.1, 266.1, 554.12, 704.17, 735.6, 765.4, 767.4, 796.1, 807.1, 978.3, 1016.11
make up accounts 628.8
makeup artist 704.23, 1016.12
makeup brush 1016.11
make up for 338.4, 481.5, 624.11, 658.4, 790.6
make up for lost time 162.2, 330.13, 392.7, 401.5
make up leeway 162.2
makeup man 548.12
make up one's mind 359.7, 371.16, 375.24, 946.11, 953.19
make up the pack 758.5
make up to 161.9, 343.8, 587.12, 624.11, 894.9
make use of 387.10, 387.14, 387.16, 480.19, 621.4
make void 445.2
make war 458.13
make war on 457.14, 458.14
make water 12.14
make waves 105.14, 322.4, 451.3, 453.3, 868.4
make way 182.21, 292.13
make way for 164.6, 368.6, 862.4, 1014.7
make way into 189.8
make-weight 768.4
makeweight 297.4, 338.2
make welcome 585.9
make well 396.15
make whoopee 582.21, 743.24
make whoopie 487.2
make with 725.8
make work 889.5
makework 724.2, 725.4
make worse 119.2, 393.9
make young 301.8
making (n) 78.1, 262.5, 266.1, 472.1, 892.1, 892.2, 893.4 (a) 677.17
making a clean breast 351.3
making again 78.1
making a leg 155.2
making amends 658.1
making a mockery of the law 674.3
making a mountain out of a molehill 355.2
making an end 307.1, 307.8
making anew 78.1
making a part of 772.5
making blind 30.1
making distinctions 944.1
making do 892.1
making good 481.2, 658.1
making instrumental 387.8
making it quits 658.1
making it with 75.7
making light of 252.5
making love 75.7, 562.2
making no bones about it 535.1
making once more 78.1
making oneself scarce 368.4
making out 562.2
making over 78.1
making public 351.1
making ready 405.1
making right 396.6, 658.1
makings 472.3
makings, the 413.4
makings and fixings 796.2
making scenes 93.9
making the scene 33.1
making up 262.5, 465.3, 658.1
making use of 387.8
mala 498.5
Malacca cane 273.2
Malachi 684.1
maladaptation 638.1
maladapted 638.3

maladjusted 414.19, 638.3, 789.7
maladjustment 92.14, 414.1, 638.1, 789.3
maladminister 389.4, 414.13
maladministration 389.1, 414.6
maladroit 250.7, 414.20
maladroitness 250.3, 414.1, 414.3
malady 85.1, 96.5
mala fides 645.5
malaise 26.1, 85.1, 85.9, 96.1, 108.1, 112.3, 126.1, 128.1, 917.1
malapert (n) 142.5 (a) 142.10
malapertness 142.2
malaprop 975.7
malapropism 489.8, 531.2, 975.7
malapropos 789.7, 844.6, 996.5
malaria 1001.4
malarial 85.61
malarkey 520.3
Malayan 312.2
Malaysian 312.2
malconformation 265.3
malcontent (n) 108.3, 115.8, 327.5, 1012.9 (a) 108.7
malcontented 108.7
mal de mer 85.30
maldistribution 477.2
mal du pays 112.5
male (n) 75.1, 76.4 (a) 76.12
male alto 58.6, 709.5
male being 76.4
male bonding 582.2, 587.2
male chauvinism 590.1, 980.4
male chauvinist 590.2, 980.5
male-chauvinistic 590.3
male chauvinist pig 980.5
malediction 513.1, 1000.4
maledictory 513.8
malefaction 655.2
malefactor 144.14, 593.1, 660.8
malefactory 655.5
malefic 144.20, 1000.12
maleficence 144.5
maleficent 144.20
male gamete 305.11
male homosexual 75.15
male line 560.4
maleness 75.1, 76.1, 303.2
male organs 2.13
male person 76.4
male prostitute 562.12
male rhyme 720.9
male sex 76.2
male sexuality 76.2
male soprano 709.5
male suffrage 609.17
male superiority 76.2
malevolence 103.1, 144.4, 589.3, 1000.1
malevolent (n) 593.1 (a) 144.19, 589.10, 1000.7, 1000.12
malevolent influence 1000.4
male witch 690.5
malfeasance 322.1, 389.1, 414.6, 638.1, 655.1, 655.2
malfeasant (n) 144.14, 593.1 (a) 655.5
malfeasor 144.14, 593.1, 660.8
malform 265.7
malformation 265.3, 638.1, 870.3
malformed 265.12, 870.13, 1015.8
malfunction (n) 393.1, 410.5, 638.1, 1003.2 (v) 393.25
malfunctioning 393.37, 410.18
malice 103.1, 144.5, 589.3
malice aforethought 144.5
malice prepense 144.5
malicious 144.20, 589.10
malicious defamation 512.2
malicious gossip 552.8
maliciousness 144.5
malicious parody 512.5
malign (v) 144.15, 512.9 (a) 82.7, 144.20, 308.23, 671.21, 1000.12
malignance 144.5, 308.9, 1000.5
malignancy 82.3, 144.5, 308.9, 1000.5
malignant 82.7, 85.61, 144.20, 308.23, 589.10, 671.21, 1000.12
malignant catarrh 85.41
malignant catarrhal fever 85.41
malignant growth 85.39
malignant pustule 85.41
malignant tumor 85.39
malignity 103.1, 144.5, 308.9, 589.3, 671.1, 1000.5
malinger 340.7, 368.9
malingerer 340.5, 357.6, 368.3
malingering (n) 368.2 (a) 368.15
malism 125.6
malison 513.1
malist 125.7
mall 383.2, 736.2, 739.1
malleability 324.1, 433.3, 570.5, 854.1, 867.1, 894.5, 1014.2, 1047.2
malleable 433.13, 570.18, 854.6, 867.5, 894.15, 923.12, 1014.15, 1047.9
mallet 715.4
malleus 2.10
malnourishment 992.6
malnutrition 270.6, 992.6
malobservation 342.1
malodor 71.1
malodorous 64.7, 69.9, 71.5, 80.23, 98.18
malodorousness 64.3
malodourousness 71.2
malperformance 340.1, 414.4
malposition 160.3
malpractice 389.1, 414.6, 638.1, 655.1
malt 66.3
Maltese cat 311.20
maltose 66.3
maltreat 389.5, 1000.6
maltreatment 389.2
malt sweetener 66.3
malt syrup 66.3
malum 655.2
malversation 389.1, 638.1, 655.1
malware 1042.11
mam 560.12
mama 560.12
mama's boy 16.6, 77.10, 427.4
mamelon 283.6
mamelonation 283.6
mammal 311.3
mammalian (n) 311.3 (a) 283.19, 311.40
mammary 283.19
mammary gland 283.6
mammate 283.19
mammatus 319.8
mammer 525.8
mammiform 283.19
mammilla 283.6
mammillary 283.19
mammillation 283.6
mammography 91.12
mammon 618.1, 728.1
mammoth (n) 257.14, 311.4 (a) 247.7, 257.20
mammy 560.12, 1008.8
Man, The 575.15
man (n) 76.3, 76.4, 104.12, 138.6, 304.1, 312.1, 312.5, 563.7, 577.4, 616.8, 743.17 (v) 385.8, 460.9
Man, the 312.3
man, the 417.1
mana 18.1, 678.1
man-about-town 413.17, 500.9, 578.7, 582.16
manacle (n) 428.4 (v) 19.10, 428.10
manacled 428.16
man after one's own heart 104.15
manage 182.14, 328.9, 385.12, 387.10, 387.12, 407.4, 409.12, 573.8, 612.11, 635.4, 765.5, 856.5, 889.5, 995.4, 1070.7
manageability 433.4, 889.3, 1014.2
manageable 433.14, 633.7, 889.10, 1014.15
manageableness 1014.2
manageable price 633.2
managed care 91.21
managed currency 609.4, 728.1
managed prices 630.5
management 249.3, 328.2, 387.2, 387.8, 573.1, 574.3, 574.11, 575.14, 612.1, 635.1, 889.1, 1008.2
management consultant 573.7
management consulting 573.7
management demands 727.1
management engineering 573.7
management information system 1042.2
management theory 573.7
manage oneself 321.4
manager 574.1, 575.6, 730.1, 745.2, 754.2, 889.4
managerial 417.15, 573.12, 889.12
managership 573.4
managery 573.1
manage somehow 409.12
manage the price of 630.11
manage with 995.4
managing (n) 573.1 (a) 573.12, 612.18
managing director 574.3
managing editor 554.2, 555.4
man among men, a 659.4
mañana 839.1
man and wife 563.9
man and woman 563.9
manas 689.18
man-at-arms 461.6
man at the plate 745.2
man breast 283.6
man cave 197.17
man-centered 312.13
manchild 302.5
manciple 385.6
mandant 232.1
mandarin (n) 141.7, 575.15, 921.1, 929.1 (a) 570.17
mandate (n) 232.1, 417.1, 417.12, 420.2, 469.1, 594.1, 613.8, 615.1 (v) 420.8, 963.8
mandated 420.12
mandatedness 963.1
mandated territory 232.1
mandatee 232.1
mandating 420.13
mandatoriness 963.1
mandatory (n) 232.1 (a) 419.4, 420.12, 424.11, 641.15, 767.9, 953.27, 963.12
mandatory primary 609.15
mandatory referendum 613.8
mandible 2.12
mandibles 292.4, 474.4
mandibular 292.22
mandolinist 710.5
mandragora 22.10
mandrake 22.10
mandrel 915.5
manducate 8.27
manducation 8.1
manducatory 8.32
mane 3.2, 3.4
man-eater 8.16, 311.29, 593.5
maneater 308.11
man-eating 8.31
man-eating shark 311.29
manege 1070.1
manège 177.6
manes 678.12, 919.4, 988.1
maneuver (n) 84.2, 328.3, 415.3, 458.4, 753.3, 889.2, 995.2 (v) 182.46, 328.5, 381.9, 415.10, 573.8, 889.5
maneuverability 889.3, 1014.2
maneuverable 889.10, 1014.15
maneuverer 381.7, 415.7
maneuvering 381.5, 415.4
maneuvering room 430.4
maneuvering space 430.4
maneuvers 415.4, 458.4
man fish 678.10
man Friday 577.3, 616.7
man from Mars 1075.8
manful 76.12, 492.16
manfulness 76.1, 492.1
manganese 7.11
mange (n) 85.41 (v) 8.20
manger 197.2
mangle 287.6, 802.14
mangled 393.27, 795.5
mango 42.2
mangy 661.12
manhandle 15.12, 176.11, 176.12, 389.5
man-hater 103.4, 590.2
man-hating (n) 590.1 (a) 590.3

man-haul 905.4
man-haulage 905.1
man-hauled 905.6
man-hauling 905.1
man higher up 610.7
manhood 14.1, 76.1, 76.3, 303.2, 492.1
man-hour 725.4, 824.2
manhunt 382.1
mania 92.16, 100.6, 101.3, 926.1, 926.12
mania a potu 926.9
maniac (n) 926.15 (a) 105.25, 926.30
maniacal 105.25, 926.28, 926.30
maniacal excitement 926.7
manic 105.20, 926.26, 926.28, 926.30
manic condition 105.1
manic-depression 926.5
manic-depressive (n) 926.17 (a) 926.28
manic-depressive disorder 926.5
manic-depressive psychosis 92.14
manic psychosis 926.12
manic state 105.1
manicure (n) 1016.10 (v) 79.20
manicurist 1016.12
manifest (n) 628.3, 871.5 (v) 292.12, 348.5, 351.4, 501.17, 517.17, 957.8 (a) 31.6, 348.8
manifestable 348.13
manifestation 31.1, 33.1, 348.1, 349.1, 351.1, 501.4, 517.3, 957.1, 1052.8
manifestative 348.9
manifest destiny 458.11, 609.5
manifested 348.13
manifesting 348.9
manifest itself 351.8
manifestness 31.2, 221.1, 348.3
manifesto (n) 334.1, 352.2, 673.3, 953.4 (v) 334.5
manifestoed 334.9
manifest oneself 33.8
manifold (n) 785.4 (v) 785.8 (a) 783.3, 883.8, 884.6
manifoldness 783.1, 884.1
manikin 258.5, 349.6
Manila folder 195.1
man in the batter's box 745.2
man in the box 745.2
man in the moon 1073.12
man in the street 606.5
man in the street, the 606.1, 864.3, 998.7
man in the White House, the 575.7
mani-pedi (n) 1016.10 (v) 79.20
maniple 461.22
manipulability 433.4
manipulable 387.23, 433.14
manipulatability 433.4, 889.3
manipulatable 433.14, 889.10
manipulate 73.6, 184.37, 354.17, 387.10, 387.16, 415.10, 573.8, 889.5
manipulated 354.30
manipulated market 737.6
manipulated variable 1041.9
manipulate the market 737.25
manipulating 73.2
manipulation 73.2, 75.8, 381.5, 387.8, 415.4, 573.1, 737.20, 889.1, 1041.7
manipulational 889.12
manipulative 381.13, 387.19, 415.12
manipulator 357.2, 415.7, 889.4, 894.6
manipulatory 381.13, 387.19, 415.12
manism 980.4
manist 980.5
Manitou 677.2
manitou 678.1
man-killer 308.11
man-killing 308.24
mankind 76.3, 312.1
manlihood 76.1
manlike 76.12, 312.14
manlikeness 76.1
manliness 76.1, 303.2, 492.1
manling 302.5
manly 76.12, 492.16, 644.13
manly art of self-defense 457.9
manly vigor 76.2
manmade 336.8, 354.26, 892.18
manmade lake 241.1
man mountain 15.7
manna 10.8, 449.3, 472.7, 478.7
manna from heaven 472.7, 478.7
manna in the wilderness 449.3
manned 385.13, 460.14
manned flight 1075.1
manned rocket 1075.2
manned station 1075.5
mannequin 349.6, 786.5
manner 33.3, 206.1, 321.1, 373.1, 384.1, 532.2, 765.4, 809.3, 866.1
mannered 321.7, 500.15, 533.9, 536.3
manneredness 533.3
mannerism 354.3, 500.1, 500.2, 532.2, 533.3, 865.4, 927.2
mannerist 500.7, 532.3
mannerless 505.5
mannerlessness 505.1
mannerliness 504.3
mannerly 504.15
manner of articulation 524.12
manner of preparation 11.2
manner of speaking 524.7, 529.1, 532.2, 536.1
manner of working 384.1
manners 321.1, 373.1, 504.3, 580.3
mannified 76.14
mannish 76.12, 76.14
mannishness 76.1
man of action 330.8
man of all work 577.9
man of blood 308.11
man of commerce 730.1
man of courage 492.7
man of deeds 330.8
man of experience 413.17
man of few words 344.5
man of genius 413.13
man of God 699.2
man of good will 143.8
man of his word 644.8
man of honor 644.8
man of intellect 921.1
man of iron 134.3
man of learning 929.3
man of letters 547.15, 718.4, 929.3, 946.7
man of men 659.4
man of parts 413.12
man of property 470.3
man of science 928.11
man of straw 349.6, 500.7, 764.2, 998.7
man of the cloth 699.2
man of the family 76.10
man of the house 470.2, 575.1
man of the people 606.5
man of the world 304.2, 413.17, 562.12, 578.7
man-of-war 180.6
man-of-war's man 183.4
manometer 1067.7
man on the make 562.12
manor 471.6
manor farm 1069.8
manor house 228.5, 228.7
manorial 228.32, 471.9
man-overboard buoy 397.6
man-o'-war 180.6
manpower 18.4, 18.9
manqué 410.18
man's best friend 311.16
manse 228.5, 703.7
manservant 577.4
man's estate 303.2
mansion 228.7, 1073.20
mansional 228.32
man-sized 257.16
man-sized job 1013.2
man-sized meal 8.8
manslaughter 308.2
manslayer 308.11
mansplain 341.10
mansplaining 341.4
manstopper 462.19
manstopping bullet 462.19
man-talk 523.10
mantel 901.14
mantelpiece 901.14
mantelshelf 901.14
man the barricades 460.9
man the garrison 460.9
man the trenches 460.9
mantic (n) 962.2 (a) 962.11
mantilla 5.26
mantis 311.35
mantle (n) 295.2, 417.9, 647.1, 702.2 (v) 5.40, 41.5, 105.19, 139.8, 152.14, 295.19, 320.5
mantled 5.45, 295.31
mantled in darkness 1027.13
mantle of snow 1023.8
mantle oneself with 376.4
mantlerock 1059.1
mantling 41.3, 139.5, 295.1, 647.2
mantology 962.2
man-to-man 535.3, 582.24, 587.19
man-to-man offense 752.3
mantra 696.3
manual 554.8, 554.10, 711.17
manual alphabet 49.3
manual art 712.2
manual labor 725.4
manual of instruction 554.10
manual training 568.3
manual transmission 1040.9
manual worker 577.3
manubial column 549.12
manufactory 739.3
manufacturable 892.20
manufactural 892.14
manufacture (n) 266.1, 405.1, 892.2, 893.1 (v) 354.18, 892.8, 1043.4
manufactured 354.29, 892.18
manufactured book 554.3
manufacturer 892.7
manufacturing (n) 892.2 (a) 892.14
manufacturing center 208.7
manufacturing plant 739.3
manufacturing quarter 739.3
manufacturing town 739.2
manumission 431.1
manumit 431.4
manumitted 430.21
manumitted slave 430.11
manumitter 592.2
manumitting 592.4
man up 134.5
man upstairs 575.4, 997.11
manure (n) 12.4, 890.4 (v) 890.8
manure pile 80.10
manuscript (n) 547.3, 547.10, 548.4, 554.6 (a) 547.22
manustupration 75.8
man with hair on his chest 76.6
man without a country 160.4, 586.4
many, a 884.3
many 247.8, 780.7, 783.4, 847.4, 883.7, 884.6, 991.7
many, the 606.2
many and various 783.4
many-colored 35.16, 47.9
many-faceted 799.4
many hats 413.3
many-hued 47.9
many irons in the fire 330.5
manyness 884.1
many-sided 218.7, 413.25, 797.14, 854.6
many-sidedness 218.1, 413.3
many times 847.4
Maoism 611.5, 860.2
Maoist (n) 611.13, 860.3 (a) 611.21, 860.6
map (n) 159.5, 216.4, 349.1, 381.3 (v) 159.11, 349.8, 381.10, 1036.17, 1043.4
maple 66.3
maple sugar 66.3
maple syrup 66.2, 66.3
maple syrup urine disease 85.22
mapmaker 159.5, 300.9
mapmaking 159.5
map out 381.10, 405.6
mapped 300.13, 381.12
mapper 159.5
mapping 381.1, 1036.8

map projection 159.5
maquis 461.16
mar 265.7, 393.10, 414.11, 1004.4, 1015.5
marabout 584.5
marais 243.1
marantic 270.20
maraschino cherries 10.40
marasmic 270.20
marasmus 85.9, 270.6
marathon (n) 261.2 (a) 827.11
maraud 482.17
marauder 483.6
marauding (n) 482.6 (a) 482.22
marble (n) 47.6, 282.2, 287.3, 715.2, 1046.6 (v) 47.7 (a) 37.7, 1046.10
marbled 47.12, 47.15
marbled paper 47.6
marblehearted 94.12, 144.25
marbleheartedness 94.3
marbleize 47.7
marbleized 47.15
marblelike 1046.10, 1059.11
marbles 743.16, 759.8
marbly 1059.11
marcando 708.25
marcato 708.25
marcel (n) 3.15 (v) 3.22
marcel wave 3.15
marcescence 393.4
marcescent 393.45
march (n) 162.1, 177.10, 177.13, 211.3, 211.5, 231.2, 333.2, 708.12 (v) 177.30, 211.10, 333.5
march against 459.17
march away 188.6
marcher 178.6
marches 211.1, 211.5
march in double-quick time 174.8
marching 177.8
marching band 710.12
marching orders 909.5
march in quick time 174.8
marchioness 608.6
marchland 211.5
March Madness 747.1
march of events 831.4
march off 188.6
march of time 821.4
march on 162.3
march out 190.12
march out of step 789.5
march past 812.7
march-past 812.3
march tempo 709.24
march to a different drummer 333.4
march under the banner of 509.13
march upon 459.17
march up to the cannon's mouth 492.10, 493.6, 1006.7
march with 223.12
Marconi-rigged 180.17
Mardi Gras 95.3, 743.4
mare 77.9, 236.1, 311.10, 757.2
mare's nest 356.7, 797.6, 799.2, 810.3
marge (n) 211.4 (v) 211.10
marged 211.12
margin (n) 158.3, 211.4, 224.1, 261.1, 430.4, 438.3, 738.10, 780.2, 993.5 (v) 211.10
marginal 211.11, 998.16
marginal affair, a 998.6
marginalia 254.2, 549.4
marginality 998.1
marginalization 998.1
marginalize 137.4, 998.12
marginal land 234.1
marginal matter, a 998.6
marginal note 549.4
marginate (v) 211.10 (a) 211.12
marginated 211.12
margined 211.12
margin of error 164.1
margin of lift 184.26
margin purchaser 737.11
margin up 737.23
margrave 608.4
margravine 608.6
Maria 758.2
Mariana Trench 275.4, 275.5
marigold 728.8
marigraph 238.15
marijuana smoker 87.21
marimbaist 710.6
marina 1009.6
marinade 397.9
marinate 397.9
marinating 192.7, 397.2
marination 797.2
marine (n) 183.4, 461.27, 1043.3 (a) 182.57, 240.8
marine animal 311.29
marine archeology 842.4
marine biologist 240.7
marine biology 240.6
Marine Corps 461.21, 461.28
Marine Corps noncommissioned officer 575.19
marine engineer 1043.2
marine engineering 1043.1
marine fish 311.30
marine painter 716.4
marine park 228.19
mariner 178.1, 183.1, 760.2
mariner's compass 574.9
marines 461.15, 461.28
marine travel 182.1
Marinism 533.3
Marinist 533.5, 545.5
Marinistic 533.9
Mariolatry 679.5
Mariology 679.5
marionette 349.6, 743.16
marish (n) 243.1 (a) 243.3
marital 563.18
marital affinity 564.1
marital faithfulness 664.3
marital fidelity 664.3
marital relations 75.7
maritime 182.57, 240.8
maritime meteorology 317.5
Maritimer 227.11
Mark 684.2
mark (n) 211.3, 245.1, 358.2, 380.2, 517.1, 517.5, 517.10, 527.10, 662.5 (v) 487.2, 517.17, 517.19, 530.16, 546.6
mark (n) 709.12, 733.4, 750.2, 759.22, 809.3, 865.4, 887.2, 957.1, 997.1, 1004.3 (v) 713.9, 749.7, 752.4, 780.6, 865.10, 865.11, 946.9, 957.8, 964.7, 983.6, 1004.6
mark boundaries 210.4
mark down 549.15, 630.11, 633.6
markdown 633.4
marked 247.10, 249.12, 517.24, 662.16, 713.11, 865.13, 964.9, 997.19
marked down 633.9
marked off 776.6
marked-off 802.20
marked resemblance 784.4
marked trail 753.1
marked with the crow's foot 303.16
marker 517.10, 549.12, 550.1, 712.18, 751.3
marker beacon 517.15
marker buoy 1036.7
market (n) 230.8, 731.1, 731.7, 733.3, 734.1, 736.1, 736.2, 739.1 (v) 731.16, 731.17, 733.8, 734.8 (a) 734.13
market, the 737.1
marketability 734.7
marketable 734.14
market economy 731.7
marketer 730.2, 733.5
market expansion 731.10
market gardener 1069.6
market gardening 1069.2
market index 737.1
market indicator 731.1
marketing (n) 731.1, 733.1, 734.2 (a) 734.13
marketing research 734.2
marketize 731.15
market leader 731.1
market maker 737.10
market overt 736.2
marketplace 230.8, 463.1, 736.2
marketplace, the 731.1
market price 630.1, 738.9
market-rate housing 228.1
market research 734.2, 938.14
market researcher 938.18
market-research survey 938.14
market share 731.1
marketspace 731.1
market town 230.1
market-trading 737.19
market value 630.2, 738.9
marking 517.5, 647.1, 713.2, 749.6, 865.4
marking off 802.1
marking the occasion 487.1
mark of Cain 661.6
mark off 210.4, 300.11, 381.10, 477.9, 517.19, 780.6, 865.10
mark of office 647.1
mark of signature 527.10
mark out 210.4, 300.11, 381.10, 517.19, 780.6, 865.10
mark out a course 381.8
mark out for 477.9
mark paid 627.3
marksman 413.11, 461.9, 904.8
marksmanship 413.1, 744.1
markswoman 904.8
Mark 10 1074.10
mark the cards 759.26
mark the interface 944.4
mark the periphery 210.4
mark the time 832.11
mark time 130.8, 173.7, 821.6, 832.11, 846.12
mark up 251.4, 630.11
markup language 1042.13
mark with a red letter 487.2
marl (n) 234.1, 742.3, 890.4 (v) 890.8
marlinespike 906.4
marly 234.5
marmalade 10.40
marmelize 412.9, 604.14, 902.17
marmoreal 37.7, 715.6
marmoreal repose 173.1
maroon (v) 370.5 (a) 41.6
marooned 370.8, 1013.27
marplot 1012.8
marquee 295.6, 352.7, 704.18
Marquess of Queensbury rules 754.1
marquetry 47.4
marquis 608.4
marquisate 608.9
Marquis de Sade, the 144.14
marquise 608.6
marred 265.12, 393.28, 1004.8, 1015.6
marriable 303.12
marriage 75.2, 563.1, 563.3, 797.5, 800.1, 805.1
marriageability 14.1, 563.2
marriageable 14.3, 303.12, 563.20
marriageableness 14.1, 563.2
marriage act 75.7
marriage bed 563.1
marriage broker 563.12
marriage bureau 563.12
marriage ceremony 563.3
marriage certificate 549.6
marriage connection 564.1
marriage contract 436.3
marriage counselor 466.5
marriage license 443.6
marriage money 478.9
marriage on the rocks 566.1
marriage portion 478.9
marriage proposal 562.8
marriage relationship 564.1
marriage sacrament 563.1
marriage song 563.3
marriage vow 436.3
marriage vows 563.3
married 563.18, 563.21, 775.9, 800.13, 805.6
married couple 563.9
married love 104.1
married man 76.10, 563.7
married name 527.5
married state 563.1
married status 563.1
married up 775.9
married woman 77.5, 77.7, 563.8
marrow 10.20, 196.5, 208.2, 767.2
marrowless 16.12, 19.19
marrow-sky 975.7

marry 563.14, 563.15, 775.6, 800.5, 805.3, 805.4
marry off 563.14
marry up 775.6
Mars 458.12, 1073.9
marsh 80.12, 243.1
marshal (n) 575.17, 743.20, 1008.15 (v) 405.6, 769.8, 800.5, 808.9, 957.12
marshaled 808.14
marshaling 458.2, 647.2, 770.1, 807.1, 808.1
marshal one's forces 405.6
marshal one's ideas 931.10
marshal's baton 273.2
marshfire 1019.13, 1025.13
marshiness 1065.1
marshland 243.1
marshy 243.3, 1065.15
Mars ship 1075.2
marsupial (n) 311.3 (a) 311.40
marsupialian 311.3
mart 230.8, 736.1, 736.2
martello 272.6, 460.6
martello tower 272.6, 460.6
martial 458.20
martial art 744.1
martial arts 457.10, 760.3
martialism 458.10
martial law 458.9, 612.4
martial music 458.11, 708.12
martial spirit 492.1
Martian 870.4, 1075.8
martinet 575.13
martingale 1012.7
Martin Luther 684.3
Martin Luther King 543.6
Martin Luther King Jr 921.2
martlet 647.2
martyr (n) 96.11, 679.1, 1011.7 (v) 26.7, 96.18, 308.13
martyrdom 26.6, 96.7, 308.1, 604.2, 652.1
martyred 26.9, 307.29, 652.5, 679.6
martyrization 26.6, 308.1
martyrize 26.7, 96.18, 308.13
martyrized 26.9
martyrizing 26.10
martyrologic 719.6
martyrological 719.6
martyrology 307.13, 719.1
marvel (n) 122.1, 122.2 (v) 122.5
marveling (n) 122.1 (a) 122.9
marvelment 122.2
marvelous 122.10, 247.10, 870.14, 999.15
marvelousness 122.3, 870.2, 999.2
marvy 999.13
Marxian 1052.12
Marxian socialism 611.5, 611.6
Marxism 611.5, 611.6, 952.7, 1052.6
Marxism-Leninism 611.5
Marxist (n) 611.13, 611.14, 860.3, 1052.7 (a) 611.21, 860.6, 1052.12
Marxist-Leninist (n) 611.13 (a) 611.21
mary 87.11
Mary Baker Eddy 684.3
maryjane 87.11
Maryland 89.2
mary warner 87.11
Masan 988.1
mascara 1016.11
mascaraed 1016.22
mascle 647.2
mascot 691.5
masculine (n) 76.4, 530.10 (a) 76.12
masculine caesura 720.7
masculineness 76.1
masculine rhyme 720.9
masculinity 75.1, 76.1, 303.2
masculinize 76.11
masculism 980.4
masculist 980.5
mash (n) 10.4, 104.3, 1063.2 (v) 439.8, 1047.6, 1051.9, 1063.5
mashed potato 10.35
masher 500.9, 562.12, 1051.7, 1063.4
mashiness 1063.1
mashing 1051.4
mash note 562.13
mash-up 718.1
masjid 703.2
mask (n) 5.9, 295.2, 344.3, 346.2, 356.11, 376.1, 705.2, 715.3, 1008.3 (v) 295.19, 346.6, 354.16
masked 295.31, 346.13
masked ball 705.2
masker 357.7
masking 295.1, 346.1, 787.1
masking tape 803.4
mask of death 307.11
masochism 75.11
masochist 75.16
mason 716.6
masonry 715.1, 1054.2
Masorah 683.5
Masoretic 683.12
masque 356.11, 705.2
masquerade (n) 5.9, 349.4, 354.3, 356.11, 705.2 (v) 346.8
masquerade as 349.12, 354.22
masquerade ball 705.2
masquerader 357.7
masquerading 346.13
Mass 696.8, 701.8
mass (n) 244.1, 247.3, 257.1, 257.10, 257.11, 269.2, 297.5, 386.1 (v) 159.15 (a) 297.20, 606.8
mass (n) 708.17, 763.1, 770.4, 770.9, 770.10, 792.6, 803.5, 883.2, 1045.6 (v) 770.16, 770.18, 800.5, 803.6
massacre (n) 308.4, 671.3 (v) 308.17, 412.9
massacrer 308.11
mass action 450.1
massage (n) 1044.3 (v) 73.8, 91.24, 1044.6, 1047.6
massage one's ego 95.11
massage parlor 665.9
massager 1044.4
massage the ego 511.6
massage therapist 1044.4
massage therapy 1044.3
massaging 73.2, 1044.3
mass attack 459.1
Mass book 701.10
mass burial 309.1
mass communications 343.5
mass destruction 308.4
massed 770.21, 803.10
mass energy 1038.15
masses 247.4, 250.2
masses, the 606.2
masses of 884.3
masseur 1044.4
masseuse 1044.4
mass extermination 308.4
mass grave 309.16
massif 237.1, 237.6
massify 244.4, 247.5
massiness 297.2
massing 800.1, 803.1
massive 247.7, 257.19, 269.8, 297.16, 297.17, 763.7, 1045.12
massiveness 257.9, 297.2
massive open online course 567.5
mass killing 308.1
mass-luminosity law 1073.8
mass mailing 553.1
mass market 734.1
mass marketing 731.13
mass media 551.5, 555.3
mass meeting 770.2
mass migration 188.1
mass movement 886.9
mass murder 308.1, 308.4
mass noun 530.5
mass number 1038.4, 1060.5
mass of, a 884.3
mass of the people, the 606.2
massotherapist 1044.4
massotherapy 1044.3
mass-produce 892.11
mass-produced 892.18
mass production 892.3
mass spectrograph 1038.12
mass spectrography 1038.1
mass spectrometer 1038.12
mass spectrometry 1038.1
mass suicide 308.5
massy 247.7, 257.19, 297.16, 1045.12
mast 180.13, 272.6, 901.2
mastaba 309.16
Master 76.7, 648.3
master (n) 183.7, 249.4, 302.5, 337.2, 411.2, 413.13, 470.2, 571.1, 571.8, 575.1, 575.3, 575.6, 648.6, 712.9, 716.1, 726.6, 892.7, 921.1, (v) 412.10, 432.9, 521.7, 570.9, 612.14, 928.12 (a) 249.14, 612.17, 997.24
master bedroom 197.7
master carpenter 726.6
master chief petty officer 575.19
master chief petty officer of the Navy 575.19
master class 541.6
master control desk 1034.7
master craftsman 726.6, 892.7
masterdom 417.7
mastered 412.17, 432.15
masterful 141.11, 413.22, 417.16, 1002.9
masterfulness 141.3, 417.3
master gunnery sergeant 575.19
master hand 413.13
masterhood 417.7
master key 292.10
masterly 413.22, 1002.9
master mariner 183.3
mastermind (n) 381.6, 413.13, 921.1, 929.3 (v) 573.8
master of 413.27, 469.9, 928.19
master of ceremonies 574.4, 704.23, 743.20, 1034.23
master of style 532.3
master of the house 575.1
master of the revels 574.4, 743.20
Master of the Rolls 596.3
master of the situation 411.2
master oneself 412.7, 668.6
master one's feelings 106.7
masterpiece 122.2, 413.10, 712.9, 893.1, 999.5, 1002.4, 1016.6
master plan 381.1
master's degree 648.6
master's degree candidate 572.8
master sergeant 575.18, 575.19
mastership 249.3, 413.1, 417.7, 573.4, 612.2
master-slave relationship 432.1
master's oral 938.2
master spirit 413.13, 662.9, 892.7, 997.10
master spirit of the age 921.1
master stroke 328.3, 413.10, 415.3
masterstroke 122.2
master switch 292.10
masterwork 413.10, 712.9, 893.1, 1002.4
master workman 726.6
mastery 249.3, 405.4, 411.1, 412.1, 413.1, 417.7, 570.1, 612.2, 894.1, 928.3
mastery of skills 570.1
masthead (n) 517.13 (v) 604.9
mastic 295.25
masticate 8.27, 1047.6, 1063.5
masticated 1063.6
masticating 8.32
mastication 8.1, 1063.3
masticatory 8.32
mastodon 257.14, 311.4
mastodonic 257.20
mastoid process 2.10
masturbate 75.22
masturbation 75.8
masturbatory 140.8
mat (n) 3.4, 211.4, 213.5, 295.9, 463.1, 750.3, 901.20 (v) 740.6, 1027.10 (a) 36.7, 1027.17
matador 308.11, 461.4
mat burn 1020.6
match (n) 349.5, 457.3, 563.1, 743.9, 744.1, 748.1, 751.3, 752.3, 754.3, 790.4, 873.2, 1021.5, 1026.1 (v) 203.4, 203.5, 215.4, 257.15, 506.6, 563.14, 770.18, 778.4, 784.7, 788.6, 790.5, 836.4, 873.5, 943.4, 943.7
match a bet 759.25

matchable 943.8
matchbook 1021.5
match coins 759.23
match data 943.6
match dissolve 706.6
matched 563.21, 800.13, 873.6, 873.8
matched up 873.8
match findings 943.6
matching (n) 457.3, 563.1, 943.1 (a) 35.16, 784.11
matching pair 784.5, 873.2
matching set 784.5
match in the powder barrel 886.3
matchless 249.15, 999.16, 999.17, 1002.6
matchlessness 999.2
matchmaker 563.12
match oneself against 457.16
match play 751.3
match-play tournament 750.1
match point 748.2
match race 457.12
matchstick 1021.5
match up 563.14, 873.5, 943.4
matchup 563.1, 784.3, 873.2, 943.1
match up with 790.5, 943.7
matchwood 16.7, 1050.2
mate (n) 183.7, 349.5, 563.6, 588.3, 588.4, 616.2, 769.4, 784.3, 790.4 (v) 75.21, 563.15, 873.5
mated 563.21, 800.13, 873.8
mateless 565.7
mater 560.12
materfamilias 77.7, 560.11, 575.2
material (n) 4.1, 196.5, 386.1, 763.2, 1052.2 (a) 33.11, 663.6, 695.16, 763.6, 767.9, 775.11, 957.16, 997.17, 997.23, 1052.10, 1055.4
material, the 2.1
material assets 471.7
material basis 600.6
material body 1052.3
material costs 626.3
material culture 312.10
material engineer 1043.2
material engineering 1043.1
material fallacy 936.3
material grounds 957.1
materialism 663.2, 695.2, 952.4, 1052.6
materialist (n) 695.10, 1052.7 (a) 1052.12
materialistic 663.6, 695.16, 724.15, 1052.12
materiality 761.1, 763.1, 775.4, 997.1, 1052.1, 1052.2
materialization 33.1, 348.1, 689.6, 763.4, 831.1, 892.4, 988.1, 1052.8
materialize 31.4, 33.8, 221.8, 262.8, 348.5, 348.6, 761.12, 763.5, 831.6, 892.10, 941.9, 1052.9
materializing (n) 33.1 (a) 348.9
material logic 935.2
material means 1054.1
materialness 221.1, 1052.1
material part 937.1
material point 997.6
material resources 1054.1
materials 386.1, 928.9, 1054.1
material thing 1052.4
material things 471.2
material wealth 618.1
material world 1052.2
materia medica 86.4, 86.34
materiate 1052.10
matériel 385.4, 386.1, 462.1, 1054.1
maternal 104.26, 226.5, 560.17
maternal ancestor 560.11
maternal love 104.4
maternalness 560.3
maternity 559.1, 560.3
maternity clothes 5.2
maternity leave 20.2
maternity ward 197.25
maternize 449.12
mates 873.2
matey 587.20
mateyness 587.5
math 1017.1
mathematic 1017.1
mathematical 973.17, 1017.22
mathematical element 1017.1
mathematical logic 935.2
mathematically exact 973.17
mathematically probable 968.6
mathematical notation 349.1
mathematical physicist 1017.16
mathematical point 258.7
mathematical precision 973.5
mathematical probability 968.2
mathematician 1017.16
mathematics 1017.1
maths 1017.1
matin 314.5
matinal 314.5
matinee 315.1, 582.10, 704.12
matinee idol 104.15, 707.2
mating 75.7, 78.3
mating call 60.1, 562.5
mating cry 60.1
mating instinct 75.5, 104.2
matins 314.1, 696.8
matman 461.3
mat of hair 3.2
matriarch 77.7, 304.3, 560.11, 575.2, 842.8
matriarchal 612.16
matriarchate 612.5
matriarchic 612.16
matriarchical 612.16
matriarchy 77.1, 612.5
matriclan 559.4
matriculate 549.15, 570.11
matriculation 549.14
matrifocal 560.17
matrilateral 559.6
matrilineage 559.1
matrilineal 559.6
matriliny 559.1
matrimonial 563.18, 701.18
matrimonial agency 563.12
matrimonial agent 563.12
matrimonial connection 564.1
matrimonial union 563.1
matrimony 563.1, 701.4
matrisib 559.1
matrix 262.1, 786.6, 886.7, 1058.7
matrix player 759.21
matroclinous 559.6, 560.19
matrocliny 559.1, 560.6
matron 77.5, 304.3, 563.8, 575.2
matronage 77.1
matronal 77.13
matronhood 77.1
matronize 1008.19
matronlike 77.13
matronliness 77.1
matronly 77.13, 303.14
matron of honor 563.4
matronship 77.1
matronym 527.5
matte 714.5, 1027.5
matted 3.24, 294.7, 799.4, 810.14
matted hair 3.2
matte finish 1027.5
matter (n) 2.24, 12.3, 12.6, 196.5, 244.1, 375.1, 404.1, 547.10, 548.4, 724.1, 763.2, 766.3, 831.3, 937.1, 1052.2, 1054.1, 1055.1 (v) 12.15, 997.12
matter, the 1013.3
matter at hand 404.1
mattering (n) 12.6 (a) 12.21
matter in hand 937.1
matter little 998.11
matter of chance 759.2
matter of concern 997.5
matter of consequence 997.5
matter of course 373.3, 373.4
matter of fact 117.2, 761.3, 831.2
matter-of-fact 117.8, 499.6, 535.3, 721.5, 987.6
matter-of-factness 117.2, 499.1, 535.1, 721.2, 987.2
matter of ignorance 930.6
matter of importance 997.5
matter of indifference 998.6
matter of interest 983.2
matter of life and death 963.4, 997.3
matter of moment 831.3
matter of necessity 963.4
matter of no consequence 998.6
matter of no importance 998.6
matters 831.4
matters in hand 724.2
matte shot 714.8
Matthew 684.2
mattify 1027.9
mattress 901.20
mattress money 728.14, 729.15
maturate 14.2, 407.8, 861.5
maturated 407.13
maturation 14.1, 259.3, 301.6, 303.2, 303.6, 392.2, 407.2, 861.1
maturational 861.8
maturative 861.8
mature (v) 14.2, 259.7, 303.9, 304.6, 392.10, 407.8, 623.7, 794.6, 861.5, 892.8, 892.12, 1002.5 (a) 14.3, 259.12, 303.12, 303.13, 304.7, 405.16, 407.13, 413.28, 623.10, 794.9, 1002.9
mature age 303.2
mature belief 953.5
matured 407.13, 413.28, 794.9, 1002.9
mature judgment 363.1, 953.5
mature man 304.1
maturement 301.6
matureness 303.2
maturescence 14.1
maturescent 14.3
mature student 572.1
mature thought 931.5
mature woman 304.1
maturing (n) 14.1, 259.3 (a) 861.8
maturity 303.1, 303.2, 405.4, 407.2, 623.1
matutinal 314.5
matzo balls 10.33
maudlin 88.31, 93.21, 923.8
maudlinness 93.8
maul 389.5, 393.13, 671.11, 754.4, 902.16
mauled 96.23
mauler 754.2
mauling 902.3
maulstick 712.18
Mau-Mau 860.6
maunder 525.9, 538.9, 922.12
maundering (n) 525.4, 538.3 (a) 538.13, 922.22
mausoleum 309.16, 549.12
mauve (n) 46.1 (a) 46.3
Mauve Decade 824.5
mauvy 46.3
maven 413.11, 422.3, 496.6, 866.3, 920.9, 928.11
maverick (n) 311.6, 327.5, 361.6, 868.3, 870.4 (a) 868.6
mavis 710.23
maw 2.12, 2.18, 292.4
mawkish 64.7, 66.6, 93.21
mawkishness 66.1, 93.8
Mawworm 693.3
max 794.3, 794.5
max, the (n) 249.3 (a) 247.13
maxed 87.24
maxed-out 16.18, 21.10, 388.5, 393.36
maxillae 474.4
maxillary 292.22
maxim 419.2, 422.2, 529.1, 869.4, 952.2, 953.2, 974.1
maximal 198.11, 249.13, 991.7
maximize 251.4, 387.15
maximum (n) 198.2, 249.3, 794.5, 991.2 (a) 198.11, 247.6, 249.13
maximum dissemination 352.4
maximum-security detention 429.3
maximum-security facility 429.8
maximum-security imprisonment 429.3
maximum-security prison 429.8
maximum speed 174.3
max out 388.3, 993.10
maxwell 1032.7
Maxwell-Boltzmann distribution law 968.2
Maxwell triangle 35.7

may 18.11, 443.13
maya 691.2, 976.1
Mayan archaeology 842.4
Mayday 400.1
mayfly 828.5
mayhem 393.1
mayonnaise 10.12
mayor 575.16
mayoralty 417.7, 417.10, 594.3
mayorship 417.7, 594.3
Maypole 273.1
may the best man win 124.3
Maytime 313.2
Mazda 677.5
maze (n) 799.2, 985.3 (v) 971.13, 985.7
mazed 926.26, 971.24, 985.14
mazuma 728.2
mazy 164.7, 238.24, 279.7, 281.6, 799.4, 854.7
McCarthyism 389.3
McCoy, the 973.4
McGuffin 706.6
me 865.5
mea culpa 113.4, 658.2
mead 310.8
meadow 243.1, 310.8
meadow land 310.8
meadow nymph 678.9
meadows and pastures 233.1
meadowy 310.42
meager 248.6, 258.13, 270.14, 270.17, 885.5, 992.10
meager diet 515.2
meagerness 248.1, 270.5, 885.1, 992.2
meal 8.5, 10.4, 10.34, 1051.5
mealie 310.29
mealiness 1051.1
meal offering 150.2
meals 10.6
meal ticket 449.3, 478.8, 729.10
mealtime 11.6
mealy 36.7, 1051.11
mealymouth 138.3, 357.8
mealymouthed 138.14, 354.32, 511.8, 693.5
mealymouthedness 138.2, 354.6, 693.1
mean (n) 246.1, 467.3, 819.1 (v) 133.11, 348.5, 380.4, 517.17, 518.8, 519.4, 957.8 (a) 110.20, 137.10, 138.13, 144.20, 144.26, 154.3, 213.10, 246.3, 248.6, 250.7, 484.8, 497.15, 606.8, 651.6, 661.12, 819.4, 980.10, 992.10, 998.21, 999.13, 1005.9, 1013.17
mean a lot 518.8
mean as a junkyard dog 110.20, 144.26
mean business 359.8
mean calorie 1019.19
meander (n) 279.3, 281.1, 799.2 (v) 164.4, 177.23, 238.16, 281.4, 914.4
meandering (n) 281.1, 538.3, 914.1 (a) 164.7, 177.37, 204.20, 238.24, 279.7, 281.6, 799.4, 914.7
meandering stream 238.1
meandrous 281.6
mean high water 272.8
meanie 660.5
meaning (n) 133.6, 341.1, 380.1, 517.3, 518.1, 519.2, 526.14, 887.2 (a) 518.10
meaningful 133.15, 517.23, 518.10, 544.10
meaningfulness 133.6, 518.5, 544.1
meaningful relationship 104.17
meaningless 344.8, 391.9, 520.6, 810.12
meaninglessness 344.1, 391.2, 520.1, 998.1
mean life 827.1
mean low water 274.2
mean mind 980.1
mean-minded 980.10
mean much 997.12
meanness 110.3, 137.1, 138.1, 144.5, 154.1, 248.1, 250.3, 484.2, 497.1, 497.5, 651.2, 661.3, 980.1, 992.2, 998.2, 1005.3
mean nothing 520.4, 522.10
means 384.1, 384.2, 386.2, 471.7, 728.14, 995.2, 1040.1
mean sea level 201.3
mean semitone 709.20
means of access 189.5
means of carrying 179.1
means of communication 343.1
means of dealing 387.2
means of propulsion 904.1
means of transport 179.1
means of transporting 179.1
mean solar time 832.3
mean something 518.8
meanspirited 154.3, 980.10
meanspiritedness 154.1
means to an end 384.2, 449.1, 995.2
mean streets 230.6
meant 380.8, 518.11, 519.7
mean time 832.3
meantime 826.2
mean to imply 519.4
mean to say 519.4
mean to suggest 519.4
mean trouble 514.2, 1000.6
mean well 143.12
mean what one says 359.8
meanwhile 826.2
meany 593.1
measly 85.61, 661.12, 998.18
measurability 300.7
measurable 300.14, 1017.25
measure (n) 158.1, 244.1, 244.2, 245.1, 257.1, 257.2, 267.1, 300.1, 300.2, 328.3, 477.5, 517.1, 533.2, 673.3, 708.4, 708.24, 709.12, 709.22, 720.6, 720.7, 720.10, 889.2, 995.2 (v) 177.20, 244.4, 257.15, 300.10, 788.7, 946.9, 1017.17, 1017.18, 1043.4
measure against 943.4
measured 244.5, 300.13, 533.8, 668.9, 709.28, 720.17, 781.5, 850.7
measuredness 533.2
measured words 399.1
measure for measure 338.1, 506.3, 649.1, 658.1, 863.1
measureless 823.3, 884.10
measurelessness 823.1
measurement 244.1, 257.1, 300.1, 946.3, 1017.9
measurement of variables 1041.7
measure off 300.11
measure one's length 194.8
measure out 300.11, 477.8
measurer 300.9
measures 296.1, 384.1, 494.3
measure signature 709.12
measure swords with 457.17
measure time 821.6, 832.11
measure twice cut once 970.12
measure up 405.15
measure up to 790.5, 943.7, 991.4
measuring (n) 300.1 (a) 300.12
measuring instrument 300.2
measuring rod 300.2
measuring stick 300.2
measuring worm 311.38
meat (n) 2.13, 8.5, 10.1, 10.13, 10.39, 75.4, 75.7, 196.5, 449.3, 557.2, 767.2, 792.6, 937.1, 997.6 (v) 8.18
meat and potatoes 518.1, 767.3
meat-and-potatoes 997.23
meat cut 10.13
meat-eater 8.16, 671.10
meat-eating 8.31
meathead 924.4
meatheaded 922.17
meatheadedness 922.4
meathooks 474.4
meatiness 257.8, 518.5
meat juice 1061.2
meatless 668.10
meatless day 515.3
meat market 736.2
meat stew 10.11
meat substitute 10.13
meatus 2.23
meaty 257.18, 518.10
mecca 100.11, 208.4
mechanic 185.6, 396.10, 607.9, 726.6, 759.22, 1040.12, 1043.2
mechanical 781.5, 963.14, 1039.7, 1040.14
mechanical aid 1040.3
mechanical binding 554.14
mechanical bird 181.6
mechanical device 1040.1, 1040.3
mechanical drawing 712.4, 712.12
mechanical effects 706.5
mechanical engineer 1043.2
mechanical engineering 1039.6, 1043.1
mechanically precise 973.17
mechanical man 1041.12
mechanical means 1040.1
mechanical oscillation 916.1
mechanical refrigeration 1024.1
mechanical vector 85.44
mechanical wave 916.4
mechanician 396.10, 1040.12
mechanics 18.7, 413.7, 1039.1
mechanic's lien 438.5
mechanism 384.3, 384.4, 413.7, 1040.3, 1040.4, 1052.6
mechanist 1052.12
mechanistic 1039.7, 1040.14, 1052.12
mechanization 1040.1
mechanize 1040.13
mechanized 1039.7, 1040.14
mechanizing 1040.1
medal 646.6, 647.1, 715.3
medalist 413.15
medallion 646.6, 715.3
Medal of Honor 646.6
medal play 751.3
medal winner 413.15
meddle 214.7, 422.5, 981.4, 1012.10
meddler 214.4, 422.3
meddlesome 214.9, 981.6
meddlesomeness 214.2, 981.1
meddle with 214.7
meddling (n) 214.2 (a) 214.9
Medea 690.9
Medellin cartel 732.4
medevac 90.11
media 343.5, 347.1
media campaign 609.13
media center 558.1
media circus 552.3
media event 831.2
media happening 831.2
media hype 552.3
medial 213.10, 246.3, 392.15, 819.4
median (n) 246.1, 819.1 (a) 213.10, 246.3, 819.4
median strip 213.5
mediant 709.15
media personality 1035.13
media player 50.11
media resource center 558.1
mediary 213.4
mediaspeak 523.9
media studies 343.1
mediate 213.6, 384.7, 465.8, 466.6
mediating (n) 466.1 (a) 384.8, 466.8
mediation 384.3, 465.1, 466.1, 677.14
mediative 466.8, 677.16
mediator 213.4, 384.4, 466.3, 466.5, 576.4, 670.3
mediatorial 384.8, 466.8
mediatorship 466.2
mediatory 466.8, 677.16
mediatrix 466.3
medicable 396.25
Medicaid 83.5, 90.1, 611.7
medical 90.15
medical attendant 90.4
medical attention 91.14
medical care 83.5, 90.1, 91.1, 91.14
medical center 208.7
medical diathermy 91.5
medical doctor 90.4
medicalese 523.10
medical ethics 636.1
medical examiner 90.4, 307.17
medical Greek 523.10

medical history 91.10
medical insurance 83.5
medical jurisprudence 673.7
medical library 558.1
medical man 90.4
medical management 83.5
medical practice 90.1, 90.13
medical practitioner 90.4
medical profession 90.1
medical specialty or branch 90.1
medical test 91.12
medical treatment 91.1, 91.14
medical waste 391.4
medicament 86.4
medicamentation 91.14
Medicare 83.5, 90.1, 611.7
medicate 86.38, 90.14, 91.25
medicating 86.39
medication 86.4, 91.1, 91.14
medicative 86.39
medicinal (n) 86.4 (a) 86.39
medicinal herbs 86.4
medicinal plant 310.3
medicine (n) 86.4, 88.14, 90.1 (v) 91.25
medicine ball 725.7
medicine man 690.7
medicines 91.1
medicine wolf 311.19
medico 90.4
medico-legal medicine 673.7
medicopsychology 92.4
medieval 842.13
medievalism 842.4
medievalist 842.5
medieval literature 547.12, 718.1
medieval mode 709.10
mediocre 246.3, 250.7, 414.15, 819.4, 869.9, 1003.4, 1005.7
mediocreness 1005.1
mediocritization 246.1
mediocritize 246.2
mediocrity 246.1, 250.3, 414.1, 414.7, 869.2, 998.7, 1003.1, 1005.1, 1005.5
medio-passive 530.14
meditate 380.5, 931.12, 931.17, 1053.6
meditated 380.8, 935.21
meditate over 931.13
meditate upon 931.13
meditating 931.21, 983.17
meditation 92.6, 92.19, 329.1, 691.3, 696.4, 931.2, 931.6, 933.1, 983.3
meditation retreat 228.27
meditative 329.6, 931.21, 983.17, 985.11
mediterranean 207.7, 819.4
Mediterranean subrace 312.2
medium (n) 35.8, 196.5, 209.4, 213.4, 246.1, 384.4, 466.3, 467.3, 554.4, 576.4, 689.13, 704.18, 712.18, 726.1, 763.2, 1053.4 (a) 11.8, 213.10, 246.3, 819.4, 1005.7
medium business 731.1
medium frequency 1034.12
mediumism 689.5
mediumistic 689.24
medium of exchange 728.1
medium of transportation 179.1
medium-rare 11.8
medium shot 714.8
medium wave 1034.11
medius 73.5
medley (n) 708.33, 770.13, 797.6 (a) 35.16, 47.9, 797.14
medley of colors 47.1
medulla 208.2
medullary 1047.11
medullary sheath 2.14
Medusa 690.9
meed 338.1, 477.5, 624.3
meed of praise 509.5
meek 134.10, 137.11, 139.9, 433.15, 464.10
meekhearted 137.11
meek-minded 137.11
meekness 134.2, 137.1, 139.1, 433.5, 464.4
meek soul 16.6
meek-spirited 137.11
meep (n) 53.5 (a) 58.13
meerschaum 89.6
meet (n) 457.3, 582.8, 743.9, 755.2, 770.2 (v) 169.2, 216.8, 223.11, 332.9, 434.2, 451.5, 457.18, 492.10, 770.16, 770.17, 800.11, 831.8, 867.3, 902.13, 991.4 (a) 167.5, 496.9, 579.5, 649.7, 843.9, 995.5
meet a bet 759.25
meet adversity 1011.9
meet and right 649.7
meet an obligation 641.11
meet around the conference table 541.10
meet boldly 492.10
meet-cute 1035.2
meet eyeball to eyeball 216.8, 223.11
meet face to face 216.8
meet God 692.7
meet halfway 465.10, 466.6, 468.2
meet head-on 215.4, 223.11, 451.5, 453.3, 492.10, 900.6
meeting (n) 169.1, 223.4, 457.3, 541.5, 582.8, 582.9, 696.8, 770.2, 800.1, 902.3 (a) 169.3, 223.17, 770.21, 800.16, 899.4
meeting ground 467.3
meeting halfway 468.1
meetinghouse 197.4, 703.1
meeting of minds 332.5, 788.3
meeting of the minds 455.1, 899.1
meeting place 228.27, 582.9, 800.1
meeting point 169.1, 800.1
meeting room 197.4
meeting up 223.4
meetness 496.2, 649.1, 843.1
meet one at every turn 221.7, 993.8
meet one-on-one 216.8
meet one's commitments 624.13
meet one's death 307.18
meet one's end 307.18
meet one's fate 307.18
meet one's Maker 307.20
meet one's obligations 624.13
meet one's Waterloo 412.12
meet one's wishes 95.6
meet requirements 942.10, 991.4
meet squarely 216.8
meet the expense of 626.7
meet the eye 31.4, 983.11
meet the gaze 31.4
meet the needs of 107.6
meet the requirements 405.15
meet tye eye 33.8
meet up 223.11, 800.11
meet-up 169.1
meet up with 223.11, 831.8, 941.3
meet with 223.11, 831.8, 941.3
meet with a loss 473.4
meet with approval 509.15
meet with attention 983.11
meet with foul play 308.21
meet with success 409.7
meg 728.8
mega 257.20, 997.17
mega- 997.9
megabit 1042.14
megabucks 618.3
megabyte 1042.14, 1042.18
megacosm 1073.1
megacurie 1037.6
megacycles 1034.12
megadeath 307.5, 459.1
megadebt 623.1
megadose 86.6
Megaera 152.10, 680.10
megaflop 410.2
megagamete 305.10
megahertz 1034.12
megalith 549.12
megalomania 140.4, 926.12
megalomaniac 926.17
megalopolis 230.1
megamall 739.1
megamillionaire 618.7
meganucleus 305.7
megaphone 48.8
megasporangium 305.13
megaspore 305.13
megasporophyll 310.28
megastar 409.6, 662.9, 707.6, 997.8
megastore 385.6, 386.6, 736.1
me generation 651.1
me generation, the 838.1
megrim 26.5, 364.1
megrims 85.41, 112.6
Meilewagon 1074.10
meiosis 305.16
melancholia 92.14, 96.6, 112.5, 926.5
melancholia attonita 926.5
melancholiac 112.13
melancholia hypochrondriaca 926.5
melancholia religiosa 926.5
melancholic (n) 92.12, 112.13, 926.15 (a) 112.23, 118.11
melancholiness 112.5
melancholy (n) 96.6, 110.8, 112.5, 118.3, 931.3 (a) 110.24, 112.23, 118.11
Melanesian race 312.2
mélange 797.6
melanian 38.10
melanic 38.10
melanin 38.6
melanism 38.1, 38.5
melanistic 38.10
melanization 38.5
melanize 38.7
melanochroi 312.2
melanoma 85.35
melanosis 38.5
melanotic 38.10
melanous 38.10
melba toast 10.30
Melchior 921.5
Melchizedek priesthood 699.10
meld (n) 797.5, 805.1 (v) 778.5, 797.10, 805.3
melding 778.2, 805.1
meld into 805.3
melee 457.5, 810.4
melic 708.48
meliorate 392.7, 392.9, 852.6, 852.7
melioration 392.1, 852.1
meliorative 392.15
meliorism 392.5
meliorist 392.6
melioristic 392.16
melisma 708.27
melliferous 66.5
mellifluence 708.2
mellifluent 66.5, 708.48
mellifluous 66.5, 97.6, 708.48
mellifluousness 97.1, 708.2
mellisonant 708.48
mellophone 711.11
Mellotron 711.1
mellow (v) 303.9, 407.8, 861.5, 1047.6, 1047.7 (a) 35.22, 54.10, 88.31, 97.6, 303.13, 407.13, 708.48, 1047.8
mellowed 303.13
mellowing 303.6, 1047.5
mellowness 54.1, 97.1, 1047.1
mellow out 20.7
mellow wisdom 920.5
mellowy 1047.8
mellow yellows 87.10
melodic 708.48
melodic interval 709.20
melodic line 708.4
melodic minor 709.6
melodics 709.1
melodious 708.48
melodiousness 708.2
melodist 710.13, 710.20
melodize 708.35, 708.46
melodizer 710.20
melodrama 93.9, 704.5
melodramatic 93.19, 105.32, 355.4, 704.33
melodramatics 93.9, 704.2
melodramatist 704.22
melodramatize 704.28
melody 708.2, 708.4
melody part 708.22
melon 310.4, 609.36, 738.7
Melpomene 704.5, 986.2
melt (n) 1023.8 (v) 34.2, 93.14, 145.4, 145.5, 828.6, 1020.21, 1064.5

meltability 1064.2
meltable 1020.31, 1064.9
melt away 34.2, 252.6, 762.6
melt down 192.16, 671.14, 1020.21, 1064.5
meltdown 395.4, 671.5, 671.6, 1011.2
melted 113.9, 1020.31, 1064.6
meltemi 318.8
melting (n) 34.1, 1020.3, 1064.1 (a) 34.3, 104.26, 145.7, 1064.7
melting mood 115.2
meltingness 104.2
melting point 1019.3, 1019.11
melting pot 797.1, 797.9, 858.10
melting pot, the 232.3
melt in one's mouth 63.4
melt in tears 115.12
melt in the air 52.9
melt into one 805.3
melt like snow 828.6
melt the heart 93.14, 145.5
meltwater 1023.8, 1065.3
member 2.7, 617.11, 793.4
member in good standing 617.11
member of academy 571.1
member of a learned profession 726.4
Member of Congress 610.3
Member of Parliament 610.3
member of the bar 597.1
member of the clergy 726.4
member of the entitlement generation 651.3
member of the human family 312.5
member of the human race 312.5
member of the intelligentsia 929.1
member of the laity 726.5
member of the me generation 651.3
member of the middle class 607.6
member of the upper class 607.4
member of the working class 726.2
members 617.12
membership 582.6, 617.12, 772.1
members in Christ 687.3
members of the bar 597.4
membrana 2.6
membrana propria 2.6
membrana serosa 2.6
membrana tympana 2.6
membrane 2.6, 296.2
membraneous labyrinth 2.10
membranous 2.27
meme 1042.18, 1042.19
memento 549.12, 989.6
memento mori 307.2, 989.6
Memento of the Dead 309.4
memo 549.4
memo book 549.11
memoir 549.4, 556.1, 719.1, 989.3
memoirs 719.1, 989.6
memorabilia 549.2, 719.1, 989.6, 997.5
memorability 989.7, 997.2
memorable 989.24, 997.19
memorandum 549.4, 989.5
memorandum book 549.11
memorial (n) 549.1, 549.4, 549.12, 719.1, 989.6 (a) 309.22, 487.3, 989.26
memorial arch 549.12
memorial column 549.12
memorialist 719.3
memorialization 487.1
memorialize 440.10, 487.2
memorial park 309.15
memorial record 549.12
memorials 719.1, 989.6
memorial service 309.4
memorial statue 549.12
memorial stone 549.12
memorial tablet 549.12
memoried 989.21
memories 989.6
memorization 570.1, 989.3
memorize 570.8, 704.32, 989.16
memorizing 989.3
memory 92.29, 487.1, 549.10, 662.7, 837.4, 989.1, 1042.7
memory bank 1042.7
memory book 549.11
memory card 1042.7
memory chip 1042.7
memory culture 373.2
memory gap 990.2
memory lapse 990.1
memoryless 990.9
memorylessness 990.1
memory like a sieve 990.1
memory loss 990.2
memory obstruction 990.3
memory span 989.2
memory stick 1042.7
memory trace 92.29, 932.1, 989.1
memory training 989.8
Memphis dominoes 759.8
men 18.9, 76.3, 577.11
menace (n) 514.1, 1006.1 (v) 133.10, 514.2, 840.2, 1000.6
menace to health 82.1
menacing 133.16, 514.3, 840.3, 1006.9
ménage 228.2, 559.5, 573.6
menage a trois 876.1
menagerie 228.19, 770.11
mend (n) 392.1 (v) 83.7, 392.7, 392.9, 396.14, 741.4
mendable 396.25
mendacious 354.34
mendaciousness 354.8, 645.3
mendacity 354.8, 354.11, 645.3
Mendelianism 560.6
Mendelism 560.6
Mendel's law 560.6
mender 396.10
mend fences 894.12
mendicancy 440.6, 619.2
mendicant (n) 331.11, 440.8, 667.2, 699.16 (a) 440.16, 619.8, 667.4
mendicant friar 440.8
mendicantism 667.1
mendicant order 440.8
mendicity 440.6
mending (n) 392.1, 396.6, 741.1 (a) 392.15
mend one's fences 609.38
mend one's manners 504.10
mend one's ways 392.9, 858.12
menfolk 76.3
menfolks 76.3
menhir 309.16, 517.10, 549.12
menial (n) 577.2, 726.2 (a) 138.13, 577.14
menialness 138.1
Ménière's disease 85.15
Ménière's syndrome 85.15
meninges 2.6
meningitis 85.25
meninx 2.6
Menippean satire 489.1
menisciform 279.11
meniscoid 279.11, 283.15
meniscoidal 279.11
meniscus 279.5
menopausal 303.14, 891.4
menopause 303.4, 303.7
menorah 696.10
mensal (n) 703.12 (a) 8.31, 11.6
mensch 659.1
men's chorus 710.16
men's clothing 5.1
men's course 753.1
menses 12.9
men's lib 431.1
men's marker 751.1
men's room 12.10
menstrual 12.24, 850.8
menstrual discharge 12.9
menstrual epact 832.5
menstruate 12.18
menstruating 12.24
menstruation 12.9
menstruum 1064.4
mensurability 300.7
mensurable 300.14, 1017.25
mensural 300.12
mensurate 300.10
mensuration 300.1, 300.8
mensurational 300.12
mensurative 300.12
men's wear 735.3
menswear 5.1
mental (n) 926.17 (a) 919.7, 926.27, 931.21, 978.7
mental ability 920.2
mental abuse 144.11
mental acquisitiveness 981.1
mental act 931.1
mental age 920.1
mental alertness 920.2
mental arithmetic 1017.10
mental attitude 978.1
mental balance 925.1
mental blankness 933.1
mental blindness 30.1
mental block 933.1, 990.3
mental body 689.17
mental breakdown 92.14
mental capability 920.2
mental capacity 919.1, 920.1
mental case 926.15, 926.17
mental climate 978.5
mental composure 106.2
mental cruelty 144.11
mental cultivation 570.1
mental culture 570.1
mental defective 924.8, 926.15
mental defectiveness 922.9
mental deficiency 922.9, 926.1
mental derangement 926.1
mental disease 926.1
mental disorder 92.14, 926.1
mental dissociation 92.20, 926.4
mental disturbance 926.1
mental effort 931.1
mental equilibrium 925.1
mental exercise 931.1
mental faculty 919.1
mental fatigue 21.1
mental genius 413.12
mental giant 413.12
mental grasp 920.1, 928.3
mental handicap 922.9
mental health 83.1, 925.1
mental health day 222.4, 857.3
mental home 926.14
mental hospital 926.14
mental hygiene 81.2, 925.1
mental illness 92.14, 926.1
mental image 932.1, 986.6
mental impression 932.1
mental instability 926.1
mental institution 926.14
mentalist 689.15
mentality 919.1, 920.1, 920.9
mental labor 570.3, 931.1
mental lapse 922.9
mental linking 92.33
mentally blind 30.9
mentally challenged 922.22
mentally defective 922.22
mentally deficient 922.22, 926.26
mentally handicapped 922.22
mentally ill 926.28
mentally retarded 922.22
mentally sick 926.28
mentally sound 925.4
mental object 932.1
mental outlook 27.7, 978.2
mental philosophy 92.1
mental picture 932.1, 986.6
mental poise 925.1
mental presentation 986.6
mental process 931.1
mental processes 92.1
mental ratio 920.1
mental representation 986.6
mental reservation 127.4, 959.1
mental retardation 922.9
mental set 978.3
mental shock 92.17
mental sickness 926.1
mental state 978.4
mental states 92.1
mental strain 21.1, 128.3
mental telepathist 689.15
mental telepathy 689.9
mental test 92.8, 92.9
mental void 922.6
mental weakness 922.1
mentation 931.1
menticide 858.5
mention (n) 524.3, 551.1, 646.4 (v) 524.24, 865.11, 983.10

mention confidentially 551.11
mention in passing 983.10
mention privately 345.9, 551.11
mention to 551.8
Mentor 921.2
mentor (n) 405.5, 413.11, 422.3, 571.1, 921.1 (v) 568.11
mentorship 422.1
menu 8.5, 8.14, 871.2, 871.5, 965.3, 1042.18
menuboard 8.14
menue viande 10.13
meow 60.2
meperidine 86.12
Mephisto 680.4
Mephistopheles 680.4
Mephistophelian 654.13
mephitic 71.5, 80.23, 82.7, 98.18, 1000.12, 1067.9
mephitis 71.1, 1001.4, 1067.1
meprobamate 86.12
merbromin 86.21
mercantile 730.12, 731.22
mercantile business 731.1
mercantile marine 180.10, 461.27
mercantilism 731.13
mercantilistic 731.22
Mercator projection 159.5
Mercator sailing 182.2
Mercedes-Benz 249.4
mercenary (n) 461.17, 577.3 (a) 100.27, 458.20, 615.20, 645.23
mercer 5.33
merchandisability 734.7
merchandisable 734.14
merchandise (n) 385.2, 735.1 (v) 731.16, 731.17, 734.8
merchandiser 730.2
merchandising (n) 731.2, 734.2 (a) 734.13
merchant (n) 385.6, 730.2 (a) 731.22
merchantable 734.14
merchant flag 647.7
merchant fleet 180.10, 461.27
merchantman 180.1
Merchant Marine 461.21
merchant marine 180.10
merchant marine 461.27
merchant navy 180.10, 461.27
merchantry 730.11, 731.1
merchant ship 180.1
merciful 143.13, 145.7, 427.7, 677.17
mercifulness 145.2, 427.1
merciless 146.3, 671.21
mercilessness 146.1, 671.1
mercurial 174.15, 330.17, 362.9, 364.6, 782.3, 854.7, 985.17, 1058.17
mercuriality 362.1, 364.3, 782.1, 854.2, 985.5
mercurial mind 920.2
mercurialness 364.3
Mercurochrome 86.21
mercurous 1058.17
Mercury 1073.9
Mercury 353.1
mercury 174.6
mercury 574.7, 854.4, 1019.20
mercury barometer 317.8
mercury bath 79.9
mercury fulminate 462.15
mercury-vapor light 1025.19
mercy 143.1, 143.7, 145.1, 427.1, 465.2
mercy flight 184.9
mercy killer 308.11
mercy killing 308.1
mercy seat 595.5
mere (n) 241.1, 243.1 (a) 248.8, 798.6
mere breath 764.3
mere caricature 787.1
mere chance 768.2
mere child 416.3, 657.4
mere child's play 1014.3
mere cosmetics 376.1
mere counterfeit 787.1
mere existence 761.6
mere externals 33.2
mere facade 500.1
mere farce 489.1
mere few 885.2
mere hint 784.4
merely adequate 246.3
merely cosmetic 206.7, 276.5, 992.9
merely exist 761.10
merely glimpsed 32.6
merely nominal 762.9
merely reactive 903.9
merely surface 276.5
merely symptomatic 992.9
merely theoretical 951.13
mere matter 1055.1
mere noise 61.2, 520.1
mere nothing, a 998.6
mere nothing 248.5
mere notion 951.5
mere occasion 376.1
mereology 935.2
mere rhetoric 545.1, 936.3
mere scratch 276.1
mere shadow 270.7, 764.3, 784.4, 1027.3
mere show 500.1
mere skin and bones 270.17
mere subsistence 992.5
mere suggestion 551.4
mere talk 540.3
mere technicality 998.6
mere theory 951.1
mere things 471.2
meretricious 354.27, 497.11, 501.20, 545.8, 665.28, 998.21
meretriciousness 33.2, 354.3, 497.2, 501.3, 545.1, 998.2
mere trickle, a 992.9
meretrix 665.16
mere tropism 761.6
mere twist of the wrist 1014.3
mere wreck 393.8
merge 169.2, 367.7, 450.3, 770.16, 778.5, 797.10, 800.5, 800.11, 805.3
merged 800.13, 805.5
merge in 796.3
merge into 805.3, 858.17
merger 169.1, 450.2, 778.2, 797.1, 800.1, 805.1
merging (n) 800.1 (a) 169.3, 805.7
meridian (n) 159.5, 198.2, 231.3, 314.4, 1073.16 (a) 198.11, 314.6
meridian devil 314.4
meridian of life 303.4
meridiem 314.4
meridional 161.14, 198.11
meringue 10.40, 320.2
meringue pie 10.41
merit (n) 997.1, 999.1 (v) 639.5
merited 639.9, 649.7
meritedness 639.1
meriting 639.10
meritless 998.22
meritlessness 998.2
meritocracy 572.8, 612.4
meritorious 509.20, 639.10, 662.15
meritoriousness 509.7
merits 639.3
merkin 3.14
Merlin 690.6
merlon 289.3
mermaid 182.12, 240.3, 678.10
merman 182.12, 240.3, 678.10
merocrine 13.8
merogenesis 78.6
merogenetic 78.16
merriment 109.5, 116.1, 489.4, 582.3, 743.3
merriness 109.5
merry 88.31, 109.15, 743.28
merry-andrew 707.10
merry as a cricket 109.15
merry as the day is long 109.15
merry chase 410.5
merry dancers 1025.16
merry-go-round 743.7, 743.15, 915.4
merrymaker 743.18
merrymaking (n) 95.3, 582.3, 743.3 (a) 743.28
merrythought 691.6
merry widow 566.4
mesa 236.1, 237.1, 237.3, 272.4
mésalliance 563.1
mesc 87.13
mesdames 77.8
meserole 87.11
mesh (n) 170.3, 777.3, 799.2, 1042.16 (v) 170.7, 356.20, 480.17, 777.6, 800.6
meshed 170.11
meshes 170.3, 356.13
meshing (n) 777.3 (a) 788.10
meshuga 926.27
meshugana 926.16
meshugga 926.27
meshuggenah 870.4
meshwork 170.3
meshy 170.11
mesial 246.3, 819.4
mesilla 236.1
Mesmer 22.9
mesmeric 22.24, 377.8, 983.20
mesmeric sleep 22.7
mesmerism 22.8
mesmerist 22.9
mesmerization 22.8
mesmerize 22.20, 377.7, 691.7, 894.11, 983.13
mesmerized 122.9, 691.12, 983.18
mesmerizer 22.9, 357.1
mesmerizing 983.20
mesne (n) 470.2 (a) 213.10, 466.8
mesne lord 470.2
mesoderm 2.4, 305.4
mesogaster 2.18
mesometeorology 317.5
mesomitosis 305.16
mesomorph 92.12
mesomorphism 92.11
mesomorphy 92.11
meson 258.8, 1037.4
mesothorium 1037.5
mesotron 1037.4
mess (n) 8.5, 10.6, 80.7, 197.11, 244.2, 247.4, 263.1, 410.6, 414.5, 477.5, 770.7, 797.6, 799.2, 810.3, 985.3, 1013.5, 1015.4 (v) 8.18, 80.17, 811.2
mess about with 340.9
message 343.1, 352.6, 551.1, 552.4, 553.2, 1034.20
message-bearer 353.1
message board 1042.18
message center 353.1
message from the sponsor 352.6
messagerie 347.13
message service 353.1
messaging 347.4
Messalina 665.15
mess around 998.15
mess around with 214.7, 340.9
messed up 393.29, 799.4, 810.14
messed-up 414.22
messenger (n) 133.4, 353.1, 551.5, 553.7, 576.2, 576.5, 577.3, 816.1 (v) 176.15
messenger boy 353.4
messenger of doom 399.4
messenger of God 679.1
messenger RNA 305.9
mess hall 8.17, 197.11
Messiah 677.10
messiah 574.6
messianic 677.16
Messier catalog 1073.8
messieurs 76.7
messiness 80.1, 263.1, 340.3, 810.6
messing 8.1
messing around 998.9
messmate 588.3
messroom 197.11
Messrs 76.7
mess sergeant 575.18
mess steward 183.6
messuage 471.6
mess up 80.17, 263.3, 393.11, 414.12, 799.3, 811.2
mess with 214.7
messy 80.22, 340.12, 810.15
mestee 797.8
mestiza 797.8
mestizo 797.8
metabolic 2.31, 262.10, 852.12
metabolic disease 85.22
metabolic process 2.20, 7.12
metabolic rate 2.20
metabolism 2.20, 7.12, 852.3
metabolize 7.18, 852.8
metachronism 833.1

metachronistic 833.3
metacriticism 723.1
metadataknowledge 551.1
metagalactic space 1073.3
metagalaxy 1073.1
metage 300.1
metagenesis 78.6, 852.3
metagenetic 78.16
metagram 489.8
metal (n) 647.2, 1058.3, 1060.2 (a) 1058.16
metalanguage 523.13
metalbearing 1058.16
metalcraft 712.2
metal foil 1058.3
metalinguistic 523.19
metal leaf 1058.3
metalleity 1058.3
metallic (n) 1058.3 (a) 58.15, 1058.16
metallic conduction 1032.14
metallic element 1058.3
metallicity 1058.3
metalliferous 1058.16
metalliform 1058.16
metal-like 1058.17
metallike 1058.16
metalline 1058.16
metallograph 714.3
metallography 1058.11
metalloid (n) 1058.3, 1060.2 (a) 1058.16
metalloidal 1058.16
metallo-organic 1058.16
metallorganic 1058.16
metallurgical 1058.18
metallurgical chemistry 1058.11
metallurgical engineer 1043.2, 1058.12
metallurgical engineering 1058.11
metallurgist 1058.12
metallurgy 1058.11
metalware 735.4, 1058.3
metalwork 712.16, 1058.3
metalworker 726.8
metalworks 739.4
metamathematics 1017.1
metamer 35.7
metameric 1060.9
metamerize 1060.8
metamerous 1060.9
metamitosis 305.16
metamorphic 783.3, 852.12, 854.6
metamorphic rock 1059.1
metamorphism 852.3
metamorphose 852.8, 854.5, 858.11
metamorphosed 852.10
metamorphosis 852.3, 858.1, 1059.8
metanoia 685.4
metaphase 305.16
metaphor 784.1, 862.2, 943.1
metaphoric 519.10
metaphorical 517.23, 518.10, 519.10, 536.3
metaphorical meaning 518.1
metaphorical sense 519.2
metaphorize 536.2, 943.4
metaphrase 341.3
metaphrast 341.7
metaphrastic 341.16
metaphysic 689.23
metaphysical 689.23, 720.16, 1053.7
metaphysical idealism 1053.3
metaphysician 689.12, 921.1, 952.8
metaphysicist 689.12
metaphysics 689.3, 761.7
metaplasm 305.6
metapsychics 689.4
metapsychism 689.4
metapsychist 689.12
metapsychology 689.4
metapsychosis 689.8
metasomatism 852.3
metasomatosis 852.3
metastasis 205.3, 852.3
metastasized 852.10
metastatic 176.18, 852.12
metastatical 176.18
metastatic tumor 85.39
metathesis 205.3, 852.3
metathesize 176.10
metathetic 176.18
metathetical 176.18
mete (n) 211.3 (v) 300.10, 477.8, 478.12
metempsychosis 1052.8
metempsychosis avatar 852.3
meteor 828.5, 1073.15
meteor crater 1073.15
Meteor Deep 275.5
meteor dust 1073.15
meteor dust impacts 1075.10
meteoric 251.8, 828.8, 1025.34, 1073.25
meteoric particles 1075.10
meteoric shower 1073.15
meteoric success 409.3
meteorite 1073.15
meteorite crater 237.7
meteorites 1075.10
meteoritic 1073.25
meteoritic crater 237.7
meteoritics 1073.19
meteoroid 1073.15
meteorolite 1073.15
meteorologic 317.13
meteorological 317.13
meteorological instrument 317.8
meteorological satellite 1075.6
meteorological tower 1074.7
meteorologist 185.4, 317.6, 1071.2
meteorology 317.5, 1071.1
meteors 1075.10
meteor shower 1073.15
meteor swarm 1073.15
meteor trail 1073.15
meteor train 1073.15
mete out 244.4, 477.8, 478.12, 643.6
meter (n) 300.2, 300.9, 709.22, 720.6, 720.7, 850.2, 1032.21 (v) 300.10
meterable 300.14
metered 300.13
metered mail 553.4
meter maid 1008.15
meter-reading 300.2
metes 211.1
metes and bounds 211.1
meth 87.4
meth addiction 87.1
methamphetamine 86.9, 87.4
methamphetamine hydrochloride 86.9
methanol 756.1
methedrine user 87.21
methhead 87.21
• **method** 321.1, 381.1, 381.5, 384.1, 413.7, 807.3
Method acting 704.8
Method actor 707.2
methodical 580.10, 781.5, 807.6, 850.6
methodicalness 807.3, 850.1
method in one's madness 415.3
methodization 808.2
methodize 381.8, 808.10
methodized 381.12, 808.14
methodologist 867.2
methodology 321.1, 381.1, 384.1, 807.3
methods 321.1
methol 89.5
Methuselah 304.2, 842.8
metic 227.4
meticulous 339.12, 425.6, 434.4, 495.9, 580.10, 644.15, 766.9, 973.16, 983.15
meticulous attention 983.4
meticulousness 339.3, 425.1, 495.1, 644.2, 973.5
métier 413.4, 724.6, 865.4, 866.1, 928.1
me time 584.3, 1009.5
meting out 643.2
métis 797.8
métisse 797.8
metonym 526.1
metonymy 862.2
me-too 336.9
me-tooer 336.4
me-tooism 332.2, 336.1, 578.5, 899.1
metoposcopist 198.9
metoposcopy 198.9, 341.8
metric 300.12, 709.28, 720.17
metrical 300.12, 709.28, 720.17
metrical accent 720.7
metrical foot 720.7
metrical form 720.6
metrical group 720.7
metrical pattern 720.6
metrical unit 720.7
metrication 300.1
metrics 524.10, 709.22, 720.6
metric system 300.1
metrist 720.13
metrize 300.10
metro (n) 230.1 (a) 230.11
métro 179.14
metrology 300.8
metron 720.7
metronome 711.22, 916.9
metronome mark 709.12
metronomic 832.15, 850.7
metronomical 832.15
metronomic mark 709.12
metropolis 208.7, 230.1, 231.5
metropolitan (n) 227.6 (a) 230.11
metropolitan area 230.1, 231.5
metropolitanate 417.7
metropolitanship 417.7
metrosexual 75.14
metta 143.1
mettle 17.4, 359.3, 492.5, 978.3
mettlesome 17.13, 105.28, 359.14, 492.17
mettlesomeness 359.3, 492.5
mew (n) 228.26, 1009.5 (v) 60.2, 212.5, 429.12
mewed 212.10
mewl 60.2
mewling infant 302.9
mews 228.20
mew up 212.5, 429.12
Mexican standoff 779.1, 790.3, 857.2
mezuzah 696.10
mezzanine 197.23, 704.15
mezzanine floor 197.23
mezzo 819.4
mezzolith 842.6
mezzolithic 842.20
mezzo-rilievo 715.3
mezzo-soprano (n) 58.6, 709.5 (a) 58.13
mezzo staccato 708.30
mezzotint (n) 35.7 (a) 713.12
mho 1032.14
miaow 60.2
miasma 71.1, 1001.4, 1067.1
miasmal 71.5, 82.7, 98.18, 1067.9
miasmatic 82.7, 1067.9
miasmic 71.5, 82.7, 98.18, 1067.9
micaceous 1058.15
Micah 684.1
Micawber 340.5
Micawberish 846.17
Micawberism 846.5
Michael 679.4
Mickey 25.3, 87.6, 88.9
Mickey Finn 25.3, 87.6, 88.9
Mickey Mouse (n) 498.3, 998.4 (a) 248.6, 497.10, 998.18, 998.21, 1005.9, 1014.13
micro 258.12
microaggression 330.7
microanalysis 801.1
microbe 85.42, 258.7, 305.2
microbial 258.15
microbial degradation 1072.2
microbic 258.15
microbicide 86.21, 1001.3
microbiological 1068.4
microbiology 1068.3
microbody 305.5
microbrew 88.16
microburst 318.1
microcard 549.10
microcentrum 305.5
microchemical 1060.9
microchip 258.7, 1033.8, 1042.3
microcircuit 1033.8
microclimate 317.3
microclimatic 317.13
microclimatologic 317.13

microclimatologist 317.6
microclimatology 317.5
microcomputer 1042.2
micro-cook 11.5
microcopy (n) 714.5, 785.4 (v) 785.8
microcosm 258.6
microcosmic 258.14
microcosmical 258.14
microcosmos 258.6
microcurie 1037.6
microdose 86.6
microdot 549.10
microecology 1072.1
microeconomics 731.7
microelectronic 1033.15
microelectronics 1033.1
microelectronics device 1042.2
microelement 1060.2
microevolution 861.3
microfiche 549.10, 714.5, 785.4
microfilm (n) 549.10, 714.5, 714.10 (v) 714.14, 785.8
microfloppy 1042.6
microform 785.4
microgamete 305.10
micrography 258.1, 547.1
microgroove 290.1
microhabitat 228.18
micro-instrumentation 1075.7
microlith 842.6
micrometeorite 1073.15
micrometeoroid 1073.15
micrometeorology 317.5
micrometrically precise 973.17
microminiaturization 258.1
micromorph 258.5
micronization 1051.4
micronize 1051.9
micronucleus 305.7
micronutrient 7.11, 1060.2
microorganic 258.15
microorganism 85.42, 258.7, 305.2
micropetrography 1058.10
microphone 50.9, 1034.4
microphonic 50.16
microphotocopy 714.5
microphotograph 714.3
micropig 311.9
micropolitan 227.6
microprint 714.5
microprocessor 1042.2
microradiograph 714.3
microscope 29.1
microscopic 29.10, 258.14, 973.17
microscopical distinctness 31.2, 348.3, 521.2
microscopically distinct 521.11
microscopic distinction 944.3
microscopics 29.7
microscopic scrutiny 983.4
microscopist 29.8
microscopy 29.7, 258.1
microsecond 824.2, 830.3
Microsoft disk operating system 1042.12
microsporangium 305.13
microspore 305.13
microsporophyll 310.28
microstate 232.1
microtelephonic 347.21
microtome 802.7
microvolume 258.6
microwave (n) 1032.10, 1034.11 (v) 11.5
microwave diathermy 91.5
microwave link 1035.9
microwave relay station 1034.6
microwaving 11.2
microzoan 258.15
microzoic 258.15
micrypyle 310.28
micturition 12.5
mid 524.30, 819.4
mid-air 272.15
mid-air collision 184.20
Midas 618.8
Midas touch 618.5, 1010.3
midcareer 162.1, 172.2
midchannel 238.1
midcourse (n) 162.1, 819.2 (a) 819.4
midcourt 747.1, 748.1
midday (n) 314.4, 819.1 (a) 314.6
midday sun 1019.7, 1025.10
midden 80.10, 370.4, 391.6
mid-distance 819.2
middle (n) 208.2, 246.1, 530.14, 819.1 (v) 208.9, 819.3 (a) 208.11, 213.10, 466.8, 819.4
middle age 303.1, 303.4
middle-aged 303.14, 304.7
Middle Ages 824.5
middle-age spread 257.8
Middle America 207.3, 231.7, 606.1, 607.5, 1005.5
Middle American (n) 867.2 (a) 207.7
Middle Atlantic 231.7
middlebrow 930.7
middle class 607.5, 1005.5
middle-class 607.10, 1005.8
middle class, the 606.1
middle-class type 867.2
middle course 246.1, 467.3
middle distance 223.2, 819.2
middle-distance running 755.2
middle ear 2.10
Middle Earth 986.10, 986.11
Middle East 231.6
middle echelon 246.1
middle-echelon 246.3
middle finger 73.5
middle ground 246.1, 467.3, 468.1, 819.2
middle-ground 246.3
middle-income group 607.5
middle latitude sailing 182.2
middle level 246.1
middle life 303.4
middleman 213.4, 385.6, 466.3, 576.4, 730.2
middle management 574.11
middle marker 751.1
middlemost 208.11, 819.4
middle name 527.3, 527.4
middleness 208.1
middle of nowhere, the 261.4
middle of the road 246.1, 467.3, 611.2, 819.2
middle-of-the-road 246.3, 467.7, 611.18, 819.4
middle-of-the-roader 611.10, 670.4
middle-of-the-roadism 611.2
middle order 607.5
middle path 670.1
middleperson 213.4
middle point 246.1
middle position 208.1, 246.1
middle reliever 745.2
middlescence 303.4
middlescent 303.14
middle school 567.4
middle state 246.1
middle voice 530.14
middle way 467.3, 668.1, 670.1, 819.2
middleweight 297.3
Middle West 231.7
middle years, the 303.4
middling 246.3, 819.4, 1005.7
middlingness 1005.1
middy 183.4
Mideast 231.6
midfield 819.4
midfielder 752.2
midfield stripe 746.1
midge 258.5, 258.7, 311.32
midget (n) 258.5 (a) 258.13
midget-car racing 756.1
midget hockey 749.1
midgut 2.18
MIDI 711.22
Midland 523.7
midland (n) 207.3 (a) 207.7
midland 819.4
Midland dialect 523.7
midlands 207.3
mid-level 246.3
midlife 303.14
midlife crisis 92.15, 303.4, 303.7
midmost (n) 819.1 (a) 208.11, 819.4
midnight (n) 315.6, 819.1 (a) 38.8, 315.9
midnight-blue 45.3
midnight hours 315.6
midnight snack 8.6, 315.6
midnight supper 8.6, 315.6
midoceanic ridge 240.5
midpassage 162.1
midpoint 208.2, 246.1, 819.1
mid position 208.1
Midrash 683.5
midriff 2.18, 213.5, 819.1
mid-season 313.9
midsection 213.5
midsemester 938.2
midshipman 183.4, 572.6
midshipmate 183.4
midships 819.4
midst 819.1
midstream (n) 238.1, 819.2 (a) 819.4
midsummer (n) 313.3, 1019.7 (a) 313.9
midsun 314.4
midterm 938.2
midtown (n) 230.6 (a) 230.11
mid-Victorian (n) 500.11, 842.8 (a) 500.19, 842.13
midway (n) 819.2 (a) 467.7, 819.4
Midwest 231.7
Midwesterner 227.11
midwife 90.8, 384.4
midwinter (n) 313.6 (a) 313.9
mid-year 819.4
midyear 824.2, 938.2
mien 33.3, 33.4, 206.1, 321.1
miff (n) 152.7 (v) 96.13, 152.24
miffed 96.21, 152.27
miffiness 110.3, 110.5
miffy 110.20, 110.21
might 15.1, 18.1, 247.1, 417.2
might and main 18.1, 725.1
might be 966.4
mightiness 15.1, 18.1, 247.1, 417.2
might of arms 458.1
mighty 15.15, 18.12, 247.6, 257.20, 417.15, 662.18
mighty, the 15.6
mighty effort 725.1
mighty in battle 18.12
Mighty Joe Young 87.1
mighty like 784.15
mighty mezz 87.11
migraine 26.5, 85.9, 85.25
migrainous 26.12
migrant 178.5, 190.10, 311.27, 726.2
migrant worker 178.5, 726.2, 1069.5
migrate 177.22
migration 177.4, 188.1
migrational 177.37
migrations 177.2
migrator 178.5
migratory (n) 178.2 (a) 177.37
migratory bird 311.27
migratory laborer 1069.5
migratory worker 178.5, 1069.5
mikado 575.9
mike 50.9
mike fright 127.3, 139.4
milady 77.5, 648.2
milch 1061.5
milcher 311.6
mild 65.2, 97.11, 143.14, 427.7, 433.15, 670.10, 1019.24, 1047.8
mild as milk 670.10
mild as milk and water 670.10
mild as mother's milk 670.10
milden 1047.6
mildew (n) 71.2, 393.6, 1001.2 (v) 393.22
mildewed 71.5, 393.42, 842.14
mildewy 71.5
mildly radical 611.20
mild-mannered 143.14, 427.7, 433.15
mild-manneredness 433.5
mildness 65.1, 143.2, 427.1, 433.5, 670.1
mild radical 611.12
mileage 261.1, 267.1, 387.4, 624.5, 995.1
mile long, a 267.7
mile off, a 787.5
milepost 273.4, 517.4, 517.10
miles away 261.2
miles gloriosus 501.10, 502.5

miles per hour 174.1
milestone 517.10, 997.6
milieu 209.1, 209.3, 231.1, 463.1, 722.4
militance 692.3
militancy 330.1, 458.10
militant (n) 330.8, 461.1, 692.4 (a) 330.17, 458.20, 459.30
militant Muslimism 675.13
militarism 458.10, 609.5, 612.4
militarist 461.5
militaristic 458.21
militarization 458.9
militarize 458.19
militarized 458.22
military 458.20
military, the 461.20
military academy 567.6
military affairs 458.5
military aircraft 181.9
military ally 232.1
military attaché 576.6
military band 458.11
military base 458.4
military bearing 136.2
military burial 309.1
military chaplain 699.2
military court 595.4
Military Cross 646.6
military defense 460.2
military dictatorship 458.9
military duty 458.8
military establishment, the 461.20
military government 612.4
military governor 575.12
military hardware 462.1
military honor 646.6
military-industrial complex 462.1
military intelligence 576.12, 938.9
military-intelligence man 576.9
militaryism 458.10
military issue 385.4
military law 673.5
military leader 575.17
military man 461.6
military march 708.12
military medal 646.6
military music 708.12
military obligation 458.8
military officer 575.17
military operation 458.1
military operations 458.4, 458.5
military orders 458.7
military pilot 185.3
military police 1008.17
military policeman 1008.15
military prison 429.8
military professional 726.4
military rations 515.2
military rocket 1074.3
military science 458.5
military service 458.8
military spirit 492.1
military strategy 458.5
military surplus 256.4
military tactics 458.5
military time 832.3
military title 527.3
military training 461.6, 568.3
military woman 461.6
militate 889.7
militate against 451.4, 900.6
militia 461.24
militiaman 461.6
milium 1004.1
milk (n) 2.24, 10.49, 13.2, 37.2, 1061.2 (v) 192.12, 387.16, 480.21, 480.24, 1070.7 (a) 1061.5
milk a he-goat into a sieve 391.8
milk and honey 1010.1
milk and water 16.7
milk-and-water 16.17, 65.2
milk a scene 704.31
milk bar 8.17
milk chocolate 10.40
milk cow 311.6
milk dry 486.4
milked 704.33
milker 311.6
milkiness 37.1, 1030.2, 1061.1
milking 192.3
milk it 704.31
milk-livered 491.10
milkmaid 1070.2
milk of human kindness 999.9
milk of magnesia 86.17
milk product 10.48
milk run 184.11
milkshake 10.49
milk sickness 85.31
milksop 16.6, 77.10, 491.5, 924.1
milksopism 491.1
milksoppiness 491.1
milksoppish 491.10
milksoppishness 491.1
milksoppy 491.10
milk the ram 391.8
milk-toast 326.5
milktoast 65.2, 433.14
milk tooth 2.8
milk train 179.14
milkwagon 179.2
milk-white 37.7
milky 16.17, 37.7, 1030.4, 1061.5
Milky Way, the 1073.6
mill (n) 728.7, 739.3, 1040.3, 1040.6, 1051.7 (v) 289.4, 770.16, 892.9, 915.12, 1040.13, 1051.9
mill about 915.12
mill around 915.12
milldam 1012.5
milled 892.18, 1051.11
millenarian (n) 124.5 (a) 124.11
millenarianism 124.2
millenary 882.30
millennial (n) 302.1 (a) 882.30, 986.23
millennialism 124.2
millennialist 124.5
millennialistic 124.11
millennials 302.2
millennian 124.5
millennium 824.2, 882.10, 986.11, 1010.4
millennium bug 1042.18
millepede 882.10
millet seed 258.7
milliard 882.12
millicurie 1037.6
milligram 882.10
milliliter 882.10
millimeter 223.2, 882.10
milliner 5.37
millinery 5.25, 5.32
milling (n) 892.2, 1051.4 (a) 770.22
million, a 884.4
million (n) 882.11 (a) 884.6
million, the 606.2
millionaire 618.7
millionairess 618.7
millionfold 884.10
millions 618.2
millionth 882.31
millipede 311.32
millisecond 824.2, 830.3
millpond 241.1
millpool 241.1
millrace 238.4
mill run 238.4
millstone 297.7, 1051.7
millstone around one's neck 96.8, 996.2, 1012.6
millstream 238.1
mill town 739.2
milord 648.2
Milquetoast 16.6
milquetoast (n) 362.5, 433.4, 491.5 (a) 326.5, 433.14
milt 305.11
Milwaukee goiter 2.19
milzbrand 85.41
mime (n) 336.4, 349.4, 707.2 (v) 336.6, 349.12, 517.21, 704.29
mimeo 785.8
mimeograph (n) 548.1 (v) 548.14, 785.8
mimeograph copy 785.5
mimeography 785.2
mimer 336.4, 707.2
mimesis 336.1, 349.4, 704.8
mimetic 336.9, 349.13
mimetism 336.2
mimic (n) 336.4, 707.2 (v) 336.6, 349.12, 517.21, 784.7 (a) 336.9
mimicked 784.10
mimicker 336.4
mimicking 349.4, 704.8, 784.1
mimicry 336.2, 349.4, 704.8
miming 349.4, 704.8
mimish 349.13
mimographer 704.22
mimsy 560.12
minacious 514.3
minaret 272.6
minatory 399.7, 514.3
minauderie 500.2
mince (n) 10.13, 177.12 (v) 177.28, 500.14, 525.7, 600.12, 802.13, 1051.9
mince it 500.14
mincemeat 10.13
mince no words 535.2
mincer 802.7
mince the truth 344.7
mince words 344.7
mincing 500.18
mincing no words 535.1
mincing steps 175.2, 177.12
Mind 677.6
mind (n) 48.1, 92.28, 100.1, 323.1, 380.1 (v) 152.13, 325.3, 326.2, 339.6, 494.7
mind (n) 689.18, 919.1, 919.4, 953.6, 978.3, 978.4, 983.1, 989.1 (v) 983.6, 989.9, 1008.19
mind-altering drug 86.13, 87.3
mind-bending drug 86.13
mind-blind 30.9, 922.14
mind-blindness 30.1
mindblindness 922.2
mind-blowing 105.30, 122.12, 976.10
mind-blowing drug 87.3
mind body 689.17
mind-boggler 522.8, 938.10
mind-boggling 25.9, 122.12, 127.28, 823.3, 955.10
mind cure 92.5
mind deafness 49.1
minded 324.5, 375.30, 978.8
minder 1008.5
mind-expanding 86.46, 976.10
mind-expanding drug 87.3
mind-expansion 976.7
mindful 143.16, 339.10, 434.4, 494.8, 928.15, 983.15, 989.21, 989.23
mindfulness 143.3, 339.1, 494.1, 928.2, 983.1
mindful of 928.16
mindful of others 143.16
mindless 102.7, 144.18, 144.26, 311.39, 497.12, 671.21, 922.13, 923.10, 930.12, 972.16, 982.3
mindless brutality 144.11
mindlessness 102.2, 497.3, 671.1, 922.1, 923.1, 930.2
mindless of 340.11
mind like a blotter 570.5
mind like a sieve 990.1
mind map 349.1
mind-matter theory 952.6
mind-numbing 25.9, 117.6, 122.12, 127.28
mind of one's own, a 359.4
mind of one's own 361.1
mind one's business 339.7, 494.7, 724.10, 983.8
mind one's manners 504.10
mind one's own business 430.16, 982.2
mind one's P's and Q's 321.5, 339.7, 504.10
mind overthrown 926.1
mind pain 26.2
mind reader 689.15
mind reading 689.9
mind's content 931.4
mind's core 919.3, 931.4
mindset 380.1, 765.2, 953.6, 978.3, 978.4
mind's eye 986.1, 989.1
mindsickness 926.1
mind-stuff theory 952.5
mind the store 724.10
mind unhinged 926.1
mind what one is doing 339.7

mine (n) 284.4, 356.12, 386.4, 460.5, 462.20, 618.4, 739.4, 886.6, 1058.6 (v) 192.10, 275.9, 284.15, 393.15, 395.18, 459.24, 460.9, 480.21, 892.9, 1058.14
mined 892.18
mine host 585.5
minelayer 180.6
mine of information 929.3
mine of wealth 618.4
mine out 1058.14
miner 192.9, 284.10, 461.14, 1058.9
mineral (n) 1058.1, 1058.2 (a) 1055.4, 1058.15
mineral aggregate 1058.1
mineral-bearing material 1058.2
mineral deposit 1058.7
mineralization 1058.1
mineralize 1058.13
mineralized 1058.15
mineral kingdom 809.4, 1055.1, 1058.1
mineralogical 1058.18
mineralogical chemistry 1058.10
mineralogist 1058.12
mineralogy 1058.10
mineraloid 1058.1
mineral oil 1056.4
mineral resources 1058.1
mineral spring 91.23
mineral water 10.49, 1065.3
mineral world 1055.1, 1058.1
Minerva 458.12
mine ship 180.6
minestra 10.10
minesweeper 180.6
minethrower 462.21
mineworker 1058.9
minginess 484.2, 651.2
mingle 797.10
mingled 797.14
mingle-mangle (n) 797.6 (v) 797.10
minglement 797.1
mingle waters 238.16
mingle with 582.17
mingling 797.1
mingy 484.8, 651.6
mini (n) 258.4, 258.6 (a) 258.12
miniate 41.4
miniature (n) 258.6, 349.5, 712.10, 712.14 (a) 248.6, 258.12
miniature golf 751.1
miniatureness 258.1
miniaturist 716.4
miniaturization 252.1, 252.5, 258.1, 260.1
miniaturize 258.9, 260.7
miniaturized 252.10, 258.12, 260.12
miniaturized version 258.6
minibike 179.8
mini-black hole 1073.8
miniboom 731.10
mini-break 20.4
minicomputer 1042.2
minié ball 462.19
minification 252.5
minifloppy 1042.6
minify 252.9, 258.9
minikin (n) 998.5 (a) 258.12
minim (n) 248.2, 258.7, 709.14, 709.21 (a) 250.8
minimal 250.8, 258.12, 885.6, 991.6
minimal force 462.22
minimalistic 250.8
minimart 736.1
minimifidian (n) 695.11 (a) 695.19, 955.8
minimifidianism 695.5, 955.1
minimization 252.5, 950.1
minimize 252.9, 258.9, 512.8, 950.2, 998.12
minimized 252.10
minimizing (n) 512.1 (a) 512.13
minimum (n) 248.2, 885.3, 991.1 (a) 250.8, 991.6
minimum flying speed 184.31
minimum free form 526.1
minimum-security detention 429.3
minimum-security facility 429.8
minimum-security imprisonment 429.3
minimum-security prison 429.8
minimum wage 624.4
minimus 73.5
mining 192.1, 275.8, 284.11, 892.2, 1058.8
mining and metallurgy 1043.1
mining claim 1058.8
mining engineer 1043.2, 1058.12
mining engineering 1058.10
mining geology 1058.10
minion 104.15, 138.3, 384.4, 577.1, 616.8
miniseries 706.1, 1035.2
mini specs 29.3
minister (n) 575.16, 576.2, 576.6, 699.2 (v) 701.15
ministerial 384.8, 449.20, 573.14, 576.17, 612.18, 698.13
ministering 384.8, 449.20, 577.14
ministering angel 592.1, 678.12
ministering spirits 679.2
minister of music 710.18
minister of state 575.16
minister of the Gospel 699.2
minister plenipotentiary 576.6
minister resident 576.6
minister to 91.24, 384.7, 449.18, 577.13, 1008.19
ministrant (n) 592.1 (a) 449.20
ministration 449.1, 577.12
ministry 449.1, 575.14, 577.12, 594.4, 613.3, 698.2, 699.1, 1008.2
ministry, the 698.1
minisupercomputer 1042.2
mink farm 1070.5
Minkowski universe 158.6
Minkowski world 158.6
minnesinger 710.14, 720.12
Minnie Mouse launcher 1074.10
minnow 258.4, 311.29
minny 258.4, 311.29
minor (n) 302.1, 568.8, 709.15 (a) 250.6, 301.10, 998.17
minor arts 712.1
minor basilica 703.1
minor chord 709.17
minor criticism 510.4
minor deities, the 678.1
minor detail 766.3
minor details 998.4
minor element 1060.2
minor in 570.15, 866.4
minor interval 709.17, 709.20
minority (n) 19.2, 250.1, 301.3, 312.2, 793.1, 885.3 (a) 885.7
minority, the 885.3
minority government 612.4
minority group 617.4, 885.3
minority interests 609.31
minority leader 610.3
minority opinion 333.1
minority position 333.1
minority prejudice 980.4
minority report 333.1
minority rights 642.3
minority rule 612.4
minority voice 333.3
minor key 709.15
minor league 745.1
minor matter, a 998.6
minor mode 709.10
minor operations 458.4
minor orders 698.10, 699.4
minor party 609.24
minor planet 1073.9
minor poet 720.12
minor premise 935.7
Minor Prophets 683.3, 684.1
minor role 704.10
minors, the 745.1
minor scale 709.6
minor second 709.20
minor suit 758.3
minor surgery 91.19
minor wrong 655.2
Minos 596.4, 649.4, 682.5
minstrel (n) 708.34, 710.13, 710.14, 720.12 (v) 708.38
minstrel show 708.34
mint (n) 247.4, 472.3, 618.3, 739.3, 739.4, 786.6 (v) 262.7, 728.28, 841.5, 892.12 (a) 390.12, 841.9, 1002.8
mintage 728.1, 728.24, 892.1, 893.1
mint condition 83.2, 841.1, 1002.2
minted 262.9, 892.19
minter 728.25
minting 728.24
mint leaves 728.6
mintmaster 728.25
minuend 255.6
minus (n) 255.6, 255.7 (v) 255.10 (a) 473.8, 762.8, 911.5, 1032.35
minus acceleration 175.4
minuscular 258.12, 546.8
minuscule (n) 548.6 (a) 258.12, 546.8
minus sign 255.6
minus some buttons 926.27
minute (n) 628.5, 824.1, 824.2, 830.3, 832.2 (v) 549.15, 628.8 (a) 258.11, 339.12, 766.9, 865.12, 998.17
minute attention 983.4
minuted 549.17
minute hand 517.4
minutemen 461.24
minuteness 248.1, 258.1, 339.3
minuteness of detail 766.4
minutes 549.4, 549.7, 719.2
minute steak 10.18
minutia 258.7, 766.3
minutiae 248.2, 258.7, 766.3, 865.6, 998.4
minuting 549.14
minx 77.6, 142.5, 302.4, 322.3
minyan 696.9, 700.1
miracle 122.2, 870.8
miracle drug 86.4, 86.29
miracle-worker 690.5
miraculous 122.10, 690.14, 870.16
miraculousness 122.3, 870.7
mirage 33.5, 132.1, 356.1, 976.6
mire (n) 80.8, 80.12, 243.1, 1062.8 (v) 80.15, 243.2
mire down 243.2
miriness 80.1, 1062.4
mirish 243.3
mirror (n) 29.6, 229.1, 659.4, 786.1, 786.4, 1002.4 (v) 336.5, 349.11, 784.7, 873.5
mirror image 873.4
mirror-image 264.4
mirror image, the 779.2
mirroring 336.1, 349.5
mirror neurons 93.4
mirror of the mind 989.1
mirror of the soul, the 524.1
mirror system 29.2
mirth 109.5, 743.1
mirthful 109.15
mirthfulness 109.5
mirthless 112.21
mirthlessness 112.2
mirth-loving 109.15
miry 80.22, 243.3, 1062.14
mirza 608.7, 648.3
Mirza Ali Muhammad of Shiraz 684.4
misadminister 414.13
misadministration 414.6
misadventure 1011.2
misadvise 569.3
misadvised 569.5, 923.10
misalliance 563.1, 776.2, 789.3
misallied 789.7
misallocation 477.3
misally 789.5
misandrist (n) 590.2 (a) 590.3
misandry 103.1, 590.1
misanthrope 103.4, 590.2
misanthropic 590.3
misanthropism 103.1, 590.1
misanthropist 103.4, 590.2
misanthropy 103.1, 590.1
misapplicability 776.2
misapplication 342.1, 389.1, 776.2, 936.1, 975.1
misapply 342.2, 389.4, 486.6, 936.8, 975.12
misappreciate 948.2
misappreciation 948.1

misapprehend 342.2, 975.13
misapprehended 342.3
misapprehension 342.1, 975.3
misappropriate 389.4
misappropriation 389.1
misarrange 811.2
misarrangement 811.1
misattributed memory 990.2
misbegot 674.7
misbegotten 265.12, 674.7, 870.13, 1015.8
misbehave 321.4, 322.4, 654.8, 655.4
misbehave oneself 322.4
misbehaving 322.5
misbehavior 321.2, 322.1, 655.1
misbelief 688.2, 955.1, 976.1
misbelieve 688.8, 955.5
misbeliever 688.5
misbelieving 688.10
miscalculate 948.2, 975.9, 975.12
miscalculation 948.1, 975.3
miscall 527.12, 975.12
miscarriage 410.5, 975.3
miscarriage of justice 650.4
miscarried 410.18
miscarry 410.15, 911.4
miscarrying (n) 410.5 (a) 410.18
miscegenate 563.15, 797.13
miscegenation 563.1, 797.4
miscegenetic 563.19
miscellanea 554.7, 557.4, 770.13
miscellaneous 797.14, 945.6
miscellaneous drugs 86.32
miscellany 554.7, 557.4, 770.13, 797.6
mischance 1011.2
mischief 322.2, 322.3, 393.1, 456.1, 996.2, 1000.3
mischief-loving 322.6
mischief-maker 322.3, 375.11, 593.2
mischievous 322.6, 680.18, 1000.12
mischievousness 322.2, 1000.5
miscible 797.16
miscitation 342.1
miscite 342.2, 354.16, 975.12
miscited 975.19
miscolor 350.3, 354.16
miscoloring 350.1, 354.9
miscommunication 344.1
miscomputation 948.1
miscompute 948.2
misconceive 342.2, 975.13
misconceived 342.3
misconception 342.1, 975.3, 976.1
misconduct (n) 322.1, 389.1, 414.6, 655.1 (v) 414.13, 975.12
misconducted 414.21
misconduct oneself 322.4
misconjecture (n) 948.1 (v) 948.2
misconnection 776.2
misconstruction 265.2, 342.1, 354.9, 531.2, 948.1, 975.1
misconstrue 265.6, 342.2, 948.2, 975.10
misconstrued 342.3
miscount (n) 975.3 (v) 975.12
miscreant 144.14, 660.4
miscreated 674.7
miscreation 870.6
miscue (n) 414.5, 975.4 (v) 414.11, 975.13
misdate (n) 833.1 (v) 833.2
misdated 833.3
misdating 833.1
misdeal (n) 975.3 (v) 975.12
misdeed 655.2
misdeem 342.2, 948.2
misdemean 322.4, 654.8
misdemeanant 660.8
misdemeaning 655.1
misdemeanist 660.8
misdemean oneself 322.4, 655.4
misdemeanor 322.1, 655.2, 674.4
misdesignate 527.12
misdiagnosis 91.12
misdirect 265.6, 356.16, 414.13, 569.3
misdirected 414.21, 569.5
misdirecting 569.6
misdirection 265.2, 350.1, 356.2, 414.6, 569.1
misdo 654.8, 655.4, 975.12
misdoing 322.1, 655.1, 975.1
misdoubt (n) 153.2, 955.2 (v) 153.3
misdraw 350.4
misdrawing 350.1
misease (n) 96.1, 98.5 (v) 98.14
miseducate 569.3
miseducative 569.6
mise en place 381.1
mise-en-scène 209.2, 704.13, 704.19, 706.4
misemploy 389.4, 975.12
misemployment 389.1
miser 484.4
miserable 26.10, 96.26, 112.21, 661.12, 998.21, 1011.13
miserable lot 1011.1
miserableness 661.3, 998.2
miserable wretch 660.2
Miserere 696.3
miserliness 484.3, 885.1, 992.2
miserly 100.27, 484.9, 885.5, 992.10
misery 26.1, 96.6, 112.2, 112.10, 115.1
misery in the head 26.5
misesteem 948.2
misestimate 948.2, 950.2
misestimation 948.1, 950.1
misevaluate 948.2
misevaluation 948.1
misexplain 342.2
misexplanation 342.1
misexplicate 342.2
misexplication 342.1
misexposition 342.1
misexpound 342.2
misfeasance 322.1, 389.1, 414.6, 655.1, 655.2, 975.1
misfeasor 593.1, 660.8
misfield 975.12
misfire (n) 410.5, 414.5 (v) 410.13, 911.4
misfit 774.2, 789.4, 868.3
misfiting 789.8
misfortune 1011.2
misfortuned 844.6, 1011.14
misgive 127.10, 955.6
misgiving (n) 113.2, 126.1, 127.4, 128.1, 133.2, 955.2 (a) 126.7, 127.24
misgovern 414.13
misgovernment 414.6
misguidance 350.1, 356.2, 414.6, 569.1
misguide 356.16, 414.13, 569.3
misguided 414.21, 569.5, 923.10
misguiding 569.6
mishandle 389.4, 389.5, 414.13
mishandling 389.1, 414.6
mishap 1011.2
mishegas 926.2
mishit 414.5
mishmash 797.6, 810.3
Mishnah 683.5
Mishnaic 683.12
misidentification 975.3
misidentify 975.13
misinform 350.3, 356.16, 569.3, 936.9
misinformation 350.1, 356.2, 569.1
misinformed 569.5, 930.13
misinforming 569.6
misinstruct 569.3
misinstructed 569.5, 930.13
misinstruction 569.1
misinstructive 569.6
misintelligence 342.1
misinterpret 265.6, 342.2, 948.2, 975.10, 975.13
misinterpretable 342.4
misinterpretation 265.2, 342.1, 948.1, 975.1
misinterpreted 342.3
misjoinder 789.3
misjoining 789.3
misjudge 342.2, 948.2
misjudgment 342.1, 948.1, 975.1, 975.3
misknowledge 569.1
mislaid 160.11
mislay 160.7, 473.4
mislaying 160.3
mislead 354.19, 356.16, 569.3, 645.14, 654.10, 665.20
misleader 357.1
misleading (n) 356.2, 569.1 (a) 356.21, 569.6, 976.9
misled 569.5
mislikable 99.7
mislike 99.3
mislocation 160.3
mismanage 389.4, 414.13, 975.12
mismanaged 414.21
mismanagement 389.1, 414.6
mismarried 789.7
mismarry 789.5
mismatch (n) 776.2, 789.3 (v) 789.5
mismatched 789.7, 791.4
mismatching 776.2
mismatchment 789.3
mismate 789.5
mismated 789.7
misname 527.12
misnomer (n) 527.9 (v) 527.12
misocainea 853.3
misogamic 565.6
misogamist 565.2, 565.3
misogamy 103.1, 565.1
misogynic 590.3
misogynist 103.4, 565.2, 590.2
misogynistic 590.3
misogynous 565.6, 590.3
misogyny 103.1, 565.1, 590.1
misoneism 853.3
misoneistic 853.8
misopedia 103.1
mispaint 350.4
mispainting 350.1
misperceive 948.2
misperception 948.1
misplace 160.7, 473.4
misplaced 160.11, 789.7, 810.13, 868.7
misplaced modifier 531.1
misplacement 160.3
misplay (n) 975.3 (v) 745.5, 975.12
misprint (n) 975.3 (v) 975.12
misprision 655.1, 950.1, 975.1
misprision of felony 655.1
misprision of treason 363.2, 645.7, 655.1
misprizal 950.1
misprize 157.3, 950.2
misprized 99.9, 950.3
misprizing 950.1
mispronounce 525.11
mispronounced 525.12
mispronunciation 525.5, 975.7
misproportion 265.3
misproportioned 265.12, 1015.8
misput (v) 160.7 (a) 160.11
misputting 160.3
misquotation 342.1, 350.1, 975.3
misquote 342.2, 350.3, 354.16, 975.12
misquoted 265.11, 342.3, 975.19
misread (v) 342.2, 948.2, 975.12 (a) 342.3
misreading 342.1, 948.1
misread the situation 948.2
misreckon 948.2
misreckoning 948.1
misrecollect 990.5
misrecollected 990.8
misreference 776.2
misrelation 776.2
misremember 990.4, 990.5
misremembered 990.8
misremembrance 990.2
misrender 265.6, 342.2
misrendering 342.1
misreport (n) 350.1, 975.3 (v) 350.3, 354.16, 975.12
misreported 975.19
misrepresent 265.6, 342.2, 350.3, 354.16, 936.9
misrepresentation 265.2, 342.1, 350.1, 354.9
misrepresented 265.11, 342.3
misrule (n) 414.6, 418.2, 810.2 (v) 414.13
Miss 77.8

miss (n) 77.8, 302.6, 410.4, 750.2, 975.3 (v) 340.7, 410.14, 473.4, 911.4, 984.2, 990.7, 992.7, 1003.3
Missa 701.8
miss a beat 127.10, 916.12
missa brevis 708.17
missal book 701.10
missal stand 703.12
Miss America 1016.7
miss an opportunity 844.5
missa solemnis 708.17
missay 525.11
missaying 489.8, 531.2, 975.7
miss by a mile 911.4, 975.10, 1003.3
missed 340.14
missed chance 1011.2
miss emma 87.14
misshape (n) 265.3 (v) 263.3, 265.7
misshapen 265.12, 810.12, 870.13, 1015.8
misshapenness 263.1, 265.3, 1015.2
missile (n) 462.18, 904.5, 1074.3 (a) 904.15
missile engineer 1074.11
missile engineering 1074.1
missile guidance 1041.7
missile program 1074.1
missilery 462.1, 462.3, 1074.1
missile science 1074.1
missile testing 1074.1
missing 34.4, 222.11, 762.8, 795.4, 992.13
missing link 813.1, 842.7
missing person 222.5
mission (n) 184.11, 380.2, 404.2, 458.4, 576.13, 615.1, 641.1, 703.1, 724.2, 724.6, 866.1, 886.9 (v) 615.10
mission accomplished 407.1
missionary (n) 699.6, 858.9 (a) 692.11
missionary apostolic 699.6
missionary rector 699.6
mission control 1074.7
mission creep 641.1
missioner 699.6
mission kill 462.22
mission statement 334.1, 381.1, 404.1
Mississippi marbles 759.8
missive 553.2
miss morph 87.14
miss nothing 983.8
miss one's aim 410.14
miss one's footing 414.11
miss one's mooring 911.4
miss one's turn 844.5
miss on the low side 950.2
Missouri marbles 759.8
Missouri meerschaum 89.6
miss out 844.5, 911.4, 1003.3
misspeak 525.11, 975.14
misspeaking 525.5
misspeak oneself 975.14
misspell 975.12
misspelling 546.4, 975.7
misspend 486.6
misspent 486.9
miss stays 182.30, 911.4
misstate 350.3, 354.16, 354.19
misstated 975.19
misstatement 350.1, 354.9, 975.3
misstep 655.2, 975.4
miss the boat 844.5, 846.7, 911.4
miss the bus 911.4
miss the chance 844.5
miss the mark 410.14, 911.4, 1003.3
miss the market 737.23
miss the point 342.2, 975.10
miss the time 844.3
miss the truth 975.10
Miss Universe 1016.7
missus 77.8
Miss USA 1016.7
Miss World 1016.7
missy 77.6, 302.6
mist (n) 316.1, 319.3, 522.3, 764.3, 985.3, 1065.4 (v) 32.4, 319.7, 985.7
mistakable 342.4, 971.17
mistake (n) 410.4, 414.5, 975.3 (v) 342.2, 975.13
mistaken 342.3, 975.18
mistake oneself 975.10
mistake-prone 414.20
mistaking 342.1, 975.1
mistaught 569.5, 930.13
mistbow 316.8
mist concentrate sprayer 1065.8
misteach 350.3, 569.3
misteaching (n) 350.1, 569.1 (a) 569.6
misted 985.13
Mister 76.7, 648.3
Mister Fix-it 577.9
misterm 527.12
misthink 948.2
mistime 833.2, 844.3
mistimed 833.3, 844.6
mistiming 833.1
mistiness 32.2, 263.1, 270.4, 319.4, 522.3, 764.1, 971.4, 1065.1
mist over 319.7
mistral 318.8
mistranslate 342.2
mistranslation 342.1
mistreat 389.5, 1000.6
mistreatment 389.2
Mistress 648.4
Mistress 77.8
mistress 104.13, 470.2, 571.2, 575.2
mistress 665.17, 921.1
mistress of ceremonies 743.20
mistress of the house 575.2
mistrial 598.5
mistrust (n) 153.2, 494.2, 955.2 (v) 153.3, 955.6
mistrusted 955.12
mistrustful 494.9, 955.9
mistrustfulness 494.2, 955.2
mistrusting 955.9
mist up 319.7
misty 32.6, 263.4, 270.16, 316.11, 319.10, 522.15, 971.19, 985.13
misty-moisty 316.11
misty rain 316.1
misunderstand 342.2, 975.13
misunderstandable 342.4
misunderstanding 342.1, 456.2, 975.3
misunderstand one another 456.8
misunderstood 99.9, 342.3
misusage 389.1, 531.2, 975.7
misuse (n) 265.2, 387.1, 389.1, 393.2, 975.3 (v) 265.6, 387.16, 389.4, 393.12, 486.4, 975.12
misused 432.16
misuse of words 342.1
misuse power 389.4
misvaluation 948.1
misvalue 948.2
mite 248.2, 258.7, 302.3, 311.32, 311.36, 728.8, 992.5
mite different, a 787.4
miter (n) 647.4, 800.4 (v) 800.8
mitered 278.6
miticide 1001.3
mitigate 16.10, 120.5, 145.4, 252.8, 600.12, 670.6, 670.9, 852.6, 852.7, 959.3
mitigated 298.11, 959.10
mitigating 120.9, 670.14, 959.7
mitigating circumstances 600.5
mitigation 16.5, 120.1, 145.1, 252.1, 600.5, 670.2, 852.1
mitigative 120.9, 959.7
mitigator 670.3
mitigatory 959.7
mitochondrion 305.5
mitosis 305.16
mitt 759.10
mitten 5.31
mittens 754.1
mittimus 429.4
mitts 474.4, 754.1
mitzvah 143.7, 419.2
mix (n) 706.6, 797.6, 1013.5 (v) 405.7, 796.3, 797.10, 805.3, 945.3
mixable 797.16
mix-and-match 784.11
mixblood 797.8
mixed 539.4, 797.14, 805.5, 1003.4
mixed bag 770.13, 797.6
mixed blessing 971.1
mixed-blood 797.8
mixed cadence 709.23
mixed chorus 710.16
mixed doubles 748.1
mixed drink 8.4, 10.49, 88.9
mixed farming 1069.1
mixed foursome 751.3
mixed greens 10.37
mixed larceny 482.2
mixed marriage 563.1
mixed martial arts 457.10
mixed media 712.16
mixed message 789.2
mixed signal 789.2
mixed tape 770.13
mixed times 709.24
mixed up 799.4, 810.16
mixed-up 922.18, 985.12
mixed vegetables 10.35
mixen 80.10
mixer 10.49, 88.9, 582.16, 705.2, 797.9, 1034.7, 1034.24, 1035.11
mixing 797.1, 1034.16, 1035.3
mixing room 1034.7
mix it up 456.12, 457.13, 754.4
mix it up with 457.17
mixologist 88.19
mixolydian mode 709.10
mix oneself up with 214.7
mixture 86.4, 405.3, 770.13, 780.1, 796.1, 797.1, 797.5, 805.2, 1064.3
mixture of colors 47.1
mixum-gatherum 804.1
mix up 522.12, 797.10, 799.3, 810.9, 811.3, 945.3, 975.13, 985.7
mix-up 810.2, 985.3
mix with 582.17
mizu ame 66.3
mizu-ame 66.3
mizuame 66.3
mizzle (n) 316.1 (v) 316.10
mizzly 316.11
Mlle 77.8
Mme 77.8
Mmes 77.8
mneme 989.1
mnemonic 989.21
mnemonic device 989.8
mnemonics 989.8
mnemonization 989.8
Mnemosyne 989.1
mnemotechnics 989.8
mnemotechny 989.8
mo 828.3
moan (n) 52.4, 115.3 (v) 52.14, 108.6, 115.10, 115.13, 115.16, 318.20
moaner 108.4, 115.8, 115.9
moanful 115.19
moaning (n) 52.8, 115.1 (a) 115.18
moaning Minnie 112.13
moat 212.4, 224.2, 290.2, 460.5, 1012.5
mob 617.1, 617.6, 770.3, 770.4, 884.3
mob, the 606.2, 660.10
mobile (n) 712.9, 715.2 (a) 172.7, 607.10, 854.6
mobile call 347.13
mobile camera 1035.10
mobile home 179.19, 228.17
mobile militia 461.24
mobile phone 347.4
mobile telephone 347.4
mobile trailer unit 1036.6
mobile transmitter 1034.5
mobile unit 1035.7
mobile vulgus 606.2
mobility 172.3, 607.1, 854.1
mobilization 172.1, 387.8, 405.1, 458.7, 458.9, 615.7, 770.1
mobilize 172.6, 405.6, 458.18, 458.19, 615.17, 770.18, 800.5
mobilized 405.16
mobilizer 886.4
mobilizing 387.8
Mobius strip 812.2

mob law 418.2
mobocracy 418.2, 612.4
mobocratic 418.6
mob rule 418.2, 612.4
mobster 483.4, 593.1, 660.9
moc 5.27
moccasin 5.27
mock (n) 156.2, 157.1, 354.13, 508.2 (v) 156.5, 157.3, 349.12, 356.14, 489.13, 508.9, 621.4 (a) 336.8, 354.26, 784.10, 862.8
mock court 595.2
mocker 336.4
mockery 156.2, 336.2, 354.5, 508.1, 508.6, 508.7, 998.5
mockery of justice 650.4
mock-heroic 488.6, 720.16
mocking (n) 621.2 (a) 508.12
mockingbird 336.4, 710.23
mock moon 1025.14
mock-serious 354.26
mock sun 1025.14
mock-up 336.3, 786.5, 942.2
mod 578.11, 841.13
modal 384.8, 765.6
modal auxiliary 530.4
modality 262.1, 384.1, 384.3, 765.1
modal scale 709.6
mode 262.1, 384.1, 530.11, 532.2, 578.1, 709.10, 765.1, 765.4, 935.6
model (n) 262.1, 300.2, 336.3, 337.2, 349.5, 349.6, 659.4, 662.9, 709.11, 767.2, 785.3, 786.1, 786.4, 809.3, 869.4, 932.2, 1016.7 (v) 262.7, 715.5 (a) 509.20, 786.8, 869.8, 1002.9
model after 336.7
model child 867.2
modeled 262.9, 715.7
modeler 716.6
model home 767.2, 785.2
modeling 262.5, 336.1, 715.1
modeling clay 715.4
modeling language 1042.13
modeling tool 715.4
model on 336.7
model oneself on 786.7
modem 347.18, 1042.8, 1042.9
mode of expression 524.7, 532.2
mode of operation 384.1
mode of procedure 384.1
mode of speech 524.7
mode of succession 479.2
mode of worship 701.3
moderate (n) 611.10, 670.4 (v) 175.9, 210.5, 252.9, 466.6, 670.6, 959.3 (a) 106.14, 175.10, 246.3, 427.7, 467.7, 611.18, 633.7, 668.9, 670.10, 819.4, 999.20, 1005.7
moderate breeze 318.4
moderated 210.7, 959.10
moderateness 248.1, 427.1, 467.3, 611.2, 633.1, 668.1, 670.1, 1005.1
moderate position 611.2
moderate price 633.2
moderating 670.2
moderating influence 466.4
moderation 106.4, 210.2, 252.4, 466.1, 467.3, 668.1, 670.1
moderationism 670.1
moderationist 611.10, 668.4, 670.4
moderatism 611.2
moderatist 611.10, 670.4
moderative 670.2
moderato 708.55
moderator 213.4, 466.4, 596.1, 670.3
modern (n) 841.4 (a) 578.11, 838.2, 841.13
modern art 712.1
modern dance music 708.8
modern dancer 705.3
modern-day 838.2
modern generation 841.4
modern history 719.1
modernism 841.3
modernist 720.12, 841.4
modernistic 841.13
modernity 838.1, 841.3
modernization 841.3
modernize 841.6
modernized 841.13
modernizer 841.4
modernizing 841.13
modern jazz 708.9
modern language 523.1
modern logic 935.2
modern man 841.4
modernness 841.3
modern times 838.1
modest 137.10, 139.9, 250.6, 325.7, 344.10, 633.7, 652.5, 664.5, 1005.7
modestness 633.1, 1005.1
modest price 633.2
modest violet 139.6
modesty 137.1, 139.1, 325.2, 344.3, 652.1, 664.2, 1005.1
modicum 248.2, 477.5, 793.3, 797.7
modifiability 854.1
modifiable 854.6, 858.18
modification 524.12, 780.4, 852.1, 959.1
modificator 852.5
modificatory 959.7
modified 852.10, 959.10
modified leaf 310.19
modifier 530.2, 852.5
modify 780.6, 852.7, 959.3
modifying 959.7
modish 5.46, 578.12, 841.13
modishness 578.2
modiste 5.36
modular 793.7, 796.5
modular assembly 892.3
modular house 228.5
modular production 892.3
modulate 524.28, 670.6, 852.6, 852.7, 959.3
modulated 959.10
modulation 524.6, 670.2, 709.2, 852.1, 1034.14
modulator 670.3
modulator-demodulator 1042.9
modulatory 959.7
module 568.8, 793.1, 796.2, 872.4, 1075.2
modus operandi 384.1, 765.4
modus ponens 935.6
modus tollens 935.6
modus vivendi 321.1, 465.5, 765.4
mogul 575.9, 753.1, 997.8, 1023.8
moguled trail 753.1
mogul racer 753.2
mogul skiing 753.1
Mohammed 684.4
Mohammedan (n) 675.23 (a) 675.31
Mohammedanism 675.13
Mohawk 1016.14
Mohs' scale 1046.6
moider 971.12, 985.7
moidore 728.4
moiety 477.5, 617.2, 793.3, 819.2, 875.2
moil (n) 725.4, 725.5, 917.1 (v) 725.14, 915.12
moiler 726.2
moiré (n) 47.6 (a) 47.10
moiré pattern 47.2
moist 1061.4, 1065.15, 1065.16
moisten 1065.12
moistening (n) 1065.6 (a) 1065.18
moist gangrene 85.40
moistiness 1065.1
moistness 1065.1
moisture 12.7, 316.1, 1061.1, 1065.1
moistureless 1066.7
moistureproof 1066.11
moisturize 1065.12
moisturizer 1065.3
moisturizing 1056.10
moisty 1065.15
mojo 87.9
moke 311.15
molar 2.8
molar weight 297.5
molasses 66.2, 66.3, 803.4, 1062.5
mold (n) 85.42, 234.1, 262.1, 266.1, 310.4, 337.2, 393.6, 767.4, 785.6, 786.6, 809.3, 865.4, 978.3, 1001.2 (v) 262.7, 393.22, 715.5, 742.6, 867.3, 892.8, 986.14
moldability 433.3, 570.5, 1047.2
moldable 433.13, 570.18, 1047.9
molded 262.9, 715.7, 892.18
molded plastic 1054.6
molder (n) 716.6 (v) 67.4, 173.8, 393.22, 806.3, 842.9
molder away 393.22, 806.3
moldering (n) 393.7 (a) 173.12, 393.42, 806.5, 842.14
moldiness 71.2
molding 262.5, 266.1, 715.1, 785.6, 892.2
molding compounds 1054.6
mold to the figure 803.8
moldy 71.5, 393.42, 842.14
mole 30.4, 85.39, 283.3, 517.5, 551.6, 901.4, 1004.1, 1009.6, 1012.5
molecular 258.14
molecular cloud 1073.8
molecular death 85.2
molecular heat 1019.1
molecular mass 1060.5
molecular physics 1038.1
molecular volume 1060.5
molecular weight 297.5, 297.8, 1060.5
molecule 248.2, 258.8, 1038.7, 1052.2, 1060.2
mole-eyed 28.13
molehill 237.4, 770.10, 998.5
Moleskine 549.11
molest 96.13, 389.5, 1000.6
molestation 75.11, 96.2, 389.2
molester 96.10
molesting 389.2
mole trap 356.12
mollification 120.1, 465.1, 670.2, 1047.5
mollified 1047.8
mollifier 670.3
mollify 120.5, 465.7, 670.7, 1047.6
mollifying (n) 1047.5 (a) 465.12, 670.15, 1047.16
mollusc 10.25, 311.29
molluscan 311.50
molluscoid 311.50
mollusk 10.25, 311.3, 311.31
mollycoddle (n) 16.6, 77.10, 427.4 (v) 427.6
mollycoddling 427.3
molossus 720.8
Molotov cocktail 462.20
molt (n) 2.5 (v) 6.10, 473.5
molten 1019.27, 1020.31, 1064.6
molting 6.2, 473.2
molybdenum 7.11
mom 560.12
mom-and-pop store 736.1
mome 924.1
moment 417.4, 824.1, 824.2, 828.3, 830.3, 894.1, 902.1, 997.1
momentaneous 830.4
momentaneousness 830.1
momentariness 828.1, 830.1
momentary 828.7, 830.4, 850.8
momentary success 409.3
momently 850.8
moment of force 902.1
moment of illumination 934.1
moment of truth 824.1, 843.5, 971.6, 997.4
momentous 417.15, 831.10, 894.13, 997.17
momentousness 997.4
momentum 172.1, 172.2, 174.1, 902.1
mom food 8.8
momma 77.6
mommy 560.12
mommy's boy 561.3
mommy's girl 561.3
Mommy track 724.6
momus 510.9
monachal 565.6, 698.14, 703.16
monachism 565.1, 667.1, 698.4
monad 258.8, 763.3, 872.3, 1052.2
monadal 872.11
monadic 872.7, 872.11

monadism 761.1
monadnock 237.4
monandrous 563.19
monarch 575.8, 997.10
monarchal 417.17, 612.16
monarchial 417.17, 612.16
monarchic 417.17, 612.16
monarchical 417.17, 612.16
monarchical government 612.4
monarchism 611.4, 612.7
monarchist 611.9
monarchy 612.4, 612.8
monasterial 698.14, 703.16
monastery 703.6
monastic (n) 565.2, 699.16 (a) 565.6, 698.14, 703.16
monasticism 565.1, 667.1, 698.4
monatomic 1038.18, 1060.10
monaural system 50.11
mondain 578.7
mondaine 578.7
Monday 832.4
monde 578.6
monetarism 952.7
monetary 728.30, 729.20, 731.23
monetary cycle 731.10
monetary denomination 728.1
monetary penalty 603.3
monetary policy 731.7
monetary unit 728.1
monetary value 630.2
monetization 728.23
monetize 728.26
money 618.1, 728.1
moneybag 729.15
moneybags 618.7
money belt 729.15
money broker 620.3, 729.11, 730.9
money changer 729.11, 730.9
money changing 729.5
money chest 729.13
money clip 729.15
money dealer 729.11
money dealing 729.5
moneyed 618.14
moneyed capital 728.15
moneyed person 618.7
moneyer 728.25
moneygetting 472.1
money going out 626.2
moneygrubber 100.12, 484.4, 651.3
moneygrubbing (n) 100.8, 472.1 (a) 100.27
money-hungry 100.27
money in hand 728.18
money in the bank 472.6
money-laundering 673.2
moneylender 620.3, 729.11
moneylending 620.1
moneyless 619.9
moneylessness 619.2
money-mad 100.27
moneymaker 249.4, 729.10
moneymaking (n) 472.1 (a) 387.22, 472.16, 624.21, 724.15
moneyman 729.9
money manager 628.7
money market 728.16, 729.4
money market account 729.14
money-market fund 737.16
money-market trading 737.19
money matters 729.1
moneymonger 620.3, 729.11
money of account 728.21
money order 728.11
money pit 992.1
money player 759.21
money-raising 621.1
money rider 757.2
moneys 728.14
money-saving 635.6
money-spinner 729.10
money's worth 630.2, 633.3
money to burn 618.1, 993.2
moneywise 728.30
monger 730.2
mongering 552.7
Mongolian 312.2
mongolianism 922.9
mongolism 922.9
Mongoloid 312.2
mongoloid 922.22
mongrel (n) 311.18, 660.6, 797.8 (a) 797.15
mongrelism 797.4
mongrelization 797.4
mongrelize 797.13
monied 618.14
moniker 527.3
monikered 527.14
monism 798.1, 802.1, 952.5
monistic 872.7
monistic idealism 1053.3
monition 379.1, 399.1, 422.1, 551.3
monitor (n) 48.5, 399.4, 422.3, 551.5, 571.4, 574.2, 938.17, 1034.24, 1035.13, 1042.9 (v) 570.11, 938.24, 1034.26
monitorial 399.7, 422.8
monitoring 339.4, 1035.3
monitoring booth 1034.7
monitor room 1034.7
monitory (n) 422.1 (a) 133.15, 379.5, 399.7, 422.8, 551.18
monitory letter 422.1
monk 311.22, 565.2, 699.16
monkery 698.4
monkey (n) 152.6, 311.22, 336.4, 358.1, 508.7, 728.8, 759.22 (v) 998.15
monkey around 998.15
monkey business 356.5
monkeying 998.9
monkeying around 998.9
monkey on one's back 87.1
monkeyshines 489.5, 489.10
monkey suit 5.7
monkey tricks 489.5
monkey with 214.7
monkey-wrench 393.15
monkey-wrenching 393.1, 395.3
monkhood 698.4
monkish 499.9, 565.6, 698.14
mono 50.11
monocase 872.1
monochord 708.3, 711.22
monochordist 710.7
monochromatic 35.16, 872.11
monochromatic film 714.10
monochromatism 30.3
monochrome (n) 35.7 (a) 35.16, 712.21
monochrome monitor 1042.9
monochromic 35.16
monochromist 716.4
monocle 29.3
monocled 29.11
monoclinous 75.31
monocot 310.3
monocotyl 310.3
monocotyledon 310.3
monocratic 417.15, 417.16, 612.16
monocular 28.12, 29.9
monodic 708.49
monodist 542.2
monodrama 542.1
monodramatic 542.4
monodramatist 704.22
monody 115.6, 542.1, 708.3, 708.21
monogamist 563.11
monogamous 563.19
monogenesis 78.6
monogenetic 78.16
monogram 517.11, 527.10, 546.1
monogrammed 517.24
monograph 556.1
monographer 547.15, 556.3, 718.4
monographic 556.6
monographist 556.3
monogynist 563.11
monogynous 563.19
monolatry 675.5
monolingual 872.11
monolith 549.12, 1059.1
monolithic 781.5, 798.6, 1059.12
monolithism 781.1
monologic 542.4
monological 542.4
monologist 542.2, 707.2
monologize 542.3
monologue 542.1, 704.7, 781.2
monology 542.1
monomachy 457.7
monomania 926.13, 983.3
monomaniac (n) 926.18 (a) 926.33
monomaniacal 926.33, 983.17
monomeric 1060.9
monomerous 1060.9
monometallism 728.21
monometer 720.7
mononymous 527.14
monophonic 708.49
monophonic system 50.11
monophony 708.21
monophthong 524.12
monophthongal 524.30
monopolist (n) 428.6, 651.3 (a) 469.11
monopolistic 469.11
monopolization 469.3
monopolize 469.6, 480.19, 651.4, 733.7, 737.26, 983.13
monopolized 983.17
monopolize one's attention 983.13
monopolize the conversation 542.3
monopolize the thoughts 931.20
monopolizing 469.11
monopoly 428.1, 469.3, 737.20, 773.3
monorail 179.14, 383.8
monosaccharide 7.5
monoscope 1035.11
monosodium glutamate 397.4
monosome 305.8
monostich 720.10
monosyllabic 523.23
monosyllable 526.1
monotasking 872.1
monotelephonic 347.21
monotheism 675.5
monotheist 675.16
monotheistic 675.25
monotonal 50.15
monotone (n) 50.2, 781.2, 812.2, 849.4 (a) 50.15, 849.15
monotonic 50.15
monotonous 118.9, 781.6, 812.8, 849.15
monotonousness 118.2, 781.2
monotony 50.2, 118.1, 781.2, 812.1, 849.4
monotype (n) 713.4 (v) 548.15
monovalence 1060.4
monovalent 1060.10
Monroe Doctrine 609.5
monsieur 76.7
Monsignor 648.5
monsignor 699.9
monsoon 313.1, 316.4
mons pubis 2.13
monster (n) 127.9, 144.14, 257.11, 257.14, 593.6, 671.9, 870.6, 1015.4 (a) 247.7, 257.20
monster of cruelty 144.14
monstrance 309.16, 703.11
monstrosity 257.7, 265.3, 870.1, 870.3, 870.6, 1015.4
monstrous 247.7, 257.20, 265.12, 654.16, 661.12, 671.21, 870.13, 923.11, 993.16, 1000.9, 1015.8
monstrous lie 354.12
monstrousness 257.7, 661.3, 870.3, 923.3, 993.1
mons veneris 2.13
montage 712.10, 714.3
montane 237.8
Montezuma's revenge 12.2, 85.29
month 824.2
monthlies 12.9
monthlong 827.12
monthly (n) 555.1 (a) 849.13, 850.8
monthly epact 832.5
monthly payments 624.1
month off 20.3
month of Sundays 827.4
month-to-month 849.13
monticle 237.4
monticule 237.4
monticuline 272.18
monticulous 272.18
Montjoie 458.7
Montreal offense 749.3

monument 272.6, 309.17, 349.6, 517.10, 549.12, 842.6
monumental 247.7, 257.20, 272.14, 715.6
monumentalism 257.7
monumentalize 829.5
monumental mason 716.6
monumental record 549.12
moo 60.2
moocah 87.14
mooch 440.15, 480.19
moocha 5.19
mooch around 331.12
moocher 331.11, 440.8, 585.6
mooching (n) 440.6, 480.1 (a) 440.16
mooch off 368.12
moo-cow 311.6
mood 530.11, 722.4, 935.6, 978.4
mood-altering 362.10
mood disorder 92.14
mood drug 86.46
mood elevation 86.46
moodiness 110.5, 110.8, 112.8, 364.2, 854.2
moodish 110.24, 112.25
moodishness 110.8
mood music 708.7
mood ring 498.6
moodscape 33.6
mood swing 362.2, 364.3
mood swings 854.3, 926.5
moody 110.24, 112.25, 364.5, 854.7
Moog synthesizer 711.1
moolah 728.2
moon (n) 824.2, 854.4, 1026.1, 1073.11 (v) 6.7, 331.12, 985.9
moon, the 261.4
moon around 331.12
moon base 1075.5
moonbeam 1025.11
moon-blind 30.2
moon blindness 30.2
mooncalf 924.1
moon dog 1025.14
moon-eyed 28.12
moonfaced 257.18
moonglow 1025.11
mooning (n) 6.2, 985.2 (a) 985.11
moonless 1027.13
moonlessness 1027.1
moonlight (n) 1025.11 (v) 88.30, 724.12
moonlighting 724.5
moonlight requisition 480.1
moonlike 279.11
moonlit 1025.39
moon orbit 1075.2
moonraking (n) 985.2 (a) 985.11
moonrise 1025.11
moonshade 1028.3
moon-shaped 279.11
moonshine (n) 88.14, 88.18, 354.14, 520.3, 936.3, 1025.11 (v) 88.30, 732.7
moonshiner 88.19, 732.4
moon-shining 732.1
moon ship 1075.2
moon station 1075.5
moonstruck 926.26
Moon's type 30.6
Moon type 30.6
moony 985.11
moor (n) 236.1, 237.1, 237.3, 243.1, 310.8 (v) 159.17, 182.15, 186.8, 428.10, 800.7, 855.8
moorage 1009.6
moored 855.16
mooring 159.7, 180.16, 186.2
mooring buoy 180.16
mooring mast 184.24
moorings 180.16, 1009.6
Moorish 198.6
moorish 243.3
moorland 236.1, 237.1, 243.1, 272.3, 310.8
moors 233.1, 272.3
moory 243.3
moose 311.5
moose call 517.16
mooshy 1047.13
moot (v) 439.5, 935.16 (a) 598.21, 951.13, 955.12, 958.8, 971.17
moota 87.11
moot case 938.10
mooter 935.12
moot point 938.10
mop (n) 3.4 (v) 79.18, 79.19, 265.8
mop and mow 265.8
mopboard 199.2
mope (n) 112.13, 331.8 (v) 110.14, 112.16, 112.17
mope around 110.14
moped 179.8
moper 331.8
mopery 331.4
mopes 110.10, 112.6
mopey 110.24, 112.25, 583.5
mopheaded 3.24
mopheadedness 3.1
mopiness 110.8, 112.8
moping 110.24, 112.25
mopish 110.24, 112.25, 583.5
mopishness 110.8, 112.8, 583.1
mopped up 407.11
moppet 302.3
mopping 79.5
mopping down 79.5
mopping up 79.5
mops 560.12
mop-squeezer 758.2
mop the floor with 604.10
mop up 79.18, 79.19, 407.6
mop up the floor with 412.9
mopus 728.2
mora 524.11, 720.7
moraine 237.4, 237.5, 256.2
moral (n) 399.1, 419.2, 529.1, 568.7, 974.1 (a) 636.6, 641.13, 644.13, 653.5
moral badness 1000.1
moral bankruptcy 636.4
moral blemish 654.2
moral censor 636.5
moral certainty 953.5, 970.1
moral climate 636.1, 978.5
moral code 636.1, 952.2
moral compass 568.7, 636.3
moral courage 359.4
moral delinquency 636.4, 654.1
morale 450.1, 636.3, 653.1, 978.4
morale booster 109.1
morale-boosting 109.16
morale-sapping 112.30
moral excellence 644.1, 653.1
moral fiber 359.4, 636.3, 653.1
moral flaw 654.2
moral insanity 92.15, 926.3
moralism 419.2
moralistic 419.4, 422.8, 636.6
morality 568.7, 636.3, 653.1
moralization 568.7
moralize 568.16
moralize upon 946.14
moral lesson 568.7
morally polluted 654.14
morally weak 654.12
moral of the story 399.1
moral philosophy 636.2
moral pollutedness 654.5
moral pollution 654.5
moral precept 419.2
moral principles 636.1
moral rectitude 653.1
morals 636.1, 636.3, 952.2
moral sense 636.5
moral strength 644.1
moral support 449.2, 901.1
moral turpitude 636.4, 645.2, 654.5
moral victory 411.1
moral virtue 653.1
moral weakness 16.2
morass 243.1, 799.2, 810.2, 1013.4
moratorium 625.2, 846.2
moratory 846.16
morbid 85.55, 85.60, 127.30, 981.5
morbid anxiety 112.4
morbid curiosity 981.1
morbid drive 926.13
morbid excitability 128.1
morbid growth 85.39
morbidity 82.3, 85.1, 85.3
morbidly curious 981.5
morbidly sensitive 495.12
morbidness 85.3
morbid sensibility 495.4
morbific 82.5
morbus 85.1
morceau 248.3, 556.1
mordacious 17.14, 144.23
mordacity 17.5, 144.8
mordancy 17.5, 68.1, 144.8, 544.3
mordant (n) 1020.15 (a) 17.14, 68.6, 144.23, 489.15, 544.11
mordent 708.27, 709.18
more (n) 883.1 (a) 253.10, 883.7
more dead than alive 21.10
more desirable 371.25
more distant 261.10
more frightened than hurt 127.25
more fun than a barrel of monkeys 743.27
more guts than brains 493.3
more heat than light 152.5
more in sorrow than in anger 148.6
more matter and less art 535.1
morendo 708.53
more of the same 118.1
mores 373.1, 373.2, 580.3, 978.5
mores, the 579.2
moresque (n) 498.2 (a) 498.12
more than a match for 15.19, 249.12
more than doubtful 969.3
more than enough 991.2, 993.2, 994.1
more than expected 131.10
more than flesh and blood can bear 98.25, 105.30
more than half 883.2
more than meets the eye 32.1, 345.5, 518.1, 519.2
more than one 883.7
more than one bargained for 131.10
more than one can afford 632.11
more than one can shake a stick at 884.3, 991.2
more than one can tell 884.10
more than one knows what to do with 993.2
more than one really wants to know 993.4
more than you can shake a stick at 884.10
more truth than poetry 761.2, 973.1
morganatic 563.19
morgue 309.9
moribund 85.54, 307.32, 331.20
moribundity 307.8
morigeration 138.2
morigerous 138.14
Mormon (n) 675.22 (a) 683.14
Mormonism 675.14
morn 314.1
morning (n) 314.1 (a) 314.5
morning after 88.1
morning after, the 839.1
morning-after pill 86.23
morning coat 5.11
morning devotions 696.8
morning dew 1065.4
morning dress 5.11
morning prayers 696.8
morning room 197.5
morning services 696.8
morning sickness 85.9
morning star 1073.4
morningtide 314.1
morning time 314.1
morning twilight 314.3
morntime 314.1
moron 924.8
moronic 922.22, 923.8
moronism 922.9
moronity 922.9
morose 110.24, 112.25, 583.5
moroseness 110.8, 112.8, 583.1
morph 87.14, 262.6, 526.3
morpheme 262.6, 518.6, 523.14, 526.3
morphemic 262.11, 518.12, 526.22

morphemic analysis 526.3
morphemics 262.6, 526.3
Morpheus 22.11
morphia 22.10
morphine 22.10, 86.12
morphine addiction 87.1
morphine habit 87.1
morphing 1042.18
morphinism 87.1
morphogenesis 262.5
morphogeny 262.5
morphologic 262.11
morphological 262.11, 266.6, 523.19, 526.22
morphological individual 305.2
morphologist 523.15
morphology 262.6, 266.1, 526.3, 530.1
morphophoneme 524.12
morphophonemic 523.19, 526.22
morphophonemic analysis 526.3
morphophonemics 524.13, 526.3
morphophonology 524.13
morphotic 262.9
Morris 311.20
morris 366.1
morrow 314.1
morrow, the 839.1
Morse code 523.11
morsel 8.2, 10.8, 248.3, 793.3
mors thymica 85.2
Morta 964.3
mortal (n) 312.5 (a) 307.33, 308.23, 312.13, 828.7
mortal blow 308.10, 820.4
mortal cinch 759.3, 759.10
mortal fear 127.1
mortal flesh 312.1
mortal horror 99.2
mortality 307.12, 308.9, 312.1, 312.8, 828.1
mortality committee 307.17
mortality rate 307.12
mortality table 968.2
mortal lock 759.3, 970.2
mortally ill 85.56, 307.32
mortalness 307.12
mortal remains 307.15
mortals 312.1
mortal sin 654.3, 655.2
mortar (n) 462.21, 858.10, 1054.2 (v) 295.25, 459.22
mortar and pestle 1051.7
mortarboard 647.1
mortgage (n) 438.4 (v) 438.10
mortgage bond 438.5
mortgage broker 730.9
mortgage company 620.4
mortgaged 438.13, 623.8
mortgage deed 438.4
mortgaged to the hilt 623.8
mortgagee 438.7, 620.3, 622.4
mortgage holder 620.3, 622.4
mortgage points 620.1, 623.3
mortgage shark 357.3
mortgaging 621.1
mortgagor 438.6, 623.4
mortician 309.8
mortification 85.40, 96.4, 98.6, 137.2, 658.3, 667.1
mortification of the flesh 113.4
mortified 85.60, 96.22, 137.14, 393.40
mortify 96.15, 98.13, 137.4, 393.22
mortifying 98.21, 137.15
mortify oneself 658.6, 668.6
mortify one's flesh 658.6
mortify the flesh 668.6
mortise 777.6, 800.8
mortise and tenon 800.4
mortised 777.9
mortmain 471.5
mortuary (n) 309.9 (a) 307.28, 309.22
mortuary roll 307.13
mortuum vadium 438.4
Mosaic 683.11
mosaic (n) 47.4 (a) 47.14
mosaic 712.10, 712.16
Mosaic Law, the 683.3
Moses 684.1
mosey 175.6
mosey along 188.7
mosh pit 704.16
Moslem (n) 675.23 (a) 675.31
Moslemism 675.13
mosque 703.2
mosquito 311.32, 311.36, 311.37
mosquito fleet 461.27
moss 310.4
mossback 842.8, 853.4
mossbacked 303.18
Mössbauer effect 1038.6
moss-covered 310.42
moss-grown 310.42, 842.14
moss-trooper 483.6
mossy 310.42
most (n) 249.3, 792.6, 883.2 (a) 247.13, 249.13, 883.9
most distant 261.12
Most Excellent, the 648.8
most favored nation 731.1
Most Honorable, the 648.8
mostly cloudy 319.8
Most Noble, the 648.8
most recent 841.14
Most Reverend, the 648.8
most sincerely 820.5
most unkindest cut of all 156.2
most valuable player 413.15
most wanted 660.9
Most Worshipful, the 648.8
Most Worthy, the 648.8
mot 489.7, 974.1
Motazilite 675.23
mote 248.2, 258.7, 298.2, 460.6, 774.2, 1051.6
motel 228.16, 739.1
motet 696.3, 708.17
moth 311.32, 1001.2
mothball 71.3
mothballed 386.15
mothball fleet 461.27
moth-eaten 117.9, 303.18, 393.42, 842.14
Mother 648.5
mother (n) 660.5, 886.4, 892.7 (v) 818.14, 1008.19
mother (n) 77.7, 559.3, 560.11 (v) 78.8, 449.16 (a) 226.5
motherboard 1042.3
Mother Carey's chicken 133.5, 311.27
Mother Carey's goose 311.27
mother complex 92.22
mother country 232.2
Mother Earth 1073.10
mother figure 92.31
mother fixation 92.21
motherhood 559.1, 560.3
mother image 92.31
mothering 449.3
mother-in-law 564.2, 750.2
motherkin 560.12
motherkins 560.12
motherland 228.2, 232.2
motherless 19.18, 307.34, 584.12
motherlessness 584.4
motherlike 560.17
motherliness 560.3
mother lode 618.4
mother love 104.4
motherly 560.17
motherly eye 1008.2
Mother Nature 677.8
mother of all 349.7, 767.3
mother-of-pearl (n) 47.6, 1025.18 (a) 35.22, 47.10
mother-of-pearl cloud 1025.18
mother of the Muses 989.1
mother's boy 16.6, 77.10
mother's darling 16.6, 77.10
mother ship 180.1, 1075.2
mothership 560.3
mother's milk 2.24
mother's side 560.4
mother's skirts 346.4
mother superior 575.2, 699.17
mother surrogate 92.31
mother symbol 92.30
mother tongue 523.3
mother wit 919.2, 920.1
motif 211.7, 498.7, 708.24, 722.4, 937.1
motile 172.7, 854.6
motility 172.3, 854.1
motion (n) 84.2, 172.1, 177.1, 330.1, 439.2, 517.14, 613.9, 745.2, 889.2, 896.2, 1040.4 (v) 517.21
motion-detecting 172.7
motion detection 172.1
motion detector 172.1
motion discomfort 85.30
motion for summary judgment 598.12
motion from 163.2
motionless 173.13, 329.6, 331.17
motionlessness 173.2, 331.1
motion picture 706.1, 714.8
motion-picture 706.9
motion-picture actor 707.4
motion-picture camera 714.11
motion-picture camera person 706.5
motion-picture company 706.4
motion-picture editing 706.6
motion-picture fan 704.27
motion-picture film 549.10, 714.10
motion-picture genre 706.1
motion-picture industry 706.1
motion-picture photography 706.5, 714.1
motion-picture projector 714.12
motion pictures 706.1
motion-picture screen 706.7
motion-picture script 706.3
motion-picture set 706.4
motion-picture show 706.1
motion-picture studio 706.4
motion-picture theater 706.7
motions 321.1
motion sickness 85.30
motion study 832.9
motion to 517.21
motivate 172.6, 375.12, 886.11, 902.11
motivated 375.30, 570.18
motivating 375.25
motivating force 17.6
motivation 172.1, 375.2, 570.5
motivational 172.7, 375.25
motivator 17.6, 375.10, 375.11, 574.7, 886.4
motive (n) 375.1, 376.1, 380.1, 708.24, 937.1 (a) 172.7, 375.25, 902.23, 904.14
motive force 92.28, 892.7
motiveless 364.5
motivelessness 364.2, 364.3
motive power 17.6, 172.3, 902.1, 904.1, 1040.3
motivity 172.3
mot juste 533.1
motley (n) 5.9, 704.6, 707.10 (v) 47.7 (a) 35.16, 47.9, 47.12, 780.7, 782.3, 797.14, 945.6
motley fool 707.10
motleyness 782.1
motocar 179.9
motocross 744.1
motocycle 179.8
motor (n) 179.9, 858.10, 1040.3 (v) 177.33 (a) 172.7
motor abreaction 92.25
motorbike 179.8
motorboat (n) 180.1, 180.4 (v) 182.13
motorboating 50.13, 182.1
motorbus 179.13
motorcade 812.3
motorcar 179.9
motor coach 179.13
motor court 228.16
motorcycle (n) 179.8 (v) 177.33
motorcycle messenger 353.1
motorcycler 178.11
motorcycle race 457.12
motorcycling 177.6, 744.1
motorcyclist 178.11
motor-driven 1040.14
motorhead 178.12
motor home 228.17
motor hotel 228.16
motorial 172.7
motoric 172.7
motoring 177.6
motor inn 228.16
motorist 178.10

motorize 1040.13
motorized 1039.7, 1040.14
motorized vehicle 179.9
motorizing 1040.1
motor launch 180.4
motor lodge 228.16
motorman 178.12
motormouth 540.4
motor neuron 2.14
motor neuron disease 85.25
motor oil 1056.4
motor paralysis 85.27
motorscooter 179.8
motor ship 180.2
motorship 180.1
motor skill 84.2
motor-speed control system 1041.5
motor sport 744.1, 756.1
motor vehicle 179.9
Motrin 86.12
motte 310.15, 460.6
mottle (n) 47.3, 517.5 (v) 47.7, 517.19
mottled 47.12
mottledness 47.3
mottlement 47.3
motto 529.1, 647.2, 937.2, 974.1, 974.4
moue 110.9, 265.4
mound (n) 237.4, 549.12, 745.1, 770.10, 1012.5 (v) 770.19
mount (n) 193.1, 237.6, 311.10, 311.13, 757.2, 901.10 (v) 75.21, 172.5, 177.34, 184.39, 191.5, 193.8, 193.11, 193.12, 200.8, 251.6, 272.10, 272.12, 704.28, 912.7
mount a coup d'état 327.7
mountain 237.6, 247.3, 272.4, 283.3
mountain artillery 462.11
mountain bike (n) 179.8 (v) 177.33
mountain biker 178.11
mountain-building 237.6
mountain chain 237.6
mountain climber 193.6
mountain climbing 760.6
mountain country 237.1
mountain dew 88.18
mountain-dwelling 272.17
mountained 272.18
mountaineer 178.1, 193.6, 227.10
mountaineering 760.6
mountain flax 1022.5
mountain goat 311.8
mountain lake 241.1
mountain lion 311.21
mountain man 227.10
mountain meteorology 317.5
mountain nymph 678.9
mountainous 237.8, 247.7, 257.20, 272.18
mountainous country 237.1
mountainousness 257.7
mountain oyster 10.20
mountain range 237.6, 272.4
mountains 237.1
mountainside 237.2
mountain skiing 753.1
Mountain Standard Time 832.3
mountain stream 238.1
mountain system 237.6
Mountain time 832.3
mountaintop 198.2, 237.6
mountain troops 461.23
mountain wind 318.1
mount an attack 459.17
mount an offensive 459.17
mountebank 357.6, 707.1
mountebankery 354.7, 356.4
mounted infantryman 461.12
mounted policeman 178.8, 1008.15
mount guard 1008.20
Mounties 1008.17
mounting (n) 172.2, 193.1, 251.1, 704.13, 901.10 (a) 172.8, 193.14, 272.14, 632.12
Mount Olympus 681.9
mount one's high horse 141.8
mount Pegasus 720.14
mount the barricades 327.7
mount the ladder of success 409.10
mount the throne 417.14, 615.13
mount up to 630.13, 792.8
mourn 98.14, 112.17, 115.10
mourner 115.8, 309.7
mourners' bench 703.14
Mourner's Kaddish 696.4
mournful 98.20, 112.26, 115.19, 309.22
mournfulness 98.5, 112.11
mourning (n) 115.1, 115.7 (a) 115.18
mourning band 115.7
mourning ring 115.7
mouse 77.6, 85.38, 139.6, 258.4, 491.5, 1042.4
mouse-brown 40.3
mouse-colored 39.4
mouse-dun 40.3
mouse-eared 48.15
mouse-gray 39.4
mousehound 311.22
mouselike 311.44
mouse pad 1042.18
mouse potato 1042.18
mouser 311.20
mousetrap 356.12, 1074.10
mousiness 39.1, 139.4
mousse (n) 10.40, 10.46, 320.2, 1062.5 (a) 298.10
mousseux 320.6
mousy 36.7, 39.4, 51.10, 127.23, 139.12, 311.44, 491.10
mouth (n) 2.12, 2.18, 8.16, 142.4, 242.1, 292.4, 524.18 (v) 8.27, 73.9, 265.8, 354.23, 524.19, 525.9, 543.10
mouth bow 711.10
mouthbreather 924.4
mouthbreeder 311.30
mouthfeel 944.1
mouthful 8.2, 545.3, 794.3
mouth harp 711.10
mouth honor 693.2
mouthing 354.6, 525.4, 693.2
mouthlike 292.22
mouth off 142.8, 502.7
mouth organ 711.10
mouthpiece 347.4, 466.3, 551.5, 576.5, 597.3, 711.6, 754.1
mouth-to-mouth resuscitation 2.21
mouthwash 72.3, 79.17, 86.22
mouth-watering (n) 13.3 (a) 8.33, 63.8, 63.10, 100.30, 377.8
mouthy 545.9
mouton 10.16
moutonnée 283.15
movability 172.3, 854.1, 894.5
movable 176.18, 854.6, 894.15
movable-do system 709.7
movable feast 20.4
movableness 172.3
movables 229.1, 471.2
move (n) 328.3, 403.2, 415.3, 759.13, 889.2, 995.2 (v) 93.14, 105.12, 145.5, 159.17, 162.2, 172.5, 172.6, 176.11, 177.18, 321.4, 328.4, 375.12, 422.6, 439.5, 734.8, 894.7, 902.11, 904.9
move ahead 216.10
move along 177.18
move aside 164.6
move away 168.2, 188.6
move back 163.6
move behind 166.3
moved 93.23, 105.20, 375.30
move forward 162.2
move heaven and earth 360.5, 403.5, 403.15, 794.8
move in 159.17, 225.7, 472.10, 894.12
move in a circle 914.5
move in on 472.10
move into 225.7, 404.3
moveless 173.13
movement 12.2, 12.4, 84.2, 172.1, 177.1, 328.3, 330.1, 458.4, 517.14, 609.33, 708.24, 709.22, 712.7, 720.7, 722.4, 770.3, 886.9, 896.2, 1040.4
movement of air 318.1
movements 321.1, 1040.4
move off 168.2, 188.6
move on 177.18
move one's bowels 12.13
move one to 375.22
move out 188.6
move over 172.5
move quickly 401.5
mover 178.2, 375.10, 726.1, 759.22, 886.4, 892.7
mover and shaker, a 894.6
mover and shaker 375.10, 997.8
movers and shakers 249.5
moves 321.1
move smoothly 287.9
move the goalposts 645.13
move to action 375.12
move to tears 145.5
move to the side 164.6
move up 162.4
move up in the world 162.4, 409.10, 1010.7
move with the times 841.6
movie (n) 706.1 (a) 706.9
movie actor 707.4
movie buff 866.3
moviedom 706.1
moviegoer 221.5, 704.27
movie house 706.7
moviemaker 706.4
movie palace 706.7
movies 706.1
movies, the 706.1
movie screen 706.7
movie star 707.4
movie studio 706.4
movie theater 706.7
moving (n) 172.1, 177.1, 375.2 (a) 93.22, 98.20, 105.30, 145.8, 162.6, 172.7, 177.36, 375.25, 544.14, 902.23
moving backwards 172.2
moving on 172.2
moving part 385.4
moving parts 1040.4
moving pictures 706.1
moving-picture show 706.1
moving road 238.1
moving spirit 375.9, 375.10
moving staircase 912.4
moving stairway 912.4
mow (n) 110.9, 265.4, 386.7, 770.10 (v) 265.8, 268.6, 287.5, 1069.19
mow down 308.17, 395.19, 913.5
mowed 268.9
mown 268.9
moxa 1020.15
moxie (n) 17.3, 18.1, 330.2, 359.3, 413.1, 492.3 (a) 330.17
MP3 1042.18
Mr 76.7
Mr. and Mrs. 563.9
Mr. and Mrs. Nobody 998.7
Mr. Big 997.11
Mr. Brown 606.5
Mr. Cool 565.3
Mr. Fixit 396.10
MRI scan 91.9
Mr. Justice 596.1
Mr. Moneybags 618.7
Mr. Nice Guy 143.8, 659.2
Mr. Nobody 606.5
Mr. Right 104.16
Mrs 77.8
Mrs. Brown 606.5
Mrs. Grundy 495.7, 579.1, 579.3, 867.2
Mrs. Malaprop 975.7
Mr. Smith 606.5
Mrs. Smith 606.5
Mrs. Warren's profession 665.8
Mr. Universe 15.6
Mr. X 528.2
Ms 77.8, 648.4
MSG 397.4
Ms. Right 104.16
mubblefubbles 96.6
much (n) 247.3, 991.2 (a) 247.8, 991.7
much acclaimed 662.16
muchacha 302.6
muchacho 302.5
much-admired 155.11
much ado about nothing 355.2, 998.3
much at fault 510.25

much at one 784.14, 943.8
much cry and little wool 998.3
much esteemed 662.15
much in evidence 31.7, 247.10, 348.8, 662.17
muchness 247.1, 884.3, 991.2
much obliged 150.5
much of a muchness (n) 994.1 (a) 784.14, 943.8
much on one's plate 330.5
much sought-after 100.30, 578.11
much the same 784.14, 790.8
much to answer for 656.1, 674.4
much to be desired 100.30, 995.5
much to be regretted 113.10
mucidness 1062.3
muciferous 1062.13
mucific 1062.13
mucilage 803.4, 1056.2, 1062.5
mucilaginous 1062.12
mucilaginousness 803.3, 1062.2
mucinous 1062.13
muck (n) 80.7, 80.8, 890.4, 1062.8 (v) 80.15
muck about 998.15
muck about with 340.9
muck around 340.9, 998.15
mucked up 393.29, 799.4, 810.16
mucker 497.6, 660.2
muckety-muck 997.9
muckhole 1062.9
muckiness 80.2, 1062.4
mucking around 998.9
muckrake 512.10
muckraker 512.6, 946.7
muckraking 512.2, 609.14
muck up 80.15, 393.11, 799.3, 811.3, 975.15
muck-up 975.6
muckworm 484.4
mucky 80.23, 1062.14
mucoid 1056.9, 1062.13
mucosity 1062.3
mucous 2.33, 1062.13
mucous membrane 2.6
mucousness 1062.3
mucro 285.3
mucronate 285.9
mucronated 285.9
mucronation 285.1
muculent 1062.13
mucus 2.24, 13.2, 80.7, 803.4, 1056.2, 1062.5
mud 80.6, 243.1, 1059.6, 1062.8
muddiness 36.2, 38.3, 80.1, 1062.4
muddle (n) 263.1, 410.6, 522.7, 810.2, 985.3 (v) 263.3, 414.11, 799.3, 810.9, 811.3, 945.3, 971.13, 971.15, 985.7
muddle along 162.4, 414.10
muddle away 486.5
muddled 88.31, 810.16, 922.18, 971.25, 985.13
muddlehead 924.4
muddleheaded 922.18, 985.13
muddleheadedness 922.5, 985.3
muddlement 985.3
muddle through 162.4, 409.12
muddy (v) 80.15, 971.15 (a) 36.7, 38.11, 80.22, 243.3, 522.15, 1062.14
muddybrained 922.18
muddy the waters 917.10
mudflat 243.1, 276.2
mudger 357.9, 936.7
mudguard 1008.3
mudhole 284.3, 1062.9
mudhook 180.16
mudlark 178.3
mudpack 1016.11
mud puddle 1062.9
mudroom 197.13
mudsill 901.9
mudslide 194.4
mudsling 512.10
mudslinger 512.6
mudslinging 512.2, 609.14
mudslinging campaign 609.14
muezzin 699.12
muff (n) 414.5, 414.9, 975.6 (v) 414.11
muffed 414.21
muffer 414.9
muffin 10.31
muffing 414.4
muffin top 283.3
muffle (n) 51.4, 283.8 (v) 15.14, 16.11, 51.8, 51.9, 295.19, 345.8
muffled 52.17, 295.31, 519.5
muffled drum 309.5
muffled drums 115.6
muffled tone 52.2
muffle kiln 742.5
muffler 51.4
muffle up 345.8
muff one's cue 414.11, 975.15
muff one's lines 414.11, 975.15
mufti 5.8, 465.6, 699.12
mug (n) 216.4, 292.4, 358.2, 508.7, 593.4, 714.3 (v) 265.8, 459.15, 482.16, 671.11, 704.31, 714.14
mugger 459.12, 483.5, 572.10, 593.4, 671.9
mugginess 1019.6, 1065.2
mugging 459.1, 482.3
muggle 572.7, 606.5
muggles 87.11
muggy 1019.28, 1065.15
muggy weather 1019.7
mugient 60.6
mug shot 714.3
mugwump 362.5, 363.4, 430.12, 467.4, 609.28
mugwumpery 362.1, 467.1, 609.26
mugwumpian 362.9, 363.12, 609.45
mugwumpish 362.9, 363.12, 609.45
mugwumpism 362.1, 467.1, 609.26
Muhammad 684.4
Muhammadan (n) 675.23 (a) 675.31
Muhammadanism 675.13
mulberry 46.3
mulch (n) 890.4 (v) 890.8, 1069.17
mulct (n) 603.3 (v) 356.18, 603.5
mule 87.21, 271.5, 311.15, 361.6, 732.5, 797.8
mule deer 311.5
mule-jenny 271.5
mule skinner 178.9
muleteer 178.9
mule train 812.3
muley cow 311.6
muley head 311.6
muliebral 77.13
muliebrity 77.1, 77.2
muliebrous 77.14
mulish 311.45, 361.8
mulishness 361.1
mull 66.4, 1020.17
mullah 699.12
muller 1051.7
mullet 647.2, 882.1
mulligan 10.11
mulligan stew 10.11
mulligrubs 110.10, 112.6
mullion 273.4
mullioned 170.11
mull over 931.13
multiangular 278.11
multibillionaire 618.7
multicasting 1035.2
multicellular 305.19
multicellularity 305.4
multicolor (n) 35.4, 47.1 (a) 47.9
multicolored 35.16, 47.9
multicolorous 47.9
multiculti (n) 782.1 (a) 782.3
multicultural 782.3, 783.4, 797.14
multiculturalism 782.1, 783.1, 797.1
multiculturism 782.1, 797.1
multicurie 1037.6
multidisciplinary 928.15
multiduplication 251.1
multiethnic 783.4, 797.14
multifaceted 218.7, 797.14
multifamily (n) 225.3 (a) 225.15
multifarious 780.7, 783.3, 799.4, 884.6
multifariousness 783.1, 884.1
multiflorous 310.38
multifold 783.3, 883.8, 884.6
multifoldness 884.1
multifoliate 310.41
multiform 783.3
multiformity 783.1
multifunctional 783.4
multigenerational 561.7
multigrain 1051.12
multigraph 548.14, 785.8
multi-gym 84.1
multi-jet 181.3
multilateral 218.7, 278.11
multilaterality 218.1
multilateral symmetry 264.1
multilateral trade 731.1
multilayer 799.4
multilayered 799.4
multilevel 799.4
multilevel marketing 347.13
multilevel sales 347.13
multilingual 523.16
multiloquence 540.1
multiloquent 540.9
multiloquious 540.9
multiloquy 540.1
multimedia 552.1, 1042.18
multimedia CD 549.10
multimedia computer 1042.2
multimillionaire 618.7
multimillionairess 618.7
multinational 797.14
multinomial 883.8
multinucleate 305.21
multiparity 1.1
multiparous 78.15
multipartite 802.20
multiparty politics 609.1
multiparty system 609.24
multipath transmission 1034.16
multiphase 783.3
multiple (n) 883.4 (a) 783.3, 883.8, 884.6
multiple-choice 862.8
multiple-choice test 938.2
multiple-disk clutch 1040.10
multiple-feed closed loop 1041.6
multiple fruit 10.38
multiple-guess test 938.2
multiple image 1035.5
multiple-missile warhead 1074.3
multiple party system 609.24
multiple personality 92.20
multiple projector 1074.10
multiple sclerosis 85.25
multiple warhead 1074.3
multiplex (n) 706.7 (a) 783.3
multiplex transmission 1034.16
multipliable 1017.25
multiplicand 883.4
multiplication 78.2, 883.4, 890.2, 1017.2
multiplication table 883.4
multiplicity 783.1, 884.1
multiplied 251.7, 883.8
multiplier 883.4
multiplier channels 1041.6
multiply 78.8, 251.6, 883.6, 884.5, 890.7, 1017.18
multiply by four 880.2
multiply by three 877.2
multiply by two 874.3
multiplying (n) 883.4 (a) 251.8
multiply out 1017.18
multiprocessor 1042.2
multi-prop 181.2
multipurpose 783.4
multiracial 782.3, 797.14
multisegmental 802.20
multistage 296.6
multistage flight 1075.1
multistage rocket 1074.5, 1075.2, 1075.9
multistory 272.14
multitheism 675.5
multitheist 675.16
multitrack player 50.11
multitrack recorder 50.11
multitrack sound system 50.11
multitude 247.3, 770.4, 884.3
multitude, the 606.2
multitudinal 884.6
multitudinous 247.8, 884.6
multitudinousness 884.1
multivalence 1060.4

multivalent 1060.10
multivocal 539.4
multivocality 539.1
multiword expression 529.1
multiword lexical unit 529.1
multtasking 330.5
mum (n) 51.1 (a) 51.12, 344.9
mumble (n) 52.4, 525.4 (v) 8.27, 52.10, 524.25, 525.9
mumblecore 706.2
mumbling (n) 52.4, 525.4 (a) 52.18
Mumbo Jumbo 680.9
mumbo jumbo 356.5, 520.2, 522.3, 523.9
mumbo jumbo 689.1, 691.4, 691.5
mummer 357.7, 707.1, 707.2
mummery 354.6, 356.11, 580.4, 693.1, 704.8
mummification 307.15, 309.3, 397.3, 1066.3
mummified 397.13, 1066.9
mummify 309.21, 397.10, 1066.6
mummy 307.15, 560.12, 1066.2
mummy-brown 40.3
mummy case 309.11
mummy chamber 309.16
mummylike 303.18
mumpish 110.24, 112.25
mumpishness 110.8, 112.8
mumps 110.10, 112.6
mumsy 560.12
munch (n) 8.2 (v) 8.27
munchies 8.2
munchies, the 100.7
munching 8.1
mundane 686.3, 695.16, 721.5, 987.5, 1005.8
mundane, the 686.2
mundane astrology 1073.20
mundane house 1073.20
mundaneness 695.2
mundivagant 177.36
mundunugu 690.7
mung 80.7
mungy 810.15
municipal 230.11
municipal building 230.5
municipal clerk 550.1
municipal council 423.1
municipal government 230.1
municipality 230.1, 594.4
municipal library 558.1
munificence 485.1
munificent 485.4
muniments 549.5, 957.1
munition (n) 385.4 (v) 385.8
munitions 385.4, 386.1, 462.1
munitions of war 462.1
munitions plant 739.3
Munsell chroma 35.6
Munsell scale 35.7
muon 258.8
mural (n) 712.10 (a) 213.11
murder (n) 307.5, 308.1, 308.2 (v) 308.16, 414.11
murdered 414.21
murderer 308.11, 593.1, 593.3
murderous 144.26, 308.24, 671.21
murderous frenzy 926.7
murderous insanity 926.7
murderousness 671.1
murder the King's English 525.11, 531.3
murder the Queen's English 525.11, 531.3
murder wholesale 308.17
muricate 285.10, 285.14
murk (n) 112.7, 522.3, 1027.2 (v) 38.7, 1027.9 (a) 1027.15
murkiness 38.3, 112.7, 522.3, 971.4, 1027.2
murksome 1027.15
murky 38.11, 112.24, 522.15, 971.19, 1004.10, 1027.15, 1027.17
murmur (n) 52.4, 115.3 (v) 52.10, 115.15, 238.18, 318.20, 524.25, 525.9
murmuration 52.4, 770.6
murmured 52.16
murmuring (n) 52.4, 115.4, 525.4 (a) 52.18, 108.7
murmurish 52.18
murmurous 52.18
Murphy's Law 759.6, 843.3
murshid 699.12
muscle (n) 15.2, 725.1, 769.5 (v) 15.12, 902.12 (a) 2.26
muscle-bound 15.16
musclebound 425.7
muscle-bound between the ears 922.17
muscle craps 759.8
muscle disease 85.10
muscle-flexing (n) 514.1 (a) 514.3
muscle in 214.5
muscle man 15.6, 15.7, 593.4, 671.10
muscle pill 86.32
muscle power 18.1
muscle relaxant 86.12
muscle-relaxant 86.45
muscles 2.3
muscles, the 2.3
muscle sense 24.5
muscling 902.3
muscular 2.26, 15.16
muscular disease 85.10
muscular disorder 85.10
muscular dystrophy 85.25
muscularity 15.2
musculature 2.3, 15.2
Muse 920.8
muse (n) 375.9, 720.11 (v) 524.24
muse (n) 985.2, 986.2 (v) 931.12, 985.9
museful 931.21, 985.11
musefulness 985.2, 986.8
Muse of history 719.1
museology 386.9
muse on 931.13
muse on other things 985.9
muse over 931.13
Muses, the 375.9, 710.22, 720.11
Muses: Calliope 986.2
musette 711.9
museum 386.9, 397.7, 770.11
museum piece 712.9, 842.6, 870.5
mush (n) 93.8, 216.4, 292.4, 1063.2 (v) 177.30
mushhead 924.4
mushiness 93.8, 922.8, 1063.1
mushroom (n) 10.35, 87.19, 310.4 (v) 14.2, 251.6, 259.7, 282.7, 890.7 (a) 40.3
mushroom cloud 1038.16
mushrooming 251.8
mush through 184.40
mushy 16.17, 93.21, 1062.12, 1063.6
music 568.3, 708.1, 708.28, 709.1
musica ficta 708.20
musical (n) 706.2, 708.34 (a) 704.33, 708.47, 708.48, 720.18
musical beds 645.5
musical box 711.15
musical chairs 854.3
musical comedy 708.34
musical copy 708.28
musical drama 708.34
musical ear 48.3, 708.31
musical flair 708.31
musical instrument 711.1
musicality 48.3, 708.2, 708.31, 709.1
musicalize 708.35, 708.46
musically inclined 708.47
musicalness 708.2
musical notation 349.1, 708.28
musical note 709.14
musical occasion 708.32
musical performance 708.33
musical phrase 708.24
musical program 708.33
musical quality 708.2
musical score 708.28
musical sense 708.31
musical sentence 708.24
musical sound 708.2
musical stage 708.34
musical talent 708.31
musical theater 704.1, 708.34
musical thought 720.1
music appreciation 708.1
music box 711.15
music buff 710.21
music critic 547.15, 718.4
music criticism 723.1, 946.2
music director 710.17
music drama 708.34
music fan 710.21
music festival 708.32
music-flowing 708.48
music hall 197.4, 704.14
musician 707.1, 710.1
musicianly 708.47
musicianship 708.31
music in space 717.1
musicless 61.4
musiclike 708.48
music lover 710.21
music-loving 708.47
music lyre 711.22
music-mad 708.47
music maker 710.1
music-making 708.30
musicmonger 710.21
musico 710.1
music of the soul 720.1
music of the spheres 708.3, 1073.4
music of the spheres, the 807.1
musicographer 710.20
musicography 709.1
musicologist 710.20
musicology 709.1
musicophile (n) 710.21 (a) 708.47
music paper 708.28
music roll 708.28, 711.12
music school 567.7
music stand 711.22
music teacher 710.20
music theater 704.1, 708.34
music theory 708.1, 709.1
music-tongued 708.48
music variety 708.1
music video 706.1, 708.32
music wire 711.20
musing (n) 931.2, 931.3, 985.2, 986.8 (a) 931.21, 985.11
musing on the past 837.4
musk 13.2, 70.2
musk deer 311.5
musket 462.10
musketeer 461.9, 904.8
musketry 459.8, 462.1, 462.3, 904.2
muskiness 70.1
musk ox 311.6
musky 70.9
Muslim (n) 675.23 (a) 675.31
Muslim calendar 832.8
Muslim fundamentalism 675.13
Muslim fundamentalist 675.23
Muslimism 675.13
Muslim militant 675.23
Muslim rulers 608.7
muslin 180.14
muss 811.2
mussed up 810.14
mussel 311.29
mussitate 52.10
Mussulman 675.23
muss up 811.2
mussy 810.15
must (n) 71.2, 88.17, 641.1, 963.2, 1001.2 (v) 641.4, 963.10 (a) 75.28, 420.12, 641.15
mustache 3.11
mustached 3.25
mustachio 3.11
mustachioed 3.25
mustachios 3.11
mustang 311.10
mustard (n) 10.12 (a) 43.4
mustard plaster 86.33
mustard seed 258.7
mustardy 68.7
mustard-yellow 43.4
mustee 797.8
muster (n) 458.7, 615.7, 770.1, 871.6 (v) 172.6, 387.14, 420.11, 458.18, 615.17, 770.16, 770.18
muster courage 492.12
muster in 615.17
mustering 615.7
mustering in 615.7
mustering out 465.6

muster one's resources 458.19
muster out 771.8
muster roll 871.6
muster up 375.13, 420.11
must have 963.9
must-have (n) 963.2 (a) 767.9
mustiness 71.2, 117.3
must item 963.2
must-read 718.1
must-see 122.10
musty 71.5, 75.28, 117.9, 393.42, 842.14
mutability 307.12, 782.1, 828.1, 854.1
mutable 307.33, 362.9, 782.3, 828.7, 854.6
mutant (n) 671.9, 852.3 (a) 671.21, 852.10
mutate 782.2, 852.6, 852.7
mutated form 852.3
mutation 265.3, 524.13, 852.3
mute (n) 51.3, 51.4, 309.7, 524.12, 707.7, 711.22 (v) 16.11, 51.9 (a) 51.12, 344.9, 525.13, 1055.5
mute button 51.4
muted 35.22, 52.17, 524.30
muted ecstasy 985.2
mutedness 52.2
muteness 51.2, 344.2, 525.6
mute witness 957.1
mutilate 255.10, 265.7, 393.13, 802.14
mutilated 265.12, 393.27, 795.5
mutilation 85.38, 255.3, 265.3, 393.1, 802.2
mutineer (n) 327.5, 418.3 (v) 327.7
mutineering 327.11
mutinous 325.5, 327.11, 418.5
mutinousness 325.1, 327.3
mutiny (n) 327.4, 418.1, 453.1 (v) 327.7, 453.3
mutism 51.2, 525.6
mutt 311.18, 924.3
mutter (n) 52.4, 115.3, 525.4 (v) 52.10, 115.15, 318.20, 524.25, 525.9
muttering (n) 52.4, 525.4 (a) 52.18, 108.7
mutton 10.16, 311.7
mutton chop 10.19
muttonchop 10.16
muttonchops 3.8
muttonhead 924.4
muttonheaded 922.17
muttonheadedness 922.4
mutual 450.5, 476.9, 769.9, 777.11, 863.5
mutual adjustment 788.4
mutual admiration 863.1
mutual affinity 100.3, 587.5
mutual agreement 437.1
mutual approach 169.1
mutual assistance 449.1, 450.1
mutual attraction 100.3, 775.1, 907.1
mutual company 1008.4
mutual concession 468.1
mutual-defense treaty 437.2
mutual friend 588.1
mutual fund 729.4, 737.16, 738.2
mutual help 449.1
mutual induction 1032.15
mutualism 450.1
mutuality 450.1, 455.1, 777.1, 863.1
mutually approaching 169.3
mutually commit 437.5
mutual regard 587.3
mutual replacement 863.1
mutual repulsion 908.1
mutual respect 587.3
mutual support 863.1
mutual supportiveness 455.1
mutual transfer 863.1
mutual understanding 332.5, 788.2
muzhik 606.6
muzzle (n) 2.11, 51.4, 283.8, 292.4, 428.4 (v) 19.10, 51.8, 428.8, 428.10
muzzle oneself 51.5
muzzy 88.33, 525.12, 922.18, 985.13
muzzy speech 525.1
mwah 562.4
my dear lady 77.8
my dear man 76.7
my dear sir 76.7
my dear woman 77.8
myelic 2.26
myelin sheath 2.14
my good lady 77.8
my good man 76.7
my humble self 865.5
My Lady 648.2
My Lord 648.2
my man 588.4
myocardial infarction 85.19
myoid 2.26
myon 2.3
myopathy 85.10
myopia 28.3
myopic 28.11, 922.14, 923.10
myrcia oil 70.2
myriad, a 884.4
myriad (n) 882.10, 991.2 (a) 884.6
myriads 991.2
myriapod 311.31, 311.32
myriorama 33.7
myriotheism 675.5
myriotheist 675.16
myrmidon 577.1, 577.3, 616.8
myrrh 70.2, 70.4
myself 865.5
mystagogue 689.11
mysteries: baptism 701.4
mysterious 122.11, 345.11, 346.11, 522.17, 522.18, 539.4, 689.23, 870.15, 930.16, 971.27
mysteriousness 122.3, 522.6, 870.7
mystery 122.3, 345.5, 522.6, 522.8, 689.1, 701.3, 706.2, 870.7, 930.6, 971.3
mystery of mysteries 345.5
mystes 699.15
mystic (n) 689.11 (a) 519.5, 522.18, 683.13, 689.23
mystical 522.18, 683.13, 689.23
mystical experience 683.10
mystical intuition 683.10
mysticism 683.10, 689.1, 692.1
mystic transport 691.3
mystification 346.1, 522.3, 569.1, 689.1, 936.1
mystificator 936.7
mystified 971.25, 1013.24
mystifier 936.7
mystify 522.12, 569.3, 936.9, 971.13
mystifying 569.6, 971.27
mystique 662.6, 675.2, 953.6
mytacism 525.5
myth 354.10, 842.2, 986.5
mythic 678.15, 986.21
mythical 354.29, 662.16, 678.15, 722.8, 870.14, 986.21
mythical lore 678.14
mythical monsters 127.9
mythical national championship 746.1
mythicalness 870.2
mythicism 678.14
mythicization 986.2
mythicize 722.7
mythicized 986.21
mythicizer 986.12
mythification 986.2
mythified 986.21
mythifier 986.12
mythify 722.7
mythmaker 722.5, 986.12
mythological 678.15, 722.8, 842.12, 986.21
mythologist 678.14
mythologize 354.18, 722.7
mythology 678.14, 842.2
mythomane 357.9
mythomania 354.8
mythomaniac 357.9
mythopoeia 986.2
mythopoeic 722.8
mythopoet 722.5, 986.12
mythopoetic 722.8
mythopoetical 722.8
mythos 722.4
myxomatosis 85.41
n 930.6, 1017.3
nab 429.16, 472.9, 480.18
nabab 575.9, 575.12
nabbing 480.2
nabob 575.12, 618.7, 997.8
nachos 10.9
nacre 47.6, 1025.18
nacré 47.10
nacred 47.10
nacreous 35.22, 47.10, 1025.37
nacreous clou 1025.18
nacreousness 47.2, 1025.18
nacry 47.10
nada 762.2
nadir 199.1, 211.3, 274.4
nadiral 199.8
nads 2.13, 142.3
nag (n) 96.10, 110.12, 311.10, 311.12, 757.2 (v) 96.13, 375.14, 440.12, 510.16, 989.19
nag at 440.12
nagged 989.23
nagging (n) 440.3, 510.4 (a) 110.22, 440.18, 510.23, 989.25
naggy 110.22
nagual 678.1
Nahum 684.1
naiad 678.10
NAIA Tournament 747.1
naif 953.9
naïf 358.1, 416.3
nail (n) 285.4 (v) 472.9, 480.14, 480.17, 604.14, 800.8, 989.11
nail-biter 1012.4
nail-biting (n) 128.1, 130.3 (a) 126.7, 128.11
nail down 855.7, 957.10, 970.11
nailed down 957.20, 970.20
nailed it 409.14
nailhead 198.4
nail it 407.4, 407.7, 409.7
nail one's colors to the mast 359.8
nail polish 1016.11
nails 15.8, 474.4, 1046.6
nail up 800.8
naive 301.10, 416.5, 499.7, 923.12, 930.11, 953.22, 954.9
naïve 1006.16
naiveness 416.1
naïveness 954.2
naïve realism 1052.6
naivete 954.2
naiveté 301.3, 657.2, 1006.3
naïveté 416.1, 499.2
naivety 416.1, 954.2
naked 6.14, 31.6, 292.17, 348.10, 499.8, 798.7, 1006.15
naked ape 312.7
naked ape, the 312.5
naked as a jaybird 6.14
naked as a worm 6.14
naked as the day one was born 6.14
naked eye 2.9, 27.9, 31.3
naked fact 761.3
naked force 424.2
nakedness 6.3, 499.3, 1006.3
naked steel 1040.2
naked to 897.6
naked truth, the 973.3
namaste 155.2, 585.4, 820.5
namby-pamby (n) 16.6, 93.8, 491.5 (a) 16.14, 93.21, 500.18, 1005.7
namby-pambyism 93.8
namby-pambyness 65.1, 93.8
name (n) 526.1, 527.3, 662.1, 662.9, 997.8 (v) 371.19, 517.18, 527.11, 615.11, 865.11, 957.13, 1017.17 (a) 997.17
nameable 865.13
name and address 553.9
name a price 630.11
name-calling 512.2
named 371.26, 527.14, 814.5
name day 832.4, 850.4
name-dropper 141.7, 606.7, 651.3
name for office 371.19
name in bright lights 352.4
nameless 528.3, 661.14
namelessness 528.1
name names 865.11
name of the game 518.1

name of the game, the 196.5, 767.3, 997.6
namesake 527.3
name to conjure with 662.2
naming (n) 371.8, 517.3, 527.2, 615.2 (a) 517.23
Namtar 680.5
nana 560.16
Nanak 684.4
nance 75.15, 77.10
nancy 77.10
nanny 77.9, 311.8, 1008.8
nanny goat 77.9, 311.8
nanodegree 567.5
nanofamous 352.4
nanoid 258.13
nanoscience 1068.3
nanosecond 824.2, 830.3
nanosized 258.12
naos 703.4
nap (n) 22.3, 294.1 (v) 22.13, 740.6
Napaea 678.9
napalm bomb 462.20
napery 4.1, 8.13, 735.3
naphtha launch 180.4
napiform 279.17
napkin 8.13
napoleon 728.4
Napoleonic Code 673.5, 673.8
nappe 238.11
napping 22.21, 930.12, 984.8, 985.11
nappy 3.27, 88.31, 294.7
Naraka 682.1
narc 576.10, 1008.15
narcism 140.1
narcissism 75.11, 104.1, 140.1, 651.1
narcissist 75.16, 140.5, 651.3
narcissistic 104.26, 140.8, 140.10, 651.5
Narcissus 140.5, 1016.9
narcist 140.5
narcistic 140.8, 140.10
narcohypnosis 22.6, 22.7
narcohypnotic 22.24
narcolepsy 22.6
narcoleptic 22.21
narcoma 22.6
narcose 22.21
narcosis 22.6, 25.1, 94.2, 94.4
narcoterrorism 732.1
narcotic (n) 25.3, 87.3 (a) 22.23, 25.9, 86.45, 670.16
narcotic addiction 87.1
narcotic drug 86.5
narcotics 732.3
narcotics abuse 87.1
narcotics addict 87.21
narcotics agent 576.10
Narcotics Anonymous 87.1
narcotics pusher 732.4
narcotics smuggling 732.2
narcotics traffic 732.1
narcotic stupor 22.6
narcotic trance 22.6
narcotization 22.6, 25.1
narcotize 22.20, 25.4, 94.8, 120.5, 670.6
narcotized 22.21, 25.6, 25.8, 87.23, 94.9
narcotizing (n) 120.1, 670.2 (a) 25.9
narcous 22.21
nard 1056.3
nares 69.5, 283.8
nargileh 89.6
naris 2.11, 69.5
nark (n) 551.6 (v) 551.13
narrate 719.5, 722.7
narratio 598.7
narration 349.2, 719.2, 722.1, 722.2, 722.3
narrational 719.7, 722.9
narrative (n) 719.2, 722.1, 722.2, 722.3 (a) 719.7, 720.16, 722.9
narrative history 719.1
narrative literature 722.1
narrative poem 720.4
narrative poetry 722.1
narrator 718.4, 722.5
narrishkeit 520.2
narrow (n) 242.1, 270.3 (v) 210.5, 260.7, 270.11, 428.9, 798.4, 866.4, 959.3 (a) 210.7, 270.14, 339.12, 484.9, 500.19, 524.30, 619.7, 773.9, 980.10, 992.10
narrow brush 223.4
narrowcast (n) 771.1 (v) 771.4, 1034.25
narrow down 159.11
narrow escape 369.2
narrow gauge 270.1, 270.3
narrow-gauge 270.14
narrow-gauged 270.14, 980.10
narrowhearted 980.10
narrow house 309.16
narrowing (n) 260.1, 270.2, 773.1, 798.2 (a) 428.12
narrowing gap 169.1
narrowish 270.14
narrow margin 780.2
narrow means 619.1
narrow-minded 980.10
narrow-mindedness 980.1
narrowness 270.1, 484.3, 500.6, 773.3, 980.1, 992.2
narrow place 260.1
narrows 242.1, 270.3
narrow seas 242.1
narrow-souled 980.10
narrow-spirited 980.10
narrow squeak 223.4, 369.2
narrow sympathies 980.1
narrow the gap 167.3, 169.2
narrow views 980.1
narrow-waisted 270.16
narrowy 270.14
narthex 197.19, 703.9
nary one 222.6, 762.4
nasal (n) 524.12 (a) 2.32, 524.30, 525.12
nasal accent 525.1
nasal cavity 2.11, 69.5, 292.5, 524.18
nasal discharge 85.9
nasality 524.8
nasalization 525.1
nasalize 525.10
nasalized 524.30
nasal organ 2.11
nasal tone 525.1
nasal twang 525.1
nascence 818.4
nascency 1.1, 818.4
nascent 818.15
nastiness 64.3, 80.2, 98.1, 98.2, 144.5, 505.1, 666.4, 1000.2
Naströnd 682.3
nasty (v) 80.17 (a) 64.7, 80.23, 98.18, 144.20, 505.6, 666.9, 1000.9
nasty blow 96.5, 1011.2
nasty crack 489.7
nasty look 510.8
nasty spot 1006.1
natal 1.4, 226.5, 818.15
natal day 850.4
natal tongue 523.3
natant 182.58
natation 182.11, 760.8
natator 182.12
natatorial 182.58
natatorium 743.12, 760.8
natatory 182.58
nates 217.4
nation 227.1, 232.1, 312.1, 559.4
nation, the 606.1
national (n) 227.4, 232.7 (a) 312.16, 559.7, 606.8, 864.14
National Advisory Committee for Aeronautics 184.7
national anthem 458.11
National Archives 549.3
national assembly 613.1
National Association of Intercollegiate Athletics 747.1
national bank note 728.5
National Basketball Association 747.1
national chairperson 610.12
national championship 746.1
National Collegiate Athletic Association 747.1, 752.1
National Collegiate Athletic Association Tournament 747.1
national convention 609.8
national debt 623.1, 731.9
national defense 460.2
national deficit 623.1
national emergency 458.9
National Federation of State High School Athletic Associations 755.1
national flag 647.7
National Football League 746.1
national forest 310.13, 397.7
national government 612.1, 612.3
National Guard 461.24, 461.25
National Hockey League 749.1
national holiday 20.4
national honor 458.11
national income 627.1
National Invitational Tournament 747.1
nationalism 232.6, 591.2, 609.5, 952.7
nationalist 232.7, 591.3
nationalistic 591.4
nationality 226.1, 227.1, 232.1, 232.6, 312.1, 591.2
nationalization 226.3, 469.2, 476.3, 480.5, 611.6, 731.7
nationalize 476.7, 480.20, 611.16
national language 523.4
national leader 610.2
national leadership 609.3
National League, the 745.1
national library 558.1
national literature 547.12, 718.1
national militia 461.24
national newspaper 555.2
national park 397.7
national pastime, the 745.1
national production of goods and services 892.1
national seashore 397.7
national security 438.1
national service 458.8
national socialism 612.7
national style 498.7
national territory 158.4
national treasure 999.5
National Union Catalog 558.4
National Wildlife Service 397.5
nationhood 232.6
nation-state 232.1
nation-statehood 232.6
nationwide 864.14
native (n) 227.3, 232.7 (a) 226.5, 406.13, 416.6, 499.7, 767.8
Native American 312.3
native-born 226.5
native-born citizenship 226.2
native-bornness 226.1
native cleverness 920.2
native environment 228.18
native heath 228.1
native hue of resolution, the 359.1
native land 228.2, 232.2
native language 523.3
native metal 1058.3
native mineral 1058.2
nativeness 226.1
native soil 232.2
native speaker 523.17
native speech 523.3
native tendency 934.2
native to 767.8
native tongue 523.3
native to the place 226.5
native to the soil 226.5
native wit 920.1
nativism 226.1
nativity 1.1, 226.1, 818.4, 1073.20
Nativity, the 1.1
natter (n) 540.3 (v) 524.20, 540.5
nattiness 578.3
natty 578.13, 807.8
Natura 677.8
natural (n) 409.2, 413.12, 709.14, 759.11, 870.4, 924.8 (a) 349.15, 406.13, 416.6, 499.7, 533.6, 535.3, 559.6, 581.3, 767.8, 784.16, 798.6, 869.8, 934.6, 973.15
natural affection 104.4
natural astrology 1073.20
natural-born 226.5
natural-born fool 924.8
natural child 561.5

natural childbirth 1.1
natural color 35.1
natural death 307.6
natural development 861.1
natural empathy 93.4
natural endowment 413.4
natural fatherhood 560.2
natural fiber 271.1
natural flavor 62.1
natural food 7.3
natural gender 530.10
natural gift 413.4
natural growth 861.1
natural harbor 242.1
natural hexachord 709.8
natural hierarchy 809.4
natural history 1068.3
natural history museum 386.9
natural idiot 924.8
natural impulse 365.1
natural instinct 934.2
naturalism 416.2, 869.1, 973.7, 1052.6
naturalist (n) 1052.7, 1068.2 (a) 1052.12
naturalistic 349.14, 349.15, 869.8, 973.15, 1052.12
naturalistic description 349.2
naturalistic humanism 312.11
naturalization 187.7, 226.3, 373.7, 858.1
naturalize 226.4, 373.9, 858.11
naturalized 226.6, 373.15, 858.19
naturalized citizen 227.4
naturalized citizenship 226.3
natural lake 241.1
natural language 523.1
natural language processing 1042.20
natural law 869.4
natural light 1025.10
natural-looking 406.13
natural magic 690.1
natural man 406.3
natural mineral 1058.1, 1058.2
natural minor 709.6
natural motherhood 560.3
naturalness 406.3, 416.2, 499.2, 533.1, 535.1, 581.1, 798.1, 869.1, 973.7
natural parent 560.8
natural philosophy 1018.1
natural poker 759.10
natural politeness 580.3
natural radioactivity 1037.1
natural realism 1052.6
natural realist 1052.7
natural resource 1054.1
natural right 642.1
natural rights 430.2
natural satellite 1073.11
natural science 928.10, 1018.1
natural selection 861.3
natural state 406.3
natural tendency 934.2
natural to 767.8
natural virtues 653.3
natural weapon 462.1
natural wit 920.1
natural world 1052.2
natural world, the 1072.1
Nature 677.8
nature 406.3, 416.2, 767.4, 809.3, 865.4, 978.3, 1052.2, 1073.1
nature book 554.8
nature boy 206.1
Nature Conservancy 397.5
nature conservancy 397.1
nature conservation 397.1
nature girl 206.1
nature in the raw 406.3
naturelike 416.6
nature-lover 1072.3
nature of the beast, the (n) 767.4 (a) 349.15
nature of things, the 765.2
nature preserve 310.13
nature's nobleman 659.1
nature tourism 177.1
nature trail 383.2
nature worship 675.6, 697.1
nature worshiper 697.4
naturism 6.3, 675.6, 869.1
naturist 6.3
naturistic 6.14, 869.8
naturopathic 90.15
naturopathy 90.13
naught, a 998.6
naught 762.2
naughtiness 322.1, 327.1, 654.4
naughty 322.5, 327.8, 654.16
naughty bits 2.13
naughty child 427.4
Naughty Nineties 824.5
naughty word 513.4, 526.6
nausea 85.9, 85.30, 96.1, 99.2, 909.8
nauseant (n) 64.3, 79.17, 86.17, 86.18 (a) 64.7
nauseate 64.4, 98.11
nauseated 85.57, 96.20
nauseating 64.7, 80.23, 98.18
nauseation 85.30
nauseous 64.7, 85.57, 96.20
nauseousness 64.3, 80.2, 98.2
nautch girl 705.3, 707.1
nautical 182.57, 240.8
Nautical Almanac 832.7
Nautilus 84.1
Navajo loom 740.5
naval 182.57
naval academy 567.6
naval air station 184.22
naval cadet 183.4
Naval Construction Battalion 461.27
naval court 595.4
naval forces 461.27
naval intelligence 576.12
naval-intelligence man 576.9
naval militia 461.27
naval noncommissioned officer 575.19
naval officer 183.7, 575.19
naval operations 458.4
naval pilot 185.3
naval reserve 461.27
Naval Reservist 183.4
naval vessel 180.6
naval war 458.1
navar 184.6, 1036.2
navarch 575.19
nave 208.2, 703.9, 915.5
navel 208.2
navicert 549.6
navicular 284.16
naviform 284.16
navigability 182.1
navigable 182.59
navigable airspace 184.32
navigable river 238.1
navigable water 182.10
navigate 159.11, 161.7, 177.21, 182.13, 182.14, 184.36
navigate in space 1075.12
navigating 182.1
navigating officer 183.7
navigation 159.3, 159.8, 161.1, 182.1, 184.6, 573.1
navigational 159.19, 182.57
navigational satellite 1075.6
navigation and ranging 1036.2
navigation bar output 1042.18
navigation of empty space 1075.1
navigation system 517.10, 573.1
navigator 183.1, 183.6, 183.7, 185.4, 574.7
navigator-bombardier trainer 181.10
navvy 284.10, 726.2
Navy 461.21
navy 461.27
navy 89.7, 180.10
navy-blue 45.3
Navy Cross 646.6
navy man 461.6
navy officer 575.19
navy plug 89.7
Navy Seals 461.15
navy serviceperson 183.4
navy woman 461.6
nay 335.1, 371.6, 442.1, 935.14
naysay 335.3, 955.5
naysayer 452.3, 789.4, 955.4
naysaying (n) 335.1, 779.1 (a) 335.5, 779.6
Nazarene 675.17
Nazarite 675.17
naze 283.9
Nazism 612.7
Nazi swastika 647.6
NCAA football 746.1
NCAA Tournament 747.1
Neanderthal (n) 497.7 (a) 497.12
Neanderthalism 497.3
neap (n) 238.13, 274.2 (a) 274.7
neap tide 238.13, 274.2
near (v) 167.3, 223.7, 784.7, 839.6, 840.2 (a) 167.4, 220.4, 223.14, 270.14, 484.9, 587.19, 775.8, 784.14, 840.3
near as the bark on a tree 484.9
near at hand 840.3
near-blindness 28.2
nearby 223.15
near collision 184.20
near death 85.56, 307.32
near-death experience 307.1
near duplicate 784.3
Near East 231.6
near-equal 784.15
nearer 223.18
nearest 223.19
near future 839.1, 840.1
near go 369.2
nearing (n) 167.1 (a) 167.4, 223.14, 839.8, 840.3
nearish 223.14
near likeness 784.4
nearly die laughing 116.8
nearly duplicate 784.7
nearly duplicated 784.10
nearly reduplicated 784.10
nearly reproduce 784.7
nearly reproduced 784.10
nearly simultaneous 830.4
nearly the same 784.14
near miss 223.2, 369.2
near-miss 184.20, 223.4, 410.4
nearmost 223.19
nearness 167.1, 221.1, 223.1, 270.1, 484.3, 587.5, 775.1, 784.1
near one's end 307.32
near relation 559.2
near rhyme 720.9, 784.6, 849.4
near side 220.1
nearsighted 28.11, 922.14, 980.10
nearsightedness 27.1, 28.3, 922.2, 980.1
near-simultaneity 830.1
near-simultaneousness 830.1
near squeak 369.2
near-term 828.8
near the limit of hearing 52.16
near the mark 223.14
near the seat of power 894.14
near the surface 276.5
near the threshold of hearing 52.16
near thing 223.4, 369.2
neat (n) 311.6 (a) 180.20, 264.5, 413.22, 533.6, 535.3, 578.13, 798.7, 807.8, 999.13
neat as a button 807.8
neat as a pin 807.8
neaten 808.12
neat-fingered 413.23
neat-handed 413.23
neatherd 1070.3
neatness 533.1, 578.3, 807.3
neato 999.13
neat profit 472.3
neat weight 297.1
neb 283.8, 285.3
nebbies 87.5, 87.15
nebbish 16.6, 764.2, 998.7
Nebiim 683.3
nebula 1025.15, 1073.7
Nebula of Lyra 1073.7
Nebula of Orion 1073.7
nebular 1073.25
nebular hypothesis 1073.7, 1073.18
nebulose 1073.25
nebulosity 319.4, 1073.7
nebulosus 319.8
nebulous 319.8, 522.15, 864.11, 1073.25
nebulous stars 1073.7
necessarian (n) 964.5 (a) 964.10
necessarianism 964.4
necessaries 963.2
necessariness 963.1

necessary (n) 12.10 (a) 424.11, 641.15, 963.12, 963.13, 963.15, 970.13
necessary, the 728.2, 963.2
necessitarian (n) 964.5 (a) 963.15, 964.10
necessitarianism 964.4
necessitate 424.5, 886.12, 963.8, 964.7
necessitated 887.6
necessitation 963.1
necessities 963.2
necessitous 619.8, 963.12
necessitousness 619.2
necessitude 963.1
necessity 424.1, 619.2, 761.2, 963.1, 963.2, 963.7, 964.1, 970.1
necessity money 728.1
neck (n) 10.15, 260.1, 270.3, 800.4, 901.2 (v) 562.15, 604.17
neck and neck 223.14
neck-and-neck 790.7, 836.5
neck-and-neck race 790.3
neckband 280.3
necking 562.2
necklace 280.3, 498.6
necklace, the 604.6, 605.5
neck of the woods 231.1
neck tackle 746.3
necktie 5.31, 280.3
necktie party 604.6
neckwear 5.31
necrologic 719.6
necrological 309.22, 549.18, 719.6
necrologue 307.13
necrology 307.13, 549.12, 719.1
necromancer 689.13, 690.5
necromancy 689.5, 690.1
necromantic 690.14, 870.16
necrophilia 75.11
necrophiliac 75.16
necropolis 309.15
necropsy 307.17
necroscopy 307.17
necrose 393.22
necrosed 393.40
necrosis 85.9, 85.40
necrotic 393.40
necrotic tissue 85.40
nectar 10.8, 66.2
nectareous 63.8, 66.5
nectarize 66.4
nectar of the gods 88.13
nectarous 63.8, 66.5
nectary 310.28
neddy 311.15
née 1.4
need (n) 100.1, 619.2, 795.2, 963.2, 992.4 (v) 619.5, 963.9, 963.10, 992.7
need a break 21.5
need-based 619.9
need clarification 522.10
need doing 963.9
needed 963.13
need explanation 522.10
need for 963.2
needful 963.13
needful, the 728.2, 963.2
needfulness 963.3
neediness 619.2
needing 100.21, 795.4, 992.13
needle (n) 17.6, 50.11, 237.6, 285.3, 285.5, 310.11, 310.19, 517.4, 574.9 (v) 96.13, 285.6, 292.15, 375.15, 490.6, 741.4
needle, the 605.5
needle bath 79.8, 1065.8
needle bearing 915.7
needled 96.24
needlelike 285.9
needleman 741.2
needle park 87.20
needlepoint 741.1
needle-pointed 285.9
needler 741.2
needles 460.3
needle scar 1004.1
needle-sharp 285.9
needless 391.10, 993.17
needlessness 391.1, 993.4
needle valve 239.10
needle-witted 920.14
needlewoman 741.2
needlework 741.1
needleworker 5.34, 741.2
needling 375.5
needly 285.9
need no explanation 348.7
need no prodding 439.10
needs must 963.10
need to 963.10
need translation 522.10
needy 619.8, 619.10
needy, the 619.3
ne'er a one 222.6, 762.4
ne'er-do-well (n) 331.9, 660.2 (a) 331.19
nefarious 654.16, 661.12, 1000.9
nefariousness 654.4, 661.3, 1000.2
negate 16.11, 335.3, 395.13, 442.3, 451.6, 789.5, 900.7, 955.5, 958.4
negated 958.7
negating (n) 335.1 (a) 900.9
negation 92.24, 335.1, 395.6, 442.1, 451.1, 762.1, 789.1, 900.2, 958.1
negational 335.5
negativate 900.7
negative (n) 255.6, 335.1, 442.1, 444.2, 713.5, 714.10, 785.5, 786.6 (v) 335.3, 395.13, 442.3, 444.5, 900.7, 958.4 (a) 125.16, 335.5, 442.6, 451.8, 762.8, 779.6, 789.6, 1017.23, 1032.35
negative, the 935.14
negative acceleration 175.4
negative answer 442.1
negative attitude 335.1
negative campaign 609.14
negative charge 1032.5
negatived 958.7
negative euthanasia 308.1
negative feedback 1041.6
negative geotropism 297.5
negative income tax 624.4
negative misprision 655.1
negativeness 335.1, 451.2, 762.1, 779.1
negative outlook 950.1
negative pole 1032.8
negative reinforcement 92.26
negative response 903.1
negative space 762.1
negative taxis 460.1
negative transference 92.33
negative tropism 460.1
negative valence 1060.4
negative veto 444.2
negativism 92.23, 125.6, 335.1, 453.1, 1012.1
negativist 125.7, 452.3, 1012.8
negativistic 125.16
negativity 335.1, 762.1
negatory 335.5
negatron 1033.3
neglect (n) 340.1, 390.1, 408.1, 414.6, 435.1 (v) 157.6, 340.6, 390.4, 408.2, 435.3
neglected 151.5, 340.14, 391.10, 408.3
neglecter 340.5
neglectful 340.10
neglectfulness 340.1
neglecting 340.10
négligé 5.20
negligee 5.20, 5.21
negligence 102.2, 340.1, 365.3, 406.2, 414.6, 426.1, 435.1, 810.6, 975.2, 984.1
negligent (n) 340.5 (a) 102.7, 340.10, 406.15, 414.21, 426.4, 435.5, 810.15, 975.17, 984.6
negligent homicide 308.2
negligibility 998.1
negligible 248.6, 258.10, 998.17
negotiability 889.3, 966.2
negotiable 629.5, 728.31, 889.10, 966.7
negotiable instrument 728.5, 728.11
negotiable instruments 622.3
negotiable note 728.5
negotiable paper 728.11
negotiant 466.3, 576.4
negotiate 366.5, 409.12, 437.6, 466.6, 541.10, 629.3, 731.18
negotiate a loan 620.5, 621.3
negotiate a peace 465.9
negotiated points 727.1
negotiated settlement 437.1
negotiating table 541.5
negotiation 731.3, 731.4
negotiation points 727.1
negotiations 541.5
negotiator 466.3, 576.4, 727.4
negotiatress 466.3
negotiatrix 466.3
Negro 312.3
negus 575.9
neigh 60.2
neighbhorhood 209.8
neighbor (n) 223.6, 588.1 (v) 223.9, 223.13 (a) 223.16
neighborer 223.6
neighborhood 209.1, 223.1, 227.1, 231.1
neighborhood newspaper 555.2
neighborhood watch 1008.17
neighboring 209.8, 223.15, 223.16
neighborlike 587.15
neighborlikeness 587.1
neighborliness 585.1, 587.1
neighborly 449.22, 582.22, 585.11, 587.15
neither fish nor fowl 363.10
neither here nor there 776.8, 790.8
neither hide nor hair 762.4
neither hot nor cold 102.6, 467.7
neither more nor less 790.8
neither one thing nor the other 65.2, 102.6, 467.7
nekton 311.29
nektonic 311.53
Nembutal 86.12
Nemesis 152.10, 649.4, 680.5, 1073.8
nemesis 507.3, 604.1, 649.1, 1001.1
nemmies 87.15
neocolonialism 609.5, 612.4
Neo-Darwinism 861.4
neofascism 612.7
neoformalist criticism 723.1
Neo-Hegelian 952.12
neoism 841.2
Neo-Lamarckism 861.4
neolith 842.6
neolithic 842.20
neological 526.21, 841.7
neologism 526.8, 841.2, 841.4, 852.4
neologist 526.18, 841.4
neologistic 841.7
neologize 841.5, 852.9
neology 526.8, 841.2, 841.4
neomycin 86.29
neonatal 301.12, 818.15, 841.9
neonate 302.9, 841.4
neonism 841.2
neon light 1025.19
neophilia 841.2
neophiliac 841.2
neophyte 572.9, 692.4, 818.2, 841.4, 858.7, 930.7
neophytic 841.7
neoplasm 85.39
Neoplatonic 952.12, 1053.8
Neoplatonism 1053.3
Neoplatonist 1053.4
Neoplatonistic 1053.8
neoprene 1048.3
Neo-Pythagorean 952.12
neoteric (n) 841.4 (a) 841.13
neoterical 526.21
neoterism 526.8, 841.4, 852.4
neoterist 526.18, 841.4
neoterize 841.5, 852.9
nepenthe 990.1
nephalism 668.2
nephalist 668.4
nephalistic 668.10
Nephelococcygia 319.1, 986.11
nephelognosy 319.5
nephelometer 319.6
nepheloscope 319.6
nephesh 919.4
nephew 76.10, 559.3
nephological 319.8, 319.11
nephologist 319.5

nephology 317.5, 319.5
nephritic 85.61
nephritis 85.24
nephroid 279.16
ne plus ultra 198.2, 249.3, 794.5, 1002.3, 1002.4
nepotism 609.35, 650.3
Neptune 183.1, 240.3, 678.10, 1073.9
nerd 413.14, 572.10, 866.3, 924.3
nerdish 920.14
nerdlike 920.14
nerdy 920.14
Nereid 240.3, 678.10
Nereus 240.3
nerf 756.4
neritic 276.6
nerval 24.10
nerve (n) 2.14, 142.3, 359.6, 492.1, 855.1 (v) 15.13, 492.15 (a) 2.30
nerve agent 1001.3
nerve cell 2.14
nerve center 208.5, 767.5
nerve-deafness 49.1
nerve disease 85.25
nerve ending 24.4
nerve fiber 2.14
nerve-jangling 128.15
nerveless 16.12, 19.19, 25.6, 129.2
nervelessness 129.1
nerve oneself 492.12
nerve-racking 128.15, 1006.12
nerve-rending 128.15
nerves 2.14, 128.1
nerve-shaking 128.15
nerve-shattering 830.5
nerves of steel 129.1, 492.1, 855.1
nerves on edge 128.11
nerve-stretching 128.15
nerve trunk 2.14
nerve-trying 128.15
nerviness 492.5, 917.1
nervosity 128.1, 544.3, 917.1
nervous 2.30, 24.10, 24.12, 105.28, 126.7, 127.23, 128.11, 917.16
nervous as a cat 128.11
nervous breakdown 85.8, 92.14, 128.4
nervous disorder 92.14
nervous exhaustion 21.2, 85.8
nervous expectation 130.3
nervous Nellie 126.3
nervousness 24.3, 105.10, 126.1, 127.5, 128.1, 135.1, 544.3, 917.1
nervous prostration 21.2, 85.8, 128.4
nervous stomach 128.1
nervous strain 126.1, 128.3
nervous system 2.14
nervous tension 126.1, 128.3
nervous wreck 128.5, 393.8
nervy 15.15, 128.11, 142.10, 492.18, 917.16
nescience 930.1
nescient 930.11
ness 237.2, 283.9
nest (n) 228.1, 228.2, 228.25, 302.10, 884.3, 886.8 (v) 121.10, 159.17, 225.7
nest-building 311.48
nest egg 386.3, 494.3, 728.14, 1008.4
nester 227.9
nesting (n) 225.1 (a) 311.48
nestle 22.19, 121.10, 562.17, 1008.18
nestling (n) 302.10, 311.27, 562.1, 818.2 (a) 841.7
Nestor 304.2, 921.2
nestor 422.3
net (n) 5.26, 170.3, 255.8, 292.8, 297.1, 356.13, 472.3, 627.1, 748.1, 749.1, 751.3, 893.2, 1034.8 (v) 170.7, 356.20, 429.15, 472.8, 472.12, 480.17, 627.4, 740.6, 1012.11 (a) 256.7
Net, the 1042.19
net asset 386.2
net assets 471.7
net-cord ball 748.2
net-court judge 748.2
net earnings 624.4
nether 274.8
nether cheeks 217.5
nethermost 199.7
nethermost level 199.1
nether region 199.1, 199.4
nether side 199.1
netherworld 275.3, 682.1
net income 624.4, 627.1
net interest 623.3
netizen 1042.19
netlike 170.11
net loss 473.3
net national product 892.1
net profit 472.3
net receipts 627.1
net result 887.1
net revenue 472.3
netspeak 1042.19
nett 297.1
netted 170.11
netting 170.3, 429.6
nettle (n) 3.9, 285.5 (v) 96.13, 152.24, 375.17
nettled 96.21, 152.27
nettle rash 85.36
nettly 285.10
netty 170.11
net weight 297.1
network (n) 170.3, 551.5, 770.3, 1034.8, 1042.16 (v) 384.6, 450.3, 731.19, 770.18, 800.11
networkable 347.21
network adapter 1042.3
network affiliations 1034.8
network card 1042.18
network commercial 352.6
networker 450.1
networking 450.1
network interface card 1042.18
network show 1034.18
network stations 1034.8
network television 1035.1
net worth 471.7, 630.2, 728.14
neural 2.30, 24.10
neural computer 1042.2
neural disease 85.25
neuralgia 85.25
neuralgic 85.61
neural net 1042.2, 1042.16
neural network 1042.2, 1042.16
neural network chip 1042.3
neurasthenia 85.8, 128.4
neurasthenic 92.39, 128.14
neurilemma 2.6
neuritic 85.61
neurocomputer 1042.2
neuroeconomics 731.7
neurologic 24.10
neurological 2.30, 24.10, 90.15
neurological disease 85.25
neuron 2.14
neuropathy 85.25
neuroplasticity 2.15
neuropsychiatric 92.37
neuropsychiatrist 92.10
neuropsychiatry 92.3
neurosis 92.14, 92.16, 112.4, 128.4, 926.3
neurotic (n) 110.11, 926.15 (a) 92.39, 926.28
neurotic disorder 92.14
neuroticism 92.14
neuroticize 92.36
neurotic reaction 92.16
neuter (n) 75.9, 467.4, 530.10 (v) 19.12, 255.11 (a) 75.29, 102.6, 329.6, 467.7
neutered 75.29
neutering 19.5
neuterness 75.9
neuter verb 530.4
neutral (n) 430.12, 467.4, 609.28, 670.4, 1040.9 (a) 16.17, 36.7, 39.4, 75.29, 102.6, 329.6, 430.22, 467.7, 609.45, 649.9, 864.11, 979.12
neutral color 35.6
neutral ground 467.3, 819.2
neutral hue 36.1
neutralism 329.1, 467.1, 609.5, 609.26
neutralist nation 232.1
neutrality 102.1, 329.1, 368.1, 430.9, 467.1, 649.3, 670.1, 979.5
neutralization 900.2
neutralize 670.8, 900.7, 1060.8
neutralizer 900.3, 1060.3
neutralizing 900.9
neutralness 102.1, 329.1
neutral-smelling 72.5
neutral territory 465.5, 467.3
neutral tint 36.1, 39.1
neutral zone 749.1, 1041.10
neutrino 258.8
neutrodyne 1034.28
neutron 1038.6
neutron bomb 462.20
neutron factory 1038.13
neutron number 1038.4
neutron reaction 1038.8
neutron star 1073.8
névé 1023.5
never a one 222.6, 762.4
never be forgotten 989.13
never cease 823.2, 829.6, 856.3
never-ceasing 829.7
never die 829.6
never-dying 829.9
never end 823.2, 829.6
never-ending 812.8, 829.7
never-endingness 829.1
never-fading 829.9
never feel better 83.6
never finish 538.8
never forget 150.3
never free from 373.17
never hear the last of 849.9
never idle 330.22
Neverland 986.11
never learn 923.6
never let go 474.6
never let on 345.7
neverness 222.1, 822.1
never-never (n) 622.1, 624.1 (a) 986.19
never-never land 986.11
never nod 339.8
never occur to one 984.5
never on time 846.16
never pass 829.6
never say die 15.10, 124.7, 359.8, 360.4, 453.4, 856.5
never sleep 339.8
never stoop 136.4
never-tiring 360.8
never-to-be-equaled 249.15
never to be erased from the mind 989.25
never to be forgotten 989.25, 997.19
never to return 837.7
never touch 668.7
nevus 85.39, 283.3, 517.5, 1004.1
new 253.10, 337.5, 374.4, 390.12, 578.11, 838.2, 841.7
New Age 870.7
New-Age Traveler 868.3
new arrival 774.4, 818.2
new ball game 841.2
new beginning 856.2, 858.2
new-begotten 841.9
newbie 572.9
new birth 396.3, 685.4, 858.2
new black 5.1
new blood 189.4
newborn (n) 818.2 (a) 1.4, 301.12, 841.9
newborn babe 416.3, 657.4
newbornness 841.1
new boy 189.4, 572.9
new broom 330.8, 610.11
new-built 841.9
new-coined 841.9
newcomer 189.4, 572.9, 774.4, 818.2
New Deal 609.6
New Deal Era 824.5
new departure 337.2, 818.1
new driver 178.10
newel 273.4
newel-post 901.8
New England 231.7
New England dialect 523.7
New Englander 227.11
New England Transcendentalism 1053.3
newest 841.14
newest of the new 841.14

new face 189.4
newfangle 841.10
newfangled 841.10
newfangled contraption 841.2
newfangled device 841.2
newfangled expression 526.8
newfangledness 841.1
newfangleness 841.1
new-fashioned 841.14
newfashioned 578.11, 841.13
new flame 104.11
new-fledged 301.10, 841.9
newfound 841.9, 892.19
New Frontier 609.6
new generation 302.2, 561.1, 841.4
new girl 189.4
new-grown 841.9
new guard 211.4, 216.2
new high 249.3
new hope 396.3
new humanism 312.11
New Jerusalem 681.3
new kid 189.4, 774.4
new kid on the block 841.4
new-laid 841.9
new lease on life 396.3
new left 609.24, 611.4
new life 685.4
new look 841.2
new look, the 578.1
newly come 841.12
newly rich (n) 606.7 (a) 606.8
newlywed (n) 563.5 (a) 563.21
newlyweds 104.17, 563.9
new-made 841.9
new man 841.4, 858.7
new mathematics 1017.1
new meaning 526.8
new media 552.1
new-mint 841.5
new mintage 893.1
new-minted 841.9, 892.19
new-mintedness 841.1
new-model (v) 858.12 (a) 841.9
new money 618.1
new moon 1073.11
new morality 75.18
new-mown 841.9
new music, the 708.9
newness 337.1, 374.1, 838.1, 841.1
newness to 374.1
new new thing 578.5
new order 852.2
New Orleans 708.9
new pence 728.8
new person 774.4, 858.7
new phase 852.4
new philharmonic pitch 709.4
new realism 1052.6
news 551.1, 552.1, 555.2
news agency 552.1
news analyst 556.4
news anchor 1034.23, 1035.2
newsbreak 552.3, 1034.18
news brief 552.5
newscast (n) 1034.18, 1035.2 (v) 1034.25
newscaster 1034.23, 1035.13
news commentator 1034.23
news conference 541.5, 552.4
news coverage 552.1
news editor 555.4
new sense 526.8
newsfeed 552.5
newsflash 1034.18
newsgather 552.11
news gathering 552.1
newsgroup 1042.19
new-shaped 841.9
newshawk 555.4
newshound 555.4
newsiness 552.1
news item 552.3
news kiosk 736.3
new slant 932.5
newsletter 552.1, 555.1
newsmagazine 552.1
newsman 555.4
news media 552.1
news medium 552.1
newsmonger 551.5, 552.9
newsmongering 552.7
newspaper 552.1, 555.2
newspaperese 523.10
newspaperish 555.5
newspaperman 547.15, 552.9, 555.4, 718.4
newspaper of record 555.2
newspaper publishing 555.3
newspaperwoman 555.4
newspaper writing 547.2, 718.2
newspapery 555.5
newspeak 523.10
newspeople 555.4
newsperson 552.9, 555.4
news photographer 555.4
newsreader 1035.13
news release 552.4
news report 552.5
newsserver 552.1
news service 552.1
news show 1035.2
newsstand 736.3
news stirring 552.6
new start 858.2
newswire 555.3
newswoman 555.4
newsworthiness 552.1
newsworthy 552.13
newswriter 555.4
newsy 343.10, 540.9, 552.13, 552.14
newt 311.26
new take 578.5, 852.1, 932.5
new term 526.8
New Testament 683.4
New-Testament 683.11
new theology 675.10
new to 374.4, 414.17
Newtonian telescope 1073.17
Newtonian universe 1073.1
new twist 932.5
New Wave 708.10
new wine 88.17
new woman 858.7
new word 526.8
New World 231.6
new world order 609.37
new wrinkle 841.2, 932.5
new-wrought 841.9
New Year's resolution 492.5
New York minute 174.6, 824.2
New York point 30.6
New York's finest 1008.16
New York Stock Exchange 737.7
next 223.16, 223.19, 815.4
next-beside 218.6
next best 1005.4
next best thing 862.2
next big thing 364.1, 409.3, 578.5
next-day 839.8, 840.3
next-door neighbor 223.6
next friend 1008.6
next in line 479.5
next level 407.2, 472.3
next life 835.1
next of kin 559.2
next period 839.1
next to 551.14
next to nothing (n) 248.5 (v) 633.5
next world, the 839.2
nexus 812.2, 843.4
nexus of cause and effect 886.3
n-gram 526.1
Niagara 238.11
nib 283.8, 285.3, 820.2
nibble (n) 8.2, 62.6 (v) 8.18, 8.26, 954.6, 998.14
nibble at 375.15, 510.16
nibble away 393.21
nibble away at 375.15
nibbler 8.16
nibbles 10.2, 10.9
nibbling (n) 8.1 (a) 8.32
Nibelung 258.5
niblet 8.2
nice 63.8, 97.6, 143.13, 339.12, 495.11, 496.8, 637.3, 644.15, 766.9, 944.7, 973.17, 983.15, 999.12
nice body 1016.3
nice ear 48.3
nice guy 659.2
nice hunk of change 618.3
nice-looking 1016.18
Nicene Creed 676.2
niceness 97.1, 143.1, 339.3, 495.3, 496.1, 637.2, 973.5, 999.1
niceness of distinction 944.1
nice piece of work 810.2
nice predicament 1013.4
nicety 339.3, 495.3, 496.1, 780.2, 944.1, 973.5
niche 197.3, 231.2, 284.7, 346.4, 724.4, 894.4
niche in the hall of fame 662.7
niche market 731.1
niche product 731.1
nick (n) 289.1, 429.9, 517.5, 548.6 (v) 289.4, 429.16, 482.16, 517.19
nicked 289.5
nickel (n) 728.7, 728.20 (a) 1058.17
nickel-and-dime (v) 998.14 (a) 248.6, 998.18
nickel-dime 998.14
nickelic 1058.17
nickeline 1058.17
nickelodeon 50.11
nickelous 1058.17
nickel plate 295.13
nickel-plate 295.26
nickel-plated 295.33
nickels and dimes 728.19
nicker 60.2
nick joint 759.19
nicknack 498.4
nickname (n) 527.7 (v) 527.11
nicknaming 527.2
nick of time 843.5
nicotia 89.9
nicotine 89.1, 89.9
nicotine addict 87.21
nicotine addiction 87.1, 89.10
nicotine patch 86.33
nicotinic 89.15
nicotinism 89.10
nictating 28.11
nictitate 28.10
nictitating membrane 2.9, 27.9
nictitation 28.7
nidicolous 311.48
nidificant 311.48
nidifugous 311.48
nidor 71.1
nidorous 71.5
nidus 228.25, 886.8
niece 77.7, 559.3
niello 38.7
Nielsen rating 1035.2
nieve penitente 1023.5
niff 71.1
niffy (v) 71.4 (a) 71.5
Niflheim 682.3
Niflhel 682.3
niftiness 578.3
nifty 578.13, 999.13
niggard (n) 484.4 (a) 484.8
niggardliness 484.2, 651.2, 885.1, 992.2
niggardly 484.8, 651.6, 885.5, 992.10
niggerhead 554.14
niggle (n) 510.4 (v) 510.16, 998.14
niggling (n) 510.4 (a) 248.6, 510.23, 983.15, 998.20
nigh (v) 223.7 (a) 220.4, 223.14, 839.8
nigher 223.18
nighest 223.19
nighish 223.14
nighness 223.1
nigh side 220.1
night (n) 38.4, 315.4, 1027.1 (a) 315.9
night and day 215.2
night-black 38.8, 1027.13
nightblind 28.11
night blindness 30.2, 85.33
nightcap 8.4, 22.10, 88.9, 188.4
night-clad 1027.13
night-cloaked 1027.13
nightclothes 5.21
nightclub 88.20, 704.14, 705.4, 743.13
night crawler 311.38
night-dark 38.8, 1027.13
night dew 1065.4
nightdress 5.21
night-enshrouded 1027.13

nightfall 315.2
night-fallen 315.9
night fighter 181.9
night-filled 1027.13
night glow 1025.2
nightgown 5.21
nighthawk 669.3
night-hid 1027.13
nightie 5.21
nightingale 710.23
night letter 347.14
nightlife 743.3
nightlight 494.3
nightlong 315.9, 827.12
nightly 315.9, 850.8
night-mantled 1027.13
nightmare 96.7, 127.9, 986.9
nightmarish 127.28
night operations 458.4
night-overtaken 315.10
night prayer 696.8
nightowl 669.3
night shift 825.3
nightshirt 5.21
night soil 12.4, 890.4
night song 696.8
night spot 704.14, 743.13
night terror 986.9
nighttide 315.4
nighttime (n) 315.4 (a) 315.9
night trader 737.10
night-veiled 1027.13
night vision 27.1
nightwalk 177.26, 177.32, 346.9
nightwalker 178.7, 311.38
nightwalking (n) 177.9, 177.17 (a) 177.38
night-wandering (n) 177.9 (a) 177.38
night watchman 1008.10
nightwear 5.21
nihil 762.2
nihilism 125.6, 418.2, 611.4
nihilist (n) 125.7, 395.8, 418.3, 593.5, 611.12 (a) 395.26
nihilistic 125.16, 395.26, 418.6, 611.20, 671.19
nihility 762.1, 998.6
nihil obstat 443.6
nil 762.2
Nilometer 238.15
Nilotic race 312.2
nimbies 87.5
nimble 174.15, 330.18, 339.14, 413.23, 920.14
nimble-fingered 413.23
nimble-footed 174.15, 413.23
nimble mind 920.2
nimbleness 330.3, 339.5, 413.2, 920.2
nimbleness of wit 920.2
nimble wit 489.1
nimble-witted 489.15, 920.14
nimble-wittedness 489.2, 920.2
nimbose 319.8
nimbosity 319.4
nimbostratous 319.8
nimbostratus 319.2
nimbus 319.2, 662.6, 1025.14
nimby 87.15
nimiety 993.1
Nimrod 382.5, 904.8
Nina from Carolina 882.5
Nina Nina ocean liner 882.5
Nina Ross the stable hoss 882.5
nincompoop 924.3
nine 617.7, 745.2, 758.2, 882.5
Nine, the 710.22
nine days' wonder 122.2, 409.3, 828.5, 882.5
ninefold 882.21
9-hole course 751.1
9 holes 751.3
900 number 347.4
nine of diamonds 758.2
nine of hearts 757.2
911 398.1
nine-part time 709.24
ninepins 750.1
nine points of the law 469.1
niner 882.5
nine-spot 758.2
Nineteenth Amendment 431.1
nineteenth hole 751.1
nine tenths of the law 469.1
nine-to-five (n) 373.5 (a) 373.14
ninety 882.7
ninja 461.6
ninny 924.3
ninnyhammer 924.3
ninnyism 922.3
ninth 882.21
ninth degree 198.2
ninth inning 820.3
Ninth of Av 515.3
nip (n) 8.2, 8.4, 26.2, 62.2, 62.6, 68.2, 88.7, 248.3, 260.2, 474.2, 793.5, 1023.1 (v) 26.7, 68.5, 88.24, 169.2, 174.9, 188.10, 255.10, 260.8, 268.6, 395.12, 474.6, 480.14, 482.16, 1023.10, 1024.11
nip and tuck 790.7
nip at the heels of 96.13
niphablepsia 30.1
nip in 33.8
nip in the air 1023.3
nip in the bud 308.13, 379.4, 395.12, 1012.13
nip off 188.10
nipped 260.12, 268.9
nipped at 96.24
nipped waist 260.1
nipper 302.3
nippers 29.3, 474.4
nippiness 68.2, 1023.1, 1023.3
nipping (n) 8.3 (a) 1023.14
nipping wind 318.7
nipple 239.6, 283.6
nippled 283.19
nippy 68.7, 1023.14, 1023.16
nippy wind 318.7
nip up 480.14
nirvana 25.2, 102.3, 173.1, 681.8, 933.1, 990.1
nirvanic 25.8, 102.8, 933.4
nisse 678.8
Nissen hut 228.9
nisus 380.1
Nisus and Euryalus 588.6
nit 311.36, 510.4
nitery 743.13
nitpick 510.15, 936.9
nitpicker 495.6, 510.9, 936.7
nitpicking (n) 510.4, 936.5 (a) 936.14
nitpicky 510.23, 936.14
nitrate (n) 890.4 (v) 1060.8
nitro 756.1
nitrogen 7.11, 890.4
nitroglycerin 462.14
nitroglycerine 462.14
nitromethane 756.1
nitrous oxide 86.15
nitty-gritty 761.4
nitty-gritty, the 196.5, 761.3, 767.3
nitwit 924.2
nitwitted 922.17
nival 1023.18
niveous 37.7, 1023.18
nix (n) 335.1, 442.1, 678.10, 762.1, 762.3 (v) 335.3, 444.5
nixie 678.10
Nixon Doctrine 609.5
nizam 575.9
n number 1017.6
no (n) 335.1, 371.6, 442.1, 935.14, 1017.3 (v) 335.3
no-account 391.11, 895.3
Noah's ark 797.6
no allegiance 430.5
no alternative 963.6
no attributable cause 972.3
Noatun 681.10
no avail 391.9
nob 578.7
nobble 96.13, 356.14, 375.23, 389.7, 482.16
nobbling 356.5, 375.3, 389.3
nobby 578.13, 999.13
no bearing 520.1
no beauty 1015.4
no beauty queen 1015.4
Nobel Prize 646.2
no better than she should be 665.26
no big deal 998.3
no biggie 998.3
nobility 136.2, 247.2, 249.5, 301.6, 417.7, 501.5, 544.6, 607.2, 608.1, 608.2, 644.1, 652.2, 662.5
no bill 600.1
no-bill 600.9
noble (n) 608.4 (a) 136.12, 141.11, 247.9, 501.21, 544.14, 608.10, 644.13, 652.6, 662.15, 855.17, 997.19, 999.12
Noble, the 648.8
noble ambition 100.10
noble animal, the 312.5
noble art of self-defense 457.9, 754.1
noble birth 608.2
noble experiment 942.1
noble gas 1060.2, 1067.2
nobleman 608.4
noble metal 1058.3, 1060.2
noble-minded 652.6
noble-mindedness 652.2
nobleness 608.2, 652.2
noble savage 416.3
noble science, the 754.1
noblesse 608.1
noblesse d'épée 608.1
noblesse de robe 608.1
noblesse oblige 504.2
noblewoman 608.6, 659.1
nobody, a 998.7
nobody 222.6, 764.2, 1005.5
nobody home 926.27, 927.6
nobody on earth 222.6
nobody one knows 998.7
nobody present 222.6
nobody's fool 920.14, 956.5
nobody's patsy 956.5
nobody special (n) 1005.5 (a) 1005.8
nobody's sucker 956.5
nobody under the sun 222.6
no-brainer 1014.4
no brain surgeon (n) 414.7, 1005.5 (a) 1005.8
no can do (n) 19.2 (v) 19.8
no chance 759.6, 967.1, 972.10
no charge (n) 634.1 (a) 634.5
no chicken 304.1
no children under 17 admitted 706.1
no choice 371.3, 428.3, 963.6
nock (n) 289.1 (v) 289.4
no claim 640.1
no common ground 787.1
no conjuror 414.7
no contest 412.3
no credit to 661.14
noctambulant 177.38
noctambulate 177.32
noctambulation 177.9
noctambule 178.7
noctambulism 177.9
noctambulist 178.7
noctambulous 177.38
noctivagant 177.38
noctivagation 177.9
noctograph 30.6
nocturnal 315.9
nod (n) 22.6, 155.2, 332.2, 420.5, 441.1, 443.1, 509.1, 517.15, 551.4, 585.4, 913.3 (v) 155.6, 202.6, 332.8, 340.6, 441.2, 517.22
nod, the 332.4, 517.15
nodal 283.17, 803.10
nodality 803.1
nod assent 332.8, 441.2
nodding (n) 331.6 (a) 22.21, 87.23, 202.10, 331.20, 984.8, 985.11
nodding acceptance 123.1
nodding to its fall 393.46
noddle 198.7, 919.6
noddy (n) 924.3 (a) 87.24
node 283.5, 916.4, 1013.7, 1045.6
noded 283.17
no-deposit 388.6
no-deposit-no-return 388.6
no depth 276.1
nodiform 283.17
nod of approval 509.1
nod of assent 332.2
nod off 22.16
nod of recognition 585.4
nodose 288.8
nodosity 283.5
nod through 340.6

nod to 585.10
nod to its fall 395.22
nodular 283.17, 288.8
nodulated 283.17
nodulation 283.5
nodule 283.5
noduled 283.17
nodulus 283.5
no dumbbell 920.14
nodus 1013.7
no ear 48.3
no easy task 1013.2
no end of (n) 247.4, 884.3, 991.2 (a) 267.7, 823.3, 884.10
no end of a fellow 659.1
no end to 267.7, 884.10
no end to to 823.3
noesis 928.2, 931.1
noetic 919.7, 920.12, 931.21, 935.18
no exit 125.2
no expectation 131.1
no few 884.6
no flies on 415.12
no-fly zone 444.1
no friend 589.6
no frills 499.3, 798.1, 987.2
no-frills 252.10, 499.8, 533.6, 767.9, 798.6
no future 125.1
noggin 2.7, 198.7, 919.6
no go (n) 410.1 (a) 391.9
no-go 125.14
no-go area 444.1
no-good (n) 660.2 (a) 391.11
no great matter 998.6
no great shakes (n) 414.7, 1005.5 (a) 248.6, 998.16, 998.22, 1005.8
no hassle 464.2
no holds barred 430.4
no hope 125.1
no hurry 175.1
no imitation 973.4
noise (n) 50.1, 53.3, 61.2, 520.1, 522.7, 551.7, 810.5, 1034.21, 1035.5 (v) 50.14, 53.9
noise abatement 52.2
noise about 352.10
noiseful 53.13
noisefulness 53.2
noise interference 1034.21
noiseless 51.10
noiseless foot of Time 821.3
noiselessness 51.1
noisemaker 53.6
noise pollution 82.1
noiseproof 15.20
noisette 10.39
noisiness 53.2, 59.5
noising 352.1
noisome 64.7, 69.10, 71.5, 82.5, 98.18, 1000.9, 1000.12
noisomeness 71.2, 82.1, 98.2, 1000.2, 1000.5
noisy 53.13, 59.10, 503.4
noix 10.39
no joke 997.3
no laughing matter 997.3
no life 307.1
nolition 325.1
nolle prosequi 598.7, 601.2
no-load fund 737.16
no longer among us 222.11
no longer present 222.11
no longer with us 222.11
no love is lost between 589.8
no love lost 589.4
nol pros 598.7
nol-pros 390.4
noma 85.40
nomad (n) 178.4 (a) 177.37
nomadic 177.37
nomadism 177.3
nomadization 177.3
nomadize 177.23
no man 222.6
no-man's-land 444.1, 463.2
no matter what 864.6
no matter who 864.7
nombril point 647.2
nom de guerre 527.8
nom de plume 527.8
nom de théâtre 527.8
no mean 413.22
nomen 527.3, 527.6
nomenclator 554.9, 871.4
nomenclatural 527.17
nomenclature 523.9, 527.1
nominal (n) 530.5 (a) 517.23, 527.15, 530.17, 580.7, 633.7
nominal charge 633.2
nominal head 575.5
nominalism 865.1
nominalness 633.1
nominal partner 616.2
nominal price 633.2
nominal rate 738.5
nominal value 738.9
nominate 371.19, 527.11, 576.15, 609.41, 615.11
nominated 371.26
nominating convention 609.8
nomination 371.8, 417.12, 609.11, 615.2, 698.10
nominative (n) 530.9 (a) 527.15, 527.16
nominee 615.9
nomistic 673.12
no modest violet 140.5
nomography 673.7
nomology 673.7
no more 34.4, 307.29, 762.11, 837.7
no more and no less 991.1
nomothetic 673.12
no-movement exercise 84.2
Nona 964.3
nonacceptance 372.1, 442.1
nonaccomplishment 408.1, 410.1
nonachievement 408.1
nonacid (n) 1060.3 (a) 1060.9
nonacknowledgment 151.1
nonactual 986.21
nonadherence 435.1
nonadherent 435.5, 804.4
nonadhesion 804.1
nonadhesive 804.4
nonadmission 773.1
nonage 301.3
nonagenarian 304.2, 882.7
nonaggression 464.4, 467.1
nonaggression pact 437.2, 464.7
nonaggressive 331.19, 464.10
nonagon 882.5
nonagonal 882.21
nonagreement 333.1
nonalcoholic 516.4
nonalcoholic beer 88.16
nonalcoholic beverage 10.49
nonaligned 430.22, 467.7, 982.3
nonaligned nation 232.1, 430.12, 467.4
nonalignment 430.9, 467.1, 611.2
nonamazedness 123.1
nonamazement 123.1
nonambiguity 970.1
nonambiguous 970.13
no-name 528.1
nonappearance 32.1, 222.4
nonapproval 372.1
nonary 882.21
nonassent 333.1
nonassertive 344.10
nonassimilation 774.1
nonastonishment 123.1
nonattendance 222.4
nonattendant 222.11
nonbeing 762.1
nonbelief 955.1
nonbeliever 695.11, 955.4
nonbelieving 955.8
nonbelligerent 464.5
nonbinding arbitration 466.2, 727.1
nonbiodegradable 1055.4
nonbiological 1055.4
nonbook 554.1
nonbreakable 1049.5
noncanonical writings 683.3
non-caring 25.6
non-Catholic (n) 675.20 (a) 675.28
nonce, the 838.1
nonce word 526.8
nonchalance 94.4, 102.2, 106.5, 123.1
nonchalant 94.13, 102.7, 106.15, 123.3
non-Christian (n) 688.6 (a) 688.10
noncivilized 497.12, 671.21
nonclastic rock 1059.1
nonclerical 700.3
nonclerics 700.1
noncoercion 430.3
noncoherent 804.4
noncohering 802.20
noncohesion 804.1
noncohesive 802.20, 804.4
noncollegiate 568.20
noncom 575.18
noncombatant (n) 464.5 (a) 464.10
noncombative 464.10
noncombustible 1022.9
noncombustive 1022.9
noncommissioned officer 461.8, 574.2
noncommitment 467.1
noncommittal 494.8
noncommitted 467.7
noncommunicability 122.4
noncommunicable 122.13
noncommunicableness 122.4
noncompassion 980.2
non-compete 210.9
noncompetitive 450.5
noncompletion 408.1
noncompliance 327.1, 435.1, 442.1, 868.1
noncompliant 435.5
non compos (n) 926.15 (a) 926.26
non compos mentis 926.26
noncompound 872.7
nonconceiving 930.12
nonconcern 340.2
nonconcurrence 333.1, 868.1
nonconducting 1032.36
nonconductive 1032.36
nonconductor 1032.14
nonconform 868.4
nonconformability 789.2
nonconformable 868.5
nonconformance 435.1, 868.1
nonconforming 327.8, 333.6, 435.5, 868.5
nonconformism 782.1, 868.1
nonconformist (n) 327.5, 333.3, 430.12, 688.5, 789.4, 868.3, 870.4, 927.3 (a) 581.3, 782.3, 789.9, 900.8
nonconformity 204.1, 327.1, 333.1, 430.10, 435.1, 688.1, 774.1, 780.1, 782.1, 789.2, 865.1, 868.1, 900.1, 927.1
nonconnotative 520.6
nonconscious 1055.5
nonconsent 333.1, 442.1
nonconsenting 442.6
nonconsideration 372.1
nonconstitutional 674.6
nonconsummation 408.1
nonconsummation of marriage 566.1
noncontiguous 802.20
noncontingency 970.1
noncontingent existence 761.5
noncontingent free will 430.6
noncontinuance 813.1
noncontinuous 813.4
nonconvergence 203.1
nonconvergent 203.6
noncooperating 327.9
noncooperation 327.1, 442.1, 451.1, 451.2, 453.1, 456.1
noncooperative 327.9, 451.8, 453.5
noncooperator 327.5, 452.3
noncreative 891.5
noncritical mass 1038.10
nondeciduous 310.39
nondenominational 675.27, 864.14
nondenotative 520.6
nondescript 65.2, 263.4, 499.6
nondevelopment 406.4
nondifferentiation 778.1
nondischarge of debts 625.1
nondischarging 408.1
nondisclosure 344.1
nondisclosure agreement 428.1
non-discretionary 419.4
nondiscrimination 843.2
nondiscriminatory 781.5, 945.6

nondissent 433.1
nondissenting 433.12
nondivergence 203.1
nondivergent 203.6
nondivisible 1045.13
nondrinker 516.1, 668.4
nondrinking 516.3
nondrying oil 1056.1
nondurable 828.7
nondutiable 630.16
none 696.8, 762.4
none at all 762.4
nonecclesiastical 700.3
none else 872.3
nonelastic 1046.12
nonelectrolyte 1032.25
nonemotional 94.9
nonemployment 390.1
nonendurance 135.2
nonennial 850.4
nonentity 16.6, 222.6, 606.5, 762.1, 764.2, 998.7, 1005.5
none other 778.3
no nerves 129.1
nones 696.8, 832.4
nonessential (n) 768.2, 998.4 (a) 391.10, 766.7, 768.4, 776.7, 993.17, 998.17
nonesuch 122.2, 999.8
none the worse for wear 397.13, 1002.8
none to spare 992.1
nonevent 831.2
non-exclusive 772.7
nonexecution 408.1
nonexercise 390.2
nonexistence 222.1, 762.1
nonexistent 34.4, 222.11, 762.8, 986.19, 992.11
nonexpectant 131.9
nonexpectation 131.1
nonextension 1053.1
nonexteriority 1053.1
nonexternality 1053.1
nonfactual 986.21
nonfeasance 327.1, 340.1, 408.1, 414.6, 435.1, 655.2, 674.3
nonfeasor 660.8
nonfertile 891.4
nonfiction 547.10
nonfiction prose 721.1
nonfiction writer 547.15, 718.4
nonfilterable virus 85.42
nonfinite verb form 530.4
nonflammability 1022.1
nonflammable 1022.9
nonfood 10.1
nonformal 5.47, 523.20, 523.21, 581.3, 782.3, 810.15, 868.6
nonformal agreement 436.2
nonformal English 523.5
nonformalization 782.1
nonformal language 523.5, 523.6, 523.9
nonformalogue 541.6
nonformal speech 523.5
nonformal standard speech 523.5
nonfriction 1056.6
nonfruition 891.1
nonfulfillment 408.1, 435.1, 992.1
nonfunctional 391.14
nonfunctional addition 498.1
nonfunctional adjunct 498.1
nonfunctioning 391.14
nongerminal 891.5
nongratification 96.1
nongregarious 583.5
nonhabitable 586.8
nonhappening 762.1
nonhazardous 1007.5
nonhistorical 986.21
nonhuman 870.15
nonillion, a 884.4
nonillion 882.13
nonimitation 337.1
nonimmune 1006.15
nonimmunity 1006.3
nonimpact printer 1042.9
noninflammability 1022.1
noninflammable 1022.9
noninhabitance 222.2
noninsular 979.8
noninsularity 979.1
nonintellectual 930.13
nonintention 972.3
noninterference 340.1, 430.9, 609.4
noninterfering 340.10
nonintermission 847.2
noninterruption 847.2
nonintervention 368.1, 430.9, 467.1, 609.4
noninterventionist 853.8
nonintimidation 430.3
nonintoxicating 516.4
noninvasive 853.8
noninvasive therapy 91.1
noninvasive treatment 91.1
noninvolved 467.7
noninvolvement 329.1, 368.1, 430.9, 467.1
non-Islamic 688.10
non-Jew 688.6
non-Jewish 688.10
non-Jewish man 688.6
non-Jewish woman 688.6
nonjudgmental 945.5
nonjuror 868.3
nonkosher 80.20
nonlegal 674.6
non-lethal weapon 462.22
nonliability 601.2
nonlicit 674.6
nonlinear 813.4
nonlinear calibration 1041.7
nonlinearity 813.1
nonlinear system 1041.5
nonliterality 536.1
nonliteralness 536.1
nonliving 1055.5
nonliving matter 1055.1
nonmalignant 999.21
nonmalignant tumor 85.39
nonmandatory 324.7
nonmanual worker 577.3
nonmarveling 123.1
nonmaterial 1053.7
nonmedical therapist 90.9
nonmedical therapy 91.2
nonmelodious 61.4
non-member 773.3, 774.3
nonmeritorious 640.9
nonmetal 1058.3, 1060.2
nonmetallic 1058.16
nonmetricalf 721.4
nonmilitant 464.10
nonministerial 700.3
non-Mohammedan (n) 688.6 (a) 688.10
nonmoral 654.11
non-Mormon (n) 688.6 (a) 688.10
non-Moslem (n) 688.6 (a) 688.10
non-Muham-madan 688.10
non-Muhammadan 688.6
nonmusical 61.4
non-Muslim (n) 688.6 (a) 688.10
nonnative citizen 227.4
nonnative speaker 523.1
nonnegative 1017.23
nonnegotiable demand 421.1
nonnuclear weapons 462.1
no-no 444.1, 513.4, 967.1
nonobedience 327.1
nonobjective 980.12
nonobjectivity 767.1
nonobservance 435.1, 442.1, 695.1, 868.1, 984.1
nonobservant 435.5, 695.15, 868.5
nonoccupancy 222.2
nonoccupation 222.2
nonoccurrence 222.1, 762.1
nonodorous 72.5
nonofficial 971.21
no nonsense 499.3, 987.2
no-nonsense 499.8, 920.13
nonopacity 1029.1
nonopaque 1029.4
nonopposal 433.1
nonopposing 433.12
nonopposition 433.1
nonordained 700.3
nonordained persons 700.1
nonorganic 1055.4
nonorganic matter 1055.1
nonorthodox 688.9
nonpareil 122.2, 249.4, 659.4, 999.8
nonparticipation 329.1
nonpartisan (n) 430.12, 467.4, 609.28 (a) 430.22, 467.7, 609.45
nonpartisan ballot 609.19
nonpartisan election 609.15
nonpartisanism 467.1, 609.26
nonpartisan primary 609.15
nonpastoral 700.3
nonpayer 625.5
nonpaying 625.10
nonpayment 625.1
nonperformance 340.1, 408.1, 435.1
nonperishable 855.18
nonpermanent 828.7
nonpermissible 444.7
nonperson 222.6, 764.2, 998.7
nonphysical 1053.7
nonplus (n) 971.3, 1013.7 (v) 958.5, 971.13, 1012.15
nonplussed 971.25, 1013.24
nonpoetic 721.4
nonpoisonous 999.21
nonpolluted 79.25
nonporous 1045.12
nonpracticing 695.15
nonpreparation 406.1
nonpreparedness 406.1
nonprescription drug 86.4
nonpresence 222.1, 762.1
nonprevalence 390.1
nonproducing 891.4
nonproductive 891.4
nonprofessional (n) 726.5 (a) 724.17
nonprofessionalism 724.9
nonprofit 617.16
nonprofit-making 617.16
nonprogressive 611.17, 853.8
nonprohibitive 443.14
nonprolific 891.4
nonproneness to disease 83.4
nonprone to disease 83.14
non-pros 601.4
nonprosecution 601.2
non prosequitur 601.2
nonpublic 872.8
nonpuncturable 293.13
nonrational 93.19, 311.39
nonrationalness 93.9
nonrealism 350.1
nonrealistic 986.21
nonreality 762.1
nonrealization 930.2
nonrecognition 151.1, 930.2
nonrecognitive 151.4
nonrecognized 151.5
nonrecyclable 388.5
nonrecyclable item 388.2
nonrecyclable resource 388.2
nonreligious 695.15, 700.3
nonreligiousness 695.1
nonremittal 625.1
nonremunerated business expenses 626.3
nonremunerative 391.12
nonrenewable 388.5, 473.7
nonrenewable energy 1021.1
nonrenewable fuel source 1021.1
nonrenewable resource 388.2, 1021.1
nonrepentance 114.2
nonrepresentationalism 350.1
nonresidence 222.2
nonresident 222.12
nonresilience 1046.2
nonresiliency 1046.2
nonresilient 1046.11
nonresistance 134.2, 329.1, 433.1, 609.5
nonresistant (n) 464.5 (a) 433.12
nonresister 464.5
nonresisting 433.12
nonresistive 433.12, 1047.8
nonresistiveness 1047.1
nonresonance 52.4
nonresonant 52.17
nonrestoration 473.1
nonrestriction 340.1
nonrestrictive 340.10, 430.25
nonreturnable 855.17
nonreusable 388.5
nonreusable item 388.2
nonrevealing 346.15
nonreversible 855.17

nonreversible reaction 1038.8
nonrigid 1047.8
nonrigidity 1047.1
nonsacred 686.3
nonsalable 734.15
nonsanctioned behavior 322.1
nonsatisfaction 96.1, 992.1
nonscheduled airline 184.10
nonscholastic 568.20
nonscientific 936.11
nonsectarian 675.27, 864.14
nonseminal 891.5
nonsense (n) 520.2, 923.1, 923.3 (a) 720.16
nonsense talk 540.3
nonsense verse 720.3
nonsensical 520.7, 923.11
nonsensicality 520.1, 923.3
nonsequential 813.4
non sequitur 813.1, 936.3
nonserial 813.4
nonseriality 813.1
non-sexist 979.12
nonsexist 781.5
nonsexualness 75.9
nonsingle 883.7
nonsingleness 883.1
nonsked 184.10
nonsmoker 668.4
nonsmoking 89.15
non-smoking car 179.15
nonsmoking section 89.13
nonsocialistic 611.23
nonspecific 864.11, 971.19
nonspiritual 663.6, 1052.10
nonspirituality 663.2
nonstandard language 523.6
nonstarter 250.2, 410.2, 410.8, 764.2, 1011.7
nonsteroidal anti-inflammatory drug 86.12
nonstop 812.8, 829.7
non-stop flight 184.9
nonstop talker 540.4
nonstretchable 1046.12
nonstrictness 426.2
nonsubjective 768.3
nonsubjectivity 768.1
nonsubsistence 762.1
nonsubsistent 762.8
nonsubstantial 764.5
nonsuccess 410.1
nonsuit 598.7
nonsurgical therapy 91.1
nonsurgical treatment 91.1
nonsusceptibility to disease 83.4
nonsusceptible to disease 83.14
nonsymmetric 265.10
nonsymmetrical 265.10, 810.12
nonsymmetry 810.1
nonsystematic 810.12
nontaxable 630.16
nonterminating 829.7
nonterminous 829.7
nontoxic 999.21
nontransferability 855.4
nontransferable vote 371.6
nontranslucency 1031.1
nontranslucent 1031.3
nontransparent 1031.3
non-U 606.8
nonunderstanding (n) 922.2 (a) 922.14
nonuniform 782.3, 783.4, 787.4, 810.12, 813.4, 851.3, 854.6
nonuniformity 288.1, 782.1, 783.1, 787.1, 791.1, 810.1, 813.1, 851.1, 854.1
non-UN international organization 614.3
nonunion 802.1
nonunion shop 727.3
nonunique 883.7
nonuniqueness 883.1
nonuple 882.21
nonuple time 709.24
nonuse 390.1, 414.1
nonutilitarian 391.14
nonvenomous 999.21
nonverbal 712.21
nonverbal agreement 437.1
nonviable 307.32
nonvintage wine 88.17
nonviolence 329.1, 464.4, 670.1
nonviolent 464.10, 670.10
nonviolent change 861.1
nonviolent protest 333.2
nonviolent resistance 134.2, 329.1
nonvirulent 999.21
nonvital 768.4
nonvitalness 768.2
nonvolatile oil 1056.1
nonwelcome 586.1
nonwelcoming 586.1
nonwonder 123.1
nonwondering 123.1
nonworker 331.11
noodle (n) 2.7, 198.7, 919.6, 924.4 (v) 931.13
noodle around 931.13
noodlehead 924.4
noodles 10.33
noodling 931.2
noodling around 931.2
nook 197.3, 278.2, 284.7, 346.4
nookie 75.4, 75.7
nooky 75.4
noological 919.7
noology 934.1
noon (n) 198.2, 314.4 (a) 314.6
noonday (n) 314.4 (a) 314.6
noonday demon 112.3
noonday light 1025.10
no one 222.6
nooning 314.4
noonish 314.6
noonlight 314.4, 1025.10
noonlit 314.6
noontide 314.4
noontide light 1025.10
noontime 314.4
noose (n) 280.2, 356.13, 605.5 (v) 356.20, 480.17, 604.17, 740.6
noose, the 604.6
noosphere 305.1, 306.7, 317.2, 932.2
no other 778.3, 872.3
no picnic (n) 997.5, 1006.1 (a) 1013.17
no place higher 198.2
no prize (n) 414.7, 1005.5 (a) 1005.8
no prize package (n) 414.7, 1005.5 (a) 1005.8
nor' 161.3
Nordic skiing 753.1
Nordic subrace 312.2
nor'easter 318.8
no regrets 114.2
no remorse 114.2
no resemblance 787.1
no rhyme or reason 810.1
no-risk 494.8
norm 246.1, 300.2, 373.4, 419.2, 636.1, 659.4, 869.4
normal (n) 184.18, 200.2, 246.1, 277.2 (a) 246.3, 278.7, 349.15, 373.13, 637.3, 807.6, 864.12, 869.8, 925.4, 1005.8
normal, the 869.3
normalcy 869.1, 925.1
normal gigantism 257.5
normal hill 753.1
normality 637.2, 864.2, 869.1, 925.1, 1005.2
normalization 546.4, 808.2, 869.5
normalize 781.4, 808.10, 869.6
normalized 808.14
normalized text 341.2
normal loop 184.16
normalness 864.2, 869.1, 925.1, 1005.2
normal order of things, the 869.3
normal pitch 709.4
normal spin 184.15
normal unemployment 331.3
normative 373.13, 419.4, 637.3, 786.8, 869.8, 869.9
normativeness 637.2
normative system 636.1
norms 636.1, 978.5
Norns 964.3
no rocket scientist (n) 414.7, 1005.5 (a) 1005.8
no room for error 494.1
no room to spar 794.11
no room to swing a cat 258.3
Norris Division 749.1
Norroy 575.20
Norroy and Ulster 575.20
Norroy and Ulster King of Arms 575.20
Norroy King of Arms 575.20
Norse and Germanic deities 678.4
North 231.7
north (n) 161.3 (a) 161.14
North America 231.6, 235.1
North American Soccer League 752.1
North and South 758.3
North Atlantic Treaty Organization 437.2
northbound 161.14
North Central region 231.7
Northeast 231.7
northeast (n) 161.3 (a) 161.14
northeaster 318.8
northeasterly 161.14
northeastern 161.14
Northener 227.11
norther 318.8
northerly 161.14
northern 161.14
Northern Hemisphere 231.6
northern lights 1025.16**northernmost** 161.14
northing 161.3**northland** 231.7
northlander 227.11
Northman 227.11
North Pole 215.2, 261.4, 1023.4
north pole 1032.8
North Ryukyu Trench 275.5
North Star 574.8, 1073.4
northward 161.3
Northwest 231.7
northwest (n) 161.3 (a) 161.14
northwester 318.8
northwesterly 161.14
northwestern 161.14
north wind 318.8
nor'wester 318.8
no say 895.1
no say-so 895.1
no scholar 930.7
nose (n) 2.11, 69.5, 216.3, 239.9, 283.8, 312.5 (v) 69.8, 73.8, 214.7, 938.35, 981.4
nose around 938.31
nose around for 981.3
nosebag, the 8.1, 10.2
nosebleed 12.8
nose candy 87.7
nose cone 1075.2
nose count 1017.11
nose-dive 367.6, 633.6
nosedive (n) 184.13, 194.3, 367.1, 410.3, 633.4 (v) 184.41, 194.8
nose down 184.40
nose for news, a 552.1
nosegay 310.25, 770.7, 770.8
nose guard 1008.3
noseguard 746.2
noseholes 69.5, 283.8
nose into 182.41, 938.23, 981.4
nose job 90.2
nose out 411.3, 412.6, 938.35, 941.6, 981.3
nose over 184.43
noseover 184.18
nose-piercing 69.10
nose ring 280.3, 498.6
nose tackle 746.2
nose-tickling 68.6
nose-tweaking 454.1
nose up 184.40, 184.43
nose-up 184.18
nosey 214.9
Nosey Parker 214.4
nosh (n) 8.7, 10.2 (v) 8.26
no-show 222.5
nosh-up 8.8
nosiness 981.1
nosing 69.3
no skin off one's nose 248.6, 998.16
no slouch 330.8, 413.11, 413.14, 659.2, 999.5
no-smoking area 72.2
no sooner said than done 1014.13

no spring chicken 304.1
nostalgia 93.8, 100.4, 100.5, 112.5, 989.3
nostalgia for the past 842.4
nostalgic 93.21, 100.23, 112.23, 837.8, 989.21
nostalgy 112.5
no stomach for 325.1
nostomania 93.8, 100.5
nostomanic 93.21
Nostradamus 399.4
no stranger to 373.16, 928.16
nostril 2.11, 239.13, 292.5
nostrils 69.5, 283.8
no strings 430.27
no strings attached 430.27
nostrum 86.2
no such a thing 787.5
no such thing (n) 762.2, 780.3 (a) 787.5
no sweat 1014.4
nosy 214.9, 938.38, 981.6
nosy Parker 981.2
not a bad idea 932.6
not abide 451.3, 510.11
notabilia 997.5
notability 247.2, 662.5, 662.9, 997.2, 997.8
not a bit 762.4
not a bit alike 787.5
not a bit of it 787.5
notable (n) 662.9, 997.8 (a) 247.10, 348.12, 662.16, 865.13, 989.24, 997.19
not a blessed one 762.4
not a blessed soul 222.6
not able to help 963.10
not able to keep from 963.10
not a breath of air 173.16
not accept 335.4, 444.4, 956.3
not accept compromise 360.2
not accept defeat 360.2
not accord with 780.5
not a Chinaman's chance 972.10
not add up 975.8
not admit 335.4, 955.5
not a dream 761.2
not a few 884.6
not affect 94.5
not affordable 632.11
not agree 333.4
not a hair out of place 807.8
not a hope in hell 125.1
not a leaf stirring 173.16
not a living soul 222.6
not all it is cracked up to be 911.5
not all it's cracked up to be 1003.4
not allow 444.4
not allowed 444.7
not allow oneself to believe 956.3
not all there 922.17, 922.22, 926.27
not amiss 999.20
not amount to a damn 998.11
not amount to a hill of beans 998.11
not amount to anything 998.11
not an iota not a jot 762.4
not answer 911.2
not anticipate 131.4
not any 762.4
not a one 762.4
not a patch on 250.7
not a peep 51.1
not a pin to choose 963.6
not appreciate 151.3
not approach 250.4
not approve 510.10
not a prayer 125.1, 972.10
not apropos 998.16
notarization 332.4
notarize 332.12
notarized 332.14
notarized statement 334.3, 549.6
notary 332.7, 550.1
notary public 332.7, 550.1
not a sausage 762.4
not a shadow of a suspicion 762.4
not a single one 222.6
not a single person 222.6
not a snowball's chance in hell 972.10
not a soul 222.6
not a sound 51.1
not a speck 762.4
not a stitch 6.3
not a stitch on one's back 6.3
not a stitch to one's name 6.3
not as young as one used to be 303.17
notate 349.8, 530.16
notation 341.5, 349.1, 517.1, 549.4, 628.5, 708.28, 709.12, 1017.2, 1017.3
not at issue 776.7
not at risk 1007.4
not attend 984.2
not attend to 340.6
not a whit 762.4
not back down 453.4
not bad 107.12, 999.20
not bargain for 131.4
not bat an eye 855.11
not bat an eyelash 855.11
not be a bit surprised 130.5
not be able 19.8
not be able to abide 99.3
not be able to account for 522.11
not be able to bear 99.3
not be able to call one's time one's own 330.10
not be able to dispense with 963.9
not be able to do without 963.9
not be able to endure 99.3
not be able to hear oneself think 53.9
not be able to make head or tail of 971.9
not be able to say much for 510.12
not be able to sit down 135.4
not be able to stand still 135.4
not be able to swallow 956.3
not be affected by 94.5
not be all there 922.12, 926.20
not bear 444.4
not bear inspection 1003.3
not bear with 444.4, 510.11
not beat about the bush 535.2
not be at home to 157.5, 442.5, 586.5
not be behindhand 843.8
not be born yesterday 413.19
not be caught flatfooted 843.8
not be caught looking 843.8
not be content with 451.3
not be entitled to 640.5
not be found 762.5
not be good for 82.4
not be in existence 762.5
not-being 762.1
not be in it 972.14
not be in one's right mind 926.20
not be in pigtails 303.9
not believe 955.5
not believe one's ears 122.5
not believe one's eyes 122.5
not believe one's senses 122.5
not be like 780.5
not be likely 969.2
not be met with 762.5
not be one's cup of tea 99.3
not be on time 846.7
not be ready 406.6
not be right in the head 926.20
not be surprised 130.5
not be taken in by 956.3
not be too visible 494.7
not be up to 414.10
not be versed 414.10
not be with it 930.8
not blink an eye 123.2
not blow one's cover 494.7
not boggle at anything 954.5
not born yesterday 413.28, 920.14, 956.5
not bothered 982.3
not breathe 173.7
not breathe a word 51.5, 344.6, 345.7
not bright 922.13
not brook 444.4, 510.11
not budge 329.2, 361.7, 855.11
not budge an inch 855.11
not buy 442.3, 955.5, 956.3
not buy into 956.3
not care 102.4, 982.2
not care a damn 102.4
not care a straw about 102.4, 998.12
not care for 99.3, 340.6
not care if one does 324.3
not care less 94.5, 102.4, 982.2
not care much for 156.4
not care to 325.3
not carry a tune 61.3
notch (n) 224.2, 237.5, 245.1, 284.6, 289.1, 517.5 (v) 284.14, 289.4, 517.19
not charmed 99.8
notched 284.17, 289.5
not chicken feed 997.5
notching 289.2
not choke on 954.6
notch one up 409.9
not chopped liver 997.18
not come 222.7
not come amiss 995.3
not come near 250.4
not come off 410.9
not come to grips with 368.13
not come to the point 936.9
not come up to 250.4, 992.8
not come up to expectation 132.3
not come up to par 1003.3
not come up to scratch 1003.3
not come up to snuff 1003.3
not come up to the mark 410.9, 1003.3
not coming 640.9
not coming back 837.7
not comparable 250.7, 787.6
not compare 250.4
not compare with 787.2, 943.7
not complain 107.5
not comply 868.4
not compute 520.4
not concern 776.4
not condone 444.4, 510.11
not conform 327.6, 868.4
not confound 944.6
not connect with 776.4
not consent 442.3
not consider 340.6, 933.2
not considered 372.3
not convey anything 520.4
not cost anything 633.5
not count 998.11
not countenance 444.4, 510.11
not count the cost 485.3
not crack a smile 111.2
not cramp someone's style 430.17
not cricket 638.3, 650.10, 868.6
not cry over spilled milk 114.3
not cut it 19.8, 992.8, 1003.3
not cut out for 414.19
not cut the mustard 19.8, 250.4, 992.8
not dare to say one's soul is one's own 432.12
not dare to show one's face 137.9
not deep 276.5
not deny 332.11
not deserving belief 955.10
not destroy 397.8
not dirty one's hands 495.8
not distinguish 975.13
not do by halves 407.7
not do justice to 950.2
not done 11.9, 638.3, 650.10, 868.6
not drunk 516.3
not dry behind the ears 301.10, 414.17
note (n) 27.2, 60.1, 209.3, 254.2, 341.5, 517.1, 524.3, 549.4, 549.6, 553.2, 556.1, 628.5, 662.5, 708.4, 709.4, 709.14, 709.20, 728.5, 728.11, 928.2, 978.4, 983.1, 997.1 (v) 517.17, 524.24, 549.15, 628.8, 983.6
no tea party 997.5, 1006.1
not easy 1011.13, 1013.17
not eat 515.4
notebook 549.11, 554.1
notebook computer 1042.2

note broker 729.11, 730.9
noted 662.16, 871.9
note discounting 728.16
note down 549.15
noteholder 622.4
not endanger 397.8
not endure 444.4, 510.11
not enough 992.9
not enough room to swing a cat 258.3, 429.7
not enough to count 885.2
not enough to cover 625.3
not enough to matter 885.2
not enough to shake a stick at 885.2
not entail 776.4
not enter one's head 933.2, 984.5
not enter one's mind 933.2
note of alarm 400.1
note of explanation 341.5
note of hand 728.11
notepad 549.11
note paper 547.4
not equal to 414.19
notes 554.12, 719.2
note shaving 728.16
note similarities and differences 943.4
notes of a scale 709.14
note to self 989.19
noteworthiness 997.2
noteworthy 247.10, 865.12, 870.14, 997.19
not exist 762.5
not expect 131.4
not expend 397.8
not expose oneself 494.7
not face up to 362.7, 368.13
not fail 644.9
not fair 650.10
not fall for 956.3
not feeling like 325.5
not feel like 325.3
not feel like anything 85.46
not figure 520.4, 975.8
not fill the bill 108.5, 911.2
not find it in one's heart to 325.3
not find one's way to first base 922.12
not firm 845.8
not fit for man or beast 586.8
not fit for mixed company 666.9
not fit to be seen 1015.6
not fit to drink 64.8
not fit to eat 64.8
not flag 15.10
not flinch from 492.10
not following 936.11, 958.8
not for all the tea in China 632.10
not for attribution 345.14
not foresee 131.4
not forget 983.5
not-for-profit 617.16
not for publication 345.14
not for real 870.11
not for release 345.14
not for the record 345.14
not found 222.11
not get 522.11
not get all choked up over 510.10
not get along 456.8
not get involved 340.6, 430.16
not get involved in 329.4
not get it 522.11
not get off base 326.2
not get out of line 326.2
not get started 175.8
not get to first base 410.10
not give a crap 102.4
not give a damn 102.4
not give a damn about 998.12
not give a dime a dozen for 998.12
not give a hoot 102.4, 998.12
not give a thought to 340.6
not give away 345.7
not give it another thought 148.5, 984.4
not give it a second thought 148.5, 984.4
not give one the time of day 583.4, 586.5
not give the time of day 368.6
not give the time of day to 99.3
not give two hoots 102.4
not give two hoots for 998.12
not give up 15.10, 360.4, 453.4
not give up the ship 360.4
not go along with 444.4
not go for 510.10, 956.3
not good enough 108.9, 510.24
not go off half-cocked 329.2
not go off the deep end 428.7
not go on all fours with 780.5
not go out on a limb 494.7
not go too far 428.7
not guesswork 761.3
not guilty 148.7, 657.6
not hack it 19.8, 132.3, 250.4, 410.10, 911.2, 992.8, 1003.3
not half a chance 972.9
not half bad 999.20
not hard to look at 1016.21
not have 442.3, 444.4
not have a care in the world 109.6
not have a chance 967.4, 972.14
not have a Chinaman's chance 972.14
not have a clue 414.10
not have a clue not have idea one 930.10
not have a dry thread 1065.11
not have a hair out of place 106.6
not have a leg to stand on 640.5, 936.8
not have all one's marbles 922.12, 926.20
not have a moment to call one's own 330.10
not have a moment to spare 330.10, 401.8
not have anything to do with 451.7
not have a penny 619.5
not have a penny to bless oneself with 619.5
not have a prayer 972.14
not have a selfish bone in one's body 652.3
not have a sou 619.5
not have a word to say 51.5
not have a word to say for oneself 137.9
not have both oars in the water 926.20
not have enough sense to come in out of the rain 922.12
not have it 19.8, 911.2
not have it in one 414.10
not have one dollar to rub against another 619.5
not have the first idea 522.11, 930.10
not have the foggiest 930.10
not have the heart to 325.3
not have the knack 414.10
not have the least idea 930.10
not have the remotest idea 930.10
not have the slightest idea 522.11, 930.10
not have the stomach for 99.3
not have the stomach to 325.3
not have time 844.3
not hay 997.18
not hear a word 984.2
not hearken 327.6
not hear of 372.2, 442.3, 444.4, 510.10
not heed 327.6, 340.6, 984.2
not held against one 148.7
not hesitate 359.10
not hesitate to 324.3
nothing, a 998.6, 998.7
nothing 222.3, 762.1, 762.2, 764.2
nothingarian (n) 467.4 (a) 467.7
nothingarianism 467.1
nothing at all 762.2
nothing but skin and bones 270.17
nothing else 872.3
nothing in excess 668.1, 670.1
nothing in particular 998.6
nothing like 787.5
nothing loath 324.6, 441.4
nothingness 25.2, 158.1, 222.3, 762.1
nothing of the kind (n) 780.3 (a) 787.5
nothing of the sort 787.5
nothing on earth 762.2
nothing special (n) 1005.5 (a) 1005.8
nothing to boast of 998.6
nothing to brag about 1005.7
nothing to do 331.2
nothing to do with 895.1
nothing to do with the case 776.7
nothing to hide 657.1
nothing to it 1014.13
nothing to say about 895.1
nothing to signify 998.6
nothing to sneeze at 997.3, 999.5
nothing to speak of 998.6
nothing to think twice about 998.6
nothing to write home about (n) 998.6 (a) 250.6, 1005.7
nothing under the sun 762.2
nothing whatever 762.2
nothing worth speaking of 998.6
not hold a candle to 250.4
not hold back 485.3
not hold it against one 600.12
not hold one's breath 125.9, 134.4
not hold together 975.8
not hold up 975.8
not hold up in the wash 975.8
not hold water 975.8
not hold with 442.3, 451.7, 510.10
notice (n) 27.2, 352.2, 352.3, 352.4, 352.6, 399.1, 421.1, 551.1, 556.2, 928.2, 946.2, 983.1 (v) 27.12, 941.5, 983.6
noticeability 348.4
noticeable 24.14, 31.6, 247.10, 300.14, 348.8, 348.12
notice board 352.2, 549.10, 551.1
notice to mariners 400.1
notification 343.2, 352.2, 399.1, 551.1
notificational 399.7
notifier 551.5
notify 133.13, 399.5, 551.8
notifying 399.7
no time 822.1, 828.3
no time at all 822.1
no time to be lost 401.1
not implicate 776.4
not imply 776.4
not included 773.7
not in error 973.13
not in it 250.7, 773.7
not in one's right mind 926.26
not in residence 222.12
not interfere 430.16
not in the habit of 374.4
not in the mood 325.5
not in the picture 773.7
not in the same league with 250.7
not in time 844.6
not involve 776.4
not involve oneself 430.16
notion 364.1, 365.1, 380.1, 381.1, 932.1, 951.5, 952.2, 953.6
notional 364.5, 932.9, 951.13, 952.10, 986.18, 986.19, 986.20
notionalist 951.7
notioned 932.10
notions 735.6
notions counter 736.6
notiony 986.20
no title 640.1
not keep 327.6
not keep faith 645.12
not keep troth 645.12
not kid oneself 956.3
not know 930.10
not know any better 930.8
not know any of the answers 930.8
not know beans 930.8

not know chalk from cheese 930.8
not know enough to come in out of the rain 930.8
not know from Adam 930.10
not know from the man in the moon 930.10
not know how 414.10
not know one's interest 414.14
not know one's own mind 362.6
not know on which side one's bread is buttered 414.14
not know the first thing about 930.8
not know the half of it 930.10
not know the score 930.8
not know the time of day 930.8
not know the way home 930.8
not know up from down 930.8
not know what it is all about 930.8
not know what o'clock it is 930.8
not know what one is about 414.14
not know what's what 930.8
not know what to make of 122.5, 522.11, 971.9
not know what to say 122.5
not know when one is beaten 409.13
not know when one is licked 856.5
not know when to stop 669.5, 669.6
not know where one's next meal is coming from 619.5
not know where one stands 362.6, 971.9
not know where to turn 1013.11
not know whether one is coming or going 971.9, 1013.11
not know whether one stands on one's head orheels 971.9
not know which way is up 930.8
not know which way to turn 971.9, 1011.9
not kosher 645.16, 650.10, 868.6
not leave a leg to stand on 19.10, 958.4
not let a word escape one 51.5
not let go 926.25
not let it bother one 134.7
not let it get one down 15.10, 134.6
not let it go further 345.7
not let out a peep 51.6
not let the grass grow under one's feet 330.16
not let the right hand know what the left is doing 345.7
not lift a finger 329.2, 340.8, 442.3
not lift a hand 329.2
not like (v) 99.3 (a) 780.7
not listen 327.6, 984.2
not listen to the voice of the siren 359.9
not live to eat 668.6
not live up to expectation 132.3
not long for this world 307.32, 395.28
not look a gift horse in the mouth 150.3
not look back 165.2, 359.10
not look backward 114.3
not look for 131.4
not look for trouble 329.4
not look like 787.2
not lose a moment 401.5
not lose sight of 983.9
not lying down 453.5
not mad 925.4
not make an issue of 134.7
not make any difference 998.11
not make a peep 51.5
not make a sound 51.5
not make head or tail of 522.11
not make it 19.8, 132.3, 250.4, 410.10, 911.2, 911.3, 992.8, 1003.3
not make out 911.2
not make sense 520.4, 522.10
not make the course 911.2
not make the cut 19.8, 250.4, 911.2, 992.8, 1003.3
not make the grade 19.8, 250.4, 410.9, 911.2, 1003.3
not make waves 329.4, 670.5
not many 885.4
not matter 998.11
not matter to 102.5
not mean a thing 520.4
not mean what one says 520.5
not measure up 250.4, 911.2, 1003.3
not measure up to expectation 132.3
not measuring up 911.1
not meddle 430.16
not meddle with 368.6
not meriting belief 955.10
not mince words 644.12
not mind 102.4, 327.6
not mind if one does 324.3
not mind one's business 214.7
not mingle 583.4
not miss a beat 916.12
not miss a trick 339.7, 983.8
not mix 583.4
not mix up 944.6
not move a foot 329.2
not move a muscle 173.7
not moving 734.15
not much 885.5
not much for looks 1015.6
not much of a bargain 1005.5
not much to boast of 1005.7
not much to look at 1015.6
not new 842.18
not notice 984.2
not observe 327.6
not occur 762.5
not of the earth 692.9
not of this world 692.9, 768.3, 986.19
not one 222.6
not one of us 774.3
not one's cup of tea 99.7
not oneself 85.56
not one's sort 99.7
not on speaking terms 589.11, 589.13
not on the job 984.8
not on the scoreboard 412.16
not open one's mouth 51.5, 344.6
not opinion 761.3
not oppose 332.11
notoriety 348.4, 352.4, 654.5, 661.2, 662.1
notorious 348.12, 645.17, 661.10, 662.16, 666.6, 928.27, 1000.9
notoriousness 348.4, 352.4, 662.1, 666.2, 1000.2
not our sort 774.3
not outstanding 640.9
not overlook a bet 794.8, 983.8
not part with 474.6
not pass 410.9
not pass muster 1003.3
not pay 625.6
not penetrate 522.10
not perfect 1003.4
not permit 444.4
not permitted 444.7
not play fair 650.6
not playing with a full deck 922.17
not play with a full deck 926.20
not possible 967.7
not present 222.11
not pretend to say 930.10
not proceed with 390.4
not proved 958.8
not pull fair 368.9
not pull one's punches 425.5
not pull one's weight 368.9
not pursue 390.4
not put a foot wrong 409.8
not put it past 130.10
not put up with 444.4, 451.3, 510.11
not qualify 992.8, 1003.3
not quite right 85.56
not rare 847.4
not reach 911.2
not reach to 911.2
not real 762.9
not realize one's expectations 132.4
not receive 157.5
not refuse 441.2
not register 520.4, 522.11, 984.5
not related 998.16
not relate to 776.4
not relax 403.15
not relax one's concern 983.8
not remember 990.5
not resemble 787.2
not resist 433.6, 670.5
not respect 156.4
not respectable 322.5
not rest 403.15
not right 926.26, 975.16
not right in the head 922.22, 926.27
not rightly know 930.10
not ring any bells 520.4
not ring true 354.15
not rock the boat 329.4, 670.5
not say a word 344.6
not say boo 51.6
not see 30.8
not see an inch beyond one's nose 922.12, 980.6
not see beyond one's nose 980.6
not see coming 131.4
not see eye-to-eye 789.5
not see the wood for the trees 522.11
not-self 768.2
not shown 958.8
not show up 222.7
not shrink from 492.10
not shut one's eyes 23.3
not signify 998.11
not sign off on 510.10
not singular 883.7
not sixteen ounces to the pound 922.17
not slacken 403.15
not sleep a wink 23.3
not so bad 999.20
not so dumb 920.12
not soil one's hands 495.8
not so many 885.6
not so much 885.6
not so you could tell it 787.5
not spare oneself nor anyone else 425.4
not spare the horses 401.6
not speak 51.5
not speak well of 512.8
not square 975.8
not square with 780.5
not stand 103.5
not stand a chance 972.14
not stand a snowball's chance in hell 972.14
not stand for 444.4, 510.11
not stand in the way of 1014.7
not stand on ceremony 581.2
not stand the sight of 103.5
not stand up 975.8
not stick one's neck out 494.7
not stir 173.7, 329.2
not stir a step 173.7
not stomach 99.3, 103.5, 444.4
not stop 812.4
not stop to think 401.7
not stretch 911.2
not strike one's colors 360.4
not submit 453.4
not suffer 444.4, 510.11
not suffice 911.2
not surprised 130.11
not swallow 955.5, 956.3
not sweat it 107.5, 1014.12
not take care of 340.6
not take it as a joke 152.13
not take kindly to 510.10
not take lying down 453.3
not take "no" for an answer 360.2, 361.7
not take no for an answer 375.14, 421.8
not take upon oneself to say 930.10
not tamper 430.16
not tell 345.7
not tell apart 784.7
not tell one from the other 784.7

not that sort 780.8
not that you would know it 787.5
not the ghost of a chance 125.1
not there 985.11
not the right sort 774.3
not the same 780.8
not the same thing at all 787.5
not the thing 638.3
not the type 780.8
not thick on the ground 885.5
not think 340.6, 933.2
not think much of 99.3, 510.10
not think of 131.4, 442.3, 933.2
not think twice about 102.4
not thrust oneself forward 139.7
not tightly wrapped 926.27
not to be believed 955.10
not to be borne 98.25
not to be changed 855.17
not to be compared 250.7, 787.6, 943.9
not to be deflected 359.12
not to be depended 645.19
not to be depended on 971.20
not to be distinguished 945.6
not to be doubted 970.16
not to be endured 98.25
not to be expected 870.10
not to be had 967.9, 992.11
not to be had at any price 992.11
not to be had for love or money 632.10, 967.9, 992.11
not to be handled without gloves 80.20
not to be improved 1002.6
not to be minuted 345.14
not to be mistaken 31.7, 348.8
not to be moved 361.9, 855.15
not to be overlooked 997.18
not to be quoted 345.14
not to be recommended 996.5
not to be relied on 971.20
not to be relied upon 645.19
not to be shaken 359.12
not to be sneezed at 371.25, 997.18
not to be sniffed 371.25
not to be thought of 125.14, 372.3, 510.24, 967.7
not to be trifled with 425.6
not to be trusted 645.19
not tolerate 444.4, 510.11
not to one's taste 99.7
not too shabby 999.13
not to the purpose 776.7
not touch 368.6, 390.5, 668.7
not touch with a ten-foot pole 261.7, 368.6
not trouble oneself with 984.2
not trouble one's head about 984.2
not true 354.25, 975.16
not true to 645.20
not turn a hair 94.5, 106.6, 106.9, 123.2
not turning over 734.15
not turn the other cheek 453.3
not turn up 222.7
not understand 522.11
not unlike 784.10
not up to 414.19
not up to expectation 108.9, 132.6
not up to it 992.9
not up to one's hopes 132.6
not up to scratch 19.15, 1000.9, 1005.10
not up to snuff 19.15, 108.9, 992.9, 1000.9, 1005.10
not up to specification 1005.10
not up to standard 1005.10
not up to the mark 1000.9, 1005.10
Notus 318.2
not use 390.5
not used to 374.4
not use up 397.8
not utter a word 51.5
not vital 998.17
not wait for an invitation 439.10
not wait to be asked 439.10
not want any part of 157.4
not want any part of not have any part of 510.10
not want anything to do with 442.5
not wash 975.8
not waste 397.8
not weaken 15.10
not well-founded 764.8
not what it is cracked up to be 911.5
not what it's cracked up to be 354.26
not what one used to be 16.12, 414.18
not whisper a word 345.7
not willing to hear of 442.6
not within the memory of man 870.14
not with it 930.12, 984.7
not words but action 328.1
not work 19.7, 410.9
not worry 107.5
not worth a damn 391.11
not worth a dime 391.11, 998.18
not worth a hill of beans 391.11, 998.18
not worth a red cent 391.11, 998.18
not worth a second thought 998.18
not worth a thought 391.11
not worth beans 998.18
not worth bubkes 391.11, 998.18
not worth having 391.11
not worth mentioning 391.11
not worth saving 390.10
not worth speaking of 391.11
not worth the pains 391.11
not worth the paper it's written on 391.11
not worth the powder and shot 391.11
not worth the powder to blow it to hell 391.11
not worth the trouble 391.11
not worthwhile 391.11
not write off 979.7
not yield an inch 361.7
nought beside 872.3
noumenon 761.1, 932.1, 932.2
noun 530.5
noun determiner 530.6
noun phrase 529.1, 530.5
nourish 7.17, 8.19, 306.11, 375.21, 449.16
nourishing (n) 7.1 (a) 7.21, 8.31, 81.5
nourish in one's bosom 93.11
nourishment 7.1, 10.3, 449.3
nous 677.7, 919.1, 920.2
nouveau riche 497.6, 606.7, 618.7, 841.4
nouveau-riche 606.8
nouvelle 337.5
nouvelle cuisine 10.1, 11.1
nova 1073.8
novation 862.1
Novaya Zemlya 1023.4
novel (n) 554.1, 722.3 (a) 337.5, 841.11
novelettish 722.8
novelettist 547.15, 718.4, 722.5
novel idea 932.5
novelist 547.15, 718.4, 722.5
novelistic 722.8
novelize 547.21, 718.6, 722.7
novelized 722.8
novelties 735.6
novelty 337.1, 578.5, 841.1, 841.2, 852.4
novel writing 718.2
novel-writing 547.2
novemdecillion 882.13
novena 696.8, 882.5
novenary 882.21
novercal 559.6
novice 572.9, 699.17, 818.2, 930.7
novice at, a 414.17
novice driver 756.2
noviciate 572.9
novitiate 572.9, 818.2
Novocain 86.15
novocaine 86.15
now (n) 838.1 (a) 841.13
now, the 838.1
nowadays 838.1
no water 276.1
no way 125.2
no way in hell 967.1
no way out 125.2
Now Generation, the 838.1
nowhere 261.4
nowhereness 222.1
nowheresville 261.4
nowhere to be found 222.11, 762.8
nowhere to turn 1013.6
no-win 125.14, 410.18
no-win situation 410.1, 1013.5, 1013.7
nowness 838.1, 841.1
no woman 222.6
no-work job 725.4
noxious 64.7, 69.10, 71.5, 82.5, 82.7, 98.18, 144.20, 1000.12
noxiousness 82.1, 82.3, 98.2, 144.5, 1000.5
noxious stench 71.1
nozzle 239.9, 283.8, 1065.8
np 728.8
N pole 1032.8
NREM sleep 22.5
nth degree 794.5
nth power 794.5
nt wt 297.1
nuance 245.1, 519.2, 780.2, 944.3
nuanced 944.7
nub 196.5, 208.2, 283.3, 294.1, 767.2, 997.6
nubber 745.3
nubbin 258.4, 283.3
nubbiness 288.1
nubble 283.3
nubbled 283.17
nubbliness 288.1
nubbly 283.17, 294.7
nubby 283.17, 294.7
nubilate 319.7
nubilation 319.4
nubile 14.3, 301.13, 303.12, 563.20
nubility 14.1, 563.2
nubilous 319.8, 319.10
nucleal 305.21
nuclear 208.12, 305.21, 819.4, 1038.19
nuclear atom 1038.4
nuclear bomb 462.20
nuclear energy 17.1, 1038.15
nuclear envelope 305.7
nuclear family 559.5, 617.2
nuclear fission 1038.8
nuclear force 1038.6
nuclear fuel 1038.10
nuclear furnace 1038.13
nuclear fusion 1038.9
nuclear isomer 1038.5
nuclear magnetic resonance 1038.6
nuclear particle 258.8, 1038.6
nuclear physicist 1038.3
nuclear physics 1033.1, 1038.1
nuclear power 18.4, 1038.15
nuclear-powered submarine 180.9
nuclear power plant 1032.19, 1038.14
nuclear radiation 1037.1
nuclear reactor 1038.13
nuclear resonance 1038.6
nuclear submarine 180.9
nuclear war 458.1
nuclear warhead 462.20, 1074.3
nuclear weapons 462.1
nuclear winter 395.6, 458.1, 459.1, 1037.1
nucleary 305.21
nucleate 208.12, 305.21
nucleation 208.8, 316.5
nucleization 1038.8
nucleize 1038.17
nucleolar 305.21
nucleolate 305.21
nucleolated 305.21
nucleolus 305.7
nucleon 1038.6
nucleonics 1038.1
nucleon number 1038.4

nucleosynthesis 1038.6
nucleotide 305.9
nucleus 196.5, 208.2, 208.3, 258.8, 305.7, 767.2, 819.1, 886.7, 1038.6
nuclide 1038.4
nude (n) 712.9, 712.14 (a) 6.14, 499.8
nude, the 6.3
nudge (n) 223.5, 517.15, 551.4, 902.2 (v) 172.6, 223.10, 375.15, 440.12, 517.22, 902.12, 989.19
nudging (n) 440.3 (a) 223.17
nudish 6.13
nudism 6.3
nudist (n) 6.3 (a) 6.14
nudity 6.3, 499.3
nudnik 96.10
nudzh (n) 96.10 (v) 96.13
nuff said 399.1
nugacious 19.15, 248.6, 391.11, 998.19
nugaciousness 248.1, 391.2, 998.3
nugacity 248.1, 391.2, 923.1, 998.3
nugae 998.4
nugatory 19.15, 248.6, 391.11, 998.19
nugget 257.10, 728.20
nuisance 96.2, 96.10, 118.4
nuisance call 347.13
nuisance value 1012.1
nuke (n) 1038.16 (v) 11.5, 308.14, 395.10, 459.23, 762.7
nuked 395.29
null 222.14, 520.6, 762.8
null and void 222.14, 445.3
nullification 335.2, 395.6, 445.1, 609.4, 900.2
nullifidian (n) 695.11 (a) 695.19, 955.8
nullifidianism 695.5, 955.1
nullifier 900.3
nullify 335.4, 395.13, 445.2, 625.9, 900.7
nullifying 900.9
nulli secundus 249.15
nullity 520.1, 762.1, 764.2, 998.6
nullius filius 561.5
nulomoline 66.3
numb (v) 25.4, 94.8, 120.5, 1023.10 (a) 25.6, 94.13, 102.7, 331.20
numbed 25.6, 94.13
number, a 884.2
number (n) 244.2, 356.9, 530.8, 554.5, 704.7, 709.22, 724.6, 793.2, 1017.3, 1017.6 (v) 244.4, 792.8, 801.7, 1017.17
numberable 1017.25
number among 772.3
number count 759.11
number-cruncher 1017.15
number-crunching 1042.1
numbered 713.11
numbered print 713.5
numbered with the dead 307.29
numbering (n) 1017.9 (a) 772.6
numberless 884.10
numberlessness 823.1
number lottery 759.14
number off 244.4, 1017.17
number one (n) 12.5, 411.2, 865.5 (a) 612.17, 997.24
number-one 1002.6
number one buzz 1016.14
number present 221.4
numbers 244.1, 709.22, 720.6, 720.7, 746.4, 884.3, 1017.1
numbers game 759.14
numbers pool 759.14
numbers runner 759.20
Number 10 Downing Street 228.5
number three buzz 1016.14
number two (n) 12.2, 12.4, 576.1 (v) 12.13
number work 1017.10
numbing (n) 120.1 (a) 25.9, 86.47, 120.9, 1023.14
numbness 25.1, 85.27, 94.4
numbnuts 924.4
numen 678.12
numerable 300.14, 1017.25
numeracy 928.5, 1017.2
numeral (n) 1017.3 (a) 1017.23
numerary 1017.22, 1017.23
numerate (v) 1017.17 (a) 570.16
numeration 1017.9
numerative 300.12, 1017.23, 1017.24
numerator 1017.7, 1017.12
numeric 1017.22, 1017.23
numerical 1017.22, 1017.23
numerical order 807.2
numero 1017.3
numero uno 997.24
numerous 247.8, 257.16, 883.7, 884.6, 991.7
numerous as the hairs on the head 884.6
numerous as the sands 884.6
numerous as the stars 884.6
numerousness 247.3, 883.1, 884.1, 991.2
numinous 122.11, 522.13, 662.19, 677.17, 685.7, 690.14, 870.15
numinous, the 685.2
numinousness 122.3, 522.1, 662.6, 685.1, 870.7
numismatic 728.30
numismatics 728.22
numismatist 728.22
numismatologist 728.22
numismatology 728.22
nummary 728.30
nummular 728.30
numskull 924.4
numskulled 922.17
numskulledness 922.4
numskullery 922.4
nun 517.10, 565.2, 699.17
nunatak 237.6
Nunc Dimittis 696.3
nunciate 353.3
nuncio 353.1, 576.6
nuncle 559.3
nuncupate 524.23
nuncupative 524.29, 957.16
nunks 559.3
nunky 559.3
nunnery 703.6
nunnish 565.6
Nuprin 86.12
nuptial (v) 563.14 (a) 75.25, 563.18, 701.18
nuptial apartment 563.3
nuptial bond 563.1
nuptial mass 563.3
nuptials 563.3
nuptial song 563.3
nuptial tie 563.1
Nuremberg defense 600.2
nurse (n) 90.8, 90.10, 1008.8 (v) 8.19, 91.24, 449.16, 474.7, 568.13, 1008.19
nurse a grudge 589.8
nurse an idea 931.16
nursemaid 577.8, 1008.8
nurse one's revenge 507.5
nurse practitioner 90.10
nurse resentment 152.12
nursery 197.7, 197.25, 567.2, 739.1, 753.1, 886.8, 1069.11
nursery, the 301.5
nurserymaid 1008.8
nurseryman 1069.6
nursery school 567.2, 568.5
nursery school child 572.3
nurse's aide 90.11
nurse's signal 400.1
nurses' station 197.25
nurse's uniform 5.7
nursing care 90.1
nursing home 91.21, 1009.4
nursing sister 90.10
nursling 302.9
nurtural 449.20
nurturance 449.3, 1008.2
nurture (n) 7.1, 10.3, 449.3, 568.3, 1008.2 (v) 7.17, 8.19, 339.9, 375.21, 392.9, 449.16, 474.7, 568.13, 1008.19, 1070.6
nurture a belief 953.13
nurture a feeling 93.10
nurture an idea 931.16
nurture the hope 124.6
nurturing 568.3, 1008.2
nut (n) 10.39, 101.5, 310.31, 866.3, 870.4, 926.16, 926.18, 927.4 (v) 1069.19
nutate 916.10
nutation 916.1
nutational 916.15
nutball 926.16
nutbar 926.16
nut-brown 40.3
nutcase 926.16
nuthouse 926.14
nutman 759.21
nutmeg grater 1051.7
NutraSweet 66.2
nutrient (n) 7.3 (a) 7.21
nutrify 7.17, 8.19
nutrilite 7.3
nutriment 7.3, 10.3
nutrition 7.1, 8.1, 11.1
nutritional disease 85.11
nutritionist 7.15, 90.11
nutritious 7.21, 8.31, 81.5
nutritiousness 7.2
nutritive (n) 7.3 (a) 7.21
nutritiveness 7.2
nutritive value 7.1
nutriture 449.3
nuts (n) 2.13, 759.3, 759.10 (a) 926.27
nuts, the 999.7
nuts about 101.11, 104.30
nuts and bolts 767.3, 818.6, 987.2, 1040.4
nutshell (n) 248.2, 557.1 (a) 268.9, 557.6
nutso (n) 926.16 (a) 926.27
nuts on 101.11
nuts over 101.11
nutter 926.16
nuttiness 923.1, 926.2
nutting 1069.15
nut to crack 522.8
nutty 63.9, 923.9, 926.27, 927.6
nutty about 104.30
nutty as a fruitcake 926.27
nuzzle 73.8, 562.17
nuzzling 562.1
nwah 562.19
nyanza 241.1
nyctalopia 30.2
nyctalopic 28.11, 30.9
nylon 4.1
nylons 5.28
nylon string 711.20
nymph 302.12, 305.14, 311.32, 678.9
nympha 302.12
nymphae 2.13
nymphal 678.18
nymphean 678.18
nymphet 302.8, 665.14, 678.9
nymphic 678.18
nymphlike 678.18
nymphlin 678.9
nympho 665.14
nymphomania 75.5, 75.11, 665.5
nymphomaniac 75.16, 665.14
nymphomaniacal 665.29
nystagmic 28.11
nystagmus 28.1
nystatin 86.29
O 87.16, 280.2
oaf 414.8, 416.3, 924.5
oafdom 922.3
oafish 414.20, 922.15
oafishness 414.3, 922.3
oak 15.8, 1046.6
oak leaf 647.5
Oaks 757.1
oar 180.15, 183.5, 760.2
oarlock 906.3, 915.5
oarsman 183.5, 760.2
oasis 241.1
oath 334.4, 436.1, 513.4
oath breaking 354.9
oath of allegiance 334.4
oath of office 334.4
oath of secrecy 345.3
oath-taking 332.3
oatmeal 40.3
oats 10.4
Obadiah 684.1
Obamacare 609.6
obcordate 279.15
obduction 295.1

obduracy 94.3, 114.2, 144.10, 361.1, 361.2, 425.2, 654.6, 1046.1
obdurate 25.6, 114.5, 144.25, 361.10, 425.7, 654.17, 1046.10
obdurateness 94.3, 425.2
obeah 675.6, 690.1, 691.5
obeah doctor 690.7
obeahism 675.6, 690.1
obedience 134.2, 326.1, 433.1, 867.1
obediency 326.1
obedient 134.10, 326.3, 433.12, 434.4, 641.13, 867.5
obeisance 138.2, 155.2, 326.1, 433.1, 913.3
obeisant 138.14, 155.10, 433.16
obelisk 272.6, 549.12
Oberon 678.8
obese 257.18, 257.23
obesity 257.5, 257.8
obesity diet 7.13
obey 134.7, 326.2, 433.6
obeying the law 434.1
obey one's impulse 365.7
obey the law 434.2
obey the rules 326.2
obfuscate 263.3, 346.6, 522.12, 569.3, 1027.9
obfuscated 346.11, 519.5, 522.15, 1027.13
obfuscation 522.3, 569.1, 936.1, 1027.6
obfuscatory 263.4, 346.15, 522.15, 569.6
obit 307.13
obiter dictum 213.2
obituarist 309.7
obituary (n) 307.13, 549.12, 719.1 (a) 309.22, 549.18
object (n) 380.2, 518.2, 530.2, 761.2, 763.3, 1052.4 (v) 333.5, 453.3, 510.10, 789.5
object case 530.9
object code 1042.13
objectification 206.4, 986.6
objectify 206.5, 986.15
objecting 333.7, 453.5
object in mind 380.2
objection 325.2, 333.2, 453.1, 510.1, 598.12, 600.2, 1012.4
objectionability 98.2, 108.2
objectionable 98.18, 108.10, 510.24
objectionableness 98.2
objectionable person 660.1
objectional 98.18
objective (n) 29.2, 323.1, 380.2 (a) 94.9, 649.9, 761.15, 768.3, 973.13, 979.12, 982.3, 1052.10
objective behavior 321.1
objective case 530.9
objective existence 761.2
objective idealism 1053.3
objectively true 973.13
objective prism 29.2
objective truth 973.1
objective witness 970.8
objectivity 94.1, 644.3, 768.1, 979.5, 982.1
objectless 972.16
object lesson 399.1, 568.7, 786.2
object libido 92.28
object of art 712.9
object of compassion 96.11
object of note 997.5
object of one's affections 104.9
objector 333.3, 452.3
object program 1042.11
object to 325.3, 510.10
objet d'art 712.9
objet trouvé 715.2
objurgate 510.17
objurgation 510.5
objurgatory 510.22
oblast 231.5
oblate spheroid 282.2, 746.2
oblation 8.4, 478.4, 696.7
oblation cloth 703.10
obligate (v) 436.5, 641.12 (a) 641.16
obligated 436.8, 623.9, 641.16
obligate oneself 404.3
obligate running 84.2
obligating 420.13
obligation 143.7, 150.1, 404.1, 424.1, 436.2, 438.1, 623.1, 641.1, 959.2, 963.1
obligative 530.11
obligatoriness 963.1
obligatory 420.12, 424.11, 641.15, 963.12
obligatory gate 753.1
oblige 143.9, 424.5, 427.6, 449.19, 641.12, 963.8
obliged 150.5, 641.16
obliged to 641.16, 897.6
obligement 424.1, 963.1
obliging (n) 427.3 (a) 143.16, 427.8, 443.14, 504.13
obligingness 143.3, 427.2
oblique (n) 204.7 (v) 204.9 (a) 161.14, 170.9, 204.13, 218.6, 538.14, 914.7
oblique angle 204.7, 278.2
oblique case 530.9
oblique figure 204.7
oblique line 204.7
oblique motion 172.2
obliqueness 204.1, 538.5
obliquitous 204.13
obliquity 164.1, 204.1, 654.3
obliterate 395.16, 625.9, 990.6
obliterated 395.28, 990.8
obliteration 395.7, 625.2, 773.2, 990.1, 1044.2
obliviate 984.4
oblivion 25.2, 94.2, 340.2, 933.1, 990.1
oblivious 22.22, 25.8, 94.10, 340.11, 933.4, 984.7, 985.11, 990.9
obliviousness 25.2, 94.2, 984.1, 990.1
oblong 267.9, 278.9
oblongated 267.9
oblongitudinal 267.9
oblongness 267.1
obloquy 510.4, 513.2, 661.4
obnoxious 98.18, 661.12, 1000.9
obnoxiousness 64.3, 98.2, 661.3, 1000.2
obnubilate 319.7, 1027.9
obnubilation 1027.6
oboist 710.4
obovate 280.12
obovoid 282.9
obscene 98.18, 497.11, 513.8, 523.21, 665.29, 666.9
obscene language 513.3, 523.9
obscene literature 547.12, 718.1
obscenity 80.7, 98.2, 497.2, 513.3, 513.4, 526.6, 665.5, 666.4
obscurant 1027.18
obscurantism 522.3, 569.1, 930.1, 936.1
obscurantist 936.7
obscuration 346.1, 522.3, 569.1, 971.4, 1027.6
obscure (n) 1027.1 (v) 30.7, 263.3, 295.19, 319.7, 346.6, 522.12, 569.3, 936.9, 971.15, 1027.9, 1031.2 (a) 32.6, 263.4, 346.11, 522.15, 539.4, 661.14, 689.23, 971.19, 1027.13, 1031.3
obscured 30.10, 295.31, 346.11, 519.5, 522.15, 1027.13
obscurement 346.1, 1027.6
obscure point 522.8
obscuring (n) 295.1 (a) 30.11, 295.35, 346.15, 569.6, 1027.18
obscurity, an 998.7
obscurity 32.2, 263.1, 522.3, 538.1, 971.4, 1027.1, 1031.1
obsecration 440.2, 696.4
obsequial 309.22
obsequies 309.4
obsequious 138.14, 155.10, 433.16, 511.8
obsequiousness 138.2, 155.2
observability 31.1
observable 31.6, 348.8
observable behavior 321.1
observable universe 1073.1
observance 27.2, 326.1, 339.4, 373.1, 434.1, 437.4, 487.1, 580.4, 692.1, 701.3, 867.1, 983.1
observances 504.7
observant 339.13, 434.4, 641.13, 692.8, 953.21, 983.15
observation 27.2, 434.1, 524.3, 932.1, 938.9, 953.6, 983.1, 1073.17
observational astronomy 1073.19
observational comedy 489.1
observation deck 27.8, 197.22
observation flight 184.11
observation point 27.8, 31.3
observation post 27.8
observation tower 272.6
observatory 27.8, 1073.17
observatory on the moon 1075.5
observe 27.12, 27.13, 326.2, 434.2, 437.9, 487.2, 524.24, 580.5, 701.14, 867.3, 938.24, 983.6
observe etiquette 504.10
observe protocol 504.10
observer 185.3, 918.1, 938.17, 1073.22
observe the formalities 580.6
observe the golden rule 652.4
observe the lex talionis 506.6
observe the proprieties 579.4
observing 983.15
obsess 98.16, 680.16, 691.9, 926.25, 983.13, 988.6, 989.13
obsessed 93.18, 93.23, 359.16, 691.13, 926.33, 983.17, 988.10, 989.23
obsessed by 93.23
obsessed with 93.23
obsessing 926.34, 983.20, 989.25
obsession 424.1, 691.2, 926.13, 983.3, 988.5
obsessional 926.34
obsessive 926.34, 983.20, 989.25
obsessive compulsion 926.13
obsessive-compulsive disorder 92.15
obsess on 92.36
obsess the mind 931.20
obsidian 38.4
obsolesce 390.9, 842.9
obsolescence 390.1
obsolescent 390.10, 837.10
obsolete (n) 526.12 (a) 19.17, 390.10, 762.11, 837.7, 842.15
obsoleteness 390.1
obsoletion 390.1
obsoletism 390.1, 526.12
obstacle 293.3, 379.2, 1012.4
obstacle course 84.2
obstacle race 457.12
obstetric 90.15
obstetrical 90.15
obstetrics 1.1
obstinacy 15.1, 325.1, 327.2, 359.1, 360.1, 361.1, 425.2, 451.2, 453.1, 803.3, 895.2
obstinate 15.15, 327.8, 359.11, 360.8, 361.8, 425.7, 451.8, 453.5, 454.7, 803.12, 895.4
obstinateness 361.1
obstinate pride 136.1
obstipate 293.7
obstipated 293.11
obstipation 293.3
obstreperous 53.13, 59.10, 327.10, 361.12, 454.7, 671.19
obstreperousness 53.2, 327.2, 361.4, 671.3
obstruct 175.9, 293.7, 451.3, 460.10, 846.8, 1012.12
obstructed 293.11, 846.16
obstructer 1012.4, 1012.8
obstructing (n) 749.6 (a) 1012.17
obstruction 175.4, 293.3, 751.1, 846.2, 1012.1, 1012.4
obstructionism 451.2, 1012.1
obstructionist (n) 452.3, 1012.8 (a) 846.17
obstructionistic 846.17
obstructive (n) 452.3 (a) 451.8, 453.5, 846.17, 1012.17
obstruent 1012.17
obtain 176.16, 192.14, 472.8, 479.6, 761.8, 864.10, 886.11
obtainability 966.3
obtainable 472.14, 966.8
obtainableness 966.3
obtain a divorce 566.5
obtain a return 472.12

obtain by fair means or foul 384.6
obtainer 479.3
obtaining 373.13
obtainment 472.1
obtain under false pretenses 356.18
obtention 472.1
obtest 440.11, 696.13, 957.12
obtestation 440.2, 696.4
obtrude 214.5, 909.13
obtrude on 478.20
obtrude upon 640.7
obtrusion 214.1, 909.1
obtrusive 140.11, 142.9, 214.8, 348.12, 501.20
obtrusiveness 140.4, 142.1, 214.2, 348.4, 501.3, 643.1
obtund 25.4, 94.7, 286.2, 670.6
obtundent 286.3
obtundity 286.1
obtuse 25.6, 94.9, 286.3, 335.5, 922.16
obtuse angle 278.2
obtuseness 25.1, 94.1, 286.1, 922.3
obtusenss 335.1
obumbrate (v) 1027.9 (a) 1027.16
obumbrated 1027.16
obumbration 1027.6
obverse (n) 215.3, 216.1, 784.3 (a) 215.5, 779.6
obverse, the 779.2
obvert 779.5
obviate 1012.14
obviation 1012.2
obviative 530.7
obvious 31.7, 348.8, 521.11, 970.15
obvious clue 351.2
obviousness 31.2, 348.3
obvious truth 974.2
occasion (n) 376.1, 766.1, 831.2, 843.2, 886.1, 963.2 (v) 886.10
occasional 766.7, 831.9, 843.11, 848.3, 886.13
occasional cause 886.3
occasional help 577.11
occasionalness 848.1
occasional poet 720.12
occasional rain 316.1
occasional showers 316.1
Occident 231.6
occident 161.3
occidental 161.14
occipital 217.10
occiput 217.1
occision 308.3
occlude 293.6, 293.7, 1012.12
occluded 293.9
occluded front 317.4
occlusion 85.6, 293.1, 293.3, 317.4, 1012.1
occlusive (n) 524.12 (a) 524.30, 1012.17
occult (v) 295.19, 346.6, 1027.9 (a) 345.11, 346.11, 519.5, 522.16, 689.23, 870.15, 988.7, 1053.7
occult, the 345.5, 870.7, 1053.1
occultate 1027.9
occultation 34.1, 295.1, 346.1, 1027.8
occulted 295.31, 1027.13
occulting 1027.6
occulting light 400.1
occultism 345.5, 689.1, 1053.1
occultist 689.11, 1053.4
occult meaning 519.2
occult phenomena 1053.1
occupancy 225.1, 469.1
occupant 227.2, 470.4
occupation 225.1, 328.1, 469.1, 480.4, 724.1, 724.6, 889.1
occupational 724.16
occupational disease 85.32
occupational hazard 85.32
occupational medicine 90.13
occupational therapist 90.8
occupational therapy 91.1
occupation force 461.23
occupation layer 296.1
occupiable 225.15
occupied 225.12, 330.21, 724.15, 931.22, 983.17
occupier 227.2, 227.7, 470.4
occupy 221.7, 225.7, 469.4, 480.19, 724.10, 772.3, 931.20, 983.13
occupy a certain position 765.5
occupy a post 609.42, 724.14
occupying 469.9
occupy oneself 724.10
occupy oneself with 889.5, 983.5
occupy oneself with engage oneself with 724.11
occupy one's time 724.10
occupy the attention 983.13
occupy the chair 573.11
occupy the mind 931.20
occupy the mind with 931.11
occupy the thoughts 931.20
occupy time 821.6
occur 221.6, 761.8, 831.5, 931.18
occur often 847.3
occurrence 33.1, 221.1, 761.1, 766.1, 831.2, 864.2
occurring 831.9
occur to 931.18
occur to one's mind 931.18
ocean 240.1, 240.2, 247.3
ocean air 317.2
ocean bed 275.4
ocean blue 240.1
ocean bottom 199.4, 275.4
ocean breeze 318.4
ocean burning 390.3
ocean deeps and trenches 240.1
ocean depths 240.1, 275.4
ocean floor 240.5, 275.4
oceanfront (n) 234.2 (a) 234.7
ocean-going 240.8
oceangoing 182.57
ocean greyhound 180.5
Oceania 231.6
oceanic 182.57, 240.8
oceanic island 235.2
oceanic ridge 237.6, 240.5
oceanic rise 237.6
oceanic sediment 1059.6
oceanic trench 240.5
Oceanid 240.3, 678.10
ocean incineration 390.3
ocean lane 182.10
ocean liner 180.5
ocean main 240.1
ocean nymph 678.10
ocean of emptiness 1073.3
oceanographer 240.7, 300.9, 1071.2
oceanographic 240.8, 275.15, 300.12
oceanographical 240.8, 300.12
oceanographic research ship 180.1
oceanographic science 1071.1
oceanography 240.6, 275.6, 1071.1
ocean pollution 1072.2
ocean sea 240.1
oceanside (n) 234.2 (a) 234.7
ocean swell 238.14
ocean travel 182.1
ocean trip 182.6
Oceanus 240.3, 678.10
ocelot 47.6, 311.21
ocherish 42.2, 43.4
ocherous 42.2, 43.4
ochery 42.2, 43.4
ochlocracy 418.2, 612.4
ochlocratic 418.6
ochre 40.1
ochreous 42.2, 43.4
ochroid 42.2, 43.4
Ockham's razor 484.1
OCR device 1042.4
octachord 882.4
octad 882.4
octadic 882.20
octagon 882.4
octagonal 278.10, 882.20
octahedral 278.10, 882.20
octahedron 882.4
octal (n) 882.4 (a) 882.20
octal system 1017.4
octameter 720.7, 882.4
octan 882.20
octangular 882.20
octaploid 882.20
octastich 720.10
octastyle 882.20
octastylos 882.4
Octateuch 683.3, 882.4
octave 709.9, 709.20, 720.10, 882.4
octave scale 709.6
octave species 709.10
octavo 554.4, 882.4
octennial 850.4
octet 450.1, 708.18, 720.10, 882.4, 1033.3
octet theory 1038.2
octillion 882.13
octodecillion 882.13
octodecimoo 554.4
octofid 882.20
octofoil 647.2
octogenarian 304.2, 882.7
octonary (n) 882.4 (a) 882.20
octoroon 797.8
octosyllabic 882.20
octuple 882.20
ocular 27.20, 29.9
ocular inspection 27.6
ocular spectrum 976.5
oculist 29.8, 90.4
oculus 2.9, 27.9
OD 308.22
od 22.8
odalisque 432.7, 665.15
odd 256.7, 787.4, 848.3, 870.11, 872.9, 926.26, 927.5, 1017.23
oddball (n) 774.2, 789.4, 870.4, 927.4 (a) 870.11, 927.6
odd duck 870.4
odd fellow 870.4, 927.4
odd fish 870.4
oddity 870.3, 870.4, 870.5, 927.1
odd job 724.2
odd-job man 577.4
odd lot 738.3
odd-lot dealer 737.10
odd man out 333.3, 1011.7
oddment 998.5
oddments 256.1, 735.1, 770.13, 797.6
odd moments 402.1
oddness 926.1
odd person 927.3
odds 249.2, 759.1, 759.6, 780.1, 791.1, 966.1, 968.1, 972.7
odds and ends 256.1, 735.6, 770.13, 793.3, 797.6
odds board 759.17
odds maker 759.6
odds-on (n) 972.8 (a) 968.6
odds-on chance 972.8
odds-on favorite 757.2
odd-toed ungulate 311.5
odd trick 758.3
odenum 2.18
odeum 704.14
odiferous 69.9
Odin 458.12
odious 80.23, 98.18, 99.7, 103.8, 661.12, 1000.9
odiousness 64.3, 80.2, 98.2, 1000.2
odist 720.12
odium 103.1, 661.4
odontalgia 26.5
odontoid 285.14
odor 69.1, 70.1, 865.4
odorant 69.9
odorate 70.9
odorator 70.6
odored 69.9
odoriferous 69.9, 70.9
odorization 69.3
odorize 69.7, 70.8
odorizer 70.6
odorizing 69.3, 70.5
odorless 72.5
odorlessness 72.1
odor of sanctity 685.1, 692.2
odorous 69.9, 70.9, 71.5
odorousness 69.2, 71.2
odyl 22.8
odylic 22.24
odylic force 22.8
Odysseus 178.2
odyssey 177.2
Oedipus complex 92.22
oenologist 88.19
oenomania 88.3
oenophile 496.6

oenophilist 88.11
Oerlikon 462.12
oersted 1032.9
o'er top 272.11
œufs 10.26
œufs à la coque 10.26
œufs brouillés 10.26
œufs pochés 10.26
œufs sur le plat 10.26
oeuvre 547.12, 718.1, 893.1
œuvres 554.7
of a certain age 303.15
of age 259.12, 303.12, 563.20
of a kind 784.11, 1005.7
of all descriptions 783.4
of all kinds 783.4
of all manner of colors 47.9
of all sorts 783.4
of all the colors of the rainbow 47.9
of all types 783.4
of all work 387.20
of a low order of importance 998.16
of a mind to 375.30
of another sort 780.8
of a piece 332.15, 781.5, 784.11, 788.9, 798.6
of a place 231.9
of a size 784.11
of a sort 780.8, 1005.7
of bad faith 645.20
of belief 953.23
of choice 249.12, 371.25, 496.7
of cleanly habits 79.25
of common ancestry 775.10
of common descent 775.10
of common occurrence 847.4
of concern 997.18
of concernment 997.18
of consequence 997.18
of consummate art 712.20
of counsel 597.6
of design 380.8
of different orders 943.9
of easy virtue 654.12, 665.26
of evil portent 133.16
off (n) 757.3 (v) 308.14, 395.12 (a) 61.4, 219.4, 331.18, 393.41, 787.4, 848.3, 870.11, 926.26, 926.31, 975.16, 1003.4, 1005.10
off-again-on-again 851.3, 854.7
off-air 549.17
of faith 953.27
offal 10.20, 80.9, 391.4
off-and-on 848.3
of fatal omen 133.16
off-balance 160.12, 791.5, 985.12
off-base 322.5, 638.3, 844.6, 975.17
offbeat (n) 709.26 (a) 787.4, 868.6, 870.10
off Broadway 704.1
off-center 160.12, 265.10, 791.5
off chance 966.1, 972.9
off-color 35.21, 85.56, 638.3, 666.7
off course 204.13
off-course 164.8
offcut 548.3
off day 414.5
off-duty 331.18
of feeling 93.17
offend 98.11, 152.21, 156.5, 655.4, 1015.5
offend against the law 674.5
offender 660.8
offender's tag and monitor 428.4
offending Adam, the 663.2
offend one's aesthetic sensibilities 1015.5
offend the ear 58.11
offend the eye 1015.5
offend the nostrils 71.4
offense 152.2, 152.11, 156.2, 435.2, 459.1, 655.1, 655.2, 674.3, 674.4, 747.3, 749.3, 754.3
offenseless 657.6
offenselessness 657.1
offense to the nostrils 71.1
offensive (n) 459.1 (a) 64.7, 71.5, 98.18, 156.8, 458.20, 459.30, 497.10, 505.6, 666.9, 1000.9, 1015.11
offensive board 747.1
offensive capacity 459.8
offensive linemen 746.2
offensiveness 64.3, 71.2, 98.2, 505.1, 666.4, 1000.2, 1015.2
offensive odor 71.1
offensive platoon 746.2
offensive team 746.2
offensive to ears polite 534.2
offensive to gentle ears 497.10
offensive warfare 458.1
offensive weapons 462.1
offensive zone 749.1
offer (n) 403.2, 439.1, 478.1 (v) 324.4, 371.21, 403.6, 439.4, 478.12, 733.9, 745.5, 939.4, 957.12
offer a good prospect 968.4
offer aid 449.11
offer an explanation 600.11
offer a prayer 696.13
offer a resolution 439.5
offer as a plea 600.10
offer at a bargain 734.10
offer bait to 377.5
offered 324.7
offer excuse for 600.11
offer felicitations 149.2
offer for sale 734.10
offer in defense 600.10
offer in exchange 862.4
offering 439.1, 478.4, 478.6, 658.3, 696.7, 745.3
offering no delight 99.7
offering price 738.9
offer itself 931.18
offer of marriage 562.8
offer of parley 465.2
offer one cannot refuse 375.7
offer one's compliments 149.2
offer one's congratulations 149.2
offer oneself 439.10, 485.3
offer resistance 451.4, 453.3
offer sacrifice 696.15
offer thanks 150.4
offer the expectation 968.4
offer to buy 733.9
offertory 478.6, 696.3, 696.7, 708.17
offertory hymn 696.3, 708.17
offertory sentence 708.17
offer to the public 352.14
offer up 385.7, 439.4, 745.5
offer up an oblation 696.15
of few words 344.9
off food 100.25
off-grid 1032.36
off-guard 340.10, 984.8
offhand 106.15, 340.11, 365.11, 365.12, 581.3
offhanded 581.3
offhandedness 106.5, 340.2, 581.1
offhand shot 365.4
off hours 331.2
off-hours (n) 20.4 (a) 20.10
office (n) 143.7, 197.6, 387.5, 449.1, 580.4, 594.4, 615.1, 696.8, 701.3, 724.3, 724.5, 739.7, 739.8 (v) 573.8
office-bearer 575.15, 610.11
office-block ballot 609.19
office boy 353.4, 577.5
office building 739.1
office furniture 229.1
office girl 577.5
officeholder 575.15, 610.11
office hours 824.2
Office of Naval Research 184.7
office of power 417.10
Office of the Dead 309.4
office park 739.1, 739.7
office pool 759.5
officer (n) 574.3, 575.15, 575.17, 1008.15 (v) 612.11
officer of the court 597.1
officer of the day 575.17
officer of the deck 183.7
officer of the watch 183.7
officer worker 577.3
offices 449.1
office seeker 610.9
office suite 739.7
office temporary 726.2
office worker 726.2
official (n) 574.3, 575.15, 576.3, 746.1, 746.3, 747.3, 748.2, 751.3, 752.3, 754.3 (a) 417.15, 419.4, 549.17, 580.7, 612.16, 612.18, 724.16, 970.18
official bulletin 352.3
official classification 345.3
official count 609.21
official document 549.5
officialdom 249.5, 575.14
officialese 523.10, 609.37
officialism 612.10
official jargon 609.37, 612.10
official journal 549.8
official language 523.4
official oath 334.4
official observer 751.3
official report 549.7
official residence 228.5
officiai scorekeeper 747.3
official scorer 550.1, 745.2
official secrecy 345.3
official spokesman 576.5
official spokesperson 576.5
official spokeswoman 576.5
officiary 575.15
officiate 466.6, 573.11, 701.15, 724.13, 745.5, 746.5, 946.12
officiating 573.14
officiation 573.3
officinal 86.4
officious 214.9, 330.24
officiousness 214.2, 330.9, 981.1
offing 261.3, 839.1
off in one's reckoning 975.18
off in the clouds 985.11
off in the upper story 926.27
offish 141.12, 344.10, 583.6
offishness 141.4, 583.2
off-key 61.4
off limits 444.7
off-limits 210.8
off-load 298.6, 909.23
off-loading 909.6
off market 737.5
off-message 164.7
off note 61.1
off-off-Broadway 704.1
off oneself 308.22
off one's feed 85.56
off one's guard 131.9, 930.12, 984.8
off one's head 926.27, 926.31
off one's nut 926.27
off one's rocker 926.27
off one's stride 985.12
off-peak 252.10
off-pitch 61.4
offprint 548.3, 785.5
off-putting 379.5, 589.10, 908.4
off-roading 756.2
off-road race 457.12
off-road racing 744.1
off-road vehicle 179.9
offscourings 80.9, 256.1, 391.4, 606.3
off-scum 256.2, 320.2, 606.3
off-season (n) 313.1 (a) 313.9
offset (n) 338.2, 548.1, 548.3, 561.4, 779.2, 900.3 (v) 338.5, 670.8, 779.4, 900.7 (a) 900.9
offset lithography 548.1, 713.3
offset printing 548.1
offsetting (n) 338.1, 900.2 (a) 338.6, 900.9
offshoot 171.4, 254.1, 302.11, 310.20, 561.4, 617.4, 617.10, 675.3, 793.4, 887.1, 893.3
offshore 261.11
offshore rights 231.1
offshore station 1034.6
offshore wind 318.10
off side 219.1
offside 749.3, 752.3
offspring 302.3, 559.5, 561.1, 561.3, 835.2, 887.1, 893.1
off-target 164.8, 265.10
off the beam 638.3
off the beaten track 584.8, 870.10
off the bottle 516.3
off-the-cuff 365.12
off the field 19.17
off the grid 1032.36
off the hinges 926.27

off the hook 148.7
off-the-peg clothes 5.4
off-the-rack 5.48, 405.19, 830.4, 892.18
off-the-rack clothes 5.4
off the rails 975.16
off the record 345.14
off-the-shelf 892.18
off the subject 776.7
off the top of one's head 365.12, 406.8
off the track 926.27, 971.24, 975.16
off-the-wall 131.10, 870.11, 926.27
off-time 826.1
off-tone 35.21, 61.4
off to one side 218.6
off-topic 776.7
off-track betting 759.4
off-track betting parlor 759.19
off-trail skiing 753.1
of full age 303.13
off-white 37.8
off-whiteness 37.1
off with 6.6
off-work 331.18
off-year 844.2
of general application 387.18
of general utility 387.18
of gentle blood 607.10, 608.10
of good breed 607.10, 608.11
of good cheer 109.11, 124.10
of good comfort 107.7, 121.13
of good constitution 83.12
of good credit 622.8
of good family 608.11
of good hope 124.10
of good omen 133.17
of good physique 15.16
of gourmet quality 63.8
of great cost 632.11
of great price 632.10
of happy portent 133.17
of heart 93.17
of help 387.18
of humble birth 606.8
of ill omen 133.16
of importance 997.18
of interest 997.18
of like mind 450.5, 788.9
of little brain 922.13
of little importance 998.16
of little or no consequence 998.16
of long duration 827.10
of long standing 827.10, 842.12
of loose morals 665.26
of mark 247.10, 662.16, 997.19
of marriageable age 303.12, 563.20
of moment 997.18
of no account 248.6, 895.3, 998.16
of no avail 391.9
of no concern 998.16
of no consequence 998.17
of no earthly use 391.11
of no effect 410.18
of no force 19.15
of no great importance 998.16
of no importance 998.16
of no matter 998.16
of no purpose 391.9
of no significance 998.16
of note 662.16, 997.18
of no use 391.9
of old 842.10
of one accord 332.15
of one mind 332.15, 455.3, 788.9
of one's own 469.8
of opposite polarity 908.4
of other times 842.13
of powerful physique 15.16
of preference 371.25
of promise 124.12, 133.17
of quality 496.7
of rank 608.10
of record 549.17
of repute 662.15
of ripe age 303.13
of sentiment 93.17
of service 387.18
of significance 997.18
of small importance 998.16
of small number 885.4
of sorts 780.8, 1005.7
of soul 93.17
of sound mind 925.4
oftenness 847.1
oftentime 847.4
of that ilk 775.9
of that kind 775.9
of that order 257.24
of that sort 775.9
of the belief 953.21
of the best 496.7
of the best sort 999.15
of the blood 559.6
of the cloth 698.17
of the deepest dye 38.8
of the earth 312.13
of the essence 767.9
of the faith 687.7
of the first degree 999.17
of the first rank 997.24
of the first water 496.7, 999.15
of the folk 842.12
of the highest type 249.13, 999.15
of the people 606.8
of the same hue 784.11
of the same kidney 778.7
of the same mind 332.15, 455.3, 788.9
of the same stripe 784.11
of the true faith 687.7
of the war party 458.21
oft-repeated 847.4
of two minds 362.9
of unsound mind 926.26
of use 387.18
of value 387.22
of vital importance 997.23
of weight 997.18
of yesterday 841.12
of yore 842.10
ogdoad 882.4
ogham 546.2
ogive 279.4
ogle (n) 27.5, 562.9 (v) 27.14, 27.15, 562.20, 918.5
ogle at 27.14
ogler 918.1
ogre 127.9, 593.6
ogreish 680.17
ogress 127.9, 593.6
ohm 1032.13
ohmage 1032.13
ohmic resistance 1032.13
ohms 1032.13
oik 924.5
oil (n) 86.11, 511.1, 712.13, 1021.1, 1025.20, 1056.1 (v) 91.25, 287.5, 385.9, 511.6, 1014.7, 1021.8, 1056.8
oil-and-vinegar 10.12
oilcan 1056.7
oil-colorist 716.4
oiled 88.33, 287.12
oiler 183.6
oilfield 386.4
oil-fired 1021.9
oil-fired power plant 1032.19
oil heat 1019.1
oil-heat 1020.17
oil-heated 1020.29
oiliness 287.1, 354.6, 504.5, 511.2, 693.1, 1056.5
oiling 1014.5, 1056.6
oil one's cross one's palm 375.23
oil one's tongue 540.6
oil on troubled waters 86.1
oil paint 35.8
oil painter 716.4
oil painting 35.12, 712.3, 712.13
oil-powered 1021.9
oil-proof 293.12
oil refinery 739.3
oil rig 386.4
oil slick 295.12, 296.2
oilstone 285.7
oil-temper 1046.7
oil-tempered 1046.15
oil the palm 378.3
oil the tongue 511.5
oil-tight 293.12
oil well 386.4
oily 287.12, 354.32, 504.17, 511.8, 1056.9
oily calm 173.5
oily-tongued 504.17, 511.8
oink 60.3
oink out 8.25
ointment 25.3, 86.11, 701.5, 728.2, 1056.3
Oisin 178.2
OK (n) 332.2, 441.1, 443.1, 509.1 (v) 443.9, 509.9 (a) 973.16, 999.13, 999.20
OK, the 332.4
okapi 311.5
okay (n) 441.1, 443.1 (v) 441.2, 443.9 (a) 107.12, 973.16, 999.13, 999.20
okay, the 332.4
okey-dokey 441.1
okrug 231.5
Oktoberfest 743.4
oktostylos 882.4
old 303.16, 390.10, 413.28, 837.10, 842.10, 842.13
old, the 304.4
Old Adam, the 663.2
old age 303.1, 303.5, 842.1
old-age and survivors insurance 611.7
old-age assistance 611.7
old-age insurance 478.8
old army game, the 356.9
old as Adam 842.10
old as God 842.10
old as history 842.10
old as Methuselah 303.16, 842.10
old as the hills 303.16, 842.10
old as time 842.10
old bach 565.3
old bag 110.12, 304.3
old ball and chain 563.6
old bat 110.12
old believer 842.8
old bone 1050.2
old boy 572.8
old-boy network 617.6, 770.3
old campaigner 413.16, 461.19, 610.1
old chap 304.2
old clothes 5.5
old-clothesman 730.10
old codger 304.2
old college spirit, the 617.13
old college try 403.1
old country, the 231.6, 232.2
old crony 588.3
old dame 304.3
old days 837.2
old dodo 842.8
old dog 304.2
old dog at, an 413.28
old duffer 304.2
olde 499.8
olden 837.10, 842.10
olden days 837.2
old enough to know better 303.12
olden time, the 837.2
olden times 837.2
older (n) 304.5 (a) 304.7, 834.4, 842.19
older generation 304.4
oldest (n) 304.5 (a) 842.19
olde-worlde 499.8
Old Faithful 1019.10
old-fangled 842.16
The Old Farmer's Almanac 832.7
old fart 924.9
old-fashioned 390.10, 504.14, 842.16, 853.8
old-fashioned civility 504.6
old-fashioned courtesy 504.6
old-fashionedness 842.3, 853.3
old flame 104.11
old fogy 842.8, 853.4, 924.9
old-fogy 842.17
old-fogyish 842.17, 853.8
old-fogyishness 842.3
old folks' home 1009.4
old fud 924.9
old geezer 304.2
old gent 304.2
old gentleman 304.2
Old Glory 647.7
old goat 665.11

old gold 42.2
old granny 304.3
old guard 842.1
old hand 413.16
old hand at, an 373.16
old hat 117.9, 842.16
old heave-ho, the 909.1
old Homo 842.7
oldie 489.9, 842.6
old joke 489.9, 974.3
old lady 304.3, 563.8
Old Lady of Threadneedle Street, the 729.14
old left 611.4
old-line 611.17, 853.8, 855.13
old liner 842.8
old maid 77.5, 304.3, 495.7, 500.11, 565.4
old-maidenish 565.7
old-maidish 500.19, 565.7
old-maidishness 500.6
old man 104.12, 304.2, 560.13, 563.7, 575.4, 842.8
Old Man, the 183.7, 575.17
old man, the 560.9, 560.10
old man of the sea, the 240.3, 678.10
old master 712.9, 716.1
old money 618.1
Old Mug 646.3
oldness 303.5, 842.1
old nobility 608.1
old order 842.1
Old Paar 304.2
old paper 1050.2
old party 304.2
old pro 413.16, 726.4
old salt 183.3, 413.16
old saw 974.3
old school (n) 853.4 (a) 842.16
old school tie 647.1, 853.3
old sea dog 183.3, 413.16
old soldier 368.3, 461.19
old soldiers' home 1009.4
old song 974.3
old song and dance 974.3
Old South 231.7
old stager 413.16
oldster 304.2
old story 974.3
old story, the 837.2
old style 842.1
Old Testament 683.3
Old-Testament 683.11
Old Testament prophet 684.1
old thing 842.6
old-time 842.10
old-time country music 708.11
old-timer 304.2, 842.8
old-time religion 687.2
old-timer one of the old guard 413.16
old times 837.2
old-timey 842.10, 842.16
old-timey music 708.11
old trooper 461.19
old trot 304.3
old turkey 489.9
old warhorse 413.16
old wheeze 489.9
old wife 304.3
old wives' tale 354.10, 954.3
old woman 304.3, 495.7, 560.16, 563.8, 842.8
old woman, the 560.12
old-womanish 77.14
Old World 231.6
old-world 504.14, 842.13
oleaginous 287.12, 504.17, 1056.9
oleaginousness 504.5
oleic 1056.9
olent 69.9
oleoresin 1057.1
olericultural 1069.21
olericulture 1069.2
olericulturist 1069.6
olfaction 69.3, 69.4
olfactive 69.12
olfactories 69.5
olfactory 69.12
olfactory area 69.5
olfactory cell 69.5
olfactory nerve 2.11
olfactory nerves 69.5
olfactory organ 69.5, 283.8
olfactory pit 69.5
olfactory sense 69.4
olibanum 70.4
olid 71.5
oligarch 575.13
oligarchal 612.16
oligarchic 612.16
oligarchical 612.16
oligarchy 612.4
olio 10.11, 797.6
olivaceous 44.4
olive 44.4
olive branch 465.2
olive-brown 40.3
olive-drab 40.3
olive-green 44.4
olla 10.11
olla podrida 10.11, 797.6
-ology 928.10
olykoek 10.44
Olympian 94.13, 141.12, 272.14, 344.10, 649.9, 681.12
Olympian detachment 141.1, 649.3
Olympian heights 272.2
Olympian loftiness 141.1
Olympic Games 747.1, 749.1, 754.1
Olympic games 457.3
Olympic lifting 744.1
Olympic medal winner 413.15
Olympics 457.3
Olympic skating 760.7
Olympic swimming 760.8
Olympus 681.9
ombrograph 316.7
ombrographic 316.12
ombrology 316.9
ombrometer 316.7
ombrometric 316.12
ombudsman 466.3
omega 820.1
omelet 10.26
omelette 10.26
omen (n) 133.3, 399.3, 962.1 (v) 133.9
omertà 51.2
ominous 133.16, 514.3, 962.12, 1000.12, 1011.14
ominousness 133.6, 1000.5
omission 255.5, 340.1, 408.1, 414.6, 435.1, 655.2, 773.1, 795.2, 975.4, 992.4
omit 255.12, 340.7, 773.4
omitted 222.11, 340.14
omneity 1073.1
omnibus (n) 179.13, 554.7 (a) 772.7, 792.9, 794.10
omnibus bill 613.9
omnicompetence 18.3
omnicompetent 18.13
omnidirectional range 184.6
omnifarious 783.3
omnifariousness 783.1
omniform 783.3
omniformal 783.3
omniformity 783.1
omnigenous 783.3
omnipotence 18.3
omnipotent 18.13, 677.17
omnipotent ruler 575.13
omnipresence 221.2, 794.1
omnipresent 221.13, 677.17, 794.10, 864.14
omni-range 184.6
omniscience 928.6
omniscient 677.17, 928.15
omniscient observer 722.6
omnium-gatherum 770.13, 797.6
omnivore 8.16, 311.3, 672.3
omnivorism 8.1
omnivorous 8.31, 100.27, 672.6
omnivorousness 8.1, 672.1
omophagia 8.1
omophagic 8.31
omophagist 8.16
omophagous 8.31
omophagy 8.1
omphalic 208.11
omphalos 208.2
on 87.25, 831.9
on a bed of roses 1010.12
on a business footing 731.20
on a downer 252.10
on a first-name basis 587.18
on a first-name basis with 587.18
on a footing 790.7
on-again off-again 813.4
on a good footing 587.18
on-air 549.17
on a leash 326.5
on a level 790.7
on a level playing field 790.7
on all fours 177.39, 788.9
on all sides 209.10
on all tongues 552.15
on an even keel 180.19, 790.9
onanism 75.7, 75.8
on a par 790.7
on a plate 1014.13
on a rock 855.13
on a roll 759.27
Onassis 618.8
on a string 326.5
on a wing and a prayer 124.12
on bad terms 589.12, 589.13
on bedrock 855.13
on bended knee 138.14, 155.9, 155.10, 433.16, 696.16
on bended knees 440.16
on board 221.12, 800.13
onboarding 373.7, 405.1
on book 341.17, 641.17
on call 387.20
once 837.10
once in a lifetime 848.2
once-in-a-lifetime chance, a 843.3
once over 938.3
once-over, the 27.6
once-over-lightly 276.1, 938.5
on cloud nine 95.17, 109.11
oncoming (n) 167.1, 818.1 (a) 162.6, 167.4
on credit 620.6
on dead center 855.15
on deck 221.12, 387.20
on deposit 438.12
on-dit 552.6
on duty 330.21
1 872.3
one (n) 312.5, 872.3 (a) 244.5, 563.21, 677.17, 778.7, 792.9, 805.5, 872.7
one accord 332.5
one all over 130.14
one and all (n) 792.3, 864.4 (a) 864.15
one and indivisible 792.9
one and one 87.22
one and only (n) 872.3 (a) 872.9
one and the same (n) 778.3 (a) 778.7
one another 777.4
one-armed bandit 759.16
on easy street 1010.12
one bone and one flesh 563.21
one C 882.8
one chance in a million 972.9
on edge 105.28, 128.11, 130.12, 135.6
one-dimensional 276.5, 998.16
one-dimensional wave 916.4
one-eyed 28.12
one-eyed jack 758.2
one-eyed king 758.2
one flesh 563.1, 563.9
one for luck 188.4
one for the book 409.4, 997.5
one for the books 122.2
one for the road 88.9, 188.4
one-fourth 881.2
one-gas-station town 230.3
one-hit wonder 828.1
one-horse 248.6, 250.6, 258.10, 998.18
one-horse town 230.3
180-degree change 859.1
180-degree shift 859.1
one hundred thousand 882.10
one in a hundred 662.9
one in a million 249.4, 662.9, 870.5, 972.6, 999.6
one in a thousand 122.2, 249.4, 659.4, 870.5, 999.6
one in a way 122.2
one in ten thousand 659.4
oneirocritic 341.7
oneirocriticism 341.8

oneirology 341.8
one jump ahead 216.10
one-line octave 709.9
one-liner 489.6, 489.7
one-man 872.8
one-man band 430.12, 584.5
one man one vote 609.17
one-man rule 612.8
one-man show 542.1
one mind 332.5
oneness 455.1, 778.1, 788.1, 792.1, 798.1, 865.1, 872.1
one-nighter 704.11
one-night stand 75.7, 704.11
one-of-a-kind 780.8
one of the people 606.5
one of us 617.11
one-on-one (n) 747.3 (a) 215.5, 216.10, 312.15, 535.3, 587.19
one or two 884.2
one pair 758.4
one-parent family 559.5
one-party rule 612.8
one-party system 609.24
one percent, the 607.2
one-percent, the 607.2
one-person 872.8
one-piece 872.11
one-piece suit 5.29
one-pointedness 537.1, 931.3
on equal footing 790.7
on equal terms 790.7
one-quarter 881.2
oner 122.2
onerous 98.24, 297.17, 725.18, 996.7, 1012.18, 1013.18
onerousness 98.8, 297.2, 725.5, 1013.1
one's adieus 188.4
one's all 403.4, 471.1
one's ancestors 307.16
one sandwich short of a picnic 926.2
one's back, nerve, and sinew 725.1
one's best 403.4, 504.8
one's best effort 403.4
one's best endeavor 403.4
one's betrothed 563.6
one's betters 249.5
one's blind side 954.1
one's bones 2.2
one's crowd 582.5
one's cup of tea 371.5
one's damndest 403.4
one's darndest 403.4
one's day in court 598.1
one's due 639.2
oneself 865.5
oneself again 396.24
one's fathers 307.16
one's fill 991.2
one's friend 12.9
one's hat 38.4
one's heart of hearts 931.4
one-shot 848.2
one-sided 218.7, 265.10, 650.11, 872.11, 980.12
onesidedness 650.3, 980.3
onesie 5.30
one-size 872.11
one's level best 403.4
one's lot 963.7
one small difficulty 1012.4
one's move 825.2
one's native ground 232.2
one's native soil 232.2
one's own choice 323.1
one's own devices 430.3
one's own discretion 323.1
one's own initiative 323.1
one's own man 430.22
one's own sweet time 402.1
one's own way 430.3
one's own will 323.1
one's pen 547.2, 718.2
one's promised 563.6
one';s say 825.2
one's set 582.5
one-star general 575.17
one-step 705.5
one-step rocket 1074.5
one-stop 223.15, 387.20
one-story 296.6
one's turn 825.2
one's two cents' worth 422.2, 524.3
one's utmost 403.4
one's word is one's bond 644.9
one thing after another 812.2
one-third 878.2
1-3-strike pocket 750.1
one-time 814.5, 848.2
onetime 837.10
one-time offer 848.1
one too many 993.2
one-to-one 312.15
one-touch (n) 268.5, 830.3 (a) 268.8
one-track mind 926.13
one-trick pony 413.12
one-up 216.10
one-upmanship 249.2, 415.1, 457.2
one up on 249.12
on even ground 790.7
on even terms 790.7
on everyone's lips 662.16, 928.27
on everyone's tongue 662.16, 928.27
one voice 332.5
one-way 161.12
one-way communication 343.1
one wheel in the sand 926.2
one who will not set the Thames on fire 414.7
one who wrote the book, the 413.14
one-woman 872.8
one-woman show 542.1
1X 257.4
one you can hang the wash on 745.3
on familiar terms 587.19
on file 549.17, 809.8
on fire 93.18, 101.9, 105.22, 375.31, 1019.27
on foot 330.19, 405.23, 761.13, 831.9, 889.11
on form 807.7
on friendly terms 587.18
on-go 162.1
ongoing (n) 162.1, 172.2 (a) 162.6, 392.15, 831.9, 889.11
on good terms 587.18
on guard 339.13, 494.8, 494.9, 983.15
on hand 221.12, 387.20, 469.8
on hands and knees 177.39
on hold 340.14, 846.16
on holiday 222.12, 402.5
oni 988.1
on ice 429.21, 965.8, 970.20
on intimate terms 587.19
on in years 303.16
on leash 428.13
on leave 222.12
online bookseller 554.16
on-line catalog 558.4
online degree 567.5
online edition 555.2
online journal 549.11
online selling 734.2
online service 1042.16
online service provider 1042.19
online shopping 733.1
online system 1042.16
on loan 620.6
onlooker 223.6, 918.1
onlooking 918.7
only 872.9
only a few 885.2
only-begotten 872.9
only choice 371.3, 963.6
only have eyes for 104.19
only human 312.13
only yesterday 837.1
on-message 343.9, 352.18, 380.8
onomasiological 526.20
onomastic 526.20, 527.17
onomastician 526.15
onomasticon 554.9
onomastics 526.14, 527.1
onomatologic 526.20
onomatology 527.1
onomatope 526.17
onomatopoeia 336.1, 526.17
onomatopoeic 336.9, 349.13, 526.20, 720.18
onomatopoeic word 526.17
onomatopoetic 336.9
on one's back 19.16
on one's beam-ends 19.16
on one's belly 433.16
on one's deathbed 307.32
on one's drop-dead list 589.13
on one's guard 339.13, 494.8
on one's hands 734.15, 993.17
on one's head 641.17, 656.3
on one's high horse 141.9
on one's knees 137.13, 138.14, 155.10, 433.16, 440.16, 696.16
on one's last legs 16.18, 21.10, 303.18, 307.32, 393.36
on one's marrow-bones 440.16
on one's marrowbones 137.13, 138.14, 433.16
on one's mettle 105.20
on one's payroll 894.15
on one's plate 404.7
on one's toes 339.14
on one's uppers 619.8
on one's word 436.7
on one's word of honor 436.7
on opposite sides 215.5
on paper 547.22
on parole 431.10
on pension 448.3
on pins and needles 126.7, 130.12
on probation 572.13
on record 549.17
on relief 619.8
onrush 172.2, 238.4
onrushing 172.8, 174.15, 238.24, 401.9
on sabbatical leave 222.12
on schedule 130.14
onset 459.1, 548.1, 818.1
onshore breeze 318.4
onshore wind 318.10
on short commons 210.7, 992.12
on short rations 210.7
on shpilkes 126.7, 135.6
onside kick 746.3
onslaught 459.1, 510.7, 671.3, 902.3
on slippery ground 1006.12
on solid ground 1007.6
on speaking terms 587.18
on standby 130.11
on stilts 912.9
on stream 405.22
on sufferance 443.16
on sure ground 1007.6
on tap 387.20
on target 973.16
on task 931.21
on tenterhooks 126.7, 130.12, 971.25
on terms of equality 790.7
on terra firma 1007.6
on the agenda 381.12, 404.7
on the alert 339.14
on the anvil 381.12, 404.7, 405.22
on the anxious seat 126.7
on the attack 459.30
on the back burner 340.14, 846.16
on the ball 339.14, 920.13, 983.15
on the barricades 453.5
on the beam 928.17
on the beat 836.6
on the Bill Daley 757.6
on the blink 391.14, 393.38, 810.13
on the Book 436.7
on the books 549.17
on the bread line 619.8
on the brink 1006.11
on the button 788.10, 973.16
on the calendar 381.12
on the carpet 381.12
on the chinstrap 757.6
on the contrary 131.10
on the corner 665.28
on the critical list 85.56
on the decline 393.46
on the descendant 194.11
on the docket 381.12
on the dole 619.8
on the double 401.11

on the downgrade 194.11, 393.46, 414.18
on the downward track 393.46
on the edge 619.7
on the edge of tears 115.21
on the face of the earth 761.13
on the fence 467.7, 609.45
on the fire 405.22, 889.11
on the fritz 391.14, 393.38, 810.13
on the go 330.21
on the good side of 587.18
on the grid 1032.30
on the guarded list 85.56
on the high side 949.3
on the hook 641.17
on the hop 330.21
on the horizon 130.13, 840.3
on the horns of a dilemma 971.25, 1013.23
on the hot seat 1006.13, 1013.22
on the house 634.5
on the increase 251.8
on the inside 429.21
on the in with 587.18
on the job 330.21, 339.14, 983.15
on-the-job training 568.3
on the jump 330.21
on the lam 368.16
on the lap of the gods 840.3
on the left 611.19
on the level 644.14
on the lift 392.15
on the lookout 339.13
on the lookout for 130.11, 938.38
on the loose 369.11, 430.21, 743.28
on the low side 950.3
on the make 100.28, 330.21
on the mark 161.13, 405.16
on the mend 392.15
on the money 161.13, 788.10, 973.16
on the move 330.21
on the needle 87.25
on the nose 161.13, 973.16
on the offensive 458.22, 459.30
on the order of 784.10
on the outs 589.12, 589.13
on the pad 378.4, 645.23
on the pavé 665.28
on the qui vive 339.14
on the rack 26.9, 96.25
on the rag 12.24
on the ragged edge 128.11, 619.7
on the rampage 671.20
on the receiving end 479.9
on the right scent 941.10
on the right side of 587.18
on the right track 941.10
on the rise 251.8, 392.15
on the road 222.12
on the rocks 566.7, 625.11, 1013.27
on the run 330.21
on the safe side 494.8, 1007.4
on the same footing 790.7
on the same level 790.7
on the same plane 790.7
on the shady side 303.15
on the shelf 256.7, 340.14, 390.10, 565.7
on the shelves 734.15
on the sick list 85.56
on the sidelines 467.7
on the skids 393.46, 412.14
on the slide 252.11
on the spot 401.9
on-the-spot 830.4, 1006.13, 1013.22
on the square 644.14
on the street 552.15
on the streets 665.28
on the surface 276.5
on the take 378.4
on the throne 894.14
on the tip of one's tongue 990.8
on the town 665.28, 743.28
on the track 166.5
on the trail 166.5
on the trail of 941.10
on the trigger 24.12
on the up and up 416.5
on the up-and-up 409.14, 644.14, 973.13
on the upbeat 392.15
on the upgrade 392.15
on the upswing 251.8, 392.15
on the uptake 24.12
on the verge 1006.11
on the wagon 516.3, 668.10
on the wane 16.21, 252.11, 393.46
on the warpath 110.26, 458.22, 459.30, 671.16
on the watch 339.13, 983.16, 1008.23
on the watch for 130.11
on the water wagon 668.10
on the way 405.22
on the way out 393.46
on the wrong track 923.10
on thin ice 1006.12
on this side of the grave 306.12
on tippytoe 177.39
on tiptoe 130.12, 177.39, 346.14
on to (v) 551.14 (a) 928.16
ontogenesis 861.3
ontogenetic 861.8
ontogeny 861.3
ontology 527.1, 761.7, 801.4, 807.2, 808.4
on top 339.14, 409.14
on top of 428.11, 983.15, 1008.23
on top of the heap 409.14, 1010.12
on top of the world 95.17, 109.11
on tour 177.36, 222.12
onus 641.1, 643.3, 656.1, 661.6, 957.3, 1012.6
on vacation 222.12, 402.5
on velvet 1010.12
on visiting terms 587.18
onward 162.6
onward course 162.1, 238.4
on welfare 619.8
oöcyte 305.12
oodles 247.4, 884.3, 991.2
oöecium 305.12
oof 728.2
oofless 619.10
ooftish 728.2
oofy 618.15
oögenesis 78.6
oögenetic 78.16
oögonium 305.12
oompah 54.11
oomph 17.3, 18.1, 330.2, 997.1
oops 909.27
oops up 909.27
oösperm 305.14
oösphere 305.12
oöspore 305.14
ooze (n) 13.1, 80.8, 190.6, 1062.8 (v) 13.5, 190.15, 1065.11
ooze out 369.10
ooziness 1062.4
oozing (n) 190.6 (a) 13.7, 1065.17
oozy 190.20, 1062.14
op 1008.16
opacity 522.3, 922.3, 1031.1
opal 47.6
opalesce 47.8, 1025.26
opalescence 47.2, 1025.18, 1030.2
opalescent 35.22, 47.10, 1025.37, 1030.4
opaline 47.10, 1030.4
opalize 47.8
opaloid 47.10
opaque (v) 1031.2 (a) 522.15, 922.15, 1031.3
opaque color 35.8
opaqueness 1031.1
ope 292.11
Op-Ed column 556.2
open (v) 224.4, 259.6, 292.11, 351.4, 704.28, 818.12 (a) 31.6, 167.5, 187.16, 206.7, 222.15, 236.2, 259.11, 292.17, 343.10, 348.10, 352.17, 402.5, 416.5, 430.23, 430.27, 485.4, 524.30, 535.3, 585.11, 644.17, 804.4, 894.15, 897.5, 966.8, 971.18, 979.10, 1006.15
open, the 206.3
openable 292.21
open a campaign 458.16
open a can of worms 1013.14
open account 622.2
open-air 206.8, 317.12
open air, the 206.3
open-air theater 704.14
open an account with 731.17
open and aboveboard 644.14
open-and-shut 348.8, 964.8, 970.20
open-and-shut case 957.3, 970.2
open an offensive 459.17
open arms 187.1, 187.3, 585.2, 585.4
open as day 348.10
open a show 704.28
open a show cold 704.28
open book 521.1
open-book test 938.2
open card 759.10
opencast 1058.6
open cluster 1073.5, 1073.8
open conflict 456.1
open country 158.4, 236.1
open cut 1058.6
open discussion 541.6
open door 187.3, 585.1, 609.5
open-door policy 609.5
open-eared 48.14, 983.15
open-ended 408.3, 430.27, 793.7
open-end fund 737.16
open enemy 589.6
opener 292.10, 818.5
openers 759.10, 818.3
open-eyed 122.9, 339.13, 981.5, 983.15
open-faced 644.17
open field 430.4
open fire (n) 1019.13 (v) 459.22, 818.12
open forum 423.3, 463.1, 541.6
open fracture 85.38
open frame 750.2
open gate 753.1
open grave 309.16
open hand 485.1
openhanded 143.15, 478.22, 485.4, 652.6
openhandedness 485.1, 652.2
open heart 485.1
openhearted 416.5, 485.4, 585.11, 644.17
openheartedness 416.1, 485.1, 585.1, 644.4
open her up 174.9
open hostilities (n) 458.1 (v) 457.13, 458.14
opening 33.1, 187.3, 189.5, 190.9, 222.2, 224.2, 292.1, 348.2, 383.3, 724.5, 818.1, 843.2
opening episode 816.2
opening gun 816.2
opening lead 758.3
opening move 818.3
opening night 704.12
opening price 738.9
opening shot 816.2
opening up 292.1
opening wedge, an 189.5
opening wedge 187.3, 818.1
open into 858.17
open juncture 524.9
open-letter proof 713.7
open mandate 443.4
open market 430.9, 731.7, 736.2, 737.1
open mike 704.7
open mind 979.3
open-minded 430.25, 894.15, 979.10
open-mindedness 430.10, 894.5, 979.3
openmouthed 59.10, 122.9, 131.12, 292.18, 981.5, 983.15
openness 167.2, 187.9, 206.1, 343.3, 348.3, 416.1, 535.1, 540.1, 644.4, 772.1, 894.5, 897.2, 966.3, 979.3, 1006.3
openness to sensation 24.2
openness to sight 348.3
open one's big fat mouth 844.4
open one's big mouth 844.4
open one's eyes 23.4, 122.5, 131.7, 351.4, 977.2

open one's eyes to 551.14
open one's heart 145.3
open one's heart to 93.11
open one's lips 524.21
open one's mind to 979.7
open one's mouth 524.21
open order 458.2
open out 292.11, 538.7
open Pandora's box 804.3, 810.9, 1013.14
open place 222.2
open poker 759.10
open post 222.2
open primary 609.15
open quarrel 456.5
open question 971.8
open road 1014.3
open road, the 177.3
open rupture 456.4
open sea 240.1
open season 313.1, 389.3
open secret 551.1
open sequence 1041.6
open-sequence system 1041.5
open sesame 292.10, 517.12, 691.4, 894.6
open shop 727.3
open sight 29.5
open source 1042.19
open space 158.4, 292.1, 430.4
open stance 751.3
open-textured 1029.4
open the door to 187.10, 405.12, 443.9, 585.7, 818.12, 886.11, 897.3, 959.5, 966.5, 1006.7, 1014.7
open the draft 1020.22
open the eyes 568.10
open the eyes to 941.8
open the floodgates 443.12, 909.24
open the light 1025.29
open the lock 940.2
open the mind 568.10
open the possibility of 897.3
open the purse 485.3, 626.5
open the throttle 174.10
open the way 405.12, 1014.7
open the way for 966.5
open throttle 174.3
open to 897.6, 966.8
open to all 348.10
open to criticism 510.25
open to doubt 955.10, 971.17
open to error 971.22
open to question 971.17
open to reproach 510.25
open to solution 940.3
open to suspicion 955.10
open to the public 352.17
open to view 31.6
open universe 1073.1
open up 259.6, 292.11, 348.6, 351.4, 351.7, 352.11, 430.19, 439.5, 818.12, 1014.7
open up on 459.22, 510.14
open up the possibility of 966.5
open war 456.1, 458.1
open warfare 458.1
open wound 1001.1
opera 704.14, 708.28, 708.34
opéra ballet 708.34
operability 387.3, 889.3, 966.2
operable 387.23, 889.10, 966.7, 995.6
opéra bouffe 708.34
opera buffa 708.34
opera festival 708.32
opera glasses 29.4
operagoer 710.21
opera house 704.14
opera lover 710.21
operant (n) 726.1, 889.4 (a) 889.11
operant conditioning 92.26
opera score 708.28
opera season 313.1
opera singer 710.13
operatable 889.10
operate 90.14, 91.24, 182.14, 328.4, 381.9, 387.10, 737.23, 889.5, 889.7
operate at a loss 623.6
operate on 91.24, 889.6
operatic 704.33, 708.50
operatic aria 708.15
operatic libretto 722.1
operatic music 708.6
operatic overture 708.26
operatic singing 708.13
operatic tenor 709.5
operating (n) 172.1 (a) 328.10, 889.11
operating budget 626.3
operating costs 626.3
operating expense 626.3
operating room 197.25
operating speed 184.31
operating system 1042.12
operating theater 197.4, 197.25
operating theatre 90.2
operation 90.2, 91.19, 172.1, 328.1, 328.3, 387.5, 387.8, 404.1, 458.4, 731.4, 889.1, 892.5
operational 328.10, 889.9, 889.11, 889.12
operational definition 1017.9
operational gain 1032.17
operationalization 328.2
operationalize 387.11
operational purpose 387.5
operations 328.1, 458.4, 889.1
operations research 381.1, 968.2
operative (n) 576.9, 576.10, 726.1, 889.4 (a) 18.12, 328.10, 387.21, 889.9
operative dentist 90.6
operativeness 889.3
operative surgeon 90.5
operator 90.5, 330.8, 347.9, 381.7, 610.6, 726.1, 737.11, 889.4, 1042.17
operator gene 305.9
operculum 295.5, 295.15
operetta 708.34
operon 305.9
operose 339.11, 725.18, 1013.17
operoseness 725.5
operosity 725.5
ophidian (n) 311.25 (a) 311.47
ophiolater 697.4
ophthalmic 2.28, 27.20, 29.9
ophthalmic disease 85.14
ophthalmologic 29.9
ophthalmological 29.9
ophthalmologist 29.8
opiate 22.10, 25.3, 87.3
opiatic 86.45
opine 524.24, 946.8, 951.10, 953.11
opinion 422.1, 932.1, 946.3, 952.2, 953.6, 978.1
opinionated 361.8, 970.22, 980.12
opinionatedness 361.1, 970.6
opinionative 970.22
opinioned 970.22
opinionist 333.3, 970.7
opinion poll 938.14
opinion sampler 938.16
opinion sampling 938.14
opinion survey 938.14
opium 22.10
opium addict 87.21
opium addiction 87.1
opium den 87.20
opium habit 87.1
opiumism 87.1
opium user 87.21
opossum 311.22
oppidan (n) 227.6 (a) 230.11
opponent (n) 452.1, 461.1, 589.6 (a) 451.8
opportune 788.10, 843.9, 995.5
opportuneness 843.1, 995.1
opportunism 100.10, 843.2
opportunist (n) 363.4, 381.7, 651.3 (a) 381.13
opportunistic 363.12, 381.13, 651.5
opportunity 825.2, 843.2, 972.1
opposable 944.9
oppose 215.4, 333.4, 335.4, 451.3, 453.3, 454.3, 510.10, 779.4, 900.6, 943.4, 1012.10
oppose change 853.6
opposed 215.5, 325.5, 451.8, 510.21, 779.6, 1011.13
opposed to change 853.8
opposer 452.3
opposing (n) 215.1, 451.1, 453.1, 943.1 (a) 215.5, 333.6, 335.5, 451.8, 510.21, 779.6, 900.8, 1011.13
opposing party 452.1
opposing side 452.1
opposite (n) 205.4, 779.2 (a) 215.5, 216.11, 335.5, 451.8, 779.6, 1011.13
opposite, the 779.2
opposite as black and white 779.7
opposite as day and night 779.7
opposite as fire and water 779.7
opposite as light and darkness 779.7
opposite as the poles 779.7
opposite camp 452.1
opposite extreme, the 779.2
opposite-field hit 745.3
oppositeness 779.1
opposite number 779.2, 790.4
opposite pole 779.2
opposite poles 215.2
opposite response 903.1
opposites 215.2
opposite sex 779.2
opposite side 215.3, 452.1
opposite term 779.2
opposite tide 238.13
opposition 215.1, 325.1, 333.1, 451.1, 453.1, 510.1, 779.1, 780.1, 789.1, 900.1, 943.1, 1012.1
opposition, the 452.1, 589.6
oppositional 451.8, 779.6, 900.8
oppositionist 452.3
opposition party 609.24
opposition to change 853.3
opposition voice 333.3
oppositive 451.8, 779.6
opposure 215.1, 451.1, 510.1, 900.1
oppress 98.16, 112.18, 112.19, 297.13, 389.7, 432.9, 612.15, 725.16, 1011.8
oppressed 112.20, 297.18, 432.14, 432.16
oppression 96.8, 112.3, 173.6, 297.7, 389.3, 428.2, 612.9
oppression of spirit 112.3
oppressive 98.24, 112.30, 173.16, 297.17, 417.16, 428.11, 725.18, 1012.18, 1013.18, 1019.28
oppressive heat 1019.5
oppressiveness 98.8, 173.6, 297.2, 725.5, 1013.1, 1019.6
oppressor 575.13
opprobrious 661.11
opprobrium 156.1, 513.2, 661.4
oppugn 451.6, 456.11, 457.21, 779.4, 900.6
oppugnance 451.2, 779.1, 900.1
oppugnancy 451.1, 451.2, 457.1, 458.10, 779.1, 789.1, 900.1
oppugnant 451.8, 779.6, 900.8
oppugnation 451.2
opsimath 572.1
opsonin 2.25
opt 371.13
Optacon 30.6
optant 371.7
optative (n) 530.11 (a) 100.21
opt for 371.13
optic (n) 2.9, 27.9 (a) 2.28, 27.20, 29.9
optical 2.28, 27.20, 29.9
optical astronomy 1073.19
optical character reader 1042.4
optical character recognition 1042.4
optical character recognition device 1042.4
optical device 29.1
optical disk 549.10, 1042.6
optical disk memory 1042.7
optical effects 706.5
optical fiber 29.1
optical illusion 976.5
optical instrument 29.1
optical observatory 1073.17
optical physics 29.7
optical scanner 1042.4
optician 29.8
optic nerve 2.9

optics 29.7, 1025.22
optimal 999.16
optimate 608.4
optime 572.7
optimism 109.1, 124.2, 130.2
optimist 124.5
optimistic 109.11, 124.11, 130.11
optimisticalness 124.2
optimize 999.11
optimum (n) 999.8 (a) 999.16
option 371.2, 430.6, 733.2, 737.21
optional 324.7, 371.22
optional dividend 738.7
optionality 371.2
optional primary 609.15
optional referendum 613.8
optometrical 29.9
optometrist 29.8, 90.4
optometry 29.7
optophone 30.6
opt out 868.4
opt-out 584.1
opt out of society 584.7
opulence 618.1, 991.2
opulency 618.1, 991.2
opulent 618.14, 991.7
opus 547.10, 554.1, 708.5, 893.1
opuscule 554.1, 893.1
opusculum 554.1
or 647.2
oracle (n) 921.1, 962.7, 974.1 (v) 970.10
oracle of Dodona 962.7
oracular 962.11, 970.22
oraculate 970.10
oracy 524.4
oral (n) 938.2 (a) 292.22, 343.9, 524.29, 842.12
oral agreement 332.1
oral cavity 2.12, 292.4, 524.18
oral communication 524.1
oral contraceptive 86.23
oral examination 938.2
oral faculty, the 524.1
oral-genital stimulation 75.7
oral history 547.12, 719.1
orally 343.12
oral method 49.3
oral record 719.1
oral sex 75.7
oral surgeon 90.6
oral tobacco 89.7
oral tradition 842.2
orange (n) 35.13, 42.1 (a) 42.2
Orange Bowl 746.1
orange cubes 87.10
orange-hued 42.2
orangeish 42.2
orangeness 42.1
orange-red 42.2
orangery 310.12, 1069.11
orange sunshine 87.10
orangey 42.2
orange-yellow 42.2
oranginess 42.1
orans 696.9
orant 696.9
orate 543.10
oration 543.2
orator 543.6
oratorical 543.12
oratorio 708.17
oratorio society 710.16
oratorium 703.3
oratory 543.1, 544.1, 703.3
orb (n) 2.9, 27.9, 231.2, 282.2, 647.3, 724.4, 1073.4 (a) 282.9
orbed 282.9
orbicular 282.9
orbicularity 282.1
orbicularness 282.1
orbiculate 282.9
orbiculated 282.9
orbiculation 282.1
orbit (n) 231.2, 245.2, 280.2, 282.2, 383.1, 724.4, 894.4, 914.1, 914.2, 1073.16, 1075.2, 1075.9 (v) 280.10, 914.5
orbital 280.11, 914.7
orbiter 1075.2, 1075.6
orbiting 914.1
orbiting astronomical observatory 1073.17
orbiting geophysical observatory 159.8
orbiting observatory 1075.6
orbiting solar observatory 1073.17
orbit the earth 1075.12
orblet 282.2
orblike 282.9
orblikeness 282.1
orb of day 1073.13
orb of night 1073.11
orby 282.9
orchard 310.12, 310.14
orcharding 1069.2
orchardist 1069.6
orchardman 1069.6
orchestra 48.6, 704.15, 704.16, 710.12
orchestra circle 704.15
orchestral 708.51
orchestra leader 710.17
orchestral musician 710.3
orchestral score 708.28
orchestra pit 704.16
orchestrate 708.46
orchestration 573.1, 708.5, 709.2
orchestrator 710.20
orchestrina 711.15
orchestrion 711.15
orchid 46.3
Orcus 682.3, 682.5
ordain 191.4, 420.8, 477.9, 613.10, 615.11, 673.9, 698.12, 964.7
ordained 698.17, 964.9
ordainment 615.2, 698.10
ordeal 26.6, 96.9, 690.3, 942.2
ordeal by fire 690.3
order (n) 245.2, 384.1, 419.1, 420.1, 421.1, 464.2, 527.1, 533.2, 559.4, 607.1, 617.2, 617.3, 617.5, 646.5, 646.6, 673.3, 675.3, 765.3, 807.1, 808.1, 809.2, 809.5, 815.1, 869.1, 946.5, 1068.1 (v) 296.5, 420.8, 421.5, 440.9, 573.8, 807.4, 808.8, 809.6, 894.8, 946.13
order about 420.8
order around 420.8, 612.15
ordered 533.8, 781.5, 807.6, 808.14, 809.8, 850.6
ordered around 432.16
orderedness 533.2
ordering 573.1, 607.1, 808.1, 808.2
orderless 263.4, 810.12, 971.19
orderlessness 263.1
orderliness 464.2, 803.2, 807.3
orderly (n) 90.11, 577.5 (a) 464.9, 533.8, 580.10, 781.5, 803.11, 807.6, 808.14, 850.6, 869.8
orderly officer 575.17
order of battle 458.2
order of being 809.4
order of business 871.6
order of magnitude 257.1
order of succession 815.1
order of the day 381.1, 831.4, 965.3
Order of the Purple Heart 646.6
order of things, the 809.4
order of worship 701.3
orders 568.6, 698.10
order up 420.11, 421.5
ordinal 809.7, 812.9, 1017.23
ordinance 419.2, 420.4, 673.3, 701.3
ordinand 699.4
ordinariness 497.5, 499.1, 864.2, 869.2, 1005.2
ordinary (n) 8.11, 647.2 (a) 246.3, 250.6, 373.13, 497.14, 499.6, 606.8, 721.5, 847.4, 864.12, 869.9, 1005.8
ordinary, the 869.3
ordinary clay 312.5
ordinary folk 606.1
ordinary Joe 606.5, 864.3
ordinary language 523.5
ordinary man 606.5
ordinary people 606.1
ordinary person 312.5
ordinary run 864.3
ordinary run of things 373.4
ordinary seaman 183.1
ordinary speech 523.5
ordinate (n) 300.5 (v) 615.11
ordination 187.2, 615.2, 698.10, 808.2
ordnance 462.1, 462.11
ordnance rocket 1074.3
ordo calendar 832.8
ordure 12.4, 80.7
ordurous 80.23
ordurousness 80.2
ore 406.5, 1058.2
oread 678.9
ore-bearing 1058.15
ore bed 1058.7
ore chute 1058.7
orectic 100.21
ore-forming 1058.15
Oregon jargon 523.11
organ 384.4, 555.1, 617.10, 711.13, 793.4
organelle 305.5
organ-grinder 710.9
organic 7.21, 8.31, 266.6, 305.17, 767.8, 1060.9
organic being 305.2
organic chemical 1060.2
organic chemist 1060.7
organic chlorine 1001.3
organic complex 2.1
organic evolution 861.4
organic farming 1069.1
organic fertilizer 890.4
organic matter 305.1, 1052.2
organic nature 305.1
organic phosphate insecticide 1001.3
organic remains 307.15
organic sediment 1059.6
organic structure 266.1
organic unity 792.1, 872.1
organism 2.1, 266.1, 305.2, 763.3
organismal 266.6, 763.6
organismic 266.6, 305.17, 763.6
organist 710.8
organization 262.2, 266.1, 305.2, 381.1, 461.22, 617.1, 617.8, 675.3, 739.1, 796.1, 807.1, 808.2, 892.4
organizational 266.6, 617.17, 808.15
organization insignia 647.5
organization man 867.2
organize 262.7, 266.5, 381.8, 573.8, 727.9, 796.3, 805.4, 808.10, 892.10
organized 88.33, 305.17, 381.12, 808.14
organized baseball 745.1
organized basketball 747.1
organized crime 660.10, 732.1
organized crime family 660.10
organized football 746.1
organized labor 727.2
organized matter 305.1
organized militia 461.24
organized reserves 461.25
organized skiing 753.1
organized strike 727.5
organized tennis 748.1
organizer 381.6, 727.4, 808.5, 892.7
organ loft 703.9
organ manual 711.17
organ of Corti 2.10
organ of thought 919.6
organ of vision 2.9, 27.9
organometallic 1058.16
organ player 710.8
organ point 709.15
organ stop 711.19
orgasm 75.7, 105.8, 917.6
orgasmic 75.27, 105.25, 671.23, 917.19
orgastic 75.27
orgiastic 105.25, 663.6, 665.24, 669.9
orgone theory 92.2
orgy 88.5, 105.8, 669.2
oriel 197.3
Orient 231.6
orient (n) 161.3 (v) 161.11
orient (v) 373.9 (a) 1025.30
oriental 161.14

Oriental calm 106.2
orientate 161.11, 373.9
orientated 373.15
orientation 159.3, 161.1, 161.4, 373.7
oriented 159.18, 373.15
orienteering 159.3
orienter 422.3
orient oneself 161.11
orient the chart 161.11
orient the map 161.11
orifice 190.9, 292.1
orificial 292.22
oriflamme 647.7
origami 291.4, 712.2
origin 526.16, 818.1, 818.4, 886.5
original (n) 337.2, 547.10, 786.1, 868.3, 870.4, 886.5 (a) 199.8, 226.5, 337.5, 390.12, 767.9, 816.4, 818.15, 841.7, 841.11, 868.6, 886.14, 973.15, 986.18
originality 337.1, 841.1, 868.1, 868.2, 986.3
original jurisdiction 594.1
original screenplay 706.3
original sin 655.2, 655.3
original thought 337.2
original title 469.1
originate 337.4, 818.10, 818.13, 886.10, 892.12, 986.14
originated 892.19
originate from 887.5
originate in 887.5
originating 892.1
origination 818.1, 818.4, 886.5, 892.1, 893.1
originative 886.13, 892.16, 986.18
originator 886.4, 892.7
origin story 413.9
oriole 710.23
orismological 527.17
orismology 527.1
orison 696.4
orle 647.2
Ormazd 677.5
ornament (n) 254.4, 498.1, 536.1, 545.4, 646.1, 646.5, 708.24, 708.27, 709.18 (v) 253.4, 498.8, 545.7
ornamental 498.10, 712.20
ornamental border 1069.10
ornamental composition 498.7
ornamental grass 310.5
ornamentalist 716.11
ornamental motif 498.7
ornamental style 498.7
ornamental theme 498.7
ornamental tree 310.10
ornamentation 498.1, 545.4, 717.2, 993.4
ornamented 498.11, 536.3
ornamentist 716.11
ornate 498.12, 545.11
ornateness 498.2, 545.4
orneriness 110.3, 144.5, 327.2, 335.1, 361.3, 451.2, 779.1, 900.1
ornery 110.20, 144.20, 327.10, 335.5, 361.11, 451.8, 779.6, 789.6, 900.8
ornithopter 181.6
orogenesis 237.6
orogenic 237.8
orogeny 237.6, 912.1
orographic 237.8
orography 237.6
orological 237.8
orology 237.6
orometric 237.8
orotund 545.8
orotundity 501.7, 545.1
orphan (n) 256.3, 370.4 (v) 307.27 (a) 307.34
orphanage 1009.4
orphan drug 86.4
orphaned 307.34
Orpheus 710.22
orrery 1073.17
or steal 384.6
orthicon 1035.10
orthochromatic film 714.10
orthodiagonal (n) 200.2 (a) 200.12, 278.7
orthodiagram 91.9
orthodiagraphy 1037.8
orthodondist 90.6
orthodontic 90.15
Orthodox 675.30
orthodox (n) 687.4 (a) 687.7, 692.8, 867.6
orthodox 373.13, 425.7, 579.5
orthodox, the 687.4
orthodox Christian 687.4
Orthodox Christianity 675.7
orthodoxian 687.4
orthodoxical 687.7
orthodoxism 687.1
orthodoxist 687.4
Orthodox Jew 675.21, 687.4
Orthodox Judaism 675.12
orthodox medicine 90.13
orthodoxness 687.1
orthodox sleep 22.5
Orthodoxy 675.9
orthodoxy 425.2, 675.1
orthodoxy 687.1, 867.1
orthoepist 523.15, 524.14
orthoepy 524.13
orthogamy 78.3
orthogenesis 78.6
orthogenetic 78.16
orthogonal 200.12, 278.7, 278.9
orthogonality 200.1, 278.1
orthogonal projection 712.5
orthographer 523.15
orthographic 546.8
orthographic projection 712.5
orthographize 546.7
orthography 546.4
orthometric 278.7
orthopedic 90.15
orthopter 181.6
orts 256.1, 391.4
orzo 10.36
os 237.5
Oscar 646.2
oscillate 202.8, 362.8, 847.3, 850.5, 854.5, 916.10
oscillating 202.9, 362.10, 847.5, 916.15
oscillating current 916.1
oscillating universe 1073.1
oscillating universe theory 1073.18
oscillation 362.2, 847.2, 850.2, 854.3, 916.1
oscillator 916.9
oscillatory 362.10, 850.7, 916.15
oscillograph 916.8
oscillometer 916.8
oscilloscope 916.8, 1036.1
oscine 311.48
oscine bird 311.27
oscitancy 22.1, 292.2, 331.6
oscitant 22.21, 292.18
oscitate 292.16
oscitation 22.1, 292.2
osculate 223.10, 562.19
osculation 223.5, 562.4
osculatory 223.17
O-shaped 914.7
Osiris 682.5
osmidrosis 71.1
osmose 187.13
osmosis 187.6
osmotic 187.17
osseous 2.26, 1046.10
Ossian 178.2
ossicular 2.26
ossiferous 2.26
ossific 1046.10
ossification 1046.5
ossified 2.26, 1046.13
ossify 94.6, 1046.7
ossuarium 309.9, 309.12, 309.16
ossuary 309.9, 309.12, 309.16
osteal 2.26
ostensible 33.11, 348.12, 354.27, 376.5, 957.20, 976.9
ostensible motive 376.1
ostensible partner 616.2
ostensorium 703.11
ostent 33.1, 501.1
ostentation 348.2, 348.4, 354.3, 498.2, 501.1, 545.1
ostentatious 498.12, 501.18, 545.8
ostentatious complexity 545.1
ostentatious devotion 354.6
ostentatiousness 501.1
ostentatious profundity 545.1
osteomalacia 85.33
osteopath 90.9
osteopathic 90.15
osteopathy 73.2
ostiarius 699.4
ostiary 1008.12
ostium 2.23
ostracism 510.1, 586.3, 773.2, 909.4
ostracization 586.3, 909.4
ostracize 510.10, 586.6, 773.4, 909.17
ostrich 986.13
ostrich feathers 5.10
otalgia 26.5, 85.15
OTB 759.19
OTC drug 86.4
Othello's flaw 153.1
other (n) 780.3 (v) 449.12 (a) 253.10, 776.6, 780.8, 841.8, 862.8
other, the 768.2, 773.3, 774.3
other America, the 619.3
other continuums 158.6
other-directed 92.41, 375.30, 867.5
other-directedness 92.11, 867.1
other-direction 375.2
other end of the spectrum 779.2
other extreme, the 779.2
other face 215.3
other from 780.8
other half 563.6
other half, the 607.7
otherness 768.1, 774.1, 780.1
others 256.3
other self 588.1, 865.5
other side 215.3
other side, the 307.1, 589.6, 779.2
other side of the coin 205.4
other side of the coin, the 215.3, 779.2
other side of the picture, the 215.3
other side of the tracks, the 230.6
other than 780.8
other way around, the 779.2
other way round, the 205.1
otherwise 780.8
other woman 104.11, 665.17
otherwordly 692.9
otherworld, the 839.2
other-worldliness 692.2
otherworldliness 870.7, 1053.1
otherworldly 681.12, 870.15, 986.24, 1053.7, 1073.26
otic 2.28, 48.13
otic disease 85.15
otic disorder 85.15
otiose 331.18, 391.12, 391.14, 402.5, 993.17, 998.19
otioseness 391.1
otiosity 331.2, 391.1, 391.2, 402.2
otography 48.9
otolaryngology 48.9
otological 48.13
otology 48.9
otoneurology 48.9
otopathic 48.13
otopathy 48.9
otoplasty 48.9
otorhinolaryngology 48.9
otosclerosis 85.15
otoscope 48.9
otoscopic 48.13
otoscopy 48.9
ottava 709.9
ottava alta 709.9
ottava bassa 709.9
ottava rima 720.9
oubliette 429.8
ouch 26.2
ought 641.1
ought to 641.3
Ouija 689.6
Ouija board 689.6
ounce 248.2
ouphe 678.8, 680.8
ourselves 865.5
our times 838.1
oust 447.4, 909.13, 909.15
ouster 909.1, 909.2, 909.11

ousting 447.2, 909.1, 909.2
out (n) 190.9, 600.4, 745.3 (v) 351.8, 547.21, 1022.7 (a) 22.22, 25.8, 88.32, 160.9, 206.7, 348.11, 390.10, 787.4, 842.16, 870.11, 975.16, 1022.11
outachieve 249.9
outage 795.2
out and about 206.8
out-and-out 247.12, 794.10, 960.2
out-and-out lie 354.12
out at elbows 619.8
out at the elbows 393.32, 810.15
out at the heels 393.32, 619.8, 810.15
out-back 584.8
outback (n) 158.4, 233.2, 261.4, 891.2 (a) 233.9
outbalance 297.14
outbid 731.18
out board 347.8
outboard cruiser 180.4
outbound 190.19
out-bowed 283.13
outbrave 492.11
outbrazen 492.11
outbreak 105.9, 190.1, 327.4, 671.6, 818.1
outbred 78.17
outbreed 78.8
outbreeding 78.2
outbuilding 228.9, 228.12, 228.20, 254.3
outburst 59.2, 105.9, 152.9, 190.3, 671.6, 909.7, 1019.14
outburst of anger 152.9
outburst of laughter 116.4
outcast (n) 160.4, 584.5, 586.4, 773.3, 774.3, 870.4 (a) 160.10, 584.12, 586.10
outcaste 586.4
outcast of society 586.4
outcasts 606.4
outclass 249.9, 412.6
outclassed 250.7
out cold 22.22, 25.8, 88.32, 331.20
outcome 190.9, 831.1, 887.1, 893.1, 940.1
outcrop (n) 31.1 (v) 33.8
outcropping (n) 31.1 (a) 31.6
outcry (n) 53.3, 59.4, 115.3, 734.4 (v) 59.8
outdare 454.3, 492.11
outdate 842.9
outdated 390.10, 842.16
outdistance 249.10, 261.5
outdo 249.9, 412.6, 999.11
outdone 412.14
outdoor 206.8
outdoor game 743.9
outdoors 206.3
outdoorsman 206.1
outdoor sport 744.1
outdoorswoman 206.1
outdoor tennis 748.1
outdoor theater 704.14
outed 75.30
outer 206.7
outer ear 2.10, 48.7
outer face 206.2
outer layer 206.2
outer markings 211.1
Outer Mongolia 261.4
outermost 206.7
outermost reaches of space 1073.3
outerness 206.1
outer planet 1073.9
outer side 206.2
outer skin 206.2
outer space 158.1, 261.4, 275.3, 1073.3
outer station 1075.5
outerwear 5.13
outface 492.11
outfall 190.4, 190.9
outfield 743.11, 745.1
outfielder 745.2
outfield stands 745.1
outfight 412.6
outfigure 415.11
outfit (n) 5.2, 5.9, 385.4, 461.22, 471.3, 617.6, 617.7, 707.11, 770.3, 770.12 (v) 5.41, 385.8
outfitted 385.13
outfitter 5.33, 5.35
outfitting 385.1
outflank 415.11
outflow (n) 190.4, 238.4, 626.2 (v) 190.13
outflowing (n) 190.4 (a) 190.19
out-focus-dissolve 706.6
out for 938.38
out for bear 938.38
out for oneself 146.3
out for the count 25.8
outfox 415.11
out from under 120.10, 298.11
outgate 190.9
outgeneral 412.6, 415.11
outgo (n) 190.2, 190.9, 626.2 (v) 249.9
outgoer 190.10
outgoing (n) 190.2 (a) 92.41, 190.19, 343.10
outgoingness 92.11, 343.3
outgoings 190.8, 626.2
out-group 770.3, 773.3
outgrow 14.2, 259.7
outgrowth 14.1, 85.39, 259.3, 887.1, 893.1, 893.3
outguard 216.2, 1008.9
outguess 415.11
outguessing 415.5
outgun 249.9
outgunned 19.14
out-Herod Herod 503.3, 543.10
outhouse 12.10, 228.9, 254.3
out in front 409.14, 757.6
outing 177.5, 351.1
out in left field 868.6
out in the cold 340.14
out in the open 1006.15
outjump 249.9
outland (n) 206.3 (a) 774.5
outlander 774.3
outlandish 122.10, 206.9, 497.12, 534.2, 774.5, 776.6, 870.11, 986.20
outlandishness 870.3
outlast 540.7, 827.8
outlaw (n) 586.4, 593.1, 660.9, 773.3, 774.3, 870.4 (v) 444.3, 586.6, 773.5, 909.17 (a) 674.6
outlawed 444.7, 586.10, 674.6
outlawing 773.2, 909.4
outlawry 674.1, 773.2, 909.4
outlaw strike 727.5
outlay (n) 626.2 (v) 626.5
outleap 249.9
outlet 92.25, 190.9, 242.1, 292.1, 369.1, 383.3, 734.1
outlet pass 747.3
outlet store 736.1
outlie 209.6, 261.5
out like a light 22.22
outline (n) 206.2, 211.2, 262.2, 381.3, 556.1, 557.1, 785.7, 801.4 (v) 211.9, 349.9, 381.11, 405.6, 557.5, 801.7
outlined 211.14
outlines 211.1, 818.6
outlining (n) 801.2 (a) 211.14
outlive 827.8
outlook (n) 27.7, 27.8, 31.3, 33.6, 130.4, 639.1, 839.1, 952.2, 968.1, 978.2 (v) 492.11
outlook over 31.3
outlying 206.7, 261.9, 261.10, 768.3
outlying picket 1008.9
outmaneuver 249.9, 356.14, 412.6, 415.11
outmaneuvering 415.5
outmarch 249.9
outmatch 411.5
outmatched 19.14, 414.19, 992.9
out-migrant 178.5, 190.10
out-migrate 177.22, 188.17, 190.16
out-migration 177.4, 190.7
outmoded 390.10, 842.16
outmost 206.7
outnumber 884.5
out of 16.18, 369.11, 388.5, 473.8, 992.13
out of accord 456.15, 789.6
out of action 19.17, 820.9
out of a job 331.18
out of all bounds 993.16
out-of-body experience 689.6
out of bounds (n) 746.3, 751.1 (a) 210.8, 444.7, 632.12, 993.16
out-of-bounds 747.3, 749.6
out of breath 21.12
out of business 625.11
out of character 789.7
out of circulation 428.13, 429.19
out of commission 19.17, 173.13, 390.10, 393.38, 765.7
out of condition 393.37, 414.18
out of contact 94.9
out of control 430.24
out of countenance 96.22, 132.5, 137.14, 661.13
out of danger 1007.6
out-of-date 390.10, 833.3, 842.16
out-of-dateness 842.3
out of debt 624.23
out-of-door 206.8
out-of-doors 206.8
out-of-doors, the 206.3
out of employ 331.18
out of fashion 842.16
out of favor 99.9, 661.13
out of focus 32.6
out of form 414.18
out of funds 619.9
out of gas 16.12, 19.13
out of gear 19.17, 160.9, 393.37, 810.13
out of hand 361.12, 430.24
out of harm's way 1007.6
out of harness 331.18
out of humor 108.7, 110.17, 112.21
out of it 19.17, 22.21, 25.8, 250.7, 923.9, 930.12, 984.7
out of its element 789.7
out of joint 160.9, 393.37, 789.7, 802.21, 810.13
out of keeping 789.7, 868.7
out of kelter 393.38
out of kilter 393.38, 765.7, 810.13
out of left field 131.10
out of line 789.7, 844.6, 868.7, 975.17
out-of-line 322.5, 638.3
out of luck 1011.14
out of one's bearings 971.24
out of one's control 963.12
out of one's depth 19.14, 414.19, 522.14, 967.8, 1013.21
out of one's element 160.11
out of one's gourd 926.27
out of one's hands 963.12
out of one's head 926.27, 926.31
out of one's mind 926.26
out of one's mind with fear 127.27
out of one's misery 307.29
out of one's power 430.24
out of one's reckoning 131.10, 971.24
out of one's senses 926.26
out of one's skull 926.27
out of one's teens 303.12
out of one's tree 926.27
out of one's wits 105.25
out of order (n) 638.1 (a) 391.14, 393.37, 638.3, 765.7, 810.13, 868.7, 996.5
out-of-order 322.5
out of phase (n) 916.4 (a) 844.6
out of pitch 61.4
out of place 160.11, 789.7, 810.13, 868.7, 996.5
out of plumb 204.15, 975.17
out-of-pocket 473.8, 619.7, 992.13
out-of-pocket expenses 626.3
out of practice 414.18
out of print 992.11
out of proportion 789.7, 789.8, 791.4
out of range 32.5
out of reach 261.9, 967.9
out of season 313.9, 789.7, 833.3, 842.16, 992.11
out of service 393.37
out of shape 265.12, 414.18

out of sight 32.5, 34.4, 97.9, 222.11, 632.12, 993.16, 999.13
out of sight out of mind 990.8
out of sorts 85.56, 110.17, 112.21
out of square 204.15, 975.17
out of steam 410.16
out of step 868.7
out of stock 992.10, 992.11
out of style 842.16
out of sympathy 99.8
out of sync 164.7, 393.38, 456.15, 844.6
out of temper 110.17
out of the Ark 842.10
out of the battle 19.17
out of the blue 131.10
out of the closet 348.10
out of the common 870.10
out of the frying pan and into the fire 119.4
out of the habit of 374.4
out of the hole 624.23, 729.18
out of the mind 990.8
out of the money 757.6
out of the ordinary 870.10, 997.19
out of the pale 870.10
out of the picture 34.4, 250.7
out of the question 125.14, 372.3, 967.7
out of the red 624.23, 729.18
out of the running 19.17, 132.6, 250.7
out-of-the-way 131.10, 164.7, 261.9, 584.8, 776.7, 776.8, 848.3, 868.6, 870.10, 914.7
out of the woods 120.10, 1007.6, 1010.14
out of the world 307.29
out-of-the-world 584.8
out of this world 97.9, 247.13, 870.10, 993.16, 999.13, 999.15
out of time 789.7
out of tone 61.4
out of touch 94.9
out of training 414.18
out of true 975.17
out of tune 61.4, 393.37, 456.15, 780.7, 789.7, 810.13, 868.7
out of turn 868.7
out of use 390.10, 842.16
out of whack 391.14, 393.38, 765.7, 789.6, 810.13
out of work 331.18
out of working order 393.37
out on 643.7
out on a limb 1006.15, 1013.22
out on bail 431.10
out on strikes 745.5
out on the town 743.28
outpace 174.13, 249.9
outpatient 85.43
outpatient care 90.1
outperform 249.9
outplace 447.4, 909.19
outplacement 447.2, 909.5
outplay 249.9, 415.11
outpoint 249.9, 412.6
outpoise 297.14
outpost 211.5, 216.2, 233.2, 261.4, 1008.9
outposts 209.1
outpour (n) 190.4, 538.2, 909.7 (v) 190.13, 909.25
outpouring (n) 190.4, 991.2 (a) 190.19
output 472.5, 627.1, 893.2
output device 1042.3, 1042.9
output lag 1041.11
output measurement 1041.7
output pulse 1035.4
output signal 1036.11
output voltage 1033.7
outrage (n) 156.2, 389.2, 650.4, 655.2, 1000.3 (v) 152.21, 156.5, 389.5, 435.4, 1000.6
outrageous 156.8, 632.12, 640.9, 661.11, 671.16, 923.11, 993.16, 1000.9
outrageousness 632.4, 923.3, 993.1, 1000.2
outrange 249.9, 261.5
outrank 249.11, 814.2
outré 923.11
outreach 249.9, 267.5, 356.14, 415.11
outride 182.40, 249.9
outrider 769.5, 1008.9
outrigger 906.4
outright 247.12, 794.10, 960.2
outright possession 469.1
outrival 249.9
outroar 53.8
outrun (n) 753.1 (v) 174.13, 249.9, 412.6
outsail 174.13, 412.6
outset (n) 818.1 (v) 188.8
outshine 249.9, 412.6
outshone 250.7
outshout 53.8
outside (n) 33.2, 206.2, 206.3, 759.12 (a) 206.7, 206.8, 768.3, 774.5
outside chance 966.1, 972.9
outside hope 966.1
outside in 205.7
outside interest 724.7
outside left 749.5, 752.2
outside loop 184.16
outside market 737.7
outside-of-the-foot pass 752.3
outside pickup 1034.17
outsider 773.3, 774.3, 870.4
outside right 749.5, 752.2
outside roll 184.14
outside the box 868.6
outside the gates 586.10
outside the pale 586.10
outsize (n) 257.5 (a) 247.7, 257.23
outsized 257.23
outskirts 209.1, 211.1, 211.5, 230.1, 230.6, 261.4
outsmart 356.14, 415.11
outsmarting 415.5
outsoar 247.5
outsource 437.5
outsourcing 726.1
outspeak 540.7
outspell 546.7
outspoken 343.10, 416.5, 430.23, 524.31, 644.17
outspokenness 343.3, 416.1, 644.4
outspread (v) 171.5, 259.6, 269.4 (a) 259.11
outstanding 206.7, 247.9, 247.10, 249.12, 249.13, 256.7, 283.14, 348.12, 623.10, 662.17, 997.19
outstanding accounts 628.1
outstanding debt 623.1
outstanding feature 997.7
outstandingness 247.2, 348.4, 662.5
outstare 492.11
outstay 827.8
outstep 249.9
outstretch 259.6, 261.5, 267.5, 269.4
outstretched 259.11
outstretched hand 465.2
outstrip 165.2, 174.13, 247.5, 249.9
outstrip the wind 174.8
outta 16.18, 388.5
outtake 552.3, 557.3, 793.3
out-talk 375.23
outtalk 540.7
out the window 473.7
out to lunch 922.17, 923.9, 926.27, 927.6, 984.6, 990.9
outtop 198.10, 272.11
outtopping 198.12, 272.14, 272.19
outvie 249.9, 457.18
outward 33.11, 206.7, 580.7, 768.3
outward appearance 33.2, 206.1
outward-bound 188.18, 190.19
outward-facing 206.7
outwardness 206.1, 768.1
outward show 33.2, 354.3
outwear 827.8
outweigh 249.6, 297.14
outwit 249.9, 356.14, 415.11
out with 351.5, 524.22
out with it 351.7
outwitting 356.1, 415.5
outworn 390.10, 842.15
oval (n) 280.6, 743.11, 755.1, 757.1 (a) 280.12
Oval Office 610.1
oval window 2.10
ovarian 2.29, 13.8
ovary 2.13, 310.28
ovate 280.12
ovation 487.1, 509.2, 704.7
oven 742.5, 1019.11, 1020.10
ovenbake 11.5
oven-baked 11.7
oven-fresh 841.9
oven-ready 405.19
oven-roasting 11.2
ovenware 735.4
over (v) 626.5 (a) 249.12, 256.7, 272.19, 820.9, 837.7, 993.18
overabound 993.8
overabundance 993.2
overabundant 993.19
overaccentuate 997.14
overaccumulation 993.2
overachievement 993.6
overachiever 330.8
overachieving 993.6
overact 500.12, 704.31, 993.10
overacted 500.15, 704.33, 993.21
overacting 704.8
overactive 330.24
overactivity 330.9
overadorned 545.9
overadornment 993.4
overage 256.4, 993.5
overall 770.23, 772.7
overall length 267.1
overallotment 477.3
overalls 5.18
overambitious 101.12
overambitiousness 101.3
over and above 993.18
over and done with 820.9
overanxiety 101.3, 126.1
over-anxious 101.12, 126.7
overanxiousness 101.3
overappraisal 949.1
overappraise 949.2
overappreciative 509.18
overapprehensive 126.7
overarch 198.10, 272.11, 295.30
overarched 295.36
overarching 198.12, 272.14, 295.36
overassess 949.2
overassessment 632.5, 949.1
overattentive 138.14
overawe 127.18, 155.7, 612.15
overawing 127.28
overbalance (n) 297.1, 791.1 (v) 249.6, 297.14, 791.3
overbalanced 791.5
overbear 249.6, 412.8, 612.15
overbearance 417.3
overbearing (n) 417.3 (a) 141.9, 417.16
overbearingness 141.1, 417.3
overbearing pride 141.1
overbig 257.23, 993.16
overbigness 257.5
overblown 303.15, 355.4, 545.8, 993.20
overbold 492.21, 493.7
overboldness 492.4, 493.1
overbook 965.4
overbooking 965.1
overborne 412.14, 432.16
overbounteous 993.19
overbounteousness 993.2
overbridge 383.9
overbright 35.20
overbrim 238.17, 993.8
overbrimming 993.3
overburden (n) 297.2, 297.7, 993.3 (v) 297.13, 993.15, 1011.8
overburdened 126.9, 297.18, 993.20
overburdening 297.7
overburdensome 98.24
overcalculate 949.2
overcalculation 949.1
overcareful 494.11
overcarefulness 494.4
overcareless 493.7
overcarelessness 493.1
overcarry 993.10
overcarrying 993.6

overcast (n) 184.32, 319.4, 1027.6 (v) 319.7, 1027.9 (a) 319.8, 1027.14
overcaution 494.4
overcautious 494.11
overcautiousness 494.4
overcharge (n) 92.34, 632.5, 993.3 (v) 355.3, 545.7, 630.12, 632.7, 993.15
overcharged 105.30, 297.18, 545.11, 993.20
overcloud 319.7, 1027.9
overclouded 319.8
overclouding 1027.6
overcoat 5.13
overcomable 966.7
overcome (v) 128.10, 249.6, 411.5, 412.7 (a) 88.32, 105.26, 112.29, 128.14, 412.14
overcome oneself 412.7
overcome one's resistance 375.23
overcoming (n) 412.1 (a) 105.30, 411.7, 412.18
overcommend 511.7
overcommendation 511.3
overcompensate 481.5, 791.3
overcompensation 92.23, 791.1
overconfidence 493.1, 970.5
overconfident 493.7, 970.21
overconfiding 954.8
overconscientious 495.12, 644.15
overconscientiousness 495.4, 644.2
overconsumption 8.1
overcooked 11.8
overcopious 993.19
overcopiousness 993.2
overcount 949.2
overcredulity 954.1
overcredulous 954.8
overcredulousness 954.1
overcritical 495.12, 510.23
overcriticalness 495.4, 510.4
overcrop 1069.17
overcropping 1069.13
overcrossing 383.9
overcrowd 884.5
overcrowded 794.11, 884.9, 993.20
overcultivate 1069.17
overcultivation 1069.13
overcurious 981.5
overdemonstrative 93.17
overdesirous 101.12
overdevelop 14.2, 259.7, 993.10, 993.13
overdeveloped 14.3, 257.23, 259.12, 993.16
overdevelopment 257.5, 993.1
overdevout 692.11
overdevoutness 692.3
overdistend 993.13
overdistension 993.7
overdo 355.3, 669.5, 910.4, 993.10
overdoing 669.1, 993.6
overdoing it 355.1
overdo it 511.6, 511.7
overdone 11.8, 355.4, 500.15, 532.5, 545.8, 993.21
overdose (n) 993.2, 994.3 (v) 85.47, 308.22, 993.14, 994.4
overdraft 623.2, 625.3
overdramatic 93.19
overdramatize 704.31
overdraw 350.3, 350.4, 355.3, 486.7, 623.6, 993.13
overdrawing 350.1, 993.7
overdrawn 355.4, 993.21
overdrawn account 625.3
overdraw one's account 486.7
overdress 5.42
overdressed 5.46
overdrive 725.16, 993.10
overdriven 21.11
overdue 130.13, 833.3, 846.16
overeager 101.12, 493.8
overeagerness 101.3, 401.2, 493.2
over-easy 10.26
overeat 672.5
overeater 8.16
overeating 8.1, 672.1
overelaborate (v) 993.10 (a) 498.12, 533.9, 545.8
overelaborateness 498.2
overelaboration 533.3
overelegance 498.2, 533.3
overelegant 498.12, 533.9
overemotional 93.19, 105.28
overemotionalism 93.9
overemphasis 355.1, 993.6
overemphasize 350.3, 355.3, 993.10, 997.14
overemphasized 355.4
overemphatic 355.4
overenthusiasm 101.3, 493.2, 926.11
overenthusiastic 101.12, 493.8, 926.32
overequip 993.14
overesteem 511.7, 949.2
overestimate (n) 949.1 (v) 355.3, 511.7, 949.2
overestimated 355.4, 949.3
overestimation 355.1, 511.3, 949.1
overexcite 105.12
overexcited 105.26
overexercise (n) 993.6 (v) 993.10
overexert 725.10, 993.10
overexertion 330.9, 725.2, 993.6
overexpand 993.13
overexpansion 993.7
overexpend 993.10
overexpenditure 993.6
overexposed 355.4, 897.5
overextend 725.10, 993.13
overextended 897.5
overextend oneself 404.6
overextension 330.9, 725.2, 993.7
overexuberant 993.19
overfall 238.14
overfalls 238.13
overfastidious 495.12
overfastidiousness 495.4
overfat 257.23
overfatigue 21.4
overfatigued 21.11
overfatness 257.5
overfed 257.23, 672.7, 993.20, 994.6
overfeed 993.15, 994.4
overfill 794.7, 993.15, 994.4
overfilling 994.7
overfine 764.6
overfleshed 257.23
overflight 184.18
overflow (n) 238.6, 256.2, 538.2, 991.2, 993.3 (v) 238.17, 884.5, 910.7, 991.5, 993.8
overflowed 1065.17
overflowing (n) 238.6, 910.1 (a) 247.8, 538.11, 884.9, 991.7, 993.20
overflowing eyes 115.2
overflow with 884.5
overflow with energy 17.11
overflow with gratitude 150.3
overfraught 297.18, 993.20
overfreight 993.3
overfreighted 297.18, 993.20
overfrugal 484.7
overfull 794.11, 993.20, 994.6
overfullness 993.3, 994.2
overfurnish 993.14
overgarment 5.12
overgenerosity 486.1
overgenerous 486.8, 993.19
overgenerousness 486.1
overglaze 742.3
overgo 910.4
overgoing 910.1
overgorge 672.5, 994.4
overgorged 672.7, 994.6
overgreat 355.4, 993.16
overgreatness 993.1
overgreediness 100.8
overgreedy 100.27
overgrow 14.2, 259.6, 259.7, 310.34, 910.5, 993.8
overgrown 14.3, 247.7, 257.23, 259.12, 310.43, 910.10, 993.16
overgrowth 14.1, 257.5, 259.3, 910.1, 993.1
overhang (n) 202.3 (v) 202.7, 272.11, 295.30, 840.2
overhanging (n) 202.3 (a) 202.11, 840.3
overhappiness 95.2
overhappy 95.17
overhastiness 365.2, 845.2
overhasty 365.9, 845.8
overhaul (n) 396.6, 938.3 (v) 174.13, 396.14, 628.9, 938.24, 1017.21
overhauling 396.4, 396.6, 938.3
overhead 295.6, 626.3
over head and ears in 983.17
over head and ears in love 104.28
overhear 48.11, 551.14, 551.15
overhearer 48.5
overhearing 48.2
overheat 1020.17
overheated 1019.25, 1020.29
overheated economy 731.7
overheating 1019.6
overheaviness 257.5
overheavy 257.23
overhot 1019.25
overhung 202.11
overimportance 993.6
overindulge 669.5, 672.5, 993.10
overindulged 672.7
overindulgence 426.2, 427.3, 669.1, 672.1, 993.1
overindulgent 426.5, 427.8, 669.7
overindulging 669.7
overinterpret 341.10
overinvolved 545.8
overirrigation 1069.13
overjoyed 95.17
overjoyful 95.17
overjoyfulness 95.2
overjump 249.9, 366.5, 910.4
overkill 355.1, 459.1, 991.2, 993.6
overking 575.8
overlabor 993.10
overlabored 498.12
overlade 993.15
overladen 297.18, 993.20
overlap (n) 295.4, 788.1, 993.4 (v) 295.30, 788.6
overlap dissolve 706.6
overlapping (n) 295.4 (a) 295.36, 775.9
overlapping grip 751.3
overlarge 257.23, 355.4, 993.16
overlargeness 257.5, 993.1
overlaud 511.7
overlaudation 511.3
overlavish (v) 993.14 (a) 486.8, 993.19
overlavishness 993.2
overlay (n) 295.4 (v) 295.19, 545.7
overlayer 295.4, 296.1
overlaying 295.1
overleap 249.9, 366.5, 910.4
overliberal 486.8, 993.19
overliberality 486.1
overlie 295.30
overline 937.2
overload (n) 297.7, 993.3 (v) 297.13, 545.7, 993.15, 1011.8
overloaded 297.18, 545.11, 993.20
overlong 827.11
overlook (n) 27.8 (v) 134.7, 148.4, 157.6, 216.9, 272.11, 340.6, 443.10, 573.10, 691.9, 938.24, 979.7, 984.2
overlook distinctions 945.3
overlooked 148.7, 340.14
overlooker 574.2
overlooking (n) 148.1, 340.1, 443.2 (a) 272.14
overlooking no possibility 494.8
overlook no possibility 494.6
overlook nothing 360.5
overlord 575.1, 575.8, 997.10
overlordship 417.6, 469.2
overluxuriance 993.2
overluxuriant 993.19
overlying 295.36
overly permissive 340.10
overman 574.2
overmaster 412.7, 432.9, 612.15
overmastered 105.26, 412.14, 432.15
overmastering 105.30, 412.18

overmatch 249.9, 412.7
overmatched 412.14
overmatching 412.18
overmeasure (n) 993.2, 993.5 (v) 949.2
overmeticulous 495.12
overmeticulousness 495.4
overmodest 500.19
overmodesty 500.6
overmost 198.11
overmuch (n) 993.1 (a) 993.16, 993.19
overmuchness 993.1, 993.2
overnice 495.12, 500.18, 533.9
overniceness 495.4, 500.5, 533.3
overnicety 495.4
overnight sensation 409.4
overnumerous 993.19
overnumerousness 993.2
overofficious 214.9
over one's head 522.14, 992.9
overopenness to persuasion 954.1
overornamentation 498.2
overornamented 498.12
overornate 498.12
overparticular 495.12
overparticularity 495.4
overpass (n) 170.2, 383.3, 383.9, 910.1 (v) 177.20, 249.6, 249.10, 910.4, 993.9
overpassed 910.10
overpassing 910.1
overpatriotic 591.4
overpatriotism 591.2
overpay 632.8
overpermissive 426.5, 427.8
overpermissiveness 426.2, 427.3
overpious 692.11
overpiousness 692.3
overplay 249.9, 993.10
overplayed 704.33, 993.21
overplay one's hand 993.10
overplenteous 993.19
overplenteousness 993.2
overplentiful 993.19
overplentifulness 993.2
overplenty (n) 993.2 (a) 993.19
overplump 257.23
overplumpness 257.5
overplus (n) 256.4, 993.5 (a) 993.18
overpoise 297.14
overpopulated 993.19
overpopulation 993.2
overpopulous 993.19
overpower 15.9, 53.8, 412.7
overpowered 105.26, 412.14
overpowering 15.19, 105.30, 412.18
overpraise (n) 509.5, 511.3 (v) 355.3, 509.12, 511.7
overpraised 355.4
overpraising 509.18
overprecise 495.12, 500.18
overpreciseness 500.5
overpresumptuous 142.9
overprice 632.7, 949.2
overpriced 632.12
overprint 548.14
overprize 511.7, 949.2
overprizing 511.3
overproduce 892.11
overproduction 892.5
overprofusion 993.2
overprolific 993.19
overproud 140.8
overproudness 140.1
overprovender 993.14
overprovide 993.14
overprovision 993.14
overrate 949.2
overrated 355.4, 949.3
overrating 949.1
overreach 355.3, 356.14, 415.11, 910.4, 993.9
overreaching 356.1, 993.6
overreach oneself 404.6, 993.10
overreact 24.6, 355.3, 993.10
overreaction 92.16, 355.2, 926.11, 949.1, 993.6
overreact to 949.2
overreckon 949.2
overreckoning 949.1
overrefined 24.12, 495.12, 500.18, 533.9, 936.10
overrefinement 495.4, 500.5, 533.3, 580.2
overreliance 130.1
overreligious 692.11, 926.32
overreligiousness 692.3, 926.11
overridden 412.14
override 249.9, 295.30, 412.10, 445.2, 612.15, 910.7
overriding 997.24
overrighteous 692.11
overrighteousness 692.3
overripe 64.7, 303.15
overripeness 64.3, 1063.1
overrule 445.2, 612.13
overruling 249.14, 417.16, 997.24
overrun (n) 910.1, 993.5 (v) 221.7, 238.17, 259.6, 310.34, 480.19, 548.16, 910.4, 910.6, 910.7, 993.8, 993.9 (a) 310.43, 910.10
overrunning 221.3, 238.6, 459.6, 910.1, 910.2
oversaturate 994.4
oversaturated 994.6
oversaturation 994.1
overscatter 771.4
overscrupulous 495.12, 644.15
overscrupulousness 495.4, 644.2
oversea 261.11
overseas 222.12, 261.11
overseas bar 647.5
overseas operations 458.4
oversee 573.10
overseeing (n) 889.1 (a) 573.13
overseer 574.2
overseership 573.4
oversell 355.3, 993.14
oversensibility 24.3
oversensible 24.12
oversensitive 24.12, 110.21, 495.12
oversensitiveness 24.3, 110.5
oversensitivity 110.5, 495.4
oversentimental 93.21
oversentimentalism 93.8
oversentimentality 93.8
oversentimentalized 93.21
overset (n) 205.2, 993.5 (v) 182.44, 205.6, 395.20, 412.7
oversexed 75.25
overshaded 1027.16
overshading 1027.6
overshadow 249.8, 272.11, 319.7, 1027.9
overshadowed 1027.16
overshadowing 1027.6
overshadowment 1027.6
overshine 1025.28
overshoes 5.27
overshoot (n) 184.18 (v) 184.43, 910.4, 993.9
overshooting 355.1
overshoot the field 910.4
overshoot the mark 910.4, 993.9
oversight 340.1, 435.1, 573.2, 612.1, 889.1, 975.4, 984.1, 1008.2
oversimple 406.12, 798.10
oversimplicity 406.4, 798.3
oversimplification 406.4, 798.3
oversimplified 798.10
oversimplify 798.4
oversimplifying 798.3
oversize (n) 257.5 (a) 257.23
oversized 158.11, 257.23
overskip 366.5
oversleep 22.13, 844.5, 846.7
oversmoke 38.7, 319.7
oversold 355.4
oversoon 845.8
oversoul 677.7
oversow 771.4
overspeak 355.3
overspend 486.7, 623.6, 632.8, 993.10
overspending 486.1
overspent 21.11
overspill (n) 993.3 (v) 993.8
overspread (v) 221.7, 295.19, 771.4, 910.5, 910.6, 993.8 (a) 910.10
overspreading 221.3, 295.1, 910.1, 910.2
oversqueamish 495.12
oversqueamishness 495.4
overstate 350.3, 354.16, 355.3, 949.2
overstated 355.4
overstatement 350.1, 355.1, 949.1
overstay 846.15
overstay the market 737.23
overstep 640.7, 910.4, 910.9, 993.9
overstep one's bounds 640.7
overstep one's rights 640.7
overstepping 910.3
overstep the bounds 910.4, 910.9
overstep the mark 910.4
overstimulated 105.26
overstock (n) 993.2, 993.5 (v) 993.14
overstocked 993.20
overstory 296.1
overstout 257.23
overstoutness 257.5
overstrain (n) 21.1, 725.2, 993.6, 993.7 (v) 21.4, 725.10, 993.10, 993.13
overstrained 21.11, 993.21
overstraining 993.7
overstress (n) 725.2 (v) 355.3, 993.10, 997.14
overstressed 355.4
overstressing 355.1
overstretch 993.13
overstretched 993.21
overstretching 993.7
overstride 910.4, 910.8
overstrung 128.11
overstudy 993.10
overstuff 295.28, 993.15, 994.4
overstuffed 295.34, 794.11, 993.20, 994.6
oversubtle 495.12, 936.10
oversubtlety 495.4, 936.1
oversufficiency 993.2
oversufficient 993.19
oversupplied 993.20
oversupply (n) 633.4, 993.2, 993.5 (v) 993.14
oversure 493.7, 970.21
oversureness 493.1, 970.5
overswarm 221.7, 910.6, 993.8
overswarming 221.3, 910.2
oversweet 66.6
oversweetness 66.1
overt 348.10
overt act 328.3
overtake 88.23, 174.13, 835.3
overtaken 88.33
overtaking 174.4
overtalkative 540.9
overtalkativeness 540.1
overtarry 846.15
overtask 725.16, 993.10
overtax 297.13, 389.5, 632.7, 725.10, 725.16, 993.10
overtaxation 630.9
overtaxed 297.18
overtaxing 297.7, 725.2, 993.6
overtechnical 522.14
overtender 24.12
overtenderness 24.3
over-the-counter drug 86.4
over-the-counter market 737.7
over the hill 303.15, 414.18
over-the-hill gang 304.4
over the hump 1007.6, 1010.14
over the moon 109.11
over the top 355.4
overthrow (n) 205.2, 395.3, 412.1, 418.1, 447.2, 852.2, 860.1, 913.2, 958.2 (v) 205.6, 327.7, 395.20, 412.7, 418.4, 447.4, 852.7, 860.4, 913.6, 958.5
overthrowal 447.2, 958.2
overthrowing 417.12
overthrown 395.28, 412.14, 958.7
overthrow one's mind 926.24
overthwart 170.9, 451.8
overtime 747.3, 749.3, 825.3
overtime pay 624.4, 624.6
overtime period 747.3, 749.3, 752.3

overtimid 491.10
overtimorous 491.10
overtire 21.4
overtired 21.11
overtiredness 21.1
overtness 348.3
overtone 50.2, 209.3, 518.1, 519.2, 709.16
overtop 14.2, 198.10, 247.5, 249.6, 259.7, 272.11
overtopping 198.12, 247.9, 272.14, 272.19
overtrain 993.10
overtrick 758.3
overtrustful 954.8
overtrustfulness 954.1
overtrusting 954.8
overture (n) 439.1, 708.26, 816.2 (v) 439.7
overturn (n) 205.2, 395.3, 412.1, 860.1, 913.2 (v) 182.44, 205.6, 395.20, 412.7, 860.4, 913.6, 958.5
overturned 412.14, 958.7
over-under 759.2
overuse (n) 389.2, 993.6 (v) 389.5, 993.10
overvaluation 949.1
overvalue 949.2
overvalued 949.3
overview 27.6, 557.1
overwariness 494.4
overwarm 1019.25
overwary 494.11
overwearied 21.11
overweary (v) 21.4 (a) 21.11
overweening (n) 141.2, 142.1, 970.5 (a) 140.8, 141.10, 142.9, 493.7, 970.21, 993.16
overweeningness 141.2, 142.1, 493.1, 970.5
overweening pride 140.1, 141.1
overweigh 297.14
overweight (n) 257.5, 297.1, 993.3 (v) 297.13, 297.14, 993.15 (a) 257.18, 257.23, 297.16
overweightage 297.1
overweighted 297.18, 993.20
overweighting 297.7
overwhelm 15.9, 53.8, 112.19, 122.6, 174.13, 221.7, 238.17, 367.7, 395.21, 412.8, 432.9, 459.20, 884.5, 910.7, 958.5, 993.14, 1065.14
overwhelmed 24.12, 105.26, 112.29, 122.9, 238.25, 412.14, 910.10
overwhelming (n) 221.3, 238.6, 910.1 (a) 15.19, 105.30, 122.12, 412.18, 884.9, 957.16
overwhelming defeat 412.3
overwinter 313.8
overwise 140.11
over with 820.9
overwork (n) 993.6 (v) 389.5, 725.10, 725.13, 725.16, 993.10
overworked 498.12, 864.16
overwritten 993.21
overwrought 21.11, 105.26, 355.4, 498.12, 545.8, 993.21
overzealous 101.12, 361.8, 493.8, 692.11, 926.32
overzealousness 101.3, 361.1, 401.2, 493.2, 692.3, 926.11
ovicell 305.12
ovicular 305.23
oviduct 2.23
oviform 280.12
ovine 311.45
oviparous 305.23
ovipyriform 279.14
ovoid (n) 280.6 (a) 280.12, 282.9
ovular 305.23
ovulating 305.12
ovulation 305.12
ovule 280.6, 305.12, 305.15, 310.28
ovum 75.7, 305.12, 886.7
owe 623.5, 897.3
owe a grudge 589.8
owed 623.10, 639.7
owe it to 641.4
owe it to oneself 641.4
owe money 623.5
Owenism 611.6
Owenite 611.14
owe one no thanks 151.3
owing 623.10, 639.7, 888.6
owl 133.5, 311.27
owlish 570.17
owllight 315.3
owl's light 315.3
own (v) 332.11, 351.7, 469.5 (a) 469.8
own accord 430.7
own account 430.7
own authority 430.7
own-brand 517.24
own choice 430.7
own discretion 430.7
owned 469.8
owner 470.2, 575.3, 757.2
ownership 469.2
own free will 430.7
own hook 430.7
owning (n) 351.3, 469.1 (a) 469.9
owning up 351.3
own initiative 430.7
own-label 517.24
own oneself in the wrong 113.7, 351.7
own power 430.7
own responsibility 430.7
own say-so 430.7
own sweet way 430.7
own up 351.7
own volition 430.7
own way 430.7
ox 15.8, 311.6, 414.8
oxbow (n) 279.3 (a) 279.10
oxbow lake 241.1
oxcart 179.3
oxen 311.6
Oxford comma 857.4
Oxford gray 39.4
oxfords 5.27
oxgoad 375.8
oxidate 1020.24
oxidation 393.6, 1020.5
oxide 1058.1
oxidization 393.6, 1020.5
oxidize 393.21, 1020.24, 1060.8
oxyacetylene 1067.9
oxyacetylene torch 1020.14
oxyacid 1060.3
oxychromatin 305.7
oxygen 7.11
oxygenate 317.11, 1067.8
oxygenation 317.9
oxygenization 317.9
oxygenize 317.11
oxygenous 1067.9
oxygonal 278.8
oxymoron 539.1, 779.3, 789.2, 967.1, 1013.7
oxymoronic 779.8, 789.8, 936.11, 967.7
oxytone 524.30
oxytonic 524.30
oyster 39.1, 311.29
oyster cracker 10.30
oyster stew 10.11
ozone 317.1
ozonic 1067.9
P 87.17
p 728.8
pa 560.10
pablum 65.1
pabulum 10.3
pace (n) 172.4, 177.11, 177.12 (v) 165.2, 177.27, 177.28, 177.34, 182.53, 300.10
paced start 756.3
pace lap 756.3
pacemaker 574.6
pace off 300.11
pace out 300.11
pacer 311.14, 757.2
pacesetter 574.6, 574.7, 757.2
pace the floor 135.4
Pachen Lama 575.9
pachyderm 311.4
pachydermatous 94.12
pachydermous 311.46
pacifiable 465.13
pacific 106.13, 173.12, 433.15, 464.9, 464.10, 465.12
pacification 465.1, 465.5, 670.1, 670.2
pacificator 464.6, 466.5, 670.3
pacificatory 465.12, 466.8
pacificism 464.4
pacificist 464.6
Pacific Northwest 231.7
Pacific plate 235.1
Pacific Standard Time 832.3
Pacific time 832.3
pacifier 86.12, 466.5, 670.3
pacifism 329.1, 464.4, 670.1
pacifist (n) 464.6, 466.5 (a) 464.10
pacifistic 464.10, 670.10
pacify 120.5, 173.8, 465.7, 670.7
pacifying 465.12, 670.15
pacing 757.1
pack (n) 181.13, 195.1, 244.2, 247.4, 293.5, 714.10, 758.2, 770.3, 770.5, 770.8, 884.3, 1012.6 (v) 159.15, 176.12, 196.7, 212.9, 293.7, 295.20, 354.17, 770.18, 770.20, 794.7, 884.5, 965.5, 993.15, 1012.12, 1045.9
<number>-pack-a-day habit 87.1
package (n) 212.2, 770.8, 792.3, 805.1 (v) 212.9, 295.20, 770.20
package bargaining 731.3
package cruise 177.5
packaged 212.12, 295.31, 770.21
packaged book 554.3
package deal 731.4, 792.3, 805.1
package design 717.5
packaged goods 735.7
packaged house 266.2
package-express 176.15
package holiday 20.3, 177.5
packager 554.2
package service 353.1
package tour 20.3, 177.5
packaging 212.2, 397.2
pack a punch 15.9
pack away 159.15, 386.10
packed 212.12, 293.11, 354.30, 770.22, 794.11, 855.16, 884.9, 965.8, 993.20, 1045.12
packed caucus 609.9
packed deal 965.2
packed in 1045.12
packed jury 965.2
packed like sardines 770.22, 794.11, 1045.12
packed lunch 8.6
packet 87.20, 180.1, 195.1, 618.3, 770.8
packet boat 353.6
packet ship 353.6
packhorse 311.13
pack ice 1023.5
pack in 189.7, 191.7, 770.18, 1045.9
packing 159.6, 196.3, 212.2, 293.5
packinghouse 739.3
pack it in 475.3
pack journalism 552.1
pack of cigarettes 89.5
pack of dogs 311.16
pack off 908.3, 909.18
pack of lies, a 354.11
pack of nonsense 520.2
pack of troubles 96.8
pack on 182.20
pack on sail 174.11, 182.20
pack rat 770.15
pack the deal 356.18, 965.5
pack train 812.3
pact 437.1
paction 437.2
Pactolus 618.5
pactum 436.2
pad (n) 52.3, 199.5, 213.5, 228.4, 311.14, 517.7, 547.4, 549.11, 901.20, 1008.3 (v) 52.15, 120.5, 177.26, 177.27, 196.7, 538.8, 794.7, 849.8
padded 538.12
padded bras 5.24
padded cell 926.14
padding 177.17, 196.3, 254.4, 293.5, 538.6, 849.3, 993.4, 1008.3, 1047.5
paddle (n) 177.12, 180.15, 605.2, 917.9 (v) 177.28, 182.53, 604.14, 917.10, 1065.12
paddleboat 180.1
paddlefoot 178.6, 461.10

paddle one's own canoe 430.20, 872.6
paddle steamer 180.1
paddle wheel 759.16, 904.6
paddling 604.4, 604.5
paddock 311.26, 757.1
paddy 1069.9
paddy field 1069.9
paddy wagon 179.11
padishah 575.9
padlock (n) 428.5 (v) 293.6
padnag 311.14
padre 699.2, 699.5
padrone 575.1
paean 116.2, 150.2, 509.5, 696.3, 708.17
paean of cheers 116.2
paella 10.11
paeon 720.8
paesan 588.4
paesano 227.5, 588.4
pagan (n) 688.7, 695.11 (a) 688.11, 695.19, 697.7, 930.13
pagan deity 678.2
pagan divinity 678.2
pagandom 688.4
paganish 688.11
paganism 688.4, 697.1, 930.3
paganistic 688.11
pagano-Christian 688.11
pagano-Christianism 688.4
paganry 688.4
page (n) 554.12, 577.5, 793.2, 1054.5 (v) 420.11, 1017.17
pageant 33.7, 451.1, 501.4
pageantry 33.7, 501.4
pageboy 1016.14
page numbering 1017.9
page printer 1042.9
page proof 548.5
page through 938.26
pageview 1042.19
paginate 1017.17
pagination 1017.9
pagoda 272.6, 703.2
Pago Pago 261.4
pahoehoe 1059.1
paid 615.20, 624.22
paid helper 577.2
paid holiday 20.3, 222.4
paid in full 624.22
paid time off 222.4, 857.3
paid-up 624.22
paid vacation 20.3, 222.4
paillasse 901.20
pain (n) 10.28, 26.1, 85.9, 96.2, 96.5, 96.10, 98.1, 98.5, 118.5, 643.1 (v) 26.7, 96.17, 98.14
pained 26.9, 26.11, 96.23
painful 26.10, 98.20, 725.18, 1013.18
painful fact 761.3
painfulness 26.1, 96.1, 98.5
pain in the ass 96.2, 96.10, 118.5
pain in the neck 26.6, 96.2, 96.10, 118.5
pain killer 86.12
painkiller 25.3
pain-killing 120.9
painless 1014.13
pain pill 86.12
pain reliever 25.3
pain-relieving 86.40
pains 339.2, 604.1, 725.1
pains and punishments 604.1
painstaking (n) 339.2 (a) 339.11, 725.18
painstakingly match 943.5
painstakingness 339.2
paint (n) 35.8, 295.12, 311.11, 712.18, 758.2, 1016.11 (v) 35.14, 295.24, 349.8, 349.9, 498.8, 498.9, 712.19, 1016.15
paint a picture 712.19
paintbox 712.18
paintbrush 712.18
painted 35.17
painted pony 311.11
painted woman 665.16
painter 311.21, 716.4
painterliness 712.8
painterly 712.20
painter of the soul 720.12
painter's cream 712.18
pain threshold 26.1
paint in bright colors 986.16
painting 35.12, 712.3, 712.13, 712.16, 713.1
paint in glowing colors 498.8, 545.7
painting the lily 355.1
paint in its true colors 644.11
paint oneself into a corner 414.14, 1013.12
paint pretty pictures of 986.16
paint-skin 758.2
paint the lily 993.12
paint the town red 88.28, 743.24
paint up 35.14
paintwork 35.12
painty 712.21
pair (n) 179.5, 784.5, 873.2, 873.3 (v) 75.21, 770.18, 800.5, 805.4, 873.5 (a) 1017.23
pair, the 873.7
paired 563.21, 769.9, 800.13, 805.6, 873.8
paired off 873.8
paired up 873.8
pairing 75.7, 800.1, 873.1
pair off 246.2, 563.15, 805.4, 873.5
pair of glasses 29.3
pair of pants 5.18
pair of spectacles 29.3
pair of stairs 193.3
pair of suspenders 202.5
pair of tongs 1020.12
pair of trousers 5.18
pair of twins 873.4
pair of winks 828.3
pairs skating 760.7
pair up 873.5
paisano 227.5
pajamas 5.21
pal (n) 588.4 (v) 582.18
palace 228.7
palace revolution 860.1
paladin 460.7, 492.7
palaeotype 548.15
palaeotypographical 548.20
palaeotypography 548.1
palaestra 463.1
palaestral 743.30
palafitte 241.3
palais 228.7
pal around with 582.18
palatability 63.1
palatable 8.33, 63.8, 100.30, 107.12
palatableness 63.1
palatalization 524.12
palatalized 524.30
palate 62.1, 62.5, 524.18, 944.1
palatial 228.32, 501.21
palatial residence 228.7
palatinate 232.1
palatine 575.12
palaver (n) 511.1, 520.2, 524.1, 540.3, 541.2, 541.5 (v) 511.5, 540.5, 541.10
palaverer 541.7
palazzo 228.7
pale (n) 211.1, 212.3, 231.2, 231.4, 273.6, 647.2 (v) 32.4, 36.5, 36.6, 37.5, 105.19, 127.11, 212.7 (a) 32.6, 35.22, 36.7, 37.8, 85.54, 117.6, 307.28
palea 295.16
pale a ghost 127.26
pale around the gills 36.7
pale as a corpse 36.7
pale as a ghost 36.7
pale as death 36.7, 127.26
pale-blue 45.3
pale color 35.3
paled 21.8, 212.10
paleethnology 842.4
pale-faced 36.7
pale horse 307.2
paleness 32.2, 36.2, 37.1, 117.1, 307.11
paleoanthropology 312.10
paleoethnography 842.4
paleoethnology 312.10
paleographer 523.15, 547.14
paleographic 523.19
paleographical 523.19
paleography 341.8, 523.13, 546.3, 547.3
paleolith 842.6
paleolithic 842.20
paleological 842.20
paleology 842.4
paleonanthropology 842.4
paleontology 842.4, 1068.3
paleornithology 842.4
paleozoology 842.4
pale rider 307.2
palette 712.18
palette knife 712.18
pale-yellow 43.4
palfrey 311.13
palilalia 525.3
palilogy 538.2
palimony 478.8
palimpsest 395.7, 547.11
palindrome 205.3, 489.8
palindromic 205.7
paling 36.3, 212.3, 212.4
palingenesis 78.1, 396.3
palinode 363.3
palinody 363.3
palisade (n) 200.3, 212.4, 237.2, 273.6 (v) 212.7, 460.9
palisades 200.3
palish 35.22
pall (n) 295.2, 309.14, 345.3 (v) 118.6, 994.4
palladium 1008.3
Pallas's cat 311.21
pallbearer 309.7
palled 118.11
pallet 901.20
palliate 120.5, 600.12, 670.6, 959.3
palliation 120.1, 600.5, 670.2
palliative (n) 86.10, 600.5, 670.3 (a) 86.40, 120.9, 600.13, 670.16, 959.7, 959.10
palliative care 83.5, 197.25
pallid 36.7, 117.6, 127.26
pallidity 36.2
pallidness 36.2
palliness 587.5
pallium 647.4
pallor 35.1, 36.2, 117.1, 307.11
pally (n) 588.4 (a) 587.20
palm (n) 474.4, 646.3 (v) 73.6, 480.13, 482.13
palmaceous 310.39
palmate 171.8, 310.39
palmated 171.8
palmer 178.1, 699.16
palmetto barrens 310.13
palmiped 170.12
palmist 962.4
palmistry 962.2
palm off 862.4
palm off on 643.7
palm oil 375.7, 478.5, 728.2
palm reader 962.4
palm-reading 962.2
palms 249.3, 646.3
palm-shaped 284.16
palmy 1010.13
palomino 311.11
palooka 461.2, 754.2, 757.2
Palookaville 230.3
palp 73.4
palpability 73.3, 348.3, 763.1, 1052.1
palpable 24.14, 73.11, 297.19, 348.8, 763.6
palpable presence, a 894.6
palpate 73.6
palpating 73.2
palpation 73.2
palpitant 55.7, 916.18
palpitate 55.4, 105.18, 916.12, 917.12
palpitating 916.18
palpitation 55.1, 105.5, 127.5, 916.3, 917.4
palpus 3.10, 73.4
palsgrave 608.4
palship 587.2
palsied 85.61, 303.18, 917.17
palsiness 587.5
palsy (n) 85.25, 85.27, 917.2 (v) 25.4 (a) 587.20
palsy-walsiness 587.5
palsy-walsy (n) 588.4 (a) 587.20
palter 344.7, 936.9
palterer 357.9, 936.7

paltering (n) 936.5 (a) 936.14
paltriness 651.2, 661.3, 992.2, 998.2
paltry 258.10, 651.6, 661.12, 992.10, 998.21, 1005.9
paludal 243.3
paludous 243.3
pal up with 582.18, 587.11
pal with 582.18
paly 647.2
pampa 236.1, 310.8
pampas 236.1, 310.8
pamper 427.6, 449.16
pampered 427.9
pampered darling 427.4
pampering 427.3
pamper oneself 651.4
pamphlet 352.8, 554.11
pamphleteer (n) 547.15, 718.4 (v) 547.21, 718.6
Pan 678.11
Pan 890.5
pan (n) 195.1, 216.4 (v) 11.5, 510.14
pan 1058.14
pan 714.14
panacea 86.3
panacean 86.39
panache 3.16, 501.3
Panama hat 5.25
panatella 89.4
pan-broil 11.5
pan-broiled 11.7
pan-broiling 11.2
pancake (n) 10.45 (v) 184.43
pancake engine 181.1
pancake house 8.17
pancake landing 184.18
pancake makeup 1016.11
Panchen Lama 699.14
panchromatic 714.17
panchromatic film 714.10
pancratiast 411.2
pancreas 2.16, 2.17, 7.8
pancreatic 13.8
pancreatic digestion 2.17, 7.8
pancreatic juice 2.17, 7.8, 13.2
panda car 179.11
pandect 556.1, 557.1, 673.5
Pandects of Justinian 673.8
pandemia 85.5
pandemic (n) 85.5 (a) 85.62, 864.12
pandemoniac 671.18, 682.8
pandemonic 682.8
Pandemonium 682.1
Pandemonium 986.11
pandemonium 53.3, 671.2
pandemonium 810.5
pander (n) 665.18 (v) 497.9, 665.21
panderer 665.18
pandering 665.8
pander to 138.8, 449.18, 577.13
pandiculation 22.1, 292.2
pandit 571.1
Pandora's box 96.8, 1000.3, 1013.3
pandowdy 10.41
pandybat 605.2
pane 10.28, 292.7, 296.2, 1029.2
panegyric (n) 509.5 (a) 509.16
panegyrical 509.16
panegyrist 509.8
panegyrize 509.12
panel (n) 213.5, 296.2, 423.1, 423.3, 541.6, 596.5, 598.11, 770.2 (v) 598.16
panelboard 1041.16, 1054.3
panel den 665.9
panel discussion 541.6
paneling 1054.3
panelist 543.4
panel show 1035.2
panel switching 347.7
panel truck 179.12
panelwork 1054.3
panfish 311.29
pan for gold 1058.14
pan-fried 11.7
pan-fry 11.5
pan-frying 11.2
pang 26.2, 96.5, 113.2
Pangaea 235.1
pangenesis 78.6
pangenetic 78.16
Panglossian 124.11
pangs 26.2, 113.2
pangs of conscience 113.2
panhandle 440.15
panhandler 331.11, 440.8
panhandling 440.6
panic (n) 127.1, 128.1, 489.6, 737.22 (v) 127.12, 127.16, 412.8
panic button 400.1
panic fear 127.1
panicked 127.27, 128.14, 412.14
panicky 127.27, 128.11, 491.10
panicle 310.27
panic-monger 127.8
panic-mongering 127.7
panic-prone 127.27, 491.10
panic room 197.17
panic-stricken 127.27
panic-struck 127.27
panic terror 127.1
panisc 678.11
panisca 678.11
paniscus 678.11
panjandrum 502.5, 997.8
panning (n) 508.1, 510.4 (a) 508.12
panoplied 460.13
panoply 460.3, 770.4
panorama 33.6, 33.7, 712.10
panoramic 772.7, 864.13
panoramic shot 714.8
panoramic sight 29.5
pan out 887.4
panpsychism 689.4, 1053.3
panpsychist (n) 689,12, 1053.4 (a) 1053.8
panpsychistic 1053.8
pansexual 75.14
pan shot 714.8
pansophic 928.21
pansophy 928.6
pansy 16.6, 75.15, 77.10
pansyish 16.14
pansy-purple 46.3
pansy-violet 46.3
pant (n) 2.21 (v) 21.5, 105.18, 524.25, 1019.22
pant after 100.18
Pantalone 707.10
Pantaloon 707.10
pantaloon 304.2
pantalooned 5.45
pantaloons 5.18
pant for 100.16
pantheism 675.5, 952.5
pantheist 675.16
pantheistic 675.25
pantheon 678.1, 703.2
pantheonic 703.15
panther 311.21
panther piss 88.14
panting (n) 21.3, 105.5 (a) 2.32, 21.12, 101.8, 401.10
pantisocracy 612.4
pantometer 278.4
pantomime (n) 349.4, 517.14, 707.2 (v) 349.12, 517.21, 704.29
pantomimic 517.25
pantomiming 349.4, 704.8
pantomimist 707.2
pantophagist 8.16
pantophagous 8.31
pantophagy 8.1
pantry 197.14, 197.15, 386.8
pants 5.18
pantsman 562.12
panty girdle 5.23
pantyhose 5.28
pantywaist 16.6, 77.10
panzer attack 459.4
panzer warfare 459.1
pap 7.13, 10.3, 283.6, 560.10, 1062.5
papa 76.10, 560.10
papacy 417.7, 698.2, 698.6
Papagayo wind 318.8
papal 698.15
Papal Court 595.3
papalism 675.8
papality 698.6
paparazzo 555.4, 714.2
paper (n) 37.2, 270.7, 547.4, 547.10, 549.5, 555.2, 556.1, 634.2, 709.12, 728.11, 1054.5 (v) 295.23
paperback 554.3
paper bag 40.1
paper-bound book 554.3
Paperbound Books in Print 558.4
paper credit 622.3
paper cut 85.38
paper doll 743.16
paper folding 712.2
paper-folding 291.4
paperiness 270.4, 270.5
paper money 728.5
paper over 346.6, 354.16
paper profits 472.3
paper pulp 1063.2
papers 226.3, 549.2, 549.5
paper stock 1054.5
paper-thin 764.7
paper tiger 500.7
paper trail 549.2, 549.5
paper war 457.1, 935.4
paperweight 297.6
papery 16.14, 270.16, 393.35, 764.7, 1050.4
papery-skinned 303.18
Paphian (n) 665.16 (a) 665.26
papilla 283.6
papillary 283.19
papilloma 283.3
papillose 283.19
papillote 10.19, 281.3
papish 675.29, 698.15
papism 675.8
papist (n) 675.19 (a) 675.29, 698.15
papistic 698.15
papistical 675.29, 698.15
papistry 675.8
papoose 302.9
pappose 3.25
pappus 3.8, 3.9
pappy (n) 560.10 (a) 65.2
Pap smear 91.12
Pap test 91.12
Papuan race 312.2
papula 85.37
papular rash 85.36
papule 85.37
papulous 283.19
papyrus 547.4, 547.11
par (n) 246.1, 738.9, 751.3, 790.1 (v) 751.4 (a) 790.7
parable 784.1
parabola 279.2
parabolic 279.13, 722.8
parabolical 279.13, 722.8
parabolic orbit 1073.16
paraboloid 279.13
paracasein 1045.7
parachronism 833.1
parachronistic 833.3
parachute (n) 181.13, 397.6, 1008.3 (v) 184.47, 194.5, 367.6
parachute approach 184.18
parachute badge 647.5
parachute flare 517.15
parachute jump 181.13, 367.1
parachute jumper 185.8, 367.4
parachutist 185.8
Paraclete, the 121.5, 677.12
parade (n) 33.7, 177.10, 383.2, 501.4, 812.3 (v) 177.29, 177.30, 348.5, 501.17, 812.7
parade ground 463.1
parade one's wares 501.16
paradiddle 55.1
paradigm 526.3, 786.1
paradigmatic 526.22, 786.8
paradigm shift 363.1
paradisaic 681.12
paradisaical 681.12
paradisal 97.9, 681.12, 986.23
Paradise 839.2
paradise 27.8, 95.2, 397.7, 704.15, 743.14, 986.11, 1069.10
paradisiac 97.9, 681.12
paradisiacal 97.9, 681.12
paradisic 97.9, 681.12
paradisical 97.9, 681.12
paradoctor 185.8
parador 228.15
paradox 522.9, 779.3, 789.2, 936.3, 967.1, 1013.7
paradoxical 779.8, 789.8, 967.7
paradoxical sleep 22.5
paraeducator 571.4
paraffin 1025.20, 1056.4

paraffinic 1056.9
parafoil 181.13
paraglider 181.13
paragon 249.4, 413.13, 659.4, 786.4, 999.8, 1002.4, 1016.7
paragraph (n) 529.1, 554.13, 556.1, 793.2 (v) 532.4
paragrapher 555.4
paragraphist 555.4
paralambdacism 525.5
paralinguistic communication 524.7
parallel (n) 159.5, 203.2, 231.3, 460.5, 784.3, 790.4 (v) 203.4, 775.6, 784.7, 788.6, 790.5, 943.4, 943.7 (a) 161.14, 203.6, 218.6, 769.9, 775.9, 784.11, 943.8
parallel bar 203.2
parallel bars 725.7
parallel column 203.2
parallel dash 203.2
parallelepiped 203.2
parallelepipedal 203.6
parallelepipedon 203.2
paralleler 203.2
parallel evolution 861.3
parallel fifths 709.20
parallel file 203.2
parallelinervate 203.6
paralleling 203.6, 784.11
parallel intervals 709.20
parallelism 203.1, 218.1, 264.1, 769.1, 784.1, 788.1, 790.1, 943.1
parallelistic 203.6
parallelization 203.1
parallelize 203.5, 775.6
parallel line 203.2
parallel-line scanning 1035.3
parallel octaves 709.20
parallelodrome 203.6
parallelogram 203.2
parallelogrammatical 203.6
parallelogrammical 203.6
parallelograph 203.3
parallelometer 203.3
parallelotropic 203.6
parallelotropism 203.1
parallel port 1042.3
parallel processing 1042.3
parallel rule 203.3
parallel ruler 203.3
parallel sailing 182.2
parallel series 203.2
parallel slalom 753.3
parallel slalom course 753.1
parallel-time chart 757.4
parallel trench 203.2
parallel universe 689.2
parallel vector 203.2
paralogical 936.11
paralogism 935.6, 936.3
paralogist 936.6
paralogize 936.8
paralysis 85.9, 85.27, 329.1
paralysis of authority 674.1
paralytic (n) 85.45 (a) 85.61, 329.6
paralytic rabies 926.6
paralyzation 85.27paralyze 19.10, 25.4, 94.8, 122.6, 127.17
paralyzed 19.16, 88.33, 127.26, 329.6
paralyzing 127.29
paramagnet 907.3
paramagnetic 1032.31
paramagnetism 1032.7
paramecium 258.7
paramedic 90.11, 185.8, 367.4
parameter 300.2, 959.2
parameters 211.1, 766.2
parametric 766.8, 959.8
paramilitary 458.20
paramnesia 990.2
paramount (n) 575.1, 575.8, 997.10 (a) 198.11, 249.14, 612.17, 997.24, 999.16
paramountcy 249.3, 997.1, 999.2
paramour 104.11, 665.17
paranoia 92.14, 92.20, 926.4
paranoiac (n) 926.17 (a) 926.28
paranoiac psychosis 926.4
paranoid (n) 926.17 (a) 926.28
paranoid personality 92.20
paranoid psychosis 926.4
paranoid schizophrenia 926.4
paranormal 689.23, 870.15
paranormal, the 689.2, 870.7
paranormality 870.7
paranymph 563.4, 576.1, 616.6
parapet 1012.5
paraphernalia 385.4, 471.2
paraphilia 75.11
paraphiliac 75.16
paraphrase (n) 336.3, 341.3 (v) 336.5, 341.13
paraphrast 341.7
paraphrastic 341.16
paraphrenia 926.4
paraplegia 85.27
paraplegic 85.45
paraprofessional 571.4, 616.6
parapsychological 1053.7
parapsychologist 689.12
parapsychology 689.4
paraquat 1001.3
pararhotacism 525.5
pararhyme 720.9
paraselene 1025.14
parasite 138.5, 166.2, 310.4, 311.3, 311.36, 311.37, 331.11, 432.6, 769.6
parasite drag 184.27
parasitic 138.14, 331.19, 480.26, 899.4
parasitic drag 184.27
parasitic plant 310.4
parasitic vowel 524.12
parasitism 138.2, 899.1
parasitize 138.12
parasol 295.7, 1028.1
parasympathetic nervous system 2.14
parataxis 530.2
paratrooper 185.8, 367.4
paratroops 461.15, 461.23
paratuberculosis 85.41
parawing 181.13
parboil 11.5, 1020.20
parboiled 11.7
parboiling 11.2
Parcae 964.3
parcel (n) 244.2, 471.6, 770.8, 793.1, 884.2 (v) 212.9, 244.4, 477.6, 770.20, 802.18
parceled 212.12, 477.12
parceling 477.1
parceling out 477.2
parcel of land 231.4, 1069.9
parcel out 477.8, 802.18, 808.9
parcel post 553.4
parcel up 770.20, 802.18
parch 260.9, 1019.22, 1020.24, 1066.5, 1066.6
parched 100.26, 260.13, 1020.30, 1066.7, 1066.9
parchedness 1066.1
parching (n) 260.3, 1020.5 (a) 1019.25
parchment 547.4, 547.10, 547.11, 549.5, 1050.2, 1066.2
parchmenty 393.35
parcourse exercise 84.2
pard 588.4, 616.2
pardner 588.4, 616.2
pardon (n) 145.1, 148.2, 464.7, 465.2, 601.1 (v) 145.4, 148.3, 601.4
pardonable 600.14
pardonableness 600.7
pardonable pride 136.1
pardoned 148.7
pare 6.8, 252.7, 255.10, 633.6, 802.11
pared-down 252.10
pare down 252.7
paregoric (n) 86.12 (a) 86.45
parent (n) 560.8, 886.4 (v) 449.16 (a) 560.17
parentage 560.1
parental 104.26, 560.17, 1008.23
parental guidance suggested 706.1
parental instinct 104.4
parental leave 20.2
parental love 104.4
parental unit 559.1
parent complex 92.22
parent element 1038.10
parent fixation 92.21
parentheses 191.2
parenthesis 164.1, 205.3, 213.2, 813.1
parenthesize 212.8, 530.16
parenthetic 813.4
parenthetical 213.9, 776.7, 843.11
parenthetical remark 213.2
parenthood 560.1
parenting 449.3
parent language 523.2
parentless 307.34
parents strongly cautioned 706.1
paresis 85.27
paresthesia 74.1
pareunia 75.7
parfait 10.47
par-5 hole 751.1
par for the course (n) 373.4, 964.1 (a) 246.3, 349.15, 864.12
par-4 hole 751.1
parfum 70.2
parfumerie 70.2
parfumeur 70.5
parfumoir 70.6
parget 35.14, 295.25
pargeting 295.1
parhelic circle 1025.14
parhelic ring 1025.14
parhelion 1025.14
pariah 584.5, 586.4, 870.4
pariah dog 311.18
paries 213.5
parietal 212.11, 213.11
parietes 213.5
pari-mutuel 757.4, 759.4, 759.17
pari-mutuel machine 759.17
paring 296.3, 793.3
paring down 798.2
parings 256.1, 391.4
parish 231.5, 698.8, 700.1
parish council 423.1
parishioner 696.9, 700.2
parishioners 700.1
parish priest 699.5
parish records 549.2
parish register 549.2
parish rolls 549.2
parity 738.9, 784.1, 790.1, 1042.18
parity of exchange 728.9
park (n) 212.3, 310.7, 310.8, 310.13, 397.7, 743.14, 745.1 (v) 159.12, 159.17
Parker House roll 10.31
park forest 310.13
parking garage 197.27
parking lot 197.27
parking orbit 1075.2, 1075.9
Parkinsonism 85.25
Parkinson's disease 85.25
park in space 1075.12
parkland 310.8, 310.13
park of artillery 462.2
park oneself 913.10
parkour 84.2
parky 1023.12
parlance 523.1, 524.2, 532.1
parlando (n) 708.30 (a) 708.53
parlay (n) 759.3 (v) 251.4, 759.25
parley (n) 422.1, 465.2, 541.5 (v) 541.8, 541.10
parleyer 541.7
parliament 613.1
parliamentarian 612.16
parliamentarianism 612.7
parliamentarism 612.7
parliamentary (n) 179.14 (a) 612.16, 613.11
parliamentary agent 609.32
parliamentary government 612.4
parliamentary train 179.14
parlor 197.5, 739.1
parlor Bolshevik 611.12
parlor car 179.15, 197.10
parlor game 743.9
parlormaid 577.8
parlor pink 611.12
parlous 1006.9
parlous straits 1013.4
Parmenidean 952.12
Parnassian (n) 720.12 (a) 720.16
Parnassus 720.11

parochial 231.9, 698.13, 773.9, 980.10
parochial church council 423.4
parochial council 423.4
parochialism 773.3, 980.1
parochial school 567.8
parodic 508.14
parodist 489.12
parody (n) 336.1, 336.3, 350.2, 489.1, 508.6 (v) 336.5, 350.3, 508.11, 512.12, 621.4
parol (n) 524.2 (a) 524.29
parole (n) 431.2, 436.1, 523.1 (v) 431.5
parolee 429.11
paronamasia 784.6
paronomasia 489.8, 539.1
paronychia 85.37
paronym 526.4, 526.7
paronymic 526.20
paronymous 526.20
paroxysm 26.2, 85.6, 105.9, 152.8, 671.5, 917.6, 926.7
paroxysmal 26.10, 671.23
paroxytonic 524.30
parquet 47.4, 199.3, 704.15
parquet circle 704.15
parquetry 47.4
parr 311.29
parrot (n) 118.1, 336.4, 867.2 (v) 336.6, 849.7, 989.16
parroted 849.12
parroting 849.1, 874.1
parrotlike 118.9, 336.9, 538.11, 849.14
parrot-nosed 279.8
parrotry 336.2
parry (n) 760.4 (v) 344.7, 368.8, 460.10, 754.4, 936.9, 958.5, 1012.14
parrying 344.4, 754.3, 936.5
parse 530.16, 801.7
parsec 1073.3
parsecs 261.1
Parsee 675.32
parser 1042.13
Parsi 697.4
Parsiism 697.1
parsimonious 484.7, 635.6, 992.10
parsimoniousness 484.1, 484.2, 635.1
parsimony 484.1, 635.1, 992.2
parsing 530.1, 801.2
parson 699.2
parsonage 228.5, 703.7
parson's nose 10.23
part (n) 196.1, 231.1, 244.2, 267.2, 387.5, 471.4, 477.5, 554.13, 704.10, 708.22, 708.24, 708.28, 724.3, 765.4, 766.3, 793.1, 796.2 (v) 224.3, 292.11, 307.18, 477.6, 566.5, 771.8, 802.8, 802.19 (a) 793.7, 795.4, 875.5
partake 8.20, 62.7, 476.5, 480.13, 898.3
partake in 476.5, 476.6
partake of 8.20, 476.5, 784.7
partake of the Lord's Supper 701.14
partaker 8.16, 476.4, 480.11
partaking (n) 476.1, 582.6 (a) 476.8
part and parcel 796.2
part company 171.5, 456.10, 771.8, 789.5, 802.19
parted 224.6
parted from 473.8
parterre 704.15
parterre boxes 704.15
parthenogenesis 78.6
parthenogenetic 78.16
Parthenope 377.4
Parthian shot 188.4, 508.2, 524.3, 817.1
par-3 hole 751.1
partial (n) 50.2 (a) 617.19, 650.11, 793.7, 795.4, 875.5, 980.12, 1003.4
partial blindness 28.1, 30.1
partial darkness 1027.2
partial eclipse 1027.8, 1028.1, 1073.13
partialism 980.3
partiality 100.3, 104.1, 371.5, 617.13, 650.3, 980.3
partially true 265.11
partial sightedness 28.1
partial to 100.22, 104.29
partial tone 50.2
partial truth 354.11
partibility 802.1
partible 802.26
participant (n) 476.4 (a) 476.8
participate 221.8, 476.5, 898.3
participate in 476.5
participating 476.8
participating mortgage 438.4
participation 221.4, 476.1, 582.6, 772.1
participative 476.8
participator 476.4
participatory 476.8
participatory democracy 476.2
participial 530.17
participle 530.3
particle 248.2, 258.7, 530.3, 793.3, 1051.5, 1051.6
particle accelerator 1038.11
particle physicist 1038.3
particle physics 1038.1
parti-color (n) 47.1 (v) 47.7 (a) 47.9
parti-colored 35.16, 47.9
particular (n) 766.3, 793.1, 831.2, 957.5 (a) 339.12, 371.23, 477.13, 495.9, 766.9, 809.7, 865.12
particular, the 865.3
particular choice 371.5
particularism 865.1
particularity 339.3, 495.1, 766.4, 865.1, 865.4, 872.1
particularization 349.2, 766.5, 780.4, 865.7, 935.3
particularize 538.7, 766.6, 780.6, 865.9, 957.13, 973.11
particular lien 438.5
particularness 339.3, 495.1
particulars 349.2, 865.6
particulars, the 761.4
particulate (n) 1051.5 (a) 1051.11
particulates 1051.5
parties litigant 598.11
par time 757.4
parting (n) 188.1, 188.4, 307.1, 771.3, 802.1, 802.2 (a) 188.18, 802.25
parting cup 88.9
parting of the ways 456.4, 789.1
parting shot 188.4, 508.2, 817.1, 939.2
parting words 188.4
parti pris 650.3, 947.1
partisan (n) 166.2, 461.16, 588.1, 609.27, 616.9 (a) 456.17, 609.44, 617.19, 650.11, 980.12
partisan election 609.15
partisanism 609.1, 609.25, 617.13, 650.3, 675.4
partisan politics 609.1
partisanry 609.25
partisanship 456.3, 609.25, 617.13, 650.3, 980.3
partisan spirit 456.3
partition (n) 213.5, 477.1, 802.1, 875.3 (v) 213.8, 477.6, 782.2, 802.18
partitioned 213.11, 802.20
partitioning 477.1
partitionment 477.1
partitive 793.7
partlet 311.28
partly 875.5
partly cloudy 319.8
partly sunny 1019.24, 1025.30
part music 708.18
partner (n) 476.4, 563.6, 588.3, 616.2, 758.3, 769.4 (v) 450.3, 770.18, 805.4
partnered 563.21
partner in crime 610.8, 616.3, 616.4
partnership 450.2, 476.1, 597.4, 617.1, 769.2
partners with 805.6
part of speech 523.14, 526.1, 530.3
parton 258.8
parts 196.1, 231.1, 413.4, 763.2, 919.2
part singing 708.18
parts of the Mass 701.8
part song 708.18
part-time (n) 825.3 (a) 848.3
part-time worker 577.3, 726.2
parturiency 78.5
parturient 78.18, 818.15
parturition 1.1, 818.4
part with 390.7, 475.3, 478.21
party (n) 95.3, 332.7, 347.11, 476.4, 487.1, 582.11, 598.11, 599.5, 609.24, 617.4, 675.3, 743.4, 743.6, 770.2, 770.3, 901.1 (v) 95.14, 487.2, 582.21, 669.6, 743.24 (a) 609.44, 617.19
party animal 669.3
party boat 180.1
party boss 610.1
party chairperson 610.12
party chieftain 610.1
party-column ballot 609.19
party-crash 582.18
party crasher 582.16
party doctrine 609.4
party down 487.2, 582.21
party dress 5.10
party emblem 609.19
partyer 669.3
party faithful 609.27
party girl 669.3
partygoer 669.3
party hack 609.27, 610.4
party-hearty 669.7
partying (n) 582.3 (a) 487.3
party in power 609.24
party leader 610.1
party line 347.17, 381.4, 609.4
party machine 609.24
party man 609.27
party member 609.27
party philosophy 609.4
party platform 609.7
party politics 609.1, 609.25
party pooper 112.14, 1012.9
party principle 609.4
party spirit 617.13
party time 582.11
party to, a (n) 476.4 (a) 898.4
party to a suit 598.11, 599.5
party wall 213.5
party wheelhorse 609.27
party whip 610.3
party woman 609.27
parulis 85.37
par value 630.2, 738.9
parvenu (n) 606.7, 618.7, 841.4 (a) 606.8
parvenu and arriviste 497.6
parvenuism 497.4
pas 245.1
paschal 701.18
pas de deux 873.4
pash 104.3
pashadom 417.7, 608.9
pashalic 417.7
pashaship 608.9
pasquil 512.5
pasquin 512.5
pasquinade (n) 512.5 (v) 512.12
pasquinader 512.7
pass (n) 237.5, 237.7, 270.3, 284.9, 356.6, 383.3, 439.2, 443.7, 459.3, 634.2, 746.3, 747.3, 749.3, 749.6, 752.3, 758.3, 765.1, 843.4, 904.3, 914.2, 1006.1, 1013.4 (v) 12.12, 34.2, 174.13, 176.10, 177.18, 246.2, 249.10, 307.18, 332.12, 343.7, 371.15, 387.13, 395.23, 409.7, 446.2, 478.13, 522.11, 613.10, 629.3, 746.5, 747.4, 749.7, 752.4, 759.25, 762.6, 820.7, 821.5, 828.6, 831.5, 837.6, 904.10, 910.8, 930.10, 942.10, 991.4, 993.9, 999.11
pass a bad check 728.28
passable 107.12, 999.20, 1005.7
passableness 246.1, 999.3, 1005.1
passage 2.23, 162.1, 172.2, 177.1, 177.4, 182.6, 189.5, 197.18, 237.7, 239.1, 328.3, 383.3, 554.13, 557.3, 613.5, 708.24, 709.18, 793.2, 858.1
passage at 457.4

passage grave 309.16
passage-making 182.1
passage of arms 457.4, 935.4
passage of time 821.4
passageway 189.5, 197.18, 239.1, 292.1, 383.3
pass all bounds 993.10
pass along 162.2, 176.15, 343.7
pass and re-pass 916.13
pass around 477.8, 771.4
pass as 349.10
pass away 34.2, 307.18, 390.9, 395.23, 762.6, 820.7, 828.6
pass-back 749.6
pass ball 747.3
pass belief 955.7
passbook 628.4
pass by 157.6, 372.2, 821.5, 910.8, 984.2
pass by in silence 600.12
passcode 517.12
pass completion 746.3
pass comprehension 522.10
pass current 953.20
passé 837.7, 842.15
passed 371.26, 837.7
passed away 307.29, 762.11, 837.7
passed ball 745.3
passed by 340.14
passed on 307.29
passed out 88.32
passed over 340.14
passed-over 773.7
passed up 340.14
passeggiare 177.29
passeggiata 177.10
passel 244.2, 884.2
passenger 178.1
passenger steamer 180.5
passenger train 179.14
passe-partout 292.10
passer 746.2, 828.4
passerby 178.1, 828.4, 918.1, 957.6
passerelle 704.16
passerine 311.48
passerine bird 311.27
passe-temps 743.1
pass for 349.10, 349.12, 354.22
pass from center 746.3
pass from mouth to mouth 352.16
pass from sight 34.2
pass from the sublime to the ridiculous 923.6
pass holder 634.3, 704.27
passibility 24.3
passible 24.12
passing (n) 34.1, 188.1, 307.1, 307.8, 446.1, 613.5, 747.3, 749.3 (a) 34.3, 172.8, 177.36, 246.3, 401.9, 828.7, 831.9
passing around 477.2
passing away 307.1, 307.8
passing belief 955.10
passing bell 115.6, 309.6
passing by (n) 372.1 (a) 918.7
passing fancy 104.3, 364.1, 828.5
passing game 747.3
passing gas 909.10
passing over 307.1
passing play 746.3
passing strange 122.10, 870.11
passing the buck 415.5
passing up 372.1, 668.2
passing word 551.3
pass in review 989.15
pass interception 746.3
pass in the dark 991.4
pass into 858.17
pass into history 837.6
pass into one's hands 479.8
passion 17.2, 75.5, 93.2, 96.5, 96.7, 100.1, 100.2, 101.2, 104.1, 105.8, 152.10, 323.1, 544.5, 671.2, 708.17, 886.9, 926.12, 983.2
passionate 17.13, 75.27, 93.18, 101.9, 104.25, 105.22, 105.29, 110.25, 544.13, 671.22, 983.16
passionate friendship 587.8
passionateness 93.2, 101.2
passionless 94.9, 102.8
passionlessness 94.1, 102.3
passive (n) 530.14 (a) 94.13, 134.10, 173.14, 329.6, 433.12, 464.10, 467.7, 933.4, 982.3
passive-aggression 329.1
passive-aggressive 329.6, 459.30
passive algolagnia 75.11
passive euthanasia 308.1
passiveness 94.4, 134.2, 173.1, 173.4, 329.1, 433.1, 467.2, 982.1
passive resistance 134.2, 327.1, 329.1, 453.1
passive resister 333.3, 392.6, 464.6
passive self-annihilation 329.1
passive smoking 89.10
passive voice 530.14
passivism 329.1
passivity 94.4, 123.1, 134.2, 173.1, 173.4, 329.1, 331.6, 368.2, 433.1, 933.1, 982.1
passivize 173.8
pass judgment 946.13
passkey 292.10
pass light 1029.3
passman 572.7
pass muster 509.15, 867.4, 942.10, 991.4
pass off 831.5, 862.4
pass off as 350.3
pass on 162.2, 176.10, 307.18, 332.12, 343.7, 478.18, 629.3, 629.4
pass one by 984.5
pass oneself off as 645.11
pass one's lips 524.27
pass one's time in 724.11
pass one's word 436.4
pass out 25.5, 34.2, 88.27, 190.12, 307.19, 352.14, 478.13, 771.4
pass out of sight 34.2
pass out of the picture 34.2, 762.6
Passover (n) 8.9 (a) 701.18
pass over 148.4, 176.10, 177.20, 340.6, 340.7, 340.8, 478.13, 629.3, 773.4, 910.8, 938.24, 984.2
pass over Jordan 307.20
pass over lightly 340.8, 938.26
pass pattern 746.3
passport 443.7, 517.11, 549.6
pass receiver 746.2
pass rush 746.3
pass sentence 598.20, 946.13
pass sentence on 602.3
pass the buck 176.10, 368.9, 415.11, 643.7, 645.12
pass the eyes over 938.24
pass the fingers over 73.6
pass the hat 440.14, 440.15
pass the spring 313.8
pass the time 331.13, 724.10, 761.10
pass the time of day 343.6, 541.9, 585.10
pass the word around 352.10
pass through 177.20, 189.8, 831.8
pass through one's head 931.18
pass through one's mind 931.18
pass time 821.6
pass to the order of the day 390.6
pass under review 541.11, 938.24
pass understanding 522.10
pass under the name of 527.13
pass up 157.6, 340.7, 372.2, 668.7
pass upon 332.12
pass water 12.14
pass with flying colors 409.7
password 292.10, 517.12, 527.3, 1042.18
past (n) 530.12, 837.1 (a) 34.4, 837.7, 837.9, 837.10, 842.15
past, the 719.1, 821.1, 837.1
pasta 10.33
past age 837.3
pasta salad 10.37
past bearing 98.25
past comprehension 522.13
past danger 1007.6
past dispute 970.16
past due 833.3
paste (n) 10.33, 354.13, 498.3, 498.5, 797.5, 803.4, 902.5, 1062.5, 1063.2 (v) 412.9, 803.9, 902.15, 902.16
pasteboard 758.2
pastel (n) 35.3, 712.12, 712.18 (a) 35.22, 36.9
pastel color 35.3
pastelist 716.2, 716.3
pastel painting 712.12
pastels 35.8
pastel shade 35.3
paste on 253.4
pastern 199.5
pasteurization 79.3
pasteurize 79.24
pasteurized 79.27
past expectation 131.10
past experience 413.9
past history 837.1
past hope 125.15
pasticcio 336.1, 336.3, 621.2, 712.9
pastiche (n) 336.1, 336.3, 621.2, 712.9, 784.1, 785.1, 797.6 (v) 336.5
pastille 70.4, 86.7
pastime 724.7, 743.1
pastiness 36.2, 1062.2, 1063.1
pasting 412.3
past life 78.1
past master 413.13, 417.7, 892.7
past one's prime 303.15
pastor 699.2
pastorage 698.1, 698.2, 699.1, 703.7, 1008.2
pastoral (n) 712.11 (a) 233.6, 416.6, 464.9, 698.13, 720.16
pastoral care 698.1
pastoralist 720.12
pastoralization 233.4
pastoralize 233.5
pastoral poet 720.12
pastoral simplicity 233.3
pastoral staff 273.2, 647.4, 702.3
pastorate 698.1, 698.2, 703.7, 1008.2
pastorship 698.2, 1008.2
pastose 712.21
past participle 530.3, 530.4, 837.5
past perfect (n) 530.12 (a) 837.9
past perfect tense 837.5
past performance 757.4
pastposting 356.10
past praying for 125.15, 654.18
past progressive tense 837.5
pastrami 10.14
past recall 990.8
past recollection 990.8
pastry 10.41
pastry chef 11.3
pastry cook 11.3
pastry shell 295.14
past tense 837.5
past time 834.1
past times 837.1
pasturage 10.4, 310.8
pasture (n) 8.1, 10.4, 310.8, 1069.8 (v) 8.18
pasture grass 310.5
pasture land 310.8
pastureland 310.8
pasture on 8.28
pasturing 8.1
past use 390.10
pasty 36.7, 65.2, 1047.9, 1047.12, 1062.12, 1063.6
PA system 50.11
pat (n) 52.3, 257.10, 562.5, 902.7 (v) 52.15, 562.16, 902.18 (a) 788.10, 855.15, 928.26
patch (n) 47.3, 86.33, 231.4, 248.3, 517.5, 647.5, 1004.3, 1025.5, 1069.9 (v) 340.9, 396.14
patcher-up 466.5
patchiness 795.1, 851.1, 1003.1
patchouli 70.2, 70.4
patch test 91.15
patch things up 465.8
patch together 340.9, 892.8

patch up 340.9, 396.13, 396.14, 466.7
patch up a friendship 465.8
patch up a quarrel 465.8
patchwork 47.4, 797.6
patchwork quilt 47.6, 295.10
patchy 47.13, 393.32, 795.4, 797.14, 813.4, 851.3, 1003.4
pat-down search 938.15
pate 10.9, 198.7, 919.6
pâté 10.21
patency 348.3
patent (n) 210.3, 430.8, 443.1, 443.5, 471.4, 642.2, 703.10, 1008.3 (v) 210.5, 397.8, 443.11, 1008.18 (a) 31.7, 348.8, 970.15
patented 210.7, 443.17, 471.8, 1008.21
patentee 479.4
patent log 174.7
patent medicine 86.2, 86.4
patentness 31.2, 348.3
patent note 709.14
patent space 548.7
pater 560.9, 560.10
paterfamilias 76.10, 560.9, 575.1
paterissa 273.2, 702.3
paternal 104.26, 560.17
paternal ancestor 560.9
paternal domicile 228.2
paternalism 612.8
paternalistic 612.16
paternal love 104.4
paternalness 560.2
paternal roof 228.2
paternity 559.1, 560.2
paternity leave 20.2
Paternoster 696.4
paternoster 691.4
path 184.33, 383.1, 383.2, 517.8, 567.5, 1032.4
path-breaking 816.4
pathenogenicity 82.1
pathetic 93.22, 98.20, 145.8, 998.21
pathetic fallacy 312.9
pathfinder 178.1, 405.5, 816.1
pathless 293.10
path of least resistance 383.1
pathogen 85.42
pathogenic 82.5, 85.53, 85.62
pathognomonic 517.23
pathognomonical 517.23
pathognomy 341.8
pathological 85.55, 85.60, 90.15, 308.24
pathological condition 85.1
pathological drinker 88.11
pathological drunkenness 88.3, 926.3
pathological intoxication 926.3
pathological liar 357.9
pathological lying 354.8
pathological personality 92.13
pathologist 307.17
pathology 85.1, 1068.3
pathos 93.5, 98.5, 112.1, 145.1
Pathsounder 30.6
pathway 383.2
patience 106.1, 134.1, 148.1, 360.1, 427.1, 979.4
patience of Job 134.1, 360.1
patient (n) 85.43, 942.7 (a) 106.10, 134.9, 148.6, 360.8, 427.7, 979.11
patient as Job 134.9, 360.8
patientness 134.1
patina 35.7, 44.2, 287.2, 296.2
patinaed 35.22, 44.5
patinate 44.3
patinated 44.5
patination 44.2
patinize 44.3
patinized 44.5
patinous 44.5
patio 197.21
patisserie 10.41
patissier 11.3
patois 523.7, 523.9
pat one on the back 149.2
pat oneself on the back 502.8
pat on the back (n) 149.1, 492.8, 509.6 (v) 121.6, 375.21, 492.15, 509.14
pat on the head 562.16
patria 232.2
patriarch 76.10, 304.2, 560.9, 575.1, 699.10, 842.8
patriarchal 303.16, 560.17, 612.16, 842.11
patriarchal basilica 703.1
patriarchate 417.7, 612.4
patriarchate of Alexandria 675.9
patriarchate of Antioch 675.9
patriarchate of Constantinople 675.9
patriarchate of Jerusalem 675.9
patriarchic 612.16
patriarchical 612.16
patriarchs 560.7
patriarchy 76.3, 417.7, 612.4
patrician (n) 607.4, 608.4 (a) 607.10, 608.10
patriciate 607.2
Patrick Division 749.1
patriclan 559.4
patrifocal 560.17
patrilateral 559.6
patrilineage 559.1
patrilineal 559.6
patriliny 559.1
patrimonial 471.9, 560.19
patrimony 479.2
patriot 232.7, 591.3
patrioteer 591.3
patriotic 591.4
patriotics 591.2
patriotism 104.1, 591.2
patrisib 559.1
patroclinous 559.6, 560.19
patrocliny 559.1, 560.6
patrol (n) 1008.1, 1008.10 (v) 177.20, 1008.20
patrol boat 180.6
patrol car 179.11
patroling 1008.1
patroller 1008.10
patrolman 1008.10, 1008.15
patrol wagon 179.11
patron 221.5, 304.2, 385.6, 478.11, 575.1, 592.1, 616.9, 704.26, 729.10, 733.4, 1008.5
patronage 449.4, 509.4, 609.36, 731.6, 733.3, 1008.2
patroness 478.11, 704.26, 1008.5
patronization 141.1, 729.2
patronize 137.8, 141.8, 449.15, 729.16, 731.17
patronizer 733.4
patronizing (n) 141.1 (a) 141.9
patronizing attitude 141.1
patrons 731.6
patron saint 679.1
patronym 527.5
patroon 575.1
patsy 358.2, 759.22, 862.3, 954.4
patte 199.5
patter (n) 52.3, 55.1, 316.1, 523.9, 704.8, 734.5 (v) 52.15, 55.4, 316.10, 523.18, 540.5, 704.29, 902.16
patterer 524.17, 540.4
pattern (n) 92.32, 262.1, 266.1, 300.2, 321.1, 337.2, 373.3, 373.5, 381.3, 498.7, 659.4, 709.11, 767.2, 786.1, 932.2 (v) 47.7 (a) 720.16
pattern after 336.7
pattern baldness 6.4
pattern bargaining 731.3
pattern-bomb 459.23
patterned 262.9, 266.6
patterning 266.1, 717.4
patternlessness 972.1
pattern on 336.7
patter of tiny feet 1.1
patter the tongue 524.19
patty 10.41
patty shell 10.41
patulous 259.11
pauciloquy 344.2
paucity 885.1, 992.3
Paul 684.2
Pauline Epistles 683.4
Paul Pry 214.4, 981.2
Paul-Pry 214.7
Paul Revere 353.1
paunch 2.18
paunched 257.18
paunchiness 257.8
paunchy 257.18
pauper 619.4
pauperism 619.2
pauperization 619.2
pauperize 619.6
pauperized 619.8, 992.12
pause (n) 20.2, 158.8, 325.2, 524.9, 709.12, 709.21, 813.2, 826.1, 846.2, 857.3, 857.4 (v) 20.8, 325.4, 362.7, 813.3, 826.3, 857.9
pause for station identification 1034.19
pave 295.22, 1043.4
pavé (n) 199.3, 295.9 (v) 498.9
paved 295.31
pavement 199.3, 295.9, 383.6, 901.6, 1054.2
pavement artist 716.4
pavement epithelium 2.4
pave over 295.22
paver of the way 405.5
pavestone 383.6
pave the way 405.12, 1014.7
pave the way for 845.6
pavilion 228.9
paving 199.3, 383.6, 1054.2
paving brick 383.6
paving material 1054.2
paving stone 383.6, 1054.2
Pavlovian conditioning 92.26
Pavlovian psychology 92.2
Pavlovian reaction 963.5
Pavlovian response 934.2
pavonian 45.3, 47.10
pavonine 45.3, 47.10
paw (n) 2.7, 199.5 (v) 73.6
pawed-over 842.18
pawkiness 920.3
pawky 415.12, 920.15
pawmark 517.7
pawn (n) 250.2, 384.4, 438.2, 743.17 (v) 438.10, 621.3
pawnbroker 620.3, 620.4, 622.4, 730.9
pawnbrokery 620.4
pawnbroking 620.1
pawned 438.12
pawning 863.2
pawn off 862.4
pawn off as 350.3
pawnshop 620.4
paw print 517.7
paws 474.4
Pax 696.4
pax 464.1
Pax Dei 465.5
Pax Romana 464.1, 465.5
pay (n) 604.1, 624.4 (v) 328.6, 387.17, 472.13, 506.5, 604.10, 624.10, 626.5, 627.4, 632.8, 831.8
pay a backhanded compliment 156.4
payable 623.10, 639.7
pay a call 12.12
pay a compliment 509.14
pay addresses to 587.12
pay a lefthanded compliment 156.4
pay and allowances 624.4
pay as you go 624.17
pay-as-you-go 624.1
pay at sight 624.17
pay attention 48.10, 339.6, 983.8
pay attentions to 504.11
pay attention to 562.21, 983.5
pay a visit 582.19
pay back 338.4, 481.5, 506.5, 624.11, 658.4, 863.4
payback 338.1, 624.2, 627.1, 738.7
pay back in full measure 506.7
payback time 338.1
pay cash 624.17
pay cash down 624.17
pay cash on delivery 624.17
pay cash on the barrelhead 624.17
paycheck 624.4
pay close attention 983.8
pay COD 624.17
pay conscience money 481.5

pay court to 138.9, 562.21, 587.12
pay damages 481.5
payday 624.4
pay dearly 632.8
pay dirt 1058.7
pay divine honors to 696.11
pay down 506.5
payee 479.3
pay envelope 624.4
payer 624.9
payess 3.5
pay exorbitantly 632.8
pay for 624.18, 729.16
pay heed 983.8
pay heed to 339.6
pay homage to 155.5, 696.11
pay honor to 646.8
pay in 624.10
pay in advance 624.17
pay in full 624.13
paying (n) 624.1 (a) 472.16, 624.21
paying attention 494.1
paying back 481.2
paying guest 227.8, 470.4
paying mind 494.1
paying off 624.1
paying out 477.2, 624.1
paying the bills 624.8
paying up 624.1
pay in installments 624.10
pay in kind 624.11
pay interest 472.13
pay lip service 693.4
payload 196.2, 462.16, 1074.3, 1075.9
paymaster 624.9, 729.12
payment 375.7, 604.1, 624.1, 624.4, 626.1
payment in kind 624.1
payment in lieu 624.2
payments 626.2
pay mind to 983.5
pay more than it's worth 632.8
pay no attention 157.6, 933.2, 984.2
pay no attention to 327.6
pay no mind 933.2, 984.2
pay no regard to 157.6, 435.3, 984.2
pay off 182.23, 182.29, 378.3, 387.17, 472.13, 506.5, 624.13, 627.4, 887.5
payoff 378.2, 624.1, 820.1, 887.1
pay-off, the 356.10
payoff, the 767.3
pay off old scores 506.7
pay off the head 182.23
payola 375.7, 378.2
pay old debts 624.12
pay on 624.10
pay one in his own coin 624.11
pay one in one's own currency 506.6
pay one's addresses to 562.21
pay one's court to 562.21
pay one's debt to society 429.18
pay one's dues 641.10, 658.4
pay one's last respects 115.10
pay one's own way 136.4, 430.20
pay one's respects 504.11
pay one's share 624.18
pay one's way 624.18
pay out 477.8, 604.10, 624.12, 624.14, 626.5
payout 627.1, 738.7
payout ratio 738.7
pay over 624.15
pay packet 624.4
pay-per-view movie 706.1
pay phone 347.4
pay raise 446.1
pay regard to 646.8, 983.5
pay reparations 396.13, 481.5
pay respect to 155.5
payroll 624.4
payroll padding 993.4
pay slip 624.4
pay spot cash 624.17
pay station 347.4
pay strict attention 983.8
pay stub 624.4
pay suit to 562.21
pay television 1035.1
pay the bill 624.13, 624.18, 624.19
pay the bills 478.19
pay the costs 624.18
pay the debt of nature 307.18
pay the debt to nature 307.18
pay the forfeit 658.4
pay the penalty 658.4
pay the piper 604.20, 624.18
pay the shot 624.13
pay through the nose 632.8
pay too much 632.8
pay to the tune of 624.16
pay tribute 150.4, 432.12, 509.12, 646.8
pay tribute to 155.5
pay up 478.14, 506.5, 624.13, 624.16
p-block 1060.2
PBX operator 347.9
PCP 87.18
pea 310.4
peabrain 924.4
pea-brained 922.13
peace 51.1, 87.18, 121.2, 173.1, 455.1, 464.1, 465.5, 788.1, 807.1
peaceable 173.12, 433.15, 464.9, 464.10, 587.15, 670.10
peaceable kingdom 464.1
peaceableness 433.5, 464.4, 587.1
peace agreement 464.7
peace and quiet 464.2
peace feelers 465.2
peaceful 106.12, 121.11, 173.12, 228.33, 287.10, 455.3, 464.9, 670.10
peaceful change 861.1
peaceful coexistence 464.4, 609.5
peaceful death 307.6
peaceful end 307.6
peacefulness 106.2, 121.2, 173.1, 287.1, 464.2
peaceful protest 333.2
peaceful sleep 22.4
peacekeeper 466.5
peacekeeping force 465.1
peacekeeping mission 465.5, 466.1
peace lover 464.6, 466.5
peace-loving 464.10
peacemaker 464.6, 466.5, 670.3
peacemaking 465.1
peacemonger 464.6
peacemongering 465.1
peace movement 464.1, 670.1
peace negotiator 466.5
peacenik 464.6
peace offensive 609.5
peace offer 465.2
peace offering 465.2, 478.4, 658.1, 658.3, 696.7
peace officer 1008.15
Peace of God 465.5
peace of God 464.3
peace of heart 464.3
peace of mind 106.2, 107.1, 464.3
peace of soul 464.3
peace of spirit 464.3
peace overture 465.2
peace pipe 89.6, 465.2
peace sign 465.2
peace talks 148.1
peace that passeth all understanding, the 106.2
peacetime (n) 464.1 (a) 464.9
peace treaty 464.7
peach (n) 310.4, 999.7, 1016.8 (v) 351.6, 551.13 (a) 42.2
peaches-and-cream 35.22
peach fuzz 3.8, 294.3
peachiness 294.3
peachlike 287.10
peachy 3.27, 999.13
peachy keen 999.13
peachy-keen 999.13
peacock (n) 47.6, 76.8, 136.3, 140.5, 311.27, 501.10 (v) 500.13, 501.15
peacock-blue 45.3
peacockery 500.3, 501.8
peacockish 140.11, 501.23
peacockishness 500.3, 501.8
peacocklike 47.10
Peacock throne 417.11
peacocky 140.11, 501.23
peafowl 311.27
peag 728.3
pea-green 44.4
peahen 77.9, 311.27
pea in the shoe 96.3, 1001.1
peak (n) 198.2, 237.6, 238.14, 272.4, 285.4, 524.12, 731.10, 794.5, 1002.3 (v) 85.48, 198.10, 238.22 (a) 198.11
peaked 85.54, 198.13, 270.20
peakedness 85.3, 270.5
peak experience 92.27
peaking 731.10
peaking circuit 1041.6
peaks 237.1
peaky 85.54, 270.20
peal (n) 53.5, 54.3, 56.4, 56.5 (v) 53.7, 53.10, 54.8, 56.9
pealing (n) 54.3 (a) 53.11, 54.13, 56.12
peal of laughter 116.4
peal of thunder 56.5
peal ringing 54.3
pean 647.2
peanut 258.4
peanut brittle 1050.2
peanut gallery 27.8, 704.15
peanut politician 610.4
peanut politics 609.1
peanuts 728.19, 998.4
pear 310.4
pearl (n) 37.2, 282.3, 659.1, 999.5 (a) 37.8, 39.4
pearl diver 367.4
pearl-diver 79.15
pearl diving 367.3
pearl-gray 39.4
Pearl Harbor 459.2
pearlike 279.14
pearliness 37.1, 47.2, 1025.18, 1030.2
pearlish 47.10
pearl-like 1025.37
pearls of wisdom 422.2
pearl-white 37.8
pearly 35.22, 37.8, 39.4, 47.10, 1025.37, 1030.4
pearly gates 87.10
pearly-white 37.8
pearly whites 2.8
pear-shaped 279.14
peart 413.23
peasant 227.10, 497.6, 606.6, 1069.5
peasant farmer 1069.5
peasant holder 1069.5
peasant revolt 327.4
peasantry 233.3
pease cod 310.30
peas in a pod 784.5
pea soup 319.3
peasouper 319.3
pea-soup fog 319.3
pea-soupy 319.10
peat bog 243.1
peat moss 890.4
peaty 1021.9
peavey 906.4
pebble (n) 248.2, 1059.4, 1059.6 (v) 295.22
pebbled 1051.12, 1059.12
pebble-dash 295.25
pebblestone 1059.4
pebbly 1051.12, 1059.12
peccability 654.1
peccable 654.12
peccadillo 655.2
peccancy 654.3, 655.2, 656.1, 975.1, 1000.1
peccant 82.5, 85.60, 393.40, 654.16, 656.3, 975.16, 1000.7
peccant humor 12.6
peck (n) 247.3, 247.4, 902.7 (v) 8.26, 902.18
peck at 8.26, 510.16
pecker 283.8
pecking 8.1
pecking order 607.1, 807.2, 809.4
peckish 100.25
peckishness 100.7
peck of troubles 96.8, 1013.3
Pecksniff 357.8, 693.3

Pecksniffery 354.6
Pecksniffian 354.33
pecten 285.4
pectoral 283.19
pecularity 532.2
peculate 389.4
peculation 389.1
peculator 483.1
peculiar 312.15, 517.23, 780.8, 780.9, 809.7, 865.13, 870.11, 927.5
peculiar expression 529.1
peculiarity 373.3, 500.2, 517.1, 865.4, 870.3, 927.1
peculiarization 865.7
peculiarize 865.9
peculiar thing 870.5
peculiar trait 500.2
pecuniary 728.30, 729.20, 731.23
pecuniary aid 478.8
pecuniary obligation 897.1
pecuniary resources 728.14
pedagese 523.10
pedagogic 571.11
pedagogical 568.19, 571.11
pedagogics 568.1
pedagogist 571.1
pedagogue 571.1
pedagogy 568.1
pedal (n) 906.4 (v) 177.33, 904.9 (a) 199.9
pedal extremity 199.5
pedaling 177.6
pedal point 709.15
pedal pushers 5.18
pedals 711.17
pedal wheel 742.4
pedant 545.5, 867.2, 929.5
pedantic 500.18, 545.8, 568.19, 570.17, 571.11, 580.7, 867.6, 928.22
pedantical 580.7
pedanticism 580.2
pedantism 580.2, 928.5
pedantry 500.5, 580.2, 928.5
peddle 734.9
peddler 730.5
peddler's cart 736.6
peddling 734.2
pederast 75.16
pederasty 75.11
pedes 199.5
pedestal 901.8
pedestrian (n) 178.6 (a) 117.6, 118.9, 177.36, 414.15, 721.5
pedestrian crosswalk 170.2
pedestrianism 177.8, 414.1, 721.2
pedestrianize 117.5, 177.27, 414.10, 721.3
pedestrian light 1026.4
pedestrian mall 736.2
pedi 199.5
pediatric 90.15
pedicab 179.8
pedicel 310.21, 901.8
pedicular 910.11
pediculosis 910.2
pediculous 910.11
pedicure (n) 1016.10 (v) 79.20
pedicurist 1016.12
pedigree 549.9, 560.5, 608.2
pedio 199.5
pedophilia 75.11
pedophiliac 75.16
peduncle 310.21, 901.8
pee, a 12.5
pee (n) 12.5 (v) 12.14
pee in one's pants laughing 116.8
peek (n) 27.4 (v) 27.13, 981.4
peekaboo 1029.4
peek store 759.19
peel (n) 295.3, 296.2, 460.6 (v) 6.8, 255.10, 802.14
peeled 6.14
peeled eye 27.10, 339.4
peeler 707.1, 1008.16
peeling (n) 6.2, 295.3 (a) 6.18
peel off 184.37, 802.9
peel-off 749.3
peel out 222.10, 368.11
peel tower 460.6
peep (n) 27.4, 52.3 (v) 27.13, 60.5, 938.28, 981.4
pee-pee (n) 12.5 (v) 12.14
peeper 2.9, 27.9
peepers 29.3
peephole 27.8
peeping 58.14
Peeping Tom 918.1, 981.2
peep into the future 961.5
peep of day 314.2
peep out 33.8
peep sight 29.5
peer (n) 588.3, 608.4, 790.4 (v) 27.13, 981.3
peerage 608.1, 608.9, 617.3
peer at 938.24
peeress 608.6
peer group 617.3, 617.6, 770.3, 790.4, 836.2
peer into 938.23
peerless 249.15, 999.16, 1002.6
peerlessness 999.2
peer out 33.8
peer pressure 375.3
peer-to-peer 312.15, 617.19
peesash 318.12
peeve (n) 103.3, 115.4, 589.5 (v) 96.13, 152.24
peeved 96.21, 152.27
peevish 108.7, 110.22, 115.19, 589.10
peevishness 108.1, 110.2, 110.6, 115.4, 589.5
peevish person 108.3
pee-wee 302.3
peewee (n) 258.4 (a) 258.11
Pee Wee football 746.1
pee-wee hockey 749.1
peg (n) 2.8, 8.4, 88.7, 245.1, 273.6, 283.3, 293.4, 904.3 (v) 175.7, 177.28, 725.14, 800.8, 904.10, 989.11
peg along 177.27
peg away 330.15, 725.14
peg away at 360.3, 510.13
peg down 428.10
pegged market 737.6
pegged pants 5.18
pegging (n) 904.2 (a) 725.17
peg out 16.9, 307.19, 395.23
peg the market 737.25
peg to hang on 376.1
pejorative 108.7, 156.8, 512.13
pelagic 182.57, 240.8
pelagic zone 240.4, 275.4
pelf 472.3, 618.1, 728.1
pelham 1012.7
pellagra 85.33
pellet (n) 282.2, 462.19 (v) 459.27
pellicle 2.6, 295.12, 296.2
pell-mell 105.4, 810.4
pellucid 521.11, 533.6, 1025.31, 1029.4, 1030.5
pellucidity 521.2, 533.1, 1029.1, 1030.2
pelt (n) 3.2, 4.2, 295.3, 902.4 (v) 316.10, 459.27, 902.16, 904.10, 904.12
peltate 279.19
pelt down 316.10
pelter 757.2
pelting 316.11
pelting rain 316.2
peltry 4.2
pelvis 2.13
pemmican 10.13
pen (n) 196.6, 212.3, 429.7, 429.8, 547.1, 547.13, 712.18, 718.3 (v) 212.5, 429.12, 547.19, 718.6
penal 604.22
penal code 673.5
penal colony 429.8
penal course 751.1
penal institution 429.8
penal interest 623.3
penalization 603.1, 604.1
penalize 598.20, 602.3, 603.4, 604.9
penal measures 603.1
penal retribution 603.1, 604.1
penal servitude 604.2
penal settlement 429.8
penalty 598.9, 603.1, 604.1, 746.3, 749.3, 749.6, 751.3, 752.3, 1012.6
penalty area 752.1
penalty bench 749.1
penalty box 749.1
penalty bully 749.6
penalty kick 752.3
penalty-kick mark 752.1
penalty killer 749.2
penalty shot 749.6
penalty spot 752.1
penance 113.4, 603.1, 658.3, 701.4
pen-and-ink 547.1, 712.12
penates 678.12
pence 728.8
penchant 100.3, 371.5, 896.1
pencil (n) 712.18, 1025.5 (v) 517.19, 547.19, 712.19
pencil drawing 712.12
pencil driver 718.3
penciled 547.22
pencil in 712.19
pencil-pusher 547.13
pencil-pushing 547.1
pencraft 547.2, 547.3, 718.2
pend 202.6
pendant 202.4, 254.1, 784.3
pendency 202.1
pendent 202.9, 971.18
pending 202.9, 202.11, 821.7, 971.18
pendragon 575.9
pen-driver 547.13
pendulant 202.9
pendular 202.9, 916.15
pendulate 362.8, 854.5, 916.10
pendulating 362.10
pendulation 362.2, 854.3, 916.1
penduline 202.9
pendulosity 202.1
pendulous 202.9, 916.15
pendulousness 202.1
pendulum 812.2, 916.9
pendulum motion 850.2
pendulum wheel 916.9
Penelope's web 391.3
peneplain 236.1
penetrability 521.1, 966.3, 1006.4
penetrable 292.21, 521.10, 966.8, 1006.16
penetralia 207.2
penetrant 93.24
penetrate 68.5, 93.14, 189.8, 191.3, 221.7, 292.15, 521.5, 521.9, 797.11, 941.8, 989.13, 1023.10
penetrated with 93.23
penetrate into the mind 931.19
penetrate to the bone 1023.10
penetrating 15.22, 17.14, 58.14, 68.6, 69.10, 93.24, 105.31, 144.23, 275.11, 544.11, 920.16, 1023.14
penetrating eye 27.10
penetrating look 27.5
penetratingness 68.1
penetration 189.1, 191.1, 221.3, 292.3, 797.2, 920.4, 944.2
penfold 429.7
penial 2.29
penicillin 86.29
penile 2.29
penile erection 75.5
pen in 212.5
peninsula 235.1, 283.9
peninsular 283.20
penis 2.13
penis envy 154.1
penitence 113.4, 658.2, 658.3, 696.7
penitent (n) 113.5 (a) 113.9, 696.16
Penitente 667.2
penitent form 703.14
penitential 113.9, 338.6, 658.7, 667.4
penitential act 658.3
penitential exercise 658.3
penitential prayer 696.4
penitentiary (n) 429.8, 699.5 (a) 113.9
penman 547.13, 718.3, 718.4
penmanship 547.3
penna 3.16
pen name 527.8
pennant 400.1, 647.7
pennate 3.27, 3.28

penne 10.33
penned 212.10, 547.22
penned in 429.19
penner 547.13, 718.3
penniless 473.8, 619.9
penniless man 619.4
pennilessness 619.2
penning 429.1
pennon 647.7
pennoncel 647.7
Pennsylvania Dutch 523.7
Pennsylvania German 523.7
penny 728.7, 728.8, 998.5
penny-a-liner 547.16, 718.5
penny-ante 248.6, 250.6, 391.11
penny bank 729.13
penny loafers 5.27
penny pincher 484.4
penny-pinching (n) 484.3 (a) 484.9
pennywise 484.7, 635.6
penny-wise and pound-foolish 484.7, 486.8
pennyworth 630.2, 633.3
penological 604.22
penologist 604.8
penology 604.1, 673.7
pen pal 553.8
pen pusher 718.3
penpusher 550.1
pen-pushing 547.1
penscript 547.3, 547.10
pensile 202.9
pensileness 202.1
pensility 202.1
pension (n) 228.15, 478.8, 729.3 (v) 447.4, 478.19
pensionable age 303.5
pensionary (n) 432.6, 479.4 (a) 478.26
pensione 228.15
pensioned 448.3
pensioned off 390.10, 448.3
pensioner 432.6, 479.4, 572.7, 577.3
pension fund 728.14
pensioning 448.1
pensioning off 390.1, 447.2, 448.1
pension off 390.8, 447.4, 448.2, 478.19, 909.19
pension plan 728.14
pension program 624.6
pensive 111.3, 112.23, 931.21, 931.22, 985.11
pensiveness 112.5, 931.3, 986.8
penstock 239.3, 239.11
pent 429.19
pentachord 709.8, 882.1
pentacle 882.1
pentad (n) 882.1 (a) 882.17
pentadic 882.17
pentagon 882.1
pentagonal 278.10, 882.17
Pentagonese 523.10
pentagram 882.1
pentahedral 278.10
pentahedron 882.1
pentalpha 882.1
pentameter 720.7, 882.1
pentapody 720.7, 882.1
pentarchy 882.1
pentastich 720.10, 882.1
pentastyle 882.17
Pentateuch 673.8, 683.3, 882.1
pentathlon 755.2, 882.1
pentatomic 1038.18
pentatonic scale 709.6
pentavalent 882.17
pentecostalism 692.3
penthouse 228.5, 228.13, 295.6
pentobarbital 86.12
pentomic division 461.22
Pentothal 86.15
pentrough 239.3
pent-up 212.10, 428.13, 429.19
pent-up in the memory 989.22
penumbra 467.3, 1027.3
penumbral 1027.16
pen up 212.7, 429.12
penurious 484.8
penuriousness 484.2, 619.2
penury 619.2
penwoman 547.15, 718.4
peon 138.3, 432.7, 577.1, 606.6
peonage 138.1, 432.1, 577.12
peonize 432.8
people (n) 227.1, 559.2, 559.4, 559.5, 700.1 (v) 159.17, 225.9
people, the 312.1, 312.4, 606.1
people at large 227.1
people carrier 179.13
peopled 225.12
people-hater 590.2
people-hating (n) 590.1 (a) 590.3
peoplehood 232.6
people in general 606.1
people in the front office, the 574.11, 575.14
peoplement 225.2
people meter 1035.2
people of fashion 578.6
people's front 609.33
people skills 582.3
people's mandate 417.1
People's Party 609.24
people's republic 232.1
people upstairs, the 574.11, 575.14
peopling 159.7, 225.2
pep 17.3, 330.2, 544.4
pepless 331.20
pepo 10.38
pepper (n) 17.3 (v) 47.7, 63.7, 459.22, 517.19, 771.6, 904.10, 904.12
pepper-and-salt 39.5
peppercorn 998.5
peppered 47.13, 292.19, 771.10
pepper grinder 1051.7
pepperiness 68.2, 68.4, 110.4
peppering 771.1
pepper mill 1051.7
pepper spray 462.22
peppery 68.7, 110.25
pep pill 86.9
pep pills 87.4
peppiness 330.2
peppy 17.13, 330.17, 544.12
pep rally 375.4
pepsin 7.9, 7.10
pepsinate 1060.8
pep talk 375.4, 543.2
peptic 7.22
peptic digestion 2.17, 7.8
peptic ulcer 85.29
peptide 7.6
pep up 17.10, 797.12
Pepys 719.3
perambulate 177.20, 177.27, 177.29
perambulating 177.36
perambulation 177.8
perambulator 179.6
perambulatory 177.36
per capita 477.13
perceivable 31.6, 348.8
perceive 24.6, 27.12, 93.10, 521.9, 928.12, 934.4, 941.5
perceived 928.26
perceiver 918.1
percent 1017.7
percentage 375.7, 387.4, 471.4, 472.3, 477.5, 631.1, 793.1, 995.1, 1017.7, 1017.12
percentages 745.4
percept 24.1, 932.2
perceptibility 24.2, 31.1
perceptible 24.14, 31.6, 300.14, 348.8, 928.25
perception 24.1, 27.1, 93.1, 919.1, 920.4, 928.2, 932.1, 944.2
perceptive 24.11, 27.21, 920.16, 928.15, 934.5, 944.8, 986.18
perceptiveness 24.3, 944.2
perceptivity 24.3
perch (n) 228.23, 901.5 (v) 159.17, 173.10, 194.7, 225.7, 901.22
perching 311.48
perching bird 311.27
percipience 920.4
percipiency 920.4
percipient (n) 918.1 (a) 24.9, 920.16, 928.15
percolate 79.22, 190.15, 238.18, 889.7, 1064.5, 1065.11, 1065.13
percolate in 187.13, 570.7
percolate into 189.10
percolating (n) 190.6 (a) 292.20
percolation 79.4, 187.6, 189.1, 190.6, 238.7, 1064.1, 1065.3, 1065.7
percolative 190.20
percolator 79.13
percuss 902.13
percussion 53.3, 671.8, 711.16, 902.3
percussion cap 462.15
percussion instrument 711.16
percussionist 710.10
percussive 902.24
percutaneous 91.17
Percy 77.10
perdition 395.1, 473.1, 682.1
perdontist 90.6
perdurability 827.1, 829.1
perdurable 827.10, 829.7
perdure 827.6
perduring 827.10
peregrinate 177.20, 177.21, 177.23
peregrination 177.3, 177.5
peregrinations 177.2
peregrinative 177.36
peregrinator 178.2
peregrine (n) 178.2 (a) 177.36
peregrinity 177.3
peremptoriness 417.3, 970.6
peremptory 417.16, 420.12, 420.13, 641.15, 960.2, 970.22
peremptory refusal 442.2
perennate 827.6
perennial (n) 310.3, 310.33 (a) 310.44, 812.8, 827.10, 829.8, 847.5, 850.8
perenniality 827.1, 829.1
perennialize 829.5
perennialness 829.1
pererrate 164.4, 177.23
pererration 164.1
perestroika 78.1, 392.5, 396.5, 808.7, 852.1
perfect (n) 530.12 (v) 249.6, 392.11, 407.6, 820.8, 1002.5 (a) 247.12, 407.12, 430.27, 677.17, 794.10, 960.2, 973.16, 1002.6
perfecta 759.4
perfect binding 554.14
perfect cadence 709.23
perfected 392.13, 820.9, 1002.9
perfect example 767.2
perfect fool 924.1
perfect game 750.2
perfect gentleman 659.1
perfectibilism 124.2
perfectibilist 124.5
perfectibilitarian (n) 124.5 (a) 124.11
perfectible 392.17
perfecting (n) 392.4 (a) 198.12, 820.11
perfection 392.2, 407.2, 794.4, 820.1, 973.5, 1002.1, 1002.3
perfectionism 124.2, 495.1, 636.2
perfectionist (n) 124.5, 495.6, 867.2 (a) 124.11, 944.8
perfectionistic 495.9
perfections 1016.3
perfective (n) 530.13 (a) 407.11, 794.13, 820.11, 837.9
perfective aspect 837.5
perfect lady 659.1
perfect likeness 349.5
perfectly sure 970.13
perfect participle 530.3, 530.4
perfect pitch 708.31, 709.4
perfect silence 51.1
perfect specimen 1002.4
perfect storm 96.9
perfect tense 837.5
perfect usufruct 387.7
perfect wreck 393.8
perfect year 824.2
perfervid 101.9, 101.12, 926.32
perfervidness 926.11
perfidious 354.31, 645.21
perfidious Albion 232.4
perfidiousness 645.6
perfidy 645.6
perflation 317.9
perforate (v) 292.15 (a) 292.19
perforated 292.19
perforation 292.3
perforator 1040.2

perform 328.9, 348.5, 349.12, 407.4, 434.3, 704.29, 708.39, 889.5, 889.7, 892.11
performability 889.3, 966.2
performable 889.10, 966.7
perform aerobatics 184.40
performance 328.2, 328.3, 348.2, 349.4, 407.1, 434.1, 580.4, 704.8, 704.12, 708.30, 708.33, 889.1, 892.5
performance anxiety 126.1
performance art 704.2
performance artist 707.1
perform a part 704.30
perform a part in 476.5
perform a procedure 91.24
perform a rite 701.15
perform a role 704.30
perform as 724.13
perform a volte-face 163.10
perform divine service 701.15
performed 892.17
performer 500.7, 707.1, 710.1, 726.1
performing (n) 349.4, 704.8, 889.1 (a) 328.10
performing area 704.16
performing arts 704.1
performing arts school 567.7
perform magic 852.8
perform one's duty 641.10
perform service 701.15
perform surgery 90.14
perform the act of lov 75.21
perform the duties of 724.13
perform the marriage act 75.21
perfrication 1044.1
perfume (n) 70.1, 70.2, 1016.11 (v) 69.7, 70.8, 1067.8
perfumed 70.9
perfume dynamics 70.1
perfumer 70.5, 70.6
perfumery 70.2
perfuming 70.5
perfumy 70.9
perfunctoriness 102.1, 325.1, 340.2
perfunctory 102.6, 325.5, 325.6, 340.11
perfuse 91.27, 176.10, 189.10, 191.3, 221.7
perfused 221.15
perfusion 190.6, 191.1, 221.3
perfusive 221.14
pergola 197.18, 228.12
perhaps 951.4
per head 477.13
peri 678.8, 1016.9
Periander 921.4
perianth 310.28
periapt 691.5
pericardium 2.6
pericarp 295.15, 310.30
pericranium 198.8
periculous 1006.9
pericynthion 1075.2
periderm 295.3
peridium 295.3
perigee 223.3, 1073.16, 1075.2
perihelion 223.3, 1073.16
peril (n) 971.6, 1006.1 (v) 1006.6
perilous 971.20, 1006.9
perilousness 971.6, 1006.2
perilune 1075.2
perilymph 2.10
perimenopausal 303.14
perimenopause 303.4, 303.7
perimeter 209.1, 211.1
perimetric 209.8, 211.14
perimetrical 211.14
perineum 2.13
perineurium 2.6
period 12.9, 158.8, 245.1, 313.1, 529.1, 708.24, 720.7, 746.3, 749.3, 749.6, 752.3, 820.1, 821.1, 824.1, 857.4, 916.4, 1060.2, 1073.16
period furniture 229.1
periodic 313.9, 812.8, 847.5, 849.13, 850.7, 916.15
periodical (n) 352.1, 555.1 (a) 555.5, 850.7
periodicalness 850.2
periodicity 313.1, 812.2, 850.2, 916.1
periodic sentence 529.1
periodic table 1060.2
periodic table of elements 1060.2
periodic wave 916.4
period of existence 827.5
periodontal tissue 2.8, 2.12
periodontic 90.15
period piece 824.1
period style 498.7
periosteum 2.6
Peripatetic 952.12
peripatetic (n) 178.2, 178.6 (a) 177.36, 177.37, 538.13
peripateticate 177.27
peripatetic exercise 177.10
Peripateticism 952.3
peripateticism 177.10
peripatetic journey 177.10
peripatetics 177.2
Peripatetic school 952.3
peripeteia 722.4
peripheral (n) 254.4, 1042.3, 1042.9 (a) 206.7, 209.8, 211.14, 218.6, 773.8
peripheral device 1042.3
peripheral field 27.1
peripheral nervous system 2.14
peripheral speed 184.31
peripheral unit 1042.3
peripheral vision 27.1
periphery 206.2, 209.1, 211.1, 257.1
periphrase (n) 538.5 (v) 538.10
periphrasis 538.5
periphrastic 538.14
periplus 182.1
periscope 367.5
perish 34.2, 307.18, 395.23, 762.6, 842.9
perishability 828.1
perishable 307.33, 828.7
perished 762.11
perishing (n) 307.1 (a) 307.32, 1023.14
perishing with hunger 100.25
perish with the cold 1023.9
perissodactyl 311.5
peristalsis 2.17
peristyle 197.18, 273.5
peritoneal cavity 2.16
peritoneum 2.6, 2.16
periwig 3.14
periwigged 3.26
perjure 354.20
perjured 354.34, 645.18
perjure oneself 354.20, 645.12
perjurer 357.9
perjury 354.9, 598.12, 645.3
perk (n) 254.4, 375.7, 472.3 (v) 889.7 (a) 140.11
perkiness 17.4, 109.3, 140.4
perks 472.3, 478.5, 482.11, 624.6
perk up 9.2, 17.10, 83.7, 109.9, 392.7, 396.19, 912.5
perky 109.11, 109.12, 140.11, 330.17
perlative 530.9
perlustrate 938.25
perlustration 938.3
perm 1016.14
permafrost 1023.7
permanence 360.1, 827.1, 829.1, 853.1, 855.4
permanency 853.1
permanent (n) 3.15, 1016.14 (a) 35.18, 360.8, 677.17, 827.10, 829.7, 853.7, 855.17
permanent magnet 907.3
permanent residence 228.1
permanent student 929.3
permanent tooth 2.8
permanent wave 3.15
permeability 292.9, 1032.7
permeable 190.20, 292.21
permeate 221.7, 797.11, 1065.13
permeate by nature 767.6
permeated 221.15, 1065.17
permeation 221.3, 797.2, 1065.7
permissibility 443.8
permissible 443.15
permissibleness 443.8
permission 332.4, 417.12, 430.8, 441.1, 443.1
permissions editor 554.2
permission to enter 443.1
permissive (n) 530.11 (a) 340.10, 418.5, 426.5, 427.8, 430.25, 430.27, 441.4, 443.14
permissiveness 340.1, 418.1, 426.2, 427.3, 430.3, 443.2, 979.4
permit (n) 443.6 (v) 332.12, 441.2, 443.9, 966.5
permit all 426.3, 443.12
permit anything 426.3, 443.12
permit of 443.9, 966.5
permitted 430.30, 443.16
permitting 443.14
permutability 854.1, 863.3
permutable 854.6, 863.5
permutation 852.3, 863.1
permute 863.4
pernicious 308.23, 1000.12
pernicious anemia 85.33
perniciousness 308.9, 1000.5
pernicious weed 89.1
pernicketiness 495.2
pernickety 495.10
perorate 538.8, 543.10, 820.6
peroration 543.2, 817.1, 820.1, 849.2
peroxide 36.5
peroxide blond 35.9
peroxide-blond 37.9
peroxidize 1060.8
perp 593.1, 645.10, 660.9
perpend 931.12
perpendicular (n) 200.2, 277.2, 278.2 (a) 200.12, 278.7
perpendicular distance 272.1
perpendicularity 200.1, 277.1
perpetrate 328.6
perpetration 328.2
perpetrator 593.1, 645.10, 660.9, 726.1
perpetual 677.17, 812.8, 823.3, 827.10, 829.7, 847.5, 853.7
perpetual calendar 832.8
perpetual motion 172.2
perpetualness 829.1, 853.1
perpetuate 823.2, 829.5, 856.4
perpetuation 827.2, 829.4, 856.1
perpetuity 267.1, 823.1, 827.1, 829.1, 847.2
perplex (n) 799.2 (v) 122.6, 522.10, 799.3, 955.7, 971.13, 985.7, 1012.15, 1013.13
perplexed 522.14, 799.4, 971.25, 985.12, 1013.24
perplexed question 522.8
perplexing 522.17, 971.27
perplexity 522.3, 522.8, 799.1, 971.3, 985.3, 1013.7
perp walk 604.2
perquisite 254.4, 472.3, 478.5, 482.11, 624.6
perquisited 385.13
perquisites 471.2, 624.6
perquisition 938.15
perquisitor 938.18
perron 193.3
perscrutate 938.25
perscrutation 938.4
persecute 96.13, 126.5, 389.7, 604.15, 1000.6
persecuted 96.24, 126.8
persecution 96.2, 96.7, 389.3
persecution complex 92.22
persecutor 96.10
Persephassa 682.5
Persephone 682.5, 1069.4
perserving 361.8
perseverance 134.1, 359.1, 360.1, 361.1, 781.1, 817.1, 827.1, 829.1, 853.1, 856.1
perseverant 360.8
perseverate 856.5
persevere 134.5, 360.2, 361.7, 409.13, 725.13, 781.3, 827.6, 855.11, 856.5
persevering 134.9, 359.11, 360.8, 725.17
Persian sibyl 962.6
persiflage 489.7, 490.1
persist 306.11, 360.2, 421.8, 761.9, 781.3, 803.6, 827.6, 853.5, 855.11, 856.5
persistence 359.1, 360.1, 421.4, 781.1, 803.3, 827.1, 853.1, 856.1
persistency 360.1, 803.3, 853.1

persistent 54.12, 359.11, 360.8, 373.14, 421.9, 781.5, 803.12, 827.10, 853.7, 856.7, 989.25
persistent vegetative state 22.6
persist in 474.5
persisting 360.8, 827.10
persnicketiness 339.3, 495.2
persnickety 339.12, 495.10, 766.9
person 262.4, 312.5, 530.7, 704.10, 763.3, 872.4, 1052.3
person, the 2.1
persona 92.28, 216.1, 722.5, 763.3, 872.4
personable 894.13, 1016.18
personableness 1016.2
person after one's own heart 659.1
personage 312.5, 575.3, 662.9, 704.10, 997.8
persona grata 659.1
personal 312.15, 345.13, 517.24, 865.12
personal ad 352.6
personal adviser 422.3
personal aims 651.1
personal ambition 651.1
personal appearance 704.12
personal assistant 432.5
personal attack 459.1, 512.2
personal attendant 577.8
personal best 407.2
personal choice 371.5
personal computer 1042.2
personal conflict 589.1
personal correspondence 553.1
personal day 20.3
personal desires 651.1
personal digital assistant 582.8, 1042.2
personal effects 385.4, 471.2
personal equation 865.1
personal file 549.5
personal finance 729.3
personal guarantee 436.1
personal identification number 517.11
personal identity 865.1
personal initiative 430.7
personalism 651.1, 1053.3
personalistic 651.5
personality 92.28, 312.5, 763.3, 865.1, 894.1, 997.8
personality conflict 93.7
personality cult 662.6
personality disintegration 92.20
personality disorder 92.15
personality disorganization 92.20
personality tendency 92.11
personalization 780.4, 865.7
personalize 536.2, 780.6, 865.9
personalizing 780.9
personal judgment 953.6
personal letter 553.2
personal matter 345.5
personal note 549.4
personal organizer 808.5, 1042.2
personal pronoun 530.5
personal property 471.2
personal responsibility 430.7
personal shopper 733.5
personal sonar 30.6
personal space 158.7
personal stereo 50.8, 549.10
personal style 532.2, 578.1
personal time 20.3
personal time off 20.3
personal touch 478.4
personal usage 523.1
persona non grata 586.4, 660.1, 773.3
personate 349.11, 349.12, 704.30
personation 349.4, 704.8
personator 357.7
personhood 92.28, 312.5, 872.4
personification 349.4, 1052.8
personify 349.11, 536.2, 1052.9
personifying 349.13
person in charge 574.1
person in holy orders 699.2
personkind 312.1
personnel 18.9, 577.11, 726.2, 745.2, 746.2, 747.2
personnel management 573.4
person of breeding 607.4
person of consequence 662.9, 997.8
person of fashion 578.7
person of honor 644.8
person of importance 997.8
person of influence 894.6
person of mark 662.9, 997.8
person of means 618.7
person of mettle 492.7
person of note 662.9, 997.8
person of old 842.7
person of opposite sex sharing living quarters 588.1
person of renown 997.8
person of substance 618.7
person of taste 496.5
person of wealth 618.7
person of wisdom 921.1
person on the bench 596.1
person on the run 368.5
persons 312.1, 606.1
personship 865.1
persons of color 312.2
persons of the drama 707.11
person to be reckoned with, a 894.6
person to be reckoned with 997.8
person to look up to 659.4
person-to-person 312.15
person-to-person call 347.13
perspective 27.7, 31.3, 33.6, 159.2, 261.1, 712.8, 978.2
perspicacious 920.16, 928.15, 944.8
perspicaciousness 920.4
perspicacity 27.1, 920.4, 944.2
perspicuity 27.1, 348.3, 521.2, 533.1, 920.4
perspicuous 348.8, 521.11, 533.6, 920.16
perspicuousness 521.2, 920.4
perspiration 2.24, 12.7
perspiration odor 12.7
perspire 12.16, 13.5
perspiring (n) 12.7 (a) 2.33, 12.22
perspiry 12.22
persuadability 894.5, 954.2, 979.3
persuadable 894.15, 954.9, 979.10
persuadableness 894.5, 979.3
persuade 375.23, 422.6, 858.16, 894.7, 953.18, 973.9
persuaded 441.4, 953.21, 970.21
persuadedness 953.1
persuade oneself 375.24, 953.19
persuader 375.10
persuading 375.29
persuasibility 894.5, 979.3
persuasible 894.15, 923.12, 979.10
persuasion 375.3, 617.5, 675.1, 675.3, 770.3, 809.3, 858.6, 894.1, 953.5
persuasive (n) 375.7 (a) 375.29, 894.13, 953.26
persuasiveness 953.8, 973.6
pert 109.13, 140.11, 142.10, 330.17, 454.7, 666.6
pertain 775.5
pertaining 775.7, 775.11
pertain to 469.7, 775.5
perthophyte 310.4
pertinacious 360.8, 361.8, 421.9, 492.17
pertinaciousness 360.1, 421.4, 492.5
pertinacity 360.1, 361.1, 421.4, 492.5
pertinence 518.1, 775.4
pertinency 518.1, 775.4
pertinent 775.7, 775.11, 788.10
pertness 17.4, 109.3, 140.4, 142.2, 454.1, 666.2
perturb 96.16, 105.14, 810.9, 811.4, 917.10, 971.12, 985.7, 1013.13
perturbability 105.10
perturbable 105.28
perturbate 917.10
perturbation 105.4, 105.11, 126.1, 127.5, 810.1, 811.1, 917.1, 971.3, 985.3
perturbed 96.22, 105.23, 126.7, 810.13, 917.16, 971.24, 985.12, 1013.20
perturbing 105.30, 971.27
Peru-Chile 275.5
peruke 3.14
peruked 3.26
perusal 570.3, 938.3
peruse 27.14, 570.12, 938.24
Peruvian marching powder 87.7
pervade 221.7, 797.11
pervading 93.24, 221.14
pervasion 221.3, 797.2
pervasive 93.24, 221.14, 794.10
pervasiveness 794.1, 864.2
perve 75.16
perverse 110.19, 335.5, 361.11, 451.8, 779.6, 789.9, 900.8, 975.16, 1013.19
perverse fool 361.6
perverseness 361.3, 451.2, 900.1
perversion 75.11, 265.2, 342.1, 350.1, 354.9, 389.1, 393.2, 569.1, 654.5, 936.1, 975.1
perversity 110.2, 335.1, 361.3, 779.1
pervert (n) 75.16, 660.4 (v) 265.6, 342.2, 350.3, 354.16, 389.4, 393.12, 569.3, 936.8
perverted 265.11, 342.3, 354.26, 654.14, 975.16
per vigilium 23.1
pervious 190.20, 292.21, 894.15, 966.8
perviousness 292.9, 894.5, 966.3
pes 199.5
pescatarian 668.4
pescatarianism 668.2
pescetarian 668.4
peskiness 98.7
pesky 98.22, 440.18
pessary 86.23
pessimism 112.3, 125.6, 130.3, 335.1, 950.1
pessimist (n) 112.14, 125.7 (a) 125.16
pessimistic 112.22, 125.16
pest 85.5, 96.2, 96.10, 118.4, 311.32, 1001.1, 1001.2
pester 96.13, 440.12, 510.16
pestered 96.24
pesterer 96.10
pestering (n) 440.3, 510.4 (a) 98.22, 440.18
pesthole 80.11, 85.5
pesthouse 91.22
pesticide 308.11, 1001.3
pestiferous 82.5, 82.7, 85.62, 98.22
pestiferousness 85.4, 98.7
pestilence 85.5, 1001.1
pestilent 82.7, 85.62, 98.22
pestilential 82.7, 85.62, 98.22
pestle (n) 1051.7 (v) 1051.9
pestled 1051.11
pestling 1051.4
pesto 10.12
pesty 98.22, 440.18
pet (n) 104.14, 104.15, 152.7, 311.2, 562.6 (v) 73.8, 427.6, 562.15, 562.16, 1044.6 (a) 104.23
petal 310.19, 310.28
petcock 239.10
pete blower 483.3
petechia 12.8, 85.37
Peter 684.2
peter 87.6
peterman 483.3
peter out 16.9, 21.6, 132.3, 388.4, 410.13, 762.6, 820.7, 891.3, 911.3
Peter Pan syndrome 301.3, 922.11
Peter's pence 478.6
pet expression 526.9
pet food 10.4
petiole 310.21
petiolule 310.21
petiolus 310.21
petit 998.17
petit-bourgeois 607.10
petit bourgeoisie 607.6

petit déjeuner 8.6
petite 258.10
petiteness 258.1
petite noblesse 608.3
petit four 10.42
petit-four 10.42
petition (n) 440.1, 696.4 (v) 440.10, 696.13
petitionary 440.16
petitionary prayer 696.4
petitioner 440.7, 599.5, 696.9
petitioning 440.1
petition nomination 609.11
Petition of Right 430.2
petitio principii 280.2
petit-juror 596.6
petit jury 596.5
petit-juryman 596.6
petit larceny 482.2
petkins 562.6
pet name 527.7
pet peeve 103.3, 115.4, 589.5
petrescent 1059.11
Petri dish 861.1
petrifaction 1059.8
petrifactive 1046.10, 1046.14
petrification 842.6, 1046.5, 1059.8
petrified 127.26, 842.13, 1046.13, 1058.15, 1059.11
petrified forest 842.6
petrified wood 842.6
petrify 122.6, 127.17, 1046.7, 1058.13, 1059.10
petrifying 127.29, 1046.14
petrochemistry 1059.9
petrogenesis 1059.9
petrogenic 1059.11
petroglyph 842.6
petrographer 1058.12
petrography 1058.10
petrol 1025.20
petroleum 1025.20, 1056.4
petroleum jelly 1056.2
petrological 1058.18
petrologist 1058.12
petrology 1058.10, 1059.9
PET scan 91.9
pet subject 866.1
petticoat 77.13
petticoat government 612.5
pettifog 510.15, 935.16
pettifogger 357.3, 510.9, 597.1, 936.7
pettifoggery 356.4, 936.5
pettifogging (n) 356.4, 510.4 (a) 510.23, 998.20
pettiness 248.1, 250.3, 651.2, 661.3, 980.1, 998.1, 998.3
petting 73.2, 427.3, 562.2
pettish 110.22
pettishness 110.6
petty 248.6, 250.7, 651.6, 661.12, 936.14, 980.10, 998.20
petty-bourgeois 607.10
petty cash 386.3, 728.14, 728.19
petty cashbook 549.11
petty criticism 510.4
petty gambler 759.21
petty grafter 483.1
petty king 575.8
petty larceny 482.2
petty matter 766.3
petty mind 980.1
petty-minded 980.10
petty officer 575.17
petty officer first class 575.19
petty officer second class 575.19
petty officer third class 575.19
petty politics 609.1
petty theft 482.2
petty thief 483.1
petty treason 645.7
petty tyrant 575.13, 575.15
petulance 108.1, 110.6, 115.4, 364.2
petulancy 110.6
petulant 108.7, 110.22, 115.19, 364.5, 935.19
petulant person 108.3
petuntse 742.3
petuntze 742.3
pew 197.2, 703.14
pewter (n) 39.1 (a) 1058.17
pewtery 1058.17
Pfannkuchen 10.45
pffft 589.11, 762.11, 820.10
P-funk 87.9
pH 1060.3
phablet 1042.2
Phaëthon 1073.14
phage 85.42
phalansterian (n) 611.14 (a) 611.22
phalansterism 611.6
phalanx 461.22, 770.3
phallic 2.29
phallicism 75.10, 76.2, 697.1
phallic symbol 92.30
phallic worship 697.1
phallic worshiper 697.4
phallus 2.13
phantasm 356.1, 976.4, 986.5, 988.1
phantasma 976.4, 988.1
phantasmagoria 33.7, 976.4
phantasmagoric 976.9
phantasmal 976.9, 986.22, 988.7
phantasmic 988.7
phantom (n) 33.5, 37.2, 127.9, 764.3, 976.4, 986.5, 988.1 (a) 976.9, 988.7, 1053.7
phantom bug 1042.11
phantomic 988.7
phantomical 988.7
phantomlike 764.6, 988.7
phantom limb pain 26.2
phantom of the mind 976.4
pharaoh 575.9, 575.13
pharisaic 354.33, 693.5
pharisaical 354.33, 693.5
pharisaicalness 693.1
Pharisaism 675.12
pharisaism 354.6
pharisaism 693.1
pharisean 354.33
Pharisee 675.21, 693.3
pharisee 357.8, 693.3
pharmaceutical 86.4
pharmaceutical chemist 86.35
pharmaceutics 86.34
pharmaceutist 86.35
pharmacist 86.35
pharmacogenetics 560.6
pharmacognosy 86.4
pharmacokinetic metabolism 2.20
pharmacologist 86.35
pharmacology 86.34
pharmacopedia 86.37
pharmacopoeia 86.37
pharmacopolist 86.35
pharmacopsychosis 926.3
pharmacy 86.34, 86.36, 197.25
pharmafood 10.1
pharos 27.8, 517.10
pharyngeal cavity 524.18
pharyngealization 524.12
pharyngealized 524.30
pharynx 2.18, 524.18
phase 33.3, 765.2
phase adjustment 1036.8
phased 245.5
phase down 255.9, 390.4, 820.6, 857.12
phasedown 255.2; 820.1, 857.1
phase in 245.4
phase modulation 1034.14
phase out 245.4, 252.7, 390.4, 820.6, 857.12
phaseout 390.2, 820.1, 857.1
phases of the moon 854.4
phasing 245.3
phasm 33.5
phat 999.13
phatic 520.6
phatic communion 520.1
Pheidippides 353.1
phelloderm 295.3
phellum 295.3
phenacetin 86.12
phennies 87.5
phenobarbital 86.12
phenom 122.2, 409.4, 409.6, 413.12
phenomenal 122.10, 831.10, 870.14
phenomenalness 122.3
phenomenology 978.2
phenomenon 33.5, 122.2, 761.2, 831.2
phenos 87.5
phenylketonuria 85.22
pheon 647.2
pheromonal 69.9
pheromone 13.2, 69.5
Philadelphia lawyer 415.6, 597.1, 935.12
Philadelphia layout 759.16
philander (n) 562.10, 562.12 (v) 562.20, 665.19
philanderer 104.12, 562.12, 665.10
philandering 562.10
philanthropic 143.15, 478.22
philanthropical 478.22
philanthropies 143.6
philanthropism 143.4
philanthropist 143.8, 478.11, 485.2
philanthropize 478.17
philanthropy 143.4, 478.3
philharmonic (n) 708.33 (a) 708.47
philharmonic concert 708.33
philharmonic person 710.21
philharmonic pitch 709.4
philippic 510.7, 543.2
Philippine Trench 275.5
Philistine (n) 497.6, 867.2 (a) 94.12, 497.14, 695.16, 930.13
Philistinism 695.2, 930.4
philistinism 25.1, 94.3, 497.1, 497.3
philobiblist 554.18, 929.4
philologaster 523.15, 929.6
philologer 523.15
philologian 523.15
philological 518.12, 523.19
philologist 523.15, 526.15, 929.3
philologue 929.3
philology 523.13
philomath 929.3
Philomel 710.23
philosophaster 929.6, 952.8
philosophastering 952.1
philosophastry 952.1
philosophe 929.3, 952.8
philosopheme 935.7
philosopher 921.1, 929.3, 935.11, 952.8
philosopher king 921.1
philosopher's stone 86.3, 618.5, 858.10
philosophic 952.10
philosophical 106.12, 134.9, 920.18, 952.10
philosophical attitude 433.1
philosophical basis 932.4
philosophical idealism 1053.3
philosophical induction 935.3
philosophical inquiry 952.1
philosophical investigation 952.1
philosophicalness 106.2
philosophical optimism 124.2
philosophical optimist 124.5
philosophical pitch 709.4
philosophical proposition 935.7
philosophical speculation 952.1
philosophical system 952.2
philosophical unitarianism 952.5
philosophic composure 106.2
philosophic doctrine 952.1
philosophicohistorical 952.10
philosophicojuristic 952.10
philosophicolegal 952.10
philosophicopsychological 952.10
philosophicoreligious 952.10
philosophicotheological 952.10
philosophic system 952.1
philosophic theory 952.1
philosophism 936.1, 936.3
philosophist 936.6
philosophistic 936.10
philosophistical 936.10
philosophize 935.15, 952.9
philosophizer 952.8
philosophy 106.2, 932.8, 935.1, 952.1, 953.3, 1018.1
philosophy branch 952.1
philosophy of history 719.1
philosophy of the Academy 952.3
philosophy of the Garden 952.3
philosophy of the Lyceum 952.3

philosophy of the Porch 952.3
philsophy of the Stoa 952.3
philter 75.6, 691.5
phiz 216.4
phlebotomize 91.27, 192.12
phlebotomy 91.20, 192.3
Phlegethon 682.4
phlegm 2.24, 13.3, 94.4, 102.2, 331.6, 467.2
phlegmatic (n) 92.12 (a) 94.13, 123.3, 173.14, 331.20, 982.3
phlegmaticalness 94.4
phlegmaticness 94.4, 123.1
phlegmy 2.33, 1062.13
phloem 305.6
pho 10.10
phobia 103.1, 103.3, 127.1
phobic (n) 103.4 (a) 92.39, 127.22
Phoebe 1073.12
phoebe 882.1
Phoebus 1073.14
Phoebus Apollo 1073.14
phoenix 659.5
phoenixlike 78.14, 396.24
phon 50.7
phonate 524.22
phonation 524.2, 524.5
phone (n) 50.1, 347.4, 524.12 (v) 347.19
phone book 347.12, 554.9, 574.10
phone call 347.13
phone card 347.4
phonecard 622.3
phone-in show 1034.18
phone it in 222.7
phonemail 347.13
phoneme 523.14, 524.12
phonemic 523.19, 524.30
phonemic alphabet 546.3
phonemicist 523.15
phone number 347.12
phoner 347.11
phone sex 75.7
phonetic (n) 546.2 (a) 523.19, 524.30
phonetic alphabet 546.3
phonetic character 546.1
phonetic entity 524.12
phonetician 523.15, 524.14
phoneticist 523.15, 524.14
phonetic law 524.13
phonetic respelling 546.4
phonetics 48.9, 524.2, 524.13, 546.4
phonetic spelling 546.4
phonetic symbol 546.1, 546.2
phonetic transcription 546.5
phonetic unit 524.12
phonetist 524.14
phonic 48.13, 50.17, 524.30
phonics 50.5
phoniness 354.2, 500.1
phonism 24.5
phonogram 546.2
phonogramic 546.8
phonograph 50.11
phonographer 547.17
phonographic 546.8
phonograph record 50.12, 549.10
phonography 524.13, 546.4, 546.5, 547.8
phonological 523.19
phonologist 523.15
phonology 524.13, 530.1
phony (n) 336.4, 354.13, 357.6, 357.8, 500.7, 785.1, 862.2 (a) 336.8, 354.26, 354.33, 500.16, 784.10, 862.8
phony dividend 738.7
phony money 728.10
phosphate 890.4
phosphatize 1060.8
Phosphor 1073.4
phosphor 1025.13, 1026.5
phosphoresce 1025.26
phosphorescence 1025.13
Phosphorus 1073.4
phosphorus 7.11
photic 1025.41
photics 1025.22
photism 24.5
photo (n) 714.3 (a) 714.17
photoactinic 1025.41
photoactive 714.17
photobiography 714.3, 719.1
photobomb 714.14
photo bomber 214.3
photo booth 714.11
photocell 1033.11
photochemical 1060.9
photochemical process 548.1
photochromy 714.1
photochronograph 714.3
photocollotype 714.4
photocomposition 548.2
photoconduction 1032.14
photocopier 549.10
photocopy 714.5, 785.5
photodisintegration 1038.8
photodrama 706.1
photoelectric 1032.30, 1033.15
photoelectric cell 1033.11
photoelectric effect 1033.4
photoelectric emission 1033.5
photoelectricity 1033.1
photoelectric pickup 50.11
photoelectric tube 1033.11
photoelectronic 1033.15
photoelectronics 1033.1
photoemission 1025.19, 1033.5, 1035.4
photoengraving 548.1, 713.2
photo finish 757.3, 790.3
photo-finish 836.5
photofinishing 714.1
photofluorogram 714.6
photofluorograph 91.9
photofluorography 1037.8
photog 714.2
photogelatin process 548.1
photogenic 714.17, 1025.38
photogram 714.6
photogrammetrist 159.5
photogrammetry 159.5, 714.1
photograph (n) 349.2, 349.5, 712.10, 714.3, 785.5 (v) 349.8, 714.14
photograph album 554.7
photographer 555.4, 714.2, 716.5
photographer's model 786.5
photographic 712.21, 714.17
photographic memory 989.2
photographic paper 714.10
photographic realism 973.7
photographic reproduction 548.1
photographist 716.5
photography 29.7, 548.1, 706.5, 712.1, 712.16, 713.1, 714.1
photography safari 177.5
photogravure 714.1, 714.5
photojournalist 555.4, 714.2
photolithography 548.1, 713.3
photologic 1025.41
photological 1025.41
photology 1025.22
photolysis 806.2
photolytic 806.6
photolyze 806.4
photomap (n) 714.3 (v) 714.14
photometric 1025.41
photometrical 1025.41
photometry 1025.22
photomicrograph 714.3
photomontage 714.3
photomural 714.3
photon 17.7, 1025.5, 1025.21
photo-offset 548.1
photo op 352.4, 541.5, 938.11
photo opportunity 352.4, 541.5, 552.3, 831.2, 938.11
photophobia 24.3, 28.1
photophobic 28.11, 1025.42
photopia 27.1
photoplay 706.1
photoprint 714.5
photo-reconnaissance plane 181.9
photosensitive 714.17, 1025.42
photosensitive devices 1033.11
photosensitivity 1025.1, 1033.11
photosetting 548.2
photo shoot 712.16, 714.1
photosphere 1073.13
photostat (n) 714.5, 785.5 (v) 714.14, 785.8
photostatic copy 714.5, 785.5
photosynthesize 310.34
phototelegraphic 347.21
phototonus 27.1
phototopography 159.5, 714.1
phototropic 1025.42
phototube 1033.11
phototypesetter 548.2
phototypesetting machine 548.2
phototypic 548.20
phototypographic 548.20
phototypography 548.1
phototypy 548.1
photovoltaic cell 1021.7
photozincography 548.1
phrasal 518.12, 529.4
phrasal idiom 529.1
phrasal verb 529.1, 530.4
phrase (n) 518.6, 523.14, 524.3, 529.1, 554.13, 708.24, 793.2, 974.1 (v) 524.22, 532.4 (a) 529.4
phrased 532.5
phrasemake 545.6
phrasemaker 526.18, 529.3, 533.5, 545.5
phraseman 529.3, 545.5
phrasemonger 526.18, 529.3, 532.3, 533.5, 545.5
phraseogram 529.1
phraseograph 529.1
phraseology 523.1, 523.9, 526.13, 529.2
phraser 526.18, 529.3
phrase structure 530.2
phrase-structure grammar 530.1
phrasey 529.4
phrasing 529.2, 709.2
phratria 617.2
phratry 559.4, 617.2
phrenetic 926.15
phrenic 919.7, 920.12, 935.18
phrenologist 198.9
phrenology 198.9
Phrygian mode 709.10
Phrygian sibyl 962.6
Phryne 665.15
phthisic 85.61
phthisis 85.17
phubbing 497.3
phut 395.29, 762.11, 820.10
phylactery 691.5, 696.10
phyle 559.4, 617.2
phyletic 559.7, 560.18
phyllo 10.41
phylogenesis 861.3
phylogenetic 559.7, 560.18, 861.8
phylogeny 861.3
phylum 305.3, 527.1, 560.4, 809.3, 809.5, 1068.1
phys ed 84.1, 568.9
physic (n) 86.4, 86.17, 1018.1 (v) 91.24
physical (n) 938.6 (a) 663.6, 767.8, 1018.3, 1052.10
physical addiction 87.1
physical anthropology 312.10
physical body 689.18, 1052.3
physical charm 1016.3
physical checkup 938.6
physical chemist 1060.7
physical condition 83.1
physical conditioning 84.1
physical culture 568.9
physical dependence 87.1
physical development 14.1
physical education 84.1, 568.9, 725.6
physical examination 91.12, 938.6
physical fitness 83.1, 84.1
physical fitness test 84.3
physical force 424.2
physicalism 1052.6
physicality 1052.1
physical law 434.1
physical love 104.1
physically challenged 85.45
physical metallurgy 1058.11
physicalness 1052.1
physical optics 1025.22
physical part, the 2.1
physical pleasure 95.1
physical presence 221.1
physical science 1018.1
physical scientist 1052.7

physical self 2.1
physical sensibility 24.2
physical structure 2.1
physical theory 1018.1
physical therapist 90.8
physical therapy 91.1, 91.14
physical world 1052.2
physician 90.4, 90.8
physician in ordinary 90.4
physician's assistant 90.11
physicism 1052.6
physicist 1018.2, 1052.7
physicochemical 1060.9
physicomorphic 675.25
physicomorphism 675.5
physicotheological 676.4
physics 1018.1
physics branch 1018.1
physio 767.4
physiochemical 1060.9
physiochemist 1060.7
physiogenesis 861.3
physiogenetic 861.8
physiogeny 861.3
physiognomic 216.10
physiognomics 341.8
physiognomist 198.9
physiognomy 33.4, 198.9, 216.4, 262.3, 341.8
physiological 305.17
physiological individual 305.2
physiology 1068.3
physiotherapist 90.8
physique 2.1, 2.3, 15.2, 262.4, 266.1, 767.4, 1052.3
physitheism 675.5
physitheist 675.16
phytivorous 8.31
phytobiological 1068.4
phytobiologist 1068.2
phytobiology 1068.1
phytochemical 1060.9
phytogenesis 78.6
phytogenetic 78.16
phytologic 1068.4
phytological 1068.4
phytologist 1068.2
phytology 1068.1
phytophagan 8.16
phytophage 8.16
phytophagous 8.31
phytophagy 8.1
phytoplanktonic 310.37
pi (n) 548.6 (v) 548.16, 811.3
piacular 658.7
piacular offering 696.7
piaculum 658.1
piaffe 177.28, 177.34
piaffer (n) 177.12 (v) 177.28
pi a form 548.16
pianism 708.30, 708.31
pianissimo (n) 708.25 (a) 52.16, 708.53
pianist 710.7
pianiste 710.7
piano (n) 708.25, 711.12 (a) 52.16, 708.53
piano accordion 711.11
piano bar 88.20
pianofortist 710.7
piano keys 711.17
piano player 710.7
piano player roll 711.12
piano score 708.28
piano wire 711.20
piazza 197.21, 230.8
pic 237.6
pica 548.6
picador 461.4
Picardy third 709.20
picaroon 483.7
picayune (n) 998.1, 998.5 (a) 248.6, 258.10, 766.9, 936.14, 998.20
picayune critic 936.7
picayunish 248.6, 998.20
picayunishness 248.1, 998.1
piccoloist 710.4
pick (n) 371.1, 711.21, 740.3, 747.3, 902.7, 999.8 (v) 8.26, 371.13, 371.14, 472.11, 708.40, 747.4, 902.18, 1069.19
pick, the 371.1
pick a bone with 456.13
pick and choose 371.13, 495.8, 944.4, 944.5
pick and roll 747.3
pick apart 510.15
pick a quarrel 456.13, 589.8
pick at 8.26, 96.13, 375.15, 510.12, 510.16
pick clean 480.24
picked 371.26, 999.16
picked on 96.24
picker 710.5, 1069.5
picket (n) 273.6, 727.5, 727.6, 727.7, 1008.9, 1008.10, 1008.13 (v) 212.7, 333.5, 428.10, 604.15, 727.10
picketer 1008.13
picket fence 212.4
picketing 333.2, 604.2, 727.5
picket line 1008.13
Pick Four 759.14
pick holes 510.15
pick holes in 510.12, 936.9, 946.14
pickiness 495.1
picking and choosing 371.10
picking out 517.3
pickings 472.3, 482.11
picking up 480.2
picking up the check 624.8
picking up the tab 624.8
pickle (n) 10.9, 67.2, 765.1, 810.3, 971.3, 1013.5 (v) 88.23, 397.9
pickleball court 743.11
pickled 67.5, 68.9, 88.33, 386.15
pickle-herring 707.10
picklement 765.1
picklepuss 108.4, 112.13, 115.9
pickling 11.2, 397.2
pick-me-up 9.1, 86.8, 88.8
pick nits 510.15, 936.9
pick off 308.14, 904.12
pickoff 745.3
pickoff play 745.3
pick of the crop 999.8
pick on 96.13, 375.15, 510.12, 510.16
pick one's brains 482.19
pick one's steps 339.7, 494.5
pick one's way 938.32
pick out 27.12, 192.10, 255.10, 371.14, 517.18, 773.5, 773.6, 865.11, 944.4, 983.10
pick over 938.31
pickpocket 483.2
pick-pocketing 482.3
pick pockets 482.14
Pick Six 759.14
pick someone's brains 387.14
pick the bones of 480.24
pick the brains of 938.21
pick the lock 940.2
pick to pieces 395.17, 510.12, 510.15, 802.14, 936.9, 946.14
pick up 9.2, 48.11, 105.13, 109.7, 176.16, 187.12, 392.7, 396.19, 429.15, 472.9, 472.11, 480.18, 912.8, 941.5, 1036.17
pickup 50.11, 88.8, 174.4, 177.7, 251.2, 392.1, 588.1, 665.14, 1034.17, 1035.10
pick up an acquaintance with 587.10
pickup camera 1035.10
pick up information 570.6
pick up speed 174.10
pick-up sticks 743.16
pick up the check 449.12, 478.19, 624.18, 624.19
pick up the mooring 182.15
pick up the tab 449.12, 478.19, 624.18, 624.19
pickup unit man 1035.13
Pickwickian 520.7
Pickwickian sense 975.7
picky 495.9, 510.23, 766.9
picky eater 8.16
picnic (n) 8.6, 411.1, 743.2, 743.4, 1014.4 (v) 8.21
picnicker 8.16
pico 237.6
picornavirus 85.42
picot 289.4
picot edge 289.2
pictogram 349.1, 517.2, 546.2
pictograph 546.2
pictographic 349.13, 546.8
pictographic symbol 546.1
pictorial (n) 555.1 (a) 349.13, 712.21
picturable 712.21
pictural 712.21
picture (n) 349.2, 349.5, 517.1, 706.1, 712.10, 714.3, 785.1, 986.6, 1016.6, 1035.5, 1036.11 (v) 349.8, 349.9, 712.19, 986.15
picture, the 381.1, 761.4, 766.2
picture book 554.1
picture card 758.2
picture carrier 1035.4
picture channel 1035.4
picture editor 554.2
picture frame 266.4
picture gallery 386.9
picture house 706.7
picture in one's mind 986.15
picture in the mind 932.1
picture monitor 1035.13
picture noise 1035.5
picture of, the 778.3, 784.3
picture of health 83.2
picture-perfect 495.11, 1002.6
picturephone 1035.11
picture postcard 553.3
picturer 716.2
pictures, the 706.1
picture shifts 1035.5
picture show 706.1
picturesome 714.17
picturesque 498.12, 712.21, 1016.17
picture-taking 714.1
picture theater 706.7
picture to oneself 986.15
picture tube 1035.11
picturing 986.6
picturization 349.1
picturize 349.8, 712.19
piddle (n) 12.5 (v) 12.14, 331.13, 331.14, 998.14
piddler 998.10
piddling (n) 998.8 (a) 248.6, 258.10, 885.5, 998.20
piddling few 885.2
piddly 258.10, 885.5, 998.18
piddly few 885.2
pidgin (n) 523.11 (a) 523.23
pidgin English 523.11
pie 10.41, 1014.4
piebald (n) 311.11 (a) 47.12
piece 8.2, 75.4, 257.10, 261.1, 267.2, 302.8, 462.10, 472.3, 477.5, 547.10, 552.3, 556.1, 704.4, 704.10, 708.5, 712.9, 728.4, 743.17, 786.3, 793.1, 793.3
pièce de résistance 10.7, 413.10, 997.7, 999.8
piece of advice 422.2
piece of cake 1014.4
piece of eight 882.4
piece of evidence 957.1
piece of furniture 229.1
piece of gold 728.4
piece of good luck 1010.3
piece of gossip 552.7
piece of guesswork 971.8
piece of land 1069.9
piece of luck 472.7
piece of meat 75.4
piece of money 728.4
piece of news 552.3
piece of one's mind 510.6
piece of sharp practice 356.8
piece of silver 728.4
piece of the action 477.5, 793.1
piece of the pie 477.5
piece of work 724.2, 893.1
piece of writing 547.10
piece out 794.6
piece together 796.3, 800.5, 892.8
piecework 892.3
piece-worker 726.2
pie chart 381.3
piecing together 472.2, 796.1
piecrust 295.14, 1050.2
pied (n) 199.5 (a) 47.12
pied-à-terre 228.8
piedmont 237.1, 274.3
piedmont glacier 1023.5
Pied Piper of Hamelin 377.4
pie-eyed 88.33
pie graph 381.3

pie in the sky (n) 986.10 (a) 986.23
pieplant 10.35
pier 273.5, 901.4, 901.8, 1009.6
pier buttress 901.4
pierce 26.7, 93.14, 96.17, 189.8, 292.15, 393.13, 459.25, 521.9, 1023.10
pierced 292.19
pierceless 293.10
piercer 1040.2
pierce the ears 53.7, 58.11
pierce the heart 112.19
pierce to the depths 275.9
piercing (n) 292.3, 459.10 (a) 15.22, 17.14, 26.10, 53.11, 58.14, 68.6, 93.24, 105.31, 144.23, 544.11, 671.16, 920.16, 1023.14
piercing eye 27.10
piercing look 27.5
piercingness 144.8
piercing pain 26.2
piercing wind 318.7
pier glass 29.6
Pierian 720.16
Pierian Spring 720.11
Pierides 710.22, 720.11
Pierrot 707.10
pierside 1009.6
pietism 354.6, 692.1, 693.1
pietist 692.4, 693.3
pietistic 692.8, 693.5, 953.21
pietistical 693.5
pietisticalness 693.1
piety 692.1, 693.1
piezoelectric 1032.30
piffle (n) 520.3 (v) 520.5
piffling 258.10, 998.20
pig 8.16, 10.17, 80.13, 179.8, 257.12, 311.5, 311.9, 660.6, 672.3, 757.2, 810.7, 980.5, 1058.5
pigboat 180.9
pigeon (n) 311.27, 358.2 (v) 356.14, 356.18
pigeon breast 283.6
pigeon-breasted 283.19
pigeonhearted 491.10
pigeonheartedness 491.1
pigeonhole (n) 258.3, 346.4, 809.2 (v) 390.6, 613.10, 809.6, 846.9, 871.8
pigeonholed 340.14, 809.8
pigeonholes 871.3
pigeonholing 801.3, 809.1, 846.2
pigeon house 228.23
pigeon loft 228.23
pigeon post 353.6
pigeon-toed 265.12
pig farm 1070.5
pig farming 1070.1
piggery 1070.5
piggish 80.24, 100.27, 311.45, 672.6
piggishness 80.2, 100.8, 672.1
piggy 311.9
piggyback control 1041.3
piggybacking 938.9
piggyback on 901.22
piggyback rocket 1074.5
piggy bank 729.13
pighead 361.6
pigheaded 361.8
pigheadedness 361.1
pigherd 1070.3
pig-ignorant 930.11
pig in a poke 731.5, 759.2, 971.8
pig in clover 606.7
pig-keeping 1070.1
pig Latin 523.10
piglet 302.10, 311.9
pigling 302.10, 311.9
pigman 1070.3
pigmeat 10.17
pigment (n) 35.8 (v) 35.14
pigmental 35.16
pigmentary 35.16
pigmentation 35.1, 35.11
pigment deficiency 36.3
pigments 712.18
pignus judiciale 438.5
pignus legale 438.5
pig out 8.25, 672.5
pigpen 80.11, 228.11
pig's eye 758.2
pigskin 746.2
pigsticker 1040.2
pigsty 80.11, 228.11
pig sweat 88.14
pig-swill 391.4
pigtail 3.7, 89.7, 217.6, 281.2, 740.2
pigtails 1016.14
Pigwiggen 258.5
pike 237.6
pikeman 461.6
piker 178.3, 759.21
pikerish 362.11
pikestaff 273.2
pilaf 10.36
pilaster 272.6, 273.5, 901.8
pilastrade 273.5
Pilates 84.2
pile (n) 3.2, 3.9, 3.19, 247.4, 266.2, 273.6, 294.1, 310.19, 386.1, 472.3, 618.3, 770.10, 901.8, 1038.13 (v) 159.15, 770.19
pile builder 241.2
piled 386.14, 770.21
piled on 643.8
pile drive 902.12
piledriver 15.6, 894.6
pile dweller 241.2
pile dwelling 241.3
pile house 241.3
pile in 193.12
pile into 459.15
pile it on 355.3, 545.6, 993.11
pile on 770.19
pileous 3.24
pile out 23.6
piles 85.37
pile up 182.42, 386.11, 770.19
pileup 1011.2
pilfer 389.4, 482.13
pilferage 482.1
pilfered 482.23
pilferer 483.1
pilfering 389.1, 482.1
pilgarlic 660.2
pilgrim (n) 178.1, 699.16 (v) 177.21
pilgrimage (n) 177.3, 177.5, 404.2, 696.8 (v) 177.21
pilgrimlike 177.36
pilgrim's staff 273.2
pili 305.5
piling 901.4, 901.8
piling on 144.11, 389.3, 993.6
pill 86.7, 118.5, 282.2, 660.5
pill, the 86.23
pillage (n) 482.6 (v) 480.14, 482.17, 671.11
pillager 483.6
pillaging (n) 480.9, 482.6, 671.3 (a) 482.22
pillar 272.6, 273.5, 282.4, 549.12, 901.8, 1008.5
pillar box 553.6
pillarist 584.5, 699.16
pillar of society 607.6, 659.3, 997.8
pillar of strength 855.6
pillar of the church 659.3, 692.4
pillar of the community 662.9
pillar saint 584.5, 699.16
Pillars of Hercules 211.5, 261.4
pillbox 460.6
pillhead 87.21
pillory (n) 428.4, 605.3 (v) 508.8, 603.5, 604.9, 661.8, 661.9
pillorying 510.3, 661.6
pillow (n) 901.20, 1047.4 (v) 901.21
pillowcase 295.10
pillow slip 295.10
pillow talk 541.3
pill popper 87.21
pill-popping 87.2
pill pusher 86.35
pill roller 86.35
pilose 3.24
pilosis 3.1
pilosism 3.1
pilosity 3.1
pilot (n) 178.10, 183.8, 185.1, 574.7, 745.2, 757.2, 1008.3 (v) 161.7, 182.14, 184.37, 573.9, 814.2 (a) 942.11
pilotage 159.3, 182.2, 182.4, 184.1, 573.1, 630.6
pilot balloon 942.4
pilot biscuit 10.30
pilot bread 10.30
pilot burner 1020.10
pilot chute 181.13
pilot flag 517.15
piloting 161.1
pilot jack 517.15
pilot light 1020.10
pilot model 337.2, 786.5
pilot plan 942.3
pilot program 942.3
pilotry 182.4
pilotship 182.4, 184.3
pilot trainee 185.3
pilot training 184.3
pilous 3.24
pilpul 935.4
pilpulist 935.12
pilpulistic 935.19
pily 294.7
pimp (n) 660.4, 665.18 (v) 665.21
pimped-out 498.12
pimping 665.8, 732.1
pimple (n) 85.36, 85.37, 283.4, 517.7, 1004.1 (v) 288.4
pimpled 1004.8
pimply 288.6, 1004.8
pin (n) 2.7, 285.4, 293.4, 474.3, 498.6, 647.1, 750.1, 751.1, 915.5, 998.5 (v) 800.8, 913.5
pinacotheca 386.9
pinafore 5.17
pin a medal on 646.8
pinball machine 759.16
pinbrain 924.4
pin-brained 922.13
pince-nez 29.3
pincer 260.6
pincer movement 459.5
pincers 192.9, 474.4
pinch (n) 26.2, 248.2, 258.3, 260.2, 375.6, 429.6, 482.4, 619.2, 843.4, 997.4, 1006.1, 1013.4, 1013.8 (v) 26.7, 169.2, 182.25, 260.8, 429.16, 482.16, 484.5 (a) 862.8
pinch bar 906.4
pinchbar (n) 906.4 (v) 906.8
pinchbeck (n) 354.13, 498.3 (a) 354.26
pinched 210.7, 260.12, 270.20, 619.7, 1013.26
pinched-in 260.12
pinched with hunger 100.25
pinchfist 484.4
pinchfisted 484.9
pinchgut 484.4
pinch-hit 862.5
pinch-hit for 576.14
pinch hitter 576.1, 745.2, 862.2
pinching (n) 482.1, 484.1 (a) 484.9, 1023.14
pinch of snuff 89.8, 998.5
pinch pennies 484.5
pinchpenny 484.8
pinch-run 862.5
pinch runner 862.2
pinch-runner 745.3
Pindaric 720.16
pindling 258.10
pin down 159.11, 428.10, 855.7, 865.11, 913.5, 970.11
pine (n) 747.1 (v) 16.9, 85.48, 112.17, 393.18
pineapple 462.20
pine away 112.17, 393.19
pine barrens 310.13
pinecone 282.5, 310.27
pine for 100.16
pine needle 285.5, 310.19
pine over 112.17
pinery 1069.11
piney 310.39
pinfall 750.2
pinfeather 3.16
pinfold 429.7
ping 54.3
Ping-Pong 748.1
pinguedinous 1056.9
pinguefy 259.8
pinguescent 1056.9
pinguid 1056.9
pinguidity 1056.5

pinhead 198.4, 258.7, 924.4
pining (n) 100,5, 112.10 (a) 16.21, 100.23, 112.22, 393.45
pinion (n) 3.16, 793.4 (v) 428.10
pinioned 3.28
pink (n) 41.2, 83.1, 611.12, 1002.3 (v) 289.4, 292.15 (a) 41.8, 83.13, 611.20
pink-cheeked 83.13
pink elephants 926.10
pinkeye 85.14
pinkie 73.5
pinkify 41.4
pinking shears 289.2
pinkish 41.8
pinkishness 41.2
pink ladies 87.5
pinkness 41.2
pink noise 52.4
pinko 611.12
pink of perfection 1002.3
pink owsley 87.10
pink slip 447.2, 909.5
pink spiders 926.10
pink wine 88.17
pinky (n) 73.5 (a) 41.8
pin money 728.19
pinna 2.10
pinnacle 198.2, 237.6, 272.6, 794.5, 1002.3
pinnate 3.27
pinning down 865.6
PIN number 517.11
pin on 599.8, 888.4
pin one's ears back 510.18
pin oneself upon 138.11
pin one's faith on 953.10
pin one's faith to 953.15
pin one's hope upon 124.6
pinpoint (n) 159.1, 258.7 (v) 159.11, 208.10, 888.4, 1036.17 (a) 973.17
pinpoint accuracy 973.5
pinpointing 47.3, 1036.8
pinprick 26.2, 276.1, 998.5
pins 177.15
pins and needles 25.1, 26.3, 74.1, 126.1
pin spot 750.1
pinstripe (n) 47.5 (a) 47.15
pinstriper 574.3
pinstripes 5.18
pintle 915.5
pinto (n) 311.11 (a) 47.12
pint-size 248.6, 258.13
pint-sized 258.13
pintsized 258.10
pinup 714.3, 1016.8
pinup girl 1016.8
pinwheel 743.16
piny (n) 227.10 (a) 310.39
pinyin 546.5
pioneer (n) 178.1, 216.2, 227.9, 405.5, 461.14, 816.1 (v) 216.7, 337.4, 405.12, 816.3, 818.10, 852.9 (a) 337.5
pioneering (n) 405.1 (a) 216.10, 404.8, 816.4
pious 692.8, 693.5, 696.16, 953.21
pious fiction 354.11
pious fraud 693.3
piousness 692.1, 693.1
pip (n) 85.41, 310.31, 647.2, 647.5, 999.7 (v) 60.5
pip, the 85.1
pipe (n) 58.4, 89.6, 239.6, 282.4, 711.6 (v) 53.10, 58.8, 60.5, 176.14, 239.15, 318.20, 524.25, 708.38, 708.42
pipe bag 711.9
pipe bomb 462.20
pipe clay 37.4
pipe-clay 37.6
pipe cleaner 89.6
piped 239.16
piped-in music 708.28
pipe down 51.7
pipe dream 124.4, 976.1, 985.2, 986.9
pipe-dream 985.9, 986.17
pipe-dreaming (n) 985.2, 986.8 (a) 985.11, 986.25
pipelike 239.16
pipeline (n) 239.6, 551.2, 552.10 (v) 176.14
pipe off 307.19
pipe of peace 465.2
pipe organ 711.13
piper 710.4
pipe rack 89.6
pipe roll 549.1
pipes 183.7, 711.9
pipe smoke 89.1
pipe smoker 89.11
pipe tobacco 89.2
pipette (n) 192.9, 239.6, 1060.6 (v) 192.12
pipetting 192.3
pipe up 59.8, 318.19, 524.21, 708.37
pipe up a song 708.37
piping (n) 239.6 (a) 58.14, 464.9, 1010.13
piping hot 1019.25
pipingness 58.1
piping times 1010.4
pippin 999.7
pips 646.6, 1036.11
pipsqueak 258.4, 998.7
piquancy 68.1, 544.4
piquant 63.10, 68.6, 105.30, 375.27, 377.8, 544.12, 983.19
pique (n) 152.2, 152.7 (v) 96.13, 105.13, 152.24, 375.17, 375.19, 983.12
piqued 96.21, 152.27, 983.16
pique oneself 136.5
pique one's interest 983.12
piracy 482.7, 482.8
pirate (n) 183.1, 461.5, 483.7, 483.9 (v) 482.18, 482.19, 621.4
pirated 482.23
piratelike 482.21
pirate radio station 1034.6
piratical 482.21
pirating 621.2
pirouette (n) 915.2 (v) 915.9
Pisacha 680.4
pis aller 995.2, 1009.2
piscatology 382.3
piscator 382.6
piscatorial 311.49, 382.11
piscatorialist 382.6
piscatorian 382.6
piscatory 311.49, 382.11
pisciculture 1070.1
pisciform 311.49
piscina 79.12, 239.5, 703.10
piscine 311.49
pish 12.5
pismire 311.33
piste 383.2, 517.8
pistil 310.28
pistol (n) 413.14, 462.10, 999.7 (v) 308.18, 904.12
pistoleer 904.8
pistol shot 223.2
pistol-whip 604.12
pistol-whipping 604.4
piston 904.6
piston engine 181.1
piston motion 850.2
piston plane 181.2
pit (n) 48.6, 275.2, 284.2, 284.4, 284.6, 294.1, 309.16, 310.31, 463.1, 654.7, 704.15, 704.16, 737.7, 756.3, 759.19, 1004.1, 1058.6 (v) 284.14
pit, the 682.1
pit against 456.14
pit against one another 215.4
pit-a-pat (n) 52.3, 55.1, 105.5, 916.3, 917.4 (a) 916.18
pitapatation 105.5
pit area 756.3
pit boss 759.19, 759.20
pit bull 110.11, 461.2
pitch (n) 38.4, 50.2, 198.2, 204.2, 204.4, 245.1, 367.1, 524.6, 543.2, 709.4, 734.5, 745.3, 749.4, 752.1, 904.3, 917.8 (v) 159.16, 182.55, 194.5, 194.8, 200.9, 204.10, 225.11, 367.6, 375.14, 439.8, 745.5, 758.5, 904.10, 916.10, 917.15 (a) 198.11, 524.30
pitch accent 524.6
pitch and plunge 917.15
pitch and toss 182.55
pitch-black 38.8, 1027.13
pitch-blackness 1027.1
pitch camp 225.11
pitch-dark 38.8, 1027.13
pitch-darkness 1027.1
pitched 204.15, 524.30
pitched battle 457.4
pitcher 745.2, 904.7
pitcher's mound 745.1
pitchfork 904.10
pitchhole 284.3, 284.7
pitch in 8.20, 450.3, 725.15, 818.7
pitchiness 38.2
pitching (n) 904.2 (a) 916.17
pitching coach 745.2
pitching motion 745.2
pitching rotation 745.2
pitching woo 562.2
pitch into 404.3, 457.14, 459.15
pitchman 352.9, 357.3
pitch one's tent 225.11
pitch-out 745.3
pitchout 746.3
pitchperson 352.9, 357.3, 730.7
pitch pipe 711.22
pitchpole 182.44
pitch range 709.4
pitch speed 184.31
pitch upon 186.7
pitch woo 562.15
pitchy 38.8, 1027.13, 1057.3
piteous 98.20, 145.8
pitfall 356.12, 1006.5
pith 196.5, 208.2, 359.3, 492.5, 518.1, 557.2, 767.2, 997.6, 1063.2
pithiness 518.5, 537.1, 1063.1
pithless 16.12, 19.19
pithy 518.10, 537.6, 974.6, 1047.11, 1063.6
pithy saying 974.1
pitiability 98.5
pitiable 98.20, 145.8, 998.21, 1000.9
pitiableness 98.5, 998.2
pitiful 145.8, 661.11, 998.21, 1000.9
pitifulness 98.5, 998.2
pitiless 146.3, 671.21, 1025.32
pitilessness 144.10, 146.1, 671.1
pit man 737.10
pitman 1058.9
pit of Acheron 682.3
pit of one's stomach 93.3
pit-pony 311.13
pitris 678.12
pits, the 199.1, 410.2, 654.7, 1000.2, 1011.1
pit stop 846.2
Pittacus 921.4
pittance 248.2, 478.6, 728.19, 992.5
pitted 284.17, 288.6, 294.7
pitter-patter (n) 52.3, 55.1, 105.5, 316.1, 849.4, 916.3, 917.4 (v) 55.4, 316.10, 917.12
pituitary gigantism 257.5
pituitary gland 13.2
pituitous 1062.13
pituitousness 1062.3
pit viper 311.25
pity (n) 143.1, 145.1, 427.1, 638.2 (v) 145.3, 147.2
pitying 145.7, 147.3
pivot (n) 208.2, 747.3, 751.3, 800.4, 906.3, 915.5, 997.6 (v) 163.9, 915.9
pivot about 163.9
pivotal 208.11, 208.13, 819.4, 843.10, 886.13, 997.22
pivotal point 997.6
pivoting 915.1
pivot joint 800.4
pivot on 208.9, 887.5
pivot tooth 2.8
pixel 258.7
pixelated 258.12
pixelize 258.9
pixie 322.3, 678.8, 680.7
pixieish 678.17
pixilated 926.29
pixilation 926.1
pizzazz (n) 17.3, 18.1, 330.2, 544.3 (a) 330.17
pizzeria 8.17
pizzicato (n) 708.25, 708.30 (a) 708.53

pjs 5.21
placability 465.1
placable 148.6, 465.13
placard (n) 352.7 (v) 352.15
placate 465.7
placation 465.1
placative 465.12
placatory 465.12
place (n) 159.1, 159.4, 228.1, 230.8, 231.1, 245.2, 463.1, 607.1, 641.1, 724.3, 724.5, 759.4, 765.1, 807.2, 825.2, 843.2, 978.2 (v) 159.11, 159.12, 615.12, 643.4, 729.17, 757.5, 808.9, 809.6, 888.3, 941.6, 989.11
place against 943.4
place an order 421.5
place at one's disposal 439.4
place a value on 630.11, 946.9
place before 216.8
placebo 86.4
placebo effect 86.4
place card 517.11
place confidence in 953.15, 953.17
placed 159.18, 808.14, 809.8
place emphasis on 997.14
place for everything and everything in its place, a 807.3
place horse 757.2
place in office 159.16, 371.20, 615.12
place in one's way 439.4
place in status quo ante 396.11
place in the foreground 348.5
place in the sun, a 662.1
place itself 807.5
placekick 746.3, 902.9
placeman 575.15
placemat 8.13
placement 159.1, 159.6, 615.3, 808.1, 808.3, 809.1, 888.1
placement test 808.3
place name 527.3
place-names 527.1
place-naming 527.1
placenta 817.3
place of articulation 524.12
place of assignation 582.9
place of business 739.1
place of confinement 429.7
place of pilgrimage 208.7
place of residence 228.1
place of torment 682.1
place of worship 703.1
place oneself 159.17
place one's feet carefully 339.7
place on the ladder 765.1
place out at interest 729.17
place parallel to 203.5
placer 1058.7
placer claim 1058.8
placer deposit 1058.7
place reliance in 953.15
place reliance on 953.16
place responsibility for 599.8
placer gravel 1058.7
placer miner 1058.9
placer mining 1058.8
place setting 735.4
place side by side 223.13
place the ball 748.3
place the blame for 599.8, 888.4
place the blame on 599.8, 888.4
place the responsibility for 888.4
place to live 228.1
place to one's account 599.9, 622.5, 888.4
place to one's credit 622.5
place to rest one's head 228.1
place trust in 953.17
place under arrest 480.18
place under oath 334.7
place upon 888.4
place upon record 549.15
place-value notation 1017.4
place where one hangs one's hat 228.2
placid 106.12, 173.12
placidity 106.2, 173.1
placidness 173.1
placing 159.6
placing in office 159.7
plafond 295.6
plagal cadence 709.23
plagal mode 709.10
plage 234.2
plagiarism 336.1, 480.4, 482.8, 621.2, 849.1
plagiarist 336.4, 357.1, 483.9
plagiarize 336.5, 482.19, 621.4, 849.7
plagiarized 336.8, 482.23, 849.12
plagiarizer 357.1, 483.9
plagiarizing 336.1, 482.8
plagiary 336.1, 482.8, 621.2
plague (n) 85.5, 96.5, 770.6, 910.2, 1001.1 (v) 96.13, 98.15, 126.5, 440.12, 910.6, 1013.13
plagued 96.24, 126.8, 989.23, 1013.20
plague one 989.13
plaguer 96.10
plaguesome 98.22
plaguesomeness 98.7
plague spot 80.11, 85.5
plaguey 98.22, 1013.18
plaguing (n) 440.3 (a) 98.22, 126.10, 440.18, 989.25
plaid (n) 47.4 (a) 47.14
plaided 47.14
plain (n) 158.4, 201.3, 236.1, 310.8 (a) 31.7, 50.16, 65.2, 117.8, 137.10, 201.7, 228.33, 236.2, 248.8, 348.8, 416.5, 499.6, 521.11, 533.6, 535.3, 581.3, 606.8, 644.17, 721.5, 794.10, 798.6, 1014.13, 1015.6
plain as a pikestaff 31.7, 348.8
plain as day 31.7, 348.8
plain as pikestaffs 521.11
plain as plain can be 31.7
plain as the nose on one's face 31.7, 348.8
plain card 758.2
plain chant 708.22
plain clothes 5.8, 5.20
plainclothesman 576.10
plain dealing 644.4
plain English 521.2, 535.1
plain folks 606.1
plain language 521.2
plain living 668.2
plainness 31.2, 117.2, 137.1, 343.3, 348.3, 416.1, 499.1, 521.2, 533.1, 535.1, 581.1, 644.4, 721.2, 798.1, 1015.1
plains (n) 233.1, 236.1 (a) 233.6
plain sail 180.14
plain sailing 1014.1
plain sense 920.6
plainsong 696.3, 708.14, 708.20, 708.22
plain speaking 535.1, 644.4
plain-speaking 524.31, 535.3
plain speech 521.2, 535.1, 644.4
plainspoken 430.23, 524.31, 535.3, 644.17
plainspokenness 343.3, 535.1, 644.4
Plains states 231.7
plain style 521.2, 535.1
plain style, the 532.2
plain stylist 533.4
plain suit 758.3
plaint 115.3, 599.1
plaintext (n) 521.2 (a) 521.12
plaintiff 452.3, 598.11, 599.5, 935.12, 938.19
plaintive 112.26, 115.19, 115.22
plaintiveness 112.11
plain to be seen 31.7, 348.8
plain truth, the 973.3
plain vanilla 246.3, 533.6
plain-vanilla 499.8, 798.6
plain words 535.1
plain-wrap 346.6
plait (n) 3.7, 291.2, 296.2, 740.2, 1016.14 (v) 291.5, 740.6
plaited 291.7, 740.7
plaiting 740.1
plan (n) 266.1, 349.1, 380.1, 381.1, 404.1, 518.2, 722.4, 801.4, 932.1, 961.2 (v) 380.4, 380.6, 380.7, 381.8, 405.6, 808.10, 839.6, 892.12, 965.4
Plan A 381.1
plan ahead 381.8
planar 201.7
planarity 201.1
Plan B 381.1
planchette 689.6
plane (n) 181.1, 201.3, 245.1, 287.3, 1040.2 (v) 193.10, 287.5 (a) 201.7, 287.10
plane crash 1011.2
plane handlers 185.5
planeness 201.1
planer 1040.6
plane sailing 182.2
planet 1073.9
planetal 1073.25
planetarian 1073.25
planetarium 27.8, 1073.17
planetary 164.7, 280.11, 864.14, 1073.25
planetary colony 1075.8
planetary house 1073.20
planetary influence 886.3
planetary meteorology 317.5
planetary nebula 1073.7
planetary probe 1075.6
planetary science 1071.1
planetary shell 1038.4
planet Earth 1073.10
planetesimal 1073.25
planetoid 1073.9
planetoidal 1073.25
planets 964.2
planet-stricken 1011.14
planet-struck 1011.14
planetwide 864.14
plan for 380.6
plangency 54.1, 112.11
plangent 53.11, 54.10, 112.26, 115.19, 115.22
planish 287.5
planisphere 1073.17
plank (n) 271.4, 296.2, 609.7, 1054.3 (v) 159.13, 295.23
plank buttress 901.4
plank down 624.16
planking 218.1, 1054.3
plankton 258.7, 311.29
planktonic 311.53
planless 810.12
planlessness 406.1
planned 380.8, 381.12, 405.16, 839.8, 965.7
planned economy 609.4
planned obsolescence 390.1
planned parenthood 891.1
planner 381.6, 892.7
planning 381.1, 405.1, 717.4, 808.2, 965.1
planning function 381.1
plan of action 381.4
plan of attack 381.1
plan of work 381.1
planogamete 305.10
planographic printing 548.1
planography 548.1, 713.3
plan on 130.9, 380.6
planospore 305.13
plan out 380.6
plant (n) 310.3, 357.5, 385.4, 739.3 (v) 159.16, 225.9, 309.19, 346.7, 354.17, 855.9, 1069.18 (a) 1068.4
plant a mine 459.24
plant and animal life 305.1
plantar 199.9
plantation 159.7, 225.2, 228.6, 310.2, 310.12, 1069.8
plant biologist 1068.2
plant biology 1068.1
plant cell 305.4
plant disease 85.1
plant-eater 8.16
plant-eating 8.31
planted 159.18
planter 227.9, 1069.5
plant evidence 599.12
plant families 310.4
plant growth 14.1
planting 310.2, 1069.14
plant kingdom 310.1, 559.4, 1068.1
plant life 310.1
plantlife 1068.1
plantlike 310.36
plant oneself 159.17
plants 310.1, 1068.1
plant science 1068.1
plant scientist 1068.2

plant worship 697.1
plant worshiper 697.4
plaque 549.12
plaquette 715.3
plash (n) 238.8, 241.1, 316.2, 1065.5 (v) 52.11, 238.19, 316.10
plashing (n) 740.1 (a) 52.19
plashy 1062.14, 1065.16
plasm 305.1
plasma 2.24, 2.25
plasma display 1042.9
plasma engine 1074.2
plasma jet 1074.2
plasma-jet 904.17
plasma screen 1042.9
plasma substitute 2.25
plasma theory 1073.18
plasmatic 262.10, 305.18
plasmic 262.10, 305.18
plasmodesmata 305.5
plasmodium 305.4
plasmosome 305.7
plaster (n) 86.33, 715.4, 803.4, 1063.2 (v) 88.23, 91.24, 287.5, 295.24, 295.25, 459.23
plaster cast 86.33
plaster casting 715.1
plaster down 287.5
plastered 88.33, 295.31
plasters 1054.2
plasterwork 295.1
plastic (n) 622.3, 1054.6, 1057.1 (a) 262.9, 262.10, 433.13, 570.18, 715.6, 854.6, 867.5, 867.6, 894.15, 1005.8, 1047.9
plastic art 712.1, 712.16, 715.1
plastic bandage 86.33
plastic binding 554.14
plastic blocks 743.16
plastic bomb 462.20
plastic bullet 462.22
plastic explosive 462.14
Plasticine 715.4
plasticity 433.3, 570.5, 854.1, 1047.2
plasticize 1048.6
plasticizer 1054.6
plastic money 622.3
plastic person 867.2
plastic plate 548.8
plastic surgeon 90.5
plastic surgery 90.2, 91.19, 1016.10
plastic wrap 295.18
plastid 305.5
plastique 462.14
plastique bomb 462.20
plastosome 305.5
plat (n) 231.4, 291.2, 471.6, 1069.9 (v) 291.5
plat du jour 8.10
plate (n) 8.10, 235.1, 295.13, 295.15, 296.2, 517.13, 548.8, 713.6, 714.10 (v) 295.26
plate, the 745.1
plate armor 460.3
plateau 236.1, 237.1, 237.3, 245.1, 272.4, 826.1
plateaulith 842.6
plate clutch 1040.10
plated 295.33, 296.6
platen 548.9
platen press 548.9
plate proof 548.5
plater 757.2
plates 8.12
plate tectonics 235.1
plate umpire 745.3
platform (n) 201.3, 381.4, 463.1, 517.10, 609.7, 901.13 (v) 543.9
platform orator 543.6
platform oratory 543.1
platform shoes 5.27
platform speaker 543.6
platform speaking 543.1
plating 206.2, 295.13, 296.2
platinum 37.7
platinum blond 35.9
platinum-blond 37.9
platinum card 622.3
platitude 118.1, 864.8, 974.3
platitudinize 117.5
platitudinous 117.9, 864.16, 928.27, 974.6
platitudinousness 117.3
platitudinous ponderosity 545.1
Plato 921.2
Platonic 664.6, 952.12, 1053.8
Platonic form 262.1, 932.2, 1053.3
Platonic idea 262.1, 932.2
Platonic ideal 1053.3
Platonic love 104.1, 664.3
Platonic philosophy 952.3
Platonic realism 1053.3
Platonic year 824.4
Platonism 952.3, 1053.3
Platonist 1053.4
Platonistic 1053.8
platoon 461.22, 617.7, 770.3
platoon sergeant 575.18
platted 740.7
platter 549.10, 745.1
plaudit 509.2
plausibility 935.9, 936.1, 953.8, 968.3
plausible 354.27, 935.20, 936.10, 953.24, 966.6, 968.7
plausibleness 936.1
play (n) 158.3, 328.1, 430.4, 489.6, 547.10, 662.1, 704.4, 743.2, 743.5, 743.9, 744.1, 745.3, 746.3, 747.3, 748.2, 749.3, 749.6, 751.3, 752.3, 758.3, 759.1, 759.3, 1025.8 (v) 238.20, 328.4, 349.12, 354.21, 387.10, 500.12, 704.29, 708.39, 743.23, 744.2, 745.5, 748.3, 759.23, 998.14, 1025.25
playa 234.2, 236.1, 476.4
play a bunco game 356.18
playact 354.21, 500.12, 704.29
playacting 354.3, 704.8
playactor 357.1, 500.7, 707.2
play a deep game 415.9
play a desperate game 493.6
play a double game 354.24
play a double role 354.24
play against 759.25
play a joke on 489.14
play a lone hand 430.20
play along 324.3, 332.9, 441.2
play a part 349.12, 354.21, 500.12, 704.30
play a part in 328.5, 476.5
play a practical joke 489.14
play a practical joke upon 356.15
play a role 328.5, 704.30
play a role in 476.5
play around 562.20, 998.15
play around with 931.12, 942.8
play a scene 500.12
play at 328.8, 340.9, 708.39, 998.14
play at battledore and shuttlecock 863.4
play at cross-purposes 451.3
play at dice 759.23
play at hide and seek 368.7
play a trick on 356.15, 489.14
play a waiting game 134.4, 329.2
play back 50.14
play ball 450.3, 745.5, 747.4
play basketball 747.4
playbill 965.3
playbook 554.1, 704.21
play both ends against the middle 354.24, 387.16
playboy 582.16, 669.3, 743.18
playbroker 704.25
play by ear 365.8, 406.6, 708.39
play-by-play description 349.3, 766.2
play by the rules 644.9
play cards 758.5
play cat and mouse with 389.7
play construction 704.2
play date 582.7
play dirty pool 645.13
play doctor 704.22
play down 51.8, 252.9, 670.6, 950.2, 998.12
play drum 708.44
play ducks and drakes with 486.3
play dumb 51.6, 345.7
played out 16.18, 21.8, 393.36
player, a 894.6
player 452.2, 476.4, 706.4, 707.2, 710.1, 710.3, 743.18, 743.19, 751.2, 759.21, 796.2
player on the scene, a 894.6
player piano 711.12
players' bench 749.1
play fair 649.6
play fast and loose with 156.4, 340.9
play favorites 650.8
playfellow 588.3
play first fiddle 249.11, 612.14
play fixer 704.22
play follow the leader 336.7
play football 746.5
play footsie with 439.8, 587.11
play for a sucker 356.19, 387.16, 923.7
play for time, a 846.5
play for time 846.11
playful 109.14, 322.6, 489.17, 743.29
playful as a kitten 109.14
playfulness 109.4, 322.2, 489.4
play games 356.14, 415.10
play God 640.8
playgoer 704.27
play golf 751.4
playground 743.11, 743.14
playgroup 582.10
play hard to get 562.20
play havoc with 393.10, 393.13, 414.11, 1000.6
play hell 1013.14
play hell with 393.11
play hide and seek 346.8
play hob 1013.14
play hob with 393.11, 395.10, 811.3, 1000.6
play hockey 749.7
play hookey 368.10
play hooky 222.9, 368.10
play hoops 747.4
playhouse 258.3, 704.14
playing (n) 349.4, 704.8, 759.1, 998.8 (a) 1025.36
playing area 704.16
playing around 998.9
playing by ear 365.5
playing card 758.2
playing engagement 704.11
playing field 463.1, 743.11
playing God 640.3
playing kissy-face 562.2
playing kissy-huggy 562.2
playing kissy-kissy 562.2
playing kissy-poo 562.2
playing lightly over 73.12
playing off 264.2
playing off against 264.2
playing possum 336.2
playing second fiddle 432.14
playing the dozens 490.2
playing the market 737.19
playing with a full deck 925.4
playing with a loaded gun 493.6
playing with fire 493.3
playing with oneself 75.8
play it by ear 365.8
play it just right 409.8
play it like a master 409.8
play it straight 644.10
play jazz 708.43
play kissy-face 562.15
playland 704.1
play loose 747.4
playmaker 747.2, 749.2
playmate 588.3, 665.17
play merry hell with 393.11, 414.12
play mischief with 414.11, 1000.6
play musical chairs 854.5
play of colors 47.2
play off 264.3
playoff 745.1, 746.1
play off against 264.3, 338.5, 387.15
play of fancy 986.7
play-off hockey 749.3
play of light 47.2, 1025.8
play of wit 489.7
play on 387.15, 387.16, 643.7
play one false 356.14, 645.13
play one for a fool 356.14
play one for a sucker 356.14
play one's cards close to the chest 345.7

play one's cards close to the vest 345.7
play one's cards right 321.5
play one's cards well 413.20
play one's part 724.13
play one's proper role 641.10
play one's trump card 415.11
play on the feelings 105.12
play on words (n) 489.8 (v) 489.13
play opposite 704.30
play out 21.5
play peekaboo 27.13, 346.8
play politics 468.2
play possum 354.21
play pranks 489.14
playreader 704.23
playroom 197.12, 743.11
play Russian roulette 493.6
play safe 494.6, 1007.3
playscape 743.11
playschool 567.2
play second fiddle 139.7, 163.6, 168.3, 250.4, 432.12
play serve-and-volley tennis 748.3
play soccer 752.4
play stopped 746.3
play tennis 748.3
play the badger game 480.22
play the big board 729.17
play the buffoon 923.6
play the devil 1013.14
play the devil with 393.11, 414.12
play the dozens 490.5
play the drums 708.44
play the field 562.20
play the fool 322.4, 923.6
play the game 321.5, 579.4, 649.6, 867.4
play the hypocrite 354.23
play the lead 704.29
play the market 737.23
play the part of 704.30, 889.8
play the ponies 759.23, 759.25
play the pontiff 501.14
play therapy 92.6
play the same broken record 118.8
play the same old record 849.9
play the same old song 118.8
play the same old tune 118.8
play the spy 938.28
play the stock exchange 729.17
play the violin 708.41
plaything 358.1, 384.4, 743.16
plaything of fortune, the 1011.7
play through 751.4
play tight 747.4
playtime 857.3
play to the gallery 500.12, 501.16, 704.31
play tricks 489.14
play truant 222.9
play up 997.16
play upon 387.16
play up to 138.9, 511.6, 587.12
play violin 708.41
playwear 5.20
play with 931.12, 998.14
play with fire 414.14, 493.6, 1006.7
play with marked cards 356.18
play with oneself 75.22
playwright 704.22
playwriter 704.22
playwriting 547.2, 718.2
plaza 230.8, 736.2
plea 375.5, 440.2, 598.6, 600.2, 935.5
plea-bargain 437.7, 468.2
plea bargaining 598.12
pleach 740.6
pleached 740.7
plead 440.11, 598.19, 935.16, 957.12
plead diminished responsibility 600.11
pleader 375.10, 576.1, 597.1, 600.8
plead for 440.11, 600.10
plead guilty 113.7, 351.7
plead ignorance 600.11
pleading (n) 597.4, 598.6, 600.2, 935.5 (a) 440.17
pleadings 598.6
plead insanity 600.11
plead one's case 598.19, 600.10
plead one's cause 600.10
plead with 375.14
plea of self-defense 600.2
pleasance 95.1, 97.1, 743.14
pleasant 97.6, 109.11, 587.15, 708.48, 999.12, 1066.8
pleasant company 582.16
pleasantly plump 257.18
pleasantness 97.1, 109.1, 999.1
pleasant reception 585.2
pleasantry 97.1, 489.1, 489.2, 489.7, 490.1, 504.6
pleasant-sounding 708.48
pleasant stimulation 74.2
pleasant time 743.2
please 95.6, 97.5, 371.17, 427.6
pleased 95.15, 107.7
pleased as a child with a new toy 95.15
pleased as Punch 95.15
pleased with 95.15
pleased with oneself 140.12
please oneself 323.3, 430.20, 651.4
please the crowd 501.16
please the nostrils 70.7
• **pleasing** (n) 427.3 (a) 63.8, 97.6, 100.30, 496.7, 544.9, 585.12, 1016.18
pleasingness 97.1, 100.13, 1016.2
pleasing style 544.1
pleasing to the eye 1016.18
pleasurability 97.1
pleasurable 97.6
pleasurableness 97.1
pleasure (n) 95.1, 97.1, 100.1, 323.1, 371.2, 420.1, 743.1 (v) 95.6
pleasure-bent 663.5
pleasure boat 180.3
pleasure craft 180.3
pleasure dome of Kubla Khan 986.10
pleasureful 97.6
pleasurefulness 97.1
pleasure garden 743.14
pleasure-giving 97.6
pleasure in 95.13
pleasureless 96.20, 112.21
pleasure-loving (n) 95.4 (a) 95.18
pleasure oneself 743.22
pleasure principle 92.28, 95.4, 100.1, 663.1
pleasurer 743.18
pleasure-seeker 663.3, 669.3, 743.18
pleasure-seeking (n) 663.1 (a) 95.18, 663.5
pleasures of the mind 95.1
pleasure trip 177.5
pleasurist 743.18
pleat (n) 290.2, 291.2 (v) 290.3, 291.5
pleated 290.4, 291.7
pleating 291.2
pleb 606.5
plebe 572.6
plebeian (n) 606.5 (a) 497.14, 606.8
plebeianism 497.5
plebeians 607.7
plebiscite 371.6, 613.8
plebiscitum 371.6, 613.8
plebs 607.7
plectron 711.21
plectrum 711.21
pledge (n) 88.10, 334.4, 436.1, 438.2, 478.6, 617.11, 623.1 (v) 8.29, 88.29, 436.4, 438.10, 478.14, 641.12
pledge, the 668.2
pledged 334.9, 436.8, 438.12, 623.9, 641.16
pledge in marriage 436.6
pledge of allegiance 334.4
pledge of secrecy 345.3
pledge one's honor 436.4
pledge one's word 436.4
pledget 86.33
pledge the health of 88.29
pleiad 662.9
Pleiades 678.9, 1073.8
plenary 247.6, 430.27, 794.11
plenary council 423.4
plenary session 423.1
plenipotentiary 18.13, 576.17
plenipotentiary power 615.1
plenish 385.7, 385.9
plenitude 247.1, 247.3, 386.1, 794.2, 812.1, 991.2, 1002.2
plenitudinous 991.7
plenteous 884.8, 890.9, 991.7
plenteousness 890.1, 991.2
plentiful 247.8, 884.8, 890.9, 991.7, 993.19
plentifulness 890.1, 991.2
plentipotentiary 576.6
plenty (n) 247.3, 386.1, 884.1, 991.2, 993.2 (a) 991.6, 991.7
plenty good enough 991.6
plenty of notice 399.2
plenty to do 330.5
plenum 221.2, 423.1, 770.2, 794.1, 812.2, 1052.2, 1073.1
pleonasm 256.4, 538.2, 849.3, 993.4
pleonastic 538.11, 993.17
plethora 794.2, 993.2, 993.3
plethoric 259.13, 993.19, 993.20
pleura 2.6
pleuritic 85.61
plexiform 170.11
plexure 170.3
plexus 2.14, 170.3
pliability 324.1, 362.4, 433.3, 570.5, 1014.2, 1047.2
pliable 291.7, 362.12, 387.23, 433.13, 570.18, 894.15, 1014.15, 1047.9
pliancy 324.1, 426.2, 433.3, 867.1, 1014.2, 1047.2
pliant 291.7, 324.5, 426.5, 433.13, 867.5, 894.15, 1014.15, 1047.9
plica 291.1
plical 291.7
plicate (v) 291.5 (a) 291.7
plicated 291.7
plication 291.1, 291.4
plicature 291.1, 291.4
pliers 192.9, 1040.7
plight (n) 436.1, 765.1, 971.3, 1006.1, 1011.1, 1013.4 (v) 436.4
plighted 436.8
plighted bride 563.5
plighted faith 436.3
plighted love 436.3
plighted troth 436.3
plight one's faith 436.4
plight one's honor 436.4
plight one's troth 436.4, 436.6
Plimsoll line 300.6
Plimsoll mark 300.6
plinth 901.8
plod (n) 175.2 (v) 175.7, 177.28, 360.3, 725.14
plod along 175.7
plodder 175.5, 726.3
plodding (n) 360.1 (a) 117.6, 360.8, 725.17
plonk 88.17
plop 159.13, 194.6, 320.4, 367.6
plop down 194.6
plosive 524.12
plot (n) 231.4, 309.15, 309.16, 381.3, 381.5, 415.3, 471.6, 706.3, 722.4, 937.1, 1069.9 (v) 380.7, 381.9, 381.10, 415.10, 839.6, 965.4
plot a course 182.27
plot of ground 231.4
plot of land 231.4
plot out 381.10
plotted 300.13, 381.12, 839.8, 965.7
plotter 357.10, 381.7, 1042.9
plotting (n) 381.5, 965.1 (a) 381.13
plotz 802.9
plough 410.17
plow (n) 1040.8 (v) 184.40, 290.3, 1069.17
plow back into 729.17
plowboy 1069.5
plowed 290.4
plow horse 311.13

plow in 1069.17
plowing 1069.13
plow into 459.15, 510.14
plowland 1069.8
plowman 1069.5
plow the deep 182.54
plow under 1069.17
plow up 1069.17
ploy 356.6, 415.3, 743.6
ploys 894.3
pluck (n) 359.3, 492.1, 905.3 (v) 6.5, 410.17, 472.11, 480.24, 708.40, 759.26, 905.5, 1069.19
pluck a crow with 456.13
pluck by the beard 454.3
plucked stringed instrument 711.4
pluckiness 359.3, 492.5
pluckless 94.13, 491.11
plucklessness 94.4, 491.2
pluck out 192.10
pluck the beard 96.13
pluck up 192.10, 912.8
pluck up by the roots 395.14
pluck up courage 492.13
pluck up heart 492.12
pluck up one's spirits 121.7
plucky 359.14, 404.8, 492.16
plug (n) 89.7, 239.12, 293.4, 311.12, 352.4, 356.13, 509.3, 1034.20 (v) 175.7, 293.7, 295.21, 352.15, 360.3, 509.11, 725.14, 904.12
plug along 175.7, 360.3
plug-and-play 1042.18
plug at 360.3
plug away 330.15, 360.3, 725.14, 827.6, 856.3
plugged 293.11
plugged-in 838.2
plugged lie 751.3
plugged nickel 998.5
plugged up 293.11
plugger 352.9, 509.8
plugging (n) 360.1 (a) 360.8, 725.17
plug in 1032.26
plug the same theme 849.9
plug tobacco 89.2
plug-ugly 461.1, 593.4, 671.10
plug up 293.7
plum (n) 100.11, 609.36, 728.8, 738.7, 999.5 (a) 46.3
plumage 3.18, 295.3
plumaged 3.28
plumate 3.28
plumb (n) 200.2, 200.6, 297.6 (v) 200.10, 275.10, 300.10, 521.9, 938.23, 940.2 (a) 200.12, 277.6, 794.10
plumbable 521.10
plumbago 1056.2
plumb bob 200.6
plumbing 385.4
plumbless 275.12
plumblessness 275.1
plumb line 200.6, 277.2
plumb-line 200.10, 275.10
plumbness 200.1
plumb rule 200.6
plumb the depths 112.16, 275.10
plumb tuckered 21.8
plum-colored 46.3
plumcot 797.8
plume (n) 3.16 (v) 79.20, 498.9
plumed 3.28, 198.13, 498.11
plume feather 3.16
plumelike 3.27
plume of smoke 1067.1
plume oneself on 136.5
plummet (n) 200.6, 297.6, 633.4 (v) 194.5, 252.6, 367.6, 633.6
plummeting (n) 194.1, 633.4 (a) 194.11
plumose 3.28
plump (n) 52.3 (v) 159.13, 194.6, 259.8, 367.6, 371.18, 1047.6 (a) 257.18
plump as a dumpling 257.18
plump as a partridge 257.18
plump down 159.12
plump for 371.18, 449.14
plumpness 257.8
plump up 1047.6
plum-purple 46.3
plumule 3.16, 3.17, 310.23
plumy 3.27
plunder (n) 482.6, 482.11 (v) 482.17
plunderbund 617.9
plunderer 483.6
plundering (n) 482.6, 671.3 (a) 482.22
plunderous 482.22
plunge (n) 174.3, 194.3, 252.2, 367.1, 393.3, 633.4, 729.4, 737.19, 743.12, 759.2, 917.8 (v) 172.5, 174.12, 182.55, 194.5, 252.6, 297.15, 367.6, 401.5, 401.7, 633.6, 729.17, 737.23, 759.25, 917.15
plunge ahead 401.7
plunge bath 79.8, 743.12
plunged in debt 623.8
plunged in grief 112.26
plunge headlong 401.7
plunge in 191.7, 459.25
plunge into 324.3, 401.7, 404.3, 570.12, 725.15, 818.7
plunge into debt 623.6
plunge into difficulties 1013.12
plunge into dissipation 669.6
plunge in water 367.7
plunge one into despair 112.18
plunge one into sorrow 112.19
plunger 367.4, 737.11, 759.21
plunge the world into war 458.14
plunging (n) 172.2, 367.3 (a) 172.8, 194.11, 200.12, 204.18, 275.12
plunging back 746.2
plungingness 200.1
plunk (n) 52.3, 902.5 (v) 52.15, 159.13, 194.6, 367.6, 708.40, 902.15
plunk down 194.6, 624.16
plunk down the money 624.17
pluperfect (n) 530.12, 837.5 (a) 837.9
plural (n) 530.8 (a) 883.7
plural, the 883.1
pluralism 612.7, 782.1, 783.1, 797.1, 883.1, 952.6
pluralistic 612.16, 782.3, 797.14, 883.7
pluralistic idealism 1053.3
plurality 792.6, 883.1, 883.2
pluralization 883.3
pluralize 883.5
pluralized 883.7
pluralness 883.1
plural number 883.1
plural system 609.18
plural vote 371.6
plurative 883.7
plurification 883.3
plurify 883.5
pluripresence 221.2
plus (n) 253.2, 993.5 (v) 253.4 (a) 253.10, 1032.35
pluses 386.2
plush (n) 1047.4 (a) 501.21, 1047.15
plushiness 1047.1
plushness 501.5
plushy 1047.15
plus-one (n) 104.12, 104.13, 616.2, 634.2 (v) 582.18
plus side 124.1
plus sign 253.2
plus size 257.4
plus-size 257.16
Pluto 682.5, 1073.9
plutocracy 612.4, 618.6
plutocrat 618.7
plutology 731.11
Plutonian 682.8
Plutonic 682.8
plutonic rock 1059.1
plutonium bomb 462.20
Plutus 618.8
pluvial 316.11
pluviograph 316.7
pluviographic 316.12
pluviography 316.9
pluviometer 316.7, 317.8, 1065.10
pluviometric 316.12
pluviometry 316.9
pluvioscope 316.7
pluvioscopic 316.12
pluviose 316.11
pluviosity 316.2, 1065.1
pluvious 316.11
ply (n) 291.1, 296.2 (v) 73.6, 177.20, 182.13, 182.25, 182.30, 291.5, 387.10, 439.9, 440.12, 725.8
plyboard 1054.3
plying 440.3
ply one's trade 724.12, 731.15
ply the oar 182.53, 725.9
ply upon 439.9
plywood 296.2, 1054.3
PM 315.1
pneuma 92.28, 306.2, 919.4
pneumatic 283.15, 317.12, 1016.18, 1039.10, 1067.9
pneumaticness 1016.3
pneumatics 317.5, 1039.5, 1067.2
pneumatogram 552.4
pneumatological 1039.10
pneumatometer 1067.7
pneumatophanic 348.9
pneumatophany 348.1
pneumatostatics 1039.5
pneumonia 85.16
pneumonic 2.32, 85.61
pneumonoultramicroscopicsilicovolcanoconiosis 545.3
poach 11.5, 382.9, 482.13
poached 11.7
poached eggs 10.26
poached fish 10.24
poacher 382.5, 483.1, 483.8
poaching 11.2, 482.1
poachy 243.3
pochette 195.2
pock (n) 85.37, 283.4, 284.6, 294.1, 1004.1 (v) 284.14
pocked 47.13, 284.17, 294.7
pockedness 288.1
pocket (n) 184.32, 195.2, 284.2, 728.14, 729.15, 746.3, 750.2, 760.1 (v) 134.8, 159.15, 212.5, 474.5, 480.13, 613.10, 627.3 (a) 258.12
pocket billiards 760.1
pocket book 554.3
pocketbook 549.11, 729.15
pocket borough 609.16
pocket change 728.19
pocket computer 1042.2
pocket edition 258.6
pocket lighter 1021.4
pocket money 728.19
pocket notebook 549.11
pocket picking 482.3
pocket-size 258.12
pocket-sized 258.12
pocket the affront 134.8, 148.4
pocket veto 444.2, 613.7
pockiness 288.1, 294.2
pockmark (n) 284.6, 1004.1 (v) 284.14
pockmarked 47.13, 284.17
pocky 47.13, 85.61, 288.6
pococurante 102.7
pococurantism 102.2
PO'd 152.30
pod (n) 87.11, 295.16, 310.30, 770.5 (v) 6.9
podagra 85.22
podagric 85.61
podcasting 343.5, 352.1
podesta 596.2
podex 217.4
podginess 257.8, 268.2
podgy 257.18, 268.10
podiatrist 90.9
podium 901.13
Podunk 230.3
poem 547.10, 720.4, 1016.6
poem without words, a 712.10
poesy 720.1, 720.3, 720.5, 720.11
poet 547.15, 718.4, 720.12, 986.12
poetaster 720.13
poetastering 720.3
poetastery 720.3
poetcraft 720.2
poetess 720.12
poetic 720.16, 986.24

poetical 720.16, 986.24
poetic diction 720.2
poetic genius 720.11
poetic image 986.6
poetic imagery 986.6
poetic imagination 986.2
poeticism 720.2
poeticize 720.14
poetic justice 649.1, 720.2
poetic language 720.2
poetic license 430.1, 720.2
poetico-mystical 720.16
poetico-mythological 720.16
poetico-philosophic 720.16
poetic prose 721.1
poetics 720.2, 723.3
poeticule 720.13
poetic works 720.5
poet-in-residence 227.2
poetize 720.14
poet laureate 720.12
poetlike 720.16
poetling 720.13
poetress 720.12
poetry 544.2, 720.1
poetryless 721.5
po-faced 99.8, 500.19, 510.22, 522.20, 980.10
pogrom 308.4
poignancy 17.5, 68.1, 98.5, 544.3, 544.4
poignant 17.14, 24.13, 26.10, 68.6, 93.24, 98.20, 544.11, 544.12
poikilotherm 311.24
poikilothermic 1023.20
poikilothymia 926.5
point (n) 17.5, 159.1, 161.1, 165.1, 198.2, 216.2, 237.6, 245.1, 248.2, 258.7, 278.2, 283.9, 285.3, 380.1, 387.4, 387.5, 489.6, 517.5, 518.1, 518.2, 530.15, 548.6, 715.4, 748.2, 749.2, 749.3, 749.6, 752.3, 766.3, 816.1, 820.2, 824.1, 857.4, 872.4, 937.1, 1008.10, 1040.2 (v) 161.5, 161.7, 285.7, 297.15, 517.19, 530.16, 896.3
point, the 997.6
pointable 161.13
point a moral 568.16
point-and-click 714.1, 1042.4
point-and-shoot 714.1
point at 161.5, 508.8, 517.18, 983.10
point at issue 937.1, 938.10
point-blank 535.3
point-blank refusal 442.2
point break 916.4
point-by-point comparison 943.2
point champain 661.6
pointed 278.6, 285.9, 489.15, 518.10, 537.6, 974.6, 997.21
pointedness 285.1, 537.1
pointer 311.17, 517.4, 551.3, 574.7
point guard 747.2
pointillage 47.3
pointillé (n) 554.15 (a) 47.13
pointillism 47.3
pointillistic 47.13
point in common 784.3
point indirectly to 519.4
pointing 517.3
pointing out 517.3
pointing to (n) 517.3 (a) 599.13
pointing with pride and viewing with alarm 609.37
point in question 937.1, 938.10
pointless 117.6, 125.13, 286.3, 391.9
pointlessness 117.1, 391.2
point man 216.2, 577.3, 749.2, 816.1
point of a pin 258.7
point of articulation 524.12
point of character 865.4
point of contact 73.1
point of convergence 169.1, 208.4
point of departure 188.5
point of difference 780.2
point of etiquette 580.3
point of honor 644.2
point of interest 997.5
point of likeness 784.3
point of no return 843.5
point of purchase 731.1
point of reference 159.2
point of repose 826.1
point of the chin 216.6
point of time 832.4
point of vantage 27.7
point of view 27.7, 932.1, 952.2, 953.6, 978.2
point-of-view 722.5
point out 517.18, 865.11, 983.10
point out to 161.6
point person 552.1, 574.6, 577.3
point player 747.2
points 620.1, 623.3, 662.3
points of the compass 161.3
point spread 759.2
point tense 530.12
point the finger at 599.7
point the finger of scorn 508.8
point the way 161.6
point to 133.11, 161.5, 517.18, 888.4, 896.3, 957.8, 983.10
point to be solved 522.8
point to from afar 519.4
point to one 888.4
point-to-point navigation 182.2
point-to-point race 757.1
point up 997.14
pointy 285.9
pointy-head 929.1
poise (n) 33.4, 106.3, 321.1, 517.14, 790.1, 970.5 (v) 193.10, 790.6
poised 106.13, 790.9, 900.9, 970.21
poison (n) 82.3, 88.14, 308.11, 1000.3, 1001.3 (v) 80.17, 85.52, 308.13, 393.12, 1000.6, 1037.10
poisoned 85.60, 1037.11
poisoner 308.11
poisoning 85.31, 308.1, 393.2, 604.6
poisonous 64.7, 82.7, 1000.12
poisonous plant 1001.6
poisonousness 82.3, 1000.5
poison-pen letter 512.4
poison-pen writer 512.7
poison pill 738.6
poisson 10.24
poitrine d'agneau 10.16
poitrine de veau 10.15
poivre 63.7
poke (n) 195.2, 517.15, 729.15, 770.8, 902.2, 902.4 (v) 175.6, 331.14, 375.15, 517.22, 902.12, 902.14, 938.31
poke about 938.23
poke along 175.6
poke around 938.31, 938.32
poke at 73.6, 459.16
poke full of holes 958.4
poke fun at 489.13, 508.8
poke in 191.7
poke into 938.23
poke one's nose in 214.7, 981.4
poke out 283.10
poker 758.4, 759.10, 1020.12
poker bet 759.3
poker dice 759.8
poker face 94.1, 123.1, 344.3, 522.5
poker-faced 522.20
poker hand 758.4, 759.10
pokerlike 1046.11
poke the fire 1020.22
pokey 429.9
pokiness 117.1, 175.1, 258.1, 661.3, 998.1
poking 175.10, 938.38
pokunt 678.1
poky (n) 429.9 (a) 117.6, 175.10, 258.10, 661.12, 810.15, 998.18
pol 610.1
polar 215.5, 820.12, 1032.31
polar coordinates 300.5
polar easterlies 318.9
polar front 317.4
Polaris 574.8, 1073.4
Polaris submarine 180.9
polarity 215.1, 264.1, 451.2, 779.1, 873.1, 1032.8
polarity of opinion 456.2
polarization 215.1, 456.2, 908.1, 1032.8
polarize 215.4
polarized one-on-one 215.5
polarizing 456.17
polar lights 1025.16
Polaroid 714.3, 714.11
Polaroid film 714.10
Polaroid glasses 29.3
polar opposite, the 779.2
polar opposites 215.2
polar opposition 215.1
polar ray 1025.16
polar star 574.8, 1073.4
polar vortex 318.8
pole (n) 180.13, 180.15, 198.2, 261.4, 272.6, 273.1, 273.3, 756.3, 820.2, 901.8, 915.5, 1032.8, 1054.3 (v) 904.9
poleax 308.18, 395.11
polecat 71.3, 311.22, 660.6
pole horse 311.13
polemic (n) 456.5, 457.1, 935.4, 935.12 (a) 110.26, 935.19
polemical 110.26, 456.17, 935.19
polemicist 935.12
polemicize 935.16
polemics 541.6, 935.4
polemist 935.12
polemize 935.16
pole position 249.2, 756.3, 814.1
poles 215.2
poles apart 780.7
poles asunder 780.7
pole-sitting 333.2
polestar 208.4, 574.8, 907.3, 1073.4
pole vault 366.1
pole vaulter 366.4
pole vaulting 366.3
police (n) 1008.17 (v) 808.12, 1008.18, 1008.20
police band 1034.13
police blotter 549.11
police captain 1008.15
police car 179.11
police citation 646.6
police commissioner 1008.15
police constable 1008.15
policed 1008.21
police department 1008.1
police detective 576.10
police dog 311.16
police force 1008.17
police headquarters 230.5
police inquiry 938.4
police inspector 1008.15
police interrogation 938.13
police investigation 938.4
police lieutenant 1008.15
policeman 1008.15
police matron 1008.15
police officer 1008.15
police officer's uniform 5.7
police photograph 714.3
police sergeant 1008.15
police state 612.4
police station 230.5
police up 808.12
police-up 808.6
police van 179.11
police whistle 400.1, 517.15
policewoman 1008.15
Polichinelle 707.10
policing 1008.1
policy 328.3, 381.4, 609.4, 920.7, 1008.4
policyholder 438.7
policymaker 381.6, 574.3, 610.7
policyspeak 523.9
polio 85.27
poliomyelitis 85.27
polis 230.1, 232.1
poli-sci 609.2
polish (n) 79.17, 287.2, 287.4, 392.3, 496.1, 504.4, 533.1 (v) 287.7, 392.11, 1044.8
polished 287.11, 392.13, 407.12, 496.8, 504.16, 533.6, 1002.9, 1025.33
polishing 392.4, 1044.2
polish of 820.8
polish off 308.14, 407.4, 820.6
Polish Power 609.31
polish the apple 138.9
polish the platter 8.24
polish up 392.11, 570.14, 989.18

polite 504.13
polite act 504.6
polite behavior 504.3
polite commendation 509.6
polite deportment 504.3
polite literature 547.12, 718.1
politeness 24.3, 504.1, 580.3
polite society 578.6
politesse 504.1, 580.3
politic 413.22, 415.12, 494.8, 609.43, 920.19, 995.5
political 609.43, 612.16
political action committee 609.31, 617.4, 894.6
political action committee politics 609.1
political activism 330.1
political activist 330.8
political agenda 609.13
political asylum 1009.1
political behavior 609.2
political belief 953.3
political canard 609.14
political conservatism 853.3
political convention 609.8
political correctness 609.4
political corruption 609.29
political dabbler 610.4
political detainee 429.11
political doubletalk 609.37
political-economical 731.23
political economist 731.12
political economy 609.2, 731.11
political election 371.9
political faith 953.3
political front 609.33
political geography 609.2
political government 612.1
political hack 610.1, 610.4
political hopeful 610.9
political influence 415.4, 609.29
political intrigue 609.34
political jargon 609.37
political leader 610.1
political leadership 609.3
politically correct 609.43
politically incorrect 609.43
political machine 609.24, 617.1
political map 159.5
political organization 612.1
political party 609.24, 612.1, 617.4
political patronage 609.36
political philosopher 610.12
political philosophy 609.2, 953.3
political police 1008.17
political principles 612.7
political prisoner 429.11
political realist 415.8
political science 609.2
political scientist 609.2
political system 612.1
political theory 609.2
political worker 610.12
politicaster 610.4
politician 413.11, 415.8, 575.15, 610.1, 610.4
politicization 609.1
politicize 609.38, 611.16
politick 609.38
politicking 609.12
politicness 995.1
politico 610.1
politico-commercial 609.43
politico-diplomatic 609.43
politico-ecclesiastical 609.43
politico-economic 609.43, 731.23
politico-ethical 609.43
politico-geographical 609.43
politico-judicial 609.43
politico-military 609.43
politico-moral 609.43
politico-religious 609.43
politico-scientific 609.43
politico-social 609.43
politico-theological 609.43
politics 415.2, 609.1, 609.2
polity 232.1, 381.4, 609.1, 609.4, 612.1, 920.7
polity, the 606.1
polka dot 47.3, 517.5
polka-dot 47.13
poll (n) 198.7, 371.6, 609.20, 609.21, 871.6, 938.14 (v) 268.6, 371.18, 549.15, 938.29, 1017.17
pollard (n) 310.10 (v) 268.6
pollarded 268.9
pollarded tree 310.10
pollbook 609.20
polled 268.9
pollen (n) 305.11, 310.28, 1051.5 (v) 78.10
pollen count 85.34, 1051.5
pollen grain 310.28
pollen sac 310.28
pollen tube 310.28
poller 938.16
pollex 73.5
pollinate 78.10, 890.8
pollination 78.3, 890.3
polling 371.6
polling booth 609.20
polling place 609.20
polling station 609.20
pollinization 78.3
pollinize 78.10
pollinosis 85.34
polliwog 183.2, 302.10, 311.26
poll-parrot 336.4
polls 609.20
pollster 938.16, 1017.15
pollutable 80.20
pollutant 1001.3
pollute 80.17, 85.51, 88.23, 389.4, 389.5, 393.10, 393.12, 694.5, 797.12, 1000.6
polluted 80.20, 82.5, 88.33, 654.14, 1004.10
pollution 80.4, 82.1, 389.1, 393.2, 694.2, 797.3, 1000.3, 1072.2
pollution of the aquifer 1072.2
pollutive 80.23, 82.7, 393.44
polly 336.4
Pollyanna 124.5
Pollyannaish 109.11, 124.11
Pollyannaism 124.2
Pollyanna optimism 124.2
polly-parrot 336.4
polo ground 743.11
Polonian 494.8
Polonius 422.3
polo pony 311.13
poltergeist 680.7, 689.6, 988.1
poltergeistism 689.6
poltroon (n) 491.6 (a) 491.12
poltroonery 491.3
poltroonish 491.12
poltroonishness 491.3
poltroonism 491.3
polyandrist 563.11
polyandrium 309.15
polyandrous 563.19
polychrest 86.3
polychromatic 35.16, 47.9
polychromatism 47.1
polychrome (n) 35.4, 47.1 (v) 47.7 (a) 47.9, 712.21
polychromic 47.9
polychromist 716.4
polychromize 47.7
polycot 310.3
polycotyl 310.3
polycotyledon 310.3
polydipsia 100.7
polyester 4.1
polygamist 563.11
polygamous 563.19
polygenesis 861.3
polygeny 861.3
polyglot 523.16
polygonal 278.11
polygraph 92.8
polygraphic 547.25
polygynist 563.11
polygynous 563.19
polyhedral 218.7, 278.11
polyhistor 929.3
polyhistorian 929.3
polyhistoric 928.21
polyhistory 928.6
Polyhymnia 710.22, 720.11, 986.2
polymath (n) 413.12, 929.3 (a) 928.21
polymathic 928.21
polymathy 570.4, 928.6
polymer 1054.6
polymerase 7.10
polymeric 1060.9
polymerize 1060.8
polymerous 1060.9
Polymnia 710.22
polymorphic 783.3
polymorphism 783.1
polymorphous 783.3
polymorphous perversity 75.5
polymyxin 86.29
Polynesian race 312.2
polynomial 883.8
polyonymy 527.1
polyp 85.37
polypeptide 7.6
polyphagia 672.1
polyphagic 672.6
Polyphemus 15.6
polyphone 524.12
polyphonic 524.30, 708.52
polyphonic music 708.18
polyphonic prose 721.1
polyphonism 708.20
polyphonous 524.30
polyphony 708.20
polyploid 305.21
polyploidy 305.8
polysaccharide 7.5
polysaccharose 7.5
polysemant 539.2
polysemantic 539.4
polysemous 539.4, 971.16
polysemousness 539.1, 971.5
polysemy 539.1
polysyllabic 523.23, 545.10
polysyllabic profundity 545.1
polysyllabism 545.3
polysyllable 526.1, 526.10
polysynthetic 523.23
polytechnic 567.5
polytheism 675.5
polytheist 675.16
polytheistic 675.25
polytonic 523.23
polytropic 364.6
polyunsaturated fat 7.7, 1056.1
polyvalence 1060.4
polyvalent 1060.10
poma 753.1
pomade (n) 1056.3 (v) 1056.8
pomander 70.6
pomatum 1056.3
pome 10.38
pome fruit 310.4
pomiculture 1069.2
pomme de terre 10.35
pommel (n) 901.18 (v) 604.12, 902.16
pommel horse 760.5
pommes frites 10.35
Pomona 1069.4
pomp 33.7, 501.6, 580.1, 812.3
pompadour (n) 1016.14 (v) 3.22
pomp and circumstance 501.6
pom-pom 462.12
pomposity 140.4, 501.7, 545.1, 545.2, 580.1, 970.5
pompous 500.17, 501.22, 502.10, 534.3, 545.8, 580.8, 970.21
pompousness 500.3, 501.7, 534.1, 545.1, 923.2
pompous prolixity 545.1
ponce 500.9, 665.18
pond 241.1
ponder 362.7, 931.12
ponderability 297.1, 763.1
ponderable 297.19, 763.6
pondering (n) 931.2 (a) 931.21
ponderosity 297.1
ponderous 117.6, 257.19, 297.16, 297.17, 414.20, 534.3, 1013.19
ponderousness 117.1, 257.9, 297.1, 414.3, 534.1, 1013.9
ponder over 931.13
pondlet 241.1
pondlike 241.5
pondy 241.5
pone 10.29
pong (n) 71.1 (v) 69.6, 71.4
pongy 71.5
poniard 459.25
pontiff 699.9
pontific 501.22, 698.15, 970.18
pontifical 501.22, 698.15, 970.22
pontificalia 702.1
pontificality 417.7, 501.7

pontificals 702.1
pontificate (n) 417.7, 698.2, 698.6 (v) 501.14, 545.6, 946.14, 970.10
pontification 501.7, 545.1, 970.6
Pontius Pilate 596.4
pontoon 180.11
pontoon bridge 383.9
pony (n) 258.4, 311.10, 341.3, 728.8, 757.2 (a) 258.12
ponycart 179.3
Pony Express 553.4
pony-express rider 353.1
ponytail 3.5, 1016.14
pony-trek 177.34
pony-trekking 177.6
pony up 478.14, 624.16
pooch (n) 311.16 (v) 283.11
pooched 283.16
poof (n) 75.15 (a) 34.4
poofter 75.15
pooh 508.9
poohed 21.8
pooh-pooh 157.6, 508.9, 955.5
pooh-poohеr 955.4
pooh-pooh theory 523.13
pooka 678.8
pool 241.1, 617.9, 728.14, 737.17, 743.12, 758.4, 759.5, 760.1
pool hall 743.11, 760.1
pooling 208.8, 450.1
pooling of resources 450.1
pool one's interests 805.4
pool one's interests with 450.4
poolroom 743.11
poolside 241.5
pool table 760.1
poonghie 699.14
poop (n) 12.4, 17.3, 18.1, 217.7, 551.2 (v) 21.6
pooped 16.12, 21.8, 331.20, 393.36
pooped out 21.8
poo-poo 12.4
poop out 16.9, 21.6, 410.13, 911.3
poopsy 104.10
poopsy-woopsy 104.10
poopy 92.39
poor 16.15, 137.10, 270.20, 414.15, 510.21, 619.7, 661.12, 885.5, 936.12, 992.10, 992.12, 998.21, 1005.9
poor, the 606.4, 619.3
poor as a church mouse 619.7
poor behavior 321.2
poor bet 972.9
poorboy 10.32
poor creature 660.2
poor custody 340.1
poor devil 96.11, 619.4, 660.2
poor diction 534.1
poor ear 48.3
poor excuse 376.1, 600.4
poor farm 1009.4
poor fist 547.6
poor guardianship 340.1
poor health 82.1, 85.3
poorhouse 1009.4
poor husbandry 406.2
poor imitation 787.1
poor in spirit 137.11
poorish 16.15
poor judgment 948.1
poor likeness 350.2
poorling 619.4
poor lookout 972.9
poor loser 412.5
poorly argued 936.12
poorly off 619.7
poor man's roulette 759.8
poor-mouth 512.9, 950.2
poorness 137.1, 270.5, 619.1, 661.3, 998.2, 1005.3
poor opinion 510.1
poor outlook 969.1
poor performance 414.5
poor person 619.4
poor possibility 969.1, 972.9
poor prognosis 972.9
poor prospect 969.1, 972.9
poor quality 1005.4
poor-quality 1000.9
poor reputation 661.1
Poor Richard's Almanac 832.7
poor show 414.5
poor sight 28.1
poor-sighted 28.11
poor sport 412.5
poor stewardship 340.1, 389.1
poor taste 497.1
poor timing 844.2
poor tool 16.6
poor track record 406.1
poor turnout 885.2
poor unfortunate 1011.7
Pooterish 497.6
poove 75.15
pop (n) 10.49, 52.3, 56.3, 497.1, 560.10, 560.14, 708.7, 756.1, 842.8 (v) 52.15, 56.8, 87.22, 283.11, 745.5 (a) 497.14
pop at 459.22
pop concert 708.33
pop culture 497.1
pope 699.9
popedom 417.7, 698.2, 698.6
popehood 417.7
popeism 675.8
popery 675.8
popeship 417.7
pope's nose 10.23
popeyed 28.12, 122.9, 283.16
popeyes 2.9, 27.9, 28.6
pop fly 745.3
pop for 478.19, 624.18
pop hero 662.9
pop in 189.7, 191.3
pop into one's head 989.15
popish 675.29, 698.15
popliteal space 2.7, 177.14
pop literature 547.12, 718.1
pop music 708.7
pop musician 710.2
popo 217.5
pop off 307.19
pop one's cherry 665.20
pop one's cork 105.17, 926.22
pop out 745.5
popover 10.31
poppers 87.5
poppet 302.3, 562.6
poppied 87.23
pop pills 87.22
popping 56.11
popping of the question 562.8
popple (n) 238.14 (v) 238.22
pop psychology 92.1
poppy 22.10
poppycock 520.3, 923.1
poppycockish 520.7
pop quiz 938.2
pops 560.10, 708.33, 842.8
pop the question 440.9, 440.14, 562.22
populace 227.1
populace, the 312.1, 312.4, 606.1
popular 100.29, 104.23, 373.13, 476.9, 497.14, 509.19, 578.11, 606.8, 662.16, 700.3, 864.12, 869.9
popular acceptance 662.1
popular authority 417.1
popular belief 953.6, 954.3
popular concert 708.33
popular crowd 617.6
popular favor 662.1
popular front 609.24, 609.33
popular hero 662.9
popular idol 662.9
popularity 104.1, 509.2, 578.2, 662.1
popularization 497.8
popularize 341.10, 497.9, 521.6
popular literature 547.12, 718.1
popular mandate 417.1
popular music 708.7
popular musician 710.2
popular prices 633.2
popular regard 104.1
popular song 708.7
popular taste 497.1
popular tune 708.7
popular vote 609.18, 609.22
populate 159.17, 225.9
populated 225.12
population (n) 159.7, 225.2, 227.1 (a) 606.8
population, the 312.4, 606.1
populational 606.8
population drift 771.3
population explosion 251.2
population statistics 227.1, 312.10
population study 312.10
Populist Party 609.24
populous 225.12, 770.22, 884.9
pop up 33.8, 33.9, 131.6, 186.6, 193.9, 745.5, 831.6, 972.11
pop-up 745.3
Pop Warner football 746.1
porc 10.17
porcelain (n) 742.2 (a) 742.7
porcelain clay 742.3
porch 189.6, 197.21, 703.9
porcine 257.18, 311.45
porcupine 311.22
pore (n) 2.23, 190.9, 292.1, 292.5 (v) 27.14
pore over 27.14, 570.12, 938.24
poriferous 292.20
pork 10.17, 609.36
pork barrel 375.7, 482.11, 609.36, 729.13, 863.2
pork-barreling 609.34
pork-barrel legislation 609.34
pork-barrel politician 610.6
pork-barrel politics 609.1
pork chop 10.19
porker 257.12, 311.9
pork out 672.5
porky 257.18
porn (n) 547.12, 666.4, 718.1 (a) 665.29
porno (n) 666.4 (a) 665.29
porno film 666.4
pornographic 665.29, 666.9
pornographic art 666.4
pornographic literature 547.12, 666.4, 718.1
pornographomania 666.4
pornography 547.12, 666.4, 718.1
porn star 665.14
porose 292.20
porosity 292.1, 292.8
porous 190.20, 292.20
porousness 292.8
porphyritic 1059.12
porphyry 1059.1
porpoise (n) 311.29 (v) 184.40
porpoising 184.13
porraceous 44.4
porridge 1062.5, 1063.2
port (n) 33.4, 184.22, 186.5, 190.9, 220.1, 321.1, 1009.1, 1009.6, 1042.3 (a) 220.4
portability 258.1
portable 176.18, 258.12
portable classroom 567.10
portable field unit 1036.6
portable television 1035.11
portage 630.6
portal 189.5, 189.6, 197.19
portal site 1042.18
portal-to-portal pay 624.4
portal vein 2.23
portative 176.18
portcullis 1012.5
porte-cochere 189.6
porte-monnaie 729.15
portend 133.10, 399.6, 962.10
portending 133.16
portent 133.3, 133.6, 399.2
portentous 133.16, 399.8, 870.14, 997.20
portentousness 133.6
porter 178.13, 577.5, 1008.12
porter's lodge 228.9
portfire 1021.4
portfolio 417.9, 549.1, 554.17, 738.2
portico 189.6, 197.19, 273.5, 383.3
port in a storm 1009.1
portion (n) 8.10, 86.6, 87.20, 244.2, 267.2, 477.5, 478.9, 793.1, 793.5, 964.2 (v) 477.6, 802.18
portion control 7.13
portioned out 477.12
portioning 477.1
portion off 477.9
portion out 477.8
portliness 257.8
portly 257.18

portmanteau 526.11
portmanteau word 526.11, 539.2
portmantologism 526.11
port of call 1009.6
port of embarkation 188.5
portrait 349.2, 349.5, 712.14, 714.3, 785.1
portrait bust 349.6
portraitist 716.4
portrait painter 716.4
portrait statue 349.6
portraiture 349.1, 349.2, 712.14
portray 349.8, 349.9, 349.12, 704.30, 712.19
portrayal 349.1, 349.2, 349.4, 704.8, 712.14, 722.1
portrayer 716.2
portraying 349.13
portraying in the mind 986.6
portreeve 575.16, 1008.15
portside 220.1
portsider 220.3, 745.2
port tack 220.1
Portuguese roll 10.31
port-wine 41.6
port-wine mark 1004.1
port-wine stain 517.5, 1004.1
posada 228.15
pose (n) 321.1, 354.3, 500.3, 517.14 (v) 159.12, 439.5, 500.13, 951.12
pose against 215.4
pose a question 938.20
pose as 349.12, 354.22
pose for effect 500.13
Poseidon 183.1, 240.3, 678.10
pose over against 215.4
pose problems 1013.10
poser 357.6, 357.8, 500.8, 522.8, 693.3, 938.10, 1013.7
poseur 336.4, 357.6, 357.8, 500.8
posh 501.21, 578.13, 607.10, 632.11
poshness 501.5
posiness 533.3
posing 349.4, 354.3, 500.3
posing against 215.1, 264.2
posing over against 215.1, 264.2
posit 159.12, 951.12
position (n) 159.1, 159.3, 245.2, 334.1, 524.3, 607.1, 609.4, 662.4, 724.3, 724.5, 753.3, 756.3, 765.1, 807.2, 809.2, 935.5, 935.7, 953.6, 978.1, 978.2 (v) 159.11
positional 159.19
positional notation 1017.4
positioned 159.18
positioning 159.6
position line 159.3
position of attention 200.1
position paper 334.1, 352.2, 381.4, 556.1, 609.7, 801.3, 953.4
position statement 801.3
positive (n) 714.5, 785.5 (a) 247.12, 334.8, 361.13, 449.21, 761.15, 788.9, 953.21, 960.2, 970.13, 970.21, 970.22, 997.21, 1017.23, 1032.35
positive charge 1032.5
positive declaration 334.1
positive discrimination 371.3, 843.2
positive fact 761.3
positive feedback 1041.6
positive geotropism 297.5
positively right 973.17
positive misprision 655.1
positive mood 324.1
positiveness 334.2, 361.5, 970.1, 970.5, 970.6
positive note 1010.3
positive philosophy 1052.6
positive pole 1032.8
positive ray 1033.5
positive reinforcement 92.26
positive relation 775.1
positive self-image 140.1
positive statement 334.1
positive transference 92.33
positive valence 1060.4
positivism 970.6, 987.2, 1052.6
positivist (n) 361.6, 970.7, 987.3, 1052.7 (a) 1052.12
positivistic 970.22, 987.6, 1052.12
positron emission tomography 91.9
posologist 86.35
posology 86.34
posse 461.22, 770.3, 938.15, 1008.17
possess 469.4, 480.13, 680.16, 691.9, 926.25, 928.12, 988.6
possess authority 18.11, 249.11, 417.13
possessed 95.17, 105.25, 469.8, 691.13, 926.29, 926.33, 988.10
possessed of 469.9
possessed with a demon 926.29
possessed with the devil 926.29
possess free and clear 469.4
possess incriminating evidence 957.15
possessing (n) 469.1 (a) 469.9, 926.34
possession 106.3, 232.1, 359.5, 387.7, 469.1, 480.1, 690.1, 691.2, 746.3, 926.1, 926.13, 988.5
possessions 471.1, 618.1
possessive 469.10, 651.5
possessive case 530.9
possessiveness 651.1
possessive noun 530.5
possessive pronoun 530.5
possess one of the facts 551.8
possess oneself 134.4
possess oneself of 480.19
possess one's soul in patience 134.4
possessor 470.1
possessorship 469.2
possessory 469.10
possess outright 469.4
possess sexually 480.15
possibility 519.1, 897.1, 966.1, 968.1, 972.8
possibility upon a possibility 971.8
possible 519.5, 966.6, 1017.23
possible, the 966.1
possible action 371.2
possible choice 371.2
possibleness 966.1
possible outcome 887.1
possibles 728.2
possible solution 940.1
possum 311.22
post (n) 159.2, 273.4, 273.5, 353.1, 460.6, 547.10, 553.4, 617.10, 724.5, 736.1, 747.3, 757.1, 901.8, 1054.3 (v) 159.12, 174.8, 176.15, 352.15, 401.5, 438.10, 549.15, 551.9, 553.12, 615.10, 624.16, 628.8, 871.8 (a) 553.14
postage 553.5
postage meter 553.5
postage stamp 553.5
postal 553.14
postal card 553.3
postal clerk 353.5, 553.7
postal code 553.9
postal order 728.11
postal service 553.7
postal services 553.4
postal system 553.7
postal union 553.7
post-and-beam construction 266.2
postbag 553.6
postbellum 464.9, 835.5
post bills 352.15
post boat 353.6
postbox 553.6
postboy 178.8, 353.1
post car 353.6
postcard 553.3
postcenal 835.5
postcibal 835.5
post coach 353.6
postcode 553.9
postdate (n) 832.4, 835.1 (v) 832.13, 833.2
postdated 833.3
postdating 833.1, 835.1
post day 553.4
post-determiner 530.6
postdiluvial 835.5
postdiluvian 835.5
posted 159.18, 438.12, 549.17, 928.18
poster 352.7, 353.6
poster child 786.4
posterial 217.10
posterior (n) 217.1, 217.4 (a) 217.9, 815.4, 835.4
posteriority 815.1, 835.1
posteriormost 217.9
posterity 559.2, 561.1, 817.4, 835.2
postern (n) 217.1 (a) 217.9
postern door 217.1
postexist 839.7
postexistence 839.2
postface 817.1
post factum 835.4
postfix (n) 817.1 (v) 253.4
post-formatted word processor 1042.11
postgrad 572.8
postgraduate (n) 572.8 (a) 568.19, 572,12
postgraduate school 567.5
post-horse 311.13, 353.6
posthumous 307.35, 835.5
posthypnotic suggestion 22.8
postilion 178.8
post-industrial 835.5
posting 159.6, 549.14, 615.2
Post-it Note 549.11
postlapsarian 654.12, 663.6, 835.5
postlapsarian nature 663.2
postlude 817.1
postman 353.5, 553.7
postmark 553.5
postmaster 353.5, 553.7
postmeridian 315.7
post meridiem 315.1
post-millennial 835.5
postmistress 353.5
postmodern 835.5, 841.13
postmodernism 841.3
postmortal 307.35
postmortem (n) 307.17 (v) 938.24 (a) 307.35
postmortem examination 307.17
postmortuary 307.35
postmundane 307.35
postnatal 1.4
post-obit 307.35
postobituary 307.35
post office 353.1, 553.7
post-office car 353.6
post-office clerk 553.7
post-office order 728.11
postpaid 624.22
post parade 757.3
postpartum depression 92.14, 926.5
postpone 390.6, 846.9
postponed 846.16
postponed payment 624.1
postponement 846.4, 857.3
post position 757.3
postposition 815.1
post-positional 530.17
postpositional 815.4
postpositive 815.4
postprandial 8.31, 11.6, 835.5
post production 706.6
postremogeniture 479.2
postrider 353.1
postscript 254.2, 817.1
post-season game 746.1
post time 757.3
posttonic 524.30
post-traumatic 92.39
post-traumatic stress disorder 92.17
postulant 440.7, 572.9, 699.17
postulate (n) 761.3, 767.2, 816.2, 935.7, 951.3, 952.2, 974.2 (v) 439.5, 951.9, 951.12
postulated 935.22, 951.14
postulation 935.7, 951.3
postulational 951.14
postulatory 951.13
postulatum 935.7
post up 352.15, 549.15, 628.8, 747.4

post-up 747.3
posture (n) 33.4, 321.1, 354.3, 517.14, 953.6, 978.1 (v) 500.13
posture maker 500.8
posturer 500.8
posturing 500.3
posturist 500.8
post-viral fatigue syndrome 21.1
postwar 464.9, 835.5
posy (n) 310.24, 310.25, 509.6, 770.7, 770.8 (a) 500.15, 501.18, 533.9
pot (n) 2.19, 87.11, 195.1, 247.4, 618.3, 646.3, 742.2, 758.4, 759.5 (v) 191.3, 212.9, 742.6, 904.12, 1069.18
potable (n) 10.49, 88.13 (a) 8.34
potage 10.10, 10.10
potash 890.4
potassium 7.11
potation 8.3, 8.4, 10.49, 88.5, 88.7, 88.13
potato 10.35
potato cellar 197.17
potato chip 10.30
potato crisp 10.30
potato head 924.4
potato masher 1063.4
potato race 457.12
potato salad 10.37
potato skins 10.9
potbellied 257.18, 283.15
potbelly 2.19, 257.12
potboiler 547.16, 718.5
pot companion 88.11, 588.5
potence 18.1, 76.2, 417.2
potency 15.1, 17.1, 18.1, 75.2, 76.2, 417.2, 894.1
potent 15.15, 18.12, 75.25, 76.13, 417.15, 894.13
potentate 575.8
potential (n) 413.4, 530.11, 966.1, 1032.12 (a) 519.5, 966.6
potential cautery 1020.15
potential difference 1032.12
potential energy 17.1
potentiality 18.2, 519.1, 966.1
potful 618.3
potgut 2.19
pot-gutted 257.18
pothead 87.21
pother (n) 105.6, 330.4, 810.4, 971.3, 985.3 (v) 96.13, 971.12, 985.7, 1013.13
potherb 310.4
potherbs 10.35
pothole 284.3
potholed 288.6
potholed road 288.2
pothook 1020.12
pothookery 547.7
pothooks 547.7
pothooks and hangers 547.7
pothouse 88.20
pot hunter 381.7
potion 8.4, 86.6, 88.7, 691.5
potlatch 701.9
potluck (n) 8.6, 759.2, 972.4 (a) 365.12
pot of gold 618.4
pot party 87.20
pot plant 310.3, 310.24
potpourri 70.6, 708.33, 770.13, 797.6
pot roast 10.13
pots and pans 11.4
potsherd 391.4, 793.3
potshoot 904.12
potshot (n) 759.2, 904.4 (v) 904.12
potted 88.33
potted version 557.1
potter (n) 716.7, 742.2 (v) 331.13, 998.14
potter away 486.5
potterer 331.8, 998.10
pottering 998.8
potter's clay 742.3
potter's earth 742.3
potter's field 309.15
potter's wheel 742.4, 858.10
pottery 712.16, 739.3, 742.1, 742.2, 1050.2
pottery design 717.5
pottiness 926.2
potting 742.1
potting shed 1069.11
potty (n) 12.11 (a) 926.27
potty-chair 12.11
potty-trained 373.15
potty training 12.11
pot-valiance 88.1
pot-valiancy 88.1
pot-valiant 88.34
pot-valor 88.1, 492.1
pot-valorous 88.34
pot-walloper 79.15
pouch (n) 195.2 (v) 283.11
pouched 283.16
pouching 283.15
poulard 311.28
poult 311.28
poultice (n) 86.33, 1063.2 (v) 91.24, 120.5
poultry 10.22, 311.28
poultry farm 1070.5
pounce (n) 194.1, 366.1, 367.1 (v) 194.5, 366.5, 367.6
pounce on 366.5, 367.6
pounces 474.4
pounce upon 131.7, 366.5, 367.6, 459.14, 480.16
pound (n) 55.1, 228.21, 429.7, 728.8, 902.4 (v) 26.8, 55.4, 182.55, 393.13, 429.12, 459.14, 708.44, 849.10, 902.16, 1051.9
pound a beat 1008.20
poundage 257.2, 297.1, 630.7
pound away 360.3, 725.14
pound cake 10.42
pounder 1051.7
pound-foolish 486.8
pound-foolishness 486.1
pound in 191.7
pounding (n) 55.1, 1051.4 (a) 55.7
pound net 356.13
pound out 340.9, 547.21, 708.39, 718.6, 892.8
pound sovereign 728.4
pounds, shillings, and pence 728.1
pound the ear 22.14
pound the pavement 177.23
pour (n) 238.5, 316.2 (v) 176.17, 190.13, 238.16, 316.10, 478.12, 909.25, 991.5
pour a broadside into 459.22
pour balm into 120.5, 670.7
pour balm on 465.7
pour balm upon 1056.8
pourboire 993.5
pour cold water on 379.4, 428.8
pour down 194.5
pour down the drain 486.4
pour forth 524.22, 540.5, 909.25
pour in 189.9
pouring 238.24, 316.11
pouring rain 316.2
pour it on 174.9, 330.14, 725.13
pour it on thick 355.3, 509.11, 511.6
pour money into 729.17
pour oil on 120.5, 1056.8
pour oil on the blaze 456.14
pour oil on the fire 105.12, 119.2, 375.17
pour oil on troubled waters 173.8, 464.8, 465.7, 670.7
pour on 295.24, 478.15, 1065.14
pour one's heart out 120.7, 524.21
pour on the coal 174.10
pour out 190.13, 238.17, 909.25
pour out blood like water 308.15
pour out the vials of one's wrath 152.16
pour over 238.17
pour water into a sieve 391.8, 486.4
pour water on 428.8
pour with rain 316.10
pousse-café 88.9
pou sto 159.2, 901.5
pout (n) 110.9, 265.4 (v) 110.15, 265.8, 283.11
pouts 110.10
POV camera 714.11
poverty 619.1, 992.3
poverty line 619.2
poverty-stricken 619.8
poverty subculture 606.4
POW camp 429.8
powder (n) 86.4, 462.14, 1016.11, 1051.5 (v) 188.7, 771.6, 1051.9, 1051.10 (a) 1051.11
powder and shot 462.13
powder barrel 462.2
powder charge 1074.8
powdered 771.10, 1051.11
powdered sugar 66.2, 66.3
powder grain 1074.8
powderiness 1051.1
powdering 1051.4
powder keg 462.2, 514.1, 1006.1
powderman 1058.9
powder metallurgy 1058.11
powder puff 1016.11
powder room 12.10
powder snow 1023.8
powder train 812.2
powdery 1051.11
power (n) 15.1, 17.1, 18.1, 232.1, 247.1, 249.3, 359.4, 384.2, 413.4, 417.1, 417.2, 417.5, 544.3, 594.1, 612.2, 618.3, 642.1, 883.4, 894.1, 902.1, 997.8 (v) 902.11 (a) 1040.14
power base 384.2, 894.4, 901.1
power behind the throne 415.8, 610.6, 894.6
powerboat 180.4
power breakfast 8.6, 423.3
power broker 609.30
powerbroker 415.8, 610.6, 894.6
power cable 1032.21
power cell 1075.4
power cord 1032.21
power couple 15.6
power cruiser 180.4
power cut 1032.20
power dinner 8.6
power dive 184.13, 367.1
power-dive 184.41
power down 857.12, 1032.26
power dressing 5.10
power-driven 1039.7, 1040.14
powered 1040.14
powered flight 184.1, 184.9
power elite 249.5, 997.8
power elite, the 575.14
power failure 1032.20
power for good 143.8
powerful 15.15, 18.12, 247.6, 417.15, 544.11, 894.13
powerful emotion 93.2
powerful like 784.15
powerfulness 15.1, 18.1, 417.2
power game 748.2
power grab 480.2
power grid 1032.19
power hitter 745.2
powerhouse 15.7, 330.8, 1032.19
power-hunger 100.10
power-hungry 100.28
powerless 16.12, 19.13, 895.3
powerless, the 606.4
powerlessness 19.1, 895.1
powerlifting 744.1
power load 1032.18
power loss 1032.20
power lunch 8.6, 423.3
power nap 22.3
power of attorney 615.1, 862.1
power of expression, the 532.2
power off 184.38
power of mind 920.1
power of mind over matter 689.6
power of reason 919.1
power of sight 27.1
power of speech, the 524.1
power of thought 920.1
power pack 18.1
powerpacked 18.12
power plant 184.25, 739.3, 1032.19, 1040.3
power play 749.3
power politics 609.1
powers 413.4, 679.3
power-sharing (n) 476.1, 612.7, 772.1 (a) 476.9
powers of darkness 680.1

power source 1032.2, 1040.3
power spin 184.15
power station 739.1, 1032.19
powers that be 249.5, 894.6
powers that be, the 575.14, 610.11, 612.3
powerstriding 84.2
power structure 18.1, 245.2, 249.5, 607.1, 809.4
power structure, the 575.14
power struggle 18.1
power supply 1032.2
power to act 615.1
power tool 1040.1
power train 1040.4
power up 1032.26
power user 1042.18
power vacuum 19.1, 418.1
power walk 177.27
power-walk 84.4
power walker 178.6
powerwalking 84.2
power wheel 742.4
power worker 1032.22
power yoga 84.2
powwow (n) 423.3, 541.5, 609.8 (v) 541.10
pox, the 85.18
P-plane 1074.4
PR 33.2
practicability 387.3, 889.3, 966.2
practicable 889.10, 966.7, 995.6
practicableness 1014.2
practical 387.18, 387.23, 724.15, 889.9, 889.10, 920.18, 956.5, 966.7, 987.6, 995.6, 1014.15
practical ability 413.1
practical consequence 518.1
practicality 387.3, 920.6, 966.2, 987.2, 1014.2
practical joke 489.10
practical joker 322.3, 357.1
practical knowledge 413.9, 928.1
practical mind 920.6
practical-minded 987.6
practical-mindedness 987.2
practicalness 987.2
practical nurse 90.10
practical person 987.3
practical piece 704.17
practical politics 609.1
practical scientist 928.11
practical skill 413.9
practical test 942.3
practical utility 387.3
practical wisdom 920.6
practice (n) 321.1, 328.1, 373.1, 373.3, 384.1, 413.9, 434.1, 568.3, 570.3, 597.4, 701.3, 724.6, 725.6, 889.1, 942.3, 1017.2 (v) 84.4, 328.4, 328.8, 384.5, 387.10, 434.3, 568.13, 570.12, 704.32, 724.11, 725.8, 744.2, 849.8
practice a profession 724.12
practice at the bar 597.5
practiced 413.26, 413.28
practice dentistry 90.14
practiced hand 413.13
practice domesticity 228.31
practice fraud upon 356.18
practice game 942.3
practice landing 184.18
practice law 597.5
practice medicine 90.14
practice nonviolence 670.5
practice of medicine 90.13
practice on one's credulity 356.15
practice run 942.3
practice self-control 670.5
practice self-denial 670.5
practice spiritualism 689.21
practice surgery 90.14
practice teacher 571.4
practice the golden rule 143.11
practice upon 942.8
practice what one preaches 434.2, 644.9
practicing (n) 849.2 (a) 328.10, 434.4, 692.8
practicing Christian 675.17
practitioner 90.8, 413.13, 726.1
prado 383.2
praedial 471.9
praedium 471.6
praelector 543.5, 571.7
praenomen 527.6
praepostor 571.4
praetor 596.2
praetorian guard 1008.14
pragmatic 920.18, 987.6, 995.6
pragmatical 387.18, 987.6, 995.6
pragmaticism 387.6, 987.2, 1052.6
pragmatic logic 935.2
pragmatism 387.6, 942.1, 987.2, 1052.6
pragmatist 987.3
prairie (n) 158.4, 201.3, 236.1, 310.8 (a) 233.6
prairie dog 311.22
prairie fire 1019.13
prairie oyster 10.20
prairies 233.1
prairie schooner 179.2
prairie squirrel 311.22
prairie wolf 311.19
praise (n) 149.1, 150.2, 509.5, 511.1, 646.4, 696.2 (v) 149.2, 509.12, 511.5, 646.8, 696.12
praise and glorify God 692.6
praise Father, Son, and Holy Ghost 696.12
praise God 696.12
praise God from whom all blessings flow 696.12
praise meeting 696.8
praiser 509.8
praise the Lord 696.12
praise to excess 509.12
praise to the skies 509.12, 511.5
praiseworthiness 509.7
praiseworthy 509.20
Prajnaparamita Sutra 683.9
pralltriller 709.18
pram 179.6
prana 306.2, 689.18, 919.5
pranayama 84.2
prance (n) 177.12, 366.2 (v) 177.28, 177.34, 366.6, 501.15, 705.5
prancer 311.10, 311.14
prancing (n) 366.3 (a) 366.7
prandial 8.31
prang (n) 184.20 (v) 184.44
prank (n) 489.10 (v) 5.42, 498.8
prankish 322.6, 489.17
prankishness 322.2, 489.4
pranksome 322.6, 489.17
pranksomeness 322.2, 489.4
prankster 322.3, 489.12
prank up 498.8
pranky 322.6, 489.17
prat 217.5
prate (n) 520.2, 540.3 (v) 520.5, 540.5
prater 540.4
pratfall 194.3, 410.3, 975.6
pratie 10.35
prating (n) 540.3 (a) 540.10
pratique 443.7
prattle (n) 520.2, 524.1, 540.3 (v) 520.5, 540.5, 541.9
prattler 540.4
prattling 540.10
praxis 321.1, 328.1, 373.1, 373.3
pray 440.10, 440.11, 696.13
prayer 440.2, 696.4, 696.8, 696.9
prayer book 554.1, 701.10
prayer carpet 703.10
prayerful 440.16, 692.8, 696.16
prayerful hope 124.1
prayerfulness 692.1
prayer mat 703.10
prayer meeting 696.8
prayer of thanks 150.2
prayer rug 703.10
prayers 696.8
prayer wheel 696.4
pray for quarter 433.8
praying (n) 696.4 (a) 696.16
pray over 696.13
preach 422.6, 543.11, 568.16
preacher 543.5, 551.6, 571.7, 699.3
preachification 543.3
preachify 543.11
preachiness 422.1
preaching (n) 375.3, 422.1, 543.1, 543.3 (a) 568.18
preaching friar 699.3
preachment 375.3, 543.3, 568.7
preach to the choir 391.8, 993.12
preach to the converted 993.12
preachy 422.8
preadamite (n) 842.7 (a) 842.11
Preakness Stakes 757.1
preamble (n) 816.2 (v) 814.3
preamp 50.10
preamplifier 50.10
preannounce 133.13
preapprehend 133.10
preapprehension 133.1, 934.3, 947.1
prearrange 381.8, 405.6, 437.5, 965.4
prearranged 405.16, 965.7
prearrangement 381.1, 405.1, 965.1
pre-Aryan 834.5
prebendal stall 698.2
prebendaryship 698.2
prebend stall 698.2
precarious 971.20, 1006.12
precariousness 971.6, 1006.2
precative 440.16, 440.17, 696.16
precatory 440.17, 696.16
precaution (n) 494.3, 1008.3 (v) 399.6
precautional 399.8, 494.10
precautionary 399.8, 494.10
precautionary steps 1008.3
precautioning 399.2
precautions 494.3
precautious 494.10
precautiousness 494.3
precede 165.2, 249.11, 814.2, 816.3, 818.10, 834.3
precede and follow 212.8
precedence 165.1, 245.2, 249.1, 417.4, 814.1, 834.1, 997.1
precedency 814.1, 834.1
precedent (n) 337.2, 786.1, 816.1, 834.2, 901.6, 946.5 (a) 165.3, 814.4
precedential 786.8
preceding (n) 165.1, 814.1 (a) 165.3, 814.4, 816.4, 834.4, 837.11
precentor 574.6, 710.18
precept 419.1, 420.3, 422.1, 673.3, 932.4, 952.2, 953.2, 974.1
preceptist 422.3
preceptive 419.4, 420.13, 568.18, 953.21, 953.27
preceptor 571.1
preceptorial 571.11
preceptorship 571.10
preceptress 571.2
precession 814.1, 834.1
precessional 165.3, 814.4
pre-Christian 834.5
précieuse (n) 500.10, 533.5 (a) 533.9
précieux (n) 533.5 (a) 533.9
precinct 212.3, 223.1, 231.2, 231.5, 463.1, 609.16
precinct captain 610.12
precinct house 230.5
precinct leader 610.12
precincts 209.1, 231.1
preciosity 500.5, 533.3, 580.2
precious (n) 562.6 (a) 104.23, 247.12, 500.18, 533.9, 580.10, 632.10
precious as the apple of one's eye 632.10
precious few 885.4
precious heart 562.6
precious little 885.4, 992.9
precious metal 728.20, 1058.3
preciousness 500.5, 533.3, 580.2, 632.2
precious rascal 660.3
precious stone 498.6, 1059.7
precip 316.1
precipice 200.3, 237.2
precipitance 365.2, 401.2, 493.2, 830.2

precipitancy 365.2, 401.2, 493.2, 830.2, 845.2
precipitant 401.9, 401.10, 493.8, 830.5
precipitate (n) 256.2, 887.1, 1045.5 (v) 194.5, 297.15, 316.10, 401.4, 913.5, 1045.11 (a) 174.15, 365.9, 401.10, 406.8, 493.8, 830.5, 845.8
precipitateness 365.2, 493.2, 830.2
precipitate oneself 194.8
precipitation 174.1, 256.2, 316.1, 317.4, 365.2, 401.2, 493.2, 845.2, 913.2, 1045.5, 1065.3
precipitation hardening 1046.4
precipitin 86.27
precipitous 200.12, 204.18, 401.10, 493.8, 830.5
precipitousness 200.1, 204.6, 401.2, 493.2
précis (n) 268.3, 557.1, 849.2 (v) 849.8
precise (v) 973.11 (a) 339.12, 495.9, 580.10, 766.9, 865.12, 944.7, 973.17
preciseness 339.3, 495.1, 580.2, 973.5
precisian (n) 495.6, 867.2, 929.5 (a) 500.18, 580.10
precisianism 339.3, 425.2, 495.1, 500.5, 580.2, 687.5
precisianist (n) 495.6, 867.2 (a) 687.8
precisianistic 339.12, 495.9, 500.18, 687.8, 867.6
precision 339.3, 495.1, 533.1, 973.5
precision focusing 1036.8
precision instrument 1040.1
precisionism 339.3, 500.5
precisionist (n) 929.5 (a) 580.10
precisionistic 339.12, 500.18
precision-production control 1041.8
precision tool 1040.1
precititous 913.12
preclassical 834.5
preclude 444.3, 773.4, 1012.14
precluded 773.7
preclusion 444.1, 773.1, 1012.2
preclusive 444.6, 773.9, 1012.19
precocial 311.48
precocious 845.8
precociousness 845.2
precocity 845.2
precognition 928.3, 934.1, 961.3
precognitive 934.5, 961.7
precognizable 962.13
precognizant 961.7
precognize 961.6
preconceive 947.2
preconceived 947.3
preconceived notion 964.1
preconceived opinion 964.1
preconception 947.1, 980.3
preconceptual 947.3
preconcert 964.6, 965.4
preconcerted 965.7
preconcertedness 965.1
preconclude 947.2
preconcluded 947.3
preconclusion 947.1
precondemn 980.7
precondition 405.9
preconization 420.5
preconize 420.11
preconscious (n) 92.28 (a) 92.42
preconsider 380.7
preconsideration 380.3, 947.1, 961.2
preconsidered 380.9
precontrive 965.4
precontrived 965.7
precook 11.5
precooked 405.19
precooked foods 10.5
precooked frozen meal 8.6
precultural 834.5
precursive 133.15, 399.8
precursor 133.4, 165.1, 216.2, 227.9, 399.3, 814.1, 816.1, 834.2, 845.4, 852.5, 892.7
precursory 133.15, 165.3, 399.8, 814.4, 818.16
predacean 8.16
predacious 8.31, 480.26, 482.22
predaciousness 480.9
predacity 480.9
predate 832.13, 834.3
predating 834.1
predator 311.3, 480.12
predators 311.1
predatory 480.26, 482.22
predecease 307.21
predecessor 816.1
predecessors 560.7
predecide 947.2, 964.6
predecided 947.3, 964.8
predecision 947.1
predeliberate 380.7
predeliberated 380.9
predeliberation 380.3, 961.2
predella 703.12, 901.14
predesign 965.4
predesigned 965.7
predestinarian 964.5
predestinarianism 964.4
predestinate (v) 964.6 (a) 964.8
predestination 964.1, 970.1
predestinationist 964.5
predestine 964.6, 964.7
predestined 963.15, 964.8, 970.13
predetermination 380.3, 947.1, 963.7, 964.1, 970.1
predetermine 380.7, 947.2, 964.6
predetermined 380.9, 947.3, 964.8, 970.13
predeterminism 964.4
predicament 765.1, 963.4, 971.3, 1006.1, 1011.1, 1013.4
predicant 699.3
predicate (n) 334.1, 530.2, 530.4 (v) 334.5, 951.12
predicate adjective 530.3
predicated 334.9
predicated on 959.9
predication 334.1
predicational 334.8
predicative 334.8
predict 130.6, 133.9, 839.6, 961.5, 962.9, 972.12
predictability 123.1, 130.1, 850.1, 962.8, 968.2, 970.4
predictable 373.14, 855.12, 961.8, 962.13, 968.6, 970.17
predictable error 975.2
predictableness 130.1
predictable response 903.1
predictable within limits 968.6
predicted 130.13, 133.14, 839.8, 962.14
prediction 133.1, 839.1, 961.1, 962.1
predictional 962.11
predictive 133.15, 962.11
predictor 962.4
predictory 962.11
predigest 7.18
predigestion 2.17, 7.8
predikant 699.3
predilection 100.3, 104.1, 371.5, 896.1, 947.1, 978.3, 980.3
predispose 894.7
predisposed 324.5, 947.3, 978.8
predisposition 371.5, 896.1, 947.1, 978.3
predispositional 947.3
predominance 249.1, 417.6, 894.1
predominance of Aquarius 316.4
predominancy 249.1, 417.6
predominant 249.14, 612.17, 864.12, 894.14, 997.24
predominate (v) 249.6, 612.14, 864.10 (a) 612.17
predominating 864.12, 869.9
predomination 417.6
pre-educate 568.14
pre-education 568.4
preemie 302.9
preeminence 247.2, 249.1, 417.4, 417.6, 662.5, 997.1, 999.2
pre-eminent 18.13
preeminent 198.11, 249.14, 417.15, 997.24
preempt 480.19, 814.2, 845.6
preemption 480.4, 733.2, 814.1
preemptive 494.10, 814.4
preemptive strike 459.1
preen 79.20, 498.8
preengage 615.14
preengagement 615.4
preen oneself 136.5
preestablish 964.6
preestablished 964.8
preexist 834.3
preexistence 834.1
preexistent 834.4
pre-existing condition 85.1
prefab (n) 266.2 (a) 405.19, 892.18
prefabricate 892.8
prefabricated 405.19, 892.18
prefabricated house 228.5
prefabrication 266.2, 892.2
preface (n) 216.1, 554.12, 793.2, 816.2 (v) 814.3
prefatory 814.4, 818.16
prefect 571.4, 574.3
prefectship 417.7
prefecture 417.7, 417.10
prefer 100.14, 371.17, 439.4, 439.5, 446.2, 650.8, 978.6
preferable 371.25
prefer a petition 440.10
prefer charges 598.15, 599.7
preference 100.3, 104.15, 371.1, 371.5, 650.3, 765.4, 814.1, 978.3
preference for the best 496.1
preference primary 609.15
preferences 866.1
preference share 738.3
preferential 371.25
preferential shop 727.3
preferential system 609.18
preferential treatment 449.5, 650.3
preferential voting 371.6, 609.18
preferment 162.1, 371.5, 392.1, 446.1, 449.5, 698.10
prefer one's own company 583.4
preferred 371.25
preferred provider 90.1
preferring 371.25
prefer to 371.17
prefiguration 133.3, 962.1
prefigurative 133.15, 962.11
prefigure 133.11, 349.11, 951.10, 962.9
prefigured 133.14
prefigurement 349.1, 962.1
prefigurer 962.4
prefiguring (n) 962.1 (a) 962.11
prefix (n) 216.1, 254.2, 526.3, 816.2 (v) 253.4, 814.3
prefixal 526.22
prefixation 253.1, 526.3, 814.1
prefixed 818.16
prefixture 816.2
preformed 405.19
pregame 818.15
pregenital fixation 92.21
preggers 78.18
preglacial 842.11
pregnability 1006.4
pregnable 19.18, 1006.16
pregnancy 78.5, 518.5, 818.4, 843.1, 890.1
pregnancy test 91.12
pregnant 78.18, 518.10, 818.15, 843.10, 886.14, 890.9, 986.18
pregnant imagination 986.3
pregnant moment 824.1, 843.5
pregnant of good 124.12
pregnant with meaning 133.15
preheat 1020.17
preheated 1020.29
preheating 1020.1
prehend 928.12
prehended 928.26
prehensibility 521.1
prehensible 521.10, 928.25
prehensile 474.9, 928.15
prehensile tail 474.4
prehensility of mind 920.1
prehension 474.1, 480.2, 928.3
prehensive 931.21

prehistoric 834.5, 837.10, 842.11
prehistoric animal 842.7
prehistoric anthropology 842.4
prehistoric man 842.7
prehistoric races 312.2
prehistory 837.3
prehuman (n) 842.7 (a) 842.11
preindicate 133.11
preindicated 133.14
preindication 133.3
preindicative 133.15
preinstruct 568.14
preinstruction 568.4
prejudge 947.2, 980.7
prejudged 947.3
prejudging 947.3
prejudgment 947.1, 980.3
prejudicate 980.7
prejudication 947.1
prejudicative 947.3
prejudice (n) 371.5, 896.1, 947.1, 980.3, 996.2 (v) 980.9, 1000.6
prejudice against 980.9
prejudiced 980.12
prejudice the issue 980.9
prejudicial 947.3, 996.6, 1000.12
pre-K 567.2
prekindergarten 567.2
prelacy 575.14, 698.2, 698.9, 699.1
prelapsarian 657.6, 834.5
prelapsarian state 657.1
prelatehood 698.2
prelateship 698.2
prelatial 698.13
prelatic 698.13
prelatical 698.13
prelature 698.2
prelect 543.11
prelection 543.3
prelibation 961.4
prelim 938.2
preliminaries 405.1, 554.12, 814.1, 845.1
preliminary (n) 405.1, 816.2, 818.5 (a) 814.4, 816.4, 818.16
preliminary act 405.1
preliminary approach 439.1
preliminary convention 609.8
preliminary examination 938.2, 938.5
preliminary measure 405.1
preliminary sign 399.3
preliminary signal 399.3
preliminary step 405.1
preliminary study 556.1
preliminary token 399.3
preloved 387.24
prelude (n) 708.26, 814.1, 816.2 (v) 814.3
preludial 814.4, 818.16
prelusive 814.4
premarital 563.18, 665.27
premarital relations 665.7
premarital sex 665.7
premature 844.6, 845.8
premature acceptation 954.1
premature baby 302.9
premature death 307.4
premature judgment 947.1
prematureness 845.2
prematurity 844.1, 845.2
premaxilla 292.4
premeditate 380.7, 965.4
premeditated 380.9, 381.12, 965.7
premeditation 380.3, 961.2, 965.1
premenstrual syndrome 92.14
premier (n) 575.7, 610.2 (a) 818.17, 997.24
premiere (n) 704.12 (v) 704.28
premier performance 704.12
premiership 417.7, 417.10, 573.4
premillenarian 834.5
premillennial 834.5
premise, a 973.2
premise (n) 761.3, 816.2, 834.2, 901.6, 932.4, 935.5, 935.7, 951.3, 952.2, 953.2 (v) 814.3, 931.16, 935.15
premised 951.14
premises 231.1, 957.1
premissable 951.15
premium (n) 254.4, 478.5, 623.3, 624.6, 627.1, 631.1, 758.3 (a) 632.11
premolar 2.8
premonish 399.6
premonition 133.1, 399.2, 689.8, 934.3, 961.3
premonitor 133.4
premonitory 133.15, 399.8, 962.12
premonitory chill 133.3
premonitory shiver 133.3
premonitory sign 133.3, 399.3
premonitory symptom 133.3, 399.3
premundane 834.5
prenatal 818.15
prenotification 399.2
prenotify 399.6
prenotion 947.1
prenup 436.3
prenuptial 563.18
prenuptial agreement 436.3, 437.1
prenuptial contract 436.3
preoccupancy 469.1
preoccupation 360.1, 469.1, 480.4, 926.13, 931.3, 983.3, 985.2
preoccupied 360.8, 926.33, 931.22, 983.17, 984.7, 985.11, 990.9
preoccupy 480.19, 926.25, 931.20, 983.13
preoccupying 926.34
preoption 371.1
preordain 964.6
preordained 963.15, 964.8
preorder 965.4
preordered 965.7
preordering 965.1
preordination 964.1
pre-owned 387.24
preowned clothing 5.5
prep (n) 405.1 (v) 405.6
prepacked 212.12
prepaid 624.22
preparation 86.4, 385.1, 405.1, 568.1, 568.3, 709.2, 725.6, 845.1, 961.1
preparationist 405.5
preparative 405.20
preparator 405.5
preparatory 405.20, 814.4, 818.16
preparatory instruction 405.1
preparatory measure 405.1
preparatory school 405.1, 567.4
preparatory step 405.1
preparatory study 405.1
prepare 11.5, 385.7, 385.8, 405.6, 547.21, 568.13, 718.6, 892.8
prepare against 494.6
prepare a meal 11.5
prepared 130.11, 385.13, 405.16, 413.26, 961.7
prepared and ready 405.16
prepared for 405.18
preparedness 339.1, 405.4, 609.5, 845.1
prepared speech 543.2
prepared text 543.2
prepare food 11.5
prepare for 405.11, 494.6
prepare for the evil day 405.11
prepare oneself 405.13, 570.11
preparer 405.5
prepare the ground 405.12
prepare the way 405.12, 1014.7
prepare to 405.10
preparing (n) 405.1 (a) 840.3
prepay 624.10
prepayment 624.1
prep cook 11.3
prepense 380.9
prepollent 612.17, 894.14
preponderance 249.1, 417.6, 883.2, 894.1
preponderancy 883.2
preponderant 249.14, 612.17, 894.14
preponderate (v) 249.6, 612.14 (a) 612.17
preponderous 612.16, 883.8
preposition 530.3
prepositional (n) 530.9 (a) 530.17
prepositional phrase 529.1
prepositioned 159.18
prepositive 818.16
prepossess 480.19, 980.9
prepossessed 926.33, 980.12
prepossessing 97.7, 377.8
prepossession 371.5, 469.1, 480.4, 926.13, 947.1, 980.3
preposterous 632.12, 640.9, 923.11, 955.10, 967.7, 986.20
preposterousness 632.4, 923.3
prepotence 249.1, 417.6
prepotency 18.1, 249.1, 417.6
prepotent 18.12, 612.17, 894.14
prepped 405.16
preppie 572.3
prepping 405.1
preprandial 8.31, 11.6
preprocessor language 1042.13
prep school 405.1, 567.4
prep schooler 572.3
prepublication 961.1
prequel 816.1, 816.2
Pre-Raphaelite 842.5
Pre-Raphaelitism 842.4
prerecord 50.14
preregistration 549.14
pre-Renaissance 834.5
prerequire 963.9
prerequirement 963.2
prerequisite (n) 405.1, 567.5, 959.2, 963.2 (a) 405.20, 963.13
preresolution 380.3
preresolve 380.7
preresolved 380.9
prerevolutionary 834.5
prerogative 249.1, 417.1, 642.1
prerogative of office 642.1
pre-Roman 834.5
pre-Romantic 834.5
presage (n) 133.1, 961.3, 962.1 (v) 133.9, 962.9
presaged 133.14, 962.14
presageful 133.15, 133.16, 962.11
presagefulness 133.6
presagement 133.1
presager 133.4, 962.4
presaging (n) 962.1 (a) 133.15, 962.11
presbyopia 28.4
presbyopic 28.11
presbyter 699.4, 699.5
presbyterate 698.2
presbytery 423.4, 698.2, 699.1, 703.7, 703.9
preschool (n) 567.2, 568.5 (a) 567.13
preschool child 572.3
preschooler 302.9, 572.3
prescience 961.3, 964.1
prescient 961.7
prescribe 86.38, 90.14, 420.9, 422.5, 573.8, 643.6, 673.9
prescribed 210.7, 373.13, 419.4, 869.8
prescribed form 373.4, 701.3, 869.4
prescribing 643.2
prescript (n) 419.1, 420.3, 673.3, 974.1 (a) 419.4, 420.12
prescription 86.1, 210.2, 373.1, 419.1, 419.3, 420.3, 469.1, 642.1, 673.3, 869.4
prescription drug 86.4
prescriptive 373.13, 419.4, 420.12, 420.13, 773.9, 842.12, 869.9
preseason 313.1
presence, a 894.6
presence 33.4, 33.5, 221.1, 321.1, 761.1, 976.4, 988.1
presence chamber 197.20
presence of mind 106.3
presence room 197.20
present (n) 478.4, 530.12 (v) 348.5, 371.21, 385.7, 439.4, 478.12, 524.22, 532.4, 587.14, 634.4, 704.28, 957.12 (a) 221.12, 761.13, 838.2
present, the 821.1, 838.1

presentable 478.23, 999.20, 1016.18
present a bold front 492.10
present-age 838.2
present age, the 838.1
present a petition 440.10
present a position paper 352.12
present arms 155.5
presentation 33.1, 33.7, 348.2, 439.1, 478.1, 478.4, 551.1, 582.15, 587.4, 698.10, 704.12, 722.1
presentational 348.9
presentation graphics 1042.11
presentation of the case 598.8
present a true bill 598.15
present-day 838.2, 841.13
present day, the 838.1
present difficulties 1013.10
presented 532.5
presenteeism 221.1
presenter 478.11
present hour, the 838.1
presentiment 93.1, 133.1, 399.2, 934.1, 934.3, 961.3, 962.1
presenting arms 155.2
present itself 33.8, 831.6, 931.18
present itself to the mind 931.18
present juncture, the 838.1
presentment 348.2, 349.1, 478.1, 598.3, 704.12
present minute, the 838.1
present moment 221.1
present moment, the 838.1
presentness 838.1, 841.1
present no difficulties 1014.10
present occasion, the 838.1
present one's case 598.19
present oneself 33.8, 221.11, 439.10, 504.11
present oneself to view 33.8
present participle 530.3, 530.4, 838.1
present perfect 530.12
present tense 838.1
present the appearance of 33.10
present time 838.1
present-time 838.2, 841.13
present to 216.8
present to the eye 31.4
present to the eyes 31.6
present to the mind 989.22
preserval 397.1
preservation 386.5, 397.1, 474.1, 677.13, 829.4, 853.2, 1008.1
preservationist 397.5, 1072.3
preservative (n) 397.4 (a) 397.12, 853.8
preservative medium 397.4
preservatory 397.12
preserve (n) 10.40, 397.7, 1009.1 (v) 386.12, 397.8, 397.9, 474.5, 829.5, 853.6, 856.4, 1008.19
preserve a balance 467.6
preserved 386.15, 397.13
preserve from oblivion 829.5
preserve in an archive 549.15
preserve one's dignity 136.7
preserve one's honor 136.7
preserver 397.5
Preserver, the 677.3
preserving (n) 11.2 (a) 397.12
preset 437.5, 964.6
preshowing 962.1
preshrink 260.9
preshrinkage 260.3
preshrinking 260.3
preshrunk 260.13
preside 573.11, 585.8, 594.5
preside at the board 573.11, 594.5
presidency 249.3, 417.7, 417.10, 573.4
president 571.8, 574.3, 575.7, 610.2
president-elect 371.12, 610.11
presidential 612.16
presidential election 609.15
presidential palace 228.5
presidential papers 549.2
presidential preference primary 609.15
presidential primary 609.15
presidential timber 610.9
President of the United States 575.7
presidentship 417.7
preside over 573.11, 612.11
presiding 573.14
presiding officer 574.5, 596.1
presign 133.11
presignal 133.11
presignaled 133.14
presigned 133.14
presignificant 133.15
presignification 133.3
presignificative 962.11
presignified 133.14
presignify 133.11
presignifying (n) 133.3, 962.1 (a) 962.11
presigning 962.1
pre-Socratic 952.12
press (n) 192.9, 260.2, 375.6, 548.9, 548.11, 554.2, 615.7, 770.4, 902.2, 997.4 (v) 260.8, 287.6, 297.11, 375.14, 401.4, 421.8, 424.6, 439.9, 440.12, 480.20, 562.18, 615.17, 725.10, 747.4, 902.12, 1045.9
press, the 551.5, 552.1, 555.3
press agency 552.1
press agent 352.9, 704.25
press-agent 352.15
press-agentry 352.5
press association 552.1
press baron 555.4
press box 552.1
press card 517.11
press charges 598.15, 599.7
press conference 541.5, 552.4, 938.11
press corps 555.4
press corps, the 552.1
press down 112.18, 297.11, 913.4, 1012.11
press drill 1040.6
pressed 401.11
pressed flower 310.25
pressed for time 401.11
press forward 162.4
press gallery 552.1
press hard upon 297.13
press her 174.11
press in 189.7, 191.7, 214.5, 284.14
pressing (n) 192.7, 375.5, 440.3 (a) 375.25, 421.9, 424.10, 997.22
pressingness 421.4, 963.4
pressing out 192.1
press into service 387.14
pressman 548.12, 555.4
press notice 352.4
press objections 333.5
press of business 330.5
press officer 551.5, 576.5
press of sail 180.14
press on 162.2, 162.4, 330.13, 401.4, 401.5, 821.5, 856.5
press one hard 459.19
press one's hand 585.10
press one's luck 972.12, 1006.7
press one's suit 562.21
press onward 162.4
press opportunity 938.11
press order 554.5
press out 192.16
press pass 517.11
press photographer 714.2
press proof 548.5
press release 352.3, 552.4
pressroom 548.11
press secretary 551.5
press the attack 459.17
press the flesh 585.10
press the panic button 127.11
press to the bosom 562.18
press to the ground 297.11
press upon 439.9, 478.20
pressure (n) 73.2, 96.2, 128.3, 260.2, 297.7, 375.5, 375.6, 417.4, 421.4, 424.3, 440.3, 894.1, 902.2, 963.4, 997.4, 1011.1 (v) 375.14, 424.6, 440.12
pressure altitude 184.35
pressure control 1041.8
pressure-cooking 11.2
pressure gauge 1067.7
pressure group 375.11, 609.31, 617.4, 894.6
pressure-group politics 609.1
pressureless space 1073.3
pressure nozzle 239.9
pressure point 208.3
pressure suit 184.21, 1075.11
pressurization 260.1
pressurize 260.8
pressurizing 260.1
presswork 548.9
prestidigitate 976.8
prestidigitation 356.5, 976.2
prestidigitator 357.2, 690.6, 707.1
prestige 155.1, 249.1, 417.4, 607.1, 662.4, 894.1, 997.2
prestige dialect 523.4
prestigious 155.11, 417.15, 662.15, 894.13, 997.19
prestissimo (n) 708.25 (a) 708.55
presto (n) 708.25, 709.24 (a) 708.55, 830.4, 852.13
presto chango 852.13
prestressed concrete 1054.2
presumable 951.15, 968.6
presumableness 951.6
presume 124.6, 130.5, 142.7, 519.4, 640.6, 772.4, 946.8, 947.2, 951.10, 953.11, 968.5
presumed 130.13, 519.7, 947.3, 951.14
presume on 640.7
presume upon 387.16, 643.7
presuming 141.10, 142.9, 640.11
presumption 124.1, 130.1, 141.2, 142.1, 214.2, 493.3, 519.2, 640.2, 772.2, 947.1, 951.3, 953.6, 968.1
presumptive 951.14, 957.16, 968.6
presumptive evidence 968.1
presumptive heir 479.5
presumptiveness 951.6
presumptive right 642.1
presumptuous 141.10, 142.9, 214.9, 493.9, 640.11
presumptuousness 141.2, 142.1, 214.2, 493.3, 640.2, 643.1
presupposal 947.1, 951.3
presuppose 519.4, 640.7, 772.4, 947.2, 951.10
presupposed 519.7, 947.3
presupposition 519.2, 772.2, 816.2, 935.7, 947.1, 951.3, 952.2
presurmise (n) 947.1 (v) 947.2, 951.10
presurmised 947.3
preteen (n) 301.6, 302.1, 302.8 (a) 301.13
preteens 301.2
pretend 354.21, 376.3, 500.12, 640.6
pretended 354.26, 376.5, 500.16
pretender 357.6, 357.8, 500.7, 640.4
pretending 354.3
pretend not to see 157.6
pretend to 403.8, 421.6, 640.8
pretend to be 349.12, 354.22
pretense 33.2, 354.3, 376.1, 500.1, 501.1, 642.1, 886.2
pretension 354.3, 376.1, 500.1, 501.1, 545.1, 642.1
pretensions 501.2
pretentious 500.15, 501.18, 502.12, 533.9, 545.8
pretentiousness 500.1, 501.1, 533.3, 545.1
preterhuman 870.15
preterit (n) 530.12, 837.5 (a) 837.9
preterite 530.12
preterition 837.5
preteritive 837.9
pretermit 340.7
preternatural 870.15
preternaturalism 689.2, 870.7
preternormal 870.15
pretersensual 689.24, 870.15
pretext (n) 354.3, 369.4, 376.1, 415.5, 886.2, 935.5 (v) 376.3
pretexted 376.5
pretonic 524.30
pretreat 405.6
pretreated 405.16
pretreatment 405.1

prettification 1016.10
prettify 498.8, 1016.15
prettiness 1016.1
pretty 1016.17
pretty as a picture 1016.17
pretty boy 75.4
pretty good 999.20
pretty kettle of fish 810.2
pretty lies 511.1
pretty much the same 784.15
pretty pass 1013.4
pretty penny, a 632.3
pretty penny 618.2, 632.1
pretty pickle 1013.5
pretty piece of business 810.2
pretty predicament 1013.4
pretty-pretty 498.12
pretty up 5.42, 1016.15
pretty wit 489.1
pretypified 133.14
pretypify 133.11, 349.11
pretzel 10.30
prevail 249.6, 409.7, 411.3, 612.14, 761.8, 781.3, 827.6, 864.10
prevailing 249.14, 318.21, 373.13, 411.7, 831.9, 864.12, 869.9, 894.14, 991.7
prevailing belief 953.6
prevailing northwesterlies 318.9
prevailing sentiment 953.6
prevailing southwesterlies 318.9
prevailing taste 578.1
prevailing westerlies 318.9
prevailing wind 318.1, 318.9
prevail on 375.23
prevail over 411.5
prevail upon 375.23
prevail with 375.23
prevalence 373.6, 578.2, 847.1, 869.2, 991.2
prevalent 373.13, 578.11, 612.17, 761.13, 831.9, 847.4, 864.12, 894.14, 991.7
prevaricate 344.7, 354.19, 936.9
prevaricating 344.11, 354.34
prevarication 344.4, 354.9, 354.11, 936.5
prevaricator 357.9, 362.5, 936.7
prevenience 839.1, 845.1
prevenient 814.4, 839.8, 845.7, 845.8
prevent 444.3, 1012.14
preventable 368.14
preventative (n) 86.20, 900.3 (a) 1012.19
prevention 368.1, 444.1, 1012.2
preventive (n) 86.20, 900.3, 1008.3 (a) 86.42, 444.6, 494.10, 773.9, 1008.23, 1012.19
preventive custody 429.5, 429.6
preventive dentist 81.3
preventive dentistry 81.2
preventive detention 429.3
preventive measure 494.3, 1008.3
preventive medicine 81.2, 83.5, 90.13
preventive step 494.3
preventive war 459.1
preventive warfare 458.1
pre-Victorian 834.5
preview (n) 27.3, 704.12, 706.1, 961.1 (v) 704.28
previous 814.5, 834.4, 837.10, 845.8, 845.10
previously owned 387.24, 842.18
previousness 834.1
previous question 613.9
previous state 834.1
previse 839.6, 845.6
prevision 839.1, 845.1, 961.1
previsional 839.8, 845.7
prewar 834.5
prewarn 399.6
prewarning 399.2
prexy 574.3
prey 96.11, 100.11, 104.9, 380.2, 382.7
prey on 8.28, 98.16, 482.17
prey on the mind 98.16
prey to blind fear 127.27
prey to malaise 96.20
prey upon 8.28, 98.16, 482.17
priapic 665.29
priapism 665.6
Priapus 665.11, 678.11, 890.5
price (n) 603.1, 623.3, 624.3, 630.1, 632.2, 738.9, 759.6 (v) 630.11
price cap 211.3
price ceiling 630.4
price controls 630.5
price cut 631.1, 633.4
price-cutting 631.1
priced 630.14
price determination 630.3
priced to go 633.9
price fall 633.4
price-fixing 630.5
price freeze 630.5
price-gouging 632.5
price index 630.4, 731.9
priceless 488.5, 632.10
pricelessness 488.1, 632.2
price level 630.4
price list 630.1
pricemaker 759.6
price of money, the 620.1, 623.3
price out of the market 632.6
price point 630.1
price range 630.1
price reduction 631.1, 633.4
prices current 630.1
price support 449.3, 478.8
price supports 609.4, 630.5
price tag 517.13, 630.1
pricey 632.11
priceyness 632.1
pricing 630.3
prick (n) 26.2, 285.3, 375.8, 517.5, 660.5 (v) 26.7, 74.5, 96.17, 285.6, 292.15, 375.15, 517.19, 1070.8
prick-eared 48.15
pricking (n) 292.3, 375.5 (a) 285.10
pricking of heart 113.2
prickle (n) 74.1, 285.3, 285.5, 803.4 (v) 74.5, 285.6
prickles 74.1
prickliness 24.3, 105.10, 110.5, 285.1
prickling (n) 74.1 (a) 74.8
prickly 24.12, 74.8, 105.28, 110.21, 285.10
prickly heat 85.36
prick one's balloon 137.4
prick song 708.22
prick up one's ears 981.3
prick up the ears 48.10, 983.7
pricky 285.10
pride 136.1, 140.2, 141.1, 501.6, 654.3, 655.3, 770.5, 970.5, 999.5
pride and joy 999.5
prideful 136.8
pridefulness 136.1
pride of bearing 136.2
pride of place 136.2, 249.1
pride oneself 136.5
prier 214.4
priest 565.2, 699.4, 699.5, 699.10, 699.11
priestcraft 698.2
priestery 699.1
priest hole 1009.5
priesthood 698.1, 698.3, 699.1
priestish 698.13
priestism 698.3
priestly 698.13
priest-ridden 698.13
priestship 698.1
prig 141.7, 500.11
priggery 141.6
priggish 141.14, 495.9, 500.19, 510.22
priggishness 141.6, 495.1, 500.6, 510.4
priggism 141.6
prim 500.19, 580.9
prima ballerina 707.6
primacord 462.15
primacy 249.3, 417.6, 698.2, 997.1, 999.2
prima donna 707.6, 710.13, 997.10
prima-donnaish 110.21, 364.5
prima-donnaism 364.2
primal (n) 818.3 (a) 199.8, 249.14, 337.6, 416.6, 767.8, 767.9, 798.6, 818.15, 886.14
primal chaos 418.2
primal ignorance 930.1
primal matter 1052.2
primal scream 58.4
primal stupidity 922.1
primaries 3.18
primariness 798.1
primary (n) 35.7, 609.15, 818.3 (a) 199.8, 216.10, 249.14, 337.6, 767.9, 798.6, 818.15, 886.14, 997.24
primary burial 309.1
primary care 90.1
primary chord 709.17
primary color 35.7
primary digestion 2.17, 7.8
primary education 568.5
primary election 371.9, 609.15
primary form 709.11
primary pigment 35.7
primary rainbow 316.8
primary receiver 746.2
primary school 567.3
primary schooler 572.3
primary storage 1042.7
primary stress 524.10
primary trainer 181.10
primary treatment 90.1
primatal 698.13
primate 311.3, 311.22, 842.7
primateship 698.2
primatial 698.13
primatical 698.13
primavera 313.2
primaveral 301.10
prime (n) 303.2, 313.2, 314.2, 696.8, 818.3, 999.8, 1010.4 (v) 35.14, 295.24, 405.9, 568.11, 904.12 (a) 216.10, 249.14, 337.6, 798.6, 818.15, 834.4, 842.11, 997.24, 999.16, 1017.23
prime coat 35.8
prime cost 626.3
primed 405.16, 413.26, 928.18
primed for 405.18
prime example 786.4
prime factor 883.4
prime focus 208.4
prime interest rate 623.3
prime interval 709.20
prime investment 729.4
prime issue 997.6
prime meridian 231.3
prime minister 575.7, 610.2
prime-ministership 417.7
prime-ministry 417.7
Prime Mover 677.2
prime mover 375.10
prime mover 726.1, 886.4, 892.7, 1040.3
prime of life 301.1, 303.2, 303.4
prime of the morning 314.2
prime of the year 313.2
primer 35.8, 462.15, 554.10, 568.5, 818.6
prime rate 623.3
prime song 696.8
prime suspect 599.6
prime time 1035.2
prime-time show 1035.2
primeval 818.15, 837.10, 842.11, 886.14
primeval forest 310.12, 310.13
priming 35.8, 35.12, 462.15, 568.4
primitive (n) 227.3, 416.3, 526.2, 842.7 (a) 199.8, 226.5, 337.6, 416.6, 497.12, 767.9, 798.6, 818.15, 837.10, 842.11, 886.14
primitive art 712.1
primitive faith 687.2
primitiveness 798.1, 842.1
primitive religion 675.6
primitive self 92.28, 934.2
primitive settler 227.3
primitivity 798.1
primness 500.6, 580.1
primo 886.14, 999.18
primogenial 842.11
primogenital 818.15
primogenitary 818.15, 842.19
primogenitors 560.7

primogeniture 303.3, 479.2, 842.1
primordial 842.11
primordialism 842.1
primordiality 842.1
primp 5.42, 498.8, 1016.15
primp up 498.8
primrose 41.8, 43.4
primrose-colored 43.4
primrose path 383.1
primrose-yellow 43.4
primus inter pares 249.4
prince 575.8, 608.7, 659.1
Prince Charming 104.12
prince consort 575.8, 608.7
princedom 417.7, 608.9
princelet 608.7
princelike 417.17, 608.10
princeliness 136.2, 652.2
princeling 608.7
princely 136.12, 417.17, 485.4, 501.21, 608.10, 652.6
Prince of Wales Conference 749.1
Prince of Wales's feathers 647.3
prince regent 575.11, 608.7
princeship 417.7, 608.9
princes of India 608.7
princess 575.10, 608.8
princesse 608.8
principal (n) 249.4, 571.8, 575.3, 707.6, 728.15, 997.10 (a) 249.14, 818.17, 997.24
principal character 704.10
principal idea 932.4
principalities 679.3
principality 231.5, 232.1, 417.6, 417.7, 679.1
principal keeper 429.10
principate 232.1
principia 818.6
principium 419.2
principle 375.1, 419.2, 767.2, 869.4, 886.1, 886.9, 901.6, 952.2, 953.2, 974.2
principled 644.13, 953.21
principle of desire 689.18
principle of equivalence 158.6
principle of faith 953.2
principle of indeterminacy 972.1
principle of relativity 158.6
principles 381.4, 636.1, 644.1, 818.6, 952.2
principles of behavior 636.1
principles of conduct 636.1
principles of professional practice 636.1
prink 5.42, 498.8, 500.14
prink out 354.16
prink up 498.8
print (n) 284.6, 517.7, 548.3, 548.6, 712.10, 713.5, 714.5, 785.5, 887.2 (v) 349.8, 517.19, 548.14, 713.9, 714.15, 728.28, 855.9
printed 547.22, 548.19, 713.11
printed book 554.3
printed circuit 1033.8
printed circuit board 1042.3
printed matter 547.10, 548.10
printed word 547.10
printer 547.18, 548.12, 554.2, 1042.9
printers 548.11
printer's copy 548.4
printer's devil 548.12, 577.5
printer's error 975.3
printer's imprint 554.12
printer's reader 548.13
printery 548.11
print formatter 1042.11
printhead 572.1
printing 349.1, 352.1, 546.5, 547.4, 548.1, 554.5, 713.1
printing equipment 548.8
printing machine 548.9
printing office 548.11
printing paper 714.10
printing plate 548.8, 713.6
printing press 548.9
printing surface 548.8
print journalism 552.1, 555.3
printmaker 716.8
printmaking 548.1, 712.16, 713.1, 713.5
print media 551.5
print media, the 555.3
print medium 555.3
print order 554.5
printout 547.10
print press, the 555.3
print run 554.5
print shop 548.11
printwheel printer 1042.9
printworker 548.12
prinz 608.7
prior (n) 699.16 (a) 165.3, 814.4, 834.4, 837.10
priorate 703.6
prior consultation 494.1
prioress 699.17
prioritization 807.1
prioritize 808.8, 997.14
priority 165.1, 216.1, 249.1, 417.4, 814.1, 815.1, 834.1, 997.1
priority mail 553.4
prior right of purchase 733.2
prior state 834.1
priory 703.6
prism 29.2
prismal 47.9
prismatic 35.16, 47.9, 278.11
prismatical 47.9
prismoid 278.11
prison 429.8
prisonbreak 369.1
prison camp 429.8
prison cell 429.8
prisoner 429.11, 599.6
prisoner before the court 599.6
prisoner of conscience 429.11
prisoner of war 429.11
prisoner-of-war camp 429.8
prisoner-of-war stockade 429.8
prison fare 515.2
prison farm 429.8
prison guard 429.10
prison house 429.8
prison pallor 36.2
prison term 825.4
prison ward 197.25
priss 500.11
prissiness 77.2, 339.3, 495.1, 500.6, 580.1
prissy 77.14, 339.12, 495.9, 500.19, 580.9
pristine 79.25, 337.6, 390.12, 406.13, 416.6, 657.6, 792.10, 798.6, 841.7, 842.11, 886.14, 1002.8
pristineness 406.3, 657.2, 841.1
prittle-prattle (n) 540.3 (v) 541.9
privacy 345.2, 584.1, 872.2, 1009.5
private (n) 461.8 (a) 207.6, 293.9, 312.15, 345.13, 480.25, 584.9, 767.7, 865.12, 872.8
private aims 651.1
private aviation 184.1
private branch exchange 347.8
private company 730.1
private conference 345.2
private desire 651.1
private detective 576.10
private dick 576.10
private enterprise 611.8
private-enterprise 611.23
private-enterprise economy 731.7
privateer (n) 183.1, 461.5, 483.7 (v) 482.18
privateering 482.7
private exchange 347.8
private eye 576.11
private first class 461.8
private flying 184.1
private housing 228.1
private information 551.2
private instructor 571.5
private investigator 576.10
private knowledge 928.1
private law 673.5
private line 347.17
privately held corporation 739.1
private matter 345.5
private ownership 611.8
private parts 2.13
private pilot 185.1
private place 1009.5
private practice 90.13
private room 197.25
privates 2.13
private sector 611.8, 731.7
private-sector housing 228.1
private soldier 461.8
private space 158.7
private teaching 568.1
private tutor 571.1
private world 583.2
privation 473.1, 480.6, 619.2
privatism 584.1, 651.1
privatistic 584.9, 651.5
privatization 584.1, 731.7
privatize 611.16
privilege (n) 249.1, 430.8, 642.2 (v) 443.11
privileged 345.13, 345.14, 430.30, 443.17, 618.14
privileged, the 607.2
privileged class 618.6
privileged communication 345.5
privileged information 345.5, 551.2
privileged question 613.9
privity 345.5, 928.1
privy (n) 12.10, 197.26, 228.9 (a) 345.12, 345.13
privy council 423.1, 613.3
privy parts 2.13
privy seal 647.3
privy to 928.16
prix fixe 630.5
prize (n) 100.11, 482.11, 549.12, 646.2, 906.1, 906.4, 999.5, 999.8 (v) 104.20, 155.4, 300.10, 630.11, 906.8, 946.9, 997.13 (a) 999.16
prized 104.23, 155.11, 630.14
prizefight (n) 457.9, 754.3 (v) 754.4
prizefighter 754.2
prizefighting 457.9, 754.1
prizeman 413.15
prize out 192.10
prize ring 463.1, 754.1
prize sap 358.2, 924.3
prizetaker 413.15
prizewinner 409.6, 413.15
pro (n) 413.11, 726.4, 759.21, 935.14 (a) 509.17, 724.16
proactive 17.13, 330.23
proactiveness 17.2
pro-am 751.1
pro and con 935.19
probabilism 968.1
probabilities 130.4
probability 130.1, 839.1, 896.1, 897.1, 962.1, 966.1, 968.1, 972.1, 972.8
probability curve 968.2
probability density function 968.2
probability distribution 968.2
probability function 968.2
probability theory 968.2
probabilize 968.4
probable 130.13, 839.8, 897.5, 962.13, 966.6, 968.6, 972.18
probable cause 968.1
probable error 968.2, 975.2
pro basketball 747.1
probate (n) 478.10 (v) 957.11
probation 942.2
probational 572.13
probationary 572.13, 942.11
probationer 90.10, 572.9, 818.2
probationist 90.10, 572.9
probative 942.11, 957.16
probatory 942.11
probatum 970.1
probe (n) 90.10, 938.4, 938.15, 942.4, 1074.6, 1075.6 (v) 275.10, 300.10, 938.23, 938.25, 942.9, 952.9
prober 938.16
probing (n) 275.6, 275.8, 938.1, 938.12 (a) 938.38
probity 644.1, 653.1
problem 96.2, 522.8, 937.1, 938.10, 971.3, 1003.2, 1013.3
problematic 955.10, 971.17, 971.27, 1013.18

problematical 955.10, 971.17, 971.27
problematicness 972.1
problem drinker 88.11
problem drinking 88.3
problem-oriented language 1042.13
problems in living 92.14
problem-solve 940.2
pro bono practice 597.4
Proboscidea 311.4
proboscidean 311.4
proboscis 2.11, 283.8
Pro Bowl 746.1
pro bowling 750.1
procacious 142.10, 666.6
procacity 142.2, 666.2
procaryotic cell 305.4
procedural language 1042.13
procedure 321.1, 373.4, 381.1, 381.4, 384.1, 889.2
proceed 162.2, 321.4, 328.4, 328.5, 384.5, 821.5
proceed from 887.5
proceeding (n) 321.1, 328.3, 384.1, 831.3, 889.2 (a) 162.6
proceedings 330.1, 549.7, 598.1, 831.4
proceeds 472.3, 472.5, 627.1, 893.2
proceed to 404.3
proceed with 328.5
proceleusmatic 720.8
procerity 257.1, 272.1
process (n) 328.3, 384.1, 815.1, 889.2 (v) 3.22, 405.6, 714.15, 892.9, 1043.4, 1054.7
process art 712.1
process control 1041.8
process-control system 1041.5
processed 405.16, 892.18
processed food 10.1
processing 397.2, 405.1, 858.1, 892.2, 1041.7
processing solution 714.13
procession 812.3, 815.1
processional march 708.12
process lag 1041.11
process loop 1041.6
process of time 821.4
processor 1042.2
process photography 706.5
process server 420.7
process shot 714.8
process variable 1041.9
procès-verbal 598.7
prochein ami 1008.6
pro-choice 86.23
prochronism 833.1
prochronistic 833.3
proclaim 133.13, 334.5, 352.13, 420.8, 524.23, 834.3, 970.10
proclaim at the crossroads 352.13
proclaimed 352.17
proclaimer 353.3
proclamation 334.1, 352.2, 420.4
proclamatory 352.18
proclitic 254.2, 526.3, 526.4
proclivity 100.3, 371.5, 896.1, 978.3
proconsul 575.12
proconsulate 417.7, 417.10
proconsulship 417.7
procrastinate 329.5, 340.7, 362.7, 368.13, 827.9, 846.11
procrastinating 329.6, 340.10, 846.17
procrastination 175.3, 329.1, 340.1, 340.3, 827.2, 846.5
procrastinative 175.11, 331.19, 846.17
procrastinator 175.5, 340.5
procrastinatory 175.11, 846.17
procreant 78.15
procreate 14.2, 78.8, 259.7, 818.14, 890.7, 892.12
procreation 14.1, 75.7, 78.2, 78.6, 259.3
procreative 75.25, 78.15, 818.15
procreative drive 104.2
procreativeness 890.1
procreator 560.8, 890.4
procrustean 425.7
Procrustean bed 605.4
Procrustean law 869.4
proctor 571.4, 574.2, 574.4, 597.1
proctoring 339.4
proctorship 573.4
procumbency 201.2
procumbent 201.8
procurability 966.3
procurable 966.8
procurableness 966.3
procural 472.1
procurance 472.1
procuration 472.1, 615.1
procurator 574.4, 576.1, 597.1
procure 176.16, 192.14, 375.22, 472.8, 665.21, 733.7, 886.11
procure materials 1054.7
procurement 385.1, 472.1
procurer 385.6, 479.3, 665.18
procuress 665.18
prod (n) 375.8, 902.2 (v) 73.6, 375.15, 440.12, 902.12
prod at 96.13, 375.15, 440.12
prodding 375.5
prodigal (n) 486.2 (a) 355.4, 406.15, 486.8, 538.11, 654.12, 669.7, 884.9, 991.7, 993.19
prodigality 355.1, 486.1, 538.2, 654.1, 669.1, 991.2, 993.2
prodigal returned 113.5
prodigal son 113.5, 486.2, 859.3
prodigal's return 186.3
prodigiosity 870.5
prodigious 122.10, 247.7, 257.20, 870.14, 870.16
prodigiousness 122.3, 247.1, 257.7, 870.2
prodigy 122.2, 249.4, 413.12, 413.13, 870.5, 870.8, 999.6
prodroma 399.3
prodromal 399.8
prodromata 399.3
prodrome 399.3
prodromic 399.8
produce (n) 10.35, 10.38, 472.5, 627.1, 735.7, 893.2 (v) 13.5, 267.6, 328.6, 348.5, 407.4, 547.21, 704.28, 718.6, 886.10, 890.7, 892.8, 892.13, 957.12, 986.14
produce an instance 957.13
produced 262.9, 892.17
producer 574.1, 704.23, 706.4, 726.1, 886.4, 892.7
producible 892.20
producing (n) 892.2 (a) 890.10
producing again 78.1
producing anew 78.1
producing once more 78.1
product 472.5, 735.2, 883.4, 887.1, 893.1, 1017.6
product design 717.5
productible 892.20
production 266.1, 267.4, 328.3, 348.2, 407.1, 472.5, 547.10, 554.1, 704.12, 704.13, 708.5, 890.2, 892.1, 892.2, 893.1, 893.2
productional 892.14
production company 706.4
production editor 554.2
production line 739.3, 770.14, 892.3
production metallurgy 1058.11
production tour 704.11
productive 18.14, 472.16, 538.11, 890.9, 892.16, 986.18, 991.7
productive capacity 890.1
productive effect 892.5
productive effort 892.5
productiveness 18.1, 251.1, 890.1, 892.5, 991.2
productivity 18.1, 538.2, 890.1, 986.3
product liability 641.2
product placement 352.5
proem 816.2
proemial 814.4, 818.16
proemium 816.2
proenzyme 7.10
profanation 389.1, 638.2, 694.2
profanatory 694.6
profane (v) 80.17, 389.4, 393.12, 513.6, 694.4 (a) 513.8, 686.3, 694.6, 695.16
profane, the 686.2
profane language 513.3
profaneness 686.1, 694.2
profane oath 513.4
profane swearing 513.3
profanity 513.3, 513.4, 686.1, 694.2
profanum vulgus 606.2
profess 334.5, 354.21, 376.3, 953.12
professed 332.14, 334.9, 376.5
professed motive 376.1
profession 332.3, 334.1, 376.2, 724.4, 724.6, 953.7, 957.2
professional (n) 413.11, 726.4 (a) 413.22, 413.26, 568.19, 724.16
professional association 90.13
professional athlete 743.19
professional baseball 745.1
professional basketball 747.1
Professional Bowlers Association 750.1
professional bowling 750.1
professional boxing 754.1
professional class 607.5
professional consultant 422.3
professional development 567.5, 568.8
professional engineer 726.7
professional ethics 636.1
professional football 746.1
professional forces 461.20
professional gambler 759.21
professional golf 751.1
Professional Golfers Association of America 751.1
professional hockey 749.1
professionalism 724.8
professional killer 308.11, 461.17
professional librarian 558.3
professional librarianship 558.2
professional mourner 309.7
professional musician 710.1
professional name 527.8
professional policing 1008.1
professional politician 610.1
professional practitioner 726.4
professional skating 760.7
professional soccer 752.1
professional soldiers 461.23
professional standing 724.8
professional status 724.8
professional student 570.1
professional title 527.3
Professional Women's Bowling Association 750.1
professional wrestling 457.10
profession of arms 458.5
profession of confession 953.7
profession of faith 953.7
professor 413.11, 543.5, 571.1, 571.3, 759.21
professorate 571.9, 571.10
professordom 571.9
professor emeritus 571.3
professorhood 571.10
professorial 570.17, 571.11
professoriate 571.9, 571.10
professorlike 571.11
professors 571.9
professorship 571.10
proffer (n) 439.1 (v) 439.4, 478.12, 939.4, 957.12
proffer aid 449.11
proffered 324.7
proffer oneself 439.10
proficiency 18.2, 405.4, 413.1, 928.6, 999.1
proficient (n) 413.11 (a) 18.14, 405.17, 413.22, 1002.9
proficient in 413.27, 928.19
profile (n) 211.2, 218.1, 262.2, 349.2, 381.3, 712.14, 719.1 (v) 211.9
profile drag 184.27
profiling 801.1
profit (n) 375.7, 387.4, 472.3, 995.1, 999.4 (v) 387.17, 472.12, 995.3, 999.10
profitability 387.3, 449.10, 472.4, 995.1

profitable 387.18, 387.22, 449.21, 472.16, 624.21, 995.5, 999.12
profitableness 472.4, 999.1
profit by 387.15, 843.8
profiteer (n) 480.12 (v) 387.16, 632.7
profiteering 632.5
profiterole 10.41
profitless 391.12, 996.6
profitlessness 391.2
profit margin 472.4
profits 251.3, 472.3, 627.1
profit sharing 476.2
profit-sharing (n) 624.6 (a) 476.9
profit taking 737.19
profit-taking 737.5
profligacy 486.1, 654.5, 665.3
profligate (n) 660.4, 665.10 (a) 486.8, 654.14, 665.25
profluence 238.4
profluent 238.24
pro football 746.1
profound 93.24, 247.12, 257.20, 275.11, 522.16, 920.17, 920.18, 928.21
profoundest 275.16
profound idiocy 922.9
profound knowledge 928.6
profoundness 275.1, 522.2, 920.5
profound secret 345.5
profound sense 93.1
profound sleep 22.5
profound thought 931.3, 983.3
profundity 257.6, 275.1, 522.2, 920.5
profuse 355.4, 485.4, 486.8, 538.11, 884.9, 991.7
profuseness 355.1, 486.1, 538.2, 884.1, 991.2
profusion 247.3, 486.1, 538.2, 884.1, 991.2
profusive 538.11, 991.7
profusiveness 538.2
progenitiveness 890.1
progenitor 560.8
progenitors 560.7
progenitorship 560.1
progenitress 560.8
progenitrix 560.8
progeny 559.5, 561.1
prognathous 283.14
prognosis 91.13, 130.4, 946.5, 962.1
prognostic (n) 91.13, 133.3 (a) 133.15, 962.11
prognosticate 124.6, 962.9, 972.12
prognosticated 133.14
prognostication 91.13, 133.3, 962.1
prognosticative 133.15, 962.11
prognosticator 962.4
prognosticatory 962.11
prognostics 91.11
pro golf 751.1
program (n) 84.2, 352.2, 381.1, 404.1, 609.6, 609.7, 708.33, 755.2, 871.6, 965.3, 1042.11 (v) 381.8, 568.12, 871.8, 965.6, 1041.20, 1042.21
program director 1034.23
programma 352.2, 965.3
programmable 1042.22
programmable read-only memory 1042.7
programmatic 1042.22
programmed 871.9
programmed instruction 568.1
programmed selling 737.19
programmer 726.7, 1034.23, 1042.17
programming 1042.13, 1074.9
programming language 1042.13
program of action 381.1
program of music 708.33
program of operation 965.3
program suite 1042.11
program trading 738.1
progress (n) 162.1, 172.2, 177.1, 177.5, 182.9, 392.1, 856.1, 858.1, 861.1 (v) 162.2, 172.5, 177.18, 251.4, 392.7, 409.10, 861.5, 1010.7
progressing 162.6, 177.36, 392.15, 861.8
progression 162.1, 392.1, 807.2, 812.2, 815.1, 856.1, 861.1, 1017.8
progressionist 392.6
progressism 392.5
progressist 392.6
progressive (n) 220.1, 392.6, 611.11 (a) 162.6, 172.8, 220.4, 245.5, 392.15, 392.16, 611.19, 812.9, 815.4, 841.13
progressive change 852.1
progressive dinner 8.6
progressive jazz 708.9
progressive lens 29.2
progressive lenses 29.3
progressiveness 162.1, 392.5, 611.3
progressive openers 759.10
Progressive Party 609.24
progressive proof 548.5
progressive sorites 935.6
progressive taxation 630.9
progressive tense 530.12
progressivism 392.5, 611.3
progressivist (n) 392.6, 611.11 (a) 392.16
progressivistic 611.19
progressivity 162.1
progress of time 821.4
prohibit 428.7, 444.3, 773.4, 967.6, 1012.14
prohibited 444.7, 773.7, 967.7
prohibiting 444.6
prohibition 428.1, 444.1, 516.1, 668.3, 773.1, 1012.2
Prohibition Era 824.5
prohibitionism 668.3
prohibitionist (n) 668.5 (a) 668.11
prohibitive 428.11, 444.6, 632.12, 773.9, 1012.19
prohibitory 444.6
prohibitory injunction 444.1
project (n) 380.1, 381.2, 404.1, 724.2, 839.1 (v) 202.7, 206.5, 283.10, 348.7, 349.11, 380.4, 381.8, 714.16, 839.6, 904.11, 1074.13
projected 380.8, 381.12, 839.8
projectile (n) 462.18, 904.5 (a) 904.15
projectile rocket 1074.3
projecting 202.11, 283.14
projection 92.23, 159.5, 202.3, 206.4, 283.2, 285.4, 348.2, 349.1, 381.2, 381.3, 704.8, 904.2
projection printing 714.5
projection television 1035.11
projection tube 1035.11
projector 381.6, 462.21, 704.18, 714.12, 1074.10
projector tube 1074.10
project over 202.7
prolate 280.12
prolate spheroid 282.2
prolative 530.9
prole 606.5, 726.2
prolegomena 816.2
prolegomenon 556.1, 816.2
prolepsis 816.2, 833.1
proles 607.7
proletarian (n) 606.5, 607.9, 726.2 (a) 607.10
proletariat 607.7
pro-life 86.23
proliferate 78.8, 251.6, 883.6, 890.7, 991.5
proliferated 251.7
proliferating 251.8, 884.9
proliferation 78.2, 251.1, 883.4, 890.2
proliferous 890.9
prolific 538.11, 884.9, 890.9, 986.18
prolificacy 538.2, 890.1, 986.3
prolificate 890.8
prolificity 538.2, 890.1
prolificness 890.1
prolix 118.9, 267.8, 538.12, 540.9, 827.11, 993.17
prolixity 118.2, 267.4, 538.2, 540.1, 993.4
prolixness 267.4
proloctor 576.5
prolocutress 576.5
prolocutrix 576.5
prologize 814.3
prologue 704.7, 793.2, 816.2
prolong 267.6, 827.9, 846.9, 856.4
prolongate 267.6
prolongated 267.8
prolongation 118.1, 267.4, 815.1, 827.2, 846.4, 856.1
prolonged 118.9, 267.8, 827.11
prolong the agony 26.7, 96.18
prom 705.2, 708.33, 770.2
prom dress 5.11
promenade (n) 177.10, 383.2, 705.2, 812.3 (v) 177.29, 812.7
promenade concert 708.33
prominence 31.2, 247.2, 272.1, 283.2, 348.4, 417.4, 662.5, 997.2
prominent 31.7, 247.9, 272.14, 283.14, 348.12, 417.15, 662.17, 997.19
prominent belly 2.18
promiscuity 665.4, 810.1, 945.1
promiscuous 340.12, 665.26, 797.14, 810.12, 945.5, 972.16
promiscuousness 810.1, 945.1
promise (n) 124.1, 133.3, 334.4, 436.1, 437.1, 962.1 (v) 124.9, 133.12, 436.4, 437.5, 968.4
promised 130.13, 133.14, 436.8, 437.11, 563.18
promised land 986.11
Promised Land, the 986.11
promise in marriage 436.6
promise of harm 514.1
promise ring 498.6
promising 124.12, 133.17, 968.6
promissory 436.7
promissory note 436.2, 728.11
promitosis 305.16
promo 352.5, 509.3
promontory 283.9
promote 162.5, 352.15, 375.12, 384.7, 392.9, 446.2, 449.17, 509.11, 995.3
promoter 352.9, 381.6, 509.8, 616.9, 704.26
promoting (n) 352.5 (a) 384.8, 449.20, 509.17
promotion 162.1, 352.5, 392.1, 446.1, 449.5, 509.3, 734.2, 912.2
promotional 352.18, 449.21, 509.17
promotional film 706.1
promotional material 352.8, 551.1
prompt (n) 551.4, 989.5 (v) 375.13, 375.22, 422.6, 551.10, 894.7, 989.19 (a) 101.8, 174.15, 324.5, 330.18, 339.14, 401.9, 441.4, 845.9
prompt book 704.21
promptbook 704.21
prompted 375.30
prompter 375.10, 704.23, 989.5
prompter's box 704.16
prompting (n) 375.2, 989.5 (a) 375.27
promptitude 174.1, 330.3, 339.5, 441.1, 845.3
promptness 101.1, 174.1, 324.1, 330.3, 339.5, 401.2, 441.1, 845.3
promptorium 871.4
prompt the mind 989.19
promulgate 352.10, 352.13, 420.8, 437.9
promulgated 352.17
promulgation 352.1
promulgatory 348.9, 352.18
pronate 205.5
pronation 205.1
prone (v) 913.11 (a) 201.8, 274.7, 324.5, 433.16, 897.5, 968.6, 978.8
proneness 201.2, 274.1, 896.1, 897.1
prong 171.4, 238.3, 285.3
pronged 171.10, 285.9

pronominal 530.17
pronoun 530.5
pronounce 334.5, 352.12, 420.8, 524.22, 946.13
pronounced 31.7, 247.12, 334.9, 348.12, 524.29
pronouncedness 348.4
pronounce judgment 602.3, 946.13
pronounce man and wife 563.14
pronouncement 334.1, 352.2, 420.4, 524.3, 946.5
pronounce on 946.13
pronounce sentence 598.20, 602.3
Pronuba 563.13
pronunciamento 352.2, 420.4
pronunciation 524.5, 524.13
pronunciative 970.22
-proof 1007.5
proof (n) 334.3, 348.1, 548.5, 551.1, 713.7, 785.5, 935.1, 942.2, 957.1, 957.3, 957.4 (v) 15.14, 548.14 (a) 15.20
proof against 94.12, 453.5
proof before letter 713.7
proofer 548.12
proof of purchase 627.2, 957.4
proof of the pudding, the 957.3
proof positive 348.1, 957.3
proofread 548.17
proofreader 548.13, 554.2, 938.17
proofroom 548.11
proof sheet 548.5
prop (n) 704.17, 901.2, 904.6 (v) 15.13, 449.12, 901.21 (a) 184.49
propaedeutic (n) 405.1, 568.5 (a) 405.20, 568.18, 814.4
propaganda 352.4, 354.11, 569.2
propagandism 569.2
propagandist 569.2
propagandistic 569.6
propagandize 354.16, 569.4, 953.18
propagate 78.8, 352.10, 771.4, 890.7
propagated 352.17
propagation 78.2, 352.1, 771.1, 890.3
propagative 78.15
propagator 890.4, 1069.6
propagatory 352.18
propel 172.6, 375.12, 902.11, 904.9
propellant (n) 904.6, 1021.1, 1067.6, 1074.8, 1075.9 (a) 172.7, 904.14
propeller (n) 904.6 (a) 184.49
propeller plane 181.2
propeller race 184.30
propelling (n) 904.1 (a) 172.7, 904.14
propelling charge 1074.8
propensity 100.3, 413.5, 896.1, 978.3
proper 247.12, 387.18, 495.9, 496.9, 533.7, 579.5, 637.3, 639.8, 649.7, 664.5, 687.7, 865.13, 973.16, 995.5
proper claim 642.1
proper fraction 1017.7
proper name 527.3
properness 496.2, 637.2, 649.1
proper noun 527.3, 530.5
proper occasion 843.3
proper piloting 182.4
proper task 641.1
proper thing 373.1, 578.1
proper thing, the 637.1, 649.2
proper thing to do, the 637.1
propertied 469.9, 471.8
propertied person 470.3
properties 471.1, 706.4
proper time 843.3
property 386.2, 469.1, 471.1, 471.6, 517.1, 618.1, 704.17, 767.4, 865.4
propertyless 619.9
property line 213.5
property owner 470.3
property-owning 469.9
property right 469.2, 642.1
property rights 469.1
property roll 871.6
property tax 630.9
prop-fan (n) 904.6 (a) 904.17
prophase 305.16
prophecy 683.10, 839.1, 962.1
prophesied 839.8, 962.14
prophesier 962.4
prophesy 839.6, 962.9
prophesying 962.1
prophet 684.1, 689.14, 962.4, 986.13
prophetess 962.4
prophetic 683.11, 962.11
prophetical 962.11
prophetic revelation 683.10
prophet of doom 125.7, 399.4, 962.4
Prophets, the 683.3
prophylactic (n) 86.20, 86.23, 900.3, 1008.3 (a) 79.27, 86.42, 494.10, 1008.23, 1012.19
prophylactic psychiatry 92.3
prophylactic psychology 81.2
prophylactodontia 81.2
prophylactodontist 81.3
prophylaxis 81.2, 86.20
propinquant 223.15
propinque 223.14
propinquity 223.1, 559.1, 775.1
propinquous 223.15
propitiable 465.13
propitiate 465.7, 658.4, 696.15
propitiation 465.1, 658.1, 677.14, 696.6
propitiative 465.12, 677.16
propitiator 466.5
propitiatory 465.12, 658.7, 677.16, 696.16
propitiatory gift 465.2
propitious 124.12, 133.17, 449.22, 843.9
propitious moment 843.3
propitiousness 133.8, 843.1
prop-jet 181.2
proponent 600.8, 935.12
proportion (n) 158.1, 245.1, 257.1, 264.1, 477.5, 533.2, 790.1, 807.1, 943.1, 943.3, 1017.2, 1017.7, 1017.12 (v) 257.15, 264.3, 477.7, 788.7, 790.6
proportionability 943.3
proportionable 107.11, 775.8
proportional 158.10, 245.5, 477.13, 775.8
proportional band 1041.10
proportional control 1041.8
proportionality 264.1, 777.1
proportional notation 709.12
proportional representation 371.6, 609.18
proportionate (v) 264.3, 477.7 (a) 107.11, 477.13, 775.8, 788.9, 790.7, 991.6
proportionateness 943.3
proportioned 264.4
proportions 257.1
proposal 371.8, 380.1, 381.2, 422.1, 439.2, 562.8, 951.2
propose 371.19, 380.4, 422.5, 439.5, 440.14, 562.22, 951.12
proposed 380.8
proposed explanation 951.2
proposition (n) 334.1, 381.2, 404.1, 422.1, 439.2, 935.7, 951.2, 951.3, 952.2, 974.2 (v) 439.8
propositional 935.22
propositional calculus 935.2
propositional function 935.7
propound 422.5, 439.5, 951.12
propoxyphene 86.12
propped 901.24
propping 901.23
proprietary (n) 86.4, 469.2, 470.2 (a) 210.7, 469.10, 471.8
proprietary drug 86.4
proprietary information 210.3
proprietary medicine 86.4
proprietary name 86.4
proprietary rights 469.1
proprieties 580.3, 637.2
proprieties, the 579.2
proprietor 227.7, 470.2
proprietorship 469.2
proprietress 470.2
proprietrix 470.2
propriety 495.1, 496.1, 496.2, 533.1, 579.1, 637.2, 649.1, 664.2, 788.5, 843.1, 869.1, 995.1
prop root 310.22
props 706.4
propsmaster 704.23
propsmistress 704.23
propulsion 18.4, 902.1, 904.1
propulsion charge 1074.8
propulsive 904.14
propulsor 904.6
propulsory 904.14
prop up 449.12
propwash 184.30
propylaeum 189.6, 197.19
pro rata 477.13, 630.14
prorate 477.7, 630.12
prorated 477.13
prorogation 846.4
prorogue 846.9
pros 935.5
prosaic 117.8, 499.6, 535.3, 721.5, 724.15, 987.5
prosaicism 117.2, 721.2, 974.3, 987.1
prosaicness 117.2, 499.1, 535.1, 721.2, 987.1
prosaism 117.2, 721.2, 974.3, 987.1
pros and cons 935.5
proscenium 216.1, 704.16
proscenium arch 704.16
proscenium boxes 704.15
proscenium stage 704.16
proscribe 428.7, 444.3, 513.5, 586.6, 602.3, 773.4, 909.17
proscribed 210.7, 773.7
proscription 210.2, 428.1, 444.1, 513.1, 586.3, 602.1, 909.4
proscriptive 444.6, 602.5
prose (n) 117.2, 721.1, 974.3 (v) 117.5, 721.3 (a) 117.8, 721.4
prosecutable 598.21
prosecute 328.8, 437.9, 598.13
prosecute a suit against 598.13
prosecute at law 598.13
prosecute to a conclusion 360.5, 407.6
prosecuting attorney 597.1
prosecution 437.4, 598.1, 599.1
prosecution, the 599.5
prosecutor 599.5
prosecutorial 598.21, 599.13
prose fiction 721.1, 722.1
proselyte (n) 363.5, 572.2, 692.4, 858.7 (v) 858.16
proselyter 858.9
proselytism 858.6
proselytization 858.6
proselytize 858.16, 953.18
proselytizer 858.9
proseminar 568.8
prose poetry 721.1
proser 118.4
prose rhythm 721.1
Proserpina 682.5
Proserpine 682.5
prose run mad 545.1
prose style 721.1
prose writer 547.15, 718.4
prosiness 117.2, 499.1, 535.1, 721.2, 987.1
prosing 117.8, 535.3, 721.5, 987.5
pro soccer 752.1
prosodic 720.17
prosodical 720.17
prosodic form 720.6
prosodic pattern 720.6
prosodics 524.10
prosodion 708.17
prosody 524.10, 709.22, 720.6
prospect (n) 27.3, 31.3, 33.6, 124.1, 130.1, 639.1, 733.4, 839.1, 961.1, 966.1, 968.1 (v) 1058.14
prospecting 1058.8
prospection 961.1
prospective 130.13, 167.4, 839.8
prospector 1058.9
prospects 130.4, 639.1
prospectus 380.1, 381.2, 557.1, 871.6, 961.2, 962.1, 965.3
prosper 409.7, 1010.7
prospering 1010.13

prosperity 409.1, 618.1, 731.10, 1010.1, 1010.4
Prospero 976.2
prosperous 133.17, 409.14, 618.14, 1010.12
prosperous issue 409.1
prosperousness 133.8, 618.1, 1010.1
prostatic 13.8
prostatic fluid 13.2
prosthodontic 90.15
prosthodontist 90.6
prostitute (n) 665.16 (v) 389.4, 393.12 (a) 665.28
prostituted 665.28
prostitute oneself 665.21
prostitution 389.1, 393.2, 665.8, 732.1
prostrate (v) 19.10, 21.4, 112.19, 128.10, 395.19, 412.10, 696.11, 913.5, 913.11 (a) 19.16, 21.10, 85.59, 112.28, 112.29, 128.14, 138.14, 155.10, 201.8, 274.7, 412.17, 433.16, 692.10, 913.12
prostrate before 696.16
prostrated 112.28, 112.29, 128.14, 274.7, 412.17, 913.12
prostrated by grief 112.26
prostrate oneself 138.7, 155.6, 913.9, 913.11
prostrate oneself before 433.10
prostrating grief 112.10
prostration 16.1, 21.2, 85.8, 96.6, 112.10, 138.2, 155.2, 201.2, 260.4, 274.1, 395.3, 433.3, 696.1, 696.4, 913.3
prosy 117.8, 499.6, 535.3, 721.5, 987.5
prosyllogism 935.6
protagonist 616.9, 704.10, 707.6
protanopia 30.3
protasis 816.2
protean 783.3, 854.6
protean actor 707.2
proteanism 783.1
protect 397.8, 449.11, 458.17, 460.8, 1007.3, 1008.18
protected 210.7, 345.13, 397.13, 460.12, 1007.4, 1008.21
protected anchorage 1009.6
protected area 397.7
protecting 1008.23
protection 378.2, 397.1, 428.1, 429.5, 443.7, 449.1, 460.1, 494.3, 609.4, 1007.1, 1008.1
protectionism 428.1, 609.4
protectionist 428.6
protection racket 480.8, 732.1
protective (n) 86.20 (a) 86.42, 397.12, 460.11, 1008.23
protective clothing 1008.3
protective coating 1008.1
protective coloration 336.2, 356.11
protective coloring 295.3
protective covering 295.15, 460.3
protective custody 429.5, 429.6, 1008.1
protective mimicry 336.2
protectiveness 397.1, 1008.1
protective tariff 428.1
protective umbrella 1008.3
protector 460.7, 575.11, 1008.5
protectorate 232.1, 417.7
protectorship 417.7, 1008.2
protectress 1008.5
protégé 432.6
proteid 7.6
proteiform 783.3, 854.6
protein 7.6
protein plastic 1054.6
protein structure 7.6
pro tempore arrangement 365.5
pro tempore measure 365.5
proteolysis 806.2
proteolytic 806.6
proteolytic enzyme 7.9
protest (n) 115.4, 325.2, 333.2, 334.1, 453.1, 510.1, 625.1, 868.1 (v) 333.5, 334.5, 451.3, 453.3, 454.3, 510.10, 625.6, 868.4
Protestant (n) 675.20 (a) 675.28
protestant (n) 333.3 (a) 333.7
Protestant Christianity 675.7
Protestant ethic 675.10
Protestantism 675.10
protestation 333.2, 334.1, 376.1
protest demonstration 333.2
protested bill 625.1
protester 333.3, 452.3
protesting 333.7, 453.5
protesting too much 511.8
protest too much 376.3, 511.7, 993.10
Proteus 783.1, 854.4
prothalamium 563.3
prothesis 703.12, 814.1
prothetic vowel 524.12
prothonotary 550.1
prothymia 101.1, 135.1
protist 311.3
protium 1038.5
protochordate 311.31
protocol 91.14, 373.1, 419.2, 437.1, 437.2, 580.3, 761.3, 928.1, 965.3
protocolary 419.4
protocolic 419.4
protocol proposition 928.1
protocol sentence 928.1
protocol statement 761.3, 928.1
protogenic 886.14
protohistoric 834.5, 842.11
protohistory 837.3
protohuman (n) 842.7 (a) 842.11
proto-industrial 233.6
proton 258.8, 1038.6
proton gun 1038.8
proton number 1038.4
proton reaction 1038.8
protoplasm 305.4
protoplasmic 262.10, 305.18
protostar 1073.8
prototypal 337.6, 786.9
prototype 262.1, 300.2, 337.2, 786.1, 932.2, 1002.4
prototypic 786.9
prototypical 786.9
prototyping 337.2
protozoal 311.50
protozoan (n) 311.3, 311.31 (a) 258.15, 311.50
protozoic 311.50
protozoon 85.42, 258.7, 311.31
protract 267.6, 538.8, 827.9, 846.9, 856.4
protracted 118.9, 267.8, 538.12, 827.11, 856.7
protraction 118.1, 267.4, 827.2, 846.4, 856.1
protractor 278.4
protrude 190.11, 283.10
protrudent 283.14
protruding 283.14
protruding belly 2.18
protrusible 283.14
protrusile 283.14
protrusion 202.3, 283.2
protrusive 283.14
protuberance 283.2, 294.1
protuberancy 283.2
protuberant 283.14
protuberate 283.10
protuberating 283.14
proud 136.8, 140.9, 141.9, 501.21, 970.21
proud, the 136.3
proud as a peacock 136.8
proud as Lucifer 136.8
proud as Punch 136.8
proud bearing 136.2
proud-blooded 136.8
proud flesh 85.39
proudful 136.8
proudhearted 136.8
proudling 136.3
proud-looking 136.8
proud-minded 136.8
proudness 136.1, 141.1, 501.5
proud-spirited 136.8
provability 957.7, 970.3
provable 761.15, 957.19, 970.15
provable fact 761.3
prove 548.14, 887.4, 942.8, 957.10, 957.11, 970.12, 1017.21
prove acceptable 991.4
proved 942.12, 957.20, 970.20, 973.13
proved fact 970.1
proved reserve 386.3
proved reserves 386.3
prove false 645.13
prove infertile 891.3
proven 644.19, 957.20, 973.13
provenance 886.5
provender (n) 10.1, 10.4, 10.5, 385.2 (v) 385.9
provenience 886.5
provenient 167.4
proven reserve 386.3
prove one's point 957.10
prove out 973.8
proverb (n) 529.1, 974.1 (v) 974.5
proverbial 928.27, 974.6
proverbial saying 974.1
proverbs 974.1
prove that black is white and white black 936.8
prove the contrary 958.4
prove to be 887.4, 957.10, 973.8
prove true 957.10, 973.8
prove up 548.14
provide 385.7, 478.15
provide against 405.11, 494.6
provide against a rainy day 405.11
provide a grubstake 385.9
provide a hedge 494.6
provide a rationale 935.15
provide capital for 729.16
provided 385.13, 405.16
provided for 618.14
provide for 7.17, 306.11, 385.7, 405.11, 478.15, 478.18, 494.6, 729.16, 959.5, 1008.19
provide for a rainy day 386.12, 405.11
provide money for 729.16
Providence 964.3
providence 494.3, 635.1, 677.13, 920.4, 920.7, 961.1
provident 405.20, 494.10, 635.6, 920.16, 920.19, 961.7
providential 478.24, 677.17, 843.9, 961.7, 1010.14
provider 385.6
provide the basis 405.12
provide with a roof 225.10
providing 385.1
province 231.2, 231.5, 232.1, 233.1, 641.1, 698.8, 724.3, 724.4, 928.10
provinces 233.1
provincial (n) 227.10, 575.12, 606.6 (a) 231.9, 233.6, 523.22, 606.8, 980.10
provincial court 423.4
provincialism 233.3, 523.7, 980.1
provinciality 233.3
provincial legislature 613.1
provincial parliament 613.1
provincial police 1008.17
proving (n) 957.4 (a) 942.11
proving ground 942.5, 1074.7
proving out 957.4
provision (n) 10.1, 385.1, 405.1, 421.2, 449.3, 478.1, 494.3, 862.1, 959.2, 961.1, 995.2, 1008.4 (v) 8.18, 385.9, 386.11
provisional 405.20, 494.10, 766.7, 826.4, 862.8, 862.9, 942.11, 959.8, 971.20, 995.7
provisional government 612.4
provisionality 862.1, 959.1, 995.1
provisionally accept 951.10
provisionalness 862.1
provisioned 385.13
provisioner 385.6
provisioning 385.1
provisionment 386.1
provision of capital 729.2
provisions 10.5, 385.2, 386.1, 959.2
proviso 210.2, 421.2, 613.9, 959.2
provisonally agree to 951.10
provisory 826.4, 959.8
provitamin 7.4
provocateur 375.11
provocation 96.3, 98.7, 105.11, 119.1, 152.11, 375.4, 375.7, 886.3

provocative 63.10, 100.30, 105.30, 119.5, 375.27, 377.8, 589.10, 983.19
provocativeness 100.13
provoke 96.13, 96.14, 98.15, 105.13, 119.2, 142.8, 152.24, 375.13, 375.17, 456.14, 589.7, 886.11, 983.12
provoked 96.21, 119.4, 152.27
provoker 375.11
provoking 98.22, 105.30, 375.27, 544.13, 983.19
provokingness 98.7
provost 571.8, 574.3, 699.9
provostry 417.7
provostship 417.7
prow 216.3
prowess 413.1, 492.1, 492.6
prowl (n) 345.4 (v) 177.23, 177.26, 346.9
prowl after 382.9, 938.30
prowl car 179.11
prowler 483.1
prowling (n) 177.17, 345.4 (a) 346.14
proximal 223.14
proximate (n) 530.7 (v) 167.3 (a) 167.4, 223.14, 775.8, 815.4
proximate analysis 801.1
proximate cause 886.3
proximation 167.1
proximity 223.1, 775.1
proxy (n) 371.6, 576.1, 609.19, 609.23, 615.1, 862.2 (a) 862.8
proxy voting 609.18
Prozac 87.3
PR person 352.9
prude 500.11
prudence 339.4, 494.1, 635.1, 653.3, 670.1, 920.7, 961.1, 995.1
prudent 339.13, 494.8, 635.6, 670.10, 920.19, 961.7
prudent, the 921.3
prudent administration 635.1
prudential 635.6, 920.19
prudentialism 920.7
prudential judgment 920.5
prudentialness 494.1
prudery 500.6
prudish 495.9, 500.19
prudishness 495.1, 500.6
prune 255.10, 268.6, 802.11, 1069.17
pruned 268.9, 537.6
prune-faced 110.23, 303.16
prunes and prisms 500.1
pruning 537.4, 1069.13
prurience 75.5, 100.6, 665.5, 981.1
pruriency 75.5, 100.6, 665.5
prurient 75.27, 100.24, 665.29, 981.5
prurient interest 981.1
pruriginous 74.10
prurigo 74.3
pruritus 74.3, 85.9, 917.5
pry (n) 214.4, 906.1, 906.4, 981.2 (v) 27.13, 214.7, 906.8, 938.31, 981.4
pry around 938.32
prying (n) 981.1 (a) 214.9, 938.38, 981.6
pry into 938.23
pry loose from 480.22
pry open 292.14
pry out 192.10, 192.14, 906.8, 938.22, 938.34, 941.4
Przewalsky's horse 311.10
psalm (n) 696.3, 708.14, 708.17 (v) 708.38
Psalm Book 701.11
psalmbook 554.1, 701.11
psalmic 708.50
psalmodial 708.50
psalmodic 708.50
psalmody 696.3, 708.17
Psalms, the 701.11
psalm singer 710.13
psalter 554.1, 701.11
Psalter, the 701.11
psalterer 710.5
Psaltery, the 701.11
pseud 357.10
pseudo 336.8, 354.26, 354.32, 784.14
pseudo-event 831.2
pseudohermaphrodite (n) 75.17 (a) 75.31
pseudohermaphroditic 75.31
pseudohermaphroditism 75.12
pseudologist 357.9
pseudologue 357.9
pseudology 354.8
pseudonym 527.8
pseudonymous literature 547.12, 718.1
pseudosyllogism 935.6, 936.3
pseudotuberculosis 85.41
psittacine 311.48
psoriasis 85.35
psych 811.4, 940.2
psychagogy 92.26
psychalgia 26.2
psychasthenic 92.39
psyche 92.28, 919.4
psychedelic (n) 86.13, 87.3 (a) 86.46, 976.10
psychedelic drug 86.13, 87.3
psychedelic show 33.7
psyched up 405.16
psychiatric 92.37, 92.38
psychiatric care 92.35, 926.19
psychiatric evaluation 92.7
psychiatric hospital 926.14
psychiatric social worker 92.10
psychiatric treatment 92.35
psychiatric ward 926.14
psychiatrist 92.10, 926.19
psychiatry 92.3, 926.19
psychic (n) 689.13, 962.4 (a) 689.24, 919.7, 988.7, 1053.7
psychical 689.24, 870.15, 919.7, 988.7, 1053.7
psychically blind 30.9
psychical research 689.4, 1053.1
psychic apparatus 92.28
psychic blindness 30.1
psychic energy 92.28
psychicism 689.4, 1053.1
psychicist 689.12
psychic monism 689.4
psychic phenomena 689.6
psychic research 689.4, 1053.1
psychics 689.4, 1053.1
psychism 689.4, 1053.1, 1053.3
psychist 689.12, 1053.4
psycho (n) 92.13, 926.16, 926.17 (a) 926.27
psychoactive 86.46
psychoactive chemical 87.3
psychoactive drug 86.13, 87.3
psychoanalysis 92.6
psychoanalyst 92.10
psychoanalytic 92.38
psychoanalytical 92.38
psychoanalytic method 92.6
psychoanalytic therapy 92.6
psychoanalyze 92.36
psychobabble 92.1, 523.10
psychobiological 92.37
psychobiologist 92.10
psychocatharsis 92.25
psychochemical (n) 87.3 (a) 86.46
psychochemist 92.10
psychodiagnosis 92.7
psychodiagnostic 92.38
psychodiagnostics 92.7
psychodrama 92.25
psychodynamic 92.37
psychogalvanic skin response 92.8
psychogalvanometer 92.8
psychogenetic 92.37
psychogenic 92.37
psychognosis 92.6
psychognosy 92.6
psychogram 92.8
psychograph 92.8
psychographer 92.10
psychographist 689.13
psychography 92.8, 689.6
psychokinesia 926.7
psychokinesis 689.6
psychokinetic 689.24
psycholinguistic 523.19
psychologic 919.7
psychological 92.37, 919.7
psychological addiction 87.1
psychological adjustive reactions 92.23
psychological block 92.24
psychological counselor 92.10
psychological defenses 460.1
psychological dependence 87.1
psychological evaluation 92.7
psychological hedonism 663.1
psychological logic 935.2
psychological me 92.28
psychological measurement 92.8
psychological medicine 92.3, 92.4
psychological moment 824.1, 843.5
psychological practitioner 92.10
psychological profile 92.6, 92.8
psychological school 92.2
psychological screening 92.8
psychological space 158.7
psychological stress 92.17
psychological support 901.1
psychological symptom 92.18
psychological test 92.9
psychological theory 92.2
psychological time 821.1
psychological trauma 92.17
psychological warfare 127.6, 458.1
psychologism 92.1, 935.2
psychologist 92.10
psychologize 92.36
psychology 92.1, 312.10, 978.1
psychology branch 92.1
psychology of depths 92.6
psychometer 92.8, 689.14
psychometric 92.37
psychometrics 92.8
psychometrist 689.14
psychometry 92.8, 689.8
psych oneself up 405.13
psychoneurological 92.37
psychoneurosis 92.14
psychoneurotic 92.39, 926.28
psychoneurotic disorder 92.14
psychonosema 92.14
psychopath 308.11, 926.17
psychopathia sexualis 926.3
psychopathic 92.37, 308.24, 926.28
psychopathic case 926.17
psychopathic condition 926.3
psychopathic hospital 926.14
psychopathic killer 926.15
psychopathic personality 92.15, 926.3, 926.17
psychopathic ward 926.14
psychopathist 92.10
psychopathological 92.37
psychopathological personality 92.13
psychopathologist 92.10
psychopathology 926.3
psychopathy 92.15, 926.3
psychopathyfunctional nervous disorder 92.14
psychophysical 92.37
psychophysicist 92.10
psychophysiological 92.37
psychophysiologist 92.10
psychorrhagy 689.6
psychosensory 689.24
psychosexual 92.37
psychosexual disorder 75.11
psychosis 92.14, 926.3
psychosocial 92.37
psychosocial medicine 92.4
psychosomatic 92.37
psychosomatic medicine 92.4
psychosomatic pain 26.2
psychosomatic symptom 92.18
psychosophy 689.4
psychosurgery 92.35
psychosynthesis 92.27
psychotaxis 92.23
psychotechnical 92.37
psychotechnologist 92.10
psychotheism 675.5
psychotheist 675.16
psychotherapeutic 92.38
psychotherapeutics 92.5
psychotherapeutist 92.10
psychotherapist 92.10, 926.19
psychotherapy 91.1, 92.5, 926.19

psychotic (n) 926.17 (a) 92.37, 926.28
psychotomimetic 86.46
psychotomimetic drug 87.3
psychotropic drug 87.3
psych out 128.10, 940.2
psychrometer 1065.10
psychrometry 1065.9
psych up 17.10, 375.19
psyhical phenomena 689.6
PT boat 180.6
ptisan 86.4
Ptolemaic universe 1073.1
ptomaine poisoning 85.31
P2P 312.15
ptyalism 13.3
ptyalize 13.6
pub 8.17, 88.20
pub crawl 88.6
pub-crawl 88.28, 743.24
puberty 14.1, 301.6
pubes 3.2
pubescence 3.2, 14.1, 294.3, 301.6
pubescent (n) 302.1 (a) 3.24, 14.3, 294.8, 301.13, 1047.14
pubic hair 2.13, 3.2
pubic region 2.13
public (n) 88.20, 166.2, 227.1, 376.1, 733.3 (a) 206.7, 312.16, 352.17, 476.9, 497.14, 606.8, 864.12, 928.27
public, the 312.4, 606.1
public-access television 1035.1
public-access TV 1035.1
public acclaim 662.1
public address 543.2
public-address system 50.11
public administration 609.2
public affairs 609.1
publican 88.19, 630.10
public assistance 478.8, 611.7
publication 343.2, 348.1, 352.1, 548.1, 551.1, 554.1, 771.1
publicational 352.18
publications 928.9
public baths 79.10
public belief 953.6
public broadcasting 1034.16, 1035.1
public charge 432.6
public choice 757.2
public communication 555.3
public company 730.1, 737.15
public consciousness 352.4
public crib 729.13
public debt 623.1
public declaration 352.2
public defender 597.1
public dishonor 661.1
public domain 469.2
public employee 575.15
public enemy 589.6, 593.1, 660.9
public enemy number one 589.6
public entertainer 707.1
public exposure 31.2
public eye 352.4
public figure 662.9
public forum 352.4
public funds 729.13
public good 387.4
public health 81.2
public health doctor 81.3
public-health medicine 90.13
public health physician 81.3
public house 88.20
public housing 225.3, 228.1
public image 33.2, 500.1
publicist 352.9, 555.4, 556.4
publicity 352.4, 551.1, 662.1
publicity agent 352.9, 704.25
publicity man 704.25
publicity manager 704.25
publicity story 352.4
publicity stunt 352.4
publicization 352.5
publicize 352.15, 552.11
publicizer 352.9
publicizing 351.1, 352.5
public knowledge 352.4, 551.1
public library 558.1
public man 610.2
publicness 352.4
public notice 352.2, 352.4
public nuisance 96.2, 96.10
public office 575.14
public official 575.15, 610.11
public opinion 609.29, 946.3, 953.6
public-opinion poll 938.14
public ownership 476.2, 611.6
public park 743.14
public policy 609.4
public press, the 555.3
public print, the 555.3
public property 471.1
public prosecutor 597.1
public radio 1034.16
public recognition 352.4
public records 549.2
public relations 352.4
public relations handout 352.8
public relations officer 352.9, 551.5
public relations person 352.9
public relations release 352.8
public relations specialist 352.9
public report 352.4
public safety 1008.1
public school 567.4
public sector 731.7
public-sector housing 228.1
public servant 575.15, 610.11
public service 143.6
public service announcement 352.3, 1035.2
public speaker 543.4, 543.6
public speaking 543.1
public speech 543.2
public spirit 591.1
public-spirited 591.4, 652.6
public square 463.1
public statement 352.2
public telephone 347.4
public television 1035.1
public till 482.11, 729.13
public tit 609.35
public tranquility 464.1
public transportation 179.1, 179.13
public treasury 729.13
public trough 482.11, 609.35, 729.13
public utility 1040.3
public walk 383.2
public weal 999.4
public welfare 143.5, 478.8
public woman 610.2
public works 143.5
public worship 696.8
publish 351.5, 352.10, 548.14, 673.10, 771.4
publish abroad 352.10
publish a manifesto 352.12
published 352.17
publisher 551.5, 554.2
publishers 548.11
publisher's catalog 558.4, 871.3
publisher's list 558.4, 871.3
publishing 352.1, 548.1, 555.3
publishing house 548.11, 554.2
publishing industry, the 555.3
publish the banns 436.6
puca 678.8
puce 41.6, 46.3
Puck 678.8, 680.7
puck 302.4, 322.3
puck 680.7
pucker (n) 105.6, 126.1, 291.3, 985.3 (v) 260.7, 291.6
puckered 260.12, 291.8
puckering 260.1
pucker up 260.7
puckery 291.8
puck-handle 749.7
puck handling 749.3
puckish 322.6, 680.18
puckishness 322.2
pudding 10.40, 10.46, 1047.4, 1062.5, 1063.2
puddinghead 924.4, 930.7
pudding stone 1059.1
puddle 241.1, 1062.9
puddle jumper 181.2
puddle-jumping 184.10
pudency 139.4, 344.3, 664.2
pudenda 2.13
pudginess 257.8, 268.2
pudgy 257.18, 268.10
pudibund 139.12
pudibundity 139.4
pudibundness 139.4
pudicity 139.4, 664.2
puerile 301.11, 406.11, 922.24
puerilism 922.11
puerility 301.2, 301.4, 922.11, 923.2
Puerto Rico Trench 275.5
puff (n) 2.21, 10.41, 89.10, 259.2, 318.3, 320.2, 352.4, 355.1, 509.3, 1016.11, 1047.4 (v) 21.5, 87.22, 89.14, 259.4, 318.19, 352.15, 355.3, 502.6, 509.11, 509.12, 511.7, 909.24 (a) 355.4
puff and blow 21.5
puff away 87.22
puffball 310.4
puffed 320.6, 355.4
puffed out 259.13
puffed up 136.10, 140.11, 259.13, 949.3
puffed-up with pride 136.10
puffer 509.8
puffery 355.1
puffiness 257.8, 259.2, 283.2
puffing (n) 259.2, 283.1 (a) 2.32, 21.12, 509.17
puffing out 283.1
puffing up 355.1
puff like a grampus 21.5
puff of air 318.3, 524.12
puff of smoke 1067.1
puff of wind 318.3
puff out 259.5
puff pastry 10.41
puff piece 545.3
puff up 140.7, 251.5, 259.4, 259.5, 509.12
puffy 257.18, 259.13, 318.21
pug (n) 199.5, 461.2, 517.7, 754.2 (a) 268.10
pugged 268.10
pugilism 457.9, 754.1
pugilist 461.2, 754.2
pugilistic 458.20
pugmark 517.7
pugnacious 456.17, 458.20
pugnaciousness 458.10
pugnacity 152.5, 456.3, 458.10
pug-nosed 265.12
puisne 301.15, 835.4
puissance 18.1, 417.2
puissant 15.15, 18.12, 417.15
pujari 699.13
puke (n) 909.8 (v) 99.4, 909.27
pukes 85.30
pukes, the 909.8
puking 909.8
pukish 85.57
puky 80.23, 85.57
pulchritude 1016.1
pulchritudinous 1016.17
Pulcinella 707.10
pule 60.2, 115.14
puling 60.6, 115.19
puling infant 302.9
Pulitzer Prize 646.2
pull (n) 8.4, 18.1, 88.7, 249.1, 548.5, 725.2, 894.2, 905.1, 905.2, 907.1 (v) 8.29, 89.14, 164.5, 182.53, 192.10, 267.6, 428.7, 548.14, 725.10, 751.4, 905.4, 907.4
pull a boner 414.12, 975.15
pull about one's ears 913.5
pull a face 265.8
pull a fast one 415.11
pull a fast one on 356.14
pull a gun on 459.21
pull ahead 249.10
pull a lone oar 430.20
pull an all-nighter 570.14
pull an el foldo 293.8
pull an oar 476.5
pull apart 510.15, 802.14
pull a proof 548.14
pull around 396.15, 396.20
pull a stunt 356.19, 489.14
pull a trick 356.19, 489.14
pull at the forelock 585.10
pull at the heartstrings 112.19
pull at the leash 135.4
pull away 168.2, 368.8, 802.8

pull back 163.5, 163.6, 168.3, 325.4, 362.7, 368.8, 802.8, 903.7
pullback 163.2, 252.4, 903.3
pull by the sleeve 989.19
pull clear 368.8
pull different ways 456.8
pull down 395.19, 472.9, 479.6, 624.20, 913.4, 913.5
pulldown 1042.18
pulled 267.8
pulled meat 10.13
pullet 302.10, 311.28
pulley 1040.5, 1040.7
pull for 403.9
pull hitter 745.2
pull in 168.3, 186.6, 428.7, 429.16, 857.7, 906.9
pulling (n) 8.3, 192.1, 905.1 (a) 905.6, 907.5
pulling down 472.1, 913.1
pulling no punches 666.8
pulling off 75.8
pulling out 370.1
pulling power 905.1, 907.1
pulling together 450.1
pull in one's horns 137.7, 433.8, 494.5
pull in pieces 395.17
pull into 857.7
pull it off 409.8
pull it together 808.8
Pullman 179.15
Pullman car 179.15, 197.10
pull no punches 997.14
pull off 328.6, 407.5, 409.11
pull oneself together 121.7
pull oneself up by one's bootstraps 409.10
pull oneself up by one's own boot-straps 1010.7
pull one's leg 356.15, 489.14, 508.8, 511.6
pull one's punches 210.5, 959.5
pull one's weight 476.6
pull one's wits together 931.10
pull one up short 105.14
pull out 163.6, 168.3, 184.40, 188.6, 192.10, 370.5, 370.6, 802.8
pull-out 184.13
pullout 163.2, 903.3
pull out all the stops 430.19
pull out by the roots 192.10
pull out of it 396.20
pullover 5.15
pull rank 424.8
pull ropes 894.9
pull round 396.15, 396.20
pull something 356.19
pull strings 415.10, 894.9
pull the plug on 395.11
pull the rug out from under 395.11
pull the strings 573.8, 612.12
pull the teeth of 19.9
pull the trigger 459.22
pull the wool over one's eyes 356.17
pull through 396.15, 396.20
pull together 381.8, 450.3, 788.7
pull to pieces 395.17, 510.15
pull towards 907.4
pullulate 14.2, 259.7, 310.34, 890.7, 993.8
pullulate with 884.5
pullulating 993.19
pullulation 14.1, 259.3, 310.32, 890.2
pull up 184.40, 192.10, 598.15, 857.7, 857.11
pull-up 184.13
pull up by the roots 192.10, 395.14
pull up short 131.7
pull up stakes 34.2, 188.7, 188.14, 222.10, 368.10
pull wires 415.10, 894.9
pulmonary 2.32
pulmonary artery 2.23
pulmonary vein 2.23
pulmonic 2.32
pulp (n) 1062.5, 1063.2 (v) 1047.6, 1063.5
pulpal 1063.6
pulpar 1063.6
pulped 1063.6
pulpefaction 1063.3
pulper 803.4, 1063.4
pulp fiction 722.1
pulpification 1063.3
pulpifier 1063.4
pulpify 1063.5
pulpiness 803.3, 1047.1, 1047.2, 1062.1, 1063.1
pulping 1063.3, 1065.7
pulpit 703.13, 901.13
pulpit, the 543.1, 698.1
pulpitarian 543.5
pulpit discourse 543.3
pulpiteer 543.5, 699.3
pulpiter 699.3
pulpit oratory 543.1
pulp lead 1063.2
pulplike 1063.6
pulp machine 1063.4
pulpous 1063.6
pulpousness 1063.1
pulpwood 1054.3, 1063.2
pulpy 65.2, 1047.11, 1062.11, 1062.12, 1063.6
pulsar 1073.8
pulsate 55.4, 850.5, 916.12
pulsatile 916.18
pulsating 709.28, 847.5, 916.18
pulsating star 1073.8
pulsating universe 1073.1
pulsating universe theory 1073.18
pulsation 55.1, 709.26, 847.2, 850.2, 916.3
pulsative 709.28, 916.18
pulsatory 709.28, 916.18
pulse (n) 10.35, 310.4, 709.26, 850.3, 916.3, 1036.10 (v) 54.6, 850.5, 916.12, 917.12
pulse jet 181.1
pulse-jet (n) 181.3 (a) 904.17
pulse-jet propulsion 184.25
pulse point 916.3
pulsing 54.10, 709.28, 850.7, 916.18
pulsive 902.23
pultaceous 1063.6
pulverable 1051.13
pulverableness 1051.3
pulverant 1051.11
pulverizable 1051.13
pulverization 771.1, 1051.4
pulverize 393.11, 395.17, 802.9, 802.13, 902.16, 1044.6, 1047.6, 1051.9
pulverized 1051.11
pulverizer 1051.7
pulverous 1051.11
pulverulence 1051.1
pulverulent 1051.11, 1051.13
puma 311.21
pumice (n) 79.17 (v) 287.8
pumice stone 79.17
pummel 604.12, 902.16
pummeling 754.3
pump (n) 2.16, 192.9, 759.10, 1040.3 (v) 192.12, 259.4, 892.9, 916.14, 938.21, 938.22
pump bilge 12.14
pumped 17.13
pumped up 17.13, 405.16, 949.3
pumper 1022.3
pumpernickel 40.1
pump fake 747.3
pump-fake 747.4
pump for information 938.21
pump full of lead 904.12
pump house 91.23
pumping 192.3, 938.12, 938.13
pumping iron 84.2
pump iron 84.4
pumpkin 42.2
pumpkin-colored 42.2
pumpkin head 924.4
pumpkin-headed 922.17
pumpman 1022.4
pump out 192.12, 909.23
pump-priming 609.4
pump room 91.23
pumps 5.27
pump up 17.10, 259.4, 259.5, 375.19, 949.2
pun (n) 489.8, 539.2, 784.6 (v) 489.13, 784.9
Punch 707.10
punch (n) 10.49, 17.3, 18.1, 68.2, 88.9, 544.3 (v) 284.14, 292.15, 517.19
punch (n) 713.8, 754.3, 786.6, 902.2, 902.4, 902.6, 1040.7 (v) 754.4, 902.12, 902.14
Punch and Judy 707.10
punch bowl 88.13, 284.2
punchbowl 8.12
punch cattle 1070.8
punch-drunk 985.14
puncheon 1054.3
puncher 178.8, 1070.3
punch full of holes 292.15
punch in 186.6, 284.14, 832.12
Punchinello 707.10
punching 292.3
punching bag 725.7
punch line 489.6
punch out 188.13, 832.12, 902.17
punch-out 457.4
punchout 745.3
punch the clock 832.12
punch-up 457.4
punchy 544.11, 985.14
punctate 47.13
punctated 47.13
punctilio 495.1, 580.2, 580.3, 644.2
punctilious 339.12, 434.4, 495.9, 580.10, 644.15, 807.6
punctiliousness 339.3, 495.1, 580.2, 644.2
punctual 339.12, 434.4, 644.15, 845.9
punctuality 339.3, 339.5, 845.3, 850.1
punctualness 845.3
punctuate 517.19, 530.16, 997.14
punctuated 517.24, 997.21
punctuated equilibrium 861.4
punctuation 530.15, 547.9
punctuation mark 530.15
puncture (n) 85.38, 292.3, 517.5 (v) 260.10, 292.15, 393.13, 517.19, 958.4
punctured 260.14, 958.7
puncture one's balloon 977.2
puncture proof 15.20
punctureproof 293.13
puncturer 1040.2
puncturing 292.3
pundit 413.11, 571.1, 699.13, 866.3, 929.1, 929.3
pungency 64.2, 67.1, 68.1, 69.2, 489.2, 544.4
pungent 15.22, 26.10, 64.6, 67.5, 68.6, 69.10, 70.9, 489.15, 544.12, 974.6
pungent taste 62.1
Punic faith 645.5
puniness 248.1, 258.1, 270.5, 992.2, 998.1
punish 96.18, 506.7, 603.4, 604.9
punishable 674.6
punisher 604.7
punishing 21.13, 604.22, 725.18
punishment 26.6, 506.2, 603.1, 604.1
punishment of Tantalus 515.1
punishment that fits the crime 604.1
punish oneself 113.6
punition 604.1
punitive 506.8, 507.7, 604.22
punitive damages 603.3
punitive measures 603.1
punitory 507.7, 604.22
punk (n) 302.4, 998.7, 1021.6 (a) 998.18, 1000.8, 1005.9
punkah 318.18
punk kid 302.4
punk rock 708.10
punner 489.12
punning (n) 489.8, 539.1 (a) 784.17
punster 489.12
punt (n) 746.3, 902.9 (v) 182.53, 468.2, 746.5, 759.25
punter 183.5, 746.2, 759.21
punting 759.1
punt return 746.3

puny 16.14, 258.10, 270.20, 992.10, 998.20
pup (n) 142.5, 302.5, 302.10, 311.16 (v) 1.3
pupa 302.12
pupil 2.9, 27.9, 572.1
pupilage 572.2
pupil teacher 571.4
puplike 301.11
puppet 138.3, 258.6, 349.6, 384.4, 575.5, 576.1, 576.3, 616.8, 743.16, 764.2
puppeteer 707.3
puppet government 232.1, 432.6
puppet regime 232.1
puppy 2.7, 142.5, 302.5, 302.10, 311.16, 500.9
puppy dog 311.16
puppy-dog eyes 562.9
puppy-feet 758.2
puppyfoot 758.2
puppyhood 301.2
puppyish 301.11
puppyism 500.4
puppylike 301.11
puppy love 104.3
Purana 683.8
purblind 28.13, 922.14, 980.10
purblindness 28.2, 922.2, 980.1
purchasability 645.9
purchasable 378.4, 645.23
purchase (n) 474.2, 733.1, 894.1, 901.5, 906.2, 906.6 (v) 378.3, 733.7
purchased 733.11
purchase price 630.1
purchaser 626.4, 733.5
purchasing (n) 733.1 (a) 733.10
purchasing agent 733.5
purchasing power 624.4, 733.1
purchasing public 733.3
purdah 563.10
pure 79.25, 192.18, 496.7, 499.6, 533.6, 535.3, 644.13, 653.6, 657.7, 664.4, 692.9, 792.10, 794.10, 798.6, 973.15, 1002.6
pure and simple 499.6, 798.6
pure as driven snow 657.7, 664.4
pure as the driven snow 653.6
pure being 761.1
pure-blooded 607.10, 608.11
purebred 607.10, 608.11
purebred horse 311.10
pure color 35.4, 35.7
pure democracy 612.4
puréepulp 1062.5
pure form 1053.3
pure heart 416.3
purehearted 664.4, 692.9
pureheartedness 692.2
pure in heart 664.4, 692.9
pure mathematics 1017.1
pureness 79.1, 644.1, 692.2
pureness of heart 692.2
pure science 928.10
purest type 767.2
pure white 37.7
purfle 211.10
purgation 12.2, 79.2, 92.25, 120.2, 600.1, 601.1, 658.3
purgative (n) 79.17, 86.17 (a) 79.28, 86.48, 120.9, 658.7
purgatorial 658.7, 682.8
purgatory 96.7, 429.7, 658.3, 682.1
purge (n) 12.2, 79.2, 79.17, 86.17, 120.2, 308.2, 395.6, 447.2, 773.2 (v) 79.18, 91.24, 120.6, 308.13, 308.16, 308.17, 395.14, 447.4, 600.9, 601.4, 773.5, 909.21, 909.22
purge away 120.6
purged 79.26, 773.7
purge oneself 658.6
purging (n) 79.2, 120.2, 308.2, 600.1, 601.1 (a) 79.28
purification 79.2, 79.4, 192.8, 255.1, 685.3, 798.2
purification plant 80.12
purificatory 79.28
purified 79.26, 798.7
purifier 79.13, 79.17
purify 79.18, 79.22, 255.9, 685.5, 798.4
purifying (n) 79.2 (a) 79.28, 658.7
purism 425.2, 495.1, 500.5, 533.3, 580.2, 687.5
purist (n) 361.6, 533.4, 929.5 (a) 425.7, 687.8
puristic 425.7, 495.9, 500.18, 580.10, 687.8
puritan (n) 500.11, 667.2 (a) 425.7
puritanic 425.7, 495.9
puritanical 425.7, 495.9, 500.19, 667.4, 687.8
puritanicalness 500.6, 687.5
puritanism 425.2, 495.1, 500.6, 667.1, 687.5
purity 35.6, 79.1, 499.1, 533.1, 644.1, 653.2, 657.1, 664.1, 692.2, 798.1, 872.1, 1002.1
purl (n) 52.4 (v) 52.11, 211.10, 238.21
purlieu 228.18, 228.27, 231.1, 463.1
purlieus 209.1, 223.1, 231.1
purling 52.19
purloin 482.13
purloined 482.23
purloiner 483.1
purloining 482.1
purohit 699.13
purple (n) 46.1, 647.3 (v) 46.2 (a) 46.3, 417.17, 545.11
purple, the 417.8
purple-blue 46.3
purple haze 87.10
purple hearts 87.4, 87.5
purpleness 46.1
purple pall 647.3
purple passage 536.1
purple passages 545.4
purple prose 522.7, 545.2
purplescent 46.3
purple state 609.18
purpliness 46.1
purplish 46.3
purplishness 46.1
purply 46.3
purport (n) 518.1 (v) 376.3, 380.4
purported 376.5
purportless 520.6
purpose (n) 359.1, 380.1, 387.5, 518.2 (v) 359.7, 380.4
purpose-build 892.8
purpose-built 892.18
purposed 380.8
purposeful 359.11, 380.8
purposefulness 359.1
purposeless 391.9, 520.6, 972.16
purposelessness 364.3, 391.2, 520.1, 972.3
purpose to oneself 380.4
purposive 380.8
purpurate (v) 46.2 (a) 46.3
purpure (n) 647.2 (a) 46.3
purpureal 46.3
purpurean 46.3
purpureous 46.3
purr 52.13, 95.12
purring (n) 52.7 (a) 52.20, 95.16
purse (n) 195.2, 728.14, 729.15 (v) 260.7, 291.6
purse atomizer 70.6
purse bearer 729.12
pursed 260.12, 291.8
purse-pride 136.1, 141.1
purse-proud 136.8, 141.9
purser 183.6, 185.4, 577.5, 624.9, 729.12
purse seine 356.13
purse snatcher 483.2
purse snatching 482.3
purse strings 729.1, 729.15
pursiness 257.8
pursing 260.1
pursual 166.1
pursuance 166.1, 382.1, 856.1
pursuant (n) 382.4 (a) 382.11
pursue 166.3, 328.8, 382.8, 389.7, 562.21, 861.6, 866.4, 938.30
pursue an inquiry 938.20
pursue a policy of Schrecklichkeit 127.20
pursue one's education 570.11
pursuer 101.4, 104.11, 166.2, 382.4, 599.5
pursue the arts of peace 464.8
pursue the even tenor of one's way 982.2
pursuing (n) 382.1 (a) 382.11
pursuit 104.5, 166.1, 380.1, 382.1, 724.6, 865.7, 866.1
pursuivant 166.2
pursy 257.18, 259.13, 291.8
purulence 2.24, 12.6
purulent 2.33, 12.21
purusha 919.4
purvey 385.9
purveyance 385.1
purveyed 385.13
purveyor 385.6
purview 27.1, 615.1
pus 2.24, 12.6, 80.7
pusgut 2.19
push (n) 17.3, 18.1, 330.7, 375.6, 459.1, 759.10, 843.4, 902.2, 904.1 (v) 87.22, 162.4, 172.6, 330.13, 375.14, 401.4, 403.12, 440.12, 459.17, 732.7, 751.4, 902.12, 904.9
push, the 909.1
push ahead 162.2
push along 188.7, 222.10
push around 15.12, 96.18, 612.15
push aside 372.2, 390.6, 846.9, 984.4
push-away 750.2
push back 460.10, 908.3
push-button control 1041.4
push-button plant 739.3, 1041.5
push-button telephone 347.4
push car 179.16
pushcart 179.3, 736.3, 736.6
push chair 179.7
push down 184.40, 913.4
pushdown 184.13
pushed 401.11
pushed to the extreme 355.4
pusher 87.21, 732.4
push for 375.14, 509.13
push forward 162.4, 449.17
push from one's thoughts 933.3
pushful 330.23
pushfulness 330.7
push in 189.7, 191.7, 214.5
push-in 749.6
push-in crime 482.3
pushiness 142.1, 330.7, 359.6
pushing (n) 375.5, 904.1 (a) 214.9, 330.23, 904.14
pushing down 913.1
pushingness 330.7
pushing the envelope 405.1
pushing under 913.1
pushing up daisies 307.29
push off 182.19, 188.7, 222.10, 908.3
push on 162.4, 401.4, 401.5
push one's luck 972.12, 1006.7
push one's way 162.4
push one to the wall 1013.16
push onward 162.4
push out 909.14
push out of place 160.5
pushover 16.6, 19.6, 358.2, 411.1, 954.4, 1014.4
push pass 752.3
push technology 1042.19
push the envelope 216.7, 405.12
push the panic button 127.11
push the pen 547.19
push the pencil 547.19
push through 401.4
push to the extreme 355.3
push-up bra 5.24
push up daisies 307.19
push upon 439.9, 478.20
pushy 142.9, 214.9, 330.23, 359.15
pusillanimity 491.3
pusillanimous 491.12
pusillanimousness 491.3
puslike 2.33
puss 216.4, 311.20
pussiness 12.6
pussle-gutted 257.18
pussy (n) 311.20 (a) 12.21
pussycat 311.20, 659.2, 1016.8

pussyfoot (n) 936.7 (v) 177.26, 344.7, 346.9, 368.8, 494.5, 936.9 (a) 346.14
pussyfooted 346.14
pussyfooter 936.7
pussyfooting (n) 177.17, 609.37, 936.5 (a) 936.14
pustule 85.37, 283.4, 1004.1
put (n) 737.21, 904.3 (v) 159.12, 334.5, 532.4, 643.4, 729.17, 888.3, 904.10 (a) 532.5
put a bee in one's bonnet 439.5, 551.10
put a bold face upon 124.8, 492.10
put about 163.9, 182.30, 352.10
put a bridle on one's tongue 51.5
put a bug in one's ear 551.11
put a construction on 341.9
put a crimp in 1012.16
put across 328.6, 407.5, 409.11, 521.6, 643.7
put a curse on 513.5, 691.10
put a duty on 630.12
put a false appearance upon 350.3, 354.16
put a false construction on 342.2
put a false construction upon 265.6, 350.3
put a figure on 1017.17
put a flea in one's ear 399.5, 422.5, 510.17
put a gloss upon 600.12
put a good face upon 124.8, 600.12
put a half nelson on 428.10
put a hex on 691.10
put a juju on 691.10
put all one's eggs in one basket 493.5
put all one's strength into 403.13
put a mark on 517.19
put a match to 1020.22
put a move on 439.8
Putana 680.4
put and call 737.21
put an embargo on 444.3
put an end to 308.13, 395.12, 762.7, 820.6, 857.11, 1012.13
put an end to oneself 308.22
put apart 386.12
put a penalty on 603.4
put a period to 820.6
put a question to 938.20
put around 552.11
put aside (v) 176.11, 386.12, 390.6, 773.6, 846.9, 984.4 (a) 340.14, 386.15, 390.12
put a spin on 350.3
put a spoke in one's wheel 1012.15
put a spoke in one's wheels 19.9
put a square peg into a round hole 414.14
put a stop to 857.11, 1012.13
put asunder 566.5
put at 300.11, 1017.18
put at a disadvantage 603.4, 1012.11
put at ease 107.4, 121.6
putative 888.6, 951.14
put at one's disposal 439.4
put a torch to 1020.22
put a tuck in one's tail 137.6
put away 8.22, 187.11, 308.13, 346.7, 386.10, 390.6, 407.4, 429.14, 566.5
put away for 182.35
put away thought 933.3
put a whammy on 513.5, 1000.6
put back 163.8, 182.30, 393.9, 396.11, 481.4, 908.3
put beef into it 15.12
put before 216.8, 439.5
put behind barriers 429.13
put behind bars 429.14
put behind one 390.4
put between 213.6
put beyond the pale 773.6
put by (v) 386.10, 386.12, 390.6, 397.11 (a) 386.15, 390.12
put dibs on 421.6
put down (v) 137.5, 156.6, 157.3, 159.14, 249.8, 308.13, 395.15, 412.10, 428.8, 510.12, 512.8, 549.15, 624.15, 643.4, 950.2 (a) 412.17, 428.14
put-down 137.2, 156.3
put down as 809.6
put down one's gun 465.11
put down roots 159.17
put down to 888.4
put faith in 953.10
put fire to tow 1013.14
put first things first 808.8
put for 161.9
put forth 188.8, 310.34, 352.14, 439.5, 501.17, 524.22, 725.8, 951.12
put forth buds 310.34
put forth leaves 310.34
put forth one's strength 725.9
put forward 324.4, 348.5, 439.5, 449.17, 501.17
put heads together 422.7, 450.3, 541.10, 805.4, 943.6
put hep 551.11
put hip 551.11
put hors de combat 19.9, 19.10, 412.6
put ideas into one's head 439.5
put in 159.16, 182.35, 186.8, 189.7, 191.3, 207.5, 214.6, 387.13, 615.12, 1069.18
put in a call 347.19
put in a false light 350.3
put in a good word 375.14
put in a good word for 509.11, 600.10
put in a hole 1013.15
put in an appearance 33.8, 186.6, 221.8
put in a new light 551.8
put in an order 421.5
put in an order for 440.9
put in a nutshell 557.5
put in a requisition 440.9
put in a row 812.5
put in a safe place 1008.18
put in a spot 1013.15
put in a trance 22.20, 691.7
put in a word 509.11, 524.21
put in black and white 547.19, 549.15
put in bodily fear 127.20
put in bright lights 997.14
put in commission 396.14
put in condition 396.14
put in context 766.6, 775.5
put in danger 1006.6
put in escrow 386.12, 438.10
put in fear 127.16
put in for 440.9
put in force 387.11, 437.9, 613.10, 673.9
put in good humor 109.7, 743.21
put in hock 438.10
put in inverted order 205.5
put in irons 428.10
put in isolation 773.6
put in jeopardy 1006.6
put in mind 989.19
put in mothballs 390.6
put in motion 902.11, 904.13
put in one's bad books 661.9
put in one's place 137.5
put in one's time 825.5
put in one's two cents worth 524.21
put in one's two cents' worth 946.8
put in one's two-cents worth 214.6, 334.5
put in opposition 215.4
put in order 396.14, 808.8, 809.6
put in pawn 438.10
put in phase 836.4
put in place 159.11
put in plain English 521.6
put in plain words 521.6
put in practice 328.7
put in print 548.14
put in proper fore-and-aft trim 182.49
put in rank order 946.9
put in remembrance 989.19
put in repair 396.14
put in requisition 421.5
put in shape 396.14, 405.6, 808.8
put in storage 159.15
put in suit 598.13
put in the bag 965.5
put in the foreground 997.14
put in the minutes 549.15
put in the picture 551.9
put in the place of 862.4
put in the right 568.10
put in the witness box 957.12
put in time 821.6
put into 182.35, 189.7, 341.12
put into a flutter 985.7
put into effect 328.7
put into execution 387.11
put into jail 429.14
put into one's head 551.10
put into operation 387.11
put into port 182.35, 186.8
put into practice 328.7, 328.8, 387.11
put into requisition 387.14
put into shape 405.6
put into the hands of 478.13
put into the picture 405.16
put into words 524.22, 532.4
put in trim 405.8, 808.12
put in tune 405.8, 465.8, 568.13, 708.36, 788.7
put in words 524.22, 532.4
put in words of one syllable 521.6
put in working order 405.8
put in writing 547.19, 549.15
put it 334.5
put it all behind one 465.10
put it away 8.24
put it in few words 537.5
put it out of one's thoughts 933.3
put it to 216.8, 439.5
put it up to 216.8
put life into 306.10
put money in 729.17
put new life into 9.2, 306.10
put next to 551.11
put obeah on 691.10
put off (v) 6.6, 98.11, 98.14, 182.36, 368.8, 368.13, 379.4, 846.9 (a) 99.8, 846.16
put-off 376.1
put off mortality 307.18
put off one's stride 985.6
put off the track 985.6
put off till tomorrow 340.6
put on 5.43, 5.44, 174.10, 214.5, 295.19, 354.21, 356.14, 490.6, 500.12, 501.14, 643.4, 643.6, 704.28, 912.7, 923.7
put-on (n) 354.13, 356.7, 500.1, 508.2 (a) 354.26, 500.16
put on a business basis 731.20
put on a charade 354.21
put on a drive for 509.13
put on a false face 645.11
put on a false front 354.21
put on a false scent 356.16
put on a front 354.21
put on a full-court press 725.9
put on a harbor furl 182.50
put on a high 88.26
put on airs 500.12, 501.14
put on a lead 428.10
put on alert 399.5
put on an act 354.21
put on an allowance 477.10
put on an even keel 182.49
put on a pedestal 155.4, 509.12, 511.7, 912.6, 949.2
put on a show 501.13, 704.28
put on a war footing 458.19
put on blinders 980.6
put on edge 128.9
put one foot in front of the other 360.3, 856.3
put one in his place 157.5
put one in mind of 784.7, 989.19
put one in the picture 351.4, 521.6

put one in the way of 439.4, 478.15
put one on 356.15, 489.14, 508.8, 983.10
put one on top of the world and on cloud nine 109.7
put one out 1011.8
put one out of one's misery 308.13
put one's arms around 562.18
put one's back into 403.12
put one's back into it 15.12, 330.14, 725.10
put one's back to the wall 1013.16
put one's back up 96.13
put one's cards on the table 351.7, 644.10
put oneself between disputants 466.6
put oneself down 617.14
put oneself down for 436.5, 478.14
put oneself forward 501.12
put oneself in another's shoes 336.7
put oneself in a spot 1013.12
put oneself in the hands of 953.15
put oneself out 403.11, 652.3, 725.9
put oneself out of court 414.14, 923.6
put oneself out of the way 403.11
put one's eyes out 30.7
put one's feet up 20.6, 121.8, 173.7, 329.2, 402.4
put one's finger on (n) 983.1 (v) 159.11, 517.18, 865.11, 983.10
put one's foot down 359.9, 420.10, 421.8, 442.3, 855.11
put one's foot down on 444.4
put one's foot in it 414.12, 975.15, 1013.12
put one's foot in one's mouth 414.12, 844.4, 975.15, 1013.12
put one's fur up 152.24
put one's good name in jeopardy 661.7
put one's hair up 152.24
put one's hands in one's pockets 485.3, 626.5
put one's hands on 480.14, 941.2
put one's hand to 404.3
put one's hand to the plow 404.3, 725.15
put one's head in a lion's mouth 493.6
put one's head in the lion's mouth 492.10, 1006.7
put one's heart and soul into it 725.13
put one's heart into 359.8, 403.12
put one's house in order 405.13
put one's John Hancock on 332.12
put one's life on the line 492.10
put one's mark on 332.12
put one's mind at rest on 953.18
put one's mind to 931.11
put one's money on the line 624.17
put one's money where one's mouth is 328.5, 972.12
put one's nose in 466.6
put one's nose out of joint 132.2, 137.6, 152.23, 249.8, 1012.15
put one's oar in 449.11
put one's pride in one's pocket 137.7
put one's shoulder to the wheel 404.3, 725.15
put one's tail between one's legs 127.13, 491.8
put one's trust in 124.6
put one's two cents in 214.5
put one's veto upon 444.5
put one's weight in the scale 449.14
put one's whole soul in 403.13
put one's X on 332.12
put one through his paces 942.8
put one through the wringer 604.10
put one wise 351.4, 977.2, 983.10
put on hold (v) 390.6, 846.9, 984.4 (a) 846.16
put on ice 846.9
put on layaway 622.7
put on long pants 303.9
put on more speed 174.10
put on mourning 115.17
put on notice 399.5
put on one's face 1016.15
put on one's feet 449.11
put on one's guard 399.5
put on one's hitting shoes 745.5
put on one's thinking cap 931.8
put on paper 549.15
put on parole 431.5
put on report 599.7
put on sail 174.11, 182.20
put on side 501.14
put on speed 174.12
put on spin 650.8
put on steam 174.10
put on tape 549.15
put on the agenda (v) 871.8, 965.6 (a) 871.9
put on the air 1034.25
put on the alert 400.3
put on the back burner (v) 390.6, 846.9, 984.4 (a) 846.16
put on the block 734.11
put on the brake 857.7
put on the brakes 175.9, 857.11, 1012.13
put on the dog 5.42, 501.14
put on the drag 175.9
put on the feed bag 8.20
put on the finishing touch 1002.5
put on the finishing touches 392.11
put on the gloves with 457.16
put on the grill 938.22
put on the Index 444.3, 510.13, 602.3
put on the map 159.11, 352.15, 997.16
put on the market 738.12
put on the new man 858.12
put on the rack 26.7, 604.15
put on the record 549.15
put on the retired list 909.19
put on the right track 161.6
put on the ritz 501.14
put on the scales 297.10
put on the shelf 390.6, 846.9
put on the soft pedal 51.8, 51.9
put on the spot 1006.6
put on the stage 704.28
put on the stand 598.17
put on the track 161.6
put on to 551.11
put onto 551.10
put on to something hot 551.11
put on trial 598.13, 598.18
put on weight 259.8
put out 96.15, 108.5, 127.19, 137.4, 352.11, 352.14, 395.15, 548.14, 626.5, 725.8, 811.4, 909.13, 909.15, 971.12, 985.7, 996.4, 1013.13, 1022.7
put-out 96.22, 152.27, 971.24, 985.12
putout 745.3
put out a feeler 942.9
put out at interest 729.17
put out buds 310.34
put out feelers 942.9
put out leaves 310.34
put out of action 19.9, 19.10
put out of breath 21.4
put out of business 625.8
put out of commission 19.9, 390.4
put out of countenance 96.15, 137.4, 1012.15
put out of court 412.8
put out of existence 395.12
put out of face 96.15, 137.4
put out of gear 811.2
put out of joint 160.5
put out of kilter 265.5
put out of mind 984.4
put out of one's head 984.4
put out of one's misery 145.4
put out of order 19.9
put out of place 160.5
put out of reach 967.6
put out of sight 346.6, 346.7
put out of the way 308.13, 395.12, 1013.13
put out the fire 745.5
put out the welcome mat 585.7
put out to grass 390.8
put out to pasture 8.18, 390.8, 447.4, 909.19
put out to sea 182.19
put over 407.5, 409.11, 409.12, 521.6, 643.7
put over against 943.4
put paid to 395.12, 820.6, 857.6, 857.11
put pep into it 17.10
put pressure on 424.6
put price 738.9
put queries 938.20
putrefacient 393.39
putrefaction 71.2, 393.7
putrefactive 393.39
putrefiable 393.47
putrefied 393.40
putrefy 393.22
putresce 393.22
putrescence 71.2, 393.7
putrescent 393.40
putrescible 393.47
putrid 64.7, 71.5, 80.23, 393.40, 1000.8
putridity 98.2, 393.7
putrid matter 80.7
putridness 71.2, 80.2, 98.2, 393.7
put right 161.6, 396.13
put rudder on 164.5
putsch 327.4
put six feet under 309.19
put someone's nose out of joint 153.4
put something across 356.14
put something aside 635.4
put something in the pot 478.14
put something over 356.14
put straight (v) 277.5, 392.9, 396.13, 437.8, 977.2 (a) 977.5
putt 751.4
putter (n) 751.2 (v) 331.13, 998.14
putterer 331.8, 998.10
puttering 998.8
put the arm on 621.3
put the best face on 600.12
put the best face upon 124.8
put the bite on 621.3
put the blame on 599.8, 888.4
put the cart before the horse 205.5, 342.2, 414.14
put the clamps on 428.10
put the damper on 51.8
put the evil eye on 1011.12
put the fear of God into 127.16
put the final touches on 820.8
put the finger on 551.13, 888.4
put the finisher on 820.6
put the finishing touches on 407.6, 820.8
put the finishing touches to 794.8
put the genie back into the bottle 481.4, 859.5
put the hammer down 756.4
put the heat on 514.2
put the helm hard over 182.31
put the helm to leeward 182.23
put the helm up 182.24
put the icing on the cake 407.6
put the jinx on 1011.12
put the kibosh on 19.9, 51.8, 395.11, 820.6
put the lid on 51.8, 293.6, 295.21, 345.8, 407.6, 428.8, 820.6
put the pedal to the metal 174.9
put the pressure on 938.22
put the right foot forward 494.5
put the rudder amidships 182.31
put the rudder hard left 182.31

put the rudder hard over 182.31
put the rudder right 182.31
put the screws on 424.8
put the screws to 375.23, 424.8, 632.7, 938.22
put the shot 904.10
put the skids to 412.7
put the skids under 395.11, 820.6
put the squeeze on 119.2, 514.2
put the toothpaste back into the tube 481.4, 859.5
put the touch on 440.15
put the whammy on 1011.12
put the worst face upon 125.9
put the wrong construction on things 948.2
put through 239.15, 328.6, 328.7, 407.5, 409.11, 409.12, 437.9, 613.10
put through a deal 731.19
put through channels 176.14
put through the grind 568.13
put through the mill 373.9, 568.13, 938.22
putting 159.6
putting away 346.1, 372.1
putting behind barriers 429.1
putting down 428.2, 512.1
putting green 310.7, 743.11, 751.1
putting in an appearance 33.1
putting in order 807.1
putting-off 846.4
putting on 356.1, 704.13
putting on airs 500.1, 500.3
putting oneself between 466.1
putting one's feet up 331.2
putting on the finishing touches 392.4
putting out 372.1, 1022.2
putting out the eyes 30.1
putting out to pasture 447.2
putting the best color on 600.5
putting the gloss on 392.4
putting together 472.2, 796.1
put to 800.7
put to advantage 387.15, 843.8
put to bed 22.19, 548.14
put to bed with a shovel 308.14
put to choice 371.21
put to death 308.13, 604.16
put to flight 127.21, 412.8
put together (v) 405.7, 770.18, 796.3, 800.5, 805.3, 892.8 (a) 892.18
put to good use 387.11, 387.14
put to inconvenience 996.4
put to it (v) 96.16, 1013.13 (a) 1013.20
put to music 708.46
put to one side 176.11, 984.4
put to one's last shifts 619.7
put to one's oath 334.7
put to one's shifts 619.7
put to one's wit's end 971.13
put to press 548.14
put to rest 395.13, 820.6, 958.4
put to rights 396.13, 807.5, 808.8
put to rout (v) 412.8 (a) 412.14
put to school 568.13
put to sea 182.19, 188.15
put to shame 137.4, 249.8, 661.8
put to silence 51.8
put to sleep 22.20, 25.4, 308.13
put to the blush 96.15, 137.4
put to the proof 942.8
put to the question 604.15, 938.22
put to the sword 308.18, 459.25
put to the test 942.8
put to the trouble of 996.4
put to torture 26.7
put to trial 942.8
put to trouble 996.4
put to use 387.11, 387.14
put to vote 371.21
putt-putt 751.1
put trust in 953.15
put two and two together 935.15, 946.10
putty (n) 803.4, 1047.4, 1062.5 (a) 1047.9
putty in one's hands 894.5
puttylike 1047.9
put under 22.20
put under an injunction 444.3
put under an obligation 641.12
put under arrest 429.15, 480.18
put under a spell 377.7
put under duress 424.6
put under lock and key 429.14
put under oath 334.7
put under restraint 428.7
put under security 429.14
put under surveillance 938.28
put under the ban 444.3, 586.6
put under the mattress 390.5
put under the yoke 412.10
put up (v) 159.16, 159.17, 202.8, 225.10, 251.4, 266.5, 354.21, 371.19, 385.10, 386.11, 397.11, 438.10, 439.4, 624.15, 734.10, 759.25, 892.8 (a) 438.12
put-up 354.29, 965.8
put up a bluff 354.21, 503.3
put up a bold front 454.5
put up a brave front 600.10
put up a false front 376.3
put up a fight 333.5, 453.3, 457.13
put up a front 354.21, 376.3, 500.12, 501.14, 600.10
put up a job on 599.12
put up an argument 935.16
put up and shut up 328.5
put up a roadblock 1012.12
put up as collateral (v) 438.10 (a) 438.12
put up a squawk 115.16, 333.5
put up a stink 115.16
put up a struggle 333.5, 453.3
put up bail 438.10
put up for auction 734.11
put up for sale 734.10
put-up job 354.13, 599.4, 965.2
put-up market 737.6
put up no barriers 521.4
put upon 214.5, 643.4
put-upon 96.22
put up one's dukes 453.3
put up one's hair 303.9
put upon oath 334.7
put upon one's mettle 492.15
put upon record 549.15
put up the money 729.16
put up the shutters 293.8, 1028.5
put up to 375.17
put up with 134.5, 443.10, 862.4
put up with it 433.6
put with 223.13, 253.4
put words in one's mouth 888.4
put words in someone's mouth 265.6
put words into one's mouth 350.3
putz 924.2, 924.4
put zip into it 17.10
puzzle (n) 522.8, 930.6, 971.3, 1013.7 (v) 931.9, 971.13, 1013.13
puzzled 122.9, 971.25, 1013.20
puzzlehead 924.4
puzzleheaded 922.18, 985.13
puzzleheadedness 922.5
puzzlement 122.1, 522.8, 971.3
puzzle out 931.11, 940.2
puzzle over 931.9, 971.9
puzzlepated 985.13
puzzler 522.8
puzzling 122.10, 522.17, 930.16, 971.27
puzzling problem 522.8
pwca 678.8
pwn 249.7
pwned 412.14
pycnometer 1045.8
pyelogram 91.9
pyemia 85.31
Pygmoid race 312.2
pygmy (n) 258.5, 312.3 (a) 258.13
pyjamas 5.21
pyknic 257.18
Pylades and Orestes 588.6
pylon 184.19, 272.6
pylorus 2.18
pyramid (n) 266.2, 272.6, 309.16, 549.12, 770.10, 809.4 (v) 251.4, 737.23, 770.19
pyramidal 278.11, 809.8
pyramidal peak 237.6
pyramidic 278.11
pyramid scheme 356.10
pyre 309.2, 309.9, 1019.13, 1020.11
pyretic 85.58
pyrexia 85.7, 1019.1
pyric 1019.26
pyriform 279.14
Pyriphlegethon 682.4
pyrogenesis 1020.1
pyrogenetic 1019.32
pyrogenic 1019.32
pyrogenous 1019.32
pyroglazer 716.7
pyrognostic 1019.32
pyrognostics 1019.21
pyrographer 716.8
pyrographic 1020.30
pyrolater 697.4, 1020.8
pyrolatry 697.1, 1020.7
pyrological 1019.32
pyrology 1019.21
pyrolysis 1020.5
pyrolytic 1020.30
pyrolyze 1020.24
pyrolyzed 1020.30
pyromania 1020.7
pyromaniac 1020.8
pyrometallurgy 1058.11
pyrometer 742.5
pyrometric cone 742.5
pyrometry 1019.3
pyrophile 1020.8
pyrophilia 1020.7
pyrosis 26.5
pyrotechnic 1019.32
pyrotechnical 1019.32
pyrotechnics 543.1, 1019.17, 1019.21
pyrotechnic sponge 1021.6
pyrotechny 1019.17, 1019.21
pyrrhic (n) 720.8 (a) 720.17
Pyrrhic victory 411.1
Pyrrhonian 952.12
Pyrrhonic 695.20, 952.12, 955.9
Pyrrhonism 695.6, 955.2
Pyrrhonist 695.12
Pythagorean (n) 668.4 (a) 668.10, 952.12
Pythagoreanism 668.2
Pythagorism 668.2
Pythagorist 668.4
Pythia 962.6
Pythian 962.6
Pythian oracle 962.7
Python 962.7
pythoness 962.4
pythonism 962.2
pyx 703.11
qadi 699.12
Q and A 541.2
qi 919.5
Quaalude 86.12
quack (n) 357.6 (v) 60.5 (a) 354.28
quackery 354.7, 356.4
quackish 354.28
quackishness 354.7
quackism 354.7
quack remedy 86.2
quacksalver 357.6
quackster 357.6
quad 212.3, 231.4, 548.7, 879.1
quadragenarian 882.7
Quadragesima 515.3
quadragesimal 515.5
quadrangle 212.3, 231.4, 879.1
quadrangular 278.9
quadrant 278.4, 280.8, 793.1
quadraphonic sound system 50.11
quadraple 880.3
quadrat 471.6, 548.7
quadrate (v) 879.3, 880.2 (a) 278.9
quadratic 879.4
quadrature 879.1
quadrennial 850.4
quadrennial circus 609.8
quadrennium 879.1
quadric 879.4
quadrifid 881.4
quadrifoil 879.1

quadrifoliate 881.4
quadriform 278.9, 881.4
quadrifurcate 881.4
quadrigeminal 880.3, 881.4
quadrilateral (n) 879.1 (a) 218.7, 278.9, 879.4
quadrille 879.1
quadrillion, a 884.4
quadrillion 882.13
quadrillionth 882.31
quadrinomial (n) 879.1 (a) 879.4
quadripartite 881.4
quadripartition 881.1
quadripinnate 881.4
quadriplanar 881.4
quadriplegia 85.27
quadriplegic 85.45
quadrisect 881.3
quadrisected 881.4
quadrisection 881.1
quadriserial 881.4
quadrivalence 1060.4
quadrivalent 879.4, 1060.10
quadrivial 881.4
quadrumanal 881.4
quadrumanous 881.4
quadruped (n) 311.3 (a) 879.4
quadruple (v) 880.2 (a) 880.3
quadruplet 879.1
quadruple time 709.24
quadruplex (v) 880.2 (a) 880.3
quadruplicate (n) 785.3 (v) 785.8, 880.2 (a) 880.3
quadruplication 880.1
quadruplicature 880.1
quadruplicity 879.2, 880.1
quaff (n) 8.4 (v) 8.29, 88.24
quaffable 8.34
quaffing 8.3
quaff the bitter cup 96.19
quaggy 243.3
quagma 297.5
quagmire 80.12, 243.1, 799.2, 1013.4
quagmiry 243.3
quahog 311.29
quail 127.13, 163.9, 325.4, 491.9, 903.7
quailing 491.13
quaint 488.4, 870.11
quaintness 488.1, 870.3
quake (n) 671.5, 917.3 (v) 105.18, 127.14, 917.11, 1023.9
quake in one's boots 127.10, 127.14
quake in one's shoes 127.14
Quaker-colored 39.4
Quaker-gray 39.4
Quakerism 134.2
quaking (n) 105.5, 127.5, 917.2 (a) 917.17
qualification 18.2, 210.2, 252.5, 371.11, 405.2, 405.4, 413.4, 421.2, 428.3, 600.5, 788.5, 852.1, 959.1
qualificative 959.7
qualificatory 959.7
qualified 210.7, 371.24, 405.17, 413.24, 428.15, 639.9, 788.10, 852.10, 959.10
qualifiedness 405.4
qualified veto 444.2, 613.7
qualifier 530.2
qualify 210.5, 405.8, 405.15, 409.7, 421.7, 428.9, 788.8, 852.7, 959.3, 991.4
qualifying (n) 756.3 (a) 959.7
qualifying examination 938.2
qualifying heat 756.3
qualitative 767.7, 865.13
qualitative analysis 801.1
quality 209.3, 496.1, 607.3, 608.2, 767.4, 865.4, 999.1
quality, the 607.2
quality control 938.3, 1041.8
quality-control inspector 938.17
quality loop 1041.6
quality of life 107.1, 504.1, 1010.1
quality time 821.1
qualm 85.30, 113.2, 127.4, 128.1, 325.2, 333.2, 644.2, 955.2
qualmish 85.57, 127.24, 128.11, 325.7
qualmishness 85.30, 113.2, 127.4, 128.1, 325.2
qualm of conscience 325.2, 333.2
qualms 113.2, 128.1
qualmy 85.57, 127.24
quandary 371.3, 971.3, 1013.7
quantifiability 300.7
quantifiable 300.14, 1017.25
quantification 300.1, 1017.9
quantified 244.5, 300.13
quantifier 300.9
quantify 244.4, 300.10, 1017.17
quantifying (n) 1017.9 (a) 1017.24
quantitatable 300.14
quantitate 244.4, 300.10, 1017.17
quantitated 300.13
quantitation 300.1
quantitative 244.5, 300.12
quantitative analysis 801.1
quantitative meter 720.6
quantities 247.3, 884.3, 991.2
quantitive 244.5
quantity 244.1, 244.2, 247.3, 257.2, 257.10, 300.2, 300.3, 524.11, 720.7, 1017.6
quantity control 1041.8
quantity surveyor 300.9
quantizable 300.14
quantization 300.1, 1017.9
quantize 244.4, 300.10, 1017.17
quantized 244.5, 300.13
quantizing 1017.24
quantum 17.7, 244.1, 477.5, 1025.21
quantum jump 162.1, 392.1, 852.2, 852.4, 860.1
quantum leap 162.1, 392.1, 852.2, 852.4, 860.1, 932.6
quantum mechanics 968.2, 1038.1
quantum theory 1018.1, 1038.2
quarantine (n) 212.1, 429.2, 584.1, 773.3 (v) 212.5, 212.6, 429.13, 773.6
quarantined 212.10, 429.20, 584.8, 773.8
quarantine flag 399.3, 429.2, 517.15
quark 258.8
quark model 1038.2
quarrel (n) 456.5, 457.1, 457.4, 462.6 (v) 456.11, 457.13
quarreler 452.3, 461.1
quarreling 457.1
quarrel over 457.21
quarrelsome 110.26, 456.17, 457.22, 458.20, 589.10, 935.19
quarrelsomeness 110.7, 456.3, 457.1, 458.10, 589.3, 935.13
quarry (n) 100.11, 104.9, 284.4, 380.2, 382.7, 386.4, 739.4, 886.6, 1058.6 (v) 192.10, 284.15, 1058.14
quarrying 192.1
quarryman 284.10
quarry miner 1058.9
quart 881.2
quarter (n) 145.1, 161.1, 218.1, 231.1, 647.2, 728.7, 746.3, 747.3, 752.3, 793.1, 824.2, 881.2 (v) 159.12, 225.10, 881.3 (a) 881.5
quarter at 159.17
quarterback (n) 575.4, 746.2 (v) 573.8
quarter-cut 881.4
quartered 225.14, 802.23, 881.4
quarter evil 85.41
quarter horse 757.2
quarter ill 85.41
quartering 225.3, 647.2, 881.1
quarter ladder 193.4
quarterly (n) 555.1 (a) 850.8
quarterly payments 624.1
quartermaster 183.7, 183.8, 385.6
quartern 881.2
quarter nelson 474.3
quarter note 709.14
quarter of a century 882.7
quarter points 161.3
quarter rest 709.21
quarters (n) 228.4 (v) 428.9
quarter semitone 709.20
quarterstaff 273.2
quarter step 709.20
quartet 450.1, 708.18, 879.1
quartic 879.4
quartile 879.4
quarto 554.4, 881.2
quartzose 1058.15
quasar 1073.8
quash 345.8, 395.15, 428.8
quashed 428.14
quashing 428.2
quashing of the charge 601.1
quash the charge 601.4
quash the indictment 601.4
quasi 336.8, 354.26, 527.15, 784.14
quasi-deaf 49.6
quasilinear 277.6
quasi partner 616.2
quasi-stellar radio source 1073.8
quasquicentennial 850.4
quatern 879.1
quaternary (n) 879.1 (a) 879.4
quaternion 879.1
quaternity 879.1, 879.2
quatrain 720.10
quatre 879.1
quatrefoil 879.1
quattuordecillion 882.13
quaver (n) 105.5, 525.1, 709.14, 709.19, 917.3 (v) 16.8, 105.18, 127.14, 525.7, 708.38, 917.11
quavering (n) 105.5, 917.2 (a) 525.12, 917.17
quavery 917.17
quay 1009.6
quayside 1009.6
quean 665.14
queasiness 85.30, 495.2
queasy 85.57, 495.12
queen 75.15, 77.10, 311.33, 311.34, 575.10, 608.8, 743.17, 758.2, 997.10, 999.8
queen bee 15.6, 77.9, 311.34, 575.4, 997.9
queen consort 575.10
queencraft 609.3
queen dowager 566.4
queenhood 417.8
queenlike 417.17, 608.10
queenliness 136.2
queenly 136.12, 417.17, 608.10
queen of heaven 1073.11
queen of night 1073.11
queen of spades 758.2
queen post 273.4
queen-post 901.8
queen regent 575.10, 575.11
queen regnant 575.10
Queensbury rules 754.1
Queen's English, the 523.4
queenship 417.8, 608.9, 612.4
queen size 257.4
queen-size 257.16, 257.20, 257.23
queer (n) 75.15 (v) 19.9, 393.11, 1012.16 (a) 75.30, 354.26, 870.11, 926.26, 927.5
queer duck 870.4
queered 393.29
queer fish 870.4
queer in the head 926.26, 927.5
queerness 870.3, 923.1, 926.1, 927.1
queer potato 927.4
queer specimen 870.4
queer the works 19.9
quell 395.15, 412.10, 428.8, 432.9, 670.7
quelled 412.17, 428.14, 432.15, 670.11
quelling 428.2, 432.4
quench 95.8, 379.4, 395.15, 428.8, 991.4, 1022.7
quenched 1022.11
quenching 428.2, 1022.2
quenchless 100.27, 855.18
querier 938.16, 981.2
querist 938.16, 981.2
quern 1051.7
quernstone 1051.7
querulant 108.7
querulous 108.7, 110.22, 115.19
querulousness 108.1, 110.2, 110.6, 115.4

querulous person 108.3
query (n) 938.10 (v) 938.20, 938.21, 955.6, 981.3
querying (n) 938.12 (a) 938.36
query language 1042.13
quest (n) 380.1, 382.1, 404.2, 938.15 (v) 382.8, 938.30
quest after 382.8
quester 382.4
questing 382.11
question (n) 522.8, 524.3, 613.9, 937.1, 938.10, 955.2, 971.8 (v) 343.8, 938.20, 938.21, 955.6, 971.9, 981.3
questionable 356.21, 645.16, 955.10, 969.3, 971.17
questionableness 955.3, 969.1, 971.2
question-and-answer 541.2
question-and-answer session 541.2
questionary 938.14
question at issue 938.10
question before the house 938.10
questioned 955.12
questionee 938.19
questioner 938.16, 981.2
questioning (n) 938.12 (a) 343.9, 938.36, 955.9
question in one's mind 955.2
questionist 572.7, 938.16
questionless 970.16
questionlessness 970.3
question mark 522.8, 938.10, 971.1, 971.8
questionnaire (n) 871.6, 938.14 (v) 938.29
queue (n) 3.7, 217.6, 812.2, 812.3, 817.2, 1042.18 (v) 812.6
queue up 812.6
quibble (n) 510.4, 935.4, 936.4 (v) 510.15, 935.16, 936.9
quibbler 510.9, 936.7
quibbling (n) 510.4, 936.5 (a) 510.23, 936.14
quiche 10.41
quiche Lorraine 10.41
quick (n) 177.13 (a) 101.8, 110.25, 174.15, 306.12, 324.5, 330.18, 339.14, 365.9, 401.9, 413.22, 570.18, 828.8, 830.5, 845.9, 920.14
quick, the 24.4, 152.11, 306.3, 306.4, 767.5
quick and dirty 365.12, 387.20, 995.7
quick-and-dirty 401.9
quick-and-dirty solution 995.2
quick and the dead, the 306.3
quick as a wink 174.15
quick as lightning 174.15, 830.4
quick assets 471.7
quick as thought 174.15, 830.4
quick ear 48.3
quick-eared 48.15
quicken 9.2, 17.10, 24.7, 105.13, 174.10, 306.9, 306.10, 401.4, 449.17, 1014.7
quickening (n) 17.8, 174.4, 306.6, 401.3, 1014.5 (a) 17.15, 306.13
quicken one's pace 174.10
quick exit 368.4
quick fire 847.2
quick fix 995.2
quick-freeze 397.9, 1024.11
quick-freezer 1024.5
quick freezing 1024.1
quick-freezing (n) 397.2 (a) 1024.12
quick-frozen 1024.14
quick hunch 365.1
quickie 75.7, 88.7
quick inspection 938.5
quick kick 746.3
quick look 938.5
quick-lunch counter 8.17
quick march 708.12
quick mind 570.5
quickness 101.1, 174.1, 330.3, 339.5, 365.2, 401.2, 413.1, 570.5, 845.3, 920.2
quickness of wit 920.2
quickness to take offense 110.5
quick on the draw 24.12, 330.18, 339.14, 365.9, 903.9
quick on the trigger 174.15, 330.18, 339.14, 365.9
quick on the upswing 330.18
quick on the uptake 339.14, 365.9, 903.9, 920.14
quick parts 920.2
quick pull 905.3
quick release 746.3
quicksand 243.1, 1006.1, 1013.4
quicksands 1006.5
quick-scented 69.13
quick sight 27.1, 27.4
quicksilver (n) 174.6, 854.4 (a) 330.17, 364.6, 1058.17
quickstep 177.13
quickstep march 177.13, 708.12
quick study 570.5
quick temper 110.2, 110.4
quick-tempered 110.25
quick thinking 920.2
quick-thinking 920.14
quick time 177.13
quick to take offense 110.21
quick trick 758.3
quick wit 489.1, 920.2
quick-witted 489.15, 920.14
quick-wittedness 489.2, 920.2
quid 8.2, 89.7, 728.8
quiddative 495.13
quiddity 495.5, 767.2, 936.4
quidnunc 552.9, 981.2
quid pro quo 338.2, 506.3, 777.3, 862.1, 863.1
quiesce 51.7, 173.8
quiescence 51.1, 173.1, 329.1, 331.1, 464.2, 853.1
quiescency 173.1
quiescent 51.10, 173.12, 329.6, 331.17, 464.9, 853.7
quiet (n) 20.1, 51.1, 106.2, 173.1, 464.2, 807.1 (v) 51.7, 51.8, 173.8, 670.7 (a) 20.10, 35.22, 51.10, 106.12, 139.11, 173.12, 344.9, 345.12, 433.15, 464.9, 496.7
quiet as a lamb 51.10, 464.9
quiet as a mouse 51.10, 173.12
quiet car 179.15
quiet death 307.6
quiet down 51.7
quiet ecstasy 985.2
quieten 51.7, 51.8, 173.8
quiet end 307.6
quietener 51.4, 86.12
quietening (n) 670.2 (a) 86.45, 670.15
quiet good manners 580.3
quieting 670.2
quietism 106.1, 134.2, 173.1, 329.1, 433.1, 933.1
quietist 329.6
quietistic 329.6, 933.4
quietize 15.14, 51.9
quiet life 464.2
quiet mind 106.2
quietness 51.1, 173.1, 344.2, 433.1, 464.2, 496.3
quietness of mind 106.2
quietness of soul 106.2
quiet of the grave, the 51.1
quiet of the tomb, the 51.1
quiet pleasure 95.1
quiet revolution 392.5
quiet spell 826.1
quiet taste 496.3
quietude 51.1, 106.2, 134.2, 173.1, 329.1, 344.2, 433.1, 464.2, 807.1
quietus 307.1, 395.2, 412.1, 601.1, 820.1, 820.4
quiff 3.6
quill (n) 3.16, 3.17, 285.5 (v) 291.5
quilled 291.7
quillet 936.4
quill pig 311.22
quilt 295.10
quilting 741.1
quilting bee 582.14
quinary 882.17
quincentenary 850.4
quincentennial 850.4
quincuncial 882.17
quincunx 882.1
quindecennial 882.7
quindecillion 882.13
quindecim 882.7
quindecima 882.7
quindene 882.7
quinquefid 882.17
quinquennial (n) 850.4 (a) 882.17
quinquennium 824.2, 882.1
quinquepartite 882.17
quinquepartition 882.14
quinquesect 882.15
quinquesection 882.14
quinquevalent 882.17
quintain 380.2
quintessence 192.8, 196.5, 349.7, 767.2, 999.8, 1002.4
quintessential 192.18, 349.15, 865.13, 999.16, 1002.9
quintet 450.1, 708.18, 882.1
quintillion 882.13
quintillionth 882.31
quintroon 797.8
quints 882.1
quintuple (v) 882.16 (a) 882.17
quintuple time 709.24
quintuplets 882.1
quintuplicate (v) 882.16 (a) 882.17
quip (n) 489.7, 508.2, 927.2, 936.4 (v) 489.13
quips 489.7
quipster 489.12
quire 1054.5
quirk 265.1, 364.1, 500.2, 865.4, 927.2, 936.4
quirkiness 364.2, 927.1
quirky 364.5, 927.5
quirt 605.1
quisling (n) 357.10, 363.5, 616.4, 660.9 (a) 645.22
quislingism 450.1, 645.7
quislingistic 645.22
quit (v) 188.9, 370.5, 390.4, 448.2, 506.5, 624.11, 857.6 (a) 430.31
quitclaim (n) 475.2 (v) 475.3
quit cold 370.5
quite a few (n) 884.3 (a) 884.6
quite a little 247.4
quite another thing (n) 776.3, 780.3 (a) 787.5
quite a thing 122.2
quite some 884.6
quite the lady 607.10, 608.10
quit of 430.31
quit oneself 321.4
quitrent 630.8
quits 790.7
quittance 506.2, 624.1, 624.3, 627.2, 658.1
quitter 362.5
quit the field 433.7
quit this world 307.18
quiver (n) 105.2, 105.5, 709.19, 770.8, 917.3, 917.4, 1025.8 (v) 16.8, 105.18, 127.14, 917.11, 1023.9, 1025.25
quivering (n) 105.5, 917.2, 1025.8 (a) 128.12, 130.12, 917.17, 1025.36
quiver like a rabbit 127.14
quiver of terror 127.5
quivers 128.2
quivery 128.12, 917.17, 1025.36
Quivira 986.11
qui vive 339.4
Quixote 986.13
quixotic 986.24
quixotic ideal 124.4
quixotism 986.7
quixotize 986.16
quixotry 986.7
quiz (n) 938.2, 938.12 (v) 938.21, 981.3
quizmaster 938.16
quiz show 1035.2
quizzee 938.19
quizzer 938.16
quizzical 488.4, 490.7, 508.12, 938.36, 981.5
quizzicalness 488.1
quizzing (n) 938.12 (a) 938.36
quizzing glass 29.3
quod 429.9
quodlibet 936.4, 938.10
quoin 278.2, 548.2, 901.7

quoit 280.3, 904.5
quondam 837.10
Quonset hut 228.9
quorum 770.2
quota 210.2, 477.5, 793.1, 1017.7
quotation 529.1, 630.1, 738.9, 849.1, 957.5
quotation board 737.7
quotation book 554.7
quotation noun 530.5
quote (n) 529.1 (v) 212.8, 524.23, 849.7, 865.11, 957.13
quote a price 630.11
quote chapter and verse 766.6, 957.13
quoted 849.12
quoted price 630.1, 738.9
quote oneself 849.8
quote out of context 342.2, 350.3
quotidian 850.8, 864.16
quotient 1017.12
quotum 1017.7
Qur'an 673.8, 683.6
R 704.16
Ra 1073.14
rabbet (n) 290.1, 800.4 (v) 290.3, 800.8
rabbeted 290.4
Rabbi 648.5
rabbi 571.1, 575.1, 616.9
rabbi 699.11, 921.1
rabbin 699.11
rabbinate 698.1, 698.2, 699.1
rabbinic 570.17, 683.12, 698.13
rabbinical 698.13
rabbinism 675.12
Rabbinist 675.21
rabbit 311.23, 890.6
rabbit's foot 691.5
rabbity 127.23, 491.10
rabble 497.6, 606.3, 770.4
rabblement 606.3
rabble-rouse 543.10
rabble-rouser 375.11, 543.4
rabble-rousing (n) 375.4, 543.1 (a) 375.28
Rabelaisian 508.13, 513.8, 666.9
Rabelaisianism 666.4
rabid 105.25, 152.32, 926.30, 926.32
rabidness 926.1, 926.11
rabies 85.41, 926.6
raccoon 311.22
race (n) 174.3, 238.1, 238.4, 239.2, 312.1, 401.1, 457.12, 559.4, 560.4, 743.9, 753.1, 755.2, 756.1, 756.3, 757.3, 809.2, 809.3 (v) 174.8, 174.10, 401.5, 457.19, 756.4, 757.5
race against the clock 1006.8
race against time (n) 843.4 (v) 821.6, 1006.8
racebook 759.19
race card 757.3
racecourse 743.11, 753.1, 757.1
race extermination 308.4
race hatred 103.1, 773.3, 980.4
racehorse 311.14, 757.2
raceme 310.27
race meeting 757.3
race memory 92.29, 934.2
race-murder 308.4
race-nag 757.2
race of man 312.1
race one's motor 105.17
race prejudice 980.4
racer 174.5, 311.14, 753.2, 756.1
race relations 980.4
race rider 757.2
race snobbery 980.4
race suicide 308.5
race through the mind 931.18
racetrack 757.1
racewalk 177.27
racewalker 178.6
racewalking 755.2
race with 457.19
rachitic 85.61, 265.12
racial 559.7
racial discrimination 980.4
racial diversity 797.1
racialism 103.1, 980.4
racialist (n) 103.4, 980.5 (a) 980.12
racial majority 312.2
racial memory 92.29, 842.2, 989.1
racial minority 312.2
racial profiling 801.1
racial segregation 773.3
racial supremacist 980.5
racial unconscious 92.28
raciness 68.2, 544.4, 666.3
racing (n) 457.11 (a) 238.24
racing association 756.1
racing bike 179.8
racing car 756.1
racing colt 757.2
racing driver 756.2
racing engine 756.1
racing equipment 757.1
racing establishment, the 757.1
racing form 757.4
racing fuel 756.1
racing sailor 183.1
racing secretary 757.2
racing stream 238.1
racing stud 757.2
racing tires 756.1
racing world, the 757.1
racism 103.1, 980.4
racist (n) 103.4, 980.5 (a) 773.9, 980.12
rack (n) 175.2, 177.12, 386.6, 395.1, 605.4, 725.2, 1040.9 (v) 26.7, 96.18, 177.28, 604.15, 632.7, 725.10
rack, the 26.6, 96.7, 604.2
rackabones 311.12
rack and pinion 1040.9
rack-and-pinion railroad 179.14
rack and ruin 395.1
racked 26.9, 93.23, 96.25
racker 311.14
racket (n) 53.3, 55.3, 356.8, 415.3, 671.2, 724.6, 732.1, 748.1, 759.13, 810.4, 810.5, 1048.3 (v) 53.9
racket court 743.11
racketeer 480.12, 483.4, 593.1, 660.9, 732.4
racket flip 748.2
racketiness 53.2
racketing 743.3
rackets, the 660.10, 732.1
rackety 53.13
racking 26.10, 98.23
rack of lamb 10.16
rack one's brains 522.11, 931.9, 989.20
rack rent (n) 630.8, 632.3 (v) 632.7
rack-rent 632.5
rack-renter 480.12
rack time 22.3
rack up 395.17
rack up the rents 632.7
racon 184.19, 1036.7
raconteur 722.5
racy 68.7, 68.8, 544.12, 666.7, 983.19
rad (n) 1037.6 (a) 122.10
radar 182.2, 184.6, 1032.10, 1033.1, 1036.1
radar antenna 1036.1
radar astronomer 1073.22
radar astronomy 1036.9, 1073.19
radar beacon 184.19, 1036.7
radar beacon buoy 1036.7
radar bombsight 1036.2
radar defenses 460.2
radar detector 1036.5
radar dome 1036.2
radar engineer 1036.14
radar fence 1036.9
radar gun 1032.10
radar highway patrol 1036.5
radar interference 1036.12
radar jamming 1036.13
radarman 185.3, 1036.14
radar marked beacon 1036.7
radar navigation 159.3, 1036.8
radar part 1036.1
radar reflector 1036.1
radarscope 1036.1
radar screen 1036.9
radar set 1036.1
radar signal 1036.11
radar speed meter 1036.5
radar station 1036.6, 1075.5
radar technician 1036.14
radar-telephone relay 1036.8
radar telescope 1073.17
radar tracking station 1074.7, 1075.5
raddle (n) 170.3 (v) 41.4, 740.6
raddled 88.33, 740.7
radiable 1037.12
radial (n) 171.1 (a) 158.10, 169.3, 171.9
radial engine 181.1
radial motion 172.2
radiance 109.1, 171.2, 662.6, 1016.5, 1025.1, 1025.4
radiancy 1025.1, 1025.4
radiant (n) 915.5, 1073.15 (a) 95.16, 109.11, 662.19, 677.17, 1016.20, 1025.30
radiant energy 1025.1, 1037.1
radiant heat 1019.1
radiant point 1073.15
radiant splendor 1025.4
radiate (v) 109.6, 171.6, 771.4, 1025.23, 1034.25, 1036.15 (a) 171.9
radiate cheer 109.6
radiated 171.9
radiate heat 1019.22
radiate out 171.6
radiating (n) 171.1 (a) 169.3, 171.9
radiating out 171.1
radiation 91.7, 171.2, 771.1, 1025.1, 1025.5, 1037.1, 1037.3, 1075.10
radiation in the visible spectrum 1025.1
radiation physicist 1037.9
radiation physics 1037.8
radiation therapy 91.6
radiative 171.9
radiator 1037.5
radiator coolant 1024.8
radiattore 10.33
radical (n) 220.1, 392.6, 526.3, 546.2, 611.12, 886.5, 901.6, 1038.7 (a) 199.8, 220.4, 247.13, 392.16, 611.20, 767.8, 794.10, 860.5, 886.14, 1017.23
radical change 852.2, 860.1
radical group 1060.2
radicalism 392.5, 611.4, 993.1
radicalization 611.4
radicalize 611.16
radical reform 392.5
radical right 611.9
radical rightism 611.4
radicated 310.36
radiciflorous 310.38
radiciform 310.36
radicle 310.22
radicular 310.36
radiferous 1037.11
radio (n) 347.3, 551.5, 552.1, 1033.1, 1034.1, 1034.3 (v) 347.20, 1034.25 (a) 347.21, 1034.28
radioacoustics 50.5, 1034.2
radioactivate 1037.10
radioactivated 1037.11
radioactive 1037.11
radioactive decay 393.6
radioactive dust 1038.16
radioactive element 1037.5
radioactive emanation 1037.1
radioactive isotope 1038.5
radioactive particle 1037.4
radioactive radiation 1037.1
radioactive waste 1037.5, 1038.13
radioactivity 1037.1
radioactivity detection identification and computation 1037.1
radio amateur 1034.24
radio astronomer 1073.22
radio astronomy 1073.19
radio audience 1034.22
radio beacon 182.2, 184.19, 517.15
radio beam 184.19
radio bearing 159.3
radiobiologist 1037.9
radiobiology 1037.8

radiobroadcast (n) 1034.18 (v) 1034.25
radiobroadcaster 1034.23
radio broadcasting 1034.16
radiocalcium 91.8
radiocarbon 91.8, 1037.5
radiocarbon dating 832.1, 1037.1
radiocast (n) 1034.18 (v) 1034.25
radiocaster 1034.23
radiocasting 1034.16
radio channel 1034.13
radiochemical 1060.9
radiochemist 1037.9
radiochemistry 1037.8
radio circuit 1034.9
radio communication 343.5
radio communications 1034.1
radio compass 574.9, 1036.4
radio compass station 1036.6
radio control 1041.2, 1041.4
radiocopper 1037.5
radio detection 1036.1
radiodetector 1037.7
radio direction finder 574.9, 1036.4
radiodynamic 1039.9
radiodynamics 1041.2
radio electrician 1034.24
radio electronics 1034.2
radioelectronics 1033.1
radioelement 91.8, 1037.5
radio engineer 1034.24
radio engineering 1034.2
radio frequency 847.1, 1034.12
radio-frequency (n) 1034.15 (a) 1034.28
radio-frequency amplifier 1034.10
radio-frequency circuit 1034.9
radio-frequency echo 1036.11
radio-frequency pulse 1036.10
radio-frequency signal 1034.10
radio-frequency stage 1034.10
radio galaxy 1073.6
radiogenic 1034.28
radiogoniometer 278.4, 1036.4
radiogoniometry 1034.2
radiogram 91.9, 347.14, 714.6
radiograph (n) 91.9, 714.3, 714.6 (v) 714.14
radiographer 90.11, 716.5
radiography 91.7, 714.1, 1037.8
radioiodine 91.8, 1037.5
radioisotope 91.8, 1037.5, 1038.5
radio journalism 552.1
radio links 1034.8
radio listener 1034.22
radiolocating 1036.1
radiolocation 1036.1
radiolocator 1036.1, 1036.4
radiological physics 1037.8
radiologist 90.4, 1037.9, 1038.3
radiology 91.7, 1037.8, 1038.1
radiolucence 1037.1
radiolucency 1037.1
radiolucent 1037.12
radioluminescence 1025.13, 1037.2
radioluminescent 1037.11
radio marker 184.19
radio mast 272.6
radiometallographer 1037.9
radiometallography 1037.8
radiometry 1037.8
radiomicrophone 50.9, 1034.4
radio mirror 1075.5
radiomobile 1034.5
radio navigation 159.3, 182.2, 184.6
radio-navigational trainer 181.10
radionics 1033.1
radio observatory 1073.17
radio operator 183.6, 1034.24
radiopacity 1037.1
radiopaque 1037.12
radioparent 1037.12
radiopathology 1037.8
radioperson 1034.24
radiophone 347.5
radiophonics 50.5
radio-phonograph combination 50.11
radiophotograph 347.15
radiophotography 347.3
radiopotassium 91.8
radio program 1034.18
radio range station 184.19
radio receiver 1034.3
radio relay station 1034.6, 1075.5
radio repairman 1034.24
radioscope 1037.7
radioscopy 91.7, 1037.8
radiosensibility 1037.1
radiosensitive 1037.12
radiosensitivity 1037.1
radio set 1034.3
radio signal 1034.10
radio silence 51.1, 1034.10
radiosodium 91.8
radiosonde 317.8
radiosonic 1034.28
radio spectrum 1032.10
radio station 1034.6
radiostereoscopy 1037.8
radiosterilize 79.24
radiosurgery 91.5
radio technician 1032.22, 1034.24
radiotechnology 1034.2, 1037.8
radiotelegram 347.14
radiotelegrapher 347.16, 1034.24
radiotelegraphic 347.21
radiotelegraphy 347.3, 1034.1
radiotelephone 347.5
radiotelephony 347.3, 1034.1
radio telescope 1034.3, 1073.17
radiotherapeutics 91.6
radiotherapist 90.11
radiotherapy 91.6, 1037.8
radiothermy 91.5
radiothorium 1037.5
radio transmission 1034.16
radio transmitter 1034.4
radiotransparency 1037.1
radiotransparent 1037.12
radiotrician 1034.24
radio tube 1033.10
radio wave 916.4, 1032.10, 1034.11
radium 91.8, 1020.15, 1037.5
radiumize 91.26, 1037.10
radium paint 1037.5
radium-proof 1037.12
radius 158.2, 169.1, 171.2, 257.1, 269.3, 277.2, 280.2
radius vector 277.2
radix 310.22, 886.5
radome 1036.2
raff 391.5, 606.3
raffish 497.13
raffle 759.14
raffle off 759.23
raffle wheel 759.16
raft (n) 180.11, 247.4, 618.3 (v) 176.13
rafting 760.2
rag (n) 4.1, 5.3, 180.14, 555.2, 704.20, 708.8, 709.24 (v) 510.19, 708.43, 749.7
rag, the 356.10
raga 709.10
ragamuffin 178.3
rag-and-bone man 730.10
ragbag 770.8, 797.6
ragboat 180.3
rage (n) 105.8, 152.8, 152.10, 578.5, 671.1, 671.2, 926.7, 926.12 (v) 105.16, 152.15, 318.19, 503.3, 671.11, 926.20
rage, the 578.4
ragged 58.15, 96.24, 288.7, 393.32, 782.3, 810.15
ragged edge 211.4
raggedness 288.1, 782.1
raggedy 393.32, 810.15
raggedy-ass 393.32, 810.15
ragger 357.1
ragging (n) 440.3, 490.3, 508.1, 749.3 (a) 508.12
raging (n) 671.1 (a) 105.25, 152.32, 318.22, 503.4, 671.18, 926.30
raging fire 1019.13
raging passion 105.8, 152.10
ragman 178.3, 730.10
rag on 489.13
rag out 5.39, 5.42
ragout 10.11
ragpicker 178.3
rag pulp 1063.2
rags 4.1, 5.1, 5.5, 256.1, 391.4, 759.10
rags-to-riches 1010.12
ragtag 606.3
rag, tag, and bobtail 606.3
ragtag and bobtail 606.3
ragtime (n) 708.8, 709.24 (a) 709.29
ragtime musician 710.2
ragtimey 709.29
rag trade 578.7
rag trade, the 5.32
rag up 5.39, 5.42
rah 116.2
raid (n) 459.4, 482.6, 737.20 (v) 459.20, 482.17
raider 459.12, 483.6
raiding 482.6
raid the market 737.25
rail (n) 212.4, 270.7, 383.7, 757.1 (v) 212.7
rail at 508.9, 510.19
railbird 757.2
railed 212.10
railer 512.6
railhead 216.2
rail in 212.5, 429.12
railing (n) 212.4 (a) 508.12
raillery 490.1, 508.1
rail line 383.7
rail off 212.5
railriding 604.2
railroad (n) 383.7, 750.2, 1043.3 (v) 401.4, 902.12
railroaded 401.11
railroader 178.13
railroad flat 228.13
railroading 902.3
railroad line 383.7
railroad man 178.13
railroad through 613.10
railroad train 179.14
railroad tunnel 383.3
railroad yard 739.3
railway 383.7
railway car 179.15
railway guard 1008.9
railway line 383.7
railway mail car 353.6
raiment (n) 5.1 (v) 5.39
raimented 5.45
raimentless 6.13
rain (n) 316.1, 1035.5, 1065.3 (v) 194.5, 316.10, 478.12, 991.5, 1065.14
rainbow (n) 35.7, 35.13, 47.1, 47.6, 133.5, 279.5, 316.8, 782.1, 1025.14, 1025.18 (a) 35.16, 782.3
rainbowed 47.10
rainbowlike 47.10, 1025.37
rainbow of colors 47.1
rainbowy 47.10
rain buckets 316.10
rain bullfrogs 316.10
rainburst 316.2
rain cats and dogs 316.10, 991.5
rain check 970.2
raincoat 5.13
rain daggers 316.10
rain dance 701.9
rain doctor 316.5
rain down 194.5, 316.10
raindrop 282.3, 316.1
rainfall 316.1, 1065.1
rain forest 1009.1
rain gauge 316.7, 317.8, 1065.10
rain gear 5.13
raininess 316.1, 316.4, 1065.1
rainless 1066.8
rainmake 316.10
rainmaker 185.1, 316.5
rainmaking 316.5
rain on one's parade 393.11
rain on one's picnic 393.11
rainout 857.3
rain pitchforks 316.10
rainproof 293.12, 1066.11
rains 316.4
rains on one's parade 112.18
rainspout 316.2, 318.13

rainstorm 316.2, 671.4
rainsuit 5.13
rain tadpoles 316.10
raintight 293.12, 1066.11
rain water 1065.3
rainwater 316.1
rainwear 5.13
rain wind rose 318.15
rainy 316.11, 318.22, 1065.15
rainy day 316.4, 1011.6
rainy-day policy 494.3
rainy season 313.1, 316.4
rainy weather 316.4, 317.3
raise (n) 251.1, 272.2, 446.1, 758.4, 759.10 (v) 158.9, 200.9, 251.4, 259.4, 266.5, 283.12, 298.7, 343.8, 375.19, 392.9, 446.2, 524.22, 568.13, 615.17, 662.13, 690.11, 770.18, 818.11, 892.8, 892.9, 912.5, 1069.16, 1070.6
raise a clamor 53.9, 59.8
raise a cry 517.22
raise a din 53.9
raise a hand 453.3
raise a hand against 451.3, 459.14
raise a howl 115.16, 333.5
raise a hue and cry 53.9, 59.8, 400.3
raise a hue and cry against 510.13
raise a hullabaloo 53.9
raise a laugh 743.21
raise aloft 200.9
raise an alarm 400.3
raise an objection 333.4, 510.10
raise apprehensions 127.15
raise a question 955.6
raise a ruckus 810.11
raise a rumpus 810.11
raise a siege 465.9
raise a stink 115.16
raise a stink about 333.5
raise a warning flag 133.10
raise Cain 53.9, 152.15, 810.11
raised 251.7, 259.10, 283.18, 892.17, 892.18, 912.9
raised arms 411.1
raised doughnut 10.44
raised in a barn 497.13
raised ranch 228.5
raise expectation 133.12
raise expectations 124.9
raise eyebrows 661.7
raise from the dead 396.16
raise ghosts 690.11
raise hell 53.9, 152.15, 743.24, 810.11, 985.7, 1013.14
raise hob with 395.10
raise hope 124.9
raise merry hell 1013.14
raise money 621.3
raise objections 333.5
raise one's eyebrows 99.5, 510.10, 517.22
raise one's eyebrows at 372.2
raise one's gorge 152.22
raise one's hackles 152.17
raise one's hand against 457.14
raise one's hopes 124.9
raise one's pay 446.2
raise one's sights 100.20, 162.4
raise one's voice 348.6
raise one's voice against 333.5, 510.13, 599.10
raiser 892.7, 1069.5
raise sand 810.11
raise some eyebrows 131.7
raise the curtain 351.4
raise the devil 53.9, 152.15, 810.11
raise the dickens 810.11
raise the drawbridge 1009.7
raise the elbow 88.25
raise the hue and cry 382.8
raise the hunt 382.8
raise the roof 53.9, 58.8, 152.15, 509.10, 810.11
raise the spirits 109.7
raise the stakes 759.24
raise the temperature 1020.17
raise to a fever pitch 105.12
raise to more than one 883.5
raise to the power of 1017.18
raise up 200.9, 375.19, 912.5
raise up the voice 59.9
raisin-colored 46.3
raising (n) 200.4, 259.1, 568.3, 892.2, 912.1, 1069.12 (a) 298.17
raising bee 582.14
raising of temperature 1020.1
raison d'être 380.2, 886.9
rajaship 417.8
rake (n) 204.2, 270.7, 285.4, 562.12, 665.10, 1040.8 (v) 79.21, 204.10, 459.22, 665.19, 938.33, 1069.17
rakehell (n) 665.10 (a) 665.25
rakehellish 665.25
rakehelly 665.25
rake in 472.9, 479.6
rake it in 472.12, 618.10
rake off 472.9
rake-off 477.5, 624.7
rakeoff 472.3
rake out 192.10
rake over the coals 510.18
rake up 472.9
rake up one side and down the other 510.18
rake up the past 989.10
raking 204.15
raking-down 510.6
raking-over 510.6
raking over the coals 510.6
rakish 501.19, 665.25
rakishness 665.3
rakshasa 680.6
rale 56.2
râle 57.1
rallentando (n) 708.25 (a) 708.54
rally (n) 333.2, 396.8, 457.3, 458.7, 609.12, 738.9, 743.10, 748.2, 770.2 (v) 333.5, 375.17, 392.8, 396.19, 396.20, 449.11, 458.18, 490.5, 508.9, 770.16, 770.18, 808.9, 957.12
rally around 770.16
rallying (n) 490.1, 508.1 (a) 508.12
rallying cry 59.1, 375.4, 458.7, 517.16
rallying point 228.27
rally round 450.4, 807.5
ralph 909.27
ralph up 909.27
ram (n) 76.8, 311.7 (v) 182.41, 902.12
Ramadan 515.3
ramage 310.20
Ramanandi 699.13
ramark 1036.7
ramate 310.41
ramble (n) 177.3, 177.10 (v) 164.4, 177.23, 522.10, 538.9, 926.20, 984.3, 985.9
ramble on 540.5
rambler 178.2, 310.33
rambling (n) 164.1, 177.3, 538.3, 538.4 (a) 164.7, 177.37, 522.13, 538.13, 851.3, 854.7, 926.31, 985.10
ramblingness 522.1
rambunctious 671.20
ram down 902.12, 1045.9
ram down one's throat 424.8, 478.20
ramen 10.10
ramification 171.3, 171.4, 259.1, 310.20, 782.1, 793.4, 799.1, 875.1
ramified 310.41, 782.3, 799.4, 875.6
ramify 171.7, 251.5, 259.6, 782.2, 799.3, 875.4
ram in 191.7, 794.7
ram-jet 904.17
ramjet 181.1, 181.3
ram-jet propulsion 184.25
ramming 902.3
ramose 310.41
ramous 171.10, 310.41
ramp (n) 184.23, 193.3, 204.4, 356.9, 753.1 (v) 105.16, 193.11, 200.8, 356.19, 366.6, 671.11
rampage (n) 810.4 (v) 671.11
rampageous 671.20
rampancy 538.2
rampant 193.14, 200.11, 418.5, 430.24, 671.19, 864.12, 912.9, 991.7
rampantness 864.2
rampant will 418.1
rampart 460.4, 901.4, 1012.5
ramping 105.25
ram pressure 184.25
ramp up 251.5, 770.19
ramp-up 251.1
ramrodlike 1046.11
ramrod-stiff 1046.11
ramrod straight 200.11
ramshackle 16.16, 393.33
Ramwat 699.13
ranch (n) 228.6, 739.1, 1070.5 (v) 1069.16, 1070.6
ranch dressing 10.12
rancher 1070.2
rancheria 1070.5
ranchero 1070.2
ranchhand 1070.2
ranch house 228.5
ranching 1070.1
ranchman 1070.2
rancho 228.6, 1070.5
rancid 64.7, 71.5, 393.41
rancidity 64.3, 71.2, 393.7
rancidness 64.3, 71.2, 393.7
rancor 103.1, 144.7, 152.3, 507.2, 589.4
rancorous 144.22, 152.26, 507.7, 589.10
randan 88.6, 743.6
R and D 942.1
R and D establishment 942.5
R and D worker 942.6
randem 179.5
randiness 665.5
random (n) 972.4 (a) 810.12, 945.6, 971.19, 972.16
random access 1042.8, 1042.18
random-access memory 1042.7
randomicity 810.1, 972.1
random motion 172.2
randomness 810.1, 870.1, 945.2, 971.1, 972.1, 972.3
random sample 793.1, 942.4, 972.1
random shot 759.2, 972.4
random testing 938.6
R and R 9.1, 20.2
randy (n) 743.6 (a) 75.27, 665.29
range (n) 27.1, 31.3, 48.4, 158.2, 161.1, 228.18, 237.1, 237.6, 245.1, 257.1, 261.1, 310.8, 430.4, 463.1, 709.6, 812.2 (v) 158.9, 177.20, 177.23, 257.15, 808.9, 809.6, 812.5
ranged 458.22, 808.14
range finding 1036.8
range horse 311.10
range of error 975.2
range of meaning 518.1
range of motion 158.2
range of vision 31.3
range oneself on the side of 449.13
range oneself with 450.4
range out 261.5
range over 177.20
ranger 397.5, 1008.6, 1069.7
rangers 461.15
range the coast 182.39
range the world 177.21
range through 177.20
range with 450.4
ranging (n) 809.1, 1036.1, 1036.9 (a) 177.37
rangy 272.16
rani 575.10
rani- 311.26
rank (n) 245.2, 417.4, 461.22, 607.1, 608.2, 662.4, 765.1, 807.2, 809.2, 812.2 (v) 249.11, 257.15, 808.11, 809.6, 812.5, 814.2, 946.9, 946.15 (a) 64.7, 68.8, 71.5, 80.23, 247.12, 288.6, 310.43, 393.41, 654.16, 661.12, 666.8, 1000.9
rank amateur 929.6
rank and file 461.23, 607.7
rank-and-file 606.8
rank and file, the 606.1
rank beneath 250.4
rank card 758.2
ranked 300.13, 808.14, 809.8
rank first 249.11

rank high 155.7
ranking (n) 607.1, 808.3, 809.1, 946.3 (a) 249.14, 417.15, 997.24
rankle 12.15, 26.7, 152.24, 393.22, 989.13
rankled 152.26, 989.23
rankle in the breast 989.13
rankling (n) 12.6, 26.4, 152.3 (a) 12.21, 26.11, 989.25
rank low 156.4, 157.3
rankness 64.3, 68.3, 71.2, 80.2, 393.7, 538.2, 654.4, 661.3, 666.3, 1000.2
rank-order 946.9
rank-ordering 946.3
rank out 156.6, 249.11
rank-out 156.3
ranks 461.23, 530.2
ranks of the homeless, the 619.3
rank under 250.4
ransack 482.17, 938.33
ransacker 938.18
ransacking 482.6, 938.15
ransack one's brains 931.9
ransom (n) 398.1, 481.3 (v) 396.12, 398.3, 481.6
ransomed 431.10
rant (n) 503.1, 520.2, 545.2 (v) 105.16, 152.15, 503.3, 543.10, 671.11, 704.31, 926.20
rant and rave 105.16, 152.15
ranter 503.2, 543.4, 693.3
ranting (n) 926.8 (a) 105.25, 152.32, 503.4, 926.30, 926.31
rantipole 493.4
rap (n) 52.3, 56.1, 510.4, 541.6, 602.1, 902.4, 902.7, 998.5 (v) 52.15, 56.6, 510.14, 541.11, 902.16, 902.18
rapacious 100.27, 480.26, 672.6
rapaciousness 100.8, 480.9
rapacity 100.8, 480.9, 672.1
rape (n) 75.11, 480.3, 482.6, 665.6, 671.3 (v) 480.15, 665.20, 671.11
raper 665.12
rape trauma syndrome 92.17
Raphael 679.4
rapid (n) 238.10 (a) 174.15, 204.18, 847.5
rapid deployment force 461.15
rapid-eye-movement sleep 22.1
rapid fire 459.9, 847.2
rapid-fire 459.29
rapid glance 27.4
rapidity 174.1, 401.2, 845.3, 847.2
rapid recurrence 847.2
rapid-response 174.15
rapids 238.10, 671.6
rapid slalom pole 753.3
rapid slope 204.4, 237.2
rapid succession 847.2
rapier 462.5
rapierlike 489.15
rapine 482.6, 671.3
rapist 75.16, 593.1, 665.12, 671.9
rap music 708.7
rap on the knuckles (n) 510.5, 604.3 (v) 510.17
rap out an oath 513.6
rappee 89.8
rappel (n) 194.1 (v) 194.7
rapping (n) 524.1, 541.1 (a) 56.11
rapport 97.1, 455.1, 587.3, 775.1, 788.1
rapporteur 576.5
rapprochement 455.1, 465.3, 587.3
rapscallion 322.3, 497.6, 660.3
rap session 541.6
rap sheet 428.1
rap shot 714.8
rap singer 710.13
rapt 95.17, 360.8, 931.22, 983.18, 985.11
rapt attention 48.1, 983.3, 983.4
rapt in wonder 122.9
raptor 311.27, 480.12
raptorial 474.9, 480.26
rapture 95.2, 104.2, 105.8, 691.3
raptured 95.17
rapturous 95.17
rara avis 870.4
rare 11.9, 122.10, 249.12, 270.16, 299.4, 406.10, 780.8, 848.2, 870.10, 885.5, 992.11, 997.19
rare bird 870.4
rare book 554.6
rare-earth element 1058.3, 1060.2
rare-earth metal 1058.3
rarefaction 299.2
rarefactional 299.5
rarefactive 299.5
rarefied 16.19, 248.7, 270.16, 299.4, 764.6
rarefy 16.11, 259.4, 270.12, 299.3, 764.4
rare gas 1060.2, 1067.2
rare good humor 109.2
rare metal 1058.3
rareness 299.1, 848.1, 870.2, 992.3
raring to 101.8
rarin' to go 135.6
rarity 122.2, 270.4, 299.1, 317.1, 848.1, 870.2, 870.5, 885.1, 992.3
rascal 322.3, 497.6, 660.3
rascality 645.2
rascally 645.17
rascalry 645.2
rase 201.6, 395.19, 913.5
rash (n) 85.9, 85.36 (a) 365.9, 401.10, 493.7
rash conviction 954.1
rasher 296.2, 793.3
rash impulse 375.6
rashness 365.2, 401.2, 493.1
rasorial 311.48
rasp (n) 58.3 (v) 26.7, 58.10, 96.14, 1044.7
raspberry 59.1, 333.1, 508.3, 510.8
raspiness 58.2
rasping (n) 1044.2 (a) 26.13, 58.16, 1044.10
raspings 391.4, 1051.5
Rasputin 894.6
raspy 58.16
rassle 457.13
rassler 461.3
rassling 457.10
Rastafarian 675.24
Rastafarianism 675.14
raster 1035.11
rat (n) 3.13, 357.10, 551.6, 660.5, 727.8 (v) 351.6, 551.13, 727.11, 957.9
ratable 300.14, 630.15
ratables 630.9
rataplan 55.1, 916.3
rat-a-tat 55.1, 916.3
ratatouille 10.35
ratchet 285.4
ratchet-jaw 540.4
ratchet up 912.5
rate (n) 172.4, 245.2, 623.3, 630.1, 630.2, 1017.7 (v) 244.4, 300.10, 510.17, 510.19, 630.11, 639.5, 809.6, 814.2, 946.9, 946.15
rate action 1041.3
rated 300.13, 630.14, 809.8
rate determination 1041.7
rated movie 706.1
rate highly 997.13
rate low 156.4, 157.3
rate of exchange 728.9
rate of interest 623.3
rate of pay 624.4
ratepayer 624.9
rates 630.9
rath 460.6
rather 371.17
rathole 80.11, 228.11
rathskeller 88.20
ratification 332.4, 441.1, 443.3, 957.4
ratified 332.14, 371.26, 437.11
ratifier 332.7
ratify 332.12, 371.15, 441.2, 443.11, 855.8, 957.11
ratifying 441.4
rating 245.2, 300.1, 510.5, 510.7, 622.1, 630.3, 706.1, 809.1, 809.2, 946.3
ratings 1035.2
rating system 706.1
ratio 245.1, 477.5, 919.1, 943.3, 1017.7, 1017.12
ratiocinate 931.11, 935.15
ratiocination 920.1, 931.1, 935.1
ratiocinative 920.18, 931.21, 935.18
ratiocinator 935.11
ratiocinatory 935.18
ration (n) 244.2, 477.5 (v) 477.8, 477.10
rational 919.7, 920.12, 920.18, 925.4, 931.21, 935.18, 935.20, 979.10, 987.6, 1017.23
rational animal 312.7
rational calorie 1019.19
rationale 341.4, 352.2, 375.1, 886.2, 935.5
rational faculty 919.1
rational ground 886.2
rational horizon 201.4
rationalism 935.1
rationalist 935.11
rationalistic 341.15
rationality 919.1, 920.1, 920.6, 925.1, 935.1, 935.9, 987.2
rationalization 92.23, 381.1, 600.1, 808.2, 809.1, 935.1, 936.1, 951.2, 952.2
rationalize 341.10, 381.8, 600.9, 808.10, 809.6, 935.15, 936.8
rationalized 381.12
rationalizer 935.11
rationalizing (n) 935.1 (a) 341.15
rational motive 375.1
rationed 210.9
rationing 428.1, 477.1
rations 10.6, 386.1
ratite 311.27
ratlike 311.44
ratline down 182.48
rat poison 88.14, 1001.3
rat race 330.5, 391.2, 457.2, 725.4, 915.2
rat race, the 118.1
ratsbane 1001.3
rat's nest 797.6, 799.2, 810.3
rat's-tail 3.7, 217.6
rat-tail 3.7
rattail 217.6
rattan 605.2, 1054.4
rat-tat 55.1
rat-tat-tat 55.1
rattattoo 55.1
ratter 311.16, 311.20
ratting 363.2, 370.2
rattle (n) 53.3, 53.6, 55.3, 540.4, 759.9 (v) 16.10, 55.6, 105.14, 520.5, 540.5, 902.12, 985.7
rattle around 55.6
rattle away 524.20
rattleboned 270.17
rattlebones 270.8
rattlebox 53.6
rattlebrain 924.7
rattlebrained 922.19, 985.16
rattled 985.12
rattlehead 924.7
rattleheaded 922.19, 985.16
rattle off 849.7, 989.16
rattle on 540.5
rattlepate 924.7
rattlepated 985.16
rattler 179.14
rattle the windows 53.7
rattletrap 393.8
rattletybang 55.3
rattling (n) 55.3 (a) 55.8
rattly 55.8
rattrap 356.12
ratty 311.44, 393.32, 910.11
raucid 58.15
raucity 58.2
raucous 58.15, 61.4
raucous happiness 116.1
raucousness 58.2
raunch 666.4
raunchiness 497.2, 666.3
raunchy 497.11, 666.9, 1000.8
rauwolfia 86.12
ravage (n) 395.1, 482.6, 665.6, 910.2 (v) 393.12, 395.10, 482.17, 665.20, 910.6

ravaged 21.9, 393.42, 395.28, 806.5, 910.11
ravaged with age 303.18, 842.17
ravagement 482.6, 806.1
ravager 483.6, 665.12
ravages of time 393.5, 806.1, 821.3
ravage with fire and sword 395.10
ravaging (n) 482.6 (a) 395.26, 482.22
Ravana 680.4
rave (n) 582.12 (v) 101.7, 105.16, 152.15, 503.3, 671.11, 926.20
rave about 101.7
rave against 510.19
ravel (n) 799.2 (v) 798.5, 799.3, 940.2
raveled 799.4
ravel out 940.2
raven (n) 38.4, 133.5 (v) 100.19, 482.17, 672.4 (a) 38.8
raven-black 38.8
raven-haired 38.13
ravening 100.25, 100.27, 480.26, 671.18
ravenous 100.25, 100.27, 480.26, 672.6
ravenousness 100.8, 480.9, 672.1
raven-tressed 38.13
rave on 101.7, 105.16, 503.3
raver 503.2
rave review 509.3
rave-up 582.12
ravine 237.7, 284.9
raving (n) 926.8 (a) 105.25, 152.32, 503.4, 671.18, 926.30, 926.31, 1016.21
raving beauty 1016.8
raving lunatic 926.15
raving mad 152.32, 926.30
ravioli 10.33
ravish 95.10, 393.12, 480.15, 482.17, 665.20
ravished 95.17, 105.25
ravished away 95.17
ravisher 483.6, 665.12
ravishing 97.7, 105.30, 377.8, 1016.20
ravishingness 1016.5
ravishment 95.2, 105.8, 480.3, 482.6, 665.6
raw (n) 24.4 (a) 6.14, 11.9, 26.11, 35.20, 301.10, 318.23, 406.10, 406.11, 414.17, 497.11, 513.8, 666.8, 841.7, 930.11, 1023.14
raw, the 6.3
raw bar 8.17
rawboned 270.17
raw data 770.11
raw deal 650.4, 1011.1, 1011.5
raw food 10.37
rawhide (n) 4.2, 605.1 (v) 604.12
rawhiding 604.4
raw material 263.2, 406.5, 1052.2, 1054.1
raw nerve 24.4, 152.11
raw nerve endings 128.4
raw nerves 128.4
rawness 301.3, 406.4, 414.2, 497.2, 666.3, 841.1, 930.1, 1023.1
raw recruit 461.18, 572.9, 818.2
raw sienna 40.1
raw sugar 66.2
raw umber 40.1
raw weather 1023.3
raw wind 318.7
ray (n) 171.2, 277.2, 916.4, 1025.5, 1037.3 (v) 171.6
rayed 171.9
ray-finned fish 311.30
ray flower 310.27
raying out 171.1
rayless 30.9, 1027.13
ray of hope 124.3
ray of light 1025.5
ray of sunshine 124.5, 1025.10
ray out 171.6
raze 201.6, 395.16, 395.19, 913.5
razed 201.7
raze to dust 395.19
raze to the ground 395.19, 913.5
razing 395.5
razorback 311.9
razor clam 311.29
razor-edge 285.2
razor-edged 285.8
razor-sharp 415.12
razor strap 605.1
razor temper 1046.4
razz (n) 59.1, 508.3 (v) 490.6, 508.10
razzia 459.4, 482.6
razzing (n) 59.1, 490.3, 508.1 (a) 508.12
razzledazzle 501.3
razzmatazz 501.3
RDF station 1034.6
reabsorb 187.15
reabsorption 187.8
reach (n) 48.4, 158.2, 242.1, 245.1, 257.1, 261.1, 267.1, 928.1 (v) 48.12, 145.5, 158.9, 177.19, 182.35, 186.6, 186.7, 343.8, 378.3, 478.13, 790.5, 991.4
reach a better place 307.20
reachable 966.8
reachableness 966.3
reach a compromise 468.2
reach an accord 332.10
reach an agreement 332.10
reach an all-time low 762.6
reach a new low 633.6
reach an understanding 332.10
reach a parting of the ways 456.10
reach back 163.5
reach boiling point 152.17
reach for the sky 100.20
reaching 186.1
reaching flashing point 1020.4
reaching flashpoint 1020.4
reaching high 100.9
reaching one's full growth 14.1
reach its season 407.8
reach land 182.38, 186.8
reach manhood 303.9
reach maturity 407.8
reach-me-down 842.18
reach-me-downs 5.5
reach of mind 920.1
reach one's destination 186.6
reach one's ears 551.15
reach one's goal 409.8
reach one's majority 303.9
reach one's nostrils 69.6
reach orgasm 75.24
reach out 158.9, 261.5, 267.5, 343.8, 523.18, 524.22
reach out to 343.8
reach safety 1009.8
reach the age of consent 303.9
reach the breaking point 993.13
reach the depths 112.16, 393.17, 1011.11
reach the ear 48.12
reach the ear of 48.12
reach the nadir 852.6
reach to 261.6
reach toward 162.4
reach twenty-one 303.9
reach voting age 303.9
reach womanhood 303.9
react 93.11, 903.5, 939.4
reactance 1032.13
reacting 903.9
reaction (n) 92.14, 93.1, 163.1, 184.25, 453.1, 611.1, 887.2, 900.1, 903.1, 939.1, 953.6 (a) 904.17
reactionariness 611.1
reactionarism 611.1
reactionarist 611.9
reactionary (n) 108.3, 219.1, 327.5, 611.9, 842.8, 903.4 (a) 163.11, 219.4, 611.17, 859.7, 900.8, 903.9
reactionaryism 611.1
reaction engine 181.1, 1074.2
reaction formation 92.24
reactionism 611.1
reactionist (n) 108.3, 611.9, 903.4 (a) 611.17
reaction motor 181.1, 1074.2
reaction propulsion 184.25, 1074.8
reactivate 17.12, 396.11, 458.19
reactivation 17.9, 396.1, 458.9
reactive 903.9
reactor 1038.13
reactor engine 1038.14
reactor pile 1038.13
read 341.9, 521.8, 543.10, 548.17, 570.12, 942.9
readability 518.5, 521.1, 521.3
readable 518.10, 521.10, 521.12, 983.19
read a lecture 543.11
read a lecture to 510.17
read a lesson 568.16
read a sermon 543.11
read between the lines 341.9, 341.10, 941.8
read copy 548.17
read easily 521.4
reader 352.6, 543.5, 543.7, 548.13, 554.1, 554.10, 555.4, 571.3, 571.7, 572.1, 699.4, 1042.4
readers 29.3
readership 571.10
read for 570.15
readied 385.13, 405.16
read in 928.19
readiness 101.1, 324.1, 330.3, 339.5, 387.3, 405.4, 413.1, 415.1, 441.1, 570.5, 845.1, 845.3, 896.1, 961.1
readiness of feeling 24.2
readiness of speech 524.4
readiness to serve 326.1
reading 300.2, 341.1, 341.2, 543.2, 570.3, 928.5, 1036.11
reading desk 703.13, 901.15
reading enthusiast 572.1
reading glasses 29.3
reading in 698.10
reading list 871.1
reading matter 547.10, 548.10
reading notice 352.6
reading room 558.1
reading stand 901.15
reading, writing, and arithmetic 568.5
read into 341.9, 341.10
read in view of 341.9
readjust 858.14
readjustment 92.27, 858.4
read law 570.15
read like a book 413.19
read loud and clear 521.8
readmission 187.8
readmit 187.15
read one 521.8
read oneself in 698.11
read one's hand 962.9
read one's lines 704.32
read one's mind 689.22
read-only memory 1042.7
read out 773.4, 909.14
readout 300.2
read out of 447.4, 909.19
read palms 962.9
read someone like a book 521.9, 941.8
read tea leaves 962.9
read the banns 436.6
read the future 962.9
read the meter 300.10
read the riot act 420.10, 510.17
read up 570.12
read up on 570.12, 570.14, 938.31
read with 570.11
read-write head 1042.3
read/write memory 1042.7
ready (v) 396.14, 405.6, 568.13 (a) 101.8, 130.11, 324.5, 330.18, 339.14, 387.20, 405.16, 413.22, 415.12, 441.4, 570.18, 845.9, 961.7
ready, the 728.18
ready and willing 101.8, 324.5
ready at hand 223.15
ready-built 405.19
ready cash 728.18
ready-cut 405.19
ready-dressed 405.19
ready for 405.18, 897.6
ready for another round 9.4
ready for anything 405.16, 413.25

ready for bed 22.21
ready-formed 405.19, 892.18
ready for more 9.4
ready-for-wear 405.19, 892.18
ready-furnished 405.19
ready grasp 570.5
readying 405.1, 568.3
ready-made (n) 5.4 (a) 5.48, 405.19, 892.18
ready-mixed 405.19
ready money 728.18
ready oneself 570.11
ready oneself to 405.10
ready pen 547.2, 718.2
ready-prepared 892.18
ready reckoner 1017.11
ready reply 939.1
ready reserves 461.25
ready to believe 954.8
ready to burst 105.20, 794.11, 993.20
ready-to-cook 405.19
ready to cry 115.21
ready to die for 652.5
ready to drop 21.7, 21.10
ready-to-wear (n) 5.4 (a) 5.48, 405.19, 830.4, 892.18
ready up 405.6
ready wit 489.1, 920.2
reaffiliation 450.2, 805.1
reaffirm 849.8
reaffirmation 849.2
reagent 1060.2
real 471.9, 761.15, 763.6, 970.15, 973.13, 973.15, 1017.23
real estate 231.4, 234.1, 471.6
real estate agent 730.9
real estate broker 730.9
real estate loan 438.4
realign 203.5, 808.13, 852.7
realignment 808.7, 852.1
realism 869.1, 973.7, 987.2, 1052.6
real issue 997.6
realist (n) 987.3, 1052.7 (a) 987.6, 1052.12
realistic 349.14, 349.15, 724.15, 784.16, 869.8, 920.18, 953.24, 956.5, 973.15, 987.6, 1052.12
realistic description 349.2
realisticness 987.2
realistic representation 973.7
reality 761.2, 831.2, 970.3, 973.1
reality check 761.2
reality show 1035.2
reality television 1035.2
reality TV 1035.2
realizability 966.2
realizable 966.7, 995.6
realization 33.1, 206.4, 349.1, 349.4, 407.1, 472.1, 794.4, 831.1, 892.4, 892.5, 928.2, 941.1, 989.4
realize 206.5, 328.6, 349.11, 407.4, 472.12, 521.7, 551.14, 728.29, 734.12, 886.10, 892.10, 892.11, 928.12, 986.15, 989.11
realized 407.10, 928.26
realized ideal, the 932.2
realize on 472.12
realize profit 472.12
realizer 892.7
real lady 644.8
real-life 349.14
reallocate 808.13
reallocation 477.3
really into 928.17
really old 303.18
really something 122.2
realm 231.2, 232.1, 724.4, 809.3, 809.4
real man 76.6
real McCoy, the 973.4
real meaning 518.1
realm of possibility 966.2
realm of possibility, the 966.1
realm of the impossible, the 967.1
realm of the mind, the 158.7
realness 973.7
real person 659.1
Realpolitik 609.1
realpolitik 415.2, 609.2
real presence 701.7
real property 234.1, 471.6
real tennis 748.1
real thing, the 104.1, 761.2, 973.4
real time 821.1, 1042.18
realtor 730.9
realty 471.6
real wages 624.4, 731.8
real world 987.2, 1052.2
real world, the 973.1
ream (n) 1054.5 (v) 75.22, 292.15, 510.18
ream ass 510.18
reaming 356.9, 510.6
reaming-out 510.6
ream out 292.15, 510.18
reanimate 9.2, 17.12, 306.9, 396.16
reanimated 9.4
reanimation 9.1, 396.3
reap 268.6, 472.8, 1069.19
reap and carry 1069.19
reaped 268.9
Reaper 307.2
reaper 1069.5
reaping 1069.15
reappear 849.11, 850.5
reappearance 849.1, 850.2, 856.2
reappearing 78.14, 396.24, 849.13
reapportionment 477.1
reappraisal 931.5, 938.7
reappraise 931.15, 938.27
reap profit 472.12
reap revenge 507.6
reap the benefit of 387.15
reap the fruits of 639.6
reap vengeance 507.6
reap where one has sown 639.6
rear (n) 209.2, 217.1, 217.2, 217.5, 817.2 (v) 182.55, 193.8, 200.8, 200.9, 247.5, 272.10, 449.16, 568.13, 892.8, 892.9, 912.5, 1069.16, 1070.6 (a) 217.9
rear admiral 575.19
rear aloft 200.9
rear area 217.2
rear cushion 750.1
reared 912.9
rear end 217.1, 217.5, 817.2
rear-end 902.13
rear guard 217.2, 1008.9
rearing (n) 200.4, 449.3, 568.3, 912.1, 1069.12 (a) 193.14, 200.11, 912.9
rear its head 33.8
rearmost 217.9
rearrange 808.13, 858.12
rearrangement 808.7
rear-screen projection 706.5
rear up 193.8, 200.8, 912.5
rearview mirror 29.6
rearward (n) 217.1 (a) 217.9
reason (n) 341.4, 375.1, 600.6, 886.2, 919.1, 920.6, 925.1, 935.1, 935.5, 935.9, 940.1, 957.1 (v) 541.11, 931.8, 935.15, 946.10, 951.10, 952.9
reasonability 600.7, 935.9, 968.3
reasonable 600.14, 633.7, 670.12, 920.12, 920.18, 925.4, 935.20, 968.7, 987.6
reasonable charge 633.2
reasonable ground 968.1
reasonable hope 968.1
reasonableness 600.7, 633.1, 920.6, 925.1, 935.1, 935.9, 987.2
reasonable presumption 968.1
reasonable price 633.2
reason about 541.11
reason behind 886.2
reasoned 931.21, 935.21
reasoner 935.11
reason for 886.2
reason for being 380.2, 886.9
reason ill 936.8
reason in a circle 936.8
reasoning (n) 919.1, 931.1, 935.1 (a) 919.7, 920.18, 935.18
reasoning animal 312.7
reasoning faculty 919.1
reasoning power 920.1
reasoning together 935.5
reasonless 365.10, 922.13, 923.10, 926.26, 936.11
reasonlessness 922.1, 923.2, 926.1, 936.2
reason out 931.11
reason speciously 936.8
reason that 946.10
reason the point 541.11
reason to believe 957.1
reason why 886.2
reason with 541.10
reassemble 396.18
reassembling 396.5
reassembly 396.5
reassert 849.8
reassertion 849.2
reassess 630.11
reassurance 121.4, 492.8, 901.1, 970.8
reassure 121.6, 124.9, 492.15, 970.11
reassured 970.21
reassurement 970.8
reassuring 121.13, 124.12
reastiness 71.2
rebarbative 64.7, 98.18, 1015.11
rebarbativeness 98.2
rebate (n) 255.7, 631.1 (v) 631.2
rebatement 631.1
rebbe 699.11
rebegin 856.6
rebeginning 856.2
rebegun 856.7
rebehold 938.27
rebeholding 938.7
rebel (n) 108.3, 327.5, 418.3, 860.3, 868.3 (v) 327.7, 333.5 (a) 327.11
rebellion 327.4, 333.2, 418.2, 453.1, 868.1
rebellious 108.7, 327.11, 333.6, 418.5, 453.5
rebelliousness 108.1, 327.3, 454.1
rebel yell 454.2, 458.7, 517.16
rebirth 78.1, 396.3, 685.4, 849.1, 858.2
reboant 54.12
reboation 54.2
reborn 396.24, 685.9, 692.10, 858.19
rebound (n) 54.2, 163.4, 747.3, 903.2, 1048.1 (v) 54.7, 163.9, 747.4, 903.6, 1048.5
rebounding 54.12, 903.10
rebroadcast 1034.18
rebuff (n) 157.2, 372.1, 412.2, 442.2, 453.1, 903.2, 908.2 (v) 157.5, 372.2, 442.5, 453.2, 460.10, 908.3
rebuffed 372.3
rebuild 78.7, 396.18, 852.7
rebuilding 78.1, 396.5
rebuilt 852.10
rebuke (n) 510.5 (v) 510.17
reburial 309.1
rebus 522.9
rebut 451.6, 600.10, 939.5, 958.5
rebutment 451.1
rebuttal 451.1, 598.6, 600.2, 939.2, 958.2
rebutter 939.2
rebuy 733.7
rebuying 733.1
recadency 394.1
recadent 394.5
recalcitrance 325.1, 327.2, 361.4, 451.2, 453.1, 868.1, 900.1
recalcitrancy 325.1, 327.2, 361.4, 453.1
recalcitrant (n) 903.4 (a) 325.5, 327.10, 361.12, 451.8, 453.5, 868.5, 900.8, 903.10
recalcitrate 453.3, 903.6
recalcitration 327.2, 453.1, 903.2
recalescence 1020.1
recalescence point 1019.3
recalibration 300.1
recall (n) 445.1, 613.8, 989.3 (v) 420.11, 445.2, 989.9, 989.19
recall dose 86.6
recalled 989.22
recalling 989.3
recall knowledge of 989.11
recall of ambassadors 456.4
recall to life 396.16
recall to mind 989.9

recant 335.4, 363.8, 372.2, 445.2, 475.3
recantation 335.2, 363.3, 372.1, 442.1, 445.1, 475.1
recanted 475.5
recanting 335.5
recap (n) 268.3, 557.2, 849.2, 1017.11 (v) 268.6, 295.29, 396.14, 1017.19
recapitulate 268.6, 849.8, 1017.19
recapitulation 268.3, 557.2, 849.2, 1017.11
recapitulative 849.14
recapitulatory 849.14
recapture (n) 481.3 (v) 481.6, 989.9
recast 78.7, 852.7, 858.12
recce 938.8
recco 938.8
recede 163.5, 168.2
recedence 168.1, 433.2
recedent 168.4
receding (n) 168.1 (a) 168.5
receipt (n) 11.4, 86.1, 187.1, 419.3, 479.1, 627.1, 627.2, 939.1 (v) 627.3
receipted 624.22
receipt in full 627.2
receipt in full of all demands 627.2
receipts 471.1, 472.3, 627.1, 628.1
receivable 187.16, 623.10
receivables 624.1, 627.1
receival 479.1
receive 187.10, 332.8, 479.6, 480.13, 585.7, 627.3, 772.3, 953.10, 1036.17
receive absolution 658.6, 701.17
receive a false impression 975.10
receive an impression 93.10
receive Christ 692.7
receive credit 622.7
received 332.14, 373.13, 479.10, 509.19, 579.5, 687.7, 842.12, 953.23, 970.18
received meaning 518.4
Received Pronunciation 523.4
Received Standard 523.4
received wisdom 920.5
receive instruction 570.11
receive pleasure from 95.13
receiver 195.1, 347.2, 347.4, 479.3, 692.4, 729.12, 732.6, 745.2, 746.2, 1034.3
receiver of stolen goods 732.6
receiver of stolen property 479.3
receive royally 585.9
receiver part 1034.3, 1035.11
receivership 625.3
receive the Sacrament 701.14
receiving (n) 187.1, 479.1 (a) 479.9
receiving end, the 479.3
receiving set 1034.3
recency 841.1
recense 392.12, 547.19
recension 392.4, 547.10
recent 837.10, 841.12
recentness 841.1
recent past 837.1
recept 932.1
receptacle 195.1
receptibility 187.9
receptible 187.16
reception 187.1, 189.1, 479.1, 480.1, 582.10, 585.2, 770.2, 772.1, 953.1, 1034.21
reception area 197.20
receptionist 585.5, 1008.12
reception room 197.20
receptive 24.9, 24.11, 93.20, 187.16, 324.5, 479.9, 570.18, 585.11, 587.16, 894.15, 979.10, 1047.9
receptive mood 324.1
receptiveness 24.2, 187.9, 324.1, 585.1, 894.5, 979.3, 1047.2
receptivity 24.2, 187.9, 324.1, 570.5, 979.3
receptor 24.5
recess (n) 20.2, 197.3, 284.7, 346.4, 402.1, 584.1, 826.1, 857.3, 1009.5 (v) 20.8, 284.14, 826.3, 846.9, 857.9
recessed 284.16
recesses 207.2
recession 163.1, 168.1, 284.7, 331.3, 433.2, 731.10, 1011.6
recessional (n) 708.17 (a) 168.4
recessional march 708.12
recessionary 168.4
recession-proof 1007.5
recessive 163.11, 168.4, 859.7
recessive character 560.6
recess of the memory 989.1
recewinptacle 310.28
Rechabite (n) 668.4 (a) 668.10
Rechabitism 668.2
recharge 17.12, 396.16
recharged 9.4
recharge one's batteries 9.2, 331.16
réchauffé 849.12, 1020.29
recheck (n) 938.7 (v) 938.27, 970.12
recherché 578.13, 870.10
recidivate 163.5, 205.5, 394.4, 654.9, 859.4
recidivation 163.1, 363.2, 394.2, 859.1
recidivism 163.1, 205.1, 361.4, 363.2, 394.2, 654.1, 694.1, 859.1
recidivist (n) 363.5, 394.3, 660.4, 694.3, 859.3 (a) 205.7, 361.12, 654.12, 694.6, 695.18, 859.7
recidivistic 205.7, 361.12, 654.12, 694.6, 695.18, 859.7
recidivous 394.5, 859.7
recipe 11.4, 86.1, 419.3
recipience 187.9
recipiency 187.9
recipient (n) 479.3 (a) 187.16, 479.9
reciprocal (n) 784.3, 1017.12 (a) 450.5, 476.9, 506.8, 777.10, 850.7, 863.5, 916.19, 1017.23
reciprocality 777.1, 863.1
reciprocal trade 731.1
reciprocate 450.3, 455.2, 506.4, 777.7, 863.4, 916.13
reciprocated 863.5
reciprocating (n) 1043.3 (a) 863.5
reciprocation 506.1, 777.1, 863.1, 916.5
reciprocatist 777.4
reciprocative 777.10, 863.5, 916.19
reciprocator 777.4
reciprocatory 863.5
reciprocity 450.1, 455.1, 777.1, 863.1
recital 543.2, 568.7, 708.33, 722.1, 722.2, 849.2
recitalist 710.1
recitation 543.2, 568.7
recitationist 543.7
recitation room 567.11
recitativo 708.16
recite 524.23, 543.10, 719.5, 722.7, 849.8, 989.16, 1017.19
recited by rote 849.12
reciter 543.7, 707.2, 722.5
recite the rosary 696.13
reck 339.6
reckless 102.7, 174.15, 340.11, 365.9, 493.8, 923.10
reckless expenditure 486.1
recklessness 102.2, 340.2, 365.2, 486.1, 493.2, 923.2
reckless spending 486.1
reckon 300.10, 380.6, 946.9, 951.10, 953.11, 1017.18
reckonable 1017.25
reckon at 1017.18
reckoner 628.7, 1017.11, 1017.15
reckoning 244.2, 253.3, 624.5, 628.2, 628.3, 946.3, 1017.2, 1017.6, 1017.10, 1017.11
reckoning of, a 1017.13
reckon on 130.6, 380.6, 953.16
reckon up 1017.19
reckon up to 792.8
reckon with 624.12, 983.9
reclaim 396.12, 449.11, 481.6, 858.12, 858.14
reclaimable 396.25, 858.18
reclaiming 480.7, 481.3
reclamation 396.2, 481.3, 658.1, 858.2, 858.4, 859.1
reclamatory 658.7
réclame 352.4, 662.1
reclination 201.2, 274.1
recline 20.6, 201.5, 913.11
recline on 901.22
reclining (n) 201.2, 274.1 (a) 201.8
recluse (n) 584.5, 927.3 (a) 584.10
reclusion 584.1
reclusive 584.9, 584.10, 872.8, 927.5, 982.3
reclusiveness 344.3, 982.1
recognition 150.2, 332.3, 509.3, 639.2, 662.1, 722.4, 928.2, 941.1, 989.4
recognitor 596.6
recognizability 31.2, 521.1
recognizable 31.6, 31.7, 928.25
recognizance 436.2, 438.2
recognize 27.12, 150.4, 332.11, 646.8, 928.12, 941.5, 989.11
recognized 332.14, 479.10, 579.5, 842.12, 928.26
recoil (n) 163.4, 325.2, 506.1, 887.2, 900.1, 903.2, 903.3 (v) 99.5, 127.13, 163.9, 325.4, 368.8, 903.6, 903.7, 1048.5
recoiling 903.10
recollect 989.9
recollectable 989.24
recollected 106.13, 837.8, 989.22
recollecting 989.3
recollection 837.4, 989.1, 989.3
recollective 989.21
recombinant DNA technology 305.9
recommence 856.6
recommenced 856.7
recommencement 856.2
recommend (n) 509.4 (v) 375.14, 422.5, 439.5, 509.11
recommendability 995.1
recommendable 995.5
recommendation 422.1, 509.4
recommendatory 422.8
recommended 509.19
recommended daily allowance 7.1
recommended daily vitamins and minerals 7.1
recommending 509.17
recommend itself 509.15
recommit 429.17, 481.4
recommitment 429.4, 481.1
recompense (n) 338.1, 396.6, 481.2, 506.2, 624.3, 658.1 (v) 338.4, 396.13, 481.5, 506.5, 624.10, 658.4
recompenser 624.9
recompensing 506.8, 658.7
recompensive 338.6, 506.8
recompose 396.11, 396.18
recomposition 396.1, 396.5
recon 938.8
reconcilable 788.9
reconcile 465.8, 466.7, 658.4, 788.7, 867.3
reconciled 107.7, 134.10
reconcilement 107.1, 465.3, 788.4, 867.1
reconcile oneself to 134.7
reconciler 466.5
reconciliation 107.1, 465.3, 788.4, 867.1
reconciliatory 465.12
recondite 346.11, 522.16, 689.23
reconditeness 522.2
recondition 396.14, 396.17, 858.14
reconditioning 396.4, 858.4
reconnaissance 184.11, 938.8
reconnaissance fighter 181.9
reconnaissance mission 184.11
reconnaissance pilot 185.3
reconnaissance rocket 1075.2
reconnect 223.11, 343.8, 775.5
reconnoiter (n) 938.8 (v) 27.13, 177.20, 938.28
reconnoiterer 576.9

reconnoitering 938.8
reconsider 931.15, 938.27
reconsideration 931.5, 989.3
reconstitute 78.7, 396.11, 396.18, 808.13
reconstitution 78.1, 396.1, 808.7
reconstruct 78.7, 396.18, 852.7, 989.9
reconstruction 78.1, 396.5
Reconstruction Era 824.5
Reconstructionism 675.12
Reconstructionist (n) 675.21 (a) 675.30
reconstructive 78.14
reconversion 396.1, 465.6, 858.1, 859.1
reconvert 396.11, 465.11, 858.11
recook 1020.17
recooked 1020.29
record (n) 50.12, 249.3, 405.4, 549.1, 719.1, 832.9, 957.1, 1042.15, 1042.18 (v) 50.14, 349.8, 547.19, 549.15, 719.4, 1035.15
record, the 549.7
record album 50.12
recordation 549.14
recordative 549.16
record book 554.9, 628.4
record book, the 745.4
record-breaker 249.4
record-breaking 999.17
record changer 50.11
record clerk 550.1
recorded 549.17, 871.9
recorder 549.10, 549.13, 550.1, 628.7, 719.3
record holder 413.15
record hop 705.2
recording (n) 50.12, 336.3, 549.1, 549.14, 719.1, 785.4 (a) 549.16
recording angel 679.1
recording barometer 317.8
recording instrument 549.10
recording instruments 549.14
recording secretary 547.13
recording system 50.11
recordist 550.1
record keeper 550.1
record keeping 549.14, 1041.7
record-keeping 549.1
record of the past, the 719.1
record pirate 483.7
record player 50.11
records 757.4
record-size 257.23
record vote 371.6
recount (n) 609.21, 1017.11 (v) 719.5, 722.7, 849.8, 1017.19
recountal 722.1, 722.2, 849.2
recounter 722.5
recounting 349.3, 722.1, 722.2, 849.2, 1017.11
recoup (n) 338.1, 481.3, 624.2 (v) 338.5, 396.12, 481.6, 624.11
recoupment 481.3, 624.2
recourse 384.3, 1009.2
recourses 384.2
re-cover 295.29
recover 83.7, 392.8, 396.12, 396.20, 398.3, 481.6, 858.14
recoverability 396.9
recoverable 396.25, 859.7
recover knowledge of 989.11
recover one's balance 925.2
recover one's equilibrium 925.2
recover one's sanity 925.2
recovery 392.1, 396.2, 396.8, 398.1, 481.3, 731.10, 858.4
recovery room 197.25
recovery time 821.1
recreancy 363.2, 645.5, 694.1
recreant (n) 363.5, 491.6, 660.4, 694.3 (a) 363.11, 491.12, 645.17, 645.20, 694.6
re-create 78.7, 396.18, 852.7
recreate 9.2, 743.21
recreated 9.4
re-creation 78.1, 396.5, 852.1
recreation 9.1, 743.1
recreational 9.3, 743.27
recreational drug 87.3
recreational karate 760.3
recreational vehicle 179.19, 228.17
recreation room 197.12
recreation vehicle 179.19
re-creative 78.14
recreative 9.3, 743.27
recriminate 599.11
recriminated 599.15
recrimination 599.3
recriminatory 506.8, 599.13
rec room 197.12
recrudesce 856.6
recrudescence 394.1, 396.3, 856.2, 858.2
recrudescent 394.5, 396.24
recruit (n) 461.18, 572.9, 774.4, 818.2 (v) 253.5, 385.7, 387.14, 396.11, 396.16, 396.19, 458.18, 615.14, 615.17
recruiting 387.8, 458.8, 615.4, 615.7
recruitment 387.8, 458.7, 458.8, 615.4, 615.7
recruit one's strength 15.13, 396.19
recrystallization 1059.8
rectangle 879.1
rectangular 267.9, 278.7, 278.9
rectangular coordinates 300.5
rectangularity 278.1
rectifiable 396.25
rectification 338.1, 392.4, 396.6
rectified 798.7
rectify 79.22, 277.5, 338.4, 392.12, 396.13, 658.4, 788.7, 867.3
rectifying 338.6
rectilineal 277.6
rectilinear 277.6
rectilinearity 277.1
rectitude 644.1, 653.1
recto 219.1, 554.12
rector 571.8, 574.1, 699.2
rectorate 417.7, 698.2
rectoress 575.2
rectorship 417.7, 698.2
rectory 228.5, 698.9, 703.7
rectum 2.18
recumbence 201.2
recumbency 201.2, 274.1
recumbent 201.8, 204.15, 274.7
recuperate 83.7, 392.8, 396.19, 481.6
recuperation 396.8, 481.3
recuperative 396.23
recuperatory 396.23
recur 847.3, 849.11, 850.5, 989.14
recurrence 394.1, 812.2, 849.1, 850.2
recurrent 373.14, 812.8, 847.4, 849.13, 850.7, 989.25
recurring 373.14, 847.4, 849.13, 850.7
recursion 186.3
recursive 849.14
recur to 387.14, 394.4, 859.6
recur to the mind 989.14
recurvate 279.7
recurvated 279.7
recurvation 279.1
recurvature 279.1
recurve 279.6
recurved 279.7
recurving 279.7
recurvity 279.1
recusance 333.1, 868.1
recusancy 327.1, 333.1, 868.1
recusant (n) 333.3 (a) 327.8, 333.6, 868.5
recyclable 387.18, 387.23, 396.25
recycle 396.12
recycling bin 391.7
Red 611.13, 611.21, 860.3
red (n) 35.13, 41.1, 611.12, 860.3 (a) 11.9, 26.11, 41.6, 139.13, 406.10, 611.20
red, the 623.2
redact 392.12
redaction 392.4
red alert 399.3, 843.4
red ant 311.33
redargue 958.4
redargution 958.1
red as a beet 41.6
red as a hot coal 41.6
red as a live coal 41.6
red as a lobster 41.6
red as a turkey-cock 41.6
red as blood 41.7
red as fire 41.6
red-assed 152.30
red-bait 980.8
red-baiting 389.3
redbaiting 980.4
red-bearded 41.10
red blindness 30.3
red blood cell 2.25
red-blooded 15.15, 492.17
Red Book 549.8
red bug 311.36
redcap 178.13, 577.5
red card 752.3
red carpet 155.2
red-carpet 580.8
red carpet, the 580.1
red cent 728.7, 998.5
redcoat 461.7
red-colored 41.6
red-complexioned 41.9
red corpuscle 2.25
red-crested 41.10
red-crowned 41.10
red deer 311.5
redden 41.4, 41.5, 105.19, 139.8, 152.14
reddened 41.6
reddening (n) 41.3, 139.5 (a) 41.11
reddish 41.6
reddish-amber 41.6
reddish brown 41.1
reddish-brown 40.4, 41.6
reddish-gray 41.6
reddishness 41.1
reddish-orange 42.2
reddish-yellow 42.2
reddition 481.1
red-dog 746.5
red-dyed 41.6
rede 422.1
redecorate 498.8
redecorating 396.4
redecoration 498.1, 852.3
redeem 396.12, 398.3, 449.11, 481.6, 624.13, 624.18, 658.4, 685.6, 858.12, 862.4
redeemability 396.9
redeemable 396.25, 398.4, 623.10, 639.7
redeemed 148.7, 431.10, 679.6, 685.9, 692.10, 858.19
redeemedness 685.4
redeemed soul 679.1
Redeemer 677.10
redeemer 592.2
redeeming 481.7, 592.4, 658.7
redeeming feature 865.4
redeem one's pledge 434.2, 624.13, 641.11, 644.9
redemption 148.2, 396.2, 398.1, 481.3, 658.1, 677.14, 685.4, 858.2, 859.1
redemptional 481.7
redemptive 481.7, 592.4, 658.7, 677.16
redeploy 858.12
redeployment 808.7
redesign (n) 78.1, 852.1 (v) 78.7, 852.7
redevelop 78.7, 396.11
redevelopment 78.1, 396.1
red-eye 184.9
red-eyed 28.13, 115.21
red eyes 28.2
red face 96.4, 139.5
red-faced 41.9, 137.14, 139.13
red flag 152.11, 399.3, 517.15
red-flag 175.9
red-fleshed 41.9
red giant 1073.8
red-green blindness 30.3
red-haired 41.10
red-handed 656.3
redhanded 308.24
red-handedness 656.1
red hands 656.1
red hat 647.4
redhead 35.9
redheaded 41.10
red heat 1019.5
red herring 10.24, 356.11, 391.3, 415.3, 998.6

red-hot 93.18, 101.9, 105.22, 671.22, 759.27, 1019.25
red-hued 41.6
redial 347.4
red ink 473.3
red-ink 41.4
redintegrate 396.11
redintegration 396.1
red in the face 139.13
redirect 573.8
redirect examination 938.13
redirecting 573.12
redirection 573.1
rediscover 941.2
rediscovery 941.1
redispose 808.13
redisposition 808.7
redistribute 808.13
redistribution 477.2
redivivus 396.24
red-letter 997.21
red-letter day 20.4, 487.1, 832.4
red light 333.1, 379.2, 399.3, 400.1, 444.2, 517.15, 1026.4
red-light district 230.6, 665.9
red line 749.1
red-looking 41.6
red meat 10.13
redneck (n) 103.4, 227.10, 497.6 (a) 233.8, 497.13
redness 28.2, 41.1, 1019.12
redo 78.7, 498.8, 849.7, 858.11
redoing 78.1, 498.1
redolence 69.1, 70.1
redolent 69.9, 70.9, 989.21
red-orange 42.2
redouble 251.5, 849.7, 874.3
redoubled 849.12
redouble one's efforts 403.11
redoubling 251.2, 849.1
redoubtable 127.30
redound 887.4
redound to 896.3
redound to one's honor 662.14
redound to the honor of 509.15
red-pencil 41.4
Red Planet, the 1073.9
red-polled 41.10
redraft 392.12
red rag 152.11
red rag to a bull 152.11
redress (n) 338.1, 396.6, 481.1, 481.2, 624.3, 658.1 (v) 396.13, 481.5, 506.5, 624.11, 658.4
redress an injustice 649.5
redress a wrong 649.5
redressing 658.7
red ribbon 646.5
red ribbon of the Legion of Honor 646.5
red shift 160.1
redskin 758.2
red state 609.18
red tape 373.5, 612.10, 846.2, 1012.4
red-tapeism 612.10, 846.2
redtapeism 373.5
red-tapery 612.10, 846.2
red-tapist 575.15
red-tufted 41.10
reduce 16.10, 16.11, 85.50, 120.5, 137.5, 244.4, 252.7, 255.9, 258.9, 260.7, 268.6, 270.13, 412.10, 432.9, 447.3, 619.6, 631.2, 633.6, 670.6, 798.4, 801.6, 913.4, 959.3, 1060.8
reduced 16.19, 85.54, 137.13, 252.10, 274.7, 412.17, 432.15, 619.7, 633.9, 885.6, 913.12
reduced-calorie 7.21
reduced-calorie diet 7.13
reduced circumstances 619.1
reduced-fat 7.21
reduced-fat diet 7.13
reduced in health 85.54
reduced price 633.2
reduced rates 633.2
reduced sail 180.14
reduced sight 28.1, 30.1
reduced to a skeleton 393.35
reduced to dire straits 1013.26
reduced to jelly 128.14
reduced to powder 1051.11
reduced vowel 524.11
reduce sail 182.50
reduce the temperature 670.6
reduce to 858.11
reduce to ashes 309.20, 1020.22, 1020.25
reduce to dust 1051.9
reduce to elements 801.6
reduce to essentials 798.4
reduce to jelly 128.10
reduce to order 808.8
reduce to powder 1051.9
reduce to rubble 395.17
reduce to silence 958.5
reduce to the ranks 604.9, 913.5
reduce to unity 872.5
reduce to writing 549.15
reduce weight 270.13, 298.6
reducibility 260.5
reducible 260.11
reducing (n) 270.9 (a) 270.21, 670.14
reducing diet 7.13
reductin to dust 1051.4
reduction 16.5, 120.1, 252.1, 255.2, 260.1, 268.3, 432.4, 447.1, 631.1, 633.4, 670.2, 858.1, 913.1, 936.1, 1017.2
reduction in forces 447.2, 635.2
reductionism 406.4
reductionistic 406.12
reduction of armaments 465.6
reduction of expenses 635.2
reduction of government spending 635.2
reduction of spending 635.2
reduction of temperature 1024.1
reduction to ashes 309.2
reduction to elements 801.1
reduction to parts 801.1
reduction to powder 1051.4
reductive 252.11, 255.13, 406.12, 798.10, 987.6
reductivism 798.3
redundance 993.4
redundancy 117.3, 118.2, 256.4, 390.1, 391.1, 538.2, 551.7, 849.3, 993.2, 993.4
redundant 256.7, 391.10, 538.11, 778.7, 849.14, 993.17
red-up 808.6
reduplicate 778.6, 785.8, 849.7, 874.3
reduplicated 778.7, 849.12
reduplication 785.2, 785.3, 849.1, 874.1
reduplicative 849.14
redux 396.24
red, white, and blue 647.7
red wine 88.17
red zone 746.1
reebok 311.5
re-echo 55.1
reecho (n) 54.2, 849.1 (v) 54.7, 336.5, 849.7, 939.4
reechoed 849.12
reechoing 54.10, 54.12, 849.14, 939.6
reed 16.7, 239.6, 310.5, 310.21, 462.6, 711.6, 711.8
reediness 58.1
reed instrument 711.8
reedition 78.1
reeducate 568.10, 858.14
reeducation 92.26, 568.1, 858.4
reedy 58.14
reef (n) 235.2, 276.2, 283.9 (v) 175.9, 182.50
reef down 494.6
reefed sail 180.14
reefer 87.12, 179.15, 1024.4
reef one's sails 182.50
reef point 180.14
reefs 1006.5
reefy 276.6
reek (n) 71.1, 1020.16, 1067.1 (v) 69.6, 71.4, 190.15, 909.24, 1019.23, 1067.8
reeking (n) 71.1 (a) 15.22, 69.10, 71.5, 1019.27, 1067.9
reek of piety 354.23
reeky 69.10, 71.5, 1067.9
reel (n) 906.7, 915.2, 916.6, 917.8 (v) 88.27, 182.55, 238.21, 906.9, 915.11, 916.10, 917.15
reel back 903.7
reel in 382.10, 906.9
reeling (n) 915.1 (a) 88.31, 915.14, 916.17
reel off 540.5, 849.7, 989.16
reembodiment 1052.8
reembody 805.3, 1052.9
reenact 396.11
reenactment 396.1
reenlist 825.5
reenter 849.11, 850.5, 856.6, 989.14
reentrance 186.3, 856.2
reentry 163.1, 186.3, 849.1, 850.2, 1075.2, 1075.9
reestablish 78.7, 396.11, 856.6
reestablishment 78.1, 396.1, 856.2
reeve 574.4, 575.16, 1008.15
reevoke 989.9
re-examination 849.1, 931.5, 938.7
re-examine 931.15, 938.27
reexamine 849.7
reexperienced 837.8
reexperiencing 837.4
ref 754.3
refabricate 396.18
refabrication 396.5
refashion 78.7, 396.18, 858.12
refashioning 78.1, 396.5
refection 8.5, 9.1, 10.3
refectory 8.17, 197.11
refer 888.3
referable 775.7, 888.6
referee (n) 466.4, 596.1, 747.3, 749.3, 751.3, 752.3, 754.3, 946.6 (v) 466.6, 946.12
refereeship 466.2
reference (n) 33.3, 509.4, 518.1, 530.15, 775.4, 888.2, 957.5 (v) 957.14
reference book 554.1, 554.9, 554.9, 574.10
reference editor 554.2
reference list 871.3
reference mark 530.15
reference point 159.2
reference sign 517.1
reference system 978.2
reference to 888.1
referendum 371.6, 609.15, 613.8
referent 518.1
referential 518.10, 519.6, 536.3
referred to 888.6
referring 775.7
refer to 387.14, 422.7, 517.18, 518.8, 524.24, 541.10, 775.5, 888.4, 957.14, 983.10
refill 396.11, 794.6
refinance 729.16
refine 24.7, 79.22, 192.16, 255.9, 764.4, 798.4, 892.9, 1020.21
refine a distinction 780.6
refined 24.12, 79.26, 294.8, 339.12, 392.13, 495.11, 496.8, 504.16, 533.6, 764.6, 798.7, 892.18, 944.7, 973.17, 1002.9
refined discrimination 944.1
refined hearing 48.3
refined palate 496.6, 944.1
refined taste 496.1
refinement 79.4, 192.8, 255.1, 294.3, 339.3, 392.2, 392.3, 495.3, 496.1, 504.4, 533.1, 780.2, 798.2, 944.1, 973.5
refiner 79.13
refinery 79.13, 739.3, 739.4
refine upon 392.9
refining 892.2, 1020.5
refit 396.17, 852.7
reflate 632.9
reflation 632.3
reflationary 632.12
reflect 279.6, 336.5, 349.11, 524.24, 931.12, 989.9, 1036.16
reflectance 1025.9
reflect discredit upon 512.8, 661.8
reflected light 1025.9
reflected signal 1034.10
reflect honor 662.14
reflecting 920.19, 931.21
reflection 279.3, 336.1, 349.5, 510.4, 512.4, 524.3, 661.6, 785.7, 903.1, 920.7, 931.2, 932.1, 989.3, 1025.9, 1036.11

reflection nebula 1073.7
reflective 920.19, 931.21
reflectiveness 920.7, 931.3
reflect on 931.13
reflector 29.6, 1073.17
reflect over 931.13
reflect upon 510.13
reflex (n) 92.26, 365.1, 785.7, 887.2, 903.1, 934.2 (v) 279.6 (a) 163.12, 365.11, 903.9, 934.6, 963.14
reflex action 903.1, 963.5
reflexive (n) 530.14 (a) 365.11, 903.9, 963.14
reflexive pronoun 530.5
reflexive verb 530.4
refloat 298.8
reflowing (n) 172.2 (a) 172.8
refluence 163.1, 163.3, 172.2, 238.12, 238.13, 903.1
refluent 172.8, 238.24, 903.9
reflux 163.1, 163.3, 172.2, 238.12, 238.13, 903.1
reforest 1069.18
reforestation 310.13, 1069.3, 1069.14
reforestational 310.40
reforested 310.40
Reform (n) 675.10 (a) 675.30
re-form 78.7, 396.18, 858.12
reform (n) 392.5 (v) 113.7, 392.9, 396.11
reform (n) 852.1, 858.2 (v) 685.6, 852.7, 858.12
reformable 858.18
reformat 262.7, 783.2
re-formation 78.1
reformation 113.4, 392.5, 396.1, 396.5, 685.4, 852.1, 858.2
reformational 392.16
Reformationism 675.10
Reformationist (n) 675.20 (a) 675.28
re-formative 78.14
reformative 392.16
reformatory (n) 429.8, 567.9 (a) 392.16
reformatting 783.1
Reformed 675.28
reformed 392.13
reformed 852.10, 858.19
Reformed believer 675.20
reformer 392.6, 610.1, 858.9
reformism 392.5
reformist (n) 392.6 (a) 392.16
reformistic 392.16
Reform Jew 675.21
Reform Judaism 675.12
reform oneself 392.9
reform politician 610.1
reform politics 609.1
reform school 429.8, 567.9
refound 78.7
refract 164.5
refracted 164.8
refractile 164.8
refraction 164.2, 1036.12
refractive 164.8
refractor 1073.17
refractoriness 325.1, 327.2, 361.4, 451.2, 453.1, 868.1
refractory (n) 742.2 (a) 325.5, 327.10, 361.12, 451.8, 453.5, 742.7, 868.5
refractory brick 742.2
refractory clay 742.3
refrain (n) 708.4, 708.24, 720.10, 817.1, 849.5 (v) 329.3, 390.5, 668.7, 857.6
refrain from 668.7
refraining 368.1, 668.2
refrainment 668.2
refrangible 164.8
refreeze 1024.11
refreezing 1024.1
refresh 9.2, 15.13, 317.11, 396.16, 396.17, 743.21, 1024.10
refreshed 9.4
refresher 88.8
refresher course 568.8
refreshful 9.3
refreshing (n) 9.1 (a) 9.3, 81.5, 86.44
refreshment 8.5, 9.1, 10.3, 15.5, 317.9, 396.3, 396.4
refreshments 8.7
refresh one's memory 989.19
refresh the inner man 8.20, 9.2, 88.24
refresh the memory 989.18
refresh the memory of 989.19
refrigerant (n) 1024.7 (a) 1024.12
refrigerate 397.9, 1023.10, 1024.10
refrigerated 386.15
refrigerating engineer 1024.9
refrigerating engineering 1024.9
refrigerating machine 1024.5
refrigerating plant 1024.5
refrigeration 397.2, 1024.1
refrigeration anesthesia 1024.2
refrigeration ship 180.1
refrigerative 1024.12
refrigerator 11.4, 1024.4
refrigerator car 179.15, 1024.4
refrigerator cookie 10.43
refrigerator-freezer 1024.4
refrigerator truck 1024.4
refrigeratory (n) 1024.4 (a) 1024.12
reft 802.23
refuel 1021.8
refuge 187.1, 346.4, 376.1, 397.7, 1008.1, 1009.1
refugee 160.4, 190.10, 368.5, 774.3
refulgence 662.6, 1025.4
refulgency 662.6, 1025.4
refulgent 1025.32
refulgentness 662.6
refund (n) 255.7, 481.2, 624.2, 631.1 (v) 481.5, 624.11, 631.2
refundment 624.2
refurbish 396.17, 498.8
refurbishing 396.4
refurbishment 396.4, 498.1
refusal 325.1, 333.1, 335.1, 372.1, 442.1, 444.1, 451.1, 733.2, 908.2
refusal to be amazed 123.1
refusal to be awed 123.1
refusal to be impressed 123.1
refusal to believe 955.1, 956.1
refusal to speak 51.2
refuse (n) 80.9, 256.1, 370.4, 390.3, 391.4 (v) 325.3, 335.3, 372.2, 442.3, 444.3, 908.3
refuse comment 344.6
refuse consent 442.3
refused 372.3
refuse heap 80.10
refusenik 327.5
refuse oneself 668.6
refuse point-blank 442.3
refuse summarily 442.3
refuse to accept 335.4
refuse to acknowledge 157.6
refuse to admit 335.4, 955.5
refuse to associate with 586.5
refuse to be impressed 123.2
refuse to believe 956.3
refuse to bow down 453.4
refuse to conform 333.4
refuse to consider 372.2
refuse to cooperate 327.6
refuse to credit 955.5
refuse to give credence to 955.5
refuse to pay 625.6
refuse to receive 442.5, 586.5
refuse to recognize 157.6
refuse to shed blood 464.8
refusing oneself 668.2
refutability 971.2
refutable 958.10, 971.17
refutal 958.2
refutation 335.2, 598.6, 600.2, 935.5, 939.2, 958.2
refutative 939.6, 958.6
refutatory 958.6
refute 335.4, 600.10, 939.5, 958.5
refuted 958.7
refuting 335.5, 600.13, 958.6
reg 419.2, 673.3, 869.4
regain 481.6
regain consciousness 306.9
regaining 481.3
regain one's composure 106.7
regain one's freedom 566.5
regal 136.12, 417.17, 608.10, 999.12
regale (n) 8.9, 9.1, 95.3 (v) 7.17, 8.18, 8.24, 9.2, 95.8, 743.21
regalement 8.1, 8.5, 9.1, 95.3, 743.1
regalia 5.10, 5.11, 647.1, 647.3, 702.1
regaling (n) 8.1 (a) 9.3
regality 136.2, 417.1
regard (n) 27.2, 27.3, 33.3, 104.1, 143.3, 155.1, 339.1, 587.3, 662.3, 766.3, 775.4, 978.2, 983.1 (v) 27.13, 104.20, 143.10, 155.4, 339.6, 434.2, 775.5, 931.17, 946.8, 953.11, 983.6
regard before 371.17
regarded highly by 587.18
regardful 143.16, 155.8, 339.10, 434.4, 494.8, 509.16, 983.15
regardfulness 143.3, 339.1, 494.1, 983.1
regardless 102.7, 340.11, 982.3, 984.6
regardlessness 102.2, 340.2, 982.1, 984.1
regardless of consequences 454.7
regards 155.3, 504.8, 585.3, 820.5
regard studiously 570.12
regard with indulgence 148.4
regatta 457.12, 743.10, 760.2
regelate 1024.11
regelation 1024.1
regency 417.7, 612.1, 612.4, 615.1
regeneracy 396.3
regenerate (v) 78.7, 396.16, 685.6, 858.12 (a) 685.9, 692.10
regenerated 685.9, 692.10, 858.19
regenerateness 396.3
regeneration 78.1, 392.5, 396.3, 677.15, 685.4, 858.2
regenerative 78.14
Regenerator, the 677.3
regenesis 78.1, 396.3
regent 575.11
regentship 417.7, 615.1
reggae 708.11
regift 478.12
regime 7.13, 91.14, 612.1
regime change 609.21
regimen 7.13, 91.14, 612.1
regiment (n) 461.22, 770.3 (v) 425.4, 643.6, 808.9
regimental tie 647.1
regimentation 425.1, 643.2, 808.1
regimented 432.16
regiminal 7.23
Regin 258.5
region 159.1, 231.1, 231.5, 234.1, 722.4
regional 159.19, 231.8, 523.22
regional accent 523.7, 524.8
regional dialect 523.7
regional forecast 317.7
regionalism 523.7
regional language 523.1
regional theater 704.1
register (n) 50.3, 158.2, 549.1, 549.4, 549.11, 549.14, 550.1, 628.4, 709.4, 709.6, 711.19, 832.9, 871.1, 1042.3 (v) 48.12, 210.5, 349.8, 397.8, 521.5, 549.15, 570.11, 704.29, 788.6, 871.8, 1008.18
register a complaint 115.15
registered 210.7, 549.17, 871.9
registered engineer 1043.2
registered lobbyist 609.32
registered mail 553.4
registered nurse 90.10
registered representative 737.10
registered trademark 210.3, 517.13
registered voter 609.23
registering rocket 1074.6
register of deaths 307.13
register with 788.6
registrar 549.3, 549.13, 550.1, 628.7

registration 549.14, 871.7
registrational 549.16
registration document 549.5
registry 549.1, 549.3, 549.4, 549.11, 549.14, 628.4, 832.9, 871.1, 871.7
registry office 549.3
règlement 419.2
regnal 612.17
regnancy 417.5, 417.8, 612.1
regnant 612.17, 864.12, 894.14
regolith 234.1, 1059.1
regrate 733.7
regrater 730.2
regress (n) 163.1, 859.1 (v) 163.5, 172.5, 175.9, 217.8, 393.16, 394.4, 859.4
regression 92.21, 92.23, 163.1, 172.2, 393.3, 394.1, 859.1
regressive 163.11, 172.8, 393.45, 394.5, 859.7
regressive sorites 935.6
regressive taxation 630.9
regret (n) 113.1 (v) 113.6, 658.6
regretful 113.8, 132.5
regretfulness 113.1
regretless 114.4
regretlessness 114.1
regrets 113.1, 658.2
regrettable 98.20, 113.10, 1000.9
regrettableness 98.5
regretting 113.1
regroup 858.12
regrowth 310.2
regs 869.4
regular (n) 221.5, 609.27, 733.4, 745.2 (a) 245.5, 247.12, 264.4, 287.10, 349.15, 373.13, 373.14, 781.5, 794.10, 807.6, 847.5, 850.6, 869.9, 1005.8
regular army 461.23
regular as clockwork 807.6, 850.6
regular buyer 733.4
regular canoness 699.17
regular customer 221.5, 733.4
regular dividend 738.7
regular forces 461.20
regular guy 606.5
regularity 264.1, 287.1, 781.2, 807.1, 847.2, 850.1, 869.1
regularization 264.2, 808.2, 869.5
regularize 264.3, 781.4, 808.10, 869.6
regularized 808.14
regular joe 606.5
regularness 850.1
regular old fogy 842.8
regular payments 624.1
regular play 916.5
regulars 461.23, 746.2
regular wave motion 850.2
regular year 824.2
regulate 573.8, 612.11, 673.9, 781.4, 788.7, 808.10, 894.8
regulate by 959.3
regulated 808.14
regulating 573.12, 612.17
regulation (n) 419.2, 420.3, 573.1, 573.3, 612.1, 673.3, 788.4, 808.2, 869.4 (a) 373.13, 419.4, 869.9
regulations 1012.4
regulative 573.12, 612.17
regulative first principle 932.2
regulator 1041.14
regulator gene 305.9
regulatory 573.12, 612.17
regulus 1058.5
regurgitate 238.16, 849.7, 909.26, 1063.5
regurgitated 849.12, 1063.6
regurgitation 238.12, 568.2, 849.1, 909.8
rehabilitate 396.11, 600.9, 858.12, 858.14
rehabilitation 92.27, 396.1, 600.1, 858.4, 859.1
rehabilitative 600.13
rehabilitator 858.9
rehash (n) 849.2, 849.5, 1017.11 (v) 341.13, 849.8, 1017.19
rehearsal 568.3, 704.13, 722.1, 722.2, 849.1, 849.2, 942.3, 1017.11
rehearse 568.13, 704.32, 719.5, 722.7, 849.8, 942.8, 1017.19
rehearsed 704.33
rehearse in extenso 538.7
reheat 1020.17
reheated 1020.29
reheat the ashes 396.16
Reichian psychology 92.2
reidentification 989.4
reidentify 989.11
reification 763.4
reify 763.5
reign (n) 417.5, 612.1, 894.1 (v) 612.13, 864.10
reigning 612.17, 864.12
reigning beauty 1016.7
reign of Saturn 1010.4
reign of Spirit, the 681.5
reign of St. Swithin 316.4
reign of terror 127.7, 612.9, 860.1
reimbursable 481.7
reimburse 481.5, 624.11
reimbursement 481.2, 624.2
rein (n) 428.1, 428.4 (v) 428.7
reincarnate 849.7, 1052.9
reincarnation 396.3, 685.4, 849.1, 852.3, 1052.8
reindeer 311.5
reindoctrinate 858.15
reindoctrination 568.2, 858.5
reinfect 85.51
reinforce 15.13, 251.5, 253.5, 449.12, 901.21, 957.11, 1046.9
reinforced 251.7, 1046.13
reinforced concrete 1054.2
reinforcement 15.5, 92.26, 251.2, 253.1, 254.1, 385.1, 901.1, 901.2, 916.4, 957.4
reinforcements 449.8, 461.25
rein in 175.9, 428.7
reinless 418.5, 430.24
reinquire 938.27
reinquiry 938.7
reins 573.5
reinsman 178.9
reins of government 612.2
reinspire 396.16
reinstall 396.11
reinstate 396.11, 600.9
reinstatement 396.1, 600.1, 859.1
reinstation 396.1
reinstitute 78.7, 396.11
reinstitution 78.1, 396.1
reinstruct 858.14
reinstruction 858.4
reintegrate 396.11
reinvent oneself 346.8, 365.7
reinvest 396.11, 729.17
reinvestiture 396.1
reinvestment 396.1
reinvigorate 9.2, 15.13, 301.8
reinvigoration 9.1, 15.5
reissue (n) 78.1, 548.3, 849.2, 849.5 (v) 78.7, 548.14, 728.26, 849.8
reiterant 849.14
reiterate (v) 849.8, 856.5 (a) 849.12
reiterated 849.12
reiteration 538.2, 849.2, 874.1, 974.3
reiterative 538.11, 849.14
reiterativeness 538.2
reject (n) 370.4, 390.3 (v) 335.3, 372.2, 390.7, 442.3, 444.3, 451.6, 451.7, 510.10, 586.6, 773.4, 909.13, 909.26, 955.5, 956.3
rejectamenta 390.3
reject authority 418.4
rejected 99.10, 108.10, 372.3, 390.11, 586.10, 909.30, 955.12, 958.7
rejection 92.24, 99.1, 157.2, 333.1, 372.1, 390.3, 442.1, 444.1, 451.1, 510.1, 586.3, 773.1, 908.2, 909.1, 955.1
rejective 372.4, 442.6, 909.30
rejig 938.27
rejigger 78.7, 437.8, 808.13, 858.11, 938.27
rejiggering 78.1
rejoice 109.7, 116.5
rejoice in 95.13
rejoice in a seller's market 1010.9
rejoice in the name of 527.13
rejoice the heart 109.7
rejoice with one 149.2
rejoicing (n) 116.1, 487.1 (a) 109.15, 116.10
rejoin 939.4, 939.5
rejoinder 939.1, 939.2
rejoining 939.6
rejuvenate 301.8, 396.16
rejuvenating 9.3
rejuvenation 9.1, 396.3
rejuvenescence 396.3
rekindle 396.16, 1020.22
relapse (n) 163.1, 363.2, 394.1, 858.1, 859.1 (v) 163.5, 205.5, 393.16, 394.4, 654.9, 858.13, 859.4
relapsing 394.5, 654.12
relatability 1016.2
relatable 775.8
relate 524.23, 552.11, 719.5, 722.7, 775.6, 784.7, 943.4, 1017.19
relate at large 538.7
related 559.6, 775.9, 775.10, 784.13
related by blood 775.10
related form 784.3
relatedness 775.1, 775.4
related word 518.6, 526.1
relate in extenso 538.7
relate to 343.8, 775.5
relate to emotionally 93.11
relating (n) 93.5, 722.1, 943.1 (a) 775.7
relation 518.1, 559.1, 722.1, 722.2, 722.3, 775.1, 898.1, 943.1
relational grammar 530.1
relations 75.7, 559.2, 559.5, 775.1, 831.4
relationship 104.5, 559.1, 775.1
relationship by blood 775.3
relative 775.7, 943.8
relative bearing 161.2
relative density 1045.1
relative electron affinity 1033.3
relative heading 161.2
relative humidity 317.4, 1065.2
relative incidence 847.1
relative magnitude 1073.8
relative pitch 708.31
relative pronoun 530.5
relatives 559.2, 559.5
relatives-in-law 564.2
relative velocity 174.1
relative wind 318.10
relativism 775.2, 943.1, 971.1
relativistic 775.7
relativity 158.6, 775.2, 777.1, 971.1
relativity theory 1018.1
relativize 775.6
relator 722.5
relaunch 849.7
relax 20.7, 106.7, 120.5, 120.6, 121.8, 145.4, 175.9, 581.2, 670.9, 743.21, 743.22, 804.3, 857.9, 959.5, 1047.6, 1047.7
relaxation 16.5, 20.1, 120.1, 252.1, 331.2, 426.1, 670.2, 743.1, 804.2, 1047.3, 1047.5
relaxation of tension 120.1, 465.1
relaxed 106.15, 120.10, 121.12, 129.2, 173.12, 175.10, 340.10, 402.6, 426.4, 581.3, 804.5, 933.4, 1047.10
relaxedness 402.2, 426.1, 581.1, 1047.3
relaxing (n) 16.5, 120.1, 670.2 (a) 120.9, 121.11, 670.14, 1047.16
relax one's grip 475.4
relax one's hold 475.4
relax the condition 959.5
relay (n) 825.3 (v) 176.10
relay link 1035.9
relay man 745.2
relay racing 755.2

relay station 1034.6, 1035.9
relay transmitter 1035.9
release (n) 120.2, 307.1, 352.3, 369.1, 398.1, 430.8, 431.2, 443.1, 475.1, 551.1, 552.4, 601.1, 627.2, 750.2, 771.3 (v) 13.5, 120.6, 398.3, 430.14, 431.5, 431.7, 443.9, 475.4, 601.4, 771.8, 802.10, 909.19
released 307.29, 430.21, 430.30, 431.10, 475.5
release from prison 431.5
release therapy 92.25
releasing 431.3
relegate 478.16, 773.4, 909.17
relegated 773.7
relegate to a place 159.11
relegation 478.2, 773.1, 909.4
relent 145.4, 433.6, 670.5, 1047.7
relenting 670.2
relentless 146.3, 330.22, 359.11, 360.8, 361.9, 425.7, 847.5, 963.15
relentlessness 146.1, 330.6, 359.1, 360.1, 361.2, 425.2, 963.7
relevance 518.1, 775.4, 788.5
relevant 775.9, 775.11, 788.10, 889.9, 957.16
relevant fact 957.1
relevant instance 786.2
reliability 644.6, 855.1, 953.8, 970.4
reliable 644.19, 855.12, 953.24, 957.16, 970.17, 1007.5
reliance 124.1, 130.1, 616.9, 901.1, 953.1
reliance in 953.1
reliance on 953.1
reliant 953.22
relic 549.1, 696.10, 842.6, 842.8, 989.6
relic area 523.7
relic of the past 842.6
relics 256.1, 307.15
relict 256.1, 256.3, 566.4
relief 86.1, 120.1, 121.4, 143.5, 143.7, 145.1, 211.2, 283.2, 298.3, 449.1, 449.3, 449.8, 478.8, 611.7, 712.16, 715.3, 825.2, 826.1, 862.2
relief-carving 713.1
relief map 574.10
relief of tension 92.25
relief payments 478.8
relief pitcher 745.2
relief printing 548.1
relieve 86.38, 120.5, 121.6, 298.6, 449.11, 478.17, 745.5, 825.5, 862.5, 1014.9
relieved 120.10, 298.11
relieve of 480.21
relieve oneself 12.12, 120.7, 524.21
relieve one's mind 933.3
reliever 745.2
relieve the mind of 985.6
relieving (n) 480.6 (a) 120.9, 121.13, 298.16
relievo 715.3
relight 396.16, 1020.22
religion 675.1, 676.1, 692.1, 953.3
religioner 675.15
religionism 692.1, 693.1
religionist 675.15, 692.4, 693.3
religiosity 354.6, 692.1, 692.3, 693.1
religious 339.12, 644.15, 675.25, 676.4, 685.7, 692.8, 973.17
religious belief 675.1
religious believer 953.9
religious ceremony 580.4
religious discourse 543.3
religious education 676.1
religious faith 675.1
religious fasting 515.1
religious holiday 850.4
religious humanism 312.11
religious humbug 693.3
religious hypocrite 693.3
religiously exact 973.17
religious-minded 692.8
religious-mindedness 692.1
religiousness 692.1
religious order 675.3, 699.1
religious painter 716.4
religious person 699.16
religious prophets 962.4
religious rites 487.1, 701.3
religious sacrifice 308.1
religious school 567.8
religious study 676.1
religious truth 687.1
relinquish 370.7, 390.4, 433.8, 448.2, 475.3, 857.6
relinquished 390.10, 475.5
relinquishment 370.3, 390.2, 433.2, 448.1, 475.1, 857.1
relinquish one's life 307.18
reliquary 309.16, 549.12, 703.4, 703.11
reliquiae 307.15
relish (n) 62.1, 63.2, 63.3, 68.2, 93.2, 95.1, 100.2, 100.7 (v) 8.20, 62.7, 63.5, 95.13
relishing 8.1
relived 837.8
reliving 837.4
relocate 159.17, 160.6, 176.11
relocation 160.2
relucent 1025.31
reluct 327.7
reluctance 139.3, 175.1, 325.1, 453.1, 1032.13
reluctant 99.8, 139.12, 175.10, 325.6, 453.5
reluctate 327.7
reluctivity 1032.13
relume 1020.22, 1025.28
relumine 1025.28
relying 953.22
rely on 124.6, 387.14, 901.22, 953.16, 953.17
rely on fortune 759.24
rely upon 953.16
remain 173.7, 221.6, 225.7, 256.5, 827.6, 853.5, 856.3
remain aloof 329.4
remain anonymous 346.8
remain at a distance 261.7
remain at peace 464.8
remain celibate 565.5
remainder (n) 255.8, 256.1, 793.1, 835.1, 993.5, 1017.12 (v) 734.8
remainderman 479.5
remain firm 359.9, 453.4, 855.11
remain incommunicado 584.7
remain indelibly impressed on the memory 989.13
remaining 225.13, 256.7, 827.10, 853.7, 856.7, 993.18
remain in one's memory 989.13
remain in possession of the field 411.3
remain in situ 173.10
remain in the shade 139.7
remain motionless 173.7
remain neutral 102.5, 467.5
remain on one's hands 993.8
remains 256.1, 307.15, 390.3, 549.1, 842.6
remain seated 173.10
remain unmoved 94.5
remain valid 973.8
remake (n) 849.5 (v) 78.7, 396.18, 852.7
remaking 78.1, 396.5, 852.1
remand (n) 429.4, 481.1 (v) 429.17, 478.16, 481.4
remanding 478.2
remandment 481.1
remand school 567.9
remanent 256.7
remark (n) 213.2, 512.4, 524.3, 556.2, 983.1 (v) 524.24, 983.6
remarkable 122.10, 247.10, 870.14, 997.19
remarkableness 122.3, 870.2, 997.2
remarkably like 784.15
remark upon 341.11, 556.5
remarque proof 713.7
remarriage 563.1
remarry 563.15
remediability 396.9
remediable 396.25
remedial 86.39, 120.9, 396.22, 449.21, 568.18
remedial measure 86.1
remediless 125.15
remedilessness 125.3
remedy (n) 86.1, 120.1, 338.1, 396.6, 396.7, 449.1, 900.3 (v) 86.38, 91.24, 396.13, 396.15, 449.11
remedy an injustice 649.5
remember 143.10, 989.9, 989.19
rememberability 989.7
rememberable 989.24, 997.19
remember as if it were yesterday 989.9
remember clearly 989.9
remembered 837.8, 989.22
remember everything 989.9
remembering (n) 989.3 (a) 989.23
remember Pearl Harbor 458.7
remember the Alamo 458.7
remember the Maine 458.7
remembrance 487.1, 549.12, 662.7, 837.4, 989.1, 989.3, 989.5, 989.6
remembrance of things past 837.4
remembrancer 989.5
remembrances 504.8
remi- 180.15
remiges 3.18
remigrate 177.22, 190.16
remigration 177.4, 186.3, 190.7
remilitarization 458.9
remilitarize 458.19
remind 989.19
reminder 549.4, 989.5
remindful 989.21
remind one of 784.7, 989.19
reminisce 989.10
reminiscence 837.4, 989.3
reminiscences 719.1
reminiscent 837.8, 989.21
remise 430.14
remiss 331.19, 340.10, 426.4, 846.17
remissibility 600.7
remissible 600.14
remission 120.1, 148.2, 252.2, 255.2, 481.1, 601.1, 670.2, 857.3
remission of sin 148.2
remissness 331.5, 340.1, 426.1, 846.5
remit (n) 601.3 (v) 120.5, 145.4, 148.3, 176.15, 252.8, 429.17, 430.14, 478.16, 481.4, 601.4, 624.10, 670.5, 670.9
remittance 478.8, 624.1
remittance man 190.10
remittance woman 190.10
remitted 148.7, 624.22
remit the penalty of 601.4
remitting 481.1
remnant (n) 256.1 (a) 256.7
remodel 396.18, 858.12
remodeled 852.10
remodeling 396.4, 396.5
remold 78.7
remonetization 728.23
remonetize 728.26
remonstrance 333.2, 379.1, 422.1, 453.1
remonstrant 333.7, 422.8
remonstrate 333.5, 379.3, 422.6, 453.3
remonstration 333.2
remonstrative 333.7, 422.8
remonstratory 422.8
remora 803.4, 1012.7
remorse 113.1, 656.1
remorseful 113.8
remorsefulness 113.1
remorseless 114.4, 146.3
remorselessness 114.1, 146.1
remorse of conscience 113.1
remote (n) 573.5 (a) 141.12, 261.8, 344.10, 583.6, 584.8, 651.5, 776.8
remote access 966.3
remote age 837.3
remote cause 886.3
remote control 573.5, 1041.4
remote-control 1041.25
remote-controlled 1041.25
remote distance 261.3
remote future 839.1

remote handling 1041.4
remotely like 784.15
remotely related distantly related 559.6
remoteness 141.4, 261.1, 344.3, 583.2, 651.1
remote past 837.3
remote pickup 1034.17
remote-pickup unit 1034.5
remote possibility 966.1, 972.9
remoter 261.10
remote resemblance 784.4
remote sensing 159.3
remotest 261.12
remotest corner of the world 261.4
remote time 837.3
remount (n) 311.13 (v) 193.12
removable 176.18, 255.13
removable disk 1042.6
removable drive 1042.5
removal 6.1, 120.2, 160.1, 188.1, 192.1, 255.1, 308.2, 390.3, 447.2, 773.2, 802.1, 909.1, 909.5, 909.6
removal to Abraham's bosom 681.11
remove (n) 158.8, 245.1 (v) 6.5, 6.6, 120.6, 176.11, 188.9, 192.10, 255.9, 308.16, 390.7, 395.14, 447.4, 773.5, 802.10, 909.13, 909.19, 909.22
remove all doubt 957.10, 970.11
remove all restrictions 443.12
removed 261.8, 344.10, 583.6, 584.8, 776.6, 802.21, 872.8
removed from the record 148.7
remove friction 1014.7
remove from life 308.13
remove from office 447.4
removing the veil 351.1
REM sleep 22.1, 22.5
remunerate 396.13, 481.5, 624.10
remuneration 481.2, 624.3, 624.4
remunerative 387.22, 472.16, 624.21
remunerativeness 472.4
remunerator 624.9
remuneratory 387.18, 472.16, 624.21
renaissance 396.3
Renaissance literature 547.12, 718.1
Renaissance man 413.3, 413.11, 929.3
Renaissance versatility 413.3
Renaissance woman 413.3, 413.11, 929.3
renal disease 85.24
renascence 78.1, 396.3, 858.2
renascent 78.14, 396.24
rencontre 223.4, 457.3
rend 26.7, 393.13, 395.17, 480.22, 802.11
rend asunder 802.11
render 192.16, 328.6, 341.12, 343.7, 349.8, 349.9, 437.9, 478.12, 478.13, 624.10, 708.39, 858.11, 1020.21
renderable 341.17
render accounts 628.8
render a service 143.12
render assistance 449.11
render blind 30.7
render credit 150.4
renderer 716.2
rendering 192.7, 341.2, 349.1, 349.2, 708.30
rendering-up 628.2
render lip service 354.23
render recognition 150.4
render service to 449.18
render thanks 150.4
render up 475.3
rendezvous (n) 582.9, 770.2, 1075.9 (v) 770.16
rend from 192.15, 480.22
rending (n) 192.6, 802.2 (a) 98.23
rendition 192.7, 341.2, 349.1, 349.2, 481.1, 708.30
rend the air 53.7, 59.9
rend the eardrums 53.7
rend the ears 53.7, 58.11
rend the firmament 53.7
rend the heart 112.19
rend the skies 53.7
renegade (n) 357.11, 363.5, 694.3, 858.8 (a) 363.11, 435.5, 694.6, 858.20
renegadism 694.1
renegado 363.5
renegate 363.5
renege 363.8, 370.5, 435.3, 442.4, 445.2, 645.12, 858.13
reneging 163.2, 363.3, 445.1
renew 9.2, 105.13, 396.16, 396.17, 841.5, 849.7, 852.7, 856.6, 858.12
renewable 396.25, 858.18
renewable energy 17.1, 1021.1, 1021.7
renewable fuel source 1021.1
renewal 9.1, 394.1, 396.3, 396.4, 849.1, 852.1, 856.2, 858.2
renewed 9.4, 396.24, 685.9, 841.8, 852.10, 856.7, 858.19
renew one's strength 9.2, 396.19
reniform 279.16
renig 445.2
renigging 445.1
renitence 325.1, 453.1, 1046.2
renitency 325.1, 453.1, 900.1, 1046.2
renitent 325.6, 453.5, 900.8, 1046.11
rennin 7.10
renounce 335.4, 363.8, 370.7, 372.2, 390.4, 433.8, 475.3, 668.8, 857.6
renounced 372.3, 390.10, 475.5
renouncement 363.3, 370.3, 372.1, 390.2, 668.1
renounce the throne 448.2
renovate 78.7, 392.11, 396.17, 481.6, 841.5
renovation 78.1, 396.4
renovator 396.10
renown 247.2, 352.4, 662.1, 997.2
renowned 247.9, 662.16
renownless 661.14
rent (n) 85.38, 224.2, 615.6, 630.8, 802.4 (v) 224.4, 225.7, 228.31, 292.11, 615.15, 615.16 (a) 224.7, 393.27, 802.23
rental 615.6, 630.8
rental car 179.13
rental library 558.1
rental movie 706.1
rent boy 562.12
rent charge 630.8
rent control 630.5
rented 615.20
renter 227.8, 470.4
rent gouger 470.3
rentiers 331.11
rent out 615.16
rent-payer 470.4
rent-roll 630.8
renunciation 335.2, 363.3, 370.3, 372.1, 390.2, 433.2, 475.1, 668.1, 857.1, 858.3, 958.2
renunciation of the world 584.1
renunciative 335.5, 363.12, 372.4
renunciatory 335.5, 363.12
reoccupation 481.3
reoccupy 481.6
reoccur 849.11, 850.5
reoccurrence 849.1, 850.2
reoccurring 850.7
reopen 856.6
reopened 856.7
reopening 856.2
reor 808.13
reorder 808.13
reordering 808.7
reorg (n) 78.1 (v) 78.7
reorganization 78.1, 808.7
reorganizational 78.14
Reorganization Objective Army Division 461.22
reorganize 78.7, 808.13
reorientation 92.26
reovirus 85.42
repair (n) 396.6, 765.3 (v) 392.11, 396.14, 658.4
repairable 396.25
repairer 396.10
repairing 396.6
repairman 396.10
repair shop 739.5
repair to 177.25
repairwoman 396.10
repairwork 396.6
repair worker 726.2
reparability 396.9
reparable 396.25
reparation 338.1, 396.6, 465.2, 481.2, 624.3, 658.1
reparative 338.6, 396.22, 481.7, 506.8, 624.21, 658.7
reparatory 396.22, 481.7, 658.7
repartee 489.7, 541.1, 541.2, 863.1, 939.1
reparteeist 489.12
repartition 477.1
repas 8.5
repast 8.5
repatriate (n) 160.4 (v) 481.4, 858.14
repatriation 481.1, 858.4
repave 295.22
repay 338.4, 472.13, 481.5, 506.5, 624.11
repaying 624.21
repay in kind 506.6
repayment 338.1, 481.2, 624.2
repeal (n) 445.1 (v) 395.13, 445.2
repealed 445.3
repeat (n) 849.5, 849.6, 874.2 (v) 78.7, 336.5, 352.10, 849.7, 849.11, 850.5, 874.3, 989.16
repeat by heart 989.16
repeated 847.5, 849.12
repeated figure 498.7
repeated sounds 849.4
repeater 462.10, 609.23, 859.3
repeating (n) 609.18 (a) 849.14
repeat like a broken record 849.7
repeat like a parrot 989.16
repeat offender 593.3
repeat oneself 849.7
repeat order 849.6
repeat performance 849.6, 874.2
repeat verbatim 849.7
repeat word for word 849.7
repel 64.4, 98.11, 99.6, 372.2, 379.4, 442.5, 453.2, 460.10, 908.3, 1012.14
repelled 96.20
repellence 98.2, 453.1, 908.1, 1015.2
repellency 98.2, 453.1, 908.1, 1015.2
repellent 98.18, 379.5, 453.5, 908.4, 1015.11
repelling (n) 908.1 (a) 908.4, 1015.11
repent (v) 113.7 (a) 177.39, 311.47
repentance 113.4, 658.3
repentant 113.9, 658.7
repenting 658.7
repent in sackcloth and ashes 658.6
repercuss 903.6
repercussion 671.8, 708.30, 887.2, 900.1, 903.2
repercussive 54.12, 903.10
repertoire 386.1, 704.9
repertory 386.1, 386.6, 704.9, 871.1, 1017.11
repertory company 707.11
repertory drama 704.1
repertory theater 704.1
repetend 849.5
repetition 78.1, 117.3, 118.2, 336.1, 785.3, 847.2, 849.1, 850.1, 856.1, 874.1
repetitional 849.14
repetitionary 849.14
repetition for effect 538.2
repetition for emphasis 538.2
repetitious 849.14, 856.7
repetitiousness 849.4
repetitive 373.14, 538.11, 781.6, 812.8, 849.14, 856.7
repetitiveness 118.2, 538.2, 849.4
repetitive strain injury 85.38

rephrase 341.13
repine 113.6, 115.10
repining (n) 113.1 (a) 113.8
replace 396.11, 447.4, 835.3, 862.5, 909.19
replaceable 388.6, 862.10
replacement 396.1, 447.2, 817.4, 835.2, 862.1, 862.2
replacement cost 626.3
replacement part 386.3
replant 91.24
replay 849.6
replaying 849.6
replenish 385.7, 396.11, 794.6
replenishment 385.1
replete 794.11, 991.7, 993.20, 994.6
repleteness 991.2
repletion 794.2, 991.2, 993.3, 994.1
replevin (n) 438.2, 481.3 (v) 480.20, 481.6
replevy (n) 438.2, 481.3 (v) 480.20, 481.6
replica 336.3, 349.5, 778.3, 785.3
replicable 336.10
replicate 785.8, 873.5, 874.3
replicated 873.6, 874.4
replication 560.6, 874.1, 939.1, 939.2
replier 939.3
reply (n) 343.1, 506.1, 553.2, 600.2, 903.1, 939.1 (v) 553.11, 600.10, 903.5, 939.4
reply by return mail 553.11
replying 939.6
reply to 343.8
repo 481.3
report (n) 53.5, 56.1, 349.3, 352.2, 352.4, 549.7, 551.1, 552.6, 556.2, 662.1, 671.7, 696.3, 709.14, 946.2 (v) 221.11, 343.7, 352.12, 551.8, 552.11, 599.7, 719.4, 719.5, 722.7, 946.13
reportage 552.1, 555.3
report card 549.7
reported 352.17, 552.15
reporter 550.1, 551.5, 552.9, 555.4, 576.5
report for duty 221.11
reportorial 552.13, 555.5
repose (n) 20.1, 22.2, 173.1, 201.2, 402.1, 670.1 (v) 20.6, 159.10, 159.14, 173.7, 201.5, 953.17
repose confidence in 953.15
reposeful 121.11, 173.12, 670.13
reposefulness 121.2
repose in 761.11, 953.15
repose on 901.22, 953.16
repose on one's laurels 329.2
repose upon 959.6
reposing 173.12, 201.8, 307.29
reposit 159.14, 386.10
reposition 159.6
repository 195.1, 386.6, 588.1, 729.13
repossess 481.6
repossessing 480.7
repossession 480.7, 481.3
repoussé (n) 715.3 (a) 283.18, 715.7
reprehend 510.13, 510.17
reprehensibility 656.1, 1000.1
reprehensible 510.25, 654.16, 656.3, 1000.9
reprehension 510.3, 510.5
represent 216.7, 341.10, 348.5, 349.8, 349.9, 466.6, 576.14, 704.30, 862.5, 986.15
representation 33.7, 336.3, 348.2, 349.1, 349.2, 349.7, 354.3, 371.6, 517.1, 597.4, 704.8, 712.10, 785.1, 785.3, 862.1, 932.1
representational 349.13, 349.14
representational film 706.1
representative (n) 349.7, 517.1, 576.1, 610.3, 786.2, 862.2 (a) 349.13, 349.14, 517.23, 576.16, 786.8
representative art 712.1
representative democracy 612.4
representative fraction 159.5
representative government 612.4
representativeness 349.7
representative of the press 555.4
representative realism 1052.6
representative town meeting 613.1
representing 349.13, 597.6
representing in the mind 986.6
represent oneself to be 349.12, 354.22
repress 106.8, 286.2, 345.8, 428.8, 444.3, 474.5, 612.15, 1012.10
repress a smile 111.2
repressed 344.10, 428.14, 990.9
repression 92.24, 344.3, 345.3, 428.2, 444.1, 474.1, 990.3, 1012.1
repressive 417.16, 428.11, 444.6, 1012.17
repress one's desires 668.6
reprieve (n) 120.2, 145.1, 148.2, 601.3, 846.2 (v) 120.6, 145.4, 601.5
reprieved 148.7
reprimand (n) 510.5, 661.6 (v) 510.17, 604.9, 661.9
reprint (n) 548.3, 785.5, 849.2, 849.5 (v) 78.7, 548.14, 849.8
reprinting 78.1
reprisal 506.2, 507.1, 603.1
reprise 837.4, 849.6
repro 548.3, 785.3, 785.5, 874.1
reproach (n) 510.5, 599.1, 661.5, 661.6 (v) 510.13, 599.7, 661.8
reproachability 656.1
reproachable 510.25, 656.3
reproachableness 656.1
reproached 599.15
reproachful 510.22
reproachfulness 510.4
reproachless 657.6
reproachlessness 657.1
reproach oneself 113.6
reprobacy 645.2, 654.3, 654.5, 695.4
reprobate (n) 660.4 (v) 510.13, 602.3 (a) 645.17, 654.14, 654.16, 686.3, 695.18
reprobate, the 660.11
reprobation 510.3, 510.5, 686.1
reprobative 510.22
reproduce 14.2, 78.7, 259.7, 306.10, 778.6, 785.8, 849.7, 874.3, 890.7
reproduce after one's kind 78.8
reproduced 849.12, 874.4
reproduce in kind 78.8
reproduction 14.1, 78.1, 78.2, 259.3, 336.3, 712.10, 785.2, 785.3, 849.1, 874.1, 890.2
reproduction proof 548.5, 785.5
reproductive 2.29, 78.14, 78.15
reproductive cell 305.10
reproductive drive 104.2
reproductive organs 2.13
reproductive urge 886.7
reprography 785.2
reproof 510.5
repro proof 548.5, 785.5
reprovability 656.1
reprovable 510.25, 656.3
reprovableness 656.1
reproval 510.5
reprove 510.17
reproving look 510.8
reptant 177.39, 311.47
reptatorial 177.39
reptile (n) 311.3, 311.24, 660.6 (a) 177.39, 311.47
reptilelike 311.47
Reptilia 311.24
reptilian (n) 311.24 (a) 311.47, 661.12
reptilian brain 311.24
reptilian-brain 311.47
reptiliform 311.47
reptiloid 311.47
republic 232.1, 612.4
Republican 609.27
republican 612.16
republicanism 612.7
republicanize 611.16
Republican Party 609.24
republic of letters 547.12, 718.1
repudiate 335.4, 363.8, 372.2, 442.3, 625.6, 773.4
repudiated 372.3
repudiation 333.1, 335.2, 363.3, 372.1, 442.1, 625.1, 773.1
repudiative 335.5, 363.12, 955.8
repudiatory 363.12
repugnance 64.3, 98.2, 99.2, 103.1, 325.1, 451.2, 589.3, 779.1, 789.1, 900.1, 1015.2
repugnancy 451.2, 1015.2
repugnant 98.18, 335.5, 451.8, 589.10, 779.6, 789.6, 900.8, 1015.11
repulse (n) 157.2, 372.1, 412.2, 442.2, 453.1, 903.2, 908.2 (v) 157.5, 372.2, 442.5, 453.2, 460.10, 908.3
repulsed 372.3
repulsion 99.2, 453.1, 908.1
repulsive 71.5, 80.23, 98.18, 908.4, 1000.9, 1015.11
repulsive force 908.1
repulsiveness 64.3, 71.2, 80.2, 98.2, 1000.2, 1015.2
repulsor 181.4
repurchase (n) 733.1 (v) 733.7
repurpose 387.10
reputability 644.1, 662.2
reputable 644.13, 662.15, 894.13, 997.19
reputableness 662.2
reputation 662.1, 997.2
reputative 519.7, 951.14
repute (n) 662.1, 731.6, 894.1, 997.2 (v) 951.10
reputed 951.14
request (n) 439.2, 440.1, 696.4 (v) 440.9
request the pleasure of one's company 440.13
request the presence of 440.13
requiem 115.6, 309.4, 708.17
requiem mass 309.4, 708.17
require 420.9, 421.5, 424.5, 630.12, 641.12, 772.4, 886.12, 963.9, 992.7
require an answer 938.20
required 420.12, 424.11, 641.15, 887.6, 963.13
required course 568.8
required visit 582.7
requirement 421.1, 568.8, 963.2
requisite (n) 959.2, 963.2 (a) 963.13
requisiteness 963.3
requisition (n) 420.5, 421.1, 440.1, 480.4, 963.2 (v) 420.11, 421.5, 440.9, 480.19
requisitioned 421.10
requisitorial 421.10
requisitory 421.10
requital 481.2, 506.2, 624.3
requite 396.13, 481.4, 481.5, 506.5, 624.11, 863.4
requited 863.5
requitement 624.3
reredos 703.10
reroute 182.30
rerun 849.5, 1034.18
rescension 341.4
rescind 255.12, 445.2
rescinded 445.3
rescinding 445.1
rescindment 445.1
rescission 255.3, 445.1
rescript 392.4, 420.4, 553.2, 673.3, 939.1
rescription 392.4, 939.1
rescuable 398.4
rescue (n) 143.7, 369.1, 398.1, 431.1, 449.1 (v) 396.12, 398.3, 431.4, 449.11
rescued 431.10
rescue dog 311.16
rescuer 397.5, 398.2, 592.2
reseal 293.6
resealed 293.9
research (n) 938.4 (v) 570.6, 938.25, 938.31, 942.8
research and development 942.1
research and development establishment 942.5
research center 739.6, 942.5

researcher 572.1, 938.18, 942.6, 951.7
research facility 739.6, 942.5
research fellowship 571.10
research installation 739.6
researchist 938.18
research laboratory 739.6, 942.5
research monograph 556.1
research paper 556.1
research park 739.6
research rocket 1074.6
research satellite 1075.6
research science 928.10
research station 1075.5
research worker 938.18, 942.6
resect 802.11
resection 802.2
resell 734.8
resemblance 349.5, 784.1, 785.1
resemblant 349.13, 784.10
resemble 784.7, 943.7
resembling 784.10
resene 1057.1
resent 152.12, 154.2
resentful 96.21, 108.7, 110.22, 152.26, 154.3, 589.10
resentfulness 110.6, 152.1, 154.1
resenting 152.26
resentment 93.7, 108.1, 152.1, 154.1, 589.4
reserpine 86.12
reservation 325.2, 333.2, 397.7, 421.2, 494.2, 615.4, 955.2, 959.1, 965.1
reserve (n) 51.1, 139.3, 212.3, 344.3, 386.3, 397.7, 537.1, 576.1 (v) 386.12, 390.5, 477.9, 615.14, 846.9, 965.4 (a) 390.12, 862.8
reserved 139.11, 344.10, 386.15, 537.6, 872.8
reservedness 344.3
reserve fleet 461.27
reserve forces 449.8, 461.20
reserve fund 386.3
reserve militia 461.24
reserve oneself 139.7
reserves 386.3, 449.8, 461.25, 617.7, 728.14, 862.2
reserve status 458.8
reserve supply 386.3
reservoir (n) 195.1, 241.1, 386.3, 386.6 (v) 386.10
reset 285.7, 1069.18
reset action 1041.3
resetting 1069.14
res gestae 328.3
reshape 78.7, 852.7, 858.12
reshaping 78.1, 852.1
reshuffle 437.8, 808.13
reside 159.17, 225.7
reside in 761.11
residence 225.1, 228.1
residencer 227.2
residency 225.1
resident (n) 90.4, 227.2, 470.4, 576.6, 699.7 (a) 225.13, 767.7
residential 228.32
residential area 230.6
residential district 230.6
residentiary (n) 227.2, 699.7 (a) 225.13, 228.32
resident maide 227.2
resident physician 90.4
resider 227.2
residing (n) 225.1 (a) 225.13, 228.32
residual (n) 256.1 (a) 256.8
residual magnetism 1032.7
residual schizophrenia 926.4
residuary 256.8
residue 80.9, 256.1, 893.3, 1017.12
residuum 256.1
resign 163.6, 370.7, 390.4, 433.6, 448.2, 475.3, 478.13
resignation 94.4, 106.2, 107.1, 134.2, 163.2, 370.3, 390.2, 433.1, 448.1, 475.1
resigned 94.13, 107.7, 134.10, 390.10, 433.12
resignedness 94.4, 106.2, 433.1
resigning 163.2
resign one's being 307.18
resign oneself 433.6
resign oneself to 134.7
resign one's life 307.18
resile 903.6
resilience 109.3, 854.1, 903.2, 1047.2, 1048.1
resiliency 109.3, 1047.2, 1048.1
resilient 109.12, 396.23, 854.6, 903.10, 1047.9, 1048.7
resin (n) 70.4, 803.4, 1057.1 (v) 1057.2
resinate (n) 1057.1 (v) 1057.2
resinic 1057.3
resinize 1057.2
resinoid (n) 1057.1 (a) 1057.3
resinous 1057.3
resin plastic 1054.6
resiny 1057.3
resist 451.3, 451.4, 453.2, 900.6, 1012.10
resistance 83.4, 92.23, 92.24, 184.27, 325.1, 327.4, 361.4, 451.1, 453.1, 460.1, 461.16, 900.1, 1012.1, 1032.13, 1033.9, 1044.1, 1046.1, 1049.1
resistance band exercise 84.2
resistance capacitance 1032.16
resistance fighter 461.16
resistance movement 327.4, 453.1
resistance to belief 956.1
resistance to change 853.3
resistance training strength training 84.2
resistant 15.20, 83.14, 325.5, 333.6, 361.12, 453.5, 900.8, 1046.10, 1049.4
resist believing 956.3
resist control 418.4
resist entreaty 442.3
resister 392.6, 452.3
resisting 361.12, 453.5
resistive 453.5, 1046.10
resistiveness to belief 956.1
resistless 15.19, 963.15
resistlessness 15.4
resist persuasion 442.3
resist temptation 653.4
resojet 904.17
resojet propulsion 184.25
resolute 101.9, 359.11, 360.8, 403.16, 492.17
resoluteness 359.1, 492.5
resolution 31.2, 101.2, 323.1, 359.1, 360.1, 380.1, 393.6, 403.1, 439.2, 465.4, 492.5, 613.5, 708.24, 709.2, 801.1, 801.2, 802.5, 806.1, 820.1, 858.1, 940.1, 946.1, 946.5
resolutive (n) 1064.4 (a) 1064.8
resolvable 858.18, 940.3
resolve (n) 359.1, 380.1 (v) 323.2, 359.7, 380.4, 403.5, 465.8, 801.6, 801.7, 820.6, 940.2, 946.11
resolved 359.11
resolvedness 359.1
resolved upon 359.16
resolve into 858.11
resolve itself 858.17
resolvent (n) 1064.4 (a) 806.5, 1064.8
resolve upon 371.16
resolving 940.1
resonance 50.1, 54.1, 903.1, 916.1, 916.4
resonance frequency 916.1, 916.4
resonancy 54.1
resonant 54.10, 720.18, 916.15
resonant cavity 54.5
resonant chamber 54.5
resonant frequency 916.1, 916.4
resonate 54.6, 916.10
resonating 54.10
resonator 54.5
resorb 187.15
resorbence 187.8
resorbent 187.17
resort 228.7, 228.15, 228.27, 384.3, 743.13, 995.2, 1009.2
resorts 384.2
resort to 177.25, 221.10, 387.14
resort to arms (n) 458.1 (v) 458.15
resound (n) 54.2 (v) 48.12, 50.14, 53.7, 54.7, 849.11
resounder 54.5
resounding (n) 54.2 (a) 53.11, 54.12
resoundingness 54.1
resounding triumph 409.3
resound in the ears 53.7
resound the praises of 509.12, 696.12
resource 386.2, 386.3, 386.4, 413.1, 995.2, 1009.2
resourceful 381.13, 404.8, 413.22, 413.25, 415.12, 986.18
resourcefulness 413.1, 415.1
resources 384.2, 386.2, 471.7, 728.14
respect (n) 27.2, 33.3, 155.1, 434.1, 504.1, 509.1, 587.3, 641.1, 662.3, 766.3, 775.4, 978.2, 983.1 (v) 143.10, 155.4, 434.2, 509.9, 696.11, 775.5, 997.13
respectability 644.1, 1005.1
respectable 644.13, 662.15, 999.20, 1005.7
respectable citizen 659.3
respected 155.11, 662.15
respectful 155.8, 434.4, 504.13, 509.16, 641.13
respectfully 820.5
respectfully yours 820.5
respectfulness 504.1
respective 477.13, 777.11, 865.12
respectless 144.18, 340.11
respectlessness 144.3
respects 155.3, 504.8
respiration 2.21
respirator 91.19
respiratory 2.32
respiratory disease 85.16
respiratory system 2.22
respire 306.8
respite (n) 20.2, 120.1, 120.2, 601.3, 826.1, 846.2, 857.3 (v) 601.5
resplendence 501.5, 662.6, 1016.5, 1025.4
resplendency 662.6, 1025.4
resplendent 662.19, 1016.20, 1025.32
respond 24.6, 93.11, 553.11, 600.10, 863.4, 903.5, 939.4
respondence 903.1, 939.1
respondent (n) 599.6, 939.3 (a) 903.9, 939.6
responder 758.3, 939.3
responding 903.9, 939.6
responding note 709.14
respond to 93.11, 321.6, 343.8, 455.2, 777.7, 788.6
respond to stimuli 24.6
response 24.1, 93.1, 93.5, 343.1, 518.1, 600.2, 696.3, 708.23, 708.24, 887.2, 903.1, 939.1
responser 939.3
response to stimuli 24.1
responsibility 130.4, 573.2, 615.1, 641.2, 644.6, 888.1, 889.1, 897.1
responsible 623.9, 641.17, 644.19, 897.5
responsible for 641.17, 897.6
responsibleness 641.2
responsible person 574.1
responsion 939.1
responsive 24.9, 24.12, 93.20, 324.5, 343.9, 894.15, 903.9, 939.6, 1047.9, 1048.7
responsiveness 24.3, 93.5, 324.1, 894.5, 1047.2, 1048.1
responsivity 324.1
responsory 696.3
responsory report 708.23
rest (n) 20.1, 20.2, 51.1, 173.1, 193.5, 256.1, 307.1, 402.1, 464.2, 709.12, 709.21, 857.3, 901.2, 906.3 (v) 20.6, 159.10, 159.14, 173.7, 182.16, 256.5, 329.2, 598.19, 670.7, 857.9, 959.6
rest and be thankful 107.5, 173.7
rest and recreation 9.1, 20.2

rest assured 124.6, 953.10, 953.14, 970.9
restate 341.13, 849.8
restatement 341.3, 849.2
restaurant 8.17, 197.11
rest easier 120.8
rest easy 107.5, 375.24
rest from one's labors 20.6
restful 20.10, 121.11, 173.12, 464.9, 670.15
restfulness 20.1, 121.2, 173.1, 464.2
restful sleep 22.4
rest hard upon 297.13
rest home 91.21, 1009.4
restimulate 396.16
restimulation 396.3
restimulative 396.22
rest in 761.11, 953.15
rest in confidence 953.14
resting 173.12
resting bitch face 144.4
resting bud 310.23
resting easy 121.12, 307.29
resting of the case 598.8
resting place 309.16, 820.1, 901.2
resting point 826.1, 906.3
Rest in Peace 309.18
rest in the arms of Morpheus 22.13
restitute 338.4, 396.11, 396.13, 481.4, 624.11, 658.4
restitution 338.1, 396.1, 465.2, 481.1, 600.1, 624.2, 624.3, 658.1, 859.1
restitutional 658.7
restitutive 396.22, 481.7, 506.8, 658.7
restitutory 396.22, 481.7, 658.7
restive 105.27, 108.7, 135.6, 325.6, 327.10, 361.8, 361.12
restiveness 108.1, 135.1, 327.2, 361.1, 361.4, 1046.1
restless 23.7, 105.27, 108.7, 135.6, 330.20, 854.7, 917.16
restlessness 23.1, 105.5, 108.1, 135.1, 172.1, 330.4, 854.2, 917.1
restless soul 988.1
restless spirit 988.1
restock 385.7, 1054.7
rest on 297.11, 901.22, 953.16, 959.6
rest one's case 598.19
rest on one's laurels 107.5, 331.15
rest on one's oars 20.6, 173.7, 331.15, 857.9
rest on the shoulders of 641.7
restorability 396.9
restorable 396.25
restoral 396.1
restoration 7.14, 78.1, 392.1, 396.1, 481.1, 481.3, 600.1, 858.4, 859.1
restorative (n) 17.6, 86.1, 86.8 (a) 78.14, 86.39, 86.44, 396.22, 481.7
restore 7.20, 9.2, 78.7, 396.11, 449.11, 481.4, 481.6, 600.9, 858.14
restored 9.4, 120.10, 837.8
restore harmony 465.8
restorer 396.10
restore self-respect 858.12
restore to health 396.15, 396.16
restoring 481.1
restrain 210.5, 424.4, 428.7, 428.10, 429.12, 670.6, 959.3, 1012.10
restrainable 433.14
restrained 139.11, 212.10, 344.10, 428.13, 496.7, 533.6, 668.9, 670.11
restrainedness 496.3, 535.1
restraining 424.10, 428.11
restraining hand 670.3
restrain oneself 106.7, 210.5, 428.7, 668.6
restraint 92.24, 106.3, 139.3, 210.2, 252.4, 325.2, 344.3, 359.5, 415.1, 424.1, 428.1, 428.4, 429.1, 432.1, 496.3, 533.1, 668.1, 670.1, 1012.1
restraint of trade 428.1, 731.1
restraints 428.4
restrengthen 15.13
restrengthening 15.5
restrict 210.5, 270.11, 428.9, 429.12, 477.9, 866.4, 959.3
restricted (n) 706.1 (a) 210.7, 210.8, 270.14, 345.11, 428.15, 429.19, 866.5, 959.10
restricted information 345.5
restrictedness 270.1, 885.1
restricted practice 90.13
restricted theory of relativity 158.6
restricting (n) 210.2 (a) 210.9, 428.12, 959.7
restriction 210.2, 270.1, 428.3, 429.1, 444.1, 773.1, 959.1, 1012.1
restrictionist 428.6
restrictions 747.3
restrictive 210.9, 428.12, 773.9, 959.7, 1012.17
restrictive convenant 444.1
restrict oneself 668.6
restrict to 477.9
restrict to home 428.9
restroom 12.10, 79.10, 197.26
restructure 78.7, 808.13, 852.7
restructuring 78.1, 396.5, 808.7, 852.1
rest satisfied 107.5
rest stop 857.2
restudy (n) 570.3 (v) 570.12, 989.18
restudying 570.3
rest upon 297.11
rest upon one's oars 329.2, 368.9
rest with 641.7, 959.6
result (n) 831.1, 887.1, 893.1, 940.1 (v) 831.7, 835.3, 887.4
resultant (n) 887.1 (a) 831.9, 887.6
result from 887.5
resulting 887.6
resume 481.6, 849.8, 849.11, 856.6
résumé 557.2, 719.1, 849.2
resumed 856.7
resumption 481.3, 849.1, 856.2
resupinate (v) 205.5 (a) 205.7
resupination 205.1
resupine 201.8
resupply 385.1
resurface 295.22, 849.11, 850.5, 989.14
resurfacing 849.1, 850.2
resurge 306.9
resurgence 396.3
resurgent 78.14, 396.24
resurrect 78.7, 306.9, 396.16
resurrected 396.24
resurrection 78.1, 396.3, 681.11
resurrectionism 482.10
resurrectionist 483.1
resuscitate 105.13, 306.9, 396.16, 449.11, 856.6
resuscitation 396.3, 856.2
retable 703.12, 901.14
retablo 703.12
retail (n) 734.1 (v) 352.10, 731.16, 734.8, 771.4, 849.8 (a) 731.22, 734.13
retailable 734.14
retail dealer 730.2
retailer 385.6, 730.2
retail goods 735.1
retail gossip 552.12
retailing (n) 385.1, 731.2, 734.2 (a) 734.13
retail merchant 730.2
retail park 730.2, 739.1
retail price 630.1
retail price index 630.4, 731.9, 733.1
retail seller 730.2
retail store 736.1
retail therapy 733.1
retain 386.12, 474.5, 615.14, 855.7, 856.4, 928.13, 989.12, 989.16
retained 386.15, 989.22
retainer 138.6, 577.1, 624.5
retaining (n) 615.4 (a) 474.8
retaining fee 624.5
retaining wall 901.4
retainment 474.1, 615.4
retain the memory of 989.12
retake (n) 481.3, 706.5, 714.8 (v) 481.6
retaking 481.3
retaliate 338.4, 459.17, 506.4, 507.4, 863.4
retaliation 338.1, 506.1, 507.1, 603.1, 639.3, 863.1
retaliative 506.8
retaliatory 338.6, 506.8, 507.7, 863.5
retard 175.9, 428.7, 846.8, 1012.10
retardance 846.2
retardant 453.5
retardation 175.4, 428.1, 846.2, 922.9, 1012.1
retardative 453.5
retarded 175.12, 428.13, 846.16, 922.22
retardee 846.6
retardment 175.4, 922.9, 1012.1
retch 99.4, 909.26, 909.27
retching 909.8
retell 722.7, 849.8
retelling 722.1, 722.2, 849.2
retention 397.2, 442.1, 474.1, 803.3, 989.2
retention bonus 254.4
retentive 474.8, 803.12, 989.21
retentive memory 989.2
retentive mind 989.2
retentiveness 474.1, 989.2
retentivity 474.1, 989.2
rethink 931.15, 938.27
rethinking 931.5, 938.7
reticence 51.1, 139.3, 344.3, 494.2
reticency 344.3
reticent 344.10, 872.8
reticle 170.3
reticular 170.11
reticulate 47.15, 170.11
reticulated 170.11
reticulation 47.5, 170.3, 812.2
reticule 170.3
reticulum 170.3, 305.4
retiform 170.11
retimber 1069.18
retimbering 1069.14
retina 2.9
retinal 27.20
retinue 577.11, 769.6
retiracy 448.1
retire 22.17, 139.7, 163.6, 168.2, 188.9, 284.12, 344.6, 390.8, 447.4, 448.2, 583.4, 584.7, 624.13, 909.19
retired 345.13, 390.10, 402.5, 448.3, 584.8, 837.10
retired list 871.1
retired professor 571.3
retired reserves 461.25
retirees 304.4
retire from office 448.2
retire from sight 34.2, 346.8
retire from the world 584.7
retire into one's shell 139.7
retire into the shade 250.5, 583.4
retirement 163.2, 168.1, 188.1, 344.3, 345.2, 390.1, 402.1, 447.2, 448.1, 584.1, 624.1, 909.5
retirement age 303.5
retirement benefits 478.8
retirement community 1009.4
retirement fund 728.14
retirement home 1009.4
retirement plan 728.14
retirement village 1009.4
retiring 139.11, 168.5, 284.16, 344.10
retiring disposition 139.3, 325.2
retold 849.12
retold story 489.9, 974.3
retool 392.12, 1040.13
retooling 1040.11
retort (n) 489.7, 506.1, 599.3, 858.10, 900.5, 939.1, 1067.6 (v) 506.4, 939.4
retort an accusation 599.11
retouch 354.17, 392.11
retrace 938.27, 989.9

retrace one's steps 163.8, 938.27
retract 168.3, 335.4, 363.8, 445.2, 475.3
retractable 168.6
retractation 168.1, 335.2, 363.3
retracted 475.5
retractile 168.6
retractility 168.1
retraction 168.1, 255.2, 335.2, 363.3, 445.1, 475.1
retrahent 168.6
retral 163.11, 217.10
retread (n) 396.4 (v) 396.14, 458.19
retreading 396.4
retreat (n) 163.2, 168.1, 188.1, 197.8, 228.12, 252.2, 315.2, 346.4, 369.1, 433.2, 584.1, 584.6, 703.6, 859.1, 903.3, 1009.4, 1009.5 (v) 163.6, 168.2, 188.9, 204.10, 284.12, 362.7, 491.8, 903.7
retreating 168.5, 284.16
retreating market 737.5
retreat into 207.5
retreat into one's mind 931.12
retreat into one's shell 346.8
retreat into one's thoughts 931.12
retreatism 125.6
retreatist 125.7
retreat to immaturity 92.21
retreat to one's ivory tower 584.7
retrench 252.7, 255.9, 268.6, 428.7, 635.5
retrenched 252.10
retrenchment 252.4, 255.2, 268.3, 428.1, 635.2
retrial 598.5
retribution 481.2, 506.2, 604.1, 624.3
retributive 338.6, 481.7, 506.8, 604.22, 624.21
retributive justice 604.1, 649.1
retributory 506.8, 624.21
retrievability 396.9
retrievable 396.25
retrieval 396.2, 398.1, 481.3, 1042.8
retrieve (n) 481.3 (v) 176.16, 396.12, 398.3, 481.6
retriever 311.17
retro (n) 392.1, 396.3, 852.1 (a) 719.6, 837.8, 837.12
retroaction 163.1, 338.2, 859.1, 903.1
retroactionary 903.9
retroactive 163.11, 837.12, 859.7, 903.9
retrocede 163.5, 168.2, 859.4
retrocedence 168.1
retrocedent 168.4
retrocession 163.1, 393.3, 859.1
retrocessive 163.11
retro-chic 5.46
retro-fashion 5.1
retrofit 392.11
retrofitting 392.4
retroflection 163.1, 205.1
retroflex 163.5, 279.6
retroflexion 163.1, 205.1
retrogradation 163.1, 393.3, 859.1
retrograde (v) 163.5, 393.16, 393.18, 859.4 (a) 163.11, 217.9, 393.45, 779.7, 859.7
retrogress 163.5, 172.5, 217.8, 393.16, 393.18, 859.4
retrogression 163.1, 172.2, 393.3, 859.1
retrogressive 163.11, 172.8, 393.45, 859.7
retrorocket 1074.2, 1075.2, 1075.9
retrorse 859.7
retrospect (n) 989.3 (v) 989.9
retrospection 837.4, 989.3
retrospective (n) 348.2, 837.4 (a) 837.8, 837.12, 989.21
retrospective falsification 990.2
retroussé 193.15, 268.10, 279.9
retroverse 859.7
retroversion 205.1, 859.1
retrovert 859.4
retroverted 205.7
retrovirus 85.42
retrusion 163.1
retry 874.2
retund 286.2
return (n) 163.1, 186.3, 394.1, 396.8, 472.3, 481.1, 506.1, 624.2, 624.3, 738.7, 748.2, 849.1, 850.2, 859.1, 893.2, 903.1, 939.1, 1036.11 (v) 54.7, 163.5, 163.8, 396.11, 481.4, 627.4, 748.3, 849.11, 850.5, 859.4, 863.4, 939.4, 1036.16
returnable 859.7, 863.5
return answer 939.4
return a true bill 599.7
return a verdict 946.13
return a verdict of not guilty 601.4
return beam 1035.4
return blow for blow 506.6
returnee 859.3
return evil for evil 506.6
return for answer 939.4
returning (n) 859.1 (a) 849.13, 939.6
return like for like 506.6
return match 849.6
return of evil for evil 506.2
return on investment 738.7
returns 472.3, 549.7, 609.21, 627.1, 871.6
return signal 1036.11
return thanks 150.4, 696.13
return the compliment 506.4, 506.6, 863.4
return the favor 863.4
return the like 506.6
return to 221.9, 394.4, 856.6, 859.6
return to dust 307.18
return to life 306.9
return to mind 989.14
return to normal 396.1
return to reality (n) 977.1 (v) 977.3
return to the earth 307.18
return to the fold (n) 859.1 (v) 859.4
return to the soil 233.5
return to the starting point 914.5
reunion 465.3, 582.10
reunite 465.8
re-up 825.5
reupholster 295.29
reusable 387.18, 387.23
reuse 387.10
rev 174.10, 756.4
revalence 864.2
revaluate 931.15, 938.27
revaluation 728.23, 931.5, 938.7
revalue 728.26
revamp 392.12, 396.17, 852.7
revampment 392.4
revanche 507.1
revanchism 507.1
revanchist (n) 507.3 (a) 507.7
reveal 292.12, 348.5, 351.4, 351.5, 517.17, 861.7, 941.4, 1029.3
reveal a secret 351.6
revealed 31.6, 348.10, 351.9, 683.11
revealed truth 973.3
reveal gradually 861.7
revealing (n) 351.1 (a) 351.10, 1029.4
revealment 351.1
reveal oneself 33.8, 351.7
reveille 23.2, 314.1, 517.16
revel (n) 88.5, 95.3, 487.1, 743.6 (v) 88.28, 116.5, 743.24
Revelation 683.4
revelation 31.1, 33.1, 131.2, 348.1, 351.1
revelation 683.10, 861.2, 934.1, 941.1
revelational 348.9, 351.10, 683.11
revelatory 348.9, 351.10
reveler 88.11, 743.18
revel in 95.13
reveling 743.3
revel master 743.20
revelment 743.3
revelry 95.3, 582.3, 743.3
revels 743.3
revenant (n) 127.9, 988.1 (a) 849.13
revenge (n) 338.1, 506.2, 507.1 (v) 507.4
revengeful 506.8, 507.7
revengefulness 507.2
revenue 627.1
revenue enhancement 630.9
revenuer 630.10
revenue stream 472.3
reverberant 54.10, 54.12
reverberate 48.12, 50.14, 54.7, 849.11, 939.4
reverberating 54.10, 54.12
reverberation 54.2, 903.1, 939.1
reverberator 54.5
reverberatory (n) 742.5 (a) 54.12
reverberatory kiln 742.5
revere 104.20, 155.4, 696.11
revered 104.23, 155.11, 662.15
Reverence 648.2
reverence (n) 155.1, 155.2, 692.1, 696.1, 913.3 (v) 155.4, 696.11
reverenced 155.11
Reverend 648.5
reverend (n) 699.2 (a) 155.12, 662.15
Reverend, the (n) 699.2 (a) 648.8
reverend mother, the 699.17
reverend seriousness 580.1
reverend sir 304.2
reverent 155.9, 692.8, 696.16
reverential 155.9, 692.8, 696.16
reverential regard 155.1
reverie 92.19, 931.3, 985.2, 986.9
reversal 163.3, 205.1, 335.2, 342.1, 362.2, 363.1, 394.1, 412.2, 445.1, 473.1, 852.1, 858.1, 859.1, 1011.3
reversal of fortune 1011.3
reverse (n) 163.3, 205.4, 215.3, 217.1, 363.1, 394.1, 412.2, 859.1, 1011.3, 1040.9 (v) 163.7, 182.34, 205.5, 342.2, 445.2, 779.5, 858.11, 859.4 (a) 215.5, 779.6
reverse, the 779.2
reverse-angle shot 714.8
reverse-commute 724.10
reverse commuter 178.1
reversed 163.12, 205.7, 342.3
reversed feedback 1041.6
reverse discrimination 650.3
reverse-engineer 1043.4
reverse engineering 717.5
reverse equity 438.4
reverse gears 335.4
reverse image, the 779.2
reverseless 855.17
reversement 184.16
reverse mortgage 438.4
reverse oneself 335.4, 363.6, 852.7
reverse one's field 163.7
reverse order 807.2
reverse overlap 751.3
reverse shot 714.8
reverse split 738.2
reverse turn 184.16
reverse vending machine 736.4
reversibility 396.9
reversible 396.25, 859.7
reversible reaction 1038.8
reversification 523.1
reversing 163.3, 205.1
reversion 92.23, 163.3, 205.1, 394.1, 396.1, 479.2, 629.2, 859.1
reversional 481.7, 859.7
reversionary 481.7, 859.7
reversioner 479.5, 859.3
reversionist 363.5, 394.3, 859.3
reverso 554.12
revert 163.5, 205.5, 217.8, 394.4, 849.11, 859.4
reverted 205.7
revertible 481.7, 859.7
reverting 859.1
revert to 387.14, 394.4, 859.6
revest 396.11

revet 295.23
revetment 295.12
review (n) 541.6, 555.1, 556.2, 557.1, 557.2, 570.3, 722.1, 722.2, 723.2, 812.3, 849.2, 931.5, 938.3, 938.7, 946.2, 989.3 (v) 541.11, 556.5, 570.12, 570.14, 849.8, 931.15, 938.24, 938.27, 946.14, 989.9, 989.18
reviewer 547.15, 556.4, 704.27, 718.4, 723.4, 938.17, 946.7
review in retrospect 989.9
review of things past 989.3
revile 508.9, 510.19, 512.10, 513.7
revilement 510.7, 512.2, 513.2
reviling 510.22
revisable 392.17
revisal 392.4
revise (n) 392.4, 548.5 (v) 78.7, 392.12, 547.19, 938.27
revised edition 392.4
Revised Standard Version 683.2
Revised Version 683.2
revise one's thoughts 931.15
reviser 555.4
revision 78.1, 392.4, 938.7
revisional 78.14, 392.16
revisionism 392.5, 611.5, 868.2
revisionist (n) 392.6, 611.13 (a) 392.16, 611.21
revisit 221.9
revisory 392.16
revitalization 17.8
revitalize 396.16
revival 9.1, 17.8, 78.1, 392.1, 396.3, 481.3, 692.3, 696.8, 837.4, 852.1, 856.2, 858.2
revivalism 692.3
revivalist 696.9, 699.6
revival meeting 696.8
revive 9.2, 15.13, 78.7, 105.13, 109.9, 306.9, 392.11, 396.16, 396.20, 449.11, 481.6, 849.7, 852.6, 852.7, 856.6, 989.9
revived 9.4, 396.24, 837.8, 852.10
reviver 88.8
revivescence 9.1, 396.3
revivescency 9.1, 396.3
revivification 9.1, 15.5, 396.3, 852.1
revivify 9.2, 396.16
reviving 86.44
reviviscent 396.23
revocation 335.2, 445.1
revocative 335.5
revocatory 335.5
revoke (n) 445.1 (v) 335.4, 395.13, 445.2
revoked 445.3
revokement 445.1
revolt (n) 327.4, 453.1, 727.5, 852.2, 860.1, 900.1 (v) 98.11, 327.7, 453.3, 727.10, 860.4
revolt at 99.5
revolted 96.20
revolter 327.5
revolting 98.18, 1015.11
revolute 327.7
revolution (n) 205.2, 327.4, 392.5, 417.12, 418.2, 802.3, 850.3, 852.2, 860.1, 914.2, 915.1, 1073.16 (v) 327.7
revolutional 327.11
revolutionariness 860.2
revolutionary (n) 327.5, 392.6, 611.12, 671.9, 860.3 (a) 327.11, 337.5, 392.16, 611.20, 671.19, 852.10, 860.5, 860.6, 900.8
Revolutionary calendar 832.8
revolutionary change 852.2
revolutionary junta 860.3
revolutionary war 860.1
revolution control 1041.8
revolutionism 611.4, 860.2
revolutionist (n) 327.5, 418.3, 611.12, 860.3 (a) 611.20, 860.6
revolutionize 327.7, 337.4, 852.7, 852.9, 860.4
revolutionizer 860.3
revolutions 915.3
revolutions per minute 915.3
revolve 205.5, 850.5, 914.5, 915.9, 931.13
revolve around 208.9
revolver 462.10
revolve upon 959.6
revolving (n) 931.2 (a) 915.14
revolving bookcase 554.17
revolving bookstand 554.17
revolving door 915.4
revolving on 959.9
revolving stage 704.16
revs 915.3
revulsion 205.1, 903.1
revulsionary 860.5
revulsive 860.5, 903.9
rev up 405.13
revved up 405.16
reward (n) 307.1, 375.7, 506.2, 624.3, 646.2 (v) 506.5, 624.10
rewardful 624.21
rewarding 97.6, 387.22, 472.16, 624.21
rewardingness 472.4, 999.1
rewardless 391.12
rewarm 396.16
rewed 563.15
rewilding 397.1
reword 341.13, 849.8
rewording 341.3
rework 78.7, 392.12
reworking 78.1
rewrite (n) 392.4 (v) 392.12, 547.19
rewrite man 555.4
rewriter 555.4
rewriting 392.4, 547.2, 718.2
reynard 311.19, 415.6
rez-de-chaussée 197.23
RF amplification 1034.15
RF amplifier 1034.10
RF pulse 1036.10
RF signal 1034.10
RF stage 1034.10
RGB monitor 1042.9
Rhadamanthus 596.4, 649.4, 682.5
rhamphoid 279.8
Rh antigen 86.27
rhapsode 710.14, 720.12
rhapsodic 95.17, 720.16
rhapsodical 95.17, 720.16
rhapsodist 101.4, 710.14, 720.12, 986.13
rhapsodize 101.7, 986.16
Rhesus factor 2.25
rhetor 532.3, 543.6, 543.8
rhetoric 532.1, 532.2, 543.1, 544.1, 545.1, 568.3
rhetorical 543.12, 545.8
rhetoricalness 545.1
rhetorical question 938.10
rhetorician 532.3, 543.6, 543.8, 545.5
rhetorize 532.4
rhetorizer 532.3
rheum 2.24, 13.2, 85.9
rheumatic (n) 85.43 (a) 85.61
rheuminess 1061.1
rheumy 2.33, 13.7, 1061.4
Rh factor 2.25, 86.27
rhinal 2.32
rhinarium 283.8
rhinestone 498.6
rhino 311.4
rhinoceros 311.4
rhinoceros hide 94.3
rhinovirus 85.42
rhizanthous 310.38
rhizoid 310.36
rhizome 310.22, 310.33
Rh-negative 2.25
rhombal 278.9
rhombic 278.9
rhombohedral 278.9
rhomboid (n) 204.7 (a) 278.9
rhomboidal 278.9
rhombus 204.7
rhonchus 57.1
rhotacism 524.13, 525.5
Rh-positive 2.25
Rh-type 2.25
rhubarb 10.35, 53.4, 456.6, 457.4, 935.4
rhumb 161.3
rhumbline sailing 182.2
rhyme (n) 720.1, 720.4, 720.9, 784.6, 849.4 (v) 720.15, 784.9
rhymed 849.15
rhymer 720.13
rhyme royal 720.9, 720.10
rhyme scheme 720.9
rhymester 720.13
rhyming 720.18, 784.17, 849.15
rhyming dictionary 720.9
rhyming slang 523.21
Rhynchocephalia 311.24
rhythm 524.10, 533.2, 709.22, 720.7, 850.2, 916.3
rhythm-and-blues 708.9
rhythmic 708.49, 709.28, 720.17, 850.7, 916.18
rhythmical 709.28, 720.17, 850.7
rhythmical accent 709.25
rhythmical accentuation 709.25
rhythmical stress 524.10
rhythmic pattern 524.10, 709.22
rhythmic phrase 709.22
rhythmic play 916.5
rhythmics 709.1
rhythmometer 711.22
rialto 230.8, 736.2
riant 109.11
rib 283.3, 563.8
ribald (n) 497.6 (a) 497.11, 513.8, 666.9
ribaldness 497.2
ribaldry 497.2, 513.3, 666.4
riband 646.5
ribband 271.4
ribbed 290.4, 294.7
ribbing 490.3
ribbon (n) 271.4, 549.12, 646.5, 1025.5 (v) 498.9
ribbon of light 1025.5
ribby 745.4
rib cage 2.2
ribonucleic acid 305.9
ribosomal RNA 305.9
ribosome 305.5
rib roast 10.14, 10.15
ribs 10.17
rib tickler 489.6
rice 10.36
rice paddy 1069.9
rice paper 1050.2
ricer 1063.4
rice syrup 66.3
rich 8.33, 35.19, 54.10, 63.9, 66.6, 488.5, 498.12, 618.14, 632.10, 708.48, 890.9, 983.19, 991.7, 1056.9
rich, the 618.6
rich and powerful 618.14
Richard Roe 527.8
rich as Croesus 618.14
rich-colored 35.19
richen 618.9, 890.8
richener 890.4
richening 890.11
riches 618.1
rich-flavored 63.9
rich harvest 991.2
rich imagination 986.3
richling 618.7
rich lode 618.4
richly deserve 639.5
richly deserved 639.9
rich man 611.15, 618.7
rich man's panic 737.22
rich media 1042.19
richness 35.4, 54.1, 63.2, 488.1, 498.2, 618.1, 632.1, 890.1, 991.2, 1056.5
richness of meaning 539.1
rich ore 406.5
rich person 618.7
rich-rich 618.15
rich soil 890.6
rich uncle 618.4
rich vein 406.5, 991.2
rich woman 618.7
rick (n) 386.1, 386.6, 770.10 (v) 770.19
ricketiness 16.3, 303.5, 804.2
ricketish 16.16
rickets 85.33
rickettsia 85.42
rickety 16.16, 85.61, 265.12, 303.18, 804.5
rickrack 289.2
ricksha 179.3
ricochet (n) 903.2 (v) 859.5, 903.6

rictus 265.4, 917.3
rid 430.31
riddance 369.1, 475.1, 773.2
riddle (n) 79.13, 170.3, 522.7, 522.9, 808.5, 930.6, 971.3 (v) 292.15, 308.18, 517.19, 522.10, 773.6, 808.11, 904.12, 940.2
riddled 292.19
riddle of the Sphinx 522.9, 799.2
riddling (n) 79.4, 940.1 (a) 522.17
ride (n) 177.7, 457.12, 743.15 (v) 96.13, 156.6, 177.33, 177.34, 182.16, 182.40, 182.54, 490.6, 508.8, 901.22
ride a broomstick 690.10
ride and tie 916.13
ride a storm 182.40
ride at anchor 182.16, 331.16
ride bareback 177.34
ride down 910.7
ride easy 182.16
ride for a fall 493.6
ride full tilt against 459.18
ride hard 177.34
ride hawse full 182.16
ride herd 417.13, 425.4, 612.14
ride herd on 573.10, 1008.19, 1070.8
ride high 298.8
ride it out 855.11
ride off in all directions at once 105.16
ride on a rail 604.15, 909.14
ride out 182.40, 757.5, 1007.2
ride out a storm 182.40
ride over 612.15, 910.7
rider 178.8, 253.1, 254.2, 311.13, 613.9, 757.2
ride roughshod 424.7
ride roughshod over 412.10, 612.15, 910.7
ride shank's mare 177.27
ride shotgun 1008.18
ride the beam 184.37
ride the gravy train 402.4, 1010.10
ride the high horse 141.8
ride the hobnail express 177.27
ride the pine 747.4
ride the sea 182.54
ride the shank's pony 177.27
ride the shoeleather 177.27
ride the skies 184.36
ride to a fall 661.7
ride to hounds 382.9
ridge (n) 198.2, 198.7, 217.3, 237.5, 272.4, 283.3, 291.3, 317.4 (v) 283.12, 291.6
ridged 291.8
ridgeline 237.5
ridgeling 757.2
ridgepole 198.1, 295.6
ridge runner 227.10
ridic 488.5
ridicule (n) 142.2, 156.1, 157.1, 490.1, 508.1, 510.2, 512.5 (v) 142.7, 156.4, 157.3, 489.13, 508.8, 510.12, 512.12
ridiculing 156.7, 508.12, 510.22, 512.13
ridiculous 488.4, 923.11, 955.10, 967.7
ridiculously like 784.15
ridiculousness 488.1, 923.3
riding 177.6, 231.5
riding at anchor 173.13
riding horse 311.13
rid of 430.31
rid oneself of 374.3, 390.7, 475.3, 773.5
ridonkulous 488.5
rife 552.15, 864.12, 864.13, 884.9, 991.7
rifeness 864.2, 884.1
riff (n) 238.10, 708.27 (v) 708.43, 909.19
riffle (n) 238.10, 238.14 (v) 811.3
riffraff 80.9, 391.5, 497.6, 606.3
rifle (n) 461.6, 461.9, 462.10 (v) 290.3, 482.17, 938.33
rifle ball 462.19
rifled 290.4
rifleman 461.6, 461.9, 904.8
rifler 483.6
rifling 290.1, 482.6
rift (n) 224.2, 237.7, 456.4, 802.4, 1003.2, 1004.1 (v) 292.11 (a) 224.7
rift valley 237.7
rig (n) 5.2, 5.6, 5.9, 179.5, 179.12, 180.12, 385.4, 575.9 (v) 5.41, 354.17, 381.9, 385.8, 965.5
rigamarole 520.2
rigatoni 10.33
rig for diving 182.47
rigged 180.17, 354.30, 385.13, 965.8
rigged game 965.2
rigged jury 965.2
rigged market 737.6
rigged-out 5.45
rigger 185.6, 1032.22
rigging 180.12, 271.3, 381.5, 385.4, 737.20, 901.2
right (n) 219.1, 417.1, 430.2, 471.4, 600.6, 609.24, 611.9, 637.1, 639.2, 642.1, 649.1, 653.1, 737.21, 973.5 (v) 396.13, 788.7, 808.8 (a) 219.4, 277.6, 496.9, 579.5, 637.3, 644.13, 649.7, 687.7, 788.10, 925.4, 973.16, 995.5
right-about 163.3, 363.1
right about-face 859.1
right-about-face (n) 163.3, 363.1 (v) 163.10
right-about turn 363.1
right amount 991.1
right and proper 637.3, 649.7
right angle 200.2, 278.2
right-angle 200.12, 278.7
right-angled 200.12, 278.7
right-angledness 200.1, 278.1
right-angular 200.12, 278.7
right-angularity 200.1
right ascension 300.5
right as rain 644.14, 1002.8
right back 752.2
right belief 687.1
right bower 758.2
right brain 2.15
right conduct 653.1
right defenseman 749.2
right doctrine 687.1
righteous 637.3, 644.13, 653.5, 692.9
righteous, the 692.5
righteous indignation 152.4
righteousness 637.2, 644.1, 653.1, 692.2
right fence 750.2
right field 219.1
right fielder 745.2
right forward 747.2
rightful 637.3, 639.8, 649.7, 673.11, 973.15
rightful authority 417.1
right fullback 749.5
rightfulness 637.1, 649.1, 673.1
rightful succession 417.12
right guard 747.2
right half 752.2
right halfback 749.5
right hand 576.1, 616.7
right-hand 218.7, 219.4, 449.21
right-handed 219.5
right-handedness 219.2
right-hander 219.3, 745.2
right-hand man 432.5, 577.3, 577.4, 616.7
right-hand pitcher 745.2
right-hand woman 616.7
Right Honorable, the 648.8
righting 658.7
right in the head 925.4
rightism 611.1, 853.3
rightist 611.9, 853.4
right itself 396.21
right joint 759.19
right line 277.2
right mind 925.1
right-minded 644.13
rightminded 637.3, 653.5
rightmindedness 637.2
right moment 843.5
right mood 324.1
rightmost 219.4
rightness 219.2, 496.2, 637.1, 637.2, 649.1, 687.1, 843.1, 973.5, 995.1
right of angary 480.5
right-of-center 219.4, 265.10, 611.17
right of common 471.4
right of eminent domain 480.5
right of entry 471.4
right of preemption 733.2
right of put and call 737.21
right of the strong, the 424.2
right of use 387.7
right of way 383.3
right-of-way 249.1, 383.5
right people 578.6
right people, the 894.2
right person for the job 413.14
Right Reverend 699.2
Right Reverend, the 648.8
rights 430.2
right side 219.1
right side of, the 587.3
right smart spell 827.4
rights of citizenship 642.3
rights of man 642.3
rights of minorities 642.3
rights of women 642.4
right sort 659.1
right stuff, the 413.4
right taste 63.1
right thing, the 637.1, 649.2, 653.1
right things, the 579.2
right thing to do, the 637.1
right thinking 496.2, 935.10
right-thinking 496.9, 579.5, 637.3, 653.5, 687.7
right-to-life 86.23
right to vote 371.6, 609.17
right wing 219.1, 611.1, 611.9
right-wing 219.4, 611.17, 853.8
right-wing conspiracy 609.24
right-winger 219.1, 609.27, 611.9, 853.4
right-wingish 219.4
right wingman 749.2
right word, the 533.1
right word at the right time 533.1
right word in the right place, the 533.1
righty 219.3, 745.2
rigid 15.18, 339.12, 361.9, 425.7, 580.9, 853.7, 855.15, 973.17, 1046.11
rigid airship 181.11
rigid control 92.24
rigid discipline 425.1
rigidification 1046.5
rigidified 1046.13
rigidify 1046.9
rigidity 359.2, 361.2, 425.2, 853.1, 855.3, 973.5, 1046.2
rigidness 425.2, 580.1, 1046.2
rigid supports 630.5
rigling 757.2
rigmarole 520.2
rigor 17.5, 339.3, 425.2, 667.1, 671.1, 917.2, 973.5, 1011.1, 1013.1, 1023.1, 1046.2
rigorism 361.2
rigorist 425.7
rigoristic 425.7, 667.4
rigor mortis 307.1
rigorous 17.14, 339.12, 361.9, 425.7, 667.4, 671.16, 973.17, 1011.13, 1013.17, 1023.14
rigorousness 339.3, 425.2, 973.5, 1013.1
rig out 5.41, 385.8
rig-out 5.2
rig the market 737.25
rig up 5.41, 385.8
Rig-Veda 683.8
rile 96.13, 152.24, 917.10
riled 96.21, 152.27
riled up 152.28
rilievo stiacciato 715.3
rill 238.1
rillet 238.1
rim (n) 211.4, 237.2, 280.4 (v) 211.10
rim clutch 1040.10
rime 1023.7
rimed 1023.17
rime frost 1023.7
rime-frosted 1023.17

rime-gray 39.4
rime riche 720.9
rimming 211.11
rim of the horizon 201.4
rimose 290.4
rimple (n) 291.3 (v) 291.6
rimpled 291.8
rind 206.2, 276.1, 295.3, 296.2
rinderpest 85.41
rindle 238.1
ring (n) 54.3, 280.2, 280.3, 283.3, 347.13, 463.1, 498.6, 617.1, 617.6, 647.1, 647.4, 754.1, 1025.14, 1038.7 (v) 53.7, 54.8, 188.13, 209.7, 347.19
ring, the 457.9, 754.1
ring a bell 903.8
ring around the moon 133.5, 1025.14
ring around the sun 1025.14
ring bearer 563.4
ring changes 54.8, 783.2
ring doorbells 609.40
ringdove 710.23
ring down the curtain 704.28
ringe 211.10
ringed 209.11, 210.6
ringent 292.18
ringer 357.6, 862.2
ring false 354.15
ring finger 73.5
ring in 186.6, 818.11, 832.12, 862.4
ringing (n) 54.3 (a) 53.11, 54.13
ringing in the ear 54.3
ringing of the ear 54.3
ringing up 253.3
ring in the ear 48.12, 54.8
ring in the ears 53.7
ringleader 375.11, 574.6, 610.7
ringlet 3.5, 280.5, 281.2
ringlike 280.11
ringliness 280.1
ringmaster 575.4, 704.23, 707.3
ring nebula 1073.7
ring off 347.19, 857.6
ring one's praises 509.12
ring out 832.12
ring peals 54.8
rings 725.7
ring-shape 280.1
ring-shaped 280.11
ringside 27.8
ringside seat 27.8, 223.6
ring the bell 409.9
ring the changes 780.5, 852.7, 854.5
ring the tocsin 400.3
ringtone 54.4, 55.1
ring true 973.9
ring up 347.19
ring up the curtain 704.28
ring with the praises of 509.15
ringy-dingy 347.13
rink 743.11, 749.1, 750.3
rinky-dink 998.21
rinse (n) 79.5, 79.17 (v) 79.19, 1065.13
rinse off 79.19
rinse out 79.19
rinsing 79.5, 1065.6
rinsings 391.4
riot (n) 327.4, 418.2, 457.5, 489.6, 671.3, 810.4, 991.2 (v) 310.34, 327.7, 457.13, 671.11, 810.10
riot control agent 462.22
rioter 327.5, 461.1
riot in 95.13
rioting 671.3
riot of color 35.4, 47.1
riotous 310.43, 327.11, 418.5, 430.24, 669.8, 671.19, 991.7, 993.19
riotous living 669.2
riotousness 322.1, 327.3, 430.3, 991.2
riot police 1008.17
rip (n) 85.38, 88.6, 156.3, 238.13, 403.3, 665.10, 802.4 (v) 96.18, 156.6, 174.9, 292.11, 393.13, 480.22
rip apart 802.14
riparial 234.7
riparian 234.7
riparious 234.7
rip cord 181.13
ripe (v) 407.8 (a) 133.17, 303.13, 405.16, 407.13, 413.28, 563.20, 794.9, 843.9, 1002.9
ripe age 303.2
ripe for instruction 570.18
ripe idea 931.5
ripen 12.15, 14.2, 259.7, 303.9, 392.10, 407.8, 861.5, 1002.5
ripened 303.13, 413.28, 1002.9
ripeness 303.2, 405.4, 407.2, 563.2, 843.1
ripening (n) 303.6, 392.2, 861.1 (a) 301.10
ripen into 858.17
ripe old age 303.5
riper years 303.2
ripe wisdom 920.5
rip from 480.22
rip into 457.14, 459.15, 510.14
rip off 482.16, 632.7
rip-off 354.13, 356.7
ripoff (n) 356.9, 482.4, 632.5 (a) 480.25
rip on 156.6
rip open 224.4, 292.11, 292.14, 351.4
riposte (n) 489.7, 600.2, 760.4, 939.1 (v) 600.10, 903.5, 939.4
rip out 192.10
rip out an oath 513.6
ripped 87.24, 88.33, 96.25
ripped off 482.23
ripping (n) 192.6, 802.2 (a) 999.13
ripping bar 906.4
ripping out 160.1, 192.1
ripple (n) 52.5, 238.10, 238.14, 288.2, 291.3, 403.3 (v) 52.11, 291.6, 917.10
rippled 291.8
ripple effect 171.1, 171.2, 221.3, 259.1, 771.1, 886.3
ripple of applause 52.5
ripple of laughter 52.5
rippling 52.19
ripply 288.6
riprap 901.6
rip-roaring 53.13, 671.18
rip-roaring drunk 88.33
riptide 238.13
rip to pieces 802.14
rip to shreds 802.14
rip up 112.19, 793.6
ris de veau 10.15
rise (n) 33.1, 193.1, 200.5, 204.6, 237.2, 237.4, 238.14, 251.1, 272.2, 392.1, 446.1, 861.1, 886.5, 903.1 (v) 23.6, 33.8, 53.7, 172.5, 193.8, 200.8, 204.10, 238.22, 251.6, 272.10, 298.9, 327.7, 409.10, 818.13
rise above 134.7, 247.5, 272.11, 411.5
rise again 306.9
rise and fall 238.22
rise and shine 23.6
rise from 887.5
rise from the grave 306.9
rise in the mind 931.18
rise in the world 409.10, 1010.9
risen from the ranks 606.8
rise of the tide 238.13
rise on the hind legs 200.8
riser 193.5
rise to a point of order 333.4
rise to mind 931.18
rise to the fly 903.5, 954.6
rise to the occasion 328.7, 365.8, 409.13, 991.4
rise to the surface 190.11
rise up 193.8, 200.8, 272.12, 327.7
rise up in arms 327.7, 458.15
rishi 921.1
risibility 116.4, 489.11
risible 109.15, 488.4
rising (n) 33.1, 85.37, 172.2, 193.1, 200.5, 204.6, 283.4, 327.4 (a) 172.8, 193.14, 204.17, 251.8
rising action 722.4
rising generation 302.2, 561.1
rising ground 204.6, 272.2
rising market 737.4
rising of the curtain 33.1, 818.1
rising prices 630.4, 632.3
rising star 707.2, 707.6
rising terminal 524.9
rising tide 238.13
rising to the surface 190.1
rising vote 371.6
risk (n) 729.4, 759.2, 971.6, 972.1, 1006.1 (v) 729.17, 759.24, 972.12, 1006.6, 1006.7
risk all 493.6
risk assuming 951.11
risk capital 728.15, 737.19
riskful 1006.10
riskiness 971.6, 1006.2
risking 759.1
riskless 1007.5
risklessness 1007.1
risk one's life 1006.7
risk one's neck 972.12, 1006.7
risk stating 951.11
risk-taking (n) 454.1, 492.4, 972.1 (a) 493.9
risky 666.7, 759.27, 971.20, 972.15, 1006.10
risky thing 759.2
risotto 10.36
risqué 513.8, 666.7
ritardando (n) 708.25 (a) 708.54
rite 373.1, 487.1, 580.4
ritenuto 708.25
rite of confession 351.3
rite of passage 580.4, 701.9
rites 504.7
ritornel 849.5
ritornello 708.24
ritual (n) 373.1, 373.5, 580.1, 580.4, 701.3 (a) 580.8, 701.18
ritual bathing 701.9
ritual cleaning 701.9
ritual contamination 80.4
ritual impurity 80.4
ritualism 580.2, 701.1
ritualist 701.2
ritualistic 580.8, 701.18
ritualistic manual 701.10
rituality 580.1, 701.1, 701.3
ritualization 701.1
ritualize 580.5, 701.14
ritual killing 308.1
ritually clean 79.25
ritually contaminated 80.20
ritually immerse 79.19
ritually impure 80.20
ritually pure 79.25
ritually unclean 80.20
ritual murder 308.1
ritual observance 487.1, 701.3
rituals 504.7
ritual suicide 308.5
ritual uncleanness 80.4
ritziness 501.5
ritz it 501.14
ritzy 501.21, 578.13
rival (n) 452.2, 461.1, 589.6 (v) 451.4, 457.18, 790.5, 943.7, 999.11 (a) 451.8, 457.23
rivaling 249.12, 457.23
rivalrous 457.23
rivalrousness 457.1
rivalry 154.1, 451.2, 457.2
rive 224.4, 292.11, 802.11
riven 224.7, 802.23, 875.6
river 238.1, 238.5
riverain 234.7
riverbed 199.4, 239.2
river boulder 1059.5
river gambler 759.21
riverhead 238.2, 886.6
river horse 311.4
riverine 182.58, 234.7, 238.23
riverlike 238.23
river of death 307.3
River of Fire 682.4
River of Forgetfulness 682.4
river of oblivion 990.1
River of Wailing 682.4
River of Woe 682.4
river pilot 574.7
riverscape 33.6, 712.11
riverside (n) 234.2 (a) 234.7
riverway 239.2
rivery 238.23
rivet 800.8
riveted 855.14, 983.18
riveting 377.8, 983.20
rivet one 377.6

rivet one's attention 983.11
rivet one's eyes upon 27.15
riviera 234.2
rivose 281.6
rivulation 281.1
rivulet 238.1
rivulose 281.6
RNA 560.6
roach 87.12, 311.36
roach paste 1001.3
roach powder 1001.3
road 182.10, 242.1, 383.1, 383.5, 1009.6
road agent 483.5
roadbed 383.7, 901.7
roadblock 379.2, 1012.5
roadbook 574.10
road circuit 756.1
road course 756.1
road dog 588.4
road hog 178.10, 651.3
road horse 311.13
roadhouse 228.15, 743.13
roadkill 1006.3
road map 574.10
road racing 744.1
road rage 105.9
roads 242.1, 1009.6
roadside cafe 8.17
roadside stand 736.3
roadstead 242.1, 1009.6
roadster 311.13
road test 942.3
road-test 942.8
road to hell 654.7
road to ruin, the 395.1
road to wrack and ruin, the 395.1
road trip 177.5
road warrior 178.1, 730.4
roadway 383.5, 383.7
road-weary 177.41
roadwork 84.2
roadworthiness 1007.1
roadworthy 176.18, 1007.7
roam (n) 177.3 (v) 177.23
roamer 178.2
roaming (n) 177.3 (a) 177.37
roan (n) 311.11 (a) 40.4
roanoke 728.3
roar (n) 53.3, 56.4, 59.1 (v) 53.9, 56.9, 59.6, 60.2, 116.8, 318.20, 524.25, 671.11, 704.31
roarer 311.12
roaring 56.12, 105.25
roaring drunk 88.33
roaring fire 1019.13
roaring forties 231.3, 318.9
roaring mad 152.30
roaring success 409.4
roaring trade 1010.5
Roaring Twenties 824.5
roar like a bull 59.6
roar of laughter 116.4
roar with laughter 116.8
roast (n) 10.7, 10.13, 487.1 (v) 11.5, 156.6, 490.6, 508.8, 510.20, 938.22, 1019.22, 1020.17 (a) 11.7
roast beef 10.14
roasted 11.7
roaster 311.28, 1019.8
roasting (n) 11.2, 490.3, 508.1, 510.4, 510.6 (a) 508.12, 1019.25
roasting hot 1019.25
rob 482.14
robbed of 473.8
robbed of illusion 977.5
robber 483.1, 483.5, 593.1
robber baron 730.1
robbery 473.1, 482.3
robbing 482.3
robe (n) 5.3, 5.21, 295.10, 702.2 (v) 5.39
robed 5.45
robe of royalty 647.3
robe of state 647.3
robes 5.1, 702.1
robes of office 647.3
robing 5.1
Robin Goodfellow 680.7
Robin Hood 143.8, 478.11
robin's-egg blue 45.3
robocall 347.19
robomb 1074.4
rob one of ease 126.4
rob one of one's illusions 977.2
rob one of rest 126.4
rob one of sleep 126.4
roborant (n) 86.8 (a) 81.5, 86.44
robot 349.6, 1040.4, 1041.12, 1041.18
robot bomb 1074.4
robot control 1041.3
robot-control 1041.20
robot factory 739.3, 1041.5
robotics 1042.20
robotization 1041.1, 1041.3
robotize 1041.20
robotized 1041.22
robotlike 781.5
robot satellite 1075.6
robot specialist 1041.19
robot system 1041.5
rob Peter to pay Paul 862.4
robust 15.15, 17.13, 83.12
robust health 83.2
robustious 15.15, 83.12
robustness 15.1, 17.4, 83.3
robustuous 83.12
Rochdale cooperative 617.1
rock (n) 15.8, 87.7, 87.20, 462.18, 708.10, 855.6, 916.6, 917.8, 1008.5, 1046.6, 1059.1, 1059.6 (v) 93.15, 105.14, 182.55, 670.7, 916.10, 917.15 (a) 708.51, 1059.11
rockabilly 708.10
rock-and-roll 708.10
rock-and-roll singer 710.13
rock bottom 199.1, 901.6
rock-bottom 199.7, 274.8, 275.12, 275.16, 633.9
rock-bottom prices 633.2
rockbound 288.7, 425.7
rockbound coast 234.2, 1006.5
rock climber 193.6
rock climbing 760.6
rock cycle 1059.8
rocked 902.24
Rockefeller 618.8
rocker 79.13, 122.2, 713.8, 916.9
rocket (n) 174.6, 181.4, 193.7, 462.18, 517.15, 1043.3, 1074.2, 1074.3, 1075.2 (v) 193.9, 193.10, 1074.12 (a) 904.17
rocket bomb 1074.4
rocketborne 1075.13
rocket debris 1075.10
rocketeer 1074.11, 1075.8
rocket engine 1074.2, 1075.4
rocket engineer 185.6, 1074.11
rocket engineering 1074.1
rocketer 1074.11
rocket exhaust 1074.2
rocket firing 1074.9
rocket fuel 87.18
rocket glider 181.12
rocket gun 1074.10
rocketing up 193.1
rocket laboratory 1074.6
rocket launcher 462.21, 1074.10
rocket launching 1074.9
rocket motor 181.1, 1074.2
rocket pilot 1075.8
rocket plane 181.4
rocket power 18.4, 184.25
rocket program 1074.1
rocket-propelled 184.50, 904.16
rocket propulsion 184.25, 1074.8, 1075.9
rocket research 1074.1
rocketry 462.3, 1074.1, 1075.1, 1075.9
rocket science 1074.1
rocket scientist 413.12, 929.1, 1074.11
rocket ship 181.4, 1075.2
rocket society 1075.9
rocket technician 1074.11
rocket technology 1074.1
rocket testing 1074.1
rocket thruster 1074.2, 1075.2
rocket to the moon 1075.12
rock face 760.6
rock festival 708.32
rock-fill dam 1012.5
rock formation 1059.1
rock-hard 361.9, 1046.10
rock-hardness 1046.1
rock hound 1071.2
rock hounding 1071.1
rock hunter 1071.2
rock hunting 1071.1
Rockies 231.7
rockiness 85.1
rocking 670.15, 916.17
rocking chair 229.1, 916.9
rocking horse 743.16
rocking stone 916.9
rock-jock 193.6
rocklike 361.9, 853.7, 855.12, 1046.10, 1059.12
rockman 1058.9
rock music 708.10
rock musician 710.2
rock 'n' roll 708.10
rock 'n' roll musician 710.2
Rock of Gibraltar 855.6, 1009.1
rock oil 1056.4
rock on 322.4
rock out 708.38
rock pile 604.2
rock plant 310.33
rock-ribbed 361.9, 1059.12
rocks 2.13, 728.2, 1006.5
rocks ahead 1006.1
rock singer 710.13
rock solid 853.7
rock-steady 129.2
rock-strewn 1059.12
rock-studded 1059.12
rock the boat 868.4
rock the sky 53.7
rock to sleep 22.20, 670.7
rockweed 310.4
rocky 16.16, 21.7, 85.56, 288.7, 1006.11, 1046.10, 1059.12
Rocky Mountain canary 311.15
rococo (n) 498.2 (a) 498.12, 870.13, 986.20
rod 273.1, 417.9, 462.10, 605.2, 647.3, 1040.5
rodent (n) 311.3 (a) 311.44
rodential 311.44
rodenticide 1001.3
rodeo 770.1
rodlike 1046.11
rodman 593.4
rod of empire 647.3
rodomontade (n) 502.1, 503.1, 520.2, 545.2 (v) 543.10
rods 1038.13
rod vision 27.1
roe 10.24, 77.9, 305.15, 311.5
roebuck 311.5
roe deer 311.5
roentgen 1037.6
roentgenize 91.26
roentgenogram 91.9, 714.6
roentgenograph (n) 91.9, 714.6 (v) 714.14
roentgenography 1037.8
roentgenology 1037.8
roentgenoscopy 1037.8
rogation 440.2, 696.4
Roget's 526.13, 554.9, 871.4
rogue 311.12, 322.3, 660.3, 757.2
roguery 322.2, 645.2
rogue's badge 30.5
rogues' gallery 714.3
rogue's march 909.5
rogue wave 238.14
roguish 322.6, 489.17, 645.17
roguishness 322.2, 489.4, 645.2
roid rage 152.10
roil (n) 917.1, 1031.1 (v) 96.13, 152.24, 810.10, 915.12, 917.10
roiled 96.21, 1031.3
roiledness 1031.1
roily 810.13, 1031.3
roister 503.3, 743.24, 810.10
roisterer 503.2
roistering 503.4
roisterous 503.4, 671.20
Roland 492.7
Roland for an Oliver, a 506.3
role 387.5, 704.10, 706.3, 724.3, 765.4
role model 659.4, 1002.4
role-model 786.4
role-play 349.12, 704.30
role-player 357.1
role-playing 704.8
role-playing game 743.9
role reversal 163.3, 852.1, 858.1

roll (n) 10.31, 55.1, 56.4, 177.12, 184.14, 238.14, 267.2, 281.2, 282.4, 549.1, 549.5, 714.10, 728.17, 759.9, 770.8, 871.6, 915.1, 916.6, 917.8 (v) 54.7, 55.4, 56.9, 60.5, 89.14, 162.2, 177.18, 177.28, 182.55, 184.40, 201.6, 238.22, 282.7, 287.5, 287.6, 287.9, 482.16, 904.9, 915.10, 915.13, 916.10, 917.15, 1014.10
roll about 850.5
roll around 850.5
roll back 252.7, 635.5
rollback 163.1, 252.4, 631.1, 635.2
roll bar 756.1
roll by 821.5
roll cage 756.1
roll call 613.6, 871.6
rolled 201.7
rolled into one 872.10
roller 86.33, 238.14, 282.4, 287.4, 745.3, 915.4, 916.4, 1051.7
roller bandage 86.33
roller bearing 915.7, 1040.5
rollerblade 177.35
Rollerblading 744.1
roller coaster 743.15
rollercoaster (n) 854.4 (a) 854.6
roller hockey 744.1
roller-skate 177.35
roller skates 179.21
roller skating 744.1
roll flat 201.6
rollick (n) 743.5 (v) 116.5, 503.3, 743.23
rollicker 743.18
rollicking 109.14, 503.4, 671.20
rollicksome 109.14
rollicksomeness 109.4
rollicky 109.14
roll in 186.6, 472.13, 669.4, 991.5
roll-in 749.6
rolling (n) 162.1, 184.13, 904.2, 915.1, 1035.5 (a) 54.10, 56.12, 237.8, 272.18, 281.10, 915.14, 916.17
rolling bones 759.8
rolling country 237.1, 272.3
rolling friction 1044.1
rolling in it 618.15
rolling in money 618.15
rolling-key clutch 1040.10
rolling on 162.1
rolling pin 282.4
rolling stock 179.14
rolling stone 178.2, 852.1, 854.4, 915.4
roll in it 618.12
roll in the aisles 116.8
roll in the dirt 80.14
roll in the dust 432.9
roll in the lap of luxury 1010.10
roll in the mud 80.14
roll into one 800.5, 805.3, 945.3
roll it 818.7
roll logs 613.10
roll of coins 728.4
roll of the dead 307.13
roll of the dice 759.2
roll of the wheel 759.2
roll on 162.2, 162.3, 177.18, 821.5
roll-on roll-off ship 180.1
roll on the tongue 62.7
roll out 23.6, 348.5
rollout 184.8
roll out the red carpet 155.5, 187.10, 585.9, 646.8
roll over 729.17
roll over and play dead 354.21
rolls 549.1
roll smooth 287.5
Rolls-Royce 249.4
roll the bones 759.23
roll the stone of Sisyphus 391.8
roll under the tongue 95.13
roll up 260.8, 770.20, 915.10
roll up into a ball 260.8
roll up one's sleeves 405.13, 725.15
roll with the punches 106.9, 134.7
Rolodex 871.7
roly-poliness 257.8
roly-poly (n) 257.12 (a) 257.18
Roman 546.8
Roman 675.29
roman 548.6
roman 722.3
Roman alphabet 349.1
Roman archaeology 842.4
Roman calendar 832.8
Roman candle 517.15
Roman Catholic (n) 675.19 (a) 675.29
Roman Catholic Church 675.8
Roman Catholicism 675.8
romance (n) 104.5, 706.2, 986.5, 986.7 (v) 104.18, 722.7, 986.16
romancer 722.5, 986.13
Romanche Trench 275.5
Roman Christianity 675.7
romancing 986.24
romancist 722.5
Roman Corinthian 198.6
Roman Doric 198.6
Roman eagle 647.6
Romanesque 198.6
Roman holiday 308.4
Roman Ionic 198.6
Romanism 675.8
Romanist 675.19
romanization 546.5
Roman-nosed 279.8
Roman numerals 1017.4
romantic (n) 986.13 (a) 93.21, 104.26, 722.8, 986.24
romantic bond 104.5
romantic comedy 1035.2
romanticism 93.8, 104.2, 986.7
romanticist 986.13
romanticize 986.16
romanticized 722.8, 986.24
romanticized version 354.10
romanticizing (n) 986.7 (a) 986.24
romantic lead 704.10, 706.3, 707.2
romantic lighting 1027.2
romantic love 104.2
romantic melancholy 112.5
romantic tie 104.5
romcom 1035.2
Rome 675.8
romedy 1035.2
Romeo 104.12
Romeo and Juliet 104.17
Romish 675.29
romp (n) 76.9, 302.8, 411.1, 743.5, 757.3 (v) 109.6, 116.5, 366.6, 743.23
rompers 5.30
romp home 411.4
romp in 757.5
rompish 76.14, 109.14, 743.29
rompishness 109.4
romp through 401.5
rondeau 280.9, 708.19
rondelet 280.9
rondelle 280.2
rondino 280.9, 708.19
rondo 280.9, 708.19
rondo form 709.11
rondoletto 708.19
rondure 279.1, 280.2, 282.2
rood 170.4
rood altar 703.12
rood arch 703.10
rood cloth 703.10
rood loft 703.9
rood screen 703.10
rood spire 703.9
rood stair 703.9
rood steeple 703.9
rood tower 703.9
rood tree 170.4
roof (n) 198.1, 228.1, 228.2, 228.5, 295.6 (v) 295.21
roofage 295.6, 1054.2
roof-deck 295.6
roofed 198.13, 295.31
roofed-in 295.31
roofed-over 295.31
roof garden 295.6
roof in 295.21
roofing 295.6, 1054.2
roof of the world, the 237.6
roof over 295.21
roof over one's head 228.1
roofpole 198.1, 295.6
rooftop 198.1, 295.6
rooftree 228.2, 295.6
rook (n) 743.17, 759.22 (v) 356.19, 759.26
rookery 80.11, 228.23, 886.8
rookie 461.18, 572.9, 774.4, 818.2
room (n) 158.3, 197.1, 224.1, 228.4, 228.13, 257.2, 430.4, 843.2 (v) 225.7, 225.10
room and board 385.3
room-and-pillar mining 1058.8
room decoration 498.1
room decorator 716.11
roomer 227.8, 470.4
roomette 179.15, 197.10
room for improvement 1003.1
roominess 121.2, 158.5
rooming house 228.15
roomlet 197.3
roommate 227.8, 588.3
rooms 228.4, 228.13
room temperature 1019.3
room-temperature 1019.24
room to be 158.7
room together 225.7
room to spare 158.3
room to swing a cat 158.3, 430.4
roomy 121.11, 158.11, 269.6, 317.12
roorback 552.6, 609.14
roost (n) 228.4, 228.23 (v) 159.17, 173.10, 225.7
rooster 76.8, 311.28
roosting place 228.23
root (n) 310.11, 310.22, 526.2, 526.3, 886.5, 901.6 (v) 310.34, 855.9, 855.10, 938.31
root around 938.23
root cellar 386.8
root crop 1069.15
rooted 373.18, 767.8, 842.12, 855.13, 855.16
rooted belief 953.5
rootedness 855.1
rooted to the spot 122.9
rooter 101.5, 509.8
root for 492.15, 509.10
root from the sidelines 375.16
root in 199.6
rooting out 192.1, 395.6
rootin'-tootin' 926.31
rootless 872.8
rootlessness 160.1, 584.4, 828.1, 854.2
rootlet 310.22
rootle up 941.4
rootlike 310.36
root mean square 883.4
root of all evil 728.1
root on 375.16
root out 160.6, 192.10, 255.10, 395.14, 773.5, 938.34
roots 312.1, 559.4
rootstock 310.22
root tuber 310.22
root up 160.6, 192.10, 395.14, 941.4
root vegetable 10.35, 310.4
rope (n) 4.1, 89.4, 271.2, 430.4, 605.5, 745.3 (v) 428.10, 480.17, 800.9
rope, the 604.6
rope bridge 383.9
roped off 429.20
rope enough to hang oneself 430.4
rope in 356.19, 377.5
rope ladder 193.4
rope off 210.4, 429.13
rope of sand 16.7
rope railway 383.8
ropes 754.1, 894.3
rope's end 605.1
rope tow 753.1
rope walk 271.5
ropewalk 739.3
ropeway 383.8
ropework 180.12, 271.3
ropiness 1045.1, 1062.2
roping 180.12, 271.3
roping horse 311.10
ropy 271.7, 1045.12, 1062.12

roric 1065.15
roriferous 1065.15
ro-ro 180.1
rosary 696.4
rosary beads 696.10
rosbif 10.14
Roscius 707.2
rose (n) 41.2, 239.9, 647.1, 647.2 (a) 41.8
roseate 41.8, 124.11
Rose Bowl 746.1
rose cold 85.34
rose-colored 41.8, 124.11
rose-colored glasses 124.2, 986.7
rosehead 239.9
rose-hued 41.8
rose oil 70.2
rose-red 41.8
rosette 10.41
rose water 70.3
rosé wine 88.17
rosin (n) 1057.1 (v) 1057.2
rosinante 311.12
rosiness 41.2, 41.3, 83.1, 1019.12
rosiny 1057.3
roster 549.1, 745.2, 746.2, 747.2, 871.6, 965.3
rostral column 549.12
rostrate 279.8
rostriform 279.8
rostrum 216.3, 283.8, 703.13, 901.13
rosy 41.8, 41.9, 83.13, 109.11, 124.11, 1010.13
rosy-cheeked 41.9, 83.13
rosy era 1010.4
rosy expectation 109.1
rosy outlook 124.2
rot (n) 80.7, 85.41, 393.7, 520.3, 1001.2 (v) 393.22
Rota 595.3
rota 549.1
rota 850.3, 871.6, 965.3
rotary (n) 170.2, 914.2, 915.2 (a) 172.8, 850.7, 914.7, 915.15
rotary engine 181.1
rotary photogravure 548.1
rotary press 548.9
rotary storm 318.13
rotary telephone 347.4
rotary-wing aircraft 181.5
rotate 172.5, 184.38, 205.5, 850.5, 915.9
rotating 915.14
rotation 184.8, 745.2, 812.2, 815.1, 850.3, 915.1, 1073.16
rotational 172.8, 850.7, 915.15
rotational axis 1073.16
rotational motion 915.1
rotational period 1073.16
rotative 915.15
rotator 915.4
rotatory 172.8, 915.15
rot away 393.22
rote 989.3
rote learning 989.3
rote memory 989.3
rote recitation 849.1
rotgut 88.14
Rothschild 618.8
rôti 10.13
rotisserie 915.4
rotisserie league 745.1
rotocraft 181.5
rotodyne 181.5
rotogravure 548.1
rotogravure press 548.9
rotor 904.6, 915.4
rotor plane 181.5
rototill 1069.17
rotten 16.15, 64.7, 71.5, 80.23, 98.19, 393.40, 645.16, 654.14
rotten apple 660.2
rotten borough 609.16
rotten break 1011.5
rotten deal 650.4
rotten egg 71.3
rotten luck 972.1, 1011.5
rottenness 64.3, 71.2, 80.2, 98.2, 393.7, 654.5, 1000.2
rotten smell 71.1
rotten temper 110.1
rotten to the core 16.15, 393.40, 654.14
rotter 660.7
rotting 393.39, 393.40
rotund 257.18, 282.8, 283.13
rotundity 257.8, 279.1, 282.1
rotundness 282.1
roué 665.10
rouge (n) 41.1, 41.1, 1016.11 (v) 41.4
rouged 41.9
rough (n) 288.2, 381.3, 461.1, 497.6, 593.3, 751.1 (v) 288.4, 389.5 (a) 17.14, 58.15, 64.6, 68.6, 144.24, 238.24, 288.6, 294.6, 406.12, 497.11, 505.7, 671.16, 671.20, 782.3, 851.3, 917.20, 1013.17
rough, the 406.4
roughage 7.3
rough air 288.1
rough-and-ready 406.8, 497.12
rough-and-tumble (n) 810.4 (a) 671.20
rough as a cob 288.7
rough-cast 288.6
roughcast (v) 262.7, 288.4, 295.25, 340.9 (a) 262.9, 406.12
rough diamond 406.5, 659.1
rough draft 712.12, 942.2
rough edges 408.1
roughed-out 262.9
roughen 288.4, 294.4, 917.10
rough go 1013.2
rough going 1011.1
rough-grained 288.6
rough guess 951.4
rough-hew 288.4
roughhew 262.7, 340.9
rough-hewn 288.6
roughhewn 262.9, 406.12
roughhouse (n) 322.1, 810.4 (v) 322.4, 810.11
rough idea, a 223.1
rough idea 784.3
rough in 381.11
rough it 225.11
rough measure 300.1
roughneck (n) 497.6, 593.4 (a) 497.13
roughness 17.5, 58.2, 68.1, 144.9, 184.32, 288.1, 294.2, 406.4, 497.2, 497.4, 505.3, 534.1, 671.1, 851.1
rough out 262.7, 340.9, 381.11
rough outline 712.12
rough patch 1011.6
roughrider 178.8
rough sea 238.14
rough sketch 942.2
rough up 288.4, 389.5, 393.13, 604.14, 902.17
rough usage 387.1
rough water 238.14
rough weather 671.4
rough wine 88.17
roulade (n) 709.18 (v) 708.38
rouleau 282.4, 728.4, 770.8
roulette 759.12
roulette bet 759.3
roulette table 759.16
roulette wheel 759.16
rouncy 311.13
round (n) 10.14, 88.7, 193.5, 231.2, 245.1, 280.2, 280.9, 373.5, 383.1, 462.13, 708.19, 724.4, 744.1, 751.3, 754.3, 812.2, 825.2, 850.3, 914.2, 915.2 (v) 163.9, 279.6, 280.10, 282.6, 914.5, 914.6, 915.9, 1017.17 (a) 280.11, 282.8, 533.6, 644.17, 794.11, 914.7
round, the 118.1
round a bend 914.6
roundabout (n) 170.2, 743.15, 914.2, 914.3, 915.2, 915.4 (a) 204.13, 206.7, 209.8, 281.6, 538.14, 799.4, 914.7
roundaboutness 538.5, 914.1
roundabout way 383.4, 914.3
round a corner 914.6
round-and-round 172.8
round a point 182.30, 914.6
round as a ball 282.8
round down 1017.17, 1017.19
rounded 280.11, 282.8, 283.15, 286.3, 524.30
rounded out 282.8
rounded up 770.21
roundel 280.2
roundelay 708.19
rounder 178.3, 665.10, 669.3
round-faced 257.18
roundhouse 197.27, 739.5
rounding 554.14, 914.1
rounding down 1017.10
rounding off 407.2, 1017.10
rounding out 407.2
rounding up 1017.10
roundlet 280.5
round lot 738.3
roundness 279.1, 280.1, 282.1, 644.4
round of applause 509.2
round of drinks 88.7
round off 407.6, 1017.17, 1017.19
round of pleasure 743.7
round of pleasures 95.3
round of visits 582.7
round out 282.6, 283.11, 407.6, 794.6, 1017.17
round pace 174.1
round robin 914.2
round-robin tournament 750.1
rounds 914.2
rounds, the 743.7
round-shouldered 265.12
roundsman 1008.10, 1008.15
round sum 728.13
roundtable 423.3
round the bend 926.27
round-the-clock 812.8
round top 295.8
round trade 737.19
round transaction 737.19
round trip 177.5, 280.3, 745.3, 914.2
round tripper 745.3
round up 472.9, 770.18, 1017.19, 1070.8
roundup 770.1
round window 2.10
roupiness 58.2
roupy 58.15
rouse 17.10, 23.4, 23.5, 105.12, 192.14, 375.19
roused 105.20
rouser 375.11
rousing (n) 23.2 (a) 9.3, 17.15, 247.11, 375.27
Rousseauistic 124.11
Rousseauistic optimism 124.2
roustabout 183.6, 183.9, 726.2
rousting out 23.2
roust out 23.5
rout (n) 163.2, 412.2, 606.3, 769.6, 770.4, 884.3, 917.1 (v) 412.8
route 383.1
routed 412.14
route march 177.10
route-march 177.30
router 757.2, 1042.8, 1042.9
routine (n) 84.2, 373.5, 384.1, 704.7, 807.1, 812.2, 1042.11 (a) 246.3, 373.14, 807.6, 847.4, 864.12
routineness 847.1, 864.2
routinization 808.2
routinize 384.5, 808.10
routinized 808.14
rout out 909.14
rove (n) 177.3 (v) 164.4, 177.23
rover 178.2, 483.7
roving (n) 177.3, 538.3 (a) 164.7, 177.37, 538.13, 854.7
roving eye 562.12
row (n) 53.4, 296.1, 456.6, 671.2, 810.4, 812.2, 917.1 (v) 53.9, 182.13, 182.53, 456.12, 904.9
row away 182.53
rowboat 760.2
row-de-dow 456.6
rowdiness 322.1
row dry 182.53
rowdy (n) 322.3, 461.1, 497.6, 593.3 (a) 53.13, 322.5, 497.13, 671.20
rowdydow 53.4
rowdyish 322.5, 497.13
rowdyism 322.1, 497.4

rowel 375.8
rower 183.5, 760.2
row house 228.5
rowing 182.1, 760.2
rowing crew 617.7
rowing machine 84.1, 725.7
rowing with one oar in the water 926.27
rowlock 906.3, 915.5
Roxburgh 554.15
royal (n) 554.4, 575.8 (a) 136.12, 417.17, 999.12
royal and ancient, the 751.1
royal-blue 45.3
Royal Canadian Mounted Police 1008.17
royal charter 642.1
royal crown 647.3
royal flush 758.4
royal grant 443.5
Royal Highness 648.2
royal insignia 417.8
royalism 611.4, 612.7
royalist 611.9
Royal Majesty 648.2
Royal Marine 183.4
Royal Marines 461.28
Royal Navy 461.27royal pain 96.2
royal personage 575.8
royal prerogative 417.1
royal purple 46.3
royal road 1014.1
royal seat 417.11
royal standard 647.7
royal tennis 748.1
royalties 627.1
royalty 417.8, 575.8, 608.1, 608.2, 624.4, 624.7
rpm 174.1
ruach 919.4
rub (n) 73.1, 223.5, 456.1, 456.7, 843.4, 1013.8, 1044.1 (v) 26.7, 73.8, 91.24, 223.10, 287.7, 349.8, 490.6, 1044.6, 1066.6
rub-a-dub 55.1
rub against 73.8, 1044.7
rub along 995.4
rubato 708.30, 709.18, 709.24
rub away 255.9, 1044.7
rubbed 287.11
rubbed out 395.29
rubber (n) 86.23, 395.9, 758.3, 1047.4, 1048.3 (v) 981.3, 1048.6 (a) 1048.8
rubber ball 1048.3
rubber band 1048.3
rubber bandage 86.33
rubber-band duckpin 750.1
rubber-band duckpin bowling 750.1
rubber-block print 713.5
rubber bridge 758.3
rubber bullet 462.22
rubber check 623.2, 625.3, 728.10
rubber dinghy 397.6
rubberiness 854.1, 1047.2, 1047.3
rubberize 1048.6
rubberized 1048.8
rubberlike 1048.8
rubberneck (n) 178.1, 918.3, 981.2 (v) 27.15, 177.21, 267.5, 918.6, 981.3 (a) 918.7
rubbernecker 178.1, 918.3, 981.2
rubbernecking (n) 27.5, 918.4, 981.1 (a) 981.5
rubberneck tour 177.5, 918.4
rubber plate 548.8
rubber room 926.14
rubber room work 725.4
rubber stamp (n) 332.4, 417.1, 509.1 (v) 332.12
rubber-stamp 332.9
rubbery 16.12, 854.6, 1047.10, 1048.8
rubbing (n) 73.2, 349.5, 785.2, 785.4, 1044.1 (a) 223.17, 1044.9
rubbing against 1044.2
rubbing away 1044.2
rubbing off 1044.2
rubbing out 308.2, 1044.2
rubbing together 1044.2
rubbish (n) 80.9, 256.1, 370.4, 391.5, 520.2, 606.3, 998.4 (v) 156.6, 510.13
rubbish heap 391.6
rubbishy 520.7, 998.21
rubble 391.5, 1059.1
rubble car 179.16
rubblestone 1059.1
rub down 1044.6, 1070.7
rubdown 1044.3
rube (n) 414.9, 416.3, 606.6, 924.5 (a) 233.8
rubefacient (n) 41.3 (a) 41.11
rubefaction 41.3
rubefy 41.4
Rube Goldberg contraption 799.2
rub elbows with 582.17
rubescence 41.3
rubescent 41.11
rube town 230.3
rubiate 41.6
rubicund 41.6, 41.9
rubicundity 41.1, 1019.12
rubification 41.3
rubificative 41.11
rubiginous 40.4, 41.6
rub in 997.14
rub it in 96.13, 119.2
rub noses 73.8
rub off 393.20
ruboff 1044.2
rub off corners 867.3
rub off rub out 1044.7
rub of the green 751.1
rub of the green, the 972.1
rub on 162.3, 175.7
rub one's eyes 122.5
rub one's fur the wrong way 96.14
rub one's hands 116.5
rub one's nose in it 96.13
rub one the wrong way 96.14
rubor 41.1
rub out 255.12, 308.14, 395.16
rubric (n) 419.2, 557.1, 673.3, 809.2, 937.1, 937.2 (v) 41.4 (a) 41.6, 419.4
rubrical 41.6, 419.4
rubricate 41.6
rubricity 41.1
rubricose 41.6
rubrific 41.11
rub salt in the wound 96.14, 119.2, 393.9
rub shoulders with 582.17
rub the lamp 690.10
rub the picture off a nickel 484.5
rub the print off a dollar bill 484.5
rub the right way 138.10
rub the ring 690.10
rub the wrong way 99.6, 288.5
rub up 392.11, 989.18, 1044.8
ruby (n) 41.1 (a) 41.6
ruby-colored 41.6
ruby-red 41.6
ruche 291.1
ruched 291.8
ruching 291.1
ruck (n) 290.1, 291.3, 606.3, 770.4, 864.3, 884.3 (v) 291.5, 291.6
rucked 291.8
ruckle (n) 55.3 (v) 55.6, 291.6
ruck up 291.5
ruckus 53.4, 456.6, 671.2, 810.4
ruction 53.4, 456.6, 810.4
rudder 573.5
rudderpost 217.7
ruddied 41.6
ruddiness 41.1
ruddle 41.4
ruddy 41.6, 41.9, 83.13, 139.13, 513.10
ruddy-complexioned 41.9
ruddy cup, the 88.13
ruddy-faced 41.9
rude 58.15, 83.12, 98.18, 142.10, 406.12, 497.11, 505.4, 534.2, 606.8, 930.13
rude awakening 23.2, 977.1
rude health 83.2
rude justice 649.1
rudeness 58.2, 98.2, 142.2, 406.4, 497.2, 505.1, 534.1
rude reproach 508.2
rudiment 305.14, 901.6
rudimental 258.13, 406.12, 818.15
rudimentary 199.8, 258.13, 406.12, 818.15, 886.14
rudiments 568.5, 818.6
rue (n) 113.1, 145.1 (v) 113.6, 115.10
rueful 98.20, 112.26, 113.8, 145.7, 145.8
ruefulness 112.11, 145.2, 656.1
ruesome 145.8
rue the day 113.6
rufescence 41.3
rufescent 41.6
ruff (n) 55.1, 758.3 (v) 291.5
ruffian 322.3, 461.1, 497.6, 593.3
ruffianism 322.1, 497.4
ruffianly 322.5, 497.13
ruffle (n) 55.1, 105.4, 211.7, 291.1, 985.3 (v) 55.4, 96.13, 105.14, 152.24, 288.5, 291.5, 708.44, 811.2, 917.10, 985.7
ruffled 96.21, 105.23, 281.6, 288.6, 291.7, 810.14, 917.16, 985.12
ruffled feathers 589.2
ruffled feelings 589.2
ruffle one's feathers 152.24
ruffles and flourishes 708.27
rufosity 41.1
RU-486 86.23
rufous 40.4, 41.6
rufous-brown 40.4
rufulous 41.6
rug 3.14, 199.3, 295.9, 295.10, 901.20
rug ape 302.9
rug designer 716.9
rugged 15.15, 83.12, 144.24, 288.7, 291.8, 425.6, 763.7, 1013.17
rugged health 83.2
rugged individualism 430.5, 611.8
rugged individualist 430.12
ruggedness 15.1, 83.3, 288.1, 425.1, 1013.1, 1049.1
rug joint 759.19
rugose 288.7, 291.8
rugosity 288.1
rugous 288.7, 291.8
rug rat 302.9
rugrat 302.1
ruin (n) 393.8, 395.1, 412.1, 473.1, 625.3, 806.1, 842.6 (v) 393.10, 395.10, 412.6, 625.8, 665.20, 671.11, 1012.15
ruinate 395.10
ruination 393.1, 395.1, 806.1
ruined 125.15, 393.28, 393.33, 395.28, 412.14, 625.11, 842.14
ruiner 395.8
ruining 395.26
ruinous 393.33, 395.26, 395.28, 806.5, 810.15, 842.14, 1011.15
ruinousness 393.1
ruins 256.1, 393.8, 842.6
rule (n) 246.1, 249.3, 277.3, 300.2, 373.4, 381.4, 417.5, 419.2, 420.3, 420.4, 612.1, 673.3, 752.3, 786.1, 869.4, 894.1, 935.6, 974.2 (v) 249.11, 417.13, 420.8, 573.8, 612.13, 864.10, 894.8, 946.13
rule against 444.3, 444.5
rulebook 869.4
rulebook slowdown 727.5
rule by terror 127.7
ruled out 293.9, 444.7
ruled-out 967.7
rule of action 419.2
rule of behavior 869.4
rule of conduct 419.2
rule of deduction 935.6
rule off 300.11
rule of law 612.7
rule of might 424.2
rule of the sword 612.4
rule of three 1017.7
rule of thumb 300.2, 942.1
rule out 255.10, 293.6, 395.16, 444.3, 967.6, 1012.14

rule over 612.13
ruler 249.4, 277.3, 575.6, 575.8, 605.2, 610.2
ruler-straight 161.12, 277.6
rules of conduct 580.3
rules of engagement 458.1, 458.5
rules of language 530.1
rules of war 458.5
rule the roost 612.14
rule with an iron fist 612.15
rule with an iron hand 425.4
rule with a rod of iron 425.4, 612.15
ruling (n) 420.4, 673.3, 946.5 (a) 18.12, 249.14, 417.15, 612.17, 864.12, 894.14
ruling circle 997.8
ruling circles 249.5, 607.2
ruling class 249.5, 417.7, 575.14, 607.2
ruling out 293.1, 444.1, 959.1
ruling passion 926.13
rum (n) 88.13 (a) 870.11, 999.13
rumaki 10.9
rumble (n) 50.13, 53.3, 53.4, 54.2, 56.4, 457.4, 552.6 (v) 54.7, 56.9, 524.25
rumble seat 217.1
rumbling (n) 54.2 (a) 54.12, 56.12
rumbustious 671.20
rumhound 88.12
ruminant (n) 311.3 (a) 8.32, 311.45, 931.21
ruminate 8.27, 931.12
ruminate over 931.13
ruminating 8.32, 931.21
rumination 8.1, 931.2
ruminative 931.21
rummage (n) 938.15 (v) 938.33
rummager 938.18
rummage sale 734.3
rummy 88.12
rum one 870.4
rumor (n) 354.11, 551.4, 552.6 (v) 352.10, 552.11
rumor about 352.10
rumored 552.15
rumored about 552.15
rumor mill 354.11
rumormonger 552.9
rump 10.15, 217.4, 256.1
rumple (n) 291.3 (v) 288 5, 291.6, 294.4, 811.2, 917.10
rumpled 291.8, 810.14
rumpus (n) 53.4, 456.6, 671.2, 810.4 (v) 53.9
rumpus room 197.12
rumrunner 732.5
rumrunning 732.2
rumshop 88.20
run (n) 85.38, 161.1, 172.2, 174.3, 177.4, 177.5, 182.6, 184.9, 228.26, 238.1, 238.4, 246.1, 267.2, 373.5, 383.1, 383.2, 430.1, 457.12, 704.11, 708.27, 709.18, 745.3, 751.3, 755.2, 812.2, 856.1, 864.3, 893.4, 896.2 (v) 12.15, 84.4, 158.9, 172.5, 174.8, 177.18, 177.22, 182.13, 182.14, 182.22, 182.54, 223.11, 238.16, 368.10, 371.19, 382.9, 393.13, 401.5, 548.14, 573.8, 573.9, 609.39, 610.13, 732.8, 746.5, 753.4, 757.5, 821.5, 827.6, 889.5, 889.7, 897.4, 902.12, 1020.21, 1042.21, 1064.5, 1070.6
run about 177.23
runabout 178.2
run abreast 203.4, 790.5
run a chance 759.24
run a comparison 943.4
run across 223.11, 941.3
run a deficit 623.6
run afoul 98.15
run afoul of 182.41, 457.15, 902.13
run after 138.8, 138.9, 176.16, 382.8, 587.12
run against 451.3, 900.6, 902.12
run a game 759.23
run a game on 356.19
runagate 368.5
run a good chance 968.4, 972.13
run aground 182.42, 1011.10
run a household 228.31
run along 188.12
run amok 671.15, 810.10, 926.20
run an experiment 942.8
run a race 457.19
run a risk 972.12, 1006.7
run around 330.12
runaround, the 368.1, 415.5
run around in circles 330.12, 410.14
run around like a chicken with its head cut off 105.16, 330.12
run a sample 942.8
run a specimen 942.8
run at (n) 459.1 (v) 459.18
run a taut ship 425.4
run a temperature 85.47, 105.17, 1019.22
run a tight ship 425.4
run a tilt 457.13
run a tilt at 457.13, 459.18
run away 188.12, 368.10
runaway (n) 368.5, 369.5 (a) 368.16, 369.11
run away from 188.12, 368.10
runaway tongue 540.1
runaway victory 411.1
run away with 368.10, 482.13, 482.20
run back 163.6
runback 746.3
run batted in 745.4
run before 133.13
run before one can walk 414.14
run broadside on 182.41
run by 341.10
run circles around 249.9, 412.9
run counter 958.5
run counter to 335.4, 451.3, 779.4, 900.6
rundle 193.5, 238.1, 915.4
run down 21.5, 85.48, 173.8, 182.41, 393.17, 429.15, 480.18, 512.8, 910.7, 938.35, 941.2, 950.2
run-down 21.7, 85.54, 393.33, 393.36
rundown (n) 184.3, 557.2 (a) 16.18
run-down neighborhood 230.6
run down the latitude 182.51
run dry 388.4
rune 349.1, 546.2, 690.1
run end on 182.41
run for 161.9, 182.35
run for it 368.10
run for office 371.19, 609.39, 610.13
run for one's life 188.12, 368.10
run for one's money 457.2
run foul of 457.15
run from 182.36
rung 193.5, 245.1, 282.4
rung of the ladder 843.2
run head and head 182.41
run head-on 182.41
runic 720.16
runic alphabet 546.3
runic character 546.2
run in 182.41, 191.7, 213.6, 429.16, 480.18
run-in (n) 456.6 (a) 373.15
run in circles 19.7, 391.8
run in opposition to 779.4
run in pursuit of 382.8
run interference for 449.13, 1014.7
run in the blood 767.6
run in the family 767.6
run in the head 931.20, 989.13
run into 223.11, 902.13, 941.3
run into a brick wall 857.7
run into a corner 1013.16
run into a stone wall 132.4
run into danger 1006.6
run into debt 621.3, 623.6
run into money 632.6
run into port 1009.7
run into the ground 993.10
run in with 182.35
run it by again 849.7
run its course 820.7, 821.5
run it up the flagpole 403.10
run it up the flagpole and see who salutes 942.8
runlet 238.1
run like a scared rabbit 174.9
run like mad 174.9
run low 252.6
run mad 926.20
run mad after 100.18
run neck and neck 174.14
runnel 238.1, 239.2
runner 174.5, 179.20, 239.4, 310.20, 353.1, 577.3, 732.5, 745.2, 757.2, 793.4
runner-up 411.2
runnerup 132.6
runniness 1061.1
running (n) 12.6, 84.2, 172.1, 573.1, 573.2, 609.10, 755.2, 889.1, 1020.3, 1064.1 (a) 172.8, 174.15, 238.24, 547.22, 812.8, 812.9, 838.2, 864.12, 889.11
running away 222.4, 368.4
running back 746.2
running broad jump 366.1
running commentary 556.2
running dive 182.8, 367.1
running down 173.3, 512.1
running engagement 457.4
running event 457.12, 755.2
running fight 457.4
running for office 609.10
running game 747.3
running head 517.13, 937.2
running high jump 366.1
running horse 757.2
running in 480.2
running in the blood 767.8
running it up the flagpole 942.1
running jump 366.1
running livestock 1070.1
running mad 105.25
running mate 610.9
running on 540.9
running-out of the sands 307.7
running out of time 822.1
running over 991.7, 993.20
running play 746.3
running rigging 180.12
running sore 1001.1
running start 249.2, 818.1, 845.1
running time 824.2, 827.3
running title 517.13, 554.12, 937.2
running total 1017.6
running wild 926.30
runny 190.20, 1061.4
run of, the 430.1
run of events 831.4
run off 188.12, 368.10, 482.13, 548.14, 909.14
runoff 190.4, 609.15, 1065.3
run off at the mouth 520.5, 540.5, 856.5
runoff election 609.15
runoff primary 609.15
run off with 482.20
run of luck 972.1, 1010.3
run-of-mill 1005.8
run of the cards 972.1
run of the mill 864.3
run-of-the-mill 1005.8
run of the mill, the 869.3
run of things 831.4
run on 162.3, 540.5, 812.4, 821.5, 827.6, 856.3
run on a bank 625.3
run one hard 1011.8
run on in a groove 373.12
run on like a mill race 540.5
run on the rocks 182.42
run out (v) 21.5, 190.12, 190.13, 369.10, 388.4, 395.23, 538.8, 820.7, 821.5, 909.13, 909.14 (a) 837.7, 842.15
run out a rope 182.15
run out of gas 16.9, 410.16, 704.28, 911.2
run out of patience 135.5
run out of steam 911.2
run out of time 821.6
run out of town 909.14
run out on 370.5
run over 238.17, 570.13, 849.8, 910.7, 931.13, 938.24, 991.5, 1017.17

run parallel 203.4
run parallel to 899.3
run prow on 182.41
run ragged 21.8
run rings around 249.9, 412.9
run riot 327.7, 669.6, 671.15, 810.10, 910.5, 993.8
run roughshod over 412.10
runs 12.2
runs, the 85.29
run scared 491.8
run short 911.2, 992.8
run short of 992.7
run side by side 203.4
run smack into 223.11
run smoothly 1014.10
runt 258.4, 998.7
run the chance 897.3, 1006.7
run the eye over 570.13, 938.24
run the fingers over 73.6
run the gauntlet 492.10
run the hazard 1006.7
run the risk 759.24, 897.3, 1006.7
run through 221.7, 292.15, 459.25, 486.3, 570.13, 626.5, 704.32
run-through 557.2, 704.13, 938.3
run through like King Charles's head 849.11
run time 824.2, 827.3
runtiness 258.1
run to 261.6, 440.11, 630.13, 790.5, 792.8
run to earth 429.15, 480.18, 938.35
run together 169.2
run to seed (v) 310.34, 393.19, 395.24, 473.6, 891.3, 1011.11 (a) 303.18, 414.18, 486.9
run to waste 393.19, 473.6
run true to form 781.3, 867.4
run true to type 781.3
runty 258.13, 274.7
run under bare poles 182.50
run up 251.6, 365.8, 816.3, 892.8
run-up 405.1, 814.1, 816.2, 961.2
run up a bill 623.6
run up against 223.11, 831.8, 941.3
run up an account 623.6
run up a score 623.6
run up a tab 623.6
run upon 223.11
run up to 405.13
runway 184.23, 383.2
runway lights 184.19
run wide 757.5
run wide open 174.9
run wild 430.19, 671.15, 810.10
run with 407.4, 582.18, 769.7
run with it 328.5
run with the hare and hunt with the hounds 354.24
run with the pack 332.9
run with the wind 182.22
rupia 85.36
rupture (n) 85.38, 224.2, 456.4, 802.4 (v) 224.4, 292.14, 393.13, 393.23, 802.12
ruptured 393.27, 802.24
rupture oneself 403.14
rural 233.6, 416.6, 1069.20
rural district 233.1
rural economics 1069.1
rural economist 1069.5
rural economy 1069.1
rural idiocy 930.3
ruralism 233.3
ruralist 227.10
ruralization 233.4
ruralize 233.5
rural market 733.3
rural route 553.9
rural route carrier 353.5
ruse 356.6, 376.1, 415.3
rush (n) 87.1, 105.2, 105.3, 172.2, 174.1, 174.3, 238.4, 238.9, 310.5, 401.1, 421.1, 459.1, 671.6, 845.2, 998.5 (v) 174.8, 238.16, 401.4, 401.5, 459.18
rush about 330.12
rush against 459.1
rush ahead 174.12
rush along 401.4
rush around 330.12
rush at 459.18
rushbuckler 502.5
rush candle 1026.2
rushed 401.11, 845.8
rush hour 293.3
rush in 214.5
rushing (n) 449.5 (a) 172.8, 174.15, 238.24
rush into 401.7
rushlight 1026.2
rush of emotion 105.2
rush order 421.1
rush through 401.5
rush to the assistance of 449.11
rush up on one 840.2
rusk 10.30
russet 40.4, 41.6
russety 40.4
Russian 89.2
Russian bath 79.8
Russian bear 647.6
Russianism 523.8
Russian Orthodox Church 675.9
rust (n) 310.4, 393.6, 1001.2 (v) 40.2, 41.4, 393.21, 842.9 (a) 40.4, 41.6
rust away 393.22
rust belt 231.7
rustbucket 180.1
rust-cankered 393.43
rust-colored 40.4
rust-eaten 393.43
rustic (n) 227.10, 606.6, 1069.5 (a) 233.6, 535.3, 798.6, 1069.20
rusticate 233.5, 584.7, 909.17
rusticated 233.8
rustication 233.4, 584.1, 909.4
rusticity 233.3, 798.1
rustic region 233.1
rustic style 535.1
rustiness 406.1, 414.1
rustle (n) 52.6 (v) 52.12, 482.13
rustler 483.8
rustle up 11.5, 365.8, 385.7, 405.7, 892.8
rustling (n) 52.6 (a) 52.18
rustproof 15.20
rustre 647.2
rust-red 41.6
rust-worn 393.43
rusty 40.4, 41.6, 303.18, 374.4, 393.43, 406.12, 414.18, 842.14
rusty-dusty 217.5
rut (n) 75.5, 105.7, 284.3, 290.1, 373.5, 383.2 (v) 75.20, 290.3
ruth 145.1, 656.1
Rutherford theory 1038.2
ruthful 145.7
ruthfulness 145.2
ruthless 144.26, 146.3, 671.21
ruthlessness 144.11, 146.1
rutilant 1025.30
rutilous 1025.30
rutted 288.6, 290.4
rutting 75.28
ruttish 75.28
rutty 75.28, 288.6, 290.4
S 279.11
Sabaism 697.1
Sabaist 697.4
Sabbatarian (n) 667.2, 701.2 (a) 434.4, 667.4, 687.8
Sabbatarianism 667.1, 687.5, 701.1
Sabbath 20.5, 690.3, 701.12
Sabbath-breaker 694.3
sabbatical (n) 20.3, 222.4, 402.1 (a) 20.10
sabbatical leave 20.3
sabbatical year 20.3
sabbatism 687.5, 701.1
sabbatist 701.2
saber (n) 462.5 (v) 459.25
saber fencing 760.4
saber rattling 458.10
saber-rattling (n) 514.1, 591.2 (a) 458.21, 514.3
Sabir 523.11
sable (n) 38.1, 38.4, 647.2 (a) 38.8, 40.3
sabotage (n) 393.1, 395.3 (v) 19.9, 393.15, 451.3, 1012.15
saboteur 357.11
sabulosity 1051.2
sabulous 1051.12
sac 195.2
saccharide 7.5
sacchariferous 66.5
saccharification 66.2
saccharify 66.4
saccharin 66.2
saccharine 66.5, 66.6
saccharinity 66.1
saccharinize 97.5
sacellum 703.3
sacerdotal 580.8, 698.13
sacerdotalism 698.3
sac fly 745.3
sachem 575.9, 610.7, 997.8
sachet 70.6
sack (n) 195.2, 482.6, 745.1, 746.3, 770.8 (v) 159.15, 212.9, 480.17, 482.17, 671.11, 746.5, 770.20, 909.20
sack, the 901.19, 909.5
sackcloth 115.7, 288.2
sackcloth and ashes 115.7, 658.3
sacker 483.6
sacking 482.6, 671.3
sack out 22.14, 22.18
sack race 457.12
sack time 22.2, 22.3
sack up 22.18
sacrament 701.3
Sacrament, the 701.7
sacramental (n) 701.3 (a) 701.18
sacramental anointment 701.5
sacramentalism 701.1
sacramentalist 701.2
sacramental offering 696.7
sacramentarian (n) 701.2 (a) 701.18
sacramentarianism 701.1
sacrament chapel 703.3
sacrament cloth 703.10
sacrament of marriage 563.1
sacrament of matrimony 563.1
Sacrament Sunday 701.7
sacrarium 703.3, 703.4, 703.5, 703.9
Sacra Romana Rota 595.3
sacred 677.17, 685.7, 708.50
sacred, the 685.2
sacred article 701.10
sacred calling 698.1
sacred canon 683.1
Sacred College 699.1
sacred cow 697.3, 997.9
sacred language 523.2
sacred memory 662.7
sacred music 708.17
sacredness 685.1
sacred Nine 710.22
sacred object 701.10
sacred text 683.7
sacred texts 683.1
sacred tongue 523.2
sacred unction 701.5
sacred writings 683.1, 683.7
sacrifice (n) 308.1, 473.1, 475.1, 652.1, 658.3, 696.7 (v) 308.13, 473.4, 475.3, 478.21, 652.3, 696.15, 734.8, 745.5
sacrificed 475.5
sacrifice fly 745.3
sacrifice oneself 324.4
sacrifice oneself for 509.13
sacrificial 633.9
sacrificial lamb 324.1
sacrificing 652.5
sacrilege 638.2, 694.2
sacrilegious 638.3, 694.6
sacrilegiousness 694.2
sacrilegist 694.3
sacristy 703.9
sacrosanct 685.7
sacrosanctity 685.1
sacrosanctness 685.1
sad 35.22, 38.9, 39.4, 96.20, 98.20, 112.20, 112.24, 145.8, 661.11, 998.21, 1000.9, 1011.14
sad case 660.2
sadden 112.18, 145.5

saddened 112.20
saddening 98.20
sad disappointment 132.1
saddle (n) 237.5, 417.10, 901.17 (v) 297.13, 800.10, 1070.7
saddleback 237.5
saddle blanket 295.11
saddlecloth 295.11
saddled 297.18, 641.16
saddle horse 311.13
saddle of mutton 10.16
saddle on 888.4
saddler 311.13
saddle shoes 5.27
saddle stitching 554.14
saddle with 253.4, 599.9, 641.12, 643.4, 888.4, 1012.11
saddling 297.7, 888.1
Sadducee 675.21
Sadduceeism 675.12
sad-eyed 112.20
sad-faced 112.20
sadhearted 112.20
sadheartedness 112.1
sadism 75.11, 144.11
sadist 75.16, 96.10, 144.14, 604.7
sadistic 144.26
sadistic cruelty 144.11
sadness 38.2, 96.6, 98.5, 112.1, 998.2
sad of heart 112.20
sadomasochism 75.11
sadomasochist 75.16
sad sack 16.6, 414.8, 660.2, 1011.7
sad story 115.4
sad times 1011.6
sad-voiced 112.20
sad work 340.3, 414.5
safari 177.5
safari park 228.19, 743.14
safe (n) 346.4, 729.13 (a) 494.8, 1007.4, 1008.21
safe and sound 1007.4
safe bet 966.1
safeblower 483.3
safeblowing 482.5
safebreaker 483.3
safebreaking 482.5
safe-conduct 443.7
safecracker 483.3
safecracking 482.5
safe-deposit box 195.1, 346.4, 729.13
safe distance 368.1, 1007.1
safe district 609.16
safeguard (n) 386.3, 443.7, 460.6, 494.3, 1007.1, 1008.3, 1008.14 (v) 460.8, 1008.18
safeguarded 1008.21
safeguarding (n) 1008.1 (a) 1008.23
safe hands 1008.2
safe haven 1009.1
safehold 460.6, 1009.1
safe house 346.4, 1009.4, 1009.5
safekeeper 397.5, 1008.5
safekeeping 386.5, 397.1, 429.5, 1007.1, 1008.1
safeness 494.1, 1007.1
safe passage 443.7
safe room 197.17
safe sex 75.7
safe to eat 8.33
safety 746.2, 746.3, 1007.1, 1008.1, 1008.3
safety belt 397.6, 1008.3
safety catch 428.5
safety curtain 704.16
safety-deposit box 729.13
safety first 494.1
safety glass 296.2, 1008.3
safety in numbers 1007.1
safety island 1009.3
safety light 1025.19
safety loop 181.13
safety match 1021.5
safety net 494.3, 1008.3
safety plug 1008.3
safety rail 1008.3
safety shoes 1008.3
safety switch 1008.3
safety valve 190.9, 494.3, 1008.3
safety zone 1009.3
saffron 42.2, 43.4
saffron-colored 43.4
saffron-yellow 43.4
sag (n) 194.2, 202.2, 633.4, 737.5 (v) 182.29, 194.6, 202.6, 252.6, 279.6, 633.6
saga 719.2
sagacious 413.28, 920.16, 928.15, 961.7
sagaciousness 920.4
sagacity 413.9, 920.4, 920.5, 961.1
sagaman 722.5
sagamore 575.9
sage (n) 413.13, 921.1, 962.7 (a) 920.17
sageness 920.5
sagging (n) 252.1 (a) 21.7, 194.11, 202.10
sagging in folds 202.10
sagging market 737.5
saggy 202.10
sagittal 285.11
sagittate 285.11
sagittiform 285.11
sag to leeward 182.29
Sahara 891.2, 1019.11
Saharan 1066.7
sahib 575.1, 648.3
said 524.29, 814.5
saignant 11.9
sail (n) 180.3, 180.14, 182.6 (v) 177.35, 182.13, 182.19, 182.54, 184.36, 1014.10
sail against the wind 182.24
sail away 182.19
sail away from 182.36
sail before the wind 182.22
sailboarder 760.2
sailboarding 760.2
sailboat 180.3, 760.2
sail by the wind 182.24
sail close-hauled 182.25
sail closer to the wind 182.25
sail close to the wind 182.25
sail coastwise 182.39
sail down the wind 182.22
sailer 180.3
sail fine 182.25
sail for 161.9, 182.35
sail free 182.22
sail full and by 182.25
sailing 177.16, 182.1, 184.1, 760.2
sailing boat 180.3
sailing cruiser 180.3
sailing master 183.7, 183.8
sailing ship 180.3
sailing vessel 180.3
sailing yacht 180.3
sail into 182.41, 457.14, 459.15, 725.15
sail into the teeth of the wind 182.24
sail into the wind's eye 182.24
sail locker 386.6
sail loft 197.6
sail near the wind 182.25
sail off the wind 182.22
sail on the wind 182.24
sailor 178.1, 183.1, 760.2
sailorman 183.1
sailors' snug harbor 1009.4
sailplane (n) 181.12 (v) 184.36
sail-planing 184.1
sail round 182.13
sail the ocean blue 182.13
sail the sea 182.13
sail through 1014.8
sail too close to the wind 182.25
sail too near the wind 493.5, 1006.7
sail to the windward of 182.24
sail to windward 182.24
sail under false colors 346.8, 354.22, 645.11
sail with the wind 182.22
sail with the wind abaft the beam 182.22
sail with the wind aft 182.22
sail with the wind quartering 182.22
saint (n) 653.2, 659.6, 679.1, 684.2, 692.4 (v) 662.13, 685.5, 698.12
sainted 307.29, 662.18, 679.6, 685.8, 912.9
sainthood 685.3, 692.2
sainting 662.8, 685.3
saintlike 653.5, 692.9
saintlikeness 653.1, 692.2
saintliness 653.1, 692.2
saintly 97.9, 653.5, 679.6, 685.8, 692.9
Saint Nicholas 678.13
Saint Nick 678.13
saint's day 701.12, 832.4, 850.4
saintship 692.2
Saint-Simonian (n) 611.14 (a) 611.22
Saint-Simonianism 611.6
Saint-Simonism 611.6
saint's legend 719.1
sake 375.1, 380.1
salaam (n) 155.2, 585.4, 913.3 (v) 155.6, 913.9
salaams 585.3
salability 734.7
salable 734.14
salableness 734.7
salacious 75.27, 665.29, 666.9
salaciousness 665.5, 666.4
salacity 665.5, 666.4
salad 10.7, 10.37, 797.6
salad bar 8.17
salad days 301.1
salad dish 8.12
salad dressing 10.12
salade 10.37
salad fork 8.12
salamander 311.26, 678.6, 1020.12
salamandrian 311.47
salaried 624.22
salaried worker 607.6, 726.2
salaried workers 607.5
salary (n) 624.4 (v) 624.10
salary negotiations 727.1
salchow 760.7
sale 629.1, 734.1, 734.3
sale at auction 734.4
sale by auction 734.4
sale price 630.1, 633.2
sales 734.13
sales agent 730.3
sales associate 577.5
sales campaign 734.2
salesclerk 577.5, 730.3
sales engineer 730.3
sales force 730.3
salesgirl 730.3
saleslady 730.3
salesman 730.3
sales manager 730.3
salesmanship 352.5, 375.3, 734.2
salespeople 730.3
salesperson 375.10, 577.5, 730.3
sales personnel 730.3
sales pitch 734.5
sales promotion 734.2
sales resistance 734.6
salesroom 736.5
sales talk 375.3, 543.2, 734.5
sales tax 630.9
saleswoman 730.3
sales worker 726.2
sale to the highest bidder 734.4
salience 283.2, 348.4, 997.2
saliency 348.4
salient (n) 231.1, 283.2 (a) 283.14, 348.12, 997.19
salient fact 761.3
salientian 311.26
salient point 997.6
salina 241.1
saline 68.9
salinity 68.4
saliva 2.17, 2.24, 7.8, 13.3, 1056.2
salivant 13.7
salivary 13.7
salivary digestion 2.17, 7.8
salivary glands 2.17, 2.18, 7.8
salivary secretion 13.2
salivate 13.6
salivating 13.7
salivation 13.3
salivous 13.7
salle 197.1
salle à manger 197.11
salle d'attente 197.20

sallow (v) 43.3 (a) 36.7, 43.4, 43.6
sallowness 36.2, 43.2
sally (n) 177.5, 459.1, 489.7 (v) 188.8, 190.11
sally forth 188.8, 190.11
sally port 190.9, 369.3
salmagundi 797.6
salmi 10.11
salmon (n) 311.29, 366.4 (a) 41.8, 42.2
salmon-colored 41.8
salmonellosis 85.31
salmon-pink 41.8
salon 197.5, 386.9, 578.6, 582.10, 736.1, 770.3
salonist 578.7, 582.16
salonnard 578.7, 582.16
saloon 88.20, 197.9
saloon bar 88.20
salpinx 2.23
salsa 10.9, 10.12
salsiccia 10.21
salt (n) 68.4, 183.1, 397.4, 413.16, 489.1 (v) 63.7, 354.17, 397.9, 628.10 (a) 62.9, 68.9, 489.15
salt a mine 354.17
salt-and-pepper (n) 39.2 (a) 39.4, 39.5, 47.12
salt-and-pepper hair 3.3
saltant 366.7
saltation 193.1, 366.3
saltatorial 366.7
saltatory 193.14, 366.7, 917.19
salt away 386.10
salt down 386.10
salted 68.9
salt flat 236.1, 891.2
salt-free 7.21
salt-free diet 7.13
saltimbanco 357.6
saltine 10.30
saltiness 62.1, 68.4, 110.3, 489.2, 666.3
salting 397.2
salt in the wound 96.3
saltire 647.2
saltish 68.9
salt lake 241.1
salt marsh 236.1, 243.1
salt of the earth 644.8, 659.3, 997.8, 999.8
salt of the earth, the 606.1
salt pan 236.1
salt pond 241.1
salts 86.9
salt sea 240.1
salt something away 405.11
salt water 240.1, 1065.3
saltwater fish 311.30
saltwater fishing 382.3
saltwater sailer 183.1
salty 68.9, 110.20, 182.57, 489.15, 666.7
salty taste 62.1
salubrious 81.5, 86.39, 397.12
salubriousness 81.1
salubrity 81.1
salutariness 81.1
salutary 81.5, 449.21
salutation 155.2, 585.4
salutations 585.3
salutatorian 543.4
salutatory 543.2
salutatory address 543.2
salute (n) 155.2, 487.1, 585.4 (v) 155.5, 182.52, 509.12, 517.22, 524.26, 585.10
salutiferous 86.39
salvage (n) 396.2, 397.1, 398.1, 481.3, 624.3, 630.6 (v) 396.12, 398.3
salvageability 396.9
salvageable 396.25, 398.4
salvager 396.10, 398.2
salvation 396.2, 397.1, 398.1, 677.14, 685.4
salvational 592.4, 677.16
salve (n) 86.11, 478.5, 670.3, 1056.3 (v) 91.25, 120.5, 396.12, 1056.8
salving (n) 120.1, 396.2 (a) 592.4
salvo 56.3, 459.9, 487.1, 904.4, 959.1
salvor 396.10, 398.2
samadhi 102.2, 173.1, 681.8, 691.3
Samaritan 592.1
Sama-Veda 683.8
sambo 797.8
same 778.7, 781.6, 814.5
same, the 778.3, 790.3
same but different 784.14
same damn thing, the 118.1
same difference, the (n) 778.3 (a) 784.15
sameliness 118.1
same mind 332.5
sameness 117.3, 118.1, 778.1, 781.2, 784.1
same old story 849.4
same old story, the 118.1, 837.2
same old thing, the 118.1, 781.2
samesomeness 118.1
samey 781.6
Sam Hill 682.1
Samhita 683.8
Samian sibyl 962.6
samiel 318.6, 318.12
Sammael 680.4
sample (n) 62.4, 786.3, 793.1, 942.4, 942.7 (v) 62.7, 938.29, 942.8 (a) 349.15
sample ballot 609.19
sampler 62.4, 938.16
sampling 62.6, 793.1
Samson 15.6
Samson post 273.4
Samuel 684.1
samurai 608.3
sanative 86.39, 396.22
sanatory 86.39
sanctification 662.8, 677.15, 685.3
sanctified 662.18, 685.8, 692.10, 693.5
sanctify 662.13, 685.5
sanctimonious 354.33, 500.19, 692.11, 693.5
sanctimonious fraud 357.8
sanctimoniousness 354.6, 500.6, 693.1
sanctimony 354.6, 500.6, 692.1, 692.3, 693.1
sanction (n) 332.4, 417.12, 441.1, 443.3, 509.1, 673.2 (v) 332.12, 441.2, 443.11, 509.9, 673.9
sanctionable 443.15
sanctionableness 443.8
sanctioned 443.17, 673.11
sanctioned behavior 321.2
sanctioned conduct 579.2
sanctioning 441.4
sanctions 603.1
sanctitude 685.1, 692.2
sanctity 685.1, 692.2
sanctuary 212.3, 346.4, 397.7, 703.5, 703.9, 1009.1
sanctum 197.8, 584.6, 703.5, 1009.5
sanctum sanctorum 197.8, 584.6, 703.4, 703.5, 1009.5
sand (n) 1051.6, 1059.2, 1059.6 (v) 287.8, 1044.8
sandals 5.27
sandalwood 70.4
sandbag (n) 297.6 (v) 297.12, 412.9, 459.15, 759.25, 902.17, 902.20
sandbagged 412.15
sandbagger 483.5
sandbank 234.2, 235.2, 276.2, 1006.5
sandbar 234.2, 235.2, 276.2, 1006.5, 1059.2
sandblast 287.8, 1044.8
sandblasting 1044.2
sand-blind 28.11, 28.13, 30.10
sand-blindness 28.2
sand castle 16.7
sand-colored 43.4
sand column 318.13
sanddab 10.24
sand dune 234.2, 237.4, 1059.2
sander 287.4
sand flat 236.1
sand flea 311.36
sand green 751.1
sand hazard 751.1
sandhi 524.9
sand hill 1059.2
sandhill 237.4
sandhog 284.10
sandiness 1051.2
sanding 1044.2
sand in the eyes 22.1
s and m 75.11
sandman 22.11
sand painting 712.13
sandpaper (n) 288.2 (v) 287.8, 1044.8
sand pile 1059.2
sand plain 236.1
sand reef 1059.2
sands 234.2, 891.2, 1006.5
sands of the sea 1059.2
sands of time 821.3
sandspit 283.9
sandspout 318.13
sandstone 1059.1
sandstorm 318.12
sand trap 751.1
sandwich (n) 10.32 (v) 213.6, 296.5
sandwich bar 8.17
sandwich board 352.7
sandwich cookie 10.43
sandwich in 213.6
sandwiching 213.1
sandwich person 352.9
sandy 43.4, 1051.12, 1059.12, 1066.7
sane 920.12, 920.18, 925.4, 935.20, 987.6
sane-minded 925.4
sanemindedness 925.1
saneness 920.6, 925.1, 987.2
Sanforize 260.9
Sanforized 260.13
Sanforizing 260.3
sang-froid 855.1
sangfroid 106.2, 123.1, 129.1
sanguinary 2.33, 144.26, 308.24, 458.20, 671.21, 1004.11
sanguine (n) 92.12 (a) 41.7, 41.9, 109.11, 124.10, 130.11
sanguine expectation 124.1, 130.2
sanguine humor 109.1
sanguineness 109.1
sanguineous 41.7, 109.11, 144.26, 458.20
sanguineousness 144.11
sanguinity 109.1
Sanhedrin 423.1
sanies 2.24, 12.6
sanious 2.33
sanitarian 81.3
sanitarium 91.21
sanitary 79.27, 81.5
sanitary cordon 429.2
sanitary engineer 79.16
sanitary landfill 80.12, 370.4, 391.6
sanitate 79.24
sanitation 79.3, 81.2
sanitization 79.3
sanitize 79.24
sanitizer 79.17
sanity 920.1, 920.6, 925.1
sannyasi 667.2, 699.13
sansculotte 611.12
sans-culotterie 611.4
sans-culottic 860.6
sans-culottish 860.6
sans-culottism 611.4, 860.2
sans-culottist 860.3
sans pareil 249.15
sans serif 548.6
sans souci 107.7
Santa 678.13
Santa Ana 318.6
Santa Claus 478.11, 485.2, 678.13
santon 699.12
sap (n) 196.5, 358.2, 460.5, 767.2, 924.3, 1061.2 (v) 16.10, 284.15, 393.15, 395.20, 764.4
saphead 358.2, 924.3
sapheaded 922.17
sapheadedness 922.4
sapid 62.9, 63.8, 63.9
sapidity 62.1, 63.1
sapidness 63.1

sapience 920.5
sapient (n) 921.1 (a) 920.17, 920.19
sapless 16.12, 65.2, 1066.7
saplessness 65.1, 1066.1
sapling 302.1, 302.11, 310.10
saponaceous 1056.9
saponaceousness 1056.5
saponacity 1056.5
sapor 62.1
saporific 62.9
saporous 62.9
sapped 16.18
sapper 284.10, 461.14
Sapphic 720.16
sapphic 75.30, 720.16
sapphire 45.3
sapphire-blue 45.3
sapphirine 45.3
sapphism 75.10
sapphist 75.14
sappiness 301.3, 923.1, 1061.1
sapping (n) 473.2 (a) 16.20
sappy 93.21, 301.10, 923.9, 1061.4
saprobic 393.39
saprogenic 393.39
saprogenous 393.39
saprolite 1059.1
saprophilous 393.39
saprophyte 310.4
saprophytic 393.39, 899.4
saprophytism 899.1
sap the foundations 395.20
sap the foundations of 393.15
sap the strength of 16.10
sapwood 1054.3
Saratoga chop 10.19
sarcasm 489.1, 508.5
sarcastic 489.15, 508.13
sarcoma 85.39
sarcophagus 309.11
Sardanapalus 663.3
sardonic 508.13
sardonic grin 116.3, 508.4
sargasso 310.4
sargassum 310.4
sarge 575.18
sark 5.15
sarment 310.20
sarmentum 310.20
sarsen 1059.1
sarsen stone 1059.1
sartor 5.35
sartorial 5.45, 5.48
Sartrian 952.12
sash 5.19, 266.4
sashay 177.18, 177.28
sashay along 188.7
sash weight 297.6
sass (n) 142.4 (v) 142.8, 454.4
sassiness 142.2
sassy 142.10, 454.7
Satan 357.9, 680.3, 680.6, 682.5
Satanas 680.3
satanic 144.26, 654.13, 680.17, 1000.10
satanic cunning 415.1
Satanism 680.14, 690.2, 697.1
Satanist 680.15
Satanophanic 348.9
Satan's designation 680.3
Satan-worshiper 680.15
satchel 195.2
sate 95.8, 994.4
sated 331.20, 994.6
satedness 331.6, 994.2
satellite 138.6, 166.2, 232.1, 250.2, 432.6, 616.8, 769.5, 1073.11, 1075.6
satellite broadcasting 343.5, 1035.1
satellite communication 347.1
satellite debris 1075.10
satellite dish 1035.11
satellite network 1034.8
satellite publishing 555.3
satellite radio 1034.6, 1034.16
satellite relay 1035.9
satellite state 432.6
satellite status 432.2
satellite television 1035.1
satellite transmitter 1035.8
satiate 95.8, 107.4, 118.6, 794.7, 993.15, 994.4
satiated 107.9, 118.11, 794.11, 993.20, 994.6
satiating 994.7
satiation 118.3, 994.1
satiety 107.1, 118.3, 794.2, 993.3, 994.1
satin (n) 287.3, 294.3, 1047.4 (a) 294.8
sating 994.7
satininess 287.1, 294.3, 1047.1
satinlike 1047.15
satiny 287.10, 287.11, 294.8, 1047.15
satire 489.1, 508.5, 508.6, 512.5, 704.6
satiric 489.15, 508.13
satirical 489.15, 508.13, 720.16
satiric humor 508.5
satiric wit 508.5
satirist 489.12, 512.7, 720.12
satirize 508.11, 512.12
satisfaction 95.1, 107.1, 338.1, 396.6, 434.1, 457.7, 481.1, 481.2, 624.1, 624.3, 658.1, 991.1, 994.1
satisfactional 658.7
satisfactoriness 107.3, 991.1, 999.3
satisfactory 107.11, 953.26, 991.6, 999.20
satisfactory amount 991.1
satisfied 95.15, 107.7, 953.21, 994.6
satisfiedness 107.1
satisfy 8.18, 95.8, 97.5, 107.4, 427.6, 434.2, 624.10, 624.13, 658.4, 953.18, 991.4, 994.4
satisfying 97.6, 107.11, 624.21, 953.26, 994.7
satisfy oneself 970.11
satisfy oneself on that point 953.19
satisfy one's obligations 641.11
satisfy requirements 942.10
satori 173.1, 934.1
satrap 575.12
sattva 999.1
saturate 794.7, 797.11, 993.8, 993.15, 994.4, 1065.13
saturated 221.15, 794.11, 993.20, 994.6, 1065.17
saturated fat 7.7, 1056.1
saturatedness 994.1
saturation 35.4, 35.6, 221.3, 794.2, 797.2, 993.3, 994.1, 1065.2, 1065.7
saturation bombing 459.7
saturation point 794.2, 994.1, 1037.1, 1065.2
saturation raid 459.4
Saturday 832.4
Saturday night special 462.10
Saturn 1073.9
Saturnalia 743.4
saturnalia 669.2
saturnalian 669.9
saturnalia of blood 308.4
Saturnian 97.11
Saturnian age 1010.4
Saturnian meter 720.7
saturnine 112.24
satyr 75.16, 665.11, 678.11
satyriasis 75.5, 665.5
satyric 665.29
satyrism 75.5, 75.11, 665.5
sauce (n) 10.12, 88.14, 142.4, 454.1, 797.6, 797.7, 1061.2, 1063.2 (v) 63.7, 142.8
saucebox 142.6
saucer 280.2
saucer-eyed 28.12
saucer eyes 2.9, 27.9, 28.6
saucerman 1075.8
saucers 8.12
saucer-shaped 279.13, 284.16
saucier 11.3
sauciness 142.2, 454.1
saucisse 10.21
saucisson 10.21
saucy 142.10, 454.7
sault 238.10, 238.11
sauna 79.8, 79.10, 1019.11
sauna bath 79.8
saunter (n) 175.2, 177.10, 177.12 (v) 175.6, 177.23, 177.28
sauntering (n) 177.8 (a) 175.10
saurian (n) 311.24 (a) 311.47
sausage 10.21
sausage meat 10.13
saut de basque 366.1
sauté 11.5, 40.2
sautéed 11.7
sautéing 11.2
savable 398.4
savage (n) 497.7, 593.5, 671.9 (v) 96.18, 389.5, 393.13, 671.11, 1000.6 (a) 144.26, 146.3, 152.32, 308.23, 458.20, 497.12, 671.21
savaged 96.25
savagery 144.11, 497.3, 671.1, 930.3
savagism 497.3
savanna 201.3, 233.1, 236.1, 310.8
savannah 233.1, 310.8
savant 413.11, 866.3, 920.9, 921.1, 928.11, 929.3
savasana 201.2
savate 457.9
save (n) 752.3, 1042.18 (v) 386.11, 386.12, 390.5, 397.8, 398.3, 449.11, 474.5, 635.4, 685.6, 752.4, 853.6, 1007.3, 1012.14
save-all (n) 484.4 (a) 484.9
save by the bell 398.3
saved 386.15, 390.12, 397.13, 679.6, 685.9, 692.10
saved, the 692.5
saved soul 679.1
save face 136.7
save for a rainy day 386.12, 635.4
save one's bacon 398.3, 592.3, 1007.2
save one's breath 51.6, 344.6
save one's face 136.7
save one's neck 398.3, 592.3, 1007.2
save one's skin 592.3
saver 397.5, 635.3
save the day 592.3
save the necessity 430.14
save to fall back upon 386.12, 405.11
save up 386.11, 386.12, 390.5, 474.5, 635.4
saving (n) 397.1, 398.1, 635.2 (a) 397.12, 592.4, 635.6
saving clause 369.4, 613.9, 959.2
saving grace 600.5, 865.4
savingness 635.1
savings 386.3, 728.14
savings account 622.2, 728.14, 729.3, 729.14, 1008.4
savings and loan 620.4
savings and loan association 620.4
savings and loan industry 620.4
savings institution 620.4, 729.14
savior 397.5, 398.2, 592.2
Savitar 1073.14
savoir-faire 413.1, 504.3, 928.3
savor (n) 62.1, 63.2, 69.1, 93.2, 865.4 (v) 8.20, 62.7, 63.5, 63.7, 95.13
savoriness 62.1, 63.1, 97.3
savoring 8.1, 62.6
savorless 65.2
savorlessness 65.1, 96.1
savor of 62.7, 63.6
savor of wit 489.1
savorous 63.8
savory (n) 10.8 (a) 8.33, 62.9, 63.8, 68.7, 70.9, 97.10
savvy (n) 413.1, 920.2, 920.6, 928.3, 944.1 (v) 521.7, 928.12
saw (n) 289.2, 974.1, 974.3, 1040.2, 1040.6, 1040.7 (v) 708.41, 802.11
saw away at 708.39
saw bearing 915.7
sawbones 90.4, 90.5
sawbuck 728.7, 901.16
sawdust 256.1, 1051.5
sawdust game 759.8
sawdust joint 759.19
saw-edge 285.2
saw-edged 289.5

sawed-off 258.13
sawed-off shotgun 462.10
saw file temper 1046.4
sawhorse 901.16
sawlike 289.5
saw logs 22.13
sawmill 739.3
sawteeth 289.2
saw the air 517.21
sawtooth (n) 285.4, 289.2 (a) 278.6, 288.7
saw-toothed 278.6, 289.5
sawtoothed 288.7
saw wood 22.13
saxophonist 710.4
say (n) 249.3, 334.1, 371.6, 430.6, 524.3, 543.2, 825.2, 894.1 (v) 334.5, 352.12, 524.22, 524.23, 939.4, 951.10
say, the 417.1
say a few words in the right quarter 894.9
say a few words to the right person 894.9
say again 849.7, 849.8
say a good word for 509.11
say "amen" to 332.9
say amen to 332.12
say a mouthful 973.10
say aside 542.3
say a word to the wise 399.5
say aye 441.2
say by the way 524.24
say "ditto" to 332.9
sayer 524.17
say farewell 188.16
say for argument's sake 951.10
say for the hell of it 951.10
say goodbye 188.16
say goodbye to 370.5
say grace 696.13
say hello 585.10
say I do 563.15
say "I do" 436.6
say in a roundabout way 344.7, 538.10, 914.4
say in defense 600.10
saying 334.1, 524.3, 974.1
saying no to 668.2
say in reply 939.4
say it all 1017.19
say loud and clear 334.5, 524.21
say nay 333.4, 442.3, 955.5
say neither yes nor no 344.6
say no 335.3, 442.3, 668.6
say nothing 51.6
say no to 444.3, 510.10
say one's lesson 989.16
say one's prayers 696.13
say out 524.21
say out loud 334.5, 524.21
say over 849.8
say over again 849.8
say over and over 849.10
say right to one's face 454.3
say-so 334.1, 420.1, 430.6, 573.3, 894.1
say-so, the 417.1
say something nice about 509.14
say that all is for the best 124.8
say the first thing that comes into one's head 365.7
say the first thing that comes into one's mind 365.7
say the word 420.8, 443.9
say to oneself 542.3
say to one's face 492.10
say "uncle" 412.12, 433.8
say uncle 127.13
say under one's breath 345.9
say what comes uppermost 365.7
say what one thinks 644.12
say yea 441.2
say yes 436.5, 441.2
say yes to 332.8
s-block 1060.2
scab (n) 85.37, 295.3, 295.14, 727.8, 1004.1 (v) 295.27, 727.11, 1004.4
scabbed 1004.8
scabbiness 80.2, 661.3
scabby 80.23, 296.7, 661.12, 1004.8
scabies 85.35, 85.41
scabietic 85.61
scabious 296.7
scab over 295.27, 396.21
scabrous 296.7, 666.7
scabrousness 288.1
scads 247.4, 884.3, 991.2
scaffold 266.4, 605.5, 901.12
scaffolding 901.12
scag 87.9
scalar 245.5
scalawag 311.12, 660.3
scald (n) 85.38, 1020.6 (v) 393.13, 1019.22, 1020.20
scalded 393.27
scalding 1019.25
scalding hot 1019.25
scale (n) 158.2, 159.5, 193.4, 193.5, 245.1, 257.1, 295.12, 295.14, 295.15, 296.3, 297.9, 300.2, 709.6, 802.4, 812.2 (v) 6.11, 193.11, 245.4, 296.5, 459.20, 802.12
scale back 252.7, 258.9
scaleback 252.4
scaled-down 252.10, 260.12
scaled-down version 258.6
scale down 252.7, 258.9
scaledown 252.1
scale leaf 310.19
scale off 6.11
scales of justice 649.1
scale the heights 193.11
scale the walls 459.20
scale up 259.4
scaliness 288.1, 296.4
scaling 459.4, 802.3
scaling down 252.1
scallop (n) 10.19, 289.2 (v) 11.5, 281.4, 289.4
scalloped 11.7, 289.5
scalp 6.8, 737.23
scalper 730.3, 737.11
scalping 737.19
scalplock 3.7
scaly 296.7, 1051.11
scam (n) 356.9, 759.13 (v) 356.14, 356.19
scammer 357.4
scamp (n) 322.3, 660.3 (v) 340.8, 484.5
scamper (n) 174.3, 401.1 (v) 174.8, 401.5
scamper off 188.10
scamping 340.10, 484.7
scampish 322.6, 645.17
scampishness 322.2, 645.2
scan (n) 31.3, 91.9, 938.3 (v) 349.8, 570.13, 720.15, 801.7, 938.24, 938.26, 1036.17
scan conversion 1036.8
scandal 512.3, 552.8, 638.2, 654.3, 661.5, 666.2
scandalize 661.7
scandalmonger 552.9
scandalmongering 552.8
scandalous 512.13, 638.3, 654.16, 661.11, 666.6, 1000.9
scandalousness 666.2, 1000.2
scandal-plagued 661.13
scandal-ridden 661.13
scandal sheet 555.2
scandent 193.14
scanned 720.17
scanner 714.11, 1042.4
scanning (n) 91.7, 720.6, 1035.3, 1036.8 (a) 720.17
scanning beam 1035.4
scanning pattern 1035.5
scansion 720.6, 801.2
scansorial 193.14
scant (v) 210.5, 484.5 (a) 270.14, 795.4, 885.5, 992.10
scantily clad 6.13
scantiness 248.1, 258.1, 885.1, 992.2, 992.3
scantling 257.1
scant of 992.13
scant sufficiency 992.3
scanty 270.14, 795.4, 885.5, 992.10, 992.11
scape 33.6, 273.1, 712.11
scapegoat 696.7, 862.3, 870.4
scapegoating 696.7
scapegrace (n) 322.3, 660.4 (a) 322.6
scaphoid 284.16
scapi- 273.1
scapular 3.16, 702.2
scar (n) 200.3, 237.2, 517.5, 1004.1 (v) 517.19, 1004.4, 1015.5
scarab 691.5
scarabaeus 691.5
scarabee 691.5
Scaramouch 707.10
scarce 848.2, 885.5, 992.11
scarce as hen's teeth 848.2, 885.5
scarcely any 885.4
scarcely anything 998.6
scarcely heard 52.16
scarcely like 787.4
scarcely to be anticipated 969.3
scarcely to be expected 969.3
scarceness 848.1, 992.3
scarcer than hen's teeth 848.2, 992.11
scarcity 848.1, 885.1, 892.5, 992.3
scarcity price 632.3
scare (n) 127.1 (v) 127.15
scare away 127.21
scarebabe 127.9
scarecrow 127.9, 349.6, 1015.4
scarecrowish 1015.8
scared 127.22
scared rabbit 174.6
scared stiff 127.26
scared to death 127.22, 127.26
scaredy-cat 16.6, 491.5
scarehead 937.2
scaremonger 127.8
scaremongering 127.7
scare off 379.3
scare one stiff 127.15
scare one to death 127.15
scare out of one's wits 127.15, 400.3
scarer 127.9
scare spitless 127.15
scare tactic 127.7
scare tactics 127.7, 424.3, 514.1
scare the daylights out of 127.15
scare the hell out of 127.15
scare the life out of 127.15
scare the living daylights out of 127.15
scare the pants off of 127.15
scare to death frighten 400.3
scare up 472.9, 472.11
scarf (n) 5.31, 10.2, 800.4 (v) 672.5, 800.8
scarf down 8.22
scarfpin 498.6
scarfskin 2.4
scarification 517.5
scarified 1004.8
scarify 96.18, 289.4, 510.20, 517.19, 1004.4
scariness 127.2
scaring 127.28
scaring off 379.1
scarlet 41.6, 665.28
scarlet woman 665.16
scarp 200.3, 204.4, 237.2
scarper 188.12, 222.10
scarpering 222.4, 368.4
scarpines 605.4
scarred 1004.8
scary 127.23, 127.28
scat 708.13
scathe (n) 393.1 (v) 510.20, 1000.6
scatheful 1000.12
scatheless 1002.8
scathing 17.14, 144.23
scatologic 12.20, 513.8
scatological 12.20, 513.8, 523.21
scatological literature 547.12, 718.1
scatologize 513.6
scatology 513.3, 523.9, 666.4
scat singing 708.13
scatter (n) 164.2, 299.1, 771.1 (v) 164.5, 171.6, 224.3, 299.3, 412.8, 486.3, 771.4, 771.8, 802.13, 802.19, 804.3, 811.2
scatteration 771.1
scatterbrain 924.7, 985.5
scatterbrained 364.6, 810.16, 854.7, 922.19, 984.6, 985.16

scatterbrains 924.7
scattered 164.8, 224.6, 299.4, 412.14, 771.9, 802.21, 810.16, 885.5
scatteredness 299.1
scattering (n) 171.2, 299.2, 771.1, 802.3, 804.1, 885.2 (a) 771.11
scattering of the ashes 309.2
scatter pin 498.6
scatter seed 1069.18
scattersite housing 228.1
scatter to the winds 473.6, 486.3, 771.4
scattiness 984.1, 985.5
scatty 923.9, 984.6, 985.16
scavenge 79.18
scavenger 79.16, 311.3
scavenger hunt 743.9
scenario 381.2, 704.21, 706.3, 887.1, 940.1
scenarioist 704.22
scenario writer 547.15, 704.22, 718.4
scenarist 547.15, 704.22, 706.4, 718.4
scenarize 547.21, 704.28, 718.6
scend (n) 238.14, 916.4 (v) 182.55, 238.22
scene 27.3, 33.6, 152.9, 209.2, 463.1, 704.7, 704.20, 712.11
scenecraft 704.3
sceneman 704.24
scene master 704.24
scene of action 463.1
scene painter 704.24, 716.4
scene plot 704.21
scenery 33.6, 463.1, 704.20
scenery-chewing 704.33
scenes, the 704.1
sceneshifter 704.24
scenewright 704.23, 704.24, 716.4
scenic 704.33, 1016.17
scenic artist 704.24
scenic overlook 27.8
scenic route 20.3, 383.1
scenic view 33.6
scenographer 716.4
scenographic 712.21
scenography 712.5
scent (n) 69.1, 69.4, 70.1, 70.2, 517.8, 517.9, 551.4 (v) 69.7, 69.8, 70.8, 941.6
scent bag 70.6
scent ball 70.6
scent bottle 70.6
scent box 70.6
scented 70.9
scenter 70.6
scent-free 72.5
scent from afar 961.6
scent gland 69.5
scent hound 311.17
scenting 69.3
scentless 72.5
scentlessness 72.1
scent strip 70.6
scent trail 382.2
scepter 417.9, 647.3
Schadenfreude 144.6
schedule (n) 381.1, 807.1, 832.9, 871.1, 871.6, 965.3 (v) 381.8, 477.9, 626.5, 871.8, 965.6
scheduled 381.12, 871.9, 965.9
scheduled airline 184.10
scheduled flight 184.9
schedule of operation 965.3
scheduling 626.1, 832.1
Scheibler's pitch 709.4
Scheiner scale 1025.21
Schellingian 952.12
schema 349.1, 381.1, 801.4
schematic 381.14, 801.9
schematism 381.1
schematization 349.1, 381.1, 801.2
schematize 349.8, 381.8, 801.7
schematized 381.12
scheme (n) 356.6, 381.1, 381.2, 381.5, 415.3, 722.4, 801.4, 807.1, 932.1 (v) 380.7, 381.9, 415.10, 839.6, 965.4
schemed 965.7
scheme of arrangement 381.1
schemer 357.10, 381.7, 415.7
schemery 381.5
schemes 894.3
scheming (n) 381.5, 965.1 (a) 356.22, 381.13, 415.12, 494.8, 645.18
schemozzle 330.4
scherzando (n) 708.25 (a) 708.53
scherzo 708.25
scherzoso 708.53
schism 370.2, 456.4, 675.3
schismatic (n) 333.3, 363.5, 675.18 (a) 333.6, 363.12, 675.26
schismatical 333.6, 675.26
schismatism 675.4
schismatize 333.4
schist 1059.1
schiz (n) 926.17 (a) 926.28
schizo (n) 926.16, 926.17 (a) 926.27
schizoaffective disorder 926.4
schizoid (n) 92.12, 926.17 (a) 926.27, 926.28
schizoidism 92.20
schizoid personality 92.11, 92.20, 926.4
schizophasia 926.4
schizophrene 926.17
schizophrenia 92.14, 92.20, 926.4
schizophrenic (n) 926.17 (a) 926.28
schizothyme 92.12
schizothymia 92.11, 92.20, 926.4
schizothymic personality 92.11
schizotypal personality 926.4
schiz out 926.22
schizy (n) 926.17 (a) 926.28
schizzy 926.27
schlemiel 358.2, 410.8, 924.3, 1011.7
schlep (n) 177.10, 810.7 (v) 175.7, 176.12
schlimazel 1011.7
schlock 1005.6
schlocky 810.15, 1000.9
schlump 810.7
schlumpy 810.14
schmaltz 93.8
schmaltzy 93.21
schmeck 87.9
schmecker 87.21
Schmerz 112.3
schmuck 924.1
schnapps 88.13
schnorrer 440.8
schnoz 2.11, 283.8
schnozzle 283.8
schnozzola 283.8
scholar 556.3, 572.1, 866.3, 920.9, 921.1, 928.11, 929.3
scholarliness 570.4
scholarly 568.19, 570.17, 928.21, 928.28
scholarly edition 341.2
scholarship 478.8, 568.1, 570.1, 570.4, 646.7, 928.5
scholastic (n) 676.3, 929.3 (a) 567.13, 568.19, 570.17, 928.21, 928.22
scholastic institution 567.1
scholia 254.2, 549.4
scholiast 341.7, 556.4, 946.7
scholiastic 341.15
scholium 341.5, 549.4
school (n) 230.5, 311.30, 567.1, 568.1, 617.5, 675.3, 712.7, 953.3 (v) 568.10 (a) 567.13
schoolable 570.18
school age 301.1
school-aged child 572.3
school board 567.12
schoolbook 554.1, 554.10
schoolboy 302.5, 572.3
schoolboyish 572.12
school building 567.10
schoolbus 179.13
school chapel 703.3
schoolchild 572.3
school chum 588.3
school colors 35.7
school companion 588.3
schooldame 571.2
school days 301.1
schooled 928.18
school edition 554.5
school examination 938.2
schoolfellow 572.3, 588.3
school furniture 229.1
schoolgirl 302.8, 572.3
schoolgirlish 572.12
school grammar 530.1
schoolhouse 567.10
schooling 568.1, 928.4
schoolish 568.19
schoolkeeper 571.1
school kid 572.3
schoolkid 302.5
school lad 572.3
school library 558.1
schoolma'am 571.2
schoolmaid 302.8
schoolman 571.1, 676.3, 929.3
schoolmarm 571.2
schoolmarmish 571.11
schoolmaster 571.1
schoolmastering 571.11
schoolmasterish 571.11
schoolmasterlike 571.11
schoolmasterly 571.11
schoolmastery 571.10
schoolmate 572.3, 588.3
schoolmiss 302.8
schoolmistress 571.2
schoolmistressy 571.11
school of 770.5
school of philosophy 952.1
school of psychology 92.2
school of the arts 567.7
school of thought 952.1, 952.2
school oneself 570.10
school ring 498.6, 647.1
schoolroom 567.11
schoolteacher 571.1
schoolteacherish 571.11
schoolteachery 571.11
schoolwork 568.1
Schopenhauerian 952.12
Schrödinger equation 916.4
Schrödinger theory 1038.2
Schule 567.1
schuss 753.4
schvitz 1019.22
schvitzing 1019.25
sciatic 217.10
sciatica 85.25
sciatic neuritis 85.25
science 413.7, 928.4, 928.10
Science and Health with Key to the Scriptures 683.7
science fiction film 706.2
science museum 386.9
science of coins 728.22
science of discursive thought 935.2
science of human behavior 92.1
science of language 523.13
science of law 673.7
science of life, the 1068.1
science of man 312.10
science of matter 1060.1
science of measurement 300.8
science of nutrition 7.16
science of rotation 915.8
science of structure 266.1
science of substances 1060.1
science of the mind 92.1
science of war 458.5
science park 739.1
scientific 807.6, 928.28, 973.17, 987.6
scientifically exact 973.17
scientific exactitude 973.5
scientific humanism 312.11
scientific management 573.7
scientific name 527.3
scientism 987.2
scientist 928.11
scientistic 987.6
sci-fi film 706.2
scintilla 248.4, 1019.15, 1025.7
scintillant 1019.27, 1025.35
scintillate 489.13, 920.11, 1025.24
scintillating 489.15, 920.14, 1019.27, 1025.35
scintillation 489.7, 1019.15, 1025.7, 1035.5
scintillescent 1025.35
sciolism 930.5
sciolist 929.6
sciolistic 930.14

scion 191.2, 302.11, 310.20, 561.3, 793.4, 809.5
scissile 802.26, 1038.20, 1050.4
scission 802.2
scissor 802.11
scissorbill 727.8
scissors 474.3
scissors kick 760.8
scissure 224.2
sclaff 751.4
sclera 2.9
sclerosis 85.9, 1046.5
sclerotic 1046.13
scobicular 1051.11
scobiform 1051.11
scoff (n) 10.2, 156.2, 508.2 (v) 508.9, 695.14
scoff at 156.5, 327.6, 454.4, 489.13, 955.5
scoffer 695.12, 955.4
scoffing (n) 508.1, 695.6 (a) 508.12, 510.22
scofflaw 660.9
scold (n) 110.12, 510.9 (v) 60.5, 510.17
scolding 115.4, 510.5
sconce (n) 198.7, 603.3, 919.6 (v) 603.5
scone 10.31, 10.41
scooch 248.2
scooch down 913.8
scoop (n) 192.9, 284.2, 552.3, 793.3 (v) 176.17, 284.15
scoop, the 551.1, 761.4
scoop out 284.15
scoop the market 737.23
scoop up 284.15
scoot 174.9
scop 710.14, 720.12
scope (n) 27.1, 29.4, 31.3, 158.2, 245.1, 257.1, 430.4, 518.1, 673.1, 843.2 (v) 27.13
scope of mind 920.1
scope of vision 31.3
scope on 27.13
scope out 27.13, 938.24
scopolamine 86.12
scopophilia 981.1
scopophiliac (n) 981.2 (a) 981.5
scorbutic 85.61
scorch (n) 85.38, 1020.6 (v) 38.7, 40.2, 174.9, 393.13, 510.20, 1004.6, 1019.22, 1020.24, 1066.6
scorched 393.27, 1020.30, 1066.9
scorched earth 671.3
scorcher 174.5, 745.3, 1019.8
scorching (n) 1020.5 (a) 144.23, 671.22, 1019.25
scorching hot 1019.25
score (n) 224.2, 289.1, 290.1, 349.1, 375.1, 409.5, 517.5, 517.6, 623.1, 628.2, 628.3, 630.1, 704.21, 708.5, 708.28, 713.2, 747.3, 748.2, 749.3, 749.6, 750.2, 751.3, 752.3, 758.3, 882.7, 1017.6 (v) 87.22, 289.4, 290.3, 409.9, 472.8, 517.19, 708.46, 713.9, 746.5, 747.4, 748.3, 749.7, 871.8, 1017.18
score, the 761.4, 766.2, 767.3
score a breakthrough 409.10
score a bull's-eye 973.10
score a point 748.3
score a success 409.9
scoreboard 549.10
scorecard 549.10
scored 289.5, 290.4
scorekeeper 550.1
scoreless 412.16
scorer 550.1, 710.20, 749.3
scores 884.3
scoresheet 549.10
score up 1017.19
scoria 256.2, 1020.16, 1059.1
scorification 1020.5
scorify 1020.24
scoring 713.2, 751.3, 1017.9
scorn (n) 103.1, 157.1, 372.1 (v) 103.5, 157.3, 372.2, 454.4, 495.8, 589.8
scorned 372.3
scornful 103.7, 157.8, 372.4
scornful laugh 508.4
scornfulness 157.1
scornful smile 508.4
scorn to accept 157.4
scorn to receive 157.4
scorper 713.8
scorpion 311.32
scot 624.5, 630.6
scot and lot 630.6
Scotch 635.6
scotch (n) 1012.7 (v) 1012.10, 1012.15
scotch (n) 289.1, 517.5 (v) 289.4, 517.19
scotched 289.5
Scotch egg 10.26
Scotch foursome 751.3
Scotch mist 316.1, 319.3
scotch one's wheel 1012.15
Scotch tape 803.4
scot-free 369.11, 430.21, 431.10
Scot Guards 461.15
Scotist 952.12
Scotland Yard 1008.17
scotograph 714.6
scotophilia 75.11
scotophiliac 75.16
scotopia 27.1
Scotticism 523.8
Scottish thistle 647.6
scoundrel 645.10, 660.3
scoundrelism 645.2
scoundrelly 645.17
scour (n) 1044.2 (v) 79.18, 79.19, 174.8, 177.20, 287.7, 938.33, 1044.7
scourge (n) 85.5, 604.1, 605.1, 1001.1 (v) 604.12
scourge of the earth 606.3
scourging 604.4
scouring 79.5, 1044.2
scouring out 909.6
scouring pad 79.17
scouring powder 79.17
scourings 256.1, 391.4
scour out 909.22
scour the country 177.20
scout (n) 216.2, 576.9, 745.2, 816.1, 1008.10 (v) 27.13, 157.4, 177.20, 454.4, 508.9, 938.28
scouting 938.8
scout out 938.28, 938.34
scowl (n) 110.9, 152.2, 265.4, 510.8 (v) 110.15, 152.14
scowling 110.24
scrabble (n) 177.17, 547.7 (v) 177.26, 284.15, 547.20, 938.32
scrabbled 547.23
scrabble one's way up 409.10
scrabble up 193.11
scrag (n) 311.12 (v) 308.14, 459.15, 604.17, 820.6
scragged 288.7, 820.10
scraggliness 288.1
scraggly 288.7, 810.15
scraggy 258.13, 270.17, 288.7
scram 188.7, 222.10, 368.11
scramble (n) 177.17, 184.11, 330.4, 401.1, 457.4, 522.7, 797.6, 810.3, 810.4 (v) 174.8, 177.26, 330.13, 401.5, 457.13, 522.12, 746.5, 797.10, 811.3
scramblebrained 922.18, 985.16
scrambled 520.6, 522.14, 797.14
scrambled eggs 10.26
scramble for 480.16
scrambler 347.4
scramble up 193.11
scramming 368.4
scranch (n) 58.3 (v) 58.10
scrap (n) 8.2, 248.3, 258.7, 391.5, 456.6, 793.3 (v) 390.8, 456.12, 820.6
scrapbook 549.11, 554.7
scrape (n) 58.3, 85.38, 155.2, 971.3, 1013.5, 1044.2 (v) 58.10, 73.7, 155.6, 223.10, 284.15, 287.8, 393.13, 635.4, 708.41, 713.9, 1044.7
scrape along 385.12, 409.12
scrape and save 635.4
scrape by 991.4
scrape the bottom of the barrel 995.4
scrape through 369.8
scrape together 472.11, 770.18
scrape up 472.9, 770.18
scrap heap 370.4, 391.6
scrapiness 58.2
scraping (n) 635.2, 1044.2 (a) 58.16, 1044.10
scrap iron 391.4
scrapped 390.11, 820.9
scrapper 452.3, 461.1, 461.2
scrappiness 110.3, 795.1
scrapping 390.3, 457.1
scrapple 10.13
scrappy 58.16, 110.20, 110.26, 458.20, 795.4, 813.4, 851.3
scraps 256.1, 391.4
scrap the plan 365.8
scrapyard 391.6
scratch (n) 10.4, 58.3, 85.38, 276.1, 290.1, 350.2, 517.5, 547.7, 713.2, 728.2, 1004.1, 1044.2 (v) 58.10, 74.5, 284.15, 290.3, 350.4, 393.13, 395.16, 517.19, 547.20, 712.19, 713.9, 725.13, 820.6, 857.6, 1044.7 (a) 406.12
scratch-and-sniff 70.6
scratch around 938.23
scratchboard 712.18
scratch comma 204.7
scratch each other's back 863.4
scratched 290.4, 547.23
scratch feed 10.4
scratch golfer 751.2
scratch hit 1010.3
scratchiness 58.2
scratching (n) 50.13, 517.5, 713.2, 857.1, 1044.2 (a) 58.16
scratch one's back 511.5
scratch out 395.16
scratch pad 549.11
scratch player 751.2
scratch sheet 757.3
scratch test 91.15
scratch the surface 206.6, 276.4, 930.10
scratch together 472.9
scratchy 26.13, 58.16, 288.7, 547.23
scrawl (n) 522.4, 547.7 (v) 547.20
scrawled 547.23
scrawly 547.23
scrawniness 270.5, 992.2
scrawny 270.17, 992.10
screak (n) 58.4 (v) 58.8, 60.2
screaky 58.14
scream (n) 58.4, 59.1, 115.3, 489.6 (v) 58.8, 59.6, 60.2, 115.13, 318.20, 524.25
scream bloody murder 59.6, 115.16
scream blue murder 59.6
scream defiance 454.3
screamer 937.2, 975.6
screaming 35.20, 59.10, 501.20
screaming color 35.5
screaming halt 857.2
screaming meemies, the 926.10
scree 1059.1
screech (n) 58.4, 59.1 (v) 58.8, 59.6, 60.2, 60.5, 318.20, 524.25
screechiness 58.1
screeching 58.14
screechy 58.14
screed 510.7, 543.2, 547.10, 556.1
screen (n) 79.13, 170.3, 229.1, 292.8, 295.2, 346.2, 376.1, 704.20, 706.7, 808.5, 1008.3, 1028.1, 1035.11, 1042.9 (v) 79.22, 90.14, 295.19, 346.6, 460.8, 714.16, 747.4, 752.4, 773.6, 808.11, 944.4, 1008.18, 1028.5
screen, the 706.1
screen adaptation 706.3
screen block 746.3
screened 295.31, 1008.21, 1028.7
screened-in 295.31
screened-off 295.31
screen grab 1035.3
screen-grid voltage 1033.7
screening (n) 79.4, 91.12, 170.3, 295.1, 346.1, 747.3, 749.3, 808.3 (a) 295.35, 460.11, 1008.23, 1028.6

screen memory 989.1
screen name 527.8, 1042.19
screen off 212.5, 213.8, 295.19, 346.6
screen out 944.4
screen pass 746.3
screenplay 706.3
screen printing 712.16
screen proportion 706.7
screen saver 1042.11
screen test 706.5
screen time 1035.2
screenwriter 704.22, 706.4
screw (n) 265.1, 281.2, 428.6, 429.10, 605.4, 904.6 (v) 75.21, 265.5, 281.4, 356.19, 389.6, 421.5, 480.22, 484.5, 632.7, 800.8, 915.9
screw around 998.15
screwball (n) 870.4, 926.16, 927.4 (a) 926.27, 927.6
screwballs 926.27
screwdriver 1040.7
screwed up 393.29, 799.4, 810.16
screwed-up 414.22
screw in 757.5
screwiness 923.1, 926.2
screwing 75.7
screwing around 998.9
screw loose, a 926.2
screw over 389.6
screw propeller 904.6
screw-shaped 281.8
screw thread 281.2
screw through 757.5
screw-top 295.5
screw up 19.9, 393.11, 414.12, 799.3, 800.7, 811.3, 975.15, 1046.9
screwup 410.6, 414.5, 414.9, 810.2, 975.6, 985.3
screw up one's face 265.8
screw up the eyes 28.9
screwy 923.9, 926.27, 927.6
scribble (n) 350.2, 522.4, 547.7, 712.12 (v) 350.4, 547.20
scribbled 547.23
scribblemania 547.2, 718.2
scribblemaniac 547.25
scribblemaniacal 547.25
scribblement 547.7
scribbler 547.13, 547.16, 716.2, 718.3, 718.5
scribbling 547.7
scribbly 547.23
scribe (n) 547.13, 547.15, 550.1, 699.11, 718.4 (v) 547.19
scribes and Pharisees 693.3
scrim 704.20
scrimmage 457.4, 457.5
scrimmage line 746.3
scrimp 484.5, 635.4
scrimpiness 885.1, 992.2
scrimping (n) 484.1, 635.2 (a) 484.7, 635.6, 885.5
scrimption 992.5
scrimpy 885.5, 992.10
scrimshaw 715.1, 715.2
scrip 547.10, 549.5, 728.1, 728.5, 728.12
scrip dividend 738.7
script (n) 349.1, 546.3, 547.3, 547.10, 548.6, 549.5, 704.21, 706.3, 1042.13 (v) 704.28
script doctor 547.15
scripting 1042.13
scripting language 1042.13, 1042.13
scriptorial 547.22
scriptural 547.22, 683.11, 687.7
scripturalism 687.5
scripturalistic 687.8
Scripture 683.2
scripture 683.1, 683.7
scriptures 683.1
Scriptures, the 683.2
scripturient 547.25
scriptwriter 547.15, 704.22, 706.4, 718.4
scritch (n) 58.5 (v) 58.7
scrive (n) 547.3, 547.10 (v) 547.19
scrivener 547.13, 550.1
scrivenery 547.1
scrivening 547.1
scrobis 703.12
scrofulous 85.61
scroll (n) 281.2, 547.10, 547.11, 549.1, 549.5, 554.6, 711.5, 871.6 (v) 547.19
scrollable 1042.18
scroll bar 1042.18
scrolled 281.8
scrooge 484.4
scrotal 2.29
scrotum 2.13
scrounge 440.15
scrounger 440.8
scrounging (n) 440.6, 482.1 (a) 331.19, 440.16
scrub (n) 79.5, 310.9, 310.13, 310.16, 576.1, 998.7, 1044.2 (v) 79.18, 79.19, 395.12, 857.6, 1044.7 (a) 250.6
scrubbed 79.26
scrubber 79.14
scrubbiness 661.3
scrubbing 79.5, 170.3, 395.7, 857.1, 1044.2
scrubbing out 79.5
scrubbing up 79.5
scrubbly 310.39
scrubby 258.13, 310.39, 310.40, 497.15, 661.12, 998.21
scrubland 310.13
scrublike 310.39
scrub out 79.19
scrub up 79.19
scrubwood 310.16
scruffiness 80.1, 661.3
scruffy 80.22, 393.32, 661.12, 998.21
scrumpdiddlyumptious 999.13
scrumptious 63.8, 999.13
scrumptiousness 63.1
scrunch (n) 58.3, 260.2 (v) 58.10, 260.8, 1051.9
scrunch up 1051.9
scruple (n) 248.2, 325.2, 333.2, 644.2, 955.2 (v) 325.4, 333.5, 362.7, 955.6
scruples 113.2, 636.3, 644.2
scrupling 362.11
scrupulosity 113.2, 325.2, 339.3, 495.1, 644.2
scrupulous 325.7, 339.12, 434.4, 495.9, 580.10, 641.13, 644.15, 955.9
scrupulousness 113.2, 325.2, 339.3, 495.1, 580.2, 644.2, 955.2
scrutability 521.1
scrutable 521.10
scrutator 938.17
scrutatorial 938.37
scrutineer 938.17
scrutinize 27.14, 938.24, 938.25, 983.8
scrutinize comparatively 943.5
scrutinizer 938.17
scrutinizing 339.12
scrutiny 27.6, 938.3, 983.4
scuba 367.5, 760.8
scuba diver 367.4
scuba diving 367.3
scud (n) 174.3, 316.2, 318.5, 320.2 (v) 174.8, 182.54
scuff (n) 80.5, 85.38, 1044.2 (v) 177.28, 393.13, 1044.7
scuffing 1044.2
scuffle (n) 457.4, 725.3 (v) 177.28, 457.13, 725.11
scuffler 461.1, 461.3
scull (n) 180.15 (v) 182.13, 182.53
sculler 183.5, 760.2
scullery 11.4, 197.14
scullery maid 79.15, 577.8
sculling 182.1, 760.2
scullion 79.15, 577.2
sculp 715.5
sculpt 262.7, 715.5
sculpted 262.9, 715.7
sculptile 715.7
sculptitory 715.6
sculptor 715.1, 716.6
sculptor's wax 715.4
sculptress 716.6
sculptural 715.6
sculpture (n) 262.5, 349.6, 712.1, 712.16, 715.1, 715.2 (v) 262.7, 713.9, 715.5
sculptured 713.11, 715.7
sculptured glass 715.3
sculpturer 716.6
sculpturesque 715.6
sculpturing 715.1
scum (n) 80.8, 80.9, 256.2, 295.12, 296.2, 305.11, 320.2, 391.4, 497.6, 606.3 (v) 295.19, 320.5
scumble 712.19
scumbled 712.21
scummed 295.31
scumminess 80.2, 661.3
scummy 80.22, 661.12, 998.21
scum of the earth 80.9, 606.3, 660.11
scunner 93.7, 99.1, 779.1
scupper 239.5
scurf 80.7, 80.9, 296.3
scurfiness 80.2
scurfy 80.23, 296.7, 1051.11
scurrile 156.8, 512.13, 513.8, 666.9
scurrility 156.2, 508.2, 513.2, 666.4
scurrilous 144.23, 156.8, 512.13, 513.8, 666.9
scurry (n) 174.3, 401.1 (v) 174.8, 401.5
S-curve 279.3
scurviness 661.3, 1000.2
scurvy (n) 85.33 (a) 497.15, 661.12, 998.21, 1000.9
scurvy trick 356.6
scut 217.6
scutate 279.19
scutcheon 647.2
scute 295.15
scutiform 279.19
scuttle (n) 174.3, 177.12, 189.6, 401.1 (v) 174.8, 177.28, 182.44, 367.8, 395.11, 401.5, 491.8, 625.8
scuttlebutt 552.6
scutum 295.15
scut work 725.4
scuzz 80.7
scuzziness 80.1, 98.2
scuzzy 80.23, 98.18, 810.15, 998.21
Scylla and Charybdis 371.3
scyphate 284.16
scythe 279.5
scythe of Death 307.2
scythe of Time 821.3
sea 238.14, 240.1, 240.2, 247.3
sea air 317.2
sea anchor 1008.3, 1012.7
seabank 234.2
seabeach 234.2
seabed 199.4, 240.5, 275.4
Seabee 183.1, 183.4, 461.14
Seabees 461.27
sea bird 311.27
sea biscuit 10.30
seaboard 234.2
sea-bordering 211.11
seaborne 182.57
sea bottom 240.5
sea breeze 318.4
sea change 303.7, 392.1, 852.2, 858.1
seachanger 680.11
seacliff 234.2
sea clutter 1036.12
seacoast 234.2
sea cock 239.10, 293.4
sea combat naval combat 457.4
sea devil 240.3
sea dog 183.1
seadog 316.8
seafare 182.13
seafarer 183.1
seafaring (n) 182.1 (a) 182.57, 240.8
seafaring man 183.1
seafloor 275.4
sea foam 320.2
seafood 10.24
seafront (n) 234.2 (a) 234.7
seagirt 235.7
sea god 240.3
sea-going 240.8
seagoing 182.57

sea grass 310.5
sea-green 44.4
sea ice 1023.5
sea-kindly 180.18
seakindly 1007.7
sea king 483.7
seal (n) 332.4, 517.1, 517.7, 517.13, 527.10, 647.3, 713.8, 785.6, 786.6, 865.4 (v) 293.6, 332.12, 359.7, 437.7, 517.19, 517.20 (a) 40.3
sea lane 182.10, 383.1
sea lawyer 597.1
seal brown 311.11
seal-brown 40.3
sealed 293.9, 293.12, 332.14, 345.14, 437.11, 930.16
sealed book 345.5, 930.6
sealed off 429.20
sealed orders 345.5
sealed verdict 598.9
sea legs 182.3
sea lentil 310.4
sea level 201.3
seal in 293.6
sea line 201.4
sealing 437.3
sealing off 293.3
seal of approval 332.4, 509.1
seal off 293.6, 429.13
seal of secrecy 345.3
seal of the confessional 345.5
seal one's infamy 661.7
seal one's lips 51.5
seal the deal 332.10
seal the doom of 395.10
seal up 293.6, 346.7, 429.12
seam (n) 224.2, 296.1, 800.4, 1058.7 (v) 517.19
sea-maid 678.10
sea-maiden 678.10
seaman 183.1, 240.3
seamanlike 182.57
seamanlikeness 182.3
seamanliness 182.3
seamanly 182.57
seamanship 182.3, 413.1
sea margin 234.2
seamark 517.10
seamless 781.5, 812.8, 872.7
seamlessness 781.1, 812.1
sea monster 311.29
sea moss 310.4
seamount 237.6, 240.5
seamster 741.2
seamstress 5.36, 741.2
seamy 661.10
seance 691.3
séance 541.5, 689.5, 689.6, 770.2
sea nymph 240.3, 678.10
sea of flames 1019.13
sea of grass 201.3, 236.1
sea of troubles 96.8, 1011.1, 1013.3
sea operations 458.4
seapiece 712.11
sea pig 311.29
seaplane (n) 181.8 (v) 184.36
seaplane carrier 180.8
seaport 1009.6
sea post office 553.7
sear (n) 1020.6 (v) 11.5, 26.7, 260.9, 393.18, 1004.6, 1020.24, 1066.6 (a) 260.13
search (n) 938.15 (v) 382.8, 938.31, 1042.21
searchability 1042.18
search-and-destroy mission 938.15
search and rescue 381.5
search and seizure 428.4
search engine 1042.18, 1042.19
search engine optimization 1042.18
searcher 938.18
search for 938.30
search high heaven 938.33
searching (n) 382.1, 938.15 (a) 382.11, 938.38
searching investigation 938.4
search into 938.23
search mission 184.11
search one's motives 113.6
search one's soul 113.6
search out 938.30, 938.34, 941.2
search party 938.15
search through 938.31
search warrant 598.12, 938.15
seared 11.7, 654.17, 1020.30, 1066.9
seared conscience 114.2
searing (n) 11.2, 260.3, 1020.5 (a) 26.10, 1019.25
sea room 158.3, 430.4
sea rover 183.1, 483.7
seascape 33.6, 712.11
sea serpent 240.3, 311.29
seashell 295.15
seashore (n) 234.2 (a) 182.58
seasick 85.57
seasickness 85.30
seaside (n) 234.2 (a) 234.7
sea snake 311.25, 311.29
sea soldiers 461.28
season (n) 313.1, 824.1 (v) 63.7, 303.9, 373.9, 392.10, 397.9, 797.11, 959.3, 1046.7, 1049.3
season, the 313.1
seasonable 788.10, 843.9, 995.5
seasonableness 313.1, 843.1, 995.1
seasonal (n) 555.1 (a) 313.9, 317.13, 850.7
seasonal affective disorder 92.14, 313.1
seasonality 313.1, 850.2
seasonal unemployment 331.3
seasoned 68.7, 303.13, 373.15, 407.13, 413.28, 920.17, 959.10, 1046.15, 1049.6
seasoned hand 413.11
seasoned professional 726.4
seasoned understanding 920.5
seasoned veteran 413.16
seasoner 63.3
seasoning 63.3, 303.6, 373.7, 392.2, 397.2, 405.4, 413.9, 797.7, 1046.5
season of the year 313.1
season's look, the 578.1
seat (n) 159.2, 208.6, 228.1, 230.4, 417.10, 901.6, 901.17 (v) 159.12, 159.16, 855.9
seat belt 1008.3
seated 159.18
seating 158.5, 704.15
seating capacity 158.5
seat of government 230.4
seat of justice 595.5
seat of learning 567.1
seat of life 306.2
seat of power 417.10
seat of state 417.10
seat of thought 919.6
seat of war 463.2
seat oneself 913.10
sea travel 182.1
sea trip 182.6
sea turtle 311.24
seawall 901.4, 1009.6, 1012.5
seawater 1065.3
sea wave 916.4
seaway 182.10
seaweed 310.4
seaworthiness 1007.1
seaworthy 176.18, 180.18, 1007.7
sea wrack 310.4
sea zoo 228.19
sebaceous 13.7, 1056.9
sebaceous cyst 283.4, 1004.1
sebaceous gland disorder 85.35
sebaceousness 1056.5
sebiferous 13.7
sebkha 236.1
sebum 13.2, 1056.1
sec (n) 830.3 (a) 67.5
secant (n) 277.2 (a) 170.8
sec champagne 88.17
secede 327.7, 333.4, 363.7, 370.6
seceder 363.5
secern 780.6, 944.4
secernment 13.1
secession 333.1, 363.2, 370.2
secessionist (n) 363.5 (a) 363.12
seclude 429.13, 773.6
secluded 173.12, 345.13, 346.11, 584.8, 773.8
seclude oneself 583.4, 584.7, 1009.8
secluse 346.11
seclusion 345.2, 429.2, 583.3, 584.1, 773.3, 872.2
seclusionist 584.5
seclusive 583.6, 584.8, 773.9
seclusiveness 583.3
secobarbital 86.12
Seconal 86.12
seconary rainbow 316.8
second (n) 616.6, 616.9, 709.20, 745.1, 754.2, 824.2, 830.3, 1005.6 (v) 332.12, 449.13 (a) 873.6
secondaries 3.18
secondariness 250.1, 998.1
secondary (n) 35.7, 250.2, 432.5, 576.1, 768.2, 862.2 (a) 250.6, 768.4, 831.11, 862.8, 873.6, 998.16
secondary burial 309.1
secondary chord 709.17
secondary color 35.7
secondary condition 85.1
secondary digestion 2.17, 7.8
secondary disease 85.1
secondary eardrum 2.10
secondary emission 1033.5
secondary issue 738.6
secondary meaning 518.1
secondary memory 1042.7
secondary planet 1073.9
secondary plot 722.4
secondary product 893.3
secondary school 567.4
secondary schooler 572.3
secondary sense 519.2
secondary sex characteristic 2.13
secondary smoke 89.1
secondary stress 524.10
second banana 250.1, 704.10
second base 745.1
second baseman 745.2
second-base umpire 745.3
second best 1005.4
second-best 132.6, 1005.9
second birth 685.4
second chance 396.3
second childhood 303.5, 922.10
second-class 606.8, 1005.9
second-class citizens 606.4
second-class citizenship 791.1
second coming 839.3
second cousin 559.3
second crop 472.5
second-degree burn 85.38, 1019.13, 1020.6
second-degree murder 308.2
second down 746.3
second draft 547.10
second edition 785.5
seconder 332.7, 616.9
second estate 607.2
second fiddle 250.1, 250.2, 432.2
second-generation 186.9
secondhand 387.24, 842.18
secondhand clothes 5.5
secondhand smoke 89.1, 1001.4
second helping 8.10, 849.5
second home 228.8
second honeymoon 1010.4
second-honeymoon 563.16
second in command 576.1, 576.8
second-in-command 432.5
seconding 449.4
second job 724.5
second language 523.1
second lieutenant 575.17
second line of defense 461.23, 461.25
second loo 849.1
second look 938.7
second mate 183.7
second mortgage 438.4
second name 527.5
second nature 373.3
second officer 185.1
second opinion 946.3
second person 530.7
second philosophy 1018.1
second player 750.3
second prize 646.2
second rank 250.6
second-rate 250.6, 1005.9
second-rateness 1005.3
second-rater 1005.5

second reading 613.6
seconds 5.5, 8.10, 89.2, 735.2
second self 616.7, 784.3
second sex, the 77.3
second sight 24.5, 689.8, 934.1
second-sighted 689.24, 934.5
second-sightedness 934.1
second-story man 483.3
second-story thief 483.3
second-story work 482.5
second string (n) 250.1, 617.7, 862.2 (a) 250.6
second stringer 250.2
second team 617.7
second thought 817.1, 931.5
second thoughts 362.1, 362.2, 363.1, 494.2
second to none 249.15
second wind 396.3
second youth 396.3
secrecy 32.1, 345.1, 346.1, 584.1
secret (n) 345.5 (a) 32.5, 345.11, 345.15, 346.11, 522.16, 767.7
secreta 13.1
secret agent 576.9, 938.16
secretarial 547.28
Secretariat 614.2
secretariat 417.10, 594.4
secretary 547.13, 550.1, 574.3, 575.16, 576.2, 576.3, 577.3, 901.15
secretary of legation 576.6
secretary of state 575.16
Secretary of the Treasury 729.12
secret ballot 371.6
secret caucus 609.9
secret compartment 346.4
secrete 12.12, 13.5, 345.7, 346.7, 386.11, 1065.11
secret enemy 589.6
secret exit 346.5
secret grip 517.12
secret heart 207.2, 767.5
secreting 13.7
secret ink 345.6
secretion 12.1, 13.1, 346.1, 1061.1, 1065.1
secretional 13.7
secretionary 13.7
secretive 13.7, 344.8, 345.15
secretiveness 344.1, 345.1
secret language 345.6, 522.7
secret meeting 345.2
secret name 527.3
secretness 345.1
secret of the confessional 345.5
secretory 12.19, 13.7
secret partner 616.2
secret passage 346.5, 369.3
secret place 346.4, 1009.5
secret places 93.3, 207.2
secret plan 381.5
secret police 938.9, 1008.17
secret recesses of the heart 93.3
Secret Service 576.10
secret service 345.4
secret service 576.12, 938.9
secret society 617.3
secret staircase 346.5
secret thoughts 931.4
secret weapon 462.1, 997.6
secret writing 345.6, 547.1
sect 617.4, 617.5, 675.3
sectarian (n) 333.3, 675.18, 868.3 (a) 333.6, 617.19, 675.26
sectarianism 617.13, 675.4
sectarism 675.3, 675.4
Sectary 675.23
sectary (n) 166.2, 333.3, 616.9, 675.18 (a) 333.6, 617.19
sectary (n) 868.3 (a) 675.26
section (n) 231.1, 231.4, 461.22, 554.13, 708.24, 793.1, 793.2, 802.2, 809.2, 809.5 (v) 802.18
sectional 231.8, 617.19, 793.7
sectionalism 609.4, 617.13
sector 231.1, 280.8, 793.1, 1042.18
secular (n) 700.2 (a) 686.3, 695.16, 700.3, 850.8, 882.29, 987.6, 1052.10
secular, the 686.2
secular canoness 699.17
secular humanism 312.11, 686.1, 695.7
secular humanist 695.13
secular-humanistic 695.16
secularism 686.1, 695.2, 987.2, 1052.6
secularist (n) 695.11 (a) 695.16, 700.3
secularistic 695.16, 700.3
secularity 686.1
secularization 695.1
secularize 695.14
secularized 695.15
seculars 700.1
secundines 817.3
securable 966.8
securableness 966.3
secure (v) 176.16, 192.14, 293.6, 428.10, 438.9, 460.8, 472.8, 479.6, 800.7, 855.8, 857.8, 1008.18 (a) 107.8, 800.14, 855.12, 953.21, 970.17, 970.20, 970.21, 1007.4
secured 293.9, 438.11, 460.12
securement 472.1, 855.1
secureness 855.1, 970.4
secure one's object 409.8
secure place in history 662.7
securities 738.1
securities market 737.1
security 124.1, 345.3, 438.1, 855.1, 970.4, 970.5, 1007.1, 1008.1, 1010.1
security agreement 438.4
security blanket 295.10, 901.1
security camera 714.11
security clearance 443.3
Security Council 614.2
security force 1008.17
security guard 1008.9
security industry 1008.1
security risk 357.11
sedan cruiser 180.4
sedate (v) 22.20, 120.5, 670.6 (a) 106.14, 111.3, 136.12
sedated 22.21
sedateness 106.4, 111.1, 136.2
sedating 120.1, 670.2
sedation 22.6, 120.1, 670.2
sedative (n) 22.10, 25.3, 86.12, 87.3, 670.3 (a) 22.23, 86.45, 120.9, 670.16
sedative hypnotic 86.12, 87.3
sedentary 173.12, 173.14, 331.17
sedge 310.5
sedilia 703.14
sediment (n) 256.2, 1059.6 (v) 1045.11
sedimental 256.8
sedimentary 256.8
sedimentary rock 1059.1
sedimentate 1045.11
sedimentation 1045.5, 1059.8
sedition 327.3, 418.2, 645.7
seditionary (n) 375.11, 418.3 (a) 327.11
seditionist 375.11
seditious 327.11, 418.5, 645.22
seditiousness 327.3
seduce 104.22, 377.5, 654.10, 665.20
seduceability 954.2
seduceable 954.9
seducement 377.1, 665.6
seducer 104.12, 357.1, 377.4, 562.12, 665.12
seducing 377.8
seduction 377.1, 665.6
seductive 100.30, 377.8
seductiveness 100.13, 122.3, 377.2
seductress 377.4, 665.15
sedulity 330.6, 360.1
sedulous 330.22, 339.11, 360.8, 983.15
sedulousness 330.6, 339.2, 360.1
see (n) 698.8 (v) 24.6, 27.12, 221.8, 323.2, 521.9, 582.19, 759.25, 918.5, 928.12, 931.17, 941.5, 983.6, 986.15
seeable 31.6, 348.8
seeableness 31.1
see about 931.14
see action 458.17
see active duty 458.17
see after 1008.19
see ahead 839.6, 961.5, 962.9
see as it really is 941.8
see at a glance 27.12, 521.9
see badly 28.8
see beforehand 961.5
see both sides 979.7
see both sides of the question 362.7
see but one side of the question 980.6
see combat 458.17
seed (n) 305.11, 310.31, 560.4, 561.1, 758.2, 886.7 (v) 890.8, 1069.18
see daylight 521.9
seedbed 1069.11
seedbox 310.30
seedcase 310.30
seed clouds 316.10
seed coat 295.16, 310.30
seed down 1069.18
seed-eating bird 311.27
seediness 85.1, 810.6
seeding 316.5, 1069.14
seed leaf 310.19
seedling 302.11, 310.3, 310.10, 310.33
seed money 438.3
see double 28.8, 88.27
seed plant 310.3
seed plot 890.6
seed pod 310.30
seedstalk 310.21
seedtime 313.2
seedtime of life 301.1
seed tray 1069.10
seed vegetable 10.35, 310.4
seed vessel 310.30
seedy 21.7, 85.56, 393.32, 810.15, 1005.9
see eye to eye 332.9, 455.2, 788.6
see fit 371.17
seegar 89.4
see how the ball bounces 846.12
see how the cat jumps 494.6
see how the cookie crumbles 846.12
see how the land lies 494.6, 942.9
see how the wind blows 494.6
see if one can do 403.10
see in a special light 341.9
seeing (n) 27.1, 27.2, 31.2, 1073.17 (a) 27.20
seeing distinctions 944.1
seeing double 88.31
Seeing Eye dog 30.6, 311.16
seeing-eye hit 745.3
seeing glass 29.6
seeing to 889.1
see in its true colors 941.8
see in perspective 925.2
see in retrospect 989.9
see in the crystal ball 962.9
see into 521.9, 938.23
see it coming 123.2
see it out 15.10, 360.5
see it through 360.5, 794.8, 856.3, 856.5
see justice done 649.5
seek 382.8, 403.5, 440.14, 938.30, 981.3
seek a second opinion 422.7
seek asylum 1009.7
seeker 382.4, 440.7, 938.18
seek for 938.30
seeking (n) 382.1, 938.12 (a) 382.11
seek in law 598.13
seek justice 598.13
seek legal protection 598.13
seek legal redress 598.13
seek out 382.8
seek refuge 1009.7
seek-sorrow 125.7
seek the company of 587.12
seek the golden mean 670.5
seek the middle 819.3
seek to 403.8
seek to communicate 518.9
see less than is there 950.2
see life 743.24
seem 33.10
seeming (n) 33.3, 206.1, 354.3, 976.2 (a) 33.11, 206.7, 354.27, 976.9

seeming difference 780.2
seem like 33.10, 784.7
seem likely 968.4
seemliness 496.2, 533.1, 579.1, 637.2, 664.2, 995.1
seemly 496.9, 533.7, 579.5, 637.3, 664.5, 995.5
seemly, the 637.1
see more than is there 949.2
seem to be 33.10
seem true 973.9
seen, the 31.1
see nothing 984.2
see nuances 944.6
see off 188.16
See of Rome 698.6
see one alone 345.9
see one redressed 649.5
see one's way clear to 441.3
see one through 449.11
see only the good points of 949.2
see out 188.16
seep (n) 190.6 (v) 190.15, 238.18, 1065.11
seepage 187.6, 189.1, 190.6, 238.7
seep in 187.13, 189.10, 570.7
seeping (n) 238.7 (a) 1065.17
see poorly 28.8
seepproof 1066.11
seer 689.14, 918.1, 921.1, 962.4, 986.13
see red 152.18, 671.12
seeress 962.4
seesaw (n) 743.15, 777.3, 916.5, 916.9 (v) 854.5, 916.13 (a) 777.10, 916.19
seesawing (n) 854.3, 916.5 (a) 777.10
see shades of difference 944.6
see something funny 955.6
see that 970.11
seethe (n) 917.1 (v) 105.16, 152.15, 320.4, 671.12, 770.16, 915.12, 917.15, 1019.22, 1020.20, 1065.13
see the cloven hoof 941.8
see the difference 944.6
see the future 962.9
see the glass half empty 125.9
see the handwriting on the wall 845.6, 961.6
see the inside of 941.8
see the last of 390.5, 475.3, 909.13
see the light 33.8, 306.9, 352.16, 521.9, 692.7
see the light at the end of the tunnel 124.8
see the light of day 1.2, 33.8, 352.16, 818.13
see the lions 918.6
see the sights 918.6
see the special circumstances 959.5
seething (n) 671.2, 917.1, 1020.2, 1065.7 (a) 105.22, 152.29, 770.22, 1019.25
see through 521.9, 941.8
see-through 1029.4
see through rose-colored glasses 986.16
see through the press 548.14
see to 405.11, 889.5, 938.30, 983.5, 1008.19
see to it 970.11
see to the bottom of 521.9
see what can be done 403.10
see what one can do 403.10, 942.8
see where one is coming from 521.8
see which way the cat jumps 846.12
see which way the land lies 161.11
see which way the wind blows 161.11, 942.9
see with half an eye 27.12, 521.9
see with one's own eyes 27.12
Seger cone 742.5
segment (n) 277.2, 477.5, 675.3, 793.1, 793.2 (v) 801.6, 802.18
segmental 793.7, 801.9
segmental phoneme 524.12
segmentary 793.7
segmentation 801.1, 802.1
segregate 429.13, 773.6, 780.6, 802.8, 944.4
segregated 429.20, 584.8, 773.8, 776.6, 802.21
segregation 429.2, 584.1, 773.3, 780.4, 802.1, 944.3, 980.4
segregationism 944.3
segregative 773.9
segue (n) 538.4 (v) 538.9, 708.35, 815.2
seiche 238.14
seigneur 575.1, 608.4
seigneurial 471.9
seigneury 608.9
seignior 608.4
seigniorial 471.9
seignioralty 608.9
seigniory 417.7, 469.2, 608.9
seine 356.13
seisin 469.1
seismatical 916.20
seismic 671.23, 916.16
seismicity 916.7
seismic sea wave 238.14, 916.4
seismic wave 916.4
seismism 916.7
seismograph 916.8
seismographic 916.20
seismography 916.7
seismological 916.20
seismology 916.7
seismometer 916.8
seismometric 916.20
seismometry 916.7
seismoscope 916.8
seizable 928.25
seize 417.14, 429.15, 474.6, 480.14, 521.7, 640.8, 855.8, 855.10, 857.7, 910.6, 928.12
seized 800.14, 855.16, 928.26
seized of 469.9, 928.16
seized up 800.14, 855.16
seized with 93.23
seize on 371.14, 480.16, 931.16, 983.8
seize one's mind 931.19
seize power 417.14
seize the day 406.7, 486.3
seize the mantle 417.14
seize the meaning 521.7
seize the mind 931.20
seize the opportunity 843.7, 843.8
seize the present hour 843.8
seize the throne 417.14
seize up 173.7, 855.10, 857.7
seize upon 480.16
seizing 480.2
seizure 26.2, 85.6, 85.9, 105.9, 417.12, 429.6, 474.2, 480.2, 480.10, 640.3, 910.1, 917.6, 926.7
seizure of power 417.12, 480.2
selachian (n) 311.30 (a) 311.49
seldom met with 848.2, 885.5
seldomness 848.1
seldom seen 848.2, 885.5
select (n) 999.8 (v) 371.14, 517.18, 615.11, 865.11, 944.4 (a) 371.26, 495.13, 773.9, 999.16
select a jury 598.16
select committee 423.2
selected 371.26
selected passage 557.3
selected works 554.7
selectee 461.18, 615.9
selecting 371.23
selection 371.1, 417.12, 517.3, 557.3, 615.2, 808.3, 865.6
selections 557.4
selective 371.23, 495.9, 495.13, 773.9, 944.7
selective breeding 1070.1
selective hearing 49.1
selectiveness 371.10, 495.1, 495.5, 944.1
selective service 458.8, 615.7
selective transmission 1040.9
selectivity 371.10, 495.1, 495.5
selectman 575.16, 610.3
selectness 495.5
selector 371.7
selectperson 610.3
Selene 1073.12
selenium 7.11
self 92.28, 865.5
self, the 919.4
self-abasement 137.2, 652.1, 913.3
self-abasing 137.12, 652.5
self-abnegating 137.12, 326.3, 652.5, 667.4
self-abnegation 137.2, 326.1, 433.5, 652.1, 667.1, 670.1
self-abnegatory 652.5
self-absorbed 94.9, 651.5
self-absorption 94.1, 651.1, 669.1
self-abuse 75.8, 389.2
self-accusation 113.3
self-accusing 113.8
self-acting 324.7, 1041.22
self-action 324.2, 1041.1
self-active 324.7, 1041.22
self-activity 324.2, 1041.1
self-actor 1041.12
self-actualization 92.27
self-address 542.1
self-addressing 542.4
self-adhesive 803.12
self-adjusting 1041.22
self-admiration 140.1, 651.1
self-admiring 140.8, 651.5
self-admission 351.3
self-adulating 502.11
self-adulation 502.3
self-adulatory 502.11
self-advancement 651.1
self-advancer 651.3
self-advancing 651.5
self-advertisement 502.3, 651.1
self-advertising (n) 502.3 (a) 502.11, 651.5
self-advocacy 352.5
self-analysis 113.3
self-annulling 936.11
self-applauding 502.11
self-applause 502.3
self-appointed 141.10, 214.9
self-approbation 107.2, 140.1, 502.3
self-approbatory 502.11
self-approval 107.2
self-approving 140.8, 502.11
self-asserting 359.15
self-assertion 359.6
self-assertive 359.15
self-assertiveness 140.4, 359.6
self-assessment 430.5
self-assuming 140.8
self-assumption 140.1
self-assurance 106.3, 970.5
self-assured 106.13, 970.21
self-avowal 351.3
self-besot 651.5
self-boosting (n) 502.3 (a) 502.11
self-called 527.15
self-care 83.5
self-centered 94.9, 140.10, 651.5
self-centeredness 140.3, 651.1
self-centerment 140.3
self-checkout 624.4
self-christened 527.15
self-closing 1041.22
self-cocking 1041.22
self-command 106.3, 359.5
self-commitment 641.1
self-communion 931.6
self-complacence 107.2
self-complacency 107.2, 140.1
self-complacent 107.10, 140.8
self-conceit 140.4
self-conceited 140.11
self-conceitedness 140.4
self-concern 651.1
self-concession 351.3
self-condemnation 113.3
self-condemning 113.8
self-confessed 332.14, 351.10
self-confidence 106.3, 136.1, 970.5
self-confident 106.13, 136.8, 970.21
self-congratulating 140.8
self-congratulation 140.1

self-congratulatory 140.8, 502.11
self-conquest 359.5
self-conscious 139.12
self-consciousness 139.4
self-consequence 136.1
self-consideration 651.1
self-considerative 651.5
self-consistency 788.1
self-consistent 788.9, 973.14
self-consultation 931.6
self-contained 430.22, 583.5, 651.5, 802.20
self-contained underwater breathing apparatus 367.5
self-containment 430.5, 583.1, 651.1
self-content (n) 107.2, 140.1 (a) 107.10, 140.8
self-contented 107.10, 140.8
self-contentedness 107.2
self-contentness 107.2
self-contradiction 779.3, 789.2, 967.1, 975.1
self-contradictory 779.8, 789.8, 936.11, 967.7, 975.16
self-control (n) 106.3, 134.1, 359.5, 428.1, 668.1, 670.1 (v) 1041.21
self-controlled 106.13, 134.9, 359.15, 1041.22
self-convicting 113.8
self-conviction 113.3
self-cooking 1041.22
self-counsel 931.6
self-cremation 1020.5
self-debasement 113.3
self-debasing 113.8
self-deceit 976.1
self-deception 356.1, 976.1
self-deceptive 976.9
self-defeating 923.10, 967.7
self-defense 460.1, 600.2
self-defensive 460.11
self-delight 140.1
self-delighting 140.8
self-deluding 976.9
self-delusion 976.1
self-denial 359.5, 565.1, 652.1, 667.1, 668.1, 670.1
self-denying 652.5, 667.4
self-dependence 430.5
self-dependent 430.22
self-deprecating 137.12, 139.10
self-deprecation 139.2
self-depreciating 137.12, 139.10
self-depreciation 139.2
self-depreciative 139.10
self-destruct 395.18, 395.22, 414.12
self-destruction 308.5
self-destructive 308.24, 395.26
self-destructive urge 112.3
self-determination 232.6, 324.2, 424.1, 430.5, 458.11, 612.4, 1041.1
self-determined 324.7, 430.22
Self-determined, the 932.2
self-determining 324.7
self-detraction 139.2
self-devoted 651.5, 652.5
self-devotion 651.1, 652.1
self-devotional 652.5
self-diminishment 137.2
self-direct 1041.21
self-directed 1041.22
self-directing 430.22, 1041.22
self-direction 430.5, 1041.1
self-discipline 359.5, 668.1
self-disciplined 359.15
self-discovery 941.1
self-distrust 139.2
self-distrustful 139.10
self-domination 359.5
self-doubt 139.2, 955.2
self-doubting 137.12, 139.10
self-dramatization 502.3
self-dramatizing (n) 502.3 (a) 502.11
self-drive 1041.23
self-driven 1041.23
self-dumping 1041.22
self-educated 928.24
self-education 570.1
self-effacement 139.2, 652.1
self-effacing 139.10, 652.5
self-elect 141.10
self-elected 141.10
self-employed person 726.2
self-emptying 1041.22
self-endeared 140.8
self-endearment 140.1
self-esteem 136.1, 140.1, 651.1
self-esteeming 136.8, 140.8, 651.5
self-evidence 348.3
self-evident 348.8, 761.15, 957.20, 970.15
self-evident fact 761.3
self-evident truth, a 973.2
self-evident truth 974.2
self-examination 938.6
self-exile 363.3
self-existence 761.5
self-existent 677.16, 761.14
self-existing 761.14
self-explaining 348.8
self-explanatory 348.8
self-expression 359.6
self-expressive 359.15
self-expressiveness 359.6
self-fertilization 78.3
self-flagellating 113.8
self-flagellation 113.3
self-flattering 502.11
self-forgetful 652.5
self-forgetfulness 652.1
self-fulfillment 92.27
self-gifting 478.1
self-glorification 502.3
self-glorifying 502.11
self-glorious 502.11
self-glorying 502.11
self-govern 1041.21
self-governance 417.7
self-governed 430.22, 1041.22
self-governing 430.22, 612.16, 1041.22
self-governing state 232.1
self government 430.5
self-government 232.6, 359.5, 612.4, 1041.1
self-gratification 95.1, 140.1
self-gratulating 140.8, 502.11
self-gratulation 140.1, 502.3
self-gratulatory 140.8
self-hating 113.8
self-hatred 113.3
self-help 449.6
self-helpful 449.23
self-helpfulness 449.6
self-help group 449.2
self-helping 449.23
self-homicide 308.5
selfhood 865.1
self-humiliating 113.8
self-humiliation 113.3
self-hypnosis 22.7
self-identity 865.1
selfie 714.3
selfie stick 714.11
self-immolating 652.5
self-immolation 308.5, 652.1, 696.7, 1020.5
self-importance 140.1, 501.7, 970.5, 997.1
self-important 140.8, 501.22, 970.21, 997.17
self-imposed duty 641.1
self-improvement 449.6
self-improving 449.23
self-induction 1032.15
self-indulgence 95.1, 651.1, 663.1, 669.1
self-indulgent 651.5, 669.7
self-infatuated 140.8
self-infatuation 140.1
self-inflicted 643.8
self-instructed 570.16
self-instruction 568.1, 570.1
self instructional 568.18
self-interest 140.3, 651.1
self-interested 140.10, 651.5
self-interestedness 651.1
selfish 140.10, 144.18, 651.5
selfishness 140.3, 144.3, 651.1
selfism 651.1
self-isolation 651.1
self-jealous 651.5
self-jealousy 651.1
self-knowledge 928.1
self-laudation 502.3
self-laudatory 502.11
self-lauding 502.11
selfless 649.9, 652.5
selflessness 649.3, 652.1
self-lighting 1041.22
self-loading 1041.22
self-love 104.1, 140.1, 651.1
self-loving 104.26, 140.8
self-made 892.18
self-mastery 359.5, 668.1
self-medicating 86.39
self-mistrustful 139.10
self-mortification 667.1
self-motion 1041.1
self-moved 1041.23
self-movement 1041.1
self-mover 1041.12
self-moving 1041.23
self-murder 308.5
self-neglect 652.1
self-neglectful 652.5
self-neglectfulness 652.1
self-neglecting 652.5
selfness 865.1
self-obsessed 140.10, 651.5
self-obsession 140.3, 651.1
self-occupation 651.1
self-occupied 651.5
self-opening 1041.22
self-operating 1041.22
self-operative 1041.22
self-opinionated 140.11, 970.22
self-opinionatedness 970.6
self-opinioned 970.22
self-pitiful 145.9
self-pity 145.1
self-pitying 145.9
self-pleaser 651.3
self-pleasing (n) 651.1 (a) 651.5
self-possessed 106.13, 359.15
self-possession 106.3, 359.5
self-praise 502.3
self-praising 502.11
self-preservation 397.1, 460.1
self-preservative 460.11
self-priming 1041.22
self-proclaimed 141.10
self-promoting (n) 502.3 (a) 502.11, 651.5
self-promotion 502.3, 651.1
self-propelled 172.7, 904.16, 1041.23
self-propelled artillery 462.11
self-propellent 1041.23
self-propelling 1041.23
self-propulsion 1041.1
self-protection 460.1
self-protective 460.11
self-published book 554.3
self-publishing 352.1
self-puffery 502.3
self-puffing 502.11
self-punishing 113.8
self-punishment 113.3
self-reflexive 140.10
self-refuting 936.11
self-regulate 1041.21
self-regulated 1041.22
self-regulating 1041.22
self-regulating market 430.9
self-regulation 1041.1
self-regulative 1041.22
self-reining 668.1
self-reliance 136.1, 430.5, 970.5
self-reliant 136.8, 430.22, 970.21
self-renouncement 652.1
self-renouncing 652.5
self-renunciation 652.1
self-reproach 113.3
self-reproachful 113.8
self-reproachfulness 113.3
self-reproaching 113.8
self-respect 136.1, 140.1
self-respecting 136.8, 140.8
self-restrained 106.13, 359.15, 565.6
self-restraint 106.3, 359.5, 565.1, 668.1, 670.1
self-revealing 343.10
self-revelatory 343.10
self-righteous 693.5
self-righteousness 693.1
self-rising 1041.22
self-rule 476.2, 612.4
self-ruling 612.16

self-sacrifice 308.5, 652.1, 696.7
self-sacrificing 652.5
selfsame (n) 778.3 (a) 778.7
selfsameness 778.1, 872.1
self-satisfaction 107.2, 140.1
self-satisfied 107.10, 140.8
self-sealing 1041.22
self-seeker 651.3
self-seeking (n) 651.1 (a) 651.5
self-server 651.3
self-service 8.11
self-service restaurant 8.17
self-serving (n) 651.1 (a) 651.5
self-slaughter 308.5
self-solicitude 651.1
self-starter 330.8, 1041.18
self-starting 1041.22
self-steered 1041.22
self-styled 354.26, 527.15, 955.10
self-styled lawyer 597.1
self-subjection 652.1
self-subordination 652.1
self-subsistent 430.22
self-sufficiency 136.1, 140.1, 430.5, 583.1, 651.1, 991.1
self-sufficient 136.8, 140.8, 430.22, 583.5, 651.5
self-support 449.6
self-supported 449.23
self-supporting 430.22, 449.23
self-suppression 652.1
self-sustained 449.23
self-sustaining 449.23
self-sustainment 449.6
self-talk 492.8, 520.1
self-taught 570.16, 928.24
self-taught person 572.1
self-teaching (n) 568.1 (a) 568.18
self-unconscious 652.5
self-vaunting (n) 502.3 (a) 502.11
self-will 359.1, 361.1
self-willed 327.8, 361.8
selfwilled 418.5
self-winding 1041.22
self-working 1041.22
self-worship 140.1
self-worshiping 140.8
sell 352.15, 375.14, 375.23, 385.9, 629.3, 731.16, 734.8, 734.12, 737.24, 953.18
sell a pig in a poke 731.15
sell at a loss 631.2, 734.8
sell at auction 734.11
sell by auction 734.11
sell-by date 10.50
sell down the river 370.6, 551.13, 645.14
sell drugs 87.22
seller 730.3
seller's market 421.1, 992.1, 1010.5
sellers' market 632.3, 731.1, 734.1
sell for 630.13, 734.12
sell futures 737.23
sell gold bricks 356.18
selling (n) 375.3, 385.1, 734.2 (a) 734.13
selling agent 730.3
selling plater 757.2
selling point 997.7
selling price 630.1
sell like hotcakes 734.12
sell off 390.7, 475.3, 629.3, 734.8
selloff 737.5
sell on consignment 734.8
sell on credit 622.6
sell one a bill of goods 356.15
sell one down the river 551.13
sell one on 375.23, 953.18
sell one out 551.13
sell oneself 645.15, 953.19
sell one's life dearly 453.4
sell out 370.6, 390.7, 551.13, 645.14, 645.15, 734.8, 737.24
sellout 645.8, 704.12, 734.2, 734.3
sell over 734.8
sell over the counter 734.8
sell retail 734.8
sell short 512.8, 734.8, 737.24, 950.2
sell-through 734.2
sell to the highest bidder 734.11
sell under the counter 732.7
sell up 734.8
sell wholesale 734.8
selsyn 1041.13
seltzer 10.49
seltzer water 10.49
selvage 211.4, 211.7
selvedge 211.4
semanteme 526.1
semantic 517.23, 518.12, 523.19
semantic cluster 518.1
semantic content 518.1
semantic domain 518.1
semantic field 518.1
semantic history 526.16
semanticist 523.15, 526.15
semantic net 1042.2
semantic network 1042.2
semantics 518.7, 526.14
semantic space 158.7
semantic unit 518.6
semantological 518.12
semaphore 517.15
semaphore flag 517.15
semaphore telegraph 517.15
semasiological 518.12
semasiological unit 518.6
semasiologist 523.15
semasiology 518.7, 526.14
semblance 33.3, 33.5, 349.5, 354.3, 376.1, 784.1, 785.1, 976.2
semeiological 341.14
semeiology 91.11
semeiotics 91.11
sememe 518.6
sememic 518.12
semen 2.24, 13.2, 305.11
semester 824.2
semestral 850.8
semi 179.12
semiannual 850.8
semiautomatic (n) 462.10, 1041.12 (a) 1041.22
semiautomatic control 1041.4
semibreve 709.14
semibreve rest 709.21
semicelebrity 662.9, 997.2
semicircle 279.5, 280.8, 875.2
semicircular 279.11
semicircular canals 2.10
semiclassic 708.6
semiclassical music 708.6
semicolon 857.4
semiconductor 1032.14
semiconductor chip 1042.3
semiconductor circuit 1033.8
semiconductor device 1033.12
semiconductor memory 1042.7
semiconductor physics 1033.1
semiconscious 25.8
semiconsciousness 25.2
semidark (n) 1027.2 (a) 1027.15
semidarkness 1027.2
semidetached house 228.5
semidiameter 269.3
semidiaphaneity 1030.1
semidiaphanous 1030.4
semidrying oil 1056.1
semifinalist 452.2
semi-fingertip grip 750.2
semifluid (n) 1062.5 (a) 1062.11
semifluidic 1062.11
semifluidity 1062.1
semiformal dress 5.11
semigloss 35.22
semi-ignorance 930.5
semi-learning 930.5
semiliquid (n) 1061.2, 1062.5 (a) 1062.11
semiliquidity 1062.1
semiliteracy 930.4
semilunar 279.11, 1073.25
semi-matte 714.5
semimetal 1058.3, 1060.2
semimetallic 1058.16
semimicroanalysis 801.1
semimonthly 850.8
seminal 2.29, 13.7, 78.15, 305.20, 337.6, 886.14, 890.9, 890.11, 986.18
seminal fluid 13.2, 305.11
seminal imagination 986.3
seminar 541.6, 568.8
seminarian 572.5
seminarist 572.5
seminary 567.1, 567.4
seminate 1069.18
semination 1069.14
seminude 6.13
semiological 518.12
semiology 341.8, 517.2, 518.7
semiopacity 1030.1
semiopaque 1030.4, 1031.3
semiotic (n) 518.7 (a) 517.23, 518.12
semiotics 341.8, 517.2, 518.7
semiotic unit 518.6
semipellucid 1030.4, 1030.5
semipellucidity 1030.1
semi-permanent 35.18
semiprecious stone 1059.7
semi-private room 197.25
semiquaver 709.14
semiretired 402.5
semiretirement 402.1
semirigid airship 181.11
semiskilled 414.16, 414.17, 930.14
semiskilled worker 577.3
semisphere 875.2
semisynthetic antibiotic 86.41
semitone 709.20
semitonic 709.27
semitrailer 179.12, 179.19
semitranslucent 1030.5
semitransparency 1030.1
semitransparent 1030.4
semitropical 1019.24
semivisibility 32.2
semivisible 32.6
semivowel (n) 524.12 (a) 524.30
semiweekly 850.8
semiyearly 850.8
semper fi 434.4
sempervirent 827.10, 829.8, 841.7
sempiternal 829.7
sempiternity 829.1
sempster 741.2
sempstress 741.2
senary 882.18
Senate 613.2
senate 423.1
Senate committee 613.2
senator 610.3
senatorial 613.11
senatorial courtesy 613.7
senatorship 609.3
senatus consult 420.4
send (n) 238.14 (v) 95.11, 176.11, 176.15, 238.22, 343.7, 553.12, 904.13, 1034.25, 1036.15
sendable 553.14
send about one's business 372.2, 908.3, 909.14, 909.18
send abroad 190.17
send after 420.11
send a letter to 553.10
send a message 343.7, 352.12, 524.23
send an engraved invitation 440.13
send a note 553.10
send a signal 343.7, 352.12
send a statement 628.11
send away 176.15, 908.3, 909.17, 909.18
send away with a flea in one's ear 372.2
send a wire 347.20
send back 54.7, 481.4
send down 909.17
sender 347.2
send flying 412.7
send for 420.11
send forth 176.15, 352.14, 904.13, 909.25
send headlong 913.5
send-in 553.14
sending 343.2
sending back 481.1
sending to Coventry 909.4
send in one's papers 448.2
send mad 926.24
send off 176.15, 818.7, 904.13, 908.3, 909.18
send-off 188.4, 818.1

send on 176.15
send on a fool's errand 356.15
send on a mission 615.10
send one away with a flea in one's ear 442.5
send one's compliments 504.12
send one's condolences 147.2
send one's love 504.12
send one spinning 985.8
send one's regards 504.12
send one to the showers 909.20
send one up the wall 128.9
send out 615.10, 909.25, 1067.8
send out a search party 382.8
send out for 420.11
send out of one's mind 926.24
send out rays 1025.23
send packing 372.2, 908.3, 909.14, 909.18
send scuttling 127.16
send sprawling 412.7
send the wrong message 265.6, 350.3
send the wrong signal 265.6
send to Coventry 773.4, 909.17
send to Davy Jones's locker 367.8
send to glory 308.13
send to hell 682.6
send to jail 429.17
send to kingdom come 308.13
send to one's last account 308.13
send to one's Maker 308.13
send to school 568.13
send to sleep 118.7
send to the big house 429.14
send to the bottom 367.8
send to the gas chamber 604.16
send to the hot seat 604.16
send to the showers 447.4, 909.18
send up 336.6, 429.17, 489.13, 512.12
send-up 512.5
send up a prayer 696.13
send up a trial balloon 942.8, 942.9
send up the river 429.14, 429.17
send word 343.7, 551.8
senectitude 303.5, 922.10
senesce 303.10
senescence 303.5, 303.6
senescent 303.15, 303.17
seneschal 574.4, 577.10
seneschalship 417.7
seneschalsy 417.7
seneschalty 232.1
senex 304.5
senile (n) 924.9 (a) 303.18, 842.17, 922.23
senile debility 922.10
senile dementia 922.10
senile psychosis 922.10
senile weakness 922.10
senilism 922.10
senility 16.3, 303.1, 303.5, 842.1, 922.10
senior (n) 249.4, 304.5, 572.6, 575.3, 758.3 (a) 417.15, 834.4, 842.19
senior chief petty officer 575.19
Senior Circuit, the 745.1
senior citizen 304.2
senior citizenship 303.5, 842.1
senior high 567.4
senior high school 567.4
seniority 249.1, 303.3, 417.4, 842.1
senior master sergeant 575.18
senior moment 990.1
senior officer 575.17
seniors 304.4
señor 76.7
señora 77.8
señorita 77.8
sensate 24.14
sensation 24.1, 93.1, 105.2, 122.2, 409.4, 919.6
sensational 93.19, 105.32, 122.10, 501.20, 544.11, 545.8, 999.15
sensationalism 93.9, 355.1, 501.3, 545.1, 704.2
sensationalistic 93.19, 545.8
sensation level 24.2
sensaysh 409.4
sense (n) 24.1, 93.1, 209.3, 518.1, 788.3, 920.1, 920.6, 928.2, 932.1, 934.3, 935.9, 944.1, 951.5, 953.6 (v) 24.6, 93.10, 521.7, 934.4, 941.5
sense-data 24.1
sense-datum 24.1
sense-distinction 518.3
sense impression 24.1
senseless 25.6, 25.8, 144.26, 520.6, 810.12, 922.13, 923.8, 923.10, 926.26, 936.11, 1055.5
senseless brutality 144.11
senselessness 25.2, 520.1, 922.1, 923.1, 923.2, 926.1, 936.2, 1055.2
sense of direction 430.5
sense of duty 641.2
sense of hearing 48.1
sense of humor 489.11
sense of indebtedness 150.1
sense of language 532.2
sense of motion 24.5
sense of mystery 122.1
sense of obligation 150.1, 641.2
sense of place 209.3
sense of relief 120.4
sense of rhythm 708.31
sense of right and wrong 636.5
sense of sight 27.1
sense of smell 69.4
sense of taste 62.1
sense of the meeting 332.5, 788.3
sense of touch 73.1
sense of wonder 122.1
sense organ 24.5
sense perception 24.1
sense pleasure 95.1
senses 24.5, 919.2, 925.1
sensibility 17.4, 24.2, 93.1, 93.4, 920.4, 928.2, 944.1, 1047.2
sensibilize 24.7
sensible 24.11, 93.20, 150.5, 297.19, 633.7, 763.6, 920.12, 920.18, 925.4, 928.15, 935.20, 987.6
sensible, the 921.3
sensible horizon 201.4
sensibleness 24.2, 920.6, 935.9, 987.2
sensible price 633.2
sensible to 928.16
sensify 24.7
sensile 24.11
sensillum 24.5
sensimotor 24.9
sensing 934.5
sensitive 24.9, 24.12, 26.11, 93.20, 105.28, 110.21, 345.14, 495.9, 496.8, 934.5, 944.7, 979.11, 1047.9
sensitive dependence on initial conditions 886.3
sensitive ear 48.3
sensitive heart 93.6
sensitiveness 24.3, 26.4, 93.1, 93.4, 110.5, 1047.2
sensitive to 24.11, 983.16
sensitivity 24.3, 73.3, 93.4, 105.10, 110.5, 143.3, 145.1, 495.1, 944.1, 979.4
sensitivity to 896.1
sensitivity to light 27.1
sensitization 24.3
sensitize 24.7
sensitizing antibody 86.27
sensorial 24.9
sensorimotor 24.9
sensorium 24.5, 919.6
sensory (n) 919.6 (a) 24.9, 663.5
sensory aid 30.6
sensory cell 2.14
sensory experience 24.1
sensory neuron 2.14
sensory organ 24.5
sensory overload 985.1
sensory paralysis 85.27
sensory pattern 92.32
sensual 75.25, 663.5, 665.29
sensualism 95.1, 663.1
sensualist (n) 663.3 (a) 663.5
sensualistic 663.5
sensuality 24.1, 75.2, 663.1, 665.5
sensualize 663.4
sensualness 663.1
sensual pleasure 95.1
sensuosity 24.1
sensuous 24.9, 97.7, 663.5
sensuous desire 75.5
sensuousness 24.1, 97.2, 663.1
sensuous pleasure 95.1
sent 95.17
sentence (n) 523.14, 524.3, 529.1, 598.9, 602.1, 793.2, 946.5, 974.1 (v) 602.3, 946.13
sentence adverb 530.3
sentenced 602.6
sentence fragment 531.1
sentence modifier 530.2
sentence of death 307.1
sentence structure 530.1
sentential function 935.7
sententious 422.8, 518.10, 537.6, 545.8, 974.6
sententious expression 974.1
sententiousness 518.5, 537.1, 545.1
sentience 23.1, 24.2
sentiency 24.2
sentient 23.8, 24.11, 93.17
sentiment 93.1, 93.8, 104.1, 932.1, 952.2, 953.6, 978.1
sentimental 93.21, 104.26, 923.8
sentimental attachment 104.1
sentimentalism 93.8
sentimentality 93.8, 104.2
sentimentalize 93.13, 97.5
sentimentalized 93.21
sentiment analysis 1042.18
sentinel 399.4, 1008.10
sentry 399.4, 1008.10
sentry box 228.9
sepal 310.19, 310.28
separability 802.1
separable 780.7, 802.26, 944.9
separate (v) 79.22, 171.5, 211.8, 213.8, 224.3, 292.11, 429.13, 456.10, 456.14, 566.5, 771.8, 773.6, 780.6, 793.6, 801.6, 802.8, 802.19, 808.11, 944.4 (a) 584.8, 780.7, 802.20, 872.8
separated 224.6, 261.8, 429.20, 566.7, 584.8, 589.11, 773.8, 776.6, 780.7, 802.21, 872.8
separatedness 261.1
separate forcibly 909.19
separate from the service 431.5
separate identity 865.1
separate maintenance 566.1
separateness 776.1, 780.1, 780.4, 802.1, 804.1, 872.2
separate off 171.5, 802.8
separate oneself 261.7, 333.4
separate out 773.6, 944.4
separate returns 630.9
separate the men from the boys 944.4
separate the sheep from the goats 371.14, 944.4
separate the wheat from the chaff 371.14, 944.4
separating 802.25
separation 79.4, 171.1, 213.5, 261.1, 429.2, 456.4, 566.1, 584.1, 709.14, 771.3, 773.3, 780.4, 801.1, 802.1, 944.3
separation anxiety 584.3
separation from the service 431.2
separationism 773.3, 944.3
separation of attention 985.1
separatism 802.1
separatist (n) 333.3, 363.5 (a) 363.12
separative 773.9, 780.9, 802.25, 806.5
separator 192.9, 802.7
separatrix 204.7
sepia (n) 40.1 (a) 40.3
seppuku 308.5
sepsis 85.31
sept 559.4, 560.4, 809.2
septal 213.11
septemfid 882.19
septempartite 882.19
septemvir 882.3
septenary 882.19
septendecillion 882.13
septennial 850.4

septet 450.1, 708.18, 720.10, 882.3
septic 80.20, 82.5, 85.60, 85.62, 393.39
septicemia 85.20, 85.31
septicopyemia 85.31
septic poisoning 85.31
septic tank 80.12
septillion 882.13
septimal 882.19
septuagenarian 304.2, 882.7
septuagenary 882.28
septuagesimal 882.28
Septuagint 683.2, 882.3
septulum 213.5
septum 213.5
septuor 708.18
septuple 882.19
septuple time 709.24
sepulcher 309.16
sepulchral 54.11, 309.22
sepulture (n) 309.1 (v) 309.19
sequacious 138.14, 815.4, 887.6, 1047.9
sequacity 1047.2
sequel 166.1, 815.1, 817.1, 835.2, 887.1
sequela 817.1, 887.1
sequelae 817.1, 835.2, 887.1
sequelant 817.1
sequence 166.1, 296.4, 803.2, 807.2, 812.2, 815.1, 835.1, 887.1
sequence flashers 184.19
sequence of ideas 931.4
sequence of phonemes 524.2
sequence of thought 931.4
sequent (n) 817.1, 887.1 (a) 803.11, 812.9, 815.4, 835.4, 887.6
sequential 803.11, 812.9, 815.4, 887.6, 935.23
sequential access 1042.8, 1042.18
sequentialness 803.2
sequester 386.12, 480.20, 802.8
sequestered 173.12, 345.13, 346.11, 584.10, 773.8, 802.21, 982.3
sequester oneself 584.7, 872.6, 1009.8
sequestrate 480.20
sequestrated 173.12, 584.10
sequestration 345.2, 386.5, 429.2, 480.5, 584.1, 598.4, 802.1, 872.2
sequin 498.4
sequitur 817.1
serac 1023.5
seraglio 563.10
serai 563.10
seraph 679.1
seraphic 104.24, 653.5, 679.6, 692.9
seraphical 692.9
seraphicalness 692.2
seraphim 679.1, 679.3
sere 393.31, 393.35, 891.4, 1066.9
serenade (n) 562.7, 708.14 (v) 562.21, 708.38
serenader 710.14
serendipitous 972.15
serendipity 941.1, 972.1
serene 106.12, 464.9, 670.13, 1025.31
Serene Highness 648.2
Serene Majesty 648.2
serenity 106.2, 107.1, 173.1, 329.1, 464.2, 670.1, 781.1
serf 138.3, 432.7, 577.1, 606.6
serfdom 138.1, 432.1, 577.12
serfhood 432.1
sergeant 575.18, 575.19, 1008.15
sergeant at arms 1008.15
sergeant-at-arms 183.7
sergeant first class 575.18
sergeant from K Company 758.2
sergeant major 575.18, 575.19
sergeant major of the army 575.18
sergeant major of the Marine Corps 575.19
Sergey Brin and Larry Page 618.8
serial (n) 554.13, 555.1, 1034.18, 1035.2 (a) 555.5, 803.11, 812.9, 815.4, 850.7
serial comma 204.7, 857.4
serial interface 1042.3
seriality 803.2
serialization 554.7, 815.1
serial killer 308.11
serial killing 308.2
serial number 517.11
serial order 807.2
serial port 1042.3
serial printer 1042.9
serial rape 480.3
serial sex 75.7
seriate 812.9
sericeous 1047.15
series 166.1, 554.5, 554.7, 749.1, 770.12, 809.5, 812.2, 815.1, 850.3, 1017.8, 1035.2
series of penalty kicks 752.3
serif 548.6
serigrapher 716.8
serigraphy 712.16, 713.4
serio-comic 488.6
serious 101.9, 106.14, 111.3, 247.6, 359.11, 544.14, 931.21, 997.20, 1006.9
serious drinker 88.11
serious drinking 88.2, 88.4
serious literature 547.12, 718.1
serious money 618.3
serious music 708.6
seriousness 101.2, 106.4, 111.1, 359.1, 997.3
sermon 510.5, 543.3, 568.7
sermoner 543.5, 699.3
sermonette 543.3
sermonist 543.5, 699.3
sermonize 543.11, 568.16
sermonizer 543.5, 699.3
sermonizing 422.1
sermons 422.1
serosa 2.6
serosity 1061.1
serotherapeutics 91.15
serotherapy 91.15
serous 2.33, 13.7
serous fluid 2.24
serous membrane 2.6
serpent 311.25, 357.10, 660.6
serpentiform 281.7, 311.47
serpentile 311.47
serpentine (n) 47.6 (v) 281.4 (a) 164.7, 238.24, 279.7, 281.6, 281.7, 311.47, 415.12
serpent kame 237.5
serpentlike 281.7, 311.47
serpentoid 311.47
serrate (v) 289.4 (a) 278.6, 288.7, 289.5
serrated 288.7, 289.5
serration 285.1, 288.2, 289.2
serried 770.22, 812.8, 1045.12
serriform 289.5
serrulated 289.5
serrulation 289.2
serum 2.24, 2.25, 86.27, 91.18
serum death 85.2, 307.5
serum gamma globulin 86.27
serum therapy 91.15
servant 138.6, 384.4, 432.5, 432.7, 577.2, 616.6, 692.4, 726.2
servant girl 577.8
servanthood 577.12
servant of God 699.2
servantry 577.11
serve (n) 748.2, 904.3 (v) 75.21, 107.6, 250.4, 328.4, 384.7, 385.9, 387.17, 420.11, 449.18, 458.17, 478.12, 577.13, 724.13, 748.3, 758.5, 788.8, 896.3, 904.10, 991.4, 995.3, 999.10
serve an apprenticeship 570.11
serve and volley 748.3
serve-and-volley 748.2
serve as 349.10
serve as proxy 862.5
serve at one's pleasure 326.2
serve in one's stead 576.14
serve in the capacity of 724.13
serve Mammon 688.8
serve notice 551.8
serve notice on 598.15
serve one out 604.10
serve one right 506.5, 604.9, 639.6, 649.5
serve one's every need 577.13
serve one's need 387.17
serve one's purpose 384.7, 387.17, 995.3
serve out 477.8
server 577.5
serve the purpose 991.4
serve time 429.18, 825.5
service (n) 8.10, 8.11, 143.7, 180.12, 326.1, 384.3, 387.3, 387.4, 397.1, 432.2, 449.1, 458.8, 461.21, 577.12, 580.4, 696.8, 701.3, 724.2, 748.2, 904.3 (v) 75.21, 396.14
service, the 461.20
serviceability 387.3, 449.10
serviceable 384.8, 387.18, 387.23, 449.21
serviceable life 827.1
service academy 567.6
service ace 748.2
service break 748.2
service ceiling 184.32
service charge 630.6
service economy 731.7
service fee 630.6
service life 827.1
service line 748.1
service-line umpire 748.2
serviceman 396.10, 461.6
service mark 210.3
service medal 646.6
service of lessons and carols 708.32
service of music 708.33
service of song 708.32
serviceperson 461.6
service provider 1042.19
services 461.20
service school 567.6
service stripe 647.5
servicewoman 396.10, 461.6
service worker 726.2
servicing 78.3, 396.6
serviette 8.13
servile 138.13, 250.6, 432.13, 432.16, 433.12, 433.16, 577.14
servility 138.1, 155.2, 250.1, 326.1, 432.1, 433.3
serving (n) 8.10, 180.12 (a) 328.10, 449.20, 577.14
serving a sentence 429.21
serving girl 577.8
serving man 577.4
serving spoon 8.12
serving suggestion 8.10
servitial 577.14
servitium 326.1
servitor 572.7, 577.2
servitorial 577.14
servitorship 432.2, 577.12
servitress 577.8
servitude 432.1, 577.12
servo 1041.13
servo control 1041.3, 1041.14
servo-control 1041.20
servo-controlled 1041.24
servo engineer 1041.19
servo engineering 1041.2
servo instrumentation 1040.11, 1041.1
servolab 1041.5
servo laboratory 1041.5
servomechanical 1041.24
servomechanics 1041.2
servomechanism 1040.4, 1041.13
servomotor 1041.13
servo regulator 1041.14
servo system 1041.5
sesquicentenary 882.8
sesquicentennial 850.4, 882.8
sesquipedal 267.7, 545.10
sesquipedalia 526.10
sesquipedalian (n) 526.10 (a) 267.7, 534.3, 545.10
sesquipedalianism 534.1, 545.3
sesquipedalian word 545.3
sesquipedality 534.1, 545.3
session 423.4, 541.5, 770.2, 824.2
Sessrymnir 681.10
sestet 708.18, 720.10, 882.2
Set 680.5

set (n) 159.3, 161.1, 172.2, 238.4, 262.1, 302.11, 554.5, 617.6 (v) 78.12, 159.12, 159.16, 161.5, 161.7, 173.10, 194.6, 238.16, 262.7, 285.7, 396.21, 405.9, 420.9, 477.9, 548.16, 643.4 (a) 117.9, 159.18, 210.6, 285.8, 359.12, 361.8, 373.13, 373.18, 381.12, 405.16
set (n) 704.19, 706.4, 744.1, 745.3, 758.3, 770.3, 770.12, 784.5, 792.3, 803.1, 809.2, 896.2, 978.3, 1034.3 (v) 708.46, 788.7, 800.7, 803.6, 855.9, 865.11, 896.3, 1045.10, 1046.8, 1069.18 (a) 800.14, 803.10, 855.13, 855.14, 970.20, 1046.13
seta 3.2, 288.3
set about 403.6, 404.3, 725.15, 818.7
set above 371.17
set abroach 818.11
setaceous 288.9
set a course 818.8
set afire 375.18
set afloat 886.10, 904.13
set against (v) 338.5, 456.14, 589.7, 943.4 (a) 451.8, 589.10
set against one another 215.4
set agoing 818.11
set a good example 321.5
setal 3.24
set alight 1020.22
set a limit 944.4
set an anchor watch 182.16
set an arbitrary price on 630.11
set an end point 210.5
set a new mark 411.3
set an examination 938.24
set an example 786.7
set apart (v) 213.8, 224.3, 255.10, 386.12, 477.9, 477.11, 685.5, 773.6, 780.6, 802.8, 865.10, 944.4 (a) 685.8, 773.8
set a pick 747.4
set a precedent 834.3
set a price 630.11
set a quota 210.5, 244.4
setarious 288.10
set aside (v) 176.11, 255.10, 386.12, 390.6, 445.2, 477.9, 773.6, 802.8, 846.9, 959.5, 984.4 (a) 445.3
set astir 105.12, 375.19
set a stopping place 210.5
set at 404.3, 725.15
set a task 568.17
set at defiance 327.6, 435.4, 454.4, 492.10
set at each other's throat 589.7
set at ease 107.4, 120.7, 121.6
set at hazard 759.24
set at intervals (v) 224.3 (a) 224.6
set at large 431.4
set at liberty 430.14, 431.4
set at little 950.2
set at naught 157.3, 327.6, 435.4, 950.2, 998.12
set at odds 456.14, 589.7
set at one's throat 456.14
set a trap for 346.10, 356.20
set at rest (v) 957.10, 970.11 (a) 407.10, 820.9
set at variance 456.14
set a value on 946.9
set back (v) 127.18, 175.9, 284.14, 393.9, 428.7, 1012.10 (a) 175.12
setback 132.1, 163.1, 175.4, 394.1, 412.2, 473.1, 758.3, 1011.3, 1012.1
set before 216.8, 371.17, 371.21, 439.5
set before oneself 380.4
set boundaries 210.4
set by 386.12, 390.6, 846.9
set by the ears 456.14
set conditions 421.7, 959.3
set criteria 959.3
set designer 704.23
set down (v) 137.5, 159.14, 334.5, 510.17, 549.15 (a) 137.13
set-down 510.6
setdown 137.2
set down as 953.11
set down for 953.11
set down for hearing 598.13
set down to 888.4
set dressing 706.4
set eyes on 27.12
set fire to 105.12, 1020.22
set foot in 177.25, 189.7, 221.8
set foot on dry land 186.8
set for 405.18
set form 373.4, 869.4
set forth 188.8, 348.5, 349.9, 439.5, 524.22, 818.8, 937.3, 951.12, 957.8
set forward 188.8, 404.3, 449.17
set free 398.3, 431.4, 601.4
set going 902.11, 904.13
set great store on 124.6
set gun 356.12
set her down 184.43
set hurdles 568.17
setiform 288.10
set in 191.3, 284.14, 318.19, 818.7, 855.9
set in concrete (v) 420.9 (a) 420.12
set in contrast 943.4
set in motion 172.6, 375.12, 437.9, 902.11, 904.13
set in one's ways 361.8, 373.18
set in opposition 943.4
set in order 808.8
set in print 548.16
set in stone 855.7
set in the tablets of memory 989.17
set in towards 161.9
set limits 780.6, 959.3
set little by 950.2, 998.12
set mind 361.1
set naught by 327.6, 435.4
set news afloat 352.10
set no store by 950.2, 955.5, 998.12
set of beliefs 952.2
set of bells 54.4
set of clothes 5.6
set of conditions 766.2
set off 188.8, 211.10, 300.11, 338.5, 375.18, 477.9, 498.8, 671.14, 779.4, 780.6, 886.10, 944.4, 1016.15
setoff 188.2, 338.2, 548.3, 631.1, 779.2
set off against 943.4
set off for 161.9
set off to advantage 1016.15
set off to good advantage 1016.15
set of furniture 229.1
set of postulates 951.3
set of rooms 228.13
set of the current 896.2
set of three 876.1
set of two 873.2
set of values 952.2
set on (v) 199.6, 375.17, 456.14, 459.14 (a) 100.22, 359.16
set one back 630.13
set one back on his heels 857.11
set on edge 96.14, 288.5
set one's back against the wall 359.9
set one's cap at 562.21
set one's cap for 100.14, 562.21
set one's compass for 161.9
set one's course for 161.9
set one's dignity aside 137.8, 141.8
set one's dignity to one side 137.8, 141.8
set oneself against 442.3, 451.3, 510.10
set one's face against 157.5, 442.3
set one's foot down 442.3
set one's foot down on 444.4
set one's hand and seal 332.12
set one's hand to 404.3, 725.15
set one's heart against 451.3, 510.10
set one's heart on 100.17, 421.8
set one's heart upon 359.8
set one's house in order 405.11, 658.4
set one's jaw 359.8
set one's mind at ease 106.6, 107.4, 120.7
set one's mind at rest 106.6, 107.4, 120.7
set one's mind upon 359.8, 421.8
set one's seal 332.12
set one's shoulder to the wheel 359.8
set one's sights 100.20
set one's sights on 380.4
set one's teeth 359.8
set one's teeth on edge 67.4, 96.14, 128.9
set one's thoughts on 983.5
set one's wits to work 892.12
set one up in business 449.11
set on fire 105.12, 375.18, 1020.22
set on foot 818.11, 886.10, 904.13
set on its base 200.9
set on its beam ends 205.6
set on its ears 205.6
set on its feet 200.9
set on one's feet 9.2, 396.15
set on one's legs 9.2, 396.15
set on the straight and narrow 858.12
setose 288.9
setous 288.9
set out 188.8, 381.10, 498.8, 532.4, 808.9, 818.7, 818.8
setout 188.2
set out for 161.9
set over against 215.4, 338.5, 943.4
set phrase 529.1
set piece 580.4
set point 748.2, 1041.10
set purpose 380.1
set right (v) 161.6, 338.4, 396.13, 568.10, 658.4, 788.7, 977.2 (a) 977.5
set sail 182.20, 188.8, 818.7
set side by side 223.13
set speech 543.2
set square 200.6, 278.4
set store by 953.10, 997.13
set straight 161.6, 277.5, 392.9, 396.13, 437.8, 510.17, 858.12, 977.2
set task 568.7
set temper 1046.4
setter 311.17
set term 529.1
set terms 421.7
set the alarm 832.11
set the brain to work 931.8
set the date 832.13
set the echoes ringing 53.7
set the fashion 578.9
set the law at defiance 674.5
set the law at naught 674.5
set the limit 210.4
set the mind to 983.5
set the mood 865.10
set theory 935.2
set the pace 165.2, 786.7, 865.10
set the price tag too high 632.7
set the record straight 420.10
set the river on fire 409.10
set the stage 704.28
set the style 578.9
set the table on a roar 116.9, 743.21
set the teeth on edge 58.11
set the time 832.11
set the tone 578.9, 865.10
set the wits to work 931.8
set the world on fire 409.10
setting (n) 8.13, 159.1, 209.2, 223.1, 463.1, 498.7, 548.2, 704.19, 708.5, 709.2, 722.4, 766.2, 901.10, 1045.4, 1046.5, 1069.14 (a) 194.11
setting apart 685.3
setting aside 445.1, 477.3
setting at liberty 431.1
setting conditions 959.1
setting free 431.1, 601.1
setting-free 369.1
setting hen 311.28
setting in motion 375.2, 818.1, 818.5
setting-off 375.2

setting right 396.6, 658.1
setting sun 315.2
setting-up 818.1, 892.4
settle 159.17, 184.41, 186.6, 194.6, 194.7, 225.9, 297.15, 308.14, 359.7, 395.11, 412.9, 437.8, 465.7, 465.8, 466.7, 468.2, 604.10, 624.13, 629.3, 808.10, 855.9, 863.4, 867.3, 946.11, 957.10, 958.5, 970.11
settle accounts 506.7, 604.9, 624.13
settle accounts with 624.12
settled 159.18, 225.12, 359.12, 373.18, 412.15, 437.11, 624.22, 820.9, 855.13, 855.14, 957.20, 970.20
settled belief 970.5
settle differences 465.8
settled in habit 373.18
settled judgment 953.5
settledness 359.2, 373.6
settle down 159.17, 184.43, 194.6, 303.9, 670.5, 855.10
settled principle 419.2, 974.2
settled purpose 380.1
settled upon 359.16
settle for 107.5, 863.4
settle for less 107.5
settle in 186.6, 225.9
settle into 858.17
settle it 457.17
settlement 159.7, 225.2, 232.1, 437.1, 465.4, 468.1, 471.4, 478.9, 617.2, 624.1, 624.2, 629.1, 957.3
settlement of differences 465.4
settle on 194.10, 332.10, 359.7, 478.17, 629.3
settle one's differences 465.10
settle one's hash 412.9, 604.10
settle one's mind 946.11
settle preliminaries 405.6
settler 189.4, 227.9, 478.11, 774.4, 820.4, 958.3
settle the land 182.37
settle the matter 946.11, 957.10
settle the score 338.5, 506.7, 604.10
settle to rest 20.6
settle to sleep 22.16
settle up 624.13
settle upon 371.16, 478.17, 888.4
settle up with 506.7
settle with 437.8, 506.7, 604.9, 624.12
settling 159.6, 159.7, 629.1
settling price 738.9
settlings 256.2
set to 404.3, 456.11, 800.7, 818.7
set-to 456.6
setto 935.4
set to music 708.46
set to one side 176.11
set to rights 396.13, 396.14, 808.8
set to the account of 888.4
set toward 896.3
set to work 725.15
setula 3.2, 288.3
setule 288.3
set up 9.2, 152.24, 159.16, 200.9, 381.8, 385.8, 396.13, 449.11, 599.12, 624.19, 662.13, 729.16, 818.11, 886.10, 892.8, 892.10, 912.5, 965.5
set-up 965.8
setup 266.1, 381.1, 766.2, 796.1, 807.1, 965.2, 1014.4
set up barriers 429.13
set-up board 1041.16
set up for 354.22
set up housekeeping 159.17
set up in business 159.17, 724.12, 729.16
set upon 459.14
set upon on all sides 459.19
set up shop 159.17, 328.8, 724.12, 725.15, 818.8
set with thorns 1013.17
seven 758.2, 882.3
seven ages of man 303.1
seven-card stud 758.4, 759.10
Seven Cities of Cibola 618.4, 986.11
seven deadly sins 654.3, 882.3
sevenfold 882.19
seven-footer 272.7
seven-league boots 691.6
seven-part time 709.24
seven sacraments 701.4
Seven Sages 921.4
seven seas 882.3
seven seas, the 240.1
Seven Sisters 1073.8
seven-spot 758.2
seventeen-year locust 311.35
seventh (n) 709.20 (a) 882.19
Seventh Avenue 5.32
seventh heaven 95.2, 198.2, 681.4
seventieth 882.28
Seventy 699.10
seventy 882.7
72 holes 751.3
Seven Wise Masters 921.4
Seven Wise Men of Greece 921.4
Seven Wonders of the World 882.3
7-yard line 749.4
sever 780.6, 802.11, 944.4
severable 477.12, 780.7, 802.26
several (n) 883.1, 884.2 (a) 477.13, 780.7, 783.4, 865.12, 883.7, 884.7
severalfold 883.7
severalization 780.4
severalize 780.6, 944.4
severalty 802.1
severance 773.2, 780.4, 802.2
severance pay 624.4
severe 17.14, 26.10, 68.6, 144.24, 417.16, 425.6, 499.9, 505.7, 535.3, 671.16, 798.6, 973.17, 1013.17, 1023.14
severe check 1011.3
severe clear 31.2, 184.32
severed 802.23
severe thunderstorm warning 400.1
severe thunderstorm watch 400.1
severity 17.5, 68.1, 144.9, 425.1, 499.4, 505.3, 535.1, 671.1, 798.1, 973.5, 1013.1, 1023.1
sew 741.4, 800.8
sewage 12.3, 12.4, 80.9, 391.4
sewage farm 80.12
sewan 728.3
sewed up 407.11, 965.8, 970.20
sewer (n) 80.12, 239.5, 284.5, 654.7, 741.2, 741.3 (a) 513.8
sewerage 12.3, 12.4, 80.9
sewing 554.14, 741.1
sewing machine 741.3
sewing room 197.13, 739.8
sewn up 407.11
sew up 396.14, 407.6, 741.4, 820.6, 965.5
sex (n) 75.1, 75.7, 104.1 (v) 75.19 (a) 75.25
sex act 75.7
sex addict 75.16
sexagenarian 304.2, 882.7
sexagenary (n) 882.7 (a) 882.27
Sexagesima 882.7
sexagesimal 882.27
sexagesimo-quarto 882.7
sex appeal 75.3, 377.2
sex chromosome 305.8, 560.6
sex crime 75.11
sex criminal 75.16
sexdecillion 882.13
sex discrimination 590.1, 980.4
sex drive 75.2
sexed 75.25
sex education 75.2
sexed-up 75.27, 498.12, 665.29
sexennial 882.18
sex fiend 75.16
sex god 75.4
sex goddess 75.4, 1016.7
sexiness 75.2, 75.3, 97.2, 104.2, 377.2, 665.5, 1016.3
sex-intergrade 75.17
sexism 75.10, 590.1, 980.4
sexist (n) 590.2, 980.5 (a) 590.3, 650.10, 773.9, 980.12
sex kitten 75.4, 1016.8
sexless 75.29
sexlessness 75.9
sex life 75.2
sexlike 75.25
sex object 75.4, 104.9
sexologist 75.18
sexology 75.18
sex organs 2.13
sexpartite 882.18
sex pervert 75.16
sexploitation 666.4
sex psychopath 75.16
sex queen 75.4
sex shop 75.7
sex-starved 75.27
sex study 75.18
sex symbol 665.15
sext 314.4, 696.8
sextant 182.2, 278.4, 280.8
sextant altitude 184.35
sextennial 850.4
sextet 450.1, 708.18, 720.10, 882.2
sextillion 882.13
sexting 347.4
sextipartite 882.18
sextipartition 882.14
sextodecimo 554.4
sexton 309.8
sextuple (v) 882.16 (a) 882.18
sextuple time 709.24
sextuplets 882.2
sextuplex 882.18
sextuplicate 882.16
sexual 2.29, 75.25, 104.25, 305.20, 562.23, 665.29
sexual abnormality 75.11
sexual abstention 565.1
sexual abstinence 565.1, 668.2
sexual abuse 75.11
sexual activity 75.2
sexual advance 439.2
sexual approach 439.2
sexual assault 480.3, 665.6
sexual attraction 75.3
sexual attractiveness 75.3
sexual climax 75.7, 917.6
sexual commerce 75.7
sexual congress 75.7
sexual counselor 75.18
sexual customs 75.18
sexual desire 75.5, 100.1, 100.6, 323.1, 1019.2
sexual deviance 75.11
sexual deviation 75.11
sexual discrimination 773.3
sexual disorder 92.14
sexual excitement 105.7
sexual fantasy 75.8, 92.23
sexual freedom 75.18
sexual harassment 75.11
sexual innocence 664.1
sexual instinct 75.2
sexual intercourse 75.7, 562.1
sexual inversion 75.10
sexual invitation 439.2
sexualism 75.2
sexual itch 665.5
sexuality 75.2, 665.5
sexualize 75.19
sexual liberation 75.18
sexual longing 75.5
sexual love 104.1
sexually abstinent 565.6, 668.10
sexually continent 565.6
sexually excited 105.22
sexually innocent 664.4
sexually transmitted disease 85.18
sexual magnetism 75.3
sexual maturity 14.1
sexual morality 75.18
sexual mores 75.18
sexual nature 75.2, 75.10
sexual normality 75.10
sexual offense 75.11
sexual orientation 75.10
sexual overture 439.2
sexual passion 75.5
sexual pathology 75.11, 92.15, 926.3
sexual perversion 75.11
sexual pervert 75.16
sexual pleasure 95.1
sexual possession 480.3
sexual power 76.2
sexual practices 75.18

sexual preference 75.10
sexual prejudice 75.10
sexual psychopathy 75.11, 92.15
sexual relations 75.7
sexual revolution 75.18
sexual stereotyping 590.1
sexual surrogate 75.18
sexual union 75.7
sexual urge 75.2
sex up 498.8
sexy 75.25, 75.27, 97.7, 97.8, 100.30, 377.8, 665.29, 999.13
sexy body 1016.3
Seyfert galaxy 1073.6
shabbiness 250.3, 484.2, 633.1, 661.3, 810.6, 998.2, 1000.2
shabby 80.25, 250.7, 391.11, 393.32, 484.8, 633.7, 661.12, 810.15, 998.21, 1000.9, 1005.9
shabby-genteel 606.8
shack 228.9
shackle (n) 428.4, 1012.7 (v) 428.10, 429.12, 1012.11
shackled 428.16
shack up 75.21, 563.17
shacky 393.33, 806.5, 810.15
shade (n) 35.1, 35.6, 245.1, 248.4, 797.7, 919.4, 976.4, 988.1, 1008.1, 1027.3, 1028.1 (v) 35.14, 38.7, 319.7, 346.6, 712.19, 1027.9, 1028.5
shaded 1027.16, 1028.7
shadeless 1025.32
shade of difference 780.2, 944.3
shade off 245.4
shader 1028.1
shades 29.3, 1028.2
shades below 682.1
shades of death 307.1
shade tree 310.10
shadiness 645.1, 1027.3
shading (n) 38.5, 245.3, 712.8, 1027.6, 1035.3, 1035.5 (a) 1028.6
shadow (n) 133.3, 138.6, 166.2, 245.1, 248.4, 256.1, 270.7, 270.8, 349.5, 588.1, 712.8, 764.3, 784.3, 785.7, 919.4, 976.4, 988.1, 1008.1, 1027.3, 1028.1 (v) 27.13, 35.14, 38.7, 133.9, 166.3, 319.7, 346.9, 349.11, 522.12, 938.35, 1027.9, 1028.5
shadow-box 754.4
shadowboxing 457.9, 754.1
shadow cabinet 613.3
shadow economy 731.7
shadowed 1027.16, 1028.7
shadowed forth 971.19
shadow figure 712.14
shadow forth 133.9, 349.11
shadowgram 714.6
shadowgraph 714.6
shadowgraphist 716.5
shadowiness 32.2, 1053.1
shadowing (n) 166.1, 295.1, 346.3, 382.1, 938.9, 1027.6 (a) 1028.6
shadowless 1025.32
shadow of a shade, the 248.5
shadow of death 307.1, 307.2
shadow of doubt 955.2
shadow of one's former self 393.3
shadowy 32.6, 522.15, 764.6, 971.19, 988.7, 1027.16, 1053.7
shady 645.16, 661.10, 1027.16, 1028.7
shady character 415.6
shady dealings 732.1
shady past 661.6
shady reputation 661.1
shady side, the 303.5
shaft (n) 3.17, 239.13, 272.6, 273.1, 275.2, 284.4, 462.6, 549.12, 901.8, 1040.5, 1058.6 (v) 389.6
shaft grave 309.16
shaft horse 311.13
shag (n) 3.2, 3.4, 89.2, 294.1 (v) 176.16
shagged 3.24, 288.6
shagginess 3.1
shaggy 3.24, 288.6, 294.7, 810.14
shaggy dog story 488.3
shaggy-dog story 489.6
shah 575.9
Shaitan 680.4
shaitan 318.12
shake (n) 10.49, 525.1, 709.19, 830.3, 917.3, 917.4, 938.15, 1054.3 (v) 16.8, 16.10, 105.14, 105.18, 127.14, 127.15, 127.18, 128.10, 131.8, 295.23, 303.10, 368.7, 374.3, 437.7, 525.7, 585.10, 705.5, 708.38, 902.12, 916.10, 916.11, 916.14, 917.10, 917.11, 938.33, 1023.9
shake a leg 330.14
shake all over 127.14
shake down 192.15, 480.22, 938.33, 942.8
shakedown 192.6, 480.8, 938.15, 942.3
shakedown artist 480.12
shakedown cruise 182.6, 942.3
shake hands 148.5, 223.7, 437.7, 465.10, 585.10, 731.19
shake hands and kiss babies 609.40
shake hands on 332.10, 436.5
shake hands with 587.10
shake hands with oneself 502.8
shake in one's boots 127.14, 917.11
shake it up 401.6
shake like an aspen leaf 105.18, 917.11
shake like jelly 116.8
shaken 105.23, 128.14, 131.13, 917.16, 985.12
shaken up 917.16
shake off 368.7, 431.8, 909.21
shake off the yoke 369.6
shake one's faith 955.7
shake one's fist at 454.3, 514.2
shake one's hand 149.2
shake one's head 335.3, 442.3
shake one's head at 510.10
shake on it 332.10, 436.5, 731.19
shake out 808.13
shakeout 773.2, 801.3, 808.3, 944.3
Shaker (n) 668.4 (a) 668.10
shaker 759.16, 797.9, 917.9
Shakerism 668.2
shakes 85.7, 105.5, 128.2, 1023.2
shakes, the 917.2, 917.3, 926.10
shake the lead out 401.6
shake the windows 53.7
shake up 16.10, 23.5, 105.14, 510.13, 808.13, 917.10, 1047.6
shakeup 808.7, 995.2
shake up a hornet's nest 917.10
shake with laughter 116.8
shakiness 16.1, 16.3, 374.1, 804.2, 971.6, 1006.2
shaking (n) 105.5, 916.2, 917.2 (a) 128.12, 525.12, 917.17
shaking of hands 465.3
shaky 16.16, 127.23, 128.12, 303.18, 374.4, 525.12, 764.7, 804.5, 917.17, 971.20, 1006.11, 1023.16
shaky ground 1006.2
shaky health 85.3
shale 1050.2
shale oil 1056.4
shallow (v) 276.3 (a) 248.6, 274.7, 276.5, 922.20, 930.14, 998.19
shallow-bottomed 276.5
shallow-brained 922.20
shallow-draft 276.5
shallow-headed 922.20
shallow-hulled 276.5
shallow-minded 922.20
shallow-mindedness 922.7
shallowness 206.1, 274.1, 276.1, 922.7, 930.5, 984.1, 998.3
shallow-pated 922.20
shallow-rooted 276.5
shallow-rooting 276.5
shallows 276.2, 1006.5
shallow-sea 276.6
shallow structure 530.2
shallow water 276.2
shallow-witted 922.20
shallow-wittedness 922.7
sham (n) 295.10, 354.3, 354.13, 356.7, 357.6, 376.1, 500.1, 501.4 (v) 354.21, 500.12 (a) 336.8, 354.26, 500.16
shaman (n) 90.9, 690.7 (a) 690.14
shamaness 690.8
shamanic 690.14
shamanism 90.13, 91.2, 675.6, 689.1, 690.1
shamanist (n) 690.7 (a) 690.14
shamanistic 690.14
shamanize 690.10
Shamash 1073.14
shamble (n) 175.2, 177.12 (v) 175.7, 177.28
shambles 308.3, 308.12, 395.1, 463.2, 810.3
shame (n) 96.4, 113.1, 137.2, 638.2, 654.3, 661.5, 664.2 (v) 98.13, 137.4, 661.8
shame culture 373.2
shamed 137.14, 661.13
shamefaced 113.8, 137.14, 139.12
shamefacedness 96.4, 113.1, 127.3, 137.2, 139.4
shamefast 113.8, 137.14, 139.12
shamefastness 113.1, 137.2, 139.4
shameful 113.8, 638.3, 654.16, 661.11, 1000.9
shamefulness 113.1, 661.2, 1000.2
shameless 114.4, 142.11, 501.20, 638.3, 645.16, 654.17, 666.6
shameless falsehood 354.12
shamelessness 114.1, 142.2, 501.3, 666.2
shammer 357.6
shampoo (n) 79.5, 79.17, 1016.11 (v) 79.19
shampooing 79.5
shamrock 647.1, 876.1
shamus 1008.16
shanghai 424.7, 480.14, 482.20
shanghaier 483.10
shanghaiing 482.9
Shangri-la 986.11
shank 2.7, 10.14, 10.15, 177.14, 273.6, 548.6
shank of the afternoon 315.2
shank of the evening 315.2
shanks 177.15
shank's mare 177.8
shank's pony 177.8
shantey 708.14
shanti 464.3
shantih 106.2
shanty 228.9
shantytown 230.6
shapable 1047.9
shape (n) 33.3, 33.5, 84.1, 262.1, 262.4, 266.1, 765.2, 765.3, 765.4, 809.3, 865.4, 976.4, 988.1 (v) 262.7, 262.8, 381.8, 742.6, 796.3, 867.3, 892.8, 986.14
shape a course 182.27, 381.8
shape after 336.7
shaped 262.9, 266.6, 381.12, 892.18
shaped note 709.14
shapeless 263.4, 522.15, 810.12, 854.7, 870.9, 971.19, 1015.8
shapelessness 263.1, 522.3, 538.1, 971.4, 1015.1
shapeliness 264.1, 1016.3
shapely 264.5, 1016.18
shape-memory alloy 1058.4
shape of things, the 765.2
shaper 892.7, 1040.6
shapes 211.2
shape-shifter 680.11
shapeshifter 783.1
shapeshifting 783.1
shape the hair 3.22
shape up 262.8, 392.7, 765.5, 796.3, 807.5
shapewear 5.22
shaping (n) 262.5, 266.1, 717.4, 796.1, 808.1, 892.2 (a) 677.17, 986.18
shaping imagination 986.2
shaping-up 796.1

sharav 318.8
shard (n) 391.4, 793.3 (v) 1050.3, 1051.9
sharded 1051.11
sharding 1051.4
share (n) 244.2, 477.5, 738.3, 793.1 (v) 93.11, 343.7, 476.6, 477.6, 793.6
shareable 343.11
share account 622.2
share and share alike (v) 476.6, 477.6, 875.4 (a) 476.9
sharebroker 737.10
share certificate 622.3
sharecrop 1069.16
sharecropper 1069.5
sharecropping 476.2, 1069.1
shared 777.11
shared pair 1033.3
shared sense 332.5
shared workspace 739.7
shareholder 476.4, 737.14
share in 476.6
share in one's grief 147.2
share ledger 738.2
share one's bed and board 563.17
share one's sorrow 147.2
share out 793.6
share-out 477.1
shareowner 737.14
share power 772.3
sharer 476.4
shares 738.2
shareware 1042.11
share with 343.7, 477.6
sharing (n) 93.5, 343.2, 455.1, 476.1, 477.1, 582.6 (a) 476.8, 777.11
sharing of grief 147.1
sharing of sorrowsorrow 147.1
sharing out 477.1
sharing quarters 225.1
shark 311.29, 357.4, 413.11, 480.12, 593.5, 759.21
sharkish 144.26, 311.49, 480.26
sharkishness 480.9
sharklike 311.49
sharp (n) 357.3, 413.11, 709.14, 759.21 (a) 17.14, 24.13, 26.10, 58.14, 61.4, 64.6, 68.6, 69.10, 93.24, 98.20, 105.31, 144.23, 204.18, 278.6, 285.8, 330.18, 339.14, 356.22, 415.12, 489.15, 505.7, 578.13, 671.16, 920.14, 1023.14
sharp air 1023.1
sharp as a razor 285.8
sharp as a tack 920.14
sharp as a two-edged sword 285.8
sharp as broken glass 285.8
sharp-cornered 278.6
sharp ear 48.3
sharp-eared 48.15
sharp edge 285.2
sharp-edged 285.8
sharpen 24.7, 67.4, 105.13, 119.2, 251.5, 285.7, 1040.13
sharpen a distinction 780.6
sharpened 285.8
sharpener 1040.2
sharpening 119.1
sharpen one's tools 405.13
sharpen the wits 568.10
sharper 357.3, 759.21
sharp eye 27.10, 339.4
sharp-eyed 27.21, 339.13
sharp-freeze 1024.11
sharp-freezer 1024.5
sharp freezing 1024.1
sharp-freezing 1024.12
sharp frost 1023.7
sharp-frozen 1024.14
sharpie 357.4, 759.21
sharpish 17.14, 144.23, 1023.12
sharp look 27.5
sharpness 17.5, 31.2, 58.1, 61.1, 64.2, 67.1, 68.1, 68.2, 98.5, 144.8, 285.1, 330.3, 339.5, 415.1, 489.2, 505.3, 578.3, 671.1, 920.2, 1023.1
sharp-nosed 69.13
sharp pain 26.2
sharp-pointed 285.9
sharp practice 356.4, 645.3
sharps and flats 709.15
sharp-set 100.25, 285.8
sharpshoot 904.12
sharpshooter 461.9, 904.8
sharpshooting 459.9
sharp sight 27.1
sharp-sighted 27.21
sharp taste 62.1
sharp tongue 110.4, 144.7
sharp-tongued 505.7
sharp weapon 462.8
sharp wind 318.7
sharp-witted 920.14
sharp-wittedness 920.2
sharp words 456.5
sharpy 413.11, 578.7
shastra 683.8
shatter 395.17, 802.13, 926.24, 1050.3, 1051.9
shatterable 1050.4
shattered 393.27, 802.24
shattered mind 926.1
shattered nerves 128.4
shattered silence 53.3
shattering (n) 771.1, 802.3, 1051.4 (a) 247.12
shatter one's hopes 125.11
shatterproof 15.20, 1049.5
shatter the peace 53.7
shattery 16.14, 1050.4
shavasana 201.2
shave (n) 1016.14 (v) 6.8, 223.10, 255.10, 268.6, 287.5, 356.19, 633.6, 728.27
shaved 268.9
shaven 6.17
shaver 302.3
shavetail 575.17
shaving 6.4, 270.7, 296.3, 793.3
shaving mirror 29.6
shavings 256.1, 391.4
shaw 310.14
shay 179.4
she 77.4, 865.5
sheaf 770.8
shear 6.5, 255.10, 268.6, 480.24
sheared 268.9, 802.23
shear off 255.10, 802.11
shears 1040.8
sheath 295.17
sheathe (n) 296.2 (v) 5.39, 295.20, 295.23
sheathed 212.12, 295.31
sheathe the sword 465.11
sheathing (n) 295.1, 295.17, 1054.3 (a) 295.35
sheathing board 1054.3
she-bear 77.9
shed (n) 184.24, 197.27, 228.9, 386.6 (v) 6.10, 473.5
shed a luster 662.14
shed blood 12.17, 308.15, 458.13
shed crocodile tears 354.23
shedding (n) 6.2, 473.2 (a) 6.18
she-devil 110.12, 593.7, 680.6
shed ink 547.19
shed light upon 341.10, 1025.28
shed luster on 1025.28
shed new light upon 551.8
shed of 430.31
shed tears 115.12
shedu 680.6
sheen 1025.2
sheeny 1025.33
sheep 37.2, 311.5, 311.7, 336.4, 696.9, 700.1, 867.2
sheepdip 79.9, 88.14, 1001.3
sheep dog 311.16, 1008.11
sheep farm 1070.5
sheepherder 1070.3
sheepherding 1070.1
sheepish 113.9, 139.13, 311.45
sheeple 606.2
sheeplike 311.45
sheepman 1070.2, 1070.3
sheep rot 85.41
sheep's eyes 100.4, 562.9
sheepskin 549.6
sheer (n) 164.1, 204.3 (v) 164.3, 182.30, 204.9 (a) 200.12, 204.18, 248.8, 794.10, 798.7, 1029.4
sheer chemistry 963.5
sheer cliff 200.3
sheer drop 200.3
sheerness 200.1, 1029.1
sheer off 164.6, 368.8, 903.7
sheer precipice 200.3
sheet 37.2, 295.10, 296.2, 555.2, 793.2, 1054.5
sheet anchor 494.3, 1008.3
sheet ice 1023.5
sheeting 295.10, 1054.3
sheet lightning 1025.17
sheet metal 1058.5
sheet music 708.28
sheet of fire 1019.13
sheet of galaxies 1073.6
sheet of rain 316.1
sheetwork 548.1
shegets 688.6
she-goat 77.9, 311.8
sheik 104.12
sheikh 575.9, 608.7, 699.12
sheikhdom 417.7
shekels 728.2
shelf 195.1, 276.2, 296.1, 386.6, 901.14
shelf ice 1023.5
shelf life 827.1
shelf-room 386.5
shelfworn 393.31
shelfy 276.6
she-lion 77.9
shell (n) 2.2, 2.10, 5.15, 180.1, 206.2, 266.4, 284.2, 295.14, 295.15, 295.16, 460.3, 462.17, 462.19, 704.16, 1038.4 (v) 6.9, 192.13, 459.22
shellac (n) 88.14 (v) 35.14, 412.9
shellacked 88.33, 287.11, 412.15
shellacking 35.12, 411.1, 412.3
shellback 183.3, 413.16
shell carver 716.6
shell company 737.16
shelled 295.31
shellfish 10.25
shell game 356.10
shelling 192.4
shell-like 279.18
shell money 728.3
shell out 478.12, 624.14, 626.5
shellproof 15.20
shells 1033.3
shell-shaped 279.18
shell shock 92.17
shell-shocked 985.14
shelter (n) 228.4, 295.2, 1008.1, 1009.3 (v) 225.10, 1008.18
shelter cabin 197.9
sheltered 173.12, 1008.21
sheltering 295.35, 1008.23
shelter under 376.4
shelty 311.10
shelve 204.10, 390.6, 846.9
shelved 340.14
shelving 204.15
shelving beach 204.4
shelvy 204.15
shemozzle (n) 53.4, 456.6, 810.3, 810.4, 917.1, 985.3 (v) 368.11
shenanigans 356.5, 489.5, 489.10
Sheol 682.1
shepherd (n) 311.16, 574.7, 699.2, 769.5, 1008.6, 1070.3 (v) 573.9, 769.8, 1008.19, 1070.8
shepherded 770.21
shepherdess 1070.3
shepherding 573.4, 770.1, 1008.1
shepherd's dog 311.16
shepherd's pie 10.11
shepherd's staff 273.2
sherbet 10.47
sherif 608.7
sheriff 1008.15
sheriffalty 231.5, 417.7, 594.4
sheriffcy 417.7
sheriffdom 417.7
sheriffry 594.4
sheriffwick 231.5, 594.4
Sherlock Holmes 576.10
Shetland 311.10
Shetland pony 311.10
she-wolf 110.12, 593.7, 671.9
Shia 675.23
shiatsu 91.14
shibboleth 517.12, 526.9

shield (n) 295.2, 295.15, 647.2, 1008.3 (v) 295.19, 460.8, 1008.18
shielded 295.31, 1008.21
shielding (n) 295.1, 1008.1 (a) 295.35, 460.11, 1008.23
shieldlike 279.19
shield-shaped 279.19
shift (n) 5.16, 160.1, 164.1, 356.6, 415.3, 825.3, 852.1, 858.1, 995.2 (v) 164.3, 172.5, 176.11, 182.30, 362.8, 368.8, 415.9, 645.11, 852.6, 854.5, 858.11, 936.9
shift about 645.11
shift ballast 182.49
shifted meaning 518.1
shift for oneself 430.20
shiftiness 345.4, 356.3, 415.1, 645.1, 854.2, 971.6
shifting (n) 164.1, 854.3, 936.5 (a) 164.7, 177.37, 854.7, 971.20
shifting course 164.1
shiftingness 854.3, 971.6
shifting sands 854.4
shifting scene 33.7
shifting trust 629.2
shifting use 629.2
shift into 858.17
shiftless 331.19, 406.15
shiftlessness 331.5, 406.2
shift off 368.8, 846.9
shift of structure 531.1
shift of tense 531.1
shift shape 783.2
shift the blame 643.7, 645.12
shift the goalposts 645.13
shift the responsibility 643.7, 645.12
shift the scene 852.7
shift with 862.4
shifty 345.12, 345.15, 356.22, 368.15, 415.12, 645.16, 645.21, 854.7, 971.20
Shi'ism 675.13
Shi'ite 675.23
Shiite 675.31
shikker (n) 88.12 (a) 88.31
shiksa 688.6
shill (n) 357.5, 733.6 (v) 733.9
shillelagh 273.2
shilling 728.8
shilly-shally (n) 362.2, 362.3, 362.5 (v) 175.8, 362.7, 362.8, 914.4 (a) 362.10
shillyshallyer 362.5
shilly-shallying (n) 362.2, 362.3 (a) 175.11, 362.10, 362.11
shillyshallying 175.3
shimmer (n) 1025.7 (v) 1025.24
shimmering (n) 1025.7 (a) 1025.35
shimmer with heat 1019.22
shimmery 1025.35
shimmy 705.5
shin (n) 2.7, 177.14 (v) 193.11
shindig 582.12, 705.2, 770.2
shindy 53.4, 456.6, 582.12, 705.2, 810.4
shine (n) 88.18, 104.1, 287.2, 1025.2, 1025.10 (v) 31.4, 287.7, 392.11, 501.13, 544.7, 662.10, 1016.16, 1025.23, 1044.8
shine a light 1025.29
shine at 413.18
shine brightly 1025.23
shined 1025.33
shine forth 1025.23
shine in 413.18
shine out 31.4
shiner 85.38
shine some light on 351.4
shine upon 449.14, 1025.28
shine up to 587.12
shingle (n) 1051.6, 1054.3, 1059.3 (v) 3.22, 295.23, 295.30, 296.5
shingled 295.36, 1051.12, 1059.12
shingles 85.25, 295.6, 1054.2
shingly 1051.12, 1059.12
shin guard 1008.3
shin guards 752.1
shininess 1025.2
shining (n) 1044.2 (a) 662.19, 1016.20, 1025.30, 1025.33
shining example 659.4, 786.4
shining light 1025.2
shining ones, the 678.2
Shining Path Guerrilla 461.16
shinny 749.4
shinny up 193.11
shin pads 749.4
shinplaster 728.5
Shintoism 675.14
Shintoist (n) 675.24 (a) 675.32
Shintoistic 675.32
shinty 749.4
shiny 79.25, 287.11, 1025.30, 1025.33
ship (n) 180.1, 181.1, 181.11 (v) 176.13, 176.15
ship biscuit 10.30
ship broker 730.9
ship chandlery 180.12
shipload 196.2
shipman 183.1
shipmanship 182.3
shipmaster 183.7
shipmate 588.3
shipment 196.2
ship oars 182.53
ship off 176.15
ship of the desert 311.5
ship of the line 180.6
ship of war 180.6
shipping 180.10
shipping lane 383.1
ship route 182.10
ships 180.10
ship's carpenter 183.6
ship's cooper 183.6
shipshape 180.20, 807.8
shipshape and Bristol fashion 180.20, 807.8
ship's husband 574.1
ship's log 549.11
ship's papers 549.5
ship's ropes 271.3
ship's tailor 183.6
ship's watch 832.6
ship's writer 183.6
ship that passes in the night 828.5
shipwreck (n) 395.4, 1011.2 (v) 182.42, 395.10
shipwrecked 1013.27
shipyard 739.1, 739.3, 1009.6
shire 231.5
shiretown 230.4
shirk (n) 368.3 (v) 331.12, 340.7, 368.9
shirker 340.5, 368.3
shirking (n) 368.2 (a) 340.11, 368.15
shirr 11.5, 291.6
shirred 11.7
shirred eggs 10.26
shirring 11.2
shirt (n) 5.15, 752.1 (v) 5.40
shirt-sleeve diplomacy 609.5
shirt tackle 746.3
shirtwaist 5.15
shiv 1040.2
shivah 701.9
shivaree 53.3
shiver (n) 105.2, 105.5, 248.3, 793.3, 917.3 (v) 105.18, 127.14, 802.13, 917.11, 1023.9, 1050.3
shivered 802.23
shivering (n) 917.2, 1023.2 (a) 128.12, 917.17, 1023.16
shivers 74.4, 85.7, 105.5, 127.5, 128.2, 1023.2
shivers, the 917.2
shiver to death 1023.9
shivery 127.23, 128.12, 917.17, 1023.16, 1050.4
shizzle 520.3
shnockered 88.33
shoal (n) 276.2, 311.30, 770.5, 884.3 (v) 276.3 (a) 274.7, 276.5
shoaliness 276.1
shoalness 276.1
shoals 1006.5
shoal water 276.2
shoaly 276.6
shoat 302.10, 311.9
shock (n) 3.4, 22.6, 85.9, 85.26, 96.5, 131.3, 671.8, 770.7, 902.3, 917.3, 1011.2, 1032.6 (v) 98.11, 105.14, 127.17, 131.8, 917.11, 1032.26
shock absorber 670.3, 1048.3
shock and awe 458.4
shocked 131.13
shocker 131.2
shockheaded 3.24
shockheadedness 3.1
shocking 98.19, 127.30, 131.11, 247.12, 661.11, 830.5, 1000.9
shocking pink 35.5
shock jock 1034.23
shock pad 213.5
shockproof 1049.4
shock-resistant 1049.4
shock tactic 131.2
shock tactics 459.1, 459.2
shock therapy 92.35
shock treatment 92.35
shock troops 461.15
shock wave 184.31, 671.5, 916.4
shod 5.45
shoddiness 16.2, 633.1, 661.3, 810.6, 998.2, 1000.2
shoddy (n) 354.13, 391.5 (a) 340.12, 354.26, 391.11, 393.32, 633.7, 661.12, 810.15, 998.21, 1000.9
shoe 5.40
shoebie 5.1
shoeblack 577.5
shoed 5.45
shoegazer 710.2
shoe last 786.6
shoemaker 5.38
shoemaking 5.32
shoes 5.27, 756.1
shoeshine boy 577.5
shoeshiner 79.14
shoestring catch 745.3
shoestring district 609.16
shoestring margin 738.10
shogun 575.9
shoo 909.21
shoo-in 409.2, 411.2, 757.3, 970.2
shook 131.13, 985.12
shook up 128.12
shookup 16.12
shoot (n) 177.5, 238.10, 239.3, 302.11, 310.20, 561.4, 740.3, 1058.7, 1074.9 (v) 26.8, 87.22, 91.28, 174.8, 182.53, 182.54, 191.7, 308.18, 310.34, 349.8, 382.9, 459.22, 604.16, 671.14, 706.8, 714.14, 747.4, 749.7, 751.4, 904.12, 1025.23, 1074.13
shoot a brick 747.4
shoot ahead 174.12, 249.10, 330.13
shoot ahead of 910.8
shoot at 459.22, 904.12
shoot back 939.4
shoot ballast 182.49
shoot craps 759.23
shoot down 308.18, 395.11, 820.6, 904.12
shoot down in flames 19.10, 393.11, 395.11, 820.6
shoot-em-up 706.2
shooter 714.2, 904.8
shoot from the hip 135.4, 365.7, 644.10, 947.2
shoot full of holes 958.4
shooting (n) 26.2, 308.1, 382.2, 459.8, 604.6, 749.3, 904.2 (a) 26.10
shooting circle 749.4
shooting gallery 87.20
shooting guard 747.2
shooting iron 462.10
shooting pain 26.2
shooting script 704.21, 706.3
shooting star 133.5, 828.5, 1073.15
shooting up 87.2, 193.1
shooting war 458.1
shoot into space 1075.12
shoot it out with 457.17
shoot off at an angle 204.9
shoot off one's mouth 503.3, 520.5, 524.20, 540.5
shoot out 283.10
shootout 459.8, 749.3, 752.3

shoot out rays 1025.23
shoot par 751.4
shoot questions at 938.21
shoot straight 644.10
shoot straight with 649.5
shoot the breeze 524.20, 541.8
shoot the bull 520.5
shoot the sun 182.51
shoot the works 359.8, 360.7, 403.14, 407.7, 493.6, 972.12
shoot to death 308.18
shoot up 14.2, 87.22, 193.9, 251.6, 259.7, 272.12, 283.10, 310.34
shoot-up 87.20
shop (n) 724.4, 736.1, 739.1, 739.7, 759.19 (v) 551.13, 733.8
shopaholic 733.5
shop around 371.13, 733.8, 944.5
shop around for 938.30
shop assistant 577.5, 730.3
shop at 731.17
shopboard 736.6
shop clerk 730.3
shop floor 726.2, 739.1, 739.3
shopfront 206.2
shopkeeper 385.6, 730.2
shoplift 482.13
shoplifter 483.1
shoplifting 482.1
shopmate 616.5
shoppable 733.10
shopper 195.2, 733.5
shopping 733.1
shopping around 733.1
shopping-bag lady 331.10, 619.4
shopping-cart lady 619.4
shopping-cart woman 619.4
shopping center 208.7, 230.6, 736.2
shopping complex 736.2
shopping list 733.1, 871.1
shopping mall 736.2, 739.1
shopping plaza 736.2
shopping spree 733.1
shop steward 727.4
shoptalk 523.9, 523.10
shop till one drops 733.8
shop window 206.2
shopwindow 1029.2
shopworn 393.31
shoran 182.2, 184.6, 1036.3
shore (n) 211.4, 218.1, 234.2 (v) 449.12, 901.21 (a) 182.58, 234.7
shorebird 311.27
shore boulder 1059.5
shored 901.24
shored up 901.24
shorefront (n) 234.2 (a) 234.7
shore leave 20.3
shoreless 823.3
shoreline (n) 234.2 (a) 234.7
shore patrol 1008.17
shoreside 234.7
shore up 15.13, 449.12, 901.21, 1046.9
shoreward 234.7
shoring 901.23
shorn 252.10
shorn of 473.8
short (n) 179.10, 706.1, 737.12 (v) 1032.26 (a) 248.6, 258.10, 268.8, 274.7, 344.9, 505.7, 537.6, 619.7, 795.4, 828.8, 911.5, 992.13, 1003.4
short account 737.12
shortage 795.2, 911.1, 992.4, 1003.1
short allowance 992.5
short and sweet 268.8, 537.6, 828.8
short answer 508.2, 939.1
short ballot 609.19
shortbread 10.41
short-breathed 21.12
shortcake 10.30, 10.42
shortchange 356.18
shortchanger 357.3
short-circuit 1032.26
shortcoming 791.1, 911.1, 992.4, 1003.1, 1003.2
short commons 10.6, 515.2, 992.5
shortcut (n) 223.2, 268.5, 277.2, 383.1 (v) 268.7 (a) 268.9
short distance 223.2
short division 1017.12
short duration 828.1
shorten 252.7, 255.9, 258.9, 260.7, 268.6, 537.5, 557.5
shortened 260.12, 268.9, 537.6, 557.6
shortened version 557.1
shortener 268.4
shortening 255.2, 260.1, 268.3, 537.4
shorten sail 182.50, 494.6
shorter 252.10
shortest 250.8
shortest way 268.5
shortfall 795.2, 911.1, 992.1, 992.4
short fuse 110.2, 110.4
shorthand (n) 523.11, 546.2, 547.8 (a) 547.22, 547.27
shorthanded 992.9, 992.12
short-hop airline 184.10
short interest 737.12
short-legged 268.11
short life and a merry one, a 743.2
short list 871.1
short-list 871.8
short-lived 828.7
short-livedness 828.1
short measure 795.1, 911.1
short memory 990.1
short memory span 990.1
short message service 347.4
short message system 347.4
short movie 706.1
shortness 110.2, 258.1, 268.1, 274.1, 344.2, 505.3, 537.1, 828.2
shortness of breath 21.3, 85.9
short odds 759.6
short of 911.5, 992.13
short of breath 21.12
short of cash 619.7
short of funds 619.7
short of luck 1011.14
short of money 619.7
short of wind 21.12
short on 619.10
short on looks 1015.6
short-order cook 11.3
short pants 5.18
short period 1060.2
short piece 223.2
short range 223.2
short-range 223.14
short range aid to navigation 1036.3
short rations 515.2
short reliever 745.2
short run 704.4
shorts 5.18, 737.12, 752.1
short sale 737.19
short score 708.28
short seller 737.12
short shorts 5.18
short shrift 146.1, 442.2
short side 737.12
short sight 28.3
shortsighted 28.11, 922.14, 923.10, 980.10
shortsightedness 28.3, 922.2, 980.1
short spell 828.3
short-staffed 992.9
short step 223.2
short-stop 714.13
shortstop 745.2
short-stop bath 714.13
short story 722.3
short story writer 547.15, 718.4
short-story writer 722.5
short-story writing 547.2, 718.2
short subject 706.1
short supply 992.1
short temper 110.2, 110.4
short-tempered 110.25
short-term 828.8
short-termed 828.8
short-term memory 989.1
short time 268.1, 828.3
short-time 828.8
short version 557.1
short vowel 524.11
shortwave (n) 1034.11 (v) 1034.25 (a) 1034.28
shortwave band 1034.13
shortwave broadcasting 1034.16
shortwave diathermy 91.5
shortwave signal 1034.10
shortwave station 1034.6
short way 223.2
short weight 356.8, 795.1
short-weight 297.1
shortweight 356.18
short-winded 21.12
short-windedness 21.3
short-winged 268.11
short-witted 922.13
shorty 258.4
short yardage 746.3
shot (n) 56.3, 86.6, 87.20, 88.7, 91.16, 156.3, 174.6, 403.3, 462.19, 630.6, 706.5, 714.3, 714.8, 745.3, 747.3, 748.2, 749.3, 752.3, 759.3, 759.9, 793.5, 904.4, 904.8, 951.4, 1074.9 (a) 47.9, 128.14, 393.29, 395.29, 820.10
shot down 820.10
shot down in flames 820.10
shotgun (n) 462.10 (v) 308.18
shotgun approach 401.1
shotgun marriage 436.3
shotgun pattern 771.1
shotgun quiz 938.2
shotgun wedding 563.3
shot in the arm, a 9.1
shot in the arm 86.8
shot in the dark 759.2, 951.4
shot put 904.3
shot-putter 904.7
shot silk 47.6
shotten 393.36
shot through 47.9, 221.15, 292.19
shot to pieces 128.14
should 641.3, 963.10
shoulder (n) 10.15, 283.3, 548.6, 800.4, 901.2, 901.4, 901.14 (v) 901.21, 902.12
shoulder a gun 458.17
shoulder arms 405.13, 458.17
shoulder bag 729.15
shoulder block 746.3
shoulder gun 462.10
shouldering 902.3
shoulder patch 647.5
shoulder sleeve insignia 647.5
shoulder-to-shoulder 223.14
shoulder weapon 462.10
shout (n) 59.1, 116.2, 116.4 (v) 53.7, 59.6, 116.6, 116.8, 348.7, 352.13
shout at the top of one's voice 59.9
shout down 53.8, 910.7
shout from the housetops 352.13
shout hallelujah 116.6
shout hosanna 116.6
shouting (n) 53.3 (a) 59.10
shouting match 53.3
shout of laughter 116.4
shout out 59.7, 59.8
shout-out 59.1, 116.2, 332.3
shoutout 524.3
shove (n) 902.2, 904.1 (v) 172.6, 732.7, 902.12, 904.9
shove aside 164.6
shove away 372.2
shove in one's oar 214.5
shovel (n) 1040.2, 1040.8 (v) 176.17, 284.15
shovel it in 672.4
shove off 182.19, 182.36, 188.7, 222.10, 307.19
shoving (n) 904.1 (a) 904.14
shoving match 457.4
show (n) 33.2, 33.7, 206.4, 348.2, 354.3, 376.1, 500.1, 501.4, 517.3, 704.4, 704.12, 736.2, 759.4, 976.2 (v) 31.4, 33.8, 161.6, 206.5, 341.10, 348.5, 351.4, 517.17, 568.10, 714.16, 757.5, 957.8, 957.10
show a bold front 454.5, 492.10
show a clean pair of heels 368.10

show a deficit 623.6
show a direction 896.3
show a lack of respect for 156.4
show a leg 23.6
show a light pair of heels 368.10
show-and-tell 348.2
show a percentage 472.13
show a profit 472.13
show a proper spirit 649.6
show aptitude for 413.18
show a tendency 896.3, 968.4
show biz 704.1, 743.13
showboat (n) 501.11, 704.14 (v) 413.20, 501.16
show business 704.1, 743.13
show card 352.7
showcase (n) 348.2, 704.12, 736.6, 1029.2 (v) 348.5
showcased 348.13
showcasing (n) 348.2 (a) 348.9
show compassion 652.3
show compunction 658.6
show consideration 670.8
show disrespect for 156.4
show distaste for 99.5
show dog 311.16
showdown 759.10, 779.1
shower (n) 79.8, 79.12, 316.1, 991.2, 1065.5, 1065.8 (v) 79.19, 316.10, 478.12, 991.5
shower bath 79.8, 79.12, 1065.8
shower curtain 79.12
shower down 316.10
shower down upon 478.15, 485.3
shower gel 79.17
shower head 79.12, 239.9, 1065.8
showeriness 1065.1
showerproof 1066.11
shower room 79.12
showers 79.12
shower stall 79.12
showery 316.11
show expertise 413.20
show fight 453.3, 454.3
show forth 348.5
show girl 707.1
show good faith 644.9
show horse 757.2
show-horse 311.14
show how 341.10, 568.10
show ignorance 922.12
show improvement 392.7
showiness 501.3, 545.1
showing (n) 33.1, 206.4, 348.2, 517.3 (a) 6.12, 31.6, 348.9, 351.10
showing for all to see 31.7
showing forth 348.1, 348.2
showing-forth 33.1
showing-off 501.4
showing up 351.1
showing-up 33.1
show in the best colors 600.12
show its colors 351.8
show its face 351.8
show kindness 143.9
showman 704.23
showmanship 501.4, 704.3
show marks of age 303.11
show mercy 148.4, 601.4, 670.8
shown 348.13, 957.20
show no amazement 123.2
show no appetite 8.26
show no mercy 146.2
shown up 958.7
show off 348.5, 500.12, 501.16
showoff 140.5, 501.11
showoffy 501.19
show of hands 371.6
show of joy 116.1
show one his place 157.5
show one's age 303.11
show one's authority 417.13
show one's cards 351.7
show one's colors 182.52, 348.6, 351.7, 517.22
show oneself 33.8
show one's face 33.8, 221.8
show one's hand 351.7
show one's ignorance 414.10
show one's mind 348.6
show one's teeth 152.14, 454.3
show one's true colors 348.6, 351.7, 941.9
show one the door 909.20
show one the gate 909.20
showpiece 786.1, 1002.4
show pity 670.8
showplace 786.1
show preference 650.8
show promise 133.12
show remorse 658.6
show respect for 155.5
showroom 197.24, 736.5
show sensitivity 670.8
show signs of 33.10, 133.11, 957.8
show signs of life 306.9, 396.20
show someone the door 908.3
showstopper 409.4
show sufficient grounds for 600.9
show talent for 413.18
show the color of one's money 624.15
show the door 372.2, 909.18
show the gate 909.18
show the heels 368.10
show the ropes 568.10
show the way 161.6, 165.2, 341.10, 816.3
show the white feather 491.8
show through 31.4, 1029.3
show-through (n) 1029.1 (a) 1029.4
show to best advantage 600.12
show up 31.4, 33.8, 186.6, 221.8, 249.8, 351.4, 831.6, 941.9, 958.4, 977.2
show up late 846.7
show what one has 501.16
show what's what 958.5
show wisdom 935.17
showy 501.19, 545.8
shpilkes 126.1
shrapnel 462.19
shred (n) 248.3, 793.3 (v) 802.14, 1051.9
shredded 802.23, 1051.11
shredder 1051.7
shredding 50.13, 1051.4
shred of comfort 121.4
shrew 110.12
shrewd 413.28, 415.12, 920.15, 928.15
shrewdness 415.1, 920.3
shrewish 110.22, 361.12, 456.17
shrewishness 110.6, 361.4, 456.3
shriek (n) 53.5, 58.4, 59.1, 116.4 (v) 53.10, 58.8, 59.6, 115.13, 116.8, 318.20, 524.25
shrieking 35.20, 58.14
shrieky 58.14
shrievalty 231.5, 417.7, 594.4
shrift 148.2, 351.3
shriftless 654.18, 695.18
shriftlessness 695.4
shrill (n) 58.4 (v) 58.8 (a) 58.14, 61.4
shrillness 58.1
shrimp (n) 258.4, 998.7 (v) 382.10
shrimpiness 258.1
shrine (n) 309.16, 549.12, 703.4 (v) 212.5
shrined 662.18
shrink (n) 92.10 (v) 26.8, 127.13, 139.7, 168.2, 168.3, 252.6, 252.7, 260.9, 325.4, 368.8, 393.18, 473.5, 903.7
shrinkability 260.5
shrinkable 260.11
shrinkage 252.1, 252.3, 255.2, 260.3, 473.2
shrink back 903.7
shrinker 92.10
shrink from 99.5
shrinking (n) 252.1, 260.3, 325.2 (a) 127.23, 139.11, 168.5, 325.7, 344.10
shrinkingness 127.3
shrinking violet 139.6
shrink-wrap 212.9, 800.9
shrink-wrapped 212.12
shrink-wrapping 212.2
shrive 148.3, 601.4, 701.17
shrivel 260.9, 303.10, 393.18, 1066.6
shriveled 258.13, 260.13, 270.20, 303.18, 393.35, 1066.9
shriveled up 260.13
shriveling (n) 260.3 (a) 393.45
shriven 148.7
shrive oneself 658.6
shroom 87.19
shroud (n) 295.2, 309.14, 901.2 (v) 5.39, 295.20, 346.6, 1008.18
shrouded 295.31
shrouded in darkness 1027.13
shrouded in mystery 522.18
shrouded spirit 988.1
shrouding (n) 295.1 (a) 295.35
shroud lines 181.13
shrub 310.9, 310.16
shrubbery 310.9
shrubby 310.39, 310.40
shrubland 310.13
shrublike 310.39
shrubwood 310.16
shrug (n) 517.14 (v) 134.7, 433.6, 517.21
shrug it off 134.7
shrug off 102.4, 390.7, 433.6, 950.2, 984.4
shrug one's shoulders at 157.3, 510.10
shrug the shoulders 517.21
shrunk 252.10, 258.13, 260.13
shrunken 252.10, 258.13, 260.13, 393.35, 473.7
shtarker 593.4, 671.10
shtick 704.7
shuck (n) 295.16 (v) 6.9
shudder (n) 105.2, 105.5, 917.3 (v) 847.3, 917.11, 1023.9
shudder at 99.5, 103.5
shuddering (n) 99.2, 847.2, 917.2 (a) 917.17
shudder of the flesh 133.2
shuffle (n) 175.2, 177.12, 344.4, 862.1, 936.4, 985.3 (v) 177.28, 705.5, 758.5, 797.10, 811.3, 854.5, 862.4, 936.9
shuffle along 175.6, 177.27
shuffled 810.13, 985.12
shuffle off 368.12
shuffle off this mortal coil 307.18
shuffle out of 368.7, 369.9
shuffler 936.7
shuffle the cards 852.7
shuffling (n) 758.1, 811.1, 854.3, 936.5 (a) 175.10, 846.17, 854.7, 936.14
shul 703.2
shumai 10.24
shun 157.7, 368.6, 668.7
shun companionship 583.4
shunning 368.1
shunt (n) 904.1 (v) 164.6, 176.11, 904.9
shunted 340.14
shunting off 368.1
shush (n) 57.1 (v) 51.8, 57.2, 345.8
shushing 57.1
shut (v) 293.6, 857.12 (a) 293.9
shut away 429.12
shut down 293.8, 428.8, 625.7, 857.8, 857.12
shutdown 293.1, 331.3, 857.1
shut down on 51.8
shuteye 22.2
shut fast 293.12
shut in (v) 212.5, 429.12 (a) 584.10
shut-in (n) 85.43, 584.5 (a) 85.54, 212.10, 331.18, 428.15, 429.19
shut it down 727.10
shut mind 980.1
shut of 430.31
shut of day 315.2
shut off (v) 802.8, 857.12, 1012.12 (a) 584.8, 802.21
shut-off 756.3
shut one's bazoo 51.6
shut one's doors 625.7
shut one's ears 49.4
shut oneself up 584.7
shut one's eyes to 30.8, 148.4, 443.10, 979.7, 984.2
shut one's mouth 51.5

shut out (v) 293.6, 412.9, 444.3, 773.4, 1012.12 (a) 412.16
shut-out 293.9, 773.7
shutout 412.3
shutter (n) 295.4 (v) 293.8, 1028.5
shutterbug 714.2, 716.5
shutter dam 1012.5
shutter speed 714.9
shut the door 293.6
shut the door in one's face 442.5
shut the door on 444.3
shut the door upon 586.5
shut the eyes of one's mind 980.6
shut the gate 756.4
shut tight 1012.12
shutting 293.1
shutting down 293.1, 428.2
shutting out 293.1
shutting post 273.4
shutting up 293.1
shuttle (n) 179.14, 181.1, 184.10, 740.5, 916.9, 1075.2 (v) 850.5, 916.13
shuttlecock (n) 916.9 (v) 916.13
shuttle crew member 1075.8
shuttle diplomacy 609.5
shuttle flights 1075.1
shuttle raid 184.11, 459.4
shuttle rocket 1075.2
shuttle service 184.10
shuttle train 179.14
shut up (v) 51.6, 212.5, 293.6, 293.8, 429.12, 958.5 (a) 584.10
shut up shop 857.8
shy (n) 368.1, 903.3, 904.3 (v) 127.12, 127.13, 131.5, 164.6, 168.3, 325.4, 362.7, 368.8, 903.7, 904.10, 936.9 (a) 127.23, 139.12, 168.5, 325.7, 494.9, 795.4, 872.8, 955.9, 992.13
shy at 325.4, 459.28
shy away 168.2, 368.8, 903.7
shy away from 127.13, 362.7, 368.6
shylock 620.3
shylocking 620.1, 732.1
shyness 127.3, 139.4, 325.2, 368.1
shy of 992.13
shy of belief 956.4
shy off 164.6
shyster 357.3, 415.6, 597.3, 660.3
sialagogic 13.7
sialagogue 13.3
sialoid 13.7
sialorrhea 13.3
siamese 239.6
siamese connection 239.6
siamese joint 239.6
Siamese twins 873.4
sib (n) 559.2 (a) 559.6
Siberia 261.4, 1023.4
Siberian 1023.14
Siberian tiger 311.21
sibilance 57.1
sibilancy 57.1
sibilant (n) 524.12 (a) 57.3, 524.30
sibilate 57.2, 524.25
sibilation 57.1, 525.1
sibling (n) 559.2 (a) 559.6
sibship 559.1
sibyl 962.6
sibyllic 962.11
sibylline 962.11
sic at 456.14
siccant 1066.10
siccative (n) 712.18, 1066.4 (a) 1066.10
siccity 1066.1
sick 85.56, 112.28, 118.11, 926.26
sick, the 85.43
sick abed 85.59
sick and tired of 118.11, 994.6
sick as a dog 85.56
sick at heart 112.28
sick bay 91.21
sick berth 91.21
sick building syndrome 85.32
sicken 82.4, 85.47, 85.50, 98.11, 393.16
sicken at 99.4
sickened 96.20
sickener 64.3, 994.3
sickening (n) 393.1 (a) 64.7, 98.18
sick fancy 986.5
sick headache 26.5
sick humor 489.1
sickie 926.16
sick-in 727.5
sick in the head 926.26
sickish 85.56
sickishness 85.1
sick joke 489.6
sickle 279.5
sick leave 222.4
sicklelike 279.11
sickle of Death 307.2
sickle-shaped 279.11
sickliness 36.2, 85.3
sick list 871.1
sickly 36.7, 85.54
sickly hue 36.2
sickly-sweet 66.6
sickly-sweetness 66.1
sick market 737.3
sick mind 926.1
sickness 85.1, 926.1
sickness insurance 611.7
sicko 926.16
sick of 118.11, 994.6
sick on each other 589.7
sick-out 857.2
sickout 727.5
sick person 85.43
sick personality 92.13
sick puppy 75.16
sick to one's stomach 85.57
sick unto death 85.56
sick up 909.26
sic on 375.17, 456.14
siddur 701.10
side (n) 10.7, 33.3, 140.4, 204.4, 211.4, 218.1, 277.2, 501.2, 502.1, 503.1, 560.4, 617.4, 704.10, 750.3, 752.2, 935.14, 978.2 (v) 176.11, 211.10, 218.4 (a) 204.13, 218.6, 848.3
side against 442.3, 451.3, 510.10, 779.4
sidearm 745.5
sidearms 462.1
sideband 1034.14
sidebar 254.1, 552.3
sidebar comment 597.1
side benefit 624.4
sideboard 1054.3
sideburns 3.8, 218.1, 1016.14
side-by-side 218.6, 223.14
side chain 1038.7
side-chain theory 91.15
side-channel 239.2
side chapel 703.3
sided 218.7
side dish 8.10, 10.7
sidedness 218.1
side door 218.1, 346.5, 383.4
side effect 254.1, 817.3, 887.1
side entrance 218.1
side frequency 1034.14
side-glance 27.4, 562.9
side horse 725.7, 760.5
side interest 724.7
side issue 254.1
sidekick 588.4, 610.8, 616.2, 769.5
sidekicker 616.2
side ladder 193.4
sidelight 551.1, 1025.1
sideline (n) 211.4, 724.7, 735.1, 746.1, 747.1, 748.1, 749.4 (v) 390.6
sideline crew 746.1
sidelined 340.14
sideling 204.15, 218.6
sidelining 724.7
sidelong 204.13, 204.15, 218.6
sidelong look 27.3
sideman 616.6
side note 254.2
side order 10.7
side partner 588.3, 616.2
side path 383.4, 538.4
sidepod 756.1
sider 616.9
sideral 1073.25
sidereal 1073.25
sidereal time 832.3
sidereal universe 1073.1
sidereal year 824.2
side remark 213.2
siderite 907.3, 1073.15
side road 383.4, 538.4
siderolite 1073.15
side room 197.20
sides 704.21
side scene 704.20
side sewing 554.14
sideshow 907.2
sideslip (n) 184.13, 194.4 (v) 177.35, 184.40, 194.9, 218.5
sideslip landing 184.18
sidesman 616.6
sidesplitter 489.6
sidestep (n) 164.2, 368.1, 903.3 (v) 164.6, 218.5, 344.7, 368.8, 468.2, 903.7, 936.9
side-stepping 368.1
sidestepping 903.3, 936.5
side street 383.4
sidestroke 182.11
side suit 758.3
sideswipe (n) 902.3 (v) 223.10, 902.13
side-talk 490.1
side to side 205.1
sidetrack (n) 538.4 (v) 164.6
sidetracked 340.14, 538.13
sidetracking 368.1
side-view 218.1
sidewalk 383.2
sidewalk salesman 730.5
sidewalk superintendent 918.1
sideward 172.8, 218.6
sideward motion 172.2
sidewards 218.6
sideway 218.6
sideways 172.8, 218.6
sideways motion 172.2
side-wheeler 180.1
sidewheeler 311.14
side whiskers 3.8
sidewise 172.8, 218.6
sidewise motion 172.2
side with 332.9, 371.14, 449.13, 450.4
siding 218.1, 1054.2, 1054.3
siding with the enemy 363.2
sidle (n) 177.12 (v) 164.6, 177.26, 177.28, 204.10, 218.5
sidle up to 167.3
sidling 177.17
Sidney 608.5
siege 212.1, 459.5
siege artillery 462.11
siegecraft 458.5
siege engine 462.11
siege mentality 460.1
sierra 237.6
Sierra Club 397.5
Sierras 231.7
siesta 22.3, 315.1
sieve (n) 79.13, 170.3, 292.8, 802.7, 808.5 (v) 79.22, 773.6, 808.11, 944.4
sievelike 292.20
sievelikeness 292.8
sieve out 944.4
sieving 79.4
siffle 57.1
sift 79.22, 371.14, 541.11, 773.6, 801.8, 808.11, 938.23, 944.4
sifted 1051.11
sifter 79.13, 808.5
sifting 79.4, 801.3, 808.3
sifting out 801.3
sift out 944.4
sigh (n) 2.21, 52.4, 52.8 (v) 52.10, 52.14, 115.10, 318.20, 524.25
sigh for 100.16
sighing 52.8
sigh of relief 120.4
sight (n) 24.5, 27.1, 27.3, 29.5, 31.3, 33.6, 33.7, 122.2, 247.4, 953.6, 978.2, 1015.4 (v) 27.12
sight bill 728.11
sight bite 793.3
sight draft 728.11
sighted 27.20
sightedness 27.1
sight for sore eyes, a 100.11

sight for sore eyes 1016.6
sight gag 489.6
sighthole 27.8, 29.5
sighthound 311.16
sight-impaired 28.11
sighting 941.1
sight land 182.38
sightless 30.9, 32.5
sightless, the 30.4
sightless eyes 30.1
sightlessness 30.1
sightline 27.1, 31.3
sightliness 1016.2
sightly 1016.18
sight on 161.5
sight-saver type 30.6
sightsee 177.21, 918.6
sightseeing (n) 918.4 (a) 918.7
sightseeing excursion 918.4
sightseeing tour 177.5, 918.4
sightseeing trip 177.5
sightseer 178.1, 918.3, 981.2
sight-unseen transaction 971.8
sigil 332.4, 517.1, 517.7, 517.13, 527.10
sigillography 647.1
sigmatism 57.1
sigmoid 279.11
sigmoidal 281.6
sigmoid flexure 2.18
sign (n) 91.13, 133.3, 352.7, 517.1, 517.15, 518.6, 523.11, 546.1, 551.4, 709.12, 862.2, 870.8, 957.1, 1017.3 (v) 49.4, 332.12, 437.7, 438.9, 517.22, 546.6
signal (n) 517.1, 517.15, 551.4, 551.7, 647.7, 756.3, 1036.11 (v) 182.52, 343.7, 517.22, 551.10 (a) 247.10, 347.21, 997.19
signal beacon 517.15, 1019.13
signal bell 517.15
signal-caller 746.2
signal display 1036.11
signaler 399.4
signal fades 1036.12
signal fire 517.15
signal flag 517.15
signal flare 1026.3
signal gong 517.15
signal gun 517.15
signaling 343.2, 343.5, 347.1
signalize 487.2, 517.22, 662.12, 957.8
signalizing 517.23
signal lamp 517.15
signal lantern 517.15
signal light 517.15
signalling 343.1
signalman 399.4
signal mast 517.15
signal modulation 1036.8
signal-noise ratio 1034.10
signal of distress 400.1
signal post 517.15
signal rocket 517.15
signal shot 517.15
signal siren 517.15
signal-to-noise ratio 1035.5
signal tower 517.15
signal whistle 517.15
sign and seal 332.12
sign a petition 440.10
signatory 332.7
signature 332.4, 437.3, 517.1, 517.11, 527.10, 554.12, 554.14, 578.1, 709.12, 793.2, 865.4, 888.2, 1034.19, 1042.18
sign away 629.3
signboard 352.7, 517.4
signed 332.14, 437.11, 517.24, 1017.23
signed agreement 437.1
signed and sealed 332.14
signed edition 554.6
signed, sealed, and delivered 407.11, 437.11
signer 332.7
signet 332.4, 517.7, 517.13, 527.10, 647.3
signet ring 498.6
sign for 438.9
signific 518.12
significance 133.6, 518.1, 518.5, 662.5, 887.2, 997.1
significancy 518.5
significant (n) 518.6 (a) 133.15, 517.23, 518.10, 662.17, 889.9, 957.16, 997.17
significant fact 761.3
significant form 262.1
significantness 518.5
significant other 104.11, 588.1
signification 517.3, 518.1
significative 517.23, 518.10
significs 518.7
signified 133.14
signify 133.11, 517.17, 518.8, 865.11, 957.8, 997.12
signifying 517.23
signify nothing 520.4, 998.11
sign in 186.6
signing 437.3, 517.14
signing bonus 254.4
signing-off 332.4
sign language 49.3, 517.14, 523.11, 525.6
sign manual 527.10
sign off 347.20, 1034.25
sign-off 857.1
sign off on 332.12, 371.15, 441.2, 509.9
sign of the cross 696.5
sign of the three balls 620.4
sign of the times 133.3, 896.2
sign on 191.4, 347.20, 476.5, 615.14, 615.17, 617.14, 1034.25
sign one's death warrant 308.20, 602.3
sign one's note 438.9
sign one's own death warrant 308.22
sign on the dotted line 332.12, 436.5
signor 76.7
signora 77.8
signore 76.7
signorina 77.8
signorino 76.7
sign out 188.13
sign over 629.3
sign painter 352.9, 716.4
signpost (n) 273.4, 517.4 (v) 161.5
signposted 517.24
signs 85.1, 517.8
signs and portents 870.8
signs of life 396.3
sign up 191.4, 404.3, 615.14, 615.17, 617.14, 825.5
sign up for 615.14
sike 238.1
Sikh 675.24
Sikhism 675.14
silage 10.4
Silas Marner 484.4
silence (n) 51.1, 173.1, 344.2, 464.2 (v) 19.10, 51.8, 308.18, 395.15, 412.7, 428.8, 958.5
silence cloth 51.4
silenced 412.14
silence of the grave, the 51.1
silence of the tomb, the 51.1
silencer 51.4
silencing 395.6
silent (n) 706.1 (a) 51.10, 344.9, 519.9
silent as a post 51.10
silent as a stone 51.10
silent as the grave 51.10
silent as the tomb 51.10
silent bit 706.3
silent consent 441.1
silent film 706.1
silent majority 607.5, 617.4, 1005.5
silent majority, the 609.33
silentness 51.1
silent partner 616.2
silent person 49.2
silent poetry 712.13
silent policeman 283.3
silent prayer 696.4
silent treatment 909.4
silenus 678.11
silhouette (n) 211.2, 262.2, 712.12, 712.14, 785.7, 1027.3 (v) 211.9
silicate 1058.1
silicic 1058.15
silicon 7.11
silicon chip 1033.8, 1042.3
silicone 1056.2
Silicon Valley 231.7
silique 310.30
silk 4.1, 287.3, 294.3, 1047.4
silken 287.11, 1047.15
silken repose 22.2, 173.1
silkiness 287.1, 294.3, 1047.1
silklike 1047.15
silks 5.9
silk-screen artist 716.8
silk-screen printing 548.1, 713.4
silk stocking 607.3, 608.4
silk-stocking 578.16
silk-stocking district 609.16
silk-stocking politics 609.1
silkworm 271.5
silky 271.7, 287.10, 287.11, 294.8, 1047.15
sill 901.6, 901.9
silliness 923.1, 998.3
silly (n) 924.6 (a) 520.7, 923.8, 985.14, 998.19
silly Billy 924.6
silly grin 116.3
silly season, the 313.3
silly smile 116.3
silo 386.7, 1074.10
siloed 802.20
silt 256.2, 1059.6
silted up 293.11
silt up 276.3, 293.7
silvan 310.40
silver (n) 8.12, 37.1, 37.2, 39.1, 728.1, 728.20 (v) 37.5, 39.3 (a) 37.7, 39.4, 544.8, 1058.17
Silver Age 824.5
silver-bearded 39.5
silver bullion 1058.3
silver cat 311.20
silver ceiling 724.1, 909.5
silver certificate 728.5
silver dollar 728.7
silvered 37.7, 39.4
silver frost 1023.7
silver-gray 39.4
silver hair 3.3
silver-headed 39.5
silveriness 37.1, 39.1
silvering 37.3
silver iodide 316.5
silver jubilee 850.4
silver lining 124.2
silver medal 646.2
silver mine 1058.6
silver plate 8.12, 295.13
silver-plate 295.26
silver-plated 295.33, 1058.17
silver-print drawing 712.12
silver screen 706.7
silver screen, the 706.1
silver standard 728.21
Silver Star Medal 646.6
silver-toned 708.48
silver tongue 544.1
silver-tongued 544.8, 708.48
silver-tongued orator 543.6
silver-voiced 708.48
silverware 8.12, 735.4
silver wedding anniversary 850.4
silvery 37.7, 39.4, 708.48, 1058.17
silvery hair 3.3
silvery moon 1073.11
silvicultural 310.40, 1069.21
silviculture 310.13, 1069.2, 1069.3
silviculturist 1069.7
SIM 347.4
simba 311.21
SIM card 347.4
simian 311.22
similar 775.8, 784.10, 943.8
similarity 775.1, 784.1, 943.3
similarize 784.8, 788.7
simile 784.1, 943.1
similitude 349.5, 784.1, 784.3, 785.1, 943.1
similize 536.2, 943.4
simmer (n) 1020.2 (v) 11.5, 152.15, 320.4, 671.12, 1019.22, 1020.20
simmer down 106.7
simmered 11.7

simmering (n) 11.2, 1020.2 (a) 105.29, 152.29, 1019.25
simoleons 728.2
simon-pure 354.33, 798.6, 973.15
simoom 318.6, 318.12
simous 265.12
simp 924.8
simpatico 455.3, 587.15
simpático 587.15
simper (n) 116.3 (v) 116.7, 500.14
simpering 500.18
simple 35.22, 137.10, 228.33, 248.8, 416.5, 496.7, 499.6, 521.11, 533.6, 535.3, 581.3, 761.15, 767.9, 798.6, 872.7, 922.22, 930.11, 954.9, 973.15, 1014.13
simple as ABC 1014.13
simple assault 459.1
simple carbohydrate 7.5
simple diet 668.2
simple existence 761.6
simple fact 761.3
simple fruit 10.38
simple harmonic motion 916.1
simplehearted 416.5
simpleheartedness 416.1
simple idea 932.2
simple interest 623.3
simple larceny 482.2
simple machine 1040.5
simple matter 1014.3
simple measure 709.24
simpleminded 416.5, 922.22
simplemindedness 416.1, 922.3, 922.9
simpleness 137.1, 416.1, 499.1, 535.1, 798.1, 922.9, 930.1, 954.2
simple protein 7.6
simple radical 1038.7
simple reflex 92.26
simples 86.4
simple soul 358.1, 416.3
simple-speaking 535.3
simple time 709.24
simpleton 924.8, 930.7
simpletonian 922.22
simpletonianism 922.3
simple truth 761.3, 973.1
simple truth, the 973.3
simple variable 1041.9
simplewitted 922.22
simple-wittedness 922.9
simplicity 117.2, 233.3, 252.1, 416.1, 496.3, 499.1, 521.2, 533.1, 535.1, 581.1, 798.1, 872.1, 922.9, 930.1, 954.2, 1014.1
simplification 341.3, 341.4, 798.2, 858.1, 1014.6
simplified 252.10, 798.9
simplify 252.7, 341.10, 499.5, 521.6, 798.4, 1014.7
simplism 406.4, 798.3
simplistic 406.12, 798.10, 987.6
simulacrum 33.3, 349.5, 354.3, 354.13, 784.3, 785.1, 976.2
simulate 336.5, 354.21, 500.12, 621.4, 784.7
simulated 354.26, 500.16, 784.10
simulation 336.1, 354.3, 621.2, 784.1
simulative 336.9, 349.13
simulator 336.4
simulcast (n) 1034.18, 1035.2 (v) 1034.25, 1035.14
simultaneity 769.1, 830.1, 836.1, 899.1
simultaneous 769.9, 830.4, 836.5
simultaneousness 769.1, 836.1
sin (n) 38.4, 654.3, 655.1, 655.2, 975.1 (v) 654.8, 655.4, 975.9
sin against the Holy Ghost 655.2
sinapism 86.33
sincere 101.9, 359.11, 416.5, 644.17, 973.15
sincere friendship 587.8
sincerely 820.5
sincerely yours 820.5
sincerest form of flattery, the 336.1
sincere thanks 150.2
sincerity 101.2, 359.1, 416.1, 644.4, 973.7
sin city 891.2
sinecure 1014.3
sine qua non 196.5, 959.2, 963.2, 997.6
sinew 2.3, 15.2, 18.1, 544.3
sine wave 916.5
sine-wave 916.19
sinewed 544.11
sinewiness 15.2, 544.3
sinewless 16.12, 19.19
sinews 15.2
sinewy 15.16, 544.11, 1049.4
sinful 638.3, 654.16, 655.5, 695.17, 1000.7
sinfulness 638.1, 654.4, 695.3, 975.1, 1000.1
sing (n) 708.32 (v) 60.5, 95.12, 109.6, 116.5, 318.20, 351.6, 524.25, 551.13, 708.38, 720.14, 957.9
singable 708.48
sing a different tune 363.6, 858.11
sing a familiar tune 117.5
sing along 708.38
singalong 708.13
sing deathless songs 720.14
singe (n) 1020.6 (v) 38.7, 1004.6, 1020.24
singed 38.11, 1020.30
singeing 1020.5
singer 707.1, 707.6, 710.1, 710.13
singfest 708.32
sing for one's supper 619.5
sing-in 708.32
sing in chorus 455.2, 708.38, 788.6
singing (n) 708.13, 708.32 (a) 60.6, 95.16, 708.50
singing bird 710.23
singing club 710.16
singing society 710.16
singing voice 710.13
sing in the shrouds 318.20
single (n) 565.2, 745.3, 872.4 (v) 745.5 (a) 565.7, 798.6, 865.13, 872.7
single blessedness 565.1, 872.2
single-blind experiment 942.1
single combat 457.7
single-crust pie 10.41
singled-out 371.26
single entry 628.5
single-entry accounting 628.6
single-entry bookkeeping 628.6
single file 812.2
single-foot 177.12
singlefoot 177.28
single-footer 311.14
single girl 565.4
single-handed 872.8
singlehearted 416.5, 644.14
singleheartedness 416.1
singlehood 565.1
single instance 872.4
single-issue group 609.31, 894.6
single-issue politics 609.1
single-jet 181.3
single man 565.3
single-member constituency 609.16
single-member district 609.16, 609.18
single-minded 359.11, 360.8, 416.5, 983.17
single-mindedness 359.1, 360.1, 416.1, 983.3
single mordent 709.18
singleness 430.5, 565.1, 584.3, 798.1, 802.1, 872.1, 872.2
singleness of heart 416.1
singleness of purpose 360.1
single out 371.14, 865.11, 983.10
single parent 559.5
single-parent family 559.5
single-prop 181.2
single reed 711.8
single-reed instrument 711.8
single rhyme 720.9
singles 748.1
single sap 460.5
singles bar 88.20
single sideband 1034.14
single space 224.1
single-stage rocket 1074.5
single state 565.1
single-step rocket 1074.5
single story 296.6
single system 609.18
singleton 872.4
single track 270.3
single-track 270.14
single transferrable vote 609.18
singletree 170.5
single voice 332.5
single vote 371.6
single woman 77.5
singling-out 865.6
sing one's own praises 502.6
sing out 59.8
sing praises 696.12
sing small 137.7
singsong (n) 781.2, 849.4 (a) 61.4, 118.9, 849.15
singstress 710.13
sing the blues 112.15, 115.10, 115.11
sing the praises of 509.12, 696.12, 708.38
sing the same old song 118.8, 849.9
sing the same old tune 118.8, 849.9
sing to a different tune 852.7
singular (n) 530.8 (a) 122.10, 865.12, 865.13, 870.11, 872.7, 872.9, 927.5
singularity 865.1, 865.4, 870.3, 872.1, 927.1, 1073.8
sinister 133.16, 204.13, 220.4, 645.16, 1000.7, 1011.13
sinister influence 894.6
sinisterness 133.6
sinistral 204.13, 218.7, 220.4, 220.5
sinistrality 220.2
sinistration 220.2
sinistrocerebral 220.4
sinistrocular 220.4
sinistrodextral 219.6
sinistrogyrate 220.4
sinistrogyration 220.2
sinistromanual 220.5
sinistrorse 220.4
sink (n) 79.12, 80.12, 239.5, 284.2, 654.7 (v) 16.9, 21.5, 34.2, 85.48, 112.16, 112.18, 168.2, 172.5, 182.44, 194.6, 252.6, 275.9, 284.12, 284.15, 297.15, 303.10, 367.7, 367.8, 393.11, 393.17, 395.11, 410.11, 625.8, 729.17, 751.4, 828.6, 913.4, 1011.10, 1011.11
sinkable 367.9
sinkage 194.2, 275.7, 275.8
sink away 34.2
sink back 394.4
sink down 194.6
sinker 10.30, 10.44, 297.6
sinkhole 284.3, 654.7, 913.1, 1065.3
sink in 93.15, 243.2, 521.5, 931.19, 989.13
sinking (n) 172.2, 275.8, 367.2, 913.1 (a) 16.21, 168.5, 172.8, 194.11, 297.18, 303.17, 307.32, 393.45
sinking fast 307.32
sinking fund 386.3
sinking-fund payment 624.1
sinking heart 112.3
sinking speed 184.31
sinking stomach 127.5
sink into despair 112.16, 125.10
sink into oblivion 990.7
sink into the mind 931.19
sink like lead 367.8
sink money in 626.5, 729.17
sink of corruption 654.7
sink one 747.4
sink one's soul 112.18
sink one's teeth 983.5
sink one's teeth into it 330.11
sink with 450.4
sinless 653.7, 657.6, 1002.6
sinlessness 653.2, 657.1, 1002.1

sinner 593.1, 660.8
sin of Adam 655.3
sin of commission 655.2
sin offering 696.7
sin of omission 655.2
sin of pride 141.1
sinopia 712.12
Sino-Tibetan 523.12
sinter 256.2
sinuate 281.6
sinuation 281.1
sinuose 281.6
sinuosity 279.1, 281.1
sinuous 279.7, 281.6
sinuousness 279.1, 281.1
sinus 279.2
sinusitis 85.16
sip (n) 8.4, 62.2, 88.7, 248.4 (v) 8.29, 62.7, 88.24
siphon (n) 192.9, 239.6 (v) 176.14, 239.15
siphoning 192.3
siphon off 192.12
sipping 8.3
Sir 648.3
sir 76.7
sirdar 575.17, 648.3
sire (n) 304.5, 560.9, 648.3, 757.2, 886.4, 892.7 (v) 78.8, 818.14, 886.10
Siren 377.4
siren (n) 399.3, 400.1, 593.7, 678.10, 690.9 (a) 377.8
siren 53.6, 240.3, 377.4
sirenic 377.8
Sir Galahad 608.5
siriasis 85.28
siring 78.2
Sirius 1073.4
Sir John Mandeville 357.9
sirloin 10.14
sirocco 318.6, 318.12
sirrah 648.3
sis 559.3
siss (n) 57.1 (v) 57.2
sissification 77.11
sissified 16.14, 77.14, 491.10
sissify 77.12
sissiness 77.2
sissing (n) 57.1 (a) 57.3
sissy (n) 16.6, 77.10, 427.4, 491.5, 559.3 (a) 77.14, 491.10
sissyish 77.14
Sister 648.5
sister 699.17, 700.2, 784.3
sister 77.6, 77.7, 90.10, 559.3, 617.11
sister city 230.1
sister-german 559.3
Sister Hicks 882.2
sisterhood 559.1, 587.2, 617.3, 642.4
sister-in-law 564.2
sisterliness 587.2
sisterly 143.13, 587.15
sisterly love 143.4
sistern 559.3
sisters 700.1
sistership 559.1
sisters under the skin 784.13
sister under the skin 784.3
sistren 700.1
Sisyphean labor 408.1
Sisyphean task 408.1
Sisyphean toil 408.1
sit 78.12, 173.10, 770.17
sit around 331.12
sit at 221.8
sit at the feet of 570.11
sit back 329.2
sit bolt upright 200.8
sit by 329.3
sitcom 1035.2
sit down 159.17, 173.10, 727.10, 913.10
sit-down 8.5, 541.5, 727.5, 770.2
sit down at the bargaining table 437.6
sit-down meal 8.8
sit down on 428.8
sit-down strike 727.5, 857.2
sitdown striker 727.6
sit down together 541.10
sit down with 437.6, 541.10
site (n) 159.1, 463.1 (v) 159.11, 159.12, 159.16
sited 159.18
site map 1042.19
sit idly by 329.3
sit in 221.8, 476.5
sit-in (n) 333.2, 770.2 (v) 333.5
sit in for 862.5
siting 159.6
sit in judgment 594.5, 598.18, 946.12
sit in on 48.10
sit it out 329.2
sit on 345.8, 428.8, 476.5, 480.19, 510.18, 598.18, 901.22
sit on a barrel of gunpowder 493.6, 1006.7
sit on one's duff 329.2
sit on one's hands 329.2, 329.3
sit on the bench 250.4
sit on the dais 814.2
sit on the fence 102.5, 329.4, 362.7, 363.9, 368.8, 467.5
sit on the shelf 565.5
sit on the sidelines 329.2, 467.5
sit on the tail of 166.3
sit on the throne 612.13
sit out 222.7, 467.5
sit spin 760.7
sitter 1008.8
sit through 134.7
sit tight 329.5, 346.8, 360.4, 846.12
sitting 78.5, 541.5, 689.5, 770.2
sitting duck 358.2, 1006.3, 1014.3
sitting meditation 92.6
sitting on a powder keg 1006.13
sitting on the fence 467.3
sitting on top of the world 109.11, 409.14, 411.7
sitting position 753.3
sitting practice 92.6
sitting pretty 109.11, 409.14, 411.7
sitting room 197.5
sitting up and taking nourishment 83.10
situal 159.19
situate (v) 159.11 (a) 159.18
situated 159.18
situation 159.1, 159.6, 209.1, 724.5, 765.1, 978.2, 1013.4
situational 159.19, 765.6
situation comedy 1035.2
situation ethics 636.2
sit up 200.8, 846.12
sit up and take notice 983.8
sit up for 130.8
sit upon 345.8, 510.18
sit upon thorns 127.10
situps 84.2
situs 159.1
sit well with one 95.6
sitz bath 79.8
sitzmark 517.7
Siva 677.3
six 758.2, 882.2
six-card stud 758.4
six-eight time 709.24
six feet above contradiction 141.9
six feet under 307.29
six-figure income 618.1
sixfold (v) 882.16 (a) 882.18
six-footer 272.7
six-gun 462.10
sixie from Dixie 882.2
sixish 884.7
six of one and half a dozen of the other (n) 790.3, 963.6 (a) 778.8, 945.6
six of one and half dozen of the other 539.1
six-pack 882.2
six-part time 709.24
sixpence 728.8
six-pointed star 882.2
six-shooter 462.10, 882.2
six-spot 758.2
sixteen 882.7
16mo 554.4, 882.7
sixteenmo 554.4, 882.7
sixteenth note 709.14
sixteenth rest 709.21
sixth (n) 709.20, 882.14 (a) 882.18
sixth man 747.2
sixth sense 24.5, 689.8, 882.2, 934.1
sixtieth 882.27
sixty 882.7
60-cycle hum 50.13
sixty-four 882.7
sixty-four dollar question 522.8
64mo 882.7
sixty-fourmo 882.7
sixty-fourth note 709.14
sixty-four-thousand-dollar question 938.10
sixty-fourth rest 709.21
sixty-nine 75.7
60-point hill 753.1
6-yard box 752.1
sizable 247.7, 257.16
sizableness 257.6
sizar 572.7
size (n) 158.1, 257.1, 300.3, 803.4, 1062.5 (v) 257.15, 300.10, 808.11, 938.24
sizeable 158.11
size commodiousness 158.5
sizeism 773.3
size of it, the 765.2
size up 27.14, 300.10, 938.24, 946.9
sizing up 300.1
sizz (n) 57.1 (v) 57.2
sizzle (n) 17.3, 57.1 (v) 57.2, 87.22, 152.15, 174.9, 1019.22
sizzler 174.5, 1019.8
sizzling (n) 56.2, 57.1 (a) 57.3, 152.29, 1019.25
sizzling hot 1019.25
sjambok 605.1
ska 708.11
skald 720.12
skaldic 720.16
skanky 1000.8
skate 177.35, 287.9, 749.7
skate around 368.6, 936.9
skateboard (n) 179.21 (v) 177.35
skateboarding 744.1
skateboard park 743.11
skate on thin ice 1006.7
skate over 340.8
skaters 749.2
skates 179.21
skating 177.16, 749.3
skating rink 743.11
skedaddle (n) 368.4, 401.3 (v) 127.12, 174.9, 188.7, 222.10, 368.11, 491.8
skedaddler 368.5
skedaddling 222.4, 368.4, 491.3
skeet 904.2
skeeter 311.37
skeet shooting 744.1, 904.2
skeezy 16.14
skein 271.2, 770.6
skeletal 2.26, 270.17, 270.20
skeletology 2.2
skeleton (n) 2.2, 199.2, 211.2, 266.4, 270.7, 270.8, 307.15, 381.3, 393.8, 557.1, 901.10 (a) 2.26
skeleton at the feast 112.14
skeleton crew 992.2
skeleton in the closet 345.5, 1000.3
skeleton in the cupboard 345.5
skeleton key 292.10
skeleton staff 885.1
skell 619.4
skeptic (n) 695.12, 955.4 (a) 695.20
skeptical 695.20, 955.9, 956.4, 971.16
skepticalness 955.2
skepticism 494.2, 695.6, 955.2, 956.1
sketch (n) 349.1, 349.2, 381.3, 556.1, 557.1, 704.7, 712.12, 784.3 (v) 349.9, 381.10, 381.11, 557.5, 704.29, 712.19
sketchbook 554.1, 712.18
sketched-out 262.9
sketcher 716.3
sketch in 381.10
sketchiness 795.1, 1003.1
sketching 712.4
sketch out 262.7, 381.10, 405.6, 557.5
sketchpad 712.18

sketchy 356.21, 415.12, 795.4, 1003.4, 1006.10
skew (n) 164.1, 204.3 (v) 28.9, 164.5, 204.9, 218.5, 791.3 (a) 164.8, 204.14, 791.4
skewback 279.4
skewbald (n) 311.11 (a) 47.12
skewed 164.8, 204.14, 791.4
skewed judgment 948.1
skewer (n) 285.4 (v) 292.15, 661.9, 800.8
skewering 292.3
skew gear 1040.9
skewgee 204.14, 791.5, 810.13
skew-jawed 204.14
skewness 164.2, 204.1, 265.1
skew-whiff 204.14, 791.5, 810.13
ski 177.35, 287.9, 753.4
skiagram 714.6, 1027.3
skiagraph 714.6, 1027.3
skiagrapher 716.5
skiboggan 179.20
ski bum 178.3
ski bunny 178.3
skid (n) 194.4 (v) 177.35, 184.40, 194.9, 218.5, 287.9
skidoo 188.10
skid road 230.6
skid row 230.6
skid-row bum 331.9, 660.2
skids, the 393.1
skid to a stop 857.7
skier 753.2
skiff 180.1
ski freestyle 753.4
skiing 177.16, 753.1
skiing equipment or gear 753.1
skijoring 753.1
ski jump (n) 366.1 (v) 366.5
ski-jump 753.1
ski-jumper 753.2
ski-jumping 753.1
ski lift 383.8, 753.1, 912.4
skill 249.1, 413.1, 413.7, 892.2, 989.1
skilled 413.26
skilled hand 413.13
skilled in 413.27
skilled laborer 726.6
skilled worker 577.3, 726.6
skilled workman 413.11
skillful 413.22, 999.12
skillful gambler 759.21
skillfulness 413.1, 999.1
skill-less 414.15
skill-lessness 414.1
skills 928.4
skill set 928.4
skill with language 547.2, 718.2
skill with words 547.2, 718.2
skim (n) 177.16 (v) 73.7, 174.8, 177.35, 182.54, 194.9, 223.10, 276.4, 340.8, 472.9, 480.13, 570.13, 938.26
skimble-skamble (n) 520.2 (a) 520.7, 810.16
skimeister 753.2
skimming 73.12
skimmings 472.3
skimmington 812.3
skimobile 179.20
skim off 472.9, 480.13
skim off the cream 999.11
skim off the top 356.18
ski mountaineering 753.1
skim over 276.4, 340.8, 938.26
skimp (v) 340.8, 484.5, 635.4 (a) 992.10
skimper 340.5, 635.3
skimpiness 885.1, 992.2
skimping (n) 484.1, 635.2 (a) 340.10, 484.7, 635.6, 885.5
skimpy 885.5, 992.10
skim the surface 276.4, 340.8
skim through 938.26
skin (n) 2.4, 4.2, 86.23, 206.2, 276.1, 295.3, 295.12, 296.2, 728.7 (v) 6.8, 249.7, 393.13, 480.24, 632.7, 759.26, 802.14, 1044.7
skin, the 2.4
skin alive 249.7, 412.9, 510.20
skin and bones (n) 260.3, 270.5 (a) 393.35
skin cancer 85.35
skin color 35.1
skin coloring 35.1
skin-deep 2.27, 248.6, 276.5, 295.32
skin disease 85.35
skin-dive 367.6
skin diver 367.4
skin diving 367.3
skin effect 1032.13
skin eruption 85.9, 85.36
skin flick 666.4
skinflint 484.4
skin friction 1044.1
skinful 794.3, 994.1
skin game 356.10
skinhead 6.4, 461.1
skinlike 2.27, 295.32
skin live 604.10
skinned alive 412.15
skinner 178.9
Skinnerian psychology 92.2, 321.3
skinniness 270.5
skinning alive 510.3
skinning house 759.19
skinny 2.27, 270.17, 295.32
skinny, the 551.1, 761.4, 973.4
skinny as a rail 270.17
skinny-dip 6.7, 182.56
skinny-dipping 6.2, 760.8
skin out 188.10, 368.11
skin pop 87.22
skin-popping 87.2
skins 4.2, 728.6
skin-search 938.15
skins game 751.1
skint 619.10
skintight 5.47
skin tone 35.1
skip (n) 177.11, 366.1, 391.7, 750.3 (v) 109.6, 116.5, 177.28, 188.7, 222.9, 340.7, 366.5, 366.6, 368.11, 369.6, 705.5, 743.23
skip bail 368.10
skip-bomb 459.23
skip for joy 116.5
skip out 188.7, 368.11
skip over 340.8
skipper (n) 183.7, 575.4 (v) 573.8
skipping (n) 366.3 (a) 366.7
skip tracer 576.11
ski race 753.3
skirl (n) 58.4 (v) 58.8
skirling 58.14
skirmish (n) 457.4 (v) 457.13
skirt (n) 5.16, 75.4, 77.6, 199.2, 211.4, 302.7 (v) 211.10, 218.4, 223.10, 368.7, 914.5
skirt chaser 562.12, 665.10
skirted 211.12
skirting (n) 211.7 (a) 211.11, 218.6
skirts 211.1
skirt the shore 182.39
ski run 753.1
skis 179.21
ski slope 753.1
skit 704.7
ski tow 753.1
ski troops 461.23
skitter 177.35
skittery 127.23, 128.12
skittish 24.12, 105.28, 109.14, 127.23, 128.12, 139.12, 364.6
skittishness 105.10, 109.4, 127.3, 139.4, 364.3
skittles 750.1
skivvies 5.22
skoosh 238.20
skosh 248.2
skreak (n) 58.4 (v) 58.8
Skuld 964.3
skulduggery 356.4
skulk (n) 368.3, 770.5 (v) 346.9, 368.9, 491.9
skulk away 368.12
skulker 368.3
skulking (n) 368.2 (a) 345.12, 346.14, 491.13
skull 198.8, 307.2, 399.3
skull and crossbones 307.2, 647.1
skull cap 5.25
skull session 568.7
skunk (n) 71.3, 311.22, 660.6 (v) 412.9
skunk-drunk 88.33
skunked 412.16
skunkworks 739.6
sky (n) 198.2, 272.2, 1073.2 (v) 751.4, 912.5
sky an oar 182.53
sky-aspiring 100.28
sky atlas 1073.8
sky-blue 45.3
skybridge 383.2, 383.9
skycap 577.5
sky-colored 45.3
skydive (n) 181.13, 367.1 (v) 184.47, 367.6
skydiver 185.8, 367.4
skydiving 367.3
sky-dyed 45.3
skygodlin 791.5, 810.13
sky-high 272.15, 632.11
sky it 745.5, 747.4
skyjack 482.20
skyjacker 483.7
skyjacking 482.7
skylark (n) 193.7 (v) 743.24
skylarker 743.18
skylarking 743.3
skylight 292.7, 295.6, 1025.2
skyline 201.4
sky parlor 197.16
sky pilot 699.2
skyriding 184.1
skyrocket (n) 193.7 (v) 193.9, 193.10, 251.6, 392.7, 1074.12
skyrocketing 193.14, 251.8, 632.12
skyscape 33.6, 712.11
skyscraper 266.2, 272.6
skyscraping 272.15
sky shot 747.3
sky survey 1073.8
skysweeper 462.12
skywalk 383.2, 383.9
sky wave 1034.11
skyway 184.33
skywrite 352.15
skywriter 352.9
skywriting 184.1, 184.9
slab 296.2, 1054.3
slabber (n) 13.3 (v) 13.6
slabbiness 1062.2, 1062.4
slabby 1062.12, 1062.14
slack (n) 391.4, 1021.2 (v) 20.7, 340.7, 368.9, 670.9, 804.3, 1022.7 (a) 16.12, 94.13, 173.14, 175.10, 331.19, 340.10, 426.4, 665.26, 804.5, 810.15, 846.17, 1047.10
slacken 20.7, 120.5, 175.9, 252.8, 393.16, 670.6, 670.9, 804.3, 810.8, 846.8, 1012.10
slackened 175.12
slackening 16.5, 120.1, 175.4, 252.1, 670.2
slacker 340.5, 368.3
slacking (n) 331.4, 368.2 (a) 331.19
slack-jawed 292.18
slackminded 922.13
slackmindedness 922.1
slackness 175.1, 340.1, 426.1, 804.2, 846.5
slack off 20.7, 175.9, 670.9, 804.3
slack-off 175.4
slack-roper artist 707.3
slacks 5.18
slacktivist 340.5
slack up 20.7, 175.9, 670.9
slack-up 175.4
slackwitted 922.13
slackwittedness 922.1
slactivist 609.23
slag 256.2, 391.4, 893.3, 1020.16
slag concrete 1054.2
slake 95.8, 120.5, 670.9, 994.4
slaked 994.6
slakeless 100.27
slake one's thirst 88.24
slalom 753.3
slalom course 164.1, 753.1
slalom pole 753.3
slalom racer 753.2

slam (n) 56.1, 156.3, 409.5, 429.9, 510.4, 902.4, 902.5 (v) 56.6, 156.6, 293.6, 510.14, 902.15
slam dunk 747.4
slam into 902.13
slammer 429.9
slamming 495.4
slam the door in one's face 157.5, 368.6, 442.5
slander (n) 354.12, 512.3, 552.8 (v) 512.11
slanderer 357.9, 512.6
slanderous 512.13
slang (n) 522.7, 523.5, 523.9, 526.6 (v) 503.3 (a) 523.21
slanger 503.2
slanging 490.1
slanging match 456.5, 513.2
slangster 523.17
slangy 523.21
slant (n) 27.4, 27.7, 33.3, 164.1, 204.2, 204.7, 650.3, 722.4, 896.1, 978.2, 978.3 (v) 204.10, 218.5, 265.6, 350.3, 354.16, 650.8, 894.7, 936.9 (a) 204.15, 204.19
slant across 204.11
slanted 204.15, 265.11, 354.26, 650.11
slanting (n) 265.2, 350.1, 354.9 (a) 204.15
slant off 278.5
slant of wind 318.10
slant on things 978.2
slant rhyme 720.9, 784.6, 849.4
slantways 204.15
slantwise 204.15
slap (n) 56.1, 604.3, 902.8 (v) 56.6, 159.13, 604.11, 902.19
slap a tax on 630.12
slap-bang 401.9, 493.8
slapdash (n) 340.3 (a) 340.12, 401.9, 493.8
slapdashness 340.3
slap down 372.2, 428.8, 902.17, 908.3, 984.4
slap-happy 985.14
slaphappy 926.27
slap in the face (n) 152.11, 156.2, 442.2, 604.3 (v) 156.5
slap of the glove 454.2
slap on 253.4, 295.24
slap one down 442.5
slap one in the face 442.5
slap one's face 454.3
slap one's wrist 427.5
slap on paint 35.14
slap on the wrist 604.3
slapping 56.11, 257.21
slap shot 749.3
slapstick (n) 489.1, 704.6, 704.8 (a) 488.6, 508.14, 704.35
slapstick comedian 707.9
slapstick humor 489.1
slapstick quality 488.2
slap the face 604.11
slap the lid on 293.6
slap together 340.9, 365.8, 892.8
slap up 340.9, 365.8, 892.8
slap-up 999.13
slash (n) 85.38, 204.7, 252.4, 517.6, 631.1, 633.4, 713.2, 802.4 (v) 204.11, 289.4, 393.13, 510.20, 633.6, 802.11
slash across 204.11
slash and burn 1069.17
slashed 393.27, 633.9
slashing (n) 252.4, 713.2, 802.2 (a) 544.11
slashing one's wrists 308.5
slash the throat 308.18
slat (n) 56.1, 270.7, 271.4, 296.2, 1054.3 (v) 56.6, 917.12
slate (n) 39.1, 609.19, 965.3, 1050.2, 1054.2 (v) 295.23, 965.6
slate-colored 39.4
slated 965.9
slatelike 1059.11
slates 295.6
slather 295.24, 486.3
slatiness 39.1
slattern 80.13, 810.7
slatternliness 810.6
slatternly 810.15
slatting 56.11
slaty 39.4, 1059.11
slaughter (n) 308.1, 308.3, 395.1, 671.3 (v) 308.17, 395.12, 671.11
slaughterer 308.11
slaughterhouse 308.12
slaughtering 308.3
slaughterous 308.24
slaunch (n) 204.2 (v) 204.10
slaunchways 204.14, 791.5, 810.13
slaunchwise 204.14
slave (n) 138.3, 384.4, 432.7, 577.1, 726.3 (v) 725.13
slave ant 311.33
slave away 725.13
slave driver 574.2, 575.13
slave labor 726.3
slave-making ant 311.33
slaver (n) 13.3 (v) 13.6, 926.20
slavering 144.26, 671.18
slaver over 511.5
slavery 138.1, 432.1, 577.12, 725.4
slave to fashion 336.4
slavey 577.2, 577.9
Slavic 523.12
slaving 725.17
slavish 138.13, 432.16
slavishness 138.1
slay 95.11, 116.9, 308.13, 743.21
slay en masse 308.17
slayer 308.11
slaying 308.1
sleaze 660.5
sleazebag 660.5
sleaze factor 16.2, 810.6
sleaziness 16.2
sleazoid 660.5
sleazy 16.14
sled (n) 179.20 (v) 177.35
sledding 177.16
sled dog 311.16
sledge 179.20
sledgehammer (v) 902.16 (a) 424.12
sledgehammering 902.3
sleek (v) 287.7 (a) 287.11, 578.13, 807.8, 1010.13, 1056.9
sleeker 287.4
sleekness 287.1, 578.3, 1056.5
sleep (n) 20.1, 22.2, 25.2, 173.1, 307.1 (v) 22.13, 173.9, 340.6
sleep around 665.19
sleep at one's post 331.12
sleep-bringer 22.10
sleep-bringing 22.23
sleep-causing 22.23
sleep-compelling 22.23
sleep disorder 92.14
sleep-drowned 22.21
sleep-drunk 22.21
sleeper 22.12, 179.15
sleepers 5.21
sleep-filled 22.21
sleepful 22.21
sleep in 20.8, 22.13
sleep-inducer 22.10
sleep-inducing 22.23, 86.45
sleepiness 21.1, 22.1, 331.6
sleeping 22.22, 173.14, 307.29, 519.5, 984.8
sleeping around 665.4
sleeping bag 901.20
sleeping beauty 22.12
sleeping car 179.15
sleeping chamber 197.7
sleeping fire 1019.13
sleeping partner 616.2
sleeping pill 25.3, 86.12
sleeping place 228.1
sleeping policeman 283.3, 1012.1
sleeping porch 197.21
sleeping potion 86.12
sleeping room 197.7
sleeping sickness 22.6
sleeping tablet 25.3, 86.12
sleeping together 75.7
sleeping with 75.7
sleep-inviting 22.23
sleep it off 396.19, 516.2
sleepland 22.2
sleepless 23.7, 339.13, 339.14, 360.8
sleepless eye 339.4
sleeplessness 23.1, 339.5
sleep like a log 22.13
sleep like the dead 22.13
sleep mode 1042.18
sleep off 20.8**sleep of the dead, the** 22.5
sleep of the just 22.4
sleep on 846.9
sleep on a volcano 493.6, 1006.7
sleep out 225.11
sleep over 20.8
sleep-producer 22.10
sleep-producing 22.23
sleep-provoker 22.10
sleep-provoking 22.23
sleep sofa 229.1
sleep soundly 22.13
sleep-swollen 22.21
sleep-tempting 22.23
sleep through 340.6
sleep together 75.21
sleep upon 931.14
sleepwalk (n) 177.9 (v) 177.32
sleepwalker 22.12, 178.7
sleepwalking (n) 22.2, 92.19, 177.9 (a) 177.38
sleepwear 5.21
sleep with 75.21
sleep with one eye open 339.8
sleep with one's ancestors 307.26
sleep with one's fathers 307.26
sleep with the Lord 307.26
sleepy 22.21, 331.20
sleepyhead 22.12, 175.5
sleepy time 315.4
sleet (n) 1023.5 (v) 1023.11
sleety 1023.14
sleigh (n) 179.20 (v) 177.35
sleight 356.4, 356.6, 415.3
sleight of hand 356.5, 356.6, 976.2
sleight-of-hand artist 707.1
sleight-of-hand performer 357.2
sleight-of-hand trick 356.6
slender 270.14, 270.16, 992.10, 998.19, 1016.18
slender as a thread 270.16
slenderish 270.16
slenderize 270.13
slenderizing (n) 270.9 (a) 270.21
slender means 619.1
slenderness 270.1, 270.4, 992.2, 998.3
sleuth 576.10
sleuthhound 576.11
sleuthing 938.4
slew (n) 247.4, 770.7, 884.3 (v) 182.30
slice (n) 8.2, 296.2, 472.3, 477.5, 793.1, 793.3, 802.4 (v) 477.6, 751.4, 793.6, 802.11
slice of life 349.2, 973.7
slicer 802.7
slice the melon 477.6
slice up 477.6, 793.6
slicing 477.1, 802.2
slick (n) 295.12, 296.2 (v) 287.7, 1056.8 (a) 287.11, 287.12, 356.22, 413.22, 415.12, 544.8, 807.8, 920.15, 1056.9
slick as a whistle 413.22, 415.12, 544.8, 807.8
slick chick 1016.8
slick citizen 415.6
slick down 287.7
slicked up 5.46
slicker (n) 5.13, 287.4, 357.4, 413.17 (v) 356.19
slickness 287.1, 504.5, 544.1, 920.3, 1056.5
slick on 1056.8
slicks 756.1
slickster 415.6
slick up 5.42
slidder 194.9
sliddery 287.12
slide (n) 177.16, 194.4, 287.3, 369.3, 711.6, 714.3, 714.5, 743.15 (v) 177.35, 194.9, 287.9, 393.17, 821.5, 1014.10
slide back 394.4
slide down 194.9
slide into 858.11, 858.17
slide off 368.12

slide out of 368.9, 369.9
slide projector 714.12
slides 5.27
slide show 714.3
slide viewer 714.12
sliding (n) 177.16 (a) 393.45
sliding block tackle 752.3
sliding friction 1044.1
sliding scale 624.4
sliding tackle 752.3
slight (n) 156.2, 157.2, 435.1 (v) 156.5, 157.6, 340.8, 454.4, 512.8, 984.2, 984.4 (a) 16.14, 258.10, 270.16, 276.5, 299.4, 992.10, 998.19
slighted 340.14
slighter 512.6
slightest 250.8
slighting (n) 340.1, 512.1 (a) 340.10, 512.13
slight knowledge 928.7, 930.5
slight-made 270.16
slightness 16.2, 248.1, 258.1, 270.4, 270.5, 276.1, 299.1, 992.2, 998.1, 998.3
slight over 454.4
slight stretching 354.11
slight wrong 655.2
slim (n) 270.8 (v) 270.13 (a) 270.16, 885.5, 992.10
slim chance 972.9
slim down 270.13
slime (n) 80.7, 80.8, 660.5, 1062.8 (v) 80.15
slimeball 660.5
sliminess 511.2, 1062.2, 1062.3
slimming 270.21
slimming down 270.9
slimmish 270.16
slimnastics 84.2
slimness 270.4, 992.2, 998.3
slim odds 966.1
slim pickings 992.2
slimy 80.23, 511.8, 1062.12, 1062.14
sling (n) 86.33, 462.9, 904.3 (v) 202.8, 904.10
sling at 459.28
slingbacks 5.27
sling bag 195.2
slinger 904.7
slinging 904.2
sling psychrometer 1065.10
slings and arrows of outrageous fortune, the 1011.4
slingshot 462.9, 743.16
slingstone 1059.4
sling the lead 275.10
slink (n) 177.12 (v) 177.26, 281.4, 346.9, 491.9
slink in 214.5
slinkiness 281.1, 345.4
slinking (n) 177.17 (a) 345.12, 491.13
slink off 368.12
slinky 270.16, 345.12, 491.13
slip (n) 180.16, 194.4, 258.4, 270.7, 270.8, 295.10, 302.1, 302.6, 302.11, 310.20, 368.1, 410.4, 414.5, 548.5, 549.10, 655.2, 742.3, 975.4, 1009.6, 1062.8 (v) 177.35, 182.54, 194.9, 287.9, 393.17, 410.11, 410.14, 414.11, 478.12, 654.9, 821.5, 975.9, 1011.11
slip, the 415.5
slip a punch 754.4
slip away 222.8, 368.12, 369.9, 837.6
slip back 163.5, 393.16, 394.4, 859.4
slip by 837.6
slipcase 554.14
slipcover 554.14
slip down 194.9
slip friction 1044.1
slip friction clutch 1040.10
slip in 189.7, 191.3, 213.6, 214.5
slip into 5.43
slip off 6.6, 222.8
slip of the pen 975.4
slip of the tongue 975.4
slip on 5.43, 5.44
slip one a Mickey 25.4
slip one a Mickey Finn 25.4
slip one over on 356.14
slip one's cable 307.19
slip one's mind 990.7
slip out 222.8
slip out of 6.6, 368.9, 368.12, 369.9
slippage 194.4, 393.3, 795.2, 992.1
slippered ease 20.1, 331.2
slipperiness 287.1, 415.1, 645.1, 971.6, 1006.2, 1056.5
slippers 5.27
slippery 287.12, 356.22, 368.15, 415.12, 645.16, 645.21, 971.20, 1006.12, 1056.9
slippery Anne 758.2
slippery as an eel 287.12, 356.22, 368.15, 415.12, 645.18, 971.20
slippery slope 886.3
slipping (n) 177.16, 754.3 (a) 307.32, 393.45, 414.18
slipping away 307.32
slipping back 859.1
slipping-in 213.1
slippy 287.12, 1006.12
slipshod 340.12, 426.4, 531.4, 810.15
slipshod construction 534.1
slipshoddiness 340.3
slipshoddy 340.12
slipshodness 340.3, 810.6
slipstream 184.30
slip the cable 368.10
slip the collar 369.6
slip through 369.9
slip through one's fingers 369.9
slip through one's hands 369.9
slip 'twixt cup and lip 410.4
slip up 410.14, 975.9
slipup 410.4, 975.4
slit (n) 224.2, 290.1, 802.4 (v) 224.4, 290.3, 292.11, 393.13, 802.11 (a) 224.7, 290.4, 393.27, 802.23
slither (n) 177.12, 177.16, 194.4 (v) 177.28, 177.35, 194.9
slithering (n) 177.16 (a) 311.47
slither off 368.12
slithery 287.12, 1062.12
slitting 802.2
slit trench 460.5
sliver 248.3, 296.2, 774.2, 793.3
Sloane Ranger 578.7
slob 340.5, 414.9, 810.7, 1023.5, 1062.8
slobber (n) 13.3, 511.2 (v) 13.6, 922.12, 926.20, 1065.12
slobbering 922.22
slobber over 93.13, 511.5
slobbery 511.8
slobbiness 1062.4
slobbish 414.20
slobby 810.14, 810.15, 1062.14
slob ice 1023.5
slob land 243.1
sloe (n) 38.4 (a) 38.8
sloe-black 38.8
sloe-colored 38.8
slog (n) 177.10, 902.4 (v) 177.28, 360.3, 725.14, 902.15
slogan 458.7, 526.9, 529.1, 974.4
slog away 360.3
slogger 726.3
slogging (n) 360.1 (a) 360.8, 725.17
slog on 827.6, 856.3
slog toward 162.4
sloka 974.1
slop (n) 80.8, 80.9, 93.8, 391.4, 1062.8, 1062.9 (v) 238.17, 1065.12
slope (n) 204.2, 204.4, 237.2, 753.1 (v) 204.10
sloped 204.15
slope up 193.13
sloping 204.15
slop on paint 35.14
sloppiness 93.8, 340.3, 414.4, 426.1, 804.2, 810.6, 1062.4
sloppy 5.47, 80.23, 93.21, 340.12, 414.20, 426.4, 804.5, 810.15, 1062.14, 1065.16
sloppy Joe 810.7
slops 5.5, 10.4, 80.9, 391.4
slosh (n) 238.8, 1023.8, 1062.8, 1065.5 (v) 52.11, 238.17, 238.19, 1065.12
sloshed 88.33
sloshiness 1062.4
sloshing 52.19
sloshy 1062.14
slot (n) 224.2, 292.1, 530.2, 759.16 (v) 224.4
slot and filler 530.2
slotback 746.2
sloth 94.4, 96.6, 102.2, 112.3, 125.2, 173.4, 175.1, 329.1, 331.5, 331.6, 654.3, 655.3, 770.5
slothful 175.10, 331.19
slothfulness 331.5, 331.6
slot machine 736.4, 759.16
slotman 555.4
slots, the 759.16
slotted 290.4, 292.19
slouch (n) 175.2, 177.12, 331.8, 414.8 (v) 177.28, 194.6, 331.12
slouch around 331.12
sloucher 331.8
slouchy 175.10
slough (n) 2.5, 80.9, 85.40, 243.1, 1013.4, 1062.9 (v) 6.10, 390.7
sloughing off 473.2
slough of despond 96.6, 112.3
slough off 6.6, 6.10, 134.7, 473.5
sloughy 6.18, 1062.14
sloven 80.13, 340.5, 810.7
slovenliness 80.1, 340.3, 810.6
slovenly 80.22, 340.12, 531.4, 810.15
slovenly performance 340.3
slovenry 340.3
slow (v) 175.9 (a) 117.6, 175.10, 325.6, 331.19, 331.20, 402.6, 846.16, 846.17, 848.2, 922.16
slow and careful steps 494.1
slow as death 175.10
slow as molasses 175.10
slow as molasses in January 175.10
slow as slow 175.10
slow burn 152.1, 152.3
slow-burning 1019.27
slow-cooking 11.2
slow-crawling 175.10
slow-creeping 175.10
slow death 759.15
slow development 846.2
slow down 20.7, 175.9, 428.7, 635.5, 670.6, 727.10, 756.4, 846.8, 1012.13
slowdown 175.4, 252.2, 635.2, 727.5, 731.10, 846.2
slow driver 756.2
slowed down 428.13
slowed-down 175.12
slower than the seven-year itch 175.10
slow-foot (n) 175.5 (a) 175.10
slow-footed 175.10
slow-gaited 175.10
slow goer 175.5
slow-going 175.10
slowing 175.4
slowing down 175.4, 428.1
slowing up 175.4
slow lane 175.1
slow learner 572.4
slow-legged 175.10
slow march 175.2, 177.13
slow market 737.3
slow motion 175.2
slow-moving 175.10
slowness 117.1, 175.1, 177.12, 325.1, 331.5, 331.6, 402.2, 846.2, 846.5, 848.1, 922.3
slowness to act 494.1
slowness to commit oneself 494.1
slowness to make one's move 494.1
slow off the mark 846.17
slow on the draw 846.16
slow on the uptake 846.16
slow-paced 175.10
slow pile 1038.13
slowpoke 175.5
slow-poky 175.10
slow roller 745.3
slow-running 175.10
slow-sailing 175.10

slow start 175.1
slow starter 175.5, 846.6
slow-stepped 175.10
slow surface 748.1
slow time 177.13, 832.3
slow to 325.6
slow to act 494.8
slow to commit oneself 494.8
slow to make one's move 494.8
slow track 846.3, 846.5
slow up 175.9
slow-up 846.2
slowup 175.4
slow-winged 175.10
slow-witted 922.16
slow-wittedness 922.3
sloyd 568.3
slubber 80.16, 1004.6
slubberer 414.8
slubber over 340.8
sludge 80.8, 391.4, 1023.5, 1062.8
sludginess 1062.4
sludgy 80.23, 1062.14
slue (n) 204.3 (v) 204.9
slug (n) 8.4, 175.5, 331.8, 462.19, 548.2, 548.7, 728.12, 793.5, 902.5 (v) 754.4, 902.15
slug-abed 846.6
slugabed 22.12, 331.7
slugfest 754.3
sluggard 175.5, 331.8
sluggardy 175.1
slugger 745.2, 754.2
slugging average 745.4
slugging percentage 745.4
sluggish 94.13, 102.7, 173.14, 175.10, 238.24, 331.20, 402.6, 846.17, 922.16
sluggishness 16.1, 94.4, 175.1, 331.6, 922.3
sluice (n) 190.9, 239.2, 239.5, 239.11 (v) 79.19, 1065.14
sluice gate 239.11
sluice out 79.19, 190.13
slum 80.3, 80.11, 230.6
slumber (n) 22.2, 173.1 (v) 22.13, 173.9
slumberer 22.12
slumbering 22.22, 173.14
slumberland 22.2
slumberless 23.7
slumberous 22.21
slumbery 22.21
slum clearance 396.4
slumdog 619.4
slum-dwellers 606.4
slumlike 80.25
slumlord 470.3
slummer 918.3
slumminess 80.3
slummy 80.25, 393.33
slump (n) 194.2, 252.2, 393.3, 633.4, 731.10, 737.5, 911.1, 1011.6 (v) 194.6, 393.17, 633.6, 911.2
slump down 194.6
slumpflation 632.3
slumpflationary 632.12
slumping 393.45
slums 230.6
slums, the 80.11
slur (n) 512.4, 661.6, 708.30, 709.12 (v) 340.8, 512.9, 512.11, 661.9, 1004.6
slurb 230.1
slur over 340.8, 346.6, 600.12
slurp (n) 8.4, 187.4 (v) 8.30, 187.12
slurp up 187.13
slurring 340.10
slurry 797.6
slush 80.8, 93.8, 540.1, 1023.8, 1062.8
slush fund 478.5, 609.35
slushiness 1062.4
slushy 1023.14, 1062.14
slut 77.9, 80.13, 311.16
slut's wool 1051.5
sluttish 810.15
sluttishness 80.1, 340.3, 810.6
sly 345.12, 415.12, 494.8, 920.15
slyboots 415.6
sly dog 415.6
sly look 27.3
slyness 345.4, 415.1, 920.3
sly suggestion 512.4
smack (n) 56.1, 62.1, 62.3, 87.9, 248.4, 403.3, 562.4, 604.3, 797.7, 865.4, 902.4, 902.8 (v) 56.6, 62.7, 562.19, 604.11, 902.14, 902.19
smack down 372.2, 428.8, 902.17, 908.3, 984.4
smackdown 132.1
smacker 728.7
smackhead 87.21
smacking 17.13, 330.17
smacking of 784.10
smack into 902.13
smack of 63.6, 784.7
smack one down 442.5
smack-sack 87.21
smack the lips 63.5, 95.13
small 137.10, 248.6, 250.7, 258.10, 270.16, 651.6, 661.12, 980.10, 992.10, 998.17
small amount 244.2
small arms 462.1
small-batch 250.8
small beer 88.16, 998.4, 1005.5
small-beer 998.20
small business 731.1
small businessman 730.1
small calorie 1019.19
small cap 548.6
small capital 548.6
small caps 548.20
small chance 759.6, 969.1, 972.9
small change 728.19, 998.4
small circle 1073.16
small claims court 595.2
smallclothes 5.22
small computer systems interface 1042.3
small craft advisory 317.7
small-craft advisory 400.1
small-craft warning 400.1
smaller 252.10, 885.6
smallest 250.8
small fish 998.10
small fortune 884.3
small fry 258.4, 302.2, 998.7
small game 311.1, 382.7
small hope 125.1, 966.1
small hours 315.6, 846.1
small hours, the 314.3
small intestine 2.18
smallish 258.10
smallishness 258.1
small-lettered 546.8
small matter, a 998.6
small-minded 980.10
small-mindedness 980.1
smallness 137.1, 248.1, 250.3, 258.1, 651.2, 661.3, 885.1, 980.1, 992.2, 998.1
small number 885.2
small octave 709.9
small plate 8.6, 62.4
small potato 998.7
small potatoes 606.4, 998.5, 998.7, 1005.5
small press 554.2
small price tag 633.2
small print 959.2
small scale 258.1
small-scale 250.6, 250.8, 258.12
small screen 1035.1
small screen, the 1035.1
small share 477.5
small-sized 258.12
small slam 758.3
small-souled 980.10
small space 210.2, 828.3
small talk 540.3, 541.4, 552.7
small-time 250.7, 998.18
small town 230.1
small-town 230.11
small voice 52.4
smaragdine 44.4
smarm 354.6, 504.5, 511.2, 693.1
smarminess 354.6, 504.5, 511.2
smarminesss 693.1
smarmy 138.14, 354.32, 504.17, 511.8, 693.5
smart (n) 26.3 (v) 26.8, 93.14, 152.12 (a) 142.10, 330.18, 339.14, 489.15, 508.12, 578.11, 578.13, 807.8, 920.14
smart alec 140.5
smart aleck 140.5, 142.6
smart-aleckiness 508.1
smart-alecky 140.11, 142.10, 508.12
smart as a fox 920.15
smart as a whip 920.14
smart ass 921.6
smart-ass (n) 140.5, 142.6 (a) 140.11, 142.10, 508.12
smart bomb 462.20
smart building 266.2
smart card 292.10, 622.3
smart cookie 413.14
smart crack 489.7
smart drug 86.4
smarten 498.8
smarten up 498.8
smart guy 142.6
smarting (n) 26.3 (a) 26.11
smart lawyer 597.1
smart money 624.3
smart mouth 140.5
smartmouth 142.6
smartness 330.3, 339.5, 489.2, 508.1, 578.3, 920.2
smart operator 737.11
smart pace 174.1
smartphone 347.4
smart quotes 530.1
smarts 919.1, 920.2, 920.6
smart saying 489.7
smart set 578.6
smarty (n) 142.6 (a) 140.11
smarty-pants 142.6
smash (n) 395.4, 409.4, 410.3, 412.1, 671.8, 737.5, 902.3, 902.4, 999.7, 1011.2, 1063.2 (v) 238.22, 395.17, 395.19, 412.10, 428.8, 748.3, 802.13, 902.13, 1047.6, 1051.9, 1063.5
smash all opposition 958.5
smashed 87.24, 88.33, 393.27, 412.17, 428.14
smasher 1063.4
smash hit 409.4, 413.8, 999.7
smash in 214.5
smashing (n) 395.5, 428.2, 554.14, 902.3, 1051.4 (a) 902.24, 999.13
smashing defeat 412.3
smash into 902.13
smashmouth (n) 746.3 (v) 744.2
smash the atom 1038.17
smash up 802.13, 902.13
smashup 395.4, 1011.2
smatter 930.10, 998.14
smatterer 929.6, 998.10
smattering (n) 248.4, 930.5, 998.8 (a) 930.14
smattering of ignorance 930.5
smattering of knowledge 930.5
smaze 319.3
smear (n) 80.5, 512.2, 661.6, 1004.3 (v) 35.14, 38.7, 80.16, 295.24, 412.9, 512.10, 661.9, 1004.6, 1056.8
smear campaign 512.2, 609.14
smearing 412.3
smear on 295.24
smear word 512.2
smell (n) 24.5, 69.1, 69.4, 248.4 (v) 24.6, 69.6, 69.8, 71.4, 941.6
smellable 69.11
smell a rat 955.6
smell around 938.31
smell bad 71.4
smeller 2.11, 283.8
smell-feast 138.5
smellfungus 108.3, 115.8, 510.9, 946.7
smell good 70.7
smelliness 69.2, 71.2
smelling (n) 69.3, 69.4 (a) 69.9, 71.5
smelling bottle 70.6
smelling salts 86.9
smell in the wind 961.6
smell land 182.38
smell-less 72.5
smell-lessness 72.1
smell like a rose 70.7
smell of 69.6, 69.8
smell of decay 71.1
smell of rotten eggs 71.4
smell of the lamp 545.6

smell out 938.35
smellsome 69.9
smell sweet 70.7
smell up 71.4
smelly 69.9, 71.5
smelt 192.10, 892.9, 1020.21
smelted 892.18
smelter 192.9, 739.4, 1020.11
smelting 892.2, 1020.5
smidgen 248.2
smile (n) 116.3, 585.4 (v) 95.12, 109.6, 116.7
smile at 508.8
smile brightly 116.7
smile on 371.14
smiles of fortune 1010.2
smile upon 449.14
smiley 1042.18
smiley face 95.2
smiling (n) 116.3 (a) 95.16, 109.11
smiling sleep 22.4
smirch (n) 38.5, 80.5, 661.6, 1004.3 (v) 38.7, 80.16, 512.10, 661.9, 1004.6
smirched 38.11, 80.21, 665.23, 1004.10
smirching 38.5
smirchy 80.22
smirk (n) 116.3, 508.4 (v) 116.7, 500.14
smirking (n) 508.1 (a) 95.16, 508.12
smirky 95.16, 508.12
smitch 248.2
smite 93.15, 459.16, 604.12, 902.14
-smith 413.11
smith 726.8, 892.7
smithereen 248.3, 793.3
smithery 739.4
smithy 739.4
smitten 104.27
smitten with 104.29
smitten with death 307.29
smock 5.17
smog (n) 319.3, 1001.4, 1067.1 (v) 319.7
smoggy 319.10, 1067.9
smoke (n) 38.4, 87.11, 89.1, 89.3, 89.10, 764.3, 828.5, 1001.4, 1020.16, 1067.1 (v) 38.7, 80.15, 87.22, 89.14, 152.15, 249.7, 319.7, 397.9, 909.24, 1004.6, 1019.23, 1066.6, 1067.8
smoke agent 178.13
smoke and mirrors 354.14, 356.1, 356.5, 375.3
smokechaser 1022.4
smoke-cure 397.9
smoke-curing 397.2
smoke detector 1019.1
smoked fish 10.24
smoked glass 1028.4
smoked glasses 1028.2
smoked herring 10.24
smoke-dry 397.9, 1066.6
smoked salmon 10.24
smoke-fog 319.3
smoke-free 72.5, 89.15
smoke-free area 72.2, 89.13
smoke-gray 39.4
smoke-haze 319.3
smokehole 1020.11
smoke jumper 367.4
smokejumper 1022.4
smokeless 72.5
smoke like a chimney 87.22, 89.14
smoke like a furnace 89.14
smoke marijuana 87.22
smoke opium 87.22
smoke out 909.14
smokeout 668.2
smoke pipe 239.14
smokeproof 293.12
smoker 87.21, 89.11, 89.13, 179.15
smokes 89.3
smoke screen 356.11, 376.1
smokeshaft 239.14
smoke signal 517.15
smokestack (n) 239.14 (a) 892.14
smoke the peace pipe 465.9
smoketight 293.12
smoke tobacco 87.22
Smokey the Bear 397.5
smokiness 38.3, 39.1
smoking (n) 11.2, 87.1, 87.2, 89.10, 397.2, 1067.5 (a) 89.15, 1019.27, 1067.9
smoking car 89.13, 179.15
smoking compartment 179.15
smoking gun 517.9, 957.3
smoking habit 87.1, 89.10
smoking hot 1019.25
smoking room 89.13, 197.14
smoking-room 666.9
smokings 89.3
smoking tobacco 89.3
smoky 38.11, 39.4, 80.22, 1004.10, 1067.9
smolder 105.16, 152.15, 173.9, 519.3, 1019.22, 1019.23
smoldering 152.29, 173.14, 1019.27
smoldering fire 1019.13
smolt 311.29
smooch (n) 562.4, 661.6 (v) 562.15, 562.19
smooching 562.2
smooth (n) 287.3, 709.14 (v) 201.6, 277.5, 286.2, 287.5, 294.4, 465.7, 670.7, 781.4, 1014.7, 1044.6, 1044.8 (a) 6.17, 173.12, 201.7, 277.6, 287.10, 294.8, 415.12, 504.17, 511.8, 533.8, 540.9, 544.8, 544.9, 781.5, 812.8, 1014.13, 1056.9
smooth as a billiard ball 287.10
smooth as glass 287.11
smooth as satin 287.10
smooth as silk 287.10
smooth as velvet 287.10
smooth citizen 415.6
smooth customer 415.6
smooth down 287.5, 465.7, 670.7
smoothed 286.3
smoothed out 201.7
smoothen 201.6, 670.7
smoothened 201.7
smoother 287.4
smoother-over 466.5
smooth-faced 6.17
smoothie 10.49, 357.4, 415.6
smoothing 1014.5, 1044.2
smoothing of the way 449.5
smoothing out 1014.5
smoothing the way 1014.5
smooth it over 465.8
smoothness 201.1, 286.1, 287.1, 294.3, 504.5, 533.1, 544.1, 544.2, 781.2, 812.1, 850.1, 1014.1, 1056.5
smooth one's feathers 465.7
smooth operator 415.6
smooth out 201.6, 287.5, 465.7, 781.4
smooth over 465.7, 600.12, 670.7
smooth road 1014.1
smooth-running 1014.14
smooth sailing 1014.1
smooth-shaven 6.17, 287.10
smooth-sounding 533.8
smooth-spoken 504.17, 511.8, 544.8
smooth-surfaced 287.10
smooth talk 354.6
smooth talker 415.6
smooth temper 106.1
smooth-textured 287.10
smooth the path 405.12
smooth the road 405.12
smooth the ruffled brow of care 120.7
smooth the way 1014.7, 1056.8
smooth the way for 966.5, 968.4
smooth tongue 354.6
smooth-tongued 504.17, 511.8, 544.8
smooth wine 88.17
smoothy 415.6
smorgasboard 770.13
smorgasbord 8.6, 8.9, 8.17, 10.9
smörgasbord 10.32
smother 106.8, 295.20, 307.23, 308.19, 345.8, 395.15, 428.8, 670.6, 1019.22, 1022.7
smotheration 307.5, 308.6, 1022.2
smothered 52.17, 345.11, 428.14
smothering 307.5, 308.6, 345.3, 428.2, 1022.2
smouch (n) 1004.3 (v) 80.16
Smriti 683.8
smudge (n) 38.5, 80.5, 661.6, 1004.3, 1020.16, 1067.1 (v) 38.7, 80.16, 1019.23
smudged 80.21
smudge fire 1019.13
smudginess 38.3
smudging 38.5
smudgy 38.11, 80.22
smug 107.10, 140.8, 500.19, 504.17, 578.13
smuggle 732.8
smuggled goods 732.3
smuggle in 213.6
smuggler 732.5
smuggling 732.2
smugness 107.2, 140.1, 500.6, 504.5
smut (n) 38.4, 38.5, 80.5, 80.6, 80.7, 256.2, 310.4, 666.4, 1001.2, 1004.3, 1020.16, 1051.5 (v) 38.7, 80.16
smutch (n) 38.5, 80.5, 661.6, 1004.3 (v) 38.7, 80.16
smutching 38.5
smutchy 80.22
smut-free 79.25
smutless 79.25
smutted 393.42
smuttiness 38.3, 666.4
smutty 38.11, 80.22, 393.42, 666.9
Smythe Division 749.1
Smyth sewing 554.14
snack (n) 8.7, 793.3 (v) 8.18, 8.26
snack bar 8.17
snackette 793.3
snacking 8.1
snaffle (n) 1012.7 (v) 472.9
snafu (n) 799.2, 810.2, 975.6, 985.3 (v) 393.11, 799.3, 811.3, 1012.16 (a) 810.16
snafued 393.29, 414.22, 799.4
snag (n) 2.8, 285.4, 421.3, 1003.2, 1013.8 (v) 472.9, 480.17
snagged 288.7
snaggle 285.4
snaggled 285.14, 288.7
snaggletooth 2.8, 285.4
snaggle-toothed 285.14
snaggy 288.7, 810.14
snags 1006.5
snail 10.25, 175.5, 311.29
snail-like 175.10
snail mail 553.4
snail-paced 175.10
snail's pace 175.2
snake (n) 311.25, 357.10, 660.6 (v) 164.4, 177.26, 281.4, 905.4, 905.5
snakebite 1001.5
snake charmer 707.3
snake eyes 873.3
snake in the grass 357.10, 1000.3, 1006.5
snake juice 88.13
snakelike 281.7, 311.47
snake medicine 88.14
snake oil 86.2
snake pit 799.2
snakes 926.10
snake-shaped 281.7
snakes in the boots 926.10
snake worship 697.1
snake worshiper 697.4
snakiness 281.1
snaking 177.17
snakish 311.47
snaky 164.7, 281.6, 281.7, 311.47, 415.12
snap (n) 17.3, 56.2, 68.2, 714.3, 746.3, 759.11, 902.7, 998.5, 1014.4, 1023.3, 1048.1 (v) 56.7, 60.4, 152.14, 293.6, 393.23, 524.25, 714.14, 800.8, 802.12, 902.14, 902.18, 904.10 (a) 365.9, 365.11, 401.9, 406.8
snap at 152.16, 480.16
snap back 903.5, 903.6, 1048.5
snap decision 365.4
snap house 759.19
snap judgment 365.4

snap of the fingers 998.3
snap one's fingers at 157.3, 327.6, 454.4, 998.12
snap one's fingers at the law 674.5
snap out of it 109.9, 396.20
snapper 53.6, 759.11
snappers 87.5
snappiness 68.2, 174.1
snapping (n) 56.2 (a) 56.10
snappish 110.19
snappishness 110.2
snappy 17.13, 68.7, 174.15, 330.17, 330.18, 1023.14
snappy comeback 489.7, 939.1
snappy dresser 578.7
snappy pace 174.1
snap roll 184.14
snapshoot 714.14
snap shooter 716.5
snap shot 365.4
snapshot (n) 714.3 (v) 714.14
snapshotter 716.5
snap the thread 857.10
snap to it 401.6
snap up 17.10, 480.14
snap vote 371.6
snare (n) 356.13, 377.3, 1006.5 (v) 356.20, 480.17, 482.16
snarf 8.22
snaring 377.1
snarl (n) 58.3, 265.4, 456.5, 799.2 (v) 58.9, 60.4, 152.14, 318.20, 356.20, 524.25, 799.3, 811.3, 1012.11
snarled 799.4, 810.14
snarled up 393.29
snarling 60.6
snarling dog 1006.5
snarl up 393.11, 799.3, 811.3
snarl-up 799.2, 810.3
snatch (n) 480.2, 793.3, 905.3 (v) 101.6, 480.14, 482.13, 482.20, 905.5
snatch at 101.6, 480.16
snatch defeat from the jaws of victory 412.12
snatcher 483.10
snatch from 480.22
snatch from the jaws of death 396.15, 398.3
snatching 480.2, 482.1, 482.9
snatch up 480.14
snatchy 813.4, 851.3
snazzy 501.19, 578.13
sneak (n) 491.6, 660.3 (v) 177.26, 346.9, 491.9, 732.8
sneak attack 356.3, 459.2
sneakers 5.27
sneak in 214.5, 617.14
sneakiness 345.4, 356.3, 415.1
sneaking (n) 177.17 (a) 345.12, 346.14, 491.13
sneaking suspicion 951.5
sneak joint 759.19
sneak off 368.12
sneak out 222.8
sneak out of 368.9, 369.9
sneak preview 706.1, 928.7
sneak thief 483.1
sneak thievery 482.1
sneak through 369.9
sneaky 345.12, 356.22, 415.12, 491.13
sneer (n) 157.2, 508.4 (v) 508.9
sneer at 157.3, 508.9
sneering (n) 508.1 (a) 157.8, 508.12
sneeshing 998.5
sneeze (n) 2.21, 57.1 (v) 57.2
sneeze at 157.3, 984.4
sneezing 57.1, 85.9
sneezy 2.32
snick 248.3
snicker (n) 116.4, 508.4 (v) 116.8
snicker at 508.8
snickering (n) 508.1 (a) 508.12
snide 144.21, 512.13, 589.10
sniff (n) 2.21, 57.1, 157.2, 187.5, 551.4 (v) 57.2, 69.8, 87.22, 187.12, 941.6
sniffable 69.11
sniff at 157.3
sniffer 87.21
sniffiness 141.6, 157.1
sniffing (n) 69.3, 87.2 (a) 57.3
sniffle (n) 2.21, 57.1, 187.5 (v) 57.2, 187.12
sniffling 2.32, 57.3
sniffly 2.32
sniff out 938.35, 941.6
sniffy 2.32, 141.14, 157.8
snifter 88.7
snigger (n) 116.4, 508.4 (v) 116.8
snigger at 508.8
sniggering (n) 508.1 (a) 508.12
sniggle (n) 356.13 (v) 356.20, 480.17
sniglet 342.1
snip (n) 183.6, 248.3, 258.4, 258.7, 793.3 (v) 802.11
snipe (n) 89.5 (v) 459.22, 904.12
snipe at 459.22, 510.14
snipe hunt 391.3
sniper 461.9, 904.8
sniping 115.4, 459.9
snippet 248.3, 258.4, 258.7, 557.3, 793.3
snippets 557.4
snippy 141.14, 505.7
snips 183.6
snirtle 116.4
snit 105.6, 152.8, 926.7
snitch (n) 551.6 (v) 482.16, 551.13
snitcher 551.6
snitching 482.1
snivel (n) 693.1 (v) 115.12, 354.23, 693.4
sniveler 115.8, 693.3
sniveling (n) 115.2 (a) 115.21, 138.14, 693.5
snob 141.7
snobbery 141.6, 495.5
snobbiness 141.6
snobbish 141.14, 157.8, 495.13, 773.9
snobbishness 141.6, 157.1, 495.5, 773.3
snobbism 141.6, 495.5
snobby 141.14, 157.8, 495.13
snooker 760.1
snookums 104.14, 562.6
snooky 104.14
snoop (n) 48.5, 214.4, 981.2 (v) 214.7, 981.4
snooper 214.4, 981.2
snoopiness 981.1
snooping (n) 981.1 (a) 981.6
snoopy 214.9, 981.6
snoose 89.8
snoot 141.7, 283.8
snootful 794.3
snootiness 141.6, 157.1
snooty 141.14, 157.8
snooze (n) 22.3 (v) 22.14
snoozle 22.2
snoozy 22.21
snop 87.11
snore (n) 2.21, 54.1, 57.1, 58.3 (v) 22.13, 54.6, 57.2, 58.9
snoring (n) 2.21, 54.1 (a) 2.32, 57.3
snorkel 239.6, 367.5, 1022.3
snorkel diver 367.4
snorkeling 367.3, 760.8
snort (n) 8.4, 57.1, 58.3, 87.20, 88.7, 116.4, 157.2, 508.4, 793.5 (v) 57.2, 60.3, 87.22, 116.8, 524.25
snort at 157.3
snorting (n) 87.2, 508.1 (a) 2.32, 508.12
snot 2.24, 80.7
snot-nosed 142.10
snotnose kid 302.4
snottiness 141.6, 157.1, 1062.3
snotty 141.14, 157.8, 1062.13
snout 2.11, 239.9, 283.8
snow (n) 37.2, 87.7, 356.9, 1023.8, 1035.5, 1047.4 (v) 356.14, 478.12, 1023.11
snowball (n) 770.9, 1023.8 (v) 251.6, 259.5, 282.7
snowballing (n) 251.1 (a) 251.8
snowball's chance in hell, a 967.1
snowbank 1023.8
snow banner 1023.8
snow-bearded 1023.18
snow bed 1023.8
Snow Belt 231.7
snowberg 1023.5
snow blanket 1023.8
snow-blanketed 1023.18
snow blast 1023.8
snow-blind (v) 30.7 (a) 28.13, 30.10
snow-blinded 30.10
snow blindness 30.1
snowblink 1025.9
snow-blown 1023.18
snowboard (n) 179.21 (v) 177.35, 753.4
snowboarder 753.2
snowboarding 753.1
snowbound 428.15, 1023.19
snowbridge 1023.8
snowcap 1023.8
snowcapped 1023.18
snowcapped peak 237.6
snow-clad 1023.18
snow climbing 760.6
snowcold 1023.14
snow cover 1023.8
snow-covered 1023.18
snow-crested 1023.18
snow-crowned 1023.18
snow-crystal 1023.8
snowdrift 770.10, 1023.8
snow-drifted 1023.18
snow drifter 87.21
snow-driven 1023.18
snow dust 1023.8
snow eater 318.6
snowed 87.24
snowed-in 1023.19
snowed under 105.26
snow-encircled 1023.18
snowfall 1023.8
snow-feathered 1023.18
snow fence 1023.8
snowfield 1023.8
snowflake 1023.8
snow flurry 1023.8
snowhouse 1023.8
snow-hung 1023.18
snow ice 1023.5
snow in 1023.11
snowiness 37.1, 664.1
snow job 356.9, 375.3
snow-laden 1023.18
snowland 1023.8
snowlike 1023.18
snow line 1023.8
snow-lined 1023.18
snow-loaded 1023.18
snowman 349.6, 1023.8
snow mantle 1023.8
snow-mantled 1023.18
snowmelt 1023.8, 1065.3
snowmobile 179.20
snowmobiling 744.1
snowpack 1023.8
snow-peaked 1023.18
snow pellets 1023.6
snow-robed 1023.18
snowscape 712.11, 1023.8
snowshed 1023.8
snowshoes 179.21
snow shower 1023.8
snow showers 319.3
snow-skier 753.2
snow-skiing 753.1
snowslide 194.4, 1023.8
snowslip 194.4, 1023.8
snow slush 1023.8
snows of yesteryear 828.5
snow-sprinkled 1023.18
snow squall 1023.8
snow-still 1023.18
snowstorm 671.4, 1023.8, 1035.5
snow-tipped 1023.18
snow-topped 1023.18
snow under 412.8, 1023.11
snow-white 37.7
snowwoman 349.6
snow wreath 1023.8
snowy 37.7, 313.9, 664.4, 1023.18
snub (n) 156.2, 157.2, 368.1, 908.2 (v) 156.5, 157.5, 268.6, 428.7, 442.5, 908.3, 909.17, 1012.10 (a) 268.9
snubbed 268.9, 372.3
snubbiness 268.2
snubbing post 273.4

snub in 428.7
snub-nosed 265.12, 268.10
snuff (n) 2.21, 57.1, 89.8, 187.5 (v) 57.2, 69.8, 187.12, 308.14, 1022.7
snuff bottle 89.8
snuffbox 89.8
snuff-brown 40.3
snuff-colored 40.3
snuff dipper 89.11
snuffed 1022.11
snuffer 89.11
snuff in 187.12
snuffing 69.3, 1022.2
snuffing out 395.6
snuffle (n) 2.21, 57.1, 187.5, 693.1 (v) 57.2, 69.8, 187.12, 354.23, 525.10, 693.4
snuffler 357.8, 693.3
snuffling (n) 69.3, 354.6 (a) 2.32, 57.3, 525.12
snuffly 2.32
snuffman 89.12
snuff out 395.15, 1022.7
snuff up 187.12
snuffy 2.32, 80.22, 89.15
snug (v) 121.9 (a) 121.11, 180.18, 228.33, 293.12, 344.9, 583.5, 807.8, 1007.7
snug as a bug in a rug 95.15, 121.11
snug down 121.9, 182.50
snuggery 197.3, 228.8
snuggle 73.8, 121.10, 562.17
snuggle down 20.6
snuggle up to 121.10, 587.11
snuggling 562.1
snug harbor 1009.1
snugness 121.2, 803.3
snug together 121.10
snug up 121.9
snye 238.12, 239.2
so 784.12
soak (n) 88.12, 1065.7 (v) 79.19, 192.16, 632.7, 902.15, 993.15, 1064.5, 1065.13
soakage 1065.7
soak away 79.19
soaked 88.33, 794.11, 993.20, 1065.17
soaker 88.11, 316.2
soak in 187.13, 189.10, 521.5, 570.7
soaking (n) 79.5, 88.1, 192.7, 797.2, 1064.1, 1065.7 (a) 187.17, 1065.17, 1065.18
soaking rain 316.2
soaking through 1065.7
soaking-up 570.2
soaking wet 1065.17
soak out 79.19
soak up 8.30, 187.13, 570.7, 1066.5, 1066.6
soaky 1065.17
so-and-so 528.2
soap (n) 79.17, 1016.11, 1035.2, 1047.4, 1056.2 (v) 79.19, 511.6, 1056.8
soapbox (n) 901.13 (v) 543.9
soap box, the 543.1
soapboxer 543.6
soapbox orator 543.6
soapbox oratory 543.2
soapbox racing 744.1
soap bubble 320.1
soaped 287.12
soap flakes 79.17
soapiness 1056.5
soaping 79.5
soap in the mouth 568.3
soap opera 93.8, 1034.18, 1035.2
soap salve 511.1
soapsuddy 320.7
soap suds 320.2
soapsudsy 320.7
soap the way 1056.8
soapy 287.12, 320.7, 504.17, 511.8, 1056.9
soar 172.5, 184.36, 193.10, 247.5, 272.10
soarer 193.6
soaring (n) 172.2, 184.1, 193.1 (a) 172.8, 184.50, 247.9, 272.14
soaring costs 632.3
soaring heights 272.2
soaring plane 181.12
sob (n) 75.16, 115.3 (v) 52.14, 115.12, 318.20, 524.25, 525.9
sobbing (n) 52.8, 115.2 (a) 115.21
sober (v) 670.6 (a) 35.22, 38.9, 39.4, 106.14, 111.3, 136.12, 516.3, 535.3, 668.9, 670.10, 761.15, 920.18, 925.4, 931.21, 997.20
sober as a judge 111.3, 516.3
sober down 106.7, 670.5, 670.6
sober fact 761.3
sobering 997.20
sober-minded 106.14, 111.3, 920.18, 987.6
sober-mindedness 106.4, 111.1, 920.6, 987.2
soberness 38.2, 39.1, 106.4, 111.1, 516.1, 535.1, 668.1, 920.6
sober off 516.2
sober reality 761.2
sober senses 925.1
sober-sided 111.3
sobersided 106.14, 987.6
sobersidedness 106.4, 111.1, 987.2
sobersides 106.4, 111.1, 668.4
sober truth 761.3
sober truth, the 973.3
sober up 516.2, 670.6, 925.2
so big 257.24
sobriety 38.2, 106.4, 111.1, 136.2, 516.1, 668.1, 670.1, 920.6, 925.1
sobriquet 527.7
sob story 93.8, 115.4, 600.4
socage 469.1
so-called 354.26, 376.5, 527.15, 955.10
soccer 752.1
soccer field 743.11, 752.1
soccer football 752.1
soccer game 752.3
soccer mom 77.7
soccer pitch 752.1
soccer player 752.2
soccer shoes 752.1
soccer team 752.2
sociability 321.2, 343.3, 540.1, 581.1, 582.1, 587.1
sociable (n) 582.10 (a) 343.10, 540.9, 581.3, 582.22, 587.15, 617.17
sociableness 582.1
social (n) 582.10 (a) 312.13, 312.16, 476.9, 582.22, 617.17
social activity 582.4
social affair 582.10
social anthropology 312.10, 606.1
social assistance 449.2
social barrier 980.4
social behavior 321.2, 321.3
social bias 607.1
social bonding 582.6
social butterfly 582.16
social call 582.7
social category 607.1
social circle 582.5
social class 582.5, 607.1, 617.2
social climber 606.7
social climbing 100.10
social-climbing 100.28
social code 580.3
social conduct 580.3
social conscience 636.5
social consciousness 591.1
social convention 373.1, 579.1, 580.3
social critic 512.6, 946.7
social Darwinism 611.4, 861.4
social Darwinist 611.9
social democracy 612.4
social democrat 611.14
social-democratic 611.22
Social Democratic Party 609.24
social differentiation 607.1
social director 743.20
social discrimination 980.4
social disease 85.18
social distinction 607.3
social drinker 88.11
social drinking 88.4
social ethics 636.1
social evolution 861.4
social fabric, the 606.1
social full-dress uniform 5.11
social gamut 607.1
social gathering 582.10
social grace 582.1
social graces 580.3
social group 607.1
social hour 582.10
social incompatibility 583.1
social inequality 607.1
social insect 311.32
social insurance 611.7
social intercourse 343.1, 541.1, 582.4
socialism 476.2, 611.6, 612.7, 952.7
socialist (n) 611.14 (a) 611.22
socialist economy 731.7
socialistic 476.9, 611.22
Socialist Party 609.24
socialist realism 973.7
socialite (n) 578.7, 607.4 (a) 607.10
sociality 582.1
socialization 392.3, 476.3, 480.5
socialize 392.9, 476.7, 480.20, 582.17, 611.16
socialized medicine 83.5, 611.7
socializing 476.2
social justice 607.1
social ladder 607.2
social life 476.2, 582.4
social lion 582.16, 662.9
social lubricant 88.13
socially incompatible 583.5
socially mobile 607.10
socially prominent 578.16
social maladjustment 92.14
social media 1042.19
social-minded 582.22
socialmindedness 582.1
social mobility 607.1, 852.1
social network 607.1
social norm 246.1
social order 612.1
social order, the 606.1
social outcast 586.4
social parasite 331.11
social prejudice 980.4
social pressure 609.29
social prestige 607.3
social procedures 580.3
social psychiatry 92.3
social psychology 312.10
social pyramid 607.1
Social Register 549.9
Social Register 607.2, 608.1
social register 578.6
social relations 582.4
social responsibility 591.1
social round 582.7
social scale 607.1
social science 321.3, 928.10
social scientist 928.11
social season 313.1
social security 143.5, 478.8, 611.7, 1008.4
Social Security number 517.11
social service 143.5
social services 449.3
social set 582.5
social skill 582.3
social status 607.1
social stratification 607.1
social structure 607.1
social studies 312.10
social system 607.1, 617.2
social usage 579.1, 580.3
social welfare 143.5, 611.7
social whirl 582.7
social work 143.5
social worker 143.8, 726.4
societal 312.13, 312.16, 476.9, 606.8
society (n) 227.1, 312.1, 373.2, 578.6, 582.6, 606.1, 617.1, 617.2, 617.3, 675.3, 700.1, 769.2 (a) 617.17
society, the 606.1
societyese 523.10
socioeconomic 731.23
socioeconomic background 607.1
socioeconomic status 607.1
sociolinguistic 523.19

sociologese 523.10
sociological 312.13
sociological adjustive reactions 92.23
sociologist 312.10
sociology 312.10
sociopathic 926.28
sociopathy 92.15
socius 617.11
sock (n) 704.6, 754.3, 902.5, 902.6 (v) 5.40, 754.4, 902.15
sock away 386.10, 390.5
sockdolager 820.4, 958.3
sockeroo 409.4
socket 284.2
socking 754.3
socks 5.28
socle 901.8
so cold one could spit ice cubes 1023.16
Socrates 921.2
Socratic 952.12
Socratic induction 938.12
Socratic method 938.12
sod 234.1, 310.6
soda 10.49, 1022.3
soda cracker 10.30
soda fountain 8.17
soda jerk 577.7
sodality 450.2, 587.2, 617.3
soda pop 10.49
soda water 10.49, 1065.3
sodbuster 1069.5
sodden (v) 1065.13 (a) 11.9, 88.31, 1065.17
soddenness 1065.1
sod house 228.5
sodium 7.11
sodium cyclamate 66.2
sodium hyposulfite 714.13
sodium light 1025.19
sodium salicylate 86.12
sodium thiopental 86.15
sodium thiosulfate 714.13
Sodom 654.7
sodomist 75.16
sodomite 75.16
sodomize 75.22
sodomy 75.7
sofa 229.1, 901.19
sofa bed 229.1
sofar 182.2
so foggy the seagulls are walking 319.10
so forget oneself 137.8, 141.8
soft 16.12, 19.13, 35.22, 52.16, 77.14, 93.20, 93.21, 104.26, 121.11, 145.7, 298.12, 375.30, 414.18, 426.5, 427.7, 433.15, 443.14, 464.9, 491.10, 516.4, 524.30, 670.10, 922.21, 954.9, 1014.13, 1047.8, 1062.12, 1063.6
soft as a baby's bottom 1047.8
soft as a kiss 1047.8
soft as a whisper 1047.8
soft as clay 1047.8
soft as dough 1047.8
soft as putty 1047.8
soft as silk 1047.15
soft binding 554.14
softblowing wind 318.4
soft-boiled eggs 10.26
soft-bound book 554.3
soft chancre 85.37
soft color 35.3
soft-colored 35.22
soft-core pornography 666.4
soft count 759.11
soft-cover 554.3
soft currency 728.1
soft diet 7.13
soft drink 10.49
soft drug 87.3
soft eighteen 759.11
soften 16.11, 32.4, 51.9, 77.12, 93.14, 120.5, 145.4, 145.5, 600.12, 670.6, 670.8, 959.3, 1047.6
softened 35.22, 52.17, 113.9, 670.11, 959.10, 1047.8
soft energy 1021.7
softening (n) 16.5, 120.1, 600.5, 670.2, 1047.5 (a) 120.9, 670.14, 959.7, 1047.16
softening-up 1047.5
soften the blow 670.8
soften up 16.10, 459.19, 511.6, 894.7, 1047.6
softer sex, the 77.3
soft focus 32.2
soft food 7.13
soft goods 735.3
soft hail 1023.6
soft hand 759.11
softhead 924.1
softhearted 93.20, 143.13, 145.7
softheartedness 93.6, 143.1, 145.2
soft hexachord 709.8
soft-hued 35.22
soft ice cream 10.47
softie 16.6
soft in the head 922.17, 922.21
soft kill 462.22
soft landing 1075.2, 1075.9
soft lenses 29.3
softling 16.6
soft market 737.5
softness 16.1, 19.1, 35.3, 52.1, 93.6, 121.2, 294.3, 298.1, 426.2, 427.1, 491.1, 922.8, 954.2, 1047.1, 1063.1
softness of heart 143.1
soft palate 524.18
soft pedal 51.4
soft-pedal 51.8, 51.9, 600.12, 950.2
soft-pedaled 52.16
soft phrases 511.1
soft place in one's heart 93.6
soft porn 547.12, 666.4, 718.1
soft rock 708.10
soft sculpture 715.1
soft sell 375.3, 734.2
soft-shell crab 311.29
soft skill 928.4
soft sleep 22.4
soft soap 354.6, 375.3, 504.5, 511.1
soft-soap 354.23, 375.14, 440.12, 511.6
soft-soaper 511.4
soft-soaping 440.18, 511.8
soft-sounding 52.16
soft-speaking 524.31
soft-spoken 504.17, 524.31
soft spot 24.4, 145.2, 896.1, 1003.2, 1006.4
soft spot in one's heart 104.1
soft tongue 504.5
soft touch 358.2
soft underbelly 16.4
soft underbelly, the 1006.4
soft voice 52.4
soft-voiced 52.16
software 1042.11
software engineer 1042.17
software package 1042.11
soft water 1065.3
softwood (n) 1054.3 (a) 310.39
softwood tree 310.10
soft words 504.5, 562.5
softy 16.6
sogginess 1065.1
soggy 1065.17
so hot you can fry eggs on sidewalk, the 1019.25
soi-disant 141.10, 354.26, 527.15
soigné 5.46, 578.12, 578.13
soignée 578.12, 578.13
soil (n) 80.5, 231.1, 234.1 (v) 12.13, 80.16, 512.10, 654.10, 661.9, 665.20, 1004.6
soil, the 233.1
soilage 80.5
soil conservation 397.1
soiled 80.21, 665.23, 1004.10
soiledness 665.1
soil-free 79.25
soiling 80.4
soil one's hands 80.16, 137.8, 141.8, 661.7
soilure 80.5
soily 234.5
soiree 582.10, 770.2
sojourn (n) 225.5 (v) 225.8
sojourner 227.2, 828.4
sojourning 225.1, 225.5
sojournment 225.5
soke 231.5
Sökkvabekk 681.10
Sol 1073.14
solace (n) 120.1, 121.4, 743.1 (v) 120.5, 121.6, 743.21
solacement 121.4
solacer 121.5
solano 318.6
solar 1073.25
solar battery 1075.4
solar cell 1021.7
solar collector 1021.7
solar corona 1025.14, 1073.13
solar disk 1073.13
solar eclipse 1027.8, 1073.13
solar energy 17.1, 1021.1, 1021.7, 1025.10
solar farm 17.1
solar flare 1025.6, 1073.13
solar halo 1025.14
solar heat 1019.1
solar-heat 1020.17
solar-heated 1020.29
solarium 197.5, 1019.11
solar mirror 1075.5
solar particle 1037.4
solar physicist 1073.22
solar physics 1073.19
solar plexus 2.14
solar power 18.4, 1021.7
solar-powered 1032.30
solar prominence 1025.6, 1073.13
solar radiation 1020.1, 1021.1, 1073.13
solar rays 1025.5
solar spectrum 35.7
solar system 1073.9
solar therapy 91.4
solar tide 238.13
solar time 832.3
solar ultraviolet detector 1075.7
solar wind 1073.13
solar X-ray detector 1075.7
solar year 824.2
so last year 842.16
solatium 624.3, 624.6
sold 734.14
solder (n) 715.4 (v) 715.5, 800.5, 803.9, 1020.24
soldering iron 715.4
soldering torch 1020.14
soldier (n) 311.33, 368.3, 461.6, 660.10 (v) 368.9, 458.17
soldiering 368.2
soldierlike 458.20, 492.16
soldierly 458.20, 492.16
soldierly quality 492.1
soldierly virtues 492.1
soldier of fortune 461.17
soldier on 360.3, 856.3
soldiership 458.5
soldier's medal 646.6
soldiery 461.23
sold on 95.15, 953.21
sold out 734.14
sole (n) 10.24, 199.2, 199.5 (a) 565.7, 872.7, 872.9
solecism 531.2, 534.1, 936.3, 975.5, 975.7
solecistic 497.11, 531.4, 534.2
solecistical 531.4
solecize 531.3
solemn 106.14, 111.3, 112.24, 117.6, 136.12, 155.9, 297.16, 487.3, 501.22, 544.14, 580.8, 692.8, 696.16, 701.18, 997.20
solemn affirmation 334.4
solemn declaration 334.4, 436.1, 953.4
solemness 111.1
solemnity 106.4, 111.1, 112.7, 117.1, 136.2, 297.1, 501.6, 544.6, 580.1, 580.4, 701.3, 997.3
solemnization 437.3, 487.1, 580.4, 701.1
solemnize 437.7, 487.2, 580.5, 701.14
solemnly mark 487.2
solemn mockery 693.2
solemn oath 334.4
solemn observance 487.1, 701.1
solemn promise 436.1
solemn secret 345.5
solemn silence 51.1

solemn word 334.4, 436.1
soleness 872.2
solenoid 907.3
sol-fa (n) 708.13, 709.7 (v) 708.38
sol-fa exercise 708.13
sol-fa syllables 709.7
solfège 708.13
solfeggio 708.13, 709.7
solicit 439.7, 440.14
solicit advice 422.7
solicitant 100.12, 440.7
solicitation 375.3, 440.5, 609.13, 665.8
solicit attention 983.11
soliciting 665.8
solicitor 440.7, 597.1, 730.6
solicitous 24.12, 126.7, 143.16, 339.10, 504.13, 983.17
solicitousness 24.3, 143.3, 504.1
solicitude 24.3, 126.1, 143.3, 339.1, 494.1, 504.1, 983.2
solicit votes 609.40
solid (n) 1045.6 (a) 15.18, 332.15, 644.20, 729.18, 763.6, 763.7, 770.22, 794.9, 853.7, 855.12, 872.7, 970.17, 973.14, 999.13, 1045.12, 1046.10
solidarity 450.1, 455.1, 794.1, 872.1
solid as a rock 15.18, 855.12
solid body 1045.6
solid bottom 901.6
solid carbon dioxide 1023.5
solid citizen 607.6
solid comfort 121.1
solid fuel 1021.1, 1074.8, 1075.9
solid ground 901.6
solidification 260.1, 803.1, 805.1, 872.1, 1045.3, 1046.5
solidified 260.12, 803.10, 1046.13
solidify 260.7, 803.6, 805.3, 1045.9, 1046.8
solidity 15.3, 729.7, 763.1, 794.1, 853.1, 855.1, 855.3, 872.1, 970.4, 973.6, 1045.1, 1046.1
solidness 1045.1
solid rock 901.6
solid rocket booster 1075.9
solid-state device 1033.12
solid-state memory 1042.7
solidus 204.7, 802.4
solid waste 370.4, 391.4, 893.3
solid waste disposal 390.3
solid-waste incinerator 1020.13
soliloquist 542.2
soliloquize 542.3
soliloquizer 542.2
soliloquizing 542.4
soliloquy 542.1, 704.7
solipsism 1053.3
solipsistic 865.12, 1053.8
solitaire 584.5
solitariness 344.3, 584.3, 872.2
solitary (n) 429.8, 584.5, 870.4 (a) 584.11, 872.7, 872.8, 927.5
solitary confinement 429.3, 429.8
solitude 584.3, 872.2
solitudinarian 584.5
solmizate 708.38
solmization 708.13, 709.7
solo (n) 184.9, 542.1, 708.4, 708.15, 711.17 (v) 184.37 (a) 872.8
solo flight 184.9
soloist 710.1
soloistic 542.4
Solomon 596.4, 921.2
Solomon Trench 275.5
Solon 921.4
solon 610.2, 610.3
solo part 708.4
solstice 313.7
solstitial 313.9
solstitial colure 1073.16
solubility 1064.2
solubilization 1064.1
solubilize 1064.5
soluble 940.3, 1064.9
solubleness 1061.1, 1064.2
solution 341.4, 405.3, 709.2, 940.1, 995.2, 1061.2, 1064.1, 1064.3
solvable 940.3
solve 341.10, 940.2, 1017.18, 1064.5
solvency 622.1, 729.7
solvent (n) 79.17, 270.10, 1061.2, 1064.4 (a) 624.23, 729.18, 806.5, 1064.8
solvent abuse 87.1
solving 940.1
soma 2.1, 1052.3
somatic 1052.10
somatical 1052.10
somatic cell 305.4
somatic death 85.2, 307.1
somatist 92.10
somatoform disorder 92.14
somatopsychic 92.37
somatosensory 24.9
somatotype 2.1, 92.11, 767.4
somatous 1052.10
somber (n) 1027.4 (v) 1027.9 (a) 35.22, 38.9, 39.4, 110.24, 111.3, 112.24, 133.16, 1027.14, 1027.17
somberness 38.2, 39.1, 111.1, 112.7, 1027.4, 1027.5
sombrous 38.9, 112.24, 1027.14
sombrousness 1027.4
some (n) 244.3, 883.1 (a) 244.5, 883.7
somebody 312.5, 662.9, 997.8
some five or six 884.7
some hope 968.1
someone 312.5
somersault (n) 205.2 (v) 182.44
somerset 205.2
Somerset House 549.3
something 244.3, 761.2, 763.3, 997.9, 1052.4
something between 104.5
something between the lines 519.2
something else (n) 122.2, 780.3, 999.7 (a) 787.5, 999.13
something else again (n) 776.3, 780.3, 999.7 (a) 787.5
something extra 249.2, 254.4, 478.5, 993.5
something for a rainy day 256.4
something for good measure 254.4
something for something 863.1
something in hand 386.3
something in reserve 249.2, 386.3
something in return 506.3
something into the bargain 254.4
something like 784.10
something missing 1003.2
something more comfortable 5.20
something of the sort 943.8
something of value 338.2
something or other 1052.4
something out of nothing 355.3
something out of one's system 120.3
something rotten in the state of Denmark 1000.3
something special 997.5
something the cat dragged in 1015.4
something to be desired 100.11
something to brag about 122.2
something to chew on 931.7
something to fall back on 386.3
something to get one's teeth into 931.7
something to shout about 122.2
something to spare 993.5
something to that effect 943.8
something to write home about 122.2, 997.5
sometime 837.10, 848.3
somewhat 244.3
somewhere else 985.11
some Zs 22.3
sommelier 577.7
somnambulant 22.24, 177.38
somnambular 177.38
somnambulate 177.32
somnambulation 177.9
somnambulator 178.7
somnambule 178.7
somnambulic 22.24
somnambulism 22.2, 92.19, 177.9
somnambulist 22.12, 178.7
somnambulistic hypnosis 22.7
somnifacient (n) 22.10, 25.3 (a) 22.23, 86.45
somniferous 22.23, 86.45
somniloquist 22.12
somniloquy 22.2
somnipathy 22.7
somnolence 22.1, 331.6
somnolency 22.1
somnolent 22.21, 331.20
Somnus 22.11
somnus 22.2
son 76.10, 559.3, 561.3
sonance 50.1
sonant (n) 524.12 (a) 524.30
sonar 182.2, 275.6
sonata allegro 709.11
sonata form 709.11
sonation 50.4
sone 50.7
son et lumière 33.7
song 708.4, 708.13, 708.14, 720.1
song and dance 356.9, 704.7
song-and-dance act 708.34
song and dance man 707.1
songbird 311.27, 710.13, 710.23
songbook 554.1, 708.28
songfest 708.32
song form 709.11
songful 708.48
song hit 708.7
song leader 710.18
songlike 708.48
song of the Sirens, the 377.3
song-play 708.34
songsmith 710.20
song sparrow 710.23
songster 708.28, 710.13, 710.23
songstress 710.13
song stylist 710.13
songwriter 710.20
songwriting 547.2, 718.2
sonhood 561.6
sonic 50.17
sonic barrier 184.31
sonic boom 50.6, 53.3, 184.31
sonics 50.6
sonic speed 174.2
sonic wall 50.6, 184.31
soniferous 50.15
sonification 50.4
son-in-law 564.2
sonlike 561.7
sonly 561.7
sonneteer 720.12
sonny 302.5, 561.3
sonny boy 302.5
Son of God 677.10
son of the soil 606.6
sonogram 91.9
sonometer 711.22
sonority 53.1, 54.1, 524.12
sonorous 50.15, 53.11, 54.10, 545.8, 708.48
sonorousness 53.1, 54.1
sonovox 524.16
sons 561.1
sonship 561.6
sons of Belial 660.11
Sons of God 679.2
sons of men 660.11
sons of the devil 660.11
sooner 227.9
soon to be 840.3
soot (n) 38.4, 38.6, 80.6, 256.2, 1020.16, 1051.5 (v) 38.7, 80.15
sooth 973.1
soothe 120.5, 173.8, 465.7, 670.7
soother 86.12, 670.3
soothful 670.15
soothing (n) 86.10, 120.1, 465.1, 670.2 (a) 86.40, 86.45, 120.9, 465.12, 670.15, 1056.10
soothingness 106.2
soothing syrup 86.12, 670.3, 1056.3
soothing words 147.1
soothsay (n) 133.3, 962.1 (v) 962.9
soothsayer 962.4
soothsaying 962.1
sootiness 38.3

sooty 38.11, 80.22
sop (n) 16.6, 378.2, 924.1 (v) 1065.13
soph 572.6
sophic 920.12
sophism 936.1, 936.3
sophist 921.1, 935.11, 936.6, 952.8
sophister 572.7, 936.6
sophistic 354.32, 936.10
sophistical 354.32, 415.12, 936.10, 952.10
sophistical reasoning 936.1
sophisticate (n) 413.17 (v) 354.17
sophisticated 413.28, 496.8, 578.13, 956.5, 977.5
sophistication 413.9, 496.1, 928.4, 936.1, 956.2
sophistry 354.5, 415.1, 569.1, 935.1, 936.1, 936.3, 952.1
sophomore 572.6, 757.2
sophomoric 572.12, 930.14
sophomorical 572.12, 930.14
sophrosyne 668.1
sopor 22.6, 94.4
soporific (n) 22.10 (a) 22.21, 22.23, 86.45, 94.13
soporifousness 94.4
soppiness 1065.1
sopping (n) 1065.7 (a) 1065.17, 1065.18
soppingness 1065.1
sopping wet 1065.17
soppy 93.21, 1065.17
soprano (n) 58.6, 708.22, 709.5 (a) 58.13, 708.50
soprano-alto-tenor-base 708.18
soprano clef 709.13
soprano part 708.4
soprano spinto 709.5
sop to Cerberus 378.2
so quiet that one might hear feather drop, a 51.10
so quiet that one might hear pin drop, a 51.10
sorbent 187.17
sorbet 10.47
sorcerer 680.15, 689.16, 690.5, 976.2
sorceress 690.8
sorcerize 690.10
sorcerous 690.14
sorcery 680.14, 689.10, 690.1, 962.2, 976.2
sordellina 711.9
sordes 80.7, 606.3
sordid 80.25, 100.27, 484.8, 661.10, 810.15, 1000.9
sordidness 80.3, 100.8, 484.2, 810.6, 1000.2
sordine 51.4
sordino 51.4
sordo 52.17, 708.53
sore (n) 26.4, 85.9, 85.37, 96.5 (a) 26.11, 98.20, 152.26, 152.30, 589.10, 1011.15
sore as a boil 152.30
sore beset 1013.20
sore disappointment 132.1
sorehead 108.4, 110.11, 115.9
soreheaded 110.20
soreheadedness 110.3
sorely disappointed 132.5
sorely pressed 1013.26
soreness 24.3, 26.4, 96.5, 152.3, 152.5, 589.4
sore point 24.4, 152.11, 456.7
sore spot 24.4, 26.4, 96.5, 152.11
sore throat 85.9
sorghum 66.2, 66.3
sorghum syrup 66.3
sorites 935.6
soritical 935.22
sorority 450.2, 587.2, 617.3
sorority house 228.15
sorority sister 617.11
sorority woman 617.11
sorosis 10.38
sorption 187.6
sorrel (n) 311.11 (a) 40.3
sorriness 113.1, 998.2
sorrow (n) 96.8, 112.10, 113.1, 115.1 (v) 98.14, 112.17, 112.19, 115.10
sorrow-beaten 112.27
sorrow-blinded 112.27
sorrow-burdened 112.27
sorrow-clouded 112.27
sorrowed 112.26
sorrowful 98.20, 112.26, 115.19
sorrowfulness 98.5, 112.11
sorrowing (n) 112.10, 115.1 (a) 112.26, 115.18
sorrow-laden 112.27
sorrowless 114.4
sorrowlessness 114.1
sorrow-shot 112.27
sorrow-sick 112.27
sorrow-sighing 112.27
sorrow-sobbing 112.27
sorrow-stricken 112.27
sorrow-struck 112.27
sorrow-torn 112.27
sorrow-wasted 112.27
sorrow with 147.2
sorrow-worn 112.27
sorrow-wounded 112.27
sorry 112.21, 113.8, 497.15, 661.11, 998.21
sorry for oneself 145.9
sorryish 112.21
sorry lot 660.4
sorry plight 1013.4
sort (n) 767.4, 809.3 (v) 257.15, 801.8, 808.11, 809.6, 944.4
sortable 788.10, 843.9, 995.5
sorted 808.14, 809.8
sorter 808.5
sortie 184.11, 459.1
sortilege 690.1
sorting 801.3, 808.3, 809.1
sorting office 553.7
sorting out 801.3, 808.3, 940.1
sortition 759.1
sort out 381.8, 437.8, 465.8, 798.5, 801.8, 808.8, 808.11, 931.11, 940.2, 944.4, 970.11
sort with 582.17, 769.7, 788.6
sorus 305.13
SOS 400.1
so-so 107.12, 246.3, 1005.7
sot (n) 88.11 (a) 359.12
so thick you can cut it with a knife 319.10
sot on 359.16
sotted 88.31
sottedness 88.1
sottish 88.35, 922.15
sottishness 88.2, 922.3
sotto voce 708.53
sou 998.5
soubrette 577.8, 706.3, 707.2
sou'easter 318.8
soufflé (n) 10.26, 320.2 (a) 298.10, 320.6
souffléed 320.6
sough (n) 52.4, 239.5, 243.1 (v) 52.14, 318.20
soughing 52.8
sought-after 100.29, 100.30, 578.11, 662.16
soul 92.28, 93.2, 93.3, 196.5, 207.2, 306.2, 312.5, 689.18, 708.11, 763.3, 767.2, 767.5, 865.1, 872.4, 919.4, 920.8
soul-baring 343.10
soul-blind 30.9
soul-blindness 30.1
soul body 689.17
soul-crushing 661.11
soul-destroying 308.24
soul food 10.1
soulful 93.17
soul in glory 679.1
soul kiss 562.4
soulless 94.9, 144.26, 311.39, 1055.5
soullessness 94.1
soul man 710.2
soul mate 104.11, 563.6, 784.3
soul mates 104.17
soul of kindness 143.1
soul of the dead 988.1
soul of wit, the 537.1
soul pain 26.2
Soul Principle 677.6
souls 227.1
soul-search 938.24
soul-searching 113.3
soul-sick 112.28
souls in hell 680.1
soulster 710.2
soul-stirring 105.30
sound (n) 50.1, 242.1, 942.4 (v) 33.10, 48.12, 50.14, 53.10, 54.7, 54.8, 275.10, 300.10, 367.6, 524.22, 708.42, 938.23, 942.9 (a) 15.18, 83.11, 687.7, 729.18, 763.7, 855.12, 920.18, 925.4, 935.20, 970.17, 973.14, 987.6, 999.12, 1002.7, 1007.5
sound abroad 352.10
sound-absorbing material 51.4
sound a fanfare 487.2
sound a knell 54.8
soundalike 784.17
sound an alarm 517.22
sound and fury 936.3
sound-and-light show 33.7
sound a retreat 163.6
sound as a dollar 15.18, 83.11, 729.18
sound asleep 22.22
sound a sour note 61.3
sound a tattoo 53.10, 55.4, 708.44
sound barrier 50.6, 174.2, 184.31
sound bite 489.7, 529.1, 551.3, 552.3, 557.3, 793.3
soundboard 54.5, 711.5
sound box 54.5
sound card 1042.3
sound carrier 1035.4
sound channel 1035.4
sound control 1034.16
sound critical judgment 496.1
sound economy 731.7
sounded 50.15, 524.29
sound effects 1034.18
sound-effects man 1034.23
sound engineer 704.24, 1034.24, 1035.13
sound engineering 1043.1
sounder 347.2, 942.4
sound evidence 935.10
sound film 706.1, 714.10
sound hole 711.5
sounding (n) 50.4, 275.6 (a) 50.15, 54.12, 54.13
sounding board 54.5
sounding out 942.2
soundings 275.6
sound intensity 50.1
sound intensity level 50.1
sound in the ear 48.12
sound in tune 708.35
sound in wind and limb 83.11
sound judgment 920.7
soundless 51.10, 275.12
soundlessness 51.1
sound like 33.10, 784.7
sound man 704.24, 1034.23, 1035.13
sound mind 925.1
sound-minded 925.4
soundmindedness 925.1
sound mind in a sound body, a 925.1
sound mixer 704.24
sound monitor 1035.13
soundness 15.3, 83.2, 687.1, 729.7, 763.1, 855.1, 920.6, 925.1, 935.9, 970.4, 973.6, 999.1, 1002.2
soundness of doctrine 687.1
soundness of judgment 920.7
soundness of mind 925.1
sound off 59.8, 334.5, 502.7, 503.3, 524.20, 524.21
sound of mind and body 83.11
sound of one's voice 48.4
sound of trumpets 53.5
sound-on-film 714.10
sound out 942.9
soundproof (v) 15.14 (a) 15.20
soundproofing 51.4, 52.2
sound-proofing insulation 51.4
sound propagation 50.1
sound reasoning 935.10
sound reduction 52.2
sound reproduction system 50.11
sound sense 935.9
sound shift 524.13
sound sleep 22.5

sound stage 706.4
soundstripe 714.10
sound system 50.11
sound taps 53.10
sound the alarm 399.5, 400.3
sound the call to arms 458.18
sound the death knell of 395.12
sound the horn 53.10, 708.42
sound the keynote 865.10
sound the last post 115.10
sound the note of preparation 405.6
sound the praises of 509.12, 696.12
sound the tocsin 400.3
sound the trumpet 517.22
sound-thinking 987.6
sound together 708.35
sound track 714.10
sound truck 50.11
sound true 973.9
sound understanding 920.5
sound wave 50.1, 916.4
sound woman 1035.13
soup 8.10, 10.10, 184.32, 270.7, 714.13, 1061.2, 1062.5
soup-and-fish 5.11
soupbone 745.3
soupçon 62.3, 248.4, 258.7, 797.7
soup de jour 10.7
soup du jour 10.7, 865.2
souped-up 1039.7
souper 8.6
soup of the day 10.7
soup spoon 8.12
soup-strainer 3.11
soup-to-nuts 792.4
soup up 15.13, 251.5
soupy 319.10, 1062.12
sour (n) 67.1, 67.2 (v) 67.4, 110.16, 119.2 (a) 61.4, 62.9, 64.6, 67.5, 68.6, 98.17, 108.7, 110.23, 393.41, 589.10
sour as vinegar 67.5
sour balls 67.2
source 238.2, 375.1, 386.4, 551.5, 818.4, 886.5
source book 554.9
source code 1042.13
source of aesthetic pleasure 1016.1
source of delight 1016.1
source of light 1026.1
source of supply 386.4
source program 1042.11
sour cherry 67.2
sour cream 67.2
sourdine 51.4
sourdough 67.2, 1058.9
sourdough bread 10.28
soured 67.5, 110.23, 119.4, 132.5, 393.41
sour grapes 512.1
sourgrass 67.2
souring 67.3, 119.1
sourish 67.5
sourishness 67.1
sour milk 67.2
sourness 61.1, 62.1, 64.2, 67.1, 68.1, 108.1, 110.1, 589.4
sour note 61.1
sour pickle 67.2
sourpuss 108.4, 112.13, 115.9, 1012.9
sour-sweet 66.5
sour taste 62.1
sour-tempered 110.23
sous chef 11.3
souse (n) 88.12, 367.2, 1065.7 (v) 88.23, 88.25, 367.7, 1065.13
soused 88.33, 1065.17
sousing 367.2, 1065.7
South 231.7
south (n) 161.3 (a) 161.14
South America 231.6, 235.1
southbound 161.14
Southeast 231.7
southeast (n) 161.3 (a) 161.14
Southeast Asia Treaty Organization 437.2
southeaster 318.8
southeasterly 161.14
southeastern 161.14
souther 318.8
southerly 161.14
southerly buster 318.8
southern 161.14
Southern dialect 523.7
Southerner 227.11
Southern Hemisphere 231.6
Southernism 523.8
southern lights 1025.16
southernmost 161.14
Southern twang 523.7
southing 161.3
southland 231.7
southlander 227.11
southpaw (n) 220.3, 745.2 (a) 220.5
South Pole 215.2, 261.4, 1023.4
south pole 1032.8
South Sandwich Trench 275.5
South Seas, the 261.4
southward 161.3
Southwest 231.7
southwest (n) 161.3 (a) 161.14
South West African People's Organization guerrilla 461.16
southwester 318.8
southwesterly 161.14
southwestern 161.14
south wind 318.8
souvenir 989.6
sou'wester 318.8
sovereign (n) 575.8, 728.4 (a) 18.13, 249.14, 417.17, 430.22, 612.17, 677.17
sovereign contempt 157.1
sovereign nation 232.1
sovereign nationhood 232.6
Sovereign of the Seas 232.4
sovereign princess 575.10
sovereign queen 575.10
sovereign remedy 86.1
sovereign state 232.1
sovereign statehood 232.6
sovereignty 232.6, 249.3, 417.5, 417.6, 417.8, 469.2, 573.4, 612.1
soviet 423.1, 613.1
Soviet hammer and sickle 647.6
sow (n) 77.9, 311.9, 1058.5 (v) 771.4, 1069.18
sow broadcast 486.3, 771.4, 1069.18
sow chaos 671.11
sow confusion 804.3, 810.9
sow disorder 671.11
sow dissension 456.14
sower 1069.5
sowing 771.1, 1069.14
sowing with salt 671.3
sow one's oats 562.20
sow one's wild oats 322.4, 430.19, 665.19, 669.6, 743.24
sow terror 671.11
sow the sand 391.8
sow the seed 405.12
sow the seeds of 886.10
sow the wind and reap the whirlwind 507.6, 604.19
soy candle 1026.2
soyfood 10.13
soy sauce 10.12
sozzled 88.33
spa 79.10, 84.1, 91.23, 228.27
space (n) 158.1, 158.7, 184.32, 197.2, 224.1, 231.1, 245.1, 257.2, 261.1, 292.1, 430.4, 548.7, 708.29, 709.12, 821.1, 824.1, 843.2, 1073.3 (v) 224.3, 808.9 (a) 158.10, 1073.26
Space Age 824.6
space age 841.3, 1075.1
space-age 841.13
space airport 1075.5
spaceband 548.7
space between 224.1
space blanket 295.10
spaceborne 1075.13
space bullets 1075.10
space cadet 87.21, 926.16
space capsule 1075.2
space charge 1033.6
space continuum 158.1
spacecraft 1075.2
space crew 1075.8
space crew member 1075.8
spaced 87.24, 224.6
space dock 1075.5
space docking 1075.2
space doctor 1075.8
spaced out 25.8, 224.6
spaced-out 923.9, 990.9
space engineering 1075.1
space exploration 1075.1
spacefaring 1075.13
space flight 1075.1
space heater 1020.10
space helmet 1075.11
space island 1075.5
space junk 1075.10
space laboratory 1075.5
space lattice 1038.7
spaceman 1075.8
space medicine 1075.1
space mirror 1075.5
space navigation 1075.1
space observatory 1075.5, 1075.6
space opera 706.2
space out (v) 224.3 (a) 87.24
space platform 1075.5
spaceport 1075.5
spaceport station 1075.5
space probe 1075.6
space research 1075.1
space rocket 1075.2
space satellite 1075.6
space science 1071.1, 1075.1
spaceship 181.4, 1075.2
Spaceship Earth 1073.10
space shuttle 181.1, 1075.2
space station 1075.5
spacesuit 1075.11
space technology 1075.1
space terminal 1075.1
space-time (n) 158.6, 821.1 (a) 158.10
space-time continuum 158.6
space tourism 1075.1
space travel 1075.1
space traveler 1075.8
spacetraveling 1075.13
space-walk 1075.12
spacewalk 1075.1
spacewoman 1075.8
spacework 818.6
spaceworld 158.6
spacey 87.24
spacial 158.10
spacing 548.7
spacious 158.11, 247.7, 257.17, 269.6
spacious mind 979.1
spaciousness 158.5, 257.6
spacious of mind 979.8
spade (n) 1040.8 (v) 176.17, 284.15, 1069.17
spade beard 3.8
spades 758.2
spadework 405.1, 725.4
spadix 310.27
spado 75.9
spaetzle 10.33
spaghetti 10.33
spaghetti junction 170.2
spaghettini 10.33
spaghetti western 706.2
spahi 461.12
spall 1059.4
spam (n) 732.1, 1042.19 (v) 732.7
span (n) 158.8, 179.5, 223.2, 261.1, 267.1, 269.1, 279.4, 383.9, 824.1, 828.3, 873.2 (v) 158.9, 267.5, 269.4, 295.30, 300.10, 800.5, 873.5
spancel (n) 428.4 (v) 428.10
spandex 1048.3
spangle (n) 1025.7 (v) 47.7, 498.9, 1025.24
spangled 47.13, 498.11, 1025.39
Spanglish 523.10
spangly 498.11, 1025.35
spaniel 138.3, 311.17
Spanish bayonet 285.5
Spanish fly 75.6
Spanish inquisition 389.3
Spanish windlass 906.7
spank (n) 902.8 (v) 510.17, 604.12, 902.16, 902.19
spanking (n) 510.5, 604.4 (a) 17.13, 257.21, 330.17, 841.10
spanking new 841.10
spanking pace 174.1
spanning 295.36

span of meaning 518.1
spar (n) 180.13, 273.3, 457.9, 906.4 (v) 456.11, 457.13, 754.4, 935.16
spar buoy 517.10
spar down 182.48
spare (n) 750.2, 993.5 (v) 145.4, 148.3, 329.3, 390.5, 397.8, 430.14, 475.3, 478.21, 601.4, 626.7, 668.7 (a) 253.10, 256.7, 270.17, 386.15, 390.12, 402.5, 535.3, 635.6, 798.6, 848.3, 862.8, 992.10, 993.17, 993.18
spare a thought for 983.5
spared 148.7, 397.13, 430.30
spare diet 515.2, 668.2
spare leave 750.2
spareness 270.5, 535.1, 992.2
spare no effort 403.15, 725.9
spare no expense 485.3
spare none 308.17
spare no pains 403.15
spare nothing 485.3
spare one's words 51.5
spare part 386.3
spareribs 10.17
spare room 158.3
spares 862.2
spare the price 626.7
spare the rod 427.5, 427.6
spare time 402.1
sparetime 848.3
spare-time activity 724.7
spare tire 2.19, 993.2
sparge (n) 1065.5, 1065.8 (v) 1065.12
sparger 1065.8
sparging 1065.6
sparing (n) 148.2, 635.2 (a) 148.6, 484.7, 635.6, 668.9, 992.10
sparingness 635.1
sparingness of words 344.2
sparing of words 344.9
sparing the rod 427.3
spark (n) 17.3, 248.4, 375.9, 375.10, 500.9, 886.3, 1019.15, 1025.7 (v) 375.12, 375.18, 562.21, 886.10, 1019.22, 1025.24
sparker 375.10, 1021.4
spark frequency 1034.12
sparking (n) 375.9 (a) 1019.27
sparkle (n) 17.3, 320.3, 544.4, 1019.15, 1025.7 (v) 109.6, 320.4, 489.13, 920.11, 1025.24
sparklers 27.9
sparkling 95.16, 109.11, 320.6, 489.15, 544.12, 1016.20, 1025.35
sparkling water 10.49
sparkling wine 88.17
spark off 375.18, 886.10
spark of life 306.2
sparkplug 17.6, 375.10, 1021.4
sparks 183.6, 347.16
sparring 754.3
sparring helmet 754.1
sparring partner 754.2
sparse 771.9, 848.2, 885.5, 992.11
sparseness 885.1, 992.3
sparsity 848.1, 885.1, 992.3
Spartan (n) 134.3, 344.5 (a) 134.9, 425.6, 499.9, 535.3, 537.6, 668.10, 992.10
Spartan fare 668.2, 992.6
Spartanic 425.6
Spartanism 425.1
Spartan simplicity 499.4
spasm 26.2, 85.6, 85.9, 96.5, 105.9, 330.4, 671.5, 860.1, 917.6, 926.7
spasmatic 26.10
spasmic 26.10, 851.3
spasmodic 26.10, 671.23, 782.3, 810.12, 813.4, 851.3, 854.7, 917.19
spasmodical 851.3
spasm of terror 127.5
spasms 917.2
spastic (n) 85.43, 924.8 (a) 671.23, 851.3, 917.19, 922.17, 922.22, 923.8
spastic aphonia 525.6
spasticity 851.1
spat (n) 456.5, 561.2 (v) 456.11
spate 238.4, 238.5, 247.3, 247.4, 316.2, 671.6, 770.4, 991.2, 993.2
spate of words 540.1
spathe 310.19, 310.28
spatial 158.10
spatial extension 158.1
spatiotemporal 158.10, 1052.10
spatter (n) 55.1, 1004.3, 1065.5 (v) 80.18, 316.10, 771.6, 1004.5, 1065.12
spatter-dash 295.25
spattered 771.10, 1004.9
spattering (n) 47.3, 771.1, 1065.6 (a) 55.7
spatula 712.18, 715.4
spat-upon 99.9
spavined 393.30
spawn (n) 302.10, 305.15, 561.2 (v) 1.3, 78.9, 892.12, 892.13
spawning 78.2
spay 255.11
spaying 255.4
spaz 924.8
spazzed-out 112.29
spazz out 128.8
spazzy 922.17
speak 50.14, 182.52, 334.5, 343.6, 420.8, 517.22, 523.18, 524.19, 524.24, 524.26, 543.9
speak at length 538.8
speak before one thinks 351.6
speak drunkenly 525.9
speakeasy 88.20
speaker 50.8, 524.17, 543.4, 574.5, 576.5
Speaker of the House 610.3
speakerphone 347.4
speaker's platform 901.13
speaker's stand 901.13
speaker system 50.8
speaker unit 50.8
speak fair 524.26
speak falsely 354.19
speak for 216.7, 551.8, 576.14, 600.10
speak for Buncombe 502.6
speak for itself 348.7, 521.4, 957.8
speak highly of 509.11
speak ill of 512.8
speak ill of behind one's back 512.11
speak incoherently 525.9
speaking (n) 343.1, 524.1, 524.2, 543.1 (a) 133.15, 524.31, 784.16
speaking in tongues 520.2
speaking out 334.2
speaking part 704.10
speaking-to 510.6
speaking trumpet 48.8
speaking tube 239.13
speaking voice 524.7
speak in high terms of 509.11
speak inopportunely 844.4
speak in privacy 345.9
speak in riddles 522.10
speak in tongues 520.5, 522.10
speak of 133.13, 517.17
speak off the cuff 365.8
speak on 551.8
speak one's mind 334.5, 348.6, 524.21, 644.12
speak one's piece 334.5, 348.6, 524.21
speak out 334.5, 348.6, 492.10, 524.21, 644.12
speak plainly 535.2, 644.12
speak poorly 525.7
speak slightingly of 512.8
speak soothing words 147.2
speak the truth 644.11
speak thickly 525.7
speak through one's nose 525.10
speak to 510.18, 524.26
speak too late 844.4
speak too soon 844.4
speak to the winds 391.8
speak true 644.11
speak under one's breath 52.10
speak up 334.5, 348.6, 492.10, 524.21
speak up for 600.10
speak volumes 521.4, 957.8
speak warmly of 509.11
speak well of 509.11
speak with 541.8
speak with forked tongue 354.19
speak words of wisdom 422.5
spear (n) 310.19, 310.20, 310.21, 462.8 (v) 292.15, 459.25, 480.17
spear-carrier 707.7
spearhead (n) 216.2 (v) 165.2, 216.7, 814.2
spearlike 285.12
spearman 461.6
spear side 559.2, 560.4
spear-thrower 462.9
special (n) 179.14, 555.2, 735.2, 866.2 (a) 572.12, 766.9, 780.8, 809.7, 865.12, 997.19
special, the 865.3
special affinity 587.5
special article 556.1
special assistant 616.6
special case 430.8, 773.3, 780.3, 865.2, 959.1
special character 1042.18
special circumstance 959.1
special committee 423.2
special consideration 983.4
special correspondent 555.4
special court-martial 595.4
special day 116.1
special delivery 553.4
special demurrer 598.6, 600.2
special dividend 738.7
special edition 555.2
special ed student 572.4
special education 567.1
special education student 572.4
special effects 706.5
special favor 642.2, 894.2
special forces 461.5, 461.15, 461.20
special full-dress uniform 5.11
special handling 553.4
special interest 609.31, 865.7, 983.2
special-interest group 375.11, 609.31, 894.6
special-interest lobby 609.32
special-interest pressure 609.29
special interests 894.6
specialism 866.1, 928.6
specialist (n) 90.4, 413.11, 413.13, 737.10, 866.3 (a) 866.5
specialistic 866.5
specialist seven 575.18
speciality 413.4, 724.4, 865.2, 866.1
specialization 724.6, 780.4, 865.7, 866.1
specialize 210.5, 780.6, 865.9, 865.11, 866.4
specialized 866.5
specialized drug 86.4
specialized knowledge 928.6
specialized or tutelary deities 678.4
specialized player 749.2
specialize in 328.8, 570.15, 866.4
specializer 866.3
special judge 596.1
special jury 596.5
special knowledge 928.6
special library 558.1
special need 19.2
special needs 19.2
special needs student 929.3
specialness 865.2, 959.1
special offer 633.3
special ops 461.15
special order 420.1
special partner 616.2
special permission 443.1
special pleading 600.2, 935.5, 936.1
special police 1008.17
special privilege 430.8
special providence 678.12
special-purpose buoy 517.10
special-purpose tube 1033.10
special relativity theory 1018.1
special request 440.1
special student exceptional student 572.4
special team 746.2

special theory of relativity 158.6
special treatment 449.5, 959.1
specialty 10.7, 568.8, 724.4, 724.6, 796.2, 865.2, 865.4, 866.1, 928.10
specialty of the house 865.2
special verdict 598.9
special weapons and tactics 1008.17
speciation 861.3
specie 728.1, 728.4
species 527.1, 559.4, 809.3, 809.5, 1068.1
specific (n) 86.1 (a) 210.6, 766.9, 809.7, 865.12
specific, the 865.3
specific activity 1037.1
specificality 865.2
specifically provide 421.7
specification 210.1, 349.2, 517.3, 599.1, 766.5, 780.4, 865.6, 959.1, 959.2
specifications 865.6
specificative 959.8
specific gravity 297.5, 1045.1
specific heat 1019.1
specificity 766.4
specificness 865.2
specific reluctance 1032.13
specific remedy 86.1
specifics, the 761.4
specified 959.8
specify 210.4, 517.18, 527.11, 766.6, 780.6, 865.11, 937.3, 983.10
specifying 865.6
specimen 62.4, 349.7, 786.3
specimen type 869.4
speciosity 936.1
specious 354.27, 376.5, 500.16, 936.10, 976.9
specious appearance 976.2
speciousness 33.2, 354.3, 936.1
specious reasoning 935.1, 936.1
speck (n) 47.3, 248.2, 258.7, 517.5, 774.2, 1004.3, 1051.6 (v) 47.7, 517.19, 771.6, 1004.5
specked 47.13, 771.10
speckle (n) 47.3, 517.5, 1004.3 (v) 47.7, 517.19, 771.6, 1004.5
speckled 47.13, 771.10, 1004.9
speckledy 47.13
speckliness 47.3
speckly 47.13, 1004.9
specky 47.13
specs 29.3
spectacle 33.7, 122.2, 501.4
spectacled 29.11
spectacles 29.3
spectacular 122.12, 501.20, 501.24, 704.33
spectate 918.5
spectating 918.7
spectator 48.6, 221.5, 479.3, 704.27, 759.21, 918.1, 957.6
spectatorial 918.7
spectator sport 918.4
spectatress 918.1
spectatrix 918.1
specter 33.5, 127.9, 678.5, 976.4, 988.1
specter-haunted 988.10
specterlike 988.7
spectral 35.16, 47.9, 976.9, 988.7, 1053.7
spectral color 35.7
spectral ghost 988.1
spectrogram 714.7
spectrograph 714.7, 1073.17
spectrography 35.10, 1073.19
spectroheliogram 714.7
spectroheliograph 1073.17
spectrohelioscope 1073.17
spectrometer 29.1
spectrometry 29.7, 35.10
spectrophotometry 29.7
spectroradiometry 1037.8
spectroscope 29.1, 1073.17
spectroscopy 29.7, 35.10, 1073.19
spectrum 35.7, 35.13, 47.1, 47.6, 158.2, 812.2, 976.5, 1034.12
spectrum analysis 35.10
spectrum color 35.7
spectrum-luminosity diagram 1073.8
speculate 729.17, 737.23, 759.23, 931.12, 951.9, 962.9
speculation 729.4, 737.19, 759.1, 759.2, 931.2, 951.1, 951.4, 952.2, 962.1
speculative 759.27, 931.21, 951.13, 971.17, 1006.10
speculativeness 931.3, 951.6, 971.6
speculator 737.11, 759.21, 951.7, 951.8, 952.8, 962.4
speculum 3.18, 29.6
speech (n) 343.1, 352.2, 523.1, 524.1, 532.1, 541.2, 543.2, 722.4 (a) 343.9, 524.29
speech abnormality 92.18
speech act 343.1, 524.2
speech circuit 343.1
speech community 227.1, 312.1, 523.7, 524.8
speechcraft 543.1
speech defect 524.8, 525.1
speech difficulty 525.1
speech disability 525.1
speecher 543.4
speechification 543.1, 543.2
speechifier 543.4
speechify 543.9
speech impediment 524.8, 525.1
speeching 543.1, 543.2
speech island 523.7
speechless 51.12, 131.13, 344.9
speechlessness 51.2, 344.2
speechmaker 543.4
speechmaking 543.1
speech melody 524.6
speech organ 524.18
speech origins 523.13
speech situation 343.1
speech sound 50.1, 524.12, 546.3
speech synthesis 1042.20
speech therapist 90.8
speech therapy 524.8, 525.1
speech tune 524.6
speechwriter 543.8, 610.12
speed (n) 87.4, 174.1, 401.1, 401.2 (v) 172.5, 174.8, 401.4, 449.17, 1014.7
speed along 401.4
speedboat 180.4
speed bump 283.3, 1012.1, 1012.5
speed calling 347.4
speed-dating 104.5, 440.5
speed demon 174.5
speed-dialing 347.13
speeder 174.5, 178.10
speed freak 87.21
speed hump 283.3
speediness 174.1, 330.3, 845.3
speeding 401.3, 449.5, 1014.5
speed limit 210.2, 428.3
speed maniac 174.5
speed of light 174.2
speed of sound 50.6, 174.2, 184.31
speedometer 174.7, 1041.18
speed on 375.16
speed on its way 401.4
speed over the bottom 174.1
speed over the ground 184.31
speed skating 760.7
speed sprayer 1065.8
speedster 174.5
speed tool 1040.1
speed up 174.10, 401.4
speedup 174.4, 251.2
speedwalk 177.27
speedwalker 178.6
speedway 756.1
speedwriting 547.8
speedy 174.15, 330.18, 401.9, 828.8, 830.5, 845.9
spell (n) 20.2, 158.8, 690.1, 691.1, 824.1, 824.3, 825.1, 825.2, 850.3, 954.3, 1000.4 (v) 133.11, 377.7, 518.8, 546.7, 691.7, 825.5, 862.5
spell backward 546.7
spellbind 377.7, 544.7, 691.7, 983.13
spellbinder 543.6, 690.9
spellbinding (n) 690.1 (a) 377.8, 544.8, 690.14, 691.11, 983.20
spellbound 122.9, 691.12, 983.18, 986.25
spellcasting 690.1
spell-caught 691.12
spellchecker 1042.18
spell checking 975.7
spell-checking 392.4
spellcraft 690.1
spell down 546.7
spelldown 546.4
spelled 546.8, 986.25
speller 554.10
spellful 377.8
spelling 546.4
spelling bee 457.3, 546.4
spelling book 554.10
spelling match 546.4
spelling-out 766.5
spelling pronunciation 546.4
spelling reform 546.4
spell off 825.5, 862.5
spell of nerves 128.1
spell of rain 316.4
spell of work 825.3
spell out 341.10, 521.6, 546.7, 766.6, 861.6, 865.9
spell phonetically respell phonetically 546.7
spell-struck 691.12
spell trouble 133.10, 514.2, 1000.6
spence 386.8
Spencerian 952.12
Spencerianism 861.4
spend 387.13, 388.3, 486.4, 626.5, 724.10, 831.8
spendable 388.6
spend-all 626.4
spendall 486.2
spend a penny 12.14
spend as if money grew on trees 486.3
spender 486.2, 626.4
spending 388.1, 626.1
spending money 728.19
spending plan 635.2
spendings 626.2
spend like a drunken sailor 486.3
spend money as if it were going out of style 486.3, 626.5
spend money like a drunken sailor 626.5
spend money like water 486.3
spend more than one has 486.7
spend oneself 403.5
spend one's time in 724.11
spend the time 724.10
spendthrift (n) 486.2, 626.4 (a) 486.8
spendthrift of one's tongue 540.4
spend time 821.6
spend what one hasn't got 486.7
spendy 632.11
Spenserian stanza 720.10
spent 16.18, 21.10, 388.5, 393.36, 486.9, 624.22
sperm 13.2, 75.7, 305.11
spermagonium 305.11
spermary 2.13
spermatic 2.29, 13.7, 78.15, 305.20
spermatic fluid 305.11
spermatid 305.11
spermatiophore 305.11
spermatium 305.11
spermatize 78.10
spermatocyte 305.11
spermatogonium 305.11
spermatophore 305.11
spermatophyte 310.3
spermatozoa 305.11
spermatozoal 305.20
spermatozoan 305.20
spermatozoic 78.15, 305.20
spermatozoid 305.11
spermatozoon 305.11, 886.7
sperm bank 890.1
sperm cell 305.11
sperm donor 76.10
spermic 305.20
spermicidal jelly 86.23
spermicide 86.23

spew (n) 238.9, 671.6, 909.8 (v) 13.6, 190.13, 238.20, 671.13, 909.25, 909.26
spew out 190.13
sphacelate 393.22
sphacelated 85.60, 393.40
sphacelation 85.40
sphacelus 85.40
sphere (n) 158.1, 231.2, 245.2, 282.2, 463.1, 724.4, 809.3, 928.10, 1073.4 (v) 282.7
sphereic 282.9
spherelike 282.9
sphere of influence 894.4
sphere-shaped 282.9
spheres of influence 609.5
spherical 158.10, 282.9
spherical coordinates 300.5
sphericality 282.1
sphericalness 282.1
spherical sailing 182.2
sphericity 282.1
spheriform 282.9
spherify 282.7
spheroconic 282.12
spheroid (n) 281.2, 282.2 (a) 282.9
spheroidal 282.9
spheroidal galaxy 1073.6
spheroidicity 282.1
spheroidity 282.1
spherosome 305.5
spherule 282.2
sphery 1073.25
sphincter 280.2
sphinxlike 522.17
sphragistics 647.1
sphygmomanometer 1061.3
spiccato (n) 708.25, 708.30, 709.14 (a) 708.53
spice (n) 63.3, 68.2, 70.1, 797.7 (v) 63.7
spiced 68.7
spiceless 65.2
spice of wit 489.1
spiciness 68.1, 68.2, 70.1, 666.3
spick and span 79.26
spiculate (v) 285.7 (a) 285.9
spicule 285.5
spiculum 285.5
spicy 68.6, 68.7, 70.9, 666.7, 983.19
spicy taste 62.1
spider 271.5, 311.32
spider crab 311.29
spider's web 271.1
spider web 271.1
spidery 16.16, 270.17
spiel (n) 734.5 (v) 352.15, 520.5, 524.20, 543.10
spieler 352.9, 357.3, 543.4, 704.23, 730.7
spiffed up 5.46
spiffiness 578.3
spiffing 999.13
spiff up 5.42
spiffy 578.13, 999.13
spigot 239.10, 293.4
spike (n) 179.5, 285.5, 293.4, 310.27, 310.29, 758.2 (v) 19.9, 292.15, 459.25, 797.12, 1012.15
spiked 285.9
spike heels 5.27
spikelet 285.5, 310.27
spikenard 1056.3
spike one's guns 19.9, 1012.15
spike team 179.5
spiking 797.3
spiky 285.9
spile (n) 273.6, 293.4 (v) 293.7
spilehole 239.13
spill (n) 194.3, 205.2, 238.6, 293.4, 1021.4 (v) 238.17, 351.6, 351.7, 486.4
spillage 238.6
spill blood 12.17, 308.15, 458.13
spillbox 239.2
spill ink 547.19
spill it 351.7
spill one's guts 351.7, 551.13
spill out 238.17
spill over 238.17, 910.5, 993.8
spillover 238.6
spill stream 238.1
spill the beans 351.4, 351.6, 551.13
spillway 239.2
spin (n) 33.3, 177.7, 184.15, 265.2, 350.1, 650.3, 748.2, 760.7, 896.1, 915.1, 915.2 (v) 163.9, 172.5, 184.40, 238.21, 271.6, 915.9, 915.11
spina bifida 85.25
spinach 17.6
spinal 2.26
spinal cord 2.14
spin a long yarn 538.8
spin control 265.2, 350.1
spindle 915.5
spindle fibers 305.5
spindle-legged 270.18
spindlelegs 270.8
spindle-shanked 270.18
spindleshanks 270.8
spindle-shaped 285.12
spindle side 559.2, 560.4
spindle temper 1046.4
spindling 270.17
spindly 16.16, 270.17
spin doctor 352.9, 375.10, 466.3, 551.5, 576.5
spindrift 320.2, 1065.5
spin-dry 1066.6
spine 237.5, 237.6, 283.3, 285.5, 901.2
spine-chilling 105.32
spined 285.9
spineless 16.12, 362.12, 433.15, 854.7
spinelessness 362.4, 433.5
spines 460.3
spin in 184.44
spininess 285.1, 288.1
spin like a top 915.11
spinner 271.5, 356.13, 740.4
spinneret 271.5
spinner of yarns 357.9, 722.5
spinney 310.14
spinning (n) 915.1 (a) 915.14, 985.15
spinning frame 271.5
spinning head 985.4
spinning jenny 271.5
spinning-off 892.4
spinning out 856.1
spinning-out 827.2
spinning wheel 271.5, 740.5
spin off 886.12, 887.5, 890.7
spinoff 254.1, 817.3, 887.1, 893.3
spin of the wheel 972.4
spin one's wheels 19.7, 391.8, 410.14
spinosity 285.1
spinous 285.9
spin out 267.6, 538.8, 540.5, 827.9, 846.9
spinster 77.5, 271.5, 565.4
spinsterhood 565.1
spinsterish 565.7
spinsterlike 565.7
spinsterly 565.7
spinstress 565.4
spiny 285.9, 1013.17
spiny lobster 311.29
spiracle 190.9, 239.13
spiral (n) 184.13, 279.2, 281.2, 914.1, 915.2, 1073.6 (v) 184.40, 193.8, 914.5, 915.9 (a) 281.8, 914.7, 915.15
spiral binding 554.14
spiral fracture 85.38
spiral galaxy 1073.6
spiraling (n) 914.1, 915.1 (a) 193.14, 632.12
spiraling prices 632.3
spiraling up 193.1
spiralize 285.7
spiralling 915.15
spiral loop 184.16
spiral nebula 1073.6
spiral notebook 549.11
spiral staircase 193.3
spiral upward 193.10
spirant (n) 524.12 (a) 524.30
spire (n) 198.2, 272.6, 285.4, 310.19, 310.21 (v) 193.8, 193.10, 272.10
spirillum 85.42
spiring 272.14
Spirit 677.6
spirit (n) 17.4, 93.2, 93.3, 101.1, 101.2, 109.4, 192.8, 196.5, 209.3, 306.2, 330.2, 330.7, 359.3, 492.5, 518.1, 544.4 (v) 375.20
spirit 678.5, 689.5, 689.18, 764.3, 767.2, 767.4, 767.5, 919.4, 920.8, 978.4, 988.1
spirit animal 221.1, 375.9
spirit away 482.20
spirit control 988.5
spirited 17.13, 101.8, 101.9, 109.14, 330.17, 492.17, 544.12
spiritedness 17.4, 109.4, 330.2
spiritful 492.17
spirit guide 221.1, 375.9
spirit gum 704.17
spirit-haunted 988.10
spiritism 689.1, 689.5
spiritist 689.13
spiritistic 689.24
spiritize 689.20, 1053.6
spiritless 94.9, 94.13, 112.22, 117.6, 491.11
spiritlessness 94.1, 94.4, 112.3, 117.1, 491.2
spirit manifestation 689.6
Spirit of God, the 677.12
spirit of the age 896.2, 978.5
spirit of the air 678.6
spirit of the earth 678.6
spirit of the sea 240.3
spirit of the time 896.2, 978.5
Spirit of Truth, the 677.12
spirit rapper 689.13
spirit rapping 689.6
spirits 10.49, 88.9, 88.13, 109.4, 678.1, 978.4
spirits of the air 680.1
spirit-stirring 105.30
spiritual 685.7, 689.24, 692.9, 870.15, 919.7, 978.7, 988.7, 1053.7
spiritual awakening 685.4
spiritual being 919.4
spiritual blindness 30.1
spiritual body 689.17
spiritual cleansing 685.4
spiritual climate 978.5
spiritual director 699.5
spiritual father 699.5
spiritual healer 90.9
spiritual healing 91.2
spiritual humbug 693.3
spiritualism 689.5, 1053.3
spiritualist (n) 689.13, 1053.4 (a) 1053.8
spiritualistic 689.24, 1053.8
spirituality 681.5, 692.1, 692.2, 1053.1
spiritualization 689.19, 1053.5
spiritualize 689.20, 764.4, 1053.6
spiritual leader 699.5
spiritual love 104.1
spiritually blind 30.9
spiritually cleansed 685.9
spiritually purified 685.9
spiritual marriage 565.1
spiritual-minded 692.9
spiritual-mindedness 692.2
spiritualness 1053.1
spiritual presence 221.1
spiritual purification 685.4
spiritual rebirth 685.4, 858.6
spiritual void 96.1
spiritual wife 665.17
spirituous 88.37, 764.6
spirituousness 1053.1
spirit up 375.20
spiritus 919.4
spiritus frumenti 88.13
Spiritus Mundi 842.2
spirit world 1053.1
spirit writing 689.6
spirochete 85.42
spiroid 281.8
spirometer 1067.7
spissitude 1045.1, 1062.2
spit (n) 2.24, 13.3, 57.1, 238.9, 283.9, 285.4, 915.4, 1020.12, 1056.2 (v) 13.6, 56.7, 57.2, 60.4, 152.14, 238.20, 292.15, 316.10, 459.25
spit and image 349.5, 778.3, 873.4

spit and polish 79.1, 339.3, 376.1, 425.1, 495.1
spit-and-polish 339.12, 425.6, 495.9
spite 103.1, 144.6, 589.3, 589.5
spiteful 110.19, 144.21, 589.10
spitefulness 103.1, 144.6, 589.3
spitfire 110.12, 330.8, 671.10
spit it out 351.7
spit on 103.5
spit on one's hands 405.13, 725.15
spitting 13.3, 56.2
spitting distance 223.2
spitting image 349.5, 778.3, 873.4
spittle 13.3, 1056.2
spit up 13.6, 909.26
spit-up 909.30
spit upon 157.4
spiv 331.11
spivvish 331.19
spizzerinctum 17.3, 492.3
splash (n) 47.3, 52.5, 238.8, 501.4, 517.5, 1004.3, 1065.5 (v) 52.11, 80.18, 238.19, 501.13, 771.6, 997.16, 1004.5, 1065.12
splashdown 1075.2, 1075.9
splashed 771.10, 1004.9
splashing (n) 1065.6 (a) 52.19
splash of color 35.4
splash of rain 316.1
splashy 501.19, 1062.14, 1065.16
splash zone 240.4
splat (n) 56.1, 1054.3 (v) 56.6
splatter (n) 316.1, 1004.3, 1065.5 (v) 55.4, 80.18, 771.6, 1004.5, 1065.12
splattered 771.10, 1004.9
splattering 1065.6
splay (n) 259.1, 771.1 (v) 171.5, 201.5, 259.6, 292.11, 771.4 (a) 201.8, 259.11
splayed 171.8, 201.8, 259.11
splay-foot 199.5
splayfoot 265.3
splayfooted 265.12
splaying (n) 171.1 (a) 259.11
splay out 292.11
spleen 2.16, 96.1, 110.1, 112.5, 118.3, 144.7, 152.3
spleeny 110.19
splendacious 501.21
splendent 662.19, 1025.32
splendid 501.21, 662.19, 999.12, 999.15, 1016.20, 1025.32
splendidness 501.5, 999.2, 1016.5
splendiferous 501.21, 999.15, 1016.20
splendiferousness 501.5, 999.2, 1016.5
splendor 501.5, 662.6, 1016.5, 1025.4
splendorous 662.19, 1016.20, 1025.32
splendorousness 1016.5
splendrous 662.19, 1016.20
splendrousness 1016.5
splenetic 13.8, 110.19, 112.23, 118.11, 152.26
splenic fever 85.41
splice (n) 800.1, 800.3 (v) 563.14, 740.6, 800.5, 800.9
spliced 563.21, 775.9, 800.13
splice the main brace 88.25
splicing 563.1, 800.1, 800.3
spliff 87.20
spline 271.4
spline clutch 1040.10
splint (n) 86.33 (v) 91.24
splinter (n) 248.3, 270.7, 617.4, 774.2, 793.3, 802.4 (v) 802.13
splintered 802.23
splinter group 617.4
splintering 802.3
splinter party 609.24
splintery 1050.4
split (n) 224.2, 292.1, 456.4, 566.1, 738.2, 750.2, 802.4, 1004.1 (v) 116.8, 188.7, 222.10, 224.4, 292.11, 368.11, 393.23, 395.17, 456.10, 477.6, 566.5, 802.8, 802.11, 802.12, 802.18, 806.3, 806.4, 1004.4 (a) 224.7, 393.27, 566.7, 802.23, 875.6, 1004.8
split decision 754.3
split down the middle (v) 246.2, 819.3, 873.5 (a) 873.6
split fifty fifty (v) 873.5 (a) 873.6
split fifty-fifty 477.6
split hairs 780.6, 936.9, 944.4
split infinitive 526.6
split in two 875.4
split-level 228.5
split off 171.5, 224.3, 333.4, 802.8
split-off 224.6
split one's head 53.7
split one's sides 116.8
split open 292.14
split personality 92.20, 926.4
split "S" 184.13
split schedule 825.3
split second 830.3
split-second 830.4
split shift 825.3
split the atom 1038.17
split the difference 246.2, 468.2, 476.6
split the ear 48.12
split the eardrums 49.5, 53.7
split the ears 49.5, 53.7, 58.11
split the lungs 59.9
split the sheets 566.5
split the throat 59.9
split ticket 609.19
splitting (n) 477.1, 802.2, 806.2 (a) 671.16
splitting down the middle 873.1
splitting fifty-fifty 873.1, 875.1
splitting headache 26.5
splitting in two 875.1
splitting the atom 1038.8
splitting-up 802.1
split up 477.6, 566.5, 771.8, 789.5, 802.18, 802.19
split-up 566.1, 771.3, 802.1
split upon a rock 1011.10
split with laughter 116.8
splotch (n) 47.3, 517.5, 1004.3 (v) 47.7, 80.18, 517.19, 1004.5
splotched 47.13, 1004.9
splotchy 47.13, 1004.9
splurge (n) 486.1, 501.4 (v) 501.13, 626.5
splurgy 501.19
splutter (n) 55.1, 57.1, 503.1, 917.4 (v) 55.4, 57.2, 503.3, 525.9, 917.12
spluttering 55.7, 917.18
spoil (n) 482.11 (v) 67.4, 389.4, 393.10, 393.22, 414.11, 427.6, 482.17, 1012.15, 1015.5
spoilage 393.6, 393.7
spoiled 64.7, 393.28, 393.40, 395.28, 414.21, 427.9, 1015.6
spoiled brat 302.4, 427.4
spoiled child 104.15, 427.4
spoiled rotten 427.9
spoiler 483.6, 756.1
spoiler alert 706.1
spoil for 100.16
spoiling (n) 393.1, 427.3, 482.6 (a) 427.8
spoiling for 100.22
spoil one 143.10
spoils 472.3, 482.11
spoilsman 610.5
spoilsmonger 610.5
spoils of office 482.11, 609.35
spoilsport 108.3, 112.14, 1012.9
spoils system 609.35
spoilt 393.28
spoke 171.2, 193.5, 1012.7
spoked 171.9
spoke in one's wheel 1012.7
spoken 523.20, 524.29
spoken for 421.10
spoken language 523.1, 523.5, 524.2
spoken word 50.1
spoken word, the 524.2
spokes 169.1
spokesman 466.3, 543.4, 551.5, 576.5
spokespeople 466.3, 551.5, 576.5
spokesperson 466.3, 543.4, 543.7, 551.5, 576.5
spokeswoman 466.3, 543.4, 551.5, 576.5
S pole 1032.8
spoliate 482.17
spoliation 395.1, 473.1, 482.6
spoliative 395.26
spoliator 483.6
spoliatory 482.22
spondaic 720.17
spondee 720.8
spondulicks 728.2
sponge (n) 79.5, 79.8, 86.33, 88.12, 138.5, 187.6, 292.8, 298.2, 311.29, 311.31, 395.9, 1063.2 (v) 79.19, 138.12, 187.13, 395.16, 634.4, 1065.12, 1066.6
sponge bath 79.8
sponge cake 10.42
sponge down 79.19
spongelike 292.20
sponge off 79.19
sponge off of 138.12
sponge on 138.12
spongeous 187.17
sponge out 395.16
sponger 138.5, 331.11, 440.8, 634.3
sponge rubber 1048.3
sponge up 8.30, 1066.5
sponginess 1047.1, 1047.2, 1063.1
sponging (n) 79.5, 138.2, 187.6 (a) 138.14, 331.19
sponging house 429.8
spongy 187.17, 292.20, 1047.11, 1063.6
sponsion 438.8
sponsor (n) 438.6, 616.9, 729.10 (v) 438.9, 449.15, 641.9, 729.16
sponsorship 438.8, 449.4, 729.2
spontaneity 324.2, 365.4
spontaneous 324.7, 365.11, 406.8, 934.6, 1041.22
spontaneous combustion 1020.5, 1020.9
spontaneous generation 78.6
spontaneousness 324.2, 365.4
spontaneous reaction 934.2
spontaneous response 903.1
spontaneous sense 934.1
spoof (n) 356.7, 489.1 (v) 356.15
spoofer 357.1
spoofery 356.1
spoofing 356.1
spook (n) 988.1 (v) 127.15, 811.4, 988.6
spooked 127.22, 988.10
spookiness 127.2, 988.4
spookish 988.9
spooky 127.31, 988.9, 988.10
spoon 176.17, 562.15
spoondrift 320.2
spoonerism 489.8, 526.4, 531.2, 975.7
spoon-feed 449.16
spoon-feeding 568.1
spoon food 7.13
spoonful 248.2
spooning 562.2
spoonlike 284.16
spoon meat 7.13
spoon out 477.8
spoons 8.12
spoon victuals 7.13
spoor 69.1, 517.8, 517.9, 551.4
sporadic 85.62, 771.9, 782.3, 810.12, 851.3, 885.5
sporadicalness 851.1
sporadicity 851.1
sporal 305.20
sporangium 305.13
spore 85.42, 305.13, 1051.5
spore mother cell 305.13
spork 8.12
sporocarp 305.13
sporocyst 305.13
sporocyte 305.13
sporogenesis 78.6
sporogenous 78.16, 305.20
sporogonium 305.13
sporoid 305.20
sporophore 305.13
sporophyte 305.13, 310.3
sporous 305.20

sport (n) 382.2, 412.5, 489.6, 490.1, 500.9, 743.2, 743.16, 744.1, 759.21, 789.4, 852.3 (v) 5.44, 382.9, 501.17, 743.23, 759.23
sport clothes 5.20
sportful 743.29
sportiness 501.3
sporting (n) 382.2, 759.1 (a) 649.8, 743.30
sporting chance 759.2, 972.8
sporting dog 311.17
sporting goods 735.3, 735.4
sporting house 228.28, 665.9, 759.19
sporting man 759.21
sportive 109.14, 322.6, 489.17, 743.29
sportiveness 109.4, 322.2, 489.4
sport jumper 367.4
sport karate 760.3
sport of fortune, the 1011.7
sport of kings, the 457.11, 757.1
sports (n) 743.8, 744.1 (a) 743.30
sports activity 744.1
sports bar 88.20
sports bet 759.3
sports book 554.8, 759.19
sports bra 5.24
sports broadcasting 1035.1
sports card 743.16
sportscast (n) 1034.18 (v) 1034.25
sportscaster 1034.23
sports dome 197.4
sports drink 10.49
sports editor 555.4
sports journalism 547.2
sportsman 382.5, 743.19, 759.21
sportsmanlike 649.8
sportsmanlikeness 649.2
sportsmanliness 649.2
sportsmanly 649.8
sportsmanship 457.2, 649.2
sports parachutist 185.8
sportsplex 197.4
sports psychology 744.1
sports reporter 551.5, 552.9
sports science 744.1
sportswear 5.1, 5.20, 735.3
sportswoman 382.5, 743.19
sportswriter 552.9
sportula 478.5
sporty 5.47, 501.19
sposhy 1062.14
spot (n) 47.3, 80.5, 88.7, 159.1, 248.2, 352.6, 517.5, 661.6, 704.18, 750.1, 765.1, 774.2, 843.4, 1004.3, 1013.5, 1034.20, 1036.11 (v) 27.12, 47.7, 80.16, 80.18, 159.11, 159.16, 517.19, 771.6, 941.5, 989.11, 1004.5, 1036.17
spot announcement 1034.20
spot card 758.2
spot cash 624.1
spot check 938.6
spot commercial 352.6
spot grain 738.11
spot in one's heart 93.6
spotless 79.25, 644.13, 653.6, 657.7, 664.4, 1002.6
spotlessness 79.1, 653.2, 657.1, 664.1, 1002.1
spotlight (n) 352.4, 704.18, 1025.19 (v) 348.5, 997.14, 1025.28
spotlighted 348.12
spotlighting 348.4
spot news 552.3
spot of lunch 8.7
spot of sleep 22.3
spot of trouble 1013.4
spot-on 788.10
spot pickup 1034.17
spot remover 1004.3
spots 738.11
spot sale 737.19
spot starter 745.2
spottable 941.10
spotted 47.13, 80.21, 159.18, 654.12, 771.10, 1004.9
spottedness 47.3
spotter 576.9, 576.11, 1008.10
spottiness 47.3, 851.1
spotting 159.6, 941.1
spotty 47.13, 813.4, 851.3, 885.5, 1004.9
spotty market 737.1
spousal 563.18
spousal abuse 144.11, 389.2
spousals 563.3
spouse 563.6
spousehood 563.1
spouseless 565.7
spouse swapping 75.7
spout (n) 190.9, 193.1, 238.9, 239.8, 316.2, 909.7 (v) 190.13, 238.20, 540.5, 543.10, 671.13, 704.31, 909.25
spouter 238.9, 543.4
spout off 524.20, 540.5
spout out 59.7, 190.13
spouty 243.3
Sprachgefühl 532.2
spraddle 259.6
spraddled 259.11
spraddling 259.11
sprain (n) 85.38, 96.5 (v) 393.13
sprangle 259.6
sprangled 259.11
sprangling 259.11
sprawl (n) 194.3, 201.2, 257.5, 259.1, 771.3 (v) 20.6, 194.8, 201.5, 259.6, 267.5
sprawled 201.8
sprawling 201.8, 259.11
sprawl out 194.8
sprawly 259.11
spray (n) 70.6, 238.9, 310.20, 310.25, 320.2, 459.9, 770.7, 793.4, 904.4, 1065.5, 1065.8, 1067.6 (v) 238.20, 1065.12, 1067.8
spray can 1065.8
sprayer 1065.8
spray gun 712.18
spray hitter 745.2
spraying 1065.6
spray nozzle 239.9
spray paint 35.8
spray tan 1016.10
spread (n) 8.5, 8.9, 10.1, 158.1, 171.1, 230.1, 251.1, 257.1, 259.1, 269.1, 295.10, 352.1, 352.6, 737.21, 771.1, 937.2 (v) 158.9, 171.5, 171.6, 176.10, 251.6, 259.6, 269.4, 292.11, 352.10, 352.16, 552.11, 771.4, 864.9 (a) 201.8, 251.7, 259.11, 352.17, 771.9
spread about 352.16
spread a report 352.10
spread around 352.10
spread a shadow over 1027.9
spread city 230.1
spread eagle 647.2, 647.5
spread-eagle 171.7, 194.8, 201.5, 913.5
spread far and wide 352.10
spread foundation 266.3
spreadhead 937.2
spreading (n) 171.1, 259.1, 352.1, 771.1 (a) 85.62, 158.11, 251.8, 259.11, 771.11
spreading abroad 352.1
spreading like a cancer 251.8
spreading like wildfire 251.8
spreading out 171.1
spreading the word 352.1
spreading too thin 993.7
spread it on thick 355.3, 509.11
spread light 1025.23
spread like wildfire 259.6, 352.16
spread on 295.24
spread oneself 201.5, 502.7, 585.8, 725.9
spread oneself too thin 669.5, 725.10, 993.10
spread one's wings 783.2
spread on the record 549.15
spread out 171.5, 259.6, 269.4, 292.11, 771.4
spread-out 269.6
spreadout 259.11
spread over 295.19, 910.5
spread sail 182.20
spread shade over 1027.9
spreadsheet 808.5, 871.1, 1042.11
spreadsheeting 1042.11
spread sideways 269.4
spread sidewise 269.4
spread the toils 356.20
spread with 295.24
spree (n) 88.5, 486.1, 743.6 (v) 88.28, 743.24
sprezzatura 142.1, 340.2
sprig 302.1, 302.11, 310.11, 310.20, 793.4
sprightliness 17.4, 109.4, 330.2
sprightly 109.14, 330.17, 413.23, 489.15
sprightly wit 920.2
spring (n) 162.1, 193.1, 241.1, 313.2, 366.1, 375.1, 386.4, 770.6, 886.6, 903.2, 1048.1, 1048.3 (v) 174.8, 265.5, 366.5, 395.18, 430.14, 431.5, 903.6, 1048.5 (a) 313.9, 904.17
spring a leak 393.23
spring allergy 85.34
spring a mine under 131.7
spring apart 802.9
spring a surprise 131.7
spring back 903.6, 1048.5
springboard 188.5, 1048.3
springbok 311.5
spring break 20.3
spring chicken 311.28
spring-clean 79.18
spring-cleaning 79.2
spring corn 1023.8
springe 356.13, 1006.5
spring fever 331.5
spring for 478.19, 624.18
spring forward 162.2
spring from 887.5
spring gun 356.12
springhead 886.6
springiness 109.3, 330.3, 1047.2, 1048.1
springing (n) 366.3, 431.2 (a) 193.14, 366.7, 903.10
springlike 44.4, 313.9
spring open 292.11
spring rains 316.4
springs 228.27, 901.20
spring snow 1023.8
spring tide 238.13, 272.8
springtide 313.2
springtide of life 301.1
springtime 313.2
springtime of life 301.1
spring to one's feet 200.8
spring up 14.2, 33.9, 193.9, 259.7, 818.13, 831.6
spring upon 131.7, 480.16
spring water 10.49, 1065.3
springwood 1054.3
springy 330.18, 903.10, 1047.9, 1048.7
springy step 109.3
sprinkle (n) 316.1, 1065.5 (v) 47.7, 316.10, 701.16, 771.6, 1065.12
sprinkled 47.13, 771.10, 885.5
sprinkler 239.6, 1022.3, 1065.8
sprinkler head 239.9, 1022.3, 1065.8
sprinkler system 1022.3
sprinkling 248.4, 701.6, 771.1, 797.7, 885.2, 1065.6
sprinkling system 1065.8
sprint (n) 174.3 (v) 174.8
sprinter 174.5, 311.14
sprint racing 755.2
sprit 310.20, 901.2
sprite 678.8, 680.7, 988.1
spriteliness 306.1
spritz (n) 238.9 (v) 238.20, 316.10, 1065.12
spritzer 10.49
spritzing 1065.6
sprocket 285.4
sprout (n) 302.11, 310.20, 561.4, 606.7 (v) 14.2, 259.7, 272.12, 310.34
sprout from 887.5
sprout hair 3.20
sprouting (n) 14.1, 259.3, 310.32 (a) 14.3, 259.12
sprout up 14.2, 259.7, 310.34
sprout wings 3.21
spruce (v) 79.18, 392.11, 808.12 (a) 5.46, 79.26, 264.5, 578.13, 807.8

spruced up 5.46
spruceness 578.3
spruce up 5.42, 392.11, 498.8, 808.12
sprue 239.4
sprung 265.10, 393.27, 430.21, 802.24
sprung rhythm 720.7
spry 330.17, 330.18, 413.23
spryness 330.3, 413.2
spud 10.35
spumante 320.6
spume (n) 238.14, 298.2, 320.2, 1065.5 (v) 320.5
spumescence 320.3
spumescent 298.10, 320.6
spumose 320.7
spumous 298.10, 320.7
spumy 298.10, 320.7
spunk 17.2, 305.11, 330.7, 359.3, 492.3, 1021.6
spunkiness 110.4, 359.3, 492.5
spunkless 94.13, 491.11
spunklessness 94.4, 491.2
spunk up 152.19
spunky 110.25, 359.14, 492.18
spun-out 538.12, 827.11
spun yarn 271.2
spur (n) 237.6, 283.9, 285.4, 310.11, 375.8, 793.4 (v) 285.7, 375.15, 401.4, 1070.8
spur gear 1040.9
spurious 354.26, 500.16, 674.7, 975.19
spuriousness 354.2
spurn (n) 157.2 (v) 156.5, 157.4, 372.2, 495.8, 586.5, 908.3, 909.17
spurned 99.10, 372.3
spurning 157.2, 372.1, 908.2
spur-of-the-moment 365.12, 401.9
spur-of-the-moment response 903.1
spur on 375.15, 375.16
spurred 405.16
spurring 375.5
spurs 646.6
spurt (n) 174.3, 193.1, 238.9, 330.4, 671.6, 828.3, 909.7 (v) 174.12, 190.13, 193.9, 238.20, 401.5, 909.25
spurtle (n) 238.7, 238.9 (v) 238.18, 238.20
spurt of rain 316.1
sputter (n) 55.1, 57.1, 503.1, 917.4 (v) 55.4, 57.2, 410.16, 503.3, 525.9, 917.12
sputtering 55.7, 917.18
sputtery 917.18
sputum 13.3
spy (n) 551.6, 576.9 (v) 27.12, 938.28, 941.5, 981.4
spy-catcher 576.9
spycraft 938.9
spy glass 29.4
spyhole 27.8
spying 27.2, 938.9
spymaster 576.9
spy on 27.13
spy out 938.28, 938.34
spy plane 181.9
spy satellite 1075.6
squab 311.27
squabble (n) 456.5 (v) 456.11, 935.16
squabble over 457.21
squabbler 461.1
squabbling 457.1
squad 461.22, 617.7, 745.2, 746.2, 747.2, 749.2, 752.2, 770.3
squad car 179.11
squadron 461.22, 461.27, 461.29
squalid 80.25, 661.12, 810.15, 1000.9
squalidity 80.3
squalidness 80.3, 810.6, 1000.2
squall (n) 59.1, 318.5, 318.11, 671.4 (v) 59.6, 60.2, 115.13, 318.19, 524.25
squall line 317.4, 318.11
squally 318.21, 319.8
squalor 80.3, 661.3, 810.6, 1000.2
squama 296.3
Squamata 311.24
squamous 296.7
squander 388.3, 473.5, 486.3, 626.5
squandered 473.7, 486.9
squanderer 486.2
squander in dribs and drabs 486.5
squandering 388.1, 486.1
squandermania 486.1
squander one's money in riotous living 669.6
square (n) 200.6, 212.3, 230.7, 230.8, 231.4, 277.3, 842.8, 867.2, 879.1, 883.4 (v) 200.10, 338.5, 481.5, 624.13, 658.4, 788.6, 790.6, 873.5, 879.3, 1017.18 (a) 117.9, 257.18, 264.4, 278.9, 644.14, 649.7, 790.7, 842.17, 867.6, 973.17
square accounts 506.7, 604.9, 624.13
square away 182.20, 277.5, 437.8
square circle 754.1
square dance 705.2, 879.1
squared circle 463.1
Square Deal 609.6
square deal 649.2
square-dealing 644.14, 649.8
squared off 779.6
squared-off 264.4
square footage 257.1
square-John 117.9
square meal 8.8
square measure 300.4
squareness 117.3, 200.1, 278.1
square odds 759.6, 972.7
square off 453.3, 457.14, 789.5
square one 818.1, 858.2, 860.1
square oneself with 624.12
square peg in a round hole, a 789.4
square peg in a round hole 868.3
square-rigged 180.17
square ring 754.1
square root 883.4
square sail 180.14
square shooter 644.8
square-shooting 644.14, 649.8
square stance 751.3
square the yards 182.20
square things 658.4
square up 200.10, 277.5, 338.5, 457.14
square up to 216.8, 454.3, 492.10
square with 788.6
square with the evidence 973.8
square with the facts 973.8
square yardage 257.1
squaring (n) 481.2, 658.1, 788.4, 879.1 (a) 658.7
squaring of the circle 522.9
squaring the circle 799.2
squash (n) 57.1, 748.1, 1062.8, 1063.2 (v) 51.8, 57.2, 345.8, 395.15, 428.8, 802.13, 913.4, 958.5, 1047.6, 1051.9, 1063.5
squash court 743.11
squashed 201.7, 428.14
squashed flat 201.7
squashiness 1062.4, 1063.1
squashing 428.2
squash racquets 748.1
squash tennis 748.1
squashy 1047.13, 1062.14, 1063.6
squat (n) 228.11, 762.3, 913.3 (v) 159.17, 225.7, 274.5, 469.4, 913.8 (a) 257.18, 258.13, 268.10, 274.7
squat down 913.8
squatness 257.8, 268.2, 274.1
squat on 469.4, 480.19
squatter 227.9, 470.4, 774.4
squatterdom 469.1
squatter's right 469.1
squattiness 257.8, 268.2, 274.1
squatting 225.1, 469.1
squattish 268.10
squatty 257.18, 268.10, 274.7
squaw 77.5, 77.6, 563.8
squawk (n) 58.4, 115.5, 333.2 (v) 58.8, 59.6, 60.5, 108.6, 115.16, 333.5, 524.25, 551.13
squawk box 50.11
squawking (n) 115.5 (a) 58.15
squawky 58.15
squeak (n) 58.4 (v) 58.8, 60.2, 524.25
squeak by 223.10, 369.8
squeaker 369.2
squeakiness 58.1
squeaking 58.14
squeak through 369.8
squeaky 58.14
squeaky-clean 79.25, 644.13, 653.6, 657.7, 657.8
squeaky-cleanness 79.1
squeal (n) 53.5, 58.4, 59.1 (v) 53.10, 58.8, 59.6, 60.2, 351.6, 524.25, 551.13, 957.9
squealer 551.6
squeals 50.13
squeamish 85.57, 325.7, 495.10
squeamishness 85.30, 495.2
squeegee 79.14
squeeze (n) 100.12, 104.11, 258.3, 260.2, 474.2, 482.11, 562.3, 770.4, 1012.1, 1013.5 (v) 192.15, 260.8, 293.6, 342.2, 421.5, 424.8, 480.22, 562.18, 1012.12, 1045.9
squeeze box 711.11
squeezed 260.12, 619.7
squeezed dry 1066.9
squeezed shut 293.9
squeeze in 189.7, 191.7, 213.6, 214.5
squeeze one's hand 585.10
squeeze out 192.16, 293.6
squeeze out a living 619.5
squeeze play 745.3
squeezer 260.6
squeeze shut 293.6, 1012.12
squeezing 192.7, 260.2, 342.1
squeezing out 192.1
squeg 916.10
squelch (n) 57.1, 958.2 (v) 51.8, 57.2, 345.8, 395.15, 428.8, 958.5
squelched 428.14
squelcher 958.3
squelchiness 1062.4
squelching 428.2
squelchy 1047.13, 1062.14, 1063.6
squib 489.1, 508.6, 512.5
squibbler 745.3
squib kick 746.3
squid 10.24, 356.13
squiffy 88.33
squiggle (n) 281.2, 517.6 (v) 281.4
squinch (n) 28.5 (v) 28.9
squinch-eyed 28.11
squint (n) 28.5, 204.1, 265.4 (v) 27.18, 28.9
squint-eyed 28.11, 154.3
squint eyes 28.6
squinting 28.11, 204.14
squinting construction 539.2
squint media 552.1
squint the eye 28.9
squinty 28.11
squire (n) 104.12, 470.2, 577.5, 608.4, 769.5 (v) 562.21, 769.8
squirearchy 608.3
squirm (n) 917.7 (v) 105.18, 135.4, 139.8, 917.14
squirming 135.6, 917.21
squirm out of 369.9, 600.11
squirmy 135.6, 917.21
squirrel 386.11
squirrel away 386.10, 386.11, 390.5
squirrel cage 373.5
squirrel cage, the 118.1
squirrel something away 405.11
squirrelly 927.6
squirt (n) 238.9, 258.4, 909.7, 998.7 (v) 238.20, 909.25
squirt gun 1065.8
squish (n) 57.1 (v) 57.2, 802.13
squishy 1047.13, 1062.14, 1063.6
squit 998.7
squiz 27.4
squushy 1047.13

Sr (n) 76.7, 304.5 (a) 842.19
sruti 683.8
S-shaped 279.11
S sleep 22.5
stab (n) 26.2, 85.38, 403.3, 459.3, 942.2, 951.4 (v) 26.7, 96.17, 292.15, 393.13, 459.25
stabbing (n) 459.10 (a) 17.14, 26.10, 105.31, 144.23
stabbingness 144.8
stabbing pain 26.2
stabile (n) 712.9, 715.2 (a) 855.12
stabilify 855.7
stabilitate 855.7
stability 15.3, 359.2, 360.1, 670.1, 763.1, 781.1, 812.1, 827.1, 829.1, 853.1, 855.1, 925.1, 970.4
stabilization 855.2
stabilize 670.7, 781.4, 855.7
stabilized 855.13
stabilizer 670.3
stab in the back (n) 459.2, 645.8 (v) 512.11
stable (n) 80.11, 228.20, 386.6, 770.3, 1070.5 (v) 212.5, 225.10 (a) 15.18, 360.8, 644.20, 670.11, 763.7, 781.5, 812.8, 827.10, 853.7, 855.12, 970.17, 1007.5
stableboy 1070.2
stabled 225.14
stable equilibrium 855.1
stableman 1070.2
stable state 855.1
stab one in the back 645.13
stab to death 308.18
stab wound 85.38
staccato (n) 55.1, 708.25, 708.30, 709.14, 847.2, 916.3 (a) 55.7, 708.53, 847.5, 916.18
stack (n) 239.14, 247.4, 386.1, 386.6, 554.17, 770.10 (v) 159.15, 354.17, 770.19
stack deck 356.18
stacked 770.21, 965.8, 1016.18
stacked deck 965.2
stack of bones 270.8, 311.12
stack room 386.6
stacks 197.6
stack the cards 356.18, 965.5
stack the deck 965.5
stack up (n) 184.18 (v) 765.5, 770.19
stack up with 784.7, 790.5, 943.7
stadium 197.4, 463.1, 704.14, 746.1, 755.1
Stadt 230.1
stadtholder 575.12
staff (n) 273.2, 417.9, 423.1, 449.8, 571.9, 577.11, 647.1, 702.3, 708.29, 709.12, 901.2, 901.8 (v) 385.8
staffed 385.13
staff member 577.3
staff officer 575.17
staff of life 10.1
staff of life, the 10.28
staff of office 417.9
staff sergeant 575.18, 575.19
staff work 458.4
stag (n) 76.8, 311.5, 366.4, 737.11 (v) 737.23
stag dance 705.2
stage (n) 209.2, 296.1, 463.1, 704.16, 824.1, 901.12, 901.13 (v) 704.28
stage, the 704.1
stage box 704.15
stage business 704.8
stagecoach 179.2
stage coachman 178.9
stagecraft 704.3
stage crew 704.24
staged 245.5, 704.33
stage design 717.5
stage direction 704.21
stage directions 704.8
stage director 704.23
stage-diver 710.2
stagedom 704.1
stage door 704.16
stage-door Johnny 704.27
stage fright 127.3, 128.1, 525.6
stagefright 139.4
stagehand 704.24
stageland 704.1
stage left 704.16
stage lighting 704.18
stagelike 704.33
stage management 704.13
stage manager 704.23
stage name 527.8
stage of life 303.1
stage performance 704.12
stage performer 707.2
stage play 704.4
stage player 707.2
stage presence 704.8
stage presentation 704.12
stage right 704.16
stagery 704.3
stagese 523.10
stage set 209.2, 463.1, 704.19
stage setting 209.2, 704.19
stage show 33.7, 704.4
stagestruck 704.33
stage technician 704.24
stage whisper 52.4
stage world 704.1
stageworthy 704.33
stag film 666.4
stagflation 632.3, 731.10
stagflationary 632.12
stagger (n) 177.12, 851.1, 917.8 (v) 88.27, 105.14, 122.6, 127.15, 131.8, 177.28, 194.8, 204.12, 362.6, 854.5, 917.15, 955.7
stagger along 175.6, 188.7
stagger belief 122.8, 955.7
staggered 122.9, 131.13, 204.20
staggerer 131.2
staggering (n) 177.8 (a) 122.12, 131.11, 175.10, 851.3
staggering belief 955.10
staggering blow 1011.2
staggering drunk 88.31
stagger on 856.3
staggers 85.41
staggery 16.16
staginess 501.4, 704.2
staging 245.3, 704.13, 901.12
stagnancy 173.4, 329.1
stagnant 82.5, 173.14, 329.6, 331.20
stagnant market 737.3
stagnant water 241.1
stagnate 173.9, 329.2, 891.3
stagnating 329.6, 331.20
stagnation 173.4, 329.1
stag night 487.1
stag party 487.1
stag the market 737.23
stagy 500.15, 501.24, 704.33
staid 106.14, 111.3, 987.5
staidness 106.4, 111.1, 580.1, 987.1
stain (n) 35.8, 80.5, 517.5, 661.6, 1004.3 (v) 35.14, 80.16, 517.19, 661.9, 1004.6
stained 35.17, 80.21, 1004.10
stained glass 47.6, 712.10, 1028.4
stained-glass ceiling 980.4, 1012.1
stained glass window 712.10
staining 35.11, 35.12
stainless 79.25, 644.13, 657.7, 664.4, 1002.6
stainlessness 79.1, 644.1, 657.1, 664.1, 1002.1
stainless steel 1040.2
stainless-steel ware 8.12
stain remover 1004.3
stair 193.5, 245.1
staircase 193.3
staircase wit 844.1
stair-climbing machine 84.1
stairs 193.3
stairway 193.3
stake (n) 231.5, 273.6, 438.3, 471.4, 477.5, 605.5, 729.2, 758.4, 759.3 (v) 438.10, 729.16, 759.25, 1006.7
stake, the 1020.5
stake a claim 421.6
stakeboat 188.5
staked 438.12
stake one's claim 480.13
stake out 27.13, 210.4, 938.28
stakeout 938.9
staker 729.10
stakes 759.5
staking 759.1
staking one's claim 480.1
stalactite 295.14
stalagmite 295.14
stale (n) 12.5 (v) 12.14 (a) 65.2, 117.9, 393.41, 842.14
stalemate (n) 173.3, 293.3, 329.1, 790.3, 857.2, 1013.6 (v) 857.11
stalemated 790.7
staleness 65.1, 71.2, 96.1, 117.1, 117.3, 842.3
Stalinism 611.5, 612.8
Stalinist (n) 611.13 (a) 611.21
Stalin organ 1074.10
stalk (n) 177.5, 177.12, 273.1, 310.21, 901.8, 938.15 (v) 96.13, 98.16, 177.28, 346.9, 346.10, 382.9, 501.15, 938.35
stalker 101.4, 382.5, 660.9
stalking (n) 345.4, 382.1, 382.2, 938.15 (a) 514.3
stalking horse 384.4
stalking-horse 311.13, 346.3, 376.1, 610.9
stalk vegetable 310.4
stall (n) 184.13, 197.2, 228.9, 228.20, 703.14, 704.15, 736.3, 846.5 (v) 184.45, 410.16, 846.11, 857.7, 1012.10, 1012.13
stall for time 846.11
stallion 76.8, 311.10, 757.2
stall landing 184.18
stall off 846.11, 1012.10
stalwart (n) 15.6, 492.7, 609.27, 616.9 (a) 15.15, 83.12, 257.18, 492.16
stalwartness 15.1, 492.1
stamen 310.28
stamina 15.1, 359.3, 360.1, 492.5, 856.1, 1049.1
stammel 41.6
stammer (n) 525.3 (v) 139.8, 525.8, 656.2
stammering (n) 139.4, 525.3, 849.3 (a) 139.12, 525.13
stammer out 59.7, 525.8
stamp (n) 262.1, 332.4, 517.1, 517.7, 517.13, 548.3, 548.6, 553.5, 713.8, 767.4, 785.6, 786.6, 809.3, 865.4, 902.10, 978.3 (v) 93.16, 177.28, 262.7, 284.14, 517.19, 517.20, 548.14, 728.28, 855.9, 902.22, 989.17
stamped 262.9, 332.14, 713.11
stampede (n) 127.1 (v) 127.12, 127.16, 401.4, 412.8
stampeded 412.14
stamped on the memory 989.22
stamping 554.14, 728.24
stamping ground 228.27, 231.1, 463.1, 894.4
stamping grounds 228.18
stamping one's foot 152.8
stamp of approval 332.4, 509.1
stamp on 93.16
stamp one's foot 152.15
stamp out 255.10, 395.15, 762.7, 1022.7
stance 33.4, 334.1, 517.14, 745.2, 751.3, 754.3, 901.5, 935.5, 953.6, 978.1
stance fatigue 21.1
stanch 293.7, 428.8
stanchion 273.4, 901.8
stand (n) 159.2, 173.3, 310.2, 310.12, 334.1, 453.1, 704.11, 736.3, 857.2, 901.5, 901.8, 901.15, 978.2, 1013.6 (v) 134.5, 159.10, 159.17, 173.7, 200.7, 221.6, 453.2, 453.3, 609.39, 626.7, 761.8, 827.6, 853.5, 991.4
stand a chance 897.3, 966.4, 972.13
stand aghast 122.5, 127.10
stand a good chance 966.4
stand alone 872.6
stand-alone 430.22, 802.20
stand aloof 157.7, 261.7, 329.4, 344.6, 368.6, 442.3, 583.4, 802.8
stand and be counted against 451.3

stand apart 780.5, 802.8, 872.6
standard (n) 245.1, 273.4, 300.2, 310.10, 419.2, 647.7, 659.4, 786.1, 869.4, 901.8, 942.2 (a) 246.3, 373.13, 419.4, 687.7, 786.8, 863.5, 864.12, 869.9, 945.6, 970.18
standard article 735.2
standard band 1034.13
standard-bearer 574.6, 574.7, 610.7
standard behavior 373.1
standardbred 757.2
standard deviation 968.2, 975.2
standard dialect 523.4
Standard English 523.4, 530.1
standard issue 5.2, 5.7
standard-issue 1005.8
standardization 863.3, 869.5, 892.3
standardize 781.4, 808.10, 869.6
standardized 808.14
standardized test 92.9
standard language 523.4
Standard Metropolitan Statistical Area 230.1
Standard Model 1038.2
standardness 864.2
standard of comfort 731.8
standard of life 731.8
standard of living 731.8
standard of perfection 1002.4
standard of value 728.21
standard operating procedure 373.4, 807.1, 869.4
standard phrase 529.1
standard pitch 709.4
standard price 630.1
standard procedure 373.4, 419.2
standards 636.1, 952.2
standard time 832.3
standard transmission 1040.9
standard usage 373.1
standard work 554.1
stand around 331.12
stand aside 448.2, 802.8
stand at attention 155.5, 200.7, 983.14
stand at bay 453.3
stand at parade rest 200.7
stand at the head 165.2, 814.2, 818.10
stand away 261.7
stand back 163.6
stand back of 438.9, 449.13
stand behind 449.13
stand behind of 438.9
stand by 223.9, 223.12, 405.14, 449.13
standby 386.3, 616.9, 707.7
standby reserves 461.25
stand by the side of 460.8
stand clear of 261.7
stand condemned 602.4
stand down 370.5, 448.2, 465.9, 857.7, 857.8
stand-down 465.5, 857.3
stand drinks 624.19
stand easy 121.8
standee 704.27
stand erect 200.7
stand fair to 133.12, 897.3, 968.4, 972.13
stand fast 173.7, 216.8, 359.9, 453.4, 855.11
stand firm 173.7, 359.9, 361.7, 453.4, 855.11
stand first 165.2, 814.2, 818.10
stand for 134.5, 182.35, 334.5, 443.10, 517.17, 517.18, 518.8
stand for office 609.39
stand forth 31.4
stand from 182.36
stand guard 1008.20
stand high 155.7
stand-in 576.1, 704.10, 707.7, 817.4, 862.2
stand in awe of 127.10, 155.4
stand in a white sheet 658.6
stand in back of 449.13
stand in dread of 127.10
stand in for 576.14, 862.5
stand in for the land 182.38
stand in front 216.7
standing (n) 159.2, 245.2, 607.1, 609.10, 622.1, 662.4, 765.1, 827.1, 853.1, 901.5 (a) 173.14
standing against 451.1
standing apart 872.2
standing army 461.23
standing at attention 155.2, 200.4
standing broad jump 366.1
standing committee 423.2
standing custom 373.1
standing down 370.3
standing forces 461.20
standing for office 609.10
standing high jump 366.1
standing joke 489.6
standing jump 366.1
standing matter 548.4
standing mute 51.2
standing on end 200.4
standing on its base 200.4
standing on its feet 200.4
stand in good stead 384.7, 449.17
standing order 673.3, 869.4
standing orders 373.4
standing ovation 509.2
standing place 901.5
standing rigging 180.12, 901.2
standing room 704.15
standing room only 794.11
standing to 897.6
standing treat 624.8
standing up 200.11
standing upright 200.4
standing water 241.1, 1065.3
standing wave 238.14, 916.4
stand in need of 963.9
stand in one's own light 414.14
stand in the place of 349.10
stand in the stead of 576.14, 862.5
stand in the way 1012.12
stand in the way of 1012.15
stand in with 450.4
stand like a post 173.7
stand mute 51.5, 344.6
stand neuter 467.5
stand no nonsense 359.9
stand of arms 462.1
stand off 182.36, 261.7
standoff (n) 779.1, 790.3, 857.2, 972.7, 1013.6 (a) 141.12, 344.10, 583.6
stand off and on 182.30, 182.36
standoffish 141.12, 344.10, 583.6, 804.4, 872.8
standoffishness 141.4, 261.1, 344.3, 583.2, 804.1
stand off stand 168.2
stand of timber 310.13
stand on 334.5, 421.8, 641.5, 901.22, 959.6
stand on ancient ways 853.6
stand on a straight course 182.28
stand on ceremony 580.6
stand on course 182.28
stand one 630.13
stand one in good stead 387.17
stand one in hand 387.17
stand on end 200.8, 200.9
stand one's ground 359.9, 453.3, 453.4, 855.11
stand one's watch 825.5
stand on one's own 430.20
stand on one's own two feet 136.4, 430.20
stand on one's rights 323.3
stand on tiptoe 27.15, 272.10
stand on tiptoes 267.5
stand opposed 215.4
stand opposite 215.4
stand out 31.4, 247.5, 283.10, 348.7, 997.12
standout (n) 249.4, 659.4, 662.9 (a) 247.9, 997.19
stand out from the shore 168.2
stand over 573.10, 612.11, 846.9
stand over against 780.5
stand pat 361.7, 759.25, 853.6, 855.11
standpat (n) 361.6, 611.9, 853.4 (a) 329.6, 611.17, 853.8, 855.15
standpatter 361.6, 611.9, 853.4
standpattism 329.1, 611.1, 853.3
standpipe 272.6
standpoint 27.7, 159.2, 978.2
stand ramrod-straight 200.7
stand ready 405.14
stand responsible for 641.6
stand revealed 351.8
stands 27.8, 745.1
stand sentinel 1008.20
stand shoulder to shoulder 450.3
stand shoulder to shoulder with 450.4
stand side by side 218.4
stand sponsor for 641.9
stand still 173.7, 853.6
standstill 173.3, 293.3, 329.1, 857.2, 1013.6
stand still for 134.6
stand surety 438.9
stand the gaff 134.6, 359.9
stand the test 942.10, 973.8
stand the test of time 761.9, 827.6
stand to 624.19
stand to gain 897.3
stand together 450.3, 788.6, 805.4
stand to lose 897.3
stand to one's engagement 434.2, 641.11
stand to reason 935.17
stand treat 624.19
stand trial 598.19
stand under 831.8
stand up 15.10, 193.8, 200.7, 200.8, 360.4, 453.2, 942.10, 973.8, 991.4
stand-up (n) 704.7 (a) 200.11, 492.18
standup 359.12
stand up against 453.3, 492.10
stand up and be counted 348.6, 371.18, 492.10
stand-up comedian 489.12, 707.9
stand-up comedy 489.1, 704.8
stand-up comedy act 704.7
stand-up comic 489.12, 707.9
stand-up fight 457.4
stand up for 438.9, 600.10
stand up for Jesus 692.7
stand upon 421.8
stand upon one's rights 421.8
stand upright 200.7, 200.9
stand up straight 136.4, 200.7
stand up to 216.8, 453.3, 454.3, 492.10, 641.11
stand up to it 604.20
stand up with 450.4, 805.4
stand with 450.4
stand with arms akimbo 454.5
stanky 69.9
Stanley Cup 749.1
St. Anthony 584.5
St. Anthony's fire 85.31
stanza 708.24, 720.10, 754.3
stapes 2.10
staphylococcus 85.42
staple (n) 386.4, 735.2, 736.2, 1054.1 (v) 800.8 (a) 855.14
staple item 735.2
staples 735.1
stapling 554.14
star (n) 208.4, 249.4, 409.6, 413.14, 646.5, 646.6, 647.5, 662.9, 706.4, 707.6, 997.10, 999.6, 1073.8 (v) 249.11, 704.28, 704.29, 997.12, 997.14, 997.15 (a) 249.14
star atlas 1073.8
starboard (n) 219.1 (a) 219.4
starboard tack 219.1
starbright 1025.30, 1025.39
starburst galaxy 1073.6
star catalog 1073.8
starch (n) 7.5, 17.3, 1062.5 (v) 1046.9 (a) 580.9
star chart 1073.8
starched 580.9, 1046.11
starchiness 580.1, 1046.3
starching 1046.5
starch sweetener 66.3
starchy 580.9, 1046.11, 1062.12
star cloud 1073.8
star cluster 1073.5, 1073.8
star-crossed 133.16, 1011.14
starcrossed life 1011.4

star-crossed lovers 104.17
stardom 409.3, 662.5, 997.2
stardust 87.7
stare (n) 27.5 (v) 27.15, 122.5, 981.3
stare at 27.15
stare down 27.15, 454.3, 492.11
stare-down 454.1
stare hard 27.15
stare in the face 216.8
stare one in the face 31.4, 348.7, 839.6, 840.2
stare openmouthed 122.5
stare out 27.15, 454.3, 492.11
stare out of countenance 492.11
starets 575.1
stargaze 985.9
stargazer 1071.2, 1073.22, 1073.23
stargazing (n) 985.2, 1073.19 (a) 985.11
staring 31.7, 348.12
staring contest 454.1
star in the firmament 409.6
stark 247.12, 248.8, 499.9, 535.3, 798.6
stark blind 30.9
starkers 6.14
stark-mad 926.26
stark-naked 6.14
starkness 499.3, 499.4, 535.1, 798.1
stark-raving mad 926.30
stark-staring 247.12, 348.12
stark-staring mad 926.26
starless 1027.13
starlessness 1027.1
starlet 706.4, 707.4
starlight 1025.12
starlike 285.15, 1025.30
starlit 1025.39
star of David 882.2
star of stage and screen 707.2
star-pointed 285.15
star populations 1073.8
star quality 377.1
starred 997.21
starring role 704.10
starry 1025.30, 1025.39, 1073.25
starry-eyed 95.16, 986.24
starry-eyed over 101.11
starry heaven 1073.2
starry host 1073.4
starry orbs 2.9, 27.9
starry sphere 1073.2
stars 964.2, 1026.1
stars, the 1073.4
Stars and Bars 647.7
Stars and Stripes 647.7
star-shaped 285.15
starshine 1025.12
star-spangled 1025.39, 1073.25
Star-Spangled Banner 647.7
starstruck 704.33
star-studded 1025.39, 1073.25
start (n) 131.3, 188.2, 188.5, 211.3, 249.2, 756.3, 757.3, 818.1, 905.3 (v) 127.12, 131.5, 188.8, 366.5, 382.9, 393.23, 439.5, 756.4, 757.5, 802.9, 818.7, 904.13
start all over 856.6
start an action 598.13
start aside 127.12, 131.5, 366.5
start back 903.7
started 182.61
starter 8.10, 10.7, 10.9, 62.4, 745.2, 818.2, 1026.1
starter home 818.1
starters 757.3, 818.3
start going 818.11, 904.13
start in 725.15, 818.7
starting 188.2
starting block 755.1
starting blocks 188.5
starting gate 188.5, 753.1
starting grid 756.3
starting gun, the 188.2
starting line 188.5, 211.3
starting lineup 745.2, 746.2
starting pistol, the 188.2
starting pitcher 745.2
starting place 188.5
starting point 188.5, 211.3, 818.1
starting post 188.5
starting rotation 745.2
startle 122.6, 127.12, 127.15, 131.5, 131.8, 400.3
startled 127.25, 131.13, 400.4
startler 131.2
startle reflex 92.26
startle the echoes 53.7
start line 755.1
startling 122.12, 127.28, 131.11, 830.5
startlingness 127.2
startling resemblance 784.4
startlish 105.28, 127.23
startlishness 127.3
start off 188.8, 818.7, 904.13
start-off 188.2, 818.1
start on 188.8
start out 188.8, 818.7
start over 849.7
start something 216.8, 454.6
start the ball rolling 818.11, 904.13
start up 33.9, 193.9, 283.10, 366.5, 818.7, 818.8, 818.11, 904.13
startup 818.2, 841.2
starvation (n) 307.5, 515.1, 992.4 (a) 992.10
starvation diet 515.2, 992.6
starvation wages 992.5
starve 100.19, 307.23, 308.13, 484.5, 619.5
starved 100.25, 270.20, 393.35, 992.12
starved-looking 270.20
starveling (n) 619.4 (a) 270.20, 619.8, 992.12
starving 100.25, 992.12
starving black hole 1073.8
Star Wars 460.2
starwatching 1073.19
star worship 697.1
star worshiper 697.4
stash (n) 346.4 (v) 346.7, 386.10
stasis 173.4, 329.1, 853.1
stat (n) 714.5, 785.5 (v) 785.8
statal 765.6
state (n) 231.5, 232.1, 501.5, 501.6, 765.1 (v) 334.5, 352.12, 524.23, 532.4, 865.11, 953.12 (a) 312.16
state a grievance 333.5
state assembly 613.1
state capitalism 611.8
state chairperson 610.12
state convention 609.8
statecraft 609.3
stated 210.6, 334.9, 352.17, 855.14, 959.8, 970.20
stated belief 953.3
stated cause 886.2
stated requirement 421.1
stated value 738.9
state fair 743.4
state forest 310.13, 397.7
state government 612.1
state guard 461.24
statehood 232.6
statehouse 613.4
state legislature 613.1
stateless 160.10
stateless person 160.4, 178.5, 368.5
state library 558.1
stateliness 136.2, 501.5, 544.6
state lottery 759.14
stately 136.12, 501.21, 544.14, 580.8
stately home 228.7
state medicine 611.7
statement 334.1, 349.3, 352.2, 524.3, 549.7, 551.1, 598.7, 628.3, 708.24, 871.5, 935.7, 957.2, 1017.11
statement covering the facts 951.2
statement of belief 953.4
statement of defense 598.6, 600.2
statement of fact 349.3
statement of facts 598.7
statement of principles 334.1, 953.4
statement under oath 334.3
statemonger 610.4
state of affairs 766.2, 831.4
state of affairs, the 765.2
state of emergency 843.4
state of expectancy 130.1
state of grace 657.1, 685.3
state of matrimony 563.1
state of mind 765.2, 978.4
state of nature 6.3, 406.3, 416.2
state of nerves 128.1
state of peace 464.1
state of suspense 130.3, 971.1
state of the art 765.2, 841.3
state-of-the-art 841.14
state of the exchequer 729.6
state of the market 731.1
state of things 831.4
state of undress 6.3
state of war 458.1, 589.3
state one's case 957.9
state ownership 469.2, 476.2
state paper 549.8
state park 397.7
state police 1008.15, 1008.17
state positively 334.5
state prison 429.8
state racing commission 757.1
stateroom 197.9, 197.10
States, the 232.3
state secret 345.5
state senator 610.3
state's evidence 351.2
stateside 232.3
statesman 413.11, 610.2
statesmanlike 413.22, 609.43, 610.14
statesmanly 610.14
statesmanship 466.1, 609.3
state socialism 611.6
state socialist 611.14
statesperson 413.11, 610.2
states' rights 609.4
stateswoman 610.2
state tax 630.9
state trooper 1008.15
state troopers 1008.17
statewide 864.14
static (n) 50.13, 57.1, 520.1, 810.5, 1034.21 (a) 173.13, 173.14, 329.6, 331.17, 853.7, 1032.30, 1039.8
static ceiling 184.32
static cling 1032.3
static electricity 1032.3
static field 1032.3
static firing 1074.1
static friction 1044.1
statics 18.7, 1039.2
static warfare 458.1
station (n) 159.2, 245.2, 607.1, 662.4, 724.5, 765.1, 809.2, 1070.5 (v) 159.12
stationary 173.13, 329.6, 331.17, 853.7, 855.15
stationary dive 182.8, 367.1
stationary front 317.4
stationary rings 760.5
station break 1034.19
stationed 159.18
stationery 547.4, 1054.5
station house 230.5
station identification 1034.19
stationing 159.6
station interference 1034.21
stationmaster 178.13
station-to-station call 347.13
statism 612.7
statistical 968.6, 1017.22, 1017.24
statistical communication 1041.7
statistical independence 968.2
statistically improbable 969.3
statistically probable 968.6
statistical mechanics 968.2
statistical prediction 962.1
statistical probability 968.2, 972.1
statistical survey 938.14
statistician 628.7, 1017.15, 1017.16
statistics 745.4, 746.4, 757.4, 968.2, 1017.14
stats 746.4
stats and numbers 745.4
statuary (n) 349.6, 715.1, 716.6 (a) 715.6

statue 349.6, 712.9, 715.2
statuelike 173.13, 715.6
statuelike repose 173.1
statuesque 136.12, 272.16, 715.6, 1016.18
statuette 349.6
stature 272.1, 417.4, 662.4
status 159.2, 245.2, 607.1, 662.4, 765.1, 807.2, 809.2
status group 607.1
status in quo 765.1, 765.2, 766.2
status quo 765.1, 766.2
status-quo 853.8
status quo, the 765.2
status seeker 606.7
status seeking 100.10
status symbol 100.11, 607.2
status system 607.1
statutable 673.11
statute 444.1, 673.3
statute book 673.5
statute law 673.5
statute of limitations 211.1
statutory 419.4, 673.11
statutory lien 438.5
statutory next of kin 479.5
statutory rape 480.3
statutory referendum 613.8
St. Augustine's summer 313.5
staunch 15.18, 293.12, 359.12, 587.21, 644.20, 687.8, 970.17
staunch belief 953.5
staunch friend 588.2
staunch friendship 587.8
staunchness 15.3, 359.2, 587.7, 644.7, 687.5, 970.4
stave 193.5, 273.2, 708.29, 709.12, 720.10, 901.2, 1054.3
stave in 292.14
stave off 460.10, 1012.14
stay (n) 20.2, 225.5, 601.2, 846.2, 857.2, 857.3, 901.2, 1012.2, 1012.7 (v) 173.7, 175.9, 225.7, 225.8, 256.5, 293.7, 601.5, 803.6, 827.6, 846.8, 846.9, 846.12, 853.5, 856.3, 857.6, 857.11, 901.21, 1012.13
stay ahead of the game 635.4
stay alert 983.8
stay aloof 261.7
stay at 159.17
stay at home 583.4, 584.7
stay-at-home (n) 584.5 (a) 173.15, 584.10
stay at it 856.3
stay awake 23.3
stay away 222.7
stay away in droves 222.7
stay briefed 551.16
stay current 841.6
stay detached from 368.6
stayed 901.24
stay employed 724.12
stayer 757.2
stay for 130.8
stay friends with 587.13
stay in 225.7, 346.8
staying (n) 225.1, 1012.2 (a) 225.13, 827.10, 853.7, 856.7
staying over 225.1
staying power 15.1, 360.1, 856.1, 1049.1
stay in hiding 346.8
stay in line 326.2, 867.4
stay in one's shell 583.4
stay in shape 83.6
stay inshore 223.12
stay in soundings 182.39
stay in the background 346.8, 494.7
stay in the shade 346.8
stay it out 15.10, 360.4, 453.4
stay late 846.7
stay near 223.12
stay of execution 846.2
stay on 827.6, 856.3
stay on an even keel 467.6
stay one's hand 329.3, 370.7
stay on one's heels 223.12
stay on one's tail 223.12
stay on the beam 161.10
stay on the treadmill 330.15
stay out 586.5
stay over 225.8
stayover 225.5
stay put 173.7, 803.6, 855.11
stays 5.23
stay the course 360.4, 827.6, 855.11
stay the distance 15.11, 360.4
stay too long 118.7
stay up 846.12
stay up for 130.8
stay up into the small hours 846.7
stay up late 846.7
stay within one's means 635.4
stay with it 360.4, 856.3
stay young 83.6
St. Cecilia 710.22
stead 159.1, 159.4
steadfast 359.12, 360.8, 587.21, 644.20, 781.5, 827.10, 853.7, 855.12, 970.17
steadfast faith 953.5
steadfastness 359.2, 360.1, 587.7, 644.7, 781.1, 827.1, 853.1, 855.1, 970.4
steadiness 106.1, 129.1, 359.2, 360.1, 670.1, 763.1, 781.1, 812.1, 847.2, 850.1, 855.1, 970.4
steading 228.6, 1069.8
steady (n) 104.11 (v) 670.7, 855.7 (a) 106.10, 129.2, 359.12, 360.8, 644.20, 763.7, 781.5, 807.6, 812.8, 829.7, 847.5, 850.7, 855.12, 856.7, 970.17, 1007.5
steady as a rock 129.2
steady hand 413.1
steady-handed 129.2
steady-handedness 129.1
steady market 737.1
steady-nerved 129.2
steady nerves 129.1, 855.1
steady state 812.1, 855.1, 1041.9
steady state theory 1073.18
steady-state universe 829.4, 1073.1
steady stream 812.3
steady temper 106.1
steak 10.14, 10.18
steakhouse 8.17
steak knife 8.12
steal (n) 633.3, 747.3 (v) 177.26, 346.9, 480.13, 482.13, 621.4, 747.4
stealage 482.1
steal along 177.26
steal a march 249.10
steal a march on 216.7, 415.11, 845.6
steal a march upon 165.2
steal away 368.12
stealer 483.1
steal in 214.5
stealing (n) 177.17, 482.1 (a) 346.14
stealings 482.11
steal one's stuff 336.5, 621.4
steal one's thunder 1012.15
steal on the ear 52.9
stealth 345.4, 415.1
Stealth Bomber 181.9
steal the show 704.29
steal the spotlight 704.29
Stealth Fighter 181.9
stealthiness 345.4, 415.1
stealthy 345.12, 346.14, 415.12
steal up on 131.6
steam (n) 17.3, 18.1, 1019.10, 1043.3, 1065.3, 1067.1 (v) 11.5, 12.16, 152.15, 152.23, 182.13, 909.24, 1019.22, 1020.17, 1020.20, 1067.8 (a) 904.17
steam bath 79.8, 1019.11
steamboat (n) 180.2 (v) 182.13
steam-clean 79.18
steamed 11.7, 152.30
steamed up 105.20
steamed up about 101.11
steamer 180.2, 311.29
steamer lane 182.10
steamer track 182.10
steam heat 1019.1
steam-heat 1020.17
steam-heated 1020.29
steaminess 1019.10
steaming (n) 11.2, 182.1, 1067.5 (a) 93.18, 105.22, 152.29, 1067.9
steaming up 105.11
steam in line 182.46
steam in line of bearing 182.46
steam launch 180.4
steam pipe 1020.10
steam power 18.4
steam-propelled 904.16
steamroll 201.6, 401.4
steamroller (n) 424.2, 1051.7 (v) 201.6, 395.19, 412.9, 424.8, 902.12 (a) 424.12
steamrollering 902.3
steamroller methods 613.6
steam room 79.10
steamship 180.2
steam shovel 284.10
steam up 105.12, 405.9
steam whistle 53.6
steamy 75.27, 93.18, 105.22, 1019.28, 1067.9
steatopygia 257.8
steatopygic 257.18
steatopygous 257.18
steatopygy 257.8
steed 311.10, 311.13
steel (n) 15.8, 39.1, 462.5, 1040.2, 1046.6, 1054.2 (v) 15.13, 94.6, 1046.7 (a) 425.7, 1058.17
steel Age 824.5
steel-cage construction 266.2
steel construction 266.2
steeled 1046.13
steeled against 94.12
steel-gray 39.4
steeliness 146.1, 359.2, 361.2, 1046.1
steeling 1046.5
steellike 1046.10
steel mill 739.4
steel mirror 29.6
steel-nerved 129.2
steel oneself 114.3, 359.8, 492.12
steel one's heart 146.2
steel plate 713.6
steel string 711.20
steel-trap 920.14
steel wool 288.2
steelworker 726.2
steelworks 739.4
steely 15.15, 39.4, 94.12, 146.3, 359.12, 361.9, 425.7, 763.7, 1046.10, 1058.17
steelyard 739.4
steep (n) 200.3, 237.2 (v) 192.16, 797.11, 1064.5, 1065.13 (a) 200.12, 204.18, 632.11, 993.16, 1013.17
steeped 1065.17
steeped in iniquity 654.14
steeped in vice 654.11
steeping 11.2, 192.7, 797.2, 1063.3, 1064.1, 1065.7
steeple 272.6, 285.4
steeplechase (n) 366.1, 366.3, 757.1 (v) 366.5
steeplechaser 178.8, 311.14
steepled 272.14
steeplejack 193.6
steeplejack course 757.1
steepness 200.1, 204.6, 632.1
steep price 632.3
steep slope 204.4, 237.2
steer (n) 75.9, 76.8, 311.6, 551.3 (v) 161.6, 161.7, 182.14, 573.9
steerable 161.13
steerage 182.4
steerageway 182.9
steer a middle course 467.6, 468.2
steer an even course 670.5
steer a straight course 161.10
steer away from 182.36
steer between 467.6
steer clear of 157.7, 164.6, 261.7, 368.6, 586.5
steerer 574.7
steer for 161.9
steering 161.1, 573.1, 1041.7
steering committee 574.11
steering oar 180.15
steering wheel 573.5
steer joint 759.19
steerman 574.7
steersman 183.8

steer toward 182.35
steeve 1045.9
stegophilist 193.6
stela 549.12
stele 549.12
stellar 249.14, 704.33, 1073.25
stellar association 1073.5
stellar birth 1073.8
stellar cosmogeny 1073.18
stellar evolution 1073.8
stellar group 1073.5
stellar magnitude 1073.8
stellar photometry 1073.19
stellar population 1073.5
stellar populations 1073.8
stellar statistics 1073.19
stellary 1073.25
stellate 285.15
stellular 285.15
St. Elmo's fire 1019.13, 1025.13
St. Elmo's light 1025.13
stem (n) 171.4, 216.3, 239.6, 273.1, 310.21, 526.3, 548.6, 559.4, 560.4, 886.5, 901.8 (v) 162.2, 171.7, 216.8, 451.4, 857.11
stem cell therapy 305.9
stem from 887.5
stemma 560.5
stems 177.15
stem the current 451.4, 857.11
stem the flood 451.4
stem the tide 451.4, 857.11
stem vegetable 10.35
stemware 1029.2
stench 69.1, 71.1
stench bomb 462.20
stench of decay 71.1
stenchy 71.5
stencil (n) 548.1, 712.10, 713.4 (v) 712.19
stencil printing 713.4
stenographer 547.17, 550.1
stenographic 547.27
stenographical 547.27
stenography 523.11, 547.8
stenopeic 270.14
stenosed 270.15
stenosis 260.1
stenotype 547.8
stenotypist 547.17
stentorian 53.12, 59.10
stentorious 53.12
stentorophonic 53.12
step (n) 172.4, 177.11, 177.12, 193.5, 223.2, 245.1, 296.1, 328.3, 403.2, 517.7, 709.20, 889.2, 995.2 (v) 174.9, 177.27, 300.10
step aerobics 84.2
step along 174.9
step aside 164.6, 368.8, 448.2, 802.8
step back, a 996.2
step back 368.8
step backward, a 996.2
stepbrother 559.3, 564.3
step-by-step change 861.1
step-by-step switching 347.7
stepchild 561.3, 564.3
step dancer 705.3
stepdaughter 561.3, 564.3
step down 252.7, 1032.26
stepfather 560.9, 564.3
step flight 1075.1
step forward 162.2, 439.10
step in 189.7, 466.6
step into 479.7
step into the breach 324.3, 439.10, 466.6
step into the limelight 501.12
step into the place of 815.2
step into the shoes of 479.7, 815.2, 835.3, 862.5
stepladder 193.4
step lively 174.9, 330.13
stepmother 560.11, 564.3
step off 300.11, 307.19
step of time 821.4
step on 910.7
step on it 174.9, 401.6
step on one's corns 96.14
step on one's dick 975.15
step on one's pecker 414.12
step on one's schvantz 414.12
step on one's toes 152.21, 156.5
step on the gas 17.12, 174.9
step out 743.24
step out of 6.6
step out of line 327.6, 654.9, 688.8
step over 910.8
stepparent 560.8
steppe 158.4, 201.3, 236.1, 310.8
steppe cat 311.21
stepped-up 119.4, 251.7
steppeland 310.8
stepper 174.5, 311.14
steppes 233.1
stepping down 370.3
stepping in 466.1
stepping-stone 193.5, 383.9, 843.2
stepping-stones 193.3
stepping-up 119.1
step rocket 1074.5
steps 193.3, 384.1, 494.3
steps and measures 494.3
stepsister 559.3, 564.3
stepson 561.3, 564.3
stepstone 383.9
step stool 193.5
step terrace 901.13
step to the fore 501.12
step to the front 501.12
step up (n) 446.1 (v) 119.2, 167.3, 174.10, 251.5, 409.10, 1032.26
step-up 174.4, 251.2, 446.1
step up the ladder 446.1
step up to the plate 745.5
stercoraceous 12.20
stercoral 12.20
stercorous 12.20
stereo 50.11
stereobate 901.6
stereo headset 50.8
stereophonic 50.16
stereophonic system 50.11
stereopticon 714.12
stereoscopic 29.10, 158.10
stereoscopy 29.7
stereotype (n) 373.3, 548.8 (v) 548.15, 781.4, 855.9, 864.9
stereotyped 117.9, 373.14, 864.12, 945.6
stereotyped behavior 373.3
stereotyper 548.12
stereotypic 548.20
stereotypical 864.12
stereotyping 373.1, 864.1, 864.8
stereotypist 548.12
stereotypy 548.1
sterile 19.15, 79.27, 117.6, 391.12, 891.4
sterileness 891.1
sterility 79.1, 117.1, 891.1
sterilization 79.3, 397.2
sterilize 19.12, 79.24, 255.11
sterilized 79.27
sterling (n) 728.1 (a) 644.13, 728.30, 973.15, 999.15
sterling character 644.1
stern (n) 217.1, 217.5, 217.7 (a) 144.24, 361.9, 425.6
stern ladder 193.4
sternness 144.9, 361.2, 425.1
sternpost 217.7
stern truth, the 973.3
sternutation 2.21, 57.1
sternutative 2.32
sternutatory 2.32
sternway 163.1, 172.2, 182.9
steroid 7.7
steroid rage 105.9, 152.10
sterol 7.7
stertor 2.21, 53.3, 57.1, 58.3
stertorous 2.32, 58.15
stertorousness 58.2
stethoscope 48.8, 48.9
stevedore 183.9
stew (n) 10.11, 88.12, 105.6, 126.1, 135.1, 152.7, 185.4, 330.4, 577.5, 665.9, 665.16, 797.6, 971.3, 985.3, 1013.5 (v) 11.5, 88.23, 126.6, 135.4, 152.14, 152.15, 671.12, 1019.22, 1020.20
steward (n) 183.6, 185.4, 385.6, 574.4, 576.3, 577.5, 577.10, 729.12, 757.2, 1008.6 (v) 387.12
stewardess 183.6, 185.4, 577.5
stewardship 339.4, 387.2, 573.4, 1008.2
stewbum 88.12
stewed 11.7, 88.33
stewed fruit 10.38
stewing (n) 11.2, 1020.2 (a) 152.26
stewing chicken 311.28
stew in one's own juice 152.14
stew over 931.9
stews 228.28, 665.9
St. George 458.7
Stheno 690.9
sthula sharira 689.18
stick (n) 87.12, 180.13, 270.8, 273.1, 273.2, 605.2, 711.22, 749.4, 901.2, 1054.3, 1066.2 (v) 15.11, 134.6, 159.12, 173.7, 285.6, 292.15, 356.19, 359.9, 360.7, 393.13, 410.16, 453.4, 459.25, 632.7, 800.8, 803.6, 855.7, 855.10, 857.7, 971.14
stickable 803.12
stick around 453.4
stick at 325.4, 362.7
stick at nothing 359.10
stick-at-nothing 359.13
stick by 449.13
stick close 803.8
stick closer than a brother 803.8
sticker 285.5, 517.13, 522.8, 630.1, 803.4
sticker price 630.1
sticker shock 632.3
stick fast 173.7, 359.9, 855.10
stick figure 712.4
stick for 630.12
stick-handle 749.7
stick handling 749.3
stick in 191.3, 213.6
stickiness 803.3, 1019.6, 1062.2, 1065.2
sticking (n) 459.10, 800.3, 803.1 (a) 362.11, 803.10, 856.7
sticking one's nose in 214.2
sticking out 283.14, 348.12
sticking point 439.3
sticking power 15.1
sticking together 803.1
stick in one's craw 98.11, 152.24
stick in one's crop 98.11
stick in one's gizzard 98.11
stick in one's throat 98.11
stick insect 311.35
stick in the mind 989.13
stick in the mud 243.2
stick-in-the-mud (n) 175.5, 331.8, 361.6, 853.4, 867.2 (a) 173.15
stick it 360.7
stick it out 134.6, 360.7, 453.4, 492.14, 855.11, 856.5
stickle 325.4, 361.7, 362.7
stickle for 457.20
stick-legged 270.18
sticklegs 270.8
stickler 361.6, 495.6, 575.13
stick like a barnacle 803.8
stick like a leech 474.6, 803.8
stick like a limpet 803.8
stick like a second skin 803.8
stick like a wet T-shirt 803.8
stick like glue 803.8
stick like the shadow of 166.3
stickling (n) 325.2 (a) 325.7, 362.11
stick of wood 1054.3
stick on a Band-Aid 376.4
stick one's foot in it 414.12, 975.15
stick one's long nose into 214.7
stick one's neck out 493.5, 1006.7
stick one's nose in 214.7, 844.4, 981.4
stick out 31.5, 283.10, 348.7, 360.4
stickout 249.13, 662.17
stick out a mile 348.7
stick out like a sore thumb 31.4, 348.7
stick out over 202.7
stickpin 498.6
sticks 177.15, 749.6

sticks, the 233.1, 261.4
sticks and stones 1054.2
stick shift 1040.9
stick someone up 482.14
stick to 421.8, 474.6
stick together 800.5, 803.6, 803.9, 973.8
stick to it 360.7, 856.5
stick-to-it-ive 330.22, 803.12
stick-to-itive 360.8
stick-to-it-iveness 15.1
stick-to-itiveness 360.1, 803.3
sticktoitiveness 15.1
stick to one's colors 359.9
stick to one's guns 359.9, 360.4, 361.7, 453.4, 492.14, 855.11
stick to one's knitting 724.10
stick to the facts 644.11, 987.4
stick to the letter 973.11
stickum 803.4
stick up 200.8, 283.10, 482.16, 912.5
stickup 482.4
stick up for 449.13, 600.10
stickup job 482.4
stickup man 483.5
stick with 643.4
stick with it 359.9, 360.7, 853.6, 856.5
sticky (n) 549.11 (a) 12.22, 93.21, 803.12, 1013.17, 1019.28, 1062.12, 1065.15
sticky-fingered 482.21
sticky fingers 482.4, 482.12
sticky mess 1062.5
sticky weather 1019.7
sticky wicket 1013.5
stiff (n) 178.3, 307.15, 311.12, 331.9, 607.9, 660.2, 726.2, 759.11 (v) 389.6 (a) 88.33, 117.6, 180.18, 307.30, 361.9, 414.18, 414.20, 425.7, 534.3, 580.9, 632.11, 993.16, 1046.11, 1049.4
stiff-arm 908.3
stiff as a board 1046.11
stiff as a poker 1046.11
stiff as buckram 1046.11
stiff backbone 136.2
stiff-backed 136.8
stiff breeze 318.4
stiff climb 204.4
stiffen 15.13, 1032.26, 1046.9, 1049.3
stiffened 251.7, 1046.13
stiffener 901.2
stiffening 1046.5
stiffen one's backbone 492.12
stiff market 737.1
stiff neck 136.3, 361.1
stiff-necked 136.8, 361.8, 500.19
stiff-neckedness 136.1, 361.1, 500.6, 687.5
stiff-necked pride 136.1, 141.1
stiffness 117.1, 361.2, 425.2, 580.1, 632.1, 1046.3, 1049.1
stiffness of posture 200.1
stiff opposition 451.1
stiff price 632.3
stiff temper 361.2
stiff upper lip 492.5
stifle 51.8, 106.8, 308.19, 345.8, 395.15, 428.8, 670.6, 1012.12, 1019.22, 1022.7
stifled 52.17, 345.11, 428.14, 525.12
stifling (n) 308.6, 345.3, 395.6, 428.2, 1022.2 (a) 69.10, 173.16, 1012.17, 1019.28
stigma 85.37, 310.28, 517.5, 661.6, 1004.3
stigmatic 1004.10
stigmatiferous 1004.10
stigmatism 661.6
stigmatization 661.6
stigmatize 512.10, 517.18, 517.19, 661.9, 1004.6
stigmatized 1004.8, 1004.10
stile 193.3, 273.4
stiletto 459.25
still (n) 51.1, 88.21, 714.3, 1067.6 (v) 51.8, 670.7 (a) 51.10, 173.12, 173.13, 287.10, 307.29, 464.9
still alarm 400.1
still around 256.7
still as a mouse 173.13
still as a statue 173.13
still as death 51.10, 173.12
stillbirth 307.6
stillborn 1.4, 307.29, 410.18
still breathing 306.12
still-fish 382.10
still hunt 382.2, 938.15
still-hunt 346.10, 382.9, 938.30
stillicide 238.7
stilling 670.15
stillish 173.12
still life 712.9, 712.10
still-life painter 716.4
stillness 51.1, 173.1, 464.2
still photograph 714.3
stillroom 386.8
still small voice within 636.5
stillstand 173.3
still water 241.1
still wine 88.17
still with us 306.12
stilly 51.10, 173.12
stilt 270.8
stilted 501.22, 534.3, 545.8, 580.9, 912.9
stiltedness 534.1, 545.1, 580.1
stilt house 241.3
stilt-legged 270.18
stimulant (n) 17.6, 86.8, 86.9, 87.3 (a) 375.27
stimulate 9.2, 17.10, 24.7, 75.23, 105.13, 192.14, 375.12, 983.12
stimulate attention 983.10
stimulated 9.4, 105.20, 375.30
stimulating 9.3, 17.15, 75.26, 86.44, 105.30, 375.27, 544.13, 983.19, 1023.12
stimulation 9.1, 17.8, 105.1, 105.11, 375.2, 375.4, 375.7, 1038.8
stimulation fatigue 21.1
stimulative (n) 375.7 (a) 9.3, 17.15, 86.44, 105.30, 375.27
stimulator 17.6, 375.10
stimulatory 9.3, 17.15, 105.30, 375.27
stimulus 17.6, 105.11, 375.7, 886.1, 986.2
stimulus-response psychology 92.2
sting (n) 17.5, 26.3, 68.2, 74.1, 285.3, 356.9, 375.8, 759.13, 1001.5 (v) 26.7, 68.5, 74.5, 93.14, 96.17, 152.21, 285.6, 356.19, 375.15, 632.7
stinger 1001.5
stinginess 484.3, 651.2, 885.1, 992.2
stinging (n) 26.3, 74.1 (a) 17.14, 26.10, 26.13, 68.6, 105.31, 144.23, 285.10
stinging defeat 412.4
sting of conscience 113.2
stingy 484.9, 651.6, 885.5, 992.10
stink (n) 69.1, 71.1 (v) 69.6, 71.4
stinkard 71.3, 660.5
stink ball 71.3
stink bomb 71.3, 462.20
stink cat 311.22
stinker 71.3, 89.4, 660.5
stink eye 144.4
stinkeye 27.5
stink-eyed 154.3
stinking 64.7, 69.9, 71.5, 98.18, 1000.8
stinking drunk 88.33
stinkingness 71.2
stink in the nostrils 71.4, 98.11
stinko 88.33
stink of 991.5
stink out 71.4
stinkpot 71.3, 180.4
stink to heaven 71.4
stink to high heaven 71.4
stink up 71.4
stinky 69.9, 1000.8
stint (n) 245.1, 428.3, 724.2, 825.3 (v) 210.5, 428.9, 484.5
stinted 428.15, 992.10
stinting (n) 484.1 (a) 484.7, 668.9
stintless 485.4
stipe 310.21
stipend 478.8, 624.5
stipendiary (n) 479.4 (a) 478.26
stipple (n) 47.3, 713.2 (v) 35.14, 47.7, 713.9
stippled 47.13
stippledness 47.3
stippling 35.12, 47.3, 713.2
stipula 310.19
stipulate 421.7, 437.5, 865.11, 951.10, 959.4
stipulated 437.11, 761.15, 951.14, 959.8
stipulate for 421.7, 457.20
stipulating 865.6
stipulation 421.2, 437.1, 865.6, 959.2
stipulatory 959.8
stipule 310.19
stir (n) 105.4, 172.1, 330.1, 330.4, 429.9, 810.4, 917.1 (v) 23.4, 24.7, 93.14, 105.12, 105.14, 172.5, 330.11, 330.12, 375.19, 671.12, 915.12, 917.10
stir about 330.11, 330.12
stir bird 429.11
stir-crazy 926.2
stir-fried 11.7
stir-fry 11.5
stir-frying 11.2
stir in 797.10, 805.3
stirk 311.6
stirless 173.16
stirlessness 173.6
Stirling 1043.3
stir of air 318.3
stir one's bile 152.24
stir one's stumps 174.9, 330.11, 401.6
stirp 305.12
stirpiculture 1070.1
stirps 559.4, 560.4
stirred 105.20
stirred up 105.20, 917.16
stirrer 917.9
stirring (n) 105.11, 172.1, 375.4 (a) 105.30, 172.7, 330.19, 375.27, 544.13, 831.10
stirring up 105.11
stirring-up 375.4
stirrup 2.10, 901.18
stirrup cup 88.9, 188.4
stir the blood 105.12, 152.24
stir the embers 105.12, 375.17, 396.16
stir the feelings 105.12
stir the fire 1020.22
stir the pot 456.14
stir up 105.12, 152.24, 375.17, 375.19, 797.10, 917.10
stir up a hornet's nest 1013.14
stir up trouble 456.14
stitch (n) 26.2, 248.3, 793.3, 800.4 (v) 741.4, 800.8
stitcher 5.34
stitchery 741.1
stitching 741.1
stitch in the side 26.2
stitch in time, a 845.1
stitch of work 725.4
stitch up 741.4
stithy 739.4
St. Luke's summer 313.5
St. Martin's summer 313.5
stoa 197.19
stochastic 971.19, 972.16
stochastic independence 968.2
stochastics 972.1
stochastic variable 968.2
stock (n) 10.10, 310.21, 311.1, 312.1, 384.2, 386.1, 471.7, 477.5, 508.7, 559.4, 560.4, 704.1, 704.9, 735.1, 738.2, 886.5, 953.1, 1054.1, 1054.5, 1058.7, 1061.2 (v) 385.7, 1054.7 (a) 117.9, 373.13, 869.9, 974.6
stockade 429.8, 460.4, 1009.3
stockbreeder 1070.2
stockbreeding 1070.1
stockbroker 730.9, 737.10
stock brokerage 737.9
stockbrokerage 737.18
stockbroker belt 230.1
stockbroking 737.18
stock-car racing 756.1
stock certificate 738.4
stock character 704.10, 706.3

stock clerk 385.6
stock company 707.11, 737.15, 1008.4
stock dealer 737.10
stock dealing 737.18
stock dividend 738.7
stocked 386.14
stock exchange 737.7, 739.1
stock-exchange broker 737.10
stock farm 1070.5
stock farming 1070.1
stockfeed 1070.5
stockholder 737.14
stockholder of record 737.14
stockholding 738.3
stockholdings 738.3
stock horse 311.10
stockiness 257.8, 268.2
stocking 5.40
stocking cap 5.25
stockings 5.28
stocking the mind 570.1
stock insurance company 737.15
stock in trade 384.2, 386.2
stock-in-trade 385.4, 386.1, 471.7, 735.1
stock issue 738.6
stockjobber 737.10
stockjobbery 737.18, 737.19
stockjobbing 737.18, 737.19
stockkeeper 1070.2
stock ledger 738.2
stock list 738.2
stockman 1070.2
stock market 729.4, 737.1, 737.7
stock market index 630.4
stock market quotations 630.1
stock-market trading 737.19
stock of words 526.13
stock option 737.21
stockowner 737.14
stock part 704.10
stock phrase 974.3
stockpile (n) 386.1, 386.3, 770.9, 770.11 (v) 386.11, 770.19
stockpiled 386.14
stockpiling 770.9
stock price index 737.1
stock raiser 1070.2
stock raising 1070.1
stockroom 386.6
stocks 428.4, 605.3
stocks and bonds 438.1, 738.1
stock saying 974.1
stock split 738.2
stock-still 173.13
stocktaking 300.1, 628.6, 946.3
stock the mind 570.6
stock ticker 737.7
stock up 386.11, 1054.7
stocky 257.18, 268.10
stockyard 308.12
stodge 243.2
stodginess 117.1, 842.3, 1062.2
stodgy 117.6, 842.17, 1062.12
stogie 89.4
Stoic 668.10
stoic (n) 134.3 (a) 25.6, 94.13, 106.10, 134.9, 148.6, 173.12
stoic 855.12
stoical 94.13, 106.10, 134.9, 173.12
stoic calm 106.2
Stoicism 636.2, 668.2
Stoicism 952.3
stoicism 855.1
stoicism 94.4, 102.1, 106.1, 134.1, 433.1
Stoic philosophy 952.3
stoke 1020.22, 1021.8
stoker 178.13, 183.6
stoke the fire 1020.22
stoke up 1020.17
stolen 482.23
stolen goods 482.11, 732.3
stolen property 732.3
stolid 106.10, 173.12, 855.12, 982.3, 987.5
stolidity 106.1, 855.1, 922.3, 982.1, 987.1
stolidness 855.1
stolon 310.20
stoma 292.1, 292.5
stomach (n) 2.18, 62.1, 100.7 (v) 134.8, 443.10
stomachache 26.5, 85.29
stomachachy 26.12
stomachal 2.31
stomach cancer 85.29
stomach condition 85.29
stomach flu 85.29
stomach gas 1067.3
stomachic 2.31
stomach poison 1001.3
stomp (n) 902.10 (v) 177.28, 902.22
stomping ground 228.27
stomping grounds 228.18
stone (n) 310.31, 383.6, 462.18, 498.6, 549.12, 713.6, 1046.6, 1054.2, 1059.1, 1059.6 (v) 88.23, 295.23, 308.18, 459.27, 604.16 (a) 1059.11
Stone Age 824.5
Stone Age man 842.7
stone-blind 30.9
stone-blindness 30.1
stone broke 619.10
stone carving 715.1
stone-cold 307.30, 1023.14
stone-cold sober 516.3
stone crab 311.29
stonecraft 712.2
stone: crystal 1059.7
stonecutter 550.1, 716.6
stonecutting 715.1
stoned 25.8, 87.24, 88.33
stone-dead 307.30
stone-deaf 49.6
stone-deafness 49.1
stone face 94.1
stone-faced 111.3
stone fruit 10.38, 310.4
stone-ground 1051.11
stone in one's path 1012.4
stonelike 1046.10, 1059.12
stoneman 548.12
stone proof 548.5
stones 142.3
stoneshot 904.4
stone's throw 223.2
stone to death 308.18
stone wall 212.4, 1012.5
stonewall 51.6, 415.11, 450.3, 846.8, 1012.10
stonewalling 51.2
stoneware 735.4
stonework 1054.2
stoniness 94.3, 1046.1
stoning 308.1, 459.11, 604.6
stony 94.12, 288.7, 619.10, 1046.10, 1059.12
stony-faced 111.3
stonyhearted 94.12, 144.25
stonyheartedness 94.3
stooge (n) 138.4, 166.2, 358.1, 384.4, 412.5, 575.5, 577.1, 616.8, 707.2 (v) 704.29
stook 770.7
stool (n) 12.2, 12.4, 12.11 (v) 12.13, 351.6, 551.13
stoolie 357.5, 551.6
stool pigeon 357.5, 551.6
stool softener 86.17
stoop (n) 194.1, 197.21, 367.1, 913.3 (v) 137.8, 138.7, 141.8, 194.5, 367.6, 433.10, 661.7, 913.8
stoop down 913.8
stooped 274.7
stooping from one's high place 137.3
stop (n) 173.3, 186.5, 225.5, 293.3, 293.4, 524.12, 530.15, 846.2, 857.2, 857.4, 1012.2, 1012.7, 1013.6 (v) 51.9, 127.18, 173.8, 225.8, 293.7, 374.2, 374.3, 390.4, 410.16, 460.10, 668.8, 820.6, 846.8, 857.6, 857.7, 857.11, 1012.13
stop-and-go 813.4
stop-and-go light 1026.4
stop at nothing 359.10
stop bath 714.13
stop breathing 307.18
stop by 582.19
stopcock 239.10
stop cold 857.11
stop dead 857.7, 857.11
stop dead in one's tracks 820.6, 857.11
stop for breath 20.8
stopgap (n) 293.4, 365.5, 995.2 (a) 365.12, 862.8, 995.7
stop in 582.19
stop in one's tracks 127.18, 308.18, 857.7, 904.12
stoplight 517.15, 1026.4
stop, look, and listen 339.8, 494.7
stop looking 27.19
stop moving 173.7
stop off 582.19
stopoff 225.5
stop on a dime 857.7
stop one's ears 49.4, 984.2
stop one's mouth 51.8
stop over 225.8, 582.19
stopover 225.5
stoppage 85.6, 173.3, 293.3, 820.1, 846.2, 857.2, 1012.2
stop payment 625.6
stopped 293.11, 524.30, 846.16
stopped up 293.11
stopper (n) 293.4, 295.5, 745.2, 752.2, 820.4 (v) 293.7, 295.21
stopping 225.1, 293.5, 857.1, 1012.2
stopping place 186.5, 820.1, 857.2
stopping time 822.1
stopple (n) 293.4 (v) 293.7
stop rank 711.19
stop short 857.7, 857.11, 911.2
stop talking 51.7
stop the breath 308.19
stop the clock 853.6
stop the mouth of 958.5
stop to consider 362.7, 971.10
stop up 293.7, 1012.12
stopway 184.23
stop work 20.8
storage 158.5, 159.6, 386.5, 386.6, 397.2, 630.6, 1042.7
storage battery 1032.21
storage device 1032.21
storage space 386.5
store (n) 195.1, 386.1, 386.3, 386.6, 397.7, 472.3, 736.1, 739.1, 759.19, 770.11, 953.1, 1054.1 (v) 159.15, 385.7, 386.10, 390.6, 1054.7
store away 346.7, 386.10
store-bought 5.48, 733.11
store-bought clothes 5.4
store-boughten 733.11
store clerk 730.3
store clothes 5.4
store credit 622.1
stored 386.14, 390.12
store detective 576.10
storefront 206.2
storehouse 386.6, 729.13
storehouse of words 554.9
store in the mind 989.12
storekeeper 385.6, 730.2
store of knowledge 928.4, 928.9
storeroom 197.14, 197.16, 386.6
stores 10.5, 386.1
store up 386.11
storied 722.9
storier 722.5
storified 722.9
storify 722.7
stork, the 1.1
storm (n) 105.9, 152.9, 318.11, 400.1, 459.6, 671.4, 770.4 (v) 105.16, 152.15, 318.19, 459.20, 503.3, 671.11
storm along 174.9
storm and stress 418.2
storm blown over, the 464.1
stormbound 428.15
storm cave 1009.3
storm cellar 197.17, 1009.3
storm center 208.2, 671.4
storm cloud 319.2
storm clouds 133.5, 1006.1, 1011.6
storm cone 400.1
storm flag 400.1
storm-force 318.22
storm in 214.5
storm in a teacup 998.3

storminess 671.2
storming (n) 459.6 (a) 105.25, 152.32, 318.22, 459.29, 503.4, 671.18
storm petrel 311.27, 399.3
stormproof 293.12, 1066.11
storm shelter 346.4
storm surge 272.8, 916.4
stormtight 293.12, 1066.11
storm tracking 1036.9
storm trooper 461.16
storm troops 461.15, 461.23
storm warning 317.7, 400.1
storm watch 317.7
storm wind 318.11
stormy 105.29, 318.22, 319.8, 671.18, 1027.14
stormy petrel 133.5, 311.27, 399.3, 816.1
stormy weather 316.4, 317.3, 671.4, 1011.6
stormy winds 318.11
story (n) 197.23, 296.1, 354.10, 354.11, 489.6, 549.1, 552.3, 552.7, 706.3, 719.1, 719.2, 722.3, 722.4 (v) 354.19
story, the 1017.6
storyboard 706.3
storybook (n) 554.1 (a) 986.24
storyline 722.4
story of mankind, the 719.1
storyteller 357.9, 547.15, 718.4, 722.5
storytelling 722.1, 722.2
story writer 547.15, 718.4
stot 76.8, 311.6
stoup 703.10
stout 15.15, 15.18, 83.12, 257.18, 492.16, 763.7
stout fellow 659.2
stout heart 492.5
stouthearted 492.16
stoutheartedness 492.1
stoutness 15.1, 15.3, 257.8, 492.1, 763.1
stove 742.5, 1020.10
stove black 38.6
stove in 292.14
stove lifter 1020.12
stovepipe 239.14
stove poker 1020.12
stovewood 1021.3, 1054.3
stow 159.15, 386.10, 390.6
stowage 158.5, 159.6, 196.2, 257.2, 386.5
stow away 346.7, 386.10
stowaway 774.4
stow down 386.10
STP 87.19
strabismal 28.11
strabismic 28.11
strabismus 28.5
Strad 711.5
straddle (n) 737.21 (v) 158.9, 177.28, 819.3, 901.22, 910.8
straddle the fence 362.7, 363.9, 467.5
straddling the fence 467.3
Stradivari 711.5
Stradivarius 711.5
strafe (n) 459.9 (v) 459.22
strafing 184.11, 459.7
straggle 164.4, 166.4, 177.23, 177.28, 217.8, 267.5
straggler 178.2
straggling 177.37, 267.8, 771.9, 810.12
straggly 771.9, 810.12
straight (n) 75.13, 277.2, 758.4 (a) 161.12, 277.6, 516.3, 644.14, 644.17, 644.19, 653.5, 794.10, 798.7, 812.8, 867.6, 960.2, 973.16
straight-ahead 161.12
straight and narrow, the 653.1
straightarm 746.3
straight arrow 644.8
straight-arrow 644.14
straight as an arrow 277.6
straight as an edge 277.6
straight as a ruler 277.6
straightaway (n) 277.2, 756.3 (a) 161.12, 277.6
straight backbone 136.2
straight ball 750.2
straight chain 1038.7
straight course 277.2, 856.1
straight-cut 277.6
straightedge 277.3
straighten 277.5, 867.3
straighten oneself out 392.9
straighten out 277.5, 392.9, 392.12, 437.8, 466.7, 510.17, 757.5, 940.2
straighten up 200.8, 277.5, 808.12
straighten up and fly right 392.7
straight face 94.1, 111.1, 123.1, 344.3, 522.5
straight-faced 111.3
straight flush 758.4
straightforward 161.12, 499.7, 521.11, 533.6, 535.3, 644.17, 798.8, 1014.13
straightforwardness 499.2, 521.2, 533.1, 535.1, 644.4
straight from the horse's mouth 970.18
straight-from-the-shoulder 644.17
straight-front 277.6
straightlacedness 361.2
straight line 277.2
straight-lined 277.6
straight man 489.12
straightness 277.1
straight of it, the 973.4
straight-out 535.3, 644.17, 960.2
straight part 704.10
straight person 707.2
straight poker 759.10
straight sailing 1014.1
straight scoop, the 973.4
straight shooter 644.8
straight-shooting 644.14
straight-side 277.6
straight skinny, the 551.1
straight stretch 277.2
straight thinking 931.1
straight-thinking 987.6
straight ticket 609.19
straight truth, the 973.3
straight-up 200.12
straight-up-and-down 200.12, 973.16
straight up-and-downness 200.1
straightway 161.12
strain (n) 21.1, 85.38, 96.5, 126.1, 128.3, 312.1, 403.1, 532.2, 559.4, 560.4, 589.1, 708.4, 708.24, 720.10, 725.2, 809.2, 809.3, 905.2, 978.3, 993.6, 993.7, 1013.1, 1048.2 (v) 79.22, 190.15, 265.6, 325.4, 354.16, 393.13, 403.5, 725.10, 993.13
strain at 362.7
strain at a gnat and swallow a camel 923.6, 936.9
strained 126.7, 128.13, 265.11, 589.9, 725.18, 776.8
strained relations 456.1, 589.2
strainer 79.13, 292.8
strain every nerve 403.13, 725.10
strain every nerve and sinew 725.10
strain for 403.9
straining (n) 79.4, 190.6, 265.2, 354.9, 725.2, 993.7 (a) 21.13, 362.11, 725.17, 725.18
strain one's attention 983.8
strain one's credulity 955.7, 969.2
strain one's ears 48.10, 983.7
strain one's eyes 27.15
strain the muscles 725.10
strain the sense 342.2
strain the throat 59.9
strain the truth 354.19
strain the vocal cords 59.9
strain the voice 59.9
strait (n) 242.1, 270.3, 843.4, 1006.1, 1013.4 (a) 210.7, 270.14
straiten 210.5, 212.6, 270.11
straitened 210.7, 619.7, 992.10, 1013.26
straitened circumstances 619.1
straitjacket (n) 428.4 (v) 428.10
straitlaced 425.7, 495.9, 500.19, 687.8, 867.6, 980.10
straitlacedness 361.2, 495.1, 500.6, 687.5, 980.1
straitness 270.1
straits 242.1, 619.1, 1013.4
strait-waistcoat 428.4
strake 271.4
strand (n) 234.2, 271.1 (v) 182.42
stranded 855.16, 1013.27
strand flat 236.1
strange 122.10, 774.5, 776.6, 841.11, 870.11, 926.26, 927.5, 930.16
strange, the 930.6
strange attraction 886.3
strange duck 927.4
strangeness 522.6, 780.1, 841.1, 870.1, 870.3, 870.7, 926.1, 927.1, 1038.6
stranger 773.3, 774.3
stranger to, a 374.4, 414.17, 930.12
strange thing 870.5
strange to 930.11
strangle 19.10, 260.7, 293.6, 307.23, 308.19, 395.15, 428.8, 604.16, 1012.12
strangled 58.15, 260.12, 293.11, 525.12
stranglehold 428.4, 474.2, 474.3, 1012.1
strangler 308.11, 604.7
strangling (n) 307.5, 308.6, 428.2, 604.6 (a) 1012.17
strangulate 260.7, 293.6, 1012.12
strangulated 260.12, 293.9, 293.11
strangulation 260.1, 270.2, 293.3, 307.5, 308.6, 395.6, 604.6
strap (n) 271.4, 605.1, 737.21 (v) 91.24, 285.7, 428.10, 604.12, 800.9
straphang 177.18
straphanger 178.1
straphanging 177.1
strapless 6.13
strapped 210.7, 428.16, 619.7, 619.10
strapper 15.7
strapping (n) 604.4 (a) 15.15, 15.16, 257.18
strata 296.1, 530.2
stratagem 356.6, 376.1, 381.5, 415.3, 995.2
stratagemical 381.13
strategian 381.6
strategic 381.12, 415.12
strategic air force 461.29
strategic bomber 181.9
strategic bombing 459.7
strategic course 751.1
strategic defense initiative 460.2
strategic materials 1054.1
strategic nuclear weapon 462.1
strategic plan 381.1
strategic withdrawal 163.2
strategist 375.11, 381.6, 415.7, 610.6
strategized 381.12
strategy 381.1, 415.3, 458.4, 745.3, 746.3, 747.3, 748.2, 754.3
strath 284.9
straticulate 296.6
stratification 296.4, 607.1, 809.1
stratificational grammar 530.1
stratified 296.6, 809.8
stratified rock 1059.1
stratiform 296.6, 319.8
stratify 296.5
stratocracy 612.4
stratocumulus 319.2
stratosphere 272.2
stratospheric 317.12
stratous 319.8
stratovision 1035.9
stratum 296.1, 317.2, 607.1, 809.2
stratus 319.2
straw (n) 10.4, 239.6, 256.1, 298.2, 310.21, 998.5 (a) 43.4
strawberry blond 35.9
strawberry-blond 37.9

strawberry fields 87.10
strawberry mark 517.5, 1004.1
strawberry roan 311.11
straw boss 574.2
straw-boss 573.10
straw-colored 43.4
straw hat 704.1
straw hat circuit 704.1
straw in the wind 399.3, 517.9
straw man 500.7, 575.5
straw poll 371.6
straw that breaks the camel's back, the 135.3
straw that broke the camel's back 886.3
straw to show the wind 942.4
straw vote 371.6, 942.4
stray (n) 160.4, 178.3 (v) 164.4, 177.23, 538.9, 654.9, 688.8, 975.9, 984.3, 985.9 (a) 164.7, 870.9, 972.16
stray from the path 688.8
straying (n) 164.1, 177.3 (a) 177.37, 870.9, 975.16
streak (n) 47.5, 174.6, 267.3, 270.7, 290.1, 517.6, 767.4, 978.3, 1025.5, 1025.17 (v) 47.7, 290.3, 517.19
streaked 47.15, 170.11
streaking 47.5, 517.6
streak of lightning 174.6
streak of luck 1010.3
streaky 47.15
stream (n) 172.2, 184.30, 238.1, 238.4, 239.1, 318.1, 812.3, 896.2, 991.2, 1025.5 (v) 172.5, 177.18, 238.16, 316.10, 770.16, 991.5
stream action 238.1
stream bed 238.1, 239.2
stream channel 238.1
stream conservation 397.1
stream course 238.1
stream down 316.10
streamer 647.7, 937.2, 1025.5
streamer aurora 1025.16
streamers 1025.15
stream forth 33.8
streaming 172.8, 238.24, 316.11, 804.5, 1025.30
streaming light 1025.4
streamlet 238.1
streamlike 238.23
streamline (n) 277.2 (v) 392.11, 798.4, 841.6
streamlined 286.3, 798.9, 841.13
streamline flow 1061.1
streamliner 179.14
streamlining 798.2, 1014.5
stream of air 318.1, 524.12
stream of consciousness 92.28, 92.33, 349.2, 542.1, 722.6, 931.4
stream of fashion 578.1
stream of light 1025.5
stream of time 821.4
stream pollution 1072.2
streams of rain 316.1
streams of sweat 12.7
stream the log 182.48
streamway 239.2
streamy 238.23
street 383.5
Street, the 737.8
street artist 716.1
streetcar 179.17
streetcar suburb 230.1
street certificate 738.4
street cred 187.2
street credibility 187.2
street drug 87.3
street entertainer 356.10
street fight 457.4
street fighter 461.2
streetfighter 461.1
street floor 197.23
street food 10.1
street-front 206.2
streetlight 1025.19
street market 736.2
street musician 710.1
street of fallen women 665.9
street organ 711.14
street people 584.4, 619.3
street performer 356.10
street person 331.10, 619.4
street singer 710.14
street-smart 928.16
street smarts 928.3
street sweeper 79.16
street theater 704.1
street urchin 178.3
street value 630.2
streetwalk 665.21
streetwalker 665.16
street-walking 665.8
streetwalking (n) 732.1 (a) 665.28
streetwise 928.16
strength 15.1, 17.1, 18.1, 68.3, 83.3, 244.1, 247.1, 359.4, 413.4, 417.2, 544.3, 763.1, 1046.1, 1049.1
strengthen 7.17, 15.13, 18.10, 251.5, 251.6, 253.5, 957.11, 1046.9, 1049.3
strengthened 251.7, 1046.13
strengthening (n) 15.5, 251.2, 957.4, 1046.5 (a) 86.44
strengthless 16.12
strengthlessness 16.1
strength of character 359.5
strength of mind 359.4
strength of purpose 359.4
strength of will 15.1
strenuosity 330.6
strenuous 17.13, 330.22, 725.18, 1013.17
strenuousness 17.1, 330.6, 725.5, 1013.1
strepitant 53.13
strepitous 53.13
streptococcus 85.42
streptomycin 86.29
stress (n) 92.17, 96.2, 96.5, 126.1, 128.3, 334.1, 375.6, 524.10, 720.7, 725.2, 902.2, 997.4, 1011.1 (v) 725.10, 902.12, 997.14
stress accent 524.10
stress and strain 128.3, 725.2
stress arsis 709.25
stressed 92.39, 524.30, 997.21
stressed out 16.18, 26.9
stress fracture 85.38
stressful 21.13, 1011.13
stressfulness 725.2
stress management 92.27
stress of life 96.5, 1011.1
stress pattern 524.10
stress test 84.3, 91.12
stretch (n) 158.2, 158.8, 177.10, 261.1, 267.1, 355.1, 725.2, 725.6, 743.11, 824.1, 825.1, 825.4, 993.7, 1048.1, 1048.2 (v) 84.4, 158.9, 259.4, 259.5, 267.5, 267.6, 355.3, 604.17, 725.10, 991.4, 993.13, 1048.4 (a) 1048.7
stretchability 1048.1
stretchable 1048.7
stretch away to 261.6
stretched 267.8, 355.4
stretched out 267.8
stretched-out 259.11, 827.11
stretched tight 128.13
stretcher 901.19
stretch fabric 1048.3
stretch forth a helping hand 449.11
stretch forth one's hand 328.5
stretchiness 1048.1
stretching 22.1, 84.2, 259.2, 267.4, 354.9, 355.1, 993.7, 1048.2
stretching everywhere 823.3
stretching of the truth 354.11
stretching one's luck 493.3
stretching out 267.4
stretching-out 827.2
stretch limo 179.13
stretch marks 2.4
stretch of the imagination 986.5
stretch oneself 267.5
stretch oneself too thin 404.6
stretch one's luck 493.6
stretch out 158.9, 261.5, 267.5, 267.6, 538.8, 827.9, 846.9
stretch the legs 177.29
stretch the meaning 342.2
stretch the point 355.3
stretch the truth 354.16, 354.19, 355.3
stretch to 261.6
stretchy 22.21, 259.9, 1048.7
stretto (n) 708.25 (a) 708.53
streusel 198.3
strew 771.4
strewing 771.1
strewn 771.9
stria 47.5, 290.1
striatal 47.15
striate (v) 47.7, 290.3, 517.19 (a) 47.15
striated 47.15, 290.4
striation 47.5, 290.1, 517.6
striature 47.5
stricken 93.23, 96.26, 112.29, 128.14
stricken dumb 51.12
stricken in years 303.18
stricken with amnesia 990.9
strict 339.12, 417.16, 425.6, 495.9, 644.15, 687.8, 973.17
strict attention 983.4
strict constructionism 341.1, 609.4
strict constructionist 341.7
strict discipline 425.1
strict interpretation 687.5
striction 260.1
strictly on the up-and-up 973.13
strictness 270.1, 339.3, 425.1, 495.1, 687.5, 867.1, 973.5
strict neutrality 467.1
strict settlement 471.4
stricture 260.1, 270.2, 510.3, 510.4, 1012.1
stride (n) 172.4, 177.11, 177.12, 261.1, 708.9 (v) 177.27, 177.28, 901.22
stridence 58.1
stridency 17.5, 53.2, 58.1, 61.1
strident 17.14, 58.12, 61.4
strident-voiced 58.12
stride piano 708.9
stridor 53.2, 58.1, 61.1, 524.8
stridulant 58.12
stridulate 58.7
stridulation 58.1, 58.5, 60.1
stridulous 58.12
stridulousness 58.1
strife 456.5, 457.1
striga 47.5, 288.3
strigal 288.9
strigate 47.15, 288.9
strigose 47.15, 288.9
strike (n) 173.3, 327.4, 333.2, 409.5, 459.1, 459.4, 727.5, 750.2, 857.2, 941.1 (v) 93.15, 255.12, 327.7, 333.5, 459.14, 459.17, 548.14, 604.11, 727.10, 857.8, 902.13, 902.14, 904.12, 931.18, 931.19, 941.2
strike a bad patch 1013.12
strike a balance 246.2, 297.10, 467.6, 468.2, 624.13, 628.8, 670.5, 790.6
strike a bargain 332.10, 437.7, 468.2, 731.19
strike a blow 328.5
strike against 902.13
strike a happy medium 246.2
strike a light 1020.22, 1025.29
strike all of a heap 122.6, 131.8
strike an attitude 500.13
strike a pose 500.13
strike a responsive chord 903.8
strike a rich vein 1010.11
strike a sour note 61.3
strike at 459.16, 902.14
strike at the root of 395.14
strike back 506.4
strike blind 30.7
strikebreaker 363.5, 727.8
strike camp 188.14
strike dead 122.6, 308.18
strike down 395.12, 445.2
strike dumb 51.8, 122.6, 127.17
strike fire 903.8
strike hard 93.15
strike home 24.8, 93.15, 903.8
strike in with 450.4
strike it lucky 1010.11
strike it rich 618.10, 1010.11
strike mute 51.8
strike off 255.10, 255.12, 365.8, 773.5

strike off the roll 447.4
strike off the rolls 909.19
strike oil 1010.11
strike on 941.3
strike one 931.18, 983.11
strike one as 33.10
strike one as funny 743.21
strike one right 95.6
strike one's fancy 95.6, 104.22
strike one's flag 433.8
strike out 188.8, 255.12, 395.16, 410.10, 745.5, 892.12
strikeout 745.3
strike out at 459.16, 510.14
strike out for 161.9
strike out for oneself 430.20
strike pay 624.4
striker 727.6, 752.2
striker of poses 500.8
strike root 159.17, 310.34, 855.10
strike root in 894.12
strike tent 188.14
strike terror into 127.17
strike the death knell of 308.20
strike the eye 31.4, 33.8, 348.7
strike the first blow 457.14
strike the mind 931.18
strike up 708.37
strike up a conversation 541.8
strike up a friendship 587.10
strike up a tune 708.37
strike upon 186.7, 194.10
strike up the band 708.37
strike while the iron is hot 843.8
strike with awe 122.6
strike with wonder 122.6
strike zone 745.3
striking (n) 255.5, 728.24 (a) 18.12, 105.30, 122.10, 247.10, 348.12, 544.11, 997.19
striking alteration 860.1
striking circle 749.4
striking down 445.1
strikingly like 784.15
strikingness 348.4
striking out 255.5
striking resemblance 784.4
striking success 409.3
string (n) 5.29, 193.5, 267.3, 271.2, 524.2, 617.7, 711.5, 711.20, 770.3, 793.2, 812.2, 812.3, 959.2 (v) 708.36, 812.4
string along 166.3, 356.14, 511.6
string along with 450.4
string alphabet 30.6
string bikini 5.29
string choir 711.2
stringed instrument 711.2
stringency 17.5, 144.9, 425.1, 885.1
stringent 17.14, 144.24, 425.6
stringer 555.4
stringhalt 85.41
stringiness 1049.1, 1062.2
stringing out 267.4, 856.1
string instrument 711.2
string musician 710.5
string out 267.6, 538.8, 812.5, 846.9, 856.4
string pulling 417.2
string quartet 708.18
strings 421.3, 710.12, 711.2, 894.3
strings attached 421.3
string-saver 635.3
string section 710.12
string theory 1018.1
string together 812.4
string to it, a 959.2
string up 604.17
stringy 271.7, 1049.4, 1062.12
striola 47.5
striolate 47.15
strip (n) 184.23, 267.2, 267.3, 271.4, 517.6, 737.21, 757.1 (v) 6.5, 6.7, 6.8, 255.10, 480.24, 798.4, 802.14, 909.19
strip away 6.5, 255.10
strip bare 6.5, 351.4, 480.24
strip city 230.1
strip clean 480.24
strip club 228.28
strip down 798.4
stripe (n) 47.5, 267.3, 517.6, 647.5, 767.4, 809.3, 902.8, 978.3 (v) 47.7, 517.19, 604.12
striped 47.15, 170.11
striped snake 174.6
stripes 604.4, 646.6
strip for action 405.13
striping 47.5, 517.6
stripling 302.1, 841.4
strip mall 736.2
strip mine 1058.6
strip mining 1058.8
strip naked 6.5
strip off 255.10
strip of office 447.4
strip of rank 447.3, 447.4
strip one of one's illusions 977.2
stripped 6.12, 473.7, 619.8
stripped bare 6.12
stripped down 798.9
stripped of 473.8
stripped of illusion 977.5
stripped of reputation 661.13
stripped to the buff 6.14
stripper 6.3, 705.3, 707.1, 802.7
stripping 6.1, 6.2, 351.1, 473.1, 473.2, 798.2, 802.3, 802.6, 909.4
stripping away 798.2
stripping bare 6.1, 351.1
stripping down 798.2, 802.6
stripping of rank 447.1
strip poker 758.4
strip-search 6.5
striptease 6.2
stripteaser 6.3, 705.3, 707.1
stripteuse 707.1
strip to the buff 6.7
stripy 47.15
strive 403.5, 457.13, 725.11
strive about 457.21
strive against 451.3, 451.4, 453.3
strive for 403.9, 457.20
strive to 403.8
strive with 457.17
striving (n) 380.1, 403.1 (a) 457.22, 725.17
strobe 704.18
strobe light 704.18, 1025.7, 1025.19
strobile 310.27
stroboscope 704.18
stroboscopic 1025.36
stroboscopic light 1025.7
stroke (n) 73.1, 85.6, 85.27, 96.5, 328.3, 403.2, 415.3, 509.6, 517.6, 671.5, 725.4, 748.2, 751.3, 830.3, 902.4, 917.6, 995.2 (v) 73.8, 95.11, 375.21, 387.16, 511.6, 1044.6
stroke above, a 249.12
stroke it 756.4
stroke of death 307.4
stroke of genius 375.9
stroke of lightning 1025.17
stroke of luck 1010.3
stroke of policy 415.3, 995.2
stroke of the hour 832.2
stroke of the pen 547.1
stroke of wit 489.7
stroke of work 725.4
stroke play 751.3
strokes 95.1, 511.1, 751.3, 901.1
stroking 73.2, 95.1, 511.1, 1044.3
stroll (n) 175.2, 177.10, 177.12 (v) 175.6, 177.23, 177.28
stroller 178.2, 179.6, 707.2
strolling (n) 177.8 (a) 175.10, 177.36, 177.37
strolling gait 177.12
strolling minstrel 710.14
strolling player 178.2, 707.2
strong 15.15, 17.13, 18.12, 68.7, 68.8, 69.10, 71.5, 83.12, 88.37, 247.6, 393.41, 524.30, 544.11, 763.7, 894.13, 1049.4
strong, the 15.6
strong argument 935.10
strong arm 18.1, 461.1, 1008.5
strong-arm (n) 906.5 (v) 15.12, 424.8 (a) 424.12
strongarm 643.6
strong arm, the 424.3
strong-armer 461.1
strong-arm man 15.7, 461.1, 593.4, 727.7
strong-arm tactics 424.3
strong as a horse 15.15, 83.12
strong as a lion 15.15
strong as an ox 15.15, 83.12
strong as brandy 15.15
strong as strong 15.15
strong bid 403.2
strongbox 386.6, 729.13
strong demand 421.1
strong drink 88.13
strong feeling 93.2
strong flair 413.4
strong flavor 68.1
strong-flavored 68.8
strong force 1038.6
strong hand 425.3
strongheaded 361.8
strongheadness 361.1
stronghold 460.6, 1009.1
strong horse 757.2
strong in 413.27, 928.19
strong interaction 1038.6
strong language 513.3, 544.3
strong liquor 88.13
strongly worded 334.9
strong man 15.6
strong market 737.1
strong-minded 359.15, 920.12
strong-mindedness 359.4
strong-nerved 129.2
strong nerves 129.1
strongness 68.3
strong point 413.4, 460.6, 866.1, 935.10
strong pull 725.1
strong relief 348.4
strong right arm 432.5
strong right hand 616.7
strong room 729.13
strongroom 386.6
strong safety 746.2
strong-scented 69.10
strong silent type 344.5
strong-smelling 69.10
strong suit 413.4
strong-tasting 68.8
strong waters 88.13
strong-willed 15.15, 359.15, 361.8
strong wind 318.11
strong woman 15.6
strontium 1038.5
strop (n) 271.4 (v) 285.7
strophe 720.10
stroppy 152.30
strown 771.9
struck all of a heap 122.9, 131.13
struck down 445.3
struck jury 596.5
struck with 104.29
struck with surprise 131.12
structural 266.6, 518.12, 523.19, 530.17, 808.15, 892.15
structural drag 184.27
structural engineer 1043.2
structural engineering 717.1, 1043.1
structural framework 266.2
structural gene 305.9
structural grammar 530.1
structural meaning 518.1
structural outline 801.4
structural polysaccharide 305.6
structure (n) 2.2, 228.5, 262.1, 266.1, 266.2, 294.1, 521.2, 530.2, 722.4, 796.1, 807.1 (v) 266.5, 796.3
structured 262.9, 266.6
structureless 263.4
structuring 266.1, 796.1, 808.1
strudel 10.41
struggle (n) 403.1, 457.1, 457.4, 725.3 (v) 403.5, 457.13, 725.11, 917.15, 1013.11
struggle against 451.4
struggle along 725.14
struggle for 403.9, 457.20
struggle on 725.14
struggler 461.1
struggle to the death 457.6
struggle up 193.11

struggle with 457.17
struggling 457.22, 725.17
strum 708.40
strummer 710.5
strumpet 562.11
strung out 25.8, 87.24, 267.8
strut (n) 177.12, 501.8 (v) 177.28, 454.5, 501.15
strut one's stuff 413.20, 501.16, 704.29
strutter 501.10
strutting (n) 501.8 (a) 501.23
St. Simeon Stylites 584.5
stub 89.5, 217.6, 256.1, 517.13, 820.2
stubbed 268.10
stubbiness 268.2
stubble 3.8, 256.1, 288.3, 391.4
stubbled 3.25, 288.9
stubbliness 3.1
stubbly 3.25, 288.9
stubborn 360.8, 361.8, 425.7, 454.7, 803.12, 1046.12, 1049.4
stubborn as a mule 361.8
stubborn fact 761.3
stubbornness 325.1, 327.2, 360.1, 361.1, 425.2, 803.3, 1046.3, 1049.1
stubby 268.10
stub one's toe 414.12
stub one's toe on 941.3
stub out 1022.7
stucco 295.25
stuccoed 295.31
stuccowork 295.1
stuck 800.14, 803.10, 855.16, 971.26, 1013.24, 1013.27
stuck fast (v) 453.4 (a) 855.16, 1013.27
stuck-in-the-mud 853.8
stuck on 104.30
stuck on oneself 140.12
stuck-up 140.11, 141.9, 157.8
stuck-upness 140.4
stuckupness 141.1
stuck with 643.8
stud (n) 75.4, 76.5, 76.8, 273.6, 283.3, 311.10, 517.7, 562.12, 757.2, 759.10 (v) 47.7, 288.4, 771.6
studbook 549.9, 554.9
studded 47.13, 283.17, 288.8, 288.9, 294.7, 498.11, 771.10, 884.9, 1025.39
student 572.1, 818.2, 929.3
student assistant 571.4
student glider 181.12
studentlike 572.12
studentship 572.2
student teacher 571.4
stud farm 1070.5
stud horse 757.2
studhorse 76.8, 311.10
studied 380.8, 533.9, 935.21
studiedness 533.3
studier 572.1
studio 197.6, 712.17, 739.1, 1034.6
studio apartment 228.13
studio audience 48.6
studio plant 1034.6
studious 570.17, 572.12, 928.21, 931.21, 983.17
studiousness 570.4, 983.3
stud muffin 75.4
stud poker 758.4, 759.10
study (n) 91.12, 197.6, 380.1, 541.6, 556.1, 568.8, 570.3, 712.9, 712.12, 739.7, 739.8, 928.10, 931.2, 931.3, 938.3, 983.3, 985.2, 1009.5 (v) 403.5, 541.11, 570.12, 931.12, 938.24, 983.8, 989.16
study for 570.15
study group 570.1
study hall 570.1
studying (n) 570.3 (a) 931.21, 983.17
study in still life 712.10
study of living things, the 1068.1
study of the past 719.1
study one's part 704.32
study to 403.8
study to be 570.15
study up 570.14
study up on 570.14
study with 570.11
stuff (n) 4.1, 196.5, 385.4, 745.3, 763.2, 767.2, 1052.2, 1054.1 (v) 8.19, 8.25, 196.7, 293.7, 397.10, 672.4, 794.7, 993.15, 994.4
stuff, the 18.2, 413.4
stuff and nonsense 520.2, 923.3
stuffed 259.13, 293.11, 397.13, 794.11, 993.20, 994.6
stuffed animal 743.16
stuffed eggs 10.26
stuffed shirt 501.9
stuffed to the gills 994.6
stuffed up 293.11, 993.20
stuff in 191.7
stuffiness 71.2, 117.1, 173.6, 361.2, 361.3, 500.6, 501.7, 842.3, 923.2, 980.1, 987.1, 1019.6
stuffing (n) 10.27, 191.2, 196.3, 254.4, 293.5, 397.3 (a) 672.6
stuffings 2.19, 207.4
stuff oneself 8.25, 672.4, 672.5
stuff that dreams are made of 299.1, 976.4
stuff the mind 570.6
stuff the mind with 989.17
stuff up 293.7
stuff with knowledge 568.11
stuffy 71.5, 117.6, 173.16, 361.9, 361.11, 500.19, 501.22, 842.17, 867.6, 980.10, 987.5, 1019.28
stuffy weather 1019.7
stultification 923.5
stultified 331.20
stultify 428.8, 900.7, 923.7
stultifying 428.11, 900.9
stultify oneself 414.14, 923.6
stultiloquence 520.2
stumble (n) 194.3, 410.3, 414.5, 917.8, 975.4 (v) 194.8, 362.6, 414.11, 525.8, 917.15, 975.9
stumble across 941.3
stumblebum 414.9
stumblebunny 414.9
stumble into 941.3
stumble on 186.7, 941.3
stumble upon 186.7
stumbling 525.13
stumbling block 1012.4
stumbling stone 1012.4
stumbling upon 941.1
stump (n) 256.1, 712.18, 793.3, 820.2, 901.13 (v) 175.7, 177.28, 543.9, 609.40, 610.13, 971.14, 1012.15
stump,the 543.1
stumped 971.26, 1013.24
stumper 522.8, 610.10, 938.10
stump excursion 609.13
stumpiness 268.2, 274.1
stumping 609.12
stumping tour 609.13
stump it 177.27
stump orator 543.6, 610.10
stump oratory 543.2
stumps 177.15
stump speaker 610.10
stump speaking 543.1
stump speech 543.2
stump the country 609.40
stump up 624.16
stumpy 265.12, 268.10, 274.7
stun 25.4, 49.5, 53.7, 94.8, 122.6, 127.17, 131.8
stung 96.23
stun gun 462.10, 462.22
stunned 25.7, 25.8, 49.6, 127.26
stunner 122.2, 1016.8
stunning 25.9, 30.11, 122.12, 127.28, 127.29, 131.11, 999.13, 1016.21
stunt (n) 328.3, 704.8 (v) 184.40, 268.6
stunted 258.13, 406.12, 795.4, 992.10
stuntedness 258.1, 274.1
stunt flier 185.1
stunt flying 184.13
stunting 184.13
stunt man 185.1
stuntman 576.1, 704.10
stunt person 492.7, 704.10
stuntwoman 185.2, 576.1, 704.10
stupa 272.6, 309.16, 549.12, 703.4
stupe (n) 86.33, 924.4 (v) 120.5
stupefaction 94.4, 122.1, 331.6
stupefied 25.7, 94.13, 122.9, 127.26
stupefied with boredom 118.12
stupefy 25.4, 94.8, 122.6, 127.17
stupefying 25.9, 127.28, 127.29, 870.14
stupefyingly boring 118.10
stupendous 122.10, 247.7, 257.20, 870.14
stupendousness 122.3, 247.1, 257.7, 870.2
stupid 922.15, 923.8
stupid grin 116.3
stupidhead 924.4
stupidheaded 922.17
stupidity 922.3, 923.1, 923.4, 975.5
stupidness 922.3
stupid person 924.2
stupid thing 923.4
stupor 22.6, 25.2, 92.19, 94.4, 331.6
stuporific 118.10
stuporose 22.21
stuporous 22.21, 331.20
stuporous melancholia 926.5
stuporousness 331.6
stuporous with boredom 118.12
sturdiness 15.1, 15.3, 763.1, 1049.1
sturdy 15.15, 15.18, 83.12, 763.7
sturdy as an ox 15.15
sturm and drang 418.2
stutter (n) 525.3 (v) 525.8
stuttering (n) 525.3, 847.2, 849.3 (a) 525.13, 847.5
Stuttgart pitch 709.4
St. Vitus's dance 85.25, 917.2
sty 80.11, 85.14, 85.37, 228.11, 1004.1
Stygian 682.8, 1027.13
Stygian creek 682.4
Stygian darkness 1027.1
Stygian gloom 1027.1
Stygian shore 307.3
style (n) 5.1, 33.3, 262.1, 310.28, 321.1, 371.5, 384.1, 413.1, 498.7, 527.3, 532.2, 578.1, 712.7, 713.8, 753.3, 754.3, 765.4, 809.3, 866.1 (v) 5.42, 527.11, 532.4
style-conscious 578.13
style-consciousness 578.3
styled 527.14, 532.5
Sty Leger 757.1
style guide 530.1
styleless 842.16
style of recipe 11.2
style of writing 532.2
styler 716.9, 717.6
style sheet 530.1
style sheet language 1042.13
style the hair 3.22
styling 527.2, 717.4
styling gel 1056.3
styling mousse 1056.3
stylish 5.46, 413.22, 578.12
stylishness 500.1, 578.2
stylist 532.3, 716.9, 717.6
stylistic 532.5
stylistic analysis 532.2
stylistics 532.2
stylite 584.5, 699.16
stylization 580.1
stylize 580.5
stylized 355.4, 580.7, 712.20
stylobate 901.6
stylographic 547.22
stylographical 547.22
stylography 547.3
stylus 50.11
stymie (n) 751.3 (v) 1012.13
stymied 1013.24
styptic (n) 260.6 (a) 260.11
styptic pencil 260.6
Styx 307.3, 682.4
suasibility 894.5
suasible 894.15
suasion 375.3, 894.1
suasive 375.29, 894.13
suave 287.10, 504.17

suaveness 504.5
suave-spoken 504.17
suavity 287.1, 504.5
sub (n) 10.32, 180.9, 571.5, 576.1, 745.2, 746.2, 862.2 (a) 250.6
subacid 67.6
subacidity 67.1
subacidulous 67.6
subaerial deposit 234.1
subahdar 575.12
subalpine 272.18
subaltern (n) 250.2, 575.17, 577.3 (a) 250.6
subaqueous 275.14
subassembly plant 739.3
subastral 234.4
subatomic 258.14, 1038.18
subatomic particle 258.8
subaudibility 52.1
subaudible 51.10, 52.16
subbase 901.8
subbasement 197.17
subcaste 617.2
subcategory 809.2
subclass 809.2, 809.5
subcommittee 423.2, 576.13
subconscious (n) 92.28, 919.3 (a) 92.42, 689.24
subconscious drive 934.2
subconscious knowledge 934.1
subconscious mind 92.28, 919.3
subconscious perception 934.1
subconscious self 865.5
subconscious urge 934.2
subcontinent 235.1
subcontract 437.5
subcontraoctave 709.9
subcutaneous (n) 91.17 (a) 2.27
subdeacon 699.4
subdeb 578.7
subdebutante 302.8, 578.7
subdiaconus 699.4
subdialect 523.7
subdiscipline 568.8, 724.4
subdivide 801.6, 802.18, 809.6, 875.4, 944.4
subdivided 802.20
subdivision 225.3, 793.1, 801.1, 802.1, 809.1, 809.2, 875.1
subdivisional 809.7
subdivisions 196.1
subdominant 709.15
subdual 411.1, 412.1, 428.2, 432.4, 670.2
subduct 255.9
subduction 255.1
subdue 51.9, 120.5, 412.10, 428.8, 432.9, 670.6, 670.7, 1047.6
subdued 35.22, 52.16, 52.17, 112.22, 344.10, 412.17, 428.14, 432.15, 433.15, 496.7, 670.11
subduedness 52.1, 344.3, 496.3
subduement 120.1
subduer 411.2
subduing (n) 411.1, 412.1 (a) 120.9, 670.14, 1047.16
subeditor 555.4
subfamily 523.1, 809.5
subfolder 1042.18
sub for 862.5
subforeman 574.2
subfusc 1027.15
subfuscous 1027.15
subgenus 809.5
subgroup 793.1, 809.2
subhead (n) 937.2 (v) 937.3
subheading 937.2
subhuman 144.26, 311.39
subjacency 274.1
subjacent 274.8
subject (n) 227.4, 432.7, 530.2, 568.8, 570.3, 708.24, 722.4, 726.1, 937.1, 938.19, 942.7 (v) 432.8 (a) 250.6, 432.13
subject case 530.9
subjected 432.14
subject for thought 931.7
subject heading 527.3, 809.2, 937.2
subjecthood 226.2, 432.2
subjection 250.1, 432.1, 433.1
subjective 92.40, 767.7, 919.7
subjective certainty 970.5
subjective idealism 1053.3
subjective inspection 931.6
subjective speculation 931.6
subjectivism 1053.3
subjectivity 767.1
subject line 937.2
subject matter 518.1, 937.1
subject-matter jurisdiction 594.1
subject of thought 937.1
subject oneself 652.3
subject to (v) 643.4 (a) 897.6, 959.9
subject to a fee 630.12
subject to a tax 630.12
subject to close scrutiny 938.25
subject to death 307.33
subjoin 253.4, 815.3
subjoinder 524.3
subjoined 253.9
sub judice 598.21, 958.8
subjugate 412.10, 432.8, 480.19, 612.15
subjugated 412.17, 432.14
subjugation 412.1, 432.1, 480.4
subjugator 411.2
subjunction 815.1
subjunctive 530.11
subkingdom 809.5
sublation 255.1
sublative 530.9
sublease (n) 469.1, 615.6 (v) 615.15, 615.16
subleased 615.20
subleaser 227.8
sublessee 227.8, 470.4
sublet (v) 615.15, 615.16 (a) 615.20
sublieutenant 575.17
sublimate (n) 192.8, 256.2 (v) 79.22, 106.8, 1067.8
sublimated 990.9
sublimation 79.4, 92.23, 990.3, 1067.5
sublime (v) 79.22, 1067.8 (a) 97.9, 247.9, 272.14, 544.14, 652.6, 662.18, 677.17, 912.9, 997.19, 1016.20
sublime, the 532.2
sublimeness 1016.5
sublime style, the 532.2
subliminal (n) 92.28 (a) 92.42, 934.6
subliminal self 92.28, 865.5
sublimity 247.2, 272.1, 544.6, 652.2, 662.5, 1016.5
sublineation 517.6
sublittoral 240.4
sublunar 234.4
submachine gun 462.10
submarine (n) 10.32, 180.9, 367.5 (a) 275.14
submarine badge 647.5
submarine canyon 240.5
submarine mountain 237.6
submariner 183.1
submediant 709.15
submerge 182.47, 194.6, 238.17, 367.7, 1065.14
submerged 32.5, 275.14, 519.5, 913.12, 1065.17
submerged coast 234.2
submerged in 898.5, 983.17
submerged mind 92.28
submergence 182.8, 194.2, 275.7, 367.2, 913.1
submergible 367.9
submerging 194.11
submerse 367.7
submersed 275.14, 1065.17
submersible (n) 180.9 (a) 367.9
submersion 238.6, 275.7, 367.2, 983.3, 1065.6
subminiature 258.12
submission 134.2, 155.2, 326.1, 433.1, 439.1, 441.1
submission to fate 134.2
submission to necessity 134.2
submission to the inevitable 134.2
submissive 134.10, 137.11, 138.13, 155.10, 326.3, 332.13, 432.16, 433.12, 441.4, 867.5, 1047.9
submissiveness 134.2, 137.1, 138.1, 155.2, 326.1, 433.3, 1047.2
submit 250.5, 326.2, 334.5, 371.19, 422.5, 433.6, 439.4, 439.5, 441.3, 1047.7
submittal 433.1
submit to 134.7, 433.9
submit to arbitration 727.9
submit to disgrace 512.8
submit to indignity 512.8
submit with a good grace 134.7
submultiple (n) 883.4 (a) 1017.23
subnormal 870.9, 922.22
subnormality 250.3, 870.1, 922.9
subnuclear 1038.18
subnuclear particle 1038.6
suborder 809.2, 809.5
subordinacy 250.1, 432.2
subordinary 647.2
subordinate (n) 250.2, 432.5, 577.1, 577.3, 768.2, 809.2 (v) 432.8, 808.11 (a) 250.6, 432.13, 768.4
subordinate clause 529.1
subordinated 432.14
subordinate oneself 652.3
subordinate role 432.2
subordinating conjunction 530.3
subordination 250.1, 432.2, 807.2, 808.3, 867.1
suborn 378.3, 886.11
subornation 378.1
subpanation 701.7
subpar 1000.9
subplot 706.3, 722.4
subpoena (n) 420.6, 598.2 (v) 420.11, 598.14
subrace 312.1
subrent 615.6
subrogate 862.5
subrogation 862.1
subroutine 1042.11
subscribe 449.14, 478.14, 617.15
subscriber 332.7, 347.11, 478.11
subscribership 332.4
subscribe to 332.8, 332.12, 438.9, 788.6
subscript 254.2, 817.1
subscription 332.4, 478.1, 478.6, 527.10
subscription book 554.5
subscription edition 554.5
subscription television 1035.1
subsense 519.2
subsequence 815.1, 835.1, 839.1
subsequent 815.4, 835.4
subserve 250.4, 384.7, 886.12
subservience 138.1, 250.1, 332.2, 432.2, 433.3
subservience to the facts 973.5
subserviency 138.1, 432.2
subservient 138.13, 250.6, 384.8, 387.21, 432.13, 433.12, 433.16, 449.20
subset 793.1, 809.2
subshell 1038.4
subside 172.5, 173.8, 194.6, 252.6, 297.15, 393.17
subsidence 173.3, 194.2, 194.4, 252.2
subsidiary (n) 768.2 (a) 387.21, 449.20, 478.26, 768.4
subsidiary office 739.7
subsidiary sense 519.2
subsiding (n) 172.2 (a) 173.12, 194.11, 252.11, 393.45
subsidization 385.1, 449.3, 478.8
subsidize 385.7, 449.12, 478.19, 624.19, 729.16, 901.21
subsidized 478.26
subsidizer 478.11
subsidy 385.1, 449.3, 478.8, 624.8, 729.2, 901.1
subsist 8.20, 256.5, 306.8, 385.12, 761.8, 827.6, 853.5
subsistence (n) 385.3, 449.3, 761.1 (a) 992.10
subsistence farming 1069.1
subsistence level 619.2
subsistent 761.13
subsistent form 932.2
subsist in 761.11
subsisting 761.13
subsoil 234.1

subsonic 50.17, 184.49
subsonic flight 184.1
subsonic jet 181.3
subsonics 50.6
subsonic speed 174.2
subspecialty 568.8
subspecies 312.1, 793.1, 809.5
substance 196.5, 244.1, 518.1, 557.2, 600.6, 618.1, 728.14, 761.2, 763.1, 763.2, 767.2, 792.6, 937.1, 997.6, 1052.2
substance abuse 87.1
substance metabolism 2.20
substance of life 919.5
substances 1054.1
substandard 108.9, 523.20, 1005.10
substandard language 523.6
substandard usage 523.6
substantial 257.16, 417.15, 518.10, 729.18, 761.15, 763.6, 767.9, 855.12, 894.13, 970.17, 973.14, 991.6, 997.17, 1045.12, 1052.10
substantialism 1052.6
substantiality 761.1, 763.1, 855.1, 970.4, 973.6, 991.2, 1052.1
substantialization 1052.8
substantialize 1052.9
substantially true 973.13
substantial meal 8.8
substantialness 763.1, 991.2
substantiatable 957.19
substantiate 334.6, 766.6, 942.8, 957.11, 1052.9
substantiated 957.20, 973.13
substantiating 334.8, 957.18
substantiation 334.3, 763.4, 957.4, 970.8, 1052.8
substantify 1052.9
substantival 530.5
substantive (n) 530.5 (a) 530.17, 763.6, 767.9, 997.23
substantive basis 600.6
substantive point 997.6
substituent 862.9
substitutable 862.10
substitute (n) 92.31, 576.1, 707.7, 745.2, 746.2, 817.4, 862.2 (v) 862.4 (a) 862.8
substituted 862.9
substitute for 576.14, 862.5
substitute teacher 571.5
substitution 92.23, 338.1, 862.1, 862.2
substitutional 862.9
substitutionary 862.9
substitutive 862.9
substrative 274.8
substratum 199.1, 274.4, 296.1, 901.6, 1052.2
substruction 266.3, 901.6
substructural 266.6
substructure 266.3, 901.6
subsume 772.4
subsumed 772.5
subsuming 796.4
subsumption 772.2
subsurface water 1065.3
subteens 301.2
subtenant 470.4
subtend 215.4
subterfuge 345.1, 346.1, 356.1, 356.6, 376.1, 415.3, 936.5
subterrane 275.2, 284.5
subterranean 275.13
subterranean river 238.1
subterranean water 1065.3
subterraneity 275.1
subterraneous 275.13
subtext 519.2
subtile 248.7, 764.6, 920.15, 944.7
subtility 270.4, 299.1, 764.1, 920.3
subtilization 299.2
subtilize 270.12, 299.3, 764.4, 944.4
subtilty 920.3
subtitle (n) 554.12, 937.2 (v) 937.3
subtle 35.22, 248.7, 270.16, 299.4, 339.12, 415.12, 495.11, 496.8, 764.6, 799.4, 920.15, 944.7, 973.17
subtle body 689.17
subtle color 35.3
subtle distinction 780.2, 944.3
subtle influence 894.1
subtleness 415.1
subtle odor 69.1
subtlety 299.1, 339.3, 415.1, 495.3, 496.1, 496.3, 764.1, 780.2, 799.1, 920.3, 936.1, 944.1, 973.5
subtle wit 489.1
subtonic 709.15
subtotal 253.2
subtract 255.9, 802.8, 1017.18
subtracted 222.11
subtraction 222.1, 252.1, 255.1, 802.1, 1017.2
subtractive 255.13, 1017.25
subtractive color 35.8
subtrahend 255.6
subtreasury 729.13
subtribe 809.5
subtropical 1019.24
subtropics 231.3, 1019.11
subungulate 311.4, 311.5
suburb 230.1
suburban 209.8, 230.11, 607.10, 1005.8
suburbanite 227.6
suburban market 733.3
suburbia 230.1, 230.6, 607.5, 1005.5
suburbs 209.1, 230.6
subvalent electrons 1033.3
subvariety 809.5
subvene 901.21
subvention (n) 385.1, 449.3, 478.8, 901.1 (v) 449.12
subventionize 449.12
subversion 205.2, 327.3, 395.3, 418.2, 645.7, 858.5, 860.1, 958.2
subversionary 395.26
subversive (n) 327.5, 357.11, 418.3, 611.12, 860.3 (a) 327.11, 395.26, 611.20, 645.22, 852.10, 860.5
subversiveness 327.3, 645.7
subversivism 645.7
subvert 205.6, 327.7, 393.15, 395.20, 852.7, 858.15, 958.5
subway 179.14, 284.5, 383.7
subzero 1023.14
subzero weather 1023.3
sucanat 66.3
succedaneum 862.2
succeed 407.4, 409.7, 411.3, 629.4, 704.28, 815.2, 817.5, 835.3, 862.5, 1010.7
succeed in 409.12
succeeding 166.5, 409.14, 815.4, 835.4
succeed to 479.7
succeed to the throne 417.14
succeed with 409.11
success 249.1, 407.1, 409.1, 409.6, 411.1, 704.4, 1010.1
successful 409.14, 411.7, 1010.12
successful advocate 600.8
successfulness 409.1
succession 417.12, 479.2, 560.4, 561.1, 629.2, 812.2, 815.1, 835.1, 862.1
successional 812.9
succession of thought 931.4
succession of time 821.4
successive 812.9, 815.4, 835.4
successiveness 812.1, 815.1
successless 410.18
successlessness 410.1
successor 166.2, 256.3, 479.5, 817.4, 835.2, 862.2
success story 409.3
succinct 268.8, 537.6, 974.6
succinctness 268.1, 537.1
succor (n) 86.1, 449.1, 449.3 (v) 449.11, 592.3
succorer 592.1
succubus 127.9, 680.6
succulence 63.1, 97.3, 1061.1, 1063.1
succulent (n) 310.4, 310.33 (a) 8.33, 63.8, 97.10, 983.19, 1061.4, 1063.6
succulent fruit 10.38
succumb 21.5, 25.5, 307.18, 395.23, 412.12, 433.6
succumb to 433.9
succussatory 916.20, 917.17
succussion 917.2
succussive 916.20, 917.17
such 784.3
such-and-such 528.2
such as 784.12
suchlike (n) 784.3 (a) 784.12
suchness 767.4
suck (n) 8.4, 88.7, 187.5 (v) 8.29, 75.22, 75.23, 187.12, 192.12
suck dry 387.16, 388.3, 480.24, 486.4
sucked dry 891.4
sucked into 898.5
sucker (n) 302.11, 310.20, 358.2, 733.4, 759.22, 924.4, 954.4 (v) 387.16
sucker for 101.5
suckering 356.9
sucker-punch 459.15
suck face 562.15
suck hind tit 432.12
suck in 8.29, 187.12, 377.5
sucking 187.5, 192.3
sucking face 562.2
sucking hind tit 432.14
sucking up 138.2
suck into 898.2
suckle 8.19, 8.29, 187.12, 449.16
suckling 302.9
suckling pig 311.9
suck off 75.22, 75.23
suck one's blood 388.3
suck out 192.12
suck the blood from 387.16
suck up 8.29, 187.12, 192.12
suck up to 138.9, 511.6, 587.12, 983.5
sucralose 66.2
sucrose 66.3
sucrovert 66.3
suction 187.5, 192.3, 894.2
sud 320.5
sudarium 79.10, 691.5
sudation 12.7
sudatorium 79.10
sudatory (n) 79.10 (a) 12.22, 13.7
sudden 131.10, 365.9, 401.10, 830.5
sudden change 852.2
sudden death 85.2, 307.4
sudden death overtime 749.3
sudden-death overtime 746.3
sudden development 131.2
sudden impulse 375.6
sudden infant death syndrome 85.2
sudden insight 928.2
suddenness 365.2, 401.2, 830.2
sudden pull 905.3
sudden thought 365.1
sudden turn 131.2
suddy 320.7
Sudoku 522.8, 522.9
sudor 12.7
sudoresis 12.7
sudoric 12.22
sudorific (n) 86.30 (a) 12.22, 1019.25
suds (n) 88.16, 320.2 (v) 320.5
sudsy 320.7
sue 440.10, 440.14, 562.21, 598.13
sue for 440.14
sue for divorce 566.5
suet 10.14
suety 1056.9
suffer 26.8, 85.46, 96.19, 134.5, 433.6, 443.10, 604.19, 831.8
sufferable 107.13
sufferance 134.1, 443.2
suffer an eclipse 34.2
suffer anguish 96.19
sufferer 85.43, 96.11
suffer for 604.19
suffer hanging 604.18
suffer hearing loss 49.4
suffering (n) 26.1, 96.5 (a) 26.9, 443.14
suffering angst 96.20
suffering dread 96.20
suffering from amnesia 990.9

suffering nausea 96.20
suffer loss 473.4
suffer memory loss 990.4
suffer misfortune 1011.10
suffer pangs of jealousy 153.3
suffer the consequences 604.19
suffer the penalty 604.19
suffice 107.6, 387.17, 991.4
suffice to oneself 430.20
sufficiency 18.2, 107.3, 991.1, 999.3
sufficient 107.11, 973.14, 991.6, 999.20
sufficient for 991.6
sufficientness 991.1
sufficing 107.11, 991.6
suffix (n) 254.2, 526.3, 817.1 (v) 253.4, 815.3
suffixal 526.22
suffixation 253.1, 526.3, 815.1
suffixed 815.4
sufflate 259.4
sufflated 259.13
sufflation 259.2
suffocate 307.23, 308.19, 395.15, 428.8, 1012.12, 1019.22
suffocated 428.14
suffocating (n) 428.2 (a) 69.10, 173.16, 1019.28
suffocation 307.5, 308.6, 395.6
suffragan 616.6
suffrage 371.6, 476.1, 609.17, 696.4
suffragette 77.5, 609.17, 642.5
suffragettism 609.17
suffragism 609.17
suffragist (n) 609.17, 642.5 (a) 609.43
suffuse 221.7, 797.11
suffused 221.15, 1025.30
suffused with light 1025.39
suffusing 221.14
suffusion 139.5, 221.3, 797.2
suffusive 221.14
Sufi 675.23
Sufism 675.13
sugar (n) 7.5, 66.2, 66.3, 87.10, 104.10, 562.6, 728.2 (v) 66.4
sugar beet 66.3
Sugar Bowl 746.1
sugar-bun 104.10
sugar cane 66.3
sugarcoat 66.4
sugar-coated 66.5
sugarcoating 66.2
sugar daddy 104.12, 478.11
sugared 66.5
sugar-free 7.21
sugar-free diet 7.13
sugariness 66.1
sugaring off 66.2
sugar invert 66.3
sugar loaf 66.2
sugar lump 66.2
sugar-making 66.2
sugar off 66.4
sugar refinery 739.3
sugar substitute 66.2
sugary 66.5
suggest 133.12, 422.5, 439.5, 517.17, 518.8, 519.4, 551.10, 784.7, 957.8, 989.19
suggested 519.7
suggestibility 894.5
suggestible 894.15
suggestion 92.26, 248.4, 422.1, 439.2, 512.4, 517.3, 517.9, 519.2, 551.4, 797.7, 894.1, 951.5
suggest itself 931.18
suggestive 517.23, 518.10, 519.6, 544.10, 666.7, 957.16, 989.21
suggestiveness 133.6, 518.5
suggestive of 784.10
suicidal 96.26, 112.22, 308.24, 395.26, 923.10
suicidal despair 96.6, 112.3
suicide 307.5, 308.5
suicide attack 459.1
suicide-bomb 308.17, 459.23
suicide bomber 671.9
suicide bombing 308.5, 459.7
suicide king 758.2
suicide pact 308.5
suicide plane 181.9
sui generis 249.15, 337.5, 780.8, 870.10
suing 562.7
suit (n) 5.6, 440.2, 440.5, 562.7, 574.3, 598.1, 599.1, 696.4, 752.1, 758.2, 758.3, 770.12, 997.9 (v) 5.41, 95.6, 107.6, 405.8, 788.8, 867.3, 991.4
suitability 371.11, 405.4, 496.2, 637.2, 788.5, 843.1, 995.1
suitable 371.24, 496.9, 637.3, 788.10, 843.9, 991.6, 995.5
suitableness 405.4
suitable occasion 843.3
suitable time 843.3
suit and service 326.1
suit at law 598.1
suitcase 195.1
suite 228.13, 229.1, 769.6, 770.12
suited 405.17, 413.24, 788.10
suitedness 405.4
suite of applications 1042.11
suite of rooms 228.13
suiting 788.10
suit in law 598.1
suit of armor 460.3
suit of clothes 5.6
suit one down to the ground 107.6
suit oneself 430.20
suit one's purpose 387.17
suitor 100.12, 104.11, 104.12, 440.7, 598.11, 599.5
suit service 326.1
suit the action to the word 328.7
suit the occasion 995.3
suit the time 843.6
suit up 5.43
sulcate 290.4
sulcated 290.4
sulcation 290.1
sulcus 290.1
sulfa 86.29
sulfacid 1060.3
sulfa drug 86.29
sulfanilamide 86.29
sulfate (n) 890.4, 1058.1 (v) 1060.8
sulfate pulp 1063.2
sulfathiazole 86.29
sulfatize 1060.8
sulfide 1058.1
sulfite pulp 1063.2
sulfonamide 86.29
sulfonate 1060.8
sulfur 7.11
sulfur-colored 43.4
sulfur dioxide 71.3
sulfuric 1058.15
sulfurous 71.5, 682.8, 1058.15
sulfur-yellow 43.4
sulk (n) 325.1 (v) 110.14
sulker 110.11
sulkiness 108.1, 110.8, 112.8, 325.1, 361.1, 361.3
sulks 110.10, 112.6, 325.1
sulky 108.7, 110.24, 112.25, 325.5, 361.8, 361.11
sullage 80.9, 1020.16
sullen 38.9, 110.24, 112.25, 325.5, 361.8, 361.11, 583.5
sullen looks 110.9
sullenness 38.2, 110.8, 112.8, 325.1, 361.1, 361.3, 583.1
sullen rabies 926.6
sullens 110.10
sullied 80.21, 665.23
sulliedness 665.1
Sullivanian psychology 92.2
sully 80.16, 80.17, 512.10, 654.10, 661.9, 665.20
sultan 575.9
sultana 10.30
sultanate 232.1, 417.8
sultanship 417.8
sultriness 1019.6
sultry 666.9, 1019.28
sultry weather 1019.7
sum (n) 244.1, 244.2, 253.2, 518.1, 557.2, 728.13, 792.2, 1017.6 (v) 253.6, 1017.18, 1017.19
sum and substance 196.5, 518.1, 557.2, 792.2, 792.3
Sumerology 842.4
sumless 823.3
summariness 268.1, 537.1, 845.3
summarization 268.3
summarize 268.6, 557.5, 849.8, 1017.19
summary (n) 268.3, 557.2, 598.8, 849.2, 1017.11 (a) 268.8, 537.6, 845.9
summary court-martial 595.4
summary execution 604.6
summary justice 649.1
summary negative 442.2
summate 1017.19
summation 253.2, 268.3, 557.2, 598.8, 1017.6, 1017.11
summational 253.8
summative 253.8
summer (n) 313.3, 1019.7 (v) 313.8, 821.6 (a) 313.9
summer course 568.8
summer day 1019.8
summer heat 1019.5
summerhouse 228.12, 1069.11
summer lightning 1025.17
summerlike 44.4, 313.9
summerly 313.9
summer-session course 568.8
summer soldier 357.8
summer solstice 313.3, 313.7
summer stock 704.1
summer theater 704.1
summertide 313.3
summer time 832.3
summertime 313.3
summerwood 1054.3
summery 44.4, 313.9, 1019.24
summing 1017.11
summing up 598.8, 849.2, 1017.11
summit 198.2, 237.6, 249.3, 541.5, 794.5, 1002.3
summit, the 997.8
summital 198.11
summit conference 541.5
summitry 541.5
summon 377.6, 420.11, 440.13, 615.17, 690.11, 770.17
summoner 420.7
summon forth 192.14, 420.11
summons (n) 420.5, 440.4, 517.16, 598.2, 615.7 (v) 420.11, 598.14
summons of death 307.1
summon spirits 690.11
summon up 105.12, 192.14, 375.13, 420.11, 986.15, 989.9
summon up courage 492.12
sumo 457.10
sum of things 1073.1
sump 80.12, 239.5, 241.1, 243.1, 284.4
sumpter 311.13, 311.15
sumpter horse 311.13
sumpter mule 311.15
sumption 935.7
sumptuary 728.30
sumptuary law 444.1
sumptuary ordinance 444.1
sumptuosity 632.1
sumptuous 501.21, 632.11
sumptuousness 501.5, 632.1
sum total 792.2
sum up 268.6, 849.8, 1017.19
sum up one's case 598.19
sun (n) 824.2, 1026.1, 1073.13 (v) 1020.19, 1066.6
sunbaked 1019.24, 1066.9
sunbath 91.4
sunbathe 1019.22, 1020.19
sunbeam 1025.10
Sunbelt 231.7
sunblind 1028.1
sunblock 1056.3
sunbreak 1025.10
sunburn (n) 1019.12, 1020.6 (v) 40.2
sunburned 40.4, 41.9, 1020.30
sunburst 1025.10
suncatcher 1028.4
sundae 10.47
sun dance 701.9
Sunda Trench 275.5
Sunday (n) 20.5, 701.12, 832.4 (v) 20.9

Sunday best 5.10
Sunday brunch 8.6
Sunday clothes 5.10
Sunday drive 177.7
Sunday driver 175.5, 178.10
Sunday-go-to-meeting clothes 5.10
Sunday-go-to-meetings 5.10
Sunday painter 998.10
Sunday paper 555.2
Sunday school 567.8
sunder 395.17, 566.5, 771.4, 802.11
sunderance 802.2
sundered 224.7
sundial 832.6
sun dog 1025.14
sundown 315.2
sundowner 88.9, 178.3, 660.2
sun-dried 1066.9
sundries 735.6, 770.13, 797.6
sun-dry 1020.19, 1066.6
sundry 783.4, 797.14, 884.7
sunfisher 311.10, 366.4
sunglasses 5.31, 29.3, 1028.2
sun helmet 1008.3
sunk 284.16, 393.29, 913.12
sunken 275.14, 284.16, 913.12
sunken part 284.6
sunk fence 290.2
sunk in oblivion 990.8
sunk relief 715.3
sunless 1027.13
sunlessness 1027.1
sunlight 1025.10, 1073.13
sunlit 1025.39
sun lounge 197.5
Sunna 683.6
Sunni (n) 675.23 (a) 675.31
Sunni Muslim 687.4
sunniness 97.4, 109.1
sunning 1066.3
Sunnism 675.13
Sunnite (n) 675.23 (a) 675.31
sunny 97.11, 109.11, 124.11, 1019.24, 1025.30
sunny side 97.4
sunny-side up 10.26
sunny weather 1019.7
sun oneself 1020.19
sun parlor 197.5
sunporch 197.5
sunproof 1028.7
sunray 171.2
sunrise 161.3, 314.2
sunrise watch 825.3
sunroof 1028.4
sunroom 197.5
sunscald 1020.6
sunscreen 1028.4
sunset 34.1, 161.3, 315.2
sunset glow 1025.2
sunset of one's days 303.5
sunshade 295.7, 1028.1
sunshine 87.10, 95.2, 1010.4, 1025.10, 1073.13
sunshine-yellow 43.4
sunshiny 1019.24, 1025.30
sunshiny weather 1019.7
sun shower 316.1
sun spark 1025.10
sun specs 29.3
sunspot 1073.13
sunspot cycle 1073.13
sunstroke 85.28
suntan 40.2, 1020.19
suntan lotion 1056.3
suntanned 40.3
sunup 314.2
sun worship 697.1
sun-worship 1020.19
sun worshiper 697.4
sup (n) 8.4, 62.2, 88.7, 248.4 (v) 8.21, 8.29, 62.7, 88.24
supe 707.7
super (n) 554.4, 707.7 (a) 249.12, 999.13, 999.15
superability 966.2
superable 966.7
superabound 910.4, 993.8
superabundance 247.3, 538.2, 890.1, 991.2, 993.2
superabundant 247.8, 538.11, 884.9, 890.9, 991.7, 993.19
superadd 253.4, 253.5
superadded 253.9, 768.4
superaddition 253.1, 254.4, 768.2
superager 882.7
superaltar 703.12, 901.14
superannuate (v) 390.8, 390.9, 447.4, 448.2, 842.9, 909.19 (a) 390.10
superannuated 390.10, 448.3, 837.10, 842.13
superannuation 303.5, 390.1, 447.2, 448.1, 842.3
superb 247.9, 501.21, 999.15
superbazooka 1074.10
superbia 141.1
superbness 999.2
Super Bowl 746.1
Super Bowl championship 746.1
supercalifragilisticexpialidocious 122.10
supercalifratilistic 122.10
supercargo 180.1, 574.1
supercharge 794.7, 993.15
supercharged 794.12, 993.20
supercharger 756.1
superchilled 1023.14
superchip 1042.3
supercilious 141.13, 157.8
superciliousness 141.5, 157.1
supercity 230.1
superclass 809.5
supercluster 1073.5
supercoil 305.9
supercomputer 1042.2
superconducting magnet 907.3
superconductivity 1032.14
superconductor 1032.14
super-cooled 1024.13
supercooled 1023.14
super-cooling 1024.1
supercurious 981.5
superdelegate 371.7, 609.28
super-duper 999.13
super-easy 1014.13
superego 92.28, 636.5, 865.5
Super-8 714.10
supereminence 662.5, 999.2
supereminent 249.14, 662.18, 999.15
supererogation 993.6
supererogative 993.17
supererogatory 253.10, 993.17
superessive 530.9
superexcellence 999.2
superexcellent 999.15
superfamily 809.5
superfancy 501.21
superfetate (v) 78.11 (a) 78.18
superfetation 78.4, 253.1
superficial 33.11, 117.6, 158.10, 206.7, 248.6, 276.5, 401.9, 580.7, 922.20, 930.14, 992.9, 998.19
superficial extension 158.1
superficiality 33.2, 117.1, 206.1, 276.1, 922.7, 930.5, 984.1, 998.3
superficially sound 936.10
superficial soundness 936.1
superficies 33.2, 206.2, 276.1
superfine 501.21, 999.15
superfineness 999.2
superfluity 247.3, 256.4, 498.3, 538.2, 768.2, 993.4
superfluous 253.10, 256.7, 391.9, 768.4, 993.17
superfluousness 391.1, 768.2, 993.4
superflux 538.2, 993.2
super G 753.3
supergalaxy 1073.6
super giant slalom 753.3
super giant slalom course 753.1
supergovernment 612.6
supergrass 87.18
supergravity 297.5
superheat (n) 1019.1 (v) 1020.17
superheated 1020.29
superheated air 1019.9
superheatedness 1019.1
superheating 1020.1
superheavy element 1060.2
superhelix 305.9
superhero 15.6, 662.9, 786.4
superheterodyne 1034.28
superheterodyne circuit 1034.9
superhigh frequency 1034.12
superhuman 677.16, 870.15
superhumanity 870.7
superimpose 295.19
superimposed 295.36
superimposition 295.1
superimpregnated 78.18
superimpregnation 78.4
superincumbence 295.1
superincumbency 297.7
superincumbent 202.11, 295.36, 297.17
superinduce 886.11
superinfect 85.51
superintend 573.10
superintendence 573.2, 573.4
superintendency 573.4
superintendent (n) 574.2, 1008.15 (a) 573.13
superior (n) 249.4, 575.3 (a) 141.9, 247.10, 249.12, 272.19, 417.15, 997.17, 999.14
superior court 595.2
superioress 699.17
superiority 18.1, 247.1, 249.1, 417.6, 814.1, 870.1, 910.1, 997.1, 999.1
superiority complex 92.22
superior planet 1073.9
superjoined 253.9
super-jumbo 257.16
superjunction 253.1
superlative (n) 355.1, 999.8 (a) 247.12, 249.13, 272.14, 355.4
Superman 15.6
superman 249.4, 997.10
supermarket 736.1
supermassive black hole 1073.8
supermicrocomputer 1042.2
superminicomputer 1042.2
supernal 272.14, 272.15, 681.12
supernatant 298.14
supernational 312.16
supernatural 677.16, 689.23, 870.15, 988.7, 1053.7
supernatural, the 689.2, 870.7
supernatural being 677.1, 678.5
supernaturalism 689.2, 870.7, 1053.1
supernaturalist 689.11
supernaturality 870.7
supernaturalness 870.7
supernatural virtues 653.3
supernature 870.7
supernormal 870.15
supernormalness 870.7
supernova 1073.8
supernova remnant 1073.8
supernumerary (n) 707.7, 768.2 (a) 253.10, 768.4, 993.18
superorder 809.5
superordinate 809.2
superordination 807.2, 808.3
superpatriot 591.3, 980.5
superpatriotic 591.4, 980.12
superpatriotism 591.2, 980.4
superphosphate 890.4
superphysical 870.15
superphysicalness 870.7
superpose 253.4, 295.19
superposed 253.9
superposition 253.1, 295.1
superpower 232.1, 894.6
super-pumper 1022.3
superrefraction 1036.12
supersaturate 993.15, 994.4
supersaturated 993.20, 994.6
supersaturation 993.3, 994.1
superscribe 547.19, 553.13
superscript 254.2
superscription 553.9, 937.2
supersecret 345.11
supersedable 862.10
supersede 862.5
superseded 390.10
superseder 862.2
superseding 862.1
supersedure 862.1
supersensible 689.24, 870.15
supersensible, the 689.2, 870.7
supersensibleness 870.7
supersensitive 24.12
supersensitivity 24.3
supersensual 689.24, 870.15
supersession 862.1

supersessive 862.9
supersize (v) 247.5 (a) 247.7
supersized 247.7
supersmart card 622.3
supersonic 50.17, 174.16, 184.49
Supersonic Age 824.6
supersonic flight 184.1, 184.9
supersonic flow detection 1041.7
supersonic jet 181.3
supersonics 50.6
supersonic speed 174.2
supersonic transport 181.3
superspecies 809.5
super speedway 756.1
superstar (n) 249.4, 409.6, 413.14, 662.9, 707.6, 997.10, 999.6 (a) 249.14
superstardom 997.2
superstition 954.3
superstitious 954.8
superstitiousness 954.3
superstore 736.1
superstorm 105.9
superstratum 198.1, 206.2, 296.1
superstring theory 1018.1
superstructural 266.6
superstructure 266.2
supersubtle 495.12
supersubtlety 495.4
supersymmetry theory 1038.2
supertanker 180.1
supertonic 709.15
supertransuranic element 1060.2
superunified theory 1018.1
superuser 866.3
supervene 253.7, 835.3
supervenience 835.1
supervenient 768.4
supervention 835.1
supervise 417.13, 573.10, 612.11
supervising 573.13
supervision 573.2, 612.1
supervisor 574.2, 575.16
supervisorship 417.7, 573.4
supervisory 573.13, 612.18
supervisory control 1041.3
superweed 87.18
superwoman 77.5, 997.10
supinate 205.5, 913.5, 913.11
supination 205.1, 913.3
supine 94.13, 201.8, 274.7, 331.20, 433.12
supineness 94.4, 201.2, 274.1, 331.6, 433.1
supper 8.6
supper club 88.20
suppertime 315.2
supplant 447.4, 862.5
supplantation 447.2, 862.1
supplanter 862.2
supplanting 447.2, 862.1
supple (v) 1047.6 (a) 363.10, 413.25, 854.6, 1047.9
supplement (n) 191.2, 254.1, 768.2, 817.1 (v) 253.5
supplemental 253.10, 768.4
supplementary 253.10, 768.4
supplementary reserves 461.25
supplementation 253.1, 254.1
supplement one's income 635.4
suppleness 854.1, 1047.2
suppletion 253.1
suppliant (n) 440.7, 696.9 (a) 440.16, 696.16
supplicant (n) 440.7, 696.9 (a) 440.16, 696.16
supplicate 440.11, 696.13
supplicating 440.16
supplication 440.2, 696.4
supplicative 440.16
supplicator 696.9
supplicatory 440.16, 696.16
supplied 385.13
supplied with drugs 87.25
supplier 385.6
supplies 10.5, 385.2, 386.1
supply (n) 384.2, 385.1, 386.2, 1054.1 (v) 385.7, 405.8, 478.15
supply base 386.6
supply chain 991.3
supply clergy 699.2
supply depot 386.6
supplying 385.1, 478.1
supplying electricity 1032.24
supply line 385.1
supply minister 699.2
supply of short-term funds 728.16
supply on hand 386.1
supply preacher 699.2
supply-side economics 731.7, 731.11
support (n) 10.3, 121.4, 332.1, 384.2, 386.2, 397.1, 449.1, 449.3, 449.8, 450.1, 478.8, 509.1, 616.9, 624.8, 707.7, 729.2, 901.1, 901.2, 957.4 (v) 15.13, 121.6, 124.9, 134.5, 332.12, 385.7, 397.8, 449.12, 478.19, 492.15, 509.11, 592.3, 600.10, 609.41, 624.19, 626.7, 704.30, 729.16, 901.21, 957.11, 1008.19
supportability 957.7
supportable 107.13, 957.19
supported 509.19, 901.24
supporter 166.2, 202.5, 221.5, 332.6, 460.7, 478.11, 588.1, 616.9, 729.10, 901.2
support fleet 461.27
support group 449.2
supporting 199.8, 509.17, 592.4, 901.23, 957.18
supporting actor 616.6, 706.4, 707.7
supporting actress 706.4, 707.7
supporting cast 707.7, 707.11
supporting character 704.10
supporting evidence 957.4
supporting instrumentalist 616.6
supporting player 616.6, 706.4
supporting role 704.10
supportive 121.13, 124.12, 587.21, 901.23, 957.18
supportive relationship 901.1
supportive therapy 901.1
support life 306.11
support oneself 385.12
support service 731.6
support services 449.3, 901.1
support troops 461.20
supposable 951.15, 986.26
supposal 935.7, 951.3
suppose 519.4, 946.8, 951.10, 953.11, 968.5, 986.14
supposed 519.7, 951.14
supposer 951.8
supposing 951.3
supposition 519.2, 932.1, 947.1, 951.3, 952.2, 953.6
suppositional 951.14, 971.17
supposititious 354.26, 951.14, 976.9, 986.19
supposititiousness 951.6
suppositive 951.14
suppress 106.8, 345.8, 395.15, 412.10, 428.8, 432.9, 444.3, 474.5, 612.15, 670.6, 670.8, 1012.10
suppressed 344.10, 345.11, 412.17, 428.14, 432.14, 990.9
suppressed desire 92.24
suppression 92.24, 344.3, 345.3, 395.6, 428.2, 432.4, 444.1, 474.1, 990.3, 1012.1
suppressive 417.16, 428.11, 444.6, 1012.17
suppurate 12.15, 393.22
suppurated 2.33
suppurating 2.33, 393.40
suppuration 2.24, 12.6, 85.37, 393.2, 1061.1
suppurative 2.33, 12.21, 393.40
supralittoral 240.4
supramundane 870.15
supranational 312.16
supranational government 612.6
supranatural 870.15
supranaturalism 689.2, 870.7
supranature 870.7
suprapartisan leadership 609.3
suprasegmental 524.6
suprasegmental phoneme 524.6
supremacy 249.3, 417.6, 894.1, 997.1, 999.2
supreme 18.13, 198.11, 249.13, 413.22, 417.15, 612.17, 677.17, 997.24, 999.16
Supreme Being 677.2
Supreme Court 613.2
supreme principle 677.7
supreme principle of pure reason 932.2
supreme soul 677.7
Supreme Soul, the 677.3
supremist 249.4, 417.10
surbase 901.8
surcease 20.2, 120.2, 857.1
surcharge (n) 297.7, 632.5, 993.3 (v) 628.10, 632.7, 993.15
surcharged 993.20
surcingle 901.18
surcoat 5.13
surd (n) 524.12, 883.4 (a) 49.6, 524.30, 1017.23
surdimutism 49.1
surdomute 49.2
sure 130.11, 438.11, 644.19, 953.21, 957.16, 963.15, 970.13, 970.17, 970.21
sure as can be 970.14
sure as death 963.15, 970.14
sure as death and taxes 963.15, 970.14
sure as fate 963.15, 970.14
sure as God made little green apples 970.14
sure as hell 970.14
sure as shooting 970.14
sure as the devil 970.14
sure bet 409.2, 970.2, 972.8
sure card 970.2
sure-enough 970.13, 973.13, 973.15
surefire 409.14, 970.17
sure-fire proposition 409.2
surefooted 413.23
sure loser 1011.7
sureness 644.6, 953.1, 963.7, 970.1, 970.5
sure of oneself 970.21
sure sign 517.1, 957.3
sure success 409.2
sure thing 409.2, 759.3, 970.2, 972.8
surety 438.1, 438.2, 438.6, 953.1, 970.1, 970.5, 1007.1
sure winner 411.2
surf (n) 238.14, 320.2, 916.4 (v) 177.35, 182.13, 1042.21
surface (n) 158.1, 198.1, 206.2, 276.1, 294.1, 748.1 (v) 31.4, 182.47, 186.6, 190.11, 193.9, 295.22, 348.6, 348.7, 351.8 (a) 33.11, 158.10, 206.7, 276.5, 580.7, 992.9
surface appearance 33.2
surface cooler 1024.3
-surfaced 294.5
surfaced 295.31
surface-effect ship 179.22
surface extension 158.1
surface mail 553.4
surface measure 300.4
surface resistance 1032.13
surface-scratching 930.5
surface show 33.2
surface structure 530.2
surface texture 294.1
surface-to-air missile 462.18
surface-to-surface missile 462.18
surface wave 916.4
surface wind 318.1
surfacing (n) 182.8, 190.1, 193.1, 199.3 (a) 190.18
surfboard 180.11
surfboarding 182.11
surf bum 178.3
surfeit (n) 993.3, 994.1 (v) 794.7, 993.15, 994.4
surfeited 794.11, 993.20, 994.6
surfeitedness 994.2
surfeiter 994.3
surfeiting 994.7
surfer 760.2, 1042.19
surfer shorts 5.18, 5.29
surfing 182.11, 760.2
surf shorts 5.29
surge (n) 53.1, 193.1, 238.4, 238.14, 251.1, 770.4, 915.2, 916.4 (v) 53.7, 190.13, 193.8, 238.16, 238.20, 238.22, 770.16, 915.11

surge back 238.16
surge of emotion 105.2
surge of sound 53.1
surgeon 90.5
surgery 90.2, 91.19, 197.25, 802.2
surgical 90.15
surgical diathermy 91.5
surgical intervention 91.19
surgical measure 91.19
surgical operation 91.19
surgical strike 459.1
surgical technique 91.19
surgical treatment 91.19
surging 238.24
surgy 238.24, 281.10
surliness 110.8, 505.3
surly 110.24, 505.7
surmisable 951.15
surmise (n) 951.3, 951.4 (v) 951.10, 953.11
surmiser 951.8
surmount 193.11, 193.12, 198.10, 272.11, 411.5, 412.7
surmountability 966.2
surmountable 966.7, 1006.16
surmounting 198.12
surname 527.5
surpass 249.6, 249.10, 993.9, 999.11
surpassing 122.11, 247.12, 249.12, 999.16
surpassingness 122.3
surplice 702.2
surplus (n) 255.8, 256.4, 910.1, 993.5 (v) 909.19 (a) 253.10, 256.7, 993.18
surplusage 256.4, 993.5
surplusing 909.5
surprisal 131.2, 459.2
surprise (n) 122.1, 131.2, 459.2 (v) 122.6, 131.7, 459.14
surprise attack 459.2
surprised 122.9, 131.12, 406.8
surprise ending 131.2
surprise package 131.2
surprise party 131.2
surprise quiz 938.2
surpriser 131.2
surprising 122.12, 131.11, 830.5
surreal 870.11, 976.9
surrealistic film 706.1
surrebut 939.5
surrebuttal 939.2
surrebutter 939.2
surrejoin 939.5
surrejoinder 939.2
surrender (n) 370.3, 433.2, 468.1, 475.1, 478.1, 629.1 (v) 16.9, 370.7, 433.8, 468.2, 475.3, 478.13, 629.3
surrendered 475.5
surrender one's life 307.18
surreptitious 345.12, 346.14, 356.22
surreptitiousness 345.4, 356.3
surrogacy 862.1
surrogate 92.31, 576.1, 862.2
surrogate motherhood 560.3
surrogate parent 560.8
surround (n) 209.1, 209.2, 223.1, 766.2, 901.10 (v) 158.9, 207.5, 209.6, 210.4, 211.8, 212.5, 280.10, 295.20, 459.19, 914.5
surrounded 209.10, 210.6
surrounding (n) 209.5 (a) 209.8, 212.11, 766.8
surrounding conditions 766.2
surroundings 209.1, 223.1, 228.18
surround sound 50.11
surveillance 27.6, 339.4, 346.3, 573.2, 938.9
survey (n) 27.6, 31.3, 300.1, 556.1, 557.1, 770.1, 938.3, 938.14 (v) 27.14, 159.11, 300.10, 556.5, 938.24, 938.29, 983.8, 1043.4
surveyed 300.13
surveying 159.8, 300.1
surveyor 300.9, 574.2, 938.18
surveyor's compass 574.9
surveyor's measure 300.4
survivability 827.1
survival 256.1, 827.1, 842.6, 856.1
survival kit 405.3
survival of the fittest 861.4
survive 256.5, 306.11, 385.12, 396.20, 827.6, 827.8, 839.7, 856.4, 856.5
surviving 256.7
survivor 256.3, 306.4
survivors' accounts 719.1
Surya 1073.14
susceptibility 18.2, 24.2, 93.1, 93.4, 104.2, 570.5, 894.5, 896.1, 897.2, 1006.3, 1047.2
susceptible 24.11, 93.20, 570.18, 894.15, 897.5, 1006.15, 1047.9
susceptible prone to 897.6
susceptive 24.11
susceptive to 897.6
susceptivity 24.2, 897.2
sushi 10.24
sushi bar 8.17
sus linguae 975.4
suspect (n) 599.6, 938.19 (v) 153.3, 951.10, 953.11, 955.6 (a) 955.10, 955.12, 971.17
suspected 955.12
suspecting 494.9, 955.9, 956.4
suspectitiousness 153.2
suspend 120.6, 202.8, 445.2, 447.4, 846.9, 857.10, 909.19
suspended 173.14, 202.9, 390.12, 813.4
suspended animation 25.2, 331.1
suspended cadence 709.23
suspender 202.5
suspenders 202.5
suspend judgment 979.7
suspend operations 20.8
suspense 126.1, 130.3, 173.4, 202.1, 971.1
suspenseful 105.30, 126.7, 130.12, 971.18
suspensefulness 971.1
suspension 20.2, 120.2, 202.1, 331.1, 390.2, 445.1, 447.2, 709.2, 773.2, 813.2, 846.2, 857.3, 909.5, 1064.3
suspension bridge 383.9
suspension of civil rights 458.9
suspension of disbelief 953.1
suspension of hostilities 465.5
suspensive 105.30
suspensive veto 444.2, 613.7
suspensory 901.23
suspensory veto 444.2, 613.7
suspicion 153.2, 248.4, 258.7, 494.2, 551.4, 797.7, 934.3, 951.5, 955.2, 956.1
suspicion of a suspicion, the 248.5
suspicious 153.5, 494.9, 645.16, 955.9, 955.10, 956.4, 971.17
suspiciousness 153.2, 494.2, 955.2, 956.1
suspiration 2.21
sussed 24.11
sussultatory 916.20
sustain 7.17, 8.18, 15.13, 134.5, 298.8, 397.8, 449.12, 449.16, 600.10, 827.6, 831.8, 856.4, 901.21, 957.11
sustainable 396.25, 957.19
sustainable energy 397.1
sustainable living 397.1
sustain a part 704.30
sustained 847.5, 853.7, 856.7, 901.24
sustained action 856.1
sustained activity 856.1
sustained note 709.14
sustainer 616.9, 901.2, 1034.18
sustaining (n) 901.1 (a) 901.23
sustaining pedal 54.5
sustaining program 1034.18
sustainment 449.3, 847.2, 901.1
sustenance 7.1, 10.1, 10.3, 449.3, 856.1, 901.1
sustentation 449.3, 901.1
sustentative 901.23
susurrant 52.18
susurrate 52.10, 525.9
susurration 52.4, 525.4
susurrous 52.18
susurrus 52.4
sutler 385.6
sutra 419.2, 974.1
Sutta Pitaka 683.9
suttee 308.5, 696.7, 1020.5
sutteeism 308.5, 696.7
suture 271.1, 741.1, 800.4
suzerain 575.8
suzerainship 417.6, 417.7
suzerainty 417.6, 417.7
svarabhakti vowel 524.12
svelte 270.16
Svengali 22.9, 894.6
swab 79.18, 79.19, 1066.6
swabber 79.14, 183.4
swabbie 183.4
swabbing 79.5
swabby 183.1
swack (n) 902.5 (v) 88.23
swacked 88.33
swacked on 104.30
swaddle (n) 5.30 (v) 5.39, 295.20, 800.9
swaddling clothes 5.30
swaddy 461.7
swag (n) 194.2, 202.2, 204.2, 279.2, 482.11, 916.6 (v) 194.6, 202.6, 204.10, 279.6, 916.10 (a) 202.10
swag-bellied 257.18
swagbelly 2.19, 257.12
swagger (n) 177.12, 501.8, 502.1, 503.1 (v) 177.28, 501.15, 502.6, 503.3
swaggerer 142.5, 461.1, 501.10, 503.2
swaggering (n) 501.8 (a) 142.11, 501.23, 503.4
swagger stick 273.2
swagman 178.3, 660.2, 732.6
swagsman 178.3, 732.6
swain (n) 100.12, 104.12, 769.5 (v) 562.21
swale 243.1, 274.3, 310.8
swallow (n) 8.2, 174.6, 187.4 (v) 8.22, 134.6, 134.8, 148.4, 187.11, 363.8, 388.3, 953.10, 954.6
swallow an insult 134.8
swallow anything 954.6
swallow hook, line, and sinker 954.6
swallowing 187.4
swallow it 433.6
swallow one's dust 166.3
swallow one's medicine 604.20
swallow one's pride 137.7
swallow one's words 525.9
swallowtail 647.7
swallow the bitter pill 604.20
swallow the pill 433.6
swallow up 388.3, 395.10
swallow whole 954.6
swamp (n) 80.12, 243.1, 1013.4 (v) 238.17, 395.21, 993.14, 1065.14
swamped 238.25, 1013.27, 1065.17
swamp-growing 243.3
swampiness 1065.1
swampish 243.3
swampland 243.1
swampy 243.3, 1065.15
swan 37.2, 311.27
swan dive 367.1
swanherd 1070.3
swank (n) 501.2, 501.8 (v) 501.14, 501.15 (a) 501.21, 578.13
swanker 501.10
swankiness 501.5, 578.3
swanking stick 273.2
swankness 578.3
swanky 501.21, 578.13
swansdown 3.19, 1047.4
swan song 188.4, 307.9, 403.3, 704.12, 708.33, 817.1, 820.1
swan-white 37.7
swap (n) 56.1, 731.5, 862.1, 863.2 (v) 56.6, 731.15, 862.4, 863.4
swap horses 731.15
swapped 863.5
swapping 731.2, 863.2
swapping spit 562.2
swap places with 862.5
swap shop 736.1

swap spit 562.15
sward 310.6
swardy 310.42
swarf 296.3
swarm (n) 177.4, 770.6, 884.3, 910.2 (v) 177.22, 770.16, 910.6, 993.8
swarming (n) 177.4, 910.2 (a) 221.15, 770.22, 884.9, 890.9, 993.19
swarmingness 884.1, 890.1
swarm over 910.5
swarm spore 305.13
swarm up 193.8
swarm with 221.7, 884.5, 910.6, 991.5
swart 38.9, 38.10
swarth 38.2
swarthiness 38.2, 1027.1
swarthy 38.9, 38.10
swartness 38.2
swash (n) 238.8, 239.2, 501.8, 501.10, 1065.5 (v) 52.11, 238.19, 501.15, 1065.12
swashbuckle 501.15, 503.3
swashbuckler 461.1, 501.10, 502.5, 503.2
swashbucklering (n) 501.8 (a) 501.23
swashbucklery 501.8, 503.1
swashbuckling (n) 501.8 (a) 501.23, 503.4
swash channel 239.2
swasher 501.10, 503.2
swashing (n) 1065.6 (a) 501.23, 503.4
swashy 1065.16
swastika 170.4, 647.1, 691.5
swat (n) 902.5 (v) 902.15
swatch 786.3
swath 812.2
swathe 5.39, 295.20, 800.9
swathed 295.31
SWAT team 461.15, 1008.1, 1008.17
sway (n) 204.2, 249.3, 417.5, 417.6, 612.1, 894.1, 894.3, 916.6, 917.8 (v) 182.55, 202.8, 204.9, 204.10, 375.22, 375.23, 393.24, 612.13, 854.5, 894.7, 916.10, 917.15, 980.9
swayable 894.15
swayableness 894.5
swayback 265.3
sway-backed 265.12
swayed 650.11, 980.12
swaying (n) 916.2 (a) 894.14, 916.17
swear 334.6, 334.7, 436.4, 513.6, 694.5, 953.12, 957.9
swear and affirm 332.12
swear at 513.7
swear by 953.16
swear by bell, book, and candle 334.6
swearer 957.6
swear falsely 354.20
swear in 334.7, 598.17
swearing 334.3, 513.3
swearing off 475.1
swear like a trooper 513.6
swear off 374.3, 475.3, 668.8
swear on the Bible 334.6
swear the truth 334.6
swear till one is blue in the face 334.6, 513.6
swear to 332.12, 334.6
swear to a belief 953.12
swear to God 334.6, 953.12
swear to goodness 334.6
swear word 513.4, 526.6
sweat (n) 2.24, 12.7, 127.5, 128.2, 135.1, 330.4, 725.4, 985.3 (v) 12.16, 13.5, 127.10, 130.8, 135.4, 238.18, 403.5, 725.13, 725.16, 1019.22, 1065.11
sweat and slave 725.13
sweat and stew 135.4
sweat bath 79.8, 91.4
sweat blood 403.5, 725.10
sweat bullets 127.10
sweat card 759.11
sweater 5.15, 759.21
sweat gland 292.5
sweatiness 1065.2
sweating (n) 12.7, 238.7 (a) 12.22, 13.7, 725.17, 1019.25
sweat it 130.8, 725.11
sweat it out 15.11, 130.8, 135.4, 846.13
sweat like a horse 12.16
sweat like a pig 12.16
sweat like a trooper 12.16
sweat of one's brow 725.4
sweat of one's brow, the 12.7
sweat out 130.8
sweat over 931.9
sweatpants 5.18
sweat room 79.10
sweatshop 739.3
sweatshop labor 726.3
sweaty 2.33, 12.22, 13.7, 1019.25
Swedish bath 79.8
Swedish pancake 10.45
sweep (n) 27.1, 33.6, 79.16, 158.2, 164.1, 177.16, 180.15, 279.3, 759.14 (v) 73.7, 79.23, 158.9, 174.9, 177.20, 177.35, 238.17, 279.6, 411.4, 482.17, 904.9, 1014.10, 1036.17
sweep along 904.9
sweep aside all obstacles 411.4
sweep away 395.14
sweeper 79.16, 752.2
sweeping (n) 177.16 (a) 772.7, 794.10, 860.5, 864.13, 971.19
sweeping change 860.1
sweepingness 864.2, 971.4
sweepings 256.1, 391.4
sweeping statement 864.8
sweep off one's feet 104.22, 122.7, 377.7, 858.16
sweep of time 821.4
sweep out 79.18, 79.23, 909.22
sweeps 1035.2
sweep shot 749.3
sweepstake 759.14
sweepstakes 646.2, 759.14
sweep the strings 708.40
sweep under the carpet 346.6
sweep under the rug 346.6
sweep up 79.23, 193.8
sweet (n) 10.40, 66.1, 562.6 (a) 35.22, 62.9, 66.5, 70.9, 79.25, 97.6, 104.24, 122.11, 143.13, 143.14, 533.8, 708.48
sweet and pungent 66.5
sweet and sour 66.5
sweet as a rose 70.9
sweet as honey 66.5
sweet as sugar 66.5
sweetbread 10.15, 10.20
sweet by-and-by, the 839.1
sweeten 66.4, 79.18, 97.5
sweetened 66.5
sweetener 66.2, 375.7, 478.5
sweetening 66.2, 375.7
sweetening agent 66.2
sweeten the kitty 478.14
Sweet Fanny Adams 762.3
sweet-flowing 708.48
sweetheart (n) 104.9, 104.14, 562.6, 659.2, 999.7 (v) 562.21
sweetheart contract 727.3
sweetie 104.10, 562.6, 659.2
sweetie-pie 104.10
sweetish 66.5
sweetishness 66.1
sweetkins 562.6
sweetmeat 10.40
sweet nature 143.2
sweetness 62.1, 66.1, 97.1, 104.6, 143.2, 533.2, 708.2
sweetness and light 93.8
sweetness of life 95.1
sweet nothings 511.1, 562.5
sweet on 104.30
sweet patootie 104.10
sweet reason 935.1, 935.9
sweet reasonableness 134.1
sweet revenge 507.1
sweets 10.40, 66.2, 104.10, 562.6
sweet savor 70.1
sweet-scented 70.9
sweet science, the 754.1
sweet shop 66.1
Sweet 16 747.1
sweet sixteen 301.14
sweet sleep 22.4
sweet smell 70.1
sweet-smelling 70.9
sweet-sounding 708.48
sweet-sour 66.5
sweet spot 748.1
sweet stuff 10.40
sweet talk 354.6, 375.3, 504.5, 511.1, 562.5
sweet-talk 354.23, 375.14, 562.14
sweet talker 415.6
sweet-talking 504.17
sweet taste 62.1
sweet temper 143.2
sweet-tempered 143.14
sweet tongue 504.5
sweet tooth 66.1, 100.7
sweet-voiced 708.48
sweet wine 88.17
sweet words 504.5, 511.1
swell (n) 53.1, 136.1, 237.4, 238.14, 259.2, 500.9, 607.4, 608.4, 709.12, 711.17 (v) 53.7, 105.18, 140.7, 238.22, 251.6, 259.4, 259.5, 283.11, 501.14, 993.13 (a) 501.21, 578.13, 999.13
swelled 259.13
swelled head 140.4
swelled-headed 140.11
swelled-headedness 140.4
swellhead 140.5
swellheaded 136.10
swelling (n) 53.1, 85.37, 251.1, 259.2, 283.4, 993.7 (a) 251.8, 283.15, 545.9
swelling utterance 545.1
swell it 501.14
swell out 259.5, 283.11
swell the ranks of 253.5, 617.14
swell up 259.5, 283.11
swell with emotion 105.18
swelter (n) 12.7, 1019.6 (v) 12.16, 1019.22
swelterer 1019.8
sweltering 1019.25
sweltering heat 1019.5
sweltry 1019.25
swept 238.25
swept-back 217.12
swept clean 148.7
swept up 983.17
swerve (n) 164.1, 204.3, 278.2 (v) 164.3, 182.30, 204.9, 278.5, 368.8, 852.6, 903.7
swerving (n) 164.1 (a) 164.7
swift 174.15, 330.18, 401.9, 828.8, 830.5, 845.9
swift as an arrow 174.15
swiftie 376.1
swiftness 174.1, 330.3, 401.2, 828.2, 845.3
swift rate 174.1
swig (n) 8.4, 88.7 (v) 8.29, 88.25
swigger 88.11
swigging 8.3
swill (n) 8.4, 10.4, 80.9, 88.7, 391.4, 1062.8 (v) 8.29, 88.25
swillbelly 88.12
swillbowl 88.12
swill down 187.11
swiller 88.11
swilling (n) 8.3, 88.4 (a) 88.35
swillpot 88.12
swill up 187.13
swim (n) 182.11 (v) 182.56
swim, the 578.1
swim against the current 162.4, 868.4, 1013.11
swim against the tide 333.4, 868.4, 900.6
swim fins 367.5
swim in 95.13
swimmer 182.12
swimming (n) 84.2, 182.11, 760.8, 985.4 (a) 182.58, 985.15
swimming bath 743.12
swimming costume 5.29
swimming eyes 115.2
swimming hole 241.1, 743.12
swimming of the head 985.4
swimming pool 743.12, 760.8
swimming suit 5.29
swimming trunks 5.29
swimming upstream 900.1
swimnastics 84.2
swimsuit 5.29

swim trunks 5.29
swim upstream 162.4, 333.4, 868.4, 900.6
swimwear 5.29
swim with 450.4
swim with the current 867.4
swim with the stream 331.15, 332.9, 1014.12
swindle (n) 354.13, 356.8, 482.1 (v) 356.18, 482.13, 632.7
swindler 357.3, 415.6, 483.1, 660.9
swindle sheet 626.3
swindling 356.1
swine 80.13, 311.5, 311.9, 660.6, 663.3, 810.7
swine dysentery 85.41
swineherd 1070.3
swing (n) 158.3, 177.12, 202.2, 430.4, 459.3, 707.7, 708.9, 709.22, 720.7, 743.15, 751.3, 896.2, 902.4, 916.6, 916.9, 917.8 (v) 163.9, 177.28, 182.55, 202.6, 202.8, 328.6, 407.4, 409.12, 604.18, 626.7, 665.19, 708.43, 854.5, 915.9, 916.10, 916.11, 916.13, 917.15 (a) 708.51
swingable 966.7, 995.5
swingaround 163.3
swing at 459.16, 954.6
swing district 609.16
swinge 604.14, 1020.24
swingeing 604.5
swinger 578.7, 665.10
swing from one thing to another 362.8, 363.6
swinging (n) 75.10, 164.1, 202.1, 665.4, 915.1, 916.6 (a) 202.9, 916.17
swinging both ways 75.10
swinging in the wind 160.10
swinging post 273.4
swing into action 321.4, 328.5, 404.3, 818.7
swing in with 450.4
swing it 328.6, 409.8
swingletree 170.5
swingman 747.2
swing musician 710.2
swing of the pendulum 916.6
swing on 459.16
swing open 292.11
swing round 163.9, 182.30
swings 738.9
swing shift 825.3
swing the stern 182.30
swing toward 896.3
swing vote 609.28
swingy 709.29
swinish 80.24, 100.27, 311.45, 663.6, 669.7, 672.6
swinish multitude 606.3
swinishness 80.2, 100.8, 663.2, 669.1, 672.1
swipe (n) 482.4, 510.4, 902.4 (v) 482.16, 902.14
swipeable 482.23
swipe at 459.15, 902.14
swipe card 292.10
swiped 482.23
swipes 88.16
swiping 482.1
swirl (n) 105.4, 238.12, 281.2, 330.4, 915.2, 917.1 (v) 238.21, 281.4, 915.11, 917.10
swirling (n) 105.4, 915.1 (a) 915.14
swirl the senses 985.8
swirly 915.15
swish (n) 57.1, 77.10 (v) 52.11, 52.12, 57.2, 747.4
swishing 52.19
Swiss army knife 462.5
Swiss bank account 728.14
Swiss cheese 284.6
Swiss cross 647.6
Swiss Guards 461.15
switch (n) 3.13, 131.2, 310.11, 310.20, 605.2, 722.4, 793.4, 852.1, 858.1, 862.1, 863.2 (v) 164.6, 176.10, 363.7, 604.12, 731.15, 858.11, 862.4, 863.4
switchback 204.8, 756.3
switchblade 462.5
switchboard 347.8, 704.16
switchboard operator 347.9
switched 863.5
switched-on 17.13, 87.24, 101.11, 105.20, 578.11, 983.18
switcheroo 862.1
switch hitter 745.2
switching 604.4, 1035.3
switching circuit 1041.6
switchman 178.13
switch off 857.12, 1032.26
switch off the light 1027.11
switch on 1032.26
switch on the light 1025.29
switch over 363.7, 858.11
switchover 852.1, 858.1
swivel (n) 915.5 (v) 163.9, 915.9
swivel-eyed 28.12
swivel eyes 28.6
swiveling 915.1
swivet 105.6, 985.3
swollen 85.60, 136.10, 251.7, 257.18, 259.13, 283.16, 501.22, 502.12, 545.9, 794.11, 993.20
swollen belly 2.18
swollen diction 545.1
swollen head 140.4
swollen-headed 140.11
swollenness 259.2, 283.4, 545.1
swollen with pride 136.10
swoon (n) 22.6, 25.2 (v) 25.5
swoop (n) 194.1, 367.1 (v) 194.5, 367.6
swoop down 367.6
swoop down on 459.14
swoop down upon 480.16
swoosh 52.6
sword (n) 461.1, 462.5, 1040.2 (v) 459.25
sword, the 424.3, 458.1, 459.10
sword in hand 460.14
swordlike 285.13
sword of Damocles 127.7, 514.1, 1006.2
swordplay 457.8
swordplayer 461.1
sword side 559.2, 560.4
sword side, the 76.3
swordsman 461.1
swordsmanship 457.8
sword swallower 707.3
sworn 334.9, 436.8
sworn and affirmed 332.14
sworn enemy 589.6
sworn evidence 957.2
sworn off 668.10
sworn statement 334.3, 549.6, 953.4, 957.2
sworn testimony 334.3, 957.2
sworn to 332.14, 334.9
swot (n) 726.3 (v) 570.12
swotter 572.10
swotting 570.3
swot up 989.18
sybarite 663.3
sybaritic 663.5
sybaritism 663.1, 669.2
syconium 10.38
sycophancy 138.2, 511.1, 645.6
sycophant 138.3, 511.4, 616.8
sycophantic 138.14, 511.8
sycophantical 138.14
syllabary 349.1, 546.3
syllabic (n) 546.1 (a) 524.30
syllabicate 546.7
syllabic character 546.1
syllabic meter 720.6
syllabic nucleus 524.12
syllabic peak 524.12
syllabic symbol 349.1
syllabify 546.7
syllabize 546.7
syllable (n) 524.12, 526.1, 720.10 (v) 546.7
syllabogram 546.1
syllabus 557.1, 568.8, 871.1
syllogism 935.3, 935.6
syllogist 921.1, 935.11, 952.8
syllogistic 935.22
syllogistical 935.22
syllogistic reasoning 935.3
syllogize 935.15
syllogizer 935.11
sylph 270.8, 678.6, 678.8
sylphid 678.8
sylphidine 678.17
sylphine 678.17
sylphish 678.17
sylphlike 270.16, 678.17
sylphy 678.17
sylvan 233.9, 310.40
sylvan deity 678.11
sylvatic 310.40
symbiosis 450.1, 769.1, 800.1, 899.1
symbiotic 450.5, 788.9, 899.4
symbiotical 450.5
symbol (n) 92.29, 92.30, 349.1, 517.2, 518.6, 546.1, 647.1, 709.12, 786.2, 862.2, 1017.3 (v) 517.18
symbolic 349.13, 517.23, 518.10, 518.12, 519.10, 523.23
symbolical 517.23, 519.10, 546.8
symbolic logic 935.2
symbolic meaning 518.1
symbolics 689.1, 701.1
symbolic system 517.2
symbolism 92.30, 517.2, 519.2, 689.1, 701.1
symbolist 720.12
symbolistic 517.23
symbolization 92.30, 349.1, 517.2, 990.3
symbolize 349.8, 517.18, 518.8, 536.2
symbolizing 349.13
symbol list 517.2
symbological 517.23
symbology 517.2
symbol-using animal 312.7
symmetric 264.4
symmetrical 264.4, 533.8, 807.6
symmetricalness 264.1
symmetrization 264.2
symmetrize 264.3, 775.6, 781.4
symmetry 264.1, 533.2, 777.1, 788.1, 790.1, 807.1
sympathetic 24.12, 93.20, 121.13, 143.13, 145.7, 147.3, 455.3, 775.9, 907.5, 979.11
sympathetic chord 93.5
sympathetic ink 345.6
sympathetic magic 690.1
sympathetic nervous system 2.14
sympathetic response 93.5
sympathetic vibration 903.1
sympathies 93.1
sympathique 587.15
sympathize 145.3, 455.2
sympathizer 588.1, 616.9
sympathize with 93.11, 121.6, 145.3, 147.2
sympathizing 143.13, 145.7
sympathy 24.3, 93.5, 100.3, 121.4, 143.1, 145.1, 147.1, 449.4, 455.1, 587.3, 775.1, 907.1, 979.4
sympathy strike 727.5
symphonic 708.49, 708.51
symphonic conductor 574.6, 710.17
symphonic form 709.11
symphonic music 708.6
symphonious 708.49
symphonist 710.3, 710.20
symphonize 708.35, 708.39
symphony 455.1, 708.3, 710.12
symphony concert 708.33
symphysis 800.4
symphystic 805.7
symposiast 556.3
symposium 8.3, 88.5, 423.3, 541.6, 554.7, 770.2
symptom 91.13, 399.3, 517.1, 551.4, 957.1
symptomatic 517.23, 957.16, 992.9
symptomaticness 517.3
symptomatize 957.8
symptomatologic 517.23
symptomatological 341.14, 517.23
symptomatology 85.1, 91.11, 341.8
symptomize 517.17
symptom of emotional disorder 92.18
symptomology 85.1
symptoms 85.1
synagogal 703.15
synagogical 703.15

synagogue 703.2
synaposematic mimicry 336.2
synapse 2.14
synaptic 2.30
sync (n) 455.1, 788.1, 836.1 (v) 788.7, 836.4
synchro 1041.13
synchromesh 1040.9
synchronal 836.6
synchronic 769.9, 788.9, 836.6, 899.4
synchronicity 689.6
synchronism 708.3, 769.1, 788.1, 836.1, 899.1
synchronization 708.3, 788.4, 836.1
synchronize 708.35, 788.7, 790.6, 808.10, 832.11, 836.4, 899.2
synchronized 708.49, 769.9, 788.9, 808.14, 836.6
synchronized shifting 1040.9
synchronized sleep 22.5
synchronized swimming 760.8
synchronizer 1035.11
synchronizing 706.6
synchronizing pulse 1035.4
synchronizing signal 1035.4
synchronous 708.49, 788.9, 836.6, 899.4
synchronous machine 1041.13
synchronous motor 1041.13
synchrotron radiation 1037.2
synchysis 205.3
syncline 291.1
Syncom 1035.9
syncopate 708.43
syncopated 708.51, 709.29
syncopated music 708.8
syncopation 708.8, 709.24
syncope 25.2, 268.3, 537.4, 709.24
syncopic 537.6
syncrasy 805.1
syncretic 797.14
syncretism 675.4, 797.1, 805.1, 945.1
syncretistic 805.5
syncretize 797.10, 805.3
syncretized 805.5
syncytium 305.4
syndeton 530.2
syndic 575.16, 596.2
syndicalism 418.2, 611.4, 860.2
syndicalist (n) 395.8, 418.3, 860.3 (a) 611.20, 860.6
syndicalistic 418.6
syndicate (n) 423.1, 617.1, 617.9 (v) 805.3
syndicate, the 660.10, 732.1
syndicated program 1035.2
syndication 805.1
syndrome 85.1, 85.9
synecdoche 862.2
syneresis 260.1, 537.4, 796.1, 805.1
synergetic 450.5, 899.4
synergic 450.5, 899.4
synergical 450.5
synergism 450.1
synergistic 450.5, 899.4
synergistical 450.5
synergize 450.3, 899.2
synergy 450.1, 899.1
synesthesia 24.5, 92.33
synfuels 1021.1
synizesis 260.1
synod 423.1, 423.4, 698.8, 770.2
synodal 423.5
synodic 423.5
synodical 423.5
synonomicon 554.9
synonym 518.6, 526.1, 778.3, 790.4
synonymity 778.1
synonymous 778.8
synonymousness 778.1
synonymy 778.1, 784.1
synopsis 268.3, 557.1
synopsize 268.6, 557.5
synopsized 537.6
synoptic 268.8, 772.7
synoptical 268.8
Synoptic Gospels 683.4
synovia 1056.2
syntactic 523.19
syntactical 523.19, 530.17
syntactic analysis 530.2
syntactic meaning 518.1
syntactics 530.2
syntactic structure 529.1, 530.1, 530.2
syntagm 529.1
syntax 523.14, 530.2, 808.1
synthesis 778.2, 796.1, 805.1, 935.3
synthesize 778.5, 796.3, 805.3, 935.15
synthesized 805.5
synthesizer 711.1, 935.11, 951.7
synthetic (n) 1054.6 (a) 336.8, 354.26, 523.23, 784.10, 935.22
synthetical 336.8, 935.22
synthetic antibiotic 86.41
synthetic fabric 1054.6
synthetic fuels 1021.1
synthetic fur 4.2
syntheticness 354.2
synthetic plasma 2.25
synthetic resin 1057.1
synthetic rubber 1054.6
synthetic textile 1054.6
syntone 92.12
syntonic personality 92.27
syntony 92.11
syph 85.18
syph, the 85.18
syphilis 85.18
syphilitic 85.61
syringe (n) 1065.8 (v) 79.19, 1065.12
syrinx 524.18
syrup 66.2, 86.4, 803.4, 1062.5
syrupiness 66.1, 1062.2
syrupy 66.5, 1062.12
system 381.1, 384.1, 767.4, 807.1, 807.3, 1073.1
systematic 781.5, 807.6, 850.6
systematical 850.6
systematically terrorize 127.20
systematicalness 850.1
systematicness 807.3
systematics 527.1, 1068.3
systematization 381.1, 808.2
systematize 262.7, 381.8, 808.10
systematized 381.12, 808.14
system component 1041.14
system engineering 1041.2
systemic 1001.3
systemic insecticide 1001.3
systemless 810.12
system of belief 953.3
system of beliefs 675.1
system of discourse 978.2
system of government 612.1
system of ideas 932.8
system of knowledge 928.9
system of laws 673.4
system of oral communication 523.1
system of psychology 92.2
system of theories 932.8
system of values 373.2
system operator 1042.17
systems analysis 1041.2
systems analyst 1041.19, 1042.17
systems design 1041.2
systems engineer 1041.19, 1042.17
system software 1042.12
system software specialist 1042.17
systems planning 1041.2
systems program 1042.12
systems programmer 1042.17
system stabilization 1041.7
systole 260.1, 850.3, 916.3
systole and diastole 916.5
syzygy 223.3, 720.7, 1073.9
T 170.4
T & A 75.25
tab (n) 283.3, 628.3, 630.1, 704.20, 817.2 (v) 517.20, 615.11
tabac 89.1
tabacism 89.10
tabacosis 89.10
tabagism 89.10
Tabasco sauce 10.12
tabbing 615.2
tabby (n) 47.2, 311.20, 552.9 (v) 47.7 (a) 47.15
tabby cat 311.20
tabernacle 703.2
tabernacular 703.15
tabes 85.9, 270.6
tabetic 85.61, 270.20, 393.45
tabid 85.61, 270.20
tablature 349.1, 708.28
table (n) 8.5, 10.1, 201.3, 229.1, 236.1, 237.3, 272.4, 296.2, 381.3, 549.1, 801.4, 808.4, 871.2, 901.15, 1017.11 (v) 390.6, 613.10, 846.9
tableau 33.7, 712.10
tableau curtain 704.20
tableau vivant 33.7
tablecloth 8.13
table cover 8.13
table decoration 498.1
table decorator 716.11
table d'hote 11.6
table d'hôte 8.11
table game 743.9
table lamp 229.1
tableland 236.1, 237.1, 237.3, 272.4
tablelike 201.7
table linen 4.1, 8.13
table manners 580.3
table mat 8.13
table mountain 237.3, 272.4
table napkin 8.13
table of contents 554.12, 801.4, 871.2
table of elements 1060.2
table of organization 808.4
table of prothesis 703.12
table of the Lord 703.12
table pad 8.13
tables 182.2
table service 8.11
table setting 498.1
tablespoon 8.12
table sugar 66.3
tablet 86.7, 296.2, 549.11, 549.12, 1042.2, 1042.4
table talk 541.4
tablet computer 1042.2
table tennis 748.1
table the motion 390.6
table-thumping (n) 334.2 (a) 334.8
table tipping 689.6
tablets of the memory 989.1
tableware 8.12, 735.4
tablier 5.17
tabling 613.6, 846.4
tabloid (n) 555.2 (a) 105.32
tabloidese 552.1
tabloidesque 552.14
tabloid journalism 552.1
tabloid press 552.1
tab of 1017.13
taboo (n) 444.1, 773.1 (v) 444.3, 773.4 (a) 444.7, 523.21
tabooed 773.7
taboo language 523.9
taboo word 526.6
taborer 710.10
tabs 87.10
tabular 201.7, 809.8
tabula rasa 222.3, 395.7, 860.1, 919.4, 930.1, 933.1
tabulate 549.15, 809.6, 871.8
tabulated 871.9
tabulation 549.14, 809.1, 871.7
tacan 184.6
tachometer 174.7
tachycardia 85.9, 85.19, 916.3
tachygrapher 547.17
tachygraphy 547.8
tachytelic 861.8
tachytely 861.3
tacit 51.11, 519.8
tacit agreement 436.2
tacit consent 441.1
tacitness 51.1
taciturn 51.10, 344.9, 537.6
taciturnity 51.1, 344.2, 537.1
tack (n) 161.2, 164.1, 271.3, 285.4, 384.1, 385.5, 757.1, 1005.3 (v) 164.3, 182.30, 800.8, 852.6
tack down wind 182.22
tackiness 497.1, 661.3, 803.3, 810.6, 1005.3, 1062.2

tackle (n) 180.12, 271.3, 385.4, 385.5, 471.3, 746.2, 746.3, 749.6, 752.3, 906.6, 912.3 (v) 328.8, 387.12, 403.7, 404.3, 451.5, 725.15, 746.5, 749.7, 752.4, 906.9
tackling 180.12
tack on 253.4
tack together 800.5
tacky 16.14, 98.17, 393.32, 497.10, 501.20, 661.12, 803.12, 810.15, 1005.9, 1062.12, 1065.15
tact 24.3, 143.3, 413.1, 504.1, 934.1, 944.1
tactful 24.12, 143.16, 413.22, 504.13, 944.7
tactfulness 24.3, 143.3, 413.1, 504.1, 944.1
tactic 415.3, 995.2
tactical 381.12, 415.12
tactical air force 461.29
tactical bombing 459.7
tactical evolutions 184.13
tactical maneuvers 184.13, 415.4
tactical nuclear weapon 462.1
tactical plan 381.1
tactical police 1008.17
tactical support bomber 181.9
tactical unit 461.22
tactician 375.11, 381.6, 415.7
tactics 321.1, 328.3, 381.1, 415.4, 458.4, 747.3
tactile 24.14, 73.10, 73.11, 715.7
tactile cell 73.4
tactile corpuscle 73.4
tactile hair 3.10, 73.4
tactile organ 73.4
tactile process 3.10, 73.4
tactile sense 73.1
tactility 73.3
taction 73.1, 223.5
tactless 25.6, 144.18, 340.11, 505.6, 945.5
tactlessness 25.1, 340.2, 505.1, 945.1
tactor 73.4
tactual 73.10, 73.11
tactual sensation 73.1
tad 302.3
tadpole 302.10, 311.26
tae bo 760.3
taedium vitae 112.3, 118.3
tae kwon do 760.3
taenia 271.4
taeniate 271.7
taeniform 271.7
taffrail log 174.7
tag (n) 248.3, 517.13, 527.3, 728.12, 817.1, 817.2, 820.2, 974.4 (v) 166.3, 253.4, 477.9, 517.20, 527.11
tag after 166.3
tag along 166.3
tag end 820.2
tagged element 91.8
tagger atom 1038.4
tagging 477.3, 938.9
tagline 489.6, 974.4
tagmeme 530.2
tagmemic 530.17
tagmemic analysis 530.1
tag on 253.4
tag sale 734.3
tagtail 138.6
tahar 79.25
taiga 243.1, 310.12
tail (n) 3.7, 166.2, 217.1, 217.1, 217.5, 217.6, 254.2, 382.4, 554.12, 793.4, 817.2, 820.2 (v) 27.13, 166.3, 815.2, 938.35 (a) 217.9, 217.11, 820.12
tail away 168.2
tailback 746.2
tailband 554.14
tailcoat 5.11
tailed 217.11
tail end 211.3, 217.1, 820.2
tail-end (n) 793.3 (a) 820.12
tail feather 3.16
tail first 205.7
tailgate 166.3, 223.12, 815.2
tailgate picnic 8.6
tailgating 815.4
tail gunner 185.4
tail in a gate 1013.5
tailing (n) 166.1, 382.1, 938.9 (a) 382.11
tailing off 252.1
tail-landing 184.18
tailless jet 181.3
taillike 217.11
tail off 16.9, 168.2, 252.6, 252.8, 762.6
tailor (n) 5.35, 741.2 (v) 5.41, 262.7, 741.4, 788.7
tailored 5.48, 262.9, 788.10
tailoress 5.35
tailoring 5.32, 741.1
tailor-made 5.48
tailor-make 5.41
tailpiece 217.1, 217.6, 254.1, 708.24, 817.2
tailrace 239.2
tail rhyme 720.9
tails 5.11, 215.3, 759.2
tailspin 184.15, 410.3
tail wagging the dog 205.1, the
tailwind 184.32, 318.1, 318.10, 449.5
taint (n) 85.4, 661.6, 797.7, 865.4, 1003.2, 1004.3 (v) 80.17, 85.51, 393.12, 661.9, 694.5, 1000.6, 1004.6
tainted 80.21, 82.5, 85.60, 393.41, 654.14, 665.23, 1004.10
taintedness 665.1
tainting 694.2
taintless 657.7, 664.4, 1002.6
taintlessness 657.1, 664.1, 1002.1
take (n) 251.3, 341.4, 472.3, 480.10, 482.11, 627.1, 706.5, 714.3, 714.8, 852.1, 893.2, 939.1 (v) 8.20, 85.47, 134.8, 148.4, 176.12, 341.9, 409.7, 433.6, 472.8, 479.6, 480.13, 480.15, 480.17, 482.13, 521.7, 621.4, 772.4, 805.3, 951.10, 953.11
take aback 127.19, 131.7, 131.8
take a back seat 139.7, 163.6, 168.3, 250.4, 432.12
take a backseat 652.3
take a bath 79.19, 473.4, 625.7
take a break 20.8, 826.3, 857.9, 857.10
take a breather 857.9
take a careful look 27.14
take account of 628.9, 959.5, 983.9, 1017.18
take a chance 759.24, 972.12, 1006.7
take a close look 27.14
take a course 182.28
take a crack 403.7
take a crack at 459.15, 818.9
take a crap 12.13
take action 328.5
take action stations 182.49
take a cursory view of 938.26
take a dare 454.6
take a decision 371.16
take a dig at 508.9
take a dim view of 99.5, 510.10
take a dislike to 99.3
take a dive 356.18
take a drop 88.24
take a drop too much 88.26
take advantage of 387.15, 387.16, 643.7, 843.8
take advice 422.7
take a fall 194.8
take a fancy to 100.14, 104.21
take a favorable turn 392.8, 396.19, 1010.7
take a flier 737.23, 759.24
take a flight 184.36
take a fling 459.16
take a flop 194.8
take a fresh lease on life 396.19
take after 336.7, 784.7
take a further look 938.27
take a gamble on 759.24
take a gander 27.13
take a glance at 27.17
take a hand in 476.5
take a hard line 425.5
take a hard line with 510.17
take a header 194.8, 367.6
take a heading 161.7
take a holiday 20.9
take a husband 563.15
take aim 161.5
take aim at 380.4, 459.22
take a journey 177.21
take a joyride 177.33
take alarm 127.11
take a leaf from someone's book 621.4
take a leaf out of one's book 336.5, 336.7
take a leak 12.14
take a leap in the dark 493.5, 759.24
take a leave of absence 20.9, 222.8
take a liberty 156.4, 640.7
take a licking 604.19
take a liking to 104.21
take a lively interest 981.3
take all of 480.19
take a load off 121.8
take a load off one's feet 20.6
take a load off one's mind 120.7
take a long 27.14
take a look 27.13
take a look at 27.13
take amiss 152.13, 342.2
take a moment 20.8
take an active part in 476.5
take a nap 20.8, 22.13
take an approach to 341.9
take an assumed name 346.8
take an aversion to 103.5
take and do 328.6
take a new lease on life 396.19
take a new turn 852.6
take an interest 339.6, 898.3
take an interest in 104.18, 981.3, 983.5
take a nosedive 252.6, 367.6, 393.17
take another loo 938.27
take another look 849.7
take an overdose 308.22
take a part 704.30
take apart 395.17, 802.14, 802.15
take a peek 27.13
take a peep 27.13
take a percentage 631.2
take a photograph 714.14
take a picture 714.14
take a poke at 459.15
take a pop at 459.22
take a potshot 904.12
take a powder 34.2, 188.7, 368.11
take a pratfall 194.8
take a premium 631.2
take a punch at 902.14
take a rain-check 329.2
take a random sample 942.9
take a reading 300.10
take a recess 20.8, 846.9, 857.9
take a reef 635.5
take a rest 20.8
take arms 457.13, 458.15
take a rubbing 349.8
take a runout powder 188.7
take as a matter of course 123.2
take as a model 336.7
take as an article of faith 953.13
take as an excuse 376.3
take as a precondition 951.10
take as a reason 376.3
take a scunner to 99.3
take as demonstrated 946.10
take a second look 938.27
take a set 1046.8
take as gospel truth 953.10
take a shine to 100.14, 104.21
take a shortcut 268.7
take a shot 403.7
take a shot at 404.3, 459.15, 459.22, 818.9
take aside 345.9, 524.26
take a side road 164.3
take a sight 182.51
take as it comes 123.2
take as one 945.3
take a spill 194.8
take as proved 946.10
take a squint at 27.17
take a stab 403.7

take a stab at 942.8
take a stand 348.6
take a straw vote 942.9
take a stretch 177.29
take a Sunday drive 177.33
take a swing at 459.15
take a swipe at 459.15, 510.14
take at face value 953.10
take at one's word 953.10, 953.17
take a trip 177.21
take a trip to the showers 745.5
take a tumble 194.8
take a turn 852.6
take a turn for the better 392.8, 396.19
take a turn for the worse 119.3, 393.17
take a voyage 182.13
take a walk 177.29, 430.17
take away 176.11, 255.9, 1017.18
takeaway 8.6
take away from 480.21
take a whack 328.5
take a whack at 403.7, 818.9, 942.8
take a whiff of 69.8
take a whizz 12.14
take a wife 563.15
take a wrong turn 164.4, 410.15
take back 335.4, 363.8, 481.4, 481.6, 658.5
take-back 481.3
take back to the old drawing board 938.27
take bearings 182.51
take before the judge 598.13
take birth 818.13
take by assault 480.14
take by storm 411.4, 459.20, 480.14
take by surprise 131.7
take by the beard 156.5
take by the hand 449.11
take by the lapel 524.26
take by the lapels 440.12
take by the throat 480.14
take captive 429.15, 432.8
take care 339.7, 494.7, 983.8
take care of 308.14, 328.9, 339.9, 378.3, 407.4, 573.10, 577.13, 604.10, 889.5, 1008.19
take care of number one 651.4
take care of numero uno 651.4
take center stage 501.12
take chances 759.24, 1006.7
take charge 18.11, 417.14
take-charge 17.13
take-charge guy 330.8
take charge of 1008.19
take charge of one's destiny 323.3
take cognizance of 983.9
take comfort 121.7
take command 417.14, 573.8
take counsel 541.10
take counsel of one's pillow 931.14
take counsel with 541.8
take courage 492.13
take cover 346.8, 1009.7
take cover under 376.4
take credit 622.7
take cuttings 1069.17
take dead aim at 459.22
take delight in 95.13
take doing 963.9
take down 137.5, 395.19, 510.17, 549.15, 802.15, 913.4, 913.5
take down a notch 432.9
take down a notch or two 137.5
take down a peg 137.5, 432.9, 913.4, 913.5
take down a rung 137.6
take down in shorthand 547.19
take effect 889.7
take evasive action 368.7, 368.8
take exception 333.4, 510.15
take exception to 510.10
take fire 105.16, 152.19, 578.8, 1020.23
take five 20.8, 826.3, 857.9
take flight 188.6, 368.10
take for 951.10, 953.11
take for a ride 308.14, 356.19
take for a sucker 356.19
take for better or for worse 563.15
take for gospel 953.10
take for granted 123.2, 130.5, 340.6, 519.4, 640.7, 951.10, 953.10
take form 262.8, 807.5
take for oneself 480.19
take for one's own 509.13
take French leave 222.9, 368.10
take fright 127.11
take from 252.7, 255.9, 480.21
take good care 339.7
take great satisfaction 95.12
take half a loaf 107.5
take heart 109.9, 121.7, 124.7, 492.13
take heart of grace 492.13
take heed 339.7, 494.7, 983.8
take heed at one's peril 494.7
take heed of 339.6, 983.9
take hold 330.11, 894.12
take hold of 480.14, 803.6, 983.5
take hold of one 373.10
take holy orders 698.11
take home 472.9, 479.6
take-home 731.8
take-home examination 938.2
take-home income 624.4
take-home pay 624.4, 627.1, 731.8
take-home work 724.2
take hope 121.7
take horse 177.34
take ill 85.47, 152.13
take in 8.22, 27.12, 48.11, 158.9, 187.10, 187.13, 189.7, 221.8, 268.6, 356.14, 385.10, 479.6, 480.18, 521.7, 570.7, 585.7, 772.3, 772.4, 800.5, 918.5, 953.18
take-in 472.3, 627.1
take in a reef 494.6
take in bad part 152.13
take in exchange 731.15
take in good part 134.7
take in hand 404.3, 449.16, 568.13
take in one's arms 562.18
take in sail 175.9, 182.50, 670.5
take in stride 123.2, 134.7
take in the sights 918.6
take into account 772.3, 959.5, 983.9
take into consideration 772.3, 959.5, 983.9
take into custody 429.15, 480.18
take into employment 615.14
take into one's service 615.14
take in tow 449.11, 905.4
take in vain 694.5
take issue 333.4
take issue with 335.4, 451.3, 457.21
take it 15.11, 134.6, 433.6, 951.10, 953.11, 991.4
take it all 469.6, 480.19
take it as given 951.10
take it coast to coast 747.4
take it easy 20.6, 106.7, 331.15, 494.5, 857.9, 1014.12
take it in one's stride 1014.12
take it into one's head 931.16, 951.10
take it like a man 134.6
take it lying down 134.8, 433.6
take it on 328.5, 403.5
take it on the chin 15.11, 134.6, 410.10, 433.11
take it on the lam 188.7, 368.11, 369.6
take it or leave it 102.5, 963.11, 982.2
take it out of 16.10, 21.4, 137.4
take it out of one's hide 604.14
take it out of one's skin 604.14
take it out on 152.16
take it out on someone 152.20
take it slow 20.7, 175.6, 494.5
take its place 807.5
take its rise 818.13
take its rise from 887.5
take it that 341.9
take kindly to 332.8, 332.9, 441.2, 509.9
take leave 20.9, 188.6, 188.16, 222.8
take leave of 370.5
take leave of one's senses 923.6, 926.21
take legal action 673.9
take lessons 570.11
take liberties 142.7, 640.7
take liberties with 156.4
take life 308.13
take life easy 20.6
take marriage vows 436.5
take measures 328.5, 405.6, 494.6
take medicine 91.29
take merit to oneself 502.8
taken aback 131.13, 406.8
take narrow views 980.6
taken as 951.14
taken away 222.11, 307.29
taken by God 307.29
taken by surprise 131.12, 406.8
taken down a notch 137.14
taken for granted 130.13, 130.14, 519.8, 951.14
taken ill 85.56
take no account of 340.6, 984.2, 998.12
take no denial 361.7, 421.8, 424.5
taken off 307.29, 784.10
take no interest in 102.4, 982.2
taken on 404.7
take no note of 157.6, 984.2
take no notice of 157.6, 984.2
take no part in 329.4, 668.7
take no prisoners 308.17
take no stock in 955.5
take note 983.6
take note of 983.9
take no thought of 340.6
take no thought of the morrow 406.7
take no thought of tomorrow 406.7
take notice 122.7, 983.6
take notice of 27.12, 983.9
take nourishment 8.20
taken over 691.13
taken unawares 131.12, 406.8
taken up 985.11
taken up with 983.17
taken with 95.15, 104.29
take oath 598.17
take odds 759.25
take off 6.6, 184.38, 188.7, 193.10, 255.10, 308.13, 336.6, 349.12, 392.7, 395.12, 489.13, 512.12, 517.21, 631.2, 784.7, 802.10, 818.7
takeoff 184.8, 188.2, 188.5, 193.1, 336.1, 489.1, 508.6, 512.5, 784.1, 818.1
take off after 166.3, 382.8
take off a high 516.2
takeoff booster 1074.5
take offense 152.13, 589.8
take off for 161.9
take off from work 222.8
take office 417.14, 615.13
take off on 336.6, 508.11
take off one's hands 479.6
take off one's hat to 155.5, 509.14
take off one's hat to one 646.8
take off one's shoes 20.6
takeoff power 184.8
takeoff ramp 1074.10
takeoff rocket 184.8, 1074.5
takeoff run 184.8
takeoff speed 184.31
takeoff strip 184.23
take off weight 270.13
take on 112.17, 115.16, 126.6, 152.15, 328.8, 387.12, 403.7, 404.3, 451.4, 451.5, 457.16, 459.17, 479.6, 615.14, 621.4, 725.15
take on a number 87.22
take on credit 953.10
take one back 989.19
take one over 373.10
take one's bearings 161.11
take one's breath away 105.15, 122.7, 127.15, 131.8

take one's business to 731.17
take one's case to the public 352.11
take one's chance 759.24
take one's choice 371.13
take one's constitutional 177.29
take one's cue from 422.7
take one's death 85.47
take one's departure 188.6
take one's ease 20.6, 331.12, 402.4
take oneself away 188.6
take oneself off 188.6
take one's foot off the gas 175.9
take one's hands off 475.3
take one's hat off to 585.10
take one's head off 152.16
take one's last breath 307.18
take one's last sleep 307.18
take one's leave 188.6, 802.8
take one's leisure 331.12, 402.4
take one's life away 308.13
take one's life in one's hand 1006.7
take one's life in one's hands 492.10
take one's measure 946.9
take one's medicine 433.6, 604.20
take one's oath 332.12, 334.6, 957.9
take one's oath upon 953.16
take one's opinions ready-made 980.7
take one's own course 430.20
take one's own life 308.22
take one's own sweet time 175.8, 402.4
take one's picture 714.14
take one's place 812.6
take one's pleasure 743.22
take one's position 159.17
take one's punishment 604.20
take one's sabbatical 20.9
take one's stand 159.17, 359.9, 453.3, 855.11
take one's stand against 451.3, 453.3
take one's stand upon 421.8, 935.16
take one step at a time 494.5
take one's time 175.8, 331.12, 331.14, 402.4, 846.12
take one's turn 825.5
take one's word 953.17
take one's word for 953.10, 953.16
take one up on 332.8, 441.3, 454.6, 951.10
take on faith 953.10
take on oneself 436.5
take on over 101.7
take on too much 404.6, 725.10, 993.10
take on trust 953.10, 982.2
take on up on 371.15
take on weight 259.8
take order 807.5
take orders 326.2, 698.11
take out 192.10, 255.10, 308.14, 762.7, 769.8, 820.6
takeout 8.6, 8.17
take out after 166.3, 382.8, 510.13
take out from under wraps 351.4
take out insurance 494.6
take out membership 617.14
take out of mothballs 458.19
takeout service 8.11
take over 417.14, 472.10, 479.6, 480.19, 621.4, 640.8, 805.3, 815.2
take-over 17.13
takeover 417.12, 480.4, 737.19, 805.1
takeover bid 737.19
take over for 825.5
take pains 339.7, 403.11
take part 221.8, 476.5
take part in 476.5
take part with 450.4
take pen in hand 547.19
take pills 87.22
take pity on 145.4
take pity upon 145.4
take place 831.5
take pleasure in 95.13
take position 184.37
take possession 472.10, 480.13
take possession of 480.19
take potluck 759.24
take precautions 494.6, 1007.3
take precedence 249.11, 814.2
take pride 136.5
take prisoner 429.15, 480.18
taker 479.3, 480.11
take rank 807.5, 812.6
take refuge 1009.7
take refuge in 376.4
take residence at 159.17
take rest 20.6
take revenge 506.7, 507.4
take rise 818.13
take risks 492.9
take root 159.17, 310.34, 373.10, 853.5, 855.10, 894.12
take shame 137.9
take shape 262.8, 807.5
take shelter 1009.7
take ship 188.15
take short 131.7
take sick 85.47
take sides 935.16
take sides with 449.13, 450.4
take silk 597.5
take snuff 89.14
take some doing 1013.10
take someone for a fool 950.2
take someone for an idiot 950.2
take soundings 182.51, 275.10
take special pains 403.11
take steps 328.5, 494.6
take steps and measures 494.6
take stock 628.9, 1017.21
take stock in 953.10
take stock of 27.14, 931.11, 938.24
take ten 20.8, 826.3, 857.9
take the air 177.24, 184.36
take the airline 161.10, 268.7
take the attitude 978.6
take the average 246.2
take the backtrack 163.7
take the bait 903.5, 954.6
take the bite out 286.2, 670.6
take the bit in one's teeth 323.3, 361.7
take the bit in the teeth 843.7
take the bitter with the sweet 107.5, 134.5, 433.6
take the blame 641.9
take the breath away 1016.16
take the bull by the horns 359.8, 403.6, 404.3, 492.10, 843.7
take the cake 249.7, 411.3
take the chair 573.11
take the chance 843.7
take the chances of 759.24
take the chill off 1020.17
take the consequences 604.20
take the count 410.10, 412.12
take the cudgels against 459.14
take the cure 91.29
take the dimensions of 300.10
take the edge off 16.10, 286.2, 670.6
take the edge off of 465.7
take the fall 604.20
take the fall for 862.6
take the fancy of 104.22
take the field 458.15, 609.39, 745.5
take the first step 818.10
take the floor 524.21, 543.9, 613.10
take the good the gods provide 107.5
take the grand tour 918.6
take the ground 182.42
take the ground from under 958.4, 977.2
take the heart out of 112.18
take the heat for 641.6, 641.9
take the helm 417.14, 573.9
take the initiative 818.10
take the last count 307.19
take the law in one's own hands 418.4
take the law into one's own hands 323.3, 435.4, 674.5
take the lead 165.2, 216.7, 417.14, 573.8, 612.14, 818.10
take the liberty 640.6
take the lid off 292.12, 351.4
take the life of 308.13
take the limelight 997.12
take the line of least resistance 433.10, 1014.12
take the long view 839.6
take the long way around 914.4
take the Lord's name in vain 513.6
take the mantle of 815.2
take the mean 468.2
take the measure 938.24
take the measure of 300.10
take the mind off of 985.6
take the next step 817.5
take the offensive 458.15, 459.14
take the opportunity 843.7
take the part of 449.13
take the place of 835.3, 862.5
take the pledge 668.8
take the plunge 359.8, 818.10
take the rap 604.20
take the rap for 641.6, 641.9, 862.6
take the reciprocal course 163.7
take the reins into one's hand 417.14
take the reins of government 417.14
take the responsibility 641.9
take the risk 759.24
take the road 177.21
take the shadow for the substance 975.10
take the shape of 33.10, 867.3
take the shine out of 137.6, 249.8
take the stage 704.29
take the stand 334.6, 598.17
take the starch out of 137.6, 379.4
take the sting out 286.2, 670.6
take the sting out of 120.5, 465.7
take the strain 906.9
take the stump 543.9, 609.40
take the throne 615.13
take the trouble 324.3
take the veil 584.7, 698.11
take the vows 436.5
take the wheel 573.9
take the wind out of 260.10, 977.2
take the wind out of one's sails 19.10, 112.18, 137.6, 173.11, 379.4, 958.5, 1012.15
take the words out of one's mouth 845.6
take the wraps off 351.4
take the wrong way 342.2
take things as they come 106.9, 134.7, 331.15
take thought of 339.6
take time 821.6, 846.12
take time by the forelock 843.8, 845.5
take time off 222.8
take time out 20.8
take time to catch one's breath 20.7
take time to smell the flowers 402.4
take time to smell the roses 402.4
take to 100.14, 104.21, 328.8, 373.11, 387.14
take to account 599.7
take to arms 458.15
take to be 951.10
take to court 598.13
take to drink 88.24
take to drinking 88.24
take to flight 188.12, 368.10
take to heart 93.11, 93.12, 152.13, 207.5, 953.10
take to like a duck to water 1014.8
take to mean 341.9
take to one's arms 562.18
take to one's heels 188.12, 368.10
take to pieces 395.17

take to task 510.17, 599.7, 604.9
take to the air 184.36, 184.38
take to the airways 184.36
take to the bosom 474.7
take to the cleaners 249.7, 473.4, 480.24
take to the hustings 609.40
take to the road 177.23
take to the stump 609.40
take to wife 563.15
take trouble 339.7, 403.11
take turns 825.5
take umbrage 152.13, 589.8
take unawares 131.7
take under active consideration 931.14
take under advisement 931.14
take under consideration 931.14
take under one's wing 449.13, 592.3, 1008.19
take up 187.13, 328.8, 371.15, 404.3, 449.15, 472.10, 472.11, 480.19, 509.13, 541.11, 556.5, 624.13, 724.11, 770.18, 772.3, 818.9, 912.8, 983.13
take up a collection 770.18
take up again 856.6
take up and pay off 624.13
take up an inquiry 938.20
take up arms 457.13, 458.15
take up arms against 459.14
take up a side 935.16
take up front 480.13
take up membership 617.14
take up one's abode 159.17, 225.7
take up one's option 371.13
take up one's quarters 159.17
take up one's thoughts 931.20
take up one's time 724.10
take upon oneself 404.3, 640.6, 641.9
take upon one's shoulders 404.3, 641.9
take up residence 159.17
take up the cause of 449.13
take up the cudgels 457.14, 458.15
take up the cudgels for 449.13, 509.13
take up the gauntlet 454.6, 458.15
take up the sword 458.15
take up time 821.6
take up with 541.10, 582.18, 587.10
take vows 698.11
take what comes 134.5, 359.9, 492.14
take what is coming to one 604.20
take wing 177.22, 184.36, 188.6, 368.10
take with a grain of salt 955.6, 959.5
take wrong 342.2, 975.10
taking (n) 479.1, 480.1, 480.3, 621.2, 805.1, 910.1 (a) 85.62, 97.7, 100.30, 377.8, 480.25
taking a part 704.8
taking apart 802.6
taking a role 704.8
taking away 255.1, 473.1, 480.1
taking by storm 459.6
taking down 802.6
taking exception 510.4
taking from under wraps 351.1
taking in 187.1, 480.2
taking-in 570.2
taking into custody 480.2
taking leave 222.4
taking measures 405.1
taking odds 759.1
taking off 193.1
taking-off 784.1
taking office 615.3
taking of life 308.1
taking on 615.4
taking over 417.12, 480.4
taking place 831.9
taking possession 480.1
taking precedence 814.1
takings 627.1
taking the cure 87.1
taking the waters 1065.9
taking the wraps off 351.1
taking ways 482.12
talapoin 699.14
talbotype (n) 714.4 (v) 714.14
talbotypist 716.5
talcum 1016.11
talcum powder 1016.11
tale 354.11, 552.7, 719.2, 722.3, 1017.6
talebearer 551.6, 552.9
talebearing (n) 552.7 (a) 552.14
talent 18.2, 413.4, 413.12, 712.6, 920.2, 920.8
talented 413.29, 920.14
talented person 413.12
talents 413.4
talent scout 615.5, 704.27, 745.2
tale of woe 115.4
talesman 596.6
taleteller 552.9, 722.5
tale-telling 722.1, 722.2
taletelling (n) 552.7 (a) 552.14
tale unfold, a 722.7
talion 506.3
talipedic 265.12
talipes 265.3
talisman 691.5, 696.10
talismanic 690.14
talk (n) 523.1, 524.1, 532.1, 541.2, 543.2, 543.3, 552.6, 552.7, 568.7 (v) 343.6, 351.6, 517.17, 523.18, 524.19, 541.9, 541.11, 543.9, 552.12
talk a blue streak 524.20
talk about 133.13, 541.11
talk against time 846.11
talk around 375.14
talkathon 543.2, 613.6
talkative 343.10, 351.10, 524.31, 538.12, 540.9
talkatively 343.12
talkativeness 343.3, 538.2, 540.1
talkative person 540.4
talk away 540.5
talk back 142.8, 939.4
talk big 355.3, 502.7, 545.6
talk de haut en bas 141.8
talk dirty 513.6
talk double Dutch 522.10
talk down 184.43, 540.7
talk down to 137.8, 141.8
talked about 552.15
talked-about 662.16, 928.27
talked-of 662.16, 928.27
talkee-talkee 523.11, 540.3
talker 524.17, 541.7, 543.4
talkfest 541.2
talk highfalutin 545.6
talk in circles 538.10, 914.4
talk incoherently 525.7
talking (n) 343.1, 524.1 (a) 524.31
talking book 30.6
talking down 184.19
talking-down system 184.19
talking head 413.11, 1035.13
talking machine 524.16
talking out of 379.1
talking point 935.5
talking shop 541.2
talking through one's nose 525.1
talking-to 510.6
talking to hear oneself talk 520.1
talking to oneself 542.4
talk in superlatives 355.3
talk into 375.23
talk it out 120.7
talk jockey 1034.23
talk nonsense 520.5, 540.5
talk of 541.11
talk off the top of one's head 365.8, 951.11
talk of the town 552.6, 662.1
talk on 540.5
talk one deaf and dumb 540.6
talk one into a fever 540.6
talk one's ear off 540.6
talk oneself hoarse 540.5
talk oneself out of breath 540.5
talk one's head off 540.6
talk one to death 538.8, 540.6
talk one up 509.12
talk out 541.11
talk out of 379.3
talk out of both sides of one's mouth at once 873.5
talk out of turn 351.6, 844.4
talk over 375.23, 541.10, 541.11, 953.18
talk over the back fence 552.12
talk radio 1034.18
talk shop 541.11
talk show 1034.18, 1035.2
talk-show host 1034.23
talk someone's ear off 524.20
talk tête-à-tête 541.9
talk the hind leg off a mule 540.6
talk through 953.18
talk through one's hat 520.5
talk till one is blue in the face 540.5, 540.6
talk to 510.18, 524.26
talk together 541.8
talk to hear one's head rattle 540.5
talk to in private 345.9, 524.26
talk too much 540.5, 993.11
talk to oneself 542.3
talk to the wall 542.3
talk turkey 535.2, 541.11
talk up 953.18
talk with 541.8
talk with one in private 541.9
talky 540.9
tall 257.16, 267.7, 272.16, 502.12, 545.8, 955.10
tall as a maypole 272.16
tall corn, the 233.1
tall dark and handsome 1016.17
tallied 871.9
tallness 257.6, 272.1
tall order 1013.2
tallow 37.2, 1056.1
tallow candle 1026.2
tallow dip 1026.2
tallow-faced 36.7
tallowy 1056.9
tall ship 180.3
tall story 354.11, 355.1, 502.2
tall tale 354.11
tall talk 355.1, 502.2, 545.1
tally (n) 517.13, 549.7, 628.2, 784.3, 788.1, 871.1, 1017.6, 1017.9 (v) 253.6, 778.4, 788.6, 871.8, 1017.17, 1017.18, 1017.19
tallyho 59.3
tallying 1017.9
tally of 1017.13
tally sheet 871.1
tally up 1017.19
tally with 867.3
Talmud 683.5
Talmudic 683.12
Talmudism 675.12
Talmudist 675.21
taloned 199.9, 474.9
talons 417.5, 474.4, 612.2
talus 204.4, 237.2, 1059.1
tamable 433.14
tamableness 433.4
tamanoas 678.1
tamasic 930.12
tame (v) 373.9, 432.11, 670.6, 1070.7 (a) 173.14, 228.34, 433.15, 670.10
tamed 228.34, 432.15, 433.15
tameless 671.21
tameness 433.4, 433.5
tamer 1070.2
taming 373.7, 432.4
Tammanism 609.1
Tammany Hall 609.1, 609.24
tamp 284.14, 902.12
tampered with 354.30
tampering 354.9
tamper-proof 1049.4
tamper-resistant 293.9, 1049.4
tamper-resistant packaging 293.4
tamper with 214.7, 354.17, 378.3, 797.12
tamp in 191.7
tampon 86.33, 191.2, 293.5
tan (v) 40.2, 397.10, 405.6, 604.14, 1020.19 (a) 40.3
tan-colored 40.3
tandem 179.5, 750.2, 873.2

tandem bicycle 179.8
tan-faced 40.3
tang 62.1, 68.2, 865.4, 1001.5
tangelo 797.8
tangency 223.5
tangent (n) 164.1, 169.1, 223.6, 277.2 (a) 169.3, 223.17
tangential 169.3, 223.16, 223.17
tangerine 42.2
tangerine-colored 42.2
tangibility 73.3, 348.3, 763.1, 1052.1
tangible 24.14, 73.11, 348.8, 763.6, 1052.10
tangible, the 763.2
tangible assets 471.7
tangibles 471.7
tanginess 68.2
tangle (n) 799.2 (v) 356.20, 480.17, 799.3, 898.2, 1012.11
tangled 799.4
tangled in 898.5
tangled skein 799.2
tanglement 799.1
tangle up with 480.17
tangle with 457.17
tangly 799.4
tangram 522.9
tangy 67.5, 68.7
tank (n) 241.1, 386.6, 429.8, 429.9 (v) 212.9, 965.5
tankage 257.2
tank attack 459.4
tank corpsman 461.13
tank crewman 461.13
tanked 87.24, 88.33
tanked-up 88.33
tanker 180.1, 461.13
tanker ship 1075.2
tank job 965.2
tank suit 5.29
tank top 5.29
tank up 88.25
tanned 40.3, 405.16
tanner 728.8
tannery 739.3
tanning 397.3, 604.5
tanning booth 1016.10
tanning cream 1056.3
tan one's hide 604.14
tan-skinned 40.3
tantalization 132.1, 377.1
tantalize 104.22, 132.2, 377.6, 983.12
tantalized 983.16
tantalizer 377.4
tantalizing 63.10, 97.7, 100.30, 105.30, 132.6, 377.8, 983.19
tantalizingness 97.2
tantamount 777.10, 790.8
tantara 53.5
tantarara 53.5
Tantra 683.8
tantric sex 75.7
tantrist 683.15
tantrum 152.8
Tao 807.1
tao 919.5
Taoism 675.14
Taoist (n) 675.24 (a) 675.32
Taoistic 675.32
Tao Té Ching 683.7
tap (n) 52.3, 56.1, 73.1, 190.9, 239.6, 239.10, 293.4, 310.22, 902.7 (v) 48.10, 52.15, 56.6, 73.6, 176.14, 192.12, 292.11, 292.15, 480.21, 708.44, 902.18
tapas 8.6, 8.10, 62.4
Tap City 619.10
tap-dance 705.5, 846.11, 936.9
tapdance 365.8, 368.8
tap dancer 705.3
tap dancing 344.4, 846.5
tape (n) 50.12, 86.33, 271.4, 549.10, 754.1, 803.4, 820.1 (v) 50.14, 549.15, 800.5, 1035.15
tape cartridge 50.12
tape cassette 50.12
taped 800.14, 970.20
tape deck 50.11
taped program 1034.18
tape drive 1042.5
taped show 1035.2
tapeline 271.4
tape measure 271.4
taper (n) 270.2, 1021.4, 1026.1, 1026.2, 1026.7 (v) 169.2, 270.11, 285.7 (a) 270.15
tape reader 1042.4
tape-record 50.14, 549.15
tape recorder 50.11, 549.10
tape recording 50.12
tapered 245.5, 270.15, 285.9
tapering (n) 245.3, 270.2 (a) 270.15, 285.9
tapering off 252.1
taper off 175.9, 245.4, 252.6, 857.12
taper to a point 285.6
tapestry 47.6, 712.10, 712.16
tapeworm 100.7, 311.38
tapioca 10.46
tapioca snow 1023.6, 1023.8
tap out 410.9, 473.4, 625.7
tap out the rhythm 708.44
tapped out 395.29, 473.8, 619.10
tapper 1069.7
tapping (n) 192.3 (a) 56.11
tapping machine 1040.6
taproom 88.20
taproot 310.22, 886.5
taps 53.5, 309.5, 315.4, 517.16, 820.1
tapster 88.19
tapstress 88.19
tap water 10.49, 1065.3
tar (n) 38.4, 87.16, 183.1, 803.4, 1054.2 (v) 295.22, 295.24
taradiddle 354.11
tar and feather 604.15
tar-and-feathering 604.2
tarantara 53.5
tarantula 311.32
tar-black 38.8
tardiness 175.3, 833.1, 846.1
tar distiller 87.21
tardy 175.12, 833.3, 846.16
tares 391.4
target 100.10, 380.2, 508.7, 1038.8
target audience 733.3
target date 211.3, 843.5
target day 459.13
target image 1036.11
target planet 1075.1
targetshooter 904.8
target shooting 744.1
target sport 744.1, 744.1
target values 1041.10
Targum 683.5
tariff 773.4
tariff wall 428.1
tarlet 10.41
tarmac 383.6
tarmacadam 383.6
tarn 241.1
Tarnhelm 691.6
tarnish (n) 661.6, 1004.3 (v) 36.5, 80.17, 512.10, 661.9, 1004.6
tarnished 80.21, 1004.10
Tarnkappe 691.6
Tarot cards 962.3
Tarot reading 962.2
tarpan 311.10
tarpaulin 295.9
tarradiddle 354.11
tarriance 846.3
tarry (v) 173.7, 175.8, 827.6, 827.7, 846.12, 856.3 (a) 38.8
tarry for 130.8
tarrying (n) 175.3, 331.4, 846.3 (a) 175.11
tarsus 2.7, 177.14
tart (n) 10.41, 665.14 (a) 17.14, 64.6, 67.5, 68.6, 144.23
tartan 47.4, 647.1
Tartar 110.11
Tartarean 144.26, 682.8
tartar sauce 10.12
Tartarus 682.3
tarte 10.41
tartish 67.5
tartishness 67.1
tartness 17.5, 64.2, 67.1, 144.8
tart taste 62.1
Tartuffe 357.8, 693.3
Tartuffery 354.6, 693.1
Tartuffian 693.5
Tartuffish 693.5
Tartuffism 354.6, 693.1
tarvia 383.6
Tarzan 15.6
Taser 462.22
tash 3.11
task (n) 404.1, 568.7, 615.1, 643.3, 724.2, 725.4 (v) 599.7, 643.4, 725.16
task bar 1042.18
taskbar 1042.18
tasked 599.15
task force 461.22, 461.27
task group 461.27
tasking 643.1
taskmaster 574.2
task the mind with 989.17
task with 599.9
tastable 62.8
taste (n) 8.2, 24.5, 62.1, 62.4, 100.2, 100.7, 248.4, 371.5, 495.1, 496.1, 533.1, 786.3, 865.4, 944.1 (v) 8.20, 24.6, 62.7, 63.5, 831.8, 942.8
taste bud 62.5
taste buds 2.12
taste bulb 62.5
taste cell 62.5
tasteful 496.7, 533.6, 712.20
tastefulness 496.1, 533.1
taste goblet 62.5
taste good 63.4
taste hair 62.5
taste in the mouth 62.1
tasteless 16.17, 65.2, 117.6, 497.10, 534.2, 661.12
tastelessness 65.1, 96.1, 117.1, 497.1, 534.1, 661.3
taste like 63.6
taste like ashes in the mouth 96.12
tastemaker 496.6, 578.7
taste of 62.7, 63.6
taste perception 62.1
taster 62.4
taste test 62.4
taste treat 62.4
tastiness 63.1, 97.3
tasting (n) 8.1, 8.3, 62.6 (a) 8.32
tasting menu 10.1
tasty 62.9, 63.8, 97.10
tater 10.35, 745.3
tat-tat 55.1
tat-tat-tat 55.1
tatter (n) 248.3, 793.3 (v) 393.20
tatterdemalion 178.3
tattered 393.32, 802.23, 810.15
tatters 5.5
tattle (n) 552.7 (v) 351.6, 551.12, 552.12
tattle on 351.6
tattler 551.6, 552.9
tattletale (n) 551.6, 552.9 (a) 551.19
tattling 351.2
tattoo (n) 53.5, 55.1, 399.3, 517.5, 847.2, 902.4, 904.4, 1004.3 (v) 47.7, 316.10, 517.19
tattoo mark 517.5
tatty 393.32
taught 928.18
taunt (n) 156.2, 454.2, 508.2 (v) 142.7, 156.5, 508.9
taunting (n) 508.1 (a) 508.12
taunt with 599.7
taupe (n) 39.1 (a) 39.4, 40.3
taurine 311.45
tauromachy 457.4
taut 128.13, 130.12, 180.20, 1046.11
tauten 906.9
tautness 128.3, 1046.2
tautologic 391.10
tautological 391.10, 778.7, 849.14, 993.17
tautologism 849.3
tautologize 849.8
tautologous 538.11, 849.14, 993.17
tautology 391.1, 538.2, 849.3, 993.4
tautonym 527.3
taut ship 425.3
tavern 8.17, 88.20, 228.15, 743.13
taw 405.6
tawdriness 501.3, 810.6, 998.2
tawdry 501.20, 998.21
tawed 405.16

tawny 40.3
tax (n) 421.1, 630.9, 643.3, 993.6 (v) 297.13, 599.7, 630.12, 643.4, 725.10, 725.16
taxable 630.15
taxable goods 630.9
taxable income 624.4, 630.9
taxable property 630.9
tax assessor 630.10
taxation 630.9
tax avoidance 630.9
tax base 630.9
tax benefit 478.8
tax-bracket creep 630.9
tax burden 630.9
tax cheat 625.5
tax code 630.9
tax collector 630.10, 770.15
tax credit 622.1
tax-deductible 630.16
tax deduction 630.9
tax dodger 368.3, 625.5
tax dodging 368.2
taxed 297.18, 599.15
taxer 630.10
taxes 630.9
tax evader 368.3, 625.5
tax evasion 368.2, 625.1, 630.9
tax-exempt 630.16
tax exemption 630.9
tax-exempt status 630.9
tax farmer 630.10
tax-free 630.16
tax haven 630.9
taxi (n) 179.13 (v) 177.33, 184.38
taxicab 179.13
taxi dancer 705.3
taxidermist 397.5
taxidermy 397.3
taxidriver 178.10
taxiing 184.8
taxing (n) 297.7, 421.1, 599.1, 643.1, 725.2 (a) 421.9
taxiway 184.23
tax law 630.9
tax lien 438.5
tax man 770.15
taxman 630.10
tax one's energies 725.9
taxonomic 527.17, 809.7, 871.9
taxonomical 809.7
taxonomist 801.5
taxonomy 305.3, 527.1, 801.3, 801.4, 807.2, 808.3, 808.4, 809.1, 1068.3
taxpayer 624.9, 630.10, 659.3
taxpayer funds 729.13
taxpayer money 729.13
tax preparer 550.1, 628.7
tax relief 630.9
tax return 630.9
tax roll 871.6
tax sale 734.3
tax shelter 630.9
tax structure 630.9
tax with 599.9
tax withholding 630.9
tax write-off 478.8, 630.9
T-bar 753.1
tea 8.6, 10.49, 87.11, 582.13
tea bag 292.8
tea break 8.7, 20.2
tea caddy 8.12
teach 568.10
teachability 570.5
teachable 137.10, 570.18
teachable moment 570.5
teachableness 137.1, 570.5
teach a lesson 568.10
teach an old dog new tricks 568.10
teacher 405.5, 422.3, 568.1, 571.1, 575.1, 699.10, 726.4
Teacher, the 677.4
teacherish 571.11
teacherlike 571.11
teacher of rhetoric 543.8
teacher's aide 571.4
teachership 571.10
teacher's pet 16.6, 104.15
teachery 571.11
teach fishes to swim 993.12
teach-in (n) 333.2 (v) 333.5
teaching (n) 419.1, 568.1, 568.7, 675.1, 953.2, 974.1 (a) 568.18
teaching and research institution 567.1
teaching assistant 571.4
teaching fellow 571.4
teaching hospital 91.21
teaching institution 567.1
teaching intern 571.4
teaching staff 571.9
teach one a lesson 604.9
teach oneself 570.10
teach one's grandmother to suck eggs 993.12
teach the basics 568.10
teach the rudiments 568.10
teachy 571.11
tea cozy 8.12
tea dance 705.2
tea garden 8.17
teahouse 8.17
tea-leaf reading 962.2
team (n) 179.5, 617.7, 745.2, 746.2, 747.2, 749.2, 750.3, 751.2, 770.3, 873.2 (v) 617.14, 873.5
teamed 805.6
teamed up 873.8
team effort 730.1
team game 744.1
teammate 588.3, 616.5
team player 450.1, 616.5
team spirit 450.1, 455.1
teamster 178.9, 178.10
team tennis 748.1
team up 450.3, 587.11, 873.5
team up with 450.4, 617.14, 805.4, 899.3
team with 805.4
teamwork 450.1
Tea Party 609.24
tea-planter 1069.5
tear (n) 2.24, 85.38, 88.6, 115.2, 802.4 (v) 13.5, 26.7, 174.8, 174.9, 292.11, 393.13, 401.5, 671.11, 802.11
tear along 174.9
tear apart 395.17, 510.15, 802.14
tear around 330.12, 671.11
tear ass 401.6
tear asunder 395.17
tear away 174.9
tear bottle 115.2
tear down 395.19, 510.15, 512.9, 802.15
teardrop 2.24, 115.2, 202.4, 282.3
tear from 192.15, 480.22
tearful 112.26, 115.21
tearful eyes 115.2
tearfulness 112.11, 115.2
tearing (n) 192.6, 802.2 (a) 2.33
tearing down 395.5
tearing out 192.1
tearing passion 105.8, 152.10
tearing up root and branch 395.6
tear into 725.15
tearjerker 93.8
tearjerking 93.21, 145.8
tearlike 2.33
tear limb from limb 604.15, 802.14
tear loose 431.7
tear off 174.9, 188.10, 328.6, 401.6, 708.38
tear off the mask 351.4
tear oneself away 188.6
tear one's hair 115.11, 846.13
tearoom 8.17
tear open 292.11, 292.14
tear out 188.10, 192.10
tears 13.2, 115.2
tear the cover off 745.5
tear to pieces 395.17, 510.15, 802.14
tear to rags 802.14
tear to shreds 395.17
tear to tatters 395.17, 802.14
tear up 112.19, 395.13, 793.6
tear up one's mortgage 624.13
tear up the earth 152.15
tear up the road 174.9
tear up the track 174.9
teary 2.33, 93.21, 115.21
tease (n) 96.10, 132.1, 357.1 (v) 96.13, 132.2, 377.6, 440.12, 490.5
teased 96.24
teaser 96.10, 352.6, 357.1, 377.4, 704.20, 1013.7
tea service 8.12
tea set 8.12
tea shop 8.17
teasing (n) 440.3, 490.2 (a) 98.22, 132.6, 377.8, 440.18, 489.15, 490.7, 508.12
teaspoon 8.12
tea strainer 8.12
tea-table talk 541.4
teated 283.19
tea things 8.12
teatime 8.6
teats 283.6
tec 576.11, 1008.16
techie 726.7, 866.3, 1042.17
technic 413.7, 928.1
technical 413.26, 724.16, 866.5, 928.28, 998.17, 998.20
technical adviser 413.11
technical brilliance 413.1
technical difficulty 1012.6
technical expert 866.3
technical flaw 674.1
technicality 369.4, 526.5, 799.1, 866.1, 998.6
technical jargon 545.3
technical knockout 754.3
technical know-how 413.7
technical knowledge 413.7
technically superb 413.22
technical mastery 413.1
technical rehearsal 704.13
technical run 704.13
technical sergeant 575.18
technical skill 413.1, 413.7
technical support 449.3, 731.6
technical term 526.5
technical worker 726.2, 726.7
technical writer 547.15, 718.4
technical writing 547.2, 718.2
technician 413.11, 726.6, 726.7, 866.3, 1042.17, 1043.2
technicological 928.28
technicology 928.10
Technicolor 35.4, 706.5
technicolored 35.16
technics 413.7, 928.1, 928.10
technique 384.1, 413.1, 413.7, 712.8, 753.3, 928.1
technobabble 523.9, 523.10
technocracy 612.4
technocrat 928.11
technological 928.28
Technological Age 824.6
technological politics 609.1
technological revolution 860.1
technological unemployment 331.3
technologist 726.7, 928.11
technology 413.7, 928.4, 928.10
technospeak 523.9, 523.10
tech rehearsal 704.13
tech run 704.13
tech support 449.3, 731.6
tectonic 266.6, 717.7
tectonic plate 235.1
tectonics 266.1, 717.1
tectrices 3.18
teddy bear 349.6, 743.16
Te Deum 696.3
tedge 239.4
tedious 117.6, 118.9, 781.6, 849.15, 1005.7
tediousness 96.1, 117.1, 118.2, 1005.1
tedious work 725.4
tedium 96.1, 118.1, 849.4
tee 751.1
teed off 152.30
teed up 405.16
tee-hee (n) 116.4 (v) 116.8
teeing ground 751.1
teem 251.6, 770.16, 890.7, 991.5, 993.8
teeming (n) 890.2, 910.2 (a) 78.18, 221.15, 538.11, 770.22, 884.9, 890.9, 910.11, 986.18, 991.7, 993.19
teeming imagination 986.3
teeming loins 890.1
teemingness 538.2, 884.1, 890.1, 991.2
teeming rain 316.2

teeming womb 890.1
teem over 910.5
teem with 221.7, 884.5, 991.5
teenage (n) 301.7 (a) 301.14
teenaged 301.14
teenagehood 301.7
teenager 302.1
teener 302.1
teenish 301.14
teens 301.7, 882.7
teeny 258.11
teenybopper 302.1, 302.7, 867.2
teen years 301.7
teeny-weeny 258.11
tee off 152.23, 751.4, 818.7
tee-off 751.3
tee off on 459.15, 510.14
teeter (n) 916.5, 916.9 (v) 16.8, 362.8, 854.5, 916.13
teeterboard 916.9
teetering (n) 854.3, 916.5 (a) 16.16
teeter on the edge 1006.8
teeter-totter (n) 743.15, 916.5, 916.9 (v) 854.5, 916.13
teeter-tottering 854.3, 916.5
teetery 16.16
teetery-bender 916.9
teeth 2.8, 2.12, 17.5, 37.2, 474.4, 524.18
teethless 286.4
teeth ridge 524.18
teetotal 668.10
teetotaler 516.1, 668.4
teetotalism 668.2
teetotalist 668.4
tee up 405.6, 751.4
tefillin 696.10
Teflon bullet 462.19
Teflon-coated 1008.23
Teflon coating 1008.1
teg 311.7
tegmen 295.3
tegmental 295.32
tegmentum 295.3
tegument 295.3
tegumental 295.32
tegumentary 295.32
Tehuantepecer 318.8
Tehuantepec wind 318.8
tektite 1073.15
tel 237.4
Telamon 901.3
telamon 273.5
telamones 273.5
tele-action 1041.4
telebanking 729.3
telebet 759.3
telecamera 1035.10, 1075.7
telecast (n) 1035.2 (v) 352.10, 1035.14 (a) 352.17
telecasting 352.1, 1035.3
telecentric system 29.2
telecommunication 343.5, 347.1, 1034.1
telecommunicational 347.21
telecommunications 517.15
telecommute 724.10
telecommuter 726.2
teleconference 347.13, 541.5
telecopier 347.15
telefilm 1035.2
telegenic 1035.16
telegram (n) 347.14, 552.4 (v) 347.20
telegraph (n) 347.2, 347.14 (v) 347.20
telegraph agency 552.1
telegraph cable 347.17
telegrapher 347.16
telegraphese 523.10
telegraphic 347.21, 537.6
telegraphics 347.2
telegraphist 347.16
telegraph line 347.17
telegraph operator 347.16
telegraph pole 273.1
telegraph recorder 347.2
telegraphy 347.2
Teleia 563.13
telekinesis 689.6
telekinetic 689.24
telemarket 734.8, 734.9
telemarketing 347.13, 734.2
telemechanic 1041.25
telemechanics 1041.2, 1041.4
telemechanism 1041.4
telemeeting 423.3, 541.5
telemeter 1041.4
telemetered 1041.25
telemetering 300.1, 1041.4
telemetric 1041.25
telemetry 300.1, 1041.4, 1074.1
teleological 380.8
teleology 380.2, 886.3
teleost fish 311.30
telepathic 343.9, 689.24, 934.5, 961.7
telepathic dream 689.9
telepathic hallucination 689.9
telepathic transmission 689.9
telepathist 689.15
telepathize 689.22
telepathy 343.1, 689.9, 962.2
telephone (n) 347.4 (v) 347.19
telephone area 347.12
telephone book 347.12, 554.9, 574.10
telephone booth 347.4
telephone box 347.4
telephone call 347.13
telephone directory 347.12, 554.9, 574.10, 871.4
telephone engineering 347.4
telephone exchange 347.7, 347.12
telephone extension 347.4
telephone kiosk 347.4
telephone line 347.17
telephone market 737.7
telephone mechanic 347.10
telephone mechanics 347.4
telephone number 347.12
telephone office 347.7
telephone operator 347.9
telephone pole 273.1
telephoner 347.11
telephone receiver 347.4
telephone set 347.4
telephone tower 272.6
telephonic 347.21
telephonic engineer 347.10
telephonics 347.4
telephonist 347.9
telephony 347.4
telephoto (n) 347.15, 714.3 (a) 714.17
telephotograph 347.15, 714.3
telephotographic 347.21, 714.17
teleplay 1035.2
teleport 689.20
teleportation 689.6
telepreacher 699.3
teleprinter 347.2
teleprinter exchange 347.2
teleran 184.6, 1036.2
telerecord 1035.15
telergy 689.9
telescope (n) 29.4, 1073.17 (v) 260.10, 268.6
telescope word 526.11
telescopic 27.21, 29.10
telescoping 268.3
telescopist 29.8
telescopy 29.7
telescreen 1035.11
teleshopping 733.1
telesthesia 689.6, 689.9
telestial kingdom 681.6
telethon 478.9, 1035.2
Teletype (v) 347.20 (a) 347.21
teletypewriter 347.2
televangelist 543.5, 699.6, 858.9
teleview 1035.15
televiewer 918.1, 1035.12
televise 352.10, 1035.14
televised 352.17
televising 1035.3
television 347.3, 551.5, 552.1, 1033.1, 1035.1
televisional 1035.16
televisionary 1035.16
television audience 1035.12
television broadcast 1035.2
television camera 1035.10
television channel 1035.4
television drama 1035.2
television engineer 1035.13
television evangelist 699.6
television journalism 552.1
television mast 272.6, 1035.8
television performer 1035.2
television personality 1035.2
television radar air navigation 1036.2
television receiver 1035.11
television recording 1035.11
television repairperson 1035.13
television selling 734.2
television set 1035.11
television show 1035.2
television studio 1035.6
television technician 1035.13
television tower 1035.8
television tube 1033.10
television viewer 918.1
televison evangelism 543.3
televison evangelist 543.5
televison preacher 699.3
televisor 1035.8, 1035.11
televisual 1035.16
telework 724.10
teleworker 726.2
telex (n) 347.2, 347.14 (v) 347.20
telic 380.8
tell (n) 237.4 (v) 93.15, 343.7, 351.5, 524.22, 551.8, 552.11, 719.5, 722.7, 894.10, 957.8, 989.11, 997.12, 1017.17
tell a good story 489.13
tell a lie 354.19
tell all 351.7
tell apart 944.6
tell a story 722.7
tell a thing or two 510.18
tell a white lie 354.19
tell confidentially 345.9
teller 551.5, 729.11
teller of tales 722.5
teller's check 728.11
tell for one's ears only 345.9
tell fortunes 962.9
tell how 341.10
tell idle tales 552.12
tell in advance 399.6
telling (n) 343.2, 722.1, 722.2, 1017.9 (a) 18.12, 105.30, 544.11, 894.13, 957.16, 997.19
tell in glowing terms 545.7
telling off 510.7
tell it like it is 644.12
tell its own story 348.7
tell its own tale 348.7, 521.4
tell it to the judge 598.19
tell more than one wants to know 993.10
tell off 510.18, 604.10
tell on 351.6, 551.13
tell once and for all 399.5, 551.8
tell one a secret 345.9
tell one's beads 696.13
tell oneself 542.3
tell one thing from another 944.6
tell one to one's face 216.8
tell one where to get off 453.2
tell secrets 351.6
telltale (n) 351.2, 517.9, 551.4, 551.6, 552.9 (a) 517.23, 551.19, 957.17
tell tales 351.6
telltale sign 351.2, 517.1
tell tales out of school 351.6
tell the future 962.9
tell the meaning of 341.10
tell the news 552.11
tell the truth 351.7, 644.11, 977.2
tell the truth and shame the devil 644.11
tell the truth, the whole truth, and nothing but the truth 644.11
tell the world 524.23
tellurian (n) 312.5 (a) 234.4, 312.13
telluric 234.4
Tellus 1073.10
tell where to get off 510.18
tell which is which 944.5
telly 1035.1, 1035.11
telophase 305.16
telos 375.1, 380.2
telpher 383.8
telpher line 383.8
telpher ropeway 383.8
telpherway 383.8

Telstar 1035.9
temblor 671.5
temerarious 493.7
temerariousness 493.1
temerity 493.1
temp 726.2, 1019.3
temper (n) 15.3, 110.4, 152.6, 767.4, 978.3, 978.4, 1046.4 (v) 15.13, 303.9, 670.6, 797.11, 959.3, 1046.7, 1049.3
tempera 35.8, 712.13
temperament 709.4, 767.4, 978.3
temperamental 110.21, 364.5, 767.8, 978.7
temperamentalness 110.5, 364.2
temperance 106.4, 516.1, 653.3, 668.1, 670.1
temperance society 516.1
temperate 106.13, 106.14, 516.3, 668.9, 670.10, 1019.24, 1023.12
temperateness 668.1, 670.1
Temperate Zone 231.3
temperature 1019.3
temperature control 1041.8
temperature-humidity index 317.4, 1019.3
temperature wind rose 318.15
tempered 303.13, 670.11, 959.10, 1046.15, 1049.6
tempered in fire 1046.15
tempered semitone 709.20
temperer 670.3
tempering (n) 15.5, 303.6, 405.4, 413.9, 670.2, 797.7, 1046.4, 1046.5 (a) 670.14
temper one's zeal 102.4
temper tantrum 152.8
temper the wind to the shorn lamb 120.5, 145.4, 670.8, 1008.18
tempest 105.9, 318.11, 671.4
tempest in a teacup 355.3
tempest in a teapot 355.2, 998.3
tempestuous 105.24, 105.29, 318.22, 671.18
tempestuousness 105.10, 671.2
tempestuous wind 318.11
template 786.6
temple 218.1, 703.2
templelike 703.15
temple of the Holy Ghost 687.3
tempo 709.24, 821.1, 916.3
tempo mark 709.12
temporal 686.3, 695.16, 700.3, 821.7, 828.7, 832.15, 1052.10
temporal, the 686.2
temporality 1052.6
temporalty 700.1
temporariness 828.1, 995.1
temporary (n) 726.2 (a) 821.7, 826.4, 828.7, 862.8, 959.8, 971.20, 995.7
temporary arrangement 365.5, 465.5
temporary employee 726.2
temporary expedient 995.2
temporary lodger 828.4
temporary measure 365.5
temporary stay 225.5
temporary truce 465.5
temporization 846.5
temporize 363.9, 368.13, 827.9, 846.11
temporizer 363.4, 651.3
temporizing 363.10
tempo rubato 709.24
tempt 104.22, 375.22, 377.6, 654.10
temptation 100.11, 377.1
tempted 100.21
tempter 375.10, 377.4
tempt fate 403.10, 493.6, 923.6, 1006.7
tempt fortune 759.24
tempting 63.10, 97.7, 100.30, 377.8
temptingness 97.2
tempt Providence 1006.7
temptress 377.4, 665.15
tempt the appetite 63.4
tempt the gods 493.6
10 1016.3
10, a 1002.4
ten 758.2, 882.6, 1016.8
tenability 107.3, 953.8
tenable 107.12, 460.15, 953.24
Tenach 683.3
tenacious 359.11, 360.8, 361.8, 474.8, 492.17, 803.12, 1049.4, 1062.12
tenaciousness 360.1, 361.1, 474.1, 492.5, 803.3, 1062.2
tenacious of life 306.12
tenacity 15.1, 359.1, 360.1, 361.1, 474.1, 492.5, 803.3, 1049.1, 1062.2
tenancy 225.1, 469.1
tenant (n) 227.2, 227.8, 470.4 (v) 225.7
tenantable 225.15
tenant at sufferance 470.4
tenant at will 470.4
tenanted 225.12
tenant farmer 1069.5
tenant for life 470.4
tenant for years 470.4
tenant from year to year 470.4
tenantless 222.15
tenantry 469.1
ten best-dressed 578.7
ten cents 728.7
ten-cent store 736.1
Ten Commandments 636.1, 673.8, 882.6
tend 161.7, 297.15, 339.9, 577.13, 896.3, 983.6, 1008.19, 1070.7
tendance 577.12
tendency 100.3, 161.1, 371.5, 413.5, 767.4, 896.1, 968.1, 978.3
tendential 650.11, 896.4
tendentious 650.11, 896.4
tendentiousness 650.3
tender (n) 577.5 (v) 439.4, 478.12, 624.10 (a) 24.12, 26.11, 35.22, 93.20, 104.26, 143.13, 145.7, 180.18, 298.12, 301.10, 339.10, 427.7, 791.5, 1047.8
tender age 301.1
tender conscience 636.5
tender-conscienced 644.15
tender feeling 93.6, 104.1
tenderfoot 461.18, 572.9, 757.2, 774.4, 818.2, 930.7
tender heart 93.6
tenderhearted 93.20, 143.13, 145.7
tenderheartedness 93.6, 143.1, 145.2
tenderize 1047.6
tenderizing 1047.5
tenderloin 10.14, 230.6, 665.9
tender loving care 339.1, 449.2, 449.3
tender mercies 146.1
tenderness 24.3, 26.4, 93.4, 93.6, 96.5, 145.2, 298.1, 301.1, 427.1, 1047.1
tenderness of heart 143.1
tender one's congratulations 149.2
tender one's resignation 448.2
tender passion 104.1
tender rocket 1075.2
tender spot 24.4, 96.5, 152.11, 456.7
tender thanks 150.4
tending 896.4
ten-dollar bill 728.7
ten-dollar gold piece 728.4
tendon 2.3, 271.2
tendril 271.1, 281.2, 310.20, 793.4
tend to a point 169.2
tend to go 161.7, 297.15
tend to show 957.8
tend toward 371.17, 978.6
tenebrific 1027.13
tenebrious 1027.13
tenebrose 1027.13
tenebrosity 1027.1
tenebrous 1027.13, 1027.16
tenebrousness 1027.1
tenement 80.11, 228.13, 228.14
tenement district 230.6
tenement of clay 307.15
tenements 471.6
tenet 419.2, 952.2, 953.2
tenfold 882.22
ten-gallon hat 5.25
ten million 882.11
tenne 647.2
tenner 728.7, 728.8
tennis 748.1
tennis ball 748.1, 1048.3
tennis bum 178.3
tennis competition 748.1
tennis court 287.3, 743.11, 748.1
tennis match 748.2
tennis racket 748.1
tennis shoes 5.27
tenno 575.9
ten o'clock scholar 846.6
tenor (n) 58.6, 161.1, 518.1, 708.22, 709.5, 765.4, 767.4, 785.4, 896.2 (a) 58.13, 708.50
tenor clef 709.13
tenor octave 709.9
ten-percenter 704.25
tenpin 750.1
tenpin bowling 750.1
tenpins 750.1
tense (n) 530.12, 821.1 (v) 260.8, 725.10, 1046.9 (a) 105.27, 126.7, 128.13, 130.12, 524.30, 589.9, 1046.11
ten-second rule 747.3
tensed up 126.7
tensed-up 128.13
tenseness 128.3, 1046.2
tense readiness 135.1
tense up 126.6, 128.6, 1046.9
tensile 1048.7
tensileness 1047.2
tensility 1047.2
tension (n) 126.1, 128.3, 456.1, 589.1, 725.2, 993.7, 997.4, 1032.12, 1046.2, 1048.2 (v) 1046.9
tension fatigue 21.1
tensity 1046.2
tensive 725.18
ten-spot 728.7, 758.2
ten-strike 750.2
tent (n) 86.33, 295.8 (v) 225.11
tentacle 3.10
tentacles 474.4
tentaculum 73.4
tentage 295.8
tentation 403.2
tentative (n) 403.2 (a) 175.10, 362.11, 403.16, 494.8, 826.4, 862.8, 930.11, 938.37, 942.11, 971.20, 995.7
tentative approach 439.1
tentative contact 223.5
tentative examination 938.5
tentative explanation 951.2
tentatively suggest 951.11
tentative method 942.1
tentativeness 175.1, 362.3, 494.1, 942.1
tentative poke 73.1
tented 295.31
tented field 463.3
tenterhooks 126.1
tentfly 295.4
tenth (n) 882.14 (a) 882.22
ten thousand 882.10
tenting 225.4
tent meeting 696.8
tent pole 273.1
tenuity 270.4, 299.1, 764.1
tenuous 248.7, 258.14, 270.16, 299.4, 764.6, 804.4
tenuousness 258.2, 299.1, 764.1
tenure 469.1, 724.5, 824.3, 825.4
tenured 469.9
tenure in 471.5
tenure in chivalry 469.1
tenure in office 825.4
tepee 228.10, 295.8
tepefy 1020.17
tepid 102.6, 1019.24
tepidarium 79.10, 1019.4
tepidity 1019.4
tepidness 102.1, 1019.4
teratic 1015.8
teratism 870.1, 870.3, 870.6, 1015.4
teratogenic 870.13
teratoid 870.13
teratology 265.3
terbit 1042.14

tercentenary 850.4, 882.8
tercentennial 850.4, 882.8
tercet 709.14, 720.10, 876.1
terebrant pain 26.2
terebrating pain 26.2
terebration 292.3
terefah 80.20
tergal 217.10
tergiversant (n) 363.5 (a) 344.11, 363.11
tergiversate 344.7, 362.8, 854.5, 936.9
tergiversating (n) 363.1 (a) 344.11, 363.11
tergiversation 344.4, 362.1, 363.1, 936.5
tergiversator 362.5, 363.5, 936.7
teriyaki sauce 10.12
term (n) 211.3, 518.6, 526.1, 529.1, 820.1, 821.1, 824.2, 824.3, 825.4 (v) 527.11
termagant 110.12, 593.7, 671.9
termed 527.14
terminable 210.10
terminal (n) 186.5, 383.7, 524.9, 820.1, 857.2, 1042.9 (a) 85.54, 85.56, 125.15, 210.10, 211.11, 261.12, 307.32, 308.23, 407.9, 820.12, 1011.15
terminal bud 310.23
terminal case 85.43, 125.8, 307.14
terminal date 211.3
terminal degree 648.6
terminal disease 85.2
terminal illness 85.2
terminal moraine 237.5
terminal point 186.5
terminal speed 184.31
terminal velocity 174.2
terminate 407.6, 820.6, 857.6, 887.4
terminated 407.11, 820.9
terminate the account 737.24
terminating (n) 820.1 (a) 820.11, 820.12
termination 407.2, 820.1, 857.1
terminative (n) 530.9 (a) 407.9, 820.12
terming 527.2
terminological 527.17
terminology 523.9, 527.1, 871.4
terminus 186.5, 211.3, 383.7, 407.2, 820.1, 857.2
termite 311.33
termiticide 1001.3
termless 823.3
termlessness 823.1
term of imprisonment 429.3
term paper 556.1
terms 421.2, 465.4, 959.2
terms of endearment 562.5
terms of reference 766.2
tern 877.3
ternal 877.3
ternary (n) 876.1 (a) 877.3, 1017.23
ternary form 709.11
ternate 877.3
ternion 876.1
Terpsichore 710.22, 986.2
terpsichore 705.1
terpsichorean (n) 705.3 (a) 704.33, 705.6
Terra 1073.10
terra 234.1, 1073.10
terrace 197.22, 201.3, 901.13
terraced 296.6
terra cotta 715.2, 742.3
terra-cotta 40.4
terra firma 199.3, 234.1, 901.6
terrain 158.4, 228.18, 231.1, 234.1, 463.1
terra incognita 234.1, 930.6
Terramycin 86.29
terran 312.5
terrapin 311.24
terraqueous 234.4
terrarium 228.24
terrene 234.4
terrestrial 234.4, 695.16, 1073.25
terrestrial globe 1073.10
terrestrial guidance 1075.2
terrestrial kingdom 681.6
terrestrial planet 1073.9
terrestrial telescope 29.4
terrible 98.19, 127.30, 247.11, 638.3, 1000.9, 1015.11
terribleness 98.3, 127.2, 1000.2, 1015.2
terrible thing 638.2
terrific 127.30, 247.11, 999.15
terrified 127.26
terrify 127.17
terrifying 127.29
terriginous 240.8
territorial 231.8
territorial army 461.25
territoriality 231.1
territorial jurisdiction 594.1
territorial militia 461.24
territorial reserves 461.25
territorial waters 231.1
territory 158.4, 231.1, 231.5, 232.1, 234.1, 894.4
terror (n) 127.1, 127.9, 593.4, 671.10 (a) 127.29
terror-bearing 127.29
terror-breathing 127.29
terror-breeding 127.29
terror-bringing 127.29
terror-crazed 127.26
terror-driven 127.26
terror-fraught 127.29
terrorful 127.29
terror-giving 127.29
terror-haunted 127.26
terror-inspiring 127.29
terrorism 127.7, 327.4, 424.3, 612.9, 655.2, 671.1, 860.2
terrorist (n) 127.8, 308.11, 395.8, 459.12, 461.5, 461.16, 461.17, 593.1, 671.9, 860.3 (a) 860.6
terrorist attack 459.1, 459.7
terroristic 127.29, 424.12, 514.3, 671.19, 860.6
terroristic tactics 127.7
terrorist killing 308.2
terrorization 127.7
terrorize 127.20, 424.7, 514.2, 612.15, 671.11
terrorizing (n) 127.7 (a) 127.29, 514.3
terror-ridden 127.26
terror-riven 127.26
terror-shaken 127.26
terror-smitten 127.26
terror-stricken 127.26, 127.27
terror-striking 127.29
terror-struck 127.26
terror suspect 429.11
terror tactics 127.7
terror-troubled 127.26
terse 344.9, 533.6, 537.6
terseness 268.1, 344.2, 533.1, 537.1
tertian 850.8
tertiaries 3.18
tertiary (n) 35.7 (a) 877.4
tertiary chord 709.17
tertiary color 35.7
tertiary school 567.5
tertiary stress 524.10
tertium quid 878.2
tervalence 1060.4
tervalent 1060.10
terza rima 720.9
terzet 708.18
terzetto 708.18, 876.1
tessellate (v) 47.7, 191.8 (a) 47.14
tessellated 47.14
tessellation 47.4, 191.1
tessera 191.2
tesserae 47.4
tessitura 709.4
test (n) 91.12, 295.15, 300.2, 457.3, 938.2, 942.2 (v) 62.7, 938.21, 942.8, 970.12 (a) 942.11
testa 295.3, 295.15
testable 970.15
testaceous 2.27, 295.32
Testament 683.2
testament 478.10
testamentary 478.25
testamur 549.6
test animal 942.7
testate (n) 478.11 (a) 478.25
testator 478.11
testatrix 478.11
test ban 464.7, 465.6
test case 598.1, 942.2
test drive 938.1
test-drive 938.24
test driver 942.6
tested 587.21, 644.19, 942.12, 970.20
testee 942.7
tester 938.17, 942.6
testes 2.13
test flight 184.9, 942.3
test hop 184.9
testicles 2.13
testicular 2.29
testifier 957.6
testify 334.6, 517.17, 598.17, 957.9
testify against 551.12
testify to 957.8
testimonial (n) 352.6, 487.1, 509.4, 549.6, 549.12, 957.2 (a) 549.18
testimonial banquet 487.1
testimonial dinner 487.1
testimonium 957.2
testimony 334.3, 598.8, 957.2
testiness 110.2, 935.13
testing (n) 938.6, 942.1 (a) 938.37, 942.11
testing ground 1074.7
test instrument vehicle 1074.6
test oath 334.4
teston 728.8
test one another 457.18
test out 942.8, 942.9
test paper 938.2
test pattern 1035.5
test pilot 185.1, 942.6
test rocket 1074.6
test run 942.3
test the waters 403.10, 942.9
test tube 858.10, 1060.6
test-tube baby 78.3
testy 110.19, 935.19
tetanus 85.6
tetany 85.6
tetched 926.27
tetchiness 24.3, 110.5
tetchy 24.12, 110.21
tête-à-tête (n) 541.3 (a) 582.24, 873.7
tête de veau 10.15
tether (n) 428.4 (v) 428.10, 800.10, 855.8
tethered 428.16, 855.16
téton 283.6
tetrachord 709.8
tetrachordal scale 709.6
tetractinal 879.4
tetracycline 86.29
tetrad (n) 879.1 (a) 879.4
tetradic 879.4
tetragon 879.1
tetragonal 278.9
tetragram 879.1
tetragrammaton 879.1
tetrahedral 218.7, 278.9
tetrahedral kite 181.14
tetrahedron 879.1
tetralemma 1013.7
tetralogy 879.1
tetrameter 720.7
tetraphony 879.1
tetraploid 880.3
tetrapody 720.7, 879.1
tetrarch 575.8, 575.12
tetrarchic 417.17
tetraseme 720.7
tetrastich 720.10
tetratheism 675.5
tetratheist 675.16
tetratomic 1038.18
tetravalence 1060.4
tetravalent 879.4, 1060.10
tewel 1020.10
Texan 502.5
Texas fever 85.41
Texas Leaguer 745.3
Texas tea 87.11
Texas tower 27.8, 517.10
text 341.2, 349.1, 518.6, 547.10, 547.12, 548.10, 554.10, 554.12, 704.21, 708.28, 718.1, 793.2, 937.1, 974.1

textbook (n) 554.1, 554.10 (a) 687.7
textbook editor 554.2
text edition 554.5
text editor 1042.11
texter 547.18
text file 1042.15
textile (n) 4.1 (a) 740.7
textile design 717.5
textile designer 716.9
textile fabric 4.1
textiles 735.3
texting 347.4, 547.1, 553.1
text message 552.4, 553.4
text messaging 347.4, 553.1
textual 683.11, 687.7
textual critic 341.7, 946.7
textual criticism 341.8
textualism 973.5
textualist 687.4
textuality 973.5
textuary (n) 687.4 (a) 683.11
textural 266.6, 294.5
texture 4.1, 170.3, 266.1, 294.1, 740.1
textured 288.6, 294.5
text-walking 347.4
Thais 665.15
thalassic 240.8
thalassographer 240.7
thalassographic 240.8
thalassographical 240.8
thalassography 240.6
thalassometer 238.13
Thales 921.4
Thalia 704.6, 986.2
thallophyte 310.3
thallus 310.20
thanatosis 22.6
thang 866.1
thank 150.4
thankful 150.5
thankfulness 150.1
thank God 150.3
thankless 98.17, 99.9, 151.4
thanklessness 151.1
thankless task 725.4
thankless wretch 151.2
thank offering 150.2, 696.7
thank one's lucky stars 116.5, 150.3
thank one's stars 116.5, 150.3
thanks 150.2, 696.4
thanksgiving 150.2, 696.4
thank you 150.2
thank-you-ma'am 283.3
that 865.14
that applies 831.9
that be 838.2
thatch (n) 3.4 (v) 295.23
that is 831.9, 838.2
that is to be 840.3
that one 865.14
that or nothing 963.6
that time 12.9
that will be 840.3
thaumatology 870.8
thaumaturge 690.5
thaumaturgia 690.1
thaumaturgic 690.14, 870.16
thaumaturgical 690.14, 870.16
thaumaturgics 690.1
thaumaturgism 690.1
thaumaturgist 690.5
thaumaturgy 690.1, 870.8
thaw (n) 1020.3 (v) 145.4, 1020.21, 1047.6, 1064.5
thawable 1064.9
thawed 1064.6
thawer 318.6
thawing (n) 1020.3, 1064.1 (a) 1064.7
thaw out 1020.21
thearchy 612.4
theater 197.4, 209.2, 212.3, 463.1, 463.2, 567.11, 704.14, 743.13
theater, the 704.1
theatercraft 704.3
theatergoer 221.5, 704.27, 918.2
theater-in-the-round 704.14, 704.16
theaterlike 704.33
theater of cruelty 704.1
theater of operations 458.1, 463.2
theater of the absurd 704.1
theater of war 463.2
theater person 704.23
theater world 704.1
theatregoers 48.6
theatre stall 704.15
theatric 93.19, 501.24, 704.33
theatrical (n) 707.2 (a) 93.19, 105.26, 500.15, 501.24, 704.33
theatrical film 706.1
theatricalism 704.2
theatricality 93.9, 704.2
theatricalize 93.13, 704.28
theatrical makeup 704.17
theatrical performance 704.12
theatricals 704.2
theatrical season 313.1
theatrician 704.23
theatricism 704.2
theatrics 93.9, 348.4, 501.4, 704.2
theatromania 704.1
theatron 704.14
theatrophobia 704.1
thecal 295.32
thé dansant 705.2
theft 480.1, 482.1, 482.3
theism 675.5, 692.1
theist 675.16, 692.4
theistic 675.25, 692.8
them 575.14, 865.5
thematic 849.13, 937.4
thematic development 722.4
theme 498.7, 517.11, 526.3, 556.1, 708.24, 722.4, 937.1
theme park 743.14
theme restaurant 8.17
theme song 517.11, 1034.19
theme tune 517.11
Themis 649.4
themselves 865.5
then 837.10
theocracy 612.4, 698.7
theocratic 612.16, 698.16
theocratist 698.16
Theocritean 720.16
theodolite 278.4
theogony 678.1
theologer 676.3
theologian 676.3
theological (n) 676.3 (a) 676.4
theological student 676.3
theological virtues 653.3
theologician 676.3
theologism 676.1
theologist 676.3
theologizer 676.3
theologue 676.3
theology 675.1, 676.1
theology branch 676.1
theopantism 675.5
theopathic 692.10
theophania 683.10
theophanic 348.9
theophany 33.1, 348.1, 683.10, 988.1
theophoric 675.25
theopneustia 683.10
theopneustic 683.11
theopneusty 683.10
theorbist 710.5
theorem 935.7, 974.2
theoretic 951.1, 951.7
theoretical 932.9, 951.13, 952.10
theoretical basis 951.1
theoretical chemist 1060.7
theoretical construct 951.1
theoretical economics 731.11
theoretical justification 951.1
theoreticalness 951.6
theoretical structure 951.1
theoretician 723.4, 951.7
theoretics 951.1
theoric 951.1
theorist 951.7
theorization 951.1
theorize 723.5, 931.16, 935.15, 951.9
theorizer 951.7
theory 709.1, 932.1, 951.1, 951.2, 953.6
theory of criticism 723.3
theory of everything 1018.1
theory of evolution 861.4
theory of games 968.2
theory of history 719.1
theory of knowledge 952.1
theory of literature 723.3
theory of probability 972.1
theory of relativity 158.6
theosophical 689.23
theosophist (n) 689.11 (a) 689.23
theosophy 689.1
theotherapist 90.9
theotherapy 91.2
theow 432.7
therapeusis 91.1
therapeutic 86.39, 90.15, 449.21
therapeutics 91.1
therapeutist 90.8
therapist 90.8, 92.10
theraputant 86.4
therapy 90.1, 91.1, 396.7, 449.1
therblig 573.7
thereness 221.1
theriac (n) 86.3, 86.26 (a) 86.39
theriaca 86.26
theriacal 86.39
therianthropic 311.39
therioanthropic 312.14
theriolater 697.4
theriomorphic 311.39
theriotheism 675.5
theriotheist 675.16
therm 1019.19
thermae 79.10, 1019.10
thermal (n) 317.4, 1019.9 (a) 1019.24, 1019.25
thermal barrier 1075.2
thermal cracking 1020.5
thermal detector 1019.20
thermal imaging 91.7
thermal printer 1042.9
thermal radiation 1019.1
thermal spring 1019.10
thermal unit 1019.19
thermantidote 318.18
thermic 1019.24, 1019.25
thermic fever 85.28
thermion 1033.3
thermionic 1033.15
thermionic effect 1033.4
thermionic emission 1033.5
thermionic grid emission 1033.5
thermionics 1038.1
thermionic tube 1033.10
thermionic tube circuit 1033.8
thermocautery 1020.15
thermochemical 1019.32, 1060.9
thermochemistry 1019.21
thermochromism 1019.12
thermodynamic 1019.32
thermodynamical 1019.32
thermodynamics 1019.21
thermoelectronic 1033.15
thermoform 262.7
thermogenesis 1020.5
thermograph 317.8, 1019.20
thermology 1019.21
thermoluminescence 1025.13
thermolysis 806.2
thermolytic 806.6
thermometer 317.8, 1019.20
thermometry 1019.3
thermonuclear 1038.19
thermonuclear arsenal 462.2
thermonuclear attack 459.1
thermonuclear bomb 1038.16
thermonuclear explosion 1038.16
thermonuclear fusion 1038.9
thermonuclear power 18.4, 1038.15
thermonuclear reaction 1038.8, 1038.9
thermonuclear warhead 1074.3
thermonuclear weapons 462.1
thermoplastic (n) 1054.6 (a) 1020.31
thermoplasticity 1020.3
thermosetting plastic 1054.6
thermostat 1019.20
thermotelephonic 347.21
thermotherapy 91.4
thermotics 1019.21
therolater 697.4
Thersites 512.6
thersitical 144.23, 513.8
thesaurus 526.13, 554.9, 871.4

these 865.14
these days 838.1
Theseus and Pirithoüs 588.6
thesis 556.1, 709.25, 720.7, 850.3, 935.7, 937.1, 951.3, 952.2
thespian (n) 707.2 (a) 704.33
Thespian art 704.2
Thetis 240.3, 678.10
theurgist 690.5
theurgy 690.1
thew 2.3, 15.2
thewiness 15.2
thews 15.2
thewy 15.16
they 575.14, 773.3, 865.5
thick (n) 94.3, 819.1 (v) 269.5, 1045.10 (a) 58.15, 269.8, 310.43, 525.12, 587.19, 884.9, 922.15, 955.10, 1045.12, 1062.12
thick as flies 884.9
thick as hail 884.9
thick as thieves 587.19
thick-bodied 269.8
thickbodied 257.18
thick-brained 922.16
thick-coming 847.4, 849.13, 884.9
thick consistency 1045.1
thicken 251.4, 269.5, 1045.10, 1046.8, 1062.10
thickened 1045.14, 1062.12
thickener 803.4
thickening 1045.4, 1062.2
thick enough to be cut with a knife 1045.12
thicket 310.15, 770.7
thick-girthed 257.18, 269.8
thick glasses 29.3
thick-growing 1045.12
thickhead 924.4
thick-headed 922.16
thick-headedness 922.3
thick hide 25.1, 295.15
thick-lensed glasses 29.3
thick lenses 29.3
thicknecked 269.8
thickness 58.2, 269.2, 296.1, 1045.1, 1062.2
thickness of speech 525.2
thick of hearing 49.6
thick of things 819.1
thick on the ground 847.4, 884.8
thick-packed 1045.12
thick-pated 922.16
thickset (n) 310.15 (a) 15.16, 257.18, 268.10, 269.8, 1045.12
thick shade 1027.3
thick skin 25.1, 94.3, 295.15, 460.3
thick-skinned 25.6, 94.12
thickskull 924.4
thick-skulled 922.16
thick space 548.7
thick-spread 1045.12
thick-spreading 1045.12
thick squall 318.11
thickwit 924.2
thick with 884.9
thick-witted 922.16
thick-wittedness 922.3
thief 483.1, 593.1, 660.9
thief in the night 307.2
thief of time, the 846.5
thieve 482.13
thievery 482.1
thieving (n) 482.1 (a) 482.21
thievish 480.25, 482.21
thievishness 482.12
thigh 2.7, 10.23, 177.14
thigh-slapper 489.6
thigh trap 752.3
thill 273.1
thiller 311.13
thill horse 311.13
thimbleful 248.2
thimblerig (n) 356.10 (v) 356.18
thimblerigger 357.3
thimblerigging 356.10
thimblewit 924.4
thin (v) 16.11, 255.9, 260.9, 270.12, 299.3, 771.5, 1064.5, 1069.17 (a) 58.14, 65.2, 248.7, 258.14, 260.13, 270.16, 276.5, 299.4, 764.6, 885.5, 955.10, 992.10, 1029.4
thin air 317.1, 764.3
thin as a rail 270.17
thin away 270.12
thin-bellied 270.17
thin-bodied 270.16
thin-cheeked 270.19
thin down 270.12, 270.13
thin edge 1013.4
thin end of the wedge 818.1
thin-faced 270.19
thin-featured 270.19
thin-fleshed 270.17
thing, the 578.4, 637.1
thing 104.5, 328.3, 371.5, 724.1, 761.2, 763.3, 765.4, 766.3, 831.3, 866.1, 1052.4
thingamabob 1052.5
thingamajig 1052.5
thing done 328.3
thing for, a 896.1
thing-in-itself 761.1
thing of beauty 1016.6
thing of interest 997.5
thing of naught 762.2, 764.2, 998.6
things 5.2, 385.4, 471.2
things as they are 973.1
things going against one 1011.1
things to be done 965.3
things to do 724.2
thing to be desired, a 999.5
thingum 1052.5
thingumadad 1052.5
thingumadoodle 1052.5
thingumajig 1052.5
thingumajigger 1052.5
thingumaree 1052.5
thingummy 1052.5
thingy 1052.5
thin ice 1006.1
think 130.5, 339.6, 380.4, 931.8, 951.10, 953.11
thinkability 966.1
thinkable 966.6, 986.26
thinkableness 966.1
think about 931.11
think affirmatively 124.8
think ahead 839.6, 961.5
think aloud 542.3
think back 989.9
think beforehand 961.5
think best 371.17
think better of 113.7, 931.15
think better of it 163.7, 363.6
think dependable 953.17
think downbeat 125.9
thinker 920.9, 921.1, 929.1, 935.11, 951.7, 952.8
think fit 323.2, 371.17
think good 323.2
think hard 931.9, 989.20
think highly of 155.4, 997.13
think ill of 510.10
think improbable 131.4
thinking (n) 931.1, 953.6 (a) 919.7, 931.21
thinking aloud (n) 931.1 (a) 542.4
thinking machine 1041.17
thinking on one's feet 365.5
thinking out 931.1
thinking over 931.5
thinking power 920.1
thinking through 931.1
thinking too late 844.1
think it over 931.14
think laterally 384.6
think likely 968.5
think little of 157.3, 359.10, 510.10, 950.2, 984.2, 998.12
think much of 104.20, 155.4, 997.13
think negatively 125.9
think no more of 148.5, 984.4
think nothing of 157.3, 359.10, 950.2, 984.2, 998.12, 1014.12
think of 143.10, 931.16, 946.8, 989.9
think one is it 140.6
think one's head off 931.9
think only of oneself 651.4
think only of others 652.3
think on one's feet 365.8, 401.5
think out 892.12, 931.11
think out loud 542.3
think over 931.13
think piece 352.1, 556.1
think positively 124.8
think proper 323.2, 371.17
think reliable 953.17
think tank 942.5
think that way about 130.10
think the best of 124.8
think the moon is made of green cheese 954.5
think the world of 104.20
think the worst of 125.9
think through 931.11
think twice 494.5, 971.10
think twice about 362.7
think unlikely 131.4
think up 892.12, 986.14
think well of 155.4, 509.9, 997.13
think well of oneself 140.6
think worlds of 104.20
thin-legged 270.18
thin margin 738.10
thinned 16.19, 299.4, 771.9
thinned-out 299.4, 771.9
thinner 35.8, 270.10, 1064.4
thinness 65.1, 270.4, 299.1, 764.1, 885.1, 922.7, 992.2, 1029.1
thinning (n) 16.5, 260.3, 299.2, 771.1, 1069.13 (a) 1064.8
thinning-out 299.2, 771.1
thinnish 270.16
thin off 270.12
thin out 16.11, 255.9, 270.12, 299.3, 771.5, 1069.17
thin-set 270.16
thin skin 24.3, 93.1, 110.5
thin-skinned 24.12, 110.21
thin space 548.7
thin-spun 270.16, 294.8
thin wine 88.17
third (n) 709.17, 709.20, 745.1, 878.2, 1005.6 (v) 878.3 (a) 877.4
third base 745.1
third-base coach 745.2
third baseman 745.2
third-base umpire 745.3
third-best 132.6
third-class 1005.9
third-degree, the 938.13
third-degree 938.22
third-degree burn 85.38, 1019.13, 1020.6
third dimension, the 269.2
third down 746.3
third estate, the 606.1
third estate 607.5
third-estate 606.8
third eye 689.8
third force 430.12, 467.4, 611.2
third-force 430.22, 467.7
third market 737.7
third mate 183.7
third mortgage 438.4
third officer 185.1
third part 878.2
third party 466.4, 609.24
third person 530.7
third-person past narrator 722.6
third-person present narrator 722.6
third planet 1073.10
third player 750.3
third rail 938.10
third rank 250.6
third-rate 250.6, 1005.9
third-rateness 1005.3
third-rater 1005.5
third reading 613.6
thirds 478.9
third-stream jazz 708.9
third string (n) 250.1, 617.7, 862.2 (a) 250.6
third stringer 250.2
third wave 1042.1
third wheel 769.5
Third World 231.6, 619.3
third world 430.12, 467.4
third-world 430.22, 467.7
third-world nation 232.1
thirst (n) 100.6, 100.7, 896.1, 1066.1 (v) 100.19, 1066.5

thirst after 100.18
thirst for 100.16, 100.19
thirst for knowledge (n) 100.1, 981.1 (v) 570.12
thirst for learning 570.5
thirstiness 100.7, 1066.1
thirsting 100.24, 100.26, 1066.7
thirst quencher 10.49
thirst-quencher 8.4
thirsty 100.24, 100.26, 187.17, 1066.7
thirsty for knowledge 570.18
thirsty soul 88.11
thirteen 882.7
thirteenth 882.25
thirtieth of February, the 822.2
thirty-eight 462.10
35mm 714.10
thirty-second clock 746.3
thirty-second note 709.14
thirty-second rest 709.21
thirty-second rule 747.3
thirty-something 302.1
thirty-thirty 462.10
thirty-two 462.10, 882.7
32mo 882.7
thirty-twomo 882.7
30-year mortgage 438.4
this 865.14
this afternoon 315.1
this AM 314.1
this and no other 865.14
this big 257.24
this day 838.1
this day and age 838.1
this hour 838.1
this instant 838.1
this man's army 461.23
this moment 838.1
this morning 314.1
this one 865.14
this point 838.1
this second 838.1
this single 865.14
this size 257.24
this stage 838.1
thistle 285.5, 647.1
thistledown 3.19, 298.2, 1047.4
thistly 285.10
thither 261.10
thole 906.3
tholepin 906.3
Thomist 952.12
Thomistic 952.12
Thompson submachine 462.10
Thomson's hypothesis 1038.2
thong 5.29, 271.4, 605.1
Thor 56.5, 316.6, 1025.17
thoracic 283.19
thoracic duct 2.23
thoracic viscera 2.16
thoracolumbar nervous system 2.14
thorax 283.6
Thorazine 86.12
thorn 96.8, 285.5, 803.4, 1001.1
thorniness 285.1, 288.1
thorn in the side 96.8, 1001.1
thorny 285.10, 1013.17
thorny problem 1013.7
thorough 247.12, 339.11, 339.12, 373.18, 407.12, 494.8, 794.10
thorough bass 708.22
thoroughbred (n) 311.10, 607.4, 608.4, 757.2 (a) 607.10, 608.11
Thoroughbred Racing Association 757.1
Thoroughbred Racing Protective Bureau 757.1
thoroughgoing 247.12, 339.11, 339.12, 794.10, 1002.9
thoroughgoingness 339.2
thoroughness 339.2, 494.1, 766.4, 794.1
thorough-paced 794.10, 1002.9
thoroughpaced 339.12
thorp 230.2
those 865.14
those left 256.3
those on the inside 575.14
thou 882.10
thought (n) 130.1, 143.3, 174.6, 248.4, 422.1, 524.3, 797.7, 919.1, 931.1, 932.1, 952.2, 953.6, 983.1 (a) 931.21
thought-challenging 983.19
thought control 428.1, 612.9
thought disorder 92.18, 926.4
thought disturbance 92.18
thoughted 932.10
thoughtfree 933.4
thoughtfreeness 933.1
thoughtful 111.3, 143.16, 339.10, 504.13, 920.19, 931.21
thoughtfulness 111.1, 143.3, 339.1, 504.1, 920.7, 931.3
thought-inspiring 983.19
thoughtless 144.18, 340.11, 365.10, 406.15, 414.15, 923.8, 923.10, 933.4, 984.6, 985.16
thoughtlessness 144.3, 340.2, 365.3, 406.2, 414.1, 923.1, 923.2, 933.1, 984.1, 985.5
thought-out 413.30, 935.21
thought pattern 931.1
thought-provoking 951.13, 983.19
thought reader 689.15
thoughts 931.4
thought transference 689.9
thousand, a 884.4
thousand (n) 882.10 (a) 884.6
thousand and one, a 884.4
thousand-dollar bill 728.7
thousand dollars 728.7
thousandfold 882.30
thousand million 882.12
thousands 618.2
thousandth 882.30
thou-shalt-not 444.1
thrall 432.1, 432.7, 577.1
thralldom 432.1, 577.12
thrash 26.7, 412.9, 604.12, 773.6, 902.16
thrash about 917.15, 971.9
thrashing 412.1, 604.4
thrash out 541.11, 801.8, 935.16
thrash over 849.9
thrash soundly 604.13
thrasonic 502.10
thrasonical 502.10
thread (n) 4.1, 16.7, 271.1, 812.2 (v) 812.4
threadbare 117.9, 393.31
threading machine 1040.6
threadlike 270.16, 271.7
thread one's way 162.4
threads 5.1
thready 271.7
threat 399.1, 454.2, 514.1, 1006.1
threaten 127.20, 133.10, 399.5, 514.2, 839.6, 840.2, 1000.6
threatened 133.14, 1006.13
threatening 85.53, 133.16, 514.3, 840.3, 1006.9
threateningness 514.1
threatful 514.3
threatfulness 514.1
threat to health 82.1
3 876.1
three (n) 758.2, 876.1 (a) 876.3
three-alarm 15.22, 1019.25
three-alarm fire 1019.13
three-bagger 745.3
three-ball match 751.3
three-base hit 745.3
three bricks shy of a load 922.17, 926.27
three-by-four 1054.3
three cheers 116.2
three-color 47.9
three-colored 47.9
three-color printing 548.1
three-cornered 878.4
3-D (n) 714.1 (a) 29.10
3-D display 1036.11
three-dimensional 29.10, 158.10, 269.8, 714.17, 878.4
three-dimensional photography 714.1
three-dimensional wave 916.4
3-D movie 706.1
3D printer 714.3
3D printing 714.1
three-em space 548.7
three-finger grip 750.2
threefold (v) 877.2 (a) 877.3
threefoldness 876.2, 877.1
three-footed 878.4
three-forked 878.4
three-four time 709.24
3G 347.4
three-hole ball 750.1
300 game 750.2
360 858.1
360-degree 792.11
360-degree change 858.1
three-in-hand 179.5
three-in-one 677.17, 876.3
Three Kings 921.5
Three Kings of Cologne 921.5
three-legged race 457.12
three-level 296.6
3-merous 878.4
three-mile limit 211.5, 231.1
Three Musketeers, the 588.6
threeness 876.2
three of a kind 758.4
three-part breath 2.21
three-parted 878.4
three-part harmony 708.3
three-part time 709.24
threepence 728.8
threepenny bit 728.8
three-personed 677.17
three-piecer 867.2
three-ply 296.6, 877.3
three-pointer 747.3
three-pointing 1036.8
three-point play 747.3
three-pronged 878.4
three-quarter nelson 474.3
three-quarter-round stage 704.16
three-quarter time 709.24
three R's 568.5
threescore 882.7
threescore and ten 882.7
threescore years and ten 303.5
three-second rule 747.3
three sheets to the wind 88.33
three-sided 218.7, 878.4
threesome 751.2, 876.1
three-spot 758.2
threespot 876.1
three squares 8.8
three-stage rocket 1074.5
three-star general 575.17
three-step approach 750.2
three-step delivery 750.2
three strikes 602.1, 604.1
3-3-4 offense 752.3
three-up 179.5
three-wheeler 179.8
Three Wise Men 921.5
3X 257.4
three-year-old 757.2
thremmatology 1069.1, 1070.1
threnode 115.6
threnodic 115.22
threnody 115.1, 115.6
threpsology 7.16
thresh 773.6, 902.16
threshold (n) 189.6, 197.19, 211.3, 901.9 (a) 211.11
threshold of sensation 24.2
thresh out 541.11
thresh over 849.9
thrice happy 95.16
thrift 620.4, 635.1
thrift industry 620.4
thriftiness 635.1
thrift institution 620.4
thriftless 406.15
thriftlessness 406.2
thrift shop 635.1, 736.1
thrift store 635.1, 736.1
thrifty 635.6
thrill (n) 26.2, 74.1, 105.2 (v) 26.8, 74.5, 74.6, 95.10, 105.15, 105.18
thrilled 95.15, 105.20
thriller 706.2
thrilling 97.7, 105.30
thrill killer 308.11
thrill of fear 127.5
thrill to 105.18
thrill to death 95.11, 105.15
thrill to pieces 95.11, 105.15
thrilly 105.30
thrippence 728.8
thrive 14.2, 17.11, 259.7, 1010.8
thriving 14.3, 259.12, 890.9, 1010.13

thriving condition 1010.1
throat 2.18, 270.3
throat cavity 524.18
throatiness 58.2
throaty 54.11, 58.15, 525.12
throb (n) 26.5, 55.1, 105.5, 709.26, 916.3, 917.4 (v) 26.8, 54.6, 55.4, 105.18, 916.12, 917.12
throbbing (n) 26.5, 55.1, 105.5, 916.3 (a) 26.12, 54.10, 55.7, 709.28, 916.18
throbbing ache 26.5
throbbing pain 26.5
throe 26.2
throes 26.2, 85.6, 96.5, 113.2, 917.6
throes of death 307.8
thromboembolism 85.6
thromboplastin 1045.7
thrombosis 85.6
throne, the 417.8
throne (n) 12.11, 417.11, 647.3 (v) 615.12, 662.13
throned 662.18
throne of God 681.4
throne room 197.20
thrones 679.3
throng (n) 770.4, 884.3 (v) 770.16
thronged 884.9
throng in 214.5
thronging 884.9
throng with 884.5
throttle 19.10, 51.8, 308.19, 428.8, 480.14
throttle down 175.9
throttling 308.6, 428.2
through (v) 31.4 (a) 407.11, 820.9
through-and-through 794.10
through-pass 749.3
throughput 893.2, 1041.11
through with 820.9
throw (n) 759.9, 904.3 (v) 1.3, 159.13, 742.6, 745.5, 811.4, 904.10, 913.5, 965.5, 971.14
throw a bean ball 745.5
throw about 182.30
throw a curve 131.7, 415.11
throw a fight 356.18
throw a fit 152.15
throw a game 356.18
throw a lot of weight 894.10
throw a monkey wrench in the machinery 19.9
throw a monkey wrench in the works 846.8
throw a monkey-wrench in the works 393.15
throw a monkey wrench into the works 1012.15
throw a party 582.21, 585.8
throw a pass 439.8
throw a pot 742.6
throw a scare into 127.16
throw a sop to 378.3
throw a stone at 510.13, 599.10
throw at 459.28
throw away 372.2, 388.3, 390.7, 486.3, 704.31, 909.13, 909.21, 998.12
throwaway (n) 352.8, 370.4, 388.2, 390.3 (a) 106.15, 365.11, 388.6, 581.3, 768.4, 1014.13
throwaway culture 388.2
throwaway item 388.2
throwaway psychology 388.2
throw away the opportunity 844.5
throw away the prepared text 365.8
throw away the scabbard 359.8
throw away the speech 365.8
throw a wet blanket on 379.4, 670.6
throw a wrench in the machinery 19.9, 1012.15
throw back 939.4
throwback 163.1, 394.1, 859.2, 1011.3
throw blind fear into 127.16
throw caution to the wind 492.10, 493.5, 1006.7
throw cold water 1012.10
throw cold water on 379.4, 670.6
throw doubt upon 955.6
throw down 395.19, 395.20, 913.5
throw down one's arms 433.8
throw down the gauntlet 216.8, 453.2, 458.14
throw dust in one's eyes 30.7, 356.17
thrower 904.7
throw for a loop 131.7
throw for a loss 412.9
throw forth 671.13
throw good money after bad 486.6
throw in 191.3, 213.6
throw-in 747.3, 752.3
throwing 904.2
throwing arm 745.3
throwing aside 370.1
throwing away 370.1, 372.1, 388.1
throwing-in 213.2
throwing in the towel 433.2
throwing one's hat in the ring 609.10
throwing open 292.1
throwing out 372.1, 909.1
throwing overboard 370.1, 909.2
throwing shade (n) 372.1 (a) 372.4
throwing spear 462.8
throwing sport 744.1
throwing-stick 462.9, 462.18
throw in one's face 216.8
throw in one's teeth 599.9
throw in prison 429.14
throw in the cooler 429.14
throw in the sponge 370.7
throw in the tank 429.14
throw in the towel 370.7, 412.12, 433.8
throw into a hissy-fit 96.15
throw into a snit 811.4
throw into a tizzy 96.15, 811.4, 985.7
throw into chaos 985.7
throw into confusion 96.15, 811.4, 985.7
throw into disorder 395.10
throw in together 450.3
throw into jail 429.14
throw into the shade 249.8, 346.6
throw into the street 909.15
throw in with 450.4, 805.4
throw light upon 341.10, 1025.28
throw money around 486.3, 626.5
throw money away 626.5
throw mud at 512.10
thrown 742.7, 971.26
thrown away 704.33
thrown for a loss 412.15
thrown into the shade 250.6
thrown over 99.10
thrown together 797.14
throw off 6.6, 6.10, 160.6, 340.9, 365.8, 374.3, 431.8, 524.22, 802.8, 909.21, 909.24
throw off all disguise 351.7
throw off balance 791.3
throw off course 160.5
throw off one's guard 985.6
throw off the scent 356.16, 368.7, 985.6
throw off the track 356.16, 368.8
throw off the trail 356.16, 368.8
throw of the dice 759.2, 972.1
throw one a curve 356.16
throw one a curve ball 356.16
throw one at 902.14
throw one back 88.24
throw one for a loss 1012.15
throw one's arms around 562.18
throw oneself at one 439.7
throw oneself at someone's mercy 145.6
throw oneself at the feet of 138.7, 145.6, 433.10, 440.11
throw oneself at the head of 562.21
throw oneself into 570.12
throw oneself into the arms of 1009.7
throw oneself on one's knees 155.6
throw oneself on the mercy of the court 113.7, 351.7, 598.19
throw one's hat in the ring 609.39
throw one's money away 486.3
throw one's weight around 375.14, 417.13, 894.9
throw one's weight into the scale 375.14, 894.9
throw on one's beam ends 122.6, 131.8, 1012.15
throw on paper 547.21, 718.6
throw on the junk heap 390.8
throw on the market 737.24
throw open 292.11
throw open to 187.10
throw out 372.2, 390.7, 802.8, 909.13, 909.25
throw out a feeler 942.9
throw out a smoke screen 346.6
throw out of gear 19.9, 160.5
throw out of joint 160.5, 802.16
throw out of order 811.2
throw out one's chest 454.5
throw out on one's ear 909.13
throw out the baby with the bath water 486.4
throw out the baby with the bathwater 486.6
throw out the window 390.7
throw over 370.5, 390.7, 395.20
throw overboard 390.7, 773.5, 909.13
throw seeds 745.5
throw smoke 745.5
throw something together 11.5
throw stick 462.9, 462.18
throw the book at 599.7, 604.10
throw the bull 520.5
throw the first stone 599.10
throw the gauntlet 454.3
throw the glove 454.3
throw the helve after the hatchet 486.6
throw the rascals out 860.4
throw the spotlight on 352.15
throw together 340.9, 365.8, 472.9, 797.10
throw to the dogs 390.7
throw to the wolves 370.5, 390.7, 604.10
throw under the jailhouse 429.14
throw up 370.7, 475.3, 909.26, 912.5
throw up one's hands in despair 112.16, 125.10
throw up one's hands in horror 127.11
throw up to one 599.9
thrum (n) 55.1 (v) 52.13, 55.4, 708.40, 708.44
thrummer 710.5
thrumming (n) 52.7 (a) 52.20, 55.7
thrush 710.23
thrust (n) 17.2, 18.4, 174.4, 457.1, 459.3, 760.4, 792.6, 902.2, 904.1, 1074.8, 1075.9 (v) 159.13, 459.17, 902.11, 902.12, 904.9
thrust and parry 457.13
thrust aside 984.4
thrust at 459.16
thrust back 908.3
thrust bearing 915.7
thrust down 913.4
thruster 1074.2, 1075.2
thrust in 189.7, 191.7, 213.6, 214.5
thrusting (n) 902.3 (a) 459.29, 902.23
thrusting under 913.1
thrust in the face of 599.9
thrust oneself forward 501.12
thrust oneself upon 214.5
thrust out 158.9, 909.13, 909.17
thrust out one's lower lip 110.15
thrust over 202.7

thrust stage 704.16
thrust to one side 984.4
thrust upon 439.9, 478.20
Thruthheim 681.10
Thruthvang 681.10
Thrymheim 681.10
thud (n) 52.3 (v) 52.15
thug 308.11, 461.1, 483.4, 593.3, 616.8, 660.9
thuggee 308.2
thuggery 308.2
thuggism 308.2
Thule 261.4, 820.2
thumb (n) 73.5 (v) 73.6, 177.31, 754.4
thumb a ride 177.31
thumb down 510.10, 909.17
Thumbelina 258.5
thumb index 871.7
thumbing 177.8
thumbing a ride 177.8
thumbing-down 909.4
thumbmark 517.7
thumbnail review 946.2
thumbnail sketch 557.1
thumb one's nose at 157.3, 327.6, 454.4
thumb one's nose at the consequences 493.6
thumb one's way 177.31
thumbprint 517.7
thumbscrew (n) 260.6, 605.4 (v) 604.15
thumbscrews 96.7
thumbs down 333.1, 586.3
thumbs-down 442.1, 444.2, 510.1, 909.4
thumbs up 509.1
thumbs-up 332.2, 443.1
thumb through 570.13, 938.26
thump (n) 52.3, 902.4 (v) 52.15, 55.4, 604.12, 708.44, 902.14, 902.16
thumped-in landing 184.18
thumper 257.11
thump in 184.43
thumping (n) 55.1 (a) 55.7, 247.11, 257.21
thump out 55.4
thump the tub for 352.15, 449.14, 509.13
thunder (n) 53.3, 54.2, 56.5 (v) 53.7, 56.9, 352.13, 524.25
thunder against 510.19, 513.5
thunder along 174.9
thunder and lightning 47.9
thunder at the top of one's voice 59.9
thunderball 1025.17
thunderbolt 131.2, 174.6, 1025.17
thunderbox 12.11
thunderclap 53.3, 56.5, 131.2
thunder cloud 319.2
thundercloud 133.5, 399.3
thundercrack 56.5
thunderer 53.6
thunder forth 352.13
thundergust 316.3, 318.11
thunderhead 133.5, 319.2, 399.3
thunderheaded 319.8
thundering (n) 54.2, 56.5, 513.1 (a) 15.22, 53.11, 54.12, 56.12, 257.21
thunderlike 56.12
thunder mug 12.11
thunder of applause 509.2
thunderous 53.11, 56.12
thunderousness 53.2
thunderpeal 56.5
thundershower 316.3
thundersquall 316.3, 318.11
thunderstorm 56.5, 316.3, 671.4
thunderstroke 56.5, 1025.17
thunderstruck 122.9
thundery 56.12
thurible 70.5, 70.6, 696.10
thurifer 70.5, 701.2
thuriferous 70.9
thurification 70.5
thurify 70.8
Thursday 832.4
thwack (n) 56.1, 902.4 (v) 56.6, 604.11, 902.14
thwart (v) 132.2, 412.11, 857.11, 900.7, 1012.15 (a) 170.9, 204.19
thwarted 132.5
thwarter 1012.8
thwarting 415.5, 900.2, 1012.3
thymic 13.8
thymic death 85.2
thyroidal 13.8
thyroxin 13.2
thyrse 310.27
thyrsus 273.2, 310.27
tiara 498.6, 647.3, 647.4
Tiburtine sibyl 962.6
tic 28.5, 28.7, 128.1, 265.4, 917.3, 926.13
tick (n) 52.3, 55.2, 245.1, 311.32, 311.36, 311.37, 517.5, 622.1, 830.3 (v) 52.15, 55.5, 517.19, 889.7, 916.12
tick away 52.15, 55.5, 821.5
tick by 821.5
ticked 152.30
ticked off 152.30
ticker 2.16, 347.2, 737.7, 832.6
ticker market 737.1
ticker tape 549.10, 737.7
ticket (n) 443.1, 443.7, 517.13, 549.6, 609.19, 630.1, 728.12 (v) 517.20
ticket collector 704.23
ticketless 443.7
ticket of admission 443.1
ticket office 739.7
ticket-of-leave man 429.11
ticket-of-leaver 429.11
ticket scalper 730.3
ticking (n) 55.2, 172.1 (a) 55.7
ticking-off 510.6
ticking package 1006.5
tickle (n) 74.2 (v) 74.6, 95.10, 105.15, 375.17, 377.6, 743.21, 902.18, 983.12
tickled 95.15, 743.26, 983.16
tickled pink 95.15, 109.15, 743.26
tickled to death 95.15, 109.15, 743.26
tickle one's fancy 104.22, 377.6, 983.12
tickle pink 95.6, 95.11, 743.21
tickler 382.6, 989.5
tickle the fancy 743.21
tickle the palate 63.4
tickle the palm 378.3, 624.16
tickle to death 95.11, 743.21
tickliness 74.2
tickling (n) 74.2 (a) 73.12, 74.9, 377.8, 983.19
ticklish 24.12, 74.9, 110.21, 971.20, 1006.12, 1013.17
ticklish business 1006.2
ticklish issue 456.7
ticklishness 24.3, 74.2, 110.5, 971.6, 1006.2
ticklish spot 1013.5
tickly 74.9
tick off 152.23, 517.19
ticktack (n) 53.6, 55.2 (v) 55.5
ticktick 55.2
tick-tock 118.2
ticktock (n) 55.2 (v) 55.5, 916.12
ticky-tacky 16.14
tidal 182.58, 234.7, 238.24
tidal amplitude 238.13
tidal bore 238.14
tidal current 238.13
tidal current chart 238.13
tidal flat 236.1, 238.13
tidal flats 276.2
tidal flood 238.13
tidal flow 238.13
tidal plain 236.1
tidal pond 241.1
tidal pool 238.13, 241.1
tidal power 1021.7
tidal range 238.13
tidal stream 238.13
tidal wave 238.14, 609.21, 671.5, 916.4
tidbit 8.2, 10.8, 62.4, 552.8
tidbits 10.9
tiddler 258.4
tiddliness 88.1, 985.4
tiddly 88.31, 985.15
tide 238.4, 238.13, 240.1, 821.1
tide chart 238.13
tide gate 238.13, 239.11
tide gauge 238.13
tideland (n) 234.2, 238.13 (a) 234.7
tidemark 300.6, 517.10
tide of time 821.4
tide over 1007.2
tide race 238.13
tiderip 238.13
tide table 238.13
tidewater (n) 234.2, 238.13 (a) 242.2
tide wave 238.14
tideway 238.13
tidiness 79.1, 807.3
tidings 552.1
tidy (v) 79.18, 808.12 (a) 79.26, 257.16, 807.8, 999.20
tidy step 261.2
tidy sum 247.4, 618.2, 884.3
tidy up 808.12
tidy-up 808.6
tie (n) 5.31, 213.4, 438.1, 457.12, 644.7, 647.1, 709.12, 775.1, 790.3, 800.1, 836.3, 857.2 (v) 424.4, 428.10, 641.12, 775.6, 790.5, 800.5, 800.9, 855.8
tie bar 498.6
tiebreaker 748.2, 752.3
tie clasp 498.6
tie clip 498.6
tied 428.16, 641.16, 775.9, 790.7, 800.13, 836.5, 855.16
tied down 428.16
tie down 428.10
tied score 790.3
tied to mother's apron strings 301.12
tied to one's apron strings 326.5, 432.16
tied up 330.21, 428.16, 623.8
tied up in 898.5
tie-dye 35.14
tie-dyed 35.17
tie-dyeing 35.11
tie hand and foot 19.10, 428.10
tie in 450.3
tie-in 450.2, 734.1, 775.1, 800.1
tie in knots 799.3, 811.3
tie-in sale 734.1
tie into 459.15, 510.14
tie in with 775.5, 805.4
tie off 855.8
tie one down 428.7
tie one in knots 971.12
tie one on 88.26
tie one's hands 424.4, 428.7, 428.10, 1012.11, 1012.15
tiepin 498.6
tier 296.1, 812.2
tierce 696.8, 876.1, 878.2
tie rod 800.4
Tierra del Fuego 261.4, 1023.4
ties of affection 455.1
ties of blood 559.1
tie tac 498.6
tie tack 498.6
tie the hands of 19.10
tie the knot 563.14, 563.15, 800.5
tie the nuptial knot 563.14
tie the wedding knot 563.14
tie up 182.15, 186.8, 428.10, 450.3, 469.6, 800.9, 855.8
tie-up 450.2, 727.5, 800.1, 805.1, 846.2
tie up one's money in 729.17
tie up with red tape 846.8
tiff (n) 152.7, 456.5 (v) 456.11
tiffin 8.6
tigella 310.21
tiger 311.21, 492.7, 593.5, 671.9
tiger cat 311.20
tigerish 311.42
tigerlike 311.42
tiger milk 88.14
tiger mother 77.7
tiger parent 559.1
tiger sweat 88.14
tight 15.20, 88.33, 180.20, 270.14, 293.12, 484.9, 537.6, 800.14, 803.11, 807.8, 885.5, 1046.11
tight-assed 583.6
tight discipline 425.1
tighten 119.2, 210.5, 260.8, 428.9, 800.7, 906.9, 1046.9

tight end 746.2
tightened 251.7
tightening (n) 251.2, 260.2 (a) 251.8
tighten one's belt 635.5, 667.3, 668.6
tighten the screws 119.2
tighten up 119.2
tightfisted 484.9
tightfistedness 484.3
tight grip 474.2
tight hand 425.3
tight-knit 800.13, 1045.12
tight-lipped 51.10, 344.9
Tight Little Island 232.4
tight money 728.16
tightness 270.1, 484.3, 773.3, 803.3, 885.1, 1046.2
tight one 457.3
tight purse strings 484.3, 635.1
tight rein 425.3
tightrope 1013.4
tightrope walker 707.3
tightrope walking 454.1, 492.4, 493.3, 971.6
tights 5.9
tight ship 425.3
tight spot 258.3, 1013.5
tight squeeze 270.1, 369.2, 619.1, 1013.5
tightwad 484.4
tighty whities 5.22
tigon 797.8
tigress 77.9, 110.12, 593.7, 671.9
tiki torch 1025.19
tile (n) 383.6, 742.2, 1054.2 (v) 295.23
tile painter 716.7
tile-red 41.6
tiles 295.6, 1054.2
tiling 295.9, 742.2, 1054.2
till (n) 482.11, 729.13 (v) 1069.17
tillage 1069.1
tiller 573.5, 1040.8, 1069.5
tiller of the soil 606.6, 1069.5
tillicum 588.4
tilling 1069.13
till the soil 1069.17
tilt (n) 100.3, 204.2, 371.5, 457.3, 896.1 (v) 194.8, 204.10, 457.13, 896.3, 904.10
tilt at 459.18
tilt at windmills 19.7, 391.8, 923.6
tilted 204.15
tilter 461.1
tilth 1069.1
tilting 204.15
tilting ground 463.1
tilting of the scales 791.1
tilt the scales 297.10
tilt toward 100.14, 371.17
tilt with 457.17
tiltyard 463.1
timbale 10.41
timber 180.13, 273.3, 310.10, 310.13, 1054.3
timbered 310.40
timbering 1054.3
timberland 310.12, 310.13
timberline 237.2, 310.12
timberman 1069.7
timbers 233.2
timber topper 366.4
timber topping 366.3
timber tree 310.10
timber wolf 311.19
timberwork 1054.3
timbre 50.3, 524.7
Timbuktu 261.4
Time 821.2
time, the 832.2, 838.1
time (n) 824.1, 824.3, 824.4, 825.2, 825.3, 825.4, 832.2, 832.4, 843.2 (v) 832.11, 836.4
time 402.1, 709.24, 821.1
time ahead 839.1
time allotment 211.3
time and a half 478.5
time and motion study 573.7, 832.9
time and tide 821.4
time at bat 825.2
time at one's command 402.1
time at one's disposal 402.1
time being, the 838.1
time bill 728.11
timebinding 821.1
time bomb 462.20, 1006.1
timebomb 514.1
time book 832.9
timecard 832.9
time chart 832.9
time constants 1041.11
time constraint 210.2
time-consuming 267.7, 827.11
time control 1041.8
time-critical 843.10
time delay 1041.11
time discount 631.1
time draft 728.11
time drawing on 839.5
time exposure 714.9
time flow 821.4
time frame 211.3, 381.1, 821.1, 824.1
timeframe 821.4
time gap 824.1
time hanging heavily on one's hands 118.1
time-honored 155.11, 155.12, 373.13, 842.12
time-honored practice 373.1
time immemorial 827.4, 837.3
time in 186.6, 832.12
time interval 224.1
time just ahead 839.1
timekeeper 300.9, 550.1, 749.6, 754.3, 832.6, 832.10
timekeepers 749.3
timekeeping (n) 832.1 (a) 832.15
time killer 331.8
time lag 813.1, 824.1, 846.2
time lead 1041.11
timeless 677.17, 822.3, 829.7, 842.10
timelessness 822.1, 829.1
time limit 210.2, 211.3
timeline 832.9
timeliness 843.1, 995.1
timely 843.9, 995.5
time management 821.1
time-motion study 573.7
time of day 832.2
time off (n) 20.3, 222.4, 402.1, 826.1, 857.3 (v) 825.5
time of life 303.1
time of night 832.2
time of one's life, the 116.1
time of one's life 743.2
time of the month 12.9
time of year 313.1
time on one's hands 118.1, 331.2, 402.1
time out (n) 20.2 (v) 832.12
timeout 826.1, 857.3
time out of mind 837.2
time out of time 822.1
time pattern 709.24
timepiece 832.6
timepleaser 651.3
timer 747.3, 832.6, 832.10
time-release capsule 86.7
times, the 831.4, 838.1
times 1017.18
time-saving 635.6
time-saving device 449.9
time scale 832.9
time's caravan 821.4
time-scarred 842.14
time schedule 832.9
time scheme 381.1
time-sensitive 843.10
timeserver 138.3, 357.10, 363.4, 651.3
timeserving (n) 138.2 (a) 138.14, 363.10
time's forelock 843.2
times gone by 837.1
time-share 228.31
time-sharer 227.8
time-sharing 228.15
time sheet 832.9
time signal 832.2
time signature 709.12, 709.24
time sink 821.1
time slot 824.3
times of old 837.2
times of yore 837.2
time-space 158.6
timespan 303.1, 821.1, 824.1
times past 837.1
time spirit 896.2
time stamp 832.6
time study 573.7, 832.9
time's winged chariot 821.3
timetable 381.1, 832.9, 871.6
time ticket 832.9
time to burn 402.1
time to catch one's breath 20.2
time to come 839.1
time to kill 402.1
time to oneself 402.1
time to spare 402.1, 845.1
time travel 821.1
time warp 158.6, 813.1, 821.1
time waster 331.8
timewise 821.7
time without end 829.2
timeworn 117.9, 303.18, 393.31, 842.14
time zone 832.3
timid 127.23, 139.12, 362.11, 491.10
timidity 127.3, 139.4, 491.1
timidness 139.4, 491.1
timing 413.1, 709.24, 788.1, 832.1
timing pulse 1035.4
timing step 750.2
timocracy 618.6
Timon 590.2
timoneer 574.7
Timonism 590.1
Timonist (n) 590.2 (a) 590.3
Timonistic 590.3
Timon of Athens 584.5, 618.8
timorous 127.23, 139.12, 491.10
timorousness 127.3, 139.4, 491.1
timothy 10.4
timpanist 710.10
tin (n) 728.2 (v) 212.9, 397.11 (a) 354.26, 1058.17
tin can 180.7
tinct (n) 35.1, 797.7 (v) 35.14 (a) 35.17
tinction 35.8, 35.11
tinctorial 35.16
tincture (n) 35.1, 35.8, 248.4, 647.2, 797.7 (v) 35.14, 797.11
tinctured 35.17
tincture of iodine 86.21
tinder 1021.6
tinderbox 1021.6
tinder fungus 1021.6
tine 285.3
tin ear 48.3
tin-eared 48.15
tined 285.9
tin foil 295.18
tinfoil 1036.13
ting (n) 52.3, 54.3 (v) 54.8
ting-a-ling 54.3
tingaling 52.3
tinge (n) 35.1, 35.6, 62.3, 248.4, 519.2, 797.7 (v) 35.14, 797.11, 894.7
tinged 35.17
tingent 35.16
tinging 35.11
tingle (n) 26.3, 54.3, 74.1, 105.2 (v) 17.11, 26.8, 54.8, 74.5, 105.18
tingle with excitement 105.18
tingling (n) 26.3, 54.3, 74.1, 105.2 (a) 26.11, 54.13, 74.8, 105.20
tingling nerves 128.4
tingly 74.8, 105.20
tin god 104.15, 575.13, 662.9, 997.9
tinhorn (n) 759.21, 1005.5 (a) 998.18
tinhorn gambler 759.21
tininess 248.1, 258.1
tink (n) 54.3 (v) 54.8
tinker (n) 396.10 (v) 396.14, 808.13, 998.14
tinkerer 396.10, 998.10
tinkering 808.2, 998.8
tinker's damn, a 998.5
tinker up 396.14
tinker with 808.13
tinkle (n) 52.3, 54.3, 347.13 (v) 12.14, 52.15, 54.8
tinkling (n) 54.3 (a) 54.13

tinkly 54.13
tinned 212.12
tinned goods 735.7
tinning 212.2, 397.2
tinnitis 54.3
tinny 58.15, 1005.9, 1058.17
Tin Pan Alley 708.7
tin pan alley 230.6
tinpot 998.21
tinsel (n) 33.2, 354.13, 498.3, 1025.7 (v) 498.9, 1025.24 (a) 354.26, 354.27
tinseled 1025.39
tinselly 1025.35
tint (n) 35.1, 35.6, 713.2, 797.7 (v) 35.14, 712.19
tintamarre 53.3
tinted 35.17
tinting 35.11
tintinnabular 54.13
tintinnabulary 54.13
tintinnabulate 54.8
tintinnabulation 54.3
tintinnabulous 54.13
tintinnabulum 54.4
tint tool 713.8
tintype (n) 714.4 (a) 714.17
tinware 735.4
tiny 248.6, 258.11
tiny bit 248.2
tiny house 228.5, 228.17
tip (n) 150.2, 198.2, 204.2, 285.3, 422.2, 478.5, 524.18, 551.3, 624.6, 820.2, 902.7, 993.5 (v) 182.43, 198.10, 204.10, 295.21, 399.5, 551.11, 902.18
tip-crowning 198.11
tipi 228.10
tip in 213.6
tip it in 747.4
tip off 399.5, 551.11
tip-off 399.1, 517.1, 517.9, 551.3, 551.4
tip of the iceberg 32.1, 248.2, 248.4, 517.1
tip over 205.6, 482.16
tipped 198.13, 204.15
tippiness 791.1
tipping (n) 554.14 (a) 204.15
tipping-in 213.1
tipping point 407.2
tipple (n) 8.4 (v) 8.29, 88.24
tippler 88.11
tippling (n) 8.3, 88.4 (a) 88.35
tippy 791.5
tippytoe (n) 177.17 (v) 177.26 (a) 177.39
tip sheet 757.4
tipsification 88.1
tipsify 88.23
tipsiness 88.1
tipstaff 1008.15
tipster 551.5, 962.5
tipsy 88.31, 204.15
tip the balance 205.5, 297.10, 852.7
tip the hat to 250.5, 585.10
tip the scale 886.12
tip the scales 297.10
tiptoe (n) 177.17 (v) 177.26, 346.9, 494.5 (a) 177.39
tiptoeing (n) 177.17 (a) 177.39
tiptop (n) 198.2 (a) 198.11, 249.13, 999.18
tip well 485.3
tirade (n) 115.3, 510.7, 538.2, 543.2 (v) 115.13
tiramisu 10.41, 10.42
tire (n) 280.4 (v) 5.39, 21.4, 21.5, 98.16, 118.6
tired 5.45, 21.7, 118.11, 393.36, 974.6
tired-armed 21.7
tired cliché 864.8
tired-eyed 21.9
tired-faced 21.9
tired-looking 21.9
tired market 737.3
tiredness 16.1, 21.1, 118.3
tired of 118.11, 994.6
tired of living 118.11
tired out 21.10
tired phrase 974.3
tired to death 21.10, 118.11
tired-winged 21.7
tireless 330.22, 360.8
tirelessness 330.6, 360.1
tire out 21.4
tires 756.1
tiresome 21.13, 98.22, 118.10, 721.5
tiresomeness 98.7, 118.2
tiresome work 725.4
tire to death 21.4, 118.6
tiring 21.13, 118.10, 725.18
Tir-na-n'Og 681.9
tisane 86.4
Tisiphone 152.10, 680.10
tissu 4.1
tissue (n) 4.1, 170.3, 266.1, 305.1, 740.1 (v) 740.6
tissue paper 295.18
Titan 1073.14
Titan 15.6
titan 257.13
titaness 257.13
Titania 678.8
titanic 247.7, 257.20
titanism 257.5
titbit 10.8
tit for tat 338.2, 506.3, 777.3, 862.1, 863.1
tit-for-tat 777.10
tithable 630.15
tithe (n) 478.6, 630.9, 882.6, 882.14 (v) 630.12 (a) 882.22
tither 478.11
tithing 478.1
titian 40.4, 41.6, 41.10
titian-red 41.6
titillate 74.6, 95.10, 105.15, 377.6, 743.21, 983.12
titillated 743.26, 983.16
titillating 377.8, 743.27, 983.19
titillation 74.2, 95.1, 105.2
titillative 74.9, 97.7, 377.8, 743.27
tit in the wringer 1013.5
titivate 5.42, 79.20, 354.16, 498.8, 1016.15
titivated 354.26, 1016.22
title (n) 469.1, 469.2, 471.4, 527.3, 554.1, 554.12, 642.1, 648.1, 751.1, 809.2, 937.2 (v) 527.11, 937.3
titled 527.14, 608.10
titled aristocracy 608.1
title deed 549.5
title deeds and papers 957.1
titled person 608.4
titleholder 413.15, 470.2
title of address 527.3
title of honor 648.1
title of respect 527.3
title page 517.13, 554.12, 937.2
title role 704.10
titmouse 258.4
Titoism 611.5
Titoist (n) 611.13 (a) 611.21
titrate 801.6
titration 801.1
tits on a boar 768.2, 993.4
titted 283.19
titter (n) 52.5, 116.4 (v) 116.8
tittle 248.2, 258.7, 517.5, 530.15
tittle-tattle (n) 540.3, 541.4, 552.7 (v) 540.5, 541.9, 552.12
tittle-tattler 552.9
tittup 177.28, 177.34
titubant 525.12
titular 527.15, 612.17, 648.7
titulary 648.7
Tiu 458.12
Tivoli 743.14
Tiw 458.12
tizzy 105.6, 985.3
TLC 449.3
T-man 576.10
tmesis 205.3
toad 138.3, 311.26
toadeat 138.7
toadeater 138.3
toadeating (n) 138.2 (a) 138.14
toadish 311.47
toad stabber 1040.2
toad sticker 1040.2
toadstool 310.4
toady (n) 138.3, 332.6 (v) 138.7
toadying (n) 138.2, 332.2 (a) 138.14
toadyish 138.14
toadyism 138.2
toady to 138.8
to-and-fro (n) 916.5 (v) 916.13 (a) 916.19
to-and-fro motion 916.1
toast (n) 8.4, 88.10, 487.1, 500.10 (v) 8.29, 11.5, 40.2, 88.29, 1019.22, 1020.17 (a) 40.3, 97.8
toast-brown 40.3
toasted 11.7
toaster pastry 10.41
toaster strudel 10.41
toasting (n) 11.2 (a) 1019.25
toastmaster 743.20
toasty 1019.24
to a turn 1002.9
tobacco (n) 89.1 (a) 89.15
tobacco addiction 89.10
tobacco belt 233.1
tobaccoey 89.15
tobaccoism 89.10
tobacco juice 89.7
tobaccolike 89.15
tobacconist 89.12
tobacco pipe 89.6
tobacco pouch 89.6
tobaccoshop 89.12
tobacco smoke 89.1
tobacco store 89.12
tobacco user 89.11
to-be 839.8
to be counted on 644.19, 970.17
to be counted on one's fingers 885.4
to be depended upon 644.19, 970.17
to be desired 100.30, 995.5
to be expected 130.14
to be had 472.14, 966.8
to be preferred 371.25
to be reckoned on 644.19, 970.17
to be reckoned with 894.13
to be relied upon 644.19, 970.17
to be seen 31.6, 348.8
to be trusted 644.19
to blame 510.25, 641.17, 656.3
toboggan (n) 179.20 (v) 177.35
tobogganing 177.16
to burst forth 105.29
toccata form 709.11
Tocharian 523.12
to come 167.4, 839.8, 840.3, 965.9
tocsin 399.3, 400.1
TO'd 152.30
today 838.1
today's special 865.2
toddle (n) 177.12 (v) 175.6, 177.28, 188.7
toddle along 175.6
toddle off 175.6
toddler 302.9
toddler-friendly 1014.15
toddling (n) 177.8 (a) 175.10
to dedicate oneself to 359.8
to die for 100.30
to-do 105.4, 330.4, 355.1, 810.4, 917.1
to-do list 871.1
toe 2.7, 199.2, 199.5
toe-curling 98.21
toed 199.9
toehold 474.2, 474.3, 901.5, 906.2
toe jump 760.7
toe the line 326.2
toe the mark 326.2, 867.4
toe-to-toe 779.6
to explode 105.29
toff 500.9
toffee 10.40
toffee-nosed 141.14
to fit the pocketbook 633.7
toft 212.3, 228.2, 228.6, 471.6, 1069.8
tofu 10.13, 10.48
tog 5.39
together (v) 770.18 (a) 106.13, 455.3, 925.4
togetherness 455.1, 587.5
togged 5.45
toggery 5.1
toggle 800.8
toggle joint 800.4

to-go 8.6, 8.11
to-go meal 8.6
tog out 5.39, 5.42
togs 5.1
tog up 5.42
to hand 387.20
toheroa 311.29
tohubohu 418.2, 810.3
toil (n) 724.2, 725.4 (v) 724.12, 725.14, 1012.11
toil and moil 725.14
toil and trouble 725.4
toil away 725.13
toiler 607.9, 726.2
toilers 607.7
toilet (n) 12.10, 12.11, 197.26, 759.19 (a) 513.8
toilet goods 735.6
toiletries 735.6, 1016.11
toilet room 12.10
toilette 5.1
toilet training 12.11
toilet water 70.3
toiling 725.17
toiling class 607.7
toils 356.13
toilsome 21.13, 725.18, 1013.17
toilsomeness 725.5, 1013.1
toilworn 21.7
toivel 79.19
toke (n) 87.20 (v) 87.22
token (n) 133.3, 517.2, 517.12, 517.13, 518.6, 549.1, 728.12, 862.2, 865.4, 957.1, 989.6 (v) 133.11, 348.5 (a) 633.7, 862.8
token gesture 354.6
tokening 133.3
tokenism 354.6
token of remembrance 989.6
token payment 438.2
token punishment 604.3
toker 87.21
tokoloshe 680.7
tolerability 107.3, 999.3
tolerable 107.13, 999.20, 1005.7
tolerableness 999.3, 1005.1
tolerance 87.1, 134.1, 148.1, 427.1, 430.4, 430.10, 443.2, 772.1, 975.2, 979.4
tolerant 134.9, 143.13, 143.16, 148.6, 427.7, 430.25, 443.14, 467.7, 979.11
tolerate 134.5, 329.4, 427.5, 430.16, 443.10, 979.7
tolerated 443.16
tolerating 134.9, 443.14, 979.11
toleration 134.1, 143.3, 430.10, 443.2, 772.1, 979.4
tolerative 134.9
toll (n) 54.3, 630.6, 630.9 (v) 54.8
tollbooth 228.9
toll bridge 383.9
toll call 347.13
toll-free call 347.13
tollhouse 228.9
tolling (n) 54.3, 309.6 (a) 54.13
tolling of the knell 309.6
toll the knell 115.10
tom 76.8, 311.20, 311.28
tomahawk 745.5
Tomahawk missile 462.18
tomato 10.35, 77.6, 302.7
tomato sauce 10.12
tomb (n) 309.16, 549.12 (v) 309.19
tomblike 309.22
tomblike silence 51.1
tomb of unknown soldier 549.12
tombola 759.14
tombolo 234.2, 276.2
tomboy 76.9, 302.8
tomboyish 76.14
tomboyishness 76.1
tombstone 549.12
tombstone marking 309.18
tomcat 76.8, 311.20
Tom, Dick, and Harry 606.1, 998.7
tome 554.1, 554.4
tomentose 3.24
tomfool (n) 924.1 (v) 923.6
tomfoolery 489.5, 923.1
Tommy 461.7
Tommy Atkins 461.7
tommy gun 462.10
tommyrot 520.3
Tom o' Bedlam 926.15
tomomania 91.19
tomorrow 839.1
Tom Swifty 489.8
Tom Thumb (n) 258.5 (a) 258.13
tom-tom 55.1
tomtom 708.44
tom turkey 76.8, 311.28
ton 247.3, 578.1, 578.2
tonal 50.15, 523.23, 524.30, 708.48, 709.27
tonalist 710.21
tonality 50.3, 708.2, 709.3, 709.4, 709.15, 1025.19
tonant 56.12
tone (n) 15.2, 35.1, 35.6, 50.2, 84.1, 93.1, 209.3, 321.1, 384.1, 524.6, 524.7, 708.2, 709.3, 709.4, 709.14, 709.20, 712.8, 722.4, 767.4, 896.2, 978.4, 1048.1 (v) 15.13, 35.14, 894.7 (a) 523.23
tone arm 50.11
tone block 709.6
tone cluster 709.6
tone color 50.3
tone control 1034.16
toned 35.17
toned down 252.10
tone-deaf 49.6
tone deafness 49.1
tone-deafness 945.1
tone down 36.5, 51.9, 252.9, 670.6, 708.36, 1027.10, 1047.6
toneless 36.7, 50.15, 61.4
tonelessness 36.1, 50.2
tone measurer 711.22
tone of one's voice 517.15
tone of voice 524.7
tone painting 709.2
tone poet 710.20
tone quality 50.3
tone row 709.6
tonesetter 578.7
tone up 392.11, 708.36
Tonga Trench 275.5
tongs 1020.12
tongue (n) 2.12, 10.20, 54.4, 62.1, 62.5, 273.1, 283.9, 523.1, 524.2, 524.18 (v) 73.9, 708.42
tongue in cheek (n) 354.5 (a) 354.32
tongue-in-cheek 489.15, 511.8
tongue-lash 510.19
tonguelash 510.17
tongue-lashing 510.7
tongueless 51.12
tonguelessness 51.2
tonguelike 62.10
tongue-tie 51.8
tongue-tied 51.12, 344.9
tongue twister 50.1, 160.1
tonic (n) 9.1, 10.49, 17.6, 86.8, 88.8, 709.15 (a) 9.3, 17.15, 81.5, 86.44, 396.22, 524.30, 709.27
tonic accent 524.6
tonic chord 709.17
tonicity 1048.1
tonic key 709.15
tonic major 709.15
tonic minor 709.15
tonic sol-fa 708.13, 709.7
tonic spasm 85.6
tonic water 10.49
toning 35.16
tonitruant 53.11, 56.12
tonitruous 53.11, 56.12
tonnage 180.10, 196.2, 257.2, 297.1, 630.7
tonsure 6.4
tonsured 6.17
tonsured cleric 699.2
tontine 759.14
tonus 1048.1
Tony 646.2
tony 501.18
too bad 661.11, 1000.9
too big 257.23
too big for one's britches 140.11, 501.23
too clever by half 415.12
too close for comfort 1006.9
too close to call 790.7
too early 845.8
too few (n) 885.2 (a) 885.4, 992.9
too few to mention 885.2
too frugal 484.7
too funny 488.5
too killing for words 488.5
tool (n) 138.3, 384.4, 576.3, 759.16, 1040.1 (v) 174.9, 713.9, 1040.13
too late 844.6
toolbar 1042.18
toolbox 195.1, 356.6
tooled 713.11
tooling 713.2, 1040.11
tooling up 1040.11
tooling-up 892.2
too little 992.9
too little too late 992.1
toolkit 1042.18
tools and machinery 735.4, 1039.1
tools of the trade 384.2
tool temper 1046.4
tool up 405.13, 1040.13
too many 993.2
too many cooks 414.4
too many irons in the fire 993.6
too much (n) 669.1, 993.1, 993.2 (a) 98.25, 247.13, 355.4, 669.7, 993.16
too much at once 993.6
too much for 967.8
too-muchness 669.1, 993.1
too much of a good thing 993.2, 994.1
too much on one's mind 985.1
too much on one's plate 985.1, 993.6
too much with us 118.9
to one's advantage 387.18
to one's fancy 97.6
to one's liking 97.6
to one's profit 387.18
to one's taste 63.8, 97.6
too quick on the draw 845.8
too quick on the uptake 845.8
too soon 844.6, 845.8
too soon off the mark 845.8
toot (n) 53.5, 87.7, 88.6 (v) 53.10, 87.22, 708.42
tooter 710.4, 711.6
tooth (n) 2.8, 62.1, 285.3, 285.4, 288.1 (v) 289.4, 294.4
toothache 26.5
toothachy 26.12
toothbrush 3.11
tooth decay 85.40
tooth doctor 90.6
toothed 285.9, 285.14, 288.7, 289.5, 474.9
tooth fairy 478.11
tooth for a tooth, a 506.3, 863.1
toothful grin 116.3
toothhold 474.2
toothless 286.4
toothlessness 286.1
toothlike 285.14, 289.5
toothpaste 79.17, 86.22
tooth powder 79.17, 86.22
tooth pulp 1063.2
tooth-shaped 289.5
toothsome 63.8, 100.30
toothsomeness 63.1
toothy 285.14
tooting one's own horn 502.1
tootle (n) 53.5 (v) 53.10, 708.42
toot one's own horn 140.6, 502.6, 502.7
toots 77.6
tootsie 104.10
tootsie-pie 104.10
tootsy 199.5
tootsy-wootsy 104.10
top, the 575.14, 997.8
top (n) 198.1, 198.2, 206.2, 282.5, 295.5, 295.6, 295.8, 743.16, 794.5, 915.4, 1002.3 (v) 198.10, 249.6, 249.8, 272.11, 295.21, 751.4, 993.9 (a) 198.11, 249.13, 632.11
to paint the lily 545.7
toparchy 232.1
topaz-yellow 43.4
top banana 249.4, 575.4, 704.10
top billing 704.10
top brass 574.11, 575.14, 575.17, 997.8

topcoat 5.13, 296.1
top cow 76.8, 311.6
top dog 249.4, 411.2, 575.4, 997.11
top-drawer 198.11, 999.18
top-dress 890.8, 1069.17
top dressing 890.4
tope (n) 272.6, 309.16, 549.12, 703.4 (v) 88.24
top-echelon 198.11, 249.13
toper 88.11
top executive 730.1
top-flight 198.11
topflight 249.14, 999.18
top floor 198.1
topful 794.11
top gallery 27.8
top gun 575.4
top-heavy 257.18, 791.5
top-heavy market 737.1
Tophet 682.1
top-hole 999.18
top horse 76.8, 311.10, 757.2
topi 87.17
topiarist 1069.7
topiary 310.9
topic 518.1, 722.4, 937.1, 938.10
topical 231.9, 838.2, 841.13, 937.4
topical anesthetic 86.15
topicality 838.1
topical outline 557.1
topic for discussion 937.1
topic of the day 552.6, 937.1
toping (n) 88.4 (a) 88.35
topknot 3.7, 3.16, 198.4
topknotted 3.29
topless 6.13, 6.14, 6.16, 198.14, 272.14
topless dancer 6.3, 705.3
toplessness 6.3
top-level 198.11, 249.13
toploftical 157.8
toploftiness 141.1, 157.1, 272.1
top-lofty 141.9
toplofty 157.8, 272.14
top man on the totem pole 997.11
topmost 198.11, 249.13, 272.19, 997.24
topmost point 237.6
topnotch 249.13, 999.18
topnotcher 413.14, 999.6
top off 198.10, 385.9, 407.6, 794.6, 794.7, 1021.8
top of one's bent, the 403.4
top of the heap, the 999.8
top of the inning 745.3
top of the line, the 249.5, 999.8
top of the line 249.13
top-of-the-line 249.13, 999.16
top of the milk 249.5
top of the world 198.2
topographer 159.5, 300.9
topographic 159.19, 231.8, 300.12
topographical 231.8, 300.12
topography 159.5, 159.8
topological 1017.22
topologist 1017.16
topology 159.8
toponym 527.3
toponymic 527.17
toponymics 526.14, 527.1
toponymous 527.17
toponymy 527.1
top out 407.6
topped 198.13
top people 249.5, 997.8
topping (n) 198.3 (a) 198.12, 249.12, 272.14, 999.18
topping off 407.2
topping-off 794.4
topple 194.8, 393.24, 395.22, 418.4, 913.5
topple down 194.8, 393.24
topple over 194.8, 205.6, 393.24
top price 630.4
top priority 814.1
toprank 997.24
top-ranking 198.11
tops (n) 999.8 (a) 999.18
top secret 345.11
top-secret information 345.5
top sergeant and topkick 575.18
top shape 83.2
top-shelf 999.14
topside 198.1
topsides 198.1
topsoil 234.1, 296.1
topspin 748.2
top spot 249.3
topsy-turvify 205.6
topsy-turviness 205.1, 810.3
topsy-turvy (v) 205.6 (a) 205.7, 810.16
topsy-turvydom 205.1
top-ten 997.19
top up 196.7, 198.10, 794.7
tor 237.6
Torah 673.8, 683.3, 683.5
torch (n) 1020.14, 1021.4, 1026.1, 1026.3 (v) 1020.22
torchbearer 574.6
torched 1020.30
torcher 1020.8
torchiere 1026.6
torch job 1020.7
torchlight 1025.19
torchlit 1025.39
torch race 457.12
torch singer 710.13
torch song 708.14
toreador 461.4
torero 461.4
toreutic 715.7
toreutics 715.1
toric lenses 29.3
to rights 807.7
torment (n) 26.6, 96.7, 96.10, 98.4, 126.2, 604.2, 1001.1 (v) 26.7, 96.13, 96.18, 98.12, 112.19, 126.5, 144.15, 389.7, 1000.6, 1013.13
tormented 26.9, 96.24, 126.8
tormenter 144.14
tormenting (n) 389.3 (a) 26.10, 98.22, 98.23, 126.10
tormentingness 98.4
torment of Tantalus 100.7
tormentor 96.10, 704.20
torn 93.23, 393.27, 393.32, 589.11, 802.23
tornadic 105.29, 318.22, 915.15
tornado 105.9, 318.13, 671.4
tornado warning 317.7, 400.1
tornado watch 317.7, 400.1
Toronto offense 749.3
torose 283.17
torpedo (n) 308.11, 462.18, 593.4, 1074.3, 1074.4 (v) 395.11, 459.22, 904.12
torpedo bomber 181.9
torpedoman 183.6
torpid 94.13, 173.14, 331.20, 853.7
torpidity 94.4, 329.1, 331.6
torpidness 94.4, 329.1, 331.6
torpor 18.5, 25.2, 94.4, 173.4, 175.1, 329.1, 331.6, 853.1
torque 280.3, 498.6
Torquemada 144.14
torrefaction 1020.1
torrefy 1020.24, 1066.6
torrent 174.6, 238.5, 671.6
torrential 238.24, 316.11
torrential downpour 316.2
torrential rain 316.2
torrent of rain 316.2
torrid 1019.25
torrid heat 1019.5
torridity 1019.5
torridness 1019.5
Torrid Zone 231.3, 1019.11
torse 647.2
torsion 164.2, 265.1, 281.1
torsional 265.9, 281.6
torsion fracture 85.38
torso 2.1, 1052.3
tort 655.2, 674.4
torte 10.42
tortellini 10.33
torticollis 265.3
tortile 281.6, 281.7
tortilla 10.29
tortoise 175.5, 311.24
tortoiselike 175.10
tortoiseshell (n) 47.6 (a) 47.10, 47.13
tortoiseshell cat 311.20
tortoise's pace 175.2
Tortoise which Supports the Earth, The 901.3
tortoni 10.47
tortuosity 265.1, 279.1, 281.1, 545.1
tortuous 265.10, 279.7, 281.6, 545.8
tortuousness 279.1, 281.1, 545.1, 799.1
torture (n) 26.6, 96.7, 98.4, 164.2, 389.3, 604.2 (v) 26.7, 96.18, 98.12, 144.15, 164.5, 265.6, 265.7, 342.2, 604.15, 1000.6
tortured 26.9, 93.23, 96.25, 265.11
torturer 96.10, 144.14, 604.7
torturesomeness 98.4
torture the law to one's own purposes 674.5
torturing 164.2, 265.2, 342.1
torturous 26.10, 98.23
torturousness 98.4
torus 310.28
Tory 611.9
Toryism 611.4
tosh 520.3
to spare 256.7, 390.12, 993.17
toss (n) 759.2, 904.3, 917.8, 938.15, 972.7 (v) 105.18, 159.13, 182.55, 238.22, 759.23, 904.10, 916.10, 917.15, 938.33
toss a monkey-wrench in the works 393.15
toss and tumble 182.55, 917.15
toss and turn 23.3, 105.18, 917.15
toss aside 370.5
toss at 459.28
toss down 8.29
tossdown 88.24
tossed salad 10.37
tosser 904.7
tossing (n) 904.2 (a) 916.17
tossing a coin 759.1
tossing and turning 23.1
tossing-in 213.2
tossing one's hat in the ring 609.10
toss of a coin 759.2
toss off 8.29, 88.24, 340.9, 365.8
toss one's cookies 909.27
toss one's drink 88.24
toss one's hat in the ring 609.39
toss one's lunch 909.27
toss out 340.9, 365.8, 909.13
toss overboard 390.7
tosspot 88.11
toss the head 141.8
toss together 340.9, 797.10
toss-up 609.15, 759.2, 857.2, 971.8, 972.7
tot (n) 8.4, 302.3 (v) 253.6, 792.8
total (n) 244.2, 253.2, 792.2, 1017.6 (v) 253.6, 393.11, 395.17, 792.8, 1017.19 (a) 247.6, 247.12, 671.17, 770.23, 772.7, 792.9, 794.9, 794.10, 864.14, 960.2, 1002.7
total abstinence 668.2
total agreement 332.5
total approach 792.5
total assets 471.7, 728.14
total attention 983.4
total blindness 30.1
total change 852.2, 860.1
total command 928.6
total commitment 359.1
total compensation 624.4
total darkness 38.2, 1027.1
total defeat 412.3
total eclipse 1027.8, 1073.13
totaled 87.24, 393.29, 806.5, 820.10
total effect 33.3
total environment 209.1
total immersion 701.6
total impression 33.3
totaling 1017.10
totalitarian 417.15, 612.16
totalitarian government 612.4
totalitarianism 612.4, 612.8
totalitarian regime 612.4
totalitarian threat 458.11
totality 792.1, 792.5, 794.1, 864.4, 1073.1

totality of associations 518.1
totality of being 1073.1
totalization 253.3
totalizator 759.17
totalize 253.6
totalizer 759.17
totalizing 253.3
total lack 222.1
total loss 393.8, 395.4, 410.2, 473.1
totally absorbed 983.17
totally committed 671.22
totally self-assured 141.11
total mastery 928.6
total memory 989.2
total recall 989.2
total resources 471.7
total self-assurance 141.2
total silence 51.1
total situation 766.2
total skepticism 955.2
total support 449.3
total theater 704.1
total up 253.6, 1017.19
total up to 630.13
total victory 411.1
total war 457.6, 458.1
tote (n) 195.2, 759.17 (v) 176.12, 253.6, 792.8
tote bag 195.2
tote board 759.17
totem 517.2, 559.4, 678.12, 696.10, 697.3
totemic 559.7
totemic group 617.2
totemism 675.6, 690.1, 697.1
totemist 697.4
totemistic 697.7
totemize 697.5
totem pole 273.1, 517.2
tote up 253.6, 1017.19
tote up to 792.8
to the front 662.17
to the life 784.16
to the manner born 607.10
to the point 537.6, 775.11, 788.10
to the purpose 387.20, 775.11, 788.10
tother (n) 780.3 (a) 862.8
to the side 218.6
toting 1017.10
toting up 253.3
tots 302.2
totter (n) 177.12, 917.8 (v) 16.8, 177.28, 194.8, 303.10, 362.8, 393.24, 854.5, 917.15
totteriness 1006.2
tottering (n) 177.8, 854.3, 916.5 (a) 16.16, 175.10, 194.11, 303.18, 393.46
tottering on the brink of the grave 307.32
totter on the brink 1006.8
totter to one's fall 393.24
tottery 16.16, 303.18, 393.33, 1006.11
totting 1017.10
tottyhead 924.4
tot up 253.6, 1017.19
tot up to 792.8
touch, the 440.1, 440.5
touch (n) 24.5, 73.1, 223.5, 248.4, 294.1, 343.1, 413.1, 413.6, 498.7, 517.15, 519.2, 708.30, 797.7, 902.7 (v) 24.6, 73.6, 93.14, 145.5, 223.10, 440.15, 517.22, 621.3, 775.5, 790.5, 902.18
touchable 73.11
touchableness 73.3
touch a chord 93.14
touch and go 759.2, 971.8, 972.7
touch-and-go 971.16, 1006.12
touch a nerve 24.8
touch a nerve ending 24.8
touch a raw nerve 96.14
touch a raw spot 24.8
touch a soft spot 24.8, 96.14
touch a sore spot 24.8
touch a sympathetic chord 93.14
touch a tender spot 96.14
touch base with 541.9
touch bottom 112.16, 393.17, 1011.11
touch down 184.43, 194.7
touchdown 184.18, 409.5, 746.3
touchdown rate of descent indicator 184.19
touched 93.23, 113.9, 926.26
touched in the head 926.26
touched up 392.13
touch elbows with 582.17
touchhole 239.13
touchiness 24.3, 105.10, 110.5, 456.1, 456.3, 1006.2
touching (n) 73.2, 223.5 (a) 93.22, 98.20, 145.8, 223.17
touching down 184.18
touching up 392.4
touch in passing 340.8
touch lightly 73.7
touch line 752.1
touch of conscience 113.2
touch off 375.18, 671.14, 1020.22
touch on 524.24, 957.8, 983.10
touch one's heart 93.14
touch on the raw 24.8, 93.14
touchpoint 2.4
touchscreen 1042.4
touch shoulders with 582.17
touchstone 300.2, 942.2
touch the cap 585.10
touch the hat 585.10
touch the wind 182.25
touch-tone telephone 347.4
touch to the quick 24.8, 93.14
touch up 392.11, 712.19
touch upon 73.7, 276.4, 340.8, 556.5, 775.5, 938.26
touch upon in passing 938.26
touch upon lightly 340.8, 938.26
touch where it hurts 24.8, 96.14
touch wood 124.7
touchwood 1021.6
touchy 24.12, 105.28, 110.21, 456.17, 1006.12
touchy-feely 73.11
tough (n) 15.7, 461.1, 593.4, 671.10 (a) 15.18, 361.10, 425.6, 492.17, 522.14, 671.16, 725.18, 763.7, 803.12, 827.10, 999.13, 1013.17, 1046.10, 1049.4, 1062.12
tough act to follow, a 249.4
tough act to follow 413.11, 999.6
tough as leather 1049.4
tough as nails 1049.4
tough break 1011.5
tough cookie 108.3
tough customer 108.3, 671.10
toughen 15.13, 1046.7, 1046.9, 1049.3
toughened 1046.13, 1049.6
toughening (n) 15.5, 1046.5 (a) 1046.14
tough grind 725.5
tough guy 15.7, 671.10
toughie 15.7, 1013.2
tough it out 15.11, 134.6, 216.8, 360.7, 453.3, 855.11
tough job 1013.2
tough lineup to buck 1013.2
tough love 449.2
tough luck 972.1, 1011.5
tough-minded 956.5
tough-mindedness 956.1
toughness 15.1, 359.3, 361.2, 425.1, 492.5, 763.1, 803.3, 1013.1, 1046.1, 1049.1, 1062.2
tough nut to crack 522.8, 938.10, 1013.2
tough one 1013.2
tough policy 609.5
tough proposition 522.8, 1013.2
tough row to hoe 1011.1, 1013.2
toupee 3.14
toupeed 3.26
tour (n) 177.5, 383.1, 704.11, 750.1, 751.1, 825.3, 825.4, 914.2, 918.4 (v) 177.21
tourbillion 915.2
tourbillon 318.13
tour conductor 574.7
tour de force 328.3, 413.10, 999.5
tour director 574.7
tourer 178.1
tour group 918.3
tour guide 574.7
touring (n) 177.1 (a) 177.36
touring bicycle 179.8
touring bike 179.8
touring company 707.11
touring skier 753.2
tourism 177.1
tourist 178.1, 918.3
tourista 12.2
tourist center 208.7
tourist class 177.5
tourist guide 178.1, 769.5
tourist hotel 228.15
touristic 177.36
touristical 177.36
touristry 177.1
tourist season 177.5
touristy 177.36
tour jeté 366.1
tournament 457.3, 743.10, 744.1, 747.1, 748.1, 750.1, 751.1, 752.1
tournament bridge 758.3
tournedo 10.18
tourney (n) 457.3, 743.10 (v) 457.13
tourniquet 86.33, 260.6, 293.5
tour of duty 825.3
tousle 811.2
tousled 810.14
tousled hair 3.2
tously 810.14
tout (n) 509.8, 551.5, 730.7, 759.20, 962.5 (v) 355.3, 509.11, 734.9
touted 355.4
touter 509.8, 730.7, 962.5
touting (n) 355.1 (a) 509.17
tout le monde 864.4
tow (n) 905.2 (v) 905.4
towage (n) 630.6, 905.1 (a) 905.6
towbar 905.1
tow car 905.1
tow-colored 43.4
towel 1066.6
tower (n) 27.8, 228.7, 266.2, 272.6, 460.6, 517.10, 1008.5 (v) 14.2, 193.8, 247.5, 259.7, 272.10
tower above 247.5, 249.6, 272.11
tower block 228.14
towered 272.14
towering 247.9, 257.20, 272.14
towering heights 272.2
towering inferno 1019.13
toweringness 257.6
towering passion 105.8, 152.10
towering rage 105.8, 152.10
tower of Pisa 204.2
tower of silence 309.16
tower of strength 15.6, 460.6, 855.6, 1008.5
tower over 249.6, 272.11
tower projector 1074.10
towery 272.14
tow-haired 37.9, 43.5
towhead 35.9
tow-headed 43.5
towheaded 37.9
towing (n) 905.1 (a) 905.6
towing cable 905.1
towing path 383.2
town (n) 230.1, 231.5 (a) 230.11
town clerk 550.1
town council 423.1
town crier 353.3
towner 227.6
townfolks 227.6
town green 230.5
town hall 230.5, 595.6
townhome 228.5
townhouse 228.5
townie 227.2, 227.6, 606.6
town library 558.1
town meeting 423.3, 476.2, 541.6, 613.1
town-meeting democracy 612.4
townscape 33.6, 712.11
townsfolk 227.6
township 230.1, 231.5
townsman 227.6
townspeople 227.6
townsperson 227.6
town square 230.5
townswoman 227.6

town talk 552.6
towny 227.6
towpath 383.2
towrope 905.1
toxemia 85.20, 85.31
toxic (n) 1001.3 (a) 64.7, 80.20, 82.7, 144.20, 1000.12
toxicant (n) 88.13, 1001.3 (a) 82.7
toxicity 82.3, 1000.5
toxicology 1001.3
toxic waste 391.4, 1001.3
toxic waste dump 391.6
toxiferous 82.7
toxin 391.4, 1000.3, 1001.3
toxin-antitoxin immunization 91.15
toxophilite 904.8
toy (n) 258.6, 358.1, 364.1, 384.4, 498.4, 508.7, 743.16, 998.5 (v) 562.14, 998.14 (a) 258.12
toyboy 100.12
toy dog 311.16
toying (n) 998.8 (a) 364.6
toy soldier 743.16
toy with 930.10, 931.12, 998.14
trace (n) 69.1, 248.4, 256.1, 258.7, 349.5, 517.9, 549.1, 797.7, 1036.11 (v) 349.8, 381.11, 517.19, 547.19, 712.19, 785.8, 938.35, 941.2
traceable 888.6
trace amount 258.7
trace down 938.35, 941.2
trace element 7.11, 1060.2
trace fossil 842.6
trace of an idea 951.5
trace out 349.8, 546.7
trace over 349.8
tracer 91.8, 462.19, 1037.5, 1038.4
tracer atom 1037.5, 1038.4
tracer bullet 462.19
tracer element 1037.5
tracer investigation 1037.8
tracery 170.3, 279.2
traces 517.8
trace the derivation of 888.5
trace the origin of 888.5
trace to 888.5
trachea 2.22
tracheal 2.32
trachoma 30.1
trachytic 1059.12
tracing 349.5, 712.12, 785.2, 785.4
tracing paper 547.4, 712.18
track (n) 161.1, 182.7, 373.5, 383.1, 383.2, 383.7, 407.1, 457.11, 517.8, 551.4, 572.11, 743.11, 755.1, 756.1, 756.3, 757.1, 887.3, 1004.1 (v) 177.20, 382.9, 835.3, 938.35
trackage 383.7
track and field 744.1, 755.1
trackball 1042.4
track conditions 757.1
track down 159.11, 938.35, 941.2
tracked vehicle 179.18
tracker 382.4
tracking 382.1, 1036.8
tracking down 382.1
tracking station 1036.6, 1074.7, 1075.5
trackless 293.10
trackless trolley 179.17
track lighting 1025.19
track location or call 757.1
track meet 755.2
track of 1017.13
track racing 744.1
track record 328.3, 405.4, 407.1, 719.1, 757.4
track sports 457.11
tract 158.2, 225.3, 231.4, 554.11, 556.1, 1069.9
tractability 324.1, 433.3, 1047.2
tractable 324.5, 433.13, 867.5, 1014.15, 1047.9
tractableness 324.1
tractate 556.1
tractation 556.3
tractator 556.3
tract house 228.5
tractile 1047.9
tractility 1047.2
traction 905.1, 906.2, 907.1
tractional 905.6
traction engine 179.18
tractive 905.6
tractive power 905.1
tract of time 821.3
tractor 179.18
tractor trailer 179.12
trad 708.9
trade (n) 724.4, 724.6, 731.1, 731.2, 731.5, 731.6, 733.3, 863.2 (v) 629.3, 731.15, 737.23, 854.5, 863.4 (a) 731.22
trade acceptance 728.11
trade agreement 437.2
trade association 617.9
trade at 731.17
trade away 629.3
trade barrier 773.4
trade book 554.1
trade center 208.7
trade cycle 731.10
traded 863.5
trade deficit 731.10
trade discount 631.1
traded-off 863.5
trade down 338.4
trade edition 554.5
trade editor 554.2
trade fair 736.2
trade gap 731.10
trade in 731.15, 731.16
trade-in 731.5
trade-in price 630.2
trade journal 555.1
trade language 523.11
trade-last 509.6, 511.1
trade magazine 555.1
trademark 210.3, 500.2, 517.13, 527.3, 888.2
trademark name 517.13
trade name 210.3, 517.13, 527.3
trade off 338.4, 731.15, 863.4
trade-off 338.2, 468.1, 777.3
tradeoff 863.1
trade on 387.15
trade on margin 737.23
trade paperback 554.3
trader 730.2
trade route 383.1
trades 318.9
trade secret 345.5
tradesfolk 730.11
trade sight unseen 731.15
tradesman 730.2
tradesmen 730.11
tradespeople 730.11
trades union 727.2
trades unionism 727.1
trades unionist 727.4
tradeswoman 730.2
trade union 727.2
trade unionism 727.1
trade unionist 727.4
trade up 338.4, 733.7
trade-up 734.2
trade winds 318.9
trade with 731.17
trading (n) 629.1, 731.2, 737.19, 854.3, 863.2 (a) 731.22
trading card 743.16
trading post 736.1, 736.2
trading stamp 631.1
tradition 373.1, 419.2, 675.1, 719.2, 842.2, 954.3
traditional 373.13, 419.4, 579.5, 687.7, 719.6, 842.12
traditional grammar 530.1
traditionalism 687.1, 842.2, 867.1
traditionalist (n) 842.8 (a) 867.6
traditionalistic 687.7, 867.6
traditionality 842.2
traditional jazz 708.9
traditional logic 935.2
traduce 512.11
traducement 512.3
traducer 512.6
traffic (n) 343.1, 731.1 (v) 731.15
traffic circle 170.2, 914.2, 915.2
traffic cone 282.5
traffic in 731.16, 731.17
traffic in women 732.1
traffic jam 293.3, 1012.1
trafficker 730.2
trafficking 731.2
traffic lane 383.1
traffic light 517.15, 1026.4
traffic officer 1008.15
traffic of the stage 704.1
traffic signal 517.15
traffic with 343.6, 731.17
tragedian 704.22, 707.8
tragedienne 707.8
tragedy 704.5, 1011.2
tragic 98.19, 704.34, 720.16, 1011.15
tragic drama 704.5
tragic flaw 704.5, 1006.4
tragic hero 492.7
tragic irony 704.2
tragic muse 704.5
tragico-comic 488.6
tragicomic 488.6, 704.34
tragicomical 704.34, 704.35
tragus 2.10
trail (n) 69.1, 84.1, 383.2, 517.8, 753.1, 817.2, 887.3 (v) 166.3, 166.4, 175.8, 202.6, 217.8, 382.9, 835.3, 905.4, 938.35
trail after 166.3
trail away 252.6
trail behind 166.4, 217.8
trail bike 179.8
trailblaze 216.7, 816.3
trailblazer 178.1, 216.2, 405.5, 816.1
trailblazing (n) 405.1 (a) 216.10, 337.5, 816.4
trailbreaker 178.1, 816.1
trail car 179.19
trailer 179.19, 228.17, 352.6, 382.4, 747.2, 817.2
trailer court 228.17
trailerload 196.2
trailer park 228.17
trailer trash 250.2, 660.2
trailer truck 179.12
trail-hike 177.30
trail hiking 177.8
trailing (n) 166.1, 382.1, 938.9 (a) 166.5, 382.11
trailing off 252.1
trail off 252.6, 762.6
trailsman 178.6
train (n) 179.14, 217.1, 461.22, 769.6, 812.2, 812.3, 817.2 (v) 161.5, 373.9, 568.13, 570.11, 744.2, 905.4, 1070.7
trainable 161.13, 570.18
trainableness 570.5
trainband 461.24
train bearer 563.4
trainbearer 166.2, 577.5
trainboy 178.13
trained 373.15, 413.26, 928.18
trainee 461.18, 572.1, 818.2
trainer 181.10, 405.5, 571.6, 754.2, 757.2, 1070.2
train guard 1008.9
training 373.7, 405.1, 568.1, 568.3
training camp 744.1
training film 706.1
training manual 568.6
training mission 184.11
training school 429.8, 567.9
trainload 196.2
trainman 178.13
trainmaster 178.13
train of thought 931.4
train robber 483.5
trainspotter 101.4, 178.13
trainspotting 27.2, 382.1
train upon 161.5
traipse (n) 177.10 (v) 175.6, 177.23, 177.27, 177.28
traipsing (n) 177.3 (a) 177.37
trait 373.2, 517.1, 865.4
trait behavior 321.1
trait-complex 373.2
traitor 327.5, 357.10, 363.5, 645.10, 660.9, 858.8
traitorous 327.11, 363.11, 645.22, 858.20
traitorousness 327.3
traits 33.4
traject (n) 383.1, 383.3 (v) 904.9
trajectile 904.15
trajection 904.2

trajectory 172.2, 383.1, 1073.16, 1074.9, 1075.9
tram 179.17, 383.8
tramcar 179.17
trammel (n) 428.4, 1012.7 (v) 428.10, 1012.11
trammeled 428.16
trammels 428.4
tramontane (n) 318.8, 774.3 (a) 261.11
tramp (n) 177.10, 178.3, 331.9, 440.8, 660.2, 828.4, 870.4 (v) 175.7, 177.23, 177.30
tramper 178.6
tramping 177.8
trample 902.22, 910.7
trampled 432.16
trample down 412.10, 432.9, 612.15, 910.7
trample in the dust 412.10, 432.9
trample on 432.9, 435.4, 910.7
trample out 395.15
trample underfoot 395.15, 412.10, 432.9, 435.4, 612.15, 910.7
trample upon 435.4
trampling down 432.4
trampoline 725.7, 1048.3
trampolining 760.5
trampy 998.21
trance (n) 22.6, 22.7, 25.2, 92.19, 691.3, 985.2, 990.1 (v) 22.20, 691.7
tranced 986.25
trance speaking 689.6
trance writing 689.6
tranche 10.18
tranche de bœuf 10.18
trank 87.3
tranqued 87.24
tranquil 106.12, 173.12, 464.9, 670.13, 933.4
tranquility 20.1, 106.2, 781.1
tranquilization 465.1, 670.2
tranquilize 106.6, 120.5, 173.8, 465.7, 670.6, 670.7
tranquilizer 25.3, 86.12, 670.3
tranquilizing (n) 670.2 (a) 86.45, 670.15
tranquillity 51.1, 173.1, 464.2, 670.1, 807.1, 933.1
tranquillity of mind 933.1
transact 328.9, 437.9
transact business 724.12
transact business with 731.17
transaction 328.2, 328.3, 437.1, 437.4, 731.4, 831.3
transactional analysis 92.6
transactions 549.7, 775.1
transalpine 261.11
transanimation 852.3
transarctic 261.11
transatlantic 261.11
transcalency 1019.18
transcalent 1019.31
transcend 247.5, 249.6, 993.9, 999.11
transcendence 122.3, 249.1, 677.1, 685.1, 858.1
transcendency 249.1
transcendent, the 685.2
transcendent 122.11, 249.12, 677.16
transcendental (n) 1053.3 (a) 249.12, 522.16, 681.12, 870.15, 986.24, 1017.23, 1073.26
transcendental essence 761.1
transcendental idealism 1053.3
transcendentalism 689.2, 870.7
transcendentalist 689.11
transcendental meditation 92.6
transcendental object 1053.3
transcendent essence 932.2
transcendent idea 932.2
transcendentness 122.3
transcendent nonempirical concept 932.2
transcendent universal 932.2
transcending 122.11, 249.12
transcontinental 261.11
transcribe 341.12, 546.6, 547.19, 708.46, 785.8
transcribed 546.8
transcriber 547.13
transcript 336.3, 547.10, 549.7, 708.28, 785.4
transcription 50.12, 341.3, 546.5, 547.10, 708.5, 708.28, 709.2, 785.2, 785.4
transcription turntable 50.11
transdisciplinary 568.19
transducer 858.10
transect 873.5, 875.4
transection 170.1
transept 170.5, 703.9
transequatorial 261.11
transeunt 190.18
transfer (n) 343.2, 629.1, 785.4 (v) 176.10, 343.7, 478.13, 615.10, 629.3
transferability 343.4
transferable 176.18, 343.11, 629.5
transferable vote 371.6
transferase 7.10
transference 92.33, 160.2, 343.2, 629.1
transfer of right 176.10
transfer orbit 1075.9
transfer property 176.10
transferral 615.2
transferred 518.10
transferred meaning 518.1
transferred sense 519.2
transfer RNA 305.9
transfiguration 852.3
transfigure 392.9, 852.8
transfigured 392.13
transfigurement 852.3
transfinite 1017.23
transfinite number 1017.5
transfix 292.15, 459.25, 855.7
transfixation 292.3
transfixed 122.9, 855.16
transfixion 292.3, 459.10
transforation 292.3
transform 392.9, 852.8, 858.11
transformable 858.18
transformation 392.5, 704.20, 852.3, 858.1, 1017.2
transformational generative grammar 530.1
transformational grammar 530.1
transformation rule 935.6
transformation scene 704.20
transformed 392.13, 852.10, 858.19
transformer 852.5, 858.10
transformism 852.3
transfusable 176.18
transfuse 91.27, 176.10, 221.7, 797.11
transfuse the sense of 341.12
transfusion 91.18, 221.3
transgender 75.2, 75.14
transgress 327.6, 435.4, 655.4, 674.5, 910.9, 975.9
transgression 327.1, 435.2, 655.1, 655.2, 674.3, 910.3
transgressive 327.8
transgressor 593.1, 660.8
transhumance 1070.1
transience 268.1, 307.12, 764.1, 828.1, 854.1
transiency 828.1
transient (n) 178.1, 178.4, 227.8, 828.4 (a) 34.3, 177.37, 190.18, 268.8, 307.33, 764.5, 828.7, 854.6
transient cause 886.3
transient guest 227.8, 828.4
transient lodging 225.3
transientness 828.1
transient state 1041.9
transilience 860.1
transilient 860.5
transistor 1033.12, 1042.3
transistor circuit 1033.8
transistor hearing aid 48.8
transistorized 1033.15
transistor physics 1033.1
transit (n) 170.1, 177.1, 278.4, 858.1 (v) 177.20
transit circle 278.4
transiting 170.1
transit instrument 278.4
transition 706.6, 852.1, 858.1
transitional 172.7, 858.18
transition element 1060.2
transition mission 184.11
transition sound 524.12
transition strip 184.23
transitive (n) 530.4 (a) 530.17, 828.7
transitive verb 530.4
transit lounge 197.20
transitoriness 828.1, 854.1
transitory 177.37, 828.7, 854.6
transits 177.2
transit station 1075.5
transit theodolite 278.4
translatability 341.6
translatable 341.17
translate 176.10, 341.12, 852.8
translated 852.10
translate into action 328.7
translation 341.3, 681.11, 852.3
translational 341.16
translative (n) 530.9 (a) 341.16
translator 341.7
translator's error 342.1
transliterate 341.12, 546.6
transliterated 546.8
transliteration 341.3, 546.5
translocate 176.10
translocation 160.2, 852.3
translucence 1025.3, 1030.2
translucency 1025.3, 1030.2
translucent 521.11, 1025.31, 1030.5
translucid 1025.31, 1030.5
translucidity 1030.2
translunar 1073.25
transmarine 261.11
transmigrant 177.37
transmigrate 177.22, 1052.9
transmigration 177.4, 852.3, 1052.8
transmigrations 177.2
transmigratory 177.37
transmissibility 343.4
transmissible 176.18, 343.11
transmission 343.2, 347.1, 551.1, 629.1, 1034.16, 1040.9
transmissional 343.9
transmission line 347.17
transmission of light 1029.1, 1030.2
transmissive 176.18
transmit 176.10, 176.15, 343.7, 478.18, 629.3, 1034.25, 1036.15
transmit light 1029.3
transmittability 343.4
transmittable 176.18, 343.11
transmittal 343.2, 629.1
transmitter 347.2, 347.4, 1034.4, 1035.8
transmitter part 1034.4, 1035.8
transmitter signal 1036.11
transmitter truck 1035.7
transmitting station 1034.6
transmogrification 852.3
transmogrifier 852.5
transmogrify 852.8
transmontane 261.11
transmundane 261.11, 681.12, 870.15, 986.24, 1053.7, 1073.26
transmutable 858.18
transmutate 852.6
transmutation 852.3, 858.1
transmute 852.8, 858.11
transmuted 852.10
transnational 864.14
transoceanic 261.11
transom 170.5, 201.1, 217.7, 239.13
transonic 50.17, 174.16
transonic barrier 50.6
transpacific 261.11
transparence 1029.1
transparency 521.2, 644.4, 714.3, 714.5, 1029.1
transparent 32.5, 521.11, 644.17, 1025.31, 1029.4
transparent color 35.8
transparent substance 1029.2
transpartisan leadership 609.3
transperson 75.2
transphysical 689.24
transphysical science 689.3
transpicuity 521.2
transpicuous 521.11, 1029.4
transpicuousness 1029.1
transpierce 292.15, 459.25
transpiration 1065.3

transpire 190.15, 351.8, 831.5
transplace 176.10
transplant (n) 191.1, 739.3 (v) 91.24, 176.10, 191.8, 1069.18
transplantation 191.1, 1069.14
transpolar 261.11
transponder 1036.7, 1041.4
transpontine 261.11
transport (n) 95.2, 105.8, 691.3 (v) 95.10, 176.12, 377.7, 909.17
transportable 176.18
transportation 909.4
transportational 179.23
transportation center 208.7
transportation engineer 1043.2
transportation engineering 1043.1
transportative 176.18
transported 95.17, 105.25, 985.11
transportive 176.18
transposable 176.18
transposal 205.1, 863.1
transpose 176.10, 205.5, 708.46, 779.5, 863.4
transposed 205.7, 863.5
transposition 205.1, 852.3, 863.1
transputer 1042.3
transsexual 75.14, 75.17
transsexualism 75.12
transsexuality 75.10, 75.12
transship 176.15
transshipment 160.2
transsonic 50.17
transsonic barrier 174.2
transsonic speed 174.2
transubstantiate 852.8
transubstantiation 701.7, 852.3, 858.1
transudation 12.1, 12.3, 13.1, 190.6
transudative 12.19, 190.20
transudatory 13.7
transude 12.12, 13.5, 190.15
transuranic element 1060.2
transversal (n) 170.5, 277.2 (a) 170.9
transverse (n) 170.5, 204.7 (v) 170.6 (a) 170.9, 204.19
transverseness 204.1
transverse wave 916.4
transversion 170.1
transvestite (n) 75.16 (a) 75.30
transvestitism 75.11
trap (n) 292.4, 346.3, 356.12, 377.3, 747.3, 752.3, 1006.5 (v) 356.20, 382.9, 480.17, 752.4
trapdoor 369.3
trapeze 725.7
trapeze artist 707.3
trapezohedral 278.9
trapezoid 278.9
trapezoidal 278.9
trapfall 356.12
trapper 382.5
trappings 5.2, 385.4, 385.5, 471.2, 498.3
Trappism 667.1
Trappist (n) 667.2 (a) 667.4
traps 471.3
trapshooter 904.8
trap shooting 744.1, 904.2
trash (n) 80.9, 370.4, 391.5, 520.2, 606.3, 759.10, 998.4 (v) 156.6, 510.13
trash can 391.7
trash collector 79.16
trash compactor 391.7
trasher 510.9, 512.6
trashing 322.1, 510.3
trash pile 391.6
trash talk 115.4
trashy 391.11, 520.7, 998.21
trattoria 8.17
traulism 525.3
trauma 85.26, 85.38, 92.17
trauma center 91.21
traumatic 393.27
traumatic memory 92.29
traumatic trace 92.29
traumatism 85.26, 92.17
traumatize 26.7, 93.15, 393.13
traumatized 26.9, 926.28
travail (n) 1.1, 725.4 (v) 1.3, 725.14, 886.10
travel (n) 162.1, 172.2, 177.1 (v) 162.2, 172.5, 177.18, 177.21
travel agency 177.5
travel book 554.8
travel bureau 177.5
travel by air 184.36
travel by airline 184.36
travel by water 182.1
travel companion 769.5
traveled 177.40
traveler 178.1, 730.4
traveler's check 728.11
travel guide 178.1
travel in a groove 373.12
travel in a rut 373.12
traveling (n) 177.1 (a) 172.7, 177.36
traveling agent 730.4
traveling person 730.4
traveling salesman 730.4
traveling wave 238.14, 916.4
travel in space 1075.12
travel-jaded 177.41
travel light 177.21
travel literature 547.12, 718.1
travelogue 543.3
travel over 177.20
travel report 317.7
travels 177.2
travel-sated 177.41
travel shot 714.8
travel sickness 85.30
travel-soiled 177.41
travel-stained 177.41
travel talk 543.3
travel the open road 177.23
travel through 177.20
travel-tired 177.41
travel-weary 177.41
travel with 769.7
travel-worn 177.41
traversal 170.1, 451.2
traverse (n) 170.5, 204.8 (v) 170.6, 177.20, 182.13, 204.12, 451.3, 451.6, 753.4 (a) 170.9
traverse a yard 182.48
traverse sailing 182.2
travesty (n) 265.2, 336.3, 350.2, 355.1, 489.1, 508.6 (v) 336.5, 350.3, 355.3, 508.11
trawl (n) 356.13 (v) 382.8, 905.4
trawler 180.1, 382.6
trawlerman 382.6
treacherous 354.31, 356.22, 645.21, 971.20, 1006.11
treacherousness 356.3, 645.6, 971.6
treachery 354.4, 645.6, 971.6, 1006.2
treacle 66.2, 66.2, 66.3, 1062.5
treacliness 1062.2
treacly 93.21, 1062.12
tread (n) 172.4, 177.11, 177.12, 193.5, 245.1 (v) 177.27, 902.22
tread close upon 166.3
treading 177.8
treading down 432.4
treading water 182.11
treadle (n) 906.4 (v) 904.9
treadmill, the 118.1, 781.2
treadmill (n) 84.1, 373.5, 605.3, 725.4, 849.4 (a) 118.9
treadmill test 84.3
tread on air 95.12
tread on eggs 339.7
tread on one's toes 96.13
tread on the heels of 835.3
treads and risers 193.3
tread the boards 704.29
tread underfoot 412.10, 432.9
tread upon 612.15, 910.7
tread warily 339.7
tread water 173.7, 182.56, 329.2
treason 363.2, 645.7, 858.3
treasonable 327.11, 363.11, 645.22, 858.20
treasonableness 327.3
treasonist 357.10
treasonous 363.11, 645.22
treasure (n) 386.1, 413.10, 618.1, 728.14, 770.11, 999.5, 1016.8 (v) 104.20, 155.4, 386.11, 474.7, 989.12, 997.13
treasure chest 941.1
treasured 104.23, 386.14
treasure house 386.6
treasure-house 729.13
treasure hunt 472.1
treasure hunter 381.7
Treasure Island 986.11
treasurer 574.3, 624.9, 729.12
treasure room 386.6
treasures 561.1
treasure trove 472.6, 941.1
treasure up 386.11, 474.7
treasure up in the heart 93.11
treasure up in the memory 989.12
treasury 386.1, 386.6, 557.4, 728.14, 728.18, 729.13, 770.11
treasury agent 576.10
treasury bill 728.11
treasury check 728.11
treasury note 728.5
treasury of information 928.9
treasury of words 554.9
treat (n) 8.5, 10.8, 95.3, 478.4, 624.8 (v) 86.38, 90.14, 91.24, 321.6, 387.12, 405.6, 541.11, 556.5, 624.19, 889.6
treatable 396.25
treat as routine 123.2
treated 405.16
treated like dirt under one's feet 432.16
treat gently 339.7
treatise 556.1
treat like dirt under one's feet 432.10
treatment 90.1, 91.1, 91.14, 387.2, 405.1, 541.6, 556.1, 706.3, 712.8
treatment center 91.21
treatment room 197.25
treat of 556.5, 775.5
treat to 624.19
treat unequally 650.8
treat well 143.9
treat with 437.6, 466.6
treat with contempt 454.4
treat with disrespect 156.4
treat with indignity 156.5
treat with reserve 955.6
treaty 437.2
treaty of peace 465.5
treaty partner 232.1
treaty port 1009.6
treble (n) 58.6, 708.4, 708.22, 709.5 (v) 877.2 (a) 58.13, 708.50, 876.3, 877.3
treble clef 709.13
trebleness 876.2, 877.1
trebuchet 462.9, 605.3
tredecillion 882.13
tree (n) 180.13, 310.10, 560.5, 605.5 (v) 1013.13, 1013.16
tree-covered 310.40
treed 1013.25
tree farm 310.12, 1069.8
tree farmer 1069.7
tree farming 1069.3
tree frog 311.26
tree-hugger 1072.3
treeless plain 891.2
treelike 171.10, 310.39
tree line 237.2, 310.12
tree litter 310.17
tree nursery 310.12
tree nymph 678.9
tree of knowledge 928.8
tree of knowledge of good and evil 928.8
tree ring 310.11
treescape 712.11
tree-shaped 171.10
tree surgeon 1069.7
tree toad 311.26
tree veld 236.1, 310.13
tree worship 697.1
tree worshiper 697.4
tree zone 310.12
tref 80.20
trefoil 876.1
trehalose 66.3
treillage 170.3
trek (n) 177.4, 177.5 (v) 177.21, 177.22
trekker 178.1, 178.5
trekking 177.36
trellis (n) 170.3 (v) 170.7

trelliswork 170.3
tremble (n) 105.5, 709.19, 917.3 (v) 16.8, 105.18, 127.14, 128.6, 917.11, 1023.9
tremble in one's boots 127.14
tremble in the balance 971.11
tremble like an aspen leaf 127.14
tremble on the verge 1006.8
trembles 128.2
trembling (n) 105.5, 917.2 (a) 127.23, 128.12, 917.17
trembling in the balance 1006.12
trembly 128.12, 917.17
tremelloid 1062.12
tremellose 1062.12
tremendous 127.30, 247.7, 257.20, 999.15
tremendousness 247.1, 257.7
tremolando (n) 709.19 (a) 708.53
tremolant 709.19
tremolo (n) 709.19 (v) 708.38
tremoloso 708.53
tremor 105.2, 105.5, 525.1, 709.19, 917.3
tremor of excitement 105.2
tremulant 128.12
tremulous 127.23, 128.12, 525.12, 917.17
tremulousness 917.2
trench (n) 224.2, 239.1, 275.4, 284.9, 290.2, 346.4, 460.5, 1009.3 (v) 214.5, 224.4, 239.15, 284.15, 290.3
trenchancy 17.5, 68.1, 144.8, 544.3, 920.4
trenchant 17.13, 17.14, 68.6, 144.23, 544.11, 920.16
trench artillery 462.11
trenched 290.4
trencherman 8.16, 672.3
trencherwoman 672.3
trenches 460.6
trench warfare 458.1
trend (n) 161.1, 172.2, 238.4, 578.1, 896.2 (v) 161.7, 164.3, 238.16, 896.3
trend downward 194.5
trendlessness 810.1, 971.1, 972.1
trendsetter 496.6, 578.7, 841.4
trend upwards 193.13
trendy 578.11, 578.15, 841.13, 928.17
trepan 292.15
trepanning 292.3
trephine 292.15
trephining 292.3
trepidacious 126.7
trepidant 127.23
trepidation 105.5, 127.5, 128.1, 917.1
trepidity 105.5, 127.5, 917.1
très bon 999.12
tres chic 5.46
trespass (n) 214.1, 435.2, 640.3, 655.1, 655.2, 674.3, 910.3 (v) 214.5, 435.4, 640.8, 655.4, 674.5, 910.9
trespasser 189.4, 214.3
trespassing 214.1, 640.3, 674.3
trespass on 214.5
trespass upon 214.5
tress 3.5
tresses 3.4
tressure 647.2
trestle 383.7, 901.16
trestle and table 901.16
trestle board 901.16
trestle table 901.16
trestlework 901.16
trestling 901.16
trey 758.2, 876.1
triable 674.6
triad 876.1
triadelphous 878.4
triadic 876.3
triadical 876.3
triage 808.3
trial (n) 96.2, 96.9, 403.2, 405.1, 457.3, 530.8, 598.5, 942.1, 942.2, 1011.1 (a) 403.16, 876.3, 942.11
trial and error 403.2, 942.1
trial-and-error 942.11
trial at the bar 598.5
trial attorney 597.1
trial balance 628.2
trial balloon 938.10, 942.2, 942.4
trial by jury 598.5
trial by law 598.5
trial court 595.2
trial impression 548.5
triality 876.2
trial lawyer 597.1
trial marriage 75.18
trialogue 541.2, 876.1
trial run 942.3
trials and tribulations 96.9
triangle 54.4, 104.5, 277.3, 605.3, 876.1
triangle player 710.11
triangular 278.8, 876.3, 878.4
triangular bandage 86.33
triangular division 461.22
triangulate (v) 159.11, 300.10 (a) 878.4
triangulated 300.13
triangulation 159.8, 300.1, 1036.8
triangulation stations 1036.6
triannual 876.3
triarch 878.4
triarchy 612.4
triathlon 744.1, 755.2
triatomic 1038.18
Triavil 86.12
tribade 75.14
tribadism 75.10
tribadistic 75.30
tribady 75.10
tribal 559.7, 606.8
tribalism 559.4, 612.4
tribal system 612.4
tribasic 1038.18
tribe 559.4, 617.2, 770.3, 809.3, 809.5
tribesman 559.2
tribespeople 559.2
tribrach 720.8
tribulation 96.9, 1011.1
tribunal (n) 423.1, 595.1, 901.13 (a) 595.7
tribunate 417.7
tribune 596.2, 901.13
tributary (n) 238.3 (a) 432.13
tributary sea 240.2
tribute 421.1, 478.4, 487.1, 509.5, 624.5, 630.9, 646.4, 888.2
tribute band 710.12
trice 830.3
tricennial 850.4
tricentenary 850.4
trice up 1046.9
trichinopoly 89.4
trichoid 3.23
trichoschistic 510.23, 936.14
trichoschistism 510.4, 936.5, 944.3
trichotomize 878.3
trichotomous 878.4
trichotomy 878.1
trichroism 47.1
trichromatic 47.9
trichromatism 47.1
trichromic 47.9
trick (n) 328.3, 356.6, 373.3, 376.1, 381.5, 413.6, 415.3, 489.10, 500.2, 532.2, 758.3, 825.3, 865.4, 927.2, 976.1, 995.2 (v) 356.14, 356.15, 415.9, 489.14
tricked out 498.11
tricked-out 5.45
tricker 357.2
trickery 356.4, 356.5, 415.3, 489.4, 498.3
trickiness 356.1, 415.1, 489.4, 645.1
tricking 356.1
trickish 322.6, 356.21, 356.22, 415.12, 489.17
trickishness 489.4
trickle, a 992.9
trickle (n) 190.5, 238.7, 885.2 (v) 190.14, 238.18
trickle away 393.19
trickle down 190.14
trickle-down economics 731.11
tricklet 238.7
trick of behavior 500.2
trick of eyesight 976.5
trick or treat 690.3
trick out 5.42, 354.16, 498.8, 545.7
trick question 938.10
trick rider 178.8
tricksiness 489.4
tricks of the trade 356.6, 384.2
trickster 357.2, 415.6
tricksy 322.6, 356.21, 489.17, 578.13
trick up 5.42, 498.8
tricky 356.21, 356.22, 415.12, 489.17, 645.16, 645.18, 645.21, 1013.17
tricky spot 1006.1, 1013.5
tricolor (n) 647.7 (a) 47.9
tricolored 47.9
tricorn (n) 876.1 (a) 878.4
tricornered 878.4
tricuspid 878.4
tricycle 179.8
tridachna 311.29
trident (n) 171.4, 876.1 (a) 878.4
tridental 878.4
tridentate 878.4
tridentlike 171.10
Trident submarine 180.9
tried 413.28, 587.21, 644.19, 942.12, 970.20
tried and true 413.28, 587.21, 644.19, 842.12, 942.12
tried-and-trueness 587.7
triedness 587.7
triennial (n) 310.3, 850.4 (a) 850.8
triennium 876.1
trifid 878.4
trifle (n) 248.5, 764.2, 766.3, 998.5 (v) 276.4, 331.13, 340.7, 562.14, 923.6, 998.14
trifle away 486.5
trifler 331.8, 340.5, 929.6, 998.10
trifles 998.4
trifle with 156.4, 340.9
trifle with the truth 354.19
trifling (n) 331.4, 998.8 (a) 248.6, 258.10, 276.5, 936.14, 998.19
trifling amount 248.2
triflingness 923.1, 998.3
trifloral 878.4
triflorate 878.4
triflorous 878.4
trifocals 29.3
trifold 876.3, 877.3
trifoliate 878.4
triforium 703.9
triforking 171.3
triform 876.3
trifurcate (v) 171.7, 878.3 (a) 171.10, 878.4
trifurcated 171.10
trifurcation 171.3, 878.1
trig 180.20, 264.5, 578.13, 807.8
trigamist 563.11
trigger (n) 886.3 (v) 375.18, 671.14, 886.10, 1036.17
trigger a mine 459.24
trigger film 706.1
trigger-happy 128.12, 458.20
triggering 375.2
triggering pulse 1035.4
triggering signals 1036.8
trigger man 308.11, 593.4
trigger off 375.18, 886.10
trigger point 407.2
trigger pulse 1036.10
triglyceride 7.7
trigonal 278.8, 878.4
trigonoid 878.4
trigonometric 1017.22
trigonometrical 1017.22
trigonometrician 1017.16
trigonometry 278.3
trigrammatic 878.4
trig up 808.12
trihedral 218.7, 878.4
trihedron 876.1
trike 179.8
trilateral 218.7, 278.8, 878.4
trilateral symmetry 264.1

trilemma 1013.7
trilevel 296.6
trilingual 523.16
triliteral 878.4
trill (n) 524.8, 709.19 (v) 52.11, 60.5, 190.14, 708.38
trillando 708.53
trillet 709.19
trilleto 709.19
trilling 52.19
trillion 882.13, 1017.5
trillionfold 884.10
trillo 709.19
trilocial 877.3
trilogic 877.3
trilogy 876.1
trim (n) 5.1, 84.1, 405.4, 498.1, 765.3, 1016.14 (v) 3.22, 182.49, 211.10, 268.6, 363.9, 405.6, 412.9, 467.5, 498.8, 510.18, 604.14, 633.6, 800.7, 802.11, 808.12, 906.9 (a) 180.19, 180.20, 264.5, 533.6, 578.13, 807.8
trim away 252.7, 802.11
trim by the head 182.49
trim by the stern 182.49
trimerous 878.4
trimester 824.2, 876.1
trimetallic 1058.16
trimeter 720.7
trimmed 180.17, 211.12, 268.9, 412.15, 498.11
trimmer 357.10, 363.4, 467.4, 867.2
trimming (n) 211.7, 254.4, 412.1, 467.1, 498.1, 554.14 (a) 363.10
trimness 578.3, 807.3
trim one's sails to the breeze 867.4
trim sail 182.20
trim ship 182.49
trim size 554.4, 554.12
trim to 788.7
trim up 182.49, 808.12
trim-up 808.6
Trimurti 677.9
trinal 876.3, 877.3
trine (n) 876.1 (a) 876.3, 877.3
trinitrotoluene 462.14
trinitrotoluol 462.14
Trinity 677.9
trinity 876.1, 876.2
trinket 498.4, 743.16, 998.5
trinomen 527.3
trinomial (n) 876.1 (a) 527.17
trinomialism 527.1
trinomial name 527.3
trio 450.1, 708.18, 876.1
trionym 876.1
trip (n) 87.2, 177.5, 184.9, 194.3, 414.5, 655.2, 770.5, 975.4, 976.1, 986.5 (v) 87.22, 174.8, 177.28, 194.8, 356.20, 366.6, 412.7, 414.11, 654.9, 671.14, 705.5, 743.23, 913.5, 975.9, 986.17
tripack 714.10
triparted 878.4
tripartite 878.4
tripartition 878.1
tripe 10.20, 520.3
tripedal 878.4
tripersonal 677.17
tripes 2.19, 207.4
tripetalous 878.4
triphibian 181.8
triphthong 524.12, 876.1
triphthongal 524.30
Tripitaka 683.9
triple (n) 745.3 (v) 251.5, 745.5, 877.2 (a) 876.3, 877.3
triple-A 745.1
triple axel 760.7
triple-check 970.12
Triple Crown 757.1
triple crown 647.4
triple crown 876.1
triple-decker 876.1
triple meter 720.6
tripleness 876.2
triple play 745.3
triple plume 647.3
triplet 709.14, 709.24, 720.10, 876.1
triple threat 876.1
triple time 709.24
triple-tongue 708.42
triple whammy 1000.4
triplex 876.3, 877.3
triplicate (n) 785.3, 877.1 (v) 785.8, 877.2 (a) 877.3
triplication 877.1
triplicity 876.2, 877.1
triplopy 876.1
tripod 876.1, 1020.12
tripodic 878.4
tripod of the Pythia 962.7
tripody 720.7
trip one up 96.13, 1012.15
tripos 938.2
trip over 194.8, 941.3
trip over one's own feet 414.11
trip over one's tongue 975.14
tripped up 406.8
tripper 87.21, 178.1
tripping (n) 976.7 (a) 87.24, 533.8, 544.9
tripping over 941.1
trippy 87.24
trip the light fantastic 705.5
Triptolemus 1069.4
trip to Mars 1075.1
trip to the moon 1075.1
triptych 549.11, 712.10, 876.1, 878.1
trip up 137.5, 356.20, 412.7, 811.4, 913.5, 975.15, 985.6
tripwire 1006.5
triquetral 878.4
triquetrous 218.7, 878.4
trireme 876.1
trisaccharide 7.5
Trisagion 696.3
trisect 878.3
trisected 878.4
trisection 878.1
triseme 720.7, 876.1
triskelion 876.1
trismus 85.6
Tristan and Isolde 104.17
tristful 112.23
tristfulness 112.5
tristich 720.10
trisul 876.1
tritanopia 30.3
trite 117.9, 373.14, 864.16, 928.27, 974.6, 998.19
trite expression 864.8
trite joke 489.9
triteness 117.3, 998.3
trite saying 974.3
tritheism 675.5
tritheist 675.16
tritheistic 675.25
tritical 974.6
triticism 974.3
tritium 1038.5
tritium nucleus 1038.6
Triton 240.3, 678.10
tritone 709.20
triton nucleus 1038.6
tritrate 1060.8
triturable 1051.13
triturate 1051.9
triturated 1051.11
trituration 1051.4
triturator 1051.7
triumph (n) 116.1, 409.3, 411.1, 487.1, 502.4 (v) 249.7, 409.13, 411.3, 502.9
triumphal 136.11, 411.7
triumphal arch 549.12
triumphalism 411.1, 501.1
triumphant 409.14, 411.7, 502.13
triumpher 411.2
triumph over 411.5, 412.6
triumvirate 450.1, 612.4, 876.1
triune 677.17, 876.3
triunity 876.1, 876.2
trivalence 1060.4
trivalent 1060.10
trivet 876.1, 1020.12
trivia 248.2, 551.1, 998.4
trivial 248.6, 250.7, 276.5, 391.11, 768.4, 936.14, 998.19
trivial affair, a 998.6
triviality 248.1, 250.3, 276.1, 391.2, 768.2, 923.1, 998.3, 998.5
trivialization 923.5, 936.1
trivialize 276.4, 998.12
trivialized 156.9
trivial matter 766.3
trivialness 998.3
trivia question 938.10
triviata 998.4
troat 60.2
trochaic 720.17
troche 86.7
trochee 720.8
trochilic 915.15
trochilics 915.8
trodden 201.7
troglodyte 497.7, 842.7
troglodytic 497.12
troglodytism 497.3
troika 179.20, 450.1, 876.1
Trojan horse 357.11, 1042.11
Trojan-horse 645.22
Trojan sibyl 962.6
trolatitious 536.3
troll (n) 708.19 (v) 382.10, 708.38, 904.9, 905.4, 915.10
troller 382.6
trolley 179.16, 179.17
trolley bus 179.17
trolley car 179.17
trolling (n) 127.6, 915.1 (a) 514.3, 915.14
trollop 660.4, 665.14, 810.7
trombonist 710.4
tromp 177.28
troop 461.22, 770.3, 770.5
troop carrier 181.9
trooper 461.6, 461.12, 461.30, 1008.15
troopers 1008.17
troops 18.9, 461.23
troops of the line 461.23
troop transport 181.9
trope 536.1
trope of comparison 943.1
trophoplasm 305.4
trophy 100.11, 411.1, 549.12, 646.3, 748.1, 989.6, 999.5
trophy wife 607.4
tropic 231.3
tropical 1019.24
tropical cyclone 318.11, 671.4
tropical disease 85.32
tropical fish 311.29, 311.30
tropical fruit 10.38, 310.4
tropical heat 1019.5, 1019.6
tropical storm 318.11, 671.4
Tropic of Cancer 231.3
Tropic of Capricorn 231.3
tropics 231.3, 1019.11
tropism 896.1
tropologic 536.3
tropological 341.14, 519.10, 536.3
tropology 341.8
tropospheric 317.12
trot (n) 174.3, 177.12, 304.3, 341.3, 849.4 (v) 174.8, 177.34, 188.7
troth (n) 436.1, 436.3, 644.7 (v) 436.4, 436.6
trothless 645.20
trothlessness 645.5
trot out 348.5
trots, the 85.29
trots 12.2
Trotskyism 611.5
Trotskyist (n) 611.13, 860.3 (a) 611.21, 860.6
Trotskyite (n) 611.13, 860.3 (a) 611.21, 860.6
trotter 199.5, 311.14, 757.2
trotters 177.15
trotting 757.1
Trotting Horse Club 757.1
troubadour 178.2, 710.14, 720.12
trouble (n) 96.2, 96.8, 126.1, 593.3, 643.1, 725.1, 810.4, 996.3, 1011.1, 1012.6, 1013.3 (v) 96.16, 98.15, 105.14, 126.4, 640.7, 811.4, 917.10, 996.4, 1013.13
troubled 96.21, 96.22, 105.23, 126.7, 917.16, 1013.20
troubled mind 926.1
trouble-free 1002.6, 1007.5

troublemaker 327.5, 375.11, 593.2
trouble man 396.10
trouble one for 440.9
trouble oneself 126.6, 137.8, 141.8, 403.11
trouble one's head 126.6
trouble one's head about 931.11, 983.5
trouble-plagued 1013.20
troubles 126.2, 1011.1
troubleshooter 396.10, 466.3
troubleshooting 396.6, 466.1
troublesome 98.22, 126.10, 725.18, 996.7, 1011.13, 1012.17, 1013.18
troublesomeness 98.7, 725.5, 996.3, 1013.1
trouble spot 458.1
troubling 98.22, 105.30
troublous 671.18, 917.16, 1011.13
trough (n) 184.32, 238.14, 239.1, 239.3, 284.2, 284.9, 290.2, 916.4 (v) 284.15, 290.3
troughed 290.4
troughing 239.1
trough line 184.32
troughway 239.1
trounce 249.7, 412.9, 510.20, 604.12
trounced 412.15
trouncing 412.1, 604.4
troupe (n) 617.7, 707.11, 770.3 (v) 704.29
trouper 707.2
trousered 5.45
trousers 5.18
trousseau 5.2
trout pout 144.4
trouvère 710.14, 720.12
trouveur 720.12
trovatore 710.14, 720.12
trove 472.6, 941.1
trover 472.1, 481.3
trow 953.11
trowel (n) 1040.2, 1040.8 (v) 284.15
troy weight 297.8
truancy 222.4, 368.2, 368.4
truant (n) 222.5, 368.3, 368.5, 660.2 (a) 222.13
truantism 222.4
truce 465.5, 857.3
truce flag 465.2
Truce of God 465.5
truck (n) 179.12, 195.1, 343.1, 391.5, 471.3, 731.1, 735.7, 775.1 (v) 176.13, 731.15
truck car 179.16
truck driver 178.10
trucker 178.10
truck farmer 1069.5
truck gardener 1069.6
truck gardening 1069.2
trucking shot 714.8
truckle 138.7
truckler 138.3
truckle to 138.8, 433.10
truckling (n) 138.2 (a) 138.14
truckload 196.2
truckman 178.9, 178.10
truck stop 739.1
truck trailer 179.12, 179.19
truculence 110.7, 144.11, 458.10, 505.3
truculent 144.26, 458.20, 505.7
trudge (n) 175.2, 177.10 (v) 175.7, 177.28
trudgen 182.11
trudging (n) 177.8 (a) 175.10
true, the 973.1
true (v) 788.7 (a) 277.6, 359.12, 434.4, 587.21, 644.16, 644.19, 644.20, 687.7, 761.15, 970.13, 973.13
true air peed 184.31
true as gospel 973.13
true bearing 161.2
true being 767.5
true believer 687.4, 953.9
true bill 598.3, 599.1
true blue 644.7, 644.8
true-blue 587.21, 644.13, 644.20, 687.7, 842.12
true-blueness 587.7
true Christian 659.3
true church, the 687.3
true course 161.2, 184.34
true-dealing 644.13
true-devoted 644.13
true directions 161.3
true-disposing 644.13
true faith 687.2
true fruit 10.38
true grit 359.3, 492.5
true heading 161.2, 184.34
truehearted 644.13
true horizon 201.4
truelove 104.1, 104.9
true meaning 518.1
true-meaning 644.16
trueness 359.2, 587.7, 644.7, 973.1, 973.5
true north 161.3
truepenny 644.8
true skin 2.4
true-souled 644.13
true-speaking 524.31, 644.16
true-spirited 644.13
true to form 349.15, 865.13
true to life 349.14, 784.16, 973.15
true-to-lifeness 973.7
true to nature 973.15
true-tongued 644.16
true to one's colors 644.20
true to one's word 644.16, 970.17
true to reality 973.15
true to the facts 973.13
true to the letter 973.15
true to the spirit 973.15
true to type 349.15
true up 788.7
truism 864.8, 974.2
truistic 117.9, 864.16, 928.27
trull 665.14
Truman Doctrine 609.5
Trump 618.8
trump 249.6
trump 659.2, 995.2
trump card 843.2, 894.1, 997.6
trumped-up 354.29
trumped-up charge 599.4
trumped-up story 354.11
trumpery (n) 498.3, 520.2, 998.4 (a) 998.21
trumpet (n) 53.5, 282.5, 665.14 (v) 53.10, 352.13, 501.17, 509.12, 524.25, 708.42
trumpet blare 53.5
trumpet blast 53.5
trumpet call 53.5, 458.7, 517.16
trumpeter 710.4
trumpet forth 352.13, 501.17
trumpet major 710.4
trumpet of doom 839.3
trumpet-tongued 53.12
trumpet-voiced 53.12
trump hand 249.2
trumps 758.3
trump suit 758.3
trump up 354.18
trump up a charge 599.12
truncate 255.10, 265.7, 268.6
truncated 265.12, 537.6, 557.6, 795.5
truncation 255.2, 265.3, 268.3, 537.4
truncheon (n) 417.9, 462.4 (v) 604.12
truncheoning 604.4
trundle 904.9, 915.10
trundling 915.1
trunk 2.1, 195.1, 282.4, 283.8, 310.11, 310.21, 347.17, 901.8, 1052.3
trunk cabin 197.9
trunk call 347.13
trunk line 347.17
trunks 5.29
trunnion 915.5
truss (n) 770.8 (v) 770.20, 800.9
trussing 800.3
truss up 19.10, 770.20
trust (n) 124.1, 471.4, 615.1, 617.9, 622.1, 737.16, 953.1, 970.5 (v) 124.6, 478.16, 622.6, 953.10, 953.17
trustability 644.6
trustable 644.19
trusted 953.23
trusted friend 588.2
trustee 429.11, 470.5, 479.3, 479.4, 576.3, 729.12
trusteeship 615.1
Trusteeship Council 614.2
truster 692.4, 953.9
trustful 416.5, 587.21, 953.22, 954.8
trustfulness 416.1, 954.1
trust fund 386.3, 737.16
trust implicitly 953.17
trust in 953.15, 953.17
trustiness 644.6
trusting 416.5, 953.22, 954.8
trustingness 416.1, 954.1
trust in God 692.6
trusting soul 358.1, 954.4
trustless 645.19
trust mortgage 438.4
trust officer 729.11
trust one's good right arm 430.20
trust one's word 953.10
trust to 953.16
trust to chance 759.24
trust utterly 953.17
trustworthiness 644.6, 953.8, 970.4
trustworthy 587.21, 644.19, 953.24, 970.17, 1007.5
trusty (n) 429.11, 644.8 (a) 587.21, 644.19, 953.22, 953.24, 970.17
trusty friend 588.2
Truth 677.6
truth, a 973.2
truth, the 687.1, 973.3
truth 644.3, 761.2, 970.1, 973.1, 974.2
truth-bearing 644.16
truth-declaring 644.16
truth-desiring 644.16
truth-filled 644.16
truthful 644.16, 973.13
truthfulness 644.1, 644.3, 973.1
truth-function 935.7
truth-guarding 644.16
truthless 354.25, 354.34
truthlessness 354.1, 354.8
truth-loving (n) 644.3 (a) 644.16
truth of the matter, the 761.4, 973.3
truth of the matter 761.3
truth-passing 644.16
truth-seeking 644.16
truth serum 86.15
truth-speaking (n) 644.3 (a) 644.16
truth table 935.7
truth-telling (n) 644.3 (a) 644.16
truth to life 973.7
truth to nature 973.7
truth to the letter 973.7
truth-value 935.7
try (n) 62.2, 403.3, 942.2 (v) 62.7, 79.22, 403.6, 403.12, 598.18, 942.8, 946.12
try a case 598.18
try again 403.12
try and 403.8
try and try 403.12
try and try again 360.2
try anything once 403.10
try conclusions 457.13, 457.18, 935.16
try conclusions with 457.16, 457.17
tryer-out 942.6
try for 403.9
try for a miracle 967.5
try hard 403.12
try in all its phases 938.25
trying (n) 942.1 (a) 16.20, 21.13, 98.24, 938.37, 942.11, 1011.13, 1013.18
trying conclusions 457.2
trying it on 942.1
trying it out 942.1
trying-out 942.1
try it for size 942.8
try it on 403.6, 942.8

try on 5.43, 5.44, 942.8
try one 1011.8
try one another 457.18
try one out 942.8
try one's best 403.13
try one's damndest 403.14
try one's darndest 403.14
try one's fortune 759.23
try one's hand 403.6, 403.10
try one's luck 403.10, 759.23
try one's patience 96.13, 98.14, 440.12
try one's strength 942.8
try one's utmost 403.13
try on for size 403.7
try out 405.6, 704.28, 744.2, 942.8
tryout 48.2, 405.1, 704.12, 942.3
try out under controlled conditions 942.8
trypanosome 85.42
trypsin 7.10
try square 200.6
tryst 104.5, 582.9
trysting place 582.9
try the chance 759.24
try the issue 457.18
try the patience of a saint 96.13
try to 403.8
try to be in two places at once 967.5
try to bribe 378.3
try to catch the wind in a net 967.5
try to change the leopard's spots 967.5
try to fetch water in a sieve 967.5
try to find 938.30
try to gather grapes from thorns 967.5
try to get blood from a turnip 967.5
try to get figs from thistles 967.5
try to make a silk purse out of a sow's ear 967.5
try to make bricks from straw 967.5
try to make cheese of chalk 967.5
try to reach 100.20
try to recall 989.20
try to weave a rope of sand 967.5
try until one is blue in the face 403.12
T-shirt 5.15
T square 200.6, 277.3
T-square 278.4
tsunami 238.14, 671.4, 671.5, 916.4
tsures 96.8
tub (n) 79.8, 79.12, 179.10, 180.1, 257.12 (v) 79.19
tubal 239.16
tubate 239.16
tubbed 79.25
tubbiness 257.8
tubbing 79.6
tubby 257.18, 268.10
tube, the 1035.1
tube (n) 179.14, 239.6, 282.4, 916.4, 1033.10 (v) 176.14
tubed 239.16
tubelike 239.16
tube of electric force 1032.3
tuber 10.35, 310.22, 310.33
tubercle 85.37, 283.3, 310.22
tubercular 85.61, 283.17
tubercule 283.3
tuberculin test 91.15
tuberculosis 85.5, 85.17
tuberculous 85.61, 283.17
tuberose 283.17
tuberosity 283.1, 283.2
tuberous 283.17, 310.36
tuberousness 283.1, 283.2
tuberous root 310.22
tuber vegetable 310.4
tube-shaped 282.11
tubiform 239.16
tubing 239.6
tub of lard 257.12
tub-thump 543.10
tub-thumper 543.4
tub-thumping 352.5, 543.2
tubular 239.16, 282.11
tubulation 239.6
tubule 239.6
tubulet 239.6
tubulure 239.6
tuchis 217.5
tuck (n) 10.2, 90.2, 291.1, 746.3, 753.3 (v) 291.5
tuck away 8.22, 187.11, 390.5
tucked 291.7
tucked-in 772.5
tucker (n) 5.17, 10.1, 10.6 (v) 21.6
tuckered 21.8
tuckered out 21.8
tucker out 21.6
tuck in 8.22, 22.19, 121.9, 191.3
tuck in a reef 494.6
tuck into 8.22, 672.4
tuck one's tail 137.7
tuck up 20.6, 291.5
Tuesday 832.4
tufa 1059.1
tuff 1059.1
tuft 3.6, 3.8, 3.16, 310.2, 770.7
tufted 3.29, 310.42
tufthunter 606.7, 651.3
tufthunting 141.6
tufty 3.24
tug (n) 725.2, 905.2, 907.1 (v) 725.10, 905.4, 907.4
tug at the heart 93.14
tug at the heartstrings 93.14, 500.12
tugging (n) 905.1 (a) 905.6, 907.5
tug-of-war 457.4, 905.1
tuition 568.1
tuitional 568.18
tuitionary 568.18
tum 2.19
tumble (n) 194.3, 410.3, 810.3, 917.8 (v) 105.18, 182.55, 194.8, 395.22, 412.12, 811.3, 913.5, 915.13, 917.15, 945.3
tumbled 810.14
tumbledown 16.16, 194.11, 393.33
tumbledown shack 228.11
tumble dryer 1066.4
tumble for 954.6
tumble on 941.3
tumble over 194.8
tumbler 8.12, 707.3
tumbler bearing 915.7
tumbler-dry 1066.6
tumble to 521.9, 551.14, 931.16, 941.8
tumbling 760.5
tumefacient 259.13
tumefaction 259.2, 283.4
tumefy 259.5
tumesce 75.20
tumescence 251.1, 259.2, 283.4
tumescent 283.16, 545.9
tumid 259.13, 283.16, 501.22, 545.9
tumidity 259.2, 283.4, 545.1
tumidness 259.2, 545.1
tummy 2.19, 819.1
tummyache 26.5
tumor 85.9, 85.39, 283.4
tumorigenic 85.61
tumorous 85.61, 283.16
tum-tum 2.19
tumult 53.3, 105.4, 330.4, 671.2, 810.4, 917.1
tumultuation 917.1
tumultuous 53.13, 105.24, 503.4, 671.18
tumultuousness 53.2, 671.2
tumulus 237.4, 309.16
tun 257.12
tunable 708.48
tuna wagon 179.10
tundra 236.1, 1023.4
tune (n) 708.2, 708.3, 708.4, 709.4 (v) 405.8, 708.35, 708.36, 788.7, 808.10, 808.13
tuned 708.49
tuned in 981.5
tune down 252.7, 1034.27
tuneful 708.48
tunefulness 708.2
tuneful Nine 710.22
tune in 1034.27, 1036.17
tuneless 61.4
tunelessness 61.1
tune off 1034.27
tune one's lyre 720.14
tune out 773.4, 984.2, 1034.27
tuner-inner 1034.22
tunesmith 710.20
tunester 710.1
tune up 708.36, 808.10, 808.13, 1034.27
tuneup 808.2
tuning 392.4, 405.2, 709.4, 808.2
tuning bar 711.22
tuning fork 711.22
tuning peg 711.5
tuning pipe 711.22
tunk 52.3
tunnel (n) 228.26, 239.1, 284.5, 383.3, 460.5 (v) 275.9, 284.15, 1043.4
tunneler 284.10
tunneling 275.8
tunnel of time 827.3
tunnel vision 28.1, 30.1, 980.1
tun of flesh 257.12
tup 76.8, 311.7
tupik 228.10
tuppence 728.8, 998.5
turbid 810.13, 1031.3, 1061.4, 1062.14
turbidity 917.1, 1031.1, 1061.1, 1062.4
turbidness 1031.1, 1062.4
turbinado sugar 66.2, 66.3
turbinal 281.8
turbinate 281.6, 281.8
turbination 281.2, 915.1
turbine 904.6
turbocharger 756.1
turbofan (n) 181.1 (a) 904.17
turbojet (n) 181.1, 181.3, 1043.3 (a) 184.49, 904.17
turbojet propulsion 184.25
turboprop (n) 181.1, 181.2, 1043.3 (a) 904.17
turbopropeller 904.17
turbo-propeller plane 181.2
turbulence 105.4, 184.29, 184.32, 288.1, 671.2, 810.1, 917.1, 1061.1
turbulent 53.13, 105.24, 318.22, 327.11, 330.20, 671.18, 810.13, 917.16
turbulent flow 174.2, 184.29, 1061.1
turd 12.4, 660.5
turf, the 457.11, 757.1
turf 228.1, 231.1, 310.6, 310.33, 463.1, 724.4, 757.1, 894.4
turf accountant 759.20
turf battle 456.11
turf consultant 759.20
turf horse 311.14
turflike 310.42
turfman 174.5, 757.2
turf sport, the 757.1
turf track 757.1
turf war 456.5
turfy 310.42
turgescence 259.2, 283.4, 545.1
turgescency 283.4
turgescent 283.16, 545.9
turgid 259.13, 283.16, 501.22, 534.3, 545.9
turgidity 259.2, 283.4, 501.7, 534.1, 545.1, 993.7
turgidness 259.2
turistas 12.2
turkey 10.22, 311.28, 410.2, 410.8, 704.4, 750.2
turkey-cock 76.8, 311.28
turkey farm 1070.5
turkey gobbler 76.8, 311.28
turkey shoot 1011.1, 1014.4
Turkish 89.2
Turkish bath 79.8
Turkish baths 79.10
turmoil 105.4, 418.2, 671.2, 810.3, 810.4, 917.1

turn (n) 33.4, 100.3, 131.3, 143.7, 158.8, 164.1, 177.5, 177.10, 184.13, 204.3, 262.1, 265.1, 279.3, 328.3, 413.5, 704.7, 709.18, 731.4, 737.19, 753.3, 756.3, 825.2, 825.3, 843.4, 850.3, 852.1, 859.1, 896.1, 914.1, 914.2, 915.2, 978.3 (v) 67.4, 161.5, 161.7, 163.9, 164.3, 182.30, 204.9, 265.5, 279.6, 281.4, 286.2, 753.4, 850.5, 852.6, 854.5, 859.5, 896.3, 914.6, 915.9
turn a blind eye 134.8, 773.4, 984.2
turn a blind eye to 148.4, 340.6
turn about 163.9, 205.5, 859.5
turnabout 163.3, 363.1, 363.5, 852.1, 859.1
turn acid 67.4
turn a cold shoulder to 340.8
turn a cold shoulder upon 157.5
turn a corner 914.6
turn a deaf ear 49.4, 146.2, 361.7, 773.4
turn a deaf ear to 442.3, 984.2
turn against 645.15, 858.13
turn a hand 725.12
turn and turn about 825.5
turn an honest penny 472.12
turn a penny 472.12
turn a pirouette 915.9
turn a pot 742.6
turn around 163.9, 379.3, 392.7, 859.5, 915.9
turnaround 163.3, 363.1
turn aside 164.3, 164.6, 379.4, 460.10, 538.9, 852.6, 903.7, 1012.14
turn aside provocation 134.8
turn a somersault 205.6
turn ass over tincups 205.6
turn away 164.6, 372.2, 379.4, 909.18
turn away from 27.19, 157.5, 368.6, 984.4
turn a willing ear 441.2
turn awry 265.5
turn back 163.8, 164.6, 182.30, 849.11, 858.11, 859.5, 908.3
turn back the clock 301.8, 853.6, 859.5
turn back time 967.5, 989.9
turn blue in the face 105.19
turn bottom side up 205.6
turn cloak 363.7
turncoat (n) 357.10, 363.5, 858.8 (a) 645.22
turn color 105.19, 127.11
turn down 205.5, 291.5, 442.3
turndown 442.1
turn down the volume 670.6
turned 393.41
turned around 163.12, 971.24, 985.15
turned-off 102.7, 510.21
turned on 105.20
turned-on 95.15, 101.11, 105.20, 983.16
turned-out 5.45
turned-up 193.15, 268.10, 279.9
turn for 413.5
turn for the better 392.1
turn from 379.4
turn gray 303.10
turn green with envy 154.2
turn head over heels 205.6
turn in 22.18, 205.5, 645.14
turn in an alarm 400.3
turn informer 551.12
turning (n) 67.3, 164.1, 279.3, 281.1, 914.1, 915.1 (a) 164.7, 281.6, 915.14
turning around 379.1
turning away 372.1
turning back 205.1
turning backwards 205.1
turning down 442.1
turning front to back 205.1
turning head over heels 205.2
turning inside out 205.1
turning into 858.1
turning inward 205.1
turning on 959.9
turning one's coat 363.2
turning out 372.1
turning over 205.1, 475.1, 938.15
turning over in the mind 931.2
turning point 722.4, 843.4, 843.5, 997.4, 997.6
turning traitor 363.2
turning turtle 205.2
turning upside down 205.1, 938.15
turn in one's badge 448.2
turn in one's uniform 448.2
turn in one's weapons 465.11
turn inside out 205.5, 938.33
turn into 341.12, 761.12, 852.6, 858.11
turn into money 734.8
turn into the opposite 205.5
turn inward 205.5
turnip 832.6
turniplike 279.17
turnip-shaped 279.17
turnkey 429.10
turnkey operation 1042.18
turn king's evidence 551.12
turn left 164.3
turn loose 431.5
turn of events 831.2
turn of expression 529.1, 536.1
turn off 98.11, 379.4, 857.12, 909.19, 1032.26
turnoff 908.2
turn off the juice 1032.26
turn off the light 1027.11
turn of mind 978.3
turn of phrase 529.1
turn of the cards 759.2
turn of the screw 251.2
turn of the table 759.2
turn of the tide 163.3, 843.4, 859.1
turn of the wheel 759.2
turn of thought 489.7
turn of work 825.3
turn on 105.12, 375.17, 375.18, 375.19, 818.11, 887.5, 959.6, 1032.26
turn on a dime 163.9
turn one away 442.5
turn one on 983.12
turn one's attention from 984.4
turn one's back on 156.4, 188.9, 340.8, 370.6, 372.2, 442.3
turn one's back upon 157.5, 163.8, 368.6, 370.5, 586.5, 984.4
turn one's coat 363.7, 645.15, 852.7, 858.13
turn one's face to the wall 125.10
turn one's hand to 328.8, 724.11
turn one's head 104.22, 122.7, 136.6, 140.7, 377.7, 923.7
turn one's stomach 64.4
turn one's tail upon 370.5
turn one's tracks to 177.25
turn on her heel 182.30
turn on one's heel 157.5
turn on the heat 424.8
turn on the juice 1032.26
turn on the light 1025.29
turn on the tap 909.24
turn on the waterworks 115.12
turn on to 105.18
turn out 5.41, 23.6, 205.5, 372.2, 385.8, 765.5, 831.7, 887.4, 909.13, 909.15, 909.19, 973.12
turnout 5.2, 179.5, 221.4, 770.2
turn out bag and baggage 909.15
turn out of doors 909.15
turn out of house and home 909.15
turn out that way 130.10
turn out to be 761.12, 887.4
turn out well 887.4, 1010.7
turn over 176.10, 182.44, 205.5, 205.6, 475.3, 478.13, 629.3, 734.8, 931.13
turnover 10.41, 205.2, 734.1, 746.3, 747.3
turn over a new leaf 392.9, 852.7, 858.12
turn over in one's grave 510.10
turn over in the mind 931.13
turn over one's knees 510.17
turn over the leaves 570.13, 938.26
turn pale 36.6, 105.19, 127.11
turnpiker 178.3
turn queen's evidence 551.12
turn red 41.5, 105.19, 139.8
turn right 164.3
turn round 163.9, 915.9
turn sour 67.4, 132.3
turnspit 577.2, 1020.12
turn state's evidence 351.6, 551.12, 957.9
turnstile 189.6
turn swords into plowshares 465.11
turntable 50.11
turn tail 163.6, 163.9, 368.10, 491.8
turntail 363.5
turn the attention to 983.5
turn the back upon 27.19
turn the balance 894.12
turn the corner 396.19, 852.6
turn the edge of 286.2
turn the eyes 27.13
turn the mind to 931.11
turn the other cheek 134.8, 148.4, 465.9
turn the point of 286.2
turn the scale 205.5, 886.12, 894.12
turn the shoulder 157.5
turn the stomach 98.11
turn the tables 205.5, 852.7, 894.12
turn the tables upon 506.4
turn the thoughts to 931.11
turn the tide 852.7
turn thumbs down 586.6
turn thumbs down on 442.3, 444.5, 510.10, 773.4, 909.17
turn to 328.8, 387.14, 404.3, 725.15, 818.7, 858.17, 983.5
turn to account 387.15, 472.12, 843.8
turn to advantage 387.15
turn to a lake 1065.14
turn to a sea 1065.14
turn to good account 387.15, 843.8
turn to good advantage 387.15
turn to naught 762.6
turn to nothing 762.6
turn to one's advantage 472.12
turn to profit 387.15, 472.12
turn topsy-turvy 205.6
turn to stone 1059.10
turn to the right-about, a 363.1
turn to the right-about (n) 163.3 (v) 163.10
turn to the side 164.6
turn to use 387.14, 387.15
turn traitor 858.13
turn turtle 182.44, 194.8, 205.6
turn under 291.5
turn up 33.8, 131.6, 159.11, 186.6, 193.13, 221.8, 291.5, 831.6, 941.4, 941.9, 972.11
turn up missing 222.7
turn upon 161.5
turn up one's nose 99.5, 495.8
turn up one's nose at 157.4, 372.2, 510.10, 984.4
turn up one's toes 307.19
turn upon one's heel 163.9
turn up roses 1010.11
turn upside down 205.5, 205.6, 852.7, 938.33
turn upside-down 395.10
turn up trumps 409.9
turn white 36.6, 303.10
turn yellow 43.3
turpentine 35.8
turpitude 645.2, 654.5
turquoise 45.3
turquoise-blue 45.3
turret 272.6
turreted 272.14
turtle 311.24
turtledoves 104.17
turtlelike 175.10
Tuscan 198.6
tush 2.8, 217.5
tushy 217.5
tusk (n) 2.8 (v) 459.26

tusked 285.14
tusker 311.9
tussle (n) 456.5, 457.3, 457.4, 725.3 (v) 457.13, 725.11
tussler 461.1
tussock 310.2, 770.7
tutee 572.1
tutelage 432.3, 449.4, 568.1, 571.10, 572.2, 1008.2
tutelar god 678.12
tutelary 1008.23
tutelary genius 678.12
tutelary god 678.12
tutelary spirit 678.12
tutor (n) 405.5, 571.1, 571.3, 571.5 (v) 568.11
tutorage 568.1, 571.10
tutorer 571.5
tutorhood 571.10
tutorial 571.11
tutoring 568.1
tutorship 568.1, 571.10
tutti 53.3, 708.24
tutti-frutti 10.40
tutti passage 708.24
tutu 5.9
tu-whit tu-whoo 60.5
tux 5.11
tuxedo 5.11
tuyere 1020.10
TV 1035.1, 1035.11
TV band 1035.4
TV camera 714.11
TV campaign 609.13
TV dinner 8.6
TV evangelism 543.3
TV evangelist 543.5, 699.6
TV lights 1025.4
TV mobile 1035.7
TV movie 706.1
TV performer 1035.2
TV personality 1035.2
TV preacher 699.3
TV set 1035.11
TV show 1035.2
TV station 1035.6
TV viewer 918.1
twaddle (n) 520.2, 540.3 (v) 520.5, 540.5
twaddler 118.4
twaddling 520.7
twaddly 520.7
twain (n) 873.2 (a) 873.6
twang (n) 58.3, 524.8, 525.1 (v) 58.9, 524.25, 525.10, 708.40
twanger 710.5
twanging 58.3
twanging nerves 128.4
twangy 524.30, 525.12
twattle (n) 540.3 (v) 540.5
tweak (n) 26.2, 260.2, 780.4, 852.1, 905.3 (v) 26.7, 260.8, 905.5
tweaking 852.1
tweak the devil's nose 493.6
tweak the nose 96.13, 454.3
tweed (n) 288.2 (a) 40.3, 288.6
tweedle (n) 53.5 (v) 53.10, 708.38, 708.42
tweedledee 708.38
Tweedledum and Tweedledee 790.3, 873.4
tweedy 288.6, 294.7, 570.17, 571.11
tweenage 301.7
tweenager 301.6, 302.1
tweeny 577.8
tweet 60.5
Tweeting 1042.19
tweezers 192.9
tweezing 1016.14
twelfth 882.24
twelve 882.7
twelve good men and true 596.5
12-hour clock 832.3
1200 hours 314.4
twelve men in a box 596.5
twelve-mile limit 211.5, 231.1
12mo 554.4, 882.7
twelvemo (n) 258.6, 554.4, 882.7 (a) 258.12
twelvemonth 824.2
twelve o'clock 314.4
twelve-o'clock 314.6
12-step group 449.2
twelve-tone scale 709.6
twentieth 882.26
twentieth-century 841.13
twenty 882.7
twenty-dollar bill 728.7
twenty-dollar gold piece 728.4
twenty-five 882.7
twenty-five cents 728.7, 881.2
twenty-five percent 881.2
25-yard line 749.4
twenty-four 882.7
twenty-four carat 973.15
24-hour 223.15
twenty-four-hour 812.8
24-hour clock 832.3
24-hour surveillance 938.9
24mo 882.7
twenty-fourmo 882.7
twenty-four-second rule 747.3
24/7 966.1
24/7/365 966.1
twenty-one 759.11
twenty-something 302.1
twenty-twenty 27.21
20/20 vision 27.1
twenty-two 462.10
twerp 660.5, 924.3
twice as ugly 31.7
twice-told 117.9, 849.12
twice-told tale 489.9, 974.3
twiddle 73.6
twiddle one's thumbs 329.2, 331.12
twiddle-twaddle 520.2
twig (n) 302.11, 310.11, 310.20, 793.4 (v) 27.12
twigginess 270.5
twiggy (n) 270.8 (a) 270.17, 310.41
twilight (n) 314.3, 315.3, 1025.10, 1027.2 (a) 315.8
twilight glow 1025.2
twilight of one's days 303.5
twilight vision 27.1
twilighty 315.8
twilight zone 539.1, 971.8
twilit 315.8
twill 291.5, 740.6
twilled 291.7, 294.7
twin (n) 349.5, 778.3, 784.3, 785.1, 790.4 (v) 778.4, 873.5, 874.3 (a) 769.9, 778.7, 784.11, 873.6
twine (n) 271.2 (v) 281.4, 740.6
twine around 209.7
twined 740.7
twinge (n) 26.2, 96.5 (v) 26.8
twinge of conscience 113.2, 333.2, 636.5, 644.2
twining (n) 740.1 (a) 740.8
twin-jet 181.3
twink 830.3
twin killing 745.3
twinkle (n) 830.3, 1025.7 (v) 1025.24
twinkle of an eye 27.4, 830.3
twinkletoes 705.3
twinkling (n) 830.3, 1025.7 (a) 1025.35
twinkling of an eye 830.3
twinkly 1025.35
twinned 775.9, 873.6, 874.4
twinning 873.1, 874.1
twin-prop 181.2
twins 784.5, 873.4
twin screws 904.6
Twin stars 873.4
twin-tailboom jet 181.3
twin town 230.1
twirl (n) 238.12, 281.2, 915.2 (v) 281.4, 915.11, 915.12
twirling 915.14
twist (n) 3.7, 33.3, 87.12, 89.7, 164.1, 204.3, 254.4, 265.1, 281.2, 722.4, 896.1, 927.2, 978.3, 980.3, 1004.1 (v) 26.7, 164.4, 164.5, 204.9, 265.5, 265.6, 265.7, 271.6, 281.4, 350.3, 354.16, 393.12, 740.6, 915.9, 915.12, 936.9, 980.9, 1004.4
twist and turn 105.18, 164.4, 281.4, 415.9, 914.4, 917.14
twist arms 424.8
twist around one's little finger 432.10, 612.14, 894.11
twisted 26.9, 265.10, 265.11, 354.26, 799.4, 927.5, 980.12, 1004.8
twistedness 265.1
twisted rope 271.2
twister 10.44, 318.13, 915.2
twisting (n) 164.2, 265.2, 281.1, 342.1, 350.1, 740.1 (a) 164.7, 281.6
twisting course 164.1
twisting downward 915.1
twisting the knife in the wound 96.3
twisting the lion's tail 609.5
twisting upward 915.1
twist one's arm 375.14, 375.23, 424.8, 514.2, 894.7
twist the knife 119.2
twist the knife in the wound 96.14
twist the law to one's own ends 674.5
twist the meaning 342.2
twist the meaning of 350.3
twist the words 342.2
twisty 204.20, 281.6
twit (n) 508.2, 924.4 (v) 60.5, 490.5, 508.9, 599.7, 708.38
twitch (n) 26.2, 830.3, 905.3, 917.3 (v) 26.8, 105.18, 905.5, 917.13
twitchety 917.19
twitching (n) 128.1, 917.5 (a) 917.19
twitch of conscience 113.2
twitchy 128.12, 917.19
twitter (n) 105.5, 105.6, 490.4, 917.1, 917.3 (v) 60.5, 105.18, 708.38, 917.11
twitteration 105.6
twittery 128.12
twitting (n) 490.2, 508.1 (a) 490.7, 508.12
2 873.2
two, the (n) 873.2 (a) 873.7
two (n) 88.7, 758.2, 873.2 (a) 873.6
two-alarm fire 1019.13
two-bagger 745.3
two-base hit 745.3
two-base shot 745.3
two-bit (n) 610.4 (a) 998.18
two bits 728.7, 881.2
two-by-four (n) 1054.3 (a) 258.10, 998.18
two cents 998.5
two-color 47.9
two-colored 47.9
two-color printing 548.1
two-dimensional 158.10, 873.6, 998.16
two-dimensional wave 916.4
two-dollar bill 728.7
two-dollar broker 737.10
two-dollar word 526.10, 545.3
two dozen 882.7
two-edged 285.8, 539.4
two-edged sword 777.1
two-faced 354.31, 356.22, 645.21, 873.6
two-facedness 354.4, 645.6, 873.1
twofer 634.2
two-finger grip 750.2
two-fisted 76.13
two-fisted man 76.6
twofoldness 873.1
two-foot octave 709.9
two-for-a-cent 998.21
two-for-a-penny 998.21
two-four time 709.24
two-handed 413.25
two-handed grip 748.2
two-hole ball 750.1
two-horned 279.11
two-level 296.6
two-line octave 709.9
two-minute gun 400.1
two-minute warning 746.3
twoness 873.1
two of a kind 784.5
two of spades 758.2
two or three 884.2
two-page spread 352.6
two pairs 758.4
two-part harmony 708.3
two-part time 709.24

two-party 609.44
two-party system 609.24
two peas in a pod 778.1
two-pence 728.8
twopence 998.5
twopenny 998.21
twopenny-halfpenny 998.21
two-piece suit 5.29
two-ply 296.6, 873.6
two-point landing 184.18
twoscore 882.7
two shakes 828.3, 830.3
two shakes of a lamb's tail 828.3, 830.3
two-sided 218.7, 539.4, 873.6
twosome 751.2, 873.2
two-spot 728.7, 758.2
two-stage rocket 1074.5
two-star general 575.17
two-step 705.5
two-story 296.6
2000 Guineas 757.1
two-time 354.24, 356.14, 645.12, 645.14
two-time loser 859.3
two-timer 357.3, 357.10, 660.9
two-timing 645.20, 645.22
two-tone 47.9
two-toned 47.9
two-way 777.11, 863.5, 873.6
two-way communication 343.1
two-way traffic 863.1
two weeks 882.7
two-wheeler 179.3
two whoops and a holler 223.2
2X 257.4
two-year-old 757.2
tycoon 575.9, 618.7, 730.1, 997.8
tying 800.3
tying the knot 563.1
tying up 186.2
tyke 302.3, 311.18
Tylenol 86.12
tympanic cavity 2.10
tympanic membrane 2.6, 2.10
tympanism 259.2
tympanist 710.10
tympanites 259.2
tympanitis 85.15
tympanum 2.6, 2.10
tympany 259.2
tymp stick 711.16
typal 349.15, 809.7
type (n) 133.3, 262.1, 300.2, 349.7, 371.5, 517.2, 518.6, 548.6, 767.4, 786.1, 786.2, 809.3, 866.1, 870.4, 978.3 (v) 547.19, 809.6
Type A (n) 92.12 (a) 92.41
Type A behavior 321.1
Type B (n) 92.12 (a) 92.40
Type B behavior 321.1
type body 548.6
typecase 548.6
type class 548.6
type-cutting 713.2
typed 547.22
typeface 548.6
typeform 548.8
typefounders 548.6
typefoundry 548.6
Type II diabetes 85.21
type in 548.6
type into 548.6
type lice 548.6
type of construction 717.2
type page 554.12
typescript 547.10, 548.4
typeset 548.19
typesetter 548.12, 554.2
typesetting 548.2
typesetting machine 548.2
type shank 548.6
type size 548.6
type species 786.1
type specimen 349.7, 786.1
type stem 548.6
type up 548.6
typewriting 547.1
typewritten 547.22
Typhoid Mary 85.44
Typhon 680.5
typhonic 318.22
typhoon 318.11, 318.13, 671.4
typhoonish 318.22
typic 349.15
typical 349.15, 517.23, 786.8, 809.7, 865.13, 869.8
typical case 786.2
typical example 786.2
typicality 349.7, 869.1
typical man 606.5
typicalness 349.7
typification 349.7, 767.2
typify 133.11, 517.18
typifying 349.13
typing 547.1
typing paper 547.4
typist 547.18
typist's error 975.3
typo 975.3
typographer 548.12
typographic 548.20
typographical 548.20
typographical error 975.3
typographic design 717.5
typography 548.1, 712.16
typolithography 548.1
typologic 809.7
typological 809.7
typology 809.1
typonym 527.3
Tyr 458.12
tyrannical 417.16
tyrannicalness 417.3
tyrannize 96.18, 432.9, 612.15
tyrannized 432.16
tyrannize over 612.15
tyrannous 98.24, 417.16
tyranny 424.2, 432.1, 612.4, 612.8, 612.9
tyranny of the majority 612.4
tyrant 575.13
tyro 572.9, 818.2
tyro at, a 414.17
tyronic 374.4
tzimmes 53.4
U 141.11, 608.11
uber 198.11, 249.13
Übermensch 659.4
uberous 890.9
uberty 890.1
ubicity 159.1
ubiety 221.1
ubiquitous 221.13, 677.17, 794.10, 849.13, 864.14
ubiquity 221.2, 794.1, 864.2
U-boat 180.9
U-boot 180.9
udder 283.6
udographic 316.12
udometer 316.7, 317.8
udometric 316.12
udomograph 316.7
UFO sighting 689.6
uglification 1015.1
uglified 1015.6
uglify 1015.5
uglifying 1015.1
ugliness 58.2, 98.1, 110.3, 1015.1
ugly 98.17, 110.20, 1006.9, 1015.6
ugly as hell 1015.6
ugly as sin 1015.6
ugly as the wrath of God 1015.6
ugly customer 110.11, 593.4, 671.10
ugly duckling 1015.4
ugly wind 318.11
uhlan 461.12
UK, the 232.4
ukase 352.2, 420.4
ulcer 85.29, 85.37
ulcerate 393.12
ulcerated 85.60, 393.40
ulceration 85.37
ulcerative 85.60
ulcerous 85.60
uliginous 243.3
ullage 795.2
ulotrichous 3.24
ulterior 253.10, 261.10, 345.11, 774.5
ulterior motive 375.1, 947.1
ultimacy 820.2
ultimate (n) 1002.3 (a) 198.11, 261.12, 407.9, 420.12, 820.11, 820.12, 831.11, 839.8
ultimate aim 380.2
ultimate analysis 801.1
ultimate cause 886.3
ultimate fighting 760.3
ultimateness 839.4
ultimate purpose 380.2, 387.3, 387.5
ultimate truth 973.1
Ultima Thule 261.4, 820.2
ultimation 439.3
ultimatum 399.1, 421.1, 439.3, 959.2
ultimogeniture 479.2
ultra (n) 611.12 (a) 247.13
ultrabasic rock 1059.1
ultracentrifuge 802.7
ultraconservatism 611.1, 611.4, 853.3
ultraconservative (n) 611.9, 853.4 (a) 611.17, 611.20, 853.8
ultracrepidarian 522.13
ultracritical 495.12, 510.23
ultraelementary 1038.18
ultraelementary particle 1038.6
ultrafashionable 578.14
ultra-high-definition television 1035.1
ultra-high frequency 1034.12
ultra-high-frequency station 1034.6
ultraism 611.4
ultraist (n) 611.12 (a) 611.20
ultraistic 611.20
ultra-large crude carrier 180.1
ultramafic rock 1059.1
ultramarine (n) 45.1 (a) 45.3, 261.11
ultramasculine 76.13
ultramasculinity 76.2
ultramicroscopic 258.14
ultramodern 841.13
ultramontane (n) 675.19, 774.3 (a) 261.11, 675.29, 698.13
ultramontanism 675.8, 698.3
ultramundane 261.11
ultranationalism 591.2, 980.4
ultranationalist (n) 232.7, 591.3, 980.5 (a) 591.4, 980.12
ultranationalistic 591.4
Ultra-Panavision 706.7
ultrareligious 692.11
ultrashortwave diathermy 91.5
ultrasmart 578.14
ultrasonic 50.17, 174.16
ultrasonic diathermy 91.5
ultrasonic flow detection 1041.7
ultrasonic frequency 50.6
ultrasonics 50.6
ultrasonic spectacles 30.6
ultrasonic speed 174.2
ultrasonography 91.9
ultrasound 50.1, 91.9, 91.12
ultrastylish 578.14
ultra-ultra 247.13, 841.13
ultraviolent radiation 1032.10
ultraviolet astronomy 1073.19
ultraviolet heat 1019.1
ultraviolet light 1025.1
ultra-violet radiation 1037.1
ultraviolet ray 1025.5
ultrazealous 101.12, 926.32
ultrazealousness 926.11
ululant 58.14, 60.6, 115.19
ululate 58.8, 60.2, 115.12, 115.13
ululating 58.14
ululation 53.3, 58.4, 60.1, 115.1, 115.3
Ulysses 178.2
umami 62.1
umbel 310.27
umber 40.3
umber-brown 40.3
umber-colored 40.3
umbilical 208.11
umbilicus 208.2
umbra 1027.3
umbrage 152.2, 310.18, 1027.3
umbrageous 1027.16
umbrageousness 1027.3
umbral 1027.16
umbrella (n) 181.13, 184.11, 295.7, 1008.3, 1028.1 (a) 772.7
umlaut 524.13
umpirage 466.2
umpire (n) 466.4, 596.1, 745.3, 747.3, 748.2, 749.6, 946.6 (v) 466.6, 745.5, 946.12
umpire crew 745.3

umpire in chief 745.3
umpteen 884.2, 884.4
umpteenth 882.25
unabashed 142.11, 492.20, 666.6
unabated 15.21, 247.14, 671.17
unabating 360.8
unabbreviated 794.9
unabetted 872.8
unabject 114.5
unabjectness 114.2
unable (n) 19.6 (a) 19.14, 414.19
unable to believe one's eyes 122.9
unable to believe one's senses 122.9
unable to forget 989.23
unable to go on 21.10
unable to keep the wolf from the door 619.7
unable to make ends meet 619.7
unable to meet one's obligations 625.11
unable to pay one's creditors 625.11
unable to say "boo" to a goose 491.11
unable to say "no" 362.12
unable to show one's face 661.13
unabridged 267.7, 792.12
unaccented 52.16, 524.30
unacceptability 98.2, 108.2
unacceptable 108.10, 510.24, 586.9
unacceptable person 586.4, 660.1
unacceptance 335.1
unaccepted 688.9
unaccepting 108.7
unaccessibility 967.3
unaccessible 967.9
unaccommodating 108.7, 144.18, 505.4
unaccommodatingness 144.3
unaccompanied 802.20, 872.8
unaccomplished 408.3, 414.16
unaccountability 418.1, 971.1
unaccountable 418.5, 430.30, 522.18, 854.7, 870.12, 971.16, 972.16
unaccountableness 522.6
unaccounted for 34.4, 346.12
unaccustomed 374.4
unaccustomedness 374.1, 414.2
unaccustomed to 414.17
unachievability 967.2
unachievable 967.8
unachieved 408.3
unacknowledged 151.5, 528.3
unacquaintance 374.1, 414.2, 930.1
unacquaintance with evil 657.2
unacquainted 930.11
unacquaintedness 414.2
unacquainted with 374.4, 414.17
unacquainted with evil 657.6
unacquirability 967.3
unacquirable 967.9
unacquisitive 652.5
unacquisitiveness 652.1
unactionable 598.21
unactive 331.17
unactual 762.9, 976.9, 986.19
unactuality 762.1, 976.2
unadaptable 868.5
unadapted 406.9, 414.19, 789.7
unadherence 804.1
unadhesive 804.4
unadhesiveness 804.1
unadjustable 868.5
unadjusted 414.19
unadmonished 131.9
unadorned 248.8, 416.6, 499.8, 533.6, 535.3, 798.6
unadorned meaning 518.1
unadornedness 499.3, 535.1
unadorned simplicity 533.1
unadorned style 521.2, 535.1
unadorned truth, the 973.3
unadorned truth 973.1
unadornment 499.3, 798.1
unadult 301.10
unadulterated 79.25, 499.8, 798.7, 960.2, 973.15, 1002.6
unadulteration 499.3, 798.1, 973.7
unadvantageous 996.6
unadventurous 494.8, 494.11
unadventurousness 494.4
unadvised 131.9, 365.11, 923.10
unaesthetic 1015.6, 1015.10
unaestheticism 497.1
unaestheticness 497.1, 1015.1
unaffability 344.3
unaffable 344.10
unaffectation 416.2
unaffected 94.11, 361.9, 416.6, 496.7, 499.7, 533.6, 535.3, 581.3, 644.18, 895.5, 973.15
unaffectedness 416.2, 499.2, 533.1, 535.1, 581.1, 973.7
unaffectionate 94.9, 144.16
unaffectionateness 144.1
unaffiliated 776.6
unafraid 492.19, 970.21
unafraidness 492.2
unagitated 106.11, 173.12
unagreeable 586.9
unaided 872.8
unaided eye 2.9, 27.9
unailing 83.10
unalarmed 492.19
unalert 984.8
unalertness 984.1
unalienable 767.7
unalienable rights 430.2
unaligned 467.7
unaligned nation 232.1, 467.4
unalignment 467.1
unalike 787.4
unallayed 15.21, 671.17
unallied 776.6
unallowable 650.12
unallowed 444.7, 674.6
unalloyed 671.17, 794.10, 798.7
unalloyed happiness 95.2
unalloyed truth, the 973.3
unalluring 98.17
unalterability 361.2, 855.4, 1046.3
unalterable 361.9, 855.17, 1046.12
unalterative 855.17
unaltered 853.7, 855.17, 960.2
unaltruistic 144.17
unamazed 123.3
unamazedness 123.1
unamazement 123.1
unambiguity 521.2, 970.1
unambiguous 521.11, 970.13
unambiguous assent 332.5
unambiguously 334.8
unambiguousness 521.2
unambitious 102.8, 139.9
unambitiousness 102.3, 139.1
unamenable 895.4
unamiability 144.1, 589.1
unamiable 99.8, 144.16, 589.9
unamicable 589.9
unamusing 117.7
unanalyzable 872.7
unanalyzed mass 406.5
unanchored 182.61, 802.22
unangelic 312.13, 654.12, 695.17
unangelical 695.17
unangelicalness 654.1, 695.3
unanimated 94.11, 1055.5
unanimity 332.5, 788.3
unanimous 332.15, 788.9
unanimous decision 754.3
unanimously elected 371.26
unanimousness 332.5
unannounced 131.10
unannounced examination 938.2
unanswerable 430.30, 970.15
unanswered 957.21
unanticipated 131.10, 830.5
unanticipating 131.9
unanticipation 131.1, 830.2
unanticipative 131.9
unanxious 102.7
unanxiousness 102.2
unappalled 492.20
unapparel 6.7
unappareled 6.13
unapparent 32.5, 346.12, 930.16
unappealing 98.17
unappealingness 98.1
unappeasable 100.27, 507.7
unappeasableness 507.2
unappeased 100.27
unappetizing 64.5, 65.2, 98.17
unapplied 390.12
unappreciated 99.9
unappreciation 151.1
unappreciative 151.4, 510.21
unappreciativeness 151.1
unappreciatory 151.4
unapprehended 930.16
unapprehending 922.14
unapprehendingness 922.2
unapprehensive 492.19
unapprehensiveness 492.2
unapprized 930.11
unapproachability 344.3, 583.2, 967.3
unapproachable 249.15, 261.9, 344.10, 583.6, 967.9
unapproached 249.15
unapproved 688.9
unapproving 510.21
unapt 414.15, 789.7
unaptness 414.1, 996.1
unarguable 970.15
unarm 19.9, 465.11
unarmed 406.9, 1006.14
unarmed combat 457.4
unarmored 1006.14
unaroused 173.14
unarraignable 657.8
unarraignableness 657.3
unarranged 406.8, 810.12
unarray 6.7
unarrayed 499.8
unarticulated 51.11
unartificial 416.6, 499.7
unartificialness 416.2
unartistic 1015.10
unary 872.7
unascertainable 967.9
unascertainableness 967.3
unascertained 930.16, 958.8
unashamed 114.4, 666.6
unashamedness 114.1
unasked 99.11, 324.7, 340.14, 586.9
unasked-for 99.11
unaspiring 102.8, 139.9, 987.5
unassailability 15.4
unassailable 15.19
unassertive 433.12
unassertiveness 433.1
unassimilable 82.6
unassisted 872.8
unassisted eye 2.9, 27.9
unassociated 776.6, 802.20
unassumed 644.18, 973.15
unassuming 139.9, 416.6, 499.7, 581.3, 644.18, 973.15
unassumingness 139.1, 416.2, 499.2
unassured 971.23
unassuredness 971.3
unastonished 123.3
unastonishment 123.1, 130.1
unastounded 123.3
unatoned 114.6
unattach 802.10
unattached 430.21, 565.7, 802.20
unattached female 565.4
unattached male 565.3
unattackable 15.19
unattackableness 15.4
unattainability 967.2, 967.3
unattainable 967.8, 967.9
unattained 408.3
unattended 802.20, 872.8, 1006.14
unattended to 340.14
unattestable 958.9
unattested 958.8, 971.21
unattired 6.13
unattracted 102.8
unattractive 98.17, 1015.6
unattractiveness 98.1, 1015.1
unaustere 426.5
unausterenes 426.2
unauthentic 354.26, 688.9, 936.11, 971.21, 975.19
unauthenticated 958.8, 971.21
unauthenticity 354.2, 688.1, 971.6
unauthoritative 688.9, 895.3, 971.21, 975.19

unauthoritativeness 688.1, 895.1, 971.6
unauthorization 674.1
unauthorized 444.7, 674.6
unauthorized absence 222.4
unavailability 967.3
unavailable 967.9
unavailing 19.15, 391.9, 391.13
unavenged 148.7
unaverse 324.6
unavoidable 963.15
unavoidable casualty 963.7
unavoidableness 963.7
unawakened 22.22
unaware 25.8, 94.10, 131.9, 930.12
unawareness 25.2, 94.2, 922.2, 930.2, 984.1
unaware of 930.12
unawed 123.3, 492.20
unbaked 406.10
unbalance (n) 791.1, 926.1 (v) 791.3, 926.24
unbalanced 160.12, 650.9, 791.5, 926.26
unbalanced mind 926.1
unballast 298.6
unballasting 298.3
unbandage 802.10
unbandaged 802.22
unbar 431.6, 1014.7
unbarring 431.2
unbased 936.13
unbashful 492.19
unbashfulness 492.2
unbated 15.21, 285.9
unbathed 80.20
unbearable 26.10, 98.25, 247.12
unbearableness 98.9
unbeatable 15.19, 249.15
unbeatableness 15.4
unbeaten 390.12, 411.8, 841.7
unbeauteous 1015.6
unbeautiful 1015.6
unbeautifulness 1015.1
unbecoming 497.10, 661.11, 666.5, 789.7
unbecomingness 497.1
unbefitting 789.7, 844.6, 996.5
unbegotten 762.10
unbeguileful 644.18
unbeguiling 644.18
unbegun 406.8
unbehaving 322.5
unbeheld 32.5
unbeholdable 32.5
unbeing 762.1
unbeknown 930.16
unbelief 688.3, 695.5, 955.1
unbelievability 955.3
unbelievable 870.12, 955.10
unbelievableness 955.3
unbelieve 955.5
unbeliever 688.6, 694.3, 695.11, 955.4
unbelieving 688.10, 695.19, 955.8
unbelievingness 955.1
unbellicose 464.10
unbelligerent 464.10
unbeloved 99.10
unbend 20.7, 277.5, 670.9, 1047.7
unbending 277.6, 359.12, 361.9, 425.7, 1046.12
unbendingness 361.2, 425.2, 1046.3
unbeneficient 144.17
unbenevolent 144.17
unbenevolentness 144.2
unbenign 144.16
unbenignant 144.16
unbenignity 144.1
unbenignness 144.1
unbent 277.6
unbeseeming 497.10
unbesmirched 79.25
unbesotted 979.10
unbesought 324.7
unbewildered 123.3
unbias 649.3
unbiased 649.9, 979.12, 982.3
unbiasedness 649.3, 979.5
unbiased observer 466.4
unbiddability 361.4
unbiddable 361.12
unbidden 99.11, 324.7, 586.9
unbigoted 430.25, 979.8
unbigotedness 430.10, 979.1
unbind 431.6, 802.10
unbinding 431.2
unblamability 657.3
unblamable 657.8
unblamableness 657.3
unblameworthiness 657.3
unblameworthy 657.8
unblemished 79.25, 644.13, 657.7, 664.4, 1002.6
unblemishedness 657.1, 664.1
unblenching 129.2, 492.20
unblended 798.7
unblessed 686.3, 1011.14
unblessedness 686.1
unblessed with 992.13
unblindfold 977.2
unblinking 129.2, 339.14, 492.20
unblinking eye 339.4
unblock 292.12, 1014.7
unblotted 79.25, 664.4
unblottedness 664.1
unblown 406.12
unblushing 142.11, 654.17, 666.6
unboastful 139.9
unboastfulness 139.1
unboat 186.8
unboiled 406.10
unbolt 292.12, 431.6, 802.10
unbolted 802.22
unbolting 431.2
unbooked 930.13
unbookish 930.13
unbook-learned 930.13
unborn 762.10
unbosoming 351.3
unbosom oneself 351.5, 351.7
unbothered 107.8
unbought 634.5, 734.15
unbound 430.27, 430.28, 431.10, 802.22
unbounded 430.27, 677.17, 823.3
unbowed 15.21, 277.6, 411.8, 492.20
unbrace 16.10, 128.10, 670.9
unbraid 798.5
unbreakability 1049.1
unbreakable 15.18, 1049.5
unbreakableness 1049.1
unbreatheable 345.11
unbreathed 519.9
unbridgeable 967.8
unbridle 431.6
unbridled 418.5, 430.24, 665.25, 669.7, 671.19, 993.16
unbridledness 665.3
unbridling 431.2
unbriefed 930.13
unbroken 161.12, 277.6, 287.10, 430.29, 781.5, 812.8, 847.5, 1002.8
unbrokenness 201.1, 781.1, 794.1, 812.1
unbroken sleep 22.5
unbruised 1002.8
unbuckle 431.6, 802.10
unbuckled 802.22
unbuckle one's belt 20.6
unbuckling 431.2
unbuild 395.17
unbuilding 802.6
unburden 120.7, 298.6, 909.23
unburdened 298.11, 430.26
unburdening (n) 120.3, 298.3, 1014.6 (a) 298.16
unburdening oneself 351.3
unburden one's conscience 351.7
unburden one's mind 351.7
unburdensome 1014.13
unburnable 1022.9
unburnableness 1022.1
unbury 192.11
unbusinesslike 414.16
unbutton 802.10
unbuttoned 802.22
unbuttoned ease 20.1
unc 559.3
uncage 431.6
uncaged 430.21
uncaging 431.2
uncalculated 365.11
uncalculatedness 365.4
uncalculating 365.10, 644.17, 644.18
uncalled-for 99.11, 142.10, 324.7, 391.10, 993.17
uncamouflaged 348.11
uncandid 354.32, 645.18
uncandidness 354.5, 645.3
uncandor 354.5, 645.3
uncanniness 127.2, 307.11, 988.4
uncanny 122.11, 127.31, 307.28, 988.9
uncanonical 688.9
uncanonicalness 688.1
uncanonicity 688.1
uncap 292.12
uncared-for 99.9, 340.14
uncaring (n) 340.2, 982.1 (a) 25.6, 94.13, 340.11
uncase 6.7, 292.12
uncased 6.12, 6.13
uncasing 6.2
uncatholic 980.10
uncatholicity 980.1
uncaught 802.22
uncaused 972.15
uncautious 984.8
unceasing 812.8, 829.7, 847.5, 856.7
unceasingness 829.1, 856.1
uncelebrated 661.14
uncensored 430.28
uncensorious 509.18
uncensurability 657.3
uncensurable 657.8
uncensurableness 657.3
uncentered 160.12
unceremonious 581.3
unceremoniousness 581.1
uncertain 32.6, 362.9, 539.4, 759.27, 775.7, 851.3, 854.7, 955.9, 971.16, 1006.11
uncertainness 971.1
uncertainty 32.2, 130.3, 362.1, 539.1, 759.2, 775.2, 851.1, 854.2, 955.2, 971.1, 972.1, 975.2, 1006.2
uncertainty principle 968.2, 971.1, 972.1
uncertified 958.8, 971.21
unchain 431.6, 802.10
unchained 430.28, 802.22
unchaining 431.2
unchallengeable 767.7
unchallenged 332.15, 970.16
unchangeability 361.2, 853.1, 855.4
unchangeable 361.9, 781.5, 853.7, 855.17
unchangeableness 853.1, 855.4
unchanged 781.5, 853.7, 855.17
unchanging 677.17, 781.5, 847.5, 853.7, 855.17
unchangingness 853.1
unchaperoned 340.14
uncharacterized 864.11
unchariness 493.1
uncharitable 144.17, 980.10
uncharitableness 144.2, 980.2
uncharm 977.2
uncharmed 977.5
uncharted 930.16
unchartered 444.7, 674.6
unchary 493.7
unchaste 654.12, 663.5, 665.23, 666.9
unchasteness 665.1
unchastity 562.10, 654.1, 663.1, 665.1, 666.1
unchecked 418.5, 430.24, 443.16, 644.17, 853.7, 971.21
unchecked enthusiasm 101.3
unchecked will 418.1
uncheerful 112.21, 125.16
uncheerfulness 112.2, 125.6
uncheery 112.21
uncherished 99.10
unchivalrous 651.6
unchristian 144.26, 688.10
unchristianity 688.3
unchristianliness 695.3
un-Christliness 695.3
unchronological 833.3

unchurch 447.4
unchurching 447.2
uncial 546.8
unciform 279.8
uncinate 279.8
uncirculated 841.9
uncircumcised 688.10
uncircumscribed 430.27, 823.3, 960.2
uncircumscribedness 960.1
uncircumspec 340.10
uncivil 497.12, 505.4
uncivilized 144.26, 497.12, 671.21
uncivilizedness 497.3
unclad 6.13
unclarity 522.3
unclasp 475.4, 802.10
unclasped 802.22
unclassical 534.2
unclassified 348.10, 810.12, 930.16
uncle 76.10, 559.3, 620.3
unclean 80.20, 654.12, 665.23, 666.9, 680.17, 1000.9
uncleanliness 80.1, 665.1
uncleanly 80.20
uncleanness 80.1, 654.1, 665.1, 1000.2
unclear 32.6, 52.16, 263.4, 522.15, 522.19, 971.19
unclearness 32.2, 52.1, 263.1, 522.3, 971.4
unclench 292.12
Uncle Sam 232.5, 612.3
unclever 414.15
uncleverness 414.1
unclinch 802.10
unclinched 802.22
unclipped 792.11
uncloak 6.5, 351.4
uncloaking 351.1
unclog 292.12, 909.22, 1014.7
unclogged 292.17, 430.26
unclogging 909.6
unclose 292.12
unclosed 292.17
unclot 1064.5
unclothe 6.7
unclothed 6.13
unclothing 6.1, 6.2, 802.6
unclotted 1061.4, 1064.6
unclotting 1064.1
unclouded 31.6, 348.11, 1025.31, 1029.4
uncloudedness 1029.1
unclubbability 583.1
unclubbable 583.5
unclubbableness 583.1
unclutch 292.12, 475.4
unclutter 798.5, 1014.9
uncluttered 798.6
uncluttering 798.2, 1014.6
uncoached 414.16
uncoded 521.12
uncoerced 324.7, 430.24
uncogency 776.1
uncogent 776.7
uncoherent 804.4
uncohesive 804.4
uncohesiveness 804.1
uncoil 798.5, 861.7
uncollected accounts 628.1
uncollectible 625.1
uncollectibles 623.1
uncolored 36.7, 973.15
uncombed 497.12, 810.14
uncombined 798.7
un-come-at-able 967.9
un-come-at-ableness 967.3
uncomeliness 1015.1
uncomely 1015.6
uncomfortable 96.22, 98.20
uncomfortableness 96.1
uncommendable 510.24
uncommensurability 787.1
uncommensurable 787.6
uncommensurableness 787.1
uncommensurate 787.6
uncommercial 391.12
uncommitted 430.21, 467.7, 494.8
uncommitted voter 609.28
uncommon 247.10, 841.11, 848.2, 870.10, 992.11
uncommonly like 784.15
uncommonness 841.1, 848.1, 870.2, 992.3
uncommunicative 51.10, 344.8, 345.15, 494.8, 522.20, 583.5
uncommunicativenes 344.1
uncommunicativeness 345.1, 346.1, 494.1, 522.5, 583.1
uncompact 299.4
uncompanionability 583.1
uncompanionable 583.5
uncomparability 787.1
uncomparable 787.6
uncomparableness 787.1
uncompassability 967.2
uncompassable 967.8
uncompassionate 25.6, 144.16, 146.3
uncompassionateness 144.1, 146.1
uncompassioned 144.16, 146.3
uncompelled 324.7, 430.24
uncompensated 625.12
uncompetitive 450.5
uncomplaining 107.7, 134.10, 433.12
uncomplainingness 134.2
uncomplaisant 144.18, 442.6, 505.4
uncompleted 408.3, 795.4
uncomplex 499.8
uncomplexity 499.3, 1014.1
uncompliant 327.9, 435.5, 442.6, 868.5
uncomplicated 499.8, 798.8, 1014.13
uncomplicatedness 499.3, 1014.1
uncomplicating 1014.6
uncomplication 499.3
uncomplimentary 510.21
uncomplimentary remark 156.2, 512.4
uncomplying 327.8, 442.6
uncompounded 798.7
uncomprehending 922.14, 930.11
uncompressed 299.4
uncompromising 361.9, 425.7
uncompromisingness 361.2, 425.2
unconcealed 31.6, 348.11
unconceived 762.10, 933.5
unconceptualized 933.5
unconcern 94.4, 102.2, 106.5, 982.1
unconcerned 25.6, 94.13, 102.7, 106.15, 982.3
unconcocted 406.8, 973.15
unconcrete 764.5
unconcreteness 764.1
uncondemned 148.7
uncondensed 792.12
unconditional 430.27, 443.16, 794.10, 960.2
unconditionality 960.1
unconditional love 104.4
unconditioned 430.27, 960.2
unconditioned free will 430.6
unconditioned reflex 92.26
uncondoning 980.11
unconducive 391.14
unconfident 955.8, 971.23
unconfined 430.27
unconfirmability 971.1
unconfirmable 958.9, 971.16
unconfirmed 958.8, 971.21
unconfirmed report 552.6
unconformability 789.2
unconformable 780.7
unconforming 435.5, 868.5
unconformism 782.1
unconformist 868.3
unconformity 780.1, 782.1, 789.2, 868.1
unconfused 521.11
unconfutability 970.3
unconfutable 970.15
unconfuted 957.21, 973.13
uncongealed 1061.4
uncongenial 99.7, 344.10, 583.5, 789.6
uncongeniality 344.3, 583.1, 789.3
unconnected 522.13, 776.6, 802.20, 804.4, 813.4, 936.11
unconnectedness 522.1, 776.1
unconned 340.16
unconquerable 15.19, 360.8
unconquerableness 15.4
unconquered 411.8, 430.29
unconscienced 645.16
unconscientious 340.13, 645.16
unconscientiousness 340.4, 645.1
unconscionable 247.12, 632.12, 645.16, 650.12, 671.16, 993.16
unconscionableness 632.4, 650.5, 993.1
unconscious (n) 92.28 (a) 22.22, 25.8, 92.42, 94.10, 365.11, 689.24, 930.12, 934.6, 963.14, 972.17, 984.7, 985.11, 1055.5
unconscious drive 934.2
unconscious knowledge 934.1
unconscious memory 92.29
unconscious mind 92.28
unconsciousness 22.2, 25.2, 94.2, 922.2, 930.2, 984.1, 1055.2
unconscious of 930.12
unconscious urge 934.2
unconsecrated 695.15
unconsecration 695.1
unconsenting 325.5, 442.6
unconsidered 340.14, 340.15, 340.16, 365.11, 923.10, 933.5
unconsolability 112.12
unconsolable 112.28
unconsolidated 804.4
unconstitutional 674.6
unconstitutionality 674.1
unconstrained 343.10, 430.24, 581.3, 644.17, 669.7
unconstrainedness 581.1
unconstraint 343.3, 430.3, 581.1, 644.4, 669.1
unconsumed 256.7, 390.12
unconsummated 408.3
uncontaminated 416.6, 1002.6
uncontentious 464.10
uncontentiousness 464.4
uncontested 332.15, 953.23, 970.16
uncontinence 665.2
uncontinent 665.24
uncontradicted 332.15, 957.21, 970.16
uncontrite 114.5
uncontriteness 114.2
uncontrived 406.8, 416.6
uncontrol 418.1, 430.3, 669.1
uncontrollability 361.4, 963.7
uncontrollable 105.25, 361.12, 926.30, 963.15
uncontrollable person 1006.1
uncontrolled 418.5, 430.24, 669.7, 854.7
uncontrolled growth 257.5
uncontrolled spin 184.15
uncontroversial 970.16
uncontroverted 332.15, 957.21, 970.16
unconventional 581.3, 868.6, 927.5
unconventionality 581.1, 868.2, 927.1
unconversable 344.8
unconversableness 344.1
unconversance 374.1
unconversant 414.17, 930.11
unconversant with 374.4, 414.17
unconversational 344.8
unconverted 695.18, 955.8
unconvince 379.3
unconvinced 955.8, 971.16
unconvincedness 955.1
unconvincibility 956.1
unconvincible 956.4
unconvincing 955.10
unconvincingness 955.3
uncooked 406.10
uncooperative 144.18, 327.9, 361.8, 442.6, 451.8, 453.5
uncooperativeness 327.1, 361.1, 451.2, 453.1
uncoordinated 414.20
uncopied 337.6, 973.15
uncordial 144.16, 586.7, 589.9
uncordiality 144.1, 589.1
uncordialness 586.1
uncork 292.12

uncorking 292.1
uncorrectness 975.2
uncorroborated 958.8, 971.21
uncorrupt 644.13, 653.7, 664.4
uncorrupted 644.13, 653.7, 657.6, 798.7
uncorruptedness 653.2, 657.2
uncorruptness 653.2, 664.1
uncountable 884.10, 971.16
uncountable noun 530.5
uncounted 884.10, 971.18
uncounterfeited 973.15
uncount noun 530.5
uncouple 802.8
uncoupled 566.7
uncourageous 491.11
uncourageousness 491.2
uncourteous 505.4
uncourtesy 505.1
uncourtliness 505.1
uncourtly 505.4, 534.2
uncouth 98.18, 233.7, 414.20, 497.12, 534.2, 666.8
uncouthness 414.3, 497.3, 534.1, 666.3
uncover 6.5, 192.11, 292.12, 351.4, 585.10, 941.4
uncovered 6.12, 292.17, 1006.14
uncovering 6.1, 192.2, 351.1, 941.1
uncover oneself 33.8
uncowed 492.20
uncreated 761.14, 762.10
uncreated being 761.5
uncreative 891.5
uncreativeness 987.1
uncredited 151.5
uncredulous 956.4
uncredulousness 956.1
uncringing 492.20
uncritical 326.3, 340.13, 509.18, 945.5, 954.8
uncritical acceptance 954.1
uncriticalness 340.4, 945.1, 954.1
uncriticizing 509.18, 945.5
uncropped 792.11
uncrown 447.4
uncrystallized 845.8
uncs 559.3
unction 86.11, 511.2, 677.15, 692.3, 693.1, 701.5, 1056.3, 1056.6
unctional 1056.9
unctiousness 1056.5
unctuosity 1056.5
unctuous 354.32, 504.17, 511.8, 692.11, 693.5, 1056.9
unctuousness 354.6, 504.5, 511.2, 693.1, 1056.5
uncullibility 956.2
uncullible 956.5
uncultivated 233.7, 406.12, 406.14, 497.12, 891.4, 930.13
uncultivatedness 497.3
uncultivation 233.3, 406.4, 497.3
uncultured 233.7, 406.12, 497.12, 606.8, 930.13
unculturedness 497.3
uncurbed 418.5, 430.24
uncurl 277.5
uncurled 277.6
uncurtain 292.12
uncurtained 348.11
uncurved 277.6
uncustomary 870.10
uncut 263.5, 406.12, 792.11, 794.9
undamaged 397.13, 792.10, 1002.8, 1007.4
undamaging 999.21
undampable 855.18
undamped 54.12, 1066.7
undangerous 1007.5
undaring 491.11, 494.8, 987.5
undarkened 348.11
undaunted 360.8, 492.20
undauntedness 492.2
undazed 123.3
undazzled 123.3, 979.12
undead, the 680.6
undebauched 653.7, 664.7
undebauchedness 653.2
undeceitful 644.18
undeceitfulness 644.5
undeceivability 956.2
undeceivable 956.5
undeceive 977.2
undeceived 928.16, 977.5
undeceiving 644.18, 977.4
undecennary 882.23
undecennial 882.23
undeception 977.1
undeceptive 644.18
undeceptiveness 644.5
undecided (n) 430.12 (a) 362.9, 971.18
undecided issue 971.8
undecidedness 362.1, 971.1
undecided voter 609.28
undecillion 882.13
undecipherability 522.4
undecipherable 522.19
undecked 499.8
undeclared 519.9
undecorated 499.8
undecorative 1015.10
undefaced 1002.8
undefeated 411.8
undefended 1006.14
undefiled 79.25, 644.13, 657.6, 657.7, 664.4, 664.7
undefiledness 657.2, 664.1
undefinability 522.6
undefinable 122.13, 522.18
undefined 32.6, 263.4, 528.3, 677.17, 945.6, 971.19
undeflectability 855.1, 963.7
undeflectable 359.12, 855.17, 963.15
undeflected 277.6
undeformed 1002.8
undeft 414.15
undeftness 414.1
undegenerate 653.7
undegenerateness 653.2
undelectability 98.1
undelectable 98.17
undeliberate 365.11
undeliberated 365.11, 406.8
undeliberateness 365.4
undelicious 98.17
undelighted 99.8
undeludable 956.5
undeluded 928.16
undemanding 426.5, 945.5
undemandingness 426.2
undemolished 1002.8
undemonstrable 958.9
undemonstratable 958.9
undemonstrated 958.8, 971.21
undemonstrative 344.10
undemonstrativeness 344.3
undemoralized 653.7
undeniability 970.3
undeniable 247.12, 761.15, 970.15
undeniable fact 761.3
undenied 957.21, 973.13
undenominational 675.27
undependability 364.3, 645.4, 854.2, 971.6, 1006.2
undependable 364.6, 645.19, 854.7, 971.20, 1006.11
undeplored 99.9
undepraved 653.7
undepravedness 653.2
under 274.8
under a charm 122.9
underachiever 572.4
under a cloud 599.15, 661.13, 955.11, 955.12
under a cloud of suspicion 599.15
underact 704.31
underacted 704.33
underactivity 331.1
underage (n) 795.2, 911.1 (a) 301.10
underaged 301.10
underallotment 477.3
under an eclipse 346.11
under an error 975.18
under any other name 527.15
under arms 460.14
under arrest 428.15, 429.22
under a spell 691.12
under a strain 128.13
under attack 599.15
underbed 901.20
underbedding 901.20
underbelly 2.18, 199.1, 1003.2
underbid 731.18
underbodice 5.24
underbrace 901.21
underbreath 52.4
underbrush 310.17
underbuilding 266.3, 901.6
under canvas 295.31
undercarriage 199.2, 901.6
undercast 184.32
undercharge 630.12
underclass, the 607.8, 619.3, 1011.7
underclass 606.4
underclassman 572.6
under close arrest 429.22
underclothed 6.13
underclothes 5.22
underclothing 5.22
undercoat (n) 35.8, 296.1 (v) 35.14, 295.24
undercoating 35.8, 35.12
undercolor 35.1
undercommitment 911.1, 992.1
undercommitted 911.5
under construction 405.22
under control 326.3, 428.13, 1022.11
undercooked 11.9, 406.10
undercover 295.31, 345.12, 346.11, 346.14, 1007.6
undercover activity 345.4
undercover man 576.9
undercovert 346.4
undercroft 266.3
undercrossing 170.2
undercurrent 52.4, 93.1, 238.4, 318.1, 451.1, 519.2, 900.4, 1006.5
undercut 734.8, 958.4
undercutting 749.6
under detention 429.22
underdevelop 795.3
underdeveloped 406.12, 795.4
underdeveloped nation 232.1, 619.3
underdevelopment 795.1
under discipline 428.13
underdog 410.8, 412.5
underdone 11.9, 406.10
underdress 5.42
underdressed 5.47
underemployment 331.2, 331.3
underestimate (n) 950.1 (v) 950.2
underestimated 950.3
underestimation 950.1
underfed 100.25, 270.20, 515.5, 992.12
under fire 599.15
under-five player 707.4
underframe 901.10
undergarment 5.22
undergird 15.13, 199.6, 449.12, 901.21, 957.11
undergirding 254.1, 901.6, 957.4
undergirdle 5.23
underglaze 742.3
undergo 626.7, 831.8
undergo a change 852.6
undergo an eclipse 34.2
undergo a personality change 858.12
undergo deprivation 473.4
undergo privation 473.4
undergo schooling 570.11
undergo treatment 91.29
undergrad 572.6
undergraduate (n) 572.6 (a) 572.12
underground (n) 179.14, 275.2, 333.1, 346.5, 357.11, 461.16 (a) 275.13, 333.6, 345.12, 346.11
underground activity 345.4
underground fighter 461.16
underground film 706.1
underground literature 547.12, 718.1
undergroundness 275.1
underground railroad 346.5
underground river 238.1
underground route 346.5
underground water 1065.3
undergrow 795.3

undergrown 258.13, 268.10, 795.4, 992.10
undergrowth 310.17
underhand 345.12, 356.22, 645.16
under hand and seal 436.7, 437.11
underhand dealing 345.4, 356.4
underhanded 345.12, 356.22, 645.16
underhandedness 345.4, 356.3, 645.1
under house arrest 346.11, 429.22
underived 337.5
underlay 296.1
underlayer 199.1, 296.1
underlease 469.1
underlessee 470.4
underlet (v) 615.15, 615.16 (a) 615.20
underlie 199.6, 274.5, 519.3, 901.21
underline (n) 517.6 (v) 517.19, 997.14
underlined 997.21
underlinen 5.22
underling 250.2, 432.5, 577.1
underlining 517.6
under lock and key 429.21, 1007.6
underlying 199.8, 519.5, 767.9
underlying level 274.4
underlying meaning 519.2
underlying reason 886.2
underlying structure 530.2
undermanned 992.12
undermeaning 519.2
undermention 519.2
undermine 16.10, 19.10, 393.15, 395.20, 418.4, 958.5
undermine one's faith 955.7
undermine one's reason 926.24
undermining 460.5, 958.2
undermost 199.7
underneath 199.1
undernourish 270.12
undernourished 270.17, 270.20, 992.12
undernourishment 270.5, 992.6
undernutrition 270.5, 992.6
under oath 436.7
under obligation 150.5, 641.16
under one's command 432.14
under one's eyes 31.6
under one's hand 547.22
under one's hat 345.14
under one's orders 432.14
under one's thumb 138.13, 326.5, 432.14, 894.15
under one's wing 1008.22
underpaid 625.12
underparent 559.1
underpass 383.3
underpay 625.6
underpin 901.21
underpinning 199.2, 266.3, 901.6
underpinnings 177.15
underplay 252.9, 670.6, 704.31, 998.12
underplayed 252.10, 704.33
underplaying 252.1
underplot 381.5
underprepared 131.9, 844.6
underprice 633.6, 950.2
underpriced 950.3
under privilege 345.14
underprivileged, the 606.4, 607.8, 619.3
underprivileged 250.6, 619.8, 1011.14
underprize 950.2
underproduce 892.11
underproduction 892.5
underprop 901.21
under protest 333.7
underrate 950.2
underrated 950.3
underrating 950.1
underreckon 950.2
underreckoning 950.1
under restraint 428.13, 429.19
under revision 405.22
underripe 406.11
underscore (n) 517.6 (v) 517.19, 997.14
underscored 334.9, 997.21
underscoring 517.6
undersea 240.8, 275.14
undersecretary 432.5, 575.16
under security 345.11
under security restrictions 345.11
undersell 734.8
underselling 631.1
underset 901.21
undersexed 75.29
undershoot (n) 184.18 (v) 184.43
undershrubs 310.17
underside 199.1, 199.2
undersign 332.12, 438.9
undersigned, the 332.7
undersize (n) 258.1 (a) 258.13
undersized 258.13, 270.17
undersong 696.8, 708.22, 849.5
understaffed 992.9
understand 341.9, 521.7, 928.12, 951.10
understandability 521.1
understandable 521.10, 928.25
understandableness 521.1
understand by 341.9
understanding, the 921.3
understanding (n) 332.5, 436.2, 437.1, 455.1, 468.1, 587.3, 788.2, 919.1, 920.1, 928.3 (a) 134.9, 145.7, 455.3, 920.12, 920.16, 928.15
understand one another 455.2
understate 350.3, 354.16, 950.2
understated 35.22, 496.7
understatement 350.1, 496.3
understood 519.8, 842.12, 928.26, 951.14
understory 296.1
understrapper 250.2, 432.5, 577.1
understratum 296.1
understruction 266.3, 901.6
understructure 266.3, 901.6
understudy (n) 576.1, 704.10, 707.7, 862.2 (v) 576.14, 704.29
understudy for 862.5
undersupplied 992.9
under suspicion 599.15, 955.12
undertake 328.8, 403.6, 404.3, 436.5, 437.5, 725.15
undertaken 404.7, 437.11
undertake operations 458.16
undertaker 309.8
undertaker's establishment 309.9
undertaking 328.3, 403.2, 404.1, 436.2, 437.1, 438.2, 724.1
undertaxation 630.9
undertenancy 469.1
undertenant 470.4
under the aegis of 1008.22
under the auspices of 1008.22
under the ban 444.7
under the ban of secrecy 345.11
under-the-counter 345.12, 674.6
under the harrow 26.9, 96.25
under the heel 432.14
under the impression 953.21
under the influence 87.23, 88.31
under the lash 432.14
under the protection of 1008.22
under the seal of secrecy 345.11
under the shadow of one's wing 1008.22
under the shield of 1008.22
under the sun 761.13
under the surface 519.5
under the table 88.32
under-the-table 345.12, 674.6
under the weather 85.56
under the wing of 1008.22
underthings 5.22
undertone 50.2, 52.4, 209.3, 518.1, 519.2
undertow 238.4, 451.1, 1006.5
underused 390.12
underutilized 390.12
undervaluation 950.1
undervalue 950.2
undervalued 99.9, 950.3
undervaluing 252.5
undervaluing of self 139.2
underwater 240.8, 275.14
underwater archeology 842.4
underwater craft 180.9
underwater explorer 240.7
underway 404.7, 405.22, 831.9
underwear 5.22
underweight (n) 270.5, 297.1 (a) 270.17, 298.13
underwhelm 94.5
underwood 310.17
Underworld, the 839.2
underworld, the 660.10
underworld 275.3, 682.1
under wraps 345.11, 346.11
underwrite 332.12, 436.4, 438.9, 1008.18
underwriter 332.7, 438.6, 1008.4
underwriting 438.1
underwritten 332.14, 436.8
undescried 340.15
undeserved 640.9, 650.9
undeservedness 640.1
undeserving 640.9
undeservingness 640.1
undesignated 528.3
undesigned 365.11, 972.17
undesignedness 365.4
undesigning 416.6, 644.18
undesirability 98.1, 108.2, 996.1
undesirable (n) 586.4, 660.1 (a) 98.17, 108.10, 586.9, 996.5
undesired 99.11
undesirous 99.11, 102.8
undesirousness 102.3
undespairing 124.10
undestined 971.19
undestroyable 855.18
undestroyed 853.7, 1002.8
undetached 650.11, 980.12
undetachment 650.3, 980.3
undetectability 32.1, 258.2
undetectable 32.5
undetected 346.12
undetermined 362.9, 958.8, 971.18, 971.19, 972.15
undeterminedness 362.1, 971.1
undeveloped 263.4, 301.10, 406.12, 414.17, 795.4, 841.7, 1003.4
undevelopment 301.3, 406.4, 1003.1
undeviating 161.12, 277.6, 781.5, 855.17, 973.17
undeviatingness 781.1
undeviation 118.1, 781.2
undevised 406.8
undevoured 668.10
undevout 695.15
undevoutness 695.1
undexterous 414.15
undexterousness 414.1
undies 5.22
undifferenced 798.6
undifferent 778.7
undifferentiable 798.6
undifferentiated 778.7, 781.5, 798.6, 812.8, 864.11, 945.6
undifferentiating 945.5
undifferentiation 778.1, 781.2, 812.1
undiffident 492.19
undigested 406.11
undignified 497.10, 534.2
undiluted 798.7
undiminished 15.21, 247.14, 792.11, 794.9
undine 240.3, 678.6, 678.10
undiplomatic 340.11
undirected 164.7, 810.12, 972.16
undirtied 79.25
undiscerned 340.15
undiscernible 32.5, 522.15
undiscerning 30.9, 922.14, 923.10, 945.5
undiscerningness 922.2
undischarged 408.3
undisciplined 327.8, 418.5, 669.7, 854.7
undisclosable 345.11
undisclosed 32.5, 345.11, 346.12, 930.16
undisclosing 346.15
undiscouraged 360.8
undiscoverability 967.3
undiscoverable 930.16, 967.9
undiscovered 346.12, 930.16
undiscreet 945.5

undiscriminated 945.6
undiscriminating 102.7, 945.5
undiscriminatingness 945.1
undiscriminative 945.5
undiscriminativeness 945.1
undisguise 416.2
undisguised 31.6, 348.11, 644.18, 973.15
undisguising 416.6, 644.18, 973.15
undismayed 492.20
undispassionate 650.11, 980.12
undispassionateness 650.3, 980.3
undisputed 953.23, 970.16
undissembled 644.18
undissembling 416.6, 644.18
undissimulated 644.18
undissimulating 416.6, 644.18
undissipated 664.7
undissolute 653.7, 664.7
undissoluteness 653.2
undistinguishable 945.6
undistinguishableness 945.2
undistinguished 137.10, 661.14, 945.6
undistinguishedness 137.1
undistorted 277.6, 973.15
undistributed costs 626.3
undistributed middle 936.3
undisturbable 106.10
undisturbed 94.9, 106.11, 107.8, 173.12
undiversified 781.5
undividable 800.15, 1045.13
undivided 792.11, 800.13, 872.7
undivided attention 360.1, 983.4
undividedness 794.1, 872.1
undivinable 971.16
undivined 131.10
undivulgable 345.11
undivulged 345.11, 346.12, 930.16
undo 6.6, 128.10, 292.12, 395.11, 395.13, 395.17, 412.6, 802.10, 804.3, 859.5, 900.7, 940.2
undoable 967.8
undogmatic 979.10
undoing 395.1, 412.1, 802.6, 900.2
undomesticated 430.29, 671.21
undone 112.29, 125.15, 127.26, 128.14, 340.14, 395.28, 408.3, 412.14, 802.22
undoubted 953.23, 970.16, 973.13
undoubtful 953.21
undoubting 953.21, 954.8, 960.2, 970.21
undrape 6.7, 292.12, 351.4
undraped 6.13
undreamed-of 870.10, 933.5
undress (n) 5.20, 6.2, 499.3 (v) 6.7
undressed 6.13, 499.8
undressing 6.2
undried 1065.15
undrinkable 64.8
undrooping 360.8
undrunk 516.3
undrunken 516.3
undrunkenness 516.1
undue 632.12, 638.3, 640.9, 650.9, 993.16
undue excitability 128.1
undue liberty 640.2
undueness 632.4, 640.1, 650.1, 993.1
undulancy 916.2
undulant 279.7, 281.10, 850.7, 916.16
undulate (v) 184.40, 238.22, 281.4, 850.5, 916.11 (a) 281.10
undulated 281.10
undulating 237.8, 281.10, 916.16
undulation 238.14, 281.1, 850.2, 916.2
undulative 281.10
undulatory 281.10, 850.7, 916.16
unduly neglected 151.5
undumbfounded 123.3
undupability 956.2
undupable 956.5
unduplicated 337.6
undurable 828.7
unduteous 327.8
unduteousness 327.1
undutiful 327.8, 694.6, 695.15
undutifulness 327.1, 694.1, 695.1
undying 829.9, 855.18, 856.7
undying fame 662.7
undying friendship 587.8
undyingness 829.3
uneager 102.8
uneagerness 102.3
unearned 640.9
unearned income 627.1
unearned increment 640.1
unearned run 745.3
unearth 192.10, 941.4
unearthing 192.2, 941.1
unearthliness 307.11, 692.2, 870.7, 1053.1
unearthly 307.28, 681.12, 692.9, 774.5, 870.11, 870.15, 955.10, 988.9, 1053.7
unease 96.1, 108.1, 126.1, 917.1
uneasiness 96.1, 108.1, 126.1, 127.5, 128.1, 135.1
uneasy 96.20, 96.22, 105.27, 108.7, 126.7, 128.11, 135.6, 917.16
uneasy truce 465.5
uneatable 64.8
uneaten 668.10
uneating 515.5
uneatness 810.6
uneconomical 406.15
unedged 286.3
unedified 930.13
uneducated 523.20, 930.13
uneducated speech 523.6
uneffectible 967.8
uneffeminate 76.12, 76.14
unelaborate 499.9
unelaborateness 499.4
unelevated 274.7
unembarrassed 430.26, 666.6
unembarrassedness 666.2
unembellished 416.6, 499.8, 721.5
unembellishedness 721.2
unembellishment 499.3
unembodied 1053.7
unemotional 25.6, 94.9
unemotionalism 94.1
unemployability 391.1
unemployable, the 331.11, 606.4
unemployable 331.18, 391.14
unemployed, the 331.11
unemployed 173.13, 331.18, 390.12, 402.5
unemployment 331.2, 331.3
unemployment compensation 611.7
unemployment insurance 331.3, 478.8, 611.7
unemployment rate 731.9
unenciphered 521.12
unencoded text 521.2
unencumbered 298.11, 430.26
unending 812.8, 829.7, 856.7
unendowed 19.14, 414.16
unendurability 98.9
unendurable 98.25
unenduring 828.7
unengaged 430.21
unengaging 98.17
unengagingness 98.1
unenhanced 248.8
unenjoyable 98.17, 117.7
unenlightened 30.9, 930.11
unenlightenment 30.1, 930.3
unenslaved 430.29
unenterprising 331.19, 494.8
unentertaining 117.7
unenthralled 430.29
unenthusiasm 325.1
unenthusiastic 102.8, 325.6
unentitled 640.9
unentitledness 640.1
unentitlement 640.1
unenvied 156.9
unequable 782.3
unequal 650.9, 780.7, 782.3, 791.4, 851.3
unequaled 249.15
unequalize 791.2
unequal to 992.9
unequal treatment 650.3
unequipped 406.9, 414.19
unequitable 650.9
unequivocal 247.12, 430.27, 521.11, 644.17, 960.2, 970.13
unequivocalness 521.2, 970.1
unerring 653.7, 970.19, 973.17
unerringness 970.4
unerroneous 973.13
unerroneousness 973.1
unerudite 930.13
unescorted 872.8
unessential (n) 768.2 (a) 391.10, 766.7, 768.4, 776.7, 993.17, 998.17
unestablished 160.10, 958.8, 971.18
unethical 645.16, 654.11
uneuphonious 534.2
uneuphoniousness 534.1
uneven 288.6, 650.9, 782.3, 791.4, 851.3, 1003.4
unevenness 288.1, 782.1, 791.1, 851.1, 1003.1
uneven parallel bars 760.5
uneventful 117.7, 118.9
unexacting 340.13, 426.5, 945.5
unexactingness 340.4
unexaggerated 973.15
unexamined 340.16
unexampled 249.15, 337.6, 870.14
unexcelled 249.15
unexceptionability 107.3, 657.3
unexceptionable 107.12, 509.20, 657.8, 953.24, 970.15, 973.16, 999.20
unexceptionableness 657.3
unexceptional 869.8, 1005.8
unexceptionality 1005.2
unexcessive 670.12
unexcessiveness 670.1
unexcitability 94.1
unexcitableness 106.1
unexcited 106.11
unexciting 65.2, 117.7
unexcused absence 222.4
unexecuted 408.3
unexempt from 641.17
unexercised 390.12
unexhausted 9.5, 15.21
unexistent 762.8
unexisting 762.8
unexpansive 344.10
unexpansiveness 344.3
unexpected 131.10, 830.5, 870.10, 870.12, 969.3, 972.15
unexpectedness 131.1, 830.2
unexpecting 131.9
unexpended 390.12
unexpended balance 386.3
unexpensive 633.7
unexperience 414.2
unexperienced 414.17
unexperiencedness 414.2
unexplainable 522.18
unexplainableness 522.6
unexplained 346.12, 930.16
unexplained death 85.2
unexplored 340.16, 346.12, 930.16
unexplored territory 930.6
unexposed 346.12, 930.16
unexpressed 51.11, 519.9
unexpressive 522.20
unexpressiveness 522.5
unexpurgated 792.12, 794.9
unextended 1053.7
unextendibility 1046.3
unextendible 1046.12
unextensibility 1046.3
unextensible 1046.12
unextinguished 671.17, 1019.27
unextravagance 670.1
unextravagant 670.12
unextreme 670.12
unextremeness 670.1
unfabricated 973.15
unfacile 414.15
unfact 354.10
unfactual 975.16, 975.17
unfactualness 975.2

unfaded 15.21, 1002.8
unfading 35.18, 827.10, 829.9, 853.7
unfailing 360.8, 644.20, 853.7, 970.17
unfailing grip 360.1
unfair 650.10
unfair advantage 791.1
unfair discrimination 791.1
unfairly neglected 151.5
unfairness 650.2
unfaith 645.5
unfaithful 435.5, 645.20
unfaithfulness 104.5, 645.5
unfaithworthiness 645.4, 971.6
unfaithworthy 645.19, 971.20
unfaked 973.15
unfallacious 973.13
unfallaciousness 973.1
unfallen 653.7, 657.6
unfallen state 657.1
unfalse 644.19, 973.13
unfalseness 644.6, 973.1
unfaltering 129.2, 359.13, 360.8, 970.21
unfamed 661.14
unfamiliar, the 930.6
unfamiliar 841.11, 870.10, 930.11, 930.16
unfamiliarity 374.1, 414.2, 841.1, 930.1
unfamiliar with 374.4, 414.17
unfanatical 979.8, 979.10
unfanciful 973.15, 987.5
unfancifulness 987.1
unfanciness 499.4
unfancy 499.9
unfashionable 842.16, 868.6
unfashionableness 842.3
unfashioned 263.5, 406.12
unfasten 802.10, 804.3
unfastened 802.22
unfastidious 945.5
unfastidiousness 945.1
unfathomable 275.12, 522.13, 823.3
unfathomableness 275.1, 522.1
unfathomed 275.12, 930.16
unfathomed deeps 275.3
unfatigued 9.5
unfaultable 1002.6
unfavorable 133.16, 451.8, 510.21, 844.6, 962.12, 996.6, 1000.7, 1011.13
unfavorable balance of payments 623.2
unfavorableness 133.7, 844.1, 1000.1
unfavorable trade balance 623.2
unfavorable wind 184.32
unfearful 492.19
unfearfulness 492.2
unfearing 492.19
unfearingness 492.2
unfeasibility 967.2
unfeasible 967.8
unfecundated 891.4
unfed 100.25, 515.5, 992.12
unfeeling (n) 25.1, 94.1, 144.10 (a) 25.6, 94.9, 144.25, 146.3, 1055.5
unfeelingness 25.1, 94.1, 146.1, 1055.2
unfeigned 644.18, 973.15
unfeigning 416.6, 499.7, 644.18, 973.15
unfelicitous 534.2
unfelt 25.6
unfeminine 76.14, 505.6
unfertile 891.4
unfertileness 891.1
unfetter 431.6, 802.10
unfettered 430.28, 802.22
unfettering 431.2
unfictitious 973.15
unfictitiousness 973.7
unfilled 100.25, 222.15
unfinical 340.13
unfinicalness 340.4
unfinish 406.4
unfinished 263.4, 406.12, 408.3, 414.16, 795.4, 1003.4
unfinishedness 406.4
unfirm 16.15
unfirmness 16.3
unfit (v) 19.9 (a) 19.14, 85.54, 391.14, 406.9, 414.19, 638.3, 789.7, 844.6, 996.5
unfit for human consumption 64.8
unfitness 19.2, 391.1, 406.1, 414.1, 638.1, 789.3, 844.1, 996.1
unfitted 19.14, 406.9, 414.19, 789.7
unfittedness 406.1, 414.1
unfitting 497.10, 638.3, 789.7, 844.6, 996.5
unfittingness 497.1, 638.1, 844.1, 996.1
unfit to live in 586.8
unfix 802.10
unfixed 802.22, 854.7, 958.8, 971.18
unfixedness 854.2
unflagging 15.21, 330.22, 360.8
unflagging efforts 360.1
unflappability 106.1, 855.1
unflappable 106.10, 359.12, 855.12
unflattering 644.18, 973.15
unflavored 65.2
unflawed 1002.6
unfledged 301.10, 406.11, 414.17, 841.7
unfledgedness 406.4, 414.2
unfleshly 1053.7
unflexible 1046.12
unflinching 129.2, 359.13, 360.8, 492.20, 855.12
unflustered 106.11
unfold 259.6, 292.12, 341.10, 348.5, 351.4, 538.7, 861.7, 887.4
unfold a tale 722.7
unfolded 259.11
unfolding (n) 33.1, 310.26, 341.4, 348.2, 351.1, 538.6, 861.2 (a) 861.8
unfoldment 33.1, 310.26, 348.2, 351.1, 861.2
unfollowing 1042.19
unfoolable 956.5
unforbearance 135.2, 980.2
unforbearing 135.7, 980.11
unforbidden 443.16
unforced 324.7, 430.24
unforced error 748.2
unforcedness 324.2
unforeseeable 131.10, 971.16, 972.15
unforeseeableness 131.1, 971.1
unforeseen, the 131.1
unforeseen 131.10, 830.5, 972.15
unforeseen attack 459.2
unforewarned 131.9
unforgettable 989.25, 997.19
unforgivable 650.12, 654.16
unforgivableness 650.5
unforgivable sin 654.3, 655.2
unforgiving 146.3
unforgivingness 146.1
unforgoable 963.13
unforgotten 989.22
unform 263.3
unformed 263.5, 301.10, 406.12
unformedness 263.1
unforseeing 923.10
unfortified 798.7, 1006.14
unfortunate (n) 1011.7 (a) 133.16, 410.18, 844.6, 996.5, 1011.14
unfortunateness 133.7, 844.1, 996.1, 1011.4
unfortunate time 844.2
unfortunate woman 665.16
unfoul 292.12, 909.22
unfouling 909.6
unfounded 354.25, 764.8, 936.13, 958.8, 975.19, 976.9
unfrail 83.10
unfrank 354.32, 645.18
unfrankness 354.5, 645.3
unfree 432.14
unfreeze 1020.21
unfreight 120.7
unfreighting 298.3
unfrequent 848.2
unfrequented 584.8
unfrequentness 848.1
unfriended 19.18, 584.12
unfriendliness 98.1, 451.1, 458.10, 583.1, 586.1, 589.1
unfriendly (n) 452.1, 589.6 (a) 98.17, 99.8, 451.8, 458.20, 583.5, 586.7, 589.9
unfrightened 492.19
unfrock 447.4, 661.8, 909.19
unfrocking 447.2, 909.4
unfrozen 1019.24
unfrozen hydrometeor 316.1
unfructified 891.5
unfructuous 891.4
unfrugal 669.7
unfruitful 891.4
unfruitfulness 891.1
unfuddled 516.3
unfulfilled 96.20, 108.7, 408.3
unfulfilled pledge 623.1
unfulfilling 108.9
unfulfillment 108.1, 408.1
unfunded debt 623.1
unfunny 117.7
unfurbished 499.8
unfurl 351.4, 861.7
unfurl a banner 182.52
unfurl a flag 517.22
unfurl an ensign 182.52
unfurling 861.2
unfurl sail 182.20
unfurnished 406.9
unfussiness 340.4, 499.4
unfussy 340.13, 499.9
ungag 431.6
ungagged 430.28
ungagging 431.2
ungainliness 414.3, 1015.1
ungainly 414.20, 1013.19, 1015.9
ungallant 491.11, 505.4
ungallantness 491.2, 505.1
ungarbed 6.13
ungarment 6.7
ungarmented 6.13
ungarnished 499.8
ungarrisoned 1006.14
ungenerosity 484.3
ungenerous 144.17, 154.3, 484.9, 651.6, 980.10
ungenerousness 144.2, 154.1, 651.2, 980.2
ungenial 144.16, 344.10, 583.5, 589.9
ungeniality 144.1, 583.1, 589.1
ungenteel 497.10, 505.6, 606.8
ungentility 497.1
ungentle 144.24, 505.6, 671.21
ungentlemanlike 505.6
ungentlemanliness 505.1
ungentlemanly 505.6
ungentleness 144.9, 671.1
ungenuine 336.8, 354.26, 354.32
ungenuineness 354.2
ungermane 776.7
ungermaneness 776.1
ungetatable 261.9
ungettable 967.9
ungettableness 967.3
ungifted 19.14, 414.16, 922.13
ungiving 361.9, 1046.12
ungivingness 361.2
unglorified 661.14
unglue 802.10, 804.3
unglued 128.14, 802.22
ungodliness 654.1, 694.1, 695.3
ungodly 654.12, 695.17, 955.10, 1000.10
ungood 654.12
ungoodness 654.1
ungovernability 361.4
ungovernable 361.12, 418.6
ungoverned 418.5, 430.24, 430.29
ungraced 1015.9
ungraceful 414.20, 534.2, 1015.9
ungracefulness 414.3, 534.1, 1015.1
ungracious 144.16, 151.4, 505.4, 586.7
ungraciousness 144.1, 505.1, 586.1
ungraded 810.12
ungrammatic 531.4
ungrammatical 531.4
ungrammaticalness 531.1
ungrammaticism 531.2

ungraspability 522.1
ungraspable 522.13
ungrateful 151.4
ungratefulness 151.1
ungrateful wretch 151.2
ungratification 96.1
ungratified 96.20, 108.7
ungratifying 108.9
ungregarious 583.5, 872.8
ungregariousness 583.1
ungrieving 114.4
ungrounded 764.8, 936.13
ungrown 406.11
ungrudging 324.6, 441.4, 485.4
ungrudgingness 324.1, 441.1
ungrumbling 324.6
unguals 474.4
unguarded 340.10, 365.10, 416.5, 644.17, 972.17, 984.8, 1006.14
unguardedness 416.1
unguent (n) 86.11, 1056.3 (v) 1056.8 (a) 1056.9
unguentary 1056.9, 1056.10
unguentous 1056.9
unguentum 86.11, 1056.3
unguessed 131.10
unguessing 131.9
unguided 930.13, 972.17
unguiform 279.8
unguiltiness 657.1
unguilty 657.6
unguinous 1056.9
ungula 199.5
ungulant 311.5
ungulate (n) 311.3, 311.5 (a) 199.9, 311.45
ungullibility 956.2
ungullible 956.5
unhabitability 586.2
unhabitable 586.8
unhabituated 374.4
unhabituatedness 374.1
unhallow 80.17, 694.4
unhallowed 686.3
unhallowedness 686.1
unhamper 1014.9
unhampered 343.10, 430.26, 960.2
unhampering 1014.6
unhand 431.5, 475.4
unhandcuff 431.6
unhandicapped 430.26
unhandiness 414.3, 996.3, 1013.9
unhanding 431.2
unhandled 390.12, 841.7
unhandseled 841.7
unhandsome 1015.6
unhandsomeness 1015.1
unhandy 414.20, 844.6, 996.7, 1013.19
unhappiness 96.1, 108.1, 112.2, 510.1
unhappy 96.20, 108.7, 112.21, 510.21, 844.6, 996.5, 1011.14
unhappy about 113.8
unhappy lot 1011.1
unharbored 160.10
unhardened 16.12, 374.4
unharmed 1002.8, 1007.4
unharmonious 61.4, 456.15, 589.9, 789.6
unharmoniousness 61.1, 456.1, 789.1
unharness 431.6
unharnessing 431.2
unharsh 426.5
unharshness 426.2
unhastiness 402.2
unhasty 402.6
unhatched 406.8
unhazardous 1007.5
unhealthful 82.5, 85.53
unhealthfulness 82.1
unhealthiness 82.1, 85.3, 1000.1, 1000.5, 1006.2
unhealthy 36.7, 82.5, 85.54, 85.55, 1000.7, 1006.11
unhealthy conditions 80.3
unhearable 51.10
unheard 930.16
unheard-of 122.10, 661.14, 841.11, 870.10, 930.16
unhearing 49.6, 930.12
unheated 1023.13
unheaviness 298.1
unheavy 298.10
unheeded 340.15
unheedful 144.18, 340.11, 984.6
unheedfulness 144.3, 340.2, 984.1
unheeding 340.11, 984.6
unhelpful 144.18, 391.14
unhelpfulness 144.3, 391.1
unheralded 131.10
unheroic 491.11
unheroicness 491.2
unhesitant 359.13
unhesitating 359.13, 960.2, 970.21
unhewn 263.5, 406.12
unhidden 31.6, 292.17, 348.11
unhidebound 979.8
unhideboundness 979.1
unhindered 430.26
unhinge 160.5, 802.16, 926.24
unhinged 128.11, 160.9, 926.26
unhinging 160.1
unhistorical 833.3
unhitch 802.10
unhitched 802.22
unhoaxability 956.2
unhoaxable 956.5
unhobble 431.6
unhobbling 431.2
unholiness 686.1, 695.3
unholy, the 686.2
unholy 686.3, 695.17, 1000.10
unholy alliance 617.1
unholy dread 127.1
unholy joy 144.6
unholy mess 810.3, 1013.5
unhonored 156.9, 661.14
unhook 802.10
unhoped for 131.10
unhopeful 125.12
unhopefulness 125.1
unhorse 160.6
unhorsing 160.2
unhospitable 586.7
unhospitableness 586.1
unhostile 464.10, 587.15
unhostility 587.1
unhouse 909.15
unhoused 160.10
unhuman 144.26, 870.15
unhurried 175.10, 402.6
unhurried ease 331.2
unhurriedness 175.3, 402.2
unhurt 1002.8, 1007.4
unhurtful 999.21
unhygienic 80.20, 82.5
uniangulate 872.11
Uniate 675.19
Uniate Rites 675.8
Uniatism 675.8
unibivalent 872.11, 875.7
unibranchiate 872.11
unicameral 613.11, 872.11
unicameral legislature 613.1
unicellular 305.19, 872.11
unicellularity 305.4
unicorn 179.5, 647.2
unicuspid 872.11
unideaed 933.4
unideal 987.6
unidealism 721.2, 987.2
unidealistic 721.5, 987.6
unidealized 987.5
unidentate 872.11
unidentical 787.4
unidentified 528.3, 930.16
unidentified flying object 1075.3
unidigitate 872.11
unidimensional 872.11
unidirectional 161.12, 872.11
unidirectional signal 1034.10
unific 872.12
unification 450.2, 778.2, 800.1, 805.1, 872.1
unified 872.10, 1045.13
unified field theory 1018.1, 1038.2
unified theory 951.1
uniflorous 310.38, 872.11
unifoliate 872.11
unifoliolate 872.11
uniform (n) 5.7, 647.1, 752.1 (v) 5.41 (a) 264.4, 287.10, 781.5, 788.9, 798.6, 807.6, 812.8, 850.6, 872.7, 945.6
Uniform Code of Military Justice 673.5
uniformed 5.45
uniformity 264.1, 287.1, 781.1, 788.1, 798.1, 807.1, 812.1, 850.1, 855.1, 867.1, 872.1, 945.2
uniformize 781.4
uniform resource locator 1042.18
uniform with 784.10
unify 778.5, 800.5, 805.3, 872.5
unifying 872.12
unigenital 872.11
uniglobular 872.11
unilateral 218.7, 872.11
unilateral disarmament 465.6
unilateralism 218.1
unilateralist 218.7, 872.11
unilaterality 218.1
unilateral trade 731.1
unilinear 872.11
uniliteral 872.11
unilluminated 930.11, 1027.13
unilobed 872.11
unilobular 872.11
unilocular 872.11
unimaged 933.5
unimaginability 967.1
unimaginable 122.10, 870.12, 955.10, 967.7
unimaginative 117.8, 535.3, 721.5, 987.5
unimaginativeness 117.2, 535.1, 721.2, 987.1
unimagined 933.5, 973.15
unimitated 337.6, 973.15
unimodular 872.11
unimolecular 872.11
unimpaired 83.11, 792.10, 1002.8
unimpassioned 94.9, 106.11, 117.8, 721.5
unimpeachability 644.1, 657.3, 970.3, 973.5
unimpeachable 644.13, 657.8, 953.24, 970.15, 973.16
unimpeachableness 644.1, 657.3
unimpeded 430.26
unimportance 137.1, 248.1, 998.1
unimportant 137.10, 248.6, 998.16
unimposing 139.9
unimpress 94.5
unimpressed 94.11, 123.3
unimpressibility 94.1
unimpressible 94.9
unimpressibleness 123.1
unimpressionability 855.1, 895.2
unimpressionable 94.9, 855.12, 895.4
unimpressionableness 94.1
unimpressive 998.17
unimpressiveness 998.1
unimproved 414.16
unindagated 340.16
unindebted 624.23, 729.18
unindebtedness 729.7
unindictable 657.8
unindictableness 657.3
unindividual 945.6
unindividualized 945.6
unindulgent 135.7, 980.11
uninebriate 516.3
uninebriated 516.3
uninebriatedness 516.1
uninebriating 516.4
uninebrious 516.3
uninfatuated 979.10
uninfected 79.27
uninflammability 1022.1
uninflammable 1022.9
uninfluenceability 895.2
uninfluenceable 895.4
uninfluenced 324.7, 649.9, 895.5, 979.12
uninfluential 895.3
uninfluentiality 895.1
uninformed 131.9, 930.11
uninfringeable 767.7
uninhabitability 586.2
uninhabitable 586.8

uninhabited 222.15
uninhabited region 233.2
uninhibited 430.24, 665.25, 669.7
uninhibitedness 430.3
uniniquitous 653.7
uniniquitousness 653.2
uninitiated 414.16, 930.11
uninitiated in 414.17
uninjured 1002.8
uninjurious 999.21
uninjuriousness 999.9
uninquiring 982.3
uninquisitive 982.3
uninquisitiveness 982.1
uninsightful 930.12
uninspired 94.11, 987.5
uninspiring 117.7
uninstructed 930.13
unintellectual 922.13, 930.13, 933.4
unintellectualism 930.4
unintellectuality 922.1, 930.4
unintelligence 414.1, 922.1, 923.2, 930.1, 933.1
unintelligent 414.15, 922.13, 930.11
unintelligentsia 930.7
unintelligibility 522.1, 810.1
unintelligible 522.13, 525.12
unintelligible speech 525.4
unintended 365.11, 972.17
unintentional 365.11, 963.14, 972.17
unintentiveness 984.1
unintentness 984.1
uninterested 94.13, 102.7, 118.12, 982.3
uninterestedness 982.1
uninteresting 117.7
uninterestingness 117.1
unintermission 847.2
unintermitted 812.8, 847.5
unintermittedness 812.1
unintermittent 812.8, 847.5
unintermitting 360.8, 812.8, 829.7, 847.5
uninterpretability 522.6
uninterpretable 522.18
uninterrupted 161.12, 221.13, 277.6, 360.8, 803.11, 812.8, 829.7, 847.5
uninterrupted course 812.1, 856.1
uninterrupted extension 158.1
uninterruptedness 812.1, 856.1
uninterruption 812.1, 847.2
unintimidated 492.20
unintoxicated 516.3
unintoxicatedness 516.1
unintoxicating 516.4
unintrepid 491.11
unintrepidness 491.2
uninuclear 872.11
uninured 374.4
uninvented 973.15
uninventive 891.5, 987.5
uninventiveness 987.1
uninvestigated 340.16, 930.16
uninvited 99.11, 324.7, 586.9
uninvited guest 214.3, 585.6
uninviting 64.5, 98.17, 99.7
uninvitingness 98.1
uninvolved 430.21, 467.7, 798.8, 982.3
uninvolvement 982.1
uniocular 872.11
union 169.1, 223.3, 450.2, 455.1, 563.1, 617.1, 775.1, 778.2, 788.1, 800.1, 800.4, 805.1, 899.1
union contract 437.1, 727.3
union contractor 727.4
Union Flag 647.7
unionism 727.1
unionist 727.4
unionization 727.1
unionize 727.9, 805.4
unionized worker 727.4
Union Jack 647.7
Union List of Serials 558.4
union local 727.2
union member 727.4
union officer 727.4
union organizer 727.4
union pipes 711.9
union shop 727.3
unipart 872.11
unipartite 872.11
unipolar 872.11
unique, the 865.3
unique 122.10, 249.15, 337.5, 780.8, 841.11, 848.2, 865.12, 865.13, 870.10, 872.7, 872.9
uniqueness 337.1, 848.1, 865.1, 870.2, 872.1
unirritable 106.10
unirritableness 106.1
unisex 872.11
unisex clothing 5.1
unisexual 872.11
unison (n) 332.5, 455.1, 708.3, 788.1, 836.1 (a) 836.5
unisonance 708.3, 788.1
unisonant 708.49, 788.9
unison interval 709.20
unisonous 708.49, 788.9, 836.5
unit 461.22, 763.3, 872.3, 872.4
Unitarian 675.20
unitariness 802.1
unitary 805.5, 872.7, 872.10
Unit Citation 646.6
unit cost 626.3
unite 169.2, 450.3, 563.14, 770.16, 778.5, 792.7, 800.5, 800.11, 805.3, 872.5, 899.2
united 455.3, 800.13, 805.5, 872.10, 899.4
united action 450.1, 899.1
united front 450.1
United Kingdom 232.4
United Nations 232.1, 612.6, 614.1
United Nations agency 614.2
United Nations peacekeeping force 465.1, 466.5
United States 232.3
United States court 595.2
United States Field Hockey Association 749.4
United States Golf Association 751.1
United States Government 613.2
United States Navy 461.27
United States of America 232.3
United States Ship 180.6
United States Tennis Association 748.1
unite efforts 450.3
unite in 796.3
unite in holy wedlock 563.14
unite in marriage 563.14
unite in sexual intercourse 75.21
unite with 253.4, 450.4, 805.4
uniting (n) 253.1, 872.1 (a) 169.3, 805.7, 872.12, 899.4
unit insignia 647.5
unitive 805.5, 805.7, 872.7
unitize 792.8, 801.6, 802.9, 805.3, 872.5
unitized 805.5
unitizing 805.7
unit of being 1052.2
unit of flux 1025.21
unit of light 1025.21
unit of measurement 1032.1
unit of weight 297.8
unit pricing 630.3
units 18.9
unit trust 737.16
unity 455.1, 778.1, 781.1, 792.1, 792.5, 794.1, 798.1, 872.1, 1045.2
univalence 1060.4
univalent 872.11, 1060.10
univalent chromosome 305.8
universal (n) 932.2, 1053.3 (a) 772.7, 792.9, 794.10, 823.3, 864.14, 869.9, 1073.24
universal accord 332.5
universal agreement 332.5
universal assent 332.5
universal church 687.3
universal concept 932.2
Universal Ego, the 677.3
universal ego 677.7
universal essence 932.2
universality 772.1, 792.5, 794.1, 823.1, 864.1, 945.2
universalization 864.1
universalize 864.9
universal joint 915.6
universal language 523.1
universal law 869.4
universal life force 677.7
universally admitted 928.27
universally recognized 928.27
universal peace 464.1
universal remedy 86.3
universal ruin 395.1
Universal Self, the 677.3
universal self 677.7
universal solvent 1064.4
universal suffrage 609.17
universal symbol 92.30
universal time 832.3
universal tongue, the 708.1
universal truth 974.2
universe 794.1, 978.2, 1073.1
universe of discourse 978.2
university (n) 567.5 (a) 567.13
university hospital 91.21
university library 558.1
university student 572.5
univocal 521.11, 872.11, 970.13
univocal assent 332.5
univocality 970.1
univocity 872.1, 970.1
UNIX 1042.12
unjam 1014.7
unjaundiced 979.12
unjelled 845.8
unjoined 802.20, 804.4, 810.12, 813.4
unjoint 160.5, 802.16
unjointed 160.9
unjointing 160.1
unjoyful 112.21
unjoyfulness 112.2
unjust 638.3, 650.9
unjustifiability 650.5
unjustifiable 650.12
unjustified 640.9
unjust legal disability 650.3
unjustness 650.1
unjust representation 350.1
unkempt 288.6, 497.12, 810.15
unkennel 351.4, 909.15
unkind 144.16, 1000.7
unkindliness 144.1
unkindly 144.16
unkindness 144.1, 1000.1
unkink 277.5
unknit (v) 802.10, 804.3, 806.3 (a) 802.22
unknitting 804.1
unknot 431.7, 798.5
unknottable 799.5
unknotting 431.3, 798.2
unknowability 522.1
unknowable, the 930.6
unknowable 522.13, 930.16
unknowing (n) 930.1 (a) 930.11, 930.12
unknowingness 930.1
unknown, the 839.2, 930.6
unknown 346.11, 528.3, 661.14, 930.16
unknown depths 275.3
unknown quantity 528.1, 930.6
Unknown Soldier 528.1
unlabored 406.12, 533.6
unlace 802.10
unlaced 802.22
unlade 298.6, 909.23
unladen 430.26
unlading 298.3
unladylike 505.6
unlamented 99.9
unlapsed 657.6
unlapsed state 657.1
unlash 182.48, 431.6
unlashing 431.2
unlatch 292.12, 431.6
unlatching 431.2
unlawful 444.7, 638.3, 650.9, 674.6
unlawful entry 214.1, 482.5
unlawful killing 308.2
unlawful love 104.5
unlawfulness 638.1, 650.1, 674.1
unlawful seizure 640.3
unlawful sexual intercourse 75.7, 75.11
unlax 20.7

unlearn 990.6
unlearned 930.13, 934.6
unlearned capacity 934.2
unlearnedness 930.4
unleash 431.6, 802.10, 804.3
unleash destruction 395.10
unleashed 802.22
unleashing 431.2
unleash the hurricane 395.10
unleavened 798.7
unlettered 930.13
unletteredness 930.4
unlevel 288.6
unliable 430.30
unliberal 980.10
unlicensed 444.7, 674.6
unlicentious 664.7
unlicked 263.5, 301.10, 406.12, 497.12
unlicked cub 263.2, 406.5
unlighted 1027.13
unlikable 64.5, 98.17, 99.7, 103.8
unlike 780.7, 787.4, 943.9
unlikelihood 969.1, 972.9
unlikeliness 969.1
unlikely 969.3
unlikeness 780.1, 787.1
unlimber 1046.12
unlimberness 1046.3
unlimited 18.13, 430.27, 669.7, 677.17, 823.3, 960.2
unlimitedness 960.1
unlinked 776.6
unlisted number 347.12
unlit 1027.13
unliterary 523.20, 930.13
unlitigable 598.21
unlivability 586.2
unlivable 586.8
unlive 658.4
unliveliness 117.1
unlively 117.6
unload 120.7, 298.6, 633.6, 734.8, 737.24, 909.23, 1014.9
unloading 120.3, 298.3, 909.6
unloath 324.6, 441.4
unloathness 324.1, 441.1
unlock 292.12, 341.10, 431.6, 940.2
unlocking 341.4, 431.2
unlooked-for, the 131.1
unlooked for 131.10
unlooked-for 830.5, 969.3, 972.15
unloose 431.6, 802.10
unloosen 431.6, 802.10
unloosened 802.22
unloosing 431.2
unloquacious 344.9
unloquaciousness 344.2
unlovable 99.7
unloved 99.10
unloveliness 1015.1
unlovely 1015.6
unloving 94.9, 144.16
unloyal 435.5, 645.20
unloyalty 645.5
unluckiness 133.7, 1011.4
unlucky 133.16, 759.27, 844.6, 1011.14
unlucky day 844.2, 964.2
unlucky hour 844.2
unmade 406.8, 762.10
unmagnanimousness 651.2
unmaimed 1002.8
unmake 395.17
unmaking 395.5
unmalleability 361.4, 1046.3
unmalleable 361.12, 1046.12
unman 16.10, 19.12, 127.15, 128.10, 255.11, 432.9, 612.15
unmanacle 431.6
unmanacling 431.2
unmanageability 361.4, 414.3, 1013.9
unmanageable 361.12, 1013.19
unmaneuverable 1013.19
unmanful 491.10
unmanfulness 491.1
unmangled 1002.8
unmanifested 519.5
unmanliness 77.2, 491.1
unmanly 77.14, 491.10
unmanned 19.19, 127.26, 128.14, 222.15, 432.16, 491.10
unmanned satellite 1075.6
unmannered 505.5
unmannerliness 505.1
unmannerly 505.5
unmanufactured 406.8
unmarked 79.25, 340.15, 1002.8
unmarketable 734.15
unmarking 984.6
unmarred 1002.8
unmarried (n) 565.2 (a) 565.7
unmarried man 565.3
unmarried state 565.1
unmarried woman 77.5, 565.4
unmarry 566.5
unmarveling 123.3
unmask 351.4
unmasking 351.1
unmastered 430.24
unmatchable 249.15, 999.16
unmatched 249.15, 787.4, 999.16, 999.17
unmated 565.7
unmatured 414.17, 845.8
unmeaning 520.6
unmeaningness 520.1
unmeant 972.17
unmeasurability 823.1
unmeasurable 823.3
unmeasured 430.24, 430.27, 669.7, 823.3, 884.10
unmeasured in one's praise 509.18
unmediated apprehension 934.1
unmediated perception 934.1
unmeditated 365.11, 845.8, 972.17
unmeet 650.9, 996.5
unmeetness 650.1, 996.1
unmellowed 301.10, 406.11
unmelodious 61.4
unmelodiousness 61.1
unmelted 114.5, 1023.13
unmentionability 122.4
unmentionable 122.13, 661.12
unmentionables 5.22
unmentioned 519.9
unmerciful 144.25, 146.3
unmercifulness 144.10, 146.1
unmerited 640.9, 650.9
unmeritedness 640.1
unmeriting 640.9
unmet 256.7
unmethodical 810.12, 851.3
unmethodicalness 851.1
unmeticulous 340.13, 945.5
unmeticulousness 340.4, 945.1, 948.1
unmetrical 851.3
unmilitant 464.10
unmilitary 464.10
unminded 340.15
unmindful 25.6, 25.8, 102.7, 144.18, 151.4, 340.11, 930.12, 982.3, 984.6, 990.9
unmindfulness 102.2, 144.3, 340.2, 930.2, 982.1, 984.1, 990.1
unmindful of 930.12
unmingled 798.7
unmirthful 112.21
unmirthfulness 112.2
unmissable 31.7
unmissed 99.9, 340.15
unmistakable 31.7, 348.8, 521.11, 960.2, 970.13
unmistakableness 348.3, 521.2, 970.1
unmistakable sign 957.3
unmistakably 334.8
unmistaken 973.13
unmitigability 125.3
unmitigable 125.15
unmitigated 247.12, 247.14, 671.17, 794.10, 852.10, 960.2
unmix 798.5
unmixed 671.17, 798.7, 1002.6
unmixedness 798.1
unmodest 666.6
unmodestness 666.2
unmodifiability 855.4
unmodifiable 855.17
unmoldable 361.12
unmoldableness 361.4
unmolested 1007.4
unmoneyed 619.7
unmoor 182.18
unmoored 182.61
unmoral 654.11
unmorality 636.4, 654.1
unmotivated 972.16
unmourned 99.9
unmovability 855.3, 895.2
unmovable 855.15, 895.4
unmoved 94.11, 102.6, 123.3, 173.12, 173.13, 361.9, 895.5
unmoving 173.13, 329.6, 855.15
unmuddied 79.25
unmurmuring 332.13, 433.13, 441.4, 867.5
unmusical 49.6, 61.4
unmusicality 61.1
unmusicalness 49.1, 61.1
unmutilated 1002.8
unmuzzle 431.6
unmuzzled 430.24, 430.28
unmuzzling 431.2
unnameable 122.13
unnameableness 122.4
unnamed 528.3
unnatural 144.25, 354.26, 500.15, 533.9, 870.9, 927.5
unnaturalism 870.1
unnaturalness 144.10, 500.1, 533.3, 870.1, 927.1
unnavigable 276.6
unneat 810.15
unnecessariness 993.4
unnecessary 391.10, 768.4, 993.17
unnecessary repetition 849.4
unnecessary surgery 91.19
unnecessity 391.1
unneeded 391.10, 993.17
unnegotiable 967.8
unneighborliness 586.1
unneighborly 586.7
unnerve 16.10, 19.12, 127.15, 128.10
unnerved 16.12, 19.19, 127.26, 128.14
unnerving 16.20, 127.28, 128.15
unnervous 106.10, 129.2
unnervousness 106.1, 129.1
unneutral 650.11
unneutrality 650.3
unnew 842.18
unnodding 339.14, 360.8
unnotable 661.14
unnoted 340.15, 661.14
unnoteworthiness 998.1, 1005.2
unnoteworthy 998.17, 1005.8
unnoticed 32.5, 340.15, 661.14
unnoticing 984.6
unnoting 984.6
unnourishing 992.10
unnumbered 823.3, 884.10
unnumbered bank account 728.14
unnutritious 82.6, 992.10
unoaked 62.9
unobjectionability 107.3
unobjectionable 100.30, 107.12, 600.14, 657.8, 999.20
unobjectionableness 100.13
unobjective 650.11
unobliging 144.18
unobligingness 144.3
unobnoxious 999.21
unobnoxiousness 999.9
unobscure 348.11
unobscured 348.11, 1025.31
unobservance 435.1, 984.1
unobservant 435.5, 984.6
unobserved 32.5, 340.15
unobserving 30.9, 984.6
unobstructed 292.17, 430.26
unobstructed vision 27.1
unobtainability 967.3
unobtainable 967.9
unobtainableness 967.3
unobtrusive 139.9, 345.12, 496.7
unobtrusiveness 139.1, 496.3
unoccupiable 586.8
unoccupied 222.15, 331.18, 402.5, 933.4
unofficial 581.3, 674.6, 971.21
unofficial wife 665.17
unopen 293.9
unopened 293.9
unopinionated 979.10

unopinionatedness 979.5
unopinioned 979.10
unopposed 332.15
unordered 263.4, 810.12
unordinariness 870.2
unordinary 870.10
unorganic 1055.4
unorganized 263.4, 406.8, 810.12, 1055.4
unorganized matter 1055.1
unoriginal 117.9, 336.8, 891.5, 987.5
unoriginality 117.3, 987.1
unornamental 1015.10
unornamentation 499.3
unornamented 499.8
unornate 499.9
unorthodox 688.9, 782.3, 789.9, 868.6, 975.16
unorthodox medicine 90.13
unorthodoxness 688.1
unorthodoxy 688.1, 780.1, 782.1, 789.2, 868.2, 975.1
unostentatious 139.9
unostentatiousness 139.1
unovercomable 967.8
unowed 640.9
unowing 624.23, 640.9
unpacific 458.20
unpack 351.4, 909.23
unpaid 623.10, 625.12
unpaid accounts 628.1
unpaid-for 634.5
unpaid work 724.7
unpainstaking 340.13
unpaired 872.9
unpalatability 64.1, 98.1
unpalatable 64.5, 98.17
unpalatableness 64.1
unpalatalized 524.30
unparagoned 249.15
unparalleled 249.15, 870.14, 999.16
unpardonability 650.5
unpardonable 650.12, 654.16
unpardonable sin 655.2
unparochial 979.8
unparochialism 979.1
unparticular 340.13, 945.5
unparticularness 340.4, 945.1
unpassable 293.13
unpassionate 94.9, 106.10
unpassionateness 94.1, 106.1
unpatient 135.6
unpatientness 135.1
unpayable 625.13, 632.11
un-PC 609.43
unpeaceable 458.20
unpeaceful 458.20, 917.16
unpeacefulness 458.10
unpeered 249.15
unpen 431.6
unpenning 431.2
unpeople 909.16
unpeopled 222.15
unpeopling 909.3
unperceivability 32.1
unperceivable 32.5
unperceived 32.5, 340.15, 346.12, 930.16
unperceiving 30.9, 930.12
unperceptive 25.6, 922.14
unperceptiveness 25.1, 340.2, 922.2
unperfected 795.4, 1003.4
unperfectedness 1003.1
unperfidious 644.19
unperfidiousness 644.6
unperforable 293.13
unperforated 293.10
unperformability 967.2
unperformable 967.8
unperformed 408.3
unperilous 1007.5
unpermissible 444.7
unperson 222.6, 764.2
unpersuadability 895.2, 956.1
unpersuadable 361.13, 895.4, 956.4
unpersuadableness 361.5
unpersuade 379.3
unpersuaded 971.16
unpersuadedness 955.1
unpersuasibility 956.1
unpersuasible 956.4
unpersuasiveness 895.1, 955.3
unperturbability 982.1
unperturbed 94.9, 106.11, 107.8, 173.12
unphilanthropic 144.17
unphilosophical 936.11
unphysical 1053.7
unpierceable 293.13
unpierced 293.10
unpigmented 36.7
unpin 802.10, 804.3
unpinned 802.22
unpitiful 146.3
unpitying 146.3
unplace 160.6
unplaced 160.10
unplacement 160.2
unplagued 107.8
unplain 32.6, 522.15, 971.19
unplainness 32.2, 522.3
unplanned 406.8, 972.17
unpleasant 64.5, 98.17, 99.7, 1000.7
unpleasantness 96.1, 98.1, 456.1, 1000.1
unpleasant smell 71.1
unpleasing 64.5, 98.17, 1015.6
unpleasingness 98.1, 1015.1
unpleasure 96.1, 108.1
unpliability 1046.3
unpliable 895.4, 1046.12
unpliant 1046.12
unplowed 891.4
unplug 292.12
unplumbed 823.3, 930.16
unpoetic 987.5
unpoetical 535.3, 721.5, 987.5
unpoeticalness 535.1, 721.2, 987.1
unpointed 286.3
unpolished 233.7, 288.6, 406.12, 414.16, 497.12, 534.2
unpolishedness 406.4
unpolite 505.4
unpoliteness 505.1
unpolitic 923.10, 996.5
unpolluted 79.25
unpopular 99.9, 108.9, 661.14
unpopulated 222.15
unpositive 979.10
unpossessed of 992.13
unpossessive 652.5
unpossessiveness 652.1
unposted 930.11
unpracticability 967.2
unpractical 986.24
unpracticalness 986.7
unpracticed 374.4, 406.12, 414.17
unpracticed in 414.17
unpracticedness 374.1, 414.2
unpragmatic 967.8
unpraiseworthy 510.24, 661.10
unprecarious 1007.5
unprecedented 122.10, 337.5, 337.6, 848.2, 870.14
unprecipitate 494.8
unprecipitateness 494.1
unprecise 340.13, 975.17
unpreciseness 340.4, 945.1, 975.2
unpredetermined 971.19
unpredictability 131.1, 364.3, 851.1, 854.2, 870.1, 971.1, 972.3, 1006.2
unpredictable 131.10, 364.6, 768.4, 854.7, 969.3, 971.16, 972.15, 1006.11
unpredictableness 131.1, 870.1
unpredictable person 1006.1
unpredicted 131.10, 830.5
unpregnant 891.5
unprehensive 930.12
unprejudiced 979.12
unprejudicedness 979.5
unpremeditated 365.11, 406.8, 845.8, 972.17
unpremeditation 365.4
unprepared 131.9, 301.10, 340.11, 406.8, 414.16, 845.8, 984.8
unprepared for 131.10
unpreparedness 131.1, 340.2, 406.1, 846.1
unprepossessed 979.12
unprepossessing 1015.7
unprepossessingness 98.1, 1015.1
unpressured 324.7
unpresuming 139.9
unpresumptuous 139.9
unpresumptuousness 139.1
unpretended 644.18, 973.15
unpretending 139.9, 228.33, 416.6, 499.7, 644.18, 973.15
unpretendingness 416.2
unpretentious 137.10, 139.9, 416.6, 499.7, 652.5, 798.6
unpretentiousness 137.1, 139.1, 416.2, 499.2, 581.1, 798.1
unprettiness 1015.1
unpretty 1015.6
unprevalence 390.1
unpreventability 963.7
unpreventable 963.15
unprevented 430.26
unprimed 406.8, 414.16
unprincipled 645.16
unprintable 666.9
unprized 99.9, 950.3
unprocessed 406.12
unproclaimed 519.9
unprocurable 967.9
unprocurableness 967.3
unproduced 762.10
unproductive 391.12, 891.4
unproductiveness 391.2, 891.1
unproductivity 891.1
unprofessional 414.16
unprofessionalism 414.2
unprofessionalness 414.2
unproficiency 414.1
unproficient 414.15
unprofitability 391.2, 996.1
unprofitable 391.12, 996.5, 996.6
unprofitableness 391.2, 996.1
unprofound 276.5, 922.20
unprofoundness 922.7
unprofundity 922.7
unprogressive 611.17, 853.8
unprogressiveness 611.1, 853.3
unprohibited 443.16
unprohibitive 443.14
unprolific 891.4
unpromising 133.16, 969.3
unprompted 324.7, 972.17
unpronounced 51.10, 519.9
unpropitious 133.16, 451.8, 844.6
unpropitiousness 133.7, 844.1
unprosecutable 598.21
unprosperous 619.7, 1011.14
unprosperousness 619.1, 1011.4
unprotected 19.18, 1006.14
unprotectedness 19.4, 1006.3
unprovability 971.1
unprovable 958.9, 971.16
unproved 936.12, 958.8, 971.21, 975.16
unproven 958.8
unprovided 406.9, 992.12
unprovidedness 406.1
unprovidential 1011.14
unproviding 406.15
unprovincial 979.8
unprovincialism 979.1
unprovoked 640.9
unprovoked assault 459.1
unpublishable 345.14
unpublished 519.9
unpugnacious 464.10
unpugnaciousness 464.4
unpunctilious 340.13
unpunctiliousness 340.4
unpunctual 340.13, 833.3, 846.16
unpunctuality 340.4, 833.1, 846.1
unpure 80.20
unpureness 80.1
unpurposed 972.17
unquailing 492.20
unqualification 406.1, 992.1
unqualified 19.14, 247.12, 406.9, 414.19, 430.27, 789.7, 794.10, 960.2, 973.15, 992.9, 1002.7
unqualifiedness 406.1, 960.1
unqualified truth, the 973.3
unquantifiable 884.10
unquelled 411.8, 430.29, 671.17
unquenchable 100.27, 855.18
unquenched 671.17, 1019.27

unquestionability 348.3, 970.3
unquestionable 247.12, 767.7, 953.24, 970.15, 973.13
unquestioned 953.23, 970.16
unquestioning 960.2
unquestioning belief 954.1
unquiet (n) 330.4 (a) 96.20, 105.27, 135.6, 330.20, 917.16
unquietness 126.1, 135.1
unquivering 129.2
unquotable 345.14
unravel 192.10, 341.10, 431.7, 798.5, 802.9, 804.3, 940.2
unraveled 804.4
unraveling 431.3, 804.1, 940.1
unravelment 192.1
unreachable 967.9
unreachableness 967.3
unreached 911.5
unread 930.13
unreadability 522.4
unreadable 522.19
unreadiness 131.1, 340.2, 406.1, 414.2, 846.1
unready 131.9, 340.11, 406.8, 844.6, 846.16, 984.8
unreal 354.26, 762.9, 764.6, 976.9, 986.19
unreal hope 124.4
unrealism 986.7
unrealistic 762.9, 986.19, 986.24
unreality 762.1, 967.1, 976.2, 986.7, 1053.1
unrealizability 967.2
unrealizable 967.8
unrealized 32.5, 408.3
unrealizing 930.12
unrealness 354.2
unreason 923.2
unreasonable 364.5, 632.12, 650.12, 923.10, 926.32, 936.11, 993.16
unreasonableness 632.4, 923.2, 936.2, 993.1
unreasoning 93.19, 365.10, 922.13, 933.4
unreasoning impulse 934.2
unreasoningness 93.9
unrecalled 990.8
unrecanting 114.5
unreceived 688.9
unreceptive 586.7, 895.4
unreceptiveness 586.1, 895.2
unreckonability 823.1
unreckonable 823.3, 884.10, 971.16
unreclaimable 388.5
unrecognition 990.2
unrecognizable 32.6, 346.13
unrecognized 151.5, 391.10
unrecognizing 151.4
unrecollectable 990.10
unrecollected 990.8
unrecompensed 625.12
unreconstructed 361.12, 430.29, 611.17, 853.8
unrecorded 519.9
unredeemable 654.18
unredeemed 686.3, 695.18
unredeemedness 695.4
unreduced 247.14, 792.11
unreel 861.7
unrefined 233.7, 288.6, 294.6, 406.12, 497.12, 505.6, 534.2, 930.13
unrefined mineral 1058.2
unrefinement 233.3, 294.2, 406.4, 497.3, 534.1
unreflecting 365.10, 923.10
unreflective 923.10
unrefreshed 21.7
unrefusing 441.4
unrefutability 970.3
unrefutable 957.21, 970.15
unrefuted 957.21, 973.13
unregarded 156.9, 340.14, 340.15
unregeneracy 695.4
unregenerate 361.8, 654.18, 686.3, 695.18
unregenerateness 361.1, 686.1
unregistered bank account 728.14
unregretful 114.4
unregretfulness 114.1
unregretted 99.9, 114.6
unregretting 114.4
unregular 851.3
unregulated 443.16, 674.6
unrehearsed 365.12
unreined 418.5, 430.24
unrelatable 776.6
unrelated 776.6, 787.6
unrelatedness 776.1
unrelational 776.6
unrelaxed 128.13, 1046.11
unrelaxing 360.8
unrelenting 360.8, 361.9, 425.7, 538.12, 847.5
unrelenting attention 983.4
unrelentingness 361.2, 425.2
unreliability 364.3, 645.4, 854.2, 955.3, 971.6, 1006.2
unreliable 364.6, 645.19, 854.7, 955.11, 971.20, 975.19, 1006.11
unrelievability 125.3
unrelievable 125.15
unrelieved 222.14, 247.12, 781.6, 812.8
unrelievedness 118.2, 201.1, 812.1
unreligious 695.15
unreligiousness 695.1
unreluctance 324.1, 441.1
unreluctant 324.6, 441.4
unremarkable 1005.8
unremarkableness 1005.2
unremarked 340.15, 661.14
unremarking 984.6
unrememberable 990.10
unremembered 990.8
unremembering 990.9
unremitting 330.22, 360.8, 812.8, 829.7, 847.5, 855.17, 856.7
unremittingness 360.1, 856.1
unremorseful 114.4, 146.3
unremorsefulness 114.1, 146.1
unremunerated 625.12
unremunerative 391.12
unrenowned 661.14
unrepeatable 666.9
unrepeatable expressions 513.3
unrepeated 872.9
unrepentance 114.2
unrepentant 114.5
unrepented 114.6
unrepenting 114.5
unrepining 107.7, 114.4
unreplenished 992.12
unrepressed 343.10, 430.24
unrepression 343.3
unreproachful 509.18
unreproduced 337.6
unrequested 324.7
unrequired 324.7, 391.10
unrequited 151.5, 625.12
unresemblance 787.1
unresemblant 787.4
unresembling 787.4
unresented 148.7
unresentful 148.6
unresentfulness 148.1
unreserve 343.3, 430.3, 644.4
unreserved 343.10, 416.5, 430.24, 644.17, 794.10, 960.2
unreservedness 343.3, 960.1
unresistant 433.12
unresisting 134.10, 433.12
unresolved 256.7, 362.9
unrespectability 661.2
unrespectable 661.10
unrespected 156.9
unresponding 94.9
unresponsive 94.9, 144.25, 895.4
unresponsiveness 94.1, 144.10, 895.2
unrest 105.5, 172.1, 917.1
unrestful 105.27
unrestorable 855.17
unrestorableness 855.4
unrestored 21.7
unrestrained 93.18, 343.10, 364.5, 418.5, 426.4, 430.24, 644.17, 665.24, 669.7, 854.7, 993.16
unrestrainedness 993.1
unrestraint 343.3, 418.1, 418.2, 426.1, 430.3, 644.4, 665.2, 669.1
unrestricted 247.14, 292.17, 343.10, 430.27, 794.10, 960.2
unrestrictedness 960.1
unrestriction 343.3
unrestrictive 430.25
unretained 990.8
unretarded 247.14
unreticence 343.3
unreticent 343.10
unreturnable 855.17
unreturnableness 855.4
unrevealable 345.11
unrevealed 32.5, 345.11, 346.12, 930.16
unrevealing 346.15
unrevenged 148.7
unrevengeful 148.6
unrevengefulness 148.1
unrevered 156.9
unrewarded 151.5, 625.12
unrewarding 391.12, 996.6
unrhymed poetry 720.9
unrhythmical 851.3
unriddle 940.2
unriddling 940.1
unrig 802.15
unrighteous, the 660.11
unrighteous 638.3, 654.12, 695.17
unrighteousness 638.1, 654.1, 695.3
unrightful 650.9
unrigorous 340.10, 340.13, 936.12, 975.17
unrigorousness 340.1, 340.4, 975.2
unripe 67.5, 301.10, 406.11, 414.17, 844.6, 845.8, 930.11
unripe acceptation 954.1
unripened 406.11
unripeness 67.1, 301.3, 406.4, 414.2, 844.1, 930.1
unrisky 1007.5
unrivaled 249.15
unrobed 6.13
unroll 292.12, 351.4, 861.7
unrolling 861.2
unromantic 721.5, 973.15, 987.6
unromanticalness 987.2
unromanticism 721.2
unromanticized 987.5
unroot 192.10
unrooting 192.1
unrough 287.10
unroughened 287.10
unrounded 524.30
unrueful 114.4
unruefulness 114.1
unruffled 94.11, 106.11, 173.12, 287.10, 781.5
unruffledness 106.2, 781.1
unruing 146.3
unruliness 327.2, 361.4, 418.2, 430.3, 671.3
unruly 327.10, 361.12, 418.6, 430.24, 671.19
unrumpled 287.10
unsacred 686.3, 694.6
unsacredness 686.1
unsaddle 160.6, 447.4
unsaddling 160.2, 298.3
unsafe 1006.11
unsafeness 1006.2
unsaid 51.11, 519.9
unsaintliness 654.1, 695.3
unsaintly 654.12, 695.17
unsalable 734.15
unsalutariness 82.1
unsalutary 82.5
unsalvability 125.3
unsalvable 125.15
unsalvageability 125.3
unsalvageable 125.15
unsameness 787.1
unsanctified 686.3
unsanctified love 104.5
unsanctioned 444.7
unsanctioned behavior 322.1
unsanctitude 686.1
unsanctity 686.1, 694.1
unsane 926.26
unsaneness 926.1
unsanitary 82.5
unsated 100.27
unsatisfaction 96.1, 108.1
unsatisfactoriness 108.2, 992.1

unsatisfactory 108.9, 132.6, 992.9
unsatisfied 75.27, 96.20, 100.27, 108.7
unsatisfying 108.9, 132.6, 992.9
unsaturated fat 7.7, 1056.1
unsaved 686.3
unsavoriness 64.1, 65.1, 98.1, 645.1, 661.2
unsavory 64.5, 65.2, 98.17, 645.16, 661.10
unsavory reputation 661.1
unsay 363.8
unsaying 363.3
unscanned 340.16
unscared 492.19
unscarred 1002.8
unscathed 1002.8, 1007.4
unscented 72.5
unscholarliness 930.4
unscholarly 930.13
unscholastic 930.13
unschooled 414.16, 930.13
unschooledness 414.1, 930.4
unscientific 936.11
unscientificness 936.2
unscoured 80.20
unscramble 798.5, 940.2, 1014.9
unscrambling 341.3, 798.2, 940.1, 1014.6
unscratched 1002.8
unscreen 351.4
unscreened 348.11, 1006.14
unscrew 802.10
unscrewed 802.22
unscriptural 688.9
un-Scripturality 688.1
unscrubbed 80.20
unscrupulous 340.13, 645.16
unscrupulousness 340.4, 645.1
unseal 292.12
unsearchable 522.13
unsearchableness 522.1
unsearched 340.16
unseasonable 789.7, 833.3, 844.6, 996.5
unseasonableness 844.1, 996.1
unseasoned 65.2, 301.10, 374.4, 406.11, 414.17
unseat 160.6, 447.4, 802.16
unseating 160.2, 447.2
unseconded 872.8
unsecretive 343.10
unsecretiveness 343.3
unsecurable 967.9
unsecurableness 967.3
unseduceability 956.2
unseduceable 956.5
unseeable 32.5, 258.14
unseeableness 32.1
unseeing, the 30.4
unseeing 30.9, 923.10, 930.12
unseeingness 30.1
unseemliness 497.1, 534.1, 638.1, 666.1, 996.1
unseemly 497.10, 534.2, 638.3, 666.5, 789.7, 996.5
unseen, the 32.1
unseen 32.5, 340.15, 346.12
unseizability 522.1
unseizable 522.13
unselective 945.5
unselectiveness 945.1
unselfassured 971.23
unself-confident 139.10
unselfconfident 971.23
unselfish 485.4, 649.9, 652.5
unselfishness 485.1, 649.3, 652.1
unself-reliant 139.10
unselfreliant 971.23
unsensible 923.10
unsensibleness 923.2
unsentimental 987.6
unsentimentality 987.2
unseparated 800.13
unsepulcher 192.11
unserious 354.32
unseriousness 354.5
unserviceability 391.1
unserviceable 391.14
unsettle 105.14, 160.6, 810.9, 811.4, 917.10, 985.7
unsettled 105.23, 105.27, 160.10, 330.20, 362.9, 810.13, 851.3, 854.7, 917.16, 926.26, 958.8, 971.18, 985.12
unsettledness 362.1, 854.2
unsettlement 362.1, 985.3
unsettling (n) 160.2 (a) 105.30
unsevere 426.5
unsevered 792.11
unsevereness 426.2
unsex 255.11
unsexed 19.19, 75.29
unsexual 75.29
unshackle 431.6
unshackled 430.28, 431.10
unshackling 431.2
unshaded 348.11
unshakable 855.12
unshakable nerves 855.1
unshakableness 359.2, 855.1
unshakeable 326.3
unshaken 15.21, 94.11, 129.2, 359.12
unshaken confidence 953.5
unshakiness 129.1
unshaky 129.2
unshape 263.3
unshaped 263.5
unshapeliness 1015.1
unshapely 1015.8
unshapen 263.5
unsharp 286.3
unsharpened 286.3
unsharpness 286.1
unshatterable 1049.5
unshattered 1002.8
unshaved 3.25
unshaven 3.25
unsheathe 6.7, 292.12, 351.4
unsheathed 6.12
unsheathe one's weapon 458.15
unsheltered 1006.14
unshielded 1006.14
unshifting 853.7
unship 909.23
unshod 6.15
unshorn 3.24, 792.11
unshown 958.8
unshrinking 129.2, 324.6, 343.10, 359.13, 492.20
unshrinkingness 492.2
unshroud 351.4
unshut 292.12
unshy 492.19
unshyness 492.2
unsick 83.10
unsickly 83.10
unsifted 340.16
unsighted 30.9
unsightliness 1015.1
unsightly 810.15, 1015.6
unsigned 1017.23
unsignificancy 520.1
unsignificant 520.6
unsilent 343.10
unsimilar 787.4
unsimilarity 787.1
unsimulated 973.15
unsincere 645.18
unsincereness 645.3
unsinew 16.10
unsinful 653.7
unsinfulness 653.2
unskeptical 954.8
unskepticalness 954.1
unskilled 414.16
unskilled in 414.17
unskilled labor 725.4
unskilled laborer 726.2
unskilled worker 577.3
unskillful 250.7, 414.15, 1000.7
unskillfulness 250.3, 414.1, 1000.1
unslakeable 100.27
unslaked 100.27
unsleeping 23.7, 330.22, 339.14, 360.8
unsmiling 111.3, 112.21
unsmirched 79.25
unsmooth 288.6
unsmoothness 288.1
unsmudged 79.25
unsnap 802.10
unsnapped 802.22
unsnarl 277.5, 431.7, 798.5, 808.8, 1014.9
unsnarling 431.3, 798.2, 1014.6
unsociability 344.1, 583.1, 589.1, 590.1
unsociable 344.8, 583.5, 589.9, 590.3
unsociableness 583.1
unsocial 583.5
unsoftened 114.5, 671.17
unsoiled 79.25, 657.7, 664.4
unsoiledness 664.1
unsold 734.15
unsoldierlike 491.11
unsoldierly 491.11
unsolicited 324.7, 340.14
unsolicitous 25.6, 102.7, 340.11, 505.6
unsolicitousness 25.1, 102.2, 340.2, 505.1
unsolicitude 340.2, 505.1
unsolid 16.15, 764.5, 971.20
unsolidity 764.1, 971.6, 1047.1
unsolvable 522.18, 799.5
unsolved 346.12
unsophisticate 416.3
unsophisticated 406.12, 416.5, 499.8, 798.7, 954.9
unsophisticatedness 416.1
unsophistication 416.1, 499.3, 798.1, 954.2
unsorriness 114.1
unsorrowful 114.4
unsorrowing 114.4
unsorry 114.4
unsorted 810.12
unsorted mess 406.5
unsought 324.7
unsound 16.15, 85.54, 85.55, 688.9, 729.19, 764.7, 923.10, 926.26, 936.12, 971.20, 1003.4, 1006.11
unsounded 51.10, 275.12
unsound mind 926.1
unsoundness 16.3, 85.3, 688.1, 923.2, 926.1, 936.2, 971.6, 1003.1, 1006.2
unsoundness of mind 926.1
unsown 406.14, 891.4
unsparing 144.24, 330.22, 425.6, 485.4
unsparingness 330.6
unsparing of self 652.5
unspeak 363.8
unspeakability 122.4, 685.1
unspeakable, the 685.2
unspeakable 98.19, 122.13, 156.8, 654.16, 661.12, 685.7, 870.14
unspeakableness 98.2
unspecific 975.17
unspecificity 975.2
unspecified 528.3, 864.11, 971.19
unspecious 973.15
unspeciousness 973.7
unspectacular 1005.8
unspell 690.12, 977.2
unspelled 977.5
unspeller 689.11, 690.7
unspelling 977.1
unspent 390.12
unspied 346.12
unspin 940.2
unspinning 940.1
unspiritual 663.6, 695.16, 1052.10
unspirituality 663.2, 695.2
unspoiled 247.12, 397.13, 416.6, 792.10, 798.7, 1002.8
unspoiledness 233.3, 416.2, 798.1
unspoken 51.11, 345.11, 519.9
unspoken accusation 599.1
unspoken agreement 436.2
unspoken consent 441.1
unsporting 650.10
unsportsmanlike 650.10
unsportsmanlikeness 650.2
unsportsmanliness 650.2
unsportsmanly 650.10
unspotted 79.25, 644.13, 657.7, 664.4, 1002.6
unspottedness 79.1, 644.1, 653.2, 664.1
unspurious 973.15
unspuriousness 973.7
unstable 16.15, 782.3, 791.5, 828.7, 854.7, 971.20, 1006.11
unstable as water 854.7
unstableness 854.2

unstaffed 222.15
unstaid 854.7
unstained 79.25, 644.13, 664.4
unstainedness 664.1
unstatutory 674.6
unsteadfast 645.20, 854.7, 971.20
unsteadfastness 645.5, 854.2, 971.6
unsteadiness 16.3, 782.1, 851.1, 854.2, 971.6, 1006.2
unsteady 16.16, 782.3, 791.5, 851.3, 854.7, 917.18, 971.20, 1006.11
unsteady market 737.1
unsteel 145.4, 145.5, 1047.6
unstern 426.5
unsternness 426.2
unstick 802.10, 804.3
unstinted 485.4
unstintedness 794.1
unstinting 485.4
unstirred 94.11, 106.11
unstirring 173.12, 173.16
unstop 292.12
unstoppable 963.15
unstopped 292.17, 812.8, 847.5
unstopper one's ears 983.7
unstopping 292.1
unstraightforward 645.16
unstraightforwardness 645.1
unstrain 670.9
unstrained 129.2
unstrap 431.6, 802.10
unstrapping 431.2
unstrengthen 16.10
unstressed 52.16, 121.12, 524.30
unstrict 426.5
unstrictness 426.2, 430.3
unstring 16.10, 61.3, 127.15, 128.10, 670.9
unstruck 94.11
unstructured 263.4, 263.5, 538.11
unstructuredness 538.1
unstrung 16.12, 127.26, 128.14, 1047.10
unstuck 802.22
unstudied 340.16, 365.11, 406.8, 523.20, 581.3
unstudiedness 365.4
unstudious 930.13
unstudiousness 930.4
unsturdiness 16.3
unsturdy 16.15
unsubduable 15.19
unsubdued 411.8, 430.24, 430.29, 671.17
unsubject 430.29, 430.30
unsubmissive 327.9, 361.12, 453.5, 868.5
unsubmissiveness 327.1, 361.4
unsubstanced 764.5
unsubstantial 16.14, 16.15, 32.5, 299.4, 762.9, 764.5, 936.12, 971.20, 976.9, 1053.7
unsubstantiality 16.2, 16.3, 32.1, 299.1, 764.1, 885.1, 971.6, 976.2, 988.1, 1053.1, 1053.2
unsubstantialization 689.19
unsubstantialize 689.20, 1053.6
unsubstantialness 764.1, 1053.1
unsubstantiatable 958.9
unsubstantiated 958.8
unsubtle 945.5
unsuccess 410.1
unsuccessful 410.18
unsuccessfulness 410.1
unsuccessive 813.4
unsufficing 992.9
unsuggestibility 895.2
unsuggestible 895.4
unsuitability 108.2, 391.1, 406.1, 497.1, 638.1, 789.3, 844.1, 992.1, 996.1
unsuitable 108.10, 391.14, 497.10, 638.3, 789.7, 844.6, 996.5
unsuitableness 406.1, 497.1, 638.1
unsuitable time 844.2
unsuited 406.9, 789.7
unsuitedness 406.1
unsullied 79.25, 406.13, 644.13, 657.7, 664.4
unsulliedness 664.1
unsung 99.9, 519.9, 661.14
unsung hero 492.7
unsupplied 992.12
unsupportable 936.13, 958.9
unsupported 872.8, 936.13, 958.8
unsupported by evidence 958.8
unsuppressed 343.10, 430.24
unsuppression 343.3
unsure 645.19, 930.11, 971.16, 971.20, 971.23, 1006.11
unsureness 971.1, 971.6, 1006.2
unsure of oneself 139.10, 971.23
unsurmountable 15.19, 967.8
unsurpassable 249.15
unsurpassed 249.15, 999.16
unsurpassedness 999.2
unsurprise 123.1
unsurprised 123.3, 130.11
unsurprisedness 123.1
unsusceptibility 94.1, 855.1, 895.2
unsusceptible 94.9, 855.12, 895.4
unsuspected 930.16, 953.23
unsuspecting 131.9, 930.12, 953.22, 954.8, 1006.14
unsuspectingness 954.1
unsuspicious 416.5, 953.22, 954.8
unsuspiciousness 416.1, 954.1
unsustainable 936.13, 958.9
unsustained 936.12, 936.13, 958.8
unswayable 895.4
unswayableness 895.2
unswayed 649.9, 895.5, 979.12
unswear 363.8
unsweet 67.5
unsweetened 67.5
unsweetness 67.1
unswept 80.20
unswerving 161.12, 277.6, 359.12, 360.8, 644.20
unswerving attention 360.1
unswervingness 277.1
unsymmetric 265.10
unsymmetrical 265.10, 810.12
unsymmetry 265.1, 810.1
unsympathetic 25.6, 94.9, 144.16, 146.3, 451.8
unsympatheticness 94.1, 144.1, 146.1
unsympathizing 144.16, 146.3
unsynchronized 456.15
unsynthetic 973.15
unsyntheticness 973.7
unsystematic 782.3, 810.12, 851.3
unsystematicness 851.1
untaciturn 343.10
untaciturnity 343.3
untactful 340.11, 945.5
untactfulness 945.1
untainted 79.25, 397.13, 416.6, 657.7, 664.4, 1002.6
untaintedness 664.1
untaken 222.15
untalented 19.14, 414.16, 922.13
untalkative 344.9
untalkativeness 344.2
untalked-of 519.9
untamable 361.12
untamableness 361.4
untamed 327.10, 430.29, 497.12, 671.21
untangle 431.7, 798.5, 940.2
untangling 431.3, 940.1
untapped 390.12
untarnished 79.25, 644.13, 664.4
untarnishedness 664.1
untasteful 64.5, 98.17, 497.10
untastefulness 64.1, 497.1
untasty 64.5
untaught 414.16, 930.13
untaxed 634.5
untaxing 298.3
unteachability 922.3
unteachable 922.15
untellable 345.11
untempered 671.17
untenability 108.2, 955.3
untenable 19.18, 108.10, 936.13
untenableness 936.2, 955.3
untenacious 804.4
untenacity 804.1
untenantable 586.8
untenanted 222.15
untended 222.15, 340.14
unterrified 492.19
Unterseeboot 180.9
untested 958.8
untether 431.6
untethering 431.2
unthanked 151.5
unthankful 151.4
unthankfulness 151.1
unthanking 151.4
unthawed 1023.13
unthinkability 967.1
unthinkable 955.10, 967.7
unthinking 144.18, 340.11, 365.10, 922.13, 923.10, 933.4, 954.8, 963.14, 972.17
unthinkingness 340.2
unthinking response 903.1, 934.2
unthorough 1003.4
unthoughtful 144.18, 365.10, 923.10
unthoughtfulness 144.3, 365.3, 923.2
unthought-of 340.15, 870.10, 933.5, 972.17
unthread 798.5
unthreatened 1007.4
unthriftiness 406.2
unthrifty 406.15, 669.7
unthrone 447.4
untidiness 80.1, 263.1, 340.3, 810.6
untidy 80.22, 340.12, 810.15
untie 431.6, 802.10
untied 182.61, 430.28, 431.10, 802.22
untie one's hands 431.6
untie the knot 566.5
untie the purse strings 485.3
untilled 406.14, 891.4
untilled ground 406.5
untimeliness 844.1, 845.2, 846.1, 996.1
untimely 789.7, 844.6, 845.8, 846.16, 996.5
untimely end 307.4
untimid 492.19
untimidness 492.2
untimorous 492.19
untimorousness 492.2
untinged 798.7
untipsy 516.3
untired 9.5
untiring 360.8, 1049.4
untogether 810.12
untogetherness 810.1
untold 345.11, 519.9, 823.3, 884.10, 971.18
untolerating 980.11
untormented 107.8
untorn 1002.8
untouchability 94.1, 791.1
untouchable (n) 586.4 (a) 94.9, 99.9, 261.9, 444.7, 685.7
untouched 94.11, 114.5, 390.12, 406.13, 792.10, 798.7, 841.7, 930.16, 1002.8, 1007.4
untouched by evil 657.6
untouchedness 794.1
untouristed 222.15, 370.8
untoward 133.16, 844.6, 1000.7, 1011.13
untraced 346.12
untracked 346.12
untractable 1046.12
untrained 374.4, 406.12, 414.16
untrainedness 414.1
untrammeled 418.5, 426.4, 430.26, 665.25
untraveled 173.15, 584.8
untreacherous 644.19
untreacherousness 644.6
untreatable 964.9
untreated 406.12
untreated mineral 1058.2
untremulous 129.2
untremulousness 129.1
untried 414.17, 841.7, 958.8
untrimmed 499.8, 644.18
untrodden 293.10, 390.12, 841.7

untroubled 106.11, 107.8, 173.12, 464.9
untroublesome 433.14, 1014.15
untroublesomeness 433.4, 1014.2
untrue 354.25, 354.34, 435.5, 645.20, 975.16
untrueness 354.1, 645.5, 975.1
untruism 354.11
untruss 431.6
untrussing 431.2
untrust 153.2
untrustful 955.9
untrustiness 645.4
untrusting 955.9
untrustworthiness 645.4, 971.6, 1006.2
untrustworthy 645.19, 971.20, 1006.11
untrusty 645.19
untruth 354.1, 354.11, 975.1
untruthful 354.34, 645.18
untruthfulness 354.8, 645.1, 645.3, 975.1
untunable 61.4
untune 61.3, 810.8
untuned 61.4
untuneful 61.4
untunefulness 61.1
unturned 277.6
untutored 414.16, 930.13
untwine 798.5
untwist 798.5, 940.2
untwisting 940.1
untying 431.2
ununderstandability 522.1
ununderstandable 522.13
ununiform 288.6, 782.3, 810.12
ununiformity 288.1, 810.1
unusability 391.1
unusable 391.14
unused 256.7, 374.4, 390.12, 841.7, 993.18
unusedness 374.1
unused to 374.4, 414.17
unusual 841.11, 848.2, 868.5, 870.10
unusualness 841.1, 848.1, 851.1, 870.2
unutilized 256.7, 390.12
unutterability 122.4, 685.1
unutterable, the 685.2
unutterable 122.13, 345.11, 685.7
unutterable sin 655.2
unuttered 51.11, 345.11, 519.9
unvaliant 491.11
unvaliantness 491.2
unvalidated 958.8, 971.21
unvalorous 491.11
unvalorousness 491.2
unvalued 99.9, 950.3
unvanquished 411.8, 430.29
unvariable 855.17
unvariableness 850.1
unvariation 118.1, 781.2
unvaried 781.5, 853.7
unvarnished 416.6, 499.8, 535.3, 644.18, 973.15
unvarnished truth, the 973.3
unvarying 118.9, 781.5, 847.5, 853.7, 855.17
unveering 161.12
unveil 6.5, 292.12, 351.4
unveiled 6.12
unveiling 348.2, 351.1, 818.5
unvenerated 156.9
unvented 173.16, 293.9
unventilated 173.16, 293.9
unveracious 354.34
unveraciousness 354.8
unveracity 354.8
unveridical 354.34
unverifiability 971.1
unverifiable 958.9, 971.16
unverified 951.13, 958.8, 971.21
unverified report 552.6
unverified supposition 951.4
unversed 414.17, 930.11
unversed in 414.17
unversified 721.4
unvexed 107.8
unviable 307.32, 967.8
unviewed 32.5
unvigilant 984.8
unvirginal 665.23
unvirtuous 654.12, 665.23
unvirtuousness 654.1, 665.1
unvisited 584.8
unvocalized 51.11
unvoiced 51.10, 519.9
unwaivable 960.2
unwakened 22.22
unwanted 99.11, 586.9
unwanted person 660.1
unwanton 664.7
unwariness 416.1, 493.1, 984.1
unwarmed 1023.13
unwarned 131.9, 1006.14
unwarrantability 650.5
unwarrantable 650.12, 674.6
unwarranted 632.12, 640.9, 674.6, 936.13, 971.21
unwarranted demand 643.1
unwarrantedness 640.1
unwary 340.10, 416.5, 493.7, 984.8
unwashed 80.20
unwasteful 635.6
unwastefulness 635.1
unwatched 340.14, 1006.14
unwatchful 340.10, 984.8
unwatchfulness 984.1
unwatered 1066.7
unwavering 129.2, 360.8, 855.12, 970.21
unwaveringness 781.1
unweakened 15.21
unweakening 15.21
unweaned 374.4
unwearied 9.5, 330.22, 360.8
unwearying 360.8
unweave 798.5, 940.2
unweaving 940.1
unwed 565.7
unwedded 565.7
unwedded to an opinion 979.10
unwed state 565.1
unweeded 310.43
unweighability 298.5
unweighable 298.18
unweighableness 298.5
unweighed 340.16
unweight 120.7
unweighting 120.3
unwelcome 98.17, 99.11, 586.9
unwelcome guest 214.3
unwell 85.56
unwept 99.9
unwhetted 286.3
unwhisperable 122.13, 345.11
unwholesome 82.5, 85.55
unwholesome joy 144.6
unwholesomeness 82.1, 85.3, 1000.1
unwicked 653.7
unwickedness 653.2
unwieldiness 257.9, 297.2, 414.3, 534.1, 996.3, 1013.9
unwieldy 257.19, 297.17, 414.20, 534.3, 996.7, 1013.19
unwilled 365.11, 963.14
unwilledness 963.5
unwilling 325.5, 379.5, 442.6, 963.14
unwillingness 325.1, 442.1
unwilling to accept 956.4
unwilling to forgive and forget 507.7
unwilling to let bygones be bygones 507.7
unwincing 492.20
unwind 20.7, 106.7, 798.5, 861.7
unwinding 331.2, 861.2
unwinking 339.14, 360.8
unwinking eye 339.4
unwiped 80.20
unwisdom 922.1, 923.2
unwise 922.13, 923.10, 996.5
unwiseness 922.1, 923.2, 996.1
unwise step 923.4
unwish 445.2
unwished 99.11
unwithered 15.21, 1002.8
unwitnessed 32.5
unwitting 930.12, 963.14, 972.17
unwitting disclosure 351.2
unwittingness 930.2
unwitty 117.7
unwomanly 76.14
unwon 412.13
unwondering 123.3
unwont 374.4
unwonted 374.4, 870.10
unwontedness 374.1, 870.2
unworkability 967.2
unworkable 391.14, 967.8, 996.5
unworked 406.12, 406.14
unworldliness 692.2, 870.7, 1053.1
unworldly 681.12, 692.9, 870.15, 1053.7
unworn 15.21, 1002.8
unworried 107.8
unworthiness 998.2
unworthy (n) 660.1 (a) 640.9, 654.16, 998.22
unworthy of belief 955.10
unworthy of consideration 998.22
unworthy of one 661.11
unworthy of regard 998.22
unworthy of serious consideration 998.19
unworthy person 660.1
unwrap 6.6, 292.12, 351.4
unwrapping 351.1
unwrinkled 287.10
unwritten 519.9, 524.29, 842.12
unwritten agreement 436.2
unwritten constitution 673.6
unwritten law 373.1, 673.5
unwrought 406.12
unyielding 15.19, 146.3, 359.12, 361.9, 425.7, 453.5, 763.7, 855.15, 895.4, 963.15, 1046.12
unyieldingness 146.1, 359.2, 361.2, 425.2, 855.3, 963.7, 1046.3
unyoke 431.6, 802.8
unyoking 431.2
unzealous 325.6
unzip 802.10
unzipped 802.22
up (n) 251.1 (v) 193.8, 251.4, 259.4, 446.2, 912.5 (a) 23.8, 109.11, 124.11
up against 215.5, 453.5
up against it 1006.13, 1013.26
up-anchor 182.18, 188.15
up and about 83.10
up-and-coming 330.23
up-and-comingness 330.7
up and die 307.18
up and do 328.6
up-and-down 200.11, 200.12, 916.19
up-and-downness 200.1
up and go 188.7
up and going 889.11
up-and-up 644.14
Upanishad 683.8
uparching 193.14
up a stump 1013.25
up a tree 1011.14, 1013.22, 1013.25
upbear 298.8, 449.12, 901.21
upbeat (n) 392.1, 709.26, 850.3 (a) 124.11
upbend (n) 193.2 (v) 193.13
upborne 901.24
upbraid 510.17
upbraiding 510.5
upbringing 568.3
upbuoy 912.5
upbuoying 912.1
up card 759.10
upcast (n) 193.2, 912.1 (v) 193.13, 912.5 (a) 193.15, 912.9
upcharge 729.16
upchuck 99.4, 909.27
upclimb (n) 193.1, 204.6 (v) 193.11
upclimber 193.6
upcoming (n) 193.1 (a) 167.4, 193.14, 840.3
upcountry (n) 207.3, 233.2 (a) 207.7, 233.7, 233.9, 261.9, 584.8
upcurve (n) 193.2 (v) 193.13
upcurving 279.9
upcycle 387.10
update (n) 552.5 (v) 832.13, 841.6
updating 841.3
updive 366.5
updo 1016.14

updraft 193.1, 317.4, 318.1
upend 200.9, 395.20
upended 200.11
upflung 912.9
up for 405.18
up for grabs 971.18
up-front 216.10, 535.3, 644.17, 818.17
upgo (n) 193.1, 204.6 (v) 193.8
upgoing (n) 193.1 (a) 193.14
upgrade (n) 193.1, 204.6, 392.1 (v) 392.9, 396.17, 446.2, 912.7 (a) 193.14, 204.17
upgraded 392.13
upgrading 446.1
upgrow 193.8, 272.12
upgrowth 14.1, 193.1, 259.3
upheaval 105.9, 395.3, 671.5, 852.2, 912.1
upheave 193.8, 200.8, 200.9, 395.10, 912.5
upheaving 671.23
upheld 901.24
uphelm 182.24
uphill (n) 193.1, 204.6 (a) 193.14, 204.17, 725.18, 1013.17
uphillward 193.14
uphill work 725.5, 1013.2
uphoist 912.5
uphold 298.8, 397.8, 449.12, 509.9, 600.10, 901.21, 912.5, 957.11
upholder 332.7, 460.7, 616.9, 901.2
upholding (n) 901.1 (a) 901.23
upholster 295.28
upholstered 295.34
upholstering 295.1
upholstery 295.1
uphorse 194.7
up in arms 405.16, 453.5, 456.16
up in the air 971.18
up in the world 1010.12
up in years 303.16
upkeep (n) 397.1, 449.3, 901.1 (v) 449.12, 901.21
upland (n) 236.1, 237.1, 272.3 (a) 233.6, 237.8, 272.17
upland area 237.1
uplands 233.1, 237.1, 272.3
upleap (n) 193.1, 366.1 (v) 193.9, 366.5
uplift (n) 193.1, 204.6, 392.1, 912.1 (v) 109.8, 200.9, 298.8, 392.9, 662.13, 912.5
uplifted 193.15, 272.14, 912.9
uplifting (n) 200.4, 912.1 (a) 109.16, 912.10
upload (n) 1042.18 (v) 1042.21
upmarket 632.11
upmost 198.11, 272.19
up on 413.27, 928.18, 928.19
upon a course 182.28
up one's pay 446.2
upon oath 436.7
upped 259.10
upper, an 9.1
upper (n) 105.3 (a) 249.12, 272.19
upper arm 2.7, 906.5
upper-atmospheric wind 318.1
upper bracket 618.1
upper case 548.6
uppercase 546.8, 548.20
upper chamber 613.1
upper circles 607.2, 608.1
upper class, the 606.1
upper class 249.5, 607.2, 608.1
upper-class 607.10
upper classes 607.2
upperclassman 572.6
upper crust 249.5, 578.6, 607.2, 608.1
upper-cruster 607.4, 608.4
upper cut 578.6, 607.2, 608.1
upper deck 745.1
upper extremity 198.2
upper frequencies 1034.12
upper hand 249.2, 417.6, 894.1
Upper House 613.2
upper house 613.1
upper-income 618.14
upper-income group 607.2
upper limit 211.3
upper middle class 607.5
upper mordent 708.27
uppermost 198.11, 249.13, 272.19, 997.24
uppermost height 198.2, 272.2
upper partial tone 709.16
upper reaches 237.2
upper respiratory disease 85.16
uppers 87.4
upper side 198.1
upper slopes 237.2
upper story 198.1, 919.6
upper ten 608.1
upper ten thousand 608.1
upping 193.1, 251.1, 259.1, 392.1, 446.1, 912.1
uppish 141.9, 142.9
uppishness 141.1, 142.1
uppity 141.9, 142.9
uppityness 141.1, 142.1
upraise 200.9, 298.8, 912.5
upraised 200.11, 912.9
upraising 200.4
uprear 200.8, 200.9, 912.5
upreared 200.11, 272.14, 912.9
uprearing (n) 200.4, 912.1 (a) 272.14
upright (n) 200.2, 273.4, 901.8 (v) 200.9 (a) 200.11, 277.6, 644.13, 653.5, 912.9
uprighteous 644.13
uprightness 200.1, 644.1
uprisal 193.1
uprise (n) 193.1, 200.5, 204.6, 272.2 (v) 193.8, 200.8, 204.10, 272.10, 272.12
uprising (n) 193.1, 200.5, 204.6, 327.4 (a) 193.14, 204.17
up-river 207.7
uproar 53.3, 59.4, 105.4, 355.2, 671.2, 810.4
uproarious 53.13, 105.24, 671.18
uproariousness 53.2
uproot 160.6, 192.10, 395.14
uprooted 160.10
uprooting (n) 160.1, 192.1, 395.6 (a) 192.17
uprush 193.1, 318.1
ups 87.4
ups and downs 916.5, 972.5
ups and downs of life 972.5, 1011.1
upscale 607.10, 618.15, 1010.12
upscale items 735.1
upscale rich 632.11
upselling 894.1
upset (n) 126.1, 160.2, 205.2, 395.3, 671.2, 810.1, 860.1, 917.1, 958.2, 971.3, 985.3, 1012.3 (v) 96.15, 96.16, 105.14, 126.4, 126.5, 128.10, 182.44, 205.6, 395.20, 412.7, 791.3, 810.9, 811.4, 860.4, 917.10, 958.5, 971.12, 985.7, 1012.15 (a) 96.22, 105.23, 105.26, 128.14, 412.14, 810.13, 917.16, 958.7, 971.24, 985.12
upset one's applecart 1012.15
upset stomach 85.9
upset the apple cart 393.11, 868.4
upset the apple-cart 811.2
upset the boat 182.44
upsetting (n) 958.2 (a) 105.30, 126.10, 971.27
upshoot (n) 193.1 (v) 14.2, 193.9, 259.7
upshot 887.1, 940.1
upside 198.1
upside-down 205.7, 810.16
upside-down cake 10.42
upside-down flag 400.1
upside-downness 205.1
upslope 193.1
upsloping 193.14
upspeak 523.7
upspear 14.2, 193.9, 259.7, 310.34
upspin 193.8
upspring (n) 366.1 (v) 14.2, 193.9, 259.7, 366.5
upsprout 14.2, 259.7, 310.34
upstage (n) 704.16 (v) 157.5, 704.29 (a) 141.9
upstairs maid 577.8
upstanding 200.11, 644.13
upstandingness 644.1, 653.2
upstart (n) 142.5, 497.6, 606.7, 841.4 (v) 193.9 (a) 606.8
upstartness 497.4
upstream 193.8
upsurge (n) 193.1, 193.2, 251.1, 251.2 (v) 193.8
upsurgence 193.1
upswarm 193.8
upsweep (n) 193.1, 193.2 (v) 193.13
upsweeping 279.9
upswing 193.1, 251.1, 392.1
uptake 939.1
up the ante 759.24
up the creek 1011.14, 1013.22
up the kazoo (v) 994.5 (a) 991.7
up the river 428.15, 429.21
up the spout 762.11
up-the-wall 926.27
upthrow (n) 912.1 (v) 912.5
upthrown 912.9
upthrust 912.1
uptick 193.1, 251.1, 259.1, 392.1, 731.10
uptight 128.13, 867.6
up to (v) 18.11 (a) 18.14, 405.18, 413.24, 991.6
up-to-date 578.11, 838.2, 841.13, 928.18
up-to-datish 578.11, 841.13
up to expectations 130.14
up to no good 645.16, 654.16
up to one's ears in 898.5, 983.17
up to one's ears in debt 623.8
up to one's elbows in 330.21, 898.5, 983.17
up to one's eyeballs in 330.21
up to one's neck in 330.21, 898.5
up to par 637.3, 999.19
up to scratch 807.7, 999.19
up to snuff 413.24, 807.7, 991.6, 999.19
up to standard 999.19
up to the ass in 991.7
up to the mark 413.24, 991.6, 999.19
up-to-the-minute 578.11, 838.2, 841.13, 841.14
up to the notch 999.19
uptown (n) 230.6 (a) 230.11
uptrend 193.2, 251.1, 392.1
up-trending 172.8
upturn (n) 193.2, 205.2, 251.1, 396.8, 731.10 (v) 193.13, 205.6
upturned 193.15
upward 172.8, 193.14
upward looking 100.9
upward-looking 100.28
upwardly mobile 607.10
upward mobility 392.1, 607.1, 852.1, 1010.1
upward motion 172.2
upwards of 884.7
upward strabismus 28.5
upwind (v) 184.43, 193.8 (a) 161.14
uraeus 647.3
Urania 986.2
uranic 1073.25
uranium 1038.5
uranographer 1073.22
uranographist 1073.22
uranography 1073.19
uranologist 1073.22
uranology 1073.19
uranometrist 1073.22
uranometry 1073.19
Uranus 1073.9
urban (n) 230.1 (a) 230.11
urban center 230.6
urban complex 230.1
urban corridor 230.1
urbane 230.11, 496.9, 504.13, 582.22
urban ghetto 230.6
urbanist 716.10, 717.3
urbanite 227.6
urbanity 496.2, 504.1, 504.6, 582.1
urbanization 230.1
urban legend 678.14
urban market 733.3
urban myth 678.14, 842.2

urbanologist 717.3
urbanology 230.10
urban planner 716.10, 717.3
urban planning 230.10
urban poor, the 619.3
urban renewal 396.4
urban sprawl 230.1, 771.3
urban studies 230.10
urbs 230.1
urchin 178.3, 302.4
Urdur 964.3
urea 12.5
urete 2.23
urethra 2.16, 2.23, 292.5
urge (n) 100.1, 365.1, 375.6 (v) 375.14, 401.4, 421.8, 422.6, 440.12
urge along 375.16
urge as a motive 376.3
urgency 375.6, 421.4, 440.3, 814.1, 963.4, 997.4
urgent 375.25, 401.9, 421.9, 440.18, 544.13, 830.4, 963.12, 997.22
urgent need 963.4
urge on 375.16
urge on the mind 568.12
urger 375.11
urge reasons for 600.10
urge upon 439.9
urging 375.5, 440.3
Uriah Heep 357.8
uric acid 12.5
uricotelic metabolism 2.20
Uriel 679.4
urinal 12.10, 12.11
urinalysis 91.12
urinary 2.33, 12.20
urinary tract 2.16
urinate 12.14
urination 12.5
urinative 12.20
urine 2.24, 12.5
urinometer 1045.8
urn 309.12, 742.2
urn burial 309.1
urnfield 309.15
urodele 311.26
uroscopy 91.12
urp 909.27
ursine 311.43
urtext 786.1
urticaria 85.34, 85.36
urtication 26.3, 74.1
US 232.3
USA 232.3
usability 387.3
usable 387.23
usage 373.1, 373.3, 387.1, 387.2, 518.4, 523.1, 526.1, 529.1, 532.1
U.S. Air Force 461.29
U.S. Air Force Reserve 461.25
U.S. Army Reserve 461.25
USB drive 1042.5
U.S. Cabinet 423.1, 613.2
U.S. Coast Guard Reserve 461.25
U.S. Customs Service 630.10
U.S. dry measure 300.4
use (n) 373.1, 373.3, 387.1, 387.3, 387.4, 387.5, 393.5, 471.4, 518.2, 626.1, 999.4 (v) 87.22, 321.6, 328.8, 384.5, 387.10, 387.12, 387.16, 626.5, 725.8
use advisedly 944.5
use a last resort 995.4
use a light hand 427.5
use a light rein 427.5
use an experimental sample 942.9
use as a doormat 432.10
use as a meal ticket 138.12
use body language 517.21
use-by date 10.50
used 387.24, 473.7, 486.9, 842.18
used to 373.15, 373.16, 373.17
used up 16.18, 21.8, 388.5, 393.36, 473.7
use every trick in the book 339.7, 407.7, 794.8
use faulty grammar 531.3
use food stamps 619.5
use force 15.12
use force upon 424.4
use for one's own ends 387.16
useful 384.8, 387.18, 449.21, 889.10, 995.5, 999.12
useful consciousness 184.21
useful life 827.1
useful lift 184.26
usefulness 387.3, 449.10, 995.1, 999.1, 999.4
use hindsight 989.9
use ill 387.16
use inappropriate grammar 531.3
use irregularly 87.22
use language 523.18
useless 19.15, 391.9, 410.18, 996.6
uselessness 19.3, 391.1, 410.1, 996.1, 998.2
use loosely 945.4
Usenet 1042.19
use nonformal speech 523.18
use occasionally 87.22
use of words 523.1, 532.1
use one's endeavor 403.10
use one's fine Italian hand 415.9
use one's good offices 143.12, 466.6
use one's head 920.10, 931.8
use one's imagination 986.14
use one's influence 894.9
use one's noggin 931.8
use one's noodle 931.8
use one's option 371.13
use one's palate 944.5
use one's wits 920.10
user 87.21, 387.7, 387.9
use reason 935.15
user fee 630.6
user-friendly 1014.15
username 1042.18
use sign language 49.4
use some elbow grease 403.5, 725.9
use strong language 513.6
use terror tactics 127.20
use the backboard 747.4
use the mails 553.10
use the mind 931.8
use the occasion 843.7
use time 821.6
use to advantage 387.15
use to the full 387.15
use unadvisedly 945.4
use up 21.4, 387.13, 388.3, 486.4
use violence 424.7
usher (n) 563.4, 577.5, 704.23, 769.5, 1008.12 (v) 769.8
usherer 704.23
usherette 704.23
usher in 814.2, 816.3, 818.11, 834.3
usher into the world 892.13
using (n) 387.8, 473.2 (a) 87.25, 387.19
using as a means 387.8
using as a tool 387.8
using one's head 931.1
using one's noodle 931.1
using up 387.1, 388.1, 473.2
U.S. liquid measure 300.4
U.S. Marine Corps Reserve 461.25
U.S. Naval Reserve 461.25
US of A 232.3
usual, the 869.3
usual 246.3, 349.15, 373.13, 373.14, 781.6, 807.6, 847.4, 864.12, 869.9, 1005.8
usualness 847.1, 864.2, 869.2
usual suspects 850.1
usucapion 469.1
usucapt 469.4
usucaption 469.1
usufruct 387.7
usurer 620.3
usurious 632.12
usurp 417.14, 480.19, 640.8, 910.9
usurpation 417.12, 480.4, 640.3, 910.3
usurp authority 418.4
usurper 575.13, 640.4
usurp power 418.4
usurp the crown 417.14
usurp the prerogatives of the crown 417.14
usurp the throne 417.14
usury 620.1, 623.3, 732.1
utensil 195.1, 1040.1
utensils 385.4
uterine 2.29, 559.6
uterine brother 559.3
uterine kin 559.2
uterine sister 559.3
uteromania 665.5
uteromaniac 665.14
uteromaniacal 665.29
uterus 2.13, 886.7
utile 384.8, 449.21
utilitarian 387.18, 724.15
utilitarianism 143.4, 387.6, 636.2, 952.7
utility (n) 387.3, 449.10, 1040.3 (a) 862.8
utility man 576.1
utility person 707.2
utility player 745.2, 862.2
utility pole 273.1
utility program 1042.11
utility room 197.13
utility woman 576.1
utilizability 387.3
utilizable 387.23
utilization 387.1, 387.8
utilize 384.5, 387.10, 1054.7
utmost (n) 794.5 (a) 247.13, 249.13, 403.16
utmost extent 794.5
utmost height 198.2
Utopia 986.11
utopia 124.4
utopia 986.11, 1010.4
utopian (n) 124.5, 392.6, 986.13 (a) 124.11, 392.16, 986.23
utopianism 124.2, 392.5, 952.7, 986.7
utopianist 986.13
utopianize 986.16
utopianizer 986.13
utopian socialism 611.6
utopian socialist 611.14
utopist 392.6
ut, re, mi, fa, sol, la 709.7
utricle 2.10
utter (v) 351.5, 523.18, 524.22, 728.26, 728.28, 771.4 (a) 247.12, 794.10, 960.2, 1002.7
utter a caveat 399.5
utter a judgment 946.13
utter a mot 489.13
utterance 334.1, 343.1, 518.6, 524.2, 524.3, 524.5, 526.1, 529.1
utterance string 524.2
utter darkness 1027.1
utter defeat 412.3
uttered 524.29
utterer 524.17
uttering 524.5
utterly attentive 360.8
utterly detest 103.5
uttermost (n) 794.5 (a) 247.13
utter rout 412.4
utter threats against 514.2
U-turn 163.3, 279.3, 363.1, 852.1
uturuncu 680.12
UVA 1032.10
UVB 1032.10
uvula 2.12, 202.4, 524.18
uxorial 563.18
uxorious 104.26, 563.18
uxoriousness 104.1
Uzi submachine gun 462.10
V 171.4, 882.1
vacancy 222.2, 724.5, 762.1, 922.6, 933.1
vacant 222.14, 522.20, 922.19, 933.4, 990.9
vacant post 222.2
vacate 188.9, 222.8, 370.5, 445.2, 448.2, 475.3
vacation (n) 20.3, 222.4, 402.1, 445.1, 826.1, 857.3 (v) 20.9, 222.8
vacational 20.10
vacation home 228.8
vacation time 624.6
vacatur 445.1
vacay 20.3

vaccinate 91.28, 191.3
vaccination 86.28, 91.16
vaccine 86.28, 91.16
vaccine rash 85.36
vaccine therapy 91.15
vaccinotherapy 91.15
vacillate 362.8, 364.4, 854.5, 916.10, 971.10
vacillating 362.10, 364.6, 854.7, 914.7, 916.15
vacillation 362.2, 854.3, 916.1, 971.1
vacillator 362.5
vacillatory 362.10, 916.15
vacuity 222.2, 222.3, 762.1, 922.6, 930.1, 933.1, 998.3
vacuole 305.5
vacuometer 317.8
vacuous 222.14, 762.8, 922.19, 930.11, 933.4, 990.9, 998.19
vacuousness 922.6, 930.1
vacuum (n) 222.3, 762.1, 795.2, 922.6 (v) 79.23, 192.12
vacuum-clean 79.23
vacuum-pack 397.9
vacuum-packed 15.20, 212.12
vacuum pump 192.9
vacuum tube 1033.10, 1042.3
vacuum-tube circuit 1033.8
vacuum tube component 1033.10
vacuum-tube hearing aid 48.8
vade mecum 554.8
vadimonium 438.2
vadium mortuum 438.4
vadium vivum 438.4
vag 178.3, 660.2
vagabond (n) 160.4, 178.3, 660.2, 828.4 (v) 177.23 (a) 177.37
vagabondage 177.3
vagabonding 177.3
vagabondish 177.37
vagabondism 177.3
vagabondize 177.23
vagarious 364.5
vagary 204.1, 364.1, 986.5
vagina 2.13, 2.23, 292.5
vaginal 2.29, 295.32
vaginismus 85.6
vagrancy 177.3, 331.5
vagrant (n) 178.3, 331.9, 660.2 (a) 164.7, 177.37, 364.5, 854.7
vagrant impulse 365.1
vague 32.6, 263.4, 270.16, 522.15, 810.12, 864.11, 971.19, 975.17
vague appearance 32.2
vague feeling 934.3
vague generalization 864.8
vague idea 934.3, 951.5
vague memory 990.1
vagueness 32.2, 263.1, 270.4, 522.3, 764.1, 810.1, 945.2, 971.4
vague notion 930.5
vain 19.15, 125.13, 136.9, 140.8, 391.13, 502.10, 936.13, 998.19
vain attempt 410.5
vain expectation 125.4
vainglorious 140.8, 502.10
vaingloriousness 140.1, 502.3
vainglory 140.1, 502.3
vainness 140.1
vain pretensions 501.2
vain show 33.2
vair 4.2, 295.3, 647.2
vairagi 699.13
vaivode 575.12
valance 211.7
Valaskjalf 681.10
vale 237.7, 284.9, 1073.10
valediction 188.4, 543.2
valedictorian 543.4
valedictory (n) 188.4, 543.2 (a) 188.18
valedictory address 188.4, 543.2
valence 1060.4
valence electrons 1033.3
valence number 1060.5
valence shell 1033.3, 1038.4
valency 1060.4
valent 1060.10
valentine 104.9, 562.13
vale of tears 1011.1, 1073.10
vale of years, the 303.5
valet (n) 577.4 (v) 577.13
valetudinarian (n) 85.43 (a) 85.54
valetudinarianism 82.1, 85.3
valetudinary 85.54
valgus 265.3
Valhalla 681.10, 839.2
vali 575.12
valiance 492.1
valiancy 492.1
valiant (n) 492.7 (a) 492.16
valiant effort 403.1
valiant knight 492.7
valid 18.12, 673.11, 957.16, 973.14, 999.12
validatable 957.19
validate 332.12, 443.11, 673.9, 942.8, 957.11, 970.12
validated 332.14, 957.20, 973.13
validating 332.14
validation 332.4, 334.3, 673.2, 957.4, 970.8
valid contract 437.1
validity 18.1, 443.8, 673.1, 970.4, 973.6, 999.1
Valium 86.12
Valkyrie 458.12
valley 224.2, 237.7, 275.2, 284.9
valley of the shadow of death 307.3
valley wind 318.1
valor 492.1
valorization 630.5
valorize 630.11
valorous 492.16
valorousness 492.1
valuable 387.22, 632.10
valuableness 632.2
valuate 300.10, 630.11, 946.9
valuated 300.13
valuation 300.1, 630.3, 946.3
valuational 300.12
valuative 300.12
valuator 300.9
value (n) 35.6, 300.2, 387.4, 518.1, 518.2, 630.2, 632.2, 997.1, 999.1 (v) 155.4, 300.10, 630.11, 946.9, 997.13
valued 155.11, 300.13, 630.14
valued at 630.14
value-fixing 630.3
value judgment 946.3, 952.2
valueless 391.11, 998.21
valuelessness 391.2
valuer 300.9
value received 630.2
values 636.1, 712.8, 1041.10
value-setting 630.3
value system 636.1, 952.2
valuing 946.3
valval 239.17
valve 239.10, 293.4, 711.6, 1033.10, 1040.2
valved 239.17
valvelike 239.17
valvula 239.10
valvular 239.17
valvule 239.10
vamoose 188.7, 188.10, 222.10, 368.11, 369.6
vamp (n) 104.11, 377.4, 562.11, 665.15, 708.26, 708.27, 1022.4 (v) 104.22, 365.8, 377.7, 392.11
vampire 104.11, 127.9, 377.4, 480.12, 593.6, 665.15, 680.6, 690.9
vampirish 480.26
vampirism 480.8, 690.1
vamp up 392.11
van 165.1, 179.2, 179.12, 216.2, 1008.9
Van Alen Streamlined Scoring System 748.2
vandal 395.8, 593.5
vandalic 395.26
vandalish 395.26
vandalism 144.11, 322.1, 395.1, 671.1
vandalistic 395.26
vandalize 395.10, 671.11
Vanderbilt 618.8
Vandyke (n) 3.8 (v) 289.4
vandyke 548.5
Vandyke edge 289.2
vane 318.16
vanguard 165.1, 211.4, 216.2, 816.1, 841.2, 1008.9
vanilla 246.3, 499.6, 499.8, 533.6, 798.6, 1005.8
vanish 34.2, 188.9, 395.23, 762.6, 828.6
vanished 222.11, 762.11, 837.7
vanish from sight 34.2
vanishing (n) 34.1 (a) 34.3
vanishing cream 1016.11
vanishing point 34.1, 169.1, 258.7, 261.3
vanish into thin air 34.2, 828.6
vanish like a dream 828.6
vanishment 34.1
vanity 136.1, 140.1, 391.2, 502.1, 998.3
vanity case 1016.11
Vanity Fair 578.6
vanity plate 443.6
vanity press 554.2
vanload 196.2
vanquish 412.10
vanquished, the 412.5
vanquished 412.17
vanquisher 411.2
vanquishing 411.7
vanquishment 412.1
vantage 27.7, 249.2, 894.4
vantage ground 249.2, 272.2
vantage point 27.7, 249.2, 272.2
vape 87.22
vaper 89.11
vape shop 89.12
vapid 16.17, 65.2, 117.6, 721.5, 922.19, 998.19, 1005.7
vapidity 16.3, 65.1, 102.1, 117.1, 721.2, 922.6, 998.3
vapidness 117.1
vaping 87.1, 89.1
vapor (n) 319.3, 764.3, 976.1, 986.5, 1019.10, 1067.1 (v) 502.6, 503.3, 520.5, 545.6, 909.24
vaporability 1067.4
vaporable 1067.10
vaporer 503.2
vaporescent 1067.10
vaporific 1067.10
vaporimeter 1067.7
vaporiness 1067.3
vaporing (n) 501.2, 520.2 (a) 502.10, 1067.9
vaporish 1067.9
vaporizability 1067.4
vaporizable 1067.10
vaporization 1067.5
vaporize 308.18, 395.10, 395.14, 1067.8
vaporized 395.28
vaporizer 1067.6
vaporlike 1067.9
vaporous 299.4, 764.6, 986.22, 1067.9
vaporousness 1067.3
vapor pressure 1067.3
vapor tension 1067.3
vapor trail 184.30, 517.8
vapory 986.22, 1067.9
vaquero 178.8, 1070.3
vardarac 318.8
Vardhamana 684.4
Vardon grip 751.3
variability 775.2, 782.1, 783.1, 851.1, 854.2
variable (n) 1041.9 (a) 775.7, 782.3, 783.3, 851.3, 854.6, 854.7, 971.16
variable annuity 1008.4
variable field 1032.3
variable-rate mortgage 438.4
Variable Zone 231.3
variance 333.1, 443.1, 456.2, 775.2, 780.1, 789.1
variant (n) 341.2 (a) 780.7, 789.6
variant reading 341.2
variation 164.1, 708.24, 780.1, 780.4, 782.1, 783.1, 852.1, 854.2, 854.3
varicolored 47.9
varicolorous 47.9
varicose vein 2.23
varied 780.7, 783.4, 797.14
variegate 35.14, 47.7, 782.2, 783.2
variegated 35.16, 47.9, 780.7, 782.3, 854.6

variegated pattern 47.4
variegation 35.4, 47.1, 780.1, 782.1, 783.1
varietal 809.7
variety 675.3, 704.1, 770.13, 780.1, 782.1, 783.1, 809.3, 809.5, 852.1, 854.2, 883.1
Varietyese 523.10
variety shop 736.1
variety show 1035.2
variety store 736.1
variform 782.3
variolar 85.61
variolous 85.61
variorum 341.2
variorum edition 341.2
various 780.7, 782.3, 783.4, 883.7, 884.7
variousness 782.1
varmint 311.2, 311.3, 660.6
varnish (n) 79.17, 287.2, 295.12, 354.3, 376.1, 600.5, 712.18 (v) 35.14, 265.6, 287.7, 346.6, 354.16, 545.7, 600.12
varnished 287.11, 355.4
varnishing 35.12
varnishing day 348.2
varnish over 376.4
varnish resin 1057.1
Varonnian satire 489.1
varsity (n) 617.7 (a) 568.19
varsity student 572.5
Varuna 183.1, 240.3
vary 164.3, 362.8, 780.5, 780.6, 782.2, 783.2, 787.3, 789.5, 851.2, 852.6, 852.7, 854.5
varying 780.7, 782.3
vas 2.23
vascular 2.33
vascular disease 85.19
vascularity 2.23
vascularization 2.23
vascularized 2.33
vascular nevus 517.5
vascular plant 310.3
vasculature 2.23
vas deferens 2.13
vase 742.2
Vaseline 1056.2
vasiform 2.33
vasoconstrictor 86.32
vasodilator 86.32
vassal (n) 432.7, 577.1 (a) 432.13
vassalage 432.1
vassalize 432.8
vast 158.11, 247.7, 257.20
vastitude 247.1, 257.1, 257.7
vast knowledge 928.6
vastness 247.1, 257.1, 257.7, 823.1
vasty 158.11, 247.7
vat 386.6
vatic 962.11
Vatican 703.8
Vatican, the 698.6
Vatican Council 423.4
Vatican Two 423.4
vaticinal 962.11
vaticinate 962.9
vaticination 962.1
vaticinatory 962.11
vaudeville 704.1
vaudeville circuit 704.11
vaudeville theater 704.14
vaudevillian 707.1
vaudevillist 707.1
vault (n) 193.1, 197.2, 279.4, 309.16, 366.1, 386.6, 729.13, 1073.2 (v) 279.6, 366.5
vaulted 279.10
vaulter 366.4
vaulting 279.1, 279.4, 366.3, 760.5
vaulting ambition 100.10
vault of heaven 1073.2
vault up 193.9
vaunt (n) 501.4, 502.1 (v) 501.17, 502.6
vaunt-courier 353.2, 816.1
vaunter 140.5
vauntery 502.1
vaunting (n) 502.1 (a) 501.18, 502.10
veal 10.15
veal chop 10.19
veal cutlet 10.15, 10.19
veau 10.15
vector 85.4, 85.44, 161.2, 184.34, 277.2
vector for 161.10
vector in flight 184.13
Veda 683.8
Vedantic 675.32
Vedas, the 683.8
vedette 1008.10
Vedic 675.32, 683.15
Vedic chant 696.3
Vedic hymn 696.3
veejay 1034.23
veep 574.3
veer (n) 164.1, 204.3, 278.2 (v) 163.9, 164.3, 182.30, 204.9, 218.5, 278.5, 852.6
veer around 163.9
veering 164.7, 851.3
veering wind 318.10
veer off 164.6, 278.5
veer short 182.32
veg 10.35
vega 236.1, 310.8
vegan (n) 8.16, 668.4 (a) 8.31, 668.10
vegan diet 7.13
veganism 668.2
veganistic 668.10
vegeburger 10.32
vegetable (n) 10.35, 310.3, 310.4, 924.4 (a) 310.36, 329.6, 331.20, 853.7
vegetable-eating 8.31
vegetable existence 761.6
vegetable juice 10.49
vegetable kingdom 310.1, 809.4, 1068.1
vegetable life 310.1
vegetable oil 1056.1
vegetable remedies 86.4
vegetable resin 1057.1
vegetables 10.7, 10.35
vegetal 310.36
vegetarian (n) 8.16, 668.4 (a) 8.31, 310.36, 668.10
vegetarianism 7.13, 8.1, 668.2
vegetate 14.2, 173.9, 259.7, 310.34, 329.2, 761.10
vegetation 14.1, 173.4, 259.3, 310.1, 310.32, 329.1, 761.6
vegetational 310.36
vegetation daemon 678.11
vegetation spirit 310.1, 678.11, 1069.4
vegetative 310.36, 329.6, 331.20, 853.7
vegged 895.4
veggieburger 10.32
veggies 10.35
veg out 329.2
vehemence 17.5, 18.1, 93.2, 101.2, 152.10, 330.6, 544.5, 671.1
vehement 17.14, 101.9, 105.29, 330.22, 544.13, 671.16
vehicle 35.8, 179.1, 384.4, 704.4, 714.10
vehicular 179.23
vehicular tunnel 383.3
veil, the 565.1
veil (n) 5.26, 295.2, 345.3, 346.2, 376.1, 702.1, 1028.1 (v) 295.19, 345.7, 346.6, 1028.5
veiled 295.31, 519.5, 971.19, 1028.7
veiled accusation 599.1
veiled threat 514.1
veiled voice 52.2
veiler 5.26
veiling (n) 5.26, 295.1 (a) 295.35, 1028.6
veilless 348.11
veil of secrecy 345.3
vein (n) 2.23, 270.7, 296.1, 386.4, 532.2, 765.4, 767.4, 978.3, 978.4, 1058.7 (v) 47.7
veinal 2.33
veined 47.15
veinlet 2.23
veinstone 1058.7
veinule 2.23
velar (n) 524.12 (a) 524.30, 525.12
Velcro 800.3, 803.4
veld 233.1, 236.1, 310.8
veldt 233.1, 310.8
velleity 16.2, 323.1
vellicate 917.13
vellication 128.1, 917.3, 917.5
vellicative 917.19
vellum 547.4
veloce 708.55
velocipede 179.8
velocity 172.4, 174.1, 177.12
velocity peak 1074.9
veloute 10.12
velum 2.6, 524.18
velutinous 294.8, 1047.15
velvet 121.1, 287.3, 294.3, 1010.1, 1014.4, 1047.4
velvet darkness 1027.1
velvetiness 287.1, 294.3, 1047.1
velvetlike 1047.15
velvety 3.27, 287.10, 287.11, 294.8, 1047.15
vena cava 2.23
venal 100.27, 378.4, 645.23
venality 645.9
venation 2.23
vend 734.9
vendee 733.5
vendetta 456.5, 507.1, 589.4
vendibility 734.7
vendible (n) 735.2 (a) 734.14
vendibles 735.1
vending (n) 734.2 (a) 734.13
vending machine 8.17, 736.4
vendor 730.5, 736.4
vendue 734.4
veneer (n) 276.1, 295.12, 296.2 (v) 295.23
veneered 296.6
veneering 295.12
venenate 82.7, 144.22, 1000.12
venenation 85.31
veneniferous 82.7, 1000.12
venenous 82.7, 1000.12
venerability 136.2, 685.1
venerable 136.12, 155.12, 303.16, 662.15, 685.7, 842.10, 842.12
venerableness 685.1, 842.1
venerable sir 304.2
venerate 155.4, 696.11
venerated 155.11, 662.15
venerating 155.9
veneration 155.1, 692.1, 696.1
venerational 155.9, 692.8, 696.16
venerative 155.9, 692.8, 696.16
venerator 696.9
venereal 75.25, 75.26
venereal appetite 75.5
venereal desire 75.5
venereal disease 85.18
venery 75.7, 382.2, 382.7, 665.3
venesect 192.12
venesection 91.20, 192.3
vengeance 507.1, 639.3
vengeful 507.7
vengefulness 507.2
venial 600.14
veniality 600.7
venial sin 322.1, 655.2
venin 1001.3
venire 598.4
venire facias 596.5, 598.4
venire facias de novo 598.4
venire-man 596.6
venire-woman 596.6
venison 10.13
venom 82.3, 103.1, 144.7, 589.4, 671.1, 1000.3, 1001.3
venomous 82.7, 103.7, 144.22, 589.10, 671.16, 1000.12
venomousness 82.3, 144.7, 1000.5
venose 2.33
venous 2.33
venous blood 2.25
vent (n) 181.13, 190.1, 190.9, 239.13, 369.1 (v) 351.5, 909.22
ventage 190.9, 239.13
venthole 190.9, 239.13
ventiduct 239.13
ventilate 72.4, 317.11, 351.4, 351.5, 352.11, 541.11, 1024.10
ventilating shaft 239.13
ventilating system 317.10

ventilation 72.2, 317.9, 352.1, 541.6
ventilator 72.3, 239.13, 317.10, 318.18, 1024.3
venting 190.1, 909.6
vent one's anger 152.16
vent one's choler 152.16
vent one's rancor 152.16
vent one's spleen 152.16
ventose 259.13, 318.21
ventral 2.31
ventricles 2.16
ventricose 283.16
ventricular 2.31
ventricular fibrillation 916.3
ventricular tachycardia 916.3
ventriloquial 524.32
ventriloquism 524.15
ventriloquist 336.4, 524.15
ventriloquistic 524.32
ventriloquy 524.15
ventripotence 2.18
venture (n) 404.1, 729.4, 737.19, 759.2 (v) 403.6, 492.9, 640.6, 729.17, 737.23, 759.24
venture a guess 951.11
venture capital 386.2, 728.15, 737.19
ventured 404.7
venture on 403.6
venturer 759.21
venturesome 330.23, 403.16, 404.8, 492.21, 1006.10
venturesomeness 330.7, 492.4
venture to 403.8
venture to say 968.5
venture upon 403.6, 404.3
venturous 330.23, 492.21, 1006.10
venturousness 330.7, 492.4
venue 159.1, 159.2
venule 2.23
Venus 104.7, 1016.9, 1073.4, 1073.9
Venus de Milo 1016.9
Venus of Willenburg 890.5
Venus's curse 85.18
Venus's flytrap 356.12
veracious 644.16, 973.13
veraciousness 644.3
veracity 644.3, 973.1
veranda 197.5, 197.21
verb 530.4
verbal (n) 530.4 (a) 343.9, 518.12, 524.29, 526.19, 530.17, 973.15
verbal abuse 389.2
verbal adjective 530.3
verbal agreement 436.2
verbal art 547.2, 718.2
verbal contest 935.4
verbal diarrhea 538.2, 540.2
verbal engagement 935.4
verbal faculty, the 524.1
verbal fallacy 936.3
verbal icon 518.6
verbal intercourse 524.1, 541.1
verbalism 526.1, 529.1, 538.2
verbalist 541.7
verbality 538.2
verbalize 523.18, 524.22
verbalized 524.29
verbally 343.12
verbally abuse 389.4
verbal noun 530.5
verbal response 989.1
verbal thrust 508.2
verbatim 341.16, 973.15
verb complex 529.1
verbiage 532.1, 538.2
verbid 530.4
verbify 538.8
verbose 538.12, 540.9, 827.11, 993.17
verbosity 538.2, 540.1, 993.4
verboten 444.7
verb phrase 529.1, 530.4
verb sap 422.2
verbum 526.1
verbum sap 422.2
verdancy 44.1
verdant 44.4, 310.36, 310.42
verdantness 44.1
verderer 1069.7
verdict 598.9, 940.1, 946.5
verdict of acquittal 601.1
verdict of guilty 602.1
verdict of not guilty 601.1
verdigris (n) 44.2 (v) 44.3
verdigrised 44.5
verdigrisy 44.5
verdure 44.1, 310.1, 310.8
verdured 310.42
verdurous 44.4, 310.42
verecund 139.12, 344.10
verecundious 139.12, 344.10
verecundity 139.4
verge (n) 211.4, 647.1 (v) 161.7, 211.10, 896.3
verge on 223.9
verges 211.1
verge upon 223.9
verglas 1023.5
veridic 973.15
veridical 644.16, 973.15
veridicality 644.3, 973.1
veriest, the 247.12
veriest 249.13
verifiability 957.7, 970.3
verifiable 957.19, 970.15
verification 334.3, 942.2, 943.2, 957.4, 970.8
verificative 957.18
verificatory 942.11
verified 942.12, 957.20, 973.13
verify 942.8, 943.5, 957.11, 970.12, 1017.21
verifying 957.18
verisimilar 968.6, 973.15
verisimilitude 968.1, 968.3, 973.7
verism 973.7
verismo 973.7
veristic 973.15
veritable 644.14, 761.15, 794.10, 973.13
vérité 706.1
verity 644.3, 973.1
verjuice 67.1, 67.2
verklempt 359.16
vermeil 41.6
vermicelli 10.33
vermicide 86.24, 1001.3
vermicompost 80.10, 890.4
vermicular 311.52
vermiform 281.7, 311.52
vermiform appendix 2.18
vermiform process 2.18
vermifugal 86.41
vermifuge 86.24
vermilion (n) 41.1 (v) 41.4 (a) 41.6
vermin 311.3, 311.36, 606.3, 660.6
verminous 311.44, 311.51
vernacular (n) 523.2, 523.3, 523.5, 523.6, 523.9, 535.1 (a) 231.9, 497.14, 523.20, 869.9
vernacularism 523.5
vernacularize 523.18
vernacular language 523.5, 523.6
vernacular speech 523.5
vernal 44.4, 301.10, 313.9, 841.7
vernal equinox 313.2, 313.7, 1073.16
vernalize 1069.18
vernant 44.4
vernation 310.18
Verna Trench 275.5
Verner's law 524.13
veronica 691.5
verruca 85.39, 283.3, 1004.1
verrucated 283.15
verrucose 283.15
versant 237.2
versatile 364.6, 387.20, 413.25, 783.3
versatility 413.3, 782.1, 783.1
versatose 66.3
verse (n) 554.13, 708.24, 720.1, 720.4, 720.10, 793.2, 816.2, 974.1 (v) 551.8, 720.14
versecraft 720.2
versed 928.18
versed in 413.27, 928.19
verselet 720.4
versemaker 720.13
versemaking 720.2
verseman 720.13
versemonger 720.13
versemongering 720.3
versesmith 720.13
verse-writing 547.2, 718.2
versicle 696.3, 720.4
versicolor 47.9
versicolorate 47.9
versicolored 47.9
versicolorous 47.9
versification 720.2, 720.6
versifier 720.13
versify 720.14
version 336.3, 341.2, 349.2, 547.10, 675.3, 708.28, 722.3
vers-librist 720.12
verso 220.1, 554.12
vert (n) 647.2 (a) 44.4
vertebrate (n) 311.3 (a) 311.40
vertex 198.2, 278.2, 285.3
Verthandi 964.3
vertical (n) 200.2 (a) 198.11, 200.11, 204.18, 277.6
vertical circle 200.2
vertical dimension 200.5
vertical distance 272.1
vertical drop 753.1
vertical envelopment 459.5
vertical height 200.5
vertical interference 1035.5
verticalism 200.1
verticality 200.1
vertically mobile 607.10
vertical mobility 607.1, 852.1
verticalness 200.1, 204.6, 277.1
vertical rays 1019.7
vertical space 158.1
vertical synchronizing pulse 1035.4
vertical union 727.2
verticillaster 310.27
verticillate 281.8
vertiginous 915.15, 985.15
vertiginousness 985.4
vertigo 85.9, 85.15, 985.4
verve 17.2, 93.2, 101.1, 109.4, 330.2, 544.4, 986.4
Verworn theory 560.6
very beginning 845.1
very best, the 999.8
very best 999.16
very good 999.12
very high frequency 1034.12
very image 349.5, 778.3
very important person 575.4, 662.9, 894.6, 997.8, 997.9
very large crude carrier 180.1
very latest, the 841.14
Very lights 399.3
very like 784.15
very low frequency 1034.12
very many 884.6
very model, the 786.4, 973.4
very model 662.9, 1002.4
very much alive 306.12
very picture 349.5
very point 159.1
Very Reverend, the (n) 699.2 (a) 648.8
very same 778.3
very smart 920.12
very spot 159.1
very stuff 767.2
very thing, the 973.4
very thing 778.3
very top 198.2
very truth 973.1
vesicant (n) 86.31 (a) 320.6
vesicate 1020.24
vesicated 320.6
vesication 1020.5
vesicatory (n) 86.31 (a) 320.6
vesicle 283.3, 320.1, 1004.1
vesicular 320.6
Vesper 1073.4
vesper (n) 315.2, 696.8 (a) 315.8
vesperal 315.8
vespers 696.8
vespertinal 315.8
vespertine 315.8
vespiary 228.25
vessel 2.23, 180.1, 195.1
vest (n) 5.14 (v) 159.16, 478.17, 615.10
Vesta 228.30
vesta 1021.5
vestal (n) 565.2, 565.4 (a) 664.6
vestal virgin 565.4
vested 5.45, 855.13

vested authority 417.1
vested interest 471.4, 609.31, 642.1
vested right 642.1
vested with authority 417.15
vestiary 5.45
vestibule 2.10, 189.5, 197.19
vestige 256.1, 517.7, 517.9, 549.1, 797.7, 842.6
vestigial 256.7
vestigial transmission 1034.16
vest in 469.7
vesting 615.1, 629.1
vestment 5.1, 5.3, 295.2
vestmental 5.48, 702.4
vestmentary 702.4
vestmented 5.45
vestments 702.1
vest-pocket 248.6, 258.12, 268.9, 537.6
vestry 423.4, 703.9
vesture 5.1, 5.3, 702.1
vest with 478.17
vesuvian 1021.5
vet (n) 90.7, 413.16, 461.19 (v) 27.14, 392.9, 392.12, 548.17, 570.12, 938.25, 946.14
vetch 310.4
veteran (n) 304.2, 413.16, 461.19 (a) 413.28
Veterans of Foreign Wars member 461.19
veterinarian 90.7
veterinary (n) 90.7 (a) 90.15
veterinary surgeon 90.7
veto (n) 372.1, 428.1, 444.2, 613.7 (v) 444.5, 451.3, 510.10, 613.10
vetoed 444.7
veto message 613.7
veto power 613.7, 894.1
vetting, a 27.6
vex 96.13, 98.15, 126.5, 152.24, 1013.13
vexation 96.2, 126.1, 152.1, 1000.3, 1001.1
vexation of spirit 96.1, 108.1
vexatious 98.22, 119.5, 1013.18
vexatiousness 96.2, 98.7
vexed 96.21, 126.8, 152.27, 1013.20
vexed question 522.8, 1013.7
vexillology 647.7
vexillum 647.7
vexing 98.22, 119.5
V formation 184.12
V-for-victory sign 411.1
VI 882.2
viability 17.9, 107.3, 306.1, 827.1, 889.3, 966.2
viable 17.15, 107.12, 306.12, 889.10, 966.7, 997.18
viableness 966.2
viaduct 170.2, 383.9
viaggiatory 177.37
vials of hate 103.1
vials of wrath 103.1, 152.5
via media 246.1, 467.3, 611.2, 668.1, 670.1
viande 10.13
viande de boucherie 10.13
viands 10.1
viaticum 188.4, 309.4, 701.5
viator 178.1
vibes 93.1, 93.5, 209.3
vibist 710.6
vibrancy 17.4, 54.1, 916.1
vibrant 17.13, 54.10
vibraphonist 710.6
vibrate 54.6, 847.3, 916.10, 917.11
vibratile 916.15
vibratility 916.1
vibrating 54.10, 847.5, 916.15, 917.17
vibration 847.2, 916.1, 917.2
vibrations 93.5, 209.3
vibrato (n) 58.4, 709.19 (a) 58.14
vibrator 916.9, 917.9, 1044.3
vibratory 916.15
vibrio 85.42
vibrissa 3.10, 73.4
vibrograph 916.8
vibroscope 916.8
vic 358.2
vicar 576.1, 699.2, 862.2
vicarage 228.5, 698.9, 703.7
vicar general 576.1
vicariate 698.2
vicarious 862.8
vicarious authority 417.1, 615.1
vicariousness 862.1
Vicar of Bray 363.4
vicarship 698.2
vice 322.1, 576.1, 654.1, 654.2, 655.1, 674.3, 862.2
vice admiral 575.19
vice-chairman 576.8
vice-chancellor 571.8, 574.3, 576.8
vice-consul 576.6, 576.8
vice-corrupted 654.14
vice-director 576.8
vicegerent 576.1, 576.8
vice-governor 576.8
vice-king 575.12, 576.8
vice-laden 654.11
vice-legate 576.6, 576.8
vice-master 576.8
vicenary 882.26
vicennial 882.26
vice-premier 576.8
vice president 610.2
vice-president 574.3, 576.8, 862.2
vice-principal 571.8
vice-prone 654.11
vice-queen 576.8
vice-regent 576.8, 862.2
vice-reine 576.8
viceroy 575.12, 576.8
vicesimal 882.26
vice squad 1008.1
vice-warden 576.8
vicinage 209.1, 223.1, 231.1
vicinal 223.15
vicinity 209.1, 223.1, 231.1
vicious 110.25, 144.26, 654.11, 654.16, 671.21, 1000.7, 1000.12
vicious circle 280.2, 391.2, 936.1, 972.5, 1012.3
vicious cycle 391.2
viciousness 144.11, 654.1, 654.4, 655.1, 671.1, 1000.1, 1000.5
vicious reasoning 936.1
vicissitude 852.3, 854.3, 1011.1
vicissitudes 972.5
vicissitudes of fortune 972.5
vicissitudinary 854.7
vicissitudinous 854.7
Viconian 952.12
victim 85.43, 96.11, 358.1, 382.7, 412.5, 508.7, 759.22, 1011.7
victimizable 954.9
victimization 356.1, 389.3
victimize 356.18, 389.7, 415.11, 632.7
victim of fate 1011.7
victor 409.6, 411.2, 413.15
Victorian (n) 500.11 (a) 500.19, 842.13
victorious 411.7
victory 409.1, 411.1
victory arch 549.12
victory lane 756.3
victory lap 411.1, 457.12, 755.1, 756.3
victress 411.2
victrix 411.2
Victrola 50.11
victual 385.9
victualage 10.1
victualing 385.1
victualler 385.6
victuals 10.2, 10.5, 735.7
Vidar 678.11
video (n) 706.1, 1035.1 (a) 1035.16
video arcade 743.15
video calling 1042.19
video camera 714.11, 1035.10
videocamera 549.10
video card 1042.3
videocassette 1035.11
videocassette recorder 50.12, 549.10, 1035.11
videocast 352.10
videocasting 352.1
video channel 1035.4
video chat 1042.19
video-chat 1042.21
video conference 1042.19
video conferencing 1042.19
video display terminal 1042.9
video display unit 1042.9
video frequency 1035.4
video game 743.9, 743.16
video gaming 743.2
video-gazer 918.1
videogenic 1035.16
video monitor 1035.13
video-on-demand 706.1
videophone 347.4, 1035.11
video pirate 483.7
videorecorder 1035.11
videoscreen 1035.11
video selling 734.2
video signal 1035.4, 1036.11
video static 1035.5
videotape (n) 549.10, 714.10, 1035.11 (v) 549.15
videotape recorder 1035.11
video teleconference 347.13
video terminal 1042.9
vidicon 1035.10
viduity 566.3
vie 457.18, 943.7, 999.11
vie against 451.4
vie for 457.20
vielle 711.14
vier 452.2
Vietcong (n) 461.16 (a) 860.6
view (n) 27.3, 31.3, 33.3, 33.6, 380.1, 712.11, 946.3, 953.6, 978.2 (v) 27.12, 27.13, 931.17, 978.6, 983.6
viewable 31.6
view as 953.11
viewer 29.1, 479.3, 918.1, 1035.12
viewership 1035.12
viewfinder 29.5
view halloo 59.3
view in a new light 931.15
viewing 27.2
viewing audience 1035.12
vie with 451.4, 457.18, 943.7, 999.11
viewless 32.5
viewlessness 32.1
viewpoint 27.7, 31.3, 33.3, 159.2, 932.1, 952.2, 953.6, 978.2
view together 943.4
view with a jaundiced eye 153.3, 980.6
view with a scornful eye 157.3
view with disfavor 510.10
view with favor 509.9
view with indulgence 979.7
view with the mind's eye 931.17, 986.15
vigesimal 882.26
vigil 23.1, 339.4
vigilance 23.1, 339.4, 981.1, 1008.1
vigilance committee 1008.17
vigilant 23.7, 339.13, 405.16, 983.15, 1008.23
vigilanteism 604.6
vigilante justice 604.6
vigilantes 1008.17
vigil light 696.10
vigils 696.8
vigintillion 882.13
vignette 349.2, 712.12, 713.5
vigor 15.1, 17.1, 18.1, 83.3, 109.4, 544.3
vigorish 793.1
vigorous 15.15, 17.13, 18.12, 83.12, 93.18, 544.11, 1010.13, 1049.4
vigorousness 15.1, 83.3, 544.3
VII 882.3
VIII 882.4
viking 183.1, 483.7
vila 678.9
vile 64.7, 71.5, 80.23, 98.18, 497.15, 513.8, 645.17, 654.16, 661.12, 666.9, 998.21, 1000.9
vile language 513.3
vileness 64.3, 80.2, 98.2, 645.2, 654.4, 661.3, 666.4, 998.2, 1000.2
vilification 510.7, 512.2, 513.2
vilify 510.19, 512.10, 513.7, 661.9, 694.5

vilifying 510.22, 512.13
vilipend 157.3
villa 228.7
village (n) 230.2, 231.5 (a) 230.11
village council 423.1
village green 310.7
village idiot 924.5
village of the dead 309.15
villager 227.6
villain 593.1, 660.3, 704.10, 707.2
villainess 593.1, 707.2
villainous 645.17, 654.16, 1000.9
villainousness 645.2, 654.4
villainy 645.2, 654.3
ville 230.1
villein 432.7, 606.6
villeinhold 469.1
villein socage 469.1
villenage 432.1, 469.1
villose 3.24
villosity 3.1
villous 3.24
villus 2.18, 3.2
vim 17.2, 18.1, 109.4, 330.2
vin 88.17
vinaceous 41.6
vinaigrette 10.12, 70.6
Vinaya Pitaka 683.9
vincibility 1006.4
vincible 1006.16
vinculum 709.12
vindicability 600.7
vindicable 600.14
vindicate 600.9, 601.4
vindicate a claim 421.6
vindicated 148.7
vindication 600.1, 601.1
vindicative 600.13
vindicator 460.7, 507.3, 600.8
vindicatory 507.7, 600.13
vindictive 146.3, 506.8, 507.7
vindictiveness 146.1, 507.2
vin du campagne 88.17
vine 310.4
vinedresser 1069.6
vinegar 10.12, 67.2, 397.4
vinegar aspect 1015.3
vinegariness 67.1
vinegarish 67.5, 110.23
vinegary 67.5
vinegrower 1069.6
vinery 1069.10
vineyard 1069.10
Vingolf 681.10
vingt-et-un 759.11
vinicultural 1069.21
viniculture 1069.2
viniculturist 1069.6
vino 88.17
vinous 88.37
vintage 472.5
vintager 1069.6
vintage wine 88.17
vintner 88.19, 385.6
vinyasa 84.2
vinyl 50.12
violaceous 46.3
viola clef 709.13
viol and violin 711.5
violate 327.6, 389.4, 393.12, 435.4, 480.15, 665.20, 671.11, 674.5, 1000.6
violate grammar 531.3
violate the law 674.5
violation 327.1, 389.1, 389.2, 435.2, 480.3, 638.1, 638.2, 665.6, 671.3, 674.3, 674.4, 747.3
violation of law 674.3
violative 327.8
violator 665.12
violence 17.5, 105.10, 144.11, 152.10, 389.2, 424.3, 671.1
violent 17.14, 105.25, 105.29, 424.12, 671.16, 926.30
violent blow 318.11
violent change 860.1
violent death 307.5, 308.8
violent exercise 725.6
violet (n) 35.13, 46.1 (a) 46.3
violet-blindness 30.3
violet ray 1025.5
violet shift 160.1
violinist 710.5
violist 710.5
violoncellist 710.5
VIP 409.6
vipassana 92.6
viper 311.25, 660.6
viperiform 311.47
viperine 311.47
viperish 311.47
viperlike 311.47
viperoid 311.47
viperous 311.47
vipery 311.47
VIP's, the 249.5
viraginous 76.14
virago 76.9, 110.12, 593.7, 671.9
viral marketing 734.2
viral video 1042.19
virescence 44.1
virescent 44.4
virgate 1046.11
virgin (n) 302.8, 565.2, 565.4, 657.4 (a) 233.9, 390.12, 406.13, 565.7, 664.4, 664.6, 792.10, 798.7, 841.7, 891.4, 930.16, 1002.8
virginal 301.10, 406.13, 565.7, 664.6, 841.7
virgin forest 310.12
Virginia 89.2
Virginia deer 311.5
virginity 406.3, 565.1, 664.3, 841.1
virgin land 233.2
virgin soil 406.5
virgin state 565.1
virgin territory 233.2
virgo intacta 565.4
virgule 204.7, 517.6
virid 44.4
viridescence 44.1
viridescent 44.4
viridity 44.1
virile 76.13, 492.16
virileness 76.2
virilism 76.2
virility 18.1, 76.2, 303.2, 492.1
virilize 76.11
virion 85.42
viripotent 76.13
virtu 496.4, 712.6, 712.9
virtual 519.5, 966.6
virtual classroom 567.5
virtual company 739.1
virtual environment 1042.1
virtuality 519.1, 966.1
virtualize 1042.21
virtual memory 1042.7
virtual office 617.10, 739.7
virtual reality 1042.1
virtual storage 1042.7
virtue 18.1, 492.1, 608.2, 636.3, 644.1, 653.1, 664.1, 999.1
virtueless 654.12
virtues 679.3
virtuosa 710.1
virtuose 708.47
virtuosic 708.47
virtuosity 249.1, 413.1, 496.4, 708.31
virtuoso (n) 249.4, 413.13, 496.6, 710.1, 999.6 (a) 413.22, 708.47
virtuous 644.13, 653.5, 664.4, 999.12
virtuousness 644.1, 653.1, 664.1, 999.1
virulence 17.5, 18.1, 82.3, 144.7, 152.3, 308.9, 589.4, 671.1, 1000.5
virulency 82.3
virulent 17.14, 82.7, 144.22, 152.26, 308.23, 589.10, 671.16, 1000.12
virus 85.4, 85.42, 258.7, 305.2, 1001.3, 1042.18
visa (n) 332.4, 443.7, 527.10, 549.6 (v) 332.12
visage 33.4, 216.4
visagiste 704.23
visagraph 30.6
vis à vis 790.4
vis-à-vis (n) 779.2 (v) 215.4 (a) 779.6
viscera 2.16, 93.3, 207.4
visceral 93.17, 207.6
visceralness 93.9
visceral skeleton 2.2
viscid 803.12, 1045.12, 1049.4, 1062.12
viscidity 803.3, 1045.1, 1049.1, 1062.2
viscose 803.12, 1062.12
viscosity 803.3, 1045.1, 1062.2
viscount 608.4
viscountcy 608.9
viscountess 608.6
viscountship 608.9
viscounty 608.9
viscous 269.8, 803.12, 1045.12, 1062.12
viscousness 1045.1, 1062.2
vise 260.6, 1040.7
visé 332.4
viselike 474.8
Vishnu 677.3
visibility 31.1, 184.32, 348.3
visibility unlimited 31.2
visibility zero 31.2, 184.32
visible, the 31.1
visible 24.14, 27.20, 31.6, 33.11, 348.8
visible horizon 31.3, 201.4
visibleness 31.1
visible radiation 1025.1, 1032.10
visible spectrum 1025.5, 1032.10
vis inertiae 18.5
vision (n) 27.1, 33.5, 124.4, 356.1, 976.4, 986.5, 986.6, 986.9, 988.1, 1016.6 (v) 986.15
visional 986.19
visionariness 986.7
visionary (n) 101.4, 124.5, 952.8, 986.13 (a) 124.11, 976.9, 986.24
visioned 986.18
visioning 27.1
visionless 30.9
vision quest 375.9
visit (n) 541.3, 582.7 (v) 177.25, 189.7, 221.8, 541.9, 582.19
visitant 178.2, 189.4, 585.6
visitation 85.6, 582.7, 938.3, 1001.1
visitations of providence 677.13
visitator 938.17
visitatorial 938.36
visiting 582.7
visiting card 517.11
visiting fireman 178.1
visiting hours 210.2, 1025.10
visiting professor 571.3
visitor 178.1, 189.4, 221.5, 227.8, 585.6, 828.4, 938.17
visitor from another planet 870.4
visitorial 938.36
visit upon 604.9, 643.5
visit with 541.8
vis major 963.7
vis mortua 18.5
visor 5.25, 356.11, 1028.2
visored 1028.7
Visotoner 30.6
vista 31.3, 33.6
vista of time 827.3
VistaVision 706.7
visual (n) 349.1 (a) 2.28, 27.20, 31.6
visual acuity 27.1
visual aid 449.2
visual arts 712.1
visual-aural range 184.6
visual defect 85.14
visual display unit 1042.9
visual examination 27.6
visual field 27.1
visual flight 184.1
visual flight rules 184.1
visual flying 184.1
visual handicap 28.1
visual humor 489.1
visual image 986.6
visuality 31.1
visualization 90.13, 932.1, 986.6
visualize 931.17, 986.15
visual joke 489.6
visually handicapped 28.11
visually impaired 28.11
visual magnitude 1073.8
visual memory 989.1

visual organ 2.9, 27.9
visual range 31.3
visual sense 27.1
visual tracking station 1074.7
vis vitae 18.5, 306.2
vis vitalis 306.2
vis viva 18.5
vita 719.1
vital 18.12, 83.12, 101.8, 109.14, 305.17, 306.12, 544.11, 827.10, 963.13, 997.23
vital body 689.17
vital center 207.2, 208.5
vital concern 997.5
vital energy 306.2
vital flame 306.2, 919.5
vital fluid 2.25, 306.2
vital force 17.4, 306.2, 689.18, 886.7, 919.5
vital impulse 92.28, 934.2
vital interest 997.5
vitality 15.1, 17.1, 17.4, 18.1, 83.3, 101.1, 109.4, 306.1, 544.3, 1049.1
vitalization 17.8, 306.6
vitalize 17.10, 109.7, 306.10
vitalizer 17.6
vitalizing 17.15
vitalness 963.3
vital principle 17.4, 306.2, 767.5, 886.7, 919.5
vitals 2.16, 207.2, 207.4, 767.5
vital signs 396.3
vital soul 919.5
vital spark 306.2, 919.5
vital spirit 306.2, 919.5
vital statistics 1017.14
vitamin 7.4
vitamin complex 7.4
vitamin deficiency 992.6
vitamin deficiency disease 85.33
vitamin-deficiency disease 85.11
vitaminization 7.14
vitaminize 7.20
vitaminologist 7.15
vitaminology 7.16
vitamin shot 86.8
vitamin supplement 7.4
vitascope 714.12
vitello 10.15
vitellus 305.15
Vitharr 678.11
Vithi 681.10
vitiate 393.12, 654.10, 900.7
vitiated 654.14
vitiating 900.9
vitiation 393.2, 900.2
viticultural 1069.21
viticulture 1069.2
viticulturist 1069.6
vitiligo 37.1
vitreosity 1029.1
vitreous 1029.5, 1046.10
vitreous humor 2.9
vitreousness 1029.1
vitrescence 1029.1
vitric 1029.5
vitrics 1029.2
vitrifaction 1046.5
vitrification 1046.5
vitrified 1046.13
vitriform 1029.5
vitrify 1029.3, 1046.7
vitrine 1029.2
vitriol 144.7, 589.4
vitriolic 17.14, 68.6, 144.22, 589.10
vitrotype 714.4
vittles 10.2
vituperate 510.19, 513.7
vituperation 510.7, 513.2
vituperative 505.7, 510.22, 513.8
viva 938.2
vivace 708.55
vivacious 17.13, 101.8, 109.14, 330.17, 544.12
vivaciousness 330.2
vivacissimo 708.55
vivacity 17.4, 101.1, 109.4, 306.1, 330.2, 544.4
vivacity of imagination 986.4
vivarium 228.24
viva voce 343.12, 524.29
viva-voce communication 524.1
viva voce examination 938.2
viva voce vote 371.6
vivid 17.13, 24.13, 35.19, 101.8, 349.13, 349.14, 544.10, 989.22, 1025.32
vivid description 349.2
vivid image 986.6
vivid imagination 986.4
vividness 35.4, 544.1, 544.4, 1025.4
vivification 9.1, 306.6
vivified 306.12
vivify 9.2, 306.10
vivifying 17.15, 306.13
viviparous 311.40
vivisect 802.17
vivisection 802.5
vixen 77.9, 110.12, 593.7, 671.9
vixenish 110.22
vixenishness 110.6
vixenly 110.22
vizard 356.11
vizier 575.12
vizierate 417.7
viziership 417.7
vocable 524.2, 524.12, 526.1
vocabular 526.19
vocabulary (n) 523.9, 526.13, 527.1, 554.9, 871.4 (a) 526.19
vocal 524.29, 708.50
vocal bands 524.18
vocal chink 524.18
vocal communication 524.1
vocal cords 524.18
vocal folds 524.18
vocalic (n) 524.12 (a) 524.30
vocalism 524.2, 708.13
vocalist 710.13
vocalization 524.2, 524.5, 708.13
vocalize 524.22, 708.38
vocalized 524.29
vocalizer 710.13
vocal minority 617.4
vocal music 708.13
vocal organ 524.18
vocal processes 524.18
vocal score 708.28
vocal style 524.7
vocation 375.1, 698.1, 724.6, 865.7, 866.1
vocational 724.16
vocational education 568.3
vocational guidance 422.1
vocational training 568.3
vocative 530.9
voce 524.7, 709.5
voce di petto 709.5
voce di testa 709.5
voce velata 52.2
vociferance 59.5
vociferant 59.10
vociferate 59.8
vociferating 59.10
vociferation 53.3, 59.4
vociferous 53.13, 59.10
vociferousness 53.2, 59.5
vocoder 524.16
vocoid (n) 524.12 (a) 524.30
voder 524.16
vogue (n) 578.1, 662.1 (a) 578.12
vogue word 526.9
voguish 578.12
voguishness 578.2
voice (n) 371.6, 509.1, 524.2, 524.7, 524.12, 524.18, 530.14, 576.5, 708.22, 709.5, 710.13 (v) 352.10, 524.22, 708.36
voice box 524.18
voice coil 50.8
voice communication 524.1
voiced 50.15, 524.29, 524.30
voiced consonant 524.12
voiced sound 524.12
voiceful 524.29
voiceless 51.12, 524.30
voicelessness 51.2, 525.1
voiceless sound 524.12
voiceless speech 525.6
voicemail 347.13
voicemail box 553.6
voice of conscience 113.2, 636.5
voice of the tempter, the 377.3
voice over 719.5
voiceover 1034.23
voice part 708.22
voiceprint 517.11
voice qualifier 524.7
voice quality 524.7
voice recognition 549.10, 1042.1
voices 710.16
voice vote 371.6
voicing 524.5, 524.12
void, the 1073.3
void (n) 158.1, 222.3, 224.2, 762.1 (v) 12.13, 255.12, 395.13, 445.2, 900.7, 909.22 (a) 222.14, 445.3, 762.8
void above, the 1073.3
voidance 12.2, 445.1, 909.6
voiding (n) 395.6, 445.1, 900.2, 909.6 (a) 900.9
voidness 222.2
void of 992.13
void of truth 354.25
voiturier 178.9
volaille 10.22
volant 184.50
volatile (n) 1067.1 (a) 298.10, 364.6, 828.7, 854.7, 922.20, 985.17, 1067.10
volatile inhalant 87.3
volatile oil 70.2, 1056.1
volatility 298.1, 364.3, 828.1, 922.7, 985.5, 1067.4
volatilizable 1067.10
volatilization 771.1, 1067.5
volatilize 771.5, 1067.8
volation 184.1
vol-au-vent 10.41
volcan 671.6
volcanic 93.18, 105.28, 105.29, 110.25, 671.24
volcanic crater 237.7
volcanic island 235.2, 240.5
volcanic lake 241.1
volcanic mountain 237.6
volcanic neck 237.6
volcanic rock 1059.1
volcanic spine 237.6
volcanic water 1019.10
volcanic wind 318.6
volcanism 237.6
volcano 237.6, 671.6
volcanology 1019.21
volitant 184.50
volitate 184.36
volitation 184.1
volitational 184.50
volition 323.1, 371.1
volitional 323.4, 371.22
volitive 323.4, 371.22
volley (n) 56.3, 459.9, 462.6, 904.4 (v) 748.3
volleying 56.12
volplane (n) 184.13 (v) 184.36
volplaning 184.1
Volstead Act 668.3
volt 1032.12
voltage 1032.12
voltage drop 1032.20
voltage loss 1032.20
voltage pulse 1035.4
voltage saturation 1033.7
voltaic 1032.30
voltametric 1032.30
volte-face (n) 163.3, 363.1, 858.1 (v) 163.10
volubility 540.1
voluble 540.9
volume 53.1, 158.1, 247.3, 257.1, 257.2, 554.1, 554.4, 554.5, 554.13
volume control 1034.16
volume engineer 1034.24
volume measure 300.4
volume-produce 892.11
volume-produced 892.18
volume production 892.3
volume resistance 1032.13
volumetric 158.10
volumetric analysis 801.1
voluminous 158.11, 247.7, 257.17
voluminousness 257.6
volumize 253.5
Völund 726.8
voluntariness 324.2
voluntarism 324.2

voluntary (n) 708.26, 816.2 (a) 323.4, 324.7, 371.22, 380.8
voluntaryism 324.2
voluntary jurisdiction 594.1
voluntary muscle 2.3
voluntary poverty 619.1, 667.1
voluntary resignation 448.1
voluntary simplicity 499.4, 798.1
volunteer (n) 324.2, 726.2 (v) 324.4, 439.10, 476.5 (a) 324.7
volunteer army 461.26
volunteer fireman 1022.4
volunteer forces 461.20, 461.26
volunteering 324.2, 458.8
volunteerism 324.2
volunteer militia 461.26
volunteer navy 461.26
volunteers 461.26
volunteer work 724.7
volupté 95.1
voluptuary 663.3
voluptuous 75.25, 97.7, 663.5
voluptuousness 75.2, 95.1, 97.2, 663.1
volutation 915.1
volute (n) 281.2 (a) 281.8
voluted 281.8
volution 281.2, 915.1
vomit (n) 86.18, 909.8 (v) 99.4, 238.20, 671.13, 909.26
vomit forth 190.13, 238.20
vomiting 85.9, 85.30, 909.8
vomition 909.8
vomitive (n) 86.18 (a) 86.49, 909.30
vomitory (n) 190.9 (a) 909.30
vomit out 238.20
vomiturition 909.8
vomitus 909.8
vomity 64.7, 80.23, 1000.8
voodoo (n) 675.6, 690.1, 690.7, 691.5, 1000.4 (v) 377.7, 691.9 (a) 690.14
voodooism 675.6, 690.1
voodooist 690.7
voodooistic 690.14
voortrekker 178.1
voracious 100.25, 100.27, 672.6
voraciousness 100.8, 672.1
voracity 100.8, 672.1
Vorlage 753.3
Vorspeise 10.9
vortex 105.4, 184.30, 238.12, 281.2, 318.11, 330.4, 915.2
vortical 238.24, 915.15
votary 100.12, 101.4, 166.2, 616.8, 616.9, 692.4, 696.9
votary candle 1026.2
votary offering 150.2
vote, the 609.17
vote (n) 371.6, 509.1, 609.18, 613.6 (v) 371.18, 476.5, 609.41
vote affirmatively 441.2
vote against 451.3
vote aye 441.2
vote down 442.3, 510.10
vote for 332.8
vote in 371.20
vote in the negative 442.3
vote nay 442.3, 451.3
vote negatively 442.3
vote of confidence 953.4
vote of no confidence 955.2
vote out 372.2
voter 371.7, 609.23
voter-preference survey 938.14
vote with one's feet 188.17
voting 371.6, 476.1, 609.18
voting age 303.2
voting booth 609.20
voting machine 371.6, 609.18, 609.20
voting right 371.6
voting with one's feet 188.1
votive 436.7
votive candle 696.10
votive offering 478.6, 696.7
vouch (n) 334.1, 334.3 (v) 334.6, 436.4, 957.9
vouched 334.9
vouched for 334.9
voucher 509.4, 549.6, 627.2, 728.11, 957.6
vouch for 334.6
vouching 334.3
vouchsafe 137.8, 141.8, 443.9, 478.12
vouchsafed 478.24
vouchsafement 443.1, 478.1
vouchsafer 478.11
voussoir 279.4
vow (n) 334.4, 436.1 (v) 334.6, 436.4, 953.12
vowed 334.9
vowel (n) 524.12 (a) 524.30
vowel gradation 524.12
vowellike 524.30
vowel mutation 524.12
vowel point 546.1
vowel quantity 524.11
vows of poverty 619.1
vox pop 332.5, 953.6
vox populi 332.5, 953.6
voyage (n) 177.5, 182.6 (v) 177.20, 177.21, 182.13
voyager 178.1
voyaging 182.1
voyagings 177.2
voyeur 75.16, 981.2
voyeurism 75.11, 981.1
voyeuristic 981.5
V-particle 1037.4
V-shaped 171.10, 278.6
V-sign 411.1
vug 284.2
vugg 284.2
vugh 284.2
Vulcan 726.8
vulcanize 1020.24, 1048.6
vulcanized 1049.6
vulgar 250.6, 497.10, 501.20, 505.6, 523.20, 523.21, 534.2, 606.8, 661.12, 666.8
vulgar fellow 497.6
vulgar fraction 1017.7
vulgarian 497.6, 618.7
vulgarism 497.1, 526.6, 534.1
vulgarist 497.6
vulgarity 250.3, 497.1, 505.1, 513.4, 534.1, 661.3, 666.3
vulgarization 497.8
vulgarize 393.12, 497.9, 521.6
vulgar language 513.3, 523.9
vulgar masses, the 606.2
vulgarness 497.1, 501.3
vulgar taste 497.1
vulgar tongue 523.6
Vulgate 683.2
vulgate (n) 523.6 (a) 523.20
vulgus 497.6, 606.1
vulnerability 19.4, 406.1, 897.2, 1006.4, 1050.1
vulnerable 19.18, 406.11, 894.15, 897.5, 1006.16, 1050.4
vulnerableness 1050.1
vulnerable place 1003.2
vulnerable point 16.4, 1006.4
vulnerable to 897.6
vulnerary 86.11
vulpine 311.41, 415.12
vulture 480.12
vulturine 480.26
vulturous 480.26
vulva 2.13
vulval 2.29
vulvar 2.29
V-weapon 1074.4
vying (n) 451.2, 457.1, 457.2 (a) 457.23
wack 926.16, 927.4
wackadoodle 924.7
wacked 926.27
wackiness 923.1, 926.2
wacko (n) 926.16, 927.4 (a) 927.6
wacky 923.9, 926.27, 927.6
wad (n) 247.4, 257.10, 618.3, 728.17, 770.7, 770.9 (v) 196.7, 794.7
wadding 196.3, 293.5
waddle (n) 175.2, 177.12 (v) 175.6, 177.28
waddling (n) 177.8 (a) 175.10
waddy 462.18, 1070.3
wade 182.56
Wade-Giles system 546.5
wade in 189.7
wade into 216.8, 459.15, 725.15
wade knee-deep in blood 308.15
wade through 570.12, 725.14
wadi 237.7, 238.1, 239.2, 284.9
wading 182.11
wading bird 311.27
wading pool 743.12
wads 618.3
wad up 260.8
wafer 10.30, 270.7, 296.2, 701.7
wafer chip 1042.3
wafer-thin 270.16, 1050.4
waffle (n) 10.45, 368.1, 520.3 (v) 340.8, 344.7, 362.8, 368.13, 467.5, 520.5, 854.5
waffle house 8.17
waffler 357.9, 936.7
wafflestompers 5.27
waffling (n) 344.4, 362.2, 936.1 (a) 344.11, 362.10, 854.7
waft (n) 318.3 (v) 176.12, 298.8, 318.19
waft on the ear 52.9
wafture 69.1
wag (n) 322.3, 489.12, 916.6, 917.7 (v) 916.10, 916.11, 917.14
wage (n) 624.4 (v) 328.8
wage contract 437.1
wage control 624.4
waged 624.22
wage earner 577.3, 726.2
wage earners 607.7
wage freeze 624.4
wage peace 464.8
wager (n) 759.3, 971.8 (v) 759.24, 759.25
wage reduction 624.4
wagerer 759.21
wagering 759.1
wage rollback 624.4
wages 624.4
wages after taxes 624.4
wage scale 624.4
wage slave 726.2
wages plus fringe benefits 624.4
wage war 457.13, 458.13
wageworker 726.2
waggery 322.2, 489.4
waggish 322.6, 489.17, 743.29
waggishness 322.2, 489.4
waggish trick 489.10
waggle (n) 751.3, 916.6, 917.7 (v) 916.10, 917.14
waggle the beard 335.3
waggon 179.2, 179.15
Wagnerian tenor 709.5
wagon 179.2, 179.11
wagoner 178.9
wag one's finger 422.6
wagonload 196.2
wagonman 178.9
wagon tongue 273.1
wag the beard 335.3
wag the tongue 524.19
wagwit 489.12
Wahabiism 675.13
Wahhabi 675.23
wahine 77.5
waif 160.4, 178.3, 370.4
waifish 270.17
waifs and strays 178.3, 370.4
wail (n) 58.4, 115.3 (v) 58.8, 60.2, 115.13, 318.20, 524.25
wailful 115.19
wailing (n) 115.1 (a) 58.14, 60.6, 115.18
wail of woe 115.3
wain 179.2
wainscot (n) 196.3, 199.2 (v) 196.7
waist 5.15, 819.1
waistband 5.19
waistcloth 5.19
waistcoat 5.14
waist-deep 275.11
waistline 819.1
wait (n) 710.14, 846.2 (v) 130.8, 134.4, 577.13, 846.12
wait about 130.8
wait and see 329.2, 846.12
wait-and-see 134.10
wait-and-see attitude, a 329.1
wait-and-see attitude 494.1
wait around 130.8, 134.4
wait a second 846.12
waiter 577.7
waiter on Providence 331.8, 340.5
wait for 130.8
wait for something to turn up 846.12

wait impatiently 135.4, 846.13
waiting (n) 130.3, 846.3 (a) 130.11, 577.14, 840.3
waiting concealed 346.14
waiting for 130.11
waiting for the bomb to drop 127.23
waiting game 134.1, 329.1
waiting in the wings 839.8
waiting it out 134.1
waiting list 871.1
waiting maid 577.8
waiting on 577.14
waiting room 197.20
wait it out 134.4
wait on 130.8, 138.8, 504.11, 577.13, 769.7, 769.8
wait one's turn 134.4
wait on hand and foot 138.8, 577.13
wait out the market 737.23
waitperson 577.7
waitress 577.7
waitron 577.7
wait to see how the cat jumps 362.7
wait to see how the wind blows 362.7
wait up 846.12
wait up for 130.8
wait upon 130.8, 138.8, 504.11
waive 370.7, 372.2, 390.4, 390.5, 443.9, 445.2, 475.3, 846.9, 959.5
waived 390.12, 475.5
waiver 370.3, 390.2, 443.1, 445.1, 475.2, 601.2, 959.1
waiving 445.1
wakan 678.1
wake (n) 23.1, 182.7, 184.30, 217.1, 309.4, 517.8, 582.10, 817.2, 887.3 (v) 23.4, 23.5, 105.12, 115.10
wakeful 23.7, 339.14
wakefulness 23.1, 339.5
wakeless sleep 22.5
waken 23.5, 105.12, 375.19
wakening 23.2
wake someone up 23.5
wake up 23.4, 23.5, 105.12, 375.19, 521.9, 977.2
wake-up call 23.2
wake up to 521.9
waking dream 976.4
waking time 314.1
Waldensian (n) 667.2 (a) 667.4
Waldensianism 667.1
waldgrave 608.4
wale 85.37, 283.3, 294.1, 1004.1
wali 575.12
walk, the 755.2
walk (n) 175.2, 177.10, 177.12, 231.2, 383.1, 383.2, 457.12, 463.1, 724.4, 724.6, 745.3, 914.2 (v) 84.4, 175.6, 177.27, 369.7, 411.4, 430.18, 431.9, 727.10, 745.5
walkability 918.4
walk all over 432.10, 612.15
walk a middle path 467.6
walk a tightrope 1013.11
walk away 188.9, 249.10, 370.5, 984.4
walkaway 411.1
walk away from 188.9, 390.7, 475.3
walk away with 411.4
walkboy 588.4
walker 178.6, 179.6
walk hand in hand with 582.17
walk humbly with one's God 692.6
walk in 189.7
walk-in closet 197.15
walk in darkness 30.8, 930.9
walking (n) 84.2, 177.8, 755.2 (a) 177.36
walking bass 708.9
walking dead man 988.1
walking encyclopedia 413.11, 920.9, 929.3
walking excursion 177.10
walking gentleman 707.7
walking into the sunset 820.1
walking lady 707.7
walking meditation 92.6
walking on eggs 177.17
walking papers 447.2, 909.5
walking part 704.10
walking phallus 665.10
walking skeleton 270.8
walking stick 273.2, 901.2
walking the plank 604.2
walking tour 177.10, 918.4
walk in lockstep 326.2, 867.4
walk in one's sleep 177.32
walk in the shoes of 336.7
walk into 472.8
walkist 178.6
walk off 249.10
walk-off 190.10
walk off with 411.4, 482.13
walk off with the game 411.4
walk of life 724.6, 765.1
walk of shame 75.7
walk on 910.7
walk-on 704.10, 707.7
walk on air 95.12, 109.6
walk on eggs 494.5
walk on eggshells 339.7, 494.5, 1013.11
walk on hot coals 1013.11
walk on thin ice 494.5
walk on tiptoe 494.5
walk on water 967.5
walk out 190.12, 566.5, 727.10, 857.8
walkout 188.1, 370.2, 727.5, 857.2
walk out on 190.12, 370.5
walk over 411.4, 612.15, 910.7
walkover 411.1, 1014.4
walk over the course 1014.11
walkscore 918.4
walk the earth 306.8
walk the floor 126.6
walk the straight path 653.4
walk the tightrope 492.9
walk the tracks 177.23
walk the walk 641.10
walk the waters 182.54
walk through 704.32
walk-through 704.13
walk through the valley of the shadow of death 307.20
walk-up 405.1, 814.1, 816.2
walkup 228.13
walkway 383.2
wall (n) 200.3, 212.4, 213.5, 237.2, 1012.5 (v) 212.7, 460.9
Wallace's Trotting Register 757.1
walled 212.10, 213.11, 295.31
walled-in 212.10, 295.31
wallet 729.15
walleye 28.5
walleyed 28.12
walleyes 28.6
wall in 212.5, 295.23, 429.12
walling 1054.2
walling in 429.2
walling-in 212.1
walling off 429.2
walling up 429.2
wall off 213.8, 429.13, 773.6
wall of secrecy 345.3
wall of silence 345.3
wall of water 238.5
wallop (n) 17.3, 902.5 (v) 604.14, 902.15, 902.17, 917.15
walloping (n) 604.5 (a) 257.21
wallow (n) 243.1, 917.8 (v) 182.55, 665.19, 913.9, 915.13, 917.15
wallow in 95.13, 669.4
wallowing in it 618.15
wallow in ignorance 930.8
wallow in the mire 80.14, 665.19
wallow in wealth 618.12
wall painting 712.10
wallpaper 295.23, 295.24
Wall Street 737.1, 737.7, 737.8
Wall Street banking 729.1
Wall Streeter 729.9, 737.10
Wall Streetese 523.10
wall telephone 347.4
wall-to-wall 772.7, 781.6, 794.10, 812.8
wall-to-wall carpet 295.9
wall-to-wall carpeting 295.9
wall up 212.5, 295.23, 429.12
walnut 40.3
walnut-brown 40.3
Walpurgis Night 690.3
walrus mustache 3.11
Walter Mitty 985.2
Waltonian 382.6
waltz (n) 1014.4 (v) 411.4, 705.5
waltz home 411.4
waltzing Matilda 177.3
waltz off with 411.4
waltz through 1014.8
waltz time 709.24
wamble 177.28, 915.9, 916.10
wamperjawed 204.14
wampum 498.6, 728.2, 728.3
wampumpeag 728.3
wan (v) 36.6 (a) 21.9, 36.7, 307.28, 331.20, 1027.17
wand 417.9, 647.1, 691.6, 962.3, 1042.4
wander 164.4, 177.23, 538.9, 688.8, 926.20, 975.9, 984.3, 985.9
wanderer 178.2, 774.3, 828.4, 1073.9
wander from 473.4
wander from the subject 538.9, 984.3
wandering (n) 164.1, 177.3, 538.3, 926.8 (a) 164.7, 177.37, 538.13, 810.12, 851.3, 854.7, 870.9, 926.26, 926.31, 985.10
wandering course 164.1
Wandering Jew 160.4, 178.2
Wandering Jew, the 774.3
wandering minstrel 178.2, 710.14
wandering pain 26.2
wandering path 164.1
wanderings 177.2
wandering scholar 178.2
wandering spirit 988.1
wandering star 1073.9
Wanderjahr 177.3
wanderlust 177.3
wander off 164.4
wanderyear 177.3
wand of office 417.9
wane (n) 34.1, 173.3, 252.2, 393.3 (v) 16.9, 34.2, 168.2, 172.5, 173.8, 252.6, 303.10, 393.17
wanga 675.6, 690.1, 691.1
wangateur 690.7
wangle 192.14, 375.23, 381.9, 415.10
wangle into 375.23
wangle out of 192.14
wangler 381.7
wangling 381.13
waning (n) 173.3, 252.1, 260.1 (a) 34.3, 168.5, 173.12, 252.11, 303.17, 393.45
waning crescent moon 1073.11
waning moon 1073.11
wank 75.8
Wankel 1043.3
wankered 87.24
wannabe (n) 100.12 (a) 100.28**wannabee** 100.12, 440.7, 610.9
wanness 36.2, 307.11
want (n) 100.1, 222.1, 619.2, 795.2, 963.2, 992.4, 1003.1 (v) 100.14, 250.4, 619.5, 795.3, 911.2, 963.9, 992.7, 992.8
want ad 352.6
wantage 795.2, 992.4
want doing 963.9
wanted 100.29, 585.12, 963.13
wanter 100.12
want everything 651.4
want everything just so 495.8
want for 795.3, 911.2, 992.8
wanting (n) 100.1 (a) 100.21, 222.11, 473.8, 762.8, 795.4, 911.5, 992.9, 992.13, 1003.4
want in the worst way 100.17
want list 871.1
want nothing to do with 99.3
wanton (n) 665.10, 665.14 (v) 562.14, 665.19, 669.6, 743.24 (a) 364.5, 430.24, 493.8, 654.12, 665.26, 854.7
wanton cruelty 144.11

wantonness 430.3, 493.2, 654.1, 665.4, 854.2
want to 100.15
want to know 938.20, 981.3
want with all one's heart 100.17
wapentake 231.5
wapiti 311.5
war (n) 457.1, 458.1, 458.3, 458.5 (v) 457.13, 458.13
warble 60.5, 524.25, 708.38
warbler 311.27, 710.13, 710.23
warbling 708.13
war bride 563.5, 563.8
war chest 728.14
war clouds 458.9
war correspondent 555.4
warcraft 458.5
war crime 655.2
war cry 59.1, 454.2, 458.7, 517.16
ward (n) 197.25, 231.5, 429.5, 432.6, 460.1, 460.6, 609.16, 1008.2 (v) 460.8
war dance 701.9
warden 429.10, 574.3, 575.16, 1008.6, 1008.12
wardenship 1008.2
warder 429.10, 1008.6, 1008.9
ward heeler 166.2, 609.27, 610.8
ward off 368.8, 460.10, 908.3, 1012.14
ward of the state 432.6
war dog 461.5
ward politics 609.1
wardrobe 5.2, 197.15
wardrobe basic 5.2
wardrobe master 704.23
wardrobe mistress 704.23
wardroom 197.20
wardship 19.2, 432.3, 1008.2
ware 735.2
war economy 458.9
war effort 458.9
warehouse (n) 386.6, 736.1, 736.2 (v) 159.15, 386.10
warehouse club 386.6
warehoused 386.15
warehouse store 386.6, 736.1
warehousing 159.6, 386.5
wareroom 736.1, 736.5
wares 735.1, 893.1
warfare 457.1, 458.1
war fever 458.10
war footing 458.9
war game 458.4
war god 458.12
war goddess 458.12
war hawk 461.5
warhead 462.16, 1074.3
warhorse 311.10, 311.13, 413.16, 461.19, 461.30, 610.1
war hound 461.5
wariness 339.4, 415.1, 494.2, 955.2, 956.1
warlike 457.22, 458.20, 458.21
warlikeness 458.10
warlike spirit 458.10
warlock 690.5
warlord 575.12, 575.13
war-loving 458.21
warm (v) 17.10, 41.4, 105.12, 1020.17 (a) 35.16, 41.6, 93.18, 101.9, 105.22, 121.11, 143.13, 223.14, 544.13, 585.11, 587.16, 618.15, 941.10, 1019.24
warmaking 458.1
warm-and-fuzzy 95.15, 121.13
warm assent 332.1
warm as toast 1019.24
warm-blooded 1019.29
warm-blooded animal 311.3
warm bodies 227.1
warm body 872.4, 1052.3
warm color 35.2, 35.6
warm-complexioned 41.9
warm-down 84.2
warmed 1020.29
war medal 646.6
warmed-over 117.9, 849.12, 1020.29
warmed-over cabbage 489.9, 994.3
warmed up 849.12, 1020.29
war memorial 549.12
warmer 1019.11, 1020.10
warm feeling 104.1
warm friendship 587.8
warm front 317.4, 1019.7
warm fuzzy 95.1
warm heart 93.6
warmhearted 93.20, 143.13, 145.7, 585.11, 587.16
warmheartedness 93.6, 143.1, 585.1, 587.6
warming (n) 1020.1 (a) 1020.26
warming-up 818.3
warmish 1019.24
warmness 121.2, 585.1, 587.6, 1019.1
warmonger 461.5
warmongering (n) 458.10 (a) 458.21
warm over 117.5, 396.16, 1020.17
warm spring 91.23, 1019.10
warm temper 110.4
warmth 17.4, 35.2, 93.2, 93.5, 93.6, 95.1, 101.2, 143.1, 544.5, 585.1, 587.6, 1019.1
warm the blood 105.12
warm the cockles of one's heart 95.6
warm the cockles of the heart 95.8
warm the spirits 109.7
warmth of color 35.2
warmth of feeling 93.2
warmth of heart 143.1
warm to 587.10
warm up 84.4, 396.16, 405.9, 405.13, 818.8, 1020.17
warm-up 84.2, 405.1, 816.2
warm up to 93.11
warm weather 1019.7
warm welcome 585.2
warm work 725.5
warn 133.10, 379.3, 399.5, 400.3, 421.5, 422.6, 514.2
warn against 399.5
warn away 379.3, 399.5, 422.6
warner 399.4
warning (n) 379.1, 399.1, 405.1, 421.1, 422.1, 514.1, 551.3 (a) 133.15, 399.7, 422.8
warning cry 60.1
warning piece 399.1
warning sign 399.3
warning signal 399.3
warning track 745.1
warn off 379.3, 399.5, 422.6
war of independence 458.1
war of national liberation 860.1
war of nerves 127.6, 127.7, 569.2
war of the elements 671.4
war of words 456.5, 457.1, 935.4
warp (n) 164.1, 204.3, 265.1, 740.3, 896.1, 978.3, 1004.1 (v) 164.5, 182.48, 265.5, 350.3, 354.16, 393.12, 852.6, 896.3, 980.9, 1004.4 (a) 174.16
warpage 740.1
war paint 1016.11
warp and weft 266.1, 740.1
warp and woof 266.1, 740.1
warpath 458.1, 458.10
warped 265.10, 354.26, 650.11, 654.14, 980.12, 1004.8
warped conception 976.1
warped judgment 948.1
warping 164.2
war pipes 711.9
warplane 181.9
war plans 458.4
warp out 368.11
warp speed 174.2
warrant (n) 332.4, 334.4, 417.12, 420.6, 438.1, 443.3, 443.6, 549.6, 598.2, 600.6, 615.1, 627.2, 642.2, 673.2, 728.11 (v) 18.10, 332.11, 332.12, 334.6, 436.4, 438.9, 443.11, 600.9, 615.10, 673.9, 953.12, 957.9, 957.11
warrantability 649.1
warrantable 443.15, 600.14, 649.7
warrantableness 443.8, 600.7
warranted 332.14, 334.9, 436.8, 438.11, 443.17, 639.9, 649.7, 673.11, 970.20
warrantedness 649.1
warrantee 438.7
warranteed 1007.5
warranting 332.14
warrant officer 575.17, 575.19
warrantor 438.6
warranty 436.1, 438.1, 443.3, 549.6
war-ravaged 458.22
warren 80.11, 284.5, 890.6
Warren Buffett 618.8
warring (n) 458.1 (a) 61.5, 457.22, 458.20
warrior 459.12, 461.6, 492.7
warrioress 461.6
Warsaw Pact 437.2
war scare 458.9
warship 180.6
war song 458.11
war spirit 458.10
wart 85.39, 258.4, 283.3, 1004.1
warthog 311.9
wartime 458.1
wartime footing 458.9
war-torn 458.22
warty 283.15
war vessel 180.6
war whoop 59.1, 454.2, 458.7, 517.16
war widow 256.3, 566.4
wary 339.13, 415.12, 494.9, 955.9, 956.4
war zone 458.1, 463.2
wash (n) 35.8, 79.5, 79.6, 182.7, 184.30, 238.8, 243.1, 712.13, 790.3, 836.3, 857.2 (v) 35.14, 52.11, 79.19, 238.19, 758.5, 973.8, 1065.13
wash-and-wear 5.4
washateria 79.11
wash away 79.19, 168.2, 255.9, 395.14, 395.16
wash barrel 79.12
washbasin 79.12
washboard 79.12, 288.2, 383.6
wash boiler 79.12
washbowl 79.12
wash coat 35.8
wash-colored 35.17
washday 79.6
washdish 79.12
wash down 8.29
wash drawing 712.13
washed 35.17, 79.26, 238.25
washed-out 19.15, 36.7, 393.34
washed sale 737.20
washed up 395.29, 407.11, 820.9, 820.10
washed-up 21.8
washer 79.12, 79.15
washerman 79.15
washerwoman 79.15
washery 79.11
washhouse 79.11
washing 79.5, 79.6, 238.8, 737.20
washing machine 79.12
washing out 395.7
washing pot 79.12
washing powder 79.17
Washington 612.3
Washingtonese 523.10, 609.37
washing up 79.5
washman 79.15
wash money 673.9
wash one's hands of 370.7, 442.3, 475.3, 510.10
wash one's sins away 685.5
wash out 36.5, 79.19, 410.17
washout 79.5, 184.3, 238.6, 395.4, 410.2, 410.5, 410.8, 750.2
wash over 238.17
washpot 79.12
washroom 12.10, 79.10, 197.26
wash sale 737.20
wash sales 737.25
washshed 79.11
washstand 79.12
washtub 79.12
wash up 79.19

washup 79.5
washwoman 79.15
washy 65.2
wasp 110.11, 311.32, 311.34
waspish 110.19
waspishness 110.2
wasp's nest 228.25
wasp waist 260.1
wasp-waisted 260.12, 270.16
wassail (n) 88.5 (v) 88.28
wassailer 88.11
wastage 388.1, 391.4, 393.4, 473.2
waste (n) 12.3, 80.9, 252.3, 256.1, 370.4, 388.1, 391.4, 393.4, 395.1, 473.2, 486.1, 806.1, 891.2, 893.3 (v) 34.2, 85.48, 252.6, 260.9, 308.14, 388.4, 393.19, 395.10, 395.12, 473.5, 486.4, 762.7, 820.6 (a) 233.9, 891.4
waste away 34.2, 85.48, 252.6, 260.9, 303.10, 388.3, 393.19, 806.3
wastebasket 391.7
wastebin 391.7
wasted 16.18, 260.13, 270.20, 388.5, 393.35, 395.28, 473.7, 486.9, 619.10, 820.10, 891.4
wasted away 260.13
wasted breath 391.3
wasted effort 391.3
waste disposal 390.3
waste disposal unit 391.7
wasted labor 391.3
wasted loins 891.1
waste effort 486.4
wasteful 395.26, 486.8
wastefulness 388.1, 486.1
wasteland 233.2, 891.2
waste matter 12.3, 391.4
waste no words 344.6, 535.2, 537.5
waste of breath 391.3
waste of effort 391.3
waste of energy 391.3
waste of labor 391.3
waste of time 391.3
waste one's breath 391.8
waste one's effort 19.7, 391.8, 410.14
wastepaper 391.4
wastepaper basket 391.7
waste product 370.4, 391.4, 893.3
waster 486.2
wastes of outer space 158.1
waste stream 391.4
waste the opportunity 844.5
waste the precious hours 331.13
wastethrift 486.2
waste time 175.8, 331.13
waste time in regret 113.6
wastewater 370.4, 391.4
wasteyard 391.6
wasting (n) 85.3, 85.9, 260.3, 308.2, 393.4, 806.1 (a) 252.11, 303.17, 393.45, 395.26
wasting away 388.1, 393.4, 806.1
wastrel 178.3, 331.9, 370.4, 486.2, 660.2
wat 703.2
watch (n) 27.2, 183.6, 339.4, 770.6, 825.3, 832.6, 1008.10 (v) 27.13, 130.8, 221.8, 339.8, 918.5, 938.28, 981.3, 983.6, 1008.19, 1008.20
watch and wait 130.8, 329.2
watch and ward 339.4, 1008.2
watch crystal 1029.2
watchdog 311.16, 1008.11
watcher 918.1, 981.2, 1008.10
watch fire 517.15, 1019.13
watch for 130.6
watch for one's moment 134.4
watchful 23.7, 339.13, 983.15, 1008.23
watchful eye 27.10, 339.4, 1008.1
watchfulness 339.4, 981.1, 1008.1
watchful waiting 329.1
watch glass 1029.2
watching 27.2, 339.4
watching and waiting 329.1
watching for 130.11
watching one's calories 7.13
watching one's weight 7.13
watchkeeper 1008.10
watchlist 937.1, 983.2
watchmaker 832.10
watch-making 832.1
watchman 1008.10
watchman's rattle 400.1, 517.15
watch meeting 696.8
watch movement 832.6
watch night 696.8
watch-night service 696.8
watch officer 183.7
watch one's calories 7.19
watch oneself 1007.3
watch one's step 339.7, 494.7
watch one's weight 7.19, 8.20, 270.13
watch out 339.8, 494.7, 983.8, 1007.3
watch out for 130.6, 1008.19
watch over 1008.19
watch television 1035.15
watch the clock 832.11
watchtower 27.8, 272.6, 517.10
watch TV 1035.15
watchword 458.7, 517.12, 974.4
watchworks 832.6, 1040.4
water (n) 10.49, 12.5, 12.7, 16.7, 712.13, 854.4, 1022.3, 1029.2, 1052.2, 1061.2, 1065.3 (v) 13.5, 16.11, 252.8, 270.12, 299.3, 393.12, 771.5, 797.12, 1065.12, 1070.7
water bed 229.1
water bird 311.27
water biscuit 10.30
waterblink 1025.9
waterboarding 458.4
water-borne 182.57, 182.60
water buffalo 311.6
water cannon 462.22
water carrier 239.2
water channel 239.2
water closet 12.10, 12.11, 197.26
water cloud 319.2
watercolor (n) 712.13 (v) 35.14
watercoloring 35.12
watercolorist 716.4
watercolor paint 35.8
watercolor painthin 712.3
watercolor paper 712.18
water conservation 397.1
water-cool 1024.10
water-cooled 1024.13
watercooler 1024.3
watercooler moment 540.3
watercourse 238.1, 239.2
watercraft 179.1, 180.1
water cure 91.3
water cycle 1065.3
water diet 515.2
water diviner 690.5, 962.3
water dog 183.1, 311.17
water down 16.11, 252.8, 270.12, 299.3, 393.12, 771.5, 797.12
water-drinker 668.4
water-driven 1021.9
water-dwelling 182.58
watered 16.19, 47.10, 65.2, 270.16, 299.4, 771.9, 992.10
watered-down 16.19, 65.2, 252.10, 270.16, 299.4, 771.9
watered silk 47.6
water exercise 84.2
waterfall 194.1, 238.11
waterflood 238.5
water flow 238.4
waterfowl 311.27
waterfront 234.2
water furrow 239.2
water gap 237.5, 239.2
water gate 239.2, 239.11
water gauge 238.15
water god 678.10
water-growing 182.58
water gun 1065.8
water hazard 751.1
water hole 751.1
waterhole 88.20
water ice 10.47
wateriness 16.3, 270.4, 1061.1, 1065.1
watering (n) 16.5, 299.2, 771.1, 797.3, 1065.6 (a) 13.7, 1065.18
watering can 1065.8
watering down 797.3
watering-down 16.5, 299.2, 771.1
watering hole 88.20, 241.1
watering place 79.10, 91.23, 228.27
waterish 1065.16
waterless 1066.7
waterlessness 1066.1
water level 201.3
waterline 300.6
water-living 182.58
waterlog 1065.13
waterlogged 1065.17
waterlogging 1065.7
Waterloo 412.1
water-loving 182.58
water main 239.7
waterman 183.5
watermark 300.6, 517.5, 517.10
water meadow 243.1, 274.3, 310.8
water nymph 678.10
water of life 88.13
water out 87.22
water parting 272.5
water pipe 89.6
water pistol 1065.8
waterplane 181.8
water plug 239.12
water pocket 241.1
water pollution 82.1, 1072.2
water power 17.1, 18.4, 1021.7
waterproof (v) 15.14 (a) 180.18, 293.12, 1066.11
water-repellent 293.12
water-resistant 293.12
waterscape 33.6, 712.11
watershed 237.5, 238.1, 272.5
watershoot 238.11
waterside 234.2
waterskiing 182.11, 744.1
water sky 1025.9
water-soak 1065.13
watersoaked 1065.17
waters of Lethe 990.1
waters of oblivion 990.1
water softener 79.17
water-soluble 1064.9
water spirit 678.6, 678.10
waterspout 239.8, 316.2, 318.13
water sprite 240.3, 678.10
water-sprite 678.6
water supply 1065.3
water system 1065.3
water table 1065.3
water therapy 91.3
watertight 15.20, 180.18, 293.12, 1066.11
watertight integrity 1066.1
watertightness 1066.1
water torture 458.4
water tower 272.6
water travel 182.1
water under the bridge 837.1
water vapor 1065.3, 1067.1
water-washed 238.25
water wave 238.14
waterway 182.10, 238.1, 239.2
water wings 397.6
water witch 690.5, 962.3
water witcher 962.3
water witching 962.3
waterworks 239.2, 1065.3
watery 13.7, 16.17, 65.2, 270.16, 992.10, 1061.4, 1065.16
watery grave 307.5
WATS line 347.17
Watsonian psychology 321.3
wattage 18.1, 1032.18
wattle (n) 170.3, 202.4 (v) 740.6
wattle and daub 170.3, 1054.2
watts 1032.18
waul (n) 58.4, 60.1 (v) 58.8, 59.6, 60.2

wave (n) 3.15, 238.14, 281.1, 585.4, 916.2, 916.4, 916.6 (v) 3.22, 238.22, 281.5, 348.5, 501.17, 517.22, 916.10, 916.11, 917.12
wave a flag 517.22
wave aside 372.2, 773.4, 984.4
wave a wand 690.10, 690.13
wave down 857.11
wave equation 916.4
wave gauge 916.8
wavelength 916.4, 1034.11
wavelet 238.14
wavelike 850.7
wave mechanics 1038.1
wavemeter 916.8
wave motion 916.2, 916.4
wave number 916.4
wave off 773.4
wave one aside 157.5
wave pool 743.12
wave power 1021.7
waver (n) 916.6, 917.4 (v) 325.4, 362.8, 782.2, 854.5, 916.10, 917.12, 1025.25
waverer 362.5
wavering (n) 362.2, 782.1, 854.3, 916.1 (a) 362.10, 782.3, 851.3, 854.7, 916.15, 917.18, 971.16, 1025.36
wavering flame 1019.13
wavering light 1025.8
wavery 782.3, 854.7, 917.18, 1025.36
wave the arms 517.21
wave the bloody shirt 152.24, 375.17, 458.18, 507.5
wave the hand 517.22
wave theory 1018.1
wave the white flag 433.8, 465.9
waving (n) 281.1, 916.2 (a) 916.16
waving of the bloody shirt 458.10
waving the bloody shirt 375.4
wavy 279.7, 281.10, 854.7
wax (n) 37.2, 50.12, 79.17, 152.8, 287.2, 1047.4, 1056.1, 1056.2 (v) 14.2, 33.8, 251.6, 259.7, 287.7, 861.5, 1056.8
wax and wane (n) 916.5 (v) 854.5, 916.13
wax candle 1026.2
waxed paper 295.18
waxen 36.7, 1056.9
wax figure 349.6
waxiness 1056.5
waxing (n) 251.1, 1016.14 (a) 251.8
waxing crescent moon 1073.11
waxing moon 1073.11
wax modeler 716.6
waxwork 349.6
waxworks 386.9
waxy 152.30, 1047.9, 1056.9
way, a 261.1
way 158.3, 161.1, 162.1, 182.9, 189.5, 239.1, 321.1, 373.1, 373.3, 381.1, 383.1, 384.1, 413.6, 430.4, 532.2, 765.4, 767.4, 856.1, 866.1
way back when 837.3
waybill 871.5
wayfare 177.18, 177.21, 177.23
wayfarer 178.1
wayfaring (n) 177.3 (a) 177.36
wayfinding 159.6
waygoose 743.4
way in 189.5
way it is, the 765.2
way it looks, the 896.2
way it shapes up, the 765.2
way it was, the 837.2
Wayland 726.8
waylay 346.10
wayleave rent 630.8
wayless 293.10
way of, the 384.1
way of acting 321.1
way of couching 532.1
way of dealing 387.2
way of escape 369.4
way off 787.5
way-off 261.8
way of gentleness, the 760.3
way of harmony of the spirit, the 760.3
way of holding oneself 517.14
way of it, the 765.2, 767.4
way of life 321.1, 371.5, 373.1, 765.4, 866.1
way of looking at things 978.2
way of putting 341.1, 532.1
way of saying 524.7
way of seeing 341.1
way of speaking 529.1, 536.1
way of the empty hand, the 760.3
way of the foot and fist, the 760.3
way of the world, the 765.2
way of things, the 765.2, 831.4
way of thinking 931.1, 953.6, 978.1
way of understanding 341.1
way one feels, the 978.1
way out (n) 190.9, 369.4, 381.5, 600.4 (a) 787.5
way-out 247.13, 841.13, 868.6
way over to one side 650.11
ways 261.1, 321.1, 384.2
ways and means 384.2
ways of the fathers 842.2
way station 213.1
way the ball bounces, the 972.1
way the cards fall, the 972.1
way the cookie crumbles, the 765.2, 766.2, 972.1
Way, the Truth, and the Life, the 677.10
way the wind blows, the 896.2
way things are, the 765.2, 838.1, 869.3
way things are done, the 373.4
way things fall, the 972.1
way things go, the 765.2, 831.4, 896.2
way train 179.14
wayward 327.8, 361.11, 364.5, 654.12, 665.26, 854.7
waywardness 327.1, 361.3, 654.1, 665.4, 854.2
way-weary 21.7, 177.41
way with, a 413.5
way with words 524.4, 532.2
wayworn 21.7, 177.41
way you are, the 312.8
wayzgoose 743.4
W chromosome 305.8
weak 16.12, 19.13, 21.7, 32.6, 36.7, 52.16, 65.2, 270.16, 303.18, 312.13, 362.12, 426.4, 491.10, 524.30, 654.12, 764.7, 894.15, 895.3, 922.21, 936.12, 1006.16
weak as a baby 16.13
weak as a chicken 16.13
weak as a child 16.13
weak as a drink of water 16.13
weak as a kitten 16.13, 19.13
weak as a mouse 16.13
weak as a rained-on bee 16.13
weak as milk and water 16.13
weak as water 16.13
weak economy 731.7
weak ego 139.2
weaken 16.9, 16.10, 19.9, 21.4, 85.48, 85.50, 252.8, 270.12, 286.2, 393.9, 395.20, 670.6, 764.4, 771.5
weakened 16.18, 21.7, 85.54, 252.10, 393.27, 771.9
weakening (n) 16.5, 252.1, 393.1, 771.1 (a) 16.20
weaker sex, the 77.3
weaker vessel, the 77.3
weaker vessel 77.5
weak-eyed 28.13
weak force 1038.6
weakhearted 491.10
weakheartedness 491.1
weak interaction 1038.6
weak in the upper story 922.21
weak-kneed 362.12, 433.15, 491.10
weak-kneedness 491.1
weak knees 491.4
weakliness 16.1, 85.3
weakling 16.6, 19.6, 362.5, 491.5
weak link 16.4, 1003.2, 1006.4
weakly 16.12, 85.54
weak market 737.1
weak-minded 362.12, 922.21
weak-mindedness 362.4, 922.8
weakness 16.1, 16.4, 19.1, 21.1, 32.2, 36.2, 52.1, 65.1, 93.6, 100.2, 100.11, 104.1, 270.4, 312.8, 362.4, 426.1, 491.1, 654.2, 866.1, 894.5, 895.1, 896.1, 897.1, 922.8, 954.2, 1003.2, 1006.4
weaknesses human flesh is heir to, the 312.8
weakness of the flesh 312.8, 654.2
weak place 16.4
weak point 16.4, 654.2, 936.3, 1003.2, 1006.4
weak safety 746.2
weaksauce 98.20
weak side 16.4, 654.2
weak sister 16.6, 77.10, 491.5
weak soul 16.6
weak stress 524.10
weak tool 16.6
weak-voiced 52.16
weak will 362.4
weak-willed 362.12
weal (n) 1004.1, 1010.1 (v) 60.2
weald 236.1
wealth 471.7, 472.3, 618.1, 991.2, 1010.1
wealthiness 618.1
wealthy, the 618.6
wealthy 618.14, 991.7, 1010.12
wealthy man 618.7
wealthy woman 618.7
wean 374.2, 858.16
weaner 302.10
wean from 379.4
weanling 302.9, 757.2
wean oneself from 374.3
weapon 285.2
weaponless 1006.14
weapon of mass destruction 462.1
weaponry 462.1
weapons 462.1
wear (n) 5.1, 387.1, 393.5, 806.1, 1044.2 (v) 5.44, 21.4, 118.6, 182.30, 252.6, 393.20, 473.5, 500.12, 827.6, 1044.7
wearable computer 1042.2
wear a hair shirt 113.6, 658.6, 667.3
wear a mask 346.8
wear and tear 252.3, 393.5, 806.1
wear an earnest frown 111.2
wear away 16.9, 34.2, 252.6, 255.9, 388.3, 393.20, 473.5, 820.7, 1044.7
wear blinkers 30.8
wear down 21.4, 375.23, 393.20, 894.7
wearer of the cap and bells 707.10
wear horns 665.22
wearied 21.7, 118.11
weariful 21.7, 21.13, 112.24, 118.10, 118.11
wearifulness 21.1, 112.7, 118.2, 118.3
weariless 360.8
weariness 16.1, 21.1, 118.3, 331.6
weariness of life 112.3
wearing (n) 255.1, 473.2 (a) 21.13, 98.24, 118.10
wearing a hairshirt 113.4
wearing apparel 5.1
wearing a sackcloth 113.4
wearing a sackcloth and ashes 113.4
wearing away 252.3, 255.1, 388.1, 473.2, 1044.2
wearing down 388.1
wearing her apron high 78.18
wearisome 21.13, 98.22, 112.24, 118.10, 725.18
wearisomeness 98.7, 112.7, 118.2
wearisome sameness 118.1
wear more than one hat 413.21
wear mourning 115.17
wear off 393.20, 820.7
wear on 21.4, 118.6, 827.7
wear one down 98.16

wear one's heart on one's sleeve 416.4
wear one's heart upon one's sleeve 348.6
wear out 21.4, 98.16, 393.20
wear out one's welcome 118.7
wear ragged 393.20
wear rose-colored glasses 124.8
wear sackcloth 658.6
wear sackcloth and ashes 658.6
wear ship 182.30
wear short 182.32
wear the cloth 698.11
wear the crown 417.13, 612.13
wear the horn 665.22
wear the look of 33.10
wear the pants 417.13, 612.14, 894.8
wear the uniform 458.17
wear thin 16.9, 117.4
wear upon 21.4, 118.6
wear upon one 98.16
wear well 83.6, 827.6
weary (v) 21.4, 21.5, 98.16, 118.6 (a) 21.7, 112.24, 118.11, 331.20
weary-footed 21.7
weary for 100.16
wearying 21.13, 98.24, 118.10
weary-laden 21.7
weary-looking 21.9
weary of life 112.22
weary round, the 118.1
weary to death 21.4
weary unto death 21.10, 118.11
weary-winged 21.7
weary-worn 21.7
weasel (n) 27.11, 179.20, 311.22, 344.5 (v) 344.7, 363.8, 539.3, 551.13, 903.7
weaseling out 163.2
weaselly 344.11
weasel out 344.7, 903.7
weasel word 519.2, 539.2
weasel-worded 344.11
weasel words 344.4
weather, the 854.4
weather (n) 184.32, 218.3, 317.3 (v) 182.24, 182.40, 393.20, 855.11, 1007.2 (a) 218.6
weather anchor 218.3
weather balloon 317.8
weather-battered 393.34
weather-beaten 393.34
weather-bitten 393.34
weatherboard (n) 218.3, 1054.3 (v) 295.23
weather-bound 846.16
weatherbound 428.15
weather bow 218.3
weather bureau 317.6
weathercock 317.8, 318.16, 363.4, 854.4, 942.4
weather conditions 184.32, 317.3
weather deck 218.3
weather-eaten 393.34
weathered 35.22, 36.7, 393.34
weather eye 27.10, 182.3, 339.4
weather forecast 317.6, 317.7
weather forecaster 317.6
weatherglass 317.8
weather-going tide 218.3
weather helm 218.3
weathering 36.3, 393.5
weather instrument 317.8
weatherly 180.18
weather man 1071.2
weatherman 317.6
weather map 317.4
weatherologist 317.6
weatherology 317.5
weather out 409.13
weather pattern 317.3
weatherproof (v) 15.14 (a) 15.20
weather prophet 317.6, 962.4
weather radar 317.8
weather rail 218.3
weather report 317.6, 317.7
weather-reporting network 317.6
weather roll 218.3
weather satellite 317.8, 1075.6
weather-scarred 393.34
weather science 317.5
weather scientist 317.6
weather sheet 218.3
weather ship 317.6
weather side 161.2, 218.3
weather situation 317.3
weather station 317.6
weather system 316.1, 317.3
weather tack 218.3
weather the storm 182.40, 396.20, 409.13, 855.11, 1007.2
weather vane 317.8, 318.16, 854.4, 942.4
weather-wasted 393.34
weather wheel 218.3
weather-wise 962.11
weatherworn 393.34
weave (n) 4.1, 170.3, 266.1, 294.1, 740.1 (v) 740.6
weave one's way 162.4
weave peace between 465.8
weaver 740.4, 740.5
weaverbird 740.4
weaver finch 740.4
weaving (n) 170.3, 740.1, 851.1 (a) 740.8, 851.3
weazen 260.9, 1066.6
weazened 260.13, 1066.9
weazen-faced 270.19
weazeny 270.20
Web 1042.19
web (n) 4.1, 170.3, 266.1, 271.1, 548.9, 740.1 (v) 170.7, 740.6
webbed 170.12, 740.7
webbing 170.3, 740.1
webby 170.12
weber 1032.7
web-footed 170.12
weblike 170.12
Weblog 547.12, 1042.19
web of deceit 415.4
web of intrigue 381.5
web page 1042.19
web press 548.9
website 1042.19
website ad 352.6
webster 740.4
Webster's 554.9
webwork 170.3, 799.2
webzine 555.1
wed (v) 563.14, 563.15, 775.6, 800.5, 805.3, 805.4 (a) 775.9, 805.6
wedded 563.18, 563.21, 775.9, 800.13, 805.6
wedded bliss 563.1
weddedness 563.1
wedded pair 563.9
wedded state 563.1
wedded status 563.1
wedded to 104.29
wedded to poverty 667.4
wedded wife 563.8
wedding 563.3, 580.4, 800.1, 805.1
wedding anniversary 487.1, 850.4
wedding attendant 563.4
wedding band 498.6
wedding bells 563.3
wedding canopy 563.3
wedding ceremony 563.3
wedding clothes 5.2
wedding crasher 214.3, 582.16
wedding knot 563.1
wedding march 708.12
wedding party 563.4
wedding planner 563.4
wedding service 563.3
wedding song 563.3
wedding veil 563.3
wedeln 753.3
wedge (n) 10.32, 293.5, 546.2, 1040.7 (v) 800.8, 855.8, 906.8
wedged 800.14, 855.16
wedge in 189.7, 191.7, 213.6
wedge kick 760.8
wedge-shaped 270.15
wedgeshaped 278.8
Wedgwood-blue 45.3
wedlock 563.1
Wednesday 832.4
wee 258.11
wee bit 248.2
weed, the 89.1
weed (n) 87.11, 310.3, 774.2 (v) 255.9, 1069.17
weed-choked 310.43
weediness 16.3
weeding 1069.13
weed killer 1001.3
weed out 87.22, 192.10, 773.5, 1069.17
weed-ridden 310.43
weeds 115.7, 391.4, 566.3
weedy 310.36, 310.43
week 824.2, 882.3
weekday 824.2
weekend (n) 20.3 (v) 20.9, 821.6
weekend warrior 461.7
weeklong 827.12
weekly (n) 555.1, 555.2 (a) 849.13, 850.8
weekly newspaper 555.2
weekly payments 624.1
week off 20.3
week-to-week 849.13
ween 953.11
weeny 248.6
weenybopper 302.7
weep (n) 190.6 (v) 12.12, 12.15, 13.5, 112.17, 115.12, 190.15, 202.6, 238.18, 316.10, 1065.11
weeper 115.8
weep for 115.10, 145.3, 147.2
weepiness 115.2
weeping (n) 12.6, 13.1, 115.2, 190.5, 190.6 (a) 115.21, 202.9, 1065.17
weeping and wailing and gnashing of teeth 112.11
weep over 115.10
weep with 147.2
weepy 115.21, 190.20
wee small hours 315.6
wee small voice 636.5
wee thing 258.4
wee tot 302.3
weevil 311.36
weevily 64.7, 311.51, 393.42
wee-wee (n) 12.5 (v) 12.14
weft 4.1, 170.3, 740.3
weftage 294.1, 740.1
we-group 617.6
weigh 297.10, 300.10, 801.8, 894.10, 931.12, 943.4, 946.9, 997.12
weighable 297.19
weigh against 943.4
weigh anchor 182.18, 188.15, 802.10
weigh down 297.12, 1011.8, 1012.11
weighed 935.21
weighed down 112.20, 297.18
weighed upon 112.20
weigh heavy 297.10
weigh heavy on 297.13, 612.15, 1011.8
weigh heavy upon 112.18
weigh in 33.8, 189.7, 297.10, 946.8
weigh-in 297.9, 757.3
weigh in for 449.14
weighing 297.9, 801.3, 920.7, 931.2, 943.1, 946.3
weighing anchor 186.2
weighing down 297.7
weighing-in 297.9, 757.3
weighing instrument 297.9
weighing-out 297.9
weighing up 946.3
weigh in the balance 297.10
weigh in with advice 422.5
weigh lightly 298.6
weigh on 297.11, 297.13, 1011.8
weigh one down 297.13
weigh one thing against another 362.7
weigh out 297.10
weigh-out 297.9
weight (n) 18.1, 84.1, 96.8, 297.1, 297.6, 300.3, 417.4, 580.1, 643.3, 725.7, 754.2, 894.1, 973.6, 997.1, 1012.6 (v) 297.10, 297.12, 794.7
weight control 1041.8
weight down 98.16, 297.12
weight down with 643.4
weight down with ornament 545.7
weighted 297.18
weighted down 112.20, 297.18

weigh the pros and cons 362.7
weightiness 98.8, 111.1, 297.1, 417.4, 997.3
weighting 643.1
weighting down 297.7, 643.1
weightless 298.10, 764.5
weightlessness 298.1, 1075.10
weight-lift 84.4
weightlifting 84.2, 744.1
weight-loss diet 7.13
weight of burden 112.1
weight problem 257.8
weight room 84.1
weight-train 84.4
weight training 84.2, 744.1
weight-watch 270.13
weight-watching 270.9
weight with 643.4
weighty 98.24, 111.3, 247.7, 297.16, 417.15, 544.14, 894.13, 957.16, 973.14, 997.20
weighty dignity 580.1
weigh up 300.10, 801.8, 946.9
weigh upon 98.16, 112.18, 297.11, 297.13
weigh with 894.7
weir 190.9, 239.11, 1012.5
weird (n) 964.2 (a) 122.11, 127.31, 307.28, 870.11, 923.11, 927.6, 988.9
weirded out 96.22
weirdie 926.16, 927.4
weirdness 127.2, 307.11, 522.6, 870.3, 923.1, 988.4
weirdo 870.4, 926.16, 927.4
Weirds 964.3
Weird Sisters 690.8, 964.3
Weismannism 560.6, 861.4
Weismann theory 560.6
welcome (n) 186.4, 187.1, 187.9, 332.1, 485.1, 585.2 (v) 187.10, 332.8, 585.9, 897.4 (a) 97.6, 585.12
welcome as the roses in May 97.6, 585.12
welcome mat 585.2
welcomeness 97.1
welcome release 307.6
welcome sight, a 100.11
welcome with open arms 585.9
welcoming (n) 187.1, 187.9, 585.2 (a) 187.16, 585.11, 587.16
welcoming address 543.2
welcoming arms 187.1
weld (n) 800.4 (v) 715.5, 775.6, 800.5, 803.9, 1020.24
welded 775.9
welder 1020.14, 1040.3
welder's mask 1008.3
welding torch 715.4, 1020.14
welfare (n) 143.5, 449.3, 478.8, 611.7, 999.4, 1010.1 (a) 143.15
welfare aid 478.8
welfare capitalism 611.7
welfare cases 606.4
welfare client 619.4
welfare clients 619.3
welfare families 619.3
welfare payments 478.8, 611.7
welfare rolls 619.3
welfare state 143.5, 611.7, 612.4
welfare stater 611.11
welfare statism 143.5, 611.7
welfare statist (n) 143.8 (a) 143.15
welfare work 143.5
welfare worker 143.8
welfarism 143.4, 143.5, 611.7
welfarist 143.15
welfaristic 143.15
welkin 317.2, 1073.2
well (n) 241.1, 275.2, 284.4, 386.4, 886.6 (v) 190.13, 238.20 (a) 83.10
well-adjusted 373.15, 405.17
well-advised 920.19
well-affected 143.17, 449.22, 587.15
well-affectedness 587.1
well afford 618.11, 626.7
well-aimed 161.13
well-appointed 385.14
well-argued 935.20
well-armed 385.14, 460.14
well-arranged 712.20
well-aware 570.16
well-balanced 106.13, 264.4, 855.12, 920.18
well-balanced mind 106.3
well-behaved 504.15
well-being 83.1, 95.1, 107.1, 121.1, 999.4, 1010.1
well-beloved (n) 104.9 (a) 104.23
well-blended 708.49
wellborn 607.10, 608.11
well-bred 504.16, 607.10, 608.11
well-brought-up 504.16
well-built 15.16, 763.7, 892.18, 1016.18
well-cared-for 807.8
well-chosen 496.7, 533.7, 788.10
well-chosen moment 843.3
well-composed 712.20
well-connected 608.11, 894.14
well-conserved 397.13
well-considered 155.11, 413.30
well-constructed 763.7, 892.18
well-content 107.9
well-contented 107.9
well-contrived 413.30
well-cooked 11.8
well-coordinated 413.22
well-defined 31.7, 521.11
well-deserved punishment 604.1
well-deserving 509.20
well-designed 413.30
well-developed 14.3, 259.12, 303.13
well-devised 413.30
well-directed 161.13
well-disposed 143.15, 143.17, 324.5, 449.22, 509.17, 587.15
well-disposedness 143.4
well-doer 143.8
well-done 11.8, 413.22
well-drawn 349.14
well-dressed 5.46, 578.13
well-educated 928.20
well-equipped 385.14
well-established 763.7, 855.13, 970.15
well-expressed 533.7
well-favored 264.5, 1016.18
well-fed 257.18
well-filled 991.7
well-fitted 385.14, 405.17, 413.24
well-fixed 618.15
well-flavored 63.9
well-formed 264.5, 530.17, 1016.18
well-formedness 530.1
well-found 385.14, 991.7
well-founded 763.7, 855.13, 935.20, 953.26, 970.13, 970.15, 973.14
well-furnished 385.14, 991.7
well-greased 1014.14
well-groomed 578.13, 807.8
well-grounded 763.7, 855.13, 928.20, 935.20, 970.15, 973.14
well-grounded hope 124.1, 968.1, 972.8
well-grouped 712.20
wellhead 886.6
well-heeled 618.15, 1010.12
well-inclined 324.5, 509.17
well-informed 928.20
well-intended 587.15
well-intentioned 143.17, 449.22, 587.15
well-invented 413.30
well-judged 920.19
well-kempt 807.8
well-kept 397.13, 807.8
well-knit 15.16, 83.12, 763.7
well-known 117.9, 662.16, 761.15, 928.27
well-known fact 761.3
well-laid 413.30
well-liked 104.23
well-lit 1025.39
well-lubricated 1014.14
well-made 264.5, 763.7, 892.18, 1016.18
well-mannered 504.15, 580.8
well-marked 31.7
well-meaning 143.17, 449.22, 587.15, 999.21
well-meant 143.17, 449.22, 587.15, 999.21
well-muscled 15.16
well-natured 143.14
wellness 83.5
wellness center 91.21
wellness program 83.5
well-off, the 618.6
well-off 618.14
well-oiled 88.33, 1014.14
well-ordered 807.6
well out 190.13
well out of 369.11
well over 238.17
well-paid 618.14, 1010.12
well-paying 472.16
well-placed 161.13
well-planned 413.30
well-pleased 107.9
well-posted 928.20
well-prepared 405.16
well-preserved 301.9, 397.13
well-pronounced 31.7
well-proportioned 264.5, 1016.18
well-provided 385.14, 991.7
well provided for 618.14
well-put 533.7
well-qualified 405.17, 413.24
well-rated 622.8
well-read 928.20
well-read in 928.19
well-reasoned 413.30, 935.21
well-received 95.15
well-recognized 928.27
well-regulated 807.6
well-regulated mind 106.3
well-resolved 31.7
well-rooted 855.13
well-rounded 413.25
well-rounded periods 533.1
well said 155.1
well-said 343.10
well-satisfied 107.9
well-scrubbed 79.25
well-set 15.16, 264.4, 855.13
well-settled 855.13
well-set-up 15.16, 264.4
well-shaped 264.5, 1016.18
well-situated 618.14
well-speaking 544.8
well-spent 387.22
well-spoken 504.15, 524.31, 544.8
wellspring 386.4, 818.4, 886.6
well-stacked 1016.18
well-stocked 385.14, 991.7
well-suited 405.17, 413.24
well-supplied 385.14
well-thought-of 155.11, 509.19, 662.15
well thought-out 920.18
well-thought-out 413.30, 935.20
well-thumbed 387.18
well-timed 843.9, 995.5
well-timed opportunity 843.3
well-to-do, the 618.6
well-to-do 618.14
well-to-do in the world 618.14
well-traveled 177.40
well-tried 413.28, 942.12
well-trodden 373.14
well-turned 5.46, 544.10
well turned-out 5.46
well-turned-out 578.13
well-turned periods 533.1
well-understood 928.27
well-upholstered 257.18
well up on 413.27
well-used 387.18
well-varied 712.20
well-versed 413.27, 570.16, 928.18, 928.20
well-washed 79.25
well water 1065.3
well-weighed 413.30
well-wisher 143.8, 588.1, 616.9
well-worked-out 413.30
well-worn 117.9, 373.14, 393.31
well-worn groove 290.1, 373.5
well worth the money 633.7
welsh 363.8, 368.9, 445.2, 625.6
Welsh daffodil 647.6
welsher 368.3, 625.5
welshing 368.2, 445.1
Welsh leek 647.6
welt (n) 85.37, 211.7, 283.3, 1004.1 (v) 604.14
Weltanschauung 978.5

welter (n) 810.3, 917.8 (v) 182.55, 913.9, 915.13, 917.15
weltering 1065.17
welter in one's own blood 308.21
welterweight 297.3
Weltschmerz 112.3, 118.3, 125.6
wemless 657.7
wen 85.39, 283.4, 1004.1
wench 77.6, 302.6, 577.8, 665.14
wenching 665.3
wend 172.5, 177.18
wend one's way 162.4, 172.5, 177.18
wentletrap 311.29
were-animals 680.12
wereass 680.12
werebear 680.12
wereboar 680.12
werecalf 680.12
werecat 680.12
werecrocodile 680.12
werefolk 680.12
werefox 680.12
werehare 680.12
werehyena 680.12
werejaguar 680.12
wereleopard 680.12
werelion 680.12
weretiger 680.12
werewolf 127.9, 593.6, 680.12
wergild 624.3
weskit 5.14
West 231.6, 231.7
west (n) 161.3 (a) 161.14
westbound 161.14
West Coast 231.7
West End 230.6
wester (n) 318.8 (v) 161.8
westerly (n) 318.8 (a) 161.14
Western 706.2
western 161.14
Western Christianity 675.7
Westerner 227.11
Western grip 748.2
Western Hemisphere 231.6
Western imperialism 458.11
Westernism 523.8
westernmost 161.14
western swing 708.11
westing 161.3
westland 231.7
westlander 227.11
Westminster chimes 54.4
Westmorland wrestling 457.10
West Side 230.6
westward 161.3
west wind 318.8
wet (n) 88.7, 316.1, 316.4, 611.11, 1065.1 (v) 12.14, 1065.12 (a) 220.4, 316.11, 611.19, 1061.4, 1065.15
wetback 178.5, 368.5
wet behind the ears 301.10, 406.11, 414.17
wet blanket 112.14, 118.4, 379.2, 1012.9, 1022.3
wet down 1065.12
wet dream 75.8
wether 76.8, 311.7
wetland (n) 234.2, 243.1 (a) 234.7, 243.3
wetlands 234.2, 276.2
wetlands conservation 397.1
wet moon 1073.11
wetness 12.7, 1061.1, 1065.1
wet noodle 452.3
wet nurse 1008.8
wet-nurse 8.19, 449.16
wet one's pants laughing 116.8
wet one's whistle 8.29, 88.25
wet rot 393.7
wet season 316.4
wet snow 1023.8
wet squib 410.5
wet suit 5.29, 367.5
wettedness 1065.1
wetting (n) 1065.6 (a) 1065.18
wetting agent 1065.3
wetting down 1065.6
wetting-out agent 1065.3
wettish 1065.15
wettishness 1065.1
wet to the skin 1065.17
wetware 1042.17
wet weather 316.4
wet with sweat 12.22
whack (n) 56.1, 403.3, 604.3, 825.2, 902.4, 942.2 (v) 56.6, 604.11, 902.14
whack down 913.5
whacked out 21.8
whacking 247.11, 257.21
whack off 75.22
whale (n) 257.11, 257.12, 257.14, 311.29 (v) 382.10, 604.12, 604.14
whaleboat 180.1
whalebone 1048.3
whale of a difference, a 780.1
whaler 180.1, 183.1, 382.6
whale the tar out of 604.14
whaling (n) 604.5 (a) 257.21
whaling fleet 180.10
wham (n) 56.1 (v) 56.6, 902.15
whammy (n) 27.5, 144.4, 513.1, 691.1, 691.5, 1000.4 (v) 1011.12
whap (n) 56.1 (v) 56.6
wharf 1009.6
wharfage 630.6
wharf hand 183.9
what 864.6
what bodes 839.2
what can be done 966.1
what can be seen 31.1
what can never be 967.1
what cannot be 967.1
what cannot happen 967.1
whatchamacallit 528.2
whatchy 1052.5
what-d'ye-call-'em 528.2
what-d'ye-call-it 528.2
whate'er 864.6
whatever 864.6
whatever comes 972.1
whatfor, the 886.2
what-for 510.6, 604.1
what happens 831.4
what has to one's name 471.2
what have you 864.4, 864.6
what is coming to one 639.2
what is comprised 196.1
what is condign 506.2
what is contained 196.1
what is destined 839.2
what is done 373.1, 579.1, 579.2, 580.3, 637.1
what is due 506.2
what is fated 839.2
what is included 196.1
what is in the books 839.2
what is merited 506.2
what is owing 639.2
what is possible 966.1
what is proper 637.1
what is read between the lines 518.1, 519.2
what is revealed 31.1
what is right 637.1, 649.1
what is to come 839.1
what is written 839.2
what it is about 937.1
what it's all about 767.3, 997.6
what it takes 18.2, 413.4
what looms 839.2
what makes it tick 207.4, 889.2, 1040.4
what makes it work 1040.4
what makes one tick 767.5
what may be 966.1
what might be 966.1
what must not be 650.1
what one can call one's own 471.1, 471.2
what one can do 966.1
what one does 579.1, 580.3
what one has coming 639.2
what one has earned 639.2
what one has to one's name 471.1
what one is about 724.1
what one is doing 724.1
what one is entitled to 639.2
what one is responsible for 641.1
what one is up to 321.1
what one is worth 471.7
what one may well call 527.14
what one merits 639.2
what ought not be 650.1
what ought to be 637.1
what ought to be done 641.1
what's coming to one 506.2, 604.1, 639.3
what's happening 130.3, 831.2, 841.2
what's-her-name 528.2
what's-his-face 528.2
what's-his-name 528.2
whatshisname 528.2
what should be 637.1
what should not be 650.1
what's in 841.2
what's in it for one 375.7, 387.4
whatsis 1052.5
whatsit 1052.4, 1052.5
what's-its-name 528.2, 1052.4
whatsoe'er 864.6
whatsoever 864.6
what's up 130.3
what's what 761.3, 761.4, 973.4
what the doctor ordered 81.5
what-you-may-call-'em 528.2
what-you-may-call-it 528.2
what you see is what you get 1042.18
what-you-see-is-what-you-get 1042.11
what you will 797.6, 864.6
whatzit 528.2
wheal 85.37
wheat 10.4
wheat belt 233.1
wheat field 1069.9
wheat pit 737.7
wheedle 375.14, 440.12, 511.5
wheedler 375.10, 511.4
wheedling (n) 375.3, 440.3, 511.1 (a) 375.29, 440.18, 511.8
wheel, the 573.1
wheel (n) 179.8, 280.2, 573.5, 605.4, 742.4, 756.1, 759.12, 850.3, 904.6, 915.2, 915.4, 997.9, 1040.7 (v) 163.9, 177.33, 363.6, 850.5, 914.5, 915.9, 915.11
wheel about 163.9
wheel and axle 1040.5
wheel and deal 894.9
wheel around 850.5
wheelbarrow 179.3
wheelbase 257.1, 267.1
wheelchair 179.7
wheelchair-bound 85.54
wheeler 311.13
wheeler-dealer 330.8, 415.6, 610.6, 894.6
wheelhorse 311.13, 609.27, 610.1
wheelhouse 356.6, 745.3, 865.4
wheeling (n) 914.1, 915.1 (a) 850.7, 915.14
wheeling and dealing 731.2
wheelman 183.8
wheel of chance 964.2
wheel of fortune 759.16, 854.4, 964.2, 972.2
wheels 2.7, 177.15, 179.10, 1040.4
wheel-shaped 914.7
wheelsman 183.8
wheels of justice, the 594.2
wheels within wheels 799.2, 1040.4
wheeltrack 290.1
wheel well 759.12
wheelwork 1040.4
wheelworks 1040.4
wheeze (n) 2.21, 57.1, 489.6 (v) 21.5, 57.2
wheezing 2.32, 21.12, 57.3
wheezy 2.32, 57.3
whelk 85.37, 311.29
whelm 221.7, 238.17, 367.7, 395.21, 412.8, 910.7, 993.14, 1065.14
whelmed 238.25, 412.14, 910.10, 1065.17
whelming 221.3, 238.6, 910.1
whelp (n) 302.5, 302.10, 311.16, 660.6 (v) 1.3
whelped 1.4
whelping 1.1
when day is done 315.2
when hell freezes over 822.2
when push comes to shove 843.5
when the balloon goes up 843.5

whereabout 159.1
whereabouts 159.1
whereas 959.2
whereases 421.3
wherefore, the 886.2
where it's at 761.3, 765.2, 767.3, 841.2, 973.4, 997.6
whereness 221.1
where one is 978.2
where one is at home 228.1
where one is coming from 518.1, 978.2
where one lives 24.4, 152.11, 208.2, 228.1, 767.5
where one resides 228.1
where one sits 978.2
where one stands 27.7, 978.2
where the action is 208.6
where the buck stops 641.1
where the earth meets the sky 261.3
where the rubber meets the road 767.3
where the shoe pinches 24.4, 1013.8
wherewith, the 728.1
wherewith 384.2
wherewithal, the 728.1
wherewithal 384.2, 728.14
wherryman 183.5
whet (n) 10.9, 375.7 (v) 24.7, 105.13, 251.5, 285.7, 375.17
whet one's interest 983.12
whet the appetite 63.4, 377.6
whet the knife 405.13
whey 1061.2
wheyface 36.2, 37.1
wheyfaced 36.7, 37.7
whichever (n) 864.6 (a) 864.15
whichsoever 864.15
whicker 60.2
whiff (n) 69.1, 318.3, 517.9, 551.4, 797.7 (v) 69.8, 318.19, 410.10, 745.5
whiffable 69.11
whiffet 318.3, 998.7
whiffing 69.3
whiffle 318.19
whiffletree 170.5
Whig Party 609.24
while, the 826.2
while (n) 158.8, 821.1, 824.1, 826.2 (v) 387.13
while away 387.13, 486.5
while away the time 331.13, 743.22, 821.6
whim 364.1, 927.2, 986.5
whimper (n) 115.3 (v) 52.14, 115.12, 115.14
whimpering (n) 115.2 (a) 52.18, 115.19, 115.21
whimsical 364.5, 488.4, 489.15, 854.7, 927.5, 971.16, 986.20
whimsicality 364.2, 489.3, 851.1, 854.2, 927.1, 971.1
whimsicalness 364.2, 488.1, 489.3
whimsy 364.1, 364.2, 927.1, 986.5
whim-wham 364.1, 498.4, 743.16, 998.5
whine (n) 58.4, 115.3, 524.8 (v) 52.14, 58.8, 60.2, 115.14, 524.25, 525.10
whiner 108.3
whining (n) 52.8, 115.4 (a) 58.14, 60.6, 115.19
whinny 60.2
whiny 108.7, 115.19
whip (n) 178.9, 375.8, 605.1, 610.3, 743.15, 902.8 (v) 249.7, 320.5, 375.15, 401.4, 412.9, 604.12, 902.16, 902.19, 917.10, 1047.6, 1062.10, 1070.8
whip along 375.16, 401.4
whip away 188.10
whip hand 249.2, 417.6, 894.1
whip in 191.3, 770.18
whip into shape 407.6, 807.5, 808.8, 1002.5
whip kick 760.8
whiplash 85.38, 605.1
whiplash injury 85.38
whip off 188.10
whip on 375.16, 902.11
whip oneself 725.10
whip-out 728.2
whipped 320.6, 412.15
whipped cream 10.40
whipped up 105.20
whipper-in 382.5
whippersnapper 142.5, 302.4, 998.7
whipping 180.12, 412.1, 604.4
whipping boy 862.3
whipping post 605.3
whipping up 105.11
whipping-up 375.4
whippletree 170.5
whippy 1047.9
whipsaw 737.25
whip-smart 920.12
whip something up 11.5
whip stall 184.13
whipstall 184.15
whip up 105.12, 365.8, 375.17, 480.14, 917.10
whir (n) 915.1 (v) 52.13
whirl (n) 105.4, 177.7, 238.12, 281.2, 330.4, 743.7, 915.2 (v) 163.9, 172.5, 238.21, 281.4, 915.11
whirlabout (n) 915.4 (a) 915.15
whirlblast 318.13
whirler 915.4
whirligig (n) 743.15, 854.4, 915.4 (v) 915.11 (a) 915.15
whirligig beetle 740.4
whirligig of time 821.3
whirling (n) 915.1 (a) 915.14
whirling dervish 915.4
whirl like a dervish 915.9, 915.11
whirlpool (n) 238.12, 915.2 (v) 915.11
whirlpool bath 79.8, 84.1, 91.3, 1044.3
whirlpool nebula 1073.7
whirl the mind 985.8
whirlwind 105.9, 318.13, 915.2
whirlwindish 915.15
whirlwindy 915.15
whirly 915.15
whirlybird 181.5
whirring (n) 52.7 (a) 52.20
whish (n) 57.1 (v) 52.12, 57.2
whisk (n) 902.7, 917.9 (v) 79.23, 174.9, 176.12, 320.5, 902.18, 917.10
whisker 3.20
whiskered 3.25, 288.9
whiskerless 6.17
whiskers 3.8, 288.3
whiskery 3.25, 288.9
whiskey 88.13
whisper (n) 52.4, 73.1, 525.4, 551.3, 551.4, 552.6 (v) 52.10, 318.20, 345.9, 352.10, 524.22, 524.25, 525.9, 551.11 (a) 52.18
whisper about 352.10
whispered 52.16, 552.15
whispered about 552.15
whispering (n) 52.4, 525.4 (a) 52.18
whispering campaign 512.4, 552.8, 609.14
whisper in the ear 52.10, 345.9, 551.11
whisper-soft 1047.8
whisper sweet nothings 562.14
whispery 52.18
whistle (n) 53.5, 53.6, 57.1, 58.4, 400.1, 517.16 (v) 53.10, 57.2, 58.8, 60.5, 109.6, 116.5, 318.20, 708.38, 708.42
whistle at 508.10
whistleblower 551.6
whistle for 440.9
whistle-pig 311.22
whistler 311.12
whistles 50.13
whistle-stop (n) 230.3 (v) 609.40
whistle-stop campaign 609.13
whistle-stopper 610.10
whistle-stopping 609.12
whistle the ball dead 746.5
whistling (n) 57.1 (a) 58.14
whit 248.2
white (n) 37.1, 87.7, 305.15 (v) 37.5, 37.6 (a) 36.7, 37.7, 79.25, 222.14, 303.16, 657.7, 664.4
white ant 311.33
white as alabaster 37.7
white as a lily 37.7
white as a sheet 36.7, 37.7, 85.56, 127.26
white as bone 37.7
white as chalk 37.7
white as driven snow 657.7, 664.4
white as snow 37.7
white-bearded 303.16
white blood cell 2.25
white book 352.2, 549.8, 551.1
white bread 607.5
white-bread 499.8, 607.10, 798.6, 867.6, 869.8
white-bread type 867.2
white-bready 499.8, 867.6, 869.8
white cane 30.6
whitecap 238.14, 916.4
white chocolate 10.40
white collar 607.10
white-collar crime 655.2
white-collar intellectual 929.1
white-collar thief 483.1
white-collar worker 577.3, 607.6, 726.2
white-collar workers 607.5
white corpuscle 2.25
white cross 307.2
white crosses 87.4
white-crowned 303.16
whited sepulcher 33.2, 354.13, 357.8, 693.3
white dwarf 1073.8
white elephant 96.8, 1012.6
white elephant sale 734.3
white feather 491.4, 491.5
white fish 10.24
white flag, the 433.2
white flag 465.2, 517.15, 647.7, 756.3
white foam 238.14
white frost 1023.7
white girl 87.7
white goods 735.3, 735.4
white hair 3.3
white-haired 37.9, 303.16
white hairs 303.5
Whitehall 612.3
whitehead 1004.1
white-headed 303.16
white heat 1019.5
white hole 1073.8
white horse 238.14, 916.4
white-hot 101.9, 671.22, 1019.25
White House 610.1
White House, the 228.5
white knight 460.7
white-knuckle 126.7, 128.11
White Ladies of Normandy 988.2
White Lady 988.2
white lady 87.7
White Lady of Avenel 988.2
white lead 1063.2
white lie 354.11
white light 1025.10
white lightning 88.14, 88.18
white list 107.1, 332.1
white-liver 491.5
white-livered 491.10
whitelivered 16.12
white-liveredness 491.1
white magic 690.1
white man 312.3
white meat 10.13, 10.23
white mule 88.18
whiten 36.5, 36.6, 37.5, 79.18, 105.19
whitened 36.8, 37.7, 79.25
whitener 36.4, 37.4, 79.17
whiteness 36.3, 37.1, 79.1, 657.1, 664.1, 1019.12
white night 23.1
whitening 36.3, 37.3, 37.4
whitening agent 37.4
white noise 52.4, 57.1
white out 32.3, 35.14
whiteout 1023.8
white paper 352.2, 549.8, 551.1
white person 312.3
white plague 85.5, 85.17
white potato 10.35
White Power 609.31
white power 980.4

white race 37.1, 312.2
white rainbow 316.8, 1025.14
white rice 10.36
whites, the 2.24
whites 5.11
white sauce 10.12
white-skinned 36.7
white slave 665.16
white slaver 665.18
white slavery 732.1
white space 158.3, 762.1
white squall 318.11
white stick 30.6
white stuff 87.7, 87.9, 87.14
white supremacist 103.4, 980.5
white supremacy 980.4
white-tailed deer 311.5
white tie 5.11
white tie and tails 5.11
whitetop 295.8
white trash 250.2, 660.2
whitewash (n) 33.2, 35.8, 37.4, 79,17, 350.1, 376.1, 412.3, 600.5 (v) 35.14, 37.6, 206.6, 346.6, 354.16, 600.12, 601.4
whitewashed 412.16
whitewasher 600.8
whitewashing 35.12, 37.3, 412.3, 600.5
whitewash job 354.13
white water 238.10
whitewater (n) 320.2 (a) 238.24
whitewater ahead 1006.1
whitewater rafting 760.2
white wedding 563.3
white wine 88.17
whitewing 79.16
white with age 303.16
white woman 312.3
whiting 37.4
whitish 36.9, 37.8
whitishness 37.1
whitlow 85.37
Whitney 618.8
whittle (n) 1040.2 (v) 262.7, 802.11
whittle away 252.7, 393.20
whittled 262.9
whittle down 252.7
whittler 716.6
whittling 715.1
whity 37.8
whiz (n) 57.1, 413.14, 999.7 (v) 52.13, 57.2, 174.9
whiz about 330.12
whizbang 249.4, 999.7
whizgig 53.6
whiz kid 409.6, 413.12
whiz-kid 413.22
whiz off 188.10
whizz, a 12.5
whizz (n) 12.5 (v) 12.14
whizzer 53.6
whizzing (n) 52.7 (a) 52.20
whoever 864.7
whole, the 792.3, 794.5
whole (n) 196.1, 244.1, 772.1, 792.1, 864.4, 1017.6 (a) 83.11, 772.7, 792.9, 794.9, 872.7, 960.2, 1002.7, 1007.4, 1017.23
whole amount 792.2
whole animal 792.4
whole ball of wax 792.4
whole bit, the 794.3
whole bit 792.4
whole blood 2.25
whole body 227.1
whole bunch 792.4
whole caboodle 792.4
whole-cloth 872.7
whole deal 792.4
whole different ball game, a 776.3
whole different ball game 780.3
whole different story, a 776.3
whole gale 318.11
whole grain 310.5
wholehearted 359.11
whole hog, the 794.5
whole hog 792.4
whole-hog 794.10
whole kit and boodle 792.4
whole kit and caboodle 792.4
whole megillah 792.4
whole mess 792.4
wholeness 792.1, 792.5, 794.1, 865.1, 872.1, 999.1, 1002.2
whole nine yards, the 766.2
whole nine yards 792.4
whole note 709.14
whole nother 780.8
whole nother thing, a 776.3
whole nother thing 780.3
whole offering 696.7
whole other thing, a 780.3
whole people, the 606.1
whole people 227.1
whole picture, the 766.2
whole range, the 792.3
whole rest 709.21
wholesale (n) 734.1 (v) 731.16, 734.8 (a) 731.22, 734.13, 794.10, 864.13, 945.5, 991.7
wholesale house 736.1
wholesale murder 308.4
wholesale price index 630.4, 733.1
wholesaler 213.4, 730.2
wholesaling (n) 731.2, 734.2 (a) 734.13
whole schmear 792.4
whole shebang 792.4
whole shooting match 792.4
whole show 792.4
whole shtick 792.4
whole slew 247.4
wholesome 81.5, 83.11, 925.4
wholesomeness 81.1, 83.2, 869.1, 925.1
whole spectrum, the 792.3
whole step 709.20
whole story, the 761.4
whole story 1017.6
whole-tone scale 709.6
whole truth and nothing but the truth, the 973.3
whole wheat 310.5
whole wide world 1073.1, 1073.10
whole works 792.4
whomever 864.7
whomp (n) 56.1, 604.3, 902.3, 902.5 (v) 56.6, 412.9, 604.11, 902.13
whomping 412.3
whomp up 262.7, 340.9, 365.8, 892.8
whomso 864.7
whomsoever 864.7
whoop, a 223.2
whoop (n) 59.1 (v) 59.6, 60.5
whoop and a holler, a 223.2
whoopdedoo 283.3
whoopee 116.1, 743.3
whoop it up 53.9, 582.21, 743.24, 810.11
whoop it up about 101.7
whoops 975.6
whoosh (n) 57.1 (v) 57.2
whop (n) 56.1, 902.5 (v) 56.6, 412.9, 604.14, 902.15
whopper 257.11, 354.12, 355.1
whopping (n) 412.3 (a) 257.21
whorl (n) 281.2, 310.28 (v) 281.4
whorled 281.6, 281.8
whoso 864.7
whosoever 864.7
Who's Who 549.9
whup 412.9
why, the 886.2
why 522.8
why and wherefore, the 886.2
whyfor, the 886.2
wibble-wabble 916.13
wick 230.2, 1026.7
wicked, the 660.11
wicked 122.10, 144.20, 638.3, 654.16, 655.5, 695.17, 1000.7, 1013.17
wicked bad 999.18
wicked good 999.18
wicked imitation 508.6
wickedness 144.5, 638.1, 654.4, 655.1, 695.3, 1000.1
wicked pastiche 508.6
wicked ways 654.4
wicker 170.3
wickerwork 170.3
wicket dam 1012.5
wickiup 228.10
wide 158.11, 257.17, 269.6, 524.30, 864.13, 975.16, 979.8
wide-angle 269.7
wide area network 1042.19
wide area telecommunications service 347.17
wide-awake 23.8, 339.14, 920.13
wide berth 368.1, 430.4, 1007.1
wide-bodied 269.7
wide-body 269.7
wide-extended 864.13
wide-extending 864.13
wide-eyed 122.9
wide-flung 864.13
wide knowledge 928.6
widely apart 780.7
widely known 928.27
widely read 928.20
wide margin 780.2
wide-minded 979.8
wide-mindedness 979.1
widen 158.9, 251.6, 259.4, 259.5, 259.6, 269.4, 864.9
widened 251.7, 259.10
wideness 257.6, 269.1
widening 251.1, 259.1
widen the distance 168.2
wide of the mark 164.8, 776.7, 975.16
wide of the point 776.7
wide-open 259.11, 292.17, 430.27
wide-open spaces 158.4, 233.1, 236.1
wide-open speed 174.3
wide place in the road 230.3
wide-ranging 158.11, 269.6, 864.13, 979.8
wide-reaching 864.13
wide reading 570.3
wide receiver 746.2
wide-ribbed 269.7
wide-scale 269.6, 864.13
widescreen (n) 706.7 (a) 269.7
wide-set 269.7
widespread 158.11, 259.11, 269.6, 373.13, 771.9, 864.13
widespreadness 864.2
widest dissemination 352.4
wide-stretching 864.13
wide-toothed 269.7
wide world 1073.1
widget 1052.5
widow (n) 77.7, 256.3, 566.4 (v) 307.27, 566.6
widowed 307.34, 566.7
widower 76.10, 256.3, 566.4
widowered 566.7
widowerhood 566.3
widowership 566.3
widowhood 566.3
widowish 566.7
widowlike 566.7
widowly 566.7
widowman 566.4
widow's dower 478.9
widow's mite 478.6, 992.5
widow's peak 3.6, 3.7
widow's walk 295.6
widow's weeds 115.7, 566.3
widow woman 566.4
width 158.1, 257.1, 269.1
wield 73.6, 387.10, 916.11
wieldable 1014.15
wieldableness 1014.2
wield authority 417.13, 612.11
wieldiness 1014.2
wield power 18.11
wield the baton 708.45
wield the scepter 612.13
wield the sword 458.13
wieldy 1014.15
wiener 10.21
wiener roast 8.6
Wiener Schnitzel 10.19
wienie roast 8.6
Wiesner theory 560.6
wife 77.5, 77.7, 563.8
wifehood 563.1
wife in all but name 563.8
wife in name only 563.8
wifeless 565.7
wifely 104.26, 563.18
wife of one's bosom 563.8
wife swapping 75.7
WiFi (n) 1042.16 (a) 1034.28
wifty 426.4
wig 3.14

wigged 3.26, 926.27
wigger 926.16
wiggle (n) 917.7 (v) 105.18, 177.28, 917.14
wiggle out of 369.9
wiggler 302.12
wiggle the finger at 517.21
wiggling 917.21
wiggly 917.21
wiggy 926.27
wight 872.4
wigmaker 704.23
wig out 87.22, 105.17, 128.8, 152.20, 926.22
wigout 926.10
wig-wag 517.21
wigwag (n) 517.15, 916.5 (v) 916.11, 916.13
wigwag flag 517.15
wigwam 228.10, 295.8
wiki 1042.19
wild (n) 891.2 (a) 101.12, 105.25, 105.29, 152.32, 233.9, 311.39, 327.10, 361.12, 430.24, 493.8, 493.9, 497.12, 665.25, 671.18, 671.19, 671.20, 671.21, 923.11, 926.30, 985.10, 986.20
wild about 101.11, 104.30
wild-and-woolly 497.12
wild animals 311.1
wild-ass 493.9
wild beast 671.9
wild beasts 311.1
wild boar 311.9
wild card 758.2
wild-card poker 759.10
wildcat (n) 311.21, 593.7 (a) 418.5, 1006.10
wildcat strike 727.5
wildcatter 1058.9
wildcraft 1069.15
wildebeest 311.5
wilderness (n) 158.4, 233.2, 799.2, 891.2 (a) 233.9
wilderness preserve 397.7
wilderness settler 227.10
wildest dream 976.4
wildest dreams 986.5
wild-eyed 105.25, 671.18, 926.32
wild fire 1025.13
wildfire 1019.13
wildflower 310.24
wild for 100.22
wildfowl 311.27
wild-goose chase 125.8, 382.1, 391.3, 410.5
wild growth 257.5
wild guess 951.4, 971.8
wild horse 311.10
Wild Hunt 988.2
wild imagination 986.4
wilding 671.3
wildlife 311.1
wildlife conservation 397.1
wildlife sanctuary 397.7
wild-looking 105.25, 926.32
wild man 493.4, 593.5
wildness 327.2, 361.4, 430.3, 493.2, 497.3, 665.3, 671.2, 923.3
wild oats 493.2, 743.2
wild rice 10.36
wilds 233.2, 891.2
wild shot 714.8
wild to 100.22
wild water 238.10
wild West 231.7, 233.2
wild-West 233.9
wildwood 310.13
wile (n) 354.4, 356.6, 415.3 (v) 387.13
wiles 415.1
wiliness 415.1, 920.3
will (n) 100.1, 323.1, 359.1, 359.4, 371.1, 380.1, 420.1, 478.10 (v) 323.2, 359.7, 478.18
will and bequeath 478.18
will and pleasure 100.1, 371.2
will and will not 362.8
willed 324.5
willed action 328.1
willed activity 328.1
willful 327.8, 361.8, 380.8, 418.5
willful disobedience 327.1
willful misconception 356.1
willfulness 361.1, 418.1
willi 678.9
William Jennings Bryan 543.6
willies 128.2
willing 323.4, 324.5, 326.3, 403.16, 441.4, 570.18
willing ear 324.1
willing heart 324.1
willinghearted 324.5
willing humor 324.1
willing mind 324.1
willingness 324.1, 441.1, 570.5, 896.1
willingness to believe 954.1
willingness to learn 570.5
willingness to serve 326.1
williwaw 318.11
will of Allah 963.7
will of Heaven 964.2
will of iron 359.4
will of one's own, a 359.4
will of one's own 361.1
will of steel 359.4
will-o'-the-wisp 356.1, 976.1, 976.6, 1019.13, 1025.13
willowiness 1047.2
willowy 270.16, 291.7, 1047.9
will power 323.1
willpower 359.4
will to 478.18
will-with-the-wisp 1025.13
wilt 12.16, 16.9, 21.4, 21.5, 85.48, 393.18
wilted 12.22, 393.35
wilting (n) 393.4 (a) 21.7, 393.45
wily 356.22, 415.12, 920.15
wily device 415.3
wimp 16.6, 19.6, 362.5, 491.5
wimpiness 19.1, 19.4, 362.4, 895.1
wimpish 16.12, 19.13, 326.5, 362.12, 491.10, 895.3
wimpishness 19.1, 362.4, 895.1
wimple (n) 291.3 (v) 291.6
wimpled 288.6
wimp out 362.7, 468.2, 491.8, 858.13
wimpy 16.12, 19.13, 362.12, 491.10, 895.3
win (n) 411.1, 754.3, 759.4 (v) 249.7, 375.23, 411.3, 472.8, 757.5
win around 375.23
win away 858.15
win back 396.12
win by a fluke 411.3
win by a nose 411.3
wince (n) 903.3 (v) 26.8, 127.13, 168.3, 325.4, 903.7
winch (n) 906.7 (v) 906.9
Winchester disk 1042.6
wind (n) 2.21, 174.6, 318.1, 520.3, 711.6, 909.9, 909.10, 1067.3 (v) 21.4, 53.10, 164.4, 182.30, 279.6, 281.4, 317.11, 356.20, 405.9, 708.42, 915.9 (a) 904.17
windage 158.3
wind aloft 318.1
wind arrow 318.15
windbag 502.5, 540.4
windblown 318.23, 810.14
wind boat 180.3
windboat 180.3
windbound 428.15
windbreak 1008.1
windburn 1020.6
windcatcher 318.18
wind chill 318.7
wind chill factor 318.7
windchill factor 317.4, 1023.3
wind cone 184.19, 317.8, 318.16
wind direction 318.15
wind down 252.6, 762.6, 857.12
wind-dried 1066.9
winded 21.12
wind eddy 318.13
windedness 21.3
wind energy 17.1, 1021.1
wind-equator 318.9
windfall 472.6, 999.5
windfall money 472.6
windfall profit 472.6
wind farm 1021.7
wind flapper 181.6
wind force 318.15
wind gap 237.5
wind gauge 174.7, 317.8
wind gust 318.5
wind in 906.9
wind in and out 204.12
wind indicator 184.19, 318.16
windiness 259.2, 317.3, 318.14, 540.1, 1067.3
winding (n) 281.1 (a) 164.7, 281.6
winding sheet 309.14
winding staircase 193.3
wind instrument 711.6
wind-instrumentalist 710.4
windjammer 180.3, 183.1, 502.5, 540.4
windlass (n) 906.7, 912.3 (v) 906.9
windless 173.16
windlessness 173.5
wind marker 318.15
windmill 181.5, 756.1
windmill tower 272.6
wind of change 133.2
window 27.8, 292.1, 292.7, 1029.2, 1036.13, 1042.9
window bay 292.7
window case 266.4
window casing 266.4
window cleaner 79.14
window decorator 716.11
window dresser 716.11
window dressing 33.2, 216.1, 354.3, 498.1
window-dressing 206.1
windowed 292.19
window fan 318.18
window frame 266.4, 292.7
window glass 292.7
window ledge 292.7, 901.9
windowlight 1029.2
window mirror 29.6
window of opportunity 292.1, 843.2, 843.3
windowpane 292.7, 1029.2
window-rattling 53.11
window-shop 733.8
window-shopper 733.5
window-shopping 733.1
windowsill 292.7, 901.9
window treatment 295.2
windpipe 2.22
wind player 710.4
wind power 1021.7
wind-powered 1021.9
windproof 293.12
wind-propelled 904.16
wind rose 318.15
windrow 812.2
windsail 318.18
windsailor 183.1
windscoop 318.18
windscreen 1008.3
wind shear 184.32, 318.1, 318.10, 318.11
windshield 1008.3
wind shift 318.1
wind-shift line 317.4, 318.11
windship 180.3
wind sleeve 317.8, 318.16
windsock 174.7, 184.19, 317.8, 318.16
winds of change, the 852.5
wind speed 317.4
wind-speed indicator 318.16
wind sprint 84.2
windstorm 318.11, 671.4
wind strength 317.4
windsurf 182.13
windsurfer 760.2
windsurfing 182.11, 760.2
windswept 318.23
windtalker 576.9
windtight 293.12
wind tunnel 239.13
wind up 405.9, 407.6, 820.6, 857.12, 887.4
windup 407.2, 745.3, 820.1
wind vane 318.16
windward (n) 218.3 (v) 182.17 (a) 218.6
windward ebb 218.3
windward flood 218.3
windwards 218.3
windward side 218.3
windward tide 218.3

windy (n) 502.5 (a) 259.13, 299.4, 318.21, 502.12, 538.12, 540.9, 545.9, 764.6, 998.19
wine (n) 10.49, 88.17 (a) 41.6
wine and dine 7.17, 8.18
win easily 1014.11
wine bar 88.20
winebibber 88.11
winebibbery 88.4
winebibbing (n) 8.3, 88.4 (a) 88.35
wine cellar 197.17, 386.6
wine-colored 41.6
wine cooler 1024.3
wine expert 88.19
wineglass 8.12
winegrower 88.19
wine list 871.5
wine lover 496.6
winemaker 88.19
wine merchant 88.19
wine of the country 88.17
wine press 88.21
wine-red 41.6
winery 88.21, 739.3
wine shop 88.20
wine steward 577.7
win freedom 369.7
win friends 587.10
win friends and influence people 587.10, 894.7
wing (n) 10.23, 254.3, 461.29, 617.4, 617.10, 704.20, 770.3, 793.4, 1008.2 (v) 19.9, 176.12, 184.36, 393.14, 409.10
wingback 746.2
wing bay 3.18
wingcut 704.20
wingding 582.12, 743.6
wing drag 184.27
winged 174.15
winged insect 311.32
winger 749.2, 752.2
wing formation 184.12
wing half 749.5
winging (n) 184.1 (a) 184.50
wing it 365.8, 704.29, 1014.8
win going away 411.4
wing one's way 174.8, 184.36
wing out ballast 182.49
wingover (n) 184.16 (v) 184.40
wings 704.16
wingspan 257.1
win hands down 411.4, 1014.11
win horse 757.2
win in a canter 411.4
win in a walk 1014.11
wink, the 517.15
wink (n) 22.3, 27.4, 509.1, 517.15, 551.4, 830.3 (v) 28.10, 517.22
wink at 30.8, 148.4, 441.2, 443.10, 979.7, 984.2
winker 28.7
winking (n) 28.7, 443.2 (a) 28.11
winkle out 192.10, 192.14, 938.34, 941.4
wink of an eye, the 828.3
wink of sleep 22.3
winner 249.4, 330.8, 409.2, 409.6, 411.2, 757.2, 999.5
winning (n) 411.1, 472.1 (a) 97.7, 100.30, 104.24, 377.8, 411.7, 757.6, 759.27, 894.13
winning chance 972.8
winningness 97.2, 377.2
winnings 251.3, 472.3, 627.1
winning streak 411.1
winning ways 104.6, 377.2, 411.1
winnow (n) 79.13 (v) 79.22, 317.11, 371.14, 773.6, 801.8, 944.4
winnower 79.13
winnowing 79.4, 801.3, 944.3
winnowing basket 79.13
winnowing fan 79.13
winnowing machine 79.13
winnowing-out 773.2
winnow out 773.6
winnow the chaff from the wheat 944.4
wino 88.12
win one's heart 104.22
win one's spurs 409.7, 411.3
win one's wings 409.7, 411.3
win on points 754.3
win out 409.13, 411.3
win over 375.23, 858.16, 953.18, 973.9
winsome 97.7, 104.24, 109.11, 377.8
winsomeness 97.2, 104.6, 109.1, 377.2
Winston Churchill 543.6
winter (n) 313.6, 1023.3 (v) 313.8, 821.6 (a) 313.9
winterbound 1023.14
winterbourne 238.1, 239.2
winter break 20.3
winter-gray 39.4
winterlike 313.9, 1023.14
winter of discontent 1011.6
winter of one's days 303.5
winter sleep 22.2
winter solstice 313.6, 313.7
winter sport 744.1
winter storm advisory 400.1
winter storm watch 400.1
wintertide 313.6
wintertime 313.6
winter weather advisory 400.1
winter wind 318.7
wintery 313.9, 1023.14
win the affections of 104.22
win the battle 411.3
win the day 411.3
win the laurels 411.3
win the love of 104.22
win the prize 411.3
win the regard of 587.13
win the start 845.6
win through 409.13, 411.3
wintriness 1023.3
wintry 313.9, 1023.14
wintry mix 319.3
wintry weather 1023.3
wintry wind 318.7, 1023.3
winy 88.37
wipe (n) 34.1 (v) 79.18, 1066.6
wipe away one's tears 147.2
wipe away the tears 121.6
wiped away 148.7
wiped out 21.8, 395.29, 473.8, 619.10, 820.10
wipe off 79.18
wipeoff 34.1
wipe off old scores 658.4
wipe off the face of the earth 308.17
wipe off the map 395.14, 395.16
wipe out 255.10, 308.14, 308.17, 395.14, 395.16, 625.8, 625.9, 762.7, 820.6
wipeout 34.1
wiper 183.6
wiper-out 395.8
wipe the plate clean 672.4
wipe the slate clean 148.3, 601.4, 625.9, 658.4
wipe the smile off one's face 111.2
wipe up 79.18
wipe up the floor with 604.10
wiping down 79.5
wiping out 395.7
wiping up 79.5
wire, the 356.10
wire (n) 271.2, 347.14, 756.1, 820.1, 1032.21 (v) 347.20, 800.9, 1032.26
wire cable 271.2
wire chief 347.16
wire communication 343.5, 347.1
wired 48.14, 87.24, 93.18, 93.23, 105.28, 128.11, 970.20, 1042.22
wired radio 347.3
wiredrawn 270.16, 294.8
wired wireless 347.3
wireframe 1042.18
wire house 737.9
wire joint 759.19
wireless (n) 347.3, 347.5, 1034.1, 1034.3 (v) 1034.25 (a) 347.21, 1034.28
wireless communication 347.1
wireless compass 1036.4
wireless network 1042.16
wireless set 1034.3
wireless telegraphy 347.3
wireless telephone 347.5
wireless telephony 347.3
wire line 347.17
wireman 347.16, 1032.22
Wirephoto 347.21
wirephoto 347.15
wirephoto 714.3
wire-pull 894.9
wire-puller 381.7, 415.7, 609.30, 610.6, 894.6
wire pulling 417.2
wire-pulling 381.5, 415.4, 609.29, 894.3
wire recording 50.12
wire rope 271.2
wire ropeway 383.8
wires 894.3
wire service 347.2, 552.1, 555.3
wire stitching 554.14
wiretap (n) 549.10, 938.9 (v) 48.10
wiretapping 48.2, 938.9
wire up 1032.26
wire wave communication 347.3
wireway 383.8
wire wheel 756.1
wiry 15.16, 270.17, 271.7, 1049.4
wisdom 920.5, 928.3, 974.1, 995.1
wisdom literature 547.12, 718.1, 974.1
wisdom tooth 2.8
wise, the 921.3
wise (n) 33.3, 384.1 (a) 920.17, 928.15, 928.21, 935.20, 956.5, 995.5
wiseacre 921.6
wise as an owl 920.17
wise as a serpent 920.17
wiseass (n) 140.5, 142.6 (a) 140.11, 142.10, 508.12
wise as Solomon 920.17
wise beyond one's years 920.17
wisecrack (n) 489.7 (v) 489.13
wisecracker 489.12
wise expression 974.1
wise fool 921.6
wiseguy 142.6, 660.9, 921.6
wisehead 921.6
wise in one's generation 920.17
wise in one's own conceit 140.11, 930.14
wise in the ways of the world 413.28
wiseling 921.6
Wise Lord, the 677.5
wise man 920.9, 921.1, 929.1
wise man of Chelm 921.6
wise man of Gotham 921.6
Wise Men of the East 921.5
wiseness 920.5
wisenheimer 142.6, 921.6
wisent 311.6
wise old man 921.1
Wise One, the 677.5
wise person 921.1
wiser head 670.3
wise saying 974.1
wise to 928.16, 928.18
wise up 551.9
wise up to 941.8
wise woman 921.1
wish (n) 100.1, 100.11, 323.1, 440.1 (v) 100.14, 124.7, 323.2, 371.17, 440.9
wishbone 10.23, 171.4, 691.6
wish book 549.11
wish-bringer 691.6
wished-for 100.29, 585.12
wisher 100.12
wish for 100.16, 440.9
wishful 100.23
wish-fulfilling 986.24
wish fulfillment 100.1, 986.7
wish-fulfillment 92.23
wish-fulfillment fantasy 92.23, 986.7
wishfulness 100.4
wishful thinker 986.13
wishful thinking 92.23, 100.4, 124.2, 356.1, 954.1, 976.1, 986.7, 986.9
wish-giver 691.6

wishing 100.21
wishing bone 691.6
wishing cap 691.6
wishing stone 691.6
wishing well 691.6
wish list 549.11, 871.1, 965.3
wish one joy 149.2, 504.12
wish one luck 504.12
wish to 100.15
wish to goodness 100.14
wish very much 100.14
wish well 143.11
wishy-washiness 16.3, 65.1
wishy-washy 16.17, 65.2, 854.7, 1005.7
wisp 3.5, 258.4, 770.7, 1025.13
wispiness 16.2, 270.4
wisp of smoke 1067.1
wispy 16.14, 270.16
wistful 100.23, 112.23, 113.8, 931.21
wistful eye 100.4
wistfulness 100.4, 112.5, 113.1, 931.3
wit 413.1, 415.1, 489.1, 489.12, 920.1
witch (n) 110.12, 127.9, 304.3, 593.7, 671.9, 690.8, 1015.4 (v) 377.7, 691.9 (a) 690.14
witch-charmed 691.13
witchcraft 690.1
witch doctor 90.9, 690.7
witched 691.13
witchery 97.2, 377.1, 690.1, 691.2, 870.7
witches' chorus 61.2
witches' coven 690.8
witches' Sabbath 690.3, 701.9, 810.5
witch-finder 690.7
witch fire 1019.13, 1025.13
witch-held 691.13
witch-hunt 389.3, 938.4
witch-hunter 690.7
witch-hunting 389.3
witching (n) 962.3 (a) 97.7, 377.8, 691.11
witching hour, the 315.6
witching hour 690.3
witching stick 962.3
witching time of night, the 315.6
witchlike 690.14
witch of Agnesi 279.2
witch of Endor 690.8
witch stick 962.3
witch-struck 691.13
witchwoman 690.8
witchwork 690.1
witchy 690.14
Wite-Out 37.4
with 582.18
with a bellyful 994.6
with a bump for 413.29
with a collar on 320.7
with a flair 413.29
with a handful of thumbs 414.20
with a head on 320.7
with a kick 68.7, 88.37
with a liking for 100.22
with all good wishes 820.5
with all my love 820.5
with a mind like a sieve 990.9
with an ear for 413.29
with an ear for music 708.47
with an eye for 413.29
with an interval 224.6
with a nose for 69.13
with a right to 639.10
with a soul possessed in patience 134.9
with a weather eye open 339.13
with a whole skin 1007.4
with a yellow streak 491.10
with bated breath 130.12, 971.25
with bats in the belfry 926.27
with both feet on the ground 987.6
with both oars in the water 925.4
with chattering teeth 1023.16
with child 78.18
with clean hands 657.6, 657.8
with crow's feet 303.16
withdraw 87.22, 163.6, 168.2, 168.3, 188.9, 192.10, 255.9, 333.4, 362.7, 363.8, 370.5, 445.2, 802.8, 872.6
withdrawal 87.1, 92.23, 94.1, 163.2, 168.1, 188.1, 192.1, 333.1, 344.3, 363.3, 370.1, 445.1, 448.1, 584.1, 729.14, 773.2, 802.1, 872.2, 982.1
withdrawal of attention 985.1
withdrawal sickness 87.1
withdrawal symptoms 87.1
withdrawal syndrome 87.1
withdraw from 448.2
withdraw from the field 433.7
withdrawing (n) 168.1, 172.2, 370.3 (a) 168.5
withdrawing room 197.5
withdrawment 163.2
withdrawn 92.40, 94.13, 344.10, 345.13, 583.6, 584.8, 872.8, 982.3
withdrawnness 94.4, 344.3, 583.2
withdraw one's support 370.6
withdraw the charge 601.4
with enough of 994.6
wither 85.48, 252.6, 260.9, 303.10, 393.18, 1066.6
wither away 85.48, 393.19
withered 260.13, 270.20, 303.18, 393.35, 1066.9
withered loins 891.1
withering (n) 252.1, 260.3, 393.4, 1066.3 (a) 144.23, 157.8, 393.45, 395.26
withering away 252.1
withering look 27.5
wither on the vine 393.18
with eyes rolling 118.12
with eyes suffused in tears 115.21
with folded hands 440.16
with half a mind to 375.30
withheld 386.15
withhold 345.7, 386.12, 428.7, 442.4, 484.6, 668.7
withhold assent 333.4
withholding 442.1
within easy reach 633.7
within means 633.7
within range of 897.6
within reach 221.12, 633.7, 966.8
within sight 221.12
with intervals 224.6
within the law 673.11
within the range of possibility 966.6
within the realm of possibility 966.6
within the scope of the law 673.11
within these four walls 345.14
with it 838.2, 928.17
with-it 578.11
withitness 578.2
with joined hands 440.16
with love 820.5
with low resistance 85.54
with muscles tense 130.12
withness and togetherness 769.1
with news value 552.13
with nothing inside 222.14
with nothing on 6.14
with one consent 332.15
with one foot in the grave 303.18, 307.32
with one's back to the wall 1013.25
with one's eyes open 339.13, 977.5
with one's eyes peeled 339.13
with one's fill of 994.6
with one's head in the clouds 986.24
with one voice 332.15
with open eyes 339.13
without a clue 971.24
without airs 137.10
without a name 528.3
without a nerve in one's body 129.2, 855.12
without any weight 895.3
without a penny to bless oneself with 619.9
without a pot to piss in 619.10
without appeal 420.12
without a sou 619.9
without a stitch 6.14
without a stitch on one's back 6.14
without a stitch to one's name 6.14
without a tremor 129.2
without a will of one's own 362.12
without basis 936.13, 958.8
without being 762.8
without benefit of clergy 674.7
without body 1053.7
without bottom 275.12
without bound 823.3
without brain one 922.17
without care 107.7
without charge 634.5
without choice 963.12
without content 222.14
without difference 778.7
without distinction 778.7, 945.6
without-doors 206.8
without end 267.7, 823.3, 829.7, 884.10
without equal 249.15
without exception 772.7, 960.2
without faith 955.8
without foundation 764.8, 936.13
without grounds 958.8
without hope 125.12
without issue 891.4
without life 307.29
without limit 823.3, 884.10
without measure 823.3
without mercy 146.3
without merit 598.21
without nerves 855.12
without number 823.3
without omission 772.7
without one dollar to rub against another 619.9
without parallel 249.15
without price 632.10
without reason 936.11
without remorse 645.16
without reproach 657.6
without reserve 960.2
without rhyme or reason 520.6, 936.11
without shame 645.16
without sound basis 936.13
without strings 430.27, 443.16
without suspicion 953.22
without vital functions 307.29
without warning 131.10
with overflowing eyes 115.21
with peace 820.5
with regards 820.5
withstand 451.3, 453.2, 453.3
withstanding (n) 453.1 (a) 453.5
with swimming eyes 115.21
with tearful eyes 115.21
with tears in one's eyes 115.21
with the beat 836.6
with the birds 845.7
with the Lord 307.29
with the saints 307.29
with voice 371.24
with voice and vote 371.24
with vote 371.24
with watery eyes 115.21
with young 78.18
witless 922.13, 923.8, 923.10, 926.26, 930.12, 985.16
witlessness 922.1, 923.1, 923.2, 926.1, 985.5
witling 489.12, 921.6, 924.2
witness (n) 549.6, 551.5, 598.11, 677.15, 918.1, 938.19, 957.2, 957.6 (v) 27.12, 221.8, 334.6, 692.6, 918.5, 957.9
witnessable 31.6
witness box 595.6
witnesses' accounts 719.1
witnessing (n) 27.2 (a) 692.8
witness list 598.12
witness stand 595.6
witness to 957.8, 957.9
wits 919.2, 925.1
wit's end 1013.6
Wittgensteinian 952.12

witticism 489.7, 974.1
wittiness 488.1, 489.2
witting 380.8
witty 488.4, 489.15
witty repartee 939.1
witty retort 939.1
wive 563.15
wizard (n) 413.13, 690.5, 976.2 (a) 999.13
wizardlike 690.14
wizardly 690.14
wizardry 413.1, 690.1
wizen (n) 2.18, 2.22 (v) 260.9, 303.10, 393.18, 1066.6 (a) 260.13
wizened 258.13, 260.13, 270.20, 303.18, 393.35, 1066.9
wizen-faced 270.19
wobble (n) 851.1, 917.3 (v) 177.28, 362.8, 854.5, 916.10, 917.11
wobble about 362.8, 854.5
wobbler 356.13, 362.5
wobbliness 16.3
wobbling (n) 362.2 (a) 851.3
wobbly 16.16, 362.10, 851.3, 917.17
Woden 458.12
wodge 257.10
woe 96.6, 96.8, 98.5, 112.10, 115.1, 1000.3, 1001.1
woebegone 96.26, 98.20, 112.22, 115.19
woebegoneness 98.5
woeful 96.26, 98.20, 112.26, 1000.9, 1011.15
woefulness 96.6, 98.5, 112.11
woesome 96.26, 98.20, 112.26, 1000.9
woesomeness 96.6, 98.5, 112.11
wold 236.1, 237.1, 272.3, 310.8
wolf (n) 8.16, 61.1, 311.19, 562.12, 665.10, 671.9, 672.3 (v) 8.23, 672.4
wolf at the door 619.2
wolf down 8.23, 187.11, 672.4
wolf-gray 39.4
wolfing (n) 8.1 (a) 672.6
wolf in one's stomach 100.7
wolf in sheep's clothing 357.6
wolfish 100.25, 144.26, 311.41, 480.26
wolfishness 100.8, 480.9
wolflike 311.41
Wolf-man 127.9
wolf ticket 510.5
wolf trap 759.19
wolf whistle 562.5
wolf-whistle (n) 58.4 (v) 58.8
wolverine 311.22
woman 77.3, 77.5, 304.1, 312.5, 563.8, 665.17
woman among women, a 659.4
woman chaser 562.12, 665.10
woman-hater 103.4, 590.2
woman-hating (n) 590.1 (a) 590.3
womanhood 14.1, 77.1, 77.3, 303.2
woman in the street, the 606.1
womanish 77.13, 77.14
womanishness 77.1, 77.2
womanism 642.4, 980.4
womanist 642.5, 980.5
womanity 77.1
womanization 77.11
womanize 77.12, 665.19
womanizer 665.10
womanizing 665.3
womankind 77.3, 312.1
womanlike 77.13
womanlikeness 77.1
womanliness 77.1, 303.2
womanly 77.13
womanness 303.2
woman of action 330.8
woman of courage 492.7
woman of easy virtue 665.14
woman of genius 413.13
woman of God 699.2
woman of her word 644.8
woman of honor 644.8
woman of parts 413.12
woman of straw 349.6
woman of the cloth 699.2
woman of the family 77.7
woman of the town 665.16
woman of the world 304.3, 578.7
woman of women 659.4
woman's editor 555.4
woman's intuition 934.1
woman-suffragist 609.17
woman-talk 523.10
woman-to-woman 535.3, 582.24, 587.19
woman upstairs 575.4
womb 2.13, 886.7
womb of time, the 839.1
womb-to-tomb security 611.7
women 77.3, 577.11
womenfolk 77.3
womenfolks 77.3
women's chorus 710.16
Women's Christian Temperance Union 668.5
women's clothing 5.1
women's college 567.5
women's course 753.1
Women's International Bowling Congress 750.1
women's lib 431.1, 642.4
women's libber 77.5, 642.5
women's liberation 431.1, 642.4
women's liberation activist 642.5
women's liberationist 642.5
women's liberation movement 642.4
womens' marker 751.1
women's movement 642.4
women's rightist 642.5
women's rights 642.4
women's room 12.10
womenswear 5.1
wommera 462.9
wonder (n) 122.1, 122.2, 131.2, 870.5, 870.8, 999.6 (v) 122.5, 930.10, 931.12, 971.9
wonder drug 86.4, 86.29
wonderful 122.10, 247.10, 870.14, 999.15
wonderfulness 122.3
wonderful thing 122.2
wondering 122.9
Wonderland 986.11
wonderland 986.11
wonderless 123.3
wonderlessness 123.1
wonderment 122.1, 122.2
wonders of the world 122.2
wonder-stricken 122.9
wonder-struck 122.9
wonder whether 930.10, 971.9
Wonder Woman 15.6
wonderwork 870.8
wonder-worker 690.5
wonder-working 870.16
wondrous 122.10, 870.16
wondrousness 122.3, 870.2
wondrous strange 122.10, 870.11
wonkiness 16.3, 1006.2
wonkish 204.14
wonky 16.16, 204.14, 393.38, 1006.11
wont (n) 373.1, 373.3 (v) 373.9, 373.11 (a) 373.15
wonted 373.13, 373.15, 869.9
wontedness 373.6
wonting 373.1
wontless 374.4
wonton 10.33
woo 104.18, 377.5, 440.14, 562.21
wood 310.13, 759.21, 1021.3, 1054.3
wood-block 713.12
woodblock 713.5
wood-block printing 548.1
wood-burning 1021.9
wood carver 716.6
wood carving 349.6
woodcarving 715.1, 715.2
wood chopper 1069.7
woodchuck 311.22
woodcraft 712.2, 1069.3
woodcraftsman 1069.7
woodcut 704.20, 712.16, 713.5
woodcutter 1069.7
wooded 310.40
wooden 117.6, 522.20, 922.16
wood engraver 716.8
wood engraving 713.5
woodenhead 924.4
woodenheaded 922.17
woodenheadedness 922.4
wooden horse 605.3
wooden kimono 309.11
woodenness 117.1
wooden overcoat 309.11
wooden racket 748.1
wooden shoes 5.27
woodenware 735.4
woodhick 227.10, 606.6
wood instrument 711.8
woodland (n) 233.1, 234.1, 310.12, 310.13 (a) 233.9, 310.40
woodlander 227.10, 1069.7
woodlands 233.2
woodlet 310.14
wood lot 310.14
woodman 227.10, 1069.7
wood model 786.5
woodnote 60.1
wood nymph 678.9
woodpile 1021.3
woodprint 713.5
wood pulp 1063.2
woods 233.2, 310.13, 711.8
woods and fields 233.1
woodsman 227.10, 1069.7
woodsy 310.40
wood tick 311.37
woodwind 710.12, 711.8
woodwind choir 711.8
woodwind instrument 711.8
woodwinds 710.12
woodwind section 710.12
woodwork 712.2
woodworking 712.2
woody 310.40
woody plant 310.33
wooer 104.11
woof (n) 4.1, 294.1, 740.3 (v) 60.2
woofing 514.1
wooing 104.5, 377.1, 440.5, 562.7
wool 3.2, 4.1, 37.2, 1047.4
woolens 5.22
woolgather 984.3, 985.9
woolgathering (n) 984.1, 985.2 (a) 984.8, 985.11
woolliness 3.1
woolly 3.24, 294.7, 1047.14
woolly bear 133.5
woolly-haired 3.24
woolly-headed 3.24
woolly mammoth 311.4
woolsack 417.10, 595.5
Woolworth 750.2
woomp 1035.5
woomping 50.13
wooziness 985.4
woozy 985.14
Worcestershire sauce 10.12
Word, the 677.11, 683.2
word (n) 334.1, 334.4, 349.3, 420.1, 436.1, 518.6, 523.14, 524.2, 524.3, 526.1, 551.1, 552.1, 552.4, 957.2, 974.1 (v) 524.22, 532.4
wordage 532.1
word arrangement 530.2
wordbook 554.9
word-bound 344.9
word boundary 524.9
word class 523.14, 526.1
word-coiner 526.18
wordcraft 543.1
word-deaf 49.6
word deafness 49.1
word dressing 532.1
worded 532.5
word element 526.3
word form 526.4
word formation 526.3
word-for-word 341.16, 973.15
word-for-word translation 341.3
word game 522.8, 743.9
word garment 532.1
word "go," the 818.1
word-group 529.1
word history 526.16
wordhoard 526.13
wordiness 538.2

wording 529.2
word in the ear 422.2, 551.3
wordless 51.11, 51.12, 344.9, 519.9
wordlessness 51.2, 344.2
word letter 546.2
wordlist 871.4
Word Made Flesh, the 677.11
word nerd 526.18, 554.18
word of advice 399.1, 422.2
word of command 420.1
word of explanation 341.5
Word of God, the 683.2
word of honor 334.4, 436.1
word of mouth 524.2
word-of-mouth success 704.4
word order 530.2
word origin 526.16
word painter 547.15, 718.4, 722.5
word painting 349.2
word-painting 986.6
word-perfect 973.15
word picture 349.2
wordplay 489.8
word power 524.4
word processor 1042.11
words 456.5, 457.1, 523.1, 524.1, 526.13, 532.1, 541.2
words from the sponsor 352.6
word-slinger 540.4, 547.13, 718.3
wordsmanship 547.2, 718.2
wordsmith 413.11, 526.15, 532.3, 547.15, 718.4
words of one syllable 535.1
words of wisdom 422.2, 974.1
wordspinner 545.5
word stock 526.13
word stress 524.10
word to the wise 399.1, 422.2, 551.3
word-usage 532.1
wordy 538.12
work (n) 328.1, 328.3, 387.5, 404.1, 460.4, 547.10, 547.12, 554.1, 704.4, 708.5, 712.9, 718.1, 724.1, 724.2, 724.6, 725.4, 889.1, 893.1, 1012.5 (v) 262.7, 320.4, 328.4, 330.10, 387.10, 407.4, 724.12, 725.12, 725.16, 797.10, 886.10, 889.5, 889.7, 892.11, 894.7, 940.2, 991.4, 995.3, 1060.8, 1069.17
workability 854.1, 889.3, 966.2
workable 889.10, 940.3, 966.7, 995.6
work a change 852.7
work a cure 396.15
workaday 373.14, 499.6, 724.15
work against 900.6
work against the clock 401.8
work against time 401.8, 821.6
workaholic (n) 330.8 (a) 330.22
work area 739.1
workaround 995.2, 1042.18
work as 889.8
work as a team 450.3
work at 328.8, 724.12
work away 725.14
workbench 739.1, 739.8, 901.15
workboat 180.1
workbook 549.11, 554.10
work both sides of the street 354.24
work buddy 616.5
work clothes 5.1
workday 499.6, 724.15
work day and night 725.13
work double hours 725.13
worked out 381.12
worked up 93.23, 105.20, 152.28
worked up into a lather 105.20
worker 311.33, 311.34, 577.3, 607.9, 726.1, 726.2, 759.22
worker of evil 593.1
worker of ill 593.1
workers 607.7
workers' comp 624.3
work evil 1000.6
workfellow 588.3, 616.5
workfolk 726.2
work for 449.18, 577.13, 724.12
work force 18.9, 726.2
work for wages 624.20
work from home 724.10
workgirl 726.2
workgroup 1042.19
workgroup computing 1042.16
workhand 726.2
work hard 725.13
work-harden 1049.3
workhorse 311.13, 726.3
workhouse 1009.4
work in 189.7, 213.6, 214.5, 772.3
working (n) 172.1, 328.1, 387.8, 889.1, 940.1, 1069.13 (a) 298.17, 328.10, 330.21, 724.15, 725.17, 889.11
working capital 728.15
working class (n) 607.7 (a) 607.10
working day, the 373.5
working dog 311.16
working drawing 381.3
working girl 607.9, 726.2
working hypothesis 951.2, 995.2
working into a lather 105.11
working lunch 423.3
working man 607.9, 726.2
working memory 989.1
working model 349.6
working mother 77.5
working on 375.3
working-out 538.6, 940.1
working out a deal 731.3
working people 607.7
working person 607.9
working plan 381.1
working principle 419.2
working proposition 995.2
working rule 419.2
workings 284.4, 328.1, 889.1, 1040.4, 1058.6
workings of the mind 931.1
working space 739.1
working stiff 607.9, 726.2
working together 450.1
working up 105.11
working wife 77.5
working without a net 493.6
working woman 77.5, 607.9, 726.2
work in progress 380.1, 724.2
work into 105.12
work into a stew 152.18
work into a sweat 152.18
work late 725.13
work-life balance 467.3
work like a beaver 725.13
work like a cart horse 725.13
work like a coal heaver 725.13
work like a dog 725.13
work like a galley slave 725.13
work like a horse 725.13
work like a machine 1014.10
work like a slave 725.13
work like a Trojan 725.13
work load 477.5
workload 641.1, 725.4
work magic 690.10
workman 607.9, 726.2, 892.7
workmanlike 413.22, 999.20
workmanship 413.1, 892.2
workmate 588.3, 616.5
workmen's compensation 611.7, 624.3
workmen's compensation insurance 611.7
work night and day 725.10
work of a master 893.1
work of an artist 893.1
work of a past master 893.1
work of art 413.10, 712.9
work off 395.11
work of Penelope 391.3, 408.1
work of reference 554.9
work on 375.14, 387.16, 440.12, 643.7, 889.6, 894.9
work oneself into a lather 105.17, 135.4, 152.18
work oneself into a sweat 105.17, 135.4
work oneself up 105.17
work one's fingers to the bone 725.13
work one's head off 725.13
work one's head to the bone 931.9
work one's shift 825.5
work one's tail off 360.7
work one's way 162.4
work one's way up 193.11, 409.10
work out 84.4, 328.7, 381.8, 407.4, 437.8, 538.7, 744.2, 861.6, 887.4, 931.11, 935.15, 940.2, 1017.18
workout 84.2, 725.6, 942.3
work out a deal 731.18
work out beforehand 380.7
work out right 940.2
workout room 84.1
work over 392.12, 604.14, 604.15, 902.17
work overtime 725.13
workpeople 726.2
work permit 443.6
workplace 197.6, 739.1
work relations 727.1
workroom 197.6, 739.1
works, the 254.4, 792.4
works 2.16, 143.6, 207.4, 328.3, 547.12, 718.1, 739.3, 739.4, 1040.4
work schedule 725.4
work shift 825.3
work shoes 5.27
workshop 739.1, 942.5
work-shy 846.17
workshy 331.19
worksite 739.1
workspace 739.1
work station 739.1, 1042.2
workstation 1042.9
work stoppage 727.5, 857.2
work-study 568.3
worktable 739.1
work the ball around 747.4
work the land 1069.16
work together 450.3
work to one's advantage 995.3
worktop 739.1
work to rule 857.8
work-to-rule 727.5
work to to windward 182.25
work toward 896.3
work under pressure 401.8
work up 105.12, 152.24, 375.17, 381.8, 917.10
workup 91.12
work up into a lather 105.12
work up into a passion 152.25
work upon 387.16
workweek 824.2
work well 409.7, 1014.10
workwoman 726.2
work wonders 409.7
world, the 312.4, 831.4, 1073.10
world 247.3, 722.4, 978.2, 1073.1
World Almanac 832.7
World Bank 620.4, 729.14
world-beater 249.4, 413.14, 999.6
world beyond the grave 839.2
World Boxing Association 754.1
World Boxing Council 754.1
world champion 413.15
world-class 249.14, 662.16, 997.24, 999.14, 1002.6
world-class performer 413.13
World English 523.4
World Federalism 612.6
world government 612.1, 612.6
world language 523.1
world leader 417.8, 575.8
worldliness 686.1, 695.2, 987.2, 1052.6
worldling 312.5, 695.10
worldly, the 686.2
worldly 413.28, 686.3, 695.16, 987.6, 1052.10
worldly minded 695.16
worldly-mindedness 695.2
worldly wisdom 413.9
worldly-wise 413.28
world of, a 884.3
world of commerce, the 731.1
world of discourse 978.2
world of fashion 578.6
world of finance 729.1
world of good 999.4
world of the dead 682.1
world of trade, the 731.1
world politics 609.5
world population 312.1

world power 232.1, 249.3
world principle 677.7
World Reason 677.7
world-record holder 413.15
worlds apart 780.7
world-self 677.7
World Series 745.1
world-shaking 997.17, 997.20
worlds of 884.3
world soul 677.7
world spirit 677.7
world, the flesh, and the devil, the 686.2
world to come, the 839.2
world travel 177.1
world traveler 178.1
world turned upside-down, the 205.1
worldview 792.3, 932.8, 953.3, 978.5
world war 458.1
world-weariness 118.3, 331.6
world-weary 112.22, 118.11, 331.20
worldwide 864.14
worldwideness 864.1
World Wide Web 347.18, 1042.19
world-wise 413.28
world without end 823.1, 1073.1
worm (n) 311.3, 311.31, 311.38, 660.6, 1001.2 (v) 175.6, 177.26, 281.4
worm along 175.6, 177.26
wormburner 745.3
worm-eaten 393.42
worm farm 311.38
worm farming 1070.1
worm gear 1040.9
worm in 213.6, 214.5
worming 177.17
worm in the apple 1000.3, 1001.2
wormlike 281.7, 311.52
worm medicine 86.24
worm oneself in 138.10
worm oneself into 189.7
worm one's way 162.4, 177.26
worm one's way into 189.10
worm out 192.14, 941.4
worm out of 192.14, 369.9, 600.11, 938.21
worm's-eye view 27.7, 33.6
wormwood 64.2, 67.2
wormy 80.23, 311.52, 393.42, 910.11
worn 16.18, 21.7, 21.9, 117.9, 252.10, 393.31, 806.5, 842.14, 842.18
worn away 388.5, 473.7
worn clothes 5.5
worn-down 21.7, 393.31
worn out 21.10
worn-out 16.18, 388.5, 390.10, 393.36, 806.5
worn ragged 393.31
worn thin 117.9
worn to a frazzle 16.18, 21.7, 393.36
worn to a shadow 21.7, 270.20, 393.35
worn to rags 393.31
worn to the bone 393.31
worn to the bones 393.35
worn to the stump 393.31
worn to threads 393.31
worried 96.24, 126.8, 1013.20
worriedness 126.2
worried sick 126.8
worried stiff 126.8
worried to a frazzle 126.8
worrier 126.3
worries 126.2
worries and cares 126.2
worriment 96.2, 126.2
worrisome 98.22, 126.10
worrisomeness 98.7
worry (n) 96.2, 126.2, 127.4, 1013.3 (v) 96.13, 96.16, 98.15, 126.5, 126.6, 1013.13
worry along 409.12
worry at 96.13
worry beads 498.5
worrying (n) 126.2 (a) 98.22, 126.10
worry oneself 126.6
worry oneself sick 126.6
worry one's head about 126.6
worrywart 112.14, 125.7, 126.3
worse 119.4, 393.27, 852.10
worse and worse 119.4
worse for, the 393.27
worse for liquor, the 88.31
worse for wear, the 303.18, 393.31, 393.33, 473.7
worsen 96.14, 119.2, 119.3, 393.9, 393.16, 852.6, 852.7
worsened 119.4, 393.27
worsening (n) 96.3, 119.1, 393.1, 393.3, 852.1 (a) 393.45
worse off 393.27
worse-off 119.4
Worship 648.2
worship (n) 104.1, 155.1 (v) 104.20, 155.4
worship (n) 692.1, 696.1 (v) 696.11
worshiped 155.11
worshiper 101.4, 675.15, 696.9
worshipful 155.9, 155.12, 662.15, 692.8, 696.16, 842.12
worshipfulness 692.1
worship idols 697.6
worshiping (n) 696.1 (a) 155.9, 696.16
worship mammon 618.13
worship the almighty dollar 618.13
worship the golden calf 618.13, 697.6
worship the ground one walks on 155.4
worst, the 1000.3
worst (v) 249.7, 412.6 (a) 1000.9
worst case 125.1
worst-case 112.30, 125.12
worsted 412.14
wort 310.4
worth (n) 387.4, 471.7, 518.2, 630.2, 632.2, 728.14, 997.1, 999.1 (a) 469.9, 630.14
worth a bundle 618.15
worth a great deal 618.14
worth a king's ransom 632.10
worth a pretty penny 632.10
worth having 100.30
worthiness 136.2, 371.11, 644.1
worth its weight in gold 632.10
worthless 391.11, 996.6, 998.21, 998.22, 1000.9
worthless as tits on a boar 391.11
worthless fellow 660.2
worthlessness 391.2, 996.1, 998.2, 1000.2
worth one's salt 662.15
worth one's while 995.5
worth the money 633.7
worthwhile 387.22, 472.16, 995.5
worthwhileness 995.1
worthy (n) 659.1, 662.9, 997.8 (a) 136.12, 371.24, 413.24, 509.20, 632.10, 639.9, 644.13, 662.15
worthy of 639.10
worthy of faith 953.24
wot 928.12
Wotan 458.12
wot not of 930.10
wot of 928.12
would as leave 324.3
would as lief 324.3
would as lief as not 324.3
would as soon 371.17
would-be (n) 100.12 (a) 100.28, 141.10, 527.15
would-be gentleman 606.7
would be glad of 100.14
would fain do 100.14
would fain have 100.14
would rather 371.17
would rather not 325.3
wound (n) 85.38, 96.5 (v) 26.7, 96.17, 152.21, 393.13, 1000.6
wounded 26.9, 96.23
wounded pride 137.2
wounding 98.17
woundingess 98.1
wound string 711.20
wound to the quick 96.17
wound up 407.11, 837.7
woven 170.12, 294.7, 740.7
wow (n) 409.4, 489.6, 999.7 (v) 95.11, 743.21
wow factor 999.2
wowser 409.4, 500.11, 999.7
wrack (n) 310.4, 395.4 (v) 395.10
wracked 93.23
wracked with age 303.18
wrack the nerves 58.11
wraith 976.4, 988.1, 988.3
wraithlike 270.20, 988.7
wraithy 988.7
wrangle (n) 456.5 (v) 456.11, 935.16, 1070.8
wrangle over 457.21
wrangler 452.3, 461.1, 572.7, 935.12, 1070.3
wrangling (n) 457.1, 935.4 (a) 456.17
wrap, a 820.1
wrap (n) 5.20, 295.10, 295.18 (v) 5.39, 209.6, 212.5, 212.9, 291.5, 295.20, 770.20, 800.9, 820.6
wrap about 295.20
wrap around 295.20
wrap in plain brown paper 346.6
wrap oneself in 376.4
wrapped 209.10, 212.12, 295.31
wrapped in 983.17
wrapped in clouds 346.11
wrapped in mystery 522.18
wrapped in thought 931.22, 985.11
wrapped up 407.11, 770.21
wrapped up in 104.29, 898.5, 983.17
wrapped up in oneself 651.5
wrapper 5.20, 295.18, 554.14
wrapping (n) 212.2, 295.1, 295.18 (a) 209.8, 295.35
wrapping paper 295.18
wrapping up 407.2
wraps 345.3, 346.2
wrap up 5.39, 295.20, 407.6, 557.5, 770.20, 800.9, 820.6
wrap-up 407.2
wrapup 268.3, 557.2, 849.2
wrath 152.5, 507.1, 655.3
wrathful 152.28, 507.7
wrathfulness 152.5
wrath of God, the 507.1, 639.3
wrathy 152.28
wrawl 58.8
wreak 328.6, 643.5
wreak havoc 395.10, 671.11
wreak havoc on 1000.6
wreak one's vengeance 507.4
wreath 280.2, 310.25, 646.3, 647.2, 740.2
wreathe 209.7, 498.9, 740.6
wreathed 209.10, 498.11, 740.7
wreathing 740.1
wreathlike 281.6
wreathwork 740.2
wreathy 281.6
wreck (n) 128.5, 179.10, 393.8, 395.1, 395.4, 1011.2 (v) 19.9, 182.42, 393.10, 395.10, 395.17, 671.11
wreckage 395.5
wreck buoy 517.10
wrecked 87.24, 393.28, 395.28, 806.5, 1013.27
wrecker 395.8, 483.6, 593.5, 905.1
wreckful 1011.15
wrecking 395.5
wrecking ball 395.5
wrecking bar 906.4
wreck of one's former self 393.8
wrench (n) 26.2, 85.38, 96.5, 192.6, 265.1, 905.3, 1040.7 (v) 26.7, 265.5, 342.2, 350.3, 393.13, 480.22, 905.5
wrench from 192.15, 480.22
wrenching 192.6, 342.1
wrest (n) 192.6, 265.1 (v) 192.15, 265.5, 480.22
wrest from 192.15, 480.22
wresting 192.6
wresting out 192.1
wrestle (n) 725.3 (v) 457.13, 725.11
wrestler 461.3

wrestle with 457.17
wrestling 457.10
wrestling match 457.10
wrestling meet 457.10
wrestling ring 463.1
wrest out 192.10
wretch 96.11, 660.2
wretched 80.25, 96.26, 98.20, 112.21, 661.12, 998.21, 1000.9, 1011.13
wretched lot 1011.1
wretchedness 96.6, 112.2, 661.3, 998.2, 1000.2
wretched of the earth, the 606.4, 1011.7
wriggle (n) 917.7 (v) 105.18, 917.14
wriggle oneself into 189.7
wriggle out of 369.9, 431.8
wriggler 302.12
wriggling 917.21
wriggly 917.21
wright 726.6, 892.7
wring (n) 192.6, 265.1 (v) 26.7, 96.18, 192.16, 265.5, 281.4, 480.22
wringer 192.9
wring from 192.15, 480.22
wringing 192.6
wringing wet 1065.17
wring one's hands 115.11
wring out 192.16
wrinkle (n) 254.4, 290.1, 291.3, 578.5 (v) 260.7, 288.5, 290.3, 291.6, 294.4, 303.10, 393.18
wrinkled 260.12, 288.7, 290.4, 291.8, 303.16, 393.35
wrinkled like a prune 393.35
wrinkle one's brow 362.7, 931.12, 971.9
wrinkling 260.1
wrinkly 290.4, 291.8, 303.16
wrist 2.7, 800.4, 906.5
wristband 280.3, 498.6
wristlet 195.2, 280.3, 498.6
wrist shot 749.3
writ 549.5, 598.2
write 349.8, 349.9, 547.19, 547.21, 549.15, 553.10, 708.46, 718.6, 892.8
write a letter 553.10
write back 553.10
write between the lines 519.4
write down 547.19, 549.15
write history 719.4
write in 549.15
write-in 371.6
write in prose 721.3
write in stone 855.7
write into 549.15
write into one's will 478.18
write-in vote 371.6
write off 125.10, 148.5, 255.10, 370.7, 390.7, 445.2, 625.9, 628.8, 631.2
write-off 255.3, 445.1, 625.2, 630.9, 631.1
write oneself a man 303.9
write one's last will and testament 478.18
write one's memoirs 989.9
write one's own ticket 323.3
write out 546.7, 547.19, 549.15
write poetry 720.14
write prose 721.3
writer 547.13, 547.15, 553.8, 556.3, 718.3, 718.4, 722.5
writer-in-residence 227.2
writer's cramp 547.2
writer's itch 547.2, 718.2
write the book 413.18
write to 553.10
write up 352.15, 549.15, 552.11, 556.5
write-up 556.2
writeup 352.4
write up a report 552.11
writhe (n) 917.7 (v) 26.8, 96.19, 105.18, 265.5, 917.14
writhing 917.21
writhy 917.21
writing 343.1, 349.1, 546.1, 547.1, 547.2, 547.10, 547.12, 549.5, 554.1, 718.2
writing expert 547.14
writing frame 30.6
writing materials 547.4
Writings, the 683.3
writings 547.12
writing stamps 30.6
writing system 349.1, 546.3, 547.1, 547.9
writing table 901.15
writing tablet 549.11
writ of certiorari 598.10
writ of error 598.10
writ of summons 598.2
written (n) 938.2 (a) 420.12, 547.22, 964.9
written agreement 332.1, 437.1
written character 546.1, 547.9
written communication 553.1
written constitution 673.6
written down 549.17
written examination 938.2
written interrogatories 598.12
written language 523.4
written law 673.5
written music 708.28
written off 390.10
written on water 764.8
written unit 526.1
written word, the 547.10
written word 349.1, 549.1
wrong (n) 638.1, 650.1, 650.4, 654.3, 655.2, 674.4, 975.1, 1000.3 (v) 650.7, 1000.6 (a) 638.3, 650.9, 654.16, 655.5, 844.6, 975.16, 975.18, 996.5, 1000.7
wrong conduct 655.1
wrong construction 948.1
wrongdoer 593.1, 660.8
wrongdoing (n) 322.1, 414.6, 654.1, 655.1, 674.4, 975.1 (a) 655.5
wrong end of the stick 948.1
wrongful 638.3, 650.9, 674.6
wrongful involvement 656.1
wrongfulness 638.1, 650.1, 674.1
wrongheaded 361.11, 922.15
wrongheadedness 361.3, 922.3
wrong impression 948.1, 976.1
wrong linking 776.2
wrong move 975.4
wrong name 527.9
wrongness 638.1, 650.1, 844.1, 975.1, 996.1
wrong number 660.4
wrongo (n) 593.1, 660.1, 660.4 (a) 971.22
wrong side 220.1
wrong side of forty, the 303.4
wrong side of the tracks, the 230.6
wrong side out 205.7
wrong step 975.4
wrong time 844.2
wrong'un 356.6, 593.1, 660.4
wrong use 387.1, 389.1
wrong-way 163.12
wrong-way around 163.12
wroth 152.28
wrought 407.10
wrought iron 1058.5
wrought out 407.10
wrought up 105.20
wrought-up 152.28
wrought up by 93.23
wrung 26.9, 96.25
wry 204.14
wry face 110.9, 265.4, 1015.3
wry mouth 265.4
wryneck 265.3
wunderkind 413.12
wurf 223.2
Wurst 10.21
wussy (n) 16.6, 77.10 (a) 16.12, 19.13
WYSIWYG word processor 1042.11
X 170.4, 527.10, 528.2, 882.6
x 930.6
Xanadu 986.10
xanthic 43.4
Xanthippe 110.12
xanthism 43.2
xanthochroi 312.2
xanthochroism 43.2
xanthocyanopia 30.3
xanthoderma 43.2
xanthodermatous 43.6
xanthous 40.5, 41.10, 43.4, 43.5
X chromosome 305.8, 560.6
xenogamy 78.2
xenogenesis 78.6
xenogenetic 78.16
xenophobe 103.4
xenophobia 103.1, 773.3, 980.4
xenophobic 773.9, 980.12
xerographic copy 785.5
xerography 548.1, 785.2
xerophagia 515.2
xerophagy 515.2
xerophthalmia 85.33
xeroprinting 548.1
xerostomia 1066.1
xerox (n) 714.5, 785.5 (v) 714.14, 785.8
xerox copy 714.5, 785.5
X factor 768.1
XL 257.18
X marks the spot 159.1
x number 1017.6
X out 255.12
X-rated 665.29
X-rated movie 666.4
X-ray (n) 91.9, 714.3, 714.6, 1025.5 (v) 91.26, 714.14
X-ray astronomy 1073.19
X-ray eye 27.10
X-ray movie 91.9
X-ray photograph 714.6
X-ray photography 714.1
X-ray photometry 1037.8
X-rays 1032.10
X-ray spectrograph 1037.7
X-ray spectrometer 1037.7
X-ray spectrometry 1037.8
X-ray technician 90.11, 716.5
X-shaped 170.10
XXL 257.18
xyl- 305.6
xylem 305.6, 1052.2
xylo- 305.6
xyloglyphic artist 716.6
xyloglyphy 715.1
xylograph 713.5
xylographer 716.8
xylographic 713.12
xylophonist 710.6
xylopyrographer 716.8
xylotypography 548.1
Y 170.4, 171.4
y 930.6
yacht (n) 180.3 (v) 182.13
yachting 182.1, 760.2
yacht race 457.12
yachtsman 183.1, 760.2
yachtswoman 183.1, 760.2
yada yada 520.3
yahoo 497.6, 924.2
Yahweh 677.2
Yahwist 683.11
Yahwistic 683.11
Yajur-Veda 683.8
yak (n) 311.6, 540.3 (v) 524.20, 540.5
yakkety-yak (n) 524.1, 540.3 (v) 524.20, 540.5
yakking 524.1
yale 647.2
yammer (n) 58.4, 59.1 (v) 58.8, 59.6, 115.14
yammering 59.10
yang 76.12
Yank 461.7
yank (n) 905.3 (v) 905.5
Yankee 227.11, 523.7, 860.3
Yankee Doodle 860.3
Yankee horse trader 415.6
Yankeeism 523.8
Yankeeland 231.7, 232.3
yap (n) 59.1, 292.4 (v) 59.6, 60.2, 115.16, 524.20, 524.25
yap at 510.16
yapping (n) 115.5 (a) 59.10
yappy 59.10
Yap Trench 275.5
yarborough 758.3
yard (n) 196.6, 212.3, 728.7, 739.3, 882.10, 901.2 (v) 212.5
yardage 267.1, 746.3
yardarm 901.2
yardbird 429.11, 572.9
yard goods 735.3

yard line 746.1
yardman 178.13
yardmaster 178.13
yards 739.3
yard sale 734.3
yardstick 300.2
yard up 212.5
yard wide, a 973.15
yare 180.18
yarn 4.1, 271.2, 354.11, 489.6, 719.2, 722.3
yarn-dye 35.14
yarner 357.9
yarning 722.1, 722.2
yarn spinner 357.9, 722.5
yarn spinning 722.2
yarn-spinning 722.1
yashmak 5.26
yaw (n) 164.1 (v) 182.29, 182.30, 182.55, 184.40
yawl (n) 59.1 (v) 59.6, 60.2, 115.13
yawn (n) 292.1, 292.2 (v) 292.16
yawning (n) 22.1, 292.2, 331.6 (a) 22.21, 275.12, 292.18
yawning abyss 275.2
yawning chasm 1006.1
yawning cliff 200.3
yawning depths 275.3
yawny 22.21, 118.10
yaw off 182.29
yawp (n) 59.1, 115.3 (v) 59.6, 60.2, 115.13, 524.25
yaw-ways 204.14
Y-axis 200.1
yay big 257.24
yazzihamper 924.5
Y chromosome 305.8, 560.6
yclept 527.14
Ydalir 681.10
yea 332.2, 371.6, 441.1, 509.1, 935.14
yeah 332.2
yean 1.3
yeanling 302.10, 311.7
year 572.11, 824.2
yearbook 549.7, 549.11, 554.7, 555.1
year-daemon 1069.4
yearling 302.9, 302.10, 311.6, 757.2
yearlong 827.12
yearly 849.13, 850.8
yearner 100.12
yearn for 100.16
yearnful 100.23
yearnfulness 100.4
yearning (n) 100.5, 104.1 (a) 100.23
yearold 302.9
years 303.1, 827.4
years of discretion 303.2
years old 303.16
years on end 827.4
years that are past, the 837.1
years to come 839.1
year-to-year 849.13
yeas and nays 371.6
yea-sayer 332.6
yea-saying 332.2
yeast 852.5, 912.3
yeastiness 105.4, 298.1
yeasty 105.20, 298.10, 298.17, 320.7
yea vote 509.1
yecchy 80.23, 1000.8
yegg 483.3
yell (n) 59.1, 116.2 (v) 59.6, 115.13, 116.6, 524.25
yell at 510.19
yell bloody murder 59.6, 115.16, 333.5
yell blue murder 59.6
yelling (n) 59.1 (a) 59.10
yell oneself hoarse 116.6
yell out 59.8
yellow (n) 35.13, 43.1, 87.10, 305.15 (v) 43.3 (a) 43.4, 105.32, 153.5, 491.10
yellow-bellied 491.10
yellow-belly 491.5
yellow bile 2.24
yellow blindness 30.3
yellow book 549.8
yellow card 752.3
yellow-cheeked 43.6
yellow complexion 43.2
yellow-complexioned 43.6
yellow-dog contract 727.3
yellow dolls 87.15
yellow-eyed 153.5
yellow-faced 43.6
yellow flag 399.3, 429.2, 517.15, 647.7
yellow-green 44.4
yellow-haired 43.5
yellowish 43.4
yellowish-brown 40.3
yellowish-green 44.4
yellowishness 43.1
yellow jack 399.3, 429.2
yellow jacket 311.34
yellow jackets 87.5
yellow jaundice 43.2
yellow journalism 93.9
yellow mustard 10.12
yellowness 43.1, 491.1
yellow-orange 42.2
Yellow Pages 352.6, 574.10
yellow peril 458.11
yellow press 552.1
yellow race 43.2, 312.2
yellows 87.15
yellow skin 43.2
yellow streak 491.4
yellow stuff 728.20
yellow sunshine 87.10
yellowtail 756.2
yellowy 43.4
yelp (n) 59.1 (v) 59.6, 60.2, 115.15, 524.25
yelp at 510.19
yelping 59.10
yen 100.5, 896.1
yen for 100.16
yenta 214.4, 422.3, 552.9, 981.2
yeoman 183.6, 577.1, 577.5, 1008.14, 1069.5
yeomanly 644.13
yeoman of the guard 1008.14
yeomanry 461.24
yeoman's service 449.1
yerba 87.11
yerk (n) 902.5 (v) 902.15, 905.5
yerk out 708.37
yes (n) 332.2, 371.6, 935.14 (v) 332.8
yes-and-no answer 939.1
yes-man 138.4, 250.2, 332.6, 511.4, 616.8, 867.2
yessir 332.2
yesterday 837.1
yesteryear 837.1
yew 115.7
yield (n) 472.5, 627.1, 738.7, 893.2 (v) 16.9, 332.11, 362.7, 370.7, 385.7, 433.7, 468.2, 475.3, 478.12, 627.4, 867.3, 892.13, 1047.7, 1048.5
yield again to 394.4
yield an aroma 69.6
yield an odor 69.6
yield a profit 387.17, 472.13
yield assent 332.8, 441.2
yielded 475.5
yield hope 124.9
yielding (n) 370.3, 433.1, 468.1, 475.1, 892.6 (a) 426.5, 433.13, 890.10, 1014.15, 1047.9
yielding a return 387.22
yieldingness 433.3
yield one's breath 307.18
yield the floor 613.10
yield the ghost 307.18
yield the palm 250.5, 433.8
yield the spirit 307.18
yield to 134.7, 427.6, 433.9
yield to despair 125.10
yield to maturity 738.5
yield up 370.7
yin 77.13
Yinglish 523.10
yin yoga 84.2
yip 60.2
yippee 116.2
yippie 611.12
yips 126.1, 128.2, 917.1
yo 59.1
Yoda 920.9
Yoda-like 920.17
yodel (n) 708.13 (v) 708.38
yodeler 710.13
yodeling 708.13
Yoga 667.1
yoga 689.1, 725.6
yoga 84.2
yoga retreat 91.23, 228.27
yoga trance 691.3
yogeeism 689.1
yogi 667.2, 689.11, 699.13
yogic 800.13, 800.16
yogin 667.2, 689.11, 699.13
yogini 680.6
yogism 689.1
yogist 689.11
yogurt 10.48, 1062.5
yo-ho 59.1
yoicks 59.3
yoke (n) 428.4, 873.2 (v) 800.5, 800.10, 805.3, 805.4, 873.5, 1070.7
yoked 775.9, 800.13, 805.6, 873.8
yoked together 805.6, 873.8
yokefellow 588.3, 616.5
yokel (n) 414.8, 416.3, 497.6, 606.6, 924.5 (a) 233.8
yokeldom 233.1
yokelish 233.8, 497.13
yokelism 233.3, 497.4, 922.3
yokemate 563.6, 588.3, 616.5
yoke together 805.3, 805.4, 873.5
yoke with 643.4
yoking 800.1, 805.1, 873.1
yolk 305.15
yolked 305.23
yolky 305.23
Yom Kippur 658.3
Yom Kippur' Tishah B'Av 515.3
yon 261.10
yonder 261.10
yore 837.2
yoretime 837.2
Yorkshire 523.7
you 865.5
you and me 606.1
you-be-damned 141.13
you-be-damnedness 141.5
you do you 430.20
you-know-who 528.2
you name it 864.4
young (n) 302.2, 561.2 (a) 301.9, 841.7
young adult 302.1
young at heart 303.4
young blood 301.1, 302.2
young buck 302.5
young creature 302.6
young devil 680.7
younger (n) 302.1 (a) 301.15, 835.4
younger days 301.1
younger generation 302.2
youngest 302.1
young fogey 301.1, 303.2
young fry 302.2
young generation 561.1
young gun 301.1
young hopeful 302.1
youngish 301.9
young lady 302.6
youngling (n) 302.1 (a) 301.9
younglings 561.1
young-looking 301.9
young love 104.3
young man 104.12, 302.5
youngness 301.1
young people 302.2
young person 302.1
youngster 302.1
youngsters 561.1
young thing 302.6
Young Turk 841.4
young'un 302.1
young whippersnapper 302.4
Your Excellency 648.2
Your Highness 648.2
your honor 596.1
Your Ladyship 648.2
Your Lordship 648.2
Your Majesty 648.2
yours affectionately 820.5
yourself 865.5
yourselves 865.5
yours faithfully 820.5

yours most sincerely 820.5
yours respectfully 820.5
yours sincerely 820.5
yours truly 820.5, 865.5
youth 301.1, 302.1, 302.2, 302.5, 303.1, 818.4, 837.4, 1010.4
youth crusade 609.33
youth deficiency 303.5
youthen 301.8
youthful 83.13, 301.9
youthfulness 301.1
youthful spirits 322.2
youth hostel 228.15
youthlike 301.9
youth market 733.3
youth movement 609.33
yow 311.7
yowl (n) 59.1, 115.3 (v) 59.6, 60.2, 115.13
yowling 60.6
yo-yo 362.5, 924.3
Y-shaped 171.10, 278.6
yucca 285.5
yuck 116.4
yuck factor 64.1
yuckiness 64.1, 64.3, 80.2, 98.2
yucky 64.7, 80.23, 98.18, 99.7
yugo 318.6
Yukon 261.4
Yukon, the 1023.4
Yukon time 832.3
yuk-yuk (n) 116.4 (v) 116.8
Yule 313.6
yule log 1021.3
Yuletide 313.6
yumminess 63.1
yummy 63.8, 97.8
yuppie 618.7, 867.2
yuppify 618.12
yurt 295.8
Z 820.1
z 930.6
Zadkiel 679.4
zaftig 97.7, 257.18
zag (n) 204.8, 278.2, 916.5 (v) 204.12, 278.5
zagged 204.20
zaniness 923.1
zany 489.12, 707.10, 924.1
zanyism 923.1
zap 308.14, 395.11, 762.7, 820.6, 1035.15
Zapata mustache 3.11
zapped 395.29, 820.10
zappy 544.11
Zarathustra 684.4
Zarathustrian 675.32
Z chromosome 305.8
zeal 17.2, 93.2, 101.2, 126.1, 324.1, 671.2, 692.3, 886.9, 983.2
zealless 102.6
zeallessness 102.1
zealot 101.4, 675.15, 692.4, 870.4, 926.18
zealotic 926.32
zealotical 692.11
zealotism 101.3, 692.3, 926.11
zealotist 692.4
zealotry 101.3, 692.3, 926.11
zealous 93.18, 101.9, 126.7, 324.5, 330.22, 671.22, 692.11
zealousness 324.1, 330.6, 401.2, 671.2, 692.3
zebra 47.6, 170.2, 746.1, 746.3
zebra crossing 170.2
zebrass 797.8
zebrule 797.8
zebu 311.6
Zechariah 684.1
zeitgeist 636.1, 896.2, 978.5
zelig (n) 221.5 (a) 677.17
zemi 678.1
zenana 563.10
Zen Buddhism 675.14
Zen Buddhist 675.24
Zend-Avesta 683.7
zendician 688.6
zendik 688.6
zendikite 688.6
zenith 198.2, 249.3, 272.2
zenithal 198.11
Zephaniah 684.1
Zephyr 318.2
zephyr 318.4, 1047.4
Zephyrus 318.2
zeppelin 181.11
zerking 923.9
0 762.2
zero 759.12, 762.2, 764.2, 1019.3
zero hour 459.13, 843.5
zero in 798.4
zero in on 159.11, 208.10, 459.22, 937.3
zero option 371.3, 428.3, 963.6
zero-sum 338.6, 790.7, 900.9
zero-sum game 356.12, 421.3
zero tolerance 372.1, 442.1
zero visibility 32.1
zero weather 1023.3
zest 17.4, 63.2, 68.2, 95.1, 101.1, 109.4
zestful 9.3, 17.13, 68.7, 101.8, 109.14
zestfulness 17.4, 68.2, 101.1, 109.4
zestiness 68.2
zesty 9.3, 17.13, 68.7
zetetic (n) 938.18 (a) 938.37
Zeus 316.6
zig (n) 204.8, 278.2, 916.5 (v) 204.12, 278.5
zig and zag 415.9
zigged 204.20
ziggurat 266.2, 703.2
zigzag (n) 164.1, 204.8, 278.2, 289.3, 368.1, 916.5 (v) 164.5, 204.12, 278.5, 368.8, 916.13 (a) 164.7, 204.20, 278.6
zigzag course 164.1
zigzagged 204.20
zigzaggery 204.8
zigzagging 916.5
zigzaggy 204.20
zigzagways 204.20
zigzagwise 204.20
zilch 762.3
zillion, a 884.4
zillion (n) 882.13, 1017.5 (a) 884.6
zinc 7.11
zincograph 548.8, 713.6
zincographer 716.8
zincography 548.1
zincotype 548.8
zine 555.1
zing (n) 17.3, 174.4 (v) 174.9
zinger 421.3, 489.7
zingy 17.13, 330.17
Zion 681.3
Zionist 675.21
zip (n) 17.3, 57.1, 68.2, 109.4, 174.4, 762.3 (v) 57.2, 174.9, 270.11
zip code 553.9
zip disk 549.10
zip drive 549.10
zip file 549.10
zip gun 462.10
ziplocked 293.9
zipped 268.9
zipped up 800.14
zipper 293.6, 800.8
zippered 293.9
zipping 800.3
zip plus four 553.9
zippo 762.3
zippy 17.13, 68.7, 109.14
zip through 938.26
zip up 17.10, 293.6
zit 85.37, 1004.1
zitherist 710.5
ziti 10.33
zitzflaysh 134.2
zizz (n) 17.3, 22.3 (v) 22.14
zodiac 280.3, 1073.16, 1073.20
zodiacal 1073.25
zodiacal constellation 1073.5
zodiacal light 1025.15
zodiac signs 1073.20, 1073.30
zoetic 305.17, 306.12
zoic 311.39
zombie 988.1
zombiish 21.9
zonal 231.8
zone (n) 231.1, 231.3, 280.3, 296.1, 553.9, 819.1, 1073.16 (v) 209.7, 802.18
zoned 87.24, 209.11
zoned out 87.24
zone fossil 842.6
zone of communications 463.2
zone of no signal 184.31
zone out 27.15
zone time 832.3
zoning 444.1, 802.1
zoning law 444.1
zoning variance 443.1
zonked 25.8, 87.24, 88.33
zonked out 25.8, 87.24
zonk out 25.5
zoo 228.19, 770.11
zoobenthoic 311.53
zoobenthos 311.29
zoochemical 1060.9
zooculture 1070.1
zooerastia 75.11
zooid 305.2, 311.3
zooidal 311.39
zoolater 697.4
zoolatrous 697.7
zoologic 311.39, 1068.4
zoological 311.39, 1068.4
zoological garden 228.19
zoological park 228.19
zoologist 1068.2
zoology 1068.1, 1068.3
zoom (n) 184.13 (v) 174.8, 184.39, 193.10
zoom binoculars 29.4
zoomechanical 1039.7
zoom in 167.3
zooming 193.1
zoom in on 167.3
zoom shot 714.8
zoon 305.2
zoophilia 75.11
zoophiliac 75.16
zooplankton 311.29
zooplanktonic 311.53
zoospore 258.7, 305.13
zootechnics 1070.1
zootechny 1070.1
zootheism 675.5
zootheist 675.16
zootomy 266.1
zoril 311.22
zoris 5.27
Zoroaster 684.4
Zoroastrian (n) 675.24, 697.4 (a) 675.32
Zoroastrianism 675.14, 697.1
Zouave 461.9
zunked 87.25
zuppa 10.10
zwieback 10.30
Zwinglian (n) 675.20 (a) 675.28
Zwinglianism 675.10
zygosis 78.3
zygospore 305.13
zygote 305.14
zymogen 7.10
zymotic 85.62